T5-BSH-565

Ulrich's International Periodicals Directory 1998

36th Edition

Ulrich's International Periodicals Directory
is compiled by
R.R. Bowker
Serials Bibliography Department

Database Publishing Group
Leigh C. Yuster-Freeman, Vice President, Database Production
Andrew Grabois, Senior Managing Director, Bibliographies

Editorial
Judith Salk, Publisher and Editorial Director
Edvika Popilskis, Managing Editor
Ewa Kowalska, Maria Mucino, Senior Editors
Zhaoxia Lian, Senior Associate Editor
Egill Halldorsson, Christopher King, Associate Editors
Thomas Berry, Gerry Milligan, Virginie Raguenaud, Diane Shpiz, Assistant Editors
Mary Crouthers, O'Sheila Delgado, Editorial Coordinators

René Bernadel, Lorraine Cantillo, Terence Carlson, Maria Christopher, Michael Dalelio,
Connie Duffy, Karl Dusza, Deborah Frail, Qingye Guo, Evelyn Irvine, Jean Kontra, Bronislaw Jan Kowalski,
Margareta Leon, Dawn Lombardy-Stoecker, Karen Lombardy, Stefan Miarka, Olga Neville,
Eline van de Poel-Becker, Noreen Riley, Alina Warda, and Lisa Wilcox, Contributing Editors

Production
Doreen Gravesande, Production Director
Myriam Nunez, Managing Editor
Barbara Holton, Frank McDermott, Senior Editors

Editorial Systems Group
Gary Aiello, Vice President, Information Technology
Rhonda Vollbrecht, Project Manager, Bibliographies
Nana Rizinashvili and Robert Michniewicz, Senior Systems Analysts

Computer Operations Group
Nick Wikowski, Director, Network/Computer Operations
Jack Murphy, Supervisor

Reed Technology and Information Services
Donna Brinkmann, Account Manager

36th Edition
ULRICH'S™
INTERNATIONAL PERIODICALS DIRECTORY
1998

including
Irregular Serials & Annuals

Volume 1

Classified List of Subjects
A-D

THE BOWKER INTERNATIONAL SERIALS DATABASE

R.R. BOWKER
A Unit of Reed Elsevier Business Information
New Providence, New Jersey

Published by R.R. Bowker
A Unit of Reed Elsevier Business Information
121 Chanlon Rd., New Providence, NJ 07974

Neal Goff, Senior Vice President and Chief Operating Officer

Copyright © 1997 by Reed Elsevier Inc.
All rights reserved

Ulrich's Hotline (U.S. only): 1-800-346-6049
Editorial (Canada only, call collect): 1-908-665-2875
Serials Fax (overseas users): 908-771-7725
Serials E-mail: ulrichs@bowker.com
URL: http://www.bowker.com

Ulrich's is a trademark of Reed Properties Inc., used under license

No part of this publication may be reproduced or transmitted in any form or by any means, stored in any information storage and retrieval system, without prior written permission of R.R. Bowker, 121 Chanlon Rd., New Providence, New Jersey 07974, USA.

International Standard Book Number
5-Volume set: 0-8352-3967-5
Volume 1: 0-8352-3968-3
Volume 2: 0-8352-3969-1
Volume 3: 0-8352-3970-5
Volume 4: 0-8352-3971-3
Volume 5: 0-8352-3972-1

International Standard Serial Number
0000-0175

Library of Congress Catalog Card Number
32-16320

Printed and bound in the United States of America

No payment is either solicited or accepted for the inclusion of entries in this publication. R.R. Bowker has used its best efforts in collecting and preparing material for inclusion in this publication, but does not warrant that the information herein is complete or accurate, and does not assume, and hereby disclaims any liability to any person for the loss or damage caused by errors or omissions in this publication whether such errors or omissions result from negligence, accident or any other cause.

ISBN 0-8352-3967-5

Contents

BOWKER/ULRICH'S SERIALS LIBRARIANSHIP
    AWARD WINNERS ... vi
PREFACE ... vii
USER'S GUIDE ... ix
INTERNATIONAL STANDARD SERIAL NUMBER (ISSN) ... xviii
ABBREVIATIONS
    General Abbreviations and Special Symbols ... xx
    Money Symbols ... xxi
    Country of Publication Codes ... xxii
    Document Suppliers ... xxiv
    Micropublishers and Distributors ... xxvi
    Reprint Services ... xxx
    Wire Services ... xxxi
    Abstracting and Indexing Services ... xxxii
SUBJECT GUIDE TO ABSTRACTING AND INDEXING ... xlv
SUBJECTS ... xlvi

VOLUME 1
CLASSIFIED LIST OF SERIALS/SUBJECTS A to D ... 1

VOLUME 2
CLASSIFIED LIST OF SERIALS/SUBJECTS E to L ... 2309

VOLUME 3
CLASSIFIED LIST OF SERIALS/SUBJECTS M to Z ... 4541

VOLUME 4
CROSS-INDEX TO SUBJECTS ... 7351
CESSATIONS ... 7383
ISSN INDEX ... 7605
TITLE INDEX ... 8461
TITLE CHANGE INDEX ... 9697

VOLUME 5
REFEREED ... 9719
SERIALS AVAILABLE ON CD-ROM ... 9973
PRODUCER LISTING/SERIALS ON CD-ROM ... 10033
SERIALS AVAILABLE ONLINE ... 10037
VENDOR LISTING/SERIALS ONLINE ... 10229
INDEX TO PUBLICATIONS OF INTERNATIONAL ORGANIZATIONS ... 10263
    International Organizations ... 10263
    International Congress Proceedings ... 10275
    European Communities ... 10278
    United Nations ... 10280
CONTROLLED CIRCULATION SERIALS ... 10289

U.S. NEWSPAPERS
USER'S GUIDE ... li
ABBREVIATIONS ... liv
DAILY NEWSPAPERS — US ... 10415
WEEKLY NEWSPAPERS — US ... 10517
TITLE INDEX ... 10777
DAILY NEWSPAPER INDEX ... 10853
WEEKLY NEWSPAPER INDEX ... 10871
GEOGRAPHIC INDEX ... 10929
CESSATIONS ... 10997

Bowker/Ulrich's Serials Librarianship Award

Presented by the Serials Section
Association for Library Collections and Technical Services (ALCTS)
Division of the American Library Association (ALA)

Sponsored by R.R. Bowker

This annual award is given in recognition of distinguished and ongoing contributions to serials librarianship. Qualified individuals demonstrate leadership in serials-related activities through their participation in professional associations, groups, and/or library education programs; make significant contributions to serials literature; and, in general, strive to enhance our comprehension of the serials world.

AWARD RECIPIENTS

1985	Marcia Tuttle
1986	Ruth C. Carter
1987	James P. Danky
1988	Marjorie E. Bloss
1989	John E. Merriman
1990	Jean S. Cook
1991	Deana L. Astle/Charles A. Hamaker
1992	Linda K. Bartley
1993	Ann L. Okerson
1994	Tina Feick
1995	Peter Gellatly
1996	Jean L. Hirons
1997	Cindy Hepfer

Preface

Now in its 36th edition, **Ulrich's International Periodicals Directory** upholds its reputation for excellence in the provision of serials information. In the 65 years since it was first published, **Ulrich's** has established itself as the premier serials reference source in the world, providing serials users with essential bibliographic and access information.

Beginning with the 34th edition, the publication date of **Ulrich's** moved from August to November. Publication in November continues to enable us to provide thousands of updated prices for 1998. Most publishers establish prices for the upcoming year between May and September. Prices set and received by us later than mid-September did not get updated for this print edition. However, data are entered as received, so price changes and all other information received after mid-September will appear in subsequent quarterly CD-ROM versions of **Ulrich's** (**Ulrich's on Disc™**, formerly Ulrich's *PLUS*) and online versions (update monthly through Knight-Ridder Information, Inc./DIALOG file number 480; OVID Technologies/file name: ULRI; and LEXIS®-NEXIS®/library: BUSREF, file name: ULRICHS; and SilverPlatter Information, Inc.-SilverPlatter ERL).

As libraries, institutions, and researchers evaluate new opportunities and technologies that enable them to access individual articles on demand rather than to acquire serials in their entirety, our coverage of document delivery services has expanded to include CINDOC (CINDOC Suministro de Documentos Service), Ask*IEEE, KR SourceOne, and Linda Hall Library. We now identify 18 different document delivery services from which the full text of articles from serials listed in **Ulrich's** may be obtained (see pgs. xxiv-xxv). For a brief explanation of and contact information for these useful services, please refer to the section entitled "Document Suppliers" in the User's Guide of **Ulrich's**, pg. ix of the prefatory material of Volumes 1-4.

Further access to serials in **Ulrich's** is facilitated through the inclusion of nearly 250,000 indicators denoting coverage by some 800 abstracting and indexing services; 12,000 notations of reprint availability; over 30,000 e-mail addresses; and 22,000 URLs (Uniform Resource Locators on the World Wide Web). The number of URLs includes publisher sites as well as sites for individual journals.

Serials, whether in print or in an electronic medium, are as important as ever as primary sources of current information and topical news in all fields of endeavor. Though the printed serial is by no means on the wane, the proliferation of serials in electronic formats, whether online or on CD-ROM, continues unabated, especially with dramatically increased use of the Internet as a publishing medium. This edition of **Ulrich's** includes 8,762 serials available exclusively online or in addition to hard copy, and 2,903 serials available on CD-ROM. These serials are indicated by a notation and a bullet (●) in the main entry.

Ulrich's includes nearly 19,000 Rights & Permissions contact names, along with telephone contact information, if provided. Users anticipating forthcoming serial launches will find 51 titles announced for publication in 1998.

The 36th edition of **Ulrich's** contains information on over 156,000 serials published throughout the world, arranged under 869 subject headings. More than 112,000 entries have been updated to reflect the most current information available and nearly 7,000 serials have been added this year, some of which have since ceased or suspended publication. Included in this edition is cessation or suspension information which has been recorded in our database during the past three years for 9,586 titles. The ceased or suspended titles are preceded by a dagger (†) in the TITLE INDEX for instant identification.

Users can identify newer serials, over 3,571 of which are known to have begun publication since January 1, 1995, by looking for an upside-down solid triangle (▼) in both the CLASSIFIED LIST OF SERIALS and the TITLE INDEX. This symbol is also used to highlight forthcoming publications. In addition, more than 13,550 refereed serials notations; nearly 71,000 brief descriptions; almost 42,700 LC Classification Numbers; over 20,000 CODEN; and 4,421 vendor file names or numbers for 8,762 serials available in an online format appear in this edition.

Included in **Ulrich's** are serials that are currently available, issued more frequently than once a year and usually published at regular intervals, as well as publications issued annually or less frequently than once a year, or irregularly. Due to the vast number of serials, we have established certain criteria for inclusion, while maintaining our aim of maximum title coverage that will satisfy the widest range of use. We include all publications that meet the definition of a serial except administrative publications of governmental agencies below state level that can be easily found elsewhere, membership directories, comic books, and puzzle and game books.

This edition of **Ulrich's** is arranged within five volumes, as follows: the first three volumes comprise the CLASSIFIED LIST OF SERIALS; the fourth volume contains the CROSS-INDEX TO SUBJECTS, CESSATIONS INDEX, ISSN INDEX, TITLE INDEX, and TITLE CHANGE INDEX. The fifth volume comprises the remaining indexes: REFEREED SERIALS, SERIALS AVAILABLE ON CD-ROM, PRODUCER LISTING/SERIALS ON CD-ROM, SERIALS AVAILABLE ONLINE, VENDOR LISTING/ SERIALS ONLINE, INDEX TO INTERNATIONAL ORGANIZATIONS, and CONTROLLED CIRCULATION SERIALS, as well as the NEWSPAPERS section listing general-interest daily and weekly newspapers published in the United States.

International data inquiries are mailed annually to nearly 80,000 publishers to secure accurate and up-to-date information on current titles, new titles, title changes, and cessations. Updating of the database occurs daily using information received from publishers throughout the year and from serials research conducted in our editorial department. All post office returns are researched, and entries from publishers whose addresses cannot be verified are suspended from the file. Information about title changes, cessations, and new titles not received by the deadline for this edition will appear in **Ulrich's Update**, in the **Ulrich's Online** file as noted above, and **Ulrich's on Disc**™, the quarterly CD-ROM formerly known as Ulrich's *PLUS*. **Ulrich's Microfiche** was discontinued in 1997.

Your purchase and use of **Ulrich's** is complemented by some additional services. **Ulrich's Update**, provided free of charge, twice a year in March and July, is a supplemental service to the annual directory. The **Ulrich's Hotline** is a toll-free number that subscribers can call to get help in solving particular serials research problems and questions. Canadian users are asked to call a special number collect, and our overseas users are asked to use a designated fax number. (Please refer to page iv for our mailing address, telephone/fax numbers, and e-mail address.)

As we continue to research, plan, and implement enhancements to the **Ulrich's** database and our database maintenance system, we consider feedback from our users to be essential. Please contact us to let us know your thoughts. We want **Ulrich's** and its family of products to provide all necessary reference information quickly and effectively. Comments and suggestions are encouraged in order to help keep our directory of the highest quality. There are a wide variety of communication modes for you to select. You may write to us, send us a fax, call us on the telephone, or send us e-mail. Also, be sure to visit the R.R. Bowker Home Page on the World Wide Web at *www.bowker.com*. Look for a Home Page for **Ulrich's** in the future. Please refer to page iv for all contact information.

My sincere gratitude is extended to the entire staff of **Ulrich's** for their unflagging dedication and diligent work in updating and maintaining the serials database in preparation of the 36th edition of **Ulrich's**. Appreciation is also extended to all vendors and service suppliers for working with us to produce this directory. Finally, I would like to thank the various information specialists, serialists, national libraries, and serials publishers throughout the world who have aided us in updating **Ulrich's**. We consider their participation and interest in the dissemination of accurate and comprehensive serials information to be of tremendous value to **Ulrich's** and its users.

Judy Salk
Publisher and Editorial Director

User's Guide

This directory offers two primary access methods for locating periodicals: by subject in the CLASSIFIED LIST OF SERIALS (Volumes 1-3), and alphabetically in the TITLE INDEX (Volume 4). Ceased serials are listed in a separate CESSATIONS section (Volume 4) and are also accessible by means of the TITLE INDEX. Other indexes provide listings of selected periodicals in specific categories. These indexes, in Volume 5 unless otherwise noted, are REFEREED SERIALS, CONTROLLED CIRCULATION SERIALS, SERIALS AVAILABLE ON CD-ROM, PRODUCER LISTING/SERIALS ON CD-ROM, SERIALS AVAILABLE ONLINE, VENDOR LISTING/SERIALS ONLINE, PUBLICATIONS OF INTERNATIONAL ORGANIZATIONS, ISSN INDEX (Volume 4), and TITLE CHANGE INDEX (Volume 4). See the User's Guide in Volume 5 for a content description and use instructions for the U.S. NEWSPAPERS section.

In addition, separate subheadings for "Abstracting, Bibliographies and Statistics" under major subject headings provide convenient access to these types of publications. Page references for these subheadings are given in the "Subject Guide to Abstracting and Indexing" on p. xlv. This listing provides an overview of subjects for which abstracting and indexing publications have been identified.

The "User's Guide" is separated into three divisions for ease of use: (I) Section Descriptions, (II) Full Entry Content Description, and (III) Cataloging Rules for Main Entry Title.

Section Descriptions

CLASSIFIED LIST OF SERIALS

This is the main section of the book, containing bibliographic information for currently published serials classified by subject. Entries are arranged alphabetically by title within each subject heading. Subject cross-references in the text direct the user to the location of subheadings.

Volume 1 contains subjects A-D, from "Abstracting and Indexing" through "Drug Abuse and Alcoholism." Volume 2 contains subjects E-L, "Earth Sciences" through "Lumber and Wood." Volume 3 contains subjects M-Z, from "Machine Theory" through "Zoology."

A complete listing of the "Subjects" used in the CLASSIFIED LIST OF SERIALS appears on p. xlvi. To aid international users, this list is translated into four languages. For additional guidance on the subject classification scheme, the user should also consult the CROSS-INDEX TO SUBJECTS on p. 7351, which contains additional key word references.

Each serial is listed with full bibliographic information only once. If a serial covers several subjects, title cross-references appear under the related headings, directing the user to the heading where the full entry is listed.

New serials beginning publication in the past three years, as well as titles announced for publication in the coming year are highlighted by a ▼ in front of the title.

The "Cataloging Rules for Main Entry Title" section of this "User's Guide" explains the title cataloging rules followed in compiling **Ulrich's**.

CROSS-INDEX TO SUBJECTS

This index lists alphabetically all main subject headings in the **Ulrich's** Subject Heading File, as well as keyword references that direct users to main or subheadings where publications on those topics are likely to be found. The number following each subject term directs users to the page on which the subject begins within the CLASSIFIED LIST OF SERIALS.

A keyword may refer the user to more than one subject category. In this case, the subject references are listed in alphabetical order and are not necessarily listed in hierarchical order.

Main subject headings appear uppercased, e.g. AGRICULTURE. Subheadings contain the main subject term in uppercase and the specific subheading term in mixed case, e.g. AGRICULTURE—Agricultural Economics. The keywords, except for acronyms, are displayed entirely in mixed case.

CESSATIONS

In this section, entries for serials for which cessation was noted in the past three years are listed alphabetically by title. The cessation entry includes: title, Dewey Decimal

Classification number, former frequency of publication, publisher name and address, country-of-publication code, and, if available, other information such as ISSN, CODEN, LC number, subtitle, corporate author, year of first issue and year ceased. Titles which were originally planned as continuing series but which have closed are included in the CESSATIONS section although back issues may still be available.

If a title has "ceased" because a new title is being used, there will not be an entry in the CESSATIONS section. Instead, the entry is maintained in the CLASSIFIED LIST OF SERIALS under the new title, with a **"Formerly"** or **"Former titles"** indication.

ISSN INDEX

The ISSN INDEX lists serials in order by ISSN number. It includes all serials contained in the Bowker International Serials Database, whether current, ceased, or inactive, to which an ISSN has been assigned in our file. A dagger symbol (†) indicates that the title is ceased. If an ISSN appears twice, it usually indicates that the serial has split into two or more parts. Titles that have changed and for which new ISSNs have been assigned will show cross-references from one ISSN to the new ISSN. If no new ISSN has been assigned, the cross-reference is from ISSN to new title. Entries for inactive titles do not appear in the book.

Italicized type indicates the page number where a complete entry can be found for active titles. Titles for which cessation was noted in the last three years have a page reference to the listing in the CESSATIONS INDEX. If no page reference appears for a ceased title, it means that the cessation was noted more than three years ago and is not listed in this edition. ISSNs of inactive titles likewise do not have page references and are not listed in this book.

A full description of the ISSN and its use is provided on p. xviii.

TITLE INDEX

The TITLE INDEX is the second major access point for serials. To locate a serial by its title, the user should be familiar with title cataloging rules as described in the "Cataloging Rules for Main Entry Titles" paragraphs of this "User's Guide."

The TITLE INDEX lists all current and ceased serials included in this directory. **Boldface** type indicates the page number where the complete entry will be found; page numbers in roman type refer to related subject categories.

For serials with identical titles published within a country, the city of publication is added in parentheses, and sometimes the year of first publication is given to further distinguish the titles.

If a serial title consists of or contains an acronym, a cross-reference is provided from the full name to the acronym form of the title.

Cross-references are provided from former titles and variant titles, and from the alternate language titles of multi-language publications. Recent title changes are noted, with a reference to the current title. The TITLE INDEX also lists the country code for all serials, along with the ISSN, if known.

The ▼ used in the "Classified List of Serials" to indicate new serials also appears in this index, preceding the title. A (†) appears preceding the title if the publication has ceased.

TITLE CHANGE INDEX

The TITLE CHANGE INDEX lists former titles alphabetically with references to new titles. Page numbers indicate where bibliographic entries are listed in the CLASSIFIED LIST OF SERIALS. This index cumulates all title changes recorded in the **Ulrich's** database since the publication of the previous, or 35th, edition.

REFEREED SERIALS

This section is an alphabetical listing by title of all serials known to be refereed, or peer reviewed. It includes the publisher name, address, and telephone number, if known. The italicized number at the end of each entry is the page number where the full entry appears in the CLASSIFIED LIST OF SERIALS.

Omission of a title from this index does not mean that the journal is not peer-reviewed; nor does **Ulrich's** make any attempt to rate or judge the relative value of an individual journal's peer review process.

SERIALS AVAILABLE ON CD-ROM

This section is an alphabetical listing of all serials known to be available on CD-ROM, either in addition to hardcopy, or on CD-ROM only. It includes the publisher name, address, telephone and fax numbers, if known. It also includes the name of CD-ROM producers, when known. The italicized number at the end of each entry is the page number where the full entry appears in the CLASSIFIED LIST OF SERIALS.

PRODUCER LISTING/SERIALS ON CD-ROM

This section is an alphabetical listing of identified producers of serials on CD-ROM. Entries include the producer address, telephone and fax numbers, and an alphabetical listing of all serial titles known to be available. If known, the serial on CD-ROM product name is listed in parentheses after the serial title. All serials listed in this index also have full bibliographic entries in the CLASSIFIED LIST OF SERIALS. Consult the TITLE INDEX or the

SERIALS AVAILABLE ONLINE

This section is an alphabetical listing of all serials known to be available online, either in addition to hardcopy, or online only. Entries include publisher name, address, telephone and fax numbers, plus names of online vendors and file names or numbers if known. Certain electronic journals may not have a physical mailing address listed. The number in parentheses at the end of each entry is the page number where the full entry appears in the CLASSIFIED LIST OF SERIALS.

VENDOR LISTING/SERIALS ONLINE

This section is an alphabetical listing of identified vendors of online periodicals. Entries include addresses, telephone and fax numbers for the vendor, and an alphabetical listing of all titles known to be available, with file names or numbers, if known. All serials listed in this index also have full bibliographic entries in the CLASSIFIED LIST OF SERIALS. Consult the TITLE INDEX or the SERIALS AVAILABLE ONLINE listing for page numbers.

INDEX TO PUBLICATIONS OF INTERNATIONAL ORGANIZATIONS

Complexity of corporate author structure, as well as title page variations in multilingual texts, compound the problems in cataloging publications of international organizations. This special index is provided so that the user may have one reference point for these titles. This index consists of four sections:

International Organizations
International Congress Proceedings
European Communities
United Nations

The index contains all current titles listed in the Bowker International Serials Database. The user must consult the CLASSIFIED LIST OF SERIALS for the full bibliographic information pertaining to these titles. Page references are provided.

CONTROLLED CIRCULATION SERIALS

This section is an alphabetical listing of all serials identified as having controlled circulations. It includes the publisher name and address, telephone and fax numbers, and circulation figure, if known. The italicized number at the end of each entry is a reference to the page on which the full entry appears in the CLASSIFIED LIST OF SERIALS.

Full Entry Content Description

Basic Information
The following elements are mandatory for listing and appear in all entries: main entry title, frequency of publication, publisher address, country code, and Dewey Decimal Classification number.

Certain electronic journals may not have a physical mailing address; the URL and/or E-mail address provide a means of contacting the publication.

Dewey Decimal Classification Number
The Dewey Decimal number is printed at the top left of each entry. More than one Dewey number may have been assigned if a serial covers several subjects.

LC Classification Number
The Library of Congress classification number, if known, appears directly below the Dewey Decimal number. Shelf numbers are not included.

Country Code
The Country Code is printed at the top right of each entry following the Dewey Decimal number. A complete list of country codes used will be found on p. xxii.

ISSN
The ISSN for the main entry title is printed immediately following the country code. Not all publications have been assigned an ISSN, and lack of a number does not render a publication ineligible for listing.

CODEN
The CODEN designation, if known, is printed directly below the country code and ISSN. The CODEN is an alphanumeric code, applied uniquely to a specific publication. Devised by the American Society for Testing and Materials, it is used primarily for scientific and technical titles. New CODEN are assigned by Chemical Abstracts Service.

Title Information
The main title is printed in **boldface** and upper case as the first item in the entry. Titles are catalogued according to rules described below in the "Cataloging Rules for Main Entry Title" section. For multi-language publications, the parallel language title is also printed in upper case, immediately following the main entry title, and is separated from it by a slash.

A ▼ printed before the title indicates that the title began publishing within the past three years. This symbol also appears before titles announced for publication in the coming year.

An asterisk (*) printed after the title indicates that the information in the entry was not verified by the publisher for this edition.

USER'S GUIDE

The subtitle is printed in lower case after the title.

Variant titles or translated edition titles are given within the entry and are labeled as such.

Former titles are given at the end of the entry, along with publication dates if known. If a former title also had an ISSN, the ISSN is listed in parentheses after the former title. Many entries contain extensive former title information, providing a history of changes which may be useful for bibliographic record-keeping.

The Key Title, which is assigned at the time of ISSN assignment by the responsible center of the International Serials Data System, is given only if it is different from the main entry title.

Year First Published
The year first published is given if provided by the publisher. If information is lacking, a volume number and specific year may be provided to indicate the approximate age of the publication.

Frequency
The frequency of publication is given in abbreviated form, such as "a." for annual, "irreg." for irregular, "m." for monthly, "3/yr." for three times per year. All abbreviations used are listed in the "General Abbreviations" on p. xx.

Price
Unless otherwise indicated, the price given is the annual price for an individual subscription in the currency of the

---

SAMPLE ENTRY

(1) 930.198 490.996   **(2)** US   **(3)** ISSN I055-7644
(4) DZ991   **(5)** CODEN: JAAPL9
(6) JOURNAL OF ANARCTIC ARCHEOLOGY AND PROTOLINGUISTICS;   **(7)** international communications and research.   **(8)** (Supplement avail.)   **(9)** (Test in English, French, Polynesian languages)   **(10)** 1927.   **(11)** 2/yr.   **(12)** $39 to individuals; institutions $99 (includes supplement) (effective 1998); newsstand price: $20   **(13)** (Societe d'Archaeologie et de Linguistique Pacifiques-Society of Pacific Archaeology and Linguistics)   **(14)** W.A. Translations (Subsidiary of: Temporary Culture),   **(15)** Box 43072, Upper Montclair, NJ 07043-7072.   **(16)** TEL 908-665-2869.
(17) FAX 508-555-0010.   **(18)** TELEX 123458.   **(19)** E-mail:antarchaeol@miskaton.edu; URL http://www.miskaton.edu/.   **(20)** (Subscr. to: Department of Archaeology and Proto-Linguistics, 7 Old College Walk, Arkham, MA 01901-1011. TEL 508-555-0110. FAX 508-555-4112;
(21) Dist. in Europe by: Editions d'Erlette, Ch. de Kerangat, 56120 Plumelec, France. TEL 33-76-63-94. FAX 33-76-205).   **(22)** (Co-sponsor: Miskatonic University, Department of Archaeology and Proto-Linguistics)
(23) Eds. A.H. Whateley, J.M. Snyrnat;   **(24)** Pub. M.J. Smith.   **(25)** R&P contact: J.M. Snymat. TEL 508-555-0011.   **(26)** adv.: B&W page $400; trim 8-1/8x10;   **(27)** adv. contact: Arthur Dunwich.
(28) bk.rev; abstr; bibl.; illus., index;   **(29)** circ. 500 (paid); 500 (controlled).   **(30)** (also avail. in microform from SWZ, UMI; also avail. on diskette; back issues avail.; reprint service avail. from SWZ, UMI).
(31) Indexed: Abstr. Anthropol, Br.Archaeol.Abstr.   **(32)** (1991—), Onoma (1986—), Ref. Zh.
(33) Document type: academic/scholarly publication.
(34) •Also available online   **(35)** Vendor(s): UTOPIA (Miskatonic).
(36) Also available on CD-ROM.   **(37)** Producer(s): TEMPCULT (Miskatonic).
(38) –BLDSC (9999.000000); CIS   **(39) CCC.**
(40) Supersedes (in 1986): Miskatonic Annals of Antarctic Archaeology and Extraterrestrial Linguistics
(41) (ISSN 0055-1298).
(42) Description: Publishes archaeologic field research on prehistoric civilizations in the Pacific Islands and Antarctica, with relevant contributions discussing worldwide linguistic evidence of contacts among civilizations.
(43) *Refereed Serial*

KEY

1. Dewey Decimal Classification
2. Country Code
3. ISSN
4. LC Classification
5. CODEN
6. Main Entry Title
7. Subtitle
8. Bibliographic Note
9. Language
10. First Published
11. Frequency
12. Price
13. Corporate Author
14. Publishing Company
15. Address
16. Telephone
17. Fax
18. Telex
19. E-mail; URL
20. Subscription Address, Tel & Fax
21. Distributor Address, Tel & Fax
22. Co-sponsor
23. Editor
24. Publisher
25. Rights & Permissions Contact, Telephone
26. Advertising Rate
27. Advertising Contact
28. Special Features
29. Circulation
30. Format
31. Indexed
32. Years of Coverage
33. Document Type
34. Online Availability
35. Online Vendor/File Name
36. CD-ROM Availability
37. CD-ROM Producer(s)
38. Document Suppliers
39. Copyright Clearance Center Registration Notation
40. Title Changes
41. Former ISSN
42. Brief Description
43. Refereed

country of origin. The price in U.S. dollars may also be given in parentheses if it is provided by the publisher. No attempt is made to convert foreign currency to U.S. dollars. Separate postage information is not given, since postal rates vary widely.

Publishing Company Information
Many serials are editorially controlled by a sponsoring organization or corporate author and published by a commercial publisher. In these instances, the commercial publishing company's name and address are given, and the name of the corporate author is given in parentheses immediately preceding. In other instances, either a sponsoring organization or a commercial publishing company has sole responsibility, and only one name is given. We avoid listing printers as publishing companies, preferring the name and address of someone with editorial responsibility. For the same reason, we avoid listing distributors as publishing companies.

If no publishing company name is given, it is assumed that the publishing company name is the same as the title.

Telephone, Fax, Telex Numbers, E-mail, and Web Site Addresses
Telephone, fax, telex numbers and e-mail as well as web site addresses (URLs) are given when provided by the publisher. U.S. and Canadian numbers are given in standard North American format. Toll-free numbers within U.S. and Canada are also included, when available. Numbers in other countries are provided in the same format as supplied by the publisher, resulting in some inconsistencies (e.g. sometimes with a country and/or city code, sometimes without). Users are advised to consult an international operator before placing calls.

Subscription or Distribution Address
A second address is given only if the address for ordering subscriptions is different from the publishing company's address. Distributors are listed only if we have been informed that a particular organization is the exclusive distributor. Additional subscription and/or distribution offices of international publishers are listed, if known. Telephone and fax numbers for subscription and/or distribution offices appear if provided by the publisher.

Editor
Only one or two names are given when known, preceded by the notation "Ed." or "Eds." Advanced degrees and titles are omitted, except for medical, military and religious titles; absence of a title does not mean that the editor has none. The abbreviation "Ed.Bd." indicates editorship by three or more persons.

Publisher
Only one or two names are given when known, preceded by the notation "Pub." or "Pubs." Advanced degrees and titles are omitted, except for medical, military and religious titles; absence of a title does not mean that the publisher has none.

If the publisher is also the editor, and no publishing company name is available, the person's name is given with the notation "Ed. & Pub."

Rights and Permissions Contact
A name is given when supplied, preceded by the notation "R&P contact". The telephone number information follows, when known and different from the main number.

Advertising Rates and Contact
When provided by the publisher, the name of the advertising contact, as well as full-page advertising rates and trim size are indicated. Most dimensions are listed in millimeters, except for U.S. publications, the dimensions of which are usually in inches.

Special Features
A listing of special features may include such items as book or other types of reviews, advertising (usually meaning commercial, not classified advertising), charts, illustrations, bibliography section, article abstracts, and an annual index to the periodical's contents.

Reprint Services
If a serial is known to be available from a reprint service, a code referring to the service appears in the entry. More than one code may be listed. For a list of reprint services and a translation of the codes, please refer to p. xxx.

Circulation
All circulation figures used are approximate. Circulation is given only if provided by the publisher. The notation "controlled" indicates that the publication is available only to the qualified persons, usually members of a particular trade or profession.

Format
Formats other than standard magazine format are noted in parentheses. Other formats may be looseleaf, duplicated (mimeographed), tabloid. If a publication is available in microform, a notation is made which includes a three-letter code for the vendor, if known. A list of names, addresses, telephone and fax numbers of micropublishers begins on p. xxvi.

Abstracting and Indexing
The notation **"Indexed:"** precedes a list of abbreviations for all abstracting and indexing services known to cover the serial on a regular basis. Years of coverage immediately follow each abstracting and indexing service code, if known. The complete names of the abstracting and indexing services are listed with their abbreviations on p. xxxii. All currently published abstracting and indexing services are also listed as entries in the CLASSIFIED LIST OF SERIALS.

Document Type

Notations are included to indicate type of publication, e.g. trade publication, newsletter, or abstracting/indexing. The words "**Document type:**" appear in boldface, followed by the document type description, in entries where this information is known. More than one document type may be listed for a single publication, if applicable.

Online Availability and CD-ROM Availability

If a serial is known to be available in a full-text online format and/or on CD-ROM, a bullet symbol (●) precedes the information. Online and CD-ROM availability are noted whether they exist in addition to hardcopy or in one or both formats exclusively. Online vendors and CD-ROM producers are also listed, if known.

For a listing of serials available online, consult the SERIALS AVAILABLE ONLINE index on p. 10037. Complete names and addresses of vendors, with a listing of serials known to be available through them, are in a separate index, VENDOR LISTING/SERIALS ONLINE on p. 10229.

For a listing of serials available on CD-ROM, consult the SERIALS AVAILABLE ON CD-ROM index on p. 9973. Complete names and addresses of producers, with a list of CD-ROMs known to be available through them, are in a separate index, PRODUCER LISTING/SERIALS ON CD-ROM on p. 10033.

Document Suppliers

The **Ulrich's** database and the individual databases of the following document suppliers were matched on the presence of ISSNs. When a match was successful, the appropriate document supplier code was noted. Not all serials titles in general, or in these individual databases, have ISSNs. Therefore, the absence of one or any document supplier code in an **Ulrich's** listing does not necessarily mean the title is unavailable from one or any of these suppliers.

ADONIS™

The notation, ADONIS, appearing in a serial entry indicates the availability of that serial for document delivery through ADONIS's service, by permission from the copyright owner. Such permission is subject to change without notice.

For further information, contact: ADONIS B.V., Spuistraat 112D, 1012VA Amsterdam, The Netherlands; tel: 31-20-6262629, fax: 31-20-6261437; ADONIS USA, 350 Main St., 6th fl., Malden, MA 02148-5018, USA; tel: 800-944-6415; fax: 617-876-7022; e-mail: infousa@adonis.nl; URL: http://www.adonis.nl.

Ask*IEEE

The notation, AskIEEE, appearing in a serial entry indicates that photocopies of articles from that serial are available through IEEE's document delivery service, Ask*IEEE.

For further information, contact Ask*IEEE, 75 Varick St., 9th fl., New York, NY 10013, USA; tel: 800-949-4333 (outside US & Canada: 212-301-4100); fax: 212-301-4090; e-mail: askieee@ieee.org.

British Library Document Supply Centre

The notation, BLDSC, appearing in a serial entry indicates the availability of that serial for document delivery from the British Library Document Supply Centre, by permission from the copyright owner. The BLDSC shelfmark number, a unique identifier of each serial, is preceded by an em-dash (—) which is followed by the notation "BLDSC (0000.000000)." The format of the shelfmark is four digits, a decimal point, then six digits.

For further information about BLDSC's services, contact: Customer Services, BLDSC, Boston Spa, Wetherby, LS23 7BQ, UK; tel: 44-1937-546060; fax: 44-1937-546333; e-mail: dsc-customer-services@bl.uk.

Chemical Abstracts Service

The notation, CASDDS, appearing in a serial entry indicates the availability of that serial for document delivery through Chemical Abstracts Service Document Detective Service.

For further information, contact CAS Client Services, Document Detective Service, 2540 Olentangy River Rd., P.O. Box 3012, Columbus, OH 43210-0012, USA; tel: 800-631-1884, 614-447-3870; fax: 614-447-3648; e-mail: dds@cas.org; URL: http://www.cas.org/Support/dds.html.

CINDOC

The notation, CINDOC, appearing in a serial entry indicates the availability of that serial for document delivery through CINDOC Suminstro de Documentos Service.

For further information, contact Document Delivery Service CINDOC (Servico de Suministro de Suministro de Documentos), Joaquín Costa, 22, 28002 Madrid, Spain; fax: 34-1-5642644; e-mail: bib-icyt@bib.csic.es.

CISTI

The notation, CISTI, appearing in a serial entry indicates the availability of that serial for document delivery from the Canada Institute for Scientific and Technical Information, by permission from the copyright owner. Such permission is subject to change without notice.

For further information, contact: Client Assistant, Document Delivery, CISTI, National Research Council Canada, Ottawa K1A 0S2, Canada; tel: 800-668-1222 (Canada & US) or 613-993-9251; fax: 613-993-7619; e-mail: cisti.docdel@nrc.ca.

Congressional Information Service, Inc.

The notation, CIS, appearing in a serial entry indicates the availability of that serial for document delivery through CIS

Documents on Demand Service, by permission from the copyright owner. Such permission is subject to change without notice.

For further information, contact Congressional Information Service, Inc., 4520 East-West Hwy., Ste. 800, Bethesda, MD 20814-3389, USA; tel: 301-654-1550, 800-227-2477; fax: 301-654-4033; e-mail: EAINET@US.NET; URL: http://www.cispubs.com.

EMDOCS

The notation, EMDOCS, appearing in a serial entry indicates the availability of that serial for document delivery through EMDOCS: The EMBASE Document Delivery Service, by permission from the copyright owner. Such permission is subject to change without notice.

For further information, contact EMDOCS, 75 Varick St., 9th fl., New York, NY 10013, USA; tel: 800-282-2720 or 212-301-4003; fax: 212-301-4060; e-mail: dds@work4u.artx.com.

Engineering Information Inc.

The notation, Ei, appearing in a serial entry indicates the availability of that serial for document delivery through Ei Text, the Ei Document Delivery Service, by permission from the copyright owner. Such permission is subject to change without notice.

For further information, contact Ei Text, One Castle Point Terrace, Hoboken, NJ 07030-5996, USA; tel: 800-221-1044 (USA & Canada), 201-216-8500; fax: 201-216-8557; e-mail: eitext@ei.org; URL: http://www.ei.org.

The Genuine Article

The notation, Genuine Article, appearing in a serial entry indicates the availability of that serial for document delivery through The Institute for Scientific Information's Document Solution, by permission from the copyright owner. Such permission is subject to change without notice.

For further information, contact ISI Document Solution, 3501 Market Street, Philadelphia, PA 19104, USA; tel: 215-386-4399; fax: 215-386-4343; e-mail: tga@isinet.com.

Haworth Document Delivery Service

The notation, Haworth, appearing in a serial entry indicates the availability of that serial for document delivery through The Haworth Press's Document Delivery Service. This service is available for all Haworth journals. As the copyright holder, there will be no permission fee, but other fees are applicable.

For further information, contact Haworth Document Delivery Service, 10 Alice Street, Binghamton, NY 13904-1580, USA; tel: 800-HAWORTH; fax: 800-895-0582; e-mail: getinfo@haworth.com.

KR SourceOne

The notation, KR SourceOne, appearing in a serial entry indicates the availability of that serial for document delivery through KR SourceOne. Copyright compliance is ensured through KR SourceOne's agreements with the Copyright Clearance Center.

For further information, contact KR SourceOne, 75 Varick St., 9th fl., New York, NY 10013, USA; tel: 800-239-3458 (outside US & Canada: 212-301-4000); fax: 212-301-4060; e-mail: dds@work4u.artx.com; URL: http://www.krinfo.com/krsourceone/.

Library KNAW

The notation, KNAW, appearing in a serial entry indicates the availability of that serial for document delivery through the NIWI (Netherlands Institute of Scientific Information Services). In addition, NIWI offers free access to Medline.

For further information, contact Library NIWI Customer Service, P.O. Box 95180, 1090 HD Amsterdam, The Netherlands; tel: 31-20-4628628; fax: 31-20-6639257; e-mail: info@niwi.knaw.nl; URL: http:// www.niwi.knaw.nl.

Linda Hall

The notation, Linda Hall, appearing in a serial entry indicates the availability of that serial for document delivery from Linda Hall Library of Science, Engineering and Technology.

For further information, contact: Document Services, Linda Hall Library, 5109 Cherry St., Kansas City, MO 64110-2498; tel: 800-662-1545, or 816-363-4600; fax: 816-926-8785; e-mail: requests@lhl.lib.mo.us; URL: http://www.lhl.lib.mo.us.

Petroleum Abstracts - Document Delivery Service (PADDS)

The notation, PADDS, appearing in a serial entry indicates the availability of that serial for document delivery through PADDS document delivery service, by permission from the copyright owner. Such permission is subject to change without notice.

For further information, contact Petroleum Abstracts - Document Delivery Service, University of Tulsa, McFarlin Library, 2933 E. 6th Street, Tulsa, OK 74104-3123, USA; tel: 800-247-8678; fax: 918-631-3823; e-mail: PADDS@TUred.pa.utulsa.edu.

SWETS

The notation, SWETS, appearing in a serial entry indicates the availability of that serial's table of contents in SwetScan, and document delivery through Swets, by permission from the copyright owner. Such permission is subject to change without notice.

For further information, contact Swets & Zeitlinger BV, Heereweg 347B, P.O. Box 830, 2160 SZ Lisse, The Netherlands; tel: 31-252-435111; fax: 31-252-415888; telex: 41325; e-mail: infoho@swets.nl; URL: http://www.swets.nl.

UMI

The notation, UMI, appearing in a serial entry indicates the availability of that serial for document delivery through UMI InfoStore service, by permission from the copyright owner. Such permission is subject to change without notice.

For further information, contact UMI InfoStore, 300 N. Zeeb Rd., P.O. Box 1346, Ann Arbor, MI 48106-1346, USA; tel: 800-248-0360 (US & Canada), fax: 313-761-1032; e-mail: orders@infostore.com.

The UnCover Company

The notation, UnCover, appearing in a serial entry indicates that the material is indexed in the UnCover database. Copies of articles are available through Uncover's document delivery service if the copyright owner has granted permission. Such permission is subject to change without notice.

For further information, contact the UnCover Co., 3801 E. Florida Ave., Ste. 200, Denver, CO 80210, USA; tel: 800-787-7979 (outside US & Canada: 303-758-3030); fax: 303-758-5946; e-mail: uncover@carl.org; URL: http://www.uncweb.carl.org.

Copyright Clearance Center, Inc.

The Copyright Clearance Center, Inc. (CCC) is a not-for-profit collective licensing organization. The CCC grants permissions to institutions and individuals to photocopy works of its registered publishers upon payment of publisher set royalties. The CCC does not supply copies of registered works directly to anyone.

The boldfaced **CCC** notation appears in the entries of titles for which the CCC has been authorized by the publisher to grant photocopy permissions through its Transactional Reporting Service (TRS). Additional titles may be available for certain publishers who have authorized the CCC to grant photocopy permissions on any of their works. The same inclusive country-wide coverage is available for publishers in the following countries: Canada, the Commonwealth of Independent States, Germany, New Zealand, Norway, and Spain. To register with the CCC, please contact TRS Customer Service, 222 Rosewood Dr., Danvers, MA 01923, USA; tel: 508-750-8400; fax: 508-750-4470; URL: http://www.copyright.com/

Brief Description

A brief description of the contents and editorial focus of the publication may be provided, preceded by the word **"Description:"** at the end of the entry. These descriptions were submitted by the publisher or were written by editorial staff after examination of sample copies or publisher catalogs.

Refereed Serial

The manuscript peer review and evaluation system is utilized to protect, maintain and raise the quality of scholarly material published in serials. If a serial is known to be refereed or juried, the notation "*Refereed Serial*" appears in italics at the end of the entry. This information is generally provided by the serial publisher.

Newspaper-Specific Data Elements

Ownership

The name of the owner(s) of a newspaper is listed, usually accompanied by the owner(s) address, and telephone and fax numbers. The owner address may differ from the newspaper location address. Owner information is preceded by the notation "Owner(s):."

Wire Services

If a newspaper is known to use one or more news or photo wire services, abbreviations or names of the services used are listed in the entry. Such information is preceded by the words "Wire Service(s):." Abbreviations for wire services used are listed on page xxxi of this volume.

Pages Per Issue; Columns Per Page

When known, the number of pages per issue (pp./issue:) and/or columns per page (cols./p.:) is/are noted.

Cataloging Rules for Main Entry Title

The majority of titles in the Bowker International Serials Database were cataloged according to *Anglo-American Cataloging Rules* prior to 1978, the date of the new edition of *Anglo-American Cataloging Rules*. The new *AACR II* reflects a trend toward the Key Title concept of cataloging as used by the International Serials Data System (ISDS) and published in its *International Standard Bibliographic Description for Serials* (1974).

Because recataloging a database the size of Bowker's was not feasible, our cataloging rules were modified but not radically changed. Cross-references are provided in the TITLE INDEX from variant forms of title, such as Key Title, to aid users searching by other methods.

Whenever possible, main entry title cataloging is done from a sample of the title page of the most recent issue, according to the following rules:

Articles at the beginning of titles are omitted, or are bypassed in filing.

Serials with distinctive titles are usually entered under title. For example:

Annual Bulletin of Historical Literature
Business Week
Milton Studies

If a title consists only of a generic term followed by the name of the issuing body, or if the name of the issuing body clarifies the content of the publication, entry is under the name of the issuing body. For example:

Newsletter of the American Theological Library Association

is entered as

American Theological Library Association. Newsletter

Economic Performance and Prospects, issued by the Private Development Corporation of the Philippines

is entered as

Private Development Corporation of the Philippines. Economic Performance and Prospects

A title which consists of a subject modified generic term followed by the name of the issuing body is considered nondistinctive and is entered under the name of the issuing body. For example:

Annual Meeting Scientific Proceedings of the American Animal Hospital Association

is entered as

American Animal Hospital Association. Annual Meeting Scientific Proceedings

Government publications with nondistinctive titles are entered under the name of the government jurisdiction of the issuing body, although distinctive titles of government organizations may be entered directly under title. For example:

Great Britain. Economic and Social Research Council. Annual Report

but

Statistical Abstract of Iceland

Titles which begin with the initials of the issuing body are entered under the initials. Cross-references from the full name are provided in the TITLE INDEX.

If a geographic name is part of the name of the issuing body, entry will be under the common form of the name of the body. For example:

University of the West Indies. Vice-Chancellor's Report

not

West Indies. University. Vice-Chancellor's Report

Note, however, that government publications retain similar cataloging as government jurisdiction.

Canada. Statistics Canada. Field Crop Reporting Series

Multilingual titles are entered under the first title given on the title page, or the first title reported by the publisher if the title page is not available. Titles in other languages are entered directly after the main entry title. Cross-references are provided in the TITLE INDEX for each language title.

FILING RULES

Due to the restrictions imposed by computer filing of titles, the following special filing rules should be noted.

Articles and prepositions within titles are alphabetized as words:

Journal of the West

precedes

Journal of Theological Studies

Hyphenated words are treated as separate words:

Pre-Text

precedes

Preaching

However, words indicating compass points (northeast, southwest, etc.) are filed as one word regardless of how printed:

Southeast Asia Builder
South-East Asia Stamp Catalogue
Southeast Dragster
South East Magazine

Titles entered under corporate author or government jurisdiction are sequenced before distinctive titles that begin with the same words:

British Columbia. Ministry of Energy, Mines and Petroleum Resources. Mineral Market Update

precedes

British Columbia Catholic

Acronyms and initials are treated as such and are listed at the beginning of each letter of the alphabet. Exceptions are the abbreviations of U.N. (United Nations), U.S. (United States), Gt. Britain (Great Britain), and St. (Saint), which are filed as words:

U R A M Newsletter
United Mutual Fund Sector
U.S. Environmental Protection Agency. Clean Water: Report to Congress

Titles in excess of 36 characters which are identical may not sort sequentially. The editors suggest that users scan the entire sequence of identical titles to locate specific entries.

Diacritical marks have been omitted. The German and Scandinavian umlaut has been replaced by the letter "e" following the vowels a, e, o, and u. In Danish, Norwegian and Swedish, the letter å is sequenced as "aa" and the letter ø as "oe."

International Standard Serial Number (ISSN)

1. What is the ISSN?

An internationally accepted, concise, unique, and unambiguous code for the identification of serial publications. One ISSN represents one serial title.

The ISSN consists of seven numbers with an eighth check digit calculated according to Modulus 11 and used to verify the number in computer processing. A hyphen is printed after the fourth digit, as a visual aid, and the acronym, ISSN, precedes the number.

2. How did the ISSN evolve as an international system?

The International Organization for Standardization Technical Committee 46 (ISO/TC 46) is the agency responsible for the development of the ISSN as an international standard. The organization responsible for the administration and coordination of ISSN assignments worldwide is the ISSN International Centre in Paris, which is supported by the French government and UNESCO.

ISSNs are assigned by over 50 national centers worldwide. The National Serials Data Program (NSDP) is the U.S. national center. The centers form a network which is coordinated by the ISSN International Centre located in Paris.

The implementation of the ISSN system started with the numbering of 70,000 titles in the serials database of R.R. Bowker (*Ulrich's International Periodicals Directory* and *Irregular Serials and Annuals*). The next serials database numbering was the *New Serials Titles 1950-70* cumulation listing 220,000 titles, cumulated, converted to magnetic tape, and published by R.R. Bowker in collaboration with the Serials Record Division of the Library of Congress. These two databases were used as the starting base for the implementation of the ISSN.

3. What types of publications are assigned ISSNs?

For assignment of an ISSN, a serial is defined as a publication in print or non-print form, issued in successive parts, usually having numerical or chronological designations, and intended to be continued indefinitely.

4. How is the ISSN used?

The ISSN is employed as a component of bar codes and as a tool for the communication of basic information about a serial title and for such processes as ordering, billing, inventory control, abstracting, and indexing. In library processes, the ISSN is used in operations such acquisitions, claiming, binding, accessioning, shelving, cooperative cataloguing, circulation, interlibrary loans, and retrieval of requests.

5. May a publication have an International Standard Book Number (ISBN) and an ISSN?

Yes! Monographic series (separate works issued indefinitely under a common title, generally in a uniform format with numeric designations) and annuals or titles planned to be issued indefinitely under the same title may be defined as serials. The ISSN is assigned to the serial title, while an ISBN is assigned to each individual title or monograph in the series.

A new ISBN is assigned to each volume or edition by the publisher, while the ISSN, which is assigned by the ISSN International Centre or national ISSN centers, remains the same for each issue. Both numbers should be printed on the copyright page or other appropriate page of each volume, with their acronyms or words preceding each number for immediate identification. With the availability of both an ISSN and ISBN, the problem of defining the overlap of serials and monographs has been resolved.

SAMPLE TITLE

Advances in the Biosciences
ISSN 0065-3446

Vol. 1 Proceedings: Berlin. Schering Symposium of Endocrinology, Berlin. Ed. by Gerhard Raspe. 1969. 40.00 (ISBN 0-08-013395-9). Pergamon.

Vol. 2 Proceedings. Schering Symposium on Biodynamics & Mechanisms of Action of Steroid Hormones, Berlin. Ed. by Gerhard Raspe. 1969. 41.25 (ISBN 0-08-006942-8). Pergamon.

Vol. 3 Proceedings. Schering Workshop on Steroid Metabolism "in Vitro Versus in Vivo," Berlin. Ed. by Gerhard Raspe. 1969. 41.25 (ISBN 0-08-017544-9). Pergamon.

Vol. 4 Proceedings. Schering Symposium on Mechanisms Involved in Conception. Berlin. Ed. by Gerhard Raspe. 1970. text ed. 41.25 (ISBN 0-08-017546-5). Pergamon.

Vol. 25 Development of Responsiveness to Steroid Hormones. Alvin M. Kaye & Myra Kaye et al. LC 79-42938. 1980. 66.00 (ISBN 0-08-024949-X). Pergamon.

6. Where should the ISSN appear on the serial?

In a prominent position on or in each issue of the serial, such as the front cover, back cover, masthead, title, or copyright pages. The international standard recommendation is that the ISSN of a periodical be printed, whenever possible, in the upper right corner of the front cover.

Promotional and descriptive materials about the serial should include the ISSN.

7. When a title changes, is a new ISSN assigned?

In most instances, a new ISSN is assigned when a title changes. However, the determination is made by the ISSN International Centre or the appropriate national ISSN centers. Publishers should report all the title changes to their respective centers.

8. How does a publisher apply for an ISSN?

The publisher should contact the appropriate national ISSN center or the ISSN International Centre. Centers require bibliographic evidence of a serial, including a copy of the title page and cover. There is no charge to publishers for the assignment of ISSNs.

For full information, publishers should contact the national library or bibliographic center in the country where they are publishing. The address of the ISSN International Centre is:

ISSN International Centre
20, rue Bachaumont
75002 Paris
France
Tel: +33 (1) 44 88 22 20
Fax: +33 (1) 40 26 32 43
Telex: 219847F
E-mail: issnic@issn.org
URL: http://www.issn.org

The address for the U.S. national ISSN center is:

National Serials Data Program (NSDP)
Library of Congress
Washington, DC 20540-4160
Tel: 202-707-6452
Fax: 202-707-6333
E-mail: ISSN@loc.gov
URL: http://lcweb.loc.gov/issn/

9. What is SISAC?

SISAC stands for the Serials Industry Systems Advisory Committee. SISAC is an industry group formed to develop voluntary standardized formats for electronically transmitting serials business transaction information. SISAC provides a forum where serial (particularly journal) publishers, library system vendors, and librarians can discuss mutual concerns regarding the electronic transmission of serial information and develop cooperative solutions, in the form of standardized formats, to efficiently address these concerns. *(Reprinted with permission from SISAC.)*

10. What is the SISAC Symbol (SICI) and its relationship to the ISSN?

The Serial Item and Contribution Identifier (SICI) is a serial identification code which follows the ISSN and is a string of letters and/or numbers which uniquely identify a particular issue of a serial. Encoded in the SICI are chronological and enumeration data which identify serials by date and volume/issue numbers. According to SISAC, "the ANSI* standard extends the code down to the article level by adding location number and necessary title information, plus a record validation character. Code 128 is the bar code symbology selected by SISAC for displaying this number string in scannable form. When displayed in the Code 128 symbology, the SICI is called the SISAC symbol." The SICI is the ANSI standard; the SISAC symbol is the bar code. *(Reprinted with permission from SISAC.)*

*ANSI American National Standards Institute. Organization that coordinates the voluntary standards system in the United States. U.S. member of the International Standards Organization (ISO).

Abbreviations

General Abbreviations and Special Symbols

a.	annual	no.	number
abstr.	abstracts	pat.	patents
adv.	advertising	play rev.	play reviews (theater reviews)
approx.	approximately	pp./issue	pages per issue
avail.	available	Prof.	Professor
bi-m.	bimonthly (every two months)	Pub., Pubs.	Publisher, Publishers
bi-w.	biweekly (every two weeks)	q.	quarterly
bibl.	bibliographies	R&P	Rights & Permissions
bk.rev.	book reviews	rec.rev.	record reviews
CCC	Copyright Clearance Center	s-a.	semiannually (twice annually)
c/o	care of	s-m.	semimonthly (twice monthly)
circ.	circulation	s-w.	semiweekly (twice weekly)
cols./p.	columns per page	stat.	statistics
cum.index	cumulative index	subscr.	subscription
Cy.	county	tele.rev.	television reviews
d.	daily	3/m.	3 times a month
dance rev.	dance reviews	3/yr.	3 times a year
Dir.	Director	tr.lit.	trade literature (manufacturers' catalogues, reader response cards)
dist.	distributed		
Ed., Eds.	Editor, Editors	tr.mk.	trade marks
Ed.Bd.	Editorial Board	URL	Uniform Resource Locator
film rev.	film reviews	video rev.	video reviews
fortn.	fortnightly (every two weeks)	vol.	volume
ISSN	International Standard Serial Number	w.	weekly
illus.	illustrations	*	not updated / unverified
irreg.	irregular	●	online and / or CD-ROM availability
m.	monthly	▼	new serial
mkt.	market prices	†	ceased
music rev.	music reviews		
N.S.	New Series		

Money Symbols

SYMBOL	UNIT	COUNTRY
	afghani	Afghanistan
	peso	Argentina
	dollar	Australia
	baht	Thailand
	dollar	Belize, Bermuda, Brunei Darussalam
	franc	Belgium
	balboa	Panama
	peso	Bolivia
	birr	Ethiopia
	bolivar	Venezuela
	bonus do tesouro nacional	Brazil
	bonus do tesouro nacional fiscal	Brazil
	cordoba; dollar; peso	Nicaragua, Cayman Islands, Cuba
	dollar	Canada
	franc	New Caledonia
	peso	Chile
	colon	Costa Rica, El Salvador
	peso	Colombia
	cruzerio	Brazil
	cruzado	Brazil
	dalasi	Gambia
h.	dirham	Morocco, United Arab Emirates
	krone	Denmark
	mark	Germany
	dinar	Algeria, Jordan, Kuwait, Libya, Tunisia, Yugoslavia
	dollar; peso	various
	drachma	Greece
	emalageni	Swaziland
	shilling	East Africa, Somalia, Tanzania, Uganda
	dollar	Dominica, Grenada, St. Lucia, Eastern Caribbean
	European currency unit	European Communities/European Union
	kroon	Estonia
	escudo	Angola, Cape Verde, Mozambique, Portugal
	franc	Djibouti, France, Guadeloupe, Mali, Martinique, Monaco, Rwanda
	dollar	Fiji
	markka	Finland
	guilder; florin	Netherlands, Netherlands Antilles, Surinam
	franc	Malagasy Republic
	mark; markka	Finland
	franc	Belgium, Liechtenstein, Luxembourg, Switzerland
	franc	African Financial Community, Benin, Burkina Faso, Burundi, Cameroon, Central African Republic, Chad, Congo, Gabon, Ivory Coast, Niger, Reunion, Senegal, Togo
	forint	Hungary
	guarani	Paraguay
	gourde	Haiti
	franc	Guinea
	dollar	Guyana
	dollar	Hong Kong
	kuna	Croatia
	pound	Ireland
	dinar	Iran, Iraq
	riyal	Iran
	shekel	Israel
	krona	Iceland
	dollar	Jamaica
	dollar	Jamaica
K.	kina; kwacha; kyat	Malawi, Papua New Guinea, Union of Myanmar (Burma), Zambia
Kc.	koruna	Czech Republic
Kcs.	koruny	Czechoslovakia
kip	kip	Laos
Kr.	krona; krone	Scandinavian countries
KShs.	shilling	Kenya
L.	lempira; lira	Honduras, Italy
Le.	leone	Sierra Leone
lek	lek	Albania
lei	lei	Rumania
Lit.	lira italiana	Italy
Ls.	lats	Latvia
Lt.	litas	Lithuania
lv.	lev	Bulgaria
M.$	dollar; ringgit	Malaysia
Mex.$	peso	Mexico
MKD	denar	Macedonia
$m.n.	moneda nacional	various
mt.	metical	Mozambique
N$	new Uruguay peso	Uruguay
NC.	cedi	Ghana
NOK	krone	Norway
NT.$	dollar	Republic of China (Taiwan)
N.Z.$	dollar	New Zealand
ORI.	riyal	Oman
P.	pula; pataca; peso	Botswana, Macao, Philippines, various
PG.	peso	Guinea-Bissau
QRI.	riyal	Qatar
£	pound	Ireland, Gt. Britain, Malta
£C	pound	Cyprus
£E	pound	Egypt
£L	pound; dinar	Lebanon
£N	pound; naira	Nigeria
£S	pound	Syria
ptas.	peseta	Spain
Q.	quetzal	Guatemala
R.	rand	South Africa, Lesotho, Namibia
RD.$	peso	Dominican Republic
Rps.	rupiah	Indonesia
Rs.	riel; rial; rupee	Cambodia, India, Iran, Mauritius, Nepal, Pakistan, Seychelles, Sri Lanka
Rub.	ruble	Commonwealth of Independent States
S/	sucre; sole	Ecuador, Peru
S.	schilling	Austria
S.$	dollar	Singapore, Western Samoa
SEK	krona	Sweden
SFr.	franc	Liechtenstein, Switzerland
SI$	dollar	Solomon Islands
SK.	koruna	Slovakia
SL.	pound	Sudan
SLT	talar	Slovenia
SRI.	riyal	Saudia Arabia
$T.	dollar	Tonga
TK.	taka	Bangladesh
TL.	pound; lira	Turkey
T.T.$	dollar	Trinidad and Tobago
tugrik	tugrik	Mongolia
UM	ouguiya	Mauritania
Urg.$	peso	Uruguay
vatu	vatu	Vanuatu
VN.$	dollar	Vietnam
Won	won (hwan)	Korea
Y	yuan	People's Republic of China
Yen	yen	Japan
YRI.	rial	Yemen
Z	zaire	Zaire
Z.$	dollar	Zimbabwe
Zl.	zloty	Poland

Country of Publication Codes

This list of countries and their codes has been taken from the list used by the Library of Congress in the MARC II format, 1992. The list used here is not the complete list of the MARC II format and is limited to countries and territories with publications listed in **Ulrich's**. The states of the United States, provinces and territories of Canada, and divisions of the United Kingdom are not listed separately.

The codes are mnemonic in most cases. Special codes not in the MARC format are used for publications of two international organizations: EI for European Communities and UN for United Nations and related organizations; and KR for Ukraine.

Country Code Sequence

AA	- ALBANIA	GD	- GRENADA	NZ	- NEW ZEALAND
AE	- ALGERIA	GE	- GERMANY, EAST	PE	- PERU
AF	- AFGHANISTAN	GH	- GHANA	PG	- GUINEA-BISSAU
AG	- ARGENTINA	GI	- GIBRALTAR	PH	- PHILIPPINES
AI	- ARMENIA	GL	- GREENLAND	PK	- PAKISTAN
AJ	- AZERBAIJAN	GM	- GAMBIA	PL	- POLAND
AN	- ANDORRA	GO	- GABON	PN	- PANAMA
AO	- ANGOLA	GP	- GUADELOUPE	PO	- PORTUGAL
AQ	- ANTIGUA	GR	- GREECE	PP	- PAPUA NEW GUINEA
AS	- AMERICAN SAMOA	GS	- GEORGIA	PR	- PUERTO RICO
AT	- AUSTRALIA	GT	- GUATEMALA	PY	- PARAGUAY
AU	- AUSTRIA	GU	- GUAM	QA	- QATAR
AY	- ANTARCTICA	GV	- GUINEA	RE	- REUNION
BA	- BAHRAIN	GW	- GERMANY	RH	- ZIMBABWE
BB	- BARBADOS	GY	- GUYANA	RM	- RUMANIA
BD	- BURUNDI	HK	- HONG KONG	RU	- RUSSIA
BE	- BELGIUM	HO	- HONDURAS	RW	- RWANDA
BF	- BAHAMAS	HT	- HAITI	SA	- SOUTH AFRICA
BG	- BANGLADESH	HU	- HUNGARY	SE	- SEYCHELLES
BH	- BELIZE	IC	- ICELAND	SF	- SAO TOME E PRINCIPE
BL	- BRAZIL	IE	- IRELAND	SG	- SENEGAL
BM	- BERMUDA	II	- INDIA	SI	- SINGAPORE
BN	- BOSNIA HERCEGOVINA	IO	- INDONESIA	SJ	- SUDAN
BO	- BOLIVIA	IQ	- IRAQ	SL	- SIERRA LEONE
BP	- SOLOMON ISLANDS	IR	- IRAN	SM	- SAN MARINO
BR	- UNION OF MYANMAR (FORMERLY BURMA)	IS	- ISRAEL	SO	- SOMALIA
		IT	- ITALY	SP	- SPAIN
BS	- BOTSWANA	IV	- IVORY COAST	SQ	- SWAZILAND
BT	- BHUTAN	JA	- JAPAN	SR	- SURINAM
BU	- BULGARIA	JM	- JAMAICA	SU	- SAUDI ARABIA
BW	- BELARUS	JO	- JORDAN	SW	- SWEDEN
BX	- BRUNEI DARUSSALAM	KE	- KENYA	SX	- NAMIBIA (FORMERLY SOUTH-WEST AFRICA)
CB	- CAMBODIA	KG	- KYRGYZSTAN		
CC	- CHINA, PEOPLE'S REPUBLIC OF	KN	- KOREA, NORTH	SY	- SYRIA
CD	- CHAD	KO	- KOREA, SOUTH	SZ	- SWITZERLAND
CE	- SRI LANKA	KR	- UKRAINE	TA	- TAJIKISTAN
CF	- CONGO (BRAZZAVILLE)	KU	- KUWAIT	TC	- TURKS AND CAICOS ISLANDS
CG	- CONGO, DEMOCRATIC REPUBLIC OF	KZ	- KAZAKHSTAN	TG	- TOGO
CH	- TAIWAN (REPUBLIC OF CHINA)	LB	- LIBERIA	TH	- THAILAND
CI	- CROATIA	LE	- LEBANON	TI	- TUNISIA
CJ	- CAYMAN ISLANDS	LH	- LIECHTENSTEIN	TK	- TURKMENISTAN
CK	- COLOMBIA	LI	- LITHUANIA	TO	- TONGA
CL	- CHILE	LO	- LESOTHO	TR	- TRINIDAD & TOBAGO
CM	- CAMEROON	LS	- LAOS	TS	- UNITED ARAB EMIRATES
CN	- CANADA	LU	- LUXEMBOURG	TU	- TURKEY
CQ	- COMOROS	LV	- LATVIA	TV	- TUVALU
CR	- COSTA RICA	LY	- LIBYA	TZ	- TANZANIA
CS	- CZECHOSLOVAKIA	MC	- MONACO	UA	- EGYPT (ARAB REPUBLIC OF EGYPT)
CU	- CUBA	MF	- MAURITIUS	UG	- UGANDA
CV	- CAPE VERDE	MG	- MADAGASCAR	UI	- UNITED KINGDOM MISC. ISLANDS
CX	- CENTRAL AFRICAN REPUBLIC	MH	- MACAO	UK	- UNITED KINGDOM
CY	- CYPRUS	MJ	- MONTSERRAT	UN	- UNITED NATIONS
DK	- DENMARK	MK	- OMAN	US	- UNITED STATES
DM	- BENIN	ML	- MALI	UV	- BURKINA FASO
DQ	- DOMINICA	MM	- MALTA	UY	- URUGUAY
DR	- DOMINICAN REPUBLIC	MP	- MONGOLIA	UZ	- UZBEKISTAN
EA	- ERITREA	MQ	- MARTINIQUE	VB	- BRITISH VIRGIN ISLANDS
EC	- ECUADOR	MR	- MOROCCO	VC	- VATICAN CITY
EG	- EQUATORIAL GUINEA	MU	- MAURITANIA	VE	- VENEZUELA
EI	- EUROPEAN COMMUNITIES/ EUROPEAN UNION	MV	- MOLDOVA	VI	- U.S. VIRGIN ISLANDS
		MW	- MALAWI	VN	- VIETNAM
ER	- ESTONIA	MX	- MEXICO	WS	- WESTERN SAMOA
ES	- EL SALVADOR	MY	- MALAYSIA	XC	- MALDIVE ISLANDS
ET	- ETHIOPIA	MZ	- MOZAMBIQUE	XE	- MARSHALL ISLANDS
FA	- FAEROE ISLANDS	NA	- NETHERLANDS ANTILLES	XI	- SAINT KITTS-NEVIS
FG	- FRENCH GUIANA	NE	- NETHERLANDS	XK	- SAINT LUCIA
FI	- FINLAND	NG	- NIGER	XM	- SAINT VINCENT
FJ	- FIJI	NL	- NEW CALEDONIA	XN	- MACEDONIA
FK	- FALKLAND ISLANDS	NN	- VANUATU (NEW HEBRIDES)	XO	- SLOVAKIA
FM	- FEDERATED STATES OF MICRONESIA	NO	- NORWAY	XR	- CZECH REPUBLIC
		NP	- NEPAL	XV	- SLOVENIA
FP	- FRENCH POLYNESIA	NQ	- NICARAGUA	YE	- YEMEN, REPUBLIC OF
FR	- FRANCE	NR	- NIGERIA	YU	- YUGOSLAVIA
FT	- DJIBOUTI	NU	- NAURU	ZA	- ZAMBIA
GB	- KIRIBATI	NX	- NORFOLK ISLAND	ZR	- ZAIRE

Country Sequence

AFGHANISTAN - AF
ALBANIA - AA
ALGERIA - AE
AMERICAN SAMOA - AS
ANDORRA - AN
ANGOLA - AO
ANTARCTICA - AY
ANTIGUA - AQ
ARGENTINA - AG
ARMENIA - AI
AUSTRALIA - AT
AUSTRIA - AU
AZERBAIJAN - AJ
BAHAMAS - BF
BAHRAIN - BA
BANGLADESH - BG
BARBADOS - BB
BELARUS - BW
BELGIUM - BE
BELIZE - BH
BENIN - DM
BERMUDA - BM
BHUTAN - BT
BOLIVIA - BO
BOSNIA HERCEGOVINA - BN
BOTSWANA - BS
BRAZIL - BL
BRITISH VIRGIN ISLANDS - VB
BRUNEI DARUSSALAM - BX
BULGARIA - BU
BURKINA FASO - UV
BURUNDI - BD
CAMBODIA - CB
CAMEROON - CM
CANADA - CN
CAPE VERDE - CV
CAYMAN ISLANDS - CJ
CENTRAL AFRICAN REPUBLIC - CX
CHAD - CD
CHILE - CL
CHINA, PEOPLE'S REPUBLIC OF - CC
COLOMBIA - CK
COMOROS - CQ
CONGO (BRAZZAVILLE) - CF
CONGO, DEMOCRATIC REPUBLIC OF - CG
COSTA RICA - CR
CROATIA - CI
CUBA - CU
CYPRUS - CY
CZECH REPUBLIC - XR
CZECHOSLOVAKIA - CS
DENMARK - DK
DJIBOUTI - FT
DOMINICA - DQ
DOMINICAN REPUBLIC - DR
ECUADOR - EC
EGYPT (ARAB REPUBLIC OF EGYPT) - UA
EL SALVADOR - ES
EQUATORIAL GUINEA - EG
ERITREA - EA
ESTONIA - ER
ETHIOPIA - ET
EUROPEAN COMMUNITIES/
    EUROPEAN UNION - EI
FAEROE ISLANDS - FA
FALKLAND ISLANDS - FK
FEDERATED STATES OF MICRONESIA - FM
FIJI - FJ
FINLAND - FI
FRANCE - FR
FRENCH GUIANA - FG
FRENCH POLYNESIA - FP
GABON - GO
GAMBIA - GM
GEORGIA - GS
GERMANY - GW
GERMANY, EAST - GE
GHANA - GH
GIBRALTAR - GI
GREECE - GR
GREENLAND - GL
GRENADA - GD
GUADELOUPE - GP
GUAM - GU
GUATEMALA - GT
GUINEA - GV
GUINEA-BISSAU - PG
GUYANA - GY
HAITI - HT
HONDURAS - HO
HONG KONG - HK
HUNGARY - HU
ICELAND - IC
INDIA - II
INDONESIA - IO
IRAN - IR
IRAQ - IQ
IRELAND - IE
ISRAEL - IS
ITALY - IT
IVORY COAST - IV
JAMAICA - JM
JAPAN - JA
JORDAN - JO
KAZAKHSTAN - KZ
KENYA - KE
KIRIBATI - GB
KOREA, NORTH - KN
KOREA, SOUTH - KO
KUWAIT - KU
KYRGYZSTAN - KG
LAOS - LS
LATVIA - LV
LEBANON - LE
LESOTHO - LO
LIBERIA - LB
LIBYA - LY
LIECHTENSTEIN - LH
LITHUANIA - LI
LUXEMBOURG - LU
MACAO - MH
MACEDONIA - XN
MADAGASCAR - MG
MALAWI - MW
MALAYSIA - MY
MALDIVE ISLANDS - XC
MALI - ML
MALTA - MM
MARSHALL ISLANDS - XE
MARTINIQUE - MQ
MAURITANIA - MU
MAURITIUS - MF
MEXICO - MX
MOLDOVA - MV
MONACO - MC
MONGOLIA - MP
MONTSERRAT - MJ
MOROCCO - MR
MOZAMBIQUE - MZ
NAMIBIA (FORMERLY SOUTH-
    WEST AFRICA)- SX
NAURU - NU
NEPAL - NP
NETHERLANDS - NE
NETHERLANDS ANTILLES - NA
NEW CALEDONIA - NL
NEW ZEALAND - NZ
NICARAGUA - NQ
NIGER - NG
NIGERIA - NR
NORFOLK ISLAND - NX
NORWAY - NO
OMAN - MK
PAKISTAN - PK
PANAMA - PN
PAPUA NEW GUINEA - PP
PARAGUAY - PY
PERU - PE
PHILIPPINES - PH
POLAND - PL
PORTUGAL - PO
PUERTO RICO - PR
QATAR - QA
REUNION - RE
RUMANIA - RM
RUSSIA - RU
RWANDA - RW
SAINT KITTS-NEVIS - XI
SAINT LUCIA - XK
SAINT VINCENT - XM
SAN MARINO - SM
SAO TOME E PRINCIPE - SF
SAUDI ARABIA - SU
SENEGAL - SG
SEYCHELLES - SE
SIERRA LEONE - SL
SINGAPORE - SI
SLOVAKIA - XO
SLOVENIA - XV
SOLOMON ISLANDS - BP
SOMALIA - SO
SOUTH AFRICA - SA
SPAIN - SP
SRI LANKA - CE
SUDAN - SJ
SURINAM - SR
SWAZILAND - SQ
SWEDEN - SW
SWITZERLAND - SZ
SYRIA - SY
TAIWAN (REPUBLIC OF CHINA) - CH
TAJIKISTAN - TA
TANZANIA - TZ
THAILAND - TH
TOGO - TG
TONGA - TO
TRINIDAD & TOBAGO - TR
TUNISIA - TI
TURKEY - TU
TURKMENISTAN - TK
TURKS AND CAICOS ISLANDS - TC
TUVALU - TV
U.S. VIRGIN ISLANDS - VI
U.S.S.R. - UR
UGANDA - UG
UKRAINE - KR
UNION OF MYANMAR (FORMERLY
    BURMA) - BR
UNITED ARAB EMIRATES - TS
UNITED STATES - US
UNITED NATIONS - UN
UNITED KINGDOM - UK
UNITED KINGDOM MISC. ISLANDS - UI
URUGUAY - UY
UZBEKISTAN - UZ
VANUATU (NEW HEBRIDES) - NN
VATICAN CITY - VC
VENEZUELA - VE
VIETNAM - VN
WESTERN SAMOA - WS
YEMEN, REPUBLIC OF - YE
YUGOSLAVIA - YU
ZAIRE - ZR
ZAMBIA - ZA
ZIMBABWE - RH

Document Suppliers

ADONIS ADONIS B.V. (main office)
Spuistraat 112D
1012 VA Amsterdam
The Netherlands
Tel: 31-20-6262629
Fax: 31-20-6261437

ADONIS USA
350 Main St., 6th fl.
Malden, MA 02148-5018
USA
Tel: 800-944-6415
Fax: 617-388-8272
E-mail: infousa@adonis.nl
URL: http://www.adonis.nl

Ask*IEEE Ask*IEEE
75 Varick St., 9th fl.
New York, NY 10013
USA
Tel: 800-949-4333 (Canada & US), or 212-301-4100
Fax: 212-301-4090
E-mail: askieee@ieee.org

BLDSC British Library Document Supply Centre
Customer Services
Boston Spa, Wetherby
W. Yorkshire LS23 7BQ
England
Tel: 44-1937-546060
Fax: 44-1937-546333
E-mail: dsc-customer-services@bl.uk

CASDDS CAS Client Services
Document Detective Service
2540 Olentangy River Rd.
P.O. Box 3012
Columbus, OH 43210-0012
USA
Tel: 800-631-1884; 614-447-3870
Fax: 614-447-3648
E-mail: dds@cas.org
URL: http://www.cas.org/Support/dds.html

CINDOC CINDOC Suministro de Documentos Service
Joaquín Costa, 22
28002 Madrid
Spain
Fax: 34-1-5642644
E-mail: bib-icyt@bib.csic.es

CIS Congressional Information Service, Inc.
CIS Documents on Demand
4520 East-West Hwy., Ste. 800
Bethesda, MD 20814-3389
USA
Tel: 301-654-1550, 800-227-2477
Fax: 301-654-4033
E-mail: EAINET@US.NET
URL: http://www.cispubs.com

CISTI Canada Institute for Scientific and Technical Information
Document Delivery, CISTI
National Research Council Canada
Ottawa K1A 0S2
Canada
Tel: 800-668-1222 (Canada & US), or 613-993-9251
Fax: 613-993-7619
E-mail: cisti.docdel@nrc.ca

Ei Engineering Information Inc.
Ei Text
One Castle Point Terrace
Hoboken, NJ 07030-5996
USA
Tel: 800-221-1044 (USA & Canada), 201-216-8500
Fax: 201-216-8557
E-mail: eitext@ei.org
URL: http://www.ei.org

EMDOCS EMDOCS: The EMBASE Document Delivery Service
75 Varick St., 9th fl.
New York, NY 10013
USA
Tel: 800-282-2720, 212-301-4003
Fax: 212-301-4060
E-mail: dds@work4u.artx.com

Genuine Article The Institute for Scientific Information
ISI Document Solution
3501 Market St.
Philadelphia, PA 19104
USA
Tel: 215-386-4399
Fax: 215-386-4343
E-mail: tga@isinet.com

Haworth The Haworth Press, Inc.
Haworth Document Delivery Service
10 Alice St.
Binghamton, NY 13904-1580
USA
Tel: 800-HAWORTH
Fax: 800-895-0582
E-mail: getinfo@haworth.com

DOCUMENT SUPPLIERS

KNAW
NIWI (Netherlands Institute of Scientific Information Services)
Customer Service
P.O. Box 95180
1090 HD Amsterdam
The Netherlands
Tel: 31-20-4628628
Fax: 31-20-6639257
E-mail: info@niwi.knaw.nl
URL: http://www.niwi.knaw.nl

KR SourceOne
KR SourceOne
75 Varick St., 9th fl.
New York, NY 10013
USA
Tel: 800-239-3458 (Canada & USA), or 212-301-4000
Fax: 212-301-4060
E-mail: dds@work4u.artx.com
URL: http://www.krinfo.com/krsourceone/

Linda Hall
Linda Hall Library
Document Services
5109 Cherry St.
Kansas City, MO 64110-2498
USA
Tel: 800-662-1545, 816-363-4600
Fax: 816-926-8785
E-mail: requests@lhl.lib.mo.us
URL: http://www.lhl.lib.mo.us

PADDS
Petroleum Abstracts - Document Delivery Service
University of Tulsa, McFarlin Library
2933 E. 6th St.
Tulsa, OK 74104-3123
USA
Tel: 800-247-8678
Fax: 918-631-3823
E-mail: PADDS@TUred.pa.utulsa.edu

SWETS
Swets & Zeitlinger bv
Heereweg 347B
P.O. Box 830
2160 SZ Lisse
The Netherlands
Tel: 31-252-435111
Fax: 31-252-415888
Telex: 41325
E-mail: infoho@swets.nl
URL: http://www.swets.nl

UMI
UMI InfoStore
300 N. Zeeb Rd.
P.O. Box 1346
Ann Arbor, MI 48106-1346
USA
Tel: 800-248-0360 (USA & Canada)
Fax: 313-761-1032
E-mail: orders@infostore.com

UnCover
The UnCover Co.
3801 E. Florida Ave., Ste. 200
Denver, CO 80210
USA
Tel: 800-787-7979,
(outside US & Canada: 303-758-3030)
Fax: 303-758-5946
E-mail: uncover@carl.org
URL: http://uncweb.carl.org

Micropublishers and Distributors

ACR   **A.C.R.P.P.**
(Association pour la Conservation et la
Reproduction Photographique de la Presse)
B.P. 21
77313 Marne-La-Vallee Cedex 2
France
Tel: 33-1-60-17-68-10; **Fax:** 33-1-60-17-68-05

ADL   **Advanced Library Systems, Inc.**
100 Brickstone Sq.
P.O. Box 246
Andover, MA 01810-0005
USA
Tel: 508-470-0610; **Fax:** 508-472-1072

AFS   **Fertility and Sterility**
(no longer producer)
2140 11 Ave. S., Ste. 200
Birmingham, AL 35205-2800
USA
Tel: 205-933-8494; **Fax:** 205-930-9904

AGU   **American Geophysical Union**
2000 Florida Ave., N.W.
Washington, DC 20009
USA
Tel: 202-462-6900; **Fax:** 202-328-0566
E-mail: Serv@kosmos.agu.org

AIP   **American Institute of Physics**
500 Sunnyside Blvd.
Woodbury, NY 11797-2999
USA
Tel: 516-576-2270; **Fax:** 516-349-9704

AIR   **Aircraft Technical Publishers**
101 S. Hill Dr.
Brisbane, CA 94005-1203
USA
Tel: 415-468-1705; **Fax:** 415-468-1596
E-mail: inf@ATP.com

AJP   **American Jewish Periodical Center**
Hebrew Union College - Jewish Institute
of Religion
3101 Clifton Ave.
Cincinnati, OH 45220
USA
Tel: 513-221-1875; **Fax:** 513-221-0519

ALP   **Alpha Com**
Sportallee 6
22335 Hamburg
Germany
Tel: 49-40-51302-123; **Fax:** 49-40-51302111

AMP   **Adam Matthew Publications**
8 Oxford St.
Marlborough, Wiltshire SN8 1AP
England
Tel: 44-1672-511921; **Fax:** 44-1672-511663

AMS   **AMS Press, Inc.**
(no longer producer)
56 E. 13th St.
New York, NY 10003
USA
Tel: 212-777-4700; **Fax:** 212-995-5413

ATL   **American Theological Library
Association, Preservation Board**
820 Church St., Ste. 400
Evanston, IL 60201
USA
Tel: 847-869-7788; **Fax:** 847-869-8513
E-mail: atla.atla.com

BHP   **Brookhaven Press**
P.O. Box 2287
La Crosse, WI 54602-2287
USA
Tel: 608-781-0850; **Fax:** 608-781-3883

BIO   **BIOSIS**
2100 Arch St.
Philadelphia, PA 19103-1399
USA
Tel: 215-587-4800, 800-523-4806
Fax: 215-587-2041

BKR   **Bowker A&I Publishing**
(See: CIS)

BLC   **Bloch & Company**
P.O. Box 18058
Cleveland, OH 44118
USA
Tel: 216-371-0979

BLH   **Bell & Howell**
(Micropublishing now operated by UMI)

BLI   **Balch Institute**
Research Library
18 S. 7th St.
Philadelphia, PA 19106
USA
Tel: 215-925-8090; **Fax:** 215-925-8195
E-mail: balchlib@hslc.org

BNB   **British Library National Bibliographic Service**
Boston Spa, Wetherby
W. Yorkshire LS23 7BQ
England
Tel: 44-1937-546585; **Fax:** 44-1937-546586

BNQ   **Bibliotheque Nationale du Quebec
Section de la Reproduction**
3275 Holt
Montreal, PQ H2J 3H1
Canada
Tel: 514-873-1100; **Fax:** 514-873-9932

MICROPUBLISHERS AND DISTRIBUTORS

BWC   **Butterworth & Co., Ltd.**
88 Kingsway
London WC2B 6AB
England
Tel: 44-171-4056900; **Fax:** 44-171-4051332

CDS   **Current Digest of the Past-Soviet Press**
3857 N. High St.
Columbus, OH 43214
USA
Tel: 614-292-4234; **Fax:** 614-267-6310

CHL   **Chadwyck-Healey Ltd.**
The Quorum, Barnwell Rd.
Cambridge CB5 8SW
England
Tel: 44-1223-215512; **Fax:** 44-1223-515514
E-mail: mail@chadwyck.co.uk

Chadwyck-Healey Inc.
1101 King St.
Alexandria, VA 22314-2944
USA
Tel: 703-683-4890; **Fax:** 703-683-7589
E-mail: mktg@chadwyck.com

CIS   **Congressional Information Service, Inc.**
4520 East-West Hwy., Ste. 800
Bethesda, MD 20814-3389
USA
Tel: 301-654-1550, 800-638-8380
Fax: 301-654-4033

CLA   **Canadian Library Association**
(no longer producer)
Microfilm Department
200 Elgin St., Ste. 602
Ottawa, ON K2P 1L5
Canada
Tel: 613-232-9625; **Fax:** 613-563-9895

CLS   **CLASS**
(Cooperative Library Agency for
Systems & Services)
1415 Koll Circle, Ste. 101
San Jose, CA 95112-4698
USA
Tel: 510-444-1011; **Fax:** 510-453-5379

CMC   **Computer Microfilm Corp.**
3655 Wheeler Ave.
Alexandria, VA 22304
USA
Tel: 703-461-4400; **Fax:** 703-461-0042

CML   **Commonwealth Microfilm Products**
202 Amber St.
Markham, ON L3R 3J8
Canada
Tel: 905-415-9498; **Fax:** 905-415-9616

EDR   **Eric Document Reproduction Service**
(See: CMC)

EEE   **Institute of Electrical and Electronics Engineers Inc.**
345 E. 47th St.
New York, NY 10017
USA
Tel: 212-705-7900; **Fax:** 212-705-7682

EMP   **Emmett Publishing, Ltd.**
W. House 21, West St.
Haslemere, Surrey GU27 2AB
England
Tel: 44-1428-654443; **Fax:** 44-1428-661582

FCM   **Fairchild Books & Visuals**
7 W. 34th St.
New York, NY 10001
USA
Tel: 212-630-3880; **Fax:** 212-630-3868

GCS   **Preston Publications**
6600 W. Touhy Ave.
P.O. Box 48312
Niles, IL 60714
USA
Tel: 847-647-2900; **Fax:** 847-647-1155

GMC   **General Microfilm Co.**
(acquired by OMNISYS Corp.)

HPL   **Harvester Press Microfilm Publications Ltd.**
(Now wholly owned and operated
by Primary Source Media)

IAM   **SIAM Publications**
3600 University City Science Center
Philadelphia, PA 19104-2688
USA
Tel: 215-382-9800; **Fax:** 215-386-7999

ICS   **Editions I.C.S.**
23 Ave. Villemain
75014 Paris
France
Tel: 33-1-45392244; **Fax:** 33-1-45434680

IDC   **IDC Microform Publishers bv**
P.O. Box 11205
2301 EE Leiden
The Netherlands
Tel: 31-71-5142700; **Fax:** 31-71-5131721

IFA   **International Federation of Film Archives (FIAF)**
6 Nottingham St.
London W1M 3RB
England
Tel: 44-171-2240991; **Fax:** 44-171-2241203

ILO   **ILO Publications**
P.O. Box 753
Waldorf, MD 20604
USA
Tel: 301-638-3152; **Fax:** 301-843-0159

IMI   **Irish Microforms, Ltd.**
Unit 56
Sandyford Industrial Estate
Dublin 18
Ireland
Tel: 353-1-2893626; **Fax:** 353-1-2954270

IPC   **Institute of Paper Science & Technology, Inc.**
500 Tenth St. N.W.
Atlanta, GA 30318
USA
Tel: 404-894-5700; **Fax:** 404-894-4778

MICROPUBLISHERS AND DISTRIBUTORS

IRE   International Research and Evaluation
21098 IRE-Control Center
Eagan, MN 55121-0098
USA
Tel: 612-888-9635; Fax: 612-888-9124

ISI   Institute for Scientific Information
3501 Market St.
Philadelphia, PA 19104
USA
Tel: 215-386-0100
Fax: 215-386-6362, 215-386-2911

JOH   Johnson Reprint Microeditions
(Out of business)

JSC   J.S. Canner & Co.
(Ceased operations)
10 Charles St.
Needham Heights, MA 02194
USA
Tel: 617-449-9103; Fax: 617-449-1767

KHS   Kansas State Historical Society
Microfilm Publications
6425 S.W. Sixth Ave.
Topeka, KS 66615-1099
USA
Tel: 913-272-8681; Fax: 913-272-8682

KTO   Kraus Microform
(Micropublishing now operated by
Norman Ross Publishing, Inc.)

LCP   The Library of Congress
Photoduplication Service
Washington, DC 20540-5230
USA
Tel: 202-707-5640; Fax: 202-707-1771

LIB   Library Microfilms
1115 E. Arques Ave.
Sunnyvale, CA 94086
USA
Tel: 408-736-7444; Fax: 408-736-4397

LOP   Lomond Publications
7101 Woodville Rd.
Mt. Airy, MD 21771
USA
Tel: 301-694-0123, 800-443-6299

MCA   Microfilming Corporation of America
(Acquired by UMI;
operation phased out)

MCE   Microcard Editions
(See: CIS)

MEL   Metropolitan Library Service Agency
(MELSA)
570 Asbury St., Ste. 201
St. Paul, MN 55104-1849
USA
Tel: 612-645-5731; Fax: 612-649-3169

MIM   Elsevier Science Ltd.
The Blvd., Langford Ln.
Kidlington, Oxford OX5 1GB
England
Tel: 44-1865-843000; Fax: 44-1865-843010

MIS   Moody's Investors Service
Sales Department
99 Church St.
New York, NY 10007
USA
Tel: 212-553-0300; Fax: 212-553-4700

MML   Micromedia Limited
20 Victoria St.
Toronto, ON M5C 2N8
Canada
Tel: 416-362-5211, 800-387-2689
Fax: 416-362-6161
E-mail: info@micromedia.on.ca

MMP   McLaren Micropublishing Ltd.
P.O. Box 972, Sta. F
Toronto, ON M4Y 2N9
Canada
Tel: 416-960-4801; Fax: 416-964-3745

MUE   University Music Editions
Div. of High Density Systems, Inc.
P.O. Box 192, Ft. George Sta.
New York, NY 10040
USA
Tel: 212-569-5340, 5393; Fax: 212-569-1269

NBI   Newsbank, Inc.
58 Pine St.
New Canaan, CT 06840
USA
Tel: 203-966-1100, 800-762-8182
Fax: 203-966-6254

NRP   Norman Ross Publishing, Inc.
330 W. 58th St., Ste. 214
New York, NY 10019
USA
Tel: 212-765-8200, 800-648-8850
Fax: 212-765-2393
E-mail: inf@nross.com

NTI   National Technical Information Service
5285 Port Royal Rd.
Springfield, VA 22161
USA
Tel: 703-487-4600; Fax: 703-321-8547

NYL   New York Law Publishing Co.
345 Park Ave., S.
New York, NY 10010
USA
Tel: 212-779-9200; Fax: 212-481-8110

NYT   New York Times Information Bank
(Operation phased out)
229 W. 43rd St.
New York, NY 10036
USA
Tel: 212-556-1234

MICROPUBLISHERS AND DISTRIBUTORS

OEC   Organization for Economic Cooperation & Development, Publications & Information Center
2001 L St., N.W., Ste. 650
Washington, DC 20036-4910
USA
Tel: 202-785-6323; **Fax:** 202-785-0350

OMN   OMNISYS Corp.
32 Wexford St.
Needham Heights, MA 02194
USA
Tel: 617-444-4123; **Fax:** 617-444-5590

OMP   Oxford Microform Publication Ltd.
(Acquired by UMI)

PMC   Princeton Microfilm Corp.
P.O. Box 2073
Princeton, NJ 08543
USA
Tel: 609-452-2066, 800-257-9502
Fax: 609-275-6201

PSL   The Pretoria State Library
P.O. Box 397
Pretoria 0001
Republic of South Africa
Tel: 27-12-218931; **Fax:** 27-12-3255984

RPI   Primary Source Media
12 Lunar Dr.
Woodbridge, CT 06525
USA
Tel: 203-397-2600, 800-444-0799
Fax: 203-397-3893

RRI   Fred B. Rothman & Co.
10368 W. Centennial Rd.
Littleton, CO 80127
USA
Tel: 303-979-5657, 800-457-1986
Fax: 303-978-1457

SAL   South African Library
P.O. Box 469
Capetown 8000
Republic of South Africa
Tel: 27-21-246320; **Fax:** 27-21-244848

SAS   Society for Applied Spectroscopy
201-B Broadway St.
Frederick, MD 21701
USA
Tel: 301-694-8122; **Fax:** 301-694-6860

SOC   Societe Canadienne du Microfilm Inc. - Canadian Microfilming Co. Ltd.
464 rue Saint-Jean
Montreal, PQ H2Y 2S1
Canada
Tel: 514-288-5404; **Fax:** 514-843-4690

SWZ   Swets & Zeitlinger bv
Backsets Department
P.O. Box 810
2160 SZ Lisse
The Netherlands
Tel: 31-252-435111; **Fax:** 31-252-415888
URL: http://www.swets.nl

TMI   Tennessee Microfilms
P.O. Box 23075
Nashville, TN 37202
USA
Tel: 615-242-3632

UMI   University Microfilms International
(A Bell & Howell Company)
300 N. Zeeb Rd.
Ann Arbor, MI 48103
USA
Tel: 313-761-4700, 800-521-0600, 800-864-0019
Fax: 313-761-1203
E-mail: T.Youst@UMI.com

UPD   Updata Publications, Inc.
1736 Westwood Blvd.
Los Angeles, CA 90024
USA
Tel: 310-474-5900; **Fax:** 310-474-4095

VCI   VCH Publishers, Inc.
303 N.W. 12th Ave.
Deerfield Beach, FL 33442-1788
USA
Tel: 305-428-5566
Fax: 305-428-8201, 800-367-8247

VFN   Voltaire Foundation Ltd.
99 Banbury Rd.
Oxford OX2 6JX
England
Tel: 44-1865-284600; **Fax:** 44-1865-284610

WDS   Dawson Microfiche
(Distributor only)
Cannon House
Parkfarm Rd.
Folkestone, Kent CT19 5EE
England
Tel: 44-1303-850101; **Fax:** 44-1303-850440

WMP   World Microfilm Publications Ltd
Microworld House, 2-6 Foscote Mews
London W9 2HH
England
Tel: 44-171-2662202; **Fax:** 44-171-2662314

WSH   William S. Hein & Co., Inc.
Hein Bldg., 1285 Main St.
Buffalo, NY 14209-1987
USA
Tel: 716-882-2600, 800-828-7571
Fax: 716-883-8100

WWS   Williams & Wilkins
351 W. Camden St.
Baltimore, MD 21201
USA
Tel: 410-528-8555, 800-638-6423
Fax: 410-528-8596

Reprint Services

CIS   **Congressional Information Service, Inc.**
4520 East-West Hwy., Ste. 800
Bethesda, MD 20814-3389
USA
Tel: 301-654-1550, 800-638-8380
Fax: 301-657-3203

CMC   **Computer Microfilm Corp.**
3655 Wheeler Ave.
Alexandria, VA 22304
USA
Tel: 703-461-4400
Fax: 703-461-0042

HAW   **The Haworth Press**
10 Alice St.
Binghamton, NY 13904
USA
Tel: 607-722-5857
Fax: 607-722-1424

IRC   **International Reprint Corp.**
968 Admiral Callaghan Ln., #268
Vallejo, CA 94590
USA
Tel: 707-746-8740
Fax: 707-746-1643
E-mail: reprints@intlreprints.com

ISI   **Institute for Scientific Information**
3501 Market St.
Philadelphia, PA 19104
USA
Tel: 215-386-0100
Fax: 215-386-6362, 215-386-2911

JOH   **Johnson Reprint Microeditions**
(out of business)

KTO   **Kraus Microform**
(reprint service acquired by
Periodicals Service Co., PSC)

NRP   **Norman Ross Publishing, Inc.**
330 W. 58th St., Ste. 214
New York, NY 10019
USA
Tel: 212-765-8200, 800-648-8850
Fax: 212-765-2393
E-mail: inf@nross.com

NTI   **National Technical Information Service**
5285 Port Royal Rd.
Springfield, VA 22161
USA
Tel: 703-487-4600
Fax: 703-321-8547

PSC   **Periodicals Service Co.**
11 Main St.
Germantown, NY 12526
USA
Tel: 518-537-4700
Fax: 518-537-5899

RPI   **Primary Source Media**
12 Lunar Dr.
Woodbridge, CT 06525
USA
Tel: 203-397-2600, 800-444-0799
Fax: 203-397-3893

RRI   **Fred B. Rothman & Co.**
10368 W. Centennial Rd.
Littleton, CO 80127
USA
Tel: 303-979-5657, 800-457-1986
Fax: 303-978-1457

SCH   **Schmidt Periodicals GmbH**
Dettendorf
D 83075 Bad Feilnbach
Germany
Tel: 49-8064221
Fax: 49-8064557

SWZ   **Swets & Zeitlinger bv**
Backsets Department
P.O. Box 810
2160 SZ Lisse
The Netherlands
Tel: 31-252-43511
Fax: 31-252-415888
Telex: 41325
URL: http://www.swets.nl

UMI   **University Microfilms International**
(A Bell & Howell Company)
300 N. Zeeb Rd.
Ann Arbor, MI 48103
USA
Tel: 313-761-4700, 800-521-0600
Fax: 313-761-1203
E-mail: T.Youst@UMI.com

WDS   **Dawson Microfiche**
Cannon House
Parkfarm Rd.
Folkestone, Kent CT19 5EE
England
Tel: 44-1303-85010
Fax: 44-1303-850440

WSH   **William S. Hein & Co., Inc.**
Hein Bldg., 1285 Main St.
Buffalo, NY 14209-1987
USA
Tel: 716-882-2600, 800-828-7571
Fax: 716-883-8100

Wire Services

- Australian Associated Press Information Services
- Agence France-Press
- Algemeen Nederlands Persbureau (Netherlands Press Agency)
- Associated Press (USA)
- Associated Press of Pakistan
- Baltic News Service
- Canadian Press
- Agencia EFE (Spain)
- Knight-Ridder Financial News
- Los Angeles Times-Washington Post News Service
- New Zealand Associated Press
- New York Times News Service
- Polska Agencja Prasowa (Polish Press Agency)
- Pakistan Press International
- Reuters News Agency
- South African Press Association
- Scripps-Howard Newspaper Alliance - Scripps-Howard News Service
- Telegrafnoe Agentstvo Suverennykh Stran (Telegraphic Agency of the Sovereign Countries)
- United Kingdom News
- United Press International

Abstracting and Indexing Services

This list contains the full names of all abstracting and indexing services whose abbreviations are used in entries in the CLASSIF[IED] LIST OF SERIALS. For all currently published abstracting and indexing services, entries containing full bibliographic informatio[n] be found in the CLASSIFIED LIST OF SERIALS. Consult the TITLE INDEX for page numbers. (Bibliographic information on title[s] which cessations were noted more than three years ago are not listed in this book. To view information on such titles, one must [refer] to Ulrich's™ *on Disc* or Ulrich's Online services.)

A

A.A.P.P.Abstr.	Amino Acids, Peptides & Proteins Abstracts (Now: Cambridge Scientific Biochemistry Abstracts, Part 3: Amino Acids, Peptides & Proteins) (Ceased)
AAR	Accounting Articles
ABC	Abstracts in BioCommerce
A.B.C.Pol.Sci.	ABC Pol Sci; A Bibliography of Contents: Political Science and Government
ABI Inform.	A B I - INFORM
ABTICS	Abstracts and Book Title Index Card Services (Ceased)
A.D.& D.	Alcohol, Drugs and Driving: Abstracts and Reviews (Now: Alcohol, Drugs and Driving)
AESIS	A E S I S Quarterly (Australian Earth Sciences Information System)
A.I.Abstr.	Artificial Intelligence Abstracts (United States) (Ceased)
A.I.C.P.	Anthropological Index to Current Periodicals in the Library of the Museum of Mankind Library
A.I.D.Res.Dev.Abstr.	A.I.D. Research & Development Abstracts (Agency for International Development)
AIDS Abstr.	AIDS Abstracts
AIM	Abridged Index Medicus
A.I.P.P.	Annual Index to Poetry in Periodicals (Now: Roth's American Poetry Annual) (Ceased)
AIT Reports	A I T Reports and Publications on Renewable Energy Resources. Abstracts (Asian Institute of Technology) (Now: A I T Reports and Publications on Energy. Abstracts)
ALISA	A L I S A (Australian Library and Information Science Abstracts)
API Abstr.	A P I Abstracts: Literature (American Petroleum Institute) (Now: Technica[l] Literature Abstracts)
API Catal.	A P I Abstracts: Catalysts & Catalysis (Now: Technical Literature Abstract[s]: Catalysts - Zeolites)
API Hlth.& Environ.	A P I Abstracts: Health & Environment (Now: Technical Literature Abstract[s]: Health & Environment)
API Oil.	A P I Abstracts: Oilfield Chemicals (No[w]: Technical Literature and Abstracts: Oilfield Chemicals)
API Pet.Ref.	A P I Abstracts: Petroleum Refining an[d] Petrochemicals (Now: Technical Literature Abstracts: Petroleum Ref[ining] and Petrochemicals)
API Pet.Subst.	A P I Abstracts: Petroleum Substitutes (Now: Technical Literature Abstract[s]: Petroleum Substitutes)
API Transport.	A P I Abstracts: Transportation and Storage (Now: Technical Literature Abstracts: Transportation and Stora[ge])
A.S.& T.Ind.	Applied Science & Technology Index
ASCA	Automatic Subject Citation Alert (Now Research Alert (Philadelphia))
ASEAN Manage. Abstr.	A S E A N Management Abstracts (Association of South East Asian Nations)
ASSIA	A S S I A: Applied Social Sciences In[dex] Abstracts
ASTIS	A S T I S Bibliography (Arctic Science Technology Information System)
Abr.R.G.	Abridged Readers' Guide to Periodica[l] Literature
Abstr.Anthropol.	Abstracts in Anthropology
Abstr.Bk.Rev.Curr.Leg.Per.	Abstracts of Book Reviews in Curren[t] Legal Periodicals (Ceased)

ostr.Bulg.Sci.Med.Lit.	Abstracts of Bulgarian Scientific Medical Literature	AgroLibex	Agro-Libex
		AgroAgen	Agro-Agen
ostr.Bull.Inst.Pap.Chem.	Institute of Paper Chemistry. Abstract Bulletin (Now: Institute of Paper Science and Technology. Abstract Bulletin)	Agroforest.Abstr.	Agroforestry Abstracts
		Air Un.Lib.Ind.	Air University Library Index to Military Periodicals
		Alloys Ind.	Alloys Index
str.Crim.&en.	Abstracts on Criminology and Penology (Now: Criminology, Penology & Police Science Abstracts)	Alt.Press Ind.	Alternative Press Index
		Amer.Bibl.Slavic & E.Ear.Stud.	American Bibliography of Slavic and East European Studies
str.Engl.Stud.	Abstracts of English Studies (Ceased)	Amer.Hist.& Life	America: History & Life
str.Folk.Stud.	Abstracts of Folklore Studies (Ceased)		
str.Health are Manage. tud.	Abstracts of Health Care Management Studies (Ceased)	Amer.Hum.Ind.	American Humanities Index
		Amer.Stat.Ind.	American Statistics Index
		Anal.Abstr.	Analytical Abstracts
str.Hosp. anage.Stud.	Abstracts of Hospital Management Studies (Now: Abstracts of Health Care Management Studies) (Ceased)	Anbar	Anbar Management Services Abstracts (Now: Operations & Production Management Abstracts; Marketing & Distribution Abstracts; Personnel & Training Abstracts) (Also see: Account.& Data Proc.Abstr.; also see: Computer Abstr.; also see: Top Manage.Abstr.)
str.Hum.Comp. ter.	Abstracts in Human-Computer Interaction		
str.Hyg.	Abstracts on Hygiene and Communicable Diseases		
str.Inter.Med.	Abstracts in Internal Medicine (Now: Abstracts in Medicine and Key Word Index) (Ceased)		
		Anim.Behav. Abstr.	Animal Behavior Abstracts
str.J.Earthq. ng.	Abstract Journal in Earthquake Engineering	Anim.Breed. Abstr.	Animal Breeding Abstracts
str.Mil.Bibl.	Abstracts of Military Bibliography		
str.Musl.Rel.	European Muslims and Christian-Muslim Relations. Abstracts. (Ceased)	Anthropol.Lit.	Anthropological Literature
		Ap.Ind.	Apple Index
str.N.Amer. eol.	Abstracts of North American Geology (Ceased)	Apic.Abstr.	Apicultural Abstracts
		Appl.Ecol.Abstr.	Applied Ecology Abstracts (Now: Ecology Abstracts)
str.Pop.Cult.	Abstracts of Popular Culture (Ceased)		
str.Rural ev.Trop.	Abstracts on Rural Development in the Tropics (Ceased)	Appl.Mech.Rev.	Applied Mechanics Reviews
		Aqua.Sci.& Fish.Abstr.	Aquatic Sciences & Fisheries Abstracts (Parts 1, 2)
str.Soc. eront.	Abstracts in Social Gerontology: Current Literature on Aging		
		Aquacult.Abstr.	A S F A Aquaculture Abstracts
str.Soc.Work.	Abstracts for Social Workers (Now: Social Work Abstracts)	Archit.Per.Ind.	Architectural Periodicals Index (Now: Architectural Publications Index)
tr.Trop.Agri.	Abstracts on Tropical Agriculture		
d.Ind.	Academic Index	Arct.Bibl.	Arctic Bibliography (Ceased)
ess	Access: the Supplementary Index to Periodicals	Art & Archaeol. Tech.Abstr.	Art and Archaeology Technical Abstracts
ount.& Data oc.Abstr.	Accounting & Data Processing Abstracts (Now: Accounting & Finance Abstracts) (Also see: Anbar)	Art Ind.	Art Index
		Art.Hosp.& Tour.	Articles in Hospitality and Tourism
		Art.Int.Abstr.	Artificial Intelligence Abstracts (England) (Ceased)
ount.Ind.	Accountant's Index (Now: Accounting and Tax Index)		
		Artbibl.	Artbibliographies Current Titles
Pre.Dig.	Acid Precipitation Digest (Ceased)	Artbibl.Mod.	Artbibliographies Modern
Rain Abstr.	Acid Rain Abstracts (Now: Environment Abstracts)	Arts & Hum. Cit.Ind.	Arts & Humanities Citation Index
Rain Ind.	Acid Rain Annual Index (Now: Environment Abstracts Annual)	Ash.G.Bot.Per.	Asher's Guide to Botanical Periodicals (Now: Guide to Botanical Periodicals) (Ceased)
ust.Abstr.	Acoustics Abstracts		
.Ment. h.Abstr.	Adolescent Mental Health Abstracts (Ceased)	Asian-Pac.Econ. Lit.	Asian-Pacific Economic Literature
Eng.Abstr.	Agricultural Engineering Abstracts	Astron.& Astrophys. Abstr.	Astronomy and Astrophysics Abstracts
Ind.	Agricultural Index (Now: Biological & Agricultural Index)		
dex	Agrindex	Aus.Educ.Ind.	Australian Education Index

Aus.Leg.Mon. Dig.	Australian Legal Monthly Digest	Bibl.Ling.	Linguistic Bibliography/Bibliographie Linguistique
Aus.P.A.I.S.	Australian Public Affairs Information Service (Now: APAIS: Australian Public Affairs Information Service)	Bibl.Repro.	Bibliography of Reproduction (Now: Human Reproduction Update)
Aus.Rd.Ind.	Australian Road Index (Ceased)	Bibliogr.Bras. Odontol.	Bibliografia Brasileira de Odontologia
Aus.Sci.Ind.	Australian Science Index (Ceased)	Bio-Contr.News & Info.	Bio-Control News and Information
Aus.Speleo Abstr.	Australian Speleo Abstracts	Biodet.Abstr.	Biodeterioration Abstracts
Avery Ind. Archit.Per.	Avery Index to Architectural Periodicals	Bioeng.Abstr.	Bioengineering Abstracts
		Biog.Ind.	Biography Index
		Biol.Abstr.	Biological Abstracts

B

		Biol.& Agr.Ind.	Biological & Agricultural Index
B.C.I.R.A.	B.C.I.R.A. Abstracts of International Foundry Literature (British Cast Iron Research Association) (Now: B C I R A Abstracts on International Literature on Metal Castings Production)	Biol.Dig.	Biology Digest
		Biostat.	Biostatistica
		Biotech.Abstr.	Biotechnology Research Abstracts (Now Agricultural & Environmental Biotechnology Abstracts; Medical & Pharmaceutical Biotechnology Abstracts)
BIM	Bibliography and Index of Micropaleontology		
BMT	B M T Abstracts (British Maritime Technology)	Biwk.Pap.Rad. Chem.& Photochem.	Biweekly List of Papers on Radiation Chemistry and Photochemistry (Cea
BNI	B N I (British Newspaper Index)		
B.P.I.	Business Periodicals Index	Bk.Rev.Dig.	Book Review Digest
BPIA	Business Publications Index and Abstracts (Ceased)	Bk.Rev.Ind.	Book Review Index
		Bk.Rev.Mo.	Book Reviews of the Month (Ceased)
B.R.I.	BioResearch Index (Now: Biological Abstracts - R R M (Reports, Reviews, Meetings))	Br.Archaeol. Abstr.	British Archaeological Abstracts (Now: British and Irish Archaeological Bibliography)
BSL Biol.	Abstracts of Bulgarian Scientific Literature. Biology (Ceased)	Br.Ceram.Abstr.	British Ceramic Abstracts (Now: World Ceramics Abstracts)
BSL Econ.	Abstracts of Bulgarian Scientific Literature. Economics and Law (Ceased)	Br.Educ.Ind.	British Education Index
		Br.Geol.Lit.	British Geological Literature
BSL Geo.	Abstracts of Bulgarian Scientific Literature. Geosciences (Ceased)	Br.Hum.Ind.	British Humanities Index
		Br.Rail.Bd.	British Railways Board. Monthly Revie Technical Literature (Ceased)
BSL Indus.	Abstracts of Bulgarian Scientific Literature. Industry, Building and Transport		
		Br.Tech.Ind.	British Technology Index (Now: Abstra in New Technologies and Engineeri
BSL Math.	Abstracts of Bulgarian Scientific Literature. Mathematical and Physical Sciences (Ceased)		
		Build.Manage. Abstr.	Building Management Abstracts (Now: Construction Information File - C I F
Bangladesh Agr. Sci.Abstr.	Bangladesh Agricultural Sciences Abstracts	Bull.Anal.Ent. Med.Vet.	Bulletin Analytique d'Entomologie Mec et Veterinaire (Ceased)
Bank.Lit.Ind.	Banking Literature Index		
Behav.Abstr.	Behavioural Abstracts (Ceased)	Bull.Signal.	Bulletin Signaletique (Now: P A S C A Explore, P A S C A L Folio, P A S C Thema) (Programme Applique a la Selection et la Compilation Automa de la Literature)
Behav.Med. Abstr.	Behavioral Medicine Abstracts (Now: Annals of Behavioral Medicine)		
Ber.Biochem. Biol.	Berichte Biochemie und Biologie (Ceased)		
Bibl Agri.	Bibliography of Agriculture	Bull.Thermodyn. & Thermochem.	Bulletin of Thermodynamics & Thermochemistry (Now: Bulletin of Chemical Thermodynamics) (Ceas
Bibl.& Ind.Geol.	Bibliography & Index of Geology (see: GeoRef)		
Bibl.Cart.	Bibliographia Cartographica	Bus.Comput.Ind.	Business Computer Index
Bibl.Dev.Med.& Child Neur.	Bibliography of Developmental Medicine & Child Neurology. Books and Articles Received (Ceased)	Bus.Educ.Ind.	Business Education Index
		Bus.Ind.	Business Index

C

Bibl.Engl.Lang. & Lit.	Bibliography of English Language and Literature (Now: Annual Bibliography of English Language and Literature)	CAD CAM Abstr.	C A D - C A M Abstracts (Ceased)
		CALL	C A L L (Current Awareness—Library Literature)
Bibl.Ind.	Bibliographic Index		

ABSTRACTING AND INDEXING

.Ob.Gyn.	Combined Cumulative Index to Obstetrics and Gynecology	**Canadiana**	Canadiana
.P.	Combined Cumulative Index to Pediatrics	**Canon Law Abstr.**	Canon Law Abstracts
L.P.	Contents of Current Legal Periodicals (Now: Legal Contents) (Ceased)	**Cath.Ind.**	Catholic Periodical & Literature Index
		Ceram.Abstr.	Ceramic Abstracts
M.J.	Contents of Contemporary Mathematical Journals (Now: Current Mathematical Publications)	**Chem.Abstr.**	Chemical Abstracts
		Chem.Cit.Ind.	Chemistry Citation Index
	Current Christian Abstracts (Now: Current Thoughts & Trends)	**Chem.Eng.Abstr.**	Chemical Engineering Abstracts (Now: Process and Chemical Engineering)
DIC	Universite de Strasbourg. Centre de Recherche et de Documentation des Institutions Chretiennes. Bulletin du CERDIC (Ceased)	**Chem.Infd.**	Chemischer Informationsdienst (Now: ChemInform)
		Chem.Titles	Chemical Titles
		Chemorec.Abstr.	Chemoreception Abstracts
	Consumer Health & Nutrition Index (Ceased)	**Chicago Psychoanal. Lit.Ind.**	Chicago Psychoanalytic Literature Index (Ceased)
E.	Current Index to Journals in Education		
HL (also N.L.)	Cumulative Index to Nursing and Allied Health Literature	**Chic.Per.Ind.**	Chicano Periodical Index (Now: Chicano Index)
Abstr.	C I R F Abstracts (Now: T&D Abstracts) (Ceased)	**Child.Auth.& Illus.**	Children's Authors and Illustrators
Abstr.	C I S Abstracts (Centre International d'Information de Securite et Hygiene du Travail) (Now: Safety and Health at Work)	**Child.Bk.Rev.Ind.**	Children's Book Review Index
		Child Devel.Abstr.	Child Development Abstracts and Bibliography
		Child.Lit.Abstr.	Children's Literature Abstracts
Ind.	C I S Index to Publications of the United States Congress (Congressional Information Service)	**Chr.Per.Ind.**	Christian Periodical Index
		Coll.Stud.Pers. Abstr.	College Student Personnel Abstracts (Now: Higher Education Abstracts)
	Criminal Justice Periodical Index	**Commun.Abstr.**	Communication Abstracts
	Current Law Index	**Community Ment.Health Rev.**	Community Mental Health Review (Now: Journal of Prevention and Intervention in the Community)
	Current Literature on Aging (Now: Abstracts in Social Gerontology: Current Literature on Aging)		
		Compumath	Compumath Citation Index
S	Current Literature on Science of Science	**Comput.Abstr.**	Computer Abstracts (Also see: Anbar)
	Canadian Magazine Index (Now: Canadian Index)	**Comput.& Info. Sys.**	Computer and Information Systems Abstracts Journal
	Current Physics Index	**Comput.Bus.**	Computer Business (Ceased)
.J.	Contents of Recent Economics Journals	**Comput.Cont.**	Computer Contents (Ceased)
Abstr.	C R I Abstracts (Cement Research Institute of India)	**Comput.Dtbs.**	Computer Database
		Comput.Ind.	Computer Index
Curr.	C R I Current Contents	**Comput.Indus.Up.**	Computer Industry Update (Ceased)
		Comput.Lit.Ind.	Computer Literature Index
.	Canadian Statistics Index (Now: Directory of Statistics in Canada	**Comput.Rev.**	Computing Reviews
	Current Work in the History of Medicine	**Concr.Abstr.**	Concrete Abstracts
an	Cadscan	**Consum.Ind.**	Consumers Index
r.Ind.	California Periodicals Index	**Cont.Pg.Educ.**	Contents Pages in Education
s.Abstr.	Calcified Tissue Abstracts (Now: Calcium and Calcified Tissue Abstracts)	**Cont.Pg.Manage.**	Contents Pages in Management
		Copper Abstr.	Copper Abstracts (Now: International Copper Information Bulletin) (Ceased)
P.I.	Canadian Business Periodicals Index (Now: Canadian Index)		
		Corros.Abstr.	Corrosion Abstracts
uc.Ind.	Canadian Education Index	**Cott.& Trop.Fibr. Abstr.**	Cotton and Tropical Fibres Abstracts (Now: Cotton and Tropical Fibres)
.Ind.	Canadian Literature Index (Ceased)		
r.Ind.	Canadian Periodical Index	**Crim.Just.Abstr.**	Criminal Justice Abstracts
v.Comp.	Canadian Review of Comparative Literature (Abstracting discontinued)	**Crime Delinq. Abstr.**	Crime and Delinquency Abstracts (Ceased)
om.Per.	Canadian Women's Periodicals Index (Ceased)	**Crop Physiol. Abstr.**	Crop Physiology Abstracts

Curr.Adv. Biochem.	Current Advances in Biochemistry (Now: Current Advances in Protein Biochemistry)	Cyb.Abstr.	Cybernetics Abstracts

D

Curr.Adv.Cancer.Res.	Current Advances in Cancer Research
Curr.Adv.Cell & Devel.Biol.	Current Advances in Cell and Developmental Biology
Curr.Adv.Clin.Chem.	Current Advances in Clinical Chemistry
Curr.Adv.Ecol.Sci.	Current Advances in Ecological Sciences (Now: Current Advances in Ecological and Environmental Sciences)
Curr.Adv.Genetics & Molec.Biol.	Current Advances in Genetics and Molecular Biology
Curr.Adv.Neurosci.	Current Advances in Neuroscience
Curr.Adv.Physiol.	Current Advances in Physiology (Now: Current Advances in Endocrinology & Metabolism)
Curr.Adv.Plant Sci.	Current Advances in Plant Science
Curr.Aus.N.Z.Leg.Lit.Ind.	Current Australian and New Zealand Legal Literature Index (Ceased)
Curr.Biotech.Abstr.	Current Biotechnology Abstracts (Now: Current Biotechnology)
Curr.Bk.Rev.Cit.	Current Book Review Citations (Ceased)
Curr.Chem.React.	Current Chemical Reactions
Curr.Cont.	Current Contents consists of: Current Contents: Agriculture, Biology & Environmental Sciences Current Contents: Arts & Humanities Current Contents: Clinical Medicine Current Contents: Engineering, Computing & Technology Current Contents: Health Services Administration (Ceased) Current Contents: Life Sciences Current Contents: Physical, Chemical & Earth Sciences Current Contents: Social & Behavioral Sciences
Curr.Cont.Africa	Current Contents Africa (Ceased)
Curr.Cont.M.E.	Current Contents of Periodicals on the Middle East
Curr.Dig.Sov.Press	Current Digest of the Soviet Press (Now: Current Digest of the Post-Soviet Press)
Curr.Ind.Stat.	Current Index to Statistics
Curr.Leather Lit.	Current Leather Literature (Now: Leather Science Abstracts)
Curr.Lit.Fam.Plan.	Current Literature in Family Planning (Ceased)
Curr.Pack.Abstr.	Current Packaging Abstracts (Ceased)
Curr.Ref. Fish Res.	Current References in Fish Research
Curr.Tit.Dent.	Current Titles in Dentistry
Curr.Tit.Electrochem.	Current Titles in Electrochemistry
Curr.Tit.Ocean	Current Titles in Ocean, Coastal, Lake & Waterway Sciences (Ceased)

DAAI	Design and Applied Arts Index
DM&T	Defense Markets and Technology (Now: Aerospace Defense Markets and Technology) (Ceased)
DNP	Digest of Neurology & Psychiatry
DSH Abstr.	DSH Abstracts (Deafness, Speech and Hearing) (Ceased)
Dairy Sci.Abstr.	Dairy Science Abstracts
Data Process.Dig.	Data Processing Digest
Deep Sea Res.& Oceanogr.Abstr.	Deep Sea Research & Oceanographic Abstracts (Now: Oceanographic Literature Review)
Dent.Abstr.	Dental Abstracts
Dent.Ind.	Index to Dental Literature
Diab.Cont.	Diabetes Contents
Diab.Lit.Ind.	Diabetes Literature Index (Ceased)
Diar.Dis.Res.	Journal of Diarrhoeal Diseases Research
Djerelo	Djerelo
Doc.Geogr.	Documentatio Geographica (Now: Dokumentation zur Raumentwicklung) (Ceased)
Documentatieblad	Documentatieblad: The Abstracts Journal of the African Studies Centre Leiden (Now: African Studies Abstracts)
Dok.Arbeitsmed.	Dokumentation Arbeitsmedizin (Now: Arbeitsmedizin)
Dok.Raum.	Dokumentation zur Raumentwicklung (Ceased)
Dok.Str.	Dokumentation Strasse

E

E & P Hlth.	Exploration and Production Health, Safety and Environment
EC Ind.	EC Index (European Communities)
E.I.	E I (Excerpta Indonesica)
ELLIS	E L L I S (European Legal Literature Information Service)
ERIC	Eric Clearinghouse (See: C.I.J.E.)
Ecol.Abstr.	Ecological Abstracts
Ecol.Zoo.& Plant Sci.Abstr.	Essential Ecology, Zoology & Plant Science Abstracts
Econ.Abstr.	Economic Abstracts (Now: Key to Economic Science) (Ceased)
Educ.Admin.Abstr.	Educational Administration Abstracts
Educ.Ind.	Education Index
Educ.Tech.Abstr.	Educational Technology Abstracts
Ekist.Ind.	Ekistic Index of Periodicals
Electroanal.Abstr.	Electroanalytical Abstracts (Ceased)
Electron.& Communic.Abstr.J.	Electronics and Communications Abstracts Journal

ABSTRACTING AND INDEXING　　xxxvii

docrin.Ind.	Endocrinology Index (Ceased)
ergy Abstr.	Energy Abstracts
ergy Ind.	Energy Index (Now: Energy Information Abstracts Annual)
ergy Info. Abstr.	Energy Information Abstracts
ergy Res. Abstr.	Energy Research Abstracts
ergy Rev.	Energy Review (Santa Barbara) (Ceased)
g.Ind.	Engineering Index (Now: Engineering Index Monthly)
g.Mat.Abstr.	Engineered Materials Abstracts
tomol.Abstr.	Entomology Abstracts
viron.Abstr.	Environment Abstracts
viron.Ind.	Environment Index (Now: Environment Abstracts Annual)
viron.Per.Bibl.	Environmental Periodicals Bibliography
on.Abstr.	Ergonomics Abstracts
ro.LJI	European Legal Journals Index
ept.Child	Exceptional Child Education Abstracts
duc.Abstr.	(Now: Exceptional Child Education Resources)
erp.Bot.	Excerpta Botanica (Sections A, B)
raMED	ExtraMED
erp.Med.	Excerpta Medica
	Section 1: Anatomy, Anthropology, Embriology & Histology
	Section 2: Physiology
	Section 3: Endocrinology
	Section 4: Microbiology: Bacteriology, Mycology Parasitology and Virology
	Section 5: General Pathology and Pathological Anatomy
	Section 6: Internal Medicine
	Section 7: Pediatrics and Pediatric Surgery
	Section 8: Neurology and Neurosurgery
	Section 9: Surgery
	Section 10: Obstetrics and Gynecology
	Section 11: Otorhinolaryngology
	Section 12: Ophthalmology
	Section 13: Dermatology and Venereology
	Section 14: Radiology
	Section 15: Chest Diseases, Thoracic Surgery and Tuberculosis
	Section 16: Cancer
	Section 17: Public Health, Social Medicine and Epidemiology
	Section 18: Cardiovascular Diseases and Cardiovascular Surgery
	Section 19: Rehabilitation and Physical Medicine
	Section 20: Gerontology and Geriatrics
	Section 21: Developmental Biology and Teratology
	Section 22: Human Genetics
	Section 23: Nuclear Medicine
	Section 24: Anesthesiology
	Section 25: Hematology
	Section 26: Immunology, Serology and Transplantation
	Section 27: Biophysics, Bio-Engineering and Medical Instrumentation
	Section 28: Urology and Nephrology
	Section 29: Clinical and Experimental Biochemistry
	Section 30: Clinical and Experimental Pharmacology
	Section 31: Arthritis and Rheumatism
	Section 32: Psychiatry
	Section 33: Orthopedic Surgery
	Section 34: Plastic Surgery
	Section 35: Occupational Health and Industrial Medicine
	Section 36: Health Policy, Economics and Management
	Section 37: Drug Literature Index
	Section 38: Adverse Reactions Titles
	Section 40: Drug Dependence, Alcohol Abuse and Alcoholism
	Section 46: Environmental Health and Pollution Control
	Section 48: Gastroenterology
	Section 49: Forensic Science Abstracts
	Section 50: Epilepsy Abstracts
	Section 51: Mycobacterial Diseases, Leprosy, Tuberculosis and Related Subjects
	Section 52: Toxicology
	Section 54: AIDS
	Section 130: Clinical Pharmacology

F

F.A.C.T.	Fuel Abstracts and Current Titles (Now: Fuel and Energy Abstracts)
FAMLI	F A M L I (Family Medicine Literature Index) (Ceased)
F.R.	Fanatic Reader
Fababean Abstr.	Faba Bean Abstracts (Ceased)
Fam.Ind.	Family Index
Farm & Garden Ind.	Farm & Garden Index (Ceased)
Fed Print	Fed in Print
Fem.Per.	Feminist Periodicals
Fert.Abstr.	Fertilizer Abstracts (Ceased)
Field Crop Abstr.	Field Crop Abstracts
Film Lit.Ind.	Film Literature Index
Fish.Abstr.	Essential Fisheries Abstracts
Fluidex	Fluidex
	consists of:
	Civil Engineering Hydraulics Abstracts (Now: Fluid Abstracts: Civil Engineering)
	Current Fluid Engineering Titles (Ceased)
	Fluid Flow Measurement Abstracts (Now: Fluid Abstracts: Process Engineering)
	Fluid Power Abstracts (Now: Fluid Abstracts: Process Engineering)
	Fluid Sealing Abstracts (Now: Fluid Abstracts: Process Engineering)
	Industrial Aerodynamics Abstracts

ABSTRACTING AND INDEXING

        (Now: Fluid Abstracts: Civil Engineering)
        Industrial Jetting Report (Ceased)
        Offshore Engineering Abstracts (Now: Fluid Abstracts: Civil Engineering)
        Pipelines Abstracts (Now: Fluid Abstracts: Process Engineering)
        Pumps & Other Fluids Machinery Abstracts (Now: Fluid Abstracts: Process Engineering)
        Pumps and Turbines (Ceased)
        River and Flood Control Abstracts (Ceased)
        Solid-Liquid Flow Abstracts (Now: Fluid Abstracts: Process Engineering)
        Tribos-Tribology Abstracts (Now: Tribology & Corrosion Abstracts) (Ceased)
        World Ports and Harbours Abstracts (Now: Fluid Abstracts: Civil Engineering)
        World Ports and Harbours News (Ceased)

Food Sci.& Tech. Abstr. Food Science and Technology Abstracts
Foreign Leg.Per. Index to Foreign Legal Periodicals
Forest.Abstr. Forestry Abstracts
Forest.& Wildfire Abstr. Essential Forestry & Wildfire Abstracts
Forest Prod. Abstr. Forest Products Abstracts
Foul.Prev.Res. Dig. Fouling Prevention Research Digest (Now: H T F S Digest (Heat Transfer & Fluid Flow Service))
Fuel & Energy Abstr. Fuel & Energy Abstracts
Fut.Abstr. Future - Abstracts
Fut.Surv. Future Survey

G

G.Indian Per.Lit. Guide to Indian Periodical Literature
G.Perf.Arts. Guide to the Performing Arts (Ceased)
G.Soc.Sci.& Rel. Per.Lit. Guide to Social Sciences and Religion in Periodical Literature
Gard.Lit. Garden Literature
Gas Abstr. Gas Abstracts
Gas Process.& Ppl. Gas Processing and Pipelining
Gastroenterol. Abstr.& Cit. Gastroenterology Abstracts & Citations (Ceased)
GdIns. Guidelines
Gen.Phys.Adv. Abstr. General Physics Advance Abstracts
Gen.Sci.Ind. General Science Index
Geneal.Per.Ind. Genealogical Periodical Annual Index
Genet.Abstr. Genetics Abstracts
Geo.Abstr.H.G. (also Geo.Abstr.) Geographical Abstracts: Human Geography
Geo.Abstr.P.G. (also Geo.Abstr.) Geographical Abstracts: Physical Geography
Geol.Abstr. Geological Abstracts
Geophys.Abstr. Geophysical Abstracts (Ceased)
GeoRef Bibliography and Index of Geology (Also known as GeoRef)
Geosci.Doc. Geoscience Documentation
Geotech.Abstr. Geotechnical Abstracts
Ger.J.Psych. German Journal of Psychology (Now: European Psychologist) (Abstracting discontinued)
Graph.Arts Abstr. Graphic Arts Abstracts (Now: G A T F World)
Graph.Arts Lit. Abstr. Graphic Arts Literature Abstracts (Now: Institute of Paper Science and Technology. Graphic Arts Bulletin)

H

HMA Healthcare Marketing Abstracts
HR Rep. Human Rights Internet Reporter
HRIS H R I S Abstracts (Now: T R I S Electronic Bibliographic Data Base (Transportation Research Information Services))
Helminthol.Abstr. Helminthological Abstracts. Series A (Helminthological Abstracts)
    Helminthological Abstracts. Series B (Nematological Abstracts)
Herb.Abstr. Herbage Abstracts (Now: Grasslands and Forage Abstracts)
High.Educ.Abstr. Higher Education Abstracts
High.Educ.Curr. Aware.Bull. Higher Education Current Awareness Bulletin (Ceased)
Hisp.Amer.Per. Ind. Hispanic American Periodicals Index
Hist.Abstr. Historical Abstracts (Parts A, B)
Hlth.Ind. Health Index
HongKongiana HongKongiana
Hort.Abstr. Horticultural Abstracts
Hosp.Abstr. Hospital Abstracts (Now: Health Services Abstracts)
Hosp.Abstr.Serv. Hospital Abstracts Service (Ceased)
Hosp.Lit.Ind. Hospital Literature Index
Hospit.Ind. Hospitality Index (Now: Hospital and Health Administration Index)
Hum.Ind. Humanities Index
Human Resour. Abstr. Human Resources Abstracts
Hung.Build.Bull. Hungarian Building Bulletin (Ceased)
Hung.Lib.& Info. Sci.Abstr. Hungarian Library and Information Science Abstracts
Hwy.Res.Abstr. Highway Research Abstracts (Now: Transportation Research Abstracts) (Ceased)

I

IBM PC Ind. IBM PC Index (Personal Computer)
IBR Internationale Bibliographie der Rezensionen Wissenschaftlicher

ABSTRACTING AND INDEXING xxxix

	Literatur/International Bibliography of Book Reviews of Scholarly Literature		Key Abstracts - Rotobics & Control
			Key Abstracts - Semiconductor Devices
	Internationale Bibliographie der Zeitschriftenliteratur aus allen Gebieten des Wissens/International Bibliography of Periodicals from all Fields of Knowledge		Key Abstracts - Software Engineering
			Key Abstracts - Telecommunications
			Physics Abstracts (Alternative title: INSPEC, Section A. Represents: Science Abstracts. Section A)
J.I.S.Abstr.	I C U I S Abstracts Service (Institute on the Church in Urban Industrial Society) (Now: I C U I S Justice Ministries) (Ceased)	I.P.A.	International Pharmaceutical Abstracts
		ISMEC	I S M E C Bulletin (Information Service in Mechanical Engineering) (Now: Mechanical Engineering Abstracts)
	International Development Abstracts	Ind.Agri.Am.Lat. Caribe	Indice Agricole de America Latina y el Caribe (Ceased)
	Index to International Statistics		
	Index to Journals in Communication Studies	Ind.Amer.Per. Verse	Index of American Periodical Verse
	Inventory of Marriage and Family Literature (Now: Family Studies Database)	Ind.Artic.Jew. Stud.	Index of Articles on Jewish Studies
M.Abstr.	I M M Abstracts (Institute of Mining & Metallurgy) (Now: I M M Abstracts and Index)	Ind.Bk.Rev.Hum.	Index to Book Reviews in the Humanities (Ceased)
		Ind.Bus.Rep.	Index to Business Reports
.P.	Index to New England Periodicals	Ind.Can.L.P.L.	Index to Canadian Legal Periodical Literature
Atomind.	I N I S Atomindex (International Nuclear Information System)	Ind.Chem.	Index Chemicus
		Ind.Child.Mag.	Subject Index to Children's Magazines (Now: Children's Magazine Guide)
EC	INSPEC (The Institution of Electrical Engineers):		
	Computers & Control Abstracts (Alternative title: INSPEC, Section C. Represents: Science Abstracts. Section C)	Ind.Curr.Urb. Doc.	Index to Current Urban Documents
		Ind.Free.Per.	Index to Free Periodicals (Ceased)
	Current Papers in Computers & Control	Ind.Heb.Per.	Index to Hebrew Periodicals
	Current Papers in Electrical & Electronics Engineering	Ind.How To Do It	Index to How to Do It Information
		Ind.Hyg.Dig.	Industrial Hygiene Digest
	Current Papers in Physics	Ind.India	Index India
	Electrical & Electronics Abstracts (Alternative title: INSPEC, Section B. Represents: Science Abstracts. Section B.)	Ind.Islam.	Index Islamicus
		Ind.Jew.Per.	Index to Jewish Periodicals
		Ind.Lit.Amer. Indian	Index to Literature on the American Indian (Ceased)
	Key Abstracts - Advanced Materials		
	Key Abstracts - Antennas & Propagation	Ind.Lit.Dent.	Indice de la Literatura Dental Periodica en Castellano
	Key Abstracts - Artificial Intelligence		
	Key Abstracts - Business Automation	Ind.Little Mag.	Index to Little Magazines (Ceased)
	Key Abstracts - Computer Communication and Storage	Ind.Med.	Index Medicus
		Ind.Med.Esp.	Indice Medico Espanol
	Key Abstracts - Computing in Electronics & Power	Ind.N.Z.Per.	Index to New Zealand Periodicals (Now: Index New Zealand)
	Key Abstracts - Electronic Circuits		
	Key Abstracts - Electronic Instrumentation	Ind.Per.Art.Relat. Law	Index to Periodical Articles Related to Law
	Key Abstracts - Factory Automation	Ind.Per.Blacks	Index to Periodical Articles by and about Blacks (Now: Index to Black Periodicals)
	Key Abstracts - High-Temperature Superconductors		
	Key Abstracts - Human-Computer Interaction	Ind.Per.Lit.	Index to Indian Periodical Literature (Ceased)
	Key Abstracts - Machine Vision	Ind.Per.Negroes	Index to Periodical Articles by & about Negroes (Now: Index to Black Periodicals)
	Key Abstracts - Measurements in Physics		
		Ind.Phil.Per.	Index to Philippine Periodicals
	Key Abstracts - Microelectronics & Printed Circuits	Ind.Rheum.	Annual Index of Rheumatology (Ceased)
		Ind.S.A.Per.	Index to South African Periodicals
	Key Abstracts - Microwave Technology	Ind.Sci.Rev.	Index to Scientific Reviews
	Key Abstracts - Neural Networks		
	Key Abstracts - Optoelectronics	Ind.Sel.Per.	Index to Selected Periodicals (Now: Index to Black Periodicals)
	Key Abstracts - Power Systems & Applications		

ABSTRACTING AND INDEXING

Ind.SST.	Indice Espanol de Ciencia y Tecnologia
Ind.U.S.Gov.Per.	Index to U.S. Government Periodicals (Now: U S Government Periodicals Index)
Ind.Vet.	Index Veterinarius
Indian Lib.Sci. Abstr.	Indian Library Science Abstracts
Indian Psychol. Abstr.	Indian Psychological Abstracts (Now: Indian Psychological Abstracts and Reviews)
Indian Sci.Abstr.	Indian Science Abstracts
Indian Sci.Ind.	Indian Science Index (Ceased)
Info.Media & Tech.	Information Media and Technology (Now: Information Management & Technology)
Inform.Sci.Abstr.	Information Science Abstracts
Inpharma	InPharma (Now: InPharma Weekly)
Int.Abstr.Biol.Sci.	International Abstracts of Biological Sciences (Now: Current Awareness in Biological Sciences)
Int.Abstr.Oper. Res.	International Abstracts in Operations Research
Int.Aerosp.Abstr.	International Aerospace Abstracts
Int.Bibl.Soc.Sci.	International Bibliography of the Social Sciences: Anthropology, Political Science, Economics, Sociology (Ceased)
Int.Build.Serv. Abstr.	International Building Services Abstracts
Int.G.Class.Stud.	International Guide to Classical Studies (Ceased)
Int.Ind.Film Per.	International Index to Film Periodicals
Int.Lab.Doc.	International Labor Documentation
Int.Nurs.Ind.	International Nursing Index
Int.Packag.Abstr.	International Packaging Abstracts
Int.Polit.Sci. Abstr.	International Political Science Abstracts
Int.Sci.Rev.	International Science Review Series (Ceased)
Int.Z.Bibelwiss.	Internationale Zietschriftenschau fuer Bibelwissenschaft und Grenzgebiete
InterActions Bibl.	InterActions Bibliography (Now: Humans & Other Species)
Intl.Bibl.S.S.Econ.	International Bibliography of the Social Sciences: Economics
Intl.Bibl.S.S.Pol. Sci.	International Bibliography of the Social Sciences: Political Science
Intl.Bibl.S.S. Soc.Cult.Anthro.	International Bibliography of the Social Sciences: Anthropology
Intl.Civil Eng. Abstr.	International Civil Engineering Abstracts
Intl.Ind.TV.	International Index to Television Periodicals
Intl.Mgmt.Info.	International Management Information Business Digest (Ceased)
Intl.Polym.Sci.& Tech.	International Polymer Science and Technology
Iron & Steel Indus.Pr.	Iron and Steel Industry Profiles (Ceased)
Irr.& Drain.Abstr.	Irrigation & Drainage Abstracts

J

JAMA	JAMA: The Journal of the American Medical Association
JCT	Japan Computer Technology and Applications Abstracts (Ceased)
JTA	Japanese Technical Abstracts (Now: Japan Technology Series) (Ceased)
J.Cont. Quant.Meth.	Journal Contents in Quantitative Methods
J.Curr.Laser Abstr.	Journal of Current Laser Abstracts
Jewish Abstr.	Jewish Abstracts
J.of Abstr.Int. Educ.	Journal of Abstracts in International Education
J.of Econ.Abstr. (also: J.of Econ. Lit.)	Journal of Economic Abstracts (Now: Journal of Economic Literature)
J.of Ferroc.	Journal of Ferrocement
Jap.Per.Ind.	Japanese Periodicals Index (Humanities and Social Sciences Section; Medical Sciences and Pharmacology (Ceased); Science and Technology)
Jun.High Mag. Abstr.	Junior High Magazine Abstracts

K

Key to Econ.Sci.	Key to Economic Science (Ceased)
Key Word Ind. Wildl.Res.	Key Word Index of Wildlife Research
Kidney	Kidney (New York, 1992)

L

LAMP	L A M P (Literature Analysis of Microcomputer Publications)
LCR	Literary Criticism Register
LHTN	Library Hi Tech News
L.I.I.	Life Insurance Index (Ceased)
LISA	L I S A: Library & Information Science Abstracts
LJI	Legal Journals Index
L.R.I.	Legal Resource Index (Now: LegalTrac)
Lab.Haz.Bull.	Laboratory Hazards Bulletin
Landwirt. Zentralbl.	Landwirtschaftliches Zentralblatt (Now: Agroselekt) (Ceased)
Lang.& Lang. Behav.Abstr.	Language and Language Behaviour Abstracts (Now: Linguistics and Language Behavior Abstracts)
Lang.Teach.& Ling.Abstr.	Language Teaching and Linguistics Abstracts (Now: Language Teaching)
Law Ofc.Info.Svc.	Law Office Information Service
Lead Abstr.	Lead Abstracts (Now: Leadscan)
Left Ind.	Left Index
Leg.Cont.	Legal Contents (Ceased)
Leg.Info.Manage. Ind.	Legal Information Management Index

ABSTRACTING AND INDEXING   xli

.Per.	Index to Legal Periodicals (Now: Index to Legal Periodicals & Books)	Mich.Mag.Ind.	Michigan Magazine Index (Ceased)
.Lit.	Library Literature	Microbiol.Abstr.	Microbiological Abstracts (Sections A, B, C)
.Sci.Abstr.	Library Science Abstracts (Now: L I S A: Library & Information Science Abstracts)	Microcomp.Ind.	Microcomputer Index (Now: Microcomputer Abstracts)
g.Abstr.	Linguistics Abstracts	Microcomp. Indus.Up.	Microcomputer Industry Update (Ceased)
Automat.	Literature on Automation (Now: Excerpta Automatica)	Mid.East: Abstr. & Ind.	Middle East: Abstracts and Index
.Restr.& ur.Ind.	Lodging, Restaurant & Tourism Index	Mineral.Abstr.	Mineralogical Abstracts
		Mkt.Inform. Guide	Marketing Information Guide (Ceased)

M

		Mult.Ed.Abstr.	Multicultural Education Abstracts
DOC	Medoc: Index to U.S. Government Publications in the Medical and Health Sciences (Ceased)	Multi.Scler.Abstr.	Multiple Sclerosis Indicative Abstracts (Ceased)
DSOC	Medical Socioeconomic Research Sources (Ceased)	Music Artic. Guide	Music Article Guide (Ceased)
LSA	MELSA Messenger (Metropolitan Library Service)(Ceased)	Music Ind.	Music Index
.A.	M L A Abstracts of Articles in Scholarly Journals (Ceased)	Mycol.Abstr.	Abstracts of Mycology

N

.A. Intl.Bibl.	M L A International Bibliography of Books and Articles on Modern Languages and Literatures	NAA	N A A (Nordic Archaeological Abstracts)
		NBA	Notiziario Bibliografico di Audiologia ORL e Foniatria
.R.I.	Multi-Media Reviews Index (Now: Media Review Digest)	NRN	Nutrition Research Newsletter
		Neurosci.Abstr.	Neurosciences Abstracts (Now: CSA Neurosciences Abstracts)
.Ind.	Magazine Index		
ze Abstr.	Maize Abstracts	Neurosci.Cit.Ind.	Neuroscience Citation Index
age.Abstr.	Management Abstracts (India) (Now: Indian Management)	New Per.Ind.	New Periodicals Index (Ceased)
		New Test.Abstr.	New Testament Abstracts
age.Cont.	Management Contents	Noise Pollut. Publ.Abstr.	Noise Pollution Publications Abstracts (Ceased)
.Aff.Bibl.	Marine Affairs Bibliography		
.Sci.Cont.Tab.	Marine Science Contents Tables (Ceased)	Nonfer.Met.Alert	Nonferrous Metals Alert
k.Res.Abstr.	Market Research Abstracts	Nonwov.Abstr.	Nonwovens Abstracts
s Spectr.Bull.	Mass Spectrometry Bulletin	Nucl.Sci.Abstr.	Nuclear Science Abstracts (Now INIS Atomindex)
Sci.Cit.Ind.	Materials Science Citation Index		
.R.	Mathematical Reviews	Numis.Lit.	Numismatic Literature
.Abstr.	Medical Abstract Service (Ceased)	Nurs.Abstr.	Nursing Abstracts
.& Surg. rmat.	Medical & Surgical Dermatology	Nurs.Res.Abstr.	Nursing Research Abstracts (Ceased)
		Nutr.Abstr.	Nutrition Abstracts & Reviews (Now: Nutrition Abstracts and Reviews Series A: Human and Experimental; Nutrition Abstracts and Reviews Series B: Livestock Feeds and Feeding)
.Care Rev.	Medical Care Review		
ia Rev.Dig.	Media Review Digest		
t.Retard. str.	Mental Retardation Abstracts (Now: Developmental Disabilities Abstracts) (Ceased)		

O

Abstr.	Metallurgical Abstracts (Now: Metals Abstracts)		
		Ocean.Abstr.	Oceanic Abstracts
Abstr.Ind.	Metals Abstracts Index	Ocean.Abstr.Bibl.	Oceanographic Abstracts and Bibliography (Now: Oceanographic Literature Review)
Finish.Abstr.	Metal Finishing Abstracts (Now: Surface Treatment Technology Abstracts)		
or.& oastrophys. str.	Meteorological & Geoastrophysical Abstracts	Ocean.Ind.	Oceanic Index (Now: Oceanic Abstracts)
		Off.Tech.	Offshore Technology
		Old Test.Abstr.	Old Testament Abstracts
.Per.Ind.	Methodist Periodical Index (Now: United Methodist Periodical Index) (Ceased)	Oncol.Abstr.	Oncology Abstracts (Ceased)
		Oper.Res. Manage.Sci.	Operations Research - Management Science
t.& Market. str.	Management & Marketing Abstracts		
		Ophthal.Lit.	Ophthalmic Literature

Oral Res.Abstr.	Oral Research Abstracts (Ceased)	Phys.Ber.	Physikalische Berichte (Now: Physics Briefs - Physikalische Berichte) (Ceased)
Ornam.Hort.	Ornamental Horticulture		
Ornithol.Abstr.	Essential Ornithological Abstracts		
		Phys.Ed.Ind.	Physical Education Index
		Pig News & Info.	Pig News and Information
		Pinpointer	Pinpointer (Ceased)

P

P.A.I.S.	P A I S Bulletin (Public Affairs Information Service) (Now: P A I S International in Print)	Plant Breed. Abstr.	Plant Breeding Abstracts
		Plant Grow.Reg. Abstr.	Plant Growth Regulator Abstracts
P.A.I.S.For. Lang.Ind.	Public Affairs Information Service Foreign Language Index (Now: P A I S International in Print)	Plast.Abstr.	Plastics Abstracts (Ceased)
		Pol.Tech.Abstr.	Polish Technical Abstracts (Now: Polish Technical and Economic Abstracts) (Ceased)
PC Abstr.	P C Abstracts (Personal Computing) (Ceased)		
PCC Alert	Polymers, Ceramics, Composites Alert	Polit.Sci.Abstr.	Political Science Abstracts
PCR2	P C R2 (Personal Computer Review - Squared)	Pollut.Abstr.	Pollution Abstracts
		Pop.Mus.Per.Ind.	Popular Music Periodicals Index (Ceased)
PHRA	Poverty & Human Resources Abstracts (Now: Human Resources Abstracts)	Pop.Per.Ind.	Popular Periodical Index
		Popul.Ind.	Population Index
P.I.R.A.	P.I.R.A. Marketing Abstracts (Packaging Industry Research Association) (Now: Management and Marketing Abstracts)	Potato Abstr.	Potato Abstracts
		Poult.Abstr.	Poultry Abstracts
		Print.Abstr.	Printing Abstracts
P.L.E.S.A.	Quarterly Index to Periodical Literature, Eastern and Southern Africa	Protozool.Abstr.	Protozoological Abstracts
		Psychoanal. Abstr.	Psychoanalysis Abstracts (Now: Psychoanalytic Abstracts)
P.L.I.I.	Property & Liability Insurance Index (Ceased)		
		Psychol.Abstr.	Psychological Abstracts
P.M.I.	Photography Magazine Index (Ceased)	Psychol.R.G.	Psychological Reader's Guide (Ceased)
PMR	Popular Magazine Review (Now: Magazine Article Summaries)	Psycho-pharmacol. Abstr.	Psychopharmacology Abstracts (Ceased)
P.N.I.	Pharmaceutical News Index		
PROMT	Predicasts Overview of Markets and Technologies	Psycscan	Psycscan: Applied Psychology
		Psycscan C.P.	Psycscan: Clinical Psychology
PSI	Philanthropic Studies Index	Psycscan D.P.	Psycscan: Developmental Psychology
Packag.Sci.Tech.	Packaging Science and Technology Abstracts	Pt.de Rep.	Point de Repere (Formed by the merger of Periodex and RADAR)
Paper & Bd.Abstr.	Paper and Board Abstracts (Now: Paperbase Abstracts)	Pub.Admin.Abstr.	Public Administration Abstracts and Index of Articles (Now: Documentation in Public Administration)
Past.Care & Couns.Abstr.	Pastoral Care & Counseling Abstracts (Now: Abstracts of Research in Pastoral Care and Counseling)		

Q

Peace Res.Abstr.	Peace Research Abstracts Journal		
Per.Islam.	Periodica Islamica	Q.Abstr.	Quality Abstracts (Ceased)
Perf.Arts Biog. Master Ind.	Performing Arts Biography Master Index	Qual.Contr. Appl.Stat.	Quality Control and Applied Statistics

R

Periodex	Periodex (Now: Point de Repere)		
Pers.Lit.	Personnel Literature		
Pers.Manage. Abstr.	Personnel Management Abstracts	RADAR	Repertoire Analytique d'Articles des Revues du Quebec (Now: Point de Repere)
Petrol.Abstr.	Petroleum Abstracts		
Petrol.Energy B.N.I.	Petroleum - Energy Business News Index	RAPRA	R A P R A Abstracts (Rubber and Plastics Research Association of Great Britain)
Phil.Ind.	Philosopher's Index	R.G.	Readers' Guide to Periodical Literature
Philip.Abstr.	Philippine Abstracts (Now: Philippine Science & Technology Abstracts)	R.G.Abstr.	Readers' Guide Abstracts
		RICS	R I C S Abstracts and Reviews (Now: RICS Library Information Service Abstracts and Reviews) (Royal Institute of Chartered Surveyors)
Photo.Abstr.	Photographic Abstracts (Now: Imaging Abstracts)		
Photo.Ind.	Photography Index		

	R I L A (Repertoire International de la Litterature d'Art) (Now: BHA (Bibliography of the History of Art))	SOPODA	Social Planning, Policy and Development Abstracts
	R I L M Abstracts of Music Literature (Repertoire International de la Litterature Musicale)	SRI	Statistical Reference Index
		SSCI	Social Sciences Citation Index
	Reactions (Now: Reactions Weekly)	Saf.Sci.Abstr.	Safety Science Abstracts Journal (Now: Health and Safety Science Abstracts)
Pt.Food us.Abstr.	Reference Point: Food Industry Abstracts	Sage Fam.Stud. Abstr.	Sage Family Studies Abstracts
Sour.	Reference Sources (Ceased)	Sage Pub.Admin. Abstr.	Sage Public Administration Abstracts
Zh.	Referativnyi Zhurnal	Sage Race Rel.Abstr.	Sage Race Relations Abstracts
g.Abstr.	Refugee Abstracts (Now: Refugee Survey Quarterly)	Sage Urb.Stud. Abstr.	Sage Urban Studies Abstracts
bil.Lit.	Rehabilitation Literature (Ceased)	Sci.Cit.Ind.	Science Citation Index
Theol. str.	Religious & Theological Abstracts	Sci.Res.Abstr.	Science Research Abstracts (Now: Solid State and Superconductivity Abstracts)
nd.One	Religion Index One: Periodicals	Search	Search (Devon)
nd.Two	Religion Index Two: Multi-Author Works	Seed Abstr.	Seed Abstracts
er.	Index to Religious Periodical Literature (Now: Religion Index One: Periodicals)	Sel.J.Water.	Selected Journals on Water (Ceased)
ndex	Repindex	Sel. Water Res. Abstr.	Selected Water Resources Abstracts (Now: Water Resources Abstracts)
Educ.	Research in Education (Now: Resources in Education)	Sh.& Vib.Dig.	Shock and Vibration Digest
High.Educ. str.	Research into Higher Education Abstracts	Small Anim. Abstr.	Small Animal Abstracts (Now: Small Animals)
ur.Ctr.Ind.	Resource Center Index	So.Pac.Per.Ind.	South Pacific Periodicals Index
Appl. omol.	Review of Applied Entomology. Series A (Now: Review of Agricultural Entomology) Review of Applied Entomology. Series B (Now: Review of Medical and Veterinary Entomology)	Soc.Sci.Ind.	Social Sciences Index
		Soc.Work Res.& Abstr.	Social Work Research & Abstracts (Now: Social Work Abstracts)
		Sociol.Abstr.	Sociological Abstracts
Appl.Mycol.	Review of Applied Mycology (Now: Review of Plant Pathology)	Sociol.Educ. Abstr.	Sociology of Education Abstracts
Med.& Mycol.	Review of Medical and Veterinary Mycology	Soft.Abstr.Eng.	Software Abstracts for Engineers
		Soils & Fert.	Soils & Fertilizers
Plant Path.	Review of Plant Pathology	Solid St.Abstr.	Solid State Abstracts (Now: Solid State and Superconductivity Abstracts)
.Abstr.	Rheology Abstracts		
Abstr.	Rice Abstracts	Sorghum & Millets Abstr.	Sorghum and Millets Abstracts (Now: Sorghum and Millets)
Abstr.	Risk Abstracts		
mat.	Robomatix Reporter (Now: Robotics Abstracts) (Ceased)	South.Bap.Per. Ind.	Southern Baptist Periodical Index (Ceased)
Devel. tr.	Rural Development Abstracts	Soyabean Abstr.	Soyabean Abstracts
Ext.Educ.& bstr.	Rural Extension, Education and Training Abstracts (Ceased)	Sp.Ed.Needs Abstr.	Special Education Needs Abstracts
Recreat. .Abstr.	Rural Recreation and Tourism Abstracts (Now: Leisure, Recreation and Tourism Abstracts)	Speleol.Abstr.	Speleological Abstracts
		Sport Fish.Abstr.	Sport Fishery Abstracts (Now: Fisheries Review)
		Sports Per.Ind.	Sports Periodicals Index (Ceased)
	S	Sportsearch	Sportsearch
		Sri Lanka Sci. Ind.	Sri Lanka Science Index
	State Academies of Science Abstracts		
aterabstr.	S.A. Waterabstracts (South Africa) (Ceased)	Stat.Theor.Meth. Abstr.	Statistical Theory and Method Abstracts
	S C I M P (Selective Cooperative Index of Management Periodicals) (Ceased)	Steels Alert	Steels Alert
		Stud.Wom.Abstr.	Studies on Women Abstracts
	School Organization & Management Abstracts	Sugar Ind.Abstr.	Sugar Industry Abstracts

T

T.C.E.A.	Theoretical Chemical Engineering Abstracts (Now: Theoretical Chemical Engineering)
THA	Tobacco & Health Abstracts
TOM	T O M (Text on Microfilm)
Tech.Educ.Abstr.	Technical Education Abstracts (Now: Technical Education & Training Abstracts)
Tel.Abstr.	Telecommunications Abstracts (Ceased)
Tel.Alert	Telecommunications Alert
Telegen	Telegen Reporter (Now: Telegen Abstracts) (Ceased)
Text.Tech.Dig.	Textile Technology Digest
Therm.Abstr.	Thermal Abstracts (Now: International Building Services Abstracts)
Tob.Abstr.	Tobacco Abstracts
Top Manage. Abstr.	Top Management Abstracts (Also see: Anbar)
Tox.Abstr.	Toxicology Abstracts
Tr.& Dev.Alert	Training and Development Alert
Tr.& Indus.Ind.	Trade & Industry Index
Trans.Res.Abstr.	Transportation Research Abstracts (Ceased)
Triticale Abstr.	Triticale Abstracts (Now: Wheat, Barley and Triticale Abstracts)
Trop.Abstr.	Tropical Abstracts (Now: Abstracts on Tropical Agriculture)
Trop.Dis.Bull.	Tropical Diseases Bulletin
Trop.Oil Seeds Abstr.	Tropical Oil Seeds Abstracts (Now: Tropical Oil Seeds)

U

Urb.Aff.Abstr.	Urban Affairs Abstracts

V

Va.Hist.Abstr.	Virginia Historical Abstracts (Ceased)
Vert.File Ind.	Vertical File Index
Vet.Bull.	Veterinary Bulletin
Viol.& Abuse Abstr.	Violence & Abuse Abstracts
Virol.Abstr.	Virology Abstracts (Now: Virology and AIDS Abstracts)
Vis.Ind.	Vision Index (Ceased)
VITIS	Vitis - Viticulture and Enology Abstracts

W

WPM	World Publishing Monitor
W.R.C.Inf.	W.R.C. Information (Water Research Centre) (Now: Aqualine Abstracts)
Water Pollut. Abstr.	Water Pollution Abstracts (Now: Aquali Abstracts)
Water Resour. Abstr.	Water Resources Abstracts (Now: Hydro-Abstracts)
Weed Abstr.	Weed Abstracts
Wild Life Rev.	Wildlife Review (Ceased)
Wild.Rev.	Wildlife Review (Fort Collins)
Wildlife & Conserv.Biol. Abstr.	Essential Wildlife & Conservation Biolo Abstracts
Wom.Stud.Abstr.	Women Studies Abstracts
Work Rel.Abstr.	Work Related Abstracts (Ceased)
World Agri.Econ. & Rural Sociol. Abstr.	World Agricultural Economics & Rural Sociology Abstracts
World Alum. Abstr.	World Aluminum Abstracts
World Bank. Abstr.	World Banking Abstracts
World Bibl.Soc. Sec.	World Bibliography of Social Security
World Fish.Abstr.	World Fisheries Abstracts (Ceased)
World Surf.Coat.	World Surface Coatings Abstracts
World Text.Abstr.	World Textile Abstracts

Y

Yrbk.Assoc.Educ. & Rehab.Blind	Association for Education and Rehabilitation of the Blind and Visu Impaired. Yearbook (Ceased)

Z

Zent.Math.	Zentralblatt fuer Mathematik und ihre Grenzgebiete
Zincscan	Zincscan
Zoo.Rec.	Zoological Record

Subject Guide to Abstracting and Indexing

The 135 subject headings listed below are major subjects which contain a sub-category headed "Abstracting, Bibliographies, Statistics." This sub-category, which follows the major subject headings in the CLASSIFIED LIST OF SERIALS, identifies publications which abstract and/or index publications in the relevant subject. Bibliographies and statistical publications pertaining to the subject are also included in this sub-category. This guide will enable users to quickly locate subject areas of interest for which abstracting and indexing publications have been identified and to build profiles by combination of relevant subject areas. Page numbers refer to the first page on which the sub-category appears.

SUBJECT CATEGORY	PAGE
Advertising and Public Relations	47
Aeronautics and Space Flight	83
Agriculture	167
Alternative Medicine	299
Animal Welfare	305
Anthropology	335
Archaeology	390
Architecture	417
Art	475
Arts and Handicrafts	485
Astronomy	503
Beauty Culture	509
Beverages	530
Biography	581
Biology	634
Birth Control	859
Building and Construction	919
Business and Economics	1014
Ceramics, Glass and Pottery	1735
Chemistry	1771
Children and Youth	1861
Civil Defense	1899
Classical Studies	1909
Cleaning and Dyeing	1912
Clothing Trade	1919
College and Alumni	1980
Communications	2010
Computers	2093
Conservation	2251
Consumer Education and Protection	2259
Criminology and Law Enforcement	2283
Dance	2295
Drug Abuse and Alcoholism	2307
Earth Sciences	2324
Education	2496
Electronics	2655
Energy	2681
Engineering	2746
Environmental Studies	2959
Ethnic Interests	3051
Fire Prevention	3059
Fish and Fisheries	3081
Folklore	3093
Food and Food Industries	3131
Forests and Forestry	3167
Minerals	3179
Gardening and Horticulture	3208

SUBJECT CATEGORY	PAGE
Genealogy and Heraldry	3246
Geography	3427
Gerontology and Geriatrics	3447
Handicapped	3458
Heating, Plumbing and Refrigeration	3486
History	3518
Hobbies	3680
Home Economics	3690
Homosexuality	3702
Hospitals	3721
Hotels and Restaurants	3738
Housing and Urban Planning	3764
How-to and Do-it-Yourself	3769
Humanities: Comprehensive Works	3798
Instruments	3806
Insurance	3838
Interior Design and Decoration	3851
Jewelry, Clocks and Watches	3868
Journalism	3883
Labor Unions	3902
Law	4050
Leather and Fur Industries	4147
Leisure and Recreation	4154
Library and Information Sciences	4223
Linguistics	4318
Literary and Political Reviews	4368
Literature	4493
Machinery	4554
Mathematics	4617
Matrimony	4627
Medical Sciences	4762
Meetings and Congresses	5173
Metallurgy	5216
Meteorology	5248
Metrology and Standardization	5256
Military	5292
Mines and Mining Industry	5319
Motion Pictures	5348
Museums and Art Galleries	5369
Music	5446
Numismatics	5468
Nutrition and Dietetics	5484
Occupational Health and Safety	5502
Occupations and Careers	5518

SUBJECT CATEGORY	PAGE
Oriental Studies	5541
Packaging	5550
Paints and Protective Coatings	5556
Paleontology	5564
Paper and Pulp	5573
Parapsychology and Occultism	5579
Patents, Trademarks and Copyrights	5592
Petroleum and Gas	5628
Pets	5644
Pharmacy and Pharmacology	5700
Philately	5715
Philosophy	5760
Photography	5776
Physical Fitness and Hygiene	5793
Physics	5833
Plastics	5886
Political Science	5982
Population Studies	6060
Printing	6087
Psychology	6160
Public Administration	6201
Public Health and Safety	6255
Publishing and Book Trade	6288
Real Estate	6316
Religions and Theology	6385
Rubber	6505
Sciences: Comprehensive Works	6587
Shoes and Boots	6597
Social Sciences: Comprehensive Works	6648
Social Services and Welfare	6695
Sociology	6739
Sound Recording and Reproduction	6746
Sports and Games	6795
Technology: Comprehensive Works	6980
Textile Industries and Fabrics	6999
Theater	7018
Tobacco	7022
Transportation	7047
Travel and Tourism	7252
Veterinary Science	7285
Water Resources	7307
Women's Health	7311
Women's Interests	7370
Women's Studies	7350

Subjects

ENGLISH	FRENCH	GERMAN	SPANISH
Abstracting and Indexing Services	Services d'Analyse et d'Indexage	Referate- und Indexdienste	Servicio de Análisis e Indización
Advertising and Public Relations	Publicité et Relations Publiques	Reklamewesen und Public Relations	Relaciones Públicas y Publicidad
Aeronautics and Space Flight	Aéronautique et Astronautique	Luft- und Raumfahrt	Aeronáutica y Vuelo Espacial
Computer Applications	Applications Informatiques	Computer Anwendung	Aplicaciones para Computadoras
Agriculture	Agriculture	Landwirtschaft	Agricultura
Agricultural Economics	Agriculture Économique	Agrarökonomie	Economía Agrícola
Agricultural Equipment	Outillage Agricole	Landwirtschaftsgeräte	Equipo para la Agricultura
Computer Applications	Applications Informatiques	Computer Anwendung	Aplicaciones para Computadoras
Crop Production and Soil	Production Végétale et Terrain	Ernte und Acker	Producción de Cosecha, Tierra
Dairying and Dairy Products	Production Laitière	Milchwirtschaft	Lechería y Productos Lácteos
Feed, Flour and Grain	Pature, Farine et Grain	Futter, Mehl und Getreide	Forraje, Granos y Harina
Poultry and Livestock	Élevage	Geflügel- und Viehwirtschaft	Ganadería
Alternative Medicine	Médecine Alternative	Alternative Heilkunde	Medicina Alternativa
Animal Welfare	Protection des Animaux	Tierschutz	Protección a los Animales
Anthropology	Anthropologie	Anthropologie	Antropología
Antiques	Antiquités	Antiquitäten	Antigüedades
Archaeology	Archeologie	Archaeologie	Arqueología
Computer Applications	Applications Informatiques	Computer Anwendung	Aplicaciones para Computadoras
Architecture	Architecture	Architektur	Arquitectura
Computer Applications	Applications Informatiques	Computer Anwendung	Aplicaciones para Computadoras
Art	Art	Kunst	Arte
Computer Applications	Applications Informatiques	Computer Anwendung	Aplicaciones para Computadoras
Arts and Handicrafts	Arts et Métiers	Kunst und Handwerk	Artesanías y Obras Manuales
Astrology	Astrologie	Astrologie	Astrología
Astronomy	Astronomie	Astronomie	Astronomía
Computer Applications	Applications Informatiques	Computer Anwendung	Aplicaciones para Computadoras
Beauty Culture	Soins de Beauté	Schönheitspflege	Belleza Personal
Perfumes and Cosmetics	Parfums et Cosmétiques	Kosmetik und Parfüme	Perfumes y Cosméticos
Beverages	Boissons	Getränke	Bebidas
Bibliographies	Bibliographies	Bibliographien	Bibliografías
Biography	Biographie	Biographie	Biografía
Biology	Biologie	Biologie	Biología
Bioengineering	Biogénie	Bioingenieurwesen	Bio-ingeniería
Biological Chemistry	Biochimie	Biochemie	Bio-química
Biophysics	Biophysique	Biophysik	Biofísica
Biotechnology	Biotechnologie	Biotechnologie	Biotecnología
Botany	Botanique	Botanik	Botánica
Computer Applications	Applications Informatiques	Computer Anwendung	Aplicaciones para Computadoras
Cytology and Histology	Cytologie et Histologie	Zytologie und Histologie	Citología e Histología
Entomology	Entomologie	Entomologie	Entomología
Genetics	Génétique	Genetik	Genética
Microbiology	Microbiologie	Mikrobiologie	Microbiología
Microscopy	Microscopie	Mikroskopie	Microscopía
Ornithology	Ornithologie	Ornithologie	Ornitología
Physiology	Physiologie	Physiologie	Fisiología
Zoology	Zoologie	Zoologie	Zoología
Birth Control	Limitation des Naissances	Geburtenregelung	Control Natal
Building and Construction	Bâtiment et Construction	Bauwesen	Edificios y Construcción
Carpentry and Woodwork	Charpenterie et Menuiserie	Zimmerhandwerk und Holzbau	Carpintería y Ebanistería
Hardware	Quincaillerie	Metallbaustoffe	Ferretería
Business and Economics	Affaires et Économie	Wirtschaft und Handel	Economía y Negocios
Accounting	Comptabilité	Rechnungswesen	Contabilidad
Banking and Finance	Banque et Finance	Bank- und Finanzwesen	Bancos y Finanzas

Banking and Finance-
    Computer Applications
	Banque et Finance-
	    Applications Informatiques
		Bank- und Finanzwesen-
		    Computer Anwendung
			Bancos y Finanzas-
			    Aplicaciones para Computadoras

Chamber of Commerce
    Publications
	Publications des Chambres
	    de Commerce
		Veröffentlichungen von Handels-
		    kammern
			Publicaciones de las Cámaras de
			    Comercio

Computer Applications	Applications Informatiques	Computer Anwendung	Aplicaciones para Computadoras
Cooperatives	Coopératives	Genossenschaften	Cooperativas
Domestic Commerce	Commerce Interieur	Binnenhandel	Comercio Interno

Economic Situation and
    Conditions
	Situations et Conditions
	    Économiques
		Wirtschaftliche Situation und
		    Verhältnisse
			Condiciones y Situaciones
			    Económicas

Economic Systems and Theories,
    Economic History
	Systèmes et Théories Économiques,
	    Histoire Économique
		Ökonomische Systeme und
		    Theorien, Wirtschafts-
		    geschichte
			Sistemas y Teorías Económicos,
			    Historia de la Económia

International Commerce	Commerce International	Aussenhandel	Comercio Internacional

International Development and
    Assistance
	Aide et Développement
	    Internationaux
		Internationale Entwicklungshilfe	Desarrollo y Asistencia Inter-
			    nacional

Investments	Investissements	Investitionen	Inversiones
Labor and Industrial Relations	Travail et Relations Industrielles	Arbeits und Industrielle Beziehungen	Trabajo y Relaciones Industriales
Macroeconomics	Macroéconomie	Makroökonomie	Macroeconomía
Management	Gestion	Betriebsführung	Administración
Marketing and Purchasing	Marketing et Achats	Marketing und Kauf	Ventas y Mercadotenica
Office Equipment and Services	Matériel et Entretien de Bureaux	Büroeinrichtung und Service	Equipo y Servicios de Oficinas
Personnel Management	Gestion du Personnel	Personal Führung	Administración de Personal
Production of Goods and Services	Production de Biens et Services	Produktion	Producción de Bienes y Servicios
Public Finance, Taxation	Tresor Publique, Fiscalité	Staatsfinanzen, Steuerwesen	Finanzas Públicas e Impuestos
Small Business	Petites et Moyennes Entreprises	Kleinbetrieb	Pequeños Negocios
Trade and Industrial Directories	Annuaires de Commerce et d'Industrie	Firmenverzeichnisse	Directorios de la Industria y el Comer

SUBJECTS   xlvii

ramics, Glass and Pottery	Céramique, Verrerie et Poterie	Keramik, Glas und Töpferei	Cerámica, Vidrio y Porcelana
emistry	Chimie	Chemie	Química
Analytical Chemistry	Chimie Analytique	Analytische Chemie	Química Analítica
Computer Applications	Applications Informatiques	Computer Anwendung	Aplicaciones para Computadoras
Crystallography	Cristallographie	Kristallographie	Cristalografía
Electrochemistry	Electrochimie	Elektrochemie	Electroquímica
Inorganic Chemistry	Chimie Inorganique	Anorganische Chemie	Química Inorgánica
Organic Chemistry	Chimie Organique	Organische Chemie	Química Orgánica
Physical Chemistry	Physicochimie	Physikalische Chemie	Fisicoquímica
ldren and Youth	Enfants et Adolescents	Kinder und Jugend	Niños y Jóvenes
About	Au Sujet des	Über	Acerca
or	Pour	Für	Para
l Defense	Defense Civile	Ziviler Bevölkerungsschutz	Defensa Civil
ssical Studies	Etudes Classiques	Klassische Studien	Estudios Clásicos
aning and Dyeing	Nettoyage et Teinturerie	Reinigen und Färben	Limpieza y Tintura
thing Trade	Vêtement	Bekleidungsgewerbe	Industria del Vestido
ashions	Mode	Moden	Modas
bs	Clubs	Klubs	Clubes
ege and Alumni	Université et Diplomés	Universitäten und Hochschul-absolventen	Universidades y Exalumnos
mmunications	Communications	Nachrichtentechnik	Comunicaciones
Computer Applications	Applications Informatiques	Computer Anwendung	Aplicaciones para Computadoras
ostal Affairs	Courrier	Postwesen	Correo
adio	Radio	Rundfunk	Radio
elephone and Telegraph	Téléphone et Télégraphe	Telephon und Telegraph	Teléfono y Telégrafo
elevision and Cable	Télévision	Fernsehen und Bildfrequenzkanal	Cable y Televisión
ideo	Video		Video
mputers	Ordinateurs	Computer	Computadoras
rtificial Intelligence	Intelligence Artificielle	Künstliche Intelligenz	Inteligencia Artificial
utomation	Automation	Automatisierung	Automatización
alculating Machines	Calculateurs	Rechenmaschine	Calculadoras
ircuits	Circuits	Schaltungen	Circuitos
omputer Architecture	Architecture de la Machine	Computer Architektur	Arquitectura de las Computadoras
omputer-Assisted Instruction	Enseignement Assisté par Ordinateur	Computerunterstützter Unterricht	Enseñanza con la Ayuda de las Computadoras
omputer Engineering	Technique Informatique	Computerentwicklung	Ingeniería de las Computadoras
omputer Games	Jeux sur Ordinateurs	Computer Spiele	Juegos para Computadoras
omputer Graphics	Conception Assistée par Ordinateur	Computergraphik	Diseño a través de Computadoras
omputer Industry	Industrie Informatique	Computerbetrieb	Industria de las Computadoras
omputer Industry Directories	Annuaire de l'Industrie Informatique	Computerbetriebverzeichnisse	Directorios de la Industria de las Computadoras
omputer Industry, Vocational Guidance	Industrie Informatique, Orientation Professionnelle	Computerbetrieb Berufsberatung	Guia para la Industria de las Computadoras
omputer Music	Musique sur Ordinateur	Computer Musik	Música a través de Computadoras
omputer Networks	Réseaux d'Ordinateurs	Rechnernetz	Redes de Computadoras
omputer Programming	Programmation Informatique	Computerprogrammierung	Programación de Computadoras
omputer Sales	Ventes d'Ordinateurs	Computervertrieb	Ventas de Computadoras
omputer Security	Sécurité Informatique	Computersicherheit	Seguridad en Computadoras
omputer Simulation	Simulation sur Ordinateurs	Computersimulation	Simulación a través de Computadoras
omputer Systems	Systèmes Informatiques	Computersystemen	Sistemas de Computadoras
ybernetics	Cybernétique	Kybernetik	Cibernética
ata Base Management	Gestion de Base de Données	Datenbankverwaltung	Bases de Datos
ata Communications, Data Transmission Systems	Communication de données	Datenübertragung, Datenübertragungssystem	Comunicación y Transmisión de Datos
ectronic Data Processing	Traitement de l'Information Electronique	Elektronische Datenverarbeitung	Procesamiento Electrónico de Datos
ardware	Matériel	Hardware	Equipo Físico
ormation Science, Information Theory	Théorie de l'Information	Informationstheorie	Ciencia y Teoría de la Información
achine Theory	Théorie de Machine	Maschinetheorie	Teoría de las Máquinas
crocomputers	Micro-Ordinateurs	Mikrocomputer	Microcomputadoras
nicomputers	Mini-Ordinateurs	Minicomputer	Minicomputadoras
ersonal Computers	Ordinateurs Personnels	Persönlichecomputer	Computadoras Personales
botics	Robotique	Robotersysteme	Robótica
ftware	Logiciel	SoftwareRComputertheorie	Applicaciones de Computadora
eory of Computing	Théorie de Traitement	Textverarbeitung	Teoría de Cálculo
rd Processing	Traitement de Textes		Procesador de Textos
ervation	Conservation	Landschaftsschutz	Conservación
umer Education and Protection	Protection du Consommateur	Verbraucherswirtschaftsschutz	Protección al Consumidor
nology and Law Enforcement	Criminologie et Police	Kriminologie und Strafvollzug	Criminología y Acción Policial
mputer Applications	Applications Informatiques	Computer Anwendung	Aplicaciones para Computadoras
curity	Securité	Sicherheit	Seguridad
e	Danse	Tanz	Baile
Abuse and Alcoholism	Toxicomanie et Alcoolisme	Rauschgiftsucht und Alkoholismus	Alcoholismo y Drogadicción
Sciences	Sciences Géologiques	Wissenschaften der Erde	Ciencias Geológicas
mputer Applications	Applications Informatiques	Computer Anwendung	Aplicaciones para Computadoras
ology	Géologie	Geologie	Geología
ophysics	Géophysique	Geophysik	Geofísica
drology	Hydrologie	Hydrologie	Hidrología
eanography	Océanographie	Ozeanographie	Oceanografía
ation	Education	Bildungswesen	Educación
ult Education	Enseignement des Adultes	Erwachsenenbildung	Educación para Adultos
mputer Applications	Applications Informatiques	Computer Anwendung	Aplicaciones para Computadoras
ides to Schools and Colleges	Guides des Écoles et Colleges	Führer zur Schulen und Universitäten	Guías de Escuelas y Colegios
her Education	Enseignement Supérieur	Hochschulwesen	Educación Superior
ernational Education Programs	Programmes d'Éducation Internationale	Internationale Erziehungsprogramme	Programas Internacionales de Educación
ool Organization and Administration	Organisation et Administration de l'École	Organisation und Verwaltung von dem Schule	Administración y Dirección de Escuelas
ecial Education and Rehabilitation	Enseignement Special et Réhabilitation	Fachunterricht und Rehabilitierung	Educación Especial y Rehabilitación
ching Methods and Curriculum	Méthodes Pédagogiques et Programmes Scolaires	Lehrmethoden und Lehrplan	Métodos y Planes de Estudio

SUBJECTS

Electronics	Electronique	Elektronik	Electrónica
Computer Applications	Applications Informatiques	Computer Anwendung	Aplicaciones para Computadoras
Encyclopedias and General Almanacs	Encyclopédies et Almanachs Générales	Enzyklopädien und Allgemeine Nachschlagewerke	Enciclopedias y Almanaques Generales
Energy	Energie	Energie	Energía
Computer Applications	Applications Informatiques	Computer Anwendung	Aplicaciones para Computadoras
Electrical Energy	Energie Électrique	Elektrizitätsenergie	Energía Eléctrica
Geothermal Energy	Energie Géothermique	Thermalenergie	Energía Geotérmica
Hydroelectrical Energy	Energie Hydraulique	Hydroelektroenergie	Energía Hidroeléctrica
Nuclear Energy	Energie Nucléaire	Kernenergie	Energía Nuclear
Solar Energy	Energie Solaire	Sonnenenergie	Energía Solar
Wind Energy	Energie Eolienne	Windenergie	Energía de Viento
Engineering	Ingénierie	Ingenieurwesen	Ingeniería
Chemical Engineering	Génie Chimique	Chemieingenieurwesen	Ingeniería Química
Civil Engineering	Génie Civil	Bauingenieurwesen	Ingeniería Civil
Computer Applications	Applications Informatiques	Computer Anwendung	Aplicaciones para Computadoras
Electrical Engineering	Génie Électrique	Elektrotechnik	Ingeniería Eléctrica
Engineering Mechanics and Materials	Méchanique et Materiels	Ingenieurwesen Mechanik und Materialien	Ingeniería Mecánica y de Materiales
Hydraulic Engineering	Génie Hydraulique	Wasserbau	Ingeniería Hidráulica
Industrial Engineering	Génie Industriel	Industrieingenieurwesen	Ingeniería Industrial
Mechanical Engineering	Génie Mécanique	Maschinenbau	Ingeniería Mecánica
Environmental Studies	Science de l'Environnement	Umweltschutz	Estudios Ambientales
Computer Applications	Applications Informatiques	Computer Anwendung	Aplicaciones para Computadoras
Pollution	Pollution	Umweltverschmutzung	Contaminación
Toxicology and Environmental Safety	Toxicologie et Sécurité de l'Environnement	Toxokologie und Umweltsicherheit	Toxicología y Seguridad Ambiental
Waste Management	Gestion de Déchets	Abfallwirtschaft	Administración de Desperdicios
Ethnic Interests	Ethnologie	Allgemeine Völkerkunde	Publicaciones de Temas Étnicos
Fire Prevention	Prévention d'Incendie	Brandbekämpfung	Prevención del Fuego
Fish and Fisheries	Poisson et Pêche	Fische und Fischerei	Pesca y Pesquerías
Folklore	Folklore	Volkskunde	Folklore
Food and Food Industries	Alimentation et Industries Alimentaires	Nahrungsmittel und Lebensmittelindustrie	Alimentos e Industrias de Alimentos
Bakers and Confectioners	Boulangerie et Confiserie	Bäcker- und Konditorgewerbe	Panaderías y Dulcerías
Grocery Trade	Épicerie	Kolonialwarenhandel	Abacerías
Forest and Forestry	Forêts et Exploitation Forestière	Forstwesen und Waldwirtschaft	Bosques y Selvicultura
Lumber and Wood	Bois	Holz	Maderas
Funerals	Funérailles	Beerdigungen	Funerales
Gardening and Horticulture	Jardinage et Horticulture	Gartenpflege und Gartenbau	Jardinería y Horticultura
Florist Trade	Commerce des Fleurs	Blumenhandel	Comercio de Flores
Genealogy and Heraldry	Généalogie et Science Héraldique	Genealogie und Wappenkunde	Genealogía y Heráldica
Computer Applications	Applications Informatiques	Computer Anwendung	Aplicaciones para Computadoras
General Interest Periodicals (Subdivided by country)	Publications d'Intérêt Général (Selon pays)	Allgemeine Zeitschriften (nach Land)	Periódicos de Interés General (por país)
Geography	Géographie	Geographie	Geografía
Computer Applications	Applications Informatiques	Computer Anwendung	Aplicaciones para Computadoras
Gerontology and Geriatrics	Gérontologie	Gerontologie	Gerontología y Geriátrica
Giftware and Toys	Cadeaux et Jouets	Geschenkartikel und Spielwaren	Juguetes y Regalos
Handicapped	Handicapés	Behinderung	Descapacitados
Computer Applications	Applications Informatiques	Computer Anwendung	Aplicaciones para Computadoras
Hearing Impaired	Sourds	Schwerhörigkeit	Descapacitado del Oído
Physically Impaired	Handicapés Physiques	Körperbehinderung	Descapacitado Físicamente
Visually Impaired	Aveugles	Blindheit	Descapacitado Visualmente
Heating, Plumbing, and Refrigeration	Chauffage, Plomberie et Réfrigeration	Heizung, Kühlung und Installation	Calefacción, Plomería y Refrigeración
History	Histoire	Geschichte	Historia
Computer Applications	Applications Informatiques	Computer Anwendung	Aplicaciones para Computadoras
History of Africa	Histoire de l'Afrique	Geschichte-Afrika	Historia de Africa
History of Asia	Histoire de l'Asie	Geschichte-Asien	Historia de Asia
History of Australasia and Other Areas	Histoire de l'Australasie et Autres Pays	Geschichte-Australasien und Andere Gebieten	Historia de Australasia y Otras Areas
History of Europe	Histoire de l'Europe	Geschichte-Europa	Historia de la Europa
History of North and South America	Histoire de l'Amérique du Nord et du Sud	Geschichte-Nord- und Südamerika	Historia de América del Norte y del Sur
History of Near East	Histoire du Proche-Orient	Geschichte-Nahe Osten	Historia del Cercano Oriente
Hobbies	Passe-Temps	Hobbies	Pasatiempos
Home Economics	Gestion Domestique	Hauswirtschaft	Economía Doméstica
Homosexuality	Homosexualité	Homosexualität	Homosexualidad
Hospitals	Hôpitaux	Krankenhäuser	Hospitales
Computer Applications	Applications Informatiques	Computer Anwendung	Aplicaciones para Computadoras
Hotels and Restaurants	Hôtels et Restaurants	Hotels und Restaurants	Restaurantes y Hoteles
Computer Applications	Applications Informatiques	Computer Anwendung	Aplicaciones para Computadoras
Housing and Urban Planning	Logement et Urbanisme	Wohnungswesen und Stadtplanung	Planeación Urbana y Vivienda
Computer Applications	Applications Informatiques	Computer Anwendung	Aplicaciones para Computadoras
How-To and Do-It-Yourself	Bricolage	Selbstanfertigung	Cómo Hacerlo Usted Mismo
Humanities: Comprehensive Works	Humanités: Oeuvres d'Ensemble	Klassische Philologie	Humanidades: Obras Generales
Computer Applications	Applications Informatiques	Computer Anwendung	Aplicaciones para Computadoras
Instruments	Instruments	Instrumente	Instrumentos
Insurance	Assurances	Versicherungswesen	Seguros
Computer Applications	Applications Informatiques	Computer Anwendung	Aplicaciones para Computadoras
Interior Design and Decoration	Agencements Intérieurs et Décoration	Innenarchitektur und Innenausstattung	Diseño Interior y Ornamentación
Furniture and House Furnishings	Meubles et Articles pour la Maison	Möbel und Wohnungseinrichtung	Muebles y Articulos para el Hogar
Jewelry, Clocks and Watches	Bijouterie et Horlogerie	Schmuck und Uhren	Joyería y Relojería
Journalism	Journalisme	Journalismus	Periodismo

SUBJECTS

or Unions	Syndicalisme	Gewerkschaften	Sindicatos
Civil Law	Droit	Rechtswissenschaft	Derecho
Computer Applications	Droit Civil	Zivilrecht	Derecho Civil
Constitutional Law	Applications Informatiques	Computer Anwendung	Aplicaciones para Computadoras
Corporate Law	Droit Constitutionel	Verfassungsrecht	Derecho Constitucional
Criminal Law	Droit Commercial	Handelsrecht	Derecho Corporativo
Estate Planning	Droit Pénal	Strafrecht	Derecho Criminal
Family and Matrimonial Law	Succession	Mobiliarvermögensrecht	Planeación de Bienes Raíces
International Law	Droit Familial et Matrimonial	Ehegesetz und Familienrecht	Derecho Familial y Matrimonial
Judicial Systems	Droit International	Völkerrecht	Derecho Internacional
Legal Aid	Système Judiciaire	Gerichtswesen	Sistemas Judiciales
Maritime Law	Assistance Judiciaire	Rechtshilfe	Ayuda Legal
Military Law	Droit Maritime	Seerecht	Derecho Marítimo
ther and Fur Industries	Droit Militaire	Kriegsrecht	Derecho Militar
ure and Recreation	Maroquinerie et Fourrure	Leder und Pelz	Pieles y Cuero
ary and Information Science	Loisirs et Récréation	Freizeit und Unterhaltung	Tiempo Libre y Recreación
	Bibliothéconomie et Informatique	Bibliothek- und Informationswissenschaft	Bibliotecología y Ciencias de la Información
Computer Applications	Applications Informatiques	Computer Anwendung	Aplicaciones para Computadoras
uistics	Linguistique	Sprachwissenschaft	Lingüística
Computer Applications	Applications Informatiques	Computer Anwendung	Aplicaciones para Computadoras
rary and Political Reviews	Revues Littéraires et Politiques	Literarische und Politische Zeitschriften	Revistas Literarias y Políticas
ature	Littérature	Literatur	Literatura
dventure and Romance	Aventure et Romance	Abenteuer und Romantik	Aventura y Romance
Mystery and Detective	Mystère et Policier	Geheimnis und Detektivroman	Misterio y Novela Policiaca
oetry	Poésie	Poesie	Poesía
cience Fiction, Fantasy, Horror	Science-Fiction, Fantastisque, Horreur	Zukunftsroman, Phantasiegebilde, Grausen	Ciencia Ficción, Fantasía, Horror
hinery	Machines	Maschinenwesen	Maquinaria
omputer Applications	Applications Informatiques	Computer Anwendung	Aplicaciones para Computadoras
hematics	Mathématiques	Mathematik	Matemáticas
omputer Applications	Applications Informatiques	Computer Anwendung	Aplicaciones para Computadoras
imony	Mariage	Ehestand	Matrimonio
omputer Applications	Applications Informatiques	Computer Anwendung	Aplicaciones para Computadoras
ical Sciences	Médecine	Medizinische Wissenschaften	Ciencias Médicas
llergology and Immunology	Allergologie et Immunologie	Allergie und Immunologie	Alergología e Imunología
naesthesiology	Anesthésiologie	Anästesiologie	Anestesiología
ardiovascular Diseases	Maladies Cardiovasculaires	Kreislauferkrankungen	Enfermedades Cardiovasculares
hiropractic, Homeopathy, Osteopathy	Chiropraxie, Homéopathie, Ostéopathie	Chiropraktik, Homöopathie, Osteopathie	Quiropráctica, Homeopatía, Osteopatía
ommunicable Diseases	Maladies Contagieuses	Infektiöse Krankheiten	Enfermedades Contagiosas
omputer Applications	Applications Informatiques	Computer Anwendung	Aplicaciones para Computadoras
entistry	Dentisterie	Zahnmedizin	Odontología
rmatology and Venereology	Dermatologie et Maladies Vénériennes	Dermatologie und Geschlechtskrankheiten	Dermatología y Venereología
ndocrinology	Endocrinologie	Endokrinologie	Endocrinología
xperimental Medicine Laboratory Technique	Médecine Expérimentale, Techniques de Laboratoire	Versuchsmedizin, Laboratoriumstechnik	Medicina Experimental, Técnicas del Laboratorio
orensic Sciences	Médecine Légale	Gerichtliche Medizin	Ciencias Forenses
astroenterology	Gastroentérologie	Gastroenterologie	Gastroenterología
ematology	Hématologie	Hämatologie	Hematología
ypnosis	Hypnose	Hypnose	Hipnotismo
ternal Medicine	Médecine Interne	Innere Medizin	Medicina Interna
urses and Nursing	Personnel et Soins Infirmiers	Krankenpflege	Enfermeros y Enfermería
bstetrics and Gynecology	Obstétrique et Gynécologie	Gynäkologie und Geburtshilfe	Obstetricia y Ginecología
ncology	Cancer	Onkologie	Oncología
phthalmology and Optometry	Ophtalmologie et Optométrie	Opthalmologie und Optometrie	Oftalmología y Optometría
rthopedics and Traumatology	Orthopédie et Traumatologie	Orthopädie und Traumatologie	Ortopedia y Traumatología
torhinolaryngology	Otorhinolaryngologie	Otorhinolaryngologie	Otorinolaringología
ediatrics	Pédiatrie	Pädiatrie	Pediatría
ysical Medicine and Rehabilitation	Médecine Physique et Réhabilitation	Physikalische Heilkunde und Rehabilitation	Medicina Física y de Rehabilitación
ychiatry and Neurology	Psychiatrie et Neurologie	Psychiatrie und Neurologie	Psiquiatría y Neurología
adiology and Nuclear Medicine	Radiologie et Médecine Nucléaire	Radiologie und Nuklearmedizin	Radiología y Medicina Nuclear
espiratory Diseases	Maladies Respiratoires	Atmungskrankheiten	Enfermedades Respiratorias
eumatology	Rhumatologie	Rheumatologie	Reumatología
orts Medicine	Médecine du Sport	Sportmedizin	Medicina del Deporte
rgery	Chirurgie	Chirurgie	Cirugía
ology and Nephrology	Urologie et Néphrologie	Urologie und Nephrologie	Urología y Nefrología
ings and Congresses	Réunions et Congrès	Tagungen und Kongresse	Conferencias y Congresos
s Health	Santé de l'Homme	Gesundheit von Männern	Salud de los Hombres
s Interests	Publications d'Intérêt Masculin	Männer Interessen	Intereses Masculinos
s Studies	Études de l'Homme	Männerstudien	Estudios de los Hombres
llurgy	Métallurgie	Metallurgie	Metalurgia
omputer Applications	Applications Informatiques	Computer Anwendung	Aplicaciones para Computadoras
elding	Soudure	Schweissen	Soldadura
orology	Météorologie	Meteorologie	Meteorología
omputer Applications	Applications Informatiques	Computer Anwendung	Aplicaciones para Computadoras
ology and Standardization	Métrologie et Standardisation	Mass- und Gewichtskunde, Normung	Metrología y Normalización
omputer Applications	Applications Informatiques	Computer Anwendung	Aplicaciones para Computadoras
ry	Militaires	Militärwesen	Militares
s and Mining Industry	Mines et Resources Minières	Bergwesen und Bergbauindustrie	Minas e Industria Minera
omputer Applications	Applications Informatiques	Computer Anwendung	Aplicaciones para Computadoras
n Pictures	Cinéma	Film und Kino	Películas
ums and Art Galleries	Musées et Galleries	Museen und Kunstgalerien	Museos y Galerías del Arte
	Musique	Musik	Música
omputer Applications	Applications Informatiques	Computer Anwendung	Aplicaciones para Computadoras
ework	Travaux de Couture	Näherei	Bordado
Age	New Age	New Age	Nueva Epoca
smatics	Numismatique	Numismatik	Numismática
on and Dietetics	Nutrition et Diététique	Ernährung und Diätetik	Dietas y Nutrición
pational Health and Safety	Médecine du Travail et Prévention	Berufsgesundheitspflege und Sicherheit	Sanidad y Seguridad en el Trabajo
pations and Careers	Emplois et Carrières	Berufe	Empleos y Ocupaciones
tal Studies	Études Orientales	Orientalistik	Estudios Orientales

SUBJECTS

Packaging	Emballage	Verpackung	Empaque
Computer Applications	Applications Informatiques	Computer Anwendung	Aplicaciones para Computadoras
Paints and Protective Coatings	Couleurs et Peintures	Farben und Beläge	Pinturas y Revestimientos Protectores
Paleontology	Paléontologie	Paleontologie	Paleontología
Computer Applications	Applications Informatiques	Computer Anwendung	Aplicaciones para Computadoras
Paper and Pulp	Papier et Pulpe	Papier und Papierstoff	Papel y Pulpa
Parapsychology and Occultism	Parapsychologie et Occultisme	Parapsychologie und Okkultismus	Parapsicología y Ocultismo
Patents, Trademarks and Copyrights	Brevets, Marques Commerciales et Droits d'Auteur	Patente, Schutzmarken und Urheberrechte	Patentes, Marcas Registradas y Derechos de Autor
Petroleum and Gas	Pétrole et Gas Naturel	Petroleum und Gas	Petróleo y Gas Natural
Computer Applications	Applications Informatiques	Computer Anwendung	Aplicaciones para Computadoras
Pets	Animaux Familiers	Haustiere	Mascotas
Pharmacy and Pharmacology	Pharmacie et Pharmacologie	Pharmazie und Pharmakologie	Farmacia y Farmacología
Computer Applications	Applications Informatiques	Computer Anwendung	Aplicaciones para Computadoras
Philately	Philatélie	Briefmarkenkunde	Filatelia
Philosophy	Philosophie	Philosophie	Filosofía
Photography	Photographie	Photographie	Fotografía
Computer Applications	Applications Informatiques	Computer Anwendung	Aplicaciones para Computadoras
Physical Fitness and Hygiene	Santé Physique et Hygiène	Gesundheitszustand und Hygiene	Salud Física e Higiene
Physics	Physique	Physik	Física
Computer Applications	Applications Informatiques	Computer Anwendung	Aplicaciones para Computadoras
Electricity	Electricité	Elektrizität	Electricidad
Heat	Chaleur	Wärme	Calor
Mechanics	Mécanique	Mechanik	Mecánica
Nuclear Physics	Physique Nucléaire	Kernphysik	Física Nuclear
Optics	Optique	Optik	Optica
Sound	Son	Schall	Sonido
Plastics	Plastiques	Kunststoffe	Plásticos
Computer Applications	Applications Informatiques	Computer Anwendung	Aplicaciones para Computadoras
Political Science	Sciences Politiques	Politische Wissenschafte	Ciencias Políticas
Civil Rights	Droits Civiques	Bürgerrechte	Derechos Civiles
International Relations	Relations Internationales	Internationale Beziehungen	Relaciones Internacionales
Population Studies	Démographie	Bevölkerungswissenschaft	Demografía
Printing	Imprimerie	Druck	Imprenta
Computer Applications	Applications Informatiques	Computer Anwendung	Aplicaciones para Computadoras
Psychology	Psychologie	Psychologie	Psicología
Public Administration	Administration Publique	Öffentliche Verwaltung	Administración Pública
Computer Applications	Applications Informatiques	Computer Anwendung	Aplicaciones para Computadoras
Municipal Government	Gouvernement Municipal	Kommunalverwaltung	Gobierno Municipal
Public Health and Safety	Santé Publique et Prévention	Öffentliche Gesundheitspflege	Salud y Seguridad Pública
Publishing and Book Trade	Édition et Commerce du Livre	Verlagswesen und Buchhandel	Editoriales y Ferias de Libros
Computer Applications	Applications Informatiques	Computer Anwendung	Aplicaciones para Computadoras
Real Estate	Immobiliers	Grundbesitz und Immobilien	Bienes Raíces
Computer Applications	Applications Informatiques	Computer Anwendung	Aplicaciones para Computadoras
Religions and Theology	Religions et Théologie	Religion and Theologie	Religión y Teología
Buddhist	Bouddhisme	Buddhist	Budismo
Eastern Orthodox	Églises Orthodoxes	Orthodox	Inglesias Ortodoxas
Hindu	Hindouisme	Hindu	Hinduísmo
Islamic	Islam	Islamische	Islamísmo
Judaic	Judaisme	Jüdäistische	Judaísmo
Protestant	Protestantisme	Evangelische	Iglesia Protestante
Roman Catholic	Catholicisme Romain	Römisch-katholische	Iglesia Católica
Other Denominations and Sects	Autres	Andere Bekenntnisse und Sekte	Otras Denominaciones y Sectas
Rubber	Caoutchouc	Gummi	Caucho
Computer Applications	Applications Informatiques	Computer Anwendung	Aplicaciones para Computadoras
Sciences: Comprehensive Works	Sciences: Oeuvres d'Ensemble	Wissenschaften: Umfassende Werke	Ciencias: Obras Completas
Computer Applications	Applications Informatiques	Computer Anwendung	Aplicaciones para Computadoras
Shoes and Boots	Chaussures et Bottes	Schuhe und Stiefel	Zapatos y Botas
Singles' Interests and Lifestyles	Intérêts et Style de Vie Célibataire	Ledigenstandinteressen	Intereses y Estilos de Vida de Solteros
Social Sciences: Comprehensive Works	Sciences Sociales: Oeuvres d'Ensemble	Sozialwissenschaften: Umfassende Werke	Ciencias Sociales: Obras Completas
Social Service and Welfare	Service Social et Protection Sociale	Sozialpflege und Fürsorge	Asistencia y Bienestar Social
Sociology	Sociologie	Soziologie	Sociología
Computer Applications	Applications Informatiques	Computer Anwendung	Aplicaciones para Computadoras
Sound Recording and Reproduction	Enregistrement et Reproduction du Son	Tonaufnahme und Tonwiedergabe	Grabaciones y Reproducciones Sonoras
Computer Applications	Applications Informatiques	Computer Anwendung	Aplicaciones para Computadoras
Sports and Games	Sports et Jeux	Sport und Spiele	Deportes y Juegos
Ball Games	Jeux de Balle	Ballspiele	Juegos de Pelota
Bicycles and Motorcycles	Bicyclettes et Motocyclettes	Fahrräder und Motorräder	Bicicletas y Motocicletas
Boats and Boating	Bateaux et Canotage	Boote und Bootfahren	Barcos y Canotaje
Horses and Horsemanship	Equitation	Pferde und Reitsport	Caballos y Equitación
Outdoor Life	Vie en Plein Air	Im Freien	Vida de Campo
Statistics	Statistiques	Statistik	Estadísticas
Technology: Comprehensive Works	Technologie: Oeuvres d'Ensemble	Technologie: Umfassende Werke	Tecnología: Obras Completas
Textile Industries and Fabrics	Textiles	Textil	Telas e Industria Textil
Computer Applications	Applications Informatiques	Computer Anwendung	Aplicaciones para Computadoras
Theater	Théâtre	Theater	Teatro
Tobacco	Tabac	Tabak	Tabaco
Transportation	Transports	Transport	Transporte
Air Transport	Transport Aérien	Luftverkehr	Transporte Aéreo
Automobiles	Automobiles	Kraftfahrzeugen	Automóviles
Computer Applications	Applications Informatiques	Computer Anwendung	Aplicaciones para Computadoras
Railroads	Chemins de Fer	Eisenbahnen	Ferrocarriles
Roads and Traffic	Routes et Circulation	Strassen und Strassenverkehr	Caminos y Tráfico
Ships and Shipping	Navires et Transport Maritimes	Schiffe und Schiffahrt	Barcos y Embarques
Trucks and Trucking	Transports Routiers	Lastkraftwagen	Camiones
Travel and Tourism	Voyages et Tourisme	Reisen und Tourismus	Viaje y Turismo
Airline Inflight and Hotel Inroom	Revues pour Vol de Lignes Aériennes et pour Chambres d'Hôtels	Fluggesellschaft und Hotel Veröffentlichungen	Vuelo en Aerolínea y Cuarto de Hotel
Veterinary Sciences	Science Vétérinaire	Tierheilkunde	Veterinaria
Computer Applications	Applications Informatiques	Computer Anwendung	Aplicaciones para Computadoras
Water Resources	Ressources en Eau	Wasserwirtschaft	Recursos del Agua
Computer Applications	Applications Informatiques	Computer Anwendung	Aplicaciones de los Computadoras
Women's Health	Santé de la Femme	Gesundheit von Frauen	Salud de las Mujeres
Women's Interests	Publications d'Intérêt Féminin	Fraueninteresse	Intereses Femeninos
Women's Studies	Études de la Femme	Frauenstudien	Estudios de las Mujeres

Classified List of Serials Subjects A-D

ABSTRACTING AND INDEXING SERVICES

see also Bibliographies

A A A S ANNUAL MEETING PROGRAM - ABSTRACTS OF PAPERS. (American Association for the Advancement of Science) see *SCIENCES: COMPREHENSIVE WORKS — Abstracting, Bibliographies, Statistics*

A A C N NURSING SCAN IN CRITICAL CARE. see *MEDICAL SCIENCES — Abstracting, Bibliographies, Statistics*

A B C NEWS INDEX. see *COMMUNICATIONS — Abstracting, Bibliographies, Statistics*

A B C POL SCI; a bibliography of contents: political science and government. see *POLITICAL SCIENCE — Abstracting, Bibliographies, Statistics*

A B I - INFORM. (American Business Information) see *BUSINESS AND ECONOMICS — Abstracting, Bibliographies, Statistics*

A B I X: AUSTRALASIAN BUSINESS INTELLIGENCE; the key to Australasian business, industry and trade information. see *BUSINESS AND ECONOMICS — Abstracting, Bibliographies, Statistics*

A B S I - ABSTRACTE IN BIBLIOLOGIE SI STIINTA INFORMARII. see *LIBRARY AND INFORMATION SCIENCES — Abstracting, Bibliographies, Statistics*

A C C CURRENT JOURNAL REVIEW. (American College of Cardiology) see *MEDICAL SCIENCES — Abstracting, Bibliographies, Statistics*

A C O G CLINICAL REVIEW. (American College of Obstetricians and Gynecologists) see *MEDICAL SCIENCES — Abstracting, Bibliographies, Statistics*

A E S I S QUARTERLY. (Australasian Earth Sciences Information System) see *MINES AND MINING INDUSTRY — Abstracting, Bibliographies, Statistics*

A E T F A T INDEX; releve des travaux de phanerogamie systematique et des taxons nouveaux concernant l'Afrique au sud du Sahara et Madagascar. (Association pour l'Etude Taxonomique de la Flore d'Afrique Tropicale) see *BIOLOGY — Abstracting, Bibliographies, Statistics*

A G E REFDEX. see *EARTH SCIENCES — Abstracting, Bibliographies, Statistics*

A I D RESEARCH AND DEVELOPMENT ABSTRACTS. (U.S. Agency for International Development) see *BUSINESS AND ECONOMICS — Abstracting, Bibliographies, Statistics*

A L I S A. (Australian Library and Information Science Abstracts) see *LIBRARY AND INFORMATION SCIENCES — Abstracting, Bibliographies, Statistics*

A M F REVIEWS. (Australian Mineral Foundation) see *EARTH SCIENCES — Abstracting, Bibliographies, Statistics*

A N T E PLUS. (Abstracts in New Technologies and Engineering) see *TECHNOLOGY: COMPREHENSIVE WORKS — Abstracting, Bibliographies, Statistics*

A P A I S: AUSTRALIAN PUBLIC AFFAIRS INFORMATION SERVICE; subject index to current literature. see *PUBLIC ADMINISTRATION — Abstracting, Bibliographies, Statistics*

A R N O V A ABSTRACTS. (Association for Research on Nonprofit Organizations and Voluntary Action) see *SOCIAL SERVICES AND WELFARE — Abstracting, Bibliographies, Statistics*

A S C E PUBLICATIONS INFORMATION. (American Society of Civil Engineers) see *ENGINEERING — Abstracting, Bibliographies, Statistics*

A S F A AQUACULTURE ABSTRACTS. (Aquatic Sciences & Fisheries Abstracts) see *FISH AND FISHERIES — Abstracting, Bibliographies, Statistics*

A S S I A: APPLIED SOCIAL SCIENCES INDEX & ABSTRACTS. see *SOCIAL SCIENCES: COMPREHENSIVE WORKS — Abstracting, Bibliographies, Statistics*

A S S I A PLUS. (Applied Social Science Index & Abstracts) see *SOCIAL SCIENCES: COMPREHENSIVE WORKS — Abstracting, Bibliographies, Statistics*

A S T I S BIBLIOGRAPHY. (Arctic Science & Technology Information System) see *BIOLOGY — Abstracting, Bibliographies, Statistics*

ABRIDGED INDEX MEDICUS. see *MEDICAL SCIENCES — Abstracting, Bibliographies, Statistics*

ABRIDGED MAGAZINE INDEX. see *PUBLISHING AND BOOK TRADE — Abstracting, Bibliographies, Statistics*

050 011 US ISSN 0001-334X
ABRIDGED READERS' GUIDE TO PERIODICAL LITERATURE. 1935. m. (Sep.-May), plus a. and q. cumulations. $100. H.W. Wilson Co., 950 University Ave., Bronx, NY 10452. TEL 718-588-8400; 800-367-6770. FAX 718-367-1617. Ed. Jean Marra. **Document type:** abstracting/indexing.
Description: Indexes general interest magazines covered by the unabridged Readers' Guide.

ABSTRACT JOURNAL IN EARTHQUAKE ENGINEERING. see *ENGINEERING — Abstracting, Bibliographies, Statistics*

ABSTRACT NEWSLETTER: PROBLEM-SOLVING INFORMATION FOR STATE AND LOCAL GOVERNMENTS. see *PUBLIC ADMINISTRATION — Abstracting, Bibliographies, Statistics*

ABSTRACT NEWSLETTER: URBAN AND REGIONAL TECHNOLOGY AND DEVELOPMENT. see *HOUSING AND URBAN PLANNING — Abstracting, Bibliographies, Statistics*

ABSTRACTA IRANICA. see *HISTORY — Abstracting, Bibliographies, Statistics*

016 US ISSN 0732-8583
Z695.93
ABSTRACTING AND INDEXING SERVICES DIRECTORY. 1982. irreg. $200. Gale Research, 835 Penobscot Bldg., 645 Griswold St., Detroit, MI 48226-4094. TEL 313-961-2242; 800-877-4253. FAX 800-414-5043. E-mail: daniel__snyder@gale. com. Ed. John Schmittroth. **Document type:** directory. —CISTI.

ABSTRACTS: CELLULAR PATHOLOGY. see *MEDICAL SCIENCES — Abstracting, Bibliographies, Statistics*

ABSTRACTS IN ANTHROPOLOGY. see *ANTHROPOLOGY — Abstracting, Bibliographies, Statistics*

ABSTRACTS IN BIOCOMMERCE. see *BIOLOGY — Abstracting, Bibliographies, Statistics*

ABSTRACTS IN MARYLAND ARCHEOLOGY. see *ARCHAEOLOGY — Abstracting, Bibliographies, Statistics*

ABSTRACTS IN NEW TECHNOLOGIES AND ENGINEERING. see *TECHNOLOGY: COMPREHENSIVE WORKS — Abstracting, Bibliographies, Statistics*

ABSTRACTS IN SOCIAL GERONTOLOGY: CURRENT LITERATURE ON AGING. see *GERONTOLOGY AND GERIATRICS — Abstracting, Bibliographies, Statistics*

ABSTRACTING AND INDEXING SERVICES

ABSTRACTS OF BULGARIAN SCIENTIFIC LITERATURE. AGRICULTURE AND FORESTRY. VETERINARY MEDICINE. see *AGRICULTURE* — *Abstracting, Bibliographies, Statistics*

ABSTRACTS OF BULGARIAN SCIENTIFIC LITERATURE. INDUSTRY, BUILDING AND TRANSPORT. see *BUSINESS AND ECONOMICS* — *Abstracting, Bibliographies, Statistics*

ABSTRACTS OF BULGARIAN SCIENTIFIC LITERATURE. PHILOSOPHY, SOCIOLOGY, SCIENCE OF SCIENCES, PSYCHOLOGY AND PEDAGOGICS. see *EDUCATION* — *Abstracting, Bibliographies, Statistics*

ABSTRACTS OF BULGARIAN SCIENTIFIC MEDICAL LITERATURE. see *MEDICAL SCIENCES* — *Abstracting, Bibliographies, Statistics*

ABSTRACTS OF CHINESE GEOLOGICAL LITERATURE. see *EARTH SCIENCES* — *Abstracting, Bibliographies, Statistics*

ABSTRACTS OF CLINICAL CARE GUIDELINES. see *MEDICAL SCIENCES* — *Abstracting, Bibliographies, Statistics*

ABSTRACTS OF CURRENT LITERATURE IN TOXICOLOGY. see *ENVIRONMENTAL STUDIES* — *Abstracting, Bibliographies, Statistics*

ABSTRACTS OF EDUCATIONAL STUDIES AND RESEARCH. see *EDUCATION* — *Abstracting, Bibliographies, Statistics*

ABSTRACTS OF ENTOMOLOGY. see *BIOLOGY* — *Abstracting, Bibliographies, Statistics*

ABSTRACTS OF MILITARY BIBLIOGRAPHY. see *MILITARY* — *Abstracting, Bibliographies, Statistics*

ABSTRACTS OF MYCOLOGY. see *BIOLOGY* — *Abstracting, Bibliographies, Statistics*

ABSTRACTS OF RESEARCH IN PASTORAL CARE AND COUNSELING. see *RELIGIONS AND THEOLOGY* — *Abstracting, Bibliographies, Statistics*

ABSTRACTS OF SYMPOSIUM ON MOLECULAR SIMULATION, JAPAN/BUNSHI SHIMYURESHON TORONKAI KOEN YOSHISHU. see *CHEMISTRY* — *Abstracting, Bibliographies, Statistics*

ABSTRACTS OF SYMPOSIUM ON PEPTIDE CHEMISTRY/PEPUCHIDO KAGAKU TORONKAI KOEN YOSHISHU. see *FISH AND FISHERIES* — *Abstracting, Bibliographies, Statistics*

ABSTRACTS OF THE SYMPOSIUM ON ORGANOMETALLIC CHEMISTRY, JAPAN/YUKI KINZOKU KAGAKU TORONKAI KOEN YOSHISHU. see *CHEMISTRY* — *Abstracting, Bibliographies, Statistics*

ABSTRACTS OF THE TOKYO CONFERENCE ON INSTRUMENTAL ANALYSIS AND ANALYTIC SYSTEMS/BUNSEKI KIKI TO KAISEKI SHISUTEMU NI KANSURU TOKYO TORONKAI KOEN YOSHISHU. see *CHEMISTRY* — *Abstracting, Bibliographies, Statistics*

ABSTRACTS OF UPPSALA DISSERTATIONS IN SCIENCE. see *SCIENCES: COMPREHENSIVE WORKS* — *Abstracting, Bibliographies, Statistics*

ABSTRACTS OF WORKING PAPERS IN ECONOMICS. see *BUSINESS AND ECONOMICS* — *Abstracting, Bibliographies, Statistics*

ABSTRACTS ON THE SYMPOSIUM ON MOLECULAR STRUCTURE/BUNSHI KOZO SOGO TORONKAI KOEN YOSHISHU. see *CHEMISTRY* — *Abstracting, Bibliographies, Statistics*

016 US ISSN 1056-7496
ACADEMIC ABSTRACTS C D - R O M. (Not avail. in printed format) 1991. m. $1799 ($1399 for 10 discs). EBSCO Publishing (Subsidiary of: EBSCO Industries, Inc.), 10 Estes St., Box 682, Ipswich, MA 01938. TEL 508-356-6500; 800-653-2726. FAX 508-356-6565. E-mail: ep@epnet.com; URL: http://www.epnet.com. Ed. Melissa Kummerer. bk.rev.; index. (also avail. in magnetic tape)
Document type: abstracting/indexing.
●Also available online. Vendor(s): Ovid Technologies, Inc.
Also available on CD-ROM.
Description: Abstracts and indexes over 750 periodicals.

ACADEMIC INDEX. see *HUMANITIES: COMPREHENSIVE WORKS* — *Abstracting, Bibliographies, Statistics*

016 US ISSN 0095-5698
AI3
ACCESS: THE SUPPLEMENTARY INDEX TO PERIODICALS. 1975. 2/yr. plus a. cumulation. $197.50 (foreign $220) (effective 1997). John Gordon Burke Publisher, Inc., Box 1492, Evanston, IL 60204-1492. TEL 847-866-8625. FAX 847-866-6639. URL: http://www.nlightn.com.
Document type: abstracting/indexing.
●Also available online.
Incorporates: Monthly Periodical Index.
Description: Covers regional and city magazines, major publications in library science, as well as general interest periodicals not indexed by the Readers' Guide to Periodical Literature.

ACCOUNTING & FINANCE ABSTRACTS. see *COMPUTERS* — *Abstracting, Bibliographies, Statistics*

ACCOUNTING AND TAX INDEX. see *BUSINESS AND ECONOMICS* — *Abstracting, Bibliographies, Statistics*

ACCOUNTING ARTICLES. see *BUSINESS AND ECONOMICS* — *Abstracting, Bibliographies, Statistics*

ACOUSTICS ABSTRACTS. see *PHYSICS* — *Abstracting, Bibliographies, Statistics*

ACTA VETERINARIA JAPONICA. see *VETERINARY SCIENCE* — *Abstracting, Bibliographies, Statistics*

ADHESIVES ABSTRACTS. see *CHEMISTRY* — *Abstracting, Bibliographies, Statistics*

ADVANCE A C S ABSTRACTS. see *CHEMISTRY* — *Abstracting, Bibliographies, Statistics*

ADVANCED POLYMERS ABSTRACTS. see *CHEMISTRY* — *Abstracting, Bibliographies, Statistics*

ADVANCES IN ORTHOPAEDIC SURGERY. see *MEDICAL SCIENCES* — *Orthopedics And Traumatology*

AFRICAN STUDIES ABSTRACTS. see *SOCIAL SCIENCES: COMPREHENSIVE WORKS* — *Abstracting, Bibliographies, Statistics*

AGBIOTECH NEWS AND INFORMATION. see *BIOLOGY* — *Abstracting, Bibliographies, Statistics*

AGRICULTURAL ABSTRACTS FOR TANZANIA. see *AGRICULTURE* — *Abstracting, Bibliographies, Statistics*

AGRICULTURAL & ENVIRONMENTAL BIOTECHNOLOGY ABSTRACTS. see *AGRICULTURE* — *Abstracting, Bibliographies, Statistics*

AGRICULTURAL AND VETERINARY PRODUCT INDEX. see *AGRICULTURE* — *Abstracting, Bibliographies, Statistics*

AGRICULTURAL ENGINEERING ABSTRACTS. see *AGRICULTURE* — *Abstracting, Bibliographies, Statistics*

AGRICULTURE AND ENVIRONMENT FOR DEVELOPING COUNTRIES. see *AGRICULTURE* — *Abstracting, Bibliographies, Statistics*

AGRO-AGEN; bibliographic database. see *AGRICULTURE* — *Abstracting, Bibliographies, Statistics*

AGRO-LIBREX; bibliographic database. see *AGRICULTURE* — *Abstracting, Bibliographies, Statistics*

AGRONOMY ABSTRACTS. see *AGRICULTURE* — *Abstracting, Bibliographies, Statistics*

AL-AHRAM INDEX/KASHSHAF AL-AHRAM. see *JOURNALISM* — *Abstracting, Bibliographies, Statistics*

AIDS ABSTRACTS; international literature on acquired immunodeficiency syndrome and related retroviruses. see *MEDICAL SCIENCES* — *Abstracting, Bibliographies, Statistics*

AIDS & T B WEEKLY ABSTRACTS FROM CONFERENCE PROCEEDINGS. see *MEDICAL SCIENCES* — *Abstracting, Bibliographies, Statistics*

AIDS & T B WEEKLY ARTICLE SUMMARIES. see *MEDICAL SCIENCES* — *Abstracting, Bibliographies, Statistics*

AIR UNIVERSITY LIBRARY INDEX TO MILITARY PERIODICALS. see *MILITARY* — *Abstracting, Bibliographies, Statistics*

ALLOYS INDEX. see *METALLURGY* — *Abstracting, Bibliographies, Statistics*

ALTERNATIVE PRESS INDEX; access to movements, news, policy, theory. see *LITERARY AND POLITICAL REVIEWS* — *Abstracting, Bibliographies, Statistics*

ALUMINIUM INDUSTRY ABSTRACTS; a monthly review of the world's technical literature on aluminum. see *METALLURGY* — *Abstracting, Bibliographies, Statistics*

AMERICA: HISTORY AND LIFE. ANNUAL INDEX. see *HISTORY* — *Abstracting, Bibliographies, Statistics*

AMERICA: HISTORY AND LIFE. ARTICLE ABSTRACTS AND CITATIONS OF REVIEWS AND DISSERTATIONS COVERING THE UNITED STATES AND CANADA. see *HISTORY* — *Abstracting, Bibliographies, Statistics*

AMERICAN ASSOCIATION OF STRATIGRAPHIC PALYNOLOGISTS. ABSTRACTS OF PAPERS PRESENTED AT THE ANNUAL MEETINGS. see *EARTH SCIENCES* — *Abstracting, Bibliographies, Statistics*

AMERICAN BANKER INDEX. see *BUSINESS AND ECONOMICS* — *Abstracting, Bibliographies, Statistics*

AMERICAN CHEMICAL SOCIETY. ABSTRACTS OF PAPERS (AT THE NATIONAL MEETING). see *CHEMISTRY* — *Abstracting, Bibliographies, Statistics*

AMERICAN DRUG INDEX. see *PHARMACY AND PHARMACOLOGY* — *Abstracting, Bibliographies, Statistics*

AMERICAN HERITAGE CUMULATIVE INDEX. see *HISTORY* — *Abstracting, Bibliographies, Statistics*

AMERICAN HUMANITIES INDEX. see *HUMANITIES: COMPREHENSIVE WORKS* — *Abstracting, Bibliographies, Statistics*

011 US
AMERICAN INFORMATION NEWSLETTER. 1991. m. $48. Paradigm Co., Box 45161, Boise, ID 83711. TEL 208-322-7781. circ. 800. (back issues avail.)
Description: A newsletter of newsletters; drawn from over 500 other periodicals.

AMERICAN INSTITUTE FOR CONSERVATION OF HISTORIC AND ARTISTIC WORKS. ABSTRACTS OF PAPERS PRESENTED AT THE ANNUAL MEETING. see *ART* — *Abstracting, Bibliographies, Statistics*

AMERICAN MATHEMATICAL SOCIETY. ABSTRACTS OF PAPERS PRESENTED. see *MATHEMATICS* — *Abstracting, Bibliographies, Statistics*

AMERICAN PETROLEUM INSTITUTE. HEALTH AND ENVIRONMENTAL SCIENCES DEPARTMENT. REPORTS AND OTHER PUBLICATIONS, INDEX AND ABSTRACTS. see *PUBLIC HEALTH AND SAFETY* — *Abstracting, Bibliographies, Statistics*

AMERICAN PETROLEUM INSTITUTE. THESAURUS. see *PETROLEUM AND GAS* — *Abstracting, Bibliographies, Statistics*

AMERICAN PUBLIC OPINION INDEX. see *SOCIOLOGY* — *Abstracting, Bibliographies, Statistics*

AMERICAN WELDING SOCIETY ANNUAL MEETING. ABSTRACTS OF PAPERS. see *METALLURGY* — *Abstracting, Bibliographies, Statistics*

ANALISIS ANUAL DEL MERCADO DEL AZUCAR. see *BUSINESS AND ECONOMICS* — *Abstracting, Bibliographies, Statistics*

ANALYTICAL ABSTRACTS. see *CHEMISTRY* — *Abstracting, Bibliographies, Statistics*

ANIMAL BEHAVIOR ABSTRACTS. see *BIOLOGY* — *Abstracting, Bibliographies, Statistics*

ABSTRACTING AND INDEXING SERVICES

ANIMAL BREEDING ABSTRACTS; a monthly abstract of world literature. see BIOLOGY — Abstracting, Bibliographies, Statistics

ANIVERSARI CULTURALE; prezentari bibliografice. see HUMANITIES: COMPREHENSIVE WORKS — Abstracting, Bibliographies, Statistics

ANTHROPOLOGICAL INDEX TO CURRENT PERIODICALS IN THE LIBRARY OF THE MUSEUM OF MANKIND LIBRARY. see ANTHROPOLOGY — Abstracting, Bibliographies, Statistics

ANTHROPOLOGISCHER ANZEIGER. see ANTHROPOLOGY — Abstracting, Bibliographies, Statistics

ANYAGMOZGATASI ES CSOMAGOLASI SZAKIRODALMI TAJEKOZTATO/ABSTRACT JOURNAL FOR MATERIALS HANDLING AND PACKAGING. see TRANSPORTATION — Abstracting, Bibliographies, Statistics

APICULTURAL ABSTRACTS. see AGRICULTURE — Abstracting, Bibliographies, Statistics

APOPTOSIS (SHEFFIELD). see BIOLOGY — Abstracting, Bibliographies, Statistics

APPALACHIAN OUTLOOK; new sources of regional information. see LIBRARY AND INFORMATION SCIENCES — Abstracting, Bibliographies, Statistics

APPLIED BOTANY ABSTRACTS. see BIOLOGY — Abstracting, Bibliographies, Statistics

APPLIED HEALTH PHYSICS ABSTRACTS AND NOTES. see PHYSICS — Abstracting, Bibliographies, Statistics

APPLIED MECHANICS REVIEWS; an assessment of world literature in engineering sciences. see ENGINEERING — Abstracting, Bibliographies, Statistics

APPLIED SCIENCE & TECHNOLOGY INDEX; a cumulative subject index to English language periodicals in the fields of aeronautics and space science, computer technology and applications, chemistry, construction industry, energy resources and research, engineering, etc. see ENGINEERING — Abstracting, Bibliographies, Statistics

APPROPRIATE TECHNOLOGY INDEX. see TECHNOLOGY: COMPREHENSIVE WORKS — Abstracting, Bibliographies, Statistics

AQUALINE ABSTRACTS. see WATER RESOURCES — Abstracting, Bibliographies, Statistics

AQUATIC SCIENCES & FISHERIES ABSTRACTS. PART 1: BIOLOGICAL SCIENCES AND LIVING RESOURCES. see WATER RESOURCES — Abstracting, Bibliographies, Statistics

AQUATIC SCIENCES & FISHERIES ABSTRACTS. PART 2: OCEAN TECHNOLOGY, POLICY AND NON-LIVING RESOURCES. see WATER RESOURCES — Abstracting, Bibliographies, Statistics

AQUATIC SCIENCES & FISHERIES ABSTRACTS. PART 3: AQUATIC POLLUTION AND ENVIRONMENTAL QUALITY. see FISH AND FISHERIES — Abstracting, Bibliographies, Statistics

ARBEITSMEDIZIN. see OCCUPATIONAL HEALTH AND SAFETY — Abstracting, Bibliographies, Statistics

ARCHITECTURAL INDEX. see ARCHITECTURE — Abstracting, Bibliographies, Statistics

ARCTIC & ANTARCTIC REGIONS (COLD REGIONS). see EARTH SCIENCES — Abstracting, Bibliographies, Statistics

ART AND ARCHAEOLOGY TECHNICAL ABSTRACTS; abstracts of the technical literature on archaeology and the fine arts. see ART — Abstracting, Bibliographies, Statistics

ART INDEX. see ART — Abstracting, Bibliographies, Statistics

ART PRICE INDEX INTERNATIONAL. see PRINTING — Abstracting, Bibliographies, Statistics

ARTBIBLIOGRAPHIES CURRENT TITLES. see ART — Abstracting, Bibliographies, Statistics

ARTBIBLIOGRAPHIES MODERN. see ART — Abstracting, Bibliographies, Statistics

ARTHA SUCHI. see BUSINESS AND ECONOMICS — Abstracting, Bibliographies, Statistics

ARTS & HUMANITIES CITATION INDEX. see ART — Abstracting, Bibliographies, Statistics

ASIAN ALMANAC; weekly abstracts of Asian affairs. see POLITICAL SCIENCE — Abstracting, Bibliographies, Statistics

ASIAN-PACIFIC ECONOMIC LITERATURE. see BUSINESS AND ECONOMICS — Abstracting, Bibliographies, Statistics

ASSESSMENT REPORT INDEX. see ENERGY — Abstracting, Bibliographies, Statistics

ASSOCIATION OF SOUTHERN AFRICAN INDEXERS AND BIBLIOGRAPHERS. NEWSLETTER. see LIBRARY AND INFORMATION SCIENCES

ASTRONOMY AND ASTROPHYSICS ABSTRACTS. see ASTRONOMY — Abstracting, Bibliographies, Statistics

THE ATLANTA CONSTITUTION AND JOURNAL INDEX. see JOURNALISM — Abstracting, Bibliographies, Statistics

ATTENDERINGSBULLETIN BIBLIOTHEEK STARING-GEBOUW: LAND, BODEM, WATER. see ENVIRONMENTAL STUDIES — Abstracting, Bibliographies, Statistics

AUDIOCASSETTE & C D FINDER. see EDUCATION — Abstracting, Bibliographies, Statistics

AUSTRALASIAN RELIGION INDEX. see RELIGIONS AND THEOLOGY — Abstracting, Bibliographies, Statistics

AUSTRALIA. BUREAU OF STATISTICS. A GUIDE TO THE CONSUMER INDEX. see BUSINESS AND ECONOMICS — Abstracting, Bibliographies, Statistics

AUSTRALIA. BUREAU OF STATISTICS. INDEX TO THE HISTORICAL MICROFICHE SERIES - STATISTICAL PUBLICATIONS SINCE FEDERATION. see STATISTICS

AUSTRALIAN AND NEW ZEALAND CITATOR TO UK REPORTS. see LAW — Abstracting, Bibliographies, Statistics

AUSTRALIAN ARCHITECTURAL PERIODICALS INDEX. see ARCHITECTURE — Abstracting, Bibliographies, Statistics

AUSTRALIAN CURRENT LAW LEGISLATION. see LAW — Abstracting, Bibliographies, Statistics

AUSTRALIAN CURRENT LAW REPORTER. see LAW — Abstracting, Bibliographies, Statistics

AUSTRALIAN EDUCATION INDEX. see EDUCATION — Abstracting, Bibliographies, Statistics

AUSTRALIAN ROAD RESEARCH. see ENGINEERING — Abstracting, Bibliographies, Statistics

AUSTRALIAN SENTENCING JUDGMENTS BULLETIN. see LAW — Abstracting, Bibliographies, Statistics

AUSTRALIAN SOCIETY OF INDEXERS NEWSLETTER. see LIBRARY AND INFORMATION SCIENCES — Abstracting, Bibliographies, Statistics

AUSTRALIAN SPELEO ABSTRACTS. see EARTH SCIENCES — Abstracting, Bibliographies, Statistics

AUSZUEGE AUS PRESSEARTIKELN. see BUSINESS AND ECONOMICS — Abstracting, Bibliographies, Statistics

AUTO INDEX. see TRANSPORTATION — Abstracting, Bibliographies, Statistics

AUTOMATIZALASI, SZAMITASTECHNIKAI ES MERESTECHNIKAI SZAKIRODALMI TAJEKOZTATO/AUTOMATION, COMPUTING, COMPUTERS & MEASUREMENT ABSTRACTS. see PHYSICS — Abstracting, Bibliographies, Statistics

AUTOMOTIVE LITERATURE INDEX. see TRANSPORTATION — Abstracting, Bibliographies, Statistics

AVERY INDEX TO ARCHITECTURAL PERIODICALS. see ARCHITECTURE — Abstracting, Bibliographies, Statistics

AVIATION TRADESCAN; monthly index and abstracts. see AERONAUTICS AND SPACE FLIGHT — Abstracting, Bibliographies, Statistics

B C I R A ABSTRACTS OF INTERNATIONAL LITERATURE ON METAL CASTINGS PRODUCTION. (British Cast Iron Research Association) see METALLURGY — Abstracting, Bibliographies, Statistics

B H A. (Bibliography of the History of Art) see ART — Abstracting, Bibliographies, Statistics

B H I PLUS. (British Humanities Index) see HUMANITIES: COMPREHENSIVE WORKS — Abstracting, Bibliographies, Statistics

B M T ABSTRACTS. (British Maritime Technology Ltd.) see TRANSPORTATION — Abstracting, Bibliographies, Statistics

B N I. (British Newspaper Index) see JOURNALISM — Abstracting, Bibliographies, Statistics

BAHRAIN. EDUCATIONAL DOCUMENTATION LIBRARY. ACQUISITIONS LIST. see EDUCATION — Abstracting, Bibliographies, Statistics

BAHRAIN. EDUCATIONAL DOCUMENTATION LIBRARY. BIBLIOGRAPHIC LISTS. see EDUCATION — Abstracting, Bibliographies, Statistics

BANGLADESH AGRICULTURAL SCIENCES ABSTRACTS. see AGRICULTURE — Abstracting, Bibliographies, Statistics

BANYASZATI SZAKIRODALMI TAJEKOZTATO/MINING ABSTRACTS. see MINES AND MINING INDUSTRY — Abstracting, Bibliographies, Statistics

BARRON'S INDEX. see BUSINESS AND ECONOMICS — Abstracting, Bibliographies, Statistics

BASE DE DONNEES P A S C A L. PLAN DE CLASSEMENT. see LIBRARY AND INFORMATION SCIENCES — Computer Applications

BEIKOKU TOKKYO SHOROKU. DENKI HEN/U.S. PATENT ABSTRACTS. ELECTRICITY. see PATENTS, TRADEMARKS AND COPYRIGHTS — Abstracting, Bibliographies, Statistics

BEIKOKU TOKKYO SHOROKU. DENSHI, TSUSHIN HEN/U.S. PATENT ABSTRACTS. ELECTRONICS, COMMUNICATIONS. see PATENTS, TRADEMARKS AND COPYRIGHTS — Abstracting, Bibliographies, Statistics

BEIKOKU TOKKYO SHOROKU. DORYOKU, DORYOKU KIKAI, BUTSURYU, BUNPAI, RYUTAI NO TORIATSUKAI HEN/U.S. PATENT ABSTRACTS. POWER, POWER MACHINE, PHYSICAL DISTRIBUTION, DISTRIBUTION, LIQUID HANDLING. see PATENTS, TRADEMARKS AND COPYRIGHTS — Abstracting, Bibliographies, Statistics

BEIKOKU TOKKYO SHOROKU. KAGAKU IPPAN, ORIMONO HEN/U.S. PATENT ABSTRACTS. GENERAL CHEMISTRY, TEXTILE. see PATENTS, TRADEMARKS AND COPYRIGHTS — Abstracting, Bibliographies, Statistics

BEIKOKU TOKKYO SHOROKU. KIKAI YOSO, KIKAI KOSAKU, ZATSUKIKAI HEN/U.S. PATENT ABSTRACTS. MACHINE ELEMENTS, MACHINE CONSTRUCTION, MISCELLANEOUS MACHINES. see PATENTS, TRADEMARKS AND COPYRIGHTS — Abstracting, Bibliographies, Statistics

BEIKOKU TOKKYO SHOROKU. MUKI KAGAKU, KINZOKU, BUKI DAN'YAKU HEN/U.S. PATENT ABSTRACTS. INORGANIC CHEMISTRY, METALS, ARMAMENT AND AMMUNITION. see PATENTS, TRADEMARKS AND COPYRIGHTS — Abstracting, Bibliographies, Statistics

ABSTRACTING AND INDEXING SERVICES

BEIKOKU TOKKYO SHOROKU. OYO YUKI KAGAKU, NOSUISAN, IJUTSU HEN/U.S. PATENT ABSTRACTS. APPLIED ORGANIC CHEMISTRY, AGRICULTURE AND FISHERY, MEDICINE. see *PATENTS, TRADEMARKS AND COPYRIGHTS — Abstracting, Bibliographies, Statistics*

BEIKOKU TOKKYO SHOROKU. SOKUTEI, SEIMITSU KIKI, INSATSU, ONKYO, KYOIKU HEN/U.S. PATENT ABSTRACTS. MEASURING, PRECISION INSTRUMENT, PRINTING, SOUND RECORDING, EDUCATION. see *PATENTS, TRADEMARKS AND COPYRIGHTS — Abstracting, Bibliographies, Statistics*

BEIKOKU TOKKYO SHOROKU. YUKI KAGAKU HEN/U.S. PATENT ABSTRACTS. ORGANIC CHEMISTRY. see *PATENTS, TRADEMARKS AND COPYRIGHTS — Abstracting, Bibliographies, Statistics*

BEIKOKU TOKKYO SHOROKU. YU'YU KIKAI, KENSETSU, DOBOKU HEN/U.S. PATENT ABSTRACTS. TRANSPORTING MACHINE, CONSTRUCTION, CIVIL ENGINEERING. see *PATENTS, TRADEMARKS AND COPYRIGHTS — Abstracting, Bibliographies, Statistics*

BIBLIOGRAPHIE DE L'ALGERIE/AL-BIBLIYUGRAFYA AL-DJAZAIRIYAH. see *BIBLIOGRAPHIES*

BIBLIOGRAPHIES AND INDEXES IN MEDICAL STUDIES. see *MEDICAL SCIENCES — Abstracting, Bibliographies, Statistics*

BIBLIOGRAPHIES AND INDEXES IN SCIENCE AND TECHNOLOGY. see *SCIENCES: COMPREHENSIVE WORKS — Abstracting, Bibliographies, Statistics*

BIBLIOGRAPHY OF AGRICULTURE. see *AGRICULTURE — Abstracting, Bibliographies, Statistics*

BIBLIOGRAPHY OF AGRICULTURE. ANNUAL CUMULATIVE INDEX. see *AGRICULTURE — Abstracting, Bibliographies, Statistics*

BILTEN DOKUMENTACIJE. GRADJEVINARSTVO - VISOKOGRADNJA I ZAVRSNI RADOVI U GRADJEVINARSTVU/BULLETIN OF DOCUMENTATION. CIVIL ENGINEERING - SUPERSTRUCTURES AND FINAL WORK. see *ENGINEERING — Abstracting, Bibliographies, Statistics*

BILTEN DOKUMENTACIJE. METALURGIJA/BULLETIN OF DOCUMENTATION. METALLURGY. see *METALLURGY — Abstracting, Bibliographies, Statistics*

BILTEN DOKUMENTACIJE. POLJOPRIVREDA. BILJNA PROIZVODNJA/BULLETIN OF DOCUMENTATION. AGRICULTURAL-PLANT PRODUCTION. see *AGRICULTURE — Abstracting, Bibliographies, Statistics*

BILTEN DOKUMENTACIJE. POLJOPRIVREDA-STOCNA PROIZVODNJA/BULLETIN OF DOCUMENTATION. AGRICULTURAL-STOCKBREEDING. see *AGRICULTURE — Abstracting, Bibliographies, Statistics*

BILTEN DOKUMENTACIJE. PRERADA NEMETALNIH MINERALA-PROIZVODNJA GRADJEVINSKOG MATERIJALA/BULLETIN OF DOCUMENTATION. MANUFACTURE OF NON-METALLIC MINERAL PRODUCTS-MANUFACTURE OF CONSTRUCTION MATERIALS. see *CERAMICS, GLASS AND POTTERY — Abstracting, Bibliographies, Statistics*

BILTEN DOKUMENTACIJE. PROIZVODNJA PREHRAMBENIH PROIZVODA. PROIZVODNJA PICA/BULLETIN OF DOCUMENTATION. MANUFACTURE OF FOOD PRODUCTS. MANUFACTURE OF BEVERAGES. see *FOOD AND FOOD INDUSTRIES — Abstracting, Bibliographies, Statistics*

BILTEN DOKUMENTACIJE. RUDARSTVO I GEOLOGIJA/BULLETIN OF DOCUMENTATION. MINING AND GEOLOGY. see *MINES AND MINING INDUSTRY — Abstracting, Bibliographies, Statistics*

BILTEN DOKUMENTACIJE. SAVREMENA ORGANIZACIJA I EKONOMIJA ORGANIZACIJA UDRUZENOG RADA. see *BUSINESS AND ECONOMICS — Abstracting, Bibliographies, Statistics*

BILTEN DOKUMENTACIJE. SERIJA D1. HEMIJA I HEMIJSKA INDUSTRIJA/BULLETIN OF DOCUMENTATION. SERIES D1. CHEMISTRY AND CHEMICAL INDUSTRY. see *CHEMISTRY — Abstracting, Bibliographies, Statistics*

BILTEN DOKUMENTACIJE. SERIJA D6. ANALITICKA HEMIJA/BULLETIN OF DOCUMENTATION. SERIES D6. ANALYTICAL CHEMISTRY. see *CHEMISTRY — Abstracting, Bibliographies, Statistics*

BILTEN DOKUMENTACIJE. SERIJA S1. SAOBRACAJ/BULLETIN OF DOCUMENTATION. SERIES S1. TRAFFIC. see *TRANSPORTATION — Abstracting, Bibliographies, Statistics*

BILTEN DOKUMENTACIJE. ZASTITA NA RADU/BULLETIN OF DOCUMENTATION. SAFETY PRECAUTIONS. see *PUBLIC HEALTH AND SAFETY — Abstracting, Bibliographies, Statistics*

BIO SCIENCE ABSTRACTS. see *BIOLOGY — Abstracting, Bibliographies, Statistics*

BIOBUSINESS SEARCH GUIDE. see *BIOLOGY — Abstracting, Bibliographies, Statistics*

BIOCHEMISTRY AND BIOPHYSICS CITATION INDEX. see *BIOLOGY — Abstracting, Bibliographies, Statistics*

BIOCOMMERCE FINANCIAL ABSTRACTS. see *BIOLOGY — Abstracting, Bibliographies, Statistics*

BIOENGINEERING ABSTRACTS. see *BIOLOGY — Abstracting, Bibliographies, Statistics*

BIOETHICS LITERATURE REVIEW. see *MEDICAL SCIENCES — Abstracting, Bibliographies, Statistics*

BIOGRAPHY AND GENEALOGY MASTER INDEX. see *BIOGRAPHY — Abstracting, Bibliographies, Statistics*

BIOGRAPHY INDEX. see *BIOGRAPHY — Abstracting, Bibliographies, Statistics*

BIOLOGICAL ABSTRACTS; references, abstracts, and indexes to the world's life sciences research literature. see *BIOLOGY — Abstracting, Bibliographies, Statistics*

BIOLOGICAL ABSTRACTS CUMULATIVE INDEXES. see *BIOLOGY — Abstracting, Bibliographies, Statistics*

BIOLOGICAL ABSTRACTS - R R M; references and indexes to the world's life science reports, reviews, and meeting literature. see *BIOLOGY — Abstracting, Bibliographies, Statistics*

BIOLOGICAL ABSTRACTS - R R M CUMULATIVE INDEX. see *BIOLOGY — Abstracting, Bibliographies, Statistics*

BIOLOGICAL & AGRICULTURAL INDEX. see *BIOLOGY — Abstracting, Bibliographies, Statistics*

BIOLOGY DIGEST. see *BIOLOGY — Abstracting, Bibliographies, Statistics*

BIOPHYSICAL SOCIETY. ANNUAL MEETING. ABSTRACTS. see *BIOLOGY — Abstracting, Bibliographies, Statistics*

BIOSIS EVOLUTIONS. see *BIOLOGY — Abstracting, Bibliographies, Statistics*

BIOSIS SEARCH GUIDE (YEAR). see *BIOLOGY — Abstracting, Bibliographies, Statistics*

BIOSIS SERIAL SOURCES. see *BIOLOGY — Abstracting, Bibliographies, Statistics*

BISEIBUTSU KAGAKU BUNRUI KENKYUKAI KOEN YOSHISHU/ABSTRACTS OF ANNUAL MEETING ON MICROBIAL CHEMOTAXONOMY. see *BIOLOGY — Abstracting, Bibliographies, Statistics*

BLACK NEWSPAPER INDEX. see *ETHNIC INTERESTS — Abstracting, Bibliographies, Statistics*

BLOOD COAGULATION FACTORS; current awareness service for researchers in life sciences. see *MEDICAL SCIENCES — Abstracting, Bibliographies, Statistics*

BLOOD TRANSFUSION. see *MEDICAL SCIENCES — Abstracting, Bibliographies, Statistics*

BOLETIN DE TRADUCCIONES. see *SCIENCES: COMPREHENSIVE WORKS — Abstracting, Bibliographies, Statistics*

BOOK REVIEW INDEX; indexes all reviews in over 600 periodicals. see *PUBLISHING AND BOOK TRADE — Abstracting, Bibliographies, Statistics*

BOOK REVIEW INDEX: ANNUAL CLOTHBOUND CUMULATIONS. see *PUBLISHING AND BOOK TRADE — Abstracting, Bibliographies, Statistics*

BOOKS ON THE ENVIRONMENT AND RELATED TOPICS. see *ENVIRONMENTAL STUDIES — Abstracting, Bibliographies, Statistics*

THE BOSTON GLOBE INDEX. see *JOURNALISM — Abstracting, Bibliographies, Statistics*

BOTTOM LINE (LANSING); on alcohol in society. see *DRUG ABUSE AND ALCOHOLISM — Abstracting, Bibliographies, Statistics*

THE BRAZILIAN BOOK MAGAZINE. see *LITERARY AND POLITICAL REVIEWS — Abstracting, Bibliographies, Statistics*

BREAST DISEASES. see *MEDICAL SCIENCES — Abstracting, Bibliographies, Statistics*

BREASTFEEDING ABSTRACTS. see *MEDICAL SCIENCES — Abstracting, Bibliographies, Statistics*

BRITISH AND IRISH ARCHAEOLOGICAL BIBLIOGRAPHY. see *ARCHAEOLOGY — Abstracting, Bibliographies, Statistics*

BRITISH CERAMIC SOCIETY. TRANSACTIONS. see *CERAMICS, GLASS AND POTTERY — Abstracting, Bibliographies, Statistics*

BRITISH EDUCATION INDEX. see *EDUCATION — Abstracting, Bibliographies, Statistics*

BRITISH GEOLOGICAL LITERATURE; a bibliography and index of geology (and related topics) of the British Isles and adjacent sea areas. see *EARTH SCIENCES — Abstracting, Bibliographies, Statistics*

BRITISH HUMANITIES INDEX. see *HUMANITIES: COMPREHENSIVE WORKS — Abstracting, Bibliographies, Statistics*

BRITISH LIBRARY. DOCUMENT SUPPLY CENTRE. INDEX OF CONFERENCE PROCEEDINGS. see *MEETINGS AND CONGRESSES — Abstracting, Bibliographies, Statistics*

BRITISH LIBRARY. NAME AUTHORITY LIST. see *LIBRARY AND INFORMATION SCIENCES — Abstracting, Bibliographies, Statistics*

BRITISH PATENTS ABSTRACTS. see *PATENTS, TRADEMARKS AND COPYRIGHTS — Abstracting, Bibliographies, Statistics*

BRITISH REPORTS, TRANSLATIONS AND THESES. see *SCIENCES: COMPREHENSIVE WORKS — Abstracting, Bibliographies, Statistics*

BULLETIN D'HISTOIRE CISTERCIENNE/CISTERCIAN HISTORY ABSTRACTS. see *RELIGIONS AND THEOLOGY — Roman Catholic*

BUSINESS AND ENVIRONMENTAL ABSTRACTS. see *ENVIRONMENTAL STUDIES — Abstracting, Bibliographies, Statistics*

BUSINESS DATELINE. see *BUSINESS AND ECONOMICS*

BUSINESS INDEX. see *BUSINESS AND ECONOMICS — Abstracting, Bibliographies, Statistics*

BUSINESS PERIODICALS INDEX. see *BUSINESS AND ECONOMICS — Abstracting, Bibliographies, Statistics*

BYOIN KANRI KENKYUJO KENKYU SHUDANKAI ENDAI SHOROKU/NATIONAL INSTITUTE OF HOSPITAL ADMINISTRATION. ABSTRACTS OF THE MEETING. see *HOSPITALS — Abstracting, Bibliographies, Statistics*

C A S BIOTECH UPDATES. AGRICULTURE. (Chemical Abstracts Service) see *AGRICULTURE — Abstracting, Bibliographies, Statistics*

ABSTRACTING AND INDEXING SERVICES

C A S BIOTECH UPDATES. ANTIBODY CONJUGATES. see *CHEMISTRY — Abstracting, Bibliographies, Statistics*

C A S BIOTECH UPDATES. BIOCHEMICAL IMMOBILIZATION & BIOCATALYTIC REACTORS. see *CHEMISTRY — Abstracting, Bibliographies, Statistics*

C A S BIOTECH UPDATES. BIOSENSORS. see *BIOLOGY — Abstracting, Bibliographies, Statistics*

C A S BIOTECH UPDATES. CELL & TISSUE CULTURE. see *BIOLOGY — Abstracting, Bibliographies, Statistics*

C A S BIOTECH UPDATES. COMMERCIAL FERMENTATION. see *CHEMISTRY — Abstracting, Bibliographies, Statistics*

C A S BIOTECH UPDATES. D N A & R N A PROBES. see *BIOLOGY — Abstracting, Bibliographies, Statistics*

C A S BIOTECH UPDATES. D N A FORMATION & REPAIR. see *BIOLOGY — Abstracting, Bibliographies, Statistics*

C A S BIOTECH UPDATES. ENVIRONMENTAL BIOTECHNOLOGY. see *ENVIRONMENTAL STUDIES — Abstracting, Bibliographies, Statistics*

C A S BIOTECH UPDATES. ENZYMES IN BIOTECHNOLOGY. see *BIOLOGY — Abstracting, Bibliographies, Statistics*

C A S BIOTECH UPDATES. GENETIC ENGINEERING. see *BIOLOGY — Abstracting, Bibliographies, Statistics*

C A S BIOTECH UPDATES. NUCLEIC ACID & PROTEIN SEQUENCES. see *BIOLOGY — Abstracting, Bibliographies, Statistics*

C A S BIOTECH UPDATES. PHARMACEUTICAL APPLICATIONS. see *CHEMISTRY — Abstracting, Bibliographies, Statistics*

C A S BIOTECH UPDATES. PRODUCT PURIFICATION & SEPARATION. see *CHEMISTRY — Abstracting, Bibliographies, Statistics*

C A S BIOTECH UPDATES. SLOW-RELEASE PHARMACEUTICALS. (Chemical Abstracts Service) see *PHARMACY AND PHARMACOLOGY — Abstracting, Bibliographies, Statistics*

C A SELECTS. (Chemical Abstracts Service) see *CHEMISTRY — Abstracting, Bibliographies, Statistics*

C A SELECTS. ACID RAIN & ACID AIR. see *ENVIRONMENTAL STUDIES — Abstracting, Bibliographies, Statistics*

C A SELECTS. ACTIVATED CARBON. see *CHEMISTRY — Abstracting, Bibliographies, Statistics*

C A SELECTS. ADSORPTION. see *CHEMISTRY — Abstracting, Bibliographies, Statistics*

C A SELECTS. AIDS AND RELATED IMMUNODEFICIENCIES. see *MEDICAL SCIENCES — Abstracting, Bibliographies, Statistics*

C A SELECTS. ALKOXYLATED OLEOCHEMICALS. see *CHEMISTRY — Abstracting, Bibliographies, Statistics*

C A SELECTS. ALKYLATION & CATALYSTS. see *CHEMISTRY — Abstracting, Bibliographies, Statistics*

C A SELECTS. ALLERGY AND ANTIALLERGIC AGENTS. see *MEDICAL SCIENCES — Abstracting, Bibliographies, Statistics*

C A SELECTS. ALUMINUM - LITHIUM AND ALUMINUM - CERIUM ALLOYS. see *CHEMISTRY — Abstracting, Bibliographies, Statistics*

C A SELECTS. ANALYTICAL ELECTROCHEMISTRY. see *CHEMISTRY — Abstracting, Bibliographies, Statistics*

C A SELECTS. ANIMAL LONGEVITY AND AGING. see *BIOLOGY — Abstracting, Bibliographies, Statistics*

C A SELECTS. ANTI-INFLAMMATORY AGENTS AND ARTHRITIS. see *MEDICAL SCIENCES — Abstracting, Bibliographies, Statistics*

C A SELECTS. ANTIARRHYTHMICS. see *MEDICAL SCIENCES — Abstracting, Bibliographies, Statistics*

C A SELECTS. ANTIBACTERIAL AGENTS. see *CHEMISTRY — Abstracting, Bibliographies, Statistics*

C A SELECTS. ANTIFUNGAL & ANTIMYCOTIC AGENTS. see *BIOLOGY — Abstracting, Bibliographies, Statistics*

C A SELECTS. ANTIOXIDANTS. see *CHEMISTRY — Abstracting, Bibliographies, Statistics*

C A SELECTS. ARTIFICIAL SWEETENERS. see *FOOD AND FOOD INDUSTRIES — Abstracting, Bibliographies, Statistics*

C A SELECTS. ATHEROSCLEROSIS & HEART DISEASE. see *MEDICAL SCIENCES — Abstracting, Bibliographies, Statistics*

C A SELECTS. ATOMIC SPECTROSCOPY. see *PHYSICS — Abstracting, Bibliographies, Statistics*

C A SELECTS. AUTOMATED CHEMICAL ANALYSIS. see *CHEMISTRY — Abstracting, Bibliographies, Statistics*

C A SELECTS. BETA-LACTAM ANTIBIOTICS. see *PHARMACY AND PHARMACOLOGY — Abstracting, Bibliographies, Statistics*

C A SELECTS. BIOGENIC AMINES & THE NERVOUS SYSTEM. see *MEDICAL SCIENCES — Abstracting, Bibliographies, Statistics*

C A SELECTS. BISMUTH CHEMISTRY. see *CHEMISTRY — Abstracting, Bibliographies, Statistics*

C A SELECTS. BLOCK & GRAFT POLYMERS. see *CHEMISTRY — Abstracting, Bibliographies, Statistics*

C A SELECTS. BLOOD COAGULATION. see *MEDICAL SCIENCES — Abstracting, Bibliographies, Statistics*

C A SELECTS. CALCIUM CHANNEL BLOCKERS. see *CHEMISTRY — Abstracting, Bibliographies, Statistics*

C A SELECTS. CARBON & GRAPHITE FIBERS. see *CHEMISTRY — Abstracting, Bibliographies, Statistics*

C A SELECTS. CARBON FIBER COMPOSITES. see *CHEMISTRY — Abstracting, Bibliographies, Statistics*

C A SELECTS. CATALYST REGENERATION. see *CHEMISTRY — Abstracting, Bibliographies, Statistics*

C A SELECTS. CATALYTIC & KINETIC ANALYSIS. see *CHEMISTRY — Abstracting, Bibliographies, Statistics*

C A SELECTS. CERAMIC MATERIALS (JOURNALS). see *CERAMICS, GLASS AND POTTERY — Abstracting, Bibliographies, Statistics*

C A SELECTS. CERAMIC MATERIALS (PATENTS). see *CERAMICS, GLASS AND POTTERY — Abstracting, Bibliographies, Statistics*

C A SELECTS. CHELATING AGENTS. see *CHEMISTRY — Abstracting, Bibliographies, Statistics*

C A SELECTS. CHEMICAL ENGINEERING OPERATIONS. see *CHEMISTRY — Abstracting, Bibliographies, Statistics*

C A SELECTS. CHEMICAL INSTRUMENTATION. see *INSTRUMENTS — Abstracting, Bibliographies, Statistics*

C A SELECTS. CHEMICAL VAPOR DEPOSITION. see *CHEMISTRY — Abstracting, Bibliographies, Statistics*

C A SELECTS. CHEMILUMINESCENCE. see *CHEMISTRY — Abstracting, Bibliographies, Statistics*

C A SELECTS. CHEMISTRY OF IR, OS, RH, & RU. see *CHEMISTRY — Abstracting, Bibliographies, Statistics*

C A SELECTS. COAL SCIENCE AND PROCESS CHEMISTRY. see *CHEMISTRY — Abstracting, Bibliographies, Statistics*

C A SELECTS. COATINGS, INKS, & RELATED PRODUCTS. see *PAINTS AND PROTECTIVE COATINGS — Abstracting, Bibliographies, Statistics*

C A SELECTS. COLLOIDS (APPLIED ASPECTS). see *CHEMISTRY — Abstracting, Bibliographies, Statistics*

C A SELECTS. COLLOIDS (MACROMOLECULAR ASPECTS). see *CHEMISTRY — Abstracting, Bibliographies, Statistics*

C A SELECTS. COLLOIDS (PHYSICOCHEMICAL ASPECTS). see *CHEMISTRY — Abstracting, Bibliographies, Statistics*

C A SELECTS. COLOR SCIENCE. see *CHEMISTRY — Abstracting, Bibliographies, Statistics*

C A SELECTS. COLORANTS AND DYES. see *CLEANING AND DYEING — Abstracting, Bibliographies, Statistics*

C A SELECTS. COMPOSITE MATERIALS (CERAMIC). see *CHEMISTRY — Abstracting, Bibliographies, Statistics*

C A SELECTS. COMPOSITE MATERIALS (METALLIC). see *CHEMISTRY — Abstracting, Bibliographies, Statistics*

C A SELECTS. COMPOSITE MATERIALS (POLYMERIC). see *CHEMISTRY — Abstracting, Bibliographies, Statistics*

C A SELECTS. COMPUTERS IN CHEMISTRY. see *CHEMISTRY — Abstracting, Bibliographies, Statistics*

C A SELECTS. CONDUCTIVE POLYMERS. see *CHEMISTRY — Abstracting, Bibliographies, Statistics*

C A SELECTS. CORROSION. see *CHEMISTRY — Abstracting, Bibliographies, Statistics*

C A SELECTS. CORROSION-INHIBITING COATINGS. see *PAINTS AND PROTECTIVE COATINGS — Abstracting, Bibliographies, Statistics*

C A SELECTS. COSMETIC CHEMICALS. see *BEAUTY CULTURE — Abstracting, Bibliographies, Statistics*

C A SELECTS. CROSSLINKING REACTIONS. see *CHEMISTRY — Abstracting, Bibliographies, Statistics*

C A SELECTS. CRYSTAL GROWTH. see *CHEMISTRY — Abstracting, Bibliographies, Statistics*

C A SELECTS. DISTILLATION TECHNOLOGY. see *CHEMISTRY — Abstracting, Bibliographies, Statistics*

C A SELECTS. DRILLING MUDS. see *PETROLEUM AND GAS — Abstracting, Bibliographies, Statistics*

C A SELECTS. DRUG ANALYSIS BIOLOGICAL FLUIDS & TISSUES. see *PHARMACY AND PHARMACOLOGY — Abstracting, Bibliographies, Statistics*

C A SELECTS. DRUG & COSMETIC TOXICITY. see *PHARMACY AND PHARMACOLOGY — Abstracting, Bibliographies, Statistics*

C A SELECTS. DRUG INTERACTIONS. see *PHARMACY AND PHARMACOLOGY — Abstracting, Bibliographies, Statistics*

C A SELECTS. ELASTOMERS. see *CHEMISTRY — Abstracting, Bibliographies, Statistics*

C A SELECTS. ELECTRICALLY CONDUCTIVE ORGANICS. see *CHEMISTRY — Abstracting, Bibliographies, Statistics*

C A SELECTS. ELECTROCHEMICAL ORGANIC SYNTHESIS. see *CHEMISTRY — Abstracting, Bibliographies, Statistics*

C A SELECTS. ELECTROCHEMICAL REACTIONS. see *CHEMISTRY — Abstracting, Bibliographies, Statistics*

C A SELECTS. ELECTRODEPOSITION. see *CHEMISTRY — Abstracting, Bibliographies, Statistics*

C A SELECTS. ELECTRON & AUGER SPECTROSCOPY. see *PHYSICS — Abstracting, Bibliographies, Statistics*

C A SELECTS. ELECTRON SPIN RESONANCE (CHEMICAL ASPECTS). see *CHEMISTRY — Abstracting, Bibliographies, Statistics*

C A SELECTS. ELECTRONIC CHEMICALS & MATERIALS. see *CHEMISTRY — Abstracting, Bibliographies, Statistics*

C A SELECTS. EMULSIFIERS AND DEMULSIFIERS. see *CHEMISTRY — Abstracting, Bibliographies, Statistics*

ABSTRACTING AND INDEXING SERVICES

C A SELECTS. EMULSION POLYMERIZATION. see *CHEMISTRY — Abstracting, Bibliographies, Statistics*

C A SELECTS. ENERGY REVIEWS & BOOKS. see *ENERGY — Abstracting, Bibliographies, Statistics*

C A SELECTS. ENHANCED PETROLEUM RECOVERY. see *PETROLEUM AND GAS — Abstracting, Bibliographies, Statistics*

C A SELECTS. ENZYME ASSAYS. see *CHEMISTRY — Abstracting, Bibliographies, Statistics*

C A SELECTS. EPOXY RESINS. see *CHEMISTRY — Abstracting, Bibliographies, Statistics*

C A SELECTS. FATS & OILS. see *CHEMISTRY — Abstracting, Bibliographies, Statistics*

C A SELECTS. FERMENTATION CHEMICALS. see *CHEMISTRY — Abstracting, Bibliographies, Statistics*

C A SELECTS. FIBER OPTICS AND OPTICAL COMMUNICATION. see *PHYSICS — Abstracting, Bibliographies, Statistics*

C A SELECTS. FIBER-REINFORCED PLASTICS. see *PLASTICS — Abstracting, Bibliographies, Statistics*

C A SELECTS. FLAMMABILITY. see *CHEMISTRY — Abstracting, Bibliographies, Statistics*

C A SELECTS. FLUIDIZED SOLIDS TECHNOLOGY. see *CHEMISTRY — Abstracting, Bibliographies, Statistics*

C A SELECTS. FLUOROPOLYMERS. see *CHEMISTRY — Abstracting, Bibliographies, Statistics*

C A SELECTS. FOOD & FEED ANALYSIS. see *FOOD AND FOOD INDUSTRIES — Abstracting, Bibliographies, Statistics*

C A SELECTS. FOOD, DRUGS, & COSMETICS - LEGISLATIVE & REGULATORY ASPECTS. see *FOOD AND FOOD INDUSTRIES — Abstracting, Bibliographies, Statistics*

C A SELECTS. FOOD TOXICITY. see *CHEMISTRY — Abstracting, Bibliographies, Statistics*

C A SELECTS. FORMULATION CHEMISTRY. see *CHEMISTRY — Abstracting, Bibliographies, Statistics*

C A SELECTS. FREE RADICALS (BIOCHEMICAL ASPECTS). see *CHEMISTRY — Abstracting, Bibliographies, Statistics*

C A SELECTS. FREE RADICALS (ORGANIC ASPECTS). see *CHEMISTRY — Abstracting, Bibliographies, Statistics*

C A SELECTS. FUEL & LUBRICANT ADDITIVES. see *CHEMISTRY — Abstracting, Bibliographies, Statistics*

C A SELECTS. GASEOUS WASTE TREATMENT. see *CHEMISTRY — Abstracting, Bibliographies, Statistics*

C A SELECTS. GEOCHEMISTRY. see *CHEMISTRY — Abstracting, Bibliographies, Statistics*

C A SELECTS. HEAT-RESISTANT AND ABLATIVE POLYMERS. see *CHEMISTRY — Abstracting, Bibliographies, Statistics*

C A SELECTS. HOT-MELT ADHESIVES. see *CHEMISTRY — Abstracting, Bibliographies, Statistics*

C A SELECTS. HYPERTENSION & ANTIHYPERTENSIVES. see *MEDICAL SCIENCES — Abstracting, Bibliographies, Statistics*

C A SELECTS. IMMUNOCHEMICAL METHODS. see *MEDICAL SCIENCES — Abstracting, Bibliographies, Statistics*

C A SELECTS. INDOOR AIR POLLUTION. see *PUBLIC HEALTH AND SAFETY — Abstracting, Bibliographies, Statistics*

C A SELECTS. INFRARED SPECTROSCOPY (ORGANIC ASPECTS). see *CHEMISTRY — Abstracting, Bibliographies, Statistics*

C A SELECTS. INFRARED SPECTROSCOPY (PHYSICOCHEMICAL ASPECTS). see *PHYSICS — Abstracting, Bibliographies, Statistics*

C A SELECTS. INITIATION OF POLYMERIZATION. see *CHEMISTRY — Abstracting, Bibliographies, Statistics*

C A SELECTS. INORGANIC ANALYTICAL CHEMISTRY. see *CHEMISTRY — Abstracting, Bibliographies, Statistics*

C A SELECTS. INORGANIC & ORGANOMETALLIC REACTION SYSTEMS. see *CHEMISTRY — Abstracting, Bibliographies, Statistics*

C A SELECTS. INORGANIC CHEMICALS & REACTIONS. see *CHEMISTRY — Abstracting, Bibliographies, Statistics*

C A SELECTS. ION CHROMATOGRAPHY. see *CHEMISTRY — Abstracting, Bibliographies, Statistics*

C A SELECTS. ION-CONTAINING POLYMERS. see *CHEMISTRY — Abstracting, Bibliographies, Statistics*

C A SELECTS. ION EXCHANGE. see *CHEMISTRY — Abstracting, Bibliographies, Statistics*

C A SELECTS. ISOMERIZATION & CATALYSTS. see *CHEMISTRY — Abstracting, Bibliographies, Statistics*

C A SELECTS. LASER-INDUCED CHEMICAL REACTIONS. see *CHEMISTRY — Abstracting, Bibliographies, Statistics*

C A SELECTS. LEUKOTRIENES. see *CHEMISTRY — Abstracting, Bibliographies, Statistics*

C A SELECTS. LIQUID CRYSTALS. see *CHEMISTRY — Abstracting, Bibliographies, Statistics*

C A SELECTS. LUBRICANTS, GREASES, & LUBRICATION. see *CHEMISTRY — Abstracting, Bibliographies, Statistics*

C A SELECTS. MEMBRANE SEPARATION. see *CHEMISTRY — Abstracting, Bibliographies, Statistics*

C A SELECTS. MEMORY & RECORDING DEVICES & MATERIALS. see *CHEMISTRY — Abstracting, Bibliographies, Statistics*

C A SELECTS. METALLO ENZYMES & METALLO COENZYMES. see *CHEMISTRY — Abstracting, Bibliographies, Statistics*

C A SELECTS. MOLECULAR MODELING (BIOCHEMICAL ASPECTS). see *CHEMISTRY — Abstracting, Bibliographies, Statistics*

C A SELECTS. MONOCLONAL ANTIBODIES. see *MEDICAL SCIENCES — Abstracting, Bibliographies, Statistics*

C A SELECTS. NATURAL PRODUCT SYNTHESIS. see *CHEMISTRY — Abstracting, Bibliographies, Statistics*

C A SELECTS. NEW ANTIBIOTICS. see *PHARMACY AND PHARMACOLOGY — Abstracting, Bibliographies, Statistics*

C A SELECTS. NEW BOOKS IN CHEMISTRY. see *CHEMISTRY — Abstracting, Bibliographies, Statistics*

C A SELECTS. NEW PLASTICS. see *PLASTICS — Abstracting, Bibliographies, Statistics*

C A SELECTS. NITROGEN FIXATION. see *CHEMISTRY — Abstracting, Bibliographies, Statistics*

C A SELECTS. NONLINEAR OPTICAL MATERIALS. see *PHYSICS — Abstracting, Bibliographies, Statistics*

C A SELECTS. NOVEL NATURAL PRODUCTS. see *CHEMISTRY — Abstracting, Bibliographies, Statistics*

C A SELECTS. NOVEL PESTICIDES & HERBICIDES. see *ENGINEERING — Abstracting, Bibliographies, Statistics*

C A SELECTS. NOVEL POLYMERS FROM PATENTS. see *PATENTS, TRADEMARKS AND COPYRIGHTS — Abstracting, Bibliographies, Statistics*

C A SELECTS. NOVEL SULFUR HETEROCYCLES. see *CHEMISTRY — Abstracting, Bibliographies, Statistics*

C A SELECTS. NUTRITIONAL ASPECTS OF CANCER. see *MEDICAL SCIENCES — Abstracting, Bibliographies, Statistics*

C A SELECTS. OCCUPATIONAL EXPOSURE & HAZARDS. see *OCCUPATIONAL HEALTH AND SAFETY — Abstracting, Bibliographies, Statistics*

C A SELECTS. OLEOCHEMICALS CONTAINING NITROGEN. see *CHEMISTRY — Abstracting, Bibliographies, Statistics*

C A SELECTS. OMEGA-3 FATTY ACIDS & FISH OIL. see *CHEMISTRY — Abstracting, Bibliographies, Statistics*

C A SELECTS. OPTICAL AND PHOTOSENSITIVE MATERIALS. see *PHYSICS — Abstracting, Bibliographies, Statistics*

C A SELECTS. OPTIMIZATION OF ORGANIC REACTIONS. see *CHEMISTRY — Abstracting, Bibliographies, Statistics*

C A SELECTS. ORGANIC ANALYTICAL CHEMISTRY. see *CHEMISTRY — Abstracting, Bibliographies, Statistics*

C A SELECTS. ORGANIC OPTICAL MATERIALS. see *CHEMISTRY — Abstracting, Bibliographies, Statistics*

C A SELECTS. ORGANIC REACTION MECHANISMS. see *CHEMISTRY — Abstracting, Bibliographies, Statistics*

C A SELECTS. ORGANIC STEREOCHEMISTRY. see *CHEMISTRY — Abstracting, Bibliographies, Statistics*

C A SELECTS. ORGANO-TRANSITION METAL COMPLEXES. see *CHEMISTRY — Abstracting, Bibliographies, Statistics*

C A SELECTS. ORGANOFLUORINE CHEMISTRY. see *CHEMISTRY — Abstracting, Bibliographies, Statistics*

C A SELECTS. ORGANOMETALLICS IN ORGANIC SYNTHESIS. see *CHEMISTRY — Abstracting, Bibliographies, Statistics*

C A SELECTS. ORGANOPHOSPHORUS CHEMISTRY. see *CHEMISTRY — Abstracting, Bibliographies, Statistics*

C A SELECTS. ORGANOSULFUR CHEMISTRY (JOURNALS). see *CHEMISTRY — Abstracting, Bibliographies, Statistics*

C A SELECTS. ORGANOTIN CHEMISTRY. see *CHEMISTRY — Abstracting, Bibliographies, Statistics*

C A SELECTS. OSTEOPOROSIS & RELATED BONE LOSS. see *MEDICAL SCIENCES — Abstracting, Bibliographies, Statistics*

C A SELECTS. OXIDATION CATALYSTS. see *CHEMISTRY — Abstracting, Bibliographies, Statistics*

C A SELECTS. OXIDE SUPERCONDUCTORS. see *CHEMISTRY — Abstracting, Bibliographies, Statistics*

C A SELECTS. PAINT ADDITIVES. see *PAINTS AND PROTECTIVE COATINGS — Abstracting, Bibliographies, Statistics*

C A SELECTS. PAPER ADDITIVES. see *PAPER AND PULP — Abstracting, Bibliographies, Statistics*

C A SELECTS. PAPER & THIN-LAYER CHROMATOGRAPHY. see *CHEMISTRY — Abstracting, Bibliographies, Statistics*

C A SELECTS. PAPER CHEMISTRY. see *CHEMISTRY — Abstracting, Bibliographies, Statistics*

C A SELECTS. PESTICIDE ANALYSIS. see *BIOLOGY — Abstracting, Bibliographies, Statistics*

C A SELECTS. PHARMACEUTICAL CHEMISTRY (JOURNALS). see *PHARMACY AND PHARMACOLOGY — Abstracting, Bibliographies, Statistics*

C A SELECTS. PHARMACEUTICAL CHEMISTRY (PATENTS). see *PHARMACY AND PHARMACOLOGY — Abstracting, Bibliographies, Statistics*

C A SELECTS. PHASE TRANSFER CATALYSIS. see *CHEMISTRY — Abstracting, Bibliographies, Statistics*

C A SELECTS. PHOSPHOLIPIDS (CHEMICAL ASPECTS). see *BIOLOGY — Abstracting, Bibliographies, Statistics*

ABSTRACTING AND INDEXING SERVICES

C A SELECTS. PHOTOBIOCHEMISTRY. see *CHEMISTRY — Abstracting, Bibliographies, Statistics*

C A SELECTS. PHOTOCATALYSTS. see *CHEMISTRY — Abstracting, Bibliographies, Statistics*

C A SELECTS. PHOTOCHEMICAL ORGANIC SYNTHESIS. see *CHEMISTRY — Abstracting, Bibliographies, Statistics*

C A SELECTS. PHOTORESISTS. see *CHEMISTRY — Abstracting, Bibliographies, Statistics*

C A SELECTS. PHOTOSENSITIVE POLYMERS. see *CHEMISTRY — Abstracting, Bibliographies, Statistics*

C A SELECTS. PLASMA & REACTIVE ION ETCHING. see *CHEMISTRY — Abstracting, Bibliographies, Statistics*

C A SELECTS. PLASTIC FILMS. see *PLASTICS — Abstracting, Bibliographies, Statistics*

C A SELECTS. PLASTICS ADDITIVES. see *PLASTICS — Abstracting, Bibliographies, Statistics*

C A SELECTS. PLASTICS FABRICATION & USES. see *PLASTICS — Abstracting, Bibliographies, Statistics*

C A SELECTS. PLASTICS MANUFACTURE & PROCESSING. see *PLASTICS — Abstracting, Bibliographies, Statistics*

C A SELECTS. PLATINUM AND PALLADIUM CHEMISTRY. see *CHEMISTRY — Abstracting, Bibliographies, Statistics*

C A SELECTS. POLYACRYLATES (JOURNALS). see *CHEMISTRY — Abstracting, Bibliographies, Statistics*

C A SELECTS. POLYACRYLATES (PATENTS). see *CHEMISTRY — Abstracting, Bibliographies, Statistics*

C A SELECTS. POLYESTERS. see *CHEMISTRY — Abstracting, Bibliographies, Statistics*

C A SELECTS. POLYIMIDES. see *CHEMISTRY — Abstracting, Bibliographies, Statistics*

C A SELECTS. POLYMER BLENDS. see *CHEMISTRY — Abstracting, Bibliographies, Statistics*

C A SELECTS. POLYMER DEGRADATION. see *CHEMISTRY — Abstracting, Bibliographies, Statistics*

C A SELECTS. POLYMER MORPHOLOGY. see *CHEMISTRY — Abstracting, Bibliographies, Statistics*

C A SELECTS. POLYMERIZATION KINETICS & PROCESS CONTROL. see *CHEMISTRY — Abstracting, Bibliographies, Statistics*

C A SELECTS. PORPHYRINS. see *CHEMISTRY — Abstracting, Bibliographies, Statistics*

C A SELECTS. PROSTAGLANDINS. see *CHEMISTRY — Abstracting, Bibliographies, Statistics*

C A SELECTS. PROTON MAGNETIC RESONANCE. see *CHEMISTRY — Abstracting, Bibliographies, Statistics*

C A SELECTS. PSYCHOBIOCHEMISTRY. see *BIOLOGY — Abstracting, Bibliographies, Statistics*

C A SELECTS. QUATERNARY AMMONIUM COMPOUNDS. see *CHEMISTRY — Abstracting, Bibliographies, Statistics*

C A SELECTS. RADIATION CHEMISTRY. see *CHEMISTRY — Abstracting, Bibliographies, Statistics*

C A SELECTS. RADIATION CURING. see *CHEMISTRY — Abstracting, Bibliographies, Statistics*

C A SELECTS. RAMAN SPECTROSCOPY. see *CHEMISTRY — Abstracting, Bibliographies, Statistics*

C A SELECTS. SELENIUM & TELLURIUM CHEMISTRY. see *METALLURGY — Abstracting, Bibliographies, Statistics*

C A SELECTS. SHAPE MEMORY ALLOYS. see *CHEMISTRY — Abstracting, Bibliographies, Statistics*

C A SELECTS. SILICAS & SILICATES. see *CHEMISTRY — Abstracting, Bibliographies, Statistics*

C A SELECTS. SILOXANES & SILICONES. see *CHEMISTRY — Abstracting, Bibliographies, Statistics*

C A SELECTS. SILVER CHEMISTRY. see *METALLURGY — Abstracting, Bibliographies, Statistics*

C A SELECTS. SOLAR ENERGY. see *ENERGY — Abstracting, Bibliographies, Statistics*

C A SELECTS. SOLID STATE N M R. see *CHEMISTRY — Abstracting, Bibliographies, Statistics*

C A SELECTS. SOLVENT EXTRACTION. see *CHEMISTRY — Abstracting, Bibliographies, Statistics*

C A SELECTS. SPECTROCHEMICAL ANALYSIS. see *CHEMISTRY — Abstracting, Bibliographies, Statistics*

C A SELECTS. STEROIDS (BIOCHEMICAL ASPECTS). see *PHARMACY AND PHARMACOLOGY — Abstracting, Bibliographies, Statistics*

C A SELECTS. STEROIDS (CHEMICAL ASPECTS). see *CHEMISTRY — Abstracting, Bibliographies, Statistics*

C A SELECTS. STRESS CORROSION - METALS. see *CHEMISTRY — Abstracting, Bibliographies, Statistics*

C A SELECTS. STRUCTURE-ACTIVITY RELATIONSHIPS. see *CHEMISTRY — Abstracting, Bibliographies, Statistics*

C A SELECTS. SURFACE ANALYSIS. see *CHEMISTRY — Abstracting, Bibliographies, Statistics*

C A SELECTS. SURFACE CHEMISTRY (PHYSICOCHEMICAL ASPECTS). see *CHEMISTRY — Abstracting, Bibliographies, Statistics*

C A SELECTS. SYNFUELS. see *CHEMISTRY — Abstracting, Bibliographies, Statistics*

C A SELECTS. SYNTHETIC HIGH POLYMERS. see *CHEMISTRY — Abstracting, Bibliographies, Statistics*

C A SELECTS. SYNTHETIC MACROCYCLIC COMPOUNDS. see *CHEMISTRY — Abstracting, Bibliographies, Statistics*

C A SELECTS. THERMAL ANALYSIS. see *CHEMISTRY — Abstracting, Bibliographies, Statistics*

C A SELECTS. THERMOCHEMISTRY. see *CHEMISTRY — Abstracting, Bibliographies, Statistics*

C A SELECTS. TRACE ELEMENT ANALYSIS. see *CHEMISTRY — Abstracting, Bibliographies, Statistics*

C A SELECTS. ULTRAVIOLET & VISIBLE SPECTROSCOPY. see *CHEMISTRY — Abstracting, Bibliographies, Statistics*

C A SELECTS. VIRUCIDES & VIRUSTATS. see *BIOLOGY — Abstracting, Bibliographies, Statistics*

C A SELECTS. WATER-BASED COATINGS. see *PAINTS AND PROTECTIVE COATINGS — Abstracting, Bibliographies, Statistics*

C A SELECTS. X-RAY ANALYSIS & SPECTROSCOPY. see *PHYSICS — Abstracting, Bibliographies, Statistics*

C A SELECTS PLUS. ADHESIVES. see *CHEMISTRY — Abstracting, Bibliographies, Statistics*

C A SELECTS PLUS. AMINO ACIDS, PEPTIDES AND PROTEINS. see *BIOLOGY — Abstracting, Bibliographies, Statistics*

C A SELECTS PLUS. ANTITUMOR AGENTS. see *MEDICAL SCIENCES — Abstracting, Bibliographies, Statistics*

C A SELECTS PLUS. ASYMMETRIC SYNTHESIS & INDUCTION. see *CHEMISTRY — Abstracting, Bibliographies, Statistics*

C A SELECTS PLUS. BATTERIES & FUEL CELLS. see *CHEMISTRY — Abstracting, Bibliographies, Statistics*

C A SELECTS PLUS. CARBOHYDRATES (CHEMICAL ASPECTS). see *CHEMISTRY — Abstracting, Bibliographies, Statistics*

C A SELECTS PLUS. CARBON & HETEROATOM N M R. see *CHEMISTRY — Abstracting, Bibliographies, Statistics*

C A SELECTS PLUS. CARCINOGENS, MUTAGENS & TERATOGENS. see *MEDICAL SCIENCES — Abstracting, Bibliographies, Statistics*

C A SELECTS PLUS. CATALYSIS (APPLIED & PHYSICAL ASPECTS). see *CHEMISTRY — Abstracting, Bibliographies, Statistics*

C A SELECTS PLUS. CATALYSIS (ORGANIC REACTIONS). see *CHEMISTRY — Abstracting, Bibliographies, Statistics*

C A SELECTS PLUS. CHEMICAL HAZARDS, HEALTH & SAFETY. see *OCCUPATIONAL HEALTH AND SAFETY — Abstracting, Bibliographies, Statistics*

C A SELECTS PLUS. CONTROLLED RELEASE TECHNOLOGY. see *CHEMISTRY — Abstracting, Bibliographies, Statistics*

C A SELECTS PLUS. DETERGENTS, SOAPS, & SURFACTANTS. see *CHEMISTRY — Abstracting, Bibliographies, Statistics*

C A SELECTS PLUS. DRUG DELIVERY SYSTEMS & DOSAGE FORMS. see *PHARMACY AND PHARMACOLOGY — Abstracting, Bibliographies, Statistics*

C A SELECTS PLUS. ELECTROPHORESIS. see *CHEMISTRY — Abstracting, Bibliographies, Statistics*

C A SELECTS PLUS. ENVIRONMENTAL POLLUTION. see *ENVIRONMENTAL STUDIES — Abstracting, Bibliographies, Statistics*

C A SELECTS PLUS. ENZYME APPLICATIONS. see *CHEMISTRY — Abstracting, Bibliographies, Statistics*

C A SELECTS PLUS. FLAVORS & FRAGRANCES. see *CHEMISTRY — Abstracting, Bibliographies, Statistics*

C A SELECTS PLUS. FORENSIC CHEMISTRY. see *CHEMISTRY — Abstracting, Bibliographies, Statistics*

C A SELECTS PLUS. FUNGICIDES. see *CHEMISTRY — Abstracting, Bibliographies, Statistics*

C A SELECTS PLUS. GAS CHROMATOGRAPHY. see *CHEMISTRY — Abstracting, Bibliographies, Statistics*

C A SELECTS PLUS. GEL PERMEATION CHROMATOGRAPHY. see *CHEMISTRY — Abstracting, Bibliographies, Statistics*

C A SELECTS PLUS. HERBICIDES. see *CHEMISTRY — Abstracting, Bibliographies, Statistics*

C A SELECTS PLUS. HIGH PERFORMANCE LIQUID CHROMATOGRAPHY. see *CHEMISTRY — Abstracting, Bibliographies, Statistics*

C A SELECTS PLUS. INSECTICIDES. see *BIOLOGY — Abstracting, Bibliographies, Statistics*

C A SELECTS PLUS. LIQUID WASTE TREATMENT. see *CHEMISTRY — Abstracting, Bibliographies, Statistics*

C A SELECTS PLUS. MASS SPECTROMETRY. see *CHEMISTRY — Abstracting, Bibliographies, Statistics*

C A SELECTS PLUS. ORGANOSILICON CHEMISTRY. see *CHEMISTRY — Abstracting, Bibliographies, Statistics*

C A SELECTS PLUS. PHARMACEUTICAL ANALYSIS. see *PHARMACY AND PHARMACOLOGY — Abstracting, Bibliographies, Statistics*

C A SELECTS PLUS. PHOTOCHEMISTRY. see *CHEMISTRY — Abstracting, Bibliographies, Statistics*

C A SELECTS PLUS. POLLUTION MONITORING. see *ENVIRONMENTAL STUDIES — Abstracting, Bibliographies, Statistics*

C A SELECTS PLUS. POLYURETHANES. see *CHEMISTRY — Abstracting, Bibliographies, Statistics*

C A SELECTS PLUS. RECOVERY & RECYCLING OF WASTES. see *CHEMISTRY — Abstracting, Bibliographies, Statistics*

C A SELECTS PLUS. SOLID & RADIOACTIVE WASTE TREATMENT. see *CHEMISTRY — Abstracting, Bibliographies, Statistics*

ABSTRACTING AND INDEXING SERVICES

C A SELECTS PLUS. ULTRAFILTRATION. see *CHEMISTRY — Abstracting, Bibliographies, Statistics*

C A SELECTS PLUS. WATER TREATMENT. see *CHEMISTRY — Abstracting, Bibliographies, Statistics*

C A SELECTS PLUS. ZEOLITES. see *CHEMISTRY — Abstracting, Bibliographies, Statistics*

C I N D A; an index to the literature on microscopic neutron data. see *PHYSICS — Abstracting, Bibliographies, Statistics*

C I S FEDERAL REGISTER INDEX. (Congressional Information Service, Inc.) see *PUBLIC ADMINISTRATION — Abstracting, Bibliographies, Statistics*

C I S INDEX INDEX. see *PUBLIC ADMINISTRATION — Abstracting, Bibliographies, Statistics*

C I S INDEX TO PUBLICATIONS OF THE UNITED STATES CONGRESS. (Congressional Information Service, Inc.) see *PUBLIC ADMINISTRATION — Abstracting, Bibliographies, Statistics*

C L A S E. (Citas Latinoamericanas en Ciencias Sociales y Humanidades) see *SOCIAL SCIENCES: COMPREHENSIVE WORKS — Abstracting, Bibliographies, Statistics*

C O R E S T A; bulletin d'information. (Centre de Cooperation pour les Recherches Scientifiques Relatives au Tabac (Coresta)) see *TOBACCO — Abstracting, Bibliographies, Statistics*

C P I DIGEST; key to world literature serving the coatings, plastics, fibers, adhesives, and related industries. (Chemical Process Industries) see *PLASTICS — Abstracting, Bibliographies, Statistics*

C R I ABSTRACTS; digest of developments & research in cement, concrete, building materials and allied industries. (Cement Research Institute of India) see *BUILDING AND CONSTRUCTION — Abstracting, Bibliographies, Statistics*

C R R I ROAD ABSTRACTS. (Central Road Research Institute) see *ENGINEERING — Abstracting, Bibliographies, Statistics*

C S A NEUROSCIENCES ABSTRACTS. (Cambridge Scientific Abstracts) see *MEDICAL SCIENCES — Abstracting, Bibliographies, Statistics*

CALCIUM AND CALCIFIED TISSUE ABSTRACTS. see *BIOLOGY — Abstracting, Bibliographies, Statistics*

016　　　　　US　ISSN 0730-1367
Z1223.5.C2
CALIFORNIA PERIODICALS INDEX. 1977. a. $95 (with microfilm ed. $285). Gabriel Micrographics, Box 611, Dekalb, IL 60115. TEL 815-895-8642. Ed. Marcia Gabriel. bk.rev. (also avail. in microfilm) **Document type:** abstracting/indexing.
　　Description: Indexes more than fifty magazines published in and about California.

CANADA. STATISTICS CANADA. AIR PASSENGER ORIGIN AND DESTINATION. DOMESTIC REPORT. see *TRANSPORTATION — Abstracting, Bibliographies, Statistics*

CANADIAN EDUCATION INDEX/REPERTOIRE CANADIEN SUR L'EDUCATION. see *EDUCATION — Abstracting, Bibliographies, Statistics*

CANADIAN INCOME TAX RESEARCH INDEX. see *BUSINESS AND ECONOMICS — Abstracting, Bibliographies, Statistics*

CANADIAN INDEX. see *BUSINESS AND ECONOMICS — Abstracting, Bibliographies, Statistics*

CANADIAN JEWISH CONGRESS. NATIONAL ARCHIVES NEWSLETTER. see *ETHNIC INTERESTS*

016　　　　　US　ISSN 0008-4719
AI3
CANADIAN PERIODICAL INDEX. (Text in English, French) 1938. m. (with a. cumulation). Gale Research, 835 Penobscot Bldg., 645 Griswold St., Detroit, MI 48226-4094. TEL 313-961-2242; 800-877-4253. FAX 800-414-5043. TELEX 810-221-7086. E-mail: daniel_snyder@gale.com. bk.rev.; index, cum.index: 1948-1959. **Document type:** abstracting/indexing.
　●Also available online.
　Also available on CD-ROM.
　—CISTI.
　　Formerly: Canadian Index to Periodicals and Documentary Films.
　　Description: Covers over 400 English and French language serials from Canada and the US.

016　　　　　CN　ISSN 1196-099X
CANADIAN RESEARCH INDEX, MICROLOG/INDEX DE RECHERCHE DU CANADA, MICROLOG. (Text in English, French) 1979. m. price varies. Micromedia Ltd., 20 Victoria St., Toronto, ON M5C 2N8, Canada. TEL 416-362-5211. FAX 416-362-6161. E-mail: info@micromedia.on.ca; URL: http://www.micromedia.on.ca. Ed. Brian Terry. R&P contact: Gail Dykstra. **Document type:** abstracting/indexing.
　●Also available online.
　Also available on CD-ROM.
　—BLDSC (5759.176500); CISTI.
　　Former titles (until 1992): Microlog: Canadian Research Index (ISSN 0839-1289) & Microlog Index (ISSN 0707-3135); Publicat Index to Canadian Federal Publications (ISSN 0384-9813); Urban Canada; Canadian Urban Sources (ISSN 0917-2775); Profile Index to Canadian and Municipal Government Publications (ISSN 0316-4068).

CANON LAW ABSTRACTS; half-yearly review of periodical literature in canon law. see *RELIGIONS AND THEOLOGY — Abstracting, Bibliographies, Statistics*

CARDIOLOGIA NEL MONDO; recensioni di riviste di cardiologia di tutto il mondo. see *MEDICAL SCIENCES — Abstracting, Bibliographies, Statistics*

CARGO TODAY. see *TRANSPORTATION — Abstracting, Bibliographies, Statistics*

CARIBBEAN ABSTRACTS. see *ANTHROPOLOGY — Abstracting, Bibliographies, Statistics*

CARINDEX: SCIENCE & TECHNOLOGY. see *SCIENCES: COMPREHENSIVE WORKS — Abstracting, Bibliographies, Statistics*

CARINDEX: SOCIAL SCIENCES AND HUMANITIES. see *SOCIAL SCIENCES: COMPREHENSIVE WORKS — Abstracting, Bibliographies, Statistics*

CATALOG OF MUSEUM PUBLICATIONS AND MEDIA; a directory and index of publications and audiovisuals available from U.S. and Canadian institutions. see *MUSEUMS AND ART GALLERIES — Abstracting, Bibliographies, Statistics*

CATALOGO DE LIBROS ANTIGUOS Y MODERNOS. see *PUBLISHING AND BOOK TRADE — Abstracting, Bibliographies, Statistics*

CATALOGUE & INDEX. see *LIBRARY AND INFORMATION SCIENCES — Abstracting, Bibliographies, Statistics*

CATCHWORD AND TRADE NAME INDEX. see *TECHNOLOGY: COMPREHENSIVE WORKS — Abstracting, Bibliographies, Statistics*

CATHOLIC PERIODICAL AND LITERATURE INDEX. see *RELIGIONS AND THEOLOGY — Abstracting, Bibliographies, Statistics*

CELL CYCLE. see *BIOLOGY — Abstracting, Bibliographies, Statistics*

CENTRE FOR SPORTS SCIENCE AND HISTORY. SERIAL HOLDINGS. see *EDUCATION — Abstracting, Bibliographies, Statistics*

CENTRE INTERNATIONAL DE DOCUMENTATION ARACHNOLOGIQUE. LISTE DES TRAVAUX ARACHNOLOGIQUES. see *BIOLOGY — Abstracting, Bibliographies, Statistics*

CERAMIC ABSTRACTS. see *CERAMICS, GLASS AND POTTERY — Abstracting, Bibliographies, Statistics*

CERAMIC ABSTRACTS (C D - R O M). see *CERAMICS, GLASS AND POTTERY — Abstracting, Bibliographies, Statistics*

CEREAL SOURCE (YEAR). see *FOOD AND FOOD INDUSTRIES — Abstracting, Bibliographies, Statistics*

016　　　　　US　ISSN 1060-1465
CHARTS, GRAPHS & STATS INDEX. every 4 yrs. (with a. supplements). $54. Highsmith Press, Box 800, Fort Atkinson, WI 53538-0800. TEL 414-563-9571; 800-835-2329. FAX 414-563-4801. E-mail: hpress@highsmith.com; URL: http://www.hpress.highsmith.com. Ed. Robert Skapura; Pub. Donald Sager. R&P contact: Donald Sager. **Document type:** abstracting/indexing.
　　Description: Publishes statistics in graphic form on the most current issues.

CHEMICAL ABSTRACTS. see *CHEMISTRY — Abstracting, Bibliographies, Statistics*

CHEMICAL ABSTRACTS - APPLIED CHEMISTRY AND CHEMICAL ENGINEERING SECTIONS. see *CHEMISTRY — Abstracting, Bibliographies, Statistics*

CHEMICAL ABSTRACTS - BIOCHEMISTRY SECTIONS. see *CHEMISTRY — Abstracting, Bibliographies, Statistics*

CHEMICAL ABSTRACTS - MACROMOLECULAR SECTIONS. see *CHEMISTRY — Abstracting, Bibliographies, Statistics*

CHEMICAL ABSTRACTS - ORGANIC CHEMISTRY SECTIONS. see *CHEMISTRY — Abstracting, Bibliographies, Statistics*

CHEMICAL ABSTRACTS - PHYSICAL, INORGANIC AND ANALYTICAL CHEMISTRY SECTIONS. see *CHEMISTRY — Abstracting, Bibliographies, Statistics*

CHEMICAL ABSTRACTS SERVICE SOURCE INDEX. see *CHEMISTRY — Abstracting, Bibliographies, Statistics*

CHEMICAL INDUSTRY NOTES. see *CHEMISTRY — Abstracting, Bibliographies, Statistics*

CHEMICAL TITLES. see *CHEMISTRY — Abstracting, Bibliographies, Statistics*

CHEMINFORM. see *CHEMISTRY — Abstracting, Bibliographies, Statistics*

CHEMORECEPTION ABSTRACTS; chemical senses & applied techniques. see *CHEMISTRY — Abstracting, Bibliographies, Statistics*

CHEMTRACTS. see *CHEMISTRY — Abstracting, Bibliographies, Statistics*

CHIKIDAH-I PAYAN'NAMAHHA-YI IRAN/IRANIAN DISSERTATION ABSTRACTS. see *SCIENCES: COMPREHENSIVE WORKS — Abstracting, Bibliographies, Statistics*

CHILD DEVELOPMENT ABSTRACTS AND BIBLIOGRAPHY. see *CHILDREN AND YOUTH — Abstracting, Bibliographies, Statistics*

CHILDREN'S BOOK REVIEW INDEX. see *CHILDREN AND YOUTH — Abstracting, Bibliographies, Statistics*

CHILDREN'S LITERATURE ABSTRACTS. see *CHILDREN AND YOUTH — Abstracting, Bibliographies, Statistics*

CHILDREN'S MAGAZINE GUIDE; subject index to children's magazines. see *CHILDREN AND YOUTH — Abstracting, Bibliographies, Statistics*

CHINA AEROSPACE ABSTRACTS. see *AERONAUTICS AND SPACE FLIGHT — Abstracting, Bibliographies, Statistics*

CHINA MEDICAL ABSTRACTS (INTERNAL MEDICINE). see *MEDICAL SCIENCES — Abstracting, Bibliographies, Statistics*

CHINESE FISHERIES ABSTRACTS. see *FISH AND FISHERIES — Abstracting, Bibliographies, Statistics*

CHINESE FISHERY ABSTRACTS (ENGLISH EDITION). see *FISH AND FISHERIES — Abstracting, Bibliographies, Statistics*

ABSTRACTING AND INDEXING SERVICES

CHINESE SCIENCE ABSTRACTS. PART A; mathematics, mechanics, astronomy and space science, physics, technical sciences. see *SCIENCES: COMPREHENSIVE WORKS — Abstracting, Bibliographies, Statistics*

CHINESE SCIENCE ABSTRACTS. PART B; chemistry, life sciences, earth sciences. see *SCIENCES: COMPREHENSIVE WORKS — Abstracting, Bibliographies, Statistics*

CHINESE SCIENCE AND TECHNOLOGY ABSTRACTS. see *SCIENCES: COMPREHENSIVE WORKS — Abstracting, Bibliographies, Statistics*

CHOJU KANKEI TOKEI/ANNUAL STATISTICS OF BIRDS AND ANIMALS. see *BIOLOGY — Abstracting, Bibliographies, Statistics*

016   KO   ISSN 1226-1556
CHONGGI KANHAENGMUL KISA SAEGIN/KOREAN INDEX TO PERIODICALS. Variant spelling: Chongki Kanhaengmul Kisa Saegin. (Text in Korean) 1964. q. (with a. cumulation). free. National Assembly Library - Kukhoe Tosogwan, 1 Yoido-dong, Seoul, S. Korea. FAX 82-2-788-4298. bibl. circ. 1,100.
Document type: abstracting/indexing.
● Also available on CD-ROM.
Formerly: Kuknae Kanhaengmul Kisa Saegin.

CHRISTIAN PERIODICAL INDEX; an index to subjects, authors and book reviews. see *RELIGIONS AND THEOLOGY — Abstracting, Bibliographies, Statistics*

CHRISTIAN SCIENCE MONITOR INDEX. see *JOURNALISM — Abstracting, Bibliographies, Statistics*

CHROMATOGRAPHY ABSTRACTS. see *CHEMISTRY — Abstracting, Bibliographies, Statistics*

CITATIONS FOR SERIAL LITERATURE. see *LIBRARY AND INFORMATION SCIENCES — Abstracting, Bibliographies, Statistics*

CLIN-ALERT. see *PHARMACY AND PHARMACOLOGY — Abstracting, Bibliographies, Statistics*

CLINICAL ABSTRACTS - CURRENT THERAPEUTIC FINDINGS. see *MEDICAL SCIENCES — Abstracting, Bibliographies, Statistics*

COAL HIGHLIGHTS. see *ENERGY*

COLD SPRING HARBOR LABORATORY. ABSTRACTS OF PAPERS PRESENTED AT MEETINGS. see *BIOLOGY*

COLOUR INDEX: ADDITIONS & AMENDMENTS. see *TEXTILE INDUSTRIES AND FABRICS — Abstracting, Bibliographies, Statistics*

COMBINED CUMULATIVE INDEX TO OBSTETRICS AND GYNECOLOGY. see *MEDICAL SCIENCES — Abstracting, Bibliographies, Statistics*

COMBINED CUMULATIVE INDEX TO PEDIATRICS. see *MEDICAL SCIENCES — Abstracting, Bibliographies, Statistics*

COMMODITY YEARBOOK STATISTICAL UPDATE. see *AGRICULTURE — Abstracting, Bibliographies, Statistics*

COMMUNICATION ABSTRACTS. see *COMMUNICATIONS — Abstracting, Bibliographies, Statistics*

COMMUNICATION BOOKNOTES; recent titles in telecommunications, information & media. see *COMMUNICATIONS — Abstracting, Bibliographies, Statistics*

COMMUNITY CURRENTS; the community development information digest. see *SOCIAL SERVICES AND WELFARE — Abstracting, Bibliographies, Statistics*

COMPACTMATH - COMPACT MATHEMATICS LIBRARY. see *MATHEMATICS — Abstracting, Bibliographies, Statistics*

COMPENSATION AND BENEFITS ABSTRACTS. see *BUSINESS AND ECONOMICS — Abstracting, Bibliographies, Statistics*

COMPLEMENTARY MEDICINE INDEX. see *ALTERNATIVE MEDICINE — Abstracting, Bibliographies, Statistics*

COMPREHENSIVE MEDLINE. see *MEDICAL SCIENCES — Abstracting, Bibliographies, Statistics*

COMPUMATH CITATION INDEX. see *MATHEMATICS — Abstracting, Bibliographies, Statistics*

COMPUTER ABSTRACTS. see *COMPUTERS — Abstracting, Bibliographies, Statistics*

COMPUTER & CONTROL ABSTRACTS. see *COMPUTERS — Abstracting, Bibliographies, Statistics*

COMPUTER AND INFORMATION SYSTEMS ABSTRACTS JOURNAL; an abstract journal pertaining to the theory, design, fabrication and application of computer and information systems. see *COMPUTERS — Abstracting, Bibliographies, Statistics*

COMPUTER DATABASE. see *COMPUTERS — Abstracting, Bibliographies, Statistics*

COMPUTER LITERATURE INDEX. see *COMPUTERS — Abstracting, Bibliographies, Statistics*

COMPUTER SELECT. see *COMPUTERS — Abstracting, Bibliographies, Statistics*

COMPUTING JOURNAL ABSTRACTS. see *COMPUTERS — Abstracting, Bibliographies, Statistics*

CONCRETE ABSTRACTS. see *BUILDING AND CONSTRUCTION — Abstracting, Bibliographies, Statistics*

CONFERENCE PAPERS ANNUAL INDEX. see *MEETINGS AND CONGRESSES — Abstracting, Bibliographies, Statistics*

CONFERENCE PAPERS INDEX. see *MEETINGS AND CONGRESSES — Abstracting, Bibliographies, Statistics*

CONGRESS OF HETEROCYCLIC CHEMISTRY. BOOK OF ABSTRACTS/FUKUSOKAN KAGAKU TORONKAI KOEN YOSHISHU. see *CHEMISTRY — Abstracting, Bibliographies, Statistics*

CONSOLIDATED INDEX TO THE ZIMBABWE LAW REPORTS. see *LAW — Abstracting, Bibliographies, Statistics*

CONSTRUCTION INFORMATION FILE - C I F. see *BUILDING AND CONSTRUCTION — Abstracting, Bibliographies, Statistics*

CONSUMERS INDEX; to product evaluations and information sources. see *CONSUMER EDUCATION AND PROTECTION — Abstracting, Bibliographies, Statistics*

CONSUMERS REFERENCE DISC. see *CONSUMER EDUCATION AND PROTECTION — Abstracting, Bibliographies, Statistics*

CONTENTS. see *PHARMACY AND PHARMACOLOGY — Abstracting, Bibliographies, Statistics*

CONTENTS LIST OF SOVIET SCIENTIFIC PERIODICALS. see *SCIENCES: COMPREHENSIVE WORKS — Abstracting, Bibliographies, Statistics*

CONTENTS OF RECENT ECONOMICS JOURNALS. see *BUSINESS AND ECONOMICS — Abstracting, Bibliographies, Statistics*

CONTENTS PAGES IN EDUCATION. see *EDUCATION — Abstracting, Bibliographies, Statistics*

COOK'S INDEX; an index of cookery periodicals and cookbooks. see *HOME ECONOMICS — Abstracting, Bibliographies, Statistics*

CORE JOURNALS IN CARDIOLOGY. see *MEDICAL SCIENCES — Abstracting, Bibliographies, Statistics*

CORE JOURNALS IN CLINICAL NEUROLOGY. see *MEDICAL SCIENCES — Abstracting, Bibliographies, Statistics*

CORE JOURNALS IN DERMATOLOGY. see *MEDICAL SCIENCES — Abstracting, Bibliographies, Statistics*

CORE JOURNALS IN GASTROENTEROLOGY. see *MEDICAL SCIENCES — Abstracting, Bibliographies, Statistics*

CORE JOURNALS IN OBSTETRICS - GYNECOLOGY. see *MEDICAL SCIENCES — Abstracting, Bibliographies, Statistics*

CORE JOURNALS IN OPHTHALMOLOGY. see *MEDICAL SCIENCES — Abstracting, Bibliographies, Statistics*

CORE JOURNALS IN PEDIATRICS. see *MEDICAL SCIENCES — Abstracting, Bibliographies, Statistics*

CORE MEDLINE. see *MEDICAL SCIENCES — Abstracting, Bibliographies, Statistics*

CORROSION ABSTRACTS; abstracts of the world's literature on corrosion and corrosion mitigation. see *ENGINEERING — Abstracting, Bibliographies, Statistics*

016   US   ISSN 1054-433X
AI3
COVER STORY INDEX. 1990. every 5 yrs. (with a. supplements). $54. Highsmith Press, Box 800, Fort Atkinson, WI 53538-0800. TEL 414-563-9571; 800-835-2329. FAX 414-563-4801. E-mail: hpress@highsmith.com; URL: http://www.hpress.highsmith.com. Ed. Robert Skapura; Pub. Donald Sager. R&P contact: Donald Sager. (back issues avail.) Document type: abstracting/indexing.
Description: Publishes the major cover story articles in chronological order.

CREATIVE BOOK SELECTION INDEX. see *PUBLISHING AND BOOK TRADE — Abstracting, Bibliographies, Statistics*

CRIMINAL JUSTICE ABSTRACTS. see *CRIMINOLOGY AND LAW ENFORCEMENT — Abstracting, Bibliographies, Statistics*

CRIMINAL JUSTICE PERIODICAL INDEX. see *CRIMINOLOGY AND LAW ENFORCEMENT — Abstracting, Bibliographies, Statistics*

CRIMINOLOGY, PENOLOGY & POLICE SCIENCE ABSTRACTS. see *CRIMINOLOGY AND LAW ENFORCEMENT — Abstracting, Bibliographies, Statistics*

CROP PHYSIOLOGY ABSTRACTS. see *AGRICULTURE — Abstracting, Bibliographies, Statistics*

CULTURA IN ROMANIA; referinte bibliografice si documentare din periodice romanesti. see *HUMANITIES: COMPREHENSIVE WORKS — Abstracting, Bibliographies, Statistics*

CUMULATIVE INDEX TO NURSING & ALLIED HEALTH LITERATURE. see *MEDICAL SCIENCES — Abstracting, Bibliographies, Statistics*

CURRENT ADVANCES IN APPLIED MICROBIOLOGY & BIOTECHNOLOGY. see *BIOLOGY — Abstracting, Bibliographies, Statistics*

CURRENT ADVANCES IN CANCER RESEARCH. see *MEDICAL SCIENCES — Abstracting, Bibliographies, Statistics*

CURRENT ADVANCES IN CELL & DEVELOPMENTAL BIOLOGY. see *BIOLOGY — Abstracting, Bibliographies, Statistics*

CURRENT ADVANCES IN CLINICAL CHEMISTRY. see *CHEMISTRY — Abstracting, Bibliographies, Statistics*

CURRENT ADVANCES IN ECOLOGICAL AND ENVIRONMENTAL SCIENCES. see *ENVIRONMENTAL STUDIES — Abstracting, Bibliographies, Statistics*

CURRENT ADVANCES IN ENDOCRINOLOGY & METABOLISM. see *MEDICAL SCIENCES — Abstracting, Bibliographies, Statistics*

CURRENT ADVANCES IN GENETICS AND MOLECULAR BIOLOGY. see *BIOLOGY — Abstracting, Bibliographies, Statistics*

CURRENT ADVANCES IN IMMUNOLOGY & INFECTIOUS DISEASES. see *MEDICAL SCIENCES — Abstracting, Bibliographies, Statistics*

CURRENT ADVANCES IN NEUROSCIENCE. see *MEDICAL SCIENCES — Abstracting, Bibliographies, Statistics*

ABSTRACTING AND INDEXING SERVICES

CURRENT ADVANCES IN PLANT SCIENCE. see *BIOLOGY — Abstracting, Bibliographies, Statistics*

CURRENT ADVANCES IN PROTEIN BIOCHEMISTRY. see *BIOLOGY — Abstracting, Bibliographies, Statistics*

CURRENT ADVANCES IN TOXICOLOGY. see *ENVIRONMENTAL STUDIES — Abstracting, Bibliographies, Statistics*

CURRENT ANTARCTIC LITERATURE. see *SCIENCES: COMPREHENSIVE WORKS — Abstracting, Bibliographies, Statistics*

CURRENT AWARENESS BULLETIN. see *BUSINESS AND ECONOMICS — Abstracting, Bibliographies, Statistics*

CURRENT AWARENESS IN BIOLOGICAL SCIENCES. see *BIOLOGY — Abstracting, Bibliographies, Statistics*

CURRENT AWARENESS IN PARTICLE TECHNOLOGY. see *ENGINEERING — Abstracting, Bibliographies, Statistics*

CURRENT BIBLIOGRAPHIES ON SCIENCE AND TECHNOLOGY: BIOLOGY, PHARMACY AND FOOD SCIENCE. see *BIOLOGY — Abstracting, Bibliographies, Statistics*

CURRENT BIBLIOGRAPHIES ON SCIENCE AND TECHNOLOGY: CHEMISTRY AND CHEMICAL INDUSTRY. see *CHEMISTRY — Abstracting, Bibliographies, Statistics*

CURRENT BIBLIOGRAPHIES ON SCIENCE AND TECHNOLOGY: MECHANICAL ENGINEERING & CONSTRUCTION ENGINEERING. see *METALLURGY — Abstracting, Bibliographies, Statistics*

CURRENT BIBLIOGRAPHY ON SCIENCE AND TECHNOLOGY: CHEMISTRY AND CHEMICAL ENGINEERING (FOREIGN)/KAGAKU GIJUTSU BUNKEN SOKUHO. KAGAKU, KAGAKU KOGYO-HEN (GAIKOKU-HEN). see *CHEMISTRY — Abstracting, Bibliographies, Statistics*

CURRENT BIBLIOGRAPHY ON SCIENCE AND TECHNOLOGY: CHEMISTRY AND CHEMICAL ENGINEERING (JAPANESE)/KAGAKU GIJUTSU BUNKEN SOKUHO KAGAKU. KAGAKU KOGYO-HEN (KOKUNAI-HEN). see *CHEMISTRY — Abstracting, Bibliographies, Statistics*

CURRENT BIBLIOGRAPHY ON SCIENCE AND TECHNOLOGY: CIVIL ENGINEERING AND ARCHITECTURE/KAGAKU GIJUTSU BUNKEN SOKUHO. DOBOKU, KENCHIKU KOGAKU HEN. see *ENGINEERING — Abstracting, Bibliographies, Statistics*

CURRENT BIBLIOGRAPHY ON SCIENCE AND TECHNOLOGY: EARTH SCIENCE, MINING AND METALLURGY/KAGAKU GIJUTSU BUNKEN SOKUHO. KINZOKU KOGAKU, KOZAN KOGAKU, CHIKYU NO KAGAKU-HEN. see *EARTH SCIENCES — Abstracting, Bibliographies, Statistics*

CURRENT BIBLIOGRAPHY ON SCIENCE AND TECHNOLOGY: MECHANICAL ENGINEERING/KAGAKU GIJUTSU BUNKEN SOKUHO. KIKAI KOGAKU-HEN. see *ENGINEERING — Abstracting, Bibliographies, Statistics*

CURRENT BIBLIOGRAPHY ON SCIENCE AND TECHNOLOGY: NUCLEAR ENGINEERING/KAGAKU GIJUTSU BUNKEN SOKUHO. GENSHIRYOKU KOGAKU-HEN. see *ENGINEERING — Abstracting, Bibliographies, Statistics*

CURRENT BIBLIOGRAPHY ON SCIENCE AND TECHNOLOGY: PURE AND APPLIED PHYSICS/KAGAKU GIJUTSU BUNKEN SOKUHO. BUTSURI, OYOBUTSURI-HEN. see *PHYSICS — Abstracting, Bibliographies, Statistics*

CURRENT BIOLOGY. see *BIOLOGY — Abstracting, Bibliographies, Statistics*

CURRENT BIOTECHNOLOGY. see *BIOLOGY — Abstracting, Bibliographies, Statistics*

CURRENT CHEMICAL REACTIONS. see *CHEMISTRY — Abstracting, Bibliographies, Statistics*

CURRENT CONTENTS: AGRICULTURE, BIOLOGY & ENVIRONMENTAL SCIENCES. see *AGRICULTURE — Abstracting, Bibliographies, Statistics*

CURRENT CONTENTS: CLINICAL MEDICINE. see *MEDICAL SCIENCES — Abstracting, Bibliographies, Statistics*

CURRENT CONTENTS: ENGINEERING, COMPUTING & TECHNOLOGY. see *ENGINEERING — Abstracting, Bibliographies, Statistics*

CURRENT CONTENTS: LIFE SCIENCES. see *BIOLOGY — Abstracting, Bibliographies, Statistics*

CURRENT CONTENTS OF FOREIGN JOURNALS: MANAGEMENT & ECONOMICS. see *BUSINESS AND ECONOMICS — Abstracting, Bibliographies, Statistics*

016　　　　IS　　ISSN 0333-9858
CURRENT CONTENTS OF PERIODICALS ON THE MIDDLE EAST. (Text in Arabic, English, French, German) 1980. bi-m. $35. Tel Aviv University, Moshe Dayan Center for Middle Eastern and African Studies, Documentation Center, P.O. Box 39040, Ramat Aviv, Tel Aviv 69978, Israel. TEL 972-3-6409646. FAX 972-3-6415802. Ed. Marion Gliksberg. circ. 250. **Document type:** abstracting/indexing.
Description: Provides a comprehensive bibliography of current literature on the Middle East. Includes lists of the latest articles and analyses on economic, political and social developments in the Middle East, which examine the area from both the Middle East and Western perspectives.

CURRENT CONTENTS: PHYSICAL, CHEMICAL & EARTH SCIENCES. see *CHEMISTRY — Abstracting, Bibliographies, Statistics*

CURRENT CONTENTS: SOCIAL & BEHAVIORAL SCIENCES. see *SOCIOLOGY — Abstracting, Bibliographies, Statistics*

CURRENT DIGEST OF THE POST-SOVIET PRESS. see *POLITICAL SCIENCE — Abstracting, Bibliographies, Statistics*

CURRENT DIGEST OF THE POST-SOVIET PRESS. ANNUAL INDEX. see *POLITICAL SCIENCE — Abstracting, Bibliographies, Statistics*

CURRENT DIGEST OF THE POST-SOVIET PRESS. QUARTERLY INDEX. see *POLITICAL SCIENCE — Abstracting, Bibliographies, Statistics*

CURRENT INDEX TO JOURNALS IN EDUCATION. see *EDUCATION — Abstracting, Bibliographies, Statistics*

CURRENT INDEX TO JOURNALS IN EDUCATION SEMIANNUAL CUMULATION. see *EDUCATION — Abstracting, Bibliographies, Statistics*

CURRENT INDEX TO STATISTICS; applications - methods - theory. see *MATHEMATICS — Abstracting, Bibliographies, Statistics*

CURRENT LAW INDEX; multiple access to legal periodicals in print. see *LAW — Abstracting, Bibliographies, Statistics*

CURRENT LITERATURE IN TRAFFIC AND TRANSPORTATION. see *TRANSPORTATION — Abstracting, Bibliographies, Statistics*

CURRENT LITERATURE ON SCIENCE OF SCIENCE. see *SCIENCES: COMPREHENSIVE WORKS — Abstracting, Bibliographies, Statistics*

CURRENT MANAGEMENT LITERATURE. see *BUSINESS AND ECONOMICS — Abstracting, Bibliographies, Statistics*

CURRENT MEDICAL LITERATURE. CARDIAC IMAGING MONITOR. see *MEDICAL SCIENCES — Abstracting, Bibliographies, Statistics*

CURRENT MEDICAL LITERATURE. COLORECTAL CANCER. see *MEDICAL SCIENCES — Abstracting, Bibliographies, Statistics*

CURRENT MEDICAL LITERATURE. HYPERTENSION AND HEART FAILURE. see *MEDICAL SCIENCES — Abstracting, Bibliographies, Statistics*

CURRENT MEDICAL LITERATURE. PRIMARY CARE. see *MEDICAL SCIENCES — Abstracting, Bibliographies, Statistics*

CURRENT MEDICAL LITERATURE. PSYCHIATRY REVIEWS; recent developments in psychiatric care for General Practitioners. see *MEDICAL SCIENCES — Abstracting, Bibliographies, Statistics*

CURRENT MEDICAL LITERATURE. RESPIRATORY MEDICINE - PEER SELECTED CITATIONS. see *MEDICAL SCIENCES — Abstracting, Bibliographies, Statistics*

CURRENT MILITARY AND POLITICAL LITERATURE. see *MILITARY — Abstracting, Bibliographies, Statistics*

CURRENT OPINION IN ANAESTHESIOLOGY. see *MEDICAL SCIENCES — Abstracting, Bibliographies, Statistics*

CURRENT OPINION IN BIOTECHNOLOGY. see *BIOLOGY — Abstracting, Bibliographies, Statistics*

CURRENT OPINION IN CARDIOLOGY. see *MEDICAL SCIENCES — Abstracting, Bibliographies, Statistics*

CURRENT OPINION IN CELL BIOLOGY. see *BIOLOGY — Abstracting, Bibliographies, Statistics*

CURRENT OPINION IN COSMETIC DENTISTRY. see *MEDICAL SCIENCES — Abstracting, Bibliographies, Statistics*

CURRENT OPINION IN GASTROENTEROLOGY. see *MEDICAL SCIENCES — Abstracting, Bibliographies, Statistics*

CURRENT OPINION IN IMMUNOLOGY. see *MEDICAL SCIENCES — Abstracting, Bibliographies, Statistics*

CURRENT OPINION IN INFECTIOUS DISEASES. see *MEDICAL SCIENCES — Abstracting, Bibliographies, Statistics*

CURRENT OPINION IN NEPHROLOGY & HYPERTENSION. see *MEDICAL SCIENCES — Abstracting, Bibliographies, Statistics*

CURRENT OPINION IN NEUROLOGY. see *MEDICAL SCIENCES — Abstracting, Bibliographies, Statistics*

CURRENT OPINION IN OBSTETRICS & GYNECOLOGY. see *MEDICAL SCIENCES — Abstracting, Bibliographies, Statistics*

CURRENT OPINION IN ONCOLOGY. see *MEDICAL SCIENCES — Abstracting, Bibliographies, Statistics*

CURRENT OPINION IN OPHTHALMOLOGY. see *MEDICAL SCIENCES — Abstracting, Bibliographies, Statistics*

CURRENT OPINION IN ORTHOPEDICS. see *MEDICAL SCIENCES — Abstracting, Bibliographies, Statistics*

CURRENT OPINION IN PEDIATRICS. see *MEDICAL SCIENCES — Abstracting, Bibliographies, Statistics*

CURRENT OPINION IN PERIODONTOLOGY. see *MEDICAL SCIENCES — Abstracting, Bibliographies, Statistics*

CURRENT OPINION IN PSYCHIATRY. see *MEDICAL SCIENCES — Abstracting, Bibliographies, Statistics*

CURRENT OPINION IN PULMONARY MEDICINE. see *MEDICAL SCIENCES — Respiratory Diseases*

CURRENT OPINION IN RHEUMATOLOGY. see *MEDICAL SCIENCES — Abstracting, Bibliographies, Statistics*

CURRENT PAPERS IN ELECTRICAL & ELECTRONICS ENGINEERING. see *ENGINEERING — Abstracting, Bibliographies, Statistics*

CURRENT PAPERS IN PHYSICS; containing about 78,000 titles of research articles from the world's physics journals. see *PHYSICS — Abstracting, Bibliographies, Statistics*

CURRENT PHYSICS INDEX. see *PHYSICS — Abstracting, Bibliographies, Statistics*

CURRENT REFERENCES IN FISH RESEARCH. see *FISH AND FISHERIES — Abstracting, Bibliographies, Statistics*

ABSTRACTING AND INDEXING SERVICES

CURRENT RESEARCH IN BRITAIN. BIOLOGICAL SCIENCES. see *BIOLOGY — Abstracting, Bibliographies, Statistics*

CURRENT RESEARCH IN BRITAIN. HUMANITIES. see *HUMANITIES: COMPREHENSIVE WORKS — Abstracting, Bibliographies, Statistics*

CURRENT RESEARCH IN BRITAIN. PHYSICAL SCIENCES. see *SCIENCES: COMPREHENSIVE WORKS — Abstracting, Bibliographies, Statistics*

CURRENT RESEARCH IN BRITAIN. SOCIAL SCIENCES. see *SOCIAL SCIENCES: COMPREHENSIVE WORKS — Abstracting, Bibliographies, Statistics*

CURRENT TITLES IN DENTISTRY. see *MEDICAL SCIENCES — Abstracting, Bibliographies, Statistics*

CURRENT TITLES IN ELECTROCHEMISTRY. see *CHEMISTRY — Abstracting, Bibliographies, Statistics*

CUTTING TECHNOLOGY. see *MACHINERY — Abstracting, Bibliographies, Statistics*

C2C ABSTRACTS: JAPAN - ANALYTICAL CHEMISTRY. see *CHEMISTRY — Abstracting, Bibliographies, Statistics*

C2C ABSTRACTS: JAPAN - CERAMICS. see *CERAMICS, GLASS AND POTTERY — Abstracting, Bibliographies, Statistics*

C2C ABSTRACTS: JAPAN - CHEMICAL ENGINEERING. see *ENGINEERING — Abstracting, Bibliographies, Statistics*

C2C ABSTRACTS: JAPAN - CRYSTALLOGRAPHY. see *CHEMISTRY — Abstracting, Bibliographies, Statistics*

C2C ABSTRACTS: JAPAN - HYDROCARBONS. see *CHEMISTRY — Abstracting, Bibliographies, Statistics*

C2C ABSTRACTS: JAPAN - INORGANIC CHEMISTRY. see *CHEMISTRY — Abstracting, Bibliographies, Statistics*

C2C ABSTRACTS: JAPAN - MATERIALS SCIENCE. see *ENGINEERING — Abstracting, Bibliographies, Statistics*

C2C ABSTRACTS: JAPAN. - METALS. see *METALLURGY — Abstracting, Bibliographies, Statistics*

C2C ABSTRACTS: JAPAN - ORGANIC CHEMISTRY. see *CHEMISTRY — Abstracting, Bibliographies, Statistics*

C2C ABSTRACTS: JAPAN - PHYSICAL CHEMISTRY. see *CHEMISTRY — Abstracting, Bibliographies, Statistics*

C2C ABSTRACTS: JAPAN - PLASTICS. see *PLASTICS — Abstracting, Bibliographies, Statistics*

C2C ABSTRACTS: JAPAN - POLYMER CHEMISTRY. see *CHEMISTRY — Abstracting, Bibliographies, Statistics*

C2C ABSTRACTS: JAPAN - SURFACE CHEMISTRY. see *CHEMISTRY — Abstracting, Bibliographies, Statistics*

C2C ABSTRACTS: JAPAN - TEXTILES. see *TEXTILE INDUSTRIES AND FABRICS — Abstracting, Bibliographies, Statistics*

C2C CURRENTS: JAPAN - CHEMISTRY. see *CHEMISTRY — Abstracting, Bibliographies, Statistics*

C2C CURRENTS: JAPAN - COMPUTERS. see *COMPUTERS — Abstracting, Bibliographies, Statistics*

C2C CURRENTS: JAPAN - ELECTRONICS. see *ELECTRONICS*

C2C CURRENTS: JAPAN - MATERIALS. see *ENGINEERING — Abstracting, Bibliographies, Statistics*

DAIRY SCIENCE ABSTRACTS. see *AGRICULTURE — Abstracting, Bibliographies, Statistics*

DANSK ARTIKELINDEKS: AVISER OG TIDSSKRIFTER/DANISH INDEX OF ARTICLES: NEWSPAPERS AND PERIODICALS. see *JOURNALISM — Abstracting, Bibliographies, Statistics*

DATA JURIDICA; documentatie van juridische literatuur. see *LAW — Abstracting, Bibliographies, Statistics*

DECLASSIFIED DOCUMENTS CATALOG. see *POLITICAL SCIENCE — Abstracting, Bibliographies, Statistics*

DENKI KAGAKU KYOKAI TAIKAI KOEN YOSHISHU/ELECTROCHEMICAL SOCIETY OF JAPAN. ABSTRACTS OF ANNUAL MEETING. see *CHEMISTRY — Abstracting, Bibliographies, Statistics*

DENTAL ABSTRACTS. see *MEDICAL SCIENCES — Abstracting, Bibliographies, Statistics*

DIABETES CONTENTS. see *MEDICAL SCIENCES — Abstracting, Bibliographies, Statistics*

DIGEST OF NEUROLOGY & PSYCHIATRY. see *MEDICAL SCIENCES — Abstracting, Bibliographies, Statistics*

DIRECTORY OF AUSTRALIAN ASSOCIATIONS. see *BUSINESS AND ECONOMICS — Trade And Industrial Directories*

DIRECTORY OF PUBLISHED PROCEEDINGS. SERIES M L S - MEDICAL, LIFE SCIENCES. see *MEDICAL SCIENCES — Abstracting, Bibliographies, Statistics*

DIRECTORY OF PUBLISHED PROCEEDINGS. SERIES P C E - POLLUTION CONTROL & ECOLOGY. see *ENVIRONMENTAL STUDIES — Abstracting, Bibliographies, Statistics*

DIRECTORY OF PUBLISHED PROCEEDINGS. SERIES S E M T - SCIENCE, ENGINEERING, MEDICINE AND TECHNOLOGY. see *SCIENCES: COMPREHENSIVE WORKS — Abstracting, Bibliographies, Statistics*

DIRECTORY OF PUBLISHED PROCEEDINGS. SERIES S S H - SOCIAL SCIENCES - HUMANITIES. see *HUMANITIES: COMPREHENSIVE WORKS — Abstracting, Bibliographies, Statistics*

DIRECTORY OF SCIENTIFIC PERIODICALS OF PAKISTAN. see *SCIENCES: COMPREHENSIVE WORKS — Abstracting, Bibliographies, Statistics*

DIRECTORY OF THE CULTURAL ORGANIZATIONS OF THE REPUBLIC OF CHINA. see *EDUCATION — Abstracting, Bibliographies, Statistics*

DISSERTATION ABSTRACTS INTERNATIONAL. SECTION B: PHYSICAL SCIENCES AND ENGINEERING. see *SCIENCES: COMPREHENSIVE WORKS — Abstracting, Bibliographies, Statistics*

DISSERTATION ABSTRACTS INTERNATIONAL. SECTION C: WORLDWIDE. see *HUMANITIES: COMPREHENSIVE WORKS — Abstracting, Bibliographies, Statistics*

DIZHEN WENZHAI/SEISMOLOGICAL ABSTRACTS. see *EARTH SCIENCES — Abstracting, Bibliographies, Statistics*

DJERELO. see *SCIENCES: COMPREHENSIVE WORKS — Abstracting, Bibliographies, Statistics*

DOCUMENTATION LIST: AFRICA. see *HISTORY — Abstracting, Bibliographies, Statistics*

DOCUMENTS; revue des questions allemandes. see *HISTORY — Abstracting, Bibliographies, Statistics*

DOKUMENTATION NATUR UND LANDSCHAFT. see *CONSERVATION — Abstracting, Bibliographies, Statistics*

DOKUMENTATION PUBLIC HEALTH, OEFFENTLICHES GESUNDHEITSWESEN, GESUNDHEITSWISSENSCHAFTEN. see *MEDICAL SCIENCES — Abstracting, Bibliographies, Statistics*

DOKUMENTATION STRASSE; Kurzauszuege aus dem Schrifttum ueber das Strassenwesen. see *ENGINEERING — Abstracting, Bibliographies, Statistics*

DRUG FILE UPDATE; a current awareness index to publications on drugs and doping in sport. see *SPORTS AND GAMES — Abstracting, Bibliographies, Statistics*

E C M T STATISTICAL REPORT ON ROAD ACCIDENTS. (European Council of Ministers of Transport) see *TRANSPORTATION — Abstracting, Bibliographies, Statistics*

E F I - NYTT/E F I NEWS. (Ekonomiska Forskningsinstitutet (EFI)) see *BUSINESS AND ECONOMICS — Abstracting, Bibliographies, Statistics*

E I S; digests of environmental impact statements. see *ENVIRONMENTAL STUDIES — Abstracting, Bibliographies, Statistics*

E L L I S; a master guide to commentary on European Community law. (European Legal Literature Information Service) see *LAW — Abstracting, Bibliographies, Statistics*

020   US
E - N F A I S NOTES. (Printed format ceased in 1995.) irreg. (approx. w.). membership only. National Federation of Abstracting and Information Services, 1518 Walnut St., Ste. 307, Philadelphia, PA 19102. TEL 215-893-1561. FAX 215-893-1564. E-mail: nfais@hslc.org. **Document type:** newsletter.
● Available only online.
Supersedes: N F A I S Notes.
Description: Provides news of current developments affecting the information industry, views, comments and opinions.

E R I C IDENTIFIER AUTHORITY LIST. (Educational Resources Information Center) see *EDUCATION — Abstracting, Bibliographies, Statistics*

E R I C ON C D - R O M. (Education Resource Information Center) see *EDUCATION — Abstracting, Bibliographies, Statistics*

E U D I S E D - EUROPEAN EDUCATIONAL RESEARCH YEARBOOK. (European Documentation and Information System for Education) see *EDUCATION — Abstracting, Bibliographies, Statistics*

EARTHQUAKE ENGINEERING ABSTRACTS DATABASE. see *ENGINEERING — Abstracting, Bibliographies, Statistics*

ECO-LOG CANADIAN POLLUTION LEGISLATION. see *ENVIRONMENTAL STUDIES — Abstracting, Bibliographies, Statistics*

ECO-LOG WEEK; a report on waste management and industrial pollution control. see *ENVIRONMENTAL STUDIES — Abstracting, Bibliographies, Statistics*

ECOLOGICAL ABSTRACTS. see *BIOLOGY — Abstracting, Bibliographies, Statistics*

ECOLOGY ABSTRACTS. see *ENVIRONMENTAL STUDIES — Abstracting, Bibliographies, Statistics*

ECONOMIC DEVELOPMENT TODAY. see *BUSINESS AND ECONOMICS — Abstracting, Bibliographies, Statistics*

ECONOMY BULLETINS; a series of current awareness bulletins for researchers in biology and medicine. see *BIOLOGY — Abstracting, Bibliographies, Statistics*

ECOSOURCE. see *ENVIRONMENTAL STUDIES — Abstracting, Bibliographies, Statistics*

EDITORIALS ON FILE; newspaper editorial reference service with index. see *JOURNALISM — Abstracting, Bibliographies, Statistics*

EDUCATION INDEX. see *EDUCATION — Abstracting, Bibliographies, Statistics*

EDUCATIONAL ADMINISTRATION ABSTRACTS. see *EDUCATION — Abstracting, Bibliographies, Statistics*

EDUCATIONAL INDEX OF ARABIC PERIODICALS. see *EDUCATION — Abstracting, Bibliographies, Statistics*

EDUCATIONAL INDEX OF FOREIGN PERIODICALS. see *EDUCATION — Abstracting, Bibliographies, Statistics*

EDUCATIONAL INDICATIVE ABSTRACTS. see *EDUCATION — Abstracting, Bibliographies, Statistics*

EDUCATIONAL INFORMATION ABSTRACTS. see *EDUCATION — Abstracting, Bibliographies, Statistics*

EDUCATIONAL LEGISLATION INDEX. see *EDUCATION — Abstracting, Bibliographies, Statistics*

EDUCATIONAL SELECTIVE ABSTRACTS. see *EDUCATION — Abstracting, Bibliographies, Statistics*

ABSTRACTING AND INDEXING SERVICES

EDUCATIONAL TECHNOLOGY ABSTRACTS. see *EDUCATION — Abstracting, Bibliographies, Statistics*

EDUCATORS INDEX OF FREE MATERIALS. see *EDUCATION — Abstracting, Bibliographies, Statistics*

EKISTIC INDEX OF PERIODICALS. see *SOCIOLOGY — Abstracting, Bibliographies, Statistics*

EKONOMIKA: OTECHESTVENNAYA I ZARUBEZHNAYA LITERATURA; referativnyi zhurnal. see *BUSINESS AND ECONOMICS — Abstracting, Bibliographies, Statistics*

EKSPRESS-INFORMATSIYA. ASTRONAVTIKA I RAKETODINAMIKA. see *AERONAUTICS AND SPACE FLIGHT — Abstracting, Bibliographies, Statistics*

EKSPRESS-INFORMATSIYA. AVIASTROENIE. see *AERONAUTICS AND SPACE FLIGHT — Abstracting, Bibliographies, Statistics*

EKSPRESS-INFORMATSIYA. DETALI MASHIN. see *MACHINERY — Abstracting, Bibliographies, Statistics*

EKSPRESS-INFORMATSIYA. ELEKTRONIKA. see *ELECTRONICS*

EKSPRESS-INFORMATSIYA. GORODSKOI TRANSPORT. see *TRANSPORTATION — Abstracting, Bibliographies, Statistics*

EKSPRESS-INFORMATSIYA. ISPYTATEL'NYE PRIBORY I STENDY. see *INSTRUMENTS — Abstracting, Bibliographies, Statistics*

EKSPRESS-INFORMATSIYA. KONTROL'NO-IZMERITEL'NAYA TEKHNIKA. see *INSTRUMENTS — Abstracting, Bibliographies, Statistics*

EKSPRESS-INFORMATSIYA. KORROZIYA I ZASHCHITA METALLOV. see *METALLURGY — Abstracting, Bibliographies, Statistics*

EKSPRESS-INFORMATSIYA. KVANTOVAYA RADIOTEKHNIKA. see *COMMUNICATIONS — Abstracting, Bibliographies, Statistics*

EKSPRESS-INFORMATSIYA. NADEZHNOST' I KONTROL' KACHESTVA. see *ENGINEERING — Abstracting, Bibliographies, Statistics*

EKSPRESS-INFORMATSIYA. ORGANIZATSIYA PEREVOZOK. AVTOMATIZIROVANNYE SISTEMY UPRAVLENIA TRANSPORTOM. see *TRANSPORTATION — Abstracting, Bibliographies, Statistics*

EKSPRESS-INFORMATSIYA. PEREDACHA INFORMATSII. see *COMMUNICATIONS — Abstracting, Bibliographies, Statistics*

EKSPRESS-INFORMATSIYA. PODVODNO-TEKHNICHESKIE, VODOLAZNYE I SUDOPOD'EMNYE RABOTY. GIDROTEKHNICHESKIE SOORUZHENIYA. see *MACHINERY — Abstracting, Bibliographies, Statistics*

EKSPRESS-INFORMATSIYA. PORSHNEVYE I GAZOTURBINNYE DVIGATELI. see *ENGINEERING — Abstracting, Bibliographies, Statistics*

EKSPRESS-INFORMATSIYA. PRIBORY I ELEMENTY AVTOMATIKI I VYCHISLITEL'NOI TEKHNIKI. see *COMPUTERS — Abstracting, Bibliographies, Statistics*

EKSPRESS-INFORMATSIYA. PROMYSHLENNYI ORGANICHESKII SINTEZ. see *BUSINESS AND ECONOMICS — Abstracting, Bibliographies, Statistics*

EKSPRESS-INFORMATSIYA. PROMYSHLENNYI TRANSPORT. see *TRANSPORTATION — Abstracting, Bibliographies, Statistics*

EKSPRESS-INFORMATSIYA. PROTSESSY I APPARATY KHIMICHESKIKH PROIZVODSTV I KHIMICHESKAYA KIBERNETIKA. see *ENGINEERING — Abstracting, Bibliographies, Statistics*

EKSPRESS-INFORMATSIYA. RADIOTEKHNIKA SVERKHVYSOKIKH CHASTOT. see *COMMUNICATIONS — Abstracting, Bibliographies, Statistics*

EKSPRESS-INFORMATSIYA. SINTETICHESKIE VYSOKOPOLIMERNYE MATERIALY. see *CHEMISTRY — Abstracting, Bibliographies, Statistics*

EKSPRESS-INFORMATSIYA. SISTEMY AVTOMATICHESKOGO UPRAVLENIYA. see *COMPUTERS — Abstracting, Bibliographies, Statistics*

EKSPRESS-INFORMATSIYA. TARA I UPAKOVKA. KONTEINERY. see *PACKAGING — Abstracting, Bibliographies, Statistics*

EKSPRESS-INFORMATSIYA. TEKHNICHESKAYA KIBERNETIKA. see *COMPUTERS — Abstracting, Bibliographies, Statistics*

ELBASE; metal finishing database software. see *METALLURGY — Abstracting, Bibliographies, Statistics*

ELECTRONIC ENGINEERING INDEX. see *ELECTRONICS*

ELECTRONICS AND COMMUNICATIONS ABSTRACTS JOURNAL. see *COMMUNICATIONS — Abstracting, Bibliographies, Statistics*

ELEKTRONIKAI ES HIRADASTECHNIKAI SZAKIRODALMI/ELECTRONICS & COMMUNICATIONS ABSTRACTS. see *COMMUNICATIONS — Abstracting, Bibliographies, Statistics*

EMBASE LIST OF JOURNALS INDEXED (YEAR). see *MEDICAL SCIENCES — Abstracting, Bibliographies, Statistics*

EMENTARIO DA LEGISLACAO DO PETROLEO. see *LAW — Abstracting, Bibliographies, Statistics*

END-USE MARKETS FOR PLASTICS. see *PLASTICS — Abstracting, Bibliographies, Statistics*

ENDOTHELIUM. see *BIOLOGY — Abstracting, Bibliographies, Statistics*

ENERGIAIPARI ES ENERGIAGAZDALKODASI TAJEKOZTATO/POWER ENGINEERING ABSTRACTS. see *ENERGY — Abstracting, Bibliographies, Statistics*

ENERGY ABSTRACTS. see *ENERGY — Abstracting, Bibliographies, Statistics*

ENERGY RESEARCH ABSTRACTS. see *ENERGY — Abstracting, Bibliographies, Statistics*

ENERGY STORAGE SYSTEMS. see *ENERGY — Abstracting, Bibliographies, Statistics*

ENERGY STORAGE SYSTEMS ABSTRACTS. see *ENERGY — Abstracting, Bibliographies, Statistics*

ENGINEERED MATERIALS ABSTRACTS. see *ENGINEERING — Abstracting, Bibliographies, Statistics*

ENGINEERING INDEX ANNUAL. see *ENGINEERING — Abstracting, Bibliographies, Statistics*

ENGINEERING INDEX CUMULATIVE INDEX. see *ENGINEERING — Abstracting, Bibliographies, Statistics*

ENGINEERING INDEX MONTHLY; abstracting and indexing services covering sources of the world's engineering literature. see *ENGINEERING — Abstracting, Bibliographies, Statistics*

ENTOMOLOGY ABSTRACTS. see *BIOLOGY — Abstracting, Bibliographies, Statistics*

ENVIROFICHE. see *ENVIRONMENTAL STUDIES — Abstracting, Bibliographies, Statistics*

ENVIRONMENT ABSTRACTS. see *ENVIRONMENTAL STUDIES — Abstracting, Bibliographies, Statistics*

ENVIRONMENT ABSTRACTS ANNUAL; a guide to the key environmental literature of the year. see *ENVIRONMENTAL STUDIES — Abstracting, Bibliographies, Statistics*

ENVIRONMENTAL PERIODICALS BIBLIOGRAPHY; a current awareness bibliography featuring citations of scientific and popular articles in serial publications in the area of the environment. see *ENVIRONMENTAL STUDIES — Abstracting, Bibliographies, Statistics*

ENVIRONMENTAL PERIODICALS BIBLIOGRAPHY (C D - R O M). see *ENVIRONMENTAL STUDIES — Abstracting, Bibliographies, Statistics*

ERGA. see *OCCUPATIONAL HEALTH AND SAFETY — Abstracting, Bibliographies, Statistics*

ERGONOMICS ABSTRACTS. see *ENGINEERING — Abstracting, Bibliographies, Statistics*

ERYTHROCYTES. see *MEDICAL SCIENCES — Abstracting, Bibliographies, Statistics*

ESSAY AND GENERAL LITERATURE INDEX. see *LITERATURE — Abstracting, Bibliographies, Statistics*

ESSENTIAL ECOLOGY, ZOOLOGY & PLANT SCIENCE ABSTRACTS. see *BIOLOGY — Abstracting, Bibliographies, Statistics*

ESSENTIAL FISHERIES ABSTRACTS. see *FISH AND FISHERIES — Abstracting, Bibliographies, Statistics*

ESSENTIAL FORESTRY & WILDFIRE ABSTRACTS. see *FORESTS AND FORESTRY — Abstracting, Bibliographies, Statistics*

ESSENTIAL ORNITHOLOGICAL ABSTRACTS. see *BIOLOGY — Abstracting, Bibliographies, Statistics*

ESSENTIAL WILDLIFE & CONSERVATION BIOLOGY ABSTRACTS. see *BIOLOGY — Abstracting, Bibliographies, Statistics*

ETHNOARTS INDEX. see *ART — Abstracting, Bibliographies, Statistics*

EURO ABSTRACTS. see *TECHNOLOGY: COMPREHENSIVE WORKS — Abstracting, Bibliographies, Statistics*

EUROPEAN CONGRESS OF CARDIOLOGY. ABSTRACTS OF PAPERS. see *MEDICAL SCIENCES — Abstracting, Bibliographies, Statistics*

EXCEPTIONAL CHILD EDUCATION RESOURCES. see *EDUCATION — Abstracting, Bibliographies, Statistics*

EXCEPTIONAL HUMAN EXPERIENCE; studies of the psychic - spontaneous - imaginal. see *NEW AGE PUBLICATIONS*

EXCERPTA INFORMATICA; an abstract journal of recent literature on automation. see *COMPUTERS — Abstracting, Bibliographies, Statistics*

EXCERPTA MEDICA ABSTRACT JOURNALS. see *MEDICAL SCIENCES — Abstracting, Bibliographies, Statistics*

EXCERPTA MEDICA. SECTION 1: ANATOMY, ANTHROPOLOGY, EMBRYOLOGY & HISTOLOGY. see *MEDICAL SCIENCES — Abstracting, Bibliographies, Statistics*

EXCERPTA MEDICA. SECTION 2: PHYSIOLOGY. see *MEDICAL SCIENCES — Abstracting, Bibliographies, Statistics*

EXCERPTA MEDICA. SECTION 3: ENDOCRINOLOGY. see *MEDICAL SCIENCES — Abstracting, Bibliographies, Statistics*

EXCERPTA MEDICA. SECTION 4: MICROBIOLOGY: BACTERIOLOGY, MYCOLOGY, PARASITOLOGY AND VIROLOGY. see *MEDICAL SCIENCES — Abstracting, Bibliographies, Statistics*

EXCERPTA MEDICA. SECTION 5: GENERAL PATHOLOGY AND PATHOLOGICAL ANATOMY. see *MEDICAL SCIENCES — Abstracting, Bibliographies, Statistics*

EXCERPTA MEDICA. SECTION 6: INTERNAL MEDICINE. see *MEDICAL SCIENCES — Abstracting, Bibliographies, Statistics*

EXCERPTA MEDICA. SECTION 7: PEDIATRICS AND PEDIATRIC SURGERY. see *MEDICAL SCIENCES — Abstracting, Bibliographies, Statistics*

EXCERPTA MEDICA. SECTION 8: NEUROLOGY AND NEUROSURGERY. see *MEDICAL SCIENCES — Abstracting, Bibliographies, Statistics*

EXCERPTA MEDICA. SECTION 9: SURGERY. see *MEDICAL SCIENCES — Abstracting, Bibliographies, Statistics*

ABSTRACTING AND INDEXING SERVICES

EXCERPTA MEDICA. SECTION 10: OBSTETRICS AND GYNECOLOGY. see *MEDICAL SCIENCES — Abstracting, Bibliographies, Statistics*

EXCERPTA MEDICA. SECTION 11: OTORHINOLARYNGOLOGY. see *MEDICAL SCIENCES — Abstracting, Bibliographies, Statistics*

EXCERPTA MEDICA. SECTION 12: OPHTHALMOLOGY. see *MEDICAL SCIENCES — Abstracting, Bibliographies, Statistics*

EXCERPTA MEDICA. SECTION 13: DERMATOLOGY AND VENEREOLOGY. see *MEDICAL SCIENCES — Abstracting, Bibliographies, Statistics*

EXCERPTA MEDICA. SECTION 14: RADIOLOGY. see *MEDICAL SCIENCES — Abstracting, Bibliographies, Statistics*

EXCERPTA MEDICA. SECTION 15: CHEST DISEASES, THORACIC SURGERY AND TUBERCULOSIS. see *MEDICAL SCIENCES — Abstracting, Bibliographies, Statistics*

EXCERPTA MEDICA. SECTION 16: CANCER. see *MEDICAL SCIENCES — Abstracting, Bibliographies, Statistics*

EXCERPTA MEDICA. SECTION 17: PUBLIC HEALTH, SOCIAL MEDICINE AND EPIDEMIOLOGY. see *PUBLIC HEALTH AND SAFETY — Abstracting, Bibliographies, Statistics*

EXCERPTA MEDICA. SECTION 18: CARDIOVASCULAR DISEASES AND CARDIOVASCULAR SURGERY. see *MEDICAL SCIENCES — Abstracting, Bibliographies, Statistics*

EXCERPTA MEDICA. SECTION 19: REHABILITATION AND PHYSICAL MEDICINE. see *MEDICAL SCIENCES — Abstracting, Bibliographies, Statistics*

EXCERPTA MEDICA. SECTION 20: GERONTOLOGY AND GERIATRICS. see *GERONTOLOGY AND GERIATRICS — Abstracting, Bibliographies, Statistics*

EXCERPTA MEDICA. SECTION 21: DEVELOPMENTAL BIOLOGY AND TERATOLOGY. see *BIOLOGY — Abstracting, Bibliographies, Statistics*

EXCERPTA MEDICA. SECTION 22: HUMAN GENETICS. see *BIOLOGY — Abstracting, Bibliographies, Statistics*

EXCERPTA MEDICA. SECTION 23: NUCLEAR MEDICINE. see *MEDICAL SCIENCES — Abstracting, Bibliographies, Statistics*

EXCERPTA MEDICA. SECTION 24: ANESTHESIOLOGY. see *MEDICAL SCIENCES — Abstracting, Bibliographies, Statistics*

EXCERPTA MEDICA. SECTION 25: HEMATOLOGY. see *MEDICAL SCIENCES — Abstracting, Bibliographies, Statistics*

EXCERPTA MEDICA. SECTION 26: IMMUNOLOGY, SEROLOGY AND TRANSPLANTATION. see *MEDICAL SCIENCES — Abstracting, Bibliographies, Statistics*

EXCERPTA MEDICA. SECTION 27: BIOPHYSICS, BIO-ENGINEERING AND MEDICAL INSTRUMENTATION. see *MEDICAL SCIENCES — Abstracting, Bibliographies, Statistics*

EXCERPTA MEDICA. SECTION 28: UROLOGY AND NEPHROLOGY. see *MEDICAL SCIENCES — Abstracting, Bibliographies, Statistics*

EXCERPTA MEDICA. SECTION 29: CLINICAL AND EXPERIMENTAL BIOCHEMISTRY. see *BIOLOGY — Abstracting, Bibliographies, Statistics*

EXCERPTA MEDICA. SECTION 30: CLINICAL AND EXPERIMENTAL PHARMACOLOGY. see *PHARMACY AND PHARMACOLOGY — Abstracting, Bibliographies, Statistics*

EXCERPTA MEDICA. SECTION 31: ARTHRITIS AND RHEUMATISM. see *MEDICAL SCIENCES — Abstracting, Bibliographies, Statistics*

EXCERPTA MEDICA. SECTION 32: PSYCHIATRY. see *MEDICAL SCIENCES — Abstracting, Bibliographies, Statistics*

EXCERPTA MEDICA. SECTION 33: ORTHOPEDIC SURGERY. see *MEDICAL SCIENCES — Abstracting, Bibliographies, Statistics*

EXCERPTA MEDICA. SECTION 35: OCCUPATIONAL HEALTH AND INDUSTRIAL MEDICINE. see *MEDICAL SCIENCES — Abstracting, Bibliographies, Statistics*

EXCERPTA MEDICA. SECTION 36: HEALTH POLICY, ECONOMICS AND MANAGEMENT. see *HOSPITALS — Abstracting, Bibliographies, Statistics*

EXCERPTA MEDICA. SECTION 38: ADVERSE REACTIONS TITLES. see *MEDICAL SCIENCES — Abstracting, Bibliographies, Statistics*

EXCERPTA MEDICA. SECTION 40: DRUG DEPENDENCE, ALCOHOL ABUSE AND ALCOHOLISM. see *DRUG ABUSE AND ALCOHOLISM — Abstracting, Bibliographies, Statistics*

EXCERPTA MEDICA. SECTION 46: ENVIRONMENTAL HEALTH AND POLLUTION CONTROL. see *ENVIRONMENTAL STUDIES — Abstracting, Bibliographies, Statistics*

EXCERPTA MEDICA. SECTION 48: GASTROENTEROLOGY. see *MEDICAL SCIENCES — Abstracting, Bibliographies, Statistics*

EXCERPTA MEDICA. SECTION 49: FORENSIC SCIENCE ABSTRACTS. see *MEDICAL SCIENCES — Abstracting, Bibliographies, Statistics*

EXCERPTA MEDICA. SECTION 50: EPILEPSY ABSTRACTS. see *MEDICAL SCIENCES — Abstracting, Bibliographies, Statistics*

EXCERPTA MEDICA. SECTION 52: TOXICOLOGY. see *ENVIRONMENTAL STUDIES — Abstracting, Bibliographies, Statistics*

EXPRESS BULLETINS; a series of current awareness bulletins for researchers in biology and medicine. see *BIOLOGY — Abstracting, Bibliographies, Statistics*

EXTRAMED. see *MEDICAL SCIENCES — Abstracting, Bibliographies, Statistics*

F A I ABSTRACT SERVICE. (Fertiliser Association of India) see *AGRICULTURE — Abstracting, Bibliographies, Statistics*

F A O DOCUMENTATION - CURRENT BIBLIOGRAPHY. see *FISH AND FISHERIES — Abstracting, Bibliographies, Statistics*

F I I R O INDUSTRIAL ABSTRACTS. (Federal Institute of Industrial Research, Oshodi) see *BUSINESS AND ECONOMICS — Abstracting, Bibliographies, Statistics*

F R A N C I S. 519: PHILOSOPHIE. see *PHILOSOPHY — Abstracting, Bibliographies, Statistics*

F R A N C I S. 520: SCIENCES DE L'EDUCATION. see *EDUCATION — Abstracting, Bibliographies, Statistics*

F R A N C I S. 521: SOCIOLOGIE. see *SOCIOLOGY — Abstracting, Bibliographies, Statistics*

F R A N C I S. 523: HISTOIRE ET SCIENCES DE LA LITTERATURE. see *LITERATURE — Abstracting, Bibliographies, Statistics*

F R A N C I S. 524: SCIENCES DU LANGAGE. see *LINGUISTICS — Abstracting, Bibliographies, Statistics*

F R A N C I S. 525: PREHISTOIRE ET PROTOHISTOIRE. see *ARCHAEOLOGY — Abstracting, Bibliographies, Statistics*

F R A N C I S. 526: ART ET ARCHEOLOGIE; Proche-Orient, Asie, Amerique. see *ART — Abstracting, Bibliographies, Statistics*

F R A N C I S. 527: HISTOIRE ET SCIENCES DES RELIGIONS. see *RELIGIONS AND THEOLOGY — Abstracting, Bibliographies, Statistics*

F R A N C I S. 528: BIBLIOGRAPHIE INTERNATIONALE DE SCIENCE ADMINISTRATIVE. see *BUSINESS AND ECONOMICS — Abstracting, Bibliographies, Statistics*

F R A N C I S. 617: E C O D O C; documentation automatisee en economie generale. see *BUSINESS AND ECONOMICS — Abstracting, Bibliographies, Statistics*

F R A N C I S. 731: ECONOMIE DE L'ENERGIE. see *ENERGY — Abstracting, Bibliographies, Statistics*

FACHINFORMATION BAHN; Dokumentation der Fachliteratur. see *TRANSPORTATION — Abstracting, Bibliographies, Statistics*

FAMILY INDEX. see *SOCIOLOGY — Abstracting, Bibliographies, Statistics*

FAMILY STUDIES DATABASE. see *MATRIMONY — Abstracting, Bibliographies, Statistics*

FANATIC READER. see *GENERAL INTEREST PERIODICALS — United States*

FEDERAL JUDGMENTS BULLETIN. see *LAW — Abstracting, Bibliographies, Statistics*

FEDERAL REGISTER SUBJECT INDEX. see *LAW — Abstracting, Bibliographies, Statistics*

FEDERAL STATUTES ANNOTATIONS. see *PUBLIC ADMINISTRATION — Abstracting, Bibliographies, Statistics*

FEMINIST PERIODICALS; a current listing of contents. see *WOMEN'S STUDIES — Abstracting, Bibliographies, Statistics*

FICHIERS-PRESSE. see *JOURNALISM — Abstracting, Bibliographies, Statistics*

FIELD CROP ABSTRACTS; monthly abstract journal on world annual cereal, legume, root, oilseed and fibre crops. see *AGRICULTURE — Abstracting, Bibliographies, Statistics*

FIHRIST; index to Arabic periodical literature. see *BIBLIOGRAPHIES*

FILM LITERATURE INDEX. see *MOTION PICTURES — Abstracting, Bibliographies, Statistics*

FILMSTRIP AND SLIDE SET FINDER. see *EDUCATION — Abstracting, Bibliographies, Statistics*

FILOSOFIYA: OTECHESTVENNAYA I ZARUBEZHNAYA LITERATURA; referativnyi zhurnal. see *PHILOSOPHY — Abstracting, Bibliographies, Statistics*

FINDEX (YEAR); the worldwide directory of market research reports, studies & surveys. see *BUSINESS AND ECONOMICS — Abstracting, Bibliographies, Statistics*

FISH & FISHERIES WORLDWIDE. see *FISH AND FISHERIES — Abstracting, Bibliographies, Statistics*

FISHERIES REVIEW; an indexing service for fishery research and management. see *FISH AND FISHERIES — Abstracting, Bibliographies, Statistics*

FLOUR MILLING AND BAKING RESEARCH ASSOCIATION. ABSTRACTS. see *FOOD AND FOOD INDUSTRIES — Abstracting, Bibliographies, Statistics*

FLUID ABSTRACTS: CIVIL ENGINEERING. see *ENGINEERING — Abstracting, Bibliographies, Statistics*

FLUID ABSTRACTS: PROCESS ENGINEERING. see *ENGINEERING — Abstracting, Bibliographies, Statistics*

FOERSVARSFORSKNINGSREFERAT/DEFENCE RESEARCH ABSTRACTS. UNCLASSIFIED; oeppen del. see *CIVIL DEFENSE — Abstracting, Bibliographies, Statistics*

FOOD SCIENCE AND TECHNOLOGY ABSTRACTS. see *FOOD AND FOOD INDUSTRIES — Abstracting, Bibliographies, Statistics*

FOODINFO. see *FOOD AND FOOD INDUSTRIES — Abstracting, Bibliographies, Statistics*

FOODS ADLIBRA; key to the world's food literature. see *FOOD AND FOOD INDUSTRIES — Abstracting, Bibliographies, Statistics*

ABSTRACTING AND INDEXING SERVICES

FOODS ADLIBRA FOODSERVICE EDITION. see *FOOD AND FOOD INDUSTRIES — Abstracting, Bibliographies, Statistics*

FOODS ADLIBRA SEAFOOD EDITION. see *FOOD AND FOOD INDUSTRIES — Abstracting, Bibliographies, Statistics*

FOODSERVICE INFORMATION ABSTRACTS. see *HOTELS AND RESTAURANTS — Abstracting, Bibliographies, Statistics*

FOOTHILLS INQUIRER. see *GENEALOGY AND HERALDRY*

FOREIGN PATENTS INFORMATION BULLETIN. see *PATENTS, TRADEMARKS AND COPYRIGHTS — Abstracting, Bibliographies, Statistics*

FOREST PRODUCTS ABSTRACTS. see *FORESTS AND FORESTRY — Abstracting, Bibliographies, Statistics*

FORESTRY ABSTRACTS; compiled from world literature. see *FORESTS AND FORESTRY — Abstracting, Bibliographies, Statistics*

FUEL AND ENERGY ABSTRACTS; a summary of world literature on all scientific, technical, commercial and environmental aspects of fuel and energy. see *PETROLEUM AND GAS — Abstracting, Bibliographies, Statistics*

FURO INJEKUSHON BUNSEKI KOENKAI KOEN YOSHISHU/ABSTRACTS OF MEETING ON FLOW INJECTION ANALYSIS. see *CHEMISTRY — Abstracting, Bibliographies, Statistics*

FUTURE SURVEY; a monthly abstract of books, articles, and reports concerning trends, forecasts, and ideas about the future. see *SCIENCES: COMPREHENSIVE WORKS — Abstracting, Bibliographies, Statistics*

GALVANO-REFERATE. see *METALLURGY — Abstracting, Bibliographies, Statistics*

GARDENER'S INDEX. see *GARDENING AND HORTICULTURE — Abstracting, Bibliographies, Statistics*

GAS ABSTRACTS. see *PETROLEUM AND GAS — Abstracting, Bibliographies, Statistics*

GAS & LIQUID CHROMATOGRAPHY LITERATURE - ABSTRACTS & INDEX. see *CHEMISTRY — Abstracting, Bibliographies, Statistics*

GENE EXPRESSION. see *BIOLOGY — Abstracting, Bibliographies, Statistics*

GENE THERAPY (SHEFFIELD). see *MEDICAL SCIENCES — Abstracting, Bibliographies, Statistics*

GENERAL SCIENCE INDEX. see *SCIENCES: COMPREHENSIVE WORKS — Abstracting, Bibliographies, Statistics*

GENETICS ABSTRACTS. see *BIOLOGY — Abstracting, Bibliographies, Statistics*

GEOGRAPHICAL ABSTRACTS: HUMAN GEOGRAPHY. see *GEOGRAPHY — Abstracting, Bibliographies, Statistics*

GEOGRAPHICAL ABSTRACTS: PHYSICAL GEOGRAPHY. see *GEOGRAPHY — Abstracting, Bibliographies, Statistics*

GEOLOGICAL ABSTRACTS. see *EARTH SCIENCES — Abstracting, Bibliographies, Statistics*

GEOLOGICAL SOCIETY OF AMERICA. ABSTRACTS WITH PROGRAMS. see *EARTH SCIENCES — Abstracting, Bibliographies, Statistics*

GEOLOGICAL SOCIETY OF EGYPT. ANNUAL MEETING. ABSTRACTS OF PAPERS. see *EARTH SCIENCES — Abstracting, Bibliographies, Statistics*

GEOMECHANICS ABSTRACTS. see *EARTH SCIENCES — Abstracting, Bibliographies, Statistics*

GEOSCIENCE DOCUMENTATION; a bi-monthly journal for the study of geoscience literature. see *EARTH SCIENCES — Abstracting, Bibliographies, Statistics*

GEOTECHNICAL ABSTRACTS. see *ENGINEERING — Abstracting, Bibliographies, Statistics*

GEOTHERMAL ENERGY. see *ENERGY — Abstracting, Bibliographies, Statistics*

GEPGYARTASTECHNOLOGIAI ES SZERSZAMGEPIPARI SZAKIRODALMI TAJEKOZTATO/MECHANICAL ENGINEERING & MACHINE TOOL ABSTRACTS. see *ENGINEERING — Abstracting, Bibliographies, Statistics*

GERMANY. DEUTSCHER BUNDESTAG. WISSENSCHAFTLICHE DIENSTE. NEUE AUFSAETZE IN DER BIBLIOTHEK. see *SCIENCES: COMPREHENSIVE WORKS — Abstracting, Bibliographies, Statistics*

GESELLSCHAFT FUER BIBLIOTHEKSWESEN UND DOKUMENTATION DES LANDBAUES. MITTEILUNGEN. see *AGRICULTURE — Abstracting, Bibliographies, Statistics*

GEZINSWETENSCHAPPELIJKE DOCUMENTATIE; Jaarboek. see *POPULATION STUDIES — Abstracting, Bibliographies, Statistics*

GHANA SCIENCE ABSTRACTS. see *SCIENCES: COMPREHENSIVE WORKS — Abstracting, Bibliographies, Statistics*

GLASS TECHNOLOGY. see *CERAMICS, GLASS AND POTTERY — Abstracting, Bibliographies, Statistics*

GLEANINGS. see *RELIGIONS AND THEOLOGY — Abstracting, Bibliographies, Statistics*

GOETEBORG PSYCHOLOGICAL REPORTS. see *PSYCHOLOGY*

GOSUDARSTVO I PRAVO: OTECHESTVENNAYA LITERATURA; referativnyi zhurnal. see *LAW — Abstracting, Bibliographies, Statistics*

GOSUDARSTVO I PRAVO: ZARUBEZHNAYA LITERATURA; referativnyi zhurnal. see *LAW — Abstracting, Bibliographies, Statistics*

GOVERNMENT REPORTS ANNOUNCEMENTS & INDEX. see *PUBLIC ADMINISTRATION — Abstracting, Bibliographies, Statistics*

GOVERNMENT REPORTS ANNUAL INDEX. see *ENGINEERING — Abstracting, Bibliographies, Statistics*

GRASSLANDS AND FORAGE ABSTRACTS; monthly abstract journal on grassland husbandry and fodder crop production. see *AGRICULTURE — Abstracting, Bibliographies, Statistics*

GROWTH FACTORS & CYTOKINES - CLINICAL. see *MEDICAL SCIENCES — Abstracting, Bibliographies, Statistics*

GUARDIAN INDEX. see *JOURNALISM — Abstracting, Bibliographies, Statistics*

GUIDE TO PETROLEUM STATISTICAL SOURCES. see *PETROLEUM AND GAS — Abstracting, Bibliographies, Statistics*

GUIDE TO SOCIAL SCIENCE AND RELIGION IN PERIODICAL LITERATURE. see *SOCIAL SCIENCES: COMPREHENSIVE WORKS — Abstracting, Bibliographies, Statistics*

011   US
GUIDE TO SPECIAL ISSUES AND INDEXES OF PERIODICALS. 1962. irreg., latest 1994. Special Libraries Association, 1700 18th St., N.W., Washington, DC 20009. TEL 202-234-4700. FAX 202-234-2442. URL: htp://www.sla.org. Ed. Miriam Uhlan. **Document type:** abstracting/indexing.

GUIDE TO U S GOVERNMENT PUBLICATIONS. see *PUBLIC ADMINISTRATION — Abstracting, Bibliographies, Statistics*

GUIDELINES; a subject guide for Australian libraries. see *LIBRARY AND INFORMATION SCIENCES — Abstracting, Bibliographies, Statistics*

GUOWAI SHEHUI KEXUE LUNWEN SUOYIN/FOREIGN SOCIAL SCIENCE DISSERTATION INDEX. see *SOCIAL SCIENCES: COMPREHENSIVE WORKS — Abstracting, Bibliographies, Statistics*

HAJOZASI SZAKIRODALMI TAJEKOZTATO/SHIPPING ABSTRACTS. see *TRANSPORTATION — Abstracting, Bibliographies, Statistics*

HANDBOOK OF LATIN AMERICAN STUDIES: A SELECTED AND ANNOTATED GUIDE TO RECENT PUBLICATIONS. see *HISTORY — Abstracting, Bibliographies, Statistics*

HANDICRAFT - HOBBY INDEX; a current periodical index to doing, making, and building. see *HOW-TO AND DO-IT-YOURSELF — Abstracting, Bibliographies, Statistics*

HANGKONG WENZHAI/AERONAUTICS ABSTRACTS. see *AERONAUTICS AND SPACE FLIGHT — Abstracting, Bibliographies, Statistics*

HARRIS POLL. see *SOCIOLOGY — Abstracting, Bibliographies, Statistics*

HEALTH AND SAFETY SCIENCE ABSTRACTS. see *PUBLIC HEALTH AND SAFETY — Abstracting, Bibliographies, Statistics*

HEALTH INDEX. see *MEDICAL SCIENCES — Abstracting, Bibliographies, Statistics*

HEALTHCARE MARKETING ABSTRACTS. see *HOSPITALS — Abstracting, Bibliographies, Statistics*

HEBRAEISCHE BEITRAEGE ZUR WISSENSCHAFT DES JUDENTUMS; ein Referatenorgan. see *RELIGIONS AND THEOLOGY — Abstracting, Bibliographies, Statistics*

HELICOBACTER. see *BIOLOGY — Abstracting, Bibliographies, Statistics*

HELMINTHOLOGICAL ABSTRACTS. see *AGRICULTURE — Abstracting, Bibliographies, Statistics*

HIGH ENERGY PHYSICS INDEX/HOCHENERGIEPHYSIK-INDEX. see *PHYSICS — Abstracting, Bibliographies, Statistics*

HIGH PERFORMANCE LIQUID CHROMATOGRAPHY. see *CHEMISTRY — Abstracting, Bibliographies, Statistics*

HIGHER EDUCATION ABSTRACTS; abstracts of periodical literature, monographs and conference papers on college students, faculty and administration. see *EDUCATION — Higher Education*

011   II
THE HINDU INDEX. m. (plus a. cumulation). Rs.1500 (a. cumulation Rs.800); newsstand price: Rs.60. Kasturi & Sons Ltd., Kasturi Bldgs., 589-860 Anna Salai, Madras 600 002, India. TEL 91-44-835067. FAX 91-44-835325. **Document type:** abstracting/indexing.

HISPANIC AMERICAN PERIODICALS INDEX. see *HISTORY — Abstracting, Bibliographies, Statistics*

HISTORICAL ABSTRACTS. PART A: MODERN HISTORY ABSTRACTS, 1450-1914. see *HISTORY — Abstracting, Bibliographies, Statistics*

HISTORICAL ABSTRACTS. PART B: TWENTIETH CENTURY ABSTRACTS, 1914 TO THE PRESENT. see *HISTORY — Abstracting, Bibliographies, Statistics*

HISTORICAL ABSTRACTS. PART B: TWENTIETH CENTURY ABSTRACTS, 1914 TO THE PRESENT. ANNUAL INDEX. see *HISTORY — Abstracting, Bibliographies, Statistics*

016   CC   ISSN 0379-5853
HONGKONGIANA; an online index to Hong Kong periodicals. (Printed format ceased with 1987 edition) (Text in Chinese and English) 1978. a. HK.$200($30) Hong Kong Polytechnic Library, Hung Hom, Kowloon, Hong Kong, People's Republic of China. TEL 852-2766-6863. FAX 852-2765-8274. TELEX 38964-POLYX-HX. E-mail: lbinf@polyu.edu.hk. Ed. Nancy Ying-Ching Wong. circ. 500. (back issues avail.) **Document type:** abstracting/indexing.
●Available only online.
—BLDSC (4326.416000).
Description: Index to English and Chinese articles about Hong Kong in about 205 Hong Kong periodicals.

HORTICULTURAL ABSTRACTS; compiled from world literature on temperate and tropical fruits, vegetables, ornaments, plantation crops. see *GARDENING AND HORTICULTURE — Abstracting, Bibliographies, Statistics*

ABSTRACTING AND INDEXING SERVICES

HOSPITAL AND HEALTH ADMINISTRATION INDEX. see *HOSPITALS — Abstracting, Bibliographies, Statistics*

HUMAN RESOURCES ABSTRACTS; an international information service. see *SOCIOLOGY — Abstracting, Bibliographies, Statistics*

HUMANITIES INDEX. see *HUMANITIES: COMPREHENSIVE WORKS — Abstracting, Bibliographies, Statistics*

HUMANS & OTHER SPECIES; the quarterly journal of resources on their relationship. see *PSYCHOLOGY — Abstracting, Bibliographies, Statistics*

HUNGARIAN LIBRARY AND INFORMATION SCIENCE ABSTRACTS. see *LIBRARY AND INFORMATION SCIENCES — Abstracting, Bibliographies, Statistics*

HUNGARIAN R AND D ABSTRACTS. SCIENCE AND TECHNOLOGY. see *SCIENCES: COMPREHENSIVE WORKS — Abstracting, Bibliographies, Statistics*

I A S C - S C A D BULLETIN. (Indexing and Abstracting Society of Canada) see *LIBRARY AND INFORMATION SCIENCES*

I C S S R JOURNAL OF ABSTRACTS AND REVIEWS: SOCIOLOGY & SOCIAL ANTHROPOLOGY. (Indian Council of Social Science Research) see *ANTHROPOLOGY — Abstracting, Bibliographies, Statistics*

I C S S R RESEARCH ABSTRACTS QUARTERLY. (Indian Council of Social Science Research) see *SOCIAL SCIENCES: COMPREHENSIVE WORKS — Abstracting, Bibliographies, Statistics*

I E E E INTERNATIONAL SYMPOSIUM ON INFORMATION THEORY. ABSTRACTS OF PAPERS. see *COMPUTERS — Information Science And Information Theory*

I M F SURVEY. (International Monetary Fund) see *BUSINESS AND ECONOMICS — Abstracting, Bibliographies, Statistics*

I M M ABSTRACTS AND INDEX; a survey of world literature on the economic geology and mining of all minerals (except coal), mineral processing and non-ferrous extraction metallurgy. (Institution of Mining and Metallurgy) see *MINES AND MINING INDUSTRY — Abstracting, Bibliographies, Statistics*

I N I S ATOMINDEX. (International Atomic Energy Agency) see *PHYSICS — Abstracting, Bibliographies, Statistics*

IMAGING ABSTRACTS. see *PHOTOGRAPHY — Abstracting, Bibliographies, Statistics*

IMMUNOASSAY. see *CHEMISTRY — Abstracting, Bibliographies, Statistics*

IMMUNOLOGY ABSTRACTS. see *MEDICAL SCIENCES — Abstracting, Bibliographies, Statistics*

INDEKS SURATKHABAR MALAYSIA. see *JOURNALISM — Abstracting, Bibliographies, Statistics*

THE INDEPENDENT INDEX. see *JOURNALISM — Abstracting, Bibliographies, Statistics*

INDEX ANALYTIQUE SIGNALETIQUE BIBLIOGRAPHIQUE. see *BUSINESS AND ECONOMICS — Abstracting, Bibliographies, Statistics*

016   US   ISSN 1041-1321
Z695.93
INDEX AND ABSTRACT DIRECTORY; an international guide to services and serials coverage. 1989. biennial. $189. Ebsco Publishing (Subsidiary of: EBSCO Industries, Inc.), 10 Estes St., Box 682, Ipswich, MA 01938. TEL 508-356-6500; 800-653-2726. FAX 508-356-5640. E-mail: ep@epnet.com; URL: http://www.epnet.com. **Document type:** abstracting/indexing, directory.
—CISTI.
Description: Directory of index and abstract services, listing publisher, price and description. Journals included.

INDEX ASIA SERIES IN HUMANITIES. see *ORIENTAL STUDIES — Abstracting, Bibliographies, Statistics*

INDEX CHEMICUS. see *CHEMISTRY — Abstracting, Bibliographies, Statistics*

INDEX: FOREIGN BROADCAST INFORMATION SERVICE DAILY REPORTS: AFRICA SUB-SAHARA. see *POLITICAL SCIENCE — Abstracting, Bibliographies, Statistics*

INDEX: FOREIGN BROADCAST INFORMATION SERVICE DAILY REPORTS: CHINA. see *POLITICAL SCIENCE — Abstracting, Bibliographies, Statistics*

INDEX: FOREIGN BROADCAST INFORMATION SERVICE DAILY REPORTS: EAST ASIA. see *POLITICAL SCIENCE — Abstracting, Bibliographies, Statistics*

INDEX: FOREIGN BROADCAST INFORMATION SERVICE DAILY REPORTS: EASTERN EUROPE. see *POLITICAL SCIENCE — Abstracting, Bibliographies, Statistics*

INDEX: FOREIGN BROADCAST INFORMATION SERVICE DAILY REPORTS: LATIN AMERICA. see *POLITICAL SCIENCE — Abstracting, Bibliographies, Statistics*

INDEX: FOREIGN BROADCAST INFORMATION SERVICE DAILY REPORTS: NEAR EAST AND SOUTH ASIA. see *POLITICAL SCIENCE — Abstracting, Bibliographies, Statistics*

INDEX: FOREIGN BROADCAST INFORMATION SERVICE DAILY REPORTS: WESTERN EUROPE. see *POLITICAL SCIENCE — Abstracting, Bibliographies, Statistics*

INDEX: FOREIGN BROADCAST INFORMATION SERVICE REPORTS: CENTRAL EURASIA. see *POLITICAL SCIENCE — Abstracting, Bibliographies, Statistics*

INDEX HEPATICARUM. see *BIOLOGY — Abstracting, Bibliographies, Statistics*

INDEX INDIA. see *ORIENTAL STUDIES — Abstracting, Bibliographies, Statistics*

016   II   ISSN 0250-7595
AI19.I5
INDEX INDIANA. (Text in Roman script) 1977. a. Rs.105. Central Reference Library, Belvedere, Calcutta 700 027, India. TEL 91-33-479-1721-22. Ed. Y. Acharya. circ. 500. **Document type:** abstracting/indexing.

INDEX INDO-ASIATICUS. see *ORIENTAL STUDIES — Abstracting, Bibliographies, Statistics*

INDEX INTERNATIONALIS INDICUS. see *ORIENTAL STUDIES — Abstracting, Bibliographies, Statistics*

INDEX MEDICUS. see *MEDICAL SCIENCES — Abstracting, Bibliographies, Statistics*

015.931   NZ   ISSN 0113-6526
INDEX NEW ZEALAND. 1940. q. NZ.$225 microfiche (foreign NZ.$280); CD-ROM NZ.$2350 (effective 1997). National Library of New Zealand, P.O. Box 1467, Wellington, New Zealand. TEL 64-4-4743098. FAX 64-4-4753124. E-mail: shop@natlib.govt.nz; URL: http://www.natlib.ogvt.nz/. Ed. Mary Keyes. circ. 400 (controlled). (also avail. in microfiche; back issues avail.; reprint service avail.) **Document type:** abstracting/indexing.
●Also available online. Vendor(s): Kiwinet.
Also available on CD-ROM.
—CCC.
Formerly (until 1986): Index to New Zealand Periodicals (ISSN 0073-5957)
Description: Provides access to journal articles, theses, reports, newspapers, books and conference papers about New Zealand or the South Pacific.

INDEX OF AFRICAN SOCIAL SCIENCE PERIODICAL ARTICLES. see *SOCIAL SCIENCES: COMPREHENSIVE WORKS — Abstracting, Bibliographies, Statistics*

INDEX OF AMERICAN PERIODICAL VERSE. see *LITERATURE — Abstracting, Bibliographies, Statistics*

INDEX OF ARTICLES ON JEWISH STUDIES/RESHIMAT MA'AMARIM BE-MADA'E HA-YAHADUT. see *ETHNIC INTERESTS — Abstracting, Bibliographies, Statistics*

INDEX OF CURRENT RESEARCH ON PIGS. see *AGRICULTURE — Abstracting, Bibliographies, Statistics*

INDEX OF ECONOMIC ARTICLES IN JOURNALS AND COLLECTIVE VOLUMES. see *BUSINESS AND ECONOMICS — Abstracting, Bibliographies, Statistics*

INDEX OF FUNGI. see *BIOLOGY — Abstracting, Bibliographies, Statistics*

INDEX OF MATHEMATICAL PAPERS. see *MATHEMATICS — Abstracting, Bibliographies, Statistics*

INDEX OF MIDDLE ENGLISH PROSE. see *LITERATURE — Abstracting, Bibliographies, Statistics*

INDEX OF VETERINARY SPECIALITIES. see *VETERINARY SCIENCE — Abstracting, Bibliographies, Statistics*

INDEX OF VETERINARY SPECIALTIES. see *VETERINARY SCIENCE — Abstracting, Bibliographies, Statistics*

INDEX TO BLACK PERIODICALS. see *ETHNIC INTERESTS — Abstracting, Bibliographies, Statistics*

INDEX TO BOOK REVIEWS IN RELIGION. see *RELIGIONS AND THEOLOGY — Abstracting, Bibliographies, Statistics*

INDEX TO CHEMICAL REGULATIONS. see *CHEMISTRY — Abstracting, Bibliographies, Statistics*

INDEX TO CHINESE LEGAL PERIODICALS. see *LAW — Abstracting, Bibliographies, Statistics*

016   CH   ISSN 0378-0112
INDEX TO CHINESE PERIODICALS. Key Title: Zhonghua Minguo Qikan Lunwen Suoyin. (Text mainly in Chinese; occasionally in English) 1970. q. $75. National Central Library, 20 Chung Shan S. Rd., Taipei, Taiwan 10040, Republic of China. TEL 886-2-361-9132. FAX 886-2-311-0155. **Document type:** abstracting/indexing.
●Available only on CD-ROM.
Formed by the merger of: Index to Chinese Periodicals - Science and Technology (ISSN 0046-8894); Index to Chinese Periodicals - Humanities and Social Sciences (ISSN 0046-8886)

INDEX TO CRAFT JOURNALS. see *ARTS AND HANDICRAFTS — Abstracting, Bibliographies, Statistics*

INDEX TO CURRENT URBAN DOCUMENTS. see *HOUSING AND URBAN PLANNING — Abstracting, Bibliographies, Statistics*

INDEX TO DANCE PERIODICALS. see *DANCE — Abstracting, Bibliographies, Statistics*

INDEX TO DENTAL LITERATURE; an alphabetical author and subject index to dental literature. see *MEDICAL SCIENCES — Abstracting, Bibliographies, Statistics*

INDEX TO FEDERAL TAX ARTICLES (SUPPLEMENT). see *BUSINESS AND ECONOMICS — Abstracting, Bibliographies, Statistics*

INDEX TO FOREIGN LEGAL PERIODICALS. see *LAW — Abstracting, Bibliographies, Statistics*

INDEX TO HEBREW PERIODICALS (C D - R O M EDITION). see *BIBLIOGRAPHIES*

INDEX TO HOUSE OF COMMONS PARLIAMENTARY PAPERS. see *POLITICAL SCIENCE — Abstracting, Bibliographies, Statistics*

INDEX TO HOW TO DO IT INFORMATION; a periodical index. see *HOW-TO AND DO-IT-YOURSELF — Abstracting, Bibliographies, Statistics*

INDEX TO INDIAN ECONOMIC JOURNALS. see *BUSINESS AND ECONOMICS — Abstracting, Bibliographies, Statistics*

INDEX TO INDIAN LEGAL PERIODICALS. see *LAW — Abstracting, Bibliographies, Statistics*

INDEX TO JEWISH PERIODICALS. see *RELIGIONS AND THEOLOGY — Abstracting, Bibliographies, Statistics*

INDEX TO LEGAL CITATIONS AND ABBREVIATIONS. see *LAW — Abstracting, Bibliographies, Statistics*

INDEX TO LEGAL PERIODICALS & BOOKS. see *LAW — Abstracting, Bibliographies, Statistics*

ABSTRACTING AND INDEXING SERVICES

INDEX TO LEGISLATION IN FORCE IN ZIMBABWE; as at 1 August 1997. see *LAW — Abstracting, Bibliographies, Statistics*

INDEX TO MALAYSIAN CONFERENCES/INDEKS PERSIDANGAN MALAYSIA. see *MEETINGS AND CONGRESSES — Abstracting, Bibliographies, Statistics*

051.016   US   ISSN 0163-0466
AI3
INDEX TO NEW ENGLAND PERIODICALS; an index to selected regional publications. 1977-1982; resumed 1985. q. (with a. cumulation). $65 paperbound; hardbound $90. Diana Witt Associates, 201 Sheridan Ave., No. 5, Minneapolis, MN 55405. Ed. Diana Witt. circ. 185. (back issues avail.) **Document type**: abstracting/indexing.

INDEX TO NIGERIANA IN SELECTED PERIODICALS. see *HISTORY — Abstracting, Bibliographies, Statistics*

INDEX TO PERIODICAL ARTICLES RELATED TO LAW. see *LAW — Abstracting, Bibliographies, Statistics*

INDEX TO REPRODUCTIONS IN ART PERIODICALS. see *ART — Abstracting, Bibliographies, Statistics*

INDEX TO SCIENTIFIC & TECHNICAL PROCEEDINGS. see *SCIENCES: COMPREHENSIVE WORKS — Abstracting, Bibliographies, Statistics*

INDEX TO SCIENTIFIC REVIEWS. see *SCIENCES: COMPREHENSIVE WORKS — Abstracting, Bibliographies, Statistics*

INDEX TO SOCIAL SCIENCES & HUMANITIES PROCEEDINGS. see *SOCIAL SCIENCES: COMPREHENSIVE WORKS — Abstracting, Bibliographies, Statistics*

INDEX TO SOUTH AFRICAN PERIODICALS. see *PUBLISHING AND BOOK TRADE — Abstracting, Bibliographies, Statistics*

INDEX TO THAI PERIODICAL LITERATURE. see *SOCIAL SCIENCES: COMPREHENSIVE WORKS — Abstracting, Bibliographies, Statistics*

INDEX TO THE CODE OF FEDERAL REGULATIONS. see *PUBLIC ADMINISTRATION — Abstracting, Bibliographies, Statistics*

INDEX TO THE NATIONAL OBSERVER. see *JOURNALISM — Abstracting, Bibliographies, Statistics*

INDEX TO THE ST. PAUL PIONEER PRESS. see *JOURNALISM — Abstracting, Bibliographies, Statistics*

INDEX TO THE SPORTING NEWS. see *SPORTS AND GAMES — Abstracting, Bibliographies, Statistics*

INDEX VETERINARIUS; a classified subject and author index produced by computer processes of current literature on veterinary science with approximately 23,000 titles. see *VETERINARY SCIENCE — Abstracting, Bibliographies, Statistics*

THE INDEXER. see *LIBRARY AND INFORMATION SCIENCES*

INDEXER LOCATOR. see *LIBRARY AND INFORMATION SCIENCES*

INDIA. MINISTRY OF EDUCATION AND SOCIAL WELFARE. DEPARTMENT OF SOCIAL WELFARE. DOCUMENTATION SERVICE BULLETIN. see *SOCIAL SCIENCES: COMPREHENSIVE WORKS — Abstracting, Bibliographies, Statistics*

INDIAN DISSERTATION ABSTRACTS. see *SOCIAL SCIENCES: COMPREHENSIVE WORKS — Abstracting, Bibliographies, Statistics*

INDIAN EDUCATION ABSTRACTS. see *EDUCATION — Abstracting, Bibliographies, Statistics*

INDIAN INSTITUTE OF TECHNOLOGY, MADRAS. PH.D. DISSERTATION ABSTRACTS. see *TECHNOLOGY: COMPREHENSIVE WORKS — Abstracting, Bibliographies, Statistics*

INDIAN LIBRARY SCIENCE ABSTRACTS. see *LIBRARY AND INFORMATION SCIENCES — Abstracting, Bibliographies, Statistics*

INDIAN MANAGEMENT ABSTRACTS. see *BUSINESS AND ECONOMICS — Abstracting, Bibliographies, Statistics*

INDIAN PRESS INDEX. see *JOURNALISM — Abstracting, Bibliographies, Statistics*

INDIAN PSYCHOLOGICAL ABSTRACTS AND REVIEWS. see *PSYCHOLOGY — Abstracting, Bibliographies, Statistics*

INDIAN SCIENCE ABSTRACTS. see *SCIENCES: COMPREHENSIVE WORKS — Abstracting, Bibliographies, Statistics*

INDIAN SCIENCE INDEX. SER. B: PRE-MODERN PERIOD. see *TECHNOLOGY: COMPREHENSIVE WORKS — Abstracting, Bibliographies, Statistics*

INDICE DE ARTICULOS SOBRE EDUCACION Y ADIESTRAMIENTO. see *EDUCATION — Abstracting, Bibliographies, Statistics*

INDICE ESPANOL DE CIENCIA Y TECNOLOGIA. see *SCIENCES: COMPREHENSIVE WORKS — Abstracting, Bibliographies, Statistics*

INDICE ESPANOL DE HUMANIDADES. SERIES A: ART. see *ART — Abstracting, Bibliographies, Statistics*

016   CU   ISSN 0864-1382
INDICE GENERAL DE PUBLICACIONES PERIODICAS CUBANAS. 1970. a. $35. Biblioteca Nacional Jose Marti, Plaza de la Revolucion, Havana, Cuba. (Dist. by: Ediciones Cubanas, Obispo No. 527, Apdo. 605, Havana, Cuba) index. circ. 500. **Document type**: abstracting/indexing.
   Description: Analytical index to articles in the social sciences and on general topics published in Cuban magazines during the preceding year.

INDICE MEDICO ESPANOL. see *MEDICAL SCIENCES — Abstracting, Bibliographies, Statistics*

INDIGENOUS KNOWLEDGE INDEX. see *ANTHROPOLOGY — Abstracting, Bibliographies, Statistics*

INDONESIAN BIOLOGICAL AND AGRICULTURAL INDEX/INDEKS BIOLOGI DAN PERTANIAN DE INDONESIA. see *AGRICULTURE — Abstracting, Bibliographies, Statistics*

INDUSTRIAL ABSTRACTS FOR TANZANIA. see *TECHNOLOGY: COMPREHENSIVE WORKS — Abstracting, Bibliographies, Statistics*

INDUSTRIAL ENERGY CONSERVATION. see *ENERGY — Abstracting, Bibliographies, Statistics*

INDUSTRIAL HYGIENE DIGEST. see *OCCUPATIONAL HEALTH AND SAFETY — Abstracting, Bibliographies, Statistics*

INFORMATION MANAGEMENT AND TECHNOLOGY ABSTRACTS. see *LIBRARY AND INFORMATION SCIENCES — Abstracting, Bibliographies, Statistics*

INFORMATION SCIENCE ABSTRACTS. see *LIBRARY AND INFORMATION SCIENCES — Abstracting, Bibliographies, Statistics*

INFORMATIONSDIENST F I Z TECHNIK. LAERM. see *ENGINEERING — Abstracting, Bibliographies, Statistics*

INFORMATIONSDIENST F I Z TECHNIK. REGELUNGSTECHNIK. see *ENGINEERING — Abstracting, Bibliographies, Statistics*

INFORMATIONSDIENST PRAXISBEZOGENER LITERATUR IM WEINBAU. see *AGRICULTURE — Abstracting, Bibliographies, Statistics*

INFORMATSIIA ZA RAKOVODNI KADRI V ZDRAVEOPAZVANETO I MEDITSINSKATA NAUKA. see *PUBLIC HEALTH AND SAFETY — Abstracting, Bibliographies, Statistics*

INPHARMA WEEKLY; rapid alerts to news on drugs and drug therapy. see *PHARMACY AND PHARMACOLOGY — Abstracting, Bibliographies, Statistics*

INSPEC LIST OF JOURNALS AND OTHER SERIAL SOURCES. see *ENGINEERING — Abstracting, Bibliographies, Statistics*

016   FR   ISSN 0243-5314
INSTITUT APPERT. BULLETIN ANALYTIQUE CIE. 1946. m. 418 F. Institut Appert, Cie, 42-44 rue d'Alesia, 75014 Paris, France. Ed. Laurent Weill. bk.rev. circ. 1,200.

INSTITUTE OF PAPER SCIENCE AND TECHNOLOGY. ABSTRACT BULLETIN. see *PAPER AND PULP — Abstracting, Bibliographies, Statistics*

INSTITUTE OF PAPER SCIENCE AND TECHNOLOGY. GRAPHIC ARTS BULLETIN. see *PRINTING — Abstracting, Bibliographies, Statistics*

INSTYTUT OBROBKI SKRAWANIEM. PRZEGLAD DOKUMENTACYJNY. see *ENGINEERING — Abstracting, Bibliographies, Statistics*

INSURANCE PERIODICALS INDEX. see *INSURANCE — Abstracting, Bibliographies, Statistics*

INTELLECTUAL PROPERTY REPORTS (NORTH RYDE, 1989); consolidated index and tables. see *PATENTS, TRADEMARKS AND COPYRIGHTS — Abstracting, Bibliographies, Statistics*

INTERNATIONAL ABSTRACTS IN OPERATIONS RESEARCH. see *COMPUTERS — Abstracting, Bibliographies, Statistics*

INTERNATIONAL ASSOCIATION FOR DENTAL RESEARCH. ABSTRACTS OF THE GENERAL MEETING. see *MEDICAL SCIENCES — Abstracting, Bibliographies, Statistics*

INTERNATIONAL BIBLIOGRAPHY OF THE SOCIAL SCIENCES. SOCIAL AND CULTURAL ANTHROPOLOGY. see *ANTHROPOLOGY — Abstracting, Bibliographies, Statistics*

INTERNATIONAL BIOPHYSICS CONGRESS. ABSTRACTS. see *BIOLOGY — Abstracting, Bibliographies, Statistics*

INTERNATIONAL BUILDING SERVICES ABSTRACTS. see *HEATING, PLUMBING AND REFRIGERATION — Abstracting, Bibliographies, Statistics*

INTERNATIONAL CIVIL ENGINEERING ABSTRACTS. see *ENGINEERING — Abstracting, Bibliographies, Statistics*

INTERNATIONAL DEVELOPMENT ABSTRACTS. see *GEOGRAPHY — Abstracting, Bibliographies, Statistics*

INTERNATIONAL INDEX TO FILM PERIODICALS. see *MOTION PICTURES — Abstracting, Bibliographies, Statistics*

INTERNATIONAL INTERTRADE INDEX; new foreign products-marketing techniques. see *BUSINESS AND ECONOMICS — Abstracting, Bibliographies, Statistics*

INTERNATIONAL LABOUR DOCUMENTATION. see *BUSINESS AND ECONOMICS — Abstracting, Bibliographies, Statistics*

INTERNATIONAL LOGISTICS ABSTRACTS. see *TRANSPORTATION — Abstracting, Bibliographies, Statistics*

INTERNATIONAL NURSING INDEX. see *MEDICAL SCIENCES — Abstracting, Bibliographies, Statistics*

INTERNATIONAL PACKAGING ABSTRACTS. see *PACKAGING — Abstracting, Bibliographies, Statistics*

INTERNATIONAL PETROLEUM ABSTRACTS. see *PETROLEUM AND GAS — Abstracting, Bibliographies, Statistics*

INTERNATIONAL PHARMACEUTICAL ABSTRACTS; key to the world's literature of pharmacy. see *PHARMACY AND PHARMACOLOGY — Abstracting, Bibliographies, Statistics*

INTERNATIONAL POLITICAL SCIENCE ABSTRACTS/DOCUMENTATION POLITIQUE INTERNATIONALE. see *POLITICAL SCIENCE — Abstracting, Bibliographies, Statistics*

ABSTRACTING AND INDEXING SERVICES

INTERNATIONALE ZEITSCHRIFTENSCHAU FUER BIBELWISSENSCHAFT UND GRENZGEBIETE/INTERNATIONAL REVIEW OF BIBLICAL STUDIES. see RELIGIONS AND THEOLOGY — Abstracting, Bibliographies, Statistics

IRRIGATION AND DRAINAGE ABSTRACTS. see AGRICULTURE — Abstracting, Bibliographies, Statistics

ISLAM IN AMERICA; a quarterly survey of books, periodicals and newspapers. see RELIGIONS AND THEOLOGY — Abstracting, Bibliographies, Statistics

ISTORIYA: OTECHESTVENNAYA LITERATURA; referativnyi zhurnal. see HISTORY — Abstracting, Bibliographies, Statistics

ISTORIYA: ZARUBEZHNAYA LITERATURA; referativnyi zhurnal. see HISTORY — Abstracting, Bibliographies, Statistics

A E R I REPORTS ABSTRACTS/GENKEN KENKYU SEIKA SHOROKUSYU. (Japan Atomic Energy Research Institute) see ENERGY — Abstracting, Bibliographies, Statistics

J P G LETTER; news on English publishing in Japan and South-East Asia. (Japan Publications Guide Service) see PUBLISHING AND BOOK TRADE

JAPAN PHARMACEUTICAL ABSTRACTS. see PHARMACY AND PHARMACOLOGY — Abstracting, Bibliographies, Statistics

JAPANESE PATENTS ABSTRACTS. EXAMINED. see PATENTS, TRADEMARKS AND COPYRIGHTS — Abstracting, Bibliographies, Statistics

JAPANESE SYMPOSIUM ON PLASMA CHEMISTRY. ABSTRACT PAPERS/PURAZUMA KAGAKU GODO SHINPOJUMU ABUSUTORAK UTOSHU. see CHEMISTRY — Abstracting, Bibliographies, Statistics

JEWISH ABSTRACTS. see ETHNIC INTERESTS — Abstracting, Bibliographies, Statistics

JIEFANG RIBAO HEDINGBEN/LIBERATION DAILY BOUND INDEX. see GENERAL INTEREST PERIODICALS — China

JINKO KESSHO KOGAKKAI TOKUBETSU KOENKAI KOEN YOSHISHU/ASSOCIATION OF SYNTHETIC CRYSTAL SCIENCE AND TECHNOLOGY. ABSTRACTS OF THE SPECIAL MEETING. see CHEMISTRY — Abstracting, Bibliographies, Statistics

JISHIN KOGAKU BUNKEN MOKUROKU/BIBLIOGRAPHY OF EARTHQUAKE ENGINEERING. see EARTH SCIENCES — Abstracting, Bibliographies, Statistics

JOURNAL FOR RESEARCH IN MATHEMATICS EDUCATION. see MATHEMATICS

JOURNAL OF ABSTRACTS IN INTERNATIONAL EDUCATION. see EDUCATION — Abstracting, Bibliographies, Statistics

JOURNAL OF CURRENT LASER ABSTRACTS. see PHYSICS — Abstracting, Bibliographies, Statistics

JOURNAL OF DIARRHOEAL DISEASES RESEARCH. see MEDICAL SCIENCES — Abstracting, Bibliographies, Statistics

JOURNAL OF ECONOMIC LITERATURE. see BUSINESS AND ECONOMICS — Abstracting, Bibliographies, Statistics

JOURNAL OF HISTORICAL STUDIES. see HISTORY — Abstracting, Bibliographies, Statistics

JOURNAL OF PREVENTION AND INTERVENTION IN THE COMMUNITY; summaries, reviews & index to the world's literature in community mental health. see PSYCHOLOGY — Abstracting, Bibliographies, Statistics

JOURNAL OF REPRODUCTION AND FERTILITY. ABSTRACT SERIES. see BIOLOGY — Abstracting, Bibliographies, Statistics

JOURNALISM AND MASS COMMUNICATION ABSTRACTS; M.A., M.S., and Ph.D. theses in journalism and mass communication. see JOURNALISM — Abstracting, Bibliographies, Statistics

JUNIOR HIGH MAGAZINE ABSTRACTS. see EDUCATION — Abstracting, Bibliographies, Statistics

JUSTITIELE VERKENNINGEN. see CRIMINOLOGY AND LAW ENFORCEMENT — Abstracting, Bibliographies, Statistics

JUTA - STATE LIBRARY INDEX TO THE GOVERNMENT GAZETTE. see PUBLIC ADMINISTRATION — Abstracting, Bibliographies, Statistics

K L M LITERATUUROVERZICHT. see AERONAUTICS AND SPACE FLIGHT — Abstracting, Bibliographies, Statistics

KAGAKU SHOHO/CHEMICAL ABSTRACTS. see CHEMISTRY — Abstracting, Bibliographies, Statistics

KARTEI DER PRAKTISCHEN MEDIZIN; unabhaengige Referatenzeitschrift des in- und auslaendischen Fachschrifttums. see MEDICAL SCIENCES — Abstracting, Bibliographies, Statistics

KARUSHUMU SHINPOJUMU KOEN YOSHI/ABSTRACTS OF CALCIUM SYMPOSIUM. see BIOLOGY — Abstracting, Bibliographies, Statistics

KEESING'S RECORD OF WORLD EVENTS. see POLITICAL SCIENCE — Abstracting, Bibliographies, Statistics

KENTUCKY COLLEGE AND UNIVERSITY DEGREES AND OTHER FORMAL AWARDS (YEAR). see EDUCATION — Abstracting, Bibliographies, Statistics

KENTUCKY COLLEGE AND UNIVERSITY ENROLLMENTS (YEAR). see EDUCATION — Abstracting, Bibliographies, Statistics

KENTUCKY INDEX. see HEATING, PLUMBING AND REFRIGERATION — Abstracting, Bibliographies, Statistics

KEY ABSTRACTS - ELECTRONIC CIRCUITS. see ELECTRONICS

KEY ABSTRACTS - ELECTRONIC INSTRUMENTATION. see ELECTRONICS

KEY ABSTRACTS - MEASUREMENTS IN PHYSICS. see METROLOGY AND STANDARDIZATION — Abstracting, Bibliographies, Statistics

KEY ABSTRACTS - MICROELECTRONICS & PRINTED CIRCUITS. see ELECTRONICS

KEY ABSTRACTS - MICROWAVE TECHNOLOGY. see ELECTRONICS

KEY ABSTRACTS - NEURAL NETWORKS. see COMPUTERS — Abstracting, Bibliographies, Statistics

KEY ABSTRACTS - SEMICONDUCTOR DEVICES. see ELECTRONICS

KEY WORD INDEX OF WILDLIFE RESEARCH. see SCIENCES: COMPREHENSIVE WORKS — Abstracting, Bibliographies, Statistics

KEYWORD INDEX TO SERIAL TITLES. see LIBRARY AND INFORMATION SCIENCES — Abstracting, Bibliographies, Statistics

KIDNEY (NEW YORK, 1992); a current survey of world literature. see MEDICAL SCIENCES — Abstracting, Bibliographies, Statistics

KIKAN KEISEI KENKYUKAI KOEN YOSHISHU/JAPANESE SOCIETY FOR BASIC AND APPLIED ORGAN RESEARCH. ABSTRACTS OF THE MEETING. see BIOLOGY — Abstracting, Bibliographies, Statistics

DER KINDERARZT. see MEDICAL SCIENCES — Abstracting, Bibliographies, Statistics

KINDEX; an index to legal periodical literature concerning children. see LAW — Abstracting, Bibliographies, Statistics

KITAEVEDENIE: ZARUBEZHNAYA LITERATURA; referativnyi zhurnal. see SOCIAL SCIENCES: COMPREHENSIVE WORKS — Abstracting, Bibliographies, Statistics

KOHASZATI ES ONTESZETI SZAKIRODALMI TAJEKOZTATO/METALLURGY AND FOUNDRY ABSTRACTS. see METALLURGY — Abstracting, Bibliographies, Statistics

KOKAGAKU TORONKAI KOEN YOSHISHU/ABSTRACTS OF SYMPOSIUM ON PHOTOCHEMISTRY. see CHEMISTRY — Abstracting, Bibliographies, Statistics

KOKU KISHO NOTO/ABSTRACTS IN AVIATION METEOROLOGY. see METEOROLOGY — Abstracting, Bibliographies, Statistics

KOREA (REPUBLIC). NATIONAL STATISTICAL OFFICE. REPORT ON MINING AND MANUFACTURING SURVEY. see MINES AND MINING INDUSTRY — Abstracting, Bibliographies, Statistics

KOREAN MEDICAL ABSTRACTS. see MEDICAL SCIENCES — Abstracting, Bibliographies, Statistics

KOREAN SCIENTIFIC ABSTRACTS. see SCIENCES: COMPREHENSIVE WORKS — Abstracting, Bibliographies, Statistics

KORNYEZETVEDELMI SZAKIRODALMI TAJEKOZTATO/ENVIRONMENTAL CONTROL ABSTRACTS. see ENVIRONMENTAL STUDIES — Abstracting, Bibliographies, Statistics

KOTAI NO HANNOSEI TORONKAI KOEN YOKOSHU/ABSTRACTS OF THE MEETING ON SOLID REACTIVITY. see CHEMISTRY — Abstracting, Bibliographies, Statistics

KYOKUIKI SEIBUTSU SHINPOJUMU KOEN YOSHISHU/ABSTRACTS OF THE SYMPOSIUM ON POLAR BIOLOGY. see BIOLOGY — Abstracting, Bibliographies, Statistics

KYUSHU UNIVERSITY. RESEARCH INSTITUTE FOR APPLIED MECHANICS. ABSTRACTS OF PAPERS. see ENGINEERING — Abstracting, Bibliographies, Statistics

L I S A: LIBRARY & INFORMATION SCIENCE ABSTRACTS. see LIBRARY AND INFORMATION SCIENCES — Abstracting, Bibliographies, Statistics

L I S A PLUS. (Library and Information Science Abstracts) see LIBRARY AND INFORMATION SCIENCES — Abstracting, Bibliographies, Statistics

LANGUAGE TEACHING. see LINGUISTICS — Abstracting, Bibliographies, Statistics

LATIN AMERICAN STUDIES. VOLUME 1. see HISTORY — Abstracting, Bibliographies, Statistics

LATIN AMERICAN STUDIES. VOLUME 2. see HISTORY — Abstracting, Bibliographies, Statistics

LEADSCAN; a review of recent technical literature on the uses of lead and its products. see METALLURGY — Abstracting, Bibliographies, Statistics

LEATHER SCIENCE ABSTRACTS. see LEATHER AND FUR INDUSTRIES — Abstracting, Bibliographies, Statistics

LEFT INDEX; a quarterly index to periodicals of the left. see POLITICAL SCIENCE — Abstracting, Bibliographies, Statistics

LEGAL BIBLIOGRAPHY JOURNAL. see LAW — Abstracting, Bibliographies, Statistics

LEGAL EDUCATION DIGEST. see LAW — Abstracting, Bibliographies, Statistics

LEGAL JOURNALS INDEX. see LAW — Abstracting, Bibliographies, Statistics

LEGAL PERIODICALS IN ENGLISH. see LAW — Abstracting, Bibliographies, Statistics

LEGALTRAC. see LAW — Abstracting, Bibliographies, Statistics

LEISURE, RECREATION AND TOURISM ABSTRACTS. see TRAVEL AND TOURISM — Abstracting, Bibliographies, Statistics

LIBRARY LITERATURE; an index to library and information science publications. see LIBRARY AND INFORMATION SCIENCES — Abstracting, Bibliographies, Statistics

A

LINGUISTICS ABSTRACTS. see *LINGUISTICS — Abstracting, Bibliographies, Statistics*

LINGUISTICS AND LANGUAGE BEHAVIOR ABSTRACTS. see *LINGUISTICS — Abstracting, Bibliographies, Statistics*

LINX DATABASE. see *LAW — Abstracting, Bibliographies, Statistics*

LITERARY CRITICISM REGISTER; a monthly listing of studies in English and American literature. see *LITERATURE — Abstracting, Bibliographies, Statistics*

LITERATURINFORMATIONDIENST SCHRIFTTUM BAUWESEN: GESAMTAUSGABE. see *BUILDING AND CONSTRUCTION — Abstracting, Bibliographies, Statistics*

LITERATUROVEDENIE: OTECHESTVENNAYA LITERATURA; referativnyi zhurnal. see *LITERATURE — Abstracting, Bibliographies, Statistics*

LITERATUROVEDENIE: ZARUBEZHNAYA LITERATURA; referativnyi zhurnal. see *LITERATURE — Abstracting, Bibliographies, Statistics*

LITERATURSCHAU: MESSEN MECHANISCHER GROESSEN/BULLETIN OF ABSTRACTS: MEASUREMENT OF MECHANICAL QUANTITIES. see *ENGINEERING — Abstracting, Bibliographies, Statistics*

LITERATURSCHAU: SCHWEISSEN UND VERWANDTE VERFAHREN/WELDING AND ALLIED PROCESSES. see *METALLURGY — Abstracting, Bibliographies, Statistics*

LOCAL GOVERNMENT INDEX (NEW SOUTH WALES). see *LAW — Abstracting, Bibliographies, Statistics*

LODGING, RESTAURANT AND TOURISM INDEX. see *HOTELS AND RESTAURANTS — Abstracting, Bibliographies, Statistics*

M E D I C. (Monthly Ethical Drug Index Complication) see *PHARMACY AND PHARMACOLOGY — Abstracting, Bibliographies, Statistics*

M I M S DISEASE INDEX. see *MEDICAL SCIENCES — Abstracting, Bibliographies, Statistics*

M I M S MEDICAL SPECIALITIES. see *MEDICAL SCIENCES — Abstracting, Bibliographies, Statistics*

M I R A AUTOINFO. (Motor Industry Research Association) see *TRANSPORTATION — Abstracting, Bibliographies, Statistics*

M I R A AUTOMOBILE ABSTRACTS. (Motor Industry Research Association) see *TRANSPORTATION — Abstracting, Bibliographies, Statistics*

M I R A AUTOMOTIVE BUSINESS NEWS. (Motor Industry Research Association) see *BUSINESS AND ECONOMICS — Abstracting, Bibliographies, Statistics*

M L A INTERNATIONAL BIBLIOGRAPHY OF BOOKS AND ARTICLES ON THE MODERN LANGUAGES AND LITERATURES. (Modern Language Association of America) see *LITERATURE — Abstracting, Bibliographies, Statistics*

051 011   US   ISSN 1041-1151
MAGAZINE ARTICLE SUMMARIES; EBSCO's weekly index to periodical literature. 1984. w. $1199 for 10 discs; $1599 for m. CD-ROM; $799 for quarterly. EBSCO Publishing (Subsidiary of: EBSCO Industries, Inc.), 10 Estes St., Box 682, Ipswich, MA 01938. TEL 508-356-6500; 800-653-2726. FAX 508-356-6565. E-mail: ep@epnet.com; URL: http://www.epnet.com. Ed. Melissa Kummerer. bk.rev.; index. circ. 3,000. **Document type:** abstracting/indexing.
●Also available online. Vendor(s): Ovid Technologies, Inc. (PMRO).
Also available on CD-ROM.
  Formerly: Popular Magazine Review (ISSN 0740-3763)

MAGAZINE INDEX. see *PUBLISHING AND BOOK TRADE — Abstracting, Bibliographies, Statistics*

MAIZE ABSTRACTS. see *AGRICULTURE — Abstracting, Bibliographies, Statistics*

050.9595   MY   ISSN 0126-5040
AI3
MALAYSIAN PERIODICALS INDEX/INDEKS MAJALAH MALAYSIA. (Text in Bahasa Malaysia, Chinese, English, Tamil) 1974. s-a. National Library of Malaysia, Serials Division, 232 Jalan Tun Razak, 50572 Kuala Lumpur, Malaysia. TEL 03-2943488. FAX 03-2927502. (Subscr. to: University of Malaya Co-operative Bookshop Ltd., P.O. Box 1127, Jalan Pantai Baru, 59700 Kuala Lumpur, Malaysia) circ. 150. **Document type:** abstracting/indexing.
—BLDSC (4375.855000).
  Description: Covers articles of academic, intellectual and educational value published in Malaysian journals.

MANAGEMENT AND MARKETING ABSTRACTS. see *BUSINESS AND ECONOMICS — Abstracting, Bibliographies, Statistics*

MANAGEMENT CONTENTS; semi-monthly compilation of tables of contents from more than 320 business magazines and journals. see *BUSINESS AND ECONOMICS — Abstracting, Bibliographies, Statistics*

MANAGEMENT DEVELOPMENT ABSTRACTS. see *BUSINESS AND ECONOMICS — Abstracting, Bibliographies, Statistics*

MANAGEMENT OF CHANGE ABSTRACTS. see *BUSINESS AND ECONOMICS — Abstracting, Bibliographies, Statistics*

MARINE POLLUTION RESEARCH TITLES. see *ENVIRONMENTAL STUDIES — Abstracting, Bibliographies, Statistics*

MARITIME INFORMATION REVIEW. see *TRANSPORTATION — Abstracting, Bibliographies, Statistics*

MARKAZ-I NASHARIYAT-I 'ILMI VA FARHANGI. FIHRIST-I MUNDARIJAT-I MAJALLAH-HA-YI JARI-I/CENTER FOR SCIENTIFIC AND CULTURAL PERIODICALS. TABLE OF CONTENTS OF CURRENT JOURNALS. see *SCIENCES: COMPREHENSIVE WORKS — Abstracting, Bibliographies, Statistics*

MARKET RESEARCH ABSTRACTS. see *BUSINESS AND ECONOMICS — Abstracting, Bibliographies, Statistics*

MARKETING & DISTRIBUTION ABSTRACTS. see *BUSINESS AND ECONOMICS — Abstracting, Bibliographies, Statistics*

MARKETING UPDATE. see *BUSINESS AND ECONOMICS — Abstracting, Bibliographies, Statistics*

MASS SPECTROMETRY BULLETIN. see *CHEMISTRY — Abstracting, Bibliographies, Statistics*

MASTERS ABSTRACTS INTERNATIONAL; catalog of selected masters theses. see *EDUCATION — Abstracting, Bibliographies, Statistics*

MATERIALS INFORMATION METALLURGICAL SEARCH-IN-PRINT SERIES. see *METALLURGY — Abstracting, Bibliographies, Statistics*

MATHEMATICAL REVIEWS; a reviewing journal covering the world literature of mathematical research. see *MATHEMATICS — Abstracting, Bibliographies, Statistics*

MEAT BALANCES IN O E C D COUNTRIES. see *AGRICULTURE — Abstracting, Bibliographies, Statistics*

MECHANICAL ENGINEERING ABSTRACTS. see *ENGINEERING — Abstracting, Bibliographies, Statistics*

MEDIA REVIEW DIGEST; the only complete guide to reviews of non-book media. see *MOTION PICTURES — Abstracting, Bibliographies, Statistics*

MEDICAL & PHARMACEUTICAL BIOTECHNOLOGY ABSTRACTS. see *MEDICAL SCIENCES — Abstracting, Bibliographies, Statistics*

MEDICAL & SURGICAL DERMATOLOGY; a critical guide to world literature. see *MEDICAL SCIENCES — Abstracting, Bibliographies, Statistics*

MEDICAL BENEFITS. see *INSURANCE — Abstracting, Bibliographies, Statistics*

MEDICAL CARE RESEARCH AND REVIEW. see *PUBLIC HEALTH AND SAFETY — Abstracting, Bibliographies, Statistics*

MEDICINAL AND AROMATIC PLANTS. see *MEDICAL SCIENCES — Abstracting, Bibliographies, Statistics*

MEDICINAL AND AROMATIC PLANTS ABSTRACTS. see *MEDICAL SCIENCES — Abstracting, Bibliographies, Statistics*

MEDIFAX INDEX. see *MEDICAL SCIENCES — Abstracting, Bibliographies, Statistics*

MEDIOEVO LATINO. see *HISTORY — Abstracting, Bibliographies, Statistics*

MEDITSINSKI PREGLED. see *MEDICAL SCIENCES — Abstracting, Bibliographies, Statistics*

MEDLINE PROFESSIONAL - C D. see *MEDICAL SCIENCES — Abstracting, Bibliographies, Statistics*

MELYEPITESI ES VIZEPITESI SZAKIRODALMI TAJEKOZTATO/CIVIL ENGINEERING & HYDRAULIC ENGINEERING ABSTRACTS. see *ENGINEERING — Abstracting, Bibliographies, Statistics*

METAL POWDER REPORT. see *METALLURGY — Abstracting, Bibliographies, Statistics*

METALS ABSTRACTS. see *METALLURGY — Abstracting, Bibliographies, Statistics*

METALS ABSTRACTS INDEX. see *METALLURGY — Abstracting, Bibliographies, Statistics*

METEOROLOGICAL AND GEOASTROPHYSICAL ABSTRACTS. see *METEOROLOGY — Abstracting, Bibliographies, Statistics*

MEXICO. CENTRO DE INFORMACION TECNICA Y DOCUMENTACION. INDICE DE REVISTAS. SECCION DE EDUCACION Y COMUNICACION. see *EDUCATION — Abstracting, Bibliographies, Statistics*

MICROBIOLOGY ABSTRACTS: SECTION A. INDUSTRIAL & APPLIED MICROBIOLOGY. see *BIOLOGY — Abstracting, Bibliographies, Statistics*

MICROBIOLOGY ABSTRACTS: SECTION B. BACTERIOLOGY. see *BIOLOGY — Abstracting, Bibliographies, Statistics*

MICROBIOLOGY ABSTRACTS: SECTION C. ALGOLOGY, MYCOLOGY AND PROTOZOOLOGY. see *BIOLOGY — Abstracting, Bibliographies, Statistics*

MICROCOMPUTER ABSTRACTS. see *COMPUTERS — Abstracting, Bibliographies, Statistics*

915.6 016   US   ISSN 0162-766X
DS41
MIDDLE EAST: ABSTRACTS AND INDEX. 1978. a., latest 1993 (for the year 1992). $300. Aristarchus Publications, Box 1020, Aberdeen, WA 98520. TEL 800-435-8221. (Winter addr.: Box 12625, Tucson, AZ 85732) Ed. James Joseph Sanchez. adv.; bk.rev. **Document type:** abstracting/indexing.
●Also available online. Vendor(s): Knight-Ridder Information, Inc. (File no.248).
—BLDSC (5761.328000).
  Description: Bibliography to English language materials on the Middle East. Over 1500 journals scanned annually. Also indexes government documents, doctoral dissertations.

MILCHWISSENSCHAFT/MILK SCIENCE INTERNATIONAL; journal of nutrition research and food science. see *AGRICULTURE — Abstracting, Bibliographies, Statistics*

MILITARY SCIENCE INDEX. see *MILITARY — Abstracting, Bibliographies, Statistics*

MILK AND MILK PRODUCTS BALANCES IN O E C D COUNTRIES. see *AGRICULTURE — Abstracting, Bibliographies, Statistics*

MINERALOGICAL SOCIETY OF JAPAN. ANNUAL MEETING ABSTRACTS/NIHON KOBUTSU GAKKAI NENKAI KOEN YOSHISHU. see *EARTH SCIENCES — Abstracting, Bibliographies, Statistics*

ABSTRACTING AND INDEXING SERVICES

MINISTERIAL DOCUMENT SERVICE. see *PUBLIC ADMINISTRATION* — *Abstracting, Bibliographies, Statistics*

MONATSSCHRIFT FUER BRAUWISSENSCHAFT. see *BEVERAGES* — *Abstracting, Bibliographies, Statistics*

LE MONDE INDEX. see *JOURNALISM* — *Abstracting, Bibliographies, Statistics*

MOTOR INDUSTRY MANAGEMENT. see *TRANSPORTATION* — *Abstracting, Bibliographies, Statistics*

MULTICULTURAL EDUCATION ABSTRACTS. see *EDUCATION* — *Abstracting, Bibliographies, Statistics*

MUSE (MUSIC SEARCH). see *MUSIC* — *Abstracting, Bibliographies, Statistics*

MUSIC-IN-PRINT SERIES. see *MUSIC* — *Abstracting, Bibliographies, Statistics*

MUSIC INDEX; a subject-author guide to over 300 current international periodicals. see *MUSIC* — *Abstracting, Bibliographies, Statistics*

MUSZAKI-GAZDASAGI MAGAZIN/TECHNICAL ECONOMIC DIGEST. see *BUSINESS AND ECONOMICS* — *Abstracting, Bibliographies, Statistics*

MYCOBACTERIA. see *BIOLOGY* — *Abstracting, Bibliographies, Statistics*

N A A. (Nordic Archaeological Abstracts) see *ARCHAEOLOGY* — *Abstracting, Bibliographies, Statistics*

N A S A PATENT ABSTRACTS BIBLIOGRAPHY: A CONTINUING BIBLIOGRAPHY. SECTION 1. ABSTRACTS. see *PATENTS, TRADEMARKS AND COPYRIGHTS* — *Abstracting, Bibliographies, Statistics*

N A S S D O C RESEARCH INFORMATION SERIES. CURRENT CONTENTS OF INDIAN SOCIAL JOURNALS. (National Social Science Documentation Centre) see *LIBRARY AND INFORMATION SCIENCES* — *Abstracting, Bibliographies, Statistics*

N B O ABSTRACTS. (National Buildings Organisation) see *BUILDING AND CONSTRUCTION* — *Abstracting, Bibliographies, Statistics*

N C B I NEWS. (U.S. National Center for Biotechnology Information) see *BIOLOGY* — *Abstracting, Bibliographies, Statistics*

N C J R S DOCUMENT RETRIEVAL INDEX. (National Criminal Justice Reference Service) see *CRIMINOLOGY AND LAW ENFORCEMENT* — *Abstracting, Bibliographies, Statistics*

N D L C D - R O M LINE JAPANESE PERIODICAL INDEX. (National Diet Library) see *HUMANITIES: COMPREHENSIVE WORKS* — *Abstracting, Bibliographies, Statistics*

N E L M INDEX SERIES. (National English Literary Museum) see *LITERATURE* — *Abstracting, Bibliographies, Statistics*

THE N E S F A INDEX TO SHORT SCIENCE FICTION. (New England Science Fiction Association Inc.) see *LITERATURE* — *Abstracting, Bibliographies, Statistics*

025 US ISSN 0090-0893
CODEN: NFNLA6
N F A I S NEWSLETTER. 1958. m. $120 (foreign $135). National Federation of Abstracting and Information Services, 1518 Walnut St., Ste. 307, Philadelphia, PA 19102. TEL 215-893-1561. FAX 215-893-1564. E-mail: nfais@hslc.org. Ed. Wendy Wicks. adv.; bk.rev.; bibl.; stat.; index. circ. 600. (back issues avail.) **Indexed:** PROMT. **Document type:** trade publication, newsletter.
—BLDSC (6109.060000); CASDDS.
Formerly: National Federation of Science Abstracting and Indexing Services. Federation Newsletter (ISSN 0027-9242)
Description: News, features, and columns of interest to the abstracting and indexing community and the information industry, with member profiles and calendar listings.

025 US
N F A I S REPORT SERIES. 1989. 3/yr. price varies. National Federation of Abstracting and Information Services, 1518 Walnut St., Ste. 307, Philadelphia, PA 19102. TEL 215-893-1561. FAX 215-893-1564. E-mail: nfais@hslc.org. **Document type:** monographic series.
Description: Research reports on critical issues of interest to the information industry, including global copyright issues, economics of database production, marketing guides, statitistical information, human resources, and technological developments affecting the industry.

025 US ISSN 1062-7952
Z695.93
N F A I S YEARBOOK OF THE INFORMATION INDUSTRY (YEAR). 1992. a. $50 (effecctive 1997). (National Federation of Abstracting and Information Services) Information Today, Inc., 143 Old Marlton Pike, Medford, NJ 08055. TEL 609-654-4309. FAX 609-654-4309. Ed. Arthur W. Elias.
—CISTI.
Description: Discusses the significant events that have influenced the information industry over the past year. Reviews critical issues, national and international policies. Features new technologies, with an emphasis on compact discs.

N I C E M INDEX TO A V PRODUCERS AND DISTRIBUTORS. (National Information Center for Educational Media) see *MOTION PICTURES* — *Abstracting, Bibliographies, Statistics*

N.S.W. JUDGMENTS BULLETIN. (New South Wales) see *LAW* — *Abstracting, Bibliographies, Statistics*

N T I S ALERTS: ADMINISTRATION AND MANAGEMENT. (U.S. National Technical Information Service) see *PUBLIC ADMINISTRATION* — *Abstracting, Bibliographies, Statistics*

N T I S ALERTS: AGRICULTURE & FOOD. (U.S. National Technical Information Service) see *AGRICULTURE* — *Abstracting, Bibliographies, Statistics*

N T I S ALERTS: BEHAVIOR AND SOCIETY. (U.S. National Technical Information Service) see *SOCIOLOGY* — *Abstracting, Bibliographies, Statistics*

N T I S ALERTS: BIOMEDICAL TECHNOLOGY & HUMAN FACTORS ENGINEERING. (U.S. National Technical Information Service) see *MEDICAL SCIENCES* — *Abstracting, Bibliographies, Statistics*

N T I S ALERTS: BUILDING INDUSTRY TECHNOLOGY. (U.S. National Technical Information Service) see *BUILDING AND CONSTRUCTION* — *Abstracting, Bibliographies, Statistics*

N T I S ALERTS: BUSINESS & ECONOMICS. (U.S. National Technical Information Service) see *BUSINESS AND ECONOMICS* — *Abstracting, Bibliographies, Statistics*

N T I S ALERTS: CHEMISTRY. (U.S. National Technical Information Service) see *CHEMISTRY* — *Abstracting, Bibliographies, Statistics*

N T I S ALERTS: CIVIL ENGINEERING. (U.S. National Technical Information Service) see *ENGINEERING* — *Abstracting, Bibliographies, Statistics*

N T I S ALERTS: COMMUNICATION. (U.S. National Technical Information Service) see *COMMUNICATIONS* — *Abstracting, Bibliographies, Statistics*

N T I S ALERTS: COMPUTERS, CONTROL & INFORMATION THEORY. (U.S. National Technical Information Service) see *COMPUTERS* — *Abstracting, Bibliographies, Statistics*

N T I S ALERTS: ELECTROTECHNOLOGY. (U.S. National Technical Information Service) see *ELECTRONICS*

N T I S ALERTS: ENERGY. (U.S. National Technical Information Service) see *ENERGY* — *Abstracting, Bibliographies, Statistics*

N T I S ALERTS: ENVIRONMENTAL POLLUTION & CONTROL. (U.S. National Technical Information Service) see *ENVIRONMENTAL STUDIES* — *Abstracting, Bibliographies, Statistics*

N T I S ALERTS: FOREIGN TECHNOLOGY. (U.S. National Technical Information Service) see *TECHNOLOGY: COMPREHENSIVE WORKS* — *Abstracting, Bibliographies, Statistics*

N T I S ALERTS: GOVERNMENT INVENTIONS FOR LICENSING. (U.S. National Technical Information Service) see *TECHNOLOGY: COMPREHENSIVE WORKS* — *Abstracting, Bibliographies, Statistics*

N T I S ALERTS: HEALTH CARE. (U.S. National Technical Information Service) see *PHYSICAL FITNESS AND HYGIENE* — *Abstracting, Bibliographies, Statistics*

N T I S ALERTS: LIBRARY & INFORMATION SCIENCES. (U.S. National Technical Information Service) see *LIBRARY AND INFORMATION SCIENCES* — *Abstracting, Bibliographies, Statistics*

N T I S ALERTS: MANUFACTURING TECHNOLOGY. (U.S. National Technical Information Service) see *TECHNOLOGY: COMPREHENSIVE WORKS* — *Abstracting, Bibliographies, Statistics*

N T I S ALERTS: MATERIALS SCIENCES. (U.S. National Technical Information Service) see *ENGINEERING* — *Abstracting, Bibliographies, Statistics*

N T I S ALERTS: MATHEMATICAL SCIENCES. (U.S. National Technical Information Service) see *MATHEMATICS* — *Abstracting, Bibliographies, Statistics*

N T I S ALERTS: MEDICINE & BIOLOGY. (U.S. National Technical Information Service) see *BIOLOGY* — *Abstracting, Bibliographies, Statistics*

N T I S ALERTS: NATURAL RESOURCES & EARTH SCIENCES. (U.S. National Technical Information Service) see *CONSERVATION* — *Abstracting, Bibliographies, Statistics*

N T I S ALERTS: OCEAN TECHNOLOGY & ENGINEERING. (U.S. National Technical Information Service) see *EARTH SCIENCES* — *Abstracting, Bibliographies, Statistics*

N T I S ALERTS: PHYSICS. (U.S. National Technical Information Service) see *PHYSICS* — *Abstracting, Bibliographies, Statistics*

N T I S ALERTS: TRANSPORTATION. (U.S. National Technical Information Service) see *TRANSPORTATION* — *Abstracting, Bibliographies, Statistics*

NATIONAL ACCOUNTS OF O E C D COUNTRIES. VOLUME 1 MAIN AGGREGATES. see *BUSINESS AND ECONOMICS* — *Abstracting, Bibliographies, Statistics*

NATIONAL ACCOUNTS OF O E C D COUNTRIES. VOLUME 2 DETAILED TABLES. see *BUSINESS AND ECONOMICS* — *Abstracting, Bibliographies, Statistics*

NATIONAL CENTER FOR AGRICULTURAL UTILIZATION RESEARCH PUBLICATIONS AND PATENTS. see *AGRICULTURE* — *Abstracting, Bibliographies, Statistics*

NATIONAL NEWSPAPER INDEX. see *JOURNALISM* — *Abstracting, Bibliographies, Statistics*

NAUKOVEDENIE: OTECHESTVENNAYA I ZARUBEZHNAYA LITERATURA; referativnyi zhurnal. see *SCIENCES: COMPREHENSIVE WORKS* — *Abstracting, Bibliographies, Statistics*

NEMATOLOGICAL ABSTRACTS. see *AGRICULTURE* — *Abstracting, Bibliographies, Statistics*

NEPAL DOCUMENTATION; occasional bibliography. see *BUSINESS AND ECONOMICS* — *Abstracting, Bibliographies, Statistics*

NETHERLANDS. MINISTERIE VAN ONDERWIJS EN WETENSCHAPPEN. ONDERWIJSLITERATUUR. see *EDUCATION* — *Abstracting, Bibliographies, Statistics*

NEUROPSYCHOLOGY ABSTRACTS. see *MEDICAL SCIENCES* — *Abstracting, Bibliographies, Statistics*

NEW SOUTH WALES STATUTES ANNOTATIONS. see *LAW* — *Abstracting, Bibliographies, Statistics*

ABSTRACTING AND INDEXING SERVICES

NEW TESTAMENT ABSTRACTS; a record of current literature. see *RELIGIONS AND THEOLOGY — Abstracting, Bibliographies, Statistics*

NEW ZEALAND INSTITUTE OF VALUERS. LIBRARY CATALOGUE. see *REAL ESTATE — Abstracting, Bibliographies, Statistics*

NEWSLETTER DIGEST. see *BUSINESS AND ECONOMICS — Abstracting, Bibliographies, Statistics*

NEWSPAPER ABSTRACTS. see *JOURNALISM — Abstracting, Bibliographies, Statistics*

NIGERIAN JOURNAL OF SOCIAL SCIENCE RESEARCH ABSTRACTS. see *SOCIAL SCIENCES: COMPREHENSIVE WORKS — Abstracting, Bibliographies, Statistics*

016   NR   ISSN 0794-6406
AI3
NIGERIAN PERIODICALS INDEX. 1986. s-a. £N80($50) Committee of University Librarians of Nigerian Universities, c/o Dr. H.I. Said, The Library, Bayero University, Kano, Nigeria. Ed. B.U. Nwafor. circ. 500. (back issues avail.) **Document type:** abstracting/indexing.
    Description: Author-subject index with the entries filing in one alphabetical sequence, word-by-word, following ALA filing rules.

NIHON BAIOREOROJI GAKKAI NENKAI SHOROKUSHU/JAPANESE SOCIETY OF BIORHEOLOGY. ABSTRACTS OF THE ANNUAL MEETING. see *BIOLOGY — Abstracting, Bibliographies, Statistics*

NIHON BENTOSU GAKKAI TAIKAI/JAPANESE ASSOCIATION OF BENTHOLOGY. ABSTRACTS OF ANNUAL MEETING. see *BIOLOGY — Abstracting, Bibliographies, Statistics*

NIHON CHIKYU KAGAKKAI NENKAI KOEN YOSHISHU/GEOCHEMICAL SOCIETY OF JAPAN. ABSTRACTS OF REPORTS ON ANNUAL MEETING. see *EARTH SCIENCES — Abstracting, Bibliographies, Statistics*

NIHON CHISHITSU GAKKAI KANTO SHIBU SHINPOJUMU KOEN YOSHISHU/GEOLOGICAL SOCIETY OF JAPAN. ABSTRACTS OF KANTO BRANCH SYMPOSIUM. see *EARTH SCIENCES — Abstracting, Bibliographies, Statistics*

NIHON GYORUI GAKKAI NENKAI KOEN YOSHI/ICHTHYOLOGY SOCIETY OF JAPAN. ADVANCE ABSTRACTS FOR THE ANNUAL MEETING. see *BIOLOGY — Abstracting, Bibliographies, Statistics*

NIHON IDEN GAKKAI TAIKAI PUROGURAMU YOKOSHU/GENETICS SOCIETY OF JAPAN. ABSTRACTS OF THE ANNUAL MEETING. see *BIOLOGY — Abstracting, Bibliographies, Statistics*

NIHON JIKKEN DOBUTSU GAKKAI SOKAI KOEN YOSHISHU/JAPANESE ASSOCIATION FOR LABORATORY ANIMAL SCIENCE. ABSTRACTS OF GENERAL MEETING. see *MEDICAL SCIENCES — Abstracting, Bibliographies, Statistics*

NIHON JINRUI IDEN GAKKAI TAIKAI SHOROKUSHU/JAPAN SOCIETY OF HUMAN GENETICS. ABSTRACTS OF THE ANNUAL MEETING. see *BIOLOGY — Abstracting, Bibliographies, Statistics*

NIHON KAIBOGAKU BUNKENSHU/ABSTRACTS OF JAPANESE ANATOMY. see *MEDICAL SCIENCES — Abstracting, Bibliographies, Statistics*

NIHON KAISUI GAKKAI KENKYU GIJUTSU HAPPYOKAI KOEN YOSHISHU/SOCIETY OF SEA WATER SCIENCE, JAPAN. ABSTRACTS OF MEETING. see *EARTH SCIENCES — Abstracting, Bibliographies, Statistics*

NIHON KESSHO GAKKAI NENKAI KOEN YOSHISHU/CRYSTALLOGRAPHIC SOCIETY OF JAPAN. ABSTRACTS OF ANNUAL MEETING. see *CHEMISTRY — Abstracting, Bibliographies, Statistics*

NIHON KONCHU GAKKAI TAIKAI KOEN YOSHI/ENTOMOLOGICAL SOCIETY OF JAPAN. ABSTRACTS OF ANNUAL MEETING. see *BIOLOGY — Abstracting, Bibliographies, Statistics*

NIHON KOSEIBUTSU GAKKAI NENKAI KOEN YOKOSHU/PALAEONTOLOGICAL SOCIETY OF JAPAN. ABSTRACTS OF THE ANNUAL MEETING. see *PALEONTOLOGY — Abstracting, Bibliographies, Statistics*

NIHON KYUCHAKU GAKKAI KENKYU HAPPYOKAI KOEN YOSHISHU/JAPAN SOCIETY ON ADSORPTION. ABSTRACTS OF THE MEETING. see *CHEMISTRY — Abstracting, Bibliographies, Statistics*

NIHON MAKU GAKKAI NENKAI KOEN YOSHISHU/MEMBRANE SOCIETY OF JAPAN. ABSTRACTS OF ANNUAL MEETING. see *CHEMISTRY — Abstracting, Bibliographies, Statistics*

NIHON MUKIN SEIBUTSU NOTO BAIOROJI GAKKAI SOKAI NITTEI TO SHOROKU/JAPANESE ASSOCIATION OF GERMFREE LIFE AND GNOTOBIOLOGY. ABSTRACTS OF MEETING. see *BIOLOGY — Abstracting, Bibliographies, Statistics*

NIHON NOGAKU BUNKEN KIJI SAKUIN/JAPANESE AGRICULTURAL SCIENCES INDEX. see *AGRICULTURE — Abstracting, Bibliographies, Statistics*

NIHON RIKUSUI GAKKAI KOEN YOSHISHU/JAPANESE SOCIETY OF LIMNOLOGY. ABSTRACTS OF MEETING. see *EARTH SCIENCES — Abstracting, Bibliographies, Statistics*

NIHON SAIBO SEIBUTSU GAKKAI TAIKAI KOEN YOSHISHU/JAPAN SOCIETY FOR CELL BIOLOGY. ABSTRACTS OF THE MEETING. see *BIOLOGY — Abstracting, Bibliographies, Statistics*

NIHON SEIKAGAKKAI KINKI SHIBU REIKAI YOSHISHU/JAPANESE BIOCHEMICAL SOCIETY. KINKI BRANCH OFFICE. ABSTRACTS OF MEETING. see *FISH AND FISHERIES — Abstracting, Bibliographies, Statistics*

NIHON SEIRI JINRUI GAKKAI TAIKAI SHOROKUSHU/JAPAN SOCIETY OF PHYSIOLOGICAL ANTHROPOLOGY. ABSTRACTS OF THE MEETING. see *BIOLOGY — Abstracting, Bibliographies, Statistics*

NIHON SENSHOKUTAI KENSA GAKKAI SHOROKUSHU/JAPANESE ASSOCIATION FOR CHROMOSOME ANALYSIS. ABSTRACT OF ANNUAL MEETING. see *BIOLOGY — Abstracting, Bibliographies, Statistics*

NIHON SHOKUBUTSU BYORI GAKKAI BAIOKONTORORU KENKYUKAI KOEN YOSHI/PHYTOPATHOLOGICAL SOCIETY OF JAPAN. ABSTRACTS OF THE MEETING OF BIOCONTROL. see *BIOLOGY — Abstracting, Bibliographies, Statistics*

NIHON TANPAKU KOGAKKAI NENKAI PUROGURAMU YOSHISHU/PROTEIN ENGINEERING SOCIETY OF JAPAN. ABSTRACTS OF THE MEETING. see *FISH AND FISHERIES — Abstracting, Bibliographies, Statistics*

NIPPON DOBUTSU KODO GAKKAI TAIKAI HAPPYO YOSHISHU/JAPAN ETHOLOGICAL SOCIETY. ABSTRACTS OF MEETING. see *BIOLOGY — Abstracting, Bibliographies, Statistics*

NO NO IGAKU SEIBUTSUGAKU KONWAKAI SHOROKU/ABSTRACTS OF CONFERENCE ON MEDICINE AND BIOLOGY OF THE BRAIN. see *BIOLOGY — Abstracting, Bibliographies, Statistics*

NOISE & VIBRATION BULLETIN. see *ENVIRONMENTAL STUDIES — Abstracting, Bibliographies, Statistics*

NONWOVENS ABSTRACTS. see *PLASTICS — Abstracting, Bibliographies, Statistics*

NORWEGIAN OFFSHORE INDEX. see *PETROLEUM AND GAS — Abstracting, Bibliographies, Statistics*

NOTE US; news from Sociological Abstracts, Linguistics and Language Behavior Abstracts, and Social Planning-Policy & Development Abstracts. see *SOCIOLOGY — Abstracting, Bibliographies, Statistics*

NOTES AND ABSTRACTS IN AMERICAN AND INTERNATIONAL EDUCATION. see *EDUCATION — Abstracting, Bibliographies, Statistics*

NOTES & COMMENT. see *ENGINEERING — Abstracting, Bibliographies, Statistics*

NOTIMEX ON C D - R O M. see *JOURNALISM — Abstracting, Bibliographies, Statistics*

NOVA ANGIOLOGICAE/NOVA ANGIOROJI. see *BIOLOGY — Abstracting, Bibliographies, Statistics*

NUCLEIC ACIDS ABSTRACTS. see *BIOLOGY — Abstracting, Bibliographies, Statistics*

NURSING ABSTRACTS. see *MEDICAL SCIENCES — Abstracting, Bibliographies, Statistics*

NUTRITION ABSTRACTS AND REVIEWS. SERIES A: HUMAN AND EXPERIMENTAL. see *NUTRITION AND DIETETICS — Abstracting, Bibliographies, Statistics*

NUTRITION ABSTRACTS AND REVIEWS. SERIES B: LIVESTOCK FEEDS AND FEEDING. see *AGRICULTURE — Abstracting, Bibliographies, Statistics*

NYA BYGGREGLER. see *BUILDING AND CONSTRUCTION — Abstracting, Bibliographies, Statistics*

NYUSEN HINYU KENKYUKAI KOEN YOSHUSHU/SOCIETY FOR MAMMARY GLANDS AND LACTATION RESEARCH. ABSTRACTS OF THE MEETING. see *MEDICAL SCIENCES — Abstracting, Bibliographies, Statistics*

O E C D ECONOMIC OUTLOOK HISTORICAL STATISTICS. see *BUSINESS AND ECONOMICS — Abstracting, Bibliographies, Statistics*

O E C D INDUSTRIAL STRUCTURE STATISTICS. see *BUSINESS AND ECONOMICS — Abstracting, Bibliographies, Statistics*

O E C S CURRENT AWARENESS BULLETIN. (Organisation of Eastern Caribbean States) see *BUSINESS AND ECONOMICS — Economic Situation And Conditions*

O J INDEX. (Official Journal of the European Communities) see *POLITICAL SCIENCE — International Relations*

O N S NURSING SCAN IN ONCOLOGY. (Oncology Nursing Society) see *MEDICAL SCIENCES — Abstracting, Bibliographies, Statistics*

O R REPORTS. (Operating Room) see *HOSPITALS — Abstracting, Bibliographies, Statistics*

OBSTETRIC ANESTHESIA DIGEST. see *MEDICAL SCIENCES — Anaesthesiology*

OCCUPATIONAL HEALTH & SAFETY CURRENT CONTENTS. see *OCCUPATIONAL HEALTH AND SAFETY — Abstracting, Bibliographies, Statistics*

OCEANIC ABSTRACTS. see *EARTH SCIENCES — Abstracting, Bibliographies, Statistics*

OCEANOGRAPHIC & MARINE RESOURCES. see *EARTH SCIENCES — Abstracting, Bibliographies, Statistics*

OCEANOGRAPHIC LITERATURE REVIEW. see *EARTH SCIENCES — Abstracting, Bibliographies, Statistics*

OCEANOGRAPHICAL SOCIETY OF JAPAN. ABSTRACTS ON THE CONFERENCE/NIHON KAIYO GAKKAI TAIKAI KOEN YOSHISHU. see *EARTH SCIENCES — Abstracting, Bibliographies, Statistics*

OFFICIAL INDEX TO THE FINANCIAL TIMES. see *BUSINESS AND ECONOMICS — Abstracting, Bibliographies, Statistics*

OIKO: THE ALTERNATIVE ENVIRONMENTAL DIGEST. see *AGRICULTURE — Abstracting, Bibliographies, Statistics*

OLD TESTAMENT ABSTRACTS. see *RELIGIONS AND THEOLOGY — Abstracting, Bibliographies, Statistics*

OLDERR'S YOUNG ADULT FICTION INDEX FOR (YEAR). see *CHILDREN AND YOUTH — Abstracting, Bibliographies, Statistics*

ONCOGENES. see *MEDICAL SCIENCES — Abstracting, Bibliographies, Statistics*

ONCOGENES AND GROWTH FACTORS ABSTRACTS. see *MEDICAL SCIENCES — Abstracting, Bibliographies, Statistics*

ABSTRACTING AND INDEXING SERVICES

ONOMA. see LINGUISTICS

OPERATIONS & PRODUCTION MANAGEMENT ABSTRACTS. see BUSINESS AND ECONOMICS — Abstracting, Bibliographies, Statistics

OPERATIONS RESEARCH - MANAGEMENT SCIENCE; international literature digest service. see BUSINESS AND ECONOMICS — Abstracting, Bibliographies, Statistics

OPERATIONS RESEARCH - MANAGEMENT SCIENCE YEARBOOK. see BUSINESS AND ECONOMICS — Abstracting, Bibliographies, Statistics

OPHTHALMIC LITERATURE. see MEDICAL SCIENCES — Abstracting, Bibliographies, Statistics

OREGON COMPREHENSIVE INDEX. see LAW — Abstracting, Bibliographies, Statistics

ORGANOMETALLIC COMPOUNDS; abstracts of literature and patents relating to compounds which contain at least metal, carbon and hydrogen atoms. see CHEMISTRY — Abstracting, Bibliographies, Statistics

ORNAMENTAL HORTICULTURE. see GARDENING AND HORTICULTURE — Abstracting, Bibliographies, Statistics

P A I S INTERNATIONAL IN PRINT. (Public Affairs Information Service, Inc.) see POLITICAL SCIENCE — Abstracting, Bibliographies, Statistics

P A I S INTERNATIONAL - JOURNALS INDEXED IN (YEAR). (Public Affairs Information Service, Inc.) see SOCIAL SCIENCES: COMPREHENSIVE WORKS

P A I S SELECT. (Public Affairs Information Service, Inc.) see POLITICAL SCIENCE — Abstracting, Bibliographies, Statistics

P A S C A L. E 11: PHYSIQUE ATOMIQUE ET MOLECULAIRE. PLASMAS. see PHYSICS — Abstracting, Bibliographies, Statistics

P A S C A L. E 12: ETAT CONDENSE. see PHYSICS — Abstracting, Bibliographies, Statistics

P A S C A L. E 13: STRUCTURE DES LIQUIDES ET DES SOLIDES - CRISTALLOGRAPHIE. see CHEMISTRY — Abstracting, Bibliographies, Statistics

P A S C A L. E 27: METHODES DE FORMATION ET TRAITEMENT DES IMAGES. see PHYSICS — Abstracting, Bibliographies, Statistics

P A S C A L. E 30: MICROSCOPIE ELECTRONIQUE ET DIFFRACTION ELECTRONIQUE. see BIOLOGY — Abstracting, Bibliographies, Statistics

P A S C A L. E 32: METROLOGIE ET APPAREILLAGE EN PHYSIQUE ET PHYSICOCHIMIE. see METROLOGY AND STANDARDIZATION — Abstracting, Bibliographies, Statistics

P A S C A L. E 33. INFORMATIQUE. see COMPUTERS — Abstracting, Bibliographies, Statistics

P A S C A L. E 34. ROBOTIQUE, AUTOMATIQUE ET AUTOMATISATION DES PROCESSUS INDUSTRIELS. see COMPUTERS — Abstracting, Bibliographies, Statistics

P A S C A L. E 36: POLLUTION DE L'EAU, DE L'AIR ET DU SOL - DECHETS - BRUIT. see ENVIRONMENTAL STUDIES — Abstracting, Bibliographies, Statistics

P A S C A L. E 48: ENVIRONNEMENT COSMIQUE TERRESTRE, ASTRONOMIE ET GEOLOGIE EXTRATERRESTRE. see EARTH SCIENCES — Abstracting, Bibliographies, Statistics

P A S C A L. E 49: METEOROLOGIE, GLACIOLOGIE, PHYSIQUE DES OCEANS. see METEOROLOGY — Abstracting, Bibliographies, Statistics

P A S C A L. E 58: GENETIQUE. see BIOLOGY — Abstracting, Bibliographies, Statistics

P A S C A L. E 61: MICROBIOLOGIE: BACTERIOLOGIE, VIROLOGIE, MYCOLOGIE, PROTOZOAIRES PATHOGENES. see BIOLOGY — Abstracting, Bibliographies, Statistics

P A S C A L. E 62: IMMUNOLOGIE. see BIOLOGY — Abstracting, Bibliographies, Statistics

P A S C A L. E 63: TOXICOLOGIE. see ENVIRONMENTAL STUDIES — Abstracting, Bibliographies, Statistics

P A S C A L. E 64: ENDOCRINOLOGIE HUMAINE ET EXPERIMENTALE. ENDOCRINOPATHIES. see MEDICAL SCIENCES — Abstracting, Bibliographies, Statistics

P A S C A L. E 65: PSYCHOLOGIE, PSYCHOPATHOLOGIE, PSYCHIATRIE. see MEDICAL SCIENCES — Abstracting, Bibliographies, Statistics

P A S C A L. E 68: GENETIQUE HUMAINE. see BIOLOGY — Abstracting, Bibliographies, Statistics

P A S C A L. E 71: OPHTALMOLOGIE. see MEDICAL SCIENCES — Abstracting, Bibliographies, Statistics

P A S C A L. E 72: OTORHINOLARYNGOLOGIE. STOMATOLOGIE. PATHOLOGIE CERVICOFACIALE. see MEDICAL SCIENCES — Abstracting, Bibliographies, Statistics

P A S C A L. E 73: DERMATOLOGIE. MALADIES SEXUELLEMENT TRANSMISSIBLES. see MEDICAL SCIENCES — Abstracting, Bibliographies, Statistics

P A S C A L. E 74: PNEUMOLOGIE. see MEDICAL SCIENCES — Abstracting, Bibliographies, Statistics

P A S C A L. E 75: CARDIOLOGIE ET APPAREIL CIRCULATOIRE. see MEDICAL SCIENCES — Abstracting, Bibliographies, Statistics

P A S C A L. E 76: GASTROENTEROLOGIE, FOIE, PANCREAS, ABDOMEN. see MEDICAL SCIENCES — Abstracting, Bibliographies, Statistics

P A S C A L. E 77: NEPHROLOGIE. VOIES URINAIRES. see MEDICAL SCIENCES — Abstracting, Bibliographies, Statistics

P A S C A L. E 78: NEUROLOGIE. see MEDICAL SCIENCES — Abstracting, Bibliographies, Statistics

P A S C A L. E 79: PATHOLOGIE ET PHYSIOLOGIE OSTEOARTICULAIRES. see MEDICAL SCIENCES — Abstracting, Bibliographies, Statistics

P A S C A L. E 80: HEMATOLOGIE. see MEDICAL SCIENCES — Abstracting, Bibliographies, Statistics

P A S C A L. E 82: GYNECOLOGIE, OBSTETRIQUE, ANDROLOGIE. see MEDICAL SCIENCES — Abstracting, Bibliographies, Statistics

P A S C A L. E 83: ANESTHESIE ET REANIMATION. see MEDICAL SCIENCES — Abstracting, Bibliographies, Statistics

P A S C A L. E 84: GENIE BIOMEDICAL. INFORMATIQUE BIOMEDICALE. see MEDICAL SCIENCES — Abstracting, Bibliographies, Statistics

P A S C A L. E 89: CANCER. see MEDICAL SCIENCES — Abstracting, Bibliographies, Statistics

P A S C A L. F 17: CHIMIE GENERALE, MINERALE ET ORGANIQUE. see CHEMISTRY — Abstracting, Bibliographies, Statistics

P A S C A L. F 23: GENIE CHIMIQUE. INDUSTRIES CHIMIQUE ET PARACHIMIQUE. see CHEMISTRY — Abstracting, Bibliographies, Statistics

P A S C A L. F 24: POLYMERES - PEINTURES - BOIS. see CHEMISTRY — Abstracting, Bibliographies, Statistics

P A S C A L. F 40: MINERALOGIE. GEOCHIMIE. GEOLOGIE EXTRATERRESTRE. see EARTH SCIENCES — Abstracting, Bibliographies, Statistics

P A S C A L. F 41: GISEMENTS METALLIQUES ET NON METALLIQUES. see MINES AND MINING INDUSTRY — Abstracting, Bibliographies, Statistics

P A S C A L. F 42: ROCHES CRISTALLINES. see EARTH SCIENCES — Abstracting, Bibliographies, Statistics

P A S C A L. F 43: ROCHES SEDIMENTAIRES. GEOLOGIE MARINE. see EARTH SCIENCES — Abstracting, Bibliographies, Statistics

P A S C A L. F 44: STRATIGRAPHIE, GEOLOGIE REGIONALE, GEOLOGIE GENERALE. see EARTH SCIENCES — Abstracting, Bibliographies, Statistics

P A S C A L. F 45: TECTONIQUE, GEOPHYSIQUE INTERNE. see EARTH SCIENCES — Abstracting, Bibliographies, Statistics

P A S C A L. F 46: HYDROLOGIE. GEOLOGIE DE L'INGENIEUR. FORMATIONS SUPERFICIELLES. see EARTH SCIENCES — Abstracting, Bibliographies, Statistics

P A S C A L. F 47: PALEONTOLOGIE. see PALEONTOLOGY — Abstracting, Bibliographies, Statistics

P A S C A L. F 52: BIOCHIMIE - BIOPHYSIQUE - MOLECULAIRE - BIOLOGIE MOLECULAIRE ET CELLULAIRE. see BIOLOGY — Abstracting, Bibliographies, Statistics

P A S C A L. F 53: ANATOMIE ET PHYSIOLOGIE DES VERTEBRES. see BIOLOGY — Abstracting, Bibliographies, Statistics

P A S C A L. F 54: REPRODUCTION DES VERTEBRES, EMBRYOLOGIE DES VERTEBRES ET DES INVERTEBRES. see MEDICAL SCIENCES — Abstracting, Bibliographies, Statistics

P A S C A L. F 55: BIOLOGIE VEGETALE. see BIOLOGY — Abstracting, Bibliographies, Statistics

P A S C A L. F 56: ECOLOGIE ANIMALE, VEGETALE ET MICROBIENNE. ETHOLOGIE ANIMALE. see BIOLOGY — Abstracting, Bibliographies, Statistics

P A S C A L. F 70: PHARMACOLOGIE. TRAITEMENTS MEDICAMENTEUX. see PHARMACY AND PHARMACOLOGY — Abstracting, Bibliographies, Statistics

P A S C A L. T 205: SCIENCES DE L'INFORMATION. DOCUMENTATION. see LIBRARY AND INFORMATION SCIENCES — Abstracting, Bibliographies, Statistics

P A S C A L. T 230: ENERGIE. see PHYSICS — Abstracting, Bibliographies, Statistics

P A S C A L. T 240: METAUX - METALLURGIE. see METALLURGY — Abstracting, Bibliographies, Statistics

P A S C A L. T 260: ZOOLOGIE FONDAMENTALE ET APPLIQUEE DES INVERTEBRES. see BIOLOGY — Abstracting, Bibliographies, Statistics

P A S C A L. T 295: BATIMENT. TRAVAUX PUBLICS. see ENGINEERING — Abstracting, Bibliographies, Statistics

P A S C A L V.4 SCIENCES DE LA TERRE. see EARTH SCIENCES — Abstracting, Bibliographies, Statistics

P L N INTERNATIONAL; international philatelic literature news. see PHILATELY — Abstracting, Bibliographies, Statistics

P N I. (Pharmaceutical News Index) see PHARMACY AND PHARMACOLOGY — Abstracting, Bibliographies, Statistics

P O P S I. (Popular Song Index) see MUSIC — Abstracting, Bibliographies, Statistics

PACKAGING SCIENCE AND TECHNOLOGY ABSTRACTS/REFERATEDIENST VERPACKUNG. see PACKAGING — Abstracting, Bibliographies, Statistics

PAGINAS DE CONTENIDO. AGROPECUARIA GENERAL. see AGRICULTURE — Abstracting, Bibliographies, Statistics

PAGINAS DE CONTENIDO. ECONOMIA AGRICOLA Y DESARROLLO RURAL. see AGRICULTURE — Abstracting, Bibliographies, Statistics

PAGINAS DE CONTENIDO. FISIOLOGIA VEGETAL, GENETICA Y BIOTECHNOLOGIA. see AGRICULTURE — Abstracting, Bibliographies, Statistics

PAGINAS DE CONTENIDO. PASTOS, PRODUCCION ANIMAL Y NUTRICION. see AGRICULTURE — Abstracting, Bibliographies, Statistics

PAGINAS DE CONTENIDO. PROTECCION DE PLANTAS. see AGRICULTURE — Abstracting, Bibliographies, Statistics

ABSTRACTING AND INDEXING SERVICES

PAGINAS DE CONTENIDO. RECURSOS NATURALES Y MEDIO AMBIENTE. see *AGRICULTURE — Abstracting, Bibliographies, Statistics*

PAINT TITLES. see *PAINTS AND PROTECTIVE COATINGS — Abstracting, Bibliographies, Statistics*

PAKISTAN SCIENCE ABSTRACTS. see *SCIENCES: COMPREHENSIVE WORKS — Abstracting, Bibliographies, Statistics*

PAKISTAN VETERINARY INDEX. see *VETERINARY SCIENCE — Abstracting, Bibliographies, Statistics*

PAPERBASE ABSTRACTS. see *PAPER AND PULP — Abstracting, Bibliographies, Statistics*

PAPIRIPARI ES NYOMDAIPARI SZAKIRODALMI TAJEKOZTATO/PAPER INDUSTRY & PRINTING ABSTRACTS. see *PAPER AND PULP — Abstracting, Bibliographies, Statistics*

PAPUA NEW GUINEA. NATIONAL STATISTICAL OFFICE. ABSTRACT OF STATISTICS. see *STATISTICS*

PAPUA NEW GUINEA. NATIONAL STATISTICAL OFFICE. CONSUMER PRICE INDEX. see *STATISTICS*

PAPUA NEW GUINEA NATIONAL BIBLIOGRAPHY. see *BIBLIOGRAPHIES*

PARASITOLOGY (SHEFFIELD). see *MEDICAL SCIENCES — Abstracting, Bibliographies, Statistics*

PATENT ABRIDGMENTS SUPPLEMENT TO THE AUSTRALIAN OFFICIAL JOURNAL OF PATENTS. see *PATENTS, TRADEMARKS AND COPYRIGHTS — Abstracting, Bibliographies, Statistics*

PATENT ABSTRACTS IN ENGLISH. see *PATENTS, TRADEMARKS AND COPYRIGHTS — Abstracting, Bibliographies, Statistics*

PATENT ABSTRACTS SUPPLEMENT TO THE AUSTRALIAN OFFICIAL JOURNAL OF PATENTS. see *PATENTS, TRADEMARKS AND COPYRIGHTS — Abstracting, Bibliographies, Statistics*

PATENTS ABSTRACTS. see *PETROLEUM AND GAS — Abstracting, Bibliographies, Statistics*

PATIENT CARE MANAGEMENT ABSTRACTS. see *MEDICAL SCIENCES — Abstracting, Bibliographies, Statistics*

PEACE RESEARCH ABSTRACTS JOURNAL. see *POLITICAL SCIENCE — Abstracting, Bibliographies, Statistics*

PEAT ABSTRACTS. see *MINES AND MINING INDUSTRY — Abstracting, Bibliographies, Statistics*

PERIODICA. INDICE DE REVISTAS LATINOAMERICANAS EN CIENCIAS. see *SCIENCES: COMPREHENSIVE WORKS — Abstracting, Bibliographies, Statistics*

PERIODICA ISLAMICA; an international contents journal. see *RELIGIONS AND THEOLOGY — Islamic*

016.05   US
PERIODICAL ABSTRACTS. (Not avail. in printed format) 1988. m. price varies. U M I (Subsidiary of: Bell & Howell Company), 300 N. Zeeb Rd., Ann Arbor, MI 48106. TEL 313-761-4700; 800-521-0600. FAX 800-864-0019. URL: http://www.umi.com. (also avail. in magnetic tape) **Document type:** abstracting/indexing.
●Also available online. Vendor(s): Knight-Ridder Information, Inc., UMI.
Also available on CD-ROM.
   Formerly: Periodical Abstracts Ondisc.

PERIODICAL SOURCE INDEX. see *HISTORY — Abstracting, Bibliographies, Statistics*

PERSONNEL & TRAINING ABSTRACTS. see *BUSINESS AND ECONOMICS — Abstracting, Bibliographies, Statistics*

PERSONNEL MANAGEMENT ABSTRACTS. see *BUSINESS AND ECONOMICS — Abstracting, Bibliographies, Statistics*

PESTICIDES ABSTRACTS. see *ENVIRONMENTAL STUDIES — Abstracting, Bibliographies, Statistics*

PETROLEUM ABSTRACTS. see *PETROLEUM AND GAS — Abstracting, Bibliographies, Statistics*

PETROLEUM - ENERGY BUSINESS NEWS INDEX. see *PETROLEUM AND GAS — Abstracting, Bibliographies, Statistics*

PHILANTHROPIC STUDIES INDEX. see *SOCIAL SERVICES AND WELFARE — Abstracting, Bibliographies, Statistics*

PHILIPPINE BUSINESS AND INDUSTRY INDEX. see *BUSINESS AND ECONOMICS — Abstracting, Bibliographies, Statistics*

PHILIPPINE SCIENCE AND TECHNOLOGY ABSTRACTS. see *SCIENCES: COMPREHENSIVE WORKS — Abstracting, Bibliographies, Statistics*

PHILOSOPHER'S INDEX; an international index to philosophical periodicals and books. see *PHILOSOPHY — Abstracting, Bibliographies, Statistics*

PHOSPHORUS IN AGRICULTURE. see *AGRICULTURE — Abstracting, Bibliographies, Statistics*

PHYSICAL EDUCATION INDEX. see *PHYSICAL FITNESS AND HYGIENE — Abstracting, Bibliographies, Statistics*

PHYSICAL REVIEW ABSTRACTS. see *PHYSICS — Abstracting, Bibliographies, Statistics*

PHYSICAL REVIEW - INDEX. see *PHYSICS — Abstracting, Bibliographies, Statistics*

PHYSICS ABSTRACTS. see *PHYSICS — Abstracting, Bibliographies, Statistics*

PHYSICS AND CHEMISTRY OF GLASSES. see *CERAMICS, GLASS AND POTTERY — Abstracting, Bibliographies, Statistics*

PHYSIOTHERAPY INDEX. see *MEDICAL SCIENCES — Abstracting, Bibliographies, Statistics*

PLANT BREEDING ABSTRACTS. see *GARDENING AND HORTICULTURE — Abstracting, Bibliographies, Statistics*

PLANT GENETIC RESOURCES ABSTRACTS. see *BIOLOGY — Abstracting, Bibliographies, Statistics*

PLANT GROWTH REGULATOR ABSTRACTS. see *AGRICULTURE — Abstracting, Bibliographies, Statistics*

PLAY INDEX. see *LITERATURE — Abstracting, Bibliographies, Statistics*

POEMFINDER. see *LITERATURE — Abstracting, Bibliographies, Statistics*

POHYBOVE USTROJI. see *MEDICAL SCIENCES — Abstracting, Bibliographies, Statistics*

016   CN   ISSN 0822-8833
AI7
POINT DE REPERE; index analytique de periodiques de langue Francaise. 1973. 10/yr. Can.$205 (foreign Can.$260). Services Documentaires Multimedia Inc., 75 Port Royal E., bureau 300, Montreal, PQ H3L 3T1, Canada. TEL 514-382-0895. FAX 514-384-9139. E-mail: info@sdm.qc.ca; URL: http://www.sdm.qc.ca. Ed. Muriel du Souich. index. circ. 650. (also avail. in microfiche) **Document type:** abstracting/indexing.
●Also available online. Vendor(s): IST-INFORMATHEQUE, Inc.
Also available on CD-ROM.
   Formed by the merger of: Periodex (ISSN 0300-3663); R A D A R (ISSN 0315-2316)

POLAR AND GLACIOLOGICAL ABSTRACTS. see *EARTH SCIENCES — Abstracting, Bibliographies, Statistics*

POLISH ARCHAEOLOGICAL ABSTRACTS. see *ARCHAEOLOGY — Abstracting, Bibliographies, Statistics*

POLISH JOURNAL OF PATHOLOGY. see *MEDICAL SCIENCES — Abstracting, Bibliographies, Statistics*

POLITICAL SCIENCE ABSTRACTS. see *POLITICAL SCIENCE — Abstracting, Bibliographies, Statistics*

POLLUTION ABSTRACTS. see *ENVIRONMENTAL STUDIES — Abstracting, Bibliographies, Statistics*

POLSKA BIBLIOGRAFIA ANALITYCZNA MECHANIKI/POLISH SCIENTIFIC ABSTRACTS ON MECHANICS. see *MACHINERY — Abstracting, Bibliographies, Statistics*

POLYMER BLENDS, ALLOYS AND INTERPENETRATING POLYMER NETWORKS ABSTRACTS. see *CHEMISTRY — Abstracting, Bibliographies, Statistics*

POLYMER CONTENTS; international current awareness publication for polymer science and engineering. see *ENGINEERING — Abstracting, Bibliographies, Statistics*

011   US   ISSN 0092-9727
AI3
POPULAR PERIODICAL INDEX. 1973. s-a. $30. Robert M. Bottorff, Ed. & Pub., Box 1156, Roslyn, PA 19001. **Document type:** abstracting/indexing.

POPULATION ABSTRACTS. see *POPULATION STUDIES — Abstracting, Bibliographies, Statistics*

POPULATION INDEX. see *POPULATION STUDIES — Abstracting, Bibliographies, Statistics*

POTATO ABSTRACTS. see *AGRICULTURE — Abstracting, Bibliographies, Statistics*

POULTRY ABSTRACTS. see *AGRICULTURE — Abstracting, Bibliographies, Statistics*

PREDI-BRIEFS. see *BUSINESS AND ECONOMICS — Abstracting, Bibliographies, Statistics*

PREDICASTS BASEBOOK. see *BUSINESS AND ECONOMICS — Abstracting, Bibliographies, Statistics*

PREDICASTS COMPANY THESAURUS. see *BUSINESS AND ECONOMICS — Abstracting, Bibliographies, Statistics*

PREDICASTS F & S INDEX EUROPE. see *BUSINESS AND ECONOMICS — Abstracting, Bibliographies, Statistics*

PREDICASTS F & S INDEX INTERNATIONAL. see *BUSINESS AND ECONOMICS — Abstracting, Bibliographies, Statistics*

PREDICASTS F & S INDEX OF CORPORATE CHANGE. see *BUSINESS AND ECONOMICS — Abstracting, Bibliographies, Statistics*

PREDICASTS F & S INDEX UNITED STATES. see *BUSINESS AND ECONOMICS — Abstracting, Bibliographies, Statistics*

PREDICASTS FORECASTS. see *BUSINESS AND ECONOMICS — Abstracting, Bibliographies, Statistics*

PREDICASTS OVERVIEW OF MARKETS AND TECHNOLOGY. see *ENGINEERING — Abstracting, Bibliographies, Statistics*

PREDICASTS SOURCE DIRECTORY. see *BUSINESS AND ECONOMICS — Abstracting, Bibliographies, Statistics*

PREHLED NOVINEK VE FONDU USTREDNI ZEMEDELSKE A LESNICKE KNIHOVNY. see *AGRICULTURE — Abstracting, Bibliographies, Statistics*

PREHLEDY POTRAVINARSKE LITERATURY/SURVEY OF FOOD LITERATURE. see *FOOD AND FOOD INDUSTRIES — Abstracting, Bibliographies, Statistics*

PREVIEWS OF HEAT AND MASS TRANSFER. see *ENGINEERING — Abstracting, Bibliographies, Statistics*

PRINTING ABSTRACTS. see *PRINTING — Abstracting, Bibliographies, Statistics*

PROGRESS IN COAL STEEL AND RELATED SOCIAL RESEARCH; a European journal. see *MINES AND MINING INDUSTRY — Abstracting, Bibliographies, Statistics*

PROMOTIONAL STRATEGIES AND TACTICS ABSTRACTS. see *BUSINESS AND ECONOMICS — Abstracting, Bibliographies, Statistics*

PROTOZOOLOGICAL ABSTRACTS. see *MEDICAL SCIENCES — Abstracting, Bibliographies, Statistics*

ABSTRACTING AND INDEXING SERVICES

PRZEGLAD PAPIERNICZY/POLISH PAPER REVIEW. see *PAPER AND PULP — Abstracting, Bibliographies, Statistics*

PSYCHOANALYTIC ABSTRACTS. see *PSYCHOLOGY — Abstracting, Bibliographies, Statistics*

PSYCHOLOGICAL ABSTRACTS. see *PSYCHOLOGY — Abstracting, Bibliographies, Statistics*

PSYCHOLOGISCHER INDEX; Referatedienst ueber die psychologische Literatur aus den deutschsprachigen Laendern. see *PSYCHOLOGY — Abstracting, Bibliographies, Statistics*

PSYSCAN: APPLIED PSYCHOLOGY. see *PSYCHOLOGY — Abstracting, Bibliographies, Statistics*

PSYSCAN: CLINICAL PSYCHOLOGY. see *PSYCHOLOGY — Abstracting, Bibliographies, Statistics*

PSYSCAN: DEVELOPMENTAL PSYCHOLOGY. see *PSYCHOLOGY — Abstracting, Bibliographies, Statistics*

PSYSCAN: LEARNING DISORDERS AND MENTAL RETARDATION. see *PSYCHOLOGY — Abstracting, Bibliographies, Statistics*

PUBLIC TELEVISION TRANSCRIPTS INDEX. see *COMMUNICATIONS — Abstracting, Bibliographies, Statistics*

PURASUMIN BUNKEN MOKUROKU/BIBLIOGRAPHY OF PLASMIN. see *MEDICAL SCIENCES — Abstracting, Bibliographies, Statistics*

QLD. & N.T. JUDGEMENTS BULLETIN. (Queensland & Northern Territory) see *LAW — Abstracting, Bibliographies, Statistics*

QUALITY CONTROL AND APPLIED STATISTICS; international literature digest service. see *EDUCATION — Abstracting, Bibliographies, Statistics*

QUALITY OF WORKING LIFE NEWS & ABSTRACTS. see *BUSINESS AND ECONOMICS — Abstracting, Bibliographies, Statistics*

016.05 020 KE ISSN 1018-1555
Z3503
QUARTERLY INDEX TO PERIODICAL LITERATURE, EASTERN AND SOUTHERN AFRICA. (Text in English) 1991. q. free. U.S. Library of Congress Office, Embassy of the United States of America, P.O. Box 30598, Nairobi, Kenya. TEL 254-2-225484. FAX 254-2-217646. E-mail: lcweb@loc.gov; URL: http://lcweb.loc.gov/. **Document type:** abstracting/indexing, government publication.
  Description: Indexes selected periodicals acquired by the Nairobi office from countries in eastern and southern Africa and the Indian Ocean, including scholarly journals, articles on subject areas not found in widely available literature, and nongovernment publications for scholars of Africa.

QUEENSLAND LEGAL INDEXES. see *LAW — Abstracting, Bibliographies, Statistics*

R A P R A ABSTRACTS. see *RUBBER — Abstracting, Bibliographies, Statistics*

R A P R A ABSTRACTS - C D - R O M. see *RUBBER — Abstracting, Bibliographies, Statistics*

R A P R A REVIEW REPORTS; expert overviews covering the science and technology of rubbers and plastics. see *PLASTICS — Abstracting, Bibliographies, Statistics*

R I C S LIBRARY INFORMATION SERVICE ABSTRACTS AND REVIEWS. (Royal Institution of Chartered Surveyors) see *ENGINEERING — Abstracting, Bibliographies, Statistics*

R I L M ABSTRACTS OF MUSIC LITERATURE. (Repertoire International de Litterature Musicale) see *MUSIC — Abstracting, Bibliographies, Statistics*

R S A P NEWSLETTER. (Research Society for American Periodicals) see *BIBLIOGRAPHIES*

RADIATION RESEARCH SOCIETY. ANNUAL MEETING. see *PHYSICS — Abstracting, Bibliographies, Statistics*

RAT FUER FORMGEBUNG. LITERATURHINWEISE. see *TECHNOLOGY: COMPREHENSIVE WORKS — Abstracting, Bibliographies, Statistics*

REACTIONS WEEKLY; rapid alerts to adverse drug experience. see *PHARMACY AND PHARMACOLOGY — Abstracting, Bibliographies, Statistics*

016.05 US
Z6941
READERS' GUIDE ABSTRACTS. CD-ROM Select edition (ISSN 1076-7142); CD-ROM Mini edition (ISSN 1082-3565) CD-ROM Full Text edition (US ISSN 1076-7134) (Print edition ceased Dec. 1996) 1984. m. (9/yr. and q. versions also avail.) $1995 (9/yr. version $1495; q. version $995). H.W. Wilson Co., 950 University Ave., Bronx, NY 10452-9978. TEL 718-588-8400; 800-367-6770. FAX 718-590-1617. TELEX 4990003 HWILSON. Ed. Robert Genovesi. film rev.; play rev. (magnetic tape) **Document type:** abstracting/indexing.
● Also available online. Vendor(s): OCLC, Wilsonline (File RDG).
Also available on CD-ROM. Producer(s): SilverPlatter Information, Inc., H.W. Wilson (WILSONDISC).
  Former titles: Readers' Guide Abstracts (Select Edition); (until 1992): Readers' Guide Abstracts (School and Public Library Edition) (ISSN 1058-1219); (until 1991): Readers' Guide Abstracts (Print Edition) (ISSN 0899-1553)
  Description: Abstracting service covering general interest publications found in the Readers' Guide to Periodical Literature.

016.05 US ISSN 0034-0464
AI3.R4
READERS' GUIDE TO PERIODICAL LITERATURE. 1900. m. (plus a. cumulation); m. on CD-ROM. $200 (CD-ROM $1095). H.W. Wilson Co., 950 University Ave., Bronx, NY 10452-9978. TEL 718-588-8400; 800-367-6770. FAX 718-590-1617. TELEX 4990003HWILSON. Ed. Jean Marra. (also avail. in magnetic tape) **Document type:** abstracting/indexing.
● Also available online. Vendor(s): OCLC, Wilsonline (File RDG).
Also available on CD-ROM. Producer(s): SilverPlatter Information, Inc., H.W. Wilson (WILSONDISC).
—CISTI; Linda Hall.
  Description: Author and subject index to selected general interest periodicals of reference value in libraries.

RECHERCHES UNIVERSITAIRES SUR L'INTEGRATION EUROPEENNE/UNIVERSITY RESEARCH ON EUROPEAN INTEGRATION. see *POLITICAL SCIENCE — Abstracting, Bibliographies, Statistics*

REFERATEBLATT ZUR RAUMENTWICKLUNG. see *PUBLIC ADMINISTRATION — Abstracting, Bibliographies, Statistics*

REFERATIVNYI ZHURNAL. ASTRONOMIYA. see *ASTRONOMY — Abstracting, Bibliographies, Statistics*

REFERATIVNYI ZHURNAL. AVIATSIONNYE I RAKETNYE DVIGATELI. see *AERONAUTICS AND SPACE FLIGHT — Abstracting, Bibliographies, Statistics*

REFERATIVNYI ZHURNAL. AVTOMATIKA I VYCHISLITEL'NAYA TEKHNIKA. see *ENGINEERING — Abstracting, Bibliographies, Statistics*

REFERATIVNYI ZHURNAL. AVTOMOBIL'NYE DOROGI. see *TRANSPORTATION — Abstracting, Bibliographies, Statistics*

REFERATIVNYI ZHURNAL. AVTOMOBIL'NYI I GORODSKOI TRANSPORT. see *TRANSPORTATION — Abstracting, Bibliographies, Statistics*

REFERATIVNYI ZHURNAL. BIOLOGIYA. see *BIOLOGY — Abstracting, Bibliographies, Statistics*

REFERATIVNYI ZHURNAL. BIOLOGIYA SEL'SKOKHOZYAISTVENNYKH ZHIVOTNYKH. see *AGRICULTURE — Abstracting, Bibliographies, Statistics*

REFERATIVNYI ZHURNAL. BIONIKA - BIOKIBERNETIKA - BIOINZHENERIYA. see *BIOLOGY — Abstracting, Bibliographies, Statistics*

REFERATIVNYI ZHURNAL. DVIGATELI VNUTRENNEGO SGORANIYA. see *TRANSPORTATION — Abstracting, Bibliographies, Statistics*

REFERATIVNYI ZHURNAL. EKOLOGIYA CHELOVEKA. see *BIOLOGY — Abstracting, Bibliographies, Statistics*

REFERATIVNYI ZHURNAL. EKONOMIKA PROMYSHLENNOSTI. see *BUSINESS AND ECONOMICS — Abstracting, Bibliographies, Statistics*

REFERATIVNYI ZHURNAL. ELEKTRONIKA. see *ELECTRONICS*

REFERATIVNYI ZHURNAL. ELEKTROTEKHNIKA. see *ELECTRONICS*

REFERATIVNYI ZHURNAL. FARMAKOLOGIYA. OBSHCHAYA FARMAKOLOGIYA NERVNOI SISTEMY. see *PHARMACY AND PHARMACOLOGY — Abstracting, Bibliographies, Statistics*

REFERATIVNYI ZHURNAL. FITOPATOLOGIYA. see *BIOLOGY — Abstracting, Bibliographies, Statistics*

REFERATIVNIYA ZHURNAL. FIZIKA. see *PHYSICS — Abstracting, Bibliographies, Statistics*

REFERATIVNYI ZHURNAL. FIZIOLOGIYA I MORFOLOGIYA CHELOVEKA I ZHIVOTNYKH. see *BIOLOGY — Abstracting, Bibliographies, Statistics*

REFERATIVNYI ZHURNAL. FOTOKINOTEKHNIKA. see *PHOTOGRAPHY — Abstracting, Bibliographies, Statistics*

REFERATIVNYI ZHURNAL. GENETIKA CHELOVEKA. see *BIOLOGY — Abstracting, Bibliographies, Statistics*

REFERATIVNYI ZHURNAL. GENETIKA I SELEKTSIYA VOZDELYVAEMYKH RASTENII. see *BIOLOGY — Abstracting, Bibliographies, Statistics*

REFERATIVNYI ZHURNAL. GEODEZIYA I AEROS'EMKA. see *EARTH SCIENCES — Abstracting, Bibliographies, Statistics*

REFERATIVNYI ZHURNAL. GEOFIZIKA. see *EARTH SCIENCES — Abstracting, Bibliographies, Statistics*

REFERATIVNYI ZHURNAL. GEOGRAFIYA. see *GEOGRAPHY — Abstracting, Bibliographies, Statistics*

REFERATIVNYI ZHURNAL. GEOLOGIYA. see *EARTH SCIENCES — Abstracting, Bibliographies, Statistics*

REFERATIVNYI ZHURNAL. GORNOE DELO. see *MINES AND MINING INDUSTRY — Abstracting, Bibliographies, Statistics*

REFERATIVNYI ZHURNAL. GORNOE I NEFTEPROMYSLOVOE MASHINOSTROENIE. see *MINES AND MINING INDUSTRY — Abstracting, Bibliographies, Statistics*

REFERATIVNYI ZHURNAL. IMMUNOLOGIYA - ALLERGOLOGIYA. see *MEDICAL SCIENCES — Abstracting, Bibliographies, Statistics*

REFERATIVNYI ZHURNAL. INFORMATIKA. see *LIBRARY AND INFORMATION SCIENCES — Abstracting, Bibliographies, Statistics*

REFERATIVNYI ZHURNAL. ISSLEDOVANIE KOSMICHESKOGO PROSTRANSTVA. see *ASTRONOMY — Abstracting, Bibliographies, Statistics*

REFERATIVNYI ZHURNAL. IZDATEL'SKOE DELO I POLIGRAFIYA. see *PRINTING — Abstracting, Bibliographies, Statistics*

REFERATIVNYI ZHURNAL. KHIMICHESKOE, NEFTEPERERABATYVAYUSCHCHEE I POLIMERNOE MASHINOSTROENIE. see *HEATING, PLUMBING AND REFRIGERATION — Abstracting, Bibliographies, Statistics*

REFERATIVNYI ZHURNAL. KHIMIYA. see *CHEMISTRY — Abstracting, Bibliographies, Statistics*

REFERATIVNYI ZHURNAL. KLINICHESKAYA FARMAKOLOGIYA. see *PHARMACY AND PHARMACOLOGY — Abstracting, Bibliographies, Statistics*

REFERATIVNYI ZHURNAL. KOMMUNAL'NOE, BYTOVOE I TORGOVOE OBORUDOVANIE. see *INTERIOR DESIGN AND DECORATION — Abstracting, Bibliographies, Statistics*

REFERATIVNYI ZHURNAL. KORROZIYA I ZASHCHITA OT KORROZII. see *METALLURGY — Abstracting, Bibliographies, Statistics*

REFERATIVNYI ZHURNAL. KOTLOSTROENIE. see *ENGINEERING — Abstracting, Bibliographies, Statistics*

REFERATIVNYI ZHURNAL. LEGKAYA PROMYSHLENNOST'. see *BUSINESS AND ECONOMICS — Abstracting, Bibliographies, Statistics*

REFERATIVNYI ZHURNAL. LESOVEDENIE I LESOVODSTVO. see *FORESTS AND FORESTRY — Abstracting, Bibliographies, Statistics*

REFERATIVNYI ZHURNAL. MASHINOSTROITEL'NYE MATERIALY, KONSTRUKTSII I RASCHET DETALI MASHIN. GIDROPRIVOD. see *ENGINEERING — Abstracting, Bibliographies, Statistics*

REFERATIVNYI ZHURNAL. MATEMATIKA. see *MATHEMATICS — Abstracting, Bibliographies, Statistics*

REFERATIVNYI ZHURNAL. MEDITSINSKAYA GEOGRAFIYA. see *MEDICAL SCIENCES — Abstracting, Bibliographies, Statistics*

REFERATIVNYI ZHURNAL. MEKHANIKA. see *ENGINEERING — Abstracting, Bibliographies, Statistics*

REFERATIVNYI ZHURNAL. METALLURGIYA. see *METALLURGY — Abstracting, Bibliographies, Statistics*

REFERATIVNYI ZHURNAL. METROLOGIYA I IZMERITEL'NAYA TEKHNIKA. see *METROLOGY AND STANDARDIZATION — Abstracting, Bibliographies, Statistics*

REFERATIVNYI ZHURNAL. NASOSOSTROENIE I KOMPRESSOROSTROENIE. KHOLODIL'NOE MASHINOSTROENIE. see *ENGINEERING — Abstracting, Bibliographies, Statistics*

REFERATIVNYI ZHURNAL. OBORUDOVANIE PISHCHEVOI PROMYSHLENNOSTI. see *FOOD AND FOOD INDUSTRIES — Abstracting, Bibliographies, Statistics*

REFERATIVNYI ZHURNAL. OBSHCHIE VOPROSY PATOLOGICHESKOI ANATOMII. see *BIOLOGY — Abstracting, Bibliographies, Statistics*

REFERATIVNYI ZHURNAL. OKHRANA I ULUCHSHENIE GORODSKOI SREDY. see *ENVIRONMENTAL STUDIES — Abstracting, Bibliographies, Statistics*

REFERATIVNYI ZHURNAL. OKHRANA PRIRODY I VOSPROIZVODSTVO PRIRODNYKH RESURSOV. see *ENVIRONMENTAL STUDIES — Abstracting, Bibliographies, Statistics*

REFERATIVNYI ZHURNAL. ONKOLOGIYA. see *MEDICAL SCIENCES — Abstracting, Bibliographies, Statistics*

REFERATIVNYI ZHURNAL. ORGANIZATSIYA I BEZOPASNOST' DOROZHNOGO DVIZHENIYA. see *TRANSPORTATION — Abstracting, Bibliographies, Statistics*

REFERATIVNYI ZHURNAL. ORGANIZATSIYA UPRAVLENIYA. see *BUSINESS AND ECONOMICS — Abstracting, Bibliographies, Statistics*

REFERATIVNYI ZHURNAL. POCHVOVEDENIE I AGROKHIMIYA. see *AGRICULTURE — Abstracting, Bibliographies, Statistics*

REFERATIVNYI ZHURNAL. POZHARNAYA OKHRANA. see *PUBLIC HEALTH AND SAFETY — Abstracting, Bibliographies, Statistics*

REFERATIVNYI ZHURNAL. PROMYSHLENNYI TRANSPORT. see *MACHINERY — Abstracting, Bibliographies, Statistics*

REFERATIVNYI ZHURNAL. RADIATSIONNAYA BIOLOGIYA. see *BIOLOGY — Abstracting, Bibliographies, Statistics*

REFERATIVNYI ZHURNAL. RAKETOSTROENIE I KOSMICHESKAYA TEKHNIKA. see *AERONAUTICS AND SPACE FLIGHT — Abstracting, Bibliographies, Statistics*

REFERATIVNYI ZHURNAL. RASTENIEVODSTVO (BIOLOGICHESKIE OSNOVY). see *AGRICULTURE — Abstracting, Bibliographies, Statistics*

REFERATIVNYI ZHURNAL. SISTEMY, PRIBORY I METODY KONTROLYA KACHESTVA OKRUZHAYUSHCHEI SREDY. see *ENVIRONMENTAL STUDIES — Abstracting, Bibliographies, Statistics*

REFERATIVNYI ZHURNAL. STROITEL'NYE I DOROZHNYE MASHINY. see *ENGINEERING — Abstracting, Bibliographies, Statistics*

REFERATIVNYI ZHURNAL. SVARKA. see *METALLURGY — Abstracting, Bibliographies, Statistics*

REFERATIVNYI ZHURNAL. TEKHNICHESKAYA KIBERNETIKA. see *COMPUTERS — Abstracting, Bibliographies, Statistics*

REFERATIVNYI ZHURNAL. TEKHNOLOGICHESKIE ASPEKTY OKHRANY OKRUZHAYUSHCHEI SREDY. see *ENVIRONMENTAL STUDIES — Abstracting, Bibliographies, Statistics*

REFERATIVNYI ZHURNAL. TEKHNOLOGIYA MASHINOSTROENIYA. see *MACHINERY — Abstracting, Bibliographies, Statistics*

REFERATIVNYI ZHURNAL. TEPLO I MASSOBMEN. see *ENERGY — Abstracting, Bibliographies, Statistics*

REFERATIVNYI ZHURNAL. TOKSIKOLOGIYA. see *PHARMACY AND PHARMACOLOGY — Abstracting, Bibliographies, Statistics*

REFERATIVNYI ZHURNAL. TRAKTORY I SEL'SKOKHOZYAISTVENNYE MASHINY I ORUDIYA. see *AGRICULTURE — Abstracting, Bibliographies, Statistics*

REFERATIVNYI ZHURNAL. TRUBOPROVODNYI TRANSPORT. see *ENGINEERING — Abstracting, Bibliographies, Statistics*

REFERATIVNYI ZHURNAL. TURBOSTROENIE. see *ENGINEERING — Abstracting, Bibliographies, Statistics*

REFERATIVNYI ZHURNAL. VODNYI TRANSPORT. see *TRANSPORTATION — Abstracting, Bibliographies, Statistics*

REFERATIVNYI ZHURNAL. VOPROSY TEKHNICHESKOGO PROGRESSA I ORGANIZATSII PROIZVODSTVA V MASHINOSTROENII. see *ENGINEERING — Abstracting, Bibliographies, Statistics*

REFERATIVNYI ZHURNAL. VOZDUSHNYI TRANSPORT. see *TRANSPORTATION — Abstracting, Bibliographies, Statistics*

REFERATIVNYI ZHURNAL. VZAIMODEISTVIE RAZNYKH VIDOV TRANSPORTA I KONTEINERNYE PEREVOZKI. see *TRANSPORTATION — Abstracting, Bibliographies, Statistics*

REFERATIVNYI ZHURNAL. YADERNYE REAKTORY. see *PHYSICS — Abstracting, Bibliographies, Statistics*

REFERATIVNYI ZHURNAL. ZHELEZNODOROZHNYI TRANSPORT. see *TRANSPORTATION — Abstracting, Bibliographies, Statistics*

REFERATOVY VYBER Z ANESTESIOLOGIE A RESUSCITACE/ABSTRACTS OF ANESTHESIOLOGY AND RESUSCITATION. see *MEDICAL SCIENCES — Abstracting, Bibliographies, Statistics*

REFERATOVY VYBER Z CHIRURGIE/ABSTRACTS OF SURGERY. see *MEDICAL SCIENCES — Abstracting, Bibliographies, Statistics*

REFERATOVY VYBER Z CHOROB INFEKCNICH/ABSTRACTS OF INFECTIOUS DISEASES. see *MEDICAL SCIENCES — Abstracting, Bibliographies, Statistics*

REFERATOVY VYBER Z DERMATOVENEROLOGIE/ABSTRACTS OF DERMATOLOGY AND VENEROLOGY. see *MEDICAL SCIENCES — Abstracting, Bibliographies, Statistics*

REFERATOVY VYBER Z GASTROENTEROLOGIE/ABSTRACTS OF GASTROENTEROLOGY. see *MEDICAL SCIENCES — Abstracting, Bibliographies, Statistics*

REFERATOVY VYBER Z KARDIOLOGIE/ABSTRACTS OF CARDIOLOGY. see *MEDICAL SCIENCES — Abstracting, Bibliographies, Statistics*

REFERATOVY VYBER Z NEUROLOGIE/ABSTRACTS OF NEUROLOGY. see *MEDICAL SCIENCES — Abstracting, Bibliographies, Statistics*

REFERATOVY VYBER Z OFTALMOLOGIE/ABSTRACTS OF OPHTHALMOLOGY. see *MEDICAL SCIENCES — Abstracting, Bibliographies, Statistics*

REFERATOVY VYBER Z PEDIATRIE/ABSTRACTS OF PEDIATRICS. see *MEDICAL SCIENCES — Abstracting, Bibliographies, Statistics*

REFERATOVY VYBER Z PNEUMOLOGIE A TUBERKULOSY/ABSTRACTS OF PNEUMOLOGY AND TUBERCULOSIS. see *MEDICAL SCIENCES — Abstracting, Bibliographies, Statistics*

REFERATOVY VYBER Z PORODNICTVI A GYNEKOLOGIE/ABSTRACTS OF OBSTETRICS AND GYNECOLOGY. see *MEDICAL SCIENCES — Abstracting, Bibliographies, Statistics*

REFERATOVY VYBER Z RADIODIAGNOSTIKY/ABSTRACTS OF RADIOLOGY. see *MEDICAL SCIENCES — Abstracting, Bibliographies, Statistics*

REFERATOVY VYBER Z REVMATOLOGIE/ABSTRACTS OF RHEUMATOLOGY. see *MEDICAL SCIENCES — Abstracting, Bibliographies, Statistics*

REFERATOVY VYBER Z UROLOGIE/ABSTRACTS OF UROLOGY. see *MEDICAL SCIENCES — Abstracting, Bibliographies, Statistics*

REFERENCE POINT: FOOD INDUSTRY ABSTRACTS. see *FOOD AND FOOD INDUSTRIES — Abstracting, Bibliographies, Statistics*

REFUGEE SURVEY QUARTERLY. see *POPULATION STUDIES — Abstracting, Bibliographies, Statistics*

RELIGION INDEX ONE: PERIODICALS. see *RELIGIONS AND THEOLOGY — Abstracting, Bibliographies, Statistics*

RELIGION INDEX TWO: MULTI-AUTHOR WORKS. see *RELIGIONS AND THEOLOGY — Abstracting, Bibliographies, Statistics*

RELIGIOUS & THEOLOGICAL ABSTRACTS. see *RELIGIONS AND THEOLOGY — Abstracting, Bibliographies, Statistics*

REOROJI TORONKAI KOEN YOSHISHU/ABSTRACTS OF SYMPOSIUM ON RHEOLOGY. see *PHYSICS — Abstracting, Bibliographies, Statistics*

REPERTOIRE INTERNATIONAL DE LA PRESSE MUSICALE. see *MUSIC — Abstracting, Bibliographies, Statistics*

REPERTORY OF ARTICLES IN THE SOUTH AFRICAN ARCHIVES JOURNAL. see *LIBRARY AND INFORMATION SCIENCES — Abstracting, Bibliographies, Statistics*

016   US
RESEARCH ALERT (PHILADELPHIA). 1965. w. $280. Institute for Scientific Information, 3501 Market St., Philadelphia, PA 19104. TEL 215-386-0100. FAX 215-386-2911. (And: Brunel Science Park, Brunel University, Uxbridge UB8 3PQ, England) **Document type:** academic/scholarly publication, bibliography.
Former titles (until 1989): Automatic Subject Citation Alert; A S C A Topics.
Description: Reports on all newly published items that match personalized parameters within research specialties in the sciences, social sciences, arts and humanities.

RESEARCH INTO HIGHER EDUCATION ABSTRACTS. see *EDUCATION — Abstracting, Bibliographies, Statistics*

ABSTRACTING AND INDEXING SERVICES

RESEARCH MANUAL OF INDUSTRIAL LAW. see *LAW — Abstracting, Bibliographies, Statistics*

RESOURCES IN EDUCATION. see *EDUCATION — Abstracting, Bibliographies, Statistics*

RESOURCES IN EDUCATION ANNUAL CUMULATION. see *EDUCATION — Abstracting, Bibliographies, Statistics*

RESUMENES ANALITICOS EN EDUCACION. see *EDUCATION — Abstracting, Bibliographies, Statistics*

REVIEW OF AGRICULTURAL ENTOMOLOGY; consisting of abstracts of reviews of current literature on applied entomology throughout the world. see *AGRICULTURE — Abstracting, Bibliographies, Statistics*

REVIEW OF AROMATIC AND MEDICINAL PLANTS. see *MEDICAL SCIENCES — Abstracting, Bibliographies, Statistics*

REVIEW OF MEDICAL AND VETERINARY ENTOMOLOGY. see *VETERINARY SCIENCE — Abstracting, Bibliographies, Statistics*

REVIEW OF MEDICAL AND VETERINARY MYCOLOGY. see *BIOLOGY — Abstracting, Bibliographies, Statistics*

REVIEW OF PLANT PATHOLOGY; consisting of abstracts and reviews of current literature on plant pathology. see *BIOLOGY — Abstracting, Bibliographies, Statistics*

REVIEW - S W A P. (Sharing with a Purpose) see *PUBLIC ADMINISTRATION — Abstracting, Bibliographies, Statistics*

REVISTA DE COMPENDIOS DE ARTICULOS DE ECONOMIA. see *BUSINESS AND ECONOMICS — Abstracting, Bibliographies, Statistics*

REZA KAGAKU/ABSTRACTS OF RIKEN SYMPOSIUM ON LASER SCIENCE. see *PHYSICS — Abstracting, Bibliographies, Statistics*

RHEOLOGY ABSTRACTS. see *PHYSICS — Abstracting, Bibliographies, Statistics*

RICE ABSTRACTS. see *AGRICULTURE — Abstracting, Bibliographies, Statistics*

RISK ABSTRACTS; a quarterly journal of abstracts, reviews and references. see *ENVIRONMENTAL STUDIES — Abstracting, Bibliographies, Statistics*

RURAL DEVELOPMENT ABSTRACTS. see *PUBLIC ADMINISTRATION — Abstracting, Bibliographies, Statistics*

S.A. & W.A. JUDGMENTS BULLETIN. (South Australian & West Australian) see *LAW — Abstracting, Bibliographies, Statistics*

S A E TECHNICAL LITERATURE ABSTRACTS. (Society of Automotive Engineers) see *TRANSPORTATION — Abstracting, Bibliographies, Statistics*

S C A D BULLETIN. (Systeme Communautaire d'Acces a la Documentation) see *LAW — Abstracting, Bibliographies, Statistics*

S D C BULLETIN. (Scientific Documentation Centre Ltd.) see *PHYSICS — Abstracting, Bibliographies, Statistics*

S I R S GOVERNMENT REPORTER ON C D - R O M. (Social Issues Resources Series) see *SOCIAL SCIENCES: COMPREHENSIVE WORKS — Abstracting, Bibliographies, Statistics*

S I R S INDEX-ONLY C D - R O M. (Social Issues Resources Series) see *SOCIAL SCIENCES: COMPREHENSIVE WORKS — Abstracting, Bibliographies, Statistics*

S I R S RESEARCHER C D - R O M. (Social Issues Resources Series) see *SOCIAL SCIENCES: COMPREHENSIVE WORKS — Abstracting, Bibliographies, Statistics*

S R G CHINA MEDIA INDEX. see *COMMUNICATIONS — Abstracting, Bibliographies, Statistics*

T A R; an abstract journal. (Scientific and Technical Aerospace Reports) see *AERONAUTICS AND SPACE FLIGHT — Abstracting, Bibliographies, Statistics*

SAFETY AND HEALTH AT WORK. see *OCCUPATIONAL HEALTH AND SAFETY — Abstracting, Bibliographies, Statistics*

SAGE FAMILY STUDIES ABSTRACTS. see *SOCIOLOGY — Abstracting, Bibliographies, Statistics*

SAGE PUBLIC ADMINISTRATION ABSTRACTS. see *PUBLIC ADMINISTRATION — Abstracting, Bibliographies, Statistics*

SAGE RACE RELATIONS ABSTRACTS. see *POLITICAL SCIENCE — Abstracting, Bibliographies, Statistics*

SAGE URBAN STUDIES ABSTRACTS. see *HOUSING AND URBAN PLANNING — Abstracting, Bibliographies, Statistics*

ST. LOUIS POST - DISPATCH INDEX. see *JOURNALISM — Abstracting, Bibliographies, Statistics*

SAN FRANCISCO CHRONICLE INDEX. see *JOURNALISM — Abstracting, Bibliographies, Statistics*

SCANP. see *BUSINESS AND ECONOMICS — Abstracting, Bibliographies, Statistics*

SCHOOL ORGANISATION & MANAGEMENT ABSTRACTS. see *EDUCATION — Abstracting, Bibliographies, Statistics*

SCHWANN C D REVIEW DIGEST - CLASSICAL; the international indexing service - a guide with excerpts to English language reviews of all music recorded on compact and video laser discs. see *MUSIC — Abstracting, Bibliographies, Statistics*

SCHWANN C D REVIEW DIGEST - JAZZ, POPULAR, ETC.; the international indexing service - a guide with excerpts to English language reviews of all music recorded on compact and video laser discs. see *MUSIC — Abstracting, Bibliographies, Statistics*

SCIDEX CUMULATIVE INDEX. see *SCIENCES: COMPREHENSIVE WORKS — Abstracting, Bibliographies, Statistics*

SCIENCE & TECHNOLOGY ABSTRACTS. see *FOOD AND FOOD INDUSTRIES — Abstracting, Bibliographies, Statistics*

SCIENCE CITATION INDEX. see *SCIENCES: COMPREHENSIVE WORKS — Abstracting, Bibliographies, Statistics*

SCIENCE FICTION AND FANTASY RESEARCH INDEX. see *LITERATURE — Abstracting, Bibliographies, Statistics*

SCIENCE OF RELIGION; abstracts and index of recent articles. see *RELIGIONS AND THEOLOGY — Abstracting, Bibliographies, Statistics*

SCIENTIFIC AND TECHNICAL PUBLICATIONS IN BULGARIA. see *SCIENCES: COMPREHENSIVE WORKS — Abstracting, Bibliographies, Statistics*

SCOOP. see *ENVIRONMENTAL STUDIES — Abstracting, Bibliographies, Statistics*

SCOTTISH ABSTRACT OF STATISTICS. see *STATISTICS*

SEA GRANT ABSTRACTS; publications from the nation's Sea Grant programs. see *EARTH SCIENCES — Abstracting, Bibliographies, Statistics*

SEARCH (DEVON); the magazine index for architecture, interiors, and housing magazines. see *ARCHITECTURE — Abstracting, Bibliographies, Statistics*

SEARCHABLE PHYSICS INFORMATION NOTICES. see *PHYSICS — Abstracting, Bibliographies, Statistics*

SECOND LANGUAGE INSTRUCTION - ACQUISITION ABSTRACTS. see *LINGUISTICS — Abstracting, Bibliographies, Statistics*

SECURITE ET SANTE AU TRAVAIL. see *OCCUPATIONAL HEALTH AND SAFETY — Abstracting, Bibliographies, Statistics*

SEED ABSTRACTS. see *AGRICULTURE — Abstracting, Bibliographies, Statistics*

SEISMOLOGICAL SOCIETY OF JAPAN. PROGRAMME AND ABSTRACTS. see *EARTH SCIENCES — Abstracting, Bibliographies, Statistics*

SELECTED ENERGY STATISTICS: SOUTH AFRICA. see *ENERGY — Abstracting, Bibliographies, Statistics*

SELECTED RAND ABSTRACTS; a biannual guide to publications of the Rand Corporation. see *SCIENCES: COMPREHENSIVE WORKS — Abstracting, Bibliographies, Statistics*

SEL'SKOE KHOZYAISTVO ZA RUBEZHOM. see *AGRICULTURE — Abstracting, Bibliographies, Statistics*

SENALES; revista bibliografica. see *PUBLISHING AND BOOK TRADE — Abstracting, Bibliographies, Statistics*

SENSORY PERCEPTION AND INFORMATION PROCESSING. see *PSYCHOLOGY — Abstracting, Bibliographies, Statistics*

SERVICIO REFERATIVO DE LA CONSTRUCCION. see *BUILDING AND CONSTRUCTION — Abstracting, Bibliographies, Statistics*

SHANTOU SPECIAL ECONOMIC ZONE YEARBOOK (YEAR). see *BUSINESS AND ECONOMICS — Abstracting, Bibliographies, Statistics*

SHOKUBUTSU SOSHIKI SAIBOU BUNSHISEIBUTSU GAKKAI TAIKAI SHINPOJUMU KOEN YOSHISHU/JAPANESE SOCIETY FOR PLANT CELL AND MOLECULAR BIOLOGY. ABSTRACTS OF THE MEETING AND SYMPOSIUM. see *BIOLOGY — Abstracting, Bibliographies, Statistics*

SHORT STORY INDEX; an index to stories in collections and periodicals. see *LITERATURE — Abstracting, Bibliographies, Statistics*

SICKNESS AND WELLNESS PUBLICATIONS. see *MEDICAL SCIENCES — Abstracting, Bibliographies, Statistics*

SIGNAL'NAYA INFORMATSIYA. AKUSTIKA. see *PHYSICS — Abstracting, Bibliographies, Statistics*

SIGNAL'NAYA INFORMATSIYA. ANALITICHESKAYA KHIMIYA. see *CHEMISTRY — Abstracting, Bibliographies, Statistics*

SIGNAL'NAYA INFORMATSIYA. ATOMNOE YADRO. see *PHYSICS — Abstracting, Bibliographies, Statistics*

SIGNAL'NAYA INFORMATSIYA. ATOMY I MOLEKULY. see *PHYSICS — Abstracting, Bibliographies, Statistics*

SIGNAL'NAYA INFORMATSIYA. CHASTITSY I POLYA. see *PHYSICS — Abstracting, Bibliographies, Statistics*

SIGNAL'NAYA INFORMATSIYA. ELEKTRICHESKIE SVOISTVA TVERDYKH TEL. see *PHYSICS — Abstracting, Bibliographies, Statistics*

SIGNAL'NAYA INFORMATSIYA. ENZIMOLOGIYA. see *BIOLOGY — Abstracting, Bibliographies, Statistics*

SIGNAL'NAYA INFORMATSIYA. FIZIKA YADERNYKH REAKTOROV. see *PHYSICS — Abstracting, Bibliographies, Statistics*

SIGNAL'NAYA INFORMATSIYA. FIZIOLOGIYA I MORFOLOGIYA CHELOVEKA I ZHIVOTNYKH: KROV' I LIMFA. see *BIOLOGY — Abstracting, Bibliographies, Statistics*

SIGNAL'NAYA INFORMATSIYA. GAZY I ZHIDKOSTI. TERMODINAMIKA I STATISTICHESKAYA FIZIKA. see *PHYSICS — Abstracting, Bibliographies, Statistics*

SIGNAL'NAYA INFORMATSIYA. KATALIZ I KATALIZATORY. see *CHEMISTRY — Abstracting, Bibliographies, Statistics*

SIGNAL'NAYA INFORMATSIYA. KHIMIYA VODY. see *CHEMISTRY — Abstracting, Bibliographies, Statistics*

SIGNAL'NAYA INFORMATSIYA. KHIMIYA VYSOKIKH ENERGII. see *CHEMISTRY — Abstracting, Bibliographies, Statistics*

SIGNAL'NAYA INFORMATSIYA. KOMPOZITSIONNYE MATERIALY. see *METALLURGY — Abstracting, Bibliographies, Statistics*

ABSTRACTING AND INDEXING SERVICES

SIGNAL'NAYA INFORMATSIYA. KORROZIYA I ZASHCHITA OT KORROZII. see METALLURGY — Abstracting, Bibliographies, Statistics

SIGNAL'NAYA INFORMATSIYA. LAKI - KRASKI - ORGANICHESKIE POKRYTIYA. see PAINTS AND PROTECTIVE COATINGS — Abstracting, Bibliographies, Statistics

SIGNAL'NAYA INFORMATSIYA. MAGNITNYE SVOISTVA TVERDYKH TEL. see PHYSICS — Abstracting, Bibliographies, Statistics

SIGNAL'NAYA INFORMATSIYA. NAPOLNENNYE I ARMIROVANNYE PLASTIKI. see CHEMISTRY — Abstracting, Bibliographies, Statistics

SIGNAL'NAYA INFORMATSIYA. NEIROPEPTIDY. see MEDICAL SCIENCES — Abstracting, Bibliographies, Statistics

SIGNAL'NAYA INFORMATSIYA. NELINEINAYA OPTIKA I KVANTOVAYA ELEKTRONIKA. see PHYSICS — Abstracting, Bibliographies, Statistics

SIGNAL'NAYA INFORMATSIYA. OCHISTKA I UTILIZATSIYA OTKHODOV KHIMICHESKIKH PROIZVODSTV. see CHEMISTRY — Abstracting, Bibliographies, Statistics

SIGNAL'NAYA INFORMATSIYA. OPTIKA. see PHYSICS — Abstracting, Bibliographies, Statistics

SIGNAL'NAYA INFORMATSIYA. POVERKHNOST'. see PHYSICS — Abstracting, Bibliographies, Statistics

SIGNAL'NAYA INFORMATSIYA. RADIOFIZIKA I FIZICHESKIE OSNOVY ELEKTRONIKI. see ELECTRONICS — Abstracting, Bibliographies, Statistics

SIGNAL'NAYA INFORMATSIYA. SORBENTY. POVERKHNOSTNO-AKTIVNYE VESHCHESTVA. see CHEMISTRY — Abstracting, Bibliographies, Statistics

SIGNAL'NAYA INFORMATSIYA. STRUKTURA I DINAMIKA RESHETKI TVERDYKH TEL. see PHYSICS — Abstracting, Bibliographies, Statistics

SIGNAL'NAYA INFORMATSIYA. TEKHNIKA BEZOPASNOSTI. SANITARNAYA TEKHNIKA. see OCCUPATIONAL HEALTH AND SAFETY — Abstracting, Bibliographies, Statistics

SIGNAL'NAYA INFORMATSIYA. TOKSIKOLOGIYA LEKARSTVENNAYA. see PHARMACY AND PHARMACOLOGY — Abstracting, Bibliographies, Statistics

015.5957 SI ISSN 0377-7928
AI3
SINGAPORE PERIODICALS INDEX. (Text in Chinese, English, Malay) 1969. a. price varies. National Library Board, 91 Stamford Rd., Singapore 1778896, Singapore. TEL 65-332-3683. FAX 65-332-3684. Ed. R. Chandran. circ. 250. Document type: abstracting/indexing.
●Also available on CD-ROM.

SMALL ANIMALS. see VETERINARY SCIENCE — Abstracting, Bibliographies, Statistics

SOCIAL SCIENCES CITATION INDEX. see SOCIAL SCIENCES: COMPREHENSIVE WORKS — Abstracting, Bibliographies, Statistics

SOCIAL SCIENCES INDEX. see SOCIAL SCIENCES: COMPREHENSIVE WORKS — Abstracting, Bibliographies, Statistics

SOCIAL SERVICE ABSTRACTS. see SOCIAL SERVICES AND WELFARE — Abstracting, Bibliographies, Statistics

SOCIAL WORK ABSTRACTS. see SOCIAL SERVICES AND WELFARE — Abstracting, Bibliographies, Statistics

SOCIETY FOR RANGE MANAGEMENT. INTERNATIONAL RANGELAND CONGRESS. ABSTRACTS OF PAPERS. see AGRICULTURE — Abstracting, Bibliographies, Statistics

SOCIETY OF INDEXERS. OCCASIONAL PAPERS ON INDEXING. see LIBRARY AND INFORMATION SCIENCES

SOCIETY OF MANUFACTURING ENGINEERS. TECHNICAL DIGEST; abstracts of technical papers on microfiche and hard copy. see TECHNOLOGY: COMPREHENSIVE WORKS — Abstracting, Bibliographies, Statistics

SOCIETY OF PROPERTY OF PHYSICAL CHEMISTRY. ABSTRACTS OF MEETING/BUSSEI BUTSURI KAGAKU KENKYUKAI KOEN YOSHISHU. see CHEMISTRY — Abstracting, Bibliographies, Statistics

SOCIOLOGICAL ABSTRACTS. see SOCIOLOGY — Abstracting, Bibliographies, Statistics

SOCIOLOGY OF EDUCATION ABSTRACTS. see EDUCATION — Abstracting, Bibliographies, Statistics

SOILS AND FERTILIZERS - ABSTRACTS OF WORLD LITERATURE. see AGRICULTURE — Abstracting, Bibliographies, Statistics

SOLID STATE AND SUPERCONDUCTIVITY ABSTRACTS. see PHYSICS — Abstracting, Bibliographies, Statistics

SORGHUM AND MILLETS. see AGRICULTURE — Abstracting, Bibliographies, Statistics

SOTSIOLOGIYA: OTECHESTVENNAYA I ZARUBEZHNAYA LITERATURA; referativnyi zhurnal. see SOCIOLOGY — Abstracting, Bibliographies, Statistics

015 FJ ISSN 1011-5110
SOUTH PACIFIC PERIODICALS INDEX. 1974. irreg. $20. Pacific Information Centre, University of the South Pacific, G.P.O. Box 1168, Suva, Fiji. TEL 313900. FAX 300830. E-mail: mamtora__j@usp.ac.fj. Ed. Jayshree Mamtora. circ. 170. (also avail. in microform; back issues avail.) Document type: abstracting/indexing.
Formerly (until 1978): Bibliography of Periodical Articles Relating to the South Pacific.
Description: Articles concerned with the South Pacific regardless of origin or language.

SOUTHEAST - EAST ASIAN ENGLISH PUBLICATIONS IN PRINT. see PUBLISHING AND BOOK TRADE — Abstracting, Bibliographies, Statistics

SOYABEAN ABSTRACTS. see AGRICULTURE — Abstracting, Bibliographies, Statistics

SPANISH CULTURAL INDEX. see LITERARY AND POLITICAL REVIEWS — Abstracting, Bibliographies, Statistics

SPEECH INDEX; an index to 259 collections of orations and speeches for various occasions. see LINGUISTICS — Abstracting, Bibliographies, Statistics

SPELEOLOGICAL ABSTRACTS/BULLETIN BIBLIOGRAPHIQUE SPELEOLOGIQUE. see EARTH SCIENCES — Abstracting, Bibliographies, Statistics

SPORTS DOCUMENTATION MONTHLY BULLETIN. see EDUCATION — Abstracting, Bibliographies, Statistics

SPORTS PHYSIOLOGY AND MEDICINE. see MEDICAL SCIENCES — Abstracting, Bibliographies, Statistics

SPORTSEARCH. see SPORTS AND GAMES — Abstracting, Bibliographies, Statistics

015 CE
SRI LANKA PERIODICALS INDEX. (Text in English and Sinhalese) 1969. s-a. free on exchange to libraries and research institutes. Department of National Museums, Box 854, Sir Marcus Fernando Mawatha, Colombo 7, Sri Lanka. bibl. Document type: abstracting/indexing.
Formerly (until vol.5): Ceylon Periodical Index.

SRI LANKA SCIENCE INDEX. see SCIENCES: COMPREHENSIVE WORKS — Abstracting, Bibliographies, Statistics

STAMPS, COINS, POSTCARDS & RELATED MATERIALS; a directory of periodicals. see NUMISMATICS — Abstracting, Bibliographies, Statistics

STATE ACADEMIES OF SCIENCE ABSTRACTS. see SCIENCES: COMPREHENSIVE WORKS — Abstracting, Bibliographies, Statistics

STATE BANK OF PAKISTAN. INDEX NUMBERS OF STOCK EXCHANGE SECURITIES. see BUSINESS AND ECONOMICS — Abstracting, Bibliographies, Statistics

STATE EDUCATION JOURNAL INDEX; an annotated index to materials in the field of education. see EDUCATION — Abstracting, Bibliographies, Statistics

STATISTICAL REFERENCE INDEX. see STATISTICS

STATISTICAL THEORY AND METHOD ABSTRACTS. see MATHEMATICS — Abstracting, Bibliographies, Statistics

STEUER UND WIRTSCHAFT INTERNATIONAL. see BUSINESS AND ECONOMICS — Abstracting, Bibliographies, Statistics

STEUER UND WIRTSCHAFTSKARTEI. see BUSINESS AND ECONOMICS — Abstracting, Bibliographies, Statistics

STUDIA JEZYKOZNAWCZE. see LINGUISTICS — Abstracting, Bibliographies, Statistics

STUDIES ON WOMEN ABSTRACTS. see WOMEN'S STUDIES — Abstracting, Bibliographies, Statistics

SUBJECT INDEX TO ARTICLES IN NEWSPAPERS IN MAURITIUS. see JOURNALISM — Abstracting, Bibliographies, Statistics

SUDAN SCIENCE ABSTRACTS. see SCIENCES: COMPREHENSIVE WORKS — Abstracting, Bibliographies, Statistics

SUGAR INDUSTRY ABSTRACTS. see FOOD AND FOOD INDUSTRIES — Abstracting, Bibliographies, Statistics

SUOMEN SANOMALEHTIEN MIKROFILMIT/MICROFILMED NEWSPAPERS OF FINLAND. see JOURNALISM — Abstracting, Bibliographies, Statistics

SURFACE SCIENCE LETTERS. see PHYSICS — Abstracting, Bibliographies, Statistics

SURFACE TREATMENT TECHNOLOGY ABSTRACTS. see METALLURGY — Abstracting, Bibliographies, Statistics

SURFACE WAVE ABSTRACTS. see PHYSICS — Abstracting, Bibliographies, Statistics

SURVEY OF ANESTHESIOLOGY. see MEDICAL SCIENCES — Abstracting, Bibliographies, Statistics

SURVEY OF OPHTHALMOLOGY. see MEDICAL SCIENCES — Abstracting, Bibliographies, Statistics

SYMPOSIUM ON RADIOCHEMISTRY. ABSTRACTS OF PAPERS/HOSHA KAGAKU TORONKAI KOEN YOKOSHU. see CHEMISTRY — Abstracting, Bibliographies, Statistics

T O M. (Text on Microfilm) see EDUCATION — Abstracting, Bibliographies, Statistics

T R I S ELECTRONIC BIBLIOGRAPHIC DATA BASE. (Transportation Research Information Services) see TRANSPORTATION — Abstracting, Bibliographies, Statistics

TECHNICAL EDUCATION & TRAINING ABSTRACTS. see EDUCATION — Abstracting, Bibliographies, Statistics

TECHNICAL LITERATURE ABSTRACTS. see PETROLEUM AND GAS — Abstracting, Bibliographies, Statistics

TECHNICAL LITERATURE ABSTRACTS: CATALYSTS - ZEOLITES. see CHEMISTRY — Abstracting, Bibliographies, Statistics

TECHNICAL LITERATURE ABSTRACTS: FUEL REFORMULATION. see CHEMISTRY — Abstracting, Bibliographies, Statistics

TECHNICAL LITERATURE ABSTRACTS: HEALTH & ENVIRONMENT. see MEDICAL SCIENCES — Abstracting, Bibliographies, Statistics

TECHNICAL LITERATURE ABSTRACTS: OILFIELD CHEMICALS. see PETROLEUM AND GAS — Abstracting, Bibliographies, Statistics

ABSTRACTING AND INDEXING SERVICES

TECHNICAL LITERATURE ABSTRACTS: PETROLEUM REFINING & PETROCHEMICALS. see *PETROLEUM AND GAS* — *Abstracting, Bibliographies, Statistics*

TECHNICAL LITERATURE ABSTRACTS: PETROLEUM SUBSTITUTES. see *PETROLEUM AND GAS* — *Abstracting, Bibliographies, Statistics*

TECHNICAL LITERATURE ABSTRACTS: TRANSPORTATION & STORAGE. see *TRANSPORTATION* — *Abstracting, Bibliographies, Statistics*

TECHNICAL LITERATURE ABSTRACTS: TRIBOLOGY. see *CHEMISTRY* — *Abstracting, Bibliographies, Statistics*

TECHNOLOGY UPDATE (FOSTER CITY). see *TECHNOLOGY: COMPREHENSIVE WORKS* — *Abstracting, Bibliographies, Statistics*

TELEVISION NEWS INDEX AND ABSTRACTS. see *COMMUNICATIONS* — *Abstracting, Bibliographies, Statistics*

TEXTILE TECHNOLOGY DIGEST. see *TEXTILE INDUSTRIES AND FABRICS* — *Abstracting, Bibliographies, Statistics*

THAI ABSTRACTS, SERIES A. SCIENCE AND TECHNOLOGY. see *SCIENCES: COMPREHENSIVE WORKS* — *Abstracting, Bibliographies, Statistics*

THANATOLOGY ABSTRACTS. see *PSYCHOLOGY* — *Abstracting, Bibliographies, Statistics*

THEORETICAL CHEMICAL ENGINEERING. see *ENGINEERING* — *Abstracting, Bibliographies, Statistics*

THESAURUS OF E R I C DESCRIPTORS. see *EDUCATION* — *Abstracting, Bibliographies, Statistics*

THESIS ABSTRACTS. see *AGRICULTURE* — *Abstracting, Bibliographies, Statistics*

TIDSSKRIFTINDEKS FOR SKOLEBIBLIOTEKER. see *BIBLIOGRAPHIES*

TIMES INDEX. see *JOURNALISM* — *Abstracting, Bibliographies, Statistics*

THE TIMES LITERARY SUPPLEMENT INDEX. see *LITERATURE* — *Abstracting, Bibliographies, Statistics*

TITLE NEWS. see *INSURANCE* — *Abstracting, Bibliographies, Statistics*

TOBACCO ABSTRACTS; world literature on Nicotiana. see *TOBACCO* — *Abstracting, Bibliographies, Statistics*

TOBACCO & HEALTH ABSTRACTS. see *TOBACCO* — *Abstracting, Bibliographies, Statistics*

TOP MANAGEMENT ABSTRACTS. see *BUSINESS AND ECONOMICS* — *Abstracting, Bibliographies, Statistics*

TOPICATOR; classified article guide to the advertising/communications/marketing periodical press. see *ADVERTISING AND PUBLIC RELATIONS* — *Abstracting, Bibliographies, Statistics*

TOXICOLOGY ABSTRACTS. see *PHARMACY AND PHARMACOLOGY* — *Abstracting, Bibliographies, Statistics*

TRADESCOPE. see *BUSINESS AND ECONOMICS* — *Trade And Industrial Directories*

TRANSIT PLANNING AND RESEARCH REPORTS; an annotated bibliography. see *TRANSPORTATION* — *Abstracting, Bibliographies, Statistics*

TRAVEL & TOURISM INDEX. see *TRAVEL AND TOURISM* — *Abstracting, Bibliographies, Statistics*

TROPICAL OIL SEEDS. see *AGRICULTURE* — *Abstracting, Bibliographies, Statistics*

TSETSE AND TRYPANOSOMIASIS INFORMATION QUARTERLY. see *BIOLOGY* — *Abstracting, Bibliographies, Statistics*

TUDOMANYOS ES MUSZAKI TAJEKOZTATAS/SCIENTIFIC AND TECHNICAL INFORMATION. see *LIBRARY AND INFORMATION SCIENCES* — *Abstracting, Bibliographies, Statistics*

TURING INSTITUTE ABSTRACTS IN ARTIFICIAL INTELLIGENCE. see *COMPUTERS* — *Abstracting, Bibliographies, Statistics*

TURKISH CHAMBER OF CIVIL ENGINEERS. DIGEST (YEAR); extended summaries from Teknik Dergi/Technical Journal. see *ENGINEERING* — *Abstracting, Bibliographies, Statistics*

U I T P BIBLIO-EXPRESS. (International Union of Public Transport) see *TRANSPORTATION* — *Abstracting, Bibliographies, Statistics*

U N D O C: CURRENT INDEX. (United Nations Documents) see *POLITICAL SCIENCE* — *Abstracting, Bibliographies, Statistics*

U S A TODAY INDEX. see *JOURNALISM* — *Abstracting, Bibliographies, Statistics*

015.73053　　　US　　ISSN 1076-3163
Z1223.Z7
U S GOVERNMENT PERIODICALS INDEX. 1970-1987; resumed 1992. q. (with a. cumulation). $795 (CD-ROM $795) (effective 1995). Congressional Information Service, Inc., A member of the LEXIS-NEXIS family, 4520 East-West Hwy., Bethesda, MD 20814-3389. TEL 301-654-1550; 800-638-8380. FAX 301-654-4033. E-mail: info@cispubs.com; URL: http://www.cispubs.com. Ed. John Heffernan. **Document type**: abstracting/indexing.
●Also available on CD-ROM.
   Supersedes (1970-1987): Index to U S Government Periodicals (ISSN 0098-4604)
   Description: Provides a title, subject and author index to more than 180 periodicals issued by the U.S. federal government.

UNIFORM COMMERCIAL CODE LAW JOURNAL. see *LAW* — *Abstracting, Bibliographies, Statistics*

U.S. NATIONAL CENTER FOR HEALTH STATISTICS. CATALOG OF PUBLICATIONS. see *PUBLIC HEALTH AND SAFETY* — *Abstracting, Bibliographies, Statistics*

UNIVERSITY OF DAYTON. SCHOOL OF EDUCATION. ABSTRACTS OF RESEARCH PROJECTS. see *EDUCATION* — *Abstracting, Bibliographies, Statistics*

URBAN ABSTRACTS. see *PUBLIC ADMINISTRATION* — *Abstracting, Bibliographies, Statistics*

URBAN AFFAIRS ABSTRACTS. see *PUBLIC ADMINISTRATION* — *Abstracting, Bibliographies, Statistics*

VALIDATED ENGINEERING DATA INDEX. see *ENGINEERING* — *Abstracting, Bibliographies, Statistics*

VALLALATSZERVEZESI ES IPARGAZDASAGI SZAKIRODALMI TAJEKOZTATO/INDUSTRIAL MANAGEMENT ABSTRACTS. see *BUSINESS AND ECONOMICS* — *Abstracting, Bibliographies, Statistics*

VEGYIPARI SZAKIRODALMI TAJEKOZTATO/CHEMICAL ENGINEERING ABSTRACTS. see *CHEMISTRY* — *Abstracting, Bibliographies, Statistics*

VEREIN DEUTSCHER INGENIEURE. INFORMATIONSDIENST. INSTANDHALTUNG. see *ENGINEERING* — *Abstracting, Bibliographies, Statistics*

VERENIGING VOOR OPPERVLAKTETECHNIEKEN VAN MATERIALEN. DOCUMENTATIESERVICE. see *METALLURGY* — *Abstracting, Bibliographies, Statistics*

VERFAHRENSTECHNISCHE BERICHTE/CHEMICAL AND PROCESS ENGINEERING ABSTRACTS. see *ENGINEERING* — *Abstracting, Bibliographies, Statistics*

050 011　　　US　　ISSN 0042-4439
Z1231.P2
VERTICAL FILE INDEX; guide to pamphlets and references to current topics. 1932. m. (Sep.-July). $50. H.W. Wilson Co., 950 University Ave., Bronx, NY 10452. TEL 718-588-8400; 800-367-6770. FAX 718-590-1617. TELEX 4990003 HWILSON. Ed. Eloise Morehouse. **Document type**: abstracting/indexing.
●Also available online. Vendor(s): Wilsonline (File VFI).
—Linda Hall.

VETERINARY BULLETIN; a monthly abstract journal on veterinary science. see *VETERINARY SCIENCE* — *Abstracting, Bibliographies, Statistics*

VICTORIAN JUDGMENTS BULLETIN. see *LAW* — *Abstracting, Bibliographies, Statistics*

VICTORIAN LAW REPORTS CONSOLIDATED INDEX AND TABLES (YEARS). CUMULATIVE SUPPLEMENT. see *LAW* — *Abstracting, Bibliographies, Statistics*

VICTORIAN STATUTES ANNOTATIONS. see *LAW* — *Abstracting, Bibliographies, Statistics*

VIKRAM RESEARCH GUIDE. see *SOCIAL SCIENCES: COMPREHENSIVE WORKS* — *Abstracting, Bibliographies, Statistics*

VIOLENCE & ABUSE ABSTRACTS; current literature in interpersonal violence. see *SOCIOLOGY* — *Abstracting, Bibliographies, Statistics*

VIROLOGY AND AIDS ABSTRACTS. see *MEDICAL SCIENCES* — *Abstracting, Bibliographies, Statistics*

VISION (SHEFFIELD). see *MEDICAL SCIENCES* — *Abstracting, Bibliographies, Statistics*

VITAL TEXTILE LITERATURE. see *TEXTILE INDUSTRIES AND FABRICS* — *Abstracting, Bibliographies, Statistics*

VITIS; Berichte ueber Rebenforschung mit Dokumentation der Weinbauforschung. see *BEVERAGES* — *Abstracting, Bibliographies, Statistics*

VITIS - VITICULTURE AND OENOLOGY ABSTRACTS. see *AGRICULTURE* — *Abstracting, Bibliographies, Statistics*

VOSTOKOVEDENIE I AFRIKANISTIKA: ZARUBEZHNAYA LITERATURA; referativnyi zhurnal. see *ORIENTAL STUDIES* — *Abstracting, Bibliographies, Statistics*

THE WASHINGTON POST INDEX. see *JOURNALISM* — *Abstracting, Bibliographies, Statistics*

THE WASHINGTON TIMES INDEX. see *JOURNALISM* — *Abstracting, Bibliographies, Statistics*

WATER AND ENERGY ABSTRACTS. see *WATER RESOURCES* — *Abstracting, Bibliographies, Statistics*

WATER RESOURCES ABSTRACTS (BETHESDA). see *WATER RESOURCES* — *Abstracting, Bibliographies, Statistics*

WATER RESOURCES ABSTRACTS (C D - R O M). see *WATER RESOURCES* — *Abstracting, Bibliographies, Statistics*

WATER RESOURCES WORLDWIDE. see *WATER RESOURCES* — *Abstracting, Bibliographies, Statistics*

WEED ABSTRACTS; compiled from world literature. see *AGRICULTURE* — *Abstracting, Bibliographies, Statistics*

WEED SCIENCE SOCIETY OF AMERICA. ABSTRACTS. see *AGRICULTURE* — *Abstracting, Bibliographies, Statistics*

WELDASEARCH SELECT; selective dissemination of information. see *METALLURGY* — *Abstracting, Bibliographies, Statistics*

WELDING ABSTRACTS. see *METALLURGY* — *Abstracting, Bibliographies, Statistics*

WESTERN SOCIETY OF PERIODONTOLOGY. JOURNAL. PERIODONTAL ABSTRACTS. see *MEDICAL SCIENCES* — *Abstracting, Bibliographies, Statistics*

WHEAT, BARLEY AND TRITICALE ABSTRACTS. see *AGRICULTURE — Abstracting, Bibliographies, Statistics*

WICKS SUBJECT INDEX OF COMMONWEALTH LEGISLATION. see *LAW — Abstracting, Bibliographies, Statistics*

WILDLIFE REVIEW (FORT COLLINS); an indexing service for wildlife management. see *CONSERVATION — Abstracting, Bibliographies, Statistics*

WILDLIFE WORLDWIDE. see *BIOLOGY — Abstracting, Bibliographies, Statistics*

WILSON ABSTRACTS. see *ART — Abstracting, Bibliographies, Statistics*

WILSON APPLIED SCIENCE AND TECHNOLOGY ABSTRACTS. see *ENGINEERING — Abstracting, Bibliographies, Statistics*

WILSON BUSINESS ABSTRACTS. see *BUSINESS AND ECONOMICS — Abstracting, Bibliographies, Statistics*

WILSON EDUCATION ABSTRACTS. see *EDUCATION — Abstracting, Bibliographies, Statistics*

WILSON GENERAL SCIENCE ABSTRACTS. see *SCIENCES: COMPREHENSIVE WORKS — Abstracting, Bibliographies, Statistics*

WILSON HUMANITIES ABSTRACTS. see *HUMANITIES: COMPREHENSIVE WORKS — Abstracting, Bibliographies, Statistics*

WILSON SOCIAL SCIENCES ABSTRACTS. see *SOCIAL SCIENCES: COMPREHENSIVE WORKS — Abstracting, Bibliographies, Statistics*

WIND ENERGY ABSTRACTS; the international wind power abstracts journal. see *ENERGY — Abstracting, Bibliographies, Statistics*

WOMEN STUDIES ABSTRACTS. see *WOMEN'S STUDIES — Abstracting, Bibliographies, Statistics*

WOMEN'S STUDIES INDEX (YEAR). see *WOMEN'S STUDIES — Abstracting, Bibliographies, Statistics*

WORLD AGRICULTURAL ECONOMICS AND RURAL SOCIOLOGY ABSTRACTS; abstracts of world literature. see *AGRICULTURE — Abstracting, Bibliographies, Statistics*

WORLD CERAMICS ABSTRACTS. see *CERAMICS, GLASS AND POTTERY — Abstracting, Bibliographies, Statistics*

WORLD PUBLISHING MONITOR. see *COMPUTERS — Abstracting, Bibliographies, Statistics*

WORLD REPORT ON TECHNICAL ADVANCEMENT. see *TECHNOLOGY: COMPREHENSIVE WORKS — Abstracting, Bibliographies, Statistics*

WORLD SURFACE COATING ABSTRACTS. see *PAINTS AND PROTECTIVE COATINGS — Abstracting, Bibliographies, Statistics*

WORLD TEXTILE ABSTRACTS. see *TEXTILE INDUSTRIES AND FABRICS — Abstracting, Bibliographies, Statistics*

WORLD TRANSLATIONS INDEX. see *SCIENCES: COMPREHENSIVE WORKS — Abstracting, Bibliographies, Statistics*

WORLDCASTS: PRODUCT EDITION. see *BUSINESS AND ECONOMICS — Abstracting, Bibliographies, Statistics*

WORLDCASTS: REGIONAL EDITION. see *BUSINESS AND ECONOMICS — Abstracting, Bibliographies, Statistics*

X SEN BUNSEKI TORONKAI KOEN YOSHISHU/ABSTRACTS OF ANNUAL CONFERENCE ON X-RAY CHEMICAL ANALYSIS. see *CHEMISTRY — Abstracting, Bibliographies, Statistics*

YAZYKOZNANIE: OTECHESTVENNAYA LITERATURA; referativnyi zhurnal. see *LINGUISTICS — Abstracting, Bibliographies, Statistics*

YAZYKOZNANIE: ZARUBEZHNAYA LITERATURA; referativnyi zhurnal. see *LINGUISTICS — Abstracting, Bibliographies, Statistics*

YIXUE WENZHAI/MEDICAL ABSTRACTS. see *MEDICAL SCIENCES — Abstracting, Bibliographies, Statistics*

YUKI HANNO KAGAKU TORONKAI KOEN YOKOSHU/ABSTRACTS OF SYMPOSIUM ON ORGANIC REACTIONS. see *CHEMISTRY — Abstracting, Bibliographies, Statistics*

ZAMBIA SCIENCE ABSTRACTS. see *SCIENCES: COMPREHENSIVE WORKS — Abstracting, Bibliographies, Statistics*

011.29171 US ISSN 1066-4858
DK1
ZARUBEZHNAYA PERIODICHESKAYA PECHAT' NA RUSSKOM YAZYKE. (Text in Russian) 1981. q. $25 (foreign $35) to individuals; institutions $40 (foreign $50). Informatics & Prognostics, 1400 Shattuck Ave., Ste. 7-no.10, Berkeley, CA 94709. TEL 510-236-2935. FAX 510-233-0341. Ed. Leonid Khotin. adv. contact: Galina Gezen. circ. 150 (paid). **Document type:** abstracting/indexing.
  Formerly (until 1992): Abstracts of Soviet and East European Emigre Periodical Literature (ISSN 0738-2707)

ZEITSCHRIFT FUER LEBENSMITTEL-UNTERSUCHUNG UND -FORSCHUNG A; international journal of food research and technology. see *FOOD AND FOOD INDUSTRIES — Abstracting, Bibliographies, Statistics*

ZEITSCHRIFT FUER LEBENSMITTEL-UNTERSUCHUNG UND -FORSCHUNG B; Referate und Lebensmittelrecht. see *FOOD AND FOOD INDUSTRIES — Abstracting, Bibliographies, Statistics*

ZEITSCHRIFT FUER PFLANZENERNAEHRUNG UND BODENKUNDE/JOURNAL OF PLANT NUTRITION AND SOIL SCIENCE. see *BIOLOGY — Abstracting, Bibliographies, Statistics*

ZEITSCHRIFTENINHALTSDIENST THEOLOGIE; indices theologici. see *RELIGIONS AND THEOLOGY — Abstracting, Bibliographies, Statistics*

ZENTRALBLATT FUER GEOLOGIE UND PALAEONTOLOGIE. TEIL I: ALLGEMEINE, ANGEWANDTE, REGIONALE UND HISTORISCHE GEOLOGIE. see *EARTH SCIENCES — Abstracting, Bibliographies, Statistics*

ZENTRALBLATT FUER GEOLOGIE UND PALAEONTOLOGIE. TEIL II: PALAEONTOLOGIE. see *PALEONTOLOGY — Abstracting, Bibliographies, Statistics*

ZENTRALBLATT FUER JUGENDRECHT; Jugend und Familie - Jugendhilfe - Jugendgerichtshilfe. see *LAW — Abstracting, Bibliographies, Statistics*

ZENTRALBLATT FUER MATHEMATIK UND IHRE GRENZGEBIETE/MATHEMATICS ABSTRACTS. see *MATHEMATICS — Abstracting, Bibliographies, Statistics*

ZENTRALBLATT FUER MINERALOGIE. TEIL I: KRISTALLOGRAPHIE, MINERALOGIE. see *MINES AND MINING INDUSTRY — Abstracting, Bibliographies, Statistics*

ZENTRALBLATT FUER MINERALOGIE. TEIL II: PETROGRAPHIE, TECHNISCHE MINERALOGIE, GEOCHEMIE UND LAGERSTAETTENKUNDE. see *MINES AND MINING INDUSTRY — Abstracting, Bibliographies, Statistics*

ZEORAITO KENKYU HAPPYOKAI KOEN YOKOSHU/JAPAN ASSOCIATION OF ZEOLITE. ABSTRACTS OF ANNUAL MEETING. see *ENGINEERING — Abstracting, Bibliographies, Statistics*

ZHONGGUO GUANGXUE YU YINGYONG GUANGXUE WENZHAI/CHINESE OPTICS AND APPLIED OPTICS ABSTRACTS. see *PHYSICS — Abstracting, Bibliographies, Statistics*

ZHONGGUO NONGYE WENZHAI - NONGYE GONGCHENG/CHINESE AGRICULTURAL ABSTRACTS - AGRICULTURAL ENGINEERING. see *AGRICULTURE — Abstracting, Bibliographies, Statistics*

ZHONGGUO SHENGWUXUE WENZHAI/CHINESE BIOLOGICAL ABSTRACTS. see *BIOLOGY — Abstracting, Bibliographies, Statistics*

ZHONGGUO SHUXUE WENZHAI/CHINESE MATHEMATICS ABSTRACTS. see *MATHEMATICS — Abstracting, Bibliographies, Statistics*

ZHONGGUO WUJI FENXI HUAXUE WENZHAI/CHINESE INORGANIC ANALYTICAL CHEMISTRY ABSTRACTS. see *CHEMISTRY — Abstracting, Bibliographies, Statistics*

ZHONGGUO WULI WENZHAI/CHINESE PHYSICS ABSTRACTS. see *PHYSICS — Abstracting, Bibliographies, Statistics*

ZHONGGUO YAOXUE WENZHAI/CHINESE PHARMACEUTICAL ABSTRACTS. see *ALTERNATIVE MEDICINE — Abstracting, Bibliographies, Statistics*

ZHONGGUO YIXUE WENZHAI (ERKEXUE)/CHINA MEDICAL ABSTRACTS (PEDIATRICS). see *MEDICAL SCIENCES — Abstracting, Bibliographies, Statistics*

ZHONGGUO YIXUE WENZHAI (JIHUA SHENGYU, FUCHAN KEXUE)/CHINA MEDICAL ABSTRACTS (BIRTH CONTROL AND GYNECOLOGY). see *MEDICAL SCIENCES — Abstracting, Bibliographies, Statistics*

ZHONGGUO YIXUE WENZHAI (KOUQIANG YIXUE)/CHINA MEDICAL ABSTRACTS (STOMATOLOGY). see *MEDICAL SCIENCES — Abstracting, Bibliographies, Statistics*

ZHONGGUO YIXUE WENZHAI (NEIKE XUE). see *MEDICAL SCIENCES — Abstracting, Bibliographies, Statistics*

ZHONGGUO YIXUE WENZHAI (WEISHENGXUE). see *PHYSICAL FITNESS AND HYGIENE — Abstracting, Bibliographies, Statistics*

ZIMBABWE RESEARCH INDEX; register of current research in Zimbabwe. see *SCIENCES: COMPREHENSIVE WORKS — Abstracting, Bibliographies, Statistics*

ZINCSCAN; a review of recent technical literature on the uses of zinc and its products. see *METALLURGY — Abstracting, Bibliographies, Statistics*

ZOOLOGICAL RECORD. see *BIOLOGY — Abstracting, Bibliographies, Statistics*

ZOOLOGICAL RECORD SERIAL SOURCES. see *BIOLOGY — Abstracting, Bibliographies, Statistics*

ZUCKERINDUSTRIE; internationales Fachblatt fuer Technik, Anbau und Wirtschaft. see *FOOD AND FOOD INDUSTRIES — Abstracting, Bibliographies, Statistics*

ACCOUNTING

see Business and Economics–Accounting

ADULT EDUCATION

see Education–Adult Education

ADVENTURE AND ROMANCE

see Literature–Adventure and Romance

ADVERTISING AND PUBLIC RELATIONS

see also Business and Economics–Marketing and Purchasing

659.1 378 US
A A F COMMUNICATOR. 1976. 4/yr. free to members. American Advertising Federation, 1101 Vermont Ave., N.W., Ste. 500, Washington, DC 20005. TEL 202-898-0089. FAX 202-898-0159. E-mail: lpowers@aaf.org. Ed.Bd. circ. 5,000. **Document type** newsletter.
  Description: Advertising information on internships, current industry affairs and AAF programs for students.

ADVERTISING AND PUBLIC RELATIONS

659.2 296 US
A J P R S REPORTER. s-a. free. (American Jewish Public Relations Society) Neil Littauer & Associates, Inc., Box 431457, Miami, FL 33243. TEL 305-261-0011. Ed. Bettijane Eisenpreis. circ. 500.
 Description: For Jewish public relations professionals.

A P A MEMBER BULLETIN. (Arkansas Press Association) see JOURNALISM

659.1 GW
A U M A INFOBLAETTER; Daten und Fakten ueber Messen und Ausstellungen im In- und Ausland. m. free. Ausstellungs- und Messe-Ausschuss der Deutschen Wirtschaft e.V. - Confederation of German Trade Fair and Exhibition Industries, Lindenstr. 8, 50674 Cologne, Germany. TEL 49-221-209070. FAX 49-221-2090712. TELEX 8881507. circ. 1,500. **Document type:** newsletter.
 Formerly: A U M A Informationsblaetter.
 Description: Preliminary figures and information on trade shows and exhibitions in Germany and worldwide.

659.1 GW
A U M A - MITTEILUNGEN. m. free. Ausstellungs- und Messe-Ausschuss der Deutschen Wirtschaft e.V. - Confederation of German Trade Fair and Exhibition Industries, Lindenstr. 8, 50674 Cologne, Germany. TEL 49-221-209070. FAX 49-221-2090712. circ. 1,700. **Document type:** newsletter.
 Description: Information for AUMA members and the press regarding the work of AUMA.

659.1 DK ISSN 0903-3459
A V HAANDBOGEN MED PRODUCENTERNES KATALOG. 1987. a. Grafiske Haandboeger, Finsensvej 80, DK-2000 Frederiksberg, Denmark. TEL 45-38-88-32-22. FAX 45-38-88-30-38. Ed. Svend Erik Pedersen. adv.: B&W page DKK 9950, color page DKK 11900. circ. 7,000.

659.1 US
A W N Y MATTERS. 1988. m. membership. Advertising Women of New York, 153 E. 57th St., New York, NY 10022. TEL 212-593-1950. FAX 212-759-2865. Ed. Phylis Goldberg. adv. circ. 800. **Document type:** newsletter.
 Description: Informs members of relevant news and developments on and in the industry.

659.1 UK
ACCOUNT LIST FILE. Abbreviated title: A L F. 1987. m. £660 (effective Jul. 1996). Data Management Services Group Ltd., Ramillies House, 1-2 Ramillies St., London W1V 1DF, England. TEL 44-171-287-0030. FAX 44-171-437-4505. Pub. Lara Griffin. R&P contact: Richard Laven. adv.: page £1000; adv. contact: Julia Coombs. circ. 800 (paid). **Document type:** directory.
 ●Also available online.
 Description: Lists the top U.K. advertising agencies and advertisers, as well as media buyers, and marketing personnel in major

659.1 US ISSN 1061-1371
AD BUSINESS REPORT. 1978. m. $75. Executive Communications, Inc., 185 E. 85th St., Ste. 11-C, New York, NY 10028. TEL 212-831-3147. Ed. Sue Fulton. bk.rev. **Document type:** newsletter.
 Formerly (until 1986): New Business Report.
 Description: Covers advertising agency business development and management and growth opportunities.

659.1 332.1 US
AD IDEAS. (Avail. in 22 industry categories.) m. $395 per industry. National System, Inc., 56 Worthington Access Dr., Maryland Heights, MO 63043-3806. TEL 800-231-8179. FAX 314-205-1996. Ed. Jeff Wingbermuehle. R&P contact: Jeff Wingbermuehle. **Document type:** trade publication.
 Formerly: Ad Trends.
 Description: Provides an on-going review of trends in newspaper advertising, reprinting and commenting on current ads in specific industries. Examines design, effectiveness and other criteria, and presents advice on ad strategies and the latest advertising updates.

659.1 US
AD - MAG.* 11/yr. Advertising Club of Greater St. Louis, 305 N. Broadway, St. Louis, MO 63102-2001. TEL 314-231-4185. FAX 314-231-4188. circ. 1,200.

659.1 658 NZ ISSN 0112-6997
AD MEDIA. 1985. 11/yr. NZ.$163.12 (foreign NZ.$232.89) (effective 1997). Profile Publishing Ltd., P.O. Box 5544, Wellesley St., Auckland, New Zealand. TEL 64-9-6308940. FAX 64-9-6301046. E-mail: sprofile@iconz.co.nz. Ed. Paul Panckhurst; Pub. Reg Birchfield. adv.; bk.rev. circ. 1,475. (back issues avail.) **Document type:** trade publication.
 —BLDSC (0678.180000).
 Description: Covers advertising and media industry news and features for senior executives.

659.1 AT ISSN 0814-6942
AD NEWS. 1928. fortn. Aus.$90 (foreign Aus.$225) (effective Aug. 1996). Yaffa Publishing Group, 17-21 Bellevue St., Surry Hills, N.S.W. 2010, Australia. TEL 61-2-92812333. FAX 61-2-92812750. E-mail: yaffa@yaffa.com.au. Ed. Edward Charles; Pub. Jeremy Light. adv.: B&W page Aus.$3530, color page Aus.$4950; trim 358 x 258; adv. contact: John Morrissey. illus.; stat. circ. 6,300. **Indexed:** Bus.Ind. **Document type:** trade publication.
 Former titles (until 1984): Advertising News (ISSN 0814-6934); (until 1971): Advertising and Newspaper News (ISSN 0001-8929)
 Description: Serves the advertising, marketing and media industries nationally.

659.1 US
AD NEWS. m. Philadelphia Advertising Club, 1818 Market St., 36th Fl., Philadelphia, PA 19103. TEL 215-564-7700. Ed. Tom Quigley. tr.lit. circ. 1,200.

659.1 AT ISSN 0816-3650
AD NEWS HANDBOOK. s-a. Aus.$80 (foreign Aus.$110) (effective Aug. 1996). Yaffa Publishing Group, 17-21 Bellevue St., Surry Hills, N.S.W. 2010, Australia. TEL 61-2-92812333st. FAX 61-2-92812750. E-mail: yaffa@yaffa.com.au. Pub. Jeremy Light. adv. contact: Jodie Reid. **Document type:** directory.

659.1 384.55 US
AD - TIER NEWSLETTER.* 1981. m. membership. Cabletelevision Advertising Bureau (CAB), 830 Third Ave., Frnt. 2, New York, NY 10022-7522. TEL 212-751-7770. Ed. Lloyd Trufelman. circ. 2,100.
 Description: Information on cable advertising.

659.1 AT ISSN 0311-2225
ADBRIEF. 1972. w. Aus.$410 (effective 1996). Newsletter Information Services, P.O. Box 693, Manly, N.S.W. 2095, Australia. TEL 61-2-9777500. FAX 61-2-9773310. E-mail: hww@hww.com.au; URL: http://www.hww.com.au. Ed. Simon Canning. R&P contact: Sue Mitchell. adv. contact: Janice Garrett. bk.rev. circ. 550. **Document type:** newsletter. —CCC.
 Incorporates: Inside Advertising and Media.
 Description: Covers advertising, media news and developments.

ADBRIEF REGISTER: AGENCIES & MARKETERS. see BUSINESS AND ECONOMICS — Trade And Industrial Directories

659.1 US
ADCLUBBER.* 1918. 10/yr. membership. Advertising Club of Metropolitan Washington, 7702 Leesburg Pike, Ste. 1400, Falls Church, VA 22043-2612. adv. circ. 1,100.

659.1 US
ADCOM NET. (Print publication ceased in 1995) 1991. d. free. Publitech, Inc., Box 840, Sherborn, MA 01770. TEL 508-651-3932. E-mail: publisher@adcom.net; URL: http://www.adcom.net. Ed. Carl B.E. Shedd; Pub. Carl B.E. Shedd. R&P contact: Carl B.E. Shedd. adv. **Document type:** trade publication.
 ●Available only online.
 Supersedes (in 1996): Ad - Com Magazine (ISSN 1061-3242)

659.1 US ISSN 0001-8066
ADCRAFTER; the voice of advertising in Detroit. 1907. w. $25 ($35 including Roster) to non-members. Adcraft Club of Detroit, 2630 Book Tower, Detroit, MI 48226. TEL 313-962-7225. Ed. Robert Guerrini; Pub. William Jentzen. R&P contact: Robert Guerrini. adv. contact: William Jentzen. bk.rev.; circ. 4,550 (paid). **Document type:** trade publication.

659.1 NE ISSN 0165-0726
ADFORMATIE. 1973. w. (Thu.). fl.235. Samsom Bedrijfsinformatie B.V. (Subsidiary of: Wolters Kluwer N.V.), Postbus 4, 2400 MA Alphen aan den Rijn, Netherlands. TEL 31-172-466775. FAX 31-172-440681. **Indexed:** Child.Lit.Abstr. **Document type:** trade publication.
 —SWETS.

741.67 SP ISSN 1130-6351
ADGRAFICA. 4/yr. P. de la Bonanova 14, Torre A, 08022 Barcelona, Spain. TEL 3-211-53-04. FAX 3-417-89-60.
 Description: Covers graphic arts and visual communication.

659.1 658 UK ISSN 1353-7318
ADLINE; the marketing magazine for the regions. 1980. m. £20. Adline Publishing Ltd., 361-363 Moseley Rd., Birmingham B12 9DE, England. TEL 0121-446-4466. FAX 0121-446-4462. E-mail: tonyadline@delphi.com; amurray@cix.compulink.co.ur. Ed. Tony Murrey. circ. 11,225 (controlled). **Document type:** trade publication.

659.1 UK ISSN 0001-8295
ADMAP. 1964. 11/yr. £210 in Europe; rest of world £240 (effective 1998). N T C Publications Ltd., P.O. Box 89, Henley-on-Thames, Oxon RB9 1GB, England. TEL 44-1491-411000. FAX 44-1491-571188. Ed. Nicholas Staveley. adv.; bk.rev.; charts; illus.; stat. circ. 1,275. (back issues avail.) **Indexed:** Account.& Data Proc.Abstr., Anbar., Ind.Bus.Rep., Mark.Res.Abstr. (1966-). **Document type:** trade publication.
 ●Also available online.
 —BLDSC (0681.910000).
 Description: Gives in-depth coverage of marketing, advertising, and market research.

657 371.2 US ISSN 0884-7398
LB2351.2
ADMISSIONS MARKETING REPORT. 1985. m. $125 (effective 1997). H M R Publications Group, 3050 Presidential Dr., Ste. 111, Atlanta, GA 30340. TEL 770-457-6105. Ed. Bill Gregory; Pub. Jan Michael Lok. circ. 900. (back issues avail.) **Document type:** trade publication.
 Description: Looks at the admissions marketing programs at colleges and universities across America.

659.1 GW
ADRESS REPORT; ausgewaehlte Informationen zum Direct-Marketing. 1969. 4/yr. free. A Z Direct Marketing Bertelsmann, Carl-Bertelsmann-Str. 161, 33311 Guetersloh, Germany. TEL 05241-803197. FAX 05241-76984. TELEX 933752. bk.rev. circ. 15,000. **Document type:** newsletter.

659.1 UK ISSN 1350-1402
ADS INTERNATIONAL; the magazine for advertising creativity. 1988. q. £15 (effective 1996-1997). Creative Magazines Ltd., 35 Britannia Row, London N1 8QH, England. TEL 44-171-226-1739. FAX 44-171-226-1540. E-mail: 71333.3134@compuserve.com. Ed. Dan Foulkes; Pub. Robert T. Prior. R&P contact: Penelope Foulkes. adv.: color page £990; adv. contact: Lawrence McAlister. bk.rev.; illus. circ. 7,000. **Indexed:** DAAI. **Document type:** trade publication.
 Formerly: HotAds International (ISSN 0962-7316)

659.1 UK ISSN 0265-1300
ADVANCE; editorial features directory. 1980. bi-m. £275. Themetree Ltd., 2 Prebendal Ct., Oxford Rd., Aylesbury, Bucks. HP19 3EY, England. TEL 44-1296-428585. FAX 44-1296-436612. Ed. Leigh Rymer. circ. 1,180. (looseleaf format; back issues avail.) **Document type:** directory.
 —BLDSC (0696.693500).
 Description: Keeps track of forthcoming UK editorial features.

659.1 SA ISSN 1022-6982
ADVANTAGE. (Text in English) 1994. m. R.89. Primedia Publishing (Pty) Ltd., P.O. Box 784698, Sandton 2146, South Africa. TEL 27-11-8843857. FAX 27-11-8844677. Ed. John Farquhari; Pub. S. Sordon. adv. contact: S. Weir. illus. circ. 3,000. **Document type:** trade publication.
 Description: Overview of advertising, marketing, publishing, and the Internet.

ADVERTISING AND PUBLIC RELATIONS

659.1   NE   ISSN 0001-8856
ADVERTENTIEBLAD. 1952. w. fl.25($20) B. V. Rotadruk, Postbus 16, Axel, Netherlands. Ed. Chr. van Breemen. adv.; circ. controlled.

659.1   US   ISSN 1078-6678
HF5805
ADVERTISER & AGENCY RED BOOKS PLUS. q. $1195. National Register Publishing, A Division of Reed Elsevier Inc., 121 Chanlon Rd., New Providence, NJ 07974. TEL 908-464-6800. FAX 908-665-6688. TELEX 138 755. E-mail: info@reedref.com; URL: http://www.reedref.com. (Subscr. to: National Register Publishing, Order Dept., Box 31, New Providence, NJ 07974-9903. TEL 800-521-8110)
● Also available on CD-ROM. Producer(s): Bowker Electronic Publishing.
    Description: Features the complete databases of all three Red Books: Standard Directory of Advertisers; Standard Directory of Advertising Agencies; and Standard Directory of International Advertisers and Agencies. Provides insight into the world's top agencies, advertisers, their products, and what media they use.

659.1   US
ADVERTISERS AND THEIR AGENCIES. a. Engel Communications, Inc., 820 Bear Tavern Rd., Mountainview Corp. Pk., W. Trenton, NJ 08628. TEL 609-530-0044. adv.

659.1   UK   ISSN 0065-3578
ADVERTISER'S ANNUAL. 1925. a. £185 (effective 1997). Hollis Directories Ltd., Harlequin House, 7 High St., Teddington, Middlesex TW11 8EHXA, England. TEL 44-181-977-7711. FAX 44-181-977-1133. E-mail: adannual@hollis-pr.demon.co.uk. Ed. Nesta Hollis. adv.: B&W page £800, color page £1200; 245 x 125; adv. contact: Jerry Odlin. circ. 1,100. **Document type:** directory.
—BLDSC (0712.238000).
    Description: Lists 4,000 major UK advertisers and 12,000 brands. Includes advertising agencies and their clients; sponsorship consultants; recruitment agencies. ABC/VFD audited newspapers and periodicals; TV and radio advertising listings.

659.1   US   ISSN 0001-8899
HF5801   CODEN: ADVAAQ
ADVERTISING AGE; the international newspaper of marketing. 1930. w. $109 (effective 1997 & 1998). Crain Communications, Inc. (Chicago), 740 Rush St., Chicago, IL 60611. TEL 312-649-5417. FAX 312-280-3174. URL: http://www.adage.com. (Subscr. to: 965 E. Jefferson Ave., Detroit, MI 48207-3185. TEL 313-446-6777) Ed. David Klein. adv.: B&W page $13775. bk.rev.; charts; illus.; tr.lit. circ. 80,000. (tabloid format; also avail. in microform from UMI; microfiche from CIS; back issues avail.) Indexed: ABI Inform., Acad.Ind., B.P.I., BPIA, Bus.Ind., CAD CAM Abstr., Chic.Per.Ind., Curr.Pack.Abstr., PMR, PROMT, PSI, Resour.Ctr.Ind., SRI, Tel.Abstr., Tr.& Indus.Ind., WPM. **Document type:** newspaper, trade publication.
● Also available online. Vendor(s): Information Access Co., Lexis-Nexis (ADAGE).
—BLDSC (0712.250000); CASDDS; KR SourceOne; UMI. **CCC.**
    Incorporates: Advertising Age's Focus (ISSN 0264-1755)

659.1   US   ISSN 1072-9119
HF5801
ADVERTISING AGE'S CREATIVITY. 1987? 10/yr. $49 in U.S. (Canada $59; elsewhere $89); newsstand price: $5. Crain Communications, Inc. (New York), 220 E. 42nd St., New York, NY 10017-5806. TEL 212-210-0100. FAX 212-210-0111. (Subscr. to: 965 E. Jefferson Ave., Detroit, MI 48207. TEL 800-678-9595) circ. 30,000 (controlled). (tabloid format) **Document type:** trade publication.
    Description: Covers technological developments affecting the advertising design field.

659.1 150   US
ADVERTISING AND CONSUMER PSYCHOLOGY. irreg. Lawrence Erlbaum Associates, Inc., 10 Industrial Ave., Mahwah, NJ 07430-2262. TEL 201-236-9500; 800-926-6579. FAX 201-236-0072. E-mail: jamsel@erlbaum.com; URL: http://www.erlbaum.com. **Document type:** monograph series.

659.1   US   ISSN 0747-3168
ADVERTISING & GRAPHIC ARTS TECHNIQUES.* 1966. m. $10. Advertising Trade Publications, Inc., c/o Dan Barron, Ed., 456 Glenbrook Rd., Stamford, CT 06906-1800. TEL 212-889-6500. FAX 212-889-6504. adv.; bk.rev.; bibl.; charts; illus.; tr.lit. circ. 3,766. (back issues avail.) **Document type:** trade publication.
    Former titles: Advertising Techniques (ISSN 0001-0235); A A T: Ad Art Techniques.

659.1   US
ADVERTISING & MARKETING REVIEW. 1975. m. $18 (effective 1997). 622 Gardenia Ct., Golden, CO 80401. TEL 303-277-9840. FAX 303-278-9909. E-mail: kencuster@aol.com; URL: http://www.ad-mkt-review.com. Ed. Ken Custer; Pub. Ken Custer. adv.: B&W page $1000, color page $1100; trim 8 3/8 x 10 7/8. (back issues avail.) **Document type:** trade publication.
    Formerly: Colorado M A C News.
    Description: Serves the advertising and marketing community in Colorado and the organizations that participate in the industry.

ADVERTISING CAREER DIRECTORY. see *OCCUPATIONS AND CAREERS*

659.1   US
ADVERTISING CLUB OF NEW YORK. NEWSLETTER. q. membership only. Advertising Club of New York, 235 Park Ave. S., New York, NY 10003-1405. TEL 212-533-8080. adv. contact: Madhn Malhan. **Document type:** newsletter.

659.1   US   ISSN 0193-4457
ADVERTISING - COMMUNICATIONS TIMES; business newspaper for the advertising general industry, corporations in Philadelphia, Eastern PA., N.J., and Del. 1977. m. $39. Advertising - Communications Times Inc., 121 Chestnut St., Philadelphia, PA 19106. TEL 215-629-1666. FAX 215-923-8358. Pub. Joseph H. Ball. R&P contact: Joseph Ball. adv. contact: Mark Bruce. tr.lit. circ. 42,000. (tabloid format; back issues avail.) **Document type:** newspaper, trade publication.

659.1 340   US   ISSN 0277-9943
ADVERTISING COMPLIANCE SERVICE NEWSLETTER. 1981. bi-m. $495 (effective 1997). John Lichtenberger, Ed. & Pub., 571 Passaic Ave., Nutley, NJ 07110. TEL 201-661-3469. FAX 201-661-3469. E-mail: lawpublish@aol.com. R&P contact: John Lichtenberger. adv. contact: John Lichtenberger. **Document type:** newsletter.
    Description: Aimed at attorneys representing advertisers, advertising agencies, marketers, publishers or broadcasters. Covers the latest developments in the broad advertising law area.

659.1   US
ADVERTISING COUNCIL. ANNUAL REPORT. 1986. a. Advertising Council, 261 Madison Ave., New York, NY 10016-2303. TEL 212-992-1500. **Document type:** corporate report.
    Former titles: Report to the American People (ISSN 1061-2912); (until 1987): Advertising Council. Annual Report (ISSN 0898-3739)

659.1   US
ADVERTISING CREATIVITY NEWSLETTER. 1990. a. $19.95. Prosperity & Profits Unlimited Distribution Services, Box 416, Denver, CO 80201. TEL 303-575-5676. Ed. A. Doyle. R&P contact: A. Doyle. circ. 4,000 (paid). (looseleaf format) **Document type:** newsletter.
    Description: Covers various aspects of advertising and public relations.

659.1   UK   ISSN 0968-2163
ADVERTISING EXPENDITURE FORECASTS. 1987. 2/yr. £275 (effective 1997). Zenith Media Ltd., 15 Chitty St., London W1P 1LJ, England. TEL 44-171-255-1221. FAX 44-171-637-0476. E-mail: publications@zenithmedia.co.uk; URL: http://www.zenithmedia.co.uk. Ed. Adam Smith. **Document type:** trade publication.
    Description: Forecasts expenditure by medium in forty countries with backdata for the last ten years.

659.1   UK
THE ADVERTISING FORECAST. 1978. q. £825 (effective 1998). N T C Publications Ltd., P.O. Box 69, Henley-on-Thames, Oxon RG9 1GB, England. TEL 44-1491-411000. FAX 44-1491-571188. **Document type:** trade publication.
    Formerly: Forecast of Advertising Expenditure (ISSN 0263-8118)

ADVERTISING LAW ANTHOLOGY. see *LAW*

659.1 658   US
ADVERTISING, P R, MARKETING CURRENTS. 1990. bi-m. $24. Currents Inc., 1801 Rockville Pike, Ste. 3300, Rockville, MD 20852-1633. TEL 301-984-4000. FAX 301-984-7340. Ed. Philip Rabin. circ. 10,400.
    Description: For senior level advertising, public relations and marketing executives in the Washington, DC area; includes strategic planning information for the 1990s.

659.1   US
ADVERTISING RESEARCH FOUNDATION. TRANSCRIPT PROCEEDINGS. irreg. $75 to non-members; members $50. Advertising Research Foundation, 641 Lexington Ave., 11th Fl., New York, NY 10022. TEL 212-751-5656. FAX 212-319-5265. adv. **Document type:** proceedings.

659.1 340   US
ADVERTISING TOPICS. m. $96 included in subscr. to Do's and Don'ts in Advertising. Council of Better Business Bureaus, Publications Department, 4200 Wilson Blvd., Ste. 800, Arlington, VA 22203-1804. TEL 703-276-0100. **Document type:** newsletter.
    Description: Provides in-depth analysis and interpretation of current advertising issues; court decisions; F.T.C., F.D.A., and F.C.C. rulings; opinions; and policy statements.

659.1   US
ADVERTISING VIA TELEMARKETING SCRIPT - PRESENTATIONS NEWSLETTER. 1990. biennial. $39.95. Wellthe Publishing, c/o Prosperity & Profits Unlimited, Distribution Svcs., Box 416, Denver, CO 80201-0416. TEL 303-575-5676. Ed. A.C. Doyle. circ. 5,000. (looseleaf format) **Document type:** directory.
    Description: Covers script presentations for telemarketing to various types of businesses.

659.1   UK   ISSN 0955-0704
ADVERTISING WORKS. 1981. biennial, no.8, 1995. £40. (Institute of Practitioners in Advertising) N T C Publications Ltd., Farm Rd., Henley-on-Thames, Oxfordshire RG9 1EJ, England. TEL 01491-411000. FAX 01491-571188. **Document type:** trade publication.
—BLDSC (0712.287150).

659.1   II   ISSN 0001-8988
ADVERTLINK;* a newspaper on advertising and marketing. (Text in English) 1957. fortn. Rs.15. Dhiren Mitra, Ed. & Pub., 45 Raja Rammohan Sarani, Calcutta 700009, India. adv.; bk.rev.; bibl.; charts; illus.; mkt.; pat.; tr.lit.; tr.mk.; stat. circ. 1,653. **Document type:** newspaper.

659.1   US   ISSN 0199-4743
ADWEEK (LOS ANGELES);* western advertising news. 1919. w. BPI Communications, Inc., 5055 Wilshire Blvd., Ste. 600, Los Angeles, CA 90036. TEL 213-525-2270. FAX 213-525-2391. Ed. Mike McCarthy. adv.; bk.rev. circ. 98,831. **Document type:** trade publication.
● Also available online. Vendor(s): Knight-Ridder Information, Inc. (File no.648), Ovid Technologies, Inc. (TSAP).
—UMI.
    Formerly: M A C Western Advertising News (Media Agencies Clients).

ADVERTISING AND PUBLIC RELATIONS

659.1   US   ISSN 0199-2864
HF5801   CODEN: AWEEEM
ADWEEK (NEW YORK). (6 Regional eds.: East, Midwest, New England, Southeast, Southwest, West) 1960. w. $125 (Canada $299.60; elsewhere $280) student $68.85 (effective 1997); newsstand price: $3. B P I Communications, Inc. (New York), 1515 Broadway, New York, NY 10036. TEL 212-536-5336; 800-344-7119. FAX 212-536-1416. E-mail: adweek@adweek.com; URL: http://www.adweek.com/magazine/adweek.asp. Ed. Kevin McCormack. adv.; bk.rev.; charts; illus.; tr.lit. circ. 84,372. **Indexed:** B.P.I., Chic.Per.Ind. **Document type:** trade publication.
●Also available online. Vendor(s): Information Access Co., Knight-Ridder Information, Inc. (File no.648), Lexis-Nexis, Ovid Technologies, Inc. (TSAP). —BLDSC (0719.580800); KR SourceOne; UMI.
CCC.
    Formerly: A N N Y (Advertising News of New York) (ISSN 0001-2041)

ADWEEK AGENCY DIRECTORY. see *BUSINESS AND ECONOMICS — Trade And Industrial Directories*

ADWEEK CLIENT - BRAND DIRECTORY. see *BUSINESS AND ECONOMICS — Trade And Industrial Directories*

659.1   US
ADWEEK: MIDWEST.* 1963. w. $60. A S M Communications, Inc. (Chicago), 222 Merchandise Mart Plaza, Ste. 936, Chicago, IL 60654-1102. TEL 312-467-6500. FAX 312-321-0039. Ed. Mary Connors. adv.; tr.lit. circ. 12,899. **Document type:** trade publication.
●Also available online. Vendor(s): Information Access Co.
    Formerly: S A M (ISSN 0036-083X)

659.1   US   ISSN 0888-0840
HE5806.A11
ADWEEK: NEW ENGLAND. 1964. w. $99. Adweek L.P., 100 Boylston St., Boston, MA 02116. TEL 617-482-0876. FAX 617-482-2921. Ed. Judy Warner. adv.; illus.; stat.; circ. 9,740 (paid). (also avail. in microfiche from UMI) **Document type:** trade publication.
—UMI.
    Formerly: New England Advertising Week (ISSN 0028-4653)

659.1   US   ISSN 0746-892X
ADWEEK: SOUTHWEST.* 1979. w. $60. B P I, 3102 Maple Ave., Ste. 120, Dallas, TX 75201-1233. TEL 214-871-9550. Ed. Monica Reeves. adv.; illus. circ. 7,000. (also avail. in microform from UMI; reprint service avail. from UMI) **Document type:** trade publication.
●Also available online. Vendor(s): Information Access Co.
—UMI.
    Former titles: Adweek: Southwest Advertising News (ISSN 0194-3553); (until 1977): Southwest Advertising News; (until Oct. 1978): Southwest Advertising and Marketing (ISSN 0038-4658)

AFRICAN INTERPRETER; journal on African and Arab affairs. see *BUSINESS AND ECONOMICS*

659.1   US   ISSN 1054-7371
HF5801
AGENCY. 1990-1991; resumed Apr. 1992; ceased May 1992; resumed 1994. q. $20 to non-members. (American Association of Advertising Agencies) Decker Decker and Associates, 120 E. 38th St., New York, NY 10016. TEL 212-683-1345. FAX 212-683-1296. (Edit. addr.: 405 Lexington Ave., New York, NY 10174-1801. TEL 212-682-2500. FAX 212-953-5665) Ed. Joyce Harrington. adv. contact: Rick Splittorf. bk.rev. circ. 36,000. (back issues avail.) **Document type:** trade publication.
    Description: Covers the advertising agency business, including media, account management, research, creativity, and government issues.

659.1 330 384   US
AGENCY EXPERTISE. a. International Federation of Advertising Agencies, 1450 E. American Ln., Ste. 1400, Schaumburg, IL 60173-4973. TEL 847-330-6344. FAX 847-517-4459. E-mail: nstephen@starnetinc.com. Ed. Norval Stephens. **Document type:** newsletter.

659.1   GW   ISSN 0178-658X
AGENTUREN UND MARKEN. 1967. 4/yr. DM.460. Media Daten Verlag GmbH, Klingenweg 4, 65396 Walluf, Germany. TEL 49-6123-700-0. FAX 49-6123-700122. circ. 2,400. **Document type:** trade publication.

659.1   IT
AGENZIE E CLIENTI. 1983. 2/yr. Lit.420000 (effective 1997). Emap Publishing s.r.l., Piazza della Repubblica, 32, 20124 Milan, Italy. TEL 39-2-67151210. FAX 39-2-66980255. Ed. Adolfo Galleazzi. adv. **Document type:** directory.

659.1 387.7   CN
AIRLINE ADVERTISING PROJECT. a. £199 (effective 1997). International Air Transport Association, 2000 Peel St., Montreal, PQ H3A 2R4, Canada. TEL 514-844-6311. FAX 514-844-5286. E-mail: sales@iata.org; URL: http://www.iata.org.
    Description: Provides comparative measures of airline advertising impact in the United Kingdom on long-haul corporate travellers.

659.1   IT
AMERICA. 4/yr. Cso. Vercelli 2, 20145 Milan, Italy. TEL 2-49-82-890. FAX 2-469-65-37. Ed. Paolo Galli. circ. 3,000. **Indexed:** Bk.Rev.Dig., R.G.Abstr.

659.1   US   ISSN 1081-9568
AMERICAN ADVERTISING. 1984. q. membership. American Advertising Federation, 1101 Vermont Ave., N.W., Ste. 500, Washington, DC 20005. TEL 202-898-0089. FAX 202-898-0159. E-mail: dghernandez@aaf.org. Ed. Debra Gersh Hernandez. adv. circ. 50,000. **Document type:** trade publication.
●Also available online. Vendor(s): UMI.
—BLDSC (0809.925000).
    Description: Focuses on people, technological innovations, and creative trends within the advertising industry.

741.67   US   ISSN 1052-0236
T223.V1
AMERICAN CORPORATE IDENTITY. 1986. a. $59.95. Art Direction Book Co., Inc., 456 Glenbrook Rd., Glenbrook, CT 06906-1800. TEL 203-353-1441. FAX 203-353-1371. Ed. David E. Carter; Pub. Don Barron. circ. 6,000 (paid). **Document type:** trade publication.
    Description: Reports corporations' visual identities, such as signage, stationery, trademarks, and packaging.

741.67   US
NC1001.5
ANDY AWARDS CREATIVE BOOK. a. $25. Advertising Club of New York, 235 Park Ave. S., New York, NY 10003-1405. TEL 212-533-1570. adv. contact: Madhn Malhan. circ. 2,000.
    Formerly: Andy Awards Souvenir Journal (ISSN 0270-2525)
    Description: Showcases winners of the International Andy Award.

659.13   XR
ANNONCE; noviny po bezplatnou soukromu inzerci. 1990. 3/w. $743. Annonce Prague, Na Porici 30, 114 06 Prague 1, Czech Republic. TEL 42-24-812459. FAX 42-24-811264. Ed. Josef Kudlacek. adv. contact: Hanka Nekvapilova. circ. 60,000. (back issues avail.) **Document type:** newspaper.
    Description: Publishes personal, real estate, cars, business cooperation ads, as well as commercial and display ads.

659   FR   ISSN 0982-9822
ANNONCES. 1945. w. 464 F. Editions G. N. Carre, 36 rue de Malte, 75011 Paris, France. TEL 48-05-30-30. FAX 48-05-29-75. Ed.Bd. adv. circ. 8,000. **Document type:** newspaper.

659.1   DK   ISSN 0108-2191
ANNONCOERFORENINGS BUREAUFORTEGNELSE;* reklamebureauer, reklamekonsulenter og specialvirksomheder i Danmark med Oplysninger om ejerforhold, afregningsformer og kundeforbindelser. vol. 13, 1982. biennial. DKK 290. Dansk Annoncoer-Forening, Laederstraede 32-34, DK-1201 Copenhagen K, Denmark.
    Formerly: Fortegnelse over Reklamebureauer - Konsulenter og Specialvirksomhede i Danmark.

659.1   FR   ISSN 1242-2347
ANNUAIRE GENERAL DE LA PUBLICITE ET DE LA COMMUNICATION. 1938. a. 700 F. (effective 1997). Nouvelles Editions de la Publicite, 9 rue Leo-Delibes, 75116 Paris, France. adv. circ. 2,500.
    Former titles: Annuaire General de la Publicite (ISSN 0998-7932); Annuaire General des Publicitaires de France (ISSN 0751-6649); Groupement des Directeurs Publicitaires de France. Annuaire (ISSN 0072-7792)

659.1 658.8   SP   ISSN 0214-4905
ANUNCIOS; semanario de la publicidad. 1980. 45/yr. 53000 ptas. Publicaciones Profesionales S.A., Principe de Vergara 15, 3o izda., 28001 Madrid, Spain. TEL 34-1-4357847. FAX 34-1-5753284. Ed. Javier Castro; Pub. Luis Muniz. adv. contact: Esther Valdivia. circ. 5,000. **Document type:** trade publication.
    Description: Covers marketing and advertising.

APPAREL PRODUCTION NEWS. see *CLOTHING TRADE*

ARKANSAS PRESS ASSOCIATION DIRECTORY. see *JOURNALISM*

ARKANSAS PUBLISHER. see *JOURNALISM*

659.1   US   ISSN 0004-3109
NC997.A1   CODEN: ARTDAL
ART DIRECTION;* the magazine of visual communication. 1949. m. $29.97. Advertising Trade Publications, Inc., c/o Dan Barron, Ed., 456 Glenbrook Rd., Stamford, CT 06906-1800. TEL 212-889-6500. FAX 212-889-6504. adv.; bk.rev.; illus.; tr.lit. circ. 7,854. **Indexed:** Art Ind., Bk.Rev.Ind. (1981-), Child.Bk.Rev.Ind. (1981-), DAAI. **Document type:** trade publication.
—KR SourceOne; UnCover.
    Description: Serves the fields of advertising art, photography, typography and related graphic arts fields.

659.1   GW
ART DIRECTORS CLUB JAHRBUCH. 1965. a. Art Directors Club Verlag GmbH, Grabenstr. 2, 40213 Duesseldorf, Germany. TEL 0211-326354. FAX 0211-320190. Ed. Ingeborg Reese. adv. circ. 4,500. (back issues avail.) **Document type:** trade publication.

659.1   CC   ISSN 0257-893X
ASIAN ADVERTISING AND MARKETING;* the magazine for communication executives. (Text in English) 1986. m. HK.$280($69) Travel & Trade Publishing (Asia) Ltd., 3201 Bank of America, Central, Hong Kong, People's Republic of China. TEL 890-30677. FAX 895-2378. TELEX 76591-TPAL-HX. Ed. Susan Girdwood. circ. controlled. (back issues avail.)
    Description: Provides views on all aspects of the communication industry.

070   JA
ASIAN MEDIA DIRECTORY.* (Text in English) 1974. a. $90. Syme Media Enterprises Ltd., c/o Intercontinental Marketing Corp., I.P.O. Box 5056, Tokyo 100-30, Japan. adv. **Document type:** directory.
    Formerly: Asian Press and Media Directory.

ASSOCIATION. see *MEETINGS AND CONGRESSES*

659.14 302.23   DK   ISSN 0108-3120
AUDIO VISUELLE MEDIA. Variant title: A V M Scandinavia (Dansk Udg.). Norwegian edition: Audiovisuelle Medier (ISSN 0804-0281) 11/yr. DKK 300. Specialbladsforlaget A-S, Finsensvej 80, DK-2000 Frederiksberg, Denmark. TEL 45-38-88-32-22. FAX 45-38-88-30-38. Ed. T. Uffe Johansen. adv.; B&W page DKK 21900, color page DKK 25950; trim 265 x 360. circ. 11,164. **Document type:** newspaper.

659.1   US
AUDIT BUREAU OF CIRCULATIONS. ANNUAL MEETING. PROCEEDINGS. a. Audit Bureau of Circulations, 900 N. Meacham Rd., Schaumburg, IL 60173. TEL 847-605-0909. FAX 847-605-0483. URL: http://www.accessabc.com. circ. 100. **Document type:** proceedings.

ADVERTISING AND PUBLIC RELATIONS

659 · · · · AT · · · · ISSN 0067-1606
AUSTRALIAN ADVERTISING RATE AND DATA SERVICE. 1935. m. Aus.$3140. Reed Business Publishing Pty. Ltd. (Subsidiary of: Reed International PLC), P.O. Box 5487, W. Chatswood, N.S.W. 2057, Australia. TEL 61-2-318-3831. FAX 61-2-698-8138. Ed. Michael Rafferty. adv.
  Description: Contains comprehensive listings of all known Australian newspapers and magazines, radio and television stations, and outdoor media.

659 760 · · · · AT · · · · ISSN 1324-1613
AUSTRALIAN CREATIVE. 1995. q. Aus.$16 (foreign Aus.$50) (effective Aug. 1996). Yaffa Publishing Group, 17-21 Bellevue St., Surry Hills, N.S.W. 2010, Australia. TEL 61-2-92812333. FAX 61-2-92812750. Ed. Robyn Gower; Pub. Jeremy Light. adv.: B&W page Aus.$1890, color page Aus.$2540; trim 297 x 210; adv. contact: John Morrissey. circ. 7,008.
  Description: For creative executives and production managers in advertising agencies, design studios, production houses and marketing companies.

AUSTRALIAN JOURNAL OF COMMUNICATION. see COMMUNICATIONS

AUTO - CENTRUM. see TRANSPORTATION — Automobiles

AUTO - TIP; ogolnopolski magazyn bezplatnych ogloszen motoryzacyjnych. see TRANSPORTATION — Automobiles

659.1 · · · · CC
B & I EXHIBITION CALENDAR. (Text in English) a. Business & Industrial Trade Fairs Ltd., 18-F First Pacific Bank Centre, 51 Gloucester Rd., Wanchai, Hong Kong, People's Republic of China. TEL 852-865-2633. FAX 852-866-1770.

658.8 · · · · AT · · · · ISSN 0005-268X
B & T. (Broadcasting and Television); advertising, marketing & media weekly. 1950. w. Aus.$169. Reed Business Information, P.O. Box 5487, West Chatswood, N.S.W. 2057, Australia. TEL 61-2-93725222. FAX 61-2-93725220. Ed. Tony Burrett; Pub. Barrie Parsons. R&P contact: Barrie Parsons. TEL 61-2-93725598. adv. contact: Dennis Russell. bk.rev.; charts; illus. circ. 4,905. (back issues avail.) **Document type:** trade publication.
  Former titles: Broadcasting; Television.
  Description: Covers advertising, public relations, journalism and marketing.

659.1 · · · · AT · · · · ISSN 0810-669X
B & T YEAR BOOK. 1958. a. Aus.$159 (effective 1996). Reed Business Publishing Pty. Ltd. (Subsidiary of: Reed International PLC), P.O. Box 5487, W. Chatswood, N.S.W. 2057, Australia. TEL 61-2-318-3831. FAX 61-2-698-8138. Ed. Michael Rafferty. adv. circ. 3,500. (back issues avail.)
  Formerly: Broadcasting and Television Year Book (ISSN 0084-8093)
  Description: Comprehensive contact information for all major media, advertising and marketing services, and related industries.

B M A MEMBERSHIP DIRECTORY AND RESOURCE GUIDE. (Business Marketing Association) see BUSINESS AND ECONOMICS — Trade And Industrial Directories

659.1 · · · · US
B P A INTERNATIONAL. ANNUAL REPORT. a. B P A International, 270 Madison Ave., New York, NY 10016-0699. TEL 212-779-3200. FAX 212-725-1721. **Document type:** corporate report.
  Formerly: Business Publications Audit of Circulations. Annual Report.

B T A STUDYCARDS; publication of educational projects. (British Trades Alphabet) see EDUCATION — Teaching Methods And Curriculum

BACON'S INTERNATIONAL MEDIA DIRECTORY. see BUSINESS AND ECONOMICS — Trade And Industrial Directories

BACON'S NEWSPAPER - MAGAZINE DIRECTORY. see BUSINESS AND ECONOMICS — Trade And Industrial Directories

BANK ADVERTISING NEWS; the independent national newspaper of financial marketing. see BUSINESS AND ECONOMICS — Banking And Finance

BARTER COMMUNIQUE. see BUSINESS AND ECONOMICS — Trade And Industrial Directories

BEGA DISTRICT NEWS. see GENERAL INTEREST PERIODICALS — Australia

659 · · · · YU
BERZA (NOVI SAD). 1994. m. Compute, Ferenca Fehera 6, Novi Sad, Yugoslavia. Ed. Ildiko Otasevic.

659.1 658 · · · · AU
BESTSELLER. m. S.750. Manstein Zeitschriften Verlagsgesellschaft mbH, Brunner Feldstr. 45, A-2380 Perchtoldsdorf, Austria. TEL 43-1-86648. FAX 43-1-8664834. circ. 9,000. **Document type:** trade publication.

659.1 686.2 · · · · US · · · · ISSN 1062-7774
NC997.A1
BOARD REPORT FOR GRAPHIC ARTISTS. 1978. m. $107. Board Report Publishing Co., Inc., Box 300789, Denver, CO 80203. TEL 303-839-9058. FAX 303-839-1272. Ed. Drew Allen Miller; Pub. Drew Allen Miller. adv.; bk.rev.; index. (looseleaf format; back issues avail.) **Document type:** newsletter.
  Description: Geared toward graphic artists, designers, ad agencies and in-house art departments.

659.1 · · · · US
BODY COPY.* 1989. bi-m. $20. Breznan Publishing Company, Inc., 11190 Carpenter Rd., Flushing, MI 48433-9746. TEL 213-470-9809. Ed. David Breznan.
  Description: Provides highlights on the people working in advertising. Articles are written by industry professionals.

659.2 · · · · IT · · · · ISSN 0006-6656
BOLLETTINO D O X A. 1947. m. L.100000($100) (Istituto per le Ricerche Statistiche e l'Analisi dell'Opinione Pubblica) D O X A, S.p.A., Via Panizza, 7, 20144 Milan, Italy. TEL 39-2-48193320. FAX 39-2-48193286. Ed. Elio Brusati; Pub. Ennio Sacamon. index, cum.index. circ. 450. (processed; back issues avail.) **Document type:** bulletin.
  Description: Results of social, economic and public opinion DOXA surveys.

659.1 · · · · BS
BOTSWANA ADVERTISER. w. 5647 Nakedi Rd., P.O. Box 130, Broadhurst, Gaborone, Botswana.

659.1 658 · · · · JA
BRAIN/BUREIN. (Text in Japanese) 1961. m. 17820 Yen. Seibundo Shinkosha Publishing Co., Ltd., 1-13-7 Yayoi-cho, Nakano-ku, Tokyo 164, Japan. Ed. H. Hayakawa. circ. 40,000. (back issues avail.)

659.1 · · · · US · · · · ISSN 1064-4318
HF5801 · · · · CODEN: BANDEN
BRANDWEEK. 1980. w. $125 students $68.85 (Canada $299.60; elsewhere $280) (effective 1997); newsstand price: $3. B P I Communications, Inc. (New York), 1515 Broadway, New York, NY 10036. TEL 212-764-7300; 800-722-6658. FAX 212-536-5084. E-mail: cstogel@adweek.com; URL: http://www.brandweek.com. (And: 5055 Wilshire Blvd., Los Angeles, CA 90036) Ed. John McManus. adv.; bk.rev.; charts; illus.; stat. circ. 32,000. (also avail. in microform from UMI; back issues avail.; reprint service avail.) **Indexed:** B.P.I., BPIA, Tr.& Indus.Ind. **Document type:** trade publication.
  ●Also available online. Vendor(s): Information Access Co., Knight-Ridder Information, Inc. (File no.648), Ovid Technologies, Inc. (TSAP).
  —BLDSC (2269.980000); KR SourceOne; UMI; UnCover. **CCC.**
  Former titles (until 1992): Adweek's Marketing Week (ISSN 0892-8274); (until 1986): Adweek (National Marketing Edition) (ISSN 0888-3718); Which supersedes (in 1985): Ad Forum (ISSN 0274-6328)

BRITISH RATE AND DATA. see BIBLIOGRAPHIES

659.1 · · · · US
BULLDOG REPORTER;* an insider's report on agency and corporate media relations. (East and West Coast editions avail.) 1979. bi-w. $347. InfoCom Group, 1250 45th St., Ste. 200, Emeryville, CA 94608-2924. TEL 510-549-4300. FAX 510-549-4331. Ed. Michael Horowitz. adv.; cum.index. circ. 1,400. (back issues avail.)
  Description: Media placement newsletter for public relations professionals.

659.1 · · · · US
BURRELLE'S CLIPPING ANALYST. 1962. q. free. Burrelle's Press Clipping Service, 75 E. Northfield Rd., Livingston, NJ 07039. TEL 201-992-6600. FAX 201-992-5122. Ed. Robert C. Waggoner. bk.rev.; film rev.; charts; illus.; tr.lit.; circ. 5,000 (controlled).
  Formerly: Your Clipping Analyst (ISSN 0300-7669)

BURRELLE'S NEW ENGLAND MEDIA DIRECTORY (YEAR). see BUSINESS AND ECONOMICS — Trade And Industrial Directories

659.1 · · · · US · · · · ISSN 1070-0250
BUSINESS LIFE MAGAZINE; the business magazine of the Piedmont Triad. 1989. m. $24; newsstand price: $2.50. 4101-A Piedmont Pkwy., Greensboro, NC 27410. TEL 910-812-8801. FAX 910-812-8832. E-mail: bizlife@spyder.net; URL: http://www.spyder.net/bizlife. Ed. Lisa M. Bouchey; Pub. Robert A. Kober. R&P contact: Lisa M. Bouchey. adv.: B&W page $2230; trim 8 3/8 x 10 7/8; adv. contact: Robert Gainey. bk.rev.; software rev.; video rev. circ. 13,000. (back issues avail.) **Document type:** trade publication.
  ●Also available online.
  Description: Contains people-oriented business information.

659.1 658.8 · · · · UK · · · · ISSN 1357-1648
BUSINESS RATIO PLUS: ADVERTISING AGENCIES. 1984. a. I C C Business Publications Ltd., Field House, 72 Oldfield Rd., Hampton, Mddx. TW12 2HQ, England. TEL 44-181-783-0922. FAX 44-181-783-1940. charts; stat. **Document type:** trade publication.
  Formerly (until 1993): Business Ratio Report: Advertising Agencies (ISSN 0267-0402)
  Description: Examines the industry structure of advertising agencies, market size and trends, recent developments and prospects, and major company profiles.

659.1 · · · · UK · · · · ISSN 1356-0158
BUSINESS RATIO PLUS: PUBLIC RELATIONS CONSULTANCIES. Variant title: Public Relations Consultancies. 1987. a. I C C Business Publications (Subsidiary of: I C C Information Group), Field House, 72 Oldfield Rd., Hampton, Middlesex TW12 2HQ, England. TEL 44-181-783-0922. FAX 44-181-783-1940. **Document type:** trade publication.
  Former titles (until 1994): Key Note Report: Public Relations Consultancies (ISSN 0963-441X); (until 1989): Business Ratio Report: Public Relations Consultants (ISSN 0952-4371)

659.1 · · · · UK
BUSINESS RATIO REPORT: SIGN AND STREET FURNITURE MANUFACTURERS; an industry sector analysis. 1987. a. I C C Business Ratios Ltd. (Subsidiary of: I C C Information Group), Field House, 72 Oldfield Rd., Hampton, Mddx. TW12 2HQ, England. TEL 0181-783-0922. FAX 0181-783-1940. **Document type:** trade publication.
  Formerly (until 1992): Business Ratio Report: Signs and Street Furniture (ISSN 0952-0775)

659.1 301.16 330 · · · · US
THE BUSINESS - TO - BUSINESS MARKETER. 1977. 10/yr. $79 to non-members; members $25. Business Marketing Association, 150 N. Wacker Dr., Ste. 1760, Chicago, IL 60606. TEL 312-409-4262 FAX 312-409-4266. Ed. Rick Kean. adv.; bk.rev.; charts. illus. tr.lit. circ. 4,500. **Document type:** newsletter.
  Former titles: Business - to - Business Marketing Communications & Communicator (Alexandria, 1977) & B - P A A Communicator (ISSN 0896-7849)
  Description: Contains business-to-business marketing, advertising and public relations news.

ADVERTISING AND PUBLIC RELATIONS

659.1 US ISSN 0095-5531
HF5843
BUYERS' GUIDE TO OUTDOOR ADVERTISING. s-a. $400 (effective 1997). Competitive Media Reporting, 11 W. 42nd St., 11th Fl., New York, NY 10036. TEL 212-789-1418. **Document type:** directory.

BUZZ (ROCHESTER); perspectives on marketing technology. see *BUSINESS AND ECONOMICS — Marketing And Purchasing*

B2B E-NEWSLETTER. see *BUSINESS AND ECONOMICS*

C B D. (Corporate Business Design) see *COMMUNICATIONS*

659.1 CN
C C A B CIRCULATE. vol.4, 1973. q. Canadian Circulations Audit Board, Inc., 188 Eglinton Ave. E., Ste. 304, Toronto, ON M4P 2X7, Canada. Ed. Patrick Sweeney. circ. 4,000. **Document type:** newsletter.

659.2 BE ISSN 0778-1032
C V NEWS. Variant title: Curriculum Vitae News. (Text in Dutch) 1989. w. (50/yr.). 5500 BEF (with French translation 8000 BEF). N.V. C V, Rijkendalstraat 12, 1853 Strombeek, Belgium. TEL 32-2-2675653. FAX 32-2-2671813. Ed. Josephine Overeem. adv.: B&W page 45000 BEF. circ. 500 (paid). (back issues avail.) **Document type:** newsletter.
Description: News of the advertising, marketing and media professions.

CABLE T V ADVERTISING; newsletter on sale of commercial time by cable T V systems. see *COMMUNICATIONS — Television And Cable*

659.1 US
CABLE T V FACTS.* 1983. a. $3.50. Cabletelevision Advertising Bureau (CAB), 830 Third Ave., Frnt. 2, New York, NY 10022-7522. TEL 212-751-7770. FAX 212-832-3268.

659 070 UK ISSN 0008-2309
PN4701 CODEN: CMPGBW
CAMPAIGN; the national weekly of the communications business, embracing advertising, marketing, newspapers and magazines, television, radios and posters. 1968. w. £1.50. Haymarket Publishing Ltd., 174 Hammersmith Rd., London W6 7JP, England. TEL 44-171-413-4328. FAX 44-171-413-4013. (Subscr. to: P.O. Box 219, Woking, Surrey GU21 1ZW, England. TEL 44-1483-733800. FAX 44-1483-756792) Ed. Dominic Mills. adv.; bk.rev.; circ. 16,452 (paid). **Indexed:** Account.& Data Proc.Abstr., Anbar., DAAI, Ind.Bus.Rep., Mgmt.& Market.Abstr., Photo.Abstr., Print.Abstr. **Document type:** trade publication.
●Also available online. Vendor(s): Information Access Co., MediaStream.
—BLDSC (3016.300000). CCC.

659 AT ISSN 0816-4789
CAMPAIGN BRIEF. 1984. 10/yr. Aus.$55; newsstand price: Aus.$5. Campaign Brief Pty. Ltd., 259 Miller St., N. Sydney, N.S.W. 2060, Australia. TEL 61-2-99540042. FAX 61-2-99540263. (Subscr. addr.: P.O. Box 699 W. Perth, W.A. 6872, Australia) Ed. Michael Lynch; Pub. Michael Lynch. adv.: B&W page Aus.$1400, color page Aus.$2000; trim 330 x 240; adv. contact: Michael Lynch. circ. 5,000 (paid). (back issues avail.) **Document type:** trade publication.
Description: Focuses on creative issues in production of TV, print and cinema advertising, for everyone involved in the creative processes.

CAPELL'S CIRCULATION REPORT; the newsletter of magazine circulation. see *PUBLISHING AND BOOK TRADE*

659.1 658 US ISSN 1076-6081
ARD TALK. 1980. q. $15 (foreign $18) (effective 1997). American Business Card Club, Box 460297, Aurora, CO 80046-0297. TEL 303-690-6496. Eds. Sue & Avery N. Pitzak; Pub. Avery N. Pitzak. R&P contact: Avery N. Pitzak. adv. contact: Avery N. Pitzak. bk.rev.; circ. 500 (paid). (back issues avail.) **Document type:** newsletter.
Description: Covers facets of business cards including their use as effective tools for advertising, marketing, promotion, sales, public relations and networking.
Refereed Serial

070.5 US ISSN 0740-3119
HF5861
CATALOG AGE. 1983. m. $64 (free to qualified personnel). Cowles Business Media, 11 River Bend Dr., S., Box 4949, Stamford, CT 06907-0949. TEL 203-358-9900. FAX 203-358-5811. Ed. Laura Christiana. adv.: B&W page $2965, color page $3830; 10 7/8 x 14 1/4. bk.rev. circ. 12,200. (reprint service avail. from UMI.) **Indexed:** ABI Inform., PSI. **Document type:** trade publication.
●Also available online. Vendor(s): Information Access Co., UMI.
—BLDSC (3074.082000); KR SourceOne; UMI.

659 US ISSN 0730-9637
THE CATALOG MARKETER. 1982. fortn. $199 (foreign $244) (effective 1997). Maxwell Sroge Publishing, Inc., 522 Forest Ave., Evanston, IL 60202-3005. TEL 847-866-1890. FAX 847-866-1899. Ed. Ann Meyer. (looseleaf format; back issues avail.) **Document type:** newsletter.
Description: Offers cost-saving, money-making practical ideas on all aspects of creating and producing catalogs.

360 659.1 US ISSN 0009-1510
CHANNELS (EXETER); communications and management ideas for all organizations. 1923. m. $50. P R Publishing Co., Inc., Box 600, Exeter, NH 03833-0600. TEL 603-778-0514. FAX 603-778-1741. E-mail: prr@nh.ultranet.com. Ed. June Barber. bk.rev. (looseleaf format) **Document type:** newsletter.

659.1 US ISSN 1062-9548
CHEAP RELIEF. 1988. m. $48. 734 W. El Alba Way, Chandler, AZ 85224-2408. TEL 602-899-8984. FAX 602-899-1725. E-mail: JKelLaw@aol.com. Ed. Jean Lawrence; Pub. Jean Lawrence. R&P contact: Jean Lawrence. bk.rev.; circ. 100 (paid). (back issues avail.)
Description: Tips on how to make everything easier and cheaper in advertising, marketing and public relations.

659.1 US
CHICAGO ADVERTISING & MEDIA. s-m. K B Communications, 2240 W. 23rd Pl., Chicago, IL 60608-3904. TEL 312-847-4444. FAX 312-847-4044. Ed. Joe Brar. adv.; tr.lit. circ. 10,000.

659.1 UK ISSN 0953-7457
CHINA MEDIA BOOK;* China's advertising rates & media. 1988. biennial. £75. Anglo-Chinese Publications Ltd., 17 Belmont, Lansdown Rd., Bath, Avon BA1 5D2, England. TEL 44-1225-339516. Ed. Marcus H. Langston. circ. 1,500. **Document type:** trade publication.

CHINESE TELEPHONE DIRECTORY. see *BUSINESS AND ECONOMICS — Trade And Industrial Directories*

659.1 200 US ISSN 0744-4370
CHRISTIAN ADVERTISING FORUM.* 1981. bi-m. $18. Box 21433, Roanoke, VA 24018-0145. Ed. Stephen M. Wike. adv. circ. 2,460.

015 US ISSN 0569-6704
HF5905
CIRCULATION (YEAR). 1957. a. $189 (effective 1997). S R D S (Subsidiary of: V N U U.S.A.), 1700 Higgins Rd., Des Plaines, IL 60018. TEL 847-375-5000; 800-851-7737. FAX 847-375-5001. E-mail: kgear@srds.com; URL: http://www.srds.com. Pub. Kathleen Geary. R&P contact: Kathleen Ann Geary. adv.; stat. **Document type:** directory, trade publication.
Formerly: Newspaper Circulation Analysis (ISSN 0585-0428)
Description: Contains detailed profiles of more than 1,800 daily newspapers and newspaper groups. Provides county-by-county analyses of daily newspaper circulation figures for each state.

659.1 US ISSN 1081-1346
CLASSIFIED COMMUNICATION; the newsletter for small budget advertising. 1990. m. $33 (Canada $45; elsewhere $55). Classified Communication Inc., Box 4242, Prescott, AZ 86302. TEL 520-778-6788. FAX 520-445-0517. E-mail: classcomm@aol.com. Ed. Agnes Franz; Pub. Agnes Franz. R&P contact: Magla Gregory. bk.rev. **Document type:** newsletter.

659.1 330 384 US
CLIENT DIRECTORY AND AGENCY LIST. 1988. s-a. International Federation of Advertising Agencies, 1450 E. American Ln., Ste. 1400, Schaumburg, IL 60173-4973. TEL 847-330-6344. FAX 847-517-4459. E-mail: nstephen@starnetinc.com. Ed. Norval Stephens. index; circ. 100 (controlled). (also avail. in diskette format; back issues avail.) **Document type:** directory.

741.67 746.92 700 FR ISSN 1152-8885
COLLECTOR. 1990. q. 250 F. (outside Europe 330 F.). Editions du Triangle Rose, 45, rue Sedaine, 75557 Paris Cedex 11, France. TEL 43-57-52-05. FAX 43-57-80-40. Ed. Pascal Le Coq. adv. circ. 10,000.
Description: Devoted to mass-media images (advertising, graphic arts, fashion, contemporary art).

COLOR NEWS. see *BEAUTY CULTURE*

COMMUNICARE; journal of communication sciences. see *COMMUNICATIONS*

659.1 NE ISSN 1381-4974
COMMUNICATIE; tijdschrift over communicatiemanagement, PR en voorlichting. 1963. m. fl.165. Bohn Stafleu van Loghum B.V. (Subsidiary of: Wolters Kluwer N.V.), Postbus 246, 3990 GA Houten, Netherlands. TEL 31-3403-95711. FAX 31-3403-50903. adv. circ. 3,500. **Document type:** trade publication. —SWETS.
Formed by the 1995 merger of: Communicatief (ISSN 0922-2944) & P R en V (ISSN 0927-619X); Which was formerly (until 1991): P R en Voorlichting (ISSN 0165-7232); (until 1979): Provisorium (ISSN 0928-5342)

659.1 760 US ISSN 0010-3519
NC997.A1
COMMUNICATION ARTS. 1959. 8/yr. $53 (Canada $70; elsewhere $110) (effective 1997). Coyne & Blanchard, Inc., 410 Sherman Ave., Box 10300, Palo Alto, CA 94303. TEL 415-326-6040. FAX 415-326-1648. E-mail: ca@commarts.com; URL: http://www.commarts.com. Ed. Patrick S. Coyne. R&P contact: Jean A. Coyne. adv. contact: Michael Krigel. bk.rev.; software rev.; illus.; circ. 68,548 (paid). **Indexed:** Abstr.Bull.Inst.Pap.Chem., Art Ind., Artbibl.Mod., DAAI, Graph.Arts Lit.Abstr. **Document type:** trade publication.
—BLDSC (3359.339000); KR SourceOne; SWETS; UMI; UnCover.
Description: For designers, art directors, design firms, corporate design departments, agencies, and everyone involved in visual communications.

COMMUNICATION SOCIALIST; Zeitschrift fuer Publizistik in Kirche und Welt. see *RELIGIONS AND THEOLOGY — Roman Catholic*

COMMUNICATOR (DON MILLS). see *BUSINESS AND ECONOMICS — Marketing And Purchasing*

659.1 333.7 US
COMMUNICATOR (SCOTTSDALE). a. membership. Utility Communicators International, c/o Robert Janke, 5316 E. Kings Ave., Scottsdale, AZ 85254-1123. TEL 602-971-1989. (tabloid format)
Formerly: Communicators Showcase.
Description: Presents membership activities and news.

COMMUNICATOR'S NOTEBOOK. see *JOURNALISM*

659.1 360 US
COMMUNITY FOCUS. q. free. California Federal Bank, Corporate Communications, 135 Main St., San Francisco, CA 94105-1817. TEL 415-904-1203. Ed. Mary Rische. **Document type:** newsletter.
Description: Informs First Nationwide employees and the public about the community-service events the bank sponsors throughout the nation.

COMPENDIUM OF GOVERNMENT ISSUES AFFECTING DIRECT MARKETING. see *BUSINESS AND ECONOMICS — Marketing And Purchasing*

659 AG ISSN 0326-3185
COMUNICACION; del area latinoamericana. 1980. m. Editorial Profesionales Publicitarios, Viamonte 1653, P.B. (1055), Buenos Aires, Argentina. Ed. Juan Carlos Escalera Moya.

ADVERTISING AND PUBLIC RELATIONS

659.1   CK   ISSN 0120-1638
COMUNICACION INTEGRAL. 1974. q. Col.400($12) Entropia, Grupo de Comunicacion Empresarial Integral, Apdo. Aereo 3139, Medellin, Colombia. Ed. Humberto Lopez. adv.; bk.rev. circ. 2,500.

650 808.0666   US
CONSULTING SUCCESS. 1983. q. $35 (includes membership). Association of Professional Communication Consultants, 3924 South Troost, Tulsa, OK 74105. TEL 918-743-4793. Ed. Lu Rehling. circ. 400. (back issues avail.) **Document type:** newsletter.
    Formerly: Professional Writing Consultant.
    Description: Includes tips on managing small businesses, pricing services, marketing, what's new in the field of writing and communications consulting and networking for new members.

659.1 384   US
CONTACTS; the media pipeline for public relations people. 1970. w. $347. C A P Communications Associates, Ltd., 35-20 Broadway, Astoria, NY 11106. TEL 718-721-0508. Ed. Madeleine Gillis. cum.index. circ. 5,000. (back issues avail.)
    Description: Outlines the information needs of editors, writers and producers of magazines (consumer & trade), newspapers, TV & radio, providing contact information.

659   SP
CONTROL. 1962. m. 6000 ptas. P C Disc, S.A., Calle Ferraz 11, 1 Piso, 28008 Madrid, Spain. TEL 1-247-30-00. FAX 1-248-11-23. Ed. Francisco Javier San Roman y Perez. adv. circ. 5,000.
—CCC.
    Formerly: Control de Publicidad y Ventas (ISSN 0573-8636)

659.1   US
HF5827.4
CO-OP ADVERTISING PROGRAM SOURCEBOOK (YEAR). 1981. s-a. £350. National Register Publishing, A Division of Reed Elsevier Inc., 121 Chanlon Rd., New Providence, NJ 07974. TEL 908-464-6800. FAX 908-464-3553. TELEX 138 755. (Subscr. to: Reed Reference Publishing, Order Dept., Box 31, New Providence, NJ 07974-9903. TEL 800-521-8110) adv. circ. 2,872. pp./issue: 1500. (also avail. in magnetic tape) **Document type:** directory.
    Formerly (until 1997): Co-op Source Directory (ISSN 0736-0878)
    Description: Used to find manufacturers' co-op programs that retailers and wholesalers use to fund advertising and promotional campaigns. Details over 6,000 programs, including the way the programs work, rules for eligibility, creative materials available, timing, and reimbursement.

659.1   FR
CORRESPONDANCE DE LA PUBLICITE; quotidien d'information et de documentation professionnelles. d. 15200 F. (foreign 16500 F.) (effective 1997). Societe Generale de Presse et d'Editions, 13 av. de l'Opera, 75001 Paris, France. TEL 40-15-17-15. FAX 40-15-17-89. TELEX SOGPRESS 230023. Ed. Etienne Lacour; Pub. Marianne Berard-Quelin. adv. circ. 3,000.
    Description: Provides professional news and data on the advertising industry.

659.1 658.8   US
COUNSEL. 1974. q. membership. National Council for Marketing and Public Relations, 364 N. Wyndham Ave., Greeley, CO 80634. Ed. Geraldine Gallagher. circ. 2,000.
    Description: For marketing and public relations officials.

659.1   US   ISSN 0011-0027
COUNSELOR (LANGHORNE). 1954. m. $65. Advertising Specialty Institute, 1120 Wheeler Way, Langnorne, PA 19047. TEL 215-752-4200. FAX 215-752-9758. URL: http://www.promomart.com. Ed. Catherine S. Holnick. R&P contact: Catherine S. Holnick. adv. contact: Christine Lovell. bk.rev. circ. 8,700. **Document type:** trade publication.
    Description: Publishes news for professionals in promotional marketing and specialty advertising management who are listed with the Advertising Specialty Institute.

COVER; arts New York. see HUMANITIES: COMPREHENSIVE WORKS

CRAP HOUND. see ART

659.1   FR
CREATION. 11/yr. 15 bis, rue Ernest Renan, 92133 Issy-les-Moulineaux, France. TEL 40-93-01-02. FAX 40-93-03-44. Ed. Sylvie Deleule. circ. 17,000.
Indexed: DAAI.

659.1   US   ISSN 0737-5883
CREATIVE; the magazine of promotion and marketing. 1966. bi-m. $30. Magazines Creative, Inc., 37 W. 39th St., New York, NY 10018. TEL 212-840-0160. FAX 212-819-0945. Ed. David H. Flaserstein. adv.; bk.rev. circ. 15,000. (also avail. in microfiche from UMI)
—UnCover.
    Formerly: Creative Signs and Displays.

659.1   IE
CREATIVE. fortn. Concept & Realisation Ltd., 23 The Mews, Upper Mount St., Dublin 2, Ireland. TEL 762212. FAX 761204. Ed. Garrett Stokes.

CREATIVE MARKETING; incentives in retail promotion. see BUSINESS AND ECONOMICS — Marketing And Purchasing

659.1   US   ISSN 1064-3915
CREATIVE NEW JERSEY. 1987. bi-m. $14.95. Calsun Publications, Box 327, Ramsey, NJ 07446. TEL 201-670-8688. FAX 201-670-4484. Ed. Sally Jane Gellert. adv.: B&W page $1746; trim 9 3/4 x 16. circ. 17,882. **Document type:** trade publication.
    Description: Reports on the State's advertising industry and related businesses.

CREATIVE REVIEW. see BUSINESS AND ECONOMICS — Marketing And Purchasing

659.1   CN   ISSN 0709-7727
NC917.A1
CREATIVE SOURCE. 1979. a. Can.$65. Motion Works Group Ltd., 150 York St., Ste. 1100, Toronto, ON M5H 3S5, Canada. TEL 416-214-0083. FAX 416-361-9062. E-mail: info@creativesource.ca; URL: http://www.creativesource.ca. (Dist. by: Firefly Books, 250 Sparks Ave., Willowdale, Ont. M2H 2S4, Canada) Pub. Peter Cordy. adv. circ. 10,000. **Document type:** directory.

659.1   IT
CREATIVI E FORNITORI GUIDE. 1979. a. L.350000. Bragadin Editore s.r.l., Via Stradella 3, 20129 Milan, Italy. TEL 2-29-40-05-54. FAX 2-29-40-18-16. Ed. Lillo Perri. adv. contact: Daniele Monai. circ. 4,000. **Document type:** directory.

740   US   ISSN 0097-6075
NC997
CREATIVITY. 1971. a. $62.95. (Art Direction Magazine) Art Direction Book Co. Inc., 456 Glenbrook Rd., Glenbrook, CT 06906. TEL 203-353-1441. FAX 203-353-1371. circ. 6,700. **Document type:** trade publication.
    ●Also available online. Vendor(s): Information Access Co.
    Supersedes (1960-1965): Advertising Directions.
    Description: Examines advertising art.

659.2   US
CRISIS MANAGEMENT REPORTER; damage control when you need it. m. $190 (foreign $210). Remy Publishing Co., 350 W. Hubbard St., No. 440, Chicago, IL 60610-4011. TEL 312-464-0300. Ed. Gerald Murray. index. **Document type:** newsletter.
    Description: For the investor relations or public relations professional who may have to face answering to stockholders, government regulators, the public, and the press regarding such issues as minority group relations, labor unrest, product tampering, community protests, and financial malfeasance.

CROSS AND TALK; for communications between you and the world. see COMMUNICATIONS

D M A STATISTICAL FACT BOOK. (Direct Marketing Association) see BUSINESS AND ECONOMICS — Marketing And Purchasing

DALTONS WEEKLY; houses, shops & businesses for sale; hotel guest house & self-catering holiday accommodation advertiser. see REAL ESTATE

DANSK PRESSE. see JOURNALISM

659.1   IT   ISSN 0038-9501
DATI E TARIFFE PUBBLICITARIE; prontuario dei mezzi pubblicitari italiani. (Text in Italian) 1962. bi-m. Lit.1000000 (effective 1997). Emap Publishing s.r.l., Piazza della Repubblica, 32, 20124 Milan, Italy. TEL 39-2-67151210. FAX 39-2-66980255. adv.

659.1   US
DELANEY REPORT. 1990. w. $265 (fax $348). 149 Fifth Ave., New York, NY 10010. TEL 212-979-7881. FAX 212-979-0691. Ed. Thomas F. Delaney; Pub. Thomas F. Delaney. R&P contact: Thomas F. Delaney. (also avail. by fax) **Document type:** newsletter.
    Description: Covers news, trends in marketing, advertising, and media.

DEMEURES ET CHATEAUX. see REAL ESTATE

740   GW
DESIGN INTERNATIONAL. A AND B. (Text in English and German) 1967. q. Design International, Kaufering 57, 5330 Koenigswinter, Germany. Ed.Bd. adv.; bk.rev.; abstr.; illus.
    Formed by the 1982 merger of: Design International. Issue A (ISSN 0343-5849); Design International. Issue B (ISSN 0343-5865); Which supersedes in part: Design International (ISSN 0011-9393)

659.1   US
DIAMOND TRAIL NEWS. 1975. w. $18 in Iowa; other states $23; foreign $35. 303 Seventh Ave., Box 186, Sully, IA 50251. TEL 515-594-4488. FAX 515-594-4498. E-mail: DTNews@aol.com. Ed. Mark Davitt; Pub. Mark Davitt. R&P contact: Mark Davitt. bk.rev. circ. 1,800. (tabloid format; back issues avail.) **Document type:** newspaper.

DIRECT LINE. see BUSINESS AND ECONOMICS — Marketing And Purchasing

DIRECT MARKETING; using direct response advertising to enhance marketing database. see BUSINESS AND ECONOMICS — Marketing And Purchasing

DIRECT MARKETING ASSOCIATION. ANNUAL REPORT. see BUSINESS AND ECONOMICS — Marketing And Purchasing

DIRECT MARKETING MARKET PLACE; the networking source of the direct marketing industry. see BUSINESS AND ECONOMICS — Marketing And Purchasing

659.1 658   US
DIRECT RESPONSE SPECIALIST. 1982. m. $77 (effective 1997). Galen Stilson Ed. & Pub., Box 1075, Tarpon Springs, FL 34688-1075. TEL 813-786-1411. FAX 813-785-7049. E-mail: gstilson@mindspring.com. adv.; bk.rev. (back issues avail.) **Document type:** newsletter.
    Formerly (until 1987): Mail Order Connection.
    Description: Discusses effective response and profit techniques.

659.1 658   US   ISSN 1087-2183
DIRECTION (ALLENDALE). 1979. bi-m. $40 (foreign $50) (effective 1997). Direct Marketing Consultants, Inc., 705 Franklin Tpke., Allendale, NJ 07401-1637. TEL 201-327-9213. FAX 201-327-9213. Ed. Hugh P. Curley. R&P contact: Hugh P. Curley. adv.; bk.rev. circ. 4,927. (back issues avail.) **Document type:** newsletter.
    Description: Provides tips on how to better influence buying decisions, with emphasis on more productive and profitable use of direct mail, sales promotion, publicity and other marketing tools.

DIRECTIONS (NEW YORK). see BUSINESS AND ECONOMICS — Marketing And Purchasing

659.2   MX
DIRECTORIO M P M - AGENCIAS Y ANUNCIANTES/M P M - MEXICAN ADVERTISING AGENCIES DIRECTORY; personal y cuentas. 1964. s-a. Mex.$150($120) (effective 1997). Medios Publicitarios Mexicanos, S.A., Av. Mexico 99-103, Col. Hipodromo-Condesa, 06170 Mexico, DF, Mexico. TEL 52-5-5742858. FAX 52-5-5742668. Ed. Fernando A. Villamil. adv. circ. 1,500. **Document type:** directory.

ADVERTISING AND PUBLIC RELATIONS

DIRECTORIO M P M - MEDIOS AUDIOVISUALES/M P M - MEXICAN AUDIOVISUAL MEDIA RATES & DATA; tarifas y datos-cine, radio y televisión. (Medios Publicitarios Mexicanos, S.A.) see *ADVERTISING AND PUBLIC RELATIONS — Abstracting, Bibliographies, Statistics*

DIRECTORIO M P M - MEDIOS IMPRESOS/M P M - MEXICAN PRINT MEDIA RATES & DATA; tarifas y datos-anuncio exterior, periodicos y revistas. (Medios Publicitarios Mexicanos, S.A.) see *ADVERTISING AND PUBLIC RELATIONS — Abstracting, Bibliographies, Statistics*

DIRECTORY OF ADVERTISING AGENCIES. see *BUSINESS AND ECONOMICS — Trade And Industrial Directories*

DIRECTORY OF JAPANESE PUBLISHING INDUSTRY. see *PUBLISHING AND BOOK TRADE*

659.132   US   ISSN 0419-2923
DIRECTORY OF MAILING LIST COMPANIES.* 1955. irreg., 12th ed., 1995. $40. Todd Publications, Box 635, Nyack, NY 10960-0635. TEL 914-358-6213. Ed. Barry Klein. **Document type:** directory.
   Formerly (until 1991): Directory of Mailing List Houses.
   Description: Provides the names and addresses of more than 1,200 mailing list specialists. Includes list brokers, compilers and owners as well as list management companies, co-operative mailers, package insert programs and card deck mailers, with name of contacts, phone numbers and types of lists carried.

DIRECTORY OF MAJOR MAILERS & WHAT THEY MAIL (YEAR). see *BUSINESS AND ECONOMICS — Trade And Industrial Directories*

DIRECTORY WORLD. see *BUSINESS AND ECONOMICS — Trade And Industrial Directories*

DIRECTORY WORLD'S YELLOW PAGES INDUSTRY SOURCE BOOK. see *BUSINESS AND ECONOMICS — Trade And Industrial Directories*

DIREKT-KONTAKT BETRIEBSBEDARF. see *BUSINESS AND ECONOMICS — Marketing And Purchasing*

659.1   UK
THE DOOR-TO-DOOR MARKETING HANDBOOK. 1989. a. free. Association of Household Distributors Ltd., 36 Frogmore St., Tring, Hants. HP23 5AU, England. TEL 44-1442-890991. FAX 44-1442-890992. Ed. Shelley Radice. adv. contact: Shelley Radice. circ. 3,000 (controlled). (back issues avail.) **Document type:** directory.
   Formerly: Letterbox Marketing Handbook.
   Description: Contains a list of companies able to deliver advertising and promotional materials to households throughout the U.K., along with background information.

659.1   GW
DOPPELPUNKT. 1984. m. DM.40. Neue Toene Werner Mende Verlag oHG, Am Haag 10, 97234 Reichenberg, Germany. TEL 49-931-69469. FAX 49-931-69470. circ. 45,000. **Document type:** trade publication.

659.1 340   US
DO'S AND DON'TS IN ADVERTISING. 1949. base vol. (plus m. supplements). $350 (renewal $235) includes Advertising Topics, Newsletter. Council of Better Business Bureaus, Publications Department, 4200 Wilson Blvd., Ste. 800, Arlington, VA 22203-1804. TEL 703-276-0100. (looseleaf format)
   Description: Contains numerous Federal Trade Commission, Food and Drug Administration, Federal Communications Commission, and other agency regulations and guides. Summarizes key legal decisions, and state and federal laws affecting advertising.

659.1   BE
DOSSIER AGENCES/BUREAUDOSSIER. (Text in Dutch, French) 1977. a. 6678 BEF (foreign 11660 BEF) (effective 1995). Kluwer Business Press (Subsidiary of: Wolters Kluwer N.V.), Kouterveldstraat 2, 1831 Diegem, Belgium. TEL 32-2-7231523. FAX 32-2-7231591. Ed. Jean-Michel Stichelbaut. adv.: B&W page 95000 BEF, color page 106000 BEF; adv. contact: Gerda Bourdeaud'hui. circ. 5,000 (paid). **Document type:** trade publication, directory.

352.7 352.7   US   ISSN 0363-2830
DOWNTOWN PROMOTION REPORTER. 1976. m. $123. (Downtown Research & Development Center) Alexander Research & Communications, Inc., 215 Park Ave., S., Ste. 1301, New York, NY 10003. TEL 212-228-0246. FAX 212-228-0376. Ed. Mary Barr; Pub. Shirley Alexander. R&P contact: Mary Dalessandro. illus. **Document type:** newsletter.
   Description: Focuses on bringing more people downtown for shopping, sales and special events. Covers tested promotional ideas, public relations, increasing participation, image building, seasonal promotions and more.

659.1   BE
E D M A - GRAM. Variant title: Edmagram. 1976. 4/yr. membership. European Direct Marketing Association, 439 Avenue de Tervueren, B-1150 Brussels, Belgium. TEL 32-2-7794268. FAX 32-2-7794269. adv.: B&W page 22000 BEF; trim 297 x 210; adv. contact: Catherine de Callatay. bk.rev. **Document type:** newsletter.

659.1   US
▼**EDITOR & PUBLISHER - FREE PAPER PUBLISHER COMMUNITY, SPECIALTY & FREE PUBLICATIONS YEAR BOOK**; a media buyers guide. 1996. a. $99. Editor & Publisher Co., Inc., 11 W. 19th St., New York, NY 10011. TEL 212-675-4380. FAX 212-929-1259. E-mail: edpub@mediainfo.com; URL: http://www.mediainfo.com. Pubs. D. Colin Phillips, Christopher Phillips. R&P contact: Ian Anderson. adv. contact: Mike Dardano. **Document type:** directory.
   ●Also available on CD-ROM.
   Description: Profiles of paid and free community weeklies, non-daily newspaper groups, and specialty and niche publications in the US and Canada. Includes key personnel and contact information.

EDITOR & PUBLISHER - THE FOURTH ESTATE; spot news and features about newspapers, advertisers & agencies. see *JOURNALISM*

659.1   UK   ISSN 0268-7542
EDITORS MEDIA DIRECTORIES. VOL. 1: NATIONAL MEDIA. m. £160 (£450 for all 6 vols.) (effective 1997). Media Information Ltd., Chess House, 34 Germain St., Chesham HP5 1SJ, England. TEL 44-1494-797230. FAX 44-1494-797224. E-mail: editors@mediainfo.co.uk. Ed. Helen Buckhurst. adv. **Document type:** directory.
   Description: Access to the entire UK media, with detailed editorial listings of over 42,000 contacts and freelancers at over 14,000 publications, stations and programmes.

659.1   UK   ISSN 0268-7550
EDITORS MEDIA DIRECTORIES. VOL. 2: BUSINESS AND PROFESSIONAL. q. £160 (£450 for all 6 vols.) (effective 1997). Media Information Ltd., Chess House, 34 Germain St., Chesham HP5 1SJ, England. TEL 44-1494-797230. FAX 44-1494-797224. E-mail: editors@mediainfo.co.uk. Ed. Helen Buckhurst. adv. **Document type:** directory.

659.1   UK   ISSN 0268-7569
EDITORS MEDIA DIRECTORIES. VOL. 3: PROVINCIAL NEWSPAPERS & TOWN GUIDE. 3/yr. £160 (£450 for all 6 vols.) (effective 1997). Media Information Ltd., Chess House, 34 Germain St., Chesham HP5 1SJ, England. TEL 44-1494-797230. FAX 44-1494-797224. E-mail: editors@mediainfo.co.uk. Ed. Helen Buckhurst. adv. **Document type:** directory.

659.1   UK   ISSN 0268-7577
EDITORS MEDIA DIRECTORIES. VOL. 4: CONSUMER & LEISURE MAGAZINES. q. £140 (£450 for all 6 vols.) (effective 1997). Media Information Ltd., Chess House, 34 Germain St., Chesham HP5 1SJ, England. TEL 44-1494-797230. FAX 44-1494-797224. E-mail: editors@mediainfo.co.uk. Ed. Helen Buckhurst. adv. **Document type:** directory.

659.1   UK
EDITORS MEDIA DIRECTORIES. VOL. 5: RADIO AND T V PROGRAMMES. s-a. £120 (£450 for all 6 vols.) (effective 1997). Media Information Ltd., Chess House, 34 Germain St., Chesham HP5 1SJ, England. TEL 44-1494-797230. FAX 44-1494-797224. E-mail: editors@mediainfo.co.uk. Ed. Helen Buckhurst. adv. **Document type:** directory.
   Formerly: Editors Media Directories. Vol. 5: Broadcast Media (ISSN 0268-7585)

659.1   UK
EDITORS MEDIA DIRECTORIES. VOL. 6: FREELANCERS, WRITERS' GUILDS & LONDON CORRESPONDENTS OF FOREIGN PRESS. a. £105 (£450 for all 6 vols.) (effective 1997). Media Information Ltd., Chess House, 34 Germain St., Chesham HP5 1SJ, England. TEL 44-1494-797230. FAX 44-1494-797224. E-mail: editors@mediainfo.co.uk. Ed. Helen Buckhurst. adv. **Document type:** directory.
   Formerly: Editors Media Directories. Vol. 6: Writers' Guilds and London Correspondents of Foreign Press (ISSN 0268-7631)

659.1   US
EIGHT-SHEET OUTDOOR RATES AND ALLOTMENTS. 1970. a. $40. Waggener & Associates, Inc., Box 39, Blue Springs, MO 64015-0039. TEL 816-228-0900. FAX 816-228-0953. Ed. R.W. Waggener. adv. circ. 2,300. **Document type:** catalog.

659.1   IT   ISSN 0393-9170
ELECTRONIC MASS MEDIA AGE. 1985. m. $50. Systems Comunicazioni, Via Olanda, 6, 20083 Gaggiano (MI), Italy. TEL 02-90841814. FAX 02-90841682. Ed. M. DiPisa. adv.: B&W page L.2500000, color page L.3300000; trim 250 x 350. circ. 4,800. (tabloid format; back issues avail.)

EMPA. see *MUSEUMS AND ART GALLERIES*

659.1 658.8   AT
EQUINE OZ. m. Laurel Enterprises, E-mail: Mark.Williams@equineoz.com.au; URL: http://www.equineoz.com.au/. Ed. Mark Williams.
   ●Available only online.
   Description: Provides news, fulltext articles about equestrian events worldwide.

659.1 658   GW
ETAT-KALKULATOR. 1978. 2/yr. DM.75. Creativ Collection Verlag GmbH, Basler Landstr. 61, 79111 Freiburg, Germany. TEL 49-761-42606. FAX 49-761-42608. Ed. Matthias Prosch. adv.: B&W page DM.3500, color page DM.3000. circ. 5,000. **Document type:** trade publication.

659.1   UK   ISSN 0952-3820
EUROMARKETING. 1987. w. £255($395) Crain Communications Inc., New Garden House, 78 Hatton Garden, London EC1N 8JQ, England. TEL 44-171-457-1400. FAX 44-171-457-1440. Ed. Bill Britt. index. (back issues avail.) **Document type:** newsletter.
   ●Also available online. Vendor(s): Information Access Co.
   —CCC.
   Description: Covers the most significant news and developments in marketing, advertising and media across Europe.

659   GW   ISSN 0085-0349
HF5808.E85
EUROPA HANDBUCH DER WERBEGESELLSCHAFTEN. 1962. a. DM.178. Team Verlag GmbH und Fachzeitschriften KG, Auwanne 19, 63791 Karlstein, Germany. Ed. Horst P. Czerner. adv. circ. 2,500. **Document type:** trade publication.

659.1   UK   ISSN 0951-7758
EUROPEAN ADVERTISING & MEDIA FORECAST. 1986. 6/yr. £1190 (effective 1998). (Advertising Association) N T C Publications Ltd., P.O. Box 69, Henley-on-Thames, Oxon RG9 1GB, England. TEL 44-1491-411000. FAX 44-1491-571188. (Co-sponsor: European Advertising Tripartite) **Document type:** trade publication.
   Description: Presents data, forecasts and expert analyses covering advertising expenditures and media developments in 17 countries.

EUROPEAN MARKETING ASSOCIATION. INTERNATIONAL MARKETING AND RESEARCH CONFERENCE. JOURNAL. see *BUSINESS AND ECONOMICS — Marketing And Purchasing*

EUROPEAN MARKETING NEWSLETTER. see *BUSINESS AND ECONOMICS — Marketing And Purchasing*

ADVERTISING AND PUBLIC RELATIONS

659 338   UK   ISSN 0924-5855
EUROPEAN SIGN MAGAZINE. (Text in English, summaries in French, German) 1987. bi-m. £45 in E.U., Europe £55, elsewhere $120. Miller Freeman plc, Miller Freeman House, 30 Calderwood St., London SE18 6QH, England.
TEL 44-181-855-7777. FAX 44-181-316-3206. Ed. Karen Charlesworth. adv.: page £5250; trim 210 x 297; adv. contact: Richard Langrish. circ. 7,000. **Document type:** trade publication.
  Description: Covers all aspects of signmaking and the sign business.

659.1   FR   ISSN 1145-6167
EVENEMENTIEL.* 11/yr. 86 rue du Pdt Wilson, 92300 Levallois-Peret, France. TEL 45-45-67-66. FAX 45-45-07-37. Ed. Yves Barraud. circ. 13,000.
  Description: Dedicated to publicity through sponsorship, conventions and product launches.

659.2   US   ISSN 0271-3659
EXECUTIVE SPEAKER. 1980. m. $132 (foreign $157). Executive Speaker Co., Box 292437, Dayton, OH 45429. TEL 937-294-8493. FAX 937-294-6044. Ed. Robert O. Skovgard; Pub. Robert O. Skovgard. bk.rev.; index. **Document type:** newsletter.
  ●Also available online. Vendor(s): Lexis-Nexis.
  Description: Serves as a clearinghouse and digest for recent speeches by executives. Features examples of the best openings, closings and quotations from speeches along with a line or two of analysis that points out what made the quotation effective.

EXHIBITOR MAGAZINE; the magazine for trade show and event marketing management. see *BUSINESS AND ECONOMICS — Marketing And Purchasing*

EXPOSURE! (YAKIMA). see *COMPUTERS — Computer Networks*

FACILITIES; the bible for convention, exposition and event management. see *BUSINESS AND ECONOMICS — Management*

FASHION WATCH. see *CLOTHING TRADE — Fashions*

FASTLINE: DIXIE EDITION. see *TRANSPORTATION — Trucks And Trucking*

FASTLINE: TENNESSEE TRUCK EDITION. see *TRANSPORTATION — Trucks And Trucking*

FEATURE NEWS PUBLICITY OUTLETS. see *JOURNALISM*

659.1 332   US   ISSN 0748-1845
FINANCIAL ADVERTISING REVIEW; creative forum for the people who plan and create financial advertising programs. 1979. m. $259. Business Word Inc., 5350 S. Roslyn St., Ste. 400, Englewood, CO 80111-2125. TEL 303-290-8500; 800-328-3211. FAX 303-290-9025. E-mail: plmoore@businessword.com. Ed. Pamela Moore; Pub. Donald E.L. Johnson. circ. 1,200 (paid). (also avail. in microform from UMI; back issues avail.) **Document type:** trade publication.
  ●Also available online. Vendor(s): NewsNet.
  —UMI. **CCC.**
  Description: Covers advertising and marketing programs successfully implemented in the financial industry, with emphasis on print advertising, featuring more than 100 examples of the nation's best print, radio, outdoor and direct-mail financial advertising campaigns.

FINANCIAL SURVEY. SIGN & STREET FURNITURE MANUFACTURERS & DISTRIBUTORS; company data for success. see *BUSINESS AND ECONOMICS — Trade And Industrial Directories*

659.1   GW
FINDLING; Marktplatz fuer kostenlose private Kleinanzeigen. 1985. 2/w. Dolmen Verlag GmbH, Untertuerkheimerstr. 39-41, 66117 Saarbruecken, Germany. TEL 0681-9535-0. FAX 0681-9535-305. Ed. Axel Schindler. adv. circ. 37,976. (looseleaf format) **Document type:** consumer publication.

FREE PAPER PUBLISHER. see *PUBLISHING AND BOOK TRADE*

FREELANCE WRITER'S REPORT. see *JOURNALISM*

FREELANCERS OF NORTH AMERICA. see *PUBLISHING AND BOOK TRADE*

FRIDAY REPORT. see *BUSINESS AND ECONOMICS — Marketing And Purchasing*

FROHLINGER'S MARKETING REPORT. see *BUSINESS AND ECONOMICS — Marketing And Purchasing*

659.1   GW
G W A. 1988. a. DM.140. Gesamtverband Werbeagenturen, Friedensstr. 11, 60311 Frankfurt a.M., Germany. TEL 069-2560080.
FAX 069-236883. **Document type:** trade publication.
  Formerly: Werbeagenturen G W A.

659.1   GW
G W A YEARBOOK. 1980. a. DM.138. (Gesamtverband Werbeagenturen e.V.) Deutscher Fachverlag GmbH, Mainzer Landstr. 251, 60326 Frankfurt a.M., Germany. TEL 49-69-75952841.
FAX 49-69-75952820. **Document type:** bulletin.

659.1   AT
GEELONG NEWS. 1940. w. Geelong Newspapers P-L, 191-197 Ryrie St., Geelong, Vic. 3220, Australia. circ. 55,000.

659.1   US
GEIGER REPORT. fortn. Box 24248, Edina, MN 55424-0248. TEL 612-925-5115. Ed. Bob Geiger. circ. 350.

DIE GESCHAEFTSIDEE; Fachmagazin fuer Unternehmensgruendung und neue Maerkte. see *BUSINESS AND ECONOMICS — Small Business*

659.1 658.8   IT
GLOBAL. (Supplement to: Media Key Synthesis) 1988. 4/yr. L.20000($175) (includes Media Key and TV Key). Media Key s.r.l., Via Filippino Lippi 33 C, 20131 Milan, Italy. TEL 39-2-70638348.
FAX 39-2-2363662. Ed. Roberto Albano. adv. contact: Silvana Catazzina. circ. 9,500.

659.2   CC
GONGGONG GUANXI BAO/PUBLIC RELATIONS NEWS. (Text in Chinese) 1987. s-w. Y52 (effective 1997). Zhejiang Ribao She, 178 Tiyuchang Lu, Hangzhou, Zhejiang 310004, People's Republic of China. TEL 86-571-5152101. FAX 86-571-5176822. (Dist. overseas by: China International Book Trading Corp., P.O. Box 399, Beijing 100044, P.R. China) Ed. Xieheng Chen. R&P contact: Zhichang Tong. adv. contact: Xieheng Chen. pp./issue: 4. **Document type:** newspaper, trade publication.
  Description: Covers the latest development in China's public relations industry. Also provides case studies and relevant tips.

659.1 340   US
GOVERNMENT REPORT. 1960. 9/yr. membership. American Advertising Federation, 1101 Vermont Ave., N.W., Ste. 500, Washington, DC 20005. TEL 202-898-0089. E-mail: dghernandez@aaf.org. Ed. Debra Gersh Hernandez. circ. 3,000. (back issues avail.) **Document type:** newsletter.
  Formerly: Washington Report (Washington, 1960).
  Description: Monitors state and federal legislation and regulatory activity affecting the advertising industry.

GRAPHIC DESIGN: U S A. see *PRINTING*

GRAPHIS; international journal of visual communication. see *ART*

GRAPHIS DESIGN; international annual of design and illustration. see *ART*

659.1   VE
GUIA VENEZOLANA DE PUBLICIDAD Y MERCADEO. 1967. a. Bs.400($60) M.G. Ediciones Especializadas, S.A., Av. Maturin, No. 15, Urb. Los Cedros, El Bosque, Caracas 1050, Venezuela. Ed. Montserrat Giol. adv. circ. 2,000.

GUIDA AGENZIE. see *BUSINESS AND ECONOMICS — Trade And Industrial Directories*

659.14   UK   ISSN 0966-4874
THE GUIDE TO EUROPEAN BUSINESS MEDIA. 1991. s-a. £150. Lizard Ltd., P.O. Box 179, Tonbridge, Kent TN12 6ZU, England. TEL 44-181-948-4732. FAX 44-181-332-2833. Ed. Susan Stephens; Pub. Susan Stephens. (also avail. in diskette format; back issues avail.) **Document type:** directory.
  Description: Lists European print and broadcast media that carry business news.

016.05   NE   ISSN 0440-1875
Z6956.N45
HANDBOEK VAN DE NEDERLANDSE PERS EN PUBLICITEIT. CD-ROM edition: Nijgh Media Disc. (In 3 vols.: Gedruckte Media; Reclamedragende Media; Algemene Gegevens) 1953. 2/yr. (CD-ROM 4/yr.) fl.420.50 (effective 1996). Nijgh Periodieken B.V., Postbus 122, 3100 AC Schiedam, Netherlands. TEL 31-10-4274100. FAX 31-10-4739911. E-mail: handboek@nijgh.nl. Pub. A.J.A. van der Post. adv.: B&W page fl.3195, color page fl.5445; trim 148 x 210. bk.rev. circ. 6,728. **Document type:** directory.
  ●Also available on CD-ROM.
  Description: Provides comprehensive information on Dutch periodical publications, including advertising rates and contact names, and an index to publishing, advertising and publicity companies.

741.67   US   ISSN 8756-4513
HEALTHCARE ADVERTISING REVIEW; creative forum for the people who plan and create healthcare advertising programs. 1985. bi-m. $259. Business Word Inc., 5350 S. Rosly St., Ste. 400, Englewood, CO 80111-2125. TEL 303-290-8500; 800-328-3211. FAX 303-290-9025. E-mail: plmoore@businessword.com. Ed. Pamela Moore; Pub. Donald E.L. Johnson. circ. 1,323 (paid). (back issues avail.) **Document type:** trade publication.
  ●Also available online. Vendor(s): NewsNet.
  —**CCC.**
  Description: Covers advertising and marketing programs successfully implemented in the health care industry, with emphasis on print advertising.

HEALTHCARE P R & MARKETING NEWS. see *MEDICAL SCIENCES*

659.1   US
HIGH-TECH HOT LINE.* 1994. s-m. $249. 114 Sansome St., Ste. 1224, San Francisco, CA 94104-3823. TEL 415-421-6770.
FAX 415-421-6225. Ed. Art Garcia. **Document type:** newsletter.
  Description: Covers media relations for public relations professionals in advanced-technology fields.

659.1   US   ISSN 1070-4752
HIGH-TECH HOT SHEET.* 1987. m. $239. 114 Sansome St., Ste. 1224, San Francisco, CA 94104-3823. TEL 415-421-6220.
FAX 415-421-6225. Ed. Art Garcia. adv.; bk.rev. circ. 400. **Document type:** newsletter.
  Formerly (until May 1993): High Technology P R News.
  Description: Covers high tech media and public relations for communications pros.

659.14   UK   ISSN 0962-3590
HOLLIS EUROPE; the directory of European public relations & PR networks. 1990. a. £155 (effective 1997). Hollis Directories Ltd., Harlequin House, 7 High St., Teddington, Middlesex TW11 8EH, England. TEL 44-181-977-7711.
FAX 44-181-977-1133. E-mail: europe@hollis-pr.demon.co.uk; hollis@hollis-pr.demon.co.uk. Ed. Rosemary Sarginson; Pub. Rosemary Sarginson. adv.: B&W page £1300, color page £2250; 265 x 179. circ. 700. **Document type:** directory.
  Description: Provides a reference to public-relations consultancies across 30 countries of Western, Central, and Eastern Europe, public affairs and sponsorship contacts, public-relations contacts in Europe's leading companies, research and information soures, and services to the public-relations industry in Europe.

659.14   UK   ISSN 0073-3059
HM263
HOLLIS PRESS & PUBLIC RELATIONS ANNUAL. 1967. a. (with q. updates). £102.50 (includes updates) (effective 1997). Hollis Directories Ltd., Harlequin House, 7 High St., Teddington, Middlesex TW11 8EH, England. TEL 44-181-977-7711.
FAX 44-181-977-1133. E-mail: hollis@hollis-pr.demon.co.uk; prannual@hollis-pr.demon.co.uk; URL: http://www.hollis-pr.co.uk. Ed. Sarah Hughes; Pub. Rosemary Sarginson. adv.: B&W page £1130; 174 x 115. bk.rev.; bibl.; index. circ. 4,500. (back issues avail.) **Document type:** directory.
  ●Also available online.
  Incorporates: Contact: The U K News Contact Directory.
  Description: Provides a guide to press contacts, public relations departments, news and information sourcces, public relations consultancies, and other services to communications and the media.

ADVERTISING AND PUBLIC RELATIONS

659.14   UK   ISSN 1351-5691
HOLLIS SPONSORSHIP & DONATIONS YEARBOOK. 1993. a. £90 (not-for-profit organizations £60) (effective 1997). Hollis Directories Ltd., Harlequin House, 7 High St., Teddington, Middlesex TW11 8EH, England. TEL 44-181-977-7711. FAX 44-181-977-1133. E-mail: spons@hollis-pr.demon.co.uk; hollis@hollis-pr.demon.co.uk. adv.: B&W page £1200, color page £1750; 265 x 179. circ. 3,000. **Document type:** directory.
—BLDSC (4322.403100).
    Description: Lists companies that sponsor events and make corporate donations; also gives sponsorship opportunities in the arts, sports, charities, education and media sector.

659.14   UK   ISSN 1354-2397
HOLLIS SPONSORSHIP NEWSLETTER. 1994. m. (10/yr.). £195 (not-for-profit organizations £150) (effective 1997). Hollis Directories Ltd., Harlequin House, 7 High St., Teddington, Middlesex TW11 8EH, England. TEL 44-181-977-7711. FAX 44-181-977-1133. E-mail: newsletter@hollis-pr.demon.co.uk; hollis@hollis-pr.demon.co.uk. Pub. Rosemary Sarginson. **Document type:** newsletter.
    Description: Provides the latest news, developments, and trends, along with expert analysis, commentary, and information on the sponsorship industry.

HOME SCHOOL MARKET GUIDE; how to sell audiocassettes, books, educational toys and games, software programs, videos and other educational products to the home schoolmarket. see *EDUCATION*

659.1   GW   ISSN 0175-7989
HORIZONT (FRANKFURT). (Index in German and Russian) 1954. w. DM.214 (E.U. DM.315.60; elsewhere DM.341.50) (effective 1996). Deutscher Fachverlag GmbH, Mainzer Landstr. 251, 60326 Frankfurt a.M., Germany. TEL 49-69-7595-01. FAX 49-69-7595-2999. Ed. Fred Tamme. adv.: B&W page DM.7470, color page DM.11340; trim 286 x 390; adv. contact: Manfred Winter. bk.rev. circ. 16,851. **Document type:** trade publication.
—CCC.
    Incorporates (1954-1991): Neue Werbung (ISSN 0028-3452)
    Description: Provides information on all important processes in marketing communications.

659.1   US
I A A WORLD NEWS. 1960; N.S. 1988. bi-m. $80. International Advertising Association, 521 Fifth Ave., Rm. 1807, New York, NY 10175-0003. TEL 212-557-1133. FAX 212-983-0455. TELEX 237969. E-mail: IAA@ibnet.com. Ed. Ellen Corey. bk.rev.; charts; illus.; mkt.; tr.lit. circ. 3,000. (also avail. in microform from UMI; reprint service avail. from UMI) **Indexed:** Manage.Cont., P.A.I.S, PROMT, Tr.& Indus.Ind. **Document type:** newsletter.
—KR SourceOne.
    Formerly (until vol.7, no.1, 1994): International Advertiser (ISSN 0885-3363); Incorporates: United Nations Report; Advertising World (ISSN 0163-9412); International Marketing Report (ISSN 0198-6228)
    Description: For IAA members in international marketing and communications.

659.1   IE
I A P I BUSINESS READERSHIP SURVEY. 1987. biennial. I£50. I A P I, 8 Upper Fitzwilliam St., Dublin 2, Ireland. TEL 353-1-6765991. FAX 353-1-6614589. Ed. Ian Fox. R&P contact: Ian Fox. circ. 200. **Document type:** bulletin.

659.1 070   II   ISSN 0073-4284
I N F A PRESS AND ADVERTISERS YEAR BOOK. (Text in English) 1962. a. $100. (India News and Feature Alliance) I N F A Publications, Jeevan Deep Bldg., Parliament St., New Delhi 110 001, India. TEL 91-11-3733330. FAX 91-11-3746788. adv. contact: Anand Kumar. circ. 5,000. **Document type:** directory.
    Description: Year book on advertising, media planning, sales promotion and publicity in India.

I.P. MARK. (Informacion de Publicidad y Marketing) see *BUSINESS AND ECONOMICS — Marketing And Purchasing*

ICOGRADA MESSAGE BOARD. see *ART*

659.1 740   JA   ISSN 0019-1299
NC997.A1
IDEA; international advertising art. (Text in English, Japanese) 1953. bi-m. 23640 Yen. Seibundo Shinkosha Publishing Co., Ltd., 1-13-7 Yayoi-cho, Nakano-ku, Tokyo 164, Japan. Ed. Minoru Takita. adv.; index. circ. 32,000. (back issues avail.) **Indexed:** Artbibl.Mod., Biol.Abstr., DAAI.
—BLDSC (4362.362000); UnCover.
    Description: International graphic design magazine.

659.1   US   ISSN 0896-1441
IDEAS (DALLAS). 1950. m. membership. International Newspaper Marketing Association, 12770 Merit Dr., Ste. 330, Dallas, TX 75251. TEL 214-991-5900. FAX 214-991-3151. E-mail: inma@connect.net; URL: http://www.infi.net/inma. Ed. Tom Geddie; Pub. Earl Wilkinson. R&P contact: Earl Wilkinson. stat. circ. 1,300. (back issues avail.) **Document type:** trade publication.
    Former titles: Ideas Newsletter; I N P A Advertising Newsletter (ISSN 0019-0152)

659.1   GW   ISSN 0176-859X
IDEEN ARCHIV. 1979. m. DM.354. Bergmoser and Hoeller Verlag GmbH, Karl-Friedrich-Str. 76, 52072 Aachen, Germany. TEL 0241-9388824. FAX 0241-9388844. Ed.Bd. circ. 1,400. (looseleaf format; back issues avail.) **Document type:** academic/scholarly publication.

IKONOMICHESKI ZHIVOT. see *BUSINESS AND ECONOMICS*

INDUSTRIAL EXCHANGE & MART. see *MACHINERY*

659.1   CN
INFO PRESSE COMMUNICATIONS; le seul magazine d'affaires francophones des communications au Canada. (Text in French) 1985. m. Can.$59 (foreign Can.$125) (effective 1998). Editions Info Presse, 4316 rue St-Laurent, Montreal, PQ H2W 1Z3, Canada. TEL 514-842-5873. FAX 514-842-2422. Ed. Bruno Gautier. adv. circ. 8,000. (back issues avail.) **Indexed:** Pt.de Rep. (1989-).
    Formerly: Info Presse Canada (ISSN 0827-4711)
    Description: Trade magazine on advertising, marketing and the media in Quebec and Canada.

INFOMERCIAL WRITERS MARKET GUIDE. see *JOURNALISM*

659   IT
INFORMAZIONI E ORIENTAMENTI. bi-m. Via Marconi 67-2, 40122 Bologna, Italy. Ed. Giuliano Cazzola.

659.1   US
INSIDE IMPACT. 1987. q. $25. Impact Advertising Inc., 1546 Main St., Dunedin, FL 34698. TEL 813-736-6228. FAX 813-734-9368. Ed. Bruce Cohen. adv. circ. 4,498.

659.2   US   ISSN 1053-8828
HF5410   CODEN: IPUBEU
INSIDE P R. (Public Relations); the magazine of reputation management. 1990. m. $40 (foreign $100). Editorial Media and Marketing International, Inc., 235 W. 48th St., New York, NY 10036. TEL 212-245-8680. FAX 212-245-8699. Ed. Paul A. Holmes. adv. circ. 28,000.

659.1   AU
INSIDER. 25/yr. Insider Verlag, Coblenzlgasse 66, A-1190 Vienna, Austria. TEL 01-326054. FAX 01-327338. Ed. Inge Weinlich. circ. 3,000.

659.1   UK   ISSN 1351-4598
INSTITUTE OF PUBLIC RELATIONS. HANDBOOK (YEAR). a. £30. Kogan Page Ltd., 120 Pentonville Rd., London N1 9JN, England. TEL 44-171-278-0433. FAX 44-171-837-6348. TELEX 263088 KOGAN G. R&P contact: Linda Batman. **Document type:** directory.

659.1   FR   ISSN 0154-1617
INTER FORAIN. 24/yr. B.P. 52, 84005 Avignon Cedex, France. TEL 90-82-54-03. TELEX 432 770. Ed. Michel Pierre. circ. 27,420.
    Description: Commercial and artistic magazine relating to exhibitions, fairs and foreign festivals.

659 384.3   US
▼**INTERACTIVE ADVERTISING SOURCE.** (Includes online supplement: SRDS' URLink) 1996. q. $229 (effective 1997). S R D S (Subsidiary of: V N U U.S.A.), 1700 Higgins Rd., Des Plaines, IL 60018. TEL 847-375-5000; 800-851-7737. FAX 847-375-5004. E-mail: cnort@srds.com; URL: http://www.srds.com. adv.: B&W page $2650, color page $5830; adv. contact: Christine Pippin Northwick. **Document type:** trade publication, directory.
    Description: Compiles over 1600 online and other interactive advertising opportunities. Includes advertising rates, traffic information, key contacts and audience profiles.

659.1   CN   ISSN 1197-7825
INTERCESSOR. (Text in English) 1930. bi-m. Inter-Varsity Christian Fellowship of Canada, Unit 17, 40 Vogell Rd., Richmond Hill, ON L4B 3N6, Canada. TEL 905-884-6880. FAX 905-884-6550. E-mail: ivcfnat@hookup.net. Ed. Rob Regier; Pub. Jim Berney. R&P contact: Rob Regier. circ. 3,000. (back issues avail.) **Document type:** newsletter.

659.1   AU
INTERN. w. S.3600. Manstein Zeitschriften Verlagsgesellschaft mbH, Brunner Feldstr. 45, A-2380 Perchtoldsdorf, Austria. TEL 43-1-86648. FAX 43-1-8664870. Ed. Hans-Joergen Manstein; Pub. Hans-Joergen Manstein. circ. 1,500. **Document type:** newsletter.

659.1 330 384   US
INTERNATIONAL FEDERATION OF ADVERTISING AGENCIES. NEWSLETTER. m. International Federation of Advertising Agencies, 1450 E. American Ln., Ste. 1400, Schaumburg, IL 60173-4973. TEL 847-330-6344. FAX 847-517-4459. E-mail: nstephen@starnetinc.com. Ed. Norval Stephens. **Document type:** newsletter.

659.1   UK   ISSN 0265-0487
HF5801
INTERNATIONAL JOURNAL OF ADVERTISING; the quarterly review of marketing communications. 1982. q. £145($242) (foreign £153) (effective 1997). (Advertising Association) Blackwell Publishers Ltd., 108 Cowley Rd., Oxford OX4 1JF, England. TEL 44-1865-791100. FAX 44-1865-791347. E-mail: jnlinfo@blackwellpublishers.co.uk; URL: http://www.blackwellpublishers.co.uk/scripts/webjrnl.idc?issn02650487. Ed. Alan Wolfe. adv.; bk.rev.; charts; illus.; stat.; index, cum.index. circ. 1,000. (reprint service avail. from SWZ) **Indexed:** ABI Inform., Acad.Ind., Account.& Data Proc.Abstr., Anbar, BPIA, Bus.Ind., Cont.Pg.Manage., Lang.& Lang.Behav.Abstr., Manage.Cont., Mark.Res.Abstr. (1983-), P.A.I.S., SSCI, Tr.& Indus.Ind. **Document type:** academic/scholarly publication.
●Also available online. Vendor(s): Information Access Co.
—BLDSC (4541.575000); SWETS; UMI; UnCover. CCC.
    Formerly: Journal of Advertising (ISSN 0261-9903); Which superseded (1978-1980): Advertising Magazine; Which was formerly: Advertising; (1964-1978): Advertising Quarterly (ISSN 0001-8961)
    Refereed Serial

659.1 658.8   US
INTERNATIONAL NEWSPAPER ADVERTISING AND MARKETING EXECUTIVES. SALES AND IDEA BOOK.* s-a. International Advertising and Marketing Executives, 21525 Ridgetop Circle, Ste. 200, Sterling, VA 20166-6510. TEL 703-648-1168.

ADVERTISING AND PUBLIC RELATIONS

659.205 327 DK ISSN 0269-0357
CODEN: IPRRET
INTERNATIONAL PUBLIC RELATIONS REVIEW. (Text in English) 1976. q. 60 SFr. (effective 1993). International Public Relations Association, Ste. 1007, South Tower, 175 Bloor St. E., Toronto ON M4W 3R8. TEL 416-968-7311. FAX 416-968-6281. E-mail: rargyle@argylecomm.com. (Subscr. to: I.P.R.A., C.P. 2100, CH-1211 Geneva 2, Switzerland. TEL 41-22-791-0550. FAX 41-22-788-0336) Ed. Raymond Argyle. adv.; bk.rev. circ. 1,300. (back issues avail.) **Indexed:** Account.& Data Proc.Abstr., BPIA, IBR. **Document type:** academic/scholarly publication, trade publication.
—BLDSC (4545.405000); UnCover. **CCC.**
Formerly (until 1986): I P R A Review (ISSN 0142-7067)
Description: Serves as a forum for the critical discussion of issues in the practice of international public relations at the senior executive level, from a variety of perspectives. Examines the history, evolution and current state of the profession.
Refereed Serial

INTERNET INFOSCAVENGER; sites and insights for growing businesses. see COMPUTERS — Computer Networks

INTERNET YELLOW PAGES: BUSINESS MODELS AND MARKET OPPORTUNITIES. see BUSINESS AND ECONOMICS — Computer Applications

INTRODUCTION TO MAIL ORDER. see BUSINESS AND ECONOMICS — Small Business

INVESTOR RELATIONS NEWSLETTER. see BUSINESS AND ECONOMICS — Investments

IOWA HOME-BASED BUSINESS DIRECTORY. see BUSINESS AND ECONOMICS — Trade And Industrial Directories

659.1 IS ISSN 0792-7185
ISRAEL ADVERTISING. (Text in English) q. free. Jerusalem Marketing Group, P.O. Box 23859, Jerusalem 91237, Israel. TEL 972-50-266598. FAX 972-2-6250946. Ed. S.I. Gottlieb. adv.

IT STARTS ON THE FRONTLINE; the comprehensive communication newsletter for your school. see EDUCATION

659 US ISSN 0047-1690
JACK O'DWYER'S NEWSLETTER. 1968. w. $225. J.R. O'Dwyer Co., Inc., 271 Madison Ave., New York, NY 10016. TEL 212-679-2471. FAX 212-683-2750. Ed. Jack O'Dwyer. (looseleaf format) **Document type:** newsletter.
●Also available online. Vendor(s): Lexis-Nexis.
Formerly: Jack O'Dwyer's P R Newsletter.

659.1 700 GW ISSN 0932-6251
HF5802
JAHRBUCH DER WERBUNG/ADVERTISER'S ANNUAL; in Deutschland, Oesterreich und der Schweiz. 1964. a. DM.168 (CD-ROM DM.98) (effective 1997). E C O N Verlag GmbH, Postfach 300321, 40403 Duesseldorf, Germany. TEL 49-211-4359749. FAX 49-211-4359781. TELEX 8587327-ECON-D. Ed. Diethelm Krull. R&P contact: Cita Wendt. adv.: B&W page DM.4505, color page DM.6657; trim 165 x 265; adv. contact: Bruni Stolz. bk.rev. circ. 4,000. **Document type:** directory.
●Also available on CD-ROM.
Formerly (until 1975): Werbung in Deutschland (ISSN 0083-8012)
Description: Provides overview of advertising developments in the German speaking world.

659.1 JA
JAPAN ADVERTISING FEDERATION. AIMS AND ORGANIZATION. irreg. Japan Advertising Federation - Zennihon Kokoku Renmei, Kochiwa Bldg., 4-8-12 Ginza, Chuo-ku, Tokyo 104, Japan. TEL 03-562-2966.

659 JA ISSN 0918-4406
JAPAN MARKETING AND ADVERTISING YEARBOOK. (Text in English) 1972. a. 8000 Yen($80) Dentsu Inc., 11-10, Tsukiji 1-chome, Chuo-ku, Tokyo 104, Japan. TEL 81-3-5551-5585. Ed. Nobuo Takagi. R&P contact: Nobuo Takagi. adv. contact: Mitsuru Nomura. bk.rev.; charts; illus.; stat. circ. 10,000. (back issues avail.) **Indexed:** Key to Econ.Sci., P.A.I.S. **Document type:** directory.
Former titles (until 1991): Dentsu Japan Marketing - Advertising (ISSN 0386-6076); (until 1972): Industrial Japan (ISSN 0019-8439)

JON SULLIVAN'S RADIO PROMOTION BULLETIN; ideas and inspiration for innovative broadcasters. see COMMUNICATIONS — Radio

JONESREPORT FOR SHOPPING CENTER MARKETING. see BUSINESS AND ECONOMICS — Marketing And Purchasing

659.1 FR ISSN 0248-7004
JOURNAL DE L'AFFICHE. 1978. q. Metrobus, 15 rue du Dome, 92100 Boulogne, France.

659.1 US ISSN 0091-3367
HF5801
JOURNAL OF ADVERTISING. 1972. q. $40 (foreign $45). American Academy of Advertising, Clemson University, College of Commerce & Industry, 245 Sirrine Hall, Clemson, SC 29634-1325. E-mail: carlsol@clemson.edu; URL: http://business.clemson.edu/market/jao/. Ed. Les Carlson. R&P contact: Les Carlson. adv.; bk.rev.; charts; illus. circ. 1,700. (also avail. in microform from UMI; reprint service avail. from UMI,SCH) **Indexed:** ABI Inform., Acad.Ind., Account.& Data Proc.Abstr., Amer.Hist.& Life (1986-1987), Anbar, Arts & Hum.Cit.Ind., ASCA, B.P.I., BPIA, Bus.Ind., Commun.Abstr., Curr.Cont., Hist.Abstr. (1986-1987), Manage.Abstr., Manage.Cont., P.A.I.S., Psychol.Abstr. (1982-), Sage Fam.Stud.Abstr., Sociol.Abstr., SSCI. **Document type:** academic/scholarly publication.
●Also available online. Vendor(s): Information Access Co., Lexis-Nexis, UMI.
Also available on CD-ROM.
—BLDSC (4918.949000); Genuine Article; KR SourceOne; SWETS; UMI; UnCover. **CCC.**
Description: Contributes to the development of advertising theory and its relationship to advertising practices and processes.

659.1 US ISSN 0021-8499
HF5801 CODEN: JADRAV
JOURNAL OF ADVERTISING RESEARCH. 1960. bi-m. $100 (foreign $130) (effective 1996). Advertising Research Foundation, 641 Lexington Ave., 11th Fl., New York, NY 10022. TEL 212-751-5656. FAX 212-319-5265. URL: http://www.arfsite.org/publish.html. Ed. William A. Cook. adv.; charts; illus.; index, cum.index. circ. 4,977. (also avail. in microform from UMI; reprint service avail. from UMI, ISI) **Indexed:** ABI Inform., Acad.Ind., Anbar, ASCA, ASEAN Manage.Abstr., B.P.I., BPIA, Bus.Ind., Commun.Abstr., Cont.Pg.Manage., Curr.Cont., J.Cont.Quant.Meth., Key to Econ.Sci., Lang.& Lang.Behav.Abstr., Manage.Abstr., Manage.Cont., Mark.Res.Abstr. (1963-), Mgmt.& Market.Abstr., Oper.Res.Manage.Sci., Psychol.Abstr. (1960-), Psycscan, SCIMP (1980-), SSCI, Tr.& Indus.Ind. **Document type:** trade publication.
●Also available online. Vendor(s): Information Access Co., UMI.
—BLDSC (4918.950000); Genuine Article; KR SourceOne; SWETS; UMI; UnCover.

741.67 US ISSN 1057-7408
HF5415.32
JOURNAL OF CONSUMER PSYCHOLOGY. 1992. q. $40 to individuals (foreign $70); institutions $175 (foreign $205) (effective 1997). (Society for Consumer Psychology) Lawrence Erlbaum Associates, Inc., 10 Industrial Dr., Mahwah, NJ 07430-2262. TEL 201-236-9500; 800-926-6579. FAX 201-236-0072. E-mail: jamsel@erlbaum.com; URL: http://www.erlbaum.com. Ed. Dipankar Chakravarti. adv.: page $225; 5 x 8. **Indexed:** Psychol.Abstr. (1992-). **Document type:** academic/scholarly publication.
—BLDSC (4965.214000); SWETS; UnCover. **CCC.**
Description: Publishes original data and theoretical, methodological and review papers on the role of advertising in consumer psychology, the development and change of consumer attitudes, choice and decision processes.
Refereed Serial

659.1 US ISSN 1064-1734
HF5801
JOURNAL OF CURRENT ISSUES & RESEARCH IN ADVERTISING. 1978. 2/yr. $24 (foreign $29). C T C Press, Box 1826, Clemson, SC 29633-1826. TEL 803-654-0510. FAX 803-654-7438. Eds. Martin Leigh, Patrick Murphy. circ. 850. **Indexed:** B.P.I. **Document type:** trade publication.
—BLDSC (4965.880000); KR SourceOne; SWETS; UnCover.
Formerly (until 1992): Current Issues and Research in Advertising (ISSN 0163-3392)

659.1 658 US ISSN 1049-6491
HF5415.34 CODEN: JPRMEP
JOURNAL OF PROMOTION MANAGEMENT; innovations in planning & applied research for advertising, sales promotion, personal selling, public relations, re-seller support. 1991. s-a. $30 to individuals (Canada $39; elsewhere $42); institutions $48 (Canada $62.40; elsewhere $67.20); libraries $95 (Canada $123.50; elsewhere $133) (effective 1996-1997). Haworth Press, Inc., 10 Alice St., Binghamton, NY 13904. TEL 607-722-5857; 800-342-9676. FAX 607-722-6362. TELEX 4932599. E-mail: getinfo@haworth.com; URL: http://www.haworth.com. Ed. Fred G. Crane; Pub. Bill Cohen. R&P contact: Ruthann Heath. adv.: B&W page $300; trim 4 3/8 x 7 1/8; adv. contact: Jackie Blakeslee. (also avail. in microfiche from HAW; reprint service avail. from HAW) **Indexed:** Mgmt.& Market.Abstr. **Document type:** academic/scholarly publication.
—BLDSC (5042.768000); Haworth.
Description: Directed to professionals in advertising, public relations, and personal sales as well as academicians, teachers, and researchers.
Refereed Serial

659.2 US ISSN 1062-726X
HM263
JOURNAL OF PUBLIC RELATIONS RESEARCH. 1989. q. $45 to individuals (foreign $75); institutions $195 (foreign $225) (effective 1997). Lawrence Erlbaum Associates, Inc., 10 Industrial Dr., Mahwah, NJ 07430-2262. TEL 201-236-9500; 800-926-6579. FAX 201-236-0072. E-mail: jamsel@erlbaum.com; URL: http://www.erlbaum.com. Ed. Elizabeth Toth. adv.: page $275; 5 x 8. **Document type:** academic/scholarly publication.
—BLDSC (5043.646000); UnCover. **CCC.**
Formerly (until 1992): Public Relations Research Annual (ISSN 1042-1408)
Description: Research in public relations theory, examinations of methodology and motivations, improvements in public relations strategies, as well as critical articles on the history, ethics and philosophy of public relations.
Refereed Serial

659.1 658.8 US
KEY (BATTLEGROUND). 1960-1990; resumed 1993. m. $45. Owen Communications Corporation, Battleground, WA 98604-0010. TEL 206-887-8646. Ed. Brooks Owen. bk.rev.; stat.; tr.lit.; index. **Indexed:** Sage Pub.Admin.Abstr.
Formed by the merger of: Mail Order Product (ISSN 0162-8496) & Key; The Newsletter that Helps You Make More Money from Your Mail Order Advertising; Which was formerly: Key: The Newsletter that Helps You Make Money with Mail Order Classified Advertising (ISSN 0160-8932); And which incorporated: Mail Order Counselor. Mail Order Product incorporated (in 1987): Mail Order Information Seller.

659.1 UK
KEY NOTE MARKET REPORT: ADVERTISING AGENCIES. Variant title: Advertising Agencies. irreg., no.6, 1994. £205. Key Note Ltd., Field House, 72 Oldfield Rd., Hampton, Middlesex TW12 2HQ, England. TEL 44-181-783-0755. FAX 44-181-783-0049. **Document type:** trade publication.
●Also available online.
Also available on CD-ROM.
Formerly: Key Note Report: Advertising Agencies (ISSN 0266-1985)

659.1 UK
KEY NOTE MARKET REPORT: P R CONSULTANCIES. Variant title: P R Consultancies. irreg., no.2, 1990. £185. Key Note Ltd., Field House, 72 Oldfield Rd., Hampton, Middlesex TW12 2HQ, England. TEL 44-181-783-0755. FAX 44-181-783-1940. **Document type:** trade publication.

ADVERTISING AND PUBLIC RELATIONS

659.1 UK
KEY NOTE MARKET REVIEW: YOUTH MARKET IN THE U.K. 1994. irreg. £410. Key Note Ltd., Field House, 72 Oldfield Rd., Hampton, Middlesex TW12 2HQ, England. TEL 44-181-783-0755. FAX 44-181-783-0049. Ed. Phillippa Smith. **Document type:** trade publication.
● Also available online.
Also available on CD-ROM.

659.1 808.8 US
▼**KINGSWOOD KRANIUM.** 1995. m. Kingswood Advertising, Inc., Cricket Terrace Center, Ardmore, PA 19003. E-mail: webczar@kingswood.com; URL: http://www.kingswood.com. Ed. Adam Bailine.
● Available only online.
Description: A lighthearted humor magazine.

659.1 676 GW
KOEHLER RUNDSCHAU. 1963. 3/yr. Papierfabrik August Koehler AG, Postfach 1245, 77696 Oberkirch, Germany. TEL 49-7802-810. FAX 49-7802-81330. Ed. Erich Kraemer. circ. 3,500.

659.1 GW
KURZWELLE AKTUELL. 1977. q. DM.24. Soldi Verlag, Wilhelmstr. 24, 21073 Hamburg, Germany. TEL 040-765 32 39. Ed. Horst Ernst. circ. 3,000. (back issues avail.)

659.1 JA
KYOWA HAKKO KOGYO. ANNUAL REPORT. a. Kyowa Hakko Kogyo Co. Ltd., Shachoshitsu, 1-6-1 Ote-machi, Chiyoda-ku, Tokyo 100, Japan. FAX 03-2841968. **Description:** Features advertising art from Japan.

THE LAW OF ADVERTISING. see *LAW*

659.1 GW
LEIPZIGER MESSEJOURNAL. (Text in English) a. Leipziger Messeamt, Markt 11-15, 04109 Leipzig, Germany. Ed. Ines Schymura. **Indexed:** Key to Econ.Sci.

LESSONS OF YELLOW PAGES COMPETITION. see *BUSINESS AND ECONOMICS — Trade And Industrial Directories*

LETTRE DU SPONSORING ET DU MECENAT; le 1er support francais sur le parrainage d'entreprise. see *BUSINESS AND ECONOMICS — Marketing And Purchasing*

LEWIS LETTER ON ENERGY COMMUNICATION. see *ENERGY*

LIBRARY P R NEWS. see *LIBRARY AND INFORMATION SCIENCES*

LICENSED PRODUCT MARKETING. see *BUSINESS AND ECONOMICS — Marketing And Purchasing*

LICENSING SCOPE. see *GIFTWARE AND TOYS*

659.1 CN
LIFE COMMUNICATIONS.* 3/yr. Life Communicators Association, 40 Ellingwood Ct., Unionville, ON 3R 8B1, Canada.
Description: For advertising and public relations employees in the insurance industry.

659.1 UK ISSN 0967-0041
LIFESTYLE POCKET BOOK. a. £24. (Advertising Association) N T C Publications Ltd., Farm Rd., Henley-on-Thames, Oxfordshire RG9 1EJ, England. TEL 01491-411000. FAX 01491-571188. **Document type:** bulletin.
Description: Provides a detailed statistical profile of the British at work and play.

659.1 US ISSN 1045-9723
LINK (TROY); the magazine of the Yellow Pages medium. 1989. 10/yr. $60. Yellow Pages Publishers Association, 820 Kirts Blvd., Ste. 100, Troy, MI 48084-4836. TEL 810-244-6200. FAX 810-244-6226. E-mail: barbier@yppa.geis.com; URL: http://www.yppa.org. Ed. Charles Laughlin; Pub. James C. Logan. R&P contact: Barbara Beck. adv. contact: Barbara Beck. circ. 12,000. **Document type:** trade publication.
Description: Addresses news and issues related to the Yellow Pages advertising medium.

659.13 UK
LOOT - LIVERPOOL, CHESTER & NORTH WALES. 1988. 2/w. £100 (foreign £355) (effective 1997). Loot Enterprises Ltd., Alberton House, St. Mary's Parsonage, Manchester M3 2WJ, England. TEL 44-161-832-0066. FAX 44-161-832-0660. Ed. Marina Ronald. adv. contact: Christine Campbell. (tabloid format; back issues avail.) **Document type:** consumer publication.
Supersedes in part (in 1995): Loot - The North West Noticeboard (ISSN 1351-2552)

659.13 UK
LOOT - MANCHESTER, CHESHIRE & LANCASHIRE. 1988. 3/wk. £180 (foreign £515) (effective 1997). Loot Enterprises Ltd., Alberton House, St. Mary's Parsonage, Manchester M3 2WJ, England. TEL 44-161-832-0066. FAX 44-161-832-0660. Ed. Marina Ronald. adv. contact: Christine Campbell. circ. 62,783. (tabloid format; back issues avail.) **Document type:** consumer publication.
Supersedes in part (in 1995): Loot - The North West Noticeboard (ISSN 1351-2552)

659.13 UK
LOOT - STOKE & STAFFORDSHIRE. 1988. w. £50 (foreign £185) (effective 1997). Loot Enterprises Ltd., Alberton House, St. Mary's Parsonage, Manchester M3 2WJ, England. TEL 44-161-832-0066. FAX 44-161-832-0660. Ed. Marina Ronald. adv. contact: Christine Campbell. (tabloid format; back issues avail.) **Document type:** consumer publication.
Supersedes in part (in 1995): Loot - The North West Noticeboard (ISSN 1351-2552)

659.1 UK ISSN 0305-1765
LOUGHTON REVIEW. 1968. m. free. Monkswood Press, Caxton House, Old Station Rd., Loughton, Essex IG10 4PE, England. TEL 0181-502-0236. FAX 0181-508-2834. Ed. A.T. Harvey. circ. 17,700 (controlled). (tabloid format; back issues avail.)

659.1 384.554 US ISSN 0893-0260
LURZER'S INTERNATIONAL ARCHIVE; ads, TV and posters world-wide. Variant title: Archive Magazine. 1984. bi-m. $43.97. American Showcase Inc., 915 Broadway, 14th Fl., New York, NY 10010-7108. TEL 212-673-6600. FAX 212-673-9795. TELEX 880356. (Subscr. to: Box 6338, Syracuse, NY 13127. TEL 800-825-0061) Eds. Walter Lurzer, Ann Middlebrook; Pub. Ira Shapiro. adv. contact: Lisa Wilker. illus.; tr.lit. circ. 9,500. (video cassette; back issues avail.) **Document type:** trade publication.
Description: Presents international TV commercials and print ad campaigns. Covers 24 categories of ads.

M D - MARKETING DIGEST; Fachbereichszeitschrift der Fachhochschule fuer Wirtschaft, Pforzheim. see *BUSINESS AND ECONOMICS — Marketing And Purchasing*

659 658 US ISSN 0895-1861
M P A NEWSLETTER OF RESEARCH. 1973. irreg. free to members. Magazine Publishers of America, 919 Third Ave., New York, NY 10022. TEL 212-872-3700. FAX 212-888-4217. Ed. Kathi Love. index. circ. 18,000. (back issues avail.) **Document type:** newsletter.
Formerly: Magazine Newsletter of Research.

M P R EXCHANGE. (American Society for Health Care Marketing and Public Relations) see *HOSPITALS*

659.1 GW ISSN 0723-3361
M UND A REPORT; das Magazin fuer Messen, Events und Marketing. 1919. 8/yr. DM.135 (foreign DM.185) (effective 1997). M und A Verlag fuer Messen, Ausstellungen und Kongresse GmbH (Subsidiary of: Deutscher Fachverlag GmbH), Postfach 101528, 60015 Frankfurt a.M., Germany. TEL 49-69-759502. FAX 49-69-75951280. E-mail: muareport-redaktion@dfv.de. Ed. Klaus Goschmann. adv.: B&W page DM.4645, color page DM.5935; trim 210 x 297; adv. contact: Jutta Fautz. bk.rev.; circ. 12,515. (back issues avail.) **Document type:** trade publication.
— CCC.
Incorporates (1919-1990): M und A Info.
Description: Trade magazine for fairs, exhibitions, events, and marketing professionals.
Refereed Serial

MACCLESFIELD EXPRESS ADVERTISER. see *JOURNALISM*

659.1 US ISSN 0076-2148
HF5805
MADISON AVENUE HANDBOOK; the image makers' source. 1956. a. $59.95 (effective 1996 ed.). Peter Glenn Publications, Inc., 42 W. 38th St., Ste. 802, New York, NY 10018. TEL 212-869-2020; 888-332-6700. FAX 212-354-4099. Ed. Gregory James; Pub. Chip Brill. adv. contact: Tricia Mazzilli. circ. 9,000. **Document type:** trade publication.
Description: Specialized yellow pages for the world of advertising, commercial production, film, fashion and print and all attendant services.

659.1 GW
MAGAZIN WERBUNG SAAR. m. Werbefachverband Saar e.V., Puccinistr. 18, 66119 Saarbruecken, Germany. TEL 0681-57093.

659.1 380 UK
THE MAGAZINE HANDBOOK (YEAR). 1991. a. £25. Periodical Publishers Association, Queens House, 28 Kingsway, London WC2B 6JR, England. TEL 44-171-404-4166. FAX 44-171-404-4167. E-mail: info1@ppa.co.uk; URL: http://www.ppa.co.uk. Ed. Phil Cutts; Pub. Peter Dear. index; circ. 6,000. **Document type:** bulletin.

659.1 380 UK ISSN 0956-9855
MAGAZINE NEWS. 1989. 5/yr. Periodical Publishers Association, Queens House, 28 Kingsway, London WC2B 6JR, England. TEL 44-171-404-4166. FAX 44-171-404-4167. E-mail: info1@ppa.co.uk; URL: http://www.ppa.co.uk. Ed. Daska Davis; Pub. Nicholas Mazur. adv.: color page £1260; trim 296 x 210; adv. contact: Antony Hill. circ. 10,194. **Indexed:** WPM. **Document type:** trade publication.

MAGNET MARKETING. see *BUSINESS AND ECONOMICS — Marketing And Purchasing*

659.1 001.6 US
MAIL ADVERTISING SERVICE ASSOCIATION INTERNATIONAL. COMPUTER SURVEY. irreg. Mail Advertising Service Association International, 1421 Prince St., Ste. 200, Alexandria, VA 22314. TEL 703-836-9200.
Description: Includes computer brand, model number of hardware, language, operation system, and software applications in use.

659.1 US
MAIL ADVERTISING SERVICE ASSOCIATION INTERNATIONAL. POSTSCRIPTS. s-w. membership. Mail Advertising Service Association International, 1421 Prince St., Ste. 200, Alexandria, VA 22314. TEL 703-836-9200.
Description: Presents association and industry news. Includes member news, job listings, equipment exchange listings, meetings, postal information and industrial information.

380 659.1 US ISSN 1040-1296
MAIL ORDER PRODUCT GUIDE.* 1989. biennial. $49.50. Todd Publications, Box 635, Nyack, NY 10960-0635. TEL 914-358-6213. Ed. Barry Klein. adv. circ. 4,000. **Document type:** directory.

659.1 US ISSN 0277-7398
HM263.A1
MANAGING THE HUMAN CLIMATE; guidelines on public relations and public affairs. 1970. bi-m. $30. Philip Lesly Company, 155 N. Harbor Dr. No. 5311, Chicago, IL 60601. TEL 312-819-3590. FAX 312-819-3592. Ed. Philip Lesly. bk.rev. circ. 2,500. (back issues avail.) **Document type:** newsletter.
Description: Analyzes factors shaping public opinion; discusses how to influence public opinion.

659.1 US ISSN 0193-3116
MANHATTAN CATALOGUE. 1979. 5/yr. $5. Manhattan Catalogue, Inc., 141 Eighth Ave., New York, NY 10011. Ed. Gene Chase. circ. 20,000.

659.1 DK ISSN 0105-9424
MARKEDSFOERING. 1927. 20/yr. DKK 620($70) (effective 1997). (Dansk Markedsfoerings Forbund) Specialbladsforlaget A-S, Finsensvej 80, 2000 Frederiksberg, Denmark. Ed. Svend Erik Pedersen. adv.; bk.rev.; charts; illus.; mkt.; tr.lit.; index. circ. 8,507.
Formerly: Dansk Reklame (ISSN 0011-6459)

ADVERTISING AND PUBLIC RELATIONS

659   GW   ISSN 0085-3119
MARKEN-HANDBUCH DER WERBUNG UND ETATBETREUUNG. 1960. a. DM.145. Team Verlag GmbH und Fachzeitschriften KG, Auwanne 19, 63791 Karlstein, Germany. Ed. Horst P. Czerner. adv. circ. 2,500. **Document type:** trade publication.

659.1   US   ISSN 1061-7159
MARKETER'S GUIDE TO MEDIA. 1978. q. $60. B P I Communications, Inc. (New York), 1515 Broadway, New York, NY 10036. TEL 212-536-6508. FAX 212-536-5321. (Subscr. to: Box 2006, Lakewood, NJ 08701. TEL 800-468-2395) Ed. Tiona Grilly. adv.; charts. (back issues avail.; reprint service avail.)
—CCC.
  Former titles (until 1992): Mediaweek's Guide to Media (ISSN 1057-1280); (until 1991): Adweek's Marketer's Guide to Media (ISSN 0888-5494); (until 1986): Adweek's Media Cost Guide (ISSN 0886-2788); Media Cost Guide.
  Description: Guide to media rates, advertising opportunities, and audience demographics.

MARKETING; Zeitschrift fuer Forschung und Praxis. see BUSINESS AND ECONOMICS — Marketing And Purchasing

MARKETING & CREATIVE HANDBOOK. see BUSINESS AND ECONOMICS — Marketing And Purchasing

659.1   BE   ISSN 0779-0619
MARKETING BOOK. (Supplement to: Media & Marketing (ISSN 0777-0812)) (Text in Dutch, French) 1992. a. 3250 BEF. Editions Dupuis, S.A., 52 rue Destree, B-6001 Marcinelle, Belgium. TEL 32-71-600500. FAX 32-71-600599. adv.: B&W page 70000 BEF; adv. contact: Marie-Laurence Decoster. circ. 2,000 (paid). **Document type:** directory.
  Description: Covers all Belgian marketing, advertising and public relations agencies.

MARKETING MAGAZINE; Canada's weekly newspaper for marketing, advertising and sales executives. see BUSINESS AND ECONOMICS — Marketing And Purchasing

659.1   IE   ISSN 0332-267X
MARKETING OPINION. 1980. 12/yr. 12 Magennis Pl., Dublin, Ireland. TEL 1-719-896. FAX 1-719-562. Ed. Derek Garvey.

658   US   ISSN 1065-9994
HE8700.8
THE MARKETING PULSE; the exclusive insight provider to the entertainment, marketing, advertising and media industries. 1979. bi-m. $300 (foreign $330). Unlimited Positive Communications, Inc., 7 Innis Ave., New Paltz, NY 12561. TEL 914-255-2222. FAX 914-255-2231. E-mail: gdnem1@ix.netcom.com. Ed. Bill Harvey. R&P contact: Russ Norman. bk.rev.; charts; stat. circ. 475. (back issues avail.) **Document type:** newsletter.
  Former titles (until 1989): Media Report; Media Science Reports; Media Science Newsletter (ISSN 0194-1607).
  Description: Provides analysis of and recommendations for the marketing media, advertising, and entertainment industries. Includes news, research, and forecasting for key decision makers.

659.1   FI   ISSN 1237-6655
MARKKINOINTI JA MAINONTA. 1952. fortn. FIM 558. Oy Talentum Ab, P.O. Box 920, FIN-00101 Helsinki, Finland. TEL 358-9-148-801. FAX 358-9-685-65-51. URL: http://www.talentum.fi. Ed. Olli Manninen. adv.; bk.rev.; film rev.; charts; illus.; stat.; tr.lit. circ. 9,522. (tabloid format) **Document type:** trade publication.
  Formerly: Mainosuutiset (ISSN 0025-0864)

659.1   CC
MEDIA; Asia's media & marketing newspaper. (Text in English) 1974. bi-w. HK.$520($80) in Asia; elsewhere $100. Media & Marketing Ltd., 1002 McDonald's Bldg., 46-54 Yee Wo Street, Causeway Bay, Hong Kong, People's Republic of China. TEL 852-2577-2628. FAX 852-2576-9171. Ed. Suzanne Miao; Pub. Ken McKenzie. adv. contact: Pollyanna Wu. circ. 11,000. (tabloid format; back issues avail.) **Document type:** newspaper.
  Formerly: Media and Marketing.
  Description: Covers the advertising, media, and marketing industries in China, Hong Kong, Indonesia, Japan, Korea, Malaysia, the Philippines, Singapore, Taiwan, Thailand and Vietnam.
  Refereed Serial

659.1   BE   ISSN 0777-0812
MEDIA & MARKETING. (Supplements avail.: Marketing Book (ISSN 0779-0619); Media Plan (ISSN 0776-5738)) (Text in Dutch, French) 1984. m. 1100 BEF (effective Dec. 1994). Editions Dupuis, S.A., 52 rue Destree, B-6001 Marcinelle, Belgium. TEL 32-71-600500. FAX 32-71-600599. Ed. Xavier Dupuis. adv.: B&W page 50000 BEF, color page 65000 BEF; adv. contact: Marie-Laurence Decoster. circ. 7,500 (paid). (illus) **Document type:** trade publication.
  Former titles (until 1989): Media Magazine (ISSN 0774-8175); (until 1986): Media Marketing (ISSN 0773-6630)
  Description: Covers the Belgian and international media and marketing scene.

659.1 658.8   UK
MEDIA & MARKETING EUROPE. 1989. m. £55 (Europe £66; rest of world £79) (effective 1996). E M A P Media (Subsidiary of: E M A P Business Communications), 33-39 Bowling Green Ln., London EC1R 0DA, England. TEL 44-171-505-8314. FAX 44-171-505-8320. E-mail: traceyt@media.emap.co.uk. (Subscr. to: Readerlink, Audit House, 260 Field End Rd., Eastcote HA4 9LT, England. TEL 44-181-956-3000) Ed. Tracey Taylor. circ. 10,600. **Document type:** trade publication.
  Description: News and features for European advertisers and agencies.

659.1   AU
MEDIA DATEN; Oesterreichs Werbeagenda. s-a. Maclean Hunter GmbH, Loquaiplatz 12, A-1060 Vienna, Austria. TEL 01-59960285. FAX 01-5996021. adv.: B&W page S.18800, color page S.30140; trim 297 x 210. circ. 2,200. **Document type:** trade publication.

659.1   GW   ISSN 0933-9728
MEDIA-DATEN ANNUALS. 1987. a. DM.150. Media Daten Verlag GmbH, Klingenweg 4, 65396 Walluf, Germany. TEL 49-6123-700-0. cum.index. circ. 1,500. **Document type:** trade publication.
  Description: Advertising rates and data about annuals.

MEDIA DATEN: DEUTSCHLAND OST. see BUSINESS AND ECONOMICS — Trade And Industrial Directories

659.1 380   GW   ISSN 0946-7637
MEDIA DATEN: REGIONALE MAERKTE UND MEDIEN. 1987. 2/yr. DM.300. Media Daten Verlag GmbH, Klingenweg 4, 65396 Walluf, Germany. TEL 49-6123-700-0. FAX 49-6123-700-122. circ. 1,200 (paid). **Document type:** directory.
  Formerly (until 1994): Media Daten: Regionale Medien und Maerkte (ISSN 0934-4861)

659.1   GW   ISSN 0934-3822
MEDIA DATEN: VERBREITUNGSATLAS - ANZEIGENBLAETTER. 1978. a. DM.270 (effective 1997). Media Daten Verlag GmbH, Am Klingenweg 4a, 65396 Walluf, Germany. TEL 49-6123-700-0. FAX 49-6123-700122. circ. 1,500 (paid). **Document type:** directory.
  Formerly (until 1988): Media Daten: Anzeigenblaetter (ISSN 0170-4036)

659.1 658   NZ   ISSN 0113-2202
MEDIA DIRECTORY. 1973. s-a. NZ.$260. A G B McNair Ltd., c/o Ed. Scanlan, Ed., 129-157 Hurstmere Rd., Takapuna, Auckland, New Zealand. TEL 64-9-4862144. FAX 64-9-4863836. R&P contact: Ed Scanlan. adv. contact: Ed Scanlan. circ. 2,000 (paid). **Document type:** directory.
  Description: Directory listing all magazines, newspapers, radio stations and TV channels.

659.1 380   GW
▼**MEDIA FACTS.** 1995. m. DM.60. Media Daten Verlag GmbH, Klingenweg 4, 65396 Walluf, Germany. TEL 49-6123-700-0. FAX 49-6123-700122. **Document type:** trade publication.

659.1   IT   ISSN 0394-9575
MEDIA FORUM. (Supplement avail.: Quaderni Media) 1970. w. L.160000 includes supplement (foreign L.260000). Ediforum srl, Via Trebbia 5, 20135 Milan, Italy. TEL 2-583-00-548. FAX 2-583-00-870. Ed. Enrico Robbiati. adv.; bk.rev. circ. 9,000.

659.1 070.05   US   ISSN 0024-9793
MEDIA INDUSTRY NEWSLETTER. Abbreviated title: M I N. 1948. w. $495 (foreign $558) (effective 1997). Phillips Business Information, Inc., 1201 Seven Locks Rd., Potomac, MD 20854. TEL 301-424-3338. FAX 301-309-3847. E-mail: pbi@phillips.com; clientservices.phi@phillips.com; URL: http://www.phillips.com/pbi.htm. bk.rev.; charts; stat.; index. circ. 2,143. (looseleaf format; back issues avail.) **Document type:** newsletter.
  ●Also available online. Vendor(s): Information Access Co., NewsNet (PB14).
  —CCC.
  Formerly: Magazine Industry Newsletter.
  Description: Provides current news and information about the marketing and advertising trends in the media industry, especially magazine and newspaper publications.

659.1   UK   ISSN 0266-8688
MEDIA INTERNATIONAL. 1973. m. £42($95) to Europe; rest of world £76. Reed Business Information (Subsidiary of: Reed Elsevier group), Quadrant House, The Quadrant, Sutton, Surrey SM2 5AS, England. TEL 44-181-652-4943. FAX 44-181-652-3959. (Subscr. to: Media International, Oakfield House, Perrymount Rd., Haywards Heath, W. Sussex RH16 3BR, England. TEL 44-1444-445566) Ed. Penny Wilson; Pub. Mark Kelsey. adv. contact: Charlotte Lamp-Carlsen. bk.rev. circ. 12,502. **Indexed:** WPM. **Document type:** trade publication.
  —BLDSC (5525.258180).

659.1   US
MEDIA MARKET GUIDE. 1969. q. $645. Media Market Resources, 322 E. 50th St., New York, NY 10022. TEL 800-242-9618. FAX 212-826-3169. Ed. Robert Herbst; Pub. Martin Herbst. R&P contact: Amy Konikowsky. adv. contact: Amy Konikowsky. circ. 1,200. **Document type:** directory.

659.1 380   GW   ISSN 0945-7356
▼**MEDIA MARKET RESEARCH.** 1995. a. DM.70. Media Daten Verlag GmbH, Klingenweg 4, 65396 Walluf, Germany. TEL 49-6123-700-0. FAX 49-6123-700122. circ. 2,500 (paid). **Document type:** trade publication.

659.1 384.55   US
MEDIA MATTERS. 1986. bi-m. $150 (effective 1997). Media Dynamics, Inc., 18 E. 41st St., Ste. 1806, New York, NY 10017. TEL 212-683-7895. FAX 212-683-7684. Ed. Carol Williams; Pub. Ed Papazian. adv. contact: Sarah K. Ryan. (back issues avail.) **Document type:** newsletter, trade publication.
  Description: Provides original commentary, analyses, and forecasts on all aspects of media.

MEDIA MERGERS & ACQUISITIONS. see COMMUNICATIONS

MEDIA MOVES; the PR industry guide to changes in the media and financial sectors. see JOURNALISM

659.1   GW   ISSN 0720-3519
MEDIA PLAKAT. 1961. a. DM.260. Media Daten Verlag GmbH, Klingenweg 4, 65396 Walluf, Germany. TEL 49-6123-700-0. FAX 49-6123-700122. circ. 1,700. **Document type:** directory.
  Description: Advertising rates and prices for billboarding and outdoor advertising.

659.1   BE   ISSN 0776-5738
MEDIA PLAN. (Supplement to: Media & Marketing (ISSN 0777-0812)) (Text in Dutch, French) 1989. a. 3500 BEF. Editions Dupuis, S.A., 52 rue Destree, B-6001 Marcinelle, Belgium. TEL 32-71-600500. FAX 32-71-600599. adv.: B&W page 50000 BEF, color page 70000 BEF; adv. contact: Marie-Laurence Decoster. circ. 3,000 (paid). **Document type:** directory.
  Description: Provides data on all Belgian print and broadcast media.

ADVERTISING AND PUBLIC RELATIONS

MEDIA PROFESSIONAL. see *JOURNALISM*

659.1320948   DK   ISSN 0076-5821
Z6941
MEDIA SCANDINAVIA; a Scandinavian advertising media directory. (Text in Danish and English) 1948. a. DKK 735 (effective 1997). Danske Reklamebureauers Brancheforening - Danish Association of Advertising Agencies, Badstuestraede 20, P.O. Box 74, DK-1003 Copenhagen K, Denmark. TEL 45-33-13-44-44. FAX 45-33-11-63-03. E-mail: drb@drb.dk; URL: www.drb.dk. Eds. Finn Kern, Hans Peter Kirkegaard. adv.: B&W page DKK 1350; trim 15 x 71; adv. contact: K. Persson. circ. 2,000. **Document type:** directory.
  Former titles (until 1967): Media (ISSN 0903-5001); (until 1962): Bladlisten (ISSN 0903-4986); (until 1960): Eberlins Bladliste (ISSN 0903-4951)

659.1   GW   ISSN 0173-5993
HN460.M3
MEDIA SPECTRUM; Kommentare, Meinungen, Analysen. 1963. m. DM.126. Media Daten Verlag GmbH, Klingenweg 4, 65396 Walluf, Germany. TEL 49-6123-700-0. FAX 49-6123-700122. circ. 2,050. **Document type:** trade publication.
  —SWETS.
  Description: For media planners and other media people.

659.1   UK   ISSN 0963-0023
MEDIA WEEK. 1985. w. £85 (Europe £105; U.S. £130; elsewhere £150). E M A P Media (Subsidiary of: E M A P Business Communications), 33-39 Bowling Green Ln., London EC1R 0DA, England. TEL 44-171-505-8341. FAX 44-171-505-8363. E-mail: mweeked@media.emap.co.uk. (Subscr. to: Readerlink, Audit House, 260 Field End Rd., Eastcote, Ruislip, Mddx. HA4 9LT, England. TEL 44-181-868-4499. FAX 44-181-829-3117) Ed. Susannah Richmond; Pub. Karen Needham. adv. contact: Elizabeth Houghton. charts; stat. circ. 16,754. (back issues avail.) **Indexed:** WPM. **Document type:** trade publication.
  ●Also available online.
  —BLDSC (5525.263000).
  Description: Provides weekly news and analysis of all the important media issues facing advertisers, agencies and media owners.

659.14   UK   ISSN 1355-0055
THE MEDIAMAP (YEAR); the European Media Yearbook. (Vol. 1 of the Mediamap package; w. supplement avail.) 1990. a. £202 (outside Europe £211.50); all 3 vols. £525 (outside Europe £553) (includes w. updates). (Communications and Information Technology Research Ltd.) C I T Publications, 3 Colleton Cresc., Exeter, Devon EX2 4DG, England. TEL 01392-493444. FAX 01392-493626. E-mail: talk2us@citpubs.zynet.co.uk. Ed. Bettina Altemueller. adv.; charts; stat. **Document type:** directory.
  Description: Lists and provides details of the media giants in Europe.

659.14   UK
MEDIAMAP WEEKLY UPDATE. (Supplement to: Mediamap; Business Media Map; Marketing Media Map) w. £100 (with subscr. to any Media Map vol.); free with Mediamap package. (Communications and Information Technology Research Ltd.) C I T Publications, 3 Colleton Cresc., Exeter, Devon EX2 4DG, England. TEL 01392-493444. FAX 01392-493626. E-mail: talk2us@citpubs.zynet.co.uk. Ed. Bettina Altemueller. abstr. **Document type:** bulletin.
  Description: Monitors media developments throughout Europe.

659.1   NE   ISSN 0168-8235
MEDIAMARKT. 1975. m. Samsom Uitgeverij B.V. (Subsidiary of: Wolters Kluwer N.V.), Postbus 4, 2400 MA Alphen aan den Rijn, Netherlands. TEL 31-172-466321. FAX 31-172-435527. adv.; charts; illus. circ. 3,500. **Document type:** trade publication.
  Former titles (until 1984): Ariadne (ISSN 0922-3800); (until 1982): Ariadne - Revue der Reclame (ISSN 0165-4152); Formed by the merger of (1973-1975): M M D Ariadne (ISSN 0922-3797); Kontekst (ISSN 0922-3916); Which was formerly (1938-1972): Revue der Reclame (ISSN 0035-1881)

659.1   US
HF6146.T42
MEDIAWEEK. 1966. w. $125 student $68.85 (Canada $299.60; elsewhere $280) (effective 1997); newsstand price: $3. B P I Communications, Inc. (New York), 1515 Broadway, New York, NY 10036. TEL 212-536-5336; 800-344-7119. FAX 212-536-6594. E-mail: atorpey@adweek.com; URL: http://www.adweek.com/magazine/mediaweek.asp. Ed. Willaim Gloede. adv.: B&W page $5910; trim 8 3/8 x 10 7/8. index. circ. 18,162. (also avail. in microform from UMI; microfiche from CIS) **Indexed:** ABI Inform., Acad.Ind., B.P.I., BPIA, Bus.Ind., Manage.Cont., PROMT, SRI (until 1990), Tr.& Indus.Ind. **Document type:** trade publication.
  ●Also available online. Vendor(s): Information Access Co., Knight-Ridder Information, Inc., Lexis-Nexis, UMI.
  —BLDSC (5525.385900); KR SourceOne; UMI; UnCover. **CCC.**
  Former titles (until 1990): Marketing and Media Decisions (ISSN 0195-4296); (until 1979): Media Decisions (ISSN 0025-6900)

MEDICAL NEWS REPORT. see *BUSINESS AND ECONOMICS — Marketing And Purchasing*

MEDIEN DIALOG; Gespraech - Diskussion - Meinung - Information. see *COMMUNICATIONS — Television And Cable*

659.1   US   ISSN 0889-2776
HM263
METRO CALIFORNIA MEDIA. 1979. s-a. $165. Public Relations Plus, Inc., Box 1197, New Milford, CT 06776. TEL 800-999-8448. FAX 203-355-8048. Ed. Harold D. Hansen. circ. 2,000.
  Formerly: California Publicity Outlets.
  Description: Covers key personnel in media located in California.

659   US
METRO'S PLUS BUSINESS. 1937. m. $60 (effective 1997). Metro Creative Graphics, Inc., 33 W. 34th St., New York, NY 10001. TEL 800-223-1600. FAX 212-967-4602. TELEX 421947. Ed. Stacey Bernstein. adv. contact: Debra Weiss. tr.lit. circ. 7,000. (back issues avail.) **Document type:** trade publication.
  Description: Contains advertising news and newspaper linage-building ideas.

MIDI MEDIA. see *BUSINESS AND ECONOMICS — Marketing And Purchasing*

659.1   BL
MIDIA. 1977. a. free. Editora Rural, Rua Gabriela 333, Porto Alegre, Brazil.

659.1   IT   ISSN 0392-5498
MILLIMETRO; periodico di informazioni aziendali di marketing e di pubblicita. 1964. q. L.70000. St. Paul's International, Via Giotto 36, 20145 Milan, Italy. TEL 39-2-48071. FAX 39-2-48008247. TELEX 332232 EPI I. Ed. Giuseppe Altamore. adv.; bk.rev. circ. 5,000. **Document type:** newsletter.

MISSOURI PRESS NEWS. see *JOURNALISM*

MONDAY REPORT ON RETAILERS. see *BUSINESS AND ECONOMICS — Marketing And Purchasing*

659.1   GW
MUENCHNER SCHAUKASTERL. 1975. w. Muenchner Schaukasterl Verlag GmbH, Simplonstr. 2, 81825 Munich, Germany. TEL 089-429129. Ed. Harald Richter. circ. 50,000.

778.5   US   ISSN 0893-5440
TR505
MULTI - IMAGES. 1974. q. $40 or membership. Association for Multi-Media International, Inc., 10006 N. Dale Mabry Hwy. Ste. 204, Tampa, FL 33618-4424. TEL 813-960-1692. FAX 813-962-7911. Pub. Marilyn Kulp. adv. contact: Louis Kupl. bk.rev. circ. 1,000. **Document type:** trade publication.
  Description: Highlights multimedia events and explores trends in presentation technologies (multi-image, video, single slides and videowalls).

659.1   US   ISSN 0743-0795
MULTINATIONAL P R REPORT. 1984. m. $85. Pigafetta Press, Box 39244, Washington, DC 20016. TEL 202-244-2580. FAX 202-244-2581. Ed. John M. Reed. bk.rev. **Document type:** newsletter.
  Description: News for professionals in public relations.

659.1   US
N A D CASE REPORTS. 1973. 10/yr. $1000. Council of Better Business Bureaus, Inc., National Advertising Division, 845 Third Ave., New York, NY 10022. TEL 212-705-0100. FAX 212-832-1296. URL: http://www.bbb.org. Ed. Delayne Caldwell. circ. 5,700. **Document type:** trade publication.

N Y AUCTION ADVERTISER. see *BUSINESS AND ECONOMICS — Marketing And Purchasing*

659.1   US
NATIONAL ADVERTISING AGENCY NETWORK. MANAGEMENT REPORT.* bi-m. National Advertising Agency Network, 234 W. Delaware Ave., Pennington, NJ 08534-1603. TEL 212-481-3022.

659.1   US
NATIONAL ADVERTISING AGENCY NETWORK. STAFF REPORT.* bi-m. National Advertising Agency Network, 234 W. Delaware Ave., Pennington, NJ 08534-1603. TEL 212-481-3022.

659.1 340   US
NATIONAL ADVERTISING DIVISION CASE REPORT. 10/yr. included in subscr. to Do's and Dont's in Advertising. Council of Better Business Bureaus, Publications Department, 4200 Wilson Blvd., Ste. 800, Arlington, VA 22203-1804. TEL 703-276-0100. circ. 1,000.
  Description: A summary of cases where national advertising claims have been challenged and the issues resolved by the industry's self-regulatory body.

NATIONAL LIST OF ADVERTISERS. see *BUSINESS AND ECONOMICS — Trade And Industrial Directories*

NATIONAL NEWS. see *COMMUNICATIONS — Television And Cable*

NATIONAL RADIO PUBLICITY OUTLETS. see *COMMUNICATIONS — Radio*

659.1   GR
NEA DIMOSSIOTIS. 1958. m. Dr.3500($50) Imera Publishing Co., 61 Mihalakopoulou St., 262 21 Patras, Greece. (Subscr. to: 5 Miltiadou St., 155 62 Holargos, Athens, Greece) Ed. Andrew C. Rizopoulos. adv.; bk.rev.; stat. circ. 2,500. (back issues avail.)
  Former titles: Dimossiotis (ISSN 0012-2920); Dimossiotis-Provoli.

659.2 370   US   ISSN 1076-254X
NETWORK (ROCKVILLE). 1959. 11/yr. membership. National School Public Relations Association, 15948 Derwood Rd., Rockville, MD 20855-2123. TEL 301-519-0496. FAX 301-519-0494. circ. controlled. **Document type:** newsletter.
  Formerly: Paragraphs (ISSN 0031-1669)

659.2   US   ISSN 0077-9024
Z6953.N6
NEW YORK PUBLICITY OUTLETS. 1954. s-a. $165. Public Relations Plus, Inc., Box 1197, New Milford, CT 06776. TEL 800-999-8448. FAX 203-355-8048. Ed. Harold D. Hansen. circ. 3,000.
  Description: Covers key personnel in media located within a 50 mile radius of Columbus Circle, New York City.

659.1   US
NEWS FROM THE ADVERTISING CLUB OF GREATER HARTFORD.* 1965. 9/yr. membership. Advertising Club of Greater Hartford, Box 271803, W. Hartford, CT 06127-1803. TEL 203-561-2582. FAX 203-521-6223. Ed. B.K. Hensey.
  Description: Covers club and member activities.

659.1 681   US
NEWSMETER.* (Text in English, French) 1957. 9/yr. membership. Instrument Society of America, Montreal Section, 67 Alexander Dr., Box 12277, Research Triangle Park, NC 27709. TEL 514-489-8884. FAX 514-489-0638. Eds. John Barr, E. Hofer. adv.; bk.rev. circ. 800. (back issues avail.)

659.1 070.172   US
NEWSPAPER ASSOCIATION OF AMERICA. NEWSPAPER ADVERTISING PLANBOOK. a. Newspaper Association of America, 1921 Gallows Rd., Ste. 600, Vienna, VA 22182-3900. TEL 703-902-1600. FAX 703-917-0636. URL: http://www.naa.org.
  Supersedes (in 1992): Newspaper Advertising Bureau. Newspaper Advertising Planbook.

ADVERTISING AND PUBLIC RELATIONS

659.1 JA
NIKKEI IMAGE CLIMATE FORECAST. m.? Nihon Keizai Shimbun, Inc., 1-9-5 Ote-machi, Chiyoda-ku, Tokyo 100-66, Japan. TEL 81-3-3270-0251. FAX 81-3-5255-2661. TELEX J22308 NIKKEI. **Document type:** newsletter.
Description: Analysis of trends and consumer behavior as they affect corporate image strategies.

659.1 JA
NIKKEI RYUTSU SHIMBUN/NIKKEI MARKETING JOURNAL. (Text in Japanese) 1971. 3/w. Nihon Keizai Shimbun, Inc., 1-9-5 Ote-machi, Chiyoda-ku, Tokyo 100-66, Japan. TEL 81-3-3270-0251. FAX 81-3-5255-2661. TELEX J22308 NIKKEI. Ed. Shunsaku Ikeda. adv.: B&W page 3270000 Yen; trim 385 x 533; adv. contact: Hiroshi Sekino. circ. 335,338. **Document type:** newspaper.
Description: Japan's leading source of information on distribution market.

659 US ISSN 0279-2893
NON-STORE MARKETING REPORT. 1979. fortn. $275 (foreign $320) (effective 1997). Maxwell Sroge Publishing, Inc., 522 Forest Ave., Evanston, IL 60202-3005. TEL 847-866-1890. FAX 847-866-1899. Ed. Ann Meyer. (looseleaf format; back issues avail.) **Document type:** newsletter.
Description: Reports regularly on non-store marketing news; includes industry forecasts, in-depth research and analysis of trends, and interviews with leading executives. Also includes two Standard & Poors type profiles on publicly held mail order companies.

659.1 740 GW
NC997.A1
NOVUM. (Text in English, German) 1924. m. DM.196.80. F. Bruckmann Muenchen Verlag und Druck GmbH, Nymphenburgerstr. 86, 80636 Munich, Germany. TEL 49-89-125701. FAX 49-89-1257269. Ed. Erhard D. Stiebner. adv.; bk.rev.; abstr.; illus. circ. 12,000. **Indexed:** Art Ind., Artbibl.Mod., DAAI, IBR. **Document type:** bulletin. —BLDSC (6180.443000); KR SourceOne; SWETS; UnCover. **CCC.**
Former titles (until 1996): Novum Gebrauchsgraphik (ISSN 0302-9794); (until 1974): Novum (ISSN 0340-1987); Gebrauchsgraphik (ISSN 0016-5743)

659.2 SP ISSN 0211-2000
NUEVA PUBLICIDAD. 1970. q. 5000 ptas. (effective 1994). Asociacion Espanola de Profesionales de Publicidad, Jardin de San Federico 5, 6o, 28009 Madrid, Spain. TEL 401-15-13. circ. 2,000. **Document type:** trade publication.
Description: Covers all communications areas, including photography and graphic arts.

O C S NOUVELLES. (Office des Communications Sociales) see COMMUNICATIONS

O P M A OVERSEAS MEDIA GUIDE. (Overseas Press and Media Association) see BUSINESS AND ECONOMICS — Trade And Industrial Directories

O'DWYER'S DIRECTORY OF PUBLIC RELATIONS EXECUTIVES. see BUSINESS AND ECONOMICS — Trade And Industrial Directories

O'DWYER'S DIRECTORY OF PUBLIC RELATIONS FIRMS. see BUSINESS AND ECONOMICS — Trade And Industrial Directories

659.1 US
O'DWYER'S P R MARKETPLACE. 1987. bi-w. $24. J.R. O'Dwyer Co., Inc., 271 Madison Ave., New York, NY 10016. TEL 212-679-2471. adv. **Document type:** newsletter.
Description: Lists public relations jobs and people available.

659.2 US ISSN 1043-2957
O'DWYER'S P R SERVICES REPORT. (Public Relations) 1987. m. $40. J.R. O'Dwyer Co., Inc., 271 Madison Ave., New York, NY 10016. TEL 212-679-2471. FAX 212-683-2750. Ed. Jack O'Dwyer. adv. circ. 5,000. **Document type:** trade publication.
●Also available online. Vendor(s): Lexis-Nexis.
Description: Publishes articles on current topics and trends of interest to PR professionals, including profiles of firms, discussions of legal and financial issues.

659.2 US
O'DWYER'S WASHINGTON REPORT. 1991. bi-w. $125. J.R. O'Dwyer Co., Inc., 271 Madison Ave., New York, NY 10016. TEL 212-679-2471. FAX 212-683-2750. Ed. Jack O'Dwyer. (looseleaf format) **Document type:** newsletter.
Formerly (until 1992): O'Dwyer's F A R A Report (ISSN 1055-3304)
Description: Covers Washington, D.C. public affairs and public relations, including Foreign Agents Registrations of firms representing foreign entities.

OKLAHOMA PUBLISHER. see PUBLISHING AND BOOK TRADE

OMNIBUS. see TRANSPORTATION

659.1 SZ ISSN 0273-2033
NC1001.5
ONE SHOW; judged to be advertisings's best print, radio, TV magazine. 1977. a. $69. (One Club for Art & Copy) Rotovision S.A., Route Suisse 9, CH-1295 Mies, Switzerland. TEL 022-7553055. FAX 022-7554072. (Dist. in the U.S. by: c/o Watson-Guptill Publications, 1695 Oak St., Lakewood, NJ 08701. TEL 800-451-1741. FAX 908-363-0338) adv. circ. 8,500. **Document type:** trade publication.
Description: For copywriters and art directors on consumer print, radio and T.V. advertising chosen for its creative excellence.

659.1 US
OUTDOOR ADVERTISING ASSOCIATION OF AMERICA. NEWSLETTER. m. Outdoor Advertising Association of America, Marketing Division, 12 E. 49th St., 22nd Fl., New York, NY 10017. TEL 212-688-3667. **Document type:** newsletter.
Formerly: Institute of Outdoor Advertising. Newsletter.

659.1 US
OUTDOOR ADVERTISING EXPENDITURE REPORT. q. Outdoor Advertising Association of America, 1850 M St., N.W., Ste. 1040, Washington, DC 20036. TEL 202-833-5566. FAX 202-833-1522. (And: 12 E. 49th St., New York, NY 10017. TEL 212-688-3667) stat. **Document type:** newsletter.

659.1 UK ISSN 0048-251X
OVERSEAS ADVERTISING. vol.8, 1971. m. £17($50) per edition. New Product Newsletter Co. Ltd., 1A Chesterfield St., London W.1., England. Ed. H.R. Vaughan. adv.; illus. circ. 7,000. (also avail. in microfilm from UMI)
Incorporates: Far East (ISSN 0014-7532)

659.1 615 US
P A CER.* 9/yr. Pharmaceutical Advertising Council, 333 US Hwy 46, Ste. 8206, Fairfield, NJ 07004-2427.

659.1 UK
P E D INDUSTRIAL SELECTOR. 1976. 9/yr. Wilmington Publishing, Wilmington House, Church Rd., Dartford, Kent UA2 7EF, England. TEL 44-1322-277788. FAX 44-1322-276476. circ. 56,323. **Document type:** trade publication.

P M C OF N Y NEWSLETTER. (Premium Marketing Club of New York, Inc.) see BUSINESS AND ECONOMICS — Marketing And Purchasing

659.1 US ISSN 1081-2660
P-O-P & SIGN DESIGN. (Point-of-Purchase); products and news fo high-volume producers of displays, signs and fixtures. 1994. bi-m. $54 (effective 1997). Hoyt Publishing Co., 7400 Skokie Blvd., Skokie, IL 60077-3339. TEL 847-675-7400. FAX 847-675-7494. E-mail: hoytpub@interaccess.com. Ed. William Schober; Pub. Peter W. Hoyt. adv. contact: Kirsten Orwick. circ. 18,000. (tabloid format; back issues avail.) **Document type:** trade publication.
Description: Publishes developments and advancements in materials, processes, systems, equipment and services.

659.1 UK ISSN 0144-0446
P R BULLETIN.* no. 41, Feb. 1982. m. £8 to non-members. Dryden Works, 172-174 Brent Crescut, North Circular Rd., London NW10 7X4, England. adv.; illus.

659.2 US
P R - CHICAGO. m. 30 N. Michigan Ave., No. 508, Chicago, IL 60602-3404. TEL 312-372-7744. Ed. Carla Brock.

659.1 GW ISSN 0342-8702
P R - MAGAZIN; Informationen fuer Fuehrungskraefte in der Kommunikationsbranche. 1969. m. DM.184. Verlag Rommerskirchen und Co. KG, Bennauerstr. 60, 53115 Bonn, Germany. TEL 0228-222974. FAX 0228-214917. Ed. Thomas Rommerskirchen. adv.; bk.rev. circ. 5,000. **Indexed:** Key to Econ.Sci. —SWETS. **CCC.**

659.1 SZ
P R MAGAZIN. m. Zollinger & Partner AG, Steinacherstr. 105, CH-8804 Zurich, Switzerland. TEL 01-7812563. FAX 01-7812570. Ed. Hans Zollinger. circ. 3,000.

P R PLANNER - EUROPE. see BUSINESS AND ECONOMICS — Trade And Industrial Directories

P R PLANNER - U.K.. see BUSINESS AND ECONOMICS — Trade And Industrial Directories

659.2 US ISSN 0048-2609
P R REPORTER; weekly newsletter of public relations, public affairs & communication. 1958. w. $225. P R Publishing Co., Inc., Box 600, Exeter, NH 03833. TEL 603-778-0514. FAX 603-778-1741. E-mail: prr@nh.ultranet.com. Ed. Patrick Jackson. **Document type:** newsletter.

659.2 SZ ISSN 0033-3727
P R REVUE; Schweizerisches Magazin fuer Public Relations/periodique suisse de relations publiques. (Text in French, German and Italian) 1954. m. 185 SFr. (Schweizerische Public Relations Gesellschaft - Swiss Public Relations Society) Rheintaler Druckerei und Verlags AG, c/o Perex Communications, Helvetiastr. 45, CH-3005 Bern, Switzerland. TEL 031-3528818. Ed. Angela Kreis-Muzzulini. adv.; bk.rev. **Indexed:** Key to Econ.Sci. **Document type:** trade publication.

659.1 US ISSN 1091-5583
P R WATCH; public interest reporting on the public relations industry. 1993. q. $35 to individuals; nonprofit organizations $60; corporate $200 (effective 1997 & 1998). Center for Media & Democracy, Inc., 3318 Gregory St., Madison, WI 53711. TEL 608-233-3346. FAX 608-238-2236. URL: http://users.aol.com/srampton/center.html. Ed. John C. Stauber. bk.rev. circ. 4,000. **Document type:** newsletter.
Description: Discusses developments and trends in the public relations industry from a populist and public-interest perspective.

659.2 UK ISSN 0267-6087
P R WEEK. (Public Relations) 1984. w. £66 (Europe £99; rest of world £140). Haymarket Publishing Ltd., 174 Hammersmith Rd., London W6 7JP, England. TEL 44-171-413-4520. FAX 44-171-413-4509. E-mail: prweek@theframe.com. (Subscr. to: WDIS, Publishing House, Victoria Rd., Ruislip, Middlesex HA4 OSE, England. TEL 44-181-841-3970. FAX 44-181-845-7696) Ed. Stephen Farish. R&P contact: Mary Cowlett. adv. contact: Nick Simpson. bk.rev.; stat. circ. 16,000. (tabloid format; back issues avail.) **Document type:** trade publication.
—BLDSC (6579.243000).

659.1 US
P S A. (Public Service Advertising) 1982. q. $20. Doug Wyles Publication, Inc., 49 W. 76th St., New York, NY 10023. TEL 212-877-4800. Ed. Cyndy Floor. adv.; tr.lit. circ. 14,600.

659.1 GW
P S I NACHRICHTEN. (Text in English, French, German) 1960. bi-m. Praesent Service Institut, Neusserstr. 111, 40219 Duesseldorf, Germany. TEL 49-211-901910. FAX 49-211-9019125. Ed. M. Mueller; Pub. W. Jung. R&P contact: W. Jung. adv.: page DM.3110; trim 260 x 185; adv. contact: S. Karabulut. bk.rev.; circ. 6,500. (back issues avail.) **Document type:** bulletin.

ADVERTISING AND PUBLIC RELATIONS

659.1 330   US
PACIFIC DIALOGUE. 1982. bi-w. $196. Box 1312, New York, NY 10018-0724. TEL 203-378-2803. Ed. Robert Miko. **Document type:** newspaper.
   Description: Covers international business and corporate communications relating to the Pacific region.

070 659.2   US
PARTYLINE; the public relations media newsletter. 1960. w. $160. PartyLine Publishing, 35 Sutton Pl., New York, NY 10022. TEL 212-755-3487. FAX 212-755-3488. E-mail: byarmon@ix.netcom.com; URL: http://www.partylinepublishing.com. Ed. Morton Yarmon. circ. 1,250. (looseleaf format; back issues avail.) **Document type:** newsletter.
   Formerly (until 1990): P R A's Party Line (Public Relations Aids) (ISSN 0030-8226)
   Description: For public relations professionals.

PENN STATER. see COLLEGE AND ALUMNI

659.1   US
PERSONALS. 1975. m. $9. Customart Press, Inc., 525 North Barry Ave., Mamaroneck, NY 10543. TEL 914-698-1500. Ed. S. Allensworth. adv.; bk.rev. circ. 3,550.

PHARMA-MARKETING JOURNAL. see BUSINESS AND ECONOMICS — Marketing And Purchasing

PLAYBACK; Canada's broadcast and production journal. see COMMUNICATIONS — Television And Cable

659.1   US
POPULAR LIFE.* 1990. q. $8; newsstand price: $2. 96 Hillside Ave., Rochester, NY 14610-2411. Eds. Lamar & Mary Arp. circ. 88.
   Description: Publishes collections of advertisements from the past to criticize the social evils of consumer society today.

659.1   GW   ISSN 0935-7149
PORENTIEF; der neue Text fuer neue Texter. 1988. q. DM.40($40) Efeuweg 52, 22299 Hamburg, Germany. TEL 040-510292. Ed. Alexander Antonoff. adv.; bk.rev. circ. 1,000.

741.67 658   US   ISSN 0883-3036
PRACTICE BUILDER. 1983. m. (except Nov.-Dec. combined). $119. Evergreen Group, 18351 Jamboree Rd., Irvine, CA 92715-1011. TEL 714-253-7900. FAX 714-252-1002. E-mail: PracBuild@aol.com. Ed. Reece Franklin; Pub. Alan Bernstein. adv. contact: Tobim Smith. circ. 25,000. (back issues avail.) **Document type:** newsletter.
   Description: Covers innovative marketing and promotional strategies for healthcare professionals to help build their practices in an effective yet ethical way.

659.1   GW   ISSN 0723-9408
PRAXIS DER WERBUNG. Short title: P W. 1980. m. Suedwestdeutsche Akademie fuer Marketing und Kommunikation e.V., Koenigstr. 1B, 70173 Stuttgart, Germany. TEL 49-711-291714. Ed. Oliver Apfel. **Document type:** trade publication.

659.1   US   ISSN 1072-7531
HF5718.22
PRESENTATIONS; technology and techniques for effective communication. 1988. m. $50 (Canada $60; elsewhere $90); newsstand price: $5. Lakewood Publications Inc., 50 S. Ninth St., Minneapolis, MN 55402. TEL 612-333-0471. FAX 612-333-6526. E-mail: sheimes@presentations.com; URL: http://www.presentations.com. Ed. Eric K. Gill. adv.; bk.rev.; circ. 70,000 (controlled). (also avail. in microform from UMI) **Document type:** trade publication.
   ●Also available online.
   —BLDSC (6609.746000); KR SourceOne; UMI.
—CCC.
   Former titles (until Sep. 1993): Presentation Products (ISSN 1070-6089); (until 1992): Presentation Products Magazine (ISSN 1041-9780)
   Description: Devoted exclusively to individuals and organizations that create and deliver presentations.

PRIMA COMUNICAZIONE. see COMMUNICATIONS

PRODUKTIONSHAANDBOGEN; virksomheder med grafisk produktion - reklamevirksomhed. see PRINTING

659.1 658   US
PROFESSIONAL ADVISOR. 1977. m. $120 (effective 1997). Bernard Hale Zick, Ed. & Pub., Box 6432, Kingwood, TX 77325-6399. TEL 281-360-4719. FAX 281-361-7163. adv.; bk.rev. (back issues avail.) **Document type:** newsletter.
   Former titles: Professional Consultant (ISSN 0272-8559); Professional Consultant and Information Marketing Report; Professional Consultant and Seminar Business Report.
   Description: Covers the marketing of consulting, seminars, information products, and services.

659.1   US   ISSN 0275-9632
PROFILES IN HEALTHCARE MARKETING; idea exchange for the people who plan and create healthcare marketing and PR campaigns. 1984. bi-m. $259. Business Word Inc., 5350 S. Roslyn St., Ste. 400, Englewood, CO 80111-2125. TEL 303-290-8500; 800-328-3211. FAX 303-290-9025. E-mail: plmoore@businessword.com. Ed. Pamela Moore; Pub. Don E.L. Johnson. circ. 1,313. (back issues avail.) **Document type:** trade publication.
   ●Also available online. Vendor(s): NewsNet.
—CCC.
   Description: Provides up-close case studies of successful and not-so-successful hospital marketing and public relations campaigns. Includes reprints of actual ads, press releases, brochures, story boards, etc.

PROMAX INTERNATIONAL. see COMMUNICATIONS — Television And Cable

659.2   SP
PROMOCION DE IMAGEN. 5/yr. Juan de Austria 6, 28010 Madrid, Spain. TEL 1-447-38-04. FAX 1-200-53-85. Ed. J. Luis Santaolaya. circ. 3,500.

659.1   US   ISSN 1072-3293
PROMOTIONAL PRODUCTS BUSINESS. (Former name of issuing body: Promotional Products Association International) 1976. m. $56 to non-members (Canada & Mexico $67; elsewhere $72); free to members. Promotional Products Association International, 3125 Skyway Circle N., Irving, TX 75038-3526. TEL 972-258-3104. FAX 972-258-3012. URL: http://www.ppa.org. Ed. Tina Berres Filipski; Pub. Lindsay Schieffelin. R&P contact: Tina Berres Filipski. adv. contact: Melissa McGrath-Klusmyer. bk.rev. circ. 6,500. **Document type:** trade publication.
   Former titles: National Products Business; Specialty Advertising Business (ISSN 0195-0495)
   Description: Provides in-depth communication with association members and others in the specialty advertising and promotional product industry.

PROTECTING THE ENVIRONMENT (YEAR). see ENVIRONMENTAL STUDIES

659.1   BE   ISSN 0771-3819
PUB. (Includes supplement: Bureaudossier - Dossier Agences) (Text in Flemish, French) 1976. fortn. 6678 BEF (foreign 11660 BEF). Kluwer Business Press (Subsidiary of: Wolters Kluwer N.V.), Kouterveldstraat 2, B-1831 Diegem, Belgium. TEL 32-2-7231523. FAX 32-2-7231591. Ed. Jean-Michel Stichelbaut. adv.: B&W page 54600 BEF, color page 79800 BEF; 313 x 227; adv. contact: Gerda Bourdeaud'hui. circ. 5,000. (tabloid format) **Document type:** trade publication.
   Description: News on advertising, marketing, and other aspects of communications and media.

659.1   BE
PUB CREATIVE BOOK. (Text in Dutch, French) 1978. a. 3286 BEF (effective 1995). Kluwer Business Press (Subsidiary of: Wolters Kluwer N.V.), Kouterveldstraat 2, 1831 Diegem, Belgium. TEL 32-2-7231523. FAX 32-2-7231591. Ed. Bernard Lefevre. adv. contact: Gerda Bourdeaud'hui. circ. 2,500. **Document type:** directory.
   Former titles: Pub Creative and Print Production Book (ISSN 0778-2101); (until 1989): Pub Annuaire Creatif - Kreatief Jaarboek Pub (ISSN 0778-2098)

659.1   BE   ISSN 0778-1946
PUB MEDIABOOK. (Text in Dutch, French) 1984. a. 2968 BEF (effective Dec. 1994). Kluwer Business Press (Subsidiary of: Wolters Kluwer N.V.), Kouterveldstraat 2, 1831 Diegem, Belgium. TEL 32-2-7231523. FAX 32-2-7231591. Ed. Bernard Lefevre. adv. contact: Gerda Bourdeaud'hui. circ. 2,500.
   Description: Covers advertising and the media in Belgium and Luxembourg.

659   IT
PUBBLICITA DOMANI. 1972. 11/yr. L.60000. New International Media s.r.l., Via Lovanio 6, 20121 Milan, Italy. TEL 2-49-81-341. FAX 2-481-93-391. Ed. Enzo Argante. adv. contact: Jania Camillozzi. bk.rev. circ. 12,000. **Document type:** trade publication.

659.1 658.8   IT
PUBBLICITA ITALIA. 1989. 45/yr. L.295000. Marketing Finanza Italia s.r.l., Via Stradella 3, 20129 Milan, Italy. TEL 2-29-40-05-54. FAX 2-29-40-18-16. Ed. Lillo Perri. adv. contact: Daniele Monai. circ. 7,678. **Document type:** newspaper.

659.1   FR   ISSN 0751-5464
PUBLI 10; le journal de la publicite. 1946. fortn. 250 F. (foreign 250 F.) (effective 1997). Nouvelles Editions de la Publicite, 9 rue Leo-Delibes, 75116 Paris, France. Ed. C. Chauvet. adv.; bk.rev. circ. 5,000.
—CCC.
   Formerly: Journal de la Publicite.

PUBLIC EYE. see LIBRARY AND INFORMATION SCIENCES

659.1   UK   ISSN 0263-6166
PUBLIC RELATIONS. 1982. q. £32($65) (Institute of Public Relations) Longman Group UK Ltd., Longman House, Burnt Mill, Harlow, Essex CM20 2JE, England. TEL 44-1279-426721. FAX 44-1279-431059. (Subscr. to: Pearson Professional, P.O. Box 77, Fourth Ave., Harlow, Essex CM19 5BQ, England. TEL 44-1279-623924. FAX 44-1279-639609) Ed. J.H. Smith. adv.; bk.rev. —SWETS. CCC.

659.1   GW   ISSN 1430-5828
PUBLIC RELATIONS. 1994. a. DM.68. E C O N Verlag GmbH, Postfach 300321, 40403 Duesseldorf, Germany. TEL 49-211-4359746. FAX 49-211-4359781. adv.: B&W page DM.1280, color page DM.1940; trim 160 x 240; adv. contact: Barbara Lampe. circ. 2,500 (paid). **Document type:** directory.
   Description: Deals with the topic of quality in public relations, including the relationship between agencies and customers.

PUBLIC RELATIONS CAREER DIRECTORY. see OCCUPATIONS AND CAREERS

659.2   II   ISSN 0033-3689
HD59
PUBLIC RELATIONS JOURNAL OF INDIA. (Text in English) 1970. 5/yr. Rs.18($12) P. R. Publications, 16-199 Lane No 7 Joshi Rd., Karol Bagh, New Delhi 5, India. Ed. Roshan Lan. adv.; bk.rev.; illus.; index.

659.2   US   ISSN 0033-3697
HM263.A1
PUBLIC RELATIONS NEWS. Short title: P R News. 1944. w. $347 (foreign $410) (effective 1997). Phillips Business Information, Inc., 1201 Seven Locks Rd., Potomac, MD 20854. TEL 301-424-3338. FAX 301-309-3847. E-mail: pbi@phillips.com. Ed. Diane Schwartz. (looseleaf format) **Document type:** newsletter.
   ●Also available online. Vendor(s): Information Access Co.
—CCC.
   Description: For public relations, public affairs and communications executives. Reports public relations techniques and trends, case studies of programs and news of the industry.

ADVERTISING AND PUBLIC RELATIONS

659.2 US ISSN 0033-3700
HM263 CODEN: PREUEU
PUBLIC RELATIONS QUARTERLY. 1955. q. $49 (Canada & Mexico $54; elsewhere $61) (effective 1996). 44 W. Market St., Box 311, Rhinebeck, NY 12572. TEL 914-876-2081. FAX 914-876-2561. E-mail: hphudson@aol.com; URL: http://www.wwmedia.com/PRQ/prq.html. Ed. Howard Penn Hudson; Pub. Howard Penn Hudson. adv. contact: E.W. Hopper. bk.rev.; charts; illus.; stat.; index. circ. 6,000. (also avail. in microform from UMI; reprint service avail. from UMI) **Indexed:** ABI Inform., Account.& Data Proc.Abstr., Account.Ind. (1974-), ASEAN Manage.Abstr., B.P.I., BPIA, Bus.Ind., Commun.Abstr., Manage.Cont., Tr.& Indus.Ind.
●Also available online. Vendor(s): Information Access Co., UMI.
—BLDSC (6968.600000); KR SourceOne; SWETS; UMI; UnCover. **CCC.**
Incorporates: International Public Relations Review (ISSN 0020-8434).
Description: Articles on the theory and practice of public relations, marketing public affairs, public relations education and organizational communication.

659.2 US ISSN 0363-8111
HM263 CODEN: PREREL
PUBLIC RELATIONS REVIEW; journal of research and comment. 1975. q. (plus a. bibliography). $110 to individuals (foreign $135); institutions $245 (foreign $270) (effective 1998). J A I Press Inc., 55 Old Post Rd., No.2, Box 1678, Greenwich, CT 06830-1678. TEL 203-661-7602. FAX 203-661-0792. E-mail: jai@jaipress.com; URL: http://www.jaipress.com/jmpub.htm. (Addr. in Europe: J A I Press Ltd., 38 Tavistock St., Covent Garden, London WC2E 7PB, England. TEL 44-171-379-8834. FAX 44-171-379-8835) Ed. Ray E. Hiebert. adv.; bk.rev.; bibl. circ. 2,500. (also avail. in microform from UMI; back issues avail.; reprint service avail. from ISI,UMI) **Indexed:** ABI Inform., Arts & Hum.Cit.Ind., ASCA, B.P.I., BPIA, Bus.Ind., C.I.J.E., Commun.Abstr., Curr.Cont., Manage.Cont., P.A.I.S., SSCI, Tr.& Indus.Ind.
Document type: trade publication.
●Also available online. Vendor(s): Information Access Co.
—BLDSC (6968.680000); Genuine Article; KR SourceOne; SWETS; UMI; UnCover. **CCC.**
Description: Features in-depth analyses of measurements and evaluations, public relations education, public policy, history and bibliographies.

PUBLIC RELATIONS SOCIETY OF AMERICA DIRECTORY. see BUSINESS AND ECONOMICS — Trade And Industrial Directories

659.2 US
▼**PUBLIC RELATIONS STRATEGIST**; issue and trends that affect management. 1995. q. $48 to non-members; members $24. Public Relations Society of America, Inc., 33 Irving Pl., New York, NY 10003-2376. TEL 212-460-1468. FAX 212-995-0757. Pub. Fraser P. Seitel. adv. **Document type:** trade publication.

659.2 US
▼**PUBLIC RELATIONS TACTICS.** 1995. q. Public Relations Society of America, Inc., 33 Irving Pl., New York, NY 10003-2376. TEL 212-460-1468. FAX 212-995-0757. **Document type:** trade publication.

659.1 US
PUBLIC SERVICE ADVERTISING BULLETIN. bi-m. Advertising Council, 261 Madison Ave., New York, NY 10016-2303. TEL 212-922-1500. Ed. Joan McLaughlin. **Document type:** bulletin, catalog.

659.2 070.5 CN ISSN 0836-5024
HF3201
PUBLICATION PROFILES. 1980. a. Can.$49. Maclean-Hunter Ltd., Business Publication Division, Maclean-Hunter Bldg., 777 Bay St., Toronto, ON M5W 1A7, Canada. TEL 416-867-9500. FAX 416-867-1505. Ed. Nancy Remnant. circ. 5,215.
Formerly: Media Editorial Profile Edition (ISSN 0228-5215)
Description: Examines consumer, agriculture and business magazines in Canada.

659.1 VE
PUBLICIDAD Y MERCADEO. 1961. m. $40. M.G. Ediciones Especializadas, S.A., Av. Maturin, No. 15, Urb. Los Cedros, El Bosque, Caracas 1050, Venezuela. Ed. Montserrat Giol. adv. circ. 3,250.

659.1 US
PUBLICITY AND MEDIA RESOURCES FOR PUBLISHERS. 1958-1979; resumed 1988. biennial. $200. Association of American University Presses, Inc., 584 Broadway, Ste. 410, New York, NY 10012. TEL 212-941-6610. Ed. Chris Terry. adv.; bk.rev.; index; circ. controlled.
Former titles (until 1992): Advertising and Publicity Resources for Scholarly Books; Ad Guide: An Advertiser's Guide to Scholarly Periodicals (ISSN 0065-3586)

659.1 US
PUBLISHERS INFORMATION BUREAU REPORT; magazine advertising expenditures. (In seven industry sections: Apparel, Business-Financial, Drugs-Toiletries, Food-Beverages, General, Home-Building, Transportation-Agriculture) 1948. m. Publishers' Information Bureau Inc., 919 Third Ave., New York, NY 10022. TEL 212-872-3700. FAX 212-888-4217. adv.; mkt.; stat. (looseleaf format; also avail. in microfiche) **Document type:** trade publication.
Former titles: P I B Monthly; P I B Monthly Service - Leading National Advertisers Monthly Service; P I B Monthly (ISSN 0030-7998)

659.1 IT ISSN 0033-3999
PUBLITRANSPORT. 1961. q. free. Impresa Generale Pubblicita, Piazza Cavour 1, 20121 Milan, Italy. TEL 654651. Ed. Fabrizio del Chene de Vere. adv. circ. 4,600.
Description: Features articles on advertising displayed on public transportation.

659.1 UK
QUARTERLY SUMMARY OF BRANDS AND ADVERTISERS. 1992. q. £860. Register - Meal Ltd., 7 Harewood Ave., London NW1 6JB, England. TEL 44-171-393-5070. FAX 44-171-393-5088. R&P contact: Barbara Johnson. circ. 200 (paid). (back issues avail.) **Document type:** trade publication.

659.1 UK ISSN 0951-7766
QUARTERLY SURVEY OF ADVERTISING EXPENDITURE. 1984. q. £595 (effective 1998). (Advertising Association) N T C Publications Ltd., P.O. Box 89, Henley-on-Thames, Oxon RG9 1GB, England. TEL 44-1491-411000. FAX 44-1491-571188. **Document type:** trade publication.
Formerly (until 1987): Quarterly Review of Advertising Statistics (ISSN 0266-5646)
Description: Provides accurate, up-to-date and detailed analysis of advertising expenditure trends in the UK.

659.1 US
R A B INSTANT BACKGROUND;* profiles of 50 businesses. 1970. s-a. $50 per vol. Radio Advertising Bureau, 261 Madison Ave., 23rd Fl., New York, NY 10016-2303. TEL 212-254-4800. FAX 212-254-8713. Ed. Kenneth J. Costa. circ. 6,000.
Description: Covers all types of retail businesses in a two-page summary profile format.

659.1 DK ISSN 0109-5196
R F AVISEN. 1983. q. free. Reklamefotograf Foreningen, Noerre Voldgade 34, 1358 Copenhagen K, Denmark. illus.

R F D NEWS. see AGRICULTURE

659.1 200 US
R P R C COUNSELOR. 4/yr. membership. Religious Public Relations Council, 475 Riverside Dr., Rm. 1948A, New York, NY 10115. Ed. Linda Lawson. circ. 800. **Document type:** newsletter.
Description: Covers events within the Council and its chapters, with special emphasis on religious public relations.

RADIO ADVERTISERS' GUIDE. see COMMUNICATIONS — Radio

659.1 US
RADIO ADVERTISING BUREAU. RETAIL MARKETING KIT.* m. Radio Advertising Bureau, 261 Madison Ave., 23rd Fl., New York, NY 10016-2303. TEL 212-254-4800. FAX 212-254-8713.

RADIO CO-OP SOURCES. see COMMUNICATIONS — Radio

659.1 384.5 US
▼**RADIO - MEDIA.** 1996. w. $25 for fax version for 6 mos. Box 2501, Los Angeles, CA 90078. E-mail: radio-media@adsong.com; URL: http://via.net/~bryanf/radio-media-info. Ed. Bryan Farrish. circ. 940. (fax) **Document type:** newsletter.
●Also available online.
Description: Covers the ad-agency media planning for, and the buying and selling of, radio advertising.

659.2 US
RADIO - T V INTERVIEW REPORT; the magazine talk show producers read to find guests. 1986. s-m. Bradley Communications Corp., Box 1206, Lansdowne, PA 19050. TEL 215-259-1070. FAX 215-284-3704. Ed. Stephen Hall. adv.: page $539. bk.rev.; circ. 4,000 (controlled). (tabloid format) **Document type:** trade publication.
Description: Lists authors, experts, entrepreneurs and others available for radio and TV appearances.

659.1 004.693 US
▼**RAGAN'S INTERACTIVE PUBLIC RELATIONS.** 1995. bi-w. $279. Ragan Communications, 212 W. Superior St., Ste. 200, Chicago, IL 60610. TEL 800-878-5331. FAX 312-335-9583. E-mail: 71154.2605@compuserve.com. Ed. Steve Crescenzo. **Document type:** newsletter.
Description: Helps PR people navigate cyberspace.

659.13 CN ISSN 0706-8085
REACHING THE MANITOBA MARKET. 1977. a. free. Manitoba Community Newspapers Association, 310-275 Portage Ave., Winnipeg, MB R3B 2B3, Canada. TEL 204-947-1691. FAX 204-947-1919. URL: http://www.manitobanews.com. Ed. Emily Boitson-Murray. adv. circ. 1,500. **Document type:** bulletin.

REDAKTIONS ADRESS. see BUSINESS AND ECONOMICS — Trade And Industrial Directories

659.1 GW ISSN 0932-1543
REDEN-BERATER; Handbuch fuer erfolgreiche Reden im Betrieb, in der Oeffentlichkeit und im Privatleben. 1987. 7/yr. DM.198. Verlag Norman Rentrop, Theodor-Heuss-Str. 4, 53177 Bonn, Germany. TEL 49-228-8205-0. FAX 49-228-364411. Ed. F. Franken. (looseleaf format) **Document type:** bulletin.
Description: How-to publication on public speaking and speechwriting.

659.2 NE ISSN 0034-3218
REGELRECHT. 1955. 11/yr. free. Honeywell B.V., Marketing Division, Postbus 12683, 1100 AR Amsterdam, Netherlands. Ed. G.J.v.d. Kempen. circ. 1,500.

659.1 BE
REKLAAM IS SUCCES. 1934. w. Otterstraat 167, 2300 Turnhout, Netherlands. TEL 31-141-411411. FAX 31-141-422932. adv.: page 40680 BEF; trim 339 x 231; adv. contact: Jacobs Ine. (also avail. in diskette format) **Document type:** newspaper.

659.1 FR ISSN 0246-7143
RELATIONS PRESSE. 1965. 4/yr. Union Nationale des Attaches de Presse et Professionnels de la Communication, 9 rue de Duras, 75008 Paris, France. TEL 1-42-65-08-03. FAX 1-42-66-07-67. Ed. Remi Roland. adv. contact: Anne-Marie Reder. circ. 600. **Document type:** newspaper.

659.2 FR ISSN 0034-3811
RELATIONS PUBLIQUES INFORMATIONS. 1956. w. 1900 F. (foreign 2100 F.). (E P C I) I S E R P, 87 bis rue Carnot, 92300 Levallois-Perret, France. Ed. Philippe A. Boiry. adv.; bk.rev. circ. 1,800.

659.1 US
REMINDER PLUS. w. $22 (free to qualified personnel). Hipple Printing Co., Inc., 333 W. Dakota, Box 878, Pierre, SD 57501. TEL 605-224-7301. Ed. Terry Hipple. adv. circ. 18,800.

RENTAL MANAGEMENT. see BUSINESS AND ECONOMICS — Marketing And Purchasing

ADVERTISING AND PUBLIC RELATIONS

659.1 US
REPORT ON ELECTRIC COMMERCE. bi-w. $694 (outside N. America $853). Telecommunications Reports (Subsidiary of: Business Research Publications, Inc.), 1333 H St., N.W., Ste. 100-E, Washington, DC 20005. TEL 800-822-6338. FAX 202-842-3023. E-mail: customerservice@tr.com; URL: http://www.tr.com. **Document type:** newsletter.

RESEARCH. see BUSINESS AND ECONOMICS — Marketing And Purchasing

RESEARCHPLUS. see BUSINESS AND ECONOMICS — Marketing And Purchasing

659.1 US ISSN 0735-7087
RETAIL AD WEEK. 1941. bi-w. $385 (effective 1994). Retail Reporting Bureau, 302 Fifth Ave., New York, NY 10001. TEL 212-279-7000; 800-251-4545. FAX 212-279-7014. illus. (also avail. in microform from UMI; reprint service avail. from UMI) —UMI.
 Formerly (until 1971): Retail Advertising Week (ISSN 0034-5997)

659.1 SP ISSN 0211-3333
REVISTA INTERNACIONAL DE COMUNICACION Y RELACIONES PUBLICAS/INTERNATIONAL MAGAZINE OF COMMUNICATIONS AND PUBLIC RELATIONS. Key Title: R P Internacional de Relaciones Publicas. Short title: Relaciones Publicas. (Text in English, Spanish) 1962. q. 6000 ptas.($50) (effective 1994-95). Jose Ortega y Gasset, 50, 28006 Madrid, Spain. TEL 34-1-4022609. FAX 34-1-4022614. Ed. Fernando Lozano Dominguez. adv.: B&W page 200000 ptas., color page 275000 ptas.; trim 230 x 180; adv. contact: Paloma Almagro. bk.rev.; bibl.; charts; illus.; stat.; tr.lit.; index; circ. 30,000 (paid). (tabloid format)
 —CCC.
 Description: Presents research and disseminates knowledge in the areas of communication and public relations.

659.15 UK
S D E A DIRECTORY OF SHOPFITTINGS AND DISPLAY EQUIPMENT. 1980. a. £15. Shop and Display Equipment Association, 24 Croydon Rd., Caterham, Surrey CR3 6YR, England. TEL 44-1883-348911. FAX 44-1883-343435. Ed. Lawrence Cutler. adv. circ. 7,000. **Document type:** directory.
 Former titles: S D E A Catalogue of Shopfittings and Display; S D E A Members Catalogue of Shopfittings and Display.

S P A N CONNECTION. (Small Publishers Association of North America) see PUBLISHING AND BOOK TRADE

SAN DIEGO CREATIVE DIRECTORY. see BUSINESS AND ECONOMICS — Trade And Industrial Directories

659.1 GW ISSN 0933-016X
SCHAUFENSTER & SHOP DESIGN; Fachzeitschrift der internationalen Schaufenster- und Verkaufsraumgestaltung. (Text in Dutch, English, French, German, Italian and Spanish) 1950. m. DM.130 (effective 1997). Verlag Passavia, Vornholzstr. 40, 94036 Passau, Germany. TEL 49-851-7002-0. FAX 49-851-9320049. Ed. Peter Schwibach. adv.; bk.rev.; bibl.; illus. circ. 11,000. **Document type:** trade publication.
 —CCC.
 Formerly (until 1988): Schaufenster (ISSN 0036-5939)
 Description: Reports on trends, innovations and new products.

659.1 GW
SCHEBEN NEWS. 1987. bi-m. Scheben Scheurer und Partner, Max-Planck-Str. 22, 50858 Cologne, Germany. TEL 49-2234-18331. FAX 49-2234-183367. Ed. Mathias Scheben. circ. 500. (looseleaf format) **Document type:** newsletter.
 Formerly: Scheben Newsletter.

659.1 IT
SECONDAMANO; pentasettimanale di inserzioni gratuite. 1977. 5/wk. L.600000($370) Editrice Secondamano S.r.l., Via Argelati 1-A, 20143 Milano, Italy. TEL 2-838721. FAX 2-83872-700. TELEX 340160 SOFT I. circ. 200,000. (tabloid format)

659.2 US
▼**SELLING TO KIDS.** 1996. bi-w. $495 (foreign $530) (effective 1997). Phillips Business Information, Inc., 1201 Seven Locks Rd., Potomac, MD 20854. TEL 301-424-3338. FAX 301-309-3847. E-mail: pbi@phillips.com. Ed. Diane Schwartz. **Document type:** newsletter.
 Description: Contains practical advice on how to prosper in the constantly changing kids' marketplace.

659 US ISSN 1074-5297
SHOOT. 1960. w. $98 (Canada $205; foreign $405) (effective 1997). B P I Communications, Inc. (New York), 1515 Broadway, New York, NY 10036. TEL 212-764-7300. FAX 212-536-5321. (Subscr. to: Box 5023, Brentwood, TN 37024. TEL 615-377-3322) Ed. Peter Caranicas; Pub. Roberta Griefer. adv. contact: Neal Greenberg. circ. 14,750. (tabloid format; back issues avail.) **Document type:** trade publication.
 ●Also available online. Vendor(s): Information Access Co.
 —UMI.
 Formerly: Back Stage Shoot (ISSN 1055-9825)
 Description: For the commercial production and advertising industries. Special feature issues cover industry events such as the Clio Awards, NAB Convention, ITS Convention, and SMPTE.

659.1 NE ISSN 0929-1431
SIGN & DISPLAY. (Text in Dutch) 1989. 8/yr. Misset (Subsidiary of: Reed Elsevier plc), Postbus 4, 7000 BA Doetinchem, Netherlands. TEL 31-314-349371. FAX 31-314-363638. adv.: B&W page fl.3340, color page fl.5335; trim 230 x 300; adv. contact: Cor van Nek. circ. 4,750. **Document type:** trade publication.
 Description: For the sign and display industry in the Netherlands and Belgium.

659 US ISSN 0895-0555
SIGN BUILDER ILLUSTRATED; the how-to magazine. 1987. q. $21 (foreign $39) (effective 1997); newsstand price: $3.75. Journalistic, Inc., 4905 Pine Cone Dr., Ste. 2, Durham, NC 27707. TEL 919-489-1916; 800-638-0776. FAX 919-489-4767. E-mail: jhyatt@jayi.com; URL: http://www.signstop.com. Ed. James B. Hyatt. adv.: B&W page $1230, color page $2260; trim 7 x 10; adv. contact: Eugene Drezner. charts; illus.; stat.; tr.lit.; circ. 12,000 (controlled). (back issues avail.)
 Description: Acts as a "how-to" publication for the sign industry.

659.15 686.2 US ISSN 0893-9888
SIGN BUSINESS. 1986. m. $45 (effective 1995). National Business Media, Inc., Box 1416, Broomfield, CO 80020. TEL 303-469-0424. FAX 303-469-5730. Ed. Terry Wike. adv.: B&W page $2065; trim 8 1/8 x 10 7/8; adv. contact: Ken Higgins. circ. 20,000. **Document type:** trade publication.
 Description: For businesses engaged in the design, production, sales and maintenance of all types of interior and exterior signs.

659.1 UK
SIGN UPDATE. 1990. bi-m. £14.50($20.50) 22 Station Rd., Woodford Halse, Northants. NN11 3RB, England. TEL 44-1327-260434. FAX 44-1327-262621. Ed. Linda Hinchliffe; Pub. Roger Hinchliffe. R&P contact: Roger Hinchliffe. adv.: B&W page £495, color page £880; trim 211 x 300; adv. contact: Heather Ashton. circ. 7,080 (paid). **Document type:** trade publication.

659.13 UK ISSN 0049-0466
SIGN WORLD. 1964. m. £16.50 (foreign £23) (effective 1998) (includes Directory). A.E. Morgan Publications Ltd., Stanley House, 9 West St., Epsom, Surrey KT18 7RL, England. TEL 44-1372-741411. FAX 44-1372-744493. Ed. Mike Connolly; Pub. Terence Morgan. adv. contact: Julia Dempstar. bk.rev.; illus. circ. 2,500. **Document type:** trade publication.
 Description: Publishes articles and news of developments and products in the sign field.

659.1 CN
SIGNALS; Canada's Premier Sign Business Magazine. 1990. m. (except Jul.). Can.$36($48) (effective 1990). Noteworthy Communications, 39 Bedford Park Ave., Richmond Hill, ON L4C 2N9, Canada. TEL 905-508-7374. FAX 609-508-7376. Ed. Kevin Press; Pub. Steve Brown. adv.: B&W page Can. $1125; trim 8 1/8 X 10 7/8; adv. contact: Steve Brown. software rev.; charts; illus.; tr.lit. circ. 7,500. (back issues avail.) **Document type:** directory, trade publication.
 Description: Canada's only independent national trade magazine for the sign industry. Covers all sectors of the industry for professionals in the field.

659.1 US ISSN 0270-4757
HF5841
SIGNCRAFT. 1980. bi-m. $28. Signcraft Publishing Co., Inc., Box 60031, Ft. Myers, FL 33906. TEL 941-939-4644. FAX 941-939-0607. Ed. Tom McIltrot. adv. contact: Bill McIltrot. circ. 19,500 (paid). **Document type:** trade publication.
 —CCC.
 Description: For the commercial sign shop. Focus on design, technique, and business management.

SIGNS & SCREEN EM PORTUGUES. see PRINTING

659.15 US ISSN 0037-5063
TT360.A4
SIGNS OF THE TIMES (CINCINNATI); the national journal of signs and advertising displays. 1906. 13/yr. $36. S T Publications Inc., 407 Gilbert Ave., Cincinnati, OH 45202. TEL 513-421-2050. FAX 513-421-5144. Ed. Darek Johnson; Pub. Tod Swormstedt. adv.: B&W page $2825, color page $3775. bk.rev.; stat.; tr.lit.; index; circ. 16,000 (paid); 4,219 (controlled). (also avail. in microform from UMI; back issues avail) **Indexed:** CERDIC. **Document type:** trade publication.
 —UMI. **CCC.**
 Description: Contains articles on the design and manufacture of all types of signs.

SIGNS OF THE TIMES & SCREEN PRINTING EN ESPANOL. see PRINTING

659.1 FR
SOURCES. 1985. bi-m. 280 F. B.P. 19, 06111 Le Cannet Cedex, France. Ed. Robert Faure. adv.; bk.rev. circ. 13,000. **Indexed:** Amer.Hist.& Life (1987-1990), (1994-), Hist.Abstr. (1987-1990). (1994-).

SOUTH AFRICAN PRODUCT DIGEST; export news from South Africa. see BUSINESS AND ECONOMICS — International Commerce

SOUTH EAST MAGAZINE. see LITERARY AND POLITICAL REVIEWS

657.1 SA
▼**SOUTHERN AFRICAN PUBLIC RELATIONS JOURNAL.** Cover title: Southern African P R J. 1995. m. (11/yr.). R.131.10 (foreign R.160. Journal Workshop, P.O. Box 387, Cramerview, Bryanston 2060, South Africa. TEL 27-11-706-4978. FAX 27-11-706-22310. E-mail: saprj@icon.co.za. Ed. Karen de Wet; Pub. Karen de Wet. R&P contact: Karen de Wet. adv.: B&W page R.3795, color page R.4740; trim 190 x 250; adv. contact: Lyn Aitken. bk.rev. circ. 4,509.
 Description: Covers issues relating to public relations in southern Africa including case studies, workshops, reports, conference and seminar information, professional profiles, and features on various industry sectors.

659.1 US
SOUTHERN CALIFORNIA MEDIA DIRECTORY. (Former name of issuing body: Publicity Club of Los Angeles) 1967. a. Public Communications of Los Angeles, 1910 W. Sunset Blvd., Ste. 460, Los Angeles, CA 90026-3299. TEL 213-387-0525. FAX 213-413-4026. Ed. Diana Gentry. adv. contact: Lisa Guilford. (looseleaf format) **Document type:** directory.
 Description: Lists media outlets: newspapers, radio and television stations, bureaus and wire services.

ADVERTISING AND PUBLIC RELATIONS

659.1 371.42   UK
SPONSORSHIP FOR STUDENTS (YEAR); for all students seeking sponsorship for degree - H N D courses. a. £8.95 (1997 edition). (Careers and Occupational Information Centre) Hobsons Publishing plc., Bateman St., Cambridge CB2 1LZ, England. TEL 44-1223-460366. FAX 44-1223-301506. TELEX 81546 HOBCAM G. (Dist. by: Biblios Publishers' Distribution Services Ltd., Star Rd., Partridge Green, W. Sussex RH13 8LD, England. TEL 44-1403-710851. FAX 44-1403-711143) (Co-sponsors: Careers Research and Advisory Centre, Employment Department Group) Ed. Wendy Frankiss; Pub. David Harrington. adv. contact: Adrian Kimpton. **Document type:** directory.

SPONSORSHIP NEWS; the first magazine devoted to sponsorship. see SPORTS AND GAMES

SPORT MEDIA BUYER'S GUIDE. see SPORTS AND GAMES

STANDARD DIRECTORY OF ADVERTISERS (BUSINESS CLASSIFICATIONS EDITION). see BUSINESS AND ECONOMICS — Trade And Industrial Directories

STANDARD DIRECTORY OF ADVERTISERS (GEOGRAPHIC EDITION). see BUSINESS AND ECONOMICS — Trade And Industrial Directories

STANDARD DIRECTORY OF ADVERTISING AGENCIES; the agency red book. see BUSINESS AND ECONOMICS — Trade And Industrial Directories

STANDARD DIRECTORY OF INTERNATIONAL ADVERTISERS AND AGENCIES; the international red book. see BUSINESS AND ECONOMICS — Trade And Industrial Directories

657 658   US
STORE WINDOWS. no.8, 1995. irreg. Retail Reporting Bureau, 302 Fifth Ave., New York, NY 10001. TEL 212-279-7000; 800-251-4545. FAX 212-279-7014. (Dist. by: Van Nostrand Reinhold, 115 Fifth Ave., New York, NY 10003)
    Formerly (until no.8, 1995): Store Windows That Sell.

659.1   IT
STRATEGIA. 1973. m. Lit.150000 (effective 1997). Emap Publishing s.r.l., Piazza della Repubblica, 32, 20124 Milan, Italy. TEL 39-2-67151205. FAX 39-2-66980255. Ed. Ivana Pasian. adv.; bk.rev.; charts; illus. stat. circ. 8,623. (back issues avail.) **Indexed:** DM & T. **Document type:** trade publication.
    Description: Covers Italian and international current events.

659.1   FR   ISSN 0180-6424
STRATEGIES; le premier journal professionnel de la communication. 1971. w. 1650 F. Groupe Strategies SA, Division of the Reed Elsevier group, 15 bis, rue Ernest Renan, B.P. 62, 92133 Issy les Moulineaux Cedex, France. TEL 46-29-46-29. FAX 40-93-00-18. TELEX 202 003 F. (Subscr. to: 99 rue d'Amsterdam, 75008 Paris, France. TEL 42-80-68-55) Eds. Julie-Emile Ades, Olivier Milot. adv.; color page 31950 F. charts; illus. circ. 14,405. **Indexed:** Educ.Ind. **Document type:** trade publication.

741.67   CN   ISSN 1202-0249
STUDIO. (Includes insert: Electronic Studio) 1983. 7/yr. Can.$40. Roger Murray & Associates Inc., 124 Galaxy Blvd., Rexdale, ON M9W 4Y6, Canada. TEL 416-675-1999. Ed. Barbara J. Murray; Pub. Roger E. Murray. adv. contact: Hersh Levy. bk.rev.; illus. circ. 10,000. **Indexed:** Can.B.P.I., Can.Per.Ind., CMI.
    Formerly (until 1992): Studio Magazine (ISSN 0715-5626)
    Description: Profiles top designers, photographers and illustrators, and covers typography, design, printing, computer graphics, photo-image manipulation and pre-press technology.

659.1   SR
SURINAM. ADVERTENTIEBLAD; national gazette. s-w. $125. N.V. Drukkerij & Uitgeverij D A G, Gravenstraat 120, P.O. Box 56, Paramaribo, Surinam. TEL 597-473501. FAX 597-454782. Ed. Edward D. Findlay. adv. circ. 1,000. (tabloid format)
    Description: Publishes official notices of the Republic, including laws, licensing requirements, court decisions, balances of the Central Bank, company statutes and other official announcements.

SYMBOLE; eine Zeitschrift fuer Abzeichen, Medaillen, Ehrenzeichen und Plaketten. see BUSINESS AND ECONOMICS — Marketing And Purchasing

T V & CABLE PUBLICITY OUTLETS - NATIONWIDE. see COMMUNICATIONS — Television And Cable

TAIPEI PICTORIAL/TAIPEI HUA K'AN. see GENERAL INTEREST PERIODICALS — Taiwan

THE TARGET (WOODSIDE). see BUSINESS AND ECONOMICS — Marketing And Purchasing

659.1   KU
TARGET ADVERTISING NEWS. (Text in English) fortn. Basel Al Abduljalil, P.O. Box 27927, Safat 13001, Kuwait. TEL 965-2408105. FAX 965-2408108. adv.: color page 4750 din. circ. 50,000. **Document type:** newspaper.

TARGET MARKETING; the leading magazine for integrated database marketing. see BUSINESS AND ECONOMICS — Marketing And Purchasing

659.2 070.5   FR   ISSN 0038-9579
TARIF MEDIA. (Supplements avail.) 1961. 6/yr. 4400 F. (foreign 5300 F.) (effective 1997). Societe Tarif Media S.A., 150 rue Gallieni, 92514 Boulogne Cedex, France. TEL 33-1-41861860. FAX 33-1-41861898. Ed. Patrick Gerbault. adv.: B&W page 15300 F., color page 23200 F.; adv. contact: Philippe Gaillard. circ. 1,750. **Document type:** consumer publication.
    Description: Supplies the advertising industry with facts on French national and local press, trade, technical and professional publications, television listings. Includes advertising rates, formats, circulation, geographical and social breakdown on French media.

658   US
TELECOM INDUSTRY ADVERTISING & MARKETING FORECAST (YEAR). a. $1701 (Canada and Mexico $1715; elsewhere $1735) (effective 1997). Cowles - SIMBA Information (Subsidiary of: Cowles Business Media), 11 Riverbend Dr. S., Box 4949, Stamford, CT 06907-0949. TEL 203-358-9900; 800-307-2529. FAX 203-358-5811. E-mail: info@simbanet.com; URL: http://www.simbanet.com. **Document type:** trade publication.
    Description: Shows what the telecommunctions industry is spending on advertising and marketing, with detailed historical data and projections for all industry leaders.

TELECOMEUROPA'S MARKETING TELECOMS; newsletter for marketers of telecoms equipment and services. see COMMUNICATIONS — Telephone And Telegraph

TELEPHONE ORGANIZATION OF THAILAND. ANNUAL REPORT. see COMMUNICATIONS — Telephone And Telegraph

THE TOASTMASTER; for better listening, thinking, speaking. see COMMUNICATIONS

659.1 658.8   IT
TODAY FAX. 1989. d. L.3000000. Marketing Finanza Italia s.r.l., Via Stradella 3, 20129 Milan, Italy. TEL 2-29-40-05-54. FAX 2-29-40-18-16. Ed. Lillo Perri. circ. 4,500. (only avail. by fax) **Document type:** newsletter.

659.1 760   JA
TOKYO ART DIRECTORS ANNUAL/A D C NENKAN. (Text in English, Japanese) 1957. a. $257. (Art Directors Club of Tokyo - Tokyo Ato Direkutazu Kurabu) Bijutsu Shuppan-sha, Inaoka Bldg., 2-36 Kanda, Jinbo-cho, Chiyoda-ku, Tokyo 101, Japan. TEL 03-3234-2151. FAX 03-3234-9451. (Dist. by: Intercontinental Marketing Corp., I.P.O. Box 5056, Tokyo 100-30, Japan. TEL 81-3-3661-7458. FAX 81-3-3667-9646) adv. circ. 4,000. (back issues avail.)
    Formerly: Annual of Advertising Art in Japan (ISSN 0548-1643)

TOP 50 EUROPEAN MEDIA OWNERS. see COMMUNICATIONS

659.1 T391   US   ISSN 0145-5559
TRADESHOW.* a. Tradeshow Week, A Division of Reed Elsevier Inc., 5700 Wilshire Blvd., Ste. 120, Los Angeles, CA 90036-3659. TEL 213-965-5300. E-mail: info@reedref.com; URL: http://www.reedref.com. **Document type:** trade publication.

658.8   US   ISSN 0733-0170
TRADESHOW WEEK; since 1971, the only weekly source of news & statistics on the tradeshow industry. 1971. w. $329. Tradeshow Week, A Division of Reed Elsevier Inc., 5700 Wilshire Blvd., Ste. 12036, Los Angeles, CA 90036-3659. TEL 213-965-5335. FAX 213-965-5336. E-mail: info@reedref.com; URL: http://www.cahners.com/mainmag/tsw1.htm. (Subscr. to: R.R. Bowker., Order Dept., Box 31, 121 Chanlon Rd., New Providence, NJ 07094. TEL 800-521-8110) Ed. Darlene Gudea; Pub. Irene Sperling. adv.; s-a. index. circ. 2,500. **Document type:** trade publication.
    Description: Informs and inspires corporate exhibitors, show organizers and suppliers about the trends, news, ideas, and issues shaping the exposition industry in the US and abroad.

TRAFFIC AUDIT BUREAU. ANNUAL REPORT. see TRANSPORTATION — Roads And Traffic

TRAFFIC AUDIT BUREAU. NEWSLETTER. see TRANSPORTATION — Roads And Traffic

U K MEDIA YEARBOOK. see COMMUNICATIONS

659   US
U S AD REVIEW. q. $349 (effective 1994). Retail Reporting Bureau, 302 Fifth Ave., New York, NY 10001. TEL 212-279-7000; 800-251-4545. FAX 212-279-7000. **Document type:** trade publication.

U S REAL ESTATE REGISTER. see REAL ESTATE

UNIFORUM MONTHLY. see COMPUTERS

659.2   FR   ISSN 0066-9253
UNION DES ASSOCIATION FRANCAISES DE RELATIONS PUBLIQUES. ANNUAIRE. 1963. a. membership. Union des Association Francaises de Relations Publiques, B.P. 8, Douvrin, 62138 Haisnes, France. adv. circ. 1,500.

659.1 363.6   US
UTILITY COMMUNICATORS INTERNATIONAL. NEWSLETTER. 8/yr. membership. Utility Communicators International, c/o Robert Janke, 5316 E. Kings Ave., Scottsdale, AZ 85254-1123. TEL 602-971-1989. circ. 400. **Document type:** newsletter.
    Formerly: Public Utilities Communicators Association. Newsletter.
    Description: Includes information on advertising and public relations as well as association news and developments.

659.1 CT120   US   ISSN 1043-0261
V I P ADDRESS BOOK. (Supplement avail.: V I P Address Book Update) 1988. a. $94.95. Associated Media Companies, Ltd., Box 489, Gleneden Beach, OR 97388-0489. TEL 541-764-4233; 800-258-0615. Ed. James M. Wiggins; Pub. James M. Wiggins. R&P contact: Adele M. Cooke. adv. contact: Adele M. Cooke. index. **Document type:** directory.

659.1   US   ISSN 1043-0261
V I P ADDRESS BOOK UPDATE. (Supplement to: V I P Address Book) 1988. a. $24.95. Associated Media Companies, Ltd., Box 489, Gleneden Beach, OR 97388-0489. TEL 541-764-4233; 800-258-0615. Ed. James M. Wiggins. adv. contact: Adele M. Cooke. **Document type:** directory.

ADVERTISING AND PUBLIC RELATIONS — ABSTRACTING, BIBLIOGRAPHIES, STATISTICS

659.15 US ISSN 0745-4295
HF5801
V M & S D. (Visual Merchandising & Store Design) 1922. m. $39. (International Authority on Visual Merchandising and Store Design) S T Publications Inc., 407 Gilbert Ave., Cincinnati, OH 45202. TEL 513-421-2050; 800-925-1110. FAX 513-421-5144. Ed. Janet Groeber; Pub. Tod Swarmstedt. adv.: B&W page $3750, color page $4800; adv. contact: Gary Goins. bk.rev.; tr.lit.; index. circ. 27,689. (back issues avail.) **Indexed:** B.P.I., Key to Econ.Sci. **Document type:** trade publication.
—UMI; UnCover. **CCC.**
Former titles (until 1982): Visual Merchandising (ISSN 0094-4610); (until 1973): Display World (ISSN 0012-3803)
Description: Directed to merchandisers in retail marketing and store designers. Examines display approaches and identity systems used in stores throughout the country, also lists products used for store and window decorating.

070 SZ
VERBREITUNGSDATEN DER SCHWEIZER PRESSE. (Text in German) 1968. triennial. 170 SFr. Verband Schweizerischer Werbegesellschaften, Weinbergstr. 11, CH-8001 Zurich, Switzerland. TEL 41-1-2613033. FAX 41-1-2613044. Ed.Bd. circ. 500. (also avail. in magnetic tape) **Document type:** trade publication.
Formerly: Streudaten der Schweizer Presse.

659.1 GW
VIERTELJAHRESHEFTE FUER MEDIA- UND WERBEWIRKUNG. 1969. q. Heinrich Bauer Verlag, Burchardstr. 11, 20095 Hamburg, Germany. TEL 49-40-3019-0. FAX 49-40-326589. Ed. Gabriele Kaplitza. circ. 3,000. **Document type:** trade publication.
Formerly: Vierteljahreshefte fuer Mediaplanung.

659.1 US ISSN 0042-5915
VIEWS & REVIEWS (NEW YORK, 1937). 1937. m. $450 (effective 1994). Retail Reporting Bureau, 302 Fifth Ave., New York, NY 10001. TEL 212-279-7000; 800-251-4545. FAX 212-279-7014. illus. **Document type:** trade publication.

659.2 SA
VOX COM. (Text in English) 1991. irreg., approx a. National Public Relations Association of South Africa, c/o S.A. Communication Service, Private Bag X745, Pretoria 0001, South Africa. **Document type:** newsletter.
Supersedes (in 1993): Songusa Newsletter.

659.1 GW ISSN 0042-9538
HF5415.12.G4
W & V. (Werben und Verkaufen) 1963. w. DM.186. Europa Fachpresse Verlag GmbH (Subsidiary of: Sueddeutsche Verlag), Thomas-Dehler-Str. 27, 81737 Munich, Germany. TEL 089-67804221. FAX 089-67804180. Ed. Daniela Sakowski. adv.: bk.rev.; charts; illus.; mkt.; pat.; tr.lit.; tr.mk. circ. 22,261. (tabloid format) **Document type:** trade publication.
—SWETS. **CCC.**

659.1 US
WASHINGTON MORNING LINE. m. membership. American Council of Highway Advertisers, Box 388, Shady Side, MD 20764. TEL 301-261-9197. FAX 410-867-1764. E-mail: rico45acp@aol.com.
Description: Provides news and information of relevance and interest to members.

WEB ADVERTISING (YEAR): MARKET ANALYSIS & FORECAST. see *COMPUTERS — Computer Networks*

659.1 SZ
WERBE WOCHE. 48/yr. Verlag Media-Daten AG, Kanzleistr. 80, CH-8026 Zurich, Switzerland. TEL 41-1-2417776. FAX 41-1-2417884. Ed. Christian Wapp. circ. 4,200. **Document type:** trade publication.

659.1 AU
WERBEALMANACH. 1978. a. S.1260. Manstein Zeitschriften Verlagsgesellschaft mbH, Brunner Feldstr. 45, A-2380 Perchtoldsdorf, Austria. TEL 43-1-86648-0. FAX 43-1-8664834. Ed. Hans-Joergen Manstein. circ. 2,800. **Document type:** trade publication.

659.1 GW
WERBEARTIKEL NACHRICHTEN FUER INSIDER. (Text in English, French and German) 1983. 10/yr. DM.65. W A Verlag GmbH, Am Ringofen 6, 41334 Nettetal, Germany. TEL 02157-2072. FAX 02157-3729. Ed. Horst Kruse. circ. 4,900. (back issues avail.) **Document type:** trade publication.

659.1 GW ISSN 0930-4487
WERBEBERATER - IDEENSERVICE FUER ERFOLGREICHE WERBUNG UND OEFFENTLICHEKEITSARBEIT. 1984. m. DM.298. Verlag Norman Rentrop, Theodor-Heuss-Str. 4, 53177 Bonn, Germany. TEL 49-228-8205-0. FAX 49-228-364411. TELEX 17228309. Ed. Norman Rentrop. (looseleaf format; back issues avail.) **Document type:** bulletin.

WERBUNG AKTUELL - PRINT & PRODUKTION. see *COMMUNICATIONS*

659.1 GW
WERBUNG IN DEUTSCHLAND (YEAR). a. Zentralverband der Deutschen Werbewirtschaft, Villichgasse 17, 53177 Bonn, Germany. TEL 0228-82092-0. FAX 0228-357583. **Document type:** corporate report.

659.1 AU
WERBUNG INSIDE. 1980. w. Media Emap Verlag GmbH, Loquaiplatz 12, A-1061 Vienna, Austria. TEL 01-59960-0. FAX 01-5996021. circ. 1,000. **Document type:** trade publication.

659.1 604.6 US
WESTERN SLOPE BARGAIN HUNTER. 1970. w. $35. Savvy Publishing Co., 311 14th St., Glenwood Springs, CO 81601-3949. TEL 970-945-6235. FAX 970-945-5140. Ed. H. Cochran. adv. contact: H. Cochran. bk.rev. circ. 10,000. (tabloid format; back issues avail.) **Document type:** newspaper.
Description: Contains classified advertisements, with an emphasis on recycling, collections, local services and opportunities.

WHERE SHALL I GO TO STUDY ADVERTISING & PUBLIC RELATIONS?. see *EDUCATION — Guides To Schools And Colleges*

WHITE PAGES & DIRECTORY LISTINGS (YEAR). see *BUSINESS AND ECONOMICS — Trade And Industrial Directories*

659 US ISSN 1058-9201
HF5863
WHO'S WHO; the MASA buyers' guide to blue ribbon mailing services. 1990. a. $65. M A S A - Mail Advertising Service Association International, 1421 Prince St., Ste. 100, Alexandria, VA 22314-2806. TEL 703-836-9200. FAX 703-548-8204. Ed. Susan Groff. adv. **Document type:** directory.

WHO'S WHO IN PUBLIC RELATIONS (INTERNATIONAL). see *BIOGRAPHY*

659.1 GW
WOERKSHOP; alles, was Werbung erfolgreich macht. 1988. 4/yr. DM.50 (effective 1997). G I T Verlag GmbH, Roesslerstr. 90, 64293 Darmstadt, Germany. TEL 49-6151-8090-0. FAX 49-6151-8090144. E-mail: gitverlag@t-online.de; URL: http://www.gitverlag.com. Ed. Joerg Peter Matthes. adv.: B&W page DM.6010, color page DM.8755; trim 218 x 235; adv. contact: Helga Kritzler. illus. circ. 9,500. **Document type:** trade publication.

(YEAR) WOMEN'S VOLLEYBALL MEDIA GUIDE. see *SPORTS AND GAMES — Ball Games*

659.1 UK
WORLD DIRECTORY OF ADVERTISING AGENCIES. 1993. irreg. £255($510) (effective 1997). Euromonitor, 60-61 Britton St., London EC1M 5NA, England. TEL 44-171-251-8024. FAX 44-171-608-3149. E-mail: info@euromonitor.com; URL: http://www.euromonitor.com. (Addr. in N. America: Euromonitor International, 122 S. Michigan Ave., Ste. 1200, Chicago, IL 60603. TEL 800-577-3876. FAX 312-922-1157) **Document type:** directory.
Description: Compiles detailed information on more than 1,600 advertising agencies worldwide and lists more than 2,000 private and government trade sources.

WORLDWIDE YELLOW PAGES MARKETS (YEAR). see *BUSINESS AND ECONOMICS — Trade And Industrial Directories*

YELLOW PAGES & DIRECTORY REPORT; the newsletter for the yellow page & directory publishing industry. see *BUSINESS AND ECONOMICS — Trade And Industrial Directories*

YELLOW PAGES MARKET FORECAST (YEAR). see *BUSINESS AND ECONOMICS — Trade And Industrial Directories*

YELLOW PAGES SALES & MARKETING (YEAR). see *BUSINESS AND ECONOMICS — Trade And Industrial Directories*

YELLOW PAGES 2000: FORECAST & ANALYSIS. see *BUSINESS AND ECONOMICS — Trade And Industrial Directories*

659.1 US
YELLOW SHEET (BALLWIN).;* the practical newsletter on agency management. 1984. m. $119. Communications Management Inc., 14208 Willow Bend Park, Apt. 5, Chesterfield, MO 63017-8258. Ed. George Johnson. R&P contact: George Johnson. adv. contact: George Johnson. index. (back issues avail.) **Document type:** newsletter.
Description: For owners and managers of small advertising agencies.

659.1 GW
ZENTRALVERBAND DER DEUTSCHEN WERBEWIRTSCHAFT. SERVICE. 6/yr. Zentralverband der Deutschen Werbewirtschaft, Villichgasse 17, 53177 Bonn, Germany. TEL 0228-82092-0. FAX 0228-357583. **Document type:** bulletin.
Formerly: Zentralausschuss der Werbewirtschaft Service.

ZESZYTY PRASOZNAWCZE. see *JOURNALISM*

659.1 CC ISSN 1005-9156
ZHONGGUO GUANGGAO/CHINA ADVERTISING. (Text in Chinese) q. $19.80. (Shanghai Guanggao Zhuanghuang Gongsi) Zhongguo Guanggao Zazhishe, 284 Yan'an Donglu, Shanghai 200002, People's Republic of China. TEL 86-21-3230702. FAX 86-21-3230935. (Dist. overseas by: China International Book Trading Corp., P.O. Box 399, Beijing 100044, P.R. China; Dist. in China by: China Books & Periodicals, Inc., 2929 24th St., San Francisco, CA 94110. TEL 415-282-2994) illus. pp./issue: 48. **Document type:** academic/scholarly publication.

659.1 US
4TH MEDIA JOURNAL. 1990. m. $45. Virgo Publishing, Inc., 3300 N. Central Ave., Ste. 2500, Phoenix, AZ 85012. TEL 602-483-0014. Ed. Joyce Hemmen. circ. 25,000.
Description: Focuses on media companies and how they enter the enhanced information services telephone markets.

ADVERTISING AND PUBLIC RELATIONS — Abstracting, Bibliographies, Statistics

659.1 310 US
A B C BLUE BOOK: CANADIAN DAILY NEWSPAPERS. 1970. s-a. $45 to members only (effective 1997). Audit Bureau of Circulations, 900 N. Meacham Rd., Schaumburg, IL 60173-4968. TEL 847-605-0909. FAX 847-605-0483. URL: http://www.accessabc.com. stat.
Description: Publishes six-month circulation averages for Canadian daily newspapers.

659.1 US
A B C BLUE BOOK: CANADIAN WEEKLY NEWSPAPERS. 1969. s-a. $68 to members only (effective 1997). Audit Bureau of Circulations, 900 N. Meacham Rd., Schaumburg, IL 60173-4968. TEL 847-605-0909. FAX 847-605-0483. URL: http://www.accessabc.com. stat. (looseleaf format)
Description: Publishes six-month circulation averages for Canadian weekly newspapers.

659.1 US
A B C BLUE BOOK: U S DAILY NEWSPAPERS. 1969. s-a. $395 to members only (effective 1997). Audit Bureau of Circulations, 900 N. Meacham Rd., Schaumburg, IL 60173-4968. TEL 847-605-0909. FAX 847-605-0483. URL: http://www.accessabc.com. stat. (looseleaf format)
Description: Publishers' statements of circulation data.

ADVERTISING AND PUBLIC RELATIONS — ABSTRACTING, BIBLIOGRAPHIES, STATISTICS

659.1 US
A B C BLUE BOOK: U S WEEKLY NEWSPAPERS. 1969. s-a. $95 to members only (effective 1997). Audit Bureau of Circulations, 900 N. Meacham Rd., Schaumburg, IL 60173-4968. TEL 847-605-0909. FAX 847-605-0483. URL: http://www.accessabc.com. stat.
Description: Publishers' statements of circulation data.

659.1 US
A B C NEWS BULLETIN. 1950. q. free. Audit Bureau of Circulations, 900 N. Meacham Rd., Schaumburg, IL 60173-4968. TEL 847-605-0909. FAX 847-605-0483. URL: http://www.accessabc.com. Ed. Cleen M. O'Grady. circ. 12,352. **Document type:** bulletin.
Description: Report on ABC activities and board actions after each board meeting.

659.1 384.5 SA
A M P S METER WEEKLY REPORTS. (All Media and Product Survey) (Text in English) 1989. w. R.6900 (effective 1997). S A Advertising Research Foundation, P.O. Box 98874, 2152 Sloane Park, South Africa. TEL 27-11-463-5340. FAX 27-11-463-5010. Ed. Mike Gorton. charts. circ. 80. (also avail. in diskette format)
●Also available online.

659.1 UK ISSN 0951-774X
ADVERTISING STATISTICS YEARBOOK (YEAR). 1986. a. £95. (Advertising Association) N T C Publications Ltd., Farm Rd., Henley-on-Thames, Oxfordshire RG9 1EJ, England. TEL 01491-411000. FAX 01491-571188. **Document type:** directory.
—BLDSC (0712.285400).
Description: Guide to the advertising and media markets of the UK.

659.1 384.1 SA ISSN 0379-637X
ALL MEDIA & PRODUCT SURVEY. Short title: A M P S. (Text in English) 1975. s-a. R.1510 (effective 1996). S A Advertising Research Foundation, P.O. Box 98874, 2152 Sloane Park, South Africa. TEL 27-11-463-5340. FAX 27-11-463-5010. Ed. Mike Gorton. charts; stat.
●Also available online.
Description: Survey of consumables, usage of media products and services.

310 659.1 US
AUDIT BUREAU OF CIRCULATIONS. ANNUAL REPORT. a. free. Audit Bureau of Circulations, 900 N. Meacham Rd., Schaumburg, IL 60173-4968. TEL 847-605-0909. FAX 847-605-0483. URL: http://www.accessabc.com. circ. 15,000. (back issues avail.) **Document type:** corporate report.

659.1 US
AUDIT BUREAU OF CIRCULATIONS. PUBLISHER'S STATEMENTS. 1983. s-a. $1.95 per periodical title (effective 1997). Audit Bureau of Circulations, 900 N. Meacham Rd., Schaumburg, IL 60173-4968. TEL 847-605-0909. FAX 847-605-0483. URL: http://www.accessabc.com. stat. (looseleaf format)
Description: Publishers' statements of circulation data.

310 659.1 US
AUDIT BUREAU OF CIRCULATIONS. SUPPLEMENTAL DATA REPORTS. 1968. a. $2.75 per periodical title (effective 1997). Audit Bureau of Circulations, 900 N. Meacham Rd., Schaumburg, IL 60173-4968. TEL 847-605-0909. FAX 847-605-0483. URL: http://www.accessabc.com. (looseleaf format; back issues avail.)
Description: Audited circulation information in addition to the contents of audit reports for selected publications.

659.1 US
P88.8
BACON'S BUSINESS MEDIA DIRECTORY. (Companion to: Newspaper - Magazine Directory) 1992. a. $280 (includes s-a. update). Bacon's Publishing Company, Inc., 332 S. Michigan Ave., Chicago, IL 60604. TEL 312-922-2400. FAX 312-922-3127. Ed. Ruth Cox McFarland. **Document type:** directory.
Formerly: Bacon's Business - Financial Directory (ISSN 1058-9716)
Description: Lists 11,000 media contacts at over 1,500 business and financial news outlets of interest to publicity and public relations professionals.

659.1 US ISSN 1071-4642
HF5905 CODEN: BPUSE4
BUSINESS PUBLICATION ADVERTISING SOURCE. 1919. m. $549 (effective 1997). S R D S (Subsidiary of: V N U U.S.A.), 1700 Higgins Rd., Des Plaines, IL 60018. TEL 847-375-5000; 800-851-7737. FAX 847-375-5001. E-mail: bbesc@srds.com; URL: http://www.srds.com. Pub. Bill Besch. R&P contact: Bill Besch. adv. **Document type:** directory, bibliography.
●Also available on CD-ROM.
Formerly (until Oct. 1993): Business Publication Rates and Data (ISSN 0038-948X); Incorporates: Business Classified Rates and Data.
Description: For planners and buyers of business and classified advertising. Provides rates and data on more than 8,000 listings, along with other needed information (e.g., circulation, advertising page dimensions) in standardized segments.

659.1 016 CN ISSN 0038-9498
HF5801
CANADIAN ADVERTISING RATES AND DATA. (Supplements avail.: Publication Profiles; Ethnic Media and Markets) 1928. m. Can.$525; newsstand price: Can.$225. Maclean-Hunter Ltd., Business Publication Division, Maclean Hunter Bldg., 777 Bay St., Toronto, ON M5W 1A7, Canada. TEL 416-596-5000; 800-265-3561. FAX 416-596-5158. URL: http://www.cardmedia.com. Ed. Nancy Remnant; Pub. Gloria Gallagher. adv. circ. 4,544. **Indexed:** Key to Econ.Sci.
—CCC.
Formed by the merger of: Standard Rate and Data Service. Canadian Advertising; Standard Rate and Data Service. Canadian Media Rates and Data.
Description: Aimed at media planning and buying executives, contains rates, circulation, and closing dates.

659.1 US ISSN 1186-2955
CANADIAN CIRCULATION OF U S MAGAZINES. 1983. a. $28 to members only (effective 1997). Audit Bureau of Circulations, 900 N. Meacham Rd., Schaumburg, IL 60173-4968. TEL 847-605-0909. FAX 847-605-0483. URL: http://www.accessabc.com. Ed. Chris Hodges. stat. (looseleaf format)
Description: Provides comparative figures and circulation trends in Canadian markets.

659.1 US ISSN 1043-7495
CANADIAN NEWSPAPER CIRCULATION FACT BOOK. 1971. a. $50 (effective 1997). Audit Bureau of Circulations, 900 N. Meacham Rd., Schaumburg, IL 60173-4968. TEL 847-605-0909. FAX 847-605-0483. URL: http://www.accessabc.com. stat. circ. 344. (looseleaf format) **Indexed:** SRI.
Former titles (until 1988): Canadian Daily - Weekly Newspaper Circulation Factbook (ISSN 0278-162X); (until 1980): A B C Factbook (ISSN 0098-2520)
Description: Circulation data for all ABC-member Canadian newspapers by market, county and province.

659.1 II
CIRCULATION AUDITING AROUND THE WORLD; memorandum report by the secretary-general. 1962. a. free. International Federation of Audit Bureau of Circulations, c/o A.B.C. Wakefield House, Sprott Rd., Ballard Estate, Bombay 400-038, India. Ed. Charles S. Karnik. **Document type:** monographic series.

659.1 US ISSN 1079-9745
HF5905
COMMUNITY PUBLICATION ADVERTISING SOURCE. 1945. s-a. $95 (effective 1997). S R D S (Subsidiary of: V N U U.S.A.), 1700 Higgins Rd., Des Plaines, IL 60018. TEL 847-375-5000; 800-851-7737. FAX 847-375-5001. E-mail: kgear@srds.com; URL: http://www.srds.com. Pub. Kathleen Geary. adv.; stat. **Document type:** directory, trade publication, bibliography.
Former titles: Community Publication Source (ISSN 1071-4650); (until 1993): Community Publication Rates and Data (ISSN 0162-8887); Weekly Newspaper and Shopping Guide Rates and Data (ISSN 0162-8895); Weekly Newspaper Rates and Data (ISSN 0038-9587)
Description: Compiles information on more than 2,500 metropolitan and nonmetropolitan newspapers, including advertising rates, page sizes and formats, and circulation.

659.1 US
HF5905
CONSUMER MAGAZINE AND ADVERTISING SOURCE. 1919. m. $529 (effective 1997). S R D S (Subsidiary of: V N U U.S.A.), 1700 Higgins Rd., Des Plaines, IL 60018. TEL 847-375-5000; 800-851-7737. FAX 847-375-5001. E-mail: dobra@srds.com; URL: http://www.srds.com. Pub. David O'Brasky. R&P contact: David O'Brasky. adv.; stat. **Document type:** directory, trade publication, bibliography.
●Also available on CD-ROM.
Former titles (until 1995): Consumer Magazine and Agri-Media Source (ISSN 1071-4537); (until Oct. 1993): Consumer Magazine and Agri-Media Rates and Data (ISSN 0746-2522); (until 1983): Consumer Magazine and Farm Publication Rates and Data (ISSN 0038-9595)
Description: Provides rates and data on more than 2,500 consumer magazines, both U.S. and international. Includes information on circulation, ad page dimensions, and personnel.

310 659.1 US
COUNTY PENETRATION REPORTS; a tabulation of county circulation data for daily and weekly newspapers. 1981. a. $2.50 per state or province; entire US $120; Canada $20; US & Canada $140 for paper or diskette (effective 1997). Audit Bureau of Circulations, 900 N. Meacham Rd., Schaumburg, IL 60173-4968. TEL 847-605-0909. FAX 847-605-0483. URL: http://www.accessabc.com. circ. 56. (also avail. in diskette format)
Description: Shows county coverage of ABC-member publications.

659.1 US
DAILY NEWSPAPER CIRCULATION RATE BOOK. 1972. a. $10 to members only (effective 1997). Audit Bureau of Circulations, 900 N. Meacham Rd., Schaumburg, IL 60173-4968. TEL 847-605-0909. FAX 847-605-0483. URL: http://www.accessabc.com. stat. circ. 597.
Description: Provides single-copy and home-delivery rate data for all audited daily newspapers.

659.13209489 DK ISSN 0109-0968
DANSK FAGPRESSEKATALOG. 1984. a. DKK 275 (effective 1997). Dansk Fagpresse Service ApS, Sommerstedgade 7, DK-1718 Copenhagen V, Denmark. TEL 45-33-86-31-00. FAX 45-31-23-43-10. Ed. Kristian Nielsen. adv. contact: Kristian Nielsen. circ. 4,329. **Document type:** abstracting/indexing, catalog, directory.
●Also available on CD-ROM.
Description: Provides annual information on the media: prices, sizes, circulation and members.

659.1 016 US ISSN 1071-4561
HF5861 CODEN: DMLSES
DIRECT MARKETING LIST SOURCE. 1967. bi-m. $384. S R D S (Subsidiary of: V N U U.S.A.), 1700 Higgins Rd., Des Plaines, IL 60018. TEL 847-375-5000; 800-851-7737. FAX 847-375-5001. E-mail: rroth@srds.com; URL: http://www.srds.com. Pub. Ruth Rothseid. adv.; stat. **Document type:** directory, trade publication.
Formerly (until 1993): Direct Mail List Rates and Data (ISSN 0419-182X)
Description: Lists more than 13,000 mailing lists available, divided into three sections: business, consumer, and farm, as well as Canadian and international lists. Includes relevant rates and data.

659.1 016 MX ISSN 0185-9099
DIRECTORIO M P M - MEDIOS AUDIOVISUALES/M P M - MEXICAN AUDIOVISUAL MEDIA RATES & DATA; tarifas y datos-cine, radio y television. 1958. q. Mex.$225($120) (effective 1997). Medios Publicitarios Mexicanos, S.A., Av. Mexico 99-103, Col. Hipodromo-Condesa, 06170 Mexico, DF, Mexico. TEL 52-5-5742858. FAX 52-5-5742668. Ed. Fernando A. Villamil. adv. circ. 1,200. **Document type:** directory.
Supersedes in part (in 1974): Directorio de Medios Publicitarios Mexicanos (ISSN 0038-9528)

ADVERTISING AND PUBLIC RELATIONS — ABSTRACTING, BIBLIOGRAPHIES, STATISTICS

659.1 016　　　MX　　ISSN 0186-7792
DIRECTORIO M P M - MEDIOS IMPRESOS/M P M - MEXICAN PRINT MEDIA RATES & DATA; tarifas y datos-anuncio exterior, periodicos y revistas. 1958. q. Mex.$225($120) Medios Publicitarios Mexicanos, S.A., Av. Mexico 99-103, Col. Hipodromo-Condesa, 06170 Mexico, DF, Mexico. TEL 52-5-5742858. FAX 52-5-5742668. Ed. Fernando A. Villamil. adv.; illus. circ. 1,200. **Document type:** directory.
　Supersedes in part (in 1974): Directorio de Medios Publicitarios Mexicanos (ISSN 0038-9528)

659.1　　　US　　ISSN 1082-4634
F A S - F A X: CANADIAN DAILY NEWSPAPERS. 1970. a. $33 to non-members; members $11; diskette $57 (effective 1997). Audit Bureau of Circulations, 900 N. Meacham Rd., Schaumburg, IL 60173-4968. TEL 708-605-0909. FAX 708-605-0483. stat. circ. 1,298. (also avail. in diskette format) **Indexed:** SRI.
　Description: Six-month circulation figures for member newspapers.

659.1　　　US
F A S - F A X REPORTS: BUSINESS PUBLICATIONS. 1969. s-a. $66 to non-members; members $22; diskette $22 (effective 1997). Audit Bureau of Circulations, 900 N. Meacham Rd., Schaumburg, IL 60173-4968. TEL 847-605-0909. FAX 847-605-0483. URL: http://www.accessabc.com. (tabloid format; also avail. in diskette format; back issues avail.)
　Description: Six-month circulation figures for ABC-member business periodicals.

659.1　　　US
F A S - F A X REPORTS: MAGAZINE - FARM. 1969. s-a. $110 to non-members; members $37; diskette $37 (effective 1997). Audit Bureau of Circulations, 900 N. Meacham Rd., Schaumburg, IL 60173-4968. TEL 847-605-0909. FAX 847-605-0483. E-mail: http://www.accessabc.com. circ. 3,892. (tabloid format; also avail. in diskette format; back issues avail.) **Indexed:** SRI.
　Formerly: F A S - F A X Reports: Periodicals.
　Description: Six-month circulation information on ABC-member periodicals.

659.1　　　US
F A S - F A X: UNITED STATES AND CANADIAN WEEKLY NEWSPAPERS. 1969. s-a. $33 to non-members; members $11; diskette $57 (effective 1997). Audit Bureau of Circulations, 900 N. Meacham Rd., Schaumburg, IL 60173-4968. TEL 847-605-0909. FAX 847-605-0483. URL: http://www.accessabc.com. circ. 927. (looseleaf format; also avail. in diskette format) **Indexed:** SRI. **Document type:** directory.
　Description: Six-month circulation figures for member newspapers.

659.1　　　US
F A S - F A X: UNITED STATES DAILY NEWSPAPERS. 1969. s-a. $110 to non-members; members $37; diskette $57 (effective 1997). Audit Bureau of Circulations, 900 N. Meacham Rd., Schaumburg, IL 60173-4968. TEL 847-605-0909. FAX 847-605-0483. URL: http://www.accessabc.com. stat. (also avail. in diskette format) **Indexed:** SRI.
　Description: Six-month circulation figures for member newspapers.

659.1　　　US　　ISSN 1071-4553
P94.5.H58
HISPANIC MEDIA & MARKET SOURCE. q. $199 (effective 1997). S R D S (Subsidiary of: V N U U.S.A.), 1700 Higgins Rd., Des Plaines, IL 60018. TEL 847-357-5000; 800-851-7737. FAX 847-357-5001. E-mail: rcoop@srds.com; URL: http://www.srds.com. Pub. Robin Cooper. R&P contact: Kathleen Ann Geary **Document type:** directory, trade publication.
　Formerly (until vol.6, no.4, 1993): Hispanic Media and Markets (ISSN 1044-0933)
　Description: Provides media planners and buyers with rates and information on Hispanic media, including radio, T.V., newspapers, business and consumer publications, and direct mail lists.

070　　　US　　ISSN 1073-8002
HF5826.5
INTERNATIONAL MEDIA GUIDE. BUSINESS - PROFESSIONAL. ASIA - PACIFIC - MIDDLE EAST - AFRICA. 1971. a. $150. International Media Guide, 85 Perimeter Rd., Nashua, NH 03063-1325. TEL 603-882-9576. FAX 603-595-0437. Ed. Anita Kotelba; Pub. Joseph P. Whelton. adv.: B&W page $2250, color page $3750; trim 8 1/2 x 11 (216 x 279); adv. contact: Anita Kotelba. circ. 1,500. (also avail. in diskette format) **Document type:** directory.
　Formed by the 1991 merger of: International Media Guide. Business - Professional. Asia - Pacific (ISSN 1073-8010); Which was formerly: International Media Guide. Business - Professional Publications. Asia, Australasia and U S S R (ISSN 1073-8029); (1983-1979): Media Guide International Edition: Business - Professional Publications. Asia, Australasia and USSR (ISSN 0730-5249); And: International Media Guide. Business - Professional. Middle East - Africa (ISSN 1073-7995); Which was formerly: International Media Guide. Business - Professional Publications. Middle East - Africa (ISSN 1073-824X); (until 1984): Media Guide International Edition: Business - Professional Publications. Middle East - Africa (ISSN 0730-5265); Both of which superseded in part: Media Guide International. Business - Professional Publications Edition (ISSN 0164-1743); Which was formerly: Media Guide International. Business Publications Edition (ISSN 0098-9398); Newsmedia Guide International.

070　　　US
INTERNATIONAL MEDIA GUIDE. BUSINESS - PROFESSIONAL. EUROPE. 1971. a. $150 per vol. International Media Guide, 85 Perimeter Rd., Nashua, NH 03063-1325. TEL 603-882-9576. FAX 603-595-0437. Ed. Anita Kotelba; Pub. Joseph P. Whelton. adv.: B&W page $2250, color page $3750; trim 8 1/2 x 11 (216 x 279); adv. contact: Anita Kotelba. circ. 1,500. (also avail. in diskette format) **Document type:** directory.
　Formerly: Media Guide International. Business - Professional Publications. Europe (ISSN 0730-5273); Supersedes in part: Media Guide International. Business - Professional Publications Edition (ISSN 0164-1743); Which was formerly: Media Guide International. Business Publications Edition (ISSN 0098-9398); Newsmedia Guide International.

070　　　US　　ISSN 1069-4277
HF5826.5
INTERNATIONAL MEDIA GUIDE. BUSINESS - PROFESSIONAL. THE AMERICAS. 1971. a. $150. International Media Guide, 85 Perimeter Rd., Nashua, NH 03063-1325. TEL 603-882-9576. FAX 603-595-0437. Ed. Anita Kotelba; Pub. Joseph P. Whelton. adv.: B&W page $2250, color page $3750; trim 8 1/2 x 11 (216 x 279); adv. contact: Anita Kotelba. circ. 1,500. (also avail. in diskette format) **Document type:** directory.
　Former titles (until 1989): Media Guide International. Business - Professional Publications. Latin America (ISSN 1069-4269); International Media Guide. Business - Professional Publications. Latin America (ISSN 1069-4250); (1979-1984): Media Guide International. Business - Professional Publications. Latin America (ISSN 0730-5257); Supersedes in part: Media Guide International. Business - Professional Publications Edition (ISSN 0164-1743); Media Guide International. Business Publications Edition (ISSN 0098-9398); Newsmedia Guide International.

659.1　　　US
Z6953.8
INTERNATIONAL MEDIA GUIDE. CONSUMER MAGAZINES WORLDWIDE. 1976. a. $150. International Media Guide, 85 Perimeter Rd., Nashua, NH 03063-1325. TEL 603-882-9576. FAX 603-595-0437. Ed. Anita Kotelba; Pub. Joseph P. Whelton. adv.: B&W page $2250, color page $3750; trim 8 1/2 x 11 (216 x 279); adv. contact: Anita Kotelba. circ. 1,500. (also avail. in diskette format) **Document type:** directory.
　Former titles: International Media Guide. Consumer Magazines Edition; (until 1982): Media Guide International. Consumer Magazines Edition (ISSN 0730-238X); Media Guide International. Airline Inflight - Travel Magazines Edition; Media Guide International. Airline Inflight Magazines Edition (ISSN 0145-9864)

659　　　US　　ISSN 1070-3195
Z6941
INTERNATIONAL MEDIA GUIDE. NEWSPAPERS WORLDWIDE. 1972. a. $150. International Media Guide, 85 Perimeter Rd., Nashua, NH 03063-1325. TEL 603-882-9576. FAX 603-595-0437. Ed. Anita Kotelba; Pub. Joseph P. Welton. adv.: B&W page $2250, color $3750; trim 8 1/2 x 11 (216 x 279); adv. contact: Anita Kotelba. circ. 2,000 (paid). (also avail. in diskette format) **Document type:** directory.
　Former titles (until 1983): Media Guide International. Newspapers - Newsmagazines Edition (ISSN 0093-9447); Newsmedia Guide International; Newspapers and Newsmagazines Worldwide.
　Description: Lists ad rates and technical information on newspapers throughout the world, complete addresses with contacts.

659 314　　　IE　　ISSN 0791-3516
IRELAND. CENTRAL STATISTICS OFFICE. BUSINESS OF ADVERTISING AGENCIES. RESULTS FOR RESPONDENTS TO INQUIRY. a. I£2. Central Statistics Office, Skehard Rd., Cork, Ireland. TEL 353-21-359000. FAX 353-21-359090. E-mail: information@cso.ie; URL: http://www.cso.ie. **Document type:** government publication.
　Former titles: Ireland Central Statistics Office. Advertising Agencies Inquiry; Ireland Central Statistics Office. Business of Advertising Agencies; (until 1984): Ireland Central Statistics Office. Inquiry into Advertising Agencies Activities (ISSN 0075-0581)
　Description: Presents details of the gross amount charged by advertising agencies.

659.1　　　US
MAGAZINE MARKET COVERAGE REPORT. (Available in 2-vol. sets: indexed by publication or by market) 1983. a. $75 per individual report; 2-vol. set $130 (effective 1997). Audit Bureau of Circulations, 900 N. Meacham Rd., Schaumburg, IL 60173-4968. TEL 847-605-0909. FAX 847-605-0483. URL: http://www.accessabc.com. stat. (looseleaf format)
　Description: Matches magazine circulation to DMA or MSA markets. Includes market data.

659.1　　　US　　ISSN 1044-6079
PN4888.C59
MAGAZINE TREND REPORT. 1980. a. $70 paper or diskette (effective 1997). Audit Bureau of Circulations, 900 N. Meacham Rd., Schaumburg, IL 60173-4968. TEL 847-605-0909. FAX 847-605-0483. URL: http://www.accessabc.com. Ed. Susan Bartucci. circ. 925. (also avail. in diskette format) **Indexed:** SRI. **Document type:** trade publication.
　Description: Provides five years of circulation and ad rate figures for all ABC-audited US and Canadian consumer magazines with ad revenue.

659.1　　　US
MAIL ADVERTISING SERVICE ASSOCIATION INTERNATIONAL. PERFORMANCE PROFILES. a. $500 to non-members; members $33 (effective 1997). Mail Advertising Service Association International, 1421 Prince St., Ste. 200, Alexandria, VA 22314. TEL 703-836-9200.
　Formerly: Mail Advertising Service Association International. Sales Personnel Compensation Survey.
　Description: Annual report on operating and financial ratios for mailing service industry.

659.1　　　US
MAIL ADVERTISING SERVICE ASSOCIATION INTERNATIONAL. QUARTERLY BUSINESS OUTLOOK. q. membership. Mail Advertising Service Association International, 1421 Prince St., Ste. 200, Alexandria, VA 22314. TEL 703-836-9200.

659.1　　　US
MAIL ADVERTISING SERVICE ASSOCIATION INTERNATIONAL. WAGE AND SALARY, AND FRINGE BENEFITS SURVEY. a. $375 to non-members; members $200 (effective 1997). Mail Advertising Service Association International, 1421 Prince St., Ste. 200, Alexandria, VA 22314. TEL 703-836-9200.
　Formerly: Mail Advertising Service Association International. Wage and Salary Survey.
　Description: Report of wages and salaries in the mailing services industry.

659.1   SZ
MEDIA-DATEN (ZURICH); directory of Swiss media. 1976. s-a. $242 (effective 1997). Verlag Media-Daten AG, Kanzleistr. 80, CH-8026 Zurich, Switzerland. TEL 41-1-2417776. FAX 41-1-2417884. Ed. Otto Eisenegger. adv. circ. 2,684. **Document type:** trade publication.

MEDIA DATEN: ZEITUNGEN. see *JOURNALISM — Abstracting, Bibliographies, Statistics*

659.1   US   ISSN 1071-4529
HF5905
NEWSPAPER ADVERTISING SOURCE. 1919. m. $529 (effective 1997). S R D S (Subsidiary of: V N U U.S.A.), 1700 Higgins Rd., Des Plaines, IL 60018. TEL 847-375-5000; 800-851-7737. FAX 847-375-5001. E-mail: kgear@srds.com; URL: http://www.srds.com. Pub. Kathleen Geary. R&P contact: Kathleen Ann Geary. adv.; stat. **Document type:** directory, trade publication, bibliography.
—UnCover.
     Formerly (until 1993): Newspaper Rates and Data (ISSN 0038-9544)
     Description: Contains rates and data for newspapers in the U.S., listed by state and city.

659.1   US   ISSN 1078-7887
OUT - OF - HOME ADVERTISING SOURCE. 1990. a. $149 (effective 1997). S R D S (Subsidiary of: V N U U.S.A.), 1700 Higgins Rd., Des Plaines, IL 60018. TEL 847-375-5000; 800-851-7737. FAX 847-375-5001. E-mail: mkili@srds.com. adv. contact: Maria Kilinski. circ. 2,000. **Document type:** directory, trade publication.
     Formerly (until 1995): Advertising Options Plus (ISSN 1058-2592)
     Description: Provides advertising rates and data for "out-of-home media" in the nontraditional media marketplace.

659.1 016   US   ISSN 1071-4545
HF5905
PRINT MEDIA PRODUCTION SOURCE. 1967. q. $318. S R D S (Subsidiary of: V N U U.S.A.), 1700 Higgins Rd., Des Plaines, IL 60018. TEL 847-375-5000; 800-851-7737. FAX 847-375-5001. E-mail: bbesc@srds.com; URL: http://www.srds.com. Pub. Bill Besch. adv.; bibl. **Document type:** directory.
●Also available on CD-ROM.
     Formerly (until 1993): Print Media Production Data (ISSN 0038-9455)
     Description: Lists more than 8,700 business, consumer, and newspaper advertising opportunities, giving production information on each. Includes trim sizes, R.O.P. guidelines, insert specs, material specifications (including film and proofing requirements), personnel to contact, and issue and closing dates.

659.14
RADIO ADVERTISING BUREAU. RADIO FACTS.* a. $10 to non-members. Radio Advertising Bureau, 261 Madison Ave., 23rd Fl., New York, NY 10016-2303. TEL 212-254-4800. FAX 212-254-8713. circ. 40,000.
     Description: Statistical overview of the U.S. commercial radio industry. Includes comparison of radio advertising with that in other media.

659.1 384.5   US   ISSN 1071-4707
HF5905
RADIO ADVERTISING SOURCE. 1929. m. $405 (effective 1997). S R D S L.P. (Subsidiary of: V N U U.S.A.), 1700 Higgins Rd., Des Plaines, IL 60018. TEL 847-375-5000; 800-851-7737. FAX 847-375-5001. E-mail: rcoop@srds.com; URL: http://www.srds.com. Pub. Robin Cooper. adv. **Document type:** trade publication, directory.
     Former titles (until 1993): Radio Advertising Rates and Data & Spot Radio Rates and Data (ISSN 0038-9560)
     Description: Contains listings of radio stations arranged geographically by state and city. Includes demographic and socioeconomic data.

659.1 658   US   ISSN 1067-1641
HF5863   CODEN: BULLE7
S R D S: BULLET. (Standard Rate and Data Service); the latest in list activity. (Supplement to: Direct Marketing List Source) 1991. bi-m. free with subscr. to Direct Marketing List Source. S R D S (Subsidiary of: V N U U.S.A.), 1700 Higgins Rd., Des Plaines, IL 60018. TEL 847-375-5000; 800-851-7737. FAX 847-375-5001. E-mail: rroth@srds.com; URL: http://www.srds.com. Pub. Ruth Rothseid. adv.; stat. **Document type:** trade publication.
—CASDDS.

338.4 316.8   SA
SOUTH AFRICA. CENTRAL STATISTICAL SERVICE. CENSUS OF BUSINESS SERVICES - ADVERTISING PRACTITIONERS AND ALLIED SERVICES AND MARKETING RESEARCH SERVICES. (Report No. 83-13-01) irreg., latest 1987. R.4.40 (foreign R.4.80). Central Statistical Service - Sentrale Statistiekdiens, Private Bag X44, Pretoria 0001, South Africa. TEL 27-12-310-8911. FAX 27-12-310-8500. (Orders to: Government Printing Works, Private Bag X85, Pretoria 0001, South Africa) **Document type:** government publication.

338.4 316.8   SA
SOUTH AFRICA. CENTRAL STATISTICAL SERVICE. STATISTICAL RELEASE. CENSUS OF ADVERTISING PRACTITIONERS AND ALLIED SERVICES AND MARKETING RESEARCH SERVICES. (No. P8313) irreg., latest 1987. free. Central Statistical Service - Sentrale Statistiekdiens, Private Bag X44, Pretoria 0001, South Africa. TEL 27-12-310-8911. FAX 27-12-310-8500. **Document type:** government publication.

659.1 384.55   US   ISSN 1071-4596
HF5905
T V & CABLE SOURCE. 1947. q. $380 (effective 1997). S R D S (Subsidiary of: V N U U.S.A.), 1700 Higgins Rd., Des Plaines, IL 60018. TEL 847-375-5000; 800-851-7737. FAX 847-375-5001. E-mail: rcoop@srds.com; URL: http://www.srds.com. Pub. Robin Cooper. R&P contact: Robin cooper. TEL 310-231-4803. adv.: B&W page $4020, color page $6650. **Document type:** directory, trade publication.
     Formerly (until 1993): Spot Television Rates and Data (ISSN 0038-9552)
     Description: Aimed at planners and buyers of television advertising. Lists T.V. stations, networks, and cable systems geographically by D.M.A.s.

659.1 658.8 600   US   ISSN 1071-4588
HF5905
TECHNOLOGY MEDIA SOURCE. 1990. a. $199 (effective 1997). S R D S (Subsidiary of: V N U U.S.A.), 1700 Higgins Rd., Des Plaines, IL 60018. TEL 847-375-5000; 800-851-7737. FAX 847-375-5001. E-mail: bbesc@srds.com. Pub. Bill Besch. adv. **Document type:** directory, trade publication.
     Formerly (until 1993): S R D S Media and Market Planner. Technology Market (ISSN 1064-5721)
     Description: Contains rates and data for for more than 3,200 business and consumer publications and direct-mail lists.

384 016 659   US   ISSN 0040-9340
TOPICATOR; classified article guide to the advertising/communications/marketing periodical press. 1965. bi-m. $110 (effective 1997 & 1998). 205 S. Stewart Rd., No. 229, Mission, TX 78572-6336. TEL 956-581-4197. Ed. Norma F. Wolles; Pub. Wendell E. Wolles. circ. 150 (paid). **Document type:** abstracting/indexing.

659.1 016 657   US   ISSN 0043-4558
WHAT'S NEW IN ADVERTISING AND MARKETING. 1945. q. $20 to non-profit organizations; corporations $30; foreign $40. Special Libraries Association, Advertising and Marketing Division, c/o Johnn Patton, Suffolk Cooperative Library System, 627 N. Sunrise Service Rd., Bellport, NY 11713. TEL 516-286-1600. FAX 516-286-1647. Ed. Brady Leyser. adv.; bk.rev.; abstr.; circ. 400 (paid). (processed) **Indexed:** P.A.I.S. **Document type:** bibliography.
     Description: Lists current materials in advertising, marketing and communication.

AERONAUTICS AND SPACE FLIGHT

see also Transportation–Air Transport

629.13   US   ISSN 0882-9365
A A H S JOURNAL. 1956. q. $45 (foreign $55) (effective 1998). American Aviation Historical Society, 2333 Otis St., Santa Ana, CA 92704. TEL 714-639-1088. URL: http://cwalton.jovanet.com/aahs/. Ed. Albert Hansen. R&P contact: Albert Hansen. adv. contact: John Dzurica. bk.rev. **Indexed:** Air Un.Lib.Ind., Amer.Hist.& Life (1977-), Hist.Abstr. (1977-).
—CISTI; UnCover.
     Formerly (until 1980): American Aviation Historical Society Journal (ISSN 0002-7553)

629.4   US   ISSN 1081-6003
A A S - A I A A SPACEFLIGHT MECHANICS MEETING. PROCEEDINGS. (Part of the Advances in the Astronautical Sciences Series (ISSN 0065-3438)) 1991. a. price varies. (American Astronautical Society) Univelt, Inc., Box 28130, San Diego, CA 92198-0198. TEL 619-746-4005. FAX 619-746-3139. E-mail: 76121.1532@compuserve.com. Ed. Robert H. Jacobs; Pub. Robert H. Jacobs. R&P contact: Robert H. Jacobs. charts; illus. (microfiche; back issues avail.) **Document type:** proceedings.

629.1   US
A A S ASTRODYNAMICS CONFERENCE. PROCEEDINGS. (Part of the Advances in the Astronautical Sciences Series (ISSN 0065-3438); specialized volumes in astrodynamics; odd-year proceedings avail. from Univelt; even-year proceedings available from the AIAA.) 1975. biennial. price varies. (American Astronautical Society) Univelt, Inc., Box 28130, San Diego, CA 92198-0198. TEL 619-746-4005. FAX 619-746-3139. E-mail: 76121.1532@compuserve.com. Ed. Robert H. Jacobs; Pub. Robert H. Jacobs. R&P contact: Robert H. Jacobs. cum.index. (back issues avail.) **Indexed:** Eng.Ind., Int.Aerosp.Abstr. **Document type:** proceedings.

624.9   US
A A S - G S F C INTERNATIONAL SYMPOSIUM ON SPACEFLIGHT DYNAMICS. (Part of the Advances in the Astronautical Sciences Series (ISSN 0065-3438)) 1993. irreg., latest vol.84 (parts 1,2), 1993. price varies. (American Astronautical Society) Univelt, Inc., Box 28130, San Diego, CA 92198-0198. TEL 619-746-4005. FAX 619-746-3139. E-mail: 76121.1532@compuserve.com. Ed. Robert H. Jacobs; Pub. Robert H. Jacobs. R&P contact: Robert H. Jacobs. illus. (back issues avail.) **Document type:** proceedings.

629.4   US
A A S GODDARD MEMORIAL SYMPOSIUM. PROCEEDINGS. (Part of the Science and Technology Series (ISSN 0278-4017); Supplement to: Advances in the Astronautical Sciences Series (ISSN 0065-3438)) 1961. a. price varies. (American Astronautical Society, Inc.) Univelt, Inc., Box 28130, San Diego, CA 92198-0198. TEL 619-746-4005. FAX 619-746-3139. E-mail: 76121.1532@compuserve.com. Ed. Robert H. Jacobs; Pub. Robert H. Jacobs. R&P contact: Robert H. Jacobs. cum.index. (back issues avail.) **Document type:** proceedings.
     Description: Proceedings volumes in space disciplines and programs based on annual symposia.

629.1   US   ISSN 0730-3564
A A S HISTORY SERIES. (Supplement to: Advances in the Astronautical Sciences (ISSN 0065-3438)) 1977. irreg. (approx. 1-2/yr.); vol.18, 1995. price varies. (American Astronautical Society, Inc.) Univelt, Inc., Box 28130, San Diego, CA 92198-0198. TEL 619-746-4005. FAX 619-746-3139. E-mail: 76121.1532@compuserve.com. Ed. R. Cargill Hall. bibl.; charts; illus.; cum.index. circ. 1,250. (back issues avail.) **Indexed:** Biol.Abstr., Curr.Cont., Eng.Ind., INSPEC, Int.Aerosp.Abstr. **Document type:** monographic series, proceedings.
—BLDSC (0537.620000); CISTI; Ei.
     Description: Comprises historical volumes on space flight and related fields. Compiles monographs of proceedings, including, as a subseries, historical symposia of the International Academy of Astronautics.
Refereed Serial

AERONAUTICS AND SPACE FLIGHT

629.4 US ISSN 0065-7417
TL787
A A S MICROFICHE SERIES. (Supplement to: Advances in the Astronautical Sciences (ISSN 0065-3438)) 1968. irreg.; vol.73, 1996. price varies. (American Astronautical Society, Inc.) Univelt, Inc., Box 28130-0198, San Diego, CA 92198. TEL 619-746-4005. FAX 619-746-3139. E-mail: 76121.1532@compuserve.com. Ed. Robert H. Jacobs; Pub. Robert H. Jacobs. R&P contact: Robert H. Jacobs. bibl.; charts; illus.; cum.index: 1968-1986. circ. 100. (microfiche) **Indexed:** Chem.Abstr., Eng.Ind., INSPEC, Int.Aerosp.Abstr. **Document type:** proceedings.
—BLDSC (0537.663000).
Description: Comprises proceedings volumes on microfiche, as well as supplements to hard-copy proceedings volumes.

387.7 US
TL512
A B D. (Aviation Buyers Directory) 1949. q. $80. Air Service Directory, Inc., 105 Calvert St., Harrison, NY 10528-3138. TEL 914-835-7200. Ed. Alan H. Greenwald. adv.; circ. 20,500 (controlled). (processed) **Document type:** directory.
—CISTI.
Formerly: A B D - Aviation Business Directory (ISSN 0001-0502)

629.1 358.4 US
A G A R D BULLETIN. (Advisory Group for Aerospace Research and Development) q.? U.S. National Aeronautics and Space Administration, Scientific and Technical Information Office, CCenter for Aerospace Information, 800 Elkridge Landing Rd., Linthicum Heights, MD 21090-2934. E-mail: help@sti.nasa.gov; URL: http://www.sti.nasa.gov. (Co-sponsor: NATO Advisory Group for Research and Development) **Document type:** government publication, bulletin.
Description: Describes A.G.A.R.D. programs and lists meetings and publications.

629.1 358.4 US
A G A R D HIGHLIGHTS. s-a. U.S. National Aeronautics and Space Administration, Scientific and Technical Information Office, Center for AeroSpace Information, 800 Elkridge Landing Rd., Linthicum Heights, MD 21090-2934. E-mail: help@sti.nasa.gov; URL: http://www.sti.nasa.gov. (Co-sponsor: NATO Advisory Group for Aerospace Research and Development) **Document type:** government publication, bulletin.
Description: Presents highlights of AGARD activities.

629.1 358.4 US
A G A R D REPORTS. q. U.S. National Aeronautics and Space Administration, Scientific and Technical Information Office, Center for AeroSpace Information, 800 Elkridge Landing Rd., Linthicum Heights, MD 21090-2934. E-mail: help@sti.nasa.gov; URL: http://www.sti.nasa.gov. (Sponsor: NATO Advisory Group for Aerospace Research and Development) **Indexed:** Alloys Ind., Eng.Mat.Abstr., Met.Abstr., Met.Abstr.Ind., Nonfer.Met.Alert, PCC Alert, Steels Alert, World Alum.Abstr. **Document type:** government publication, academic/scholarly publication.
●Available only online.
Description: Lists classified AGARD publications announced in Scientific and Technical Aerospace Reports (STAR) during the preceding quarter.
Refereed Serial

629.1 358.4 US
A G A R D TECHNICAL PROGRAMME. a. U.S. National Aeronautics and Space Administration, Scientific and Technical Information, Center for AeroSpace Information, 800 Elkridge Landing Rd., Linthicum Heights, Wheeling, MD 21090-2934. E-mail: help@sti.nasa.gov; URL: http://www.sti.nasa.gov. (Co-sponsor: NATO Advisory Group for Aerospace Research and Development) **Document type:** government publication, bulletin.
Description: Presents the AGARD Technical Programme for the coming year, listing scheduled meetings and describing individual Panel Programmes.

629.1 US ISSN 0273-4508
TL875 CODEN: CPSCDO
A I A A - A S M E - A S C E - A H S STRUCTURES, STRUCTURAL DYNAMICS, AND MATERIALS CONFERENCE. COLLECTION OF TECHNICAL PAPERS. 1976. a. $180 to non-members; members $135. American Institute of Aeronautics and Astronautics, Inc., 1801 Alexander Dr., Ste. 500, Reston, VA 20191. TEL 703-264-7500. (reprint service avail. from UMI) **Indexed:** Int.Aerosp.Abstr. **Document type:** proceedings.
—CASDDS; Ei. **CCC.**
Former titles: A I A A - A S M E Structures, Structural Dynamics, and Materials Conference. Collection of Technical Papers (ISSN 0161-5750); A I A A - A S M E - S A E Structures, Structural Dynamics, and Materials Conference. Proceedings (ISSN 0160-855X)

629.1 US
A I A A ATMOSPHERIC FLIGHT MECHANICS CONFERENCE PROCEEDINGS. a. $170 to non-members; members $128. American Institute of Aeronautics and Astronautics, Inc., 1801 Alexander Dr., Ste. 500, Reston, VA 20191. TEL 703-264-7500. (reprint service avail. from UMI) **Indexed:** Int.Aerosp.Abstr. **Document type:** proceedings.

629.1 621.384 US
A I A A COMMUNICATIONS SATELLITE SYSTEMS CONFERENCE. TECHNICAL PAPERS. 1972. biennial, 13th ed., 1990. American Institute of Aeronautics and Astronautics, Inc., 1801 Alexander Dr., Ste. 500, Reston, VA 20191. TEL 703-264-7500. **Indexed:** Int.Aerosp.Abstr., VITIS. **Document type:** proceedings, academic/scholarly publication.
Description: Features research and innovations in the telecommunications field.

629.1 US ISSN 0001-1452
TL501.A688 CODEN: AIAJAH
A I A A JOURNAL; devoted to aerospace research and development. 1963. m. $500 to non-members (foreign $620); members $58 (foreign $118). American Institute of Aeronautics and Astronautics, Inc., 1801 Alexander Dr., Ste. 500, Reston, VA 20191. TEL 703-264-7500. URL: http://www.aiaa.org/publications/journal/aiaa.html. Ed. George W. Sutton. charts; illus.; index. circ. 5,000. (also avail. in microform from UMI,PMC; reprint service avail. from KTO,UMI) **Indexed:** A.S.& T.Ind., Alloys Ind., Appl.Mech.Rev., ASCA, Bibl.Ind., BMT, Chem.Abstr., Chem.Cit.Ind., Compumath, Curr.Cont., Eng.Ind., Eng.Mat.Abstr., Excerp.Med., Fluidex, Geo.Abstr., Ind.Sci.Rev., INIS Atomind., INSPEC (1968-), Int.Aerosp.Abstr., Mat.Sci.Cit.Ind., Math.R., Met.Abstr., Met.Abstr.Ind., Nonfer.Met.Alert, PCC Alert, Sci.Cit.Ind., Sh.& Vib.Dig., Sh.& Vib.Dig., Steels Alert, World Alum.Abstr., Zent.Math. **Document type:** academic/scholarly publication.
●Also available on CD-ROM.
—BLDSC (0772.610000); AskIEEE; CASDDS; CISTI; Ei; EMDOCS; Genuine Article; KR SourceOne; Linda Hall; SWETS; UnCover. **CCC.**
Formed by the merger of: A R S Journal (ISSN 0097-4056); Journal of the Aerospace Sciences (ISSN 0095-9820)
Description: Covers new theoretical developments and experimental results on aeroacoustics, aerodynamics, combustion, fundamentals of propulsion, fluid mechanics, aerospace environment, marine technology, lasers, plasmas, and magnetohydrodynamics, research instrumentation, structural mechanics and thermophysics.
Refereed Serial

629.13 629.4 US ISSN 1062-2241
TL512
A I A A MEMBERSHIP ROSTER. 1964. biennial. $79.95 to non-members; members $39.95. American Institute of Aeronautics and Astronautics, Inc., 1801 Alexander Dr., Ste. 500, Reston, VA 20191. TEL 703-264-7500. **Document type:** directory.
—CISTI.
Formerly: A I A A Roster (ISSN 0065-8693)

629.1 US ISSN 0001-1460
TL501.A688
A I A A STUDENT JOURNAL. 1963. q. $18 to non-members; members $8 (foreign $22); student members free. American Institute of Aeronautics and Astronautics, Inc., 1801 Alexander Dr., Ste. 500, Reston, VA 20191. TEL 703-264-7500. URL: http://www.aiaa.org/publications/stu-journal.html. Ed. Patrick Gouhin. adv.; bk.rev.; charts; illus. circ. 9,000. (also avail. in microform from UMI; reprint service avail. from UMI) **Indexed:** Int.Aerosp.Abstr. **Document type:** academic/scholarly publication.
—BLDSC (0772.810000); CISTI; Linda Hall; SWETS; UnCover. **CCC.**

629.1 US
A M F I INDUSTRY NEWS. 1972. bi-m. membership. Aviation Maintenance Foundation International, Box 2826, Redmond, WA 98073. TEL 360-658-8980. FAX 360-658-7274. Ed. R. Kost. adv.; bk.rev. circ. 6,000. (looseleaf format) **Document type:** newsletter.
Formerly: Aviation Maintenance Foundation. Industry News.
Description: Information and news pertaining to aviation maintenance industry.

629.13 AT ISSN 0002-2691
A O P A MAGAZINE. 1948. m. Aus.$96. Aircraft Owners and Pilots Association of Australia, P.O. Box 1065, Fyshwick, A.C.T. 2609, Australia. TEL 61-6-2804221. FAX 61-6-2391366. URL: http://www.aopa.com.au/. Ed. Mark Barnett. R&P contact: Mark Barnett. adv.; B&W page Aus.$525, color page Aus.$920; adv. contact: Cathy Montalto. bk.rev.; illus.; pat. circ. 11,000. **Document type:** trade publication.
Description: Covers all aspects of interest for general aviators.
Refereed Serial

629.132 US ISSN 0001-2084
A O P A PILOT. 1958. m. $21 to institutions. Aircraft Owners and Pilots Association, 421 Aviation Way, Frederick, MD 21701. TEL 301-695-2350. FAX 301-695-2180. URL: http://www.aopa.org/pilot/pwelcome.html. Ed. Tom Haines. Pub. Phil Boyer. R&P contact: Tom Haines. adv. contact: Denis Beran. bk.rev.; charts; illus.; stat.; tr.lit.; index. circ. 339,000. **Document type:** bulletin.
—CISTI; Linda Hall; UnCover.

629.132 US ISSN 1056-7704
TL726.2
A O P A'S AVIATION U S A. 1962. a. $24.95. Aircraft Owners and Pilots Association, 421 Aviation Way, Frederick, MD 21701. TEL 301-695-2000. Pub. Phil Boyer. R&P contact: Tom Haines. adv. contact: Denis Beran. circ. 100,000. **Document type:** directory.
—CISTI.
Incorporates: Aircraft Owners and Pilots Association. Handbook for Pilots (ISSN 0568-3785); (in 1989): A O P A's Airport U S A (ISSN 0271-065X); Which was formerly: A O P A Airport Directory (ISSN 0065-4906)

A P M BULLETIN. (Air Power Museum) see *ANTIQUES*

629.13 XR
A R T I REPORTS. (Aeronautical Research and Test Institute) (Text in English; summaries in Czech, French, German) 1960. irreg. (2-3/yr.). exchange basis only. Vyzkumny a Zkusebni Letecky Ustav, Beranovych 130, 19905 Prague 9-Letnany, Czech Republic. TEL 66311397. FAX 66310518. TELEX 121893. Ed. Ladislav Vymetal. (also avail. in microfilm; microfiche; back issues avail.) **Document type:** academic/scholarly publication.

629.1 US ISSN 1041-6706
A W A NEWS.* 1938. 6/yr. membership. Aviation - Space Writers Association, 6540 50th St., N., Oakdale, MN 55128-1708. TEL 614-221-1900. FAX 614-221-1989. adv.; bk.rev. circ. 1,500.
Former titles: Aviation - Space Writers Association Newsletter; Aviation - Space Writers Association News.

AERONAUTICS AND SPACE FLIGHT

614.85 387.7 629.1   US   ISSN 1057-5561
ACCIDENT PREVENTION. 1948. m. $80 in N. America; elsewhere $85. Flight Safety Foundation, Inc., 601 Madison St., Ste. 300, Alexandria, VA 22314-1756. TEL 703-739-6700. FAX 703-739-6708. Ed. Roger Rozelle. bk.rev.; circ. 2,400 (paid). (reprint service avail. from UMI). **Document type:** newsletter.
   Formerly (until vol.44, no.11, 1987): Accident Prevention Bulletin (ISSN 0898-5774)
   Description: Focuses on the flight deck.

629.4   UK   ISSN 0094-5765
TL787   CODEN: AASTCF
ACTA ASTRONAUTICA. (Summaries in English, French, German and Russian) 1955. s-m. fl.3976($2285) (effective 1998). (International Academy of Astronautics, FR) Elsevier Science Ltd., Pergamon, P.O. Box 800, Kidlington, Oxford OX5 1DX, England. TEL 44-1865-843000. FAX 44-1865-843010. E-mail: nlinfo-f@elsevier.nl; usinfo-f@elsevier.com; forinfo-kyf04035@niftyserve.or.jp; URL: http://www.elsevier.nl/inca:80/publications/store/3/1/0/310.pub.shtml. (Subscr. to: Elsevier Science, Regional Sales Office, P.O. Box 211, 1000 AE Amsterdam, Netherlands. TEL 31-20-4853757. FAX 31-20-4853432; Subscr. in the Americas to: Elsevier Science, Regional Sales Office, Box 945, New York, NY 10159-0945. TEL 212-633-3730. FAX 212-633-3680; Subscr. in Australasia and the Far East to: Elsevier Science (Singapore) Pte Ltd, No.1 Temasek Ave., No.17-01 Millenia Tower, Singapore 039192, Singapore. TEL 65-434-3727. FAX 65-337-2230) Ed. Jean-Pierre Marec. adv. (also avail. in microform from UMI; back issues avail.) **Indexed:** Appl.Mech.Rev., ASCA, Biol.Abstr., Chem.Abstr., Curr.Cont., Eng.Ind., Ind.Sci.Rev., INSPEC (1974-), Int.Aerosp.Abstr., Sci.Cit.Ind, SSCI. **Document type:** academic/scholarly publication, proceedings.
   —BLDSC (0596.750000); AskIEEE; CASDDS; CISTI; Ei; Genuine Article; KR SourceOne; Linda Hall; SWETS; UMI; UnCover. **CCC.**
   Supersedes (in 1974): Astronautica Acta (ISSN 0004-6205)
   Description: Publishes contributions in all fields of basic engineering, life and social sciences and space technology pertaining to the peaceful scientific exploration of space, its exploitation for human welfare and progress, and the conception, design, development and operation of earth-based or spaceborne systems.
   Refereed Serial

629.4   US   ISSN 1041-102X
TL787   CODEN: ADASED
AD ASTRA.* 1989. 6/yr. $35 to individuals; institutions $40. National Space Society, 600 Pennsylvania Ave., S.E., Ste. 201, Washington, DC 20003-4316. TEL 202-543-1900. FAX 202-546-4189. E-mail: adastra@ari.net; URL: http://www.nss.org/adastra/home.html. Ed. Richard Wagner. R&P contact: Pat Dasch. adv.; bk.rev. circ. 25,000. **Indexed:** Acad.Ind., R.G.Abstr.
   —BLDSC (0678.160000); CISTI; KR SourceOne; Linda Hall; UMI; UnCover.
   Description: Features articles on space and exploration, astronomy, satellites and technology, commercial space, and educational activities.

629.13   GW   ISSN 0001-8279
DER ADLER; Monatszeitschrift fuer Luftsport und Luftfahrt. 1926. m. DM.3.10 (foreign DM.3.40) per no. Baden-Wuerttembergische Luftfahrtverband e.V., Herdweg 77, 70193 Stuttgart, Germany. TEL 49-711-2276223. FAX 49-711-22762-44. Ed. Reinhold Putzhammer. adv.; bk.rev.; charts; illus.; index. circ. 12,000.
   —**CCC.**

ADVANCED COMPOSITES MONTHLY. see ENGINEERING — *Engineering Mechanics And Materials*

629.4   UK   ISSN 0273-1177
QB495   CODEN: ASRSDW
ADVANCES IN SPACE RESEARCH. 1981. 27/yr. fl.4294($2468) (effective 1998). (International Council of Scientific Unions, Committee on Space Research, FR) Elsevier Science Ltd., Pergamon, P.O. Box 800, Kidlington, Oxford OX5 1DX, England. TEL 44-1865-843000. FAX 44-1865-843010. E-mail: nlinfo-f@elsevier.nl; usinfo-f@elsevier.com; forinfo-kyf04035@niftyserve.or.jp; URL: http://www.elsevier.nl:80/inca/publications/store/6/4/4/644.pub.shtml. (Subscr. to: Elsevier Science, Regional Sales Office, P.O. Box 211, 1000 AE Amsterdam, Netherlands. TEL 31-20-4853757. FAX 31-20-4853432; Subscr. in the Americas to: Elsevier Science, Regional Sales Office, Box 945, New York, NY 10159-0945. TEL 212-633-3730. FAX 212-633-3680; Subscr. in Australasia and the Far East to: Elsevier Science (Singapore) Pte Ltd, No.1 Temasek Ave., No.17-01 Millenia Tower, Singapore 039192, Singapore. TEL 65-434-3727. FAX 65-337-2230) Ed. W.I. Axford. illus. (also avail. in microform from UMI) **Indexed:** ASCA, Biol.Abstr., Chem.Abstr., Deep Sea Res.& Oceanogr.Abstr., Ecol.Abstr., Geo.Abstr.H.G., Geo.Abstr.P.G., Ind.Sci.Rev., INSPEC (1982-), Int.Aerosp.Abstr., Meteor.& Geoastrophys.Abstr., Phys.Ber., Sci.Cit.Ind. **Document type:** proceedings.
   —BLDSC (0711.490000); AskIEEE; CASDDS; CISTI; Ei; EMDOCS; Genuine Article; KR SourceOne; Linda Hall; SWETS; UMI; UnCover. **CCC.**
   Formed by the merger of (1978-1980): Advances in Space Exploration (ISSN 0164-0046); (1963-1980): Life Sciences and Space Research (ISSN 0075-9422); (1960-1980): Space Research (ISSN 0371-232X)
   Description: Presents the latest scientific information in all fields of space research.
   Refereed Serial

629.4   US   ISSN 0065-3438
TL787.A6   CODEN: ADASA9
ADVANCES IN THE ASTRONAUTICAL SCIENCES. (Contains several sub-series: Guidance and Control; Astrodynamics; AAS Anniversary Conference Proceedings; Spaceflight Mechanics) 1957. irreg. (approx. 5-6/yr.); vol.93 (pts. 1-2) 1996. price varies. (American Astronautical Society) Univelt, Inc., Box 28130, San Diego, CA 92198-0198. TEL 619-746-4005. FAX 619-746-3139. E-mail: 76121.1532@compuserve.com. Ed. Robert H. Jacobs; Pub. Robert H. Jacobs. R&P contact: Robert H. Jacobs. adv.; bk.rev.; bibl.; charts; illus.; cum.index: 1957-1978; 1979-1986; 1986-1992. circ. 400. (also avail. in microfiche; back issues avail.) **Indexed:** Biol.Abstr., Chem.Abstr., Eng.Ind., INSPEC, Int.Aerosp.Abstr. **Document type:** proceedings.
   —BLDSC (0699.300000); CASDDS; CISTI; Ei; UnCover.
   Description: Proceedings of major technical conferences in the field of space. For universities, research establishments, libraries, and the aerospace industry.

629.13   IT   ISSN 0390-1173
AEREI. 1973. m. (11/yr.). L.60000. Delta Editrice s.n.c., Borgo Regale 21-5, Casella Postale 409, 43100 Parma, Italy. TEL 521-28-78-83. FAX 521-23-75-46. Ed. Corrado Barbieri. adv.; bk.rev.; illus.

AEREI MODELLISMO; mensile di attualita e tecnica modellistica. see HOBBIES

629.13   NE   ISSN 1381-8600
AERO-JOURNAAL. 1987. m. fl.60($37) (Koninklijke Nederlandse Vereniging voor Luchtvaart) Printing & Projects, Postbus 312, 7400 AE Deventer, Netherlands. TEL 31-5700-11341. FAX 31-5700-14741. (Subscr. to: KNVvL, Jozef Israelsplein 8, 2596 AS The Hague, Netherlands. TEL 31-70-3245457. FAX 31-70-3240230; Editorial addr.: Heinsiuslaan 29, 2353 SJ Leidersdorp, Netherlands. TEL 31-71-892172) adv. (also avail. in diskette format; back issues avail.)
   Description: Contains news, information, interviews, association policy statements, and other items relating to flying, including gliding and ballooning.

AERO MECHANIC. see LABOR UNIONS

629.13 629.4   PL   ISSN 0867-6720
TL500   CODEN: TLASB3
AERO-TECHNIKA LOTNICZA. 1936. m. $42. Oficyna Wydawnicza SIMP Press, Ltd., Ul. Swietokrzyska 14A, 00-050 Warsaw, Poland. (Dist. by: Ars Polona-Ruch, Krakowskie Przedmiescie 7, Warsaw, Poland; Editorial addr.: Ul. Bartycka 20, 00-716 Warsaw 36, Poland. TEL 48-22-403802) Ed. W.J. Gawrych. adv.; bk.rev. circ. 3,500. **Indexed:** Chem.Abstr., Int.Aerosp.Abstr.
   —BLDSC (0721.150000); CASDDS; CISTI; Linda Hall.
   Former titles (until 1990): Technika Lotnicza i Astronautyczna (ISSN 0040-1145); (until 1966): Technika Lotnicza (ISSN 0371-6368)
   Description: Covers air technics and history of airplane.

629.1   AG   ISSN 0001-9127
AEROESPACIO/AEROSPACE; revista nacional aeronautica y espacial - national aeronautic and space review. (Text in English, Spanish) 1931. bi-m. $48. Fuerza Aerea Argentina, Paraguay 748, Piso 3, 1057 Buenos Aires, Argentina. TEL 322-2753. FAX 0054-111-8125-6. TELEX 39-21763 AEROESPACIO. (Subscr. to: Casilla de Correo 37, Suc. 12B, 1412 Buenos Aires, Argentina) Ed. Jorge Di Paolo. adv.; bk.rev.; charts; illus.; index. circ. 24,000. (back issues avail.)
   Former titles (until 1967): Revista Nacional de Aeronautica y Espacial (ISSN 0325-3082); (until 1962): Revista Nacional de Aeronautica.
   Description: Articles on aerospace news, civil, military, entrepreneurial, sports and airborne and ground equipment, air and anti-air weapons. Includes defense matters and aerospace systems.

629.1   UK   ISSN 0265-8569
AEROGRAM. 1977. s-a. free. Cranfield University, College of Aeronautics, Cranfield, Beds. MK43 0AL, England. TEL 44-1234-750111. FAX 44-1234-751640. TELEX 825172 CITECH G. E-mail: r.g.wingrove@cranfield.ac.uk. Ed. Ron G. Wingrove. R&P contact: Ron G. Wingrove. adv.; bk.rev.; circ. 3,000 (controlled). **Document type:** academic/scholarly publication.
   —BLDSC (0721.708000).

629.13   GW   ISSN 0341-1281
TL503
AEROKURIER. 1955. m. DM.88; newsstand price: DM.8. (Deutscher Aero Club e.V.) Vereinigte Motor-Verlage GmbH und Co. KG, Leuschnerstr. 1, 70174 Stuttgart, Germany. TEL 49-711-18201. FAX 49-711-1821970. Ed. Werner Pfaendler; Pub. Peter-Paul Pietsch. adv.: B&W page DM.6000, color page DM.11100; trim 185 x 248; adv. contact: Reinhard Wittstamm. bk.rev.; bibl.; charts; illus.; stat.; tr.mk.; index. circ. 35,256. **Indexed:** Excerp.Med. **Document type:** bulletin.
   —BLDSC (0721.850000); CISTI; SWETS. **CCC.**
   Formerly: Deutscher Aerokurier (ISSN 0012-107X)
   Description: Civil aviation news, events and products for all size planes.

629.132   US
AEROLOG. q. membership. National Aviation Club, 1500 N. Beauregard St., Ste. 104, Alexandria, VA 22311-1715. TEL 703-379-1506. FAX 703-379-1507. E-mail: natavclub@aol.com. Ed. Al Sack. bk.rev. circ. 500. **Document type:** newsletter.
   Description: Details news of interest to members of the association.

AEROMILITARIA; Air-Britain military aviation historical journal. see MILITARY

629.1   IT   ISSN 0394-820X
AERONAUTICA E DIFESA. 1986. 11/yr. Lit.48000 (foreign Lit.70000) (effective 1997). Edizioni Monografie s.r.l., Casella 2446, 00100 Roma, Italy. TEL 39-6-5180534. FAX 39-6-51600013. E-mail: http://www.aerodife@tin.it. Ed. Antonio Cervone. adv.; bk.rev.; circ. 60,000 (paid).

AERONAUTICS AND SPACE FLIGHT

629.1 SA ISSN 0257-8573
AERONAUTICA MERIDIANA. (Text in English; summaries in Afrikaans, English) 1980. a. R.20($10) Aeronautical Society of South Africa, c/o School of Mechanical Engineering, University of Pretoria, 0002 Pretoria, South Africa. TEL 27-12-4202014. FAX 27-12-3421379. Ed. E.H. Mathews. circ. 1,000. (back issues avail.) **Indexed:** Ind.S.A.Per., INSPEC (1985-). **Document type:** academic/scholarly publication.
—AskIEEE; KR SourceOne.
 Formerly: Aeronautical Society of South Africa. Journal (ISSN 0250-3786)

629.13 UK ISSN 0001-9240
TL501 CODEN: AENJAK
AERONAUTICAL JOURNAL. 1897. 10/yr. £200. Royal Aeronautical Society, 4 Hamilton Pl., London W1V OBQ, England. TEL 0171-499-3515. FAX 0171-499-6230. URL: http://www.raes.org.uk/publications.html. Ed. B. Baldwin. adv. contact: C. Marot. bk.rev.; charts; illus. circ. 2,000. (also avail. in microform from PMC,UMI) **Indexed:** A.S.& T.Ind., Appl.Mech.Rev., ASCA, BMT, Br.Tech.Ind., C.I.S. Abstr., Chem.Abstr., Curr.Cont., Eng.Ind., Excerp.Med., Fluidex, Ind.Sci.Rev., INSPEC (1968-1988), Int.Aerosp.Abstr., Math.R., Met.Abstr., Sci.Cit.Ind., Sh.& Vib.Dig., Sh.& Vib.Dig., World Alum.Abstr. **Document type:** academic/scholarly publication.
—BLDSC (0725.400000); CISTI; Ei; Genuine Article; Linda Hall; SWETS; UMI; UnCover.
 Incorporates: Aeronautical Quarterly (ISSN 0001-9259)
 Description: Covers all aspects of aerospace technology and engineering.

629.1 CC ISSN 1000-8756
 CODEN: HGJIEO
AERONAUTICAL MANUFACTURING TECHNOLOGY/HANGKONG GONGYI JISHU. 1958. bi-m. $30. Beijing Hangkong Gongyi Yanjiusuo - Beijing Aeronautical Manufacturing Technology Research Institute, P.O. Box 863, Beijing 100024, People's Republic of China. TEL 5761731. FAX 5762306. TELEX 210066 BAMTI CN. (Overseas subscr. to: China National Publishing Industry Trading Corp., P.O. Box 782, Beijing 100011, P.R.C.) Ed. Feng Jinyong. adv.: B&W page $1500, color page $2500; adv. contact: Liu Zhu. circ. 80,000. **Document type:** academic/scholarly publication.
 Description: Caters to the top management of the Ministry of Aero-space Industry, the Air Force and other national defense administrations, scientific researchers, and engineers and technical personnel in China.
 Refereed Serial

629.1 UK ISSN 0269-8900
AERONAUTICAL SATELLITE NEWS. (Includes s-a. supplement: Aero Industry) 1986. bi-m. free. (International Maritime Satellite Organization) Inmarsat, 99 City Rd., London EC1Y 1AX, England. TEL 0171-728-1449. FAX 0171-728-1344. TELEX 297201 INMSAT G. E-mail: emma_kelly@inmarsat.org. Ed. Emma Kelly. adv. contact: Peter Honeywell. charts; illus.; stat.; circ. 13,000 (controlled). (back issues avail.) **Document type:** trade publication.
 Description: Promotes the development of aeronautical satellite communications.
 Refereed Serial

629.13 II ISSN 0001-9267
TL504 CODEN: JANIAK
AERONAUTICAL SOCIETY OF INDIA. JOURNAL. (Text in English) 1949. q. $70. (Aeronautical Society of India) Hindustan Publishing Corp., 4805-24, 1st Fl., Bharat Ram Rd., Darya Ganj, New Delhi 110 002, India. TEL 91-11-3254401. FAX 91-11-6863511. E-mail: hpcpd@giasdl01.vsnl.net.in. Ed. P.J. Lalvani. adv.; bk.rev.; index. circ. 1,800. **Indexed:** Appl.Mech.Rev., INSPEC, Int.Aerosp.Abstr.
—BLDSC (4677.000000); CISTI; Ei; Linda Hall; SWETS; UnCover.

629.13 BE ISSN 0065-3713
AERONOMICA ACTA. (Text in Dutch, English or French, with preliminary material also in other languages) 1959. irreg., latest 1985. price varies. Institut d'Aeronomie Spatiale de Belgique, Ave. Circulaire 3, 1180 Brussels, Belgium.

AEROPHILE. see *HOBBIES*

629.13 YU ISSN 0354-7175
▼**AEROPLAN**; vazduhoplovna istorija, tehnika i maketarstvo. 1995. bi-m. Jurist, Ul. 13 Jul 70, Niksic, Yugoslavia. Ed. Vojislav Vujovic.

629.1 UK ISSN 0143-7240
TL501
AEROPLANE MONTHLY. 1973. m. £31.20 (effective 1996). I P C Magazines, Specialist Magazine Group (Subsidiary of: Reed Elsevier group), King's Reach Tower, Stamford St., London SE1 9LS, England. TEL 44-171-261-5000. FAX 44-1444-445599. TELEX 0892084 REEDBP G. (Dist. by: Quadrant Subscription Services, Oakfield House, Perrymount Rd., Haywards Heath, W. Sussex RH16 3DH, England. TEL 44-1444-445555) Ed. Richard Riding. adv. circ. 34,079. (also avail. in microform from UMI; reprint service avail. from UMI) **Document type:** consumer publication.
—BLDSC (0729.070000); CISTI; SWETS.
 Description: Features information on old, historic and restored military and civil aircraft.

629.1 CN ISSN 0826-2713
AEROSCOPE. 1983. 4/yr. Can.$15. Publications Aeroscope Inc., C.P. 309, Succ. M, Montreal, PQ H1V 3M3, Canada. TEL 514-356-0787. FAX 514-251-8038. Ed. Jacques Beaulieu. adv. circ. 3,000.

387.7 GW ISSN 0949-7064
AEROSPACE. (Editions in English, German) 1935. 2/yr. DM.8 per no. Daimler-Benz Aerospace AG, Postfach 801109, 81663 Munich, Germany. TEL 49-89-60734651. FAX 49-89-60734655. E-mail: yza8735@dbmail.dasa.de. Ed. Manfred Knappe. adv. contact: Silvia Hromada. circ. 78,000. **Indexed:** Abstr.Mil.Bibl., INIS Atomind., Int.Aerosp.Abstr., Med.Abstr., Ocean.Abstr., Pollut.Abstr. **Document type:** trade publication.
—CISTI; Linda Hall. **CCC.**
 Formerly (until 1995): Dornier Post (ISSN 0012-5563)
 Description: Portrays the benefits of aviation, spaceflight and defense technologies and clarifies these with actual examples.

629.1 UK ISSN 0305-0831
AEROSPACE. 1945. m. £95. Royal Aeronautical Society, 4 Hamilton Pl., London W1V OBQ, England. TEL 0171-499-3515. FAX 0171-499-6230. Ed. B. Baldwin. adv. contact: C. Marot. bk.rev.; illus. circ. 19,000. **Indexed:** Alloys Ind., Br.Tech.Ind., Copper Abstr., Eng.Mat.Abstr., Int.Aerosp.Abstr., Met.Abstr.Ind., Met.Abstr., Nonfer.Met.Alert, PCC Alert, Steels Alert, World Alum.Abstr. **Document type:** trade publication.
—BLDSC (0729.837000); CISTI; Ei; Genuine Article; Linda Hall; SWETS; UMI.
 Incorporates (in 1987): Tech Air (ISSN 0040-0831); Which was formerly: Society of Licensed Aircraft Engineers and Technologists. Journal.

629.13 629.4 US ISSN 0740-722X
TL501.A688 CODEN: ASAEA4
AEROSPACE AMERICA. 1932. m. $75 to non-members (foreign $85). American Institute of Aeronautics and Astronautics, Inc., 1801 Alexander Dr., Ste. 500, Reston, VA 20191. TEL 703-264-7500. FAX 202-646-7508. URL: http://www.aiaa.org/publications/aa-magazine.html. Ed. Elaine Camhi. adv.; bk.rev.; bibl.; charts; illus.; stat.; tr.lit.; index. circ. 55,000. (also avail. in microform from UMI; reprint service avail. from UMI) **Indexed:** A.S.& T.Ind., Abstr.Mil.Bibl., Alloys Ind., Appl.Mech.Rev., ASCA, Chem.Abstr., Curr.Cont., Eng.Ind., Eng.Mat.Abstr., Excerp.Med., Ind.Sci.Rev., INIS Atomind., Int.Aerosp.Abstr., ISMEC, Met.Abstr., Met.Abstr.Ind., Noise Pollut.Publ.Abstr., Nonfer.Met.Alert, Ocean.Abstr., PCC Alert, Pollut.Abstr., Robomat. (until 1992), Sci.Cit.Ind., Sh.& Vib.Dig., SSCI, Steels Alert, World Alum.Abstr. **Document type:** academic/scholarly publication.
●Also available online. Vendor(s): Lexis-Nexis (AEROAM).
—BLDSC (0729.852000); CASDDS; CISTI; Ei; Genuine Article; KR SourceOne; Linda Hall; SWETS; UnCover. **CCC.**
 Formerly (1963-1983): Astronautics and Aeronautics (ISSN 0004-6213) *Incorporating:* A I A A Bulletin.
 Description: Provides coverage of key issues affecting the aerospace field. Includes analytical coverage of aeronautics, space, defense, design, electronics, computer applications, and science, highlighting the principal technologies involved and their implications for both industry and the individual aerospace professional.

629.1 UK
AEROSPACE AND AVIATION DOCUMENTS MICROFILE. Short title: A & A. 1982. bi-m. Technical Indexes Ltd., Willoughby Rd., Bracknell, Berkshire RG12 8DW, England. TEL 44-1344-426311. FAX 44-1344-424971. E-mail: systems@techindex.co.uk; URL: http://www.techindex.co.uk. adv. contact: Gary Kearns. **Document type:** abstracting/indexing.

629.1 JA
AEROSPACE AND DEFENCE WEEKLY.* (Text in English) w. 80000 Yen. Koku Shinbunsha - Wing Aviation Press, 30, Kanda Higshi-Konya-cho, Chiyoda-ku, Tokyo 101, Japan.

629.132 JA
AEROSPACE ANNUAL JAPAN. (Text in Japanese) 1954. a. 10000 Yen (effective Oct. 1996). Nihon Koku Kyokai, 1-18-2 Shimbashi, Minato-ku, Tokyo 105, Japan. TEL 03-3502-1206. FAX 03-3503-1375. Ed. Takeshi Ijichi; Pub. Toshiyuki Yamauchi. adv. **Document type:** directory.
 Formerly: Aviation Annual of Japan (ISSN 0389-4185)
 Description: Covers Japanese aviation policy and administration, airline business, aircraft manufacturing, air sports and self-defence air force.

629.1 SI
AEROSPACE ASIA - PACIFIC. (Text in English) 1989. m. $80 in Asia; elsewhere $90. Miller Freeman Pte. Ltd., 100 Beach Rd., 26-00 Shaw Towers, Singapore 0718, Singapore. TEL 294-3366. FAX 298-5534. Ed. Terrence Hardeman. adv.: B&W page $4920, color page $7020; trim 8 1/4 x 11 1/4. circ. 11,375 (controlled). **Document type:** trade publication.
 Formerly: Aerospace (ISSN 0129-1815)
 Description: Includes news and features for commercial aviation and defense industry buyers throughout Asia and the Pacific Rim area.

629.1 CC ISSN 1004-9711
TL289.8.C55
AEROSPACE CHINA. Chinese edition: Zhongguo Hangtian (ISSN 1002-7742) (Text in English) 1992. s-a. $50 (effective 1997). Hangtian Gongye Zong Gongsi, Xinxi Yanjiu-suo - China Aerospace Corporation, Institute for Astronautics Information, P.O. Box 1408, 1 Binhe Lu, Hepingli, Beijing 100013, People's Republic of China. TEL 86-10-6837-2847. FAX 86-10-6422-7606. TELEX 210471 IAI CN. E-mail: duyq@mimi.cnc.ac.cn; URL: http://www.iai.canet.cn. Ed. Xue Fuxing.
 Description: Covers China's space activities, achievements, science and technology, experiments, satellites and missiles.
 Refereed Serial

AERONAUTICS AND SPACE FLIGHT

629.1 — US — ISSN 0193-4546
HD9711.5.U58
AEROSPACE DAILY. vol.61, 1973. d. (5/w.). $1340 (foreign $1510). McGraw-Hill Companies, Aviation Week Group (Washington), 1200 G St., N.W., Ste. 200, Washington, DC 20005. TEL 202-383-2350. Ed. Dave Bond. **Document type:** newspaper, trade publication.
●Also available online. Vendor(s): Dow Jones News Retrieval, European Space Agency (File no.72/AEROSPACE DAILY), Knight-Ridder Information, Inc. (File nos.624,648), Lexis-Nexis (AIRDLY), NewsNet (AE29), Ovid Technologies, Inc. (TSAP).
—BLDSC (0729.856000). **CCC.**
Formerly: Missile - Space Daily.

629.1 — US — ISSN 0736-2536
TL671.2
AEROSPACE ENGINEERING MAGAZINE. 1981. m. $60 (foreign $107). Society of Automotive Engineers, 400 Commonwealth Dr., Warrendale, PA 15096-0001. TEL 412-772-7114. FAX 412-776-4026. E-mail: magazines@sae.org; URL: http://www.sae.org/PRODSERV/MAGAZINE/Aerospac.htm. Ed. Daniel J. Holt. adv. circ. 61,598. (also avail. in microfiche; microfilm; back issues avail.) **Indexed:** Alloys Ind., ASCA, Eng.Mat.Abstr., Int.Aerosp.Abstr., Met.Abstr.Ind., Met.Abstr., Nonfer.Met.Alert, PCC Alert, Steels Alert, World Alum.Abstr. **Document type:** trade publication.
●Also available online. Vendor(s): Questel Orbit Inc.
—BLDSC (0729.861000); CISTI; Ei; Genuine Article; Linda Hall; SWETS; UMI; UnCover. **CCC.**
Formerly: S A E in Aerospace Engineering.
Description: Directed to the aerospace engineer; covers advances in aerospace technology that can be applied to the design of new or improved vehicles or systems. Bibliographic article abstracts are on-line.

629.13 — UK
AEROSPACE EUROPE. 1947. a. £83.50 (rest of Europe £96; elsewhere £104) (effective 1997). Miller Freeman Information Services (Subsidiary of: United News & Media), Riverbank House, Angel Ln., Tonbridge, Kent TN9 1SE, England. TEL 44-1732-362666. FAX 44-1732-367301. URL: http://www.mfplc.com. Ed. Gwen Young. adv. contact: Elaine Soni. bk.rev. circ. 5,000. **Document type:** directory.
—CISTI.
Formerly: Aviation Europe (ISSN 0143-1145); Incorporates: Sell's British Aviation (ISSN 0080-8695)
Description: Contains information about European aviation companies in the civil and defense sectors.

629.1 — US
AEROSPACE INDUSTRIES ASSOCIATION ANNUAL REPORT. 1941. a. free. Aerospace Industries Association of America, 1250 Eye St. N.W., Ste. 1200, Washington, DC 20005. TEL 202-371-8561. FAX 202-371-8470. URL: http://www.aia-aerospace.org. Ed. Kathy Linse. circ. 3,000. **Document type:** corporate report.

629.1 — US — ISSN 0898-509X
AEROSPACE INDUSTRIES ASSOCIATION OF AMERICA. NEWSLETTER. 10/yr. Aerospace Industries Association of America, 1250 Eye St., N.W., Washington, DC 20005. TEL 202-371-8561. FAX 202-371-8470. URL: http://www.aia-aerospace.org. Ed. Kathy Linse. circ. 5,000. **Document type:** newsletter.

629.1 — JA
AEROSPACE INDUSTRY YEARBOOK. (Text in Japanese) 1974. a. 7000 Yen. Society of Japanese Aerospace Companies, Inc. - Nihon Koku Uchu Kogyokai, Hibiya Park Bldg, 8-1 Yurakucho 1-chome, Chiyoda-ku, Tokyo 100, Japan. circ. 1,000.

629.1 — JA
AEROSPACE JAPAN WEEKLY. (Text in English) 1988. w. 185000 Yen. Ikaros Publications Ltd., 3-2 Kagurazaka, Shinjuku-ku, Tokyo 162, Japan. TEL 81-3-3267-2832. FAX 81-3-3267-2787. Ed. Koji Hoashi. adv. contact: Kinsaku Endo. circ. 500. **Document type:** newsletter.
Refereed Serial

629.1 340 — US
AEROSPACE MANAGEMENT AND LAW. 1991. irreg. price varies. Praeger Publishers (Subsidiary of: Greenwood Publishing Group Inc.), 88 Post Rd. W., Box 5007, Westport, CT 06881-5007. TEL 203-226-3571. FAX 203-222-1502. **Document type:** monographic series.

629.1 — CN
AEROSPACE NEWS. 4/yr. Can.$35 to non-members (effective 1997). Aerospace Industries Association of Canada - Association des Industries Aerospatiales du Canada, 60 Queen St., Ste. 1200, Ottawa, ON K1P 5Y7, Canada. TEL 613-232-4297. FAX 613-232-1142. E-mail: aiac@fox.nstn.ns.ca. Ed. Ray Windsor. adv.: B&W half page Can.$500. circ. 2,400 (controlled). **Document type:** newsletter.
Description: Provides an overview of issues and events currently affecting the Canadian aerospace industry.

620.86 — US
AEROSPACE NEWSLETTER. 1961. bi-m. $19 to non-members; members $15. National Safety Council, Periodicals Department, 1121 Spring Lake Dr., Itasca, IL 60143. TEL 708-775-2281. Ed. Kathy Henderson; Pub. Kevin H. Axe. **Document type:** newsletter.
Formerly: Safety Newsletter: Aerospace Section (ISSN 0470-2824)
Description: Information and recommendations on various safety issues in the aerospace industry.

629 — US — ISSN 1054-7045
AEROSPACE PRODUCTS; components and systems technology. 1986. q. Phillips Publishing International Inc., 1201 Seven Locks Rd., Ste. 300, Potomac, MD 20854. TEL 301-340-1520. Ed. Dave Jensen. adv.; circ. controlled. (tabloid format)
—**CCC.**

629.13 — US — ISSN 0363-8219
AEROSPACE PROPULSION. 1963. 25/yr. $550. McGraw-Hill Companies, Aviation Week Group (Washington), 1200 G. St., N.W., Ste. 200, Washington, DC 20005. TEL 202-383-2350. Ed. Jim Mathews. bk.rev.; abstr.; charts; illus.; mkt.; pat.; stat.; tr.lit.; index. **Document type:** trade publication.
●Also available online. Vendor(s): Dow Jones News Retrieval (ASR), Knight-Ridder Information, Inc. (ASP), Lexis-Nexis (AERPRO), NewsNet (AE34).
Formerly (until 1976): Space Propulsion (ISSN 0038-6294)

629.1 — UK
AEROSPACE REVIEW. 1950. s-a. free. Smiths Industries Aerospace, 765 Finchley Rd., London NW11 8DS, England. TEL 44-181-458-3232. FAX 44-181-209-0526. E-mail: plc@smithsind.co.uk; URL: http://www.smithsind-aerospace.co.uk. (Dist. addr. in US: Publicity Dept., Smith Industries Aerospace, 4141 Eastern Ave. S.E., Grand Rapids, MI 49518-8727) Ed. S. Broadbent. R&P contact: R. Plumley. illus.; circ. 6,500 (controlled). (back issues avail.) **Indexed:** INSPEC (1980-). **Document type:** trade publication.
Former titles: Aerospace and Defence Review; Aviation Review (ISSN 0374-2490)
Description: News and technical reviews of avionics systems and equipment manufactured by Smiths Industries.

629.13 — FR — CODEN: REARAU
TL502
AEROSPACE SCIENCE AND TECHNOLOGY. (Text in English or French) 1997. 8/yr. 1210 F. institutions (outside the Americas F.1430) (effective 1998). (Office National d'Etudes et de Recherches Aerospatiales) Gauthier-Villars, 5 rue Laromiguiere, 75005 Paris, France. TEL 33-1-40466200. FAX 33-1-40466201. E-mail: gauthier.villars.publisher@mail.sgip.fr; URL: http://www.gauthier-villars.fr. (Subscr. to: Societe de Periodiques Specialises, B.P. 22, 41354 Vineuil Cedex, France. TEL 33-2-54504612. FAX 33-2-54504611) (Co-sponsor: Forschungsanstalt fur Luft-und Raumfahrt - Deutsche Gesellschaft fur Luft- und Raumfahrt) Eds. Jean Carpentier, Fred Thomas. charts; illus.; index. **Indexed:** Appl.Mech.Rev., ASCA, Cadscan, Chem.Abstr., Compumath, Curr.Cont., Eng.Mat.Abstr., Excerp.Med., Fluidex, Ind.Sci.Rev., INSPEC (1992-), Int.Aerosp.Abstr., Lead Abstr., Mat.Sci.Cit.Ind., Math.R., Met.Abstr., Met.Abstr.Ind., Nonfer.Met.Alert, PCC Alert, Steels Alert, World Alum.Abstr., Zincscan. **Document type:** academic/scholarly publication.
—AskIEEE; CASDDS; CISTI; Ei; Genuine Article; KR SourceOne; Linda Hall; SWETS; UnCover. **CCC.**
Formed by the 1997 merger of: Recherche Aerospaciale (ISSN 0034-1223) & Zeitschrift fuer Flugwissenschaften und Weltraumforschung (ISSN 0342-068X); Which was formerly: Raumfahrtforschung (ISSN 0034-0103)
Description: Covers all fields of aerospace research from fundamental research to industrial applications.
Refereed Serial

629.1 — CH
AEROSPACE TECHNOLOGY. (Text in Chinese) 1985. bi-m. Tzeng Brothers Information Group, P.O. Box 43-345, Taipei, Taiwan 110, Republic of China. TEL 2-999-2969. FAX 2-999-2989. Ed. G.L. Wang; Pub. James Y.C. Tzeng. adv.: B&W page $2000, color page $3000; trim 215 x 287; adv. contact: James Y.C. Tzeng. circ. 9,100.
Description: Covers technical developments and engineering issues in Asia-Pacific aerospace industry.

629.1 600 — US
AEROSPACE TESTING SEMINAR. PROCEEDINGS. 1975. irreg., 16th, 1996. $100 to non-members; members $70 (effective 1997). Institute of Environmental Sciences, 940 E. Northwest Hwy., Mt. Prospect, IL 60056. TEL 847-255-1561. FAX 847-255-1699. (Co-sponsor: Aerospace Corporation) **Document type:** proceedings.

001.94 — JA
AEROSPACE U F O NEWS. (Text in Japanese; summaries in English) vol.6, 1974. q. membership. (International U F O Observer Corps.) C B A International, Naka P.O. Box 12, Yokohama 231, Japan. Ed. Yusuke J. Matsumura. bk.rev.; illus. circ. 35,000.
Formerly (until 1982): U F O News.

629.1 — SI
AEROSPACE YEARBOOK. (Text in English) 1991. a. $50. Miller Freeman Pte. Ltd., 100 Beach Rd., 26-00 Shaw Towers, Singapore 0718, Singapore. TEL 65-294-3366. FAX 65-298-5534. adv.: B&W page $4900, color page $7000; trim 8 1/4 x 11 1/4. circ. 9,513. **Document type:** trade publication.
Description: Summarizes and studies the major happenings in the aviation industry over the past year.

629.1 — US
AEROTECH NEWS & REVIEW. w. E-mail: aerotech@netport.com; URL: http://www.avimall.com/aerotech/index.html.
●Available only online.
Description: Serves the aerospace industry of Southern California.

AERONAUTICS AND SPACE FLIGHT

629.13   IT   ISSN 0365-7442
TL504   CODEN: ATMSCD
AEROTECNICA, MISSILI E SPAZIO. (Text in English, Italian; summaries in English) 1920. q. L.70000 (foreign $70) (effective 1996). Associazione Italiana di Aeronautica e Astronautica, Via Golgi 40, 20133 Milan, Italy. Ed. Vittorio Giavotto. adv.; bk.rev.; abstr.; bibl.; charts; illus.; index. circ. 1,000. (also avail. in microform from UMI) **Indexed:** Chem.Abstr., Curr.Cont., Zent.Math.
—CASDDS; CISTI; Linda Hall; UnCover.
Formed by the merger of: Aerotecnica (ISSN 0001-9453); Missili e Spazio (ISSN 0026-6019); Which was formerly: Missili (ISSN 0369-2175).

387.7   CU   ISSN 0001-9461
AEROVOZ.* 1945. m. $1. Sindicato Nacional de Trabajadores de la Aviacion, Palacio de los Trabajadores, San Carlos y Penalver, Havana, Cuba. Ed. Gustavo Mas Aguilar. adv.; charts; illus. circ. 3,000.

387.7   IE   ISSN 0001-9550
AERSCEALA; staff journal of Aer Lingus. (Text in English and Irish) 1948. bi-m. free. Aer Lingus, Communications Department, Dublin Airport PA6, Dublin, Ireland. TEL 353-1-7052326. Ed. Collette Kearney. adv.; circ. 9,500 (controlled). (tabloid format) **Document type:** newsletter.
Description: Covers news and areas of interest to serving and retired airline staff.

629.132   US   ISSN 0740-1434
AG-PILOT INTERNATIONAL; aviation in agriculture worldwide. 1978. 12/yr. $29.95 in N. America; elsewhere $49.95. Graphics Plus, Box 1607, Mt. Vernon, WA 98273-1607. TEL 206-336-9737. FAX 206-336-2506. Ed. Tom J. Wood. adv.; B&W page $2380, color page $3350; trim 8 1/2 x 10 7/8. bk.rev.; bibl.; charts; illus.; stat.; tr.lit.; circ. 4,494 (paid). **Document type:** trade publication.
Description: Information on agri-aviation for ag pilots, chemical dealers and consultants.

629.1 630   US   ISSN 0745-4864
AGRICULTURAL AVIATION. 1974. 6/yr. $30 (foreign $40). National Agricultural Aviation Association, 1005 E St. S.E., Washington, DC 20003. TEL 202-546-5722. FAX 202-546-5726. Ed. Jim Boillot. adv. circ. 6,600. **Document type:** trade publication.
—CISTI.
Formerly: W A A (ISSN 0192-6845)

629.13   FR   ISSN 1166-0422
AILES MAGAZINE. (Text in French) 1984. m. 350 F.($66) (foreign 450 F.). ConceptAir, 12 rue de Bercy, 75012 Paris, France. TEL 1-40-19-90-00. Ed. Alain-Yves Berger. circ. 25,000. (back issues avail.)
Former titles (until 1991): U L M Ailes Magazine (ISSN 0764-3977); (until 1986): U L M Mag (ISSN 0756-9785)
Description: Covers light and microlight aircraft.

341.46   US
AIM - FAR (YEAR).* 1947. a. $5.70. Tab Books, (Subsidiary of: McGraw-Hill, Inc.), Box 451, Hightstown, NJ 08520-0451. adv. contact: Judith Terrill-Breuer. index. **Document type:** trade publication.
Formed by the 1991 merger of: Federal Aviation Regulations for Pilots (ISSN 0533-0963); Airman's Information Manual.

629.1 070.48   US
AIR ACCIDENTS & THE NEWS MEDIA.* 1965. irreg. $5. Aviation - Space Writers Association, 6540 50th St., N., Oakdale, MN 55128-1708. TEL 614-221-1900. FAX 614-221-1989. bk.rev. circ. 1,500.
Formerly: Air Accidents and the Newswriter.

AIR ACTUALITES; le magazine de l'Armee de l'air. see MILITARY

629.132 387.7   US   ISSN 0889-9576
AIR ALASKA;* the northern aviator's news. 1980. m. $15. Pacific Rim Publishing Co., Box 201894, Anchorage, AK 99520-1894. TEL 907-272-7500. FAX 907-279-1037. Ed. Steve Storm. circ. 10,000. (tabloid format; back issues avail.)
Description: Covers all aspects of flying and aviation in Alaska.

629.13 528   US   ISSN 0002-2160
THE AIR ALMANAC. 1937. a. price varies. U.S. Naval Observatory, Department of the Navy, Washington, DC 20392. (Subscr. also to: Superintendent of Documents, U.S. Government Printing Office, Box 371954, Pittsburgh, PA 15250-7954. TEL 202-512-1800. FAX 202-512-2250) (Co-sponsor: H.M. Nautical Almanac Office (UK)) (back issues avail.) **Document type:** government publication.
—CCC.
Description: Contains the astronomical data required for air navigation.

AIR & SPACE LAW. see TRANSPORTATION — Air Transport

AIR AND SPACE LAWYER. see LAW

629.13   US   ISSN 0886-2257
TL501
AIR & SPACE - SMITHSONIAN. 1986. bi-m. $20 (foreign $26) (effective 1997-1998). Smithsonian Institution, Air & Space Museum, 370 L'Enfant Promenade, S.W., 10th Fl., Washington, DC 20024-2518. TEL 202-287-3733. FAX 202-287-3163. URL: http://airspacemag.earthlink.edu/. Ed. George C. Larson; Pub. Ronald Walker. R&P contact: Sheila Brannum. adv. contact: Louis Kolenda. bk.rev.; bibl.; illus. circ. 350,000. **Indexed:** Access (1986-), Amer.Hist.& Life (1986-), Bk.Rev.Ind. (1992-), Child.Bk.Rev.Ind. (1992-), Hist.Abstr. (1986-), INIS Atomind. **Document type:** academic/scholarly publication, consumer publication.
—BLDSC (0774.132000); CISTI; Linda Hall; UMI; UnCover.
Description: Discusses the design and history of all types of aircraft and space vehicles.

629.1   UK   ISSN 0950-7434
AIR-BRITAIN DIGEST. 1948. q. £15 includes Air-Britain News. Air-Britain (Historians) Ltd., 1 East St., Tonbridge, Kent TN9 1HP, England. circ. 4,000.
—UnCover.
Description: Publishes articles on historical and contemporary aviation worldwide.

629.1   UK   ISSN 0950-7442
AIR-BRITAIN NEWS. 1964. m. £15 includes Air-Britain Digest. Air-Britain (Historians) Ltd., 1 East St., Tonbridge, Kent TN9 1HP, England.
Description: News on civil registers worldwide.

AIR CADET; the journal for air minded youth. see CHILDREN AND YOUTH — For

387.7   CN   ISSN 0568-3424
HE9815.A95
AIR CANADA. ANNUAL REPORT. (Text in English and French) a. Air Canada, Place Air Canada, Montreal, PQ H2Z 1X5, Canada. TEL 514-879-7766.

387.744   US   ISSN 0002-2241
AIR CLASSICS. 1963. m. $25.95 (foreign $37.95). Challenge Publications, Inc., 7950 Deering Ave., Canoga Park, CA 91304. TEL 818-887-0550. FAX 818-884-1343. E-mail: warbirdmag@aol.com. Ed. Michael O'Leary; Pub. Edwin Schnepf. R&P contact: Susan Duprey. adv. contact: Greg Lovell. bk.rev.; film rev.; charts; illus. circ. 72,119. (processed) **Indexed:** Amer.Hist.& Life, Hist.Abstr. **Document type:** consumer publication.
—CISTI.

629.13   FR   ISSN 1240-3113
TL502
AIR & COSMOS - AVIATION MAGAZINE INTERNATIONAL. 1963. w. 957 F. (foreign 1150 F.). Groupe Revenu Francais, 1 bis av. de la Republique, 75011 Paris, France. TEL 49-29-30-00. FAX 43-55-91-41. (Subscr. to: B. 540, 60732 Ste. Genevieve Cedex, France. TEL 44-03-44-19. FAX 44-07-43-36) Ed. Robert Monteux. adv.; bk.rev.; bibl.; charts; illus. circ. 20,000. **Indexed:** DM& T, Key to Econ.Sci., PROMT.
—CISTI; Linda Hall; SWETS. **CCC.**
Formed by the 1992 merger of: Air et Cosmos (ISSN 0044-6971) & Aviation Magazine International (ISSN 0005-2132); Which incorporates: Air Transport Magazine (ISSN 0002-256X)

AIR FORCE COMPTROLLER. see MILITARY

AIR FORCE MAGAZINE. see MILITARY

AIR FORCE TIMES. see MILITARY

387.7   UK   ISSN 0306-5634
UG630.A1
AIR INTERNATIONAL. 1971. m. £34.50 (foreign $62.10). Key Publishing Ltd., P.O. Box 300, Stamford, Lincs. PE9 1NA, England. TEL 44-1780-480404. FAX 44-1780-757812. E-mail: postmaster@keymags.demon.co.uk; URL: http://www.keymags.co.uk/airint/. Ed. Malcolm English. adv.; bk.rev.; bibl.; charts; illus.; s-a. index. circ. 42,283. **Indexed:** DM& T, Int.Aerosp.Abstr., PROMT. **Document type:** bulletin.
—BLDSC (0776.340000); CISTI; SWETS; UnCover.
Formerly: Air Enthusiast (ISSN 0044-6963)
Description: International military and civil aerospace news and analysis of current and historical events.

AIR JOBS DIGEST. see OCCUPATIONS AND CAREERS

387.72   US   ISSN 0002-242X
TL501
AIR LINE PILOT; the magazine of professional flight deck crews. 1932. m. $26 (foreign $40) (effective 1996). Air Line Pilots Association, A F L - C I O, 535 Herndon Pkwy., Box 1169, Herndon, VA 20172. TEL 703-481-4460. FAX 703-689-4370. E-mail: 73714.41@compuserve.com. Ed. J. Gary DiNunno. R&P contact: Susan Fager. TEL 703-481-4469. adv. contact: Lara Engebretson. bk.rev.; charts; illus.; stat.; index. circ. 65,000. (also avail. in microform from UMI; reprint service avail. from UMI) **Indexed:** Air Un.Lib.Ind. **Document type:** trade publication.
—BLDSC (0776.349600); CISTI; UMI; UnCover.
Incorporates: Tech Talk (Herndon) (ISSN 0040-0858)
Description: Covers air safety and technology, industry developments, labor union issues, airline industry regulations and economics, airline pilot profession.

629.1   US
AIR MARKET NEWS. 1982. bi-m. free to qualified personnel. General Publications, Inc., Box 480, Hatch, NM 87937-0480. TEL 505-267-1030. FAX 505-267-1920. Ed. Dixie Binning; Pub. Jennifer Prill. adv.; tr.lit.; circ. 18,500 (controlled). **Document type:** trade publication.

AIR MEDICAL JOURNAL. see MEDICAL SCIENCES

629.13   UK   ISSN 0002-2462
AIR PICTORIAL.* 1939. m. £23 (overseas £29.50). H P C Publishing, Drury Lane, St. Leonards on Sea, E. Sussex TN38 9BJ, England. TEL 0181-668-7403. FAX 0181-660-7569. Ed. Barry Wheeler; Pub. Derek Knoll. adv. contact: David New. bk.rev.; illus.; stat.; index. circ. 18,850. **Document type:** consumer publication.
—BLDSC (0776.400000).
Description: Directed to the air enthusiast to inform about all aspects of aviation.

387.7   US   ISSN 1044-016X
UG633.A1
AIR POWER HISTORY. 1954. q. $35 to individuals; institutions $45. Air Force Historical Foundation, 110 Luke Ave., Ste. 405, Bolling AFB, DC 20332-5113. TEL 202-767-5088. FAX 202-767-5527. URL: http://www.aon.af.mil/historic.html#power. Ed. Jacob Neufeld; Pub. Gen. Bryce Poe II. adv.: B&W page $300 to publishers; others $1400; adv. contact: Mark D. Mandeles. bk.rev.; bibl.; charts; cum.index: 1954-1972, 1973-1983. circ. 7,000. (also avail. in microform from UMI; reprint service avail. from UMI,ISI) **Indexed:** Abstr.Mil.Bibl., Air Un.Lib.Ind., Amer.Hist.& Life (1963-), Hist.Abstr. (1963-), So.Pac.Per.Ind. **Document type:** academic/scholarly publication.
—CISTI; UMI; UnCover.
Former titles (until 1989): Aerospace Historian (ISSN 0001-9364); Airpower History (ISSN 0277-9048)
Description: Focuses on scholarly articles on subjects focusing on any aspect of air or space history.
Refereed Serial

629.13   IT
AIR PRESS. (Text in Italian) 1959. w. L.870000 (foreign L.1000000) (effective 1995). Editoriale Aeronautica s.r.l., Via Prenestine 685, 00155 Rome, Italy. TEL 39-6-2280535. FAX 39-6-2280720. Ed. Oscar Dariz. adv.: B&W page L.2300000, color page L.3850000; adv. contact: Grazia Prunas. circ. 2,000. **Document type:** newsletter.

AERONAUTICS AND SPACE FLIGHT

629.13 US
TL501
AIR PROGRESS. 1941. 9/yr. $16.95 (foreign $24.95). Challenge Publications, Inc., 7950 Deering Ave., Canoga Park, CA 91304. TEL 818-887-0550. FAX 818-884-1343. E-mail: challpubs@aol.com; URL: http://www.challpubs.com/airprogress/about.shtml. Ed. Michael O'Leary; Pub. Edwin Schnepf. R&P contact: Susan Duprey. adv. contact: Greg Lovell. bk.rev.; charts; illus. circ. 51,127. (processed; also avail. in microform from UMI) **Indexed:** A.S.& T.Ind., Access (1975-1988), Bus.Ind., Ind.Sci.Rev., Mag.Ind., PMR, Tr.& Indus.Ind. **Document type:** consumer publication.
—BLDSC (0776.495000); KR SourceOne; Linda Hall; UnCover.
Former titles: Air Progress - Affordable Flying (ISSN 1086-4725); Air Progress (ISSN 0002-2500)

629.1 US ISSN 1044-727X
KF2406.A15
AIR SAFETY WEEK; the newsletter of air safety regulation. 1987. w. $797 (foreign $860) (effective 1997). Phillips Business Information, Inc., 1201 Seven Locks Rd., Potomac, MD 20854. TEL 301-424-3338. FAX 301-309-3847. E-mail: pbi@phillips.com. Ed. Jim Stevenson. index. (back issues avail.) **Document type:** newsletter.
●Also available online. Vendor(s): Data-Star, Information Access Co., Knight-Ridder Information, Inc., NewsNet (AE16).
—CCC.
Incorporates (1993-1997): C N S Outlook (ISSN 1072-5393); (in 1989): Air Safety Law Law and Technology (ISSN 0893-1003)
Description: Reports on developments in air safety regulation, focusing on regulatory authorities in the US.

629.1 SP ISSN 0210-9123
AIR SONIC. 1980. 12/yr. Balmes 86 entlo., 08008 Barcelona, Spain. TEL 215-87-96.
Description: Covers military, civil and sport aviation, including model aircraft.

629.1 US ISSN 0192-8740
TL725.3.T7
AIR TRAFFIC CONTROL ASSOCIATION. FALL CONFERENCE PROCEEDINGS. 1977. a. $30. Air Traffic Control Association, Inc., 2300 Clarendon Blvd., Ste. 711, Arlington, VA 22201. TEL 703-522-5717. Ed. G.A. Hartl. circ. 1,200. (back issues avail.) **Document type:** proceedings.

AIR TRAFFIC MANAGEMENT. see *TRANSPORTATION — Air Transport*

AIR TRAFFIC MANAGEMENT YEARBOOK. see *TRANSPORTATION — Air Transport*

387.7 US ISSN 0002-2543
HE9761.1
AIR TRANSPORT WORLD. 1964. m. $50. Penton Publishing Co. (Stamford) (Subsidiary of: Pittway Company), 600 Summer St., Box 1361, Stamford, CT 06904. TEL 203-348-7531. FAX 203-348-4023. URL: http://www.atwonline.com/. (Subscr. to: Box 96732, Chicago, IL 60693) Ed. J.A. Donoghue; Pub. Gere D. Coffey. R&P contact: J.A. Donoghue. adv. contact: Bill Freeman. charts; illus.; tr.lit.; index; circ. 7,654 (paid); 40,100 (controlled). (also avail. in microform from UMI; reprint service avail. from UMI) **Indexed:** B.P.I., Bus.Ind., Energy Ind., Energy Info.Abstr., Environ.Abstr., HRIS, PROMT, SRI, Tel.Abstr., Tr.& Indus.Ind. **Document type:** trade publication.
●Also available online. Vendor(s): Information Access Co., Knight-Ridder Information, Inc., UMI.
—BLDSC (0776.800000); CISTI; KR SourceOne; SWETS; UMI; UnCover. **CCC.**
Description: Reports on managerial, technical and operational advances, and developments and trends in the airline industries that supply the airlines with equipment and services.

629.13 US ISSN 1087-2701
AIRBORNE LOG; the magazine of naval sea control and maritime patrol. 1981. s-a. free. Lockheed Martin, 542642 LOCKHEED MARA, 86 S. Cobb Dr., Marietta, GA 30063-0244. TEL 770-494-2406. FAX 770-494-4809. Ed. Bob Harper. illus.; circ. 30,000 (controlled). **Indexed:** Abstr.Mil.Bibl. **Document type:** consumer publication, trade publication.
Formerly (until 1993): A S W Log; Formed by the 1990 merger of: Viking Watch & Patrol Log; Which was formerly (until 1981): Airborne A S W Log; Supersedes: Lockheed Reports (ISSN 0024-5712)
Description: Features the P-3 Orion and S-3 Viking aircraft in their maritime role. Includes related articles, interviews and news reports.

629.1 UN ISSN 0443-7926
AIRCRAFT ACCIDENT DIGEST. French edition: Recueil d'Accidents d'Aviation (ISSN 1014-4536); Spanish edition: Recompilacion de Accidentes de Aviacion (ISSN 1014-4544) (Issued as a subseries of: Air Navigation. Series F: Circulars) 1951. irreg., latest 1994. $40. International Civil Aviation Organization, Attn: Document Sales Unit, 1000 Sherbrooke St. W., Montreal, PQ H3A 2R2, Canada. TEL 514-285-8022. FAX 514-285-6769. TELEX 05-24513. (reprint service avail.)

629.13 AT ISSN 1032-9366
AIRCRAFT & AEROSPACE. 1918. m. $75. (Royal Aeronautical Society, Australian Division) Peter Isaacson Publications Pty. Ltd., 46-50 Porter St., Prahran, Vic. 3181, Australia. TEL 61-3-2457777. FAX 61-3-2457606. Ed. Gerry Carman. adv.; bk.rev.; abstr.; bibl.; charts; illus.; stat. circ. 12,453. **Indexed:** Abstr.Mil.Bibl.
—Genuine Article; SWETS.
Incorporates: Aviation News; Supersedes (in 1988, vol.68, no.6): Aircraft (ISSN 1032-9358)

AIRCRAFT ECONOMICS. see *TRANSPORTATION — Air Transport*

629.1 UK
AIRCRAFT ENGINEERING AND AEROSPACE TECHNOLOGY. 1929. 6/yr. £349 (effective 1997). M C B University Press Ltd., 60-62 Toller Ln., Bradford, W. Yorks BD8 9BY, England. TEL 44-1274-777700. FAX 44-1274-785200. E-mail: akaminska@mcb.co.uk; URL: http://www.mcb.co.uk/cgi-bin/mcb-serve/table1.txt&aeat&journal1.html. Ed. Terry Savage. adv.; bk.rev.; charts; illus.; pat.; tr.lit.; index. circ. 2,221. **Indexed:** A.S.& T.Ind., Alloys Ind., ASCA, Br.Tech.Ind., Chem.Abstr., Eng.Ind., Eng.Mat.Abstr., Excerp.Med., INSPEC (1993-), Met.Abstr., Met.Abstr.Ind., Nonfer.Met.Alert, PCC Alert, PROMT, Steels Alert. **Document type:** academic/scholarly publication.
—AskIEEE; CISTI; Ei; Genuine Article; KR SourceOne; Linda Hall; SWETS; UnCover. **CCC.**
Formerly: Aircraft Engineering (ISSN 0002-2667)

629.13 UK ISSN 0002-2675
AIRCRAFT ILLUSTRATED. 1968. m. £33 (overseas £52). Ian Allan Ltd., Coombelands House, Coombelands Ln., Addlestone, Surrey KT15 1HY, England. TEL 44-1932-855909. FAX 44-1932-854750. Ed. Allan Burney. R&P contact: Allan Burney. adv. contact: Sheila West. bk.rev.; film rev.; charts; illus.; index; circ. 35,000 (paid). (reprint service avail. from UMI) **Document type:** consumer publication.
—CCC.
Description: Contains news and features on military and civil aviation subjects.

387.732 UK ISSN 0002-2683
AIRCRAFT INDUSTRY RECORD. irreg. £245. Aviation Studies International, Sussex House, Parkside, Wimbledon, London SW19 5NB, England. TEL 44-181-946-5082. **Document type:** directory, trade publication.
Description: Compiles and lists first flight and delivery dates for thousands of aircraft, along with selected chronologies, milestones, and production runs.

629.1 US
AIRCRAFT SURVIVABILITY. q. Joint Technical Coordinating Group - Aircraft Survivability, E-mail: jtcgas@tecnet1.jcte.jcs.mil; URL: http://surviac.flight.wpafb.af.mil/curr_awar/ac__surv_newsletter/newsletters.html. **Document type:** newsletter.
●Available only online.

629.13 387.7 UK ISSN 0967-439X
AIRCRAFT TECHNOLOGY ENGINEERING & MAINTENANCE. (Supplements avail.: Quality and Training; Commuter and Regional Aircraft) 1992. bi-m. £60($120) (overseas £70). Aviation Industry Press, 31 Palace St., London SW1E 5HW, England. TEL 44-171-828-4376. FAX 44-171-828-9154. E-mail: a.i.group@pipex.com. Ed. Paul F. Copping; Pub. Paul F. Copping. R&P contact: Amanda Cooper. adv.: B&W page £1850 ($3050), color page £2870 ($4735); trim 186 x 258; adv. contact: Simon N. Barker. circ. 10,000 (controlled). (back issues avail.) **Document type:** trade publication.
Description: Covers many aspects of aircraft technology, including avionics, design, international and regional airlines, maintenance, and engineering for senior and middle management.

629.1 387.7 UN ISSN 1014-0107
AIRCRAFT TYPE DESIGNATORS/INDICATIFS DE TYPE D'AERONEF/DESIGNADORES DE TIPOS DE AERONAVE. (Text in English, French, Russian, Spanish) 1967. irreg., 24th ed., 1994. $9 (diskette version $200). International Civil Aviation Organization, Attn: Document Sales Unit, 1000 Sherbrooke St. W., Montreal, PQ H3A 2R2, Canada. TEL 514-285-8022. FAX 514-285-6769. TELEX 05-24513. (also avail. in diskette format)

387.7 332 UK ISSN 0966-0348
AIRCRAFT VALUE JOURNAL. 1992. m. £200($320). Aircraft Value Analysis Co., 41A Kilburn Rd., Belper, Derbys. DE56 1HA, England. TEL 44-1773-828872. FAX 44-1773-828603. Ed. Paul Leighton. charts; stat. (back issues avail.) **Document type:** trade publication.
Description: Reviews aircraft value by type for the aviation financing community.

797.55 AT ISSN 0158-8346
AIRFLOW. 1947. q. Aus.$2 per no. Gliding Club of Victoria, Benalla Airport, Benalla, Vic. 3672, Australia. TEL 057-621058. FAX 057-625599. Ed. Bruce Hearn. adv. circ. 500. **Document type:** newsletter.

AIRFORCE. see *MILITARY*

629.133 US ISSN 1065-9757
AIRLINER. 1992. q. $35 (free to qualified personnel). Boeing Co., Commercial Airline Group, Customer Services Division, Box 3707, M-S 2M-89, Seattle, WA 98124-2207. TEL 206-544-8237. FAX 206-544-9178. Ed. Gary Lesser.
—BLDSC (0784.536000).

AIRMAN; official magazine of the U.S. Air Force. see *MILITARY*

629.13 US ISSN 1057-963X
AIRMAN'S INFORMATION MANUAL; official guide to basic flight information and A T C procedures. s-a., plus updates 4/yr. $58 (foreign $72.50). U.S. Federal Aviation Administration, 800 Independence Ave., Washington, DC 20591. TEL 202-655-4000. (Subscr. to: Superintendent of Documents, U.S. Government Printing Office, Box 371954, Pittsburgh, PA 15250-7954. TEL 202-512-1800. FAX 202-512-2250) **Document type:** government publication.
—CISTI.
Former titles: Airman's Information Manual. Basic Flight Information and A T C Procedures; Airman's Information Manual. Part 1: Basic Flight Information and ATC Procedures; Airman's Information Manual. Part 1: Basic Flight Manual and ATC Procedures (ISSN 0002-2764)
Description: Contains the fundamentals required in order to fly in the U.S. National Airspace System; also contains items of interest to pilots concerning health and flight safety.

AIRMED. see *MEDICAL SCIENCES*

629.132 AT ISSN 1321-0564
AIRNEWS. 1950. q. Aus.$25 (membership Aus.$45). Australian Women Pilots' Association, c/o Margaret-Anne Thomas, Ed., 1-4 Campbell Rd., Deepdene, Vic. 3103, Australia. TEL 61-03-817-2826. adv.: page Aus.$400; adv. contact: Margaret-Anne Thomas. circ. 700. **Document type:** newsletter.

AERONAUTICS AND SPACE FLIGHT

387.74 US ISSN 1072-1797
AIRPORT BUSINESS. 1993. 9/yr. $48 (effective 1997). Johnson Hill Press, Inc. (Subsidiary of: Cygnus Publishing), 1233 Janesville Ave., Ft. Atkinson, WI 53538. TEL 920-563-6388. FAX 920-563-1702. Ed. John Infanger; Pub. Paul Bowers. adv. contact: Megan Granlund. charts; illus.; stat. circ. 20,100. (reprint service avail.)
—CCC.
 Formed by the 1993 merger of: F B O - Fixed Base Operator (ISSN 0893-3081) & Airport Services (ISSN 1041-4231); Which was formerly (until 1988): Airport Services Management (ISSN 0002-2829)
 Description: An on-going source of how-to information for managers of airports and airport-based businesses. Covers management, finance and funding, regulations, community relations, sales and marketing, operations, maintenance, security, fuel, and ground service.

629.13 358.4 US ISSN 1067-1048
TL685.3
AIRPOWER; the story of combat aviation. 1971. bi-m. $22 (foreign $28) (effective 1997). Sentry Books, Inc., 10718 White Oak Ave., Box 3324, Granada Hills, CA 91344. TEL 818-368-2012. Ed. Joseph V. Mizrahi. adv.: page $500. bk.rev.=; charts; illus. circ. 80,000. **Document type:** consumer publication.

AIRPOWER JOURNAL. see *MILITARY*

AIRREPORT; South Africa's aviation yearbook. see *TRANSPORTATION — Air Transport*

629.132 797 AT ISSN 0156-6016
AIRSPORT. 1968. bi-m. Aus.$85. Sport Aircraft Association of Australia, P.O. Box 169, Clifton Hill, Vic. 3068, Australia. TEL 61-3-94824716. FAX 61-3-94823936. Ed. Carolyn Dennis. adv. contact: Martin Hone. circ. 2,000. (back issues avail.) **Document type:** newspaper, trade publication.
 Description: Covers amateur aircraft construction and operation.

629.132 IT ISSN 1122-231X
ALISEI. 1992. m. L.7000 per no. (Touring Club Italiano) Touring Periodici s.r.l., Corso Italia 10, 20122 Milan, Italy. TEL 02-85261. FAX 02-8526299. Ed. Egidio Gavazzi. adv.: B&W page L.13000000, color page L.20000000. circ. 60,000. **Document type:** consumer publication.
 Description: Covers the hobby of small aircraft piloting and travel.

629.4 US ISSN 0516-9593
AMERICAN ASTRONAUTICAL SOCIETY. PROCEEDINGS OF THE ANNUAL MEETING. (Part of the Advances in the Astronautical Sciences Series (ISSN 0065-3438)) 1957. a. price varies. (American Astronautical Society, Inc.) Univelt, Inc., Box 28130, San Diego, CA 92198. TEL 619-746-4005. FAX 609-746-3139. E-mail: 76121.1532@compuserve.com. Ed. Robert H. Jacobs. cum. index. (back issues avail.) **Document type:** proceedings.

629.133 US ISSN 0733-4249
CODEN: PFASDL
AMERICAN HELICOPTER SOCIETY. ANNUAL FORUM. PROCEEDINGS. 1943. a. $180 to non-members; members $135 (effective 1997). American Helicopter Society, Inc., 217 N. Washington St., Alexandria, VA 22314. TEL 703-684-6777. FAX 703-739-9279. circ. 650. (back issues avail.) **Document type:** proceedings.
—BLDSC (1085.665000).
 Formerly: American Helicopter Society. National Forum. Proceedings (ISSN 0065-8510)

629.133 US ISSN 0002-8711
TL716.A1 CODEN: JHESAK
AMERICAN HELICOPTER SOCIETY. JOURNAL. 1956. q. $60 (foreign $75) (effective 1997). American Helicopter Society, Inc., 217 N. Washington St., Alexandria, VA 22314. TEL 703-684-6777. FAX 703-739-9279. URL: http://www.vtol.org/journal/journal/html. Ed. David Jenney. illus. circ. 7,400. **Indexed:** Appl.Mech.Rev., ASCA, Curr.Cont., Eng.Ind., INSPEC (1984-). **Document type:** bulletin.
—BLDSC (4686.350000); AskIEEE; CISTI; Genuine Article; KR SourceOne; SWETS; UnCover.

001.94 US
ANCIENT SKIES. 1974. bi-m. $12. Ancient Astronaut Society, 1921 St. Johns Ave., Highland Park, IL 60035-3178. TEL 847-295-8899. FAX 847-295-0868. Ed. Gene M. Phillips; Pub. Gene M. Phillips. R&P contact: Gene M. Phillips. adv. contact: Gene M. Phillips. bk.rev. circ. 5,000. (tabloid format; back issues avail.) **Document type:** bulletin.
 Description: Examines the search for evidence of extraterrestrial visitations to Earth in ancient times, and to civilizations in prehistory.

340 387.7 CN ISSN 0701-158X
K1
ANNALS OF AIR AND SPACE LAW/ANNALES DE DROIT AERIEN ET SPATIAL. 1976. s-a. Can.$120 (effective 1996-1997). McGill University, Centre for Research of Air and Space Law, 3661 Peel St., Montreal, PQ H3A 1X1, Canada. TEL 514-398-5095. FAX 514-398-8197. E-mail: milde__m@falaw.lan.mcgill.ca; URL: http://icarus.iasl.mcgill.ca. Ed. Michael Milde. bk.rev.=; cum.index: 1976-1987. circ. 1,200. (back issues avail.; reprint service avail. from WSH) **Indexed:** C.L.I., Ind.Can.L.P.L., L.R.I., Leg.Per. **Document type:** academic/scholarly publication, monographic series.
—BLDSC (1035.800000); CISTI; KR SourceOne; UnCover.
 Refereed Serial

629.13 US
ANNALS OF BALLOON HISTORY AND MUSEOLOGY. 1991. irreg. $30 (foreign $35). 15155 County Rd. 32, Mayer, MN 55360. TEL 612-657-2237. Ed. Paul Maravelas. bk.rev. **Document type:** academic/scholarly publication.
 Description: Scholarly essays on history of the free balloon and the collecting of related material.

ANOMALIES; observateur des parasciences. see *PARAPSYCHOLOGY AND OCCULTISM*

387.7 US ISSN 0003-5823
ANTIQUE AIRPLANE ASSOCIATION NEWS. 1953. q. $36 membership (includes APM Bulletin and International Antique Airplane Digest). Antique Airplane Association, Inc., 22001 Bluegrass Rd., Ottumwa, IA 52501-8569. TEL 515-938-2773. Ed. Robert L. Taylor; Pub. Robert L. Taylor. R&P contact: Robert L. Taylor. adv. contact: L. Reis. bk.rev.; charts; illus.; tr.lit. circ. 5,000.
 Description: Presents articles, photos and drawings of antique and classical airplanes of past and present.

629.1 BL ISSN 0103-5002
ANUARIO AEROESPACIAL BRASILEIRO/BRAZILIAN AEROSPACE YEARBOOK. (Text in Portuguese; summaries in English) 1983. a. exchange basis. Aviacao em Revista Editora, Ltda., Rua da Consolacao 1992, 10o andar, Cerqueira Cesar, 01302-000 Sao Paulo, Brazil. TEL 55-11-2570577. FAX 55-11-2570577. Ed. Ernesto Klotzel; Pub. Helcio Estrella. R&P contact: Helcio Estrella. adv.: B&W page $6300, color page $7400; trim 210 x 280; adv. contact: Francisco Carlos Alves. charts; illus.; stat. circ. 24,000. **Document type:** directory.
 Description: Contains sector analysis, performance statistics, trend indicators, data on aircraft fleets, and supply and service company listings.

629.13255 US ISSN 1086-928X
VG93
APPROACH MECH; the naval safety center's aviation magazine. 1955. bi-m. $15. U.S. Naval Safety Center, 375 A St., Norfolk, VA 23511-4399. TEL 804-444-3520. E-mail: edapprch@tecnet1.jcte.jcs.mil. (Subscr. to: Superintendent of Documents, U.S. Government Printing Office, Box 371954, Pittsburgh, PA 15250-7954. TEL 202-512-1800. FAX 202-512-2250) Ed. L.Cdr. Kenn Skaggs. charts; illus. circ. 13,000. (back issues avail.) **Indexed:** Ind.U.S.Gov.Per. **Document type:** government publication.
—BLDSC (1580.200000); CISTI; Linda Hall; UnCover.
 Formed by the 1995 merger of: Approach (ISSN 0570-4979); (1968-1995): Mech (ISSN 0025-6471)

629.1 UK ISSN 0262-4923
ARCHIVE (AIR-BRITAIN); civil aviation historical quarterly. 1980. q. £14. Air-Britain (Historians) Ltd., 1 East St., Tonbridge, Kent TN9 1HP, England. (Subscr. to: c/o 15 Mallory Close, St. Athan, South Glamorgan, CF6 9JJ, England) illus. circ. 1,500.

629.1 358.4 SZ ISSN 0252-9793
HD9743.A1
ARMADA INTERNATIONAL. (Editions in English, French and German) 1977. 6/yr. 106 SFr. (outside Europe $106) (effective 1997). Armada International AG, Thurgauerstr. 39, CH-8050 Zurich, Switzerland. TEL 41-1-3085050. FAX 41-1-3085055. Ed. Eric Biass; Pub. Mathias Schwegler. R&P contact: Peter Stierlin. adv. contact: Peter Stierlin. circ. 28,124. (reprint service avail.) **Indexed:** Abstr.Mil.Bibl., Air Un.Lib.Ind., Alloys Ind., DM& T, Eng.Mat.Abstr., Met.Abstr.Ind., Met.Abstr., Nonfer.Met.Alert, PCC Alert, PROMT, Steels Alert, World Alum.Abstr. **Document type:** trade publication.
—BLDSC (1682.400000); SWETS.
 Description: International news of weapon systems and armed forces.

629.13 UK ISSN 0004-2153
ARMAMENT DATA SHEETS. 1954. q. $320. Aviation Studies International, Sussex House, Parkside, Wimbledon, London SW19 5NB, England. TEL 44-181-946-5082. charts; cum.index. **Document type:** trade publication, directory.
 Description: Compiles data on rockets, missiles, mines, LGBs, guns, gas-fills, clusters, depth charges, sons, fire bombs, warheads, ECM, torpedoes, drones, readiness, and sonobuoys.

ARMY AVIATION. see *MILITARY*

ARMY FLIER. see *MILITARY*

387.7 US ISSN 0004-2617
ARNOLD AIR LETTER. 1950. q. $5 to non-members. Arnold Air Society, National Publications Headquarters, AFROTC Det 045, San Jose State University, One Washington Sq., San Jose, CA 95192-0051. TEL 214-886-5200. (Alt. addr.: James Handley Squadron, 830th AFROTC Det., E. Texas State University, Commerce, TX 75428) Ed. Col. Randal G. Kelly. adv.; charts; illus. circ. 7,500.

629.13 SI ISSN 0129-1289
ASIA - PACIFIC AVIATION AND ENGINEERING JOURNAL. 1976. 4/yr. $90. Singapore Institute of Aerospace Engineers, Airline House A 5F, 25 Airline Rd., Singapore 1781, Singapore. TEL 542-0688. FAX 542-9034. Ed. Poon Chia-Wee. adv. circ. 10,000. **Document type:** academic/scholarly publication, trade publication.
 Formerly (until Dec. 1987): Aircraft Engineer (ISSN 0129-9913)

ASIAN AIRLINES & AEROSPACE. see *TRANSPORTATION — Air Transport*

629.1 SI ISSN 0129-9972
ASIAN AVIATION. (Text in English) 1981. m. S.70 in Asia & Pacific $60; elsewhere $75 (free to qualified personnel). Asian Aviation Publications Pte. Ltd., 2 Leng Kee Rd., No. 04-01, Thye Hong Centre, Singapore 159086, Singapore. TEL 65-474-7088. FAX 65-479-6668. Ed. Colin Gibson. adv.; bk.rev.; circ. 10,951 (controlled). (back issues avail.) **Document type:** trade publication.
—SWETS.
 Description: Activities of the aerospace industry of the Asia-Pacific region: airlines, air forces, airports and space communications.

ASSOCIATION TECHNIQUE MARITIME ET AERONAUTIQUE, PARIS. BULLETIN. see *TRANSPORTATION — Ships And Shipping*

629.4 028.5 US
ASTRO-NEWS. 1985. q. free to members. Young Astronaut Council, 1308 19th St., N.W., Washington, DC 20036. TEL 202-682-1984. FAX 202-775-1773. Ed. Cecelia Blalock. R&P contact: Cecelia Blalock. (back issues avail.) **Document type:** newsletter.
 Description: Organizational newsletter giving updates on space-related news, program and membership activities.

AERONAUTICS AND SPACE FLIGHT

629.4   PL   ISSN 0004-623X
ASTRONAUTYKA. 1958. bi-m. $16.20. Polskie Towarzystwo Astronautyczne - Polish Astronautical Society, Ul. Z. Krasinskiego 54, 01-755 Warsaw, Poland. TEL 48-22-3082703. (Dist. by: Ars Polona-Ruch, Krakowskie Przedmiescie 7, Warsaw, Poland) Ed. Pawel Elsztein. bk.rev.; charts; illus. circ. 3,000. **Indexed:** IBR, Ref.Zh.
   Description: Popular-scientific magazine devoted to astronautics and space research.

ASTRONOMI- OCH RYMDFART. see *ASTRONOMY*

629.1 797.5   CN
ATLANTIC INFLIGHT. 1978. q. Can.$10($8) (effective 1997). Hang Gliding Association of Newfoundland, 16 Woodbine Ave., Corner Brook, NF A2H 3N8, Canada. TEL 709-785-2697. Ed. Chris Walters. R&P contact: Chris Walters. adv.; bk.rev.; stat.; tr.lit.; circ. 35 (controlled). (looseleaf format) **Document type:** newsletter.
   Description: Provides coverage of hanggliding and paragliding events in Eastern Canada.

AUSTRALIAN AEROSPACE INDUSTRY CAPABILITY DIRECTORY. see *BUSINESS AND ECONOMICS — Trade And Industrial Directories*

629.13   AT   ISSN 0004-9123
AUSTRALIAN FLYING. 1961. bi-m. Aus.$31.50 (foreign Aus.$88) (effective Aug. 1996). Yaffa Publishing Group, 17-21 Bellevue St., Surry Hills, N.S.W. 2010, Australia. TEL 61-2-92812333. FAX 61-2-92812750. E-mail: yaffa@yaffa.com.au. Ed. Paul Phelan; Pub. Tracy Yaffa. adv.: B&W page Aus.$1645, color page Aus.$2305; trim 273 x 210; adv. contact: Carol Roselli. bk.rev.; illus. circ. 10,755. **Document type:** consumer publication.
   Description: Industry magazine devoted to the needs of today's aviation professional. Covers both civil and military flying disciplines, from fixed-wing to helicopter operations.

629.13   AT   ISSN 0004-9204
AUSTRALIAN GLIDING. 1950. m. Aus.$28.80 (foreign Aus.$40.50) includes Yearbook. Gliding Federation of Australia, G.P.O. Box 1650, Adelaide, S.A. 5001, Australia. TEL 61-8-82316263. FAX 61-8-84104711. E-mail: AGeditor@gfa.on.net. Ed. Noel Matthews. R&P contact: D.E. Thomas. adv.: page Aus.$240; trim 255 x 185; adv. contact: Ray Munn. bk.rev.; charts; illus.; stat.; circ. 3,500 (paid). **Indexed:** Sportsearch (1976-). **Document type:** newsletter.
   Description: Carries world wide news, technical and semi-technical features.

629.13   AT   ISSN 0084-7364
AUSTRALIAN GLIDING YEARBOOK. 1969. a. Aus.$5. Gliding Federation of Australia, G.P.O. Box 1650, Adelaide, S.A. 5001, Australia. TEL 61-8-82316263. FAX 61-8-84104711. Ed. Noel Matthews. R&P contact: E.R.N. Thomas. adv.: page Aus.$120; trim 255 x 185; adv. contact: Ray Munn. bk.rev.; circ. 3,500 (paid).
   Description: Contains detailed information on all gliding clubs in Australia, complete gliding statistics, lists of national and international records, competition numbers, etc.

001.94   AT   ISSN 0156-742X
AUSTRALIAN INTERNATIONAL U F O FLYING SAUCER RESEARCH. 1978. q. Aus.$12 membership. Australian Flying Saucer Society, G.P.O. Box 2004, Adelaide, S.A. 5001, Australia. Ed. Colin Norris; Pub. Colin Norris. **Document type:** newsletter.

001.94   AT
AUSTRALIAN U F O BULLETIN. 1972. q. Aus.$15($20) Victorian U.F.O. Research Society, P.O. Box 43, Moorabbin, Vic. 3189, Australia. TEL 61-3-95922502. FAX 61-3-95922502. E-mail: vufors@zemail.com.au. Ed. Judith M. Magee. R&P contact: Judith M. Magee. adv.; bk.rev.; charts. circ. 500. **Document type:** bulletin.

629.13   AU   ISSN 0005-0555
AUSTROFLUG; die Luft-und Raumfahrtzeitschrift Oesterreichs. 1951. 6/yr. S.250. Horden Magazinverlag, Kettenbrueckengasse 22, A-1040 Vienna, Austria. Ed. Harald Laa. adv.; bk.rev.; illus.; tr.lit. circ. 28,000.

629.13   IT   ISSN 0005-2027
AVIA.* 1960. m. L.1500.($2.50) Aeronews, Aeroporto Fiumicino, Rome, Italy. Ed. Romano Nodari. adv.; bk.rev.; illus.

629.1   BL   ISSN 0102-4876
AVIACAO EM REVISTA/AVIATION MAGAZINE. (Text in Portuguese; summaries in English) 1938. m. (except Nov.-Dec. combined). $100 or exchange basis (effective 1997). Aviacao em Revista Editora Ltda., Rua da Consolacao 1992, 10o andar, 01302-000 Sao Paulo, Brazil. TEL 55-11-2570577. FAX 55-11-2570577. Ed. Ernesto Klotzel; Pub. Helcio Estrella. adv.: B&W page $5700, color page $6750; trim 210 x 280; adv. contact: Francisco Carlos Alves. bk.rev.; illus. circ. 24,000. **Document type:** trade publication.
   Formerly: Aviacao e Astronautica (ISSN 0005-206X)
   Description: Covers the aviation industry, airlines, airports, air cargo, training, market, technology and sport flying.

AVIACION. see *MILITARY*

629.13 629.4   AG   ISSN 0045-1177
AVIACION Y ASTRONAUTICA.* vol.11, 1971. bi-m. Arg.$25.($8.) Av. Belgrano 1735, Buenos Aires, Argentina. Ed. Gilberto Julian Riega. adv.; bibl.; charts; illus.; tr.lit.

629.13   FR
AVIAGUIDE; ou voler en Ile-de-France? 1980. s-a. 1013 Editions, 7 rue de Blaru, 78270 Jeufosse, France. TEL 30-98-92-92. FAX 30-98-93-13. Ed. Christian Sainderichin. adv.; circ. 2,500 (paid). (back issues avail.) **Document type:** directory.
   Description: Provides information on where to rent a light aircraft (or helicopter) and where to learn to pilot an aircraft as well as corresponding prices.

629.13   FR   ISSN 0005-2094
AVIASPORT; le magazine du pilote. 1954. m. 380 F. Societe d'Edition de Periodiques d'Aviation Generale, 59 av. Aristide Briand, 93190 Livry Gargan, France. TEL 43-02-10-64. FAX 43-01-83-11. Ed. Jean Molveau. adv.; bk.rev.; abstr.; charts; illus.; stat. circ. 18,000.
   —BLDSC (1837.892000).

629.13   CN
AVIATION & AEROSPACE DIRECTORY AND BUYER'S GUIDE. a. Can.$25 (U.S. $20; elsewhere $25) (effective 1997). Baxter Publishing Co., 310 Dupont St., Toronto, ON M5R 1V9, Canada. TEL 416-968-7252. FAX 416-968-7569. E-mail: aa@baxter.net; URL: http://www.baxter.net. adv. contact: Marlene Schwengers. (back issues avail.) **Document type:** directory.
   Description: Covers all aspects of the aviation and aerospace industry.

340 629.13   UK   ISSN 1352-4003
AVIATION & SPACE LAW REPORTS. 1994. m. (with a. cumulation). £295($445) includes cumulation (effective 1996). Oxford University Press, Oxford Journals, Walton St., Oxford OX2 6DP, England. TEL 01865-56767. FAX 01865-56646. (Subscr. in U.S. and Canada to: Oxford University Press Inc., 2001 Evans Rd., Cary, NC 27513. TEL 919-677-0977. FAX 919-677-1714) **Document type:** academic/scholarly publication.

629.132   US   ISSN 0147-9911
TL721.4
THE AVIATION CONSUMER. 1971. m. $84 (foreign $108) (effective 1996). Belvoir Publications, Inc., 75 Holly Hill Ln., Box 2626, Greenwich, CT 06836-2626. TEL 203-661-6111. FAX 203-661-4802. (Subscr. to: Box 420234, Palm Coast, FL 32142) Ed. Richard B. Weeghman. **Document type:** consumer publication.
   —CISTI; UnCover.

629.1   US   ISSN 0193-4597
TL501
AVIATION DAILY. vol.205, 1973. d. (5/w.). $1340 (foreign $1510). McGraw-Hill Companies, Aviation Week Group (Washington), 1200 G St., N.W., Ste. 200, Washington, DC 20005. TEL 202-383-2350. Ed. Edmund Pinto. charts; stat. (looseleaf format) **Document type:** newspaper, trade publication.
   ●Also available online. Vendor(s): Dow Jones News Retrieval, Knight-Ridder Information, Inc. (File no.624/McGRAW-HILL PUBLICATIONS ONLINE), Lexis-Nexis (AVDLY), NewsNet (AE28).
   —CCC.
   Incorporates: Regional Aviation Weekly.

629.1 374   US
AVIATION EDUCATION NEWS BULLETIN. bi-m. Aviation Distributors and Manufacturers Association, 1900 Arch St., Philadelphia, PA 19103-1498. TEL 215-564-3484. Ed. Maureen Waddington. **Document type:** newsletter.
   Description: For educators and students interested in aviation.

AVIATION EUROPE. see *TRANSPORTATION — Air Transport*

629.13 333.79   US
AVIATION FACILITIES ENERGY ASSOCIATION. ANNUAL REPORT. a. Aviation Facilities Energy Association, Atlanta Airlines Terminal Corp., Box 45171, Atlanta, GA 30320. TEL 404-530-2105.

629.13 333.79   US
AVIATION FACILITIES ENERGY ASSOCIATION. ENERGY CONSUMPTION ANALYSIS REPORT. a. Aviation Facilities Energy Association, Atlanta Airlines Terminal Corp., Box 45171, Atlanta, GA 30320. TEL 404-530-2105.

629.13   AT   ISSN 0815-4392
AVIATION HERITAGE. 1960. q. Aus.$40 (foreign Aus.$50). Aviation Historical Society of Australia, P.O. Box 2007, S. Melbourne, Vic. 3205, Australia. TEL 61-3-5800140. Eds. Bill and Judith Baker. bk.rev. (back issues avail.)
   Formerly: Aviation Historical Society of Australia. Journal (ISSN 0045-1185)
   Description: Covers Australian and Pacific Islands historical events and personalities.

387.7   NZ   ISSN 0110-5493
AVIATION HISTORICAL SOCIETY OF NEW ZEALAND. JOURNAL. 1958. a. NZ.$40. Aviation Historical Society of New Zealand, P.O. Box 12-009, Wellington 6038, New Zealand. TEL 64-4-471-4070. FAX 64-4-471-0395. Ed. C.F.L. Jenks. adv.; bk.rev.; bibl.; charts; illus.; index. circ. 400. **Indexed:** Ind.N.Z.Per. **Document type:** academic/scholarly publication.
   —CCC.

629.13   US   ISSN 1076-8858
TL515
AVIATION HISTORY. 1990. bi-m. $24 (Canada $30; elsewhere $48). Cowles History Group, 741 Miller Dr., S.E., No. D-2, Leesburg, VA 20175. TEL 703-771-9400; 800-829-3340. FAX 703-779-8345. (Subscr. to: 11 Commerce Blvd., Palm Coast, FL 32164. TEL 800-829-3340) Ed. Arthur H. Sanfelici; Pub. Thomas G. O'Keefe. adv. contact: Tamra Varda. bk.rev.; software rev.; illus.; maps. circ. 75,136. (back issues avail.) **Document type:** consumer publication.
   Former titles: Aviation (ISSN 1067-4799); Aviation Heritage (ISSN 1054-335X)
   Description: For history enthusiasts. Features man's dream of flight, from our earlies attempts to today's Mach 5 jets.

629.13   CN
AVIATION IN CANADA. (Editions in English, French) 1993. irreg. Can.$48($58) (foreign $67). Statistics Canada, Operations and Integration Division, Circulation Management, Jean Talon Bldg., 2-C12, Tunney's Pasture, Ottawa, ON K1A 0T6, Canada. TEL 613-951-7277; 800-267-6677. FAX 613-951-1584. URL: http://www.statcan.ca.
   Description: Describes the Canadian aviation industry from its earliest years to present with up to 75 years of operating and financial data and information on key markets, airports, air regulation and Canada's safety record.

629.1   UK
TL724
AVIATION INDUSTRY DEVELOPMENT. 1986. a. £55. Sterling Publications Ltd., 86-88 Edgware Rd., London W2 2YW, England. TEL 44-171-915-9600. FAX 44-171-915-9619. R&P contact: Sandy Tucker. circ. 10,000. **Document type:** trade publication.
   —BLDSC (9352.405000); CISTI.
   Former titles: World Aerospace Technology (ISSN 0959-0846); (until 1990): World Aerospace Profile (ISSN 0268-8670)

AERONAUTICS AND SPACE FLIGHT

629.1 US
TL671.9
AVIATION MAINTENANCE. 1982. 12/yr. free to qualified personnel. Phillips Business Information, Inc., 1201 Seven Locks Rd., Potomac, MD 20854. TEL 301-424-3338. FAX 301-309-3487. E-mail: pbi@phillips.com. Ed. Clifford Stoud. adv.; circ. 37,488 (controlled). **Document type:** trade publication.
—CISTI; UnCover. **CCC.**
 Formerly: Aviation Equipment Maintenance (ISSN 0745-0214)
 Description: For aviation service professionals in commercial, corporate and military aviation maintenance.

629.1 US
AVIATION MAINTENANCE FOUNDATION INTERNATIONAL. INDUSTRY REPORT. a. Aviation Maintenance Foundation International, Box 2826, Redmond, WA 98073. TEL 360-658-8980. FAX 360-658-7274. **Document type:** trade publication.

AVIATION MASTER FILE. see COMMUNICATIONS — Abstracting, Bibliographies, Statistics

629.132 US ISSN 0005-2140
AVIATION MECHANICS BULLETIN. 1953. bi-m. $35 in N. America; elsewhere $40. Flight Safety Foundation, Inc., 601 Madison St., Ste. 300, Alexandria, VA 22314-1756. TEL 703-739-6700. FAX 703-739-6708. URL: http://flightsafety.org/ aviation_mech.html. (reprint service avail. from UMI) **Document type:** trade publication.
—CISTI.
 Former titles (until 1960): Aviation; Mechanic's Bulletin.
 Description: For aviation maintenance technicians, with an emphasis on airline and corporate operations.

616.98 US ISSN 0067-2661
AVIATION MEDICAL EDUCATION SERIES. 1965. irreg. U.S. Federal Aviation Administration, Aviation Medicine Office, 800 Independence Ave., S.W., Washington, DC 20591. TEL 202-655-4000. **Document type:** government publication, monographic series.

AVIATION MEDICINE. see MEDICAL SCIENCES

387.7 US ISSN 0145-1014
AVIATION MONTHLY; monthly aviation safety summary and consumer report. 1973. m. $39. Peter Katz Productions, Inc., Box 831, White Plains, NY 10602-0831. TEL 914-949-7443. Ed. Peter J. Katz. stat.; index. circ. 18,000. (back issues avail.)
 Formerly (until 1976): M A S S Report.
 Description: Aviation accident report briefs.

387.7 US ISSN 0005-2159
AVIATION REPORTS. (Includes: Civil Tuesdays and Military Fridays) 1951. w. $1100. Aviation Studies International, Sussex House, Parkside, Wimbledon, London SW19 5NB, England.
TEL 44-181-946-5082. charts. **Document type:** directory, trade publication.
 Description: Compiles aerospace equipment and intelligence data. Covers economic, technical, and acquisition needs, government news and analysis, and trends.

629.132 US ISSN 0277-1764
AVIATION SAFETY; the twice-monthly journal of accident prevention. 1981. s-m. $84 (foreign $108) (effective 1996). Belvoir Publications, Inc., 75 Holly Hill Ln., Box 2626, Greenwich, CT 06836-2626. TEL 203-661-6111. FAX 203-661-4802. (Subscr. to: Box 420234, Palm Coast, FL 32142) Ed. Mark M. Lacagnina. **Document type:** trade publication.
—BLDSC (1838.578000); CISTI.
 Description: Offers professional and recreational pilots important safety information, tips, and related news.

629.1 US
AVIATION SPACE WRITERS ASSOCIATION. YEARBOOK AND DIRECTORY; including roster of membership. 1938. a. $95. Aviation - Space Writers Association, 6540 50th St., N., Oakdale, MN 55128-1708. TEL 614-221-1900. FAX 614-221-1989. Ed. Madeline Field. adv. circ. 1,200. **Document type:** directory.
 Formerly: Aviation Space Writers Association Manual.

387.7 UK ISSN 0005-2167
AVIATION STUDIES INTERNATIONAL. OFFICIAL PRICE LIST. 1954. q. $395. Aviation Studies International, Sussex House, Parkside, Wimbledon, London SW19 5NB, England. TEL 44-181-946-5082. charts. **Document type:** directory, trade publication.
 Description: Lists more than 1,000 new and historical prices of aircraft, ships, avionics, radio, weapons, missiles, helicopters, engines, and ACVs.

629.13 US ISSN 0005-2175
TL501
AVIATION WEEK & SPACE TECHNOLOGY. 1916. w. $84 to individuals; institutions $105. McGraw-Hill Companies, Aviation Week Group (New York), 1221 Ave. of the Americas, New York, NY 10020. TEL 212-512-3034. FAX 212-512-4225. TELEX 2323265 MGH PUBNET. E-mail: pduggan@ mcgraw-hill.com; URL: http://www.awgnet.com/ aviation/. (Subscr. to: Box 503, Hightstown, NJ 08520-9899) Ed. David M. North. adv.; charts; illus. circ. 105,000. (also avail. in microfilm from UMI) **Indexed:** A.I.Abstr., A.S.& T.Ind., ABI Inform., Abstr.Mil.Bibl., Acad.Ind., Amer.Bibl.Slavic & E.Eur.Stud., Appl.Mech.Rev., ASCA, B.P.I., BMT, Bus.Ind., CAD CAM Abstr., Chem.Abstr., DM & T, Environ.Abstr., Excerp.Med., Fluidex, Hlth.Ind., HRIS, Ind.Sci.Rev., INIS Atomind., Int.Aerosp.Abstr., Mag.Ind., Mid.East: Abstr.& Ind., Ocean.Abstr., PMR, Pollut.Abstr., PROMT, R.G., R.G.Abstr., SRI, Tel.Abstr., Tr.& Indus.Ind. **Document type:** trade publication.
●Also available online. Vendor(s): Dow Jones News Retrieval, Knight-Ridder Information, Inc. (File no.624/McGRAW-HILL PUBLICATIONS ONLINE), Lexis-Nexis, NewsNet (AE30).
Also available on CD-ROM.
—BLDSC (1838.695000); CISTI; Ei; Genuine Article; KR SourceOne; Linda Hall; SWETS; UMI; UnCover. **CCC.**
 Description: Provides current news and information related to the aviation and aerospace industry.

629.1 384.554 US
AVIATION WEEK VIDEO. q. $49.95 per no. McGraw-Hill Companies, Video Magazine Department, 1221 Ave. of the Americas, 42nd Fl., New York, NY 10020. TEL 212-512-3213. FAX 212-512-4225. adv. (video cassette)
 Formerly: Aviation Week Video Magazine.

629.13 IT ISSN 0391-7738
HE9761.9.I9
AVIAZIONE. (Includes a. directory: L'Aviazione in Italia) (Text in Italian; summaries in English) 1963. 9/yr. $109 (effective 1995). Publi & Consult S.P.A., Via Tagliamento 29, 00198 Rome, Italy.
TEL 39-6-8543603. FAX 39-6-85350021. Ed. Paolo F. Bancale. adv.: B&W page 3600 ptas., color page 5600; trim 185 x 275; adv. contact: Luana Guido. bk.rev.; abstr.; bibl.; charts; illus.; stat.; index, cum.index. circ. 14,300. **Indexed:** DM&T; PROMT. **Document type:** trade publication.
 Former titles (until 1977): Aviazione di Linea Difesa e Spazio (ISSN 0391-755X); (until 1971): Aviazione di Linea, Aeronautica e Spazio (ISSN 0391-7541); (until 1966): Aviazione di Linea (ISSN 0005-2205)

629.13 SP
AVION REVUE. 1982. m. 4800 ptas. (Europe 8000 ptas.; elsewhere 11000 ptas.). Luike - Motorpress, C. Ancora, 40, 28045 Madrid, Spain.
TEL 34-1-347-0100. FAX 34-1-347-0143. TELEX 42022 LUIK E. Ed. Jose Maria Pares; Pub. Jose Luis Samaranch. adv.: B&W page 250000 ptas., color page 360000 ptas.; trim 210 x 248; adv. contact: Miguel Munoz. illus. circ. 19,893. **Document type:** trade publication.

629.13 621.38 US ISSN 0273-7639
AVIONICS. 1977. m. free to qualified personnel. Phillips Business Information, Inc., 1201 Seven Locks Rd., Potomac, MD 20854. TEL 301-424-3338. FAX 301-309-3847. E-mail: pbi@phillips.com. Eds Dave Robb, Bill Levey. adv.; bk.rev.; charts; illus.; pat.; stat.; index; circ. controlled. (back issues avail.) **Document type:** trade publication.
—BLDSC (1839.162000); CISTI; SWETS. **CCC.**
 Description: Discusses aviation electronics in the airline, military, commuter and general aviation industries.

629.132 US
AVIONICS MAINTENANCE CONFERENCE. BOOKLET. irreg. Avionics Maintenance Conference, c/o Aeronautical Radio, Inc., 2551 Riva Rd., Annapolis, MD 21401. TEL 301-266-4116.

629.1 US
AVIONICS MAINTENANCE CONFERENCE. CONFERENCE PROGRAM. a. Avionics Maintenance Conference, c/o Aeronautical Radio, Inc., 2551 Riva Rd., Annapolis, MD 21401. TEL 301-266-4116.

629.1 US
AVIONICS MAINTENANCE CONFERENCE. CONFERENCE REPORT. a. Avionics Maintenance Conference, c/o Aeronautical Radio, Inc., 2551 Riva Rd., Annapolis, MD 21401. TEL 301-266-4116.

629.132 621.38 US
AVIONICS NEWS MAGAZINE. 1959. m. free. Aircraft Electronics Association, Box 1981, Independence, MO 64055. TEL 816-373-6565. FAX 816-478-3100. Ed. Monte R. Mitchell. adv. circ. 4,500.

629.13 US
AVIONICS NEWSLETTER. 1974. m. membership. National Avionics Society, Box 5633, Denver, CO 80217-5633. Ed. Allan J. Lundquist. adv.; bk.rev. circ. 200. (looseleaf format; back issues avail.) **Document type:** newsletter.
 Description: Review of developments in aviation and avionics systems, including satellite communication and navigation systems.

629.1 UK
B H A B INFORMATION HANDBOOK. 1972. a. £7.50 (£9 in U.S.). British Helicopter Advisory Board, Graham Ste., W. Entrance, Fairoaks Airport, Chobham, Woking, Surrey GU24 8HX, England. TEL 44-1276-856100. FAX 44-1276-856126. Ed. J.P.W. Friedberger. adv.; stat.; tr.lit. circ. 2,000. **Document type:** trade publication.
 Description: Reference guide for civil helicopter users.

629.132 GW
B L N - BAYERISCHE LUFTSPORT-NACHRICHTEN. 1962. bi-m. DM.20. (Deutscher Aero Club e.V.) Luftsport-Verband Bayern e.V., Prinzregentenstr. 120, 81677 Munich, Germany.
TEL 089-45503216. FAX 089-45503211. Ed. Juergen Woerdehoff. **Document type:** newsletter.

629.132 UK
B W P A NEWSLETTER. 1955. q. membership. British Women Pilots Association, Rochester Airport, Chatham, Kent ME5 9SD, England.
TEL 0993-779353. FAX 0580-212089. Ed. Molly White. adv.; bk.rev. circ. 500. (processed) **Document type:** newsletter.
 Former titles: B W P A Gazette; B W P A Magazine.

629.1 IS
BAAVIR. (Text in Hebrew) 1987. bi-m. Baavir Publications, P.O. Box 1173, Rehovot 76 111, Israel. TEL 03-959976.

629.13 531.64 US
BALLAST (ATLANTA). q. Aviation Facilities Energy Association, Atlanta Airlines Terminal Corp., Box 415171, Atlanta, GA 30320. TEL 404-530-2105.

BALLOON LIFE; the magazine for hot air ballooning. see SPORTS AND GAMES

387 797 US ISSN 0194-6854
BALLOONING. vol.10, 1977. bi-m. $45. (Balloon Federation of America) Ballooning Magazine, Box 400, Indianola, IA 50125. FAX 515-961-3537. E-mail: ballon-fed@bfa.ycg.org; URL: http://www.bfa. ycg.org. adv.; bk.rev.; charts; illus.; tr.lit. circ. 5,100.

629.1 UK ISSN 0961-2211
BALLOONS AND AIRSHIPS. 1990. bi-m. £19.50 (rest of world £25.50). Kelsey Publishing Ltd., Kelsey House, 77 High St., Beckenham, Kent BR3 1AN, England. TEL 44-181-658-3531. FAX 44-181-650-8035. adv. **Document type:** consumer publication.

629.1 FR ISSN 1024-5464
BAROMETRE DU TRANSPORT AERIEN/AVIATION INDUSTRY BAROMETER. (Text in English, French) 1994. q. Institut du Transport Aerien, 103 rue la Boetie, 75008 Paris, France. TEL 33-1-43593868. FAX 33-1-43594737. TELEX 642 584F. pp./issue: 40.
 Description: Analysis of current trends in the aviation industry.

AERONAUTICS AND SPACE FLIGHT

629.1   CC   ISSN 1001-5965
CODEN: BHHDE8
BEIJING HANGKONG HANGTIAN DAXUE XUEBAO/BEIJING UNIVERSITY OF AERONAUTICS AND ASTRONAUTICS. JOURNAL. (Text in Chinese; abstracts in English) 1956-1960; resumed 1980. q. Y5 per no. Beijing University of Aeronautics and Astronautics, 37 Xueyuan Rd., Haidian District, Beijing 100083, People's Republic of China. TEL 2017251. Eds. Zhang Guilian, Huang Junqin. **Document type:** academic/scholarly publication.
—BLDSC (4707.892700); AskIEEE; CASDDS; KR SourceOne.
Description: Contains original papers on aeronautics and astronautics.

629.1   IS   ISSN 0302-8194
TL527.I75
BIAF/ISRAEL AVIATION AND SPACE MAGAZINE. (Text in Hebrew; summaries in English) 1972. q. $25. (Israel Society of Aeronautics and Astronautics) Yehuda Borovik Ed. & Pub., P.O. Box 3144, Rishon le-Zion 75131, Israel. TEL 972-3-9664034. FAX 972-3-9649599. adv.; bk.rev.; bibl.; charts; illus. circ. 4,000. (back issues avail.) **Document type:** trade publication.
Description: Covers current developments in military and civil aviation and aerospace in Israel and the world, as well as historical topics.

358.4   IS   ISSN 0006-3878
BITAON HEYL HA-AVIR/ISRAEL AIR FORCE MAGAZINE. 1948. bi-m. $50. (Air Force of Israel) Ministry of Defense Publishing House, M.P.O. Box 01560, Zahal - IDF, Israel. TEL 972-3-5694153. (US addr.: International Aviation Magazine Group, Box 520849, Miami, FL 33156-0849) Ed. Marav Halperin. adv.; bk.rev.; film rev.; charts; illus.; stat. circ. 30,000. **Indexed:** PROMT.
Description: New products and technical reports for the ministry and airforce members.

629.4   UK   ISSN 0007-084X
TL790.A1   CODEN: JBISAW
BRITISH INTERPLANETARY SOCIETY JOURNAL. 1934. m. £195($351) British Interplanetary Society, 27-29 S. Lambeth Rd., London SW8 1SZ, England. Ed. L.J. Carter. bk.rev. circ. 1,500. (also avail. in microform from UMI; reprint service avail. from KTO,UMI) **Indexed:** Eng.Ind., Excerpt.Med., GeoRef., INSPEC (1968-), Int.Aerosp.Abstr., Meteor.& Geoastrophys.Abstr. **Document type:** academic/scholarly publication.
—BLDSC (4718.000000); AskIEEE; CISTI; Ei; KR SourceOne; Linda Hall; UMI; UnCover.

629.1   US   ISSN 1059-3977
BUCKEYE PIETENPOL ASSOCIATION NEWSLETTER. 1983. q. $10 (Canada & Mexico $12; elsewhere $14). Buckeye Pietenpol Association, 6364 Franks Rd., Byrnes Mill, MO 63051-1103. TEL 314-677-1669. E-mail: gmaclaren@aol.com; URL: http://users.aol.com/bpanews. Ed. Grant E. MacLaren. R&P contact: Grant E. MacLaren. adv.; bk.rev.; circ. 1,000 (paid). (back issues avail.) **Document type:** newsletter.
Description: Covers Pietenpol airplanes and their designer, Bernard H. Pietenpol.

BULLETIN OF THE ASTRONOMICAL INSTITUTES OF CZECHOSLOVAKIA. see *ASTRONOMY*

629.1   US   ISSN 0361-5065
TL609
BUOYANT FLIGHT. 1952. bi-m. $15. Lighter Than Air Society, 1436 Triplett Blvd., Akron, OH 44306-3304. Ed. Eric Brothers. bk.rev.; bibl.; illus. circ. 900. (looseleaf format; back issues avail.) **Indexed:** Sportsearch (1983-).
—CISTI.

658   US
BUSINESS AIR TODAY. m. $21.95. Heartland Aviation Group, 1003 Central Ave., Fort Dodge, IA 50501. TEL 515-955-1600; 800-247-2000. FAX 800-247-2000. circ. 40,000. **Document type:** trade publication.
Formerly: Aviators Hot Line (ISSN 0195-0347).
Description: National and international marketplace for active buyers and sellers of corporate and general aircraft, parts and services.

387.7   US   ISSN 0007-6570
BUSINESS AND COMMERCIAL AVIATION. (Supplement avail.: Annual Planning Purchasing Handbook) 1958. m. $48 in U.S.; Canada and Mexico $52; elsewhere $73 (effective 1997). McGraw-Hill Companies (Port Chester), Four International Dr., Port Chester, NY 10573. TEL 914-939-0300. FAX 914-939-1184. URL: http://www.awgnet.com/bca. (Subscr. to: Box 619, Hightstown, NJ 08520-1450) Ed. Richard N. Aarons; Pub. David W. Ewald. R&P contact: Jessica Salerno. adv. contact: Kathleen Lindh. bk.rev.; illus. circ. 50,000. (also avail. in microform from UMI) **Indexed:** A.S.& T.Ind., Bus.Ind., Ind.Sci.Rev., SRI (until 1993), Tr.& Indus.Ind. **Document type:** trade publication.
● Also available online. Vendor(s): Information Access Co., Knight-Ridder Information, Inc.
Description: Covers current industry news. Provides readers with vital information to help them operate aircraft with greater safety and efficiency. Has a strong editorial focus on how-to operations.

BUSINESS AVIATION & REGIONAL TRANSPORT. see *TRANSPORTATION — Air Transport*

629.1 658.8   UK   ISSN 0954-6723
BUSINESS RATIO REPORT: AEROSPACE INDUSTRY; an industry sector analysis. 1980. a. I C C Business Ratios Ltd., Freepost, Field House, Hampton, Mddx. TW12 1BR, England. TEL 081-783-0977. FAX 081-783-1940. charts; stat. **Document type:** trade publication.
Formerly (until 1988): Business Ratio Report: Aerospace Component Manufacturers (ISSN 0261-7293)

387.7   CN   ISSN 0007-7771
TL501
C A H S JOURNAL. 1963. q. Can.$35. Canadian Aviation Historical Society, Box 224 Sta. A, Willowdale, ON M2N 5S8, Canada. TEL 416-488-2247. Ed. W.J. Wheeler. bk.rev.; illus.; index, cum.index. circ. 1,350. **Indexed:** Amer.Hist.& Life (1990-), Hist.Abstr. (1990-). **Document type:** academic/scholarly publication.
—CISTI; UnCover.
Description: Aims to record Canada's aviation history.

629.1 745.1   US
C.A.L. - N-X-211 COLLECTORS SOCIETY. NEWSLETTER. 1989. m. $15. C.A.L. - N-X-211 Collectors Society, 727 Younkin Pkwy. S., Columbus, OH 43207-4788. TEL 614-497-9517. Ed. Bob Hatcher; Pub. Dick Hoerle. adv. contact: Dan Clemons. bk.rev.; circ. 225 (paid). (looseleaf format; back issues avail.) **Document type:** newsletter.

629.13   UY   ISSN 0797-0072
CODEN: CCIAEE
C I D A E. 1976. a. free. Direccion General de Aviacion Civil, Centro de Investigacion y Difusion Aeronautico Espacial, Carlos Ouijano 1182, 11100 Montevideo, Uruguay. TEL 598-2-981627. FAX 598-2-921258. TELEX 22631 DIRACIV UY. bk.rev. circ. 600.
—BLDSC (7804.779600).
Description: Covers doctrine, legislation and jurisprudence on aerospace issues.

629.13   UK   ISSN 0045-8732
TL787
C O S P A R INFORMATION BULLETIN. (Text in English, French) 1960. 3/yr. fl.234($144) (effective 1997). (International Council of Scientific Unions, Committee on Space Research, FR) Elsevier Science Ltd., Pergamon, P.O. Box 800, Kidlington, Oxford OX5 1DX, England. TEL 44-1865-843000. FAX 44-1865-843010. E-mail: nlinfo-f@elsevier.nl; usinfo-f@elsevier.com; forinfo-ky04035@niftyserve.or.jp; URL: http://www.elsevier.nl:80/inca/publications/store/5/8/7/587.pub.shtml. (Subscr. to: Elsevier Science, Regional Sales Office, P.O. Box 211, 1000 AE Amsterdam, Netherlands. TEL 31-20-4853757. FAX 31-20-4853432; Subscr. in the Americas to: Elsevier Science, Regional Sales Office, Box 945, New York, NY 10159-0945. TEL 212-633-3730. FAX 212-633-3680; Subscr. in Australasia and the Far East to: Elsevier Science (Singapore) Pte Ltd, No.1 Temasek Ave., No.17-01 Millenia Tower, Singapore 039192, Singapore. TEL 65-434-3727. FAX 65-337-2230) Ed. R.A. Harrison. adv. circ. 2,300. (also avail. in microfilm from UMI; reprint service avail. from UMI) **Document type:** academic/scholarly publication, bulletin.
—CISTI; UMI. **CCC.**
Description: Covers the latest developments in scientific space activities.
Refereed Serial

C 4 I NEWS. see *MILITARY*

614.85 387.7 629.1   US   ISSN 0898-5758
CABIN CREW SAFETY. 1956. bi-m. $60 in N. America; elsewhere $65. Flight Safety Foundation, Inc., 601 Madison St., Ste. 300, Alexandria, VA 22314-1756. TEL 703-739-6700. FAX 703-739-6708. Ed. Roger Rozelle. circ. 2,250. (reprint service avail. from UMI) **Document type:** newsletter.
Former titles (until vol.22, no.6, 1987): Cabin Crew Safety Bulletin; (until 1975): Cabin Crew Safety Exchange.
Description: Focuses attention on the cabin crew, especially in airline operations, but the special requirements of corporate operations are also presented.

629.1   CC   ISSN 1001-4381
CAILIAO GONGCHENG/MATERIAL ENGINEERING. (Text in Chinese) bi-m. Hangkong Hangtian Gongye-bu, 621 Yanjiusuo - Ministry of Aero-Space Industry, No.621 Institute, P.O. Box 81-62, Beijing 100095, People's Republic of China. TEL 287261.
—BLDSC (5012.229000).

629.1   UK
CAMBRIDGE AEROSPACE SERIES. irreg., vol.7, 1997. University of Cambridge, Press Syndicate, The Pitt Bldg., Trumpington St., Cambridge CB2 1RP, England. TEL 44-1223-315052. (Orders in US to: Cambridge University Press, 40 W. 20th St., New York, NY 10011-4211. TEL 212-924-3900. FAX 212-691-3239) **Document type:** monographic series.

629.13   CN   ISSN 0008-2821
CODEN: CSPJAE
CANADIAN AERONAUTICS AND SPACE JOURNAL. (Text in English or French) 1955. q. Can.$70 in N. America; elsewhere Can.$90 (effective 1997). Canadian Aeronautics and Space Institute, 130 Slater, Ste. 818, Ottawa, ON K1P 6E2, Canada. TEL 613-234-0191. FAX 613-234-9039. E-mail: casi@casi.ca; URL: http://www.casi.ca/abstracts.htm. Ed. Ian Ross. R&P contact: Ian Ross. bk.rev.; bibl.; charts; illus.; index. circ. 2,500. (also avail. in microform from UMI; back issues avail.; reprint service avail. from UMI) **Indexed:** Abstr.Mil.Bibl., Appl.Mech.Rev., Can.B.P.I., Curr.Cont., Eng.Ind., IBR, INSPEC (1971-1988), ISMEC.
—BLDSC (3016.600000); CISTI; Ei; Linda Hall; SWETS; UMI; UnCover. **CCC.**
Description: Devoted to timely reporting on a variety of topics of interest to the international aerospace community

AERONAUTICS AND SPACE FLIGHT

629.13   CN   ISSN 1198-0176
TL501   CODEN: CAVSEH
CANADIAN AVIATION & AIRCRAFT FOR SALE; Canada's leading edge of current aircraft information. 1928. bi-m. Can.$29.96 (U.S. $32; elsewhere $39). P.O. Box 47555, Hamilton, ON L8H 7S7, Canada. TEL 905-544-0560; 800-567-5966. FAX 905-544-8121. E-mail: jhminc@cml.com. (Subscr. to: Box 117, Richmond Hill, ON L4C 4X9, Canada. TEL 905-475-4145. FAX 905-940-3606) Pub. Gerry Boyar. adv. contact: John Hughes. illus. circ. 10,000. (also avail. in microfiche from MML) **Indexed**: Can.B.P.I., Can.Per.Ind., CMI, Eng.Ind., HRIS. **Document type**: directory, trade publication.
—BLDSC (3017.603000); CISTI. **CCC.**
    Formed by the 1993 merger of: Aircraft for Sale Magazine (ISSN 1189-9697) & Aviation and Aerospace (ISSN 0847-0588); Which was formed by the merger of (1928-1990): Canadian Aviation (ISSN 0008-2953); Which incorporated (1951-1964): Aircraft; And: Aerospace and Defense Technology (ISSN 0838-4835); Which was formerly (until 1987): Aerospace Canada International (ISSN 0826-4848); (1977-1983): Aerospace Canada (ISSN 0700-5768).
    Description: Covers aircraft manufacturing, including transport airplanes, light aircraft and helicopters, avionics, airlines, corporate aviation, military aviation, blue-collar aviation, aviation training, airports, airshows, space.

629.132   387.7   CN   ISSN 0527-6497
HE9769.C2
CANADIAN CIVIL AIRCRAFT REGISTER. (In 2 vols.) 1929. m. price varies. Transport Canada, Aircraft Registration, A A R R C, 200 Kent St., Ottawa, ON K1A 0N8, Canada. TEL 613-990-1118. FAX 613-990-6215. circ. 900. (also avail. in microfiche; magnetic tape; diskette format; reprint service avail.)
—CISTI.

629.132   CN
CANADIAN FLIGHT. 1964. m. Can.$40. (Canadian Owners & Pilots Association) Canadian Flight Publishing Co., P.O. Box 563, Stn. B, Ottawa, ON K1P 5P7, Canada. TEL 613-565-0881. FAX 613-236-8646. E-mail: editorial@copanational.org; advertising@copanational.org. Ed. Doris Ohlmann; Pub. Garth Wallace. R&P contact: Doris Ohlmann. adv. contact: Cathy Kennedy. circ. 17,000 (paid). (tabloid format) **Document type**: trade publication.
    Formerly: Canadian General Aviation News (ISSN 0226-5648)

629.13   CN
CANADIAN FLIGHT ANNUAL. 1955. a. Can.$5. (Canadian Owners and Pilots Association) Canadian Flight Publishing Co., P.O. Box 563, Stn. B, Ottawa, ON K1P 5P7, Canada. TEL 613-565-0881. FAX 613-236-8646. E-mail: editorial@copanational.org; advertising@copanational.org. Ed. Doris Ohlman; Pub. Garth Wallace. R&P contact: Doris Ohlman. adv. contact: Cathy Kennedy. bk.rev.; film rev.; illus. circ. 24,000. **Document type**: directory.
—CISTI.
    Supersedes (in 1995): Canadian Flight (ISSN 0008-3577)

629.132   CN   ISSN 0820-5639
CANADIAN HOMEBUILT AIRCRAFT NEWS. (Included in Canadian Flight) m. Canadian Flight Publishing Co., P.O. Box 563, Stn. B, Ottawa, ON K1P 5P7, Canada. TEL 613-565-0881. FAX 613-236-8646. Ed. Doris Ohlmann.
    Description: Contains information of interest to pilots of homebuilt aircraft.

629.13   CN   ISSN 0703-8992
G70.4   CODEN: CJRSDP
CANADIAN JOURNAL OF REMOTE SENSING. 1975. q. Can.$100 in N. America Can.$100; elsewhere Can.$110 (effective 1997). (Canadian Remote Sensing Society) Canadian Aeronautics and Space Institute, 130 Slater, Ste. 818, Ottawa, ON K1P 6E2, Canada. TEL 613-234-0191. FAX 613-234-9039. Ed. N. O'Neill. R&P contact: Ian Ross. adv.; charts; illus.; stat. **Indexed**: Excerp.Med., Geo Abstr., GeoRef., INSPEC (1978-).
—BLDSC (3035.450000); AskIEEE; CISTI; Ei; KR SourceOne; SWETS; UMI; UnCover. **CCC.**
    Description: Devoted to timely reporting on topics of interests to the international remote sensing community.

CANADIAN MUSEUM OF FLIGHT & TRANSPORTATION. MUSEUM NEWSLETTER. see MUSEUMS AND ART GALLERIES

629.132   CN   ISSN 0821-6673
CANADIAN ULTRALIGHT NEWS. (Included in Canadian Flight) 1982. m. Canadian Flight Publishing Co., P.O. Box 563, Stn. B, Ottawa, ON K1P 5P7, Canada. TEL 613-565-0881. FAX 613-236-8646. Ed. Doris Ohlmann.

629.132   US   ISSN 1048-8898
CAREER PILOT;* guiding pilots to their professional goals. 1983. m. $39 (effective 1995). Future Aviation Professionals (FAPA), 4002 Riverdale Ct., Atlanta, GA 30337-6018. TEL 404-997-8097; 800-538-5627. FAX 404-997-8111. Ed. E.F. Cudworth; Pub. W. Louis Smith. R&P contact: E.F. Cudworth. adv. contact: Ed Ray. bk.rev.; index; circ. 12,500 (paid). (back issues avail.) **Document type**: trade publication.
    Formerly (until 1989): Piloting Careers (ISSN 0745-4996)
    Description: Covers career advice and information on airlines as employers. Covers peripheral topics for pilots, such as: health, training, qualifications, finance.

629.132   919.704   NA
CARIBBEAN AVIATION AND TOURISM NEWS/NOTICIERO AERONAUTICO Y TURISMO CARIBENSE. (Text in English, Spanish) 1981. m. free. International Caribbean Federation of AeroClubs, Fosfaatweg 27, Willemstad, Curacao, Netherlands Antilles, W.I. TEL 599-9-681910. FAX 599-9625962. TELEX 390-1080 AFRO NA. Eds. Henry Veeris (English), Elba Serrano (Spanish). adv. circ. 15,000.
    Formerly: Caribbean Aviation News.

629.13   359   AT
▼**CARRIER AVIATION NEWS.** 1996. bi-m. (with d. updates). G.P.O. Box 2204, Adelaide, S.A. 5001, Australia. TEL 61-8-8276-8661. E-mail: davemc@geocities.com; URL: http://www.geocities.com/~davemc/canset.htm. Ed. David McCandless. **Document type**: newsletter.
    ●Available only online.
    Description: Contains current locations of aircraft carriers, news, features, photos, statistics, and links to all carrier sites.

629.1   CC   ISSN 1000-8829
CEKONG JISHU/MEASUREMENT & CONTROL TECHNOLOGY. (Text in Chinese) 1982. bi-m. $6. Hangkong Gongye Zonggongsi, Beijing Cekong Jishu Yanjiusuo - Aviation Industries of China, Beijing Measurement and Control Technology Research Institute, P.O. Box 2351, Beijing 100022, People's Republic of China. TEL 861-10-5026291. FAX 861-10-5005191. TELEX 210411 CIFAI CN. Ed. Ning Zhou. adv.; circ. 10,000. circ. 6,000 (paid). **Document type**: academic/scholarly publication.
—BLDSC (5413.560500).

CENTRAL EURASIA SERIAL REPORTS: AVIATION AND COSMONAUTICS. see POLITICAL SCIENCE — International Relations

629.4   FR   ISSN 0069-2034
CENTRE NATIONAL D'ETUDES SPATIALES. RAPPORT D'ACTIVITE. (Text in English or French) 1962. a. free. Centre National d'Etudes Spatiales (CNES), 18 Ave. E. Belin, 31055 Toulouse Cedex, France. FAX 33-61-28-13-27. Ed. Alain Benssoussan. R&P contact: J.L. Astor. circ. 3,500. **Document type**: corporate report.

697   US   ISSN 0745-3523
CESSNA OWNER MAGAZINE; The Cessna Owner Magazine. 1974. m. $42 membership (effective 1997). Jones Publishing Inc., Box 5000, N. 7450 Aanstad Rd., Iola, WI 54945. TEL 715-445-5000. FAX 715-445-4053. Ed. Tom Huismann. R&P contact: Jennifer Julin. adv.: B&W page $949, color page $1085; trim 7 1/8 x 10; adv. contact: Wanda Zuege. circ. 5,975. **Document type**: consumer publication.
    Description: Directed to Cessna owners and other enthusiasts about the joys and rewards of flying Cessna airplanes. Provides information on flight safety, places to fly, tips on maintenance and repairs, FAA airworthiness alerts, and service difficulty reports.

629.1   IT
CHI E CHI DELL'AERONAUTICA E DELLO SPAZIO. (Text in English, Italian) 1992. a. L.80000. Crisalide Press, Via Brusuglio 66, 20161 Milan, Italy. TEL 39-2-66221694. FAX 39-2-6461622. **Document type**: directory.

CHIKYU DENJIKI CHIKYU WAKUSEIKEN GAKKAI KAIHO/SOCIETY OF GEOMAGNETISM AND EARTH, PLANETARY AND SPACE SCIENCES. NEWS. see EARTH SCIENCES — Geophysics

CHIKYU DENJIKI CHIKYU WAKUSEIKEN GAKKAI KOENKAI KOEN YOKOSHU/SOCIETY OF GEOMAGNETISM AND EARTH, PLANETARY AND SPACE SCIENCES. PREPRINTS OF THE MEETING. see EARTH SCIENCES — Geophysics

629.1   CC   ISSN 1003-6008
CHINA AERO INFORMATION/ZHONGGUO HANGKONG XINXI. (Text in English) m. $100 (foreign $120) (effective 1998). Hangkong Hangtian Gongye-bu, Keji Qingbao Yanjiusuo - Aviation Industries of China, China Aero-Information Center, 14 Xiaoguan Dongli, P.O. Box 9816, Beijing 100029, People's Republic of China. TEL 86-10-6492-2211. FAX 86-10-6491-8417. E-mail: iag@public3.bta.net.cn; URL: http://www.iag.com. Ed. Zhu Xiaoyun. adv. contact: Zhiyuan Xiao.
●Also available online.

629.13   619.4   CC   ISSN 1000-9361
TL501   CODEN: CJAEEZ
CHINESE JOURNAL OF AERONAUTICS. Chinese edition: Hangkong Xuebao (ISSN 1000-6893) (Text in English) 1988. q. $300. Chinese Society of Aeronautics and Astronautics - Zhongguo Hangkong Xuehui, Attn: Wu Xiaoyong, 37 Xueyuan Lu, Beijing 100083, People's Republic of China. TEL 86-10-6201-7247. TELEX 22036-BUAAT-CN. (Dist. by: Allerton Press, Inc., 150 Fifth Ave., New York, NY 10011. TEL 212-924-3950. FAX 212-463-9684) Eds. Zhu Dechao, Wu Xiaoyong. adv. circ. 500. (back issues avail.) **Document type**: academic/scholarly publication.
—BLDSC (3180.290500); CISTI; Linda Hall. **CCC.**
    Description: Covers aeronautical research in China, including fluid mechanics and aerodynamics, flight dynamics and testing, aircraft propulsion systems, auto control and avionics, aerospace manufacturing and materials.

629.1   US   ISSN 0887-9680
UG633
CITIZEN AIRMAN. 1949. bi-m. $8 (foreign $10). U.S. Air Force - Reserves, HQ AFRES - PAR, 155 Second St., Robins AFB, GA 31098-1635. TEL 912-327-1773. FAX 913-327-1772. (Subscr. to: Superintendent of Documents, U.S. Government Printing Office, Box 371954, Pittsburgh, PA 15250) Ed. Cliff Tyler. circ. 80,000. (back issues avail.) **Indexed**: Air Un.Lib.Ind. **Document type**: government publication.
—UMI; UnCover.

629.1   355   US   ISSN 0009-7810
CIVIL AIR PATROL NEWS. 1968. m. $5. Civil Air Patrol Corp., Bldg. 714, Maxwell Air Force Base, AL 36112-6334. TEL 334-953-5700. FAX 334-953-4245. Ed. Jim Tynan. adv.; bk.rev. circ. 54,000. (tabloid format) **Document type**: newspaper.

CIVIL AIRCRAFT AIRWORTHINESS INFORMATION AND PROCEDURES. see TRANSPORTATION — Air Transport

629.1   PK
CIVIL AVIATION IN PAKISTAN: HALF-YEARLY NEWSLETTER. (Text in English) 1971. s-a. Department of Civil Aviation, Karachi 4, Pakistan. charts; stat. **Document type**: newsletter.
    Incorporates: Forward (ISSN 0015-8615); Forward: P I D C Journal (ISSN 0429-2405)

CIVIL AVIATION MEDICAL ASSOCIATION. BULLETIN. see MEDICAL SCIENCES

AERONAUTICS AND SPACE FLIGHT

380.5   UK   ISSN 0009-806X
CIVIL TRANSPORT DATA SHEETS. 1953. q. $295. Aviation Studies International, Sussex House, Parkside, Wimbledon, London SW19 5NB, England. TEL 44-181-946-5082. charts; mkt. **Document type:** trade publication, directory.
  Description: Compiles data on the payload, fuel, take-off weight, dimensions. and performance of 500 types of passenger and cargo commercial aircraft.

629.132   NO   ISSN 0332-9798
COCKPIT FORUM. 1973. bi-m. membership. Norsk Flygerforbund, Oksenoeystien 2, N-1324 Lysaker, Norway. TEL 47-67-58-11-85. FAX 47-67-58-11-82. Ed. Per G. Birkeland. adv.; bk.rev. circ. 1,500. **Document type:** trade publication.
  —CCC.

629.1   US   ISSN 1071-3816
CODE ONE. 1985. q. $12 (foreign $25) (effective 1997). Lockheed Martin TAS (Subsidiary of: Lockheed Martin), Mail Zone 1224, Box 748, Ft. Worth, TX 76101-0748. TEL 817-777-5542. FAX 817-777-5557. E-mail: erichehs@lmtas.com; URL: http://www.lmtas.com/codeone/codeone.html. Ed. Eric Hehs. illus. circ. 30,000. (back issues avail.)
  ●Also available online.
  Description: Covers military aviation, with particular emphasis on the F-16 family of planes.

629.4 341   US   ISSN 0069-5831
COLLOQUIUM ON THE LAW OF OUTER SPACE. PROCEEDINGS. 1958. a. $84.95 to non-members; members $64.95. (International Aeronautical Federation) American Institute of Aeronautics and Astronautics, Inc., 1801 Alexander Dr., Ste. 500, Reston, VA 20191. TEL 703-264-7500. (Co-sponsor: International Institute of Space Law) (back issues avail.; reprint service avail. from UMI) **Indexed:** Int.Aerosp.Abstr. **Document type:** academic/scholarly publication, proceedings.
  —UnCover.
  Description: Covers the latest developments in the legal aspects of astronautics, space travel and exploration.

COMBAT CREW. see *MILITARY*

629.132   US   ISSN 1063-8970
COMBAT EDGE. 1961. m. $21 (foreign $26.25) (effective 1996). U.S. Department of the Air Force, Office of Safety, HQ, Air Combat Command, Langley AFB, VA 23665-2786. TEL 804-764-3658. FAX 804-764-3102. (Subscr. to: U.S. Government Printing Office, Superintendent of Documents, Box 371954, Pittsburgh, PA 15250-7954. TEL 202-512-1800. FAX 202-512-2250) Ed. Lt. Col. Nelson L. Beard. R&P contact: Lt. Col. Nelson L. Beard. circ. 20,000. **Indexed:** Air Un.Lib.Ind. **Document type:** government publication.
  Formerly (until 1992): T A C Attack (Tactical Air Command) (ISSN 0494-3880)
  Description: Focuses on leadership and flight safety; includes weapons, ground, maintenance and general safety.

629.1   US
COMMONWEALTH OF PENNSYLVANIA. AIRPORT DIRECTORY.* a. free. Department of Transportation, Bureau of Aviation, 555 Walnut St., Harrisburg, PA 17101-1907. **Document type:** directory.

629.13   US
COMMONWEALTH OF PENNSYLVANIA AERONAUTICAL CHART.* a. free. Department of Transportation, Bureau of Aviation, 555 Walnut St., Harrisburg, PA 17101-1907.

629.13 358.4
387.71   UK   ISSN 1350-2859
CONCISE; aerospace news from the commonwealth of independent states. 1993. m. £195($335) (outside the EC £240 ($395)); by fax and e-mail £245 ($405) (outside the EC £300 ($505)). Airworty Publications International Ltd., Bassfield South, Manchester Rd., Walmersley, Bury, Lancs. BL9 5LY, England. TEL 44-1706-828811. FAX 44-1706-828300. E-mail: wuase@ben.co.uk. Pub. Steve Broadbent. circ. 100 (paid). (also avail. by fax; back issues avail.) **Document type:** newsletter.
  Description: Reports on developments in the aerospace and air transport industries in the former communist nations of Eastern Europe.
  Refereed Serial

629.1 600   US
CONFERENCE ON SPACE SIMULATION. PROCEEDINGS. irreg., 19th, 1996. $100 to non-members; members $70 (effective 1997). Institute of Environmental Sciences, 940 E. Northwest Hwy., Mt. Prospect, IL 60056. TEL 847-255-1561. FAX 847-255-1699. (Co-sponsors: American Institute of Aeronautics and Astronautics; American Society for Testing and Materials; National Aeronautics and Space Administration) **Document type:** proceedings.

629.13   US
CONTACT! (TUCSON); experimental aircraft and powerplant newsforum for designers and builders. 1990. bi-m. $20 (Canada & Mexico $27; elsewhere $29) (effective 1997). (Aeronautics Education Enterprises) Michael C. Myac, Ed. & Pub., 2900 E. Weymouth, Tucson, AZ 85716. TEL 520-881-2232. FAX 520-795-6776. circ. 1,000.
  Description: Promotes the experimental development, expansion and exchange of aeronautical concepts, information, and experience.

629.8   US   ISSN 0090-5267
QA402.3   CODEN: CDSYD6
CONTROL AND DYNAMIC SYSTEMS: ADVANCES IN THEORY AND APPLICATIONS. Key Title: Control and Dynamic Systems. a., vol.79, 1996. Academic Press, Inc., 525 B St., Ste. 1900, San Diego, CA 92101-4495. TEL 619-231-0926. FAX 619-699-6715. (Subscr. to: Order Dept., 6277 Sea Harbor Dr., 4th Fl., Orlando, FL 32887. TEL 800-321-5068) Ed. Cornelius T. Leondes. illus. (reprint service avail. from ISI) **Indexed:** Appl.Mech.Rev., Chem.Abstr., INSPEC, Zent.Math.
  —BLDSC (3461.860000); CASDDS; CISTI; Linda Hall; SWETS; UnCover. **CCC.**
  Formerly: Advances in Control Systems (ISSN 0065-2466)

629.13   UK
CONTROL COLUMN. 1967. 8/yr. £3.60($8) Control Column Publications, 127 Hawton Rd., Newark, Notts. NG24 4QG, England. Ed. Neville Franklin. adv.; bk.rev. circ. 1,200. (back issues avail.)

387.7   SZ   ISSN 0010-8073
THE CONTROLLER; journal of air traffic control. (Includes Annual Conference Proceedings) (Text in English) 1961. q. 20 SFr. International Federation of Air Traffic Controllers' Associations, P.O. Box 196, CH-1215 Geneva 15 Airport, Switzerland. TEL 022-7827983. FAX 022-664305. Ed. Terry Crowhurst. adv.: B&W page 2900 SFr.; trim 265 x 185; adv. contact: Patrick Schelling. bk.rev.; film rev.; charts; illus. circ. 5,000. **Indexed:** HRIS, INSPEC, Int.Aerosp.Abstr.
  —BLDSC (3463.100000); CISTI; SWETS.

629.1   US   ISSN 0736-4709
TL722
CORPORATE AVIATION SAFETY SEMINAR. PROCEEDINGS. 1955. a., 37th, 1992, Baltimore, MD. Flight Safety Foundation, Inc., 601 Madison St., Ste. 300, Alexandria, VA 22314-1756. TEL 703-739-6700. FAX 703-739-6708. Ed. Roger Rozelle. (reprint service avail. from UMI) **Document type:** proceedings.
  —Ei.
  Former titles (until 23rd, 1978): Corporate Aircraft Safety Seminar; (until 14th, 1969): Business Aircraft Safety Seminar.

629.4   RU   ISSN 0010-9525
QC801   CODEN: CSCRA7
COSMIC RESEARCH. English translation of: Kosmicheskie Issledovaniya (RU ISSN 0023-4206) 1963. bi-m. $1595 in US; elsewhere $1865 (effective 1998). (Russian Academy of Sciences) Maik Nauka - Interperiodica, Mezhdunarodnyi Otdel, Ul. Profsoyuznaya 90, Moscow 117864, Russia. TEL 7-95-3360066. FAX 7-95-3660666. (Dist. by: Plenum Publishing Corp., 233 Spring St., New York, NY 10013-1578, U.S.A. TEL 212-620-8468. FAX 212-463-0742) Ed. L.I. Sedov. (also avail. in microfilm from UMI; back issues avail.) **Indexed:** Appl.Mech.Rev., Energy Res.Abstr., Eng.Ind., INIS Atomind., INSPEC. **Document type:** academic/scholarly publication.
  —BLDSC (0411.075000); AskIEEE; CISTI; KR SourceOne; Linda Hall; SWETS; UMI; UnCover. **CCC.**
  Refereed Serial

COUNTDOWN TO SPACE. see *CHILDREN AND YOUTH — For*

CROSS & COCKADE INTERNATIONAL. see *MILITARY*

629.1   UK   ISSN 0263-3043
CROYDON AIRPORT SOCIETY JOURNAL. 1981. s-a. £12.50($30) membership (effective 1992). Croydon Airport Society, 193 Commonside E., Mitcham, Surrey CR4 1HB, England. TEL 44-181-648-3906. FAX 44-181-770-4750. Ed. Peter G. Cooksley. R&P contact: Peter G. Cooksley. adv. contact: Tom Samson. bk.rev.; index; circ. 800 (controlled). (back issues avail.) **Document type:** academic/scholarly publication.
  Description: Contains historical information about Croydon Airport.

629.1   GW   ISSN 0178-6326
D G L R BERICHT. irreg. Deutsche Gesellschaft fuer Luft- und Raumfahrt e.V., Godesberger Allee 70, 53175 Bonn, Germany. TEL 0228-376726. FAX 0228-374755. **Document type:** monographic series.
  —BLDSC (3579.420000).

629.13 629.4   GW   ISSN 0070-4083
D G L R JAHRBUECHER. 1952. a. price varies. Deutsche Gesellschaft fuer Luft- und Raumfahrt e.V., Godesberger Allee 70, 53175 Bonn, Germany. TEL 0228-376726. FAX 0228-374755. index.
  Formerly: Wissenschaftliche Gesellschaft fuer Luft- und Raumfahrt. Jahrbuecher.

629.13   GW   ISSN 0939-2963
TL507   CODEN: FDFREM
D L R - FORSCHUNGSBERICHTE. (Text in English or German) 1964. irreg. price varies. Deutsche Forschungsanstalt fuer Luft- und Raumfahrt e.V., Linder Hoehe, 51170 Cologne, Germany. TEL 49-2203-6010. FAX 49-2203-6013249. E-mail: werner.wilke@dlr.de; URL: http://www.dlr.de. index. **Indexed:** Appl.Mech.Rev., Chem.Abstr., Int.Aerosp.Abstr., Meteor.& Geoastrophys.Abstr., Zent.Math. **Document type:** monographic series.
  —BLDSC (4011.164700); CISTI; Ei; Linda Hall. **CCC.**
  Former titles (until 1989): D F V L R - Forschungsberichte und D F V L R - Mitteilungen (ISSN 0171-1342); (until 1978): Deutsche Luft- und Raumfahrt Forschungsberichte (ISSN 0070-4245)
  Description: New findings in the research fields of aerospace and energetics.

629.13   GW   ISSN 0938-2194
D L R - JAHRESBERICHT. 1969. a. free. Deutsche Forschungsanstalt fuer Luft- und Raumfahrt e.V., Linder Hoehe, 51170 Cologne, Germany. TEL 49-2203-6010. FAX 49-2203-6013249. E-mail: pressestelle@dlr.de; URL: http://www.dlr.de. circ. 5,000. **Document type:** corporate report.
  —CISTI; Linda Hall.
  Formerly: D F V L R Jahresbericht (ISSN 0070-3966)

629.13   GW   ISSN 0939-298X
   CODEN: MDFREV
D L R - MITTEILUNGEN. 1964. irreg. Deutsche Forschungsanstalt fuer Luft- und Raumfahrt e.V., Linder Hoehe, 51170 Cologne, Germany. TEL 49-2203-6010. FAX 49-2203-6014745. E-mail: werner.wilke@dlr.de; URL: http://www.dlr.de. **Indexed:** Meteor.& Geoastrophys.Abstr., Zent.Math. **Document type:** monographic series.
  —CASDDS; CISTI; Ei.
  Formerly: D F V L R - Mitteilungen (ISSN 0176-7739)
  Description: New findings in the DLR research fields of aerospace and energetics.

629.13   GW   ISSN 0937-0420
TL526.G3   CODEN: DLRNE2
D L R - NACHRICHTEN. 1969. 4/yr. free. Deutsche Forschungsanstalt fuer Luft- und Raumfahrt e.V., Linder Hoehe, 51170 Cologne, Germany. TEL 49-2203-6010. FAX 49-2203-6013249. E-mail: pressestelle@dlr.de; URL: http://www.dlr.de. Ed. Thomas H. Weyer. bibl.; charts; illus. circ. 10,000. **Indexed:** Appl.Mech.Rev., Fluidex, Geo.Abstr., INIS Atomind. **Document type:** bulletin.
  —BLDSC (3605.683000); CISTI; Ei; Linda Hall. **CCC.**
  Former titles: D F V L R - Nachrichten (ISSN 0011-4901); D V L - Nachrichten.
  Description: Covers all aspects of aviation and aerospace technology. Includes European space projects, reports of events, association news.

AERONAUTICS AND SPACE FLIGHT

D M S MARKET INTELLIGENCE REPORTS: AIRBORNE ELECTRONICS. (Defense Market Services) see ELECTRONICS

629.1 US
D M S MARKET INTELLIGENCE REPORTS: AIRBORNE RETROFIT AND MODERNIZATION. base vol. (plus m. updates). $1295 (effective 1997). Forecast International Inc. - D M S, 22 Commerce Rd., Newtown, CT 06470. TEL 203-426-0800. FAX 203-426-1964. E-mail: fidms@ibm.net.
●Also available on CD-ROM.
Description: Information on R & M programs for both civil and military aircraft of fixed and rotary-wing configurations.

629.1 355 US
D M S MARKET INTELLIGENCE REPORTS: AIRCRAFT: CIVIL AND MILITARY. base vol. (plus m. updates). $1395. Forecast International - D M S, 22 Commerce Rd., Newtown, CT 06470. TEL 203-426-0800. FAX 203-426-0223. E-mail: fidms@ibm.net.
●Also available on CD-ROM.
Description: Analysis of more than 200 military, commercial, business and general aviation aircraft programs.

D M S MARKET INTELLIGENCE REPORTS: ANTI-SUBMARINE WARFARE. see MILITARY

D M S MARKET INTELLIGENCE REPORTS: C 3 I. see MILITARY

629.13 355 US
D M S MARKET INTELLIGENCE REPORTS: CIVIL AIRCRAFT. base vol. (plus m. updates). $1295 (effective 1997). Forecast International Inc. - D M S, 22 Commerce Rd., Newtown, CT 06470. TEL 203-426-0800. FAX 203-426-0223. E-mail: fiaero1@ibm.net. (looseleaf format; back issues avail.)
●Also available on CD-ROM.
Description: Provides comprehensive coverage of the worldwide commercial aircraft market, from large jet transports to light general aviation fixed and rotary-wing aircraft.

D M S MARKET INTELLIGENCE REPORTS: DEFENSE AND AEROSPACE COMPANIES. see MILITARY

D M S MARKET INTELLIGENCE REPORTS: ELECTRONIC SYSTEMS. see MILITARY

D M S MARKET INTELLIGENCE REPORTS: ELECTRONIC WARFARE. see MILITARY

D M S MARKET INTELLIGENCE REPORTS: FOREIGN MILITARY MARKETS: N A T O & EUROPE. see MILITARY

D M S MARKET INTELLIGENCE REPORTS: GAS TURBINE. see MILITARY

D M S MARKET INTELLIGENCE REPORTS: MILITARY AIRCRAFT. see MILITARY

D M S MARKET INTELLIGENCE REPORTS: MISSILES. see MILITARY

D M S MARKET INTELLIGENCE REPORTS: RADAR. see MILITARY

D M S MARKET INTELLIGENCE REPORTS: SPACE SYSTEMS. see MILITARY

629.1 US
D M S MARKET INTELLIGENCE REPORTS: WORLD AIRLINE MAINTENANCE. base vol. (plus m. updates). $1995 (effective 1997). Forecast International Inc. - D M S, 22 Commerce St., Newtown, CT 06470. TEL 203-426-0800. FAX 203-426-0223. E-mail: fiaero1@ibm.net.
Description: Provides a 10-year forecast of the demand for shop visits for each type of transport aircraft by region worldwide.

629.1 US
D M S MARKET INTELLIGENCE REPORTS: WORLD COMMERCIAL AIRCRAFT - ENGINE ORDERS & OPTIONS. base vol. (plus m. updates). $945 (effective 1997). Forecast International Inc. - D M S, 22 Commerce Rd., Newtown, CT 06470. TEL 203-426-0800. FAX 203-426-0223. E-mail: montneb@ibm.net.
Description: Lists all available orders and options for commercial transport aircraft worldwide.

629.1 DK ISSN 0109-6605
DANSK RUMFORSKNINGINSTITUT. PUBLIKATIONER. irreg. Dansk Rumforskninginstitut - Danish Space Research Institut, Juliane Maries Vej 30, DK-2100 Copenhagen OE, Denmark. TEL 45-35-32-58-30. FAX 45-35-36-24-75. E-mail: username@dsri.dk; URL: http://www.dsri.dk. **Document type:** government publication.

DE L'AUTOMOBILE ET DE L'AERONAUTIQUE. see TRANSPORTATION — Automobiles

629.132 355 UK ISSN 0963-116X
DEFENCE HELICOPTER. 1982. q. $60. Shephard Press Ltd., 111 High St., Burnham, Bucks. SL1 7JZ, England. TEL 44-1628-604311. FAX 44-1628-664334. E-mail: heli-uv@shepard.co.uk. Ed. Ian Parker; Pub. Ben Dvero. adv.: B&W page £5040, color page £6720; trim 273 x 205; adv. contact: Aude Dupont-Dudley. circ. 12,207. **Document type:** trade publication.
—BLDSC (3541.615500); CISTI; SWETS.
Formerly: Defence Helicopter World (ISSN 0263-5062)
Description: Provides unclassified sources of information on military helicopters.

629.1 355 US
DEFENSE AND AEROSPACE AGENCIES BRIEFING. m. Teal Group Corp., 3900 University Dr., Ste. 220, Fairfax, VA 22030. TEL 703-385-1992. FAX 703-691-9591. (looseleaf format) **Document type:** newsletter.
Description: Traces and analyzes the activities of nearly 100 U.S. government agencies, facilities, and other contracting offices.

629.1 355 US
DEFENSE AND AEROSPACE COMPANIES BRIEFING. m. Teal Group Corp., 3900 University Dr., Ste. 220, Fairfax, VA 22030. TEL 703-385-1992. FAX 703-691-9591. (looseleaf format) **Document type:** newsletter.
Description: Reports on US and international companies, organizations, and universities that do a major portion of their business in the defense and aerospace sector.

387.8 US ISSN 0889-0404
UA23
DEFENSE DAILY. 1959. d. $1597 (foreign $1742) (effective 1997). Phillips Business Information, Inc., 120 Seven Locks Rd., Potomac, MD 20854. TEL 301-424-3338. FAX 301-309-3847. E-mail: pbi@phillips.com. Ed. Gary Crouse. charts; illus. **Indexed:** DM& T. **Document type:** newsletter.
●Also available online. Vendor(s): Information Access Co., Knight-Ridder Information, Inc., NewsNet (DE01).
—CCC.
Incorporates: Tactical Technology (ISSN 1059-0552); Former titles (until 1981): Defense - Space Business Daily; Space Business Daily News Service (ISSN 0038-6243)

DESERT AIRMAN. see MILITARY

629.1 387.7 UN ISSN 1014-0123
DESIGNATORS FOR AIRCRAFT OPERATING AGENCIES, AERONAUTICAL AUTHORITIES AND SERVICES. (Text in English, French, Russian, Spanish) 1959? irreg., 98th ed., 1996. $41 (diskette $200). International Civil Aviation Organization, Attn: Document Sales Unit, 1000 Sherbrooke St. W., Montreal, PQ H3A 2R2, Canada. TEL 514-285-8022. FAX 514-285-6769. TELEX 05-24513. (also avail. in diskette format)

629.13 UK
DIRECTED ENERGY - AVIONICS DATA SHEETS. irreg. $495. Aviation Studies International, Sussex House, Parkside, Wimbledon, London SW19 5NB, England. TEL 44-181-946-5082. **Document type:** trade publication, directory.
Formerly: Avionics Data Sheets.
Description: Compiles data on thermal weapon types, prospects, roles, and research and development; covers avionics suites for tactical, strategic, patrol, and support aircraft.

629.1 FR
DIRECTORY OF RUSSIAN SPACE INDUSTRY. 1993. a. 650 F. (European Space Agency) Sevig Press Publishing, 6 rue Bellart, 75015 Paris, France. TEL 33-1-42-73-2837. FAX 33-1-42-73-2095. illus. **Document type:** directory.
Description: Lists 100 Russian space organizations and firms. Includes a short space glossary and acronym list.

DIRITTO AEREO; rivista di dottrina, giurisprudenza e legislazione aeronautica dei trasporti intermodali e del diritto spaziale. see LAW

358.4 976 US ISSN 1061-1231
THE DISPATCH (MIDLAND); American airpower a proud heritage. 1976. q. $38. Confederate Air Force, Box 62000, Midland, TX 79711-2000. TEL 915-563-1000. FAX 915-563-8046. Ed. Tina Stewart. adv.; bk.rev.; charts; illus.; stat. circ. 7,000.
Formerly: C A F Dispatch.
Description: Covers WWII aviation history (1939-1945).

629.132 FR ISSN 0764-9185
DOCAVIA. irreg. Editions Lariviere, 12 rue Mozart, 92587 Clichy Cedex. TEL 33-1-41403360. FAX 33-1-47376498. Ed. Michel Benichou. R&P contact: Isabelle Leguillon. TEL 33-1-41403388. adv. contact: Ollivier Adda. **Document type:** monographic series.
Description: Covers aviation topics.

629.1 US ISSN 0894-1289
TL685.15
E A A EXPERIMENTER; the "how to" magazine for the aircraft builder. 1980. m. $30. Experimental Aircraft Association, Inc., Box 3086, Oshkosh, WI 54903-3086. TEL 414-426-4800. FAX 414-426-4828. Ed. Jack Cox. adv. contact: Golda Cox. bk.rev.; index. circ. 16,000. (back issues avail.) **Indexed:** Ind.How To Do It (1990-).
Formerly (until 1987): Light Plane World.
Description: Technical magazine covering home-building aircraft. Includes plans and design information, and news on ultralights and kit planes.
Refereed Serial

629.132 US
E A A TECHNICAL COUNSELOR NEWSLETTER. 1958. q. $12. Experimental Aircraft Association, Inc., Box 3086, Oshkosh, WI 54903-3086. TEL 414-426-4821. FAX 414-426-6560. Ed. Ben Owen. circ. 1,200. (looseleaf format) **Indexed:** Ind.How To Do It (1989-). **Document type:** newsletter.
Description: Provides building and repairing tips for recreational aircraft.

629.13 NE ISSN 1013-9036
E C S L NEWS. (European Centre for Space) (Text in English, French) 1989. q. free. European Space Agency, Publications Division, Keplerlaan 1, 22000 AG Noordwijk, Netherlands. TEL 31-1719-86555. FAX 31-1719-58433. TELEX 39098. Ed. D. Guyenne. illus. circ. 3,300. **Document type:** newsletter.

629.1 NE ISSN 0376-4265
TL787 CODEN: ESABD8
E S A BULLETIN. (Text in English, French) 1966. q. free. European Space Agency, Publications Division, Keplerlaan 1, 22000 AG Noordwijk, Netherlands. TEL 31-071-5153400. FAX 31-071-5655433. TELEX 39098. Eds. B. Battrick, T.D. Guyenne. bibl.; illus. circ. 25,000. **Indexed:** ASCA, Curr.Cont., Ergon.Abstr., Geo.Abstr.H.G., Geo.Abstr.P.G., INIS Atomind., INSPEC, Int.Aerosp.Abstr., Risk Abstr., Tel.Abstr. **Document type:** bulletin.
—BLDSC (3810.923300); AskIEEE; CISTI; Ei; Genuine Article; KR SourceOne; Linda Hall; UnCover.
Formerly (1968-1975): E S R O - E L D O Bulletin (ISSN 0012-799X)

629.1 355 JA ISSN 0288-5603
EA WARUDO/AIR WORLD. (Text in Japanese) 1977. m. Air World Inc., 12-8, Roppongi 4-chome, Minato-ku, Tokyo 106, Japan.

AERONAUTICS AND SPACE FLIGHT

629.13   NE   ISSN 0256-596X
EARTH OBSERVATION QUARTERLY. French edition: Observation de la Terre (ISSN 0256-2936) (French edition ceased 1995) (Text in English) 1983. q. free. European Space Agency, Publications Division, Keplerlaan 1, 22200 AG Noordwijk, Netherlands. TEL 31-1719-86555. FAX 31-1719-85433. TELEX 39098. Ed. T.D. Guyenne. illus. circ. 12,000
Indexed: Environ.Abstr., Geo.Abstr.
—BLDSC (3643.200000); CIS; EMDOCS; KR SourceOne.

629.1 613.1   US
EARTH OBSERVER. 1989. bi-m. free. U.S. National Aeronautics and Space Administration, Earth Observing System Project, Goddard Space Flight Center, Greenbelt, MD 20771. TEL 301-286-3411. FAX 301-286-1738. E-mail: cgriner@pop900.gsfc.nasa.gov; URL: http://eospso.gsfc.nasa.gov/earth_observ.html. Ed. Charlotte Griner. circ. 5,000.
Document type: government publication, newsletter.
●Also available online.

EAST DEFENCE AND AEROSPACE UPDATE. see MILITARY

ECOLOGICAL MONOGRAPHS. see ENVIRONMENTAL STUDIES

ELECTRONIC PROGRESS. see ELECTRONICS

629.133   IT
ELICOTTERI. 6/yr. Via Sanvito Silvestro 43, 21100 Varese, Italy. TEL 332-23-12-59. FAX 332-23-00-73. Ed. Giorgio Apostolo.

629.134   UK   ISSN 0013-774X
ENGINE DATA SHEETS. 1954. 3/yr. $245. Aviation Studies International, Sussex House, Parkside, Wimbledon, London SW19 5NB, England. TEL 44-181-946-5082. charts; cum.index.
Document type: directory, trade publication.
Description: Describes the design features of radial and conventional piston engines, turboprops, turbojets, fanjets, unducted fans, and liquid and solid rockets.

629.13   UK
ENGINE YEARBOOK (YEAR). a. Aviation Industry Press, 31 Palace St., London SW1E 5HW, England. TEL 44-171-828-4376. FAX 44-171-828-9154. E-mail: a.i.group@pipex.com. **Document type:** trade publication.
Description: Examines many aspects of the aircraft engine business, from manufacturing through maintenance. Also covers the specialist component and service sectors.

629.1   GW
EUROCOPTER INTERN. 1992. m. Eurocopter Deutschland GmbH, Postfach 801140, 81611 Munich, Germany. Ed. Alfred Beck. circ. 4,500.
Document type: corporate report.

629.1 621.38   FR   ISSN 0531-7444
EUROPEAN ORGANISATION FOR CIVIL AVIATION EQUIPMENT. GENERAL ASSEMBLY. ANNUAL REPORT. (Text in English and French) 1964. a. free. European Organization for Civil Aviation Equipment - Organisation Europeenne pour l'Equipement de l'Aviation Civile, 17 rue Hamelin, 75783 Paris Cedex 16, France. TEL 33-1-45057188. FAX 33-1-45057230. E-mail: eurocae@compuserve.com. circ. 200.

629.13   NE   ISSN 0379-4059
EUROPEAN SPACE AGENCY. PROCEDURES, STANDARDS AND SPECIFICATIONS SERIES. Key Title: E S A - P S S. 1978. irreg. price varies. European Space Agency, Publications Division, Keplerlaan 1, 22200 AG Noordwijk, Netherlands. TEL 31-071-5653400. FAX 31-071-5655433. TELEX 39098.
—BLDSC (3830.148000); CISTI.

629.13   NE   ISSN 0379-4075
EUROPEAN SPACE AGENCY. SCIENTIFIC AND TECHNICAL MEMORANDA. Key Title: E S A - S T M. 1964. irreg. European Space Agency, Publications Division, Keplerlaan 1, 22200 AG Noordwijk, Netherlands. TEL 31-071-5653400. FAX 31-071-5655433.
—BLDSC (3830.151000); CISTI.
Supersedes in part: E S A Scientific - Technical Reports, Notes and Memoranda; Formerly (until 1975): E S R O Scientific - Technical Reports, Notes and Memoranda.

629.13   NE   ISSN 0379-4067
CODEN: ESSTFI
EUROPEAN SPACE AGENCY. SCIENTIFIC AND TECHNICAL REPORTS. Key Title: E S A - S T R. 1964. irreg. European Space Agency, Publications Division, Keplerlaan 1, 22200 AG Noordwijk, Netherlands. TEL 31-071-5653400. FAX 31-071-5655433. TELEX 39098.
—BLDSC (3830.152000); CASDDS.
Supersedes in part: E S A Scientific - Technical Reports, Notes and Memoranda; Formerly (until 1975): E S R O Scientific - Technical Reports, Notes and Memoranda.

629.1   FR   ISSN 0765-0574
TL788.3
EUROPEAN SPACE DIRECTORY. 1986. a. 940 F. (effective 1997). Sevig Press Publishing, 6 rue Bellart, 75015 Paris, France. TEL 33-1-42732837. FAX 33-1-42732095. Ed. Dick Shirvanian. adv. contact: Anayis Khedjian. circ. 4,000. **Document type:** directory.
—BLDSC (3830.180000); CISTI.
Description: Lists 300 company profiles of European space firms and agencies.

629.13   US   ISSN 1062-8576
EXPERIMENTAL ROCKET FLYER. 1992. q. $15. California Rocketry, Box 1242, Claremont, CA 91711. TEL 800-266-6913. FAX 909-398-1877. E-mail: jjirvine@aol.com. Ed. Jerry Irvine. adv.: page $300; trim 8 1/2 x 11. bk.rev.; software rev.; charts; illus. circ. 2,000. (back issues avail.)
●Also available online.
Description: Covers experimental rocket construction, suppliers, launchings and results. Specializing in rockets traveling 20,000 to 2,000,000 feet altitude sub-orbital.

387.7   US
EXXON AVIATION NEWS DIGEST. 1947. w. (Exxon Aviation Marketing Affiliates) Exxon Company USA, Division of Exxon Corporation, Box 2180, Houston, TX 77252-2180. TEL 713-656-3636. (And: 225 E. John W. Carpenter Pkwy., Ste. 802, Irving, TX 75062-2298. TEL 214-444-1000) stat. circ. 10,000.
Formerly: Esso Aviation News Digest (ISSN 0014-0996)

629.1 387.7   CN
F A N S FACTS SHEET. (Future Air Navigation Systems) bi-m. $50 (effective 1995). International Air Transport Association, Technical Department, Avionics Section, 2000 Peel St., Montreal, PQ H3A 2R4, Canada. TEL 514-844-6311. FAX 514-844-3788. TELEX 05-267627.
Description: Intended to increase the awareness and understanding of the ICAO Future Air Navigation Systems concept and its impact on airline operations.

F M T. (Flug- und Modell-Technik) see HOBBIES

629.13   FR   ISSN 0757-4169
FANA DE L'AVIATION. 1969. m. 306 F. (foreign 372 F.) (effective 1997). Editions Lariviere, 12 rue Mozart, 92587 Clichy Cedex, France. TEL 33-1-41403366. FAX 33-1-47376498. Ed. Bertrand de Cerval. adv. contact: Ollivier Adda. bk.rev. circ. 43,000.
Former titles: Fanatique de l'Aviation; Album du Fanatique de l'Aviation.

629.13   UK   ISSN 0071-402X
FARNBOROUGH AIR SHOW (PUBLIC PROGRAMME). biennial. Society of British Aerospace Companies Ltd., 60 Petty France, London SW1H 9EU, England. TEL 44-171-839-3231. Ed. Susan Godfrey. **Document type:** catalog.

629.4   US   ISSN 0899-4161
TL787
FINAL FRONTIER;* the magazine of space exploration. 1988. bi-m. $14.95. Final Frontier Publishing, Inc., The Brooklyn College Science Fiction Society, Central Depository, Boylan Hall, Bedford Ave. and Ave. H, Brooklyn, NY 11210. TEL 612-822-9600. FAX 612-822-9640. Ed. Leonard David. adv.; bk.rev. circ. 90,000. **Document type:** consumer publication.
Description: Seeks to broaden the base of space enthusiasts among the general public, as well as to provide information to aerospace professionals.

387.7   BL   ISSN 0046-404X
FLAP INTERNACIONAL; revista latinoamericana de aviacao. 1962. m. Grupo Editorial Spagat Ltda., Rua Prof. Artur Ramos 183, 10 andar, 01454-905 Sao Paulo, SP, Brazil. TEL 55-11-8164455. FAX 55-11-2104186. Ed. Carlos Andre Spagat. adv.; charts; illus.; stat. circ. 42,000.
Description: Provides current trade information, news and articles to airline pilots and professionals related to the aeronautics field.

629.13   GW   ISSN 0015-3680
DER FLIEGER. 1921. m. DM.48. Luftfahrt-Verlag Walter Zuerl, Amselweg 6, 8031 Woerthsee-Steinebach, Germany. Ed. Walter J.A. Zuerl. adv.; bk.rev.; bibl.; charts; illus.; mkt.; tr.lit. circ. 14,000.
—CCC.
Incorporating: Luftfahrt-Zubehoer; Privatpilot.

629.13   GW   ISSN 0001-9445
FLIEGER-REVUE. 1952. m. (Gesellschaft fuer Sport und Technik) Flug Verlag GmbH, Rosenthalerstr. 36, 10178 Berlin, Germany. TEL 030-2846345. FAX 030-2827020. Ed. Matthias Gruender; Pub. Peter Stache. adv.; bk.rev.; charts; illus.; index. circ. 25,000. **Document type:** consumer publication.
—CCC.
Formerly: Aerosport.

629.1   GW
FLIEGERKALENDER. 1979. a. DM.22.50. Verlag E.S. Mittler und Sohn GmbH, Striepenweg 31, 21147 Hamburg, Germany. TEL 49-40-79713322. FAX 49-40-79713324. Ed. Hans M. Namislo. adv.: B&W page DM.2300, color page DM.3290; trim 112 x 171; adv. contact: Rainer Metzner. abstr.; charts; illus.; stat. circ. 5,500. **Document type:** academic/scholarly publication.

629.132   GW   ISSN 0170-5504
FLIEGERMAGAZIN. m. DM.86.40 (foreign DM.96); newsstand price: DM.8. Top Special Verlag GmbH, Nebendahlstr. 16, 22041 Hamburg, Germany. TEL 49-40-3470-0. FAX 49-40-34725588. Ed. Juergen Werner. adv.: B&W page DM.6210, color page DM.10550; trim 190 x 244; adv. contact: Claudia Popp. circ. 50,490. **Document type:** consumer publication.
—CCC.

629.13   US   ISSN 1087-0822
▼**FLIGHT.** 1996. bi-m. Air Age Publishing, 100 East Ridge, Ridgefield, CT 06877. TEL 203-431-9000. FAX 203-431-3000. E-mail: toma@airage.com. Ed. Tom Atwood. bk.rev.; circ. 40,000 (paid). **Document type:** consumer publication.
Description: Covers current and historic aviation and personalities.

629.13   UK   ISSN 0015-3710
TL501
FLIGHT INTERNATIONAL. 1909. w. $184. Reed Business Publishing Group (Subsidiary of: Reed Elsevier group), Quadrant House, The Quadrant, Sutton, Surrey SM2 5AS, England. TEL 44-181-652-3882. FAX 44-181-652-3840. URL: http://www.reedbusiness.com/aerospace.htm. (Subscr. to: Flight Int'l subscriptions, Reed Business, P.O. Box 302, Haywards Heath, West Sussex, RH16 3DH. TEL 01444-4455661) Ed. Allan Winn. R&P contact: Allan Winn. adv. contact: Trevor Parker. bk.rev.; charts; illus.; index. circ. 50,500. (also avail. in microform from UMI; reprint service avail. from UMI) **Indexed:** Air Un.Lib.Ind., Br.Tech.Ind., Chem.Abstr., DM& T, Eng.Ind., HRIS, Int.Aerosp.Abstr., PROMT, World Text.Abstr.
Document type: trade publication.
●Also available online. Vendor(s): Data-Star, Information Access Co., Lexis-Nexis.
—BLDSC (3951.010000); CISTI; Linda Hall; SWETS; UMI; UnCover. CCC.
Description: Provides in-depth technical reporting on world aerospace news geared toward the professional.

629.13   US   ISSN 1074-0090
FLIGHT JACKET.* 1943. w. free. Golden West Publishing, Inc., 22481 Aspan St., Lake Forest, CA 92630-1630. TEL 714-726-2939. FAX 714-830-9504. Ed. Christie Lowe. circ. 13,000. (tabloid format) **Document type:** newspaper.

AERONAUTICS AND SPACE FLIGHT

629.132 UK ISSN 0015-3737
FLIGHT SAFETY BULLETIN. 1965. q. £12 (foreign £18) (effective 1998). General Aviation Safety Council, Holly Tree Cottage, Park Corner, Nettlebed, Oxon. RG9 6DP, England. TEL 44-1491-641735. Ed. John Stewart-Smith. R&P contact: John Stewart-Smith. adv. contact: Andrew Dent. bk.rev.; illus.; stat. circ. 14,500. **Document type:** bulletin.
 Description: Contains articles, statistics, and accident details of UK general aviation accidents and incidents. Aims to foster the development of general aviation and its safety by encouraging competence among pilots and operators.

629.13 US ISSN 0898-5715
TL553.5
FLIGHT SAFETY DIGEST. m. $95 in N. America; elsewhere $100. Flight Safety Foundation, Inc., 601 Madison St., Ste. 300, Alexandria, VA 22314-1756. TEL 703-739-6700. FAX 703-739-6708. Ed. Roger Rozelle. illus. circ. 2,700. (reprint service avail. from UMI) **Document type:** trade publication.
—CISTI.
 Former titles: Flight Safety Facts and Reports (ISSN 0098-7182); Flight Safety Facts and Analysis.
 Description: Analyzes controversial industry issues, shares observations of important influences, describes the latest innovations in training, technology or management.

629.1 US
FLIGHT TEST NEWS. 1981. m. $25. Society of Flight Test Engineers, Box 4047, Lancaster, CA 93539. TEL 805-538-9715. FAX 805-538-9715. circ. 1,200. (looseleaf format; back issues avail.) **Document type:** newsletter.

629.132 US ISSN 1047-6415
FLIGHT TRAINING. 1989. m. $21.95. Smooth Propeller Company, 201 Main St., Parkville, MO 64152. TEL 816-741-5151. FAX 816-741-6458. Ed. Scott Spangler; Pub. Melissa Murphy. adv. contact: Melissa Murphy. bk.rev. circ. 80,000. (back issues avail.) **Document type:** trade publication.
 Incorporates (1968-1989): N A F I Newsletter.
 Description: Provides how-to and operational information for pilots in various stages of receiving, renewing or upgrading their certification. Covers careers, safety, techniques, regulations, and aircraft.

629.13 US
FLIGHTLINES. 10/yr. Kent Publications, Inc. (Woodmere), Box 364, Woodmere, NY 11598-0364. Pub. Bernard Kovit. adv. **Document type:** newsletter.

629.132 AT ISSN 1320-5870
FLIGHTPATH. q. Aus.$29 (foreign Aus.$82) (effective Aug. 1996). Yaffa Publishing Group, 17-21 Bellevue St., Surry Hills, N.S.W. 2010, Australia. TEL 61-2-92812333. FAX 61-2-92812750. E-mail: yaffa@yaffa.com.au. Ed. Doug Nancarrow; Pub. Tracy Yaffa. adv.: B&W page Aus.$1290, color page Aus.$1745; trim 297 x 210; adv. contact: John Cassidy. circ. 9,299. **Document type:** consumer publication.
 Incorporates: AirPower.
 Description: For pilots and aircraft owners, civil and military aircrews as well as enthusiasts who have a fascination with flight.

629.13 AU
FLUG-INFORMATIONEN. 1950. q. membership. Oesterreichisches Luftfahrt Archiv, Kreuzgasse 63, A-1180 Vienna, Austria. Ed. Reinhard Keimel. bk.rev circ. 500. **Document type:** bulletin.
 Formerly: Flugsport-Informationen (ISSN 0015-4598)
 Description: Contains information on Austrian aviation history.

629.13 GW ISSN 0015-4547
TL503
FLUG REVUE; Vereinigt mit Flugwelt International mit Flugkoerper. 1956. m. DM.78; newsstand price: DM.7. Vereinigte Motor-Verlage GmbH und Co. KG, Leuschnerstr. 1, 70174 Stuttgart, Germany. TEL 49-711-18201. FAX 49-711-1821723. (U.S. addr.: 6810 Butler Valley Rd., Korbel, CA 95550. TEL 707-668-4027. FAX 707-668-4055) Ed. Wolfdietrich Hoeveler; Pubs. Karl Vogel, Paul Pietsch. adv.: B&W page DM.8760, color page DM.16206; trim 185 x 248; adv. contact: Reinhard Wittstamm. bk.rev.; index. circ. 50,540. **Document type:** consumer publication.
—CISTI; Linda Hall; SWETS. **CCC**.
 Description: Contains research information on all aspects of air and space travel.

629.1 GW ISSN 0938-3883
FLUGPOST; Informationsdienst Luftfahrt. 1989. w. DM.680 (effective 1997 & 1998). Flugpost Verlag Peter Pletschacher, Kolpingring 3, 82041 Oberhaching, Germany. TEL 49-89-613890-0. FAX 49-89-61389010. Ed. Peter Pletschacher. **Document type:** newsletter.

629.1 GW
FLUGSICHERHEITSMITTEILUNGEN (FSM). 1972. irreg. free. Luftfahrt-Bundesamt, Postfach 3054, 38020 Braunschweig, Germany. TEL 49-531-2355-0. FAX 49-531-2355360. circ. 27,000. (back issues avail.) **Document type:** government publication.
 Description: Basic theoretical information for training of pilot students.

629.1 AU
FLUGSPORTZEITUNG. 1972. m. S.350. Verlag Karl Berger, Spratzerner Kirchenweg 51, Postfach 398, A-3101 St. Poelten, Austria. TEL 43-2742-353422. FAX 43-2742-353422. E-mail: bergfsz@noet.at; URL: http://www.noet.at/flugsportzeitung. Ed. Karl Berger. adv. contact: Karl Berger. bk.rev. circ. 2,400. **Document type:** consumer publication.

629.1 GW ISSN 0933-8454
FLUGZEUG; Aktuell-Historie-Modell. 1985. s-m. DM.51 (foreign DM.64). Flugzeug Publikations GmbH, Thomas-Mann-Str. 3, 89257 Illertissen, Germany. FAX 49-7303-964141. Ed. Gerhard Lang. R&P contact: Manfred Franzue. adv. contact: Jutta Richter. bk.rev.; charts; illus.; index. circ. 19,000. (back issues avail.) **Document type:** consumer publication.

629.1 GW
FLY AND GLIDE. 1975. m. DM.86.40 (foreign DM.96); newsstand price: DM.8. Top Special Verlag GmbH, Nebendahlstr. 16, 22041 Hamburg, Germany. TEL 49-40-3470-0. FAX 49-40-34725588. Ed. Edeltraud Erl. adv.: B&W page DM.3250, color page DM.5620; trim 190 x 244; adv. contact: Marlene Mauracher. circ. 22,017. **Document type:** consumer publication.
 Former titles: Drachenflieger Magazin (ISSN 0175-1492); Drachenflieger (ISSN 0722-8589)

FLYER. see TRANSPORTATION — Air Transport

629.13 SW ISSN 0281-8760
FLYG; flygets aarsbok. 1948-1971; resumed 1979. a. SEK 275 (effective 1997). Bevingade Ord, Martinvaegen 36, S-161 55 Bromma, Sweden. TEL 46-8-37-70-50. FAX 46-8-37-17-70. (Dist. by: Soerlins Foerlag, P.O. Box 434, S-601 05 Noerrkoeping, Sweden) Ed. P. Kristoffersson. bk.rev. circ. 5,000. **Document type:** monographic series.
 Formerly (until 1982): I Luften.
 Description: Features articles on all aspects of aviation with emphasis on recent events.

629.132 SW ISSN 0284-1215
FLYGBRANSCHEN. 1987. m. SEK 295 (effective 1991). Flygbranschen, Bollgraend 18, S-178 00 Ekeroe, Sweden.

629.132 SW ISSN 1101-3915
FLYGLEDAREN; tidning foer Svensk Flygledarfoerening. 1977. q. SEK 360 membership (effective 1990). Flygledaren, A T S, P.O. Box 54, S230 32 Malmoe-Sturup, Sweden.

629.13 SW ISSN 0081-5640
FLYGTEKNISKA FOERSOEKSANSTALTEN. MEDDELANDE - REPORT. (Text in English) 1944. irreg. price varies. A W I International AB, P.O. Box 4627, S-116 91 Stockholm, Sweden. TEL 46-8-7282500. FAX 46-8-338707. Ed. Brit Berg. **Document type:** monographic series.

629.13 US ISSN 0015-4806
TL501
FLYING. 1927. m. $24. Hachette Filipacchi Magazines, Inc., 1633 Broadway, New York, NY 10019. TEL 212-767-6953. (Subscr. to: Box 53647, Boulder, CO 80302. TEL 800-678-0797) Ed. J. Mac McClellan. adv.; bk.rev.; charts; illus.; stat.; tr.lit.; index. circ. 323,177. (also avail. in microform from UMI,MIM; reprint service avail. from UMI) **Indexed:** Abr.R.G., Bk.Rev.Ind. (1965-), Child.Bk.Rev.Ind. (1965-), Consum.Ind., Mag.Ind., PMR, R.G., R.G.Abstr., Sports Per.Ind., Sportsearch. **Document type:** consumer publication, trade publication.
 ●Also available online. Vendor(s): Information Access Co., Knight-Ridder Information, Inc., UMI.
—CISTI; KR SourceOne; Linda Hall; SWETS; UMI; UnCover.
 Description: Discusses topics in general (private and corporate) aviation and reviews new aircraft and equipment. Covers safety and flying techniques.

629.13 355 UK ISSN 0262-8201
FLYING M. vol.5, 1980. 3/yr. membership. Society of Friends of the Royal Air Force Museum, Hendon, London NW9 5LL, England. Ed. John H.C. Kenyon. adv.; bk.rev.; illus. circ. 2,300.

629.132 US ISSN 0274-5798
FLYING REVIEW MAGAZINE; aviation's forum. 1970. m. $26 (effective 1994). (United States Pilots Association) Fly Review Publications, Box 9191, Albuquerque, NM 87119. TEL 505-271-8877; 800-282-8839. FAX 505-271-8876. Ed. Bill Gilbert; Pub. James Kinlen. R&P contact: Rozanna Kinlen. adv.: page $715; 7 1/2 x 10; adv. contact: Rozonna Kinlen. bk.rev. circ. 35,000. (back issues avail.) **Document type:** consumer publication, trade publication.
 Description: Addresses all facets of aviation, features columns on flight training, soaring, air racing, new products and projects.

614.8 355 US ISSN 0279-9308
UG633
FLYING SAFETY. 1944. m. $20 (foreign $25). U.S. Air Force Safety Agency, 9700 Ave. G, S.E., Ste. 282, Kirtland AFB, NM 87117-5670. TEL 505-846-0936. FAX 505-846-2710. (Subscr. to: Superintendent of Documents, U.S. Government Printing Office, Box 371954, Pittsburgh, PA 15250-7954. TEL 202-512-1800. FAX 202-512-2250) Ed. Maj. James H. Grigsby. bk.rev.; illus.; charts. circ. 18,350. (also avail. in microform from MIM,UMI; back issues avail.; reprint service avail. from UMI) **Indexed:** Air Un.Lib.Ind., Ind.U.S.Gov.Per. **Document type:** government publication.
—BLDSC (3964.128000); CISTI; Linda Hall; SWETS; UMI; UnCover.
 Formerly (until vol.37, 1981): Aerospace Safety (ISSN 0001-9429)
 Description: Covers the many fields of flight, aircraft engineering, flight training, and safety both in the air and on the ground.

001.94 US ISSN 0898-3798
FLYING SAUCER DIGEST. 1967. 5/yr. $12. United Aerial Phenomena Agency, Box 347032, Cleveland, OH 44134-7032. Ed. Allan J. Manak. adv. contact: Allan J. Manak. bk.rev. (back issues avail.) **Document type:** newsletter.
 Formerly: U F O Journal (Cleveland).

001.94 UK ISSN 0015-4881
TL789
FLYING SAUCER REVIEW. Abbreviated title: F S R. 1955. q. £15 (overseas £18 ($35)). F S R Publications Ltd., P.O. Box 162, High Wycombe, Bucks. HP13 5DZ, England. Ed. Gordon Creighton. adv.; bk.rev. circ. 3,500. (back issues avail.) **Document type:** consumer publication.
—BLDSC (3964.145000).
 Description: Carries the latest U.F.O. reports from all parts of the English-speaking world, includes information directly translated from numerous languages worldwide.

AERONAUTICS AND SPACE FLIGHT

629.13   NO   ISSN 0332-6934
FLYNYTT. 1929. 6/yr. NOK 185 (Euroep NOK 265; elsewhere NOK 275). Norsk Aero Klubb, Tollbugaten 3, N-0152 Oslo, Norway. TEL 47-23-10-29-00. FAX 47-23-10-29-01. E-mail: flynytt@nak.no. (Co-sponsor: Norges Luftsportsforbund) Ed. Olav F. Aamoth. adv.; B&W page NOK 7900, color page NOK 10900; trim 193 x 277; adv. contact: Martin Aarestrup. bk.rev.; circ. 10,000 (controlled).
—CCC.

629.1   UK   ISSN 0262-6950
FLYPAST. 1980. m. £36 (foreign £64.80). Key Publishing Ltd., P.O. Box 300, Stamford, Lincs. PE9 1NA, England. TEL 44-1780-480404. FAX 44-1780-757812. TELEX 265871-MONREF-G. E-mail: postmaster@keymags.demon.co.uk; URL: http://www.keymags.co.uk/flypast/. Ed. Ken Delve. adv.; bk.rev.; bibl.; illus. circ. 42,070. (back issues avail.) **Document type:** bulletin.

629.132 797.5   DK   ISSN 0015-492X
FLYV. 1928. m. DKK 324 (effective 1995). (Kongelig Dansk Aeroklub) Danish General Aviation ApS, Lufthavnsvej 28, DK-4000 Roskilde, Denmark. TEL 45-31-35-45-00. FAX 45-31-35-97-68. Ed. Hans Kofoed. adv.; B&W page DKK 5750, color page DKK 9250; adv. contact: Jakob Tornvig. bk.rev.; charts; film rev.; illus.; stat.; tr.lit.; elec. circ. 8,500 (controlled). **Document type:** trade publication.
Description: Provides information about general aviation, military aviation, commercial aviation, air traffic, gliding, sport flying, home-building of aircraft and ballooning in Denmark and abroad.

001.94   US   ISSN 1054-4208
TL789.A1
FOCUS (BURBANK). 1985-1996 (Jun.). bi-m. $24. Fair Witness Project, 4219 W. Olive Ave., Ste. 247, Burbank, CA 91505. TEL 818-980-8758. Ed. William L. Moore. adv.; bk.rev. circ. 1,000. (back issues avail.) **Document type:** newsletter.
Description: Publishes well-researched, evidence-oriented articles about UFO's and similar unexplained phenomena.

387.7 629.1   US
FOR THE RECORD (ARLINGTON). Variant title: N A A Newsletter. 6/yr. $24 includes membership. National Aeronautic Association, 1815 N. Fort Myer Dr., Ste. 700, Arlington, VA 22209-1805. TEL 703-527-0226. FAX 703-527-0229. Ed. Jim Way. bk.rev. circ. 6,000. **Document type:** newsletter.
Description: Includes competition results, aviation records, membership news.

387.7   UK
FORECAST CUMULATIVE SHEETS. bi-m. $910 (with Weekly Profile $1250 and missiles; vehicles and weapons $495). Aviation Studies International, Sussex House, Parkside, Wimbledon, London SW19 5NB, England. TEL 44-181-946-5082. **Document type:** directory, trade publication.
Formerly: Forecast Data Bank Cumulative Sheets (ISSN 0015-7082)
Description: Lists and descibes civil and military airplanes, helicopters, and general-aviation aircraft individually and by type for 200 territories.

FOREIGN AIRWORTHINESS DIRECTIVES. C A A ADDITIONAL AIRWORTHINESS DIRECTIVES. see *TRANSPORTATION — Air Transport*

FORESIGHT (BIRMINGHAM). see *PARAPSYCHOLOGY AND OCCULTISM*

FORST, HOLZ UND JAGD TASCHENBUCH. see *FORESTS AND FORESTRY*

629.13   FR   ISSN 1169-7830
FRANCE. OFFICE NATIONAL D'ETUDES ET DE RECHERCHES AEROSPATIALES. ACTIVITES. English edition: France. Nation Office of Aerospace Studies and Research. Activities (ISSN 1169-7857) 1969. a. free. Office National d'Etudes et de Recherches Aerospatiales, 29 av. de la Division-Leclerc, 92322 Chatillon Cedex, France. URL: http://www.onera.fr. circ. 3,450 (1,050 English ed., 2,400 French ed.). **Document type:** corporate report.
—BLDSC (0676.461000).

629.13   FR   ISSN 0078-3781
TL502   CODEN: ORATAQ
FRANCE. OFFICE NATIONAL D'ETUDES ET DE RECHERCHES AEROSPATIALES. NOTES TECHNIQUES. (Text in French; summaries in English) 1946. irreg., approx. 15/yr. 500 F. (effective 1997). Office National d'Etudes et de Recherches Aerospatiales, 29 av. de la Division-Leclerc, 92322 Chatillon Cedex, France. URL: http://www.onera.fr. Ed. Jean-Philippe Chateau. index, cum.index: 1950-1987. circ. 230. **Indexed:** Appl.Mech.Rev. **Document type:** academic/scholarly publication.
—CASDDS; CISTI; Linda Hall.
Formerly (until 1963): France. Office National d'Etudes et de Recherches Aeronautiques. Note Technique (ISSN 0369-7614)
Description: Presents works of a high technical level with documents concerning aerodynamics, energetics, materials, structures, physics, computer sciences, automatic systems and test instrumentation.

629.13   FR   ISSN 0078-379X
TL507
FRANCE. OFFICE NATIONAL D'ETUDES ET DE RECHERCHES AEROSPATIALES. PUBLICATIONS. (Text in French; summaries in English) 1946. irreg. (approx. 5/yr.). 500 F. (effective 1997). Office National d'Etudes et de Recherches Aerospatiales, 29 av. de la Division-Leclerc, 92322 Chatillon Cedex, France. URL: http://www.onera.fr. Ed. Jean-Philippe Chateau. index, cum.index: 1947-1987. circ. 230. **Indexed:** Appl.Mech.Rev. **Document type:** academic/scholarly publication.
—CISTI; Linda Hall.
Formerly (until 1963): France, Office National d'Etudes et de Recherches Aeronautiques. Publications (ISSN 0369-7622)
Description: Results of studies and work of primary importance concerning aerodynamics, energetics, materials, structures, physics, computer sciences, automatic systems and test instrumentation.

629.1   FR   ISSN 0751-5596
FRANCE AVIATION. 1954. bi-m. 130 F. (effective Jan. 1991). Societe d'Informations et d'Editions Aeronautiques, 25 bd de Vaugirard, 75757 Paris Cedex 15, France. TEL 43-23-05-02. FAX 43-23-94-02. Ed. Thierry Do Espirito. adv.; circ. 65,000 (controlled). (tabloid format) **Document type:** newspaper.

629.1   CN   ISSN 0317-056X
FROM THE GROUND UP. 1947. irreg., latest 27th ed. Can.$33.95. Aviation Publishers Co. Ltd., P.O. Box 1361, Sta. B, Ottawa, ON K1P 5R4, Canada. TEL 613-745-2943. FAX 613-745-9851. E-mail: aviationpub@igs.net. Ed. I.L. Peppler. R&P contact: Graeme Peppler. **Document type:** academic/scholarly publication.
Description: Discusses in-depth all subjects related to aircraft operation: theory of flight, aero engines, meteorology, navigation, radio and radio navigation, air safety and aeronautical facilities.

FUERZA AEREA. see *MILITARY*

001.94   US
FUND FOR U F O RESEARCH QUARTERLY REPORT. 1980. q. $15 contribution. Fund for U F O Research, Box 277, Mt. Rainier, MD 20712. TEL 703-684-6032. Ed. Richard Hall. circ. 1,200. **Document type:** newsletter.
Description: Current scientific research into unidentified flying objects.

629.1   US
G A C I A C BULLETIN. q. U.S. Department of Defense, Guidance and Control Information Analysis Center, c/o Chalmer George, AMC Smart Weapons Management Office, Attn.: AMSMI-SW, Redstone Arsenal, AL 35898-5222. TEL 205-876-3788. URL: http://gaciac.iitri.com/bulletins.html. **Document type:** government publication.
● Available only online.

629.13   VE
GACETA AEREA/AIR GAZETTE. 1971. m. $90. Edif. La Carlota, Ofc. 8-D, Piso 8, Av. Libertador, Cruce con Acacias, Apdo. 68075, Caracas 1062A, Venezuela. Ed. Miguel Antoni. adv. circ. 4,500.

629.1   US
GASBAG. q. $28 membership. Association of Balloon and Airship Constructors, Box 90864, San Diego, CA 92169. TEL 619-581-1721. FAX 619-581-1721. URL: http://www.sdic.net/piolenc/abac.htm. Ed. F. Marc de Piolenc; Pub. F. Marc de Piolenc. R&P contact: F. Marc de Piolenc. adv. contact: F. Marc de Piolenc. bk.rev.; bibl.; illus.; circ. 100 (paid).
Incorporates (1974-1996): Aerostation (ISSN 0741-5974)
Description: Covers technology of lighter-than-air flight.

629.13   UK
GATWICK NEWS. 1982. w. £25. Malmoss Ltd., 40 The Blvd., Crawley, W. Sussex RH10 1XP, England. TEL 01293-545499. FAX 01293-521680. Ed. Jackie Pond. adv.; bk.rev.; film rev.; play rev.; stat.; tr.lit. circ. 23,000. (tabloid format; back issues avail.) **Document type:** newspaper.

629.13   US   ISSN 1052-9136
GENERAL AVIATION NEWS & FLYER. 1949. fortn. $29. Northwest Flyer, Inc., Box 39099, Tacoma, WA 98439-0099. TEL 206-471-9888. FAX 206-471-9911. URL: http://www.ganflyer.com. Ed. Kirk Gormley; Pubs. Mary Lou & Dave Sclair. R&P contact: Ben Sclair. adv. contact: Larry Price. bk.rev.; charts; illus.; stat.; tr.lit.; circ. 38,500 (paid). **Document type:** newspaper.
Former titles (until 1990): General Aviation News: The Green Sheet (ISSN 0191-927X); General Aviation (ISSN 0016-6510); Incorporates (1959-1990): Western Flyer; Sport Flyer and Whole Air.
Description: Covers the general aviation scene, from business flying to recreational activities, with technical and personality features, product reviews, air show news, and other topics of interest to plane owners, airport operators, pilots.

GLOBAL POSITIONING & NAVIGATION NEWS. see *COMMUNICATIONS — Telephone And Telegraph*

GOVERNMENT BUSINESS WORLDWIDE REPORTS. see *PUBLIC ADMINISTRATION*

GREAT BRITAIN. CIVIL AVIATION AUTHORITY. AIRWORTHINESS NOTICES. see *TRANSPORTATION — Air Transport*

GREAT BRITAIN. CIVIL AVIATION AUTHORITY. APPROVED AERIAL POSITIONS. see *TRANSPORTATION — Air Transport*

GREAT BRITAIN. CIVIL AVIATION AUTHORITY. CIVIL AVIATION PUBLICATIONS. see *TRANSPORTATION — Air Transport*

GREAT BRITAIN. CIVIL AVIATION AUTHORITY. TYPE CERTIFICATE DATA SHEETS. see *TRANSPORTATION — Air Transport*

629.1 387.7   US   ISSN 1081-406X
GREAT LAKES PILOT NEWS. 1989. bi-m. $12 (effective 1997). 1219 Van Dusen, Ann Arbor, MI 48103. TEL 313-439-8847. FAX 313-769-6471. Pub. Don Kleinschmidt. adv.; B&W page $660; 10 1/2 x 14. circ. 13,000 (controlled). **Document type:** newspaper.

001.94   US
GROUND SAUCER WATCH NEWSLETTER.* 1973. 3/yr. $4.50. Civilian Aerial Phenomena Research Organization, 1634 E. Monte Cristo Ave., Phoenix, AZ 85022-3300. Ed. William Spaulding. bk.rev.; illus. circ. 1,500. **Document type:** newsletter.

629.1   US
GROUND SUPPORT EQUIPMENT TODAY. Short title: G S E Today. 1993. bi-m. free to qualified personnel. General Publications, Inc., Box 480, Hatch, NM 87937-0480. TEL 505-267-1030. FAX 505-267-1920. Ed. George Prill; Pub. Jennifer Prill. adv. contact: Rebecca Sheer. circ. 14,000 (controlled). **Document type:** trade publication.
Description: Connects airlines, manufacturers, suppliers, airports and regulatory bodies in the ground support industry.

AERONAUTICS AND SPACE FLIGHT

629.13 FR ISSN 1266-4812
GROUPEMENT DES INDUSTRIES FRANCAISES AERONAUTIQUES ET SPATIALES. LETTRE. Key Title: Lettre G I F A S. English edition: G I F A S Newsletter (ISSN 1266-4820) (Editions in English, French) 1946. m. 220 F. (foreign 182.42 F.) (effective 1998). Groupement des Industries Francaises Aeronautiques et Spatiales, 4 rue Galilee, 75782 Paris Cedex 16, France. TEL 33-1-44431752. FAX 33-1-44431756. Ed. Patrick Guerin. charts; illus.; stat. circ. 3,500. **Document type:** newsletter.
Former titles (until 1993): Lettre Hebdomadaire - G I F A S (ISSN 1247-9802); (until 1989): Informations Aeronautiques et Spatiales. La Lettre Hebdomadaire (ISSN 0399-4864); Which supersedes in part (in 1976): Informations Aeronautiques (ISSN 0399-4856); Which was formerly (until 1976): Informations Aeronautiques Francaises (ISSN 0399-4848); (until 1956): Informations Aeronautiques (ISSN 0399-483X)

GUANGZHOU MINHANG/GUANGZHOU CIVIL AVIATION. see TRANSPORTATION — Air Transport

629.13 630 BL ISSN 0104-4958
GUIA DE AVIACAO AGRICOLA/AGRICULTURAL AVIATION GUIDE. (Text in Portuguese; summaries in English) 1992. a. Aviacao em Revista Editora Ltda., Rua da Consolacao 1992, 10o andar, 01302-000 Sao Paulo, Brazil. TEL 55-11-2570577. FAX 55-11-2570577. Ed. Ernesto Klotzel; Pub. Helcio Estrella. adv.: B&W page $4500, color page $4950; trim 210 x 280; adv. contact: Francisco Carlos Alves. circ. 10,000. **Document type:** directory.
Description: Provides information on sales, services available, fleets, companies and personnel in the industry.

629.13 BL ISSN 0104-4974
GUIA DE OFICINAS E MANUTENCAO/WORKSHOP AND MAINTENANCE GUIDE. 1991. a. Aviacao em Revista Editora Ltda, Rua da Consolacao 1992, 10o andar, 01302-000 Sao Paulo, Brazil. TEL 55-11-2570577. FAX 55-11-2570577. Pub. Helcio Estrella. adv.: B&W page $4500, color page $4950; trim 210 x 280; adv. contact: Francisco Carlos Alves. circ. 10,000. **Document type:** directory.
Description: Contains analysis, performance statistics, trend indicators, company data, services and supply listings.

629.132 BL ISSN 0104-7957
GUIA DO AEROCLUBES E AERODESPORTOS/AEROCLUBS AND AIR SPORTS GUIDE. (Text in Portuguese; summaries in English) 1990. a. Aviacao em Revista Editora Ltda., Rua da Consolacao 1992, 10o andar, 01302-000 Sao Paulo, Brazil. TEL 55-11-2570577. FAX 55-11-2570577. Ed. Ernesto Klotzel; Pub. Helcio Estrella. R&P contact: Helcio Estrella. adv.: B&W page $4500, color page $4950; trim 210 x 280; adv. contact: Francisco Carlos Alves. circ. 10,000. **Document type:** directory.
Description: Provides analyses, fleet data, company, club, manufacturer listings, air sport associations, parachuting clubs and ballon activities.

629.1 US ISSN 1057-493X
TL787.A6
GUIDANCE AND CONTROL. (Part of the Advances in the Astronautical Sciences Series (ISSN 0065-3438)) 1979. a. price varies. (American Astronautical Society) Univelt, Inc., Box 28130, San Diego, CA 92198-0198. TEL 619-746-4005. FAX 619-746-3139. E-mail: 76121.1532@compuserve.com. Ed. Robert H. Jacobs; Pub. Robert H. Jacobs. R&P contact: Robert H. Jacobs. (back issues avail.) Indexed: Eng.Ind., Int.Aerosp.Abstr. **Document type:** proceedings.

629.132 UK
GUILD NEWS. 1956. bi-m. membership. Guild of Air Pilots and Air Navigators, Cobham House, 291 Gray's Inn Rd., London WC1X 8QF, England. TEL 0171-837 3323. FAX 0171-833-3190. Ed. H.O. Field. bk.rev. circ. 2,000. (back issues avail.) **Document type:** academic/scholarly publication.
Incorporates: Guild of Air Pilots and Air Navigators. Journal.
Description: Includes records of the guild's technical and social activities.

629.1 CC ISSN 1000-4009
GUOJI HANGKONG/INTERNATIONAL AVIATION. (Text in Chinese) m. $2 per no. Hangkong Gongye Chubanshe - Aviation Industry Press, 14 Xiaoguan Dongli, Anwai, Beijing 100029, People's Republic of China. TEL 8610-4918417. FAX 8610-4918420. Ed. Xu Dekang.

629.133 387 US
H A C TECHLINE.* 1977. q. $10 (foreign $15). Historical Aircraft Corporation, Box 430, Naturita, CO 81422-0430. TEL 612-451-3283. Ed. Warren Eberspacher. R&P contact: Warren Eberspacher. adv. contact: Warren Eberspacher. bk.rev.; circ. 100 (paid). (looseleaf format; back issues avail.) **Document type:** newsletter.
Description: Covers amateur-built sport aircraft in the form of authentically scaled replicas of old civil and military aircraft.

HANG GLIDING. see SPORTS AND GAMES — Outdoor Life

629.1 CC
HANGKONG DANG'AN/AERONAUTICS ARCHIVES. (Text in Chinese) bi-m. Hangkong Hangtian-bu, Dang'an-guan - Ministry of Aero-Space Industry, Archives, P.O. Box 33, No. 11, Beijing 100712, People's Republic of China. TEL 4013322. Ed. Ju Hongfu.

629.1 CC ISSN 1000-6885
HANGKONG MOXING/MODEL AIRPLANE. (Text in Chinese) q. Zhongguo Hangkong Xuehui - Chinese Society of Aeronautics and Astronautics, 37 Xueyuan Lu, Beijing 100083, People's Republic of China. TEL 86-10-6201-7322. **Document type:** academic/scholarly publication.

629.1 CC ISSN 1000-6893
HANGKONG XUEBAO/ACTA AERONAUTICA ET ASTRONAUTICA SINICA. English edition: Chinese Journal of Aeronautics (ISSN 1000-9361) (Text in Chinese; abstracts in English) 1965. m. $4 per no. Zhongguo Hangkong Xuehui - Chinese Society of Aeronautics and Astronautics, 37 Xueyuan Lu, Beijing 100083, People's Republic of China. TEL 86-10-6201-7247. (Dist. overseas by: China International Book Trading Corp., P.O. Box 399, Beijing, P.R.C.) circ. 1,900. Indexed: Int.Aerosp.Abstr. **Document type:** academic/scholarly publication. —BLDSC (0588.200000).
Description: Covers aeronautical research in China, including fluid mechanics and aerodynamics, flight dynamics and testing, aircraft propulsion systems, autocontrol and avionics, aerospace manufacturing and materials.

629.1 387.7 CC ISSN 1000-0119
TL504
HANGKONG ZHISHI/AEROSPACE KNOWLEDGE. (Text in Chinese) 1958. m. Y182.50($39) (Zhongguo Hangkong Xuehui - Chinese Society of Aeronautics and Astronautics) Hangkong Zhishi Zazhishe - Aerospace Knowledge Press, 37 Xueyuan Lu, Beijing 100083, People's Republic of China. TEL 86-10-8201-7251. FAX 86-10-8201-7322. (Dist. overseas by: China International Book Trading Corp., P.O. Box 399, Beijing, P.R.C.) Ed. Chu Xie. R&P contact: Chu Xie. adv.: B&W page $2,000, color page $3,000; trim 208 x 279. bk.rev. circ. 320,000. (back issues avail.) **Document type:** consumer publication.
Description: Covers the aerospace field in China and abroad, providing scientific, technical, and management information. Reports on China's air force, civil aviation, and aerospace industry, and introduces aerial sports, including ultralight aircraft, airships, balloons, gliding, and parachuting.

629.1 CC ISSN 1001-1765
TL671.28 CODEN: HZGOEO
HANGKONG ZHIZAO GONGCHENG/AVIATION PRODUCTION ENGINEERING. (Text in Chinese) m. $3 per no. (China Aero-Information Center) Hangkong Gongye Chubanshe - Aviation Industry Press, 14 Xiaoguan Dongli, Anwai, Beijing 100029, People's Republic of China. TEL 8610-4922211. FAX 8610-4918420. Ed. Shen Changzhi. adv.: B&W page $2200, color page $3500; trim 8 x 10 3/4.
Description: Reports on aviation and aerospace production and marketing activities, including advanced manufacturing technology, material engineering and management.

629.1 CC ISSN 1000-7474
TL789.8.C55
HANGTIAN/ASTRONAUTICS. (Text in Chinese) bi-m. Y1.60 per no. Zhongguo Yuhang Xuehui - Chinese Astronautic Society, 2 Yuetan Beixiaojie, Beijing 100830, People's Republic of China. TEL 894602. Ed. Li Longyuan.
—SWETS.

629.1 CC ISSN 1002-6665
HANGTIAN JISHU YU MINPIN/AERONAUTIC TECHNOLOGY AND CIVIL PRODUCTS. (Text in Chinese) 1988. m. Hangkong Hangtian Gongye-bu, Keji Qingbao Yanjiu-suo - Ministry of Aero-Space Industry, Institute for Astronautics Information, 14 Xiaoguan Dongli, P.O. Box 1415, Beijing 100029, People's Republic of China. TEL 8411117. Ed. Yang Zhiqiong.

629.132 MX
HELICE. 1959. bi-m. Mex.$27. Mexican Air Line Pilots Association, c/o Capt. J.J. Castillo A., Av. Palomas 110, Lomas de Sotelo, Mexico 10, D.F., Mexico. FAX 52-5-202-25-73. TELEX 17-63-468 ASPAME. Ed. Capt. R. Rebollo. adv.; bk.rev.; charts; illus.; stat.; circ. 2,000 (controlled).

HELICOPTER ASSOCIATION INTERNATIONAL. MAINTENANCE UPDATE. see TRANSPORTATION — Air Transport

629.1 387.7 US
HELICOPTER ASSOCIATION INTERNATIONAL. PRELIMINARY ACCIDENT REPORTS AND TECHNICAL NOTES. m. $50 to non-members; members $25 (effective 1997). Helicopter Association International, 1635 Prince St., Alexandria, VA 22314-2818. TEL 703-683-4646; 800-435-4976. FAX 703-683-4745. Ed. Dick Wright. R&P contact: Dick Wright. circ. 800. **Document type:** trade publication, newsletter.
Description: Includes technical difficulty reports as well as bulletins of interest to helicopter operators.

629.133 355 UK
HELICOPTER INTERNATIONAL MAGAZINE. 1977. bi-m. £20 (outside Europe £30 or $50). Avia Press Associates, 75 Elm Tree Rd., Locking, Weston-super-Mare, Avon BS24 8EL, England. TEL 44-1934-822524. FAX 44-1934-822400. Ed. Elfan ap Rees; Pub. Elfan ap Rees. adv. contact: Julie Derrick. bk.rev.; circ. 24,490 (paid). (back issues avail.) Indexed: PROMT. **Document type:** newsletter. —BLDSC (4285.214000); CISTI; SWETS.
Formerly: Helicopter Magazine (ISSN 0143-1005)
Description: International news coverage of the military and commercial helicopter industry and operators worldwide.

629.133 US ISSN 0363-8227
HELICOPTER NEWS. 1975. bi-w. $597 (foreign $630) (effective 1997). Phillips Business Information, Inc., 1201 Seven Locks Rd., Potomac, MD 20854. TEL 301-424-3338. FAX 301-309-3847. E-mail: pbi@phillips.com. Ed. Tom Moore. bk.rev. circ. 700. **Document type:** newsletter.
●Also available online. Vendor(s): Data-Star, Information Access Co., Knight-Ridder Information, Inc., NewsNet (AE12).
—CCC.

629.133 US ISSN 1042-2048
TL716.5
HELICOPTER SAFETY. 1967. bi-m. $60 in N. America; elsewhere $65. Flight Safety Foundation, Inc., 601 Madison St., Ste. 300, Alexandria, VA 22314-1756. TEL 703-739-6700. FAX 703-739-6708. Ed. Roger Rozelle. bk.rev.; illus. circ. 2,750. (reprint service avail. from UMI) **Document type:** newsletter.
Formerly (until vol.13, no.5, 1987): Helicopter Safety Bulletin (ISSN 0898-8145)
Description: Highlights the broad spectrum of real-world helicopter operations.

AERONAUTICS AND SPACE FLIGHT

629.133   UK
HELIDATA NEWS & CLASSIFIED. 1980. bi-w. £200 (outside Europe £250 ($450)). Avia Press Associates, 75 Elm Tree Rd., Locking, Weston-super-Mare, Avon BS24 8EL, England. TEL 44-1934-822524. FAX 44-1934-822400. Ed. Elfan ap Rees; Pub. Elfan ap Rees. adv. contact: Wendy Reed. bk.rev. circ. 10,800. (looseleaf format; back issues avail.) **Document type:** newsletter.
    Formerly: HeliData (ISSN 0951-9904)
    Description: Contains helicopter news and marketing support classified covering the international military and commercial helicopter industry.

HELIPORT DEVELOPMENT GUIDE. see TRANSPORTATION — Air Transport

629.13   NE   ISSN 0018-0734
HERKENNING (THE HAGUE, 1948). journal for aircraft-, ship and A.F.V. recognition. 1948. bi-m. fl.39.50. (Koninklijke Luchtmacht - Dutch Air Force) Herkenning, Postbus 20708, 2500 ES The Hague, Netherlands. TEL 31-70-3492800. FAX 31-70-3492500. TELEX 43393 NL. E-mail: herken@bart.nl; URL: http://www.bart.nl/~bock. Ed. Elt R.W.M. van Vuuren. bk.rev.; illus. circ. 10,000. **Indexed:** CERDIC. **Document type:** government publication.

HIGH TECHNOLOGY CAREERS. see OCCUPATIONS AND CAREERS

387.7   US   ISSN 0018-2443
HISTORICAL AVIATION ALBUM.* 1965. a. price varies. Sunshine House, Box 665, Destin, FL 32540-0665. TEL 812-232-3076. Ed. Alan Abel. charts; illus.; stat.; tr.mk. circ. 3,500. (also avail. in microform from UMI) **Document type:** consumer publication.
    Description: Short stories on airplanes and aviation history. Includes production statistics.

HOBBY VOLO. see SPORTS AND GAMES

629.13   FR   ISSN 0018-4411
HOMMES VOLANTS. 1949. bi-m. 250 F. 28 rue de Navarin, 75009 Paris, France. TEL 45-26-02-75. FAX 40-16-09-51. TELEX 281 342. Ed. Rene Gardes. adv.; bk.rev.; abstr.; illus.; stat. circ. 20,000. **Indexed:** Sportsearch (1976-).

629.1 621.3   CC   ISSN 1007-2276
HONGWAI YU JIGUANG GONGCHENG/INFRARED AND LASER ENGINEERING. (Text in Chinese; summaries in English) 1972. bi-m. $120 (effective 1998). Hangtian Gongye Zong Gongsi, Tianjin Jinhang Jishu Wuli Yanjiusuo - China Aerospace Corporation, Tianjin Jinhang Technical Physics Institute, P.O. Box 225-32, Tianjin 300192, People's Republic of China. TEL 86-22-23363000. FAX 86-22-23363423. E-mail: duyq@mimi.cnc.ac.cn. (Subscr. to: An Bo, Dept. of Documentation, P.O. Box 1408, Beijing 100013, People's Republic of China. TEL 86-10-68372847. FAX 86-10-64227606) Ed. Xiong Huifeng. adv. contact: An Bo.
    Description: A scientific journal focusing on the applications of infrared and laser technology to space, satellites, tactical missiles, and other weapon systems.
    Refereed Serial

629.1   US
HORIZONS (TORRANCE). 1988. m. free. Allied-Signal Aerospace Company, 2525 W. 190th St., Torrance, CA 90504. TEL 213-512-1928. FAX 213-512-2490. Ed. Gary Lutz. circ. 56,000. (tabloid format; back issues avail.)
    Description: Covers contracts and product news, aerospace industry trends, and human interest articles for employees.

629.133   UK   ISSN 0144-3755
HOVERCRAFT BULLETIN; a monthly summary of world hovercraft news and events. 1980. m. £20 (foreign £23) (effective 1997 & 1998). Hovercraft Society, 24 Jellicoe Ave., Alverstoke, Gosport, Hants PO12 2PE, England. TEL 0705-584371. Ed. Brian J. Russell. R&P contact: Brian J. Russell. adv. contact: Brian J. Russell. bk.rev. circ. 250. **Document type:** bulletin.
    Formerly: U K H S Bulletin.

614.85 629.1   US   ISSN 1057-5545
HUMAN FACTORS & AVIATION MEDICINE. 1957. bi-m. $60 in N. America; elsewhere $65. Flight Safety Foundation, Inc., 601 Madison St., Ste. 300, Alexandria, VA 22314-1756. TEL 703-739-6700. FAX 703-739-6708. Ed. Roger Rozelle. bk.rev. circ. 2,200. (reprint service avail. from UMI) **Document type:** newsletter.
    Former titles (until vol.34, no.6, 1987): Human Factors and Aviation Medicine Bulletin (ISSN 0898-5723); (until vol.34, no.4, 1987): Human Factors Bulletin.
    Description: Allows specialists, researchers, and physicians to present information critical to the training, performance and health of aviation professionals.

363.12   UN
HUMAN FACTORS DIGEST. (Editions in English, French, Russian, Spanish) 1989. irreg., no.11, 1994. price varies. International Civil Aviation Organization, Attn: Document Sales Unit, 1000 Sherbrooke St. W., Montreal, PQ H3A 2R2, Canada. TEL 514-285-8022. FAX 514-285-6769. TELEX 05-24513. (back issues avail.)

HUNTING REVIEW. see PETROLEUM AND GAS

001.94   FR   ISSN 0246-6287
HYPOTHESES EXTRATERRESTRES; revue de l'Univers O.V.N.I. 1971. q. 50 F. G.E.O.S.-France, Saint Denis les Rebais, 77510 Rebais, France. Ed. L. Gerard. bk.rev. circ. 5,000.
    Formerly (until 1980): Extraterrestres (ISSN 0399-5216)

I A T A - I A L AIR DISTANCES. (International Air Transport Association) see TRANSPORTATION — Air Transport

387.7
TL500.5   UN   ISSN 1014-8876
I C A O JOURNAL. (Editions in English, French, Spanish) 1946. m. (10/yr.). $20. International Civil Aviation Organization, Attn: Document Sales Unit, 1000 Sherbrooke St. W., Ste. 652, Montreal, PQ H3A 2R2, Canada. TEL 514-285-8022. FAX 514-285-6769. TELEX 05-24513. E-mail: icaohq@icao.org; URL: http://www.worldyellowpages.com/icao. Ed. Eric MacBurnie. adv.; charts; illus. (also avail. in microfiche from CIS) **Indexed:** Environ.Abstr., HRIS, IIS, Int.Aerosp.Abstr., Tel.Abstr.—BLDSC (4360.220750); CISTI; Linda Hall; SWETS; UnCover.
    Former titles (until 1990): I C A O Bulletin (ISSN 0018-8778); (until 1952): I C A O Monthly Bulletin (ISSN 0256-8128); (until 1948): P I C A O Monthly Bulletin (ISSN 0256-8136)

629.13   US   ISSN 0746-2743
I C A S NEWS. 1984. q. $25 to members only. International Council of Air Shows, 1931 Horton Rd., Ste. 5, Jackson, MI 49203-5599. TEL 517-782-5886. E-mail: hgicas@aol.com; URL: http://www.airshows.org. Ed. Linda Singer. R&P contact: Linda Singer. TEL 517-782-2424. adv. contact: Linda Singer. circ. 1,800. **Document type:** trade publication.
    Description: Contains industry news, views, trends and education.

629.1   UK   ISSN 0308-7247
I C AERO REPORT. irreg. Imperial College of Science, Technology & Medicine, Department of Aeronautics, University of London, Prince Consort Rd., London SW7 2BY, England. R&P contact: Sue Clarke. **Document type:** monographic series.
—CISTI.

629.132   DK
I D A FLYAARBOG. 1975. irreg. membership. Ingenioerforeningen i Danmark, Flyvetekniisk Selskab, Vester Farimagsgade 29, DK-1780 Copenhagen V, Denmark. **Document type:** proceedings.
    Former titles (until 1995): D I F Flyaarbog (ISSN 0107-0886); (until 1976): Dansk Ingenioerforening. Flyvetekniisk Sektion. Aarbog (ISSN 0906-9402)

I E E E - A E S C O N AEROSPACE AND ELECTRONICS CONFERENCE. RECORD. see ENGINEERING — Electrical Engineering

629.1   US
I E E E - A E S S DAYTON CHAPTER SYMPOSIUM. 1979. a. price varies. (I E E E, Aerospace and Electronic Systems Society, Dayton Section) Institute of Electrical and Electronics Engineers, Inc., 345 E. 47th St., New York, NY 10017-2394. TEL 732-981-0060; 800-678-4333. FAX 732-981-9667. E-mail: customer.service@ieee.org; URL: http://www.ieee.org. (Subscr. to: 445 Hoes Ln., Box 1331, Piscataway, NJ 08855-1331)
    Former titles (1980-1984): I E E E - A E S S Symposium (Proceedings); (until 1979): I E E E - A E S S Seminar.

629.1   US
I E E E - A I A A DIGITAL AVIONICS SYSTEMS CONFERENCE. PROCEEDINGS. Variant title in alternate years: A I A A - I E E E Digital Avionics Systems Conference. Proceedings. (Publication alternates between IEEE and AIAA) 1975. biennial. price varies. (I E E E, Aerospace and Electronic Systems Society) Institute of Electrical and Electronics Engineers, Inc., 345 E. 47th St., New York, NY 10017-2394. TEL 732-981-0060; 800-678-4333. FAX 732-981-9667. E-mail: customer.service@ieee.org; URL: http://www.ieee.org. (Subscr. to: 445 Hoes Ln., Box 1331, Piscataway, NJ 08855-1331) (Co-sponsor: American Institute of Aeronautics and Astronautics) (also avail. in microfiche) **Document type:** proceedings.
    Former titles (until 1981): A I A A - I E E E Digital Avionics Systems Conference. Technical Papers; (until 1979): Digital Avionics Systems Conference (Publication); (until 1977): A I A A Digital Avionics Systems Conference (Preprints).

I E E E AEROSPACE AND ELECTRONIC SYSTEMS MAGAZINE. see ELECTRONICS

629.4
TL693   US   CODEN: NASEA9
I E E E AEROSPACE CONFERENCE. PROCEEDINGS. a. price varies. (I E E E, Aerospace and Electronic Systems Society) Institute of Electrical and Electronics Engineers, Inc., 345 E. 47th St., New York, NY 10017-2394. TEL 732-981-0060; 800-678-4333. FAX 732-981-9667. E-mail: customer.service@ieee.org; URL: http://www.ieee.org. (Subscr. to: Box 1331, 445 Hoes Lane, Piscataway, NJ 08855-1331) **Indexed:** INSPEC. **Document type:** proceedings.
—Linda Hall; UMI. **CCC.**
    Former titles (until 1997): I E E E National Aerospace and Electronics Conference. Proceedings (ISSN 0547-3578); National Aerospace Electronics Conference. Proceedings; National Aerospace and Electronics Conference. Record (ISSN 0065-373X)

629.47
TL1100   US   ISSN 0275-9306
    CODEN: PRICDT
I E E E POWER ELECTRONICS SPECIALISTS CONFERENCE. RECORD. Short title: P E S C Record. 1970. a. price varies. (I E E E, Aerospace and Electronics Systems Society) Institute of Electrical and Electronics Engineers, Inc., 345 E. 47th St., New York, NY 10017-2394. TEL 732-981-0060; 800-678-4333. FAX 732-981-9667. E-mail: customer.service@ieee.org; URL: http://www.ieee.org. (Subscr. to: Box 1331, 445 Hoes Lane, Piscataway, NJ 08855-1331) illus. **Indexed:** INSPEC.—BLDSC (4363.015000); Ei; UMI. **CCC.**
    Former titles: I E E E Power Processing and Electronics Specialists Conference. Record (ISSN 0090-2381); (until 1971): Power Conditioning Specialists Conference. Record (ISSN 0079-4414)

I E E E TRANSACTIONS ON AEROSPACE AND ELECTRONIC SYSTEMS. see ENGINEERING — Electrical Engineering

629.132   US   ISSN 0894-6620
I F R (Instrument Flight Rule); the magazine for the accomplished pilot. 1985. m. $59 (foreign $71) (effective 1996). Belvoir Publications, Inc., 75 Holly Hill Ln., Box 2626, Greenwich, CT 06836-2626. TEL 203-661-6111. FAX 203-661-4802. (Subscr. to: Box 420234, Palm Coast, FL 32142) Ed. Paul Bertorelli. adv. circ. 25,000. **Document type:** consumer publication.
—UnCover.

AERONAUTICS AND SPACE FLIGHT

629.132 US ISSN 0896-9868
I F R REFRESHER. 1987. m. $72 (foreign $84) (effective 1996). Belvoir Publications, Inc., 75 Holly Hill Ln., Box 2626, Greenwich, CT 06836-2626. TEL 203-661-6111. FAX 203-661-4802. (Subscr. to: Box 420234, Palm Coast, FL 32142) Ed. Russell Lawton. circ. 15,000. **Document type:** consumer publication.

387.7 FR ISSN 1011-615X
I.T.A. ETUDES ET DOCUMENTS/I.T.A. STUDIES AND REPORTS. (Text in English, French) 1986. bi-m. membership. Institut du Transport Aerien, 103 rue La Boetie, 75008 Paris, France. TEL 33-1-43593868. FAX 33-1-43594737. TELEX 642 584 F. charts; illus.; stat.; index, cum.index: 1961-1971. **Document type:** monographic series.
—BLDSC (4587.819000).
Formed by the 1986 merger of: I.T.A. Documents (ISSN 0248-577X) & I.T.A. Etudes.

629.1 FR ISSN 0766-2750
I.T.A. PRESS (EDITION FRANCAISE). 1986. s-m. Institut du Transport Aerien, 103 rue La Boetie, 75008 Paris, France. TEL 33-1-43593868. FAX 33-1-43594737. TELEX 642 584 F. (looseleaf format) **Document type:** newsletter.
Formerly (until 1983): Institut du Transport Aerien. Communication (ISSN 0755-5148)

629.1 FR ISSN 0766-3366
I.T.A. PRESS (ENGLISH EDITION). 1983. bi-m. Institut du Transport Aerien, 103 rue La Boetie, 75008 Paris, France. TEL 33-1-43593868. FAX 33-1-43594737. TELEX 642 584 F. **Document type:** newsletter.
Formerly (until 1984): Institut du Transport Aerien. Newsletter (ISSN 0755-513X)

629.13 FR ISSN 0018-8786
ICARE; revue de l'aviation francaise. 1957. q. 340 F. (foreign 400 F.). Syndicat National des Pilotes de Ligne Francais, Tour Essor 93 - Espace Jean Mermoz, 14 - 16, rue de Scandicci, 93500 Pantin Cedex, France. TEL 49-42-20-89. FAX 48-91-72-89. Ed. Jean Lasserre. Pub. Geoffroy Bouvet. R&P contact: Jean Lasserre. adv. contact: Jean Delattre. bk.rev.; film rev.; illus. circ. 10,000. (back issues avail.) **Document type:** academic/scholarly publication, bibliography, consumer publication.

IKOMAYAMA UCHU KAGAKUKAN NYUSU. see MUSEUMS AND ART GALLERIES

629.13 FI ISSN 0019-252X
ILMAILU. 1938. m. FIM 190. Suomen Ilmailuliitto - Finlands Flygfoerbund (Finnish Aeronautical Association), Malmi Airport, 00700 Helsinki 70, Finland. TEL 358-0-35093444. FAX 358-0-35093440. Ed. Tero Tuominen. adv.; bk.rev.; charts; illus.; circ. 10,600 (controlled).
—BLDSC (4367.500000).

IN FLIGHT U S A. see TRANSPORTATION — Air Transport

629.1 II ISSN 0376-5466
TL789.8.I5
INDIA. DEPARTMENT OF SPACE. ANNUAL REPORT. (Editions in English, Hindi) 1973. a. free. Department of Space, Antariksh Bhavan, New Bel Rd., Bangalore 560094, India. TEL 080-3334474. FAX 080-3332253. Dir. S. Krish Namurthy. circ. 5,000 (controlled). **Document type:** government publication.

629.1 II ISSN 0970-6674
INDIAN AIRMAN AND SPACEMAN. (Text in English) 1947. m. $60. A. Devi Biren Roy Trust, Roy Mansions, Behala, Calcutta 700034, India. Ed. Biren Roy. adv. contact: T.K. Ghosh. circ. 2,000.

001.94 BE
INFORESPACE. 1972. bi-m. $30. Societe Belge d'Etude des Phenomenes Spatiaux, 74 av. Paul Janson, B-1070 Brussels, Belgium. FAX 25-20-73-93. Ed.Bd. adv. contact: Michel Bougard. circ. 2,000. **Document type:** bulletin.
Description: Features research on various extra-terrestrial phenomena.

629.1 FR
INFORMATIONS SUP'AERO. 2/yr. Ofersop, 28 rue des Petites-Ecuries, 75010 Paris, France. TEL 48-24-93-39. FAX 45-23-33-58. Ed. Fernand Mary. circ. 3,000.

629.13 629.4 SP ISSN 0020-1006
INGENIERIA AERONAUTICA Y ASTRONAUTICA. 1949. q. 2500 ptas. (effective 1997). Asociacion de Ingenieros Aeronauticos, C. Hermosilla, 30 1o, 28001 Madrid, Spain. TEL 34-1-4353021. FAX 34-1-4358283. Ed. Anibal Isidoro Carmona. R&P contact: Anibal Isidoro Carmona. adv.; bk.rev.; charts; illus.; index. circ. 2,000. **Indexed:** Ind.SST. **Document type:** academic/scholarly publication.
—BLDSC (4501.810000).

629.4 CN ISSN 0823-048X
INSTITUTE FOR AEROSPACE RESEARCH. AERONAUTICAL NOTES. Key Title: Aeronautical Note. irreg. free. National Research Council of Canada, Institute for Aerospace Research, Bldg. M-16, Rm. 204, Montreal Rd., Ottawa, ON K1A 0R6, Canada. Pub. Jonathan Rath. adv. contact: Jeff Mackwood. **Document type:** government publication.
—BLDSC (0725.605000). CCC.
Formerly (until June 1990): National Aeronautical Establishment. Aeronautical Notes.

629.13 US
INSTITUTE OF NAVIGATION. NATIONAL TECHNICAL MEETING PROCEEDINGS. a. price varies. Institute of Navigation, 1800 Diagonal Rd., Ste. 480, Alexandria, VA 22314-2840. TEL 703-683-7101. FAX 703-683-7105. E-mail: meetings@ion.org. **Document type:** proceedings.
Supersedes (in 1984): National Aerospace Meeting. Proceedings.

629.1 II ISSN 0257-3423
TL501
INSTITUTION OF ENGINEERS (INDIA). AEROSPACE ENGINEERING DIVISION. JOURNAL. (Text in English) 1978. s-a. Rs.60($20) Institution of Engineers (India), Aerospace Engineering Division, 8 Gokhale Rd., Calcutta 700 020, India. TEL 91-33-2238334. FAX 91-33-2238345. TELEX 021 7885 IEIC IN. Ed. S.P. Misra. adv.; charts; illus.; index. circ. 2,000. **Document type:** academic/scholarly publication.
—CISTI; Ei; Linda Hall.
Refereed Serial

629.1 UK ISSN 0954-4100
TJ1 CODEN: PMGEEP
INSTITUTION OF MECHANICAL ENGINEERS. PROCEEDINGS. PART G: JOURNAL OF AEROSPACE ENGINEERING. bi-m. $471 in the Americas (rest of world £269) for Part G; $3483 in the Americas (rest of the world) for parts A-J (effective 1997). Mechanical Engineering Publications Ltd., Northgate Ave., Bury St. Edmunds, Suffolk IP32 6BW, England. TEL 44-1284-763277. FAX 44-1284-704006. E-mail: sales@imeche.org.uk. Ed. J. Hodgkinson. circ. 1,006. **Indexed:** A.S.& T.Ind., Alloys Ind., ASCA, Br.Tech.Ind., Compumath, Curr.Cont., Eng.Mat.Abstr., INSPEC (1989-), Met.Abstr., Met.Abstr.Ind., Nonfer.Met.Alert, PCC Alert, Steels Alert, World Alum.Abstr. **Document type:** academic/scholarly publication, proceedings.
—BLDSC (6724.900870); AskIEEE; CISTI; Ei; EMDOCS; Genuine Article; KR SourceOne; Linda Hall; SWETS; UMI. CCC.
Description: Communicates ideas on both theoretical and practical aspects of all types of civil and military air- and spacecraft and their support systems.

629.13 SZ
INTERAVIA. 1946. m. 155 SFr. (Europe $130; U.S. and Canada $130; elsewhere $150) (effective 1997). Aerospace Media Publishing SA, Swissair Center, 33 Route de l'Aeroport, Box 56, CH-1215 Geneva 15, Switzerland. TEL 41-22-7882788. FAX 41-22-7882726. Ed. Oliver Sutton; Pub. Robert Monteux. R&P contact: Madeleine Loetscher. adv. contact: Madeleine Loetscher. circ. 22,000. (back issues avail.) **Indexed:** Air Un.Lib.Ind., HRIS, INSPEC (1993-). **Document type:** trade publication.
—AskIEEE; CISTI; KR SourceOne; SWETS.
Former titles: Aerospace World; Air and Cosmos Monthly (ISSN 0983-1592)

387.7 US ISSN 0270-5176
TL553.5
INTERNATIONAL AIR SAFETY SEMINAR PROCEEDINGS. 1949? a. price varies. Flight Safety Foundation, Inc., 601 Madison St., Ste. 300, Alexandria, VA 22314-1756. TEL 703-739-6700. FAX 703-739-6708. Ed. Roger Rozelle. (also avail. in microform from UMI; reprint service avail. from UMI) **Document type:** proceedings.
—BLDSC (1086.500000); Ei.
Former titles (until 9th, 1957): Annual International Air Safety Seminar; (until 6th, 1955): Annual Air Safety Seminar.

387.7 745.1 US
INTERNATIONAL ANTIQUE AIRPLANE DIGEST. q. $36 membership (includes APM Bulletin and Antique Airplane Association News). Antique Airplane Association, Inc., 22001 Bluegrass Rd., Ottumwa, IA 52501-8569. TEL 515-938-2773. Ed. Robert L. Taylor; Pub. Robert L. Taylor. R&P contact: Robert L. Taylor. adv. contact: L. Reis. **Document type:** newsletter.
Description: Historical aviation articles, photos, aircraft company histories and biographical stories on pioneer aviators.

INTERNATIONAL AVIATION NEWS. see TRANSPORTATION — Air Transport

629.132 UN ISSN 0074-2287
INTERNATIONAL CIVIL AVIATION ORGANIZATION. AIR NAVIGATION PLAN. AFRICA - INDIAN OCEAN REGION. (Text in English, French and Spanish) 1954. irreg., 26th, 1989. $75. International Civil Aviation Organization, Attn: Document Sales Unit, 1000 Sherbrooke St. W., Montreal, PQ H3A 2R2, Canada. TEL 514-285-8022. FAX 514-285-3769. TELEX 05-24513.

629.132 UN ISSN 0074-2295
INTERNATIONAL CIVIL AVIATION ORGANIZATION. AIR NAVIGATION PLAN. CARIBBEAN AND SOUTH AMERICAN REGIONS. (Editions in English, French and Spanish) 1956. irreg., 14th, 1991. $58. International Civil Aviation Organization, Attn: Document Sales Unit, 1000 Sherbrooke St. W., Montreal, PQ H3A 2R2, Canada. TEL 514-285-8022. FAX 514-285-6769. TELEX 05-24513.
Formed by the 1968 merger of: International Civil Aviation Organization. Air Navigation Plan. Caribbean Region (ISSN 0534-8056); International Civil Aviation Organization. Air Navigation Plan. South American - South Atlantic Region (ISSN 0534-8080)

629.132 UN ISSN 0304-7652
TL500.5
INTERNATIONAL CIVIL AVIATION ORGANIZATION. AIR NAVIGATION PLAN. EUROPEAN REGION. (Editions in English, French, Russian, Spanish) irreg. (in 2 vols.), 23rd ed., 1985. $146 (includes binders). International Civil Aviation Organization, Attn: Document Sales Unit, 1000 Sherbrooke St. W., Montreal, PQ H3A 2R2, Canada. TEL 514-285-8022. FAX 514-285-6769. TELEX 05-24513. (looseleaf format)

629.132 UN ISSN 1014-0034
INTERNATIONAL CIVIL AVIATION ORGANIZATION. AIR NAVIGATION PLAN. MIDDLE EAST AND ASIA REGIONS. (Editions in Arabic, English, French, Spanish) 1967. irreg., 15th, 1989. $58. International Civil Aviation Organization, Attn: Document Sales Unit, 1000 Sherbrooke St. W., Montreal, PQ H3A 2R2, Canada. TEL 514-285-8022. FAX 514-285-6769. TELEX 05-24513.
Formerly: International Civil Aviation Organization. Air Navigation Plan. Middle East and South East Asia Regions (ISSN 0074-2317)

629.132 UN ISSN 0074-2325
INTERNATIONAL CIVIL AVIATION ORGANIZATION. AIR NAVIGATION PLAN. NORTH ATLANTIC, NORTH AMERICAN AND PACIFIC REGIONS. (Editions in English, French, Spanish) 1956. irreg., 13th, 1990. $49. International Civil Aviation Organization, Attn: Document Sales Unit, 1000 Sherbrooke St. W., Montreal, PQ H3A 2R2, Canada. TEL 514-285-8022. FAX 514-285-6769. TELEX 05-24513.
Formed by the 1967 merger of: I C A O. Air Navigation Plan. North Atlantic Region (ISSN 0534-8064); I C A O. Air Navigation Plan. Pacific Region (ISSN 0534-8072)

AERONAUTICS AND SPACE FLIGHT

INTERNATIONAL CIVIL AVIATION ORGANIZATION. ASSEMBLY. MINUTES OF THE PLENARY MEETINGS. see *TRANSPORTATION — Air Transport*

629.1   UN   ISSN 0074-2384
INTERNATIONAL CIVIL AVIATION ORGANIZATION. ASSEMBLY. REPORT OF THE TECHNICAL COMMISSION. Arabic Edition: Al-Taqrir - Al-Gamiyyat al-Umumiyyat al-Dawarat. Al-Lagnat al-Fanmiyyat (ISSN 1014-4927); French edition: Organisation de l'Aviation Civile Internationale. Assemble. Rapport et Procedes Verbaux de la Commission Technique (ISSN 1014-0387); Russian edition: Mezhdunarodnaya Organizatsiya Grazhdanskoi Aviatsii. Assambleya. Doklady i Protokoly Tekhnicheskoi Komissii (ISSN 1014-0395); Spanish edition: Organizacion de Aviacion Civil Internacional. Asamblea. Informe y Actas de la Comision Tecnica (ISSN 1014-0379) 1947. irreg., 29th, 1992. $14. International Civil Aviation Organization, Attn: Document Sales Unit, 1000 Sherbrooke St. W., Montreal, PQ H3A 2R2, Canada. TEL 514-285-8022. FAX 514-285-6769. TELEX 05-24513. **Document type:** proceedings.

629.1   UN
INTERNATIONAL CIVIL AVIATION ORGANIZATION. COMMITTEE ON AVIATION ENVIRONMENTAL PROTECTION. REPORT OF THE MEETING. (Editions in English, French, Russian, Spanish) 1986. irreg., no.2, 1991. $31. International Civil Aviation Organization, Attn: Document Sales Unit, 1000 Sherbrooke St. W., Montreal, PQ H3A 2R2, Canada. TEL 514-285-8022. FAX 514-285-6769. TELEX 05-24513. (back issues avail.)

INTERNATIONAL CIVIL AVIATION ORGANIZATION. COUNCIL. ANNUAL REPORT. see *TRANSPORTATION — Air Transport*

621.1 387.7   UN
INTERNATIONAL CIVIL AVIATION ORGANIZATION. COUNCIL TO CONTRACTING STATES ON CHARGES FOR AIRPORTS AND AIR NAVIGATION SYSTEMS. STATEMENTS. (Editions in Arabic, English, French, Russian, Spanish) irreg., 4th ed., 1992. $6. International Civil Aviation Organization, Attn: Document Sales Unit, 1000 Sherbrooke St. W., Montreal, PQ H3A 2R2, Canada. TEL 514-285-8022. FAX 514-285-6769. TELEX 05-24513.

INTERNATIONAL CIVIL AVIATION ORGANIZATION. DIGESTS OF STATISTICS. SERIES R. CIVIL AIRCRAFT ON REGISTER. see *TRANSPORTATION — Abstracting, Bibliographies, Statistics*

387.7   UN
INTERNATIONAL CIVIL AVIATION ORGANIZATION. LOCATION INDICATORS. (Text in English, French, Russian, Spanish) irreg., 80th ed., Mar. 1996. $36 (diskette edition $200). International Civil Aviation Organization, Attn: Document Sales Unit, 1000 Sherbrooke St. W., Montreal, PQ H3A 2R2, Canada. TEL 514-285-8022. FAX 514-285-6769. TELEX 05-24513. (also avail. in diskette format)

INTERNATIONAL CIVIL AVIATION ORGANIZATION. REPORT OF THE AIR NAVIGATION CONFERENCE. see *TRANSPORTATION — Air Transport*

621.1 387.7   UN
INTERNATIONAL CIVIL AVIATION ORGANIZATION. SPECIAL COMMITTEE FOR THE MONITORING AND CO-ORDINATION OF DEVELOPMENT AND TRANSITION PLANNING FOR THE FUTURE AIR NAVIGATION SYSTEM (FANS - PHASE II). REPORT OF THE MEETING. (Editions in English, French, Russian, Spanish) irreg., latest 1993. $54. International Civil Aviation Organization, Attn: Document Sales Unit, 1000 Sherbrooke St. W., Montreal, PQ H3A 2R2, Canada. TEL 514-285-8022. FAX 514-285-6769. TELEX 05-24513. **Document type:** proceedings.
   Formerly: International Civil Aviation Organization, Special Committee on Future Air Navigation Systems (FANS). Report of the Meeting.

INTERNATIONAL CIVIL AVIATION ORGANIZATION. VISUAL AIDS PANEL. REPORT OF THE MEETING. see *TRANSPORTATION — Air Transport*

629.1   US   ISSN 0730-2010
TL566
INTERNATIONAL CONGRESS ON INSTRUMENTATION IN AEROSPACE SIMULATION FACILITIES. RECORD. Key Title: I C I A S F Record. 1964. biennial. price varies. (I E E E, Aerospace and Electronic Systems Society) Institute of Electrical and Electronics Engineers, Inc., 345 E. 47th St., New York, NY 10017-2394. TEL 732-981-0060; 800-678-4333. FAX 732-981-9667. E-mail: customer.service@ieee.org; URL: http://www.ieee.org. (Subscr. to: Box 1331, 445 Hoes Lane, Piscataway, NJ 08855-1331)
   —BLDSC (4362.045300); Ei; UMI. **CCC**.
   Formerly (until 1966): International Congress on Instrumentation in Aerospace Simulation Facilities. Proceedings (ISSN 0730-1790)

629.132   US
INTERNATIONAL COUNCIL OF AIRCRAFT OWNER AND PILOT ASSOCIATIONS BULLETIN. m. free. International Council of Aircraft Owner and Pilot Associations, 421 Aviation Way, Fredrick, MD 21701. TEL 301-695-2221. FAX 301-695-2375. Ed. Steven J. Brown. **Document type:** bulletin.
   Description: Details membership activities.

629.4   US
INTERNATIONAL DEVELOPMENT IN SPACE STATION AND SPACE TECHNOLOGIES. irreg., 35th, 1984, Lausanne. $94.50 to non-members; members $64.50. (International Astronautical Federation) American Institute of Aeronautics and Astronautics, Inc., 1801 Alexander Dr., Ste. 500, Reston, VA 20191. TEL 703-264-7500. Ed. Luigi G. Napolitano. (reprint service avail. from UMI) **Document type:** academic/scholarly publication.
   Formerly: International Astronautical Federation (I A F). International Congress. Invited Papers.
   Description: Selected papers from IAF meetings.

INTERNATIONAL DIRECTORY OF CIVIL AIRCRAFT (YEAR). see *TRANSPORTATION — Air Transport*

INTERNATIONAL DIRECTORY OF MILITARY AIRCRAFT (YEAR). see *MILITARY*

629.1   US   ISSN 0364-0418
INTERNATIONAL FLIGHT INFORMATION MANUAL. a. (plus q. supplement). $59 (foreign $73.75). U.S. Federal Aviation Administration, Department of Transportation, 800 Independence Ave., S.W., Washington, DC 20591. TEL 202-655-4000. (Subscr. to: Superintendent of Documents, U.S. Government Printing Office, Box 371954, Pittsburgh, PA 15250-7954. TEL 202-512-3238. FAX 202-512-2250) (looseleaf format) **Document type:** government publication.
   Description: Used as a preflight and training guide by U.S. nonscheduled commercial carriers, business operations, and private aviators for flights beyond U.S. airspace.

631 629.132   US   ISSN 0020-675X
INTERNATIONAL FLYING FARMER. 1947. 9/yr. $25 to non-members; Canada $30; elsewhere $35 (effective 1996). International Flying Farmers, Inc., Mid-Continent Airport, Box 9124, Wichita, KS 67227-0124. TEL 316-943-4234. Ed. Deanne Earwood. R&P contact: Kathy Marsh. adv.; bk.rev.; illus.; mkt.; pat. circ. 2,000. **Document type:** trade publication.
   Description: Focuses on aviation and agriculture and on how they are intertwined. Includes profiles of members.

620.1   US   ISSN 0277-7576
TL589   CODEN: PIISEF
INTERNATIONAL INSTRUMENTATION SYMPOSIUM. 1987. a., 41st, 1995. $95 to non-members; members $76. Instrument Society of America, 67 Alexander Dr., Box 12277, Research Triangle Park, NC 27709. TEL 919-549-8411. FAX 919-549-8288. TELEX 802540 ISA DURM. E-mail: info@isa.org; URL: http://www.isa.org. (also avail. in microform from UMI; reprint service avail. from ISI,UMI) **Indexed:** INSPEC. **Document type:** proceedings.
   —BLDSC (6846.335000); CASDDS; Ei. **CCC**.
   Supersedes in part: Instrumentation in the Aerospace Industry (ISSN 0096-7238); Fundamentals of Test Measurement (ISSN 0891-4052); Fundamentals of Aerospace Instrumentation (ISSN 0094-3975); Former titles: Advances in Test Measurement. Proceedings (ISSN 0568-0204); I S A Aerospace Instrumentation Symposium. Proceedings (ISSN 0536-2008)
   Refereed Serial

370.19   US   ISSN 1050-8414
TL553.6
INTERNATIONAL JOURNAL OF AVIATION PSYCHOLOGY. 1991. q. $39 to individuals (foreign $69); institutions $200 (foreign $230) (effective 1997). Lawrence Erlbaum Associates, Inc., 10 Industrial Dr., Mahwah, NJ 07430-2262. TEL 201-236-9500; 800-926-6579. FAX 201-236-0072. E-mail: jamsel@erlbaum.com; URL: http://www.erlbaum.com. Ed. Richard S. Jensen. adv.: page $325; 5 x 8. bk.rev. **Indexed:** ASCA, Curr.Cont., Psychol.Abstr. (1991-). **Document type:** academic/scholarly publication.
   —BLDSC (4542.125500); SWETS. **CCC**.
   Description: Development and management of safe, effective aviation systems from the standpoint of the human operators.
   Refereed Serial

629.1   US
INTERNATIONAL JOURNAL OF SPACE RESEARCH. 1986. q. $225 (effective 1996). Nova Science Publishers, Inc., 6080 Jericho Tpke., Ste. 207, Commack, NY 11725-2808. TEL 516-499-3103. FAX 516-499-3146. E-mail: novasci1@aol.com. Pub. Frank Columbus. circ. 700. **Document type:** academic/scholarly publication.
   Former titles: Journal of Space Abstracts and Research; Space Abstracts on Microfiche; (until vol.4): Space Information Review (ISSN 0895-6596)

629.13   UK   ISSN 0334-0082
INTERNATIONAL JOURNAL OF TURBO AND JET ENGINES. 1983. q. $280 (effective 1997). Freund Publishing House Ltd., Chesham House, Ste. 500, 150 Regent St., London W1R 5FA, Israel. (And: P.O. Box 35010, Tel Aviv, Israel. TEL 972-3-5628540. FAX 972-3-5628538) Ed. B. Gal-Or. adv.; bk.rev. (back issues avail.) **Indexed:** ASCA, Int.Aerosp.Abstr., Met.Abstr., World Alum.Abstr. **Document type:** academic/scholarly publication.
   —BLDSC (4542.696200); CISTI; SWETS; UnCover.

629.134   US
INTERNATIONAL JOURNAL OF WEIGHT ENGINEERING. 1943. 3/yr. $30 (effective 1997). Society of Allied Weight Engineers, Inc., 5530 Aztec Dr., La Mesa, CA 91942-2110. TEL 619-465-1367. FAX 619-465-2561. Ed. Robert W. Ridenour. adv. contact: Robert W. Ridenour. illus. circ. 1,000. **Indexed:** BMT. **Document type:** academic/scholarly publication.
   —CISTI.
   Former titles: Journal of Weight Engineering; (until 1981): S.A.W.E. Journal (ISSN 0583-9270)
   Refereed Serial

629.132 387   US
VK560
INTERNATIONAL NAVIGATION ASSOCIATION. PROCEEDINGS OF ANNUAL MEETING. 1975. a. $50 to non-members. International Navigation Association, Inc., Box 2324, Arlington, VA 22202-0324. Ed.Bd. circ. 350. **Document type:** proceedings.
   Formerly: International Omega Association. Proceedings of Annual Meeting (ISSN 0278-9396)
   Description: Compendium of technical and scientific papers relating to navigation.

AERONAUTICS AND SPACE FLIGHT

629.1 US ISSN 0364-6742
TL725.A1
INTERNATIONAL NOTICES TO AIRMEN. 1973. fortn. $55 (foreign $68.75). U.S. Federal Aviation Administration, 800 Independence Ave., S.W., Washington, DC 20591. TEL 202-655-4000. (Subscr. to: Superintendent of Documents, U.S. Government Printing Office, Box 371954, Pittsburgh, PA 15250-7954. TEL 202-512-1800. FAX 202-512-2250) (back issues avail.) Document type: government publication.
  Formerly (until 1975): International Notams.
  Description: Alerts pilots traveling in U.S. airspace to temporary hazardous conditions, changes in facility operational data, and foreign entry procedures and regulations.

629.132 387.7 US
INTERNATIONAL OPERATIONS BULLETIN. 1982. q. membership only. (International Business Aviation Council) National Business Aircraft Association, 1200 18th St., N.W., Washington, DC 20036-2598. TEL 202-783-9000. FAX 202-331-8364. Ed. William H. Stine, II. bk.rev. circ. 4,000. Document type: bulletin.
  Formerly: I B A C International Update.
  Description: Timely operational information for professional aircrews of business aircraft that fly internationally.

INTERNATIONAL RADAR CONFERENCE. RECORD. see *COMMUNICATIONS*

629.1 384 US ISSN 1041-4541
TL512
INTERNATIONAL SATELLITE DIRECTORY; a complete guide to the satellite communications industry. 1982. a. $269.50 (effective 1996). Design Publishers, 800 Siesta Way, Sonoma, CA 95476-4413. URL: www.satnews.com. Ed. Silvano Payne. adv. contact. circ. 3,500. Document type: directory.
  ●Also available online.
  Also available on CD-ROM.
  —BLDSC (4548.780000); CISTI.

629.132 US
INTERNATIONAL SOCIETY OF WOMEN AIRLINE PILOTS NEWSLETTER.* q. membership. International Society of Women Airline Pilots, 2250 E. Tropicana Ave., Ste. 19-395, Las Vegas, NV 89119. circ. 450. Document type: newsletter.

629.1 UK ISSN 0958-9058
INTERNATIONAL SPACE DIRECTORY. 1989. a. Parker Publications Ltd., 42 Keephatch Rd., Wokingham, Berks RG40 1QD, England. TEL 44-118-9774000. FAX 44-118-9774001. Ed. Mary Williamson; Pub. Julie Alexander. R&P contact: Ian Parker. adv. contact: Julie Alexander. Document type: directory.

001.94 US ISSN 0730-174X
TL789.A1
INTERNATIONAL U F O REPORTER. 1976. 4/yr. $25. Center for U F O Studies, 2457 W. Peterson Ave., Ste. 6, Chicago, IL 60659-4118. TEL 312-271-3611. Ed. Jerome Clark. adv.: bk.rev. circ. 2,000.
  Formerly (until 1982): Second Look; Which incorporates: Frontiers of Science; Probe.

629.13 GW ISSN 0579-6938
INTERNATIONALER WELTKONGRESS DER U F O-FORSCHER. DOKUMENTARBERICHT. a. Ventla-Verlag, Postfach 130185, 65195 Wiesbaden, Germany.

629.13 UK ISSN 0020-9597
INTERPLANETARY NEWS; Britain's space monthly. 1957. m. £6. Interplanetary Space Travel Research Association (United Kingdom), 21 Hargwyne St., Stockwell, London SW9 9RQ, England. Ed. Mike Parry. adv.; bk.rev.; circ. controlled. (also avail. in microfiche).

001.94 US
INTERSPACE - LINK CONFIDENTIAL NEWSLETTER; the link. 1983. m. $75 (foreign $100). (National Investigation Committee on Unidentified Flying Objects) N I C U F O Publishing, 14617 Victory Blvd., Ste. 4, Van Nuys, CA 91411. TEL 818-989-5942. FAX 818-989-5942. Ed. Frank Stranges. circ. 300 (paid). (back issues avail.) Document type: newsletter.
  Description: Keeps readers current on UFOs, space, science, and metaphysical teachings.

629.13 IS
ISRAEL ANNUAL CONFERENCE ON AEROSPACE SCIENCES. PROCEEDINGS. 1958. a. $115. Technion - Israel Institute of Technology, Faculty of Aerospace Engineering, Technion City, Haifa 32000, Israel. TEL 972-4-8292260. FAX 972-4-8231848. adv.; circ. 1,000 (paid). Indexed: Appl.Mech.Rev. Document type: proceedings.
  Formerly: Israel Annual Conference on Aviation and Astronautics. Proceedings (ISSN 0075-0972)
  Refereed Serial

629.134 IT ISSN 1120-6977
VK4
ISTITUTO ITALIANO DI NAVIGAZIONE. ATTI. 1959. q. L.120000 (effective 1997-98). Istituto Italiano di Navigazione, Via Prisciano, 42, 00136 Rome, Italy. TEL 39-6-35452841. FAX 39-6-35452841. Ed. Adolfo Gambardella. adv.; bk.rev.; illus. circ. 750. Document type: academic/scholarly publication, proceedings.
  Formerly (until 1967): Istituto Italiano di Navigazione. Notiziario (ISSN 1120-6985)
  Description: Includes texts of conferences, articles about navigation, problems and proposals, as well as pertinent news articles.
  Refereed Serial

629.1 SP ISSN 0213-1250
ITAVIA. 1973. 3/yr. free. Asociacion y Colegio de Ingenieros Tecnicos Aeronauticos, Principe de Vergara 15, 28001 Madrid, Spain. Indexed: Ind.SST.

J A R AMENDMENT SERVICE TO REGULATORY DOCUMENTS. see *TRANSPORTATION — Air Transport*

629.13 IT ISSN 0394-3437
J P 4 MENSILE DI AERONAUTICA. (Jet Petrol Quattro) 1972. m. L.80000 (foreign L.95000) (effective 1997). Ed.A.I. s.r.l. (Edizioni Aeronautiche Italiane), V. Guinicelli 4, 50133 Florence, Italy. TEL 39-55-574774. FAX 39-55-570103. E-mail: edai@edai.it; URL: http://www.edai.it/edai. Ed. Paolo Gianvanni. R&P contact: Randa Eid. adv.: B&W page L.3500000, color page L.5950000; adv. contact: Vania Pistolozzi. bk.rev.; adv.; index. circ. 30,000. Document type: consumer publication.
  Description: Deals with every aspect of civilian and military aviation. Covers commercial aviation, technology and space.

629.13 GW ISSN 0021-3896
JAEGERBLATT; fuer Angehoerige von Jagd-, Nachtjagd- und Zerstoerer-Geschwader und der fliegenden Kampfverbaende der Bundeswehr-Luftwaffe. 1952. bi-m. DM.70($30) Gemeinschaft der Jagdflieger, Postfach 510811, 50944 Cologne, Germany. TEL 49-2233-21058. FAX 49-2233-280398. Ed. Johannes Mohn. adv.; bk.rev.; illus. Document type: newsletter.
  —CCC.

JANE'S AIR TRAFFIC CONTROL. see *TRANSPORTATION — Air Transport*

629.133 UK ISSN 1361-6684
JANE'S AIRCRAFT UPGRADES. 1992. a. £215 (CD-ROM £425) (effective 1997). Jane's Information Group, Sentinel House, 163 Brighton Rd., Coulsdon, Surrey CR5 2NH, England. TEL 44-181-700-3700. FAX 44-181-700-3788. TELEX 916907-JANE-G. E-mail: info@janes.co.uk; URL: http://www.janes. com/janes.html. (US subscr. to: Jane's Information Group Inc., 1340 Braddock Pl., Ste. 300, Alexandria, VA 22314-1651. TEL 703-683-3700. FAX 703-836-0029) Ed. Simon Michell; Pub. Robert Hutchinson. adv.: page £4000; trim 8 x 12; adv. contact: Richard West. (back issues avail.) Document type: directory.
  ●Also available on CD-ROM.
  —BLDSC (4646.680000).
  Formerly (until 1995): Jane's Civil and Military Aircraft Upgrades (ISSN 0969-0417)
  Description: Covers air upgrade programs for aircraft no longer in production.

629.133 UK ISSN 0075-3017
TL501
JANE'S ALL THE WORLD'S AIRCRAFT. 1909. a. £250 (CD-ROM £425) (effective 1997). Jane's Information Group, Sentinel House, 163 Brighton Rd., Coulsdon, Surrey CR5 2NH, England. TEL 44-181-700-3700. FAX 44-181-700-3788. TELEX 916907-JANES-G. E-mail: info@janes.co.uk; URL: http://www.janes.com/janes.html. (U.S. & Can. order from: Dept. DSM, 1340 Braddock Pl., Ste. 300, Box 1436, Alexandria, VA 22314-1651. TEL 703-683-3700. FAX 703-836-0029) Ed. Paul Jackson. adv. contact: Richard West. index. Document type: trade publication.
  ●Also available on CD-ROM.
  —CISTI; Linda Hall; SWETS. CCC.
  Description: Publishes technical details of all piloted aircraft, powered and unpowered, currently under development, in production or available in assembly kit production in 172 countries worldwide.

629.1 UK ISSN 0264-794X
JANE'S AVIONICS. 1982. a. £215 (CD-ROM £425) (effective 1997). Jane's Information Group, Sentinel House, 163 Brighton Rd., Coulsdon, Surrey CR5 2NH, England. TEL 44-181-700-3700. FAX 44-181-700-3788. TELEX 916907-JANES-G. E-mail: info@janes.co.uk; URL: http://www.janes. com/janes.html. (U.S. & Can. subscr. to: Dept. DSM, 1340 Braddock Pl., Ste. 300, Box 1436, Alexandria, VA 22314-1651. TEL 703-683-3700. FAX 703-836-0029) Ed. David Brinkman; Pub. Robert Hutchinson. adv. contact: Richard West. index. Document type: trade publication.
  ●Also available on CD-ROM.
  —BLDSC (4646.620000).
  Description: Covers civil and military airborne electronic equipment; provides technical details and manufacturer contact information.

JANE'S C 4 I SYSTEMS. see *MILITARY*

629.1 387.7 UK ISSN 1357-518X
JANE'S INFORMATION UPDATE. ALL THE WORLD'S AIRCRAFT. 1993. 11/yr. Jane's Information Group, Sentinel House, 163 Brighton Rd., Coulsdon, Surrey CR5 2NH, England. TEL 44-181-700-3700. FAX 44-181-700-3788. E-mail: info@janes.co.uk; URL: http://www.janes.com/janes.html. Ed. Terry Gander. Document type: bulletin.
  —BLDSC (4646.200000).

629.1 UK ISSN 0967-6481
TL512
JANE'S INTERNATIONAL A B C AEROSPACE DIRECTORY. 1936. a. £215($475) (effective 1997). Jane's Information Group, Sentinel House, 163 Brighton Rd., Coulsdon, Surrey CR5 2NH, England. TEL 44-181-700-3700. FAX 44-181-700-3788. TELEX 916907-JANES-G. E-mail: directories@janes. co.uk; URL: http://www.janes.com/janes.html. Ed. Ian Tandy; Pub. Ruth Jowett. adv.; index. Indexed: Bus.Ind., Tr.& Indus.Ind. Document type: directory.
  ●Also available on CD-ROM.
  —BLDSC (4535.085000); CISTI.
  Formerly: Interavia A B C (ISSN 0074-1116)
  Description: Lists companies, manufacturers, governmental and official organizations in all areas of aerospace-related activities. Includes company name, senior personnel, and product, service description.

629.1 UK ISSN 1352-0660
JANE'S SPACE DIRECTORY. a. £215 (effective 1997). Jane's Information Group, Sentinel House, 163 Brighton Rd., Coulsdon, Surrey CR5 2NH, England. TEL 44-181-700-3700. FAX 44-181-700-3788. TELEX 916907-JANES-G. E-mail: info@janes.co.uk; URL: http://www.janes.com/janes.html. (US and Canada order from: Marketing Dept. DSM, 1340 Braddock Pl., Ste. 300, Box 1436, Alexandria, VA 22314-1651. TEL 703-683-3700. FAX 703-836-0029) Ed. Phillip Clarke. Document type: trade publication.
  ●Also available on CD-ROM.
  —BLDSC (4647.097300).
  Former titles: Interavia Space Directory; (until 1988): Jane's Spaceflight Directory.

JAPAN AVIATION DIRECTORY. see *BUSINESS AND ECONOMICS — Trade And Industrial Directories*

JAPAN INSTITUTE OF NAVIGATION. JOURNAL/NIHON KOKAI GAKKAI RONBUNSHU. see *TRANSPORTATION — Ships And Shipping*

AERONAUTICS AND SPACE FLIGHT

629.13   JA   ISSN 0021-4663
                           CODEN: NKGAB8
JAPAN SOCIETY FOR AERONAUTICAL AND SPACE SCIENCES. JOURNAL/NIHON KOKU UCHU GAKKAI-SHI. (Text in Japanese; summaries in English) 1934. m. 1500 Yen per no. Japan Society for Aeronautical and Space Sciences - Nihon Koku Uchu Gakkai, 18-2, Shinbashi 1-chome, Minato-ku, Tokyo 105, Japan. adv.; abstr.; bibl.; charts; illus. **Indexed:** INIS Atomind., INSPEC, Int.Aerosp.Abstr., Jap.Per.Ind., JTA.
—BLDSC (4805.980000); AskIEEE; CISTI; KR SourceOne; Linda Hall. **CCC.**

629.13   JA   ISSN 0549-3811
TL501   CODEN: TJASAM
JAPAN SOCIETY FOR AERONAUTICAL AND SPACE SCIENCES. TRANSACTIONS. (Text in English) 1958. q. Japan Society for Aeronautical and Space Sciences - Nihon Koku Uchu Gakkai, 18-2, Shinbashi 1-chome, Minato-ku, Tokyo 105, Japan. abstr.; charts; illus. **Indexed:** Alloys Ind., ASCA, Chem.Abstr., Curr.Cont., Eng.Mat.Abstr., INSPEC, JCT, JTA, Met.Abstr.Ind., Met.Abstr., Nonfer.Met.Alert, PCC Alert, Steels Alert, World Alum.Abstr.
—BLDSC (8973.950000); AskIEEE; CASDDS; CISTI; Ei; KR SourceOne; Linda Hall; UnCover. **CCC.**

JOINT AVIATION AUTHORITIES. CERTIFICATION INFORMATION - PROCEDURES. see *TRANSPORTATION — Air Transport*

JOINT AVIATION AUTHORITIES. GENERAL INFORMATION - PROCEDURES. INFORMATION LEAFLETS. see *TRANSPORTATION — Air Transport*

JOINT AVIATION AUTHORITIES. MAINTENANCE INFORMATION - PROCEDURES. see *TRANSPORTATION — Air Transport*

JOINT AVIATION AUTHORITIES. NOTICE OF PROPOSED AMENDMENT SCHEME. see *TRANSPORTATION — Air Transport*

JOINT AVIATION AUTHORITIES. REGULATORY DOCUMENTS. see *TRANSPORTATION — Air Transport*

JORNADAS NACIONALES DE DERECHO AERONAUTICO Y ESPACIAL. TRABAJOS. see *TRANSPORTATION — Air Transport*

629.1 367 500   GW   ISSN 0723-7766
JOURNAL FUER U F O - FORSCHUNG. (Text in German; summaries in English) 1980. bi-m. DM.39. Gesellschaft zur Erforschung des U F O - Phaenomens - G E P e.V., Luisenstr. 4, 58511 Luedenscheid, Germany. TEL 02351-23377. FAX 02351-23335. adv.; bk.rev. circ. 400. **Document type:** bulletin.

JOURNAL OF AEROSPACE ENGINEERING. see *ENGINEERING — Civil Engineering*

387.7   US   ISSN 0021-8650
TL725.3.T7
JOURNAL OF AIR TRAFFIC CONTROL. 1958. q. $35 to non-members (foreign $45). Air Traffic Control Association, Inc., 2300 Clarendon Blvd., Ste. 711, Arlington, VA 22201. TEL 703-522-5717. Ed. Suzette Matthews. adv.; bk.rev.; film rev.; charts; illus.; index. circ. 4,000. (back issues avail.) **Document type:** trade publication.
—SWETS.
   Description: Dedicated to the progress in the art and science of air traffic control.

JOURNAL OF AIR TRANSPORTATION WORLD WIDE. see *TRANSPORTATION*

629.13   US   ISSN 0021-8669
TL501   CODEN: JAIRAM
JOURNAL OF AIRCRAFT; devoted to aeronautical science and technology. 1963. bi-m. $275 to non-members (foreign 3355); members $46 (foreign $76). American Institute of Aeronautics and Astronautics, Inc., 1801 Alexander Dr., Ste. 500, Reston, VA 20191. TEL 703-264-7500. URL: http://www.aiaa.org/publications/journals/aircraft-scope.html. Ed. Thomas M. Weeks. charts; illus.; index. circ. 3,500. (also avail. in microform from UMI; reprint service avail. from UMI) **Indexed:** Alloys Ind, Appl.Mech.Rev., ASCA, Curr.Cont., Eng.Ind., Eng.Mat.Abstr., INSPEC, Int.Aerosp.Abstr., ISMEC, Met.Abstr.Ind., Met.Abstr., Nonfer.Met.Alert, PCC Alert, Risk Abstr., Sci.Cit.Ind., Sh.& Vib.Dig., Steels Alert, World Alum.Abstr. **Document type:** academic/scholarly publication.
—BLDSC (4926.700000); CISTI; Ei; Genuine Article; Linda Hall; SWETS; UnCover. **CCC.**
   Description: Covers advanced design concepts and operating advances in aircraft. Papers on military and civilian aircraft, ground effect machines, V/STOL and supersonic and hypersonic aircraft, with emphasis on practical engineering.
Refereed Serial

629.4   US   ISSN 0021-9142
TL787.A6   CODEN: JALSA6
JOURNAL OF ASTRONAUTICAL SCIENCES. Variant title: Journal of the Astronautical Sciences. 1954. q. $140 (foreign $155) to institutions (effective 1998). American Astronautical Society (Springfield), 6352 Rolling Mill Pl., Ste. 102, Springfield, VA 22152-2354. TEL 703-866-0020. FAX 703-866-3526. E-mail: 74673-724@compuserve.com; URL: http://www.glue.umd.edu/~tkash/gms/aas.html. Ed. Kathleen Howell. cum.index: 1954-1979. circ. 1,800. (also avail. in microfilm; back issues avail.) **Indexed:** ASCA, Curr.Cont., Eng.Ind., INSPEC (1969-), Int.Aerosp.Abstr., Math.R., Nucl.Sci.Abstr., Sci.Cit.Ind. **Document type:** academic/scholarly publication.
—BLDSC (4947.450000); AskIEEE; CISTI; Ei; Genuine Article; KR SourceOne; Linda Hall; SWETS; UMI; UnCover.

JOURNAL OF FLOW VISUALIZATION AND IMAGE PROCESSING. see *ENGINEERING — Mechanical Engineering*

629.1   US   ISSN 0731-5090
TL676   CODEN: JGCODS
JOURNAL OF GUIDANCE, CONTROL, AND DYNAMICS; devoted to the technology of dynamics and control. 1978. bi-m. $285 to non-members (foreign $345); members $50 (foreign $80). American Institute of Aeronautics and Astronautics, Inc., 1801 Alexander Dr., Ste. 500, Reston, VA 20191. TEL 703-264-7500. URL: http://www.aiaa.org/publications/jornals/guidance-scope.html. Ed. Kyle T. Alfriend. charts; illus.; index. circ. 3,000. **Indexed:** A.S.& T.Ind., Appl.Mech.Rev., ASCA, Compumath, Curr.Cont., Eng.Ind., Ind.Sci.Rev., INSPEC, Int.Aerosp.Abstr., Sci.Cit.Ind., Zent.Math. **Document type:** academic/scholarly publication.
—BLDSC (4996.561000); AskIEEE; CISTI; Ei; Genuine Article; KR SourceOne; Linda Hall; SWETS; UnCover. **CCC.**
   Formerly: Journal of Guidance and Control (ISSN 0162-3192)
   Description: Covers dynamics, guidance, control, navigation, optimization, electronics, and information processing related to aeronautical and astronautical systems. Focuses on technical knowledge, exploratory developments, design criteria, and applications.
Refereed Serial

JOURNAL OF NAVIGATION. see *TRANSPORTATION — Ships And Shipping*

629.1   US   ISSN 0748-4658
TL780   CODEN: JPPOEL
JOURNAL OF PROPULSION AND POWER; devoted to aerospace propulsion and power. 1985. bi-m. $300 to non-members (foreign $360); members $42 (foreign $72). American Institute of Aeronautics and Astronautics, Inc., 1801 Alexander Dr., Ste. 500, Reston, VA 20191. TEL 703-264-7500. URL: http://www.aiaa.org/publications/journals/propulsion-scope.html. Ed. R.H. Woodward Waesche. charts; illus.; index. circ. 2,000. (also avail. in microform) **Indexed:** Appl.Mech.Rev., ASCA, Compumath, Curr.Cont., Ind.Sci.Rev., INIS Atomind., Int.Aerosp.Abstr., Sci.Cit.Ind. **Document type:** academic/scholarly publication.
—BLDSC (5042.795000); CASDDS; CISTI; Ei; Genuine Article; Linda Hall; SWETS; UnCover. **CCC.**
   Description: Covers advances in airbreathing electric and exotic propulsion, solid and liquid rockets, fuels and propellants, power generation, and the application of aerospace technology to terrestrial energy systems.
Refereed Serial

JOURNAL OF SPACE LAW. see *LAW — International Law*

629.1   JA   ISSN 0911-551X
                           CODEN: JSTSF7
JOURNAL OF SPACE TECHNOLOGY AND SCIENCE. (Text in English) 2/yr. $50. Japanese Rocket Society, c/o Business Center for Academic Societies Japan, 5-16-9 Honkomagome, Bunkyo-ku, Tokyo 113, Japan. TEL 81-3-5814-5811. FAX 81-3-5814-5822. TELEX 2722268 BCJSP. Ed. Yoshiaki Ohkami. **Document type:** academic/scholarly publication.

629.13   US   ISSN 0022-4650
TL787.A62   CODEN: JSCRAG
JOURNAL OF SPACECRAFT AND ROCKETS; devoted to astronautical science and technology. 1964. bi-m. $260 to non-members (foreign $320); members $38 (foreign $68). American Institute of Aeronautics and Astronautics, Inc., 1801 Alexander Dr., Ste. 500, Reston, VA 20191. TEL 703-264-7500. URL: http://www.aiaa.org/publications/jornals/spacecraft-scope.html. Ed. E. Vincent Zoby. charts; illus.; index. circ. 3,500. (also avail. in microform from UMI; reprint service avail. from UMI) **Indexed:** A.S.& T.Ind., Alloys Ind., Appl.Mech.Rev., ASCA, Cadscan, Chem.Abstr., Curr.Cont., Eng.Ind., Eng.Mat.Abstr., Ind.Sci.Rev., INIS Atomind., INSPEC, Int.Aerosp.Abstr., Lead Abstr., Met.Abstr., Met.Abstr.Ind., Nonfer.Met.Alert, PCC Alert, Sci.Cit.Ind., Sh.& Vib.Dig., Steels Alert, World Alum.Abstr., Zincscan. **Document type:** academic/scholarly publication.
—BLDSC (5066.100000); CASDDS; CISTI; Ei; Genuine Article; KR SourceOne; Linda Hall; SWETS; UnCover. **CCC.**
   Description: Advancement of the science and technology related to spacecraft and missile systems and their associated missions and performance through the dissemination of original archival papers describing significant advances in space sciences, and the application of space technology to other fields.
Refereed Serial

629.1   CC   ISSN 1004-4132
JOURNAL OF SYSTEMS ENGINEERING AND ELECTRONICS/XITONG GONGCHENG YU DIANZI JISHU. (Editions in Chinese, English) 1979. q. $175 (effective 1996). (Ministry of Aero-Space Industry, The Second Academy) Science Press, Marketing and Sales Department, 16 Donghuangchenggen North St., Beijing 100717, People's Republic of China. TEL 4010642. FAX 4019810. (US office: Science Press New York, Ltd., 84-04 58th Ave., Elmhurst, NY 11373. TEL 718-476-0238) Ed. Liu Kexi. **Document type:** academic/scholarly publication.
—BLDSC (5068.073500); AskIEEE; CISTI; Ei; KR SourceOne.
   Formerly (until 1990): System Engineering and Electronic Technology (ISSN 1001-506X)
   Description: Covers academic exchanges in the field of high technology, and technological developments relevant to China's space undertaking.
Refereed Serial

001.94   US   ISSN 0730-5478
TL789.A1
JOURNAL OF U F O STUDIES. 1979-1983; N.S. 1989. a. $21. Center for U F O Studies, 2457 W. Peterson Ave., Chicago, IL 60659-4118. TEL 312-271-3611. Ed. Stuart Appelle. bk.rev.; bibl.; illus. circ. 500.

AERONAUTICS AND SPACE FLIGHT

KAIJO JIEITAI KANTEI TO KOKUKISHU/J.M.S.D.F. SHIPS AND AIRCRAFT. see TRANSPORTATION — Ships And Shipping

629.1   UK
KEY NOTE MARKET REPORT: AEROSPACE. Variant title: Aerospace. irreg., no.9, 1994. £205. Key Note Ltd., Field House, 72 Oldfield Rd., Hampton, Middlesex TW12 2HQ, England. TEL 44-181-783-0755. FAX 44-181-783-0049. **Document type:** trade publication.
●Also available online.
●Also available on CD-ROM.
    Formerly: Key Note Report: Aerospace (ISSN 0954-8262)

KISHO EISEI SENTA GIJUTSU HOKOKU/METEOROLOGICAL SATELLITE CENTER TECHNICAL NOTE. see METEOROLOGY

KISHO EISEI SENTA NYUSU/METEOROLOGICAL SATELLITE CENTER NEWS. see METEOROLOGY

629.132   745.5   US   ISSN 0891-1851
KITPLANES. 1984. m. $29.95 (Canada $37.95; elsewhere $45.95) (effective 1997). Cowles Enthusiast Media, 1000 Quail St., Ste. 190, Newport Beach, CA 92660. TEL 714-477-2295. FAX 714-477-3484. (Subscr. to: Box 420262, Palm Coast, FL 32142-0262) Ed. Dave Martin; Pub. Cindy Pedersen. adv. circ. 48,000. **Indexed:** Ind.How To Do It. **Document type:** consumer publication.
    Description: Provides tips and other information to persons interested in designing, building and flying their own aircraft. Covers theory, practical application, how-to, and in-flight reports.

629.132   IS   ISSN 0792-4836
KNAFAIM. (Text in Hebrew) 1988. q. membership. Aero Club of Israel, P.O. Box 26261, Tel Aviv 63432, Israel. TEL 972-3-5175038. FAX 972-3-5177280. Ed. Arik Sinai. adv.; bk.rev. circ. 6,000.
    Formerly: Termica.

629.1   621.38   JA   ISSN 0910-5689
KOKU DENSHI GIHO/JAPAN AVIATION ELECTRONICS TECHNICAL REPORT. (Text in Japanese; summaries in English, Japanese) 1969. a. Nihon Koku Denshi Kogyo K.K. - Japan Aviation Electronics Industry, Ltd., 21-6, Dogenzaka 1-chome, Shibuya-ku, Tokyo 196, Japan.
    —BLDSC (4616.581000).

KOKU KISHO NOTO/ABSTRACTS IN AVIATION METEOROLOGY. see METEOROLOGY — Abstracting, Bibliographies, Statistics

629.13   JA   ISSN 0389-4010
KOKU UCHU GIJUTSU KENKYUJO HOKOKU/NATIONAL AEROSPACE LABORATORY. TECHNICAL REPORT. (Text in English, Japanese) 1963. irreg. Kagaku Gijutsucho Koku Uchu Gijutsu Kenkyujo - National Aerospace Laboratory, 7-44-1 Jindaijihigashi-machi, Chofu, Tokyo, Japan. TEL 0422-47-5911. FAX 0422-42-1371.
    —BLDSC (8717.410000); CISTI.
    Formerly: Koku Gijutsu Kenkyujo Hokoku (ISSN 0452-294X)

629.13   JA   ISSN 0289-260X
KOKU UCHU GIJUTSU KENKYUJO TOKUBETSU SHIRYO/NATIONAL AEROSPACE LABORATORY. SPECIAL PUBLICATION. (Text in English, Japanese) 1983. irreg. Kagaku Gijutsucho Koku Uchu Gijutsu Kenkyujo - National Aerospace Laboratory, 7-44-1 Jindaijihigashi-machi, Chofu, Tokyo, Japan. TEL 0422-47-5911. FAX 0422-42-1371.
    —BLDSC (8379.490000); CISTI.

KOKUSAI EISEI TSUSHIN JIDAI/INTERNATIONAL SATELLITE COMMUNICATIONS AGE. see COMMUNICATIONS

629.1   CC   ISSN 0254-6124
QB495   CODEN: KKXUDK
KONGJIAN KEXUE XUEBAO/CHINESE JOURNAL OF SPACE SCIENCE. (Selected English translation: Chinese Astronomy and Astrophysics (ISSN 0275-1062)) (Text in Chinese; summaries in English) 1981. q. $52.80. Science Press, Marketing and Sales Department, 16 Donghuangchenggen North St., Beijing 100717, People's Republic of China. TEL 4019642. FAX 4019810. adv. circ. 6,000. **Indexed:** INSPEC (1984-). **Document type:** academic/scholarly publication.
    —AskIEEE; CASDDS; KR SourceOne; Linda Hall.
    Description: Deals with various aspects of space sciences, including physics, chemistry, astrophysics, geology, medicine, and biology in space, space material science, space sensing, space probing technology, and analysis of space observations.
    Refereed Serial

629.4   RU   ISSN 0023-4206
QB500   CODEN: KOISAW
KOSMICHESKIE ISSLEDOVANIYA. English translation: Cosmic Research (US ISSN 0010-9525) 1963. bi-m. $152 (effective 1998). (Rossiiskaya Akademiya Nauk) Izdatel'stvo Nauka, 90 Profsoyuznaya ul., 117864 Moscow, Russia. (Dist. in U.S. by: Victor Kamkin Inc., 4956 Boiling Brook Pkwy., Rockville, MD 20852. TEL 301-881-5973. FAX 301-881-1637) Ed. L.I. Sedov. bk.rev.; index. (tabloid format) **Indexed:** Biol.Abstr., Chem.Abstr., INIS Atomind., INSPEC, Int.Aerosp.Abstr.
    —BLDSC (0092.540000); AskIEEE; CASDDS; CISTI; KR SourceOne; Linda Hall. **CCC.**

KRILA ARMIJE. see MILITARY

629.13   RU   ISSN 0130-2701
TL504
KRYL'YA RODINY/WINGS OF THE MOTHERLAND. 1950. m. $71 (effective 1998). Izdatel'stvo DOSAAF, Novo-Ryazanskaya ul. 26, 107066 Moscow, Russia. TEL 261-68-90. Ed. L.F. Yasnopol'skii. bk.rev.; bibl.; illus. circ. 80,000.
    —BLDSC (0093.800000).

629.13   SW   ISSN 0280-1078
KUNGLIGA TEKNISKA HOEGSKOLAN. FLYGTEKNISK INSTITUTIONEN. K T H AERO MEMO F I. (Text in English, Swedish) 1948. irreg. Kungliga Tekniska Hoegskolan, Institutionen foer Flygteknik - Royal Institute of Technology, Division of Aeronautics, S-100 44 Stockholm, Sweden. circ. 35. **Document type:** monographic series.
    —CISTI.

343.73   347.303   US   ISSN 0274-9319
KF2400.A15
LAWYER - PILOTS BAR ASSOCIATION JOURNAL. Key Title: L P B A Journal. 195965. q. $55. Lawyer - Pilots Bar Association, c/o Yodice Associates, 500 E St., SW, Ste. 930, Washington, DC 20024. TEL 202-863-1000. FAX 202-484-1312. Ed. Jacob I. Rosenbaum. bk.rev.; illus.; index. circ. 1,600.
    Formerly (until 1980): Legal Eagles News (ISSN 0024-0354)
    Description: Covers legal aspects of aeronautics, aviation law and regulations, product liability and aviation safety.

629.1   629.4   XR   ISSN 0024-1156
TL504
LETECTVI A KOSMONAUTIKA; polularne odborny ctrnactidenik. 1921. fortn. 109 Kc.($50.60) (effective 1996). (Aeroklub) Vydavatelstvi Magnet Press, Vladislavova 26, 113 66 Prague 1, Czech Republic. TEL 42-2-24239435. FAX 42-2-261226. Ed. Josef Fryha. adv.; bk.rev. circ. 58,000.
    —SWETS.
    Formerly: Kridla Vlasti.

629.132   US   ISSN 0278-8950
TL671.9
LIGHT PLANE MAINTENANCE; the monthly maintenance report to pilots and aircraft owners. 1987. m. $75 (foreign $87) (effective 1996). Belvoir Publications, Inc., 75 Holly Hill Ln., Box 2626, Greenwich, CT 06836-2626. TEL 203-661-6111. FAX 203-661-4802. (Subscr. to: Box 420234, Palm Coast, FL 32142) Ed. John Likokis. **Indexed:** Ind.How To Do It (1987-). **Document type:** consumer publication.
    —CISTI.

629.132   US
LLOYD'S AVIATION LAW. 1981. s-m. $435 (foreign $455). L L P Inc - Distributech, Distributech, 41-21 28th St., RM-D, Long Island City, NY 11101-3732. TEL 212-529-9500. FAX 212-529-9826. Ed. George Tompkins, Jr.
    Description: For lawyers, insurers and aviation industry executives worldwide. Contains reports and commentary on major cases in civil aviation. Analyzes U.S. and international court decisions and interprets their implications for the outcome of future cases and their application to national and international law.

387.72   UK   ISSN 0024-5798
TL501
LOG. 1937. bi-m. £14 (foreign £22) (effective Jan. 1997). British Air Line Pilots Association (B.A.L.P.A.), 81 New Rd., Harlington, Hayes, Mddx. UB3 9BG, England. TEL 44-181-476-4000. FAX 44-181-476-4077. TELEX 265871 MONREF G. E-mail: ginaalexander@balpa.org.uk. Ed. I.G. Frow. adv.; bk.rev.; charts; illus. circ. 9,000. **Document type:** trade publication.

629.1   DK   ISSN 0108-4550
LUFT- OG RUMFARTSAARBOGEN. 1982. a. DKK 240 (effective 1997). Luft- og Rumfartsforlaget, Kastanievej 4, DK-5884 Gudme, Denmark. Ed. Bent Aalbaek-Nielsen. illus. circ. 3,000.

629.13   GW   ISSN 0173-6264
TL503
LUFT- UND RAUMFAHRT. 1980. q. DM.36 (Austria & Switzerland DM.42) (effective 1997). (Deutsche Gesellschaft fuer Luft- und Raumfahrt e.V.) Aviatic Verlag GmbH Peter Pletschacher, Kolpingring 3, 82041 Oberhaching, Germany. TEL 49-89-613890-0. FAX 49-89-61389010. Ed. Peter Pletschacher. adv.; bk.rev. circ. 4,000. **Document type:** academic/scholarly publication.
    —Linda Hall. **CCC.**

629.13   US   ISSN 0015-3699
LUFTWAFFE.* 1965. m. Monch Publishing Group, 1120 Greenway Rd., Ste. 101, Alexandria, VA 22308. TEL 703-765-8711. Ed. Manfred Sadlowski. adv.; bk.rev.; illus. circ. 36,000.
    Formerly: Fliegerkurier.

729 011   US
L5 SPACE DEVELOPMENT CONFERENCE. PROCEEDINGS. (Subseries of: Science and Technology Series (ISSN 0278-4017); Supplement to: Advances in the Astronautical Sciences Series (ISSN 0065-3438)) a. varies. (National Space Society) Univelt, Inc., Box 28130, San Diego, CA 92198-0198. TEL 619-746-4005. FAX 619-746-3139. E-mail: 76121.1532@compuserve.com. Ed. Robert H. Jacobs; Pub. Robert H. Jacobs. R&P contact: Robert H. Jacobs. **Document type:** proceedings.

629.132   US   ISSN 0199-5243
M A P A LOG.* vol.4, 1981. m. (except Oct.). $20 to non-members. Mooney Aircraft Pilots Association, 10715 Gulfdale St., Ste. 285, San Antonio, TX 78216-3633. TEL 512-434-5959. FAX 512-435-2526. adv.; bk.rev.

629.1   600   GW   ISSN 0935-8099
M T U FOCUS. (Text in English, German) 1989-1995. s-a. Motoren- und Turbinen-Union Muenchen GmbH, Postfach 500640, 80976 Munich, Germany. TEL 49-89-14894332. FAX 49-89-14892172. Ed. Ingo Petermann. circ. 3,000. **Document type:** academic/scholarly publication.

001.94   US
M U F O N - INTERNATIONAL U F O SYMPOSIUM PROCEEDINGS. 1971. a. $25. Mutual U F O Network, Inc., 103 Oldtowne Rd., Seguin, TX 78155-4099. TEL 210-379-9216. FAX 210-372-9439. Eds. Walter H. Andrus, Jr., Irena Scott. circ. 1,500. **Document type:** proceedings.
    Formerly: M U F O N - U F O Symposium Proceedings.

AERONAUTICS AND SPACE FLIGHT

001.94 US ISSN 0270-6822
TL789.A1
M U F O N UFO JOURNAL. 1967. m. $30 (effective 1996). Mutual U F O Network, Inc., c/o Walter H. Andrus, Jr., 103 Oldtowne Rd., Seguin, TX 78155-4099. TEL 210-379-9216. FAX 210-372-9439. E-mail: mufonhg@aol.com. Ed. Dennis W. Stacy. adv.; bk.rev. circ. 5,000. (reprint service avail.) **Indexed:** Mag.Ind. **Document type:** bulletin.
—UnCover.
  Formerly: Skylook (ISSN 0049-0687)
  Description: News and investigations of sightings of UFO phenomena.

629.31 SW ISSN 0280-8498
MACH. 1980. q. SEK 180 in Sweden; Europe SEK 200; elsewhere SEK 210 (effective 1997); newsstand price: SEK 48. Mach, P.O. Box 5002, S-161 05 Bromma, Sweden. TEL 46008-17-88-50. FAX 46-08-17-88-55. Ed. Haakan Ahlstroem. adv. contact: May Backryd. bk.rev.; circ. 11,000 (paid). **Document type:** trade publication.
  Refereed Serial

629.1 SP
MACH 82. 6/yr. Spanish Union of Airline Pilots, Grl. Diaz Porlier 49, int. 4o, 28001 Madrid, Spain. TEL 1-402-28-35. Ed. J.A. Silva. circ. 30,000.

MANDATORY AIRCRAFT MODIFICATIONS AND INSPECTIONS SUMMARY. see *TRANSPORTATION — Air Transport*

MAPPINGS: SOCIETY - THEORY - SPACE. see *GEOGRAPHY*

MARITIME COMMAND TRIDENT. see *MILITARY*

629.1 US
MASSACHUSETTS INSTITUTE OF TECHNOLOGY. FLIGHT TRANSPORTATION LABORATORY. F T L REPORTS AND MEMORANDA. 1966. irreg. price varies. Massachusetts Institute of Technology, Department of Aeronautics and Astronautics, Flight Transportation Laboratory, Rm. 33-412, Cambridge, MA 02139. TEL 617-253-2424. Dir. Robert W. Simpson. charts; illus.
  Formerly: Massachusetts Institute of Technology. Flight Transportation Laboratory. F T L Reports.
  Refereed Serial

629.1 US
MECHANIST.* m. International Association of Machinists and Aerospace Workers, 900 Machinists Pl., Upper Marboro, MD 20772. TEL 301-967-4500.

METEOROLOGICAL SATELLITE CENTER. MONTHLY REPORT. see *METEOROLOGY*

629.1 US ISSN 0539-8703
MICHIGAN AVIATION. 1961. bi-m. free. Aeronautics Commission, 2700 E. Airport Service Dr., Capital City Airport, Lansing, MI 48906.
TEL 517-335-9283. FAX 517-321-6422. Ed. Kenneth Schaschl. bk.rev.; illus.; circ. 17,000 (controlled).

MICRO. see *ELECTRONICS*

629.13 NE ISSN 1015-1648
MICROGRAVITY NEWS FROM E S A. 1988. 3/yr. free. European Space Agency, Publications Division, Keplerlaan 1, 22000 AG Noordwijk, Netherlands. TEL 31-0071-5653400. FAX 31-071-5655433. TELEX 39098. Ed. B. Kaldeich. illus. circ. 8,000. **Document type:** newsletter.

629.1 GW ISSN 0938-0108
TL1489 CODEN: MSTYEN
MICROGRAVITY - SCIENCE AND TECHNOLOGY; international journal for microgravity research and applications. (Text in English) 1987. q. DM.516. Carl Hanser Verlag, Kolbergerstr. 22, 81679 Munich, Germany. TEL 49-89-998300. FAX 49-89-984809. (Subscr. to: Postfach 860420, 81631 Munich, Germany) Eds. G. Greger, H.J. Rath. adv.; bk.rev.; charts; illus. circ. 500. **Indexed:** Alloys Ind., ASCA, Eng.Mat.Abstr., IBR, Met.Abstr., Met.Abstr.Ind., Nonfer.Met.Alert, PCC Alert, Steels Alert. **Document type:** trade publication.
—BLDSC (5759.147500); AskIEEE; CASDDS; CISTI; Ei; Genuine Article; KR SourceOne; UnCover. **CCC.**
  Formerly: Applied Microgravity Technology (ISSN 0931-9530)
  Description: Surveys research results on microgravity and its applications in space and on earth.

629.1 796 UK ISSN 0968-3100
MICROLIGHT FLYING. 1980. bi-m. £33 to non-members. British Microlight Aircraft Association, 4-5 Lansil Way, Lancaster, Lancs. LA1 3QY, England. FAX 44-1524-841578. Ed. David Bremner; Pub. Norman Burr. R&P contact: Norman Burr. adv. contact: Amy Poole. bk.rev.; circ. 4,000 (paid). (back issues avail.) **Document type:** consumer publication.
  Formerly: Flightline (ISSN 0266-0504)

629.13 355 UK ISSN 0026-394X
MILITARY AIRCRAFT AND MISSILE DATA SHEETS. 1954. q. $245. Aviation Studies International, Sussex House, Parkside, Wimbledon, London SW19 5NB, England. TEL 44-181-946-5082. **Document type:** trade publication, directory.
  Description: Describes 2,500 designs of fighters, bombers, transports, helicopters, and trainers, listing their dimensions, engines, weights, performance and range, and production runs.

629.1 355 US ISSN 1046-9079
UG485
MILITARY & AEROSPACE ELECTRONICS. 1990. 12/yr. $99 in N. America (free to qualified personnel); elsewhere $195 by airmail (effective 1997). PennWell Publishing Co. (Nashua), 10 Tara Blvd., 5th Fl., Nashua, NH 03062-2801.
TEL 603-891-0123. FAX 603-891-0574. (Subscr. to: Box 1260, Tulsa, OK 74101. TEL 918-835-3161. FAX 918-832-9295) Ed. Bruce Raynor. circ. 48,000 (controlled). (tabloid format) **Document type:** newspaper, trade publication.
—BLDSC (5767.974500). **CCC.**
  Description: For designers, buyers and specifiers of electronic components and subsystems. Includes product and technology applications, military and defense industry news, design development briefs and new product updates.

MILITARY & COMMERCIAL FIBER BUSINESS. see *MILITARY*

629.13 355 UK
MILITARY RECORD OF ATOMIC C B R HAPPENINGS. ARMAMENT DATA SHEETS. q. $735. Aviation Studies International, Sussex House, Parkside, Wimbledon, London SW19 5NB, England.
TEL 44-181-946-5082. **Document type:** directory, trade publication.
  Formerly: Military Record of Atomic C B R Happenings (ISSN 0026-4121)
  Description: Compiles data on conventional and nuclear weapons.

MILITARY SPACE. see *MILITARY*

629.1 CC ISSN 1003-2061
MINHANG JINGJI YU JISHU/CIVIL AVIATION ECONOMICS AND TECHNOLOGY. (Text in Chinese) m. Civil Aviation Administration of China - C A A C, No. 1 Information Institute, Building 1, Room 4029, Anzhenli Erqu (2nd District), Andingmenwai, Beijing 100029, People's Republic of China. TEL 5223377. Ed. Li Xuan.

MODEL AIRPLANE NEWS. see *HOBBIES*

MODELE MAGAZINE; revue des modeles d'avions. see *HOBBIES*

MODELE REDUIT D'AVION. see *HOBBIES*

MOUNTAIN PILOT; the mountains aviation magazine. see *TRANSPORTATION — Air Transport*

629 US
MUSEUM OF FLIGHT NEWS. 1979. bi-m. $35 (effective 1997). Museum of Flight Foundation, 9404 E. Marginal Way, So., Seattle, WA 98108.
TEL 206-764-5700. FAX 206-764-5707. Ed. Hollis M. Palmer. adv.; bk.rev.; illus. circ. 15,000. (tabloid format) **Document type:** newsletter.
  Formerly: Air Museum News.

387.7 630
N A A NEWSLETTER. w. National Agricultural Aviation Association, 1005 E St. S.E., Washington, DC 20003-2847. TEL 202-546-5722.
FAX 202-546-5726. Ed. Jim Boillot. **Document type:** newsletter.

629.13 JA ISSN 0023-2726
N A L NEWS/KOGIKEN NYUSU. (Text in Japanese) 1958. m. National Aerospace Laboratory - Kagaku Gijutsucho Koku Uchu Gijutsu Kenkyujo, 7-44-1 Jindaijihigashi-machi, Chofu, Tokyo, Japan. TEL 0422-47-5911. Ed. Kingo Takasawa. abstr. **Document type:** newsletter.

629.1 371.3 US
TL521.3.R4
N A S A EDUCATIONAL HORIZONS. Variant title: N.A.S.A. Report to Educators. 1973. 3/yr. free. U.S. National Aeronautics and Space Administration, Washington, DC 20546. TEL 202-453-1533. Ed. Elsie Weigel. illus. circ. 200,000. **Indexed:** Ind.U.S.Gov.Per. **Document type:** government publication.
  Supersedes (in 1992): Report to Educators (ISSN 0883-0983); Which was formerly: N A S A Report to Educators (ISSN 0092-346X)
  Description: Enables teachers to interact with N A S A through workshops and seminars, educational publications and videotapes, and cable television and teleconferencing.

629.13 US ISSN 0077-3093
N A S A FACTS. irreg. U.S. National Aeronautics and Space Administration, Washington, DC 20546. TEL 202-755-2320. (Dist. by: Supt. of Documents, Washington, DC 20402)

N A S A FORMAL SERIES REPORTS. (U.S. National Aeronautics and Space Administration) see *SCIENCES: COMPREHENSIVE WORKS*

629.1 350 US
N A S A O NEWSLETTER. m. $70. National Association of State Aviation Officials, 8401 Colesville Rd., Ste. 505, Silver Spring, MD 20910. TEL 301-588-0587. FAX 301-585-1803. Ed. Lori Lehnerd. R&P contact: Stacey Moyeund. **Document type:** newsletter.
  Description: Reports on current aviation issues and developments, state agency activities, pertinent congressional news and general items of interest.

629.1
N A S A SCIENTIFIC AND TECHNICAL PUBLICATIONS CATALOG. a. U.S. National Aeronautics and Space Administration, Scientific and Technical Information Office, Center for AeroSpace Information, 800 Elkridge Landing Rd., Linthicum Heights, MD 21090-2934. E-mail: help@sti.nasa.gov; URL: http://www.sti.nasa.gov. **Document type:** government publication, catalog.
  Description: Lists N.A.S.A. publications from four report series entered into the S.T.I. Database during the previous year.

N A S A UNIVERSITY PROGRAMS REPORT. (U.S. National Aeronautics and Space Administration) see *EDUCATION — International Education Programs*

387.7
N B A A DIGEST. m. membership. National Business Aircraft Association, 1200 18th St., N.W., Ste. 200, Washington, DC 20036. TEL 202-783-9000. FAX 202-331-8364.
  Formerly: Business Aviation Digest.

629.1 US
N T I S ALERTS: SPACE TECHNOLOGY. w. $160 (outside N. America $225). U.S. National Technical Information Service, 5285 Port Royal Rd., Springfield, VA 22161. TEL 703-487-4650. FAX 703-321-8547. TELEX 64617. bibl. (also avail in microform from NTI) **Document type:** newsletter, government publication.

NAGOYA KOKU KISHOHYO/NAGOYA DATA OF AERONAUTICAL METEOROLOGY. see *METEOROLOGY*

AERONAUTICS AND SPACE FLIGHT

629.1   CC   ISSN 1005-2615
CODEN: NHHXEU
NANJING HANGKONG HANGTIAN DAXUE XUEBAO/NANJING UNIVERSITY OF AERONAUTICS AND ASTRONAUTICS. JOURNAL. (Text in Chinese) 1956. bi-m. $140. Nanjing Hangkong Hangtian Daxue, 29 Yudao St., Nanjing, Jiangsu 210016, People's Republic of China. TEL 025-4492492. FAX 025-4494880. TELEX 34155 NAINJ CN. Ed. Sun Pingfan. adv.; bk.rev. circ. 1,200. **Indexed:** Zent.Math. **Document type:** academic/scholarly publication.
—BLDSC (4828.679300); AskIEEE; CASDDS; KR SourceOne.
Formerly (until vol.25, no.2, 1993): Nanjing Hangkong Xueyuan Xuebao (ISSN 1000-1956)

629.1   CC   ISSN 1005-1120
NANJING UNIVERSITY OF AERONAUTICS AND ASTRONAUTICS. TRANSACTIONS. (Text in English) 1982. s-a. $60. Nanjing Hangkong Hangtian Daxue, 29 Yudao St., Nanjing, Jiangsu 210016, People's Republic of China. TEL 025-4492492. FAX 025-4494880. TELEX 34155 NAINJ CN. Ed. Sun Pingfan. adv.; bk.rev. circ. 900. **Indexed:** Zent.Math. **Document type:** academic/scholarly publication.
—BLDSC (8983.730000); AskIEEE; KR SourceOne.
Formerly (until 1993): Nanjing Aeronautical Institute. Journal (English Edition).

629.13   II   ISSN 0077-2976
NATIONAL AERONAUTICAL LABORATORY. ANNUAL REPORT. (Text in English) 1961. a. exchange basis. National Aeronautical Laboratory, P.O. Box 1779 Kodihalli, Bangalore 560017, India. (Affiliate: Council of Scientific and Industrial Research) circ. 500.
—CISTI.

016 629.1   II
NATIONAL AERONAUTICAL LABORATORY. CURRENT SCIENTIFIC AND TECHNICAL REPORTS. m. exchange basis. National Aeronautical Laboratory, P.O. Box 1779, Kodihalli, Bangalore 560017, India.

629.1   II
NATIONAL AERONAUTICAL LABORATORY. LIBRARY BULLETIN. 1980. q. exchange basis. National Aeronautical Laboratory, P.O. Box 1779, Kodihalli, Bangalore 560017, India.

629.1   II
NATIONAL AERONAUTICAL LABORATORY. RECENT MICROFICHE ADDITIONS. 1978. q. exchange basis.. National Aeronautical Laboratory, P.O. Box 1779, Kodihalli, Bangalore 560017, India. (microfiche)

629.13   II   ISSN 0077-300X
NATIONAL AERONAUTICAL LABORATORY. TECHNICAL NOTE. (Text in English) 1960. irreg., latest 1978. exchange basis. National Aeronautical Laboratory, P.O. Box 1779, Kodihalli, Bangalore 560017, India. circ. 500. **Indexed:** Appl.Mech.Rev.

NATIONAL BUSINESS AIRCRAFT ASSOCIATION. MAINTENANCE AND OPERATIONS BULLETIN. see *TRANSPORTATION — Air Transport*

NATIONAL DEFENSE. see *MILITARY*

629.13 359   US   ISSN 0028-1417
VG93
NAVAL AVIATION NEWS. 1917. bi-m. $12 (foreign $15) (effective 1997). U.S. Department of the Navy, Naval Historical Center, Bldg. 157-1 WNY, Washington, DC 20374-5059. TEL 202-433-4407. FAX 202-433-2343. URL: http://www.history.navy.mil. (Subscr. to: Superintendent of Documents, U.S. Government Printing Office, Box 371954, Pittsburgh, PA 15250-7954. TEL 202-512-1800. FAX 202-512-2250) bk.rev.; illus.; index; circ. 30,000 (controlled). (back issues avail.) **Indexed:** DM&T, Ind.U.S.Gov.Per.; PROMT. **Document type:** government publication.
—BLDSC (6063.900000); Linda Hall; SWETS; UMI; UnCover.
Description: Presents articles of interest on all phases of Navy and Marine air activity.

NAVIGATION; revue technique de navigation aerienne, maritime, spatiale et terrestre. see *TRANSPORTATION — Ships And Shipping*

629.13   US   ISSN 0028-1522
VK1   CODEN: NAVIB3
NAVIGATION (WASHINGTON). 1946. q. $45 (foreign $55) (effective 1997). Institute of Navigation, 1800 Diagonal Rd., Ste. 480, Alexandria, VA 22314-2840. TEL 703-683-7101. FAX 703-683-7105. E-mail: membership@ion.org. Ed. Ron Braff. adv.; bk.rev.; bibl.; illus.; index. circ. 3,000. **Indexed:** Air Un.Lib.Ind., Bibl.Cart., Deep Sea Res.& Oceanogr.Abstr., INSPEC (1973-), Int.Aerosp.Abstr., Math.R., Ocean.Abstr., Pollut.Abstr.
—BLDSC (6066.000000); AskIEEE; CISTI; Ei; KR SourceOne; Linda Hall; SWETS; UnCover. **CCC.**

629.132   US   ISSN 0028-1581
NAVIONEERS. 1960. bi-m. $15 to non-members. American Navion Society, 225 N. 5th St., Ste. 301, Grand Junction, CO 81501. TEL 970-243-8513. (Subscr. to: Box 1810, Lodi, CA 95241. TEL 209-339-4213. FAX 209-339-1701) Ed. Hugh Smith. R&P contact: Jerry Feather. adv. contact: Jerry Feather. illus.; cum.index: 1961-1996. circ. 1,200. (back issues avail.) **Document type:** newsletter.
Refereed Serial

NEGRO AIRMEN INTERNATIONAL NEWSLETTER. see *CLUBS*

629.1 387.7   AU
NEUE FLIEGER REVUE. 8/yr. S.252; newsstand price: S.42. (Oesterreichischen Aero-Club) Orac Zeitschriftenverlag GmbH, Brunner Feldstr. 45, A-2380 Perchtoldsdorf, Austria. TEL 43-1-8696536. FAX 43-1-8696536. E-mail: flieger@via.at; URL: http://www.via.at/flieger. Ed. Manfred Hluma. adv.: B&W page S.31800, color page S.54060; trim 185 x 250. circ. 31,500 (paid). **Document type:** consumer publication.

NEUES VON ROHDE UND SCHWARZ. see *COMMUNICATIONS*

629.13   US
NEW JERSEY AVIATION NEWS. 1962. q. free. Department of Transportation, Division of Aeronautics, 1035 Parkway Ave., CN 610, Trenton, NJ 08625-0610. TEL 609-530-2915. FAX 609-530-5719. Ed. Mike Stoddard. circ. 14,000 (controlled). **Document type:** government publication, newsletter.
Former titles: New Jersey Aviation; New Jersey Aviation News and Views; Flight Log.

614.8   NZ   ISSN 0112-8949
TL553.5
NEW ZEALAND FLIGHT SAFETY. (Supplement avail.) 1972. 2/yr. NZ.$20 (foreign NZ.$23) (effective 1992). Civil Aviation Authority of New Zealand, P.O. Box 31-441, Lower Hutt, New Zealand. FAX 64-4-5692-024. Ed. C.F.L. Jenks. illus. circ. 9,500. **Document type:** government publication.
Formerly: Flight Safety.
Description: To promote safety in the New Zealand civil aviation system by providing safety information.

614.8   NZ   ISSN 1171-1558
NEW ZEALAND FLIGHT SAFETY SUPPLEMENT. 1992. every 6 weeks. NZ.$20 (foreign NZ.$23) with parent title. Civil Aviation Authority of New Zealand, P.O. Box 31-441, Lower Hutt, New Zealand. FAX 64-4-5692-024. Ed. C.F.L. Jenks. **Document type:** government publication.
Description: Provides safety information for the New Zealand civil aviation system.

629.13   NZ   ISSN 0110-1471
NEW ZEALAND WINGS. 1932. m. NZ.$46 (Australia NZ.$60; elsewhere NZ.$73). N.Z. Wings, P.O. Box 120, Otaki, New Zealand. TEL 64-6-3644423. FAX 64-6-3647797. Ed. R.F. MacPherson. adv.: page NZ.$900; trim 285 x 210. bk.rev.; charts; illus.; stat.; circ. 6,500 (paid). (back issues avail.) **Document type:** trade publication.
—**CCC.**
Formerly: Wings (ISSN 0043-5899)
Description: Covers both civil and military aviation within New Zealand.

629.132   US
NINETY-NINE NEWS. 1929. 6/yr. $20. International Women Pilots, Box 965, Will Rogers Airport, Oklahoma City, OK 73159. TEL 405-685-7969. FAX 405-685-7985. Ed. Beyyt Rowley. adv. contact: Betty Rowley. bk.rev.; cum.index: 1929-1984. circ. 7,000. (back issues avail.) **Document type:** bibliography, directory.

629.1 630   US
NORTH AMERICAN APPLICATOR MAGAZINE. bi-m. free. Graphics Plus, Box 1607, Mt. Vernon, WA 98273-1607. TEL 360-336-9738. FAX 360-336-2506. Ed. Thomas J. Wood. R&P contact: Thomas J. Wood. adv.; bk.rev. circ. 2,940. **Document type:** trade publication.
Formed by the merger of (1982-199?): I A A F Newsletter (International Agricultural Aviation Foundation); (1986-199?): Northern Applicator Magazine; Which was formerly: Canadian Aerial Applicators Association Newsletter.

629.13 614.7   US   ISSN 0887-4301
K14
NORTHROP UNIVERSITY LAW JOURNAL OF AEROSPACE, BUSINESS AND TAXATION. 1979. a. $6. Northrop University, School of Law, 5800 W. Arbor Vitae St., Los Angeles, CA 90045. adv.; bk.rev. circ. 250. (reprint service avail. from WSH) **Indexed:** C.L.I., L.R.I., Leg.Per.
—KR SourceOne.
Formerly (until vol.5, 1985): Northrop University Law Journal of Aerospace, Energy and the Environment (ISSN 0196-1489)

629.13   US   ISSN 1057-9621
NOTICES TO AIRMEN. fortn. $208 (foreign $260.00). U.S. Federal Aviation Administration, Planning, Publications & Analysis Division, Publication Branch, ATX-420, 800 Independence Avenue, SW, Washington, DC 20591. TEL 202-655-4000. (Subscr. to: Superintendent of Documents, U.S. Government Printing Office, Box 371954, Pittsburgh, PA 15250-7954. TEL 202-512-1800. FAX 202-512-2250) (back issues avail.) **Document type:** government publication.
—CISTI.
Former titles: Airman's Information Manual. Notices to Airmen; (until May 1978): Airman's Information Manual. Part 3A: Notices to Airmen.
Description: Contains all NOTAMs.

691.1 520   IT
NOTIZIARIO U F O; Italy's international U F O news. (Text in Italian; summaries in English) 1966. bi-m. L.48000($35) Centro Ufologico Nazionale (CUN) - National Ufological Center, Via Odorico da Pordenone 36, 50127 Florence, Italy. TEL 39-55-353498. (Subscr. to: CUN, P.O. Box 823, 40100 Bologna, Italy) Ed. Roberto Pinotti. adv.; bk.rev.; film rev.; bibl.; illus. circ. 50,000. (back issues avail.)

629.1 629.4   FR   ISSN 1247-5793
TL502   CODEN: AENABS
NOUVELLE REVUE D'AERONAUTIQUE ET D'ASTRONAUTIQUE. 1943. 6/yr. 594 F. to institutions (foreign 790 F.); students 297 F. (foreign 395 F.) (effective 1997). (Association Aeronautique et Astronautique de Franceet Academie Nationale de l'Air et de l'Espace) Dunod, 5 rue Laromiguiere, 75005 Paris, France. TEL 33-1-40466200. FAX 33-1-40466201. E-mail: gauthier.villars.publisher@mail.sgip.fr; URL: http://www.gauthier-villars.fr. (Subscr. to: Societe de Periodiques Specialises, B.P. 22, 41354 Vineuil Cedex, France. TEL 33-2-54504612. FAX 33-2-54504611) Ed. J.-P. Sanfourche. adv. circ. 3,000. **Indexed:** Alloys Ind., ASCA, Eng.Mat.Abstr., Excerp.Med., INIS Atomind., INSPEC (1971-1986), Met.Abstr., Met.Abstr.Ind., PCC Alert, Steels Alert, World Alum.Abstr.
—BLDSC (6176.797200); CASDDS; CISTI; Genuine Article; Linda Hall; SWETS. **CCC.**
Formerly (until 1993): Aeronautique et l'Astronautique (ISSN 0001-9275); Incorporates: Association Aeronautique et Astronautique de France. Annuaire; Which was formerly (1961-1973): Association Francaise des Ingenieures et Techniciens de l'Aeronautique et de l'Espace. Annuaire (ISSN 0066-9245); Formerly (until 1967): Techniques et Sciences Aeronautiques (ISSN 0151-0622)

629.1   IT   ISSN 0393-1005
NOVA ASTRONAUTICA. (Text in English, Italian) 1981. q. L.90000($100) (effective 1997-98). Associazione Sviluppo Propulsione Spaziale - Association for the Development of Space Propulsion, Via N. Martoglio 22, 00137 Rome, Italy. TEL 39-6-87131068. E-mail: MD1175@mclink.it. adv.; bk.rev. circ. 900. (back issues avail.) **Document type:** newsletter.
●Also available online.
Description: Covers studies and experiments on Non Newtonian Propulsion of the new ASPS prototype SC23.

AERONAUTICS AND SPACE FLIGHT

629.4 520   RU
NOVOSTI KOSMONAVTIKI. (Text in Russian) 1991. bi-w. 150000 Rub. Video Cosmos Company, Akademika Koroleva ul., 12, stroen 3, 127427 Moscow, Russia. TEL 7-095-2833314. FAX 7-095-2833314. E-mail: cosmos@space.accessnet.ru. Ed. Igor Marinin. adv.: page $300; adv. contact: Igor Marinin. charts; illus.; stat.; circ. 1,000 (paid). (back issues avail.) **Document type:** bulletin, newsletter.
   Description: Provides news on Russian and international astronautics: manned missions, satellites, probes, launch vehicles, spacecrafts.

001.94   UK   ISSN 0262-7795
O S E A P CENTRE UPDATE. 1982. irreg. £5 (joint subscr. with O S E A P Journal). Organisation for Scientific Evaluation of Aerial Phenomena, 2 Acer Ave., Crewe, Cheshire, England. Ed. David L. Rees. bk.rev. circ. 135.

001.94   UK   ISSN 0262-5954
O S E A P JOURNAL. 1982. irreg. £5 (joint subscr. with O S E A P Centre Update). Organisation for Scientific Evaluation of Aerial Phenomena, 2 Acer Ave., Crewe, Cheshire, England. Ed. Mark A. Tyrrell. circ. 135.

ONZE LUCHTMACHT. see MILITARY

629.132   US
ORGANIZATION OF BLACK AIRLINE PILOTS. CONVENTION JOURNAL. a. Organization of Black Airline Pilots, Box 5793, Englewood, NJ 07631. TEL 201-568-8145.

629.132
ORGANIZATION OF BLACK AIRLINE PILOTS. NEWSLETTER. q. Organization of Black Airline Pilots, Box 5793, Englewood, NJ 07631. TEL 201-568-8145. **Document type:** newsletter.

971 629   CN   ISSN 0843-1566
OUTBOUND. 1969. q. free to members. Canadian Aviation Historical Society, Box 224 Sta. A, Willowdale, ON M2N 5S8, Canada. TEL 416-488-2247. bk.rev.; bibl. circ. 1,350. (back issues avail.) **Document type:** academic/scholarly publication.
—CISTI.
   Description: Covers the society's affairs and general items of aviation interest.

629.13   US   ISSN 0092-3591
TL521
OVERVIEW OF THE F A A ENGINEERING & DEVELOPMENT PROGRAMS. (Supplement to F.A.A. Report no. FAA-EM) 1974. irreg. free to qualified personnel. U.S. Federal Aviation Administration, 800 Independence Ave., S.W., Washington, DC 20591. TEL 202-655-4000. illus. **Document type:** government publication, monographic series.

629.1   JA   ISSN 0912-490X
PAIROTTO. (Text in Japanese) 1965. 3/yr. Nihon Pairotto Kyokai - Japanese Pilots Association, 4-5, Koji-machi, Chiyoda-ku, Tokyo 102, Japan.

PARACHUTIST. see SPORTS AND GAMES

PEGASUS JOURNAL. see MILITARY

001.94   FR   ISSN 1157-4704
PHENOMENA. 1991. bi-m. 150 F. S O S Ovni, B.P. 324, 13611 Aix-en-Provence Cedex 1, France. Ed. Perry Petrakis.
   Description: News magazine of current information pertaining to unidentified aerial phenomena in France and the world.

629.13   NE   ISSN 1381-1827
PILOOT EN VLIEGTUIG; het complete luchtvaart magazine. 1994. m. fl.95. Creation Station, P.O. Box 1110, 6040 KC Roermond, Netherlands. TEL 31-475-324242. FAX 31-475-324833. Ed. K. Compers. adv.: B&W page fl.2150; adv. contact: G. v.d. Borst. bk.rev.; illus. circ. 12,000. **Document type:** consumer publication.
   Description: Provides useful information for pilots and student pilots.

629.132   UK   ISSN 0300-1695
TL721.4
PILOT (CLAPHAM). 1967. m. £28.80 (foreign £37) (effective 1997); newsstand price: £2.25. Pilot Publishing Company Ltd., The Clock House, 28 Old Town, Clapham, London SW4 0LB, England. TEL 44-171-498-2506. FAX 44-171-498-6920. E-mail: 100126.563@compuserve.com; URL: http://www.hiway.co.uk/aviation/pilothom.html. (Dist. by: Comag, Tavistock Rd., W. Drayton, Middlesex UB7 7QE, England. TEL 44-1895-444055. FAX 44-1895-433605; Subscr. to: Bradley Pavilions, Bradley Stoke N., Bristol BS12 0BQ, England. TEL 44-1454-617798. FAX 44-1454-620080) Ed. James Gilbert. adv.: B&W page £1175, color page £1755; trim 279 x 216; adv. contact: Brian Harriss. bk.rev.; illus.; index; circ. 30,668 (paid). (back issues avail.) **Document type:** consumer publication.
—SWETS.

PIPER'S MAGAZINE. see TRANSPORTATION — Air Transport

629.13   US   ISSN 0032-0617
TL721.4
PLANE AND PILOT. 1965. m. $16.95. Werner Publishing Corporation, 12121 Wilshire Blvd. No. 1220, Los Angeles, CA 90025-1175. Ed. Steve Werner. adv.; bk.rev.; illus. circ. 134,000. (also avail. in microform from UMI; reprint service avail. from UMI) **Indexed:** Ind.How To Do It (1983-1987), Sportsearch. **Document type:** consumer publication.
—UMI; UnCover.
   Incorporates (in 1987): Homebuilt Aircraft; Airways (ISSN 0002-287X)

629.132   US
PLANE TALK. m. Avionics Maintenance Conference, c/o Aeronautical Radio, Inc., 2551 Riva Rd., Annapolis, MD 21401. TEL 301-266-4116.

PLANETARY REPORT. see ASTRONOMY

629.13   UK   ISSN 0032-4493
POPULAR FLYING. 1957. bi-m. membership. Popular Flying Association, Terminal Bldg., Shoreham Airport, Shoreham-by-Sea, W. Sussex BN43 5FF, England. TEL 44-1273-461616. FAX 44-1273-463390. Ed. John Catchpole. R&P contact: A. Preston. adv.: B&W page £535, color page £700; trim 297 x 210; adv. contact: John Catchpole. bk.rev.; charts; illus. circ. 8,000. **Document type:** trade publication.
—CISTI.

629.13   PL   ISSN 0373-5982
TL787.P67   CODEN: POASBE
POSTEPY ASTRONAUTYKI/PROGRESS IN ASTRONAUTICS. 1967. q. $16. Polskie Towarzystwo Astronautyczne - Polish Astronautical Society, Ul. Z. Krasinskiego 54, 01-755 Warsaw, Poland. TEL 48-22-308-2703. (Dist. by: Ars Polona-Ruch, Krakowskie Przedmiescie 7, Warsaw, Poland) Ed. Pawel Elsztein. bk.rev.; charts; illus. circ. 500. **Indexed:** Int.Aerosp.Abstr., Ref.Zh.
—CASDDS; CISTI.
   Description: Publishes original papers on astronautics.

629.13   NE   ISSN 1018-8657
TL790   CODEN: PRFUEZ
PREPARING FOR THE FUTURE: E S A TECHNOLOGY QUARTERLY. (Text in English) 1991. q. free. European Space Agency, Publications Division, Keplerlaan 1, 22000 AG Noordwijk, Netherlands. TEL 31-071-5653677. FAX 31-071-5655433. TELEX 39098. Ed. M. Perry. circ. 25,000.
—BLDSC (6607.876580); CISTI; Linda Hall.

PREVISIONS GLISSANTES DETAILLEES EN PERSPECTIVES SECTORIELLES (VOL.16): CONSTRUCTION AEROSPATIALE. see BUSINESS AND ECONOMICS — Economic Situation And Conditions

PROBE REPORT. see PARAPSYCHOLOGY AND OCCULTISM

629.1   UK   ISSN 0376-0421
TL500   CODEN: PAESD6
PROGRESS IN AEROSPACE SCIENCES; an international journal. (Text in English, French and German) 196 m. fl.1860($1069) (effective 1998). Elsevier Science Ltd., Pergamon, P.O. Box 800, Kidlington, Oxford OX5 1DX, England. TEL 44-1865-843000. FAX 44-1865-843010. E-mail: nlinfo-f@elsevier.nl, usinfo-f@elsevier.com; forinfo-kyf04035@niftyserv or.jp; URL: http://www.elsevier.nl:80/inca/publications/store/4/1/5/415.pub.shtml. (Subscr. to: Elsevier Science, Regional Sales Office, P.O. Box 211, 1000 AE Amsterdam, Netherlands. TEL 31-20-4853757. FAX 31-20-4853432; Subscr. in the Americas to: Elsevier Science, Regional Sales Office, Box 945, New York, NY 10159-0945. TEL 212-633-3730. FAX 212-633-3680; Subscr. in Australasia and the Far East to: Elsevier Science (Singapore) Pte Ltd, No.1 Temasek Ave., No.17-01 Millenia Tower, Singapore 039192, Singapore. TEL 65-434-3727. FAX 65-337-2230) Ed. Alec D. Young. (also avail. in microfilm from UMI) **Indexed:** Alloys Ind., Appl.Mech.Rev., ASCA, Eng.Mat.Abstr., INSPEC, Int.Aerosp.Abstr., Met.Abstr.Ind., Met.Abstr Nonfer.Met.Alert, PCC Alert, Steels Alert, World Alum.Abstr. **Document type:** academic/scholarly publication.
—BLDSC (6865.902000); CISTI; Ei; Genuine Articl Linda Hall; SWETS; UMI; UnCover. **CCC.**
   Formerly: Progress in Aeronautical Sciences (ISSN 0079-6026)
   Description: Focuses on the application of recent developments and research in the aerospace sciences to problems encountered in industry, research establishments and universities.
   Refereed Serial

629.13 629.4   US   ISSN 0079-6050
TL507   CODEN: PAAEA9
PROGRESS IN ASTRONAUTICS AND AERONAUTICS SERIES. (Vols. 1-8 published as Progress in Astronautics and Rocketry; Vols. 1-23 published by Academic Press) 1960. irreg., vol.142, 1994. American Institute of Aeronautics and Astronautics, Inc., 1801 Alexander Dr., Ste. 500, Reston, VA 20191. TEL 703-264-7500. Ed. A. Richard Seebass. (reprint service avail. from UMI) **Indexed:** Chem.Abstr., INSPEC, Int.Aerosp.Abstr. **Document type:** academic/scholarly publication.
—BLDSC (6865.915000); CASDDS; CISTI; Ei; Lind Hall; UnCover. **CCC.**
   Description: A series of hard-cover books, each of which is devoted to a particular, well-defined subjec in astronautical or aeronautical (aerospace) science and technology.

358.4   DK   ISSN 0033-1279
PROPEL; tidsskrift for flyvning og rumfart. 1943. m. DKK 285($12) (effective 1997). Luft- og Rumfartsforlaget - Danish Aerospace Publishers, Kastanievej 4, DK-5884 Gudme, Denmark. TEL 45-62-25-20-00. FAX 45-62-25-20-00. E-mai aerospace.publ@cybernet.dk. Ed. Bent Aalbaek-Nielsen. adv.; bk.rev.; charts; film rev.; illus. stat. circ. 6,325.

629.133   UK   ISSN 0269-4018
PROPLINER; the international review of piston-engined and turboprop transport aircraft. 1979. q. £14 (foreign £17). Propliner Magazine Ltd., 3 Castlewoods, Vale Rd., Red Lynch, Salisbury, Wiltshire SP5 2PY, England. TEL 44-1725-51385 FAX 44-1725-513857. (Subscr. to: New Roots, Sutton Green Rd., Sutton Green, Guildford, Surrey GU4 7QD, England) Ed. Tony Merton Jones. adv. contact: Tony Merton Jones. charts; illus. circ. 4,000. (back issues avail.) **Document type:** consume publication.

AERONAUTICS AND SPACE FLIGHT

629.1 520 US ISSN 1065-7738
TL787
QUEST (GRAND RAPIDS); the history of spaceflight magazine. 1992. q. $24.95 (Canada & Mexico $30; elsewhere $40). CSPACE Press, Box 9331, Grand Rapids, MI 49509-0331. TEL 616-452-5500. FAX 616-452-5538. E-mail: gswanson@vixa.voyager.net. (Alt. addr.: 123 32nd St., S.E., Grand Rapids, MI 49548-2218) Ed. Glen E. Swanson. adv. contact: Glen E. Swanson. bk.rev.; film rev.; charts; illus.; tr.lit.; circ. 3,000 (paid). (back issues avail.) Document type: academic/scholarly publication, trade publication.
  Description: Chronicles the past international achievements in the fields of both manned and unmanned spaceflight. Preserves these histories and provides a network for correspondence with others who share a similar interest.
  Refereed Serial

R & D CONTRACTS MONTHLY; a continuously up-dated sales and R & D tool for all research organizations and manufacturers. (Research & Development) see *SCIENCES: COMPREHENSIVE WORKS*

R-C MODELER. see *HOBBIES*

R E M E JOURNAL. (Royal Electrical & Mechanical Engineers) see *ENGINEERING — Mechanical Engineering*

629.135 US ISSN 0193-4422
R T C A DIGEST. 1965. bi-m. $95. (Radio Technical Commission for Aeronautics) R T C A, Inc., 1140 Connecticut Ave., N.W., Ste. 1020, Washington, DC 20036-4001. TEL 202-833-9339. FAX 202-833-9434. Ed. Caroline Cole. R&P contact: Caroline Cole. circ. 1,000. Document type: newsletter.

629.135 US
RADIO TECHNICAL COMMISSION FOR AERONAUTICS. PROCEEDINGS OF THE ANNUAL TECHNICAL SYMPOSIUM. Short title: R T C A Proceedings. 1955. a. $35. R T C A, Inc., 1140 Connecticut Ave., N.W., Ste. 1020, Washington, DC 20036-4001. TEL 202-833-9339. FAX 202-833-9434. TELEX 2407254. Ed. Caroline Cole. R&P contact: Caroline Cole. circ. 750. Document type: proceedings.
  —Linda Hall.
  Formerly: Radio Technical Commission for Aeronautics. Proceedings of the Annual Assembly Meeting (ISSN 0145-9589)

RAPID NOTICE NEWS SERVICE. see *PHILATELY*

629.13 NE ISSN 1013-9044
  CODEN: RESKEZ
REACHING FOR THE SKIES; E S A space transportation systems. (Text in English, French) 1989. q. free. European Space Agency, Publications Division, Keplerlaan 1, 22000 AG Noordwijk, Netherlands. TEL 31-071-5653403. FAX 31-071-5655433. TELEX 39098. Eds. D. Guyenne, N. Longdon. illus. circ. 20,000.
  —CISTI.

629.1 SZ
REGA. (Text in French, German, Italian) 1972. s-a. Mainaustr. 21, CH-8008 Zurich, Switzerland. TEL 41-1-3858585. TELEX 815816. URL: http://www.rega.com. Ed. Norbert Hobmeier. adv. contact: Walter Stuenzi. circ. 1,100,000. Document type: corporate report.

629.136 FR ISSN 0034-320X
REGARDS SUR LE COMITE D'ETABLISSEMENT D'ORLY SUD. 1966. q. free. Comite d'Etablissement Air France-Orly Sud, Extension Est, Batiment CRP, Aerogare d'Orly Sud, France. Ed. M. Alain Lemaitre. adv.; circ. 8,000 (controlled). (tabloid format)

629 GW
REUSS JAHRBUCH DER LUFT- UND RAUMFAHRT; German Aerospace Annual. 1951. a. DM.84.50. Suedwestdeutsche Verlagsanstalt GmbH, R1, 4-6, 68161 Mannheim, Germany. TEL 0621-3922882. FAX 0621-3922800. Ed. Tilman Reuss. adv.; bk.rev.; index. Document type: directory.
  —CISTI.
  Formerly: Jahrbuch der Luftfahrt und Raumfahrt (ISSN 0075-269X)

REVEILLE; the voice of more than 126,000 ex-servicemen and women. see *MILITARY*

629.1 US ISSN 0279-4519
REVISTA AEREA; voz aeronautica de America Latina, Espana y las Filipinas. (Text in Spanish) 1937. 10/yr. $50. Strato Publishing Co., Inc., 310 E. 44th St., Ste. 1601, New York, NY 10017. TEL 212-370-1740. FAX 212-949-6756. TELEX 221213-TTC-UR. E-mail: strato310@aol.com. Ed. Elaine Asch-Root; Pub. Elaine Asch-Root. R&P contact: Elaine Asch-Root. adv.: B&W page $6300; color page $9865; adv. contact: Ines Trevino. bk.rev.; illus.; circ. 10,200 (controlled). Document type: trade publication.
  Formerly: Revista Aerea Latinoamericana (ISSN 0034-6934)
  Description: Covers aviation and aerospace developments (military, commercial, and business) worldwide for senior Latin American business executives, government officials, and other ranking aerospace decision makers.

629.13 CK ISSN 0034-6942
REVISTA AERONAUTICA; al servicio de la aviacion colombiana. 1947. a. $28. Fuerza Aerea Colombiana, Apdo. Aereo 51097, Bogota, D.E., Colombia. Ed. Alvaro Baquero. adv.; bk.rev.; charts; illus.; index. circ. 20,000. Document type: government publication.

629.13 629.4 SP ISSN 0034-7647
TL504
REVISTA DE AERONAUTICA Y ASTRONAUTICA. 1932. m. 3480 ptas. (foreign 6400 ptas.) (effective 1995). Ministerio del Aire - Spanish Airforce, Princesa, 88, 28008 Madrid, Spain. TEL 34-1-5442819. FAX 34-1-5442612. Ed. Col. Sergio Rubiano Gomez. adv.: B&W page 40000 ptas., color page 60000 ptas. bk.rev.; circ. 10,000 (paid). Indexed: Abstr.Mil.Bibl., Ind.SST. Document type: government publication.
  —CISTI. **CCC**.
  Formerly: Revista de Aeronautica.

629.13 PO ISSN 0034-9208
REVISTA DO AR. 1937. q. Esc.1500. Aero Club de Portugal, R. General Pimenta de Castro, 4-C, 1700 Lisbon, Portugal. TEL 805317. FAX 8805572. Ed. Jose Augusto Rosa. adv.; bk.rev.; charts; illus. circ. 5,000.

629.1 FR ISSN 0065-3780
REVUE AEROSPATIALE. (Editions in English, French) 1970. m. (10/yr.). 200 F. (foreign 280 F.) (effective 1996). Pema 28, 19 bd. du Parc, 92200 Neuilly, France. FAX 45-20-98-76. TELEX 643 032 PEMAERO. Ed. Gilles Patri. adv. contact: Nicolas Van Eck. bk.rev. circ. 76,500. Document type: trade publication, consumer publication.
  —CISTI.
  Formerly (until 1983): Aerospatiale.

387.7 340 FR ISSN 1144-2158
REVUE FRANCAISE DE DROIT AERIEN ET SPATIAL. 1946. q. 440 F. (foreign 500 F.). (Association d'Etudes et de Documentation de Droit Aerien) Editions Pedone, 13, rue Soufflot, 75005 Paris, France. Ed. A. Garnault. adv.; bk.rev.; index. circ. 1,000. (reprint service avail. from SCH) Indexed: IBR.
  —BLDSC (7903.520000); SWETS. **CCC**.
  Formerly (until 1989): Revue Francaise de Droit Aerien (ISSN 0035-287Y)

REVUE GENERALE DES ROUTES ET DES AERODROMES. see *TRANSPORTATION — Roads And Traffic*

REVUE ROUMAINE DES SCIENCES TECHNIQUES. SERIE DE MECANIQUE APPLIQUEE. see *ENGINEERING — Mechanical Engineering*

629 JA ISSN 0485-2877
ROCKET NEWS. (Text in Japanese) 1957. m. 300 Yen per no. to non-members. Japanese Rocket Society - Nihon Roketto Kyokai, c/o Business Center for Academic Societies Japan, 5-16-9 Honkomagome, Bunkyo-ku, Tokyo 113, Japan. TEL 81-3-5814-5811. FAX 81-3-5814-5822. Ed. Y. Inatani. abstr. circ. 600. Document type: newsletter.

629.133 US ISSN 0191-6408
TL716.A1 CODEN: RWINEI
ROTOR AND WING INTERNATIONAL. 1967. m. $49 (foreign $80) (effective 1996). Phillips Business Information, Inc., 1201 Seven Locks Rd., Potomac, MD 20854. TEL 301-424-3338. FAX 301-309-3847. E-mail: pbi@phillips.com. Ed. David Jensen. adv.; charts; illus.; circ. controlled. Indexed: HRIS. Document type: trade publication.
  —BLDSC (8025.720000); CISTI; SWETS. **CCC**.
  Formerly: Rotor and Wing (ISSN 0035-8452)

629.13 US
ROTOR BREEZE. 1951. bi-m. free. Bell Helicopter Textron, Inc., Dept. H3, Box 482, Ft. Worth, TX 76101. Ed. Susan Green. Document type: newsletter.

ROTOR ROSTER. see *TRANSPORTATION — Air Transport*

629.133 US ISSN 1041-2735
ROTORCRAFT. 1963. 9/yr. $30 (effective 1997). Popular Rotorcraft Association, Box 68, Mentone, IN 46539-0068. TEL 219-353-7227. FAX 219-353-7227. E-mail: prahq@aol.com; URL: http://www.pra.org. Ed. Paul Abbott. adv.; bk.rev.; illus. circ. 5,000.
  Formerly (until 1988): Popular Rotorcraft Flying (ISSN 0032-4620)

629.13 US ISSN 1068-7998
TL504
RUSSIAN AERONAUTICS - IZ. V U Z. English translation of: Izvestiya Vysshikh Uchebnykh Zavedenii. Aviatsionnaya Tekhnika. 1966. q. $1080 (effective 1998). (Ministerstvo Vysshego i Srednego Spetsial'nogo Obrazovaniya, RU) Allerton Press, Inc., 150 Fifth Ave., New York, NY 10011. TEL 212-924-3950. FAX 212-463-9684. Ed. M.B. Vakhitov. bk.rev.; abstr.; charts; illus.; index. Indexed: Appl.Mech.Rev., Eng.Ind., INSPEC (1973-), Math.R. Document type: academic/scholarly publication.
  —BLDSC (0420.752000); AskIEEE; CISTI; KR SourceOne. **CCC**.
  Formerly: Soviet Aeronautics - Iz. V U Z (ISSN 0364-8117)
  Description: Presents reports on the research being conducted at Tupolev Kazan Aviation Institute. Articles may cover aerodynamics, structural mechanics, instrumentation, automation and aeronautics, and communications systems.

629.1 NE ISSN 1025-5826
RUSSIAN SPACE BULLETIN. 1994. 4/yr. $48 (effective 1998). (Association for the Advancement of Space Science & Technology) Gordon and Breach - Harwood Academic, Amsteldisk 166, 1st Fl., 1079 LH Amsterdam, Netherlands. (Subscr. to: International Publishers Distributor, Box 32160, Newark, NJ 07102. TEL 800-545-8398. FAX 215-750-6343) (Co-sponsors: Russian Space Agency; Russian Academy of Sciences, Space Research Institute) Ed. Albert Galeev.

629.13 US ISSN 0743-846X
TL697.S3
S A F E SYMPOSIUM PROCEEDINGS. a. $27.50 (foreign $30). S A F E Association, 107 Music City Circle, Ste. 112, Nashville, TN 37214. TEL 615-902-0056. FAX 615-902-0077. Ed. Russ Burton. circ. 1,000. Document type: proceedings.
  —BLDSC (6842.284000); Linda Hall.
  Refereed Serial

629.1 US
S A W E NEWSLETTER. 1966. q. $30 (includes International Journal of Weight Engineering) (effective 1997 & 1998). Society of Allied Weight Engineers, Inc., 5530 Aztec Dr., La Mesa, CA 91942-2110. TEL 619-465-1367. FAX 619-465-2561. Ed. Robert W. Ridenour. bk.rev.; circ. 1,000 (controlled). Document type: newsletter.
  Refereed Serial

629.134 FR ISSN 0750-7569
S N E C M A INFORMATIONS; journal d'information du personnel. 1953. q. free. Societe Nationale d'Etude et de Construction de Moteurs d'Aviation, 2 bd. du General Martial Valin, 75724 Paris Cedex 15, France. FAX 40-60-81-02. Ed. Nicole Spodek. bk.rev.; charts; illus.; stat.; index. circ. 22,000.
  Formerly: S N E C M A (ISSN 0036-1720)

S P A R C JIMUKYOKUHO/S P A R C NEWS. (Space Research Co-Operative Association) see *ASTRONOMY*

AERONAUTICS AND SPACE FLIGHT

629.1 387.7 US ISSN 0894-5667
TL726.2
S P A WATER LANDING DIRECTORY. (Includes Seaplane Base Directory) biennial. $37 per no. to non-members; members $18. Seaplane Pilots Association, 421 Aviation Way, Frederick, MD 21701. TEL 301-695-2083. FAX 301-695-2375. adv. circ. 3,000. **Document type:** directory.
 Formerly: Seaplane Landing Directory.
 Description: Lists landing areas and regulations by state, with descriptions of facilities and services available. Also lists bodies of water that are open or off limits.

001.94 DK
S U F O I. NEWS. (Text in English) irreg. Skandinavisk U F O Information, P.O. Box 6, 2820 Gentofte, Denmark. **Document type:** newsletter.
 Formerly: Skandinavisk U F O Information. Newsletter.

629.1 US
S U R V I A C BULLETIN. bi-m. U.S. Department of Defense, Survivability - Vulnerability Information Analysis Center, E-mail: ryan__linda@bah.com; URL: http://surviac.flight.wpafb.af.mil/curr__awar/surviac__bulletin/bulletins.html. **Document type:** government publication.
 ●Available only online.

629.13 US ISSN 0191-6319
,TL553.5 CODEN: SAFJDH
SAFE JOURNAL. 1967. q. $25 (foreign $30) (effective 1996). S A F E Association, 107 Music City Circle, Ste. 112, Nashville, TN 37214. TEL 615-902-0056. FAX 615-902-0077. Ed. Russ Burton. adv. contact: Jean Benton. bk.rev. circ. 1,000. **Indexed:** Excerp.Med., HRIS. **Document type:** trade publication.
 —BLDSC (8065.300000); CISTI; Linda Hall; UnCover.
 Description: Provides a multidisciplinary forum for sharing ideas and information on human safety.

629.133 UK ISSN 0036-2735
TL760.A1
SAILPLANE AND GLIDING. 1950. bi-m. £12.40($19) British Gliding Association, Kimberley House, Vaughan Way, Leicester LE1 4SE, England. TEL 01533-531051. FAX 01533-515939. Ed. Gillian Bryce-Smith. adv. contact: Debbie Carr. bk.rev.; charts; illus.; stat.; index. circ. 8,500. (also avail. in microfilm from UMI; reprint service avail. from UMI) **Indexed:** Sportsearch (1974-).

629.19 US
SAMOLYOT/AIRCRAFT. m. Aviation Maintenance Foundation International, Box 2826, Redmond, WA 98073. TEL 360-658-8980. FAX 360-658-7274. (Co-sponsor: Russian Aeronautical Society) adv. **Document type:** trade publication.
 Description: Covers the past, present and future of the aviation and aerospace industries in Russia; includes interviews.

SATELLITE COMMUNICATIONS. see *COMMUNICATIONS*

SAVUNMA VE HAVACILIK; defence and aerospace. see *MILITARY*

SCALE AIRCRAFT MODELLING. see *HOBBIES*

629.13 US ISSN 0278-4017
CODEN: AASTBE
SCIENCE AND TECHNOLOGY SERIES. (Contains several subseries: Space Safety and Rescue; Goddard Memorial Symposium Proceedings; L5 Space Development Conference Proceedings. Supplement to: Advances in the Astronautical Sciences Series (ISSN 0065-3438)) 1964. irreg. (approx. 4-5/yr.) vol.88, 1996. price varies. (American Astronautical Society, Inc.) Univelt, Inc., Box 28130, San Diego, CA 92198-0198. TEL 619-746-4005. FAX 619-746-3139. E-mail: 76121.1532@compuserve.com. Ed. Robert H. Jacobs. bibl.; charts; illus.; cum.index 1964-1978; 1979-1985; 1986-1992. circ. 400. (also avail. in microfiche; back issues avail.) **Indexed:** Biol.Abstr., Chem.Abstr., Curr.Cont., Eng.Ind., INSPEC, Int.Aerosp.Abstr. **Document type:** proceedings.
 —BLDSC (8134.283000); CISTI; Ei.
 Former titles (until 1976): Science and Technology (San Diego) (ISSN 0080-7451); (until 1972): A A S Science and Technology Series (ISSN 0065-7425)

SCREAMING EAGLE. see *MILITARY*

629.134 JA
SHOGEKI KOGAKU SHINPOJUMU. (Text in English, Japanese) 1974. a. Institute of Space and Astronautical Science - Uchu Kagaku Kenkyujo, 1-1, Yoshinodai 3-chome, Sagamihara-shi, Kanagawa-ken 229, Japan. FAX 0427-57-4779. Ed. Takashi Abe. **Document type:** proceedings.
 Description: Covers shock engineering.

387.7 UK ISSN 0037-4245
SHORT'S STORY. 1950. 10/yr. free. Short Brothers PLC, Airport Rd., Belfast BT3 9DZ, N. Ireland. FAX 0232-732974. TELEX 74688. Ed. Jacky McCune. charts; illus. circ. 11,000.
 Formerly: Short's Quarterly Review.

629.13 UK
SKYPORT. 1976. w. £40. Skyport Communication Ltd., The Red House, 360 Cranford Ln., Hayes, Middx. UB3 5HD, England. TEL 44-181-759-1235. FAX 44-181-759-7739. Ed. Nigel Botherway; Pub. Nigel Gotherway. adv. contact: Sunita Parrkh. bk.rev. circ. 36,000. **Document type:** newspaper.

629.13 US ISSN 1087-2698
▼**SKYPOWER**; Lockheed Martin aeronautical systems. 1995. s-a. free. Lockheed Martin, 542642 LOCKHEED MARA, 86 S. Cobb Dr., Marietta, GA 30063-0244. TEL 770-494-2406. FAX 770-494-4809. Ed. Bob Harper. circ. 30,000 (controlled). **Document type:** consumer publication, trade publication.
 Description: Targets US Air Force and foreign nation air forces. Features the C-130 Hercules, C-141 and C-5 in their various roles for the USAF and operators worldwide.

387.7 II ISSN 0970-8502
SKYWAYS; aviation magazine of Asia. (Text in English) 1947. m. $50. Aeronautical Publications of India Pvt. Ltd., Old Santacruz Airport, Bombay 400 029, India. TEL 11-6124448. FAX 22-942222. TELEX 011-71086-AWIB-IN. Ed. D.M. Heble. adv. contact: D. De St. Rotta. bk.rev.; illus. circ. 9,980.
 —CISTI.
 Formerly (until Jan. 1976): Asian and Indian Skyways (ISSN 0004-4539)

387.7 US ISSN 1051-6956
SKYWAYS; journal of the airplane 1920-1940. 1987. q. $30 (foreign $35) (effective 1997 & 1998). World War I Aeroplanes, Inc., 15 Crescent Rd., Poughkeepsie, NY 12601-4490. TEL 914-473-3679. Ed. David W. Ostrowski; Pub. Leonard E. Opdycke. adv. contact: Beverly Williams. bk.rev. circ. 1,200. (back issues avail.)
 —CISTI.
 Description: Contains information on the restoration, reproduction and modelling of airplanes, 1920-1940.

629.13 US ISSN 0197-7245
SMITHSONIAN STUDIES IN AIR AND SPACE. 1977. irreg., no.7, 1990. free. Smithsonian Institution Press, 470 L'Enfant Plaza, Ste. 7100, Washington, DC 20560. TEL 202-287-3738. FAX 202-287-3637. Ed. Don Fisher. circ. 1,600. (reprint service avail. from UMI) **Indexed:** GeoRef. **Document type:** monographic series.
 —Linda Hall.

629.133 US ISSN 0037-7503
TL760.A1
SOARING. 1937. m. $55 membership. Soaring Society of America, Inc., Box E, Hobbs, NM 88241-1308. TEL 505-392-1177. FAX 505-392-8154. URL: http://acro.harvard.edu/SSA/ssa__magazine.html. Ed. Mark Kennedy. adv.; bk.rev.; charts; illus.; stat. circ. 14,881. **Indexed:** Mag.Ind., Sports Per.Ind., Sportsearch (1974-).
 —CISTI; Linda Hall; UnCover.

629.13 BL ISSN 0037-8666
SOCIEDADE BRASILEIRA DE ESTUDOS SOBRE DISCOS VOADORES. BOLETIM. (Text in Portuguese; summaries in English) 1957. irreg. membership or exchange basis. Sociedade Brasileira de Estudos Sobre Discos Voadores, C.P. 16-017, Correio Largo do Machado, 22222-970 Rio de Janeiro, RJ, Brazil. Ed. W. Buhler. bk.rev.; illus.; stat.; cum.index: 1957-1987. circ. 400. (processed; also avail. in microfilm) **Document type:** bulletin.
 Description: Explores the phenomenon of extraterrestrial crafts landing on Earth.

629.1 UK
SOCIETY OF BRITISH AEROSPACE COMPANIES. AGENDA. m. Society of British Aerospace Companies Ltd., 60 Petty France, London SW1H 9EU, England. TEL 44-171-839-3231. Ed. Susan Godfrey. circ. 1,500. **Document type:** newsletter.
 Formerly (until 1993): S B A C News.

629.1 US ISSN 1050-9690
SOCIETY OF FLIGHT TEST ENGINEERS. ANNUAL SYMPOSIUM PROCEEDINGS. 1970. a. $50. Society of Flight Test Engineers, Box 4047, Lancaster, CA 93539. TEL 805-538-9715. FAX 805-538-9715. illus. **Document type:** proceedings.
 —BLDSC (1534.963000).

629.1 US
SOCIETY OF FLIGHT TEST ENGINEERS. NEWSLETTER. 1970. m. $25. Society of Flight Test Engineers, Box 4047, Lancaster, CA 93539. TEL 805-538-9715. FAX 805-538-9715. **Document type:** newsletter.

001.94 US
SOLAR SPACE LETTER. 1960. 6/yr. $12 (foreign $15). Box 332, Cornville, AZ 86325-0332. Ed. Robert Short. R&P contact: Robert Short. adv.; bk.rev. circ. 2,000. **Document type:** newsletter.

629.13 551.6 JA ISSN 0289-3347
SORA TO UMI/SKY AND MARINE. (Text in Japanese; summaries in English) 1980. a. 2000 Yen. Koku Uchu Riyo Suisan Kaiyo Kenkyukai - Society of Airborne, Satellite Physical and Fishery Oceanography, Tokai Daigaku Kaiyogakubu Kaiyo Kagakuka, 20-1, Orido 3-chome, Shimizu-shi, Shizuoka-ken 424, Japan.

629.132 790.1 SA ISSN 0256-0593
SOUTH AFRICAN AERONEWS. (Text in English) 1983. 11/yr. R.30($13) Aero Club of South Africa, P.O. Box 1993, Halfway House 1685, South Africa. FAX 27-11-8052765. Ed. M.A. van Ginkel. adv.; bk.rev. circ. 5,000. (back issues avail.) **Document type:** newsletter.

629.1 US ISSN 0738-0968
TL787
SPACE AGE TIMES; the international publication of space news, benefits and education. (Includes: U S S E A Update) 1974. bi-m. $26 (foreign $32). U S Space Education Association, News Operations Division, Box 249, Rheems, PA 17570-0249. TEL 717-367-5196. Ed. Stephen M. Cobaugh. R&P contact: Debra Palmisano. adv. contact: Ronald Palmisano. bk.rev.; film rev.; charts; illus.; stat., tr.lit. circ. 1,500. (back issues avail.)
 Description: Worldwide coverage of space news exploration for both the professional and the layman.

621.9 338.025 UK
SPACE AND EDUCATION. biennial (with a. updates). British National Space Centre, Dean Bradley House, Horseferry Rd., London SW1P 2AG, England. **Document type:** directory.
 Supersedes in part (in 1992): Directory of U K Space Capabilities.

629.1 338.025 UK
SPACE AND INDUSTRY; (year) directory of U K capabilities. biennial (with a. updates). British National Space Centre, Dean Bradley House, Horseferry Rd., London SW1P 2AG, England. **Document type:** directory.
 Supersedes in part (in 1992): Directory of U K Space Capabilities.

629.4 AT ISSN 1030-2166
SPACE ASSOCIATION NEWS. 1981. bi-m. Aus.$40 (foreign Aus.$60). Space Association of Australia, Inc., P.O. Box 351, Mulgrave N., Vic. 3170, Australia. TEL 61-3-97295538. E-mail: jcoleman@melb.alexia.net.au; URL: http://www.vicnet.net.au/~saa. Ed. Andrew Rennie. R&P contact: Andrew Rennie. adv. contact: Andrew Rennie. bk.rev.; circ. 200 (paid). (back issues avail.) **Document type:** bulletin.
 Description: For both specialist and lay persons interested in astronautics, spaceflight and satellites

AERONAUTICS AND SPACE FLIGHT

629.4 US ISSN 0738-9884
SPACE BUSINESS NEWS. 1984. bi-w. $697 (foreign $730) (effective 1997). Phillips Business Information, Inc., 1201 Seven Locks Rd., Potomac, MD 20854. TEL 301-424-3338. FAX 301-309-3847. E-mail: pbi@phillips.com. Ed. Gary Crouse. circ. controlled. (looseleaf format; back issues avail.) **Document type:** newsletter.
● Also available online. Vendor(s): Data-Star, Information Access Co., Knight-Ridder Information, Inc., NewsNet (AE11).
—CISTI. **CCC.**
Incorporates: Space Station News (ISSN 0895-8947); (1990-1993): Space Exploration Technology (ISSN 1052-3383) & Space Commerce Week; Which was formerly: Space Commerce Bulletin (ISSN 0743-4820).

629.13 US ISSN 0741-1731
SPACE CALENDAR. 1982. w. $79 to individuals (foreign $139); institutions $139 (foreign $199). Space Age Publishing Company, 75-5751 Kuakini Hwy., Ste. 201, Kaulua-Kona, HI 96740. TEL 808-326-2014. FAX 808-326-1825. E-mail: spaceage@ilhawaii.net. Ed. Steve Durst; Pub. Steve Durst. circ. 625. (avail. by fax; back issues avail.) **Document type:** newsletter.
● Also available online. Vendor(s): NewsNet (AE04).
Description: Covers space-related events and news worldwide.

621.38 NE ISSN 0924-8625
TK5104 CODEN: SPCCEJ
SPACE COMMUNICATIONS; an international journal. (Text in English) 1983. 4/yr. fl.440($354) (effective 1997). I O S Press, Van Diemenstraat 94, 1013 CN Amsterdam, Netherlands. TEL 31-20-6382189. FAX 31-20-6203419. E-mail: market@iospress.nl; URL: http://www.iospress.nl/html/journals.html. (In N. America: Box 10558, Burke, VA 22009-0558. TEL 703-323-5554. FAX 703-250-4705) Eds. E.W. Ashford, J.N. Pelton. adv.; illus.; index. (back issues avail.) **Indexed:** ASCA, Commun.Abstr., INSPEC, Int.Aerosp.Abstr. **Document type:** academic/scholarly publication.
—BLDSC (8361.592000); AskIEEE; CISTI; Ei; Genuine Article; KR SourceOne; Linda Hall; SWETS. **CCC.**
Formerly (until 1990): Space Communication and Broadcasting (ISSN 0167-9368)
Description: Covers all aspects of the satellite communications: technical, financial and legal.

629.1 UK
TL787
SPACE COMMUNICATIONS. 1985. bi-m. £250($84) Parker Publications Ltd., 42 Keephatch Rd., Wokingham, Berks RG40 1QD, England. TEL 44-118-9774000. FAX 44-118-9774001. Ed. Mark Williamson; Pub. Julie Alexander. R&P contact: Ian Parker. adv. contact: Julie Alexander. circ. 11,963. **Document type:** directory, trade publication.
—SWETS; UnCover.
Formerly: Space (ISSN 0267-954X)

621.47 US ISSN 1087-5654
CODEN: SSPRDD
SPACE, ENERGY AND TRANSPORTATION. 1995. q. $140 to individuals; institutions $200 (effective 1997). High Frontier, Inc., 2800 Shirlington Rd., Ste. 405, Arlington, VA 22206. TEL 703-671-4111. FAX 703-931-6432. E-mail: highfront@erols.com. Ed. Doug Frye. adv.; bk.rev.; illus.; stat.; index. circ. 250. (also avail. in microform; back issues avail.) **Indexed:** Curr.Cont., Energy Res.Abstr., Eng.Ind., INSPEC (1993-), Int.Aerosp.Abstr. **Document type:** academic/scholarly publication.
—AskIEEE; CASDDS; CISTI; Ei; Genuine Article; KR SourceOne; Linda Hall; UMI; UnCover. **CCC.**
Formed by the merger of (1989-1995): Journal of Practical Applications in Space (ISSN 1046-8757); (1980-1995): Space Power (ISSN 0883-6272); Which was formerly (1980-1986): Space Power Review (ISSN 0191-9067)
Description: Provides discussion, analysis, and important research in all areas of space travel and space exploration.

629.13 US ISSN 1048-2652
SPACE FAX DAILY. 1984. d. $195 to individuals (foreign $570); institutions $295 (foreign $670). Space Age Publishing Company, 75-5751 Kuakini Hwy., Ste. 201, Kaulua-Kona, HI 96740. TEL 808-326-2014. FAX 808-326-1825. E-mail: spaceage@ilhawaii.net. Ed. Steve Durst; Pub. Steve Durst. (also. avail. by fax) **Document type:** newsletter.
● Also available online. Vendor(s): NewsNet (AE07).
Formerly: Space Daily (ISSN 0749-6575)
Description: Provides information on the developments and technology of the space industry.

629.1 330 NE ISSN 1024-803X
HD9711.75.A1
SPACE FORUM; the international journal of space policy, science and technology for industrial applications. 1990. 4/yr. $90 (effective 1998). Gordon and Breach - Harwood Academic, Amsteldisk 166, 1st Fl., 1079 LH Amsterdam, Netherlands. URL: http://www.gbhap.com/Space__Forum/. (Subscr. to: International Publishers Distributor, Box 32160, Newark, NJ 07102. TEL 800-545-8398. FAX 215-750-6343) Ed. Peter Kleber. (also avail. in microform)
● Also available online.
Also available on CD-ROM.
—BLDSC (8361.594380). **CCC.**
Formerly (until 1996): Space Commerce (ISSN 1043-934X)
Description: Addresses issues relevant to the broad interests of the international space community in the academic, public and industrial sectors.
Refereed Serial

629.4 JA
SPACE IN JAPAN. (Text in English) biennial. 1500 Yen. Kagaku Gijiutsu-cho - Science and Technology Agency, 2-1 Kasumigaseki, 2-chome, Chiyoda-ku, Tokyo 100, Japan. TEL 03-3581-5271. (Subscr. to: Keidanren (Federation of Economic Organizations), 1-9-4 Ote-machi, Chiyoda-ku, Tokyo 100, Japan) illus.
Description: Covers Japan's space development policies, national organizations for space activities, international cooperation projects; profiles of members; addresses of related organizations; information on and brief histories of space development.

629.1 AT
SPACE INDUSTRY NEWS. Online edition (AT ISSN 1037-5759) q. C.S.I.R.O., Office of Space Science and Applications, URL: http://www.cossa.csiro.au/pubs/spins.htm. **Document type:** newsletter.
● Also available online.

341.47 NE
SPACE LAW; basic legal documents. (Text in English) 2 base vols. (plus irreg. supplements). $1271 (includes supplements 1-5). Kluwer Law International (Subsidiary of: Wolters Kluwer N.V.), Postbus 85889, 2508 CN The Hague, Netherlands. TEL 31-70-3081500. FAX 31-70-3081515. E-mail: services@wkap.nl; URL: http://www.wkap.nl. (Dist. by: Libresso Distribution Centre, P.O. Box 23, 7400 GA Deventer, Netherlands. TEL 31-570-633155. FAX 31-570-633834; In N. America: Kluwer Law International, 675 Massachusetts Ave., Cambridge, MA 02139. TEL 617-354-0140. FAX 617-354-8595) Eds. Karl-Heinz Bockstiegel, Marietta Benko. (looseleaf format) **Document type:** academic/scholarly publication.
Description: Publishes the basic legal documents relating to space law, including UN instruments, treaties and conventions, reports on past and current disputes in space law, international projects and organizations, and national legislation on space issues.

387.8 US ISSN 0038-6278
SPACE LETTER; twice-monthly letter on contracting opportunities, marketing data, and research & development with the National Aeronautics and Space Administration, plus army, navy, air force, NOAA and commercial space ventures. 1957. s-m. $225. Callahan Publications, Box 1173, McLean, VA 22101. TEL 703-356-1925. FAX 703-356-9614. Ed. Vincent F. Callahan, Jr. bk.rev.; charts; stat. **Document type:** newsletter.
Description: Provides factual information from Washington on the US multi-billion dollar National Space Program.

629.1 382 US ISSN 1046-6940
TL787
SPACE NEWS (SPRINGFIELD). 1989. 48/yr. $99 (Canada $139; elsewhere $169). Army Times Publishing Co., 6883 Commercial Dr., Springfield, VA 22159. TEL 703-750-8137. FAX 703-642-7352. URL: http://www.spacenews.com/. Ed. Lon Rains. adv. contact: Elaine Howard. charts. circ. 13,417. (tabloid format; also avail. in microform; reprint service avail. from UMI) **Document type:** newspaper.
—SWETS. **CCC.**
Description: Covers the international politics and business of the space industry.

629.1 UK ISSN 0265-9646
TL787 CODEN: SPCPEO
SPACE POLICY. 1985. q. fl.1440($828) (effective 1998). Elsevier Science Ltd., P.O. Box 800, Kidlington, Oxford OX5 1DX, England. TEL 44-1865-843000. FAX 44-1865-843010. TELEX 83111 BHPOXF G. E-mail: nlinfo-f@elsevier.nl; usinfo-f@elsevier.com; forinfo-kyf04035@niftyserve.or.jp; URL: http://butterworth-heinemann.co.uk/. (Subscr. to: Elsevier Science, Regional Sales Office, P.O. Box 211, 1000 AE Amsterdam, Netherlands. TEL 31-20-4853757. FAX 31-20-4853432; Subscr. in the Americas to: Elsevier Science, Regional Sales Office, Box 945, New York, NY 10159-0945. TEL 212-633-3730. FAX 212-633-3680; Subscr. in Australasia and the Far East to: Elsevier Science (Singapore) Pte Ltd, No.1 Temasek Ave., No.17-01 Millenia Tower, Singapore 039192, Singapore. TEL 65-434-3727. FAX 65-337-2230) Ed. Frances Brown. (also avail. in microform from UMI; back issues avail.) **Indexed:** ASCA, Curr.Cont., P.A.I.S., Polit.Sci.Abstr., SSCI, Tel.Abstr. **Document type:** academic/scholarly publication.
—BLDSC (8361.604500); CISTI; Genuine Article; SWETS; UMI; UnCover. **CCC.**
Description: Takes an interdisciplinary approach to space activities and developments in their industrial, economic, political, legal and social contexts.
Refereed Serial

629.13 US ISSN 0733-8678
SPACE PRESS. 1981. m. $50. Vernuccio Publications, 645 West End Ave., New York, NY 10025. TEL 212-724-5919. Ed. Frank V. Vernuccio, Jr. adv.; bk.rev.; charts; illus.; pat.; stat. circ. 1,000. **Document type:** newsletter.
Description: Complete coverage of all US and international space news.

629.1 381 US ISSN 0743-8982
SPACE R & D ALERT.* 1982. bi-m. $195. Aerospace Communications, c/o Jeffrey K. Manber, Ed., 519 N. Alfred St., Alexandria, VA 22314-2226. Ed. Jeffrey K. Manber. adv.; bk.rev. circ. 3,500. (back issues avail.)
● Also available online. Vendor(s): NewsNet.
Formerly: Space Journal (ISSN 0736-0789)

SPACE RESEARCH IN JAPAN. see *ASTRONOMY*

624.9 US
SPACE SAFETY AND RESCUE (YEAR). (Subseries of Science and Technology Series (ISSN 0278-4017); Supplement to: Advances in the Astronautical Sciences SSeries (ISSN 0065-3438)) 1974. a. (American Astronautical Society) Univelt, Inc., Box 28130, San Diego, CA 92198-0198. TEL 619-746-4005. FAX 619-746-3139. E-mail: 76121.1532@Compuserve.com. Ed. Robert H. Jacobs; Pub. Robert H. Jacobs. R&P contact: Robert H. Jacobs. illus. (also avail. in microfiche; back issues avail.) **Document type:** proceedings.
Formerly (until 1976): Space Rescue and Safety.

SPACE SCIENCE REVIEWS. see *ASTRONOMY*

SPACE TECHNOLOGY; industrial and commercial applications. see *TECHNOLOGY: COMPREHENSIVE WORKS*

AERONAUTICS AND SPACE FLIGHT

629.1   NE   ISSN 0924-4263
SPACE TECHNOLOGY LIBRARY. (Text in English) 1983. irreg., vol.3, 1994. price varies. Kluwer Academic Publishers, Postbus 17, 3300 AA Dordrecht, Netherlands. TEL 31-78-6392392. FAX 31-78-6392254. TELEX 29245 KAPG NL. E-mail: services@wkap.nl; URL: http://www.wkap.nl. (Dist. by: Kluwer Academic Publishers Group, P.O. Box 322, 3300 AH Dordrecht, Netherlands. TEL 31-78-6392392. FAX 31-78-6546474; N. America dist. addr.: Box 358, Accord Sta., Hingham, MA 02018-0358. TEL 617-871-6600. FAX 617-871-6528) **Document type:** monographic series.
—BLDSC (8361.660200); CISTI.
Refereed Serial

629.4   US
SPACE TIMES (SPRINGFIELD). 1962. bi-m. $65 (foreign $70) to institutions (effective 1998). American Astronautical Society (Springfield), 6352 Rolling Mill Place, Ste. 102, Springfield, VA 22152-2354. TEL 703-866-0020. FAX 703-866-3526. E-mail: 74673.724@compuserve.com. Ed. Roger Lannins. bk.rev. circ. 1,600. (back issues avail.) **Document type:** academic/scholarly publication.
—CISTI.
Formerly (until 1986): A A S Newsletter (ISSN 0001-0227)

629.1   US   ISSN 0889-6054
SPACE TODAY; covering space from earth to the edge of the universe. 1986. m. $34.95. Arcsoft Publishers, Box 179, Hebron, MD 21830-0179. TEL 410-742-9009. Ed. Anthony R. Curtis. adv.; bk.rev.; index. circ. 5,000. (back issues avail.) **Document type:** bulletin.
Description: Space news, astronomy, sciences and flights.

629.4   UK   ISSN 0038-6340
TL787   CODEN: SPFLAN
SPACEFLIGHT. 1956. m. £40($72) British Interplanetary Society, 27-29 South Lambeth Rd., London SW8 1SZ, England. Ed. G.V. Groves. adv.; bk.rev.; charts; illus.; index. circ. 8,000. (tabloid format; also avail. in microform from UMI; reprint service avail. from UMI) **Indexed:** A.S.& T.Ind., Appl.Mech.Rev., Br.Tech.Ind., Chem.Abstr., Eng.Ind., IBR, Int.Aerosp.Abstr. **Document type:** bulletin.
—BLDSC (8361.700000); CISTI; KR SourceOne; SWETS; UMI; UnCover.
Incorporates: Space Education.

629.1   US
SPACEWATCH. 1984. m. membership. United States Space Foundation, 2860 S. Circle Dr., Ste. 2301, Colorado Springs, CO 80906-4184. TEL 719-576-8000. FAX 719-576-6801. Ed. Steve Eisenhart; Pub. Richard P. Macleod. R&P contact: Steve Eisenhart. TEL 719-576-8000. adv. contact: Beth-Ann Lipskin. **Document type:** newsletter.

629.13   US   ISSN 0038-7835
SPORT AVIATION. 1953. m. $35. Experimental Aircraft Association, Inc., Box 3086, Oshkosh, WI 54903-3086. TEL 414-426-4800. URL: http://www.eaa.org/eaapublications/sportsaviation/index.html. Ed. Jack Cox. adv. contact: Golda Cox. bk.rev.; charts; illus. circ. 165,000. **Indexed:** Ind.How To Do It (1983-), PMR, Sportsearch.
—CISTI; UnCover.
Description: Covers a wide variety of aviation topics ranging from the latest homebuilt designs to personality profiles.

619.132 794   US
SPORT PILOT & ULTRALIGHTS; the magazine of recreational flying. 1984. m. $25.95 (foreign $37.95). Challenge Publications, Inc., 7950 Deering Ave., Canoga Park, CA 91304. TEL 818-887-0550. FAX 818-884-1343. E-mail: challpubs@aol.com; URL: http://www.challpubs.com/sportpilot/about.shtml. Ed. Michael O'Leary; Pub. Edwin Schnepf. R&P contact: Susan Duprey. adv. contact: Dave Gustafson. bk.rev.; illus. circ. 55,137. **Document type:** consumer publication.
Former titles: Sport Pilot Hot Kits and Homebuilts (ISSN 1040-5798); Sport Pilot (ISSN 0883-8119); Air Progress Ultralights (ISSN 0735-3871)

SPORT ROCKETRY. see *HOBBIES*

SPORTPARACHUTIST. see *SPORTS AND GAMES — Outdoor Life*

SPORTS AVIATION. see *SPORTS AND GAMES*

629.132   US   ISSN 0279-1749
TL721.4
SPORTSMAN PILOT. 1981. q. $8 (foreign $9) (effective 1997). Jack B. Cox, Ed. & Pub., Box 2768, Oshkosh, WI 54903. TEL 414-231-6657. adv.; bk.rev. circ. 3,000. **Document type:** consumer publication.

001.94   SP
STENDEK. 1970. 4/yr. $12. Centro de Estudios Interplanetarios de Barcelona, Apto. 282, Barcelona, Spain. Ed. Pedro Redon. bk.rev. circ. 1,400.
Description: Covers unidentified flying objects.

629.4   NE   ISSN 0926-7093
STUDIES IN ASTRONAUTICS. (Text in English) 1979. irreg., vol.4, 1990. price varies. Elsevier Science B.V., Books Division, P.O. Box 211, 1000 AE Amsterdam, Netherlands. TEL 31-20-4853911. FAX 31-20-4853705. TELEX 18582 ESPA NL. E-mail: nlinfo-f@elsevier.nl; usinfo-f@elsevier.com; forinfo-kyf04035@niftyserve.or.jp; URL: http://www.elsevier.nl/. (Subscr. in the Americas to: Elsevier Science, Regional Sales Office, Box 945, New York, NY 10159-0945. TEL 212-633-3730. FAX 212-633-3680; Subscr. in Australasia and the Far East to: Elsevier Science (Singapore) Pte Ltd, No.1 Temasek Ave., No.17-01 Millenia Tower, Singapore 039192, Singapore. TEL 65-434-3727. FAX 65-337-2230; Subscr. in Japan to: Elsevier Science Japan, 9-15 Higashi-Azabu 1-chome, Minato-ku, Tokyo 106, Japan. TEL 81-3-5561-5033. FAX 81-3-5561-5047) **Document type:** monographic series.
—BLDSC (8489.563000).
Refereed Serial

629.13   SU   ISSN 1319-1594
AL-SUQUR. 1978. 2/yr. free. P.O. Box 2973, Riyadh 11461, Saudi Arabia. TEL 966-1-476-6566. Ed. Hamad A. al-Saleh. **Document type:** government publication.

SURINAM. CENTRAAL BUREAU LUCHTKARTERING. JAARVERSLAG. see *GEOGRAPHY*

629.1309   SW   ISSN 1100-9837
SVENSK FLYGHISTORISK TIDSKRIFT. 1970. bi-m. SEK 230 in Sweden; other Nordic countries SEK 300; elsewhere SEK 340. Svensk Flyghistorisk Foerening, P.O. Box 10267, S-100 55 Stockholm, Sweden. Ed. Sven Stridsberg. R&P contact: Sven Stridsberg. bk.rev. circ. 3,800. **Document type:** academic/scholarly publication.
Former titles: (until 1990): Flyghistorisk Maanadsblad; (until 1971): Flyghistorisk Tidskrift.
Refereed Serial

001.94   CN   ISSN 0707-7106
SWAMP GAS JOURNAL. 1978. irreg. Can.$5($6) (foreign Can.$8). Ufology Research of Manitoba, Box 1918, Winnipeg General Post Office, Winnipeg, MB R3C 3R2, Canada. TEL 204-269-7553. E-mail: rutkows@cc.umanitoba.ca. Ed. Chris Rutkowski. bk.rev.; circ. 250 (controlled). **Document type:** bulletin.
Description: Information on unidentified flying objects and related phenomena.

621.48   US
CODEN: SNPSEG
SYMPOSIUM ON SPACE NUCLEAR SYSTEMS. PROCEEDINGS. (In 2 vols.) 1984. a. price varies. Institute for Space Nuclear Power Studies, University of New Mexico, Albuquerque, NM 87131. TEL 505-277-2813. Eds. Mohamed S. El-Genk, Mark D. Hoover. **Document type:** proceedings.
—CASDDS; CISTI.
Formerly: Space Nuclear Power Systems (ISSN 1041-2824)

629.13   IS   ISSN 0072-9302
CODEN: TIDRAR
T.A.E. REPORT. (Text in English) 1959. irreg. $20. Technion - Israel Institute of Technology, Department of Aeronautical Engineering, Haifa, Israel. TEL 04-292260. FAX 04-231848. TELEX 46406-TECON-IL. circ. 100. **Indexed:** Appl.Mech.Rev.

629.132   CN   ISSN 0316-2494
TAILSPINNER. 1972. irreg. Waterloo-Wellington Flying Club, Breslau, Ont., Canada.
Formerly: Talespinner (ISSN 0316-2540)

629.13   TS
AL-TAIRAN AL-MADANI/CIVIL AVIATION. (Text in Arabic) 1980. m. free. Civil Aviation Administration, P.O. Box 20, Abu Dhabi, United Arab Emirates. TEL 757500. Ed. Ali bin Khalfan al-Dahiri. circ. 1,000.
Description: Covers civil aviation matters in the U.A.E., including safety awareness.

629.13   UK
TECH LOG. 1970. m. membership. Association of Licensed Aircraft Engineers (1981), The Old Court House, London Rd., Ascot, Berks. SL5 7EN, England. TEL 44-1582-606620. FAX 44-1344-21340. Ed. M.A. Newman; Pub. Keith Rogers. R&P contact: Keith Rogers. TEL 44-1344-26138. adv. circ. 1,500. **Document type:** newsletter.
Description: Deals with technical and legal matters facing membership. Also covers aircraft maintenance techniques.

629.132   US   ISSN 0744-8996
TL760.A1
TECHNICAL SOARING. 1976. q. $24 membership (foreign $27); non-members $30. Technical Soaring Society of America, Inc., Box E, Hobbs, NM 88241-1308. TEL 503-392-1177. FAX 503-392-8154. E-mail: 74521.116@compuserve.com; URL: http://acro.harvard.edu/SSA/. Ed. Mark Kennedy. adv. contact: Denise Gartman. circ. 750. (back issues avail.) **Indexed:** Sportsearch (1976-). **Document type:** trade publication.
—BLDSC (8726.780000); UnCover.

629.1 620 531   US   ISSN 0193-4120
TA171
TEST ENGINEERING & MANAGEMENT. 1959. bi-m. $35 (foreign $45). Mattingley Publishing Co., Inc., 3756 Grand Ave., Ste. 205, Oakland, CA 94610. TEL 510-839-0909. FAX 510-839-2950. Ed. Eve Mattingley-Hannigan. adv.; bk.rev.; charts; illus.; tr.lit.; index. circ. 9,839. **Indexed:** Alloys Ind., Curr.Pack.Abstr., Eng.Ind., Eng.Mat.Abstr., Met.Abstr., Met.Abstr.Ind., Nonfer.Met.Alert, PCC Alert, Steels Alert, World Alum.Abstr. **Document type:** trade publication.
—CISTI; Ei.
Formerly: Test Engineering.
Description: Exchange of ideas and information among reliability, qualification testing professionals. Covers shock and vibration testing; model analysis, materials testing, climatics testing, product and package testing, automotive testing, biomedical testing, and stress screening.

629.13   NE   ISSN 0040-6023
THERMIEK. 1964. 5/yr. fl.45($20) Koninklijke Nederlandse Vereniging voor Luchtvaart, Afdeling Zweefvliegen - Royal Netherlands Aeronautical Association, Apeldoornseweg 203, 6816 SM Arnhem, Netherlands. TEL 31-26-3514515. FAX 31-26-3510446. Ed. Niels Visser. adv.: B&W page fl.990; trim 210 x 297. bk.rev. circ. 5,700.
—SWETS.
Description: Includes gliding news and activities, reports of events, championships, technical information, new designs, safety information, and lis of events.

629.132   CN
TOWLINE. irreg. (approx. 6/yr.). membership. Edmonton Soaring Club, Box 472, Edmonton, Alta. T5J 2K1, Canada. Ed. Marty Slater. circ. 100.

387.7   US   ISSN 0041-0365
TRADE-A-PLANE. 1937. 36/yr. $98. 410 W. Fourth St Crossville, TN 38555. TEL 615-484-5137. FAX 615-484-5137. TELEX 325815. adv. circ. 211,080. **Document type:** newspaper.
Description: Provides buying and selling information for general aviation.

AERONAUTICS AND SPACE FLIGHT

629.1   US   ISSN 1073-8703
CODEN: TSJOEK
THE TS A G I JOURNAL. (Text in English) 1972. q. $459 (effective 1997-1998). (Tsentralnyi Aero-Gidrodinamicheskii Institut, RU - Central Aero-Hydrodynamic Institute) Begell House Inc., 79 Madison Ave., Ste. 1205, New York, NY 10016-7892. TEL 212-725-1999. FAX 212-213-8368. E-mail: begellhouse@worldnet.att.net. Ed. Victor N. Gusev; Pub. William Begell. R&P contact: Felix Portnoy. adv. contact: Felix Portnoy. (back issues avail.) **Document type:** academic/scholarly publication.
—BLDSC (9067.433000); CISTI; Genuine Article; SWETS; UnCover. **CCC**.
Formerly (until 1994): Mechanics - Soviet Research.
Description: Publishes articles on fundamental and applied aspects of aero-hydrodynamics and dynamics of flying vehicles, stability, strength and aeroacoustics, experimental and computational research and related areas of aerospace engineering.
Refereed Serial

629.1   CC   ISSN 1001-4055
CODEN: TUJIEG
TUIJIN JISHU/JOURNAL OF PROPULSION TECHNOLOGY. (Text in Chinese) 1980. bi-m. $120. Zhongguo Hangtian Gongye Zonggongsi, Di 3 Yanjiuyuan, 31 Yanjiusho - China Aerospace Corporation, Third Research Academy, No.31 Institute, P.O. Box 7208-26, Beijing 100074, People's Republic of China. TEL 86-10-6837-6141. FAX 86-10-6837-4052. TELEX 222832 AHY CN. Ed. Yaosong Dai. adv. contact: Shijie Gong. circ. 2,000. **Indexed:** Chem.Abstr., Eng.Ind., Int.Aerosp.Abstr. **Document type:** academic/scholarly publication.
●Also available online.
—BLDSC (5042.800000); CASDDS.
Description: Carries theses, research papers, reports in theoretical studies, design, experiment, manufacture and application of propulsion technology in the field of propulsion systems for missiles, launch vehicles and spacecrafts.
Refereed Serial

TURKISH DEFENCE & AEROSPACE UPDATE. see *MILITARY*

001.94   US   ISSN 1043-1233
U F O; a forum for extraordinary theories and phenomena. 1986. bi-m. $21 (foreign $28). U F O Media Group, Box 1053, Sunland, CA 91041. TEL 818-951-1250. Ed. Vicki Cooper Ecker. adv.; bk.rev.; film rev.; bibl.; charts; illus.; pat.; stat. circ. 24,000. (back issues avail.)
Description: Journalistic and cultural view of UFO reports, theories and ideas. Covers broad range of approaches.

U F O ENCOUNTER. see *NEW AGE PUBLICATIONS*

001.94   US
U F O NEWSCLIPPING SERVICE. 1969. m. $55 (foreign $80) (effective 1996). 2 Caney Valley Dr., Plumerville, AR 72127. TEL 501-354-2558. Ed. Lucius Farish; Pub. Lucius Farish. bk.rev.; circ. 550 (paid). (back issues avail.) **Document type:** newsletter.
Description: Reports on current worldwide U.F.O. sightings.

001.94   DK   ISSN 0049-4976
U F O - NYT. 1958. q. DKK 197($39) Skandinavisk U F O Information, P.O. Box 6, 2820 Gentofte, Denmark. Ed. Kim Moeller Hansen. adv.; bk.rev.; illus. circ. 1,500. **Document type:** consumer publication.
Description: Covers unidentified flying objects.

001.94   UK   ISSN 0958-4846
J F O TIMES. 1989. 6/yr. £16 (foreign $32). British Unidentified Flying Objects Research Association Ltd. (BUFORA), 16 Southway, Burgess Hill, Sussex RH15 9ST, England. TEL 44-1444-236738. adv.; bk.rev. circ. 500.
—BLDSC (9079.920000).

001.94   US
F OLOGY. a. $6.50. Ghost Research Society, Box 205, Oak Lawn, IL 60454-0205. TEL 708-425-5163. **Document type:** directory.
Description: Contains names of individuals, groups, organizations, and UFO-related publications.

K ADDITIONAL REQUIREMENTS AND SPECIAL CONDITIONS. see *TRANSPORTATION — Air Transport*

629.1   US   ISSN 0741-4587
U S S E A UPDATE; the bulletin of important space news, politics, and information. (Included in: Space Age Times) 1980. m. $26 (foreign $32). U S Space Education Association, News Operations Division, Box 249, Rheems, PA 17570-0249. TEL 717-367-5196. Ed. Stephen M. Cobaugh. R&P contact: Debra Palmisano. circ. 1,500. (back issues avail.) **Document type:** newsletter.
Description: Provides information on space legislation, workshops and conferences.

797.55   US   ISSN 0883-7937
ULTRALIGHT FLYING!; international magazine of ultralight aviation. 1976. m. $29.95 (foreign $34.95). Glider Rider, Inc., Box 6009, Chattanooga, TN 37401. TEL 423-629-5375. FAX 423-629-5379. E-mail: ultraw@aol.com; URL: http://www.ulflyingmag.com/. Ed. Buzz Chalmers; Pub. Tracy Knauss. R&P contact: David Prestridge. adv. contact: David Prestridge. bk.rev.; circ. 16,000 (paid). **Document type:** consumer publication.
—CISTI.
Formerly: Glider Rider.
Description: For enthusiasts of ultralight and microlight aviation.

629.1   US
U.S. AERONAUTICAL INFORMATION PUBLICATION. Short title: U.S. A I P. biennial (with q. amendments). $87 (foreign $108.75). U.S. Federal Aviation Administration, 800 Independence Ave., S.W., Washington, DC 20591. TEL 202-267-3484. (Subscr. to: Superintendent of Documents, U.S. Government Printing Office, Box 371954, Pittsburgh, PA 15250-7954. TEL 202-512-1800. FAX 202-512-2250) (looseleaf format) **Document type:** government publication.
Description: Lists F.A.A. regulations and data required for safe aircraft operations in the U.S. National Airspace System.

629.13   US   ISSN 0499-9320
TL521.3.T4   CODEN: NATMA4
U.S. NATIONAL AERONAUTICS AND SPACE ADMINISTRATION. TECHNICAL MEMORANDUM. Key Title: N A S A Technical Memorandum. irreg. U.S. National Aeronautics and Space Administration, Scientific and Technical Information Office, Center for AeroSpace Information, 800 Elkridge Landing Rd., Linthicum Heights, MD 21090-2934. E-mail: help@sti.nasa.gov; URL: http://www.sti.nasa.gov. (also avail. in microfiche) **Indexed:** Alloys Ind., Biol.Abstr., Eng.Mat.Abstr., Geo.Abstr.H.G., GeoRef, Met.Abstr., Met.Abstr.Ind., Nonfer.Met.Alert, PCC Alert, Steels Alert, World Alum.Abstr. **Document type:** government publication, monographic series.
—BLDSC (6015.473500); CASDDS; CISTI; Ei.

629.13   US   ISSN 0077-3131
U.S. NATIONAL AERONAUTICS AND SPACE ADMINISTRATION. TECHNICAL NOTES. irreg. U.S. National Aeronautics and Space Administration, Scientific and Technical Information Office, Center for AeroSpacce Information, 800 Elkridge Landing Rd., Linthicum Heights, MD 21090-2934. E-mail: help@sti.nasa.gov; URL: http://www.sti.nasa.gov. **Indexed:** Appl.Mech.Rev., Biol.Abstr. **Document type:** government publication.
—CISTI.

629.132   US
UNITED STATES PILOTS ASSOCIATION NEWS. bi-m. $35. United States Pilots Association, 483 S. Kirkwood Rd., Ste. 10, St. Louis, MO 63122. TEL 314-849-8772. Ed. Bob Worthington. circ. 200 (controlled). **Document type:** newsletter.
Description: Covers activities, operations, and meetings of the association, a non-profit group of state pilot organizations and their members united for mutual support, aviation safety and education. Contains news, aviation events, and relevant legislation.

629.1   US
UNITED STATES SPACE FOUNDATION. NATIONAL SPACE SYMPOSIUM PROCEEDINGS REPORTS. 1984. a. $50. United States Space Foundation, 2860 S. Circle Dr., Colorado Springs, CO 80906. TEL 719-576-8000. FAX 719-576-8801. URL: http://www.inovatec.com/ussf.org. Ed. Steve Eisenhart; Pub. Richard P. MacLeod. R&P contact: Steve Eisenhart. TEL 719-576-8000. adv. contact: Beth-Ann Lipskin. circ. 1,400. **Document type:** proceedings.
Formerly: United States Space Foundation. National Space Symposium Reports.

629.1   UK
UNIVERSITY OF SOUTHAMPTON. DEPARTMENT OF AERONAUTICS AND ASTRONAUTICS. TECHNICAL REPORT. irreg. University of Southampton, Department of Aeronautics and Astronautics, Highfield, Southampton SO17 1BJ, England. TEL 44-1703-592322. FAX 44-1703-593058. E-mail: dm@aero.soton.ac.uk. **Document type:** monographic series.

629.13   CN
TL568.U55
UNIVERSITY OF TORONTO. INSTITUTE FOR AEROSPACE STUDIES. GRADUATE STUDIES AND RESEARCH PROGRESS REPORT. 1952-199?; resumed 1992. biennial. free. University of Toronto, Institute for Aerospace Studies, 4925 Dufferin St., North York, ON M3H 5T6, Canada. TEL 416-667-7700. FAX 416-667-7799. URL: http://www.utias.utoronto.ca. circ. 450.
—BLDSC (4207.423500); CISTI.
Formerly (until 1994): University of Toronto. Institute for Aerospace Studies. Annual Progress Report (ISSN 0082-5239)

629.1   UK   ISSN 1351-3478
UNMANNED VEHICLES HANDBOOK. 1994. a. Shephard Press Ltd., 111 High St., Burnham, Bucks. SL1 7J2, England. TEL 44-1628-604311. FAX 44-1628-664334. **Document type:** directory.
Description: Comprehensive directory of unmanned aerial vehicles, payloads and groundstations.

UTRECHT STUDIES IN AIR AND SPACE LAW. see *LAW*

629.13   XR   ISSN 0044-5355
V Z L U ZPRAVODAJ. (Text in Czech; summaries in English) 1957. 5/yr. exchange basis only. Vyzkumny a Zkusebni Letecky Ustav, Beranovych 130, Prague 9-Letnany 19905, Czech Republic. TEL 66311397. Ed. Ladislav Vymetal. charts; illus. (also avail. in microform; back issues avail.) **Indexed:** Int.Aerosp.Abstr. **Document type:** academic/scholarly publication.

629.1   II
VAYU AEROSPACE REVIEW. 1974. bi-m. $30. Society For Aerospace Studies, D-43, Sujan Singh Park, New Delhi 110 003, India. TEL 4626183. FAX 4623271. TELEX 031-63358-LTAIN. Ed. Vikramjit S. Chopra. adv.; bk.rev. circ. 20,000.

358.4   NE   ISSN 0042-3122
VEILIG VLIEGEN; flight, ground and maintenance safety journal. 1953. m. Koninklijke Luchtmacht, Afdeling Bedrijfsveiligheid Koninklijke Luchtmachtstaf - Royal Netherlands Air Force, Binckhorstlaan 135, Postbus 20703, 2500 ES The Hague, Netherlands. TEL 70-3492358. FAX 70-3492500. TELEX 43393. Ed. L. van Hof. bk.rev.; illus.; index; circ. 5,000 (controlled).
—SWETS.

629.133   US   ISSN 0042-4455
TL716.A1   CODEN: VEFLAD
VERTIFLITE. 1955. bi-m. $60 (foreign $75) (effective 1997). American Helicopter Society, Inc., 217 N. Washington St., Alexandria, VA 22314. TEL 703-684-6777. FAX 703-739-9279. URL: http://www.vtol.org/journal/. Ed. Kim Smith. adv.; illus. circ. 9,300. (processed) **Indexed:** Eng.Ind., HRIS, Int.Aerosp.Abstr. **Document type:** bulletin.
—BLDSC (9216.900000); CISTI; Linda Hall; SWETS; UnCover.

629.13   RU   ISSN 1025-6768
TL504
VESTNIK VOZDUSHNOGO FLOTA. 1918. m. $133 (effective 1998). Ul. Krasnoarmezhskaya, D.4, 125167 Moscow, Russia. TEL 7-95-214-8404. FAX 7-95-214-5680. (Dist. by: Mezhdunarodnaya Kniga, B. Yakimanka 39, 117049 Moscow, Russia. TEL 7-095-2384967. FAX 7-095-2384634) **Document type:** trade publication.
—BLDSC (0032.850000); CISTI.
Formerly (until 1995): Aviatsiya i Kosmonavtika (ISSN 0373-9821)
Description: Covers Russian military and commercial aviation.

AERONAUTICS AND SPACE FLIGHT

629.133 DK ISSN 0109-8330
VETERANFLY KLUBBEN. 1969. q. DKK 300 membership (effective 1997). K Z & Veteranfly Klubben, Nygade 12A, P.O. Box 104, DK-6200 Aabenraa, Denmark. TEL 45-74-62-22-66. FAX 45-74-62-80-69. Ed. Tine Atterman. adv. contact: Lisbeth Seemann. bk.rev.; illus. circ. 1,000. **Document type:** newsletter.
   Formerly: K Z and Veteranfly Klubben.

629.1 745.1 US ISSN 0091-6943
TL506.A1
VINTAGE AIRPLANE. 1972. m. $27. Experimental Aircraft Association, Inc., Antique Classic Division, Box 3086, Oshkosh, WI 54903-3086. TEL 414-426-4800. Ed. H.G. Frautshy. adv. contact: Golda Cox. circ. 10,000. **Indexed:** Ind.How To Do It (1990-).
   —CISTI.

629.13 NE ISSN 0042-7705
VLIEGENDE HOLLANDER. 1945. m. fl.36.50. Ministerie van Defensie, Directie Voorlichting, Postbus 20701, 2500 ES The Hague, Netherlands. TEL 31-70-3188335. FAX 31-70-31-88426. (Co-sponsor: Koninklijke Luchtmacht) Ed. Martin Zijlstra. adv.; bk.rev.; charts; illus. circ. 40,000. **Document type:** government publication.

629.132 797 FR
VOL A VOILE MAGAZINE. 1983. bi-m. 250 F. (foreign 300 F.). S E P A G, 59 ave. Aristide Briand, 93190 Livry-Gargan, France. TEL 33-1-43-02-10-64. FAX 33-1-43-01-83-11. Ed. Jean Molveau. adv.: page 8500 F.; trim 210 x 297. (back issues avail.) **Document type:** consumer publication.
   Description: Covers gliding championships, new sailplanes for glider pilots and modellers.

629.1 SP
VOLAR. 1988. 12/yr. 7200 ptas. (Europe 10236 ptas.; elsewhere 11520 ptas.) (effective 1994). Trade Zap, S.L., C. las Llamas, 5, 28707 S. Sebastian de los Reyes (Madrid), Spain. TEL 34-1-6570116. FAX 34-1-6570202. Ed. Enrique Jimenez. adv. contact: Chony Zapico. circ. 10,600. **Document type:** consumer publication.
   Description: Covers sport flying and parachuting.

629.133 IT ISSN 1121-5607
VOLARE. 1983. 11/yr. L.80000($109) Editoriale Domus, Via Grandi 5-7, 20089 Rozzano (MI), Italy. TEL 39-2-824721. FAX 39-2-8255033. Ed. Francesco Giaculli. adv.: B&W page L.8400000, color page L.12600000. circ. 26,024.

629.1 627 BE ISSN 0377-8312
CODEN: LSVDDQ
VON KARMAN INSTITUTE FOR FLUID DYNAMICS. LECTURE SERIES. (Text in English) 1965. irreg. (approx 10/yr.). 8000 BEF per no. (effective 1995). Von Karman Institute for Fluid Dynamics - Institut von Karman de Dynamique des Fluides, Chaussee de Waterloo 72, 1640 Rhode-Saint-Genese, Belgium. TEL 32-2-3581901. FAX 32-2-3582885. E-mail: biblio@vki.ac.be. Ed. Mrs. E. Crochard. (also avail. in microfiche from NTI; back issues avail.) **Document type:** monographic series.
   —BLDSC (5180.590000); CISTI; Linda Hall.

387.7 US ISSN 0736-198X
TL506.A1
W W I AERO; the journal of the early aeroplane (1900-1918). 1961. q. $30 (foreign $35) (effective 1997 & 1998). World War I Aeroplanes, Inc., 15 Crescent Rd., Poughkeepsie, NY 12601-4490. TEL 914-473-3679. Ed. Leonard E. Opdycke; Pub. Leonard E. Opdycke. adv. contact: Beverly Williams. bk.rev. circ. 2,000. (back issues avail.)
   —CISTI.
   Formerly: World War I Aeroplanes.
   Description: Covers restoration, reproduction and modelling of early airplanes, 1900-1918.

629.1 US
UG1240
WARBIRDS INTERNATIONAL. 9/yr. $21.95 (foreign $30.95). Challenge Publications, Inc., 7950 Deering Ave., Canoga Park, CA 91304. TEL 818-887-0550. FAX 818-884-1343. E-mail: warbirdmag@aol.com. Ed. Michael O'Leary; Pub. Edwin Schnepf. R&P contact: Susan Duprey. adv. contact: Greg Lovell. circ. 47,736. **Document type:** consumer publication.
   Formerly: Air Progress Warbirds International (ISSN 0885-2502)

629.1 US ISSN 0739-6538
WASHINGTON REMOTE SENSING LETTER. 1981. s-m. (m. Jan. & Aug.). $410 in N. America; elsewhere $500. Felsher Publishing Co., 1057-B National Press Bldg., Washington, DC 20045. TEL 202-393-3640. FAX 301-428-0557. (Subscr. to: Box 2075, Washington, DC 20013) Ed. Murray Felsher; Pub. Murray Felsher. bk.rev.; bibl.; stat.; tr.lit. (back issues avail.) **Document type:** newsletter.
   Description: Includes applications of satellite photography of the Earth; also covers related programs of world governments and the private sector.

629.1 387.7 US ISSN 0733-1754
TL684
WATER FLYING. bi-m. $1.50 to non-members. Seaplane Pilots Association, 421 Aviation Way, Frederick, MD 21701. TEL 301-695-2083. FAX 301-695-2375. adv.; circ. 7,000 (controlled). **Document type:** trade publication.
   Description: Covers regulatory, operational, safety, and industry developments. Includes regional reports.

629.1 387.7 US ISSN 0193-4198
TL684
WATER FLYING ANNUAL. a. $10 to non-members. Seaplane Pilots Association, 421 Aviation Way, Frederick, MD 21701. TEL 301-695-2083. FAX 301-695-2375. bk.rev. circ. 7,600. **Document type:** trade publication.
   Description: Features reports, tips, and techniques to improve flying. Includes listings of training facilities equipment.

629.13 GW ISSN 0043-2172
U3 CODEN: WHTCAK
WEHRTECHNIK, VEREINIGT MIT WEHR UND WIRTSCHAFT; Monatsschrift fuer wirtschaftliche Fragen der Verteidigung, Luftfahrt und Industrie. Key Title: Wehrtechnik. 1969. m. DM.105($78) (foreign DM.115($85)) (effective 1997). (Deutsche Gesellschaft fuer Wehrtechnik e.V.) Wehr und Wissen Verlagsgesellschaft mbH, Postfach 140261, 53057 Bonn, Germany. TEL 49-228-64830. FAX 49-228-6483-109. E-mail: 101336.245@compuserve.com. adv.; bk.rev.; charts; illus. circ. 25,000. **Indexed:** Excerp.Med., IBR. **Document type:** trade publication.
   —SWETS. **CCC.**
   Incorporates (1957-1975): Wehr und Wirtschaft (ISSN 0043-2113)
   Description: Covers defense and economics, aerospace technology and electronics.

629.1 GW
DIE WELT DER LUFTSCHIFFE. 1963. 3/yr. DM.15. Verein der Luftschiffahrt e.V., Falkentaler Steig 108, 13465 Berlin, Germany. Ed.Bd. **Document type:** bulletin.

387.7 CN
WHAT IS THE I B A C. 1981. irreg. free to members. International Business Aviation Council, c/o Edmund Stohr, Dir., 1010 Sherbrooke St. W., Ste. 1514, Montreal, PQ H3A 2R7, Canada. TEL 514-982-0260. FAX 514-982-0799. **Document type:** bulletin.

629.1 JA ISSN 0910-7800
WING; Japanese aviation news. Variant title: Wing Weekly. (Text in Japanese) 1956. w. 12,000 Yen. Koku Shinbunsha - Wing Aviation Press, Kanda Kitamura Bldg., 30 Kanda Higashi-Konya-cho, Chiyoda-ku, Tokyo 101, Japan. TEL 03-3258-9840. FAX 03-3258-5044. TELEX J27117-WINGKOKU. Ed. Hitoshi Ohashi. adv.: B&W page 380000 Yen, color page 700000 Yen; trim 280 x 393; adv. contact: Hitoshi Ohashi. circ. 32,000.
   ●Also available online. Vendor(s): NewsNet (AE06).

629.132 JA ISSN 0388-1032
WING NEWSLETTER. (Text in English) 1967. w. $1000. Koku Shinbunsha - Wing Aviation Press, Kanda Kitamura Bldg., 30 Kanda Higashi-Konya-cho, Chiyoda-ku, Tokyo 101, Japan. TEL 03-3258-0880. FAX 03-3258-5004. TELEX J27117-WINGKOKU. Ed. Hitoshi Ohashi. circ. 5,000. **Document type:** newsletter.
   ●Also available online. Vendor(s): Data-Star, Knight-Ridder Information, Inc., NewsNet.

629.13 AT ISSN 0043-5880
WINGS. 1940. q. Aus.$8 (foreign Aus.$15). Royal Australian Air Force Association, New South Wales Division, P.O. Box A2147, Sydney South, N.S.W. 2000, Australia. TEL 61-2-92672722. FAX 61-2-92645432. (Co-sponsor: Australian Flying Corps) Ed. D. Hornsey. adv.; bk.rev.; illus. circ. 10,000.
   Description: Keeps readers up-to-date on current aviation both military and civil.

629.1 358.4 PK
WINGS; world review of aviation & defence. Cover title: Monthly Wings. (Text in English) 1979. m. Rs.400 (international $80) (effective 1997). Phoenix Publications Co., 101 Muhammadi House, Chundrigar Rd., Karachi, Pakistan. TEL 92-21-2412591. FAX 92-21-2420797. TELEX 21101 WINGS PK. Ed. Javed Mushtaq; Pub. Javed Mushtaq. adv. contact: Uner Khan. bk.rev.; illus. circ. 5,000. **Document type:** trade publication.
   Description: Covers news of the aviation, air transport and defense and aerospace sectors in Pakistan and throughout the world.

629.13 358.4 US ISSN 1067-0637
WINGS (GRANADA HILLS). 1971. bi-m. $22 (foreign $28) (effective 1997). Sentry Books, Inc., 10718 White Oak Ave., Box 3324, Granada Hills, CA 91344. TEL 818-368-2012. Ed. Joseph V. Mizrahi. adv.: page $500. bk.rev.; charts; illus.; stat. circ. 80,000. (back issues avail.) **Document type:** consumer publication.

629.13
WINGS CLUB. BULLETIN. m. Wings Club, 52 Vanderbilt Ave., 18th Fl., New York, NY 10017. TEL 212-867-1770. **Document type:** bulletin.

629.13 358.4 US ISSN 0274-7405
VG93
WINGS OF GOLD. 1975. q. $35 (effective Jul. 1996). (Association of Naval Aviation, Inc.) Wings of Gold, Inc., 5205 Leesburg Pike, Ste. 200, Falls Church, VA 22041. TEL 703-998-7733; 800-666-6050. FAX 703-671-6050. Ed. Zip Rausa. R&P contact: Zip Rausa. adv. contact: George Newell. bk.rev.; circ. 10,000 (paid). **Document type:** newsletter.

WINGSPREAD RANDOLPH A F B. see *MILITARY*

629.132 384.554 US
WONDERFUL WORLD OF FLYING. 1987. q. $300. Aviation Media Inc., 50 E. 42nd St., 12th Fl., New York, NY 10017-5405. TEL 800-772-9963. FAX 212-370-4937. Pub. Stephen Kahm. adv. (video cassette; 60 mins.)
   Former titles: Wide World of Flying; A B C Wide World of Flying.

629.4 355 US
WORLD AEROSPACE & DEFENSE INTELLIGENCE. w. $495 (effective 1997). Forecast International Inc. - D M S, 22 Commerce Rd., Newtown, CT 06470. TEL 203-426-0800. FAX 203-426-0233. E-mail: finews1@ibm.net.
   Former titles (until 1990): Aerospace Intelligence (ISSN 1041-7419); (until 1985): Aerospace D M S Intelligence (ISSN 0275-2948)
   Description: Describes and analyzes significant developments in aerospace and defense. Includes current information on aircraft, electronics, ships, vehicles, ordnance, missiles, and space programs.

629.13 SA ISSN 0261-2399
WORLD AIRNEWS. 1973. m. R.70 in RSA & Namibia; elsewhere R.125 (effective 1997). T C E Publications Ltd., P.O. Box 35082, Northway 4065, South Africa. TEL 27-31-841319. FAX 27-31-837115. Ed. Tom Chalmers. R&P contact: Tom Chalmers. adv. contact: Tom Chalmers. bk.rev.; illus. circ. 12,832. **Indexed:** Ind.S.A.Per. **Document type:** trade publication.
   Incorporates: African Air Transport (ISSN 0261-2313) & Wings Over Africa (ISSN 0043-5910)
   Description: Articles, news items, photography, pertaining to commercial and avocational aviation technology and activities in Africa.

629.132 US ISSN 0888-5265
WORLD AIRSHOW NEWS. 1986. bi-m. $20 (effective 1995). Flyer Publications, Inc., Box 199, Oregon, W 53575. TEL 608-835-7063. Ed. Dave W.R. Weiman. adv.; bk.rev. illus. circ. 3,500. **Document type:** trade publication.

AERONAUTICS AND SPACE FLIGHT — ABSTRACTING, BIBLIOGRAPHIES, STATISTICS

387.7 629.13 US ISSN 0890-510X
TL537
WORLD AND UNITED STATES AVIATION AND SPACE RECORDS. a. (with q. updates). $13.95 to non-members (with updates $39). National Aeronautic Association, 1815 N. Fort Myer Dr., Ste. 700, Arlington, VA 22209-1805. TEL 703-527-0226. FAX 703-527-0229. Ed. Art Greenfield. bk.rev.
—CISTI.

629.13 US ISSN 0043-826X
TL512
WORLD AVIATION DIRECTORY. Issued with: World Space Directory. 1940. s-a. $250 (foreign $310) includes WAD Buyer's Guide & WAD Catalog Guide (effective 1997). McGraw-Hill Companies, Aviation Week Group (New York), 1221 Ave. of the Americas, New York, NY 10020. FAX 215-586-3232. TELEX 2323265 MHG PUBNET. Ed. Donna Kaulkin. adv.; pat.; index. circ. 15,000. **Document type:** directory.
●Also available on CD-ROM.
—CISTI. **CCC.**
   Incorporates (1955-1987): Aviation Week and Space Technology Marketing Directory; Which was formerly: Aviation Week and Space Technology. Buyers Guide.
   Description: Lists the people, companies, products and services in aviation, defense and aerospace.

WORLD HELICOPTER INVENTORY & FORECAST. see MILITARY

WORLD MILITARY AIRCRAFT INVENTORY & FORECAST. see MILITARY

629.1 355 US
WORLD MILITARY AVIATION (YEAR). Cover title: Naval Institute Guide to World Military Aviation. biennial, latest 1997-1998. $150. (Naval Institute) Naval Institute Press, 118 Maryland Ave., Annapolis, MD 21402. TEL 410-268-6110. FAX 410-269-7940. (Orders to: Naval Institute Press, 2062 Generals Hwy., Annapolis, MD 21401. TEL 800-233-8764) Ed. Rene J. Francillon. R&P contact: Linda Cullen. illus.
   Description: Covers military combat, transport, and rescue aircraft worldwide.

629.4 US
WORLD SPACE SYSTEMS BRIEFING. m. Teal Group Corp., 3900 University Dr., Ste. 220, Fairfax, VA 22030. TEL 703-385-1992. FAX 703-691-9591. (looseleaf format) **Document type:** newsletter.
   Description: Identifies and analyzes emerging programs and services, with an eye toward helping contractors get in on the bottom floor.

629.1 US ISSN 0737-8548
WORLD SPACEFLIGHT NEWS. m. $30. Randall M. Schuler, Ed. & Pub., Box 98, Sewell, NJ 08080. TEL 609-478-6396.

629.1 620.1 CC ISSN 1007-2330
YUHANG CAILIAO GONGYI/AEROSPACE MATERIALS & TECHNOLOGY. (Text in Chinese; summaries in English) 1971. bi-m. $120. Hangtian Gongye Zong Gongsi, Hangtian Cailiao ji Gongyi Yanjiu-suo - China Aerospace Corporation, Aerospace Research Institute of Materials and Processing Technology, P.O. Box 9200-73, Beijing 100076, People's Republic of China. TEL 86-10-68383269. FAX 86-10-64227606. E-mail: duyq@mimi.cnc.ac.cn; anb@ns.iai.canet.cn. (Subscr. to: An Bo, Dept. of Documentation, P.O. Box 1408, Beijing 100013, People's Republic of China. TEL 86-10-68372847. FAX 86-10-64227606) Ed. Li Hong.
   Description: A scientific journal focusing on aerospace materials and technology.
   Refereed Serial

629.1 CC ISSN 1000-1328
TL787
YUHANG XUEBAO/JOURNAL OF ASTRONAUTICS. (Text in Chinese) q. (Zhongguo Yuhang Xuehui - Chinese Society of Astronautics) Yuhang Xuebao Bianjibu, P.O. Box 838, Beijing 100830, People's Republic of China. (Dist. outside China by: China International Book Trading Corp., Box 399, Beijing, P.R. China) Ed. Zhuang Fenggan.
—BLDSC (4947.498000).

629.1 CC ISSN 1002-7742
ZHONGGUO HANGTIAN. English edition: Aerospace China (ISSN 1004-9711) (Text in Chinese; summaries in English) 1977. m. $240 (effective 1996). Hangtian Gongye Zong Gongsi, Xinxi Yanjiu-suo - China Aerospace Corporation, Institute for Astronautics Information, P.O. Box 1408, 1 Binhe Lu, Hepingli, Beijing 100013, People's Republic of China. TEL 86-10-6837-3440. FAX 81-10-6422-7606. E-mail: duyq@mimi.cnc.ac.cn; anb@ns.iai.canet.cn. Ed. Li Enzhong. R&P contact: An Bo. adv.: color page $4500; adv. contact: An Bo.
—BLDSC (0729.855500).
   Formerly (until Jul. 1991): Shijie Daodan yu Hangtian (ISSN 1001-4144).
   Description: Introduces both civil and military applications of space science and technology; provides the latest information on Chinese launch vehicles, satellites and rockets.
   Refereed Serial

629.1 CC ISSN 1000-758X
   CODEN: JKKJEK
ZHONGGUO KONGJIAN KEXUE JISHU/CHINESE SPACE SCIENCE AND TECHNOLOGY. (Text in Chinese) 1981. bi-m. $30 (effective 1997 & 1998). Chinese Academy of Space Technology, P.O. Box 9622, Beijing 100086, People's Republic of China. TEL 86-10-6837-8744. FAX 86-10-6837-8745. (Subscr. overseas to: Office of Chinese Newspapers and Periodicals, China International Book Trading Corp., P.O. Box 399, Beijing 100044, P.R. China. TEL 86-10-6841-3063) Ed. Shenyuan Hou. circ. 1,500. **Document type:** academic/scholarly publication.
   Description: Covers system integration and subsystem design of spacecraft, sounding rockets; astrodynamics; reentry and recovery techniques; space electronics; remote sensing from space power supply; materials used and processed in space; space medicine and biology; space environment simulation and more.
   Refereed Serial

629.1 CC ISSN 1001-5000
ZHONGGUO MINHANG XUEYUAN XUEBAO/CIVIL AVIATION INSTITUTE OF CHINA. JOURNAL. (Text in Chinese; abstracts in English) 1984. q. $10. Zhongguo Minhang Xueyuan - Civil Aviation Institute of China, Zhangguizhuang Jichang (Airport), Tianjin 300300, People's Republic of China. TEL 491750. FAX 022-493347. Ed. Zai Jian Ping. adv.: page $500; adv. contact: Yatian Li. circ. 1,000. **Document type:** academic/scholarly publication.
   Description: Covers aeronautical power and mechanical devices, aircraft maintenance, automatic control, electrical engineering, communication, air transportation, and other related disciplines.

629.13 GW ISSN 0065-2024
ZUERL'S ADRESSBUCH DER DEUTSCHEN LUFT- UND RAUMFAHRT. 1950. a. DM.64. Luftfahrt-Verlag Walter Zuerl, Amselweg 6, 8031 Woerthsee-Steinebach, Germany. Ed. Walter J.A. Zuerl. adv.; bk.rev. circ. 3,000.

AERONAUTICS AND SPACE FLIGHT —
Abstracting, Bibliographies, Statistics

629.1 358.4 US
A G A R D INDEX TO PUBLICATIONS. irreg. U.S. National Aeronautics and Space Administration, Scientific and Technical Information Office, Center for AeroSpace Information, 800 Elkridge Landing Rd., Linthicum Heights, MD 21090-2934. E-mail: help@sti.nasa.gov; URL: http://www.sti.nasa.gov. (Co-sponsor: NATO Advisory Group for Aerospace Research and Development) **Document type:** government publication, abstracting/indexing.
   Description: Lists abstracts and indexes for AGARD unclassified publications announced in STAR during the previous 3 years.

629.1 016 US ISSN 0163-4941
Z5063.A2
AERONAUTICAL ENGINEERING: A CONTINUING BIOGRAPHY WITH INDEXES. 1970. m. U.S. National Aeronautics and Space Administration, Scientific and Technical Information Office, Center for AeroSpace Information, 800 Elkridge Landing Rd., Linthicum Heights, MD 21090-2934. E-mail: help@sti.nasa.gov; URL: http://www.sti.nasa.gov. (Co-sponsor: U.S. Federal Aviation Administration) index. (back issues avail.) **Indexed:** Corros.Abstr. **Document type:** abstracting/indexing, government publication.
●Available only online.
—CISTI; Linda Hall.
   Formerly: Aeronautical Engineering: A Special Biography with Indexes.

629.13 US ISSN 0898-4425
TL501
AEROSPACE FACTS AND FIGURES. 1945. a. $35. Aerospace Industries Association of America, 1250 Eye St., N.W., Washington, DC 20005. TEL 202-371-8561. FAX 202-371-8470. URL: http://www.aia-aerospace.org. Ed. David Vadas. charts. **Indexed:** SRI. **Document type:** trade publication.
—CISTI; Linda Hall.

AEROSPACE MEDICINE AND BIOLOGY; a continuing bibliography. see MEDICAL SCIENCES — Abstracting, Bibliographies, Statistics

629.1 011 US ISSN 0899-1928
AVIATION TRADESCAN; monthly index and abstracts. 1984. m. $175 (effective 1994). Aerospace Research Group, 2812 Summit Ridge, Grapevine, TX 76051. TEL 817-488-9161. FAX 817-481-5418. Ed. Catherine Heinzer. Pub. Catherine Heinzer. R&P contact: Catherine Heinzer. circ. 500 (paid). (also avail. in diskette format; back issues avail.) **Document type:** abstracting/indexing.
   Description: Provides monthly indexing and brief abstracts for over 70 aviation-aerospace publications.

629.1 011 CC ISSN 1002-6592
CHINA AEROSPACE ABSTRACTS. Chinese edition: Zhongguo Hangkong Wenzhai (ISSN 1002-6606) (Text in English) 1988. q. $140. (Aviation Industries of China, China Aero-Information Centre) Hangkong Gongye Chubanshe - Aviation Industry Press, 14 Xiaoguan Dongli, Anwai, Beijing 100029, People's Republic of China. TEL 8610-4918404. FAX 8610-4221696. Ed. Wen Ruilin. index. **Document type:** abstracting/indexing.
●Also available online.

629.4 016 RU ISSN 0132-1668
TL787.7
EKSPRESS-INFORMATSIYA. ASTRONAVTIKA I RAKETODINAMIKA. 1960. 24/yr. $284 (effective 1998). Vsesoyuznyi Institut Nauchno-Tekhnicheskoi Informatsii (VINITI), Baltiiskaya ul., 14, Moscow A-219, Russia. (Subscr. to: Mezhdunarodnaya Kniga, Dimitrova ul. 39, 113095 Moscow, Russia).

629.13 016 RU ISSN 0207-5008
TL504
EKSPRESS-INFORMATSIYA. AVIASTROENIE. 1964. 48/yr. 59.40 Rub. Vsesoyuznyi Institut Nauchno-Tekhnicheskoi Informatsii (VINITI), Baltiiskaya ul., 14, Moscow A-219, Russia. (Subscr. to: Mezhdunarodnaya Kniga, Dimitrova ul. 39, 113095 Moscow, Russia)
—CCC.

629.1 FJ ISSN 0256-8071
FIJI. BUREAU OF STATISTICS. AIRCRAFT STATISTICS. a., latest 1992. $5 (effective 1997). Bureau of Statistics, P.O. Box 2221, Suva, Fiji. **Document type:** government publication.
   Description: Contains information on the operations of both domestic and international airlines.

387.7 FR ISSN 0181-1517
TL502
FRANCE. DIRECTION GENERALE DE L'AVIATION CIVILE. BULLETIN STATISTIQUE. 1960. a. free. Direction Generale de l'Aviation Civile, Service de Coordination Economique, Europeenne et Internationale, Bureau Statistiques, 48 rue Camille Desmoulins, 92452 Issy les Moulineaux Cedex, France. TEL 41-09-49-80. FAX 41-09-48-83. circ. 600.

AERONAUTICS AND SPACE FLIGHT — COMPUTER APPLICATIONS

629.1   CC   ISSN 1006-2130
HANGKONG WENZHAI/AERONAUTICS ABSTRACTS. (Text in Chinese) m. $190. (Aviation Industries of China, China Aero-Information Center) Hangkong Gongye Chubanshe - Aviation Industry Press, 14 Xiaoguan Dongli, Anwai, Beijing 100029, People's Republic of China. TEL 8610-4918404. FAX 8610-4918420. Ed. Qiu Zubin. **Document type:** abstracting/indexing.
Formerly: Guowai Hangkong Wenxhai - Foreign Aeronautics Abstracts (ISSN 1002-6614)

629.1   US
INDEX TO N A S A NEWS RELEASES AND SPEECHES. a. free. U.S. National Aeronautics and Space Administration, Scientific and Technical Information Office, Center for AeroSpace Information, 800 Elkridge Landing Rd., Linthicum Heights, MD 21090-2934. E-mail: help@sti.nasa.gov; URL: http://www.sti.nasa.gov. **Document type:** government publication, abstracting/indexing.
Description: Lists news releases from selected NASA agencies.

629.1 355   JA
JAPANESE MILITARY AIRCRAFT SERIALS. (Text in Japanese) a. Nihon Kokuki Kenkyukai - Japan Aviation Research Group, c/o Mr. Masataka Sato, 28-5, Hiyoshi-cho, Tokorozawa-shi, Saitama-ken 359, Japan.

629.13 016   NE   ISSN 0022-7366
K L M LITERATUUROVERZICHT. (Text in language of the periodicals) 1958. m. fl.10($30) K L M Royal Dutch Airlines, Information and Documentation Department, Postbus 7700, 1117 ZL Schiphol, Netherlands. circ. 240. **Document type:** abstracting/indexing.

MANAGEMENT (BALTIMORE); a bibliography for N A S A managers. see BUSINESS AND ECONOMICS — Abstracting, Bibliographies, Statistics

629.1   US
N A S A THESAURUS SUPPLEMENT. PART 1. HIERARCHICAL LISTING. irreg., latest no.4, Jul. 1996. U.S. National Aeronautics and Space Administration, Scientific and Technical Information Office, Center for AeroSpace Information, 800 Elkridge Landing Rd., Linthicum Heights, MD 21090-2934. E-mail: help@sti.nasa.gov; URL: http://www.sti.nasa.gov. (back issues avail.) **Document type:** government publication, abstracting/indexing.
●Also available online.
Description: Compiles aerospace engineering terms and lists any changes in their definitions. Used both when entering documents into and retrieving documents from the NASA STI database.

629.1   US
N A S A THESAURUS SUPPLEMENT. PART 2. ACCESS VOCABULARY. irreg., latest no.4, Jul. 1996. U.S. National Aeronautics and Space Administration, Scientific and Technical Information Office, Center for AeroSpace Information, 800 Elkridge Landing Rd., Linthicum Heights, MD 21090-2934. E-mail: help@sti.nasa.gov; URL: http://www.sti.nasa.gov. (back issues avail.) **Document type:** government publication, abstracting/indexing.
●Also available online.
Description: Compiles aerospace engineering terms and lists any changes in their definitions. Used both to enter and retrieve documents from the N.A.S.A. S.T.I. database.

629.1   US
N A S A THESAURUS SUPPLEMENT. PART 3. DEFINITIONS. irreg., latest 1994. U.S. National Aeronautics and Space Administration, Scientific and Technical Information Office, Center for AeroSpace Information, 800 Elkridge Landing Rd., Linthicum Heights, MD 21090-2934. E-mail: help@sti.nasa.gov; URL: http://www.sti.nasa.gov. **Document type:** government publication, abstracting/indexing.
●Also available online.
Description: Compiles aerospace engineering terms and lists any changes in their definitions. Used both to enter and retrieve documents from the N.A.S.A. S.T.I. database.

629.1 011   II
NATIONAL AERONAUTICAL LABORATORY. BIBLIOGRAPHY SERIES. m. exchange basis. National Aeronautical Laboratory, P.O. Box 1779, Kodihalli, Bangalore 560017, India. **Document type:** bibliography.

629.1 016   II
NATIONAL AERONAUTICAL LABORATORY. RECENT BOOK ADDITIONS. s-m. exchange basis. National Aeronautical Laboratory, P.O. Box 1779, Kodihalli, Bangalore 560017, India.

011   IS
NEW BOOKS RECEIVED BY THE FACULTY LIBRARY. (Text in English) 1956. q. free. Technion - Israel Institute of Technology, Faculty of Aeronautical Engineering, Kiryat Hatechnion, Haifa 32 000, Israel. Ed. Mariuca Stanciu. circ. 300.

629.3 016   RU   ISSN 0373-6407
REFERATIVNYI ZHURNAL. AVIATSIONNYE I RAKETNYE DVIGATELI. 1961. m. $139 (effective 1998). Vsesoyuznyi Institut Nauchno-Tekhnicheskoi Informatsii (VINITI), Baltiiskaya ul., 14, Moscow A-219, Russia. (Subscr. to: Mezhdunarodnaya Kniga, Dimitrova ul. 39, 113095 Moscow, Russia) **Document type:** abstracting/indexing.

REFERATIVNYI ZHURNAL. ISSLEDOVANIE KOSMICHESKOGO PROSTRANSTVA. see ASTRONOMY — Abstracting, Bibliographies, Statistics

629.3 016   RU   ISSN 0207-1371
TL787.7
REFERATIVNYI ZHURNAL. RAKETOSTROENIE I KOSMICHESKAYA TEKHNIKA. 1961. m. $174 (effective 1998). Vsesoyuznyi Institut Nauchno-Tekhnicheskoi Informatsii (VINITI), Baltiiskaya ul., 14, Moscow A-219, Russia. (Subscr. to: Mezhdunarodnaya Kniga, Dimitrova ul. 39, 113095 Moscow, Russia) **Indexed:** Chem.Abstr. **Document type:** abstracting/indexing.
—Linda Hall.
Formerly: Referativnyi Zhurnal. Raketostroenie.

629.13   US
S C A N. (Selected Current Aerospace Notices) s-m. U.S. National Aeronautics and Space Administration, Scientific and Technical Information Office, Center for AeroSpace Information, 800 Elkridge Landing Rd., Linthicum Heights, MD 21090-2934. E-mail: help@sti.nasa.gov; URL: http://www.sti.nasa.gov. circ. controlled. **Document type:** government publication, abstracting/indexing.
●Also available online.
Description: Keeps readers aware of the latest additions to the NASA STI Database, arranged in 191 aerospace-related categories.

629.13 016   US   ISSN 0036-8741
TL500   CODEN: STAEA5
S T A R. (Scientific and Technical Aerospace Reports); an abstract journal. 1963. m. U.S. National Aeronautics and Space Administration, Scientific and Technical Information Office, Center for AeroSpace Information, 800 Elkridge Landing Rd., Linthicum Heights, MD 21090-2934. E-mail: help@sti.nasa.gov; URL: http://www.sti.nasa.gov. index. (also avail. in microform from NTI,UMI,PMC; back issues avail.; reprint service avail. from UMI) **Indexed:** Chem.Abstr., Corros.Abstr., Ergon.Abstr., Fluidex, Mass Spectr.Bull., Ocean.Abstr., Photo.Abstr., Pollut.Abstr. **Document type:** government publication, academic/scholarly publication, abstracting/indexing.
●Available only online. Vendor(s): European Space Agency, Knight-Ridder Information, Inc. (File no.108).
—BLDSC (8176.600000); CASDDS; CISTI; Linda Hall; UMI.
Description: Announces abstracts and indexes reports issued by NASA and similar government agencies, as well as from universities, independent research organizations, and industry.
Refereed Serial

629.1   US
U.S. NATIONAL AERONAUTICS AND SPACE ADMINISTRATION. VIDEO CATALOG. irreg. free. U.S. National Aeronautics and Space Administration, Scientific and Technical Information Office, Center for AeroSpace Information, 800 Elkridge Landing Rd., Linthicum Heights, MD 21090-2934. E-mail: help@sti.nasa.gov; URL: http://www.sti.nasa.gov. **Document type:** catalog, government publication.
●Also available online.
Description: Lists all N.A.S.A.-produced videotapes.

629.1   CC   ISSN 1005-7870
ZHONGGUO DAODAN YU HANGTIAN WENZHAI/CHINA ASTRONAUTICS AND MISSILERY ABSTRACTS. (Text in Chinese, English) 1994. bi-m. $250 (effective 1997). Hangtian Gongye Zong Gongsi, Xinxi Yanjiu-suo - China Aerospace Corporation, Institute for Astronautics Information, P.O. Box 1408, 1 Binhe Lu, Hepingli, Beijing 100013, People's Republic of China. TEL 86-10-6837-2847. FAX 86-10-6422-7606. E-mail: duyq@mimi.cnc.ac.cn;anb@ns.iai.canet.cn. Ed. An Bo. adv.: color page $1000. index. **Document type:** abstracting/indexing.
●Also available on CD-ROM.
Description: Cites the aerospace-related books, technical papers, standards, conference papers, and journals recently produced in China.

AERONAUTICS AND SPACE FLIGHT — Computer Applications

629.131   US
COMPUTER SECURITY APPLICATIONS CONFERENCE. 1985. a. price varies. (Institute of Electrical and Electronics Engineers, Inc.) I E E E Computer Society Press, 10662 Los Vaqueros Circle, Los Alamitos, CA 90720-1264. TEL 714-821-8380. FAX 714-821-4010. Ed. Cat Harris; Pub. Matt Loeb. adv. contact: Frieda Koester. **Indexed:** INSPEC. **Document type:** proceedings.
Former titles (until 1988): Aerospace Computer Security Applications Conference; (until 1987): Aerospace Computer Security Conference.
Description: Contains technical papers and tutorials that address the application of computer security technologies in the aerospace and other environments.

E S A - I R S NEWS & VIEWS. (European Space Agency) see LIBRARY AND INFORMATION SCIENCES — Computer Applications

629.1 001.6   US
LOCKHEED M S C STAR. 1955. fortn. free. Lockheed Missiles and Space Co., Inc., Department of Public Relations, Box 3504-1111 Lockheed Way, Sunnyvale, CA 94088-3504. TEL 408-742-7441. FAX 408-743-2239. Ed. Mark van Wyk. adv.; illus. circ. 31,000. (tabloid format; back issues avail.)

629.13   US
U.S. FEDERAL AVIATION ADMINISTRATION. SYSTEMS RESEARCH AND DEVELOPMENT. REPORT F A A - R D. 1958. irreg. price varies. U.S. Federal Aviation Administration, Systems Research and Development Service, 800 Independence Ave. S.W., Washington, DC 20591. TEL 202-655-4000. (Orders to: National Technical Information Service, 5285 Port Royal Rd., Springfield, VA 22151. TEL 703-487-4630. FAX 703-321-8547) **Document type:** government publication, monographic series.

AGRICULTURAL ECONOMICS

see Agriculture–Agricultural Economics

AGRICULTURAL EQUIPMENT

see Agriculture–Agricultural Equipment

AGRICULTURE

see also Agriculture–Agricultural Economics; Agriculture–Agricultural Equipment; Agriculture–Computer Applications; Agriculture–Crop Production and Soil; Agriculture–Dairying and Dairy Products; Agriculture–Feed, Flour and Grain; Agriculture–Poultry and Livestock; Food and Food Industries; Forests and Forestry; Gardening and Horticulture

630   US   ISSN 0001-0073
A A E A BYLINE. 1924. 10/yr. membership. American Agricultural Editors Association, 1005 Congress Ave., Ste. 420, Austin, TX 78701-2415. TEL 512-474-2041. FAX 512-474-77787. Ed. Denise C. Terrell. bk.rev. circ. 600. (processed) **Document type:** newsletter, trade publication.

AGRICULTURE

A A G BIJDRAGEN. (Vakgroep Agrarische Geschiedenis) see HISTORY — History Of Europe

630 338.1 US
A A N TODAY. bi-m. American Association of Nurserymen, 1250 I St., N.W., Ste. 500, Washington, DC 20005. TEL 202-789-2900. Ed. Angela Hutcherson. **Document type:** bulletin.

333.79 US ISSN 1046-0993
A E R O SUN TIMES. 1973. q. $15 (Canada $20; foreign $25). Alternative Energy Resources Organization, 25 S. Ewing St., Ste. 214, Helena, MT 59601-5732. TEL 406-443-7272. FAX 406-442-9120. E-mail: aero@desktop.org. Ed. Sheila Habeck. R&P contact: Sheila Habeck. adv. contact: Sheila Habeck. bk.rev.; bibl.; charts; illus. circ. 700. (back issues avail.) **Indexed:** Energy Info.Abstr., New Per.Ind. **Document type:** newsletter. **Description:** Information on sustainable agriculture, renewable energy and conservation, multi-modal transportation, and community self-reliance.

630 MR
A F A A NEWSLETTER/A F A A BULLETIN D'INFORMATION. (Text in Arabic, English, French) 1978. s-a. DH.80($10) Association of Faculties of Agriculture in Africa, B.P. 8642 - Instituts, Rabat, Morocco. TEL 774702. (Affiliate: Institut Agronomique et Veterinaire Hassan II) Ed. A.O. Tantawy. adv.; bk.rev. circ. 1,000. (back issues avail.) **Document type:** newsletter.

630 CN
A F H R C FACTSHEETS. (Atlantic Food and Horticulture Research Centre) (Text in English) 3/yr. free. Agriculture Canada, Kentville Research Station, Kentville, NS B4N 1J5, Canada. TEL 902-679-5333; 97237(VR). FAX 902-679-2311. URL: http://res.agr.ca/kentville/pubs/agindex.htm. Ed. Charlie Embree. **Document type:** government publication.
●Available only online.
Supersedes in part (in 1994): Agriscope (ISSN 1181-814X)

630 GT ISSN 0001-1274
A G A. vol. 18, 1970. m. membership. Asociacion General de Agricultores, 9A. Calle 3-43, Guatemala 1, Guatemala. Ed. Mario Alvarado Rubio. circ. 1,000.

630 SP
A L S A R.* (Al Servicio de Una Agricultura Rentable) 1974. m. 700 ptas.($14) Ediciones Anel, San Vicente Ferrer 13, Granada, Spain. adv.; bibl.; illus.; stat.; circ. 25,000 (controlled). (back issues avail.)

630 658 CU ISSN 0514-9797
A N A P. 1961. m. $20 in N. America; S. America $26; Europe $29; elsewhere $41. (Asociacion Nacional de Agricultores Pequenos, Departamento de Exportacion) Ediciones Cubanas, Obispo No. 527, Apdo. 605, Havana, Cuba. Dir. Ricardo Machado. illus. circ. 90,000.
Description: Official organ of the Cuban farmers. Contains information, interviews and features about national events.

A N R EDUCATOR. (Agricultural and Natural Resources) see EDUCATION — Teaching Methods And Curriculum

638.1 US ISSN 0889-3764
SF521
A P I S. (Apicultural Information and Issues) 1983. m. free. University of Florida, Institute of Food and Agricultural Sciences, Dept. of Entomology and Nematology, Bldg. 970, Gainesville, FL 32611-0620. TEL 904-392-1801. FAX 904-392-0190. E-mail: mts@gnv.ifas.ufl.edu; URL: http://www.ifas.ufl.edu/~mts/apishtm/apis.htm. Ed. Malcolm T. Sanford. index. circ. 800. (looseleaf format) **Document type:** newsletter.
●Also available online.
Description: Focuses on the bee culture.

630 RU ISSN 0235-2443
S13
A P K: EKONOMIKA, UPRAVLENIE. (Agro-promyshlennyi Kompleks) (Text in Russian; content page in English and Russian) 1988. m. $120 (effective 1998). AgriPress, Sadovaya-Spasskaya, 18, 107807 Moscow, Russia. TEL 7-095-2071662. FAX 7-095-2072870. (Dist. by: Mezhdunarodnaya Kniga, B. Yakimanka 39, 117049 Moscow, Russia. TEL 7-095-2384967. FAX 7-095-2384634) Ed. Marlen M. Makeenko. circ. 50,000. **Document type:** academic/scholarly publication.
—BLDSC (0007.562000).
Refereed Serial

344.94043 AT ISSN 1033-9280
A Q I S BULLETIN. 1989. m. Australian Quarantine and Inspection Service, G.P.O. Box 858, Canberra, A.C.T, Australia. TEL 61-6-2725234. FAX 61-6-2724494. Ed. Carson Creagh. R&P contact: Carson Creagh. circ. 3,000. **Document type:** bulletin, government publication.
Description: Summarizes information and news from A.Q.I.S. for individuals and organizations involved in quarantine and inspection matters.

630 SA ISSN 1021-2752
A R D R I NEWS. 1980. s-a. free. University of Fort Hare, Agricultural and Rural Development Research Institute, Private Bag X1314, Alice 5700, South Africa. TEL 0404-31154. FAX 0404-31730. Ed. Barbara Morrow. bk.rev.; circ. 1,000 (controlled). **Document type:** newsletter.
Description: Provides information to practitioners and decision-makers in the area of agriculture and rural and community development, and fosters awareness of the institute's activities and resources.

630 ET
A R D U PUBLICATION. 1966. irreg. price varies. Arussi Rural Development Unit, P.O. Box 3376, Addis Ababa, Ethiopia. charts; cum.index.
Supersedes: C A D U Publications (ISSN 0069-3405)

630 310 374 301 CE
A R T I NEWS LETTER. (Text in English, Sinhala) 1973. q. free. Agrarian Research and Training Institute, 114 Wijerama Mawatha, Colombo 7, Sri Lanka. Ed. S.B.K. Bandara. adv.; abstr.; stat. circ. 1,200. (tabloid format) **Document type:** newsletter.

A S A E MONOGRAPH SERIES. (American Society of Agricultural Engineers) see ENGINEERING

630 US ISSN 0001-2351
S671 CODEN: TAAEAJ
A S A E TRANSACTIONS. Key Title: Transactions of the A S A E. (Consists of Divisional Transactions: Power & Machinery; Soil & Water; Structure & Environment; Electrical & Electronic Systems - Emerging Technologies; Food and Process Engineering) 1958. bi-m. $220 to non-members (foreign $232); members $74.50 (foreign $86.50) (effective 1997). American Society of Agricultural Engineers, 2950 Niles Rd., St. Joseph, MI 49085-9659. TEL 616-429-0300. FAX 616-429-3852. E-mail: hq@asae.org; URL: http://www.asae.org/pubs/style/trans.html. Ed. Pamela DeVore-Hansen. index, cum.index: 1907-1960, 1961-1970, 1971-1980, 1981-1985. circ. 1,800. **Indexed:** A.I.Abstr., Agri.Eng.Abstr., Anim.Breed.Abstr., ASCA, Biol.Abstr., Biol.& Agr.Ind., Chem.Abstr., Compumath, Cott.& Trop.Fibr.Abstr., Curr.Adv.Ecol.Sci., Curr.Cont., Dairy Sci.Abstr., Energy Info.Abstr., Eng.Ind., Environ.Abstr., Excerp.Med., Field Crop Abstr., Fluidex, Food Sci.& Tech.Abstr., Forest.Abstr., Forest Prod.Abstr., Geo.Abstr.H.G., Geo.Abstr.P.G., Geotech.Abstr., Herb.Abstr., Hort.Abstr., IDA, Ind.Sci.Rev., Ind.Vet., Int.Abstr.Oper.Res., Irr.& Drain.Abstr., Maize Abstr., Nutr.Abstr., Ocean.Abstr., Ornam.Hort., Pig News & Info., Potato Abstr., Rev.Med.& Vet.Mycol., Rice Abstr., Seed Abstr., Sel.Water Res.Abstr., Soils & Fert., Sorghum & Millets Abstr., Soyabean Abstr., Triticale Abstr., Trop.Oil Seeds Abstr., Vet.Bull., W.R.C.Inf., Weed Abstr., World Agri.Econ.& Rural Sociol.Abstr. **Document type:** trade publication.
—BLDSC (8894.650000); CASDDS; CIS; CISTI; Ei; EMDOCS; Genuine Article; KR SourceOne; Linda Hall; SWETS; UnCover. **CCC.**
Description: Addresses irrigation, drainage, farm buildings and equipment, agricultural machinery, biological engineering, food engineering, aquaculture, electronics, forestry and knowledge systems.
Refereed Serial

630 US ISSN 0066-0566
S1 CODEN: AASPC3
A S A SPECIAL PUBLICATION. 1963. irreg., no.57, 1994. American Society of Agronomy, Inc., 677 S. Segoe Rd., Madison, WI 53711. TEL 608-273-8080. FAX 608-273-2021. R&P contact: David M. Kral. adv. contact: Keith R. Schlesinger. **Indexed:** Biol.Abstr., GeoRef., Soils & Fert.
—BLDSC (1738.600000); CASDDS; CISTI; Ei.

630 JA ISSN 0917-1150
A T I C INFORMATION/A T I C JOHO. (Text in Japanese) 1987. 5/yr. Agricultural Development Technical Information Center - Tochi Kairyo Gijutsu Joho Senta, 34-4, Shinbashi 5-chome, Minato-ku, Tokyo 105, Japan. stat.

630 SW ISSN 0284-6160
A T L; lantbrukets affaerstidning. 1884. w. SEK 455 (effective 1996). (Lantbrukarnas Riksfoerbund - Federation of Swedish Farmers) L R F Media, P.O. Box 6044, S-200 11 Malmoe, Sweden. TEL 46-40-10-44-10. FAX 46-40-23-60-53. E-mail: alt@media.lrf.se. Ed. Olle Sjoekvist. adv. contact: Nils Adelcreutz. circ. 68,000. (tabloid format)
Formerly (until 1988): Annonsblad till Tidskrift foer Landtmaen (ISSN 0282-1451)

AARDAPPELWERELD. see BUSINESS AND ECONOMICS — Domestic Commerce

630 DK ISSN 0107-0304
AARSSKRIFT FOR TOENDER LANDBRUGSSKOLE. 1979. a. DKK 50. Toender Landbrugsskole, Vestre Omfartsvej, 6270 Toender, Denmark. illus.

638.1 FR ISSN 0373-4625
ABEILLE DE FRANCE ET L'APICULTEUR. 1922. m. 220 F. (effective 1998). Abeille de France, 5 rue Copenhague, 75008 Paris, France. TEL 33-1-45224842. FAX 33-1-42937785. Ed. Yves Vedrenne. adv.; bk.rev.; charts; illus. circ. 38,000. **Indexed:** Apic.Abstr., Apic.Abstr.
—BLDSC (0537.860000).
Formerly: Abeille de France (ISSN 0001-3137)
Description: Information of interest to apiculturists, agriculturalists, nature lovers and botanists.

638.1 FR ISSN 0765-8702
ABEILLES ET FLEURS; mensuel d'information apicole. 1953. m. 150 F. (foreign 200 F.) (effective 1996). 32 bis bd. Gambetta, 03200 Vichy, France. TEL 33-4-70984280. FAX 33-4-70982102. Ed. Michel Beraud; Pub. Aurelie Morel. R&P contact: Frederic Pichon. adv. contact: Aurelie Morel. illus. circ. 10,000. **Indexed:** Apic.Abstr. **Document type:** trade publication.
Description: Information of interest to the apiculturist.

630 SP ISSN 0210-4172
ABREGO; revista de divulgacion agraria. 1971. q. free. Enfersa, Prim, 12, 28004 Madrid, Spain. TEL (91)231 29 00. Ed. Francios Jimenez-Alfaro y Goma.

630 634 RM ISSN 1010-3589
CODEN: BASSDO
ACADEMIA DE STIINTE AGRICOLE SI SILVICE. BULETIN INFORMATIV. (Text in French) 1970. a. exchange basis. Academia de Stiinte Agricole si Silvice, Bd. Marasti 61, 71331 Bucharest, Rumania. Ed. Ileana Muresan. **Indexed:** Field Crop Abstr., Herb.Abstr., Potato Abstr. **Document type:** bulletin.
—CASDDS.

AGRICULTURE

630   FR   ISSN 0989-6988
S5   CODEN: CRAFEQ
ACADEMIE D'AGRICULTURE DE FRANCE. COMPTES RENDUS. 1761. bi-m. 620 F. (foreign 720 F.). Academie d'Agriculture de France, 18 rue de Bellechasse, 75007 Paris, France.
TEL 47-05-10-37. FAX 45-55-09-78. Ed. Andre Cauderon. bk.rev.; bibl.; charts; stat. **Indexed:** Agri.Eng.Abstr., Anim.Breed.Abstr., Biol.Abstr., Biotech.Abstr., Chem.Abstr., Dairy Sci.Abstr., Excerp.Med., Field Crop Abstr., Food Sci.& Tech.Abstr., Forest.Abstr., Forest Prod.Abstr., Helminthol.Abstr., Herb.Abstr., Hort.Abstr., Ind.Vet., INIS Atomind., Nutr.Abstr., Plant Breed.Abstr., Plant Grow.Reg.Abstr., Potato Abstr., Rev.Appl.Entomol., Rev.Plant Path., Seed Abstr., Vet.Bull., Weed Abstr. **Document type:** proceedings.
—BLDSC (3369.043000); CASDDS; Linda Hall.
Former titles (until 1986): Academie d'Agriculture de France. Comptes Rendus des Seances (ISSN 0001-3986); (until 1915): Societe Royale et Centrale d'Agriculture. Bulletin des Seances (ISSN 0151-1335)

ACCADEMIA DELLE SCIENZE DI SIENA DETTA DE FISIOCRITICI. ATTI. see *MEDICAL SCIENCES*

630   SP
ACCION COOPERATIVA. 12/yr. Plaza de los Fueros, 1, 31002 Pamplona, Spain. TEL 48-239050. FAX 48-244573. Ed. J. Sarasa Murugarren. circ. 140,000.

630   BL   ISSN 0100-560X
HD1875.P35
ACOMPANHAMENTO DA SITUACAO AGROPECUARIA DO PARANA. 1974. m. free or exchange basis. Secretaria de Estado da Agricultura, Rua dos Funcionarios 1559, Caixa Postal 464, C.E.P. 80030 Curitiba, Parana, Brazil. charts; stat. circ. 3,500.
Former titles (until 1976, vol.2, no.4): Acompanhamento da Situacao das Culturas; (until 1976, vol.2, no.3): Situacao das Culturas; (until 1975): Relatorio da Situacao das Culturas.

630   US
ACREAGE MAGAZINE. 1978. m. $5. Argus Observer, 1160 S. W. 4th St., Box 130, Ontario, OR 97914-0130. TEL 503-889-5387.
FAX 503-889-3347. Ed. Eric Ellis. adv. contact: Linda Warren. circ. 56,292. (tabloid format; back issues avail.)

630   US
ACRES U S A;* the voice for eco-agriculture. 1971. m. $20. 10802 E. 70th Terr., Raytown, MO 64133-6619. TEL 816-737-0064.
FAX 816-737-3346. (Subscr. to: Box 9547, Kansas City, MO 64133) Ed. Charles Walters, Jr. adv.; bk.rev.; charts; illus.; stat.; cum.index: 1970-1985. circ. 15,000. (tabloid format) **Indexed:** Farm & Garden Ind., New Per.Ind.

630   PL   ISSN 0860-262X
ACTA ACADEMIAE AGRICULTURAE AC TECHNICAE OLSTENENSIS. GEODAESIA ET RURIS REGULATIO/AGRICULTURAL AND TECHNICAL ACADEMY IN OLSZTYN. GEODESY AND AGRICULTURAL ARRANGEMENT. (Supplement avail.: Geodaesia et Ruris Regulatio) (Text and summaries in English, Polish) 1968. s-a. price varies. (Akademia Rolniczo-Techniczna im. M. Oczapowskiego) Wydawnictwo A R T Olsztyn, Blok 12, 10-957 Olsztyn-Kortowo, Poland.
TEL 48-89-5273310. TELEX 0526419. E-mail: artbib@moskit.art.olsztyn.pl. (Dist. by: Ars Polona-Ruch, Krakowskie Przedmiescie 7, 00-901 Warsaw, Poland. TEL 48-22-265334) Ed. Barbara Grudniewska. R&P contact: Jolanta Mieszkalska. adv. contact: Maciej Gajecki. bibl.; charts; illus.; circ. 140 (controlled). **Indexed:** AgroLibrex, Irr.& Drain.Abstr., Ref.Zh., Soils & Fert. **Document type:** academic/scholarly publication.
Formerly: Akademia Rolniczo-Techniczna. Zeszyty Naukowe. Geodezja i Urzadzenia Rolne (ISSN 0324-9174)

ACTA AGROBOTANICA. see *BIOLOGY* — *Botany*

630   HU   ISSN 0238-0161
S16.H8   CODEN: AAHUEX
ACTA AGRONOMICA HUNGARICA. (Text in English) 1950. q. $156 (effective 1998). (Magyar Tudomanyos Akademia) Akademiai Kiado Rt., P.O. Box 245, H-1519 Budapest, Hungary.
TEL 36-1-2043976. FAX 36-1-2043973. Ed. Pal Kozma. adv.; bk.rev.; bibl.; charts; illus.; maps; index. **Indexed:** Anim.Breed.Abstr., Biol.Abstr., Chem.Abstr., Cott.& Trop.Fibr.Abstr., Curr.Adv.Ecol.Sci., Curr.Cont., Field Crop Abstr., Food Sci.& Tech.Abstr., Herb.Abstr., IBR, Ind.Vet., INIS Atomind., Irr.& Drain.Abstr., Nutr.Abstr., Ornam.Hort., Plant Grow.Reg.Abstr., Seed Abstr., Sorghum & Millets Abstr., Triticale Abstr., Trop.Oil Seeds Abstr., Vet.Bull. **Document type:** academic/scholarly publication.
—BLDSC (0590.200000); CASDDS; KNAW; Linda Hall; UnCover. **CCC.**
Formerly (until 1985): Academiae Scientiarum Hungaricae. Acta Agronomica (ISSN 0001-513X)
Description: Publishes papers on applied and basic research in plant genetics, breeding, cultivation, taxonomy, physiology, biochemistry, ecology, and cenology. Covers phytotomy, phytogeography, and phytopathology. Includes zootomy, geography, pathology, biology, genetics, and breeding, soil science and virology.

630   XR   ISSN 0524-7403
                  CODEN: AUAAB7
ACTA UNIVERSITATIS AGRICULTURAE. SERIES A. FACULTAS AGRONOMICA. (Text and summaries in Czech, English) 1919. q. $20. Vysoka Skola Zemedelska, Zemedelska 1, 613 00 Brno, Czech Republic. FAX 42-05-452-11128. TELEX 62489. Ed. Jan Hradilik. charts; stat.; index. circ. 400. **Indexed:** Agri.Eng.Abstr., Anim.Breed.Abstr., Biol.Abstr., Chem.Abstr., Curr.Cont., Dairy Sci.Abstr., Excerp.Med., Fababean Abstr., Field Crop Abstr., Food Sci.& Tech.Abstr., Forest.Abstr., Helminthol.Abstr., Herb.Abstr., Hort.Abstr., Ind.Vet., Irr.& Drain.Abstr., Maize Abstr., Nutr.Abstr., Plant Breed.Abstr., Plant Grow.Reg.Abstr., Potato Abstr., Rev.Appl.Entomol., Soils & Fert., Weed Abstr. **Document type:** academic/scholarly publication.
—CASDDS; UMI.

630 338.1   XR   ISSN 0524-7446
ACTA UNIVERSITATIS AGRICULTURAE. SERIES D. FACULTAS AGROECONOMICA. (Text and summaries in Czech, English) 1965-1989; resumed 1992. q. $20. Vysoka Skola Zemedelska, Zemedelska 1, 613 00 Brno, Czech Republic. FAX 42-05-45211128. TELEX 624-89. Ed. Oldrich Rejnus. charts; stat.; index. circ. 270. **Indexed:** Anim.Breed.Abstr., Chem.Abstr., Curr.Adv.Ecol.Sci., Curr.Cont., Dairy Sci.Abstr., Excerp.Med., Field Crop Abstr., Food Sci.& Tech.Abstr., Geo.Abstr., Herb.Abstr., Hort.Abstr., Potato Abstr., Poult.Abstr., Rural Recreat.Tour.Abstr., World Agri.Econ.& Rural Sociol.Abstr.
—BLDSC (0584.356000).

630   FR   ISSN 0338-182X
ACTION AGRICOLE DE TARN ET GARONNE. (Supplement avail.: Tempe Informations (ISSN 0338-1811)) 1972. 23/yr. 420 av. de Monclar, 82017 Montauban Cedex, France. TEL 63-63-11-15. FAX 63-20-15-65. Ed. Paul Couronne. circ. 10,186.

630   FR   ISSN 0767-8711
ACTION AGRICOLE DE TOURAINE. 1944. w. 30 rue de la Prefecture, 37000 Tours, France.
TEL 47-05-54-72. FAX 47-05-58-17. Ed. Michel Gerbault. circ. 7,000.

630   FR   ISSN 0750-862X
ACTION AGRICOLE PICARDE. 1945. w. 19 bis, rue Alexandre Dumas, 80045 Amiens Cedex, France. TEL 22-95-13-50. circ. 10,224.

630   FR
ACTION PAYSANNE. 47/yr. 5 rue A. Deforges, 04100 Manosque, France. TEL 92-72-00-44.
FAX 92-72-58-73. Ed. T. Trellu. circ. 2,100.

630   CN
AD-VISER. 1965. s-m. Can.$33. 1320 36 St. N., Lethbridge, Alta. T1H 5H8, Canada.
TEL 403-328-5114. FAX 403-328-5443. Ed. Rick Gillis; Pub. Rick Gillis. R&P contact: Rick Gillis. adv. contact: Al Such. circ. 19,200. **Document type:** consumer publication.

630   US   ISSN 0172-4207
                  CODEN: ASASDF
ADVANCED SERIES IN AGRICULTURAL SCIENCES. 1975. irreg., vol.16, 1987. price varies. Springer-Verlag, 175 Fifth Ave., New York, NY 10010.
TEL 212-460-1500. FAX 212-473-6272. (Also: Berlin, Heidelberg, Tokyo and Vienna) Ed.Bd. (reprint service avail. from ISI) **Indexed:** Biol.Abstr. **Document type:** monographic series.
—BLDSC (0696.927000); CASDDS.

ADVANCES IN AGRICULTURAL BIOTECHNOLOGY. see *BIOLOGY* — *Biotechnology*

630   PL   ISSN 1230-1353
ADVANCES IN AGRICULTURAL SCIENCES. (Text and abstract in English) 1993. a. price varies. Akademia Rolnicza w Szczecinie - Agricultural University in Szczecin, Dzial Wydawnictw, Ul. Doktora Judyma 22, 71-460 Szczecin, Poland. TEL 48-91-541639. FAX 48-91-541642. TELEX 0425494 AR. Ed. Antoni Furowicz. **Indexed:** AgroAgen. **Document type:** academic/scholarly publication.
—BLDSC (0697.815000).
Refereed Serial

630   US   ISSN 0065-2113
S405   CODEN: ADAGA7
ADVANCES IN AGRONOMY. 1949. irreg., vol.61, 1997. (American Society for Agronomy, Inc.) Academic Press, Inc., 525 B St., Ste. 1900, San Diego, CA 92101-4495. TEL 619-231-0926.
FAX 619-699-6715. (Subscr. to: Order Dept., 6277 Sea Harbor Dr., 4th Fl., Orlando, FL 32887. TEL 800-321-5068) Ed. N.C. Brady. (reprint service avail. from ISI) **Indexed:** Agri.Eng.Abstr., ASCA, Bio-Contr.News & Info., Biol.Abstr., Biol.& Agr.Ind., Chem.Abstr., Crop Physiol.Abstr., Curr.Adv.Ecol.Sci., Field Crop.Abstr., GeoRef., Herb.Abstr., Hort.Abstr., Ind.Sci.Rev., Plant Breed.Abstr., Rev.Plant Path., Rice Abstr., Sci.Cit.Ind, Soils & Fert., Triticale Abstr., Weed Abstr.
—BLDSC (0698.000000); CASDDS; CISTI; KR SourceOne; Linda Hall; SWETS; UnCover. **CCC.**
Refereed Serial

630 664   UK   ISSN 0266-8017
AFRICAN FARMING AND FOOD PROCESSING. 1980. bi-m. £43.50($75) Alain Charles Publishing Ltd., Alain Charles House, 27 Wilfred St., London SW1E 6PR, England. TEL 44-171-834-7676.
FAX 44-171-973-0076. TELEX 297165 ACPLTD G. Ed. Jonquil L. Phelan. adv. contact: Cecil Coin. circ. 9,951 (paid). (back issues avail.) **Indexed:** Agri.Eng.Abstr., Field Crop Abstr., Food Sci.& Tech.Abstr., Herb.Abstr., Ind.Vet., Poult.Abstr., Rural Recreat.Tour.Abstr., Trop.Oil Seeds Abstr., World Agri.Econ.& Rural Sociol.Abstr. **Document type:** trade publication.
—BLDSC (0732.443000).
Formerly: West African Farming and Food Processing (ISSN 0143-1307)
Description: Covers the agricultural and primary food-processing industries in English-speaking nations in Africa.

AFRICAN STUDY MONOGRAPHS. see *ANTHROPOLOGY*

AFRICAN STUDY MONOGRAPHS. SUPPLEMENTARY ISSUE. see *ANTHROPOLOGY*

630   US   ISSN 0161-5408
AG ALERT. 1974. w. membership only. California Farm Bureau Federation, 1601 Exposition Blvd., FB9, Sacramento, CA 95815. TEL 916-924-4140. FAX 916-929-1680. Ed. Steve Adler. adv. contact: 45,000. (tabloid format) **Document type:** newspaper.
Description: Provides news and information on California agriculture.

630 570   US
THE AG BIOETHICS FORUM. 1988. s-a. I S U Bioethics Program, E-mail: comstock@iastate.edu; URL: http://www.iastate.edu/~grad__cikkege/bioethics. Ed. Gary Comstock.
●Also available online.
Description: Covers bioethical issues pertaining to agriculture, food, animals and the environment.

AGRICULTURE

630.24 668.6   JA   ISSN 0029-5426
CODEN: NOJID9
AG-CHEM AGE/NOYAKU JIDAI. (Text in Japanese) 1954. s-a. free. Nippon Soda Co. Ltd., New Otemachi Bldg., 2-2-1 Otemachi, Chiyoda-ku, Tokyo 100, Japan. TEL 03-3245-6178. FAX 03-3245-6289. Ed. Koji Kikkawa. adv. circ. 10,000. **Document type:** newsletter.
—CASDDS.
Description: Examines research in agricultural chemicals.

630   US   ISSN 0894-7155
AG CONSULTANT. 1945. 6/yr. $16 (effective 1997). Meister Publishing Co., 37733 Euclid Ave., Willoughby, OH 44094. TEL 216-942-2000. FAX 216-942-0662. E-mail: agc__circ@meistepubl.cam. Ed. Dick Meister. adv. contact: Ric Abernathy. bk.rev.; charts; illus.; mkt.; tr.lit. circ. 19,000. (also avail. in microform from UMI) **Indexed:** Farm & Garden Ind. **Document type:** trade publication.
—Linda Hall; UMI. **CCC.**
Former titles: Ag Consultant and Fieldman (ISSN 0199-6460); Agri-Fieldman and Consultant (ISSN 0190-2423); Agri-Fieldman; Farm Technology (ISSN 0014-8148)

630   US   ISSN 0899-7535
AG FOCUS. 1924. m. $30. Cornell Cooperative Extension Orange County Agriculture, Community Campus, Education Center, Dillon Dr., Middletown, NY 10940. TEL 914-343-1234. FAX 914-343-7471. E-mail: orange@cce.cornell.edu. Ed. Lucy T. Joyce. adv.; charts; illus.; tr.lit. circ. 800. (back issues avail.) **Document type:** newsletter.
Formerly: Orange County Farm News (ISSN 0030-4271)

630   US
AG JOURNAL. 1989. m. $1 per no. Freedom Newspapers, Inc., 1310 S. Commerce, Harlingen, TX 78550. TEL 210-430-6211. FAX 210-430-6213. Ed. Gary Long. adv.: B&W page $994.50; trim 10 x 13; adv. contact: Marcia Bleier. circ. 33,132. **Document type:** newspaper.

AG-PILOT INTERNATIONAL; aviation in agriculture worldwide. see *AERONAUTICS AND SPACE FLIGHT*

630   US
AGFOCUS. 1974. m. $59 (effective Jan. 1996). Cornell Cooperative Extension, 420 E. Main St., Batavia, NY 14020. TEL 716-343-3040. FAX 716-439-8455. (Co-sponsors: Cooperative Extension Associations) Ed. Nathan Herendeen. R&P contact: Nathan Herendeen. adv. contact: Wendy Garrett. circ. 1,000. (controlled). (back issues avail.) **Document type:** newsletter.
Former titles: AgImpact; Genesee County Trends.
Description: Covers commercial agriculture and rural land use issues.

630   FR   ISSN 0339-4409
AGRA ALIMENTATION. 1964. 45/yr. 29 rue du General Foy, 75008 Paris, France. TEL 43-87-39-59. FAX 43-87-79-11. TELEX 650 452 AGRAPRS. Ed. G. Chalencon. circ. 1,500.

630   UK   ISSN 1361-9810
AGRAFOOD EUROPE. m. £230 (rest of Europe £250; elsewhere £275) (effective 1997). Agra Europe (London) Ltd., 25 Frant Rd., Tunbridge Wells, Kent TN2 5JT, England. TEL 44-1892-533813. FAX 44-1892-544895. TELEX 95114 AGRATW G. E-mail: 100637.3460@compuserve.com. **Document type:** trade publication.
—BLDSC (0737.470000).
Formerly: European Agribusiness (ISSN 1350-4460); Supersedes (in 1992): Green Europe (ISSN 0141-2213)

630   SZ
AGRAR KOMBI. w. ASSA Schweizer Annoncen AG, Thunstr. 22, CH-3000 Berne 6, Switzerland. TEL 031-434242. FAX 031-434252. circ. 7,592.

630   AU
AGRAR POST; unabhaengige oesterreichische Zeitschrift. m. S.80 (foreign S.160); newsstand price: S.8. Agrar Post Verlag Dr. Bruno Mueller GmbH, Schulstr. 80, A-2103 Langenzersdorf, Austria. TEL 02244-4647. FAX 02244-464723. adv.; B&W page S.41600, color page S.62400; trim 200 x 260. circ. 65,000. **Document type:** trade publication.

630   GW   ISSN 0342-7900
AGRAR-UEBERSICHT; das active Magazin fuer active Landwirte. 1949. m. DM.82.80 (foreign DM.99.80). Landbuch Verlag GmbH, Kabelkamp 6, 30179 Hannover, Germany. TEL 0511-67806-0. FAX 0511-6780668. **Document type:** trade publication.
Formerly (until 1976): Ubersicht (ISSN 0497-4468)
Description: Covers all aspects of farming, including machinery, economics, marketing, crop production, animal husbandry and breeding.

630   SZ   ISSN 1022-663X
CODEN: SLWFAS
AGRARFORSCHUNG. (Text in German) 1994. 11/yr. 52 SFr. (foreign 58 SFr.). Eidgenoessische Forschungsanstalt fuer Nutztiere, CH-1725 Posieux, Switzerland. TEL 41-26-4077221. FAX 41-26-4077300. E-mail: monika.boltshauser@rap.admin.ch; URL: http://www.admin.ch/sar/zs/afo/. (Co-sponsor: Bundesamt fuer Landwirtschaft) Ed. Monika Boltshauser. adv.; bk.rev.; index. **Indexed:** Biol.Abstr., Chem.Abstr, Dairy Sci.Abstr., Field Crop Abstr., Helminthol.Abstr., Herb.Abstr., Hort.Abstr., Nutr.Abstr., Plant Breed.Abstr., Rev.Appl.Entomol., Rural Recreat.Tour.Abstr., Soils & Fert., World Agri.Econ.& Rural Sociol.Abstr. **Document type:** academic/scholarly publication.
—CASDDS; Linda Hall; SWETS.
Formed by the merger of (1887-1994): Landwirtschaftliches Jahrbuch der Schweiz (ISSN 0023-8171); (1962-1994): Schweizerische Landwirtschaftliche Forschung (ISSN 0036-763X) & Landwirtschaft Schweiz (ISSN 1013-3054); Which was formed by the merger of: Schweizerische Landwirtschaftliche Monatshefte (ISSN 0036-7648); Mitteilungen fuer die Schweizerische Landwirtschaft (ISSN 0540-4789).
Description: Swiss agricultural research journal covering animal production, plant production, environment, agricultural economics and engineering, and food.

630   US
AGRARIAN ADVOCATE. 1979. q. $15. Community Alliance with Family Farmers, Box 464, Davis, CA 95617. TEL 916-756-8518. FAX 916-756-7857. Ed. Adair Schwartz. adv.; bk.rev.; tr.lit. circ. 2,000. (tabloid format; back issues avail.) **Document type:** newsletter.
Formerly: California Agrarian Action Project. Newsletter.

630   GW   ISSN 0341-2520
AGRARINGENIEUR UND AGRARMANAGER; Zeitschrift der landwirtschaftlichen Fuehrungspraxis. (Including: Mitteilungen des Bundesverbandes der Agraringenieure e.V. (BAI) & Europa-Mitteilungen fuer Agraringenieure) 1965. m. DM.36. (Bundesverband der Agraringenieure (BAI) e.V.) B A I Verlag GmbH, Reihermoorweg 19, 30938 Burgwedel, Germany. TEL 05139-8352. adv.; bk.rev.; abstr.; bibl.; charts; illus.; stat. circ. 4,000. **Document type:** trade publication.
—CCC.
Formerly: Agraringenieur (ISSN 0002-1059)

630   NE
AGRARISCH DAGBLAD. 1987. 5/w. fl.391.20. Misset (Subsidiary of: Reed Elsevier plc), Postbus 4, 7000 BA Doetinchem, Netherlands. TEL 31-314-349371. FAX 31-314-363638. (Editorial addr.: P.O. Box 1401, 8001 BK Zwolle, Netherlands. TEL 31-38-274274. FAX 31-38-211822) Ed. Theo Leone. adv. contact: Cor van Nek. illus. circ. 25,000. (tabloid format) **Document type:** trade publication, newspaper.
Description: For farmers, managers and investors in the agricultural sector.

630   NE   ISSN 0925-837X
AGRARISCH ONDERWIJS. 1958. 20/yr. fl.25. Educatieve Partners Nederland, Postbus 666, 3990 DR Houten, Netherlands. TEL 31-3403-59771. FAX 31-3403-59700. (Editorial addr.: Twijnsterhof 32, 5709 GS Helmond, Netherlands. TEL 31-4920-10199. FAX 31-4920-16695) Ed. P.J. Boetzkes. adv.; bk.rev. circ. 1,451.
Former titles (until 1990): Land- en Tuinbouwonderwijs (ISSN 0169-0973); (until 1984): Maandblad voor het Land- en Tuinbouwonderwijs (ISSN 0024-8657)

630 340   NE   ISSN 0167-4242
AGRARISCH RECHT. 1940. m. fl.220 (effective 1996). (Instituut voor Agrarisch Recht) Uitgeverij Kluwer B.V., Postbus 23, 7400 GA Deventer, Netherlands. TEL 31-570-647111. FAX 31-570-631419. (Editorial addr.: Postbus 245, 6700 AE Wageningen, Netherlands. TEL 31-8730-24181. FAX 31-8730-24313) adv.; index. circ. 1,400. **Indexed:** ELLIS.
—SWETS.
Formerly (until 1982): Pacht (ISSN 0165-7186)

630   AU   ISSN 0002-0710
AGRARISCHE RUNDSCHAU. 1947. 6/yr. S.418 (foreign S.515). (Oesterreichische Gesellschaft fuer Land- und Forstwirtschaftspolitik) Oesterreichischer Agrarverlag GmbH, Inkustr. 1-7, A-3400 Klosterneuburg, Austria. TEL 02243-333006. FAX 02243-3330056. Ed. Ernst Scheiber. adv.; B&W page S.14300, color page S.33200; trim 185 x 262. bk.rev.; index. circ. 3,000. **Indexed:** Geo.Abstr., Rural Recreat.Tour.Abstr., World Agri.Econ.& Rural Sociol.Abstr. **Document type:** trade publication.
—BLDSC (0738.320000).

630   AU
AGRARISCHES INFORMATIONSZENTRUM. d. S.5885. Oesterreichischer Agrarverlag GmbH, Inkustr. 1-7, A-3400 Klosterneuburg, Austria. TEL 02243-333006. FAX 02243-3330056. Ed. Dr. Klaus Hoglinger. **Document type:** trade publication.

630   GW   ISSN 0172-9403
AGRARMETEOROLOGISCHER WOCHENBERICHT FUER NORDRHEIN - WESTFALEN. w. DM.30. Deutscher Wetterdienst (Bonn), Siebengebirgstr. 200, 53299 Bonn, Germany.

630 551.5   GW   ISSN 0172-0570
AGRARMETEOROLOGISCHER WOCHENHINWEIS FUER DAS GEBIET BUNDESREPUBLIK DEUTSCHLAND. 1954. w. DM.100. Deutscher Wetterdienst, Bibliothek, Postfach 100465, 63004 Offenbach a.M., Germany. TEL 49-69-80622225. FAX 49-69-80622486. circ. 360. (back issues avail.) **Document type:** government publication.

630   RU   ISSN 1023-1668
S13   CODEN: VSNLAF
AGRARNAYA NAUKA. 1956. bi-m. $101. Akademiya Sel'skokhozyaistvennykh Nauk, Sadovaya-Spasskaya, 18, 107807 Moscow, Russia. TEL 7-095-2071837. FAX 7-095-2072870. (Dist. by: Mezhdunarodnaya Kniga, B. Yakimanka 39, 117049 Moscow, Russia. TEL 7-095-2384967. FAX 7-095-2384634) Ed. V.B. Zil'berkvit. circ. 2,000. **Indexed:** Agri.Eng.Abstr., Agroforest.Abstr., Anim.Breed.Abstr., Bio-Contr.News & Info., Biol.Abstr., Chem.Abstr., Crop Physiol.Abstr., Dairy Sci.Abstr., Field Crop Abstr., Food Sci.& Tech.Abstr., Forest.Abstr., Herb.Abstr., Hort.Abstr., Ind.Vet., Irr.& Drain.Abstr., Maize Abstr., Pig News & Info., Plant Grow.Reg.Abstr., Potato Abstr., Poult.Abstr., Seed Abstr., Triticale Abstr., Vet.Bull., Weed Abstr., World Agri.Econ.& Rural Sociol.Abstr. **Document type:** academic/scholarly publication.
—CASDDS; Linda Hall.
Formerly (until 1992): Vestnik Sel'skokhozyaistvennoi Nauki (ISSN 0206-6335)
Description: Covers issues conserning agriculture. Aimed at scientists, teachers and students.

630 340   GW   ISSN 0340-840X
K1
AGRARRECHT. m. DM.278.40 (foreign DM.295.80) (effective 1997). (Deutsche Gesellschaft fuer Agrarrecht) Landwirtschaftsverlag GmbH, Huelsebrockstr. 2, 48165 Muenster, Germany. TEL 49-2501-801-0. FAX 49-2501-801-204. (Subscr. to: Postfach 480249, 48079 Muenster, Germany) Ed. Bernold Bendel. circ. 1,633. (back issues avail.) **Indexed:** Agri.Eng.Abstr., ELLIS, Excerp.Med., Forest.Abstr., IBR, Rural Recreat.Tour.Abstr., World Agri.Econ.& Rural Sociol.Abstr. **Document type:** trade publication.
—BLDSC (0738.383000). **CCC.**

AGRARSOZIALE GESELLSCHAFT. ARBEITSBERICHT. see *SOCIOLOGY*

AGRARSOZIALE GESELLSCHAFT. KLEINE REIHE. see *SOCIOLOGY*

AGRARSOZIALE GESELLSCHAFT. LAENDLICHER RAUM. RUNDBRIEF. see *SOCIOLOGY*

AGRICULTURE

AGRARSOZIALE GESELLSCHAFT. MATERIALSAMMLUNG.
see *SOCIOLOGY*

630   GW   ISSN 0179-2903
AGRARTECHNIK (WUERZBURG). 1922. m. DM.123 (foreign DM.142) (effective 1997). B L V Verlagsgesellschaft mbH, Lothstr. 29, 80797 Munich, Germany. TEL 49-89-12705-0. FAX 49-89-12705354. Ed. Peter Wiggers. adv.: B&W page DM.5130, color page DM.7398; trim 270 x 188; adv. contact: Henning Stemmler. mkt.; stat.; circ. 13,308 (controlled). **Indexed:** Agri.Eng.Abstr., Rural Recreat.Tour.Abstr., Vet.Bull., World Agri.Econ.& Rural Sociol.Abstr. **Document type:** trade publication.
—CCC.
   Former titles (until 1985): Agrartechnik International (ISSN 0179-289X); (until 1984): Agrartechnik International. Ausgabe A (ISSN 0341-695X); Landmaschinen Markt (ISSN 0023-7981).

630   HU   ISSN 0002-1105
S16.H8
AGRARTORTENETI SZEMLE/AGRICULTURAL HISTORY REVIEW; historia rerum rusticarum. (Text in Hungarian; summaries in English) 1957. q. $30. Magyar Mezogazdasagi Muzeum, P.O. Box 129, 1367 Budapest, Hungary. TEL 36-1-3430573. FAX 36-1-3439120. (Co-sponsor: Hungarian Academy of Sciences, Committee for Agricultural History and Rural Sociology) Eds. Sandor Szarnoczai, Gyorgy Feher. R&P contact: Gyorgy Feher. TEL 36-1-3438485. adv.; bk.rev.; illus.; index; circ. 500 (paid). **Indexed:** Amer.Hist.& Life (1955-), Curr.Adv.Ecol.Sci., Curr.Cont., Geo.Abstr.H.G., Hist.Abstr. (1955-), World Agri.Econ.& Rural Sociol.Abstr. **Document type:** academic/scholarly publication.
—CCC.

630   GW   ISSN 0002-1121
HD101
AGRARWIRTSCHAFT; Zeitschrift fuer Betriebswirtschaft, Marktforschung und Agrarpolitik. (Text in German; summaries in English) 1952. 10/yr. DM.183 (Europe DM.201.70; elsewhere DM.192.60) (effective 1997). (Institut fuer Landwirtschaftliche Marktforschung Braunschweig) Verlag Alfred Strothe, Mainzer Landstr. 251, 60326 Frankfurt a.M., Germany. TEL 49-69-759501. FAX 49-69-75951260. Ed. H. Buchholz. adv.; bk.rev.; bibl.; charts; mkt.; stat.; index; circ. 1,150. **Indexed:** Anim.Breed.Abstr., Biol.Abstr., Dairy Sci.Abstr., ELLIS, Field Crop Abstr., Food Sci.& Tech.Abstr., IBR, Key to Econ.Sci., Maize Abstr., Pig News & Info., Potato Abstr., Poult.Abstr., PROMT, Rural Recreat.Tour.Abstr., Soils & Fert., Soyabean Abstr., Triticale Abstr., Trop.Oil Seeds Abstr., World Agri.Econ.& Rural Sociol.Abstr. **Document type:** academic/scholarly publication.
—BLDSC (0738.600000); SWETS. CCC.

630   CN   ISSN 0705-3878
AGRI-BOOK MAGAZINE. BEANS IN CANADA. 1974. a. Can.$8 (foreign Can.$16). A I S Communications Ltd., 145 Thames Rd. W., Exeter, ON N0M 1S3, Canada. TEL 519-235-2400. FAX 519-235-0798. Ed. Peter Darbishire. adv.; illus. circ. 21,416. (also avail. in microform from MML; back issues avail.) **Document type:** trade publication.

630   CN   ISSN 0705-3878
AGRI-BOOK MAGAZINE. CORN IN CANADA. 1975. a. Can.$8 (foreign Can.$16). A I S Communications Ltd., 145 Thames Rd. W., Exeter, ON N0M 1S3, Canada. TEL 519-235-2400. FAX 519-235-0798. Ed. Peter Darbishire. adv.; illus. circ. 20,900. (also avail. in microform from MML; back issues avail.) **Document type:** trade publication.

630   CN   ISSN 0705-3878
AGRI-BOOK MAGAZINE. DRAINAGE CONTRACTOR. 1973. a. Can.$8 (foreign Can.$16). A I S Communications Ltd., 145 Thames Rd. W., Exeter, ON N0M 1S3, Canada. TEL 519-235-2400. FAX 519-235-0798. Ed. Peter Darbishire. adv.; illus. circ. 8,400. (back issues avail.) **Document type:** trade publication.
   Description: Covers agricultural land drainage.

630   CN   ISSN 0705-3878
AGRI-BOOK MAGAZINE. POTATOES IN CANADA. 1981. a. Can.$8 (foreign Can.$16). A I S Communications Ltd., 145 Thames Rd. W., Exeter, ON N0M 1S3, Canada. TEL 519-235-2400. FAX 519-235-0798. Ed. Peter Darbishire. adv.; illus. circ. 3,014. (back issues avail.) **Document type:** trade publication.

630   CN   ISSN 0705-3878
AGRI-BOOK MAGAZINE. TOP CROP MANAGER. 1984. 4/yr. Can.$24 (foreign Can.$48). A I S Communications Ltd., 145 Thames Rd. W., Exeter, ON N0M 1S3, Canada. TEL 519-235-2400. FAX 519-235-0798. Ed. Peter Darbishire. adv.; illus. circ. 30,000. (back issues avail.) **Document type:** trade publication.
   Incorporates: Seed in Canada.

630   CN   ISSN 0833-8353
AGRI-COM. (Text in French) 1983. s-m. Can.$15 (effective 1997). Union des Cultivateurs Franco-Ontariens, 2474 rue Champlain, Clarence Creek, ON K0A 1N0, Canada. TEL 613-488-2651. FAX 613-488-2541. Ed. Pierre Glaude. R&P contact: Pierre Glaude. adv. contact: Jean-Claude Clark. circ. 5,300. (tabloid format) **Document type:** newspaper.

630 658   US
AGRI-CULTURE. 1950. m. $22. Box 208, Marengo, IA 52301. TEL 319-642-5506. FAX 319-642-5509. Ed. G. Alan Sieve; Pub. Michael Simmons. R&P contact: G. Alan Sieve. adv. contact: Paul Thompson. circ. 10,000 (paid). **Document type:** newspaper.
   Formerly: Iowa County Farmer.

630   CN   ISSN 1193-8277
HD9014.C2
AGRI-FOOD PERSPECTIVES. French edition: Perspectives Agro-Alimentaire (ISSN 1193-8285) (Supplements avail.: Animal and Animal Products Outlook; Grains & Oilseeds; Horticulture & Special Crops; Milk & Dairy Products) q. Agriculture Canada, Policy Branch, 930 Carling Ave., Ottawa, ON K1A 0C7, Canada. TEL 613-995-5880. FAX 613-996-9564. TELEX 053-3283. charts; illus.; stat. circ. 4,800 (4,000 English ed., 800 French ed.). **Indexed:** Can.B.P.I., CS Ind., Food Sci.& Tech.Abstr., Poult.Abstr., World Agri.Econ.& Rural Sociol.Abstr. **Document type:** government publication.
—CISTI.
   Former titles: Canada. Agriculture Canada. Market Outlook and Analysis Division. Policy Branch. Market Commentary (ISSN 0823-4760) & Canada. Agriculture Canada. Market Commentary; (until 1982): Canada. Agriculture Canada. Marketing and Trade Division. Animal and Animal Products: Outlook.
   Description: Outlook for major Canadian food commodities.

630   CN   ISSN 1192-7704
AGRI-FOOD RESEARCH IN ONTARIO/RECHERCHE AGRO-ALIMENTAIRE EN ONTARIO. 1978. q. free. Ministry of Agriculture, Food & Rural Affairs, Education Research & Laboratories Division, 1 Stone Rd. W., Guelph, ON N1G 4Y2, Canada. TEL 519-826-4191. FAX 519-767-6240. Ed. Robyn Meerveld. illus.; index; cum.index. circ. 8,300. **Indexed:** Agri.Eng.Abstr., Field Crop Abstr., Herb.Abstr., Hort.Abstr., Soils & Fert., Weed Abstr. **Document type:** academic/scholarly publication, government publication.
—BLDSC (0738.874500).
   Former titles (until 1993): Highlights of Agricultural and Food Research in Ontario; Highlights of Agricultural Research in Ontario (ISSN 0706-5213).
   Description: Semi-technical reviews of research projects in agriculture funded by the Ministry.

630   CN
AGRI-FOOD TRADE UPDATE. q. Ministry of Agriculture, Food and Rural Affairs, Policy Analysis Branch, Legislative Bldg., Queen's Park, Toronto, ON M7A 2B2, Canada. TEL 416-326-3229. FAX 416-326-9892. Ed. Laurinda Lang. **Document type:** newsletter.
   Formerly: Ontario Ministry of Agriculture, Food and Rural Affairs. Agricultural Trade Update; Ontario. Ministry of Agriculture and Food. Agricultural Trade Update.

630   SZ
AGRI-HEBDO. w. Case Postale 247, CH-1000 Lausanne 6, Switzerland. TEL 021-6177457. FAX 021-262292. Ed. Janine Rouiler. circ. 20,200.

630   NL   ISSN 1257-0397
AGRI INFOS. 1983. bi-m. CFPF3000. Chambre d'Agriculture New Caledonia, P.O. Box 111, Noumea, New Caledonia. TEL 687-272056. FAX 687-284567. Ed. Roger Pene. adv. contact: Ann Marie Brot. circ. 3,500. **Document type:** bulletin.
   Formerly: Chambre d'Agriculture New Caledonia. Bulletin.

630   SZ
AGRI JOURNAL. (Text in French) w. Route des Arsenaux 22, CH-1700 Fribourg, Switzerland. TEL 037-242812. Ed. Beat Andrey. circ. 6,109.

AGRI MARKETING; the magazine for professionals selling to the farm market. see *AGRICULTURE — Agricultural Economics*

630 378   US   ISSN 0882-9292
AGRI-NATURALIST. 1893. 3/yr. $10. Ohio State University, College of Agriculture, 204 Agriculture Administration Bldg., 2120 Fyffe Rd., Columbus, OH 43210. TEL 614-292-0202. Ed. Robert Agunga. circ. 2,000. **Document type:** government publication.
   Former titles (until 1984): Buckeye Triune (ISSN 0274-9785); (until 1975): Ag Student (ISSN 0090-3388)
   Description: Provides students, faculty, and staff with a source of information about the College's activities.

630   US
AGRI-NEWS (BILLINGS). 1967. w. $25. Western Livestock Reporter, Inc., Box 30755, Billings, MT 59107-0759. TEL 406-259-5406. FAX 406-259-6888. Ed. Chuck Rightmire; Pub. Pat Goggins. adv.: page $1142; 11 x 16. bk.rev. circ. 18,000. (tabloid format) **Document type:** newspaper, trade publication.
   Description: Reports general agriculture news in Montana, Wyoming, and the western Dakotas.

630 658   US   ISSN 0744-5598
AGRI-NEWS (DES MOINES). 1983. 26/yr. $11. Agricultural Statistics, Federal Bldg., Rm. 833, 210 Walnut St., Des Moines, IA 50309. TEL 515-284-4340. FAX 515-284-4342. E-mail: nass-ia@nass.usda.gov; URL: http://www.nass.usda.gov/ia. Ed. Jim Sands. circ. 1,000. **Document type:** newsletter.
   Description: Provides economic information on agriculture in Iowa and nationwide, crop and livestock information for Iowa and the US.

630   US   ISSN 0745-3450
AGRI NEWS (ROCHESTER). 1976. w. $29. Post-Bulletin Company, Box 6118, Rochester, MN 55903-6118. TEL 507-285-7707. Ed. Kelly J. Boldan. R&P contact: Kelly Boldan. adv. circ. 17,698. **Document type:** newspaper.
   Description: Features news and information of importance to farm households and agribusiness in southern and central Minnesota and northern Iowa.

630   FR   ISSN 0002-1199
AGRI-PICK-UP; hebdomadaire d'information agricole. 1963. w. 470 F. 6 rue Henri Barbusse, 91210 Draveil, France. Ed. Jean P. Jamet.

AGRI-PLASTICS REPORT. see *PLASTICS*

630   US   ISSN 0887-2910
AGRI-TIMES NORTHWEST. 1984. s-m. $20 (effective 1997). J - A Publishing Corp., 211 S.E. Court, Box 189, Pendleton, OR 97801-0189. TEL 503-276-7845. FAX 503-276-7964. Ed. Virgil Rupp. adv. contact: Bill Johnson. bk.rev. circ. 3,000. **Document type:** newspaper.
   Description: Contains news of interest to farmers in eastern Washington, eastern Oregon and northern Idaho.

630   SZ
AGRI-WOCHE. w. Rte. de Chantemerle 41, Postfach 918, CH-1700 Freiburg 1, Switzerland. TEL 037-267313. FAX 037-267574. Ed. Beat Andrey.

AGRICULTURE

630 GW ISSN 0938-0337
S7 CODEN: AGRREE
AGRIBIOLOGICAL RESEARCH; Zeitschrift fuer Agrarbiologie - Agrikulturchemie - Oekologie. (Text in German; summaries in English and French) 1953. q. DM.204.50 (foreign DM.211) (effective 1997). V D L U F A Verlag, Bismarckstr. 41A, 64293 Darmstadt, Germany. TEL 49-61-5126485. FAX 49-61-51293370. E-mail: vdlufa@t-online.de. Ed. M. Kirchgessner. adv.; bk.rev.; charts; illus.; index. **Indexed:** ASCA, Biol.Abstr., Chem.Abstr., Crop Physiol.Abstr., Curr.Adv.Ecol.Sci., Curr.Cont., Dairy Sci.Abstr., Excerpt.Med., Field Crop Abstr., Food Sci.& Tech.Abstr., Herb.Abstr., Hort.Abstr., IBR, Ind.Sci.Rev., Ind.Vet., INIS Atomind., Maize Abstr., Nutr.Abstr., Rice Abstr., Sci.Cit.Ind., Seed Abstr., Sel.Water Res.Abstr., Soils & Fert., Triticale Abstr., Vet.Bull. **Document type:** academic/scholarly publication.
—BLDSC (0738.953500); CASDDS; Genuine Article; Linda Hall. **CCC.**
Formerly: Landwirtschaftliche Forschung (ISSN 0023-8147)
 Description: Contains original articles by experts in agricultural research in the fields of cattle, feed, and soil.
 Refereed Serial

630 IT
AGRICOLTORE (MILAN). 1919. 24/yr. Unione Provinciale Agricoltori di Milano, Via Ripamonti 35, 20136 Milan, Italy. TEL 39-2-583-02-096. Ed. Marcello Bosio. adv. circ. 4,500.

630 IT ISSN 0002-1202
AGRICOLTORE (PERUGIA); periodico degli agricoltori umbri. 1944. m. membership. Unione Provinciale degli Agricoltori di Perugia, Via Manzoni, 223, 06087 Ponte S. Giovanni (PG), Italy. TEL 39-75-5990584. FAX 39-75-5990485. Dir. Antonio Margiotta. adv.; bk.rev.; charts; illus.; stat. circ. 2,000. (also avail. in microform)
 Description: Provides information for agriculturalists and farmers.

630 IT ISSN 0515-6912
AGRICOLTORE BRESCIANO. 1953. w. (50/yr.). L.2500. Unione Provinciale Agricoltori di Brescia, Via Creta 50, 25100 Brescia, Italy. TEL 30-222-861. Ed. Lucio Binacchi. adv. circ. 9,000.

630 IT
AGRICOLTORE CUNEENSE. m. Unione Provinciale Agricoltori di Cuneo, 12100 Cuneo, Italy. Ed. Ettore Bandiera.

630 IT
AGRICOLTORE MONREGALESE. m. Corso Statuto 38, 12048 Mondovi, Italy. Ed. Carlo Nan.

630 IT
AGRICOLTORE VERONESE. a. Unione Provinciale Agricoltori di Verona, Via Locatelli 3, 37100 Verona, Italy.

630 IT ISSN 0002-1245
AGRICOLTURA ARETINA. 1945. m. L.800. Unione Provinciale Agricoltori di Arezzo, Corso Italia 205, Arezzo, Italy. TEL 39-575-22280. Dir. Umberto Moretti. adv. circ. 22,280.

630 IT ISSN 0002-127X
CODEN: AGITD8
AGRICOLTURA D'ITALIA. 1954. 11/yr. L.50000 (foreign L.100000) (effective 1994). (Istituto di Studi Nucleari per l'Agricoltura) Gesualdi Editore Roma, Via IV Novembre 152, 00187 Rome, Italy. TEL 06-6784964. FAX 06-6782994. Ed. Gemma Gesualdi. adv.; B&W page L.1100000, color page L.2200000; 125 x 180. charts; illus. circ. 25,000. **Indexed:** Forest.Abstr.
—CASDDS.
 Description: For farmers, breeders, and agricultural technicians. Contains news about atomic energy applied to agriculture and about all agricultural problems.

630 IT
AGRICOLTURA DEL FRIULI-VENEZIA GIULIA. vol.11, 1979. q. membership. Federazione Regionale delle Unioni Agricoltori del Friuli-Venezia Giulia, Via D. Moro 18, 33100 Udine, Italy. Ed. G. Scorzon.

630 IT ISSN 0002-1261
AGRICOLTURA DELLE VENEZIE. 1947. m. L.80000. Consulta per l'Agricoltura e le Foreste delle Venezie, Corso del Popolo 85-e, 30173 Destre (VE), Italy. bk.rev. circ. 1,500. (reprint service avail. from ISI)
 Indexed: Chem.Abstr., Plant Breed.Abstr., Sport Fish.Abstr., Wild.Rev.

630 IT
AGRICOLTURA MANTOVANA. 1946. 48/yr. L.50000. Unione Provinciale degli Agricoltori di Mantova, Piazza Martiri Belfiore 7, 46100 Mantova, Italy. TEL 39-376-369121. Ed. Pietro Guandalini. adv. circ. 4,500.

630 IT ISSN 0394-0438
CODEN: AGIPAR
AGRICOLTURA MEDITERRANEA; international journal of agricultural science. 1871. 4/yr. L.200000 (effective 1996). (Universita degli Studi di Pisa) Pacini Editore s.r.l., Via A. Gherardesca 1, 56121 Ospedaletto (Pisa), Italy. TEL 39-50-982439. FAX 39-50-983906. E-mail: pacini@cibernet.it; URL: http://www.cibernet.it/pacini. Ed. Ranieri Favilli. **Indexed:** Biol.Abstr., Chem.Abstr., Excerp.Med., Ornam.Hort., Soils & Fert.
—BLDSC (0739.811000); CASDDS.
 Formerly (until 1986): Agricoltura Italiana (ISSN 0375-8389)

630 IT ISSN 0002-1288
AGRICOLTURA NOSTRA.* 1951. m. L.1000. Ispettorato Provinciale dell'Agricoltura Pesaro, Via Giusti 5, 61100 Pesaro, Italy. bk.rev. circ. 2,500.

630 IT
AGRICOLTURA NUOVA (ROME). 1959. m. (11/yr.). L.12000. Associazione Nazionale Giovani Agricoltori - National Association of Young Farmers, Corso Vittorio Emanuele 101, Rome, Italy. TEL 39-6-6877072. TELEX 612533. Ed. Elisabetta Tufarelli. adv.; B&W page L.1100000; color page L.1500000. bk.rev. circ. 50,000.

630 IT ISSN 0002-1296
AGRICOLTURA ROMAGNOLA. 1933. q. Ispettorato Provinciale dell'Agricoltura, Forli, 47100 Forli, Italy. Ed. Salvatore Rossi. adv.; bk.rev.; mkt. circ. 5,000.

630 IT
AGRICOLTURA 2000. 12/yr. L.35000. Valentini Editore s.r.l., Via Fabio Filzi 41, 20124 Milan, Italy. TEL 39-2-66804467. FAX 39-2-6887740. Ed. Pietro Paolo Valentini. adv.; B&W page L.1300000, color page L.2400000. circ. 20,000.

631 BE
L'AGRICULTEUR.* (Text in French) 1892. w. 2300 BEF incl. Alliance Agricole. Belgische Boerenbond, Minderbroedersstraat 8, 3000 Louvain, Belgium. TEL 016-242200. FAX 016-242266. Ed. S. Minten. adv.; bk.rev. circ. 2,700.

630 FR ISSN 0293-9428
AGRICULTEUR CHARENTAIS. w. 2 av. de Fetilly, 17074 La Rochelle Cedex 09, France. TEL 46-67-25-22. TELEX AGRICHA 790 750 F. Ed. Claude Belliard. circ. 9,800.

630 FR
AGRICULTEUR D'ANJOU. m. 7 av. Jean-Joxe, B.P. 248, 49002 Angers Cedex 01, France. TEL 41-32-43-43. FAX 41-32-43-70. TELEX 720 823. Ed. Francois Merle. circ. 13,329.

630 FR ISSN 1148-8247
AGRICULTEUR DE L'AISNE. 1951. w. 38 place E. Herriot, 02007 Laon Cedex, France. TEL 33-3-23225050. FAX 33-3-23237541. Ed. J.L. Martin. adv. contact: P. Perbereau. circ. 6,600. **Document type:** newspaper.

630 FR ISSN 0758-5411
AGRICULTEUR DU LOIR ET CHER. 1944. 23/yr. 11 rue Franciale, 41001 Blois Cedex, France. TEL 54-55-89-00. FAX 54-55-88-04. TELEX 750 246. Ed. Marc Delpastre. circ. 8,100.

630 FR ISSN 1144-2484
AGRICULTEUR MODERNE DE HAUTE-NORMANDIE. 1964. m. 12 rue de la Chaine, B.P. 3030, 76041 Rouen, France. TEL 35-88-73-73. FAX 35-70-35-96. TELEX 770 821. Ed. Jacques Grancher. circ. 5,500.

630 FR ISSN 0751-6231
AGRICULTEUR NORMAND. CALVADOS. 1969. w. 490 F. Agriculteur Normand, 19 quai de Juillet, 14000 Caen, France. TEL 31-70-88-00. FAX 31-82-29-63. Ed. Francois Durand. circ. 28,507.

630 FR ISSN 0751-6266
AGRICULTEUR NORMAND. MANCHE. 1969. w. Agriculteur Normand, 19 quai de Juillet, 14000 Caen, France. TEL 31-70-88-00. FAX 31-82-29-63.

630 FR ISSN 0751-624X
AGRICULTEUR NORMAND. ORNE. 1969. w. Agriculteur Normand, 19 quai de Juillet, 14000 Caen, France. TEL 31-70-88-00. FAX 31-82-29-63.

630 FR ISSN 0758-380X
AGRICULTEUR PROVENCAL. w. Maison des Agriculteurs, 22 av. Pontier, 13626 Aix-en-Provence, France. TEL 42-21-23-18. FAX 42-23-14-18. Ed. Alain Poisson. circ. 12,000.

630 IT
AGRICULTEUR VALDOTAIN. m. Piazza Arco d'Augusto, 11100 Aosta, Italy. Ed. Callisto Savoiz.

630 FR ISSN 0339-4433
AGRICULTEURS DE FRANCE. 1867. 8/yr. 400 F. (foreign 391.77 F.) (effective 1997). Societe des Agriculteurs de France, 8 rue d'Athenes, 75009 Paris, France. TEL 33-1-44531541. FAX 33-1-44531525. Ed. Jean-Marie Coutel. adv. circ. 5,000. **Document type:** newsletter.
 Former titles (until 1965): Revue des Agriculteurs de France (ISSN 1155-0937); (until 1962): Agriculture Pratique (ISSN 0365-2688)

630 VE ISSN 0002-1326
AGRICULTOR VENEZOLANO.* vol.34, 1970. bi-m. free. Ministerio de Agricultura y Cria, Centro Simon Bolivar, Torre Norte 16o, Caracas 1010, Venezuela. charts; illus. circ. 15,000.

630 636 SP ISSN 0002-1334
AGRICULTURA; revista agropecuaria. 1929. m. 4500 ptas. Editorial Agricola Espanola, S.A., Caballero de Gracia, 24-3, 28013 Madrid, Spain. TEL 91-5211633. FAX 91-5224872. Ed. Cristobal de la Puerta Castello. adv.; bk.rev.; illus.; stat.; index. circ. 6,300. **Indexed:** Agri.Eng.Abstr., Biodet.Abstr., Biol.Abstr., Chem.Abstr., Dairy Sci.Abstr., Field Crop Abstr., Herb.Abstr., Hort.Abstr., Ind.SST, Nutr.Abstr., Triticale Abstr., Weed Abstr.
—CINDOC. **CCC.**

630 DR ISSN 0365-2750
AGRICULTURA. 1905. m. Secretaria de Estado de Agricultura y Colonizacion, Santo Domingo, Dominican Republic. Ed. Miguel Rodriguez, Jr. —Linda Hall.
 Formerly: Revista de Agricultura (ISSN 0370-3312)

630 MZ
AGRICULTURA. 1982. q. Instituto Nacional de Investigacao Agronomica, Centro de Documentacao e Informacao, C.P. 3658, Maputo 11, Mozambique. TEL 1-460100.

630 US ISSN 0002-1350
AGRICULTURA DE LAS AMERICAS. (Text in Spanish) 1952. bi-m. free to qualified personnel. Keller International Publishing Corporation, 150 Great Neck Rd., Great Neck, NY 11021. TEL 516-829-9210. FAX 516-829-7265. Ed. Victor Prieto. adv. contact: Orlando Llerandi. bk.rev.; charts; illus. circ. 38,144. (also avail. in microfilm from UMI; reprint service avail. from UMI) **Indexed:** Dairy Sci.Abstr., Field Crop Abstr., Helminthol.Abstr., Herb.Abstr. **Document type:** trade publication.
—Linda Hall; UMI. **CCC.**

630 SP ISSN 0213-3385
S253
AGRICULTURA, LA PESCA Y LA ALIMENTACION ESPANOLAS. 1963. a. 2500 ptas. Ministerio de Agricultura, Pesca y Alimentacion, Secretaria General Tecnica, Centro de Publicaciones, Paseo de la Infanta Isabel 1, 28071 Madrid, Spain. TEL 34-1-3475551. FAX 34-1-3475722. Ed. Porfirio Sanchez Rodriguez. R&P contact: Juan Carlos Palacios Lopez. illus.; charts; stat. **Document type:** government publication.
 Former titles (until 1982): Agricultura y la Pesca Espanolas en (Year) (ISSN 0212-1182); (until 1980): Agricultura Espanola (ISSN 0065-440X)

AGRICULTURE

630   PO
AGRICULTURA NOVA. 12/yr. Rua 9 de Abril 132 r-c 1-2o, 4200 Porto, Portugal. TEL 2-814944. FAX 2-817813. TELEX 28388. Ed. Adelaide Maria.

630   RM   ISSN 1220-7578
AGRICULTURA ROMANIEI. 1974. w. Ministerul Agriculturii si Alimentatiei, Calea Serban Voda, nr. 30-32, Sector 4, Bucharest, Rumania. TEL 176020. Ed. Lucian Rosca. circ. 70,000.

630   CL   ISSN 0365-2807
S15   CODEN: AGTCA9
AGRICULTURA TECNICA. (Text in Spanish; summaries in English and Spanish) 1941. q. Esc.4200($35) or exchange basis. Instituto de Investigaciones Agropecuarias, Casilla 439, Correo 3, Santiago, Chile. TEL 56-2-5417223. FAX 56-2-5417667. Ed. Nora Aedo. bk.rev.; bibl.; illus.; index. cum.index: 1965-1980. circ. 1,500. (back issues avail.) **Indexed:** Agrindex, Anim.Breed.Abstr., Bibl.Agri, Biol.Abstr., Chem.Abstr., Dairy Sci.Abstr., Field Crop Abstr., Food Sci.& Tech.Abstr., Herb.Abstr., Ind.Agri.Am.Lat.Caribe, Ind.Vet., Irr.& Drain.Abstr., Rev.Appl.Entomol., Seed Abstr., Sel.Water Res.Abstr., Sugar Ind.Abstr.
—BLDSC (0742.000000); CASDDS; Linda Hall.
Formerly (until 1942): Boletin de Sanidad Vegetal (ISSN 0716-3827)
Description: Presents the results of land and cattle studies from the institute and Chilean universities.

630   MX   ISSN 0568-2517
CODEN: ATMXAQ
AGRICULTURA TECNICA EN MEXICO. (Text in Spanish; summaries in English, Spanish) 1955. s-a. $12. Instituto Nacional de Investigaciones Forestales, Agricolas y Pecuarias, Vocalia Division Agricola, Apdo. Postal 6-882, 06600 Mexico, D.F., Mexico. Ed. Marino Gonzalez Camarillo; Pub. Matilde Marquez Sanchez. index; circ. 1,000 (controlled). (back issues avail.) **Indexed:** Anim.Breed.Abstr., Bibl.Agri., Bio-Contr.News & Info., Biol.Abstr., Chem.Abstr., Dairy Sci.Abstr., Field Crop Abstr., Herb.Abstr., Hort.Abstr., Irr.& Drain.Abstr., Potato Abstr., Rev.Appl.Entomol., Rev.Plant Path, Seed Abstr., Soils & Fert., Sorghum & Millets Abstr., Soyabean Abstr., Trop.Oil Seeds Abstr., Vet.Bull., VITIS, Weed Abstr. **Document type:** academic/scholarly publication.
—CASDDS.

630   SP
AGRICULTURA Y COOPERACION. 1983. m. 2500 ptas. Union de Cooperativas del Campo de Valencia, Plaza del Ayuntamiento, 29, entresuelo., Valencia, Spain. TEL 96-351-35-00. Ed. Leonor Juan.

630 301   SP   ISSN 0211-8394
AGRICULTURA Y SOCIEDAD. (Text in Spanish; summaries in English, French, Spanish) 1976. q. 7200 ptas. to individuals; students 5000 ptas.; foreign 9500 ptas. (effective 1997). Ministerio de Agricultura, Pesca y Alimentacion, Centro de Publicaciones, Paseo de la Infanta Isabel 1, 28071 Madrid, Spain. TEL 34-1-3475551. FAX 34-1-3475722. Ed. Juan Manuel Garcia Bartolome. R&P contact: Juan Carlos Palacios Lopez. adv.; bk.rev. circ. 2,500. **Indexed:** Ind.SST, Irr.& Drain.Abstr., Rural Devel.Abstr., Rural Recreat.Tour.Abstr., World Agri.Econ.& Rural Sociol.Abstr. **Document type:** academic/scholarly publication.
●Also available on CD-ROM.
—BLDSC (0742.410000); CINDOC. **CCC.**
Description: Covers agriculture, fishery, and food science, on theoretical and empirical levels.

630 570 615.9   II   ISSN 0970-1907
CODEN: ABRSEG
AGRICULTURAL AND BIOLOGICAL RESEARCH. (Text in English) 1985. s-a. Rs.150($50) to individuals; institutions Rs.350($80). Young Environmentalist Association, 64 Khurshed Bagh, Lucknow 226 004, India. TEL 91-522-226091. Ed. Anil Mishra. R&P contact: Anil Misnra. adv.: page Rs.2000; adv. contact: Jaya Mishra. circ. 1,000. **Indexed:** Food Sci.& Tech.Abstr. **Document type:** academic/scholarly publication.
—BLDSC (0742.710000).
Description: An international journal on agricultural and biological research including environmental and toxicological studies.
Refereed Serial

630   FI   ISSN 1239-0992
S269.F5   CODEN: ASFIEB
AGRICULTURAL AND FOOD SCIENCE IN FINLAND. (Text in English; summaries in Finnish) 1992. 6/yr. FIM 300 (foreign FIM500) or exchange basis (effective 1996). Agricultural Research Centre of Finland, Editorial Office, FIN-31600 Jokioinen, Finland. FAX 358-3-418-83-39. TELEX 6741-MTTK-SF. E-mail: sari.torkko@mtt.fi; URL: http://www.mtt.fi/mtt/afsf.htm. (Co-sponsor: Scientific Agricultural Society of Finland) Eds. Aarne Kurppa, Sari Torkko. R&P contact: Sari Torkko. charts; illus.; index. circ. 800. **Indexed:** ASCA, Curr.Cont., Food Sci.& Tech.Abstr., Int.Abstr.Biol.Sci. **Document type:** academic/scholarly publication.
—BLDSC (0742.865000); CASDDS; Genuine Article; Linda Hall; UnCover.
Formerly (until vol.5, 1996): Agricultural Science in Finland (ISSN 0789-600X)
Refereed Serial

AGRICULTURAL AND FOREST METEOROLOGY; an international journal. *see* METEOROLOGY

AGRICULTURAL & VETERINARY CHEMICALS. *see* AGRICULTURE — Crop Production And Soil

630   CH   ISSN 0300-550X
S19   CODEN: CHNHAN
AGRICULTURAL ASSOCIATION OF CHINA. JOURNAL/CHUNG HUA NUNG YEH HUI HSUEH PAO. (Text in Chinese; summaries in English) 1918; N.S. 1953. q. membership or exchange basis. Agricultural Association of China - Chung Hua Nung Yeh Hui, 14 Wenchow St., Taipei, Taiwan 106, Republic of China. Ed. Ching-Huei Kao; Pub. Mao-Ying Chiu. adv.; abstr.; cum.index. circ. 3,000. **Indexed:** ASCA, Biol.Abstr., Crop Physiol.Abstr., Curr.Adv.Ecol.Sci., Curr.Cont., Excerp.Med., Field Crop Abstr., Helminthol.Abstr., Herb.Abstr., Hort.Abstr., Lead Abstr., Maize Abstr., Pig News & Info., Plant Breed.Abstr., Plant Grow.Reg.Abstr., Rev.Appl.Entomol., Rev.Plant Path., Seed Abstr., Soils & Fert., Sorghum & Millets Abstr., Triticale Abstr., Trop.Oil Seeds Abstr., Weed Abstr., Zincscan. **Document type:** academic/scholarly publication.
—Linda Hall; UMI.

AGRICULTURAL AVIATION. *see* AERONAUTICS AND SPACE FLIGHT

AGRICULTURAL CHEMICAL NEWSLETTER. *see* CHEMISTRY — Organic Chemistry

630   KE
AGRICULTURAL DEVELOPMENT CORPORATION. ANNUAL REPORT. (Text in English) 1966. a. free. Agricultural Development Corporation, P.O. Box 47101, Development House, Nairobi, Kenya. circ. 500.

630   PK
AGRICULTURAL DEVELOPMENT IN PAKISTAN. (Text in English) 1967. a. $15. Press Corporation of Pakistan, P.O. Box 3138, Karachi 75400, Pakistan. TEL 21-455-3703. FAX 21-7736198. Ed. Saeed Hafeez. circ. 10,000.

630   US   ISSN 0732-4677
S530
THE AGRICULTURAL EDUCATION MAGAZINE. 1929. m. $10 (foreign $20). Agricultural Education Magazine, Inc., 10171 Suzanne Dr., Mechanicsville, VA 23111-4028. TEL 804-746-3538. Ed. Glenn Anderson. R&P contact: Louis Riesenberg. bk.rev.; index. circ. 4,500. (also avail. in microform from UMI; reprint service avail. from UMI) **Indexed:** Bibl.Agri., C.I.J.E., Curr.Cont., Educ.Ind., Farm & Garden Ind.
—BLDSC (0745.880000); KR SourceOne; Linda Hall; UMI; UnCover.
Formerly (until 1980): Agricultural Education (ISSN 0002-144X)

630 378   US   ISSN 1089-9030
AGRICULTURAL EDUCATORS DIRECTORY. 1952. a. $15 to libraries. Charles M. Henry Printing Co., Box 68, Greensburg, PA 15601. TEL 412-834-7600. FAX 412-836-7759. Ed. Sarah Henry. adv. contact: Jim Guilinger. circ. 12,000 (controlled). **Document type:** directory.
Formerly (until 1991): Agriculture Teachers Directory.
Description: Lists teachers of vocational agriculture in secondary and post-secondary schools, teacher educators in colleges and universities, state administrative personnel and U.S. Office of Education staff. Includes feature articles, fund raising projects and products and materials.

630   CE
AGRICULTURAL ENGINEERING. (Text in English) 1977. s-a. Rs.6($4) Agricultural Engineering Society of Sri Lanka, c/o University of Sri Lanka, Department of Agricultural Engineering, Peradeniya, Sri Lanka. **Indexed:** Field Crop Abstr., Sri Lanka Sci.Ind.

630   AT   ISSN 0044-6807
AGRICULTURAL ENGINEERING AUSTRALIA. 1970. s-a. Aus.$40 (foreign Aus.$60). Society for Engineering in Agriculture, Institution of Engineers, 11 National Circuit, Barton, A.C.T. 2600, Australia. TEL 61-6-2706555. FAX 61-6-2731488. TELEX AA62758. Ed. G. Quick. R&P contact: F. Williams. adv. contact: F. Williams. bk.rev. circ. 600. **Indexed:** Agri.Eng.Abstr., Dairy Sci.Abstr., Field Crop Abstr., Int.Abstr.Oper.Res., Seed Abstr., Triticale Abstr. **Document type:** academic/scholarly publication.
—BLDSC (0746.010000).
Refereed Serial

630 620   US   ISSN 0733-1770
AGRICULTURAL ENGINEERING INDEX (YEARS). irreg., latest vol.5. $41.25 to non-members; members $28.50 (effective 1997). American Society of Agricultural Engineers, 2950 Niles Rd., St. Joseph, MI 49085-9659. TEL 616-429-0300. FAX 616-429-3852. E-mail: hq@asae.org; URL: http://asae.org/. **Document type:** abstracting/indexing.
—**CCC.**
Description: Lists over 10,000 books, articles, and technical papers published by selected U.S. and foreign agricultural engineering technical societies during a five-year period.

630 620   TH   ISSN 0858-2114
CODEN: IAEJE5
AGRICULTURAL ENGINEERING JOURNAL. (Text in English) 1992. 4/yr. $20 to individuals (outside Asia $30); institutions $60 (outside Asia $70). Asian Association for Agricultural Engineering, c/o Division of Agricultural and Food Engineering, Asian Institute of Technology, G.P.O. Box 2754, Bangkok 10501, Thailand. TEL 66-2-524-5478. FAX 66-2-524-6200. TELEX 84276 TH. Ed. D. Gee-Clough. circ. 300.
—BLDSC (4535.648600); Ei.
Description: Covers soil and water engineering, farm machinery, farm structures, post-harvest technology, and food processing and emerging technologies.
Refereed Serial

630   II
AGRICULTURAL EXTENSION REVIEW. (Text in English) bi-m. Rs.12. Ministry of Agriculture and Rural Development, Directorate of Extension, Krishi Vistar Bhawan, Dr. K.S. Krishnan Marg, Pusa, New Delhi 110012, India. TEL 603568. adv.: page Rs.2000; 270 x 210. circ. 4,000.

AGRICULTURE

630 US ISSN 0002-1482
S1
AGRICULTURAL HISTORY. 1927. q. $32 to individuals; institutions $75; students $19 (effective July 1997). (Agricultural History Society) University of California Press, Journals Division, 2120 Berkeley Way, No. 5812, Berkeley, CA 94720-5812. TEL 510-643-7154. FAX 510-642-9917. E-mail: journal@ucop.edu; URL: http://library.berkeley.edu:8080/ucalpress/journals. Ed. R. Douglas Hurt. adv.: B&W page $275; adv. contact: Marge Dean. bk.rev.; bibl.; illus.; index; circ. 1,250 (paid). (also avail. in microform from UMI; back issues avail.) **Indexed:** Agri.Eng.Abstr., Amer.Bibl.Slavic & E.Eur.Stud., Amer.Hist.& Life (1954-), Arts & Hum.Cit.Ind., ASCA, Bibl.Agri., Biol.Abstr., Biol.& Agr.Ind., Br.Archaeol.Abstr., Chic.Per.Ind., Curr.Cont., Dairy Sci.Abstr., Environ.Abstr., Geo.Abstr.H.G., Hist.Abstr. (1954-), Hum.Ind., IBR, IDA, Plant Breed.Abstr., Ref.Sour., Soils & Fert., SSCI, Vet.Bull., World Agri.Econ.& Rural Sociol.Abstr. **Document type:** academic/scholarly publication.
●Also available online. Vendor(s): Information Access Co.
—BLDSC (0747.400000); CISTI; Genuine Article; KR SourceOne; Linda Hall; SWETS; UMI; UnCover. **CCC.**
Description: Covers economic, social, historical, political, technological and scientific developments throughout the world and throughout history as they relate to agriculture.
Refereed Serial

630 UK ISSN 0002-1490
AGRICULTURAL HISTORY REVIEW. 1953. s-a. £30 to non-members; members £15 (effective 1998). British Agricultural History Society, c/o University of Exeter, Department of Economic and Social Research, Amory Building, Rennes Dr., Exeter EX4 4RJ, England. TEL 44-1734-263286. FAX 44-1392-263305. E-mail: BAHS@Exeter.ac.uk. Ed. A.D.M. Phillips. R&P contact: E.J.T. Collins. adv.; bk.rev.; bibl.; charts; cum.index vols. 1-35. circ. 850. (also avail. in microform from UMI; back issues avail.; reprint service avail. from UMI) **Indexed:** Amer.Hist.& Life, Arts & Hum.Cit.Ind., ASCA, Br.Archaeol.Abstr., Br.Hum.Ind., Dairy Sci.Abstr., Geo.Abstr., Hist.Abstr., Mid.East: Abstr.& Ind., Soils & Fert., SSCI. **Document type:** academic/scholarly publication.
—BLDSC (0747.500000); Genuine Article; KR SourceOne; SWETS; UMI; UnCover.

AGRICULTURAL INFORMATION RESOURCE CENTERS (YEAR); a world directory. see *LIBRARY AND INFORMATION SCIENCES*

630 AT ISSN 0814-8066
AGRICULTURAL LAND BULLETIN. 1983. irreg. price varies. Department of Agriculture, Locked Bag 21, Orange, N.S.W. 2800, Australia. TEL 61-63-913433. Ed. Ling Sim. circ. 500. **Document type:** bulletin.
Description: Description and methodology of the Department of Agriculture's land classification mapping program.

AGRICULTURAL LAW (NEW YORK). see *LAW*

630 340 US
AGRICULTURAL LAW (SPRINGFIELD). 1992. q. $14 to members; non-menbers $68. Illinois State Bar Association, Illinois Bar Center, Springfield, IL 62701. TEL 217-525-1760. FAX 217-525-0712. Ed. Paul Meints. (looseleaf format; back issues avail.) **Document type:** newsletter.

630 340 US ISSN 1051-2780
KF1681.A15
AGRICULTURAL LAW DIGEST. 1989. 24/yr. $100 (foreign $120). Agricultural Law Press, 2084 W. 29th Ave., Eugene, OR 97405-1762. TEL 541-302-1667. FAX 541-302-1958. E-mail: aglaw@aol.com. Ed. Robert P. Achenbach, Jr. R&P contact: Robert P. Achenbach, Jr. adv.; s-a. index; circ. 250 (paid). (looseleaf format; back issues avail.) **Document type:** newsletter.
Description: Publishes articles on current developments in agricultural law.

630 340 US
AGRICULTURAL LAW NEWSLETTER. q. membership. Missouri Bar, AgLaw Committee, Box 119, Jefferson City, MO 65102. TEL 314-635-4128. FAX 314-635-2811. Ed. Ernest H. Van Hooser. **Document type:** newsletter.

630 338.1 US ISSN 0002-1512
AGRICULTURAL LETTER. 1949. bi-w. free. Federal Reserve Bank of Chicago, Public Information Center, Box 834, Chicago, IL 60690. TEL 312-322-5112. charts; stat.; mkt. circ. 14,300. (looseleaf format; also avail. in microfiche from CIS; reprint service avail. from CIS) **Indexed:** Amer.Stat.Ind. (1982-).

AGRICULTURAL LIBRARIES INFORMATION NOTES. see *LIBRARY AND INFORMATION SCIENCES*

630 658.8 II ISSN 0002-1555
AGRICULTURAL MARKETING; devoted to the problems of agricultural marketing in India. (Text in English, Hindi) 1958. q. Rs.40($14.40) Ministry of Rural Development, Directorate of Marketing and Inspection, New C.G.O. Bldg., N.H.IV, Faridabad 121 001, India. TEL 8212392. (Dist. by: Government of India, Dept. of Publication, Civil Lines, Delhi 110 054, India) Ed. Shri Lallan Rai. adv.; charts; illus.; mkt. circ. 450. **Document type:** government publication.
—BLDSC (0750.390000); UnCover.

630 US ISSN 0002-158X
AGRICULTURAL NEWS (LAFAYETTE). Short title: Ag News. 1917. m. $5 membership. (Cooperative Extension Association of Cayuga, Onondaga, Oswego Counties, Agricultural Division) A G Service Publications, Sentinel Heights Rd., LaFayette, NY 13084. TEL 315-677-7818. FAX 315-677-3924. (Subscr. to: 1050 W. Genesee St., Syracuse, NY 13204) Ed. Robert C. Watson. R&P contact: Keith Severson. TEL 315-963-7286. adv. contact: Robert C. Watson. charts; illus.; stat. circ. 3,000. (back issues avail.) **Indexed:** Soyabean Abstr., Weed Abstr. **Document type:** consumer publication, trade publication.
Incorporates (1915-1970): Cayuga County Farm and Home News (ISSN 0008-865X)
Description: Covers farm management, dairy, field crops, fruits and vegetables, and woodlot, nursery and greenhouse management.

AGRICULTURAL REAL ESTATE VALUES IN ALBERTA. see *REAL ESTATE*

630 CY
AGRICULTURAL REGIONS OF CYPRUS. (Text in English) 1982. irreg. £C2 per no. Ministry of Finance, Department of Statistics and Research, 13 Lord Byron Ave., Nicosia, Cyprus. TEL 357-2-302349. FAX 357-2-456712. **Document type:** government publication.
Description: Offers a comparative analysis of the agro-economic regions of Cyprus with such statistics as the availability of resources, land use, cropping patterns, levels of production and productivity.

470 UK
AGRICULTURAL RESEARCH CENTRES; a world directory of organizations and programmes. triennial. £299. Longman Group UK Ltd., Longman House, Burnt Mill, Harlow, Essex CM20 2JE, England. TEL 44-1279-442601. FAX 44-1279-444501. (Subscr. to: Pearson Professional, P.O. Box 77, Fourth Ave., Harlow, Essex CM19 5BQ, England. TEL 44-1279-623924. FAX 44-1279-639609; Dist. in U.S. and Canada by: Gale Research Inc., 10 Penobscot Bldg., Detroit, MI48277-0748) **Indexed:** Maize Abstr. **Document type:** trade publication.
Formerly: Agricultural Research Index (ISSN 0065-4531)

630 GY ISSN 0065-4523
AGRICULTURAL RESEARCH GUYANA. 1967. a. free. National Agricultural Research Institute, Mon Repos, E.C. Demerara, Guyana. TEL 592-20-2249. FAX 592-20-4481. bk.rev. circ. 150. **Indexed:** Agrindex.

630 CN ISSN 0706-425X
S155
AGRICULTURAL RESEARCH INSTITUTE OF ONTARIO. ANNUAL REPORT. (Text in English, French) 1962. a. free. Ontario Ministry of Agriculture, Food & Rural Affairs, Education, Research and Laboratories Division, 1 Stone Rd. W., 4th Fl. N.W., Guelph, ON N1G 4Y2, Canada. TEL 519-826-4191. FAX 519-826-4211. E-mail: meervel@omafra.gov.on.ca. Ed. Robyn Meerwald. circ. 900. **Indexed:** Hort.Abstr. **Document type:** government publication.
Formerly: Ontario. Agricultural Research Institute. Report (ISSN 0078-4664)
Description: Includes summaries of selected research programs in all areas of agriculture research, listings of projects funded by the Ministry, publications resulting from research completed during the period and reports on research programs and projects approved by the ARIO and funded by the Ministry.

630 600 IS ISSN 0333-578X
AGRICULTURAL RESEARCH ORGANIZATION. SCIENTIFIC ACTIVITIES. (Text in English) 1971. triennial. $25 (effective 1996). Agricultural Research Organization, Institute for Technology and Storage of Agricultural Products, Volcani Center, P.O. Box 6, Bet Dagan 50250, Israel. TEL 972-3-9683111. FAX 972-3-993998. TELEX 381746. Ed. Y. Russo Aro. circ. 2,500. **Document type:** government publication, academic/scholarly publication.

630 IS ISSN 0334-2484
AGRICULTURAL RESEARCH ORGANIZATION. SPECIAL PUBLICATIONS. (Text in English and Hebrew) 1971. every 3 yrs. $25 per no. Agricultural Research Organization, Publications Department, Volcani Center, P.O. Box 6, Bet Dagan 50250, Israel. TEL 972-3-9683216. FAX 972-3-993998. **Indexed:** Biol.Abstr. **Document type:** government publication, academic/scholarly publication.
—BLDSC (8371.830000).

630 RH
AGRICULTURAL RESEARCH TRUST (ZIMBABWE). SUMMER REPORT. Running title: A R T Summer Report. (Supplement to: The Farmer (ISSN 1011-0488)) 1981. a. Modern Farming Publications Trust, P.O. Box 1622, Harare, Zimbabwe. TEL 263-4-753278. FAX 263-4-750754. TELEX 22084 CFU ZW. adv.: B&W page Z.$5294, color page Z.$7054; trim 280 x 216; adv. contact: Michael Rook. **Document type:** trade publication.

630 RH
AGRICULTURAL RESEARCH TRUST (ZIMBABWE). WINTER REPORT. Running title: A R T Winter Report. (Supplement to: The Farmer (ISSN 1011-0488)) 1981. a. Modern Farming Publications Trust, P.O. Box 1622, Harare, Zimbabwe. TEL 263-4-753278. FAX 263-4-750754. TELEX 22084 CFU ZW. adv.: B&W page Z.$5294, color page Z.$7054; trim 280 x 216; adv. contact: Michael Rook. **Document type:** trade publication.

630 II ISSN 0253-1496
AGRICULTURAL REVIEWS. 1980. q. $60 (effective 1997 & 1998). Agricultural Research Communication Centre, 11038 Sadar, Karnal 132 001, Haryana, India. TEL 91-184-255080. Ed. A.N. Asthana. **Indexed:** Anim.Breed.Abstr., Bio-Contr.News & Info., Biol.Abstr., Chem.Abstr., Cott.& Trop.Fibr.Abstr., Dairy Sci.Abstr., Field Crop Abstr., Herb.Abstr., Hort.Abstr., Irr.& Drain.Abstr., Pig News & Info., Soils & Fert., Sorghum & Millets Abstr., Triticale Abstr., Weed Abstr. **Document type:** academic/scholarly publication.
—BLDSC (0754.120000); UnCover.
Description: Review articles reporting original research with a new theory on all aspects of plant and soil sciences, animal husbandry, and veterinary and dairy sciences.

AGRICULTURE

630 636 II ISSN 0253-150X
CODEN: ASDIDY
AGRICULTURAL SCIENCE DIGEST. 1981. q. $60 (effective 1997). Agricultural Research Communication Centre, 1130 Sadar, Karnal 132001, Haryana, India. TEL 91-184-255080. Ed. B.S. Dahiya. **Indexed:** Agroforest.Abstr., Bio-Contr.News & Info., Biol.Abstr., Chem.Abstr., Cott.& Trop.Fibr.Abstr., Field Crop Abstr., Food Sci.& Tech.Abstr., Helminthol.Abstr., Herb.Abstr., Hort.Abstr., Ind.Vet., Maize Abstr., Nutr.Abstr., Plant Breed.Abstr., Potato Abstr., Rice Abstr., Seed Abstr., Soils & Fert., Sorghum & Millets Abstr., Triticale Abstr., Trop.Oil Seeds Abstr., Vet.Bull., Weed Abstr.
—CASDDS; Linda Hall; UMI.
Description: Features original research notes and short communications on plant and soil sciences.

630 NE ISSN 0169-4901
AGRICULTURAL SCIENCE IN THE NETHERLANDS. (Text in English) 1953. triennial, 28th ed., 1994. fl.16 (outside Europe fl.25). International Agricultural Centre, Library, P.O. Box 88, 6700 AB Wageningen, Netherlands. FAX 31-317-418552. TELEX 45888 INTAS NL. circ. 5,000. (tabloid format) **Document type:** directory.

630 NR ISSN 0065-454X
AGRICULTURAL SOCIETY OF NIGERIA. PROCEEDINGS. 1962. a. free. Agricultural Society of Nigeria, c/o Dr. T.I. Ashaye, P.M.B. 5029, Ibadan, Oyo State, Nigeria. Ed. Q.B. Anthonio. adv.; bk.rev. circ. 1,000. **Document type:** proceedings.

630 TR ISSN 0368-1327
AGRICULTURAL SOCIETY OF TRINIDAD & TOBAGO. JOURNAL.* 1894. q. T.T.$14($7) Agricultural Society of Trinidad & Tobago, 44 Pembroke St., Port-of-Spain, Trinidad & Tobago, W.I. Ed. Leo C. Nanton. adv.; index. circ. 2,680. **Indexed:** Anim.Breed.Abstr., Biol.Abstr., Curr.Adv.Ecol.Sci., Curr.Cont., Dairy Sci.Abstr., Field Crop Abstr., Helminthol.Abstr., Herb.Abstr., Hort.Abstr., Plant Breed.Abstr., Rev.Plant Path., Rural Recreat.Tour.Abstr., Soils & Fert., World Agri.Econ.& Rural Sociol.Abstr.
Formerly: Agricultural Society of Trinidad & Tobago. Proceedings (ISSN 0370-2030)

AGRICULTURAL SPRAY ADJUVANTS. see *CHEMISTRY — Organic Chemistry*

631 UK ISSN 0140-4822
AGRICULTURAL SUPPLY INDUSTRY. 1971. w. £155 (foreign £190) (effective 1997). P J B Publications Ltd., 18-20 Hill Rise, Richmond, Surrey TW10 6UA, England. TEL 44-181-948-3262. FAX 44-181-332-8998. E-mail: asi@pubagvet.demon.co.uk; URL: http://www.pjbpubs.co.uk/agrow/aghome.html. Ed. Ray Cox. adv. contact: Richard Allen. bk.rev. circ. 10,000. **Indexed:** PROMT. **Document type:** newsletter.
●Also available online. Vendor(s): Data-Star, Knight-Ridder Information, Inc. (File no.129), Ovid Technologies, Inc. (PHIN).
Description: Aimed at manufacturers and distributors of agrochemicals, fertilizers, animal feeds, health products, seeds and grain.

630 UK ISSN 0308-521X
S3 CODEN: AGSYD5
AGRICULTURAL SYSTEMS. 1976. m. fl.2414($1387) (effective 1998). Elsevier Science Ltd., P.O. Box 800, Kidlington, Oxford OX5 1DX, England. TEL 44-1865-843000. FAX 44-1865-843010. E-mail: nlinfo-f@elsevier.nl; usinfo-f@elsevier.com; forinfo-kyf04035@niftyserve.or.jp; URL: http://www.elsevier.nl/. (Subscr. to: Elsevier Science, Regional Sales Office, P.O. Box 211, 1000 AE Amsterdam, Netherlands. TEL 31-20-4853757. FAX 31-20-4853432; Subscr. in the Americas to: Elsevier Science, Regional Sales Office, Box 945, New York, NY 10159-0945. TEL 212-633-3730. FAX 212-633-3680; Subscr. in Australasia and the Far East to: Elsevier Science (Singapore) Pte Ltd, No.1 Temasek Ave., No.17-01 Millenia Tower, Singapore 039192, Singapore. TEL 65-434-3727. FAX 65-337-2230) Eds. J.B. Dent, J.W. Jones. adv.; bk.rev.; charts; illus.; index. (also avail. in microform from UMI; back issues avail.) **Indexed:** Agri.Eng.Abstr., Agroforest.Abstr., Anim.Breed.Abstr., Apic.Abstr., ASCA, Bibl.Agri., Biol.Abstr., Cott.& Trop.Fibr.Abstr., Curr.Adv.Ecol.Sci., Curr.Cont., Dairy Sci.Abstr., Ecol.Abstr., Environ.Per.Bibl. (1989-), Field Crop Abstr., Forest.Abstr., Geo.Abstr.H.G., Herb.Abstr., Hort.Abstr., IDA, Ind.Sci.Rev., Ind.Vet., Int.Abstr.Oper.Res., Maize Abstr., Nutr.Abstr., Ornam.Hort., Pig News & Info., Potato Abstr., Poult.Abstr., Rice Abstr., Rural Devel.Abstr., Rural Ext.Educ.& Tr.Abstr., Sci.Cit.Ind., Soils & Fert., Soyabean Abstr., Sport Fish.Abstr., SSCI, Triticale Abstr., Vet.Bull., Weed Abstr., Wild.Rev., World Agri.Econ.& Rural Sociol.Abstr. **Document type:** academic/scholarly publication.
—BLDSC (0757.410000); EMDOCS; Genuine Article; SWETS; UnCover. **CCC**
Formerly: Agricultural Administration.
Description: Presents the results of studies concerning the whole or parts of the food chain from production to consumption.
Refereed Serial

630 320.532 KN
AGRICULTURAL WORKING PEOPLE OF KOREA.* no.30, 1973. m. Central Committee of the Union of Agricultural Working People of Korea, Pyongyang, N. Korea. charts; illus.

630 NR ISSN 0331-0965
AGRICULTURE. (Text in English) 1969. bi-m. £6($24) Joe Obateru & Co., P.O. Box 472, Okitipupa, Ondo State, Nigeria. Ed. Tayo Obateru. adv.; bk.rev. circ. 20,000.

630 II ISSN 0002-1725
AGRICULTURE AND AGRO-INDUSTRIES JOURNAL. (Text in English) 1968. m. Rs.30. Chary Publications, 14 Sidh Prasad, Ghatkopar Mahul Rd., Tilak Nagar, Bombay 400089, India. Ed. S.T. Chary. adv.; charts; mkt.; stat. circ. 4,000. **Indexed:** Excerp.Med., Food Sci.& Tech.Abstr.

630 UK
SB4 CODEN: AGINEP
AGRICULTURE & EQUIPMENT INTERNATIONAL; the journal of international crop and animal husbandry. 1949. bi-m. £45($81) (effective 1997). Research Information Ltd., 222 Maylands Ave., Hemel Hempstead, Herts. HP2 7TD, England. TEL 44-1442-213222. FAX 44-1442-259395. E-mail: resinf@globalnet.co.uk. Ed. K.W. Bean. adv.; B&W page £576; adv. contact: Kumar Patel. bk.rev.; charts; illus.; stat. circ. 4,800. (also avail. in microfilm from UMI; microfiche from UMI) **Indexed:** Abstr.Rural Dev.Trop., Agri.Eng.Abstr., Anim.Breed.Abstr., Bio-Contr.News & Info., Biol.& Agr.Ind., Biotech.Abstr., Br.Tech.Ind., Curr.Adv.Ecol.Sci., Field Crop Abstr., Food Sci.& Tech.Abstr., Herb.Abstr., Maize Abstr., Potato Abstr., Seed Abstr., Sport Fish.Abstr., Weed Abstr., Wild.Rev., World Agri.Econ.& Rural Sociol.Abstr. **Document type:** academic/scholarly publication.
—BLDSC (0759.385000); KR SourceOne; Linda Hall; SWETS; UMI; UnCover.
Formed by the 1992 merger of: Farm Equipment International; Agriculture International (ISSN 0269-2457); Which was formed by the merger of: Livestock International (ISSN 0306-8560); World Crops (ISSN 0043-8391)
Description: Publishes technical articles on agriculture and related disciplines for persons working in countries other than their own.

630 635 JA ISSN 0369-5247
CODEN: NOOEAJ
AGRICULTURE AND HORTICULTURE/NOKO TO ENGEI. (Text in Japanese) 1926. m. 17700 Yen. Seibundo Shinkosha Publishing Co. Ltd., 1-13-7 Yayoi-cho, Nakano-ku, Tokyo 164, Japan. Ed. Toshikuni Numaho. circ. 100,000. **Indexed:** Field Crop Abstr., Herb.Abstr., Hort.Abstr., Ornam.Hort., Plant Breed.Abstr., Rice Abstr., Soils & Fert.
—CASDDS.

307.72 NE ISSN 0889-048X
CODEN: AHVAEO
AGRICULTURE AND HUMAN VALUES. (Text in English) 1984. q. fl.370 to institutions; $190 to institutions in U.S. (effective 1998). Kluwer Academic Publishers, Postbus 17, 3300 AA Dordrecht, Netherlands. TEL 31-78-6392392. FAX 31-78-6392254. E-mail: services@wkap.nl; URL: http://www.wkap.nl. (Dist. by: Kluwer Academic Publishers Group, P.O. Box 322, 3300 AH Dordrecht, Netherlands. TEL 31-78-6392392. FAX 31-78-6546474; N. America dist. addr.: Box 358, Accord Sta., Hingham, MA 02018-0358. TEL 617-871-6600. FAX 617-871-6528) **Document type:** academic/scholarly publication.
—BLDSC (0759.530000); UnCover.
Refereed Serial

630 UK
AGRICULTURE AND VETERINARY SCIENCES INTERNATIONAL WHO'S WHO. (2 Vols.) 1979. irreg., 4th ed., 1990. £325. Longman Group UK Ltd., Westgate House, 6th Fl., The High, Harlow, Essex CM20 1YR, England. TEL 44-1279-442601. FAX 44-1279-444501. (Subscr. to: Pearson Professional, P.O. Box 77, Fourth Ave., Harlow, Essex CM19 5BQ, England. TEL 44-1279-623924. FAX 44-1279-639609; Dist. in U.S. and Canada by: Gale Research Inc., 10 Penobscot Bldg., Detroit, MI 48277-0748) **Document type:** directory.
Formerly: Who's Who in World Agriculture.

630 PH ISSN 0115-5067
AGRICULTURE AT LOS BANOS. (Text in English) 1961. irreg. University of the Philippines at Los Banos, Institute of Development Communication, c/o Mr. Apolinario Lantican, Manager, College of Agriculture Publications Program, Laguna 4031, Philippines. FAX 6394-3551. Ed. Maria Theresa S. Velasco. circ. 1,000. (back issues avail.) **Indexed:** Dairy Sci.Abstr., Poult.Abstr., Soyabean Abstr., Sugar Ind.Abstr. **Document type:** academic/scholarly publication.
Former titles: Research at Los Banos (ISSN 0116-4686); Agriculture at Los Banos.
Description: Contains agricultural results of research conducted at UPLB.

630 FR ISSN 0395-7152
AGRICULTURE DE GROUPE. 1953. bi-m. 198 F. (effective 1997). Groupements Agricoles pour l'Exploitation en Commun, Service de Publications, 11 rue de la Baume, 75008 Paris, France. TEL 33-1-53891228. FAX 33-1-45630932. Ed. Bernadette Weber; Pub. Pierre Lenoir. adv.
Formerly (until 1962): Union des Ententes et Communautes Rurales. Bulletin de Liaison (ISSN 0997-4164)
Description: Explores the world of agriculture; its economy, production costs, laws and regulations, choices.

630 FR ISSN 0821-2732
AGRICULTURE DE LA NIEVRE. 1981. w. Maison de l'Agriculture, Place de Chantefois, 58000 Nevers, France. TEL 86-60-30-30. Ed. Philippe Richard. circ. 7,600.

AGRICULTURE DECISIONS. see *LAW*

630 FR
AGRICULTURE DROMOISE. 1952. w. 290 F. 2 bd. Vauban, B.P. 121, 26001 Valence Cedex, France. TEL 75-42-04-00. FAX 75-42-07-88. Ed. Freddy Martin-Rosset. circ. 8,088.

AGRICULTURE

630 614.7 NE ISSN 0167-8809
S601 CODEN: AEENDO
AGRICULTURE, ECOSYSTEMS AND ENVIRONMENT. (Text in English) 1974. 15/yr. fl.2345($1348) (effective 1998). Elsevier Science B.V., P.O. Box 211, 1000 AE Amsterdam, Netherlands. TEL 31-20-4853911. FAX 31-20-4853598. TELEX 18582 ESPA NL. E-mail: nlinfo-f@elsevier.nl; usinfo-f@elsevier.com; forinfo-kyf04035@niftyserve.or.jp; URL: http://www.elsevier.nl:80/inca/publications/store/5/0/3/2/9/8/503298.pub.shtml. (Subscr. in the Americas to: Elsevier Science, Regional Sales Office, Box 945, New York, NY 10159-0945. TEL 212-633-3730. FAX 212-633-3680; Subscr. in Australasia and the Far East to: Elsevier Science (Singapore) Pte Ltd, No.1 Temasek Ave., No.17-01 Millenia Tower, Singapore 039192, Singapore. TEL 65-434-3727. FAX 65-337-2230; Subscr. in Japan to: Elsevier Science Japan, 9-15 Higashi-Azabu 1-chome, Minato-ku, Tokyo 106, Japan. TEL 81-3-5561-5033. FAX 81-3-5561-5047) Eds. T.L.V. Ulbricht, J.W. Sturrock. adv.; bk.rev.; bibl.; illus.; index. (also avail. in microform from UMI) **Indexed:** Acid Pre.Dig., Acid Rain Abstr., Acid Rain Ind., Agri.Eng.Abstr., Agroforest.Abstr., Appl.Ecol.Abstr., ASCA, Bio-Contr.News & Info., Biol.Abstr., Biol.& Agr.Ind., Biotech.Abstr., Chem.Abstr., Cott.& Trop.Fibr.Abstr., Crop Physiol.Abstr., Curr.Adv.Ecol.Sci., Curr.Cont., Dairy Sci.Abstr., Ecol.Abstr., Energy Ind., Energy Info.Abstr., Environ.Abstr., Environ.Per.Bibl. (1981-), Excerp.Med., Fababean Abstr., Field Crop Abstr., Food Sci.& Tech.Abstr., Geo.Abstr.H.G., Geo.Abstr.P.G., Herb.Abstr., IDA, Ind.Sci.Rev., Ind.Vet., Maize Abstr., Nutr.Abstr., Pollut.Abstr., Rev.Appl.Entomol., Rice Abstr., Rural Recreat.Tour.Abstr., Sci.Cit.Ind., Seed Abstr., Sel.Water Res.Abstr., Soils & Fert., Sorghum & Millets Abstr., Soyabean Abstr., Sport Fish.Abstr., SSCI, Triticale Abstr., Vet.Bull., Weed Abstr., Wild.Rev., World Agri.Econ.& Rural Sociol.Abstr., Zoo.Rec. **Document type:** academic/scholarly publication.
—BLDSC (0760.380000); CASDDS; CISTI; Ei; EMDOCS; Genuine Article; KR SourceOne; Linda Hall; SWETS; UnCover. **CCC.**
Incorporates (1979-1985): Protection Ecology (ISSN 0378-4339); **Formerly:** Agriculture and Environment (ISSN 0304-1131)
Description: Concerned with the interaction of methods of agricultural production, agroecosystems and the environment.
Refereed Serial

630 FR ISSN 1249-9951
CODEN: AGDEE7
AGRICULTURE ET DEVELOPPEMENT. (Text in French, summaries in English, French, Spanish) 1994. q. 603 F. (foreign 500 F.) (effective 1996). C I R A D - C A, B.P. 5035, 34032 Montpellier Cedex, France. TEL 67-61-59-18. FAX 67-61-59-21. Ed. Herve Saint Macary. adv. contact: Roselyne Calmel. bk.rev.; illus. circ. 2,000. **Indexed:** Geo.Abstr.H.G., Geo.Abstr.P.G. **Document type:** academic/scholarly publication.
Description: Covers all aspects of agricultural development focusing on annual crops in tropical regions: natural resources management, food and cash crops, cropping systems management.
Refereed Serial

630 FR
AGRICULTURE - HORIZON. 1893. w. 150 F. B.P. 757, 62031 Arras Cedex, France. TEL 21-50-24-74. FAX 21-24-03-93. Ed. Jean Petit. R&P contact: Jean Petit. circ. 44,477.

630 338 NZ ISSN 1172-1995
AGRICULTURE, HORTICULTURE AND FORESTRY; a directory of New Zealand contacts. 1963. a. NZ.$59.95 (Australia NZ.$85; elsewhere NZ.$105) (effective 1996). Harding McPhail, P.O. Box 2091, Palmerston North, New Zealand. TEL 64-6-357-1644. FAX 64-6-357-1648. Eds. Neal Harding, Ron McPhail. adv. circ. 1,300. **Document type:** directory.
Former titles (until 1993): Contacts in Agriculture (ISSN 0110-6902); (until 1978): Handbook of New Zealand Agriculture (ISSN 0438-5101)
Description: Lists agricultural, horticultural and forestry organizations, agencies and services in New Zealand.

630 JA ISSN 0018-3490
AGRICULTURE IN HOKKAIDO/HOKUNO. (Text in Japanese) 1934. m. newsstand price: 800Yen. Hokunokai, 1-1, Nishi 7-chome, Kita 1-jo, Chuo-ku, Sapporo-shi, Hokkaido 060, Japan. index. circ. 1,600.

630 JO
AGRICULTURE IN JORDAN/ZIRA'AT FI EL-URDON. (Text in Arabic) 1965. q. Ministry of Agriculture, P.O. Box 2099, Amman, Jordan.

630 UK ISSN 0268-876X
AGRICULTURE IN SCOTLAND. 1049. a. price varies. Scottish Office, Agriculture and Fisheries Department, Pentland House, 47 Robb's Loan, Edinburgh EH14 1TY, Scotland. (Subscr. to: H.M.S.O., 71 Lothian Rd., Edinburgh EH3 9AZ, Scotland) **Document type:** government publication.

630 AT ISSN 1326-4141
S397
AGRICULTURE WESTERN AUSTRALIA. ANNUAL REPORT. a. free. Agriculture Western Australia, Baron-Hay Court, South Perth, W.A. 6151, Australia. TEL 09-368-3333. R&P contact: G.P. Ayling. **Indexed:** Biol.Abstr. **Document type:** government publication.
Formerly: Western Australia. Department of Agriculture. Annual Report (ISSN 0726-9366)
Description: Covers research, extension and regulatory activities of the department.

630 AT
AGRICULTURE WESTERN AUSTRALIA. BULLETIN. 1905. irreg. price varies. Agriculture Western Ausralia, Baron-Hay Court, South Perth, W.A. 6151, Australia. TEL 61-9-3683333. R&P contact: G.P. Ayling. **Indexed:** Herb.Abstr. **Document type:** government publication, bulletin.
—BLDSC (2814.502000).
Formerly: Western Australia. Department of Agriculture. Bulletin (ISSN 0729-0012)
Description: Covers topics relevant to agriculture.

630 AT ISSN 1325-3379
AGRICULTURE WESTERN AUSTRALIA. TECHNICAL BULLETIN. 1969. irreg. price varies. Agriculture Western Australia, Baron-Hay Court, South Perth, W.A. 6151, Australia. TEL 61-9-3683333. Ed. M. Howes. R&P contact: G.P. Ayling. circ. 475. (back issues avail.) **Indexed:** Aus.Sci.Ind., Field Crop Abstr., Triticale Abstr. **Document type:** bulletin, government publication.
Formerly: Western Australia. Department of Agriculture. Technical Bulletin (ISSN 0083-8675)
Description: Comprehensive report of research conducted by the department.

630 SW ISSN 0044-6831
AGRIFACK. 1944. m. SEK 300 (effective 1997). Box 2062, Stockholm 10372, Sweden. TEL 46-8-613-4900. FAX 46-8-2020811. Ed. Lars-Erik Liljebaeck. adv.; bk.rev. circ. 4,711. **Document type:** newspaper.
Description: Covers agriculture, forestry, food & nutrition, economics and labor conditions.

630 SA ISSN 1021-4895
AGRIFOKUS/AGRIFOCUS. (Text in Afrikaans, English) 1992. q. Transvaalse Landbou-ontwikkelingsinstituut - Transvaal Agricultural Development Institute, Privaatsak X180, Pretoria 0001, South Africa. **Indexed:** Ind.S.A.Per., Ind.S.A.Per.

630 SX
AGRIFORUM. (Text mainly in Afrikaans, occasionally in English) 1990. m. n.$ 4.80 per no. Namibia Agricultural Union, Private Bag 13255, Windhoek 9000, Namibia. Ed. R. Erasmus. adv.; illus.

630 664 639.2
634.9 UN ISSN 0254-8801
Z5073
AGRINDEX; international information system for the agricultural sciences and technology. (Text in English, French, Spanish) 1975. m. $500. Food and Agriculture Organization of the United Nations (Rome), Via delle Terme di Caracalla, 00100 Rome, Italy. TEL 57974350. FAX 57975155. cum.index. (also avail. in magnetic tape; back issues avail.) **Indexed:** Dairy Sci.Abstr., Helminthol.Abstr., Rev.Appl.Entomol., Rural Recreat.Tour.Abstr., World Agri.Econ.& Rural Sociol.Abstr. **Document type:** bibliography.
●Also available online. Vendor(s): DIMDI, Knight-Ridder Information, Inc. (File no.203), European Space Agency (File no.29/AGRIS).
—Linda Hall.
Description: Provides references to current literature, collected from worldwide sources, relevant to research and development in the food and agriculture sectors and allied fields.

659.1 BS
AGRINEWS. 1971. m. Private Bag 003, Gaborone, Botswana. circ. 6,000.
Description: Contains technical information about agriculture and rural development.

630 SP ISSN 0211-030X
AGRISHELL; revista de fitopatologia y agricultura. 1973. 3/yr. free. Shell Espana, S.A., Barquillo, 17, 28004 Madrid, Spain. TEL 91-521-47-41. TELEX 27734 SHELL E. Ed. Alfonso Alvarez Valdes. bk.rev.; illus. circ. 10,000. **Indexed:** Ind.SST.
—**CCC.**

630 BL ISSN 0002-1784
AGRISUL. (Text in Portuguese) 1963. m. free. Instituto de Pesquisas e Experimentacao Agropecuarias do Sul, Divisao de Informacao e Divulgacao Agricolas, Caixa Postal E, Pelotas, Rio Grande do Sul, Brazil. Ed. Mancel Luis Moscareli. charts; illus. circ. 2,500. **Indexed:** Biol.Abstr.

630 US
AGRIVIEW. 24/yr. $10. Department of Agriculture, Food and Markets, 116 State St., Drawer 20, Montpelier, VT 05620-2901. TEL 802-828-2500. FAX 802-828-2361. URL: http://www.cit.state.vt.us/agric/index.htm. Ed. Justin Johnson. circ. 4,000. **Document type:** government publication.
Description: Focuses on Vermont agriculture.

630 CN ISSN 0228-5584
AGRIWEEK. 1967. w. Can.$127. Century Publishing Co., c/o Morris Dorosh, Box 444, 143 Grain Ex Bldg., Winnipeg, Man. R3C 2H6, Canada. TEL 204-943-8861. FAX 204-944-8033.
—CISTI. **CCC.**

630.2 IT
AGRO AMBIENTE. 1951. m. membership. (Federazione Nazionale Dottori in Scienze Agrarie) Iacico s.r.l., Via A. Poliziano 80, 00184 Rome, Italy. TEL 39-6-4873183. FAX 39-6-4873144. Dir. Leone Barozzi. adv.: B&W page L.1800000; adv. contact: Claudio Cutrone. bibl.; illus. circ. 23,000.
Former titles: Dottore in Scienze Agrarie e Forestali (ISSN 0393-5728); (until 1975): Dottore in Scienze Agrarie (ISSN 0012-5687)
Refereed Serial

664 IT
CODEN: AIHTEI
AGRO FOOD INDUSTRY HI-TECH. 1990. 6/yr. L.100000 to individuals; institutions L.130000; foreign $120 (effective 1995 & 1996). Teknoscienze s.r.l., Via Aurelio Saffi 23, 20123 Milan, Italy. TEL 39-2-4818118. FAX 39-2-4818070. Ed. Carla Scesa; Pub. Gianna Lorenzini. adv.; B&W page L1540; adv. contact: Michaela Carmagnola. bk.rev. circ. 7,000. **Indexed:** ASCA, Food Sci.& Tech.Abstr. **Document type:** trade publication.
—CASDDS; Genuine Article; SWETS.
Formerly (until 1991): Agro-Industry Hi-Tech (ISSN 1120-6012)
Description: Presents technical developments in the agro food industry, cosmetic, chemical, pharmaceutical, agrochemicals and nutritional fields.
Refereed Serial

AGRICULTURE

630 338.1   FR   ISSN 1166-7729
AGRO MAGAZINE; revue mensuelle technique and economique en agro-industrie et agro-alimentaire. 1937. 11/yr. 180 F. (effective 1997). Editagro, 64 rue la Boetie, 75008 Paris, France. TEL 33-1-45610406. FAX 33-1-42251770. Ed. J. Billiemaz. adv.; bk.rev.; charts; illus.; tr.lit. circ. 7,500. **Indexed:** Biol.Abstr.
—CCC.
Formerly (until 1992): Agriculture (ISSN 0002-1709)

630   CN   ISSN 0065-4655
AGRO-NOUVELLES. (Text in French) 1965. 11/yr. membership. Order of Agrologists of Quebec, 1259 Berri St., Ste. 710, Montreal, PQ H2L 4C7, Canada. TEL 514-844-3833; 800-361-3833. FAX 514-844-7462. E-mail: agronome@oaq.qc.ca; URL: http://www.iconode.ca/oaso. Ed. Johanne Fournier. R&P contact: Johanne Fournier. adv. contact: Johanne Fournier. bk.rev.; circ. controlled. **Document type:** bulletin.

630   BE   ISSN 0002-1814
AGRO-SERVICE/LANDBOUW SERVICE. (Editions in Dutch and French) 1954. bi-m. 1000 BEF. Nationale Centrale Landbouw-Service, Spastraat 8, 1040 Brussels, Belgium. Ed. M. Speeckaert. adv.; bk.rev.; charts; illus.; stat. circ. 5,000 (Dutch ed. 3,000; French ed. 2,000). **Document type:** government publication.

630   PL   ISSN 1230-1825
AGRO SERWIS. 1992. bi-m. 24 Zl. (in US $10). Biznes - Press Ltd., Ul. Swietokrzyska 20, pok. 302, 00-002 Warsaw, Poland. TEL 48-22-272401. FAX 48-22-272401. adv.: B&W page 1500 Zl.; adv. contact: Teresa Gosiorowska. bk.rev.; index. circ. 25,000. (back issues avail.)
Description: Provides information, summaries, reports, forecast for farmers, agricultural firms, students.

630   MX
AGRO-SINTESIS; agricultura-ganaderia-avicultura. 1969. m. $20. Editorial Ano Dos Mil, S.A., Indianapolis 70, 03810 Mexico, D.F., Mexico. Ed. Juan Francisco Gonzalez Inigo. adv.; bk.rev.; abstr.; illus.; stat.; tr.lit.; index. circ. 13,000. (back issues avail.)

570   CL   ISSN 0304-8802
                               CODEN: AGSUDR
AGRO SUR. (Text and summaries in English and Spanish) 1973. s-a. Esc.4000($40) or exchange basis. Universidad Austral de Chile, Facultad de Ciencias Agrarias, Casilla 567, Valdivia, Chile. TEL 56-63-221660. FAX 56-63-221460. E-mail: fmujica@valdivia.uca.uach.cl. Ed. Fernando Mujica. adv.; bk.rev.; abstr.; charts; illus.; index; circ. 250 (paid); 250 (controlled). **Indexed:** A.I.D.Res.Dev.Abstr., Agri.Ind., Agrindex, Anim.Breed.Abstr., Bibl.Agri., Biol.Abstr., Chem.Abstr., Curr.Adv.Ecol.Sci., Dairy Sci.Abstr., Field Crop Abstr., Food Sci.& Tech.Abstr., Forest.Abstr., Herb.Abstr., Hort.Abstr., IBR, Ind.Agri.Am.Lat.Caribe, Irr.& Drain.Abstr., Microbiol.Abstr., Nutr.Abstr., Plant Breed.Abstr., Potato Abstr., Rev.Appl.Entomol., Rev.Appl.Mycol., Rev.Plant Path., Soils & Fert., VITIS, World Agri.Econ.& Rural Sociol.Abstr. **Document type:** academic/scholarly publication.
—BLDSC (0764.552500); CASDDS.
Description: Includes research papers produced by the faculty and external researchers, both from Chile and neighboring countries.
Refereed Serial

630   AU
AGROBONUS; das Agrarmagazin fuer Management, Produktion und Technik. m. S.698 (foreign S.850). (Oesterreichisches Kuratorium fuer Landtechnik) Oesterreichischer Agrarverlag GmbH, Inkustr. 1-7, A-3400 Klosterneuburg, Austria. TEL 02243-33300. FAX 02243-3330056. Ed. Gabriele Luttenberger. adv.: B&W page S.18500, color page S.31100; trim 184 x 262. **Document type:** trade publication.

630   US   ISSN 0002-1822
S33   CODEN: AGBOBO
AGROBOREALIS. 1969. s-a. free. University of Alaska at Fairbanks, Agricultural and Forestry Experiment Station, Fairbanks, AK 99775. TEL 907-474-7653. E-mail: fynrpub@aurora.alaska.edu; URL: http://www.lter.alaska.edu/salrm/salrm.html. Ed. Jan Hanscom. charts; illus.; stat.; circ. 4,000 (controlled). **Indexed:** Biol.Abstr., Curr.Adv.Ecol.Sci., Curr.Cont., Environ.Abstr., Excerp.Med., Field Crop Abstr., Food Sci.& Tech.Abstr., Forest.Abstr., Forest Prod.Abstr., Herb.Abstr., Hort.Abstr., Ind.Vet., Irr.& Drain.Abstr., Maize Abstr., Nutr.Abstr., Ornam.Hort., Soils & Fert., Sport Fish.Abstr., Triticale Abstr., Vet.Bull., Wild.Rev. **Document type:** academic/scholarly publication.
—BLDSC (0764.555000); Linda Hall; UnCover.
Refereed Serial

630 668.6   XO   ISSN 0002-1830
                               CODEN: AGROB2
AGROCHEMIA/AGRICULTURAL CHEMICALS. (Text in Czech or Slovak; summaries in English) 1961. m. 96 Sk.($29) (Vyzkumny Ustav Agrochemicke Technologie) V U C H T a.s., Novelova 34, 836 03 Bratislava, Slovakia. TEL 33-14-41. FAX 42-7-594-43. (Dist. by: Slovart, nam. Slobody 6, 817 64 Bratislava, Slovakia) (Co-sponsor: Slovchemia) adv.; bk.rev.; charts; illus.; pat. circ. 5,000. (also avail. in microfilm from PMC) **Indexed:** Biol.Abstr., Chem.Abstr., Excerp.Med., Field Crop Abstr., Helminthol.Abstr., Herb.Abstr., Rev.Med.& Vet.Mycol., Soils & Fert., Weed Abstr. **Document type:** trade publication.
—CASDDS; Linda Hall.

630 668.6   PL   ISSN 0002-1849
                               CODEN: AGROD4
AGROCHEMIA; poradnik nawozenia i ochrony roslin. 1961. m. $39. Wydawnictwo Hortpress, Spolka z o.o., Ul. Zielna, paw. 106, 00-108 Warsaw, Poland. TEL 48-22-490938. (Dist. by: Ars Polona-Ruch, Krakowskie Przedmiescie 7, Warsaw, Poland) Ed. Janusz Nuckowski. adv.; bk.rev.; charts; illus.; index, cum.index. circ. 30,000. **Indexed:** Biol.Abstr., Crop Physiol.Abstr., Excerp.Med., Fababean Abstr., Field Crop Abstr., Helminthol.Abstr., Herb.Abstr., Pig News & Info., Potato Abstr., Seed Abstr., Sugar Ind.Abstr.
—CASDDS.
Description: Covers tillage, fertilization and protection of plants in the field.

630 668.6   IT   ISSN 0002-1857
S583   CODEN: AGRCAX
AGROCHIMICA; rivista internazionale di chimica vegetale, pedologia e fertilizzazione del suolo. (Text in English, French, German, Italian, Spanish) 1956. bi-m. L.300000 (effective 1998). (Universita degli Studi di Pisa, Istituto di Chimica Agraria) Gruppo Agrochimica, Via S. Michele degli Scalzi 2, 56124 Pisa, Italy. TEL 39-50-571557. FAX 39-50-598614. (Subscr. to: Industrie Grafiche, V. Lischi & Figli, Via XXIV Maggio 20, 56123 Pisa, Italy.) Ed. Prof. R. Riffaldi. adv.; bk.rev.; bibl.; index. circ. 500. (back issues avail.; reprint service avail. from ISI) **Indexed:** ASCA, Biodet.Abstr., Biol.Abstr., Cadscan, Chem.Abstr., Chem.Cit.Ind., Cott.& Trop.Fibr.Abstr., Crop Physiol.Abstr., Curr.Adv.Ecol.Sci., Curr.Cont., Dairy Sci.Abstr., Excerp.Med., Fababean Abstr., Field Crop Abstr., Forest.Abstr., Helminthol.Abstr., Herb.Abstr., Hort.Abstr., INIS Atomind., Irr.& Drain.Abstr., Lead Abstr., Maize Abstr., Plant Grow.Reg.Abstr., Seed Abstr., Sel.Water Res.Abstr., Soils & Fert., Sorghum & Millets Abstr., Triticale Abstr., Zincscan. **Document type:** academic/scholarly publication.
—BLDSC (0764.600000); CASDDS; EMDOCS; Genuine Article; Linda Hall; SWETS; UMI; UnCover.
Description: Devoted to original research in the field of plant chemistry, soil science and fertilization.
Refereed Serial

630 581   MX   ISSN 1405-3195
S539.M6
AGROCIENCIA. (Text in English, French, Spanish; summaries in English) 1966. q. Mex.$250 (foreign $70) (effective Jan. 1996). Colegio de Postgraduados, Instituto de Estudios, Investigaciones y Servicio Agripefor Chapingo S.C., Cerro del Vigilante 169, Col. Romero de Terrenos, 04310 Mexico DF, Mexico. TEL 915-5-541304. E-mail: agrocien@colpos.colpos.mx. (Subscr. to: Colegio de Postgraduados, Km. 36.5, Carretera Mexico-Texcoco, 56230 Montecillo, Mex., Mexico. TEL 91-595-47011) Ed. Jose D. Molina Galna. adv.; bk.rev.; abstr.; charts; illus.; circ. 1,500 (controlled). (back issues avail.) **Indexed:** Biol.Abstr., Field Crop Abstr., Herb.Abstr., Rural Recreat.Tour.Abstr., Soils & Fert., Triticale Abstr., Weed Abstr., World Agri.Econ.& Rural Sociol.Abstr. **Document type:** academic/scholarly publication.
Formed by the 1996 merger of: Agrociencia. Fitociencia (ISSN 0188-302X) & Agrociencia. Agua, Suelo, Clima (ISSN 0188-3089) & Agrociencia. Ciencia Animal (ISSN 0188-3038) & Agrociencia. Recursos Naturales Renovables (ISSN 0188-3062) & Agrociencia. Socioeconomica (ISSN 0188-3070); Agrociencia. Matematicas Aplicada, Estadisticas y Computacion (ISSN 0188-3054) & Agrociencia. Proteccion Vegetal (ISSN 0188-3046); Which supersedes in part (in 1990): Agrociencia (ISSN 0185-0288).
Description: Presents original papers in plant protection, animal science, crop science, animal and plant breeding, crop physiology, water resources, meteorology and microclimate, crop production, soil science, agricultural development and economics, genetic and natural resources, and forestry.
Refereed Serial

630   DR   ISSN 0376-4974
AGROCONOCIMIENTO. 1976. m. $12. Apdo. 345-2, Santo Domingo, Dominican Republic. Ed. Domingo Marte. adv.; bk.rev. circ. 10,000.
Description: Contains agricultural news and technical information.

630   CK
AGRODIARIO. 1980. m. Calle 15 no. 8-94, Of. 506, Apdo. Aereo 24215, Bogota, Colombia. TEL 281-5528. circ. 10,000.

630 634.9   NE   ISSN 0167-4366
                               CODEN: AGSYE6
AGROFORESTRY SYSTEMS. (Text in English) 1982. m. fl.1488 to institutions; $764 to institutions in U.S. (effective 1998). (International Council for Research in Agroforestry) Kluwer Academic Publishers, Postbus 17, 3300 AA Dordrecht, Netherlands. TEL 31-78-6392392. FAX 31-78-6392254. TELEX 29245 KAPG NL. E-mail: services@wkap.nl; URL: http://www.wkap.nl. (Dist. by: Kluwer Academic Publishers Group, P.O. Box 322, 3300 AH Dordrecht, Netherlands. TEL 31-78-6392392. FAX 31-78-6546474; N. America dist. addr.: Box 358, Accord Sta., Hingham, MA 02018-0358. TEL 617-871-6600. FAX 617-871-6528) Ed. H.J. von Maydell. (also avail. in microform from UMI; back issues avail.; reprint service avail. from SWZ) **Indexed:** Abstr.Rural Dev.Trop., Agroforest.Abstr., ASCA, Biol.& Agr.Ind., Curr.Adv.Ecol.Sci., Curr.Cont., Ecol.Abstr., Environ.Abstr., Environ.Per.Bibl. (1989-) Field Crop Abstr., Forest.Abstr., Forest Prod.Abstr., Geo.Abstr.H.G., Geo.Abstr.P.G., Herb.Abstr., Hort.Abstr., IDA, Int.Lab.Doc., Maize Abstr., Rural Devel.Abstr., Soils & Fert., Sport Fish.Abstr., SSCI, Wild.Rev., World Agri.Econ.& Rural Sociol.Abstr. **Document type:** academic/scholarly publication.
—BLDSC (0764.730000); Ei; EMDOCS; Genuine Article; KR SourceOne; SWETS; UMI; UnCover. **CCC**.
Description: Publishes research concerning agroforestry and other sustainable land management systems which combine agriculture, animal husbandry and trees on the same unit of land.
Refereed Serial

AGRICULTURE

630 KE ISSN 1013-9591
AGROFORESTRY TODAY. French edition: Agroforesterie Aujourd'hui (ISSN 1015-3225) 1979. q. $40 to individuals; institutions $60. International Centre for Research in Agroforestry, P.O. Box 30677, Nairobi, Kenya. TEL 254-2-521450. FAX 254-2-521001. TELEX 22048. Ed. Joan Baxter. R&P contact: Joan Baxter. adv. contact: Joan Baxter. circ. 6,000. **Indexed:** Abstr.Rural Dev.Trop., Agroforest.Abstr., Forest.Abstr., Forest Prod.Abstr. **Document type:** newsletter.
—BLDSC (0764.740000); UnCover.
Former titles (until 1989): I C R A F Newsletter and Agroforestry Review & Agroforestry Review; I C R A F Newsletter (ISSN 0255-8173)
Description: Initiates, stimulates and supports research leading to more sustainable and productive land use in developing countries through integration of trees in land use systems.

630 668.6 HU ISSN 0002-1873
CODEN: AKTLAU
AGROKEMIA ES TALAJTAN/AGROCHEMISTRY AND SOIL RESEARCH. (Text in Hungarian; summaries in several languages) 1952. q. $56 (effective 1998). (Magyar Tudomanyos Akademia, Agrokemiai Kutato Intezet) Akademiai Kiado Rt., P.O. Box 245, H-1519 Budapest, Hungary. TEL 36-1-2043976. FAX 36-1-2043973. Ed. Dr. Istvan Szabolcs. bk.rev.; bibl.; charts; illus.; maps; index, cum.index. circ. 1,500. **Indexed:** Biol.Abstr., Bull.Signal., Chem.Abstr., Curr.Adv.Ecol.Sci., Curr.Cont., Field Crop Abstr., Herb.Abstr., Irr.& Drain.Abstr., Maize Abstr., Plant Breed.Abstr., Soils & Fert., Triticale Abstr., Weed Abstr. **Document type:** academic/scholarly publication.
—CASDDS. **CCC.**

630 668.6 RU ISSN 0002-1881
S583 CODEN: AGKYAU
AGROKHIMIYA. 1964. m. $246 (effective 1998). (Rossiiskaya Akademiya Nauk) Izdatel'stvo Nauka, 90 Profsoyuznaya ul., 117864 Moscow, Russia. (Dist. by: Mezhdunarodnaya Kniga, Moscow, ul. Dimitrova D.39, Russia) (Co-sponsor: Ministerstvo Sel'skogo Khozyaistva) Ed. N.N. Mel'nikov. bk.rev.; index. **Indexed:** Apic.Abstr., Bio-Contr.News & Info., Biol.Abstr., Biotech.Abstr., Chem.Abstr., Cott.& Trop.Fibr.Abstr., Crop Physiol.Abstr., Fababean Abstr., Field Crop Abstr., Food Sci.& Tech.Abstr., Herb.Abstr., Hort.Abstr., Irr.& Drain.Abstr., Maize Abstr., Nutr.Abstr., Ornam.Hort., Plant Grow.Reg.Abstr., Potato Abstr., Rice Abstr., Seed Abstr., Soils & Fert., Sorghum & Millets Abstr., Triticale Abstr., VITIS, Weed Abstr. **Document type:** academic/scholarly publication.
—BLDSC (0005.250000); CASDDS; KNAW; Linda Hall. **CCC.**

630 DK ISSN 0906-0081
AGROLOGISK (ODENSE). 1983. m. DKK 425 (effective 1997). Dansk Agrar Forlag A-S, Tagtaekkervej 8, DK-5230 Odense M, Denmark. TEL 45-66-15-60-87. FAX 45-66-15-60-37. Ed. Knud E. Madsen. adv.; illus. circ. 5,000.
Formerly (until 1990): Agrologisk Tidsskrift Marken (ISSN 0108-8459)

630 CR ISSN 0377-9424
CODEN: AGCODV
AGRONOMIA COSTARRICENSE. Variant title: Revista de Ciencias Agricolas. 1977. s-a. Col.1000($25) Editorial de la Universidad de Costa Rica, Apdo. 75-2060, Ciudad Univ. R. Facio, 2050 San Pedro de Montes de Oca, San Jose, Costa Rica. TEL 506-25-3133. FAX 506-24-9367. TELEX UNICORI 2544. Ed. Floria Berstch H. adv. contact: Cristina Moreno Murillo. charts; illus.; index. **Indexed:** Agroforest.Abstr., Biodet.Abstr., Biol.Abstr., Chem.Abstr., Crop Physiol.Abstr., Curr.Cont., Dairy Sci.Abstr., Field Crop Abstr., Herb.Abstr., Hort.Abstr., Maize Abstr., Plant Grow.Reg.Abstr., Potato Abstr., Rev.Appl.Entomol., Rice Abstr., Soils & Fert., Soyabean Abstr. **Document type:** academic/scholarly publication.
—CASDDS; Linda Hall.

630 580 MZ ISSN 0044-6858
CODEN: AMOCBR
AGRONOMIA MOCAMBICANA. Represents: Instituto de Investigacao Agronomica de Mocambique. Comunicacoes. (Text in Portuguese; summaries in English and Portuguese) 1967. irreg, no.2, 1974. price varies. Instituto Nacional de Investigacao Agronomica, Centro de Documentacao e Informacao, C.P. 3658, Maputo 11, Mozambique. charts; illus.; stat.; index. circ. 400-500. **Indexed:** Biol.Abstr., Chem.Abstr., GeoRef.

630 BL ISSN 0365-2726
AGRONOMICO. 1949. 3/yr. $70. Instituto Agronomico, Servico de Divulgacao Tecnico-Cientifica, Caixa Postal 28, 13001-970 Campinas, Sao Paulo, Brazil. FAX 0192-31-4943. TELEX 019-1059. Ed. Angela M.C. Furlani. bk.rev.; abstr. circ. 2,000. **Indexed:** Bibl.Agri., Biol.Abstr., Chem.Abstr., Field Crop Abstr., Hort.Abstr., Maize Abstr., Ornam.Hort., Plant Breed.Abstr., Seed Abstr., Soyabean Abstr., Triticale Abstr., Trop.Abstr.
—UMI.

630 FI ISSN 0781-8718
AGRONOMILIITTO. YEARBOOK. a. Agronomiliitto - Finnish Association of Academic Agronomists, P. Makasiinkatu 6 A 8, FIN-00130 Helsinki, Finland. TEL 358-0-171-201. FAX 358-0-171-251. Ed. Juha Liuttula. **Document type:** academic/scholarly publication, catalog.

630 CI ISSN 0002-1954
AGRONOMSKI GLASNIK. (Text in Serbocroatian; summaries in English, French or German) 1938. bi-m. $26.70. Savez Poljoprivrednih Inzenjera i Tehnicara Hrvatske, Berislaviceva 6, Zagreb, Croatia. Ed. Ivan Novak. adv.; bk.rev.; abstr.; bibl.; charts; illus. **Indexed:** Biol.Abstr., Chem.Abstr., Dairy Sci.Abstr., Field Crop Abstr., Food Sci.& Tech.Abstr., Helminthol.Abstr., Herb.Abstr., Landwirt.Zentralbl., Nutr.Abstr., Plant Breed.Abstr., Ref.Zh., VITIS.
—BLDSC (0770.600000).

630 US ISSN 0065-4663
CODEN: AGRYAV
AGRONOMY: A SERIES OF MONOGRAPHS. 1949. irreg., no.33, 1992. price varies. American Society of Agronomy, Inc., 677 S. Segoe Rd., Madison, WI 53711. TEL 608-273-8080. FAX 608-273-2021. R&P contact: David M. Kral. adv. contact: Keith R. Schlesinger. **Indexed:** Biol.Abstr., Chem.Abstr. **Document type:** monographic series.
—BLDSC (0770.900000); CASDDS; CISTI.

630 RH
AGRONOMY INSTITUTE. ANNUAL REPORT. a. free. Ministry of Lands, Agriculture and Rural Resettlement, Research and Specialist Services, Information Services, P.O. Box CY594, Causeway, Harare, Zimbabwe. circ. 250. (back issues avail.)

630 US ISSN 0002-1962
S22 CODEN: AGJOAT
AGRONOMY JOURNAL. 1907. bi-m. $117. American Society of Agronomy, Inc., 677 S. Segoe Rd., Madison, WI 53711. TEL 608-273-8080. FAX 608-273-2021. E-mail: journal@agronomy.org; URL: http://www.agronomy.org/journals/aj.html. Ed. Jerry L. Hatfreld. R&P contact: David M. Kral. adv. contact: Gary A. Peterson. charts; illus.; index. circ. 9,200. (also avail. in microfilm from PMC) **Indexed:** Acid Rain Abstr., Acid Rain Ind., Agri.Eng.Abstr., ASCA, Bibl.Agri., Biol.Abstr., Biol.& Agr.Ind., Biotech.Abstr., Cadscan, Chem.Abstr., Cott.& Trop.Fibr.Abstr., Crop Physiol.Abstr., Curr.Adv.Ecol.Sci., Curr.Cont., Dairy Sci.Abstr., Environ.Per.Bibl. (1989-), Excerp.Med., Fababean Abstr., Farm & Garden Ind., Field Crop Abstr., Food Sci.& Tech.Abstr., Geo.Abstr., Herb.Abstr., Hort.Abstr., Ind.Sci.Rev., Ind.Vet., INIS Atomind., Intl.Polym.Sci.& Tech., Irr.& Drain.Abstr., Lead Abstr., Maize Abstr., Meteor.& Geoastrophys.Abstr., Nutr.Abstr., Ornam.Hort., Plant Breed.Abstr., Plant Grow.Reg.Abstr., Potato Abstr., Rev.Appl.Entomol., Rev.Med.& Vet.Mycol., Rev.Plant Path., Rice Abstr., Rural Recreat.Tour.Abstr., Sci.Cit.Ind, Sel.Water Res.Abstr., Soils & Fert., Sorghum & Millets Abstr., Soyabean Abstr., Triticale Abstr., Trop.Oil Seeds Abstr., Vet.Bull., Weed Abstr., World Agri.Econ.& Rural Sociol.Abstr., Zincscan.
—BLDSC (0771.200000); CASDDS; CISTI; Ei; EMDOCS; Genuine Article; KR SourceOne; Linda Hall; SWETS; UnCover. **CCC.**
Formerly: American Society of Agronomy. Journal (ISSN 0095-9650)
Description: Contains papers on all aspects of crop and soil sciences including crop physiology, production, and management along with their relationship to soil fertility and climatic conditions.

630 US ISSN 0568-3106
AGRONOMY NEWS. 1956. 12/yr. $12 to non-members. American Society of Agronomy, Inc., 677 S. Segoe Rd., Madison, WI 53711. TEL 608-273-8080. FAX 608-273-2021. R&P contact: David M. Kral. adv. contact: Keith R. Schlesinger.
—**CCC.**
Description: Contains information about the society members and activities. Includes news of recent developments in agronomy related fields.

630 VE
AGROPECUARIO (VENEZUELA). 24/yr. Venozolana de Prensa, Calle 5, no. 9-27, Calabozo, Estado Guarico, Venezuela. Dir. Gontran Carcia.

630 PL ISSN 1230-7866
AGROPROLOG. 1990. m. Zwiazek Przedsiebiorstw Rolnych, Ul. Wspolna 30, 00-930 Warsaw, Poland. TEL 48-22-628-7889. TELEX 812400. Ed. Bozena Kopka. circ. 40,000.

630 PO ISSN 0002-1970
CODEN: AGLSAH
AGROS; revista tecnico-cientifica. (Text in Portuguese; summaries in English) 1917. 2/yr. Esc.1020. Instituto Superior de Agronomia, Associacao dos Estudantes, Tapada da Ajuda, 1399 Lisbon Codex, Portugal. TEL 351-1-3631171. FAX 351-1-3635031. Ed. Pedro Miguel Martin. adv. contact: Parfirio Trincheiro. abstr.; charts; illus.; maps; stat. circ. 5,000. **Indexed:** Biol.Abstr., Chem.Abstr. **Document type:** academic/scholarly publication.
—CASDDS.

630 CK ISSN 0044-6882
AGROSINTESIS. 1968. m. Apdo. Aereo 24.215, Bogota, Colombia. Ed. Carlos Giraldo. adv. circ. 5,000. (also avail. in microform from UMI)

630 SP
AGROSUR. 12/yr. Alhamar 33, Edif. 11, 1a planta, 18004 Granada, Spain. TEL 58-25-43-00. FAX 58-26-03-13. Ed. R.M. Aguayo Suarez.

AGRICULTURE

630   CU   ISSN 0568-3114
CODEN: AGCUDF
AGROTECNIA DE CUBA. (Abstracts and contents page in English) 1963. q. $32 in S. America; N. America $34; elsewhere $36. Centro de Informacion y Documentacion Agropecuario, Gaveta Postal 4149, Havana 4, Cuba. (Dist. by: Ediciones Cubanas, Obispo No. 527, Apdo. 605, Havana, Cuba) **Indexed:** Agrindex, Bio-Contr.News & Info., Chem.Abstr., Field Crop Abstr., Herb.Abstr., Hort.Abstr., Maize Abstr., Plant Grow.Reg.Abstr., Potato Abstr., Rice Abstr., Seed Abstr., Weed Abstr.
—CASDDS.
   Description: Offers initiatives to the science of agronomy.

630   CI   ISSN 0002-1989
AGROTEHNICAR; Jugoslavenski list za mehanizaciju u poljoprivredi. (Text in Serbocroatian) 1965. m. $23.70. Novinski Izdavacki Zavod za Poljoprivredu, Trg Republike 3-I, 41000 Zagreb, Croatia. Ed. Mile Culjat. adv.; bk.rev. circ. 20,000.

630   CY   ISSN 0002-1997
AGROTIS/COUNTRYMAN. (Text in Greek) 1943. q. free. Press and Information Office, Nicosia, Cyprus. TEL 357-2-446981. FAX 357-2-453730. TELEX 2526 PIONIC. circ. 6,500. **Document type:** government publication.

631.091 301   BL   ISSN 0103-3816
CODEN: AGROE5
AGROTROPICA. (Text in English, French, Portuguese or Spanish; summaries in English) 1971. 3/yr. R.40($60) (effective 1997). Centro de Pesquisas do Cacau - Cacao Research Center, Caixa Postal 7, 45600-000 Itabuna, Bahia, Brazil. TEL 55-73-214-3217. FAX 55-73-2143204. TELEX 0732157 CLRC BR. (Co-sponsor: Comissao Executiva do Plano da Lavoura Cacaueira) Eds. Paulo Dos Santos Terra, Miguel Moreno Ruiz. index, cum.index: 1971-1975. circ. 650. (back issues avail.) **Indexed:** Abstr.Trop.Agri., Agri.Eng.Abstr., Agrindex, Agroforest.Abstr., Bibl.Agri., Biol.Abstr., Chem.Abstr., Excerp.Med., Food Sci.& Tech.Abstr., Hort.Abstr., Ind.Agri.Am.Lat.Caribe, Nutr.Abstr., Protozool.Abstr., Rev.Appl.Entomol., Seed Abstr., Soils & Fert., Trop.Oil Seeds Abstr.
—BLDSC (0771.856000); CASDDS; Linda Hall; UnCover.
   Formerly (until 1989): Revista Theobroma (ISSN 0370-7962)

630 660   UK   ISSN 0268-313X
AGROW; world crop protection news. 1985. 2/m. £365 (foreign £390) (effective 1997). P J B Publications Ltd., 18-20 Hill Rise, Richmond, Surrey TW10 6UA, England. TEL 44-181-948-3262. FAX 44-181-332-8998. E-mail: agrow@pjbagvet.demon.co.uk; URL: http://www.pjbpubs.co.uk/agrow/aghome.html. (Dist. by: Dasprint Ltd., 53 Lyden Grove, London SW14 4LW, England. TEL 44-181-874-4366) Ed. Jackie Bird. adv. contact: Donna Lee. circ. 14,000 (paid). **Document type:** newsletter.
●Also available online. Vendor/s: Data-Star, Knight-Ridder Information, Inc. (File No.129), Ovid Technologies, Inc. (PHIN,PHIC,PHID).
—BLDSC (0771.865000); SWETS. **CCC.**
   Description: Market information, statistics, company news, legislation and product development for the international crop protection industry.

630 334   US   ISSN 0002-2012
AGWAY COOPERATOR. 1964. 5/yr. $6. Agway Inc., Box 4741, Syracuse, NY 13221. TEL 315-479-6117. FAX 315-449-6041. E-mail: szarins@agway.com; URL: http://www.agway.com. Ed. Sue Zarins. adv.: color page $3000; trim 8 3/8 x 10 7/8; adv. contact: Sue Zarins. illus.; circ. 50,000 (controlled). **Document type:** trade publication.
●Also available online.
   Description: Covers farming in the Northeast US.

630   US   ISSN 0884-6162
AGWEEK. 1984. w. $32 (effective 1997). Knight-Ridder Inc., 303 2nd Ave. N., Grand Forks, ND 58203. TEL 701-780-1242. FAX 701-780-1188. Ed. Rona K. Johnson; Pub. Michael Maidenberg. R&P contact: Noel Letexier. adv. contact: Noel LeTexier. bk.rev. circ. 30,000. **Document type:** trade publication.
   Formerly (until 1985): Farm and Home (ISSN 8750-1783)

630   NR   ISSN 0065-471X
AHMADU BELLO UNIVERSITY. INSTITUTE FOR AGRICULTURAL RESEARCH. ANNUAL REPORT. 1962-1968; N.S. 1980. a. $20. Ahmadu Bello University, Institute for Agricultural Research, P.M.B. 1044, Samaru-Zaria, Kaduna State, Nigeria. FAX 234-69-50563. **Indexed:** Field Crop Abstr., Herb.Abstr., Rev.Plant Path. **Document type:** corporate report.
   Description: Overview and research highlights of eight research programs of the Institute for Agricultural Research in Nigeria.

630   FR   ISSN 0002-2136
AIN AGRICOLE. 1944. w. 290 F. Societe d'Editions et de Publicite Agricole du Department de l'Ain (Subsidiary of: Agri-Media), 4 Av du Champ de Foire, 01003 Bourg en Bresse, France. FAX 74-22-47-20. Ed. Alain Silvestre. adv.; bk.rev. circ. 10,000.
—**CCC.**

630   PL   ISSN 0239-9296
AKADEMIA ROLNICZA IM. HUGONA KOLLATAJA W KRAKOWIE. ZESZYTY NAUKOWE. SERIA: HISTORIA ROLNICTWA. (Text in Polish; summaries in English) 1972. a. price varies. Akademia Rolnicza im. Hugona Kollataja w Krakowie, c/o Ligia Hayto, Biblioteka Glowna AR, Al. Mickeiwicza 24-28, 30-059 Krakow, Poland. TEL 48-12-119144. FAX 48-12-336245. TELEX 322469 PL. E-mail: hayto.victoria@uci.agh.edu.pl. Ed. Zdzislaw Piskornik. circ. 120 (paid). **Document type:** academic/scholarly publication.
—BLDSC (9512.150600).
   Former titles (until 1979): Akademia Rolnicza w Krakowie. Zeszyty Naukowe. Historia Rolnictwa (ISSN 0137-1843); (until 1972): Wyzsza Szkola Rolnicza w Krakowie. Zeszyty Naukowe. Historia Rolnictwa (ISSN 0137-2068)
   Description: Covers agricultural history.

630   PL   ISSN 0239-9334
CODEN: ZNARDE
AKADEMIA ROLNICZA IM. HUGONA KOLLATAJA W KRAKOWIE. ZESZYTY NAUKOWE. SERIA: ROLNICTWO. (Text in Polish; summaries in English) 1956. a. price varies. Akademia Rolnicza im. Hugona Kollataja w Krakowie, c/o Ligia Hayto, Biblioteka Glowna AR, Al. Mickiewicza 24-28, 30-059 Krakow, Poland. TEL 48-12-119144. FAX 48-12-336245. TELEX 322469 PL. Ed. Zdzislaw Piskornik. circ. 120 (paid). **Indexed:** AgroLibrex, Chem.Abstr. **Document type:** academic/scholarly publication.
—CASDDS.
   Former titles (until 1978): Akademia Rolnicza w Krakowie. Rolnictwo (ISSN 0137-1886); (until 1972): Wyzsza Szkola Rolnicza w Krakowie. Zeszyty Naukowe. Rolnictwo (ISSN 0485-3709)
   Description: Includes papers on various fields of agriculture.

630   PL   ISSN 0137-1754
S13
AKADEMIA ROLNICZA, POZNAN. ROCZNIKI. ROLNICTWO. (Text in Polish; summaries in English) 1966. irreg. price varies. Wydawnictwo Akademii Rolniczej w Poznaniu, Ul. Witosa 45, 60-667 Poznan, Poland. TEL 48-61-487809. FAX 48-61-487802. E-mail: wgolab@owl.au.poznan.pl; URL: http://swan.au.poznan.pl/bib/bghome.html. R&P contact: Elzbieta Zagorska. TEL 48-61-487806. **Indexed:** AgroLibrex, Bibl.Agri. **Document type:** academic/scholarly publication.
   Description: Works on field and plants cultivation, genetics and breeding of plants, pedology, agro-chemistry, agro-microbiology and mechanization farming.

630   PL   ISSN 0208-8436
CODEN: RRPNDH
AKADEMIA ROLNICZA, POZNAN. ROCZNIKI. ROZPRAWY NAUKOWE. (Text in Polish; summaries in English) 1959. irreg. price varies. Wydawnictwo Akademii Rolniczej w Poznaniu, Ul. Witosa 45, 60-667 Poznan, Poland. TEL 48-61-487809. FAX 48-61-487802. E-mail: wgolab@owl.au.poznan.pl; URL: http://swan.au.poznan.pl/bib/bghome.html. R&P contact: Elzbieta Zagorska. TEL 48-61-487806. **Indexed:** AgroLibrex, Bibl.Agri., Weed Abstr. **Document type:** academic/scholarly publication, monographic series.
—BLDSC (8005.872000); CASDDS.
   Description: Covers biology, zoology, agriculture, food technology, wood technology, animal husbandry, animal breeding, horticulture, forestry, soil science, and agricultural technics.

630   PL   ISSN 0137-2149
Z5055.P6
AKADEMIA ROLNICZA W SZCZECINIE. INFORMATORY. (Text in English or Polish) 1968. irreg. price varies. Akademia Rolnicza w Szczecinie, Dzial Wydawnictw, Ul. Doktora Judyma 22, 71-460 Szczecin, Poland. TEL 48-91-541639. FAX 48-91-541642. TELEX 0425494. Ed. Antoni Furowicz. bk.rev. **Indexed:** Chem.Abstr., Field Crop Abstr., Nutr.Abstr., Potato Abstr. **Document type:** academic/scholarly publication.
Refereed Serial

630   PL   ISSN 0239-6467
CODEN: RZARB8
AKADEMIA ROLNICZA W SZCZECINIE. ROZPRAWY. (Text in Polish; abstract in English) 1966. irreg. price varies. Akademia Rolnicza w Szczecinie, Dzial Wydawnictw, Ul. Doktora Judyma 22, 71-460 Szczecin, Poland. TEL 48-91-54169. FAX 48-91-541642. TELEX 0425494. Ed. Antoni Furowicz. bk.rev. **Indexed:** AgroLibrex, Chem.Abstr., Field Crop Abstr., Nutr.Abstr. **Document type:** academic/scholarly publication.
—BLDSC (8035.205000); CASDDS.
Refereed Serial

630   PL   ISSN 0867-7964
AKADEMIA ROLNICZA WE WROCLAWIU. ZESZYTY NAUKOWE. (Includes the following subseries: Bibliografie (1427-5805); Geodezja i Urzadzenia Rolne (ISSN 0209-0511); Inzynieria Srodowiska (ISSN 1230-4484); Konferencje (1232-3071); Mechanizacja Rolnictwa (ISSN 0867-3756); Melioracja (ISSN 0137-1967); Monografie (ISSN 0867-2393); Nauki Humanistycne (ISSN 1234-8333); Rolnictwo (ISSN 0137-1959); Rozprawa Habilitacyjna (ISSN 0867-1427); Technologia Zywnosci (ISSN 0209-0503); Weterynaria (ISSN 0137-1975); Zootechnika (ISSN 0137-2017)) irreg. Akademia Rolnicza we Wroclawiu, Ul. Norwida 25, 50-375 Wroclaw, Poland. FAX 48-71-2295762295. (Subscr. to: Wydawnictwo Akademii Rolniczej, ul. Sopocka 23, 50-344 Wroclaw, Poland. TEL 48-71-211277) **Document type:** academic/scholarly publication.
—BLDSC (9512.152000).
   Formerly (until 1972): Wyzsza Szkola Rolnicza. Zeszyty Naukowe (ISSN 0867-065X)

630   PL   ISSN 1232-3071
AKADEMIA ROLNICZA WE WROCLAWIU. ZESZYTY NAUKOWE. KONFERENCJE. (Subseries of: Akademia Rolnicza we Wroclawiu. Zeszyty Naukowe (ISSN 0867-7964)) 1994. irreg. price varies. Akademia Rolnicza we Wroclawiu, Ul. Norwida 25, 50-375 Wroclaw, Poland. FAX 48-71-229576. (Subscr. to: Wydawnictwo Akademii Rolniczej, ul. Sopocka 23, 50-344 Wroclaw, Poland. TEL 48-71-211277) **Indexed:** AgroLibrex.

630   PL   ISSN 0867-2393
AKADEMIA ROLNICZA WE WROCLAWIU. ZESZYTY NAUKOWE. MONOGRAFIE. (Subseries of: Akademia Rolnicza we Wroclawiu. Zeszyty Naukowe (ISSN 0867-7964)) (Text in Polish; summaries in English) 1990. irreg. price varies. Akademia Rolnicza we Wroclawiu, Ul. Norwida 25, 50-375 Wroclaw, Poland. FAX 48-71-229576. (Subscr. to: Wydawnictwo Akademii Rolniczej, ul. Sopocka 23, 50-344 Wroclaw, Poland. TEL 48-71-211277) circ. 300. **Indexed:** AgroLibrex. **Document type:** monographic series.

630   PL   ISSN 0137-1959
CODEN: ZNARBC
AKADEMIA ROLNICZA WE WROCLAWIU. ZESZYTY NAUKOWE. ROLNICTWO. (Subseries of: Akademia Rolnicza we Wroclawiu. Zeszyty Naukowe (ISSN 0867-7964)) (Text in Polish; summaries in English) 1955. irreg. price varies. Akademia Rolnicza we Wroclawiu, Ul. Norwida 25, 50-375 Wroclaw, Poland. FAX 48-71-229576. (Subscr. to: Wydawnictwo Akademii Rolniczej, ul. Sopocka 23, 50-344 Wroclaw, Poland. TEL 48-71-211277) circ. 350. **Indexed:** Agri.Eng.Abstr., AgroLibrex, Dairy Sci.Abstr., Field Crop Abstr., Rural Ext.Educ.& Tr.Abstr. **Document type:** academic/scholarly publication.
—CASDDS.
   Formerly (until 1973): Wyzsza Szkola Rolnicza we Wroclawiu. Zeszyty Naukowe. Rolnictwo (ISSN 0520-9307)

AGRICULTURE

630   **PL**
AKADEMIA ROLNICZA WE WROCLAWIU. ZESZYTY NAUKOWE. ROZPRAWY. (Subseries of: Akademia Ronicza we Wroclawiu. Zeszyty Naukowe (ISSN 0867-7964)) 1977. irreg. price varies. Akademia Rolnicza we Wroclawiu, Ul. Norwida 25, 50-375 Wroclaw, Poland. FAX 48-71-229576. (Subscr. to: Wydawnictwo Akademii Rolniczej, ul. Sopocka 23, 50-344 Wroclaw, Poland. TEL 48-71-211277) circ. 300. Indexed: AgroLibrex. **Document type:** academic/scholarly publication.
    Former titles (until 1994): Akademia Rolnicza we Wroclawiu. Zeszyty Naukowe. Rozprawa Habilitacyjna (ISSN 0867-1427); (until 1990): Akademia Rolnicza we Wroclawiu. Rozprawy (ISSN 0209-1321)

630   **BW**
    CODEN: VBYSA6
AKADEMIYA AGRARNYKH NAVUK BELARUSI. VESTSI. (Text in Byelorussian; summaries in English) 1963. q. $59 (effective 1998). Vydavetstvo Navuka i Tekhnika, Zhodzinskaya, 18, 220067 Minsk, Belarus. TEL 39-55-17. FAX 252494. (Dist. by: Mezhdunarodnaya Kniga, B. Yakimanka 39, 117049 Moscow, Russia. TEL 7-095-2384967. FAX 7-095-2384634) Ed. I.N. Nikitchenko. bibl.; charts; illus.; index. circ. 340. Indexed: Anim.Breed.Abstr., Biol.Abstr., Field Crop Abstr., Herb.Abstr., Ind.Vet., Nutr.Abstr., Pig News & Info., Rev.Plant Path., Triticale Abstr., Vet.Bull. **Document type:** academic/scholarly publication.
—CASDDS. **CCC.**
    Formerly (until 1992): Akademiya Navuk Belarusskai S.S.R. Vestsi. Seriya Sel'skogaspadarchykh Navuk (ISSN 0321-1657)

630 581   **JA**
AKITA PREFECTURAL COLLEGE OF AGRICULTURE. BULLETIN. (Text and summaries in English and Japanese) 1975. a. Akita Prefectural College of Agriculture, 2-2 Ohgata-Mura, Akita Pref., 010-04, Japan. circ. 550. (back issues avail.) Indexed: Biol.Abstr., Excerp.Med., Field Crop Abstr., Herb.Abstr., Ind.Vet., Nutr.Abstr., Plant Breed.Abstr., Soils & Fert., Vet.Bull.

630   **NE**   ISSN 0169-0116
AKKERBOUW (DOETINCHEM). (Supplement to: Boerderij (ISSN 0006-5617)) 1971. bi-m. fl.217.50 includes Boerderij. Misset (Subsidiary of: Reed Elsevier plc), Postbus 4, 7000 BA Doetinchem, Netherlands. TEL 31-314-349371. FAX 31-314-363638. Ed. Henk E.P. Dokter. adv.; B&W page fl.3520, color page fl.5600; trim 230 x 290; adv. contact: Cor van Nek. bk.rev.; charts; illus.; tr.lit.; index. circ. 16,100. **Document type:** trade publication.
    Description: For the large arable farming specialist; information about cultural, technical, financial and mechanization aspects.

630 634.9 635   **US**   ISSN 1072-074X
ALABAMA AGRICULTURAL EXPERIMENT STATION. RESEARCH REPORT SERIES. 1983. irreg., no.7, 1991. Alabama Agricultural Experiment Station, 2 Comer Hall, Auburn University, AL 36849. TEL 334-844-4877. FAX 334-844-5892. Ed. J.R. Roberson. R&P contact: J.R. Roberson. circ. 4,000. Indexed: Bio-Contr.News & Info., Forest.Abstr., Hort.Abstr., Ornam.Hort., Potato Abstr., Weed Abstr., World Agri.Econ.& Rural Sociol.Abstr.
—Linda Hall.

630   **US**
ALABAMA FARMER. 1985. m. $12 (foreign $24). Rural Press U S A, 7701 Six Forks Rd., Ste. 120, Raleigh, NC 27615. TEL 919-676-3276; 800-477-1737. FAX 919-676-9803. (Subscr. to: Box 150001, Raleigh, NC 27624) Ed. Pam Golden. adv.; B&W page $1218. circ. 12,000. **Document type:** newspaper.
    Description: Contains national and local news about dairy products, cattle, cotton, row crops, poultry, and swine.

630   **CN**   ISSN 0702-3030
ALBERTA AGRICULTURE. ANNUAL REPORT. 1905. a. free. Department of Agriculture, Publishing Branch, 7000 113th St., Edmonton, AB T6H 5T6, Canada. TEL 403-427-2121. FAX 403-427-2861. circ. controlled.
    Former titles (until 1972): Alberta. Department of Agriculture. Annual Report (ISSN 0702-3022); (until 1969): Alberta. Water Resources Division. Annual Report (ISSN 0065-597X)

630   **CN**
ALBERTA AGROLOGIST. 1947. 5/yr. Can.$30 (effective 1997 & 1998). Alberta Institute of Agrologists, 8506 - 104 St., Edmonton, AB T6E 4G4, Canada. TEL 403-432-0663. FAX 403-439-8414. E-mail: p.ag@aia.ab.ca; URL: http://www.aia.ab.ca. Ed. Ken Davies. adv.; bk.rev.; circ. 1,300 (controlled). **Document type:** newsletter.
    Formerly: A I A Newsletter.
    Description: For professionals in the agriculture and food industry in Alberta.

630 658   **CN**   ISSN 0845-5007
ALBERTA FARM AND RANCH MAGAZINE. 1983. m. Can.$24. North Hill Publications Ltd., 4000 - 19th St., N.E., Calgary, AB T2E 6P8, Canada. TEL 403-250-6633. FAX 403-291-0502. Ed. Mike Steele. adv.; bk.rev. circ. 70,000. (back issues avail.)
    Former titles: Alberta Farmagazine (ISSN 0823-6720); Alberta Farm and Ranch Magazine.

630 658   **LU**
ALCOVIT. (Text in German) 1959. m. 800 F. Moulins de Kleinbettingen, 7 rue Laduno, L-9147 Erpeldange-Ettelbruck, Luxembourg. TEL 352-810344. FAX 352-817863. Ed. Rudy Peters. adv. circ. 10,500.
    Formerly: Conseiller Alcovit-Protector.
    Description: Covers farm management.

630   **IS**
ALEI ESEV. (Text in Hebrew) 1979. q. membership only. Weed Science Society of Israel, Department of Ornamental Horticulture, Volcani Centre, P.O. Box 6, Bet Dagan 50250, Israel. TEL 972-3-9683500. FAX 972-3-9660589. Ed. Menashe Horowitz. bk.rev. **Document type:** newsletter.

630   **PE**   ISSN 1021-1810
ALERTA AGRARIO. 1987. m. Centro Peruano de Estudios Sociales, Avda. Salaverry 818, Lima 11, Peru. TEL 51-14-336610. FAX 51-14-331744. E-mail: alerta@cepes.org.pe. Ed. Bertha Consiglieri. circ. 100,000. **Document type:** bulletin.
    Description: Reviews rural problems.

630   **UA**   ISSN 0044-7250
S19   CODEN: AAGRAF
ALEXANDRIA JOURNAL OF AGRICULTURAL RESEARCH. (Text in English; summaries in Arabic, English) 1953. 3/yr. £E39 (overseas $75) (effective 1993). University of Alexandria, Faculty of Agriculture, Alexandria, Egypt. FAX 20-3-5972780. Ed. Fawzi Abdel-Kadir. adv.; abstr.; bibl.; charts; illus.; stat. circ. 1,000. (back issues avail.) Indexed: Agroforest.Abstr., Anim.Breed.Abstr., Bio-Contr.News & Info., Biodet.Abstr., Biol.Abstr., Chem.Abstr., Cott.& Trop.Fibr.Abstr., Crop Physiol.Abstr., Dairy Sci.Abstr., Fababean Abstr., Field Crop Abstr., Food Sci.& Tech.Abstr., Forest Prod.Abstr., Herb.Abstr., Hort.Abstr., Irr.& Drain.Abstr., Maize Abstr., Nutr.Abstr., Ornam.Hort., Plant Breed.Abstr., Plant Grow.Reg.Abstr., Rev.Appl.Entomol., Rev.Plant Path., Rice Abstr., Rural Ext.Educ.& Tr.Abstr., Seed Abstr., Sugar Ind.Abstr., Triticale Abstr., Weed Abstr., Zoo.Rec. **Document type:** academic/scholarly publication.
—BLDSC (0786.940000); CASDDS; Ei.
    Description: Publishes papers in agricultural science and related subjects, including agricultural engineering, food science, floriculture and horticulture, plant pathology, forestry and wood technology, soil and water science.
    Refereed Serial

630   **US**   ISSN 1065-7673
ALFA NEWS. 1946. q. $1. Alabama Farmers Federation, 2108 E. South Blvd., Box 11000, Montgomery, AL 36191-0001. TEL 334-288-3900. FAX 334-284-3957. Ed. Mark Morrison. adv.; tr.lit. circ. 275,000. (back issues avail) **Document type:** trade publication.
    Formerly: Alabama Farm Bureau News.

ALIMARKET; informe confidencial de alimentacion y bebidas. see *FOOD AND FOOD INDUSTRIES*

ALIMARKET INFORME ANUAL. see *FOOD AND FOOD INDUSTRIES*

ALIMARKET REVISTA. see *FOOD AND FOOD INDUSTRIES*

630   **FI**
ALIMENTA. 1907. 9/yr. FIM 100 in Europe; elsewhere FIM 200. Agronomiliitto - Finnish Association of Academic Agronomists, P. Makasiinkatu 6 A 8, FIN-00130 Helsinki, Finland. TEL 358-0-171-201. FAX 358-0-171-251. Ed. Juha Liuttula. adv.: B&W page FIM 3700, color page FIM 8900; trim 185 x 270. bk.rev.; illus.; stat. circ. 4,800. Indexed: Biol.Abstr. **Document type:** academic/scholarly publication.
    Formerly (until 1996): Maatalous (ISSN 0024-8827)

630 976   **US**
ALL AROUND KENTUCKY. 1937. bi-m. $0.50 (effective 1997). Kentucky Farm Bureau Federation, Box 20700, Louisville, KY 40220. TEL 502-495-5112. FAX 502-495-5114. Ed. Gary Huddleston. adv.; B&W page $2690, color page $3290; adv. contact: Sara Plummer. illus.; circ. 376,000 (paid). (tabloid format) **Document type:** newsletter.
    Formerly (until 1995): Kentucky Farm Bureau News (ISSN 0023-0200)
    Description: Newsletter on issues affecting the farming and agricultural population of the state, with editorial column on commodities and market analysis. Also articles on travel, outdoor activities and sports in Kentucky.

630   **HU**
ALLAMI GAZDASAG/STATE FARMING. 1946. m. $26. General Direction of State Farming, Akademia u. 1-3, 1054 Budapest, Hungary. TEL 112-4617. FAX 111-4877. Ed. Mrs. P. Gorgenyi.

630   **AU**
ALLGEMEINE BAUERN ZEITUNG. q. 8.-Mai-Str. 47-11, A-9020 Klagenfurt, Austria. TEL 0463-511710. FAX 0463-502018. Ed. Horst Reichmann. circ. 32,000.

638.1   **GW**   ISSN 0002-5828
    CODEN: ADIMBW
ALLGEMEINE DEUTSCHE IMKERZEITUNG. 1967. m. DM.43 (foreign DM.45). Greiter Verlag, Untere Walkestr. 19, 78333 Stockach, Germany. TEL 07771-4055. FAX 07771-5228. adv.; charts; illus. Indexed: Apic.Abstr., Chem.Abstr., Excerp.Med. **Document type:** bulletin.
—CASDDS.
    Description: Discusses bee culture.

631   **BE**
ALLIANCE AGRICOLE.* (Text in French) w. 750 BEF includes Agriculteur. Belgische Boerenbond, Minderbroedersstraat 8, 3000 Louvain, Belgium. TEL 016-242246. FAX 016-242266. (Subscr. to: 25 rue de la Science, 1040 Brussels, Belgium) adv.; illus. circ. 19,804.

630   **AU**
ALM UND BERGBAUER. 1948. m. S.120 (foreign S.180). Oesterreichische Arbeitsgemeinschaft fuer Alm und Weide, Gilmstr. 2 - Stoecklgebaeude, A-6020 Innsbruck, Austria. TEL 43-1-512-5083908. FAX 43-1-512-5083905. Ed. Dieter Putz. adv.: page S.9000; trim 125 x 205. bk.rev. circ. 5,000. Indexed: Rural Recreat.Tour.Abstr., World Agri.Econ.& Rural Sociol.Abstr. **Document type:** bulletin.
    Formerly: Alm und Weide (ISSN 0044-7374)

ALMANAC FOR FARMERS AND CITY FOLK. see *ENCYCLOPEDIAS AND GENERAL ALMANACS*

630   **GW**   ISSN 0002-6298
DER ALMBAUER; Mitteilungen fuer Alm-, Berg- und Gruenlandbauern und ueber Forstrechte. 1948. m. DM.40 (foreign DM.45) (effective 1997). (Almwirtschaftlicher Verein Oberbayern) B L V Verlagsgesellschaft mbH, Lothstr. 29, 80797 Munich, Germany. TEL 49-89-12705-0. FAX 49-89-12705354. Ed. H. Silbernagel. adv. contact: Henning Stemmler. bk.rev.; illus. **Document type:** trade publication.
—CCC.

638.1   **AU**   ISSN 0002-6352
ALPENLAENDISCHE BIENENZEITUNG. 1912. 11/yr. S.188. Leopold Stocker Verlag, Hofgasse 5, A-8011 Graz, Austria. TEL 43-316-821636. FAX 43-316-835612. Ed. Josef Gstrein. adv. contact: Thomas Muehlbacher. bk.rev.; index. circ. 6,000. Indexed: Apic.Abstr. **Document type:** trade publication.

AGRICULTURE

630 US ISSN 8755-4941
CODEN: AAGNE7
ALTERNATIVE AGRICULTURE NEWS. 1983. m. $16 to individuals (Canada & Mexico $21; elsewhere $22) (effective 1998). Henry A. Wallace Institute for Alternative Agriculture, Inc., 9200 Edmonston Rd., Ste. 117, Greenbelt, MD 20770-1551. TEL 301-441-8777. FAX 301-220-0164. E-mail: hawiaa@access.digex.net; URL: http://www.hawiaa.org. Pub. Henry A. Wallace. circ. 1,200. (back issues avail.) **Document type:** newsletter.

630 II ISSN 0970-4671
ALTERNATIVE - APPROPRIATE TECHNOLOGIES IN AGRICULTURE. 1980. 4/yr. Rs.570($95) K.K. Roy (Private) Ltd., 55 Gariahat Rd., P.O. Box 10210, Calcutta 700 019, India. Ed. Dr. K.K. Roy. adv.; abstr.; bibl.; index. circ. 1,690.

630 US ISSN 0161-8237
AMERICAN AGRICULTURIST. 1842. m. $19.95. Farm Progress Companies (Subsidiary of: A B C Publishing Companies), 191 S. Gary Ave., Carol Stream, IL 60188. TEL 630-690-5600. FAX 630-462-2869. (Edit. addr.: 2389 North Triphammer Rd., Ithaca, NY 14850. TEL 607-257-8670. FAX 607-257-8238) Ed. Eleanor Jacobs. adv.: B&W page $3400, color page $3910; trim 7 X 10. bk.rev.; illus.; mkt.; stat.; circ. 32,382 (paid). (also avail. in microform from UMI)
—Linda Hall; UMI.
Formerly: American Agriculturist and Rural New Yorker (ISSN 0002-7219); Incorporates (in 1964): Rural New Yorker.

630 338.1 US
AMERICAN ASSOCIATION OF NURSERYMEN UPDATE. every 3 weeks. American Association of Nurserymen, 1250 I St., N.W., Ste. 500, Washington, DC 20005. TEL 202-789-2900. Ed. Angela Hutcherson. **Document type:** bulletin.

630 338.1 US
AMERICAN ASSOCIATION OF NURSERYMEN WHO'S WHO IN THE NURSERY INDUSTRY MEMBER DIRECTORY. a. $150 to non-members. American Association of Nurserymen, 1250 I St., N.W., Ste. 500, Washington, DC 20005. TEL 202-789-2900. adv. circ. 3,500. **Document type:** directory.
Former titles: American Association of Nurserymen Directory for the Nursery Industry and Related Associations; American Association of Nurserymen Membership Directory; Allied Landscape Industry Member Directory (ISSN 0098-793X)

638.1 US ISSN 0002-7626
SF521 CODEN: ABJOAS
AMERICAN BEE JOURNAL. 1861. m. $17.95 (foreign $27.50). Dadant & Sons, Inc., Hamilton, IL 62341. TEL 217-847-3324. FAX 217-847-3660. Ed. Joe M. Graham. R&P contact: Joe M. Graham. adv.: page $775; adv. contact: Joe M. Graham. bk.rev.; abstr.; charts; illus.; stat.; index; circ. 12,000 (paid). (also avail. in microfilm from PMC,UMI; reprint service avail. from UMI) **Indexed:** Apic.Abstr., ASCA, Bibl.Agri., Biol.Abstr., Chem.Abstr., Curr.Adv.Ecol.Sci., Curr.Cont., Farm & Garden Ind., Forest.Abstr., Helminthol.Abstr., Intl.Polym.Sci.& Tech., Soils & Fert., SSCI. **Document type:** trade publication.
—BLDSC (0810.750000); CASDDS; Genuine Article; Linda Hall; SWETS; UMI; UnCover. CCC.
Description: Magazine for hobby and professional beekeepers. Topics include management, honey processing, marketing, disease control.

638.1 US ISSN 0014-9438
AMERICAN BEEKEEPING FEDERATION. NEWSLETTER. 1943. bi-m. $25 (foreign $32). American Beekeeping Federation, Inc., Box 1038, Jesup, GA 31598. TEL 912-427-4233. FAX 912-427-8447. Ed. Troy H. Fore, Jr. adv. contact: Christina Wright. bk.rev. circ. 2,000. **Indexed:** Apic.Abstr. **Document type:** newsletter, trade publication.
Description: Keeps members current on activities of the organization and of happenings in the honey and beekeeping industry in the USA.

630 US ISSN 0198-8816
AMERICAN CHIANINA JOURNAL. 1973. 8/yr. $25. American Chianina Association, Box 890, Platte City, MO 64079. TEL 816-431-2808. FAX 816-431-5381. Ed. Tammy Scott. adv. contact: Terry Atchison. circ. 2,500. (back issues avail.) **Document type:** trade publication.

AMERICAN FARMER SERIES. see *LITERATURE*

630 US ISSN 0889-1893
S605.5 CODEN: AJAAEZ
AMERICAN JOURNAL OF ALTERNATIVE AGRICULTURE. 1986. q. $24 (Canada & Mexico $27; elsewhere $28) (effective 1998). Henry A. Wallace Institute for Alternative Agriculture, Inc., 9200 Edmonston Rd., Ste. 117, Greenbelt, MD 20770-1551. TEL 301-441-8777. FAX 301-220-0164. E-mail: hawiaa@access.digex.net; URL: http://www.hawiaa.org. Ed. I. Garth Youngberg; Pub. Henry A. Wallace. bk.rev. circ. 1,100. (back issues avail.) **Indexed:** ASCA, Biol.& Agr.Ind., Dairy Sci.Abstr., Ecol.Abstr., Environ.Abstr., Environ.Per.Bibl. (1989-), Field Crop Abstr., Food Sci.& Tech.Abstr., Forest.Abstr., Geo.Abstr.H.G., Geo.Abstr.P.G., Herb.Abstr., IDA, Irr.& Drain.Abstr., Maize Abstr., Rural Ext.Educ.& Tr.Abstr., Seed Abstr., Soils & Fert., SSCI, Triticale Abstr., World Agri.Econ.& Rural Sociol.Abstr. **Document type:** trade publication.
—BLDSC (0820.980000); Ei; KR SourceOne; SWETS; UnCover.
Refereed Serial

630 338 US ISSN 1089-8492
AMERICAN OSTRICH. 1987. m. $80 (foreign $120). American Ostrich Association, 3950 Fossil Creek Blvd., Ste. 200, Fort Worth, TX 76137-2745. TEL 817-232-1200. FAX 817-232-1390. E-mail: aoa@flash.net; URL: http://www.ostriches.org. Ed. Janis L. Gary. R&P contact: Janis L. Gary. adv. contact: Janis L. Gary. bk.rev. circ. 4,500. (back issues avail.) **Document type:** trade publication.
Formerly: Ostrich Report.
Description: Covers alternative agriculture.

630 US ISSN 1064-7473
AMERICAN SMALL FARM. 1992. 10/yr. $18. Magnet Communications, Inc., 21822 Sherman Way, Ste. 200, Canoga Park, CA 91303-1942. TEL 818-727-2236. FAX 818-727-1358. URL: http://www.smallfarm.com. Ed. Andrew Stevens. R&P contact: George St. Johns. adv.: B&W page $4545, color page $5885; trim 7 7/8 x 10 1/2; adv. contact: Larry Throckmorton. bk.rev.; circ. 65,000. **Document type:** consumer publication.
Description: Focuses on production agriculture by the small-acreage farmer and rancher.

630 US ISSN 0149-9890
CODEN: AAEPCZ
AMERICAN SOCIETY OF AGRICULTURAL ENGINEERS. ANNUAL MEETING PAPERS. 1957. a. $975. American Society of Agricultural Engineers, 2950 Niles Rd., St. Joseph, MI 49085-9659. TEL 616-429-0300. FAX 616-429-3852. E-mail: hq@asae.org; URL: http://asae.org/. (also avail. in microfiche) **Indexed:** Agri.Eng.Abstr., Dairy Sci.Abstr., Hort.Abstr., Ind.Vet., Irr.& Drain.Abstr., Maize Abstr., Potato Abstr., Rice Abstr., Seed Abstr., Sorghum & Millets Abstr., Sugar Ind.Abstr., Vet.Bull., World Agri.Econ.& Rural Sociol.Abstr.
—BLDSC (6369.640000); CISTI. CCC.

630 US ISSN 1061-1827
Z5074.E6
AMERICAN SOCIETY OF AGRICULTURAL ENGINEERS. COMPREHENSIVE INDEX OF PUBLICATIONS. 1979. a. $6 to non-members; members $2 (effective 1997). American Society of Agricultural Engineers, 2950 Niles Rd., St. Joseph, MI 49085-9659. TEL 616-429-0300. FAX 616-429-3852. E-mail: hq@asae.org; URL: http://asae.org/.
Formerly (until 1984): Comprehensive Index of A S A E Publications (ISSN 0889-6798)
Description: Provides a keyword listing of all publications available from the Society.

630 US ISSN 0003-116X
AMERICAN SOCIETY OF FARM MANAGERS AND RURAL APPRAISERS. JOURNAL. 1937. a. $24. American Society of Farm Managers and Rural Appraisers, 950 S. Cherry St., Ste. 508, Denver, CO 80222. TEL 303-758-3513. FAX 303-758-0190. E-mail: asfmra@aol.com. Ed. Alan L. Yoder. cum.index: nos.1-41 (1937-1977), nos.42-57 (1978-1987). circ. 4,000. **Document type:** academic/scholarly publication.
—UnCover.
Description: Contains articles of interest to farm managers, rural appraisers, agricultural consultants, and other agricultural professionals.
Refereed Serial

ANALES CIENTIFICOS. see *SCIENCES: COMPREHENSIVE WORKS*

ANDHRA PRADESH PRODUCTIVITY COUNCIL. TARGET. see *PUBLIC ADMINISTRATION*

630 UK
ANGLIA FARMER AND CONTRACTOR. m. £18 (foreign £34). B C Publications, 16C Market Pl., Diss, Norfolk IP22 3AB, England. TEL 44-1379-644200. FAX 44-1379-650480. Ed. Roger Turff. adv. contact: Jenny Holkham. circ. 7,600 (controlled). **Document type:** bulletin.
Description: Covers all aspects of agriculture.

630 CC ISSN 0517-6611
ANHUI NONGYE KEXUE/ANHUI AGRICULTURAL SCIENCE. (Text in Chinese) q. Anhui Sheng Nongye Kexueyuan - Anhui Provincial Academy of Agricultural Science, Silihe, Hefei Xijiao (West Suburb), Anhui 230031, People's Republic of China. TEL 257273. Ed. Zhang Zhengzhong.

630 FR
ANJOU AGRICOLE. w. 14 av. Joxe, 49006 Angers Cedex, France. TEL 41-88-98-53. circ. 11,293.

630 PL ISSN 0365-1118
S13 CODEN: ACEAA2
ANNALES UNIVERSITATIS MARIAE CURIE-SKLODOWSKA. SECTIO E. AGRICULTURA. (Text in English or Polish; summaries in English, French, German) 1946. a. price varies. Uniwersytet Marii Curie-Sklodowskiej, Wydawnictwo, Pl. M. Curie-Sklodowskiej 5, 20-031 Lublin, Poland. TEL 48-81-375304. FAX 48-81-336699. TELEX 0643223. Ed. Adam Szember. circ. 650. **Indexed:** Anim.Breed.Abstr., Biol.Abstr., Chem.Abstr., Excerpt.Med., Field Crop Abstr., Forest.Abstr., Herb.Abstr., Hort.Abstr., Maize Abstr., Nutr.Abstr., Plant Breed.Abstr., Rev.Appl.Entomol., Soils & Fert., Weed Abstr. **Document type:** academic/scholarly publication.
—BLDSC (0961.000000); CASDDS; CISTI; Linda Hall.

630 570 II
▼**ANNALS OF AGRI BIO RESEARCH**; an international journal of basic and applied agriculture and biology. (Text in English) 1996. a. Rs.500($60) (effective 1997). Agri Bio Research Publishers, 121 Mohalla Chaudharian, Hisar 125 001, India. TEL 91-1662-37530. Ed. B.D. Chaudhary. adv.; bk.rev. circ. 500. **Document type:** academic/scholarly publication.

630 II ISSN 0970-3179
ANNALS OF AGRICULTURAL RESEARCH. (Text in English) 1980. s-a. $150. (Indian Society of Agricultural Science) Hindustan Publishing Corp., 4805-24, 1st Fl., Bharat Ram Rd., Darya Ganj, New Delhi 110 002, India. TEL 91-11-3254401. FAX 91-11-6863511. E-mail: hpcpd@giasdl01.vsnl.net.in.

631.091 PH ISSN 0116-0710
CODEN: ATREDV
ANNALS OF TROPICAL RESEARCH. (Text in English) 1979. s-a. $30 (library $25; students $20). Visayas State College of Agriculture, Baybay, Leyte 6521-A, Philippines. TEL 53-335-2617. E-mail: visca@sat.vitanet.org. Ed. Jose R. Pardales, Jr. R&P contact: Jose R. Pardales, Jr. abstr.; index. circ. 500. (back issues avail.) **Indexed:** Anim.Breed.Abstr., Field Crop Abstr., Food Sci.& Tech.Abstr., Forest Prod.Abstr., Ind.Phil.Per., Rice Abstr., Rural Devel.Abstr., Weed Abstr., World Agri.Econ.& Rural Sociol.Abstr. **Document type:** academic/scholarly publication.
—BLDSC (1045.200000).
Refereed Serial

630 915.2 JA
ANNUAL REVIEW OF AGRICULTURE IN KINKI DISTRICT/KINKI NOGYO JOSEI HOKOKU. (Text in Japanese) 1964. a. Kinki Agricultural Administration Bureau - Kinki Nosei-kyoku, Shimochoja-machi Sagaru, Nishinotoin-dori, Kamigyo-ku, Kyoto 602, Japan.

630 IT ISSN 0304-0666
HD1970
ANNUARIO DELL'AGRICOLTURA ITALIANA. (Text in Italian; summaries in English) 1946; N.S. 1976. a. Lit.68000 (effective 1997). (Istituto Nazionale di Economia Agraria) Societa Editrice Il Mulino, Strada Maggiore 37, 40125 Bologna, Italy. TEL 39-51-256011. E-mail: riviste@mulino.it. Ed. Giuseppe Colombo. bk.rev. circ. 1,000.

AGRICULTURE

ANVIL MAGAZINE. see *METALLURGY*

ANZEIGER FUER SCHAEDLINGSKUNDE, PFLANZENSCHUTZ, UMWELTSCHUTZ. see *BIOLOGY — Entomology*

630   JA   ISSN 0003-6331
AOMORI NOGYO. (Text in Japanese) 1950. m. newsstand price: 350Yen. Aomoriken Nogyo Kairyo Fukyukai - Aomori Prefecture Agricultural Improvement and Propagation Association, Aomoriken Norinbu, 1-1 Nagashima 1-chome, Aomori-shi, Aomori-ken 030, Japan. Ed. Yotsuo Katsurahara. circ. 96,000.

638.1   IT   ISSN 0003-6455
APIACTA; an international technical magazine of apicultural and economic information. (Text in English, French, German, Spanish) 1966. q. $28 (effective 1996). "Apimondia" International Federation of Beekeepers' Associations - Federation Internationale des Associations d'Apiculture, Corso Vittorio Emanuele 101, 00186 Rome, Italy. TEL 39-6-6852286. FAX 39-6-68522868. TELEX 612533. E-mail: apimondia@mclink.it. Ed. Ms. E. Dumitrascu. adv. contact: Cristian Constantinescu. bk.rev. circ. 1,000. (also avail. in microform from UMI; back issues avail.) **Indexed:** Apic.Abstr., Biol.Abstr., Excerp.Med. **Document type:** bulletin.
—BLDSC (1567.975000); Linda Hall; SWETS.
Description: Discusses bee culture.

638.1 636.089   IT   ISSN 0518-1259
CODEN: APMOD8
L'APICOLTORE MODERNO. (Text in Italian; summaries in English, Italian) 1910. q. L.30000 (foreign L.40000) (effective 1997). Universita di Torino, Osservatorio di Apicoltura, Via Leonardo da Vinci 44, 10095 Grugliasco TO, Italy. TEL 39-11-4033893. FAX 39-11-4033894. Ed. Dr. Franco Marletto. R&P contact: Franco Marletto. adv. contact: Marco Porporato. bk.rev.; index; circ. 1,500 (controlled). (back issues avail.) **Indexed:** Apic.Abstr., Chem.Abstr., Rev.Appl.Entomol. **Document type:** academic/scholarly publication.
—BLDSC (1568.300000); CASDDS.

638.1   RM   ISSN 0378-2425
CODEN: APRODX
APICULTURA IN ROMANIA. 1925. m. $32. Asociatia Crescatorilor de Albine din Romania - Beekeeping Association from Romania, Str. Iulius Fucik nr.17, sector 2, Bucharest 70231, Rumania. TEL 137877. TELEX 11205 APIROM R. (Dist. by: Rompresfilatelia Enterprise, Press Exportation - Importation Department, P.O. Box 12-201, Calea Grivitei no.64-66, Bucharest, Rumania) Ed. Elisei Tarta. adv.; bk.rev. circ. 25,000. **Indexed:** Apic.Abstr., Biol.Abstr.
—CASDDS.
Formerly (until 1975): Apicultura (ISSN 0518-1305)

638.1   IT
APIMONDIA INTERNATIONAL BEEKEEPING CONGRESS. PROCEEDINGS. (Text in various languages) 17th, 1958. biennial, 34th, 1995, Lausanne. price varies. "Apimondia" International Federation of Beekeepers' Associations, Corso Vittorio Emanuele 101, 00186 Rome, Italy. TEL 39-6-6852286. FAX 39-6-6852286. TELEX 612533. E-mail: apimondia@mclink.it. **Document type:** proceedings.

630   SZ
APPENZOELLER BUUR. w. Engelgasse 3, CH-9050 Appenzell, Switzerland. TEL 071-871922. FAX 071-873753. Ed. Walter Koller. circ. 5,200.

630   US   ISSN 0883-8542
APPLIED ENGINEERING IN AGRICULTURE. 1985. 6/yr. $77.50 to non-members (foreign $86); members $41 (foreign $49.50) (effective 1997). American Society of Agricultural Engineers, 2950 Niles Rd., St. Joseph, MI 49085-9659. TEL 616-429-0300. FAX 616-429-3852. E-mail: hq@asae.org; URL: http://www.asae.org/. Ed. Pamela DeVore-Hansen. circ. 1,000. **Indexed:** Agri.Eng.Abstr., Anim.Breed.Abstr., Cott.& Trop.Fibr.Abstr., Dairy Sci.Abstr., Field Crop Abstr., Food Sci.& Tech.Abstr., Forest.Abstr., Forest Prod.Abstr., Herb.Abstr., Ind.Vet., Irr.& Drain.Abstr., Maize Abstr., Pig News & Info., Rice Abstr., Seed Abstr., Soils & Fert., Sorghum & Millets Abstr., Soyabean Abstr., Triticale Abstr., Vet.Bull., World Agri.Econ.& Rural Sociol.Abstr. **Document type:** trade publication.
—BLDSC (1572.350000); CISTI; Ei; SWETS; UnCover. **CCC.**
Description: Presents the latest technical developments in every area of engineering for agriculture.
Refereed Serial

630   BA
ARAB AGRICULTURE YEARBOOK/AL-ZIRA'AH AL-ARABIYYAH. (Supplement to: Arab World Agribusiness) (Text in Arabic, English) 1985. a. 17 din.($45) Fanar Publishing W L L, Bahrain Tower, 8th Fl., P.O. Box 10131, Manama, Bahrain. TEL 973-213900. FAX 973-211765. Ed. Abdul Wahed Alwani. adv.: B&W page $1925, color page $2530; trim 270 x 210. illus.; stat. circ. 12,000. **Document type:** directory.
Description: Comprehensive guide to all sectors of agriculture in the Arab world, including North Africa and Somalia, covering government ministries, farm consultancy services, international suppliers of machinery, food processing and storage equipment, investment opportunities and agricultural scientists.

630   BA
ARAB WORLD AGRIBUSINESS/AL-ZIRA'AH FI-L-ALAM AL-ARABI. (Includes supplement: Arab Agriculture Yearbook) (Text in Arabic and English) 1984. 9/yr. $65. Fanar Publishing W L L, Bahrain Tower, 8th Fl., P.O. Box 10131, Manama, Bahrain. TEL 973-213900. FAX 973-211765. Ed. Abdul Wahed Alwani. circ. 16,000. (back issues avail.) **Indexed:** Food Sci.& Tech.Abstr. **Document type:** trade publication.

630   NE   ISSN 0003-9306
CODEN: ARNLBG
ARCHIV FUER NATURSCHUTZ UND LANDSCHAFTSFORSCHUNG/ARCHIVES OF NATURE CONSERVATION AND LANDSCAPE RESEARCH. (Text and summaries in English, German) 1961. q. $112 (effective 1998). (Akademie der Landwirtschaftswissenschaften) Gordon and Breach - Harwood Academic, Amsteldisk 166, 1st Fl., 1079 LH Amsterdam, Netherlands. (Subscr. to: International Publishers Distributor, Box 32160, Newark, NJ 07102. TEL 800-545-8398. FAX 215-750-6343) Ed. Gerhard Stocker. adv.; bk.rev.; bibl.; charts; illus.; index. **Indexed:** Biol.Abstr., Chem.Abstr., Excerp.Med., Forest.Abstr., Forest Prod.Abstr., INIS Atomind., Key Word Ind.Wildl.Res., Ornam.Hort., Rural Recreat.Tour.Abstr., Seed Abstr., Soils & Fert., Weed Abstr.
—BLDSC (1621.400000); CASDDS; CISTI. **CCC.**

630   NE   ISSN 0323-5408
CODEN: APPZAJ
ARCHIV FUER PHYTOPATHOLOGIE UND PFLANZENSCHUTZ/ARCHIVES OF PHYTOPATHOLOGY AND PLANT PROTECTION. (Text in German; summaries in English, German, Russian) 1965. 6/yr. $151 (effective 1998). (Akademie der Landwirtschaftswissenschaften) Gordon and Breach - Harwood Academic, Amsteldisk 166, 1st Fl., 1079 LH Amsterdam, Netherlands. (Subscr. to: International Publishers Distributor, Box 32160, Newark, NJ 07102. TEL 800-545-8398. FAX 215-750-6343) Eds. D. Spaar, T. Wetzel. bk.rev.; charts; illus.; stat.; index. **Indexed:** Agri.Eng.Abstr., ASCA, Bio-Contr.News & Info., Biodet.Abstr., Biotech.Abstr., Chem.Abstr., Curr.Cont., Excerp.Med., Fababean Abstr., Food Sci.& Tech.Abstr., Hort.Abstr., INIS Atomind., Potato Abstr., Rev.Appl.Entomol., Seed Abstr., Soils & Fert., Triticale Abstr.
—BLDSC (1639.700000); CASDDS; CISTI; Linda Hall; SWETS. **CCC.**
Formerly (until 1972): Archiv fuer Pflanzenschutz

630   MG
ARCHIVES DU FO FI FA. (Text in French) a. Centre d'Information et de Documentation Scientifique et Technique, B.P. 6224, Antananarivo 101, Madagascar. TEL 33288.

630   FR   ISSN 0750-1536
ARDENNE AGRICOLE. 1944. w. 1 av. du Petit Bois, B.P. 416, 08105 Charleville-Mezieres, France. TEL 24-33-53-00. Ed. Albert Molie. circ. 6,000.

AL-ARDH. see *LABOR UNIONS*

630   AG
ARGENTINA. SECRETARIA DE ESTADO DE AGRICULTURA Y GANADERIA. COMUNICADO DE PRENSA. no.107, 1979. irreg. Secretaria de Estado de Agricultura y Ganaderia, Paseo Colon 922, 1063 Buenos Aires, Argentina. stat. (processed)

630   AG
ARGENTINA. SERVICIO NACIONAL DE ECONOMIA Y SOCIOLOGIA RURAL. PUBLICACION E S R. irreg. Servicio Nacional de Economia y Sociologia Rural, Paseo Colon 974, Buenos Aires, Argentina.

630   YU   ISSN 0004-1262
CODEN: APNAA2
ARHIV ZA POLJOPRIVREDNE NAUKE/JOURNAL OF SCIENTIFIC AGRICULTURAL RESEARCH. (Text in Serbocroatian; summaries in English) 1934. q. Savez Poljoprivrednih Inzenjera i Tehnicara Jugoslavije - Society of Agricultural Engineers and Technicians, Kneza Milosa 9-1, 11000 Belgrade, Yugoslavia. TEL 344-319. FAX 344-318. Ed. Zivorad Videnovic. bk.rev. circ. 1,100. **Indexed:** Anim.Breed.Abstr., Biol.Abstr., Chem.Abstr., Crop Physiol.Abstr., Curr.Adv.Ecol.Sci., Curr.Cont., Dairy Sci.Abstr., Field Crop Abstr., Food Sci.& Tech.Abstr., Herb.Abstr., Hort.Abstr., Maize Abstr., Nutr.Abstr., Pig News & Info., Plant Grow.Reg.Abstr., Rev.Plant Path., Seed Abstr., Soyabean Abstr., Triticale Abstr., Weed Abstr.
—BLDSC (5056.851000); CASDDS; Linda Hall.

630   US   ISSN 0274-7014
ARIZONA FARM BUREAU NEWS. 1948. bi-w. $25. Arizona Farm Bureau Federation, 3401 E. Elwood St., Phoenix, AZ 85040-1625. TEL 602-470-0088. Ed. Michael G. Shirra. adv.; bk.rev.; charts; illus.; pat.; stat.; tr.lit. circ. 4,000. (tabloid format; back issues avail.) **Document type:** newspaper.
Description: Covers legislative, regulatory and economic issues impacting Arizona agriculturalists.

630   US   ISSN 1071-6521
ARIZONA FARMER. 1922. 15/yr. $19.95. Farm Progress Co., Inc., 191 S. Gary Ave., Carol Stream, IL 60188. TEL 708-462-2860. Ed. Len Richardson; Pub. Allen R. Johnson. R&P contact: Len Richardson. adv. contact: Vicki Rabbiosi. bk.rev.; illus.; stat.; circ. 2,141 (paid). **Document type:** trade publication.
Former titles (until 1993): Arizona Farmer - Stockman (ISSN 8750-6432); Arizona Producer; Arizona Farmer - Ranchman (ISSN 0004-1491)

630   US   ISSN 0744-5474
ARIZONA LAND AND PEOPLE. 1949. a. free. University of Arizona, College of Agriculture, Tucson, AZ 85721. TEL 602-621-7176. Ed. S. McGinley. bk.rev. circ. 5,500. **Indexed:** Biol.Abstr., Biol.& Agr.Ind., Curr.Adv.Ecol.Sci., Curr.Cont., Energy Ind., Energy Info.Abstr., Field Crop Abstr., Herb.Abstr., Ornam.Hort. **Document type:** consumer publication.
—UMI.
Formerly: Progressive Agriculture in Arizona (ISSN 0033-0744)
Description: Highlights and describes for a key audience the programs and activities of the college.

ARKANSAS. AGRICULTURAL EXPERIMENT STATION. SPECIAL REPORTS. see *AGRICULTURE — Abstracting, Bibliographies, Statistics*

630   US
ARKANSAS FARMER. 1985. m. $12 (foreign $25). Rural Press U S A, 7701 Six Forks Rd., Ste. 132, Raleigh, NC 27615. TEL 919-676-3276; 800-477-1737. FAX 919-676-9803. (Subscr. to: Box 150001, Raleigh, NC 27624) Ed. Eva Ann Dorris; Pub. Jeff Tennant. adv.: B&W page $1009. circ. 12,500. **Document type:** newspaper.
Formerly (until 1992): Arkansas Farm and Country.
Description: Contains agricultural news and features for Arkansas' commercial farm and ranch operators.

AGRICULTURE

630   US   ISSN 0004-1890
ARKANSAS VALLEY JOURNAL. 1949. w. $38 (foreign $30). Arkansas Valley Journal, Inc., 7 W. Fifth St., Box 500, La Junta, CO 81050. TEL 719-384-8121. FAX 719-384-2867. Ed. Susan Russell; Pub. Daniel Hyatt. adv. contact: Pat R. Ptoleny. illus.; mkt.; circ. 6,323 (paid). (also avail. in microform) **Document type:** newspaper, trade publication.
  Description: Covers all aspects of agriculture in the state of Colorado.

631.8   CH
ASIAN AND PACIFIC COUNCIL. FOOD AND FERTILIZER TECHNOLOGY CENTER. EXTENSION - TECHNICAL BULLETIN. 1970. s-m. free. Asian and Pacific Council, Food and Fertilizer Technology Center, 14 Wenchow St., 5th Fl., Taipei, Taiwan, Republic of China. FAX 02-362-0478. bibl.; charts; illus.; stat.; circ. 4,300 (controlled). **Indexed:** Agri.Eng.Abstr., Anim.Breed.Abstr., Field Crop Abstr., Herb.Abstr., Hort.Abstr., Ind.Vet., Irr.& Drain.Abstr., Nutr.Abstr., Rural Devel.Abstr., Rural Recreat.Tour.Abstr., Weed Abstr., World Agri.Econ.& Rural Sociol.Abstr.

630 020   CR
ASOCIACION INTERAMERICANA DE BIBLIOTECARIOS, DOCUMENTALISTAS Y ESPECIALISTAS EN INFORMACION AGRICOLA. BOLETIN ESPECIAL. 1966. irreg. membership. Asociacion Interamericana de Bibliotecarios, Documentalistas y Especialistas en Informacion Agricola, Apdo. Postal 55, 2200 Coronado, Costa Rica. TEL 506-229-0222. FAX 506-2294741. TELEX 2144 IICA. E-mail: gpoitevi@iica.ac.cr. Ed. Ghislaine Poitevien. circ. 800.
—Linda Hall.
  Formerly: Asociacion Interamericana de Bibliotecarios y Documentalistas Agricolas. Boletin Especial (ISSN 0074-0748).
  Description: Directory of AIBDEIA corporation and individual members.

ASOCIACION INTERAMERICANA DE BIBLIOTECARIOS, DOCUMENTALISTAS Y ESPECIALISTAS EN INFORMACION AGRICOLA. BOLETIN INFORMATIVO. see *LIBRARY AND INFORMATION SCIENCES*

630   UY   ISSN 0044-9326
ASOCIACION RURAL DEL URUGUAY. REVISTA. 1872. s-m. Asociacion Rural del Uruguay, Avda. Uruguay 864, Montevideo, Uruguay. abstr.; bibl.; illus.; stat.; tr.lit. circ. 5,000.

630 070.48   FR
ASSOCIATION DES JOURNALISTES AGRICOLES. ANNUAIRE. a. Association des Journalistes Agricoles, 9 rue Papillon, 75009 Paris, France. circ. 2,000.

ASSOCIATION OF OFFICIAL SEED ANALYSTS. NEWS LETTER. see *BIOLOGY — Botany*

ATLANTIC REGION GEOGRAPHICAL STUDIES. see *GEOGRAPHY*

630   FR   ISSN 0221-508X
AURORE PAYSANNE. 24/yr. 24 rue des Ingrains, B.P. 213, 36028 Chateaurous Cedex, France. TEL 54-22-20-07. circ. 7,900.

630   GW   ISSN 0045-0049
AUSBILDUNG UND BERATUNG IN LAND- UND HAUSWIRTSCHAFT; Monatsschrift fuer Lehr- und Beratungskraefte. 1948. 11/yr. DM.64.80 (foreign DM.75.30). (Land- und Hauswirtschaftlicher Auswertungs- und Informationsdienst) Landwirtschaftsverlag GmbH, Huelsebrockstr. 2, 48165 Muenster, Germany. TEL 49-2501-801-0. FAX 49-2501-801-204. TELEX 892665-LANDV-D. (Subscr. to: Postfach 480249, 48079 Muenster, Germany) **Indexed:** Rural Recreat.Tour.Abstr., World Agri.Econ.& Rural Sociol.Abstr. **Document type:** trade publication.
—CCC.

638.1   AT   ISSN 0004-8313
AUSTRALASIAN BEEKEEPER. 1899. m. Aus.$33.50 (foreign $36) (effective 1997). Pender Beekeeping Supplies Pty. Ltd., P.M.B 19, Maitland, N.S.W. 2320, Australia. TEL 61-49-327244. FAX 61-49-327621. Ed. R. Gulliford. R&P contact: Allen Clarke. adv. contact: Joyce Gardner. bk.rev.; charts; illus.; mkt.; stat.; index; circ. 2,200 (paid). **Indexed:** Apic.Abstr, Forest.Abstr.
—UnCover.

630 330   AT
AUSTRALIAN AGRICULTURAL AND RESOURCE ECONOMICS SOCIETY. PAPERS PRESENTED AT ANNUAL CONFERENCE (MICROFICHE). 1989. a. Aus.$35($32) avail. on special order to existing subscribers and members only. (Australian Agricultural and Resource Economics Society) Blackwell Publishers Ltd., 108 Cowley Rd., Oxford OX4 1JF, England. TEL 61-3-94396833. **Document type:** proceedings.
  Formerly: Australian Agricultural Economics Society. Papers Presented at Annual Conference (Microfiche).

AUSTRALIAN AND NEW ZEALAND WINE INDUSTRY JOURNAL. see *BEVERAGES*

638.1   AT   ISSN 0045-0294
AUSTRALIAN BEE JOURNAL. 1918. m. Aus.$30. Victorian Apiarist's Association, c/o Mrs. Judy Graves, 23 McBride Rd., Upper Beaconsfield, Vic. 3808, Australia. **Indexed:** Apic.Abstr, Forest.Abstr., Forest Prod.Abstr. **Document type:** trade publication.

630   AT   ISSN 0157-3039
AUSTRALIAN CANEGROWER. 1979. fortn. (foreign Aus.$112). CANEGROWERS, 190-194 Edward St., Brisbane, Qld. 4001, Australia. TEL 61-07-38646444. FAX 61-7-38646429. Ed. Elizabeth Foley. adv. contact: Marina Rockett. bk.rev. circ. 8,100. **Indexed:** Sugar Ind.Abstr. **Document type:** trade publication.
  Description: Provides news and information for the Australian sugar industry.

630 658 338.1   AT   ISSN 1036-6474
AUSTRALIAN FARM JOURNAL. 1991. m. Aus.$59. Rural Press Magazines, P.O. Box 160, Port Melbourne, Vic. 3207, Australia. FAX 61-3-287-0999. Ed. Patrick Francis. adv. contact: Mevyn Christian. bk.rev.; illus.; index. circ. 19,500. (back issues avail.)
—UnCover.
  Formed by the merger of (1980-1991): Farm (ISSN 0725-3338); (1977-1991): Australian Rural Times (ISSN 1034-5809); Which was formerly (until 1989): National Farmer (ISSN 0155-2201)

630   AT   ISSN 0004-9409
S17   CODEN: AJAEA9
AUSTRALIAN JOURNAL OF AGRICULTURAL RESEARCH. 1950. 8/yr. Aus.$380($380) (effective 1998). (C.S.I.R.O. Australia) C.S.I.R.O. Publishing, 150 Oxford St., Collingwood, Vic. 3066, Australia. TEL 61-3-96627628. FAX 61-3-96627611. E-mail: jenny.fegent@publish.csiro.au; URL: http://www.publish.csiro.au/journals/ajar/electronic.html. Ed. J.C. Fegent. adv.; bibl.; charts; illus.; index. circ. 900. (also avail. in microform from UMI; back issues avail.) **Indexed:** Acid Rain Abstr., Acid Rain Ind., Agri.Eng.Abstr., Anal.Abstr., Anim.Breed.Abstr., Apic.Abstr., ASCA, Bibl.Agri., Biodet.Abstr., Biol.Abstr., Biol.& Agr.Ind., Biotech.Abstr., Cadscan, Chem.Abstr., Cott.& Trop.Fibr.Abstr., Curr.Adv.Ecol.Sci., Curr.Biotech.Abstr., Curr.Cont., Dairy Sci.Abstr., Ecol.Abstr., Energy Ind., Energy Info.Abstr., Environ.Abstr., Environ.Per.Bibl. (1975-), Excerp.Med., Field Crop Abstr., Food Sci.& Tech.Abstr., Geo.Abstr.H.G., Geo.Abstr.P.G., Helminthol.Abstr., Herb.Abstr., Hort.Abstr., Ind.Sci.Rev., Ind.Vet., INIS Atomind., Irr.& Drain.Abstr., Lead Abstr., Maize Abstr., Meteor.& Geoastrophys.Abstr., Nutr.Abstr., Ornam.Hort., Plant Breed.Abstr., Plant Grow.Reg.Abstr., Potato Abstr., Poult.Abstr., Rev.Appl.Entomol., Rev.Med.& Vet.Mycol., Rev.Plant Path., Rice Abstr., Sci.Cit.Ind, Seed Abstr., Sel.Water Res.Abstr., Soils & Fert., Sorghum & Millets Abstr., Sugar Ind.Abstr., Triticale Abstr., Vet.Bull., VITIS, Weed Abstr., Zincscan. **Document type:** academic/scholarly publication.
● Also available online.
—BLDSC (1802.000000); CASDDS; CIS; CISTI; Ei; EMDOCS; Genuine Article; Linda Hall; SWETS; UMI; UnCover. CCC.
  Description: Covers the physical, chemical, or biological aspects of an agricultural system with regard to the Australasian region.

630   AT   ISSN 0819-2995
AUSTRALIAN RURAL SCIENCE ANNUAL; a forum for rural thought. 1963. a. Aus.$2.50. (University of New England, Rural Science Undergraduates' Society) Percival Publishing Co. Pty. Ltd., 862-870 Elizabeth St., Waterloo, N.S.W. 2017, Australia. Ed. Deborah Streeter. adv.; bk.rev. circ. 1,500.
  Formerly (until 1987): Chiasma (ISSN 0084-8735)
  Description: Informs the public and primary producers of scientific research and development in the rural sector of Australia.

630   AU
AUSTRIA. BUNDESMINISTERIUM FUER LAND- UND FORSTWIRTSCHAFT. JAHRESBERICHT. 1959. a. free. Bundesministerium fuer Land- und Forstwirtschaft, Stubenring 1, A-1010 Vienna, Austria. TEL 43-1-711006762. FAX 43-1-711002127. circ. 1,600. **Document type:** government publication.
  Formerly: Austria. Bundesministerium fuer Land- und Forstwirtschaft. Taetigkeitsbericht (ISSN 0067-2262)

630   FR   ISSN 0988-9256
AUVERGNE AGRICOLE. w. 10-12 Au Marx Dormof, B.P. 479, 63013 Clermont-Ferrand, France. TEL 73-43-44-30. FAX 73-34-02-40. Ed. M. Francois Charles. circ. 10,500.

630   MX   ISSN 0188-7890
AVANCES EN INVESTIGACION AGROPECUARIA. (Text in English, French, Spanish; summaries in English) 1992. 3/yr. (Spanish 2/yr.; English 1/yr.). Mex.$30($40) (effective 1994). University of Colima, Coordinacion Gral. de Investigacion Cientifica, Justo Sierra 592, 28010 Colima, Mexico. TEL 331-4-11-33. FAX 331-2-75-81. E-mail: hummel@volcan.ucol.mx. (Subscr. to: Apdo. Postal 22, Colima, 28045 Colima, Mexico) Ed. Janet Hummel. charts; stat.; index. circ. 250. (back issues avail.) **Document type:** academic/scholarly publication.
  Description: Includes a wide spectrum of topics related to agriculture in the tropics. Considers economics, technology, computer technology, or anything which affects agriculture or animal production in the tropics.

630   FR   ISSN 0998-0210
AVENIR AGRICOLE DE L'ARDECHE. 1885. w. 4 av. de l'Europe Unie, B.P. 139, 07000 Privas Cedex, France. TEL 75-64-60-62. circ. 6,018.

630   FR
AVENIR AGRICOLE DE LA MAYENNE.* w. 3 rue Saint-Andre, B.P. 0325, 53003 Laval Cedex, France. TEL 43-49-56-00. FAX 43-49-56-19. Ed. D. Legoy. circ. 13,000.

630   FR   ISSN 1148-3121
AVENIR AGRICOLE ET RURAL DE LA HAUTE MARNE. w. Maison de l'Agriculture (Chaumont), 26 av. du 109e-RI, 52000 Chaumont, France. TEL 25-32-19-91. FAX 25-31-40-54. Ed. Patrice Zehr. circ. 2,600. **Document type:** newspaper.
  Former titles (until 1990): Avenir Paysan et Rural de la Haute Marne (ISSN 0154-7461); (until 1977): Avenir Paysan de la Haute Marne (ISSN 0154-7453)

630   IT   ISSN 0005-2361
AVVENIRE AGRICOLO (PARMA). 1892. m. free. Consorzio Agrario Provinciale, Viale Gramsci 26-C, 43100 Parma, Italy. TEL 0521-4981. TELEX 0521-550097. Ed. Domenico Fini. adv.; bk.rev.; illus. circ. 1,300. **Indexed:** Chem.Abstr.

630   AU   ISSN 1026-6275
B A L VEROEFFENTLICHUNGEN. 1949. irreg. varies. Bundesanstalt fuer Alpenlaendische Landwirtschaft Gumpenstein, A-8952 Irdning, Austria. TEL 43-3682-22451. FAX 43-3682-2461488. Ed. Kurt Chytil. R&P contact: Kurt Chytil. adv. contact: Eva Rainer. circ. 500. **Document type:** monographic series.
  Formerly (until 1989): Bundesanstalt fuer Alpenlaendische Landwirtschaft. Veroeffentlichungen (ISSN 1010-6146)

AGRICULTURE

630 664   UK
B B S R C NEWSLETTERS. 1967. s-a. free. Biotechnology and Biological Sciences Research Council, Polaris House, North Star Ave., Swindon, Wilts. SN2 1UH, England. TEL 44-1793-413200. FAX 44-1793-413201. Ed. Monica Winstanley. circ. 2,500. **Document type:** newsletter.
  Supersedes in part (in Apr. 1994): A F R C News (ISSN 0267-8489)
  Description: Presents research relevant to industry in food, agricultural systems, chemicals, and pharmaceuticals.

633.6   IO   ISSN 0043-0382
BALAI PENYELIDIKAN PERUSAHAAN PERKEBUNAN GULA. WARTA BULANAN. 1954. m. free to those interested in the sugar industry. Indonesian Sugar Experiment Station - Balai Penyelidikan Perusahaan Perkebunan Gula, Jalan Pahlawan 25, Pasurnan 67126, Indonesia. TEL 0343-21086. TELEX 31008-SUGEXST-PS. charts; index. circ. 500. (processed)

630   II
BALIRAJA; magazine devoted to modern commercial agriculture. (Text in Marathi) 1970. m. Rs.200. P.B. Bhosale, Ed. & Pub., 768 Sadashiv Peth, Phadtare Chowk, Pune 411 030, India. TEL 91-212-48-58-03. FAX 91-212-47-32-25. adv.: B&W page Rs.5200, color page Rs.10400; trim 230 x 170. pp./issue: 108.
  Description: Devoted to the progress of modern agriculture and rural marketing in Maharashtra.

630   BG
BANGLADESH INSTITUTE OF NUCLEAR AGRICULTURE. ANNUAL REPORT. (Text in English) 1982. a. Tk.100 (foreign $15) per no. Bangladesh Institute of Nuclear Agriculture, P.O. Box 4, Mymensingh 2200, Bangladesh. TEL 91-4401-02. Ed. M. Idris Al. circ. 100.
  Description: Covers research work on nuclear applications in agriculture.

630   BG   ISSN 0379-4296
S322.B26   CODEN: BJAGAQ
BANGLADESH JOURNAL OF AGRICULTURAL SCIENCES. (Text in English) 1974. s-a. Tk.60 individuals; Tk. 200($30) to institutions. Bangladesh Agricultural University Old Boys' Association, c/o Dept. of Soil Science, Bangladesh Agricultural University, Mymensingh, Bangladesh. (Co-sponsor: Bangladesh Agricultural University) Ed. M. Eaqub. circ. 300. **Indexed:** Biol.Abstr., Chem.Abstr., Field Crop Abstr., Food Sci.& Tech.Abstr., INIS Atomind.
—CASDDS; Linda Hall.

BANGLADESH JOURNAL OF BIOLOGICAL SCIENCES. see *BIOLOGY*

BANGLADESH JOURNAL OF EXTENSION EDUCATION. see *EDUCATION*

630   BG   ISSN 0258-7130
BANGLADESH JOURNAL OF NUCLEAR AGRICULTURE. (Text in English) 1985. a. $15. Bangladesh Institute of Nuclear Agriculture, P.O. Box 4, Mymensingh 2200, Bangladesh. TEL 4401-02. Ed. M. Idris Ali. circ. 400.
  Description: Covers research papers on nuclear applications in agriculture.

633.72   BG
BANGLADESH TEA RESEARCH INSTITUTE. ANNUAL REPORT.* (Text in English) 1973. irreg. Tk.20. Bangladesh Tea Research Institute, Srimangal, Sylhet, Bangladesh.

BAUEN FUER DIE LANDWIRTSCHAFT. see *BUILDING AND CONSTRUCTION*

630   AU   ISSN 0005-6561
DER BAUER; Mitteilungsblatt der Oberoesterreichischen Landwirtschaftskammer. 1948. w. S.450. Landwirtschaftskammer fuer Oberoesterreich, Auf der Gugl 3, A-4021 Linz, Austria. FAX 0732-690248. Ed. Heinz Krichbaumer. adv.; bk.rev. circ. 52,000. **Document type:** trade publication.

630   BE
DER BAUER; Wochenschrift fuer den praktischen Landwirt und die Familie auf dem Land. (Text in German) 1923. w. 2300 BEF. Belgische Boerenbond, Minderbroedersstraat 8, 3000 Leuven, Belgium. TEL 32-87-552446. FAX 32-87-742311. Ed. Frans Sterckx. adv.; bk.rev. circ. 2,300.

630   GW   ISSN 0936-4668
BAUERNBLATT; Schleswig-Holstein, Mecklenburg-Vorpommern und Hamburg. 1850. w. Bauernband Schleswig-Holstein, Jungfernsteig 25, 24768 Rendsburg, Germany. TEL 04331-1277-0. TELEX 04331-23701. Ed. Erich Thiesen. adv.: B&W page DM.4416, color page DM.6276; trim 276 x 198. circ. 30,000. **Document type:** newspaper.

630   SZ
BAUERNBLATT DER NORDWESTSCHWEIZ. w. Obere Steingrubenstr. 55, Postfach 63, CH-4504 Solothurn, Switzerland. TEL 065-233657. FAX 065-235893. Ed. Urs Nussbaumer. circ. 4,007.

630   SZ
BAUERNSPIEGEL. m. Postfach, CH-3053 Muenchenbuchsee, Switzerland. TEL 031-8693504. Ed. H.P. Rueb. circ. 5,000.

630   GW   ISSN 0941-2239
BAUERNZEITUNG. 1960. w. DM.94.80. Deutscher Bauernverlag GmbH, Brunnenstr. 128, 13355 Berlin, Germany. TEL 49-30-464060. FAX 49-30-46406205. adv.: B&W page DM.6944, color page DM.11656; trim 310 x 202. circ. 50,000. (tabloid format) **Document type:** newspaper.
  Formerly: Neue Deutsche Bauernzeitung.

630   SZ
BAUERNZEITUNG ZENTRALSCHWEIZ. 1867. w. 50 SFr. Luzerner Bauernverband, Postfach, CH-6210 Sursee, Switzerland. TEL 41-45-217923. FAX 41-45-217337. Ed. Alois Hodel. circ. 12,000. **Document type:** trade publication.
  Formed by the merger of (186?-1994): Landwirt (ISSN 1420-1615); (until 1994): Innerschweizer Bauernzeitung (ISSN 1420-1623); (until 1935): Urschweizer Bauernzeitung (ISSN 1420-245X)

630   NZ
BAY OF PLENTY FARMER. 1982. m. Hauraki Publishers Ltd., P.O. Box 363, Thames, New Zealand. Ed. Stephen D. Hill. adv. circ. 16,000. (tabloid format; back issues avail.)
  Description: Covers national and regional issues and events in agriculture and horticulture.

638.1   GW   ISSN 0724-8857
BAYERISCHES BIENEN-BLATT; Fachblatt fuer Bienenzucht. 1973. q. membership. Verband Bayerischer Bienenzuechter e.V., Spitzwegstr. 6, 84453 Muehldorf, Germany. TEL 08631-5363. FAX 08631-5392. Ed. Eduard Wimmer. adv.; bk.rev. circ. 5,700. **Document type:** corporate report.

630   GW   ISSN 0005-7150
BAYERISCHES LANDWIRTSCHAFTLICHES JAHRBUCH. (Supplement avail.) 1911. 8/yr. price varies. Bayerisches Staatsministerium fuer Ernaehrung, Landwirtschaft und Forsten, Ludwigstr. 2, 80539 Munich, Germany. Ed. Dr. Ullrich Keymer. bk.rev.; charts; illus.; index. circ. 2,000. **Indexed:** Anim.Breed.Abstr., Biodet.Abstr., Biol.Abstr., Chem.Abstr., Dairy Sci.Abstr., Excerp.Med., Field Crop Abstr., Food Sci.& Tech.Abstr., Geo.Abstr., Helminthol.Abstr., Herb.Abstr., Ind.Vet., Maize Abstr., Nutr.Abstr., Pig News & Info., Plant Breed.Abstr., Plant Grow.Reg.Abstr., Potato Abstr., Poult.Abstr., Rev.Appl.Entomol., Rev.Plant Path., Rural Devel.Abstr., Rural Ext.Educ.& Tr.Abstr., Rural Recreat.Tour.Abstr., Soils & Fert., Triticale Abstr., World Agri.Econ.& Rural Sociol.Abstr. **Document type:** bulletin.
—CCC.

053.1   GW   ISSN 0005-7169
BAYERISCHES LANDWIRTSCHAFTLICHES WOCHENBLATT. 1810. w. DM.173 (foreign DM.218) (effective 1997); newsstand price: DM.4.30. (Bayerischer Bauernverband) B L V Verlagsgesellschaft mbH, Lothstr. 29, 80797 Munich, Germany. TEL 49-89-12705-0. FAX 49-89-12705354. Ed. Johannes Urban. adv. contact: Henning Stemmler. bk.rev.; illus.; mkt. circ. 110,000. (looseleaf format) **Document type:** newspaper.
—CCC.

630   CK   ISSN 0120-2243
SB327
BEAN PROGRAM ANNUAL REPORT. Cover title: Beans. Spanish edition: Informe Anual del Programa de Frijol (ISSN 0120-2235) 1969. a. Centro Internacional de Agricultura Tropical, Bean Program - International Center for Tropical Agriculture, Apdo. Aereo 6713, Cali, Colombia. TEL 57-2-4450000. FAX 57-2-4450073. TELEX 05769 CIAT CO. Ed. Julia Cornegay. circ. 600 (controlled). **Document type:** corporate report.
  Description: Detailed progress report primarily for the information of research collaborators in the bean network.

630   UK
BEDFORDSHIRE AND HUNTINGDONSHIRE FARMER. m. membership. (National Farmers' Union) Eastern Counties N.F.U. Journals Ltd., 55 Goldington Rd., Bedford MK40 3LU, England. FAX 0234-50207. Ed. R. Payne. adv. circ. 2,200. (back issues avail.)

630 338.1   NE   ISSN 0927-7218
BEDRIJFSUITKOMSTEN EN FINANCIELE POSITIE; samenvattend overzicht van landbouwbedrijven tot en met boekjaar. 1977. a. fl.39. Landbouw-Economisch Instituut, Burg. Patijnlaan 19, 2585 BE The Hague, Netherlands. TEL 31-70-3308330. FAX 31-70-3615624. E-mail: postmaster@lei.dlo.nl; URL: http://www.lei.dlo.nl/lei. Ed.Bd. **Document type:** government publication.
  Formerly (until 1989): Van Bedrijfsuitkomsten tot Financiele Positie (ISSN 0921-4135)
  Description: Explores profitability and financing of Dutch agricultural holdings.

638.1   UK   ISSN 0005-7703
BEE CRAFT. 1919. m. £14.50 (foreign £15.20) (effective 1997). (British Bee-Keepers Association) Bee Craft Ltd., The Secretary, 15 West Way, Copthorne Bank, Crawley, W. Sussex RH10 3QS, England. TEL 44-1342-712119. Ed. Clare Waring. R&P contact: Clare Waring. adv. contact: Joan Gibb. bk.rev.; illus.; index; circ. 4,500 (paid). **Indexed:** Apic.Abstr. **Document type:** consumer publication.
  Description: Contains beginners' notes, practical suggestions, scientific works, seasonal checks, calendar of events, and readers' letters.

638.1   US   ISSN 1071-3190
SF521   CODEN: GLBCAK
BEE CULTURE. 1872. m. $17 (foreign $26.50) (effective 1997). A.I. Root Co., Box 706, Medina, OH 44258-0706. TEL 216-725-6677. FAX 216-725-5624. E-mail: bculture@aol.com; URL: http://www.airoot.com. Ed. Kim Flottum; Pub. John Root. R&P contact: Kim Flottum. adv. contact: Dawn Feagan. bk.rev.; charts; illus.; stat.; index; circ. 12,500 (paid). (also avail. in microform from UMI; back issues avail.; reprint service avail. from UMI) **Indexed:** Apic.Abstr., Biol.Abstr., Biol.& Agr.Ind., Chem.Abstr., Farm & Garden Ind. **Document type:** trade publication.
—KR SourceOne; Linda Hall; UMI; UnCover.
  Formerly (until 1992): Gleanings in Bee Culture (ISSN 0017-114X)
  Description: Focuses on American beekeeping, honey, and pollination.

638.1   UK   ISSN 0005-772X
    CODEN: BEWOAN
BEE WORLD. 1919. q. £40($70) (effective 1996). International Bee Research Association, 18 North Rd., Cardiff CF1 3DY, Wales. TEL 44-1222-372409. FAX 44-1222-665522. E-mail: ibra@cardiff.ac.uk. Ed. Pamela A. Munn. adv.: page £134; trim 175 x 120; adv. contact: Pamela A. Munn. bk.rev.; bibl.; charts; illus.; mkt.; index., cum.index: 1919-1949. circ. 1,200. **Indexed:** Apic.Abstr., ASCA, Bibl.Agri., Biol.Abstr., Biol.& Agr.Ind., Chem.Abstr., Curr.Adv.Ecol.Sci., Curr.Cont., Farm & Garden Ind., Helminthol.Abstr., Rev.Appl.Entomol., Sci.Cit.Ind. **Document type:** trade publication, academic/scholarly publication.
—BLDSC (1876.000000); Linda Hall; SWETS; UnCover. **CCC**.
  Description: Provides the international link between beekeeping science and practice.
  Refereed Serial

AGRICULTURE

638.1 UK ISSN 0005-7754
BEEKEEPING. 1934. 10/yr. £8.500 to non-members (overseas £11.50). Devon Beekeepers Association, c/o Brian Gant, Ed., Leaf Orchard, Grange Rd., Buckfast, Devon TQ11 0EH, England. TEL 44-1364-642233. FAX 44-1364-342233. E-mail: 106213.3313@compuserve.com. R&P contact: Brian Gant. TEL 44-1364-642233. adv. contact: Brian Gant. bk.rev.; index. circ. 1,000. Indexed: Apic.Abstr.
Description: Discusses bee culture.
Refereed Serial

638.1 UK ISSN 0256-4424
BEEKEEPING & DEVELOPMENT; the journal for sustainable beekeeping. 1983. q. £16($35) Bees for Development, Troy, Monmouth, Gwent NP5 4AB, Wales. TEL 44-1600-713648. FAX 44-1600-716167. E-mail: 100410.2631@compuserve.com. Ed. Nicola Bradbear. adv.: page £160; adv. contact: Helen Jackson. bibl.; illus.; index. circ. 4,000. (back issues avail.) **Document type:** academic/scholarly publication.
Description: Provides information on sustainable, low-technology beekeeping.
Refereed Serial

638.1 CN ISSN 0838-0937
BEEKEEPING NOTES. 3/yr. (plus irreg. updates). free. Department of Agriculture and Marketing, Kentville Agricultural Centre, Kentville, N.S. B4N 1J5, Canada. TEL 902-679-6029. FAX 902-679-6062. E-mail: drogers@kent.nsac.ns.ca. Ed. R.E.L. (Dick) Rogers. circ. 650. **Document type:** newsletter.

638.1 RH
BEELINE. 1963. q. Z.$100 (effective 1993). Zimbabwe Beekeepers Council, P.O. Box HG255, Highlands, Harare, Zimbabwe. TEL 263-4-490625. FAX 263-4-490625. E-mail: athol@msasa.samara.co.zw. Ed. Athol Desmond. adv.: B&W page Z.$136. bk.rev. circ. 400. **Document type:** academic/scholarly publication, newsletter.

630 CN
BEESCENE. q. Can.$20($30) (effective 1997). (British Columbia Honey Producers Association) BC Interior Agri Publications, RR 2, Chase, BC V0E 1M0, Canada. TEL 250-679-5362. FAX 250-679-5362. E-mail: frankay@mail.netshop.net. Ed. Fran Kay; Pub. Fran Kay. adv.: page Can.$500; trim 8 1/4 x 10 3/4; adv. contact: Fran Kay. illus.; mkt.; stat.; tr.lit.; circ. 850 (paid). (back issues avail.) **Document type:** trade publication.

638.1 US ISSN 1063-939X
BEESCIENCE. 1990. 4/yr. $30. Wicwas Press, L.L.C., Box 817, Cheshire, CT 06410-0817. TEL 203-250-7575. FAX 203-250-7575. Ed. Lawrence J. Connor. **Document type:** academic/scholarly publication.

630 NE
BEHEERSEN VAN ZIEKTEN, PLAGEN EN ONKRUIDEN. 1980. m. Misset (Subsidiary of: Reed Elsevier plc), Postbus 4, 7000 BA Doetinchem, Netherlands. TEL 31-8340-49911. FAX 31-8340-43839. TELEX 45481. Ed. S. Wit. (looseleaf format) **Document type:** trade publication.
Formerly: Akkerbouwpraktijk.
Description: Covers all aspects of crop protection, control of diseases, pests and weeds (excluding cultivation under glass) as well as approved materials, legislation and safety matters.

630 GW ISSN 0522-604X
BEHOERDEN UND ORGANISATIONEN DER LAND- FORST- UND ERNAEHRUNGSWIRTSCHAFT. irreg. (approx. a.). DM.195 (effective 1997). B. Behr's Verlag GmbH, Averhoffstr. 10, 22085 Hamburg, Germany. TEL 49-40-2270080. FAX 49-40-2201091. E-mail: behrs@behrs.de; URL: http://www.behrs.de. **Document type:** directory.

630 CC ISSN 1000-6966
BEIJING NONGYE/BEIJING AGRICULTURE. (Text in Chinese) m. Beijing Shi Nongye Ju, 19, Beisanhuan Donglu, Dewai, Beijing 100029, People's Republic of China. TEL 2012244. Ed. Li Hushan.

630 CC ISSN 0479-8007
S19
BEIJING NONGYE DAXUE XUEBAO/ACTA AGRICULTURAE UNIVERSITATIS PEKINENSIS. (Text in Chinese) q. $20. Beijing Nongye Daxue, Xuebao Bianjibu, Haidian-qu, Beijing 100094, People's Republic of China. TEL 2582244. Ed. Zeng Shimai. **Document type:** academic/scholarly publication.
—BLDSC (0588.850000).
Description: Publishes academic papers on agronomy, horticulture, plant protection, soil science and plant nutrition, animal sciences, veterinary medicine, agricultural meteorology, agricultural biology, food science, land resources and applied chemistry.

630 CC ISSN 1000-1514
CODEN: BNGXE3
BEIJING NONGYE GONGCHENG DAXUE XUEBAO/BEIJING UNIVERSITY OF AGRICULTURAL ENGINEERING. JOURNAL. (Text in Chinese) 1981. q. $80 (effective till 1995). Beijing Nongye Gongcheng Daxue, Qinghua Donglu, Beijing 100083, People's Republic of China. TEL 86-1-2017267. FAX 86-01-2016320. Ed. Li Xingchang. **Document type:** academic/scholarly publication.
Formerly (until 1986): Beijing Agricultural Mechanization College. Journal.
Description: Covers research development in the field of agriculture engineering, including agriculture mechanization, machinery, water conservation, poultry product processing, food engineering, and rural development studies.

630 CC ISSN 1001-8344
BEIJING NONGYE KEXUE/BEIJING AGRICULTURAL SCIENCE. (Text in Chinese) 1983. bi-m. Beijing Shi Nonglin Kexueyuan, Nongye Keji Qingbaosuo - Beijing Institute of Agriculture and Forestry, Institute of Agricultural Science and Technology Information, Haidian Banjing, Beijing 100081, People's Republic of China. TEL 8416644. Ed. Wang Yuanmin.

BEIKOKU TOKKYO SHOROKU. OYO YUKI KAGAKU, NOSUISAN, IJUTSU HEN/U.S. PATENT ABSTRACTS. APPLIED ORGANIC CHEMISTRY, AGRICULTURE AND FISHERY, MEDICINE. see *PATENTS, TRADEMARKS AND COPYRIGHTS — Abstracting, Bibliographies, Statistics*

630.091 636.089 GW ISSN 0301-567X
CODEN: BTLVBR
BEITRAEGE ZUR TROPISCHEN LANDWIRTSCHAFT UND VETERINAERMEDIZIN. (Text in English, French, German, Spanish; summaries in English, French, German, Spanish) 1963. 4/yr. DM.80. Institut fuer Tropische Landwirtschaft, Fichtestr. 28, 04275 Leipzig, Germany. FAX 0341-313090. adv.; bk.rev.; charts; illus. circ. 650. **Indexed:** Agroforest.Abstr., Anim.Breed.Abstr., Biodet.Abstr., Biol.Abstr., Chem.Abstr., Curr.Adv.Ecol.Sci., Curr.Cont., Dairy Sci.Abstr., Excerp.Med., Field Crop Abstr., Food Sci.& Tech.Abstr., Geo.Abstr., Helminthol.Abstr., Herb.Abstr., Hort.Abstr., IDA, Ind.Med., Ind.Vet., Plant Breed.Abstr., Poult.Abstr., Rev.Med.& Vet.Mycol., Rev.Plant Path., Rice Abstr., Rural Recreat.Tour.Abstr., Seed Abstr., Soils & Fert., Vet.Bull., Weed Abstr., World Agri.Econ.& Rural Sociol.Abstr. **Document type:** academic/scholarly publication.
—CASDDS; UnCover.
Formerly: Beitraege zur Tropischen und Subtropischen Landwirtschaft und Tropen Veterinaermedizin (ISSN 0005-8203)
Description: Contains research and communications in the fields of agrarian economy and management, agriculture and plant cultivation, soil science, animal nutrition and husbandry, veterinary hygiene, forestry and forest economics.

630 BH
BELIZE. DEPARTMENT OF AGRICULTURE. ANNUAL REPORT AND SUMMARY OF STATISTICS. 1937. a. $2. Ministry of Natural Resources, Department of Agriculture, Belmopan, Belize. stat. circ. 350. **Indexed:** Field Crop Abstr., Herb.Abstr., Rev.Plant Path.

630 NE ISSN 0160-3612
CODEN: BSARDN
BELTSVILLE SYMPOSIA IN AGRICULTURAL RESEARCH. 1977. irreg. price varies. (U.S. Department of Agriculture, Beltsville Agricultural Research Center) Kluwer Academic Publishers, Postbus 17, 3300 AA Dordrecht, Netherlands. TEL 31-78-6392392. FAX 31-78-6392254. TELEX 29245 KAPG NL. E-mail: services@wkap.nl; URL: http://www.wkap.nl. (Dist. by: Kluwer Academic Publishers Group, P.O. Box 322, 3300 AH Dordrecht, Netherlands. TEL 31-78-6392392. FAX 31-78-6546474; N. America dist. addr.: Box 358, Accord Sta., Hingham, MA 02018-0358. TEL 617-871-6600. FAX 617-871-6528) (back issues avail.) **Indexed:** Biol.Abstr., Chem.Abstr. **Document type:** proceedings.
—CASDDS; CISTI.
Refereed Serial

630.285 IS
BEN-GURION UNIVERSITY OF THE NEGEV. INSTITUTES FOR APPLIED RESEARCH. SCIENTIFIC ACTIVITIES. (Text in English) 1973. irreg., latest 1996. free. Ben Gurion University of the Negev, Institutes for Applied Research, P.O. Box 653, Beersheva 84105, Israel. TEL 972-7-6461931. FAX 972-7-6472569. E-mail: iar@bgumail.bgu.ac.il. Ed. Dorot Imber. circ. 1,500. **Indexed:** Field Crop Abstr., Herb.Abstr., Hort.Abstr. **Document type:** academic/scholarly publication.
Formerly: Ben-Gurion University of the Negev. Research and Development Authority. Applied Research Institute. Scientific Activities; Which superseded: Negev Institute for Arid Zone Research, Beer-Sheva, Israel. Report for Year (ISSN 0077-6467)
Description: Publishes short summaries of research projects conducted at the institutes, covering findings in chemistry and applications of chemical technology, and agriculture, applied biology and biotechnology.

630 GW ISSN 0005-9080
HD1951 CODEN: BERLAN
BERICHTE UEBER LANDWIRTSCHAFT. (Summaries in English, French, German) 1907. q. DM.498 (foreign DM.504) (effective 1997). (Bundesministerium fuer Ernaehrung, Landwirtschaft und Forsten) Landwirtschaftsverlag GmbH, Huelsebrockstr. 2, 48165 Muenster, Germany. TEL 49-2501-801-0. FAX 49-2501-801204. Eds. F. Quadflieg, J. Blasum. bk.rev.; charts; illus.; index. circ. 1,620. (reprint service avail. from ISI; back issues avail.) **Indexed:** ASCA, Biol.Abstr., Chem.Abstr., Curr.Adv.Ecol.Sci., Curr.Cont., Excerp.Med., Food Sci.& Tech.Abstr., Geo.Abstr., Helminthol.Abstr., IBR, Key to Econ.Sci., Maize Abstr., P.A.I.S.For.Lang.Ind., Pig News & Info., Potato Abstr., Rural Ext.Educ.& Tr.Abstr., SSCI, Triticale Abstr., World Agri.Econ.& Rural Sociol.Abstr., World Agri.Econ.& Rural Sociol.Abstr. **Document type:** academic/scholarly publication.
—BLDSC (1936.500000); CASDDS; Genuine Article; SWETS. **CCC.**

630 GW ISSN 0301-2689
CODEN: BELWAQ
BERICHTE UEBER LANDWIRTSCHAFT. SONDERHEFTE. irreg., no.205, 1991. price varies. Landwirtschaftsverlag GmbH, Huelsebrockstr. 2, 48165 Muenster, Germany. TEL 49-2501-801-0. FAX 49-2501-801204. circ. 1,600. (reprint service avail. from ISI) **Indexed:** Biol.Abstr., Curr.Cont., Int.Lab.Doc. **Document type:** monographic series.
—BLDSC (1936.505000).

630 UK ISSN 0954-9609
BERKS, BUCKS AND OXON FARMER. 1962. m. County Farmers Publications Ltd., 55 Goldington Rd., Bedford MK40 3LU, England. TEL 0234-351401. FAX 0234-328615. Ed. T. Bewley. adv. circ. 4,100.
Formerly (until 1988): Oxford and Berkshire Farmer; Incorporates: Oxford Farmer; Berkshire Farmer; Oxfordshire Farmer (ISSN 0030-7688)

630 639.2 BM
BERMUDA. DEPARTMENT OF AGRICULTURE AND FISHERIES. MONTHLY BULLETIN. 1914. m. free. Department of Agriculture and Fisheries, P.O. Box HM 834, Hamilton HM CX, Bermuda. TEL 441-236-4201. FAX 441-236-7582. Ed. LeYoni Junos. circ. 1,274. (back issues avail.) **Document type:** newsletter, government publication.
Former titles: Bermuda. Department of Agriculture, Fisheries and Parks. Monthly Bulletin; Farmers' Bulletin; Bermuda. Department of Agriculture. Agricultural Bulletin.

AGRICULTURE

630 639.2   BM
BERMUDA. DEPARTMENT OF AGRICULTURE AND FISHERIES. REPORT FOR THE YEAR. 1905. a. free (subject to availability). Department of Agriculture and Fisheries, P.O. Box HM 834, Hamilton HM CX, Bermuda. TEL 441-236-4201. FAX 441-236-7582. Ed. Diane Saunders. circ. 250. (back issues avail.) **Indexed:** Biol.Abstr., Field Crop Abstr., Herb.Abstr., Hort.Abstr., Maize Abstr., Rev.Plant Path. **Document type:** government publication.
    Former titles: Bermuda. Department of Agriculture, Fisheries and Parks. Report for the Year; Bermuda. Department of Agriculture and Fisheries. Report for the Year.

630   II   ISSN 0303-3821
BHARTIYA KRISHI ANUSANDHAN PATRIKA; quarterly research journal of plant and animal sciences. (Text in Hindi; summaries in English) 1973. q. Rs.250($50) (effective 1997). Agricultural Research Communication Centre, 1130 Sadar, Karnal 132001, Haryana, India. TEL 91-184-255080. Ed. B.S. Modi. **Indexed:** Chem.Abstr., Rice Abstr., Triticale Abstr., Weed Abstr.

630   HU
BIBLIOGRAPHIA HISTORIAE RERUM RUSTICARUM INTERNATIONALIS/INTERNATIONAL BIBLIOGRAPHY OF AGRICULTURAL HISTORY. 1964. biennial. $40. Magyar Mezogazdasagi Muzeum, P.O. Box 129, 1367 Budapest, Hungary. TEL 36-1-3430573. FAX 36-1-3439120. Eds. Peter Hajdu, Eva Voros; Pub. Gyorgy Feher. R&P contact: Gyorgy Feher. TEL 36-1-3438485. index. circ. 500. **Document type:** bibliography.
    Description: Provides data on works concerning agricultural history and related fields.

BIBLIOGRAPHIES AND LITERATURE OF AGRICULTURE. see AGRICULTURE — Abstracting, Bibliographies, Statistics

BIBLIOGRAPHY OF AGRICULTURE. see AGRICULTURE — Abstracting, Bibliographies, Statistics

BIBLIOGRAPHY OF AGRICULTURE. ANNUAL CUMULATIVE INDEX. see AGRICULTURE — Abstracting, Bibliographies, Statistics

638.1   GW   ISSN 0006-212X
DIE BIENE. 1864. m. DM.48 (foreign DM.53) (effective 1997). (Deutscher Imkerbund e.V.) D L V Deutscher Landwirtschaftsverlag Berlin, Guertelstr. 29a-30, 10247 Berlin, Germany. TEL 49-30-293974-87. FAX 49-30-29397459. adv.; bk.rev.; charts; illus.; stat. circ. 15,000. **Indexed:** Apic.Abstr. **Document type:** bulletin.

638.1   GW
DAS BIENENMUETTERCHEN. 1955. 10/yr. DM.28. Internationaler Bund der Sklaenarbienenzuechter e.V., Pommernstr. 3, 79761 Waldshut-Tiengen, Germany. TEL 05254-5889. Ed. Karl-Heinz Bosawe. adv. circ. 2,000. (back issues avail.) **Document type:** trade publication.
    Description: News for beekeepers worldwide.

638.1   AU   ISSN 0006-2146
BIENENVATER. 1869. m. S.300. Oesterreichischer Imkerbund, Georg-Coch-Platz 3-11 A, A-1010 Vienna, Austria. Ed. Hans Hutsteiner. adv.; bk.rev.; illus.; index. circ. 27,000. **Indexed:** Apic.Abstr.
    Description: Covers bee keeping.

638.1   AU   ISSN 0006-2154
BIENENWELT; Fachzeitschrift fuer den Imker. 1959. m. (11/yr.). S.188. Leopold Stocker Verlag, Hofgasse 5, A-8011 Graz, Austria. TEL 43-316-821636. FAX 43-316-835612. Ed. Simon Stolz. adv. contact: Thomas Muehlbacher. bk.rev.; illus.; index. circ. 4,000. **Indexed:** Apic.Abstr., Chem.Abstr. **Document type:** trade publication.
    —BLDSC (2022.910000).

638.1   NE   ISSN 0926-3357
BIJEN; maandblad voor imkers. 1898; N.S. 1992. 11/yr. fl.40 (effective through 1996). (Vereniging tot Bevordering der Bijenteelt in Nederland) Bijen, Postbus 198, 6720 AD Bennekom, Netherlands. TEL 31-317-422422. FAX 31-317-424180. E-mail: bijenhuis@tip.nl. (Co-sponsors: Imkersbonden ABTB Limburgse Land- en Tuinbouwbond; Bond van Bijenhouders van de Noordbrabantse Christelijke Boerenbond) Ed. J. Beetsma. R&P contact: J. Beetsma. adv.; bk.rev.; illus. circ. 9,000. **Indexed:** Apic.Abstr.
    Formed by the 1992 merger of: Bijenteelt (ISSN 0166-5820); Which was formerly (1922-1964): St. Ambrosius (ISSN 0927-6661) & Bijenteelt - Maandschrift voor Bijenteelt (ISSN 0166-6444); Which was formerly: Maandschrift voor Bijenteelt (ISSN 0024-8681)
    Description: Magazine about beekeeping, includes announcements of activities and lectures.
    Refereed Serial

630   SZ
BIO AKTUELL; Informationsbulletin fuer Biobaeurinnen und Biobauern. bi-m. 24 SFr. Forschungsinstitut fuer Biologischen Landbau, Bernhardsberg, CH-4104 Oberwil, Switzerland. (Co-sponsor: Vereinigung Schweizerischer Biologischer Landbauorganisationen) **Document type:** academic/scholarly publication.

630 574.192   US
BIO OPTIONS. 1986. q. $10 (foreign $12). 1970 Folwell Ave., 352 Alderman Hall, St. Paul, MN 55108. TEL 612-624-4217. FAX 612-625-4273. Ed. Judith Day. bk.rev. **Document type:** newsletter.
    Description: Contains articles on alternative plants and animals; covers new publications, calendar and center projects.

BIOCONTROL NEWS AND INFORMATION. see BIOLOGY

630 635   UK   ISSN 0144-8765
    CODEN: BIAHDP
BIOLOGICAL AGRICULTURE AND HORTICULTURE; an international journal of sustainable production systems. 1982. q. £59($99) to individuals; institutions £99 ($189). A B Academic Publishers, P.O. Box 42, Bicester, Oxon. OX6 7NW, England. TEL 44-1869-320949. Ed. P.J.C. Harris. adv.; bk.rev.; index. (also avail. in microform) **Indexed:** Agroforest.Abstr., ASCA, Bibl.Agri., Bio-Contr.News & Info., Chem.Abstr., Curr.Adv.Ecol.Sci., Curr.Cont., Ecol.Abstr., Environ.Per.Bibl. (1989-1994), Excerp.Med., Field Crop Abstr., Geo.Abstr.H.G., Geo.Abstr.P.G., Herb.Abstr., IDA, Irr.& Drain.Abstr., Maize Abstr., Soils & Fert., Triticale Abstr. **Document type:** academic/scholarly publication.
    —BLDSC (2074.200000); CASDDS; CISTI; Genuine Article; Linda Hall; SWETS; UnCover. CCC.
    Description: Covers the field of sustainable agriculture.

630   US
BIOLOGICAL FARMING NEWS. 1970. 5/yr. $10. 6808 Academy Pkwy. E., N.E., Albuquerque, NM 87109. TEL 505-761-1454. FAX 505-761-1458. Ed. Leland B. Taylor; Pub. Leland B. Taylor. R&P contact: Leland B. Taylor. bk.rev. circ. 25,000. **Document type:** newspaper.
    Description: Offers resources and services advocating a biological approach to agriculture as an alternative to organic or chemical farming.

630   BL   ISSN 0366-0567
    CODEN: BIOGAL
BIOLOGICO. (Text in Portuguese; summaries in English) 1935. s-a. R.7($7) Instituto Biologico, Av. Rodrigues Alves 1252, C.P. 7119, 01064-970 Sao Paulo, Brazil. TEL 55-11-5729822. FAX 55-11-5709704. Ed. Zuleide Alves Ramiro. bibl.; illus.; index. cum.index. circ. 2,000. **Indexed:** Bio-Contr.News & Info., Biol.Abstr., Biotech.Abstr., Chem.Abstr., Field Crop Abstr., Forest.Abstr., Helminthol.Abstr., Herb.Abstr., Hort.Abstr., Ind.Vet., Plant Breed.Abstr., Rev.Appl.Entomol., Rev.Plant Path., Seed Abstr., Triticale Abstr., Trop.Oil Seeds Abstr., Vet.Bull., Weed Abstr. **Document type:** academic/scholarly publication.
    —CASDDS; Linda Hall.

630 634.9   GW   ISSN 0067-5849
S231   CODEN: MBBLA9
BIOLOGISCHE BUNDESANSTALT FUER LAND- UND FORSTWIRTSCHAFT, BERLIN-DAHLEM. MITTEILUNGEN. (Text and summaries in English and German) 1906. irreg. price varies. (Biologische Bundesanstalt fuer Land- und Forstwirtschaft in Berlin-Dahlem) Blackwell Wissenschaft, Kurfuerstendamm 57, 10707 Berlin, Germany. TEL 49-30-32790628. FAX 49-30-32790610. E-mail: aboverwalt@ blackwis.de; URL: http://www.blackwis.com. illus. **Indexed:** Bio-Contr.News & Info., Biol.Abstr., Biotech.Abstr., Field Crop Abstr., Food Sci.& Tech.Abstr., Forest.Abstr., Forest Prod.Abstr., Herb.Abstr., Hort.Abstr., Plant Breed.Abstr., Rev.Appl.Entomol., Rev.Plant Path., Soils & Fert., Weed Abstr. **Document type:** bulletin.
    —BLDSC (5833.900000); Linda Hall.
    Description: Publication devoted to biological research in agriculture and forestry.

BIORESOURCE TECHNOLOGY. see BIOLOGY — Biotechnology

630   SZ
DAS BIOSKOP; Fachzeitschrift fuer Biolandbau und Oekologie. bi-m. 39 SFr. Forschungsinstitut fuer Biologischen Landbau, Bernhardsberg, CH-4104 Oberwil, Switzerland. **Document type:** academic/scholarly publication.

BIOTECH REPORTER; agricultural research - business. see BIOLOGY — Biotechnology

BIOTECHNOLOGY AND GENETIC ENGINEERING REVIEWS. see BIOLOGY — Biotechnology

BIOTECHNOLOGY IN AGRICULTURE AND FORESTRY. see BIOLOGY — Biotechnology

638.1   SW   ISSN 0006-3886
BITIDNINGEN. 1902. m. SEK 250 (effective 1997). Sveriges Biodlares Riksfoerbund (SBR), Trumpetarevaegen 5, S-59019 Mantorp, Sweden. FAX 46-582-61-16-82. E-mail: osterlund@bt. biodlarna.se. Ed. Erik Oesterlund. adv. contact: Erik Oesterlund. bk.rev.; abstr.; charts; illus.; mkt.; index. circ. 13,700.

630 634.9   GW   ISSN 0935-4344
BLICK INS HESSENLAND; Magazin fuer Landwirtschaft, Wald und Natur. 1981. q. DM.8. (Ministerium fuer Landwirtschaft, Forsten und Naturschutz) Bernecker GmbH & Co. KG, Unter dem Schoeneberg 1, 34212 Melsungen, Germany. TEL 05661-7310. Ed. Gerd Kallweit. **Indexed:** Nutr.Abstr.
    Formerly: Hessen. Minister fuer Landesentwicklung, Umwelt, Landwirtschaft und Forsten. Mitteilungen. Land und Umwelt.

630   AU   ISSN 0006-4742
BLICK INS LAND. 1966. m. (Universitaet fuer Bodenkultur Wien) S P V Printmedien GmbH, Talgasse 15, A-2753 Markt Piesting, Austria. TEL 43-1-71170-0. FAX 43-1-71170310. Ed. Klaus Orthaber. illus. circ. 240,000. **Document type:** bulletin.

631   SA
BLOEMFONTEIN AGRICULTURAL SHOW CATALOGUE. (Text in Afrikaans and English) a. Dryer Advertising, 21-25 Kruase St., P.O. Box 286, Bloemfontein, South Africa. Ed. F. de Jaeger. adv.

631   AU   ISSN 0006-5471
    CODEN: BODEA2
DIE BODENKULTUR; Journal fuer landwirtschaftliche Forschung. (Text in German; summaries in English and German) 1949. 4/yr. S.2480 (foreign S.2547). (Universitaet fuer Bodenkultur) Oesterreichischer Agrarverlag GmbH, Inkustr. 1-7, A-3400 Klosterneuburg, Austria. TEL 02243-333006. FAX 02243-3330056. Ed. Otto Steineck. adv.; bk.rev.; charts; illus. circ. 2,122. **Indexed:** Anim.Breed.Abstr., ASCA, Biodet.Abstr., Biol.Abstr., Biotech.Abstr., Chem.Abstr., Crop Physiol.Abstr., Curr.Adv.Ecol.Sci., Curr.Cont., Dairy Sci.Abstr., Excerp.Med., Field Crop Abstr., Food Sci.& Tech.Abstr., Helminthol.Abstr., Herb.Abstr., Hort.Abstr., IBR, Ind.Sci.Rev., Irr.& Drain.Abstr., Nutr.Abstr., Pig News & Info., Plant Breed.Abstr., Plant Grow.Reg.Abstr., Potato Abstr., Poult.Abstr., Rev.Plant Path., Rural Recreat.Tour.Abstr., Sci.Cit.Ind, Soils & Fert., Weed Abstr., World Agri.Econ.& Rural Sociol.Abstr.
    —BLDSC (2116.790000); CASDDS; EMDOCS.

AGRICULTURE

630   BE   ISSN 0772-7054
DE BOER & DE TUINDER. 1891. w. 1200 BEF. Belgische Boerenbond, Minderbroedersstraat 8, 3000 Leuven, Belgium. TEL 32-87-552446. FAX 32-87-742311. Ed. F. Hofkens. adv.; bk.rev. circ. 50,000. **Indexed:** Agri.Eng.Abstr., Hort.Abstr., Plant Grow.Reg.Abstr., Soils & Fert., Weed Abstr.
    Formerly: Boer (ISSN 0006-5595); Incorporating (since Jan. 1, 1976): Ons Fruitteeltblad (ISSN 0030-266X); Tuinbouwberichten (ISSN 0041-3976)

630   SA   ISSN 0259-0204
DIE BOER - THE FARMER. (Text in Afrikaans and English) 1974. m. free. South African Agricultural Union - Suid-Afrikaanse Landbou Unie, P.O. Box 1508, Pretoria 0001, South Africa. TEL 27-12-3226980. FAX 27-12-3200557. E-mail: salu@iafrica.com. Ed. Lynette van Hoven. R&P contact: Lynette van Hoven. adv.: B&W page R.4800, color page R.7980; trim 298 x 210; adv. contact: Lynette van Hoven. bk.rev.; circ. 40,000 (paid). **Document type:** newspaper.

630   NE   ISSN 0006-5617
BOERDERIJ. (Supplements avail.: Akkerbouw (ISSN 0169-0116); Varkenshouderij (ISSN 0169-0167); Veehouderij (ISSN 0169-0213)) 1915. w. fl.157.25. Misset (Subsidiary of: Reed Elsevier plc), Postbus 4, 7000 BA Doetinchem, Netherlands. TEL 31-314-349371. FAX 31-314-363638. TELEX 45481. Ed. H.E.P. Dokter. adv.: B&W page fl.7647, color page fl.9942; trim 230 x 295; adv. contact: Cor van Nek. bk.rev.; charts; illus.; mkt. circ. 80,330. **Indexed:** Excerp.Med. **Document type:** trade publication.
    —SWETS.
    Description: General agricultural trade news plus politics, technical, financial and family information.

630   SA
BOERE WEEKBLAD. (Text in Afrikaans) 1994. w. R.249.45 (foreign R.509.60) (effective 1997). Republican Press (Pty) Ltd., P.O. Box 32083, Mobeni 4060, South Africa. TEL 27-31-422041. FAX 27-31-921831. Ed. Corrie Venter. R&P contact: Roy Minnaar. TEL 27-11-7287245. adv. contact: T. Anderson. illus.
    Incorporates: Farmers Weekly (Afrikaans Edition).

BOL OG BY. see HISTORY — History Of Europe

BOLETIM METEOROLOGICO PARA A AGRICULTURA. see METEOROLOGY

630 570   SP
BOLETIN DE AGRICULTURA BIOLOGICO-DINAMICA. 1986. q. 954 ptas. Editorial Rudolf Steiner, Guipuzcoa, 11-1 izda, Madrid, Spain. TEL 34-1-2531481. Ed. Antonio Malagon Golderos. **Document type:** bulletin.

630   IT
BOLOGNA AGRICOLA. 1948. fortn. L.4000 or membership. Unione Provinciale Agricoltori di Bologna, Via Castiglione 24, 40124 Bologna, Italy. TEL 39-51-233991. FAX 39-51-228350. Ed. Antonio Ricci. adv.: page L.500000. bk.rev. circ. 13,000.

630   AG   ISSN 0084-7968
HD9044.A78
BOLSA DE CEREALES. NUMERO ESTADISTICO. 1937. a. Bolsa de Cereales, Avda. Corrientes 127, 1043 Buenos Aires, Argentina. E-mail: bolcebib@ datamarkets.com.ar; URL: http://www.bolcereales. com.

630   FR
BON CULTIVATEUR DE L'EST. 1820. m. 35 F. H. Burcier, Ed. & Pub., 6 rue des Michottes, 54000 Nancy, France. circ. 5,200.

630   NO   ISSN 0332-8414
BONDEBLADET. 1974. w. NOK 450. Norwegian Farmers Union, Schweigaardsgt. 34C, P.O. Box 9367, Groenland, N-0135 Oslo 1, Norway. TEL 47-22-05-47-67. Ed. Bendik Bendiksen. adv. contact: Hilde Elin Ranberg. charts; illus. circ. 94,000. (tabloid format; back issues avail.)
    —CCC.
    Formed by the 1974 merger of: Norges Bondeblad (ISSN 0029-1684); Produsenten.

630   NO   ISSN 0800-2126
BONDEVENNEN. 1897. w. (fortn. in summer months). NOK 360. (Felleskjoepet Rogaland Agder) Bonden, P.O. Box 208, N-4001 Stavanger, Norway. FAX 47-51-88-74-53. Ed. Oeyvind Bergoey. adv. circ. 8,300.

DE BOOMKWEKERIJ (DOETINCHEM). see GARDENING AND HORTICULTURE

630   BS   ISSN 0068-0478
BOTSWANA. MINISTRY OF AGRICULTURE. ANNUAL REPORT. (Reports available for various divisions of the Ministry of Agriculture) 1947. a. free. Ministry of Agriculture, Private Bag 0033, Gaborone, Botswana. TEL 267-328780. FAX 267-328847. TELEX 2752 SACCAR BD. Ed. Henry G. Jobeta. R&P contact: Dan B. Gombalume. **Indexed:** Field Crop Abstr., Herb.Abstr. **Document type:** government publication.

630   FR   ISSN 1257-144X
BOURBONNAIS RURAL. 1972. w. 335 F. B.P. 12, 03630 Desertines, France. TEL 70-05-10-46. FAX 70-05-35-98. Ed. Jean-Paul Bourdier. adv. contact: Jean-Paul Bourdier. circ. 10,910. **Document type:** newspaper.

631   US   ISSN 0192-4176
BRADFORD-TIOGA-SULLIVAN-POTTER-WYOMING FARM AND HOME NEWS.* 1947. m. $5 for 3 yrs. Farm & Home Publications, 10 Lourdes Rd., Binghamton, NY 13905-4293. Ed. Bernard M. Swartz. adv.; illus.; stat. circ. 2,382.

630 570   BL   ISSN 0006-8705
SB13   CODEN: BRGTAF
BRAGANTIA. (Text in English, Portuguese; abstracts in English) 1941. 2/yr. (in 1 vol., 2 nos./vol.). $70. Instituto Agronomico, Servico de Divulgacao Tecnico-Cientifica, Caixa Postal 28, 13001-970 Campinas, Sao Paulo, Brazil. TEL 55-19-2315422 ext. 118. FAX 0192-31-4943. E-mail: public@ barao.iac.br. Ed. Angela M.C. Furlani. bibl.; charts; illus.; index. circ. 1,000. **Indexed:** Bibl.Agri., Biol.Abstr., Chem.Abstr., Cott.& Trop.Fibr.Abstr., Ecol.Abstr., Field Crop Abstr., Geo.Abstr.P.G., Helminthol.Abstr., Herb.Abstr., Herb.Abstr., Hort.Abstr., Maize Abstr., Plant Breed.Abstr., Potato Abstr., Rev.Appl.Entomol., Rev.Plant Path., Rice Abstr., Seed Abstr., Soils & Fert., Soyabean Abstr., Triticale Abstr., Trop.Abstr., Trop.Oil Seeds Abstr., VITIS, Weed Abstr. **Document type:** government publication.
    —CASDDS; Linda Hall; UMI.

630   BL   ISSN 0101-5117
BRAZIL. CENTRO NACIONAL DE PESQUISA DE MANDIOCA E FRUTICULTURA TROPICAL. BOLETIM DE PESQUISA. 1981. irreg. price varies. Centro Nacional de Pesquisa de Mandioca e Fruticultura Tropical, Rua Embrapa s-n, Caixa Postal 007, 44380-000 Cruz das Almas, Bahia, Brazil. TEL 55-75-721-2120. FAX 55-75-721-1118. **Indexed:** Chem.Abstr., Plant Grow.Reg.Abstr. **Document type:** bulletin, government publication.

639.2 630   BL   ISSN 0100-8064
BRAZIL. CENTRO NACIONAL DE PESQUISA DE MANDIOCA E FRUTICULTURA TROPICAL. CIRCULAR TECNICA. 1980. irreg. price varies. Centro Nacional de Pesquisa de Mandioca e Fruticultura Tropical, Rua Embrapa s-n, Caixa Postal 007, 44380-000 Cruz das Almas, Bahia, Brazil. TEL 55-75-721-2120. FAX 55-75-721-1118. **Document type:** government publication.
    —BLDSC (3265.129000).

630   BL   ISSN 0100-8854
BRAZIL. CENTRO NACIONAL DE PESQUISA DE MANDIOCA E FRUTICULTURA TROPICAL. COMUNICADO TECNICO. 1975. irreg. price varies. Centro Nacional de Pesquisa de Mandioca e Fruticultura Tropical, Rua Embrapa s-n, Caixa Postal 007, 44380-000 Cruz das Almas, Bahia, Bahia, Brazil. TEL 55-75-721-2120. FAX 55-75-721-1118. **Indexed:** Chem.Abstr., Hort.Abstr. **Document type:** government publication, monographic series.
    —BLDSC (3397.470060).

638.1   UK   ISSN 0007-0327
BRITISH BEE JOURNAL. 1873. m. £8.40 (foreign £12 ($22.50)). British Bee Publications Ltd., 46 Queen St., Geddington, Nr. Kettering, Northants. NN14 1AZ, England. TEL 44-1536-742250. Ed. Cecil C. Tonsley. adv.; charts; illus. circ. 3,500. **Indexed:** Apic.Abstr.

630   CN   ISSN 0706-9308
BRITISH COLUMBIA. MINISTRY OF AGRICULTURE FISHERIES AND FOOD D.A.T.E. PROGRAM REPORT. 1974. a. Can.$5. Ministry of Agriculture Fisheries and Food, Extension Systems Branch, Parliament Bldgs., Victoria, BC V8W 2Z7, Canada. (Orders to: W A I R, 742 Vanalman Ave., Victoria, BC V8V 1X4, Canada) Ed. Reg Miller. circ. 1,300. **Document type:** government publication.
    Former titles: British Columbia. Ministry of Agriculture and Food D.A.T.E. Program Report; British Columbia. Ministry of Agriculture D.A.T.E. Program Report.

632.9   CN   ISSN 0228-8117
BRITISH COLUMBIA. MINISTRY OF AGRICULTURE FISHERIES AND FOOD. FIELD CROP PRODUCTION GUIDE TO WEED, DISEASE, INSECT, BIRD AND RODENT CONTROL. a. Can.$10. Ministry of Agriculture Fisheries and Food, Extension Systems Branch, Parliament Bldgs., Victoria, BC V8W 2Z7, Canada. (W A I R, 742 Vanalman Ave., Victoria, BC V8V 1X4, Canada) **Document type:** government publication.
    Former titles (until 1980): British Columbia. Department of Agriculture. Guide to Field Crop Weed, Disease, Insect, Rodent Control Recommendations (ISSN 0706-4322); (until 1978): British Columbia. Department of Agriculture. Field Crop Control Recommendations (ISSN 0706-4330); (until 1973): British Columbia. Department of Agriculture. Recommendations for Field Crops (ISSN 0706-4349); (until 1971): British Columbia. Department of Agriculture. Field Crop Recommendations (ISSN 0713-0090)

BRITISH COLUMBIA. MINISTRY OF AGRICULTURE FISHERIES AND FOOD. MUSHROOM PRODUCTION GUIDE. see GARDENING AND HORTICULTURE

BRITISH COLUMBIA. MINISTRY OF AGRICULTURE FISHERIES AND FOOD. NURSERY CROP PRODUCTION GUIDE FOR COMMERCIAL GROWERS. see GARDENING AND HORTICULTURE

630   CN   ISSN 1184-2164
BRITISH COLUMBIA AGRI DIGEST. 1985. 6/yr. Can.$10($15) (effective Jan. 1997). BC Interior Agri Publications, RR 2, Chase, BC V0E 1M0, Canada. TEL 250-679-5362. FAX 250-679-5362. E-mail: frankay@mail.netshop.net. Ed. Fran Kay; Pub. Fran Kay. adv.: page Can.$1275; trim size 11 1/2 x 17; adv. contact: Ralph Terpstra. bk.rev.; mkt, tr.lit.; circ. 7,500 (controlled). cols./p.: 6; pp./issue: 24. (tabloid format)
    Formed by the merger of: B.C. Farm Business Digest (ISSN 1184-2180) & British Columbia Dairy Digest (ISSN 1182-011X) & British Columbia Growers Digest (ISSN 1184-2172)
    Description: Focus on production and marketing technology relating to agriculture, particularly in British Columbia.

630   UK   ISSN 1364-7849
BRITISH FARMER AND GROWER MAGAZINE. q. £9.20 (Europe £12, elsewhere £18) (effective 1997). National Farmers' Union, Agriculture House, 164 Shaftesbury Ave., London WC2H 8HL, England. TEL 44-171-331-7200. FAX 44-171-331-7406. Ed. Sara Cushing. circ. 89,000. **Indexed:** Dairy Sci.Abstr., Field Crop Abstr., Food Sci.& Tech.Abstr., Herb.Abstr., Rural Recreat.Tour.Abstr., World Agri.Econ.& Rural Sociol.Abstr. **Document type:** trade publication.
    Former titles (until 1996): British Farmer (ISSN 0267-6338); (until 1985): British Farmer and Stockbreeder (ISSN 0007-0688); (until 1971): Farmer and Stock Breeder (ISSN 0425-760X)

630   CN   ISSN 0711-7590
BROADWATER MARKET LETTER; a weekly summary of farm commodity prices, management suggestions, market trends and policies. 1974. w. Can.$149($159) (fax deliv. Can.$260). DePutter Publishing Ltd., Box 43023, London, ON N6C 6A2, Canada. TEL 519-663-2224. FAX 519-663-9124. Ed. John DePutter; Pub. Jon DePutter. (also avail. by fax) **Document type:** newsletter.
    Description: Informs farmers, ranchers, and agri-business subscribers about the week's activities in local and world commodity markets.

AGRICULTURE

661.073 630.24　　IS　　ISSN 0007-2192
BROMIDES IN AGRICULTURE. (Text in English) 1960. 2/yr. free. Dead Sea Bromine Company Ltd., P.O. Box 180, Beersheva 84101, Israel. TEL 972-7-797630. FAX 972-7-297846. Ed. Yuval Cohen. bk.rev.; abstr.; charts; illus. circ. 1,500. **Indexed:** Helminthol.Abstr.

630　　US　　ISSN 0007-2834
BUCKEYE FARM NEWS. 1919. 11/yr. $5. Ohio Farm Bureau Federation, Inc., Box 479, Columbus, OH 43216. TEL 614-249-2483. FAX 614-249-2200. E-mail: farmb@ee.net; URL: http://fb.com/ohfb. Ed. Curt Dunham. adv. contact: Sharon Dilbone. bk.rev.; illus.; index; circ. 182,000 (paid). **Document type:** trade publication.
　　Formerly: Ohio Farm Bureau News.

630　　AA
BUJQESIA SOCIALISTE.* m. $3.08. Ministria e Bujqesise - Ministry of Agriculture, c/o Publishing and Information Center for Agriculture, Tirana, Albania. TELEX 4209. Ed. Faik Labinoti.

630　　AA
BUJQESTA SHQIPTARE/ALBANIAN AGRICULTURE. m. $3.08. Center of Information and Agrifood Formation, c/o Kastriot Ahmati, Ed., Rr. Skender Kosturi, Tirana, Albania. TEL 355-42-28422. FAX 355-42-28422.

630 334.683　　AA　　ISSN 0563-573X
　　　　　　CODEN: BSBUAY
BULETINI I SHKENCAVE BUJQESORE/BULLETIN DES SCIENCES AGRICOLES. (Text in Albanian; summaries in French) 1962. q. $8. Center of Information and Agrifood Formation, c/o Kastriot Ahmati, Ed., Rr. Skender Kosturi, Tirana, Albania. TEL 355-42-28422. FAX 355-42-28422. **Indexed:** Chem.Abstr., Field Crop Abstr., Hort.Abstr., Seed Abstr., Soils & Fert., Triticale Abstr.
　—CASDDS; Linda Hall.

630　　FR　　ISSN 0007-4055
BULLETIN AGRICOLE DES HAUTES PYRENEES. 1941. 10/yr. 34 Place du Foirail, 65000 Tarbes, France. TEL 62-93-55-52. Ed. Alain Fontaine. circ. 9,500.

631　　RW　　ISSN 0557-8213
BULLETIN AGRICOLE DU RWANDA/RWANDA AGRICULTURAL BULLETIN. (Text in French) 1968. 4/yr. (Ministere de l'Agriculture, de l'Elevage et des Forets) O C I R, B.P. 104, Kigali-Gikondo, Rwanda. TELEX 13. Ed. Augustin Nzindukiyimana. adv. circ. 800.

630　　BD
BULLETIN D'INFORMATION SUR LES JARDINS AGROSTOLOGIQUES DES PAYS MEMBRES DE LA C E P G L. Variant title: Bulletin d'Information I R A Z. irreg. (Communaute Economique des Pays des Grands Lacs) Institut de Recherche Agronomique et Zootechnique, B.P. 91, Citenga, Burundi. **Indexed:** P.L.E.S.A.

630　　CN　　ISSN 0007-4446
BULLETIN DES AGRICULTEURS. 1917. m. Can.$24.95 (foreign Can.$40). Maclean Hunter Ltd., Maclean Hunter Bldg., 777 Bay St., Toronto, ON M5W 1A7, Canada. TEL 514-382-4350. FAX 514-382-4356. Ed. Marc-Alain Soucy. adv.: B&W page Can.$3450, color page Can.$4395; trim 8 x 10 3/4; adv. contact: Simon Guertin. bk.rev.; circ. 35,067 (paid). (also avail. in microfiche) **Indexed:** Pt.de Rep. (1981-). **Document type:** trade publication.

630　　BS　　ISSN 0256-7512
S542.B55
BULLETIN OF AGRICULTURAL RESEARCH IN BOTSWANA. 1983. q. free. Ministry of Agriculture, Department of Agricultural Research, Private Bag 0033, Gaborone, Botswana. TEL 267-328780. FAX 267-628847. TELEX 2752 SACCAR BD. Ed. Lobisa L. Setshwaelo. R&P contact: Dan B. Gombalume. charts; bibl.; illus.; stat. circ. 250. (back issues avail.) **Indexed:** Ind.S.A.Per. **Document type:** government publication, bulletin.

630　　II
BULLETIN OF AGRICULTURE PRICES. (Text in English) w. Rs.150($54) (effective 1992, 1993). Ministry of Agriculture, Department of Economics and Cooperation, Directorate of Economics and Statistics, A-2E-3 Kasturba Gandhi Marg Barracks, New Dehli 110 001, India. TEL 11-381523. (Dist. by: Controller of Publications, Ministry of Urban Development, Civil Lines, Delhi 110 054, India) Ed. Brajesh Kumar Gautam. circ. 370.

633.1　　II　　ISSN 0007-4896
SB183　　CODEN: BUGTA2
BULLETIN OF GRAIN TECHNOLOGY. (Text in English) 1963. 3/yr. membership; non-members $15. Foodgrain Technologists' Research Association of India, Hapur, Uttar Pradesh, India. Ed. Dr. N.S. Agarwal. adv.; bk.rev.; abstr.; bibl.; charts; illus.; stat.; cum.index. circ. 750. (back issues avail.) **Indexed:** Biol.Abstr., Chem.Abstr., Excerp.Med., Field Crop Abstr., Food Sci.& Tech.Abstr., Herb.Abstr., Nutr.Abstr., Rev.Appl.Entomol., Rice Abstr., Soils & Fert.
　—CASDDS; CISTI.

638.1　　FR　　ISSN 0335-3710
　　　　　　CODEN: BTAPDO
BULLETIN TECHNIQUE APICOLE. 1973. m. 175 F. (foreign 190 F.) (effective 1997). Centre Apicole, Office pour l'Information et la Documentation en Apiculture, Echauffour, 61370 Ste. Gauburge, France. TEL 33-2-33340580. Ed. Francoise Jeanne. adv. contact: Raymond Bartlet. bk.rev.; cum.index: 1973-1995. circ. 3,000. **Indexed:** Apic.Abstr., Biol.Abstr., Sugar Ind.Abstr. **Document type:** bulletin.
　—CASDDS. CCC.

630　　IC　　ISSN 0251-2661
BUNADARRIT. 1887. a. $25 to non-members. Bunadarfelag Islands - Agricultural Society of Iceland, Box 7080, Reykjavik, Iceland. TEL 354-551-9200. FAX 354-562-3058. Ed. Jonas Jonsson. circ. 2,500. **Indexed:** Anim.Breed.Abstr., Nutr.Abstr.

630　　AU　　ISSN 1026-6267
BUNDESANSTALT FUER ALPENLAENDISCHE LANDWIRTSCHAFT. BERICHT. 1989. irreg. varies. Bundesanstalt fuer Alpenlaendische Landwirtschaft Gumpenstein, A-8952 Irdning, Austria. TEL 43-3682-22451. FAX 43-3682-2461488. Ed. Kurt Chytil. R&P contact: Kurt Chytil. adv. contact: Eva Rainer. circ. 500. (back issues avail.) **Document type:** proceedings.

630　　AU　　ISSN 0007-6244
BURGENLAENDISCHE LANDWIRTSCHAFTSKAMMER. MITTEILUNGSBLATT. 1957. m. S.60. Burgenlaendische Landwirtschaftskammer, Esterhazystr. 15, A-7001 Eisenstadt, Austria. Ed. Josef F. Scharnagl. adv.; bk.rev.; illus.; mkt.; pat. circ. 39,000.

630　　AU
BURGENLAENDISCHER AGRARKURIER. m. S.130. (Burgenlaendischer Bauernbund) Oesterreichischer Agrarverlag GmbH, Inkustr. 1-7, A-3400 Klosterneuburg, Austria. TEL 02243-333006. FAX 02243-3330056.

338.1　　UV
BURKINA FASO. SERVICE DES STATISTIQUES AGRICOLES. ANNUAIRE. 1970. a. Service des Statistiques Agricoles, Ministere de l'Agriculture et de l'Elevage, B.P. 7010, Ouagadougou, Burkina Faso. circ. 500.
　　Formerly: Upper Volta. Service des Statistiques Agricoles. Annuaire.

630　　US　　ISSN 0195-1246
BUSINESS FARMER. 1925. w. $24. Business Farmer, Inc., Box 770, Scottsbluff, NE 69361. TEL 307-532-2184. FAX 308-635-2348. Ed. Penny Yekel. adv.; bk.rev. circ. 3,300. **Document type:** newspaper.

BUSINESS RATIO PLUS: THE AGRICULTURAL EQUIPMENT INDUSTRY. see *MACHINERY*

630　　IC　　ISSN 1012-6910
　　　　　　CODEN: BUVIEE
BUVISINDI/ICELANDIC AGRICULTURAL SCIENCES. (Text in English, Scandinavian languages; summaries in English) 1969-1986; resumed 1988. irreg. (1-2/yr.). free. Rannsoknastofnun Landbunadarins - Agricultural Research Institute, Keldnaholti, IS-112 Reykjavik, Iceland. TEL 354-577-1010. FAX 354-577-1020. E-mail: gudrun@rala.is; URL: http://www.rala.is. Ed. Fridrik Palmason. circ. 600 (controlled). **Document type:** academic/scholarly publication.
　—BLDSC (4361.454000).
　　Formerly (until 1986): Islenzkar Landbunadarrannsoknir (ISSN 0368-0142)
　　Description: Publishes original research concerning Icelandic agriculture.

630　　CN
C A A R COMMUNICATOR. 1980. q. Can.$17.12 (foreign Can.$21.40) (effective 1997); newsstand price: Can.$4.28. Canadian Association of Agri-Retailers, 1090 Waverley St., Ste 107, Winnipeg, MB R3T 0P4, Canada. TEL 204-989-9300. FAX 204-989-9306. Ed. Robynne Anderson Eva. R&P contact: Robynne Anderson Eva. TEL 204-453-1965. adv. contact: Robynne Anderson Eva. circ. 3,800. (back issues avail.) **Document type:** trade publication.
　　Formerly: W F C D Communicator (ISSN 0822-8183)
　　Description: For retailers of fertilizers and chemicals in Canada, their suppliers, and manufacturers.

630　　US
C A HIGHLIGHTS. 1977. bi-m. $12 to non-members; members free. Communicating for Agriculture, 101 E. Lincoln, Box 677, Fergus Falls, MN 56538. TEL 218-739-3241. FAX 218-739-3832. E-mail: editor@cainc.org; URL: http://www.cainc.org. Ed. Steven K. Anderson. circ. 33,900. (tabloid format; back issues avail.)
　　Description: Covers rural issues, including legislative news, technological trends, agricultural business news, exchange opportunities, as well as member-related association news.

630　　UK　　ISSN 0953-5586
C A P LEGISLATION QUARTERLY. (Common Agricultural Policy) q. £290 (rest of Europe £325) (includes C A P Legislation Weekly). Agra Europe (London) Ltd., 25 Frant Rd., Tunbridge Wells, Kent TN2 5JT, England. TEL 44-1892-533813. FAX 44-1892-544895. TELEX 95114 AGRATW G. E-mail: 100637.3460@compuserve.com. (looseleaf format) **Document type:** trade publication.

630　　UK　　ISSN 1356-5508
C A P LEGISLATION WEEKLY. (Common Agricultural Policy) w. (plus q. summaries). £330 (rest of Europe £345; elsewhere £385) (includes C A P Legislation Quarterly) (effective 1997). Agra Europe (London) Ltd., 25 Frant Rd., Tunbridge Wells, Kent TN2 5JT, England. TEL 44-1892-533813. FAX 44-1892-544895. TELEX 95114 AGRATW G. E-mail: 100637.3460@compuserve.com. (looseleaf format) **Document type:** trade publication.
　　Former titles (until 1995): C A P Weekly (ISSN 0953-5594); (until 1988): Agra Europe Express Monitor (ISSN 0951-2063)
　　Description: Covers EU legislation on agricultural commodities, including information on the latest changes in levies, refunds and correctives for the main commodities; and agrimonetary comment. Quarterly summaries are indexed by commodity and provide a cumulative permanent reference.

630 341　　UK　　ISSN 0142-5633
C A P MONITOR. (Common Agricultural Policy); a continuously up-dated information service on the Common Agricultural Policy of the European Union. 1978. base vol. (plus irreg. updates). £690 (rest of Europe £745; elsewhere £805); updates (renewals only) £545 (rest of Europe £590; elsewhere £640) (effective 1997). Agra Europe (London) Ltd., 25 Frant Rd., Tunbridge Wells, Kent TN2 5JT, England. TEL 44-1892-533813. FAX 44-1892-544895. TELEX 95114 AGRATW G. E-mail: 10637.3460@compuserve.com. (looseleaf format) **Document type:** trade publication.
　—BLDSC (3050.622300).
　　Description: Provides a guide to the EU Common Agricultural Policy, explaining its operations.

AGRICULTURE

630 GY ISSN 1018-1210
C A R A P H I N NEWS. 1989. s-a. Inter-American Institute for Cooperation on Agriculture, Caribbean Animal and Plant Health Information Network, P.O. Box 10-1089, Georgetown, Guyana. TEL 5922-78791. FAX 5922-58358. E-mail: svokaty@iica.org.gy. Ed. Sandra Vokaty. R&P contact: Sandra Vokaty. adv. circ. 1,000. **Document type:** newsletter.
—BLDSC (3050.952500).
Formerly: I I C A Miscellaneous Publication (ISSN 0534-5391)

630 US ISSN 0886-3970
C A R D REPORT (AMES, 1986). 1986. q. free. Iowa State University, Center for Agricultural and Rural Development, 578 Heady Hall, Ames, IA 50011-1070. TEL 515-294-7519. FAX 515-294-6336. E-mail: card@card.iastate.edu; URL: htttp://www.ag.iastate.edu/card. Ed. Judith Pim. R&P contact: Judith Pim. circ. 6,500.
—BLDSC (3051.014500).
Description: Features agricultural policy research.

630 FR ISSN 1167-3702
C.F.C.A. ACTUALITES. bi-m. 560 F. (effective 1997). (Confederation Francaise de la Cooperation Agricole) Societe de Diffusion, d'Informations Agricoles et de Presse (SODIAP), 49 Ave. de la Grande Armee, 75116 Paris, France. TEL 33-1-44175700. FAX 33-1-44175701.

630 CK
S540.8.C45
C I A T IN PERSPECTIVE. (Each report since 1992 has distinctive title.) (Text in English) 1980. a. free. Centro Internacional de Agricultura Tropical, Distribucion de Publicaciones - International Center for Tropical Agriculture, Publications Unit, Apdo. Aereo 6713, Cali, Colombia. TEL 57-2-4450000. FAX 57-2-4450073. Eds. Nathan C. Russell, Thomas Hargrove. circ. 3,500. **Indexed:** Anim.Breed.Abstr., Biol.Abstr., Herb.Abstr., Plant Breed.Abstr. **Document type:** corporate report.
—BLDSC (3190.090000).
Formerly: C I A T Report (ISSN 0120-3169); **Supersedes:** Centro Internacional de Agricultura Tropical. Annual Report; C I A T Highlights.
Description: Presents highlights of CIAT activities.

630 600 PH ISSN 0115-0405
CODEN: CSCJDK
C L S U SCIENTIFIC JOURNAL. 1966. 2/yr. P.30($10) Central Luzon State University, c/o Estefania W. Kollin, Publications House, Munoz, Nueva Ecija, Philippines. Ed. Carminia Leabres Ramos. circ. 4,000. (back issues avail.) **Indexed:** Ind.Phil.Per. **Document type:** academic/scholarly publication.
—BLDSC (3287.027000); CASDDS.

C M S NEWS. (Clay Minerals Society) see MINES AND MINING INDUSTRY

630 641.1 PH ISSN 0116-7847
CODEN: CJANES
C M U JOURNAL OF SCIENCE. 1979. q. P.60($4) Central Mindanao University, University Town, Musuan, Bukidnon, Philippines. Ed. Herminio M. Pava. circ. 350. (back issues avail.) **Indexed:** Bio-Contr.News & Info., Dairy Sci.Abstr., Field Crop Abstr., Herb.Abstr., Ind.Phil.Per., Ind.Vet., Maize Abstr., Pig News & Info., Potato Abstr., Rural Recreat.Tour.Abstr., Seed Abstr., Soils & Fert., World Agri.Econ.& Rural Sociol.Abstr.
—CCC.
Formerly (until vol.9, 1987): C M U Journal of Agriculture, Food and Nutrition (ISSN 0115-4931)

C T F A STRAIGHT TALK. (Committee for Truth in Farmland Assessment) see CONSERVATION

630 FR
CAHIER DE CONJONCTURE DES REGIONS VITICOLES EUROPEENNES. (Text in French; summaries in English) 1968. 3/yr. 500 F. (effective 1997); newsstand price: 250 F. Institut Europeen de Conjoncture Viti-Vinicole, Ecole Nationale de Formation Agronomique, B.P. 87, 31326 Castanet Tolosan Cedex, France. TEL 33-5-61753280. FAX 33-5-61753274. Ed. Jean Dubos. R&P contact: Jean Dubos. adv. contact: Jean Dubos. circ. 400. **Document type:** bulletin.
Formerly (until 1992): Situation du Marche Vinicole (ISSN 0223-4580)

630 FR ISSN 1166-7699
CAHIERS D'ETUDES ET DE RECHERCHES FRANCOPHONES AGRICULTURES. Key Title: Agricultures (Montrouge). Variant title: Cahiers Agricultures. 1992. 6/yr. 420 F. to individuals; institutions 710 F.; students 260 F. (effective 1997). John Libbey Eurotext, 127 av. de la Republique, 92120 Montrouge, France. TEL 33-1-46730660. FAX 33-1-40840999. E-mail: marketing@jle.com. (Subscr. to: A T E I, 3 av. Pierre Kerautret, 93230 Romainville, France. TEL 33-1-48408686. FAX 33-1-48400731) Eds. Jean Semal, Didier Spire.
—BLDSC (2948.610500).
Description: Takes a multidisciplinary approach to agronmomic research and rural development.

631.091 FR ISSN 0760-579X
CAHIERS DE LA RECHERCHE - DEVELOPPEMENT. (Text in French; summaries in English, Spanish) 1983. q. 300 F. Centre de Cooperation Internationale en Recherche Agronomique pour le Developpement (CIRAD), Systemes Agroalimentaires et Ruraux, B.P. 5035, 34032 Montpellier, France. TEL 33-67-61-57-00. FAX 33-67-61-12-23. TELEX 485 221 F. E-mail: pelleceuer@cirad.fr. **Indexed:** Agroforest.Abstr., Herb.Abstr., Maize Abstr., Rice Abstr., Rural Devel.Abstr., Triticale Abstr., World Agri.Econ.& Rural Sociol.Abstr.
—BLDSC (2952.125150).

630 FR ISSN 1022-1379
CAHIERS OPTIONS MEDITERRANEENNES. 1993. irreg., vol.16, 1996. Centre International de Hautes Etudes Agronomiques Mediterraneennes, Institut Agronomique Mediterraneen de Montpellier, 3191, route de Mende, B.P. 5056, 34044 Montpellier, France. TEL 33-67046000. FAX 33-67542527.
—BLDSC (2950.537000).

630 US ISSN 0575-5298
CALIFORNIA AGRICULTURAL DIRECTORY (YEAR); including Oregon & Washington. 1963. a. $30. California Farm Bureau Federation, 1601 Exposition Blvd., FB10, Sacramento, CA 95815. TEL 916-924-4060. FAX 916-929-1680. Ed. Clark Biggs. circ. 1,000. **Document type:** directory.

630 US ISSN 0008-0845
S1 CODEN: CAGRA3
CALIFORNIA AGRICULTURE; reports of progress in research. 1947. bi-m. (foreign $12). University of California, Division of Agriculture and Natural Resources, 300 Lakeside Dr., 6th Fl., Oakland, CA 94612-3560. TEL 510-987-0044. E-mail: iorrie.mandoriao@ucop.edu; URL: http://www.ucop.edu/anrhome/cal-ag/about__ca.html. Ed. Pam Kan-Rice. charts; illus.; stat.; index. circ. 18,484. **Indexed:** Agri.Eng.Abstr., Bio-Contr.News & Info., Biol.Abstr., Biotech.Abstr., Cal.Per.Ind. (1978-), Chem.Abstr., Cott.& Trop.Fibr.Abstr., Curr.Pack.Abstr., Dairy Sci.Abstr., Energy Info.Abstr., Environ.Abstr., Excerp.Med., Field Crop Abstr., Food Sci.& Tech.Abstr., Forest.Abstr., Geo.Abstr., Helminthol.Abstr., Herb.Abstr., Hort.Abstr., INIS Atomind., Irr.& Drain.Abstr., Ocean.Abstr., Ornam.Hort., Plant Breed.Abstr., Pollut.Abstr., Poult.Abstr., Rev.Appl.Entomol., Rev.Plant Path., Rice Abstr., Rural Recreat.Tour.Abstr., Sel.Water Res.Abstr., Soils & Fert., Sport Fish.Abstr., VITIS, Weed Abstr., Wild.Rev., World Agri.Econ.& Rural Sociol.Abstr., Zoo.Rec. (until 19??). **Document type:** academic/scholarly publication.
●Also available online.
—BLDSC (3011.000000); CASDDS; CIS; Linda Hall; UMI; UnCover.
Description: Reports of progress in research by the Agricultural Experiment Station.

630 US ISSN 0164-5331
CALIFORNIA - ARIZONA FARM PRESS; timely, reliable information for Western agriculture. 1979. s-m. $30. Farm Press, Division of Intertec Publishing, Box 1420, Clarksdale, MS 38614. TEL 601-624-8503. FAX 601-627-1977. Ed. Harry Cline. R&P contact: Darrah Parker. adv. contact: Darrah Parker. circ. 24,000. **Document type:** trade publication.
—CCC.

630 US ISSN 0008-1051
CALIFORNIA FARMER; the business magazine for commercial agriculture. (In 3 editions: Northern, Southern and Central Valley) 1854. 15/yr. $19.95 (foreign $45). Farm Progress Companies (Subsidiary of: A B C Publishing Companies), 191 S. Gary Ave., Carol Stream, IL 60188. TEL 630-690-5600. FAX 630-462-2869. (Edit. addr.: 1410 Danzig Plaza, Ste. 250, Concord, CA 94520-5270. TEL 510-687-1662. FAX 510-687-4945) Ed. Len Richardson. adv.: B&W page $3400, color page $4430; trim 7 X 10. illus.; mkt.; circ. 53,013 (paid). (also avail. in microfilm from LIB) **Indexed:** Acid Rain Abstr., Acid Rain Ind., Cal.Per.Ind. (1980-), Environ.Abstr., Farm & Garden Ind.
Description: Covers farming and ranching, marketing, and legislation for farmers and ranchers in California.

630 US ISSN 0008-1124
CALIFORNIA GRANGE NEWS. 1932. m. $6.50. California State Grange, 2101 Stockton Blvd., Sacramento, CA 95817. TEL 916-454-5805. FAX 916-739-8189. Ed. J.D. Hartz. adv.; bk.rev.; illus. circ. 34,850. (tabloid format)

631 US
CALIFORNIA ORNAMENTAL CROPS REPORT. s-w. $132. (U.S. Department of Agriculture) Federal-State Market News Service, 630 Sansome St., Rm. 727, San Francisco, CA 94111. TEL 415-705-1300. FAX 415-705-1301. circ. 150. (looseleaf format; back issues avail.) **Document type:** government publication, newspaper.
Description: Presents lists of shipping points, market conditions, price ranges, product quality, and wholesale markets pertaining to cut flowers in- and out-of-state.

631 US ISSN 0194-8504
CALIFORNIA STRAWBERRY REPORT. s-w. $99 (foreign $198). (U.S. Department of Agriculture) Federal-State Market News Service, 630 Sansome St., Rm. 727, San Francisco, CA 94111. TEL 415-705-1300. FAX 415-705-1301. circ. 100. (looseleaf format; back issues avail.) **Document type:** government publication.
Description: Presents lists of shipments, market conditions, wholesale prices, product quality, and produce distribution of this fruit from and throughout the state.

630 635 UK ISSN 0954-9617
CAMBRIDGESHIRE FARMERS. 1947. m. County Farmers Publications Ltd., 55 Goldington Rd., Bedford MK40 3LU, England. TEL 0234-351401. FAX 0234-328614. Ed. D. Brown. adv.; bk.rev. circ. 3,450.
Formerly: Cambridgeshire Farmers' Journal.

630 CM ISSN 0527-4257
S19
CAMEROUN AGRICOLE, PASTORALE ET FORESTIER.* (Text in French) 1957. 6/yr. Chambre d'Agriculture et des Forets du Cameroun, B.P. L87, Parc Repiquet, Yaounde, Cameroon. adv.

630 SP
CAMP VALENCIA. 1977. m. 1000 ptas. Unio de Llavrador i Ramaders del Pais Valencia, Avellanas, 17 3o, 46003 Valencia, Spain. TEL 6-931-31-93. FAX 6-391-59-47. Ed. Eloi Casanovas. circ. 10,000.

983 CL ISSN 0008-2341
CAMPESINO. 1838. m. $20. Sociedad Nacional de Agricultura, Tenderini 187, Casilla 40-D, Santiago, Chile. TEL 2-39-6710. TELEX 240760. Dir. Patricio Montt. adv.; abstr.; illus.; stat.; index. circ. 5,000.

630 MX ISSN 0008-2473
EL CAMPO; revista mensual agricola y ganadera. 1924. m. Mex.$750. Publicaciones Armol, S.A., Mar Negro No. 147, Apdo. Postal 17-506, Mexico D.F. 11410, Mexico. Ed. Armando Palafox Flores. adv.; bk.rev. circ. 35,000.

630 332 SP ISSN 0212-2146
CAMPO; boletin de informacion agraria. 1967. q. free. Banco de Bilbao - Vizcaya, Servicio de Estudios, Gran Via 1, 48001 Bilbao, Spain. TEL 94-447 71 00. TELEX 32055 BB AC. Ed. Sabino Larrea Ereno. charts; illus.; stat.; cum.index. **Indexed:** Ind.SST.
—CINDOC.

AGRICULTURE

630 AG ISSN 0325-7940
CAMPO MODERNO Y CHACRA. 1930. m. Editorial Atlantida, S.A., Azopardo 579, 1307 Buenos Aires, Argentina. TEL 1-333-4591. TELEX 21163. Ed. Constancio C. Vigil. adv.; illus. circ. 35,000.
Former titles (until 1975): Chacra y Campo Moderno (ISSN 0325-7932); (until 1974): Chacra (ISSN 0009-0913)
Description: Covers farming and the countryside.

630 US ISSN 0211-4704
CAMPO Y MECANICA; journal of popular farm science and rural life. English edition: Furrow (ISSN 0016-3112) (Text in Spanish) 1960. 4/yr. free to qualified personnel. Deere & Company, John Deere Rd., Moline, IL 61265. TEL 309-765-8000. Ed. Jean-Claude Hiron. circ. 203,000.

638.1 CN ISSN 0576-4688
CANADIAN BEEKEEPING. 1968. 6/yr. Can.$21.40($20) (foreign Can.$60) (effective 1997). Beekeeping Industry in Canada, P.O. Box 678, Tottenham, ON L0G 1W0, Canada. TEL 905-936-4975. E-mail: warnott@bconnex.net. Ed. W.J.R. Arnott; Pub. W.J.R. Arnott. R&P contact: W.J.R. Arnott. adv.: B&W page Can.$420; adv. contact: W.J.R. Arnott. **Indexed:** Apic.Abstr. **Document type:** trade publication, consumer publication.
—BLDSC (3017.621000).

CANADIAN PAPERS IN RURAL HISTORY. see HISTORY — History Of North And South America

CANADIAN PLANT DISEASE SURVEY. see BIOLOGY — Botany

CANADIAN SOCIETY OF PLANT PHYSIOLOGISTS. BULLETIN/SOCIETE CANADIENNE DE PHYSIOLOGIE VEGETALE. BULLETIN. see BIOLOGY — Botany

630 CN ISSN 0841-209X
CANOLA GUIDE. (Supplement to: Country Guide) 1987. 7/yr. Farm Business Communications, Box 6600, Winnipeg, MB R3C 3A7, Canada. TEL 204-944-5761. FAX 204-942-8463. Ed. Bill Strautman. adv. contact: Tom Mumby. circ. 25,641. **Document type:** trade publication.
Description: Published for canola growers in western Canada interested in increasing the efficiency and profitability of their operations.

630 CC ISSN 0258-4069
CANSANG TONGBAO/SERICULTURE BULLETIN. (Text in Chinese) 1954. q. $0.50 per no. Zhejiang Cansang Xuehui - Zhejiang Sericulture Society, Huajiachi, Hangzhou, Zhejiang 310029, People's Republic of China. TEL 86-571-6041733. FAX 86-571-6049815. Ed. Xu Junliang. adv. **Document type:** bulletin.
Refereed Serial

630 634.9 US ISSN 0740-3704
CAPITAL PRESS; regional Oregon, Idaho, Washington, N. California agricultural-forest weekly. 1928. w. $36. Press Publishing Co., Box 2048, Salem, OR 97308. TEL 503-364-4431. FAX 503-370-4843. Ed. Mike Forrester. adv. contact: Greg Hains. circ. 35,000. (back issues avail.) **Document type:** newspaper.

CARETAKER GAZETTE; number 1 source for caretaker jobs! see OCCUPATIONS AND CAREERS

CASA SUI CAMPI. see LEISURE AND RECREATION

630 570 HO ISSN 0008-8692
CODEN: CEIBAR
CEIBA. (Text in English and Spanish) 1950. s-a. $30 (effective 1996). Escuela Agricola Panamericana, Adpo. 93, Tegucigalpa D.C., Honduras. TEL 504-76-6140. FAX 504-76-6242. E-mail: abelino%eapdpv@sdnhon.org.hn. Ed. Abelino Pitty. R&P contact: Abelino Pitty. adv. contact: Abelino Pitty. bk.rev.; charts; illus.; cum.index. circ. 1,000. (also avail. in microform from UMI; reprint service avail. from UMI) **Indexed:** Biol.Abstr., Chem.Abstr., Field Crop Abstr., Herb.Abstr., Hort.Abstr., Rev.Plant Path., Soils & Fert., Sport Fish.Abstr., Weed Abstr., Wild.Rev., Zoo.Rec. **Document type:** academic/scholarly publication.
—BLDSC (3097.400000); Linda Hall; UMI; UnCover.
Refereed Serial

CENICAFE. see FOOD AND FOOD INDUSTRIES

630 US ISSN 1085-4975
CENTER FOR RURAL AFFAIRS NEWSLETTER; a newsletter surveying events affecting rural America. 1974. m. free. Center for Rural Affairs, Box 406, Walthill, NE 68067. TEL 402-846-5428. FAX 402-846-5420. E-mail: HN1721@handsnet.org. Ed. Marie Powelle; Pub. Marty Strange. R&P contact: Marie Powell. circ. 7,000. **Document type:** newsletter.
Description: Covers agricultural and policy issues of interest to rural communities.

630 BL ISSN 0101-2711
CENTRAL NACIONAL DE PESQUISA DE MANDIOCA E FRUTICULTURA TROPICAL. RELATORIO TECNICO ANUAL. 1977. a. $1. Centro Nacional de Pesquisa de Mandioca e Fruticultura Tropical, Rua Embrapa s-n, Caixa Postal 007, 44380-000 Cruz das Almas, Bahia, Brazil. TEL 55-75-721-2120. FAX 55-75-721-1118. TELEX 75-2074. E-mail: cnpmf@brfapesp.bitnet. abstr.; bibl.; charts. circ. 1,000. **Indexed:** Chem.Abstr. **Document type:** government publication.
—BLDSC (7354.107800).

630 338.1 581 II ISSN 0374-7115
CENTRAL PLANTATION CROPS RESEARCH INSTITUTE. ANNUAL REPORT. (Text in English) 1970. a. free. Central Plantation Crops Research Institute, Kasaragod 671 124, KSD District, Kerala, India. TEL 91-4995-20094. FAX 91-4995-23300. TELEX 08001202 PALM IN. circ. 450. **Indexed:** Biol.Abstr. **Document type:** corporate report.

630 338.1 II
CENTRAL PLANTATION CROPS RESEARCH INSTITUTE. NEWSLETTER. (Text in English, Hindi) 1975. q. free. Central Plantation Crops Research Institute, Kasaragod 671 124, KSD District, Kerala, India. TEL 91-4995-20094. FAX 91-4995-23300. TELEX 08001202 PALM IN. Ed. A.R.S. Menon. **Document type:** newsletter.

630 581 II
CENTRAL PLANTATION CROPS RESEARCH INSTITUTE. RESEARCH HIGHLIGHTS. (Text in English) 1980. a. free. Central Plantation Crops Research Institute, Kasaragod 671 124, KSD District, Kerala, India. TEL 91-4995-20094. FAX 91-4995-23300. TELEX 08001202 PALM IN. circ. 400. **Document type:** corporate report.

630 622 636 381 AT
CENTRAL QUEENSLAND NEWS. 1937. s-w. Aus.$29.50. Central Queensland News Publishing Co., P.O. Box 259, Emerald, Qld. 4720, Australia. Ed. Peter Cliff. circ. 4,717.

630 UK
CENTRAL REGION FARMER. 1992. m. membership. West Country Magazines Ltd., Bailey Web, Dursley, Glos. GL11 4LS, England. TEL 01453-544000. FAX 01453-544577. Ed. Tom Bewley. adv. contact: Bob Wood. circ. 8,000 (paid). **Document type:** trade publication.

638.2 II ISSN 0304-6818
SF542.75.I52
CENTRAL SERICULTURAL RESEARCH AND TRAINING INSTITUTE. ANNUAL REPORT. Key Title: Annual Report - Central Sericultural Research and Training Institute. (Text in English) 1964. a. Central Sericultural Research and Training Institute, Manandavadi Rd., Sriramapura, Mysore 570008, India. FAX 91-821-520845. TELEX 0846203-CSRI-IN. E-mail: root@csrti.ernet.in. circ. 300 (controlled). **Document type:** government publication.

630 UK
CENTRAL SOUTHERN FARMER. 1964. m. County Farmers Publications Ltd., 55 Goldington Rd., Bedford MK40 3LU, England. TEL 0234-351401. FAX 0234-328614. Ed. N. Errington. adv. circ. 2,500.
Formerly: Surrey N.F.U. Journal (ISSN 0039-6176)

630 UK
CENTRE FOR AGRICULTURAL STRATEGY SERIES. irreg., vol.3, 1993. prices varies. Oxford University Press, Walton St., Oxford OX2 6DP, England. TEL 44-1865-56767. FAX 44-1865-56646. (Subscr. in US to: Oxford University Press Inc., 2001 Evans Rd., Cary, NC 27513. TEL 919-677-0977. FAX 919-677-1714) Eds. C.R.W. Spedding, L.J. Peel. (back issues avail.) **Document type:** monographic series.
Description: Profiles the state of agriculture in individual countries, with particular emphasis on the developing nations.

630 320 SW ISSN 0348-5676
CENTRE FOR DEVELOPMENT RESEARCH. PUBLICATIONS. (Text in English) 1979. irreg. SEK 180 per no. (effective 1997). Scandinavian Institute of African Studies - Nordiska Afrikainstitutet, P.O. Box 1703, Dragarbrunnsgatan 24, S-751 47 Uppsala, Sweden. TEL 018-562200. FAX 018-695629. circ. 1,500. (back issues avail.)

354.69 MG
CENTRE NATIONAL DE RECHERCHES APPLIQUES AU DEVELOPPEMENT RURAL. DEPARTEMENT DE RECHERCHES AGRONOMIQUES. RAPPORT ANNUEL. a. Centre National de la Recherche Appliquee au Developpement Rural, Departement de Recherches Agronomiques, B.P. 1690, Antananarivo, Madagascar.

630 MG
CENTRE NATIONAL DE RECHERCHES APPLIQUES AU DEVELOPPEMENT RURAL. DEPARTEMENT DE RECHERCHES AGRONOMIQUES. RAPPORT D'ACTIVITE. irreg. Centre National de la Recherche Appliquee au Developpement Rural, Departement de Recherches Agronomiques, B.P. 1690, Antananarivo, Madagascar.

630 SP
CENTRO DE EDAFOLOGIA Y BIOLOGIA APLICADA DEL SEGURA. MONOGRAFIAS. 1950. irreg. 1500 ptas. Centro de Edafologia y Biologia Aplicada del Segura, Avda. de la Fama 1, 30003 Murcia, Spain. **Document type:** monographic series.

630 MX ISSN 0084-8697
CENTRO DE INVESTIGACIONES AGRICOLAS DE TAMAULIPAS. INFORME ANUAL DE LABORES. 1968. a. free. Centro de Investigaciones Agricolas de Tamaulipas, Apdo. Postal 172, Rio Bravo, Tamaulipas, Mexico.

631.091 BL
CENTRO DE PESQUISA AGROFLORESTAL DA AMAZONIA ORIENTAL. BOLETIM DE PESQUISA. (Text in Portuguese; summaries in English, Portuguese) 1976. irreg. price varies. Empresa Brasileira de Pesquisa Agropecuaria, Centro de Pesquisa Agroflorestal da Amazonia Oriental, Caixa Postal 48, 66017-970 Belem, Para, Brazil. FAX 091-911210. TELEX COLOCAR CPATU. bibl.; charts; stat. circ. 1,000. **Indexed:** Ahstr.Trop.Agri., Agrindex, Bibl.Agri., Herb.Abstr., Ind.Vet., Protozool.Abstr., Sugar Ind.Abstr., Vet.Bull. **Document type:** bulletin.
—BLDSC (2158.130000).
Former titles (until 1992): Centro de Pesquisa Agropecuaria do Tropico Umido. Boletim de Pesquisa (ISSN 0100-8102); (until 1980): Instituto de Pesquisa Agropecuaria do Norte. Boletim Tecnico.

630 BL ISSN 0100-0845
CODEN: BTCPBW
CENTRO DE PESQUISAS DO CACAU. BOLETIM TECNICO. 1970. irreg. R.5($10) per no. (effective 1997). (Comissao Executiva do Plano da Lavoura Cacaueira) Centro de Pesquisas do Cacau, Caixa Postal 7, 45600-000 Itabuna-Bahia, Brazil. TEL 55-73-2143217. FAX 55-73-2143204. Eds. Paulo Dos Santos Terra, Miguel Moreno Ruiz. circ. 400. **Indexed:** Biol.Abstr., Soils & Fert., Weed Abstr. **Document type:** bulletin.
—Linda Hall.

AGRICULTURE

630 BL ISSN 0102-4256
SB268.B6
CENTRO DE PESQUISAS DO CACAU. INFORME DE PESQUISAS. 1963. a. (Comissao Executiva do Plano da Lavoura Cacaueira) Centro de Pesquisas do Cacau, Caixa Postal 7, 45600-000 Itabuna-Bahia, Brazil. TEL 55-73-2143217. FAX 55-73-2143204. Eds. Paulo Dos Santos Terra, Miguel Moreno Ruiz. **Indexed:** Agri.Eng.Abstr., Biol.Abstr.
—Linda Hall.
Formerly: Centro de Pesquisas do Cacau. Informe Tecnico (ISSN 0100-5065)

630 BL ISSN 0101-7411
CENTRO NACIONAL DE PESQUISA DE MANDIOCA E FRUTICULTURA TROPICAL. DOCUMENTO. 1981. irreg., no.57, 1994. Centro Nacional de Pesquisa de Mandioca e Fruticultura Tropical, Rua Embrapa s-n, 44380-000 Cruz de Almas, BA, Brazil. TEL 55-75-7212120. FAX 55-75-7211115. circ. 300.
—BLDSC (3612.112000).

630 338.1 UN ISSN 0009-0379
HN980 CODEN: CERSBM
CERES; the F A O review on agriculture and development. Spanish edition (ISSN 0251-1576); French edition (ISSN 0251-1568); Arabic edition: Siriz (ISSN 0256-1204) (Text in English) 1968. bi-m. $24. Food and Agriculture Organization of the United Nations (Rome), Via delle Terme di Caracalla, 00100 Rome, Italy. TEL 57974350. FAX 57974608. URL: http://www.fao.org. Ed. Peter Hendry. adv.; charts; illus. (also avail. in microfiche from CIS) **Indexed:** Agri.Eng.Abstr., Agroforest.Abstr., Cott.& Trop.Fibr.Abstr., Curr.Adv.Ecol.Sci., Environ.Abstr., Geo.Abstr.H.G., HR Rep., IDA, IIS, P.A.I.S., PROMT, Rural Devel.Abstr., W.R.C.Inf.
—CIS; CISTI; Linda Hall; UMI; UnCover.
Formerly: F A O Review.
Description: Offers in-depth coverage of all aspects of current issues in agriculture, forestry, fisheries, nutrition and sustainable development.

630 FR ISSN 0396-7883
CHAMBRES D'AGRICULTURE. 1929. m. (11/yr.). 480 F. (foreign 580 F.) (effective 1993). Assemblee Permanente des Chambres d'Agriculture, Maison des Chambres d'Agriculture, 9 av. Georges V, 75008 Paris, France. TEL 1-47-23-55-40. FAX 47-23-84-97. Ed. Lucien Bourgeois. **Indexed:** Food Sci.& Tech.Abstr., Geo.Abstr., Rural Recreat.Tour.Abstr., World Agri.Econ.& Rural Sociol.Abstr.
—BLDSC (3129.550000).
Former titles: Chambres d'Agriculture. Circulaire (ISSN 1155-6986); (until 1941): Agriculture en Temps de Guerre (ISSN 1155-6994); Which was formed by the merger of: Chambres d'Agriculture. Serie E, Faits et Documents (ISSN 1155-7044); Chambres d'Agriculture. Serie C, les Pouvoirs Publics (ISSN 1155-7028); Chambres d'Agriculture. Serie A, les Travaux des Chambres d'Agriculture (ISSN 1155-7001).

630 US
CHAUTAUQUA COUNTY AGRICULTURAL NEWS. 1918. m. $7.50. Cornell Cooperative Extension Association of Chautauqua County, 3542 Turner Rd., Jamestown, NY 14701-9608. TEL 716-664-9502. FAX 716-664-6327. Ed. Andrew Dufresne. adv. circ. 975. **Document type:** consumer publication.

630 UK ISSN 0954-9641
CHESHIRE FARMER. 1963. m. County Farmers Publications Ltd., 55 Goldington Rd., Bedford MK40 3LU, England. TEL 0234-351401. FAX 0234-328614. Ed. R. Bacon. adv. circ. 3,000.

630 CL
CHILE. INSTITUTO DE INVESTIGACIONES AGROPECUARIAS. MEMORIA ANUAL. 1965. a. exchange basis. Instituto de Investigaciones Agropecuarias, Casilla 439, Correo 3, Santiago, Chile. TEL 5417223. FAX 562-5417667. **Indexed:** Anim.Breed.Abstr.

630 CL ISSN 0379-5845
S193
CHILE AGRICOLA; revista de divulgacion agropecuaria. 1976. 8/yr. $70 (Europe $80) (effective 1997). Casilla 2, Correo 13, Teresa Vial 1172, Santiago, Chile. TEL 56-2-5222627. E-mail: adventur@entelchile.net. Ed. Raul Gonzalez Valenzuela; Pub. Ricardo Fonzalez Hidalgo. adv.: B&W page $770, color page $1080; adv. contact: Raul Gonzales Valenzuela. bk.rev.; index. circ. 10,000. (back issues avail.) **Document type:** trade publication.
Description: Covers agricultural economics, equipment, crop production and soil, dairying and dairy products, feed, flour, and animals.

630 658 UK
CHINA AGRICULTURE. (Text in Chinese) 1992. q. Alain Charles Publishing Ltd., Alain Charles House, 27 Wilfred St., London SW1E 6PR, England. TEL 44-171-834-7676. FAX 44-171-973-0076. TELEX 297165 ACPLTD G. Ed. Nathaniel Green. adv. contact: Marcus Langston. circ. 10,555 (paid). **Document type:** trade publication.
Description: Covers international developments for leaders in agriculture in China.

630 643.9 US ISSN 0199-0217
CHRISTMAS TREES MAGAZINE; a magazine of plantation management for Christmas tree growers. 1973. q. $12 (Canada & Mexico $16.20; elsewhere $20) (effective 1997). Tree Publishers, Inc., Box 107, Lecompton, KS 66050-0107. TEL 913-887-6324. FAX 913-887-6734. Ed. Charles W. Wright. R&P contact: Charles W. Wright. adv. contact: Alice Wright. circ. 4,868 (paid). (back issues avail.) **Document type:** trade publication.
Description: Covers various aspects of the grower's operations from planting, insect and weed control, to shearing, shaping and marketing. For Christmas tree growers, wholesale and retail.

CHUGOKU SHIKOKU NO NOGYO KISHO/AGRICULTURAL METEOROLOGY OF CHUGOKU AND SHIKOKU. see METEOROLOGY

630 BL ISSN 0045-6888
CODEN: CIAGDX
CIENCIA AGRONOMICA. (Text in Portuguese; summaries in English) 1971. s-a. $10 to individuals; institutions on exchange basis. Universidade Federal do Ceara, Centro de Ciencias Agrarias, Av. Mister Hull, Caixa Postal 12168, 60355 Fortaleza, Ceara, Brazil. TEL 55-85-243-9668. FAX 55-85-243-9513. Ed. Jackson Albuquerque. R&P contact: Jackson Albuquerque. bibl.; charts; illus. circ. 1,200. **Indexed:** Biol.Abstr., Chem.Abstr.
—CASDDS.
Refereed Serial

630 PN ISSN 0258-6452
CIENCIA AGROPECUARIA. (Text in Spanish; summaries in English) 1978. a. $3.50 (or exchange). Instituto de Investigacion Agropecuaria de Panama, Centro de Informacion Documental Agropecuaria, Apdo. 6-4391, El Dorado, Panama 6A, Panama. TELEX 3677 PG. Ed. Elizabeth de Ruiloba. abstr.; bibl.; charts. circ. 1,000. **Indexed:** Rice Abstr.

630 CL ISSN 0304-5609
CODEN: CINADC
CIENCIA E INVESTIGACION AGRARIA.* (Text in Spanish; summaries in English) 1974. 3/yr. $35 (effective 1996). Pontificia Universidad Catolica de Chile, Facultad de Agronomia, Casilla 114-D, Santiago, Chile. TEL 562-552-2375. FAX 562-552-6005. TELEX 240395 PUCVA-CL. E-mail: admest@tronador.puc.cl. Ed. Horacio Urzua. adv. contact: Eduardo Venezian. bk.rev.; stat. circ. 300. **Indexed:** Anim.Breed.Abstr., Biol.& Agr.Ind., Chem.Abstr., Crop Physiol.Abstr., Dairy Sci.Abstr., Food Sci.& Tech.Abstr., Helminthol.Abstr., Hort.Abstr., Nutr.Abstr., Plant Grow.Reg.Abstr., Soils & Fert. **Document type:** academic/scholarly publication.
—CASDDS.
Description: Original papers on agricultural research including soil sciences, crop sciences, animal sciences, fruit culture and technology, and agricultural economics.

630 636.08 BL ISSN 0103-8478
S191 CODEN: CIRUEP
CIENCIA RURAL. (Text and summaries in English, Portuguese) 1971. 3/yr. $15 (foreign $30) or exchange basis (effective 1997). Universidade Federal de Santa Maria, Centro de Ciencias Rurais, Campus Universitario, 97119-900 Santa Maria, Rio Grande do Sul, Brazil. TEL 55-55-226-2698. TELEX 552230 UFSM BR. E-mail: rudi@super.ufsm.br; URL: http://www.ufsm.br/ccr/revista/. Ed. Rudi Weiblen. adv. contact: Rudi Weiblen. bk.rev.; bibl.; charts; illus.; circ. 1,200 (controlled). **Indexed:** Chem.Abstr., Field Crop Abstr., Herb.Abstr., Ind.Vet., Seed Abstr. **Document type:** government publication.
—CASDDS.
Formerly (until 1990, vol.20): Centro de Ciencias Rurais. Revista (ISSN 0085-5901)
Refereed Serial

630 CU
CIENCIA Y TECNICA EN LA AGRICULTURA. SERIE: APICULTURA. (Table of contents and abstracts in English) 1985. a. $6 in N. and S. America; Europe $7; or exchange basis. Centro de Informacion y Documentacion Agropecuario, Gaveta Postal 4149, Havana 4, Cuba. (Dist. by: Ediciones Cubanas, Obispo No. 527, Apdo. 605, Havana, Cuba) **Indexed:** Agrindex, Sugar Ind.Abstr.

630 CU ISSN 0138-7251
S15 CODEN: CAGRD6
CIENCIAS DE LA AGRICULTURA. (Text in Spanish; summaries in English) 1966. q. $16 in N. America; S. America $18; Europe $19; elsewhere $21. (Academia de Ciencias de Cuba) Ediciones Cubanas, Obispo No. 527, Apdo. 605, Havana, Cuba. Ed. Fernando Ortega. bibl.; charts; illus. **Indexed:** Anim.Breed.Abstr., Biodet.Abstr., Chem.Abstr., Excerp.Med., Field Crop Abstr., Helminthol.Abstr., Herb.Abstr., Hort.Abstr., Ind.Vet., Irr.& Drain.Abstr., Maize Abstr., Plant Breed Abstr., Plant Grow.Reg.Abstr., Rev.Appl.Entomol., Rev.Plant Path., Seed Abstr., Soils & Fert., Soyabean Abstr., Sugar Ind.Abstr., Triticale Abstr., Vet.Bull., Weed Abstr.
—BLDSC (3198.202600).
Formerly (until 1977): Revista de Agricultura (ISSN 0034-7671)

630 MX ISSN 0084-8689
CIRCULAR C I A T. 1968. a. free. Centro de Investigaciones Agricolas de Tamaulipas, Apdo. Postal 172, Rio Bravo, Tamaulipas, Mexico.

634 CE ISSN 0255-4119
COCONUT BULLETIN. (Text in English) 1960. s-a. Rs.5($1.25) per no. Coconut Research Institute, Bandirippuwa Estate, Lunuwila, Sri Lanka. FAX 031-77195. Ed.Bd. adv.; abstr.; charts; illus.; stat.; cum.index. circ. 1,500. **Indexed:** Agroforest.Abstr., Biol.Abstr., Chem.Abstr., Field Crop.Abstr., Hort.Abstr., Indian Sci.Abstr., Sri Lanka Sci.Ind., Trop.Abstr., Trop.Oil Seeds Abstr.
Formerly (until 1983): Ceylon Coconut Planters' Review (ISSN 0009-0816)
Description: Source of information for coconut growers.

630 FJ
COCONUT TELEGRAPH. (Text in English) 1975. m. P.O. Box 249, Savusavu, Vanua Levu, Fiji. Ed. Mrs. Lema Low.
Description: Serves widely-scattered rural communities.

634 CE ISSN 0255-4100
CODEN: COCSEK
COCOS. (Text in English) 1950. a. Rs.20($5) Coconut Research Institute, Bandirippuwa Estate, Lunuwila, Sri Lanka. FAX 031-77195. Ed. M.De.S. Liyanage. adv.; bibl.; charts; illus.; cum.index every 10 yrs. circ. 500. (back issues avail.) **Indexed:** Agroforest.Abstr., Biol.Abstr., Chem.Abstr., Field Crop.Abstr., Hort.Abstr., Indian Sci.Abstr., Irr.& Drain.Abstr., Plant Breed.Abstr., Seed Abstr., Soils & Fert., Sri Lanka Sci.Ind., Trop.Abstr., Trop.Oil Seeds Abstr.
—CCC.
Formerly (until 1983): Ceylon Coconut Quarterly (ISSN 0009-0824)
Description: Technical articles and research notes on coconuts.

630 BL
COLECCAO C E D E S. GRANDES TEMAS.* 1982. irreg. Camara de Estudos e Debates Economicos e Sociais c/o Paulo Robello de Castro, Rua da Quitanda, 68 - 4o andar, 20011-030 Rio de Janeiro, RJ, Brazil.

AGRICULTURE

630 CK
COLEGA AGROPECUARIO. 1976. irreg. Sociedad de Ingenieros Agronomos de Antioquia, Calle 54 no. 45-36, Apdo. Aereos 51185, Medellin, Colombia. (Co-sponsors: Colegio de Medicos Veterinarios y Zootecnistas de Antioquia; Asociacion Nacional de Tecnologos Agropecuarios)

630 SA
COLIMPEX AGRICULTURAL EXECUPAD. (Text in Afrikaans and English) a. Colimpex Africa (Pty) Ltd., P.O. Box 5838, Johannesburg 2000, South Africa. adv.

630 FR ISSN 1159-6457
COLLECTION DOCUMENTS SYSTEMES AGRAIRES. 1986. irreg. price varies. Centre de Cooperation Internationale en Recherche Agronomique pour le Developpement (CIRAD), Systemes Agroalimentaires et Ruraux, B.P. 5035, 34032 Montpellier Cedex, France. TEL 33-67-61-57-00. FAX 33-67-61-12-23. TELEX 485 221F. E-mail: pellecuer@cirad.fr. **Indexed:** Agri.Eng.Abstr., Irr.& Drain.Abstr. **Document type:** monographic series.

630 US
COLLEGE OF AGRICULTURAL, CONSUMER AND ENVIRONMENTAL SCIENCES. RESEARCH PROGRESS. 1888. biennial. free. University of Illinois at Urbana-Champaign, College of Agricultural, Consumer and Environmental Sciences, Office of Research and Information Services, 47 Mumford Hall, 1301 W. Gregory Dr., Urbana, IL 61801. TEL 217-244-2830. E-mail: c-frank@uiuc.edu. Ed. Tina Prow. circ. 1,700. **Document type:** academic/scholarly publication.
●Also available on CD-ROM.
—CISTI; Linda Hall.
Formerly: Illinois Agricultural Experiment Station. Research Progress (ISSN 0887-7300)

630 US ISSN 0010-1729
COLORADO RANCHER AND FARMER; the magazine of Colorado agriculture. 1947. m. $19.95. Farm Progress Companies (Subsidiary of: A B C Publishing Companies), 191 S. Gary Ave., Carol Stream, IL 60188. TEL 630-690-5600. FAX 630-462-2869. (Edit. addr.: 2755 S. Locust, Ste. 217, Denver, CO 80222. TEL 303-756-1526. FAX 303-759-9540) Ed. Becky Ohlde. adv.: B&W page $1775, color page $2040; trim 7 X 10. charts;illus.; stat.; circ. 13,103 (paid). **Indexed:** Geo.Abstr.
—UnCover.
Description: Covers ranching and farming practices, marketing, and legislation for ranchers and farmers in Colorado.

630 IT ISSN 0391-6251
IL COLTIVATORE; settimanale della coldiretti. 1944. w. L.1200 per no. Confederazione Nazionale Coltivatori Diretti, Via 24 Maggio 43, 00187 Rome, Italy. TEL 39-6-4682220. FAX 39-6-4871199. Ed. Luigi Valente. adv.: B&W page L.3500000, color page L.5000000. charts; illus.; stat. circ. 600,000. (tabloid format) **Document type:** newspaper.
Description: Forum dealing with the production and distribution of field crops.

630 IT
COLTIVATORE ENNESE. 1951. bi-m. membership. Federazione Provinciale Coltivatori Diritti di Enna, Via Roma 429, 94100 Enna, Italy. Ed. Giuseppe Pergola.

630 IT
IL COLTIVATORE ITALIANO. (Supplement avail.) 1952. m. L.300 per no. Confederazione Nazionale Coltivatori Diretti, Via XXIV Maggio, 43, 00187 Rome, Italy. TEL 46821. Ed. Luigi Valente. adv.; illus.; stat. circ. 1,000,000.
Description: Features articles on the world of agriculture. Includes social cultural and political news.

630 IT
COLTIVATORE MARCHIGIANO. m. Via dell'Industria 18, 60100 Ancona, Italy. Ed. Alberto Castellucci.

630 IT
COLTIVATORE REGGIANO. 1953. 24/yr. L.500 to non-members. Federazione Provinciale Coltivatori Diretti di Reggio Emilia, Via B. Ricasoli 4, 42100 Reggio Emilia, Italy. TEL 74747. Ed. Ugo Saoncella. adv. circ. 8,300.

630 IT
COLTIVATORI CUNEESI. 1946. 26/yr. L.1500. Federazione Provinciale Coltivatori Diretti di Cuneo, Corso Giolitti 21, 12100 Cuneo, Italy. TEL 39-171-64591. FAX 39-171-697134. Ed. A. Cantamessa. adv. circ. 59,000.

630 US ISSN 0010-1877
COLUMBIA BASIN FARMER. 1957. m. $2. Basin Publishing Co., 180 E. Main, Box O, Othello, WA 99344. TEL 509-488-3345. adv.; illus.; mkt. circ. 6,400.

630 664 NE ISSN 0892-2101
CODEN: CACHEP
COMMENTS ON AGRICULTURAL AND FOOD CHEMISTRY. 1987. 6/yr. (in 1 voi., 6 nos./vol.). $230 (effective 1998). Gordon and Breach - Harwood Academic, Amsteldisk 166, 1st Fl., 1079 LH Amsterdam, Netherlands. (Subscr. to: International Publishers Distributor, Box 32160, Newark, NJ 07102. TEL 800-545-8398. FAX 215-750-6343) Ed. John W. Finley. (also avail. in microform) **Indexed:** Food Sci.& Tech.Abstr.
—BLDSC (3336.013000); CASDDS. **CCC.**

COMMODITY FUTURES FORECAST SERVICE. see BUSINESS AND ECONOMICS — Investments

630 AT ISSN 0156-2444
COMMONWEALTH SCIENTIFIC AND INDUSTRIAL RESEARCH ORGANIZATION. DIVISION OF TROPICAL CROPS AND PASTURES. RESEARCH REPORT. 1977. irreg. price varies. C.S.I.R.O., Division of Tropical Crops and Pastures, St. Lucia, Brisbane, Qld. 4067, Australia. FAX 61-7-33713946. E-mail: library@tcp.csiro.au. R&P contact: Roger K. Jones. **Indexed:** Field Crop Abstr. **Document type:** monographic series.

630 AT ISSN 0157-9711
CODEN: TATMD5
COMMONWEALTH SCIENTIFIC AND INDUSTRIAL RESEARCH ORGANIZATION. DIVISION OF TROPICAL CROPS AND PASTURES. TROPICAL AGRONOMY TECHNICAL MEMORANDUM. 1976. irreg. price varies. C.S.I.R.O., Division of Tropical Crops and Pastures, St. Lucia, Brisbane, Qld. 4067, Australia. TEL 61-7-33770209. FAX 61-7-33713946. E-mail: library@tcp.csiro.au. R&P contact: Roger K. Jones. **Indexed:** Biol.Abstr., Field Crop Abstr., Geo.Abstr., Herb.Abstr., Ind.Vet., Seed Abstr., Small Anim.Abstr., Vet.Bull. **Document type:** monographic series.
—BLDSC (9054.150000); CASDDS.

COMMUNITY TRANSPORTATION REPORTER; the magazine of community transit industry. see TRANSPORTATION

630 BL
CONFLITOS NO CAMPO - BRASIL. irreg. Comissao Pastoral da Terra, Rua 19, No. 35, Centro, Caixa Postal 749, 74001 Goiania GO, Brazil. TEL 062-224-4436. FAX 062-225-4967.

630 US ISSN 1059-8723
CONNECTICUT WEEKLY AGRICULTURAL REPORT. 1920. w. $10. Department of Agriculture, State Office Bldg., Rm. 234, Hartford, CT 06106. TEL 213-566-4845. FAX 213-566-6094. Ed. Robert Pellegrino. adv. contact: Patricia Bussa. circ. 2,200. (tabloid format)
Formerly: Connecticut Market Bulletin (ISSN 0161-5858)

630 UV
CONSTRUIRE ENSEMBLE. bi-m. 2500 Fr.CFA. Centre d'Etudes Economiques et Sociales d'Afrique, B.P. 305, Bobo-Dioulasso, Burkina Faso.

630 IT ISSN 1121-8592
CONTOTERZISTA; rivista per l'impresa agromeccanica. 1992. m. (11/yr.). L.70000 (effective 1996). Edagricole S.p.A., Via Emilia Levante 31, 40139 Bologna, Italy. TEL 39-51-492211. FAX 39-51-493660. Ed. Alberto Perdisa. adv.: B&W page L.3300000, color page L.4850000; trim 212 x 287. circ. 25,200.
Description: For and about farm-contractors.

630 334.683 CN ISSN 0315-1204
COOPERATEUR AGRICOLE. (Text in French) 1972. 9/yr. Can.$10. Cooperative Federee de Quebec, P.O. Box 500, Youville Stn., Montreal, PQ H2P 2W2, Canada. TEL 514-384-6450. E-mail: coopagri@coopfed.qc.ca; URL: http://www.coopfed.qc.ca. Ed. Patrick Dupuis; Pub. Mario Dumais. adv. contact: Andre Leger. circ. 23,293. **Document type:** trade publication.

630 334.683 IT
COOPERATIVA (MACERATA). q. Via Carducci 20, 62100 Macerata, Italy. Ed. Franco Ortenzi.

630 US ISSN 0010-8448
COOPERATIVE FARMER; a farm paper published by farmers for farmers. 1945. 9/yr. $10. (Southern States Cooperative, Inc.) Charles I. Batchelor, Ed. & Pub., Box 26234, Richmond, VA 23260. TEL 804-281-1317. FAX 804-281-1141. R&P contact: Charles I. Batchelor. adv. contact: Charles I. Batchelor. illus. circ. 175,527. **Document type:** trade publication.
Description: Informs farmers about Southern states products and services, current trends and developments in agriculture and their cooperative's policies and progress. Covers cooperation as a way of doing business.

COOPERATIVE NEWS INTERNATIONAL. see BUSINESS AND ECONOMICS — International Development And Assistance

630 II ISSN 0302-7767
HD2951
COOPERATIVE PERSPECTIVE. (Text in English) 1966. q. Rs.60 to students; institutions Rs.120; foreign $30. Vaikunth Mehta National Institute of Cooperative Management, University Rd., Poona 411 007, India. TEL 327974. FAX 327726. Ed.Bd. adv.: page Rs.1500. bk.rev.; charts; stat.; cum.index vols. 1-13. circ. 800. (back issues avail.) **Document type:** academic/scholarly publication.
—UnCover.
Formerly (Feb.-Apr. 1973): Cooperative Information Bulletin (ISSN 0009-9805)

630 334.683 IT
COOPERATORE AGRICOLO. 3/yr. Consorzio Agricolo Provinciale, 60100 Ancona, Italy. Ed. Antonio Liguori.

570 630 US ISSN 1067-585X
CORNELL FOCUS. 1968. 3/yr. free. Cornell University, Agricultural Experiment Station, 1150 Comstock Hall, College of Agriculture & Life Sciences, Ithaca, NY 14853. TEL 607-255-1876. FAX 607-255-9873. Ed. Elizabeth Bauman. charts; illus.; index; circ. 5,000 (controlled). **Indexed:** Biol.Abstr., Biol.Dig., Dairy Sci.Abstr., Environ.Abstr., Environ.Ind., Field Crop Abstr., Food Sci.& Tech.Abstr., Herb.Abstr., Hort.Abstr., Plant Breed.Abstr., Potato Abstr., Rural Recreat.Tour.Abstr., Soils & Fert., Sport Fish.Abstr., Weed Abstr., Wild.Rev., World Agri.Econ.& Rural Sociol.Abstr. **Document type:** academic/scholarly publication.
—BLDSC (3470.942400); Linda Hall; UnCover.
Former titles (until vol.20, no.4, 1991): New York's Food and Life Sciences Quarterly (ISSN 0361-5367); Farm Research (ISSN 0028-7938)

630 UK ISSN 0954-9668
CORNISH FARMER AND GROWER. 1964. m. County Farmers Publications Ltd., 55 Goldington Rd., Bedford MK40 3LU, England. TEL 0234-351401. FAX 0234-328614. Ed. Alison Best. adv. circ. 2,700.

COTTON DIGEST INTERNATIONAL. see TEXTILE INDUSTRIES AND FABRICS

COTTON: REVIEW OF THE WORLD SITUATION. see TEXTILE INDUSTRIES AND FABRICS

630 664 US ISSN 1070-0021
COUNCIL FOR AGRICULTURAL SCIENCE AND TECHNOLOGY. ISSUE PAPERS. 1993. irreg., no.197, 1996. Council for Agricultural Science and Technology, 4420 W. Lincoln Way, Ames, IA 50014-3447. TEL 515-292-2125. FAX 515-292-4512. E-mail: cast@cast-science.org. R&P contact: Richard Stuckey. **Document type:** monographic series.
—BLDSC (4584.030700).

AGRICULTURE

630 664　　US　　ISSN 0194-407X
S1
COUNCIL FOR AGRICULTURAL SCIENCE AND TECHNOLOGY. SPECIAL PUBLICATIONS. irreg., SP20, 1996. Council for Agricultural Science and Technology, 4420 W. Lincoln Way, Ames, IA 50014-3447. TEL 515-292-2125. FAX 515-292-4512. E-mail: cast@cast-science.org.
Description: Series of occasional reports on issues in food and agricultural science.

630 664　　US　　ISSN 0194-4088
**　　　　　　　　　　　CODEN: RCATEQ**
COUNCIL FOR AGRICULTURAL SCIENCE AND TECHNOLOGY. TASK FORCE REPORTS. irreg., R126, 1996. Council for Agricultural Science and Technology, 4420 W. Lincoln Way, Ames, IA 50014-3447. TEL 515-292-2125. FAX 515-292-4512. E-mail: cast@cast-science.org. **Indexed:** Food Sci.& Tech.Abstr.
Incorporates (1976-1994): Comments From C A S T (ISSN 0194-4096)
Description: Broad scientific documents written by groups of scientists.

630　　　　　US　　ISSN 0742-4566
COUNTRY CHRONICLE. 1938. w. $20. Brown County Publishing Co., Box 278, Denmark, WI 54208. TEL 414-863-2154. Ed. John Heiser. adv. circ. 14,900.
Description: Contains items of local interest.

630　　　　　US　　ISSN 0191-8907
COUNTRY FOLKS. (Avail. in 4 editions: East, West, Pennsylvania, New England) 1974. w. $25 (effective 1997). Lee Publications, Inc., 6113 State Hwy 5, Box 121, Palatine Bridge, NY 13428. TEL 518-673-3237. FAX 518-673-2699. E-mail: ctryfks@telenet.net. Ed. Janice Handy.
Description: Covers all aspects of agriculture.

COUNTRY FOLKS GROWER. see *GARDENING AND HORTICULTURE*

630　　　　　US　　ISSN 1054-9064
COUNTRY FOLKS OF PENNSYLVANIA. 1945. w. $25 (effective 1997); newsstand price: $1. Lee Publications, Inc., Box 121, Palatine Bridge, NY 13428. TEL 518-673-3237. FAX 518-673-2699. Ed. Janice Handy. adv.: B&W page $665; trim 10 1/4 x 14. bk.rev. circ. 10,465. (tabloid format; back issues avail.) **Document type:** newspaper.
Formerly (until 1990): Farm and Home News (ISSN 1040-8525)

630 640　　　　　UK
COUNTRY GARDEN & SMALLHOLDING. 1975. m. £19.95 (overseas £23.95). Broad Leys Publishing Co., Buriton House, Station Rd., Newport, Saffron Waldon, Essex CB11 3PL, England. TEL 01799-540922. FAX 01799-541367. E-mail: egs@broadleys.com; URL: http://www.3.mistral.co.uk/egs. Ed. Katie Thear; Pub. David Thear. adv. contact: Jan Ayres. bk.rev.; stat.; tr.lit.; index; circ. 21,000 (paid). (back issues avail.) **Document type:** consumer publication.
Former titles (until 1993): Home Farm (ISSN 0264-8873); Formerly (until 1983): Practical Self-Sufficiency (ISSN 0309-510X)
Description: Covers information for homesteaders, small farmers, and other people who keep poultry and livestock on a small scale. Also directed toward organic gardeners and growers.

630　　　　　CN　　ISSN 0383-7114
COUNTRY GUIDE; the farm magazine. 1882. m. (11/yr.). Can.$19.50($50) Farm Business Communications, Box 6600, Winnipeg, MB R3C 3A7, Canada. TEL 204-944-5761. FAX 204-942-8463. Ed. Dave Wreford. adv. contact: Tom Mumby. bk.rev.; charts; illus.; mkt.; pat.; stat. circ. 73,996. (also avail. in microform from UMI; microfilm from CML,SOC) **Indexed:** Can.B.P.I., CMI. **Document type:** trade publication.
—Linda Hall.

630　　　　　CN　　ISSN 0011-0183
COUNTRY LIFE IN BRITISH COLUMBIA. 1915. m. Can.$10($20) Country Life Ltd., 3308 King George Hwy., Surrey, BC V4P 1A8, Canada. TEL 604-536-7622. FAX 604-536-5677. Ed. D.M. Young. adv.; bk.rev.; illus. circ. 9,060.
Description: News and features concerning farming in B.C. covering a wide spectrum of commodities such as beef, tree fruits, and dairy.

630　　　　　US　　ISSN 0011-0205
COUNTRY LIVING (COVINGTON). 1945. m. $6. Arens Corp., 395 S. High St., Covington, OH 45318. TEL 513-473-2020. Ed. Terry A. Barton. adv.; bk.rev. circ. 17,448. (tabloid format)

630　　　　　US　　ISSN 0192-9658
COUNTRY TODAY. 1977. w. $23. Eau Claire Press Company, 611 S. Farwell, Eau Claire, WI 54702. TEL 715-833-9270. FAX 715-833-9273. Ed. Armie Hoffman; Pub. Pieter Graaskamp. R&P contact: Jim Massey. adv. contact: Mike Strauch. circ. 33,200. (also avail. in microfilm) **Document type:** newspaper.
Description: Contains agricultural news, features, market information for farmers and rural residents.

630　　　　　NZ　　ISSN 0110-9200
COUNTRY - WIDE. 1978. m. NZ.$22($33) Sweetbreeze Investments Ltd., 118 Rangitikei St., Palmerston North, New Zealand. TEL 61-6-3588033. FAX 61-6-3569022. Ed. David McLaughlin. adv. circ. 40,000. (tabloid format)
Description: Designed to promote and enhance the profitability of farmers and agribusiness.

COUNTRY WOMAN. see *WOMEN'S INTERESTS*

630　　　　　AT　　ISSN 0011-0264
COUNTRYMAN. 1885. w. Aus.$65. West Australian Newspapers, 219 St. Georges Terrace, Perth, W.A. 6000, Australia. FAX 09-482-3324. Ed. John Dare. adv.; bk.rev.; charts; illus.; stat. circ. 15,000. **Document type:** newspaper.

630　　　　　US　　ISSN 0739-4330
COUNTY AGENTS DIRECTORY; the reference book for agricultural extension workers. 1915. biennial. $23.95. Doane Agricultural Services Co., 11701 Borman St., St. Louis, MO 63146-4199. TEL 314-569-2700. FAX 314-569-1083. Ed. Kristine Myszka. circ. 3,000. **Document type:** directory.

630　　　　　UK
COURSES IN AGRICULTURE DIRECTORY. a. $27 (effective 1997). Research Information Ltd., 222 Maylands Ave., Hemel Hempstead, Herts HP2 7TD, England. TEL 44-1442-213222. FAX 44-1442-259395. E-mail: info@resinf.co.uk; URL: http://www.users.globalnet.co.uk/~resinf. **Document type:** directory.

630　　　　　SP　　ISSN 0590-0433
COYUNTURA AGRARIA. 1987. m. free. (Departamento de Agricultura, Ganaderia y Montes) Gobierno de Navarra, Fondo de Publicaciones, Navas de Tolosa 21, 31002 Pamplona, Spain. TEL 34-48-427123.

630　　　　　IT
CREMONA PRODUCE. 1968. bi-m. L.25000. Casa Editrice Cremona Produce, Via Navigatori Padani, 3, 26100 Cremona, Italy. TEL 0372-33630. FAX 0372-26610. Ed. Michele Uggeri. adv.: B&W page L.700000, color page L.1000000; adv. contact: Michele Uggeri. bk.rev. circ. 4,600.
Former titles: Cremona Produce - Cultura e Tradizione (ISSN 1120-0103); (until 1981): Cremona Produce (ISSN 1120-0375)

630　　　　　IT
CRONACHE DELL'AGRICOLTURA. 1949. m. L.3000. Unione Provinciale Agricoltori di Torino, Corso V. Emanuele 58, 10121 Turin, Italy. TEL 39-11-530616. Ed. M.G. Calzoni. adv. circ. 16,500.

630　　　　　SW　　ISSN 1100-1186
**　　　　　　　　　　　CODEN: CRSCE5**
CROP PRODUCTION SCIENCE. (Text in English) 1988. irreg. price varies. Sveriges Lantbruksuniversitettural Sciences, Institutionen foer Vaextodlingslaera - Swedish University of Agricultural Sciences, Department of Crop Production Science, P.O. Box 7043, S-750 07 Uppsala, Sweden. TEL 46-18-67-1000. FAX 46-18-67-29-09. Ed.Bd. circ. 500. **Document type:** academic/scholarly publication, monographic series.

631　　　　　II　　ISSN 0011-1872
CROPS IN INDIA. (Text in English) 1968. q. Rs.8. Agro-Service, 3491 Gali Bajrangbali, Chawri Bazar, Delhi 6, India. Ed. H.K. Tiwari. charts; stat.

630 635　　　FR　　ISSN 0263-9459
**　　　　　　　　　　　CODEN: CRUNDD**
CRUCIFERAE NEWSLETTER. (Text in English) 1976-1991; resumed 1993. a. donation. European Association for Research on Plant Breeding, INRA - Station d'Amelioration des Plantes, B.P. 29, 35650 Le Rheu, France. TEL 99-28-51-00. FAX 99-28-51-20. TELEX 740 060 F. Ed.Bd. bk.rev. circ. 500. **Indexed:** Chem.Abstr., Plant Breed.Abstr. **Document type:** newsletter.
—BLDSC (3489.871500); CASDDS.
Description: Contains research notes, news items, and information on cruciferous crops and related species.
Refereed Serial

630　　　　　SP　　ISSN 0214-8161
CUADERNOS DO AREA DE CIENCIAS AGRARIAS. 1981. a. 2000 ptas. Seminario de Estudos Galegos, Instituto Gallego de Informacion, Monte do Gozo San Marcos s-n, 15771 Santiago de Compostela (La Coruna), Spain.

CUBA. CENTRO DE INFORMACION Y DOCUMENTACION AGROPECUARIO. BOLETIN DE RESENAS. SERIE: MEJORAMIENTO ANIMAL. see *BIOLOGY — Zoology*

630　　　　　CU　　ISSN 0253-5785
**　　　　　　　　　　　CODEN: CEAGD5**
CUBA. MINISTERIO DE EDUCACION SUPERIOR. CENTRO AGRICOLA. 3/yr. $20 in N. and S. America; Europe $24. Ediciones Cubanas, Obispo No. 527, Apdo. 605, Havana, Cuba. **Indexed:** Agroforest.Abstr., Field Crop Abstr., Irr.& Drain.Abstr., Plant Grow.Reg.Abstr., Potato Abstr., Rice Abstr., Seed Abstr.
—CASDDS.

630　　　　　CU
CUBA. MINISTERIO DE LA AGRICULTURA. CENTRO DE INFORMACION Y DIVULGACION AGROPECUARIO. NOTICIERO AGROPECUARIO. SUPLEMENTO. m. Centro de Informacion y Documentacion Agropecuario, Gaveta Postal 4149, Havana 4, Cuba.

630　　　　　CU
CUBA. MINISTERIO DE LA AGRICULTURA. CENTRO DE INFORMACION Y DOCUMENTACION AGROPECUARIO. EXTRANJERAS. w. Centro de Informacion y Documentacion Agropecuario, Gaveta Postal 4149, Havana 4, Cuba.

630　　　　　CU
CUBA. MINISTERIO DE LA AGRICULTURA. CENTRO DE INFORMACION Y DOCUMENTACION AGROPECUARIO. NOTICIERO AGROPECUARIO. irreg. Centro de Informacion y Documentacion Agropecuario, Gaveta Postal 4149, Havana 4, Cuba.

CUBA. MINISTERIO DE LA AGRICULTURA. CENTRO DE INFORMACION Y DOCUMENTACION AGROPECUARIO. NOTICIERO AGROPECUARIO. SUPLEMENTO AGROMETEOROLOGICO. see *METEOROLOGY*

630　　　　　SP
CUENCA AGRARIA. 12/yr. Teruel 1, 1o, 16004 Cuenca, Spain. TEL 66-27-77-77. FAX 66-21-13-60. circ. 6,000.

630　　　　　SP　　ISSN 0011-2747
CULTIVADOR MODERNO; revista de agricultura ganaderia y mechanizacion. 1911. m. (11/yr.). 6784 ptas. (foreign 8900 ptas.). Raul Maria Mir Rague, Ed. & Pub., Escoles Pies, 45, 08017 Barcelona, Spain. TEL 93-212-43-67. FAX 93-418-92-79. adv.; bk.rev.; bibl. circ. 11,000. **Indexed:** Ind.SST.
Description: Covers agriculture with emphasis on livestock, machinery and equipment.

630　　　　　CK　　ISSN 0122-8056
CULTIVANDO AFINIDADES. (Text in Spanish) 1982. 2/yr. free. Centro Internacional de Agricultura Tropical, Unidad de Comunicaciones - International Center for Tropical Agriculture, Communications Unit, Apdo. Aereo 6713, Cali, Colombia. TEL 57-2-4450000. FAX 57-2-4450073. circ. 4,000. **Indexed:** Herb.Abstr. **Document type:** bulletin.
Formerly: C I A T International (ISSN 0120-4092)
Description: Highlights CIAT's current research activities and results and their impact on agricultural development.

AGRICULTURE

630 US ISSN 1065-1691
CULTIVAR. 1981. s-a. free. University of California at Santa Cruz, Center for Agroecology & Sustainable Food Systems, Santa Cruz, CA 95064. TEL 408-459-4140. FAX 408-459-2799. URL: http://zzyx.ucsc.edu/casfs. Ed. Martha Brown. R&P contact: Martha Brown. bk.rev. circ. 5,000. **Document type:** newsletter.
   Description: For researchers, farmers and gardeners interested in agro-ecological approaches to farming and gardening. Addresses issues related to sustainable agriculture. Reports on research and activities of the Center for Agroecology & Sustainable Food Systems.

630 US ISSN 1048-4876
HT401
CULTURE AND AGRICULTURE. 1977. s-a. $10 to individuals; institutions $25 (effective 1996). American Anthropological Association, 4350 N. Fairfax Dr., Ste. 640, Arlington, VA 22203-1621. Ed. Ann Ferguson. R&P contact: Terry Clifford. **Indexed:** Anthropol.Lit. **Document type:** academic/scholarly publication.
   —BLDSC (3491.668560).

630 UK
CUMBRIA FARMER. 1972. m. County Farmers Publications Ltd., 55 Goldington Rd., Bedford MK40 3LU, England. TEL 0234-351401. FAX 0234-328614. Ed. R. Bacon. adv. circ. 4,050.

630 UK
CUMBRIAN FARMING. q. 3 Chatsworth Sq., Carlisle, Cumbria CA1 1HB, England. TEL 01228-47144. FAX 01228-514747. Ed. Tony Thornton. circ. 8,560.

630 II
CODEN: OAREEJ
CURRENT AGRICULTURAL RESEARCH. (Text in English) 1988. q. $100 (effective 1996). Association of Agricultural Scientists, College of Agriculture Bldg., O.U.A.T., Bhubaneswar 751003, India. Ed. D. Mishra. bk.rev. circ. 300. **Indexed:** Agrindex. **Document type:** academic/scholarly publication.
   —CASDDS.
   Formerly (until 1995): Orissa Journal of Agricultural Research (ISSN 0970-728X)
   Refereed Serial

630 II ISSN 0254-1092
CODEN: CUAGEG
CURRENT AGRICULTURE. (Text in English) 1977. s-a. $45. Hindustan Publishing Corp., 4805-24, 1st Fl., Bharat Ram Rd., Darya Ganj, New Delhi 110 002, India. TEL 91-11-3254401. FAX 91-11-6863511. E-mail: hpcpd@giasdl01.vsnl.net.in.
   —BLDSC (3494.120000); CASDDS; Linda Hall.

630 631 PK
CURRENT AGRO-TECHNOLOGY FOR POTATO PRODUCTION. 1981. every 2-3 yrs. Pakistan Agricultural Research Council, Agricultural Documentation Wing, Box 1031, F-7-2, Islamabad, Pakistan. Ed. Mahfooz Ali Shah. circ. 1,000.

630 II ISSN 0256-6885
CODEN: CREEE
CURRENT RESEARCH REPORTER. (Text in English) 1985. s-a. Rs.30 to individuals (foreign $20); institutions Rs.50 (foreign $50). Mahatma Phule Agricultural University, Rahuri - 413722, Dist-Ahmednagar, Maharashtra, India. Ed.Bd. **Indexed:** Sugar Ind.Abstr.
   —CASDDS.
   Description: Publishes papers on original research in the field of agricultural science and techonology.

630 CY ISSN 1018-9475
S322.C8
CYPRUS. AGRICULTURAL RESEARCH INSTITUTE. ANNUAL REVIEW. 1962. a. free. Ministry of Agriculture, Natural Resources and the Environment, Agricultural Research Institute, P.O. Box 2016, 1516 Nicosia, Cyprus. TEL 357-2-305101. FAX 357-2-316770. E-mail: library@arinet.ari.gov.cy; URL: http://www.ari.gov.cy. Ed. S. Papachristodoulou. bk.rev. circ. 1,200. **Indexed:** Anim.Breed.Abstr., Biol.Abstr., Food Sci.& Tech.Abstr., Hort.Abstr., Rev.Appl.Entomol., Rev.Plant Path. **Document type:** monographic series, government publication.
   —BLDSC (7785.939200).
   Formerly (until 1991): Cyprus. Agricultural Research Institute. Annual Report (ISSN 0070-2307)
   Description: Outlines the year's research activities.

630 CY ISSN 0253-6749
CODEN: MRCIEJ
CYPRUS. AGRICULTURAL RESEARCH INSTITUTE. MISCELLANEOUS REPORTS. (Text in English or Greek) 1980. irreg., no.63, 1994. free. Ministry of Agriculture, Natural Resources and the Environment, Agricultural Research Institute, P.O. Box 2016, 1516 Nicosia, Cyprus. TEL 357-2-305101. FAX 357-2-316770. TELEX 4660. E-mail: library@arinet.ar.gov.cy; URL: http://www.ari.gov.cy. Ed. S. Papachristodoulou. circ. 400. **Indexed:** Dairy Sci.Abstr., Herb.Abstr., Soils & Fert. **Document type:** monographic series, government publication.

630 CY ISSN 0070-2315
CODEN: CYABAP
CYPRUS. AGRICULTURAL RESEARCH INSTITUTE. TECHNICAL BULLETIN. 1966. irreg., no.165, 1994. free. Ministry of Agriculture, Natural Resources and the Environment, Agricultural Research Institute, P.O. Box 2016, 1516 Nicosia, Cyprus. TEL 357-2-305101. FAX 357-2-316770. E-mail: library@arinet.ari.gov.cy; URL: http://www.ari.gov.cy. Ed. S. Papachristodoulou. circ. 400. **Indexed:** Anim.Breed.Abstr., Biol.Abstr., Dairy Sci.Abstr., Fababean Abstr., Field Crop Abstr., Food Sci.& Tech.Abstr., Nutr.Abstr., Seed Abstr., Soyabean Abstr., Triticale Abstr. **Document type:** monographic series, government publication.
   —BLDSC (8618.200000).

630 GW ISSN 0173-654X
D B V INFORMATIONEN. w. Deutscher Bauernverband, Godesberger Allee 142-148, 53175 Bonn, Germany. TEL 0228-8198240. FAX 0228-8198231. (looseleaf format) **Document type:** bulletin.

630 GW ISSN 0341-0412
S7
D L G - MITTEILUNGEN. 1885. m. DM.117.60 (foreign DM.134.40) (effective 1997). (Deutsche Landwirtschafts-Gesellschaft e.V.) Landwirtschaftsverlag GmbH, Huelsebrockstr. 2, 48165 Muenster, Germany. TEL 49-2501-801-0. FAX 49-2501-801-204. (Subscr. to: Postfach 480249, 48079 Muenster, Germany) Ed. H. Luedemann. bk.rev.; abstr.; illus.; stat.; index. **Indexed:** Agri.Eng.Abstr., Dairy Sci.Abstr., Excerp.Med., Fababean Abstr., Field Crop Abstr., Herb.Abstr., Ind.Vet., Maize Abstr., Plant Breed.Abstr., Plant Grow.Reg.Abstr., Rural Recreat.Tour.Abstr., Triticale Abstr., Weed Abstr., World Agri.Econ.& Rural Sociol.Abstr. **Document type:** bulletin.
   —BLDSC (3605.640000); SWETS. **CCC.**
   Formerly: Deutsche Landwirtschafts-Gesellschaft. Mitteilungen der D L G (ISSN 0341-0404); Which incorporated (in 1990): Agrar-Inform (ISSN 0863-4491); Which was formerly: Kooperation (ISSN 0023-3811)

631 GW ISSN 0340-787X
D L Z AGRARMAGAZIN; die landwirtschaftliche Zeitschrift fuer Management, Produktion und Technik. 1949. m. DM.94 (foreign DM.110) (effective 1997); newsstand price: DM.9. B L V Verlagsgesellschaft mbH, Lothstr. 29, 80797 Munich, Germany. TEL 49-89-12705-0. FAX 49-89-12705354. Ed. Dr. Willi Weber. adv. contact: Ute Kelm. bk.rev. circ. 80,000. **Indexed:** Agri.Eng.Abstr., Chem.Abstr., Rural Recreat.Tour.Abstr., World Agri.Econ.& Rural Sociol.Abstr. **Document type:** trade publication.
   —CCC.
   Formerly (until 1994): D L Z (ISSN 0011-5010)

DAKOTA COUNSEL. see *ENERGY*

630 US ISSN 1069-5397
DAKOTA FARMER. (Supplement avail.: Dairy Producer) 1927. m. Farm Progress Companies (Subsidiary of: A B C Publishing Companies), 191 S. Gary Ave., Carol Stream, IL 60188. TEL 630-690-5600. FAX 630-462-2869. (Edit. addr.: Box 430, Soiux Falls, SD 57101. TEL 605-335-7752) Ed. Gil Gullickson. adv.: B&W page $3400, color page $3910; trim 7 X 10; adv. contact: Charles Roth. circ. 45,000 (paid). **Document type:** trade publication.
   Former titles (until 1993): Dakota Grower and Rancher (ISSN 1064-6760); (until 1992): Dakota Wallace Farmer (ISSN 1048-5775)
   Description: Provides local and timely crop and livestock production practices for farm operators in the Dakotas.

638.1 DK ISSN 0900-5749
DANSK BIAVL. 1977. m. DKK 60. Danske Biavleres Landsforening D.B.L., Sjaellandsgade 4, DK-7490 Aulum, Denmark. illus. **Indexed:** Apic.Abstr.
   Former titles (until 1984): Dansk-Biavl og Miljoe (ISSN 0108-3139); (until 1981): Danske Biavl (ISSN 0106-9128)

630 DK ISSN 0904-9363
DANSK LANDBRUG. 1979. fortn. DKK 298($37.45) Vest Media A-S, Storegade 28, Skansen, 6800 Varde, Denmark. TEL 75 22 44 00. FAX 75-22-44-77. Ed. Niels Henrik Iversen. circ. 126,495. **Document type:** newspaper.
   Formerly: Jysk Landbrug.

630 US
DATA TRANSMISSION NETWORK.* d. $19.95 via FM radio antenna; small satellite $29.95; large satellite $24.95 for one month. 1 Penn Plaza, Ste. 4515, New York, NY 10119-0118. TEL 212-724-4466. (avail. through electronic transmissions only)
   Description: Allows farmers to view news, commodity futures prices, cash grain and livestock prices, and government reports.

630 PE ISSN 1017-9011
DEBATE AGRARIO. 1987. q. $40. Centro Peruano de Estudios Sociales, Avda. Salaverry 818, Lima 11, Peru. TEL 51-1-4336610. FAX 51-1-4331744. E-mail: feguren@cepes.org.pe. Dir. Fernando Eguren L. **Indexed:** Rice Abstr.
   Description: Deals with rural issues.

630 FR ISSN 0249-7336
DEFENSE AGRICOLE DE LA BEAUCE ET DU PERCHE. 1904. m. 15 place des Halles, 28004 Chartres Cedex, France. TEL 37-20-30-40. Ed. Jean-Claude Moriceau. circ. 3,373.

630 FR ISSN 1162-9908
DEFENSE PAYSANNE DU LOT. 24/yr. 430 av. Jean Jaures, 46004 Cahors Cedex, France. TEL 65-22-55-30. TELEX 533 725 AGRI LOT. Ed. M. Marchais. circ. 15,974.

630 PK
DEHI RAZAKAR. (Text in Urdu) 1969. fortn. Rs.75 (foreign Rs.200). National Farm Guide Council of Pakistan, c/o Shabaz A. Raheem, Ed., 405 Ferozepur Rd., Lahore 54600, Pakistan. TEL 92-42-5864155. FAX 92-42-5864155. Ed. Shabaz A. Raheem. circ. controlled. **Document type:** newspaper.
   Description: Discusses various aspects of agriculture, economic planning, social welfare and farm management, as well as issues such as literacy, youth development, civil defence, farm forestry and environmental safety.

630 US
DEL-MAR-VA HEARTLAND.* vol.9, 1983. 3/yr. $2 per issue. Heartland Publications, Ltd., Box 249, Denton, MD 21629. TEL 301-479-2061. Ed. Kristen Dukes. adv.; bk.rev.; illus. circ. 105,000.

630 US
DELAWARE AG NEWS. 1984. m. free. Department of Agriculture, 2320 S. DuPont Hwy., Dover, DE 19901. TEL 302-739-4811. FAX 302-697-6287. Ed. Vicki Davis. **Document type:** government publication.
   Formerly (until 1994): Delaware Agenda.
   Description: Provides news about Delaware Department of Agriculture services and activities. Includes calendar of events, legislative updates, and features on local topics.

AGRICULTURE

630   US   ISSN 0194-2964
DELMARVA FARMER. 1978. w. $14. (American Farm Publications, Inc.) American Farm Publications, Inc., 505 Brooklett Ave., Box 2026, Easton, MD 21601. TEL 410-822-3366. FAX 410-822-3366. Ed. Mark Powell. circ. 10,000.

630   CN
DELORAINE TIMES & STAR. w. Can.$23.94 locally; elsewhere Can.$35.34. D T S Publishing, Ltd., 122 Broadway St. N., P.O. Box 407, Deloraine, MB R0M 0M0, Canada. TEL 204-747-2249. FAX 204-747-2180. Ed. Ben Kroeker. circ. 1,400. (tabloid format; also avail. in microfilm) **Document type:** newspaper.
Description: Local news and photos, editorial comment, agriculture-related articles.

630   AG   ISSN 0011-7978
DELTA. 1933. fortn. Periodico Delta S.C.A., General Mitre 320, Tigre, Argentina. Eds. Julio Cesar Comte, Rosalia K. De Mikler. adv.; mkt. circ. 5,000. (tabloid format)

630   US
DELTA AGRICULTURAL DIGEST. a. $30. Farm Press, Division of Intertec Publishing, Box 1420, Clarksdale, MS 38614. TEL 601-624-8503. FAX 601-621-1977. Ed. Scott McClure; Pub. John L. Montandon. R&P contact: Darrah Parker. adv. contact: Darrah Parker. circ. 18,000. **Document type:** trade publication.
Formerly: Delta Digest.

630   US   ISSN 0011-8036
DELTA FARM PRESS. 1944. w. $30. Farm Press, Division of Intertec Publishing, Box 1420, Clarksdale, MS 38614. TEL 601-624-8503. FAX 601-627-1977. Ed. Ed Phillips; Pub. John L. Montandon. R&P contact: Darrah Parker. adv. contact: Darrah Parker. charts; stat. circ. 28,000. **Document type:** trade publication.
—CCC.

DEMOCRACIA NA TERRA. see *POLITICAL SCIENCE*

630   DK
DENMARK. MINISTERIET FOR FOEDEVARER, LANDBRUG OG FISKERI.FORSKNINGSSEKRETARIATET. KORTLAEGNING. 1976. a. Ministeriet for Foedevarer, Landbrug og Fiskeri, Forskningssekretariatet - Danish Ministry of Food, Agriculture and Fisheries, Directorate for Development, Toldbodgade 29, DK-1253 Copenhagen K, Denmark. TEL 45-33-63-73-00. FAX 45-33-63-73-33. Ed. Bettina Christiansen. circ. 400. **Document type:** catalog.
Former titles: Landbrugs- og Fiskeriministeriet, Forskningssekretariatet. Kortlaegning (ISSN 0906-1770); Landbrugets Samraad for Forskning og Forsoeg. Kortlaegning (ISSN 0105-4244)
Description: Inventory of current agricultural research projects financed by the ministry.

630   UK   ISSN 0954-9684
DERBYSHIRE FARMER. vol.27, 1973. m. County Farmers Publications Ltd., 55 Goldington Rd., Bedford MK40 3LU, England. TEL 0234-351401. FAX 0234-328614. Ed. P. Hudson. adv. circ. 2,900.

630   UA   ISSN 1110-0605
   CODEN: DIBLAR
DESERT INSTITUTE BULLETIN. (Text in English; summaries in Arabic) 1951. 2/yr. $57 (effective 1997). National Information and Documentation Centre (NIDOC), Tahrir St., Dokki, Awqaf P.O., Cairo, Egypt. TEL 20-2-3371696. Ed. M. El-Kady. adv. circ. 1,000. (reprint service avail. from IRC) **Document type:** academic/scholarly publication.
—CASDDS; Linda Hall; SWETS.
Former titles: Desert Institute Bulletin - A R E - Majallat Ma'had al-Sahra' (ISSN 0302-8038); Institut du Desert d'Egypte. Bulletin (ISSN 0020-2258)

631   US   ISSN 0046-0044
DESERT RANCHER. 1949. m. $6. (Evening News Association) Desert Sun Publishing Co., 45-140 Towne St., Indio, CA 92201. TEL 619-347-3313. Ed. Anthony Greno. adv.; illus.; stat. circ. 17,500. (tabloid format; also avail. in microform from UMI)

630   GW   ISSN 0343-3846
DEUTSCHE BAUERN-KORRESPONDENZ. 1948. m. DM.38.52. (Deutscher Bauernverband e V.) Deutscher Agrar-Verlag GmbH, Godesberger Allee 142-148, 53175 Bonn, Germany. Ed.Bd. adv.; bk.rev.; stat.; index. circ. controlled. **Indexed:** Excerp.Med., Rural Recreat.Tour.Abstr., World Agri.Econ.& Rural Sociol.Abstr. **Document type:** trade publication.

630   SZ   ISSN 0938-8818
DEUTSCHE LANDWIRT;* Monatszeitung des Verbandes Deutscher Landwirte. 1990. m. DM.30. (Verband Deutscher Landwirte) Azed Ag, Dornacherstr. 60-62, CH-4002 Basel, Switzerland. adv.; bk.rev. circ. 50,000. (back issues avail.)

630 338.91   NE
DEVELOPMENT ORIENTED RESEARCH IN AGRICULTURE. 1988. irreg., vol.5, 1994. Koninklijk Instituut voor de Tropen - Royal Tropical Institute, Mauritskade 63, 1092 AD Amsterdam, Netherlands. TEL 31-20-5688272. FAX 31-20-5688286. TELEX 15080 KIT NL. **Document type:** monographic series.
Description: Monographic studies on topics in agricultural development.

DEVELOPMENTS IN AGRICULTURAL AND MANAGED FOREST ECOLOGY. see *FORESTS AND FORESTRY*

630   UK   ISSN 0012-169X
DEVON FARMER. m. County Farmers Publications Ltd., 55 Goldington Rd., Bedford MK40 3LU, England. TEL 0234-351401. FAX 0234-328614. Ed. A. Gibson. adv. circ. 7,100.

630.24 668.6   MX
DICCIONARIO DE ESPECIALIDADES AGROQUIMICAS. 1984. a. $37 (effective Dec. 1991). Ediciones P L M, S.A. de C.V., San Bernadino 17, Col. del Valle, 03100 Mexico, D.F., Mexico. TEL 687-1766. FAX 536-5027. Ed. Luis Hochstein. adv. circ. 5,000.
Formerly: Diccionario Agroquimico.

630   FR
DICTIONNAIRE - ANNUAIRE DE L'AGRICULTURE ET DE L'AGRO-ALIMENTAIRE; organismes - dirigeants - fournisseurs. Short title: Dic-Agri. 1966. a. 980 F. (effective Apr. 1995). Editions et Publications Specialisees, 17 bis, rue Joseph-de Maistre, 75881 Paris Cedex 18, France. TEL 33-1-44-92-38-38. FAX 33-1-44-92-90-06. Ed. Olga Tarassoff; Pub. Philippe Garnier. adv. contact: Olga Tarassoff. index. circ. 15,000. **Document type:** directory.
Formerly: Dictionnaire - Annuaire de l'Agriculture.
Description: Catalogs agricultural unions, professional associations, specialized schools on the national, regional and departmental levels, as well as 3000 French and European food companies.

630   FR   ISSN 0012-2483
DICTIONNAIRE PERMANENT: ENTREPRISE AGRICOLE. 1969. 2 base vols. plus m. updates. 1240 F. for base vols. (updates 400 F.) (effective 1995). Editions Legislatives et Administratives, 80 ave. de la Marne, 92546 Montrouge Cedex, France. TEL 40-92-68-68. FAX 46-56-00-15. TELEX 632 855 F. bibl.; index, cum.index. circ. 4,000. (looseleaf format) **Indexed:** Rural Recreat.Tour.Abstr., World Agri.Econ.& Rural Sociol.Abstr.
Description: Discusses legal and fiscal problems linked with agricultural activities.

349   FR
DICTIONNAIRE PERMANENT: RURAL (DROIT SOCIAL AGRICOLE). 1956. base vol. plus m. updates. 1490 F. for base vol. (updates 620 F.) (effective 1995). Editions Legislatives et Administratives, 80 ave. de la Marne, 92546 Montrouge Cedex, France. TEL 40-92-68-68. FAX 46-56-00-15. TELEX 632 855 F. bibl.; index, cum.index. circ. 2,800. (looseleaf format)
Formerly: Dictionnaire Permanent: Rural (ISSN 0012-2505)
Description: Presents social legislation pertaining to agriculture.

630   JO   ISSN 1026-3764
   CODEN: DSNJDI
DIRASAT. AGRICULTURAL SCIENCES. (Text in Arabic, English) 3/yr. $45 (effective 1998). University of Jordan, Deanship of Academic Research, Amman, Jordan. TEL 962-6-843555. FAX 962-6-840263. E-mail: research@amra.nic.gov.jo. Ed.Bd. **Document type:** academic/scholarly publication.
—BLDSC (3589.615000); CASDDS; CISTI.
Supersedes in part (in 1996): Dirasat. Series B: Pure and Applied Sciences (ISSN 0253-424X)
Refereed Serial

630   CK
DIRECTORIO AGROPECUARIO DE COLOMBIA. biennial. Col.3000($10) (Sociedad de Agricultores de Colombia) Corporacion Editorial Interamericana, Avda. Jimenez 403 (of 907), Apdo. 14965, Bogota 1, Colombia.

DIRECTORY OF COCONUT TRADERS AND EQUIPMENT MANUFACTURERS. see *BUSINESS AND ECONOMICS — Trade And Industrial Directories*

DIRECTORY OF INTERNATIONAL COCONUT RESEARCH WORKERS. see *BUSINESS AND ECONOMICS — Trade And Industrial Directories*

630 340   IT
DIRITTO DELL'AGRICOLTURA. 1992. 3/yr. L.77000 to individuals; institutions L.100000; foreign L.110000 (effective 1993). Edizioni Scientifiche Italiane S.p.A., Via Chiatamone, 7, 80121 Naples, Italy. TEL 081-7645768. FAX 081-7646477.

630   SP   ISSN 1132-0176
DISTRIBUCION Y CONSUMO. 1984. m. (11/yr.). free. Empresa Nacional Mercasa, Paseo de la Habana, 101, 28036 Madrid, Spain. TEL 1-457-25-12. Ed. I. Olivares. circ. 10,034.
—CINDOC.
Formerly (until 1991): Mercaconsumo (ISSN 1130-8273)

630 595.7   UK   ISSN 0952-634X
DISTRIBUTION MAPS OF PESTS. 1951. s-m. £75($130) (effective 1997). CAB International, Wallingford, Oxon. OX10 8DE, England. TEL 44-1492-832111. FAX 44-1492-826090. TELEX 847964 COMAGG G. E-mail: cabi@cabi.org; URL: http://www.cabi.org. (U.S. subscr. to: CAB International, North American Office, 198 Madison Ave., New York, NY 10016. TEL 212-726-6490. FAX 212-686-7993) (looseleaf format; back issues avail.) **Document type:** academic/scholarly publication.
Description: Comprises maps giving the world distribution, together with supporting references, of a particular arthropod pest.

630   US   ISSN 0093-5271
DOANE'S AGRICULTURAL REPORT. 1938. w. $98 (includes tel. hotline) (effective 1997). Doane Information Service, 11701 Borman Dr., St. Louis, MO 63146. TEL 314-569-2700. FAX 314-564-1083. Ed. Allen Dever; Pub. Allen Dever. bk.rev. circ. 25,000. **Document type:** newsletter.
Description: Covers farm marketing and management.

334   DQ
DOMINICA. REGISTRAR OF CO-OPERATIVE SOCIETIES. REPORT.* irreg. Ministry of Agriculture, Roseau, Dominica, W.I. charts.

630   CC   ISSN 1005-9369
   CODEN: DNDXEA
DONGBEI NONGYE DAXUE XUEBAO/NORTHEAST AGRICULTURAL UNIVERSITY. JOURNAL. (Text in Chinese; abstracts in English) 1957. q. $60 (effective 1996). Dongbei Nongye Daxue, Xuebao Bianjibu, Xiangfang-qu, Harbin, Heilongjiang 150030, People's Republic of China. TEL 0451-5305988. FAX 0451-5303336. Ed. Li Wenxiong. circ. 6,000. **Document type:** academic/scholarly publication.
—CASDDS; CISTI.
Formerly (until Mar. 1994): Dongbei Nongxueyuar Xuebao - Northeast Agricultural College. Journal (ISSN 0253-228X)
Description: Covers scientific experiment results in the fields of agronomy, animal science, veterinary science, farm machinery, biotechnology, horticulture and agricultural economics.

AGRICULTURE

630   UK   ISSN 0012-5598
DORSET FARMER. 1962. m. County Farmers Publications Ltd., 55 Goldington Rd., Bedford MK40 3LU, England. TEL 0234-351401. FAX 0234-328614. Ed. R.A. MacDonald. adv. circ. 2,250.

630   RU   ISSN 0235-2451
DOSTIZHENIYA NAUKI I TEKHNIKI A P K. (Agro-Promyshlennyi Kompleks) 1987. bi-m. $150 (effective 1998). Sadovaya-Spasskaya, 18, 107807 Moscow, Russia. TEL 7-095-2072291. FAX 7-095-2072870. (Dist. by: Mezhdunarodnaya Kniga, B. Yakimanka 39, 117049 Moscow, Russia. TEL 7-095-2384967. FAX 7-095-2384634) Ed. Vladimir I. Nikiforov. circ. 1,600.
—BLDSC (0056.155000).

630   SP
DRECERA. m. 3500 ptas. Confederation and Professional Agricultural Organizations of Catalunya, Pza. Sant Josep Oriol 4, 08002 Barcelona, Spain. TEL 3-301-17-40. FAX 3-317-30-05. Ed. Ferran de Muller. circ. 60,000.
Formerly (until 1993): Forum Agrari.

630   AG
E A G PUBLICACIONES. Secretaria de Estado de Agricultura y Ganaderia, Servicio Nacional de Economia y Sociologia Rural, Paseo Colon 922, 1063 Buenos Aires, Argentina. charts; stat. (processed)
Formed by the merger of: S E A G Boletin del Maiz (ISSN 0036-1232) & S E A G Boletin del Trigo (ISSN 0036-1240) & S E A G Boletin del Algodon (ISSN 0036-1224)

THE EARLY BIRD. see *HISTORY — History Of North And South America*

630   JA   ISSN 0913-7815
EARTH/CHIJO. (Text in Japanese) 1947. Ie-No-Hikari Coop-Publishing Association, No.11, Funagawara-cho, Ichigaya, Shinjuku-ku, Tokyo 162, Japan. TEL 03-3266-9000. FAX 03-3266-9048. TELEX 22367. Ed. Takeshi Nogami.

630 200   CN   ISSN 1183-630X
EARTHKEEPING ONTARIO. 1985. bi-m. Can.$15 (U.S. Can.$20, elsewhere Can.$25). Jubilee Centre for Agricultural Research, 115 Woolwich St., 2nd Fl., Guelph, ON N1H 3V1, Canada. TEL 519-837-1620. FAX 519-824-1835. E-mail: cffomail@christianfarmers.org. Ed. John Clement; Pub. Elbert van Donkersgoed. R&P contact: John Clement. adv.; bk.rev. circ. 2,200. (back issues avail.) **Document type:** newsletter.
Formerly (until 1990): Earthkeeping (ISSN 0833-823X)
Description: Covers family farm entrepreneurs, stewardship of creation's resources, compassionate help, organizational policy development updates

630   KE   ISSN 0012-8325
S17   CODEN: EAFJAU
EAST AFRICAN AGRICULTURAL AND FORESTRY JOURNAL. 1935. q. KShs.300($30) Kenya Agricultural Research Institute, Veterubart Research Department, P.O. Box 30148, Nairobi, Kenya. TEL 254-2-444144. Ed. J.O. Mugah. adv.; bk.rev.; index, cum.index. circ. 1,000. (also avail. in microfilm; back issues avail.; reprints avail.) **Indexed:** Anim.Breed.Abstr., Biol. & Agr.Ind., Biol.Abstr., Chem.Abstr., Cott.& Trop.Fibr.Abstr., Curr.Adv.Ecol.Sci., Dairy Sci.Abstr., Field Crop Abstr., Food Sci.& Tech.Abstr., Forest.Abstr., Forest Prod.Abstr., Geo.Abstr., Helminthol.Abstr., Herb.Abstr., Hort.Abstr., IBR, Ind.Vet., Meteor.& Geostrophys.Abstr., Nutr.Abstr., P.L.E.S.A. (1987-), Plant Breed.Abstr., Poult.Abstr., Rev.Appl.Entomol., Rev.Plant Path., Soils & Fert., Sorghum & Millets Abstr., Vet.Bull., Weed Abstr. **Document type:** academic/scholarly publication.
—BLDSC (3643.850000); CASDDS; Linda Hall.
Description: Publishes original research in agriculture, veterinary science, forestry and, allied subjects.
Refereed Serial

630   UK
EAST ANGLIAN FARMER & GROWER. m. West Country Magazines, N R U, Agriculture House, Willie Snarth Rd., Newmarket, Cambs. CB8 7SN, England. TEL 44-1638-667662. FAX 44-1638-666442. Ed. R. Tuner. adv. contact: C. Newman. circ. 46,437. **Document type:** trade publication.
Formed by the Dec. 1992 merger of: Bedfordshire and Huntingdonshire Farmer and Grower & Cambridgeshire Farmer and Grower.

EAST EUROPE AGRICULTURE & FOOD. see *BUSINESS AND ECONOMICS — Trade And Industrial Directories*

630   UK
EAST OF ENGLAND SHOW CATALOGUE. 1968. a. £3. East of England Agricultural Society, East of England Showground, Peterborough PE2 6XE, England. FAX 0733-370038. Ed. Tonie Gibson. adv. circ. 6,000.

630   UK   ISSN 0954-9692
EAST RIDING FARMER. 1949. m. County Farmers Publications Ltd., 55 Goldington Rd., Bedford MK40 3LU, England. TEL 0234-351401. FAX 0234-328614. Ed. A. Hepworth. adv. circ. 2,000.

630   UK   ISSN 0012-8546
EAST SUSSEX FARMER. 1964. m. County Farmers Publications Ltd., 55 Goldington Rd., Bedford MK40 3LU, England. TEL 0234-351401. FAX 0234-328614. Ed. N. Errington. adv. circ. 1,550.

630 338.1   FR   ISSN 1273-7011
ECHO DES M.I.N.; mensuel de la filiere fruits et legumes. 1985. m. 295 F. (foreign 450 F.) (effective 1997). Echo Edition, Centre d'Affaires du M.I.N., Bat. H2, Rte. de Marseille, 84000 Avignon, France. TEL 33-4-90898560. FAX 33-4-90876184. Ed. Jean Harzig; Pub. J.L. Gregorini. R&P contact: Jean-Luc Gregorini. adv.: page 15600 F.; adv. contact: J.L. Gregorini. index. **Document type:** trade publication.
Description: Offers news on the culture and consumption of fruits and vegetables and economic analysis in the French and international market.

630   GW   ISSN 1016-5061
ECOLOGY AND FARMING. German edition: Oekologie und Landbau (ISSN 1015-2423) (Text in English) 1982. 3/yr. DM.48($30) in Europe; elsewhere DM.78($48) (effective 1997). International Federation of Organic Agriculture Movements, c/o Oekozentrum Imsbach, 66636 Tholey-Theley, Germany. TEL 49-6853-5190. FAX 49-6853-30110. E-mail: ifoam-secretary@oln.comlink.apc.org. Ed. Sue Stolton. bk.rev. (back issues avail.) **Document type:** bulletin.
Supersedes: International Federation of Organic Agricultural Movements. Bulletin (ISSN 0195-0304)
Description: Charts the progress of organic agriculture on an international basis.

ECONOMIA MONTANA - LINEA ECOLOGICA. see *FORESTS AND FORESTRY*

630   DK   ISSN 0013-2187
EFFEKTIVT LANDBRUG/PRODUCTIVE FARMING. 1970. 21/yr. DKK 275. Teknisk Forlag A-S, Skelbaekgade 4, DK-1780 Copenhagen V, Denmark. TEL 45-31-21-68-01. FAX 45-31-21-04-01. Eds. Steen Lynge Pedersen, Erik Kjaergaard Christensen. adv.: B&W page DKK 19100, color page DKK 21530; trim 360 x 266. charts; illus.; circ. 30,997 (controlled). (tabloid format)
Formerly (until 1970): Traktor- og Landbrugsbladet (ISSN 0041-0977)
Description: Focuses on independent discussions about the structure and trends of Danish agriculture and the supply, processing and marketing sectors of Danish agriculture, including information about products and methods of significance to farmers in Denmark.

630   UA   ISSN 0379-3575
                         CODEN: EJAGDS
EGYPTIAN JOURNAL OF AGRONOMY. Key Title: Al-Magallat al-Misriyyat li-l-Mahasil. (Text in English; summaries in Arabic and English) 1976. s.a. $57 (effective 1997). (Egyptian Society of Crop Science, Research Department) National Information and Documentation Centre (NIDOC), Tahrir St., Dokki, Awqaf P.O., Cairo, Egypt. TEL 20-2-3371696. Ed. M.A. Nofal. charts; illus. circ. 1,000. (reprint service avail. from IRC) **Document type:** academic/scholarly publication.
—BLDSC (3664.260000); CASDDS; Linda Hall.

630   SP   ISSN 0211-0946
EINA; unio de pagesos-baix llobregat. (Text in Catalan) 1983. bi-m. Edicions la Terra, S.L., Avda. Francesc Cambo 14, 3-B, 08003 Barcelona, Spain. TEL 34-3-2680900. FAX 34-3-2684893. Ed. Dolors Aixala. adv. contact: Josep M. Escola. circ. 600.

630   IS
EKARAI ISRAEL. irreg. free. Farmers in Israel Association, P.O. Box 209, Tel Aviv 61 001, Israel. TEL 03-252227.

630   NE   ISSN 0926-9142
EKOLAND. 1980. 11/yr. fl.85. (Stichting Ekoland) Uitgeverij van Westering, Postbus 16, 3740 AA Baarn, Netherlands. TEL 31-355423281. FAX 31-35-5424119. E-mail: uvw@hacom.nl. Ed. Harry te Walvaart. R&P contact: Jaap van Westering. adv. contact: Bert van Duinen. bk.rev. circ. 4,150. **Document type:** trade publication.
Formerly (until 1981): Boerenbrief (ISSN 0926-9150)

631.584   PL   ISSN 1426-2940
EKOLAND; kwartalnik rolnictwa ekologicznego. 1990. q. 16 Zl. (effective 1998); newsstand price: 4 Zl. Stowarzyszenie Ekoland, Osrodek Dokumentacjny Rolnictwa Ekologicznego, Ul. Piotrkowska 83, 90-423 Lodz, Poland. TEL 48-42-329765. FAX 48-42-300740. E-mail: ekoland1@podi.ld.onet.pl. Ed. Waldemar Fortuna. R&P contact: Waldemar Fortuna. adv.: page 50 Zl.; 600 x 400; adv. contact: Waldemar Fortuna. bk.rev.; abstr.; charts; illus. circ. 2,000. (back issues avail.) **Document type:** bulletin.
Description: Covers organic agriculture and horticulture. For scientists, research workers, students, farmers, gardeners, food producers.

630 637   US   ISSN 0886-9693
EMPIRE STATE FARMER. 1978. s-m. free. Journal Publishing Co., Inc., 7 Main St., Box 68, Adams, NY 13605. TEL 315-232-2141. FAX 315-232-4586. Ed. Karl A. Fowler. adv.: B&W page $480, color page $630. circ. 10,000. (back issues avail.) **Document type:** newspaper.
Formerly: North Country Farmer (Adams).

539.7 630   BL   ISSN 0100-3593
                         CODEN: ENAGDM
ENERGIA NUCLEAR E AGRICULTURA. (Text and summaries in English and Portuguese) 1979. s.a. $30. Universidade de Sao Paulo, Centro de Energia Nuclear na Agricultura, Av. Centenario 303, C.P. 96, 13400 Piracicaba SP, Brazil. Ed. Frederico Maximiliano Wiendl. bk.rev.; bibl.; charts; illus.; stat. circ. 400. (back issues avail.) **Indexed:** Agrindex, Biol.Abstr., Chem.Abstr., Excerp.Med.
—CASDDS.

ENERGY IN WORLD AGRICULTURE. see *ENERGY*

630 333.8 621.9   BL   ISSN 0100-6916
                         CODEN: EARIDM
ENGENHARIA AGRICOLA. (Text in Portuguese and English) 1971. q. R.15($14.42) Brazilian Agricultural Engineering Society, Departamento de Engenharia Rural - UNESP, Faculdade de Ciencias Agrarias e Veterinarias, Rodovia Carlos Tonnani, km 5, 14870-000 Jaboticabal SP, Brazil. TEL 55-16-3233341. Ed. Jose Renato Zanini. R&P contact: Sergio Hugo Benez. adv. contact: Walter Francisco Molina Jr. (back issues avail.) **Indexed:** Agri.Eng.Abstr., Hort.Abstr., Irr.& Drain.Abstr., Soils & Fert., Soyabean Abstr., Trop.Oil Seeds Abstr. **Document type:** academic/scholarly publication.
—CASDDS.
Description: Presents original papers in agricultural engineering.
Refereed Serial

AGRICULTURE

630   FR
ENSEMBLE. 11/yr. La Noelle, 44150 Ancenis, France. TEL 40-98-91-60. FAX 40-98-91-64. TELEX 710 645. Ed. Robert Rene. circ. 15,000.

630   334.683   FR   ISSN 1143-7588
ENTRAID' CENTRE-OUEST. 1984. 11/yr. 265 F. (effective 1997). Agropole, B.P. 129, 86004 Poitiers, France. TEL 33-5-49447448. FAX 33-5-49447446. Ed. Pascal Bordeau. adv. circ. 5,000. **Document type:** newspaper.
Description: For cooperatives and development groups of farmers.

630   FR   ISSN 0242-9063
ENTRAID'OC. 11/yr. B.P. 5, 26 place Marnac, 31520 Ramonville-Saint-Ange, France. TEL 61-75-86-30. FAX 61-75-64-28. Ed. Jean Gaffet. circ. 13,000.

630   FR   ISSN 0397-197X
ENTRAID'OUEST. 1973. 11/yr. 250 F. (effective 1997). 65 rue de Saint-Brieuc, 35042 Rennes Cedex, France. TEL 33-2-99546312. FAX 33-2-99546309. Ed. J.F. Bourblanc; Pub. Alain Hindre. adv. contact: Laurence Guilmois. bk.rev. circ. 18,000. **Document type:** newspaper.
Formerly (until 1974): Federation Departementale des C.U.M.A. d'Ille et Vilaine. Bulletin de Liaison (ISSN 0397-1988)

630   GW   ISSN 0343-6462
ENTWICKLUNG UND LAENDLICHER RAUM. (Text in English, German; summaries in English, French) 1967. bi-m. DM.60 (foreign DM.66) (effective 1996). (Deutsche Stiftung fuer Internationale Entwicklung, Zentralstelle fuer Ernaehrung und Landwirtschaft) D L G Verlags GmbH, Eschborner Landstr. 122, 60489 Frankfurt a.M., Germany. TEL 069-24788-0. FAX 069-24788480. (Co-sponsor: Deutsche Landwirtschafts-Gesellschaft e.V.) Ed. A. Wilcke. adv.; bk.rev.; abstr.; illus.; stat.; index. circ. 6,000. **Indexed:** Abstr.Rural Dev.Trop., Agri.Eng.Abstr., Excerp.Med., Geo.Abstr., IDA, Potato Abstr., Rural Devel.Abstr., Rural Ext.Educ.& Tr.Abstr., Rural Recreat.Tour.Abstr., World Agri.Econ.& Rural Sociol.Abstr. **Document type:** trade publication.
—BLDSC (3790.935000). **CCC.**
Formerly: Landwirt im Ausland (ISSN 0047-4002)

630   VE
ERA AGRICOLA; una vision alternativa del campo venezolano. q. Bs.395 (Latin America $15; elsewhere $20). Fundacion la Era Agricola, Apdo. Postal 456, Merida 5101-A, Venezuela. TEL 074-527401. FAX 074-527402. Ed. Alfredo Lascoutx. adv.; bk.rev.; illus. circ. 5,300.

630   DK   ISSN 0902-9737
ERHVERVS-JORDBRUGET. 1987. m. DKK 450 (effective 1997). Jordbrugsforlaget, Mariendalsvej 27, 2. sal, DK-2000 Frederiksberg, Denmark. FAX 45-33-12-06-03. Ed. Else Damsgaard. adv. contact: Tine Vorting. index. circ. 5,000(controlled). **Document type:** newsletter.
Incorporates (1946-1994): Landbo-nyt (ISSN 0047-3960)

630   GW   ISSN 0014-0309
ERWERBSOBSTBAU. 1959. 6/yr. DM.321 in Europe; rest of world DM.318 (effective 1998). Blackwell Wissenschaft, Kurfuerstendamm 57, 10707 Berlin, Germany. TEL 49-30-32790634. FAX 49-30-32790610. E-mail: aboverwalt@blackwis.de; URL: http://www.blackwis.com. Ed. F. Lenz. adv.; bk.rev.; charts; illus.; index. (back issues avail.) **Indexed:** Agri.Eng.Abstr., Crop Physiol.Abstr., Food Sci.& Tech.Abstr., Hort.Abstr., Plant Breed.Abstr., Plant Grow.Reg.Abstr., Rural Recreat.Tour.Abstr., Weed Abstr., World Agri.Econ.& Rural Sociol.Abstr. **Document type:** academic/scholarly publication.
—SWETS. **CCC.**

630   FR
ESPACE OUEST - ILLE ET VILAINE - COTES D'ARMOR - FINISTERE. 50/yr. Espace Ouvert, 22 av. Janvier, 35007 Rennes Cedex, France. TEL 99-29-58-88. FAX 99-31-18-19. Ed. Yves Dibout. circ. 29,000.

630   UK   ISSN 0954-9749
ESSEX FARMER. m. County Farmers Publications Ltd., 55 Goldington Rd., Bedford MK40 3LU, England. TEL 0234-351401. FAX 0234-328614. Ed. D. Brown. adv. circ. 2,600.
Formerly: Essex Farmers Journal (ISSN 0014-0945)

630   UK
ESSEX YOUNG FARMER. 10/yr. 2 East Hill, Colchester, Essex CO1 2QL, England. TEL 01206-861574. FAX 01206-862537. Ed. Tony Phelps. circ. 2,500. **Document type:** newsletter.

630   AG   ISSN 0325-1799
ESTACION EXPERIMENTAL REGION AGROPECUARIA PERGAMINO. INFORME TECNICO. (Summaries in English) 1960. irreg. exchange basis. Instituto Nacional de Tecnologia Agropecuaria, Estacion Experimental Regional Agropecuaria Pergamino, C.C.31, 2700 Pergamino, Argentina. circ. 2,000 (controlled). (also avail. in microfilm) **Indexed:** Anim.Breed.Abstr., Bibl.Agri., Dairy Sci.Abstr., Field Crop Abstr., Herb.Abstr., Irr.& Drain.Abstr., Maize Abstr., Nutr.Abstr., Pig News & Info., Plant Breed.Abstr., Poult.Abstr., Rev.Plant Path., Sorghum & Millets Abstr., Weed Abstr.
—BLDSC (4498.890000).
Formerly: Estacion Experimental Agropecuaria Pergamino. Informe Tecnico (ISSN 0020-0832)

630   BL
ESTUDOS SOCIEDADE E AGRICULTURA. 1993. irreg. Universidade Federal Rural do Rio de Janeiro, Departamento de Letras e Ciencias Sociais, Curso de Pos-graduacao em Desenvolvimento Agricola, Av. Presidente Vargas 417, 6-9 Andares, 20071-003 Rio de Janeiro RJ, Brazil. TEL 55-21-2248477.

630   ET   ISSN 0257-2605
ETHIOPIAN JOURNAL OF AGRICULTURAL SCIENCES. (Text in English) 1979. s-a. $20. P.O. Box 5509, Addis Ababa, Ethiopia. (Co-sponsors: Institute of Agricultural Research; Alemaya University of Agriculture; Addis Ababa University; Ethiopian Science and Technology Commission) Ed. Dr. Hailu Gebre-Mariam. circ. 500. **Document type:** academic/scholarly publication.
Description: Fosters scientific communication and promotes the dissemination and application of research findings through research and review articles, and short communications on agricultural development-technology; animal and crop improvement, nutrition, protection and management.

630   FR   ISSN 0983-3846
EURE AGRICOLE. 1945. w. B.P. 185, 1 bis, rue de la Justice, 27001 Evreux Cedex, France. TEL 32-39-36-72. Ed. Pierre Roussel. circ. 5,003.

630   HU   ISSN 1416-6194
AZ EUROPAI UNIO AGRARGAZDASAGA. 1993. m. free. Orszagos Mezogazdasagi Konyvtar es Documentacios Kozpont, Attila ut. 93, 1253 Budapest 13, Hungary. TEL 36-1-1568211. FAX 36-1-1569928. TELEX 22-4717. Ed. Erika Gulacsi-Papay.
Former titles (until 1996): Europai Unio Mezogazdasaga (ISSN 1218-7941); (until 1995): Ek-Agrarszemle (ISSN 1217-6230)

630   NE   ISSN 1381-2335
EUROPEAN JOURNAL OF AGRICULTURAL EDUCATION AND EXTENSION. (Text in English) 1994. 4/yr. fl.106 to individuals; institutions fl.180 (outside Europe fl.230). P.O. Box 194, 6700 AD Wageningen, Netherlands. TEL 31-317-484018. FAX 31-317-485123. E-mail: Rob.vanHaarlem@Alg.OOB.WAU.nl; URL: http://www.bib.wau.nl/ejae/. Ed. Robert van Haarlem. R&P contact: Robert van Haarlem. bk.rev.; circ. 250 (paid). (also avail. in diskette format) **Indexed:** C.I.J.E. **Document type:** academic/scholarly publication.
—BLDSC (3829.722130).
Description: Publishes articles on topical issues in agricultural higher and secondary education and extension.
Refereed Serial

630   338.91   NE
EUROPEAN PERSPECTIVES ON RURAL DEVELOPMENT. (Text in English) 1994. irreg. (Circle for Rural European Studies) Van Gorcum en Co. B.V., P.O. Box 43, 9400 AA Assen, Netherlands. TEL 31-5920-46846. FAX 31-5920-72064. **Document type:** monographic series.
Description: Discusses issues relating to different aspects of European rural development.

EXCLAIMER. see EDUCATION — Higher Education

630   UK   ISSN 0014-4797
S3   CODEN: EXAGAL
EXPERIMENTAL AGRICULTURE. 1965. q. £120($208) (effective 1998). Cambridge University Press, Edinburgh Bldg., Shaftesbury Rd., Cambridge CB2 2RU, England. TEL 44-1223-312393. FAX 44-1223-315052. TELEX 851817256. E-mail: information@cup.ac.uk; URL: http://www.cup.org/journals/jnlscat/eag/eag.html. (N. American addr.: Cambridge University Press, Journals Dept., 40 W. 20th St., New York, NY 10011. TEL 212-924-3900. FAX 212-691-3239) Ed. J.G.W. Jones. R&P contact: Linda Nicol. adv. contact: Rebecca Symons. bk.rev.; bibl.; charts; illus. (also avail. in microform from UMI; back issues avail.) **Indexed:** Agroforest.Abstr., ASCA, Biol.Abstr., Biol.& Agr.Ind., Cadscan, Chem.Abstr., Cott.& Trop.Fibr.Abstr., Crop Physiol.Abstr., Curr.Cont., Dairy Sci.Abstr., Ecol.Abstr., Field Crop Abstr., Food Sci.& Tech.Abstr., Geo.Abstr., Helminthol.Abstr., Herb.Abstr., Hort.Abstr., IDA, Ind.Sci.Rev., Ind.Vet.Irr.& Drain.Abstr., Lead Abstr., Maize Abstr., Plant Breed.Abstr., Potato Abstr., Rev.Appl.Entomol., Rev.Plant Path., Rice Abstr., Rural Recreat.Tour.Abstr., Sci.Cit.Ind., Seed Abstr., Sel.Water Res.Abstr., Soils & Fert., Sorghum & Millets Abstr., Soyabean Abstr., Triticale Abstr., Trop.Oil Seeds Abstr., Vet.Bull., Weed Abstr., World Agri.Econ.& Rural Sociol.Abstr., Zincscan. **Document type:** academic/scholarly publication.
—BLDSC (3838.600000); CASDDS; Ei; EMDOCS; Genuine Article; KR SourceOne; Linda Hall; SWETS; UMI; UnCover. **CCC.**
Description: Discusses the agronomy of crops. Includes information on the food, forage, and industrial crops of the warmer regions of the Earth.

EXPERIMENTAL & APPLIED ACAROLOGY. see BIOLOGY

630   FR   ISSN 0983-6233
EXPLOITANT AGRICOLE DE SAONE ET LOIRE. w. Maison de l'Agriculture (Macon), 59 rue du 19 Mars 1962, B.P. 522, 71010 Macon Cedex, France. TEL 85-38-50-66. FAX 85-39-46-77. TELEX 351 928. Ed. Lucette Pagnier. circ. 14,548.
Formerly (until 1947): Saone et Loire Agricole et Viticole (ISSN 0983-6225)

630   FR   ISSN 1266-1791
EXPLOITANT AGRICOLE DU GARD. 1959. w. 360 F. (effective 1998). L'Exploitant Agricole, 7 rue Bernard Aton, B. P. 144, 30011 Nimes Cedex, France. TEL 33-4-66670812. FAX 33-4-66216824. Ed. Pierre Lalanne. adv.; bk.rev.; circ. 2,200 (controlled). **Document type:** newspaper.

630   FR   ISSN 0755-284X
EXPLOITANT FAMILIAL. 1960. m. 10 F. (Federation des Syndicats Agricoles) Agence Centrale de Publicite, 100 rue de Bordeaux, 16000 Angouleme, France. TEL 45-95-01-88. FAX 45-38-37-74. Ed. Alain Giagnerot. adv. circ. 66,000.

EXPORT MARKETS FOR U.S. GRAIN AND PRODUCTS. see BUSINESS AND ECONOMICS — International Commerce

630   BL   ISSN 0014-5394
EXTENSAO EM MINAS GERAIS. fortn. free. Empresa de Assistencia Tecnica e Extensao Rural do Estado de Minas Gerais, Assessoria de Relacoes Publicas & Impresa, Av. Raja Gabaglia 1626, 1 andar, 30350-540 Belo Horizonte MG, Brazil. TEL 55-31-349-8000. FAX 55-31-349-8250. Ed. Harildo Norberto Ferreira. adv.; circ. 4,500 (controlled).

630   US
EXTENSION NEWS - ALBANY - RENSSELAER - SARATOGA - WASHINGTON COUNTIES. 1918. m. membership. Cooperative Extension Association of Albany County, Agricultural Division, Martin Rd., Voorheesville, Albany, NY 12186. TEL 518-765-3635. Ed. John E Gergen. adv.; charts; illus. circ. 5,000. (processed)
Formerly: Albany County Agriculture News (ISSN 0002-466X)

AGRICULTURE

630 628   UN   ISSN 0259-2568
F A O LAND AND DEVELOPMENT SERIES. Spanish edition: Coleccion F A O, Fomento de Tierras y Aguas (ISSN 1014-319X); French edition: Collection F A O, Mise en Valeur des Terres et des Eaux (ISSN 1014-3203) 1977. irreg., no.9, 1993. Food and Agriculture Organization of the United Nations (Rome), Viale delle Terme di Caracalla, 00100 Rome, Italy. TEL 57974350. FAX 57974608.
—BLDSC (3865.684500).

350 630   UN   ISSN 1014-6679
F A O LEGISLATIVE STUDY. (Text in English and French) 1957. irreg., no.54, 1995. price varies. Food and Agriculture Organization of the United Nations, Bernan Associates, 4611-F Assembly Dr., Lanham, MD 20706-4391. TEL 301-459-7666. FAX 301-459-0056. **Indexed:** Sport Fish.Abstr., Wild.Rev. **Document type:** monographic series.
—Linda Hall.
 Former titles (until 1986): Food and Agriculture Organization of the United Nations. Legislative Study (ISSN 0253-021X); (until 1971): F A O Legislative Series (ISSN 0071-7045)

630   UN   ISSN 0429-9353
F A O REGIONAL CONFERENCE FOR AFRICA. REPORT. French edition: Conference Regionale de la F A O pour l'Afrique. Rapport (ISSN 1014-1588) (Text in English) 1960. biennial. $12. Food and Agriculture Organization of the United Nations, Bernan Associates, 4611-F Assembly Dr., Lanham, MD 20706-4391. TEL 301-459-7666. FAX 301-459-0056.

630   UN   ISSN 1010-0997
F A O REGIONAL CONFERENCE FOR ASIA AND THE PACIFIC. REPORT. French edition: Conference Regionale de la F A O pour l'Asie et le Pacifique. Rapport (ISSN 1014-4080) (Section of: Agriculture in Asia and the Far East) (Text in English) 1949. biennial, 22nd, 1994, Beijing, China. $12. Food and Agriculture Organization of the United Nations, Bernan Associates, 4611-F Assembly Dr., Lanham, MD 20706-4391. TEL 301-459-7666. FAX 301-459-0056.
 Formerly (until 1979): F A O Regional Conference for Asia and the Far East. Report (ISSN 0427-8070)

630   UN   ISSN 1010-1403
F A O REGIONAL CONFERENCE FOR EUROPE. REPORT. French edition: Conference Regionale de la F A O pour l'Europe. Rapport (ISSN 1014-4056); Spanish edition: Conferencia Regional de la F A O para Europa. Informe (ISSN 1014-4064) biennial, 19th, 1994. $12. Food and Agriculture Organization of the United Nations, Bernan Associates, 4611-F Assembly Dr., Lanham, MD 20706-4391. TEL 301-459-7666. FAX 301-459-0056. (Co-sponsor: UN Economic Commission for Europe)

630   UN
F A O REGIONAL CONFERENCE FOR LATIN AMERICA AND THE CARIBBEAN. REPORT. 1962. biennial, 23rd, 1994. price varies (latest issue $12). Food and Agriculture Organization of the United Nations, Bernan Associates, 4611-F Assembly Dr., Lanham, MD 20706-4391. TEL 301-459-7666. FAX 301-459-0056.
 Formerly: F A O Regional Conference for Latin America. Report (ISSN 1010-1381)

630   UN   ISSN 0427-8089
HD2056.5
F A O REGIONAL CONFERENCE FOR THE NEAR EAST. REPORT. French edition: Conference Regionale de la F A O pour le Proche-Orient. Rapport (ISSN 1014-2398) (Text in English) 1962. biennial, 22nd, 1994. $12. Food and Agriculture Organization of the United Nations, Bernan Associates, 4611-F Assembly Dr., Lanham, MD 20706-4391. TEL 301-459-7666. FAX 301-459-0056.

630   UN   ISSN 0532-0313
F A O TERMINOLOGY BULLETIN. irreg., no.32, 1995. price varies. Food and Agriculture Organization of the United Nations, Bernan Associates, 4611-F Assembly Dr., Lanham, MD 20706-4391. TEL 310-459-7666. FAX 301-459-0056. **Indexed:** Food Sci.& Tech.Abstr. **Document type:** monographic series.

630.7 630   US
F F A ADVISORS MAKING A DIFFERENCE. bi-m. National F F A Organization, Box 15160, 5632 Mt. Vernon Memorial Hwy., Alexandria, VA 22309. TEL 703-360-3600. FAX 703-360-5524. Ed. Randy Bernhardt.
 Formerly: Future Farmers of America. Between Issues.

630.7 630   US   ISSN 1069-806X
F F A NEW HORIZONS. (Future Farmers of America) 1952. bi-m. $5. National F F A Organization, Box 15160, 5632 Mt. Vernon Memorial Hwy., Alexandria, VA 22309. TEL 703-360-3600. FAX 703-360-5524. Ed. Jim Scott. adv.; bk.rev.; illus. 452,000.
 Former titles (until 1990): National Future Farmer; Future Farmer; National Future Farmer (ISSN 0027-9315)
 Description: Farm education and vocations.

633.6 664.1   GW
F.O. LICHT'S INTERNATIONAL SUGAR AND SWEETENER REPORT. (Editions in English, German) 1961. 3/m. DM.1468 in US & Canada. F.O. Licht GmbH, Am Muehlengraben 22, 23902 Ratzeburg, Germany. FAX 04541-92145. Ed. Helmut Ahlfeld. adv.; charts; stat. **Indexed:** Rural Recreat.Tour.Abstr., World Agri.Econ.& Rural Sociol.Abstr. **Document type:** trade publication.
 Former titles: F.O. Licht's International Sugar Report; F.O. Licht's Europaeisches Zuckerjournal (ISSN 0014-6048)

630   BL   ISSN 0100-2694
FACULDADE DE CIENCIAS AGRARIAS DO PARA. BOLETIM. (Text in Portuguese; abstracts in English) 1972. irreg., no.25, 1996. $3 (effective 1997). Ministerio de Educacao, Faculdade de Ciencias Agrarias do Para, Servicio de Documentacao e Informacao, Caixa Postal, 917, 66077-530 Belem, Para, Brazil. TEL 55-91-2464518. TELEX 091-1892 FAGP. E-mail: fcap@supridad.com.br. Ed. Marly Sampaio. bibl.; charts; stat. **Document type:** bulletin.
 Formerly: Escola de Agronomia da Amazonia. Boletim.
 Description: Covers agriculture, forestry and veterinary science.

630 570   CK   ISSN 0304-2847
S15
FACULTAD NACIONAL DE AGRONOMIA MEDELLIN. REVISTA. Key Title: Revista Facultad Nacional de Agronomia. (Text in Spanish; summaries in English and Spanish) 1939. s-a. Col.$10000($12) (effective 1997-98). Facultad Nacional de Agronomia Medellin, Facultad de Ciencias Agropecuarias, Universidad Nacional de Colombia, Apartado 568, Medellin, Colombia. TEL 57-4-2607333 ext. 103. FAX 57-4-2300420. cum.index: 1939-1981. circ. 700. (back issues avail.) **Indexed:** Biol.Abstr., Field Crop Abstr., Forest.Abstr., Herb.Abstr., Irr.& Drain.Abstr., Plant Breed.Abstr., Rev.Appl.Entomol., Rev.Plant Path., Soils & Fert. **Document type:** academic/scholarly publication.
—BLDSC (7815.300000); Linda Hall.

630   UK   ISSN 0266-8025
FAR EASTERN AGRICULTURE. Chinese edition: Dong Nong Ye (ISSN 0950-527X) 1983. bi-m. £43.50($75) Alain Charles Publishing Ltd., Alain Charles House, 27 Wilfred St., London SW1E 6PR, England. TEL 44-171-834-7676. FAX 44-171-973-0076. TELEX 297165 ACPLTD G. Ed. Nathaniel Green. adv. contact: Marcus Langston. circ. 9,195 (paid). (back issues avail.) **Indexed:** Dairy Sci.Abstr., Field Crop Abstr., Ind.Vet., Poult.Abstr., Rev.Med.& Vet.Mycol., World Agri.Econ.& Rural Sociol.Abstr. **Document type:** trade publication.
 Description: Covers all sectors of agriculture in Southeast Asia.

630   US
FARA; journal of popular farm science and rural life. English edition: Furrow (ISSN 0016-3112) (Text in Norwegian) 1978. 4/yr. free to qualified personnel. Deere & Company, John Deere Rd., Moline, IL 61265. TEL 309-765-8000. Ed. Jean-Claude Hiron. circ. 34,500.

630   US
FARAN; a journal of popular farm science and rural life. English edition: Furrow (ISSN 0016-3112) (Text in Swedish) 1975. 4/yr. free to qualified personnel. Deere & Company, John Deere Rd., Moline, IL 61265. TEL 309-765-8000. Ed. Jean-Claude Hiron. circ. 26,500.

630   CN   ISSN 0046-3299
FARM AND COUNTRY. 1936. 18/yr. Can.$26 (foreign $99) (effective 1997). Agricultural Publishing Co., 1 Yonge St. Ste. 1504, Toronto, ON M5E 1E5, Canada. TEL 416-364-5324. FAX 416-364-5857. E-mail: agpub@inforamp.net; URL: http://www.agpub.on.ca. Ed. John Muggeridge. adv.; bk.rev. circ. 58,000. (tabloid format) **Indexed:** Can.B.P.I. **Document type:** newspaper, trade publication.

630 664   IE   ISSN 0791-6477
                                  CODEN: FFOOE4
FARM AND FOOD. 1970. 3/yr. I£12 (effective 1997). Teagasc, 19 Sandymount Ave., Dublin 4, Ireland. TEL 353-1-6688188. FAX 353-1-6688023. E-mail: corourke@hq.teagasc.ie. Ed. C.J. O'Rourke. circ. 5,500. (reprint service avail. from UMI) **Indexed:** Agri.Eng.Abstr., Anim.Breed.Abstr., Curr.Adv.Ecol.Sci., Dairy Sci.Abstr., Field Crop Abstr., Food Sci.& Tech.Abstr., Herb.Abstr., Hort.Abstr., Packag.Sci.Tech., Rural Recreat.Tour.Abstr., Sport Fish.Abstr., Weed Abstr., Wild.Rev., World Agri.Econ.& Rural Sociol.Abstr. **Document type:** academic/scholarly publication.
●Also available online.
—BLDSC (3870.870000); UnCover. **CCC.**
 Formerly: Farm and Food Research (ISSN 0046-3302); Incorporating: Farm Research News.

630   CN
FARM AND FOOD REPORT. 1978. free. Saskatchewan Agriculture and Food Library, B5 Walter Scott Bldg., 3085 Albert St., Regina, SK S4S 0B1, Canada. TEL 306-787-6933. FAX 306-787-0216. E-mail: pdc@agr.gov.sk.ca; URL: http://www.gov.sk.ca/agfood. (back issues avail.) **Document type:** government publication.
 Description: Presents general agriculture topics for farmers, such as the effect of diet on young horses, vegetable oil based fuels, and short articles on various related topics.

630 614.7   UK
FARM AND FOOD SOCIETY NEWSLETTER. 1966. 3/yr. $10. Farm and Food Society, 4 Willifield Way, London NW11 7XT, England. Ed. J. Bower. bk.rev. (back issues avail.)

630   US   ISSN 0038-3295
S113   CODEN: SDFHAT
FARM AND HOME RESEARCH; agricultural experiment station quarterly. Title varies: South Dakota Farm and Home Research. 1949. q. free. South Dakota Agricultural Experiment Station, South Dakota State University, Box 2207, Brookings, SD 57007. TEL 605-688-4149. FAX 605-688-4018. (Subscr. to: South Dakota State University Farm and Home Research, ACC, Box 2231, Brookings SD 57007) Ed. Mary Brashier. circ. 6,600. **Indexed:** ASCA, Biol.Abstr., Curr.Adv.Ecol.Sci., Curr.Cont., Dairy Sci.Abstr., Excerp.Med., Field Crop Abstr., Herb.Abstr., Nutr.Abstr., Plant Breed.Abstr.
—Linda Hall; UnCover.
 Description: Reports research done in the experiment station to assist farmers, ranchers and consumers in developing economic, human, and natural resources.

630   US   ISSN 0192-5237
FARM AND RANCH.* 1970. s-m. $10. Farm & Ranch Weekly, Inc., Box 2368, Dallas, TX 75221. TEL 817-562-2814. Ed. Bill Dutton. adv. circ. 8,200. (also avail. in microfilm from KTO)

630   US
FARM AND RANCH GUIDE. 1980. s-w. $15 (effective Oct. 1994). 4023 N. State St., Bismarck, ND 58501. TEL 701-255-4905. FAX 701-255-2312. Ed. Mark Conlon; Pub. David Borlaug. adv. contact: Cliff Meyer. circ. 46,000. **Document type:** newspaper.

AGRICULTURE

630 US
S521.5.A2
FARM & RANCH LIVING. 1979. bi-m. $16.98 (Canada $24.59; elsewhere $25.98); newsstand price: $2.99. Reiman Publications, LP, 5400 S. 60th St., Greendale, WI 53129. TEL 414-423-0100. FAX 414-423-1143. (Subscr. to: Box 997, Greendale, WI 53129) Ed. Nick Pabst. circ. 400,000 (paid). **Document type:** consumer publication.
—UMI.
Description: Offers photo-tours of farms and ranches, including visits with the owners.

630 US
FARM & RANCH NEWS. 1974. m. $12.50 (effective 1997). Farm & Ranch News, Box 160, Lithia, FL 33547-0160. TEL 813-737-6397. Ed. George Parker Jr.; Pub. George Parker Jr. adv.: page $510; trim 10 3/4 x 13 1/2; adv. contact: George Parker. mkt.; maps; tr.mk.; circ. 19,500 (paid). cols./p.: 6; pp./issue: 28. (tabloid format; back issues avail.) **Document type:** newspaper, trade publication.
Description: Includes news on rural life and agricultural issues.

FARM ANTIQUES NEWS. see *ANTIQUES*

430 US
FARM BROADCASTERS LETTER. 1953. w. U.S. Department of Agriculture, Office of Public Affairs, 14th St. & Independence Ave., S.W., Rm. 528-A, Washington, DC 20250-1300. TEL 202-720-7762. FAX 202-690-1131. Ed. Vic Powell. circ. 1,200. **Document type:** government publication.
Description: Includes information for and about farm broadcasters. Highlights developments at U.S.D.A. and in agriculture.

630 US ISSN 0197-5617
FARM BUREAU NEWS. 1921. w. $10. American Farm Bureau Federation, 600 Maryland Ave., S.W., Ste. 800, Washington, DC 20024. TEL 202-484-3600. E-mail: fbnews@fb.com; URL: http://www.fb.com/. Ed. Joan Waldoch. circ. 50,500. **Document type:** newsletter.
●Also available online.
Formerly: American Farm Bureau Federations Official News Letter (ISSN 0002-8398)
Description: Newsletter updating legislative and regulatory developments affecting farmers and ranchers.

630 US
FARM BUREAU PRESS. 1938. m. membership. Arkansas Farm Bureau Federation, 10720 Kanis Road, Little Rock, AR 72211. TEL 501-224-4400. FAX 501-228-1557. Ed. A. Audie Ayer. adv.: B&W page $2867, color page $3462; 9 3/8 x 12 1/2; adv. contact: Jim Kester. circ. 203,000 (controlled). **Document type:** newspaper.

630 US
FARM BUREAU'S RURAL ROUTE. 1930. q. membership. Wisconsin Farm Bureau Federation, Box 5550, Madison, WI 53705. TEL 608-833-8070. FAX 608-829-4256. Ed. Tom Thieding. adv. circ. 54,000. (tabloid format)
Former titles: Agventure (ISSN 0887-9133); (until 1986): Badger Farm Bureau News (ISSN 0005-3740)
Description: Contains articles about the organization's programs, activities, and views concerning public policy issues.

630 US ISSN 0896-1883
FARM CHRONICLE. 1981. w. $10.50. Lee Newspapers, Ltd., Box 460, Culpeper, VA 22701. TEL 540-829-1010. FAX 540-829-1013. Eds. Kay Wilson, June Sekell. adv. circ. 14,500. (tabloid format) **Document type:** trade publication.
Formerly: Farm and Country.
Description: Contains national and local news of interest to people in Virginia, Maryland and North Carolina.

630 UK ISSN 0144-0675
FARM CONTRACTOR AND LARGE-SCALE FARMER. 1971. m. $55. A C P Publishers Ltd., Iron Down House, Deddington, Banbury, Oxon. OX15 0PJ, England. TEL 44-1869-338936. FAX 44-1869-338578. Ed. A. Collier. adv. contact: M. Benjamin. bk.rev.; charts; illus.; stat.; tr.lit. circ. 10,167. **Indexed:** Agri.Eng.Abstr. **Document type:** trade publication.
Description: Supplies coverage of new machines, new techniques and business management for agricultural contractors and large-scale farmers.

630 CN
FARM FOCUS. vol.3, 1975. s-m. Can.$20. Fundy Group Publications, Box 128, 2 Second St., Yarmouth, NS B5A 4B1, Canada. TEL 902-742-7111. Ed. Heather Jones. adv.; illus. circ. 8,500. (tabloid format) **Document type:** trade publication.
Description: Trade journal serving the maritime province's agricultural industry.

630 CN ISSN 0705-8748
FARM GATE. 1977. m. Can.$12. North Waterloo Publishing, 15 King St., Elmira, ON N3B 2R1, Canada. TEL 519-669-5155; 800-645-7355. FAX 519-669-5928. E-mail: enews@realm.tdkcs.waterloo.on.ca. Ed. Robert Verdun. adv. contact: Hugh Weltz. circ. 21,000. **Document type:** newspaper.
Description: Information for farmers about innovations, equipment and sustainable agricultural methods.
Refereed Serial

630 PK
FARM GUIDE. Variant title: Quarterly Farm Guide. (Text in English) 1970. q. Rs.75 (foreign Rs.200). National Farm Guide Council of Pakistan, c/o Shabaz A. Raheem, Ed., 405 Ferozepur Rd., Lahore 54600, Pakistan. TEL 92-42-5864155. FAX 92-42-5864155. Ed. Shabaz A. Raheem. **Document type:** newspaper.
Description: Discusses various aspects of agriculture, farm forestry and farm management from an international perspective, as well as relevant issues such as literacy, youth development, civil defence, and environmental safety.

630 US ISSN 0191-5045
FARM IMPACT. 1975. m. free. Yelvington Publications, P.O. Drawer C, 314 E. Church St., Mascoutah, IL 62258. TEL 618-566-8282. FAX 618-566-8283. Ed. Greg Hoskins. adv. circ. 5,000. (tabloid format)

631 US ISSN 0892-8312
S671.F37
FARM INDUSTRY NEWS. 1967. 12/yr. $12.95 (foreign $24.95). Intertec Publishing Corp., Webb Division, 7900 International Dr., Ste. 300, Minneapolis, MN 55425. TEL 612-851-4684. FAX 612-851-4601. E-mail: farmindustrynews@intertec.com. Ed. Joseph Degnan. adv.; bk.rev.; illus.; tr.lit.; circ. 257,000 (controlled). **Indexed:** Farm & Garden Ind.
—UMI. CCC.
Incorporating: Farm Industry News - West (ISSN 0161-4339); Farm Industry News - Sunbelt; Which was formerly titled: Farm Industry News - South (ISSN 0161-4347); Farm Industry News - Midwest (ISSN 0199-6924); Which in 1979 superseded : Farm Industry News (ISSN 0014-7790)

630 US ISSN 0014-8008
S1
FARM JOURNAL. (Published in numerous Crop and Livestock Editions) 1877. 14/yr. plus supplements. $14.95 (foreign $30). Farm Journal, Inc., 1500 Market St., Philadelphia, PA 19102-2181. TEL 215-557-8900. URL: http://www.farmjournal.com. Ed. Sonja Hillgren. adv.; bk.rev.; illus. (also avail. in microform from UMI; reprint service avail. from UMI) **Indexed:** Bus.Ind., Mag.Ind., PMR, R.G., Tr.& Indus.Ind. **Document type:** trade publication.
—BLDSC (3878.800000); Linda Hall; UMI; UnCover.

FARM LAW. see *LAW*

630 US
FARM NEWS. 1935. m. $4. News Printing Company, 430 S. Adams, Box 1105, Marion, IN 46952. TEL 317-664-0207. Ed. V.O. Pinkerton. circ. 58,235.

630 US
FARM NEWS OF ERIE AND WYOMING COUNTIES; helping you put knowledge to work. 1914. m. $20. Agriculture Programs Cooperative Extension Associations of Erie & Wyoming Counties, 21 S. Grove St., Ste. 240, E. Aurora, NY 14052. TEL 716-652-5400. E-mail: david_weaver@cce.cornell.edu. (And: 401 N. Main St., Warsaw, NY 14569-1091) Ed. David Weaver. adv.; circ. 1,600 (paid). (tabloid format; back issues avail.)
Former Titles: Erie County Farm News; Wyoming County Farm and Home News.
Description: Adult agriculture education.

630 US
FARM TALK. 1974. w. $25. Farm Talk Publishing (Subsidiary of: H D S Corp.), 1801 S. 59 Hwy., Box 601, Parsons, KS 67357. TEL 316-421-9450. FAX 316-421-9473. Ed. Mark Parker. circ. 9,500.

630 US
FARM TIMES, INCORPORATED. 1987. m. $15 (effective 1996). Farm Times, 504 Sixth St., Rupert, ID 83350. TEL 208-436-1111. FAX 208-436-9455. Ed. Eric Goodell; Pub. Steven R. Ward. adv. contact: Steven R. Ward. circ. 25,080. **Document type:** newspaper.
Formerly (until 1994): Farm Times.
Description: Provides information about the economic and political trends affecting the rural Western family.
Refereed Serial

630 AT
FARM WEEKLY. 1921. w. Aus.$92. W.A. Primary Industry Press, P.O. Box 1268, Victoria Park East, Perth, W.A. 6101, Australia. Ed. Graham Greenwood; Pub. Patricia Seeney. R&P contact: Patricia Seeney. adv. contact: Rob Chittick. bk.rev.; charts; illus.; mkt. circ. 14,050. **Document type:** newspaper.
Former titles (until 1994): Elders Weekly & Western Farmer and Grazier (ISSN 0311-7804); (until 1974): Wesfarmers News (ISSN 0043-2865)

633.18 GY
FARMER. vol.8, 1959. q. $1. (Guyana Rice Producers Association) New Guyana Co. Ltd., Lot 8, Government Industrial Estate, East Bank, Demerara, Guyana. TEL 592-2-62471. adv.; stat. circ. 4,000. (tabloid format)
Formerly (until 1975): Rice Review (ISSN 0035-497X)

631 JM ISSN 0014-8350
FARMER. bi-m. J.$2. Jamaica Agricultural Society, N. Parade, Kingston, Jamaica, W.I. adv.; illus.; index. **Indexed:** Chem.Abstr., Hort.Abstr., Plant Breed.Abstr.

631 RH ISSN 1011-0488
THE FARMER; Zimbabwe farming news magazine. (Supplements avail.: A R T Winter Report; A R T Summer Report; Cattleman of the Year; Zimbabwe's Farming Year Book and Agricultural Inputs - Services Directory) 1930. w. (Thu.). Z.$157 (in Africa Z.$193; elsewhere Z.$218); airmail to U.S. Z.$1767) (effective 1996). (Commercial Farmers' Union) Modern Farming Publications Trust, Agriculture House, Leopold Takawira St., P.O. Box 1622, Harare, Zimbabwe. TEL 263-4-753278. FAX 263-4-750754. TELEX 22084 CFU ZW. Ed. Felicity Wood. adv.: B&W page Z.$5294, color page Z.$7054; trim 280 x 216; adv. contact: Michael Rook. bk.rev.; charts; illus.; mkt.; circ. 6,000 (paid). **Document type:** trade publication.
Formerly: Rhodesian Farmer (ISSN 0035-4775); Incorporates: Tobacco News.
Description: Disseminates information of interest to farmers in Zimbabwe, promoting the adoption, implementation and application of improved farming practices.

630 658 CN
FARMER. m. Gordon Publishing & Printing, 228 Main St., Bible Hill, NS B2N 4H2, Canada. TEL 902-895-7946. FAX 902-893-1427. Ed. Peter Heckhert. adv. circ. 2,550.

630 UK
THE FARMER. 22/yr. Chronicle House, Castle Foregate Shrewsbury, Shropshire SY1 2DN, England. TEL 0743-363222. FAX 0743-232305. Ed. A. Godding. circ. 18,291.

AGRICULTURE

630 US ISSN 1069-5400
THE FARMER. MINNESOTA. (Supplement avail.: Dairy Producer) 15/yr. $19.95. Farm Progress Companies (Subsidiary of: A B C Publishing Companies), 191 S. Gary Ave., Carol Stream, IL 60188. TEL 708-690-5600. FAX 708-462-2869. (Edit. addr.: Box 430, Sioux Falls, SD 57101. TEL 605-335-7752) Ed. Gil Gullickson. adv. contact: Charles Roth. illus. circ. 49,490. **Document type:** trade publication.
—UMI.
  Formed by the merger of (1992-1993): Minnesota Farmer (ISSN 1064-6752); Which was formerly (until 1992): Minnesota Wallaces Farmer (ISSN 1049-8214); (1992-1993): U S Agriculture (ISSN 1066-1301); Which was formed by the merger of (1935-1992): Farmer (ISSN 0896-5579); (1980-1992): Dakota Farmer (ISSN 0198-6171)
  Description: Provides timely and local crop and livestock production practices to farm operators in Minnesota.

631 II ISSN 0014-8369
FARMER AND PARLIAMENT. (Text in English, Hindi) 1966. m. Rs.60($6) Farmers' Parliamentary Forum, 215 Rouse Ave., Deen Dayal Upadhay Marg, New Delhi 110002, India. (Dist. overseas by: HPC Publishers' Distributors Pvt. Ltd., 4805-24, 1st Fl., Bharat Ram Rd., Darya Ganj, New Delhi 110 002, India. TEL 91-11-3254401. FAX 91-11-6863511) Ed. S.N. Bhalla. adv. circ. 2,000.

630 UK
FARMER BUSINESS IN WALES. 1967. 4/yr. membership. Welsh Agricultural Organisation Society Ltd., Brynawel, Box 8, Aberystwyth, Wales. Ed. J. Kendall. adv.; bk.rev. circ. 9,000.

630 658 CN ISSN 1185-2178
FARMER - RANCHER. q. Battlefords Publishing Ltd., P.O. Box 1029, N. Battleford, SK S9A 3E6, Canada. TEL 306-445-7261. FAX 306-445-3223. Ed. Lorne Cooper; Pub. Steven Dills. R&P contact: Steven Dills. adv. contact: Alana Schweitzer. circ. 15,602. (tabloid format; also avail. in microfilm from CML) **Document type:** trade publication.
  Formerly (until 1990): Northwest Farmer - Rancher (ISSN 0822-5737)

630 636 US ISSN 0739-9235
FARMER STOCKMAN OF THE MIDWEST. w. $20. Telescope, Inc., 1817 E. U.S. 81 Frontage Rd., Box 349, Belleville, KS 66935. TEL 913-527-2224. FAX 913-527-2225. Ed. Merle M. Miller; Pub. Merle Miller. R&P contact: Merle Miller. adv. contact: Merle Miller. circ. 10,000 (paid). (tabloid format) **Document type:** newspaper.

630 UK ISSN 1074-0163
FARMER TO FARMER. 8/yr. B H R Communications, County Mills, Worcester WR1 3NU, England. TEL 01905-25541. FAX 01905-723412. TELEX 338266. Ed. Sylvia Powell. **Document type:** newsletter.

630 US
FARMERS' ADVANCE. 1898. w. $31.95. Camden Publications, 331 E. Bell St., Camden, MI 49232-0008. TEL 517-368-0365. FAX 517-368-5131. Ed. John Snyder; Pub. Kurt Greenhoe. adv. contact: Jay Sliker. circ. 20,000 (paid). **Document type:** newsletter.
  Description: Farm and auction guide for Michigan, Indiana and Ohio.

630 640 US ISSN 0889-5619
FARMERS AND CONSUMERS MARKET BULLETIN. 1917. w. $10 (free in Georgia). Department of Agriculture, 19 Martin Luther King Jr. Dr., Rm. 226, Capitol Sq., Atlanta, GA 30334-4250. TEL 404-656-3722. FAX 404-651-7957. Ed. Carlton B. Moore. R&P contact: Carlton B. Moore. illus.; circ. 250,000 (controlled). (tabloid format) **Document type:** bulletin, government publication.
  Description: Provides agriculture features and stories for Georgia residents.

630 UK ISSN 0014-8393
FARMERS CLUB. JOURNAL. 1842. bi-m. £1. Farmers Club, 3 Whitehall Court, London SW1, England. Ed. D.D. Watson. adv.; bk.rev. circ. 5,000. **Indexed:** Field Crop Abstr., Geo.Abstr., Herb.Abstr., Plant Breed.Abstr., Rural Recreat.Tour.Abstr., World Agri.Econ. & Rural Sociol.Abstr.
—BLDSC (3894.200000).

630 US ISSN 0046-3337
FARMER'S DIGEST. 1937. 10/yr. $17.95 (effective 1997); newsstand price: $3.95. Lessiter Publications, Box 624, Brookfield, WI 53008-0624. TEL 414-782-4480. FAX 414-782-1252. E-mail: lesspub@aol.com. Ed. Frank Lessiter. adv.; bk.rev.; charts; illus.; cum.index. circ. 15,000. (also avail. in microform from UMI; reprint service avail. from UMI) **Indexed:** Farm & Garden Ind. **Document type:** consumer publication.
—UMI; UnCover.
  Description: Contains current information on all phases of agriculture, gathered from over 300 farm publications.

630 US
FARMERS' EXCHANGE (FAYETTEVILLE). 1987. m. free to qualified personnel. Exchange, Inc., Box 490, 408 S. Main St., Fayetteville, TN 37334. TEL 615-433-9737. FAX 615-433-0053. Ed. William F. Thomas. adv. circ. 20,000.
  Formerly: Tennessee Farmer's Exchange.

630 CH ISSN 0014-8415
FARMERS' FRIEND.* Key Title: Nong You. 1940. m. NT.$72($1.80) Box 16, Nei-Hsin, Taichung, Taiwan, Republic of China. Ed. Yen Chun Hsiung. adv.; bk.rev.; abstr.; charts; illus.; stat.; index; cum.index. circ. 18,000.

630 UK ISSN 0014-8423
FARMERS GUARDIAN. 1958. w. £45 (foreign £84). United Newspapers Publications Ltd., Olivers Pl., Fulwood Preston PR2 9ZA, England. TEL 44-1772-203800. FAX 44-1772-204939. Ed. Michael Finch. R&P contact: Michael Finch. adv. contact: Lynn Andriotis. bk.rev.; illus. circ. 54,693. (also avail. in microform) **Document type:** newspaper.
  Description: News briefs, articles, editorial, and opinions on the legislative, regulatory, health, and market forecasting issues that affect the financial and operational aspects of agricultural businesses.

630 UK
FARMERS GUIDE. 1979. m. £30. Early Bird Farming Publications Ltd., Early Bird House, 16 Orford St., Ipswich, Suffolk IP1 3NS, England. TEL 0473-218812. FAX 0473-226613. Ed. Doug Potts. adv.: B&W page £590, color page £700. circ. 16,000. **Document type:** trade publication.
  Formerly (until 1992): East Anglian Farmers Guide.
  Description: Regional farming publication for agriculture in the eastern counties.

630 US ISSN 0192-6322
FARMERS HOT LINE. 42/yr. $39.95. Heartland Ag-Business Group, Inc., 1003 Central Ave., Fort Dodge, IA 50501. TEL 515-955-1600. FAX 800-247-2000. Ed. Sandra J. Simonson; Pub. Sandra J. Simonson. R&P contact: Sandra J. Simonson. adv. contact: Lisa Ziems. circ. 40,000. **Document type:** trade publication.
  Description: For dealers, manufacturers, and other machinery purchasing decision makers. Designed to bring together buyers and sellers of farm machinery and related services.

630 RH
FARMERS' REVIEW. 1991. bi-m. Z.$10.50. Argosy Press, P.O. Box 2677, Harare, Zimbabwe. TEL 263-4-755084. FAX 263-4-752162. TELEX 26334 MODUS ZW. Ed. Desmond Kumbuka. adv. contact: Ruth P. Mahleka. **Document type:** trade publication.
  Description: Directed at the farming fraternity.

630 SA ISSN 0014-8482
FARMER'S WEEKLY. Afrikaans edition: Boere Weekblad. (Text in English) 1911. w. R.249.45 (overseas R.509.60) (effective 1997). Republican Press (Pty) Ltd., P.O. Box 32083, Mobeni 4060, South Africa. TEL 27-31-422041. FAX 27-31-426068. Ed. Corrie Venter. R&P contact: Roy Minnaar. TEL 27-11-7287245. adv. contact: T. Anderson. bk.rev.; illus.; mkt.; index. circ. 38,000. **Indexed:** Anim.Breed.Abstr., Food Sci.& Tech.Abstr., Ind.S.A.Per., INIS Atomind., Sugar Ind. Abstr. **Document type:** trade publication.
  Description: Covers all aspects of farming in South Africa.

630 UK ISSN 0014-8474
FARMERS WEEKLY. 1934. w. £57. Reed Business Publishing Ltd., Farmers Publishing Group (Subsidiary of: Reed Elsevier group), Quadrant House, The Quadrant, Sutton, Surrey SM2 5AS, England. TEL 44-181-652-4911. FAX 44-181-652-4005. TELEX 892084-REEDBP-G. Ed. Stephen Howe. R&P contact: Stephen Howe. adv. contact: Vic Bunby. circ. 99,000. **Indexed:** Agroforest.Abstr., Anim.Breed.Abstr., Dairy Sci.Abstr., Field Crop Abstr., Food Sci.& Tech.Abstr., Herb.Abstr., Hort.Abstr., Rural Recreat.Tour.Abstr., Sugar Ind.Abstr., World Agri.Econ. & Rural Sociol.Abstr. **Document type:** trade publication.
—BLDSC (3895.500000); CISTI; SWETS. **CCC.**
  Incorporates: Farmland Market (ISSN 0305-0157); Power Farming (ISSN 0032-5988)

630 US
FARMERS WEEKLY REVIEW. 1921. w. $15 (effective 1997). Farmers Weekly Review, Inc., 100 Manhattan Rd., Joliet, IL 60433. TEL 815-727-4811. FAX 815-727-5570. Ed. Patrick Cleary; Pub. P.J. Cleary. adv. contact: Debbie Werner. bk.rev.; circ. 11,250. circ. 11,000 (paid). cols./p.: 5; pp./issue: 16. (tabloid format; also avail. in microform) **Document type:** newspaper.
  Description: Includes items of regional interest, including local government and business.

630 KE
FARMER'S WORLD; Kenya's farm magazine. (Text in English and Swahili) 1977. m. (Kenya Grain Growers Co-operative Union) Oryx Publications Ltd., P.O. Box 40106, Nairobi, Kenya. adv.; charts; illus.; stat. circ. 7,500.
  Formerly: Farmer's Voice.

630 US ISSN 0091-1305
FARMFUTURES; the farm business magazine. 1972. 12/yr. $36. Farm Progress Companies, 191 S. Gary Ave., Carol Stream, IL 60188. TEL 708-690-5600. FAX 708-462-2869. (Edit. addr.: 13 Meadow Ridge, St. Peters, MO 63376. TEL 314-447-5786. FAX 314-447-5941) Ed. Stewart Reeve. adv.; bk.rev.; charts. circ. 212,000. (back issues avail.)
  Description: The business magazine of American agriculture, edited expressly for the operators of large, fulltime farming businesses.

630 AT ISSN 1038-1678
FARMING AHEAD. 1983. m. Aus.$115 (foreign Aus.$130). Kondinin Group, P.O. Box 913, Cloverdale, W.A. 6105, Australia. TEL 61-9-4783343. FAX 61-9-4783353. E-mail: kgperth@ozemail.com.au. Ed. Deborah King. R&P contact: Deborah King. adv. contact: Carole King. software rev.; mkt.; stat.; charts. circ. 29,000 (controlled). **Document type:** consumer publication.
  Former titles (until 1992): Kondinin Group Talk (ISSN 1033-9078); (until 1988): Group Talk (ISSN 0814-4613)
  Description: Covers cropping, cattle, and sheep management, pasture management, machinery - equipment evaluations, research reports, farm computing and technology, marketing and finance.

630 UK
FARMING ECHO. m. Lincolnshire Publishing Ltd., Brayford Wharf East, Lincoln LN5 7AT, England. TEL 01522-525252. FAX 01522-545759. Ed. Cliff Smith. circ. 65,000. **Document type:** bulletin.

630 UK
FARMING LIFE. 104/yr. 51-67 Donegall St., Belfast BT1 2GB, N. Ireland. TEL 0232-244441. FAX 0232-230715. Ed. David McCoy. circ. 62,000.

630 UK ISSN 0265-1645
FARMING NEWS. 1983. w. $130. Morgan-Grampian (Farming) Press Ltd. (Subsidiary of: Morgan-Grampian plc), Morgan-Grampian House, 30 Calderwood St., London SE18 6QH, England. TEL 081-855-7777. FAX 081-854-7476. Ed. Donald Taylor. adv. contact: Ian Stokes. circ. 71,000. **Document type:** trade publication.

630 CN
FARMING TODAY (SIMCOE COUNTY EDITION). 1977. m. Alliston Press Ltd., Box 280, 14 Victoria St., E., Alliston, Ont. L0M 1A0, Canada. TEL 705-435-6228. Ed. Mariellen Venhola. circ. 11,500. (tabloid format)

AGRICULTURE

630 CN ISSN 0838-8512
FARMING TODAY (WELLINGTON-WATERLOO-PERTH EDITION). 1978. s-m. $10. Wenger Publications, Box 130, Mount Forest, Ont. N0G 2L0, Canada. TEL 519-291-1660. Ed. Vaugham Douglas. circ. 15,999.

630 US ISSN 0272-3417
FARMING UNCLE; periodical for natural people and mother nature lovers. 1977. q. $5. Farming Uncle, 780 E. 185th St., No. 3d, Bronx, NY 10460-1089. Ed. Louis Toro; Pub. Louis Toro. adv.: B&W page $47.50. bk.rev.; illus.; stat. circ. 1,000. (back issues avail.) Indexed: Alt.Press Ind.
 Description: Features articles on the appreciation of nature and wildlife and its relationship to operating a self-sufficient agricultural enterprise.

630 UK
FARMING WALES/YR AMAETHWR. 1992. m. membership. National Farmer's Union, 24 Tawe Business Village, Phoenix Way, Swansea Enterprise Park, Llansamlet, Swansea SA7 9LB, Wales. TEL 44-1792-774848. FAX 44-1792-774758. Ed. Keith Jones. adv. contact: Caroline Herbert. bk.rev. circ. 14,000. **Document type:** trade publication.
 Refereed Serial

338 630 US ISSN 0093-5832
FARMLAND NEWS. 1933. w. $21 (effective 1996). Box 240, Archbold, OH 43502-0240. TEL 419-445-9456. FAX 419-445-4444. Ed. Jerry Rohrs; Pub. O. Roger Taylor. R&P contact: Jerry Rohrs. adv. contact: Doug Nutter. illus.; circ. 7,426 (paid). (tabloid format; back issues avail.) **Document type:** newspaper.
 —Linda Hall.
 Incorporated (1986-1991): Big Times (ISSN 0898-5154); **Formerly** (until 1959): Farmland (ISSN 0014-8539)
 Description: Covers farming, home, and garden management, and rural human interest.

630 UK ISSN 0014-8547
FARMWEEK. 1961. w. £32. (Ulster Farmers Union) Morton Newspapers Ltd., 14 Church St., Portadown Co. Armagh BT62 3LQ, N. Ireland. TEL 01762-339421. FAX 01762-350203. Ed. Hal Crowe. adv. contact: Diane McCartney. bk.rev.; abstr.; charts; mkt.; stat. circ. 13,800. (tabloid format) Indexed: Hort.Abstr., Seed Abstr., Weed Abstr. **Document type:** newspaper, trade publication.
 Incorporating: Farmer's Journal.

630 US ISSN 0164-8640
FARMWEEK. 1955. w. $17.95. Mayhill Publications, Inc., Attn.: Gary Thoe, Pres., 27 N. Jefferson St., Box 90, Knightstown, IN 46148. TEL 317-345-5133. Ed. Nancy Sear Foss. adv.; bk.rev. circ. 32,879. (tabloid format)
 Supersedes in part (in Sep. 1978): Eastern Indiana Farmer (ISSN 0420-3690)

630 SP
FASAGA - ANDALUCIA. 12/yr. Edif. Jerez, 74 planta 2a, 11405 Jerez de la Frontera (Cadiz), Spain. TEL 56-30-79-00.

630 BG
FASHAL. (Text in Bengali) 1965. w. 28J Toyenbee Circular Rd., Motijheel C-A, Dhaka 1000, Bangladesh. TEL 2-233099. Ed. Ershad Mazumdar. circ. 8,000.

630 US
FASTLINE: WISCONSIN EDITION. 1988-198?; resumed 1994. m. $8. Fastline Publications, 4900 Fox Run Rd., Buckner, KY 40010. TEL 502-222-0146; 800-332-7854. FAX 502-222-0615. E-mail: fastpub@aol.com. Ed. William G. Howard; Pub. William G. Howard. R&P contact: William G. Howard. circ. 22,000.
 Former titles: Farmers Fastline: Wisconsin Edition; (until 1989): Wisconsin Farmers Fastline.
 Description: Designed to the farming industry.

630 FR ISSN 0396-8936
FEDERATION NATIONALE DES AGRICULTEURS MULTIPLICATEURS DE SEMENCES. BULLETIN. 1962. 4/yr. 210 F. (foreign 355 F.) (effective 1997). Federation Nationale des Agriculteurs Multiplicateurs de SEMENCES, 74 rue Jean-Jacques Rousseau, 75001 Paris, France. TEL 33-1-44827333. FAX 33-1-44827340. Eds. Yves Bouchet, Daniel Dattee. R&P contact: Daniel Dattee. adv. contact: Catherine Guy. bibl.; stat. circ. 30,000. **Document type:** bulletin.
 —BLDSC (2512.140000).
 Description: Technical information on seed producing, means to guarantee yield and quality in producing fields, economic information on market situation, and general information on regulation and findings that may influence seed growing.

630 US ISSN 0274-7308
FENCE POST.* 1980. w. $14. John Walker, P.O. Box 448, Windsor, CO 80550-0448. TEL 303-686-5694. FAX 303-686-5694. Ed. Duane McCormick. adv. circ. 10,000.

630 SP
FERIAS, MERCADOS Y MATADEROS. 52/yr. Gran Via 49, Apdo. 125, 37001 Salamanca, Spain. TEL 23-27-05-87. FAX 23-21-00-99. Ed. E. Ferreira Carretero.

630 RU ISSN 0868-4863
FERMER. 1990. q. $55 (effective 1996). Assotsiatsiya Krest'yanskikh Khozyaistv i Sel'skokhozyaistvennykh Kooperativov Rossii, 7-ya ul. Tekstil'shchikov, 14, 109263 Moscow, Russia. circ. 30,000.

630 US ISSN 0071-4607
TP963.A1 CODEN: PFRWAD
FERTILIZER INDUSTRY ROUND TABLE. PROCEEDINGS. 1955. a. $35 per copy. Fertilizer Industry Round Table, Box 5036, Glen Arm, MD 21057. Ed. Terri Silbersack. circ. 300. **Document type:** proceedings.
 —BLDSC (6841.440000); CASDDS; Linda Hall.

630 UK
FIFE FARMER. m. Angus County Press Ltd., Forfar, Angus DD8 1BU, Scotland. TEL 01307-464899. FAX 01307-466923. Ed. Ian Wallace. adv. contact: Linda Ruston. circ. 7,000. **Document type:** trade publication.

630 FJ ISSN 0071-4844
FIJI. MINISTRY OF AGRICULTURE & FISHERIES. ANNUAL REPORT. (Text in English) 1906. a. F.$1. Ministry of Agriculture & Fisheries, Box 358, Suva, Fiji. Indexed: Field Crop Abstr., Herb.Abstr., Nutr.Abstr., Rev.Appl.Entomol., Rev.Plant Path.
 Formerly: Fiji. Department of Agriculture. Annual Report.

630 FJ
FIJI. MINISTRY OF AGRICULTURE & FISHERIES. ANNUAL RESEARCH REPORT. (Text in English) N.S. 1969. a. F.$2($3.75) per no. Ministry of Agriculture & Fisheries, Box 358, Suva, Fiji.
 Formerly: Fiji. Department of Agriculture. Annual Research Report.

630 FJ ISSN 0015-0886
S400.F5 CODEN: FJAJAB
FIJI AGRICULTURAL JOURNAL. (Text in English) N.S. 1970. s-a. F.$2. Ministry of Agriculture & Fisheries, Box 358, Suva, Fiji. Ed. Param Sivan. circ. 600. (back issues avail.) Indexed: Agroforest.Abstr., Anim.Breed.Abstr., Biol.Abstr., Chem.Abstr., Curr.Adv.Ecol.Sci., Dairy Sci.Abstr., Field Crop Abstr., Food Sci.& Tech.Abstr., Helminthol.Abstr., Herb.Abstr., Hort.Abstr., Ind.Vet., Pig News & Info., Plant Breed Abstr., Rev.Appl.Entomol., Rev.Plant Path., Rural Recreat.Tour.Abstr., So.Pac.Per.Ind., Soils & Fert., Soyabean Abstr., Vet.Bull., Weed Abstr., World Agri.Econ. & Rural Sociol.Abstr.
 —BLDSC (3925.530000); CASDDS; Linda Hall.

FINANCIAL SURVEY. AGRICULTURAL GROWERS & MERCHANTS. LONDON & SOUTH; company data for success. see *BUSINESS AND ECONOMICS — Trade And Industrial Directories*

FINANCIAL SURVEY. AGRICULTURAL GROWERS & MERCHANTS. MIDLANDS & NORTH. see *BUSINESS AND ECONOMICS — Trade And Industrial Directories*

630 338.1 NE ISSN 0921-4100
FINANCIELE POSITIE VAN DE LANDBOUW; boekjaar en vergelijkingen met voorgaande jaren. 1975. a. fl.69. Landbouw-Economisch Instituut, Burg. Patijnlaan 19, 2585 BE The Hague, Netherlands. TEL 31-70-3308330. FAX 31-70-3615624. E-mail: postmaster@lei.dlo.nl; URL: http://www.lei.dlo.nl/lei. Ed.Bd. **Document type:** government publication.
 Description: Extended data in financing of Dutch farms.

630 338 332.7 II ISSN 0015-2110
HG2051.I4
FINANCING AGRICULTURE. 1969. q. Rs.75($35) Agricultural Finance Corporation Ltd., Dhanraj Mahal, 1st Fl., Chatrapati Shivaji Maharaj Marg, Mumbai 400 001, India. TEL 91-22-202-8924. FAX 91-22-202-966. TELEX 11 85849 AFCO IN. E-mail: afcl@bom2 vsnl.net-in. Ed. Subash Chandra Wadhwa. bk.rev. circ. 3,000. Indexed: Hort.Abstr., Rural Devel.Abstr., Rural Recreat.Tour.Abstr., World Agri.Econ. & Rural Sociol.Abstr. **Document type:** consumer publication.
 —BLDSC (3927.250000).
 Refereed Serial

630 US ISSN 0747-1114
FIRELANDS FARMER. 1971. w. $20. Thomas Mezick, 211 W. Main St., New London, OH 44851. TEL 419-929-8043. FAX 419-929-3800. Ed. Cleve Canham. adv. contact: Amy Cawrse. bk.rev. circ. 4,150. (tabloid format) **Document type:** newspaper.

581 630 US ISSN 0071-5948
CODEN: FPBRAE
FLORIDA. DIVISION OF PLANT INDUSTRY. BIENNIAL REPORT. 1916. biennial. one copy free to Florida residents. Department of Agriculture and Consumer Services, Division of Plant Industry, 1911 S.W. 34th St., Box 147100, Gainesville, FL 32614-7100. TEL 904-372-3505. FAX 904-955-2301. Ed. Maeve McConnell. R&P contact: Maeve McConnell. Indexed: Biol.Abstr., Rev.Plant Path. **Document type:** government publication.
 —Linda Hall.

630 US
FLORIDA AGRICULTURAL RESEARCH. 1956. q. free. University of Florida, Institute of Food & Agricultural Sciences, Agricultural Experiment Sta., McCarty Hall, Gainesville, FL 32611-0620. TEL 904-392-1733. Ed. Chuck Woods. charts; illus.; stat. circ. 8,000. Indexed: Biol.Abstr., Chem.Abstr., Curr.Adv.Ecol.Sci., Field Crop Abstr., Herb.Abstr., Plant Breed.Abstr.
 —Linda Hall; UMI.
 Former titles (until 1987): University of Florida. Institute of Food and Agricultural Sciences. Research (ISSN 0894-0673); (until 1986): Florida Agricultural Research (ISSN 0734-8444); **Supersedes** (in 1982): Sunshine State Agricultural Research Report (ISSN 0039-5447)

630 US ISSN 0015-4091
CODEN: FGRAAE
FLORIDA GROWER AND RANCHER.* 1907. m. $35 (out-of-state $45; free to qualified personnel) (effective 1993). F.G.R., Incorporated, 1555 Howell Branch Rd., Ste. C-204, Winter Park, FL 32789-1171. TEL 407-894-6522. FAX 407-894-6511. Ed. Frank C. Garner; Pub. Sondra Abrahamson. adv. contact: Sondra Abrahamson. bk.rev.; illus. circ. 17,500. (also avail. in microform from UMI; reprint service avail. from UMI) Indexed: Chem.Abstr. **Document type:** trade publication.
 —UMI.
 Incorporates (in 1979): Florida Field Report (ISSN 0015-4075)
 Description: Covers growing, harvesting, processing, packing, shipping and marketing of Florida commodities, with emphasis on citrus, vegetables and livestock. Includes dairying, row crops, sugarcane, and forestry.

338.1 US ISSN 0046-4120
FLORIDA MARKET BULLETIN. vol.20, 1978. s-m. free. Department of Agriculture and Consumer Services, 545 E. Tennessee St., Tallahassee, FL 32308. Ed. Walter Land. adv.; illus.; tr.lit.; circ. 30,000 (controlled). (tabloid format) **Document type:** government publication.
 Formerly: Florida. Department of Agriculture and Consumer Services. Market Bulletin.
 Description: Contains news and classified ads relating to Florida agriculture.

AGRICULTURE

630 US ISSN 0015-3869
FLORIDAGRICULTURE. 1943. m. free to qualified personnel. Florida Farm Bureau Federation, 5700 S.W. 34th Ave., Gainesville, FL 32608. TEL 904-374-1521. (And: Box 147030, Gainesville, FL 32614-7030) Ed. Mary Ward. adv. contact: Tom Lampert. illus.; circ. 105,000 (paid). (tabloid format; back issues avail.) **Document type:** trade publication.
  Description: Covers FFB activities, agriculture in Florida, and environmental issues.

630 US
FOCUS ON FARMING. 1979. s-m. $8. Community Newspapers, 6 Central St., Box 591, Moravia, NY 13118-0591. TEL 315-497-1551. Ed. Bernard F. McGuerty III. adv.: B&W page $452.24; adv. contact: Janet Mulvaney. circ. 15,000 (paid). (tabloid format) **Document type:** newspaper.

630 AU ISSN 0015-525X
HD1931
FOERDERUNGSDIENST; Zeitschrift fuer Lehr- und Beratungskraefte. 1953. m. free. Bundesministerium fuer Land- und Forstwirtschaft, Stubenring 1, A-1010 Vienna, Austria. TEL 43-1-711006710. FAX 43-1-711002127. bk.rev.; charts; illus.; stat.; index; circ. 3,500 (controlled). (tabloid format) **Indexed:** Rural Ext.Educ.& Tr.Abstr., Rural Recreat.Tour.Abstr., World Agri.Econ.& Rural Sociol.Abstr. **Document type:** government publication.
—BLDSC (3985.800000).

630 VE
FOMENTO AGROPECUARIO. 1976. m. free. Banco de Venezuela, Apdo. Postal 6268, Caracas 1010, Venezuela. charts; illus.; stat.

630 VE
FONAIAP DIVULGA. 1981. 4/yr. Bs.1200($25) Fondo Nacional de Investigaciones Agropecuarias, Apdo. 2103, Maracay 2105, Venezuela. FAX 043-831423. Ed. Josefa Saavedra. adv.; bk.rev.; illus. circ. 5,000. **Indexed:** Biodet.Abstr., Hort.Abstr.

FOOD AND AGRICULTURAL LEGISLATION. see *LAW*

630 UN ISSN 0532-0208
FOOD AND AGRICULTURE ORGANIZATION OF THE UNITED NATIONS. BASIC TEXTS. (Text in English, French and Spanish) 1960. irreg. Food and Agriculture Organization of the United Nations, Bernan Associates, 4611-F Assembly Dr., Lanham, MD 20706-4391. TEL 301-459-7666. FAX 301-459-0056. **Document type:** monographic series.

630 UN ISSN 0071-6944
FOOD AND AGRICULTURE ORGANIZATION OF THE UNITED NATIONS CONFERENCE. REPORT. biennial, 27th session, 1993. price varies. Food and Agriculture Organization of the United Nations, Bernan Associates, 4611-F Assembly Dr., Lanham, MD 20706-4391. TEL 301-459-7666. FAX 301-459-0056. (also avail. in microfiche from CIS) **Indexed:** Chem.Abstr., IIS, Nutr.Abstr.

664.6 US ISSN 0739-6791
THE FOOD AND FIBER LETTER. w. $445 (foreign $495). Sparks Companies, Inc., 6708 Whittier Ave., McLean, VA 22101. TEL 703-734-8787. FAX 703-556-7865. TELEX 4993332 SCIDC. Ed. Barry Jenkins. adv.; bk.rev. (back issues avail.) **Document type:** newsletter.
  Description: Analyzes US and foreign agricultural policies and politics.

630 II ISSN 0015-6396
CODEN: FFAGDB
FOOD FARMING AND AGRICULTURE. (Text in English) 1968. m. Ed. L.K. Pandeya, Block F, 105-C New Alipore Rd., Calcutta 53, India. abstr.; bibl.; charts; illus.; stat.; cum.index. **Indexed:** Chem.Abstr., Field Crop Abstr., Herb.Abstr., Nutr.Abstr.
—CASDDS.

FOOD, ITS SCIENCE AND TECHNOLOGY. see *FOOD AND FOOD INDUSTRIES*

FOOD STRUCTURE. see *NUTRITION AND DIETETICS*

FOODWATCH UPDATE. see *CONSUMER EDUCATION AND PROTECTION*

630 AT
FORAGE. 1958. a. free. University of Melbourne, School of Agriculture, Parkville, Vic. 3052, Australia. (Co-sponsor: La Trobe University, School of Forestry) Ed.Bd. adv. circ. 1,500.

630 US
FORAGE FARMER. * q. International Silo Association, Box 560, Lafayette, IN 47902-0560. TEL 913-599-1919.

FORD ALMANAC; for farm and home. see *ENCYCLOPEDIAS AND GENERAL ALMANACS*

630 AU ISSN 0015-8224
DER FORTSCHRITTLICHE LANDWIRT. 1917. 24/yr. S.658. Leopold Stocker Verlag, Hofgasse 5, A-8011 Graz, Austria. TEL 43-316-821636. FAX 43-316-835612. Ed. Anton Stock. adv. contact: Thomas Muehlbacher. bk.rev.; index. circ. 40,000. **Document type:** trade publication.

630 581 CI ISSN 1330-2884
CODEN: FHJUDA
FRAGMENTA PHYTOMEDICA ET HERBOLOGICA. 1971. s-a. $10. Institute for Plant Protection, Faculty of Agricultural Sciences, Simunska c.25-V, 41000 Zagreb, Croatia. abstr. circ. 500. (back issues avail.) **Indexed:** Biol.Abstr., Chem.Abstr., Curr.Adv.Ecol.Sci., Weed Abstr.
—BLDSC (4032.110300); CASDDS.
  Former titles (until 1993): Fragmenta Herbologica (ISSN 1330-2906); (until 1991): Fragmenta Herbologica Jugoslavica (ISSN 0350-3615)

630 FR ISSN 1148-2168
FRANCE. MINISTERE DE L'AGRICULTURE. BULLETIN TECHNIQUE D'INFORMATION. 1945. m. 310 F. (foreign 420 F.). Ministere de l'Agriculture, 78 rue de Varenne, 75700 Paris, France. abstr.; bibl.; charts; illus.; stat. circ. 4,500. **Indexed:** Dairy Sci.Abstr., Excerp.Med. **Document type:** bulletin.
  Former titles: France. Ministere de l'Agriculture et du Developpement Rural. Bulletin Technique d'Information (ISSN 0303-1721); France. Ministere de l'Agriculture. Bulletin Technique d'Information (1945) (ISSN 0015-9646)

630 FR ISSN 0152-3295
FRANCE. MINISTERE DE L'AGRICULTURE ET DE LA FORET. BULLETIN D'INFORMATION. Cover title: B I M A. 1958. w. (40/yr.). 200 F. (foreign 300 F.). Ministere de l'Agriculture et de la Foret, Service de la Communication, 78 rue de Varenne, 75700 Paris, France. (Subscr. to: L'Imprimerie Nationale, B.P. 514, 59505 Douai Cedex, France. TEL 33-3-27937070) charts; illus.; stat. **Document type:** bulletin.
  Formerly: France. Ministere de l'Agriculture. Bulletin d'Information.
  Description: Covers the principal measures taken and decisions made by the Ministry in agricultural and social matters.

630 500 FR ISSN 0046-4899
FRANCE AGRICOLE. 1945. w. (49/yr.). 418 F. (effective 1997). C E P Groupe France Agricole, 8 Cite Paradis, 75493 Paris Cedex 10, France. TEL 33-1-40227900. FAX 33-1-48240315. Ed. Michel Collonge. adv.; bk.rev.; cum.index. circ. 200,000. **Indexed:** Agri.Eng.Abstr., Weed Abstr.
—BLDSC (4032.190000); SWETS.
  Formerly: Journal de la France Agricole.

630 GW
FREIER AGRARHANDEL. 1967. m. DM.48. (Landhandelsverband Bayern e.V.) Agrarhandelsdienst GmbH, Brienner Str. 27, 80997 Munich, Germany. TEL 089-557296. FAX 089-597077. circ. 2,900.

630 IC ISSN 0016-1209
S11
FREYR. 1904. fortn. $45. Bunadarfelag Islands - Agricultural Society of Iceland, Box 7080, Reykjavik, Iceland. TEL 354-551-9200. FAX 354-562-3058. Eds. Matthias Eggertsson, Julius Danielsson. adv.; bk.rev.; illus.; mkt.; stat. circ. 3,700.

638.1 FR ISSN 0429-7857
FRUITS ET ABEILLES. m. 70 Fr. Union des Federations Arboricoles et Apicoles, 24 rue St-Wolfgang, 67700 Weyersheim, France. Ed. Gerard Weibel. **Indexed:** Apic.Abstr.

630 CC ISSN 0429-8047
FUJIAN NONGYE/FUJIAN AGRICULTURE. (Text in Chinese) m. Y12. (Fujian Sheng Nongye Ting - Fujian Provincial Bureau of Agriculture) Fujian Nongye Bianjibu, 153 Guping Lu, Fuzhou, Fujian 350003, People's Republic of China. TEL 556106. Ed. Chen Qingshou. circ. 78,000.

630 631 CC
CODEN: FCNHAL
FUJIAN NONGYE DAXUE XUEBAO/FUJIAN AGRICULTURAL UNIVERSITY. JOURNAL. (Text in Chinese; abstracts in English) q. $24. Fujian Nongye Daxue, Jinshan, Fuzhou, Fujian 350002, People's Republic of China. TEL 0591-3741213. FAX 0591-3710251. (Dist. overseas by: China International Book Trading Corp., P.O. Box 399, Beijing, P.R.C.) Ed. Li Wenshan. adv. circ. 2,000. **Indexed:** Seed Abstr. **Document type:** academic/scholarly publication.
—CASDDS.
  Formerly (until 1994): Fujian Nongxueyuan Xuebao - Fujian Agricultural College. Journal (ISSN 0427-7082)
  Description: Covers crop production, fruit trees, tea, vegetables, flowers, bees, animal husbandry and veterinary science, food engineering, plant protection, soil and plant nutrient, as well as agricultural economics.

630 CC ISSN 0253-2301
S471.C62 CODEN: FNKED9
FUJIAN NONGYE KEJI/FUJIAN AGRICULTURAL SCIENCE AND TECHNOLOGY. (Text in Chinese) 1970. bi-m. Y18($48) Fujian Nongye Kexueyuan - Fujian Academy of Agricultural Science, 41 Hualin Lu, Fuzhou, Fujian 350003, People's Republic of China. TEL 841771. (Dist. overseas by: Jiangsu Publications Import & Export Corp., 56 Gao Yun Ling, Nanjing, Jiangsu, P.R.C.) Ed. Yang Hui. adv. **Indexed:** Hort.Abstr., Rice Abstr., Seed Abstr. **Document type:** academic/scholarly publication.
—CASDDS.

630 CC ISSN 1000-7121
FUJIAN SHENG NONGKEYUAN XUEBAO/FUJIAN ACADEMY OF AGRICULTURAL SCIENCE. JOURNAL. (Text in Chinese) 1986. q. newsstand price: Y1.20. Fujian Sheng Nongkeyuan, Qingbao Suo - Fujian Academy of Agricultural Science, Information Institute, 247 Wusi Rd., Fuzhou, Fujian 350003, People's Republic of China. TEL 86-591-784-1771. Ed. Wang Jinghui. **Document type:** academic/scholarly publication.

630 JA
FUKUI UNIVERSITY. FACULTY OF EDUCATION. MEMOIRS. SERIES 3: APPLIED SCIENCE AND AGRICULTURAL SCIENCE. (Text in Japanese; summaries in English, Japanese) a. free. Fukui University, Faculty of Education, 9-1, 3-chome, Bunkyo, Fukui 910, Japan. Ed. Terutsugu Ando. **Document type:** academic/scholarly publication.

630 VE ISSN 0029-4160
FUNDACION SERVICIO PARA EL AGRICULTOR. NOTICIAS AGRICOLAS. 1955. bi-m. $15. Fundacion Servicio para el Agricultor, Estacion Experimental de Cagua, Carretera via La Segundera Km. 3, Cagua (Estado Aragua), Venezuela. TEL (044) 79184.79234. FAX 584475607. Ed. Hector Ayala. adv.; charts; illus.; index. cum.index every 3 yrs. circ. 10,000.

630 US ISSN 0016-3112
FURROW; a journal of popular farm science and rural life. (Editions in Afrikaans, Danish, Dutch, English, French, German, Italian, Portuguese, Norwegian, Spanish and Swedish) 1895. 8/yr. free to qualified personnel. Deere & Company, John Deere Rd., Moline, IL 61265. TEL 309-765-8000. Ed. G.R. Sollenberger. illus. circ. 1,550,700. (also avail. in microform from UMI; reprint service avail. from UMI) **Indexed:** Agri.Eng.Abstr., Farm & Garden Ind., Ind.Free Per.
—Linda Hall; UMI.

630 US
FURROW (AUSTRALIAN - NEW ZEALAND EDITION). 1978. 3/yr. free. Deere & Company, John Deere Rd., Moline, IL 61265. TEL 309-765-8000. Ed. G.R. Sollenberger. circ. 40,000.

AGRICULTURE

630   US
FURROW (UNITED KINGDOM EDITION); journal of popular farm science and rural life. 1973. 4/yr. free to qualified personnel. Deere & Company, John Deere Rd., Moline, IL 61265. TEL 309-765-8000. Ed. Jean-Claude Hiron. circ. 52,000.

635   US
FUTURE FARMERS OF AMERICA. NEWSLETTER.* 6/yr. membership only. National F F A Organization, Box 15160, Alexandria, VA 22309-0160. TEL 703-360-3600. **Document type:** newsletter.
   Description: To prepare students for careers in agriculture.

630   US   ISSN 0748-1578
                             CODEN: FTRSER
FUTURES (EAST LANSING). 1967. q. single copy free. Michigan State University, Agricultural Experiment Station, 310 Agriculture Hall, East Lansing, MI 48824-1039. TEL 517-432-1555. FAX 517-355-1804. Ed. Jamie DePolo. circ. 5,000 (controlled). (reprint service avail. from ISI,UMI) **Indexed:** A.B.C.Pol.Sci., ABI Inform., Br.Rail.Bd., C.R.E.J., CLOSS, Cont.Pg.Manage., Educ.Admin.Abstr., Farm & Garden Ind., Field Crop Abstr., Herb.Abstr., Manage.Cont., Mich.Mag.Ind., Nutr.Abstr., Plant Breed.Abstr., SCIMP, Tr.& Indus.Ind., VITIS.
  —BLDSC (4060.645000); Linda Hall.
   Formerly: Michigan Science in Action (ISSN 0076-809X)

630   MX   ISSN 0187-4381
GACETA AGRICOLA. 1956. every 10 days. Mex.$2000($30) Av. La Paz 1522, Apdo. Postal 5-225, 45000 Guadalajara, Jalisco, Mexico. Ed. Francisco Sainz Ibarra. adv.; bk.rev. circ. 30,000.

630   SP   ISSN 0016-3864
GACETA RURAL; semanario de informacion agropecuaria. 1945. w. 8000 ptas. (effective 1997). Gestora Editorial Rural, S.L., Avda. de Ramon y Cajal 5, 28016 Madrid, Spain. TEL 34-1-3440462. FAX 34-1-3440463. Ed. Ana de Rojas. adv.; bk.rev.; bibl.; stat. circ. 2,500. **Document type:** newspaper.
   Description: Presents general information on agriculture in Spain.
   Refereed Serial

630 575.1   JA   ISSN 0435-1096
                             CODEN: GFSYAR
GAMMA FIELD SYMPOSIA. (Text in English; summaries in Japanese) 1962. a. exchange basis. Institute of Radiation Breeding (NIAR, MAFF), P.O. Box 3, Ohmiya-machi, Naka-gun, Ibaraki-ken 319-22, Japan. TEL 02955-2-1138. FAX 02955-3-1075. Ed.Bd. **Indexed:** Chem.Abstr., INIS Atomind.
  —BLDSC (4069.200000); CASDDS; Linda Hall.

630 636   VE   ISSN 0046-5399
GANAGRINCO; ganaderia - agricultura - industria - comercio. (Text in Spanish; summaries in English, Spanish) q. $6. Ed. Rafael Salom, Apdo. de Correos 3318, Caracas 101, Venezuela. adv.; illus.; charts. circ. 2,000.

630   PO   ISSN 0378-8032
S18   CODEN: GOSADL
GARCIA DE ORTA: SERIE DE ESTUDOS AGRONOMICOS. 1973. 2/yr. price varies. Instituto de Investigacao Cientifica Tropical, Rua da Junqueira 30, 1300 Lisbon, Portugal. TEL 351-1-3622621. FAX 351-1-3631460. E-mail: cdi@iict.pt; URL: http://www.iict.pt. (Subscr. to: Centro de Documentacao e Informacao, Rua Jua 47, 1300 Lisbon, Portugal) circ. 1,000. **Indexed:** Food Sci.& Tech.Abstr. **Document type:** academic/scholarly publication.
  —BLDSC (4069.982000); CASDDS.

GARDEN TO KITCHEN NEWSLETTER. see *NUTRITION AND DIETETICS*

630   MZ
GAZETA DO AGRICULTOR. (Text in Portuguese) m. Centro de Documentacao e Informacao do Sector Agrario, P.O. Box 1406, Maputo, Mozambique. FAX 258-1-460137. E-mail: cda@sdisa.vem.mz. Ed. Felix Alexandre Senete. **Indexed:** Field Crop Abstr., Herb.Abstr. **Document type:** bulletin, catalog.

630   IT
GAZZETTA AGRICOLA. 1945. 28/yr. Via Guidelli 10, 42100 Reggio Emilia, Italy. TEL 39-241. FAX 53-105. Ed. Marco Benati. circ. 8,000.

630   IT
GAZZETTINO AGRICOLO (PARMA). 1947. w. L.25000. Unione Provinciale Agricoltori di Parma, Piazzale A. Barezzi 3, 43100 Parma, Italy. TEL 22-546. Ed. Massimo Dall'Olio. adv.; circ. 6,500 (controlled).

630   US   ISSN 0735-696X
S451.G4
GEORGIA FARM BUREAU NEWS; the voice of Georgia farmers. 1938. m. (8/yr.). $9 to non-members. Georgia Farm Bureau Federation, Box 7068, Macon, GA 31298. TEL 912-474-8411. FAX 912-474-8750. E-mail: gfbmacon@aol.com. Ed. Jennifer Whittaker; Pub. Paul Beliveau. R&P contact: Jennifer Whittaker. adv. contact: Sara Hudson. circ. 65,000. **Document type:** trade publication.
   Description: Information on the financial, legislative, and policy issues affecting Georgia agriculture.

630   US   ISSN 0016-8254
GEORGIA FARMER. 1956. m. $12 (foreign $25). Rural Press U S A, 7701 Six Forks Rd., Ste. 132, Raleigh, NC 27615. TEL 919-676-3276; 800-477-1737. FAX 919-676-9803. (Subscr. to: Box 150001, Raleigh, NC 27624) Ed. Pam Golden; Pub. Jeff Tennant. adv.: B&W page $1346. circ. 18,000. **Document type:** newspaper.

630   US   ISSN 0016-8262
GEORGIA FUTURE FARMER. 1942. 2/yr. Future Farmers of America, Georgia Association, 1766 Twin Towers East, Atlanta, GA 30334. Ed. Curtis Corbin. circ. 18,000.

338 630   GW   ISSN 0722-8333
HE5614.5.G3
GERMANY. BUNDESMINISTERIUM FUER ERNAEHRUNG, LANDWIRTSCHAFT UND FORSTEN. AGRARBERICHT DER BUNDESREGIERUNG. 1956. a. Bundesministerium fuer Ernaehrung, Landwirtschaft und Forsten, 53107 Bonn, Germany. TEL 49-228-5293698. **Document type:** government publication.

630   GW   ISSN 0939-6586
GESTALTEN UND VERKAUFEN. m. DM.104.40 (foreign DM.125.40) (effective 1998). Bernhard Thalacker Verlag GmbH, Postfach 8364, 38133 Braunschweig, Germany. TEL 49-531-38004-0. FAX 49-531-3800425. Ed. Matthias Donners. adv.: B&W page DM.3481.60, color page DM.5551.60; trim 272 x 186; adv. contact: Bruno Steder. illus. circ. 12,278. **Document type:** trade publication.
   Formerly: Neue Blumenbindekunst.

630   CN
GESTION ET TECHNOLOGIE AGRICOLES. 1975. 9/yr. Can.$18.70. Courrier de Saint-Hyacinthe, 655 Sainte-Anne, St. Hyacinthe, PQ J2S 5G4, Canada. TEL 514-773-6028. Ed. Denis Lacasse. R&P contact: Paul Paradis. adv. contact: Paul Paradis. circ. 20,000 (paid). **Document type:** consumer publication, newspaper.

GHANA. METEOROLOGICAL DEPARTMENT. AGROMETEOROLOGICAL BULLETIN. see *METEOROLOGY*

638.1   GH
GHANA BEE NEWS. (Text in English) 1981. q. $9. Technology Consultancy Centre, University of Science and Technology, Kumasi, Ghana. Ed. Celia Till. adv.; bk.rev.; illus. circ. 1,200. (back issues avail.)

630   GH   ISSN 0046-5917
GHANA FARMER; Ministry of Agriculture review on agricultural development. 1932-1974; resumed 1978. 3/yr. Ministry of Agriculture, Information Support Unit, P.O. Box 299, Accra, Ghana. Ed. J. Agbebkewu. adv.; bk.rev. circ. 3,000. **Indexed:** Field Crop Abstr., Herb.Abstr., Hort.Abstr., Plant Breed.Abstr. **Document type:** trade publication, government publication.

630   GH   ISSN 0855-0042
S379.G4   CODEN: GJASAF
GHANA JOURNAL OF AGRICULTURAL SCIENCE. (Text in English; summaries in English, French) 1968. 3/yr. $20. (Council for Scientific and Industrial Research) National Science and Technology Press, P.O. Box M.32, Accra, Ghana. Ed. D.K. Acquaye. R&P contact: F.J.K. Adotevi. bk.rev.; index. circ. 500. **Indexed:** Anim.Breed.Abstr., Biol.Abstr., Chem.Abstr., Curr.Adv.Ecol.Sci., Dairy Sci.Abstr., Field Crop Abstr., Helminthol.Abstr., Herb.Abstr., Hort.Abstr., Ind.Vet., INIS Atomind., Nutr.Abstr., Plant Breed.Abstr., Rev.Appl.Entomol., Rev.Plant Path., Rural Recreat.Tour.Abstr., Soils & Fert., Vet.Bull., Weed Abstr., World Agri.Econ. & Rural Sociol.Abstr. **Document type:** academic/scholarly publication, government publication.
   Description: Publishes papers on agricultural science and related disciplines. Focuses on original research and new investigations into changes in subsistence agriculture.
   Refereed Serial

630   JA   ISSN 0072-4513
                             CODEN: GNKEAH
GIFU DAIGAKU NOGAKUBU KENKYU HOKOKU/GIFU UNIVERSITY. FACULTY OF AGRICULTURE. RESEARCH BULLETIN. (Text and summaries in English or Japanese) 1951. irreg., no. 28, 1969. free. Gifu Daigaku, Nogakubu - Gifu University, Faculty of Agriculture, 1-1 Yanagito, Gifu 501-11, Japan. Ed. Hironori Sakurai. circ. 750. **Indexed:** Bio-Contr.News & Info., Biol.Abstr., Chem.Abstr., Crop Physiol.Abstr., Dairy Sci.Abstr., Field Crop Abstr., Food Sci.& Tech.Abstr., Forest.Abstr., Forest Prod.Abstr., Herb.Abstr., Hort.Abstr., Ind.Vet., Nutr.Abstr., Plant Breed.Abstr., Plant Grow.Reg.Abstr., Rev.Plant Path., Rural Recreat.Tour.Abstr., Sorghum & Millets Abstr., Vet.Bull. **Document type:** bulletin.
  —BLDSC (7722.000000); CASDDS.

GINSHENG REVIEW. see *PHARMACY AND PHARMACOLOGY*

630   IT   ISSN 0304-064X
                             CODEN: GIAGA
GIORNALE DI AGRICOLTURA. 1890. w. L.76000. REDA - Edizioni per l'Agricoltura S.r.l., Via Tor Sapienza 172, 00155 Rome, Italy. TEL 39-6-2280077. Ed. B.C. Fischetti. adv.: B&W page L.2730000, color page L.4400000. circ. 61,476.

630   IT
GIOVENTU DEI CAMPI. 1977. fortn. REDA - Edizioni per l'Agricoltura S.r.l., Via Nazionale, 89-A, 00184 Rome, Italy. TEL 06-463651. Dir. Valentino Crea. adv.; bk.rev.

630   AT   ISSN 0158-3840
GIPPSLAND FARMER. 1981. m. Aus.$30. Southern Newspapers Pty., Ltd., 74-76 Mac Alister St., Sale, Vic. 3850, Australia. FAX 051-441356. Ed. David Tulloch. adv. circ. 13,000. (back issues avail.)
   Description: Concentrates on issues affecting the Gippsland farmer.

630 340   IT   ISSN 0434-040X
GIURISPRUDENZA AGRARIA ITALIANA. 1954. m. L.170000. REDA - Edizioni per l'Agricoltura S.r.l., Via Nazionale, 89-A, 00184 Rome, Italy. TEL 06-463651-2-3-4. FAX 4747206.

630   YU   ISSN 0017-0976
GLASNIK POLJOPRIVREDNE PROIZVODNJE, PRERADE I PLASMANA. (Text in Serbo-Croatian) 1952. m. 550 din. Privredni Pregled, Marsala Birjuzova 3-5, 11000 Belgrade, Yugoslavia. Ed. Slobodan Sindovic.

630   US
GLOBE ADVERTISER. 1977. w. free. Globe Gazette, 300 N. Washington Ave., Mason City, IA 50401. TEL 515-421-0546. FAX 515-421-0516. Ed. Kevi Baskins; Pub. Howard Query. adv. contact: Byron Wooten. circ. 16,303. **Document type:** newspaper.
   Former titles (until 1994): Heartland Journal (Mason City); Rural Life.

630   UK   ISSN 0954-9714
GLOUCESTERSHIRE AND NORTH AVON FARMER. 1962 m. County Farmers Publications Ltd., 55 Goldingto Rd., Bedford MK40 3LU, England. TEL 0234-351401. FAX 0234-328614. Ed. T. Bawley. adv. circ. 2,600.
   Formerly: Gloucestershire Farmer (ISSN 0017-131X)

AGRICULTURE

630.075 US
GOOD EARTH ASSOCIATION. NEWSLETTER. 1984. biennial. $5 membership (effective 1997). Good Earth Association, 202 E. Church St., Pocohontas, AR 72455-2899. TEL 870-892-9545. FAX 870-892-8681. Ed. Gladys Nelson. adv. contact: Donald Waterworth. bk.rev. circ. 500. (tabloid format) **Document type:** newsletter.
Description: News of the organization, which operates a living farm museum displaying historical farm equipment, farming data, recipes, ecology information, etc.

630 II
GRAMEEN DUNIYA. (Text in Hindi) 1973. w. Rs.200; newsstand price: Rs.3. M.M.G. Publications, 199 C.M.-I., Jhandewalan Extn., New Delhi 55, India. TEL 7779843. Ed. Sanjay Gupta; Pub. M.M. Gupta. adv. contact: Ajay Gupta. (tabloid format) **Document type:** newspaper.

630 II
GRAMLOK. (Text in Hindi) 1975. fortn. Rs.100; newsstand price: Rs.5. Gramlok Prakashan, 5-32, Patel Gali, Vishwasnagar, Shahdara, New Delhi 110032, India. TEL 2208405. Ed. Krishan Kumar; Pub. Raghunath Basak. adv. B&W page Rs.13000, color page Rs.26000; 325 x 200; adv. contact: K.R. Nair. circ. 49,415. cols./p.: 4.

630 US ISSN 0279-9391
GRANGE ADVOCATE. Key Title: Grange Advocate Aggressive for Rural Pennsylvania. 1904. every 3 wks. membership. Pennsylvania State Grange, 1604 N. Second St., Harrisburg, PA 17102. TEL 717-234-5001. Ed. James C. Mentzer. adv. circ. 24,000. **Document type:** newsletter.
Former titles: Grange Advocate for Rural Pennsylvania (ISSN 0164-4955); Pennsylvania Grange News.

630 UK ISSN 0142-5242
CODEN: GFSCDW
GRASS AND FORAGE SCIENCE. 1946. q. £196($358.50) (foreign £216) (effective 1998). (British Grassland Society) Blackwell Science Ltd., Osney Mead, Oxford OX2 0EL, England. TEL 44-1865-206206. FAX 44-1865-721205. E-mail: journals.cs@blacksci.co.uk; URL: http://www.black.co.uk. Ed. R.O. Jewiss; Pub. Allen Stevens. R&P contact: Sarah Pollard. adv. contact: Martine Cariou-Keen. bk.rev.; abstr.; charts; illus.; index. circ. 1,450. (also avail. in microform from UMI) **Indexed:** Agri.Eng.Abstr., ASCA, Biol.Abstr., Biol.& Agr.Ind., Chem.Abstr., Crop Physiol.Abstr., Curr.Adv.Ecol.Sci., Curr.Cont., Dairy Sci.Abstr., Ecol.Abstr., Field Crop Abstr., Geo.Abstr., Herb.Abstr., Ind.Sci.Rev., Ind.Vet., Int.Abstr.Oper.Res., Irr.& Drain.Abstr., Maize Abstr., Nutr.Abstr., Sci.Cit.Ind., Soils & Fert., Soyabean Abstr., Sugar Ind.Abstr., Triticale Abstr., Vet.Bull., Weed Abstr., World Agri.Econ.& Rural Sociol.Abstr. **Document type:** academic/scholarly publication.
—BLDSC (4213.320000); CASDDS; EMDOCS; Genuine Article; Linda Hall; SWETS; UMI; UnCover. CCC.
Formerly (until vol.34, 1979): British Grassland Society. Journal (ISSN 0007-0750)
Description: Disseminates the results of research and development in all aspects of grass and forage utilization and reviews the state of knowledge on relevant topics.
Refereed Serial

630 UK ISSN 0262-2394
GREAT BRITAIN. MINISTRY OF AGRICULTURE, FISHERIES AND FOOD. AGRICULTURAL STATISTICS, ENGLAND. 1972. a. price varies. H.M.S.O., 51 Nine Elms Ln., London SW8 5DR, England. TEL 44-171-873-0011. FAX 44-171-873-8247. (Co-sponsors: Ministry of Agriculture, Fisheries and Food, Department of Agriculture for Scotland; Ministry of Agriculture, N. Ireland) (also avail. in microfiche from CHL; reprint service avail. from UMI) **Document type:** government publication.
—CCC.
Supersedes in part: Agricultural Statistics, England and Wales (ISSN 0065-4558)

630 333.1 UK
GREAT BRITAIN. NATURAL RESOURCES INSTITUTE. BULLETIN. 1987. irreg. varies. Natural Resources Institute, Central Ave., Chatham Maritime, Kent ME4 4TB, England. TEL 44-1634-880088. FAX 44-1634-880066. TELEX 263907-LDN-G. E-mail: publications@nri.org; URL: http://www.nri.org. **Document type:** monographic series.
●Also available online.
Also available on CD-ROM.
—BLDSC (2674.720000).
Formerly: Great Britain. Overseas Development Natural Resources Institute. Bulletin (ISSN 0952-8245)
Description: Presents the results of research covering topics relevant to development issues in agriculture, especially sustainable resource management.

630 EI ISSN 0250-5886
HD1920.5.Z8
GREEN EUROPE; newsletter on the common agricultural policy. (Editions in Danish, French, German, Greek, Italian, Portuguese, Spanish) 1979. m. free. Commission of the European Communities, 200 rue de la Loi, B-1049 Brussels, Belgium. (Dist. by: Office for Official Publications of the European Communities, 2 rue Mercier, L-2985 Luxembourg, Luxembourg) adv. contact: Rebecca Zahn. (also avail. in microfiche from CIS) **Indexed:** Dairy Sci.Abstr., Geo.Abstr., IIS, Potato Abstr., Rural Recreat.Tour.Abstr., World Agri.Econ.& Rural Sociol.Abstr. **Document type:** newsletter.
Formerly: Newsletter on the Common Agricultural Policy.

630 US ISSN 0149-5569
GREEN MARKETS. 1977. w. $890 (foreign $1095) (effective 1997). Pike & Fischer, Inc., 4600 East-West Hwy., Ste. 200, Bethesda, MD 20814. TEL 301-654-6262. FAX 301-654-6297. Ed. Margaret Miller. (also avail. in diskette format) **Document type:** newsletter.
●Also available online.

630 US ISSN 0895-772X
GREEN MARKETS DEALER REPORT. w. $267 (effective 1995). Pike & Fischer, Inc., 4600 East West Hwy., Ste. 200, Bethesda, MD 20814. TEL 301-654-6262. FAX 301-654-6297. Ed. Margaret Miller. **Document type:** newsletter.

630 UK ISSN 0017-4092
GREENSWARD. 1962. a. £2($6) to non-members. South West Scotland Grassland Society, Auchincruive, Ayr, Scotland. Ed. David Reid. adv.; bk.rev.; abstr.; charts. circ. 800. **Indexed:** Dairy Sci.Abstr., Field Crop Abstr., Herb.Abstr.

630 BE
GROENE KRANT. 1973. m. 1000 BEF. K.L.J. Kring - Groene (B.J.B.), Waversebaan 99, Postbus 107, B-3050 Oud-Heverlee, Belgium. TEL 32-16-479999. Ed. Bart Teuwen. adv.; bk.rev. circ. 3,500. **Document type:** newspaper.

GROENTEN & FRUIT. see GARDENING AND HORTICULTURE

GROENTEN & FRUIT - VAKDEEL GLASGROENTEN. see GARDENING AND HORTICULTURE

GROENTEN & FRUIT - VAKDEEL HARD EN ZACHT FRUIT. see GARDENING AND HORTICULTURE

GROENTEN & FRUIT - VAKDEEL PADDESTOELEN. see GARDENING AND HORTICULTURE

GROENTEN & FRUIT - VAKDEEL VOLLEGRONDSGROENTEN. see GARDENING AND HORTICULTURE

631.091 CK ISSN 0122-8048
SB111.A2
GROWING AFFINITIES. (Text in English) 1982. 2/yr. free. Centro Internacional de Agricultura Tropical, Unidad de Comunicaciones - International Center for Tropical Agriculture, Communications Unit, Apdo. Aereo 6713, Cali, Colombia. TEL 57-2-4450000. FAX 57-2-4450073. TELEX 05769 CIAT. Ed. Alexandra Walter. circ. 3,000. **Indexed:** Nutr Abstr. **Document type:** bulletin.
Formerly (until 1996): C I A T International (ISSN 0120-4084)
Description: Highlights CIAT's current research activities and CIAT's relationship with other related organizations.

GROWING EDGE MAGAZINE; indoor & outdoor gardening for today's grower. see GARDENING AND HORTICULTURE

630 664 GT
GUATEMALA. MINISTERIO DE AGRICULTURA, GANADERIA Y ALIMENTACION. DIRECCION GENERAL DE SERVICIOS AGRICOLAS. MEMORIA DE LABORES. a. Ministerio de Agricultura, Ganaderia y Alimentacion, Direccion General de Servicios Agricolas, Palacio Nacional, Guatemala, Guatemala.
Description: Provides information on projects of the ministry.

GUIA DE AVIACAO AGRICOLA/AGRICULTURAL AVIATION GUIDE. see AERONAUTICS AND SPACE FLIGHT

630 CN
GUIDE DE L'AGRICULTURE DU QUEBEC. 1992. a. Can.$25. Publedition Inc., 620 Industriel Blvd., Ste.-Jean-sur-Richelieu, PQ J3B 7X4, Canada. TEL 514-856-7821. FAX 514-359-0836. Ed. Martine Breton. adv.: B&W page Can.$1030, color page Can.$1330; trim 8 1/4 x 10 7/8. circ. 5,000.

630 MW ISSN 0542-3007
S338.M28
GUIDE TO AGRICULTURAL PRODUCTION IN MALAWI. (Text in English) 1968. a. Ministry of Agriculture, Extension Aids Branch, P.O. Box 594, Lilongwe, Malawi. TEL 265-720933. (Orders to: Government Printer, P.O. Box 37, Zomba, Malawi. TEL 265-50-523155) circ. 5,000. **Document type:** government publication.

630 070 UK ISSN 0072-8969
GUILD OF AGRICULTURAL JOURNALISTS YEAR BOOK.* 1958. a. £5. Lancer Public Relations, 26 Kingsfield Ave., Ipswich, Suffolk IP1 3TA, England.

630 II ISSN 0250-5193
CODEN: GAUJDS
GUJARAT AGRICULTURAL UNIVERSITY RESEARCH JOURNAL. (Text in English) 1975. s-a. Rs.20 (foreign $8). Gujarat Agricultural University, Shahibag, Ahmedabad 380 004, India. TEL 866431. Ed. K. Janakiraman. adv. circ. 700. **Indexed:** Bio-Contr.News & Info., Biol.Abstr., Can.Per.Ind., Chem.Abstr., Cott.& Trop.Fibr.Abstr., Dairy Sci.Abstr., Field Crop Abstr., Food Sci.& Tech.Abstr., Herb.Abstr., Hort.Abstr., Irr.& Drain.Abstr., Maize Abstr., Nutr.Abstr., Plant Grow.Reg.Abstr., Rev.Appl.Entomol., Rice Abstr., Seed Abstr., Soils & Fert., Triticale Abstr., Trop.Oil Seeds Abstr., Vet.Bull., Weed Abstr. **Document type:** academic/scholarly publication.
—BLDSC (4230.240000); CASDDS.
Description: Disseminates research findings in agriculture and allied fields.

GUNMAKEN NOGYO KISHO SAIGAI SOKUHO/GUNMA PREFECTURE. NEWS OF AGRICULTURAL METEOROLOGY DISASTER. see METEOROLOGY

630 551.5 CC ISSN 1000-6427
GUOWAI NONGXUE - NONGYE QIXIANG/FOREIGN AGRICULTURE - AGRICULTURAL METEOROLOGY. (Text in Chinese) q. Zhongguo Nongye Kexueyuan - Chinese Academy of Agricultural Science, 30 Baishiqiao Lu, Beijing 100081, People's Republic of China. TEL 8314433. Ed. Zhu Lukuan.

630 UK
H S E AGRICULTURE INFORMATION SHEET. (Subseries of: H S E Information Sheet) N.S. 1996. irreg., no.1, 1996. Health & Safety Executive, Information Centre, Broad Lane, Sheffield S3 7HQ, England. TEL 44-114-2892345. FAX 44-114-2892333.
Formerly (until 1995): H S E Agriculture Sheet.
Description: Contains notes on good practices which are not compulsory but which may be helpful.

630 UK ISSN 0017-7121
HAMPSHIRE FARMER. m. County Farmers Publications Ltd., 55 Goldington Rd., Bedford MK40 3LU, England. TEL 0234-351401. FAX 0234-328614. Ed. N. Errington. adv. circ. 2,300.

AGRICULTURE

630   IC   ISSN 0251-1940
HANDBOK BAENDA. 1951. a. ISK 1400($25) Agricultural Society of Iceland, Post Box 7080, 127 Reykjavik, Iceland. TEL 354-563-0300. FAX 354-562-3058. Eds. Matthias Eggertsson, Ottar Geirsson. circ. 2,700. (back issues avail.; reprint service avail.)
Description: Contains advice and other material of interest to the farming industry in Iceland.

630 634.9   GW   ISSN 0017-7466
HANNOVERSCHE LAND- UND FORSTWIRTSCHAFTLICHE ZEITUNG. 1847. w. DM.79.80. (Landwirtschaftskammer Hannover) Landvolk-Verlag, Kabelkamp 6, 30179 Hannover, Germany. TEL 0511-67806-0. adv.; bk.rev.; illus.; mkt. circ. 48,000.
—CCC.
Description: Covers all aspects of agriculture and farming. Includes list of prices, reports of events, questions and answers and weather forecasts.

630 334.683   CN   ISSN 0381-6885
S522.C2   CODEN: HARSEI
HARROWSMITH. 1976. 6/yr. Can.$21.38 (in US Can.$25, elsewhere Can.$29). I N D A S Limited, 35 Riviera Dr., Unit 17, Markham, ON L3R 8N4, Canada. TEL 613-378-6661. Ed. Mike Webster. adv.; bk.rev.; bibl.; charts; illus.; stat.; tr.lit.; index. circ. 155,000. (also avail. in microfiche from UMI; reprint service avail. from UMI; back issues avail.)
Indexed: Can.B.P.I., Can.Per.Ind., CMI, Ind.How To Do It.
—UMI. **CCC.**

630 663   US
HARVEST (LAKEVILLE-MIDDLEBORO). 1980. bi-m. free to growers-owners. Ocean Spray, One Ocean Spray Dr., Lakeville-Middleboro, MA 02349. TEL 508-946-7246. FAX 508-947-9791. Ed. Judith Duffy. R&P contact: Judith Duffy. circ. 2,000.
Document type: newsletter.
Description: For growers in the Ocean Spray cooperative. Provides information on business, entomology, horticulture, environment and equipment.

630 658   CH   ISSN 0017-8195
S471.T28
HARVEST SEMI-MONTHLY. Key Title: Fengnian. English title varies slightly. (Text in Chinese) 1951. s-m. NT.$650 in ROC; Hong Kong and Macao $42; elsewhere $52. Harvest Farm Magazine, 14 Wenchow St., Taipei, Taiwan, Republic of China. TEL 02-362-8148. FAX 02-363-6724. Ed. Ming-Tang Kao. adv.; charts; illus.; stat.; cum.index. circ. 25,000. (tabloid format; back issues avail.)
Indexed: Bio-Contr.News & Info.
Description: For families involved in agriculture. Suggests agricultural techniques, examines production and marketing of specific crops. Coverage includes livestock, irrigation, automation, and news of the industry.

630   US   ISSN 1089-4640
HARVEST STATES AGRIVISIONS. 1927. bi-m. $4. Harvest States Cooperatives, 1667 N. Snelling Ave., Box 94594, St. Paul, MN 55164. FAX 612-641-3731. Ed. Alison Cummings. R&P contact: Alison Cummings. adv.; bk.rev.; charts; illus.; stat. circ. 13,000. (tabloid format)
Former titles (until Nov. 1992): Harvest States Journal; Co-Op Country News; Farmers Union Herald (ISSN 0014-8458)

630   II   ISSN 0017-8225
HARVESTER; agricultural engineering journal. 1968. q. Rs.40. (Indian Institute of Technology, Agricultural Engineering Society) Indian Society of Engineers, 5 Lindsay St., Calcutta 700 016, India. Ed. M.K. Diwan. adv.; bk.rev.; bibl.; charts; stat. circ. 3,100.
Description: Published with the interest of informing and edifying the prairie family.

630 300 636.089   II   ISSN 0379-4008
HARYANA AGRICULTURAL UNIVERSITY. JOURNAL OF RESEARCH. (Text in English) 1971. q. Rs.200($60) Haryana Agricultural University, Hisar 125 004, Haryana, India. Ed.Bd. adv.; abstr.; bibl.; charts. circ. 500. *Indexed:* Biol.Abstr., Chem.Abstr., Cott.& Trop.Fibr.Abstr., Field Crop Abstr., Food Sci.& Tech.Abstr., Helminthol.Abstr., Hort.Abstr., Ind.Vet., Maize Abstr., Nutr.Abstr., Pig News & Info., Plant Grow.Reg.Abstr., Potato Abstr., Rev.Appl.Entomol., Seed Abstr., Sorghum & Millets Abstr., Triticale Abstr., Vet.Bull., Weed Abstr. *Document type:* academic/scholarly publication.
Description: Contains original research articles and notes on agriculture, animal and veterinary sciences, basic sciences, social sciences and home science.

630   IS   ISSN 0017-8314
S19
HASSADEH/FIELD; a monthly review of settlement and agriculture. (Text in English, Hebrew) 1920. m. $150. G.K. Hassadeh Monthly Review Ltd., 8 Shaul Hamelech St., P.O. Box 40044, 61400 Tel Aviv, Israel. TEL 972-3-6929978. FAX 972-3-6929979. Ed. J. M. Margalit. adv. contact: Guy Klug. bk.rev.; abstr.; bibl.; charts; illus.; stat.; index; circ. 8,000 (controlled). *Indexed:* Anim.Breed.Abstr., Biol.Abstr., Chem.Abstr., Cott.& Trop.Fibr.Abstr., Crop Physiol.Abstr., Field Crop Abstr., Herb.Abstr., Hort.Abstr., Ind.Vet., Maize Abstr., Ornam.Hort., Plant Grow.Reg.Abstr., Poult.Abstr., Soyabean Abstr., Weed Abstr. *Document type:* academic/scholarly publication.
—BLDSC (4272.000000).

630   FR
HAUTE LOIRE PAYSANNE. w. Hotel Interconsulaire, Bd. Bertrand, B.P. 63, 43002 Le Puy Cedex, France. TEL 71-02-60-44. Ed. G. Assezat. circ. 5,000.

630   FR
HAUTE SAONE AGRICOLE BELFORT AGRICULTURE. w. B.P. 251, 22 place du Champ de Foire, 70005 Vesoul, France. TEL 84-76-07-36. FAX 84-76-76-36. Ed. Laurent Le Gall. circ. 6,600.

HEALTHY HARVEST. see *PUBLIC HEALTH AND SAFETY*

630   CC   ISSN 1000-1573
   CODEN: HNSBEM
HEBEI NONGYE DAXUE XUEBAO/HEBEI UNIVERSITY OF AGRICULTURE. JOURNAL. (Text in Chinese; abstracts in English) 1959. q. Y16($40) (effective 1997 & 1998). Hebei Nongye Daxue - Hebei University of Agriculture, Nanguan, Baoding, Hebei 071001, People's Republic of China. TEL 86-312-2091322. FAX 86-312-2025635. (Dist. overseas by: China International Book Trading Corp., P.O. Box 399, Beijing 100044, P.R. China) Ed. Yiyuan He. circ. 2,500. *Document type:* academic/scholarly publication.
—CASDDS.
Description: Covers crop cultivation, fruit, vegetables, and plant protection, pesticide, husbandry and veterinary, food processing and sanitation.

630   NE   ISSN 0169-7978
HEIDEMTIJDSCHRIFT. 1889. 5/yr. fl.50. Vereniging Koninklijke Nederlandse HeideMaatschappij, Postbus 33 6, 6800 LE Arnhem, Netherlands. TEL 31-26-4455146. FAX 31-26-4437827. Ed. P.R. Bas. adv.; bk.rev.; charts; illus.; index. circ. 10,000. *Indexed:* Biol.Abstr.
—BLDSC (4284.135000); SWETS.
Formerly (until 1985): Vereniging Koninklijke Nederlandsche Heide Maatschappij. Tijdschrift (ISSN 0165-0017)

630 531.64   CC   ISSN 1000-8551
S589.5   CODEN: HEXUEE
HENONG XUEBAO/ACTA AGRICULTURAE NUCLEATAE SINICA. (Text in Chinese, English; abstracts in English) 1987. q. Y10. Zhongguo Nongye Kexueyuan, Yuanzineng Liyong Yanjiusuo - Chinese Academy of Agricultural Sciences, Institute of Nuclear Energy Utilization, P.O. Box 5109, Beijing 100094, People's Republic of China. TEL 2581177. Ed. Xu Guanren. *Document type:* academic/scholarly publication.
—CASDDS; Linda Hall.
Description: Publishes researches on the use of nuclear technology in various branches of agriculture, biology and animal sciences.

630   UK   ISSN 0018-0688
HEREFORDSHIRE FARMER. 1948. m. County Farmers Publications Ltd., 55 Goldington Rd., Bedford MK40 3LU, England. TEL 0234-351401. FAX 0234-328614. Ed. P. Hudson. adv. circ. 1,900.

630   UK
HERTFORDSHIRE FARMER. 1948. m. Eastern Counties N.F.U. Journals Ltd., 55 Goldington Rd., Bedford MK40 3LU, England. Ed. D. Green. adv. circ. 2,100. (back issues avail.)

630   GW   ISSN 0723-3639
HESSENBAUER - AUSGABE NORD. 1792. w. DM.115.20 (foreign DM.186.60). Landwirtschaftsverlag Hessen GmbH, Taunusstr. 151, 61381 Friedrichsdorf, Germany. TEL 49-6172-7106-0. FAX 49-6172-710610. Ed. Joerg Ruehlemann. adv.: B&W page DM.3960, color page DM.6985; trim 192 x 275; adv. contact: Christa Schweitzer. *Document type:* trade publication.

630   GW   ISSN 0723-3647
HESSENBAUER - AUSGABE SUED. 1792. w. DM.115.20 (foreign DM.186.60). Landwirtschaftsverlag Hessen GmbH, Taunusstr. 151, 61381 Friedrichsdorf, Germany. TEL 49-6172-7106-0. FAX 49-6172-710610. Ed. Joerg Ruehlemann. adv.: B&W page DM.3960, color page DM.6985; trim 192 x 275; adv. contact: Christa Schweitzer. circ. 46,644 (paid). *Document type:* trade publication.

630   US   ISSN 0018-1471
HIGH PLAINS JOURNAL. (In 5 regional eds.: Western Kansas; Eastern Kansas & Missouri; Nebraska, Iowa & South Dakota; Colorado & Wyoming; Oklahoma, Texas, New Mexico) 1883. w. $56. High Plains Publishers, Inc., 1500 E. Wyatt Earp Blvd., Box 760, Dodge City, KS 67801-0760. TEL 316-227-7171. FAX 316-227-7173. Ed. Galen Hubbs; Pub. Duane Ross. adv. contact: Tom Taylor. bk.rev.; illus.; mkt. circ. 58,000. (tabloid format) *Document type:* consumer publication, newspaper.
Description: Covers agricultural matters throughout the entire Plains region.

630 634.9   PH
HIGHLIGHTS. (Text in English) 1982. a. Philippine Council for Agriculture, Forestry and Natural Resources Research and Development, Department of Science and Technology, Los Banos, Laguna 4030, Philippines. FAX 63-094-50016.
Formerly (until 1989): Highlights from the Philippine Agriculture, Environment, and Natural Resources Research and Development Network (ISSN 0116-9440)
Description: Summary of the proceedings of the annual regional R&D symposium.

630   US   ISSN 0018-1668
   CODEN: HARAAS
HIGHLIGHTS OF AGRICULTURAL RESEARCH. 1954. q. free. Alabama Agricultural Experiment Station, 2 Comer Hall, Auburn University, AL 36849. TEL 334-844-4877. FAX 334-844-5892. Ed. J.R. Roberson. R&P contact: J.R. Roberson. charts; illus.; stat. circ. 10,500. *Indexed:* Chem.Abstr., Curr.Adv.Ecol.Sci., Environ.Abstr., Hort.Abstr., Ind.Vet., Ornam.Hort., Poult.Abstr., Weed.Abstr.
—BLDSC (4307.530000); CASDDS; CIS; UnCover. *Refereed Serial*

630   US   ISSN 0073-2230
S1   CODEN: HILGA4
HILGARDIA; a journal of agricultural science. 1925. irreg. exchange basis only. University of California, Division of Agriculture and Natural Resources, 300 Lakeside Dr., 6th Fl., Oakland, CA 94612-3560. Ed. Janet White. circ. 1,800. *Indexed:* Bio-Contr.News & Info., Biol.Abstr., Biol.& Agr.Ind., Chem.Abstr., Curr.Adv.Ecol.Sci., Curr.Cont., Ecol.Abstr., Forest.Abstr., Forest Prod.Abstr., Geo.Abstr., Helminthol.Abstr., Ind.Sci.Rev., Irr.& Drain.Abstr., Rev.Appl.Entomol., Sci.Cit.Ind., Sel.Water Res.Abstr., Soils & Fert., VITIS. *Document type:* academic/scholarly publication.
—BLDSC (4313.000000); KR SourceOne; Linda Hall; UMI.
Description: Studies in agricultural science.

630   II   ISSN 0018-1889
HIMACHAL AGRICULTURAL NEWSLETTER. (Text in English) 1969. q. Department of Agriculture, c/o G.S. Agarval, Agricultural Information Officer, Simla, Himachal Pradesh, India. Ed. Rattan S. Himesh. charts; illus. *Document type:* newsletter.

AGRICULTURE

630   II   ISSN 0970-0595
CODEN: HJARAN
HIMACHAL JOURNAL OF AGRICULTURAL RESEARCH.
(Text and summaries in English) 1971. s-a. Rs.50 to individuals; institutions Rs.100. H.P. Agriculture University, Himachal Pradesh Krishi Vishvavidyalaya, Palampur 176 062, Himachal Pradesh, India. TEL 91-189-30406. FAX 91-1894-30511. Ed. Hirday Paul Singh. adv.; bk.rev.; circ. 300 (paid). **Indexed:** Biol.Abstr., Field Crop Abstr., Herb.Abstr., Indian Sci.Abstr., Soils & Fert.
  Description: Publishes research on agricultural, veterinary, animal and home sciences.
Refereed Serial

630   JA   ISSN 0073-229X
CODEN: HIROAO
HIROSAKI UNIVERSITY. FACULTY OF AGRICULTURE. BULLETIN/HIROSAKI DAIGAKU NOGAKUBU GAKUJUTSU HOKOKU. (Text in English or Japanese; summaries in English) 1955. s-a. exchange basis. Hirosaki Daigaku, Nogakubu - Hirosaki University, Faculty of Agriculture, 3 Bunkyo-cho, Hirosaki, Aomori-ken 036, Japan. Ed. Eiji Bekki. circ. 470. **Indexed:** Biodet.Abstr., Biol.Abstr., Chem.Abstr., Dairy Sci.Abstr., Excerp.Med., Field Crop Abstr., Food Sci.& Tech.Abstr., Herb.Abstr., Hort.Abstr., INIS Atomind., Nutr.Abstr., Plant Breed.Abstr., Rev.Plant Path. **Document type:** bulletin.
—CASDDS.

630   II   ISSN 0378-7524
HISTORY OF AGRICULTURE. 1973. q. $67. (International Association for the History of Agriculture) K.K. Roy (Private) Ltd., 55 Gariahat Rd., P.O. Box 10210, Calcutta 700 019, India. Ed. Dr. K.K. Roy. adv.; bk.rev.; index. circ. 1,980. **Indexed:** Amer.Hist.& Life (1974-), Hist.Abstr. (1974-).
—BLDSC (4317.770000).

638.1   CN
HIVE LIGHTS. 1986. q. Can.$40. Canadian Honey Council, Box 1566, Nipawin, SK S0E 1E0, Canada. TEL 306-862-3844. FAX 306-862-5122. Ed. Ted Hancock; Pub. Fran Kay. R&P contact: Ted Hancock. adv. contact: Fran Kay. bk.rev. circ. 750. (back issues avail.) **Document type:** trade publication.

630   GW   ISSN 0340-9783
CODEN: HOARDR
HOHENHEIMER ARBEITEN. 1961. irreg. (not numbered after vol.132). (Universitaet Hohenheim) Verlag Eugen Ulmer GmbH, Wollgrasweg 41, 70599 Stuttgart, Germany. TEL 49-711-4507-0. FAX 49-711-4507-120. (Subscr. to: Postfach 700561, 70574 Stuttgart, Germany) bk.rev. **Indexed:** Anim.Breed.Abstr., Chem.Abstr., Soils & Fert. **Document type:** monographic series.
—CASDDS.

HOKKAIDO KYOIKU DAIGAKU KIYO. DAI-2-BU, B. SEIBUTSUGAKU, CHIGAKU, NOGAKU-HEN/HOKKAIDO UNIVERSITY OF EDUCATION. JOURNAL. SECTION 2 B. BIOLOGY, GEOLOGY, AND AGRICULTURE. see *BIOLOGY*

HOKKAIDO NO NOGYO KISHO/HOKKAIDO JOURNAL OF AGRICULTURAL METEOROLOGY. see *METEOROLOGY*

630   JA   ISSN 0018-3415
CODEN: HKNSBV
HOKKAIDO NOGYO SHIKENJO KENKYU HOKOKU/HOKKAIDO NATIONAL AGRICULTURAL EXPERIMENT STATION. RESEARCH BULLETIN. (Text in Japanese; summaries in English) 1905. 2/yr. exchange basis. Hokkaido National Agricultural Experiment Station - Hokkaido Nogyo Shikenjo, 1 Hitsujigaoka, Toyohira-ku, Sapporo-shi, Hokkaido 062, Japan. TEL 011-851-9141. FAX 011-859-2178. (Dist. in US by: New York Agricultural Experiment Station, Geneva, NY 14456) Ed. Shigeo Komuro. circ. 1,000. (also avail. in microform) **Indexed:** Anim.Breed.Abstr., Biol.Abstr., Chem.Abstr., Field Crop Abstr., Geo.Abstr., Helminthol.Abstr., Herb.Abstr., Hort.Abstr., INIS Atomind., Maize Abstr., Nutr.Abstr., Plant Breed.Abstr., Seed Abstr., Soyabean Abstr., Triticale Abstr. **Document type:** government publication, bulletin.

630   JA   ISSN 0018-344X
CODEN: JFAGAI
HOKKAIDO UNIVERSITY. FACULTY OF AGRICULTURE. JOURNAL. (Text in English) 1902. irreg. exchange basis. Hokkaido University, Faculty of Agriculture - Hokkaido Dagaiku Nogakubu, Nishi-9-chome, Kita 9-jo, Kita-ku, Sapporo 060, Japan. Ed. Hideo Okajima. charts; illus. (also avail. in microfilm) **Indexed:** Abstr.Bull.Inst.Pap.Chem., Biol.Abstr., Chem.Abstr., Crop Physiol.Abstr., Field Crop Abstr., Herb.Abstr., Maize Abstr., Ornam.Hort., Plant Breed.Abstr., Plant Grow.Reg.Abstr., Rev.Appl.Entomol., Rev.Plant Path., Rice Abstr., Seed Abstr., Soils & Fert., Sport Fish.Abstr., Wild.Rev., Zoo.Rec. **Document type:** academic/scholarly publication.
—BLDSC (4741.900000); CASDDS; Linda Hall; UnCover.

HONEY MARKET NEWS. see *AGRICULTURE — Agricultural Economics*

638.1   US
HONEY PRODUCER MAGAZINE. 1969. bi-m. $20. (American Honey Producer Association, Inc.) Wicwas Press. L.L.C., Box 817, Cheshire, CT 06410-0584. TEL 203-250-7575. Ed. Lawrence J. Connor. adv.; bk.rev.; stat.; tr.lit. (back issues avail.) **Document type:** trade publication.
  Description: For beekeepers who commercially pollinate and produce honey.

630   US   ISSN 0018-4748
HOOSIER FARMER. 1919. bi-m. $9.75 to out-of-state non-members; members $2. Indiana Farm Bureau, Inc., 225 South East St., Box 1290, Indianapolis, IN 46206. TEL 317-692-7819. FAX 317-692-7854. Ed. Shirley Richardson. adv. circ. 240,000.

630   FR   ISSN 1147-7598
HORIZONS CENTRE ILE-DE-FRANCE (EDITION EURE ET LOIR). 1946. w. 550 F. 6 rue Francis Vovelle, B.P. 195, 28004 Chartres Cedex, France. TEL 37-28-40-93. FAX 37-34-58-39. Ed. Joannes Cote. adv.; bk.rev. circ. 16,000. (tabloid format) **Document type:** newspaper.
  Formerly: Agriculture d'Eure et Loir.

630   FR   ISSN 1147-758X
HORIZONS CENTRE ILE-DE-FRANCE (EDITION LOIR-ET-CHER). 1968. w. 15 av. de Vendome, 41000 Blois Cedex, France. TEL 54-78-51-20.
FAX 54-78-31-03. Ed. Marie-Odile Beaudoux. circ. 5,000.
  Formerly (until 1990): Information Agricole de Loir et Cher (ISSN 0337-1719)

630   FR   ISSN 1147-7563
HORIZONS CENTRE ILE-DE-FRANCE (EDITION SEINE-ET-MARNE). w. 418 av. Aristide Briand, 77350 Le Mee sur Seine, France. TEL 64-39-95-94.
FAX 64-39-62-52. circ. 5,100.
  Formerly (until 1990): Sillon de Seine et Marne (ISSN 0751-6355)

630 635   JA   ISSN 0911-6494
HOUJYOU. (Text in Japanese) 1963. a. donation. Kagawa Prefecture Agricultural Experiment Station, Busshozan-cho, Takamatsu-shi 761, Japan. TEL 81-878-89-1121. FAX 81-878-89-1125. Ed. Kazunori Obika. circ. 200. **Document type:** bulletin.

630   CC   ISSN 1000-7091
S19
HUABEI NONGXUE BAO/NORTH CHINA AGRICULTURE JOURNAL. (Text in Chinese) 1986. q. $60. Hebei Academy of Agricultural and Forestry Sciences, 24 Jichang Lu, Shijiazhuang, Hebei 050051, People's Republic of China. TEL 7042853. Ed. Wei Jiankun. circ. 5,000. **Document type:** academic/scholarly publication.

630   HU   ISSN 0864-7410
HUNGARIAN AGRICULTURAL ENGINEERING. (Text in English) 1988. a. free. (Hungarian Academy of Sciences, Agricultural Engineering Committee) Hungarian Institute of Agricultural Engineering, Tessedik S. u. 4, 2101 Godollo, Hungary. Ed. Laszlo Toth. charts; stat. **Indexed:** Food Sci.& Tech.Abstr. **Document type:** proceedings.
—BLDSC (4336.990000).

638.1   595.7   UK
I B R A CONFERENCE ON TROPICAL BEES. irreg., no.6, 1996. International Bee Research Association, 18 North Rd., Cardiff CF1 3DY, Wales.
TEL 44-1222-372409. FAX 44-1222-665522. E-mail: ibra@cardiff.ac.uk. **Document type:** proceedings.
  Formerly: International Conference on Apiculture in Tropical Climates. Proceedings.

I C A C RECORDER. (International Cotton Advisory Committee) see *TEXTILE INDUSTRIES AND FABRICS*

630   CK   ISSN 0046-9920
I C A INFORMA. 1966. q. Col.$10000($20) Instituto Colombiano Agropecuario, Apdo. Aereo 151123, El Dorado, Bogota, Colombia. FAX 2673013. circ. 1,500. **Indexed:** Biol.Abstr., Hort.Abstr. **Document type:** monographic series.
—BLDSC (4360.180000). CCC.
  Incorporates: Instituto Colombiano Agropecuario. Temas Didacticos.

631   US   ISSN 0018-8808
I C A S A L S NEWSLETTER. 1968. 2/yr. free. International Center for Arid and Semiarid Land Studies, Texas Tech Univ., Box 41036, Lubbock, TX 79409-1036. TEL 806-742-2218.
FAX 806-742-1954. Eds. Idris R. Traylor, Jr., Sonia L. Moore. bk.rev.; illus.; circ. 3,000 (controlled). **Indexed:** Geo.Abstr. **Document type:** newsletter.
—BLDSC (4360.280000).

631.6   II
I C I D JOURNAL. (Text in English or French) 1952. s-a. $30. International Commission on Irrigation and Drainage - Commission Internationale des Irrigations et du Drainage, 48 Nyaya Marg, Chanakyapuri, New Delhi 110021, India. adv.; bk.rev. circ. 2,900. **Indexed:** Agri.Eng.Abstr., Irr.& Drain.Abstr., Soils & Fert.
  Formerly: I C I D Bulletin (ISSN 0579-5427)
  Description: Contains articles on irrigation, drainage, river training and flood control.

630   US
I F A COOPERATOR. 1935. 4/yr. $1. Intermountain Farmers Association, 1147 West 2100 South, Salt Lake City, UT 84119. TEL 801-972-2122.
FAX 801-972-2186. Ed. Bonnie Humphrey. R&P contact: Bonnie Humphrey. adv. contact: Bonnie Humphrey. illus. circ. 7,250. **Document type:** consumer publication, trade publication.
  Formerly: Intermountain Farmer (ISSN 0020-5672)

I F A D UPDATE. (International Fund for Agricultural Development) see *BUSINESS AND ECONOMICS — International Development And Assistance*

630   FR   ISSN 0984-9963
I F A P NEWSLETTER. bi-m. International Federation of Agricultural Producers - Federation Internationale des Producteurs Agricoles, 21 rue Chaptal, 75009 Paris, France. TEL 45-26-05-53. FAX 48-74-72-12. TELEX 281210. circ. 1,500. **Document type:** newsletter.
  Description: News on the activities of IFAP and its member organizations throughout the world.

630   595.7   614.8   US   ISSN 0738-968X
I P M PRACTITIONER. (Integrated Pest Management); monitoring the field of pest management. 1979. m. $35 to individuals; institutions $60. Bio Integral Resource Center, Box 7414, Berkeley, CA 94707. TEL 510-524-2567. FAX 510-524-1758. Ed. William Quarles. R&P contact: William Quarles. adv.; bk.rev.; index. circ. 5,000. (back issues avail.) **Indexed:** Bio-Contr.News & Info., Forest Prod.Abstr., Gard.Lit. (1992-), Weed Abstr. **Document type:** newsletter.
—BLDSC (4567.390000).
  Description: Covers integrated pest management programs, methods, products and research.

630   US   ISSN 1073-189X
IDAHO FARMER. 1895. m. $19.95. Western Farmer-Stockman Magazines (Subsidiary of: Cowles Publishing Co.), Box 2160, Spokane, WA 99210-1615. TEL 509-459-5361.
FAX 509-459-5102. adv. contact: Richard C. Brantley. circ. 8,568 (paid). **Document type:** trade publication.
  Former titles (until 1993): Idaho Farmer - Stockman (ISSN 1041-1682); (until 1977): Gem State Rural; Western Farmer and Agricultural Age.

AGRICULTURE

630   **CL**   ISSN 0073-4675
CODEN: IDESBG
IDESIA. (Text in Spanish; summaries in English) 1970. a. $6 or exchange basis. Universidad de Tarapaca, Instituto de Agronomia, Casilla 6-D, Arica, Chile. TEL 56-58-224157. FAX 56-58-226737. TELEX 221128 UNTAR CL. Ed. Mauricio Jimenez. bk.rev.; charts; bibl.; illus.; stat. circ. 1,000. **Indexed:** Biol.Abstr., Chem.Abstr. **Document type:** academic/scholarly publication.
—CASDDS.
  Description: Covers agronomic research and scientific papers and reports.
Refereed Serial

630   **JA**   ISSN 0913-7823
IE-NO-HIKARI/LIGHT OF HOME. (Text in Japanese) 1925. m. Ie-no-Hikari Association, No.11, funagawara-cho, Ichigaya, Shinjuku-ku, Tokyo 162, Japan. TEL 03-3266-9000. FAX 03-3266-9048. Ed. Toshio Horie. circ. 1,100,000.

630   **NR**   ISSN 0331-6351
IFE JOURNAL OF AGRICULTURE. 1967. a. ₤N1.50. University of Ife, Faculty of Agriculture, Ile-Ife, Osun State, Nigeria. Ed. A.E. Akingbohungbe. bk.rev. circ. 500. **Indexed:** Rural Devel.Abstr., World Agri.Econ.& Rural Sociol.Abstr. **Document type:** academic/scholarly publication.
  Formerly (until 1979): University of Ife. Faculty of Agriculture. Annual Research Report (ISSN 0579-7195)

630   **US**   ISSN 0194-7443
ILLINOIS AGRI-NEWS. 1977. w. $20. Agri-News Publications, 426 Second St., LaSalle, IL 61301. TEL 815-223-2558. FAX 815-223-5997. Ed. Warren Pufahl; Pub. Lynn Barker. R&P contact: Lynn Barker. adv. contact: Sue Cheslic. circ. 36,000. (also avail. in microfilm; back issues avail.) **Document type:** newspaper.
  Description: Serves farm families in the state of Illinois.

630   **US**
ILLINOIS FARMWEEK. 1974. w. $75. Illinois Farm Bureau, 1701 Towanda Ave., Bloomington, IL 61701. TEL 309-557-2238. FAX 309-557-2559. Ed. David McClelland. adv. contact: Bob Standard. circ. 87,650. **Document type:** newspaper.
  Description: Covers the latest news on farm production and marketing, economics, research and legislation.

630   **US**   ISSN 0019-2201
ILLINOIS RESEARCH. 1959. s-a. free. University of Illinois at Urbana-Champaign, College of Agricultural, Consumer and Environmental Sciences, Office of Research and Information Services, 47 Mumford Hall, 1301 W. Gregory Dr., IL 61801. TEL 217-244-2830. E-mail: c-frank@uiuc.edu. Ed. Cheryl Frank. R&P contact: Cheryl Frank. charts; illus. circ. 10,000. **Indexed:** Biol.Dig., Curr.Adv.Ecol.Sci., Curr.Cont., Excerp.Med., Field Crop Abstr., Helminthol.Abstr., Hort.Abstr., Plant Breed.Abstr., Sci.Cit.Ind., Soils & Fert., Soyabean Abstr. **Document type:** academic/scholarly publication.
  ●Also available on CD-ROM.
—BLDSC (4365.500000); Linda Hall; UMI; UnCover.

638.1   **GW**   ISSN 0019-2732
CODEN: IMKRA3
IMKERFREUND; Bienenzeitung zur Wahrung und Foerderung der Interessen der Bienenzuechter. 1945. m. DM.60 (foreign DM.78) (effective 1997); newsstand price: DM.5.80. (Landesverband Bayerischer Imker e.V.) B L V Verlagsgesellschaft mbH, Lothstr. 29, 80797 Munich, Germany. TEL 49-89-12705-0. FAX 49-89-12705354. Ed. D. Kauhausen-Keller. adv. contact: Gebhard von Doering. bk.rev.; charts; illus.; mkt.; tr.lit. **Indexed:** Apic.Abstr., Biol.Abstr. **Document type:** consumer publication.
—BLDSC (4369.611000). **CCC.**

630   **US**   ISSN 0749-1573
IMPACT (ATHENS). 1890. a. free. (Georgia Agricultural Experiment Stations) University of Georgia, College of Agriculture, Division of Agricultural Communications, Athens, GA 30602. TEL 404-542-3621. Ed. Kathleen Sheridan. illus. circ. 10,000. (back issues avail.)
—BLDSC (1481.190000); Linda Hall.
  Formerly: University of Georgia. Agricultural Experiment Stations. Annual Report.

630   **II**   ISSN 0084-781X
INDIAN AGRICULTURE IN BRIEF. (Text in English) 1958. a. Rs.200($72) Ministry of Agriculture, Department of Agriculture and Cooperation, Directorate of Economics and Statistics, A-2E-3 Kasturba Gandhi Marg Barracks, New Delhi 110 001, India. TEL 11-381523. Ed. Brajesh Kumar Gautam. circ. 900. **Document type:** government publication.

630   **II**
INDIAN AGRICULTURE REVIEW. (Text in English) 1993. a. Rs.250($55) Technical Press Publications, Eucharistic Congress Bldg., No. 1, 5-1 Convent St., Colaba, Mumbai 400 039, India. TEL 91-22-2021446. FAX 91-22-2871499. TELEX 011-83479 CHEM IN. Ed. J.P. de Sousa. adv.; abstr.; charts; illus. circ. 12,000. (also avail. in microfilm from UMI; reprint service avail. from UMI) **Document type:** trade publication.

630   **II**   ISSN 0019-4336
CODEN: INAGAT
INDIAN AGRICULTURIST. (Text in English) 1957. q. Rs.160($50) (Agricultural Society of India) Calcutta University Press, Sri Sibendra Nath Kanjilal, 48 Hazra Rd., Calcutta 19, India. Ed. Dr. A.K. Sarkar. adv.; bk.rev.; abstr.; charts; illus.; index. circ. 600. **Indexed:** Bio-Contr.News & Info., Biol.Abstr., Chem.Abstr., Cott.& Trop.Fibr.Abstr., Crop Physiol.Abstr., Curr.Adv.Ecol.Sci., Field Crop Abstr., Food Sci.& Tech.Abstr., Herb.Abstr., Hort.Abstr., Irr.& Drain.Abstr., Maize Abstr., Plant Breed.Abstr., Plant Grow.Reg.Abstr., Potato Abstr., Rev.Appl.Entomol., Rice Abstr., Seed Abstr., Soils & Fert., Soyabean Abstr., Triticale Abstr., Trop.Oil Seeds Abstr., Weed Abstr.
—CASDDS; Linda Hall.
  Description: Provides forum for association and gives conference information as well as research data in the agricultural field.

638.1 595.7   **II**   ISSN 0019-4425
INDIAN BEE JOURNAL. (Text in English) 1938. q. Rs.125($45) to individuals; institutions Rs.500($110). All-India Bee Keepers Association, c/o Dept. of Zoology, Haryana Agricultural University, Hisar 125 004, India. Ed. R.C. Sihagr. adv.; bk.rev.; abstr.; charts; illus.; stat.; index. circ. 700. **Indexed:** Apic.Abstr., Biol.Abstr., Chem.Abstr., Curr.Adv.Ecol.Sci.

634   **II**   ISSN 0367-7281
INDIAN COCONUT JOURNAL. (Text in English) N.S. 1970. m. Rs.75($50) Department of Agriculture, Coconut Development Board, Ernakulam, Cochin 11, India. TELEX 0855 6736 CODE IN. Ed. Muhammad Edachal. adv.; bk.rev. circ. 2,000. **Indexed:** Agroforest.Abstr., Biol.Abstr., Food Sci.& Tech.Abstr., Hort.Abstr., Plant Breed.Abstr., Soils & Fert.
—BLDSC (4394.000000).
  Formerly: Coconut Bulletin (ISSN 0010-0145)

630   **II**
INDIAN FARMER TIMES. (Text in English) 1983. m. Rs.55. Farmers Welfare Trust Society (WAFM), 6-B, Regal Building, New Delhi-110 001, India. Ed. Jagdeesh Kodesia. adv.; bk.rev.; illus. circ. 3,500.

631   **II**   ISSN 0019-4786
S17
INDIAN FARMING. (Text in English) 1940. m. Rs.84($20) Indian Council of Agricultural Research, Krishi Anusandhan Bhavan, Pusa, New Delhi 110012, India. Ed. S.N. Tata. adv.; bk.rev.; charts; illus.; index. circ. 51,200. (also avail. in microform from UMI; reprint service avail. from UMI) **Indexed:** Agri.Eng.Abstr., Agroforest.Abstr., Anim.Breed.Abstr., Bio-Contr.News & Info., Biol.Abstr., Chem.Abstr., Cott.& Trop.Fibr.Abstr., Dairy Sci.Abstr., Excerp.Med., Field Crop Abstr., Food Sci.& Tech.Abstr., Forest.Abstr., Forest Prod.Abstr., Helminthol.Abstr., Herb.Abstr., Hort.Abstr., Ind.Vet., Maize Abstr., Nutr.Abstr., Pig News & Info., Potato Abstr., Poult.Abstr., Protozool.Abstr., Rice Abstr., Rural Devel.Abstr., Seed Abstr., Soils & Fert., Sorghum & Millets Abstr., Soyabean Abstr., Triticale Abstr., Trop.Oil Seeds Abstr., Vet.Bull., Weed Abstr., World Agri.Econ.& Rural Sociol.Abstr.
—BLDSC (4397.000000); Linda Hall; UMI.
  Description: Covers agriculture, animal husbandry and allied subjects.

INDIAN FORESTER. see *FORESTS AND FORESTRY*

INDIAN JOURNAL OF AGRICULTURAL BIOCHEMISTRY.
  see *BIOLOGY — Biological Chemistry*

630   **II**   ISSN 0971-2356
INDIAN JOURNAL OF AGRICULTURAL ENGINEERING. (Text in English) 1991. q. Rs.80($20) Indian Council of Agricultural Research, Krishi Anusandhan Bhavan, Pusa, New Delhi 110012, India. TEL 91-11-570-9003. Ed. C.S. Viswanath. adv.; bk.rev.; bibl.; charts; illus.; index. circ. 4,000. (also avail. in microfilm from UMI; reprint service avail. from UMI) **Document type:** academic/scholarly publication.
—BLDSC (4409.955000).

630   **II**   ISSN 0971-8664
INDIAN JOURNAL OF AGRICULTURAL MARKETING. (Text in English) 1986. 3/yr. £25 to individuals; institutions £45. Indian Society of Agricultural Marketing, F-5 Utkarsh Anurag Apts., Agrasen Marg, Giripeth, Nagpur 440 010, India. TEL 91-712-558-767. FAX 91-712-548-236. Ed. T. Satyanarayana. circ. 800. **Document type:** academic/scholarly publication.
Refereed Serial

630   **II**   ISSN 0367-8245
S19   CODEN: IJARC2
INDIAN JOURNAL OF AGRICULTURAL RESEARCH; journal of plant and soil science. (Text in English) 1967. q. $60 (effective 1997). Agricultural Research Communication Centre, 1130 Sadar, Karnal 132 001, Haryana, India. TEL 91-184-255080. Ed. Dr. Kirti Singh. bk.rev.; abstr. circ. 1,500. **Indexed:** Biol.Abstr., Chem.Abstr., Cott.& Trop.Fibr.Abstr., Curr.Adv.Ecol.Sci., Curr.Cont., Field Crop Abstr., Herb.Abstr., Hort.Abstr., Ind.Sci.Rev., INIS Atomind., Irr.& Drain.Abstr., Plant Breed.Abstr., Potato Abstr., Rev.Appl.Entomol., Rev.Plant.Path., Rice Abstr., Rural Recreat.Tour.Abstr., Seed Abstr., Soils & Fert., Sorghum & Millets Abstr., Soyabean Abstr., Triticale Abstr., Trop.Oil Seeds Abstr., Weed Abstr., World Agri.Econ. & Rural Sociol.Abstr.
—BLDSC (4409.980000); CASDDS; CISTI; Linda Hall; SWETS; UMI.
  Formerly: Indian Journal of Science and Industry. Section A. Agricultural Sciences (ISSN 0367-8296); Supersedes in part: Indian Journal of Science and Industry (ISSN 0019-5618)

630.2   **II**   ISSN 0019-5022
S19   CODEN: IJASA3
INDIAN JOURNAL OF AGRICULTURAL SCIENCES. (Text in English) 1931. m. Rs.240($50) Indian Council of Agricultural Research, Krishi Anusandhan Bhaven, Pusa, New Delhi 110012, India. Ed. R.S. Gupta. adv.; bk.rev.; bibl.; charts; illus.; index. circ. 2,000. (also avail. in microform from UMI; reprint service avail. from UMI) **Indexed:** Agri.Eng.Abstr., Agrindex, Agroforest.Abstr., ASCA, Bio-Contr.News & Info., Biol.Abstr., Chem.Abstr., Cott.& Trop.Fibr.Abstr., Crop Physiol.Abstr., Curr.Adv.Ecol.Sci., Curr.Adv.Genetics & Molec.Biol., Curr.Cont., Excerp.Med., Field Crop Abstr., Food Sci.& Tech.Abstr., Forest.Abstr., Forest Prod.Abstr., Helminthol.Abstr., Herb.Abstr., Hort.Abstr., INIS Atomind., Lead Abstr., Maize Abstr., Nutr.Abstr., Plant Breed Abstr., Plant Grow.Reg.Abstr., Potato Abstr., Rev.Appl.Entomol., Rice Abstr., Seed Abstr., Sel.Water Res.Abstr., So.Pac.Per.Ind., Sorghum & Millets Abstr., Soyabean Abstr., Sport Fish.Abstr., Sugar Ind.Abstr., Triticale Abstr., Trop.Oil Seeds Abstr., Weed Abstr., Wild.Rev., Zincscan, Zoo.Rec.
—BLDSC (4410.000000); CASDDS; Ei; EMDOCS; Genuine Article; Linda Hall; SWETS; UMI; UnCover.
  Description: A scientific journal containing articles based on original research.

630   **II**   ISSN 0537-197X
SB4   CODEN: IJAGAZ
INDIAN JOURNAL OF AGRONOMY. (Text in English) 1956. q. Rs.60($15) to individuals; institutions Rs.350($150). Indian Society of Agronomy, Divisior of Agronomy, Indian Agricultural Research Institute, New Delhi 110 012, India. TEL 574-2283. Ed. S.P. Singh. adv.; bk.rev. circ. 1,900. (back issues avail.) **Indexed:** Agri.Eng.Abstr., ASCA, Biol.Abstr., Chem.Abstr., Cott.& Trop.Fibr.Abstr., Curr.Cont., Field Crop Abstr., Helminthol.Abstr., Herb.Abstr., Hort.Abstr., Irr.& Drain.Abstr., Maize Abstr., Nutr.Abstr., Plant Breed.Abstr., Potato Abstr., Rev.Plant Path., Rice Abstr., Seed Abstr., Soils & Fert., Sorghum & Millets Abstr., Soyabean Abstr., Sugar Ind.Abstr., Triticale Abstr., Trop.Oil Seeds Abstr., Weed Abstr. **Document type:** academic/scholarly publication.
—BLDSC (4410.100000); CASDDS; Genuine Article; Linda Hall; SWETS; UMI.

AGRICULTURE 125

630 II ISSN 0971-2062
INDIAN JOURNAL OF DRYLAND AGRICULTURAL RESEARCH AND DEVELOPMENT. (Text in English) 1986. s-a. $50. (Indian Society of Dryland Agriculture) Hindustan Publishing Corp., 4805-24, 1st Fl., Bharat Ram Rd., Darya Ganj, New Delhi 110 002, India. TEL 91-11-3254401. FAX 91-11-6863511. E-mail: hpcpd@giasdl01.vsnl.net.in.

INDIAN JOURNAL OF HEREDITY. see *BIOLOGY — Genetics*

632 576 II ISSN 0303-6960
QL391.N4 CODEN: IJNEDT
INDIAN JOURNAL OF NEMATOLOGY. 1971. s-a. Rs.225($50) Indian Agricultural Research Institute, Nematological Society of India, Division of Nematology, c/o General Secretary, I.A.R.I., New Delhi 110 012, India. Ed. D.R. Dasgupta. adv.; bk.rev.; bibl.; charts; illus. circ. 500. (back issues avail.) **Indexed:** Agroforest.Abstr., Bio-Contr.News & Info., Biol.Abstr., Field Crop Abstr., Forest Prod.Abstr., Helminthol.Abstr., Hort.Abstr., Potato Abstr., Rice Abstr., Seed Abstr., Soils & Fert., Triticale Abstr., Weed Abstr.

630 II ISSN 0970-308X
INDIAN SOCIETY FOR COTTON IMPROVEMENT. JOURNAL. (Text in English) 1976. s-a. Rs.100($25) Indian Society for Cotton Improvement, c/o Central Institute for Research on Cotton Technology, Adenwala Rd., Matunga, Bombay - 400 019, India. Ed. V. Sundaram. **Indexed:** Indian Sci.Abstr.
—BLDSC (4768.650000).

631 II ISSN 0019-638X
S590 CODEN: JINSA4
INDIAN SOCIETY OF SOIL SCIENCE. JOURNAL. (Text in English) 1953. q. $100. Indian Society of Soil Science, Indian Agricultural Research Institute, Division of Soil Science and Agricultural Chemistry, New Delhi 110 012, India. FAX 91-11-5755529. Ed. T.D. Biswas. adv.; bk.rev.; illus.; index. circ. 2,500. **Indexed:** Agroforest.Abstr., Biol.Abstr., Chem.Abstr., Curr.Adv.Ecol.Sci., Excerp.Med., Field Crop Abstr., Geo.Abstr., Herb.Abstr., Indian Sci.Abstr., Irr.& Drain.Abstr., Maize Abstr., Potato Abstr., Rice Abstr., Soils & Fert., Sorghum & Millets Abstr., Soyabean Abstr., Sugar Ind.Abstr., Triticale Abstr., Trop.Abstr., Trop.Oil Seeds Abstr., Weed Abstr. **Document type:** academic/scholarly publication.
—BLDSC (4769.000000); CASDDS; CISTI; Linda Hall; SWETS; UnCover.

630 US ISSN 0073-6783
INDIANA. AGRICULTURAL EXPERIMENT STATION. INSPECTION REPORT. 1956. irreg. price varies. Purdue University, Agricultural Experiment Station, c/o Donna Southard, W. Lafayette, IN 47907. TEL 317-494-5962. FAX 317-496-1117.
—Linda Hall.

630 US ISSN 0073-6791
INDIANA. AGRICULTURAL EXPERIMENT STATION. RESEARCH BULLETIN. 1957. irreg. (12-15/yr.). Purdue University, Agricultural Experiment Station, c/o Donna Southard, W. Lafayette, IN 47907. TEL 317-494-5962. FAX 317-496-1117. R&P contact: Eldon Ortman. circ. 2,500. **Indexed:** Helminthol.Abstr. **Document type:** academic/scholarly publication.

630 US ISSN 0745-7103
INDIANA AGRI-NEWS. 1982. w. $15. Agri-News Publications, 420 Second St., LaSalle, IL 61301. TEL 815-223-2558. FAX 815-223-5997. Ed. Warren Pufahl; Pub. Lynn Barker. R&P contact: Lynn Barker. adv. contact: Sue Cheslic. circ. 22,000. **Document type:** newspaper.
Description: Farm and rural community magazine.

630 US ISSN 0162-7104
INDIANA PRAIRIE FARMER. 1841. m. (except Jan.-Mar., s-m.). $19.95 (outside Indiana $25). Farm Progress Companies (Subsidiary of A B C Publishing Companies), 191 S. Gary Ave., Carol Stream, IL 60188. TEL 630-690-5600. FAX 630-462-2869. (Edit. addr.: 2346 S. Lnhurst Dr., Ste. 304, Indianapolis, IN 46241-8602. TEL 317-248-0681. FAX 317-248-0828) Ed. Paul Queck. adv.: B&W page $3850, color page $4430; trim 7 X 10; adv. contact: Charles P. Roth. circ. 48,261 (paid). **Document type:** trade publication.
Description: Local and timely crop and livestock production practices are emphasized by staff editors who live and work in the area. Management, government, rural lifestyle, and economic issues are also regularly featured.

630.5 IO ISSN 0126-2920
CODEN: IARJE2
INDONESIAN AGRICULTURAL RESEARCH & DEVELOPMENT JOURNAL. (Text in English) 1979. irreg. Ministry of Agriculture, Agency for Agricultural Research & Development, 29 Jalan Ragunan, Pasar Minggu, Jakarta Selatan, Indonesia. **Indexed:** Sport Fish.Abstr., Wild.Rev., Zoo.Rec. **Document type:** academic/scholarly publication.
—UnCover.

INDUSTRIES ALIMENTAIRES ET AGRICOLES. see *FOOD AND FOOD INDUSTRIES*

630 PN
INFORMACION AGRICOLA PANAMENA. 1981. bi-m. Instituto de Investigacion Agropecuaria de Panama, Centro de Informacion Documental Agropecuaria, Apdo. 6-4391, El Dorado, Panama 6A, Panama. TELEX 3677 PG. Ed. Vielka Chang-Yau. circ. 250.

630 FR ISSN 0019-994X
INFORMATION AGRICOLE. m. 190 F. (foreign 240 F.). Federation Nationale des Syndicats d'Exploitants Agricoles, 11 rue de la Baume, 75008 Paris, France. TEL 45-63-11-77. Ed. Yves Salmon. adv.; charts; illus.; stat.; tr.lit. **Indexed:** Rural Recreat.Tour.Abstr., World Agri.Econ.& Rural Sociol.Abstr.
—BLDSC (4481.730000).

630 FR
INFORMATION AGRICOLE DU CHER. w. 3 rue Volta, 18002 Bourges Cedex, France. TEL 48-70-14-54. FAX 48-65-01-29. Ed. Maryvonne Langlois; Pub. Berry Republichin. circ. 7,100. **Document type:** newspaper.

630 FR ISSN 1157-2507
INFORMATION AGRICOLE DU RHONE. w. 4 place Gensoul, 69006 Lyon, France. TEL 78-42-65-92. FAX 78-42-61-63. Ed. Paul Lormage. circ. 9,087.

200 IT
INFORMATION BULLETIN FOR CATHOLIC RURAL ORGANIZATIONS. (Text in English, French, German, Spanish) 1965. q. $10. International Catholic Rural Association, Piazza S. Calisto 16, 00153 Rome, Italy. TEL 06-69887123. Ed.Bd. adv.; bk.rev.; cum.index. circ. 1,200. (back issues avail.) **Document type:** bulletin.

630 IT ISSN 0020-0689
L'INFORMATORE AGRARIO. 1945. w. (51/yr.). Lit.115000 (foreign L.235000) (effective 1998). Edizione L' Informatore Agrario s.r.l., Lungadige Galtarossa 23-E, 37123 Verona, Italy. TEL 39-45-597855. FAX 39-45-597510. TELEX 481117 INFAGR. Ed. Giovanni Rizzotti; Pub. Elena Rizzotti. adv.: B&W page Lit.3650000, color page Lit.5840000; adv. contact: Nino Piras. bk.rev.; charts; illus.; mkt.; stat.; index; circ. 40,111 (controlled). (tabloid format) **Indexed:** Agri.Eng.Abstr., Agroforest.Abstr., Apic.Abstr., Bio-Contr.News & Info., Fababean Abstr., Field Crop Abstr., Geo.Abstr., Herb.Abstr., Hort.Abstr., Ind.Vet., Irr.& Drain.Abstr., Maize Abstr., Ornam.Hort., Plant Breed.Abstr., Plant Grow.Reg.Abstr., Potato Abstr., Rice Abstr., Rural Recreat.Tour.Abstr., Seed Abstr., Soils & Fert., Sorghum & Millets Abstr., Soyabean Abstr., Sugar Ind.Abstr., Triticale Abstr., Weed Abstr., World Agri.Econ.& Rural Sociol.Abstr. **Document type:** newspaper.
—BLDSC (4496.750000).
Description: Covers the technical, economic and political aspects of all the branches of agriculture and breeding.

INFORMATORE FITOPATOLOGICO. see *BIOLOGY — Botany*

630 BL ISSN 0100-3364
HD1875.M5
INFORME AGROPECUARIO. 1975. m. Cr.$480($60) Empresa de Pesquisa Agropecuaria de Minas Gerais, Av. Amazonas 115, 30000 Belo Horizonte, Brazil. Ed. Gustavo de Jesus Werneck. adv. circ. 15,000. **Indexed:** Agri.Eng.Abstr., Agrindex, Agroforest.Abstr., Anim.Breed.Abstr., Dairy Sci.Abstr., Field Crop Abstr., Herb.Abstr., Hort.Abstr., IBR, Ind.Vet., Maize Abstr., Pig News & Info., Poult.Abstr., Rice Abstr., Sorghum & Millets Abstr., Sugar Ind.Abstr.
—BLDSC (4498.311000).
Formerly (until no.2, 1976): Informe Agropecuario: Conjuntura e Estatistica.

630 MX
INGENIERIA AGRONOMICA. 1975. a. Mex.$150($14) Colegio de Ingenieros Agronomos de Mexico, A.C., Sindicalismo 92, Mexico 18, D.F., Mexico. Ed.Bd. charts; illus.

630 FR ISSN 1264-9147
INGENIERIES. 6/yr. 390 F. (foreign 470 F.) (effective 1997). Librairie Lavoisier, 11 rue Lavoisier, 75384 Paris Cedex 08, France. TEL 33-1-42657167. FAX 33-1-42650246. E-mail: group@lavoisier.fr; URL: http://www.lavoisier.fr. (Subscr. to: Lavoisier Abonnements, 14 rue de Provigny, 94236 Cachan Cedex, France. TEL 33-1-47406700. FAX 33-1-47406703)

630 SP
INSTITUT AGRICOLA CATALA DE SANT ISIDRE. CALENDARI DEL PAGES. 1856. a. 750 ptas. Institut Agricola Catala de Sant Isidre, Plaza de Sant Josep Oriol, 4, 08002 Barcelona, Spain. TEL 93-301-16-36. FAX 93-317-30-05. Dir. Ferran de Muller.

630 RW
INSTITUT DES SCIENCES AGRONOMIQUES DU RWANDA. DEPARTEMENT DES PRODUCTIONS VEGETALES. COMPTE RENDU DES TRAVAUX. a. Institut des Sciences Agronomiques, Departement des Productions Vegetales, B.P. 138, Butare, Rwanda.

630 TI ISSN 0365-4761
SB29.T8
INSTITUT NATIONAL DE LA RECHERCHE AGRONOMIQUE DE TUNISIE. ANNALES. (Text in French; summaries in English) 1920. a. price varies. Institut National de la Recherche Agronomique de Tunisie, Service de Documentation, Rue Hedi Karray, 2080 Ariana, Tunis, Tunisia. TEL 230024. FAX 231693. circ. 800. **Indexed:** Anim.Breed.Abstr. **Document type:** government publication, academic/scholarly publication.
—BLDSC (0925.100000).
Description: Scientific journal publishing the results of Tunisian agricultural research and focusing on the improvement of animal and plant production in Tunisia.

630 TI ISSN 0020-238X
INSTITUT NATIONAL DE LA RECHERCHE AGRONOMIQUE DE TUNISIE. DOCUMENTS TECHNIQUES. (Text in French; summaries in English) 1963. irreg., no.107, 1991. price varies. Institut National de la Recherche Agronomique de Tunisie, Service de Documentation, Rue Hedi Karray, 2080 Ariana, Tunis, Tunisia. TEL 230024. FAX 231693. circ. 500. **Indexed:** Biol.Abstr. **Document type:** government publication.
Description: Technical journal intended to help Tunisian farmers improve crop and livestock productivity through improved management.

630 CG
INSTITUT NATIONAL POUR L'ETUDE ET LA RECHERCHE AGRONOMIQUE. RAPPORT ANNUEL. Cover title: Rapport pour l'Exercice. a. Institut National pour l'Etude et la Recherche Agronomique, B.P. 1513, Kisangani, Democratic Republic of the Congo. illus.

AGRICULTURE

631   GR   ISSN 0365-5814
SB599   CODEN: APYBAQ
INSTITUT PHYTOPATHOLOGIQUE BENAKI. ANNALES. NOUVELLE SERIE. (Text in English, French, Greek) 1935; N.S. irreg., vol.17, no.2, 1996. $40. Institut Phytopathologique Benaki - Benaki Phytopathological Institute, 8 Delta St., 145 61 Kifissia, Greece. FAX 30-1-807-7506. E-mail: schatz@leon.nreps.aziaduet.gr. Ed. D. Lascaris. R&P contact: A.S. Alivizatos. TEL 30-1-807-9603. charts; illus.; index. circ. 700. (back issues avail.) **Indexed:** Bio-Contr.News & Info., Biodet.Abstr., Biol.Abstr., Biotech.Abstr., Chem.Abstr., Helminthol.Abstr., Hort.Abstr., Maize Abstr., Plant Breed.Abstr., Potato Abstr., Rev.Appl.Entomol., Rev.Plant Path., Soils & Fert., Weed Abstr. **Document type:** academic/scholarly publication.
—BLDSC (0933.000000); CASDDS.

630 296   IS
INSTITUTE FOR AGRICULTURAL RESEARCH ACCORDING TO THE TORAH. BULLETIN. (Text in Hebrew) 1980. bi-m. IS.50. Institute for Agricultural Research According to the Torah, Nahal Soreq Municipal Building, Yad Benjamin 76812, Israel. TEL 972-8-594099. FAX 972-8-594174. Ed. Elyakim Shlanger. adv.: B&W page IS.2000. bk.rev. circ. 3,000. **Indexed:** Soils & Fert. **Document type:** bulletin.
Description: Examines religious issues affecting farmers and consumers, to foster observance of Jewish law in matters pertaining to agriculture, food production and consumerism.

630   AT
INSTITUTE FOR INTEGRATED AGRICULTURAL DEVELOPMENT. RESEARCH REPORT. 1982. biennial. free. Institute for Integrated Agricultural Development, Department of Agriculture Energy & Minerals, RMB 1145, Chiltern Valley Rd., Rutherglen, Vic. 3685, Australia. TEL 61-60-304500. FAX 61-60-304600. E-mail: belfordb@rri.agvic.gov.au. Ed. Bob Belford. circ. 1,000. **Document type:** consumer publication.
Former titles: Rutherglen Research Institute. Research Report (ISSN 0814-4990); Rutherglen, Australia. Research Station. Digest of Recent Research (ISSN 0080-5009)

INSTITUTE OF AGRICULTURE AND ANIMAL SCIENCE. JOURNAL. see *VETERINARY SCIENCE*

INSTITUTE OF BREWING. JOURNAL. see *BEVERAGES*

630   BL   ISSN 0020-3653
     CODEN: AIBOA3
INSTITUTO BIOLOGICO. ARQUIVOS. (Text in Portuguese; summaries in English) 1928. s-a. R.15($15) Instituto Biologico, Av. Rodrigues Alves 1252, C.P. 7119, 01064-970 Sao Paulo, Brazil. TEL 55-11-5729822. FAX 55-11-5709704. Ed. Zuleide Alves Ramiro. illus.; index. (also avail. in microfilm) **Indexed:** Biol.Abstr., Chem.Abstr., Curr.Adv.Ecol.Sci., Dairy Sci.Abstr., Excerp.Med., Helminthol.Abstr., Hort.Abstr., Ind.Med., Ind.Vet., Rev.Appl.Entomol., Seed Abstr., Sorghum & Millets Abstr., Trop.Oil Seeds Abstr., Vet.Bull. **Document type:** academic/scholarly publication.
—BLDSC (1687.000000); CASDDS; CISTI.

630   CK   ISSN 0538-0391
INSTITUTO COLOMBIANO AGROPECUARIO. BOLETIN TECNICO. no.45, 1977. irreg. Instituto Colombiano Agropecuario, Apdo. Aereo 151123, El Dorado, Bogota, Colombia. FAX 57-1-2673013. illus. circ. 2,500. **Indexed:** Biol.Abstr.

630 570   CK   ISSN 0018-8794
     CODEN: RCOAB2
INSTITUTO COLOMBIANO AGROPECUARIO. REVISTA I C A. (Text in English; summaries in English and Spanish) 1964. q. Col.$10000($20) or exchange basis. Instituto Colombiano Agropecuario, Produmedios, Apdo. Aereo 151123, El Dorado, Bogota, Colombia. FAX 267-30-13. bibl.; charts; illus. circ. 1,050. **Indexed:** Chem.Abstr., Cott.& Trop.Fibr.Abstr., Dairy Sci.Abstr., Field Crop Abstr., Herb.Abstr., Hort.Abstr., Ind.Vet., Maize Abstr., Nutr.Abstr., Rev.Med.& Vet.Mycol., Rev.Plant Path., Rural Recreat.Tour.Abstr., Soils & Fert., Vet.Bull., World Agri.Econ.& Rural Sociol.Abstr. **Document type:** monographic series.
—CASDDS. CCC.

630   SP   ISSN 0374-8189
INSTITUTO DE ECONOMIA Y PRODUCCIONES GANADERAS DEL EBRO. COMUNICACIONES. 1970. irreg., no.11, 1980. free. Instituto de Economia y Producciones Ganaderas del Ebro, Miguel Servet, 177, Zaragoza, Spain. circ. 500. **Indexed:** Anim.Breed.Abstr., Biol.Abstr., Bull.Signal., World Agri.Econ.& Rural Sociol.Abstr.

630   SP   ISSN 0375-3417
INSTITUTO DE ECONOMIA Y PRODUCCIONES GANADERAS DEL EBRO. TRABAJOS. 1970. irreg., no.63, 1988. free. Instituto de Economia y Producciones Ganaderas del Ebro, Miguel Servet, 177, 50013 Zaragoza, Spain. Dir. M. Ocana. circ. 500. **Indexed:** Anim.Breed.Abstr., Biol.Abstr., Bull.Signal., Ind.SST, World Agri.Econ.& Rural Sociol.Abstr.

630   MZ   ISSN 0077-1791
INSTITUTO DE INVESTIGACAO AGRONOMICA DE MOCAMBIQUE. CENTRO DE DOCUMENTACAO AGRARIA. MEMORIAS. (Text in Portuguese; summaries in English, French and Portuguese) 1966. irreg., no.5, 1974. price varies. Instituto Nacional de Investigacao Agronomica, Centro de Documentacao e Informacao, C.P. 3658, Maputo 11, Mozambique. illus.; index. circ. 500. **Indexed:** Biol.Abstr.

631.091   PO   ISSN 0871-1763
INSTITUTO DE INVESTIGACAO CIENTIFICA TROPICAL. COMUNICACOES. SERIE DE CIENCIAS AGRARIAS. 1989. irreg. price varies. Instituto de Investigacao Cientifica Tropical, Rua da Junqueira 30, 1300 Lisbon, Portugal. TEL 351-1-3622621. FAX 351-1-3631460. E-mail: cdi@iict.pt; URL: http://www.iict.pt. (Subscr to: Centro de Documentacao e Informacao, Rua Jau 47, 1300 Lisbon, Portugal) circ. 1,000. **Document type:** monographic series.

630   BL   ISSN 0103-5215
INSTITUTO DO DESENVOLVIMENTO ECONOMICO-SOCIAL DO PARA. PARA AGRARIO. 1986. s-a. free. Instituto do Desenvolvimento Economico-Social do Para, Av. Nazare 871, 66035-170 Belem, Para, Brazil. TEL 55-91-2244411. FAX 55-91-2253414. bibl.; charts; stat. **Document type:** government publication.

630   SP   ISSN 0210-3354
     CODEN: MINIB8
INSTITUTO NACIONAL DE INVESTIGACIONES AGRARIAS. MONOGRAFIAS. 1973. irreg. price varies. Ministerio de Agricultura, Pesca y Alimentacion, Instituto Nacional de Investigaciones Agrarias, Centro de Publicaciones, Paseo de la Infanta Isabel 1, 28071 Madrid, Spain. TEL 34-1-3475551. FAX 34-2-3475722. (I.N.I.A. addr.: Jose Abascal 56, 28003 Madrid, Spain. TEL 347-39-16) Ed. Carmen Perez Munoz. R&P contact: Juan Carlos Palacios Lopez. **Document type:** monographic series.
—CASDDS.

630 330.9   MX
INSTITUTO NACIONAL DE INVESTIGACIONES FORESTALES, AGRICOLAS Y PECUARIAS. FOLLETOS DE INVESTIGACION. (Text in Spanish; summaries in English and Spanish) 1979. irreg. free. Instituto Nacional de Investigaciones Forestales, Agricolas y Pecuarias, Vocalia Division Agricola, Apdo. Postal 6-882, 06600 Mexico, D.F., Mexico. Ed.Bd. charts. circ. 3,000. **Indexed:** Biol.Abstr. **Document type:** academic/scholarly publication.
Formerly (until 1985): Instituto Nacional de Investigaciones Agricolas. Folletos de Investigacion.

630   MX
INSTITUTO NACIONAL DE INVESTIGACIONES FORESTALES, AGRICOLAS Y PECUARIAS. TEMAS DIDACTICOS. 1976. irreg. free. Instituto Nacional de Investigaciones Forestales, Agricolas y Pecuarias, Vocalia Division Agricola, Apdo. Postal 6-882, 06600 Mexico, D.F., Mexico. Ed.Bd. charts. circ. 3,000. **Document type:** academic/scholarly publication.
Formerly (until 1985): Instituto Nacional de Investigaciones Agricolas. Temas Didacticos.

630   AG   ISSN 0325-1772
INSTITUTO NACIONAL DE TECNOLOGIA AGROPECUARIA. ESTACION EXPERIMENTAL REGIONAL AGROPECUARIA. BOLETIN DE DIVULGACION TECNICA. 1970. irreg. Instituto Nacional de Tecnologia Agropecuaria, Estacion Experimental Regional Agropecuaria, Casilla de Correo No. 31, 2700 Pergamino, Argentina. circ. 1,500. **Indexed:** Biol.Abstr., Dairy Sci.Abstr., Herb.Abstr., Soils & Fert., World Agri.Econ.& Rural Sociol.Abstr.
Formerly: Instituto Nacional de Tecnologia Agropecuaria. Estacion Experimental Regional Agropecuaria. Publicacion Tecnica.

630 664   PO   ISSN 0365-2971
INSTITUTO SUPERIOR DE AGRONOMIA. ANAIS. (Text in English, French and Portuguese; summaries in English and French) 1920. a. price varies. Instituto Superior de Agronomia, Tapada da Ajuda, 1399 Lisbon Codex, Portugal. FAX 351-1-3635031. TELEX 44700 ISATEL. Ed. R.P. Ricardo. circ. 900. (back issues avail.) **Document type:** academic/scholarly publication.

630 595.7 576 591   RM   ISSN 0365-575X
     CODEN: APSVBN
INSTITUTUL DE CERCETARI PENTRU PROTECTIA PLANTELOR. ANALELE/RESEARCH INSTITUTE FOR PLANT PROTECTION. ANNALS. (Text in Rumanian; summaries in English and Russian) 1965. a. 150 lei. (Academy of Agricultural and Forestry Sciences) Centrul de Material Didactic si Propag. Agricola, Cal.Serban Voda 34, Bucharest, Rumania. (Subscr. to: Research Institute for Plant Protection, bd. Ion Ionescu de la Brad no.8, 71592 Bucharest, Rumania) circ. 500. (back issues avail.) **Indexed:** Biol.Abstr., Fababean Abstr., Hort.Abstr., Potato Abstr., Rev.Appl.Entomol., Rev.Med.& Vet.Mycol., Rev.Plant Path., Triticale Abstr., Weed Abstr.
—CASDDS.

632   PL   ISSN 0020-448X
SB599
INSTYTUT OCHRONY ROSLIN. BIULETYN. (Text in Polish; summaries in English and Russian) 1957. irreg. free. Instytut Ochrony Roslin - Institute of Plant Protection, Miczurina 20, 60-318 Poznan, Poland. Eds. W. Wegorek, J.J. Lipa. illus.; index. circ. 1,000. **Indexed:** Biol.Abstr., Helminthol.Abstr., Plant Breed.Abstr., Rev.Appl.Entomol., Rev.Plant Path., Sel.Water Res.Abstr., Soils & Fert.

630   II   ISSN 0020-4919
INTENSIVE AGRICULTURE. (Text in English) 1963. bi-m. Rs.12. Ministry of Agriculture and Rural Development, Directorate of Extension, Krishi Vistar Bhawan, Dr. K.S. Krishnan Marg, Pusa, New Delhi 110012, India. TEL 603568. Ed. Shukla Hazra. adv.: page Rs.2000; 270 x 210. bk.rev.; charts; illus. circ. 12,000.
Formerly: Extension (ISSN 0421-9724)
Description: Contains information on practical aspects of farming told in a very simple language and supported by helpful pictures.

630   SW   ISSN 1100-1194
INTERNA PUBLIKATIONER. 1988. irreg. Sveriges Lantbruksuniversitet, Institutionen foer Vaextodlingslaera - Swedish University of Agricultural Sciences, Department of Crop Production Science, P.O. Box 7043, S-750 07 Uppsala, Sweden. TEL 46-18-67-10-00. FAX 46-18-67-29-09. Ed.Bd. **Document type:** academic/scholarly publication.
Description: Publishes special types of materials, including reports and tables.

630   UK   ISSN 0261-4413
INTERNATIONAL AGRICULTURAL DEVELOPMENT. 1980. bi-m. £54($97) (effective 1997). Research Information Ltd., 222 Maylands Ave., Hemel Hempstead, Herts. HP2 7TD, England. TEL 44-1442-213222. FAX 44-1442-259395. E-mail: resinf@globalnet.co.uk. Ed. John Madeley. adv.: B&W page £576. bk.rev.; illus. circ. 1,000. **Indexed:** Agri.Eng.Abstr., Apic.Abstr., Environ.Abstr., Environ.Per.Bibl. (1989-1994), Geo.Abstr., Rural Recreat.Tour.Abstr., World Agri.Econ.& Rural Sociol.Abstr. **Document type:** academic/scholarly publication.
—BLDSC (4535.648500); SWETS.
Formerly: Third World Agriculture.
Description: Forum for increasing food output in developing countries in a sustainable way.

INTERNATIONAL ASSOCIATION OF AGRICULTURAL INFORMATION SPECIALISTS. QUARTERLY BULLETIN. see *LIBRARY AND INFORMATION SCIENCES*

AGRICULTURE 127

638.1   RM   ISSN 0074-2007
INTERNATIONAL BEEKEEPING CONGRESS. REPORTS. biennial since 1963, latest 33rd, 1993, Beijing. price varies. International Federation of Beekeepers' Associations "Apimondia", 42 Ficusului Blvd., 71544 Bucharest, Rumania. TEL 40-1-6330918. FAX 40-1-63129492. TELEX 10998 IITEA R. Ed. Erika Dumitrascu. adv. contact: Paltin Nottara. **Document type:** proceedings.

630   KE
INTERNATIONAL CENTRE FOR RESEARCH IN AGROFORESTRY. ANNUAL REPORT. 1979. a. free. International Centre for Research in Agroforestry, P.O. Box 30677, Nairobi, Kenya. TEL 254-2-521450. FAX 254-2-521001. TELEX 22048. E-mail: icraf@cgnet.com. Ed. Helen Van Houten. R&P contact: Helen Van Houten. adv. contact: Helen Van Houten. circ. 3,000. **Document type:** corporate report.

INTERNATIONAL COMMISSION ON IRRIGATION AND DRAINAGE. CONGRESS REPORTS. see ENGINEERING — Hydraulic Engineering

INTERNATIONAL COMMISSION ON IRRIGATION AND DRAINAGE. REPORT. see WATER RESOURCES

INTERNATIONAL COTTON ADVISORY COMMITTEE. PROCEEDINGS. see TEXTILE INDUSTRIES AND FABRICS

338.1   FR   ISSN 0074-5863
INTERNATIONAL FEDERATION OF AGRICULTURAL PRODUCERS. GENERAL CONFERENCE PROCEEDINGS. (Editions in English, French) 1946. biennial; latest 31th. International Federation of Agricultural Producers - Federation Internationale des Producteurs Agricoles, 21 rue Chaptal, 75009 Paris, France. TEL 45-26-05-53. FAX 48-74-72-12. TELEX 281210. **Document type:** proceedings.
 Description: Report on the deliberations of IFAP biennial general conference, the World Farmers' Congress.

INTERNATIONAL FLYING FARMER. see AERONAUTICS AND SPACE FLIGHT

630 338.91   UK   ISSN 1357-9258
INTERNATIONAL INSTITUTE FOR ENVIRONMENT AND DEVELOPMENT. SUSTAINABLE AGRICULTURE PROGRAMME. GATEKEEPER SERIES. 1987. 3/yr. £3. International Institute for Environment and Development (IIED), Sustainable Agriculture Programme, 3 Endsleigh St., London WC1H 0DD, England. TEL 44-171-388-2117. FAX 44-171-388-2826. TELEX 317210 BUREAU G. **Document type:** monographic series, academic/scholarly publication.
 Description: Publishes research aimed at policy makers on promoting the development of socially and environmentally aware agriculture.

630 338.91   UK   ISSN 1358-3875
INTERNATIONAL INSTITUTE FOR ENVIRONMENT AND DEVELOPMENT. SUSTAINABLE AGRICULTURE PROGRAMME. RESEARCH SERIES. 1993. irreg., latest vol.3. £5. International Institute for Environment and Development (IIED), Sustainable Agriculture Programme, 3 Endsleigh St., London WC1H 0DD, England. TEL 44-171-388-2117. FAX 44-171-388-2826. TELEX 317210 BUREAU G. **Document type:** monographic series, academic/scholarly publication.
 Description: Reports on the collaborative research projects to promote and support the development of socially and environmentally aware agriculture.

630   NR   ISSN 1013-0322
S540.8.I57
INTERNATIONAL INSTITUTE OF TROPICAL AGRICULTURE. ANNUAL REPORT AND RESEARCH HIGHLIGHTS. French edition (ISSN 1115-8891) 1984. a. $10. International Institute of Tropical Agriculture (IITA), Oyo Rd., P.M.B. 5320, Ibadan, Oyo State, Nigeria. TEL 234-2-241-2626. TELEX 31417 TROPIB NG. E-mail: iita@cgnet.com. Ed. Kim Atkinson. **Indexed:** Irr.& Drain.Abstr., Maize Abstr. **Document type:** corporate report.
 —CISTI.
 Formed by the merger of (1976-1984): International Institute of Tropical Agriculture. Annual Report (ISSN 0257-8387); (1968-1984): International Institute of Tropical Agriculture. Research Highlights (ISSN 0331-4340)

630   II   ISSN 0254-8755
             CODEN: IJTADD
INTERNATIONAL JOURNAL OF TROPICAL AGRICULTURE. (Text in English) 1983. q. Rs.300($70) to individuals; institutions Rs.600($130). Vidya International Publishers, 8-16 New Campus, Haryana Agricultural University, Hissar 125004, Haryana, India. TEL 75354. Ed. R.D. Laura. adv.; bk.rev. circ. 1,000. (back issues avail.) **Indexed:** Biol.Abstr., Chem.Abstr., Cott.& Trop.Fibr.Abstr., Curr.Cont., Field Crop Abstr., Food Sci.& Tech.Abstr., Herb.Abstr., Hort.Abstr., Maize Abstr., Potato Abstr., Ref.Zh., Rice Abstr., Seed Abstr., Soils & Fert., Sorghum & Millets Abstr., Sugar Ind.Abstr., Triticale Abstr., Weed Abstr. **Document type:** academic/scholarly publication.
 —BLDSC (4542.696100); CASDDS; Ei; UnCover.
 Description: Original research papers, critical reviews and short communications dealing with all aspects of fundamental and applied tropical agriculture.

630 011   US
INTERNATIONAL SOCIETY OF CITRICULTURE. PROCEEDINGS. 1973. irreg. price varies. International Society of Citriculture, c/o Dir. Charlie Coggins, Department of Botany and Plant Sciences, University of California, Riverside, CA 92521-0124. TEL 909-787-4412. FAX 909-787-4437. E-mail: charles.coggins@ucr.edu. circ. 1,000. (back issues avail.) **Indexed:** Biol.Abstr., Curr.Adv.Ecol.Sci., Hort.Abstr. **Document type:** proceedings.
 Refereed Serial

INTERNATIONAL TREE CROPS JOURNAL; the journal of agroforestry. see FORESTS AND FORESTRY

630   CL
INVESTIGACION Y PROGRESO AGROPECUARIO KAMPENAIKE. 1988. irreg. $4.50 (foreign $6). Instituto de Investigaciones Agropecuarias, Estacion Experimental Kampenaike, Casilla 439, Correo 3, Santiago, Chile. circ. 1,000.

630   US   ISSN 0097-3416
             CODEN: IWRBBR
IOWA AGRICULTURE AND HOME ECONOMICS EXPERIMENT STATION. RESEARCH BULLETIN. 1911. irreg. exchange basis. Iowa State University of Science and Technology, 304 Curtiss Hall, Ames, IA 50011. TEL 515-294-5616. FAX 515-294-8662. Ed. Carol A. Greiner. charts; illus.; stat.; cum.index; circ. controlled. (back issues avail.) **Indexed:** Bibl.Agri., Biol.Abstr., Chem.Abstr., Curr.Cont., Ref.Zh. **Document type:** bulletin.
 —Linda Hall.
 Description: Includes reports of research in the agricultural and biological sciences of interest primarily to scientific and professional workers.

630   US   ISSN 0361-199X
             CODEN: IWSRBC
IOWA AGRICULTURE AND HOME ECONOMICS EXPERIMENT STATION. SPECIAL REPORT. 1936. irreg. exchange basis. Iowa State University of Science and Technology, 304 Curtiss Hall, Ames, IA 50011. TEL 515-294-5616. FAX 515-294-8662. (Co-sponsor: Iowa Cooperative Extension Service in Agriculture and Home Economics) Ed. Carol A. Greiner. charts; illus.; stat.; cum.index. (back issues avail.) **Indexed:** Bibl.Agri., Biol.Abstr., Curr.Cont., Nutr.Abstr., Ref.Zh., Sci.Cit.Ind. **Document type:** monographic series.
 —Linda Hall.
 Formerly: Agricultural and Home Economics Experiment Station. Special Report (ISSN 0097-5125)
 Description: Includes papers, technical and semitechnical reports in the agricultural and biological sciences of interest primarily to specialized audiences.

630   US   ISSN 0021-051X
IOWA FARM BUREAU SPOKESMAN. 1934. w. membership. (Iowa Farm Bureau Federation) Spokesman Press, Inc., 606 Eighth St., Grundy Center, IA 50638. TEL 319-824-5454. FAX 515-225-5419. Ed. Daryl Jahn; Pub. Charles M. Allen. adv. contact: John Doak. charts; illus.; circ. 107,486 (paid). (tabloid format) **Document type:** newspaper.

630   US
IOWA FARMER TODAY. 1984. w. $28 (effective 1995). Gazette Company, Box 5279, Cedar Rapids, IA 52406. TEL 319-398-8461. FAX 319-398-8482. E-mail: IFT@FYIowa.infi.net; URL: http://www.fyiowa.com/ift/. Ed. Lori Leonard; Pub. Stephen L. DeWitt. adv. contact: Terry Reilly. circ. 73,000. **Document type:** trade publication.
 Description: Covers Iowa's farmers and agribusiness. Contains production, policy, equipment, marketing and rural living information.

IOWA R E C NEWS. see ENERGY — Electrical Energy

630   IR   ISSN 1013-9885
             CODEN: IAGRE5
IRAN AGRICULTURAL RESEARCH/TAHQIQAT KISHAVARZAI-I IRAN. (Text in English; summaries in English, Persian) 1981. s-a. $50 to individuals; institutions $100 (effective 1998). Shiraz University, College of Agriculture, Shiraz, Iran. TEL 98-71-28193. FAX 98-71-28193. Ed. M. Khosh-Khui. R&P contact: J. Jamalian. (also avail. in microform) **Indexed:** Anim.Breed.Abstr., Biol.Abstr., Dairy Sci.Abstr., Field Crop Abstr., Helminthol.Abstr., Herb.Abstr., Hort.Abstr., Nutr.Abstr., Rev.Appl.Entomol. **Document type:** academic/scholarly publication.
 —CASDDS; Linda Hall.
 Supersedes: Iranian Journal of Agricultural Research (ISSN 0376-4524)
 Description: Publishes original research articles and notes pertaining to agricultural science.
 Refereed Serial

630   IR   ISSN 1017-5652
             CODEN: IRJADJ
IRANIAN JOURNAL OF AGRICULTURAL SCIENCES. (Text in Persian; abstracts in English) 1969. q. Rs.1000 to individuals; students Rs.800. University of Teheran, College of Agriculture, Centre for Scientific and Technical Publications, Karaj, Iran. Ed. H. Oloumi-Sadeghi. circ. 1,000. **Indexed:** Biol.Abstr., Field Crop Abstr., Irr.& Drain.Abstr., Meteor.& Geostrophys.Abstr., Seed Abstr., Soyabean Abstr., Triticale Abstr., World Agri.Econ.& Rural Sociol.Abstr.
 Formerly: University of Teheran. Agricultural College Publication.
 Description: Presents technical research studies in the agricultural sciences. Discusses ways of improving productivity in terms of crop yield and livestock.

IRANIAN JOURNAL OF PLANT PATHOLOGY/BIMARIHAYE GUIAHI. see BIOLOGY — Botany

630   IE   ISSN 0791-3001
IRELAND. CENTRAL STATISTICS OFFICE. ESTIMATED OUTPUT, INPUT AND INCOME ARISING IN AGRICULTURE. a. I£2. Central Statistics Office, Skehard Rd., Cork, Ireland. TEL 353-21-359000. FAX 353-21-359090. E-mail: information@cso.ie; URL: http://www.cso.ie. **Document type:** government publication.
 Former titles: Ireland Central Statistics Office. Agricultural Output; Ireland Central Statistics Office. Estimated Gross and Net Agricultural Output; Ireland Central Statistics Office. Estimates of the Quantity and Value of Agricultural Output (ISSN 0075-0557)

630   IE   ISSN 0791-0177
S219
IRELAND. MINISTER FOR AGRICULTURE & FOOD. ANNUAL REPORT. a. Stationery Office, Dublin, Ireland. **Indexed:** Anim.Breed.Abstr. **Document type:** government publication.
 Former titles (until 1988): Ireland. Minister for Agriculture. Annual Report (ISSN 0332-1088); (until 1977): Ireland. Minister for Agriculture and Fisheries. Annual Report (ISSN 0075-0646)

638.1   IE   ISSN 0021-1079
THE IRISH BEEKEEPER. 1947. m. £10. Federation of Irish Beekeeping Associations, St. Ives, Kilcrea Park, Magazine Rd., Cork, Ireland. TEL 021-542614. (Subscr. to: S. Reddy, Manager, 8 Tower View Park, Kildare, Ireland) Ed. E. O'Sullivan. circ. 1,200. **Indexed:** Apic.Abstr.

AGRICULTURE

630   IE   ISSN 0790-4568
IRISH COOPERATIVE ORGANIZATION SOCIETY. ANNUAL REPORT. 1895. a. I£5. Irish Cooperative Organization Society Ltd., Plunkett House, 84 Merrion Sq., Dublin 2, Ireland. TEL 353-1-6764783. FAX 353-1-6624502. Ed. Gregory Tierney. R&P contact: Gregory Tierney. circ. controlled. **Document type:** corporate report.
    Formerly: Irish Agricultural Organization Society. Annual Report (ISSN 0075-0719)

630   IE   ISSN 0021-1168
IRISH FARMERS' JOURNAL. 1948. w. I£61 (N. Ireland I£61; U.K. I£64; European Union I£140; rest of world I£174.50) (effective 1997). Agricultural Trust, Irish Farm Centre, Bluebell, Dublin 12, Ireland. TEL 353-1-4501166. FAX 353-1-4520876. Ed. Matthew Dempsey. R&P contact: Michael Moroney. adv. contact: John Gill. bk.rev. circ. 74,821. (reprint service avail. from UMI) **Document type:** newspaper, trade publication.

630   IE   ISSN 0332-2408
IRISH FARMERS MONTHLY. 1977. m. £12. Irish Food Publishers Ltd., 31 Deansgrange Rd., Blackrock, Co. Dublin, Ireland. FAX 896406. Ed. William Ryan. adv.; bk.rev. circ. 118,000.

630   IE   ISSN 0791-6833
CODEN: IAFREY
IRISH JOURNAL OF AGRICULTURAL AND FOOD RESEARCH. 1961. 2/yr. I£50 (effective 1996 & 1997). Teagasc, 19 Sandymount Ave., Dublin 4, Ireland. TEL 353-1-6688188. FAX 353-1-6688023. Ed. J.P. Hanrahan. illus.; stat.; index. circ. 1,300. **Indexed:** Agri.Eng.Abstr., Anim.Breed.Abstr., ASCA, Biol.Abstr., Chem.Abstr., Curr.Cont., Dairy Sci.Abstr., Excerp.Med., Food Sci.& Tech.Abstr., Forest.Abstr., Forest Prod.Abstr., Geo.Abstr., Helminthol.Abstr., Herb.Abstr., Ind.Sci.Rev., Nutr.Abstr., Sci.Cit.Ind., Triticale Abstr., Vet.Bull., W.R.C.Inf. **Document type:** academic/scholarly publication.
    ●Also available online.
    —BLDSC (4571.850000); CASDDS; CISTI; Genuine Article; UMI; UnCover. **CCC.**
    Incorporated (in 1991): Irish Journal of Food Science and Technology (ISSN 0332-0375);
    Formerly: Irish Journal of Agricultural Research (ISSN 0578-7483)

IRRIGATION NEWS. see WATER RESOURCES

631.7   GW   ISSN 0342-7188
S612   CODEN: IRSCD2
IRRIGATION SCIENCE. Online edition (GW ISSN 1432-1319) (Text in English) 1978. q. DM.616 (foreign DM.620.60) (effective 1998). Springer-Verlag, Heidelberger Platz 3, 14197 Berlin, Germany. TEL 49-30-82787-0. FAX 49-30-82787448. E-mail: subscriptions@ springer.de; URL: http://link.springer.de. (Subscr. in N. America to: Springer-Verlag New York, Inc., 333 Meadowlands Pkwy., Secaucus, NJ 07094. TEL 212-460-1500. FAX 212-473-6272) Ed. Gerald Stanhill. adv. (also avail. in microform from UMI; reprint service avail. from ISI) **Indexed:** Agri.Eng.Abstr., ASCA, Chem.Abstr., Cott.& Trop.Fibr.Abstr., Curr.Cont., Eng.Ind., Environ.Abstr., Herb.Abstr., Hort.Abstr., Ind.Sci.Rev., Int.Abstr.Oper.Res., Irr.& Drain.Abstr., Maize Abstr., Rice Abstr., Sci.Cit.Ind., Sel.Water Res.Abstr., Soils & Fert., Sorghum & Millets Abstr., Soyabean Abstr., Triticale Abstr., W.R.C.Inf. **Document type:** academic/scholarly publication.
    ●Also available online.
    —BLDSC (4581.580000); CASDDS; CISTI; Ei; Genuine Article; Linda Hall; SWETS; UMI; UnCover. **CCC.**
    Description: Emphasis is placed on physical and chemical aspects of water status and movement in the plant-soil-atmosphere system.

IRRIGAZIONE E DRENAGGIO. see WATER RESOURCES

630   SY
IRSHAD AL-ZIRAI. 6/yr. Ministry of Agriculture, Damascus, Syria. adv.

630   CN   ISSN 0823-7735
ISLAND FARMER. 1974. w. Island Press Ltd., P.O. Box 790, Montague, PE C0A 1R0, Canada. TEL 902-838-2515. FAX 902-838-4392. adv. contact: Barb Donnelly. circ. 2,261. (tabloid format)

ISRAEL. METEOROLOGICAL SERVICE. MONTHLY AGROCLIMATOLOGICAL REPORT. see METEOROLOGY

630   IS
ISRAEL. RURAL PLANNING AND DEVELOPMENT AUTHORITY. AGRICULTURAL AND RURAL ECONOMIC REPORT. (Text in Hebrew) a. free. Ministry of Agriculture, Rural Planning and Economic Development, P.O. Box 7011, Hakirya, Tel-Aviv, Israel. circ. 500.
    Former titles: Israel. Rural Planning and Development Authority. Agricultural and Rural Development Report; Israel. Agriculture and Settlement Planning and Development Center. Agricultural and Rural Development Report; Israel. Agricultural and Settlement Planning and Development Center. Statistical Series for the Agricultural Year (ISSN 0075-0964); Israel. Agricultural and Settlement Planning and Development Center. Statistical Series of the Budgetary Year (ISSN 0075-1294)

630 338.95694   IS   ISSN 0793-4971
ISRAEL AGRITECHNOLOGY FOCUS. (Text in English) 1993. q. IS.79($28.90) Global Link Ltd., P.O. Box 57179, Tel Aviv 61571, Israel. TEL 972-3-5628511. FAX 972-3-5628512. Ed. Nicky Blackburn; Pub. Tamara Genosar. R&P contact: Michael Eilan. adv. contact: Haim Heller. charts; illus.; stat.; tr.lit.; index. (back issues avail.) **Document type:** trade publication.
    Formerly: Focus on Israel Agritechnology.
    Description: Covers farming technology and agriculture and agricultural R&D in Israel, business ventures and investments in agriculture.

630   IT   ISSN 0021-275X
CODEN: IAGRAZ
ITALIA AGRICOLA. 1864. q. L.80000. REDA - Edizioni per l'Agricoltura S.r.l., Via Tor Sapienza 172, 00155 Rome, Italy. TEL 39-6-2280077. Ed. Boris Carlo Fischetti. adv.: B&W page L.1570000, color page L.2860000. bibl.; charts; illus.; stat.; tr.lit.; index. circ. 25,000. **Indexed:** Anim.Breed.Abstr., Biol.Abstr., Chem.Abstr., Fababean Abstr., Field Crop Abstr., Forest.Abstr., Forest Prod.Abstr., Geo.Abstr., Helminthol.Abstr., Herb.Abstr., Hort.Abstr., Ind.Vet., Maize Abstr., Ornam.Hort., Plant Breed.Abstr., Rural Recreat.Tour.Abstr., Sorghum & Millets Abstr., World Agri.Econ.& Rural Sociol.Abstr.
    —CASDDS.

630   IT   ISSN 1120-8945
S235
ITALY. ISTITUTO NAZIONALE DI STATISTICA. STATISTICHE DELL'AGRICOLTURA, ZOOTECNIA E MEZZI DI PRODUZIONE. 1940. a. L.35000 (effective 1993). Istituto Nazionale di Statistica, Via Cesare Balbo 16, Rome, Italy. FAX 39-6-46735198. circ. 1,500. **Document type:** government publication.
    Former titles (until 1985): Italy. Istituto Centrale di Statistica. Statistiche Agrarie (ISSN 1120-8937); (until 1983): Italy. Istituto Centrale di Statistica. Annuario di Statistica Agraria (ISSN 0075-1669); (until 1950): Annuario Statistico dell'Agricoltura Italiana (ISSN 1120-8929).

630.5   JA   ISSN 0579-2746
CODEN: IDNHAR
IWATE DAIGAKU NOGAKUBU HOKOKU/IWATE UNIVERSITY. FACULTY OF AGRICULTURE. JOURNAL. 1953. s-a. Iwate Daigaku Nogakubu - Iwate University, Faculty of Agriculture, Morioka 020, Iwate-ken, Japan. **Indexed:** Sport Fish.Abstr., Wild.Rev., Zoo.Rec.
    —BLDSC (4742.000000).

IWATE HORTICULTURE EXPERIMENT STATION. BULLETIN. see AGRICULTURE — Crop Production And Soil

630   JA   ISSN 1340-6108
CODEN: TARSDD
J I R C A S INTERNATIONAL SYMPOSIUM SERIES. (Text in English) 1967. a. Ministry of Agriculture, Forestry and Fisheries, Japan International Research Center for Agricultural Sciences - Norinsuisan-sho Kokusai Norinsuisangyo Kenkyu Center, Tsukuba-shi, Ibaraki-ken 305, Japan. E-mail: head@ss.jircas.affrc.go.jp; URL: http://ss.jircas.affrc.go.jp/index.sjis.html. (reprint service avail. from ISI) **Indexed:** Rice Abstr. **Document type:** government publication, proceedings.
    —BLDSC (4669.175000); CASDDS.
    Formerly (until no.26, 1993): Tropical Agriculture Research Series (ISSN 0388-9386).

630   JA   ISSN 1340-7686
J I R C A S JOURNAL; for scientific papers. (Text in English) 1971. s-a. Ministry of Agriculture, Forestry and Fisheries, Japan International Research Center for Agricultural Sciences - Norinsuisan-sho Kokusai Norinsuisangyo Kenkyu Center, Tsukuba, Ibaraki 305, Japan. TEL 0298-38-6304. E-mail: head@ss.jircas.affrc.go.jp; URL: http://ss.jircas.affrc.go.jp/index.sjis.html. Dir. Nobuyoshi Maeno.
    —BLDSC (4669.176000); UnCover.
    Formerly (until 1994): Tropical Agriculture Research Center. Technical Bulletin (ISSN 0388-9394)

630   II   ISSN 0021-3713
J N K V V NEWS. (Text in English) 1967. q. free. Jawaharlal Nehru Krishi Vishwa Vidyalaya, c/o Information and Public Relations Office, Jabalpur 482004, India. Ed. S.D.N. Tiwari. circ. 1,100.

630   II   ISSN 0021-3721
S17   CODEN: JNRJAW
J N K V V RESEARCH JOURNAL. (Text in English) 1967. q. $6. Jawaharlal Nehru Krishi Vishwa Vidyalaya, c/o Information and Public Relations Office, Jabalpur 482004, India. Ed. Dr. K.G. Nema. adv.; bk.rev. circ. 500. **Indexed:** Anim.Breed.Abstr., Biol.Abstr., Chem.Abstr., Field Crop Abstr., Herb.Abstr., Hort.Abstr., Ind.Vet., Nutr.Abstr., Plant Breed.Abstr., Rev.Appl.Entomol., Rev.Plant Path., Soils & Fert., Vet.Bull.
    —CASDDS.

630   JM
JAMAICA AGRICULTURAL SOCIETY. MINUTES OF THE HALF-YEARLY MEETING. s-a. Jamaica Agricultural Society, N. Parade, Kingston, Jamaica, W.I.

JAPAN. MINISTRY OF AGRICULTURE, FORESTRY AND FISHERIES. NATIONAL FOOD RESEARCH INSTITUTE. REPORT. see FOOD AND FOOD INDUSTRIES

630 634.9   JA   ISSN 0446-5458
JAPAN. NORIN-SHO NENPO/JAPAN. MINISTRY OF AGRICULTURE AND FORESTRY. ANNUAL REPORT. (Text in Japanese) 1953. a. 5800 Yen. (Association of Agriculture and Forestry Statistics) Government Publications Service Center, 2-1, 1-chome, Kasumigaseki, Chiyoda-ku, Tokyo 100, Japan. bk.rev.; illus.; stat. **Document type:** government publication.
    Supersedes: Norin Suisan Nenkan.

630   JA   ISSN 0021-3551
CODEN: JARJA9
JAPAN AGRICULTURAL RESEARCH QUARTERLY. Abbreviated title: J A R Q. (Text in English) 1966. q. Ministry of Agriculture, Forestry and Fisheries, Japan International Research Center for Agricultural Sciences - Norinsuisan-sho Kokusai Norinsuisangyo Kenkyu Center, Tsukuba, Ibaraki 305, Japan. TEL 0298-38-6304. FAX 0298-38-6316. TELEX 3652456-TARCJP-J. E-mail: head@ss.jircas.affrc.go.jp; URL: http://ss.jircas.affrc.go.jp/index.sjis.html. charts; illus.; stat.; index. circ. 2,000. (reprint service avail. from ISI) **Indexed:** Agri.Eng.Abstr., Agroforest.Abstr., Anim.Breed.Abstr., ASCA, Biol.Abstr., Chem.Abstr., Crop Physiol.Abstr., Curr.Cont., Dairy Sci.Abstr., Excerp.Med., Field Crop Abstr., Food Sci.& Tech.Abstr., Forest.Abstr., Forest Prod.Abstr., Helminthol.Abstr., Herb.Abstr., Hort.Abstr., Ind.Vet., Irr.& Drain.Abstr., Maize Abstr., Nutr.Abstr., Ornam.Hort., Plant Breed.Abstr., Potato Abstr., Poult.Abstr., Protozool.Abstr., Rev.Plant Path., Rice Abstr., Seed Abstr., Soils & Fert., Sorghum & Millets Abstr., Vet.Bull., Weed Abstr. **Document type:** government publication.
    —BLDSC (4647.780000); CASDDS; Genuine Article; Linda Hall; UnCover.
    Description: Disseminates information on the achievements and trends of agricultural research in Japan.

630   FR   ISSN 0396-7425
JEUNES AGRICULTEURS. 1947. m. 240 F. Centre National des Jeunes Agriculteurs, 14 rue La Boetie, 75008 Paris, France. TEL 33-1-42651751. FAX 33-1-47426284. Ed. Philippe Kroslakova. R& contact: Philippe Kroslakova. adv. contact: Philippe Clavier. **Document type:** newspaper.

AGRICULTURE

630   CC   ISSN 1002-1302
JIANGSU NONGYE KEXUE/JIANGSU AGRICULTURAL SCIENCES. (Text in Chinese; summaries in English) 1979. bi-m. (Jiangsusheng Nongye Kexueyuan - Jiangsu Academy of Agricultural Sciences) Jiangsu Nongye Kexue Bianjibu, Xiaolinwei, Nanjing, Jiangsu 210014, People's Republic of China. Ed. Ma Yikang. adv. **Document type:** academic/scholarly publication.
—BLDSC (4668.456000).

630   CC   ISSN 1000-4440
JIANGSU NONGYE XUEBAO/JIANGSU JOURNAL OF AGRICULTURAL SCIENCES. (Text in Chinese; abstracts in English) 1985. q. Y4 per no. Jiangsu Sheng Nongye Kexueyuan - Jiangsu Academy of Agricultural Sciences, Xiaolingwei, Nanjing, Jiangsu 210014, People's Republic of China. TEL 86-25-4390285. Ed. Gao Liangzhi. **Document type:** academic/scholarly publication.
●Also available on CD-ROM.
—BLDSC (4668.459000).
Description: Contains research papers on various aspects of agricultural sciences.
Refereed Serial

630   CC   ISSN 1000-5684
S19   CODEN: JNDXUEB
JILIN NONGYE DAXUE XUEBAO/JILIN UNIVERSITY OF AGRICULTURE. JOURNAL. (Text in Chinese) q. $120. Jilin Nongye Daxue - Jilin University of Agriculture, Donghuan Lunan, Changchun, Jilin 130118, People's Republic of China. TEL 86-431-4510901. Ed. Xingkui Fu. **Document type:** academic/scholarly publication.
—BLDSC (4809.594000).

630 635 634.9   DK   ISSN 0906-7043
JORD OG VIDEN; agronomer - hortonomer - forstkandidater - landskabsarkitekter. 1855. fortn. DKK 750 (foreign DKK 900) (effective 1997). Danmarks Jordbrugsvidenskabelige Kandidatforbund, Strandvejen 863, DK-2930 Klampenborg, Denmark. TEL 45-39-97-01-00. FAX 45-39-63-88-11. Ed. Marianne Tinggaard. adv.: B&W page DKK 13728, color page DKK 20728; trim 185 x 264; adv. contact: Bente Nielsen. bk.rev.; bibl.; charts; illus.; index. circ. 5,705. cols./p.: 4. **Indexed:** Field Crop Abstr., Herb.Abstr., Hort.Abstr., Soils & Fert., Weed Abstr. **Document type:** bulletin, proceedings, trade publication.
—BLDSC (4673.655000).
Former titles (until 1992): Ugeskrift for Jordbrug (ISSN 0106-0546); (until Jan. 1979): Ugeskrift for Agronomer, Hortonomer, Forstkandidater og Licentiater; Ugeskrift for Agronomer og Hortonomer; Ugeskrift for Agronomer (ISSN 0041-5774); Horticultura (ISSN 0018-5272)

630   JO
JORDAN. DEPARTMENT OF STATISTICS. AGRICULTURAL STATISTICAL YEARBOOK AND AGRICULTURAL SAMPLE SURVEY. (Text in Arabic and English) 1966. a. $15. Department of Statistics, P.O. Box 2015, Amman, Jordan. TEL 962-6-842171. FAX 962-6-833518. TELEX 24117 STATIS JO. **Document type:** government publication.

630 634.9   DK   ISSN 0107-6108
JORDBRUG OESTJYLLAND (MIDT): SAMTLIGE LANDBRUG, SKOVBRUG OG GARTNERIER. 1980. fortn. Jordbrug Oestjylland (Midt), c/o Bo Eriksson, Fussingsvej 21, 8700 Horsens, Denmark. adv.; illus.

338.1 338.3
JORDBRUG OG FISKERI; den aarlige rapport om jordbrugets og fiskeriets erhvervsmaessige forhold. (Includes supplement) 1982. a. DKK 85. Landbrugs- og Fiskeriministeriet - Ministry of Agriculture and Fisheries, Slotsholmsgade 10, DK-1216 Copenhagen K, Denmark. TEL 45-33-92-33-01. FAX 45-33-14-50-42. TELEX 27157 MINAG DK. (Dist. by: Statens Information, DK-1364 Copenhagen K) circ. 1,500. **Document type:** government publication.
Formerly (until 1994): Jordbrug (ISSN 0108-884X)
Description: Annual report from the Danish Ministry of Agriculture and Fisheries, describing the economic and political development regarding agriculture and fisheries in Denmark, the EEC and internationally.

630   SW   ISSN 0345-5718
JORDBRUKSAKTUELLT. 1962. 18/yr. SEK 80 (effective 1991). Jordbruksaktuellt, P.O. Box 8120, S-700 08 Oerebro, Sweden.

630   FR   ISSN 0021-7778
JOURNAL DE LA CORSE AGRICOLE. 1965. m. 8 F. (Mutualite Sociale Agricole de la Corse) Imprimerie Siciliano, B.P. 255, 20179 Ajaccio, Corsica, France. TEL 95-21-01-84. FAX 95-21-37-49. circ. 3,800.

630 658   FR   ISSN 0446-9739
JOURNAL DU FERMIER ET DU METAYER. 1948. m. 170 F. (effective 1997). F.N.S.E.A., Section Nationale des Fermiers et Metayers, 11 rue de la Baume, 75008 Paris, France. Ed. Sabine Lagarde. adv.

JOURNAL OF AGRICULTURAL AND ENVIRONMENTAL ETHICS. see *PHILOSOPHY*

630   US   ISSN 1049-6505
S494.5.I47   CODEN: JFOIEU
JOURNAL OF AGRICULTURAL & FOOD INFORMATION. q. $36 to individuals (Canada $46.80; elsewhere 50.40); institutions $85 (Canada $110.50; elsewhere $119.50); libraries $85 (Canada $110.50; elsewhere $119.50) (effective 1997-1998). Haworth Press, Inc., 10 Alice St., Binghamton, NY 13904. TEL 607-722-5857; 800-342-9676. FAX 607-722-6362. E-mail: getinfo@haworth.com; URL: http://www.haworth.com. Ed. Robyn Frank; Pub. Bill Cohen. R&P contact: Ruthann Heath. adv.: B&W page $300; trim 4 3/8 x 7 1/8; adv. contact: Jackie Blakeslee. (also avail. in microform from HAW,UMI; reprint service avail. from HAW) **Indexed:** Bibl.Agri., Environ.Abstr., Food Sci.& Tech.Abstr., Human Resour.Abstr., INSPEC, LISA, Lod.Restr.& Tour.Ind. **Document type:** academic/scholarly publication.
—BLDSC (4920.050000); AskIEEE; Haworth; KR SourceOne; SWETS; UnCover.
Formerly (until 1991): Journal of Food and Agricultural Info.
Description: Provides a forum for the communication of research, innovative practice, and informed opinion on all aspects of agricultural and food information.
Refereed Serial

JOURNAL OF AGRICULTURAL EDUCATION. see *EDUCATION*

630   II   ISSN 0256-6524
JOURNAL OF AGRICULTURAL ENGINEERING. (Text in English) 1964. q. Rs.400($70) Indian Society of Agricultural Engineers, Satya Mansion, Flat nos. 305-306, Community Centre, Ranjit Nagar, New Delhi 100 008, India. TEL 11-5709003. Ed. A.P. Bhatnagar. adv.; bk.rev.; bibl.; charts; illus. circ. 1,000. **Indexed:** Int.Abstr.Oper.Res., Soils & Fert.

JOURNAL OF AGRICULTURAL ENTOMOLOGY. see *BIOLOGY — Entomology*

JOURNAL OF AGRICULTURAL LENDING. see *BUSINESS AND ECONOMICS — Banking And Finance*

JOURNAL OF AGRICULTURAL METEOROLOGY/NOGYO KISHO. see *METEOROLOGY*

630   CH   ISSN 0376-477X
           CODEN: CHNCDB
JOURNAL OF AGRICULTURAL RESEARCH OF CHINA. Key Title: Zhonghua Nongye Yanjiu. (Text in Chinese and English) 1950. q. free. Taiwan Agricultural Research Institute, 189 Chung-cheng Rd., Wufeng, Taichung, Taiwan, Republic of China. FAX 866-4-333-8162. Pub. Chien-Yih Lin. **Indexed:** Bio-Contr.News & Info., Biol.Abstr., Crop Physiol.Abstr., Field Crop Abstr., Helminthol.Abstr., Herb.Abstr., Hort.Abstr., Maize Abstr., Ornam.Hort., Plant Breed.Abstr., Potato Abstr., Poult.Abstr., Rev.Appl.Entomol., Rev.Plant Path., Rice Abstr., Seed Abstr., Soils & Fert., Sorghum & Millets Abstr., Soyabean Abstr., Trop.Oil Seeds Abstr., Weed Abstr. **Document type:** academic/scholarly publication.
—BLDSC (4922.870000); CASDDS.
Formerly (until vol.23, 1974): Journal of Taiwan Agricultural Research (ISSN 0022-4847)

363.11963   US   ISSN 1074-7583
▼**JOURNAL OF AGRICULTURAL SAFETY AND HEALTH.** 1995. q. $70.50 to non-members (foreign $77.50); members $37 (foreign $44) (effective 1997). American Society of Agricultural Engineers, 2950 Niles Rd., St. Joseph, MI 49085-9659. TEL 616-429-0300. FAX 616-429-3852. E-mail: hq@asae.org; URL: http://asae.org/pubs/period.html. Ed. Pamela DeVore-Hansen. circ. 400. **Document type:** trade publication.
—BLDSC (4922.980000); UnCover.
Description: Focuses on the unique needs and concerns of safety and health as they relate to agriculture.
Refereed Serial

630   UK   ISSN 0021-8596
S3   CODEN: JASIAB
JOURNAL OF AGRICULTURAL SCIENCE. 1905. 8/yr. £306($528) (effective 1998). Cambridge University Press, Edinburgh Bldg., Shaftesbury Rd., Cambridge CB2 2RU, England. TEL 44-1223-312393. FAX 44-1223-315052. TELEX 851817256. E-mail: information@cup.cam.ac.uk; URL: http://www.cup.cam.ac.uk. (N. American addr.: Cambridge University Press, Journals Dept., 40 W. 20th St., New York, NY 10011. TEL 212-924-3900. FAX 212-691-3239) Ed. W.J. Whittington. R&P contact: Linda Nicol. adv. contact: Rebecca Symons. bk.rev.; bibl.; charts; illus.; index. (also avail. in microform from UMI,PMC; back issues avail.; reprint service avail. from SWZ) **Indexed:** Agroforest.Abstr., Anim.Breed.Abstr., Apic.Abstr., ASCA, Bibl.Agri., Bio-Contr.News & Info., Biol.Abstr., Biol.& Agr.Ind., Biotech.Abstr., CAD CAM Abstr., Chem.Abstr., Cott.& Trop.Fibr.Abstr., Crop Physiol.Abstr., Curr.Adv.Genetics & Molec.Biol., Curr.Biotech.Abstr., Curr.Cont., Dairy Sci.Abstr., Ecol.Abstr., Environ.Abstr., Environ.Per.Bibl. (1973-1994), Excerp.Med., Fababean Abstr., Field Crop Abstr., Food Sci.& Tech.Abstr., Geo.Abstr.P.G., Helminthol.Abstr., Herb.Abstr., Hort.Abstr., IDA, Ind.Sci.Rev., Ind.Vet., Int.Abstr.Biol.Sci., Irr.& Drain.Abstr., NAA, Nutr.Abstr., Pig News & Info., Plant Breed.Abstr., Plant Grow.Reg.Abstr., Potato Abstr., Poult.Abstr., Protozool.Abstr., Rev.Plant Path., Sci.Cit.Ind., Seed Abstr., Sel.Water Res.Abstr., So.Pac.Per.Ind., Soils & Fert., Sorghum & Millets Abstr., Sport Fish.Abstr., Sugar Ind.Abstr., Triticale Abstr., Trop.Oil Seeds Abstr., Vet.Bull., Weed Abstr., Wild.Rev., Zoo.Rec. **Document type:** academic/scholarly publication.
—BLDSC (4923.000000); CASDDS; CISTI; Ei; EMDOCS; Genuine Article; KR SourceOne; Linda Hall; SWETS; UMI; UnCover. **CCC.**
Description: Covers research in pure and applied sciences relating to agricultural problems.

630   IQ   ISSN 1012-3474
           CODEN: JAWPEM
JOURNAL OF AGRICULTURE AND WATER RESEARCH. PLANT PRODUCTION. (Text in Arabic, English) 1986. s-a. ID.5($15) to individuals; institutions $50. Scientific Research Council, Agricultural and Water Resources Research Center, Jadiriyah P.O. Box 2441, Baghdad, Iraq. TELEX 213976 SR IK. Ed. Semir A. Al-Shaker. circ. 500. **Indexed:** Agrindex, Biol.Abstr., Chem.Abstr., Herb.Abstr.
—CASDDS.

630   IQ   ISSN 1012-3466
           CODEN: JWAPEW
JOURNAL OF AGRICULTURE AND WATER RESOURCES RESEARCH. ANIMAL PRODUCTION. (Text in Arabic, English) 1986. s-a. ID.5($15) to individuals; institutions $50. Scientific Research Council, Agriculture and Water Resources Research Center, Jadiriyah P.O. Box 2441, Baghdad, Iraq. TELEX 213976 SR IK. Ed. Semir A. Al-Shaker. circ. 500. **Indexed:** Agrindex, Anim.Breed.Abstr., Biol.Abstr., Chem.Abstr., Ind.Vet., Poult.Abstr., Vet.Bull.
—CASDDS.

630   IQ   ISSN 1012-3482
           CODEN: JWSREQ
JOURNAL OF AGRICULTURE AND WATER RESOURCES RESEARCH. SOIL AND WATER RESOURCES. (Text in Arabic, English) 1986. s-a. ID.5($15) to individuals; institutions $50. Scientific Research Council, Agricultural and Water Resources Research Center, Jadiriyah P.O. Box 2441, Baghdad, Iraq. TELEX 213976 SR IK. Ed. Semir A. Al-Shaker. circ. 500. **Indexed:** Agri.Eng.Abstr., Agrindex, Biol.Abstr., Chem.Abstr., Herb.Abstr., Irr.& Drain.Abstr.
—CASDDS.

AGRICULTURE

630   AT   ISSN 0021-8618
S397
JOURNAL OF AGRICULTURE OF WESTERN AUSTRALIA. 1894. q. Aus.$29 (foreign Aus.$35) (effective 1996). Agriculture Western Australia, Baron-Hay Court, South Perth, W.A. 6151, Australia. TEL 09-368-3333. Ed. K.M. Howes. R&P contact: G.P. Ayling. illus.; index. circ. 8,000. (back issues avail.) **Indexed:** Anim.Breed.Abstr., Biol.Abstr., Chem.Abstr., Dairy Sci.Abstr., Field Crop Abstr., Food Sci.& Tech.Abstr., Herb.Abstr., Hort.Abstr., Ind.Vet., Irr.& Drain.Abstr., Nutr.Abstr., Plant Breed.Abstr., Rev.Appl.Entomol., Rev.Plant Path., Soils & Fert., Triticale Abstr., Vet.Bull., VITIS, Weed Abstr. **Document type:** government publication.
—BLDSC (4925.200000); Linda Hall; UnCover.
Description: Agricultural extension journal featuring research and articles concerning the agricultural industry.

JOURNAL OF AGROMEDICINE. see OCCUPATIONAL HEALTH AND SAFETY

638.1   UK   ISSN 0021-8839
CODEN: JACRAQ
JOURNAL OF APICULTURAL RESEARCH. 1962. q. £95($170) (effective 1996). International Bee Research Association, 18 North Rd., Cardiff CF1 3DY, Wales. TEL 44-1222-372409. FAX 44-1222-665522. E-mail: ibra@cardiff.ac.uk Ed. I.E. Rinderer. adv.: page £134; trim 200x 130; adv. contact: P.A. Munn. bibl.; charts; illus.; index. circ. 500. (back issues avail.) **Indexed:** Apic.Abstr., ASCA, Biol.Abstr., Chem.Abstr., Curr.Cont., Food Sci.& Tech.Abstr., Helminthol.Abstr., Rev.Appl.Entomol., Sugar Ind.Abstr. **Document type:** academic/scholarly publication.
—BLDSC (4939.600000); CASDDS; Linda Hall; SWETS; UnCover. **CCC**.
Description: Contains original scientific research on bees and beekeeping.
Refereed Serial

630   US   ISSN 1051-0834
JOURNAL OF APPLIED COMMUNICATIONS. 1990. q. $75 (effective 1996). Agricultural Communicators in Education, Box 35, Evinston, FL 32633. TEL 352-392-9588. FAX 352-392-8583. E-mail: amw@gnv.ifas.ufl.edu; URL: http://ems.ifas.ufl.edu/jac/jac.html. bk.rev.; index; circ. 740 (paid). (back issues avail.) **Document type:** trade publication.
—UnCover.
Refereed Serial

JOURNAL OF ENVIRONMENTAL SCIENCE AND HEALTH. PART B: PESTICIDES, FOOD CONTAMINANTS, AND AGRICULTURAL WASTES. see ENVIRONMENTAL STUDIES

636 575.1   IT   ISSN 0394-9257
SB123   CODEN: JGBREX
JOURNAL OF GENETICS & BREEDING. (Text in English) 1946. q. L.180000($116) (effective Jan. 1993). Istituto Sperimentale per la Cerealicoltura, Via Cassia, 176, 00191 Rome, Italy. TEL 39-6-3295705. FAX 39-6-36306022. Ed. A. Bianchi. adv.; bk.rev.; charts; illus.; index; circ. 300 (controlled). **Indexed:** Anim.Breed.Abstr., Biol.Abstr., Chem.Abstr., Cott.& Trop.Fibr.Abstr., Crop Physiol.Abstr., Curr.Adv.Genetics & Molec.Biol., Fababean Abstr., Field Crop Abstr., Food Sci.& Tech.Abstr., Forest.Abstr., Herb.Abstr., Hort.Abstr., INIS Atomind., Irr.& Drain.Abstr., Maize Abstr., Plant Breed.Abstr., Plant Grow.Reg.Abstr., Potato Abstr., Rice Abstr., Seed Abstr., Sorghum & Millets Abstr., Soyabean Abstr., Triticale Abstr. **Document type:** academic/scholarly publication.
—BLDSC (4990.200000); CASDDS; EMDOCS; SWETS.
Formerly: Genetica Agraria (ISSN 0016-6685)
Description: Focuses on biochemical and molecular genetics, genetic fundamentals of breeding, breeding methodology and genetic aspects of "in vitro" culture.
Refereed Serial

JOURNAL OF IRRIGATION AND DRAINAGE. see ENGINEERING — Civil Engineering

630 624   JA   ISSN 0287-8607
JOURNAL OF IRRIGATION ENGINEERING AND RURAL PLANNING. (Text in English) 1982. s-a. 6000 Yen. Japanese Society of Irrigation, Drainage and Reclamation Engineering - Nogyo Doboku Gakkai, Nogyo Doboku Kaikan, 34-4, Shinbashi 5-chome, Minato-ku, Tokyo, Japan. **Indexed:** Eng.Ind.

630   II   ISSN 0378-2395
CODEN: JMAUDA
JOURNAL OF MAHARASHTRA AGRICULTURAL UNIVERSITIES. (Text in English) 1976. 3/yr. Rs.400($40) Poona Agricultural College, Poona 411 005, India. TEL 327033. (Co-sponsors: Mahatma Phule Agricultural University Rahuri; Marathwada Krishi Vidyapeeth Parbhani; Konkan Krishi Vidyapeeth, Dapoli; Punjabrao Krishi Vidyapeeth, Akola) Ed. K.N. Warhal. bk.rev.; charts; illus.; stat. circ. 1,200. (back issues avail.) **Indexed:** Agri.Eng.Abstr., Biol.Abstr., Chem.Abstr., Cott.& Trop.Fibr.Abstr., Dairy Sci.Abstr., Field Crop Abstr., Forest.Abstr., Herb.Abstr., Hort.Abstr., INIS Atomind., Irr.& Drain.Abstr., Maize Abstr., Plant Breed Abstr., Plant Grow.Reg.Abstr., Potato Abstr., Rev.Appl.Entomol., Rice Abstr., Rural Ext.Educ.& Tr.Abstr., Seed Abstr., Soils & Fert., Sorghum & Millets Abstr., Soyabean Abstr., Sugar Ind.Abstr., Triticale Abstr., Trop.Oil Seeds Abstr., Weed Abstr., World Agri.Econ.& Rural Sociol.Abstr. **Document type:** academic/scholarly publication.
—BLDSC (4819.230000); CASDDS; Linda Hall.
Formerly (until 1976): Research Journal of Mahatma Phule Agricultural University (ISSN 0378-6404)
Refereed Serial

JOURNAL OF PALYNOLOGY. see BIOLOGY — Botany

630   US   ISSN 0890-8524
CODEN: JPRAEN
JOURNAL OF PRODUCTION AGRICULTURE. 1988. q. $61. American Society of Agronomy, Inc., 677 S. Segoe Rd., Madison, WI 53711. TEL 608-273-8080. FAX 608-273-2021. R&P contact: David M. Kral. adv. contact: Keith R. Schlesinger. **Indexed:** ASCA, Curr.Cont., Rice Abstr., Sel.Water Res.Abstr., SSCI.
—BLDSC (5042.656000); Ei; EMDOCS; Genuine Article; Linda Hall; SWETS; UnCover. **CCC**.
Description: Offers latest production-oriented information from a variety of agricultural fields. Some of the areas covered include: agronomy, crop science, soil science, range management, weed science, entomology, plant pathology, horticulture, and forestry.

JOURNAL OF RANGE MANAGEMENT; covering the study, management, and use of rangeland ecosystems and range resources. see BIOLOGY

630   II   ISSN 0971-1724
JOURNAL OF RESEARCH. (Text in English) 1989. s-a. Rs.25. Birsa Agricultural University, Ranchi 834 006, Bihar, India. Ed. A.A. Khan.
—BLDSC (5049.840000).
Formerly (until 1991): B A U Journal of Research (ISSN 0971-1201)

630   UK
JOURNAL OF RURAL MANAGEMENT AND HUMAN RESOURCES. vol.4, 1975. s-a. £10 to individuals; institutions £35 (effective 1997). Agricultural Manpower Society, University of Reading, Earley Gate, P.O. Box 236, Reading, Berks. RG6 2AT, England. TEL 44-1568-613175. Ed. M. Robinson. R&P contact: M. Robinson. adv. contact: M. Robinson. bk.rev. circ. 200. **Indexed:** Agri.Eng.Abstr., Dairy Sci.Abstr., Rural Ext.Educ.& Tr.Abstr., World Agri.Econ.& Rural Sociol.Abstr. **Document type:** academic/scholarly publication.
Former titles: Agricultural Manpower (ISSN 0260-2040); Journal of Agricultural Labour Science.
Description: Seeks to provide an outlet to put forward the results of new research, review papers, information, and commentary relevant to agricultural staffing.
Refereed Serial

JOURNAL OF SERICULTURAL SCIENCE OF JAPAN/NIPPON SANSHIGAKU ZASSHI. see BIOLOGY — Entomology

JOURNAL OF SOIL AND WATER CONSERVATION IN INDIA. see CONSERVATION

630 664   UK   ISSN 0022-5142
TX341   CODEN: JSFAAE
JOURNAL OF THE SCIENCE OF FOOD AND AGRICULTURE. 1950. m. $1245 (foreign $1245) (effective 1998). (Society of Chemical Industry) John Wiley & Sons Ltd., Journals, Baffins Ln., Chichester, W. Sussex PO19 1UD, England. TEL 44-1243-779777. FAX 44-1243-775878. E-mail: info-assets@wiley.co.uk; URL: http://www.wiley.co.uk. (Subscr. in the Americas to: John Wiley & Sons, Inc. 605 Third Ave., New York, NY 10158. TEL 212-850-6645. FAX 212-850-6021) Ed.Bd.; Pub. Ernest Kirkwood. adv.: B&W page £595, color page £1495; trim 297 x 210; adv. contact: Bob Kern. abstr.; bibl.; charts; illus.; index. circ. 1,250. (also avail. in microform from UMI; back issues avail.; reprint service avail. from ISI) **Indexed:** Agroforest.Abstr., Anim.Breed.Abstr., ASCA, Biol.Abstr., Biol.& Agr.Ind., Br.Tech.Ind., Cadscan, Chem.Abstr., Chem.Cit.Ind., Chem.Eng.Abstr., Cott.& Trop.Fibr.Abstr., Crop Physiol.Abstr., Curr.Adv.Biochem., Curr.Adv.Ecol.Sci., Curr.Biotech.Abstr., Curr.Cont., Dairy Sci.Abstr., Ecol.Abstr., Excerp.Med., Fababean Abstr., Field Crop Abstr., Food Sci.& Tech.Abstr., Geo.Abstr.H.G., Helminthol.Abstr., Herb.Abstr., Hort.Abstr., IDA, Ind.Med., Ind.Sci.Rev., Ind.Vet., Irr.& Drain.Abstr., Lead Abstr., Maize Abstr., Nutr.Abstr., Pig News & Info., Plant Breed.Abstr., Plant Grow.Reg.Abstr., Poult.Abstr., Rev.Plant Path., Rice Abstr., Rural Recreat.Tour.Abstr., Sci.Cit.Ind., Seed Abstr., Sel.Water Res.Abstr., So.Pac.Per.Ind., Soils & Fert., Sorghum & Millets Abstr., Soyabean Abstr., Sport Fish.Abstr., T.C.E.A., Triticale Abstr., Trop.Oil Seeds Abstr., Vet.Bull., VITIS, Weed Abstr., Wild.Rev., World Agri.Econ.& Rural Sociol.Abstr., Zincscan, Zoo.Rec. **Document type:** academic/scholarly publication.
—BLDSC (5055.000000); ADONIS; CASDDS; CISTI; Ei; EMDOCS; Genuine Article; KR SourceOne; Linda Hall; SWETS; UnCover. **CCC**.
Description: Publishes original research and critical reviews in agriculture and food science, with particular emphasis on interdisciplinary studies at the agriculture-food interface.
Refereed Serial

630   II   ISSN 0971-636X
CODEN: ARJKAQ
JOURNAL OF TROPICAL AGRICULTURE. (Text in English) 1962. s-a. Rs.150 (foreign $75) (effective 1997). Kerala Agricultural University, College of Horticulture, Vellanikkara 680 654, Trichur, Kerala, India. TEL 91-487-21822. FAX 91-487-399019. TELEX 887-268 KAU IN. (Dist. by: HPC Publisher's Distributors (Pvt.) Ltd., 4805-24, 1st Fl., Bharat Ram Rd., Darya Ganj, New Delhi 110 002, India. TEL 91-11-3254402. FAX 91-11-6863511) Ed. A.I. Jose. bk.rev.; charts; illus. circ. 500. (back issues avail.) **Indexed:** Agroforest.Abstr., Biol.Abstr., Chem.Abstr., Field Crop Abstr., Herb.Abstr., Hort.Abstr., INIS Atomind., Irr.& Drain.Abstr., Plant Breed.Abstr., Rev.Appl.Entomol., Rev.Plant Path., Rice Abstr., Rural Recreat.Tour.Abstr., Seed Abstr., Soils & Fert., Trop.Oil Seeds Abstr., Weed Abstr., World Agri.Econ.& Rural Sociol.Abstr. **Document type:** academic/scholarly publication.
—BLDSC (5070.660000); CASDDS.
Formerly (until vol.30, 1993): Agricultural Research Journal of Kerala (ISSN 0002-1628)
Refereed Serial

630   MY   ISSN 1394-9829
S3
JOURNAL OF TROPICAL AGRICULTURE AND FOOD SCIENCE. (Text in English or Malay) 1973. s-a. $40 to individuals; institutions $50. Malaysian Agricultural Research & Development Institute - Institut Penyelidikan dan Kemajuan Pertanian Malaysia, P.O. Box 12301, General Post Office, 50774 Kuala Lumpur, Malaysia. TEL 03-9437236 FAX 03-9482216. TELEX MARDI-MA-37115. Ed. Rohani Mahmood. bibl.; illus. circ. 1,000. **Indexed:** Agroforest.Abstr., Food Sci.& Tech.Abstr., Herb.Abstr., Hort.Abstr., Pig News & Info., Poult.Abstr., Rice Abstr., Soils & Fert.
—BLDSC (5373.210000); CASDDS.
Former titles (until vol.24, no.2, 1996): M A R D I Research Journal - Jurnal Penyelidikan M A R D I (ISSN 0128-0686); (until vol.15, no.2, 1987): M R D I Research Bulletin (ISSN 0126-5709)
Refereed Serial

AGRICULTURE

638.1 SZ ISSN 0368-4040
JOURNAL SUISSE D'APICULTURE. 1879. 10/yr. 48 SFr. Societe Romande d'Apiculture, c/o Joseph Girard, Parqueterie 7, CH-1680 Romont, Switzerland. Ed. Robert Fauchere. adv. circ. 4,500. **Indexed:** Apic.Abstr., Chem.Abstr. **Document type:** bulletin.
  Description: Focuses on bee culture.

630 SP
JOVENES AGRICULTORES. 1978. m. (11/yr.). 5000 ptas. (effective 1996). Asociacion Agraria Jovenes Agricultores (ASAJA), Agustin de Bethancourt, 17-2o, 28003 Madrid, Spain. TEL 34-1-5336764. FAX 34-1-5349286. Ed. Pilar Sanchez Munoz. adv.: B&W page 77000 ptas., color page 125000 ptas.; adv. contact: Fernanda Pastor. illus. circ. 22,000.

630 FR ISSN 0222-979X
JURA AGRICOLE ET RURAL. w. 455 rue du Colonel de Casteinau, B.P. 420, 39006 Lons-le-Saunier Cedex, France. TEL 84-24-44-70. Ed. Marc Derudet. circ. 4,665.

630 GW ISSN 0945-2370
S674.43.G3
K T B L ARBEITSPAPIERE. irreg., no.200, 1993. DM.20. Kuratorium fuer Technik und Bauwesen in der Landwirtschaft e.V., Bartingstr. 49, 64289 Darmstadt, Germany. TEL 06151-7001-0. FAX 06151-7001123. **Document type:** monographic series.

630 GW ISSN 0173-2811
K T B L - SCHRIFTEN. 1947. irreg, no.357, 1993. price varies. Kuratorium fuer Technik und Bauwesen in der Landwirtschaft e.V., Bartingstr. 49, 64289 Darmstadt, Germany. TEL 06151-7001-0. FAX 06151-700123. (Co-sponsor: Bundesministerium fuer Ernaehrung, Landwirtschaft und Forsten) charts; illus. circ. 800. **Indexed:** Agri.Eng.Abstr., Dairy Sci.Abstr., Excerp.Med., Geo.Abstr., Herb.Abstr., Ind.Vet., Pig News & Info., Rural Recreat.Tour.Abstr., Soils & Fert., Vet.Bull., World Agri.Econ.& Rural Sociol.Abstr. **Document type:** monographic series.
  —BLDSC (5118.768000).

630 AU
KAERNTER BAUER. 1844. w. S.400 (foreign S.500) (effective 1997). Kammer fuer Land- und Forstwirtschaft Kaernten, Museumgasse 5, A-9020 Klagenfurt, Austria. TEL 43-463-5850. FAX 43-463-5850389. Ed. Rudolf Fritzer. adv.; bk.rev.; circ. 30,000 (controlled). **Document type:** consumer publication.

630.2 JA ISSN 0374-8804
CODEN: KNKHA2
KAGAWA PREFECTURE AGRICULTURAL EXPERIMENT STATION. BULLETIN. (Text in Japanese; summaries in English and Japanese) 1949. a. donation. Kagawa Prefecture Agricultural Experiment Station - Kagawa-ken Nogyo Shikenjo, Busshozan-cho, Takamatsu-shi, Kagawa-ken, Japan. TEL 81-878-89-1121. FAX 81-878-89-1125. Ed. Kazunori Obika. circ. 600. **Indexed:** Biol.Abstr. **Document type:** bulletin.
  —BLDSC (2597.852000); CASDDS.

630 JA ISSN 0453-0853
S19 CODEN: MAKUA6
KAGOSHIMA UNIVERSITY. FACULTY OF AGRICULTURE. MEMOIRS/KAGOSHIMA DAIGAKU NOGAKUBU KIYO. 1952. a. exchange basis. Kagoshima Daigaku, Nogakubu - Kagoshima University, Faculty of Agriculture, 21-24 Korimoto 1-chome, Kagoshima 890, Japan. TEL 81-99-285-7111. FAX 81-99-285-8525. Ed. Takeomi Etoh. bibl.; charts; illus. circ. 1,000. **Indexed:** Abstr.Hyg., Biol.Abstr., Chem.Abstr., Crop Physiol.Abstr., Curr.Adv.Ecol.Sci., Excerp.Med., Field Crop Abstr., Forest.Abstr., Forest Prod.Abstr., Ind.Vet., Ornam.Hort., Plant Breed.Abstr., Rev.Med.& Vet.Mycol., Seed Abstr., Soyabean Abstr., Vet.Bull. **Document type:** academic/scholarly publication.
  —BLDSC (5592.000000); CASDDS; UnCover.

KAGOSHIMAKEN NOGYO KISHO GEPPO/KAGOSHIMA PREFECTURE. MONTHLY REPORT OF METEOROLOGY. see METEOROLOGY

338.1 US
KANSAS AGRICULTURE ANNUAL REPORT AND FARM FACTS. 1872. a. free. State Board of Agriculture, 901 S. Kansas Ave., Topeka, KS 66612-1280. TEL 913-296-3556. FAX 913-296-2247. Ed. Carole A. Jordan. illus.; stat. circ. 8,000. **Document type:** government publication.
  —Linda Hall.
  Former titles (until 1981): Kansas. State Board of Agriculture. Annual Report and Farm Facts (ISSN 0196-0954); Formed by the merger of: Kansas. State Board of Agriculture. Annual Report; Farm Facts; Formerly (until 1976): Kansas Agriculture Report (ISSN 0091-6900); Supersedes: Kansas. State Board of Agriculture. Biennial Report to the Governor.

630 US ISSN 0091-9586
KANSAS COUNTRY LIVING. 1951. m. $8.40. Kansas Electric Cooperatives, Inc., Box 4267, Topeka, KS 66604. TEL 913-478-4554. FAX 913-478-4852. Ed. Larry Freeze. adv.; tr.lit. circ. 81,890. (processed) **Document type:** consumer publication.
  Formerly: Kansas Electric Farmer (ISSN 0022-8540)

630 US ISSN 0022-8575
KANSAS FARM BUREAU NEWS.* 1947. m. (combined May-Jun., Jul.-Aug.). membership. Kansas Farm Bureau, 2627 KFB Plaza, Manhattan, KS 66502-8155. TEL 913-537-2261. Ed. John Schlageck. adv.; bk.rev.; illus. circ. 50,000.

630 US
KANSAS LIVING.* q. Kansas Farm Bureau, 2627 K F B Plaza, Manhattan, KS 66502. Ed. John Schlageck. circ. 90,000.

630.7 367 US
KANSAS 4-H JOURNAL. 1950. 10/yr. $6. Kansas 4-H Foundation Inc., Umberger Hall, Rm. 116, Kansas State University, Manhattan, KS 66506-3417. TEL 913-532-5881. FAX 913-532-6963. Ed. Rhonda Atkinson. R&P contact: Rhonda Atkinson. adv.; bk.rev. circ. 13,200. **Document type:** newsletter.
  Description: Serves as a communication link for Kansas 4-H'ers.

630 II
KARSHAKAN. (Text in Malayalam) m. Rs.150 for 2 yrs.; newsstand price: Rs.8. Rashtra Deepika Ltd., Deepika Bldg., C.M.S. College Rd., P.B. No. 7, Kottayam 686 001, India. TEL 91-481-566706. FAX 91-481-567947. TELEX 0888-203 DPKA IN. adv.: page Rs.18000; 230 x 170. circ. 40,000.
  Description: Agricultural magazine.

630 II
▼**KARSHAKASREE;** farmers' monthly. (Text in Malayalam) 1995. m. Malayala Monorama Co. Ltd., P.O. Box 26, Kottayam 686 001, Kerala, India. TEL 91-481-563646. FAX 91-481-562479. TELEX 0888-201-MNR-IN. Ed. K.M. Mathew; Pub. Jacob Mathew. adv.: B&W page Rs.10000, color page Rs.20000. circ. 45,000.

630 TH ISSN 0075-5192
CODEN: KASJAP
KASETSART JOURNAL. (Text in English or Thai) 1961. s-a. Kasetsart University, Research and Development Institute, Bangkok 10900, Thailand. Ed. S. Panichsakpatana. **Indexed:** Asian-Pac.Econ.Lit., Chem.Abstr., Field Crop Abstr., Hort.Abstr., Ornam.Hort., Plant Breed.Abstr., Rev.Plant Path., Rice Abstr., Soyabean Abstr.
  —BLDSC (5086.651000); CASDDS.

630 TH ISSN 0125-3697
KASIKORN. 1928. m. Department of Agriculture, Bangkhen, Bangkok 10900, Thailand. Ed. Udom Simaban. TEL 02-579-5369.

630 SZ
KATHOLISCHER SCHWEIZERBAUER. 14/yr. St. Galler Str. 35, CH-9327 Tuebach, Switzerland. TEL 071-411795. Ed. Notker Angehr-Zahner. circ. 198,000.

630 FI ISSN 0022-9571
KAYTANNON MAAMIES. 1952. m. FIM 414. Yhtyneet Kuvalehdet Oy, Maistraatinportti 1, FIN-00240 Helsinki, Finland. TEL 358-0-156-6524. FAX 358-0-156-6515. TELEX 121364. Ed. Paavo Tuovinen. adv.: B&W page FIM 8500, color page FIM 12700. charts; illus.; index. circ. 25,061. **Document type:** trade publication.
  Description: For the professional farmer.

630 UK ISSN 0023-0022
KENT FARMER. 1952. m. County Farmers Publications Ltd., 55 Goldington Rd., Bedford MK40 3LU, England. TEL 0234-351401. FAX 0234-328614. Ed. N. Errington. adv. circ. 3,300.

630 US ISSN 0023-0219
KENTUCKY FARMER. 1864. m. $12 (foreign $25). Rural Press U S A, 7701 Six Forks Rd., Ste. 132, Raleigh, NC 27615. TEL 919-676-3276; 800-477-1737. FAX 919-676-9803. (Subscr. to: Box 150001, Raleigh, NC 27624) Ed. Wayne Harr; Pub. Jeff Tennant. adv.: B&W page $1515. charts; illus.; mkt.; pat. circ. 22,000. **Document type:** newspaper.

630 KE
KENYA. MINISTRY OF AGRICULTURE. SCIENTIFIC RESEARCH DIVISION. ANNUAL REPORT.* 1964? a. Ministry of Agriculture, Scientific Research Division, Nairobi, Kenya. (Subscr. to: Government Printing and Stationery Dept., Box 30128, Nairobi, KE) **Indexed:** Field Crop Abstr., Herb.Abstr., Rev.Plant Path.
  Formerly: Kenya. Ministry of Agriculture. Research Division. Annual Report.

630 KE ISSN 0023-0421
KENYA FARMER. (Text in English; occasionally in Swahili) 1954. m. EAs.120. Agricultural Society of Kenya, P.O. Box 30176, Nairobi, Kenya. Ed. Fred Nyanga-Origa. adv. circ. 20,000.
  Incorporates: Mkulima wa Kenya.

KEXUE ZHIFU YU SHENGHUO/SCIENCE PROSPERITY AND LIFE. see SCIENCES: COMPREHENSIVE WORKS

630 II ISSN 0023-1088
KHETI. (Text in Hindi) 1948. m. Rs.84($20) Indian Council of Agricultural Research, Krishi Anusandhan Bhavan, Pusa, New Delhi 110012, India. Ed. Ramesh Dutta Sharma. adv.; bk.rev.; charts; illus.; index. circ. 45,100. **Indexed:** Agri.Eng.Abstr.
  Incorporates: Pashupalan (ISSN 0031-2606)
  Description: Caters to the needs of progressive farmers, research workers and students.

630.24 668.6 RU
CODEN: KSKHE7
KHIMIYA V SEL'SKOM KHOZYAISTVE. 1963. bi-m. $81. Gosudarstvennyi Agropromyshlennyi Komitet, Sadovaya-Spaskaya, 18, kom.611, 107807 Moscow, Russia. TEL 7-095-2072410. Ed. Irina I. Prokhorova. bk.rev.; bibl.; index. circ. 3,000. **Indexed:** Biol.Abstr., Biotech.Abstr., Chem.Abstr., Dairy Sci.Abstr., Field Crop Abstr., Food Sci.& Tech.Abstr., Herb.Abstr., Hort.Abstr., Maize Abstr., Nutr.Abstr., Pollut.Abstr., Potato Abstr., Poult.Abstr., Rev.Plant Path., Soils & Fert., Sugar Ind.Abstr., Weed Abstr.
  —BLDSC (0394.540000); CASDDS; Linda Hall.
  Former titles (until 1992): Khimizatsiya Sel'skogo Khozyaistva (ISSN 0235-2516); (until 1988): Khimiya v Sel'skom Khozyaistve (ISSN 0023-1185)

630 BW
S13
KHOZYAIN (MINSK). 1925. m. Soyuz Agrarnikov Belorussii, Pereulok Instrumental'nyi, 11, 220012 Minsk, Belarus. TEL 66-18-91. Ed. I.F. Kravtsov. circ. 25,500.
  Formerly (until 1991): Sel'skoe Khozyaistvo v Belorussii (ISSN 0131-6311)

630 RU ISSN 0868-7188
S13
KHOZYAIN (MOSCOW). 1963. bi-m. $67 (effective 1997). Ministerstvo Sel'skogo Khozyaistva i Prodovol'stviya, Ul. Krizhanovskogo 15, Korpus 2, kom.426, 117218 Moscow, Russia. TEL 7-95-1299870. Ed. V.N. Mikheev. circ. 7,760.
  —BLDSC (0395.355000).
  Formerly (until no.11, 1990): Agropromyshlennyi Kompleks Rossii (ISSN 0235-2613)

630 KE
KILIMO NEWS. (Text in English) 1979. q. KShs.30 (effective Jul. 1994). Ministry of Agriculture, Agricultural Information Center, P.O. Box 14733, Nairobi, Kenya. Ed. James Wahome. adv. circ. 8,000. (also avail. in diskette format) **Document type:** newsletter, government publication.
  Description: Gathers and disseminates information on recent technologies farmers in Kenya can use to boost their crop production.

AGRICULTURE

630   SU   ISSN 1018-3590
KING SAUD UNIVERSITY. JOURNAL. AGRICULTURAL SCIENCES. Key Title: Majallat Jami'at as-Malik Sa'ud, al-'Ulum al-Zira'iyyah. (Other sections avail.: Administrative Sciences, Architecture and Planning, Arts, Computer and Information Sciences, Educational Sciences and Islamic Studies, Engineering Sciences, Science) (Text in Arabic, English) 1989. s-a. $10. King Saud University, University Libraries, P.O. Box 22480, Riyadh 11495, Saudi Arabia. TEL 966-1-4676148. FAX 966-1-4676162. TELEX 401019 KSU SJ. Ed. Khalid A. Al-Hamoudi. R&P contact: Saad A. Al-Dobaian. charts; illus. circ. 2,000. **Indexed:** Food Sci.& Tech.Abstr. **Document type:** academic/scholarly publication.
—BLDSC (4810.887000).
Refereed Serial

630   JA   ISSN 0385-311X
CODEN: KCNKDK
KINKI CHUGOKU AGRICULTURAL RESEARCH/KINKI CHUGOKU NOGYO KENKYU. (Text in Japanese; table of contents in English and Japanese) 1962. s-a. 2000 Yen (effective 1991). Kinki Chugoku Agricultural Research Association, c/o Chugoku National Agricultural Experiment Station, Nishi Fukatsu-machi, Fukuyama-shi 721, Japan. FAX 81-849-24-7893. Ed. Koroh Koizumi. circ. 1,150. **Indexed:** Poult.Abstr.
—BLDSC (5096.530000).
Formerly (until 1973): Chugoku Agricultural Research (ISSN 0009-6229)

630   JA   ISSN 0919-3022
CODEN: KDNKES
KINKI DAIGAKU NOGAKU SOGO KENKYUJO HOKOKU/KINKI UNIVERSITY. INSTITUTE FOR COMPREHENSIVE AGRICULTURAL SCIENCES. BULLETIN. (Text in Japanese) 1963. a. Kinki Daigaku, Nogaku Sogo Kenkyujo, Nara 631, Japan. TEL 81-742-43-1511. FAX 81-742-43-2970. Ed. Seiji Ouchi. circ. 600. **Document type:** academic/scholarly publication.
—BLDSC (2580.263000); CASDDS.
Formerly (until 1993): Kinki Daigaku Shokuhin Kagaku Kenkyujo Hokoku - Kinki University. Research Institute for Food Science. Bulletin (ISSN 0453-8897)

630   US   ISSN 0023-1746
HD1751
KIPLINGER AGRICULTURE LETTER. 1929. fortn. $54. Kiplinger Washington Editors, Inc., 1729 H St., N.W., Washington, DC 20006. TEL 202-887-6400. FAX 202-778-8976. URL: http://www.kiplinger.com/. Ed. Melissa Bristow. **Document type:** trade publication.
●Also available online.
—CCC.
Description: News and summary forecasts for agriculturists and businesspersons who deal with agriculture.

630   II
KISAN WORLD. (Text in English) 1974. m. Rs.20($16) Sakthi Sugars Ltd., 101 Mount Rd., Guindy, Madras 600 032, India. TEL 91-422-2350212. Ed. N. Mahalingam; Pub. K.P. Ganesan. adv.; bk.rev.; illus. circ. 30,000. **Indexed:** Field Crop Abstr., Herb.Abstr. **Document type:** newspaper.

630   IR
KISHAVARAZ. vol.10, 1989. m. Rs.350 per no. F. Gulafra, Vali Asar Rd., Opp. Fatimi Rd., Blk.4, Teheran, Iran.

KISHO TO NOSAGYO/METEOROLOGY AND AGRICULTURE. see *METEOROLOGY*

630   XV   ISSN 0023-2238
KMECKI GLAS. 1943. w. 987 din.($77) (effective Mar. 1991). C Z P Kmecki Glas, Celovska 43, P.O. Box 47, 61001 Ljubljana, Slovenia. TEL 061-328670. FAX 061-321-651. Ed. Rajko Ocepek. adv. circ. 35,000.

630 570   JA   ISSN 0452-2370
CODEN: KNGKAP
KOBE UNIVERSITY. FACULTY OF AGRICULTURE. SCIENCE REPORTS. (Text in English and Japanese; summaries in English) 1953. a. exchange basis. Kobe Daigaku, Nogakubu - Kobe University, Faculty of Agriculture, 1 Rokkodai-cho, Nada-ku, Kobe-shi, Hyogo-ken 657, Japan. FAX 078-871-8450. circ. 800. **Indexed:** Biol.Abstr., Food Sci.& Tech.Abstr.
—BLDSC (8152.377000); CASDDS.

630 570   JA   ISSN 0389-0473
CODEN: KDGHBF
KOCHI UNIVERSITY. AGRICULTURAL SCIENCE. RESEARCH REPORTS. (Text in English and Japanese; summaries in English) 1968. a. free. Kochi Daigaku - Kochi University, Akebono-cho, Kochi-shi, Kochi-ken, Japan. TEL 0888-44-0111. FAX 0888-64-5200. **Indexed:** Biol.Abstr., Helminthol.Abstr., Hort.Abstr., Ornam.Hort., Rev.Plant Path. **Document type:** bulletin.
—BLDSC (7762.399500); CASDDS.

630 620   JA   ISSN 0450-6219
KOCHI UNIVERSITY. FACULTY OF AGRICULTURE. MEMOIRS. (Text in English and Japanese; summaries in English) 1956. a. free. Kochi Daigaku, Nogakubu - Kochi University, Faculty of Agriculture, Monobe, Nankoku-shi, Kochi-ken, Japan. FAX 0888-64-5200. **Indexed:** Biol.Abstr.

KOMPASS AGRIBUSINESSS AND FOOD AND BEVERAGE. see *BUSINESS AND ECONOMICS — Trade And Industrial Directories*

630.711 636.089   DK   ISSN 0109-4998
KONGELIGE VETERINAER- OG LANDBOHOEJSKOLE. HAANDBOG 1982 a DKK 30 Kongelige Veterinaer-og Landbohoejskole, Studerendes Raad, Copenhagen, Denmark. Ed. B. Rasmussen. circ. 1,500.
Formerly: Haandbog for Studerende ved Landbohoejskolen.

630   DK   ISSN 0106-8237
KONGELIGE VETERINAER- OG LANDBOHOEJSKOLE. JORDBRUGSTEKNISK INSTITUT. MEDDELELSE. irreg. price varies. D S R Boghandel, Thorvaldsensvej 40, 1871 Copenhagen V, Denmark. **Indexed:** Agri.Eng.Abstr.

KONGETSU NO TENKO TO NORIN SAGYO/MONTHLY NEWS OF WEATHER, AGRICULTURE AND FORESTRY. see *METEOROLOGY*

630   KO
CODEN: NSYPAS
KOREA (REPUBLIC). OFFICE OF RURAL DEVELOPMENT. RESEARCH REPORT. Key Title: Nongsa Siheom Yeon'gu Pogo. (Text in Korean; summaries in English) 1958. a. free. Ministry of Agriculture & Fishery, Office of Rural Development, Seodun-dong, Suweon, S. Korea. Ed. Kun Hwan Yun. circ. 1,230. (also avail. in microfiche) **Indexed:** Anim.Breed.Abstr., Excerp.Med., Hort.Abstr., Nutr.Abstr., Potato Abstr., Poult.Abstr., Vet.Bull.
—CASDDS.
Formerly: Korea (Republic). Office of Rural Development. Agricultural Research Report (ISSN 0075-6865)

KOTI. see *HOME ECONOMICS*

630   II   ISSN 0970-8650
KRISHAK JAGAT. (Text in Hindi) 1946. w. Rs.250. 43, Fire Brigade St., Sultania Rd., P.B No. 3, Bhopal 462 001, India. TEL 91-755-542466. FAX 91-755-510334. Ed. Vijay Kumar Bondriya. adv.: B&W page Rs.17000, color page Rs.34000; 420 x 280. bk.rev. circ. 45,457. **Document type:** newspaper.
Description: Coverage of agriculture, animal husbandry, dairy, poultry and other agro-industries.

630   II   ISSN 0023-4710
KRISHAK SAMACHAR. (Editions in English and Hindi) 1956. m. Rs.10($2) Bharat Krishak Samaj - Farmer's Forum, India, A-1 Nizamuddin West, New Delhi 110013, India. TEL 11-619508. Ed. K. Prabhakar Reddy. adv.; bk.rev.; abstr.; bibl.; charts; illus.; stat. circ. 12,000(English); 30,000(Hindi).

630   II
KRISHAK SANDESH. (Text in Hindi) 1987. fortn. newsstand price: Rs.2. 81-L Block, Sri Ganganagar 335001, India. TEL 24569. Ed. Santosh Sharma; Pub. Brij Bhushan Sharma. adv. pp./issue: 12.

630 634.9   SW   ISSN 0023-5350
S11
KUNGLIGA SKOGS- OCH LANTBRUKSAKADEMIENS TIDSKRIFT/ROYAL SWEDISH ACADEMY OF AGRICULTURE AND FORESTRY. JOURNAL/ACADEMIE ROYALE D'AGRICULTURE ET DE SYLVICULTURE DE SUEDE. ANNALES/KOENIGLICHE SCHWEDISCHE AKADEMIE DER LAND- UND FORSTWIRTSCHAFT. ZEITSCHRIFT. Includes: Kungliga Skogs- och Lantbruksakademiens Tidskrift. Supplement (ISSN 0075-7233) (Text in Swedish; summaries in English or German) 1862. 6/yr. SEK 100 includes irreg. supplements. Kungliga Skogs- och Lantbruksakademien - Royal Swedish Academy of Agriculture and Forestry, P.O. Box 6806, S-113 86 Stockholm, Sweden. TEL 46-87360900. FAX 322130. TELEX 19507 KSLAS. bibl.; charts; illus.; index. (back issues avail.) **Indexed:** Anim.Breed.Abstr., Biol.Abstr., Chem.Abstr., Dairy Sci.Abstr., Forest.Abstr., Forest Prod.Abstr., Ind.Vet., Nutr.Abstr., Pig News & Info., Potato Abstr., Rural Devel.Abstr., Soils & Fert., Sport Fish.Abstr., Triticale Abstr., Wild.Rev., World Agri.Econ.& Rural Sociol.Abstr. **Document type:** academic/scholarly publication.
—Linda Hall.
Former titles (until 1956): Kungl. Landtbruksakademiens Tidskrift; Kungl. Landtbruks-akademiens Handlingar och Tidskrift.

630   JA   ISSN 0023-5725
KUSUNOKI NOHO.* (Text in Japanese) 1947. m. 800 Yen($2.30) Nishimura Shoten, 1-10 Kanda-Nishiki-cho, Chiyoda-ku, Tokyo 101, Japan. Ed. Ikuo Uesugi. adv.; bk.rev.; abstr.; charts; illus.; index. circ. 800.

630   JA   ISSN 0451-1476
QP141.A1   CODEN: KDSKAF
KYOTO DAIGAKU SHOKURYO KAGAKU KENKYUSHO HOKOKU/KYOTO UNIVERSITY. RESEARCH INSTITUTE FOR FOOD SCIENCE. BULLETIN. (Text in English and Japanese; summaries in English) 1949. a. free. Kyoto University, Research Institute for Food Science - Kyoto Daigaku Shokuryo Kagaku Kenkyusho, c/o Akira Kimura, Uji, Kyoto 611, Japan. TEL 81-774-32-3111. FAX 81-774-33-3004. Ed. Makoto Kito. bk.rev. circ. 800. (back issues avail.) **Indexed:** Chem.Abstr., Curr.Adv.Ecol.Sci., Food Sci.& Tech.Abstr. **Document type:** academic/scholarly publication.
—BLDSC (2695.000000); CASDDS.

630   JA   ISSN 0075-7373
CODEN: KFGNAC
KYOTO-FURITSU DAIGAKU GAKUJUTSU HOKOKU: NOGAKU/KYOTO PREFECTURAL UNIVERSITY. SCIENTIFIC REPORTS: AGRICULTURE. (Text in Japanese) 1951. a. exchange basis only. Kyoto Prefectural University - Kyoto-furitsu Daigaku, Shimogamo Hangi-cho, Sakyo-ku, Kyoto 606, Japan. TEL 81-75-781-3131. FAX 81-75-723-2670. **Indexed:** Biol.Abstr., Crop Physiol.Abstr., Dairy Sci.Abstr., Field Crop Abstr., Food Sci.& Tech.Abstr., Forest.Abstr., Forest Prod.Abstr., Herb.Abstr., INIS Atomind., Nutr.Abstr., Plant Breed.Abstr., Rev.Appl.Entomol., Seed Abstr., Soils & Fert. **Document type:** academic/scholarly publication.
—BLDSC (8198.400000).

630   JA   ISSN 0388-2330
S405   CODEN: MAGKAO
KYOTO UNIVERSITY. COLLEGE OF AGRICULTURE. MEMOIRS/KYOTO DAIGAKU NOGAKUBU KIYO. (Text in English) 1926. s-a. exchange basis. Kyoto University, College of Agriculture - Kyoto Daigaku Nogakubu, Kitashirakawa Oiwake-cho, Sakyo-ku, Kyoto 606, Japan. FAX 075-753-6025. Ed. Kanji Nakato. circ. 700. **Indexed:** Abstr.Bull.Inst.Pap.Chem., Biol.Abstr., Dairy Sci.Abstr., Deep Sea Res.& Oceanogr.Abstr., Environ.Abstr., Food Sci.& Tech.Abstr., Forest.Abstr., Forest Prod.Abstr., Helminthol.Abstr., Herb.Abstr., Hort.Abstr., Irr.& Drain.Abstr., Plant Breed.Abstr., Rev.Appl.Entomol., Sel.Water Res.Abstr., Soils & Fert.
—CASDDS.

AGRICULTURE

630   JA   ISSN 0023-6152
CODEN: JFAKAU
KYUSHU UNIVERSITY. FACULTY OF AGRICULTURE. JOURNAL/KYUSHU DAIGAKU NOGAKUBU KIYO. (Text in English, French or German) 1923. q. exchange basis. Kyushu University, Faculty of Agriculture - Kyushu Daigaku Nogakubu, 6-10-1 Hakozaki, Higashi-ku, Fukuoka 812, Japan. Ed.Bd. bibl.; illus.; index. **Indexed:** ASCA, Biol.Abstr., Biotech.Abstr., Chem.Abstr., Curr.Adv.Ecol.Sci., Curr.Cont., Field Crop Abstr., Food Sci.& Tech.Abstr., Forest.Abstr., Forest Prod.Abstr., Helminthol.Abstr., Herb.Abstr., Hort.Abstr., Ind.Vet., Irr.& Drain.Abstr., Maize Abstr., Nutr.Abstr., Plant Breed.Abstr., Potato Abstr., Rev.Appl.Entomol., Rev.Plant Path., Soils & Fert., Soyabean Abstr., Sport Fish.Abstr., Vet.Bull., Weed Abstr., Wild.Rev., Zoo.Rec. **Document type:** academic/scholarly publication.
—BLDSC (4743.000000); CASDDS; Genuine Article; UnCover.

630   JA   ISSN 0915-499X
KYUSHU UNIVERSITY. INSTITUTE OF TROPICAL AGRICULTURE. BULLETIN/NETTAI NOGAKU KENKYU. (Text in English) 1975. a. exchange basis. Kyushu University, Institute of Tropical Agriculture - Kyushu Daigaku Nettai Nogaku Kenkyu Senta, 13 Hakazaki, Higashi-ku, Fukuoka 812-81, Japan. TEL 81-92-642-3076. FAX 81-92-642-3077. Ed. Hisashi Yahata. circ. 400. (back issues avail.) **Indexed:** Rev.Plant Path., Seed Abstr., Soils & Fert., Soyabean Abstr. **Document type:** academic/scholarly publication.
—BLDSC (2585.195000).

630   FR
L'AGRI.... 1947. w. 260 F. (foreign 400 F.) (effective 1997). 77 av. Victor Dilbiez, 66027 Perpignan Cedex, France. TEL 33-4-68850202. FAX 33-4-68852425. Ed. Jean-Pierre Cot. circ. 9,000 (paid). **Document type:** newspaper.

630   NE   ISSN 0927-6203
L T JOURNAAL. 1887. 16/yr. fl.97.50 to individuals; institutions fl.150 (effective 1994). Koninklijk Landbouwkundige Vereniging - Royal Society of Agricultural Sciences, Postbus 79, 6700 AB Wageningen, Netherlands. TEL 31-8730-83537. FAX 31-8730-83976. Ed. L.C.J. Slobbe. adv.; bk.rev.; abstr.; bibl.; charts; index; circ. 9,000 (paid). **Indexed:** Biol.Abstr., Chem.Abstr., Dairy Sci.Abstr., ELLIS, Excerp.Med., Field Crop Abstr., Food Sci.& Tech.Abstr., Geo.Abstr., Helminthol.Abstr., Herb.Abstr., Key to Econ.Sci., Nutr.Abstr., Rural Recreat.Tour.Abstr., Soils & Fert., World Agri.Econ. & Rural Sociol.Abstr. **Document type:** trade publication.
—BLDSC (5300.615000).
Former titles (until 1992): Landbouwkundig Tijdschrift (ISSN 0927-6955); (until 1983): Landbouwkundig Tijdschrift. P T (ISSN 0165-5221); Landbouwkundig Tijdschrift (ISSN 0023-7787); (until 1924): Cultura.

630   US   ISSN 0093-4909
LACKAWANNA - WAYNE - PIKE - SUSQUEHANNA FARM & HOME NEWS.* 1947. m. $5 for 3 yrs. Farm & Home Publications, 10 Lourdes Rd., Binghamton, NY 13905-4293. Ed. Bernard M. Swartz. adv.; illus.; stat. circ. 2,100.

630   UK   ISSN 0955-0011
LANCASHIRE FARMER. 1962. m. County Farmers Publications Ltd., 55 Goldington Rd., Bedford MK40 3LU, England. TEL 0234-351401. FAX 0234-328614. Ed. R. Bacon. adv. circ. 4,150.

630   US   ISSN 0023-7485
LANCASTER FARMING. 1955. w. $25 (effective 1997). 1 E. Main St., Box 609, Ephrata, PA 17522. TEL 717-394-3047. FAX 717-733-6058. Ed. Everett Newswanger; Pub. Robert Campbell. adv. contact: Gary Myer. bk.rev.; illus.; mkt. circ. 4,231,612. (tabloid format; also avail. in microform from UMI; reprint service avail. from UMI) **Document type:** newspaper, trade publication.

630   AT   ISSN 0023-7523
LAND. 1911. w. Aus.$147 (effective 1996). Land Newspaper Ltd., P.O. Box 999, North Richmond, N.S.W. 2754, Australia. TEL 61-45-70-4444. FAX 61-45-70-4649. Ed. Peter Austin. R&P contact: Ann Pender. adv. contact: Michael Boyd. bk.rev.; illus.; circ. 59,313 (paid). **Document type:** newspaper.

630   US   ISSN 0279-1633
THE LAND. 1976. w. free to qualified readers. Mankato Free Press Company, The Land, Box 3169, Mankato, MN 56002-3169. TEL 507-345-4523. E-mail: theland@ic.mankato.mn.us. Ed. Randy Frahm. R&P contact: Randy Frahm. adv.; bk.rev.; circ. 40,000. (tabloid format) **Document type:** newspaper.

LAND AKTUELL. see *POLITICAL SCIENCE*

630   UK
LAND CONTRACTOR. 4/yr. Huts Corner, Tilford Rd., Hindhead, Surrey GU26 6SF, England. TEL 0428-605360. FAX 0428-606351. Ed. Don Gomery. circ. 3,500.

630   BE
LANDBODE.* (Text in Flemish) 24/yr. Kapellelei 14, B-2510 Mortsel, Belgium. adv. circ. 5,500.

630   NE
LANDBOUW-ECONOMISCH INSTITUUT. ONDERZOEKVERSLAG. (Text in Dutch, occasionally in English) no.92, 1992. irreg., no.153, 1996. price varies. Landbouw-Economisch Instituut, Burg. Patijnlaan 19, 2585 BE The Hague, Netherlands. TEL 31-70-3308330. FAX 31-70-3615624. E-mail: postmaster@lei.dlo.nl; URL: http://www.lei.dlo.nl/lei. (back issues avail.) **Document type:** government publication.
Description: Publishes the results of statistical, econometric and environmental research on topics and issues pertaining to agriculture in the Netherlands and Europe.

630   NE   ISSN 0927-7838
HET LANDBOUWBLAD; agrarisch vakblad voor Friesland en Flevoland. 1903. w. (Sat.) fl.230. Fries-Flevolandse Land- en Tuinbouw Organisatie, Postbus 613, 8901 BK Leeuwarden, Netherlands. TEL 31-58-2133441. FAX 31-58-2126040. Ed. W. Dijkstra. adv.; B&W page fl.2156; color page fl.3556. bk.rev.; illus.; stat. circ. 16,000. cols./p.: 7. **Document type:** newspaper.
Formerly (until 1993): Fries Landbouwblad (ISSN 0016-1373)
Description: Covers agricultural, economic and social news and issues for farmers in Friesland and Flevoland.

630   SA   ISSN 0023-7779
LANDBOUWEEKBLAD. (Text in Afrikaans) 1919. w. R.260.40 (foreign R.802.05). National Magazines (Subsidiary of: National Media Ltd.), P.O. Box 1802, Cape Town 8000, South Africa. TEL 27-21-4062202. FAX 27-21-4062913. Ed. Pienaar Smit. adv.; bk.rev.; charts; illus. circ. 50,885. **Indexed:** Ind.S.A.Per., INIS Atomind. **Document type:** consumer publication.

630   SR
LANDBOUWPROEFSTATION SURINAME. JAARVERSLAG/AGRICULTURAL EXPERIMENT STATION SURINAME. ANNUAL REPORT. (Text in Dutch; summaries in English) 1903. a. fl.15. Department of Agriculture and Fisheries, Landbouwproefstation, P.O. Box 160, Paramaribo, Surinam. charts; illus.; stat. circ. 500. **Indexed:** Field Crop Abstr., Herb.Abstr., Hort.Abstr. **Document type:** government publication.

630   DK   ISSN 0900-0143
LANDBOVIRKE; tidsskrift for oekonomisk landbrug. 1967. m. Landbrugets Faelles Organisation, Lovbyvej 90, DK-8700 Horsens, Denmark. FAX 45-75-65-44-68. adv.; B&W page DKK 1700; trim 180 x 130.

630   DK   ISSN 0108-2744
LANDBRUG FYN; fynsk landbrugs eget blad. 1981. w. A R Forlaget, Postboks 40, DK-5550 Langeskov, Denmark. illus.

630.60489   DK   ISSN 0302-4946
S245
LANDBRUGSAARBOG. 1899. a. DKK 350 (effective 1997). Det Kgl. Danske Landhusholdningsselskab, Mariendalsvej 27, 2., DK-2000 Frederiksberg, Denmark. TEL 45-38-88-66-88. FAX 45-38-88-66-11. E-mail: NJF-GS@inet.uni-c.dk. Ed. Else Damsgaard.
Formerly (until 1966): Landoekonomisk Aarbog (ISSN 0105-0036)

630   DK   ISSN 0109-0240
LANDBRUGSMAGASINET. 1951. w. DKK 420. Danske Husmandsforeninger - Danish Family Farmers Association, Vester Farimagsgade 6, 1606 Copenhagen V, Denmark. TEL 33-129950. FAX 33-126362. Ed. Boerge Larsen. adv.; bk.rev.; abstr.; bibl.; charts; illus.; stat.; index. circ. 25,000. (reprint service avail.)
Formerly: Husmandshjemmet (ISSN 0018-8018)

630   SZ   ISSN 1420-5351
LANDFREUND. w. 90 SFr. Hallwag AG, Nordring 4, CH-3001 Bern, Switzerland. TEL 41-31-3323131. FAX 41-31-3314133. TELEX 912661-CH. Ed. Max Welter. circ. 14,704. **Document type:** newsletter.

630   GW   ISSN 0170-3412
LANDPOSTMAGAZIN; Monatsumschau fuer die Landwirtschaft. 1974. m. DM.9.60. Jahr-Verlag GmbH & Co., Jessenstr. 1, 22767 Hamburg, Germany. TEL 49-40-38906-0. FAX 49-40-38906302. Ed. Rolf Roosen. adv. contact: Waltraud Jante. circ. 85,600. **Document type:** trade publication.

630   DK   ISSN 0455-2741
LANDSBLADET. 1956. w. DKK 386. Danish Farmers' Union, Vester Farimagsgade 6, 1606 Copenhagen V, Denmark. TEL 45-33-112-22. FAX 45-33-11-31-48. Ed. Henrik Lisberg. adv. contact: Claus Moeller. circ. 65,618. (tabloid format)

630   FI
LANDSBYGDENS FOLK. (Text in Swedish) 1947. w. FIM 220 (effective 1997). Svenska Lantbruksproducenternas Centralfoerbund, Fredriksg. 61, SF-00100 Helsinki, Finland. TEL 358-0-694-0533. FAX 358-0-694-1358. Ed. Ulf Johansson. adv. contact: Bjarne Jansson. circ. 11,500. **Document type:** newspaper.
Formerly: Svenska Lantbruksproducenternas Centralfoerbund. Publication (ISSN 0355-0788)

LANDSCAPE HISTORY. see *HISTORY*

630   AU
LANDTECHNISCHE SCHRIFTENREIHE. irreg., no.192, 1993. S.130. Oesterreichisches Kuratorium fuer Landtechnik, Schwindgasse 5, A-1040 Vienna, Austria. TEL 0222-5053175. FAX 0222-505189116. adv. **Document type:** monographic series.

630   GW   ISSN 0023-8104
DAS LANDVOLK. s-m. DM.16. (Verband der Niedersaechsischen Landvolkes e.V.) Landbuch Verlag GmbH, Kabelkamp 6, 30179 Hannover, Germany. Ed. M. Beine. adv.; bk.rev. circ. 108,000. **Document type:** trade publication.
—CCC.
Description: Publication for farmers featuring news on agricultural economy, prices, market, production. Includes list of events.

630   UK   ISSN 1363-8300
LANDWARDS, the journal for professional engineers in agriculture, forestry, environment and amenity. 1944. q. £47 (effective 1998). Institution of Agricultural Engineers, West End Rd., Silsoe, Beds. MK45 4DU, England. TEL 44-1525-861096. FAX 44-1525-861660. E-mail: secretary@iagre.demon.co.uk; URL: http://www.cranfield.ac.uk/safe/iagre. Ed. Brian D. Whitney. R&P contact: Brian Whitney. adv. contact: Brian Whitney. bk.rev.; charts; illus.; stat.; index; circ. 2,300 (paid). (also avail. in microform from UMI) **Indexed:** Agri.Eng.Abstr., Field Crop Abstr., Int.Abstr.Oper.Res., Potato Abstr., Triticale Abstr. **Document type:** academic/scholarly publication.
—BLDSC (5153.660000); CISTI; UMI; UnCover.
Formerly (until 1996): Agricultural Engineer (ISSN 0308-5732); Which Incorporated (1938-1988): Soil and Water (ISSN 0309-023X); Which was formerly: Institution of Agricultural Engineers. Journal and Proceedings (ISSN 0020-3238)
Description: Contains conference papers, refereed scientific papers and technical articles.
Refereed Serial

AGRICULTURE

630 634.9 AU ISSN 0047-4010
DIE LANDWIRTSCHAFT; Fachzeitschrift fuer die Gesamtinteressen der Land- und Forstwirtschaft. 1971. m. S.220 (foreign S.347). (Niederoesterreichische Landes-Landwirtschaftskammer) Oesterreichischer Agrarverlag GmbH, Inkustr. 1-7, A-3400 Klosterneuburg, Austria. TEL 02243-333006. FAX 02243-3330056. Ed. Franz Gebhart. adv.; charts; illus. circ. 105,000. **Indexed:** Plant Breed.Abstr.

630 LU
LANDWIRTSCHAFT AKTUELL. m. 10 rue Principale, 9463 Stolzembourg, Luxembourg. TEL 84-67-7.

630 SZ
LANDWIRTSCHAFTLICHE ANGESTELLTE. 20/yr. Kantonsstr. 40, Postfach 181, CH-6048 Horw, Switzerland. TEL 041-485041. FAX 041-485081. Ed. Heiri Leer. circ. 923.

630 AU
LANDWIRTSCHAFTLICHE BLAETTER. w. Landeslandwirtschaftskammer fuer Tirol, Brixnerstr. 1, A-6020 Innsbruck, Austria. TEL 28721.

630 AU ISSN 1010-1330
LANDWIRTSCHAFTLICHE MITTEILUNGEN. 1884. s-m. S.150. Landeskammer fuer Land- und Forstwirtschaft in Steiermark, Hamerlinggasse 3, A-8011 Graz, Austria. TEL 43-316-80-50. FAX 43-316-80-50-512. Ed. Helmut Pieber. adv.: B&W page S.73600, color page S.80100; trim 276 x 410; adv. contact: Eveline Gruber. bk.rev. circ. 68,000. **Document type:** newspaper.
Description: Covers news and information of interest to farmers. Features crop production, livestock, market news, agricultural economics and politics. Includes calendar of events.

630 GW ISSN 0023-8163
LANDWIRTSCHAFTLICHE ZEITSCHRIFT RHEINLAND. 1833. w. DM.84. Rheinischer Landwirtschaftsverlag GmbH, Rochusstr. 18, 53123 Bonn, Germany. TEL 0228-5200635. FAX 0228-5200660. Ed. Dr. Hasso Pacyna. adv.; bk.rev.; illus.; stat. circ. 22,000. **Document type:** newsletter.
Description: Provides various agricultural information about the region: on farming, marketing, government policies, and industry. Includes association news, events, questions and answers.

630 GW
LANDWIRTSCHAFTLICHER TASCHENKALENDER FUER WESER - EMS. 1948. a. DM.5. Landwirtschaftsverlag Weser-Ems GmbH, Hindenburgstr. 29, 26122 Oldenburg, Germany. TEL 0441-75055. Ed. Heinrich von Maydell. circ. 9,000.

630 GW ISSN 0342-765X
LANDWIRTSCHAFTLICHES WOCHENBLATT WESTFALEN-LIPPE: AUSGABE A. 1844. w. DM.126 (foreign DM.225) (effective 1997). Landwirtschaftsverlag GmbH, Huelsebrockstr. 2, 48165 Muenster, Germany. TEL 49-2501-801-0. FAX 49-2501-801-204. (Subscr. to: Postfach 480249, 48079 Muenster, Germany) adv.; bk.rev. circ. 62,000. **Document type:** trade publication.
—CCC.

630 GW ISSN 0930-8377
LANDWIRTSCHAFTLICHES WOCHENBLATT WESTFALEN-LIPPE: AUSGABE B. w. DM.132 (foreign DM.231) (effective 1997). Landwirtschaftsverlag GmbH, Huelsebrockstr. 2, 48165 Muenster, Germany. TEL 49-2501-801-0. FAX 49-2501-801-204. (Subscr. to: Postfach 480249, 48079 Muenster, Germany) **Document type:** trade publication.

630 AU
LANDWIRTSCHAFTS ZEITUNG. w. (Fri.). S.480; newsstand price: S.12. O Oe Bauern- und Nebenerwerbsbauernbund, Harrachstr. 12, Postfach 441, A-4010 Linz, Austria. TEL 43-732-77386626. FAX 43-732-784067. Ed. Franz Hofer. adv.: B&W page S.68096; trim 275 x 380; adv. contact: Josef Meisinger. circ. 40,930. **Document type:** newspaper.
Formerly: Oberoesterreichische Landwirtschafts Zeitung.

630 GW ISSN 0047-4029
S7
LANDWIRTSCHAFTSBLATT WESER-EMS. 1853. w. DM.70.40. (Landwirtschaftskammer Weser-Ems GmbH) Landwirtschaftsverlag Weser-Ems GmbH, Hindenburgstr. 29, 26122 Oldenburg, Germany. TEL 0441-75055. Ed. Heinrich von Maydell. circ. 23,800.
—BLDSC (5155.665000).

LANDWORKER. see *LABOR UNIONS*

630 SW ISSN 0345-6358
LANTARBETAREN. 1908. m. SEK 100. Svenska Lantarbetarefoerbundet, P.O. Box 1104, 111 81 Stockholm, Sweden. Ed. Robert Janson. adv.; bk.rev. circ. 14,500.

630 SW ISSN 0282-4132
LANTBRUKSPRAKTIKA; med Lantbrukstekniska Kalendern. 1942. a. SEK 119 (effective 1997). Lantbrukstekniska Foerlaget, P.O. Box 150, S-711 23 Lindesberg, Sweden. TEL 46-581-15550. FAX 46-581-14400. Ed. Hans Falck. adv.: B&W page SEK 3900; adv. contact: Brita Falck.

630 SW ISSN 0023-8430
LANTMAFSTAREN. 1940. q. SEK 75($10) (effective 1993). Sveriges Lantmaestarfoerbund, c/o S. Paulsson, Koersbaersg. 6, S-234 00 Lomma, Sweden. TEL 46-413-147-89. FAX 46-413-110-23. Ed. Jan Herlitz. adv.; charts; illus. circ. 3,500.

630 SW ISSN 0023-8449
LANTMANNEN; svenskt land: tidskrift foer lantmaen. 1879. m. SEK 450. (Lantbrukarnas Riksfoerbund - Federation of Swedish Farmers) L R F Media AB, Suttungsgraend 3, S-753 19 Uppsala, Sweden. TEL 018-693040. FAX 018-693182. Ed. Lars Helgstrand. adv.; bk.rev.; charts; illus.; tr.lit.; index. circ. 13,000. **Indexed:** Chem.Abstr., Field Crop Abstr., Herb.Abstr., NAA, Plant Breed.Abstr.
Incorporates (in 1990): Jord och Skog; Which was formed by the merger of: Svenskt Land; (until 1935): Landtmannen - Tidskrift foer Landtmaen; Which was formed by the merger of: Landtmannen; (until 1917): Tidskrift foer Landtmaen.

630 BL ISSN 0023-9135
LAVOURA. 1897. bi-m. Cr.$120. Sociedade Nacional de Agricultura, General Justo 171, Rio de Janeiro, Brazil. Ed. Rufino D'Almeida Guerra Filho. adv.; bibl.; charts; illus.; stat. **Indexed:** IBR.
—Linda Hall.

630 PO
LAVRADOR. 6/yr. Avda. Aliados 107-9, Lisbon, Portugal. TEL 21021. TELEX 25108.

630 GW ISSN 0023-9917
LEBENDIGE ERDE; Zeitschrift fuer Biologisch-Dynamische Wirtschaftsweise. 1950. bi-m. DM.45 (foreign DM.50). Forschungsring fuer Biologisch-Dynamische Wirtschaftsweise e.V., Brandscheise 2, 64295 Darmstadt, Germany. TEL 49-6155-84123. FAX 49-6155-846911. adv.: page DM.620; trim 135 x 195; adv. contact: Birgit Johannssen. bk.rev. circ. 8,500. **Document type:** academic/scholarly publication.

630 IT
LEGA CONTADINA. bi-m. L.1000. Rura Grafica s.r.l., c/o Rag. Tenneriello, Via S. Angela Merici, 96, I-00198 Rome, Italy. Dir. Ricci Sante. circ. 12,500.

630 UK ISSN 0306-0160
LEICESTERSHIRE, NORTHAMPTONSHIRE & RUTLAND FARMER. 1954. m. County Farmers Publications Ltd., 55 Goldington Rd., Bedford MK40 3LU, England. TEL 0234-351401. FAX 0234-328614. Ed. S. Fisher. adv. circ. 4,100.
Formerly: Leicestershire Farmer (ISSN 0024-0656)

630 FR
LETTRE DES I T P A. (Ingenieurs et Techniciens pour l'Agriculture); hommes et agriculture. 1949. q. 50 F. Ecole Superieure d'Agriculture, B.P. 201, 27100 Val De Reuil, France. Ed. M. Havard. adv.; bk.rev.; bibl.; charts; illus.; stat. circ. 2,000.
Former titles: I T P A Letters; Hommes et Agriculture; Technique et Pratique Agricoles (ISSN 0040-1226)

630 LU ISSN 0455-8154
LETZEBURGER BAUER. (Text in German) 1944. w. 1500 Fr. to individuals; institutions 2500 Fr. Centrale Paysanne, 16 bd. d'Avranches, L-2980 Luxembourg, Luxembourg. TEL 48-81-61. FAX 400375. Ed. Guy Tabourin. adv.: B&W page 30972 Fr., color page 50972 Fr.; 275 x 435. bk.rev. circ. 8,500.
Description: Covers national and international agricultural problems.

630 BE
LEVEND LAND. 1971. m. 675 BEF. Belgische Boerenbond, Minderbroedersstraat 8, 3000 Leuven, Belgium. TEL 32-16-242165. FAX 32-16-242168. TELEX 23119 AVV B. adv.; bk.rev.

630 LY ISSN 1010-3740
CODEN: LJAGD3
LIBYAN JOURNAL OF AGRICULTURE. (Text in English) 1971. a. Al-Fateh University, Faculty of Agriculture, P.O. Box 13040, Tripoli, Libya. TEL 36010. TELEX 20629.
—CASDDS.

630 UK ISSN 0955-6893
LINCOLNSHIRE FARMER. 1925. m. County Farmers Publications Ltd., 55 Goldington Rd., Bedford MK40 3LU, England. TEL 01234-351401. FAX 01234-328614. Ed. S. Fisher. adv. circ. 4,550.
Former titles (until 1989): Lincolnshire Farmer and Record (ISSN 0955-002X); Lincolnshire Record.

LIST OF PROPRIETARY SUBSTANCES AND NONFOOD COMPOUNDS AUTHORIZED FOR USE UNDER U S D A INSPECTION AND GRADING PROGRAMS. see *PUBLIC HEALTH AND SAFETY*

LIVE ANIMAL TRADE & TRANSPORT MAGAZINE. see *TRANSPORTATION*

LIVING HISTORICAL FARMS BULLETIN. see *MUSEUMS AND ART GALLERIES*

630 US ISSN 0024-5313
LIVINGSTON COUNTY AGRICULTURAL NEWS. 1918. m. $10 (effective Oct. 1991). Cooperative Extension Association of Livingston County, Agricultural Division, 158 S. Main St., Mount Morris, NY 14510. TEL 716-658-4110. FAX 716-658-4707. Ed. David L. Thorp; Pub. David L. Thorp. R&P contact: David L. Thorp. TEL 716-658-3250. adv. contact: David L. Thorp. illus.; circ. 250 (controlled). (processed) **Document type:** newsletter.

630 NE ISSN 1380-426X
LOONBEDRIJF; periodiek gewijd aan de belangen van het loonbedrijf in agrarisch- en grondverzetwerk. 1948. m. fl.120. (Bond van Loonbedrijven voor Agrarisch en Grondverzetwerk) Stichting BovaLpers, Postbus 1156, 3600 BD Maarssen, Netherlands. TEL 31-346-565994. FAX 31-346-572958. Ed. W.J. Fournier. adv.: B&W page fl.1494, color fl.2594; trim 230 x 295. circ. 3,000. **Document type:** trade publication.
Formerly (until 1981): Loonbedrijf in Land- en Tuinbouw (ISSN 0024-6468)

630 US ISSN 0024-6735
CODEN: LOAGAZ
LOUISIANA AGRICULTURE. 1957. q. free to state residents. (Louisiana Agricultural Experiment Station, Louisiana State University, Agricultural Center, Box 25100, Baton Rouge, LA 70894-5100. TEL 504-388-2263. FAX 504-388-4524. Ed. John Tarver. charts; illus.; circ. 5,000 (controlled).
Indexed: Acid Rain Abstr., Acid Rain Ind., Agroforest.Abstr., Anim.Breed.Abstr., Biol.Abstr., Cott.& Trop.Fibr.Abstr., Curr.Adv.Ecol.Sci., Curr.Cont. Dairy Sci.Abstr., Environ.Abstr., Excerp.Med., Field Crop Abstr., Food Sci.& Tech.Abstr., Helminthol.Abstr., Herb.Abstr., Hort.Abstr., Ind.Vet., Maize Abstr., Nutr.Abstr., Ornam.Hort., Plant Grow.Reg.Abstr., Rice Abstr., Soils & Fert., Soyabean Abstr., Triticale Abstr., Weed Abstr., Zoo.Rec. **Document type:** academic/scholarly publication.
—BLDSC (5294.950000); CASDDS; CIS; UMI; UnCover.
Description: Publishes results of research in agricultural sciences.
Refereed Serial

AGRICULTURE

630 US ISSN 0024-6808
LOUISIANA FARMER. m. $12 (foreign $24). Rural Press USA, 7701 Six Forks Rd., Ste. 132, Raleigh, NC 27615. TEL 919-676-3276; 800-477-1737. FAX 919-676-9803. (Subscr. to: Box 150001, Raleigh, NC 27624) Ed. Eva Ann Dorris. adv.: B&W page $1009. circ. 12,500. **Document type:** newspaper.
   Formerly (until 1965): Louisiana Farm and Ranch (ISSN 0092-7538)

630 US ISSN 0279-8824
LOUISIANA MARKET BULLETIN. 1916. fortn. $10 for 2 yrs. Department of Agriculture and Forestry, Box 3534, Baton Rouge, LA 70821-3534. TEL 504-922-1284. Ed. Renee M. Tull. adv. circ. 25,000.
   Description: News of the Louisiana agriculture industry.

630 RH
LOWVELD RESEARCH STATIONS. ANNUAL REPORT. a. free. Ministry of Lands, Agriculture and Rural Resettlement, Research and Specialist Services, Information Services, P.O. Box 8108, Causeway, Harare, Zimbabwe. circ. 250. (back issues avail.) **Indexed:** Biol.Abstr.

630 US ISSN 0091-4460
M A F E S RESEARCH HIGHLIGHTS. 1939. q. free. Mississippi Agricultural and Forestry Experiment Station, Box 9625, Mississippi State, MS 39762. TEL 601-325-3701. FAX 601-325-1710. E-mail: bobbyr@mces.msstate.edu; URL: http://www.aac.msstate.edu/majes/highlights/. Ed. Bob Ratliff. R&P contact: Bob Ratliff. charts; illus.; index. circ. 10,000. **Indexed:** Bibl.Agri., Cott.& Trop.Fibr.Abstr., Hort.Abstr., Ornam.Hort., World Agri.Econ.& Rural Sociol.Abstr. **Document type:** government publication.
—Linda Hall.
   Formerly: Mississippi Farm. Research (ISSN 0026-6221)

630 MY ISSN 0127-4007
M A R D I REPORT. (Text in English, or Malay) irreg. (7-8/yr.), no.189, 1996. price varies. Malaysian Agricultural Research & Development Institute - Institut Penyelidikan dan Kemajuan Pertanian Malaysia, P.O. Box 12301, General Post Office, 50774 Kuala Lumpur, Malaysia. TEL 03-9437236. FAX 03-9482216. TELEX MARDI-MA-37115. Ed. Rohani Mahmood. bibl.; illus. circ. 750. **Document type:** monographic series.
   Refereed Serial

638.1 II ISSN 0970-0919
MADHUPRAPANCHA. 1981. q. Rs.10. South Kanara Bee-Keepers' Co-operative Society Ltd., No. L 386, Puttur, D.K. 574201, Karnataka, India. Ed. Srimivasa Rae. illus. circ. 1,000. (back issues avail.)

630 IO ISSN 0024-9556
MADJALAH PERTANIAN.* 1949. irreg., (4-12/yr.) free. Directorate of Agriculture Extension - Direktorat Penyuluhan Pertanian, Jalan Ragunan, Pasarminggu, Djakarta, Indonesia. Ed. Soekandar Wiriaatmadja. charts; stat. circ. 6,000.

630 II ISSN 0024-9602
S17 CODEN: MAAJAP
MADRAS AGRICULTURAL JOURNAL. (Text in English) vol.60, 1973. m. Rs.60 to individuals; institutions Rs.150. Madras Agricultural Students' Union, Tamil Nadu Agricultural University Campus, Coimbatore 641 003, India. Ed. M. Stephen Dorairaj. adv.; charts; stat. **Indexed:** Agroforest.Abstr., Bio-Contr.News & Info., Biol.Abstr., Biotech.Abstr., Chem.Abstr., Cott.& Trop.Fibr.Abstr., Crop Physiol.Abstr., Dairy Sci.Abstr., Excerp.Med., Field Crop Abstr., Food Sci.& Tech.Abstr., Herb.Abstr., Hort.Abstr., Irr.& Drain.Abstr., Maize Abstr., Plant Breed.Abstr., Plant Grow.Reg.Abstr., Rev.Appl.Entomol., Rev.Plant Path., Rice Abstr., Rural Recreat.Tour.Abstr., Seed Abstr., Soils & Fert., Sorghum & Millets Abstr., Soyabean Abstr., Triticale Abstr., Trop.Oil Seeds Abstr., Weed Abstr., World Agri.Econ.& Rural Sociol.Abstr.
—BLDSC (5331.000000); CASDDS.
   Refereed Serial

630 FR ISSN 0763-8922
MAGASIN AGRICOLE.* 1984. 10/yr. 150 F. 1 ave. Edouard Belin, 92856 Rueil-Malmaison, France. TEL 40-38-08-80. FAX 40-50-04-95. Ed. Daniel Bailly.

630 LE ISSN 0076-2369
MAGON. SERIE SCIENTIFIQUE.* (Text and summaries in English and French) 1965. irreg., no.33, 1970. free. Institut de Recherches Agronomiques, Laboratoire Regional Veterinaire, Fanar, Lebanon.

630 LE ISSN 0076-2377
MAGON. SERIE TECHNIQUE.* (Text in Arabic, English and French; summaries in English and French) 1965. irreg., no.11, 1970. free. Institut de Recherches Agronomiques, Laboratoire Regional Veterinaire, Fanar, Lebanon. **Indexed:** Biol.Abstr.

630 HU ISSN 0521-4238
S227
MAGYAR MEZOGAZDASAGI MUZEUM KOZLEMENYEI/HUNGARIAN AGRICULTURAL MUSEUM. PROCEEDINGS. (Text mainly in Hungarian; summaries in English or German) 1966. biennial. $35. Magyar Mezogazdasagi Muzeum, P.O. Box 129, 1367 Budapest, Hungary. TEL 36-1-3430573. FAX 36-1-3439120. Eds. Gyorgy Feher, Sandor Oroszi. R&P contact: Gyorgy Geher. TEL 36-1-3438485. illus. circ. 700. **Indexed:** Amer.Hist.& Life (1981-1987), (1992-), Hist.Abstr. (1981-1987), (1992-). **Document type:** proceedings.
   Description: Essays in agricultural history.

630.724 634.92 US
MAINE AGRICULTURAL and FOREST EXPERIMENT STATION. ANNUAL REPORT. 1886. a. free. Maine Agricultural and Forest Experiment Station, University of Maine, 5782 Winslow Hall, Rm. 1, Orono, ME 04469-5782. TEL 207-581-3227. E-mail: MAES2@MAINE.MAINE.EDU; URL: http://www.ume.maine.edu/~nfa/mafes/pub/ms.htm. Ed. M.R. Gross. illus. circ. 1,500. (also avail. in microfilm; back issues avail.)
   Formerly: Maine Agricultural Experiment Station. Annual Report.

630 US ISSN 1070-1516
MAINE AGRICULTURAL AND FOREST EXPERIMENT STATION. MISCELLANEOUS REPORT. 1948. irreg., no.423, 1993. free. Maine Agricultural and Forest Experiment Station, University of Maine, 5782 Winslow Hall, Rm. 1, Orono, ME 04469-5782. TEL 207-581-3227. Ed. Barbara Harrity. (also avail. in microfilm) **Indexed:** Sport Fish.Abstr., Wild.Rev.
   Formerly: Maine Agricultural Experiment Station. Miscellaneous Report (ISSN 0734-9564)

630 US ISSN 1070-1524
CODEN: TBMSEU
MAINE AGRICULTURAL AND FOREST EXPERIMENT STATION. TECHNICAL BULLETIN. 1962. irreg., vol.129, 1987. free. Maine Agricultural and Forest Experiment Station, University of Maine, 5782 Winslow Hall, Rm. 1, Orono, ME 04469-5782. TEL 207-581-3227. Ed. Barbara Harrity. (also avail. in microfilm) **Indexed:** Biol.Abstr., Dairy Sci.Abstr., Forest.Abstr., Soils & Fert., Sport Fish.Abstr., Wild.Rev., World Agri.Econ.& Rural Sociol.Abstr., Zoo.Rec. **Document type:** bulletin.
—BLDSC (8630.019000).
   Formerly (until 1994): Maine Agricultural Experiment Station. Technical Bulletin (ISSN 0734-9556)

630 635 US ISSN 0891-9194
MAINE ORGANIC FARMER AND GARDENER. 1974. q. $12 (foreign $18) (effective 1997). Maine Organic Farmers and Gardeners Association, 283 Water St., Box 2176, Augusta, ME 04338-2176. TEL 207-622-3118. E-mail: MOFOGA@Biddeford.com. Ed. Jean English. adv. contact: Janice Clark. bk.rev.; illus.; index. cum.index. circ. 5,000. (tabloid format; back issues avail.) **Document type:** newspaper, consumer publication.
   Description: News, articles, announcements, and instruction on environmental, agricultural issues, farming and gardening.

630 TS ISSN 1021-1357
MAJALLAT AL-IMARAT LIL-'ULUM AL-ZIRA'IYYAH/EMIRATES JOURNAL FOR AGRICULTURAL SCIENCES. (Text in Arabic, English) 1988. a. exchange basis. United Arab Emirates University, Faculty of Agriculture, P.O. Box 17555, Al-Ain, United Arab Emirates. TEL 971-3-635647. FAX 971-3-632384. TELEX 33521 JAMEAH EM. Ed. Nuhad J. Daghir. circ. 2,000. **Document type:** academic/scholarly publication.
   Refereed Serial

630 UG ISSN 0075-4730
MAKERERE UNIVERSITY. FACULTY OF AGRICULTURE. HANDBOOK.* 1963. irreg. Makerere University, Faculty of Agriculture, P.O. Box 7062, Kampala, Uganda.

630 UG ISSN 0075-4773
MAKERERE UNIVERSITY. FACULTY OF AGRICULTURE. TECHNICAL BULLETIN. 1962. irreg. Makerere University, Faculty of Agriculture, P.O. Box 7062, Kampala, Uganda.

630 MW
MALAWI. DEPARTMENT OF AGRICULTURAL RESEARCH. ANNUAL REPORT. a. K.10 price varies. Ministry of Agriculture, Department of Agricultural Research, Library System, P.O. Box 158, Lilongwe, Malawi. TEL 265-767222. (Orders to: Government Printer, P.O. Box 37, Zomba, Malawi. TEL 265-50-523155) **Indexed:** Anim.Breed.Abstr., Biol.Abstr., Dairy Sci.Abstr., Field Crop Abstr., Herb.Abstr., Rev.Appl.Entomol., Rev.Plant Path.
   Incorporates (in 1975): Agricultural Research Council of Malawi. Annual Report (ISSN 0065-4515); **Formerly** (1963-1969): Malawi. Department of Agriculture. Annual Report (ISSN 0076-3047)

630 639.2 MY
MALAYSIA. MINISTRY OF AGRICULTURE. TECHNICAL AND GENERAL BULLETINS. 1957. N.S. 1973. irreg. Ministry of Agriculture, Publications Officer, Wisma Tani, Jalan Mahameru, 50624 Kuala Lumpur, Malaysia. **Indexed:** Anim.Breed.Abstr., Rev.Appl.Entomol., Soils & Fert.
   Former titles: Malaysia. Ministry of Agriculture. Technical Bulletins; Malaysia. Ministry of Agriculture and Rural Development. Technical Bulletins.

630 MY ISSN 0025-1321
S17 CODEN: MAGJAL
MALAYSIAN AGRICULTURAL JOURNAL. s-a. $26 for 4 issues. Ministry of Agriculture, Publications Officer, Wisma Tani, Jalan Mahameru, 50624 Kuala Lumpur, Malaysia. Ed. S. Thamutaram. adv.; bk.rev.; charts; illus.; stat.; index; circ. 1,500 (controlled). **Indexed:** Anim.Breed.Abstr., Bio-Contr.News & Info., Biol.Abstr., Chem.Abstr., Dairy Sci.Abstr., Field Crop Abstr., Food Sci.& Tech.Abstr., Helminthol.Abstr., Herb.Abstr., Hort.Abstr., Ind.Vet., Nutr.Abstr., Plant Breed.Abstr., Rev.Appl.Entomol., Rev.Plant Path., Rural Recreat.Tour.Abstr., Soils & Fert., Trop.Oil Seeds Abstr., Vet.Bull., Weed Abstr., World Agri.Econ.& Rural Sociol.Abstr.
—BLDSC (5356.060000); CASDDS.

570 MY ISSN 0126-8643
CODEN: MABIDU
MALAYSIAN APPLIED BIOLOGY JOURNAL. 1972. s-a. $50. Malaysian Society of Applied Biology, c/o Faculty of Science, Universiti Kebangsaan Malaysia, 43600 UKM, Bangi, Selangor, Malaysia. Ed. Syed Jalaludin. R&P contact: Syed Jalaludin. adv.; bk.rev. circ. 500. **Indexed:** Anim.Breed.Abstr., Dairy Sci.Abstr., Excerp.Med. (until 19??), Field Crop Abstr., Food Sci.& Tech.Abstr., Helminthol.Abstr., Herb.Abstr., Ind.Vet., Nutr.Abstr., Sport Fish.Abstr., Vet.Bull., Wild.Rev., Zoo.Rec. **Document type:** academic/scholarly publication.
—BLDSC (5356.064000); Linda Hall; UnCover.
   Formerly (until 1977): Malaysian Agricultural Research Journal (ISSN 0126-5458)
   Refereed Serial

634 MY ISSN 0126-5601
MALAYSIAN PINEAPPLE. (Text and summaries in English) 1971. irreg. vol.2, 1972. Malayan Pineapple Industry Board, Pineapple Research Station, P.O. Box 101, Pekan Nenas, Johor, Malaysia. illus. circ. 1,500.

630 BL ISSN 0102-8901
MANCHETE RURAL. 1975. m. $42. Bloch Editores S.A., Rua do Russell 766-804, 22210-000 Rio de Janeiro, RJ, Brazil. TEL 021-5554000. FAX 021-2059998. TELEX 2121525 BLOC. Ed. Paulo Roque. circ. 70,000. **Document type:** trade publication.
   Formerly (until 1987): Agricultura de Hoje (ISSN 0100-5707)
   Description: For people who deal with agriculture, cattle raising and related industries.

136 AGRICULTURE

630　　　　CN　　ISSN 0084-3865
S147
MANITOBA AGRICULTURE YEARBOOK. 1907. a. Can.$6.42. Manitoba Agriculture, Program & Policy Analysis Branch, 810-401 York Ave., Winnipeg, MB R3C 0P8, Canada. TEL 204-945-3503. FAX 204-945-5024. Ed. Janet Honey. circ. 2,000. **Document type:** government publication.
Description: Major responsibility is to acquire and provide selected data on Manitoba agriculture for use by government, farm organizations and farmers, researchers and the general public.

638.1　　　CN　　ISSN 0708-3483
MANITOBA BEEKEEPER. 1979. q. Can.$20 (effective 1998). Manitoba Beekeepers' Association, P.O. Box 1448, Steinback, MB R0A 2A0, Canada. TEL 204-326-3763. E-mail: manbeekr@mb.sympatico.ca. Ed. Ron Rudiak. bk.rev. circ. 900. (looseleaf format) **Document type:** newsletter.
Description: Provides technical information related to honey production and beekeeping.

630　　　　CN　　ISSN 0025-2239
MANITOBA CO-OPERATOR. 1925. w. Can.$32.40 (US $75; elsewhere $130) (effective 1997). Manitoba Pool Elevators, 220 Portage Ave., P.O. Box 9800, Stn. Main, Winnipeg, MB R3C 3K7, Canada. TEL 204-934-0401. FAX 204-934-0480. E-mail: news@co-operator.mb.ca. Ed. John Morriss; Pub. John Morriss. adv.; B&W page $2886; trim 10 1/4 x 15 7/8; adv. contact: Don Wiebe. bk.rev.; circ. 13,377. circ. 21,820 (paid). (tabloid format) **Document type:** newspaper.
●Also available on CD-ROM.
Description: Features comments on local, national and international events relevant to farming. Includes news and articles of interest to farm women, 4-H reports and commodity market commentary.

630　　　　FR　　ISSN 0295-7841
MARAICHER NANTAIS. 1962. 11/yr. 22 bd. Benoni-Goullin, 44062 Nantes Cedex, France. Ed. L. Bureau. circ. 3,000.

630　　　　FR　　ISSN 0758-5691
MARNE AGRICOLE. w. Maison des Agriculteurs (Reims), Rue Leon Patoux, B.P. 326, 51061 Reims Cedex, France. TEL 26-04-74-51. TELEX MARAGRI 830 487. Ed. Pierre Flandre. circ. 8,775.

630　　　　US　　ISSN 0279-7895
MARYLAND FARMER. 1978. m. $12 (foreign $25). Rural Press U S A, 7701 Six Forks Rd., Ste. 132, Raleigh, NC 27615. TEL 919-676-3276; 800-477-1737. FAX 919-676-9803. (Subscr. to: Box 150001, Raleigh, NC 27624) Ed. Julie Gochenour; Pub. Jeff Tennant. adv.; B&W page $1218. circ. 18,000. **Document type:** newspaper.

630 635　　NZ　　ISSN 1173-6097
MASSEY UNIVERSITY. FACULTY OF AGRICULTURAL AND HORTICULTURAL SCIENCES. RESEARCH AND EXTENSION REPORT (YEARS). 1979. biennial. free. Massey University, Faculty of Agricultural and Horticultural Sciences, Palmerston North, New Zealand. TEL 64-4-3505130. FAX 64-4-3505620. E-mail: r.d.aderson@massey.ac.nz; URL: http://www.massey.ac.nz. index. **Document type:** corporate report.
Description: Provides summary of research projects, publications and extension activities within the areas of agricultural engineering, agricultural economics, animal science, plant science (including agronomy, cropping and horticulture) and soil science.

630　　　　MF
MAURITIUS. MINISTRY OF AGRICULTURE AND NATURAL RESOURCES. TECHNICAL BULLETIN. 1979. a. free. Ministry of Agriculture, Fisheries and Cooperatives, Agricultural Services, Reduit, Mauritius. TEL 454-1091. FAX 464-8749. TELEX 2124427. Ed.Bd. **Document type:** corporate report, bulletin.
Former titles: Mauritius. Ministry of Agriculture and Natural Resources. Technical Bulletin & Mauritius. Ministry of Agriculture, Fisheries and Natural Resources. Technical Bulletin; Mauritius. Ministry of Agriculture and Natural Resources and the Environment. Technical Bulletin.

630　　　　MF
S338.M3
MAURITIUS. MINISTRY OF AGRICULTURE, FISHERIES AND COOPERATIVES. ANNUAL REPORT. 1913. a. R.50. Ministry of Agriculture, Fisheries and Cooperatives, Agricultural Services, Reduit, Mauritius. TEL 454-1091. FAX 464-8749. TELEX 2124427. Ed.Bd. **Indexed:** Biol.Abstr. **Document type:** corporate report, bulletin.
Former titles: Mauritius. Ministry of Agriculture and Natural Resources. Annual Report (ISSN 0304-775X) & Mauritius. Ministry of Agriculture, Fisheries and Natural Resources. Annual Report; Mauritius. Ministry of Agriculture and Natural Resources and the Environment. Annual Report.

630　　　　MF　　ISSN 0368-9042
　　　　　　　　　CODEN: MDARA2
MAURITIUS CHAMBER OF AGRICULTURE. ANNUAL REPORT. (Text in English) 1853. a. $3 (effective 1997). Mauritius Chamber of Agriculture, P.O. Box 312, Port Louis, Mauritius. TEL 230-208-0747. FAX 230-208-1269. TELEX 4214 SUGMAUR IW. E-mail: mca312@bow.intnet.mu; URL: http://www.prosi.intnet.mu. Ed. Axel Pellegrin. circ. 1,000. **Document type:** corporate report.
Formerly: Mauritius Chamber of Agriculture. President's Report.
Description: Annual review of Mauritian sugar industry and agricultural diversification, including tea, tobacco and other crops, with a comprehensive statistical bulletin.

630 658　　MX
MAYO AGRICOLA. 1962. q. Distrito de Riego No. 38, Rio Mayo, Pesquera y Jimenez, Navojoa, Sonora, Mexico. bk.rev.; index; circ. controlled.

630　　　　MK
AL-MAZARI'. w. Ministry of Agriculture and Fisheries, P.O. Box 467, Ruwi, Muscat, Sultanate of Oman. TEL 696300. TELEX 3503. Ed. Khalid az-Zubaidi.

630　　　　IT　　ISSN 1120-6403
MEDIT. (Text in English, French) 1990. 4/yr. L.95000 (effective 1996). (International Centre of Further Study of Agriculture) Edagricole S.p.A., Via Emilia Levante 31-2, 40139 Bologna, Italy. TEL 39-51-492211. FAX 39-51-493660. Ed. Cosimo Lacirignola. adv.; B&W page L.2000000, color page L.3000000; trim 185 x 247. circ. 3,850.
—BLDSC (5534.685000).

638.1　　　FI　　ISSN 0783-3377
MEHILAINEN. (Text in Finnish; summaries occasionally in English or Swedish) 1984. bi-m. FIM 170. Suomen Mehilaishoitajain Liitto SML r.y. - Finnish Beekeepers' Association, Kasarmikatu 26 C 34, FIN-00130 Helsinki, Finland. TEL 358-0-661-281. FAX 358-0-661-283. Ed. Heikki Varttainen. adv.; B&W page FIM 3000. bk.rev.; index. circ. 4,500. (back issues avail.) **Document type:** newsletter.
Description: Focuses on beekeeping both as profession and hobby.

630　　　　IO　　ISSN 0125-9318
MENARA PERKEBUNAN. (Text in Indonesian; summaries in English) 1958. 3/yr. Rps.16500($16.50) Indonesian Biotechnology Research Institute for Estate - Pusat Penelitian Bioteknologi Perkebunan, Jl. Taman Kencana 1, P.O. Box 179, Bogor 16001, Indonesia. TEL 62-251-324048. FAX 62-251-328516. TELEX 48369-AARD-IA. charts; stat. circ. 1,000. (also avail. in microfiche from IDC) **Indexed:** Crop Physiol.Abstr., Field Crop Abstr., Forest Prod.Abstr., Herb.Abstr., Hort.Abstr., Hort.Abstr., RAPRA, Rural Recreat.Tour.Abstr., Trop.Abstr., Weed Abstr., World Agri.Econ.& Rural Sociol.Abstr. **Document type:** academic/scholarly publication.
Supersedes (1926-1957): Bergcultures.

630　　　　AG　　ISSN 0328-2708
▼**MERCOSUR AGROPECUARIO**; actualidad y perspectivas. 1995. irreg. Secretaria de Agricultura, Ganaderia y Pesca, Avda. Paseo Colon 982, 3o piso, Of. 162, 1063 Buenos Aires, Argentina. TEL 54-1-3492753. FAX 54-1-3492742.

METSATILASTOLLINEN VUOSIKIRJA/STATISTICAL YEARBOOK OF FORESTRY. see FORESTS AND FORESTRY

630　　　　RU　　ISSN 0235-7801
S13　　　　　　　　CODEN: MAZHEC
MEZHDUNARODNYI AGROPROMYSHLENNYI ZHURNAL; nauchno-proizvodstvennyi zhurnal po obmenu dostizheniyami nauki i peredovogo opyta v agropromyshlennom komplekse stran. 1957. bi-m. $68 (effective 1996). (Sovet Ekonomicheskoi Vzaimopomoshchi, Komitet po Sotrudnichestvu v Oblasti Agropromyshlennogo Kompleksa) Mezhdunarodnyi Agropromyshlennyi Zhurnal, Sadovaya-Spasskaya, 18, 107807 Moscow, Russia. TEL 7-095-2073211. FAX 7-095-2072870. (Dist. by: Mezhdunarodnaya Kniga, B. Yakimanka 39, 117049 Moscow, Russia. TEL 7-095-2384967. FAX 7-095-2384634; Dist. in U.S. by: Victor Kamkin Inc., 4956 Boiling Brook Pkwy, Rockville, MD 20852. TEL 301-881-5973) Ed. Georgii P. Rudenko. bk.rev.; charts; index. circ. 3,500. (tabloid format) **Indexed:** Anim.Breed.Abstr., Biol.Abstr., Chem.Abstr., Food Sci.& Tech.Abstr., Hort.Abstr., Maize Abstr., Nutr.Abstr., Pig News & Info., Seed Abstr., Triticale Abstr.
—BLDSC (0107.860000).
Formerly (until 1989): Mezhdunarodnyi Sel'skokhozyaistvennyi Zhurnal (ISSN 0026-1882)

630　　　　US　　ISSN 0885-6060
MICHIGAN DRY BEAN DIGEST. 1976. q. $25 (foreign $35) (effective 1997); newsstand price: $7.50 (foreign $10). Michigan Bean Shippers Association, Box 6008, Saginaw, MI 48608. TEL 517-790-3010. FAX 517-790-3747. Ed. John A. McGill. adv.; B&W page $1250, color page $1500; adv. contact: Ann M. Watters. circ. 5,500. **Indexed:** Bibl.Agri. **Document type:** consumer publication, trade publication.

630　　　　US　　ISSN 1063-598X
S451.M5
MICHIGAN FARM NEWS. 1923. 20/yr. $45 to non-members. Michigan Farm Bureau, Box 30960, Lansing, MI 48909. TEL 517-323-7000. FAX 517-323-6793. Ed. Dennis Rudat. adv. contact: Dennis Rudat. **Document type:** newspaper.
Supersedes (in part 1990): Rural Living (Lansing) (ISSN 0743-9962); Which was formerly (until 1981): Michigan Farm News (ISSN 0026-2161)

630　　　　US　　ISSN 0026-2153
MICHIGAN FARMER. 1841. m. $19.95. Farm Progress Companies (Subsidiary of: A B C Publishing Companies), 191 S. Gary Ave., Carol Stream, IL 60188. TEL 630-690-5600. FAX 630-462-2869. (Edit. addr.: 911 E. State St., Ste. H, St. Johns, MI 48879. TEL 517-224-1081. FAX 517-224-4353) Ed. Dean Peterson. adv.; B&W page $3400, color page $3910; trim 7 X 10. bk.rev.; charts; illus.; stat.; circ. 30,094 (paid). (tabloid format; also avail. in microfilm)

630　　　　IS　　ISSN 0334-7532
S542.I75
MICHKAR CHAKLAEI BEYISRAEL/ISRAEL AGRESEARCH. (Text in Hebrew) 1986. s-a. $20 (effective 1996). Agricultural Research Organization, Volcani Center, P.O. Box 6, Bet Dagan 50250, Israel. TEL 972-3-9683215. FAX 972-3-993998. TELEX 381476. Ed. Y. Rousso. **Document type:** government publication.
Refereed Serial

MICROBIOLOGICAL RESEARCH. see BIOLOGY — Microbiology

630　　　　US
MIDAMERICA FARMER GROWER. 1983. w. $21. S J S Publishing Co., Inc., 19 N. Main, Perryville, MO 63775. TEL 314-547-2244. FAX 314-547-5663. adv. circ. 24,000.
Description: For farmers in Illinois, Southwest Indiana, Missouri, Kentucky, Arkansas and Tennessee who farm 220 or more acres. Covers news, events, shows, workshops and insect and weed control.

MIDDLE EAST SCIENCE POLICY SERIES. see PUBLIC ADMINISTRATION

630　　　　UK
MID-WEST FARMER. 8/yr. Homer Rd., Hereford HR4 9UJ, England. TEL 432-274413. FAX 432-50514. Ed. Richard Winterbourn.

AGRICULTURE 137

630 635.67   SA   ISSN 1012-6775
MIELIES - MAIZE. Key Title: Mielies (Pretoria). (Text in Afrikaans, English) 1963. m. R.20.46 (effective 1996 & 1997). National Maize Producers Organization - Nasionale Mielieprodusente-Organisasie, P.O. Box 88, Bothaville, South Africa. TEL 27-565-2145. FAX 27-565-3613. (Co-sponsor: Mielieraad - Maize Board) Ed. Peter Maertens. adv.: B&W page R.3810, color page R.5260; trim 298 x 210; adv. contact: Johan van Onselen. bk.rev.; illus.; mkt.; stat. circ. 22,000. **Indexed:** GeoRef. **Document type:** trade publication.
  Incorporates: Maize News - Mielienuus (ISSN 0026-3559); **Former titles (1969-1980):** Landman (ISSN 0023-7965); Sampi-News - Sampi-Nuus.
  Description: Covers commercial, agricultural, and technical news relating to commercial grain crops and their production in the summer grain areas of South Africa.

630   BL   ISSN 0100-9974
MINISTERIO DE EDUCACAO. FACULDADE DE CIENCIAS AGRARIAS DO PARA. INFORME TECNICO. 1979. irreg., no.20, 1996. $2. Ministerio de Educacao, Faculdade de Ciencias Agrarias do Para, Servicio de Documentacao e Informacao, Caixa Postal, 917, 66077-530 Belem, Para, Brazil. TEL 55-91-2464518. FAX 55-91-2263814. TELEX 091-1892 FAGP. E-mail: fcap@supridad.com.br. Ed. Marly Sampaio. abstr.; charts; stat. **Document type:** monographic series.
  Description: Covers agriculture, forestry and veterinary science.

630   US   ISSN 0362-8167
CODEN: MXSBAE
MINNESOTA AGRICULTURAL EXPERIMENT STATION. STATION BULLETIN. 1888. irreg., approx. 8/yr. price varies. (Minnesota Agricultural Experiment Station) University of Minnesota, Coffey Hall, 1420 Eckles Ave., St. Paul, MN 55108-6068. FAX 612-625-2207. Ed. Larry A. Etkin. (also avail. in microfilm) **Indexed:** Biol.Abstr., Curr.Adv.Ecol.Sci. **Document type:** academic/scholarly publication.

630   FR   ISSN 0026-5810
MIROIR DU CENTRE; agricole, artistique, economique, universitaire. 1963. m. 30 F. Office Publicitaire du Centre, 14 Place Jourdan, 87003 Limoges, France. Dir. Camille Rivet. adv.; bk.rev.; illus.; film rev.; tr.lit. circ. 80,000.

630   US
MISSISSIPPI FARM BUREAU COUNTRY. 1922. 4/yr. $2. Mississippi Farm Bureau Federation, Box 1972, Jackson, MS 39215-1972. TEL 601-977-4153. Ed. Glynda Phillips. adv.; bk.rev.; illus. circ. 196,000. (also avail. in microfilm)
  Formerly (until 1995): Mississippi Farm Bureau News (ISSN 0026-6205)

630   US
MISSISSIPPI FARMER. m. $12 (foreign $25). Rural Press U S A, 7701 Six Forks Rd., Ste. 132, Raleigh, NC 27615. TEL 919-676-3276; 800-477-1737. FAX 919-676-9803. (Subscr. to: Box 150001, Raleigh, NC 27624) Ed. Eva Ann Dorris; Pub. Jeff Tennant. adv.: B&W page $1009. circ. 12,500. **Document type:** newspaper.

630 636   US
MISSOURI. DEPARTMENT OF AGRICULTURE. DAILY MARKET SUMMARY. 1967. d. $45. Department of Agriculture, 1616 Missouri Blvd., Box 630, Jefferson City, MO 65102. TEL 573-751-4211. FAX 573-751-2868. Ed. Sam Shelton. circ. 500. **Document type:** government publication.

630 636   US   ISSN 0279-2346
MISSOURI. DEPARTMENT OF AGRICULTURE. WEEKLY MARKET SUMMARY. 1981. w. $18. Department of Agriculture, 1616 Missouri Blvd., Box 630, Jefferson City, MO 65102. TEL 573-751-4211. FAX 573-751-2868. Ed. Sam Shelton. circ. 1,750. **Document type:** government publication.

630   US   ISSN 0026-668X
MISSOURI RURALIST. 1859. 15/yr. $19.95. Farm Progress Companies (Subsidiary of: A B C Publishing Companies), 191 S. Gary Ave., Carol Stream, IL 60188. TEL 630-690-5600. FAX 630-462-2869. (Edit. addr.: 1007 N. College Ave., Ste. 3-4, Columbia, MO 65201. TEL 573-875-5445. FAX 573-875-5447) Ed. Larry Harper. adv.: B&W page $3850, color page $4430, trim 7 X 10. bk.rev.; charts; illus.; stat.; circ. 45,118 (paid). (also avail. in microfilm)

630   UK   ISSN 0267-4637
MODERN FARMING. 1964. 3/yr. £10. Massey Ferguson, P.O. Box 62, Floor 10, Coventry CV4 9GF, England. TEL 44-1203-851221. FAX 44-1203-851182. Ed. Sandy Cox. circ. 17,130 (controlled). **Document type:** trade publication.
  Formerly (until 1985): Modern Farmer (ISSN 0047-7699)

630   II
MODERN - KHETI. (Text in Punjabi) 1987. m. Rs.24($12) Mehram, Nabha 147 201 (Patiala), India. TEL 01765-3678. Ed. Karamjit Singh. adv.: B&W page Rs.6500, color page Rs.13000; trim 265 x 205. circ. 47,721.

630   IT   ISSN 0026-9484
MONDO AGRICOLO; settimanale di tecnica, economia e politica agraria. 1950. fortn. L.50000. (Confederazione Generale Agricoltura Italiana) Societa Editrice Periodici Enotria, Corso Vittorio Emanuele 101, 00186 Rome, Italy. TEL 39-6-6852374. FAX 39-6-68308578. E-mail: immco@mbox.vol.it; URL: http://www.confagricoltura.it/. Ed. Augusto Bocchini. adv.: B&W page L.2000000, color page L.3000000. bk.rev.; illus. circ. 45,000. (tabloid format)

630   US   ISSN 0886-3075
MONTANA FARM BUREAU SPOKESMAN. 1949. q. $25 to non-members; members $5.00 (effective 1997). Montana Farm Bureau Federation, 502 S. 19th, Bozeman, MT 59718. TEL 406-587-3153. FAX 406-587-0319. E-mail: MFFarmB@AOL.com. Eds. Jake Cummins, Lorna Karn. R&P contact: Lorna Karn. adv.: B&W page $525; trim 8 1/2 x 11. circ. 7,000 (controlled). **Document type:** newsletter, trade publication.
  Supersedes (in 1985): Montana Agriculture (ISSN 0026-9905)

630   FR   ISSN 0750-2389
MOSELLE AGRICOLE. w. 64 av. Andre Malraux, 57045 Metz Cedex, France. TEL 87-63-31-33. Ed. M. Forte. circ. 14,586.

630   II   ISSN 0047-8539
CODEN: MJASAD
MYSORE JOURNAL OF AGRICULTURAL SCIENCES. 1967. q. $60. University of Agricultural Sciences, Bangalore, Communication Centre, Hebbal, Bangalore 560 024, Karnataka, India. (Dist. overseas by: HPX Publishers' Distributors Pvt. Ltd., 4805-24, 1st Fl., Bharat Ram Rd., Darya Ganj, New Delhi 110 002, India. TEL 91-11-3254401. FAX 91-11-6864511) Ed. B.S. Siddaramiah. bk.rev.; index. circ. 600. (also avail. in microfilm from UMI; reprint service avail. from ISI,UMI) **Indexed:** Agroforest.Abstr., Bio-Contr.News & Info., Biol.Abstr., Chem.Abstr., Cott.& Trop.Fibr.Abstr., Crop Physiol.Abstr., Curr.Cont., Dairy Sci.Abstr., Excerp.Med., Fababean Abstr., Field Crop Abstr., Food Sci.& Tech.Abstr., Helminthol.Abstr., Herb.Abstr., Hort.Abstr., Ind.Vet., Maize Abstr., Nutr.Abstr., Ornam.Hort., Plant Breed.Abstr., Plant Grow.Reg.Abstr., Potato Abstr., Rev.Appl.Entomol., Rev.Med.& Vet.Mycol., Rev.Plant Path., Rice Abstr., Rural Recreat.Tour.Abstr., Seed Abstr., Soils & Fert., Sorghum & Millets Abstr., Soyabean Abstr., Sport Fish.Abstr., Trop.Oil Seeds Abstr., Vet.Bull., Weed Abstr., Wild.Rev., World Agri.Econ.& Rural Sociol.Abstr., Zoo.Rec. **Document type:** academic/scholarly publication.
  —BLDSC (5997.500000); CASDDS; Linda Hall.

N A A A NEWSLETTER. (National Agricultural Aviation Association) see *AERONAUTICS AND SPACE FLIGHT*

630   UK
N A A C NEWSLETTER. 12/yr. membership. Huts Corner, Tilford Rd., Hindhead, Surrey GU26 6SF, England. TEL 44-1428-605360. FAX 44-1428-606531. Ed. J.L. Taylor. circ. 600. **Document type:** newsletter.
  Description: Contains information about all aspects of contracting operations.

630.7   US   ISSN 0149-4910
N A C T A JOURNAL. 1957. q. $25. National Association of Colleges and Teachers of Agriculture, 608 W. Vermont, Urbana, IL 61801. TEL 217-344-5738. Ed. Jack C. Everly. adv.; bk.rev.; cum.index: 1957-1965; circ. 1,500 (paid). (also avail. in microfilm from UMI; reprint service avail. from ISI,UMI) **Indexed:** Curr.Cont., Ind.Sci.Rev. **Document type:** academic/scholarly publication.
  —BLDSC (6011.330000); UMI; UnCover.
  Formerly: National Association of Colleges and Teachers of Agriculture. Journal (ISSN 0027-8602)
  Description: Presents articles and research on agricultural instruction at the college level.
  Refereed Serial

630   SA   ISSN 0028-128X
N A U N L U. (Text in Afrikaans and English) 1951. m. free. Natal Agricultural Union, P.O. Box 186, Pietermaritzburg 3200, South Africa. Ed. S. Shone. adv.; illus. circ. 9,200. **Document type:** newsletter.
  Description: News and information journal for farmers in Natal, covering activities of Natal Agriculture Union and affiliations such as farmers' association, cooperatives, producer organizations.

630   CN   ISSN 0848-8851
N B I A NEWSLETTER. (Text in English, French) 1989. q. free. New Brunswick Institute of Agrologists, P.O. Box 20280, Fredericton, NB E3B 4Z7, Canada. TEL 506-452-3260. FAX 506-452-3316. Ed. Dr. Warren K. Coleman. bk.rev.; circ. 200 (controlled). (looseleaf format; back issues avail.) **Document type:** newsletter.
  Description: For professional agrologists in Atlantic Canada.

630   US   ISSN 1055-2634
N F O REPORTER. 1956. 10/yr. $1 to members; non-members $5. National Farmers Organization, 2505 Elwood Dr., Ames, IA 50010-2005. TEL 515-292-2000; 800-247-2110. FAX 515-292-7106. E-mail: nfo@netins.net; URL: http://nfo.org. Ed. Perry Garner. R&P contact: Perry Garner. TEL 515-292-2000 ext.271. circ. 20,000. (tabloid format) **Document type:** trade publication.
  Description: Covers group marketing and price negotiation and other topics of interest to family farmers.

630   CG
N U K T A. w. 14 Chaussee de Kasenga, B.P. 3805, Lubumbashi, Democratic Republic of the Congo. Ed. Ngoy Bunduki.

NAFO - NYTT. (Norsk Naturforvalterforbund) see *LABOR UNIONS*

630   CC   ISSN 1000-2030
S19   CODEN: NNDXEI
NANJING NONGYE DAXUE XUEBAO/NANJING AGRICULTURAL UNIVERSITY. JOURNAL. (Text in Chinese) 1956-1957; resumed 1980. q. Y20. Nanjing Nongye Daxue - Nanjing Agricultural University, Weigang, Nanjing Jiangsu 210095, People's Republic of China. TEL 86-25-4432420. FAX 86-25-4431492. E-mail: Ed. Huqu Zhai. circ. 1,400 (paid). **Document type:** academic/scholarly publication.
  —BLDSC (4828.675700); CASDDS.
  Formerly (until 1985): Nanjing Agricultural College. Journal (ISSN 0465-7918)
  Description: Covers original research papers, literature reviews and brief information on different fields of agriculture science.

659.1   US
NATIONAL AGRI-MARKETING ASSOCIATION NEWS.* tortn. membership. National Agri-Markcting Association, 11020 King St., Ste. 205, Shawnee Mission, KS 66210-1201. TEL 913-492-0220. FAX 913-492-5147. bk.rev.
  Description: Includes association and industry developments, as well as employment opportunities and calendar of events.

AGRICULTURE

NATIONAL AGRICULTURAL PLASTICS CONGRESS. PROCEEDINGS. see *PLASTICS*

630 US ISSN 1045-1579
S541
NATIONAL AGRICULTURAL RESEARCH AND EXTENSION USERS ADVISORY BOARD. REPORT TO THE PRESIDENT AND CONGRESS - UNITED STATES. a. National Agricultural Research and Extension Users Advisory Board, Rm. 432-A, Admin. Bldg., USDA, 14th St. & Independence Ave., S.W., Washington, DC 20250.

630 CE
 CODEN: NASJAO
NATIONAL AGRICULTURAL SOCIETY OF SRI LANKA. JOURNAL. (Text in English) 1964. a. $18. National Agricultural Society of Sri Lanka, Faculty of Agriculture, University of Sri Lanka, Peradeniya, Sri Lanka. TEL 94-8-388041. FAX 94-8-388041. Ed. H.P.M. Gunasena. R&P contact: H.P.M. Gunasena. adv.; illus. circ. 400. **Indexed:** Biol.Abstr., Chem.Abstr., Dairy Sci.Abstr., Field Crop Abstr., Food Sci.& Tech.Abstr., Herb.Abstr., Hort.Abstr., Plant Breed.Abstr., Rev.Plant Path., Rural Recreat.Tour.Abstr., Sri Lanka Sci.Ind., Trop.Abstr., World Agri.Econ.& Rural Sociol.Abstr. **Document type:** academic/scholarly publication.
—CASDDS
 Formerly: National Agricultural Society of Ceylon. Journal (ISSN 0547-3616)

630 AT
NATIONAL COUNTRY LIFE. 1889. m. (Wool Selling Brokers Association) Country Life Newspaper Co. Ltd., G.P.O. Box 1558, Sydney 2000, N.S.W, Australia. (Co-sponsor: Stock & Station Agents Association of NSW) Ed. I. Law. adv.; bk.rev.; illus.; stat.; tr.lit. circ. 14,500. (tabloid format)
 Formerly: Country Life (ISSN 0011-0167)

630 UK
NATIONAL FEDERATION OF FRUIT AND POTATO TRADES. ANNUAL HANDBOOK AND LIST OF MEMBERS. a. £10 to non-members; members £4. National Federation of Fruit and Potato Trades Ltd., 103-107 Market Towers, 1 Nine Elms Ln., London SW8 5NQ, England. Ed. Ann M. Stirling.

635 UK
NATIONAL FEDERATION OF FRUIT & POTATO TRADES. FEDERATION NEWS. m. membership. National Federation of Fruit and Potato Trades Ltd., 103-107 Market Towers, 1 Nine Elms Ln., London SW8 5NQ, England. Ed. D.P. Mead. adv.; circ. controlled.
 Formerly (until 1983): National Federation of Fruit and Potato Trades. News and Views.

NATIONAL INSTITUTE OF AGROBIOLOGICAL RESOURCES. ANNUAL REPORT. see *BIOLOGY*

630 US ISSN 1073-0540
HD9003
NATIONAL ORGANIC DIRECTORY. 1983. a. $34.95. Community Alliance with Family Farmers, Box 464, Davis, CA 95617. TEL 916-756-8518; 800-852-3832. FAX 916-756-7857. Ed. Carol Klesow. adv. contact: Carol Klesow. circ. 2,000. **Document type:** directory.
 Former titles (until 1995): National Directory of Organic Wholesalers (ISSN 1066-2162); **Former titles:** Organic Wholesalers Directory and Yearbook - Organic Food and Farm Supplies; C A N Directory - Wholesalers of Organic Produce and Products; C A A P Directory - Wholesalers of Organic Produce and Products.

630 JA ISSN 0916-6858
 CODEN: KHYCEJ
NATIONAL RESEARCH INSTITUTE OF VEGETABLES, ORNAMENTAL PLANTS AND TEA. BULLETIN. SERIES B. (Text in Japanese; summaries in English) 1962. a. Ministry of Agriculture, Forestry and Fisheries, National Research Institute of Vegetables, Ornamental Plants and Tea, 2769 Kanaya, Haibara, Shizuoka 428, Japan. TEL 0547-45-4101. FAX 0547-46-2169. Ed.Bd. **Indexed:** Biol.Abstr., Chem.Abstr., Food Sci.& Tech.Abstr., Hort.Abstr., Plant Breed.Abstr.
—BLDSC (2643.350000); CASDDS.
 Former titles: National Research Institute of Tea. Bulletin (ISSN 0528-7820); (until 1973): Tea Research Station. Bulletin.

630 CH ISSN 0077-5819
SB13 CODEN: KTNYA8
NATIONAL TAIWAN UNIVERSITY. COLLEGE OF AGRICULTURE. MEMOIRS. Key Title: Guoli Taiwan Daxue Nongxueyuan Yanjiu Baogao. (Text in Chinese and English; summaries in English) 1936. irreg. National Taiwan University, College of Agriculture, Taipei, Taiwan, Republic of China. Ed.Bd. circ. 500. **Indexed:** Biol.Abstr., Crop Physiol.Abstr., Excerp.Med., Field Crop Abstr., Forest.Abstr., Forest Prod.Abstr., Geo.Abstr., Herb.Abstr., Hort.Abstr., Ind.Vet., Pig News & Info., Rev.Plant Path., Rice Abstr., Seed Abstr., Sel.Water Res.Abstr., Soils & Fert., Sport Fish.Abstr., Trop.Oil Seeds Abstr., Vet.Bull., VITIS, Weed Abstr., Wild.Rev., Zoo.Rec.
—BLDSC (5581.150000); CASDDS.

630 GW ISSN 0172-1631
NATUR UND RECHT; Zeitschrift fuer das gesamte Recht zum Schutze der natuerlichen Lebensgrundlagen. 1979. 12/yr. DM.454 in Europe; rest of world DM.466 (effective 1998). Blackwell Wissenschaft, Kurfuerstendamm 57, 10707 Berlin, Germany. TEL 49-30-32790634. FAX 49-30-32790610. E-mail: aboverwalt@blackwis.de; URL: http://www.blackwis.com. Ed. Claus Carlsen. bk.rev. (back issues avail.) **Indexed:** Dok.Str., IBR. **Document type:** academic/scholarly publication.
—SWETS. CCC.

630 BN ISSN 0351-4471
NAUCNA SVESKA. (Text in Serbo-Croatian; summaries in English) 1979. a. 12000 din.($40) A I P K Istrizivacko Razvojni Institut, 4 Jula 19, 78000 Banja Luka, Bosnia Hercegovina. TEL 078 42-792. Ed. Jovan Kondic. circ. 400. (back issues avail.)

630 635 YU ISSN 0350-1388
NAUKA U PRAKSI. (Text in Serbo-Croatian) 1971. q. 600 din.($60) (Institute for Scientific Work, Consulting and Engineering) P K B - Agroekonomik, d.d., 11213 Padinska Skela, Belgrade, Yugoslavia. TEL 8171-460. FAX 343-326. TELEX 72286. Ed. Mihailo Milosevic. circ. 1,000. **Indexed:** Field Crop Abstr., Herb.Abstr., Hort.Abstr.
—BLDSC (6059.150000).

630 GR ISSN 0028-1727
 CODEN: NAEPO9
NEA AGROTIKI EPITHEORISSIS; agricultural and farming review. (Text in Greek; summaries in English, French) 1947. bi-m. Dr.5000($31) to individuals; farmers and agronomists Dr.1000 ($6.50). (Committee of Greek Agronomists) Spiros Spirou Ltd., 5 Markoni St., 122 42 Athens, Greece. TEL 30-1-3472-821. FAX 30-1-3471-890. TELEX 219133 SPIR GR. Ed. George Spirou. adv. contact: George Spirou. bk.rev.; abstr.; bibl.; illus.; stat.; index. circ. 7,300. (tabloid format) **Document type:** newspaper.

630 US ISSN 0745-6522
NEBRASKA FARM BUREAU NEWS. 1960. m. membership. Nebraska Farm Bureau Federation, Box 80299, Lincoln, NE 68501. TEL 402-421-4405. FAX 402-421-4432. Ed. Cheryl Stubbendieck. adv. circ. 43,500.
 Formerly: Nebraska Agriculture.
 Description: News of state and national events and legislation affecting farmers and ranchers.

631 US ISSN 1049-1880
S1
NEBRASKA FARMER. 1859. 15/yr. $19.95. (Nebraska Farmer Co.) Farm Progress Companies (Subsidiary of: A B C Publishing Companies), 191 S. Gary Ave., Carol Stream, IL 60188. TEL 630-690-5600. FAX 630-462-2869. (Edit. addr.: 5625 O St., Ste. 5, Lincoln, NE 68510. TEL 402-489-9331. FAX 402-489-9335) Ed. Dave Howe. adv.: B&W page $3850, color page $4430; trim 7 X 10. circ. 48,295 (paid).
—Linda Hall.
 Description: Covers ranching and farming practices, marketing, legislation, and technology updates for farmers and ranchers in Nebraska.

630 US
NEIGHBOR. 1983. bi-w. $20. 309 W. 43rd St., Ste. 103, Sioux Falls, SD 57105-6805. TEL 605-335-7300. FAX 605-335-8141. E-mail: neighbor@aol.com. Ed. Sheri Poore. adv. contact: Randy Ahrendt. circ. 29,000 (controlled). **Document type:** newspaper.
 Formerly (until 1993): Tri-State Neighbor.
 Description: Regional farm news for SD, IA, MN, and NE.

630 US ISSN 0162-3974
NEIGHBORS. 1975. m. $2. Alabama Farmers Federation, 2108 E. South Blvd., Box 11000, Montgomery, AL 36191-0001. TEL 334-288-3900. FAX 334-284-3957. Ed. Mark Morrison. adv. circ. 100,000.

NEMATOLOGICA; international journal of nematological research. see *BIOLOGY — Zoology*

630 NE ISSN 0028-2928
S11 CODEN: NETMAW
NETHERLANDS JOURNAL OF AGRICULTURAL SCIENCE. (Text in English) 1953. q. fl.135 (foreign fl.170) (effective 1996). Koninklijk Landbouwkundige Vereniging - Royal Society of Agricultural Sciences, Postbus 79, 6700 AB Wageningen, Netherlands. TEL 31-8370-83537. FAX 31-8370-83976. Ed. J.J. Neeteson. adv.: B&W page fl.400. bk.rev.; abstr.; bibl.; charts; illus.; index. circ. 2,000. (also avail. in microform from UMI; reprint service avail. from UMI) **Indexed:** Agri.Eng.Abstr., Anim.Breed.Abstr., ASCA, Bio-Contr.News & Info., Biol.Abstr., Cadscan, Chem.Abstr., Cott.& Trop.Fibr.Abstr., Crop Physiol.Abstr., Curr.Adv.Ecol.Sci., Curr.Adv.Genetics & Molec.Biol., Curr.Cont., Dairy Sci.Abstr., Ecol.Abstr., Energy Ind., Energy Info.Abstr., Excerp.Med., Fababean Abstr., Field Crop Abstr., Food Sci.& Tech.Abstr., Forest.Abstr., Forest Prod.Abstr., Geo.Abstr.H.G., Geo.Abstr.P.G., Helminthol.Abstr., Herb.Abstr., Herb.Abstr., Hort.Abstr., IBR, IDA, Ind.Sci.Rev., Ind.Vet., Irr.& Drain.Abstr., Lead Abstr., Maize Abstr., Nutr.Abstr., Ornam.Hort., Pig News & Info., Plant Breed.Abstr., Potato Abstr., Poult.Abstr., Rice Abstr., Rural Recreat.Tour.Abstr., Sci.Cit.Ind., Sel.Water Res.Abstr., Soils & Fert., Sorghum & Millets Abstr., Soyabean Abstr., Sport Fish.Abstr., Sugar Ind.Abstr., Triticale Abstr., Vet.Bull., Weed Abstr., Wild.Rev., World Agri.Econ.& Rural Sociol.Abstr., Zincscan, Zoo.Rec. **Document type:** academic/scholarly publication.
—BLDSC (6077.000000); CASDDS; Ei; EMDOCS; Genuine Article; KR SourceOne; Linda Hall; SWETS; UMI; UnCover.

630 AU
NEUE AGRARZEITUNG; Magazin fuer die Bauern. (Text in German) 1920. m. S.180. (SPO - Bauern) Erwin Schwaiger Verlag GmbH, Haspingergasse 5-1, A-1080 Vienna, Austria. TEL 43-1-4030180. FAX 43-1-403018020. Ed. Karin Kopp. R&P contact: Fritz Edlinger. adv. contact: Anneliese Leifert. bk.rev. circ. 100,000. (reprint service avail.) **Document type:** trade publication.

638.1 GW
NEUE BIENENZUCHT. 1974. m. DM.26. Landesverband Schleswig-Holsteinischer Imker, Theodor-Heuss-Ring 55, 23795 Bad Segeberg, Germany. Ed. Horst Sigfert. adv.; bk.rev. circ. 4,000. **Indexed:** Apic.Abstr.
 Formerly: Bienenzucht.

630 GW ISSN 0937-9851
DIE NEUE D L. 1955. bi-m. DM.12. Bund der Deutschen Landjugend im Deutschen Bauernverband e.V., Godesbergerallee 142-148, 53175 Bonn, Germany. TEL 49-228-8198258. FAX 49-228-8198206. Ed. Jochen Heimberg. adv.: B&W page DM.1240, color page DM.3600; trim 270 x 190; adv. contact: Monika Baaken. bk.rev. circ. 11,000. **Document type:** newsletter.
 Former titles (until 1989): D L Quer (ISSN 0935-5529); (until 1988): D L Deutsche Landjugend (Ausgabe Bayern) (ISSN 0935-5510); (until 1980): Deutsche Landjugend (ISSN 0170-0642)

630 GW ISSN 0863-2847
NEUE LANDWIRTSCHAFT; Fachzeitschrift fuer Agrarmanagement. 1990. m. DM.90 (foreign DM.119) (effective 1997). D L V Deutscher Landwirtschaftsverlag Berlin, Guertelstr. 29a-30, 10247 Berlin, Germany. TEL 49-30-293974-57. FAX 49-30-29397459. Eds. Klaus Boehme, Manfred Grund. adv. **Indexed:** Sugar Ind.Abstr. **Document type:** trade publication.
 Incorporates: Feldwirtschaft (ISSN 0014-9799); Tierzucht (ISSN 0373-1677)

630 AU
NEUES LAND. 1934. w. Steirischer Bauernband, Reitschulgasse 3, A-8010 Graz, Austria. TEL 43-316-826361. FAX 43-316-826361-16. Ed. Fred Strohmeier. R&P contact: Alois Puntigam. adv. contact: Josef Trattner. bk.rev. **Document type:** bulletin.
 Formerly: Steirisches Bauernbuendler.

AGRICULTURE

630 US ISSN 0899-8434
NEVADA FARM BUREAU'S AGRICULTURE & LIVESTOCK JOURNAL. 1932. m. $1 to members only. Nevada Farm Bureau Federation, 1300 Marietta Way, Sparks, NV 89431. TEL 702-358-7737. FAX 702-358-2107. Ed. Norman F. Cardoza. R&P contact: Norman F. Cardoza. adv.; bk.rev.; illus.; circ. 8,739 (paid). **Document type:** newspaper.
Description: Provides news, features and information of interest to Nevada farmers and ranchers and other members.

630 II ISSN 0971-0647
CODEN: NEAGEP
NEW AGRICULTURIST. (Text in English) 1990. s-a. Rs.100 to individuals (foreign $50); institutions Rs.500 (foreign $125). Bioved Research Society, c/o Brijesh K. Dwivedi, General Secretary, 252A-4A Om Gayatri Nagar, Teliarganj, Allahabad 211 004, U.P., India. TEL 91-532-644069. FAX 91-532-640429. **Indexed:** Food Sci.& Tech.Abstr. **Document type:** academic/scholarly publication.
—BLDSC (6081.775000); CASDDS. **CCC.**

630 US
NEW ENGLAND FARM BULLETIN AND GARDEN GAZETTE. 1976. m. $17 (effective 1997). Jacob's Meadow, Inc., Box 67, Taunton, MA 02780-0067. TEL 508-998-5424. Ed. Pam Comstock. adv.; bk.rev.; index. circ. 17,000. **Document type:** newsletter.
Formerly: New England Farm Bulletin (ISSN 0279-9162)

630 US ISSN 0193-0923
NEW ENGLAND FARMER. 1822. m. $12 (foreign $25). Rural Press U S A, 7701 Six Forks Rd., Ste. 132, Raleigh, NC 27615. TEL 919-676-3276. FAX 919-676-9803. (Subscr. to: Box 150001, Raleigh, NC 27624) Ed. M. Moore; Pub. Jeff Tennant. adv.; B&W page $1346. bk.rev.; charts. circ. 17,000. (tabloid format; also avail. in microform from UMI; reprint service avail. from UMI) **Document type:** newspaper.

630 UK ISSN 0952-1402
NEW FARMER AND GROWER; Britain's journal for organic food production. 1983. q. £15 to individuals (foreign £17 ($26)); institutions £18 (foreign £20 ($30)) (effective 1997); newsstand price: £2.95. Soil Association, 86 Colston St., Bristol, Avon BS1 5BB, England. TEL 44-117-929-9666. FAX 44-117-925-2504. Ed. Joy McInaud. R&P contact: Tim Weisselberg. TEL 44-117-929-0661. adv.; B&W page £260, color page £500; trim 180 x 270; adv. contact: Paul Adams. bk.rev.; circ. 2,250 (paid). **Indexed:** Environ.Per.Bibl. (1990-). **Document type:** trade publication.
—BLDSC (6084.157500).
Description: Provides technical information, news, and commentary on the principles, practice, and politics of organic farming and growing.
Refereed Serial

630 US ISSN 0077-832X
S89
NEW HAMPSHIRE. AGRICULTURAL EXPERIMENT STATION, DURHAM. RESEARCH REPORTS. 1961. irreg., latest 1994. free. University of New Hampshire, Agricultural Experiment Station, Durham, NH 03824. TEL 603-862-1234. **Indexed:** Curr.Adv.Ecol.Sci., Curr.Cont. **Document type:** academic/scholarly publication.
Refereed Serial

630 US ISSN 0077-8338
NEW HAMPSHIRE. AGRICULTURAL EXPERIMENT STATION, DURHAM. STATION BULLETINS. 1888. irreg. free. University of New Hampshire, Agricultural Experiment Station, Durham, NH 03824. TEL 603-862-1234. circ. 100. **Indexed:** Curr.Adv.Ecol.Sci., Curr.Cont. **Document type:** bulletin.
—CISTI; Linda Hall.

630 US
NEW HOLLAND NEWS. 1960. 8/yr. New Holland, Inc., Box 1895, New Holland, PA 17557. TEL 717-354-1121. URL: http://www.newholland.com/na. Ed. Gary Martin. adv.; circ. 400,000 (controlled). **Indexed:** Farm & Garden Ind.
Former titles: Ford New Holland News; Sperry New Holland News.
Description: Promotional material from this agricultural and farm machinery manufacturer and retailer, with miscellaneous articles on crops, animals, farm people, and rural life.

630 US ISSN 0898-8765
NEW JERSEY FARMER. 1988. m. $10. American Farm Publications, Inc., 505 Brookletts Ave., Box 2026, Easton, MD 21601. TEL 301-822-3965. FAX 301-822-5068. Ed. Mark Powell. adv. circ. 5,000.
Description: Focuses on New Jersey's principal agricultural interests and on agri-political issues.

630 US ISSN 0028-6192
NEW MEXICO FARM & RANCH. 1944. m. $24. (New Mexico Farm & Livestock Bureau) New Mexico Farm & Ranch, Inc., 421 N. Water St., Las Cruces, NM 88001. TEL 505-526-5521. FAX 505-525-0858. Ed. Erik Ness. R&P contact: Erik Ness. adv.; bk.rev.; illus. circ. 11,010. **Document type:** trade publication.
Description: News and information on agriculture in New Mexico including legislation and farm bureau actions.

630 US ISSN 0548-5967
S93 CODEN: NEXRAX
NEW MEXICO STATE UNIVERSITY. AGRICULTURAL EXPERIMENT STATION. RESEARCH REPORT. 1955. irreg. (10-20/yr.), no.678, 1993. New Mexico State University, Agricultural Experiment Station, Drawer 3AI, Las Cruces, NM 88003-0003. TEL 505-646-2701. Ed. Terry Canup. **Indexed:** ASCA, Biol.Abstr., Curr.Adv.Ecol.Sci., Curr.Cont., Nutr.Abstr. **Document type:** academic/scholarly publication.
—Linda Hall.

630 639.2 350 AT ISSN 0156-255X
HD2155.N47
NEW SOUTH WALES. DEPARTMENT OF AGRICULTURE. ANNUAL REPORT. 1890. a. Aus.$16. Department of Agriculture, Locked Bag 21, Orange, N.S.W. 2800, Australia. TEL 61-63-913433. Ed. D. Harris. circ. 1,500. (back issues avail.) **Indexed:** Biol.Abstr.

630 AT ISSN 0369-5867
NEW SOUTH WALES. DEPARTMENT OF AGRICULTURE. SCIENCE BULLETIN. 1912. irreg. price varies. Department of Agriculture, Locked Bag 21, Orange, N.S.W. 2800, Australia. TEL 61-63-913433. Ed. E. Roberts. circ. 750.
—CISTI.
Description: Contains major research reports, reviews and monographs.

630 AT ISSN 0311-8576
CODEN: TBAWDF
NEW SOUTH WALES. DEPARTMENT OF AGRICULTURE. TECHNICAL BULLETIN. 1974. irreg. price varies. Department of Agriculture, Locked Bag 21, Orange, N.S.W. 2800, Australia. TEL 61-63-913433. Ed. E. Roberts. circ. 750.
—CASDDS; CISTI.
Description: Discusses soundly designed and executed agricultural programs or reviews.

630 US
NEW YORK FARMER. m. $12 (foreign $25). Rural Press U S A, 7701 Six Forks Rd., Ste. 132, Raleigh, NC 27615. TEL 919-676-3276; 800-477-1737. FAX 919-676-9803. (Subscr. to: Box 150001, Raleigh, NC 27624) Ed. Linda Goodwin; Pub. Jeff Tennant. adv.; B&W page $1218. circ. 17,000. **Document type:** newspaper.

630 NZ ISSN 0028-8098
NEW ZEALAND FARMER. 1882. w. NZ.$104 (Australia NZ.$200; elsewhere NZ.$330). New Zealand Rural Press Ltd., 300 Great South Rd., P.O. Box 4233, Auckland, New Zealand. E-mail: ruralprs@iconz.co.nz. Ed. H. Stringleman. adv.; bk.rev.; charts; illus.; index. circ. 15,000.
—CCC.

630 NZ ISSN 0028-8233
CODEN: NEZFA7
NEW ZEALAND JOURNAL OF AGRICULTURAL RESEARCH. 1958. q. NZ.$140($90) to individuals; institutions NZ.$300 ($200) (effective 1997). (Royal Society of New Zealand) S I R Publishing, P.O. Box 399, Wellington, New Zealand. TEL 64-4-472-7421. FAX 64-4-473-1841. E-mail: nzja@rsnz.govt.nz; URL: http://www.rsnz.govt.nz. (Subscr. addr. in US: SIR Publishing, 810 E. 10th St., Box 1897, Lawrence, KS 66044-8897, USA. TEL 913-843-1221) Ed. G.P. Sutherland. bibl.; charts; illus.; index. circ. 600. (back issues avail.) **Indexed:** Anim.Breed.Abstr., ASCA, Bio-Contr.News & Info., Biol.Abstr., Biol.& Agr.Ind., Biotech.Abstr., Chem.Abstr., Curr.Adv.Ecol.Sci., Curr.Cont., Dairy Sci.Abstr., Ecol.Abstr., Energy Ind., Energy Info.Abstr., Environ.Abstr., Excerp.Med., Field Crop Abstr., Food Sci.& Tech.Abstr., Forest.Abstr., Geo.Abstr., Helminthol.Abstr., Herb.Abstr., Hort.Abstr., Ind.Sci.Rev., Ind.Vet., Irr.& Drain.Abstr., Maize Abstr., Nutr.Abstr., Ocean.Abstr., Pig News & Info., Pollut.Abstr., Poult.Abstr., Rev.Med.& Vet.Mycol., Sci.Cit.Ind., Seed Abstr., Sel.Water Res.Abstr., Soils & Fert., Soyabean Abstr., Telegen, Triticale Abstr., Trop.Oil Seeds Abstr., Vet.Bull., VITIS, W.R.C.Inf., Weed Abstr. **Document type:** academic/scholarly publication.
—BLDSC (6092.500000); CASDDS; Ei; EMDOCS; Genuine Article; KR SourceOne; Linda Hall; SWETS; UnCover. **CCC.**
Description: Publishes papers on all aspects of animal and pastoral science relevant to temperate and sub-tropical regions.
Refereed Serial

630 NZ ISSN 0114-0671
CODEN: NZJSEF
NEW ZEALAND JOURNAL OF CROP AND HORTICULTURAL SCIENCE. 1973. q. NZ.$140($90) to individuals; institutions NZ.$300 ($200) (effective 1997). (Royal Society of New Zealand) S I R Publishing, P.O. Box 399, Wellington, New Zealand. TEL 64-4-472-7421. FAX 64-4-473-1841. E-mail: nzjch@rsnz.govt.nz; URL: http://www.rsnz.govt.nz. (Subscr. addr. in US: SIR Publishing, 810 E. 10th St., Box 1897, Lawrence, KS 66044-8897, USA. TEL 913-843-1221) Ed. S. Stanislawek. circ. 400. (back issues avail.) **Indexed:** Anim.Breed.Abstr., Apic.Abstr., ASCA, Biol.Abstr., Chem.Abstr., Crop Physiol.Abstr., Curr.Adv.Ecol.Sci., Curr.Cont., Dairy Sci.Abstr., Ecol.Abstr., Excerp.Med., Field Crop Abstr., Food Sci.& Tech.Abstr., Forest.Abstr., Forest Prod.Abstr., Geo.Abstr., Helminthol.Abstr., Herb.Abstr., Hort.Abstr., Ind.Sci.Rev., Ind.Vet., Irr.& Drain.Abstr., Nutr.Abstr., Pig News & Info., Plant Breed.Abstr., Plant Grow.Reg.Abstr., Rev.Appl.Entomol., Rev.Plant Path., Sci.Cit.Ind., Seed Abstr., So.Pac.Per.Ind., Soils & Fert., Vet.Bull., Weed Abstr., World Agri.Econ.& Rural Sociol.Abstr. **Document type:** academic/scholarly publication.
—BLDSC (6093.300000); CASDDS; CISTI; EMDOCS; Genuine Article; Linda Hall; SWETS; UnCover. **CCC.**
Formerly (until 1990): New Zealand Journal of Experimental Agriculture (ISSN 0301-5521)
Description: Publishes research papers concerned with all aspects of horticulture and crops, with a special focus on kiwifruit and apples.
Refereed Serial

630 640 US ISSN 1061-7760
NEWS & VIEWS (BELMONT). 1917. 10/yr. $6. Cornell Cooperative Extension of Allegany County, 5435A County Rd. 48, Belmont, NY 14813. TEL 716-268-7644. Ed. Paul Westfall. adv.; charts; stat. circ. 500. (back issues avail.) **Indexed:** Bibl.Agri. **Document type:** newsletter.
Former titles: Allegany County Cooperative Extension News; Allegany County Farm and Home News.

630 371.3 US ISSN 0199-4530
NEWS & VIEWS (MAYS LANDING). 1947. q. $20 (effective 1994). National Association of Extension 4 H Agents, 6260 W. Landing Hwy., Mays Landing, NJ 08330. TEL 609-625-0056. Ed. Debi Cole. adv.; bk.rev.; circ. 1,800 (paid). (back issues avail.) **Document type:** newsletter.

AGRICULTURE

630 US ISSN 0886-814X
NEWS C A S T. 1974. q. $50 (foreign $100, includes Task Force Reports and Special Publications). Council for Agricultural Science and Technology, 4420 W. Lincoln Way, Ames, IA 50014-3447. TEL 515-292-2125. FAX 515-292-4512. E-mail: cast@cast-science.org. Ed. Robert J. Ver Straeten. circ. 6,000.
  Description: News of interest to CAST members, and summaries of CAST publications.

630 US
NEWS FOR FAMILY FARMERS AND RURAL AMERICANS. 1948. 12/yr. $10 (effective 1997). Farmers Educational & Cooperative Union of America, 400 Virginia Ave., S.W., Ste. 710, Washington, DC 20024. TEL 202-554-1600. FAX 202-554-1654. Ed. Larry Mitchell. bk.rev. circ. 35,003. **Document type:** newsletter.
  Formerly: National Farmers Union Washington Newsletter (ISSN 0027-9226)

NIGERIA. METEOROLOGICAL SERVICE. AGROMETEOROLOGICAL BULLETIN. see METEOROLOGY

630 NR ISSN 0300-368X
NIGERIAN AGRICULTURAL JOURNAL. (Text in English) 1964. s-a. $8. Agricultural Society of Nigeria, c/o Dr. T.I. Ashaye, P.M.B. 5029, Ibadan, Oyo State, Nigeria. Ed. Prof. Q.B.O. Anthonio. adv.; bk.rev.; illus. circ. 1,000. **Indexed:** Biol.Abstr., Field Crop Abstr., Herb.Abstr., Plant Breed.Abstr., Rev.Plant Path., Weed Abstr. **Document type:** academic/scholarly publication.

NIHON DANI GAKKAISHI/ACAROLOGICAL SOCIETY OF JAPAN. JOURNAL. see BIOLOGY — Entomology

630 JA ISSN 0385-8634
CODEN: NDNHDH
NIIGATA DAIGAKU NOGAKUBU KENKYU HOKOKU/NIIGATA UNIVERSITY. FACULTY OF AGRICULTURE. BULLETIN. (Text in English, Japanese) 1951. a. exchange basis. Niigata Daigaku, Nogakubu - Niigata University, Faculty of Agriculture, 8050 Igarashi 2, Niigata-shi 950-21, Japan. Ed. Atsushi Suzuki. circ. 500. **Indexed:** Crop Physiol.Abstr., Excerp.Med., Field Crop Abstr., Forest.Abstr., Herb.Abstr., Pig News & Info., Plant Breed.Abstr., Plant Grow.Reg.Abstr., Potato Abstr., Rev.Plant Path., Seed Abstr., Soils & Fert., Soyabean Abstr., Weed Abstr. **Document type:** academic/scholarly publication.
  —BLDSC (2507.237000); CASDDS.
  Formerly (until 1977): Niigata Agricultural Science.

630 JA ISSN 0549-4826
NIIGATA DAIGAKU NOGAKUBU KIYO/NIIGATA UNIVERSITY. FACULTY OF AGRICULTURE. MEMOIRS. (Text in English and Japanese) 1961. a. exchange basis. Niigata Daigaku, Nogakubu - Niigata University, Faculty of Agriculture, 8050 Igarashi 2, Niigata-shi 950-21, Japan. Ed. Atsushi Suzuki. circ. 500. **Indexed:** Biol.Abstr., Chem.Abstr., Forest.Abstr., Forest Prod.Abstr., Helminthol.Abstr., Irr.& Drain.Abstr., Plant Breed.Abstr., Rev.Plant Path., Soils & Fert., VITIS. **Document type:** academic/scholarly publication.
  —BLDSC (5593.100000).

630 US ISSN 0091-9993
NO-TILL FARMER. 1972. 17/yr. $34.95 (effective 1997); newsstand price: $4. Lessiter Publications, Box 624, Brookfield, WI 53008-0624. TEL 414-782-4480. FAX 414-782-1252. E-mail: lesspub@aol.com. Ed. Frank Lessiter. adv.; bk.rev. circ. 10,000. **Indexed:** Farm & Garden Ind. **Document type:** consumer publication.
  —CCC.
  Description: For farmers who are interested in all aspects of no-till farming; from beginner level to experienced.

630 SW ISSN 0281-8205
NOETKOETT; aktuellt om svensk noetkoettsproduktion. 1982. q. SEK 190. (Nordiska Avelsfoereningen foer Biffraser) Svensk Husdjursskoetsel, Haallsta, S-631 84 Eskilstuna, Sweden. TEL 46-16-16-34-00. FAX 46-16-211-25. (Co-sponsor: Sveriges Koettproducenters Interessefoerening) Ed. Lena Widebeck. R&P contact: Britt-Marie Jafner. adv. contact: Sten Larsson. circ. 6,500. (back issues avail.) **Document type:** newspaper.
  Description: Focuses on agriculture, agricultural equipment and economics, animal feed and welfare, food and food industries.

630 570 JA ISSN 0911-9450
CODEN: NKGHEW
NOGYO KANKYO GIJUTSU KENKYUSHO HOKOKU/NATIONAL INSTITUTE OF AGRO-ENVIRONMENTAL SCIENCES. BULLETIN. (Text in English or Japanese; summaries in English) 1986. irreg. free. National Institute of Agro-Environmental Sciences - Nogyo Kankyo Gijutsu Kenkyusho, Kannondai 3-1-1, Tsukuba-shi, Ibaraki-ken 305, Japan. TEL 81-298-38-8186. FAX 81-298-38-8186. circ. 1,700. (back issues avail.) **Document type:** bulletin, academic/scholarly publication.
  —BLDSC (2640.020000); CASDDS; Linda Hall.

NOGYO KISHO KENKYU SHUROKU/COLLECTED PAPERS OF AGRICULTURAL METEOROLOGY. see METEOROLOGY

NOGYO KISHO NENPO/ANNUAL REPORT OF AGRICULTURAL METEOROLOGY. see METEOROLOGY

NOGYO SEIBUTSU SHIGEN KENKYUJO KENKYU SHIRYO/NATIONAL INSTITUTE OF AGROBIOLOGICAL RESOURCES. MISCELLANEOUS PUBLICATION. see BIOLOGY

NOGYO SEIBUTSU SHIGEN KENKYUJO NENPO/NATIONAL INSTITUTE OF AGROBIOLOGICAL RESOURCES. ANNUAL REPORT. see BIOLOGY

NOGYO SEIBUTSU SHIGEN KENKYUJO NYUSU/NATIONAL INSTITUTE OF AGROBIOLOGICAL RESOURCES. NEWS. see BIOLOGY

630 JA
NOGYO SOGO KENKYUJO NENPO/NATIONAL RESEARCH INSTITUTE OF AGRICULTURAL ECONOMICS. ANNUAL REPORT. (Text in Japanese) 1949. a. Norinsuisan-sho, Nogyo Sogo Kenkyujo - Ministry of Agriculture, Forestry and Fisheries, National Research Institute of Agricultural Economics, 2-1 Nishi-gahara 2-chome, Kita-ku, Tokyo 114, Japan. TEL 81-3-3910-3946. Ed. Kazuo Nonaka. **Document type:** government publication.
  Formerly: National Research Institute of Agriculture. Annual Report.

630 NR ISSN 0331-6742
NOMA. 1978. a. $25. Ahmadu Bello University, Institute for Agricultural Research, P.M.B. 1044, Samaru-Zaria, Kaduna State, Nigeria. FAX 234-69-50563. Ed. T.O. Fadiji. bk.rev.; charts. (processed) **Indexed:** Anim.Breed.Abstr., Biol.Abstr., Dairy Sci.Abstr., Hort.Abstr., Rev.Appl.Entomol., Rural Recreat.Tour.Abstr., Soils & Fert., World Agri.Econ.& Rural Sociol.Abstr. **Document type:** academic/scholarly publication.
  Formerly (until 1978): Samaru Agricultural Newsletter (ISSN 0036-3731)
  Description: Contains general-interest articles on agriculture.

630 CC ISSN 1002-7785
NONGCUN DASHIJIE. (Text in Chinese) bi-m. Xinhua News Agency, Nongcun Dashijie Bianjibu, 57 Xuanwumen Xidajie, Beijing 100803, People's Republic of China. Ed. Zhao Huaiqing.

630 CC ISSN 0577-5825
NONGCUN KEXUE SHIYAN/AGRICULTURAL EXPERIMENT. (Text in Chinese) m. Jilin Keji Baokan She, 8, Minkang Lu, Changchun, Jilin 130041, People's Republic of China. TEL 853243. Ed. Zhang Jiugui.

NONGCUN QINGNIAN/COUNTRY YOUTH. see CHILDREN AND YOUTH — For

630 CC ISSN 1002-6827
NONGCUN SHIYONG GONGCHENG JISHU/PRACTICAL RURAL ENGINEERING TECHNOLOGY. (Text in Chinese) 1986. bi-m. Zhongguo Nongye Gongcheng Yanjiu Shejiyuan - Chinese Research and Design Institute of Agricultural Engineering, Nongzhanguan Nanlu, Beijing 100026, People's Republic of China. TEL 5003366. Ed. Wang Songtao. **Document type:** academic/scholarly publication.

630 US
NONGMIN RIBAO/FARMER'S DAILY. (Text in Chinese) 6/w. $291.30. China Books & Periodicals, Inc., 2929 24th St., San Francisco, CA 94110. TEL 415-282-2994. FAX 415-282-0994. **Document type:** newspaper.

630 CC ISSN 1000-7741
NONGMIN WENZHAI. (Text in Chinese) m. newsstand price: Y1.50. Zhongguo Nongcun Zazhishe, No. 61 Fuxing Lu, Beijing 100036, People's Republic of China. TEL 86-10-6827-1458. Ed. Hongfei Zhou. R&P contact: Xiaochun Xu. adv. contact: Youming Dong. circ. 2,400,000.
  Description: Presents a broad selection of information and new technologies published in China's newspapers and magazines.

NONGYE HUANJING BAOHU/AGRO-ENVIRONMENTAL PROTECTION. see ENVIRONMENTAL STUDIES

NONGYE KAOGU/AGRICULTURAL ARCHAEOLOGY. see ARCHAEOLOGY

630 CC ISSN 1000-6400
S471.C6
NONGYE KEJI TONGXUN/AGRICULTURAL SCIENCE AND TECHNOLOGY BULLETIN. (Text in Chinese) m. Zhongguo Nongye Kexueyuan - Chinese Academy of Agriculture, 30 Baishiqiao Lu, Beijing 100081, People's Republic of China. TEL 8314433. Ed. Hou Liande.

630 CC ISSN 1002-4840
NONGYE QUHUA/AGRICULTURAL REGIONAL PLANNING. (Text in Chinese) 1987. bi-m. Y2 per no. Zhongguo Nongye Kexueyuan, Quhua Suo - Chinese Academy of Agricultural Sciences, Institute of Natural Resources and Regional Planning, 30 Baishiqiao Rd., Beijing 100081, People's Republic of China. TEL 01-8316560. FAX 01-831654. TELEX 222720 CAAS CN. Ed. Li Yingzhong. bk.rev. **Document type:** academic/scholarly publication.

630 CC
NONGYE ZHISHI/AGRICULTURAL KNOWLEDGE. (Text in Chinese) 1950. m. $18. Shandong Nongye Zhishi Zazhishe, 21 Minziqian Rd., Jinan, Shandong 250100, People's Republic of China. TEL 86-531-8930447. Ed. Yang Lijian; Pub. Liu Zongquan. circ. 650,000. **Document type:** academic/scholarly publication.
  Description: Introduces popular agricultural science knowledge.

630 NE ISSN 1380-4278
NOORDOOGST. 1919. w. fl.179 includes Oogst. Noordelijke Land- en Tuinbouw Organisatie, Postbus 170, 9400 AD Assen, Netherlands. TEL 31-5920-11721. FAX 31-5920-16211. adv.; illus. circ. 10,800. (tabloid format) **Document type:** trade publication.
  Former titles (until 1994): Landbode (Editie Drenthe - Groningen) (ISSN 0923-3229); Formed by the 1988 merger of: Landbode - Drents Landbouwblad (ISSN 0165-6635); Landbode - Groninger Landbouwblad; Which was formerly: Groninger Landbouwblad (ISSN 0017-4521)

630 DK
NORD- MIDT- OG VESTSJAELLANDS LANDBRUGS-NYT. w. Lolland-Falsters Erhvervsforlag ApS, Marrebaeck, 4873 Vaeggerloese, Denmark. adv. circ. 16,933.

630 NO ISSN 0029-1226
NORDEN; nord-Norges landbrukstidsskrift. 1896. 16/yr. NOK 390 (foreign NOK 450) (effective 1997). A-L Landbrukstidsskriftet Norden, Vaagenes Forskningsstasjon, N-8010 Bodoe, Norway. TEL 47-75-58-48-40. FAX 47-75-58-48-40. E-mail: norden@online.no. Ed. Haakon Renolen. adv.; bk.rev.; illus.; stat.; index. circ. 3,500. **Document type** trade publication, newsletter.

AGRICULTURE 141

630   FI   ISSN 0048-0495
                        CODEN: NOJOAO
NORDISK JORDBRUKSFORSKNING. (Text in Danish, English, Norwegian and Swedish) 1918. q. FIM 190 (effective 1996 & 1997). Nordiska Jordbruksforskares Foerening, T T S - Institutt, P.O. Box 28, FIN-00211 Helsinki, Finland. TEL 358-0-29041200. FAX 358-0-6922084. Ed. Erkki Oksanen. bk.rev. circ. 3,000. **Indexed:** Anim.Breed.Abstr., Biol.Abstr., Chem.Abstr., Crop Physiol.Abstr., Dairy Sci.Abstr., Field Crop Abstr., Herb.Abstr., Hort.Abstr., Irr.& Drain.Abstr., Plant Breed.Abstr., Plant Grow.Reg.Abstr., Potato Abstr., Seed Abstr., Triticale Abstr., Weed Abstr. **Document type:** trade publication.
—CASDDS.

630   UK   ISSN 0955-0208
NORFOLK FARMER. m. County Farmers Publications Ltd., 55 Goldington Rd., Bedford MK40 3LU, England. TEL 0234-351401. FAX 0234-328614. Ed. D. Brown. adv. circ. 2,400.
    Formerly: Norfolk Farmers' Union Gazette.

631 690   NO   ISSN 0804-676X
NORGES LANDBRUKSHOEGSKOLE. INSTITUTT FOR TEKNISKE FAG. MELDINGER/AGRICULTURAL UNIVERSITY OF NORWAY. DEPARTMENT OF AGRICULTURAL ENGINEERING. REPORTS. 1990. irreg. NOK 250. Norges Landbrukshoegskole, Institutt for Tekniske Fag, P.O. Box 5065, N-1432 Aas, Norway. TEL 47-64-94-87-94. FAX 47-64-94-88-10. TELEX 77125-NLHBI-N. circ. 2,000. **Document type:** bulletin.
    Former titles (until 1992): Noerges Landbrukshoegskole. Institutt for Tekniske Fag. Proevemelding (ISSN 0802-8524); (until 1990): Landbruksteknisk Institutt. Proevemelding (ISSN 0801-6178); (until 1986): Landbruksteknisk Institutt. Melding (ISSN 0800-7721)
    Description: Publishes results of official, required tests.

630 690   NO   ISSN 0802-8532
NORGES LANDBRUKSHOEGSKOLE. INSTITUTT FOR TEKNISKE FAG. RAPPORTER/AGRICULTURAL UNIVERSITY OF NORWAY. DEPARTMENT OF AGRICULTURAL ENGINEERING. RESEARCH REPORTS. (Text in Norwegian; summaries and captions in English) 1990. irreg. free (special issues NOK 50 to NOK 150). Norges Landbrukshoegskole, Institutt for Tekniske Fag, P.O. Box 5065, N-1432 Aas, Norway. TEL 47-64-94-87-94. FAX 47-64-94-88-10. TELEX 77125-NLHBI-N. Ed. Oluf Berentsen.
    Description: Contains reports from research projects.

630   NO   ISSN 0332-5474
NORSK LANDBRUK. 1882. s-m. NOK 690($28.80) A-S Landbruksforlaget, Boks 3647, Gamlebyen, Oslo 1, Norway. FAX 2-173881. Ed. Stein Hoset. adv. circ. 20,700. (back issues avail.) **Indexed:** Field Crop Abstr., Herb.Abstr., Hort.Abstr., Plant Breed.Abstr., Seed Abstr., Triticale Abstr.
—CCC.

630   NO   ISSN 0801-5333
                        CODEN: NOLAEU
NORSK LANDBRUKSFORSKING/NORWEGIAN AGRICULTURAL RESEARCH. (Text in Norwegian; summaries in English) 1987. q. NOK 500. Statens Fagtjeneste for Landbruket - Norwegian Agricultural Advisory Service, Moerveien 12, N-1430 Aas, Norway. TEL 47-64-94-13-65. FAX 47-64-94-37-97. Ed. Margrethe Wiig. circ. 1,550. **Indexed:** Agri.Eng.Abstr., Ornam.Hort., Poult.Abstr., Sport Fish.Abstr., Wild.Rev., Zoo.Rec.
—CCC.

NORTH AMERICAN APPLICATOR MAGAZINE. see AERONAUTICS AND SPACE FLIGHT

630 320 301   US
NORTH AMERICAN FARMER.* 1984. 12/yr. $10 to individuals (foreign $18); institutions $15 (foreign $27). North American Farm Alliance, Box 747, Coloma, MI 49038-0747. Ed. Lynne Blahnik. adv.; bk.rev. circ. 30,000.

630   US   ISSN 0744-5466
NORTH CAROLINA. DEPARTMENT OF AGRICULTURE. AGRICULTURAL REVIEW. Key Title: Agricultural Review (Raleigh). 1925. m. free. Department of Agriculture, 2 W. Edenton St., Raleigh, NC 27601. TEL 919-733-4216. E-mail: jim__knight@ncdamail.agr.state.nc.us; URL: http://www.agr.state.nc.us. (Subscr. to: Box 27647, Raleigh, NC 27611) Ed. James S. Knight. R&P contact: James S. Knight. adv. circ. 70,700. (tabloid format) **Document type:** government publication, newspaper.
—Linda Hall.
    Description: Editorial and classified advertising for farmers.

630   US   ISSN 0744-9593
NORTH CAROLINA FARM BUREAU NEWS. 1936. m. $0.50 per no. North Carolina Farm Bureau Federation, 5301 Glenwood Ave., Box 27766, Raleigh, NC 27611. FAX 919-782-1705. Ed. Chris Street. R&P contact: Janice Nofsinger. adv.: B&W page $3600; trim 8 x 10 3/4; adv. contact: Lori Smith. circ. 375,000 (paid). **Document type:** consumer publication.

630   US
NORTH CAROLINA FARMER. 1980. m. $12. Rural Press U S A, Box 150001, Raleigh, NC 27624-0001. TEL 919-621-0991; 800-477-1737. FAX 919-676-9803. Ed. Richard Davis; Pub. Jeff Tennant. adv.: B&W page $1515; adv. contact: Blake Lewis. circ. 30,000. **Document type:** newspaper.
    Supersedes: Carolina Farmer (North Carolina Edition) (ISSN 0744-2033)
    Description: Covers people and progress in agriculture, innovative farm operations, crop and livestock improvements and management, farm business, and marketing.

630   US
NORTH CAROLINA SEED LAW. 1953. irreg. free. Department of Agriculture, Box 27647, Raleigh, NC 27611. TEL 919-733-7125. URL: http://www.agr.state.nc.us. R&P contact: James S. Knight. TEL 919-733-4216. circ. controlled. **Document type:** government publication.
    Description: Provides seed law information to the North Carolina seed industry.

630 640   US
NORTH COUNTRY FARM NEWS.* 1956. m. Clinton County Cooperative Extension, 6064 State Rte. 22, Ste. 5, Plattsburgh, NY 12901-6222. Ed. Beth Spaugh. adv.; bk.rev.; circ. 900 (controlled).
    Former titles (until Jan. 1979): Extension; (until Jan. 1975): Clinton County Cooperative Extension News; Clinton County Agricultural News.
    Description: Informs agricultural producers on how to improve agricultural productivity and improve environmental quality.

603 353.9   US   ISSN 0362-9643
S99
NORTH DAKOTA. DEPARTMENT OF AGRICULTURE. BIENNIAL REPORT. 1890. biennial. free. Department of Agriculture, 600 E. Blvd., 6th Fl., Bismarck, ND 58505-0020. TEL 701-224-2231. FAX 701-224-4567. Ed. Ellen Delp. illus.; stat. circ. 600. **Document type:** government publication.
    Formerly: North Dakota. Department of Agriculture. Annual Report (ISSN 0093-8203)

630   US
NORTH IOWA FARMER. m. free. Globe-Gazette, 300 N. Washington Ave., Mason City, IA 50401. TEL 515-421-0546. FAX 515-421-0516. Ed. Kevin Baskins; Pub. Howard Query. adv. contact: Byron Wooten. circ. 10,777. **Document type:** newspaper.

630   UK   ISSN 0306-0675
NORTH RIDING AND DURHAM FARMER. WHOLE EDITION. 1962. m. County Farmers Publications Ltd., 55 Goldington Rd., Bedford MK40 3LU, England. TEL 0234-351401. FAX 0234-328614. Ed. A. Hepworth. adv. circ. 4,250.
    Incorporates: North Riding and Durham Farmer. North Riding Edition; Formerly: North Riding and Durham Farmer. Durham Edition.

630   UK
NORTH WALES FARMING NEWS.* 1973. m. £1.24. Mellison Ltd., 63 Cambrian Dr., Rhos-on-Seas, Colwyn Bay, Clwyd LL28 4TA, Wales. Ed. G.E. Walters.

630   UK
NORTH EAST FARMER. m. Agriculture House, Murton Ln., Murton, Yorks. YO1 3UF, England. TEL 01904-488432. FAX 01904-488521. Ed. Kevin Pearce. adv. circ. 2,500. **Document type:** newsletter.
    Formerly: East Riding Farmers Journal.

338.1 639.2   AT
NORTHERN TERRITORY. DEPARTMENT OF PRIMARY INDUSTRY AND FISHERIES. TECHNICAL ANNUAL REPORT. 1989. a. Aus.$8. Department of Primary Industry and Fisheries, P.O. Box 79, Berrimah, N.T. 0828, Australia. TEL 61-89-992202. FAX 61-89-992307. E-mail: graham.calley@nt.gov.au. Ed. Graham Calley. R&P contact: Graham Calley. **Document type:** academic/scholarly publication, government publication.

338.1 639.2   AT   ISSN 1032-0393
NORTHERN TERRITORY. DEPARTMENT OF PRIMARY INDUSTRY AND FISHERIES. TECHNICAL BULLETIN. 1979. irreg. Aus.$6 per no. Department of Primary Industry and Fisheries, P.O. Box 79, Berrimah, N.T. 0828, Australia. TEL 61-89-992202. FAX 61-89-992307. E-mail: graham.calley@nt.gov.au. Ed. Graham Calley. R&P contact: Graham Calley. **Document type:** government publication, monographic series.
    Former titles (until 1988): Northern Territory. Division of Primary Production. Technical Bulletin (ISSN 1031-9581); (until 1987): Northern Territory. Department of Primary Production. Technical Bulletin (ISSN 0158-2763)

630   UK   ISSN 0955-0216
NORTHUMBERLAND FARMER. 1958. m. County Farmers Publications Ltd., 55 Goldington Rd., Bedford MK40 3LU, England. TEL 0234-351401. FAX 0234-328614. Ed. A. Hepworth. adv. circ. 1,750.

630   US
NORTHWEST FARM & FIELD REPORT. 1966. m. $7.50. Lewis Publishing Co., Box 153, Lynden, WA 98264. TEL 206-354-4444. FAX 206-398-1731. Ed. Roy Neese; Pub. Michael D. Lewis. adv. contact: Pam Richardson. charts. circ. 5,000. (tabloid format; back issues avail.) **Document type:** newspaper.
    Formerly: Skagit Farmer.

051   US
NORTHWESTERN ILLINOIS FARMER; the farm family newspaper. 1867. w. $18 (effective 1996 & 1997). Northwestern Illinois Farmer, Box 536, Lena, IL 61048-0536. TEL 815-369-2811. FAX 815-369-2816. Ed. Norman C. Templin. adv.; circ. 11,500 (paid). **Document type:** newspaper.

630   NO   ISSN 0801-5341
NORWEGIAN JOURNAL OF AGRICULTURAL SCIENCES. (Text in English) 1987. q. NOK 500. Statens Fagtjeneste for Landbruket - Norwegian Agricultural Advisory Service, Moerveien 12, N-1430 Aas, Norway. TEL 47-64-94-13-65. FAX 47-64-94-37-97. Ed. Margrethe Wiig. circ. 1,350. **Indexed:** Anim.Breed.Abstr., Dairy Sci.Abstr., Hort.Abstr., Ind.Vet., Ornam.Hort., Rev.Med.& Vet.Mycol., Vet.Bull.
—UnCover.
    Description: Contains agricultural research reports.

630 900   SP   ISSN 1132-1261
HD2021   CODEN: NHAGEC
NOTICIARIO DE HISTORIA AGRARIA. (Text in Spanish; abstracts in English, Spanish) 1991. s-a. 4000 ptas.($50) to individuals; institutions 6000 ptas.($70) (effective 1996). Universidad de Murcia, Facultad de Ciencias Economicas y Empresariales, C. Ronda de Levante, 10, 30008 Murcia, Spain. TEL 34-968-761770. FAX 34-968-363831. E-mail: jcarrion@fcu.um.es. (Subscr. to: Seminario de Historia Agraria, Univ. de Zaragoza, Fac. de Ciencias Econ. y Empresariales, C. Dr. Cerrada 1, 50005 Zaragoza, Spain. TEL 34-976-233551. FAX 34-976-761841) Ed. Jose Miguel Martinez Carrion. adv. contact: Luis German. bk.rev.; bibl.; index, cum.index: 1991-1992. circ. 800. **Indexed:** Amer.Hist.& Life (1993-), Geo.Abstr.P.G., Hist.Abstr. (1993-). **Document type:** academic/scholarly publication.
—CINDOC.
    Description: Specializes on the history of agriculture, economy and rural society of Spain and Latin America.
    Refereed Serial

142 AGRICULTURE

630 FR ISSN 0299-3635
NOTRE TERROIR. 1987. 24/yr. 1 rue du Chateau, 73000 Chambery, France. TEL 33-17-36. Ed. M. Donzel. circ. 5,000.

630 UK ISSN 0955-0224
NOTTINGHAMSHIRE FARMER. 1949. m. County Farmers Publications Ltd., 55 Goldington Rd., Bedford MK40 3LU, England. TEL 0234-351401. FAX 0234-328614. Ed. S. Fisher. adv.; index. circ. 1,600. **Document type:** trade publication.
Formerly: Nottinghamshire Farmers' Journal.

630 CN
NOVA SCOTIA FEDERATION OF AGRICULTURE. ANNUAL REPORT. a. Nova Scotia Federation of Agriculture, P.O. Box 784, Truro, N.S. B2N 5E8, Canada.

630 CN ISSN 0833-8485
NOVA SCOTIA INSTITUTE OF AGROLOGISTS NEWSLETTER. q. free. Nova Scotia Institute of Agrologists, P.O. Box 550, Truro, NS B2N 5E3, Canada. TEL 902-893-6520. Eds. Laurie Eagles, Campbell Gunn. circ. 350. (looseleaf format; back issues avail.) **Document type:** newsletter.

630 338 CI ISSN 0353-7838
NOVOGRADISKI GLASNIK. 1974. s-m. Narodno Sveuciliste "Matija Antun Reljkovic", Reljkoviceva 4, 55400 Nova Gradiska, Croatia. TEL 055 63-762.
Formerly (until 1990): N G Novine (ISSN 0351-6857)

630 PL ISSN 0029-5396
S13
NOWE ROLNICTWO.* 1951. s-m. 600 Zl. Polskie Towarzystwo Nauk Agrotechnicznych, Zarzad Glowny, Ul. Akademicka 13, 20-934 Lublin, Poland. (Dist. by: Ars Polona-Ruch, Krakowskie Przedmiescie 7, Warsaw, Poland) Ed. Rudolf Kowalski. adv.; bk.rev.; bibl.; charts; illus.; stat.; index. circ. 19,000. (tabloid format)

NUCLEUS. see *ENERGY — Nuclear Energy*

630 FI ISSN 0029-6139
NUORTEN SARKA. 1945. m. (8/yr.). FIM 70. Suomen 4H-Liitto - 4H Federation in Finland, Bulevardi 28, 00120 Helsinki 12, Finland. TEL 358-0-645133. Ed. Laura-Leena Happonen. adv.; bk.rev.; film rev.; play rev.; circ. 28,500 (controlled).

630 IT
NUOVA AGRICOLTURA. 1958. m. L.25000. Confederazione Italiana Coltivatori, Via Teresa Ciceri 12, 22100 Como, Italy. TEL 39-31-264561. FAX 39-31-307655. Ed. Liliana Belli. adv.; B&W page L.2700000. circ. 100,000. **Document type:** trade publication.
Description: For farmers in the districts of Como and Lecce.

NUTRITION SOCIETY OF INDIA. PROCEEDINGS. see *NUTRITION AND DIETETICS*

630 GW ISSN 0933-4351
NYANKPALA AGRICULTURAL RESEARCH REPORT. (Text in English) 1988. irreg. DM.39. (Nyankpala Agricultural Experiment Station) Margraf Scientific Publishers, Postfach 105, 97985 Weikersheim, Germany. TEL 07934-3071. FAX 07934-8156. Ed. Cornelie Steidel. **Document type:** academic/scholarly publication.

O D I AGRICULTURAL RESEARCH AND EXTENSION NETWORK PAPERS. (Overseas Development Institute) see *BUSINESS AND ECONOMICS — International Development And Assistance*

630 SA ISSN 0029-7321
O T KANER. (Oostelike Transvaalse) (Text in Afrikaans) 1956. bi-m. membership. O T K (Koop) Bpk, P.O. Box 100, Bethal 2310, South Africa. TEL 01361-71000. FAX 01361-5776. Ed. Werner A. Ras. adv.; bk.rev.; illus.; stat. circ. 11,000. (back issues avail.)

630 SA
O V K BOERENUUS. 1993. irreg. Oos-Vrystaat Kooperasie, Posbus 96, Ladybrand 9745, South Africa. adv.; illus. **Document type:** newsletter.
Formerly: Oos-Vrystaat Boerenuus.

OBST- UND WEINBAU. see *BEVERAGES*

630 GW ISSN 0179-7077
OBSTBAU. 1976. m. Fachgruppe Obstbau im Bundesausschuss fuer Obst und Gemuese, Godesberger Allee 142-148, 53175 Bonn, Germany. **Indexed:** Agri.Eng.Abstr., Food Sci.& Tech.Abstr., Irr.& Drain.Abstr.
—BLDSC (6208.130000).

630 AU
OBSTBAU AKTUELL. 1880. q. Landesobstbauverband fuer Niederoesterreich, Lowelstr. 16, A-1010 Vienna, Austria.

630 SZ
OBWALDNER BAUERNBLATT. m. Tellenstr. 39, CH-6056 Kaegiswil, Switzerland. TEL 041-661651. Ed. Peter Krummenacher. circ. 1,050.

630 PL ISSN 0029-8239
OCHRONA ROSLIN. 1956. m. Instytut Ochrony Roslin, Ul. Miczurina 20, 60-318 Poznan, Poland. TEL 48-61-679021. FAX 48-61-676301. (Dist. by: Ars Polona-Ruch, Krakowskie Przedmiescie 7, Warsaw, Poland) Ed. Stefan Pruszynski. adv.; B&W page X.400. circ. 1,200. **Indexed:** AgroLibrex, Biotech.Abstr., Fababean Abstr., Field Crop Abstr., Forest.Abstr., Helminthol.Abstr., Herb.Abstr., Maize Abstr., Plant Grow.Reg.Abstr., Potato Abstr., Seed Abstr., Triticale Abstr., Weed Abstr.
—BLDSC (6235.120000).

630 GW ISSN 1015-2423
OEKOLOGIE UND LANDBAU. English edition: Ecology and Farming (ISSN 1016-5061) 1977. q. DM.40 (students DM.27.50) (effective 1997). (International Federation of Organic Agriculture Movements - Internationale Vereinigung Biologischer Landbaubewegungen) Stiftung Oekologie und Landbau, Postfach 1516, 67089 Bad Duerkheim, Germany. TEL 49-6322-66002. FAX 49-6322-989701. E-mail: stiftung.soel@t-online.de. Ed. Immo Luenzer. R&P contact: Helga Willer. adv. contact: Beate Dussa. bk.rev. circ. 5,000. **Indexed:** Excerp.Med. **Document type:** newsletter.
—BLDSC (6253.370500).
Formerly (until 1988): I F O A M (ISSN 0171-7456)
Refereed Serial

630 AU
OESTERREICHISCHE BAUERBUENDLER. w. S.430. (Niederoesterreichischer Bauernbund) Oesterreichischer Agrarverlag GmbH, Inkustr. 1-7, A-3400 Klosterneuburg, Austria. TEL 02243-333006. FAX 02243-3330056. Ed. Paul Gruber. circ. 90,000.

630 AU ISSN 0029-8905
OESTERREICHISCHE BAUERNZEITUNG. 1960. m. S.135. (Oesterreichischer Bauernverband) Baeuerlicher Presseverein, Castellezgasse 20-1, A-1020 Vienna, Austria. Ed. Josef Artbauer. adv.; bk.rev.; abstr.; circ. 16,000 (controlled).

630 AU
OESTERREICHISCHE WEINZEITUNG. m. S.835 (foreign S.948). Oesterreichischer Agrarverlag GmbH, Inkustr. 1-7, A-3400 Klosterneuburg, Austria. TEL 02243-333006. FAX 02243-3330056. Ed. Wolfgang Brandstetter.

630 AU
OESTERREICHISCHES RAIFFEISENBLATT. m. S.420 (foreign S.510). Oesterreichischer Agrarverlag GmbH, Inkustr. 1-7, A-3400 Klosterneuburg, Austria. TEL 02243-333006. FAX 02243-3330056. Ed. Robert Bzoch.

630 US ISSN 0078-3951
CODEN: OARBB7
OHIO AGRICULTURAL RESEARCH AND DEVELOPMENT CENTER, WOOSTER. RESEARCH BULLETIN. 1888. irreg., no.1190, 1994. free. Ohio State University, Ohio Agricultural Research and Development Center, Wooster, 1680 Madison Ave., Wooster, OH 44691-4096. TEL 330-263-3777. Ed. Joy Ann Fischer. bibl.; charts; illus. circ. 1,100. **Indexed:** Biol.Abstr., Curr.Adv.Ecol.Sci., Curr.Cont., Excerp.Med., Field Crop Abstr., Forest.Abstr., Helminthol.Abstr., Herb.Abstr., Maize Abstr., Nutr.Abstr., Plant Breed.Abstr., Rev.Appl.Entomol., Rural Recreat.Tour.Abstr., Soils & Fert., World Agri.Econ.& Rural Sociol.Abstr. **Document type:** bulletin.
—BLDSC (7730.720000); Linda Hall.
Refereed Serial

630 US ISSN 0078-396X
CODEN: OARCBA
OHIO AGRICULTURAL RESEARCH AND DEVELOPMENT CENTER, WOOSTER. RESEARCH CIRCULAR. 1888. irreg., no.298, 1994. free. Ohio State University, Ohio Agricultural Research and Development Center, Wooster, 1680 Madison Ave., Wooster, OH 44691-4096. TEL 330-263-3777. Ed. Joy Ann Fischer. bibl.; charts; illus. circ. 1,100. (back issues avail.) **Indexed:** Biol.Abstr., Curr.Adv.Ecol.Sci., Curr.Cont., Field Crop Abstr., Forest.Abstr., Forest Prod.Abstr., Herb.Abstr., Hort.Abstr., Ind.Vet., Nutr.Abstr., Plant Breed.Abstr., Rev.Appl.Entomol., Rural Recreat.Tour.Abstr., Soils & Fert., Vet.Bull., Weed Abstr., World Agri.Econ.& Rural Sociol.Abstr. **Document type:** bulletin.
—Linda Hall.
Refereed Serial

630 US ISSN 0030-0896
OHIO FARMER. 1849. 15/yr. $19.95. Farm Progress Companies (Subsidiary of: A B C Publishing Companies), 191 S. Gary Ave., Carol Stream, IL 60188. TEL 630-690-5600. FAX 630-462-2869. (Edit. addr.: 1350 W. Fifth Ave., Columbus, OH 43212. TEL 614-486-9637. FAX 614-486-4789) Ed. Tim White. adv.: B&W page $3850, color page $5980; trim 7 X 10. bk.rev.; charts; illus.; stat.; circ. 49,170 (paid). (also avail. in microfilm)

630 US ISSN 0749-4009
OHIO GRANGER. 1983. bi-m. $2. Ohio State Grange, 1031 E. Broad St., Columbus, OH 43205. TEL 614-258-9569. Ed. Bernard Shoemaker. adv.; circ. 14,500 (controlled). (processed)
Supersedes (1898?-1982): Ohio Grange (ISSN 0030-0926); Which was formerly: Ohio State Grange Monthly.

630 634.9 US ISSN 0736-8003
OHIO STATE UNIVERSITY. AGRICULTURAL RESEARCH AND DEVELOPMENT CENTER, WOOSTER. SPECIAL CIRCULAR. 1925. irreg., no.156, 1996. free. Ohio State University, Ohio Agricultural Research and Development Center, Wooster, 1680 Madison Ave., Wooster, OH 44691-4096. TEL 330-263-3775. Ed. Joy Ann Fischer. bibl.; charts; illus. circ. 2,500. (back issues avail.) **Indexed:** Cott.&Trop.Fibr.Abstr., Ornam.Hort. **Document type:** bulletin.
—BLDSC (8366.120000); Linda Hall.
Description: In-depth, specialized examinations of individual topics in various disciplines of the agricultural sciences.

630 US ISSN 1082-7854
OHIO'S COUNTRY JOURNAL. 1992. m. $12. Agri Communicators, Inc., 1515 W. Lane Ave., Columbus, OH 43221-3974. TEL 614-481-6000. FAX 614-487-8205. Ed. Tim Reeves; Pub. Ed Johnson. adv. contact: Jill Davis. circ. 16,100 (paid). (tabloid format)

630 UK
OILSEEDS AND INDUSTRIAL CROPS. 1983. q. £19. Processors & Growers Research Organisation, 34 Cavendish Rd., London NW6 7XP, England. TEL 0181-459-5330. Ed. Herbert Daybell. adv. contact: Tony Smith. circ. 12,000. **Document type:** trade publication.
Formerly: Oilseeds (ISSN 0265-0002)

630 FR ISSN 0030-1523
OISE AGRICOLE. 1915. w. 370 F. (effective Jan. 1993). Oise Peasants Organizations, Rue Frere-Gagne, B.P. 463, 60021 Beauvais Cedex, France. FAX 44-89-45-50. Ed. A. Devooght. adv.; bk.rev. circ. 6,378.

630 US ISSN 1077-1859
OKLAHOMA FARM BUREAU JOURNAL. 1947. m. $5. Oklahoma Farm Bureau, 2501 N. Stiles, Oklahoma City, OK 73105. TEL 405-273-4200. FAX 405-523-2326. Ed. Mike Nichols. R&P contact Mike Nichols. adv. contact: Mike Nichols. circ. 112,000 (controlled). (tabloid format; also avail. in microfiche) **Document type:** newspaper.
Formerly (until 1989): Oklahoma Farm Bureau Farmer (ISSN 0048-1599)
Description: Documents the impact of federal and state legislation on agricultural and rural areas.

AGRICULTURE

630 SA ISSN 0259-9341
ONS EIE. 1965. bi-m. membership. Suidwes Kooperasie Bpk - Southwest Co-operatice Ltd, P.O. Box 150, Kimberley 8301, South Africa. TEL 27-531-811578. FAX 27-531-812370. Ed. Adri Theron. adv.: B&W page R.2150, color page R.3100; trim 297 x 210; adv. contact: Adri Theron. circ. 9,000. **Document type:** trade publication.
Description: Covers agricultural and related topics.

630 NE ISSN 0030-2732
ONS PLATTELAND. 1918. w. Nederlandse Christelijke Boeren- en Tuindersbond, Postbus 74, Agro Business Park 1, 6700 AB Wageningen, Netherlands. TEL 31-8370-12514. FAX 31-8370-26628. Ed. P. van Veen. adv.; bk.rev.; illus.; mkt.; tr.lit. circ. 20,000. **Document type:** newspaper.

630 CN
ONTARIO. MINISTRY OF AGRICULTURE, FOOD AND RURAL AFFAIRS. AGRI-FOOD TRADE UPDATE. q. free. Ministry of Agriculture, Food and Rural Affairs, Policy Analysis Branch, Legislative Bldg., Queen's Park, Toronto, ON M7A 2B2, Canada. TEL 416-326-3210. FAX 416-326-9892. **Document type:** government publication.
Formerly: Ontario. Ministry of Agriculture and Food. Agri-Food Trade Update (ISSN 1183-1588)

630 CN
ONTARIO. MINISTRY OF AGRICULTURE, FOOD AND RURAL ANALYSIS. AGRI-FOOD OUTLOOK AND POLICY REVIEW. bi-m. Ministry of Agriculture, Food and Rural Analysis, Policy Analysis Branch, Legislative Bldg., Queen's Park, Toronto, ON M7A 2B2, Canada. TEL 416-326-3210. FAX 416-326-9892. Ed. Martin Jaeger. charts; stat. **Document type:** newsletter.
Formerly: Ontario. Ministry of Agriculture and Food. Agri-Food Outlook and Policy Review (ISSN 1180-2936)

630 CN
ONTARIO. MINISTRY OF AGRICULTURE, FOOD AND RURAL ANALYSIS. P D R NOTES. (Processing, Distribution and Retailing) m. Ministry of Agriculture, Food and Rural Analysis, Policy Analysis Branch, Legislative Bldgs., Queen's Park, Toronto, ON M7A 2B2, Canada. TEL 416-326-7228. FAX 416-326-7630. Ed. Kevin Grier. **Document type:** newsletter.
Formerly: Ontario. Ministry of Agriculture and Food. P D R Notes.

631 CN
ONTARIO FARMER. 1968. w. Can.$35. Bowes Publishers Ltd., P.O. Box 7400, London, ON N5Y 4X3, Canada. TEL 519-473-0010. FAX 519-473-2256. Ed. Paul Mahon; Pub. M.J. Hawkins. circ. 35,398. **Document type:** trade publication.
Formed by the merger of: Ontario Farmer (Eastern Edition) (ISSN 0831-3873); Which was formerly: Eastern Ontario Farmer (ISSN 0380-0067) & Ontario Farmer (Western Edition) (ISSN 0831-3865); Which was formerly: Western Ontario Farmer (ISSN 0049-7460)

635 NE ISSN 0923-0769
OOGST; land- en tuinbouw weekblad. Regional edition: Noordoogst (ISSN 1380-4278); G L T O Nieuws. Westweek (ISSN 0929-8290); N C B Journaal. Land & Vee. (Supplements avail.: Oogst Plus voor de Akkerbouw; Oogst Plus voor de Glastuinder; Oogst Plus voor de Veehouder) 1988. w. fl.147 (foreign fl.305). (Land- en Tuinbouw Organisatie Nederland) Stichting Agripers, Postbus 29745, 2502 LS The Hague, Netherlands. TEL 31-70-3382888. FAX 31-70-3382899. Ed. F. Visser; Pub. A.C. van der Wees. adv.: B&W page fl.7867. bk.rev.; illus. circ. 105,100. (tabloid format) **Indexed:** ELLIS. **Document type:** trade publication.
—SWETS.
Incorporates (1946-1987): Boer en Tuinder (ISSN 0006-5609)

630 II
OOSAMALA. (Text in Marathi) m. V.S. Kane, Ed. & Pub., White House, Tilak Rd., Pune 411 030, India. circ. 2,000.

630 FR ISSN 1016-121X
S5
OPTIONS MEDITERRANEENNES. SERIE A: SEMINAIRES MEDITERRANEENS. 1963. irreg., no.28, 1996. Centre International de Hautes Etudes Agronomiques Mediterraneennes, Institut Agronomique Mediterraneen de Montpellier - International Centre for Advanced Mediterranean Agronomic Studies, 3191 route de Mende, B.P. 5056, 34033 Montpellier, France. TEL 33-67046000. FAX 33-67542527. TELEX 58672 IAMZ E. Ed. M. Lasram; Pub. M. Lerin. adv.; bk.rev.; abstr.; bibl.; charts; illus. circ. 1,000. **Indexed:** Maize Abstr., Seed Abstr., Sorghum & Millets Abstr., Triticale Abstr. **Document type:** monographic series, proceedings.
Supersedes in part (in 1989): Options Mediterraneennes. Serie Etudes (ISSN 0253-1542); Which was formerly (until 1981): Options Mediterraneennes (ISSN 0025-8261); Mediterranea.

630 FR ISSN 1016-1228
OPTIONS MEDITERRANEENNES. SERIE B: ETUDES ET RECHERCHES. 1963. irreg., no.14, 1996. Centre International de Hautes Etudes Agronomiques Mediterraneennes, Institute Agronomique Mediterraneen de Montpellier - International Centre for Advanced Mediterranean Agronomic Studies, 3191 route de Mende, B.P. 5056, 34033 Montpellier, France. TEL 33-67046000. FAX 33-67542527. circ. 1,000.
Supersedes in part (in 1989): Options Mediterraneennes. Serie Etudes (ISSN 0253-1542); Which was formerly (until 1981): Options Mediterraneennes (ISSN 0025-8261); Mediterranea.

630 NE ISSN 0030-4239
ORANG PELADANG. 1912. bi-m. fl.25. Deventer Landbouwers Vereniging Nji Sri, Postbox 27, Deventer, Netherlands. Ed. Robert van Donk. adv. circ. 750. **Document type:** academic/scholarly publication.

630 US ISSN 0162-5179
OREGON FARM BUREAU NEWS. * s-m. membership only. Oregon Farm Bureau Federation, 3415 Commercial St., S.E., Ste. G, Salem, OR 97302-4668. TEL 503-399-1701. Ed. Rick Stevenson. circ. 11,000. **Document type:** newsletter.

630 US ISSN 0030-4697
OREGON GRANGE BULLETIN. * 1900. m. $10 to non-members. Oregon State Grange, 643 Union St., N.E., Salem, OR 97301-2462. TEL 503-236-1118. FAX 503-236-4018. Ed. Edward Luttrell. adv.; bk.rev.; illus.; circ. 17,500 (paid). (tabloid format) **Document type:** newspaper.

ORGANIC GROWING (ULVERSTONE). see *GARDENING AND HORTICULTURE*

630 US
ORGANIC NEWS; working to promote organic farming and gardening in New Jersey. Variant title: N O F A - N J's Organic News. q. membership. Northeast Organic Farming Association, New Jersey Chapter, 33 Titus Mill Rd., Pennington, NJ 08534. TEL 609-737-6848. adv.: page $85. circ. 3,000 (paid). pp./issue: 12. (tabloid format) **Document type:** newsletter, newspaper.
Description: Discusses the association's activities and profiles members.

631 US
ORNAMENTAL CROPS NATIONAL MARKET TRENDS. 1968. w. $96 (foreign $192). (U.S. Department of Agriculture) Federal-State Market News Service, 630 Sansome St., Rm. 727, San Francisco, CA 94111. TEL 415-705-1300. FAX 415-705-1301. circ. 175. (looseleaf format; back issues avail.) **Document type:** government publication, newsletter.
Description: Offers news briefs on production projections, price ranges, available supplies, and trading activity for decorative greens and cut flowers throughout the United States with lists of imports from abroad.

630 NZ
OTAGO SOUTHLAND FARMER. fortn. P.O. Box 45, Balclutha, New Zealand. TEL 03-418-1115. FAX 03-418-1173. Ed. I.T. Carson. circ. 17,500.

630 UK ISSN 0030-7270
CODEN: OUAGA8
OUTLOOK ON AGRICULTURE; an international review of agricultural science and technology. 1956. q. £140($245) (effective 1997). CAB International, Wallingford, Oxon. OX10 8DE, England. TEL 44-1491-832111. FAX 44-1491-826090. TELEX 847964 COMAGG G. E-mail: cabi@cabi.org; URL: http://www.cabi.org. (U.S. subscr. to: CAB International, North American Office, 198 Madison Ave., New York, NY 10016. TEL 212-726-6490. FAX 212-686-7933) bk.rev.; bibl.; charts; illus.; index. circ. 6,000. **Indexed:** Agri.Eng.Abstr., Agroforest.Abstr., Anim.Breed.Abstr., ASCA, Biol.Abstr., Biotech.Abstr., Chem.Abstr., Curr.Adv.Ecol.Sci., Curr.Cont., Dairy Sci.Abstr., Ecol.Abstr., Energy Ind., Energy Info.Abstr., Field Crop Abstr., Food Sci.& Tech.Abstr., Forest.Abstr., Geo.Abstr.H.G., Geo.Abstr.P.G., Helminthol.Abstr., Herb.Abstr., Hort.Abstr., IDA, Ind.Vet., Irr.& Drain.Abstr., Maize Abstr., Nutr.Abstr., Plant Breed.Abstr., Rev.Appl.Entomol., Rev.Plant Path., Rural Recreat.Tour.Abstr., Sci.Cit.Ind., Soils & Fert., SSCI, Sugar Ind.Abstr., Triticale Abstr., Trop.Dis.Bull., Vet.Bull., Weed Abstr., World Agri.Econ.& Rural Sociol.Abstr. **Document type:** academic/scholarly publication.
—BLDSC (6314.500000); CASDDS; Genuine Article; Linda Hall; SWETS; UMI; UnCover.
Description: Covers the entire subject area of agriculture and related disciplines, including food, forestry, horticulture, and socioeconomic and environmental considerations. The topics addressed range from molecular biology and biotechnology to socioeconomic issues in world food productivity and distribution and practical methods of crop and animal husbandry.
Refereed Serial

630 PH ISSN 0116-3140
THE P C A R R D MONITOR. 1973. bi-m. free. Philippine Council for Agriculture, Forestry, and Natural Resources Research and Development, Los Banos, Laguna 4030, Philippines. FAX 63-094-50016. TELEX 40860 PARRS PM. Ed. Zenaida C. Gibe. bk.rev. circ. 4,000. **Indexed:** Field Crop Abstr., Herb.Abstr., Ind.Phil.Per., Rural Recreat.Tour.Abstr., World Agri.Econ.& Rural Sociol.Abstr. **Document type:** newsletter, government publication.
—BLDSC (6413.450000).
Formerly (until 1982): Philippine Council for Agriculture, Forestry, and National Resources Research and Development. Monitor (ISSN 0115-0529)

630 II ISSN 0378-813X
P K V RESEARCH JOURNAL. (Punjabrao Krishi Vidyapeeth) (Text in English) 1972. s-a. Rs.75 to non-members & institutions; members Rs.50; (foreign Rs.200). Agricultural University, Akola 444 104, Maharashtra, India. TEL 58419. TELEX 0725-215 PKV IN. Ed. R.S. Bonde. **Document type:** academic/scholarly publication.
Description: Devoted to research in the field of agricultural sciences. Contains original research, research notes and review papers.

630 338.91 UK ISSN 1357-938X
P L A NOTES. (Participatory Learning and Action) 1988. 3/yr. International Institute for Environment and Development (IIED), Sustainable Agriculture Programme, 3 Endsleigh St., London WC1H 0DD, England. TEL 44-171-388-2117. FAX 44-171-388-2826.
—BLDSC (6506.505000).
Formerly: R R A Notes.
Description: Enables practitioners of participatory methodologies throughout the world to share their field experiences, conceptual reflections and methodological innovations.

630 GW ISSN 0723-0311
P S P PFLANZENSCHUTZ-PRAXIS. 1981. 4/yr. DM.57 (foreign DM.63) (effective 1996). (Deutsche Landwirtschaftsgesellschaft e.V.) D L G Verlags GmbH, Eschborner Landstr. 122, 60489 Frankfurt a.M., Germany. TEL 069-24788-0. FAX 069-24788480. **Document type:** bulletin.

AGRICULTURE

630 US ISSN 1071-6548
S449
PACIFIC FARMER. 1884. m. $19.95. Western Farmer-Stockman Magazines (Subsidiary of: Cowles Publishing Co.), Box 2160, Spokane, WA 99210-1615. TEL 509-459-5361. FAX 509-459-5102. E.W. Ramsey, Pub. Dir. adv. contact: Richard C. Brantley. bk.rev.; stat.; circ. 13,059 (paid). **Document type:** trade publication.
Former titles (until 1993): Pacific Farmer - Stockman (ISSN 1062-256X); (until 1992): Washington Farmer - Stockman (ISSN 1041-2727); (until 1971): Ranch; Horn and Hoof.

630 PH ISSN 0117-522X
PACIFIC JOURNAL OF SCIENCE AND TECHNOLOGY. 1965. s-a. P.100($25) University of Eastern Philippines, Research Center, University Town, Northern Samar 6400, Philippines. Ed. Julita R. Calonge. bk.rev. circ. 3,000. (processed; back issues avail.)
Formerly (until 1992): Researcher (ISSN 0048-7341).
Description: Publishes original scientific reports of experiments on any field of study geared toward rural development in the tropical setting, particularly the Pacific Basin.

633.51 PK ISSN 0030-9699
PAKISTAN COTTONS. (Text in English) 1958. q. Rs.26. Pakistan Central Cotton Committee, Secretary, Moulvi Tamizuddin Khan Rd., Karachi 1, Pakistan. TEL 524104-6. Ed. S. Zain Idris Mirza. adv.; charts; illus.; stat.; index. **Indexed:** Chem.Abstr., Cott.&Trop.Fibr.Abstr., Field Crop Abstr., Herb.Abstr., Irr.& Drain.Abstr., Plant Breed.Abstr., Seed Abstr., Soils & Fert., Text.Tech.Dig.
Supersedes: Pakistan Cotton Bulletin (ISSN 0479-2327)

630 PK ISSN 0251-0480
CODEN: PJARDC
PAKISTAN JOURNAL OF AGRICULTURAL RESEARCH. (Text in English) 1949. q. Rs.60. Pakistan Agricultural Research Council, P.O. Box 1031, Plot 20, G-5-1, Islamabad, Pakistan. Ed. Sabiha Amin. adv.; abstr.; charts; illus. circ. 1,000. (also avail. in microform from UMI; reprint service avail. from UMI) **Indexed:** Agri.Eng.Abstr., Anim.Breed.Abstr., Bibl.Agri., Bio-Contr.News & Info., Biol.Abstr., Biol.& Agr.Ind., Chem.Abstr., Cott.& Trop.Fibr.Abstr., Crop Physiol.Abstr., Curr.Adv.Ecol.Sci., Dairy Sci.Abstr., Entomol.Abstr., Fert.Abstr., Field Crop Abstr., Food Sci.& Tech.Abstr., Geo.Abstr.P.G., Herb.Abstr., Hort.Abstr., Ind.Vet., Irr.& Drain.Abstr., Maize Abstr., Nutr.Abstr., Plant Breed.Abstr., Plant Grow.Reg.Abstr., Potato Abstr., Rev.Appl.Entomol., Rev.Plant Path., Rice Abstr., Rural Recreat.Tour.Abstr., Soils & Fert., Sorghum & Millets Abstr., Soyabean Abstr., Sugar Ind.Abstr., Triticale Abstr., Trop.Oil Seeds Abstr., Vet.Bull., Weed Abstr., World Agri.Econ.& Rural Sociol.Abstr. **Document type:** academic/scholarly publication.
—BLDSC (6340.894500); CASDDS; Linda Hall.
Former titles: Journal of Agricultural Research; West Pakistan Journal of Agricultural Research (ISSN 0043-3179); Agriculture Pakistan (ISSN 0002-1776).

630 PK ISSN 0552-9034
S471.P16
PAKISTAN JOURNAL OF AGRICULTURAL SCIENCES. (Text in English) 1964? q. $25. Society for the Advancement of Agricultural Sciences, c/o Dept. of Soil Science, University of Agriculture, Faisalabad, Pakistan. Ed. Riaz Hussain Qureshi. adv.; bk.rev. **Indexed:** Apic.Abstr., Biol.Abstr., Chem.Abstr., Field Crop Abstr., Herb.Abstr., Weed Abstr. **Document type:** academic/scholarly publication.
—UnCover.

630 PK ISSN 1015-3055
SB610
PAKISTAN JOURNAL OF AGRICULTURE, AGRICULTURAL ENGINEERING AND VETERINARY SCIENCES. (Text in English) 1985. s-a. $40 (effective 1997). Sindh Agriculture University, Tandojam 70050, Pakistan. TEL 92-2233-8869. FAX 92-2233-300. Ed. Dr. Abdul Jabbar Malik. adv. circ. 1,000. (back issues avail.) **Indexed:** Ecol.Abstr., IDA. **Document type:** academic/scholarly publication.
Description: Original research papers in agricultural and veterinary sciences.

630 AU
PALETTE. m. S.300. Oesterreichischer Agrarverlag GmbH, Inkustr. 1-7, A-3400 Klosterneuburg, Austria. TEL 02243-333006. FAX 02243-3330056.

630 PN
PANAMA. INSTITUTO DE INVESTIGACION AGROPECUARIA. INFORME ANUAL. 1976. a. Instituto de Investigacion Agropecuaria de Panama, Centro de Informacion Documental Agropecuaria, Apdo. 6-4391, El Dorado, Panama 6A, Panama. TELEX 3677 PG. Dir. Tomas Noriega.

630 PN
PANAMA. INSTITUTO DE INVESTIGACION AGROPECUARIA. MEMORIA. FORO NACIONAL DE INFORMACION DOCUMENTAL. 1980. a. Instituto de Investigacion Agropecuaria de Panama, Centro de Informacion Documental Agropecuaria, Apdo. 6-4391, El Dorado, Panama 6A, Panama. TELEX 3677 PG. (Co-sponsor: Grupo Panameno de Informacion Agricola) Ed. Vielka Chang-Yau. circ. 300.
Formerly: Panama. Instituto de Investigacion Agropecuaria. Memoria. Reunion Panamena de Informacion Agricola.

630 PP ISSN 0256-954X
CODEN: PNGFEZ
PAPUA NEW GUINEA JOURNAL OF AGRICULTURE, FORESTRY AND FISHERIES. (Text in English) 1935. s-a. K.17.64 to Australia, Asia, Pacific (elsewhere K.24.60). Department of Agriculture and Livestock, Publication Section, P.O. Box 417, Konedobu, Papua New Guinea. TEL 675-230268. FAX 675-230279. Ed. Ray Kumar. bk.rev.; abstr.; charts; illus.; cum.index. circ. 1,200. **Indexed:** Biol.Abstr., Chem.Abstr., Curr.Adv.Ecol.Sci., Curr.Cont., Dairy Sci.Abstr., Field Crop Abstr., Forest.Abstr., Forest Prod.Abstr., GeoRef., Helminthol.Abstr., Herb.Abstr., Hort.Abstr., Ind.Vet., Nutr.Abstr., Poult.Abstr., Rev.Plant Path., Rural Recreat.Tour.Abstr., Soils & Fert., World Agri.Econ.& Rural Sociol.Abstr. **Document type:** academic/scholarly publication.
—BLDSC (6404.513450); CASDDS.
Former titles (until 1984): Papua New Guinea Agricultural Journal (ISSN 0031-1464); (until 1954): Papua and New Guinea Agriculture Gazette (ISSN 0370-078X); (until 1941): New Guinea Agricultural Gazette (ISSN 0369-3716)
Description: Publishes research papers on primary industry subjects.

630 CK ISSN 1012-7410
PASTURAS TROPICALES. (Text in English, French, Portuguese or Spanish; summaries in English, Spanish) 1979. 3/yr. Col.$15000 ($40 to developed countries; developing countries $22) (effective 1996). Centro Internacional de Agricultura Tropical, Unidad de Comunicaciones - International Center for Tropical Agriculture, Communications Unit, Apdo. Aereo 6713, Cali, Colombia. TEL 57-2-4450000. FAX 57-2-4450073. Ed. Alberto Ramirez. circ. 700. **Indexed:** Field Crop Abstr., Herb.Abstr.
Former titles: Pasturas Tropicales. Boletin; Pastos Tropicales. Boletin Informativo (ISSN 0120-1484)
Description: Accumulates scientific articles, research notes and comments about pasture research in the tropics.

630 FR ISSN 1145-6639
PAYSAN BRETON (EDITION COTES-DU-NORD). 1945. w. Groupe Interagri, 2 av. du Chalutier-sans-Pitie, B.P. 66, 22190 Plerin, France.
Supersedes in part (in 1961): Paysan Breton (ISSN 0996-1615)

630 FR ISSN 1145-6620
PAYSAN BRETON (EDITION FINISTERE). 1945. w. Groupe Interagri, 2 av. du Chalutier-sans-Pitie, B.P. 66, 22190 Plerin, France.
Supersedes in part (in 1961): Paysan Breton (ISSN 0996-1615)

630 FR ISSN 1156-8461
PAYSAN BRETON (EDITION MORBIHAN). w. Groupe Interagri, 2 av. du Chalutier-sans-Pitie, B.P. 66, 22190 Plerin, France. Ed. M. Gouerou. circ. 80,910.

630 FR
PAYSAN D'AUVERGNE. w. Maison des Paysans, R.N. 89, 63370 Marmilhat, France. TEL 73-91-23-33. Ed. Herve de Puytorac. circ. 10,166.

630 FR ISSN 0184-8550
PAYSAN DU HAUT-RHIN. 1945. w. 3 place de la Gare, B.P. 227, 68000 Colmar, France. TEL 89-41-35-32. Ed. Paul-Andre Murrisch. circ. 8,200.

630 FR ISSN 1148-7488
PAYSAN DU MIDI. 1946. w. 365 F. 4 rue Jacqueline Auriol, Parc Marcel Dessault, 34430 St. Jean de Vedas, France. TEL 33-04-67070366. FAX 33-04-67070371. Ed. M. Ponce. circ. 12,000. **Document type:** newspaper.

630 FR ISSN 0755-7027
PAYSAN LORRAIN. 1946. 50/yr. 5 rue de la Vologne, 54524 Laxou Cedex, France. TEL 83-96-51-16. FAX 83-96-31-50. Ed. Jean-Luc Masson. circ. 4,000.

630 FR ISSN 0221-0037
PAYSAN MORBIHANNAIS. 1946. 24/yr. B.P. 183, 56000 Vannes, France. circ. 14,714.

630 FR ISSN 0181-8880
PAYSAN SAVOYARD. 1945. 22/yr. 52 av. des Iles, B.P. 327, 74037 Annecy Cedex, France. TEL 50-52-82-40. circ. 6,000.

630 FR
PAYSAN TARNAIS LA MILLIASOLLE. w. B.P. 42, 81002 Albi, France. TEL 63-54-39-81. FAX 63-47-09-87. Ed. Pierre Chavanon. circ. 7,850.

630 FR ISSN 0241-9092
PAYSAN VOSGIEN. 1946. w. La Colombiere, Rue Andre-Vith, 88025 Epinal, France. TEL 29-33-01-23. circ. 3,630.

630 FR ISSN 1245-0855
PAYSANS DE LA LOIRE. 1945. w. 43 av. Albert Raimond, B.P. 50, 42272 St-Priest-en-Jarez Cedex, France. TEL 77-79-15-22. FAX 77-79-17-82. Ed. Erick Roizard. circ. 11,286.

638.1 CI ISSN 0031-3416
PCELA. 1881. m. Pcelarski Savez Hrvatske, 8 Maja 26, 41000 Zagreb, Croatia. TEL (041) 272-383. (Co-sponsor: Savez Pcelara Bosne i Hercegovine) Ed. Koviljka Majnaric. index. **Indexed:** Apic.Abstr.

638.1 RU ISSN 0369-8629
PCHELOVODSTVO. 1921. bi-m. $82 (effective 1998). Izdatel'stvo Kolos, Sadovaya-Spasskaya, 18, 107807 Moscow, Russia. TEL 7-095-2074219. FAX 7-095-2072870. (Dist. by: Mezhdunarodnaya Kniga, B. Yakimanka 39, 117049 Moscow, Russia. TEL 7-095-2384967. FAX 7-095-2384634; Dist. in U.S. by: Victor Kamkin Inc., 4956 Boiling Brook Pkwy, Rockville, MD 20852) Ed. Irina Yu. Vereshchaka. circ. 88,000. **Indexed:** Apic.Abstr., Biol.Abstr., Forest.Abstr., Sugar Ind.Abstr.
—CISTI.

630 UK
PEA & BEAN PROGRESS. 1982. 3/yr. Processors & Growers Research Organisation, 34 Cavendish Rd., London NW6 7XP, England. TEL 0181-459-5330. Ed. Herbert Daybell. adv. contact: Tony Smith. circ. 5,500. **Document type:** trade publication.
Former titles: Vegetable Grower (ISSN 0264-8857); (until 1982): Processors and Growers Research Organisation. News Letter (ISSN 0308-2504); (until 1973): Pea Growers Research Organisation. News Letter.

630 334 FI ISSN 0031-4188
S16.F5
PELLERVO. 1899. m. FIM 370. Finn Coop Pellervo, P.O. Box 77, Simonkatu 6, FIN-00101 Helsinki, Finland. TEL 358-0-4767501. FAX 358-0-6948945. Ed. Kaisu Raesaenen. adv.: color page FIM18000. circ. 51,000.

338.1 US ISSN 1043-6235
PENNSYLVANIA AGRICULTURE NEWS. 1915. q. free. Department of Agriculture, 2301 N. Cameron St., Harrisburg, PA 17110-9408. FAX 717-772-2780. Ed. Dyan L. Yingst. circ. 7,000. **Document type:** government publication.
Formerly (until Dec. 1989): Agriculture News Bulletin.

AGRICULTURE

630 US ISSN 0031-4471
S1
PENNSYLVANIA FARMER. 1877. 12/yr. $19.95. Farm Progress Companies (Subsidiary of: A B C Publishing Companies), 191 S. Gary Ave., Carol Stream, IL 60188. TEL 630-690-5600. FAX 630-462-2869. (Edit. addr.: Box 4475, Gettysburg, PA 17325. TEL 717-334-4300. FAX 717-334-3129) Ed. John Vogel. adv.: B&W page $3400, color page $3910; trim 7 X 10. bk.rev.; charts; illus.; stat.; tr.lit.; circ. 40,738. circ. 38,699 (paid).

630 IT ISSN 1120-2955
PERITO AGRARIO. 1953. 6/yr. IACICO s.r.l., Via A. Poliziano 80, 00184 Rome, Italy. TEL 39-6-4873183. FAX 39-6-4873144. Ed. Andrea Bottaro. adv.: color page L.2500000; adv. contact: Claudio Cutrone. circ. 12,000 (paid).
Refereed Serial

630 712 US ISSN 0897-7348
THE PERMACULTURE ACTIVIST. 1985. 3/yr. $19 (outside N. America $30). The Permaculture Activist, Box 1209, Black Mountain, NC 28711-1209. TEL 704-298-2812. FAX 704-298-6441. URL: http://eden.com/fineprint/40081.html. Ed. Peter Bane; Pub. Peter Bane. adv.; bk.rev.; circ. 5,000 (paid). (back issues avail.) **Indexed:** Alt.Press Ind., Environ.Per.Bibl. (1991-1993). **Document type:** trade publication.
—UnCover.
Description: Propounds the four-point ethic of permaculture: care of the earth, care of people, distribution of surplus to assist others, and limiting of consumption.

630 NE ISSN 0031-5869
PERSOVERZICHT. 1955. fortn. fl.150. Hoofdproduktschap voor Akkerbouwprodukten, Stadhoudersplantsoen 12, The Hague, Netherlands. TEL 31-70-3708319. FAX 31-70-3708444. Ed. J.C. Fraase Storm. index. circ. 600.

630 FR ISSN 0399-8533
PERSPECTIVES AGRICOLES. 11/yr. 400 F. (foreign 550 F.). Societe les Editions et Publications Agricoles Francaises, 3 rue des Freres Perier, 75116 Paris, France. TEL 64-99-22-24. FAX 64-99-33-30. (Subscr. to: 91720 Boigneville, France) Ed. Elisabeth Fabre. adv. contact: M. Seroux. circ. 21,000.
—BLDSC (6428.137400).

630 IO
PERTANI P T. 1974. m. Jalan Pasar Minggu, Kalibata, P.O. Box 247 KBY, Jakarta Belatan, Indonesia. TEL 021-793108. TELEX 47249. Ed. Ir Rusli Yahya.

630 MY
S3 CODEN: PERTDY
PERTANIKA JOURNAL OF TROPICAL AGRICULTURAL SCIENCE. (Text and summaries in English, Malay) 1978. 3/yr. $70 (effective 1996). (Agricultural University of Malaysia - Universiti Pertanian Malaysia) Universiti Pertanian Malaysia Press, Serdang, Selangor, Malaysia. FAX 03-9483745. TELEX UNIPER-37454. Ed. Ruth Kiew. adv.; bk.rev. circ. 400. (also avail. in microfilm) **Indexed:** Agrindex, Apic.Abstr., Biol.Abstr., Chem.Abstr., Crop Physiol.Abstr., Field Crop Abstr., Field Crop Abstr., Forest.Abstr., Forest Prod.Abstr., Herb.Abstr., Hort.Abstr., Ind.Vet., Irr.& Drain.Abstr., Nutr.Abstr., Packag.Sci.Tech., Poult.Abstr., Rev.Appl.Entomol., Rev.Plant Path., Rice Abstr., Rural Ext.Educ.& Tr.Abstr., Soils & Fert., Trop.Oil Seeds Abstr., Vet.Bull., Weed Abstr., World Agri.Econ.& Rural Sociol.Abstr. **Document type:** academic/scholarly publication.
—CASDDS.
Superseded in part (in 1993): Pertanika (ISSN 0126-6128)
Refereed Serial

630 BL ISSN 0100-204X
CODEN: PEABBT
PESQUISA AGROPECUARIA BRASILEIRA/BRAZILIAN JOURNAL OF AGRICULTURAL RESEARCH. (Text in Portuguese; abstracts in English) 1966. m. Cr.$48($180) (effective Dec. 1995). Empresa Brasileira de Pesquisa Agropecuaria, Servico de Producao e Informacao, Caixa Postal 040315, 70770-901 Brasilia D.F., Brazil. TEL 55-61-2739616. FAX 55-61-2724168. E-mail: vendas@spi.embrapa.br. Ed. Allert Rosa Suhet. bk.rev.; abstr.; charts; illus.; circ. 1,600 (controlled). (back issues avail.) **Indexed:** Agri.Eng.Abstr., Agroforest.Abstr., Anim.Breed.Abstr., ASCA, Biol.Abstr., Cadscan., Chem.Abstr., Cott.& Trop.Fibr.Abstr., Crop Physiol.Abstr., Curr.Adv.Ecol.Sci., Curr.Cont., Dairy Sci.Abstr., Field Crop Abstr., Food Sci.& Tech.Abstr., Helminthol.Abstr., Herb.Abstr., Hort.Abstr., Ind.Vet., Irr.& Drain.Abstr., Lead Abstr., Maize Abstr., Nutr.Abstr., Ornam.Hort., Pig News & Info., Plant Breed.Abstr., Plant Grow.Reg.Abstr., Poult.Abstr., Rev.Appl.Entomol., Rev.Plant Path., Rice Abstr., Risk Abstr., Seed Abstr., Soils & Fert., Sorghum & Millets Abstr., Soyabean Abstr., Trop.Oil Seeds Abstr., Vet.Bull., Weed Abstr., World Agri.Econ.& Rural Sociol.Abstr., Zincscan, Zoo.Rec. **Document type:** academic/scholarly publication.
—BLDSC (6428.230000); CASDDS; Genuine Article; SWETS.
Formerly (until 1978): Pesquisa Agropecuaria. Serie Agronomia; **Incorporates** (in 1978): Pesquisa Agropecuaria Brasileira. Serie Veterinaria-Zootecnia; Which was formed by the 1977 merger of: Pesquisa Agropecuaria Brasileira. Serie Veterinaria; Pesquisa Agropecuaria Brasileira. Serie Zootenia.

630 BL ISSN 0104-9070
▼**PESQUISA AGROPECUARIA GAUCHA.** 1995. s-a. $35. Fundacao Estadual de Pesquisa Agropecuaria, Secretaria da Ciencia e Tecnologia, Rua Goncalves Dias, 570, 90130-060 Porto Alegre, RS, Brazil. TEL 55-512-33-5411. FAX 55-512-337607. Ed.Bd.
Description: Publishes original articles and reviews in the fields of agronomy, renewable natural resources, veterinary and animal science and related subjects.

630 BL ISSN 0100-8501
CODEN: PAPEDJ
PESQUISA AGROPECUARIA PERNAMBUCANA. (Text in Portuguese; summaries in English) 1977. s-a. free. Empresa Pernambucana de Pesquisa Agropecuaria, Divisao de Informacao e Documentacao, Av. Gal. San Martin 1371, Bonji, 50751 Recife PE, Brazil. TEL 081-445-2200. FAX 081-227-4017. Ed. Jose Bahia de Oliveira. bk.rev. circ. 1,000. (back issues avail.) **Indexed:** Biol.Abstr., Chem.Abstr.
—CASDDS.

630 BL ISSN 0100-8161
PESQUISA EM ANDAMENTO - MANDIOCA E FRUTICULTURA. 1980. irreg. price varies. Centro Nacional de Pesquisa de Mandioca e Fruticultura Tropical, Rua Embrapa s-n, Caixa Postal 007, 44380-000 Cruz das Almas, Bahia, Brazil. TEL 55-75-721-2120. FAX 55-75-721-1118. **Indexed:** Agri.Eng.Abstr., Anim.Breed.Abstr., Protozool.Abstr.

630 540 UK
THE PESTICIDE MANUAL. 1983. irreg., vol.10, 1994. £110. British Crop Protection Council, Bear Farm, Binfield, Bracknell, Berkshire RG12 5QE, England. TEL 44-1734-341998. FAX 44-1734-341998. (Subscr. in N. America to: Blackwells Scientific, 238 Main St., Cambridge, MA 02142. TEL 617-876-7000. FAX 617-876-7022) (Co-sponsor: The Royal Society of Chemistry) Ed. Clive Tomlin. (looseleaf format) **Document type:** trade publication. ●Also available online. Vendor(s): Data-Star, Knight-Ridder Information, Inc. (File no.306).
Formerly (until 1994): Agrochemicals Handbook.
Description: Contains comprehensive data on active ingredients used in crop protection and pest control.

630 PH ISSN 0031-7454
CODEN: PHAGAU
PHILIPPINE AGRICULTURIST. (Text in English) 1911. q. $70. University of the Philippines at Los Banos, College of Agriculture, College, Laguna 4031, Philippines. TEL 2379. (Co-sponsor: Central Experiment Station) Ed. Teresita L. Rosario. bk.rev.; charts; illus.; index; circ. 25,000 (paid). **Indexed:** Anim.Breed.Abstr., Bio-Contr.News & Info., Biol.Abstr., Chem.Abstr., Cott.& Trop.Fibr.Abstr., Dairy Sci.Abstr., Excerp.Med., Field Crop Abstr., Food Sci.& Tech.Abstr., GeoRef., Helminthol.Abstr., Herb.Abstr., Hort.Abstr., Ind.Phil.Per., Ind.Vet., Maize Abstr., Nutr.Abstr., Pig News & Info., Plant Breed.Abstr., Potato Abstr., Rev.Appl.Entomol., Rev.Plant Path., Rice Abstr., Seed Abstr., Soils & Fert., Vet.Bull., VITIS, Weed Abstr., World Agri.Econ.& Rural Sociol.Abstr. **Document type:** academic/scholarly publication.
—BLDSC (6453.000000); CASDDS; Linda Hall; UnCover.
Description: Original research papers and reviews on plant, animal, soil and food sciences, agricultural biotechnology and agri-business.

630 US ISSN 0191-7935
PHOTO STAR. 1895. w. $25. 307 State St., Box B, Willshire, OH 45898. TEL 419-495-2696. FAX 419-495-2143. Ed. Judith E. Bunner. adv. contact: John Bunner. circ. 11,000. **Document type:** newspaper.

630 330.9 IT ISSN 0392-5056
PICENTINO. 1845. q. L.20000 (effective 1996). Societa Economica della Provincia di Salerno, Biblioteca Provinciale di Salerno, Via Valerio Laspro, 84100 Salerno, Italy. Ed. Luigi Postiglione. adv.; bk.rev.; bibl.; charts. circ. 500. **Document type:** academic/scholarly publication.
Description: Features financial, agricultural and historical news in the province of Salerno and surrounding areas.

636.2 UK
PIG INDUSTRY. 1985. m. £18 (foreign £34). (British Pig Association) B C Publications, 16C Market Pl., Diss, Norfolk IP22 3AB, England. TEL 44-1379-644200. FAX 44-1379-650480. Ed. Brian Chester. circ. 7,800 (controlled). **Document type:** bulletin.
Formerly: National Pig News.
Description: Contains news about the pig industry.

570 PL
SB123 CODEN: HRANAX
PLANT BREEDING AND SEED SCIENCE/HODOWLA ROSLIN I NASIENNICTWO. (Text and summaries in English) 1957. q. $120. Instytut Hodowli i Aklimatyzacji Roslin, Radzikow, 05-870 Blonie, Poland. TEL 725-3611. FAX 725-4714. TELEX 812914 IHAR PL. (Dist. by: Centrala Kolportazu Prasy i Wydawnictw, ul. Towarowa 28, Warsaw, Poland) Ed. Henryk J. Czembor. R&P contact: Roman Osinski. adv. contact: Roman Osinski. bk.rev. circ. 1,300. (reprint service avail.) **Indexed:** AgroAgen, AgroLibrex, Biol.Abstr., Chem.Abstr., Excerp.Med., Field Crop Abstr., Food Sci.& Tech.Abstr., Helminthol.Abstr., Herb.Abstr., INIS Atomind, Maize Abstr., Nutr.Abstr., Rev.Plant Path., Seed Abstr., Sugar Ind.Abstr., Triticale Abstr. **Document type:** academic/scholarly publication.
—CASDDS.
Formerly: Hodowla Roslin, Aklimatyzacja i Nasiennictwo (ISSN 0018-3040)
Description: Contains basic publications on plant breeding, seed production and such related areas as genetics, botany, physiology, biochemistry, phytopathology.

PLANT CELL, TISSUE AND ORGAN CULTURE; an international journal on in vitro culture of higher plants. see BIOLOGY — Cytology And Histology

AGRICULTURE

630   US
PLANT INDUSTRY NEWS. 1959. s-a. free. Department of Agriculture and Consumer Services, Division of Plant Industry, 1911 S.W. 34th St., Box 147100, Gainesville, FL 32614-7100. TEL 904-372-3505. FAX 904-955-2301. Ed. Phyllis Habeck. R&P contact: Maeve McConnell. circ. 11,000. **Indexed:** Chem.Abstr. **Document type:** bulletin, government publication.
  Formerly: Florida. Department of Agriculture. Division of Plant Industry. News Bulletin (ISSN 0015-4008)
  Description: Provides information on the programs, problems, regulations, and other activities of the industry.

633.7 663.9   FR   ISSN 1254-7670
CODEN: PREDED
PLANTATIONS, RECHERCHE, DEVELOPPEMENT. (Text in English and French; summaries in Spanish) 1957. bi-m. 900 F. (foreign 1100 F.) (effective 1997). C I R A D, Departement Cultures Perennes, Avenue Agropolis, B.P. 5035, 34032 Montpellier Cedex 1, France. TEL 33-4-67615800. FAX 33-4-67615513. (Subscr. to: 6 rue du General Clergerie, 75116 Paris, France. TEL 33-1-53702269. FAX 33-1-53702145) Ed. Christine Nouaille. adv.; bk.rev.; charts; illus.; stat.; index. circ. 700. (back issues avail.) **Indexed:** Agroforest.Abstr., Apic.Abstr., Biol.Abstr., Biotech.Abstr., Chem.Abstr., Crop Physiol.Abstr., Curr.Adv.Ecol.Sci., Curr.Cont., Food Sci.& Tech.Abstr., Geo.Abstr.P.G., Hort.Abstr., IDA, Maize Abstr., Plant Breed.Abstr., Plant Grow.Reg.Abstr., Rev.Appl.Entomol., Rev.Plant Path., Seed Abstr., Soils & Fert., SSCI, Weed Abstr., World Agri.Econ.& Rural Sociol.Abstr.
  —BLDSC (6524.620000); CASDDS; CISTI; Genuine Article; KR SourceOne; Linda Hall; SWETS; UMI; UnCover.
  Formed by the merger of (1957-1994): Cafe, Cacao (ISSN 0007-9510); (1946-1994): Oleagineux (ISSN 0030-2082); Which was formerly (until 1946): Bulletin des Matieres Grasses (ISSN 0366-1202)

630   MY   ISSN 0126-575X
S295   CODEN: PLTRBH
PLANTER. 1920. a. M.$150 (foreign M.$170). Incorporated Society of Planters, P.O. Box 10262, 50708 Kuala Lumpur, Malaysia. TEL 60-3-242-5561. FAX 60-3-242-6898. Ed. W.T. Perera. R&P contact: W.T. Perera. adv.; bk.rev. circ. 3500. (also avail. in microfilm; reprint service avail.) **Indexed:** Abstr.Trop.Agri., Agri.Eng.Abstr., Agroforest.Abstr., Curr.Adv.Ecol.Sci., Excerp.Med., Field Crop Abstr., Geo.Abstr., Herb.Abstr., Hort.Abstr., Rev.Plant Path., Rural Recreat.Tour.Abstr., Soils & Fert., Trop.Oil Seeds Abstr., Weed Abstr., World Agri.Econ.& Rural Sociol.Abstr. **Document type:** bulletin.
  —BLDSC (6524.800000); CASDDS.
  Refereed Serial

PLANTERS BULLETIN. see *RUBBER*

PLASTICULTURE; les plastiques dans l'agriculture - plastics in agriculture and horticulture - los plasticos en la agricultura - Kunststoffe im Landbau. see *PLASTICS*

PLATFORM; extern magazine over het beleidsterrein van het ministerie van LNV. see *ENVIRONMENTAL STUDIES*

630   NE
PLATTELANDS POST; agrarisch vakblad. 1948. m. (10/yr.) fl.30. Plattelandspost, Postbus 3, 4600 Bergen op Zoom, Netherlands. TEL 31-164-237564. FAX 31-164-247605. E-mail: wezel@pl.net. Ed. M.H.K. van Wezel. adv.: B&W page fl.700; trim 230 x 285. circ. 20,000 (paid). cols./p.: 4; pp./issue: 64. (back issues avail.) **Document type:** newspaper.

630 663 664   CI   ISSN 0352-1753
PODRAVKA; znanstveno-strucni casopis. (Text in Croatian; summaries in English) 1983. s-a. $10. R.O. Istrazivanja i Razvoj, Marinkoivca 32, 43300 Koprivnica, Croatia. TEL 043-827-144. FAX 043-827-169. TELEX 23348 YU POD KC. Ed. Ante Babic. circ. 1,000. (back issues avail.)

630   CI   ISSN 0370-0291
S13   CODEN: PJZSAZ
POLJOPRIVREDNA ZNANSTVENA SMOTRA/AGRICULTURAE CONSPECTUS SCIENTIFICUS. (Text in Serbo-Croatian; summaries in English) 1939. q. $50. Fakultet Poljoprivrednih Znanosti, Simunska 25, 41000 Zagreb, Croatia. Ed. Franjo Satovic. bk.rev. circ. 1,000. (back issues avail.) **Indexed:** Anim.Breed.Abstr., Biol.Abstr., Dairy Sci.Abstr., Field Crop Abstr., Geo.Abstr.H.G., Geo.Abstr.P.G., Herb.Abstr., Hort.Abstr., Maize Abstr., Seed Abstr., Soils & Fert., Soyabean Abstr., VITIS.
  —BLDSC (6544.180000); CASDDS.

630   XO
POLNOHOSPODARSTVO/AGRICULTURE. (Text in Czech or Slovak; contents page and summaries also in English and Russian) vol.18, 1972. m. $42. Slovenska Akademia Vied, Vyskumny Ustav Zivocisnej Vyroby, Hlohovska 2, 949 92 Bratislava, Slovakia. (Dist. by: Slovart, Nam. Slobody 6, 817 64 Bratislava, Slovakia) Ed. Jan Plesnik. bk.rev.; bibl.; charts. **Indexed:** Anim.Breed.Abstr., Biol.Abstr., Chem.Abstr., Crop Physiol.Abstr., Dairy Sci.Abstr., Excerp.Med., Fababean Abstr., Field Crop Abstr., Food Sci.& Tech.Abstr., Forest.Abstr., Helminthol.Abstr., Herb.Abstr., Hort.Abstr., Ind.Vet., Maize Abstr., Nutr.Abstr., Ornam.Hort., Pig Nowc & Info., Plant Breed Abstr., Plant Grow.Reg.Abstr., Potato Abstr., Poult.Abstr., Rev.Plant Path., Seed Abstr., Soyabean Abstr., Triticale Abstr., Vet.Bull., VITIS, Weed Abstr.
  Description: Presents research on plant and animal production, and on mechanization of agriculture, focusing primarily on Slovakia. Contains information about events in professional and scientific life in the region, and on the development of agricultural science and practice abroad.

630   368   IT
PONTE. (Text in Italian; summaries in English) 1990. a. free. Consorzio Italiano Assicuratori Grandine, Cso. Matteotti, 22, 20121 Milan, Italy. TEL 39-2-76020561. FAX 39-2-76004909. Eds. A. Grassi, E. Manetti. (reprint service avail. from SCH) **Indexed:** Arts & Hum.Cit.Ind.

630.7   II   ISSN 0032-4299
POONA AGRICULTURAL COLLEGE MAGAZINE. (Text in English, Hindi, Marathi) vol.60, 1970. irreg.? Rs.12($5) Pune Agricultural College, c/o P.L. Patil, Ed., Pune 5, India. bibl.; charts; illus. **Indexed:** Biol.Abstr., Chem.Abstr.

630   PL   ISSN 0137-6780
PORADNIK GOSPODARSKI; czasopismo rolnikow i organizacji rolniczych Wielkopolski, Pomorza i Ziemi Lubuskiej. 1889. m. $87 (effective 1998). Ul. Mickiewicza 33, 60-837 Poznan, Poland. TEL 48-61-476001. (Dist. by: Mezhdunarodnaya Kniga, B. Yakimanka 39, 117049 Moscow, Russia. TEL 7-095-2384967. FAX 7-095-2384634) Ed. Wawrzyniec Trawinski. adv. contact: Aleksandra Szymanowska. bk.rev.; illus. circ. 10,000. (back issues avail.)
  Description: Guide for farmers and their families.

630 338.1   PO   ISSN 0870-2594
PORTUGAL. INSTITUTO NACIONAL DE ESTATISTICA. ESTADO DAS CULTURAS E PREVISAO DE COLHEITAS. 1945. m. Esc.6850 (effective 1997). Instituto Nacional de Estatistica, Ave. Antonio Jose de Almeida, 1078 Lisbon, Portugal. TEL 351-1-8470050. FAX 351-1-8478578. TELEX 351-63738 PCDINE P. bk.rev.; charts; stat. circ. 1,200. **Document type:** government publication.
  Formerly: Folha Mensal do Estado das Culturas e Previsao de Colheitas (ISSN 0014-1178)
  Description: Describes the development of the major agricultural crops.

630.92021   PO   ISSN 0871-8032
PORTUGAL. INSTITUTO NACIONAL DE ESTATISTICA. INQUERITO AO GANHO DOS TRABALHADORES AGRICOLAS. 1991. s-a. Instituto Nacional de Estatistica, Ave. Antonio Jose de Almeida, 1078 Lisbon, Portugal. TEL 351-1-8470050. FAX 351-1-8478578. TELEX 351-1-63738 PCDINE P.
  Description: Provides statistical data on agricultural workers in Portugal

338.021   PO   ISSN 0871-9152
PORTUGAL. INSTITUTO NACIONAL DE ESTATISTICA. PRECOS RENDIMENTOS NA AGRICULTURA. 1991. q. Esc.2300. Instituto Nacional de Estatistica, Ave. Antonio Jose de Almeida, 1078 Lisbon, Portugal. TEL 351-1-8470050. FAX 351-1-8478578. TELEX 351-1-63738 PCDINE P.

630   PL   ISSN 0032-5457
CODEN: PNROAB
POSTEPY NAUK ROLNICZYCH. (Text in Polish; summaries in English) 1949. bi-m. 60 Zl.($20) (effective 1997). Polska Akademia Nauk, Wydzial Nauk Rolniczych i Lesnych, P.O. Box 24, Palac Kultury i Nauki, 00-901 Warsaw, Poland. TEL 48-2-6204292. FAX 48-2-6204292. (Dist. by: DABOR - Oficyna Wydawniczo-Poligraficzna, ul. Kazury 22-27, 02-795 Warsaw, Poland. TEL 48-22-6491899) Ed. Henryk Okruszko. R&P contact: Henryk Okruszko. adv.; bk.rev.; charts; illus.; index. circ. 300. **Indexed:** AgroLibrex, Anim.Breed.Abstr., Biol.Abstr., Chem.Abstr., Field Crop Abstr., Herb.Abstr., Rev.Plant Path., Rural Recreat.Tour.Abstr., World Agri.Econ. & Rural Sociol.Abstr. **Document type:** monographic series.
  —CASDDS.
  Formerly (until 1954): Postepy Wiedzy Powszechnej (ISSN 0370 2650)
  Description: Provides articles reviewing the most recent achievements in agricultural sciences.

POSTHARVEST BIOLOGY AND TECHNOLOGY. see *BIOLOGY — Biotechnology*

630   UK
POTATO MAGAZINE. 6/yr. 78-A Ashby Rd., Spilsby, Lincs PE23 5DW, England. TEL 0359-41663. FAX 0790-53556. Ed. Fid Backhouse. circ. 20,000.
  Description: Serves the potato industry, including growers and traders.

630   UK   ISSN 1365-571X
POTATO MARKETS WEEKLY. 1975. w. £840 (rest of Europe £960; elsewhere £995); by fax £950 (rest of Europe £1135; elsewhere £1300) (effective 1997). Agra Europe (London) Ltd., 25 Frant Rd., Tunbridge Wells, Kent TN2 5JT, England. TEL 44-1892-533813. FAX 44-1892-544895. TELEX 95114 AGRATW G. E-mail: 100637.3460@compuserve.com. Ed. Guy Faulkner. (also avail. by fax; back issues avail.) **Document type:** trade publication.
  —BLDSC (6565.158500).
  Formerly: Potato Markets (ISSN 0141-2221)
  Description: Contains worldwide production, price, and market information.

630   UK   ISSN 0961-7655
POTATO REVIEW. 6/yr. Docwra Manor, Guestwick, Dereham, Norfolk NR20 5QA, England. TEL 0362-84363. Ed. David Mossman. bk.rev. circ. 19,645.
  Description: Serves the potato industry with information about market trends, technical and scientific developments in the potato crop.

630   PL   ISSN 0079-4708
S13   CODEN: PTPWAX
POZNANSKIE TOWARZYSTWO PRZYJACIOL NAUK. KOMISJA NAUK ROLNICZYCH I KOMISJA NAUK LESNYCH. PRACE. (Text in Polish; summaries in English or German) 1950. irreg., vol.78, 1994. price varies. Poznanskie Towarzystwo Przyjaciol Nauk, Ul. Mielzynskiego 27-29, 61-725 Poznan, Poland. (Dist. by: Ars Polona-Ruch, Krakowskie Przedmiescie 7, Warsaw, Poland) Ed. Eugeniusz Matusiewicz. bibl.; charts; illus. **Indexed:** AgroLibrex, Chem.Abstr. **Document type:** bulletin.
  —BLDSC (6588.085000); CASDDS.

630   IE   ISSN 0332-4680
PRACTICAL FARMER. 1979. 10/yr. I£13. Green Publishing Ltd., 50 Fitzwilliam Square W., Dublin 2, Ireland. Ed. Paddy Smith. adv.; bk.rev. circ. 9,600.
  Formerly (until 1982): Farmer (ISSN 0332-2351)

AGRICULTURE

630 US ISSN 0032-6615
PRAIRIE FARMER. (Supplement avail.: Dairy Producer) 1841. 15/yr. $19.95. Farm Progress Companies (Subsidiary of: Walt Disney Co.), 191 S. Gary Ave., Carol Stream, IL 60188. TEL 630-690-5600. FAX 630-462-2869. (Edit. addr.: Box 3217, Decatur, IL 62524. TEL 217-877-9070. FAX 217-877-9695) Ed. Paul Queck. adv.: B&W page $5200, color page $5980, trim 7 X 10; adv. contact: Charles Roth. bk.rev.; charts; illus.; stat.; tr.lit.; index; circ. 74,543 (paid). (also avail. in microform from UMI; reprint service avail. from UMI) **Indexed:** Farm & Garden Ind. **Document type:** trade publication.
—UMI.
Description: General farm management magazine for farmers in Illinois, Indiana, Ohio, Michigan and Kentucky.

630 AU
PRAKTISCHE LANDTECHNIK. 1947. m. S.595 (foreign S.696). (Oesterreichisches Kuratorium fuer Landtechnik) Oesterreichischer Agrarverlag GmbH, Inkustr. 1-7, A-3400 Klosterneuburg, Austria. TEL 02243-333006. FAX 02243-3330056. Ed. Johannes Schlemmer. adv.; bk.rev. circ. 9,000.

630 XR ISSN 0862-8483
PRAMENY A STUDIE. (Text in Czech or Slovak; summaries in English, German, Russian) 1960. irreg. $9. Narodni Zemedelske Muzeum, Kostelni 44, 170 00 Prague 7, Czech Republic. TEL 25-91-19. Eds. Antonin Kubacak, Jan Rychlik. **Document type:** academic/scholarly publication.
—BLDSC (6601.370000).

630 US ISSN 1385-2256
PRECISION AGRICULTURE. Announced for publication in 1998. 3/yr. fl.480 to institutions; $280 to institutions in U.S. (effective 1998). Kluwer Academic Publishers Boston, Box 358, Accord Sta., Hingham, MA 02018-0358. TEL 617-871-6600. FAX 617-871-6528.

370 630 FR ISSN 0339-0055
PRESENCE DE L'ENSEIGNEMENT AGRICOLE PRIVE. 1975. bi-m. 55 F. Conseil National de l'Enseignement Agricole Prive, 277 rue St. Jacques, 75005 Paris, France. TEL 1-43-54-86-75. FAX 1-43-25-43-25. Ed. Jean-Bernard Contat. adv.

630 IT ISSN 0032-8057
PREVIDENZA AGRICOLA.* 1951. m. L.10000. Ente Nazionale di Previdenza e di Assistenza per gli Impiegati dell'Agricoltura, Viale Beethoven 48, 00144 Rome, Italy. TEL 39-6-460202. Ed. Donato De Leonardis. adv.: B&W page L.1520000. bk.rev.; charts; illus.; stat. circ. 25,000.

630 AT ISSN 1038-9830
PRIMARY REPORT. 1986. 11/yr. N.S.W. Farmers Association, G.P.O. Box 1068, Sydney, N.S.W. 2001, Australia. TEL 61-2-2511700. FAX 61-2-2216913. R&P contact: Donna Gersbach. adv. contact: Donna Gersbach. **Document type:** newspaper.

630 SA ISSN 1024-1558
PROAGRI. (Text in Afrikaans, English) 1994. 9/yr. $25 for 10 issues. Promedia, P.O. Box 72691, Lynnwoodridge 0040, South Africa. TEL 27-12-8090150. FAX 27-12-8090149. Ed. A.F. Rall. R&P contact: A.F. Rall. adv.: page $1650; adv. contact: Pieter Rall. circ. 40,000. **Indexed:** Ind.S.A.Per.
Description: Informs farmers on technological developments, products, and services of importance to agriculture.

630 PL ISSN 0137-6586
PROBLEMY AGROFIZYKI. (Text in Polish; summaries in English) irreg., vol.68, 1993. price varies. (Polish Academy of Sciences, Institute of Agrophysics) Ossolineum, Publishing House of the Polish Academy of Sciences, Pl. Solny 14a, 50-062 Wroclaw, Poland. TEL 48-71-343-6961. FAX 48-71-448-103. TELEX 0712771 OSS PL. Ed. Jan Glinski. **Indexed:** AgroLibrex. **Document type:** monographic series.
—BLDSC (6617.944000).
Description: Monographic and collective volumes on theoretical and practical aspects of agrophysical research.

631 TK ISSN 0032-9428
S612 CODEN: POSPBR
PROBLEMY OSVOENIYA PUSTYN'. English translation: Problems of Desert Development (US ISSN 0278-4750) (Text in Russian; contents page and summaries in English) 1967. bi-m. 66 Rub. Akademiya Nauk Turkmenistana, Institut Pustyn', Ul. Gogol, 15, 744000 Ashkhabad, Turkmenistan. TEL 25-72-57. Ed. A. Babaev. bk.rev.; abstr.; charts; illus.; index. circ. 800. **Indexed:** Biol.Abstr., Ecol.Abstr., Geo.Abstr., Geol.Abstr., GeoRef., Hort.Abstr., IDA, Zoo.Rec. **Document type:** academic/scholarly publication.
—CCC.
Description: Focuses on results of scientific research of desert territories in the former Soviet Union and abroad.

630 CN ISSN 1183-9929
PRODUCTEUR PLUS. (Text in French) 1991. 6/yr. Can.$28.44 (effective 1997). Editions Imago Inc., P.O. Box 147, Farnham, PQ J2N 2R4, Canada. TEL 514-293-8282. FAX 514-293-8554. Ed. Leonard Pigeon; Pub. Bertrand Beaumont. adv. circ. 22,290.

630 GW ISSN 0937-1583
PROFI; Magazin fuer Agrartechnik. m. DM.129 (foreign DM.156) (effective 1997). Landwirtschaftsverlag GmbH, Huelsebrockstr. 2, 48165 Muenster, Germany. TEL 49-2501-801-0. FAX 49-2501-801-204. (Subscr. to: Postfach 480249, 48079 Muenster, Germany) circ. 46,522. **Document type:** trade publication.

631.091 CK
PROGRAMA DE FORRAJES TROPICALES. INFORME BIANUAL. English edition: Tropical Forages Program Annual Report. 1975. a. Centro Internacional de Agricultura Tropical, Unidad de Comunicaciones - International Center for Tropical Agriculture, Communications Unit, Apdo. Aereo 6713, Cali, Colombia. TEL 57-2-4450000. FAX 57-2-4450073. TELEX 05769 CIAT CO. Ed. Peter Kerridge. circ. 250 (controlled). **Document type:** corporate report.
Formerly: Programa de Pastos Tropicales. Informe Anual (ISSN 0120-2391)
Description: Detailed progress report primarily for information for research collaborators in the tropical pastures network.

630 US ISSN 0033-0760
PROGRESSIVE FARMER. (Includes supplement: Rural Sportsman) 1886. m. $16 (foreign $68) (effective 1997). Southern Progressive Co., 2100 Lakeshore Dr., Birmingham, AL 35209. TEL 205-877-6000. FAX 205-877-6700. URL: http://www.pathfinder.com/PF. (Subscr. to: Box 2581, Birmingham, AL 35202. TEL 800-292-2340) Ed. Jack Odle. adv. contact: Ed Dickinson. bk.rev.; charts; illus.; stat.; tr.lit.; index. circ. 650,000. (also avail. in microform from UMI; reprint service avail. from UMI) **Document type:** consumer publication.
●Also available online.
—Linda Hall.
Description: Covers all issues affecting farmers.

630 PK
PROGRESSIVE FARMING. (Text in English) 1981. bi-m. Rs.15. Pakistan Agricultural Research Council, Sector G-5-1, P.O. Box 1031, Islamabad, Pakistan. Ed. Syed Athar Hosain. adv.; bk.rev. circ. 1,000. **Indexed:** Biol.Abstr., Chem.Abstr., Curr.Adv.Ecol.Sci., Forest.Abstr., Hort.Abstr., Nutr.Abstr., Rice Abstr.

630 UK
PROGRESSIVE YOUNG FARMER. 1978. q. £2.50. Gildea & Co. Ltd., Monkscoole House, Ste. 14D, Rathcoole, Co. Antrim BT37 9DA, N. Ireland. Ed. W.D. Morrow. adv. circ. 7,000.

630 UY
PROPAGANDA RURAL. 1902. m. Arenal Grande 1341, Montevideo, Uruguay. Dirs. Oscar Martin, Alberto R. Conde. circ. 5,000.

PROPHYTA; vakblad voor teeltmateriaal. see GARDENING AND HORTICULTURE

630 IE
PROVINCIAL FARMER. (Text in English) 1983. m. I£6. Meath Chronicle Ltd., Market Square, Navan, Co. Meath, Ireland. TEL 353-46-21442. FAX 353-46-23565. Ed. Ken Davis. adv.: B&W page I£1275, color page I£1417; trim 346 x 260; adv. contact: Paul Luddy. circ. 19,320. (tabloid format; back issues avail.)

630 II ISSN 0048-6019
S17 CODEN: JRPUAF
PUNJAB AGRICULTURAL UNIVERSITY. JOURNAL OF RESEARCH. (Text and summaries in English) 1964. q. Rs.45. Punjab Agricultural University, Ludhiana 141 004, Punjab, India. Ed. K.L. Dua. bk.rev. circ. 500. **Indexed:** Agri.Eng.Abstr., Anim.Breed.Abstr., Apic.Abstr., Bio-Contr.News & Info., Biol.Abstr., Chem.Abstr., Cott.& Trop.Fibr.Abstr., Crop Physiol.Abstr., Dairy Sci.Abstr., Field Crop Abstr., Food Sci.& Tech.Abstr., Helminthol.Abstr., Herb.Abstr., Hort.Abstr., Ind.Vet., Maize Abstr., Nutr.Abstr., Ornam.Hort., Plant Breed.Abstr., Plant Grow.Reg.Abstr., Potato Abstr., Poult.Abstr., Rev.Appl.Entomol., Rev.Plant Path., Rice Abstr., Rural Recreat.Tour.Abstr., Seed Abstr., Sorghum & Millets Abstr., Soyabean Abstr., Triticale Abstr., Trop.Oil Seeds Abstr., Vet.Bull., Weed Abstr., World Agri.Econ.& Rural Sociol.Abstr. **Document type:** academic/scholarly publication.
—CASDDS; Linda Hall.

PUNJAB FRUIT JOURNAL. see GARDENING AND HORTICULTURE

PUNJAB HORTICULTURAL JOURNAL. see GARDENING AND HORTICULTURE

630 CN ISSN 0701-6557
S159
QUEBEC (PROVINCE). MINISTERE DE L'AGRICULTURE. RAPPORT ANNUEL: MERITE AGRICOLE. 1972. a. Can.$5. Ministere de l'Agriculture, des Pecheries et de l'Alimentation Quebec, 200 Chemin Ste-/Foy, 1er etage, Quebec, PQ G1R 4X6, Canada. TEL 418-643-2673. FAX 418-646-0829. illus.
Formerly: Quebec (Province). Ministere de l'Agriculture. Rapport du Merite Agriculture.

630 CN ISSN 0714-9158
QUEBEC FARMERS ADVOCATE. 1980. m. (11/yr.). Can.$20. Le Defenseur des Agriculteurs du Quebec Inc., P.O. Box 80, Ste. Anne de Bellevue, PQ H9X 3L4, Canada. TEL 514-457-2010. FAX 514-398-7972. Ed. Susanne Brown; Pub. Hugh Maynard. adv.: B&W page Can.$650, color page Can.$1550; 10 1/4 x 13 1/2. bk.rev.; illus.; stat.; tr.lit. circ. 4,000. (tabloid format) **Document type:** newspaper.
Formerly: Quebec Farmers Association. Newsletter (ISSN 0226-7705)
Description: Provides information, news and current events for the English-speaking farmers of Quebec.

630 AT
QUEENSLAND FARMER & GRAZIER. m. Aus.$20 (free to farmers in Southern Queensland). Western Publishers Pty. Ltd., 10 Joseph St., P.O. Box 188, Toowoomba, Qld. 4350, Australia. TEL 076-324444. FAX 076-382118. Ed. Stephen Darracott. circ. 20,000.

QUICK FROZEN FOODS INTERNATIONAL. see FOOD AND FOOD INDUSTRIES

630 UK
R A S E NEWS. 1969-199? 4/yr. membership. Royal Agricultural Society of England, National Agricultural Centre, Stoneleigh, Warwickshire CV8 2LZ, England. TEL 44-1230-696969. FAX 44-1230-696900. Ed. Anne Chamberlain. adv.; bk.rev.; illus. circ. 16,000. **Document type:** newsletter.
Former titles: N A C News (ISSN 0027-8491); Farming Practice.

630 KO
R D A JOURNAL OF AGRICULTURAL SCIENCE. (Text in Korean) 1958. s-a. free. Rural Development Administration, Research Support Division, Suwon 441-707, Korea. TEL 82-331-292-4251. FAX 82-331-291-6067. Ed. Yu-Ki Hong; Pub. Young-Sun Park. adv. **Document type:** academic/scholarly publication, government publication.
Formerly (until 1993): R D A Research Reports.

AGRICULTURE

630   659   US   ISSN 0481-5084
R F D NEWS. 1958. s-m. $12. Gazette Publishing Co., Inc., 131 E. Main St., Box 367, Bellevue, OH 44811. TEL 419-483-7410. Ed. Tom Ackerman; Pub. Tom Smith. adv.; bk.rev.; tr.lit. circ. 75,705. (tabloid format) **Document type:** newspaper.

630   II
RAJASTHAN JOURNAL OF AGRICULTURAL SCIENCES. (Text in English) 1970. s-a. Rs.15. Rajasthan Agricultural Research Workers Association, Government Agricultural Research Sta., Durgapur, Jaipur, India. Ed. R.L. Mathur. bibl.; charts. **Indexed:** Biol.Abstr.

630   JA   ISSN 0388-0028
RAKUNO GAKUEN DAIGAKU KIYO. JINBUN SHAKAI KAGAKU HEN/RAKUNO GAKUEN UNIVERSITY. JOURNAL: CULTURAL AND SOCIAL SCIENCES. (Text mainly in Japanese, occasionally in English and German; summaries mainly in English) 1961. a. exchange basis. Rakuno Gakuen Daigaku - Rakuno Gakuen University, 582-1 Bunkyodai Midori-cho, Ebetsu-shi, Hokkaido 069, Japan. Ed. Kazuo Horiuchi. circ. 1,000. **Document type:** academic/scholarly publication.
Supersedes in part: College of Dairy Agriculture, Hokkaido. Journal (ISSN 0069-570X)

600   658   AT   ISSN 0812-4930
RANGE MANAGEMENT NEWSLETTER. 1975. 3/yr. Aus.$25 (foreign Aus.$30) (effective 1997). Australian Rangeland Society, 54 Broome Str., Cottesloe, W.A. 6011, Australia. TEL 61-8-89500137. FAX 61-8-89529587. Ed. Gary Bastin. R&P contact: Gary Bastim. adv. circ. 550. **Document type:** newsletter.
Description: For scientific and management groups in the pastoral industries of Australia.

RASSEGNA TECNICA DEL FRIULI VENEZIA GIULIA. see ENGINEERING — Civil Engineering

630   GW   ISSN 0486-1469
RECHT DER LANDWIRTSCHAFT; Zeitschrift fuer Landwirtschafts- und Agrarumweltrecht. 1949. m. DM.268. Agricola-Verlag GmbH, Postfach 2133, 26964 Butjadingen, Germany. **Indexed:** IBR. **Document type:** newsletter.
—CCC.

630   US
THE RECORD (GAINSVILLE). 1965. w. $20 in Florida; elsewhere $25 (effective 1997). Santa Fe Publishing Co., Inc., 620 N. Main St., Box 806, Gainsville, FL 32602. TEL 904-377-2444. FAX 904-338-1986. Ed. Richard Canaday; Pub. Constance D. Rowe. R&P contact: Constance Rowe. adv. contact: Richard Canaday. bk.rev.; circ. 6,800 (paid). **Document type:** newspaper.
Former titles: Record-Farm and Ranch; Independent Farmer and Rancher.
Description: General news and some agricultural news.

630   658   CN
RED DEER ADVOCATE PLUS. 1967. w. Can.$83.46. Canwest Publishers Ltd., 2950 Bremner Ave., Bag 5200, Red Deer, Alta. T4N 5G3, Canada. TEL 403-343-2400. FAX 403-342-4051. adv. circ. 40,457. (also avail. in microfilm from CML,SOC)

630   US   ISSN 0090-8932
RENDER; the national magazine of rendering. 1972. 6/yr. free. Editors West, 10961 Desert Lawn Dr., No. 57, Calimesa, CA 92320. TEL 714-795-4240. Ed. Frank A. Burnham. adv.; illus.; stat.; tr.lit.; circ. 7,500 (controlled). **Document type:** trade publication.
—UnCover.
Supersedes (1959-1972): Renderer (ISSN 0034-4362)

630   CC
RENSHEN YANJIU/GINSENG STUDIES. (Text in Chinese) q. Jilin Renshen Yanjiusuo - Jilin Ginseng Research Institute, 37-12, Longquan Lu, Tonghua, Jilin 134001, People's Republic of China. TEL 4835. Ed. Zhou Wenhao.

630   YU   ISSN 0354-6748
REPUBLICKI FOND ZA ZASITU, KORISCENJE, UNAPREDENJE I UREDENJE POLJOPRIVREDNOG ZEMLJISTA. BILTEN. 1994. m.? Republicki Fond za Zasitu, Koriscenje, Unapredenje i Uredenje Poljoprivrednog Zemljista, Sremska 5, Belgrade, Yugoslavia.

RESALE WEEKLY. see BUILDING AND CONSTRUCTION

630   658   US   ISSN 1061-7795
RESISTANT PEST MANAGEMENT. 1989. s-a. free. Michigan State University, B-11 Pesticide Research Center, E. Lansing, MI 48824-1311. TEL 517-355-1768. FAX 517-353-5598. E-mail: 22513mew@msu.edu; URL: http://www.msstate.edu/entomology/enthome.html. Eds. Mark E. Whalon, Robert Hollingworth. adv. contact: Andrea Coombs. bk.rev. circ. 1,600. **Document type:** newsletter.
—BLDSC (7777.541200).
Former titles: Pest Resistance Management & Pesticide Resistance Management.

630   RE   ISSN 0395-0328
REUNION AGRICOLE. m. 40 F. Chambre d'Agriculture, 24 rue de la Source, B.P. 134, 97464 Saint-Denis Cedex, Reunion. TEL 21-25-88. FAX 41-17-84. Ed. Herve Cailleaux. circ. 8,000.

630   FR
REUSSIR. 11/yr. 11 rue de la Baume, 75008 Paris, France. TEL 42-56-00-33. FAX 42-25-64-85. Ed. Phillipe Pelzer. circ. 400,000.

630   FR   ISSN 0995-6069
REVEIL LOZERE. 1969. 48/yr. Societe d'Edition et de Publication Agricole de Lozere, 9 place au Ble, 48000 Mende, France. TEL 66-49-18-92. FAX 66-49-00-52. Ed. Anselme Rousset. circ. 5,000.
Formerly (until 1989): Reveil Agricole (ISSN 0995-6077)

REVISTA A I B D A. (Asociacion Interamericana de Bibliotecarios, Documentalistas y Especialistas en Informacion Agricola) see LIBRARY AND INFORMATION SCIENCES

630   AG   ISSN 0080-2069
CODEN: RAARA2
REVISTA AGRONOMICA DEL NOROESTE ARGENTINO. 1953. irreg. Arg.$1000. Universidad Nacional de Tucuman, Facultad de Agronomia y Zootecnia, Casilla de Correos 125, 4000 San Miguel de Tucuman, Argentina. bk.rev. circ. 350. **Indexed:** Biol.Abstr., Dairy Sci.Abstr., Field Crop Abstr., Herb.Abstr., Hort.Abstr., Rev.Plant Path., Rural Recreat.Tour.Abstr., Trop.Abstr., VITIS, World Agri.Econ.& Rural Sociol.Abstr.
—CASDDS.

630   CR   ISSN 0048-7597
REVISTA AGROPECUARIA; al servicio de la agricultura y la ganaderia centroamericana. 1969. q. $6. Editora Latina Ltda., San Rafael Abajo de Desamparados, San Jose, Costa Rica. Ed. J. Luis Burgos Murillo. adv.; bk.rev.; illus. circ. 5,000. **Indexed:** Field Crop Abstr.

630   BL   ISSN 0034-737X
S15   CODEN: RCERA2
REVISTA CERES; orgao de divulgacao tecnico-cientifica em ciencias agrarias. (Text in Portuguese; summaries in English and Portuguese) 1939. bi-m. $40 or exchange basis (effective 1996). Universidade Federal de Vicosa, 36570-000 Vicosa, Minas Gerais, Brazil. TEL 55-31-8992136. FAX 55-31-8992205. Ed. Clibas Vieira. abstr.; bibl.; charts; illus.; index. circ. 1,100. **Indexed:** Agroforest.Abstr., Biol.Abstr., Chem.Abstr., Crop Physiol.Abstr., Field Crop Abstr., Herb.Abstr., Hort.Abstr., Irr.& Drain.Abstr., Maize Abstr., Plant Breed.Abstr., Seed Abstr., Soils & Fert., Soyabean Abstr., Sport Fish.Abstr., Wild.Rev., World Agri.Econ.& Rural Sociol.Abstr., Zoo.Rec. **Document type:** academic/scholarly publication.
—BLDSC (7848.000000); CASDDS; Linda Hall.
Formerly (until 1944): Ceres (ISSN 0366-5798)
Refereed Serial

630   CU   ISSN 1010-2760
REVISTA CIENCIAS TECNICAS AGROPECUARIAS. 3/yr. $21 in N. America; S. America $24; Europe $25; elsewhere $28. Instituto Superior Ciencias Agropecuarias de la Habana (ISCAH), Direccion de Informacion Cientifico-Tecnica, Apdo. Postal 18-19, San Jose de las Lajas, Havana, Cuba. (Dist. by: Ediciones Cubanas, Obispo No. 527, Apdo. 605, Havana, Cuba)

630   CU   ISSN 0034-7485
REVISTA CUBANA DE CIENCIA AGRICOLA. English edition: Cuban Journal of Agricultural Science. 1967. 3/yr. $45 (foreign $60) (effective 1997 & 1998). Instituto de Ciencia Animal, Tulipan No. 1011 e-47 y Loma, Nuevo Vedado, Havana, Cuba. TEL 537-99180. FAX 537-335382. E-mail: ICA@ceniai.cu. Ed. Manuel Valdive; Pub. Rafael Herrera. R&P contact: Dulce Maria Vento. adv. contact: Maria Teresa Perez. bk.rev.; charts; illus.; stat.; index; circ. 500 (paid). (tabloid format; also avail. in microform from UMI; reprint service avail. from UMI) **Indexed:** Anim.Breed.Abstr., ASCA, Biol.Abstr., Chem.Abstr., Curr.Adv.Ecol.Sci., Curr.Cont., Dairy Sci.Abstr., Excerp.Med., Field Crop Abstr., Food Sci.& Tech.Abstr., Helminthol.Abstr., Herb.Abstr., Ind.Agri.Am.Lat.Caribe, Ind.Vet., Nutr.Abstr., Plant Breed.Abstr., Poult.Abstr., Rice Abstr., Rural Recreat.Tour.Abstr., Soils & Fert., Sugar Ind.Abstr., Vet.Bull., Weed Abstr., Weed Abstr., World Agri.Econ.& Rural Sociol.Abstr. **Document type:** academic/scholarly publication.
—UnCover.
Description: Covers animal nutrition, genetics, pasture and forage production. Includes information about milk, beef, poultry and swine production; biochemistry, conservation, weeds and pests, soils, fertilizers and mechanization.
Refereed Serial

630   BL   ISSN 0034-7655
CODEN: RAPCAW
REVISTA DE AGRICULTURA. (Text in English, Portuguese and Spanish; summaries in English and Portuguese or Spanish) 1926. 3/yr. $60 (effective 1996). Caixa Postal 60, 13400-970 Piracicaba, Sao Paulo, Brazil. TEL 0194-22-3604. TELEX 19-1141 ESALQ-PCP. Ed. Frederico Pimentel Gomes. adv. contact: Mrs. Marli de Bem Gomes. bk.rev.; bibl.; charts; illus.; index. circ. 700. **Indexed:** Anim.Breed.Abstr., Bio-Contr.News & Info., Biol.Abstr., Chem.Abstr., Curr.Cont., Field Crop Abstr., Forest.Abstr., Forest Prod.Abstr., Helminthol.Abstr., Herb.Abstr., Hort.Abstr., Ind.Vet., Irr.& Drain.Abstr., Plant Breed Abstr., Potato Abstr., Rev.Appl.Entomol., Rev.Plant Path., Seed Abstr., Soils & Fert., Tob.Abstr., Triticale Abstr., Weed Abstr. **Document type:** academic/scholarly publication.
—BLDSC (7838.020000); CASDDS; Linda Hall.
Refereed Serial

630   PO   ISSN 0871-018X
REVISTA DE CIENCIAS AGRARIAS. 1903. 4/yr. $60 (effective 1997). Sociedade de Ciencias Agrarias, Rua Junqueira 299, 1300 Lisbon, Portugal. TEL 351-1-3633719. FAX 351-1-3622518. Ed. F. Castro Roque; Dir. R. Monjardino. adv. contact: R. Manjardino. **Document type:** academic/scholarly publication, bulletin.

REVISTA DE DERECHO Y REFORMA AGRARIA. see LAW

REVISTA DE DIREITO AGRARIO. see LAW

630   SP
REVISTA DE L'INSTITUT. 4/yr. Association of Agricultural Traders in Catalunya, Plaza de Sant Josep Oriol 4, 08002 Barcelona, Spain. TEL 3-30-11-740. FAX 3-317-30-05. circ. 3,000.

630   BL   ISSN 0100-607X
REVISTA DO SETOR DE CIENCIAS AGRARIAS. (Text in Portuguese; summaries in English, Portuguese) 1979. biennial. Universidade Federal do Parana, Sector de Ciencias Agrarias, Caixa Postal 672, 80035-050 Curitiba PR, Brazil. TEL 55-41-2535552. FAX 55-41-2535552. Ed. Vismar da Costa Lima Neto. adv.; bibl.; charts; illus. circ. 800. **Indexed:** Forest.Abstr., Forest Prod.Abstr., Nutr.Abstr., Soils & Fert. **Document type:** academic/scholarly publication.
●Also available on CD-ROM.
—BLDSC (7870.641000).
Description: Articles and scientific notes in the area of agronomy, forestry, and veterinary sciences.

REVISTA INTERNACIONAL DE SOCIOLOGIA SOBRE AGRICULTURA Y ALIMENTOS/INTERNATIONAL JOURNAL OF SOCIOLOGY OF AGRICULTURE AND FOOD. see SOCIOLOGY

AGRICULTURE

630   **CK**   ISSN 0035-0222
REVISTA NACIONAL DE AGRICULTURA. 1906. q. Col.$36000($160) or exchange basis (effective 1997). Sociedad de Agricultores de Colombia, Carrera 7a No. 24-89, Piso 44, Bogota D.E., Colombia. TEL 57-1-3415929. FAX 57-1-2844572. Ed. Gabriel Martinez-Pelaez. adv. contact: Sandra Cardona. bk.rev.; charts; illus. circ. 2,000. Indexed: Biol.Abstr., Chem.Abstr., Rice Abstr.
—BLDSC (7868.300000).
    Description: Publishes articles on all aspects of price policy, credit, land tenure reform, research extension, natural resources management, marketing, foreign trade, and public investment. Analyzes the effects of these factors on agricultural production.

581 630   **CU**   ISSN 0138-6492
REVISTA PLANTAS MEDICINALES. (Table of contents and abstracts in English) 1981. a. $6 in N. and S. America; Europe $9. Centro de Informacion y Documentacion Agropecuario, Gaveta Postal 4149, Havana 4, Cuba. (Dist. by: Ediciones Cubanas, Obispo No. 527, Apdo. 605, Havana, Cuba) abstr. Indexed: Agrindex.

630   **BL**
REVISTA REALIDAD E RURAL/RURAL REALTY. 1963. m. Cooperativa Central dos Produtores Rurais de Minas Gerais, Rua Itambe 40, Belo Horizonte, MG, Brazil. Dir. Jose P. Campos. circ. 30,000.

630   **FR**   ISSN 0999-212X
REVUE AGRICOLE DE L'AUBE. 1862. w. 2 bis rue Jeanne d'Arc, B.P. 4017, 10013 Troyes Cedex, France. TEL 25-73-30-55. FAX 25-73-12-63. Ed. G. Menuel. circ. 5,000.
    Formerly (until 1928): Revue Agricole du Comice Departmental de l'Aube (ISSN 0999-2111); (until 1902): Bulletin Agricole (ISSN 0999-2103); (until 1875): Revue Agricole du Department de l'Aube (ISSN 0999-209X)

638.1   **FR**   ISSN 0035-2853
REVUE FRANCAISE D'APICULTURE; l'abeille et le miel. 1946. 11/yr. 165 F. (foreign 215 F.). Union Nationale de l'Apiculture Francaise, 26 rue des Tournelles, 75004 Paris, France. TEL 48-87-47-15. Ed. Louis Seard. adv.; illus. Indexed: Apic.Abstr.

630   **FR**   ISSN 1145-1971
REVUE FRANCAISE DE L'AGRO-ALIMENTAIRE. (Text in French) 1964. q. 70 F. Societe Nouvelle Meridionale d'Imprimerie et d'Edition (S N M I E), Centre d'Affaires CAP SUD, Immeuble Orion, Route de Marseille, 84000 Avignon, France. TEL 90-86-03-33. FAX 90-27-05-67. Ed. Marie-Claire Forcina. adv.: B&W page 5500 F., color page 11000 F.; trim 252 x 189; adv. contact: Christian Hodapp. circ. 30,000.
    Former titles: France Agriculture (ISSN 0184-1726); Fournisseur de l'Agriculture.

630   **SZ**   ISSN 0375-1325
    CODEN: RSAGB
REVUE SUISSE D'AGRICULTURE. (Text in French; summaries in English, German and Italian) 1969. bi-m. 37 SFr. (with Revue Suisse de Viticulture, d'Arboriculture et d'Horticulture 47 SFr.). A M T R A - Association pour la Mise en Valeur des Travaux de la Recherche Agronomique, Case Postale 190, CH-1260 Nyon 1, Switzerland. TEL 022-3634151. FAX 022-3621325. Ed. Michel Magnenat. adv.: B&W page 1312 SFr.; trim 180 x 250; adv. contact: Eliane Roher. bk.rev.; illus. circ. 7,000. Indexed: Anim.Breed.Abstr., Bio-Contr.News & Info., Biol.Abstr., Biotech.Abstr., Dairy Sci.Abstr., Field Crop Abstr., Food Sci.& Tech.Abstr., Herb.Abstr., Hort.Abstr., Maize Abstr., Pig News & Info., Plant Breed.Abstr., Potato Abstr., Rev.Appl.Entomol., Rev.Plant Path., Rural Recreat.Tour.Abstr., Seed Abstr., Soils & Fert., Soyabean Abstr., Triticale Abstr., VITIS, Weed Abstr. **Document type:** academic/scholarly publication.
—BLDSC (7953.345000); Linda Hall; SWETS.
    Supersedes in part (in 1969): Agriculture Romande (ISSN 0515-7412)

630   **GW**
RHEINISCHES GENOSSENSCHAFTSBLATT. m. Genossenschaftsverband Rheinland e.V., Postfach 101562, 50455 Cologne, Germany. TEL 49-221-20140. FAX 49-221-236581. adv.; bk.rev.

630   **CN**   ISSN 0844-3823
LE RICHELIEU DIMANCHE. (Text in French) 1936. w. Can.$48($270) Promotion G.& P. Inc., 84 Richelieu St., Saint-Jean-sur-Richelieu, PQ J3B 6X3, Canada. TEL 514-347-5371. FAX 514-347-4539. Ed. Robert Paradis. adv. contact: Leopold St-Marie. circ. 32,645. cols./p.: 8. (tabloid format; also avail. in microfilm) **Document type:** newspaper.
    Formerly: Richelieu Agricole.

630   **IT**   ISSN 0391-8688
RISICOLTORE; mensile d'informazione agricole, industriali, e commerciali. 1956. m. free. Ente Nazionale Risi, Piazza Pio XI 1, 20123 Milan, Italy. FAX 02-861372. TELEX 334032. Ed. Enrico Villa. R&P contact: Enrico Villa. adv. contact: Donata Zanardo. bk.rev. circ. 30,000. **Document type:** newspaper.
    Description: Deals with rice and grain growing; includes political, technical and economic factors pertaining to agriculture.

630   **US**
RIVERSIDE COUNTY AGRICULTURE.* 1946. m. $5 to non-members. (Riverside County Farm Bureau, Inc.) Riverside County Publishing Co., 7190 Jurupa Ave., Riverside, CA 92504-1016. Ed. Robert Eli Perkins. adv.; bk.rev.; illus. circ. 3,277.
    Former titles: Riverside County Farm and Agricultural Business News (ISSN 0035-5690); Riverside County Farm Bureau News.

631.091   **IT**   ISSN 0035-6026
    CODEN: RSTTAP
RIVISTA DI AGRICOLTURA SUBTROPICALE E TROPICALE. (Text in Italian; summaries in English, Italian) 1907. q. exchange basis. Istituto Agronomico per l'Oltremare, Via Antonio Cocchi 4, Florence 50131, Italy. FAX 39-55-580314. TELEX 571549 IAO I. E-mail: rivtrop@iao.florence.it. Ed. Gian Luigi Curotti. bk.rev.; abstr.; bibl.; charts; illus.; stat.; index. circ. 1,300. Indexed: Anim.Breed.Abstr., Bio-Contr.News & Info., Biol.Abstr., Biol.& Agr.Ind., Chem.Abstr., Crop Physiol.Abstr., Curr.Adv.Ecol.Sci., Curr.Cont., Excerp.Med., Field Crop Abstr., Food Sci.& Tech.Abstr., Forest.Abstr., Forest Prod.Abstr., Geo.Abstr., Helminthol.Abstr., Herb.Abstr., Hort.Abstr., Plant Breed.Abstr., Potato Abstr., Rev.Appl.Entomol., Rev.Plant Path., Rural Devel.Abstr., Rural Recreat.Tour.Abstr., Seed Abstr., Soils & Fert., Sorghum & Millets Abstr., Trop.Abstr., Weed Abstr., World Agri.Econ.& Rural Sociol.Abstr. **Document type:** academic/scholarly publication.
—CASDDS.

630 340   **IT**   ISSN 0391-8696
RIVISTA DI DIRITTO AGRARIO. 1922. q. Lit.120000 (foreign Lit.180000) (effective 1997). (Istituto di Diritto Agrario Internazionale e Comparato) Casa Editrice Dott. A. Giuffre, Via Busto Arsizio 40, 20151 Milan, Italy. TEL 39-2-38089200. FAX 39-2-38009582. Ed. Antonio Carrozza. adv. circ. 1,800. Indexed: ELLIS, IBR.

630   **IT**   ISSN 0393-4810
RIVISTA DI POLITICA AGRARIA. (Text in English, French, German, Italian) 1953. bi-m. L.75000 (effective 1996). Edagricole S.p.A., Via Emilia Levante 31, 40139 Bologna, Italy. TEL 39-51-492211. FAX 39-51-493660. Ed. Alfredo Diana. adv.: B&W page L.1300000; 175 x 230. bk.rev.; charts; tr.lit.; index. circ. 5,500. Indexed: Geo.Abstr., P.A.I.S.For.Lang.Ind., Rural Recreat.Tour.Abstr., World Agri.Econ.& Rural Sociol.Abstr.

630 900   **IT**   ISSN 0557-1359
RIVISTA DI STORIA DELL'AGRICOLTURA. (Text in Italian; summaries in English) 1961. s-a. L.30000 (effective June 1995). Accademia dei Georgofili, Logge Uffizi Corti, 50122 Florence, Italy. TEL 39-55-212114. FAX 39-55-2302754. Ed. Giovanni Cherubini. bibl.; illus.; maps; index. pub.index: 1961-1995. circ. 1,200. (back issues avail.) **Document type:** academic/scholarly publication.
    Description: Covers history of agriculture, agricultural technologies, the rural world, and agricultural literature.
    Refereed Serial

630   **US**   ISSN 0035-7650
ROCKY MOUNTAIN UNION FARMER. 1912. bi-m. $7. Rocky Mountain Farmers Union, 10800 E. Bethany Dr., 4th Fl., Aurora, CO 80014-2632. TEL 303-752-5800. FAX 303-752-5810. E-mail: rmfu@aol.com. Ed. Melissa Elliott. Pub. Dave Carter. R&P contact: Melissa Elliott. charts; illus.; circ. 8,000 (paid). (tabloid format) **Document type:** trade publication.

630   **IT**
LA ROMAGNA AGRICOLA E ZOOTECNICA. 1915. a. free. Azienda Agraria Sperimentale Marani, Via Romea Nord 248, 48100 Ravenna, Italy. TEL 0544 451041. FAX 0544-451448. circ. 1,000.

638.1   **RM**
ROMANIA APICOLA. 1926. m. Beekeepers' Association, Str. I. Fucik 17, 70231 Bucharest, Rumania. TEL 137877. TELEX 11205. Ed. Elisei Tarta. circ. 25,000.
    Description: Review of apiculture.

630   **RU**   ISSN 0869-6128
    CODEN: DRASE8
ROSSIISKAYA AKADEMIYA SEL'SKOKHOZYAISTVENNYKH NAUK. DOKLADY. English translation: Russian Agricultural Sciences (US ISSN 1068-3674) 1936. bi-m. $81 (effective 1998). c/o Tsentral'naya Nauchnaya Sel'skokhozyaistvennaya Biblioteka, Orlikov per. 3, 107804 Moscow, Russia. TEL 7-095-2078972. FAX 7-095-2075662. (Dist. by: Mezhdunarodnaya Kniga, B. Yakimanka 39, 117049 Moscow, Russia. TEL 7-095-2384967. FAX 7-095-2384634) Ed. Nadezhda S. Markova. bk.rev.; charts; index. circ. 1,300. Indexed: Chem.Abstr., Cott.& Trop.Fibr.Abstr., Crop Physiol.Abstr., Helminthol.Abstr., Hort.Abstr., INIS Atomind., Irr.& Drain.Abstr., Nutr.Abstr., Plant Grow.Reg.Abstr., Potato Abstr., Soyabean Abstr., Triticale Abstr., Vet.Bull.
—BLDSC (0055.460000); CASDDS; Linda Hall.
    Formerly: Vsezoyuznaya Akademiya Sel'skohozyaistvennykh Nauk im. V.I. Lenina. Doklady (ISSN 0042-9244)

630   **XR**   ISSN 0370-663X
S13   CODEN: ROVYAM
ROSTLINNA VYROBA/PLANT PRODUCTION. (Text and summaries in Czech, English, Slovak) 1954. m. $170 in Europe; elsewhere $177 (effective 1997). Ustav Zemedelskych a Potravinarskych Informaci, Slezska 7, 120 56 Prague 2, Czech Republic. TEL 420-2-24257939. FAX 420-2-24253938. E-mail: uzlk@uzpi.cz. Ed. Eva Stribrna. adv.; bk.rev.; charts; illus. circ. 600. Indexed: Agri.Eng.Abstr., ASCA, Biol.Abstr., Chem.Abstr., Crop Physiol.Abstr., Curr.Adv.Ecol.Sci., Curr.Cont., Excerp.Med., Fababean Abstr., Field Crop Abstr., Food Sci.& Tech.Abstr., Helminthol.Abstr., Herb.Abstr., Hort.Abstr., Irr.& Drain.Abstr., Maize Abstr., Nutr.Abstr., Plant Breed.Abstr., Plant Grow.Reg.Abstr., Potato Abstr., Rev.Appl.Entomol., Rev.Plant Path., Seed Abstr., Soils & Fert., Sugar Ind.Abstr., Triticale Abstr., Weed Abstr. **Document type:** academic/scholarly publication.
—BLDSC (8025.300000); CASDDS; Genuine Article.

630   **UK**   ISSN 0080-4134
S3   CODEN: JRAGAY
ROYAL AGRICULTURAL SOCIETY OF ENGLAND. JOURNAL. 1839. a. £32 to non-members. National Agricultural Centre, Stoneleigh, Warks. CV8 2LZ, England. TEL 44-1230-696969. FAX 44-1230-696900. R&P contact: Alan Spedding. adv.; index. circ. 16,000. (also avail. in microform from PMC; reprint service avail. from ISI) Indexed: Agri.Eng.Abstr., Anim.Breed.Abstr., Biol.Abstr., Curr.Adv.Ecol.Sci., Dairy Sci.Abstr., Ecol.Abstr., Field Crop Abstr., Food Sci.& Tech.Abstr., Geo.Abstr.P.G., Herb.Abstr., Hort.Abstr., Ind.Vet., Nutr.Abstr., Plant Breed.Abstr., RICS, Soils & Fert., Vet.Bull., Weed Abstr., World Agri.Econ.& Rural Sociol.Abstr. **Document type:** academic/scholarly publication.
—BLDSC (4851.000000); Ei; Linda Hall; UnCover.

630   **SA**
ROYAL AGRICULTURAL SOCIETY OF NATAL. ROYAL SHOW PROGRAMME. a. R.4. Royal Agricultural Society of Natal, P.O. Box 524, Pietermaritzburg 3200, South Africa. TEL 27-331-56274. FAX 27-331-943540. adv. circ. 500.
    Formerly: Royal Agricultural Society of Natal. Royal Show Catalogue.

AGRICULTURE

630 UK
ROYAL BATH & WEST SHOW CATALOGUE. 1852. a. £2.50. Royal Bath and West of England Society, The Showground, Shepton Mallet, Somerset BA4 6QN, England. TEL 44-1749-823211. FAX 44-1749-823169. Ed. Derek I. Jarman. adv. circ. 3,000. **Document type:** catalog.
Formerly: Bath and West Show Catalogue.

630 UK
ROYAL HIGHLAND NEWS. 1969. s-a. free to members. Royal Highland and Agricultural Society of Scotland, Royal Highland Centre, Ingliston, Edinburgh EH28 8NF, Scotland. TEL 44-131-333-2444. FAX 44-131-333-5236. Ed. Nick Dougan. R&P contact: Lara Stewart. adv. contact: Lara Stewart. circ. 16,000. **Document type:** newsletter.
Former titles (until 1992): Royal Highland and Agricultural Society of Scotland. Review; Royal Highland and Agricultural Society of Scotland. Show Guide and Review.
Description: Review of the society's activities.

ROYAL TROPICAL INSTITUTE. BULLETIN. see *ANTHROPOLOGY*

RURAL BUILDER. see *BUILDING AND CONSTRUCTION*

630 US ISSN 1063-5866
RURAL CONDITIONS AND TRENDS. 1990. q. $14 (foreign $17). Department of Agriculture, Economic Research Service, ERS-NASS, 341 Victory Dr., Herndon, VA 22070. Ed. Linda M. Ghelfi. illus. **Indexed:** C.I.J.E.
Description: Analyzes statistical data obtained from a number of federal sources. Describes conditions and trends of rural America in terms of employment and unemployment, industry, earnings, income poetry, and population.

630 334 US
HD1491.U5
RURAL COOPERATIVES. 1934. q. $11 (foreign $16). U.S. Department of Agriculture, Rural Business - Cooperative Service, AG Box 3255, Washington, DC 20250-3255. TEL 202-720-6483. FAX 202-720-4641. (Subscr. to: Superintendent of Documents, U.S. Government Printing Office, Box 371954, Pittsburgh, PA 15250-7954. TEL 202-512-1800. FAX 202-512-2250) Ed. Daniel Campbell. charts; illus. circ. 7,000. (also avail. in microform from CIS; reprint service avail. from CIS) **Indexed:** Amer.Stat.Ind. (1981-), Bibl.Agri., Farm & Garden Ind., Ind.U.S.Gov.Per., P.A.I.S. **Document type:** government publication, trade publication.
—Linda Hall; UnCover.
Former titles: Farmer Cooperatives (ISSN 0364-0736); (until 1976): News for Farmer Cooperatives (ISSN 0028-9035)
Description: Directed to cooperatives' hired professional management and its elected leadership. Reports actions by cooperatives, RBS and Cooperative Services activities, and perspectives of leaders on problems, issues, and challenges facing cooperatives' member-owners.

630 330 301 US ISSN 0271-2172
HN90.C6
RURAL DEVELOPMENT PERSPECTIVES. 1984. 3/yr. $6.50 (foreign $8.15). U.S. Economic Research Service, Department of Agriculture, 1303 New York Ave., N.W., Rm. 208, Washington, DC 20005-4788. TEL 202-219-4060. E-mail: dbowers@econ.ag.gov; URL: http://www.econ.ag.gov/epubs/pdf/rdp/rdp. htm. (Dist. by: ERS-NASS, 341 Victory Dr., Herndon, VA 22070. TEL 800-999-6779; And: Superintendent of Documents, U.S. Government Printing Office, Box 371954, Pittsburgh, PA 15250-7954. TEL 202-512-1800. FAX 202-512-2250) Eds. L. Ghelfi, L. Mann. bk.rev. circ. 3,000. (also avail. in microfiche from CIS; back issues avail.; reprint service avail. from CIS) **Indexed:** Amer.Stat.Ind. (1984-), Bibl.Agri., C.I.J.E., P.A.I.S. **Document type:** government publication.
●Also available online.
—BLDSC (8052.422780); SWETS.
Description: Covers issues influencing rural development, as well as persistent and emerging problems.

338.01 AT ISSN 0812-1729
RURAL INDUSTRY DIRECTORY. 1958. a. Aus.$24.95. Department of Primary Industries and Energy, G.P.O. Box 858, Canberra, A.C.T. 2601, Australia. **Document type:** directory.
—CCC.
Former titles: Australian Agriculture, Fisheries and Forestry Directory (ISSN 0067-2106); Australian Primary Industry Organizations.

630 US ISSN 0743-9962
RURAL LIVING (LANSING). Variant title: Michigan Farm News Rural Living. 1923. q. membership. Michigan Farm Bureau, Box 30690, Lansing, MI 48909. TEL 517-323-7000. FAX 517-323-6793. Ed. Dennis Rudat. circ. 45,640. **Document type:** newspaper.
Formerly (until 1981): Michigan Farm News (ISSN 0026-2161)

RURAL PROGRESS. see *BUSINESS AND ECONOMICS — International Development And Assistance*

630 CN ISSN 1197-124X
RURAL ROOTS. 1991. w. Can.$32. Prince Albert Daily Herald, 24-10th St., P.O. Box 550, Prince Albert, SK S6V 5R9, Canada. TEL 306-764-4276. FAX 306-763-3331. E-mail: pa.dailyherald@ sasknet.sk.ca. Ed. Barb Gustafson; Pub. Bob Gibb. adv. contact: Len Haubrich. bk.rev.; circ. 6,600 (paid); 24,107 (controlled). (tabloid format; also avail. in microform) **Document type:** newspaper.
Refereed Serial

THE RURAL SOCIOLOGIST. see *SOCIOLOGY*

RURAL SOCIOLOGY; devoted to scientific study of rural and community life. see *SOCIOLOGY*

630 UK ISSN 0141-898X
RURAL TECHNOLOGY GUIDE. 1977. irreg. price varies (free to official bodies in developing countries). Natural Resources Institute, Central Ave., Chatham Maritime, Kent ME4 4TB, England. TEL 44-1634-880088. FAX 44-1634-880066. TELEX 263907-LDN-G. E-mail: publications@nri.org; URL: http://www.nri.org. **Indexed:** Field Crop Abstr., Forest.Abstr., Herb.Abstr., Rural Recreat.Tour.Abstr., World Agri.Econ.& Rural Sociol.Abstr. **Document type:** monographic series.
●Also available online.
Also available on CD-ROM.
—BLDSC (8052.640500); CISTI.
Description: Describes how to make devices or utilize appropriate technologies designed to assist rural industries and communities in developing countries.

917.5 US ISSN 1059-6305
RURAL VIRGINIA VOICE. 1983. q. $20 to individuals; institutions $50. Rural Virginia Inc., Box 105, Richmond, VA 23201-0105. Ed. Rick Cagan. adv. circ. 1,000. (back issues avail.) **Document type:** newsletter.
Description: Publishes news, articles, and letters relevant to the concerns of rural Virginians.

630.97132 CN ISSN 0700-5385
RURAL VOICE. 1975. m. $16.05 (foreign Can.$20). North Huron Publishing Company Inc., P.O. Box 429, 136 Queen St., Blyth, ON N0M 1H0, Canada. TEL 519-523-4311. FAX 519-523-9140. Ed. Keith Roulston; Pub. Keith Roulston. adv. contact: Gerry Fortune. bk.rev. circ. 15,000. (back issues avail.) **Document type:** trade publication.
Description: Addresses the people and issues central to agriculture and the family farm.

630 AG ISSN 0327-9596
HD1861
RURALIA; revista argentina de estudios agrarios. 1990. a. (Facultad Latino Americana de Ciencias Sociales (FLASCO), Programa Argentina - Area de Estudios Agrarios) Ediciones Imago Mundi, Sanchez de Loria 1821, 1241 Buenos Aires C.F., Argentina. FAX 541-775-6937. TELEX 18937 FLACS AR. (FLASCO addr.: Av. F. Lacroze 2097, Casilla 145, Suc. 26, 1426 Buenos Aires, Argentina. TEL 541-771-0978) Ed. Osvaldo Barsky.

630 US ISSN 1068-3674
S3
RUSSIAN AGRICULTURAL SCIENCES. English translation of: Rossiiskaya Akademiya Sel'skokhozyaistvennykh Nauk. Doklady (RU ISSN 0869-6128) 1976. m. $1155 (effective 1998). (Rossiiskaya Akademiya Sel'skokhozyaistvennykh Nauk, RU - Russian Academy of Agricultural Sciences) Allerton Press, Inc., 150 Fifth Ave., New York, NY 10011. TEL 212-924-3950. FAX 212-463-9684. Ed. N.S. Markova. charts; illus.; stat.; index. **Indexed:** Agri.Eng.Abstr., Agroforest.Abstr., Biol.Abstr., Excerp.Med., Field Crop Abstr., Forest.Abstr., Herb.Abstr., Ind.Vet., Irr.& Drain.Abstr., Maize Abstr., Pig News & Info., Potato Abstr., Rev.Plant Path., Rice Abstr., Soils & Fert., Triticale Abstr., Vet.Bull., W.R.C.Inf. **Document type:** academic/scholarly publication.
—BLDSC (0420.752100). CCC.
Formerly: Soviet Agricultural Sciences (ISSN 0735-2700)
Description: Covers agronomy, soil science, irrigation and erosion, plant diseases, animal breeding, fertilizers, etc.

630 FR ISSN 0338-5353
RUSTICA HEBDO.* 1928. w. 330 F. 6 Rue Laferniere, 75009 Paris, France. adv. circ. 174,862.
Formerly (until 1973): Rustica (ISSN 0338-5345)

630 636 RW
RWANDA. MINISTERE DE L'AGRICULTURE ET DE L'ELEVAGE. RAPPORT ANNUEL. a. Ministere de l'Agriculture et de l'Elevage, B.P. 621, Kigali, Rwanda.

636.08 TH ISSN 1010-3902
S A B R A O JOURNAL. (Text in English) 1969. s-a. membership. Society for the Advancement of Breeding Researches in Asia and Oceania, c/o Prof. Sumin Smutkupt, Secretary-General, Dept. of Applied Radiation & Isotopes, Faculty of Science, Kasetsart University, Bangkok 10900, Thailand.
Formerly (until 1974): S A B R A O Newsletter (ISSN 1010-4674)
Description: Devoted to the basic and practical aspects of breeding research in economic organisms.

630 UK ISSN 0953-413X
S A C DEPARTMENTAL NOTE. 1987. irreg., no.76, 1996. Scottish Agricultural College, Resource Engineering Department, W. Mains Rd., Edinburgh EH9 3JG, Scotland. **Document type:** monographic series.

338.1 UK
S A C REVIEW. 1988. a. S A C, West Mains Rd., Edinburgh EH9 3JG, Scotland. TEL 44-131-535-4000. FAX 44-131-535-4246. **Document type:** academic/scholarly publication.
Formerly: Edinburgh School of Agriculture. Annual Review (ISSN 0953-6884)

630 SA
S A CO-OP. (South Africa) 1977. m. free to members. (Northern Transvaal Co-Op Ltd.) Mediacom C C, P.O. Box 1432, Northcliff 2115, South Africa. TEL 27-11-4763702. (Co-sponsors: Sentralwes Co-op, Free State Co-op) Ed. Johann Van Zyl. adv. contact: Jana Greenall. bk.rev. circ. 22,000.
Formerly: N T K - Nuus (ISSN 0250-1236)

630 CL
S N A BOLETIN DE MERCADO. m. Sociedad Nacional de Agricultura, Tenderini 187, Casilla 40-D, Santiago, Chile. TEL 34374. TELEX 40760.

630 CL
S N A BOLETIN ECONOMICO. m. Sociedad Nacional de Agricultura, Tenderini 187, Casilla 40-D, Santiago, Chile. TEL 34374. TELEX 40760.

630 CL
S N A VOCERO AGRICOLA. m. Sociedad Nacional de Agricultura, Tenderini 187, Casilla 40-D, Santiago, Chile. TEL 34374. TELEX 40760.

630 NL ISSN 1019-6234
S P C AGRICULTURAL NEWS. French edition: Bulletin de l'Agriculture (ISSN 1025-4935) 1992. s-a. South Pacific Commission, B.P. D5, 98848 Noumea Cedex, New Caledonia. TEL 687-262000. FAX 687-263818. E-mail: spc@spc.org.nc. **Document type:** newsletter.

AGRICULTURE 151

630   GW
SAARLAENDISCHES BAUERNBLATT. fortn. Bauernbund Saar e.V., Heinestr. 2-4, 66121 Saarbruecken, Germany. TEL 62964.

630   RU
SADOVOD K.M.K. 1990. m. 0.15 Rub. per issue. Zavodoupravlenie K.M.K., Pl. Pobedy, 654000 Novokuznetsk, Kemerovskaya Oblast', Russia. Ed. M.P. Merenkov.

630   JA   ISSN 0581-2801
                                CODEN: SDNID7
SAGA DAIGAKU NOGAKUBU IHO/SAGA UNIVERSITY. FACULTY OF AGRICULTURE. BULLETIN. (Text in English and Japanese; summaries in English) s-a. exchange basis. Saga Daigaku, Nogakubu - Saga University, Faculty of Agriculture, 1 Honjo-machi, Saga-shi, Saga-ken 840, Japan. Ed. Teru Yanagita. circ. 500. (back issues avail.) **Indexed:** Biol.Abstr., Crop Physiol.Abstr., Field Crop Abstr., Helminthol.Abstr., Plant Grow.Reg.Abstr. **Document type:** academic/scholarly publication, bulletin.
—BLDSC (2507.239000).

630   SZ
ST. GALLER BAUER. w. Mattenweg 11, CH-9230 Flavil, Switzerland. TEL 071-848121. FAX 071-835210. Ed. H. Peter. circ. 11,861.

630   II
SAKSHI FARM WEEKLY. (Text in Hindi) 1964. w. Rs.65; newsstand price: Rs.1.50. Vijay Kumar Bhatia, Ed. & Pub., 38-18 East Patel Nagar, New Delhi 110 008, India. TEL 5711319. adv.: page Rs.12000. circ. 47,207. cols./p.: 5; pp./issue: 12.

630   AU
SALZBURGER BAUER. w. Schwarzstr. 19, A-5020 Salzburg, Austria. TEL 0662-870571. TELEX 633110. Ed. Enzia Hein. circ. 9,700.

630   NR   ISSN 0331-7285
SAMARU JOURNAL OF AGRICULTURAL RESEARCH. 1981. a. $30 per no. Ahmadu Bello University, Institute for Agricultural Research, P.M.B. 1044, Samaru-Zaria, Kaduna State, Nigeria. FAX 234-69-50563. Ed. A.M. Emechebe. **Indexed:** Food Sci.& Tech.Abstr., Irr.& Drain.Abstr., Maize Abstr., Rice Abstr., Seed Abstr., Soils & Fert., Sorghum & Millets Abstr., Triticale Abstr., Trop.Oil Seeds Abstr. **Document type:** academic/scholarly publication.
     Description: Publishes the results of agricultural research concerning arable savannah land.

630   NR   ISSN 0080-5769
SAMARU MISCELLANEOUS PAPERS. 1963. irreg. $20. Ahmadu Bello University, Institute for Agricultural Research, P.M.B. 1044, Samaru-Zaria, Kaduna State, Nigeria. FAX 234-69-50563. **Indexed:** Biol.Abstr., Rural Devel.Abstr., Rural Recreat.Tour.Abstr., World Agri.Econ.& Rural Sociol.Abstr. **Document type:** monographic series, academic/scholarly publication.
     Description: Publishes research papers on agricultural topics of local interest.

630   NR   ISSN 0080-5777
SAMARU RESEARCH BULLETIN. 1960. irreg. $20. Ahmadu Bello University, Institute for Agricultural Research, P.M.B. 1044, Samaru-Zaria, Kaduna State, Nigeria. FAX 234-69-50563. circ. 50. **Indexed:** Biol.Abstr. **Document type:** academic/scholarly publication.
     Description: Publishes papers by members of the institute.

631   US   ISSN 0273-6004
SAN FRANCISCO WHOLESALE ORNAMENTAL CROPS REPORT. 1968. w. $96. (U.S. Department of Agriculture) Federal-State Market News Service, 630 Sansome St., Rm. 727, San Francisco, CA 94111. TEL 415-705-1300. FAX 415-705-1301. circ. 135. (looseleaf format; back issues avail.) **Document type:** government publication.
     Description: Presents lists of price ranges and offerings of cut flowers, potted plants and greens on the flower market.

SAN JOAQUIN AGRICULTURAL LAW REVIEW. see *LAW*

638.1   FR   ISSN 0036-4568
LA SANTE DE L'ABEILLE. 1967. bi-m. 95 F. (foreign 140 F.) (effective 1998). Federation Nationale des Organisations Sanitaires Apicoles Departementales (F.N.O.S.A.D.), 33 rue Lepante, 06000 Nice, France. TEL 33-4-93922775. FAX 33-4-93850907. Ed. Jean-Paul Faucon. adv.; bibl.; charts; illus.; index. circ. 10,000. **Indexed:** Apic.Abstr., Biol.Abstr. **Document type:** newspaper.
     Description: News of interest to the apiculturist.

630   MY   ISSN 0080-6420
S322.S3
SARAWAK. DEPARTMENT OF AGRICULTURE. RESEARCH BRANCH. ANNUAL REPORT. (Text in English) 1962. a., latest 1993. M.25. Department of Agriculture, Agricultural Research Centre, Peti Sura 977, 93720 Kuching, Sarawak, Malaysia. TEL 60-82-611171. FAX 60-82-611178. E-mail: ngtt@pc.jaring.my. Ed. Ng Thai Tsiung. circ. 350. **Indexed:** Field Crop Abstr., Herb.Abstr., Hort.Abstr., Rev.Appl.Entomol., Rev.Plant Path. **Document type:** government publication.

630   IT
SARDEGNA - AGRICOLTURA 80. 1970. bi-m. L.36000 (effective 1997). Piazza Annunziata 4, 09123 Cagliari, Italy. TEL 39-70-274096. Ed. Flavio Siddi. adv.: page L.1200000. circ. 3,000.

SARMA. see *LABOR UNIONS*

630   CN   ISSN 0713-1844
SASKATCHEWAN AGRICULTURE AND FOOD. ANNUAL REPORT. 1905. a. free. Saskatchewan Agriculture and Food, Communications Branch, 3085 Albert St., Regina, SK S4S 0B1, Canada. TEL 306-787-6933. FAX 306-787-0216. E-mail: pdc@mailer.agr.gov.sk.ca; URL: http://www.gov.sk.ca/agfood. Ed. Harvey Johnson. adv. contact: Harvey Johnson. charts; illus. circ. 500. (also avail. in microfiche) **Document type:** government publication, corporate report.
     Formerly: Saskatchewan. Department of Agriculture. Annual Report (ISSN 0319-3578)

630 658   CN
SASKATCHEWAN FARM LIFE. 1982. fortn. Can.$33.68. Farm Life Publications, 75 Lenore Dr., No. 4, Saskatoon, SK S7K 7Y1, Canada. TEL 306-242-5723. FAX 306-668-6164. Ed. Larry Hiatt. adv.; circ. 160,000 (controlled). (tabloid format; back issues avail.)

SASKATCHEWAN GRAIN CAR CORPORATION. ANNUAL REPORT. see *TRANSPORTATION*

630   RM   ISSN 1220-8140
SATUL ROMANESC. w. Federation of Agricultural Companies of Rumania, Piata Presei Libere 1, 71341 Bucharest, Rumania. Ed. Titu Constantin. circ. 80,000.

630   YU   ISSN 0581-8850
SAVREMENA POLJOPRIVREDA/CONTEMPORARY AGRICULTURE; Jugoslovenski casopis za poljoprivredu. (Text in Serbo-Croatian; summaries in English) 1953. m. 120 din.($22.75) Dnevnik, Bulevar 23 Oktobra 31, Novi Sad, Yugoslavia. Ed. Miloje Saric. bibl.; charts; illus.; pat.; stat. **Indexed:** Anim.Breed.Abstr., Field Crop Abstr., Herb.Abstr., Hort.Abstr., Plant Breed.Abstr., Soils & Fert., Weed Abstr.

630 631   YU   ISSN 0350-2953
SAVREMENA POLJOPRIVREDNA TEHNIKA/ADVANCED AGRICULTURAL ENGINEERING; Jugoslovenski casopis za poljoprivrednu tehniku. (Text in Serbo-Croatian; abstracts in English) 1975. q. 200 din. (foreign 750 Din.($35)) (effective Jan. 1990). Vojvodjansko Drustvo za Poljoprivrednu Tehniku - Voivodina's Society of Agricultural Technique, Trg Dositeja Obradovica 8, 21000 Novi Sad, Yugoslavia. TELEX 39-021-59-761. (Co-sponsor: Scientific Association of Voivodina) Ed. Radovan Popov. adv.; bk.rev.

630   US
SAYRE JOURNAL. 1898. w. $24.50. 110 N. Fourth St., Box 340, Sayre, OK 73662-0340. TEL 405-928-3372. Ed. Tom Higley. adv. contact: Tom Higley. circ. 2,050 (paid). (broadsheet format; also avail. in microfilm; back issues avail.) **Document type:** newspaper.

630   SZ   ISSN 1420-0546
SCHWEIZER BAUER. 1846. 102/yr. 138 SFr. Dammweg 9, CH-3001 Bern, Switzerland. TEL 41-31-3303444. FAX 41-31-3303395. Ed. Rudolf Haudenschild. bk.rev. circ. 28,500. **Document type:** newspaper.
     Former titles (until 1901): Schweizer Bauer und Bernische Blaetter fuer Landwirtschaft (ISSN 1421-167X); (until 1897): Bernische Blaetter fuer Landwirtschaft (ISSN 1421-1548); (until 1857): Bernische Blaetter fuer Landwirtschaft, Wald- und Gartenbau (ISSN 1421-153X); (until 1849): Wochenblatt fuer Landwirtschaft und Gartenbau (ISSN 1421-1521).

630 338.1 658.8   SZ   ISSN 0377-5070
SCHWEIZER LANDTECHNIK. French edition: Technique Agricole. 12/yr. 45 SFr. (foreign 60 SFr.). Schweizerischer Verband fuer Landtechnik, Ausserdorfstr. 31, Postfach 55, CH-5223 Riniken, Switzerland. TEL 056-412022. FAX 056-416731. **Document type:** trade publication.

638.1   SZ   ISSN 0036-7540
SCHWEIZERISCHE BIENEN-ZEITUNG. 1863. m. 35 SFr. (Verein Deutschschweizerischer und Raetoromanischer Bienenfreunde) Sauerlaender AG, Laurenzenvorstadt 89, CH-5001 Aarau, Switzerland. TEL 064-268626. FAX 064-245780. TELEX 981195-SAG-CH. Ed. Berchtold Lehnherr. adv.: B&W page 1050 SFr., color page 2458.50 SFr.; trim 135 x 193. bk.rev.; charts; illus.; index. circ. 18,000. **Indexed:** Apic.Abstr., Biol.Abstr., Chem.Abstr. **Document type:** bulletin.
—BLDSC (8114.700000). **CCC.**
     Description: Features news and information on breeding, behavior, honey and pollen production of bees; includes reports and a calendar of events.

630   SZ
SCHWEIZERISCHER VERBAND INGENIEUR-AGRONOMEN UND LEBENSMITTEL-INGENIEURE. BULLETIN. (Text in French, German) q. 106.50 SFr. membership (effective 1997). Laenggasse 79, CH-3052 Zollikofen, Switzerland. TEL 41-31-9110668. FAX 41-31-9114925. E-mail: svial@pop.agri.ch; URL: http://www.agri.ch/svial. Ed. Oskar Meyer. circ. 2,500. **Document type:** bulletin.

630   BL   ISSN 0103-9016
                         CODEN: SGRIEF
SCIENTIA AGRICOLA. (Text in English, Portuguese; summaries in English and Portuguese) 1944. q. $50 or exchange basis (effective 1997). Universidade de Sao Paulo, Escola Superior de Agricultura "Luiz de Queiroz", Caixa Postal 9, 13418-900 Piracicaba, Sao Paulo, Brazil. TEL 55-19-4294311. FAX 55-19-4220244. TELEX 19-1141 EALQ. Ed.Bd. bibl. circ. 700. **Indexed:** Agrindex, Agroforest.Abstr., Bibl.Agri., Bio-Contr.News & Info., Biol.Abstr., Bull.Signal., Chem.Abstr., Cott.& Trop.Fibr.Abstr., Crop Physiol.Abstr., Field Crop Abstr., Helminthol.Abstr., Herb.Abstr., Hort.Abstr., Ornam.Hort., Plant Grow.Reg.Abstr., Seed Abstr., Soils & Fert., Sorghum & Millets Abstr., Soyabean Abstr., Sugar Ind.Abstr. **Document type:** academic/scholarly publication.
—CASDDS; UMI.
     Formerly (until 1992): Escola Superior de Agricultura "Luiz de Queiroz". Anais (ISSN 0071-1276)

630   II
SCIENTIFIC HORTICULTURE. (Text and summaries in English) a. $35. Scientific Publishers, P.O. Box 91, 5A, New Pali Rd., Jodhpur 342 001, India. TEL 91-291-33323. FAX 91-291-613480. Ed. S.P. Singh.
     Formerly (until 1992): Scientific Publishers.

630   IT   ISSN 0036-8881
SCIENZA E TECNICA AGRARIA; rivista mensile di agricoltura meridionale. 1961. m. $8.07. Associazioni Dottori in Scienze Agrarie di Bari, Via Japigia 184, 70126 Bari, Italy. Dir. Nicola Matarrese. adv.; charts; illus.; stat.; index.

638.1   UK   ISSN 0370-8918
                         CODEN: SCBKAB
SCOTTISH BEEKEEPER. 1924. m. £10 membership. Scottish Beekeepers' Association, c/o David Blair, 44 Dalhousie Rd., Kilbrachan, Renfrewshire PA10 2AT, Scotland. TEL 44-1505-702680. Ed. A.E. McArthur. R&P contact: David Blair. adv. contact: David Blair. **Document type:** newsletter.

AGRICULTURE

630   UK   ISSN 0036-9195
SCOTTISH FARMER. 1893. w. £55 (overseas £75) (effective 1996). Caledonian Magazines Ltd., The Plaza Tower, East Kilbridge, Glasgow G74 1LW, Scotland. TEL 44-135-524-6444. FAX 44-135-526-3013. Ed. A. Fletcher. adv.: bk.rev.; charts; illus.; mkt.; pat.; stat.; tr.mk. circ. 24,881. (tabloid format) **Indexed:** Ind.Vet., RICS, Vet.Bull. **Document type:** newspaper.

SEED SCIENCE AND TECHNOLOGY. see *BIOLOGY — Botany*

630
SB114.A1   US   CODEN: JSTEDV
SEED TECHNOLOGY. 1908. a. $50 (foreign $60). Association of Official Seed Analysts, Inc., Box 81152, Lincoln, NE 68501-1152. TEL 402-476-3852. Ed. Dennis Tekrony. R&P contact: Dennis Tekrony. TEL 606-257-3878. cum.index: 1908-1937, 1938-1959. circ. 400. **Indexed:** Biol.Abstr., Chem.Abstr., Crop Physiol.Abstr., Curr.Adv.Ecol.Sci., Field Crop Abstr., Herb.Abstr., Hort.Abstr., Rev.Plant Path., Seed Abstr., Soyabean Abstr., Triticale Abstr., Weed Abstr. **Document type:** academic/scholarly publication.
—BLDSC (5063.250000); CASDDS; Linda Hall; SWETS; UnCover.
Formerly: Journal of Seed Technology (ISSN 0146 3071); Which superseded (in 1976): Association of Official Seed Analysts. Proceedings (ISSN 0097-1324)
Refereed Serial

SEEDHEAD NEWS. see *BIOLOGY — Botany*

SEEDS; hope for the healing and hunger of poverty. see *SOCIAL SERVICES AND WELFARE*

630   BL   ISSN 0037-1122
CODEN: SEVAAR
SEIVA. (Text in Portuguese; summaries in English) 1940. q. Cr.$15($3) Universidade Federal de Vicosa, Diretorio Central dos Estudiantes, Vicosa, MG, Brazil. Ed.Bd. charts; illus.; index. circ. 4,000. (processed) **Indexed:** Biol.Abstr., Chem.Abstr., Field Crop Abstr., Herb.Abstr., Hort.Abstr., Plant Breed.Abstr., Rice Abstr., Soils & Fert.

630   JA   ISSN 0387-4338
SEKAI NO NORINSUISAN/WORLD AGRICULTURE, FORESTRY AND FISHERIES. (Text in Japanese) 1952. m. 6000 Yen (foreign 9000 Yen). Japan F A O Association - Kokusai Shokuryo Nogyo Kyokai, Bajichikusan-Kaikan, 1-2 Kanda Surugadai, Chiyoda-ku, Tokyo 101, Japan. TEL 81-3-3294-2425. FAX 81-3-3294-2427. Ed. Yutaka Furuya. adv. contact: Toyo Sekikawa. bk.rev. circ. 1,800. **Document type:** bulletin.
Formerly: F A O Information (ISSN 0014-5629)

SEL'SKOKHOZYAISTVENNAYA BIOLOGIYA. SERIYA BIOLOGIYA RASTENII. see *BIOLOGY*

630   GT
SEMILLAS DE PROGRESO. 1986. bi-m. Instituto Nacional de Transformacion Agraria, 8a Avenida 14-15 Zona 1, Guatemala, Guatemala.

630   IT   ISSN 0037-234X
SENTINELLA AGRICOLA; periodico cremonese di tecnica e divulgazione agraria fondato nel 1896. 1896. m. free. Servizio Provinciale Agricoltura, Foresta, Alimentazione, Via Monteverdi 17, 26100 Cremona, Italy. FAX 39-372-457167. Ed. Paolo Baccolo. adv.; bk.rev.; illus.; stat.; index. circ. 1,033. (tabloid format) **Document type:** bulletin.

SEOUL NATIONAL UNIVERSITY. FACULTY PAPERS. BIOLOGY AND AGRICULTURE SERIES. see *BIOLOGY*

630   KO   ISSN 1013-4077
S19   CODEN: SNYOEF
SEOUL NATIONAL UNIVERSITY JOURNAL OF AGRICULTURAL SCIENCES/SOUL TAE-NONGHAK YON'GU CHI. (Text in English and Korean) 1976. s-a. exchange basis. Seoul National University, College of Agriculture, 103 Seodoon-dong, Suwon 170, S. Korea. FAX 0331-293-5928. Ed.Bd. circ. 800. **Indexed:** Apic.Abstr., Field Crop Abstr., INIS Atomind., Plant Grow.Reg.Abstr. **Document type:** academic/scholarly publication.
—BLDSC (8241.815800).
Former titles (until 1988): Seoul National University. Agricultural Research (ISSN 0255-7010); Seoul National University. College of Agriculture. Bulletin.

630   US
SERIE DE INVESTIGACIONES Y DESARROLLO. Short title: S I D. (Text in Spanish) 1984. irreg. price varies. Organization of American States, Instituto Interamericano de Cooperacion Agricola - Organizacion de los Estados Americanos, 1889 F St., N.W., Washington, DC 20006-4499. TEL 202-458-3527. FAX 202-458-3534. (Dist. by: Center for Promotion and Distribution of Publications, Box 66398, Washington, DC 20035)

630   FR   ISSN 1260-0849
SESAME BULLETIN; revue bibliographique en agronomie tropicale francophone. 1977. q. 510 F. (foreign 570 F.). Centre de Cooperation Internationale en Recherche Agronomique pour le Developpement (CIRAD), B.P. 5035, 34032 Montpellier Cedex 1, France. TEL 67-61-58-00. FAX 67-61-58-20. TELEX 680762F. E-mail: sesame@cirad.fr; URL: http://www.cirad.fr. Ed. Helene Doco. R&P contact: Helene Doco. **Document type:** abstracting/indexing, academic/scholarly publication.
●Also available on CD-ROM.
Formerly (until 1995): Agritrop (ISSN 0399-1539)
Description: Lists publications, articles, theses, books and reports on tropical and Mediterranean agriculture by Francophone scientists. Subjects covered include agricultural economics and development, production systems, crop and livestock production, forestry, fisheries, agricultural engineering, natural resource management, processing of agricultural products.

630   II
SEVAGRAM/FARM WEEKLY. (Text in Hindi) 1954. fortn. Rs.70. Sevagram Journals (P) Ltd., Basant Cinema Bldg., Lalbagh P.B. No. 155, Lucknow 226001, India. Ed. B.P. Gupta. adv.: B&W page Rs.7200; 360 x 250. circ. 18,000. cols./p.: 5.

630   US   ISSN 0192-4184
SEVEN COUNTY FARM AND HOME NEWS. 1947. m. $5 for 3 yrs. Farm & Home Publications, 10 Lourdes Rd., Binghamton, NY 13905-4293. Ed. Bernard M. Swartz. adv. circ. 3,100.
Formerly: Columbia - Luzerne - Wyoming - Lycoming Farm and Home News.

052 054.1   SE
SEYCHELLOIS. (Text in English and French) 1928. d. Rs.48. (Seychelles Farmers Association) Seychellois Press Ltd., Box 32, Victoria, Mahe, Seychelles. (Co-sponsor: Seychelles Copra Association) Ed. G. de Comarmond. adv. circ. 1,800.

630   CC   ISSN 1000-193X
SHANGHAI NONGXUEYUAN XUEBAO/SHANGHAI AGRICULTURAL INSTITUTE. JOURNAL. (Text in Chinese) 1983. q. Y2.50. Shanghai Nongxueyuan - Shanghai Agricultural College, No. 31, Qishen Lu, Shanghai 201101, People's Republic of China. TEL 923010. Ed. Wu Jinkang. adv. circ. 1,000.
—BLDSC (4874.740000).

630   CC
SHANXI GUOSHU/SHANXI FRUIT TREES. (Text in Chinese) q. Shanxi Sheng Nongye Kexueyuan, Guoshu Yanjiusuo - Shanxi Academy of Agricultural Sciences, Fruit Tree Research Institute, Taigu Xian (County), Shanxi 030800, People's Republic of China. TEL 22587. Ed. Chen Keliang.

630   CC   ISSN 0488-5368
SHANXI NONGYE/SHANXI AGRICULTURE. (Text in Chinese) bi-m. Shanxi Nongye Kexueyuan - Shanxi Academy of Agricultural Sciences, 4 Wucheng Lu, Taiyuan, Shanxi 030006, People's Republic of China. TEL 775565. Ed. Guo Huarong.

630   CC   ISSN 1000-162X
SHANXI NONGYE DAXUE XUEBAO/SHANXI UNIVERSITY OF AGRICULTURE. JOURNAL. (Text in Chinese) s-a. Shanxi Nongye Daxue - Shanxi University of Agriculture, Taigu Xian (County), Shanxi 030801, People's Republic of China. TEL 22902. Ed. Chen Zhen.

630   II   ISSN 0037-3648
SHETKARI.* (Text in Marathi) 1965. m. Rs.10. Department of Agriculture, Central Bldg., Pune 411001, India. Ed. Shri D.K. Dhat. adv.; bk.rev.; charts; illus.; stat. circ. 100,000.
Supersedes: Farmer.

630   CC   ISSN 1002-4433
SHIJIE NONGYE/WORLD AGRICULTURE. (Text in Chinese) 1979. m. $30 (effective 1994). Zhongguo Nongye Chubanshe - China Agricultural Press, 2 Nongzhanguan Beilu, Beijing 100026, People's Republic of China. TEL 01-506-4142. FAX 01-5005665. Eds. Cai Shenglin, Wang Qiang. adv.: page $5000. circ. 10,000. **Document type:** academic/scholarly publication.
Description: Introduces the current advances in agriculture, animal husbandry and fishery.

630   JA   ISSN 0037-3702
S471.J32   CODEN: SNSKA3
SHIKOKU NATIONAL AGRICULTURAL EXPERIMENT STATION. BULLETIN. (Text in Japanese; summaries in English) 1953. a. exchange basis. Shikoku National Agricultural Experiment Station - Norin Suisansho Shikoku Nogyo Shikenjo, 3 Zentsuji-cho, Zentsuji-city, Kagawa-ken 765, Japan. Ed. Shigeo Oba. circ. 1,000. **Indexed:** Biol.Abstr., Chem.Abstr., Excerp.Med., Field Crop Abstr., Food Sci.& Tech.Abstr., Helminthol.Abstr., Herb.Abstr., Hort.Abstr., Plant Breed.Abstr., Rev.Plant Path., Rural Recreat.Tour.Abstr., Soils & Fert., Weed Abstr., World Agri.Econ.& Rural Sociol.Abstr. **Document type:** bulletin.
—BLDSC (2720.190100); CASDDS.

630   US   ISSN 1093-9520
SHOW ME MISSOURI FARM BUREAU. 1921. 6/yr. $5 to non-members. Missouri Farm Bureau Federation, Box 658, Jefferson City, MO 65102. TEL 314-893-1400. FAX 573-893-1470. E-mail: mo@momail.com. Ed. Chris Fennewald. adv. contact: Chris Fennewald. circ. 84,000. (also avail. in microfiche) **Document type:** trade publication.
Formerly (until 1997): Missouri F B News (ISSN 0026-6574)
Refereed Serial

630   GW
SICHER LEBEN (HANNOVER). 1965. bi-m. Hannoversche Landwirtschaftliche Berufsgenossenschaft, Im Haspelfelde 24, 30173 Hannover, Germany. TEL 0511-8073-0. FAX 0511-8073-498.

630   GW
SICHER LEBEN (SPEYER). 1965. 6/yr. Landwirtschaftliche Berufsgenossenschaft Rheinhessen-Pfalz, 67343 Speyer, Germany. TEL 06232-911205. FAX 06232-911187. Ed. Richard Binz. circ. 18,000. **Document type:** bulletin.

SICKLE & SHEAF. see *CLUBS*

630   SL
SIERRA LEONE AGRICULTURAL JOURNAL. (Text in English) 1972. s-a. Le.2($6) Sierra Leone Agricultural Society, c/o W.E. Taylor, Ed., University of Sierra Leone, Njala University College, Private Mail Bag, Freetown, Sierra Leone. adv.; bk.rev.; charts; illus. **Indexed:** Field Crop Abstr., Herb.Abstr., Rural Recreat.Tour.Abstr., World Agri.Econ.& Rural Sociol.Abstr. **Document type:** academic/scholarly publication.

630   XR   ISSN 1210-1346
SIGNALNI INFORMACE ZE SVETA ZEMEDELSTVI. 1992. s-a. $58 (effective 1997). Ustav Zemedelskych a Potravinarskych Informaci, Slezska 7, 120 56 Prague 2, Czech Republic. TEL 420-2-24257939. FAX 420-2-24253938. E-mail: uzlk@uzpi.cz. Ed. I. Fantysova. circ. 400.
Description: Provides information on world agriculture.

630   US
SILLON; a journal of popular farm science and rural life. (French edition of: Furrow (ISSN 0016-3112)) (Text in French) 1970. 4/yr. free to qualified personnel. Deere & Company, John Deere Rd., Moline, IL 61265. TEL 309-765-8000. Ed. Jean-Claude Hiron. circ. 140,000. **Indexed:** RILM.

630   FR   ISSN 0765-166X
SILLON ALPIN. 1938. 22/yr. 8 ter, rue Capitaine de Brisson, 05000 Gap, France. TEL 92-51-06-87. FAX 92-53-35-51. Ed. Michel Espitallier. circ. 2,200.

AGRICULTURE

630 BE
SILLON BELGE. Dutch edition: Landbouwleven. (Text in French) 1931. 49/yr. 1270 BEF (1275 BEF for Dutch ed.). Editions Rurales, 92 Leon Grosjeanlaan, 1140 Brussels, Belgium. TEL 02-730-3300. FAX 02-726-9134. TELEX 25882. E-mail: erulu@infoboard.be. Ed. A. Demol; Pub. Ludo Hugaerts. adv. contact: Sylvie Eyben. circ. 87,741 (44.395 Dutch ed.; 43,346 French ed.). **Document type:** newspaper.

630 FR ISSN 0152-6456
SILLON DES LANDES ET DES PYRENEES. EDITION 64. 1968. w. Societe d'Editions Agricoles du Basin de l'Adour, 124 bd. Tourasse, 64000 Pau, France. TEL 59-02-35-55. Ed. J.L. Dumontier-Beroulet. circ. 20,000.
Formerly (until 1978): Sillion des Landes et des Pyrenees (ISSN 0152-6421)

630 SZ ISSN 1420-4258
LE SILLON ROMAND. (Text in French) 1898. w. 118 SFr. Edipresse Publications SA, Av. de la Gare 33, CH-1001 Lausanne, Switzerland. TEL 41-21-3494545. FAX 41-21-3494079. Ed. Bernard Debetaz. adv.; circ. 23,675 (controlled). **Document type:** newspaper.

630 RU ISSN 0037-5322
SIL'S'KE BUDIVNYTSTVO. (Text in Ukrainian) 1951. m. 15.60 Rub. Izdatel'stvo Kniga, 125047 Moscow, Russia. illus.

630 CL ISSN 0037-5403
CODEN: SMNTAW
SIMIENTE. 1942. q. Esc.2500($30) (effective 1991). Sociedad Agronomica de Chile, Calle MacIver 120, of. 36, Casilla 4109, Santiago, Chile. TEL 384881. Ed. Gustavo Saravia Iglesias. adv.; bk.rev.; bibl.; charts; illus.; stat. circ. 2,000. **Indexed:** Biol.Abstr., Chem.Abstr., Field Crop Abstr., Herb.Abstr., Hort.Abstr., Maize Abstr., Plant Grow.Reg.Abstr., Potato Abstr., Seed Abstr., Soils & Fert., Triticale Abstr., Weed Abstr.
—CASDDS.
Description: Technical articles on agricultural science and engineering. Includes news of and for members.

630 CN ISSN 0225-7211
SIMMENTAL COUNTRY. 1973. m. Can.$38($50) (Canadian Simmental Association) Pritchett Publications, 13 4101 19th St. N.E., Calgary, AB T2E 7C4, Canada. TEL 403-250-5255. FAX 403-250-5279. Ed. Ted Pritchett. adv.: B&W page Can.$585; trim 8 3/8 x 10 3/4. circ. 4,355. **Document type:** trade publication.
Formerly (until Oct. 1979): Simmental Scene (ISSN 0318-0913)

630 US
SIMPLE LIVING. 1938. m. $22. Luna Ventures, Box 398, Suisun, CA 94585. Ed. Paul Doerr. adv.; bk.rev.; film rev.; index. (looseleaf format; also avail. in microfiche; back issues avail.) **Document type:** newsletter.
Formed by the merger of: Backwoods (ISSN 1042-7732); Which was formerly: Pioneer (ISSN 0275-8148); Owlhooters (ISSN 1042-7902); Which was formerly: Owlhooter's Gazette (ISSN 0748-402X)
Description: Covers homesteading, survival, living on small boats and RVs, treasure hunting and prospecting.

630 PO
SIMPOSIUM AGRO-PECUARIO. 4/yr. Rua Antonio Per Carrilho 38-2o, Lisbon, Portugal.

630 IO
SINAR JAYA. fortn. Jalan Sultan Aqung 67 A, Jakarta Selatan, Indonesia. Ed. Suryono Projopranoto. adv.

630 639.2 636.089 SI ISSN 0129-6485
S322.S55 CODEN: SJPIDP
SINGAPORE JOURNAL OF PRIMARY INDUSTRIES. (Text in English) 1973. s-a. S.$10. Ministry of National Development, Primary Production Department, 5 Maxwell Rd., No. 03-00, National Development Bldg., Singapore 0106, Singapore. FAX 2206068. TELEX RS-28851-PPD. Ed. May G.B. Lim. adv. circ. 500. (back issues avail.) **Indexed:** Biol.Abstr., Chem.Abstr., Hort.Abstr., Nutr.Abstr., Ornam.Hort., Poult.Abstr., Soils & Fert.
—BLDSC (8285.464000); CASDDS.

630.9489 DK ISSN 0900-3460
SKALMEJEN. 1984. q. DKK 25. Ringsted Museum og Forening, c/o Kirsten Henriksen, Koegevej 41, DK-4100 Ringsted, Denmark. illus. **Document type:** newsletter, consumer publication.

630 US
SMALL FARM NEWS. 1981. bi-m. free. Small Farm Center, University of California at Davis, Davis, CA 95616. TEL 916-752-8136. FAX 916-752-7716. Ed. Christie Wyman. bk.rev. **Document type:** newsletter.
Description: Provides information to extension workers, researchers, and operators of small farms and related businesses.

630 US ISSN 1079-9729
SMALL FARM TODAY; the how-to magazine of alternative crops, livestock and direct marketing. 1984. bi-m. $21 (foreign $31) (effective through 1998). Missouri Farm Publishing, Inc., 3903 W. Ridge Trail Rd., Clark, MO 65243-9525. TEL 573-687-3525; 800-633-2335. FAX 573-687-3148. Ed. Poul Berger; Pub. Ron Macher. adv. contact: Mark Arends. bk.rev.; illus. circ. 12,000. (back issues avail.) **Document type:** consumer publication.
Formerly (until Apr., 1992): Missouri Farm (ISSN 0892-6301)
Description: To promote and preserve small farming and rural living by providing both traditional and non-traditional farming alternatives adaptable to small acreages.

630 US ISSN 0743-9989
SMALL FARMER'S JOURNAL; featuring practical horse-farming. 1976. q. $24 (foreign $31). Small Farmers Journal, Inc., Box 1627, Sisters, OR 97759-1627. TEL 541-549-2064. FAX 541-549-4403. Ed. Lynn R. Miller. R&P contact: Lynn R. Miller. adv. contact: Suzie Clarke. bk.rev.; illus. circ. 20,000. (back issues avail.) **Document type:** trade publication.
—UnCover.

630 CN ISSN 0383-6312
SMALLHOLDER. 1974. 4/yr. Can.$14 for 6 nos. Smallholder Publishing Collective, Argenta, BC V0G 1B0, Canada. Ed.Bd. adv.; bk.rev.; bibl.; illus. circ. 700. **Document type:** newsletter.
Description: Reader's exchange on topics of interest to people living rural lifestyles; covers gardening, homestead skills and environment.

630 637 UK ISSN 0265-7473
SMALLHOLDER; the practical monthly guide for the small farmer. 1981. m. £19.95 (Europe £28.75; elsewhere £37.50) (effective 1997). Bailey Newspaper Group Ltd., Reliance House, Long St., Dursley, Glos GL11 4LS, England. TEL 44-1453-544000. FAX 44-1453-544577. (Dist. by: Diamond Magazine Dist. Ltd., Unit 7, Rother Ironworks, Fishmarket Rd., Rye, E. Sussex TN31 7LR, England. TEL 44-1797-225229. FAX 44-1797-225657) Ed. Liz Wright. R&P contact: Liz Wright. adv. contact: Linda Andrews. bk.rev.; cum.index. circ. 12,000. (back issues avail.) **Document type:** trade publication.

630 AG ISSN 0037-864X
SOCIEDAD RURAL ARGENTINA, BOLETIN. 1958. 9/yr. Arg.$20000. Sociedad Rural Argentina, Florida 460, Buenos Aires, Argentina. adv. circ. 15,000. **Document type:** bulletin.

630 YU
SOCIJALISTICKA POLJOPRIVREDA; mesecnik za poljoprivredu i zemiljoradnicko zadrugarstvo. 1950. m. Glavni Zadruzni Savez, Kneza Milosa 26-l, Belgrade, Yugoslavia. bibl.

630 301 UK ISSN 0967-0548
SOCIO-ECONOMIC SERIES. 1993. irreg. price varies. Natural Resources Institute, Central Ave., Chatham Maritime, Kent ME4 4TB, England. TEL 44-1634-880088. FAX 44-1634-880066. TELEX 263907-LDN-G. E-mail: publications@nri.org; URL: http://www.nri.org. **Document type:** monographic series.
●Also available online.
Also available on CD-ROM.
—BLDSC (6180.547900).
Description: Covers a wide range of development issues in agriculture from reviews to practical field projects.

630 XV ISSN 0350-1655
SODOBNO KMETIJSTVO. (Text in Slovenian) 1950. m. 1584 SLT($107) (effective Mar. 1991). C Z P Kmecki Glas, Celovska 43, P.O. Box 47, 61001 Ljubljana, Slovenia. TEL 061-328670. FAX 061-321-651. Ed. Rajko Ocepek. adv. circ. 1,000.
Formerly: Socialisticno Kmetijstvo.

630 NE ISSN 0167-1987
CODEN: SOTRD5
SOIL AND TILLAGE RESEARCH; an international journal on research and development concerning soil. 1981. 16/yr. fl.2400($1379) (effective 1998). (International Soil Tillage Research Organisation) Elsevier Science B.V., P.O. Box 211, 1000 AE Amsterdam, Netherlands. TEL 31-20-4853911. FAX 31-20-4853598. TELEX 18582 ESPA NL. E-mail: nlinfo-f@elsevier.nl; usinfo-f@elsevier.com; forinfo-kyf04035@niftyserve.or.jp; URL: http://www.elsevier.nl/. (Subscr. in the Americas to: Elsevier Science, Regional Sales Office, Box 945, New York, NY 10159-0945. TEL 212-633-3730. FAX 212-633-3680; Subscr. in Australasia and the Far East to: Elsevier Science (Singapore) Pte Ltd, No.1 Temasek Ave., No.17-01 Millenia Tower, Singapore 039192, Singapore. TEL 65-434-3727. FAX 65-337-2230; Subscr. in Japan to: Elsevier Science Japan, 9-15 Higashi-Azabu 1-chome, Minato-ku, Tokyo 106, Japan. TEL 81-3-5561-5033. FAX 81-3-5561-5047) Eds. A. Hadas, P.H. Groenevelt. adv.; bk.rev.; bibl.; index. (also avail. in microform from UMI; back issues avail.; reprint service avail. from SWZ) **Indexed:** Agri.Eng.Abstr., ASCA, Biol.Abstr., Chem.Abstr., Cott.& Trop.Fibr.Abstr., Curr.Adv.Ecol.Sci., Curr.Cont., Ecol.Abstr., Environ.Per.Bibl. (1981-), Excerp.Med., Field Crop Abstr., Geo.Abstr.H.G., Geo.Abstr.P.G., Herb.Abstr., IDA, Ind.Sci.Rev., Irr.& Drain.Abstr., Maize Abstr., Potato Abstr., Sci.Cit.Ind., Soils & Fert., Sorghum & Millets Abstr., Soyabean Abstr., SSCI, Triticale Abstr., Weed Abstr., World Agri.Econ.& Rural Sociol.Abstr. **Document type:** academic/scholarly publication.
—BLDSC (8321.760000); CASDDS; Ei; EMDOCS; Genuine Article; Linda Hall; SWETS; UnCover. CCC.
Description: Covers changes in the physical, chemical and biological parameters of soil environment caused by soil tillage and field traffic; the effects and interactions on crop establishment, root development and plant growth.
Refereed Serial

630 UK ISSN 0038-1314
SOMERSET FARMER. 1962. m. County Farmers Publications Ltd., 55 Goldington Rd., Bedford MK40 3LU, England. TEL 0234-351401. FAX 0234-328614. Ed. A.A. Gibson. adv. circ. 4,600.

630 AU ISSN 1018-1954
SORTENVERSUCHSERGEBNISSE. 1950. a. price varies. Bundesanstalt fuer Alpenlaendische Landwirtschaft Gumpenstein, A-8952 Irdning, Austria. TEL 43-3682-2461488. FAX 43-3682-2461488. Ed. Kurt Chytil. R&P contact: Kurt Chytil. adv. contact: Eva Rainer. circ. 250. (back issues avail.) **Indexed:** Field Crop Abstr., Plant Grow.Reg.Abstr. **Document type:** academic/scholarly publication.
—BLDSC (8328.673150).
Former titles (until 1989): Bundesanstalt fuer Alpenlaendische Landwirtschaft Gumpenstein. Versuchsergebnisse; Bundesanstalt fuer Alpine Landwirtschaft. Versuchsergebnisse.

630 SA
SOUTH AFRICA. DEPARTMENT OF AGRICULTURE. AGRICULTURAL BULLETINS. (Editions in Afrikaans and English) 1925. irreg. (10-12/yr.) price varies. Department of Agriculture, Private Bag X144, Pretoria 0001, South Africa. TEL 27-12-3197141. FAX 27-12-3232516. charts; illus.; stat. circ. 1,100. **Indexed:** Biol.Abstr., Plant Breed.Abstr. **Document type:** government publication, bulletin.
Former titles: South Africa. Department of Agriculture and Fisheries. Agricultural Bulletins; South Africa. Department of Agricultural Technical Services. Agricultural Bulletins (ISSN 0002-1393)

AGRICULTURE

630 SA
SOUTH AFRICA. DEPARTMENT OF AGRICULTURE. ANNUAL REPORT OF THE DIRECTOR-GENERAL. 1960. a. price varies. Department of Agriculture, Private Bag X144, Pretoria 0001, South Africa. TEL 27-12-3197141. FAX 27-12-3232516. R&P contact: M.A. Fourie. circ. 1,000. **Indexed:** Helminthol.Abstr., Rev.Plant Path., Weed Abstr. **Document type:** government publication.
  Former titles: South Africa. Department of Agriculture. Annual Report of the Chief; South Africa. Department of Agricultural Development. Annual Report of the Chief for Agricultural Development; South Africa. Department of Agriculture and Water Supply. Annual Report of the Superintendent-General (ISSN 1017-4575); (until 1985): South Africa. Department of Agriculture and Water Supply. Annual Report of the Head of the Department (ISSN 1010-1942); (until 1984): South Africa. Department of Agriculture. Report of the Secretary for Agricultural Technical Services; (until 1981): South Africa. Department of Agriculture and Fisheries. Report of the Secretary for Agricultural Technical Services; South Africa. Department of Agricultural Technical Services. Report of the Secretary for Agricultural Technical Services (ISSN 0081-2153).

630 SA
SOUTH AFRICA. DEPARTMENT OF AGRICULTURE. OFFICIAL LIST OF PROFESSIONAL RESEARCH WORKERS, LECTURING STAFF AND EXTENSION WORKERS IN THE AGRICULTURAL FIELD. 1965. a. free. Department of Agriculture, Private Bag X144, Pretoria 0001, South Africa. TEL 27-12-3197141. FAX 27-12-3232516. R&P contact: Ronelle Hechter. circ. controlled. **Document type:** government publication.
  Former titles: South Africa. Department of Agriculture and Fisheries. Official List of Professional Research Workers, Lecturing Staff and Extension Workers in the Agricultural Field; South Africa. Department of Agricultural Technical Services. Official List of Professional Research Workers, Lecturing Staff and Extension Workers in the Agricultural Field.

630 SA
CODEN: TCSFDR
SOUTH AFRICA. DEPARTMENT OF AGRICULTURE. TECHNICAL COMMUNICATION. 1960. irreg. price varies. Department of Agriculture, Private Bag X144, Pretoria 0001, South Africa. TEL 27-12-3197141. FAX 27-12-3232516. Ed. Ronelle Hechter. R&P contact: Ronelle Hechter. circ. 1,100. **Indexed:** Biol.Abstr., Food Sci.& Tech.Abstr., GeoRef., Rev.Plant Path. **Document type:** government publication, academic/scholarly publication.
  —CASDDS.
  Former titles (until no.238, 1994): South Africa. Department of Agricultural Development. Technical Communication (ISSN 1019-3111); (until no.220, 1990): South Africa. Department of Agriculture and Water Supply. Technical Communication (ISSN 1012-7100); (until 1984): South Africa. Department of Agriculture. Technical Communication (ISSN 0255-0164); (until 1981): South Africa. Department of Agriculture and Fisheries. Technical Communication (ISSN 0253-2840); South Africa. Department of Agricultural Technical Services. Technical Communication (ISSN 0081-217X).

638.1 SA ISSN 0038-2019
SOUTH AFRICAN BEE JOURNAL. (Text in Afrikaans, English) 1911. bi-m. R.110 (effective 1997). South African Federation of Beefarmers' Associations, P.O. Box 41, Modderfontein 1645, South Africa. TEL 27-11-8822646. E-mail: lear@ae.aeci.co.za. adv.; bk.rev.; stat. circ. 500. **Indexed:** Apic.Abstr., Bio-Contr.News & Info., Ind.S.A.Per. **Document type:** trade publication.
  —BLDSC (8332.000000).

630 600 SA ISSN 0301-603X
SOUTH AFRICAN JOURNAL OF AGRICULTURAL EXTENSION/SUID-AFRIKAANSE TYDSKRIF VIR LANDBOUVOORLIGTING. (Text and summaries in Afrikaans, English) 1972. a. R.30. South African Society for Agricultural Extension - Suid-Afrikaanse Vereniging vir Landbouvoorligting, University of Pretoria, Pretoria 0002, South Africa. TEL 27-12-420-3247. FAX 27-12-342-2713. Ed. Caj Botha. adv.; bk.rev.; bibl.; author index: vols.1-22; circ. controlled. (back issues avail.) **Indexed:** Ind.S.A.Per. **Document type:** academic/scholarly publication.
  Formerly: South African Society for Agricultural Extension. Journal.
  Description: Promotes the adoption of sound farming practices by the creation of scientific guidelines for agricultural development.

630 370 SA
SOUTH AFRICAN SOCIETY FOR AGRICULTURAL EXTENSION. CONFERENCE PROCEEDINGS/SUID-AFRIKAANSE VERENIGING VIR LANDBOUVOORLIGTING. KONFERENSIEHANDELINGE. (Text in Afrikaans, English) a. R.30. South African Society for Agricultural Extension - Suid-Afrikaanse Vereniging vir Landbouvoorligting, University of Pretoria, Pretoria 0002, South Africa. TEL 27-12-420-3247. FAX 27-12-342-2713. Ed. Caj Botha. **Document type:** proceedings.

630 US ISSN 0889-1834
SOUTH CAROLINA FARMER. m. $12 (foreign $25). Rural Press U S A, 7701 Six Forks Rd., Ste. 132, Raleigh, NC 27615. TEL 919-676-3276; 800-477-1737. FAX 919-676-9803. (Subscr. to: Box 150001, Raleigh, NC 27624) Ed. R. Davis; Pub. Jeff Tennant. adv.: B&W page £1218. circ. 11,000. **Document type:** newspaper.
  Supersedes: Carolina Farmer (South Carolina Edition) (ISSN 0893-7508)

630 US ISSN 1079-8889
SOUTH CAROLINA Y F AND F F A. 1950. q. $0.50. South Carolina Young Farmers and Future Farmers, 914A Rutledge Bldg., 1429 Senate St., Columbia, SC 29201. TEL 803-734-8426. FAX 803-734-3525. E-mail: dlaw@sde.state.sc.us. Ed. Dale A. Law. adv.; tr.lit.; circ. 8,000 (controlled). **Document type:** trade publication.
  Formerly: South Carolina Young Farmer and Future Farmer (ISSN 0038-3201)

630 US ISSN 0745-8797
SOUTH DAKOTA UNION FARMER. 1918. m. $1. Farmers Educational and Cooperative Union of America, South Dakota Division, Box 1388, Huron, SD 57350. Ed. Charles W. Groth. adv. circ. 16,007.

630 US ISSN 0194-0937
SOUTHEAST FARM PRESS. 1974. s-m. $30. Farm Press, Division of Intertec Publishing, Box 1420, Clarksdale, MS 38614. TEL 601-624-8503. FAX 601-627-1977. Ed. Glenn Rutz; John L. Montandon. R&P contact: Darrah Parker. adv. contact: Darrah Parker. stat. circ. 54,000. (tabloid format) **Document type:** trade publication.
  —CCC.

630 UK ISSN 0953-7546
SOUTH EAST FARMER. 1979. 12/yr. £15 (foreign £35) (effective 1996). Evegate Barn, Smeeth, Ashford, Kent TN25 6SX, England. Ed. Stewart Lawrie; Pub. Clive Rabson. bk.rev. circ. 9,100. **Document type:** trade publication.

630 UK
SOUTH EAST REGION N F U JOURNAL. 12/yr. Agriculture House, Sta. Rd., Liss, Hampshire GU33 7AR, England. TEL 730-893723. FAX 730-892622. Ed. Neville Errington.

630 US
SOUTHERN ORGANIC APPRENTICESHIP PROGRAM. 1982. 7/yr.? $7. Utopia Organic Gardens, Box 45, Utopia, TX 78884. TEL 512-966-3724. circ. 50.

630 US ISSN 0192-4168
SOUTHERN TIER TOWN AND COUNTRY LIVING.* 1947. m. $5 for 3 yrs. Farm & Home Publications, 10 Lourdes Rd., Binghamton, NY 13905-4293. Ed. Bernard M. Swartz. adv.; stat.; illus. circ. 2,600.

630 US ISSN 0194-0945
SOUTHWEST FARM PRESS. 1974. s-m. $30. Farm Press, Division of Intertec Publishing, Box 1420, Clarksdale, MS 38614. TEL 601-624-8503. FAX 601-627-1977. Ed. Glenn Rutz; Pub. John L. Montandon. R&P contact: Darrah Parker. adv. contact: Darrah Parker. charts; illus.; tr.lit. circ. 43,000. (tabloid format) **Document type:** trade publication.
  —CCC.

630 UK
SOUTH WEST FARMER. 1981. m. West of England Newspapers Ltd., Burrington Way, Plymouth, Devon P15 3LN, England. TEL 44-1752-777151. FAX 44-1752-780680. Ed. David Husband. adv.; bk.rev. circ. 30,000. (tabloid format)

630 SP ISSN 0210-3362
SPAIN. INSTITUTO NACIONAL DE INVESTIGACIONES AGRARIAS. TESIS DOCTORALES. 1973. irreg. free. Ministerio de Agricultura, Pesca y Alimentacion, Instituto Nacional de Investigaciones Agrarias, Centro de Publicaciones, Paseo de la Infanta Isabel 1, 28071 Madrid, Spain. TEL 34-1-3475551. (I.N.I.A. addr.: Jose Abascal 56, 28003 Madrid, Spain. TEL 34-1-3473916) Ed. Antonio Sole Orostivar. R&P contact: Juan Carlos Palacios Lopez. **Document type:** academic/scholarly publication.

630 SP
SPAIN. MINISTERIO DE AGRICULTURA, PESCA Y ALIMENTACION. BOLETIN. 1993. m. 3000 ptas. (effective 1997). Ministerio de Agricultura, Pesca y Alimentacion, Secretaria General Tecnica, Centro de Publicaciones, Paseo de la Infanta Isabel 1, 28071 Madrid, Spain. TEL 34-1-3475551. FAX 34-1-3475722. Ed. Sira Laguna Fernandez. R&P contact: Juan Carlos Palacios Lopez. illus, charts, stat. **Document type:** government publication.

630 SP
SPAIN. MINISTERIO DE AGRICULTURA, PESCA Y ALIMENTACION. INSTITUTO DE REFORMA Y DESARROLLO AGRARIO. HOJAS DIVULGADORAS. 1918. 20/yr. 600 ptas. Ministerio de Agricultura, Pesca y Alimentacion, Instituto de Reforma y Desarrollo Agrario, Centro de Publicaciones, Paseo de la Infanta Isabel 1, 28071 Madrid, Spain. TEL 34-1-3475551. FAX 37-1-3475722. (Editorial addr.: Corazon de Maria 8, 28002 Madrid, Spain. TEL 34-1-4138013) Ed. Felicisimo Gonzalez Rodriguez. R&P contact: Juan Carlos Palacios Lopez. circ. 40,000. **Indexed:** Anim.Breed.Abstr., Dairy Sci.Abstr., Field Crop Abstr., Herb.Abstr., Ind.Vet., Potato Abstr., Rev.Med.& Vet.Mycol. **Document type:** bulletin, academic/scholarly publication.
  Formerly: Spain. Ministerio de Agricultura, Pesca y Alimentacion. Servicio de Extension Agraria. Hojas Divulgadoras.
  Description: Technical bulletin for farmers.

638.1 US ISSN 0190-6798
SPEEDY BEE; the beekeepers' newspaper. 1972. m. $17.75. Fore's Honey Farms, Inc., Box 998, Jesup, GA 31545. TEL 912-427-4018. FAX 912-427-8447. Ed. Troy H. Fore, Jr. adv. contact: Donna Poythress. bk.rev. circ. 5,000. (tabloid format) **Indexed:** Apic.Abstr. **Document type:** trade publication, newspaper.
  Incorporates (1934-1974): Canadian Bee Journal (ISSN 0045-446X)
  Description: Covers the beekeeping and honey industry.

633.83 II ISSN 0970-5805
HD9210.I5
SPICE INDIA. (Editions in English, Hindi, Kannada, Malayalam, Nepali and Tamil) m.; Hindi ed. bi-m. Rs.20. Ministry of Commerce, Spices Board, K.C. Ave., St. Vincent Cross Rd., P.O. No. 1909, Ernakulam, Kochi 682 018, India. TEL 91-484-33610. FAX 91-484-331429. TELEX 0885-6534 SEPC IN. E-mail: sbhochn@giasmd01.vsnl.net.in. Ed. P.S. Sreekantan Thampi. adv.; bk.rev. circ. 3,000. **Document type:** government publication.
  Former titles: Cardamom (ISSN 0970-5449); (until Nov. 1976): Cardamom News (ISSN 0008-6274)

AGRICULTURE

633.83 II
SPICES MARKET. (Text in English) w. Rs.100. Ministry of Commerce, Spices Board, K.C. Ave., St. Vincent Cross Rd., P.B. No. 1909, Ernakulam, Kochi 682 018, India. TEL 91-484-353837. FAX 91-484-364429. TELEX 0885-6480 ELAM IN. E-mail: sbhochn@giasmd01.vsnl.net.in. Ed. P.S. Sreekantan Thampi. **Document type:** government publication.

630 UK ISSN 0955-0267
STAFFORDSHIRE FARMER. m. County Farmers Publications Ltd., 55 Goldington Rd., Bedford MK40 3LU, England. TEL 0234-351401. FAX 0234-328614. Ed. P. Hudson. adv. circ. 3,650.

630 382 US ISSN 0844-3955
STAT (BLAINE). 1988. w. $260 (foreign $340) (effective 1997). Stat Publishing, Box 8110-361, Blaine, WA 98230. TEL 604-535-8505. FAX 604-531-8818. E-mail: publisher@stat.mlnet.com; URL: http://stat.mlnet.com/stat/. Ed. Brian Clancey; Pub. P.B. Clancey. adv. circ. 1,000.
 Description: Specializes in peas, beans, lentils, canaryseed, millet, and sunflower market analysis.

630 UN ISSN 0081-4539
S401.U6 CODEN: FAONEY
STATE OF FOOD AND AGRICULTURE. Spanish edition: Estado Mundial de la Agricultura y la Alimentacion (ISSN 0251-1371); French edition: Situation Mondiale de l'Alimentation et de l'Agriculture (ISSN 0251-1460) (Text in English) 1947. a. $55. Food and Agriculture Organization of the United Nations, Bernan Associates, 4611-F Assembly Dr., Lanham, MD 20706-4391. TEL 301-459-7666. FAX 301-459-0056. (also avail. in microfiche from CIS) **Indexed:** IIS. **Document type:** monographic series.
 —BLDSC (3865.593000); CISTI; Linda Hall.

STATISTICAL YEAR BOOK OF INDONESIA. see *POPULATION STUDIES — Abstracting, Bibliographies, Statistics*

638.1 CN
STING. 1983. q. membership. Ontario Beekeepers Association, Bayfield, ON N0M 1G0, Canada. TEL 519-565-2622. FAX 519-565-5452. E-mail: ontbee@tcc.on.ca; URL: http://www.tdg.ca/ontag/bee. Ed. Pat Westlake. adv. contact: Pat Westlake. bk.rev. circ. 300. (back issues avail.) **Document type:** newsletter.
 Description: Provides updates, management techniques, meeting dates, programs, reports to advance and promote apiculture in Ontario for both hobbyists and commercial producers.

630 AT ISSN 1321-0157
STOCK AND LAND.* 1914. w. Aus.$78. Rural Press Magazines, P.O. Box 160, Port Melbourne, Vic. 3207, Australia. Eds. Don Stori, Mark Paterson; Pub. Colin Baulch. adv.; bk.rev.; mkt. circ. 15,339. (tabloid format) **Document type:** newspaper.
 Description: Business and livestock information for farmers and graziers.

STOCKMAN - GRASS FARMER. see *AGRICULTURE — Poultry And Livestock*

630 US ISSN 0097-1251
S43
STORRS AGRICULTURAL EXPERIMENT STATION. BULLETIN. 1888. irreg., no.476, 1988. Storrs Agricultural Experiment Station, Agricultural Publications, U-35, 1376 Storrs Rd., University of Connecticut, Storrs, CT 06269-4035. TEL 203-486-3336. circ. 300. **Indexed:** Biol.Abstr., GeoRef. **Document type:** bulletin.
 —BLDSC (2770.500000); CISTI; Linda Hall.

630 US ISSN 0069-8997
CODEN: CASRBU
STORRS AGRICULTURAL EXPERIMENT STATION. RESEARCH REPORT. 1964. irreg., no.85, 1992. Storrs Agricultural Experiment Station, Agricultural Publications, U-35, 1376 Storrs Rd., University of Connecticut, Storrs, CT 06269-4035. TEL 203-486-3336. circ. 300. **Indexed:** Biol.Abstr., Excerp.Med., Sport Fish.Abstr., Wild.Rev., Zoo.Rec. **Document type:** academic/scholarly publication.
 —BLDSC (7766.270000); Linda Hall.

630 DK ISSN 0908-0058
TORSTROEMS AMTS LANDBRUGS-NYT. w. Lolland-Falsters Ervervsforlag ApS, Marrebaeck, 4873 Vaeggerloese, Denmark. adv. circ. 10,323.

630 658 US ISSN 0039-4432
S1
SUCCESSFUL FARMING. 1902. m. $15. Meredith Corporation, 1716 Locust St., Des Moines, IA 50309-3023. TEL 515-284-3000; 800-374-3276. FAX 515-284-3563. E-mail: lkruse@dsm.mdp.com; URL: http://www.agriculture.com. Ed. Loren Kruse. circ. 485,000. (also avail. in microfiche from NBI) **Indexed:** R.G.Abstr. **Document type:** trade publication.
 ●Also available online. Vendor(s): Information Access Co., UMI.
 —BLDSC (8504.050000); KR SourceOne; Linda Hall; UMI; UnCover.

630 IT ISSN 1120-5857
SUEDTIROLER LANDWIRT; Fachblatt der Suedtiroler Bauern und Genossenschaften. (Text in German) 1947. s-m. L.60000. Suedtiroler Bauernbundgenossenschaft, Bolzano, Italy. TELEX 981171. Ed. L. Michael Pohl. adv.; bk.rev.; abstr.; charts; illus.; mkt.; stat.; cum.index. circ. 19,000. (also avail. in microform)
 Formerly: Landwirt (ISSN 0023-8112)

630 US ISSN 0039-467X
SUFFOLK COUNTY AGRICULTURAL NEWS. 1917. m. $25 for residents; non-residents $30. Cooperative Extension Association of Suffolk County, 246 Griffing Ave., Riverhead, NY 11901. TEL 516-727-7850. FAX 516-727-7130. Ed. William J. Sanok. adv.; bk.rev.; charts; illus.; tr.lit. circ. 1,300.
 Formerly: Suffolk County Farm News.

630 UK ISSN 0955-0275
SUFFOLK FARMER. m. County Farmers Publications Ltd., 55 Goldington Rd., Bedford MK40 3LU, England. TEL 0234-351401. FAX 0234-328614. Ed. D. Brown. adv. circ. 2,300.

630 UK
SUFFOLK SCENE. 4/yr. 30 Lower Brook St., Ipswich, Suffolk IP4 1AN, England. TEL 473-230023. FAX 473-225296. TELEX 98172. Ed. Peter Hopper. bk.rev. circ. 57,000.

630 664.1 UK ISSN 0265-7406
SB226 CODEN: SUCAEE
SUGAR CANE; the only international journal devoted solely to sugarcane agriculture. 1983. bi-m. $120. International Media Ltd., P.O. Box 26, Port Talbot, W. Glamorgan SA13 1NX, Wales. TEL 44-1639-887498. FAX 44-1639-899830. Ed. Robin Vernon. adv. contact: Mark Jones. bk.rev.; abstr.; charts; illus.; pat.; stat. circ. 750. **Indexed:** Bio-Contr.News & Info., Sugar Ind.Abstr. **Document type:** academic/scholarly publication.
 —BLDSC (8511.290000); Linda Hall.

630 US ISSN 0730-6490
TP375 CODEN: PSPCE4
SUGAR PROCESSING RESEARCH CONFERENCE. PROCEEDINGS. 1982. irreg. U.S. Department of Agriculture, Agricultural Research Service (New Orleans), Box 53326, New Orleans, LA 70153. **Indexed:** Chem.Abstr. **Document type:** proceedings.
 —CASDDS.
 Formerly: Technical Session on Cane Sugar Refining Research. Proceedings.

631.091 US ISSN 0199-8498
SUGAR PRODUCER; representing the sugar beet industry in the United States. 1976. 8/yr. $8. Harris Publishing, Inc. (Idaho Falls), 520 Park Ave., Idaho Falls, ID 83402. TEL 208-524-7000. FAX 208-522-5241. adv. circ. 20,000.

633.61 PH ISSN 0039-4769
SUGARCANE FARMERS' BULLETIN. 1964-1977; resumed 19?? bi-m. 12p. Philippine Sugar Regulatory Administration, North Ave., Diliman, Quezon City, Philippines. Ed. Antonina P. Pamaran. bk.rev.; charts; illus.; index. circ. 7,000. **Document type:** bulletin.

624 JA ISSN 0914-4218
SUIRIHO. (Text in Japanese) 1982. a. 1500 Yen. Nogyo Doboku Gakkai, Nogyo Suiri Kenkyu Bukai - Japanese Society of Irrigation, Drainage and Reclamation Engineering, Society for the Study of Agricultural Water Use, Tokyo Nogyo Daigaku Nogyo Kogakka, Tochi Kairyogaku Kenkyushitsu, 1-1, Sakuragaoka 1-chome, Setagaya-ku, Tokyo 156, Japan.

630 US
SULCO; journal of popular farm science and rural life. (Portuguese edition of: Furrow (ISSN 0016-3112)) (Text in Portuguese) 1973. 4/yr. free to qualified personnel. Deere & Company, John Deere Rd., Moline, IL 61265. TEL 309-765-8000. Ed. Jean-Claude Hiron. circ. 11,000.

630 US ISSN 0160-0680
CODEN: SUAGDL
SULPHUR IN AGRICULTURE. 1977. biennial. free to qualified personnel. Sulphur Institute, 1140 Connecticut Ave., N.W., Ste. 612, Washington, DC 20036. TEL 202-331-9660. FAX 202-293-2940. TELEX 440472. E-mail: sulphur@access.digex.net. Ed. Donald L. Messick. R&P contact: Donald L. Messick. bk.rev.; circ. 3,000 (controlled). (back issues avail.) **Indexed:** Biol.Abstr., Chem.Abstr., Field Crop Abstr., Herb.Abstr., Soils & Fert., Triticale Abstr. **Document type:** academic/scholarly publication.
 —CASDDS; Linda Hall; UnCover.
 Supersedes: Sulphur Institute Journal (ISSN 0039-4904)
 Description: Provides information about sulphur in plant and animal nutrition; the use of sulphur and sulphur compounds as soil amendments; the technology, use and marketing of sulphur-containing fertilizers; and other aspects of sulphur in agriculture.
 Refereed Serial

SUO. see *FORESTS AND FORESTRY*

630 US
SUPIMA ASSOCIATION OF AMERICA NEWSLETTER. 1954. m. free. Supima Association of America, 4141 E. Broadway Rd., Phoenix, AZ 85040. TEL 602-437-1364. FAX 602-437-0143. TELEX 5106005606 (SUPIMA PHX). E-mail: mlsupima@amug.org. Ed. Matt Laughlin. charts; stat. circ. 2,600. (looseleaf format; back issues avail.) **Document type:** newsletter.

630 US
SURCO ARGENTINA; journal of popular farm science and rural life. (Argentine edition of: Furrow (ISSN 0016-3112)) (Text in Spanish) 1959. 2/yr. free to qualified personnel. Deere & Company, John Deere Rd., Moline, IL 61265. TEL 309-752-8000. Ed. G.R. Souenberger. circ. 19,100.

630 US
SURCO LATINOAMERICANA; journal of popular farm science and rural life. (Central and South American edition of: Furrow (ISSN 0016-3112)) (Text in Spanish) 1965. 4/yr. free to qualified personnel. Deere & Company, John Deere Rd., Moline, IL 61265. TEL 309-765-8000. Ed. G.R. Souenberger. circ. 24,800.

630 US
SURCO MEXICANA; journal of popular farm science and rural life. (Mexican edition of: Furrow (ISSN 0016-3112)) (Text in Spanish) 1952. 4/yr. free to qualified personnel. Deere & Company, John Deere Rd., Moline, IL 61265. TEL 309-765-8000. Ed. Carolos MacDonado. circ. 55,000.
 Formerly: Surco John Deere.

630 SP
SURCOS DE ARAGON. 12/yr. Departamento de Agricultura, Ganaderia y Montes, Paseo Maria Agustin, Edif. Pignatelli, 50004 Zaragoza, Spain. TEL 76-22-43-00. FAX 76-47-07-48. Ed. I. Palacio Espanol.

630 SR ISSN 0039-6133
S201
SURINAAMSE LANDBOUW/SURINAM AGRICULTURE. (Text in English) 1953. irreg. (2-3/yr.) fl.15. Department of Agriculture and Fisheries, Agricultural Experiment Station, Box 160, Paramaribo, Surinam. Ed.Bd. bk.rev ; abstr ; bibl.; charts; illus.; stat.; index. cum.index. circ. 600. **Indexed:** Bibl.Agri., Biol.Abstr., Chem.Abstr., Field Crop Abstr., Herb.Abstr., Hort.Abstr., Nutr.Abstr., Plant Grow.Reg.Abstr., Protozool.Abstr., Weed Abstr. **Document type:** academic/scholarly publication.
 —BLDSC (8548.300000).

156 AGRICULTURE

630   UK
SUSTAINABLE RURAL DEVELOPMENT SERIES. irreg., no.2, 1995. CAB International, Wallingford, Oxon. OX10 8DE, England. TEL 44-1491-832111. FAX 44-1491-826090. TELEX 847964 COMAGG G. E-mail: cabi@cabi.org. (US subscr. to: CAB International, North American Office, 198 Madison Ave., N.Y. 10016. TEL 212-726-6490. FAX 212-686-7993) **Document type:** monographic series.

630 690   SW   ISSN 1104-7321
SVERIGES LANTBRUKSUNIVERSITET. INSTITUTIONEN FOER JORDBRUKETS BIOSYSTEM OCH TEKNOLOGI. SPECIALMEDDELANDE/SWEDISH UNIVERSITY OF AGRICULTURAL SCIENCES. DEPARTMENT OF AGRICULTURAL BIOSYSTEMS AND TECHNOLOGY. SPECIAL REPORT. Cover title: Specialmeddelande - J B T. (Text in Swedish; summaries in English) 1971. irreg. (5-6/yr.). Swedish University of Agricultural Sciences, P.O. Box 945, S-220 09 Lund, Sweden. TEL 46-46-11-75-10. FAX 46-46-11-31-45. circ. 300. (back issues avail.) **Document type:** monographic series.
—BLDSC (8404.955000).
Former titles (until 1994): Sveriges Lantbruksuniversitet. Insittutionen foer Lantbrukets Byggnadsteknik (LBT). Specialmeddelande (ISSN 0348-0593); (until 1977): Lantbrukshoegskolan. Institutionen foer Lantbrukets Byggnadsteknik (LBT). Specialmeddelande (ISSN 0346 7686).
Description: For scientists, consultants and teachers on research results in farm-building technology and environment.

630   SQ
SWAZILAND. MINISTRY OF AGRICULTURE. AGRICULTURAL RESEARCH DIVISION. ANNUAL REPORT. 1960. a., latest 1988. Ministry of Agriculture, Agricultural Research Division, c/o Chief Research Officer, P.O. Box 4, Malkerns, Swaziland. TEL 268-83017. TELEX 22589 WD. (back issues avail.) **Indexed:** Biol.Abstr., Field Crop Abstr., Herb.Abstr., Hort.Abstr. **Document type:** government publication.
Former titles (until 1977): University of Botswana, Lesotho and Swaziland. Agricultural Research Division. Annual Report; (until 1971): Swaziland. Ministry of Agriculture. Agricultural Research Division. Annual Report; Swaziland. Department of Agriculture. Research Division. Annual Report (ISSN 0586-125X).

354.68   SQ
SWAZILAND. MINISTRY OF AGRICULTURE. ANNUAL REPORT. 1967. a. Ministry of Agriculture, Mbabane, Swaziland. stat. **Indexed:** Anim.Breed.Abstr., Field Crop Abstr., Herb.Abstr., Hort.Abstr., Rev.Appl.Entomol. **Document type:** government publication.

630   NO   ISSN 0049-2701
CODEN: SJARB9
SWEDISH JOURNAL OF AGRICULTURAL RESEARCH. (Text in English) 1934. 4/yr. NOK 670 in Nordic countries; elsewhere $118 (effective 1997). (Sveriges Lantbruksuniversitet - Swedish University of Agricultural Sciences) Scandinavian University Press, P.O. Box 2959 Toeyen, N-0608 Oslo, Norway. TEL 47-22-57-54-00. FAX 47-22-57-53-53. E-mail: mail@scup.no; URL: http://www.scup.no. (US addr.: 875 Massachusetts Ave., Ste. 84, Cambridge, MA 02139. TEL 617-497-6515. FAX 617-354-6875) Ed. Goeran Grant. charts; stat. circ. 1,300. **Indexed:** Anal.Abstr., Anim.Breed.Abstr., ASCA, Biol.Abstr., Chem.Abstr., Curr.Adv.Ecol.Sci., Curr.Cont., Dairy Sci.Abstr., Ecol.Abstr., Energy Info.Abstr., Energy Res.Abstr., Environ.Abstr., Excerp.Med., Field Crop Abstr., Food Sci.& Tech.Abstr., Geo.Abstr., Herb.Abstr., Hort.Abstr., Ind.Vet., Maize Abstr., Nutr.Abstr., Pig News & Info., Plant Breed.Abstr., Poult.Abstr., Rev.Plant Path., Sci.Cit.Ind., Soils & Fert., Soyabean Abstr., Sport Fish.Abstr., Sugar Ind.Abstr., Triticale Abstr., Vet.Bull., Weed Abstr., Wild.Rev., Zoo.Rec. **Document type:** academic/scholarly publication.
—BLDSC (8573.890000); CASDDS; Ei; Genuine Article; Linda Hall; SWETS; UnCover. **CCC.**
Supersedes: Kungliga Lantbrukshoegskolans Annaler (ISSN 0368-7325).

630   FR
SYNDICAT AGRICOLE. w. 44 rue Jean-Sans-Peur, 59024 Lille Cedex, France. TEL 20-54-85-97. FAX 20-54-55-72. Ed. C. Durlin. circ. 16,500.

631   NE   ISSN 0928-9526
SYSTEMS APPROACHES FOR SUSTAINABLE AGRICULTURAL DEVELOPMENT. (Text in English) 1992. irreg. price varies. Kluwer Academic Publishers, Postbus 17, 3300 AA Dordrecht, Netherlands. TEL 31-78-6392392. FAX 31-78-6392254. E-mail: services@wkap.nl; URL: http://www.wkap.nl. (Dist. by: Kluwer Academic Publishers Group, P.O. Box 322, 3300 AH Dordrecht, Netherlands. TEL 31-78-6392392. FAX 31-78-6546474; N. America dist. addr.: Box 358, Accord Sta., Hingham, MA 02018-0358. TEL 617-871-6600. FAX 617-871-6528) **Document type:** monographic series.
—BLDSC (8589.323500).

630 338.1   XO   ISSN 0491-9424
SZABAD FOLDMUVES.* 1950. w. Ministerstvo Podhospodarstva a Vyzivy, Dobrovicova 12, 800 00 Bratislava, Slovakia.

SZCZECINSKIE ROCZNIKI NAUKOWE, NAUKI PRZYRODNICZE I ROLNICZE. see BIOLOGY — Botany

630   PL   ISSN 0239-8613
CODEN: ZNWNDA
SZKOLA GLOWNA GOSPODARSTWA WIEJSKIEGO. ROZPRAWY NAUKOWE I MONOGRAFIE/WARSAW AGRICULTURAL UNIVERSITY. TREATISES AND MONOGRAPHS. (Text in English or Polish) 1957. irreg. $10 per no. Szkola Glowna Gospodarstwa Wiejskiego (SGGW) - Warsaw Agricultural University, Ul. Nowoursynowska 166, 02-766 Warsaw, Poland. Ed. H. Sandner. **Indexed:** AgroLibrex. **Document type:** academic/scholarly publication, monographic series.
—CASDDS; Linda Hall.
Formerly (until 1980): Akademia Rolnicza, Warsaw. Zeszyty Naukowe. Rozprawy Naukowe (ISSN 0512-4646)

630.968 330.968   SA
T R A C ANNUAL REPORT. 1993. a. R.15. Transvaal Rural Action Committee, P.O. Box 62535, Marshalltown 2107, South Africa. TEL 27-11-8331060. FAX 27-11-8348385. E-mail: trac@wn.apc.org; URL: http://www.oneworld.org/. Ed. Stuart Maar. R&P contact: Sturt Maar. **Document type:** corporate report, newsletter.

630.968 330.968   SA   ISSN 1023-5310
T R A C NEWLETTER. (Text in English) 1983. 3/yr. R.2.50 per issue. Transvaal Rural Action Committee, P.O. Box 62535, Marshalltown 2107, South Africa. TEL 27-11-8331060. FAX 27-11-8348385. E-mail: trac@wn.apc.org; URL: http://www.oenworld.org/.

T U I A F P W INFORMATION. (Trade Union International of Agricultural, Forestry and Plantation Workers) see LABOR UNIONS

630   CH   ISSN 0494-5263
TAIWAN AGRICULTURAL RESEARCH INSTITUTE. ANNUAL REPORT. Key Title: Nianbao - Taiwan Sheng Nongye Shiyansuo. (Text in Chinese) 1946. a. Taiwan Agricultural Research Institute, 189 Chung-cheng Rd., Wufeng, Taichung, Taiwan, Republic of China. FAX 04-3338162. Ed. Ching-Liang Liaw; Pub. Chien-Yih Lin. charts; illus.; stat.
—BLDSC (8601.007000).

630 581   CH
TAIWAN AGRICULTURAL RESEARCH INSTITUTE. RESEARCH SUMMARY. irreg., latest Jun. 1975. Taiwan Agricultural Research Institute, 189 Chung-cheng Rd., Wufeng, Taichung, Taiwan, Republic of China. FAX 04-3338162. Pub. Chien-Yih Lin.

630   CC
TAIWAN NONGYE QINGKUANG/TAIWAN AGRICULTURAL INFORMATION. (Text in Chinese) q. Y3.20. Fujian Sheng Nongye Kexueyuan, Keji Qingbao Suo - Fujian Academy of Agricultural Science, Science and Technology Information Institute, 41 Hualin Lu, Fuzhou, Fujian 350003, People's Republic of China. TEL 571771. (Dist. overseas by: Jiangsu Publications Import & Export Corp., 56 Gao Yun Ling, Nanjing, Jiangsu, P.R.C.) Ed. He Shukai.

630   JA   ISSN 0082-156X
CODEN: TDNHAC
TAMAGAWA UNIVERSITY. FACULTY OF AGRICULTURE. BULLETIN. (Text in English, German and Japanese; summaries in English and German) 1960. a. available on exchange. Tamagawa University, Faculty of Agriculture - Tamagawa Daigaku Nogakubu, 6-1-1 Tamagawagakuen, Machida, Tokyo 194, Japan. **Indexed:** Biol.Abstr., Excerpt.Med., Field Crop Abstr., Herb.Abstr., Hort.Abstr., Plant Breed.Abstr., Rev.Plant Path., VITIS, Weed Abstr.
—BLDSC (2507.350000); CASDDS; Linda Hall.

630 070   GW   ISSN 0082-1845
TASCHENBUCH FUER AGRARJOURNALISTEN. 1957. a. DM.65 (effective 1997). (Verband der Agrarjournalisten) B. Behr's Verlag GmbH, Averhoffstr. 10, 22085 Hamburg, Germany. TEL 49-40-2270080. FAX 49-40-2201091. E-mail: behrs@behrs.de; URL: http://www.behrs.de. **Document type:** bulletin.

630   AT
TASMANIA. DEPARTMENT OF PRIMARY INDUSTRY & FISHERIES. ANNUAL REPORT. 1928. a. free. Department of Primary Industry & Fisheries, Corporate Marketing Unit, G.P.O. Box 192 B, Hobart, Tas. 7001, Australia. TEL 61-3-62338011. FAX 61-3-6233038. Ed. Sally Chambers. circ. 1,000. **Indexed:** Anim.Breed.Abstr., Biol.Abstr., Field Crop Abstr., Herb.Abstr., Weed Abstr. **Document type:** government publication, corporate report.
Former titles: Tasmania. Department of Primary Industry. Annual Report; Tasmania. Department of Agriculture. Annual Report (ISSN 0082-1993).

630   UK
TAYSIDE FARMER. q. Angus County Press Ltd., Forfar, Angus DD8 1BU, Scotland. TEL 01307-464899. FAX 01307-466923. Ed. Ian Wallace. adv. contact: Linda Ruxton. circ. 7,000. **Document type:** trade publication.

633.72   BG
TEA JOURNAL OF BANGLADESH.* (Text in English) 1963. s-a. Tk.7 per no. Bangladesh Tea Research Institute, Srimangal, Sylhet, Bangladesh. Ed. S.H. Chaudhury. adv.; bk.rev.; abstr.; bibl.; charts; illus.; index; cum.index. circ. 500. **Indexed:** Bangladesh Agr.Sci.Abstr., Chem.Abstr., Hort.Abstr., Soils & Fert.
Formerly: Tea Journal of Pakistan (ISSN 0040-0351).

633.72   MW
TEA RESEARCH FOUNDATION. QUARTERLY NEWSLETTER. 1952. q. $72 (rest of Africa $80; Europe, India, Middle East $81.50; elsewhere $83) (effective 1995). Tea Research Foundation of Central Africa, P.O. Box 51, Mulanje, Malawi. TEL 265-462277. Ed. A.M. Whittle. circ. 450. (back issues avail.) **Indexed:** Hort.Abstr., Plant Breed Abstr. Soils & Fert., Trop.Abstr. **Document type:** newsletter.
—BLDSC (7196.690000); SWETS.
Formerly: Tea Research Station. Quarterly Newsletter (ISSN 0040-0378)
Description: Covers tea growing and manufacturing in regions with a single rainy season.

630 664   IE   ISSN 0791-4695
TEAGASC ANNUAL REPORT. a. Teagasc, 19 Sandymount Ave., Dublin 4, Ireland. TEL 353-1-6688188. FAX 353-1-6688023. **Document type:** government publication.
Formed by the 1990 merger of: Foras Taluntais. Annual Report (ISSN 0790-7400); A C O T Annual Report (ISSN 0332-379X)

AGRICULTURE   157

630 664 IE ISSN 0791-7376
TEAGASC RESEARCH REPORT. a. I£20 (effective 1996 & 1997). Teagasc, 19 Sandymount Ave., Dublin 4, Ireland. TEL 353-1-6688188.
FAX 353-1-6688023. E-mail: corourke@hq.teagasc.ie. Ed. C.J. O'Rourke. circ. 500 (paid). **Document type:** academic/scholarly publication.
—BLDSC (7766.770500).
  Supersedes (in 1990?): Teagasc. Report; Which incorporated (in 1989): Economics and Rural Welfare Research Report (ISSN 0332-0251); (until 1971): Foras Taluntais. Rural Economics Division. Research Report (ISSN 0332-0200); (1961-1962): Foras Taluntais. Rural Economics Division. Technical Progress Report (ISSN 0429-0313); Incorporates (in 1992) Animal Production Research Report (ISSN 0332-1207); which was formerly (1960-1971): Foras Taluntais. Animal Husbandry and Dairying Division and Animal Sciences Division. Research Report (ISSN 0429-0283); And: Food Science and Technology Research Report (ISSN 0790-2999); And: Horticulture Research Report (ISSN 0790-2964); which was formerly (until 1971): Foras Taluntais. Horticulture and Forestry Division. Research Report (ISSN 0332-1258); (1960-1961): Foras Taluntais. Horticulture and Forestry Division. Technical Progress Report (ISSN 0532-1093); And: Plant Sciences and Crop Husbandry Research Report (ISSN 0790-2956); which was (until 1971): Foras Taluntais. Plant Sciences and Crop Husbandry Division. Research Report (ISSN 0332-1053); Foras Taluntais. Plant Sciences and Crop Husbandry Division. Technical Progress Report (ISSN 0429-0291); And: Soils and Grassland Production Research Report (ISSN 0790-2980); which was (until 1981): Soils Research Report (ISSN 0790-2980); (until 1971): Foras Taluntais. Soils Division. Research Report (ISSN 0332-1002); (1960-1961): Foras Taluntais. Soils Division. Technical Progress Report (ISSN 0429-0321).
  Description: Annual research report covering approximately 400 research projects in agriculture and food.

TECHNICAL AND COMMERCIAL MESSAGE. see *ENGINEERING*

TECHNISCHE UNIVERSITAET BERLIN. INSTITUT FUER SOZIALOEKONOMIE DER AGRARENTWICKLUNG. SCHRIFTENREIHE DES FACHBEREICHS. see *AGRICULTURE — Agricultural Economics*

630 634.9 FI ISSN 0355-0567
TEHO A. (Text in Finnish; summaries in English) 1946. 6/yr. FIM 190 includes Teho B (foreign FIM 240) (effective through 1998). Tyotehoseura R.Y., P.O. Box 28, Melkonkatu 16 A, FIN-00211 Helsinki, Finland. TEL 358-9-290-41200.
FAX 358-9-692-2084. E-mail: tts@tts.fi; URL: http://www.tts.fi. Ed. Tarmo Luoma. circ. 5,074. (back issues avail.) Indexed: Agri.Eng.Abstr. **Document type:** academic/scholarly publication, consumer publication.
  Description: Deals with the rationalization of work related to agriculture, forestry, ergonomics, home economics, consumer education.

TELHAN PATRIKA/OILSEEDS JOURNAL. see *CHEMISTRY — Organic Chemistry*

TELMA. see *EARTH SCIENCES*

630 CK ISSN 0049-3333
TEMAS DE ORIENTACION AGROPECUARIA; conviertase en un agricultor o ganadero progesista. 1966. bi-m. $20. Apdo. Aereo 13169, Bogota, Colombia. Ed. Ruben Ruiz Camacho. circ. 50,000.

630 FR ISSN 0338-1811
TEMPE INFORMATIONS. (Supplement to: Action Agricole de Tarn et Garonne (ISSN 0338-182X)) 1972. m. Cooperative Laiti, 420 av. de Monclar, 82017 Montauban France. TEL 63-63-11-15. FAX 63-20-15-65.
  Formerly (until 1972): Tempe Lait Informations (ISSN 0338-1803)

630 US CODEN: TFHSAT
TENNESSEE AGRI SCIENCE. 1952. q. free. University of Tennessee at Knoxville, Agricultural Experiment Station, Knoxville, TN 37901-1071.
TEL 423-974-7362. FAX 423-974-7448. E-mail: pclark@utk.edu. Ed. P.A. Clark; Pub. B.P. Reichert. R&P contact: Patricia A. Clark. charts; illus.; index. circ. 4,500. Indexed: Agri.Eng.Abstr., Anim.Breed.Abstr., Biol.Abstr., Chem.Abstr., Cott.& Trop.Fibr.Abstr., Curr.Adv.Ecol.Sci., Curr.Cont., Dairy Sci.Abstr., Field Crop Abstr., Food Sci.& Tech.Abstr., Forest.Abstr., Forest Prod.Abstr., Helminthol.Abstr., Herb.Abstr., Hort.Abstr., Ind.Vet., Maize Abstr., Nutr.Abstr., Pig News & Info., Seed Abstr., Soils & Fert., Soyabean Abstr., Vet.Bull., Weed Abstr. **Document type:** consumer publication.
—BLDSC (8790.600000); CASDDS; UnCover.
  Formerly (until 1995): Tennessee Farm and Home Science (ISSN 0040-3229)
  Description: Reports on research on agriculture and natural resources.

630 US ISSN 0040-3148
    CODEN: TUAUA3
TENNESSEE AGRICULTURAL EXPERIMENT STATION. BULLETIN. 1888. 15/yr. University of Tennessee at Knoxville, Agricultural Experiment Station, Knoxville, TN 37901-1071. TEL 423-974-7362.
FAX 423-974-7448. E-mail: pclark@utk.edu. Ed. P.A. Clark; Pub. B.P. Reichert. bibl.; charts; illus.; stat. circ. 2,000. Indexed: ASCA, Bibl.Agri., Biol.Abstr., Chem.Abstr., Curr.Adv.Ecol.Sci., Curr.Cont., Helminthol.Abstr. **Document type:** monographic series.
—Linda Hall.
  Description: Reports on agricultural research.

630 US ISSN 0162-2617
TENNESSEE FARM BUREAU NEWS. 1923. m. (except Dec. & Jan. and Jul. & Aug. combined). $5. Tennessee Farm Bureau Federation, Box 313, Columbia, TN 38402. TEL 615-388-7872. Ed. Pettus L. Read. adv.: page $4,675; 9 3/4 x 13 3/4; adv. contact: Connie Heflan. illus. circ. 176,000. **Document type:** newspaper.
  Description: Farm-consumer-rural resident publication for members of the Tennessee Farm Bureau.

630 US ISSN 0040-3245
TENNESSEE FARMER. 1950. m. $12 (foreign $25). Rural Press U S A, 7701 Six Forks Rd., Ste. 132, Raleigh, NC 27615. TEL 919-676-3276; 800-477-1737. FAX 919-676-9803. (Subscr. to: Box 150001, Raleigh, NC 27624) Ed. Wayne Harr; Pub. Jeff Tennant. adv.: B&W page $1515. illus. circ. 20,000. **Document type:** newspaper.

630 SP ISSN 0212-5684
TERRA (BARCELONA, 1983); organ d'informacion i debat U.P. (Text in Catalan) 1983. m. 3000 ptas. Edicions La Terra, S.L., Avda. Francesc Cambo 14, 3-B, 08003 Barcelona, Spain. TEL 34-3-2680900. FAX 34-3-2684893. E-mail: laterra@svt.es; URL: http://www.uniopagesos.es/unio. Ed. Humbert Roma de Asso. circ. 10,000. **Document type:** trade publication.
—CINDOC.

630 IT ISSN 0040-3768
TERRA E SOLE; agricoltura pratica e meccanica agraria. 1945. m. L.50000 (foreign L.75000($50)). IACICO S.r.L., Via A. Poliziano 80, 00184 Rome, Italy. TEL 39-6-4873183. FAX 39-6-4873144. Ed. Andrea S. Silenzi. adv.: color page L.4300000; adv. contact: Claudio Cutrone. bk.rev.; bibl.; illus. circ. 41,000. Indexed: Agri.Eng.Abstr., Field Crop Abstr., Hort.Abstr., Ornam.Hort., Potato Abstr., Rice Abstr., Soils & Fert., Weed Abstr.
  Description: Covers agronomics, machinery, and zootechnology.
  Refereed Serial

630 IT ISSN 0040-3776
TERRA E VITA. 1960. w. L.110000 (effective 1996). Edagricole S.p.A., Via Emilia Levante 31, 40139 Bologna, Italy. TEL 39-51-492211.
FAX 39-51-493660. Ed. Franco Mantovani. adv.: B&W page L.4250000, color page L.6250000; 212 x 287. bk.rev.; charts; illus.; index. circ. 98,800. Indexed: Agri.Eng.Abstr., Hort.Abstr.
  Incorporates: Raccolto (ISSN 0033-7269)
  Description: Features articles written by farmers about farming and the agricultural world.

630 FR
TERRE DAUPHINOISE. vol.32, 1977. w. 90 F. Associations Agricole de l'Isere, (Subsidiary of: Agropact), 5 rue G. Rivet, B.P. 1064, 38021 Grenoble, France. TEL 76-40-31-32.
FAX 76-33-04-82. Ed. M. Lalanne-Cloute. adv.; charts; illus.; stat.

630 CN ISSN 0040-3830
TERRE DE CHEZ NOUS. 1929. w. Can.$18. Union des Producteurs Agricoles, 555 Boul. Roland Therrien, Longueuil, Que. J4H 3Y9, Canada.
TEL 514-679-0530. FAX 514-679-5436. Ed. Andre Charbonneau. adv.; bk.rev. circ. 44,000. (tabloid format)

630 FR
TERRE DE CHEZ NOUS.* w. Societe Comtoise d'Edition et d'Information, 130 bis, rue de Belfort, B.P. 939, 25021 Besancon Cedex, France. TEL 81-80-75-77. Ed. M. Narbey. circ. 14,586.

630 SZ
TERRE VALAISANNE. 24/yr. Maison du Paysan, CH-1964 Conthey, Switzerland.
TEL 41-27-366352. Ed. Ariane Alter. circ. 4,091. **Document type:** newspaper.

630 FR ISSN 0750-8093
TERRES D'ARIEGE. (Supplement avail.: Gascon Magazine (ISSN 1245-1606)) 1953. 56/yr. 195 F. 32 av. du General de Gaulle, B.P. 7, 09001 Foix Cedex, France. TEL 61-65-20-00.
FAX 61-02-89-60. Ed. Claudes Laborde. circ. 15,785.

630 FR
TERRITOIRES EN MUTATION. 1979. irreg., latest no.37-38, 1997. prices varies (effective 1997). Universite de Montpellier (Universite Paul Valery), B.P. 5043, 34032 Montpellier Cedex 1, France. TEL 33-467-142406. FAX 33-467-142332. E-mail: serpub@alor.univ-montp3.fr. Ed. M.C. Maurel.
  Formerly: Espace Rural (ISSN 0764-7557)
  Description: Publishes the findings of the National Center for Scientific Research, geography and rural researches.

630 US
TEXAS AGRICULTURE. 1935. s-m. membership. Texas Farm Bureau, Box 2689, Waco, TX 76702-2689.
TEL 817-751-2244. FAX 817-772-1766. Ed. Mike Barnett; Pub. Gene Hall. R&P contact: Mike Barnett. adv. contact: James Gohlke. illus. circ. 104,321. (tabloid format) **Document type:** trade publication.
  Former titles: Texas Agriculture Weekly; (until 1985): Texas Agriculture (ISSN 0040-4152)

638 US
TEXAS AGRINEWS; the farm and ranch newspaper serving Texas. 1981. bi-w. $15 (free to qualified personnel). Big River Press, Inc., 1217 N. Conway, Box 353, Mission, TX 78572. TEL 210-585-4893. FAX 210-585-2304. Pub. June Brann. adv.: B&W page $1100; adv. contact: Clyde Machen. circ. 9,379 (controlled). (tabloid format; back issues avail.) **Document type:** newspaper.
  Formerly (until 1993): South Texas AgriNews.
  Description: Serves farmers, ranchers, and growers with marketing and agricultural news.

630 US ISSN 0893-8997
TEXAS F F A MAGAZINE. 1928. bi-m. $1. Texas F F A Association, 1701 N. Congress Ave., Austin, TX 78701. Ed. Jack Winterrowd, Jr. circ. 30,000. (tabloid format)
  Formerly: Texas Future Farmer (ISSN 0040-4330)

630 US
TEXAS NEIGHBORS. 1985. q. Texas Farm Bureau, Box 2689, Waco, TX 76702. TEL 817-751-2251.
FAX 817-772-3628. Ed. Mike Barnett; Pub. Gene Hall. R&P contact: Mike Barnett. adv. contact: James Gohlke. circ. 317,549. **Document type:** newspaper.
  Description: Features items of interest to bureau member families and articles on Texas lifestyles.

AGRICULTURE

630   TH   ISSN 0049-3589
CODEN: TJASBN
THAI JOURNAL OF AGRICULTURAL SCIENCE. 1968. q. $38 (effective 1992). Agricultural Science Society of Thailand, P.O. Box 1070, Kasetsart University, Bangkok 10903, Thailand. Ed. Prapandh Boonklinkajorn. adv.; charts; stat. circ. 1,000. (reprint service avail. from UMI) **Indexed:** Agri.Eng.Abstr., Agroforest.Abstr., AIT Reports, Anim.Breed.Abstr., Biol.Abstr., Chem.Abstr., Crop Physiol.Abstr., Excerp.Med., Field Crop Abstr., Food Sci.& Tech.Abstr., Geo.Abstr., Herb.Abstr., Hort.Abstr., Irr.& Drain.Abstr., Nutr.Abstr., Packag.Sci.Tech., Poult.Abstr., Rice Abstr., Rural Recreat.Tour.Abstr., Seed Abstr., Soils & Fert., Soyabean Abstr., Weed Abstr., World Agri.Econ.& Rural Sociol.Abstr. **Document type:** academic/scholarly publication.
—BLDSC (8813.970000); CASDDS.

630   SY
THAWRAH AL-ZIRAIA/AGRICULTURAL REVOLUTION REVIEW. (Text in Arabic) 1965. m. Ministry of Agrarian Reform, Damascus, Syria. adv. circ. 7,000. **Document type:** government publication.

630   UK
THREE COUNTIES FARMING REVIEW. 1986. m. free. Community Media Ltd., 12 Avon House, Brassmill Lane, Bath, Avon BA1 3JE, England. Ed. David Parker. circ. 5,500.
Formerly: Five Counties Farming Review.

630   SZ
THURGAUER BAUER. w. Thurgauisches Bauernsekretariat, CH-8570 Weinfelden, Switzerland. TEL 072-224422. FAX 054-218871. circ. 5,270.

638.1   DK   ISSN 0900-0801
TIDSSKRIFT FOR BIAVL. 1866. m. DKK 325. Danmarks Biavlerforening, Ledreborg Alle 104, 4000 Roskilde, Denmark. TEL 46-32-22-77. FAX 46-32-08-11. E-mail: dbf@posty.tele.dk. Ed. Flemming Vejsnes. adv.; bk.rev. circ. 6,500. **Indexed:** Apic.Abstr. **Document type:** newsletter.
Description: Discusses technical and political aspects of beekeeping for professionals and hobbyists.

630   DK   ISSN 0040-7119
TIDSSKRIFT FOR LANDOEKONOMI. 1831. 4/yr. DKK 275. Det Kgl. Danske Landhusholdningsselskab, Mariendalsvej 27, 2., DK-2000 Frederiksberg, Denmark. TEL 45-38-88-66-88. FAX 45-38-88-66-11. Ed. Else Damsgaard. charts; illus. circ. 1,700. **Indexed:** Geo.Abstr.

630   SP
TIERRA; del agricultor y ganadero. 1984. m. 1000 ptas. Union de Pequenos Agricultores - Union of Small Farmers, Avda. de America, 25, 4o, 28002 Madrid, Spain. TEL 1-589-72-18. FAX 1-589-75-54. Ed. Ana Vicandi. circ. 15,000.

630   CL   ISSN 0717-1609
S539.5
TIERRA ADENTRO. 1995. bi-m. Esc.16000 (America $70; elsewhere $83) or exchange basis (effective 1995). Instituto de Investigaciones Agropecuarias, Centro Regional de Investigacion La Platina, Casilla 469, Correo 3, Santiago, Chile. TEL 56-2-5417223. FAX 56-2-5417667. Ed. Silvia Altamirano. adv.; circ. 5,000 (controlled). **Indexed:** Food Sci.& Tech.Abstr. **Document type:** academic/scholarly publication.
Formed by the merger of (1980-1995): Investigacion y Progreso Agropecuario Quilamapu (ISSN 0716-6052); (1982-1995): Investigacion y Progreso Agropecuario Carillanca (ISSN 0716-5943); (1982-1995): Investigacion y Progreso Agropecuario Remehue (ISSN 0716-5951); (1980-1995): Investigacion y Progreso Agropecuario La Platina (ISSN 0716-5331); Which supersedes (1967-1977): Investigacion y Progreso Agricola (ISSN 0304-5579).
Description: Presents accounts, economic studies and practical data of interest to the land and cattle industries.

630   GT
TIKALIA. 1982. 2/yr. Q.4($10) Universidad de San Carlos de Guatemala, Facultad de Agronomia, Ciudad Universitaria, Zona 12, Apdo. Postal 1545, Guatemala C.A., Guatemala. Ed.Bd. bk.rev. circ. 1,000.

630   RU   ISSN 0021-342X
CODEN: ITSAA7
TIMIRYAZEVSKAYA SEL'SKOKHOZYAISTVENNAYA AKADEMIYA. IZVESTIYA. 1878. bi-m. $31.80. Timiryazevskaya Sel'skokhozyaistvennaya Akademiya, Timiryazevskaya ul., 48, 127550 Moscow, Russia. TEL 7-095-9762050. Ed. M. Sinyukov. charts; illus.; index. circ. 2,400. **Indexed:** Biol.Abstr., Chem.Abstr., Crop Physiol.Abstr., Field Crop Abstr., INIS Atomind., Plant Grow.Reg.Abstr., Triticale Abstr.
—BLDSC (0082.900000); CASDDS.

TOBACCO NEWS. see *TOBACCO*

TODAY IN MISSISSIPPI. see *ENGINEERING — Electrical Engineering*

630   US   ISSN 0739-0092
TODAY'S FARMER. 1908. 10/yr. $5 (effective 1997). (Midcontinent Farmers Association Incorporated) M F A, Inc., 201 Ray Young Dr., Columbia, MO 65201. TEL 573-876-5252. Ed. Chuck Lay. adv. contact: Julia Cashman. circ. 45,000. **Document type:** consumer publication, trade publication.

TOHOKU NO NOGYO KISHO/BULLETIN OF THE AGRICULTURAL METEOROLOGY OF TOHOKU DISTRICT. see *METEOROLOGY*

630   JA   ISSN 0495-7318
CODEN: TNSKAE
TOHOKU NOGYO SHIKENJO KENKYU HOKOKU/TOHOKU NATIONAL AGRICULTURAL EXPERIMENT STATION. BULLETIN. (Text in English and Japanese; summaries in English) 1950. s-a. Tohoku National Agricultural Experiment Station - Tohoku Nogyo Shikenjo, Shimo-Kuriyagawa, Morioka, Iwate-ken 020-1, Japan. TEL 81-196-43-3433. FAX 81-196-41-7794. circ. 1,130. **Document type:** bulletin.
—BLDSC (2779.500000); CASDDS.

630   JA   ISSN 0387-172X
CODEN: TNKSDZ
TOHOKU NOGYO SHIKENJO KENKYU SHIRYO/TOHOKU NATIONAL AGRICULTURAL EXPERIMENT STATION. MISCELLANEOUS PUBLICATION. (Text in English or Japanese; summaries in English) 1978. irreg., no.17, 1995. Tohoku National Agricultural Experiment Station - Tohoku Nogyo Shikenjo, Shimo-Kuriyagawa, Morioka, Iwate-ken 020-01, Japan. TEL 81-196-43-3433. FAX 81-196-41-7794. Ed.Bd. circ. 1,130. **Indexed:** Herb.Abstr., Seed Abstr., Soils & Fert., Soyabean Abstr., Triticale Abstr., World Agri.Econ.& Rural Sociol.Abstr. **Document type:** bulletin.
—BLDSC (5823.030000).
Formerly: Tohoku Nogyo Shikenjo Kenkyu Sokuho (ISSN 0495-730X)

TOKYO NOGYO DAIGAKU AISOTOPU SENTA KENKYU HOKOKU/TOKYO UNIVERSITY OF AGRICULTURE. ISOTOPE CENTER. BULLETIN. see *PHYSICS — Nuclear Physics*

630.5   JA   ISSN 0375-9202
CODEN: TNDNAG
TOKYO NOGYO DAIGAKU NOGAKU SHUHO/JOURNAL OF AGRICULTURAL SCIENCE, TOKYO NOGYO DAIGAKU. 1937. q. Tokyo Nogyo Daigaku, 1-1-1 Sakuragaoka, Setagaya-ku, Tokyo 156, Japan. Ed. Kazumori Morita. **Indexed:** Food Sci.& Tech.Abstr., Sport Fish.Abstr., Wild.Rev., Zoo.Rec. **Document type:** academic/scholarly publication.
—BLDSC (4923.025000); CASDDS; UnCover.

631.3   DK   ISSN 0563-8887
S419
TOOLS AND TILLAGE; a journal on the history of the implements of cultivation and other agricultural processes. (Text in English; summaries in German) 1968. a. DKK 100 (effective 1997). (International Secretariat for Research on the History of Agricultural Implements) Grafisk Virksomhed & Forlag A-S, Aakirkebyvej 2, DK-7400 Herning, Denmark. TEL 45-97-12-10-22. FAX 45-97-12-11-15. Ed.Bd. bk.rev.; charts; illus. **Indexed:** Amer.Hist.& Life (1980-), Br.Archaeol.Abstr., Hist.Abstr. (1980-), M.L.A., MLA Intl.Bibl., NAA, Per.Islam. (1990-).
—BLDSC (8867.200000); UnCover.

630   AU
TOP AGRAR. m. S.630. Oesterreichischer Agrarverlag GmbH, Inkustr. 1-7, A-3400 Klosterneuburg, Austria. TEL 02243-333006. FAX 02243-3330056.

630   GW   ISSN 0936-8302
TOP AGRAR: AUSGABE B. 1972. m. DM.94.80 (foreign DM.118.80) (effective 1997). Landwirtschaftsverlag GmbH, Huelsebrockstr. 2, 48165 Muenster, Germany. TEL 49-2501-801-0. FAX 49-2501-801-204. (Subscr. to: Postfach 480249, 48079 Muenster, Germany) **Document type:** trade publication.
—SWETS.

630   GW   ISSN 0936-8310
TOP AGRAR: AUSGABE R. 1972. m. DM.105 (foreign DM.129) (effective 1997). Landwirtschaftsverlag GmbH, Huelsebrockstr. 2, 48165 Muenster, Germany. TEL 49-2501-801-0. FAX 49-2501-801-204. (Subscr. to: Postfach 480249, 48079 Muenster, Germany) **Document type:** trade publication.

630   GW   ISSN 0936-8329
TOP AGRAR: AUSGABE S. 1972. m. DM.105 (foreign DM.129) (effective 1997). Landwirtschaftsverlag GmbH, Huelsebrockstr. 2, 48165 Muenster, Germany. TEL 49-2501-801-0. FAX 49-2501-801-204. (Subscr. to: Postfach 480249, 48079 Muenster, Germany) **Document type:** trade publication.

630   GW   ISSN 0342-2399
TOP AGRAR: AUSGABE S - R; das Magazin fuer moderne Landwirtschaft. 1972. m. DM.114.60 (foreign DM.138.60) (effective 1997). Landwirtschaftsverlag GmbH, Huelsebrockstr. 2, 48165 Muenster, Germany. TEL 49-2501-801-0. FAX 49-2501-801-204. (Subscr. to: Postfach 480249, 48079 Muenster, Germany) Ed.Bd. circ. 133,000. **Document type:** trade publication.
—SWETS. **CCC.**

630 658   US   ISSN 1056-0831
TOP PRODUCER. 1986. m. (10/yr.). Farm Journal, Inc., 1500 Market St., Philadelphia, PA 19102-2181. TEL 215-557-8900. Ed. Marcia Taylor. adv. circ. 225,000. **Document type:** trade publication.
Formerly: Farm Journal Extra.

630.7   JA   ISSN 0082-5360
CODEN: JFALAX
TOTTORI UNIVERSITY. FACULTY OF AGRICULTURE. JOURNAL. (Text in European languages) 1951. a. exchange basis only. Tottori Daigaku, Nogakubu - Tottori University, Faculty of Agriculture, 4-101 Koyama-Minami, Tottori 680, Japan. Ed.Bd. circ. 750. **Indexed:** Biol.Abstr., Field Crop Abstr., Forest.Abstr., Forest Prod.Abstr., Herb.Abstr., Ind.Vet., Irr.& Drain.Abstr., Plant Breed.Abstr., Seed Abstr., Sport Fish.Abstr., Triticale Abstr., Vet.Bull., Weed Abstr., Wild.Rev., Zoo.Rec. **Document type:** academic/scholarly publication.
—BLDSC (4743.400000); CASDDS.

630 634.96   AT   ISSN 0814-4540
TOWN AND COUNTRY FARMER. 1984. q. Aus.$25.60. Town and Country Farmer Publications Pty. Ltd., P.O. Box 798, Benalla, Vic. 3672, Australia. TEL 61-57-641348. FAX 61-57-641349. E-mail: tacfarmr@benalla.net.au. Eds. Glenn Hurley, Shirley Hurley. adv.; tr.lit.; index; circ. 18,000 (controlled). (back issues avail.) **Document type:** consumer publication.
Description: Covers all aspects of farm management: planning, health and weed control, plus diversifying and alternative farm production activities.

630   FR
TRAVAUX AGRICOLES DE FRANCE. m. 190 F. Federation Nationale des Entrepreneurs de Travaux Agricoles et Forestiers, 8, Villa d'Alesia, 75014 Paris, France. TEL 33-1-45-39-44-80. Ed. J.C. Michel; Pub. Gerald Fougereux.

630　　　　　　　US　　ISSN 0041-2481
　　　　　　　　　　　　　CODEN: TTCRAV
TRI-OLOGY TECHNICAL REPORT. 1962. bi-m. free.
Department of Agriculture and Consumer Services,
Division of Plant Industry, 1911 S.W. 34th St., Box
147100, Gainesville, FL 32614-7100.
TEL 904-372-3505. FAX 904-955-2301. Eds.
Wayne N. Dixon, Nancy C. Coile. R&P contact:
Maeve McConnell. **Indexed:** Bibl.Agri., Biol.Abstr.,
Cott.& Trop.Fibr.Abstr., Entomol.Abstr., Hort.Abstr.
Document type: government publication.
　—BLDSC (9050.675000).
　Description: Focuses on pathology, nematology,
botany and entomology.

631.091　　　　　　GW　　ISSN 0041-3186
TROPENLANDWIRT; Zeitschrift fuer die Landwirtschaft in
den Tropen und Subtropen. (Text in German;
summaries in English) 1899. s-a. DM.50. (Verband
der Tropenlandwirte aus Witzenhausen e.V.) Verlag
der Tropenlandwirte, Steinstr. 19, 37213
Witzenhausen, Germany. TEL 49-5542-981216.
FAX 49-5542-981313. E-mail: tropen@wiz.uni-
kassel.de. (Co-sponsors: Deutsches Institut fuer
Tropische und Subtropische Landwirtschaft; Institut
fuer Tropische Landwirtschaft) Ed. Hans Hemann.
R&P contact: Hans Hemann. adv.; bk.rev.; abstr. circ.
1,500. **Indexed:** Agroforest.Abstr., Anim.Breed.Abstr.,
ASCA, Crop Physiol.Abstr., Curr.Adv.Ecol.Sci.,
Curr.Cont., Dairy Sci.Abstr., Field Crop Abstr.,
Forest.Abstr., Helminthol.Abstr., Hort.Abstr., IBR,
Maize Abstr., Nutr.Abstr., Plant Grow.Reg.Abstr.,
Rural Devel.Abstr., Seed Abstr., Soils & Fert., VITIS,
Weed Abstr., World Agri.Econ.& Rural Sociol.Abstr.
Document type: academic/scholarly publication.
　—BLDSC (9051.450000); UnCover.
　Formerly: Deutsche Kulturpionier-Deutsche
Tropenlandwirt.

631.491　　　　　　TR　　ISSN 0041-3216
SB111.A2　　　　　　　　　CODEN: TAGLA2
TROPICAL AGRICULTURE. 1924. q. £165. University of
the West Indies, Imperial College of Tropical
Agriculture, St. Augustine, Trinidad & Tobago, W.I.
TEL 809-645-3640. FAX 809-662-1182. TELEX
24520 UWI WG. Ed. F.A. Gumbs. adv.; bk.rev.;
index. (also avail. in microfilm from UMI; microfiche
from BHP; back issues avail.) **Indexed:**
Agroforest.Abstr., Anim.Breed.Abstr., ASCA,
Bibl.Agri., Biol.Abstr., Biol.& Agr.Ind., Chem.Abstr.,
Cott.& Trop.Fibr.Abstr., Curr.Adv.Ecol.Sci., Curr.Cont.,
Dairy Sci.Abstr., Energy Ind., Energy Info.Abstr.,
Environ.Abstr., Environ.Per.Bibl. (1977-1993), Field
Crop Abstr., Food Sci.& Tech.Abstr., Forest Abstr.,
Forest Prod.Abstr., Geo.Abstr.H.G., Geo.Abstr.P.G.,
Helminthol.Abstr., Herb.Abstr., Hort.Abstr., Ind.Vet.,
Irr.& Drain.Abstr., Maize Abstr., Nutr.Abstr., Plant
Breed.Abstr., Plant Grow.Reg.Abstr., Potato Abstr.,
Poult.Abstr., Rev.Appl.Entomol., Rev.Med.&
Vet.Mycol., Rev.Plant Path., Rice Abstr., Rural
Recreat.Tour.Abstr., Sci.Cit.Ind., Seed Abstr.,
So.Pac.Per.Ind., Soils & Fert., Sorghum & Millets
Abstr., Soyabean Abstr., Sugar Ind.Abstr., Triticale
Abstr., Trop.Abstr., Trop.Oil Seeds Abstr., Vet.Bull.,
Weed Abstr., World Agri.Econ.& Rural Sociol.Abstr.
Document type: academic/scholarly publication.
　—BLDSC (9053.000000); CASDDS; EMDOCS; KR
SourceOne; Linda Hall; SWETS; UMI; UnCover.
　Incorporates: Oil Palm News (ISSN 0048-1580)
　Description: Covers all aspects of agriculture in
tropical and semi-tropical countries.
　Refereed Serial

631.091　　　　　　CE　　ISSN 0041-3224
TROPICAL AGRICULTURIST; agricultural journal of
Ceylon. (Text in English) 1881. a. $15 (effective
1995). Department of Agriculture, No. 1, Sarasavi
Mawatha, P.O. Box 05, Peradeniya, Sri Lanka.
TEL 94-8-88136. FAX 94-8-88030. (Subscr. to:
Chief Librarian, Central Library, Dept. of Agriculture,
P.O. Box 47, Peradeniya, Sri Lanka) Ed. S.
Nagarajah. adv.; bk.rev.; charts; illus.; index; circ.
850 (controlled). **Indexed:** Agri.Eng.Abstr., Biol.Abstr.,
Biotech.Abstr., Chem.Abstr., Ecol.Abstr., Field Crop
Abstr., Herb.Abstr., Hort.Abstr., IDA, Nutr.Abstr.,
Plant Breed.Abstr., Rev.Appl.Entomol., Rev.Plant
Path., Rice Abstr., Soils & Fert., Sugar Ind.Abstr.,
Weed Abstr. **Document type:** trade publication.
　Description: Promotes agricultural research in the
tropics.
　Refereed Serial

631.091　　　　　　UK　　ISSN 0041-3291
S3　　　　　　　　　　　CODEN: TROSAC
TROPICAL SCIENCE. 1959. q. £130($230) (developing
countries £65($115) (effective 1998). Whurr
Publishers Ltd., 19b Compton Terrace, London N1
2UN, England. TEL 44-171-359-5979.
FAX 44-171-226-5290. (Subscr. to: Turpin
Distribution Services Ltd., Blackhorse Rd.,
Letchworth, Herts. SG6 1HN, England. TEL
44-1462-672555. FAX 44-1462-480947; Subscr.
in N. America to: Whurr Publishers Ltd., Box 1897,
Lawrence, KS 66044-8897. TEL 913-843-1221.
FAX 913-843-1274) Ed. Geoffrey Ames. adv.: page
£300; adv. contact: Maggy Park. bibl.; charts; illus.;
stat.; index. circ. 1,300. (also avail. in microform
from UMI) **Indexed:** Agroforest.Abstr., Anal.Abstr.,
Anim.Breed.Abstr., Art & Archaeol.Tech.Abstr.,
Bibl.Agri., Biol.Abstr., Biol.& Agr.Ind., Chem.Abstr.,
Curr.Adv.Ecol.Sci., Dairy Sci.Abstr., Energy Ind.,
Energy Info.Abstr., Excerp.Med., Field Crop Abstr.,
Food Sci.& Tech.Abstr., Forest.Abstr., Forest
Prod.Abstr., Helminthol.Abstr., Herb.Abstr.,
Hort.Abstr., Int.Packag.Abstr., Maize Abstr.,
Nutr.Abstr., Packag.Sci.Tech., Plant Breed.Abstr.,
Plant Grow.Reg.Abstr., Potato Abstr., Rev.Med.&
Vet.Mycol., Rev.Plant Path., Rice Abstr., Seed Abstr.,
Soils & Fert., Vet.Bull., Weed Abstr., World
Agri.Econ.& Rural Sociol.Abstr. **Document type:**
academic/scholarly publication.
　—BLDSC (9056.600000); CASDDS; CISTI;
EMDOCS; Linda Hall; SWETS; UMI; UnCover.
　Incorporates (in 1985): Tropical Stored Products
Information (ISSN 0564-3325); Which incorporated:
Tropical Storage Abstracts (ISSN 0305-8964)
　Description: Information within the spheres of
science, technology and economics as applied to the
development of renewable resources in the tropics
and sub-tropics.
　Refereed Serial

630　　　　　　　IO　　ISSN 0126-0057
S19
TRUBUS; the magazine for the development of
agriculture and agribusiness. 1969. m.
Rps.30000($19) Yayasan Sosial Tani Membangun,
Jl. Gunung Sahari III-7, Jakarta, Indonesia.
TEL 4204402. Ed. Slamet Soeseno. adv.; bk.rev.
circ. 50,000. **Indexed:** E.I.

630　　　　　　　TU　　ISSN 1300-011X
　　　　　　　　　　　　CODEN: TJAFEL
**TURKISH JOURNAL OF AGRICULTURE AND
FORESTRY/TURK TARIM VE ORMANCILIK DERGISI.**
(Text in English, Turkish) 1976. 6/yr. $150
(effective 1996 & 1997). Scientific and Technical
Research Council of Turkey - TUBITAK - Turkiye
Bilimsel ve Teknik Arastirma Kurumu, Ataturk
Bulvari, No. 221, Kavaklidere, 06100 Ankara,
Turkey. TEL 90-312-4685300.
FAX 90-312-4271336. TELEX 43186 BTAK TR.
E-mail: bdym@tubitak.gov.tr. Ed. Cengiz Ozsavasci.
Indexed: Biodet.Abstr., Ecol.Abstr., Food Sci.&
Tech.Abstr., Geo.Abstr.H.G., Geo.Abstr.P.G., IDA,
Irr.& Drain.Abstr., Ornam.Hort., Seed Abstr.
Document type: academic/scholarly publication.
　—BLDSC (9072.466500); CASDDS.
　Formerly (until 1994): Doga Turkish Journal of
Agriculture and Forestry - Doga Turk Tarim ve
Ormancilik Dergisi (ISSN 1010-7649)
　Refereed Serial

630　　　　　　　PL
TYGODNIK ROLNIKOW - OBSERWATOR. 1990. w.
Fundacja Prasowa Solidarnosci, Al. Jerozolimskie
125-127, 00-017 Warsaw, Poland.
TEL 48-22-217419. FAX 48-22-6285727. Ed.
Tadeusz Karolak. circ. 50,000.

TYGODNIK ROLNIKOW - SOLIDARNOSC. see *LABOR
UNIONS*

630　　　　　　　II　　ISSN 0067-3471
U A S EXTENSION SERIES. 1967. irreg., no.14, 1985.
University of Agricultural Sciences, Bangalore,
Communication Centre, Hebbal, Bangalore 560
024, Karnataka, India. Ed. B.S. Siddaramiah. circ.
500. (also avail. in microform from UMI; reprint
service avail. from ISI,UMI) **Document type:**
academic/scholarly publication.

AGRICULTURE　　159

630　　　　　　　II　　ISSN 0067-348X
U A S MISCELLANEOUS SERIES. 1965. irreg., no.39,
1988. price varies. University of Agricultural
Sciences, Bangalore, Communication Centre, Hebbal,
Bangalore 560 024, Karnataka, India. Ed. K.R.
Gapanathy. circ. 500. (also avail. in microform from
UMI; reprint service avail. from ISI,UMI) **Document
type:** academic/scholarly publication.

630　　　　　　　SZ　　ISSN 1420-5106
U F A - REVUE; the magazine of Swiss agriculture. (Text
and summaries in French, German) 1958. m.
35 SFr. Fenaco Landi-Medien, Postfach 344,
CH-8401 Winterthur, Switzerland.
TEL 41-52-2642728. FAX 41-52-2132161. Ed.
Hans Peter Kurzen. adv.: B&W page 6885 SFr.,
color page 8385 SFr. bk.rev. circ. 92,354. **Document
type:** bulletin.

U.K. IRRIGATION ASSOCIATION QUARTERLY. see *WATER
RESOURCES*

630　　　　　　　US　　ISSN 0041-7637
U S FARM NEWS. 1917. bi-m. $5. U S Farmers
Association, 1407 Second Ave. S., Denison, IA
51442-2017. Ed. Bill Gudex. bk.rev. circ. 2,500.
(tabloid format) **Indexed:** Alt.Press Ind.

630　　　　　　　PH　　ISSN 0117-0155
U S M C A RESEARCH JOURNAL. 1990. 2/yr.
P.125($25) to individuals; institutions P.225($45).
University of Southern Mindanao, College of
Agriculture, Kabacan, Cotabato 9407, Philippines.
Ed. Naomi G. Tangonan. abstr.; bibl.; charts; illus.;
stat. circ. 500. (back issues avail.) **Indexed:** Food
Sci.& Tech.Abstr.
　—BLDSC (9135.100203).
　Former titles (until 1990): U S M Research
Journal; (until vol.7, no.2, 1977): M I T Research
Journal (ISSN 0302-7937)
　Description: Contains original R&D in the fields of
agricultural education and extension, agronomy,
animal science, entomology, farming system,
horticulture, plant breeding and genetics, plant
pathology and soil science.
　Refereed Serial

630　　　　　　　GW　　ISSN 0303-6340
　　　　　　　　　　　　CODEN: UETIDW
UEBERSICHTEN ZUR TIERERNAEHRUNG. 1973. irreg.
(2-4/yr.). DM.9 (members DM.7.20) (effective
1996). D L G Verlags GmbH, Eschborner Landstr.
122, 60489 Frankfurt a.M., Germany.
TEL 069-24788-0. FAX 069-24788480. Ed.Bd.
Indexed: Anim.Breed.Abstr., Chem.Abstr., Food Sci.&
Tech.Abstr., Herb.Abstr., Ind.Vet., Nutr.Abstr., Pig
News & Info., Vet.Bull. **Document type:** trade
publication.
　—BLDSC (9079.603000); CASDDS. CCC.

630　　　　　　　TZ　　ISSN 0856-0838
UKULIMA WA KISASA/MODERN FARMING. (Text in
Swahili) 1955. m. Sh.200. Ministry of Agriculture,
Publicity Section, P.O. Box 2308, Dar es Salaam,
Tanzania. TEL 255-51-29047. TELEX 41246 Kl.
Ed. Cleophas C. Rwechungura. adv. contact: Bigelwa
Kisinza. charts; illus. circ. 35,000. (tabloid format)
Document type: government publication.
　Description: Gives advice on agicultural practices.
Provides forecasts on wheat and other crop prices
along with availability of materials necessary to the
industry. Includes coverage of policies affecting the
agricultural industry.

630　　　　　　　UK
ULSTER FARMER. 1900. w. Observer Newspapers Ltd.,
Irish St., Dungannon, N. Ireland. TEL 22557. Ed. D.J.
Mallon. **Document type:** newspaper.

631　　　　　　　RW
UMUHINZI - MWOROZI. 1975. m. (Ministere de
l'Agriculture, de l'Elevage et des Forets) O C I R, B.P.
104, Kigali-Gikondo, Rwanda. Ed. William Mwizerwa.
adv. circ. 1,500.

630　　　　　　　GW　　ISSN 0934-4632
UNABHAENGIGE BAUERNSTIMME; eine Zeitung von
Baeuerinnen und Bauern. 1976. m. DM.60.
Arbeitsgemeinschaft Baeuerliche
Landwirtschaft-Bauernblatt e.V., Marienfelderstr. 14,
33378 Rheda-Wiedenbrueck, Germany.
TEL 05242-48476. FAX 05242-47838. Ed.
Friedhelm Stodieck. adv.; bk.rev. circ. 8,000. (back
issues avail.) **Document type:** newsletter.

AGRICULTURE

630   FR   ISSN 0244-8459
L'UNION AGRICOLE. 1946. w. Union Syndicale Agricole, Cite de l'Agriculture, B.P. 10, 76231 Bois-Guillaume Cedex, France. TEL 35-60-21-60. FAX 35-60-37-98. Ed. Daniel Cadet. circ. 12,114.
   Formerly (until 1980): Union Syndicale Agricole (ISSN 0247-7009)

630
UNION AGRICOLE DE LA HAUTE-VIENNE. w. 32 av. du General Leclerc, 87065 Limoges Cedex, France. TEL 55-79-89-60. FAX 55-79-15-99. Ed. Albert Robert. circ. 7,670.

630   SZ
UNION DES PRODUCTEURS SUISSES. JOURNAL. 18/yr. Union des Producteurs Suisses, Le Sasselet, CH-2523 Lignieres, Switzerland. TEL 38511953. FAX 218411621. Ed. Fernand Cuche. circ. 3,000.

630   CN   ISSN 0041-6878
UNION FARMER. 1950. q. Can.$25 to individuals; institutions Can.$35. National Farmers Union, 250-C 2nd Ave. S., Saskatoon, SK S7K 2MI, Canada. TEL 306-652-9465. FAX 306-664-6226. Ed. Ed. Carla Roppel. adv. contact: Joan Lange. bk.rev.; charts; illus. circ. 5,000. **Document type:** trade publication.

UNION HERALD. see *LABOR UNIONS*

630 370   FR   ISSN 0082-7711
UNION NATIONALE DE L'ENSEIGNEMENT AGRICOLE PRIVE. ANNUAIRE. 1968. a. 120 F. Union Nationale de l'Enseignement Agricole Prive, 14 rue Drouot, 75009 Paris, France. adv.; bk.rev.

630   BE
UNION NATIONALE DU COMMERCE DE GROS EN FRUITS ET LEGUMES. BULLETIN. bi-m. Union Nationale du Commerce de Gros en Fruits et Legumes, 3 rue de la Corderie, Centra 356, F-94596 Rungis Cedex, Belgium. TEL 6864354. TELEX 202011. **Document type:** bulletin.

630   FR   ISSN 1141-0175
UNION PAYSANNE DE LA CORREZE. 24/yr. 36 av. du Generale de Gaulle, 19000 Tulle, France. TEL 16-55-26-71-00. Ed. Henri Demontjean. circ. 8,500.

630   SQ   ISSN 1021-0873
S338.S9
UNISWA JOURNAL OF AGRICULTURE. 1992. a. R.30($10) University of Swaziland, Faculty of Agriculture, Office of the Dean, Luyengo Campus, P.O. Luyengo, Swaziland. TEL 268-83021. FAX 268-83441. TELEX 2087 WD. Ed. Stephen Kayode Subair. bk.rev. circ. 300. **Document type:** academic/scholarly publication.
   Description: Serves as a forum for agricultural development research in the SADCC region. Publishes research papers, case studies, review articles and essays as well as first hand experiences of interest to researchers.

630.8   US   ISSN 0092-1785
S21.R44   CODEN: XNRCAT
U.S. AGRICULTURAL RESEARCH SERVICE. A R S - N C. Key Title: A R S - N C Agricultural Research Service. North Central Region. 1972. irreg., no.20, 1975. U.S. Department of Agriculture, Agricultural Research Service, North Central Region, 1815 N. University St., Peoria, IL 61604-3999. illus. **Indexed:** Biol.Abstr.

U.S. DEPARTMENT OF AGRICULTURE. AGRICULTURAL STATISTICS BOARD REPORT: COLD STORAGE. see *AGRICULTURE — Abstracting, Bibliographies, Statistics*

630   US   ISSN 0065-4612
S21   CODEN: XAAHA4
U.S. DEPARTMENT OF AGRICULTURE. AGRICULTURE HANDBOOK. 1949. irreg. U.S. Department of Agriculture, Office of Public Affairs, 14th St. & Independence Ave., S.W., Washington, DC 20250-1300. TEL 202-720-2791. **Indexed:** Abstr.Bull.Inst.Pap.Chem., Bio-Contr.News & Info., Biol.Abstr., Cott.& Trop.Fibr.Abstr., Field Crop Abstr., Forest. Abstr., Forest Prod.Abstr., Maize Abstr., Triticale Abstr., Trop.Oil Seeds Abstr., World Agri.Econ.& Rural Sociol.Abstr. **Document type:** government publication.
   —CISTI.

630.82   US   ISSN 0065-4639
S21   CODEN: XAAIA7
U.S. DEPARTMENT OF AGRICULTURE. AGRICULTURE INFORMATION BULLETIN. 1949. irreg. U.S. Department of Agriculture, Office of Public Affairs, 14th St. & Independence Ave., S.W., Washington, DC 20250-1300. TEL 202-720-2791. (also avail. in microfiche from UPD) **Indexed:** Agri.Eng.Abstr., Biodet.Abstr., Biol.Abstr., Cott.& Trop.Fibr.Abstr., Dairy Sci.Abstr., Forest.Abstr., Forest Prod.Abstr., GeoRef., Irr.& Drain.Abstr., Maize Abstr., Rice Abstr., Rural Recreat.Tour.Abstr., Soils & Fert., World Agri.Econ.& Rural Sociol.Abstr. **Document type:** bulletin, government publication.

630   US   ISSN 0082-9803
S21
U.S. DEPARTMENT OF AGRICULTURE. REPORT OF THE SECRETARY OF AGRICULTURE. Key Title: Report of the Secretary of Agriculture. 1862. a. free. U.S. Department of Agriculture, Office of Public Affairs, 14th St. & Independence Ave., S.W., Washington, DC 20250-1300. TEL 202-720-2791. **Document type:** government publication.

630 658   US
U.S. DEPARTMENT OF AGRICULTURE. RURAL BUSINESS - COOPERATIVE DEVELOPMENT SERVICE. SERVICE REPORT. irreg. price varies. U.S. Department of Agriculture, Rural Business - Cooperative Service, AG Box 3255, Washington, DC 20250-3255. TEL 202-720-6483. FAX 202-720-4641. **Document type:** government publication, monographic series.
   Description: Discusses various issues in managing farm cooperatives.

630   US   ISSN 0742-9487
HD1491.U5
U.S. DEPARTMENT OF AGRICULTURE. RURAL BUSINESS - COOPERATIVE SERVICE. COOPERATIVE INFORMATION REPORTS. 1977. irreg. price varies. U.S. Department of Agriculture, Rural Business - Cooperative Service, AG Box 3255, Washington, DC 20250-3255. TEL 202-720-6483. FAX 202-720-4641. **Document type:** government publication.
   Supersedes: U.S. Department of Agriculture. Farmer Cooperative Service. Information (Series) (ISSN 0082-9765)

630   US   ISSN 0082-9811
S21   CODEN: XATBAD
U.S. DEPARTMENT OF AGRICULTURE. TECHNICAL BULLETIN. 1927. irreg. U.S. Department of Agriculture, Office of Public Affairs, 14th St. & Independence Ave., S.W., Washington, DC 20250-1300. TEL 202-720-2791. (also avail. in microfiche from UPD,PMC) **Indexed:** Agri.Eng.Abstr., Bio-Contr.News & Info., Biol.Abstr., Curr.Adv.Ecol.Sci., Field Crop Abstr., Forest.Abstr., Forest Prod.Abstr., Herb.Abstr., Hort.Abstr., Potato Abstr., Rev.Appl.Entomol., Rev.Plant Path., Soils & Fert., Weed Abstr., World Agri.Econ.& Rural Sociol.Abstr. **Document type:** bulletin, government publication.
   —BLDSC (8641.000000); CASDDS; CISTI.

630.58   US   ISSN 0084-3628
S21   CODEN: YAXAA7
U.S. DEPARTMENT OF AGRICULTURE. YEARBOOK OF AGRICULTURE. 1894. a. price varies. U.S. Department of Agriculture, Office of Public Affairs, 14th St. and Independence Ave., S.W., Washington, DC 20250-1300. TEL 202-720-2791. (also avail. in microfiche from UPD) **Indexed:** Biol.Abstr., Nutr.Abstr., Plant Breed.Abstr. **Document type:** government publication.
   —CISTI.

630   VE   ISSN 0041-8285
S542.V42   CODEN: RFAMAM
UNIVERSIDAD CENTRAL DE VENEZUELA. FACULTAD DE AGRONOMIA. REVISTA. (Text mainly in Spanish, occasionally in English or Portuguese; summaries in English, Portuguese, Spanish) 1952. q. $25 or exchange basis. Universidad Central de Venezuela, Facultad de Agronomia, Apdo. 4579, Maracay, Edo. Aragua 2101, Venezuela. TEL 58-43-462212. Ed. Gustavo Trujillo P. bibl.; charts; illus.; stat.; index. circ. 1,000. **Indexed:** Abstr.Trop.Agri., Agrindex, Biol.Abstr., Chem.Abstr., Field Crop Abstr., Food Sci.& Tech.Abstr., Herb.Abstr., Hort.Abstr., Ind.Agri.Am.Lat.Caribe, Nutr.Abstr., Plant Breed.Abstr., Rev.Appl.Entomol., Rev.Plant Path., Soils & Fert., Soyabean Abstr., Weed Abstr. **Document type:** academic/scholarly publication.
   Description: Publishes original articles on tropical agriculture, including animal and plant production, food technology and agricultural economics.
   Refereed Serial

630   VE
UNIVERSIDAD CENTRAL DE VENEZUELA. FACULTAD DE AGRONOMIA. REVISTA ALCANCE. (Text in Spanish; summaries in English) 1956. irreg., vol.40, 1991. $25 or exchange basis. Universidad Central de Venezuela, Facultad de Agronomia, Apdo. 4579, Maraca, Edo. Aragua 2101, Venezuela. Ed. Gustavo Trujillo P. abstr.; bibl.; illus. circ. 1,500. **Indexed:** Bibl.Agri., Biol.Abstr. **Document type:** academic/scholarly publication.

630   UY   ISSN 0077-1260
BFMUAW
UNIVERSIDAD DE LA REPUBLICA. FACULTAD DE AGRONOMIA. BOLETIN. 1953. irreg. exchange basis. Universidad de la Republica, Facultad de Agronomia, Casilla de Correo 1238, Avda. Garzon 780, Montevideo, Uruguay. circ. 1,000. **Indexed:** Biol.Abstr., Chem.Abstr., Forest.Abstr., Weed Abstr. **Document type:** academic/scholarly publication, bulletin.

630   AG   ISSN 0041-8676
UNIVERSIDAD NACIONAL DE LA PLATA. FACULTAD DE AGRONOMIA. REVISTA. (Text and summaries in English, Spanish) 1895. s-a. $30 or exchange basis. Universidad Nacional de la Plata, Facultad de Agronomia, C.C. 31, Calle 60 y 119, 1900 La Plata, Argentina. TEL 54-21-38168. FAX 54-21-252346. E-mail: dacaldiz@isis.unlp.edu.ar. Dir. Edgardo R. Montaldi. R&P contact: Daniel Caldiz. adv.; bk.rev.; bibl.; charts; illus.; index. circ. 1,000. (reprint service avail.) **Indexed:** Biol.Abstr., Field Crop Abstr., Herb.Abstr., Plant Breed Abstr., Rev.Appl.Entomol., Rev.Plant Path., Soils & Fert. **Document type:** academic/scholarly publication.
   —BLDSC (7808.800000).
   Description: Covers general and specific topics related to agriculture and forestry.
   Refereed Serial

630   BL   ISSN 0084-8646
UNIVERSIDADE FEDERAL DO CEARA. ESCOLA DE AGRONOMIA. DEPARTAMENTO DE FITOTECNIA. RELATORIA TECNICO. * irreg. free. Universidade Federal do Ceara, Escola de Agronomia, Departamento de Fitotecnia, Caixa Postal 354, Fortaleza, Ceara 60000, Brazil.

630   IT   ISSN 0540-049X
         CODEN: AFAGAL
UNIVERSITA CATTOLICA DEL SACRO CUORE. FACOLTA DI AGRARIA. ANNALI. (Text in Italian; summaries in English, French and Italian) 1955. s-a. Lit.90000 (foreign Lit.130000 ($93)) (effective 1997); newsstand price: Lit.53000. Vita e Pensiero, Largo Gemelli 1, 20123 Milan, Italy. TEL 39-2-72342370. FAX 39-2-72342974. TELEX 321033 UCATMI 1. Ed. Carlo Lorenzoni. adv.; abstr.; index. circ. 400. **Indexed:** Agri.Eng.Abstr., Anim.Breed.Abstr., Biol.Abstr., Chem.Abstr., Crop Physiol.Abstr., Excerp.Med., Herb.Abstr., Hort.Abstr., Nutr.Abstr., Plant Grow.Reg.Abstr., Potato Abstr., Soils & Fert., Triticale Abstr., World Agri.Econ.& Rural Sociol.Abstr. **Document type:** academic/scholarly publication.
   —BLDSC (1005.890000); CASDDS.
   Description: Publishes original research articles in areas of agronomy, agrarian chemistry and the agrarian industry.

AGRICULTURE

630   IT   ISSN 0365-799X
CODEN: AUNPAE
UNIVERSITA DEGLI STUDI DI NAPOLI. FACOLTA DI SCIENZE AGRARIE. ANNALI. (Text in Italian; summaries in English) 1966. a. L.10000 per no. Universita degli Studi di Napoli, Facolta di Scienze Agrarie, 80055 Portici Naples, Italy. charts; illus.; maps; stat. circ. 500. **Indexed:** Dairy Sci.Abstr., Forest.Abstr., Irr.& Drain.Abstr., Rev.Med.& Vet.Mycol., Soils & Fert., Sport Fish.Abstr., Wild.Rev., Zoo.Rec. **Document type:** academic/scholarly publication.
—BLDSC (1007.000000); CASDDS; CISTI; Linda Hall.
   Description: Research papers on the agrarian sciences.

630 634.9   AU   ISSN 0256-4246
UNIVERSITAET FUER BODENKULTUR IN WIEN. DISSERTATIONEN. 1972. irreg., no.45, 1996. price varies. (Universitaet fuer Bodenkultur in Wien) Oesterreichischer Kunst- und Kulturverlag, Postfach 17, A-1016 Vienna, Austria. **Document type:** academic/scholarly publication.
   Formerly: Hochschule fuer Bodenkultur in Wien. Dissertationen.

630   GW   ISSN 0075-4609
S231   CODEN: ELFLDE
UNIVERSITAET GIESSEN. ERGEBNISSE LANDWIRTSCHAFTLICHER FORSCHUNG. 1956. irreg. DM.25 per no. FB 17 - Agrarwissenschaften, Bismarkstr. 24, 35370 Giessen, Germany. TEL 0641-7029670. FAX 0641-7029669. E-mail: peter.wagner@agrar.uni-giessen.de. Ed. Peter Wagner. circ. 1,200. **Indexed:** Geo.Abstr. **Document type:** monographic series.
—CASDDS.

630   RM   ISSN 1223-494X
UNIVERSITATEA AGRONOMICA ION IONESCU DE LA BRAD. LUCRARI STIINTIFICE. SERIA AGRONOMIE. 1957. a. Universitatea Agronomica "Ion Ionescu de la Brad", Aleea M. Sadoveanu, Nr. 3, Jassy, Rumania. **Indexed:** Biol.Abstr., Chem.Abstr., Crop Physiol.Abstr., Field Crop Abstr., Herb.Abstr., Hort.Abstr., Maize Abstr., Plant Breed.Abstr., Poult.Abstr., Soils & Fert., Trop.Oil Seeds Abstr.
—BLDSC (5303.405100).
   Formerly: Institutul Agronomic Ion Ionescu de la Brad. Lucrari Stiintifice. Seria Agronomie (ISSN 0379-8364); Supersedes in part: Institutul Agronomic Ion Ionescu de la Brad. Lucrari Stiintifice. Seria Agronomie-Horticultura (ISSN 0075-3505)

630 635   RM   ISSN 1221-3608
CODEN: BIAAD4
UNIVERSITATEA DE STIINTE AGRICOLE CLUJ-NAPOCA. BULETINUL. SERIA AGRICULTURA SI HORTICULTURA. (Text in Rumanian; summaries in English) 1975. a. 35 lei($10) Universitatea de Stiinte Agricole Cluj-Napoca, Str. Manastur No. 3, 3400 Cluj-Napoca, Rumania. Ed. Leon Muntean. circ. 175. (back issues avail.) **Indexed:** Agri.Eng.Abstr., Biol.Abstr., Field Crop Abstr., Landwirt.Zentralbl., Maize Abstr., Potato Abstr., Seed Abstr., Sorghum & Millets Abstr., Soyabean Abstr., Triticale Abstr., Weed Abstr.
—BLDSC (2366.127500); CASDDS.
   Former titles (until 1992): Institutul Agronomic Cluj-Napoca. Buletinul. Seria Agricultura si Horticultura (ISSN 1220-8450); (until 1990): Institutul Agronomic Cluj-Napoca. Buletinul. Seria Agricultura (ISSN 0557-465X); Supersedes in part (in 1977): Institutul Agronomic Cluj-Napoca. Buletinul (ISSN 0378-0554)

630   RM
CODEN: LABAAQ
UNIVERSITATEA DE STIINTE AGRONOMICE. LUCRARI STIINTIFICE. SERIA A, AGRONOMIE. (Text in Rumanian; summaries in English) 1960. a. exchange basis only. Universitatea de Stiinte Agronomice si Medicina Veterinaria, Bdul. Marasti, 59, Bucharest, Sec. 1, Rumania. **Document type:** academic/scholarly publication.
—CASDDS.
   Former titles (until 1992): Institutul Agronomic Nicolae Balcescu. Lucrari Stiintifice. Seria A, Agronomie (ISSN 0521-3401); (until 1964): Institutul Agronomic Nicolae Balcescu. Lucrari Stiintifice. Seria A, Pedologie, Ingrasaminte, Chimie Agricola, Ameliorattii Agricole (ISSN 1220-1995)

630   RM
CODEN: LSABAE
UNIVERSITATEA DE STIINTE AGRONOMICE. LUCRARI STIINTIFICE. SERIA B, HORTICULTURA. (Text in Rumanian; summaries in English) 1957. a. exchange basis only. Universitatea de Stiinte Agronomice si Medicina Veterinaria, Bdul. Marasti, 59, Bucharest, Sec. 1, Rumania. Ed.Bd. **Document type:** academic/scholarly publication.
—CASDDS.
   Former titles (until 1992): Institutul Agronomic Nicolae Balcescu. Lucrari Stiintifice. Seria B, Horticultura (ISSN 0521-341X); (until 1964): Institutul Agronomic N. Balcescu. Lucrari Stiintifice. Seria B, Agrotehnica, Fitotehnie si Selectia Plantelor de Cimp di Horticole (ISSN 1220-2002); Which superseded in part (in 1960): Institutul Agronomic N. Balcescu. Anuarul Lucrarilor Stiintifice (ISSN 1220-1987)

UNIVERSITATEA DIN CRAIOVA. ANALE. SERIA: BIOLOGIE, AGRONOMIE, HORTICULTURA. see *BIOLOGY*

630   II   ISSN 0067-3455
UNIVERSITY OF AGRICULTURAL SCIENCES, BANGALORE. ANNUAL REPORT. 1965. a. Rs.50. University of Agricultural Sciences, Bangalore, Communication Centre, Hebbal, Bangalore 560 024, Karnataka, India. Ed. B.S. Siddaramiah. circ. 1,000. (also avail. in microform from UMI; reprint service avail. from ISI,UMI) **Indexed:** Biol.Abstr., Field Crop Abstr., Herb.Abstr., Hort.Abstr. **Document type:** academic/scholarly publication.

630   II
UNIVERSITY OF AGRICULTURAL SCIENCES, BANGALORE. COLLABORATIVE SERIES. (Text in English) 1968. irreg., no.3, 1976. price varies. University of Agricultural Sciences, Bangalore, Communication Centre, Hebbal, Bangalore 560 024, Karnataka, India. Ed. H.R. Gapanathy. (reprint service avail. from ISI,UMI) **Document type:** academic/scholarly publication.

630   II
UNIVERSITY OF AGRICULTURAL SCIENCES, BANGALORE. CURRENT RESEARCH. 1971. m. $30. University of Agricultural Sciences, Bangalore, Communication Centre, Hebbal, Bangalore 560 024, India. Ed. B.S. Siddaramiah. circ. 600. (reprint service avail. from ISI,UMI) **Indexed:** Agroforest.Abstr., Bio-Contr.News & Info., Biodet.Abstr., Biol.Abstr., Crop Physiol.Abstr., Fababean Abstr., Field Crop Abstr., Food Sci.& Tech.Abstr., Herb.Abstr., Hort.Abstr., Ind.Vet., Irr.& Drain.Abstr., Maize Abstr., Ornam.Hort., Plant Breed.Abstr., Plant Grow.Reg.Abstr., Poult.Abstr., Rice Abstr., Seed Abstr., Small Anim.Abstr., Soils & Fert., Sorghum & Millets Abstr., Soyabean Abstr., Sugar Ind.Abstr., Triticale Abstr., Vet.Bull., Weed Abstr., World Agri.Econ.& Rural Sociol.Abstr. **Document type:** academic/scholarly publication.

630   II
UNIVERSITY OF AGRICULTURAL SCIENCES, BANGALORE. EDUCATIONAL SERIES. (Text in English) 1969. irreg., no.9, 1987. price varies. University of Agricultural Sciences, Bangalore, Communication Centre, Hebbal, Bangalore 560 024, Karnataka, India. Ed. B.S. Siddaramiah. (reprint service avail. from ISI,UMI) **Indexed:** Rural Ext.Educ.& Tr.Abstr., World Agri.Econ.& Rural Sociol.Abstr. **Document type:** academic/scholarly publication.

630   II
UNIVERSITY OF AGRICULTURAL SCIENCES, BANGALORE. INFORMATION SERIES. (Text in English) irreg., no.8, 1979. price varies. University of Agricultural Sciences, Bangalore, Communication Centre, Hebbal, Bangalore 560 024, Karnataka, India. (reprint service avail. from ISI,UMI) **Document type:** academic/scholarly publication.

630   II
UNIVERSITY OF AGRICULTURAL SCIENCES, BANGALORE. RESEARCH MONOGRAPH SERIES. irreg., no.4, 1978. price varies. University of Agricultural Sciences, Bangalore, Communication Centre, Hebbal, Bangalore 560 024, Karnataka, India. Ed. B.S. Siddaramiah. (reprint service avail. from ISI,UMI) **Document type:** academic/scholarly publication, monographic series.

630   II
UNIVERSITY OF AGRICULTURAL SCIENCES, BANGALORE. RESEARCH REVIEW SERIES. (Text in English) 1977. irreg., latest no.8, 1988. price varies. University of Agricultural Sciences, Bangalore, Communication Centre, Hebbal, Bangalore 560 024, Karnataka, India. circ. 500. (reprint service avail. from ISI,UMI) **Document type:** academic/scholarly publication.

630   II
UNIVERSITY OF AGRICULTURAL SCIENCES, BANGALORE. TECHNICAL INFORMATION SERIES. (Text in Kannada) 1975. irreg., no.6, 1989. price varies. University of Agricultural Sciences, Bangalore, Communication Centre, Hebbal, Bangalore 560 024, Karnataka, India. (reprint service avail. from ISI,UMI) **Document type:** academic/scholarly publication.

630   II
UNIVERSITY OF AGRICULTURAL SCIENCES, BANGALORE. TECHNICAL SERIES. (Text in English) 1973. irreg., latest issue no.51, 1989. price varies. University of Agricultural Sciences, Bangalore, Communication Centre, Hebbal, Bangalore 560 024, Karnataka, India. (reprint service avail. from ISI,UMI) **Indexed:** Agroforest.Abstr., Biol.Abstr., Dairy Sci.Abstr., Field Crop Abstr., Herb.Abstr., Hort.Abstr., Potato Abstr., Rice Abstr., Rural Devel.Abstr., Sorghum & Millets Abstr., World Agri.Econ.& Rural Sociol.Abstr. **Document type:** academic/scholarly publication.

630   II
UNIVERSITY OF AGRICULTURAL SCIENCES, BANGALORE. U A S TEXTBOOK SERIES. (Text in English) 1979. irreg. University of Agricultural Sciences, Bangalore, Communication Center, Hebbal, Bangalore 560 024, Karnataka, India. Ed. B.S. Siddaramiah. (reprint service avail. from ISI,UMI) **Document type:** academic/scholarly publication.

630 636.089   TZ
UNIVERSITY OF DAR ES SALAAM. FACULTY OF AGRICULTURE, FORESTRY AND VETERINARY SCIENCE. ANNUAL RECORD OF RESEARCH. (Text in English) 1979. a. $6. Sokoine University of Agriculture, P.O. Box 3022, Mzumbe-Morogoro, Tanzania. Ed. M. Mgheni. circ. 1,000. **Document type:** academic/scholarly publication.

630   US   ISSN 0072-1271
UNIVERSITY OF GEORGIA. COLLEGE OF AGRICULTURE EXPERIMENT STATIONS. BULLETIN. irreg. free. University of Georgia, College of Agriculture Experiment Stations, Connor Hall, Athens, GA 30602. TEL 404-542-3621. Ed. Kathleen Sheridan. circ. controlled. **Indexed:** Excerp.Med. **Document type:** academic/scholarly publication, bulletin.

630   US   ISSN 0072-128X
S537   CODEN: GARRAY
UNIVERSITY OF GEORGIA. COLLEGE OF AGRICULTURE EXPERIMENT STATIONS. RESEARCH REPORTS. 1967. irreg., no.551, 1988. free. University of Georgia, College of Agriculture Experiment Stations, Connor Hall, Athens, GA 30602. TEL 404-542-3621. Ed. Kathleen Sheridan. circ. 1,500 (controlled). **Indexed:** Field Crop Abstr., Herb.Abstr., Hort.Abstr., Nutr.Abstr., Plant Breed.Abstr., Rural Recreat.Tour.Abstr., Soils & Fert., World Agri.Econ.& Rural Sociol.Abstr. **Document type:** academic/scholarly publication.
—CASDDS; Linda Hall.

630   CN
UNIVERSITY OF MANITOBA. FACULTY OF AGRICULTURAL AND FOOD SCIENCES. ANNUAL PROGRESS REVIEW. 1954. a. free. University of Manitoba, Faculty of Agricultural and Food Sciences, Winnipeg, MB R3T 2N2, Canada. TEL 204-474-9435. FAX 204-275-5128. TELEX 44370. circ. 1,000. **Document type:** academic/scholarly publication.
   Former titles: University of Manitoba. Faculty of Agriculture. Annual Progress Review: Agricultural Research, Teaching and Extension (ISSN 0832-266X); (until 1986): University of Manitoba. Faculty of Agriculture. Annual Progress Report: Agricultural Research, Teaching and Extension (ISSN 0832-2651); (until 1982): University of Manitoba. Faculty of Agriculture. Annual Progress Report: Agricultural Research and Experimentation (ISSN 0384-8884); (until 1959): University of Manitoba. Faculty of Agriculture. Progress Report on Agricultural Research (ISSN 0076-4051)

AGRICULTURE

630 US ISSN 1042-2889
CODEN: RBUREB
UNIVERSITY OF NEBRASKA. AGRICULTURAL RESEARCH DIVISION. RESEARCH BULLETIN. irreg. University of Nebraska at Lincoln, Agricultural Research Division, Institute of Agriculture and Natural Resources, Lincoln, NE 68583-0918. **Document type:** academic/scholarly publication, bulletin.

630 570 JA
S19 CODEN: BSKBAM
UNIVERSITY OF OSAKA PREFECTURE. BULLETIN. SERIES B: AGRICULTURE AND LIFE SCIENCES. (Text in Japanese and European languages) 1951. a. exchange basis. University of Osaka Prefecture - Osaka-furitsu Daigaku, 1-1 Gakuen-cho, Sakai-shi, Osaka 593, Japan. TEL 0722-52-1161. FAX 0722-52-6798. **Indexed:** Biol.Abstr., Chem.Abstr., Crop Physiol.Abstr., Field Crop Abstr., Herb.Abstr., Hort.Abstr., Ind.Vet., INIS Atomind., Irr.& Drain.Abstr., Plant Breed.Abstr., Poult.Abstr., Sel.Water Res.Abstr., Soils & Fert., Vet.Bull. **Document type:** academic/scholarly publication.
—BLDSC (2795.520000); CASDDS.
Former titles: University of Osaka Prefecture. Bulletin. Series B: Agriculture and Biology (ISSN 0366-3353); (until 1955): Naniwa University. Bulletin. Series B: Agricultural and Natural Science (ISSN 0474-7852)

630 PR ISSN 0163-8238
UNIVERSITY OF PUERTO RICO. AGRICULTURAL EXPERIMENT STATION. BULLETIN. (Text and summaries in English and Spanish) 1911. irreg. price varies. University of Puerto Rico, Agricultural Experiment Station, Box 21360, Rio Piedras, PR 00927. TEL 787-767-9705. FAX 787-758-5158. Ed. Wanda I. Lugo. circ. 1,000. (back issues avail.). **Indexed:** Biol.Abstr., Curr.Adv.Ecol.Sci., Helminthol.Abstr., Rev.Plant Path. **Document type:** academic/scholarly publication, bulletin.

630 PR ISSN 0041-994X
S542.P9 CODEN: JAUPA8
UNIVERSITY OF PUERTO RICO. JOURNAL OF AGRICULTURE. (Text and summaries in English and Spanish) 1917. q. $25 or exchange basis. University of Puerto Rico, Agricultural Experiment Station, Box 21360, Rio Piedras, PR 00927. TEL 787-767-9705. FAX 787-758-5158. Ed. Wanda I. Lugo. bibl.; illus. circ. 750. (also avail. in microform from UMI; back issues avail.; reprint service avail. from UMI,ISI) **Indexed:** Agri.Eng.Abstr., ASCA, Bio-Contr.News & Info., Biol.Abstr., Chem.Abstr., Curr.Cont., Field Crop Abstr., Food Sci.& Tech.Abstr., Geo.Abstr., Helminthol.Abstr., Herb.Abstr., Hort.Abstr., Ind.Vet., Irr.& Drain.Abstr., Maize Abstr., Nutr.Abstr., Potato Abstr., Rice Abstr., Sci.Cit.Ind., Seed Abstr., Sel.Water Res.Abstr., Sorghum & Millets Abstr., Sport Fish.Abstr., Sugar Ind.Abstr., Vet.Bull., Weed Abstr., Wild.Rev., Zoo.Rec. **Document type:** academic/scholarly publication.
—BLDSC (4925.000000); CASDDS; Genuine Article; Linda Hall; UMI; UnCover.

630 664 634.9
633.71 IQ ISSN 1017-3188
UNIVERSITY OF SALAHADDIN. COLLEGE OF AGRICULTURE. SCIENTIFIC JOURNAL "ZANCO". (Text and summaries in Arabic and English) 1983. q. ID.4($20) University of Salahaddin, College of Agriculture, Aski Kalak, Arbil, Iraq. Ed. Khusrow G. Shali. bk.rev. circ. 1,000. **Indexed:** Agri.Eng.Abstr., Bio-Contr.News & Info., Biol.Abstr., Dairy Sci.Abstr., Fababean Abstr., Field Crop Abstr., Food Sci.& Tech.Abstr., Hort.Abstr., Ind.Vet., Irr.& Drain.Abstr., Maize Abstr., Plant Grow.Reg.Abstr., Poult.Abstr., Protozool.Abstr., Seed Abstr., Soils & Fert., Sorghum & Millets Abstr., Soyabean Abstr., Triticale Abstr., Vet.Bull., Weed Abstr.
Formerly: Iraqi Journal of Agricultural Sciences "ZANCO".
Description: Presents original research papers in the fields of natural and applied sciences.

630 PH
UNIVERSITY OF THE PHILIPPINES AT LOS BANOS. AGRARIAN REFORM INSTITUTE. OCCASIONAL PAPERS. 1975. irreg. free. University of the Philippines at Los Banos, Institute of Agrarian Studies, Laguna 4031, Philippines. Ed. Honorio C. Batangantang. circ. 500. **Document type:** academic/scholarly publication.

630 JA ISSN 0370-4246
S19 CODEN: RDNGBM
UNIVERSITY OF THE RYUKYUS. COLLEGE OF AGRICULTURE. SCIENCE BULLETIN/RYUKYU DAIGAKU NOGAKUBU GAKUJUTSU HOKOKU. (Text in English or Japanese) 1954. a. free. University of the Ryukyus, College of Agriculture - Ryukyu Daigaku Nogakubu, 59 Senbaru, Nishishara-cho, Okinawa 90301, Japan. FAX 09889-5-2864. circ. 400. **Indexed:** Agroforest.Abstr., Biol.Abstr., Curr.Adv.Ecol.Sci., Forest.Abstr., Forest Prod.Abstr., Herb.Abstr., Hort.Abstr., Ind.Vet., Nutr.Abstr., Plant Breed.Abstr., Seed Abstr., Sugar Ind.Abstr., Vet.Bull., Weed Abstr. **Document type:** academic/scholarly publication, bulletin.
—BLDSC (8134.650000); CASDDS.

630 BN ISSN 0033-8583
CODEN: RPFUB6
UNIVERZITET U SARAJEVU. POLJOPRIVREDNI FAKULTET. RADOVI. (Text in Yugoslavian; summaries in Dutch, English, German) 1952. a. $20. Univerzitet u Sarajevu, Poljoprivredni Fakultet, Zagrebacka 18, Sarajevo, Bosnia Hercegovina. Ed. Taib Saric. circ. 520. **Indexed:** Anim.Breed.Abstr., Chem.Abstr., Dairy Sci.Abstr., Field Crop Abstr., Food Sci.& Tech.Abstr., Herb.Abstr., Hort.Abstr., Nutr.Abstr., Plant Breed.Abstr., Rural Recreat.Tour.Abstr., Seed Abstr., Soils & Fert., Weed Abstr., World Agri.Econ.& Rural Sociol.Abstr. **Document type:** academic/scholarly publication.
—BLDSC (7242.050000); CASDDS.

630 II
UNNAT KRISHI. (Text in Hindi) bi-m. Rs.12. Ministry of Agriculture and Rural Development, Directorate of Extension, Krishi Vistar Bhawan, Dr. K.S. Krishnan Marg, Pusa, New Delhi 110012, India. TEL 603568. adv.: page Rs.2000; 270 x 210.

630 II ISSN 0566-2540
UNNATKRISHI/PROGRESS IN AGRICULTURE. (Text in Hindi) 1961. m. Rps.5.50. Ministry of Food & Agriculture, Farm Information Unit Directorate of Extension, R.K. Puram, New Delhi 110 066, India. Ed. Vidyapati Jha. adv. circ. 20,000. **Document type:** government publication.

630 GW ISSN 0179-4132
UNSER LAND (BERLIN); das vielseitige Agrarmagazin. 1989. m. DM.84 (foreign DM.106) (effective 1997). D L V Deutscher Landwirtschaftsverlag Berlin, Guertelstr. 29a-30, 10247 Berlin, Germany. TEL 49-30-293974-80. FAX 49-30-29397459. Ed. Peter Schulz. **Document type:** trade publication.

630 GW
UNSER LAND (PASSAU). s-a. DM.42.80. Unser Land Verlags GmbH, Dr.-Hans-Kapfinger-Str. 30, 94032 Passau, Germany. TEL 0851-502344. FAX 0851-502256. adv.; bk.rev.

THE UPRIGHT OSTRICH. see BUSINESS AND ECONOMICS — Small Business

630 US ISSN 1071-653X
UTAH FARMER. 1884. m. $19.95. Western Farmer-Stockman Magazines (Subsidiary of: Cowles Publishing Co.), Box 2160, Spokane, WA 99210-1615. TEL 509-459-5361. FAX 509-459-5102. E.W. Ramsey, Pub. Dir. adv. contact: Richard C. Brantley. bk.rev.; stat.; circ. 4,193 (paid). **Document type:** trade publication.
Formerly (until 1993): Utah Farmer - Stockman (ISSN 1041-1666); Which incorporates: Pacific Dairyman (ISSN 0552-7325); **Former titles:** Utah Farmer; Desert Farmer; Rocky Mountain Agriculturalist and Irrigation Age.

630 US ISSN 0042-1502
CODEN: UTSCBA
UTAH SCIENCE. 1940. q. free. Utah Agricultural Experiment Station, Utah State University, Logan, UT 84322. TEL 801-797-2189. Ed. Kurt Gutknecht. R&P contact: Kurt Gutknecht. charts; illus.; stat.; cum.index. circ. 4,000. **Indexed:** Agri.Eng.Abstr., Biol.Abstr., Curr.Adv.Ecol.Sci., Dairy Sci.Abstr., Environ.Per.Bibl., Field Crop Abstr., Food Sci.& Tech.Abstr., Geo.Abstr., Helminthol.Abstr, Herb.Abstr., Ind.Free Per., Ind.Vet., Maize Abstr., Nutr.Abstr., Plant Breed.Abstr., Pollut.Abstr., Rev.Plant Path., Risk Abstr., Sport Fish.Abstr., Triticale Abstr., Vet.Bull., Wild.Rev., Zoo.Rec. (until 19??). **Document type:** government publication.
—BLDSC (9135.220000); Linda Hall; UnCover.
Formerly: Utah Farm and Home Science.

630 II
UTAMA KHETI BARI.* (Text in Punjabi) 1970. m. Rs.12. B 1-23-A Hauz Khas, New Delhi 16, India. adv.; charts.

630.2 GW ISSN 0724-2344
V D L - JOURNAL. 1950. 10/yr. DM.84.60 (foreign DM.96) (effective 1997). (Verband Deutscher Akademiker fuer Landwirtschaft, Ernaehrung und Landespflege e.V.) Landwirtschaftsverlag Gmbh, Huelsebrockstr. 2, 48165 Muenster, Germany. TEL 49-2501-801-0. FAX 49-2501-801-204. (Subscr. to: Postfach 480249, 48079 Muenster, Germany) Ed. Dieter Barth. adv.; bk.rev.; abstr.; charts; illus.; pat.; stat.; tr.mk.; index. circ. 6,238. (also avail. in microfilm) **Indexed:** Rural Recreat.Tour.Abstr., World Agri.Econ. & Rural Sociol.Abstr. **Document type:** academic/scholarly publication.
Former titles: V D L - Nachrichten (ISSN 0340-7810); Diplomlandwirt (ISSN 0012-3129)

630 SZ
V O L G GENOSSENSCHAFTER. 21/yr. Fenaco Landi-Medien, Postfach 344, CH-8401 Winterthur, Switzerland. TEL 41-52-2642722. FAX 41-52-2132161. Ed. Hans Peter Kurzen. adv.: B&W page 2480 SFr., color page 3300 SFr. circ. 28,162. **Document type:** trade publication.

630 SW ISSN 1100-1151
VAEXTODLING. (Text in Swedish; summaries in English) 1973. irreg. Sveriges Lantbruksuniversitet, Institutionen foer Vaextodlingslaera - Swedish University of Agricultural Sciences, Department of Crop Production Science, P.O. Box 7043, S-750 07 Uppsala, Sweden. TEL 46-18-67-10-00. FAX 46-18-67-29-09. Ed.Bd. **Indexed:** Field Crop Abstr., Hort.Abstr., Plant Breed.Abstr., Potato Abstr.
Former titles (until 1988): Sveriges Lantbruksuniversitet. Institutionen foer Vaextodling. Rapport (ISSN 0348-1034); (until 1988): Lantbrukshoegskolan. Institutionen foer Vaextodling. Rapporter och Avhandlingar (ISSN 0346-7236)

630 US
VALLEY FARMER. 1929. w. $18 35. Valley Tribune, 905 S. Henry, Bay City, MI 48706. TEL 517-893-6507. Ed. Mark Schanhals; Pub. David Hebert. adv. contact: David Hebert. circ. 2,300 (paid). (tabloid format) **Document type:** newspaper.
Description: Covers farm news and information; lists auctions.

630 LI ISSN 1021-4526
VALSTIECIU LAIKRASTIS. 1940. 2/wk. $100. Laisves pr. 60, 2056 Vilnius, Lithuania. TEL 370-2-421281. Ed. Jonas Svoba. R&P contact: Jonas Svoba. adv. contact: Ona Baublyte. circ. 110,000. **Document type:** newspaper.

630 RU
VASHI SHEST' SOTOK. (Text in Russian) 1991. fortn. 45000 Rub. Varvarka ul., 14, 103690 Moscow, Russia. TEL 7-095-2984789. FAX 7-095-2983830. adv. contact: Sergei Krasichkov. circ. 120,000.

630 FR ISSN 0335-7856
VAUCLUSE AGRICOLE. no.557, 1978. w. 30 F. Societe des Editions Vaucluse Agricole (Subsidiary of: Agropact), B.P. 734, 84034 Avignon Cedex, France. TEL 90-84-03-03. Ed. Marie Therese Chevalier. adv.; charts; illus.; stat. circ. 7,956. (tabloid format)

630 XO ISSN 0139-6064
VCELAR. 1922. m. Slovensky Zvaz Vcelarov, Svrcia ul. 14, 842 08 Bratislava, Slovakia. (Subscr. to: Slovart Gottwaldovo nam. 48, 805 32 Bratislava, Slovakia). **Indexed:** Apic.Abstr.
Description: Covers all aspects of bees and bee culture.

638.1 XR ISSN 0042-2924
VCELARSTVI. 1877. m. 30 Kc.($0.20) Cesky Svaz Vcelary, Kremencova 8, 115 24 Prague 1, Czech Republic. (Subscr. to: Artia, Ve Smeckach 30, 111 27 Prague 1, Czech Republic) Ed. Miroslav Peroutka. adv.; bk.rev.; illus. circ. 52,000. **Indexed:** Apic.Abstr., Biol.Abstr., Chem.Abstr., Forest.Abstr.

AGRICULTURE

630   JA   ISSN 0386-250X
CODEN: YSHBDP
VEGETABLE AND ORNAMENTAL CROPS RESEARCH STATION. BULLETIN. SERIES B. (Text in Japanese; summaries in English) 1977. irreg. 92 Nabeyashiki, Shimokuriyagawa, Morioka, Iwate, Japan. (Subscr. to: Morioka Branch, Vegetable and Ornamental Crops Research Station, Shimokuriyagawa, Morioka, Iwate 020-01, Japan) Ed. Katsuya Takada. circ. 800. **Indexed:** Field Crop Abstr. **Document type:** bulletin.
—CASDDS.

630   UK   ISSN 0960-863X
VEGETABLE FARMER. 1989. m. £25 (Europe £30; U.S., Canada & the Middle East £35; elsewhere £40) (effective 1997). AGA Bldgs., Lamberhurst Rd., Horsmonden, Tonbridge, Kent TN12 8DP, England. TEL 44-1892-724277. FAX 44-1892-722516. Ed. John Jarrett. adv. contact: Joseph Champneys. bk.rev. circ. 3,400.
Document type: trade publication.
Description: Covers the U.K. commercial vegetable-growing industry.

630   FR   ISSN 0983-3897
VENDEE AGRICOLE. 50/yr. Bd. Reaumur, 85013 La Roche sur Yon Cedex, France. TEL 51-36-82-04. FAX 51-36-82-13. Ed. Gilbert Metivier. circ. 14,000.

630 398   GW
VEREIN OBERPFAELZISCHES BAUERNMUSEUM. MITTEILUNGEN. 1964. a. Verein Oberpfaelzisches Bauernmuseum e.V., Regensburgerstr. 51, 92507 Nabburg, Germany. TEL 09433-521. circ. 500.

638 333.7   SP   ISSN 0210-8089
VERGEL; revista de ciencias naturales visualizada. 1975. a. 16650 ptas. (effective 1997). Ediciones y Promociones Lav, S.L., Apdo. 473, 46080 Valencia, Spain. TEL 34-6-3720262. FAX 34-6-3710516. Ed. Francisco Salvador Planes Planes. **Document type:** monographic series.

630   US   ISSN 0083-5706
VERMONT. AGRICULTURAL EXPERIMENT STATION, BURLINGTON. RESEARCH REPORT. 1951. irreg., no.59, 1990. free. Vermont Agricultural Experiment Station, Morrill Hall, Burlington, VT 05405-0106. FAX 802-656-8642. Ed. LaRae M. Donnellan.
Formerly (until 1968): Vermont. Agricultural Experiment Station, Burlington. Miscellaneous Publications Series.

630   US   ISSN 0083-5714
VERMONT. AGRICULTURAL EXPERIMENT STATION, BURLINGTON. STATION BULLETIN SERIES. 1887. irreg., no.697, 1989. free. Vermont Agricultural Experiment Station, University of Vermont, Morrill Hall, Burlington, VT 05405. FAX 802-656-8432. Ed. LaRae M. Donnellan. **Document type:** bulletin.

630   US   ISSN 0083-5722
VERMONT. AGRICULTURAL EXPERIMENT STATION, BURLINGTON. STATION PAMPHLET SERIES. 1943. irreg., no.43, 1980. free. Vermont Agricultural Experiment Station, University of Vermont, Burlington, VT 05405. FAX 802-656-8432. Ed. LaRae M. Donnellan.

630   US
VERMONT. AGRICULTURAL EXPERIMENT STATION, BURLINGTON. TECHNICAL NOTES. Title varies slightly. 1981. irreg., no.3, 1987. free. Vermont Agricultural Experiment Station, University of Vermont, Burlington, VT 05405. FAX 802-656-8432. Ed. LaRae M. Donnellan. circ. 500.

630   US
VERMONT SCIENCE NEWSLETTER. 1977. 2/yr. free. Vermont Agricultural Experiment Station, University of Vermont, Burlington, VT 05405. FAX 802-656-8432. Ed. LaRae M. Donnellan. **Document type:** newsletter.

630   GW   ISSN 0342-6769
DER VERTRIEBENE LANDVOLK. 1957. m. DM.16. Bauernverband der Vertriebenen e.V., In der Wehrhecke 1, 53125 Bonn, Germany. TEL 49-228-251392. **Document type:** bulletin.
Formerly: Vertriebene Bauer.

630   KZ   ISSN 0042-4684
CODEN: VSNKBD
VESTNIK SEL'SKOKHOZYAISTVENNOI NAUKI KAZAKHSTANA. (Text in Russian; summaries in Kazakh) 1958. m. 33.60 Rub. (Ministerstvo Sel'skogo Khozyaistva) Izdatel'stvo Kainar, Kashgarskaya ul., 64, Alma-Ata, Kazakhstan. charts; illus. circ. 1,650. **Indexed:** Biol.Abstr., Chem.Abstr., Excerp.Med., Helminthol.Abstr., Herb.Abstr., Hort.Abstr., Ind.Vet., Maize Abstr., Pig News & Info., Plant Grow.Reg.Abstr., Protozool.Abstr., Rev.Appl.Entomol., Rice Abstr., Seed Abstr., Soils & Fert., Triticale Abstr., Vet.Bull., World Agri.Econ.& Rural Sociol.Abstr.
—BLDSC (0034.500000); CASDDS; Linda Hall.

VIDA APICOLA; revista de apicultura. see FOOD AND FOOD INDUSTRIES — Bakers And Confectioners

630   PO
VIDA RURAL. 12/yr. R. Antonio Maria Cardoso, n. 15 2oC, 1200 Lisbon, Portugal. TEL 347-0163. FAX 346-9696. Ed. F. Igrejas Mendes. circ. 15,000.

630   FR   ISSN 1245-124X
VIE AGRICOLE DE LA MEUSE. 1945. 50/yr. Maison de l'Agriculture (Verdun), Places St-Paul, 55100 Verdun, France. TEL 29-83-30-30. Ed. M. Lamorlette. circ. 3,800.
Formerly (until 1971): Meuse Agricole (ISSN 1245-1231)

630 334.683   FR   ISSN 0750-4497
VIE AGRICOLE ET COOPERATIVE. 1946. 51/yr. Union Paysanne des Alpes-Maritimes, 7 place Ile de Beaute, 06300 Nice, France. TEL 93-55-32-72. FAX 93-55-93-94. Ed. E. Richaud. circ. 18,000.

630   FR
VIE CHARENTAISE.* 50/yr. Les Charmes de Crage, BP 1243, 16006 Angouleme Cedex, France. TEL 45-61-46-47. Ed. Gerard Seguin. circ. 11,540.

630   FR   ISSN 1163-5479
VIENNE RURALE. 50/yr. 99 av. de la Liberation, 86035 Poitiers Cedex, France. TEL 49-58-55-67. circ. 10,600.

630   US   ISSN 0042-6482
VIRGINIA. DEPARTMENT OF AGRICULTURE AND CONSUMER SERVICES. BULLETIN. 1900. q. free. Department of Agriculture and Consumer Services, Box 1163, Richmond, VA 23218. TEL 804-786-2373. FAX 804-371-7679. URL: http://www.state.va.us/vdacs/vdacs.htm. Ed. Maurcine Baughman. illus.; stat. circ. 4,000. **Document type:** bulletin, government publication.

630 332.64   US   ISSN 1064-4067
VIRGINIA AGRICULTURE COMMODITY NEWSLETTER. w. free. Virginia Department of Agriculture & Consumer Services, 1100 Bank St., Ste. 805, Richmond, VA 23219-3638. TEL 804-786-3947. FAX 804-371-7787. Ed. J.P. Welch. circ. 2,400. (back issues avail.) **Document type:** government publication, newsletter.
Description: Provides livestock, grain, poultry, and egg market prices for the past week to Virginia farmers and agribusinesses.

917.502   US
VIRGINIA FARM BUREAU NEWS. 1940. 10/yr. membership. Virginia Farm Bureau Federation, 12580 W. Creek Pkwy., Box 27552, Richmond, VA 23261. TEL 804-784-1234. FAX 804-784-2588. URL: http://wwww.fb.com/vfbf. Ed. Eric Miller. R&P contact: Eric Miller. TEL 804-784-1321. adv. contact: Shirley Taylor. circ. 130,000. (tabloid format) **Document type:** newspaper.
Description: Covers agriculture, consumer issues, the federation's insurance and other services.

630   US   ISSN 0746-1186
VIRGINIA FARMER. 1982. m. $12 (foreign $25). Rural Press U S A, 7701 Six Forks Rd., Ste. 132, Raleigh, NC 27615. TEL 919-676-3276; 800-477-1737. FAX 919-676-9803. (Subscr. to: Box 150001, Raleigh, NC 27624) Ed. Julie Gochenour; Pub. Jeff Tennant. adv.: B&W page $1346. circ. 18,000. **Document type:** newspaper.
Description: Contains national and local news. Covers dairy, cattle, field crops, tobacco, poultry, the family, and new products.

630   US   ISSN 0096-6088
CODEN: VPSRA3
VIRGINIA POLYTECHNIC INSTITUTE AND STATE UNIVERSITY. VIRGINIA AGRICULTURAL EXPERIMENT STATION. BULLETIN. 1981. irreg. Virginia Polytechnic Institute and State University, Virginia Agricultural Experiment Station, Blacksburg, VA 24061-0402. TEL 540-231-6986. FAX 540-231-4163. circ. 1,000. **Indexed:** Herb.Abstr., Soils & Fert. **Document type:** academic/scholarly publication, bulletin.
—BLDSC (2806.000000); CASDDS; Linda Hall.
Supersedes: Virginia Polytechnic Institute and State University. Research Division. Bulletin; Virginia Polytechnic Institute and State University Research Division. Report (ISSN 0097-1510)
Description: Reports of research conducted by the Virginia Agricultural Experiment Station on crops, soils, animal science, agricultural economics, nutrition, agricultural engineering, entomology, and other agricultural fields.

630   US
CODEN: ISVSE5
VIRGINIA POLYTECHNIC INSTITUTE AND STATE UNIVERSITY. VIRGINIA AGRICULTURAL EXPERIMENT STATION. INFORMATION SERIES. (Print edition ceased 1996) 1982. irreg. free. Virginia Polytechnic Institute and State University, Virginia Agricultural Experiment Station, College of Agriculture and Life Sciences, Blacksburg, VA 24061-0402. TEL 540-231-6986. FAX 540-231-4163. URL: http://www.web.vaes.vt.edu/VAES/Publications/vaesnumpubs.html. circ. 1,000. **Document type:** academic/scholarly publication.
●Available only online.
—Linda Hall.
Formerly: Virginia Polytechnic Institute and State University. College of Agriculture and Life Sciences. Information Series (ISSN 0742-7425)
Description: Provides reviews of scientific literature, historical progress reports, and proceedings of significant scientific symposia; presents scientific data in an informal structure.

630   RU   ISSN 0042-7020
S13   CODEN: VSNAAG
VISNYK SIL'S'KOGOSPODAR'SKOI NAUKI. (Text in Ukrainian) 1957. m. 25.80 Rub. Izdatel'stvo Kniga, 50, Gorky St., 125047 Moscow, Russia. charts; illus.; index. **Indexed:** Anim.Breed.Abstr., Biol.Abstr., Chem.Abstr., Helminthol.Abstr., Hort.Abstr., Pig News & Info., Potato Abstr., Rural Recreat.Tour.Abstr., World Agri.Econ.& Rural Sociol.Abstr.
—CASDDS; Linda Hall.

630   CN   ISSN 0703-8852
VOICE OF THE ESSEX FARMER. 1977. s-m. Can.$22. Leader Publications Ltd., Box 490, Main St., Dresden, ON N0P 1M0, Canada. TEL 519-683-4485. FAX 519-683-4355. Ed. Peter Epp. adv. circ. 3,925.

630   CN   ISSN 0715-4372
VOICE OF THE HURON FARMER. 1981-1988; resumed. s-m. Can.$24($52) Leader Publications Ltd., Box 490, Main St., Dresden, ON N0P 1M0, Canada. TEL 519-683-4485. FAX 519-683-4355. Ed. Peter Epp. circ. 4,140.

630   CN   ISSN 0700-723X
VOICE OF THE KENT FARMER. 1963. s-m. Can.$22. Leader Publications Ltd., Box 490, Main St., Dresden, ON N0P 1M0, Canada. TEL 519-683-4485. FAX 519-683-4355. Ed. Peter Epp. adv. circ. 4,350.

630   CN   ISSN 0703-8860
VOICE OF THE LAMBTON FARMER. 1962. s-m. Can.$22. Leader Publications Ltd., Box 490, Main St., Dresden, ON N0P 1M0, Canada. TEL 519-683-4485. FAX 519-683-4355. Ed. Peter Epp. adv. circ. 4,775.

630   CN   ISSN 0709-1915
VOICE OF THE MIDDLESEX FARMER. 1977. s-m. Can.$22. Leader Publications Ltd., Box 490, Main St., Dresden, ON N0P 1M0, Canada. TEL 519-683-4485. FAX 519-683-4355. Ed. Peter Epp. adv. circ. 6,925.

AGRICULTURE

630   FR   ISSN 1141-2356
LA VOIX DE LA TERRE; le journal rural du Lot-et-Garonne. s-m. (except m. Jul.-Sept.). 340 F.; newsstand price: 16 F. 9 bd. Sylvain-Dumon, 47000 Agen, France. TEL 33-5-53-47-29-50. FAX 33-5-53-47-69-16. Ed. Jean-Michel Delmas; Pub. Marie-France Bonneau. adv.; charts; illus. circ. 8,500. cols./p.: 5; pp./issue: 20. (tabloid format) **Document type:** newspaper.
   Description: Covers labor issues for farmers and agricultural workers in the Lot and Garonne region.

630   FR
VOLONTE PAYSANNE DE L'AVERYRON. w. Carrefour de l'Agriculture, 12006 Rodez, France. circ. 11,050.

630   FR   ISSN 1163-5487
VOLONTE PAYSANNE DU GERS. 1945. 20/yr. 140 F. (effective 1997). Chambre d'Agriculture, Maison de l'Agriculture, Route de Mirande, 32000 Auch, France. TEL 33-5-62617777. FAX 33-5-62617707. Ed. Jean Dauzerre. adv. contact: Jean Dauzere. circ. 18,100.

630   US
VOOR; journal of popular farm science and rural life. (Dutch edition of: Furrow (ISSN 0016-3112)) (Text in Dutch) 1970. 4/yr. free to qualified personnel. Deere & Company, John Deere Rd., Moline, IL 61265. TEL 309-765-8000. Ed. Jean-Claude Hiron. circ. 50,000.

630 179.3   XO   ISSN 0375-5010
SF55.S56   CODEN: VPVZB9
VYSKUMNY USTAV ZIVOCISNEJ VYROBY V NITRE. VEDECKE PRACE/JOURNAL OF FARM ANIMAL SCIENCE. (Text in Slovak; abstracts, tables in English) 1961. a. 500 Sk.($15) Vyskumny Ustav Zivocisnej Vyroby v Nitre - Research Institute of Animal Production at Nitra, Hlohovska 2, 949 92 Nitra, Slovak Republic. TEL 42-87-519030. FAX 42-87-519032. TELEX 87446. Ed. Ladislav Hetenyi. R&P contact: Katarina Smatanova. adv. contact: Katarina Smatanova. circ. 500. **Indexed:** Biol.Abstr. **Document type:** academic/scholarly publication.
   —CASDDS.
   Description: Provides scientific papers on all aspects of animal production in Slovak Republic.
   Refereed Serial

630   NE   ISSN 0169-345X
     CODEN: AUWPET
WAGENINGEN AGRICULTURAL UNIVERSITY PAPERS. 1984. irreg. (2-3/yr.). price varies. Agricultural University Wageningen, P.O. Box 1901, 6700 HB Wageningen, Netherlands. (Dist. by: Backhuys Publishers - Universal Book Services, P.O. Box 321, 2300 AH Leiden, Netherlands. TEL 31-71-5170208. FAX 31-71-5171856) (back issues avail.) **Indexed:** Biol.Abstr., Dairy Sci.Abstr., Ecol.Abstr., Field Crop Abstr., Forest.Abstr., Geo.Abstr.P.G., GeoRef, Herb.Abstr., Hort.Abstr., IDA, Nutr.Abstr., Plant Breed.Abstr., Rev.Appl.Entomol., Rev.Plant Path., Rural Recreat.Tour.Abstr., Soils & Fert., Sport Fish.Abstr., Wild.Rev., World Agri.Econ.& Rural Sociol.Abstr., Zoo.Rec. **Document type:** monographic series.
   —CASDDS; KNAW.
   Formed by the merger of (1918-1984): Landbouwhogeschool Wageningen. Mededelingen (ISSN 0369-0598); (1968-1984): Landbouwhogeschool Wageningen. Miscellaneous Papers (ISSN 0083-6990)

630   US   ISSN 0043-0129
S1
WALLACES FARMER. 1855. 15/yr. $19.95 in Iowa; out-of-state $30. Farm Progress Companies (Subsidiary of: A B C Publishing Companies), 191 S. Gary Ave., Carol Stream, IL 60188. TEL 630-690-5600. FAX 630-462-2869. (Edit. addr.: 6200 Aurora Ave., Ste. 609E, Urbandale, IA 50322-2838. TEL 515-278-6693. FAX 515-278-7797) Ed. Monte N. Sesker. R&P contact: Frank Holdmeyer. adv.: B&W page $5200, color page $5980; trim 7 X 10; adv. contact: Dick Kuhn. illus.; circ. 85,851 (paid); 80,000 (controlled). (also avail. in microform from UMI) **Indexed:** Farm & Garden Ind. **Document type:** trade publication.
   —Linda Hall; UMI; UnCover.

630   SZ
WALLISER BAUERNBLATT. w. Bahnhof FOB, CH-3993 Grengiols, Switzerland. TEL 028-271519. Ed. Peter Gurten. circ. 2,886.

630   CN   ISSN 1197-3625
WARREN'S FARM & RANCH DIRECTORY. 1992. a. Can.$29.95. Box 189, Bethune, SK S0G 0H0, Canada. TEL 306-638-2208. FAX 306-638-3130. Pub. Jim W. Warren. adv.: B&W page Can.$2040; trim 8 1/8 x 10 1/2. circ. 222,000. **Document type:** directory.

630   PL
WARSAW AGRICULTURAL UNIVERSITY. S G G W. ANNALS. AGRICULTURE. (Text mainly in English; occasionally in French, German or Russian; summaries in Polish) 1957. irreg. $10 per no. Szkola Glowna Gospodarstwa Wiejskiego (SGGW) - Warsaw Agricultural University, Ul. Nowoursynowska 166, 02-766 Warsaw, Poland. Ed. B. Gej. **Indexed:** Hort.Abstr., Packag.Sci.Tech. **Document type:** academic/scholarly publication.
   —Linda Hall.
   Former titles: Warsaw Agricultural University. S G G W - A R. Annals. Agriculture (ISSN 0208-5712); (until 1980): Akademia Rolnicza w Warszawie. Zeszyty Naukowe. Rolnictwo (ISSN 0511-1692)

630   UK   ISSN 0955-0283
WARWICKSHIRE FARMER. 1973. m. County Farmers Publications Ltd., 55 Goldington Rd., Bedford MK40 3LU, England. TEL 0234-351401. FAX 0234-328614. Ed. S. Fisher. adv. circ. 2,100.

630   US   ISSN 0195-0673
WASHINGTON AGRICULTURAL RECORD. 1971. w. $65. Box 25001, Georgetown Sta., Washington, DC 20007. TEL 202-333-8190. Ed. John Podewils; Pub. Robert N. Pyle. adv. contact: Robert Pyle. bk.rev. circ. 500. **Document type:** newsletter.

630   US   ISSN 1070-4442
WASHINGTON STATE GRANGE NEWS; informing Grangers since 1912. 1912. m. $4.75. Washington State Grange, Box 1186, Olympia, WA 98507-1186. TEL 360-943-9911. FAX 360-357-3548. Ed. Dave Howard. R&P contact: Pat Nikula. adv.: page $1244.64; adv. contact: Patricia Nikula. bk.rev.; illus.; stat.; circ. 49,000 (paid). cols./p.: 4; pp./issue: 20. (tabloid format; back issues avail.) **Document type:** newspaper.
   Formerly: Washington Grange News (ISSN 0043-0587)
   Description: Informs rural Washington state residents about agricultural trends, legislative news, conservation advances, and the development of cooperatives. Also provides information about the activities of the Grange in Washington.

WATER & ENERGY INTERNATIONAL. see *WATER RESOURCES*

WATER FARMING JOURNAL; America's aquaculture news monthly. see *WATER RESOURCES*

630 323   US   ISSN 1073-4813
THE WEBSTER AGRICULTURAL LETTER. 1981. s-m. $295. Webster Communications Corporation, 1530 N. Key Blvd., PH2, Arlington, VA 22209. TEL 703-525-4512. FAX 703-525-4917. E-mail: websterj@aol.com. Ed. James C. Webster. bk.rev (back issues avail.) **Document type:** newsletter.
   Formerly (until Jan. 1994): Agricultural Credit Letter (ISSN 0887-7521)

630   AT   ISSN 0043-194X
WEEKLY TIMES. 1869. w. Aus.$48.62. Herald & Weekly Times Ltd., 44-74 Flinders St., Melbourne, Vic. 3000, Australia. TEL 61-3-652-1111. FAX 61-3-652-2697. TELEX 30104. Ed. Hugh Jones. adv. contact: Michael Richards. bk.rev.; illus. circ. 87,500. (also avail. in microfilm)
   Description: Covers farming, gardening, country life.

630   UK   ISSN 0040-8050
WELSH FARMER/Y TIR. (Text in English and Welsh) vol. 3, 1973. m. £10 (foreign £12). Farmers' Union of Wales, Llys Amaeth, Queens Sq., Aberystwyth, Dyfed, Wales. TEL 44-1970-612755. FAX 44-1225-774660. Ed. G.L. Thomas. R&P contact: G.L. Thomas. adv. contact: Anna Merritt. bk.rev./ circ. 16,000 (controlled). **Document type:** newspaper.
   Former titles: Y Tir and Welsh Farmer; Y Tir.
   Description: Informs the farming community of the latest developments in agriculture.

630   UK   ISSN 0955-0291
WEST RIDING FARMER. 1957. m. County Farmers Publications Ltd., 55 Goldington Rd., Bedford MK40 3LU, England. TEL 0234-351401. FAX 0234-328614. Ed. A. Hepworth. adv. circ. 3,900.

630 634.9   US
WEST VIRGINIA. AGRICULTURAL AND FORESTRY EXPERIMENT STATION. ANNUAL REPORT. 1980. a. West Virginia University, Agricultural and Forestry Experiment Station, College of Agriculture and Forestry, Morgantown, WV 26506-6108. FAX 304-293-3740. Ed. John Luchok. circ. 3,000. **Document type:** academic/scholarly publication, corporate report.

630 634.9   US
WEST VIRGINIA. AGRICULTURAL AND FORESTRY EXPERIMENT STATION. BULLETIN. 1888. irreg. free. West Virginia University, Agricultural and Forestry Experiment Station, College of Agriculture and Forestry, Morgantown, WV 26506-6108. TEL 304-293-6368. FAX 304-293-3740. **Indexed:** Anim.Breed.Abstr., Biol.Abstr., Curr.Adv.Ecol.Sci., Curr.Cont., Herb.Abstr., Nutr.Abstr. **Document type:** monographic series.

634.9   US
WEST VIRGINIA. AGRICULTURAL AND FORESTRY EXPERIMENT STATION. CIRCULAR. no.119, 1981. irreg. West Virginia University, Agricultural and Forestry Experiment Station, College of Agriculture and Forestry, Morgantown, WV 26506-6108. TEL 304-293-6368. FAX 304-293-3740. Ed.Bd. charts. **Indexed:** Biol.Abstr., Curr.Adv.Ecol.Sci., Forest Prod.Abstr. **Document type:** newsletter.

630 634.9   US
WEST VIRGINIA. AGRICULTURAL AND FORESTRY EXPERIMENT STATION. CURRENT REPORT. 1952. irreg., no.75, 1981. free. West Virginia University, Agricultural and Forestry Experiment Station, College of Agriculture and Forestry, Morgantown, WV 26506-6108. TEL 304-293-6368. FAX 304-293-3740. Ed. Debbie Fast. circ. 5,000. **Indexed:** Biol.Abstr., Curr.Adv.Ecol.Sci., Curr.Cont., Forest Prod.Abstr., Plant Breed.Abstr. **Document type:** academic/scholarly publication.
   —Linda Hall.
   Formerly: West Virginia. Agricultural Experiment Station, Morgantown. Current Report (ISSN 0083-8381)

630 338.1   US   ISSN 0025-3545
WEST VIRGINIA. DEPARTMENT OF AGRICULTURE. MARKET BULLETIN. 1916? s-m. free. Department of Agriculture, Publications Division, State Capitol, 1900 Kanwha Blvd., E., Charleston, WV 25305-0192. TEL 304-348-3708. FAX 304-348-2203. Ed. Howard T. Knotts. adv.; illus.; mkt. circ. 64,000. **Document type:** bulletin, government publication.

630   AT
WESTERN DISTRICT FARMER. 1987. m. Aus.$18. Hamilton Spectator Partnership, P.O. Box 416, Hamilton, Vic. 3300, Australia. TEL 61-3-55721011. FAX 61-3-55723800. Ed. Helen Fry. R&P contact: Richard Beks. adv.: page Aus.$1406.30; trim 445 x 290; adv. contact: Norah Franc. charts; illus. circ. 24,000. (tabloid format) **Document type:** newspaper.
   Description: Provides information on broadacre and intensive farming for farmers within the Western District of Victoria.

630   CN   ISSN 0043-4094
WESTERN PRODUCER. 1923. w. Can.$39 (U.S. $70; elsewhere Can.$250) (effective 1997). Western Producer Publications (Subsidiary of: Saskatchewan Wheat Pool), P.O. Box 2500, Saskatoon, SK S7K 2C4, Canada. TEL 306-665-3500. FAX 306-653-1255. E-mail: newsroom@producer.com; URL: http://www.producer.com. Ed. Garry Fairbairn; Pub. Allan Laughland. R&P contact: Garry Fair. adv. contact: Darryl Thompson. bk.rev.; charts; mkt.; illus.; circ. 96,324 (paid). (also avail. in microfilm from CML,SOC) **Indexed:** Can.B.P.I. **Document type:** newspaper.
   —CISTI.
   Description: News for farms families.

AGRICULTURE

630   US
WHATCOM COUNTY FARM REVIEW. 1960. m. $23. Lewis Publishing Co., 113 N. Sixth St., Box 153, Lynden, WA 98264. FAX 360-398-1731. Ed. Calvin Bratt; Pub. Michael Lewis. adv. contact: Maggy Jones. charts; illus.; stat. circ. 14,000. (back issues avail.) **Document type:** newspaper.

630   UK   ISSN 0143-9596
WHAT'S NEW IN FARMING. 1977. m. $150. Morgan-Grampian (Farming) Press Ltd. (Subsidiary of: Morgan-Grampian plc), Morgan-Grampian House, 30 Calderwood St., London SE18 6QH, England. TEL 081-855-7777. FAX 081-854-7476. Ed. Donald Taylor. adv. contact: Alistair Fitzpatrick. circ. 48,000. **Document type:** trade publication.
—CCC.

630   CN   ISSN 1187-2179
WHO'S WHO IN BRITISH COLUMBIA AGRICULTURE. 1978. a. Can.$10. Country Life Ltd., 3308 King George Hwy., Surrey, BC V4P 1A8, Canada. TEL 604-536-7622. FAX 604-536-5677. Ed. D.M. Young. adv.
Description: A listing of personnel in government, academia, farm associations, finance, agribusiness and consulting firms involved in agriculture.

WHO'S WHO IN LIVE ANIMAL TRADE & TRANSPORT. see TRANSPORTATION

631   PL   ISSN 0137-3838
WIADOMOSCI ZIELARSKIE.* 1958. m. $18. (Stowarzyszenie Naukowo-Techniczne Inzynierow i Technikow Przemyslu Spozywczego) Wydawnictwo Hortpress, Spolka z o.o., Ul. Zielna, paw.106, 00-108 Warsaw, Poland. (Dist. by: Ars Polona-Ruch, Krakowskie Przedmiescie 7, Warsaw, Poland) (Co-sponsors: Zrzeszenie Producentow Roslin Zielarskich; Zjednoczenie Przemyslu Zielarskiego "Herbapol") circ. 9,600. **Indexed:** AgroLibrex.

630   UK   ISSN 0043-566X
WILTSHIRE FARMER. 1962. m. County Farmers Publications Ltd., 55 Goldington Rd., Bedford MK40 3LU, England. TEL 0234-351401. FAX 0234-328614. Ed. T. Bawley. adv. circ. 1,950.

630   US   ISSN 0043-6356
WISCONSIN AGRICULTURIST. 1849. 15/yr. $17.95. Farm Progress Companies (Subsidiary of: A B C Publishing Companies), 191 S. Gary Ave., Carol Stream, IL 60188. TEL 630-690-5600. FAX 630-462-2869. (Edit. addr.: 2820 Walton Commons W., Ste. 136, Madison, WI 53704-6797. TEL 608-224-1030. FAX 608-224-1044) Ed. Al Morrow. adv.: B&W page $3400, color page $3910; trim 7 X 10; adv. contact: Steven Keppy. bk.rev.; circ. 48,335 (paid). (also avail. in microfilm) **Document type:** trade publication.
—Linda Hall.
Description: Emphasizes management information for farmers.

630   US
WISCONSIN STATE FARMER. 1956. w. $15. Box 152, Waupaca, WI 54981. TEL 715-258-5546. FAX 715-258-8162. Ed. Carla Hagenow. adv. circ. 30,000.

630   UK   ISSN 0955-0305
WORCESTERSHIRE FARMER & RECORD. 1925. m. County Farmers Publications Ltd., 55 Goldington Rd., Bedford MK40 3LU, England. TEL 0234-351401. FAX 0234-328614. Ed. P. Hudson. adv. circ. 2,200.
Formerly: Worcestershire Record; **Incorporates:** Worcestershire Grower.

WORKING PAPERS ON WOMEN IN INTERNATIONAL DEVELOPMENT. see BUSINESS AND ECONOMICS — International Development And Assistance

630   US   ISSN 1052-0279
S21.F6
WORLD AGRICULTURAL PRODUCTION. 1979. m. $38. U.S. Department of Agriculture, Foreign Agricultural Service, Information Division, Rm. 5920-S, Washington, DC 20250-1000. TEL 202-720-7937. (Subscr. to: Superintendent of Documents, U.S. Government Printing Office, Washington, DC 20402. TEL 202-512-1800. FAX 202-512-2250) (also avail. in microfiche from CIS; reprint service avail. from CIS) **Indexed:** Amer.Stat.Ind. (1979-). **Document type:** government publication.
● Also available online. Vendor(s): Information Access Co.
Former titles (until 1987): World Crop Production (ISSN 1046-3224); (until 1986): Foreign Agriculture Circular. World Crop Production (ISSN 0271-3691)

630   FR   ISSN 1011-9779
WORLD FARMERS' TIMES. (Text in English) bi-m. 180 F.($30) International Federation of Agricultural Producers - Federation Internationale des Producteurs Agricoles, 21 rue Chaptal, 75009 Paris, France. TEL 45-26-05-53. FAX 48-74-72-12. TELEX 281210. (Co-sponsor: World Farmers' Times Foundation, SZ) **Indexed:** Biol.Dig., Curr.Cont., Helminthol.Abstr., IDA. **Document type:** consumer publication.
Incorporates: World Agriculture - I F A P News; Formed by the merger of: World Agriculture - Agriculture dans le Monde (ISSN 0043-8227); (1952-1980): I F A P News - F I P A Nouvelles (ISSN 0018-9650)
Description: Promotes the discussion of public policy issues in agriculture and food for decision-makers at national and international levels.

630   UN   ISSN 0259-8213
HD9275.A1
WORLD MARKET FOR DAIRY PRODUCTS. (Editions in English, French, Spanish) 1980. a. 25 Fr. General Agreement on Tariffs and Trade, Centre William Rappard, 154 rue de Lausanne, CH-1211 Geneva 21, Switzerland. TEL 022-7395208. FAX 022-739-5458. (also avail. in microfiche from CIS) **Indexed:** IIS.
Description: Survey of trade, production, consumption and price trends in fresh milk, milk powders, butter and cheeses.

WORLD METEOROLOGICAL ORGANIZATION. COMMISSION FOR AGRICULTURAL METEOROLOGY. ABRIDGED FINAL REPORT OF THE (NO.) SESSION. see METEOROLOGY

630   US   ISSN 1071-0272
WYOMING AGRICULTURE. 1938. m. $1 to members. Wyoming Farm Bureau Federation, 406 S. 21st St., Box 1348, Laramie, WY 82070. TEL 307-745-4835. FAX 307-721-7790. Ed. Suzy Noecker. R&P contact: Suzy Noecker. TEL 307-721-7728. adv. contact: Suzy Noecker. circ. 8,000 (controlled). (back issues avail.) **Document type:** newspaper, trade publication.
Description: Contains news for agriculture producers regarding production, as well as political and regulatory issues in Wyoming. Lists Wyoming Farm Bureau events.

630   CH   ISSN 1015-8367
XIANGJIAN XIAOLU. 1975. m. NT.$1000($75) Harvest Farm Magazine, 14 Wenchow St., Taipei, Taiwan, Republic of China. TEL 02-362-8148. FAX 02-363-6724. Ed. Ming-Tang Kao. adv.; charts; illus.; index. circ. 15,000. (back issues avail.)
Formerly (until 1989): Nongye Zhoukan - Agri-Week (ISSN 0379-4040)
Description: Consumer-oriented magazine that covers farm products, agriculture, tourism, food and health, and home gardening.

XIANGZHEN QIYE YU NONGCHANG GUANLI. see BUSINESS AND ECONOMICS — Small Business

630   CC   ISSN 1004-1389
XIBEI NONGYE XUEBAO/ACTA AGRICULTURAE BOREALI - OCCIDENTALIS SINICA. (Text in Chinese or English; abstracts in English) 1992. q. $16 (foreign $20). Xibei Nongye Xuebao Bianjibu, Shaanxi Sheng Nongye Kexueyuan Nei, Yangling Zheng, Xianyang, Shaanxi 712100, People's Republic of China. TEL 7088401. (Dist. overseas by: China International Book Trading Corp., P.O. Box 399, Beijing 100044, P.R. China) Ed. Qikun Wang. illus. pp./issue: 96. **Document type:** academic/scholarly publication.
Description: Covers the latest technological developments in agriculture.

630   CC   ISSN 1000-2642
                              CODEN: XNDXEQ
XINAN NONGYE DAXUE XUEBAO/SOUTHWEST AGRICULTURAL UNIVERSITY. JOURNAL. (Text in Chinese) 1985. bi-m. Xinan Nongye Daxue, Xuebao Bianjibu, Chongqing, People's Republic of China. **Document type:** academic/scholarly publication.

630   330.9   CC
XINCUN. (Text in Chinese) 1981. m. Y15 (effective 1989). Jilin Renmin Chubanshe, Qikan Bu - Jilin People's Publishing House, Stalin Dajie, P.O. Box 20, Changcun, Jilin, People's Republic of China. TEL 884490. circ. 55,000.

630   JA   ISSN 0513-1715
                            CODEN: YDNGAU
YAMAGUCHI UNIVERSITY. FACULTY OF AGRICULTURE. BULLETIN. 1950. a. Yamaguchi Daigaku, Nogakubu - Yamaguchi University, Faculty of Agriculture, 1677-1 Yoshida, Yamaguchi-shi, Yamaguchi-ken 753, Japan. Ed. Noriyuki Fujita. **Indexed:** Bio-Contr.News & Info., Biol.Abstr., Field Crop Abstr., Herb.Abstr., Ind.Vet., Plant Breed.Abstr., Rev.Plant Path., Soils & Fert., Vet.Bull. **Document type:** academic/scholarly publication, bulletin.
—CASDDS.

630   UK   ISSN 0955-0313
YORK COUNTY FARMER. 1960. m. County Farmers Publications Ltd., 55 Goldington Rd., Bedford MK40 3LU, England. TEL 0234-351401. FAX 0234-328614. Ed. A. Hepworth. adv. circ. 1,650.
Formerly: North Riding (No.2) Farmer.

630   374   US
YOUNG FARMER UPDATE. 1985. 2/yr. free. National Young Farmer Educational Association, 5632 Mt. Vernon Memorial Hwy., Box 15160, Alexandria, VA 22309. TEL 703-799-0594. FAX 703-360-5524. Ed. Sandy Coons. circ. 4,000. **Document type:** newsletter.
Description: Covers programs for adult education in agriculture and association activities.

630   US
YOUR ILLINOIS F F A. (Future Farmers of America) 1940. 3/yr. free. Illinois F F A, Box 50, Roanoke, IL 61561. TEL 309-923-7413. FAX 309-923-7618. circ. 17,000 (controlled).
Description: News about the Illinois FFA and affiliated groups for members, alumni and friends.

YUANZINENG NONGYE YINGYONG/APPLICATIONS OF ATOMIC ENERGY IN AGRICULTURE. see ENERGY — Nuclear Energy

631.091   CK   ISSN 0120-1824
YUCA BOLETIN INFORMATIVO. English edition: Cassava Newsletter (ISSN 0259-3688); French edition: Manioc Bulletin d'Information. 1977-199?; suspended. 2/yr. free to qualified personnel. Centro Internacional de Agricultura Tropical, Unidad de Comunicaciones - International Center for Tropical Agriculture, Communications Unit, Apdo. Aereo 6713, Cali, Colombia. TEL 57-2-4450000. FAX 57-2-4450073. E-mail: CIAT@CGNET.COM. Ed. Carlos Iglesias. circ. 2,200 (controlled). **Indexed:** Agri.Eng.Abstr., Curr.Adv.Ecol.Sci., Field Crop Abstr., Food Sci.& Tech.Abstr., Plant Breed.Abstr. **Document type:** newsletter.
Description: Provides progress reports from cassava researchers and developers in tropical countries, interchange of technical notes, and other news.

AGRICULTURE

630   GW   ISSN 0946-6614
Z M P AGRARMARKT; Nachrichten fuer Verbraucher und Wirtschaft. 4/wk. Zentrale Markt- und Preisberichtstelle GmbH, Rochusstr. 2, 53123 Bonn, Germany. TEL 49-228-9777173. FAX 49-228-9777179. **Document type:** bulletin.

630   GW   ISSN 0946-6630
Z M P NACHRICHTEN. 2/wk. Zentrale Markt- und Preisberichtstelle GmbH, Rochusstr. 2, 53123 Bonn, Germany. TEL 49-228-9777176. FAX 49-228-9777179. **Document type:** bulletin.

630   PK
ZARAAT. (Text in English and Sindhi) 1982. q. Rs.50. Sind Agriculture University, Zaraat Publication Committee, Tandojam, Hyderabad, Sind, Pakistan. Ed. Dr. M.Y. Panhwer. adv.; bk.rev. circ. 1,000. **Document type:** academic/scholarly publication.
    Description: Scientific information about agriculture.

630   GW   ISSN 0044-2194
HD1401
ZEITSCHRIFT FUER AGRARGESCHICHTE UND AGRARSOZIOLOGIE. 1953. s-a. DM.116 (members DM.50) (effective 1996). (Gesellschaft fuer Agrargeschichte und Agrarsoziologie) D L G Verlags GmbH, Eschborner Landstr. 122, 60489 Frankfurt a.M., Germany. TEL 069-24788-0. FAX 069-24788480. Ed. K. Herrmann. bk.rev.; charts; illus.; stat.; index. circ. 900. **Indexed:** Amer.Hist.& Life (1987-1990), (1993-), Bibl.Cart., Hist.Abstr. (1987-1990), (1993-), IBR, P.A.I.S.For.Lang.Ind., Rural Recreat.Tour.Abstr., World Agri.Econ.& Rural Sociol.Abstr. **Document type:** trade publication.
—SWETS. **CCC**.

630   GW   ISSN 0049-8599
ZEITSCHRIFT FUER AUSLAENDISCHE LANDWIRTSCHAFT/QUARTERLY JOURNAL OF INTERNATIONAL AGRICULTURE/JOURNAL TRIMESTRIEL D'AGRICULTURE INTERNATIONALE. (Text in German, English; summaries in English, French, German) 1962. q. DM.183 (foreign DM.187); members DM.148 (foreign DM.152) (effective 1996). D L G Verlags GmbH, Eschborner Landstr. 122, 60489 Frankfurt a.M., Germany. TEL 069-24788-0. FAX 069-24788480. Ed. R. Sachs. bk.rev.; abstr.; bibl.; stat.; index. circ. 600. **Indexed:** Abstr.Rural Dev.Trop., Anim.Breed.Abstr., Field Crop Abstr., Geo.Abstr.P.G., Herb.Abstr., IBR, IDA, Int.Lab.Doc., Maize Abstr., P.A.I.S.For.Lang.Ind., Potato Abstr., Rice Abstr., Rural Devel.Abstr., Rural Ext.Educ.& Tr.Abstr., Rural Recreat.Tour.Abstr., World Agri.Econ.& Rural Sociol.Abstr. **Document type:** trade publication.
—BLDSC (7191.600000); Ei; SWETS; UnCover. **CCC**.

630   XR   ISSN 0044-3883
S269.C93
ZEMEDELSKA TECHNIKA/AGRICULTURAL TECHNOLOGY; vedecky casopis. (Text in Czech, English, German, Slovak; summaries in Czech, English, Slovak) 1954. q. $51 in Europe; elsewhere $53 (effective 1997). Ustav Zemedelskych a Potravinarskych Informaci, Slezska 7, 120 56 Prague 2, Czech Republic. TEL 420-2-24257939. FAX 420-2-24253938. E-mail: uzlk@uzpi.cz. Ed. J. Vaclavickova. adv.; bk.rev. circ. 450. **Indexed:** Agri.Eng.Abstr., Dairy Sci.Abstr., Field Crop Abstr., Herb.Abstr., Ind.Vet., Pig News & Info., Plant Breed.Abstr., Seed Abstr., Triticale Abstr., World Agri.Econ.& Rural Sociol.Abstr. **Document type:** academic/scholarly publication.
—BLDSC (9499.560000).

630   XR
ZEMEDELSKE AKTUALITY/AGRICULTURAL NEWS. 1965. $60 (effective 1997). Ustav Zemedelskych a Potravinarskych Informaci, Slezska 7, 120 56 Prague 2, Czech Republic. TEL 420-2-24257939. FAX 420-2-24253938. E-mail: uzlk@uzpi.cz. Ed. I. Fantysova. circ. 1,000. **Document type:** academic/scholarly publication.
    Former titles: Zemedelske - Polnohospodarske Aktuality; (until 1989): Zemedelska Aktuality ze Sveta (ISSN 0862-2310); Zemedelsky Aktuality (ISSN 0513-9259).
    Description: Contains short articles on the latest results in the scientific and technical development in Czech Republic and abroad.

630   RU   ISSN 0044-3913
S13   CODEN: ZMLDAH
ZEMLEDELIE. 1939. bi-m. $75 (effective 1998). Sadovaya-Spasskaya, 18, 107807 Moscow, Russia. TEL 7-095-2072466. FAX 7-095-2072870. (Dist. by: Mezhdunarodnaya Kniga, B. Yakimanka 39, 117049 Moscow, Russia. TEL 7-095-2384967. FAX 7-095-2384634) Ed. Vladilen A. Ivanov. adv.; bk.rev.; bibl.; charts; illus.; stat.; index. circ. 11,170. **Indexed:** Biol.Abstr., Chem.Abstr., Field Crop Abstr., Herb.Abstr., Plant Breed.Abstr., Sorghum & Millets Abstr., Triticale Abstr.
—BLDSC (0072.000000); CASDDS; Linda Hall.

630   SZ
ZENTRALBLATT LAND- UND MILCHWIRTSCHAFT. w. Weststr. 10, CH-3000 Bern 6, Switzerland. TEL 031-449311. FAX 031-449236. TELEX 912395. Ed. Anton Haas. circ. 63,524.

630   CC   ISSN 1000-2111
         CODEN: ZNDXEE
ZHEJIANG NONGYE DAXUE XUEBAO/ZHEJIANG UNIVERSITY OF AGRICULTURE. JOURNAL. (Text in Chinese) 1956. bi-m. $60 (effective 1996 & 1996). Zhejiang Nongye Daxue - Zhejiang University of Agriculture, Huajiachi, Hangzhou, Zhejiang 310029, People's Republic of China. TEL 0571-6041733. FAX 0571-6049815. E-mail: AU lidb@Zunet.ihep.ac.cn. (Dist. overseas by: China International Book Trading Corp., P.O. Box 399, Beijing, P.R. China. FAX 8412023) Ed. Li Debao. (also avail. in microfiche; reprint service avail.) **Document type:** academic/scholarly publication.
    Description: Publishes research papers on vegetable culture, horticulture, tea science, agricultural microbiology, crop science, biotechnology, soil science and agricultural engineering.

630   CC   ISSN 0528-9017
ZHEJIANG NONGYE KEXUE/ZHEJIANG AGRICULTURAL SCIENCE. (Text in Chinese) bi-m. Zhejiang Nongye Kexueyuan - Zhejiang Academy of Agricultural Science, 48 Shiqiao Lu, Hangzhou, Zhejiang 310021, People's Republic of China. TEL 42701. (Co-sponsor: Zhejiang Nongye Daxue) Ed. Zhou Jiefang. **Indexed:** Seed Abstr. **Document type:** academic/scholarly publication.

630   CC   ISSN 1000-8047
ZHONGGUO GUOSHU/CHINA'S FRUIT TREES. (Text in Chinese) 1959. q. Y12($16) (effective 1998). Zhongguo Nongye Kexueyuan, Guoshu Yanjiusuo - Chinese Academy of Agricultural Sciences, Fruit Tree Research Institute, Wenquan, Xingcheng, Liaoning 121600, People's Republic of China. TEL 86-429-515-2273. Ed. Fengyu Zhao. adv. contact: Weiyi Weng. circ. 20,000. **Document type:** academic/scholarly publication.
—BLDSC (3180.164000).
    Description: Covers fruit production, and studies and advances of research on fruit trees.

630 951   CC   ISSN 1000-4459
S471.C6
ZHONGGUO NONG-SHI/AGRICULTURAL HISTORY OF CHINA. (Text in Chinese) 1982. q. Y12($24) (Zhongguo Nongye Yichan Yanjiushi - Institute for Chinese Agricultural Heritage) Nongye Chubanshe - China Agricultural Press, 2, Nongzhanguan Beilou, Chaoyang District, Beijing 100026, People's Republic of China. TEL 5005894. (Dist. in US by: China Books & Periodicals, Inc., 2929 24th St., San Francisco, CA 94110. TEL 415-282-2994) (Co-sponsor: Zhongguo Nongye Lishi Xuehui - Chinese Society of Agricultural History) circ. 2,000. **Indexed:** Amer.Hist.& Life (1992-), Hist.Abstr. (1992-).

ZHONGGUO NONGCUN JINRONG/CHINA RURAL FINANCE. see *BUSINESS AND ECONOMICS — Banking And Finance*

630   CC   ISSN 1002-381X
ZHONGGUO NONGJI TUIGUANG/CHINA AGRO-TECHNOLOGY EXTENSION. (Text in Chinese) 1985. bi-m. Y15. Zhongguo Nongji Tuiguang Xiehui - Chinese Agricultural Technology Extension Association, 11 Nongzhanguan Nanli, Beijing 100026, People's Republic of China. TEL 86-10-6419-4515. FAX 86-10-6502-5146. TELEX 22233 MAGR CN. (Co-sponsor: Zhongguo Nongye Jishu Tuiguang Fuwu Zongxing - National Agricultural Technology Extension & Service Center) Ed. Li Liqiu. circ. 90,000. **Document type:** government publication, newsletter.
    Formerly (until Aug. 1991): Nongji Tuiguang, Agricultural Technology Marketing.
    Description: Introduces and promotes agricultural technologies.

630 636   CC   ISSN 0578-1752
S471.C6   CODEN: CKNYAR
ZHONGGUO NONGYE KEXUE/CHINESE AGRICULTURAL SCIENCES. (Text in Chinese; abstracts in English) 1960. bi-m. $6.72 per no. Zhongguo Nongye Kexueyuan - Chinese Academy of Agricultural Sciences, 30 Baishiqiao Lu, Beijing 100081, People's Republic of China. TEL 8314433. FAX 8315645. Ed. Liu Gengling. circ. 15,000. **Indexed:** Chem.Abstr., Helminthol.Abstr. **Document type:** academic/scholarly publication.
—BLDSC (8169.300000); CASDDS; Linda Hall.

ZHONGGUO NONGYE QIXIANG/CHINESE AGRICULTURAL METEOROLOGY. see *METEOROLOGY*

630   CC   ISSN 1001-4187
ZHONGGUO TIANCAI/CHINESE BEETS. (Text in Chinese) q. Zhongguo Nongye Kexueyuan, Tiancai Yanjiusuo - Chinese Academy of Agriculture, Beet Research Institute, Hulan Xian (County), Heilongjiang 150501, People's Republic of China. Ed. Cai Bao.

630   CC   ISSN 1002-0551
ZHONGGUO TIANCAI TANGYE/CHINA BEET & SUGAR. (Text in Chinese) bi-m. (Qinggongye Bu, Tiancai Tangye Kexue Yanjiusuo - Ministry of Light Industry, Sugarbeet and Sugar Institute) Tiancai Tangye Bianjibu, 333 Xuegu Rd., Harbin, Heilongjiang 150086, People's Republic of China. TEL 86-451-6661826. FAX 86-451-6662881. Ed. Qin Wenxin. adv.: B&W page $1000, color page $4000. circ. 3,000.
    Formerly (until 1991): Tiancia Tangye - Beet and Sugar (ISSN 1000-6451)

638.1   CC   ISSN 0412-4367
ZHONGGUO YANGFENG/APICULTURE OF CHINA. (Text in Chinese) 1957. bi-m. $14 (effective 1996). Zhongguo Nongye Kexueyuan, Yangfeng Yanjiusuo - Chinese Academy of Agricultural Science, Institute of Apicultural Research, Xiangshan, Beijing 100093, People's Republic of China. TEL 81-10-6259-1473. FAX 86-10-6259-1620. Ed. Li Jiyong. adv.: page $1000; adv. contact: Ye Zhensheng. circ. 20,000 (paid). (reprint service avail.) **Document type:** academic/scholarly publication.
    ●Also available online. Vendor(s): Knight-Ridder Information, Inc.
—BLDSC (1568.540000).

630   RH
ZIMBABWE. AGRICULTURAL DEVELOPMENT AUTHORITY ANNUAL REPORT AND ACCOUNTS. a. Agricultural and Rural Development Authority, P.O. Box CY1420, Causeway, Harare, Zimbabwe. TEL 263-4-700095. FAX 263-4-705847. TELEX 22272 ZW. **Document type:** government publication.
    Formerly: Zimbabwe. Agricultural and Rural Development Authority. Annual Report and Accounts

AGRICULTURE — ABSTRACTING, BIBLIOGRAPHIES, STATISTICS

630   RH   ISSN 1017-5156
CODEN: ZIAJEO
ZIMBABWE AGRICULTURAL JOURNAL. 1903. bi-m. Z.$2. Ministry of Lands, Agriculture and Rural Resettlement, Research and Specialist Services, Information Services, P.O. Box 8108, Causeway, Harare, Zimbabwe. Ed. R.J. Fenner. adv.; bk.rev.; charts; illus.; index. circ. 1,200. **Indexed:** Anim.Breed.Abstr., Apic.Abstr., Biol.Abstr., Chem.Abstr., Curr.Adv.Ecol.Sci., Curr.Cont., Entomol.Abstr., Field Crop Abstr., Food Sci.& Tech.Abstr., Geo.Abstr., Helminthol.Abstr., Herb.Abstr., Hort.Abstr., Ind.S.A.Per., Ind.Vet., Nutr.Abstr., Plant Breed.Abstr., Rev.Appl.Entomol., Rev.Plant.Path., Rural Recreat.Tour.Abstr., Soils & Fert., Tob.Abstr., Vet.Bull., Weed Abstr., World Agri.Econ.& Rural Sociol.Abstr., Zoo.Rec. **Document type:** academic/scholarly publication.
—Linda Hall.
 Formerly: Rhodesia Agricultural Journal (ISSN 0035-4686)

630   RH   ISSN 0251-1045
S338.Z55   CODEN: ZJARDK
THE ZIMBABWE JOURNAL OF AGRICULTURAL RESEARCH. 1963. s-a. Z.$10($16) Ministry of Lands, Agriculture and Rural Resettlement, Research and Specialist Services, Information Services, P.O. Box 8108, Causeway, Harare, Zimbabwe. (Co-sponsor: Southern African Centre for Co-operation in Agricultural Research) Ed. R.J. Fenner. bk.rev.; charts; illus.; cum.index. circ. 1,000. (back issues avail.) **Indexed:** Anim.Breed.Abstr., Biol.Abstr., Chem.Abstr., Curr.Adv.Ecol.Sci., Curr.Cont., Energy Ind., Energy Info.Abstr., Entomol.Abstr., Excerp.Med., Field Crop Abstr., Food Sci.& Tech.Abstr., Forest.Abstr., Forest Prod.Abstr., Geo.Abstr., Helminthol.Abstr., Herb.Abstr., Hort.Abstr., Ind.S.A.Per., Ind.Vet., Nutr.Abstr., Plant Breed.Abstr., Rev.Appl.Entomol., Rev.Plant.Path., Soils & Fert., Tob.Abstr., Vet.Bull., Weed Abstr., Zoo.Rec. **Document type:** government publication, academic/scholarly publication.
—BLDSC (9513.240000); Linda Hall; UMI.
 Former titles (until 1980): Rhodesian Journal of Agricultural Research (ISSN 0035-4813); (until 1967): Rhodesia, Zambia and Malawi Journal of Agricultural Research (ISSN 0370-8101)

630   BA
AL-ZIRA'A FIL-ALAM AL-ARABI/AGRICULTURE IN THE ARAB WORLD. (Text in Arabic) m. Falcon Publishing, P.O. Box 5028, Manama, Bahrain. TEL 253162. FAX 259694. TELEX 8917.

630   SZ
ZUERCHER BAUER. w. Nueschelerstr. 35, CH-8023 Zurich, Switzerland. TEL 01-2117379. FAX 01-2121723. Ed. Hannes Ringger. circ. 13,000.

630   CC   ISSN 1001-7283
ZUOWU ZAZHI. (Text in Chinese) q. Zhongguo Zuowu Xuehui - Chinese Society of Crop Science, Zhongguo Nongye Kexueyuan, 30 Baishiqiao Lu, Beijing 100081, People's Republic of China. TEL 891731. Ed. Wang Hengli.
 Refereed Serial

ŻYCIE GOSPODARCZE; tygodnik spoleczno-gospodarczy. see BUSINESS AND ECONOMICS

630 310   GW
X 1 IHR PARTNER. 1967. bi-m. Profil Werbe- & Verlagsgesellschaft, Breitenweg 29-33, 28195 Bremen, Germany. Ed.Bd. circ. 5,300.

AGRICULTURE — Abstracting, Bibliographies, Statistics

B C BLUE BOOK: U S AND CANADIAN FARM PUBLICATIONS. (Audit Bureau of Circulations) see PUBLISHING AND BOOK TRADE

630 016 011   BU   ISSN 0324-1068
CODEN: VMDNAV
ABSTRACTS OF BULGARIAN SCIENTIFIC LITERATURE. AGRICULTURE AND FORESTRY. VETERINARY MEDICINE. Key Title: Veterinarno-Medicinski Nauki. 1956. q. 1.30 lv. per no. (Akademiia na Selskostopanskite Nauki) Publishing House of the Bulgarian Academy of Sciences, Acad. G. Bonchev St., Bldg. 6, 1113 Sofia, Bulgaria. (Dist. by: Hemus, 6, Rouski Blvd., 1000 Sofia, Bulgaria) bibl.; index. circ. 1,280. (reprint service avail. from IRC) **Indexed:** Agri.Eng.Abstr., Anim.Breed.Abstr., Chem.Abstr., Dairy Sci.Abstr., Field Crop Abstr., Forest.Abstr., Forest Prod.Abstr., Helminthol.Abstr., Herb.Abstr., Ind.Med., Ind.Vet., Pig News & Info., Plant Breed.Abstr., Protozool.Abstr., Rev.Med.& Vet.Mycol., Rev.Plant Path., Vet.Bull., VITIS, Weed Abstr. **Document type:** abstracting/indexing.
—CASDDS.

630   NE   ISSN 0929-7790
ACTUELE ONTWIKKELING VAN BEDRIJFSRESULTATEN EN INKOMENS. 1993. a. fl.31. Landbouw-Economisch Instituut, Burg. Patijnlaan 19, 2585 BE The Hague, Netherlands. TEL 31-70-3308330. FAX 31-70-3615624. E-mail: postmaster@lei.dlo.nl; URL: http://www.lei.dlo.nl/lei. Ed. C.J.A.M. de Bont. circ. 600. **Document type:** government publication.
 Formed by the merger of (1982-1992): Inkomensontwikkeling in de Agrarische Sector (ISSN 0921-4119); (1983-1992): Raming van de Bedrijfsuitkomsten van de Glastuinbouw- en Champignonbedrijven (ISSN 0921-4267) & Prognose cum Bedrijfsuitkomsten op Akkerbouw- en Veehouderijbedrijven (ISSN 1381-3463); Which was formerly (1975-1983): Prognose van Bedrijfsuitkomsten op Akkerbouw- en Rundveehouderijbedrijven (ISSN 0921-4143)
 Description: Provides an analysis of actual income development in Dutch agriculture.

630   NE   ISSN 0002-1075
AGRARISCH WEEKOVERZICHT. 1953. w. price varies. Landbouw-Economisch Instituut, Burg. Patijnlaan 19, 2585 BE The Hague, Netherlands. TEL 31-70-3308330. FAX 31-70-3615624. E-mail: postmaster@lei.dlo.nl; URL: http://www.lei.dlo.nl/lei. circ. 3,500. **Document type:** government publication.
 Description: Statistical data on prices of agricultural commodities, fodders, and fodder crops.

630   RM   ISSN 1223-7531
AGRICULTURA SI SILVICULTURA ROMANIEI IN PROFIL TERITORIAL/ROMANIA'S AGRICULTURE AND SYLVICULTURE AT THE TERRITORIAL LEVEL. (Text in Rumanian; table of contents in English) biennial. $18 (effective 1997). Comisia Nationala pentru Statistica - National Commission for Statistics, Bd. Libertatii 16, Sector 3, 70542 Bucharest, Rumania. TEL 40-1-6143371. FAX 40-1-3124873. **Document type:** government publication.
 Description: Presents statistics per total and at territorial level. Data on agriculture, crop areas and animal production.

630 016   TZ   ISSN 0251-2440
AGRICULTURAL ABSTRACTS FOR TANZANIA. 1978. s-a. $28. Library Services Board, National Documentation Centre, P.O. Box 9283, Dar es Salaam, Tanzania. TEL 255-51-150048-9. Ed. D.A. Sekimang'a. circ. 200.
 Formerly: Abstracting and Indexing Bulletin for Agricultural and Animal Husbandry.

630 613.1   US   ISSN 1063-1151
S494.5.B563
AGRICULTURAL & ENVIRONMENTAL BIOTECHNOLOGY ABSTRACTS. 1984. bi-m. $345 (foreign $365). Cambridge Scientific Abstracts, 7200 Wisconsin Ave., 6th Fl., Bethesda, MD 20814. TEL 301-961-6700. FAX 301-961-6720. E-mail: market@csa.com; URL: http://www.csa.com. Ed. Deborah Whitman; Pub. Ted Caris. **Document type:** abstracting/indexing.
 •Also available online. Vendor(s): Knight-Ridder Information, Inc. (File no. 76/Life Sciences Collection), STN International (LIFESCI).
 Also available on CD-ROM. Producer(s): Knight-Ridder, Inc., NISC, SilverPlatter Information, Inc.
—BLDSC (0742.760000); CISTI.
 Supersedes in part (in 1993): Biotechnology Research Abstracts (ISSN 0733-5709)
 Description: Covers basic research and applications of biotechnology techniques in the food industry, agriculture and the environment.

630 636.089   AT   ISSN 0816-1623
AGRICULTURAL AND VETERINARY PRODUCT INDEX. 1984. a. Aus.$25 (effective 1996). M I M S Australia, 48 Albany St., Crows Nest, N.S.W. 2065, Australia. TEL 02-438-3588. Ed. Linda H. Badewitz-Dodd. R&P contact: Chris Wills. adv. contact: M. McCaffrey. circ. 17,000.
 Description: Lists all chemicals and on-prescription drugs available in Australia.

630 620 016   UK   ISSN 0308-8863
Z5074.E6
AGRICULTURAL ENGINEERING ABSTRACTS. 1976. bi-m. £310($560) (effective 1997). CAB International, Walingford, Oxon. OX10 8DE, England. TEL 44-1491-832111. FAX 44-1491-826090. TELEX 847964 COMAGG G. E-mail: cabi@cabi.org; URL: http://www.cabi.org. (U.S. subscr. to: CAB International, North American Office, 198 Madison Ave., New York, NY 10016. TEL 212-726-6490. FAX 212-686-7993) circ. 450. (also avail. in diskette format; microfiche; back issues avail.) **Indexed:** Dairy Sci.Abstr., Field Crop Abstr., Herb.Abstr., Weed Abstr. **Document type:** abstracting/indexing.
 •Also available online. Vendor(s): DIMDI, European Space Agency (File nos.16 & 116 EA), Knight-Ridder Information, Inc., STN International.
—BLDSC (0746.002000).
 Description: Covers research developments in agricultural engineering and instrumentation.

338.1   CN   ISSN 1188-7516
HD1781
AGRICULTURAL FINANCIAL STATISTICS. (Text in English, French) 1990. a. Can.$45 (U.S. $54, elsewhere $63). Statistics Canada, Circulation Management, Jean Talon Bldg., 2-C12, Tunney's Pasture, Ottawa, ON K1A 0T6, Canada. TEL 613-951-7277; 800-267-6677. FAX 613-951-1584. URL: http://www.statcan.ca. circ. 400. **Document type:** government publication.
 Description: Provides a detailed picture of the performance of Canadian farms as revealed by the information compiled from tax returns of unincorporated and incorporated farmers.
 Refereed Serial

630   II
AGRICULTURAL PRICES IN INDIA. (Text in English, Hindi) 1957. a. Rs.275($16.48) Ministry of Agriculture, Directorate of Economics and Statistics, A-2E-3 Kasturba Gandhi Marg Barracks, New Delhi 110 001, India. TEL 11-381523. (Dist. by: Controller of Publications, Government of India, Civil Lines, Delhi 110 054, India) Ed. Brajesh Kumar Gautam. circ. 600. **Document type:** government publication.
 Former titles: India. Ministry of Agriculture. Directorate of Economics and Statistics. Bulletin of Agriculture Prices; Agricultural Prices in India; All India Report on Agricultural Census.

630   II   ISSN 0970-4019
AGRICULTURAL RESEARCH ABSTRACTS AND NEWSLETTER. 1973. q. Rs.200($25) (effective 1998). Agricultural Research Communication Centre, 1130 Sadar, Karnal 132 001, Hayrana, India. TEL 91-184-255080. Ed. R.D. Goel. bk.rev. **Document type:** abstracting/indexing.

630   II   ISSN 0002-1679
AGRICULTURAL SITUATION IN INDIA. (Text in English) 1948. m. Rs.100($36) Ministry of Agriculture, Directorate of Economics and Statistics, A-2E-3 Kasturba Gandhi Marg Barracks, New Delhi 110 001, India. Ed. Brajesh Kumar Gautam. bk.rev.; abstr.; charts; stat.; index. circ. 975. **Indexed:** Abstr.Rural Dev.Trop., Agri.Eng.Abstr., Agroforest.Abstr., Biodet.Abstr., Cott.& Trop.Fibr.Abstr., Dairy Sci.Abstr., Forest.Abstr., Forest Prod.Abstr., Hort.Abstr., IDA, Int.Lab.Doc., Irr.& Drain.Abstr., Maize Abstr., Pub.Admin.Abstr., Rice Abstr., Rural Devel.Abstr., Rural Ext.Educ.& Tr.Abstr., Rural Recreat.Tour.Abstr., Soils & Fert., Sorghum & Millets Abstr., Triticale Abstr., Trop.Abstr., Trop.Oil Seeds Abstr., World Agri.Econ.& Rural Sociol.Abstr. **Document type:** government publication.
—BLDSC (0755.400000).

AGRICULTURE — ABSTRACTING, BIBLIOGRAPHIES, STATISTICS

630 338.1 GR ISSN 0065-4574
AGRICULTURAL STATISTICS OF GREECE. (Text in English and Greek) 1961. a., latest 1992. $15. National Statistical Service of Greece, Statistical Information and Publications Division - Ethniki Statistiki Yperesia tes Ellados, 14-16 Lykourgou, 101 66 Athens, Greece. TEL 30-1-3289-397. FAX 30-1-3244-708. TELEX 216734 ESYE GR. (back issues avail.) **Document type:** government publication.

630 338.1 MY
AGRICULTURAL STATISTICS OF SABAH. (Text in English) 1971. a. free. Department of Agriculture, Statistics Unit, Planning Division, 88632 Kota Kinabalu, Sabah, Malaysia. TEL 088-55155. FAX 088-239046. Ed. Abdullah Sibil. charts; circ. 500 (controlled). **Document type:** government publication.

630 338.1 MY ISSN 0127-4708
HD2080.6.Z9
AGRICULTURAL STATISTICS OF SARAWAK. 1971. a., latest 1983. M.$5. Department of Agriculture, Statistics Unit, 88632 Kota Kinabalu, Sabah, Malaysia. **Indexed:** Field Crop Abstr., Herb.Abstr.

636 EI
HD9425.E8
AGRICULTURAL STATISTICS SERIES NO.2: ANIMAL PRODUCTION. (Text in English, French, German) 1975. q. $110. Statistical Office of the European Communities, Rue Alcide de Gasperi, 2920 Luxembourg, Luxembourg. TEL 43011. TELEX COMMEUR LU 3423. (Dist. in the U.S. by: Unipub, 4611-F Assembly Dr., Lanham, MD 20706-4391. TEL 800-274-4888. FAX 301-459-0056) charts; stat. (also avail. in microfiche from CIS) **Indexed:** IIS.
●Also available online.
Formerly: Statistical Office of the European Communities. Animal Production (ISSN 0250-6580); Formed by the merger of: Statistical Office of the European Communities. Monthly Statistics. Eggs; Statistical Office of the European Communities. Monthly Statistics. Meat; Statistical Office of the European Communities. Monthly Statistics. Milk.
Description: Statistics on meat, eggs and poultry, milk and milk products.

630 310 EI
AGRICULTURAL STATISTICS SERIES NO.3: EUROPEAN COMMUNITIES INDEX OF AGRICULTURAL PRICES. s-a. $100. Statistical Office of the European Communities, Rue Alcide de Gasperi, 2920 Luxembourg, Luxembourg. (Subscr. in U.S. to: Unipub, 4611-F Assembly Dr., Lanham, MD 20706-4391. TEL 800-274-4888. FAX 301-459-0056) (also avail. in microfiche from CIS) **Indexed:** IIS.
Formerly: E C Agricultural Price Indices (ISSN 0250-5967)
Description: Shows trends of monthly community producer price indices for agricultural products and the purchase of the means of agricultural production over the last 13 available months.

631.091 016 NE
SB111.A2
AGRICULTURE AND ENVIRONMENT FOR DEVELOPING COUNTRIES. (Text and summaries in English) 1975. m. fl.525 (effective 1996). Koninklijk Instituut voor de Tropen, Information, Library and Documentation - Royal Tropical Institute, Mauritskade 63, 1092 AD Amsterdam, Netherlands. TEL 31-20-5688298. FAX 31-20-6654423. TELEX 15080 KIT NL. Ed. Wiebe de Boer. adv.; bk.rev. circ. 500. (back issues avail.; reprint service avail. from KTO) **Indexed:** Agri.Eng.Abstr., E.I., Key to Econ.Sci. **Document type:** abstracting/indexing.
●Also available online. Vendor(s): Questel Orbit Inc. (TROPAG).
Also available on CD-ROM. Producer(s): SilverPlatter Information, Inc.
Former titles: Abstracts on Tropical Agriculture (ISSN 0304-5951); Tropical Abstracts (ISSN 0041-3208)
Description: Covers worldwide literature on agriculture and environment in tropical and subtropical areas of the developing world. Includes animal husbandry, crop production and soils, fertilizers, fish and fisheries, forestry and nutrition and environmental management.

630 016 II ISSN 0002-1733
AGRICULTURE CHECKLIST. 1966. bi-m. Rs.150($30) K.K. Roy (Private) Ltd., 55 Gariahat Rd., P.O. Box 10210, Calcutta 700 019, India. Ed. K.K. Roy. adv.; bk.rev.; bibl. circ. 1,000. (looseleaf format) —BLDSC (0803.581500).

338.109489 DK ISSN 0905-5142
AGRICULTURE IN DENMARK. Danish edition: Landoekonomisk Oversigt (ISSN 0107-7163) (Text in English) a. free. Danske Landboforeninger - Danish Farmers' Unions, Axelborg, 4th Fl., Vesterbrogade 4A, DK-1620 Copenhagen V, Denmark. TEL 45-33-12-75-61. FAX 45-33-32-76-62. Ed. Morten H. Knudsen. stat.
Description: Provides statistical information on the agricultural situation in Denmark, including summary coverage of topics relating to production, marketing, and economic forecasting.

630 PH
AGRIDEV WEEKLY BULLETIN. w. Department of Agriculture, Bureau of Agricultural Statistics, BEN-LOR Bldg., 1184 Quezon Ave., Quezon City, Philippines. FAX 63-2-968-966. E-mail: da-bas@gaia.psdn.org. Ed. Aurora D. Abaya. R&P contact: Romeo S. Recide. circ. 300. **Document type:** government publication, bulletin.
Formerly: Philippines. Department of Agriculture. Bureau of Agricultural Statistics. Weekly Agricultural Situation Report.
Description: Summary of agricultural situations throughout the Philippines. Weather, crop, livestock, poultry and fishery information.

630 574 628 016 PL
AGRO-AGEN; bibliographic database. (Not avail. in print format) (Text and summaries in English) 1992. q. $210 (effective 1997). Akademia Rolnicza, Poznan, Biblioteka Glowna, Ul. Witosa 45, 60-667 Poznan, Poland. TEL 48-61-487809. FAX 48-61-487802. E-mail: wgolob@owl.au.poznan.pl. (Dist. by: Madex, ul. Grunwaldzka 11, 60-782 Poznan, Poland. TEL 48-61-666066. FAX 48-61-659653) Ed. Wlodzimierz Golab. adv. contact: Wlodzimierz Golab. cum.index 1992-1997. (also avail. in diskette format) **Document type:** abstracting/indexing.
●Also available on CD-ROM.
Description: Indexes the contents of Polish journals published in English covering biology, agriculture and environment.

630 574 628 016 PL
AGRO-LIBREX; bibliographic database. (Text in English, Polish) 1992. q. $350. Akademia Rolnicza, Poznan, Biblioteka Glowna, Ul. Witosa 45, 60-667 Poznan, Poland. TEL 48-61-666066. FAX 48-61-659643. TELEX 413374. E-mail: wgolob@owl.au.poznan.pl. (Dist. by: Madex, ul. Grunwaldzka 11, 60-782 Poznan, Poland. TEL 48-61-666066. FAX 48-61-659643) Ed. Wlodzimierz Golab; Pub. Marek Marcinowski. adv. contact: Marek Marcinowski. **Document type:** abstracting/indexing.
●Available only on CD-ROM.
Description: Indexes the contents of Polish journals and series covering biology, agriculture, forestry, horticulture, animal science, wood, food, nutrition, environmental and veterinary sciences.

AGROFORESTRY ABSTRACTS. see FORESTS AND FORESTRY — Abstracting, Bibliographies, Statistics

630 016 US ISSN 0065-4671
AGRONOMY ABSTRACTS. 1950. a. $13. American Society of Agronomy, Inc., 677 South Segoe Rd., Madison, WI 53711. TEL 608-273-8080. FAX 608-273-2021. Ed. Gary A. Peterson. R&P contact: David M. Kral. adv. contact: Keith R. Schlesinger. circ. 12,500. **Indexed:** GeoRef., Plant Breed.Abstr.
—BLDSC (0771.000000). **CCC.**
Description: Includes abstracts of volunteer papers as well as invitational papers presented at the society's annual meetings.

630.01605 PL ISSN 1427-5805
▼**AKADEMIA ROLNICZA WE WROCLAWIU. ZESZYTY NAUKOWE. BIBLIOGRAFIE.** 1996. irreg. price varies. Akademia Rolnicza we Wroclawiu, Ul. Norwida 25, 50-3 Wroclaw, Poland. TEL 48-71-211277. FAX 48-71-229576. (Subscr. to: Wydawnictwo Akademii Rolniczej, ul. Sopocka 23, 50-344 Wroclaw, Poland) **Document type:** academic/scholarly publication.

630 310 US
ALASKA AGRICULTURAL STATISTICS. 1960. a. $5. Alaska Agricultural Statistics Service, Box 799, Palmer, AK 99645. TEL 907-745-4272. (Dist. by: Agricultural Statistics Board Publications, South Bldg., Rm. 5829, U.S. Department of Agriculture, Washington, DC 20250) Ed. DeLon A. Brown. **Indexed:** SRI. **Document type:** government publication.
Former titles: Alaska Agricultural Statistics Service. Agricultural Statistics (ISSN 0065-5694); (until 1962): Alaska Farm Production (ISSN 0516-4850)

630 310 US
ALASKA FARM REPORTER. m. $7. Alaska Agricultural Statistics Service, Box 799, Palmer, AK 99645. TEL 907-745-4272. (Dist. by: Agricultural Statistics Board Publications, South Bldg., Rm. 5829, U.S. Department of Agriculture, Washington, DC 20250) **Document type:** government publication.

630 551.5 US
ALASKA WEEKLY CROP WEATHER. w. (May-Oct.). $9. Alaska Agricultural Statistics Service, Box 799, Palmer, AK 99645. TEL 907-745-4272. (Dist. by: Agricultural Statistics Board Publications, South Bldg., Rm. 5829, U.S. Department of Agriculture, Washington, DC 20250) **Document type:** government publication.
Former titles: Alaska Agricultural Statistics Service. Crop Weather Report; Alaska Crop and Livestock Reporting Service. Weekly Crop-Weather.

630 FR ISSN 0243-6825
ANNUAIRE DE STATISTIQUE AGRICOLE. a. 296 F. (effective 1997). Ministere de l'Agriculture et de la Peche, Service Central des Enquetes et Etudes Statistique, 4 av. Saint-Mande, 75570 Paris Cedex 12, France. TEL 33-1-49558585. FAX 33-1-49558503. URL: http://www.agriculture.gouv.fr. Ed. G. Raulin. (also avail. in microfiche) **Document type:** government publication.

638.1 016 UK ISSN 0003-648X
CODEN: APIBAE
APICULTURAL ABSTRACTS. 1950. q. £165($295) (effective 1996). International Bee Research Association, 18 North Rd., Cardiff CF1 3DY, Wales. TEL 44-1222-372409. FAX 44-1222-665522. E-mail: ibra@cardiff.ac.uk. Ed. David Lowe. adv.: page £134; 175 x 115; adv. contact: Pamela A. Munn. bk.rev.; pat.; tr.lit.; index. cum.index: 1950-1972; 1973-1983 (microfiche). circ. 400. (also avail. in diskette format; back issues avail.) **Indexed:** Apic.Abstr, Biol.& Agr.Ind., Chem.Abstr., Forest.Abstr., Forest Prod.Abstr., Plant Breed.Abstr., Rev.Appl.Entomol. **Document type:** abstracting/indexing.
●Also available online. Vendor(s): European Space Agency (File nos.16 & 124/CAB), Knight-Ridder Information, Inc.
—BLDSC (1568.520000); Linda Hall.
Description: Reviews the world literature on bees, beekeeping, and related subjects.

338.1 318 AG ISSN 0066-7269
ARGENTINA. JUNTA NACIONAL DE CARNES. SINTESIS ESTADISTICA. Title varies; issued 1956-59, 1961-69 as: Argentine Republic. Junta Nacional de Carnes. Resena. 1934. a. Arg.$9600. Junta Nacional de Carnes, Biblioteca, San Martin 459 1 Piso, Buenos Aires, Argentina. index. circ. 2,000.

636 AG
ARGENTINA. SECRETARIA DE AGRICULTURA GANADERIA Y PESCA. SITUACION DEL MERCADO DE CARNES. English edition: Argentina. Secretariat for Agriculture Livestock and Fisheries. Market Situation and the Role of Government in the Argentinian Meat Sector. 1992. m.? Secretaria de Agricultura, Ganaderia y Pesca, Paseo Colon 922, 1o, Of. 146, 1063 Bueno Aires, Argentina. **Document type:** government publication.

338.1 318 AG
ARGENTINA. SECRETARIA DE ESTADO DE AGRICULTUR Y GANADERIA. AREA DE TRABAJO DE LECHERIA. RESENA ESTADISTICA. 1964. irreg. free. Secretaria de Estado de Agricultura y Ganaderia, Area de Trabajo de Lecheria, Paseo Colon 922, 1063 Buenos Aires, Argentina. stat. circ. 1,000. (processed; also avail. in cards)

AGRICULTURE — ABSTRACTING, BIBLIOGRAPHIES, STATISTICS

630
S37 US
CODEN: AKABA7
ARKANSAS. AGRICULTURAL EXPERIMENT STATION. RESEARCH BULLETIN. 1886. irreg. (approx. 5/yr.). Agricultural Experiment Station, Agricultural Publications, 110 Agriculture Bldg., 1 University of Arkansas, Division of Agriculture, Fayetteville, AR 72701-1201. TEL 501-575-5647. FAX 501-575-7531. URL: http://www.uark.edu/depts/agripub/publications/. circ. 1,200 (controlled). **Indexed:** Anim.Breed.Abstr., Biol.Abstr., Curr.Adv.Ecol.Sci., Dairy Sci.Abstr., Field Crop Abstr., Forest.Abstr., Forest Prod.Abstr., Herb.Abstr., Ind.Vet., Irr.& Drain.Abstr., Nutr.Abstr., Rice Abstr., Soils & Fert., Soyabean Abstr., Triticale Abstr., Weed Abstr., World Agri.Econ.& Rural Sociol.Abstr.
●Also available online.
—CASDDS; UnCover.
Formerly: Arkansas. Agricultural Experiment Station. Bulletin (ISSN 0097-3491)
Description: Reports on investigative research in agriculture, forestry and home economics.
Refereed Serial

631 US
CODEN: AKAMA6
ARKANSAS. AGRICULTURAL EXPERIMENT STATION. RESEARCH SERIES. 1949. irreg. (approx. 8/yr.). Agricultural Experiment Station, Agricultural Publications, 110 Agriculture Bldg., 1 University of Arkansas, Division of Agriculture, Fayetteville, AR 72701-1201. TEL 501-575-5647. FAX 501-575-7531. URL: http://www.uark.edu/depts/agripub/publications/. Ed.Bd. circ. 1,000. **Indexed:** Biol.Abstr., Curr.Adv.Ecol.Sci., Rice Abstr.
●Also available online.
—CASDDS; Linda Hall.
Formerly (until 1985): Arkansas Agricultural Experiment Station. Mimeograph Series (ISSN 0099-5010)
Description: Reports on agricultural, food and life sciences research.

630 US ISSN 0571-0189
CODEN: AUARAN
ARKANSAS. AGRICULTURAL EXPERIMENT STATION. SPECIAL REPORTS. 1957. irreg. (approx. 4/yr.). Agricultural Experiment Station, Agricultural Publications, 110 Agriculture Bldg., 1 University of Arkansas, Division of Agriculture, Fayetteville, AR 72701-1201. TEL 501-575-5647. FAX 501-575-7531. URL: http://www.uark.edu/depts/agripub/publications/. Ed. Raymond Barclay, Jr. circ. 1,000. (back issues avail.) **Indexed:** Biol.Abstr., Curr.Adv.Ecol.Sci.
●Also available online.
—BLDSC (8401.008000); Linda Hall.
Description: Reports on enterprise budgets, lecture series, workshops, proceedings of symposiums and survey data relating to research in agriculture, forestry and home economics.

631 011 IO
ASIAN AND PACIFIC COCONUT COMMUNITY. BIBLIOGRAPHY SERIES. irreg. Asian and Pacific Coconut Community, Wisma Bakrie, 3rd Fl., Jl. H.R. Rasuna Said, Kuningan, Jakarta 12920, Indonesia. TEL 62-21-510-073. FAX 62-21-520-5160. TELEX 62863 APCCIA. **Document type:** bibliography.
Description: Lists documents related to coconut wood, small-scale processing of coconuts and coconut-based farming systems.

630 332 AT ISSN 0810-459X
AUSTRALIA. BUREAU OF STATISTICS. AGRICULTURAL INDUSTRIES, FINANCIAL STATISTICS, AUSTRALIA. 1974. a. Aus.$29. Australian Bureau of Statistics, P.O. Box 10, Belconnen, A.C.T. 2616, Australia. **Document type:** government publication.
Description: Financial year estimates of turnover, expenditure, value added, cash operating surplus, value of selected assets, capital expenditure, indebtedness and net worth of farm businesses.

630 332 AT ISSN 1320-6443
AUSTRALIA. BUREAU OF STATISTICS. AGRICULTURAL INDUSTRIES, FINANCIAL STATISTICS, AUSTRALIA, PRELIMINARY ESTIMATES. 1989. a. Aus.$10. Australian Bureau of Statistics, P.O. Box 10, Belconnen, A.C.T. 2616, Australia. **Document type:** government publication.
Formerly (until 1993): Agricultural Industries, Financial Statistics, Australia, First Preliminary Estimates (ISSN 1037-8952)
Description: Preliminary financial year estimates of turnover, value added, cash operating surplus and indebtedness of farm businesses classified by 13 agricultural industries.

630 AT ISSN 1322-865X
AUSTRALIA. BUREAU OF STATISTICS. AGRICULTURE, AUSTRALIA. 1993. a. Aus.$29. Australian Bureau of Statistics, P.O. Box 10, Belconnen, A.C.T. 2616, Australia. **Document type:** government publication.
Description: Covers the structure of the Australian farming sector and included details of land use, crop and horticultural activity, and livestock numbers.

630 310 AT
AUSTRALIA. BUREAU OF STATISTICS. AGSTATS MANUAL. 1976. a. Australian Bureau of Statistics, P.O. Box 10, Belconnen, A.C.T. 2616, Australia. (looseleaf format; also avail. in magnetic tape; microfiche; diskette format) **Document type:** government publication.
Formerly: Agricultural Data Dissemination Services Manual.
Description: Contains information on data collected, commodity and area classifications.

AUSTRALIA. BUREAU OF STATISTICS. AUSTRALIAN WINE AND GRAPE INDUSTRY. see *BEVERAGES — Abstracting, Bibliographies, Statistics*

636 AT ISSN 0728-4047
AUSTRALIA. BUREAU OF STATISTICS. LIVESTOCK PRODUCTS, AUSTRALIA. 1981. m. Aus.$10 per no. Australian Bureau of Statistics, P.O. Box 10, Belconnen, A.C.T. 2616, Australia. **Document type:** government publication.
Description: Provides information about livestock slaughterings, meat production, milk intake by factories, receivals of wool by brokers, and exports of meat.

630 310 AT ISSN 1322-8633
AUSTRALIA. BUREAU OF STATISTICS. NEW SOUTH WALES OFFICE. PRINCIPAL AGRICULTURAL COMMODITIES, NEW SOUTH WALES, PRELIMINARY. 1981. a. Aus.$14.50. Australian Bureau of Statistics, New South Wales Office, St. Andrews House, Sydney Square, George St., Sydney, N.S.W. 2000, Australia. **Document type:** government publication.
Description: Preliminary statistics on area and production of principal cereals for grain; area intended to be sown to barley, oats and wheat for all purposes; farm stock of cereal grains; livestock numbers, shearing and wool production, lambing and intended matings.

630 310 AT ISSN 1033-4823
AUSTRALIA. BUREAU OF STATISTICS. PRINCIPAL AGRICULTURAL COMMODITIES, AUSTRALIA, PRELIMINARY, AGRICULTURAL PRODUCTION AND FARMERS' INTENTIONS FOR (NEXT) SEASON. 1981. a. Aus.$16.50. Australian Bureau of Statistics, P.O. Box 10, Belconnen, A.C.T. 2616, Australia. **Document type:** government publication.
Formerly: Principal Agricultural Commodities, Australia, Preliminary.
Description: Preliminary statistics on area and production of principal cereals for grain; area intended to be sown to barley, oats and wheat for all purposes; livestock numbers, lambing and intended matings.

630 AT ISSN 1322-8668
AUSTRALIA. BUREAU OF STATISTICS. QUEENSLAND OFFICE. AGRICULTURE, QUEENSLAND. 1993. a. Aus.$30. Australian Bureau of Statistics, Queensland Office, 313 Adelaide St., Brisbane, Qld. 4000, Australia. **Document type:** government publication.
Incorporates (1990-1993): Agriculture Statistics - Selected Small Area Data, Queensland (ISSN 1037-9124)
Description: Number, area and land utilization of agricultural establishments; numbers of cattle and sheep classified by age, sex and purpose; numbers of pigs and poultry and other livestock; beekeeping and wool statistics.

636.2 AT
AUSTRALIA. BUREAU OF STATISTICS. QUEENSLAND OFFICE. CATTLE BREEDS, QUEENSLAND. 1973. irreg., latest 1987. Aus.$10. Australian Bureau of Statistics, Queensland Office, 313 Adelaide St., Brisbane, Qld. 4000, Australia. TEL 07-222-6022. FAX 07-229-6171. TELEX AA 40271.
Description: Cattle numbers, summary of breeds, breeds by type in local government areas and statistical divisions.

630 AT ISSN 0810-7742
AUSTRALIA. BUREAU OF STATISTICS. QUEENSLAND OFFICE. VALUE OF AGRICULTURAL COMMODITIES PRODUCED, QUEENSLAND. 1963. a. Aus.$15.50. Australian Bureau of Statistics, Queensland Office, 313 Adelaide St., Brisbane, Qld. 4000, Australia. TEL 07-222-6022. FAX 07-229-6171. TELEX AA 40271. **Document type:** government publication.
Formerly (until 1980): Value of Primary Industry Commodities Produced, Excluding Mining, Queensland (ISSN 0810-7750)
Description: Presents gross and local value of crops, fruit, vegetables for human consumption, livestock slaughterings and other disposals and livestock products.

636 AT ISSN 0815-7103
AUSTRALIA. BUREAU OF STATISTICS. SHEEP AND WOOL, AUSTRALIA, PRELIMINARY. 1983. a. Aus.$10.50. Australian Bureau of Statistics, P.O. Box 10, Belconnen, A.C.T. 2616, Australia. **Document type:** government publication.
Description: Contains estimates from the Agricultural Census of sheep numbers, lambing statistics, numbers of sheep shorn and wool produced.

630 AT ISSN 1031-1939
AUSTRALIA. BUREAU OF STATISTICS. SOUTH AUSTRALIAN OFFICE. AGRICULTURE, SOUTH AUSTRALIA. 1943. a. Aus.$18. Australian Bureau of Statistics, South Australian Office, G.P.O. Box 2272, Adelaide, S.A. 5001, Australia. FAX 61-8-82377566. **Document type:** government publication.
Description: Covers the structure of the South Australian farming sector and including details of land use, crop and horticultural activity and livestock numbers.

630 AT ISSN 0729-8684
AUSTRALIA. BUREAU OF STATISTICS. SOUTH AUSTRALIAN OFFICE. PRINCIPAL AGRICULTURAL COMMODITIES, SOUTH AUSTRALIA, PRELIMINARY. 1981. a. Aus.$14. Australian Bureau of Statistics, South Australian Office, G.P.O. Box 2272, Adelaide, S.A. 5001, Australia. FAX 61-8-82377566. **Document type:** government publication.
Description: Contains preliminary statistics on production of principal cereals and legumes for grain, livestock numbers, lambing and intended matings.

630.201 AT
AUSTRALIA. BUREAU OF STATISTICS. TASMANIAN OFFICE. AGRICULTURE, TASMANIA (HOBART, 1987). 1987. a. Aus.$23. Australian Bureau of Statistics, Tasmanian Office, G.P.O. Box 66A, Hobart, Tas. 7001, Australia. illus. circ. 620. **Document type:** government publication.
Formerly: Agricultural Statistics, Tasmania (ISSN 1033-646X); Which was formed by the 1987 merger of: Agricultural Land Use and Selected Inputs, Tasmania (ISSN 0810-963X); Crops and Pastures, Tasmania (ISSN 0729-9672); Livestock and Livestock Products, Tasmania (ISSN 0810-9621); Fruit, Tasmania (ISSN 0810-9176); Which was formerly: Fruit Production, Tasmania (ISSN 0314-1667).
Description: Provides comprehensive information on Tasmanian agricultural establishments and production, vegetables, livestock, poultry and fruits, etc.

630 AT ISSN 0728-4217
AUSTRALIA. BUREAU OF STATISTICS. TASMANIAN OFFICE. PRINCIPAL AGRICULTURAL COMMODITIES, TASMANIA, PRELIMINARY. 1981. a. Aus.$12. Australian Bureau of Statistics, Tasmanian Office, G.P.O. Box 66A, Hobart, Tas. 7001, Australia. **Document type:** government publication.
Description: Contains preliminary estimates of area and production of principal crops, livestock, and lambing details.

AGRICULTURE — ABSTRACTING, BIBLIOGRAPHIES, STATISTICS

338.1   AT   ISSN 1031-0789
AUSTRALIA. BUREAU OF STATISTICS. VALUE OF AGRICULTURAL COMMODITIES PRODUCED, AUSTRALIA. 1950. a. Aus.$23. Australian Bureau of Statistics, P.O. Box 10, Belconnen, A.C.T. 2616, Australia. TEL 062-527911. FAX 062-516009. circ. 392. **Document type:** government publication.
   Formerly (until 1975): Value of Primary Production, Excluding Mining, and Indexes of Quantum and Unit Gross Value of Agricultural Production (ISSN 0312-6242)
   Description: Detailed statistics of the gross and local value of crops, pastures and grasses, fruits and nuts, vegetables, livestock slaughterings by type, and livestock products.

630   AT   ISSN 1031-0797
AUSTRALIA. BUREAU OF STATISTICS. VALUE OF PRINCIPAL AGRICULTURAL COMMODITIES PRODUCED, AUSTRALIA, PRELIMINARY. 1965. a. Aus.$10.50. Australian Bureau of Statistics, P.O. Box 10, Belconnen, A.C.T. 2616, Australia. **Document type:** government publication.
   Formerly: Value of Agricultural Commodities Produced, Australia, First Estimates.
   Description: Details the broad aggregates of gross value of production of selected crops, livestock slaughterings and livestock products.

630   AT   ISSN 0812-8634
AUSTRALIA. BUREAU OF STATISTICS. VICTORIAN OFFICE. AGRICULTURAL LAND USE AND SELECTED INPUTS, VICTORIA. 1981. a. Aus.$18. Australian Bureau of Statistics, Victorian Office, G.P.O. Box 2796Y, Melbourne, Vic. 3001, Australia. **Document type:** government publication.
   Description: Covers area and land utilization of agricultural establishments, number of agricultural establishments and number of their employees.

630   AT   ISSN 1037-9126
AUSTRALIA. BUREAU OF STATISTICS. VICTORIAN OFFICE. AGRICULTURE STATISTICS - SELECTED SMALL AREA DATA, VICTORIA. 1990. a. Aus.$16.50. Australian Bureau of Statistics, Victorian Office, G.P.O. Box 2796Y, Melbourne, Vic. 3001, Australia. **Document type:** government publication.
   Description: Summary data for major agricultural commodities (area and production of major crops, numbers of livestock) by statistical local area.

630   AT   ISSN 1036-2711
AUSTRALIA. BUREAU OF STATISTICS. VICTORIAN OFFICE. CROPS, PASTURES AND FRUIT, VICTORIA. 1989. a. Aus.$27.50. Australian Bureau of Statistics, Victorian Office, G.P.O. Box 2796Y, Melbourne, Vic. 3001, Australia. **Document type:** government publication.
   Formed by the merger of (1981-1989): Crops and Pastures, Victoria (ISSN 0812-8359); (1981-1989): Fruit, Victoria (ISSN 0812-7239)

636   AT   ISSN 0812-9525
AUSTRALIA. BUREAU OF STATISTICS. VICTORIAN OFFICE. LIVESTOCK AND LIVESTOCK PRODUCTS, VICTORIA. 1981. a. Aus.$22. Australian Bureau of Statistics, Victorian Office, G.P.O. Box 2796Y, Melbourne, Vic. 3001, Australia. **Document type:** government publication.
   Description: Contains numbers of cattle and sheep, pigs and poultry, lambing, livestock slaughterings, production of meat, livestock and dairy products, beekeeping, and wool clipped.

630   AT   ISSN 0810-0640
AUSTRALIA. BUREAU OF STATISTICS. VICTORIAN OFFICE. PRINCIPAL AGRICULTURAL COMMODITIES, VICTORIA, PRELIMINARY. 1981. a. Aus.$11.50. Australian Bureau of Statistics, Victorian Office, G.P.O. Box 2796Y, Melbourne, Vic. 3001, Australia. **Document type:** government publication.
   Description: Contains preliminary statistics on the production of principal cereals for grain, farm stocks of cereal grains, livestock numbers, shearing and wool production, and lambing and intended matings.

338.1 310   AT
AUSTRALIA. BUREAU OF STATISTICS. VICTORIAN OFFICE. VALUE OF AGRICULTURAL COMMODITIES PRODUCED, VICTORIA. 1967. a. Aus.$15.50. Australian Bureau of Statistics, Victorian Office, G.P.O. Box 2796Y, Melbourne, Vic. 3001, Australia. circ. 300. **Document type:** government publication.
   Former titles: Value of Agricultural Production, Victoria; Value of Agricultural Commodities Produced, Victoria (ISSN 1031-2927); Value of Primary Commodities Produced (Excluding Mining); Value of Primary Production.
   Description: Contains gross value of agricultural commodities produced, including cereals, legumes, hay, vegetables, grapes, livestock slaughtering, and livestock products.

AUSTRALIA. BUREAU OF STATISTICS. VITICULTURE, AUSTRALIA. see BEVERAGES — Abstracting, Bibliographies, Statistics

630   AT   ISSN 0727-517X
AUSTRALIA. BUREAU OF STATISTICS. WESTERN AUSTRALIAN OFFICE. AGRICULTURE, WESTERN AUSTRALIA. 1981. a. Aus.$16.50 per no. (effective 1996). Australian Bureau of Statistics, Western Australian Office, 30 Terrace Rd., E. Perth, W.A. 6004, Australia. **Document type:** government publication.
   Description: Contains six year summaries of agricultural land utilization, crop production, fruit production and livestock products.

630   AT   ISSN 0729-512X
AUSTRALIA. BUREAU OF STATISTICS. WESTERN AUSTRALIAN OFFICE. PRINCIPAL AGRICULTURAL COMMODITIES, WESTERN AUSTRALIA, PRELIMINARY. 1981. a. Aus.$13.50 per no. (effective 1996). Australian Bureau of Statistics, Western Australian Office, 30 Terrace Rd., E. Perth, W.A. 6004, Australia. **Document type:** government publication.
   Description: Provides preliminary statistics on production of principal crops for grain, farm stock of cereal grains, livestock numbers, shearing and wool production, lambing and intended matings.

630   AT   ISSN 0727-2170
AUSTRALIA. BUREAU OF STATISTICS. WESTERN AUSTRALIAN OFFICE. VALUE OF AGRICULTURAL COMMODITIES PRODUCED, WESTERN AUSTRALIA. 1966. a. Aus.$15.50 per no. (effective 1996. Australian Bureau of Statistics, Western Australian Office, 30 Terrace Rd., E. Perth, W.A. 6004, Australia. **Document type:** government publication.
   Description: Contains detailed statistics of the gross and local value of crops and pastures and grasses, fruits and nuts, vegetables, and livestock products.

630 314   AU   ISSN 0067-2327
AUSTRIA. STATISTISCHES ZENTRALAMT. ERGEBNISSE DER LANDWIRTSCHAFTLICHEN STATISTIK. (Subseries of: Beitraege zur Oesterreichischen Statistik) 1948. a. S.200. Oesterreichisches Statistisches Zentralamt, Hintere Zollamtsstr. 2b, A-1033 Vienna, Austria. TEL 43-1-71128-0. FAX 43-1-7156828. circ. 410. **Document type:** government publication.
   Description: Data on livestock, milk, and overall farm production.

630   AU   ISSN 0259-7977
AUSTRIA. STATISTISCHES ZENTRALAMT. LANDWIRTSCHAFTLICHE MASCHINENZAEHLUNG. (Subseries of: Beitraege zur Oesterreichischen Statistik) 1954. irreg. S.160. Oesterreichisches Statistisches Zentralamt, Hintere Zollamtsstr. 2b, A-1033 Vienna, Austria. TEL 43-1-71128-0. FAX 43-1-7156828. circ. 370. **Document type:** government publication.
   Formerly: Austria. Statistisches Zentralamt. Ergebnisse der Landwirtschaftlichen Maschinenzaehlung.
   Description: Data on stock of agricultural machinery and implements.

630 016   BG
BANGLADESH AGRICULTURAL SCIENCES ABSTRACTS. Short title: B A S A. (Text in English) 1974. biennial. Tk.50($20) Bangladesh Agricultural University Old Boys' Association, c/o Dept. of Soil Science, Bangladesh Agricultural University, Mymensingh, Bangladesh. (Co-sponsor: Bangladesh Agricultural Research Council) Ed. M. Eaqub. circ. 500.

630 338.1   NE   ISSN 1381-0219
BEDRIJFSUITKOMSTEN IN DE TUINBOUW. 1994. a. fl.51. Landbouw-Economisch Instituut, Burg. Patijnlaan 19, 2585 BE The Hague, Netherlands. TEL 31-70-3308330. FAX 31-70-3615624. E-mail: postmaster@lei.dlo.nl; URL: http://www.lei.dlo.nl/lei. Ed. A. Boers. **Document type:** government publication.

    BE   ISSN 0067-5466
BELGIUM. INSTITUT NATIONAL DE STATISTIQUE. STATISTIQUES AGRICOLES. Key Title: Statistiques Agricoles - Institut National de Statistique. Dutch edition: Landbouwstatistieken - Nationaal Instituut voor de Statistiek (ISSN 0772-7615) (Text in French) 5/yr. 1100 BEF (foreign 1380 BEF) (effective 1997). Institut National de Statistique, 44 rue de Louvain, 1000 Brussels, Belgium. TEL 32-2-5486211. FAX 32-2-5486367. Indexed: P.A.I.S.For.Lang.Ind. **Document type:** government publication.
—BLDSC (8454.080000).

630   IT   ISSN 0393-7046
BIBLIOGRAFIA AGRICOLA. 1984. s-a. free. Comune di Parma, Biblioteca A. Bizzozero, Vicolo S. Maria 5, 43100 Parma, Italy. TEL 39-521-218584. FAX 39-521-230085. E-mail: raffa@biblio.cineca.it. Ed. Raffa Flora. bk.rev. **Document type:** abstracting/indexing.

630   PL   ISSN 0208-4260
BIBLIOGRAFIA PUBLIKACJI PRACOWNIKOW W S G G W W WARSZAWIE. a. Szkola Glowna Gospodarstwa Wiejskiego (SGGW) - Warsaw Agricultural University, Ul. Nowoursynowska 166, 02-766 Warsaw, Poland. (Dist. by: Ars Polona-Ruch, Krakowskie Przedmiescie 7, 00-068 Warsaw, Poland) Ed. J. Lewandowski.

630   US   ISSN 0163-0873
BIBLIOGRAPHIES AND LITERATURE OF AGRICULTURE. 1978. irreg. price varies. U.S. Department of Agriculture, Editorial Division, Room 544-A Administration Bldg., 14th & Independence Ave. S.W., Washington, DC 20250. TEL 202-720-6046. FAX 202-720-4948. Ed. Carrie Pollard. circ. 3,000. Indexed: Hort.Abstr., Ornam.Hort., Potato Abstr., Rice Abstr., World Agri.Econ.& Rural Sociol.Abstr.
   Former titles: Bibliographies and Agricultural Library Information Notes; Bibliographies and Literature of Agriculture.

016.63 630   US   ISSN 0006-1530
Z5073
BIBLIOGRAPHY OF AGRICULTURE. 1942. m. (plus a. cumulation). $695 (foreign $795); $1295 with a. cumulation (foreign $1395) (effective 1997). (U.S. National Agricultural Library, Technical Information Systems) Oryx Press, Box 33889, Phoenix, AZ 85067-3889. TEL 602-265-2651. FAX 602-265-6250. E-mail: info@oryxpress.com; URL: http://www.oryxpress.com/. Ed. Magon Kinzie; Pub. Phyllis Steckler. R&P contact: Betsy Durkin. (also avail. in microform from UMI,BHP,PMC; back issues avail.; reprint service avail. from UMI) **Document type:** abstracting/indexing.
• Also available online. Vendor(s): CISTI.
Also available on CD-ROM. Producer(s): SilverPlatter Information, Inc.
—BLDSC (2000.000000); CISTI; Linda Hall; UMI.
   Description: Index to worldwide literature on all aspects of agriculture-related research science, including plant and animal sciences, human nutrition, and natural resources.

016.63 630   US   ISSN 1082-6408
BIBLIOGRAPHY OF AGRICULTURE. ANNUAL CUMULATIVE INDEX. 1975. a. $645 (outside N. America $695); $1295 with monthly (foreign $1395) (effective 1997). (U.S. National Agricultural Library, Technical Information Systems) Oryx Press, Box 33889, Phoenix, AZ 85067-3889. TEL 602-265-2651. FAX 602-265-6250. E-mail: info@oryxpress.com; URL: http://www.oryxpress.com. Ed. Magon Kinzie. (back issues avail.) **Document type:** abstracting/indexing.
   Formerly (until 1983): Bibliography of Agriculture Annual Cumulation (ISSN 0364-829X)

635   NE
BIBLIOGRAPHY ON SOILLESS CULTURE. 1957. biennial latest 1992. membership only. International Society for Soilless Culture, P.O. Box 52, 6700 AB Wageningen, Netherlands. TEL 31-317-413809. FAX 31-317-423457. **Document type:** bibliography.
   Description: Comprehensive summaries of current literature on soilless culture.

581 016 631.5   YU   ISSN 0351-2312
BILTEN DOKUMENTACIJE. POLJOPRIVREDA. BILJNA PROIZVODNJA/BULLETIN OF DOCUMENTATION. AGRICULTURAL-PLANT PRODUCTION. 1950. bi-m. $264. Jugoslovenski Centar za Tehnicku i Naucnu Dokumentaciju - Yugoslav Center for Technological and Scientific Documentation, Sl. Penezica-Krcuna 29-31, Box 724, 11000 Belgrade, Yugoslavia. Ed. Ljiljana Kojic-Bogdanovic. (also avail. in microfilm)
Formerly (until 1980): Bilten Dokumentacije. Biljna Proizvodnja (ISSN 0006-257X)

636.082 016   YU   ISSN 0351-2320
BILTEN DOKUMENTACIJE. POLJOPRIVREDA-STOCNA PROIZVODNJA/BULLETIN OF DOCUMENTATION. AGRICULTURAL-STOCKBREEDING. 1950. bi-m. $264. Jugoslovenski Centar za Tehnicku i Naucnu Dokumentaciju - Yugoslav Center for Technological and Scientific Documentation (YCTSD), Sl. Penezica-Krcuna 29-31, Box 724, 11000 Belgrade, Yugoslavia. Ed. Ljiljana Kojic-Bogdanovic.
Formerly: Bilten Dokumentacije. Stocna Proizvodnja i Veterinarstvo (ISSN 0006-2707)

BIOLOGICAL & AGRICULTURAL INDEX. see *BIOLOGY — Abstracting, Bibliographies, Statistics*

630   NE   ISSN 0928-8201
DE BOOMKWEKERIJ (THE HAGUE); beschouwingen over economische ontwikkelingen. 1992. irreg. fl.23.75. Landbouw-Economisch Instituut, Burg. Patijnlaan 19, 2585 BE The Hague, Netherlands. TEL 31-70-3308330. FAX 31-70-3615624. E-mail: postmaster@lei.dlo.nl; URL: http://www.lei.dlo.nl/lei. Ed.Bd. **Document type:** government publication.

630 330.9   BS   ISSN 1013-574X
BOTSWANA. MINISTRY OF AGRICULTURE. AGRICULTURAL STATISTICS. irreg. Ministry of Agriculture, Ministry of Finance and Development Planning, Private Bag 0033, Gaborone, Botswana. TEL 267-328780. FAX 267-328847. TELEX 2752 SACCAR BD. (Dist. by: Government Printer, Box 87, Gaborone, Botswana) (Co-sponsor: Central Statistics Office) Ed. Henry G. Jobeta. R&P contact: Dan B. Gomballime. **Document type:** government publication.

630 639 664   CN
BRITISH COLUMBIA. MINISTRY OF AGRICULTURE, FISHERIES AND FOOD. ANNUAL STATISTICS (YEAR). 1911. a. free. Ministry of Agriculture, Fisheries and Food, Public Affairs Branch, Statistical Services Unit, Windsor Court, 808 Douglas St., Victoria, BC V8W 2Z7, Canada. TEL 604-387-7169. FAX 604-387-9105. E-mail: agf__bcbn@galaxy.gov.bc.ca. circ. 1,000. **Document type:** government publication.
—Linda Hall.
Former titles: British Columbia. Ministry of Agriculture and Fisheries. Annual Statistics (ISSN 1180-4718); (until 1988): British Columbia. Ministry of Agriculture and Food. Agricultural Statistics Profile (ISSN 0848-4724); (until 1982): British Columbia. Ministry of Agriculture and Food. Agriculture Statistics Yearbook (ISSN 0706-1471); (until 1973): British Columbia. Department of Agriculture. Agricultural Statistics Report (ISSN 0407-2049); (until 1928): British Columbia. Department of Agriculture. Agricultural Statistics (ISSN 0319-8812)
Refereed Serial

**540 575.1   US   ISSN 0890-7528
                                  CODEN: CBAGEJ**
A S BIOTECH UPDATES. AGRICULTURE. s-w. $240 (effective 1998). Chemical Abstracts Service (Subsidiary of: American Chemical Society), 2540 Olentangy River Rd., Box 3012, Columbus, OH 43210-0012. TEL 614-447-3600. FAX 614-447-3713. TELEX 6842086. **Document type:** abstracting/indexing.
Description: Covers improvement and protection of plants of commercial interest, including genetic manipulation; biological production of agrochemicals; and hydroponics, plant cell, and tissue culture technology.

A SELECTS PLUS. FUNGICIDES. see *CHEMISTRY — Abstracting, Bibliographies, Statistics*

338.1   US
CALIFORNIA. AGRICULTURAL STATISTICS SERVICE. AGRICULTURAL STATISTICS REVIEW. SUMMARY. a. $10 (foreign $20). Agricultural Statistics Service, 1220 N St., Rm. 243, Sacramento, CA 95814. (Subscr. to: Box 1258, Sacramento, CA 95812-1258) **Document type:** government publication.
Description: Summary of over 69 crops, their acreage, production, value, ranking, and major producing counties.

**631 551.6   US   ISSN 0279-2656
S600.62.C2**
CALIFORNIA. AGRICULTURAL STATISTICS SERVICE. CROP WEATHER REPORT. 1981. w. $30 (foreign $60). Agricultural Statistics Service, 1220 N St., Rm. 243, Sacramento, CA 95814. (Subscr. to: Box 1258, Sacramento, CA 95812-1258) **Document type:** government publication.
Description: Covers weather's effect on crops, planting and harvesting, weekly and accumulated precipitation data and temperature by station.

338.1   US
CALIFORNIA. AGRICULTURAL STATISTICS SERVICE. DAIRY INDUSTRY STATISTICS. a. $10 (foreign $20). Agricultural Statistics Service, 1220 N St., Rm. 243, Sacramento, CA 95814. (Subscr. to: Box 1258, Sacramento, CA 95812-1258) Indexed: SRI. **Document type:** government publication.
Description: Provides historic and detailed data on the dairy industry.

633   US
CALIFORNIA. AGRICULTURAL STATISTICS SERVICE. FIELD CROP REVIEW. m. $15 (foreign $30). Agricultural Statistics Service, 1220 N St., Rm. 243, Sacramento, CA 95814. (Subscr. to: Box 1258, Sacramento, CA 95812-1258) **Document type:** government publication.
Description: Covers field crops such as grain, cotton, hay, and sugar beet; provides data on acreage, production, value, price, warehouse, and farm labor.

633   US
CALIFORNIA. AGRICULTURAL STATISTICS SERVICE. FRUIT AND NUT REVIEW. m. $15 (foreign $30). Agricultural Statistics Service, 1220 N St., Rm. 243, Sacramento, CA 95814. TEL 916-445-6076. (Subscr. to: Box 1258, Sacramento, CA 95814-1258) **Document type:** government publication.
Description: Covers grape, citrus, deciduous, and nut acreage, production, price and utilization.

633   US
CALIFORNIA. AGRICULTURAL STATISTICS SERVICE. GRAPE ACREAGE. a. $10 (foreign $20) (diskette $100). Agricultural Statistics Service, 1220 N St., Rm. 243, Sacramento, CA 95814. (Subscr. to: Box 1258, Sacramento, CA 95812-1258) (also avail. in diskette format) **Document type:** government publication.
Description: Provides information on acreage of grapes by year planted, variety, and county; removal data.

630   US
CALIFORNIA. AGRICULTURAL STATISTICS SERVICE. GRAPE CRUSH REPORT. 2/yr. (diskette a.) $20 (foreign $40) (diskette $100). Agricultural Statistics Service, 1220 N St., Rm. 243, Sacramento, CA 95814. (Subscr. to: Box 1258, Sacramento, CA 95812-1258) (also avail. in diskette format) **Document type:** government publication.
Description: Covers tons purchased and crushed, Brix factors, and preliminary and final prices per ton by variety and by district.

636   US
CALIFORNIA. AGRICULTURAL STATISTICS SERVICE. LIVESTOCK REVIEW. m. $15 (foreign $30). Agricultural Statistics Service, 1220 N St., Rm. 243, Sacramento, CA 95814. (Subscr. to: Box 1258, Sacramento, CA 95812-1258) **Document type:** government publication.
Description: Covers livestock inventories, intentions, and values; pasture, slaughter, and on-feed data for cattle and sheep.

635.5   US
CALIFORNIA. AGRICULTURAL STATISTICS SERVICE. POULTRY REPORT. m. $15 (foreign $30). Agricultural Statistics Service, 1220 N St., Rm. 243, Sacramento, CA 95814. (Subscr. to: Box 1258, Sacramento, CA 95812-1258) **Document type:** government publication.
Description: Covers chicken and turkey, settings, hatchings, eggs produced, inventory, value, and cold storage.

633   US
CALIFORNIA. AGRICULTURAL STATISTICS SERVICE. VEGETABLE REVIEW. 5/yr. $7 (foreign $14). Agricultural Statistics Service, 1220 N St., Rm. 243, Sacramento, CA 95814. (Subscr. to: Box 1258, Sacramento, CA 95812-1258) **Document type:** government publication.
Description: Covers the production and processing of fresh vegetables as well as market value.

631   US
CALIFORNIA. AGRICULTURAL STATISTICS SERVICE. WALNUTS, RAISINS AND PRUNES (PRICE REPORT). a. $1. Agricultural Statistics Service, 1220 N St., Rm. 243, Sacramento, CA 95814. (Subscr. to: Box 1258, Sacramento, CA 95812-1258) **Document type:** government publication.

637   US   ISSN 0892-4406
CALIFORNIA DAIRY INFORMATION BULLETIN. m. $15 (foreign $30). Agricultural Statistics Service, 1220 N St., Rm. 243, Sacramento, CA 95814. (Subscr. to: Box 1258, Sacramento, CA 95812-1258) **Document type:** bulletin, government publication.
Formerly: California. Agricultural Statistics Service. Dairy Information Bulletin (ISSN 0279-2605)
Description: Covers production, utilization, and prices of milk and dairy products.

**382 633.1   CN   ISSN 0317-4980
HD9044.C2**
CANADA. GRAIN COMMISSION. CORPORATE SERVICES. CANADIAN GRAIN EXPORTS. Key Title: Canadian Grain Exports. (Text in English, French) a. Can.$14. Grain Commission, Corporate Services, 700-303 Main St., Winnipeg, MB R3C 3G8, Canada. TEL 204-983-2793. R&P contact: Peter Kuzyk. **Document type:** government publication.
Former titles: Canada. Grain Commission. Economics and Statistics Division. Canadian Grain Exports; Canada. Board of Grain Commissioners. Canadian Grain Exports.
Description: Compiles Canadian grain export statistics by grain, grade, country of destination, and port of loading.

633.1   CN   ISSN 0832-6215
CANADA. GRAIN COMMISSION. CORPORATE SERVICES. EXPORTS OF CANADIAN GRAIN AND WHEAT FLOUR. Key Title: Exports of Canadian Grain and Wheat Flour. (Text in English, French) m. Can.$38 (foreign Can.$50) (effective 1996). Grain Commission, Corporate Services, 700-303 Main St., Winnipeg, MB R3C 3G8, Canada. TEL 204-983-2793. R&P contact: Peter Kuzyk. stat; circ. 250 (controlled). **Document type:** government publication.
Formerly: Canada. Grain Commission. Economics and Statistics Division. Exports of Canadian Grain and Wheat Flour.
Description: Canadian grain export statistics by grain, country of destination and port of loading.

**631   CN   ISSN 0575-8548
S133**
CANADA. STATISTICS CANADA. FIELD CROP REPORTING SERIES/SERIE DE RAPPORTS SUR LES GRANDES CULTURES. (Text in English and French) 1922. irreg. Can.$15 per issue (foreign $15) (effective 1998). Statistics Canada, Operations and Integration Division, Circulation Management, Jean Talon Bldg., 2-C12, Tunney's Pasture, Ottawa, ON K1A 0T6, Canada. TEL 613-951-7277; 800-267-6677. FAX 613-951-1584. URL: http://www.statcan.ca. (also avail. in microform from MML) **Document type:** government publication.
—CISTI.
Description: Details farm stocks of grain, crop area, yield and production.

AGRICULTURE — ABSTRACTING, BIBLIOGRAPHIES, STATISTICS

338.17   CN   ISSN 0383-008X
HD9254.C18
CANADA. STATISTICS CANADA. FRUIT AND VEGETABLE PRODUCTION/PRODUCTIONS DE FRUITS ET LEGUMES. (Text in English and French) 1932. s-a. Can.$62 (foreign $62) (effective 1998). Statistics Canada, Operations and Integration Division, Circulation Management, Jean Talon Bldg., 2-C12, Tunney's Pasture, Ottawa, ON K1A 0T6, Canada. TEL 613-951-7277; 800-267-6677. FAX 613-951-1584. URL: http://www.statcan.ca. (also avail. in microform from MML) **Document type:** government publication.
   Description: Provides an overview of the Canadian fruit and vegetable production sector.

636.5   CN   ISSN 0068-7189
HD9437.C2
CANADA. STATISTICS CANADA. PRODUCTION OF POULTRY AND EGGS/PRODUCTION DE VOLAILLE ET OEUFS. (Text in English and French) 1936. a. Can.$38 (foreign $38) (effective 1998). Statistics Canada, Operations and Integration Division, Circulation Management, Jean Talon Bldg., 2-C12, Tunney's Pasture, Ottawa, ON K1A 0T6, Canada. TEL 613-951-7277; 800-267-6677. FAX 613-951-1584. URL: http://www.statcan.ca. (also avail. in microform from MML) **Document type:** government publication.
—CISTI.
   Formerly: Canada. Statistics Canada. Production of Poultry and Eggs in Canada.
   Description: Presents current and historical data on the turkey, chicken, stewing hen and egg industries in Canada.

633.1   CN
CANADA GRAINS COUNCIL. STATISTICAL HANDBOOK. 1974. a. Canada Grains Council, 330-360 Main St., Winnipeg, MB R3C 3Z3, Canada. TEL 204-942-2254. FAX 204-947-0992. E-mail: dmutch@canadagrainscouncil.ca; URL: http://www.canadagrainscouncil.ca. circ. 1,500. **Document type:** bulletin.
   Description: Production, trade, prices and handlings of Canadian grains.

633.1   CN   ISSN 1201-5679
CANADIAN GRAINS INDUSTRY STATISTICAL HANDBOOK. 1974. a. Canada Grains Council, 330-360 Main St., Winnipeg, MB R3C 3Z3, Canada. TEL 204-942-2254. FAX 204-947-0992. E-mail: dmutch@canadagrainscouncil.ca; URL: http://www.canadagrainscouncil.ca. **Document type:** directory.

630   BL   ISSN 0103-6157
CENSO AGROPECUARIO. 1940. quinquennial. Fundacao Instituto Brasileiro de Geografia e Estatistica, Centro de Documentacao e Disseminacao de Informacoes, Rua General Canabarro 706, 20 andar, Maracana 20271-201 Rio de Janeiro, Brazil. TEL 55-21-2645424. FAX 55-21-2841959. **Document type:** government publication.
   Formerly (until 1970): Censo Agricola; Supersedes in part (in 1950): Recenseamento Geral do Brasil.
   Description: Contains data on farm characteristics, employed persons, livestock, and agricultural production.

630 310   CY
CENSUS OF AGRICULTURE. (Text in English) irreg. £C8 per no. Ministry of Finance, Department of Statistics and Research, 13 Lord Byron Ave., Nicosia, Cyprus. TEL 357-2-302349. FAX 357-2-456712. **Document type:** government publication.
   Description: Provides information on the structure of agricultural holdings.

630 310   US   ISSN 0082-9315
CENSUS OF AGRICULTURE: FINAL REPORTS. (Published in 4 vols.) 1840. quinquennial, latest 1992. $557 for Geographic Area Series (foreign $696.25); other reports also available. U.S. Bureau of the Census, Customer Services, Washington, DC 20233. TEL 301-457-4100. FAX 301-457-4714. URL: http://www.census.gov/. (Subscr. to: Superintendent of Documents, U.S. Government Printing Office, Box 371954, Pittsburgh, PA 15250-7954. TEL 202-512-1800. FAX 202-512-2250; Or: Bernan, 4611-F Assembly Dr., Lanham, MD 20706. TEL 301-459-7666. FAX 301-459-0056) **Document type:** government publication.
● Also available online.
Also available on CD-ROM.
   Description: Presents agricultural statistics for each state and Puerto Rico; published in 4 vols.: Vol. 1 - State and County Data (United States Summary and vols. for each state plus Puerto Rico avail.); Vol. 2 - Subject Reports; Vol. 3 - Related Survey; Vol. 4 - Census of Horticultural Specialties

630 658   CN   ISSN 0820-9030
HD9044.C2
CEREALS AND OILSEEDS REVIEW. 1978. m. Can.$138($166) (foreign $193). Statistics Canada, Operations and Integration Division, Circulation Management, Jean Talon Bldg., 2-C12, Tunney's Pasture, Ottawa, ON K1A 0T6, Canada. TEL 613-951-7277; 800-267-6677. FAX 613-951-1584. URL: http://www.statcan.ca.
   Description: Reports on supply and disposition of the four traditional major wheat exporters.

630   XR
CESKA ZEMEDELSKA BIBLIOGRAFIE/CZECH AGRICULTURAL BIBLIOGRAPHY. 1966. a. $60 (effective 1997). Ustav Zemedelskych a Potravinarskych Informaci, Slezska 7, 120 56 Prague 2, Czech Republic. TEL 420-2-24257939. FAX 420-2-24253938. E-mail: uzlk@uzpi.cz. (diskette format) **Document type:** bibliography.
   Formerly: Ceskoslovenska Zemedelska Bibliografie (ISSN 0232-0851)
   Description: Contains bibliographical citations of books and journals published in Czech Republic.

338.1   UK
CHARTERED INSTITUTE OF PUBLIC FINANCE AND ACCOUNTANCY. COUNTY FARMS STATISTICS. ACTUALS. a. £55. Chartered Institute of Public Finance and Accountancy, Statistical Information Service, 3 Robert St., London WC2N 6BH, England. TEL 44-171-543-5600. FAX 44-171-543-5700. (back issues avail.)

338.1   CL
CHILE. INSTITUTO NACIONAL DE ESTADISTICAS. ESTADISTICAS AGROPECUARIAS. (In 2 parts: Uso del Suelo; Produccion Fruticola) a. Ch.$2000 (US $13.50; elsewhere $15.90) (effective 1995). Instituto Nacional de Estadisticas, Av. Bulnes 418, Casilla 498, Correo 3 Santiago, Chile. TEL 56-2-6991441. FAX 56-2-6712169.
   Formerly (until 1985): Programa de Mejoramiento de las Estadisticas Agropecuarias.

636 310   CL
CHILE. INSTITUTO NACIONAL DE ESTADISTICAS. ESTADISTICAS PECUARIAS. 1985. s-a. Ch.$2000 (US $13.50; elsewhere $15) (effective 1995). Instituto Nacional de Estadisticas, Av. Bulnes 418, Casilla 498, Correo 3 Santiago, Chile. TEL 56-2-6991441. FAX 56-2-6712169.

633.11   CL
CHILE. INSTITUTO NACIONAL DE ESTADISTICAS. INDUSTRIA MOLINERA. TRIGO. 1978. q. Esc.1100 (US $7.50; elsewhere $8.60) (effective 1995). Instituto Nacional de Estadisticas, Av. Bulnes 418, Casilla 498, Correo 3 Santiago, Chile. TEL 56-2-6991441. FAX 56-2-6712169.

338.1 016   US
COMMODITY YEARBOOK STATISTICAL UPDATE. (Suppl. to: Commodity Year Book) 3/yr. $95 (effective 1997). Bridge Publishing, 30 S. Wacker Dr., Ste. 1810, Chicago, IL 60606. TEL 312-454-1801; 800-621-5271. FAX 312-454-0239. E-mail: crbinfo@ais.net; URL: http://www.krf.com/crb/. Eds. Bob Hafer, Ann Ingles. R&P contact: Carlene Camera. charts; mkt.; stat. (also avail. in microfiche from CIS) **Indexed:** SRI. **Document type:** trade publication.
   Formerly: Commodity Yearbook Statistical Abstract Service (ISSN 0010-3241)

630 319   NZ   ISSN 0545-7769
COMPENDIUM OF NEW ZEALAND FARM PRODUCTION STATISTICS. 1955. biennial. NZ.$2. Meat and Wool Boards' Economic Service, P.O. Box 5179, Wellington, New Zealand. FAX 64-4-712-173. circ. 4,000.

636   HO
CONSUMO PECUARIO NACIONAL. a. Secretaria de Planificacion, Coordinacion y Presupuesto, Direccion General de Estadistica y Censos, Tegucigalpa D.C., Honduras. **Document type:** government publication.

630   NE   ISSN 0921-4305
CONSUMPTIE VAN VOEDINGSMIDDELEN IN NEDERLAND. 1983. a. price varies. Landbouw-Economisch Instituut, Burg. Patijnlaan 19, 2585 BE The Hague, Netherlands. TEL 31-70-3308330. FAX 31-70-3615624. E-mail: postmaster@lei.dlo.nl; URL: http://www.lei.dlo.nl/lei. **Document type:** government publication.

633 016   UK   ISSN 0961-3528
COTTON AND TROPICAL FIBRES. (Not avail. in printed format) 1976. a. £35($60) (effective 1997). CAB International, Wallingford, Oxon. OX10 8DE, England. TEL 44-1491-832111. FAX 44-1491-826090. TELEX 847964 COMAGG G. E-mail: cabi@cabi.org; URL: http://www.cabi.org. (U.S. subscr. to: CAB International, North American Office, 198 Madison Ave., New York, NY 10016. TEL 212-726-6490. FAX 212-686-7993) Ed. A.M. Doroszenko. circ. 200. (diskette format; back issues avail.; reprint service avail.) **Indexed:** Field Crop Abstr., Herb.Abstr. **Document type:** bibliography.
● Also available online. Vendor(s): DIMDI, European Space Agency (File nos.16 & 124/CAB), Knight-Ridder Information, Inc.
   Formerly (until 1991): Cotton and Tropical Fibres Abstracts (ISSN 0308-6577)
   Description: Covers research on cotton, sisal, jute, kenaf, roselle, other tropical fibres.

COTTON: WORLD STATISTICS. see *TEXTILE INDUSTRIES AND FABRICS — Abstracting, Bibliographies, Statistics*

631 016   UK   ISSN 0306-7556
CROP PHYSIOLOGY ABSTRACTS. 1975. bi-m. £375($655) (effective 1997). CAB International, Wallingford, Oxon. OX10 8DE, England. TEL 44-1491-832111. FAX 44-1491-826090. TELEX 847964 COMAGG G. E-mail: cabi@cabi.org; URL: http://www.cabi.org. (U.S. subscr. to: CAB International, North American Office, 198 Madison Ave., New York, NY 10016. TEL 212-726-6490. FAX 212-686-7993) circ. 250. (also avail. in diskette format; microfiche; back issues avail.; reprint service avail.) **Document type:** abstracting/indexing.
● Also available online. Vendor(s): DIMDI, European Space Agency, Knight-Ridder Information, Inc., STN International.
   Description: Deals with the physiology of all higher plants of economic importance.

631   EI
CROP PRODUCTION HALF-YEARLY STATISTICS. 2/yr. $80. (Statistical Office of the European Communities) Office for Official Publications of the European Communities, Rue Alcide de Gasperi, 2920 Luxembourg, Luxembourg. (Dist. in U.S. by: UNIPUB, 4611-F Assembly Dr., Lanham, MD 20706-4391. TEL 800-274-4888. FAX 800-865-3450) (also avail. in microfiche from CIS) **Indexed:** IIS.
   Former titles: Agricultural Statistics Series No.1: Crop Production; Statistical Office of the European Communities. Crop Production (ISSN 0378-3588)
   Description: Contains most recent data on land use, arable crops (areas, yields and production) and fruit and vegetable consumption, weather conditions supply balance sheet, plant products and fruit.

CURRENT BIBLIOGRAPHIES ON SCIENCE AND TECHNOLOGY: BIOLOGY, PHARMACY AND FOOD SCIENCE. see *BIOLOGY — Abstracting, Bibliographies, Statistics*

AGRICULTURE — ABSTRACTING, BIBLIOGRAPHIES, STATISTICS

630 016   US   ISSN 0090-0508
Z5071   CODEN: CCASDR
CURRENT CONTENTS: AGRICULTURE, BIOLOGY & ENVIRONMENTAL SCIENCES. Short title: C C: A B & E S. (Includes Author Index and Address Directory, Current Book Contents, and Title Word Index) 1970. w. $730. Institute for Scientific Information, 3501 Market St., Philadelphia, PA 19104. TEL 215-386-0100. FAX 215-386-2911. (And: Brunel Science Park, Brunel University, Uxbridge UB8 3PQ, England) (also avail. in magnetic tape; diskette format) Indexed: Abstr.Bull.Inst.Pap.Chem., AESIS, Compumath, Forest.Abstr., Forest Prod.Abstr., Ind.Sci.Rev., Rev.Appl.Entomol., Sci.Cit.Ind., SSCI. **Document type:** academic/scholarly publication, bibliography.
● Also available online. Vendor(s): Knight-Ridder Information, Inc. (File no.440), Ovid Technologies, Inc. (CTOC,CBIB,AGRI).
Also available on CD-ROM.
—BLDSC (3496.126000); CASDDS; CISTI.
Formerly: C C A F V (Current Contents, Agricultural, Food and Veterinary Sciences) (ISSN 0011-3379)
Description: Tables of contents of the world's leading publications covering biology, biotechnology and applied microbiology.

310   CY   ISSN 0379-0924
CYPRUS. DEPARTMENT OF STATISTICS AND RESEARCH. AGRICULTURAL STATISTICS. (Text in English, Greek) a. £C4. Ministry of Finance, Department of Statistics and Research, 13 Lord Byron Ave., Nicosia, Cyprus. TEL 357-2-302349. FAX 357-2-456712. **Document type:** government publication.
Formerly: Cyprus. Department of Statistics and Research. Agricultural Survey.
Description: Summarizes accounts of the broad agricultural sector, with data on crop and livestock production, forestry and fishing, employment and land use.

310   CY
CYPRUS. DEPARTMENT OF STATISTICS AND RESEARCH. CENSUS OF POULTRY. (Text in English) 1982. irreg. £C0.75. Ministry of Finance, Department of Statistics and Research, 13 Lord Byron Ave., Nicosia, Cyprus. TEL 357-2-302349. FAX 357-2-456712. **Document type:** government publication.
Description: Presents number of holders, structure and size of poultry units and number of poultry; covers chickens, pigeons, rabbits and quail.

330   CN   ISSN 0317-6207
DAIRY FACTS AND FIGURES AT A GLANCE. a. Can.$3 (foreign Can.$4). Dairy Farmers of Canada, 75 Albert St., Ste. 1101, Ottawa, ON K1P 5E7, Canada. FAX 613-236-5749.
Description: Collection of tables containing statistical information on the Canadian dairy industry, as well as related international data.

637.1   US   ISSN 0098-6690
HD9275.U3
DAIRY MARKET STATISTICS: ANNUAL SUMMARY. 1965. a. $4. U.S. Department of Agriculture, Agricultural Marketing Service (Washington), Dairy Division, Washington, DC 20250. **Document type:** government publication.

637   CN   ISSN 0300-0753
DAIRY REVIEW/REVUE LAITIERE. (Text in English and French) 1932. q. Can.$119 (foreign $119) (effective 1998). Statistics Canada, Operations and Integration Division, Circulation Management, Jean Talon Bldg., 2-C12, Tunney's Pasture, Ottawa, ON K1A 0T6, Canada. TEL 613-951-7277; 800-267-6677. FAX 613-951-1584. URL: http://www.statcan.ca. (also avail. in microform from MML) **Document type:** government publication.
Incorporates (in Apr. 1995): Production and Inventories of Process Cheese and Instant Skim Milk Powder (ISSN 0705-551X)
Description: Provides a statistical summary of the dairy situation in Canada and the provinces, including farm sales of milk for fluid and manufacturing purposes.

630 016   UK   ISSN 0011-5681
DAIRY SCIENCE ABSTRACTS. 1939. m. £460($805) (effective 1997). CAB International, Wallingford, Oxon. OX10 8DE, England. TEL 44-1491-832111. FAX 44-1491-826090. TELEX 847964 COMAGG G. E-mail: cabi@cabi.org; URL: http://www.cabi.org. (U.S. subscr. to: CAB International, North American Office, 198 Madison Ave., New York, NY 10016. TEL 212-726-6490. FAX 212-686-7993) Ed. E.J. Mann. adv.; bk.rev.; abstr.; pat.; stat.; index. circ. 1,500. (also avail. in diskette format; back issues avail.; reprint service avail.) Indexed: Abstr.Hyg., Anim.Breed.Abstr., Chem.Abstr, Field Crop Abstr., Herb.Abstr., Ind.Vet., Nutr.Abstr., Rural Recreat.Tour.Abstr., Trop.Dis.Bull., Vet.Bull., World Agri.Econ.& Rural Sociol.Abstr. **Document type:** abstracting/indexing.
● Also available online. Vendor(s): DIMDI, European Space Agency, Knight-Ridder Information, Inc.
—BLDSC (3516.000000); Linda Hall.
Description: Provides information on all aspects of milk production, secretion, processing, and milk products.

637 310   NZ   ISSN 0114-975X
DAIRY STATISTICS. 1970. a. Livestock Improvement Corporation Ltd., Cnr. Ruakura & Morrinsville Rds., Private Bag 3016, Hamilton, New Zealand. TEL 64-7-8560700. FAX 64-7-8562429. Ed. Frances West. circ. 2,900. **Document type:** academic/scholarly publication.
Former titles (until 1990): New Zealand Dairy Board. Livestock Improvement Division. Annual Report (ISSN 0114-2917); (until 1988): Livestock Improvement Report (ISSN 0113-2806); Farm Production Report and Summary of Boards Work (ISSN 0111-1388)
Description: Contains statistics on New Zealand dairy industry.
Refereed Serial

DATAVIN. see BEVERAGES — Abstracting, Bibliographies, Statistics

630.20112   DK
DENMARK. DANMARKS STATISTIK. LANDBRUGSSTATISTIK. (Text in Danish; notes in English) 1936. a. DKK 191.20 (effective 1997). Danmarks Statistik, Sejroegade 11, DK-2100 Copenhagen OE, Denmark. TEL 45-39-17-39-17. FAX 45-31-18-48-01. TELEX 16236. index. **Document type:** government publication.
Formerly: Denmark. Danmarks Statistik. Landbrugsstatistik. Herunder Gartneri og Skovbrug (ISSN 0070-3559)

DENMARK. STATENS JORDBRUGS- OG FISKERIOEKONOMISKE INSTITUT. SERIE A: LANDBRUGSREGNSKABSSTATISTIK/AGRICULTURAL ACCOUNTS STATISTICS. see AGRICULTURE — Agricultural Economics

DENMARK. STATENS- JORDBRUGS OG FISKERIOEKONOMISKE INSTITUT. SERIE D: GARTNERI-REGNSKABSSTATISTIK/HORTICULTURAL ACCOUNTS STATISTICS. see AGRICULTURE — Agricultural Economics

630   BO
ENCUESTA NACIONAL AGROPECUARIA. RESULTADOS DE LA PRODUCCION AGRICOLA. a. Instituto Nacional de Estadistica, Departamento de Estadisticas Agropecuarias, Casilla de Correo No. 6129, La Paz, Bolivia.

630 310   PN   ISSN 0378-2581
HD9424.P26
ESTADISTICA PANAMENA. SITUACION ECONOMICA. SECCION 312. PRODUCCION PECUARIA. 1954. a. Bl.0.50 (effective 1997). Direccion de Estadistica y Censo, Contraloria General, Apdo. 5213, Panama 5, Panama. FAX 507-269-7294. circ. 850. **Document type:** government publication, bulletin.
Description: Presents information on cattle, pigs and chickens, including milk and egg production.

338.1   PN   ISSN 0378-2565
SB192.P2
ESTADISTICA PANAMENA. SITUACION ECONOMICA. SECCION 312. SUPERFICIE SEMBRADA Y COSECHA DE ARROZ, MAIZ Y FRIJOL DE BEJUCO. 1954. a. Bl.0.50 (effective 1997). Direccion de Estadistica y Censo, Contraloria General, Apdo. 5213, Panama 5, Panama. FAX 507-269-7294. circ. 800. **Document type:** government publication, bulletin.
Description: Presents data on the harvests of rice, corn and beans.

630 310   PN
SB87.P2
ESTADISTICA PANAMENA. SITUACION ECONOMICA. SECCION 312. SUPERFICIE SEMBRADA Y COSECHA DE CAFE Y CANA DE AZUCAR. 1954. a. Bl.0.50. Direccion de Estadistica y Censo, Contraloria General, Apdo. 5213, Panama 5, Panama. FAX 507-269-7294. circ. 700. **Document type:** government publication, bulletin.
Formerly: Estadistica Panamena. Situation Economica. Seccion 312. Superficie Sembrada y Cosecha de Cafe, Tabaco y Cana de Azucar (ISSN 0378-2573)
Description: Offers data on the harvests of coffee and sugar cane. Includes export amounts and prices.

630.021   PN   ISSN 0378-2530
S562.P33
ESTADISTICA PANAMENA. SITUACION ECONOMICA. SECCION 351. PRECIOS PAGADOS POR EL PRODUCTOR AGROPECUARIO. 1974. a. Bl.0.50 (effective 1997). Direccion de Estadistica y Censo, Contraloria General, Apdo. 5213, Panama 5, Panama. FAX 507-269-7294. circ. 700. **Document type:** government publication, bulletin.
Description: Presents prices paid for animal feed, fertilizer, pesticide, farm equipment, construction materials, veterinary care, and rice and corn seed.

338.021   PN   ISSN 0378-2611
ESTADISTICA PANAMENA. SITUACION ECONOMICA. SECCION 351. PRECIOS RECIBIDOS POR EL PRODUCTOR AGROPECUARIO. 1958. s-a. Bl.0.50 (effective 1997). Direccion de Estadistica y Censo, Contraloria General, Apdo. 5213, Panama 5, Panama. FAX 507-269-7294. circ. 800. **Document type:** government publication, bulletin.
Description: Presents prices received on the sale of agricultural products.

338.021   PN   ISSN 0378-2549
ESTADISTICA PANAMENA. SITUACION ECONOMICA. SECCION 351. PRECIOS RECIBIDOS POR EL PRODUCTOR AGROPECUARIO. COMPENDIO. 1975. a. Bl.0.50 (effective 1997). Direccion de Estadistica y Censo, Contraloria General, Apdo. 5213, Panama 5, Panama. FAX 507-269-7294. circ. 800. **Document type:** government publication, bulletin.

630.021   PN   ISSN 0378-4991
HD9014.P3
ESTADISTICA PANAMENA. SITUACION ECONOMICA. SECCION 352. HOJA DE BALANCE DE ALIMENTOS. 1960. a. Bl.0.50 (effective 1997). Direccion de Estadistica y Censo, Contraloria General, Apdo. 5213, Panama 5, Panama. FAX 507-269-7294. circ. 250. **Document type:** government publication, bulletin.
Description: Offers data on production, foreign commerce, internal resources and their usage, and consumption.

630   EI   ISSN 1024-4263
HD1920.5
EUROSTAT. STATISTICS IN FOCUS. AGRICULTURE, FORESTRY AND FISHERIES. French edition: Eurostat. Statistiques en Bref. Agriculture, Sylviculture et Peche (ISSN 1024-4271); German edition: Eurostat. Statistik Kurzgefasst. Land- und Forstwirtschaft, Fischerei (ISSN 1024-428X) (Text in English) 1991. a. 160 ECU. Statistical Office of the European Communities, Eurostat, Rue Alcide de Gasperi, 2920 Luxembourg, Luxembourg. TEL 352-4301-34526. FAX 352-4301-34415. (Dist. in the U.S. by: Unipub, 4611-F Assembly Dr., Lanham, MD 20706. TEL 800-274-4888. FAX 301-459-0056) **Document type:** government publication.
—BLDSC (8453.536720).
Formerly (until 1994): Eurostat. Rapid Reports. Agriculture, Forestry and Fisheries (ISSN 1017-5776); Which superseded in part: Eurostat. Rapid Reports. Agriculture (ISSN 1016-0221)

AGRICULTURE — ABSTRACTING, BIBLIOGRAPHIES, STATISTICS

630   EI   ISSN 1024-428X
EUROSTAT. STATISTIK KURZGEFASST. LAND- UND FORSTWIRTSCHAFT, FISCHEREI. English edition: Eurostat. Statistics in Focus. Agriculture, Forestry and Fisheries (ISSN 1024-4263); French edition: Eurostat. Statistiques en Bref. Agriculture, Sylviculture et Peche (ISSN 1024-4271) (Text in German) 1991. m. Statistical Office of the European Communities, Eurostat, Rue Alcide de Gasperi, 2920 Luxembourg, Luxembourg. TEL 352-4301-34526. FAX 352-4301-34415. (Dist. in the U.S. by: Unipub, 4611-F Assembly Dr., Lanham, MD 20706. TEL 800-274-4888. FAX 301-459-0056) **Document type:** government publication.
    Formerly (until 1994): Eurostat. Schnellberichte. Land- und Forstwirtschaft, Fischerei (ISSN 1017-5784)

630 639.3   EI   ISSN 1024-4271
EUROSTAT. STATISTIQUES EN BREF. AGRICULTURE, SYLVICULTURE ET PECHE. English edition: Eurostat. Statistics in Focus. Agriculture, Forestry and Fisheries (ISSN 1024-4263); German edition: Eurostat. Statistik Kurzgefasst. Land- und Forstwirtschaft, Fischerei (ISSN 1024-428X) (Text in French) 1991. m. Statistical Office of the European Communities, Eurostat, Rue Alcide de Gasperi, 2920 Luxembourg, Luxembourg. TEL 352-4301-34526. FAX 352-4301-34415. (Dist. in the U.S. by: Unipub, 4611-F Assembly Dr., Lanham, MD 20706. TEL 800-274-4888. FAX 301-459-0056) **Document type:** government publication.
    Formerly (until 1994): Eurostat. Statistiques Rapides. Agriculture, Sylviculture et Peche (ISSN 1017-5768)

016.6318   II   ISSN 0014-5564
F A I ABSTRACT SERVICE. (Text in English) 1962. m. $10. Fertiliser Association of India, 10 Shaheed Jit Singh Marg, New Delhi 110067, India. TEL 91-11-667144. FAX 91-11-696-0052. TELEX 031-73056. Ed. V. Sarangan. abstr. circ. 1,000. **Document type:** abstracting/indexing.

F A O DOCUMENTATION - CURRENT BIBLIOGRAPHY. see FISH AND FISHERIES — *Abstracting, Bibliographies, Statistics*

630 338.1 310   UN   ISSN 1011-8780
HD9000.4
F A O QUARTERLY BULLETIN OF STATISTICS/BULLETIN TRIMESTRIEL F A O DE STATISTIQUES/BOLETIN TRIMESTRAL F A O DE ESTADISTICAS. (Text in English, French and Spanish) 1948. q. $24. Food and Agriculture Organization of the United Nations (Rome), Via delle Terme di Caracalla, 00100 Rome, Italy. TEL 57974350. FAX 57975155. mkt.; stat.; index, cum.index. circ. 7,800. (also avail. in microfiche from CIS; back issues avail.) **Indexed:** Biol.& Agr.Ind., IIS, Key to Econ.Sci., Nutr.Abstr., P.A.I.S.For.Lang.Ind., P.A.I.S., Rice Abstr., World Bank.Abstr.
—KR SourceOne; Linda Hall.
    Former titles (unitl 1988): F A O Monthly Bulletin of Statistics (ISSN 0379-0010); F A O Monthly Bulletin of Agricultural Economics and Statistics (ISSN 0027-0229)
    Description: Provides facts and data on world food and agricultural conditions, with an analysis of the factors influencing them.

338.1 314   UK
FARM BUSINESS STATISTICS FOR SOUTH EAST ENGLAND. 1969. a. £3. University of London, Wye College, Department of Agricultural Economics, Ashford, Kent TN25 5AH, England. TEL 44-1233-812401. Ed.Bd. charts; stat. circ. 800. **Document type:** academic/scholarly publication, monographic series.

630 658   CN   ISSN 0703-7945
FARM CASH RECEIPTS. 1940. q. Can.$44($53) (foreign $62). Statistics Canada, Operations and Integration Division, Circulation Management, Jean Talon Bldg., 2-C12, Tunney's Pasture, Ottawa, ON K1A 0T6, Canada. TEL 613-951-7277; 800-267-6677. FAX 613-951-1584. URL: http://www.statcan.ca.
    Description: Presents estimates of revenue received by farmers from the sale of farm products and from direct program payments, by main commodity, cumulative by quarter for Canada and provinces.

637.1   US   ISSN 0498-2002
FEDERAL MILK ORDER MARKET STATISTICS. 1960. m. free. U.S. Department of Agriculture, Agricultural Marketing Service (Washington), Dairy Division, Washington, DC 20250. TEL 202-720-2352. stat. circ. 800. (also avail. in microfiche from CIS; reprint service avail. from CIS) **Indexed:** Amer.Stat.Ind. (1974-). **Document type:** government publication.

631.8   II   ISSN 0430-327X
FERTILISER ASSOCIATION OF INDIA. FERTILISER STATISTICS. (Text in English) 1956. a. $25. Fertiliser Association of India, 10 Shaheed Jit Singh Marg, New Delhi 110067, India. TEL 91-11-667144. FAX 91-11-696-0052. TELEX 031-73056. Ed.Bd. charts; stat.
—Linda Hall.

633 016   UK   ISSN 0015-069X
SB183
FIELD CROP ABSTRACTS; monthly abstract journal on world annual cereal, legume, root, oilseed and fibre crops. 1948. m. £605($1090) (effective 1997). CAB International, Wallingford, Oxon. OX10 8DE, England. TEL 44-1491-832111. FAX 44-1491-826090. TELEX 847964 COMAGG G. E-mail: cabi@cabi.org; URL: http://www.cabi.org. (U.S. subscr. to: CAB International, North American Office, 198 Madison Ave., New York, NY 10016. TEL 212-726-6490. FAX 212-686-7993) bk.rev.; abstr.; bibl.; index. circ. 1,300. (also avail. in diskette format; back issues avail.; reprint service avail.) **Indexed:** Anim.Breed.Abstr., Apic.Abstr., Dairy Sci.Abstr., Forest.Abstr., Helminthol.Abstr., Plant Breed.Abstr., Rev.Appl.Entomol., Rural Recreat.Tour.Abstr., Weed Abstr., World Agri.Econ.& Rural Sociol.Abstr. **Document type:** abstracting/indexing.
●Also available online. Vendor(s): DIMDI, European Space Agency, Knight-Ridder Information, Inc., STN International.
—BLDSC (3920.000000); Linda Hall.
    Description: Covers literature on agronomy, field production, crop botany, and physiology of all annual field crops, both temperate and tropical.

630 338.1   NE   ISSN 1381-0200
DE FINANCIELE POSITIE VAN DE TUINBOUW. 1994. a. fl.85. Landbouw-Economisch Instituut, Burg. Patijnlaan 19, 2585 BE The Hague, Netherlands. TEL 31-70-3308330. FAX 31-70-3615624. E-mail: postmaster@lei.dlo.nl; URL: http://www.lei.dlo.nl/lei. Ed. A. Boers. **Document type:** government publication.

630 310   FI
S242.F5
FINLAND. MINISTRY OF AGRICULTURE AND FORESTRY. INFORMATION CENTRE. STATISTICS. TIETOKAPPA. (Text in English, Finnish and Swedish) 1955. m. FIM 240. Ministry of Agriculture and Forestry, Information Centre, P.O. Box 310, FIN- 00171 Helsinki, Finland. TEL 358-9-134-211. FAX 358-9-1342-1573. Ed. Mika Tuikkanen. charts; stat. circ. 450.
    Formerly (until 1995): Finland. National Board of Agriculture. Statistics. Monthly Review of Agricultural Statistics (ISSN 0786-938X)
    Description: Publishes data on agriculture: statistics on dairies and slaughterhouses, yields, use of arable land and number of livestock.

630   US
FLORIDA AVOCADO ADMINISTRATIVE COMMITTEE. SHIPMENTS REPORT. 1954. w. Florida Avocado Administrative Committee, 18710 S.W. 288th St., Homestead, FL 33030. TEL 305-247-0848. FAX 305-245-1315. (Subscr. to: Box 900188, Homestead, FL 33090-0188) circ. 400. (back issues avail.)
    Description: Covers amount of Florida shipments, prices, California shipments, and import shipments.

630   US
FLORIDA LIME ADMINISTRATIVE COMMITTEE. SHIPMENTS REPORT. 1955. w. Florida Lime Administrative Committee, 18710 S.W. 288th St., Homestead, FL 33030. TEL 305-247-0848. FAX 305-245-1315. (Subscr. to: Box 900188, Homestead, FL 33090-0188) circ. 400. (back issues avail.)
    Description: Covers amount of Florida shipments, prices, Mexican lime totals, import totals, and California shipments.

FLOUR MILLING AND BAKING RESEARCH ASSOCIATION. ABSTRACTS. see FOOD AND FOOD INDUSTRIES — *Abstracting, Bibliographies, Statistics*

630   UN   ISSN 1014-3696
FOOD AND AGRICULTURE ORGANIZATION OF THE UNITED NATIONS. ASIA AND THE PACIFIC COMMISSION ON AGRICULTURAL STATISTICS. PERIODIC REPORT. irreg. free. Food and Agriculture Organization of the United Nations, Regional Office for Asia and the Pacific, Milawan Mansion, Phra Atit Rd., Bangkok 2, Thailand.
    Formerly: Asia and the Far East Commission on Agricultural Statistics. Periodic Report.

338.1   US
FOREIGN PRODUCTION, SUPPLY AND DISTRIBUTION OF AGRICULTURAL COMMODITIES. q. $200 per no. in US, Canada, Mexico; elsewhere $400. (Department of Agriculture) U.S. National Technical Information Service, 5825 Port Royal Rd., Springfield, VA 22161. TEL 703-487-4630. (magnetic tape)
    Description: Covers the production, import and export, and domestic use of grains, rice, dairy, poultry, livestock, oilseeds, cotton, coffee, sugar, and tobacco.

630 338.1   FR
FRANCE. MINISTERE DE L'AGRICULTURE, DE LA PECHE ET DE L'ALIMENTATION. AGRESTE INFO; la statistique agricole. m. 60 F. (foreign 120 F.) (effective 1997). Ministere de l'Agriculture, de la Peche et de l'Alimentation, Service Central des Enquetes et Etudes Statistiques, 4 av. de Saint Mande, 75570 Paris Cedex 12, France. TEL 33-1-49558585. FAX 33-1-49558503. (Subscr. to: B.P. 88, 31326 Castanet Tolosan Cedex, France) Ed. G. Raulin. (back issues avail.) **Document type:** government publication.
    Formerly: France. Ministere de l'Agriculture et de la Foret. Agreste Info (ISSN 1150-1324)
    Description: Provides information on new Agreste publications.

630 338.1   FR   ISSN 1270-265X
S229
FRANCE. MINISTERE DE L'AGRICULTURE, DE LA PECHE ET DE L'ALIMENTATION. BULLETIN. 1962. m. 440 F. (foreign 520 F.) (effective 1997). Ministere de l'Agriculture, de la Peche et de l'Alimentation, Service Central des Enquetes et Etudes Statistiques, 4 av. de Saint Mande, 75570 Paris Cedex 12, France. TEL 33-1-49558585. FAX 33-1-49558503. (Subscr. to: B.P. 88, 31326 Castanet Tolosan Cedex, France) (also avail. in microfiche) **Indexed:** Rural Recreat.Tour.Abstr., World Agri.Econ.& Rural Sociol.Abstr. **Document type:** bulletin, government publication.
    Former titles (until 1995): France. Ministere de l'Agriculture et de la Peche. Series: Bulletin (ISSN 1142-3218); France. Ministere de l'Agriculture. Service Central des Enquetes et Etudes Statistiques. Bulletin de Statistique Agricole (ISSN 0336-9919); Cahiers Mensuels de Statistique Agricole.

630   FR   ISSN 1167-4717
HD1941
FRANCE. MINISTERE DE L'AGRICULTURE, DE LA PECHE ET DE L'ALIMENTATION. CONJONCTURE GRAPH-AGRI (REGIONS). irreg., latest June, 1992. 130 F. (foreign 150 F.). Ministere de l'Agriculture, de la Peche et de l'Alimentation, Service Central des Enquetes et Etudes Statistiques, Direction des Affaires Financieres et Economiques, 4 av. de Saint Mande, 75570 Paris Cedex 12, France. TEL 33-1-49558585. FAX 33-1-49558503. (Subscr. to: B.P. 88, 31326 Castanet Tolosan Cedex, France) **Document type:** government publication.
    Formerly (until 1992): France. Ministere de l'Agriculture et de la Foret. Conjoncture Graph-Agri (Regions) (ISSN 0755-1908)

637 338.1   FR
FRANCE. MINISTERE DE L'AGRICULTURE, DE LA PECHE ET DE L'ALIMENTATION. CONJONCTURE LAIT ET PRODUITS LAITIERS. 1977. m. 178 F. (foreign 200 F.) (effective 1997). Ministere de l'Agriculture, de la Peche et de l'Alimentation, Service Central des Enquetes et Etudes Statistiques, 4 av. de Saint Mande, 75570 Paris, France. TEL 33-1-49558585 FAX 33-1-49558503. (Subscr. to: B.P. 88, 31326 Castanet Tolosan Cedex, France) **Document type:** government publication.
    Former titles: France. Ministere de l'Agriculture et de la Foret. Conjoncture Lait et Produits Laitiers; France. Ministere de l'Agriculture. Conjoncture Lait et Produits Laitiers; France. Ministere de l'Agriculture. Informations Rapides. Lait et Produits Laitiers; France. Ministere de l'Agriculture. Informations Rapides. Statistique Laitiere (ISSN 0223-4939)

AGRICULTURE — ABSTRACTING, BIBLIOGRAPHIES, STATISTICS

630 338.1　　　　　　　　FR
HD1941
FRANCE. MINISTERE DE L'AGRICULTURE, DE LA PECHE ET DE L'ALIMENTATION. DONNEES CHIFFRES AGRICULTURE. 1975. irreg. 630 F. (foreign 790 F.) for 10 nos. (effective 1997). Ministere de l'Agriculture, de la Peche et de l'Alimentation, Service Central des Enquetes et Etudes Statistiques, 4 av. de Saint Mande, 75570 Paris Cedex 12, France. TEL 33-1-49558585. FAX 33-1-49558503. **Document type:** government publication.
　Formerly: France. Ministere de l'Agriculture et de la Foret. Donnees Chiffres Agriculture; Incorporates: France. Ministere de l'Agriculture. Series "S". Production Animales (ISSN 0243-6566); France. Ministere de l'Agriculture. Series "S". Departements d'Outre-Mer (ISSN 0243-6574)

630 338.1　　　　　　　　FR
FRANCE. MINISTERE DE L'AGRICULTURE, DE LA PECHE ET DE L'ALIMENTATION. DONNEES CHIFFRES. I A A. 1978. irreg. 630 F. (foreign 690 F.) for 10 nos. (effective 1997). Ministere de l'Agriculture, de la Peche et de l'Alimentation, Service Central des Enquetes et Etudes Statistiques, 4 av. de Saint Mande, 75570 Paris Cedex 12, France. TEL 33-1-49558585. FAX 33-1-49558503. (Subscr. to: B.P. 88, 31326 Castanet Tolosan Cedex, France) **Document type:** government publication.
　Formerly: France. Ministere de l'Agriculture et de la Foret. Donnees Chiffres. I A A; Incorporates: France. Ministere de l'Agriculture. Series "S". Production Vegetale et Forestieres (ISSN 0755-3218); Incorporates in part: France. Ministere de l'Agriculture. Series "S". Industries Agricoles et Alimentaires (ISSN 0243-6647); Former titles: France. Ministere de l'Agriculture. Informations Rapides. Statistiques des Entreprises (ISSN 0243-6167); France. Ministere de l'Agriculture. Informations Rapides Agro-Alimentaires.

310 630　　　　　　　　FR　　ISSN 1274-1116
FRANCE. MINISTERE DE L'AGRICULTURE ET DE LA PECHE. AGRESTE. CAHIERS. Key Title: Agreste. Les Cahiers. (Supplement avail.) 1972. q. 464 F. (foreign 568 F.) (effective 1997). Ministere de l'Agriculture et de la Peche, Service Central des Enquetes et Etudes Statistiques, 4 av. de Saint Mande, 75570 Paris Cedex 12, France. TEL 33-1-49558585. FAX 33-1-49558503. URL: http://www.agriculture.gouv.fr. (Subscr. to: B.P. 88, 31326 Castanet Tolosan Cedex, France) (also avail. in microfiche) **Indexed:** Agri.Eng.Abstr., Geo.Abstr., IDA, Pig News & Info., Poult.Abstr., Rural Recreat.Tour.Abstr., World Agri.Econ.& Rural Sociol.Abstr. **Document type:** government publication.
　Former titles: France. Ministere de l'Agriculture et de la Foret. Agreste. Cahiers (ISSN 0998-4178); (until 1990): France. Ministere de l'Agriculture. Cahiers de Statistiques Agricoles (ISSN 0336-9943); France. Ministere de l'Agriculture et du Developpement Rural. Cahiers de Statistiques Agricoles (ISSN 0336-4178)

630 338.1　　　　　　　　FR
HD1941
FRANCE. MINISTERE DE L'AGRICULTURE ET DE LA PECHE. ANALYSES ET ETUDES. (Supplement to: Agreste. Les Cahiers (ISSN 1274-1116)) 1965. q. 568 F. (effective 1997). Ministere de l'Agriculture et de la Peche, Service Central des Enquetes et Etudes Statistiques, 4 av. Saint-Mande, 75570 Paris Cedex 12, France. TEL 33-1-49558585. FAX 33-1-49558503. URL: http://www.agriculture.gouv.fr. (also avail. in microfiche) **Indexed:** Dairy Sci.Abstr. **Document type:** government publication.
　Former titles: Ministere de l'Agriculture et de la Foret Analyses et Etudes (ISSN 0998-4186); (until 1989): France. Ministere de l'Agriculture. Collections de Statistique Agricole. Etude (ISSN 0336-5638)

634　　　　　　　　US
FRUIT STATISTICAL YEARBOOK. 1993. a. $22.50. National Peach Council, Box 11280, Columbia, SC 29211. TEL 803-253-4036. Ed. Charles Walker. **Description:** Provides comprehensive statistical information on production, marketing and sales.

314 338.1　　　　　　GW　　ISSN 0072-3681
GERMANY. STATISTISCHES BUNDESAMT. FACHSERIE 3, LAND- UND FORSTWIRTSCHAFT, FISCHEREI; REIHE 2: BETRIEBS-, ARBEITS- UND EINKOMMENSVERHAELTNISSE. (Consists of several subseries) irreg. price varies. 65180 Wiesbaden, Germany. TEL 49-611-75-1. FAX 49-611-724000. TELEX 61186-STBA-D. URL: http://www.statistik-bund.de. **Document type:** government publication.

633 338.1 314　　　　　GW
GERMANY. STATISTISCHES BUNDESAMT. FACHSERIE 3, LAND- UND FORSTWIRTSCHAFT, FISCHEREI; REIHE 3: LANDWIRTSCHAFTLICHE BODENNUETZUNG UND PFLANZLICHE ERZEUGUNG. 1961. a. DM.23 (effective 1997). Statistisches Bundesamt, 65180 Wiesbaden, Germany. TEL 49-611-75-1. FAX 49-611-724000. TELEX 61186-STBA-D. URL: http://www.statistik-bund.de. **Document type:** government publication.
　Former titles: Germany (Federal Republic, 1949-). Statistisches Bundesamt. Fachserie 3: Land- und Forstwirtschaft, Fischerei; Reihe 3: Bodennuetzung und Pflanzliche Erzeugung; Germany (Federal Republic, 1949-). Statistisches Bundesamt. Fachserie 3, Reihe 3: Pflanzliche Erzeugung; Germany (Federal Republic, 1949-) Statistisches Bundesamt. Fachserie 3, Reihe 3: Gartenbau und Weinwirtschaft.

636 338.1　　　　　　　GW
GERMANY. STATISTISCHES BUNDESAMT. FACHSERIE 3, LAND- UND FORSTWIRTSCHAFT, FISCHEREI; REIHE 4: VIEHBESTAND UND TIERISCHE ERZEUGUNG. a. DM.17.70 (effective 1997). 65180 Wiesbaden, Germany. TEL 49-611-75-1. FAX 49-611-724000. TELEX 61186-STBA-D. URL: http://www.statistik-bund.de. **Document type:** government publication.
　Formerly: Germany (Federal Republic, 1949-). Statistisches Bundesamt. Fachserie 3, Reihe 4: Tierische Erzeugung.

GERMANY. STATISTISCHES BUNDESAMT. FACHSERIE 16, LOEHNE UND GEHAELTER, REIHE 1: ARBEITERVERDIENSTE IN DER LANDWIRTSCHAFT. see BUSINESS AND ECONOMICS — Abstracting, Bibliographies, Statistics

338.1 314　　　　　　GW　　ISSN 0072-3894
GERMANY. STATISTISCHES BUNDESAMT. FACHSERIE 17, PREISE, REIHE 1: PREISE UND PREISINDIZES FUER DIE LAND- UND FORSTWIRTSCHAFT. m. DM.116.40. 65180 Wiesbaden, Germany. TEL 49-611-75-1. FAX 49-611-724000. TELEX 61186-STBA-D. URL: http://www.statistik-bund.de. **Document type:** government publication.

630　　　　　　　　GW　　ISSN 0433-860X
GESELLSCHAFT FUER BIBLIOTHEKSWESEN UND DOKUMENTATION DES LANDBAUES. MITTEILUNGEN. (Text in German; summaries occasionally in English) 1959. irreg. (2-3/yr.). DM.30($5.50) per no. Gesellschaft fuer Bibliothekswesen und Dokumentation des Landbaues, Engesserstr. 20, 76131 Karlsruhe, Germany. TEL 49-721-6625148. FAX 49-721-6625111. Ed. Heidemarie Schulz. adv.; bk.rev.; bibl.; cum.index: 1958-1973; circ. 150 (controlled). (back issues avail.) **Document type:** academic/scholarly publication.
—BLDSC (5846.600000).

633 016　　　　　　UK　　ISSN 1350-9837
SB183
GRASSLANDS AND FORAGE ABSTRACTS; monthly abstract journal on grassland husbandry and fodder crop production. 1931. m. £360($630) (effective 1997). CAB International, Wallingford, Oxon. OX10 8DE, England. TEL 44-1491-832111. FAX 44-1491-826090. TELEX 847964 COMAGG G. E-mail: cabi@cabi.org; URL: http://www.cabi.org. (U.S. subscr. to: CAB International, North American Office, 198 Madison Ave., New York, NY 10016. TEL 212-726-6490. FAX 212-686-7993) Ed. R.E. Hill. adv.; bk.rev.; abstr.; index. circ. 1,400. (also avail. in diskette format; back issues avail.; reprint service avail.) **Indexed:** Apic.Abstr., Nutr.Abstr. **Document type:** abstracting/indexing.
　●Also available online. Vendor(s): DIMDI, European Space Agency, Knight-Ridder Information, Inc., Ovid Technologies, Inc., STN International.
—BLDSC (4213.525000); Linda Hall.
　Formerly: Herbage Abstracts (ISSN 0018-0602)
　Description: Main topics covered include: management, productivity, and economics of grasslands and fodder crops; species and cultivar descriptions; fodder conservation; composition and nutritive value; botany; plant physiology; grassland ecology; and seed production, testing, and storage.

636　　　　　　　　GR　　ISSN 1107-0129
GREECE. NATIONAL STATISTICAL SERVICE. AGRICULTURAL AND LIVESTOCK PRODUCTION (YEAR). (Text in Greek) 1934. a. price varies. National Statistical Service of Greece, Statistical Information and Publications Division - Ethniki Statistiki Yperesia tes Ellados, 14-16 Lykourgou, 101 66 Athens, Greece. TEL 30-1-3289-397. FAX 30-1-3241-102. TELEX 216734 ESYE GR. (back issues avail.) **Document type:** government publication.

690　　　　　　　　　GR
GREECE. NATIONAL STATISTICAL SERVICE. REVISED AGRICULTURAL PRICE INDICES. (Text in English and Greek) 1974. irreg. latest 1994. $7. National Statistical Service of Greece, Statistical Information and Publications Division - Ethniki Statistiki Yperesia tes Ellados, 14-16 Lykourgou, 101 66 Athens, Greece. TEL 30-1-3244-748. FAX 30-1-3241-102. TELEX 216734 ESYE GR. (back issues avail.) **Document type:** government publication.
　Formerly (until 1985): Greece. National Statistical Service. Agricultural Price Indices.

630 382　　　　　　US　　ISSN 1183-3777
GREY BOOK. 1991. m. $75 (foreign $75). Stat Publishing, Box 8110-361, Blaine, WA 98230. TEL 604-535-8505. FAX 604-531-8818. E-mail: publisher@stat.mlnet.com; URL: http://stat.mlnet.com/stat/. Pub. P.B. Clancey. **Document type:** trade publication.
　Description: Specializes in export and production data for the United States, Canada and Australia with a special interest in pulses, birdseeds, and oilseeds.

HANDBOOK OF LIVE ANIMAL TRANSPORT. see TRANSPORTATION — Abstracting, Bibliographies, Statistics

AGRICULTURE — ABSTRACTING, BIBLIOGRAPHIES, STATISTICS

595.1 016   UK   ISSN 0957-6789
QL392.A1   CODEN: HEABEC
HELMINTHOLOGICAL ABSTRACTS. 1932. m. £355($620) (effective 1997). CAB International, Wallingford, Oxon. OX10 8DE, England. TEL 44-1491-832111. FAX 44-1491-826090. TELEX 847964 COMAGG G. (U.S. subscr. to: CAB International, North American Office, 198 Madison Ave., NY 10016. TEL 212-726-6490. FAX 212-686-7993) adv.; bk.rev.; abstr.; index, cum.index. circ. 1,200. (also avail. in diskette format; microfiche; back issues avail.; reprint service avail.) **Indexed:** Abstr.Hyg., Ind.Vet., Rev.Appl.Entomol., Sport Fish.Abstr., Trop.Dis.Bull., Vet.Bull., Wild.Rev., Zoo.Rec. **Document type:** abstracting/indexing.
● Also available online. Vendor(s): CISTI, DIMDI, European Space Agency (File nos.16 & 124/CAB), Knight-Ridder Information, Inc., Ovid Technologies, Inc. (VETR).
—Linda Hall.
Supersedes: Helminthological Abstracts. Series A: Animal and Human Helminthology (ISSN 0300-8339)
Description: Covers the literature on parasitic helminths: gastrointestinal nematodes, liver flukes, hydatid, trichinella, schistosomes, filariids, and taenia. Aspects covered include morphology, taxonomy, immunology, pathology, biochemistry, epidemiology, life history, control, and molecular biology.

633.1 338.1   UK   ISSN 1350-3057
HOME-GROWN CEREALS AUTHORITY. CEREALS STATISTICS. 1975. a. Home-Grown Cereals Authority, Research and Development Advisory Committee, Hamlyn House, Highgate Hill, London N19 5PR, England. TEL 0171-263-3391. TELEX 27615.

630   HU
HD1940.5
HUNGARY. KOZPONTI STATISZTIKAI HIVATAL. MEZOGAZDASAGI ELELMISZERIPARI STATISZTIKAI EVKONYV/HUNGARY. CENTRAL STATISTICAL OFFICE. YEARBOOK OF AGRICULTURAL STATISTICS. 1981. a. 185 Ft. Statisztikai Kiado Vallalat, Kaszasdulo u. 2, P.O. Box 99, 1300 Budapest 3, Hungary. TEL 36-1-180-3311. FAX 36-1-168-8635. TELEX 22-6699. (Dist. by: Kultura, P.O. Box 149, H-1389 Budapest, Hungary) stat. circ. 1,600. **Document type:** government publication.
Formerly: Hungary. Kozponti Statisztikai Hivatal. Mezogazdasagi Statisztikai Evkonyv (ISSN 0230-4066)

630 314   HU   ISSN 0238-7891
HD1940.5
HUNGARY. KOZPONTI STATISZTIKAI HIVATAL. MEZOGAZDASAGI ELELMISZERIPARI STATISZTIKAI ZSEBKONYV. a. 200 Ft. Statiqum Kiado es Nyomda Kft., Kaszasdulo u. 2, P.O. Box 99, 1300 Budapest 3, Hungary. TEL 36-1-180-3311. FAX 36-1-168-8635. TELEX 22-6699. (Subscr. to: Kultura, Box 149, 1389 Budapest, Hungary) stat. circ. 1,500. **Document type:** government publication.
Formerly: Hungary. Kozponti Statisztikai Hivatal. Mezogazdasagi Statisztikao Zsebkonyu (ISSN 0441-4683)

338.1   US   ISSN 0094-1271
S53
IDAHO AGRICULTURAL STATISTICS. 1972. a. $5. Department of Agriculture, Idaho Agricultural Statistics Service, Box 1699, Boise, ID 83701. FAX 208-334-1114. Ed. D.G. Gerhardt. circ. 2,500. (also avail. in microfiche from CIS) **Indexed:** SRI. **Document type:** government publication.

636.4 016   UK   ISSN 0568-2800
INDEX OF CURRENT RESEARCH ON PIGS. 1954. a. £40($70) (effective 1997). CAB International, Wallingford, Oxon., England. TEL 44-1491-832111. FAX 44-1491-826090. TELEX 847964 COMAGG G. E-mail: cabi@cabi.org; URL: http://www.cabi.org. (U.S. subscr. to: CAB International, North American Office, 198 Madison Ave., New York, NY 10016. TEL 212-726-6490. FAX 212-686-7993) circ. 1,300. **Indexed:** Anim.Breed.Abstr., Helminthol.Abstr., Nutr.Abstr. **Document type:** abstracting/indexing, bibliography.
● Also available online. Vendor(s): DIMDI, European Space Agency, Knight-Ridder Information, Inc., STN International.
—BLDSC (4377.750000).
Description: Contains research projects in progress throughout the world and lists publications from the previous year.

338.1 310   II
INDIA. DEPARTMENT OF RURAL DEVELOPMENT. ADMINISTRATIVE INTELLIGENCE DIVISION. PROGRESS REPORT ON SMALL FARMERS DEVELOPMENT AGENCY PROGRAMME. a. Ministry of Agriculture, Department of Rural Development, New Delhi 110 001, India. stat.

338.1 310   II
INDIA. DEPARTMENT OF RURAL DEVELOPMENT. ADMINISTRATIVE INTELLIGENCE DIVISION. SOME SPECIAL PROGRAMMES OF RURAL DEVELOPMENT. STATISTICS. a. Ministry of Agriculture, Department of Rural Development, New Delhi 110 001, India. stat.

338.1 636.5   II   ISSN 0536-8502
HD9016.I4
INDIA. MINISTRY OF AGRICULTURE. BULLETIN ON FOOD STATISTICS. (Text in English, Hindi) 1972. a. Rs.260($93.60) Ministry of Agriculture, Department of Economics and Statistics, A-2E-3 Kasturba Gandhi Marg Barracks, New Delhi 110 001, India. TEL 11-381523. Ed. Brajesh Kumar Gautam. stat. circ. 650. **Document type:** government publication.
Formerly: Studies in the Economics of Poultry Farming in Punjab.

633.2 310   II
INDIAN DEOILED CAKES EXPORTERS' PERFORMANCE MONITOR. (Text in English, French, German, Italian) 1986. m. $500. Commercial Information Services, No.1 Beena Building, 6th Road, T.P.S. IV, Bandra, Bombay 400 050, India. TEL 91-22-6426703. Ed. C. Moonjely. circ. 300.
Description: Statistics relating to quantity, prices and turnover of each participating deoiled cake exporter in India.

631.8   II
INDIAN FERTILISER STATISTICS. (Text in English) 1967. a. free. Ministry of Chemicals and Fertilisers, Economics and Statistics Division, New Delhi, India. stat.; circ. controlled. **Indexed:** Soils & Fert.

630   II   ISSN 0019-6363
INDIAN SOCIETY OF AGRICULTURAL STATISTICS. JOURNAL. (Text in English or Hindi) 1948. 3/yr. $30. Indian Society of Agricultural Statistics, P.O. Box 310, New Delhi, India. Ed. Prof. Prem Narain. adv.; bk.rev.; index. circ. 325. **Indexed:** Biol.Abstr., Biostat., Curr.Cont. (1971-), Plant Breed.Abstr., Stat.Theor.Meth.Abstr. (1971-).
—Linda Hall.

630 574 016   IO
INDONESIAN BIOLOGICAL AND AGRICULTURAL INDEX/INDEKS BIOLOGI DAN PERTANIAN DE INDONESIA. (Text in English, Indonesian) 1969. bi-m. free. National Library for Agricultural Science, Jalan Ir. Haji Juanda 20, Bogor, Indonesia. Ed. Sulastuti Sophia. circ. 1,500. **Indexed:** Biol.& Agr.Ind.
Former titles (until 1980): Index of Biology, Agriculture and Agro Economy (ISSN 0216-0803); Indonesian Biological and Agricultural Index (ISSN 0019-3593)

634.3   GW   ISSN 0946-9761
INFORMATIONSDIENST PRAXISBEZOGENER LITERATUR IM WEINBAU. 1994. q. DM.30. Bundesanstalt fuer Zuechtungsforschung an Kulturpflanzen, Institut fuer Rebenzuechtung Geilweilerhof, 76833 Siebeldingen, Germany. TEL 49-6345-41-0. FAX 49-6345-41177. E-mail: irz@geilweilerhof.suew.shuttle.de. Ed. Martin Klenert. circ. 150. **Document type:** abstracting/indexing, government publication.
● Also available online. Vendor(s): DIMDI, Knight-Ridder Information, Inc., STN International.
Description: Abstracts from journals, books, conference proceedings and reports on all aspects of technical literature on wine and grapevines in the German language.

637 016   BE   ISSN 0538-7086
INTERNATIONAL DAIRY FEDERATION. CATALOGUE OF I D F PUBLICATIONS/FEDERATION INTERNATIONALE LAITIERE. CATALOGUE DES PUBLICATIONS. (Text in English, French) 1973. a. free. International Dairy Federation, Square Vergote 41, 1030 Brussels, Belgium. TEL 32-2-7339888. FAX 32-2-7330413. bk.rev. circ. 3,000. (processed) **Document type:** catalog.

338.1   UK
INTERNATIONAL GRAINS COUNCIL. WORLD GRAIN STATISTICS (YEAR). (Text in English, French, Russian, Spanish) 1955. a. £80($125) (effective 1997). International Grains Council, One Canada Sq., Canary Wharf, London E14 5AE, England. TEL 44-171-513-1122. FAX 44-171-513-0630. E-mail: igc-fac@int-grains-council.org.uk. charts. **Document type:** trade publication.
Former titles: International Wheat Council. World Grain Statistics; (until 1987): World Wheat Statistics (ISSN 0512-3844)
Description: Compiles long-term data on production, trade, and prices of wheat, corn, barley, and other coarse grains.

631.6 016   NE   ISSN 0074-6436
    CODEN: BIIIDY
INTERNATIONAL INSTITUTE FOR LAND RECLAMATION AND IMPROVEMENT. BIBLIOGRAPHY. (Text in English) 1960. irreg., latest no.18, 1984. price varies. International Institute for Land Reclamation and Improvement, P.O. Box 45, 6700 AA Wageningen, Netherlands. TEL 31-317-490144. FAX 31-317-417187. TELEX 45888 INTAS NL. E-mail: ilri@ilri.nl. Ed. M.G. Bos. R&P contact: E.A. Rylhsen. adv. contact: E.A. Rylhsen. **Indexed:** Field Crop Abstr., Herb.Abstr., Rural Recreat.Tour.Abstr., Soils & Fert., World Agri.Econ.& Rural Sociol.Abstr. **Document type:** bibliography.

631   US   ISSN 1041-9268
IOWA CROPS & WEATHER. w. (Apr.-Nov.), m. (Dec.-Mar.). $13. Agricultural Statistics, Rm. 833 - 210 Walnut, Des Moines, IA 50309. TEL 515-284-4340. FAX 515-284-4342. Ed. Jim Sands. circ. 1,050. (looseleaf format) **Document type:** newsletter.
Description: Covers crop development and how it is affected by weather conditions in Iowa.

630   IE   ISSN 0791-301X
IRELAND. CENTRAL STATISTICS OFFICE. ADVANCE ESTIMATE OF OUTPUT, INPUT AND INCOME ARISING IN AGRICULTURE. a. I£2. Central Statistics Office, Skehard Rd., Cork, Ireland. TEL 353-21-359000. FAX 353-21-359090. E-mail: information@cso.ie; URL: http://www.cso.ie. **Document type:** government publication.

630   IE   ISSN 0791-3346
IRELAND. CENTRAL STATISTICS OFFICE. AGRICULTURAL INPUT PRICE INDEX. m. I£24. Central Statistics Office, Skehard Rd., Cork, Ireland. TEL 353-21-359000. FAX 353-21-359090. E-mail information@cso.ie; URL: http://www.cso.ie. (processed) **Document type:** government publication.
Formerly: Ireland. Central Statistics Office. Agricultural Input Price Indices.
Description: Monitors the prices of agricultural inputs

630   IE   ISSN 1393-2764
▼**IRELAND. CENTRAL STATISTICS OFFICE. AGRICULTURAL LABOUR INPUT.** 1995. a. I£2. Central Statistics Office, Skehard Rd., Cork, Ireland. TEL 353-21-359000. FAX 353-21-359090. E-mail information@cso.ie; URL: http://www.cso.ie. **Document type:** government publication.

AGRICULTURE — ABSTRACTING, BIBLIOGRAPHIES, STATISTICS

630　　　　　　　　IE　　　ISSN 0791-3354
IRELAND. CENTRAL STATISTICS OFFICE. AGRICULTURAL OUTPUT PRICE INDEX. m. I£24. Central Statistics Office, Skehard Rd., Cork, Ireland. TEL 353-21-359000. FAX 353-21-359090. E-mail: information@cso.ie; URL: http://www.cso.ie. (processed) **Document type:** government publication.
　　Formerly: Ireland. Central Statistics Office. Agricultural Output Price Indices.
　　Description: Monitors changes in the prices of agricultural outputs.

631.5 636　　　　IE　　　ISSN 0791-3524
IRELAND. CENTRAL STATISTICS OFFICE. AGRICULTURE - JUNE SURVEY - FINAL ESTIMATES. a. I£2. Central Statistics Office, Skehard Rd., Cork, Ireland. TEL 353-21-359000. FAX 353-21-359090. E-mail: information@cso.ie; URL: http://www.cso.ie. **Document type:** government publication.
　　Former titles: Ireland Central Statistics Office. June Survey - Final Estimates; Ireland Central Statistics Office. Land Utilization and Livestock Numbers; Ireland Central Statistical Office. Crops and Livestock Enumeration; (until 1984): Ireland Central Statistics Office. Crops and Pasture and Numbers of Livestock; Ireland Central Statistics Office. Crops and Livestock Numbers. (ISSN 0075-0549)

630　　　　　　　　IE　　　ISSN 0791-3141
IRELAND. CENTRAL STATISTICS OFFICE. AGRICULTURE - JUNE SURVEY - PROVISIONAL RESULTS. a. I£2. Central Statistics Office, Skehard Rd., Cork, Ireland. TEL 353-21-359000. FAX 353-21-359090. E-mail: information@cso.ie; URL: http://www.cso.ie. **Document type:** government publication.

636 314　　　　　IE　　　ISSN 0790-7729
IRELAND. CENTRAL STATISTICS OFFICE. DISTRIBUTION OF CATTLE AND PIGS BY SIZE OF HERD. biennial. I£2. Central Statistics Office, Skehard Rd., Cork, Ireland. TEL 353-21-359000. FAX 353-21-359090. E-mail: information@cso.ie; URL: http://www.cso.ie. **Document type:** government publication.
　　Description: Contains details of the number of agricultural holdings with cattle or pigs respectively and the number of cattle and pigs classified by size of herd.

630　　　　　　　　IE　　　ISSN 1393-2284
▼**IRELAND. CENTRAL STATISTICS OFFICE. ESTIMATED AREA, YIELD AND PRODUCTION OF CROPS.** 1995. a. I£2. Central Statistics Office, Skehard Rd., Cork, Ireland. TEL 353-21-359000. FAX 353-21-359090. E-mail: information@cso.ie; URL: http://www.cso.ie. **Document type:** government publication.

630　　　　　　　　IE　　　ISSN 1393-2667
▼**IRELAND. CENTRAL STATISTICS OFFICE. MEAT SUPPLY BALANCE.** 1995. a. I£2. Central Statistics Office, Skehard Rd., Cork, Ireland. TEL 353-21-359000. FAX 353-21-359090. E-mail: information@cso.ie; URL: http://www.cso.ie. **Document type:** government publication.
　　Description: Reconciles the total supplies of a product with the various uses taking account of changes in stock levels.

630　　　　　　　　IE　　　ISSN 1393-2276
IRELAND. CENTRAL STATISTICS OFFICE. PIG SLAUGHTERINGS. I£24. Central Statistics Office, Skehard Rd., Cork, Ireland. TEL 353-21-359000. FAX 353-21-359090. E-mail: information@cso.ie; URL: http://www.cso.ie. (processed) **Document type:** government publication.
　　Former titles (until 1995): Ireland. Central Statistics Office. Number and Weight of Pigs Slaughtered at Bacon Factories (ISSN 0791-3044); Ireland. Central Statistics Office. Pig Slaughterings.

636.4 314　　　　IE　　　ISSN 0791-3079
IRELAND. CENTRAL STATISTICS OFFICE. PIG SURVEY - APRIL. a. I£2. Central Statistics Office, Skehard Rd., Cork, Ireland. TEL 353-21-359000. FAX 353-21-359090. E-mail: information@cso.ie; URL: http://www.cso.ie. **Document type:** government publication.
　　Formerly: Ireland. Central Statistics Office. Pig Enumeration.

630　　　　　　　　IE　　　ISSN 0791-3095
IRELAND. CENTRAL STATISTICS OFFICE. PIG SURVEY - AUGUST. a. I£2. Central Statistics Office, Skehard Rd., Cork, Ireland. TEL 353-21-359000. FAX 353-21-359090. E-mail: information@cso.ie; URL: http://www.cso.ie. **Document type:** government publication.

630　　　　　　　　IE　　　ISSN 0791-3028
IRELAND. CENTRAL STATISTICS OFFICE. PRELIMINARY ESTIMATE OF OUTPUT, INPUT AND INCOME IN AGRICULTURE. a. I£2. Central Statistics Office, Skehard Rd., Cork, Ireland. TEL 353-21-359000. FAX 353-21-359090. E-mail: information@cso.ie; URL: http://www.cso.ie. **Document type:** government publication.

630　　　　　　　　IE　　　ISSN 0791-3036
IRELAND. CENTRAL STATISTICS OFFICE. PRODUCTION OF MILK AND MILK PRODUCTS. m. I£24. Central Statistics Office, Skehard Rd., Cork, Ireland. TEL 353-21-359000. FAX 353-21-359090. E-mail: information@cso.ie; URL: http://www.cso.ie. (processed) **Document type:** government publication.
　　Formerly: Ireland. Central Statistics Office. Production of Butter and Separated Milk Powder.

631.7 016　　　　UK　　　ISSN 0306-7327
S612
IRRIGATION AND DRAINAGE ABSTRACTS. 1975. q. £225($395) (effective 1997). CAB International, Wallingford, Oxon. OX10 8DE, England. TEL 44-1491-832111. FAX 44-1491-826090. TELEX 847964 COMAGG G. E-mail: cabi@cabi.org; URL: http://www.cabi.org. (U.S. subscr. to: CAB International, North American Office, 198 Madison Ave., New York, NY 10016. TEL 212-726-6490. FAX 212-686-7993) circ. 450. (also avail. in diskette format; back issues avail.) **Indexed:** Field Crop Abstr., Herb.Abstr. **Document type:** abstracting/indexing.
　　●Also available online. Vendor(s): DIMDI, European Space Agency, Knight-Ridder Information, Inc., STN International.
　　Description: Topics covered include: water management, irrigation of crop plants, soil-water relations, salinity and toxicity problems, environmental aspects, irrigation, drainage, plant water relations, meteorological aspects, and human and animal health.

310 338.1　　　　IS　　　ISSN 0334-2573
ISRAEL. CENTRAL BUREAU OF STATISTICS. AGRICULTURAL STATISTICS QUARTERLY. (Text in Hebrew, English) q. $25. Central Bureau of Statistics, P.O. Box 13015, Jerusalem 91130, Israel. TEL 972-2-6553400. FAX 972-2-6553325. charts; stat. **Document type:** government publication.
　　Formerly: Israel. Central Bureau of Statistics. Agricultural Statistics Monthly.

636 314　　　　　IT
SF55.I8
ITALY. ISTITUTO NAZIONALE DI STATISTICA. STATISTICHE DELLA CACCIA E DELLA PESCA. 1960. a. L.15000 (effective 1992 ed.). Istituto Nazionale di Statistica, Via Cesare Balbo 16, 00100 Rome, Italy. FAX 39-6-46735198. circ. 1,200. **Document type:** government publication.
　　Formerly: Italy. Istituto Nazionale di Statistica. Statistiche della Caccia, Pesca e Cooperazione; Which superseded in part (in 1988): Italy. Istituto Nazionale di Statistica. Statistiche della Zootecnia, della Pesca e della Caccia; Which was formerly: Italy. Istituto Centrale di Statistica. Annuario Statistico della Zootecnia, della Pesca e della Caccia (ISSN 0390-6426); (until 1975): Italy. Istituto Centrale di Statistica. Annuario di Statistiche Zootecniche (ISSN 0075-1774); Statistiche delle Macellazioni.

630 310　　　　　IV　　　ISSN 1018-2217
IVORY COAST. MINISTERE DE L'AGRICULTURE. ANNUAIRE DES STATISTIQUES AGRICOLES. 1970. a. $20 free in Ivory Coast (foreign 10,000 Fr.CFA) (effective 1998). Ministere de l'Agriculture et des Ressources Animales, Direction des Statistiques, de la Documentation et de l'Informatique, B.P. V-203, Abidjan, Ivory Coast. TEL 225-21-58-63. Ed. Acoupo Asseupi. adv. contact: Acoupo Asseupi. **Document type:** directory, government publication.
　　Formerly (until 1989): Ivory Coast. Ministere de l'Agriculture. Statistiques Agricoles.

630　　　　　　　　NE　　　ISSN 0925-9767
JAARSTATISTIEK VAN DE KUNSTMESTSTOFFEN. 1967. a. fl.22. Landbouw-Economisch Instituut, Burg. Patijnlaan 19, 2585 BE The Hague, Netherlands. TEL 31-70-3308330. FAX 31-70-3615624. E-mail: postmaster@lei.dlo.nl; URL: http://www.lei.dlo.nl/lei. Ed. A. Pronk. **Document type:** government publication.
　　Former titles (until 1980): Jaarstatistiek van de Kunstmestindustrie (ISSN 0921-4321); (until 1975): Jaarstatistiek van de Kunstmeststoffen (ISSN 0925-9775)

630　　　　　　　　NE　　　ISSN 0923-0718
JAARSTATISTIEK VAN DE VEEVOEDERS. 1971. a. fl.22. Landbouw-Economisch Instituut, Burg. Patijnlaan 19, 2585 BE The Hague, Netherlands. TEL 31-70-3308330. FAX 31-70-3615624. E-mail: postmaster@lei.dlo.nl; URL: http://www.lei.dlo.nl/lei. Ed.Bd. **Document type:** government publication.

630　　　　　　　　JA
JAPAN BANANA IMPORTERS ASSOCIATION. ANNUAL REPORT OF BANANA STATISTICS. a. Japan Banana Importers Association - Nihon Banana Yunyu Kumiai, 2-7-9 Hirakawa-cho, Chiyoda-ku, Tokyo 102, Japan. TEL 03-263-0461.

630　　　　　　　　JA
JAPAN BANANA IMPORTERS ASSOCIATION. MONTHLY BULLETIN OF BANANA STATISTICS. m. Japan Banana Importers Association - Nihon Banana Yunyu Kumiai, 2-7-9 Hirakawa-cho, Chiyoda-ku, Tokyo 102, Japan. TEL 03-263-0461.

630　　　　　　　　JA
JAPAN FRUIT GROWERS COOPERATIVE ASSOCIATION. FRUIT STATISTICS IN JAPAN.* irreg. Japan Fruit Growers Cooperative Association - Nihon Engei Nogyo Kyodokumiai Rengokai, 2-1, Tokai 3-chome, Ota-ku, Tokyo 101, Japan. TEL 03-257-3336.

338.1　　　　　　　US
KENTUCKY AGRICULTURAL STATISTICS. 1948. a. free. Department of Agriculture, Kentucky Agricultural Statistics Service, Box 1120, Louisville, KY 40201. TEL 502-582-5293. URL: http://www.usda.gov/nass/sso/ky/homepage.htm. Ed. Leland E. Brown. R&P contact: William Brannen. illus. circ. 5,000. **Indexed:** SRI. **Document type:** government publication.

316 630　　　　　KE　　　ISSN 0300-2373
KENYA. CENTRAL BUREAU OF STATISTICS. AGRICULTURAL CENSUS (LARGE FARM AREAS). (Former name of issuing body: Kenya. Ministry of Planning and National Development) irreg. price varies. Ministry of Finance and Planning, Central Bureau of Statistics, P.O. Box 30266, Nairobi, Kenya. (Subscr. to: Government Press, Haile Selaissie Ave., P.O. Box 30128, Nairobi, Kenya. TEL 254-2-334075) stat. **Document type:** government publication.

338.91 630　　　　NE　　　ISSN 0924-9745
KONINKLIJK INSTITUUT VOR DE TROPEN. ANNOTATED BIBLIOGRAPHIES SERIES. irreg. Koninklijk Instituut voor de Tropen, Information and Documentation - Royal Tropical Institute, Mauritskade 63, 1092 AD Amsterdam, Netherlands. TEL 31-20-5688272. FAX 31-20-5688286. TELEX 15080 KIT NL. **Document type:** bibliography.
　　Description: Covers literature on rural development and tropical agriculture.

630　　　　　　　　KU
KUWAIT. CENTRAL STATISTICAL OFFICE. AGRICULTURAL STATISTICS BULLETIN/KUWAIT. AL-IDARAH AL-MARKAZIYYAH LIL-IHSA'. NASHRAH AL-IHSA'AT AL-ZIRA'IYYAH. (Text in Arabic, English) 1971. a., latest for years 1994-1995. Central Statistical Office - Al-Idarah al-Markaziyyah lil-Ihsa', P.O. Box 26188, Safat 13122, Kuwait. TEL 965-2428200. FAX 965-2430464. TELEX 22468 TAKI ITET KT. **Document type:** government publication.

630　　　　　　　　NE　　　ISSN 0169-2100
LANDBOUW-ECONOMISCH INSTITUUT. JAARVERSLAG. 1942. a. Landbouw-Economisch Instituut, Burg. Patijnlaan 19, 2585 BE The Hague, Netherlands. TEL 31-70-3308330. FAX 31-70-3615624. E-mail: postmaster@lei.dlo.nl; URL: http://www.lei.dlo.nl/lei. **Document type:** government publication.

630　　　　　　　　NE　　　ISSN 0166-8129
LANDBOUW-ECONOMISCH INSTITUUT. MEDEDELINGEN. 1968. irreg., no.551, 1996. price varies. Landbouw-Economisch Instituut, Burg. Patijnlaan 19, 2585 BE The Hague, Netherlands. TEL 31-70-3308330. FAX 31-70-3615624. E-mail: postmaster@lei.dlo.nl; URL: http://www.lei.dlo.nl/lei. **Document type:** government publication.
　—BLDSC (5510.500000).

AGRICULTURE — ABSTRACTING, BIBLIOGRAPHIES, STATISTICS

630   NE   ISSN 0921-7169
LANDBOUW-ECONOMISCH INSTITUUT. PERIODIEKE RAPPORTAGE. 1982. irreg. price varies. Landbouw-Economisch Instituut, Burg. Patijnlaan 19, 2585 BE The Hague, Netherlands. TEL 31-70-3308330. FAX 31-70-3615624. E-mail: postmaster@lei.dlo.nl; URL: http://www.lei.dlo.nl/lei. **Document type:** government publication.
—BLDSC (6426.320000).

630 333.79   NE   ISSN 0929-0036
LANDBOUW, MILIEU EN ECONOMIE. 1993. a. fl.69. Landbouw-Economisch Instituut, Burg. Patijnlaan 19, 2585 BE The Hague, Netherlands. TEL 31-70-3308330. FAX 31-70-3615624. E-mail: postmaster@lei.dlo.nl; URL: http://www.lei.dlo.nl/lei. Ed.Bd. **Document type:** government publication.

630   NE   ISSN 0168-4019
LANDBOUWCIJFERS. 1954. a. fl.65. Landbouw-Economisch Instituut, Burg. Patijnlaan 19, 2585 BE The Hague, Netherlands. TEL 31-70-3308330. FAX 31-70-3615624. E-mail: postmaster@lei.dlo.nl; URL: http://www.lei.dlo.nl/lei. Ed. W. van Veen. **Document type:** government publication.
—BLDSC (5148.500000).
Description: Statistical data on income, sales, production, inputs, acreage and other features of Dutch agriculture.

338.109489   DK   ISSN 0107-7163
LANDOEKONOMISK OVERSIGT. English edition: Agriculture in Denmark (ISSN 0905-5142) (Text in Danish) 1954. a. free. Danske Landboforeninger - Danish Farmers' Unions, Axelborg, 4th Fl., Vesterbrogade 4A, DK-1620 Copenhagen V, Denmark. TEL 45-33-12-75-61. FAX 45-33-32-76-62. Ed. Morten Knudsen. stat.
Description: Presents statistical information on the agricultural situation in Denmark, with discussion of topics including production, marketing, and economic forecasts.

338.1   NE   ISSN 0168-1850
LEIDRAAD. 1983. bi-m. free. Landbouw-Economisch Instituut, Burg. Patijnlaan 19, 2585 BE The Hague, Netherlands. TEL 31-70-3308330. FAX 31-70-3615624. E-mail: postmaster@lei.dlo.nl; URL: http://www.lei.dlo.nl/lei. Ed. G.C. de Graaff. **Document type:** bibliography.
Description: Includes list of abstracts of publications, reports and studies of the institute, as well as a list of articles from other publications concerning agriculture.

LEVANTAMENTO SISTEMATICO DA PRODUCAO AGRICOLA/SYSTEMATIC SURVEY OF AGRICULTURAL PRODUCTION. see *AGRICULTURE — Agricultural Economics*

338.1   LB
LIBERIA. MINISTRY OF AGRICULTURE. PRODUCTION ESTIMATES OF MAJOR CROPS.* a. Ministry of Agriculture, Monrovia, Liberia. (Co-sponsor: Ministry of Planning and Economic Affairs)
Formerly: Liberia. Ministry of Agriculture. National Rice Production Estimates.

630 338.1   LB
LIBERIA. MINISTRY OF AGRICULTURE. STATISTICAL HANDBOOK.* triennial. Ministry of Agriculture, Monrovia, Liberia.

630   LY
LIBYA. CENSUS AND STATISTICS DEPARTMENT. AGRICULTURAL CENSUS. (Text in Arabic and English) 1974. decennial. free. Secretariat of Planning, Census and Statistics Department, P.O. Box 600, Tripoli, Libya. **Document type:** government publication.

630   MG
MADAGASCAR. MINISTERE DE LA PRODUCTION AGRICOLE ET DU PATRIMOINE FONCIER. STATISTIQUES AGRICOLES. ANNUAIRE. (Text in French) 1969. a. FMG.25595. Ministere de la Production Agricole et du Patrimoine Foncier, Service de la Methodologie et du Traitement des Informations Statistiques, B.P. 7086, Antananarivo 101, Madagascar. circ. 100.
Formerly: Malagasy Republic. Ministere de la Production Agricole et la Reforme Agraire. Statistiques Agricoles. Annuaire.
Description: Covers a variety of topics concerning agriculture in Madagascar.

338.1 630   II   ISSN 0304-6184
S280.M26
MADHYA PRADESH. DIRECTORATE OF AGRICULTURE. AGRICULTURAL STATISTICS. Key Title: Agricultural Statistics, Madhya Pradesh. (Text in English) a. Directorate of Agriculture, Bhopal, India.

630 016   HU   ISSN 0025-0198
MAGYAR MEZOGAZDASAGI BIBLIOGRAFIA. 1960. q. 1800 Ft. Orszagos Mezogazdasagi Konyvtar es Dokumentacios Kozpont, Attila ut. 93, 1253 Budapest 13, Hungary. TEL 36-1-1568211. FAX 36-1-1569219. Ed. Erika Gulacsi-Papay. bibl.; index. circ. 300.
—BLDSC (5343.600000).

633.1 016   UK   ISSN 0267-2987
MAIZE ABSTRACTS. 1975. bi-m. £310($540) (effective 1997). CAB International, Wallingford, Oxon. OX10 8DE, England. TEL 44-1491-832111. FAX 44-1491-826090. TELEX 847964 COMAGG G. E-mail: cabi@cabi.org; URL: http://www.cabi.org. (U.S. subscr. to: CAB International, North American Office, 198 Madison Ave., New York, NY 10016. TEL 212-726-6490. FAX 212-686-7993) (Co-sponsor: International Maize and Wheat Improvement Center (CIMMYT)) circ. 850. (also avail. in diskette format; back issues avail.) **Document type:** abstracting/indexing.
●Also available online. Vendor(s): DIMDI, European Space Agency, Knight-Ridder Information, Inc., STN International.
Formerly: Maize Quality Protein Abstracts (ISSN 0305-9162)
Description: Topics covered include: plant breeding and genetics, plant physiology, soil science, pests and diseases, agricultural engineering, crop science, seeds and grains, weeds and weed control, agricultural economics, and nutrition and quality.

630   MW   ISSN 0076-3292
MALAWI. NATIONAL STATISTICAL OFFICE. NATIONAL SAMPLE SURVEY OF AGRICULTURE. 1970. irreg. (approx. every 10 yrs.) K.200. National Statistical Office, Commissioner for Census and Statistics, P.O. Box 333, Zomba, Malawi. TEL 265-50-522377. FAX 265-50-523130. TELEX 44015 CENSUS MI. stat. (processed) **Document type:** government publication.
Incorporates: Malawi. National Statistical Office. Compendium of Agricultural Statistics (ISSN 0085-3011)

630 310   MY   ISSN 0127-4694
SB299.P3
MALAYSIA. DEPARTMENT OF STATISTICS. HANDBOOK OF COCOA, COCONUT AND TEA STATISTICS MALAYSIA. (Text in English) 1988. irreg., latest 1993. M.$18. Department of Statistics, Wisma Statistik, Jalan Cenderasari, 50514 Kuala Lumpur, Malaysia. TEL 60-3-2922133. FAX 60-3-2937018. **Document type:** government publication.
Formerly: Malaysia. Department of Statistics. Handbook of Oil Palm, Cocoa, Coconut and Tea Statistics Malaysia.

630   CN
MARKET TRENDS. 1986. w. free. Saskatchewan Agriculture and Food Library, B5 Walter Scott Bldg., 3085 Albert St., Regina, SK S4S 0B1, Canada. TEL 306-787-6933. FAX 306-787-0216. E-mail: pdc@agr.gov.sk.ca; URL: http://www.gov.sk.ca/agfood. circ. 400. (back issues avail.) **Document type:** government publication.
Description: Includes forecast prices of grain, trade statistics for hogs, cattle and grain, and information for farmers.

338.1   US
MASSACHUSETTS AGRICULTURE (YEAR) ANNUAL REPORT. 1972. a. free. Department of Food and Agriculture, 100 Cambridge Street, Boston, MA 02202. FAX 617-727-7235. (Co-sponsors: New England Agricultural Statistics Service; U.S. Department of Agriculture) illus.; stat. circ. 1,000. **Indexed:** SRI.
Formerly: Massachusetts Agricultural Statistics (ISSN 0092-9794)

316 630   MF
MAURITIUS. CENTRAL STATISTICAL OFFICE. DIGEST OF AGRICULTURAL STATISTICS. 1984. a. Rs.75 (effective Jun. 1995). Central Statistical Office, Toorawa Centre, Cr. S.S. R & J. Mosque Sts., Port Louis, Mauritius. TEL 230-234-5294. FAX 230-208-4011. (Subscr. to: Government Printing Office, Ramtoolah Bldg., Sir S. Ramgoolam St., Port Louis, Mauritius) **Document type:** government publication.

630 322   FR   ISSN 0259-5222
MEAT BALANCES IN O E C D COUNTRIES. irreg. price varies. Organization for Economic Cooperation and Development, 2 rue Andre-Pascal, 75775 Paris Cedex 16, France. (U.S. orders to: O.E.C.D. Publications and Information Center, 2001 L St., N.W., Ste. 650, Washington, DC 20036-4922. TEL 202-785-6323) **Indexed:** IIS.

637.1 016   GW   ISSN 0026-3788
SF221   CODEN: MILCAD
MILCHWISSENSCHAFT/MILK SCIENCE INTERNATIONAL; journal of nutrition research and food science. (Text in English and German) 1945. m. DM.346.50 (foreign DM.375) (effective 1996). Volkswirtschaftlicher Verlag (VV GmbH), Kederbacherstr. 50, 81377 Munich, Germany. TEL 49-89-7141013. FAX 49-89-7192753. Ed. R. von Funke. adv. contact: Inge Seifert. bk.rev.; abstr.; bibl.; charts; illus.; mkt.; pat.; index. circ. 1,500. (back issues avail.) **Indexed:** Agri.Eng.Abstr., Anim.Breed.Abstr., ASCA, Biol.Abstr., Biotech.Abstr., Chem.Abstr., Curr.Adv.Ecol.Sci., Curr.Cont., Curr.Pack.Abstr., Dairy Sci.Abstr., Excerp.Med., Food Sci.& Tech.Abstr., Ind.Sci.Rev., Ind.Vet., Nutr.Abstr., Pig News & Info., Rev.Plant Path., Rural Recreat.Tour.Abstr., Sci.Cit.Ind., Soils & Fert., Vet.Bull., World Agri.Econ.& Rural Sociol.Abstr. **Document type:** trade publication.
—BLDSC (5767.000000); CASDDS; Genuine Article; Linda Hall; SWETS. **CCC.**

630 322   FR   ISSN 0259-5257
MILK AND MILK PRODUCTS BALANCES IN O E C D COUNTRIES. irreg. price varies. Organization for Economic Cooperation and Development, 2 rue Andre-Pascal, 75775 Paris Cedex 16, France. (U.S. orders to: O.E.C.D. Publications and Information Center, 2001 L St., N.W., Ste. 650, Washington, DC 20036-4922. TEL 202-785-6323)

630   JA   ISSN 0029-1757
MONTHLY STATISTICS ON AGRICULTURE, FORESTRY AND FISHERIES/NORIN SUISAN TOKEI GEPPO.* m. 3600 Yen($49.50) Norinsuisan-sho, Tokei-kyoku - Ministry of Agriculture, Forestry and Fisheries, Statistics Bureau, c/o Japan Publication Trading Co., Ltd., P.O. Box 5030, Tokyo International, Tokyo 100-31, Japan. (U.S. subscr. to: 1255 Howard St., San Francisco, CA 94103)

630 664 016 011   US
N T I S ALERTS: AGRICULTURE & FOOD. w. $135 (foreign $195). U.S. National Technical Information Service, 5285 Port Royal Rd., Springfield, VA 22161. TEL 703-487-4630. FAX 703-321-8547. TELEX 64617. index. (also avail. in microform from NTI; back issues avail.)
Former titles: Abstract Newsletter: Agriculture and Food (ISSN 0364-7994); Weekly Abstracts Newsletter: Agriculture and Food; Weekly Government Abstracts. Agriculture and Food.

631.5 636   US   ISSN 0364-202X
NATIONAL AGRICULTURAL STATISTICS SERVICE. CATTLE ON FEED. m., plus b-m reports. $29 (includes s-a. Cattle Reports). U.S. Department of Agriculture, National Agricultural Statistics Service, Independence Ave., between 12th & 14th Sts., S.W., South Bldg., Rm. 4117, Washington, DC 20250. TEL 202-655-4000. (Subscr. to: ERS-NASS, 341 Victory Dr., Herndon, VA 22070. TEL 800-999-6779. FAX 703-834-0110) (also avail. in microfiche from CIS; reprint service avail. from CIS) **Indexed:** Amer.Stat.Ind. (1974-). **Document type:** government publication.
●Also available online. Vendor(s): Knight-Ridder Information, Inc.
Formerly: U.S. Crop Reporting Board. Cattle and Calves on Feed.

AGRICULTURE — ABSTRACTING, BIBLIOGRAPHIES, STATISTICS

011 630   US   ISSN 1066-257X
NATIONAL CENTER FOR AGRICULTURAL UTILIZATION RESEARCH PUBLICATIONS AND PATENTS. 1940. a. free. U.S. Department of Agriculture, Agricultural Research Service, National Center for Agricultural Utilization Research, 1815 N. University, Peoria, IL 61604. TEL 309-685-4011. bibl.; pat. circ. 700. (back issues avail.)
  Formerly: Northern Regional Research Center Publications and Patents.

630   SP
NEKAZAL ELIKAGAI SEKTOREAREN ESTATISTIKA URTEKARIA E.A.E/ANUARIO ESTADISTICO DEL SECTOR AGROALIMENTARIO C.A.P.V. (Text in Basque, Spanish) 1988. a. 1000 ptas. (Industri, Nekazaritza eta Arrantza Saila - Departamento de Industria, Agricultura y Pesca) Eusko Jaurlaritzaren Argitalpen-Zerbitzu - Servicio Central de Publicaciones del Gobierno Vasco, Duque de Wellington 2, 01010 Vitoria-Gasteiz, Spain. TEL 34-45-188000. FAX 34-45-189702.

595.1 016   UK   ISSN 0957-6797
SB998.N4   CODEN: NEABEA
NEMATOLOGICAL ABSTRACTS. 1932. q. £150($260) (effective 1997). CAB International, Wallingford, Oxon. OX10 8DE, England. TEL 44-1491-832111. FAX 44-1491-826090. TELEX 847964 COMAGG G. (U.S. subscr. to: CAB International, North American Office, 198 Madison Ave., NY 10016. TEL 212-726-6490. FAX 212-686-7993) adv.; bk.rev. circ. 1,000. (also avail. in diskette format; back issues avail.; reprint service avail.) **Indexed:** Forest.Abstr., Forest Prod.Abstr., Rev.Appl.Entomol., Vet.Bull., Zoo.Rec. **Document type:** abstracting/indexing.
  ●Also available online. Vendor(s): CISTI, DIMDI, European Space Agency (File nos.16 & 124/CAB), Knight-Ridder Information, Inc., Ovid Technologies, Inc. (CABA).
  —Linda Hall.
  Supersedes: Helminthological Abstracts. Series B: Plant Nematology (ISSN 0300-8320)
  Description: Contains abstracts of the world literature on: nematodes parasitic on plants, free-living and marine nematodes, and nematodes parasitic on insects or other invertebrates.

314   NE   ISSN 0024-8754
NETHERLANDS. CENTRAAL BUREAU VOOR DE STATISTIEK. MAANDSTATISTIEK VAN DE LANDBOUW. 1953. m. fl.25. Centraal Bureau voor de Statistiek, Prinses Beatrixlaan 428, Voorburg, Netherlands. (Dist. by: SDU - Publishers, Christoffel Plantijnstraat, The Hague, Netherlands) stat.; index. circ. 425. **Document type:** government publication.

637   NE   ISSN 0168-518X
HD9275.N2
NETHERLANDS. CENTRAAL BUREAU VOOR DE STATISTIEK. PRODUCTIE STATISTIEK VAN DE ZUIVELINDUSTRIE/NETHERLANDS. CENTRAL BUREAU OF STATISTICS. PRODUCTION STATISTICS OF THE DAIRY INDUSTRY. (Text in Dutch and English) 1952. a. fl.5.50. Centraal Bureau voor de Statistiek, Prinses Beatrixlaan 428, Voorburg, Netherlands. (Dist. by: SDU - Publishers, Christoffel Plantijnstraat 2, Postbus 20014, 2500 EA The Hague, Netherlands) **Document type:** government publication.
  Formerly: Netherlands. Centraal Bureau voor de Statistiek. Zuivelstatistiek (ISSN 0077-7528)

633.7   NE   ISSN 0168-5333
HD9056.N4
NETHERLANDS. CENTRAAL BUREAU VOOR DE STATISTIEK. PRODUKTIESTATISTIEKEN: VEEVOEDERINDUSTRIE. a. fl.6.50. Centraal Bureau voor de Statistiek, Prinses Beatrixlaan 428, Voorburg, Netherlands. (Orders to: SDU - Publishers, Christoffel Plantijnstraat, The Hague, Netherlands) **Document type:** government publication.

630   NE   ISSN 0168-3918
NETHERLANDS. CENTRAAL BUREAU VOOR DE STATISTIEK. STATISTIEK VAN DE LAND- EN TUINBOUW/NETHERLANDS. CENTRAL BUREAU OF STATISTICS. STATISTICS OF AGRICULTURE. (Text in Dutch and English) 1949. a. fl.72. Centraal Bureau voor de Statistiek, Prinses Beatrixlaan 428, Voorburg, Netherlands. (Orders to: SDU - Publishers, Christoffel Plantijnstraat 2, Postbus 20014, 2500 EA The Hague, The Netherlands) **Document type:** government publication.

338.1   US   ISSN 0077-8540
HD1775.N6
NEW MEXICO AGRICULTURAL STATISTICS. 1962. a. free. Department of Agriculture, Agricultural Statistical Service, P.O. Box 30005, Dept. 5600, Las Cruces, NM 88003-0005. (Co-sponsor: U.S. Department of Agriculture) **Indexed:** SRI. **Document type:** government publication.

633   US   ISSN 0276-8798
HD1775.N8
NEW YORK AGRICULTURAL STATISTICS. a. free. Department of Agriculture and Markets, 1 Winner's Cir., Albany, NY 12235-0001. FAX 518-453-6564. circ. 2,800 (controlled). (also avail. in microfiche from CIS) **Indexed:** SRI. **Document type:** government publication.

630   NZ   ISSN 0110-4624
S397.7
NEW ZEALAND. DEPARTMENT OF STATISTICS. AGRICULTURAL STATISTICS. a. NZ.$95. Department of Statistics, P.O. Box 2922, Wellington, New Zealand. TEL 04-495-4600. FAX 04-472-9135.
—CCC.
  Formerly: New Zealand. Department of Statistics. Statistical Report of Farm Production (ISSN 0077-9822)

630 338.1   AU   ISSN 0028-9744
NIEDEROESTERREICHISCHE LANDES-LANDWIRTSCHAFTSKAMMER. AMTLICHER MARKTBERICHT. 1922. w. S.530 (foreign S.785). Oesterreichischer Agrarverlag GmbH, Inkustr. 1-7, A-3400 Klosterneuburg, Austria. TEL 02243-333006. FAX 02243-3330056. Ed. Richard Kaiser. bk.rev.; abstr.; mkt.; index, cum.index. circ. 2,200. (looseleaf format)

630 016   JA   ISSN 0385-3012
Z5073
NIHON NOGAKU BUNKEN KIJI SAKUIN/JAPANESE AGRICULTURAL SCIENCES INDEX. (Text in Japanese) 1970. m. (plus s-a. cumulative nos.). Norin Shuisansho, Norin Suisan Gijutsu Kaigi Jimukyoku, Tsukuba Jimusho Kenkyu Johoka, 1-2, Kannondai 2-chome, Tsukuba-shi, Ibaraki-ken, Japan. **Document type:** abstracting/indexing, government publication.

634.9 016   JA   ISSN 0029-1773
NORIN TOSHO SHIRYO GEPPO. m. 6240 Yen($48) (Ministry of Agriculture, Forestry and Fisheries, Statistics and Information Department) Association of Agriculture-Forestry Statistics, Otori Building, 11-14, Megro 2-chome, Megro-ku, Tokyo 153, Japan. (Dist. overseas by: Japan Publications Trading Co., Ltd., Box 5030, Tokyo International, Tokyo 100-31, Japan; or 1255 Howard St., San Francisco, CA 94103) adv.; bk.rev.; abstr.; bibl.; index. circ. 1,400.

338.1 317   US   ISSN 0737-1624
S99
NORTH DAKOTA AGRICULTURAL STATISTICS. 1956. a. $10. North Dakota Agricultural Statistics Service, Box 3166, Fargo, ND 58108. TEL 701-239-5306. FAX 701-239-5613. Ed. Larry W. Beard. circ. 2,000. (also avail. in microfiche from CIS) **Indexed:** SRI. **Document type:** government publication.
  —Linda Hall.
  Formerly: North Dakota Crop and Livestock Statistics (ISSN 0078-1541)
  Description: Provides comprehensive crop, livestock and price statistics, including county estimates.

664.7   US
NORTH DAKOTA GRAIN AND OILSEED TRANSPORTATION STATISTICS. 1975. a. free. North Dakota State University, Upper Great Plains Transportation Institute, P.O. Box 5074, Fargo, ND 58105. FAX 701-231-1945. Ed. Kimberly Vachal. circ. 250.

630   NO   ISSN 0078-1894
HA1501
NORWAY. STATISTISK SENTRALBYRAA. JORDBRUKSSTATISTIKK/STATISTICS NORWAY. AGRICULTURAL STATISTICS. (Subseries of its Norges Offisielle Statistikk) (Text in Norwegian and English) 1937. a. NOK 95 (effective 1997). Statistisk Sentralbyraa, P.O. Box 8131 Dep., N-033 Oslo, Norway. TEL 47-22-864500. FAX 47-22-864976. circ. 1,400. **Document type:** government publication.

633.1 016   UK   ISSN 0309-135X
SF95
NUTRITION ABSTRACTS AND REVIEWS. SERIES B: LIVESTOCK FEEDS AND FEEDING. 1931. m. £395($690) (effective 1997). CAB International, Wallingford, Oxon. OX10 8DE, England. TEL 44-1491-832111. FAX 44-1491-826090. TELEX 847964 COMAGG G. E-mail: cabi@cabi.org. (U.S. subscr. to: CAB International, North American Office, 845 N. Park Ave., Tucson, AZ 85719. TEL 800-528-4841) circ. 1,700. (also avail. in diskette format; back issues avail.) **Indexed:** Anal.Abstr., Anim.Breed.Abstr., Biol.Abstr., Dairy Sci.Abstr., Field Crop Abstr., Forest.Abstr., Herb.Abstr., Ind.Vet., Rural Recreat.Tour.Abstr., Sport Fish.Abstr., Vet.Bull., Wild.Rev., World Agri.Econ.& Rural Sociol.Abstr. **Document type:** abstracting/indexing.
  ●Also available online. Vendor(s): CISTI, DIMDI, European Space Agency (File nos.16 & 124/CAB), Knight-Ridder Information, Inc., Ovid Technologies, Inc. (VETR).
  —Linda Hall.
  Supersedes in part: Nutrition Abstracts and Reviews (ISSN 0029-6619)
  Description: Covers the analysis, technology, and biochemistry of feeds.

631 011   US
OIKO: THE ALTERNATIVE ENVIRONMENTAL DIGEST. 1992. q. $20 to individuals; grassroots organizations $35; institutions $50. Box 115, Greenwood, VA 22943-0115. TEL 703-456-8232. Ed. Del Kolberg.
  Description: Covers grassroots environmental publications.

630   CN
ONTARIO. MINISTRY OF AGRICULTURE, FOOD AND RURAL AFFAIRS. AGRICULTURAL STATISTICS FOR ONTARIO (YEAR). a. Ministry of Agriculture, Food and Rural Affairs, Policy Analysis Branch, Legislative Bldgs., Queen's Park, Toronto, ON M7A 2B2, Canada. TEL 416-326-3210. FAX 416-326-9892. Ed. Bill McGee. **Document type:** government publication.
  Formerly: Ontario. Ministry of Agriculture and Food. Agricultural Statistics for Ontario (Year).

630   CN
ONTARIO. MINISTRY OF AGRICULTURE, FOOD AND RURAL ANALYSIS. FRUIT TREE CENSUS PART 1: GRAPES (YEAR). every 5 yrs. Ministry of Agriculture, Food and Rural Analysis, Policy Analysis Branch, Legislative Bldgs., Queen's Park, Toronto, ON M7A 1B6, Canada. TEL 416-326-3210. FAX 416-326-9892. Ed. Patricia Bany. **Document type:** government publication.
  Formerly: Ontario. Ministry of Agriculture and Food. Fruit Tree Census Part 1: Grapes (Year).

630   CN
ONTARIO. MINISTRY OF AGRICULTURE, FOOD AND RURAL ANALYSIS. FRUIT TREE CENSUS PART 2: TENDER FRUIT (YEAR). every 5 yrs. Ministry of Agriculture, Food and Rural Analysis, Policy Analysis Branch, Legislative Bldgs., Queen's Park, Toronto, ON M7A 2B2, Canada. TEL 416-326-3210. FAX 416-326-9892. Ed. Patricia Bany. **Document type:** government publication.
  Formerly: Ontario. Ministry of Agriculture and Food. Fruit Tree Census Part 2: Tender Fruit (Year).

630   CN
ONTARIO. MINISTRY OF AGRICULTURE, FOOD AND RURAL ANALYSIS. FRUIT TREE CENSUS PART 3: APPLES (YEAR). every 5 yrs. Ministry of Agriculture, Food and Rural Analysis, Policy Analysis Branch, Legislative Bldgs., Queen's Park, Toronto, ON M7A 2B2, Canada. TEL 416-326-3210. FAX 416-326-9892. Ed. Patricia Bany. **Document type:** government publication.
  Formerly: Ontario. Ministry of Agriculture and Food. Fruit Tree Census Part 3: Apples (Year).

AGRICULTURE — ABSTRACTING, BIBLIOGRAPHIES, STATISTICS

637 338.1　　　　　CN
HD9275.C3
ONTARIO. MINISTRY OF AGRICULTURE, FOOD AND RURAL ANALYSIS. MONTHLY DAIRY REPORT. (Annual supplement avail.) 1938. m. free. Ministry of Agriculture, Food and Rural Analysis, Policy Analysis Branch, Legislative Bldgs., Queen's Park, Toronto, ON M7A 2B2, Canada. TEL 416-326-3214. FAX 416-326-9892. Ed. Cyril Fernandes. stat. circ. 1,000. **Indexed:** CS Ind., Dairy Sci.Abstr. **Document type:** government publication.
—Linda Hall.
　Formerly: Ontario. Ministry of Agriculture and Food. Monthly Dairy Report (ISSN 0030-2872)
　Description: Production statistics for processed dairy products, stocks, milk shipments, net payments and utilization, fluid and industrial prices, quarterly retail milk prices, and trade.

634 012　　　　　CN
SB29.C2
ONTARIO. MINISTRY OF AGRICULTURE, FOOD AND RURAL ANALYSIS. SEASONAL FRUIT AND VEGETABLE REPORT. (Annual supplement avail.) 1936. q. free. Ministry of Agriculture, Food and Rural Analysis, Policy Analysis Branch, Legislative Bldgs., Queen's Park, Toronto, ON M7A 2B2, Canada. TEL 416-326-3218. FAX 416-326-9892. Ed. Patricia Bany. circ. 1,000. **Indexed:** CS Ind. **Document type:** government publication.
—Linda Hall.
　Formerly: Ontario, Ministry of Agriculture and Food. Seasonal Fruit and Vegetable Report (ISSN 0474-1560)
　Description: Statistics for fruit and vegetable producers, prices and values; fresh and processed, market sales, export and import quantities, values of nursery stock sales.

631　　　　　FR　　ISSN 1146-5085
Z5073
P A S C A L T 280: **SCIENCES AGRONOMIQUES ET FORESTIERES: PRODUCTIONS VEGETALES.** (Printed format ceased Jan. 1995) (Text in English, French) 1984. 10/yr. Centre National de la Recherche Scientifique, Institut de l'Information Scientifique et Technique, 2 allee du Parc de Brabois, 54514 Vandoeuvre-Les-Nancy Cedex, France. TEL 83-50-46-00. FAX 83-50-46-50. (Co-sponsor: Institut National de la Recherche Agronomique) Ed. Claude Patou. adv. contact: Veronique Guinvarc'h. index, cum.index. (also avail. in microfiche) **Document type:** bibliography.
●Also available online. Vendor(s): European Space Agency (File no.14), Knight-Ridder Information, Inc. (File no.144), Telesystemes - Questel.
Also available on CD-ROM.
—Linda Hall.
　Former titles: P A S C A L Thema. T 280: Sciences Agronomiques, Production Vegetales (ISSN 0761-3431); Bulletin Signaletique. Part 381: Sciences Agronomiques. Production Vegetales (ISSN 0223-4238)

630 011　　　　　CK　　ISSN 0120-4408
PAGINAS DE CONTENIDO. AGROPECUARIA GENERAL. 1976. bi-m. Col.$15000. Centro Internacional de Agricultura Tropical, Unidad de Informacion y Documentacion - International Center for Tropical Agriculture, Information and Documentation Unit, Apdo. Aereo 6713, Cali, Colombia. TEL 57-2-4450000. FAX 57-2-4450073. E-mail: e.goldberg@cgnet.com. Ed Elizabeth Goldberg. circ. 250. **Document type:** bibliography.
　Description: Contains the titles of recent articles published in major agricultural journals about agronomy, horticulture, cultivation, biology, agricultural engineering, seeds, and food technology.

338.1 011　　　　　CK　　ISSN 0120-4467
PAGINAS DE CONTENIDO. ECONOMIA AGRICOLA Y DESARROLLO RURAL. 1976. bi-m. Col.$15000 (developing countries $20). Centro Internacional de Agricultura Tropical, Unidad de Informacion y Documentacion - International Center for Tropical Agriculture, Information and Documentation Unit, Apdo. Aereo 6713, Cali, Colombia. TEL 57-2-4450000. FAX 57-2-4450073. E-mail: e.goldberg@cgnet.com. Ed. Elizabeth Goldberg. circ. 201. **Document type:** abstracting/indexing.
　Description: Titles of recent articles published in agricultural journals about economic theory, statistics, economic and rural development, econometrics, sociology, anthropology, international policy, economic policy, nutrition and food policy.

630 011　　　　　CK
PAGINAS DE CONTENIDO. FISIOLOGIA VEGETAL, GENETICA Y BIOTECHNOLOGIA. 1982. bi-m. Col.$15000 (developing countries $20). Centro Internacional de Agricultura Tropical, Unidad de Informacion y Documentacion - International Center for Tropical Agriculture, Information and Documentation Unit, Apdo. Aereo 6713, Cali, Colombia. TEL 57-2-4450000. FAX 57-2-4450073. E-mail: e.goldberg@cgnet.com. Ed. Elizabeth Goldberg. circ. 236. **Document type:** abstracting/indexing.
　Formerly: Paginas de Contenido. Fisiologia Vegetal (ISSN 0120-4416)
　Description: Contains the titles of recent articles published in major agricultural journals about botany, photosynthesis, plant breeding and biochemistry.

630 011　　　　　CK　　ISSN 0120-4440
PAGINAS DE CONTENIDO. PASTOS, PRODUCCION ANIMAL Y NUTRICION. 1982. bi-m. Col.$15000 (developing countries $20). Centro Internacional de Agricultura Tropical, Unidad de Informacion y Documentacion - International Center for Tropical Agriculture, Information and Documentation Unit, Apdo. Aereo 6713, Cali, Colombia. TEL 57-2-4450000. FAX 57-2-4450073. E-mail: e.goldberg@cgnet.com. Ed. Elizabeth Goldberg. circ. 105. **Document type:** abstracting/indexing.
　Formerly: Paginas de Contenido. Pastos, Nutricion y Produccion Animal.
　Description: Contains the titles of recent articles published in major agricultural journals about animal management, reproduction and nutrition, pastures and forage, and veterinary science.

631 011　　　　　CK　　ISSN 0120-4424
PAGINAS DE CONTENIDO. PROTECCION DE PLANTAS. 1982. bi-m. Col.$15000 (developing countries $20). Centro Internacional de Agricultura Tropical, Unidad de Informacion y Documentacion - International Center for Tropical Agriculture, Information and Documentation Unit, Apdo. Aereo 6713, Cali, Colombia. TEL 57-2-4450000. FAX 57-2-4450073. E-mail: e.goldberg@cgnet.com. Ed. Elizabeth Goldberg. circ. 254. **Document type:** abstracting/indexing.
　Description: Contains the titles of recent articles published in major agricultural journals about entomology, plant pathology, weed control, biological, chemical and cultural control.

631.4 011　　　　　CK　　ISSN 0121-8867
PAGINAS DE CONTENIDO. RECURSOS NATURALES Y MEDIO AMBIENTE. 1982. bi-m. Col.$15000 (developing countries $20). Centro Internacional de Agricultura Tropical, Unidad de Informacion y Documentacion - International Center for Tropical Agriculture, Information and Documentation Unit, Apdo. Aereo 6713, Cali, Colombia. TEL 57-2-4450000. FAX 57-2-4450073. E-mail: e.goldberg@cgnet.com. circ. 150. **Document type:** academic/scholarly publication.
　Formerly: (until 1993): Paginas de Contenido. Suelos y Nutricion de Plantas (ISSN 0120-4432)
　Description: Contains the titles of recent articles published in agricultural journals about ecology, agroforestry, sustainability, pollution, degradation and erosion of soils, land use, edaphology, agrochemistry, and fertilizers.

630　　　　　PK
PAKISTAN. FOOD AND AGRICULTURE DIVISION. AGRICULTURAL STATISTICS OF PAKISTAN. (Text in English) 1952. a. free. Ministry of Food, Agriculture and Rural Development, Food and Agriculture Division, Planning Unit, 210-H-G-6/3, Islamabad, Pakistan.
　Formerly: Pakistan. Food and Agricultural Division. Yearbook of Agricultural Statistics (ISSN 0078-8139)

630　　　　　BL　　ISSN 0103-6181
SB186.3
PESQUISA DE ESTOQUES. 1974. s-a. $50. Fundacao Instituto Brasileiro de Geografia e Estatistica, Centro de Documentacao e Disseminacao de Informacoes, Rua General Canabarro 706, 2o andar, Maracana 20271-201 Rio de Janeiro, Brazil. TEL 55-21-2645424. FAX 55-21-2841959. **Document type:** government publication.
　Former titles (until 1987): Pesquisa Especial de Armazenagem; (until 1986): Armazenagem e Estocagem a Seco e a Frio (ISSN 0101-028X)
　Description: Provides information on existing stocks of cotton, rice, beans, soyabeans, wheat and more, in storage units all over Brazil.

632.97　　　　　UK
PESTICIDE INDEX. 1984. irreg., 3rd ed., 1995. £35. British Crop Protection Council, Bear Farm, Binfield, Bracknell, Berkshire RG12 5QE, England. TEL 44-1734-342727. FAX 44-1734-341998. (Subscr. in N. America to: Blackwells Scientific, 238 Main St., Cambridge, MA 02142. TEL 617-876-7000. FAX 617-876-7022) (Co-sponsor: The Royal Society of Chemistry) Ed.Bd. **Document type:** trade publication.
　Description: Lists the generic and trade names of pesticides in use worldwide.

PESTICIDES ABSTRACTS. see ENVIRONMENTAL STUDIES — Abstracting, Bibliographies, Statistics

PHILIPPINE BUSINESS AND INDUSTRY INDEX. see BUSINESS AND ECONOMICS — Abstracting, Bibliographies, Statistics

630　　　　　PH
PHILIPPINES. DEPARTMENT OF AGRICULTURE. BUREAU OF AGRICULTURAL STATISTICS. DEVELOPMENT INDICATORS IN PHILIPPINE AGRICULTURE. a. Department of Agriculture, Bureau of Agricultural Statistics, BEN-LOR Bldg., 1184 Quezon Ave., Quezon City, Philippines. FAX 63-2-968-966. R&P contact: Romeo S. Recide. circ. 500. **Document type:** government publication.
　Description: For policy-makers and planners: for monitoring and evaluating programs related to agriculture.

630　　　　　PH
PHILIPPINES. DEPARTMENT OF AGRICULTURE. BUREAU OF AGRICULTURAL STATISTICS. LIVESTOCK AND POULTRY PERFORMANCE REPORT. a. Department of Agriculture, Bureau of Agricultural Statistics, BEN-LOR Bldg., 1184 Quezon Ave., Quezon City, Philippines. FAX 63-2-968-966. E-mail: da-bas@gaia.psdn.org. R&P contact: Romeo S. Recide. charts; stat. circ. 300. (processed) **Document type:** government publication, bulletin.
　Formerly: Philippines. Department of Agriculture. Bureau of Agricultural Statistics. Livestock, Poultry and Fishery Statistics Bulletin.
　Description: Results of the Bureau's surveys on livestock and poultry and the monitoring of animals slaughtered in abbatoirs.

630　　　　　PH
PHILIPPINES. DEPARTMENT OF AGRICULTURE. BUREAU OF AGRICULTURAL STATISTICS. RICE AND CORN SITUATION OUTLOOK. q. Department of Agriculture, Bureau of Agricultural Statistics, BEN-LOR Bldg., 1184 Quezon Ave., Quezon City, Philippines. FAX 63-2-968-966. E-mail: da-bas@gaia.psdn.org. R&P contact: Romeo S. Recide. circ. 700. **Document type:** government publication.
　Formerly: Philippines. Department of Agriculture. Bureau of Agricultural Statistics. Rice and Corn Outlook.
　Description: Rice and corn prospects for the coming quarter; includes area and production forecast of rice and corn.

630　　　　　PH
PHILIPPINES. DEPARTMENT OF AGRICULTURE. BUREAU OF AGRICULTURAL STATISTICS. SELECTED STATISTICS IN AGRICULTURE. a. Department of Agriculture, Bureau of Agricultural Statistics, BEN-LOR Bldg., 1184 Quezon Ave., Quezon City, Philippines. FAX 63-2-968-966. E-mail: da-bas@gaia.psdn.org. R&P contact: Romeo S. Recide. circ. 500. **Document type:** government publication.
　Description: Statistics on crops, livestock, poultry and fisheries; annual average process of selected commodities.

AGRICULTURE — ABSTRACTING, BIBLIOGRAPHIES, STATISTICS

633 UK ISSN 0031-8426
TP245.P5 CODEN: POPOA8
PHOSPHORUS AND POTASSIUM; covers all aspects of world phosphate and potash fertilizer industry. 1963. bi-m. £340($495) British Sulphur Publishing (Subsidiary of: C R U Publishing Ltd.), 31 Mount Pleasant, London WC1X 0AD, England. TEL 44-171-837-5600. FAX 44-171-837-0292. TELEX 918918 SULFEX G. Ed. Lynda Davies; Pub. John French. R&P contact: John French. adv. contact: Tina Firman. bk.rev.; charts; illus.; mkt.; stat.; index. circ. 599. (also avail. in microform from UMI; reprint service avail. from UMI) **Indexed:** Chem.Abstr., Fert.Abstr., I.M.M.Abstr., PROMT, Ref.Zh., Soils & Fert. **Document type:** trade publication.
—BLDSC (6465.300000); CASDDS; CISTI; Ei; Linda Hall; SWETS; UMI.

630 UK ISSN 0960-2976
PHOSPHORUS IN AGRICULTURE. 1991. a. £42($78) (World Phosphate Institute (IMPHOS)) CAB International, Wallingford, Oxon. OX10 8DE, England. TEL 44-1491-832111. FAX 44-1491-833508. TELEX 847964 COMAGG G. E-mail: cabi@cabi.org; URL: http://www.cabi.org. (U.S. subscr. to: CAB International, North American Office, 198 Madison Ave., New York, NY 10016. TEL 212-726-6490. FAX 212-686-7933) Ed. J.L. Nowland. **Document type:** academic/scholarly publication.
Description: Covers the latest research on aspects of the use and effect of phosphorus in agriculture.

631 016 UK ISSN 0305-9154
PLANT GROWTH REGULATOR ABSTRACTS. 1975. q. £215($375) (effective 1997). CAB International, Wallingford, Oxon. OX10 8DE, England. TEL 44-1491-832111. FAX 44-1491-833508. TELEX 847964 COMAGG G. E-mail: cabi@cabi.org; URL: http://www.cabi.org. (U.S. subscr. to: CAB International, North American Office, 198 Madison Ave., New York, NY 10016. TEL 212-726-6490. FAX 212-686-7933) circ. 550. (also avail. in diskette format; back issues avail.) **Document type:** abstracting/indexing.
●Also available online. Vendor(s): DIMDI, European Space Agency, Knight-Ridder Information, Inc., STN International.
Description: Deals with the role of chemicals in plant growth regulation and beneficial modification of plant growth processes.

631 314 PL ISSN 0208-9602
POLAND. GLOWNY URZAD STATYSTYCZNY. WYNIKI SPISU ROLNICZEGO. UZYTKOWANIE GRUNTOW I POWIERZCHNIA ZASIEWOW, ORAZ ZWIERZETA GOSPODARSKIE. (Subseries of its: Statystyka Polski) 1966. a. 23 Zl. Zaklad Wydawnictw Statystycznych, Al. Niepodleglosci 208, 00-925 Warsaw, Poland. TEL 48 22 25-03-45.
Formerly: Poland. Glowny Urzad Statystyczny. Uzytkowanie Gruntow i Powierzchnia Zasiewow oraz Zwierzeta Gospodarskie (ISSN 0079-2861)

630 PO ISSN 0302-5853
HD2026
PORTUGAL. INSTITUTO NACIONAL DE ESTATISTICA. ESTATISTICAS AGRICOLAS E ALIMENTARES; Continente, Acores e Madeira. (Text in Portuguese and French) 1943. a. Esc.3200. Instituto Nacional de Estatistica, Ave. Antonio Jose de Almeida, 1078 Lisbon Codex, Portugal. (Orders to: Imprensa Nacional, Casa da Moeda, Direccao Comercial, rua D. Francisco Manuel de Melo 5, 1000 Lisbon, Portugal)
Formerly (until 1964): Portugal. Instituto Nacional de Estatistica. Estatistica Agricola (ISSN 0302-4504)

338.176021 PO ISSN 0871-8997
PORTUGAL. INSTITUTO NACIONAL DE ESTATISTICA. INDICADORES DA PRODUCAO ANIMAL. 1989. q. Esc.2300. Instituto Nacional de Estatistica, Ave. Antonio Jose de Almeida, 1078 Lisbon, Portugal. TEL 351-8470050. FAX 351-8478578. TELEX 351-63738 PCDINE P.
Formerly (until 1991): Portugal. Instituto Nacional de Estatistica. Estatisticas da Producao Animal (ISSN 0871-3278)
Description: Provides statistical data on animal husbandry with an emphasis on production.

635.021 PO ISSN 0871-9004
PORTUGAL. INSTITUTO NACIONAL DE ESTATISTICA. INDICADORES DA PRODUCAO VEGETAL. 1987. q. Esc.2300. Instituto Nacional de Estatistica, Ave. Antonio Jose de Almeida, 1078 Lisbon, Portugal. TEL 351-8470050. FAX 351-8478578. TELEX 351-63738 PCDINE P.
Formerly (until 1991): Portugal. Instituto Nacional de Estatistica. Estatisticas da Producao Vegetal (ISSN 0871-1356)
Description: Provides statistical data on vegetable production in Portugal.

PORTUGAL. INSTITUTO NACIONAL DE ESTATISTICA. INQUERITO AO GANHO DOS TRABALHADORES AGRICOLAS. see *AGRICULTURE*

PORTUGAL. INSTITUTO NACIONAL DE ESTATISTICA. PRECOS RENDIMENTOS NA AGRICULTURA. see *AGRICULTURE*

630 UK ISSN 0957-7505
SB129
POSTHARVEST NEWS AND INFORMATION. 1990. bi-m. £260($455) (effective 1997). CAB International, Wallingford, Oxon. OX10 8DE, England. TEL 44-1491-832111. FAX 44-1491-826090. TELEX 847964 COMAGG G. E-mail: cabi@cabi.org; URL: http://www.cabi.org. (U.S. subscr. to: CAB International, North American Office, 198 Madison Ave., New York, NY 10016. TEL 212-726-6490. FAX 212-686-7993) Ed. A.J. Rendall-Dunn. **Indexed:** Food Sci.& Tech.Abstr. **Document type:** trade publication.
—BLDSC (6563.922000).
Description: Covers current research on postharvest technology. Provides timely news items, review articles, and abstracts of interest to researchers, administrators, and planners.

633.491 016 UK ISSN 0308-7344
POTATO ABSTRACTS. 1976. bi-m. £185($325) (effective 1997). CAB International, Wallingford, Oxon. OX10 8DE, England. TEL 44-1491-832111. FAX 44-1491-826090. TELEX 847964 COMAGG. E-mail: cabi@cabi.org; URL: http://www.cabi.org. (U.S. subscr. to: CAB International, North American Office, 198 Madison Ave., New York, NY 10016. TEL 212-726-6490. FAX 212-686-7993) circ. 350. (also avail. in diskette format; back issues avail.) **Document type:** abstracting/indexing.
●Also available online. Vendor(s): DIMDI, European Space Agency, Knight-Ridder Information, Inc., STN International.

631 UK ISSN 0266-6022
POTATO STATISTICS IN GREAT BRITAIN. 1984. a. £20. Potato Marketing Board, Broad Field House, 4 Between Towns Rd., Cowley, Oxford OX4 3NA, England. TEL 44-1865-714455. FAX 44-1865-716418. Ed. M. Plass. **Document type:** bulletin.

636.5 016 UK ISSN 0306-1582
POULTRY ABSTRACTS. 1975. m. £260($455) (effective 1997). CAB International, Wallingford, Oxon. OX10 8DE, England. TEL 44-1491-832111. FAX 44-1491-826090. TELEX 847964 COMAGG G. E-mail: cabi@cabi.org; URL: http://www.cabi.org. (U.S. subscr. to: CAB International, North American Office, 198 Madison Ave., New York, NY 10016. TEL 212-726-6490. FAX 212-686-7993) circ. 500. (also avail. in diskette format; back issues avail.) **Indexed:** Rev.Appl.Entomol. **Document type:** abstracting/indexing.
●Also available online. Vendor(s): DIMDI, European Space Agency, Knight-Ridder Information, Inc., STN International.

636.5 310 US ISSN 0565-1980
HD1751
POULTRY MARKET STATISTICS. a. $12. U.S. Department of Agriculture, Agricultural Marketing Services (Washington), Washington, DC 20250. TEL 202-720-6911. **Document type:** government publication.
Formerly: U.S. Agricultural Marketing Service. Dairy and Poultry Market Statistics.

630 011 XR
PREHLED NOVINEK VE FONDU USTREDNI ZEMEDELSKE A LESNICKE KNIHOVNY. 1971. bi-m. $18 (effective 1997). Ustav Zemedelskych a Potravinarskych Informaci, Slezska 7, 120 56 Prague, Czech Republic. TEL 420-2-24257939. FAX 420-2-24253938. E-mail: uzlk@uzpi.cz. Ed. R. Karesova. circ. 120.
Formerly: Vyber z Novych Priirustku Zahranicni Zemedelske Literatury.
Description: Reviews recently published foreign agricultural and forestry literature. Includes information about seminars, conferences and exhibitions.

338.1 CN
PRINCE EDWARD ISLAND. DEPARTMENT OF AGRICULTURE. AGRICULTURAL STATISTICS. 1966. a. Department of Agriculture, P.O. Box 2000, Charlottetown, PE C1A 7N8, Canada. TEL 902-368-4856. FAX 902-368-4857. (Co-sponsor: Statistics Canada) illus.; stat. circ. 750.

630 BL ISSN 0101-3963
S191
PRODUCAO AGRICOLA MUNICIPAL; culturas temporarias e permanentes. 1973. a. Fundacao Instituto Brasileiro de Geografia e Estatistica, Centro de Documentacao e Disseminacao de Informacoes, Rua General Canabarro 706, 2o andar, Maracana 20271-201 Rio de Janeiro, Brazil. TEL 55-21-2645424. FAX 55-21-2841959. **Document type:** government publication.
Formerly (until 1974): Levantamento da Producao Agricola Municipal (ISSN 0100-543X)
Description: Provides annual estimates on quantity, harvested area, productivity and value of production of 30 permanent and 30 temporary agricultural products.

636 BL ISSN 0101-4234
HD9424.B7
PRODUCAO DA PECUARIA MUNICIPAL. 1973. a. $50. Fundacao Instituto Brasileiro de Geografia e Estatistica, Centro de Documentacao e Disseminacao de Informacoes, Rua General Canabarro 706, 2o andar, Maracana 20271-201 Rio de Janeiro, Brazil. TEL 55-21-2645424. FAX 55-21-2841959. **Document type:** government publication.
Formerly: Levantamento do Producao Pecuaria (ISSN 0100-493X)
Description: Provides information on livestock and poultry, as well as on amount and value of milk, wool, eggs, honey, and beeswax.

318 338.1 VE
PRODUCCION AGRICOLA - PERIODO DE INVIERNO. 1965. irreg., latest issue 1976. free. Ministerio de Agricultura y Cria, Direccion de Planificacion y Estadistica, Division de Estadistica, Centro Simon Bolivar, Torre Norte 16o, Caracas 1010, Venezuela.

318 630 VE
PRODUCCION AGRICOLA - PERIODO DE VERANO. 1965. irreg., latest issue 1976. free. Ministerio de Agricultura y Cria, Direccion de Planificacion y Estadistica, Division de Estadistica, Centro Simon Bolivar, Torre Norte 16o, Caracas 1010, Venezuela.

338.1 317 PR
PUERTO RICO. OFICINA DE ESTADISTICAS AGRICOLAS. BOLETIN SEMESTRAL DE ESTADISTICAS AGRICOLAS. vol.13, 1973. s-a. free. Department of Agriculture, Agricultural Statistics Office, P.O. Box 10163, Santurce, PR 00908. circ. 450. **Indexed:** P.A.I.S.For.Lang.Ind. **Document type:** government publication.
Formerly (until 1980): Puerto Rico. Oficina de Estadisticas Agricolas. Boletin Mensual de Estadisticas Agricolas.
Description: Provides monthly and annual statistics including those on local production, prices, imports, exports, slaughter and the labor force in Puerto Rico.

630 664 CN ISSN 1192-8522
HD9014.C4
QUEBEC (PROVINCE). BUREAU DE LA STATISTIQUE. STATISTIQUES AGRO-ALIMENTAIRES. 1992. s-a. Can.$67. Bureau de la Statistique, 5800 rue St. Denis, Ste. 605, Montreal, PQ H2S 3L5, Canada. TEL 514-272-6330. Eds. Denis Belzile, Paul Provencal. adv. contact: Denis Belzile. pp./issue: 255. **Document type:** government publication.

AGRICULTURE — ABSTRACTING, BIBLIOGRAPHIES, STATISTICS

011 630   CN
QUEBEC (PROVINCE). BUREAU DE LA STATISTIQUE. STATISTIQUES DE L'AGRICULTURE, DES PECHES ET DE L'ALIMENTATION, EDITION (YEAR). 1968. a. Can.$34.95. Bureau of Statistics, 117, Rue Saint-Andre, Quebec, Que. G1K 3Y3, Canada. TEL 416-691-2401. FAX 418-643-4129. circ. 200.

630   NE   ISSN 1385-8335
RAMING VAN DE BEDRIJFSUITKOMSTEN VAN DE BEDRIJVEN MET GROENTEELT IN DE OPEN GROND, FRUIT- EN BLOEMBOLLENT. 1984. a. fl.18. Landbouw-Economisch Instituut, Burg. Patijnlaan 19, 2585 BE The Hague, Netherlands. TEL 31-70-3308330. FAX 31-70-3615624. E-mail: postmaster@lei.dlo.nl; URL: http://www.lei.dlo.nl/lei. Eds. A. Boers, W.A.H.B. Bouwman. **Document type:** government publication.
    Former titles (until 1992): Raming van de Bedrijfsuitkomsten van de Bedrijven met Groenteelt in de Open Grond, Fruit- en Bloembollenbedrijven (ISSN 1385-8327); (until 1989): Raming van de Bedrijfsuitkomsten van de Bedrijven met Groenteteelt in de Open Grond en van Fruitteeltbedrijven (ISSN 1385-8319); Which was formed by the 1987 merger of: Raming van de Bedrijfsuitkomsten van de Bedrijven met Groenteteelt in de Open Grond (ISSN 0921-4240); Raming van de Bedrijfsuitkomsten van de Fruitteeltbedrijven (ISSN 0921-4259)

636 591.15 016   RU   ISSN 0235-3105
REFERATIVNYI ZHURNAL. BIOLOGIYA SEL'SKOKHOZYAISTVENNYKH ZHIVOTNYKH. m. $396 (effective 1998). Vsesoyuznyi Institut Nauchno-Tekhnicheskoi Informatsii (VINITI), Baltiiskaya ul. 14, Moscow A-219, Russia. (Dist. by: Mezhdunarodnaya Kniga, B. Yakimanka 39, 117049 Moscow, Russia) **Indexed:** Chem.Abstr. **Document type:** abstracting/indexing.
    Formerly: Referativnyi Zhurnal. Zhivotnovodstvo (ISSN 0206-5533)

631.6 016   RU   ISSN 0034-2548
                CODEN: RZPAAV
REFERATIVNYI ZHURNAL. POCHVOVEDENIE I AGROKHIMIYA. 1960. m. $206 (effective 1998). Vsesoyuznyi Institut Nauchno-Tekhnicheskoi Informatsii (VINITI), Baltiiskaya ul., 14, Moscow A-219, Russia. (Subscr. to: Mezhdunarodnaya Kniga, Dimitrova ul. 39, 113095 Moscow, Russia) **Indexed:** Chem.Abstr. **Document type:** abstracting/indexing.
—CASDDS.

631.5 016   RU   ISSN 0202-9200
                CODEN: RZRAA7
REFERATIVNYI ZHURNAL. RASTENIEVODSTVO (BIOLOGICHESKIE OSNOVY). 1961. m. $396 (effective 1998). Vsesoyuznyi Institut Nauchno-Tekhnicheskoi Informatsii (VINITI), Baltiiskaya ul., 14, Moscow A-219, Russia. (Subscr. to: Mezhdunarodnaya Kniga, Dimitrova ul. 39, 113095 Moscow, G-200, Russia) **Indexed:** Chem.Abstr. **Document type:** abstracting/indexing.

631.3 016   RU   ISSN 0034-2602
REFERATIVNYI ZHURNAL. TRAKTORY I SEL'SKOKHOZYAISTVENNYE MASHINY I ORUDIYA. 1956. m. $399 (effective 1998). Vsesoyuznyi Institut Nauchno-Tekhnicheskoi Informatsii (VINITI), Baltiiskaya ul., 14, Moscow A-219, Russia. (Subscr. to: Mezhdunarodnaya Kniga, Dimitrova ul. 39, 113095 Moscow, Russia) **Indexed:** Agri.Eng.Abstr. **Document type:** abstracting/indexing.
—Linda Hall.

632.9 016   UK   ISSN 0957-6762
REVIEW OF AGRICULTURAL ENTOMOLOGY; consisting of abstracts of reviews of current literature on applied entomology throughout the world. 1913. m. £495($865) (effective 1997). CAB International, Wallingford, Oxon. OX10 8DE, England. TEL 44-1491-832111. FAX 44-1491-826090. TELEX 847964 COMAGG G. E-mail: cabi@cabi.org; URL: http://www.cabi.org. (U.S. subscr. to: CAB International, North American Office, 198 Madison Ave., New York, NY 10016. TEL 212-726-6490. FAX 212-686-7993) Ed.Bd. adv.; bk.rev.; index. circ. 1,850. (also avail. in diskette format; back issues avail.) **Indexed:** Abstr.Hyg., Apic.Abstr., Chem.Abstr., Field Crop Abstr., Forest.Abstr., Forest Prod.Abstr., Helminthol.Abstr., Herb.Abstr., Plant Breed.Abstr., Rev.Appl.Entomol., Rev.Plant Path. **Document type:** abstracting/indexing.
● Also available online. Vendor(s): DIMDI, European Space Agency, Knight-Ridder Information, Inc., STN International.
    Formerly: Review of Applied Entomology. Series A: Agricultural (ISSN 0305-0076)
    Description: Covers literature on insects and other pests of cultivated plants, forest trees and stored products, and beneficial arthropods such as parasites and predators.

338.1 011   GW   ISSN 0344-5267
RHEINLAND AKTUELL; Analysen - Daten - Informationen. 1977. 3/yr. free. Landwirtschaftskammer Rheinland, Endenicher Allee 60, 53115 Bonn, Germany. TEL 49-228-703223. FAX 49-228-703498. TELEX 886685-LWRH-D. Ed. Hans Peter Rehse. **Document type:** bulletin.
    Description: Presents agricultural statistics of the Rhineland area of Northrhein-Westfalen.

631 016   UK   ISSN 0141-0164
RICE ABSTRACTS. 1978. q. £205($360) (effective 1997). CAB International, Wallingford, Oxon. OX10 8DE, England. TEL 44-1491-832111. FAX 44-1491-826090. TELEX 847964 COMAGG G. E-mail: cabi@cabi.org; URL: http://www.cabi.org. (U.S. subscr. to: CAB International, North American Office, 198 Madison Ave., New York, NY 10016. TEL 212-726-6490. FAX 212-686-7993) circ. 300. (also avail. in diskette format; back issues avail.) **Document type:** abstracting/indexing.
● Also available online. Vendor(s): DIMDI, European Space Agency, Knight-Ridder Information, Inc., STN International.

630   NE   ISSN 0928-4087
SALDI VAN AKKERBOUWGEWASSEN. 1988. biennial. fl.47. Landbouw-Economisch Instituut, Burg. Patijnlaan 19, 2585 BE The Hague, Netherlands. TEL 31-70-3308330. FAX 31-70-3615624. E-mail: postmaster@lei.dlo.nl; URL: http://www.lei.dlo.nl/lei. Ed. J.H. Jager. **Document type:** government publication.

630   CN   ISSN 0702-7389
S161
SASKATCHEWAN AGRICULTURE AND FOOD. AGRICULTURAL STATISTICS. 1975. a. free. Saskatchewan Agriculture and Food Library, B5 Walter Scott Bldg., 3085 Albert St., Regina, SK S4S 0B1, Canada. TEL 306-787-6933. FAX 306-787-0216. E-mail: pdc@agr.gov.sk.ca; URL: http://www.gov.sk.ca/agfood. charts; stat. circ. 1,600. (also avail. in microfiche; back issues avail.) **Document type:** government publication.

631 016   UK   ISSN 0141-0180
SEED ABSTRACTS. 1978. m. £225($395) (effective 1997). CAB International, Wallingford, Oxon. OX10 8DE, England. TEL 44-1491-832111. FAX 44-1491-826090. TELEX 847964 COMAGG G. E-mail: cabi@cabi.org; URL: http://www.cabi.org. (U.S. subscr. to: CAB International, North American Office, 198 Madison Ave., New York, NY 10016. TEL 212-726-6490. FAX 212-686-7993) circ. 450. (also avail. in diskette format; back issues avail.) **Indexed:** Weed Abstr. **Document type:** abstracting/indexing.
● Also available online. Vendor(s): DIMDI, European Space Agency, Knight-Ridder Information, Inc., STN International.
    Description: Topics covered include seed morphology and anatomy, seed chemistry, germination, seed storage and longevity, breeding and selection, seed assessment and testing, seed regulations, seed development, seed ecology, seed production, pests and diseases, seed processing, economics, and marketing.

016.581   UK   ISSN 0959-9592
SEED PATHOLOGY AND MICROBIOLOGY. 1991. a. £35($63) (diskette £38($65)) (effective 1997). (Danish Government Institute of Seed Pathology for Developing Countries (DGISP), DK) CAB International, Wallingford, Oxon. OX10 8DE, England. TEL 44-1491-832111. FAX 44-1491-826090. TELEX 847964 COMAGG G. E-mail: cabi@cabi.org; URL: http://www.cabi.org. (U.S. subscr. to: CAB International, North American Office, 198 Madison Ave., New York, NY 10016. TEL 212-726-6490. FAX 212-686-7993) Ed. J.A. Brunt. (also avail. in diskette format) **Document type:** bibliography.
● Also available online.
—BLDSC (8218.104000).
    Description: Covers diseases affecting seeds and the microorganisms that cause them.

630 016   RU   ISSN 0134-9120
SEL'SKOE KHOZYAISTVO ZA RUBEZHOM.* 1955. m. Rossiiskaya Akademiya Sel'skokhozyaistvennykh Nauk, c/o Tsentral'naya Nauchnaya Sel'skokhozyaistvennaya Biblioteka, Orlikov per. 3, 107804 Moscow, Russia. TEL 7-095-2078972. FAX 7-095-2075662. Ed. V.D. Pannikov. adv.; abstr.; charts; illus.; index. circ. 34,200. **Indexed:** Biol.Abstr., Helminthol.Abstr.
    Formed by the 1975 merger of: Sel'skoe Khozyaistvo za Rubezhom. Rastenievodstvo (ISSN 0131-6346); Sel'skoe Khozyaistvo za Rubezhom. Zhivotnovodstvo (ISSN 0131-6338)

338.1 630 016   RU
SEL'SKOKHOZYAISTVENNAYA LITERATURA. (Text in Russian) 1948. m. 1000 Rub. per issues. Rossiiskaya Akademiya Sel'skokhozyaistvennykh Nauk, Tsentral'naya Nauchnaya Sel'skokhozyaistvennaya Biblioteka - Russian Academy of Agricultural Sciences, Central Scientific Agricultural Library, Orlikov per. 3, 107804 Moscow, Russia. TEL 7-095-2078972. FAX 7-095-2075662. TELEX 911032. Ed. V.G. Pozdnyakov. adv.; page $4000 - 10000 Rub.; adv. contact: N.P. Abbakumova. bk.rev.; abstr.; bibl.; index. circ. 1,200. (also avail. in microform) **Indexed:** Anim.Breed.Abstr., Ind.Vet., Nutr.Abstr., Vet.Bull., Weed Abstr. **Document type:** bibliography.
    Formerly (until 1992): Sel'skokhozyaistvennaya Literatura S.S.S.R. (ISSN 0037-1688)
    Description: Organ of the National Agricultural Bibliography; covers books, brochures and provides an analytical registry of serial publications and non-periodical collections of papers.
Refereed Serial

630   SE
SEYCHELLES. PRESIDENT'S OFFICE. STATISTICS DIVISION. AGRICULTURE SURVEY. irreg. Rs.60. President's Office, Department of Finance, Statistic Division, P.O. Box 206, Mahe, Seychelles. stat.

SITUATION ET STATISTIQUES MONDIALES DU SECTEUR VITICOLE. see *BEVERAGES — Abstracting, Bibliographies, Statistics*

663   FR
▼**SITUATION ET STATISTIQUES MONDIALES DU SECTEUR VITIVINICOLE EN (YEAR).** (Text in English, French) 1997. a. 135 F. Office International de la Vigne et du Vin, 18 rue d'Aguesseau, 75008 Paris, France. TEL 33-1-44948080. FAX 33-1-42669063. E-mail: OIV101675.2013@compuserve.com.
    Description: Reports on the production, import-export, and cost of vitiviniculture in the world in the previous year.

SMALL ANIMALS. see *VETERINARY SCIENCE — Abstracting, Bibliographies, Statistics*

016.6364   US   ISSN 0163-173X
SOCIETY FOR RANGE MANAGEMENT. INTERNATIONAL RANGELAND CONGRESS. ABSTRACTS OF PAPERS. 1969? a. $5 (effective 1995). Society for Range Management, 1839 York St., Denver, CO 80206. TEL 303-355-7070. FAX 303-355-5059. (back issues avail.) **Document type:** proceedings.
    Former titles (until 1979): Society for Range Management. Annual Meeting. Abstracts of Papers Presented (ISSN 0736-1416); (until 1971): American Society for Range Management. Annual Meeting. Abstracts of Papers Presented (ISSN 0886-5515)

AGRICULTURE — ABSTRACTING, BIBLIOGRAPHIES, STATISTICS

631.4 016 UK
SOILS AND FERTILIZERS. 1965. m. price varies. CAB International, Wallingford, Oxon. OX10 8DE, England. TEL 44-491-832111. FAX 44-491-833508. TELEX 847964 COMAGG G. (U.S. subscr. to: CAB International, 198 Madison Ave., New York, NY 100166. TEL 212-726-6490) Indexed: Geo.Abstr. Pollut.Abstr. Document type: bibliography.
●Also available online. Vendor(s): CISTI, DIMDI, European Space Agency, Knight-Ridder Information, Inc., Ovid Technologies, Inc.
Former titles: CAB International. Bureau of Soils. Annotated Bibliographies & Commonwealth Bureau of Soils. Annotated Bibliographies (ISSN 0305-2524)

631.8 016 UK ISSN 0038-0792
S590 CODEN: SOFEAT
SOILS AND FERTILIZERS - ABSTRACTS OF WORLD LITERATURE. 1937. m. £685($1200) (effective 1997). CAB International, Wallingford, Oxon. OX10 8DE, England. TEL 44-1491-832111. FAX 44-1491-826090. TELEX 847964 COMAGG G. E-mail: cabi@cabi.org; URL: http://www.cabi.org. (U.S. subscr. to: CAB International, North American Office, 198 Madison Ave., New York, NY 10016. TEL 212-726-6490. FAX 212-686-7993) adv.; bk.rev.; index. circ. 1,900. (also avail. in diskette format; back issues avail.) Indexed: Biol.Abstr., Chem.Abstr., Dairy Sci.Abstr., Field Crop Abstr., Forest.Abstr., Forest Prod.Abstr., Helminthol.Abstr., Herb.Abstr., Nutr.Abstr., Rev.Plant Path, Rural Recreat.Tour.Abstr., Weed Abstr., World Agri.Econ.& Rural Sociol.Abstr. Document type: abstracting/indexing.
●Also available online. Vendor(s): DIMDI.
—BLDSC (8327.000000); Linda Hall.
Description: Aimed at specialists in the land resource and fertilizer sciences.

633.1 016 UK
SORGHUM AND MILLETS. (Not avail. in printed format) a. £35($60) (effective 1997). CAB International, Wallingford, Oxon. OX10 8DE, England. TEL 44-1419-832111. FAX 44-1491-826090. TELEX 847964 COMAGG G. E-mail: cabi@cabi.org; URL: http://www.cabi.org. (U.S. subscr. to: CAB International, North American Office, 198 Madison Ave., New York, NY 10016. TEL 212-726-6490. FAX 212-686-7993) circ. 250. (diskette format; back issues avail.) Indexed: Field Crop Abstr., Herb.Abstr. Document type: bibliography.
●Also available online. Vendor(s): DIMDI, European Space Agency, Knight-Ridder Information, Inc., STN International.
Supersedes (1976-1994): Sorghum and Millets Abstracts (ISSN 0308-2970)

338.1 316.8 SA ISSN 1021-5867
SOUTH AFRICA. CENTRAL STATISTICAL SERVICE. AGRICULTURAL SURVEY. (Report No. 11-01-01) a., latest 1992. R.10 (foreign R.11). Central Statistical Service - Sentrale Statistiekdiens, Private Bag X44, Pretoria 0001, South Africa. TEL 27-12-310-8911. FAX 27-12-310-8500. (Orders to: Government Printing Works, Private Bag X85, Pretoria 0001, South Africa) Document type: government publication.

338.1 316.8 SA
SOUTH AFRICA. CENTRAL STATISTICAL SERVICE. STATISTICAL RELEASE. AGRICULTURAL SURVEY. (No. P1101) a. free. Central Statistical Service - Sentrale Statistiekdiens, Private Bag X44, Pretoria 0001, South Africa. TEL 27-12-310-8911. FAX 27-12-310-8500. Document type: government publication.
Description: Covers employment, income, current and capital expenditures, assets, and production.

338.1021 SA
SOUTH AFRICA. DEPARTMENT OF AGRICULTURE. DIRECTORATE OF AGRICULTURAL STATISTICS. ABSTRACT OF AGRICULTURAL STATISTICS/KORTBEGRIP VAN LANDBOUSTATISTIEKE. (Text in Afrikaans, English) 1958. a. free. Department of Agriculture, Directorate Agricultural Statistics, Private Bag X144, Pretoria 0001, South Africa. stat.; circ. controlled.
Former titles: South Africa. Department of Agriculture and Fisheries. Division of Economic Services. Abstract of Agricultural Statistics; South Africa. Department of Agricultural Economics and Marketing. Division of Agricultural Marketing Research. Abstract of Agricultural Statistics.

631 016 UK ISSN 0141-0172
SOYABEAN ABSTRACTS. 1978. bi-m. £170($300) (effective 1997). CAB International, Wallingford, Oxon. OX10 8DE, England. TEL 44-1491-832111. FAX 44-1491-826090. TELEX 847964 COMAGG G. E-mail: cabi@cabi.org; URL: http://www.cabi.org. (U.S. subscr. to: CAB International, North American Office, 198 Madison Ave., New York, NY 10016. TEL 212-726-6490. FAX 212-686-7933) circ. 250. (also avail. in diskette format; back issues avail.) Document type: abstracting/indexing.
●Also available online. Vendor(s): DIMDI, European Space Agency, Knight-Ridder Information, Inc., STN International.
Description: Topics covered include: breeding and selection, agronomy, physiological disorders, nitrogen fixation, physiology and biochemistry, storage and quality, nutrition and utilization, varieties and varietal resistance, fertilizers, pests and diseases, climate and environment, harvesting, food technology, and economics.

630 314.6 SP ISSN 0211-9897
SPAIN. MINISTERIO DE AGRICULTURA, PESCA Y ALIMENTACION. BOLETIN MENSUAL DE ESTADISTICA AGRARIA. (Includes special nos.) m. 6000 ptas. (foreign 9000 ptas.) (effective 1997). Ministerio de Agricultura, Pesca y Alimentacion, Secretaria General Tecnica, Centro de Publicaciones, Paseo de la Infanta Isabel 1, 28071 Madrid, Spain. TEL 34-1-3475551. Ed. Porfirio Sanchez Rodriguez. R&P contact: Juan Carlos Palacios Lopez. charts; illus.; index. Indexed: P.A.I.S.For.Lang.Ind. Document type: government publication.

630 310 SP ISSN 0212-1158
SPAIN. MINISTERIO DE AGRICULTURA, PESCA Y ALIMENTACION. SECRETARIA GENERAL TECNICA. ANUARIO DE ESTADISTICA AGRARIA. 1904. a. 5500 ptas. (effective 1995). Ministerio de Agricultura, Pesca y Alimentacion, Secretaria General Tecnica, Centro de Publicaciones, Paseo de la Infanta Isabel 1, 28071 Madrid, Spain. TEL 34-1-3475551. Ed. Porfirio Sanchez Rodriguez. R&P contact: Juan Carlos Palacios Lopez. charts. Document type: government publication.
Former titles (until 1972): Spain. Ministerio de Agricultura, Pesca y Alimentacion. Anuario Estadistico de Produccion Agricola (ISSN 0081-3419); (until 1942): Spain. Ministerio de Agricultura. Avance Estadistico.

636 EI ISSN 0254-3834
STATISTICAL OFFICE OF THE EUROPEAN COMMUNITIES. AGRICULTURAL PRICES; selected series - chronos data bank. q. $110. Office for Official Publications of the European Communities, Rue Alcide de Gasperi, 2920 Luxembourg, Luxembourg. (Dist. in the U.S. by: Unipub, 4611-F Assembly Dr., Lanham, MD 20706-4391. TEL 800-274-4888. FAX 301-459-0056) stat. (also avail. in microfiche from CIS) Indexed: IIS.
—BLDSC (0750.828000).
Formed by the merger of: Statistical Office of the European Communities. Selling Prices of Animal Products (ISSN 0378-6722); Statistical Office of the European Communities. Selling Prices of Vegetables Products (ISSN 0378-6714)
Description: Statistics on selling prices of plant products, selling prices of animal products and purchase prices of the means of agricultural production.

630 EI
STATISTICAL OFFICE OF THE EUROPEAN COMMUNITIES. STATISTICAL YEARBOOK. AGRICULTURE. (Text in English) 1961. a. $20. Office for Official Publications of the European Communities, Rue Alcide de Gasperi, 2920 Luxembourg, Luxembourg. (Dist. in the U.S. by: Unipub, 4611-F Assembly Dr., Lanham, MD 20706-4391. TEL 800-274-4888. FAX 301-459-0056) (also avail. in microfiche from CIS) Indexed: IIS.
Formerly: Statistical Office of the European Communities. Statistique Agricole (ISSN 0081-4946)

338.1 630 GW ISSN 0072-1581
STATISTISCHES JAHRBUCH UEBER ERNAEHRUNG, LANDWIRTSCHAFT UND FORSTEN DER BUNDESREPUBLIK DEUTSCHLAND. 1956. a. DM.138. Bundesministerium fuer Ernaehrung, Landwirtschaft und Forsten, 53107 Bonn, Germany. TEL 49-228-5293959. Document type: government publication.
—CCC.

338.2 633 661.2 UK ISSN 0039-4890
CODEN: SULPAW
SULPHUR; covers all aspects of world sulphur and sulphuric acid industry. 1953. bi-m. £340($495) (effective May 1997). British Sulphur Publishing (Subsidiary of: C R U Publishing Ltd.), 31 Mount Pleasant, London WC1X 0AD, England. TEL 44-171-837-5600. FAX 44-171-837-0292. TELEX 918918 SULFEX G. Ed. Martin Horeseman; Pub. John French. R&P contact: John French. adv. contact: Tina Firman. bk.rev.; charts; illus.; mkt.; stat.; index. circ. 639. (also avail. in microform from UMI; reprint service avail. from UMI) Indexed: Chem.Abstr., I.M.M.Abstr., Soils & Fert. Document type: trade publication.
●Also available online. Vendor(s): Information Access Co.
—BLDSC (8516.800000); CASDDS; CISTI; SWETS; UMI; UnCover.

338.1 310 SQ ISSN 0302-4024
SWAZILAND. CENTRAL STATISTICAL OFFICE. CENSUS OF INDIVIDUAL TENURE FARMS. 1968. a. free. Central Statistical Office, P.O. Box 456, Mbabane, Swaziland. TEL 268-43765. stat. circ. 600. (processed) Document type: government publication.

630 SW ISSN 0082-0199
SWEDEN. STATISTISKA CENTRALBYRAAN. JORDBRUKSSTATISTISK AARSBOK. (Text in Swedish; summaries in English) 1965. a. SEK 280. Statistiska Centralbyraan, Publishing Unit, S-701 89 Oerebro, Sweden. circ. 1,500.

630 314 SW ISSN 0082-0288
SWEDEN. STATISTISKA CENTRALBYRAAN. STATISTISKA MEDDELANDEN. SERIE J, JORDBRUK, SKOGSBRUK OCH FISKE. (Text in Swedish; table heads and summaries in English) 1963. irreg. SEK 2100. Statistiska Centralbyraan, Publishing Unit, S-701 89 Oerebro, Sweden. circ. 1,175.

631 II ISSN 0082-1586
TAMIL NADU. DEPARTMENT OF STATISTICS. SEASON AND CROP REPORT. (Text in English) 1902. a. Rs.5. Director of Statistics, Madras 600006, India. (Subscr. to: Government Publication Depot, 166 Anna Rd., Madras 600006, India)

631 636 TZ
TANZANIA. MINISTRY OF AGRICULTURE AND LIVESTOCK DEVELOPMENT. BULLETIN OF CROP STATISTICS. (Text in English) 1975. a. Ministry of Agriculture and Livestock Development, Planning and Marketing Division, Statistics Section, P.O. Box 9192, Dar es Salaam, Tanzania. Ed. M.S. Ravivarma. circ. 200. Document type: bulletin, government publication.
Former titles: Tanzania. Ministry of Agriculture. Bulletin of Crop Statistics; Bulletin of Crop and Livestock Statistics.

338.1 US
HD9417.T4
TEXAS AGRICULTURAL STATISTICS. (Subseries of: Texas Department of Agriculture. Bulletin) 1994. a. $30 (free to Texas farmers and ranchers). Texas Agricultural Statistics Service, Box 70, Austin, TX 78767. TEL 512-916-5581. FAX 512-916-5956. E-mail: nass-tx@nass.usda.gov; URL: http://www.io.com/~tass. (Co-sponsor: Texas Department of Agriculture) Dir. Dennis Findley. charts; illus.; mkt.; stat. circ. 2,700. Document type: government publication.
Formed by the merger of (1968-1994): Texas Livestock Statistics (ISSN 0091-1550); (1968-1994): Texas Small Grains Statistics (ISSN 0091-4673) & Texas Crop Statistics.
Description: Contains crop statistics, livestock statistics, and economic statistics.

630 001.3 016 II ISSN 0379-3990
THESIS ABSTRACTS. (Text in English) 1975. q. Rs.200($60) Haryana Agricultural University, Hisar 125 004, Haryana, India. TEL 73721. Ed. R.P. Bansal. adv. circ. 500.
—BLDSC (8820.092300).
Description: Abstracts of Master's and doctoral theses approved for degrees by the various agricultural universities and National Institutes in India.

AGRICULTURE — ABSTRACTING, BIBLIOGRAPHIES, STATISTICS

630 310   TR
TRINIDAD AND TOBAGO. CENTRAL STATISTICAL OFFICE. AGRICULTURAL REPORT. 1950. a. T.T.$15($7.50) Central Statistical Office, 35-41 Queen St., P.O. Box 98, Port-of-Spain, Trinidad & Tobago, W.I. TEL 809-623-7069. **Document type:** government publication.
    Formerly: Trinidad and Tobago. Central Statistical Office. Quarterly Agricultural Report.

633   UK   ISSN 0961-351X
TROPICAL OIL SEEDS. 1975. a. £350($60) (effective 1997). CAB International, Wallingford, Oxon. OX10 8DE, England. TEL 44-1491-832111. FAX 44-1491-826090. TELEX 847964 COMAGG G. E-mail: cabi@cabi.org; URL: http://www.cabi.org. (U.S. subscr. to: CAB International, North American Office, 198 Madison Ave., New York, NY 10016. TEL 212-726-6490. FAX 212-686-7993) circ. 250. (also avail. in diskette format; back issues avail.) **Indexed:** Field Crop Abstr., Herb.Abstr. **Document type:** bibliography.
    ●Also available online. Vendor(s): DIMDI, European Space Agency, Knight-Ridder Information, Inc., STN International.
    Formerly (until 1991): Tropical Oil Seeds Abstracts (ISSN 0308-2962)
    Description: Covers aspects of research on groundnuts, safflower, coconuts, oil palms, castor, sesame, seed oils, and other oilseed crops.

636   YU   ISSN 0041-3755
TRZISTE STOKE I STOCIHH PROIZODA;* konjunkturne informacije. (Text in Serbo-Croatian) 1962. s-m. 1000 din. Zavod za Trzisna Istrazivanja, Mose Pijade 8-I, 11001 Belgrade, Yugoslavia. Ed. Julije Drasinover. stat.; circ. controlled.

TSETSE AND TRYPANOSOMIASIS INFORMATION QUARTERLY. see *BIOLOGY — Abstracting, Bibliographies, Statistics*

315.61   TU   ISSN 1300-123X
HA1911
TURKEY. DEVLET ISTATISTIK ENSTITUSU. CIFTCININ ELINE GECEN FIYATLAR/TURKEY. STATE INSTITUTE OF STATISTICS. PRICES RECEIVED BY FARMERS. (Text in English, Turkish) 1977. a., latest 1993. $40 (effective 1996). Devlet Istatistik Enstitusu - State Institute of Statistics, Necatibey Caddesi No. 114, 06100 Ankara, Turkey. TEL 90-312-4185027. FAX 90-312-4710432. (also avail. in diskette format) **Document type:** government publication.

630   TU
TURKEY. DEVLET ISTATISTIK ENSTITUSU. GENEL TARIM SAYIMI/TURKEY. STATE INSTITUTE OF STATISTICS. GENERAL AGRICULTURAL CENSUS. (Consists of: Village Information Survey; Agricultural Holdings Survey) (Text in English, Turkish) 1941. irreg., latest 1991. $70 for Village Information Survey; $90 for Agricultural Holding Survey. Devlet Istatistik Enstitusu - State Institute of Statistics, Necatibey Caddesi No. 114, 06100 Ankara, Turkey. TEL 90-312-4185027. FAX 90-312-4170432. circ. 1,500. (also avail. in diskette format) **Document type:** government publication.

315.61   TU   ISSN 1300-1213
TURKEY. DEVLET ISTATISTIK ENSTITUSU. TARIM ISTATISTIKLERI OZETI/TURKEY. STATE INSTITUTE OF STATISTICS. SUMMARY OF AGRICULTURAL STATISTICS. (Text in English, Turkish) 1957. a. $45 (effective 1996). Devlet Istatistik Enstitusu - State Institute of Statistics, Necatibey Caddesi No. 114, 06100 Ankara, Turkey. TEL 90-312-4185027. FAX 90-312-4170432. **Document type:** government publication.

630 315.61   TU   ISSN 1300-3577
TURKEY. DEVLET ISTATISTIK ENSTITUSU. TARIMSAL URETIM DEGERI/TURKEY. STATE INSTITUTE OF STATISTICS. VALUE OF AGRICULTURAL PRODUCTION. (Text in English, Turkish) a., latest 1989. $75 (effective 1996). Devlet Istatistik Enstitusu - State Institute of Statistics, Necatibey Cad. No. 114, 06100 Ankara, Turkey. TEL 90-312-4185027. FAX 90-312-4170432. (also avail. in diskette format) **Document type:** government publication.
    Description: Provides statistical information on agricultural and animal production, including market shares and production value.

315.61   TU   ISSN 0082-6936
HA1911
TURKEY. DEVLET ISTATISTIK ENSTITUSU. TARIMSAL YAPI VE URETIM/TURKEY. STATE INSTITUTE OF STATISTICS. AGRICULTURAL STRUCTURE AND PRODUCTION. (Text in English, Turkish) 1936. a. $65 (effective 1996). Devlet Istatistik Enstitusu - State Institute of Statistics, Necatibey Caddesi No. 114, 06100 Ankara, Turkey. TEL 90-312-4185027. FAX 90-312-4170432. circ. 750. **Document type:** government publication.
    Description: Provides statistical information by province on all aspects of agricultural activity, including area under cultivation, production and yields of vegetable, fruit and tree crops, agricultural machinery, as well as apiculture, livestock and animal production and sericulture.

630   UK
U K DIRECTORY AND STATISTICS. COOPERATIVES AND FARMER CONTROLLED BUSINESSES. a. Plunkett Foundation, 23 Hanborough Business Park, Long Hanborough, Oxford OX8 8LH, England. TEL 44-1993-883636. FAX 44-1993-883576. **Document type:** trade publication.
    Formerly: Facts and Figures about Farmer Controlled Businesses in the United Kingdom.

338.109   US   ISSN 0082-9714
HD1751
U.S. DEPARTMENT OF AGRICULTURE. AGRICULTURAL STATISTICS. 1936. a. price varies. U.S. Department of Agriculture, Office of Public Affairs, 14th St. & Independence Ave., S.W., Washington, DC 20250-1300. TEL 202-720-2791. (Orders to: ERS-NASS, P.O. Box 1608, Rockville, MD 20850) (also avail. in microform from BHP; microfilm from BHP) **Document type:** government publication.
—CISTI; UMI.

338.1 310   US   ISSN 0002-1601
HD9004
U.S. DEPARTMENT OF AGRICULTURE. AGRICULTURAL STATISTICS BOARD REPORT: AGRICULTURAL PRICES. m. $38 (foreign $47.50). U.S. Department of Agriculture, Agricultural Statistics Board, Publications, South Bldg., Rm. 5829, Washington, DC 20250. TEL 202-655-4000. (Subscr. to: Superintendent of Documents, U.S. Government Printing Office, Box 371954, Pittsburgh, PA 15250-7954. TEL 202-512-1800. FAX 202-512-2250) (back issues avail.) **Document type:** government publication.
    ●Also available online. Vendor(s): Knight-Ridder Information, Inc.
    Description: Supplies comparative information on prices received by farmers for various commodities and prices paid by farmers for commodities and services, interest, taxes, and farm wage rates.

636.2   US   ISSN 0094-3819
U.S. DEPARTMENT OF AGRICULTURE. AGRICULTURAL STATISTICS BOARD REPORT: CATTLE. 1972. m. (plus s-a. reports). $29 (foreign $36.25) (includes m. Cattle on Feed). U.S. Department of Agriculture, Agricultural Statistics Board, Publications, Rm. 5829, South Bldg., Washington, DC 20250. (Subscr. to: ERS-NASS, 341 Victory Dr., Herndon, VA 22070. TEL 800-999-6779. FAX 703-834-0110; Or: Superintendent of Documents, U.S. Government Printing Office, Box 371954, Pittsburgh, PA 15250-7954. TEL 202-512-1800. FAX 202-512-2250) stat. (back issues avail.) **Document type:** government publication.
    Supersedes in part (in 1973): Agricultural Statistics Board Reports: Cattle, Sheep and Goat Inventory (ISSN 0094-3827)

636 310   US   ISSN 1076-3945
    CODEN: CHEGED
U.S. DEPARTMENT OF AGRICULTURE. AGRICULTURAL STATISTICS BOARD REPORT: CHICKENS AND EGGS. m. $39 (foreign $48.75). U.S. Department of Agriculture, Agricultural Statistics Board, Publications, Rm. 5829, South Bldg., Washington, DC 20250. (Subscr. to: Superintendent of Documents, U.S. Government Printing Office, Box 371954, Pittsburgh, PA 15250-7954. TEL 202-512-1800. FAX 202-512-2250) (back issues avail.) **Document type:** government publication.
    Former titles (until 1994): Agricultural Statistics Board Report: Eggs, Chickens and Turkeys (ISSN 0093-013X); (until 1969): U.S. Crop Reporting Board. Hatchery Production (ISSN 0093-0121)

633 310   US   ISSN 0363-8561
SB83
U.S. DEPARTMENT OF AGRICULTURE. AGRICULTURAL STATISTICS BOARD REPORT: CROP PRODUCTION. Key Title: Crop Production. m. with a. summary. $39 (foreign $48.75). U.S. Department of Agriculture, Agricultural Statistics Board, Publications, Rm. 5829, South Bldg., Washington, DC 20250. TEL 202-655-4000. (Subscr. to: Superintendent of Documents, U.S. Government Printing Office, Box 371954, Pittsburgh, PA 15250-7954. TEL 202-512-1800. FAX 202-512-2250) (also avail. in microfiche from CIS; reprint service avail. from CIS; back issues avail.) **Indexed:** Amer.Stat.Ind. (1987-), Crop Physiol.Abstr., Field Crop Abstr., Herb.Abstr., Irr.& Drain.Abstr., Maize Abstr., Plant Grow.Reg.Abstr., Rice Abstr., Seed Abstr., Soyabean Abstr., Weed Abstr. **Document type:** government publication.
    ●Also available online. Vendor(s): Knight-Ridder Information, Inc.

630 310   US   ISSN 0091-1267
U.S. DEPARTMENT OF AGRICULTURE. AGRICULTURAL STATISTICS BOARD REPORT: COLD STORAGE. 1945. m. (plus a. cumulation). $29 (foreign $36.25). U.S. Department of Agriculture, Agricultural Statistics Board, Publications, Rm. 5829, South Bldg., Washington, DC 20250. (Subscr. to: Superintendent of Documents, U.S. Government Printing Office, Box 371954, Pittsburgh, PA 15250-7954. TEL 202-512-1800. FAX 202-512-2250) (back issues avail.) **Document type:** government publication.

338.1 310   US   ISSN 0093-1446
U.S. DEPARTMENT OF AGRICULTURE. AGRICULTURAL STATISTICS BOARD REPORT: DAIRY PRODUCTS. 1972. m. (plus 5/yr. supplements) $49 (foreign $61.25). U.S. Department of Agriculture, Agricultural Statistics Board, Publications, Rm. 5829, South Bldg., Washington, DC 20250. (Subscr. to: Superintendent of Documents, U.S. Government Printing Office, Box 371954, Pittsburgh, PA 15250-7954. TEL 202-512-1800. FAX 202-512-2250) stat. (back issues avail.) **Document type:** government publication.

637.5 310   US
U.S. DEPARTMENT OF AGRICULTURE. AGRICULTURAL STATISTICS BOARD REPORT: EGG PRODUCTS. m. $20 (foreign $25). U.S. Department of Agriculture, Agricultural Statistics Board, Publications, Rm. 5829, South Bldg., Washington, DC 20250. (Subscr. to: Superintendent of Documents, U.S. Government Printing Office, Box 371954, Pittsburgh, PA 15250-7954. TEL 202-512-1800. FAX 202-512-2250) (back issues avail.) **Document type:** government publication.

338.1   US
U.S. DEPARTMENT OF AGRICULTURE. AGRICULTURAL STATISTICS BOARD REPORT: GRAIN STOCKS. q. $8.50 (foreign $10.65). U.S. Department of Agriculture, Agricultural Statistics Board, Publications, Rm. 5829, South Bldg., Washington, DC 20250. (Subscr. to: Superintendent of Documents, U.S. Government Printing Office, Box 371954, Pittsburgh, PA 15250-7954. TEL 202-512-1800. FAX 202-512-2250) stat. (back issues avail.) **Document type:** government publication.

636 310   US   ISSN 0565-2189
U.S. DEPARTMENT OF AGRICULTURE. AGRICULTURAL STATISTICS BOARD REPORT: HOGS AND PIGS. 1968. q. $10 (foreign $12.50). U.S. Department of Agriculture, Agricultural Statistics Board, Publications, Rm. 5829, South Bldg., Washington, DC 20250. URL: http://www.mannlib.cornell.edu/reports/nassr/livestock/php-bb/. (Subscr. to: Superintendent of Documents, U.S. Government Printing Office, Box 371954, Pittsburgh, PA 15250-7954. TEL 202-512-1800. FAX 202-512-2250) (back issues avail.) **Document type:** government publication.
    ●Also available online.

636 310   US   ISSN 0499-0544
U.S. DEPARTMENT OF AGRICULTURE. AGRICULTURAL STATISTICS BOARD REPORT: LIVESTOCK SLAUGHTER. m. (plus a. cumulation). $35 (foreign $43.75). U.S. Department of Agriculture, Agriculture Statistics Board, Publications, Rm. 5829, South Bldg., Washington, DC 20250. (Subscr. to: Superintendent of Documents, U.S. Government Printing Office, Box 371954, Pittsburgh, PA 15250-7954. TEL 202-512-1800. FAX 202-512-2250) (back issues avail.) **Document type:** government publication.

AGRICULTURE — ABSTRACTING, BIBLIOGRAPHIES, STATISTICS

637.1 310   US   ISSN 0026-4202
HD9282.U3
U.S. DEPARTMENT OF AGRICULTURE. AGRICULTURAL STATISTICS BOARD REPORT: MILK PRODUCTION. m. (plus a. cumulation). $23 (foreign $28.75). U.S. Department of Agriculture, Agricultural Statistics Board, Publications, Rm. 5829, South Bldg., Washington, DC 20250. E-mail: nass@nass.usda.gov; URL: http://www.mannlib.cornell.edu/reports/nassr/livestock/php-bb/. (Subscr. to: Superintendent of Documents, U.S. Government Printing Office, Box 371954, Pittsburgh, PA 15250-7954. TEL 202-512-1800. FAX 202-512-2250) (back issues avail.) **Document type:** government publication.
●Also available online.

631 310   US   ISSN 1057-7912
U.S. DEPARTMENT OF AGRICULTURE. AGRICULTURAL STATISTICS BOARD REPORT: NONCITRUS FRUITS AND NUTS. s-a. $7.50 (foreign $9.40). U.S. Department of Agriculture, Agricultural Statistics Board, Publications, Rm. 5829, South Bldg., Washington, DC 20250. (Subscr. to: Superintendent of Documents, U.S. Government Printing Office, Box 371954, Pittsburgh, PA 15250-7954. TEL 202-512-1800. FAX 202-512-2250) (back issues avail.) **Document type:** government publication.

631 310   US
U.S. DEPARTMENT OF AGRICULTURE. AGRICULTURAL STATISTICS BOARD REPORT: POTATOES AND POTATO STOCKS. 7/yr. $14 (foreign $17.50). U.S. Department of Agriculture, Agricultural Statistics Board, Publications, Rm. 5829, South Bldg., Washington, DC 20250. (Subscr. to: Superintendent of Documents, U.S. Government Printing Office, Box 371954, Pittsburgh, PA 15250-7954. TEL 202-512-1800. FAX 202-512-2250) (back issues avail.) **Document type:** government publication.
Formerly (until 1995): Agricultural Statistics Board Report: Potatoes.

636.9 310   US   ISSN 0364-2682
HD9437.U6
U.S. DEPARTMENT OF AGRICULTURE. AGRICULTURAL STATISTICS BOARD REPORT: POULTRY SLAUGHTER. m. $24 (foreign $30). U.S. Department of Agriculture, Agricultural Statistics Board, Publications, Rm. 5829, South Bldg., Washington, DC 20250. (Subscr. to: Superintendent of Documents, U.S. Government Printing Office, Box 371954, Pittsburgh, PA 15250-7954. TEL 202-512-1800. FAX 202-512-2250) (back issues avail.) **Document type:** government publication.

633 310   US   ISSN 0499-0579
U.S. DEPARTMENT OF AGRICULTURE. AGRICULTURAL STATISTICS BOARD REPORT: PEANUT STOCKS AND PROCESSING. m. $20 (foreign $25). U.S. Department of Agriculture, Agricultural Statistics Board, Publications, Rm. 5829, South Bldg., Washington, DC 20250. (Subscr. to: Superintendent of Documents, U.S. Government Printing Office, Box 371954, Pittsburgh, PA 15250-7954. TEL 202-512-1800. FAX 202-512-2250) (back issues avail.) **Document type:** government publication.

633.1 310   US   ISSN 1057-7920
U.S. DEPARTMENT OF AGRICULTURE. AGRICULTURAL STATISTICS BOARD REPORT: RICE STOCKS. q. $6.50 (foreign $8.15). U.S. Department of Agriculture, Agricultural Statistics Board, Publications, Rm. 5829, South Bldg., Washington, DC 20250. (Subscr. to: Superintendent of Documents, U.S. Government Printing Office, Box 371954, Pittsburgh, PA 15250-7954. TEL 202-512-1800. FAX 202-512-2250) (back issues avail.) **Document type:** government publication.

633 310   US   ISSN 0193-6603
U.S. DEPARTMENT OF AGRICULTURE. AGRICULTURAL STATISTICS BOARD REPORT: VEGETABLES. q. (plus a. cumulation). $11 (foreign $13.75). U.S. Department of Agriculture, Agricultural Statistics Board, Publications, Rm. 5829, South Bldg., Washington, DC 20250. (Subscr. to: Superintendent of Documents, U.S. Government Printing Office, Box 371954, Pittsburgh, PA 15250-7954. TEL 202-512-1800. FAX 202-512-2250) (back issues avail.)

636 317   US
U.S. DEPARTMENT OF AGRICULTURE. ANIMAL AND PLANT HEALTH INSPECTION SERVICE. COOPERATIVE STATE-FEDERAL BRUCELLOSIS ERADICATION PROGRAM: STATISTICAL TABLES.* a. free. U.S. Animal and Plant Health Inspection Service, 4700 River Rd., Unit 6, Riverdale, MD 20737. TEL 301-734-5240. stat.

636 317   US
U.S. DEPARTMENT OF AGRICULTURE. ANIMAL AND PLANT HEALTH INSPECTION SERVICE. COOPERATIVE STATE-FEDERAL BOVINE TUBERCULOSIS ERADICATION PROGRAM: STATISTICAL TABLES.* a. free. U.S. Animal and Plant Health Inspection Service, 4700 River Rd., Unit 6, Riverdale, MD 20737. TEL 301-734-5240. stat.

631   US
U.S. DEPARTMENT OF AGRICULTURE. RURAL BUSINESS - COOPERATIVE SERVICE. COMPARATIVE STATISTICS. a. $5. U.S. Department of Agriculture, Rural Business - Cooperative Service, AG Box 3255, Washington, DC 20250-3255. TEL 202-720-6483. FAX 202-720-4641. Ed. Daniel Campbell. **Document type:** government publication, trade publication.
Formerly: Statistics of Farmer Cooperatives (ISSN 0081-5128)
Description: Provides the latest statistics on farmer cooperatives in the U.S.

338.1 382 317   US
HD9002
U.S. FOREIGN AGRICULTURAL TRADE AND AGRICULTURAL TRADE UPDATES STATISTICAL REPORT. (Supplement to: Foreign Agricultural Trade of the United States) 1971. a. $34 (included with subscr. to Foreign Agricultural Trade of the United States). U.S. Department of Agriculture, Economics Research Service, Information Division, 1301 New York Ave., Rm. 110, Washington, DC 20005. TEL 800-999-6779. (Dist. by: ERS-NASS, 341 Victory Dr., Herndon, VA 20170) **Document type:** government publication.
Formerly: U.S. Foreign Agricultural Trade Statistical Report (ISSN 0362-0530)

338.1 382 317   US
U.S. FOREIGN AGRICULTURAL TRADE STATISTICAL REPORT. FISCAL YEAR. (Supplement to the m. Foreign Agricultural Trade of the United States) a. $29. U.S. Department of Agriculture, Economics Research Service, Information Services Division, 1301 New York Ave., Rm. 237, Washington, DC 20005. TEL 800-999-6779. URL: http://www.econ.ag.gov/. (Dist. by: ERS-NASS, 341 Victory Dr., Herndon, VA 22070) Ed. Martha R. Evans. **Document type:** government publication.

630 317   US   ISSN 0276-0193
S119
UTAH AGRICULTURAL STATISTICS. 1971. a. free. Department of Agriculture, 350 N. Redwood Rd., Box 146500, Salt Lake City, UT 84114-6500. TEL 801-538-7100. (Co-sponsor: U.S. Department of Agriculture, Utah Agricultural Statistical Service) (also avail. in microfiche from CIS) **Indexed:** SRI. **Document type:** government publication.

630   NN
VANUATU. STATISTICS OFFICE. REPORT OF THE AGRICULTURAL CENSUS. (Part I: The Results; Part II: Summary of Results) irreg., latest 1984. 1000 vatu($15) for Part I; 100 vatu ($10) for Part II (effective 1996). Statistics Office, Private Mail Bag 19, Port-Vila, Vanuatu. TEL 678-22110. FAX 678-24583. Ed. Jacob Isaiah. adv. contact: Tali Saurei. **Document type:** government publication.

630   NN
VANUATU. STATISTICS OFFICE. REPORT ON SMALL HOLDER AGRICULTURE SURVEY. 1989. a. 1000 vatu($15) (effective 1996). Statistics Office, Private Mail Bag 19, Port-Vila, Vanuatu. TEL 678-22110. FAX 678-24583. Ed. Jacob Isaiah. adv. contact: Tali Saurei. **Document type:** government publication.
Description: Contains detailed data on cocoa practices, cocoa fermenting, livestock and pastures.

338.1 318   VE
VENEZUELA. MINISTERIO DE AGRICULTURA Y CRIA. BOLETIN DE PRECIOS DE PRODUCTOS AGROPECUARIOS. (Cumulated annually) 1955. m. free. Ministerio de Agricultura y Cria, Direccion de Planificacion y Estadistica, Division de Estadistica, Centro Simon Bolivar, Torre Norte 16o, Caracas 1010, Venezuela. TEL 2-509-0111. **Document type:** bulletin, government publication.

338.1 318   VE   ISSN 0085-7653
VENEZUELA. MINISTERIO DE AGRICULTURA Y CRIA. DIRECCION DE ECONOMIA Y ESTADISTICA AGROPECUARIA. DIVISION DE ESTADISTICA. PLAN DE TRABAJO.* a. Ministerio de Agricultura y Cria, Direccion de Economia y Estadistica Agropecuaria, Division de Estadistica, Centro Simon Bolivar, Torre Norte 16o, Caracas 1010, Venezuela. **Document type:** government publication.

338.1 310   VE   ISSN 0083-5366
VENEZUELA. MINISTERIO DE AGRICULTURA Y CRIA. DIRECCION DE ECONOMICA Y ESTADISTICA AGROPECUARIA. ANUARIO ESTADISTICO AGROPECUARIO. 1961. a. free. Ministerio de Agricultura y Cria, Direccion de Planificacion y Estadistica, Division de Estadistica, Centro Simon Bolivar, Torre Norte 16o, Caracas 1010, Venezuela. **Document type:** government publication.

630 338.1   VE
VENEZUELA. MINISTERIO DE AGRICULTURA Y CRIA. DIRECCION DE PLANIFICACION Y ESTADISTICA. ESTADISTICAS AGROPECUARIAS DE LAS ENTIDADES FEDERALES. 1962. biennial. free. Ministerio de Agricultura y Cria, Direccion de Planificacion y Estadistica, Division de Estadistica, Centro Simon Bolivar, Torre Norte 16o, Caracas 1010, Venezuela. **Document type:** government publication.

634.3 011   GW   ISSN 0175-8292
VITIS - VITICULTURE AND OENOLOGY ABSTRACTS. Variant title: Vitis - V E A. 1984. 4/yr. DM.80. Bundesanstalt fuer Zuechtungsforschung an Kulturpflanzen, Institut fuer Rebenzuechtung Geilweilerhof, 76833 Siebeldingen, Germany. TEL 49-63-45410. FAX 49-63-4541177. E-mail: irz@geilweilerhof.suew.shuttle.de. Ed. Martin Klenert. index. circ. 700. **Document type:** abstracting/indexing.
●Also available online. Vendor(s): DIMDI, Knight-Ridder Information, Inc., STN International. —BLDSC (9244.120100); Linda Hall. **CCC.**
Description: Abstracts from journals, books, conference proceedings and reports on all aspects of vine and grapevine science and technology.

338.1   US   ISSN 0095-4330
S125
WASHINGTON AGRICULTURAL STATISTICS. 1973. a. free. U.S. Department of Agriculture, Agricultural Statstics Service (Olympia), Box 609, Olympia, WA 98507-0609. TEL 206-902-1940. FAX 206-902-2091. URL: http://www.usda.gov/nass/SSO/WA/homepage.htm. circ. 3,000. (also avail. in microfiche from CIS) **Indexed:** SRI. **Document type:** government publication.

WATER AND ENERGY ABSTRACTS. see *WATER RESOURCES — Abstracting, Bibliographies, Statistics*

632.58 016   UK   ISSN 0043-1729
SB611
WEED ABSTRACTS; compiled from world literature. 1954. m. £300($525) (effective 1997). CAB International, Wallingford, Oxon OX10 8DE, England. TEL 44-1491-832111. FAX 44-1491-826090. TELEX 847964 COMAGG G. E-mail: cabi@cagi.org; URL: http://www.cabi.org. (U.S. subscr. to: CAB International, North American Office, 198 Madison Ave., New York, NY 10016. TEL 212-726-6490. FAX 212-686-7993) bk.rev.; abstr.; index. circ. 2,250. (also avail. in diskette format; back issues avail.) **Indexed:** Biol.Abstr., Chem.Abstr., Field Crop Abstr., Forest.Abstr., Forest Prod.Abstr., Herb.Abstr., Ind.Vet., Rev.Appl.Entomol., Rural Recreat.Tour.Abstr., Vet.Bull., World Agri.Econ. & Rural Sociol.Abstr. **Document type:** abstracting/indexing.
●Also available online. Vendor(s): DIMDI, European Space Agency, Knight-Ridder Information, Inc., STN International.
—Linda Hall.
Description: Covers the current literature on weeds, weed control, and allied subjects.

AGRICULTURE — AGRICULTURAL ECONOMICS

632.58   US
WEED SCIENCE SOCIETY OF AMERICA. ABSTRACTS. 1956. a. Weed Science Society of America, 1508 W. University, Champaign, IL 61821-3133. TEL 217-352-4212. FAX 217-352-4241. (reprint service avail. from UMI,ISI) **Indexed:** Biotech.Abstr., Weed Abstr. **Document type:** abstracting/indexing.
   Formerly (until 1967): Weed Society of America. Abstracts (ISSN 0511-4144)

664 636   US
WEEKLY INSIDERS TURKEY REPORT AND WEEKLY HATCH REPORT. 1858. w. $173 (Canada $183) (effective 1997). Urner Barry Publications, Inc., Box 389, Toms River, NJ 08754. TEL 908-240-5330. FAX 908-341-0891. E-mail: mail@urnerbarry.com; URL: http://www.urnerbarry.com. Ed. Russell Whitman. adv. contact: Angela Cuccinello. circ. 230. (back issues avail.) **Document type:** trade publication.
   Supersedes: Weekly Insiders Turkey Letter (ISSN 0160-4910)
   Description: Contains slaughter figures, consumption patterns, U.S. Storage Stock Estimates and comparative weekly prices.

630 338.1   UK   ISSN 0262-8325
HD1930.W3
WELSH AGRICULTURAL STATISTICS. a. Welsh Office, Statistical Directorate, Publication Unit, Cathays Park, Cardiff CF1 3NQ, Wales. TEL 44-1222-825054. FAX 44-1222-825350. E-mail: statswales@gtnet.gov.uk. **Document type:** government publication.
   —BLDSC (9294.320000).
   Supersedes (in 1979): Annual Digest of Welsh Agricultural Statistics.

630 016   UK   ISSN 0265-7880
WHEAT, BARLEY AND TRITICALE ABSTRACTS. 1975. bi-m. £365($640) (effective 1997). CAB International, Wallingford, Oxon. OX10 8DE, England. TEL 44-1491-832111. FAX 44-1491-826090. TELEX 847964 COMAGG G. E-mail: cabi@cabi.org; URL: http://www.cabi.org. (U.S. subscr. to: CAB International, North American Office, 198 Madison Ave., New York, NY 10016. TEL 212-726-6490. FAX 212-686-7993) circ. 150. (also avail. in diskette format; back issues avail.) **Document type:** abstracting/indexing.
   ●Also available online. Vendor(s): DIMDI, European Space Agency, Knight-Ridder Information, Inc., STN International.
   —BLDSC (9310.505000).
   Formerly: Triticale Abstracts (ISSN 0307-7004)

636.5 338.1 920   US   ISSN 0510-4130
HD9284.U4
WHO'S WHO IN THE EGG AND POULTRY INDUSTRIES. 1929. a. $75. Watt Publishing Co., 122 S. Wesley Ave., Mt. Morris, IL 61054. TEL 815-734-4171. FAX 815-734-4201. Pub. Charles Olentine. adv.: B&W page $2250, color page $3075; trim 8 x 10 3/4; adv. contact: Anita Martin. circ. 8,000. **Document type:** trade publication.
   Description: Serves as a one step reference to the poultry industry. Lists suppliers and processors to the broiler, egg and turkey industries for business leaders who buy and sell in the poultry industry.

WOOLS OF NEW ZEALAND. STATISTICAL HANDBOOK. see *TEXTILE INDUSTRIES AND FABRICS — Abstracting, Bibliographies, Statistics*

338.1 016 301   UK   ISSN 0043-8219
WORLD AGRICULTURAL ECONOMICS AND RURAL SOCIOLOGY ABSTRACTS; abstracts of world literature. 1959. m. £465($815) (effective 1997). CAB International, Wallingford, Oxon. OX10 8DE, England. TEL 44-1491-832111. FAX 44-1491-826090. TELEX 847964 COMAGG G. E-mail: cabi@cabi.org; URL: http://www.cabi.org. (U.S. subscr. to: CAB International, North American Office, 198 Madison Ave., New York, NY 10016. TEL 212-726-6490. FAX 212-686-7993) adv.; bk.rev.; index, cum.index. circ. 1,250. (also avail. in diskette format; back issues avail.) **Indexed:** Anim.Breed.Abstr., Dairy Sci.Abstr., Field Crop Abstr., Forest.Abstr., Herb.Abstr., Key to Econ.Sci., Nutr.Abstr. **Document type:** abstracting/indexing.
   ●Also available online. Vendor(s): DIMDI, European Space Agency, Knight-Ridder Information, Inc., STN International.
   —BLDSC (9352.500000).
   Supersedes: Digest of Agricultural Economics and Marketing.

630 310   BG
YEARBOOK OF AGRICULTURAL STATISTICS OF BANGLADESH. (Text in English) 1975. a. Tk.200($35) Bureau of Statistics, Secretariat, Dhaka 2, Bangladesh. circ. 500.
   Former titles: Agricultural Statistics of Bangladesh (ISSN 0065-4566); Agricultural Yearbook of Bangladesh.
   Description: Data on major aspects of agriculture such as data on area, production and yield rate of crops.

316 630   ZA
ZAMBIA. CENTRAL STATISTICAL OFFICE. AGRICULTURAL AND PASTORAL PRODUCTION (COMMERCIAL AND NON-COMMERCIAL). 1966. a. K.3. Central Statistical Office, P.O. Box 31908, Lusaka, Zambia. TEL 260-1-211231. **Document type:** government publication.
   Supersedes in part: Zambia. Central Statistical Office. Agricultural and Pastoral Production (ISSN 0080-1305)

338.1   ZA
ZAMBIA. CENTRAL STATISTICAL OFFICE. AGRICULTURAL AND PASTORAL PRODUCTION (COMMERCIAL FARMS). a. $12. Central Statistical Office, P.O. Box 31908, Lusaka, Zambia. TEL 260-1-211231. **Document type:** government publication.
   Supersedes in part: Zambia. Central Statistical Office. Agricultural and Pastoral Production (ISSN 0080-1305)

630   ZA
ZAMBIA. CENTRAL STATISTICAL OFFICE. AGRICULTURAL AND PASTORAL PRODUCTION (NON-COMMERCIAL). 1972. a., latest 1977-78. $25. Central Statistical Office, P.O. Box 31908, Lusaka, Zambia. TEL 260-1-211231. **Document type:** government publication.
   Supersedes in part: Zambia. Central Statistical Office. Agricultural and Pastoral Production (ISSN 0080-1305)

630   ZA
ZAMBIA. CENTRAL STATISTICAL OFFICE. QUARTERLY AGRICULTURAL STATISTICAL BULLETIN. q. K.5. Central Statistical Office, P.O. Box 31908, Lusaka, Zambia. TEL 260-1-211231. **Document type:** government publication, bulletin.

338.1 316   ZA
ZAMBIA. MINISTRY OF AGRICULTURE, FOOD AND FISHERIES. ANNUAL AGRICULTURAL STATISTICAL BULLETIN. 1964-1976; resumed 1979. q. K.500($25) Ministry of Agriculture, Food and Fisheries, Statistics Section, P.O. Box 50197, 15100 Ridgeway, Lusaka, Zambia. TEL 228244. TELEX AGRIM ZA 43950. circ. 500. **Document type:** government publication, bulletin.
   Former Titles: Zambia. Ministry of Agricultural and Water Development. Quarterly Agricultural Statistical Bulletin; Zambia. Ministry of Lands and Agriculture. Quarterly Agricultural Statistical Bulletin; Zambia. Ministry of Rural Development. Quarterly Agricultural Statistical Bulletin.

ZEITSCHRIFT FUER PFLANZENERNAEHRUNG UND BODENKUNDE/JOURNAL OF PLANT NUTRITION AND SOIL SCIENCE. see *BIOLOGY — Abstracting, Bibliographies, Statistics*

630 011   CC   ISSN 1002-5103
ZHONGGUO NONGYE WENZHAI - NONGYE GONGCHENG/CHINESE AGRICULTURAL ABSTRACTS - AGRICULTURAL ENGINEERING. (Text in Chinese) 1989. bi-m. $30 (effective 1993). Beijing Nongye Gongcheng Daxue - Beijing Agricultural Engineering University, Qinghua Donglu, Beijing 100083, People's Republic of China. TEL 2017267. Ed. Lu Zhongxiao. circ. 1,000. **Document type:** abstracting/indexing.
   Description: Covers significant research literature in agricultural engineering at home and abroad.

636.5   RH
ZIMBABWE. CENTRAL STATISTICAL OFFICE. QUARTERLY POULTRY CENSUS. 1966. q. Z.$67 in Africa; Europe Z.$80; Asia Z.$83; the Americas Z.$89. Central Statistical Office, P.O. Box 8063, Causeway, Harae, Zimbabwe. circ. 70. **Document type:** government publication.

AGRICULTURE — Agricultural Economics

338.1   AT   ISSN 1031-3087
A B A R E FARM SURVEYS REPORT (YEAR). a. Aus.$34 (effective 1997). Australian Bureau of Agricultural and Resource Economics, G.P.O. Box 1563, Canberra, A.C.T. 2601, Australia. TEL 61-6-272-2211. FAX 61-6-272-2330. E-mail: deniseflamia@abare.gov.au. Ed. Andrew Wright. **Document type:** government publication.
   Description: Covers Australian major dairy industries, and farm strategies and management issues.

A I APPLICATIONS. see *ENVIRONMENTAL STUDIES — Computer Applications*

330.9   PL   ISSN 0860-2948
S469.P72
ACTA ACADEMIAE AGRICULTURAE AC TECHNICAE OLSTENENSIS. OECONOMICA/AGRICULTURAL AND TECHNICAL ACADEMY IN OLSZTYN. ECONOMICS.. (Supplement avail.: Oeconomica) (Text in Polish; summaries in English and Polish) 1959. irreg. price varies. (Akademia Rolniczo-Techniczna im. M. Oczapowskiego) Wydawnictwo A R T Olsztyn, Blok 12, 10-957 Olsztyn-Kortowo, Poland. TEL 48-89-5273310. TELEX 0526419. E-mail: artbib@moskit.art.olsztyn.pl. (Dist. by: Ars Polona-Ruch, Krakowskie Przedmiescie 7, 00-901 Warsaw, Poland. TEL 48-22-265334) Ed. Barbara Grudniewska. R&P contact: Jolanta Mieszkalska. adv. contact: Maciej Gajecki. bibl.; charts; illus.; circ. 130 (controlled). **Indexed:** AgroLibrex, Dairy Sci.Abstr., Poult.Abstr., Ref.Zh., Rural Ext.Educ.& Tr.Abstr., World Agri.Econ.& Rural Sociol.Abstr. **Document type:** academic/scholarly publication.
   Formerly: Akademia Rolniczo-Techniczna. Zeszyty Naukowe. Ekonomika (ISSN 0324-9166)

ACTUELE ONTWIKKELING VAN BEDRIJFSRESULTATEN EN INKOMENS. see *AGRICULTURE — Abstracting, Bibliographies, Statistics*

338.1   US   ISSN 1053-2692
AG EXECUTIVE. 1984. m. $78. Ag Executive, Inc., 115 E. Twyman, Box 180, Bushnell, IL 61422. TEL 309-772-2168. FAX 309-772-2167. E-mail: darrellID@aol.com. Ed. Darrell L. Dunteman; Pub. Darrell L. Dunteman. R&P contact: Darrell L. Dunteman. bk.rev.; circ. 3,362 (paid). (looseleaf format; back issues avail.; reprint service avail.) **Document type:** newsletter.
   Description: Covers agricultural finance and management issues.

630   US   ISSN 1047-4781
HD9001   CODEN: AGEXEZ
AGEXPORTER. 1937. m. $18 (foreign $22.50). U.S. Department of Agriculture, Foreign Agricultural Service, Information Division, Rm. 4638-S, Washington, DC 20250-1000. TEL 202-720-9437. FAX 202-720-3229. (Subscr. to: Superintendent of Documents, U.S. Government Printing Office, Box 371954, Pittsburgh, PA 15250-7954. TEL 202-512-1800. FAX 202-512-2250) charts; illus.; index. circ. 1,800. (also avail. in microform from MIM,UMI; microfiche from CIS; reprint service avail. from CIS,UMI) **Indexed:** Amer.Bibl.Slavic & E.Eur.Stud., Amer.Stat.Ind. (1974-), Anim.Breed.Abstr., Apic.Abstr., Bibl.Agri., Biol.Abstr., Biol.& Agr.Ind., Dairy Sci.Abstr., Farm & Garden Ind., Geo.Abstr.H.G., Hort.Abstr., Ind.U.S.Gov.Per., Intl.Mgmt.Info., Key to Econ.Sci., Mid.East: Abstr.& Ind., Potato Abstr., PROMT, Rural Recreat.Tour.Abstr., Text.Tech.Dig., Trop.Dis.Bull., World Agri.Econ.& Rural Sociol.Abstr. **Document type:** government publication.
   ●Also available online. Vendor(s): Information Access Co.
   —BLDSC (0736.259500); KR SourceOne; Linda Hall; SWETS; UMI.
   Formerly (until 1989): Foreign Agriculture (ISSN 0015-7163)

AGRICULTURE — AGRICULTURAL ECONOMICS

630 338.1   UK   ISSN 0002-1024
AGRA EUROPE. (Editions in English, French, German, Italian) 1963. w. £1030 (rest of Europe £1280; elsewhere £1340) (effective 1997). Agra Europe (London) Ltd., 25 Frant Rd., Tunbridge Wells, Kent TN2 5JT, England. TEL 44-1892-533813. FAX 44-1892-544895. TELEX 95114 AGRATW G. E-mail: 100637.3460@compuserve.com. (Subscr. addr.: Box 297044, Ft. Worth, TX 76129) Ed. Guy Faulkner. bk.rev.; mkt.; stat.; q. index. **Indexed:** Dairy Sci.Abstr., Geo.Abstr., Maize Abstr., Pig News & Info., Potato Abstr., Poult.Abstr., PROMT, Soyabean Abstr., Triticale Abstr., World Agri.Econ.& Rural Sociol.Abstr. **Document type:** trade publication.
● Also available online. Vendor(s): Information Access Co.
—BLDSC (0736.800000).
   Description: Covers European and world developments affecting the production and marketing of food and agricultural commodities.

630 658.8   UK   ISSN 0142-422X
HD9275.E86
AGRA EUROPE (LONDON). SPECIAL REPORT. irreg. price varies. Agra Europe (London) Ltd., 25 Frant Rd., Tunbridge Wells, Kent TN2 5JT, England. TEL 44-1892 533813. FAX 44-1892-544895. TELEX 95114 AGRATW G. E-mail: 100637.3460@compuserve.com. **Document type:** trade publication.
—BLDSC (0736.810000).

AGRAR-UEBERSICHT; das active Magazin fuer active Landwirte. see *AGRICULTURE*

338.1   AU
AGRARHANDEL. m. S.860 (effective 1997). Verlag Lorenz, Ebendorferstr. 10, A-1010 Vienna, Austria. TEL 43-1-4056695. FAX 43-1-4068693. Ed. Gerhard Perschler. adv.: B&W page S.16200, color page S.27900; trim 165 x 254. circ. 5,300. **Document type:** trade publication.

338.1   UK   ISSN 0065-4337
AGRARIAN DEVELOPMENT STUDIES. 1965. irreg. price varies. University of London, Wye College, Department of Agricultural Economics, Ashford, Kent TN25 5AH, England. TEL 44-1233-812401. Ed. I. Carruthers. bk.rev.; index. **Document type:** academic/scholarly publication, monographic series.

338.1   SA   ISSN 0303-1853
AGREKON (ENGLISH EDITION). Afrikaans edition (ISSN 0303-1861) 1962. q. R.75($20) to non-members in Africa (outside Africa $75) (effective 1996 & 1997). Landbou-Ekonomie Vereniging van Suid-Afrika - Agricultural Economics Association of South Africa, Posbus 12986, Hatfield 0028, South Africa. TEL 27-12-4203248. FAX 27-12-3422713. Ed. J.A. Groenewald. R&P contact: J.A. Groenewald. charts; mkt.; stat.; cum.index every 5 years. **Indexed:** Agri.Eng.Abstr., Food Sci.& Tech.Abstr., Helminthol.Abstr., Hort.Abstr., Ind.S.A.Per., Irr.& Drain.Abstr., Rural Recreat.Tour.Abstr., Soils & Fert., Triticale Abstr., World Agri.Econ.& Rural Sociol.Abstr. **Document type:** academic/scholarly publication.
—BLDSC (0738.700000).
   Description: Promotes research and discussion on agricultural economic issues related to southern Africa.
   Refereed Serial

338.1   UK   ISSN 1352-1144
AGRI-BUSINESS SCOTLAND. 1985. m. £31.15 (foreign £37.15) (effective 1997). Peebles Publishing Group Ltd., Bergius House, Clifton St., Glasgow G3 7LA, Scotland. TEL 44-141-331-1022. FAX 44-141-331-1395. Ed. Bob Carruth. adv.; bk.rev. circ. 14,000. (back issues avail.) **Document type:** trade publication.
   Formerly: Agri-Business Monthly.
   Description: Business aspects of agriculture for the progressive farmer.

630 338.1   US   ISSN 0002-1164
HG2051.U5
AGRI FINANCE. 1959. 9/yr. $36. Doane Agricultural Service Co., 11701 Borman Dr., St. Louis, MO 63146-4199. TEL 314-569-2700. FAX 314-569-1083. Ed. James R. Baxter. adv.; bk.rev.; charts; illus.; stat.; index. circ. 18,000. (also avail. in microform from UMI) **Indexed:** Farm & Garden Ind. **Document type:** trade publication.
● Also available online. Vendor(s): UMI.
—UMI; UnCover.

338.1 630   US   ISSN 0002-1180
AGRI MARKETING; the magazine for professionals selling to the farm market. 1963. 11/yr. $30. Doane Information Service, 11701 Borman Dr., St. Louis, MO 63146. TEL 314-569-2700. FAX 314-564-1083. Pub. Lynn Henderson. adv.; bk.rev.; charts; illus.; stat.; index. circ. 9,200. **Indexed:** B.P.I., Farm & Garden Ind. **Document type:** trade publication.
● Also available online. Vendor(s): UMI.
—BLDSC (0738.930000); KR SourceOne; UMI.

338.1   US   ISSN 0742-4477
HD1401   CODEN: AGRBEY
AGRIBUSINESS (NEW YORK); an international journal. 1984. bi-m. $625 (foreign $730) (effective 1998). John Wiley & Sons, Inc., Journals, 605 Third Ave., New York, NY 10158-6012. TEL 212-850-6645. FAX 212-850-6021. TELEX 12-7063. E-mail: SUBINFO@JWILEY.COM; URL: http://www.wiley.co.uk. (Overseas subscr. to: John Wiley & Sons Ltd., Baffins Ln., Chichester, W. Sussex PO19 1UD, England. TEL 44-1243-779777. FAX 44-1243-776128) Ed. James G. Beierlein. adv.: B&W page £640, color page £1515; trim 254 x 165. circ. 1,700. (also avail. in microform from UMI; back issues avail.) **Indexed:** Energy Info.Abstr., Environ.Abstr., Food Sci.& Tech.Abstr. **Document type:** academic/scholarly publication.
—BLDSC (0738.954000); KR SourceOne; SWETS; UMI; UnCover. **CCC**.
   Description: Serves the nonfarm sectors of the food and fiber system with articles that deal with the business aspects of agricultural production. For agribusiness economists, managers, and engineers, academic and industry market researchers, government analysts,and food quality technologists.
   Refereed Serial

630 338.1   IT   ISSN 0002-1229
AGRICOLTORE TREVISANO. 1945. s-m. membership. Unione Provinciale Agricoltori di Treviso, Viale Cadorna 10, Treviso 31100, Italy. Ed. Fulvio Fantini. adv.; bk.rev.; illus. circ. 6,500. **Document type:** newspaper.

338.1   IT   ISSN 0392-5617
AGRICOOP. 1971. 12/yr. L.35000 (foreign L.50000). Via Pietramellara 11, 40121 Bologna, Italy. TEL 39-51-55-76-00. FAX 39-51-55-48-13. Ed. Omer Pignatti. adv.: B&W page L.1800000, color page L.2300000. circ. 19,000.

338.1   BL   ISSN 0044-6793
HD1875.S3
AGRICULTURA EM SAO PAULO. (Text in Portuguese) 1951. s-a. $8 (foreign $16). Instituto de Economia Agricola, Av. Miguel Estefano, 3900, Caixa Postal 6802, 04301-903 Sao Paulo, Brazil. FAX 55-11-2764062. bk.rev.; stat.; cum.index; circ. controlled. **Indexed:** Chem.Abstr., Cott.& Trop.Fibr.Abstr., Field Crop Abstr., Food Sci.& Tech.Abstr., Herb.Abstr., Maize Abstr., Rural Recreat.Tour.Abstr., Soyabean Abstr., World Agri.Econ.& Rural Sociol.Abstr.
—BLDSC (0741.880000).
   Description: Covers institutional scientific production; includes technical, scientific and research articles.

338.1   UK   ISSN 0951-1865
AGRICULTURAL ADMINISTRATION RESEARCH EXTENSION NETWORK. NEWSLETTER. 1979. s-a. Overseas Development Institute, Regent's College, Inner Circle Regent's Park, London NW1 4NS, England. TEL 0171-487-7413. FAX 0171-487-7590. TELEX 94082191 ODI G. E-mail: odi@gn.apc.org. Eds. John Farrington, Diana Carney. bk.rev. circ. 1,000. **Indexed:** Abstr.Rural Dev.Trop. **Document type:** newsletter.
   Formerly: Agricultural Administration Network. Newsletter (ISSN 0260-7883)

338.1   US   ISSN 1068-2805
HD1773.A2
AGRICULTURAL AND RESOURCE ECONOMICS REVIEW. 1972. s-a. $15 (effective 1996 & 1997). Northeastern Agricultural and Resource Economics Association, c/o John Halstead, Dept. of Resource Economics, 312 James Hall, Univ. of New Hampshire, Durham, NH 03824. Ed. Linda Lee. R&P contact: John Halstead. circ. 500 (paid). **Indexed:** Rural Recreat.Tour.Abstr., World Agri.Econ.& Rural Sociol.Abstr. **Document type:** academic/scholarly publication.
—BLDSC (0743.140000); UnCover.
   Former titles (until 1992): Northeastern Journal of Agricultural and Resource Economics (ISSN 0899-367X); (until Oct. 1984): Northeastern Agricultural Economics Council. Journal (ISSN 0163-5484)

338.1   II
AGRICULTURAL BANKER. (Text in English) 1978. q. Rs.56. S.R. Suneja, Ed. & Pub., B4/29 Safdarjang Enclave, New Delhi 110 029, India. adv.; bk.rev. circ. 3,000.

338.1   NP
AGRICULTURAL CREDIT. (Text in English) q. (Agricultural Credit Training Institute) Agricultural Development Bank, Ramshah Path, Panchayat Plaza, Kathmandu, Nepal. TEL 216075. Ed. Prem Nath Ojha.

338.1   CN   ISSN 0837-2136
HG2051.C39
AGRICULTURAL CREDIT CORPORATION OF SASKATCHEWAN. ANNUAL REPORT. 1973. a. free. Agricultural Credit Corporation of Saskatchewan, Box 820, Swift Current, SK. S9H 4Y7, Canada. TEL 306-778-8455. FAX 306-778-8614. Ed. Margot Trembath. circ. 500. **Document type:** corporate report.
   Formerly: Saskatchewan FarmStart Corporation. Annual Report (ISSN 0709-325X)

338.1   MW
AGRICULTURAL DEVELOPMENT AND MARKETING CORPORATION. ANNUAL REPORT AND STATEMENT OF ACCOUNTS. a. free. Agricultural Development and Marketing Corporation (ADMARC), P.O. Box 5052, Limbe, Malawi. TEL 265-640044. stat. **Document type:** government publication.
   Supersedes: Agricultural Development and Marketing Corporation. Annual Report; Agricultural Development Corporation. Balance Sheet and Accounts; Which was formerly: Farmers Marketing Board. Balance Sheet and Accounts.

338.1   NE   ISSN 0169-5150
                         CODEN: AGECE6
AGRICULTURAL ECONOMICS. 1986. bi-m. fl.930($534) (effective 1998). Elsevier Science B.V., P.O. Box 211, 1000 AE Amsterdam, Netherlands. TEL 31-20-4853911. FAX 31-20-4853598. TELEX 18582 ESPA NL. E-mail: nlinfo-f@elsevier.nl; usinfo-f@elsevier.com; forinfo-kyf04035@niftyserve.or.jp; URL: http://www.elsevier.nl/. (Subscr. in the Americas to: Elsevier Science, Regional Sales Office, Box 945, New York, NY 10159-0945. TEL 212-633-3730. FAX 212-633-3680; Subscr. in Australasia and the Far East to: Elsevier Science (Singapore) Pte Ltd, No.1 Temasek Ave., No.17-01 Millenia Tower, Singapore 039192, Singapore. TEL 65-434-3727. FAX 65-337-2230, Subscr. in Japan to: Elsevier Science Japan, 9-15 Higashi-Azabu 1-chome, Minato-ku, Tokyo 106, Japan. TEL 81-3-5561-5033. FAX 81-3-5561-5047) Ed. B. Greenshields. bk.rev. (also avail. in microform from UMI; back issues avail.; reprint service avail. from SWZ) **Indexed:** ASCA, Bibl.Agri., Biol.& Agr.Ind., Food Sci.& Tech.Abstr., Geo.Abstr.H.G., Maize Abstr., SSCI, Triticale Abstr., Trop.Oil Seeds Abstr., World Agri.Econ.& Rural Sociol.Abstr. **Document type:** academic/scholarly publication.
—BLDSC (0745.580000); EMDOCS; Genuine Article; KR SourceOne; SWETS; UnCover. **CCC**.
   Description: Provides a focal point for the publication of work on research, extension and outreach, consulting, advising, entrepreneurship, administration and teaching, in the areas of agricultural economics.
   Refereed Serial

AGRICULTURAL FINANCE DATABOOK. see *BUSINESS AND ECONOMICS — Banking And Finance*

AGRICULTURE — AGRICULTURAL ECONOMICS

338.1 US ISSN 0002-1466
HG2051.U5
AGRICULTURAL FINANCE REVIEW. 1938. a. $10. Cornell University, Department of Agricultural Resource and Managerial Economics, 357 Warren Hall, Ithaca, NY 14853-7801. TEL 607-255-4534. FAX 607-255-1589. E-mail: elly@cornell.edu. Eds. John R. Brake, Eddy L. LaDue. charts; mkt.; stat.; index; circ. 900 (controlled). (also avail. in microfiche from CIS) **Indexed:** Geo.Abstr., Ind.U.S.Gov.Per., J.of Econ.Abstr., P.A.I.S., Rural Recreat.Tour.Abstr., SRI, World Agri.Econ.& Rural Sociol.Abstr. **Document type:** academic/scholarly publication.
—BLDSC (0746.650000); Linda Hall; UMI; UnCover.
Description: Provides a forum for research teaching and extension publication, and discussion of issues in agricultural finance.
Refereed Serial

AGRICULTURAL FINANCIAL STATISTICS. see AGRICULTURE — Abstracting, Bibliographies, Statistics

338.1 US
AGRICULTURAL LAW UPDATE. 1981. m. $50 to US and Canada; elsewhere $65. American Agricultural Law Association, School of Law, University of Arkansas, Fayetteville, AR 72701. TEL 501-575-7389. FAX 501-575-2053. Ed. Linda G. McCormick. bk.rev. circ. 1,000.
Formerly (until 1983): Agricultural Law Newsletter.

630 JO
AGRICULTURAL MARKETING/TASWIQ AL-ZIRAIY. (Text in Arabic) 1966. q. Ministry of National Economy, Department of Agricultural Marketing, Box 2097, Amman, Jordan. Ed. Fahed Al-Azeb. adv.

338.1 633 EI
AGRICULTURAL MARKETS: PRICES. (Multilingual edition) 1962. 4/yr. $155 (effective 1997). Commission of the European Communities, Directorate General Agriculture, Rue de la Loi, 200, B-1049 Brussels, Belgium. (Dist. in the U.S. by: UNIPUB, 4611-F Assembly Dr., Lanham, MD 20706-4391; in the U.K. by: H.M.S.O., Publications Centre, 51 Nine Elms Ln., London SW8 5DR, England) **Indexed:** IIS.
Formed by the 1981 merger of: Marches Agricoles. Prix: Produits Vegetaux - Agricultural Markets. Prices: Vegetable Products (ISSN 0378-4436); Marches Agricoles. Prix: Produits Animaux - Agricultural Markets. Prices: Livestock Products (ISSN 0378-4444); Marches Agricoles. Prix: Notes Explicatif.

338.1 US ISSN 0895-9781
AGRICULTURAL POLICY AND ECONOMICS ISSUES. 1978. m. Oklahoma State University, Oklahoma Cooperative Extension Service, Extension Agricultural Economics, 513 Ag. Hall, Stillwater, OK 74078. TEL 405-744-9834. FAX 405-744-8210. E-mail: lsanders@okway.okstate.edu. Ed. Larry D. Sanders. R&P contact: Larry D. Sanders. circ. 3,200. **Document type:** newsletter.

338.1 BG
AGRICULTURAL PRODUCTION LEVELS IN BANGLADESH. (Text in English) 1976. a. free. Bureau of Statistics, Secretariat, Dhaka 2, Bangladesh. Ed. A.K.M. Ghulam Rabbani. charts; stat.

338.1 UK ISSN 0065-4493
AGRICULTURAL PROGRESS. 1924. a. £15. Agricultural Education Association, c/o A.R. Staniforth, Ed., 5 Capel Close, Oxford OX2 7LA, England. adv.; bk.rev. circ. 1,000. **Indexed:** Anim.Breed.Abstr., Biol.Abstr., Dairy Sci.Abstr., Field Crop Abstr., Geo.Abstr., Herb.Abstr., Ind.Vet., Nutr.Abstr., Plant Breed Abstr., RICS, Rural Ext.Educ.& Tr.Abstr., Soils & Fert., Triticale Abstr., Vet.Bull., World Agri.Econ.& Rural Sociol.Abstr.

630 330.8 UN ISSN 1011-3363
AGRICULTURAL REVIEW FOR EUROPE. French edition: Revue Agricole pour l'Europe (ISSN 1011-159X); Russian edition: Sel'skohozjstvennyj obzor Evropy (ISSN 1014-5443) 1958. irreg., no.37, vol.1-6. price varies. (Economic Commission for Europe (ECE)) United Nations Publications, Sales and Marketing Section, Room DC2-0853, New York, NY 10017. TEL 212-963-8302; 800-253-9646. FAX 212-963-3489. E-mail: publications@un.org; URL: http://www.un.org/publications. (Or: Distribution and Sales Section, Palais des Nations, 1211 Geneva 10, Switzerland) (also avail. in microfiche from CIS) **Indexed:** Dairy Sci.Abstr., IIS, Maize Abstr., Pig News & Info., Potato Abstr., Poult.Abstr., Rice Abstr., Triticale Abstr., World Agri.Econ.& Rural Sociol.Abstr.
Former titles: Review of the Agricultural Situation in Europe at the End of (Year) (ISSN 0085-5618); Agricultural Market Review.

338.1 336 UN
AGRICULTURAL TAXATION STUDIES. no.4, 1992. irreg. Food & Agriculture Organization of the United Nations (Rome), Viale delle Terme di Caracalla, 00100 Rome, Italy. TEL 57974350. FAX 57974608.

338.1 330.8 UN ISSN 0084-6058
AGRICULTURAL TRADE IN EUROPE. 1960. a. $11. (Economic Commission for Europe (ECE)) United Nations Publications, Sales and Marketing Section, Room DC2-0853, New York, NY 10017. TEL 212-963-8300; 800-253-9646. FAX 212-963-3489. E-mail: publications@un.org; URL: http://www.un.org/publications. (Or: Distribution and Sales Section, Palais des Nations, 1211 Geneva 10, Switzerland)

338.1 331 II ISSN 0084-6066
AGRICULTURAL WAGES IN INDIA. (Text in English, Hindi) 1950. a. Rs.115. Ministry of Agriculture, Department of Agriculture and Cooperation, Directorate of Economics and Statistics, A-2E-3 Kasturba Gandhi Marg Barracks, New Delhi 110 001, India. TEL 11-381523. Ed. Brajesh Kumar Gautam. circ. 350. **Document type:** government publication.

338.1 IT ISSN 0394-5537
AGRIGIORNALE DEL COMMERCIO. 1987. 11/yr. L.63000 (effective 1996). (Compaq - Associazione Commercianti Produttori Agricoli Confcommercio) Edagricole S.p.A., Via Emilia Levante 31, 40139 Bologna, Italy. TEL 39-51-492211. FAX 39-51-493660. Ed. Alberto Perdisa. adv.: B&W page L.3100000, color page L.4500000; 230 x 324. circ. 15,200.

AGRO-CHEMICALS NEWS IN BRIEF. see AGRICULTURE — Crop Production And Soil

338.1 FR ISSN 1152-880X
AGRO-DISTRIBUTION. 1990. 10/yr. 349 F. (effective 1997). C E P Groupe France Agricole, 8 Cite Paradis, 75493 Paris Cedex 10, France. TEL 33-1-40227900. FAX 33-1-48240315. Ed. Catherine Queheille. circ. 9,000.

338.1 BL ISSN 0100-4298
AGROANALYSIS. 1977-1989; resumed 1994. m. $150 (effective 1997). (Instituto Brasileiro de Economia, Centro de Estudos Agricolas) Fundacao Getulio Vargas, Caixa Postal 62591, 22257-970 Rio de Janeiro, RJ, Brazil. TEL 55-21-5369196. FAX 55-21-5369155. Ed. Regis Norberto da Cunta Alimandro. adv. contact: Milton Gondim. circ. 10,000. **Indexed:** Food Sci.& Tech.Abstr., P.A.I.S.For.Lang.Ind., World Agri.Econ.& Rural Sociol.Abstr. **Document type:** academic/scholarly publication.
—BLDSC (0764.552900).
Description: Provides a survey of Brazilian agribusiness and how it is affected by both national and international economic policies.

338.1 630 MX ISSN 0188-3054
S565.97
AGROCIENCIA. MATEMATICAS APLICADAS, ESTADISTICA Y COMPUTACION. 1966. 3/yr. Mex.$45($20) (effective 1992). Colegio de Postgraduados, Instituto de Estudios, Investigaciones y Servicio Agripefor Chapingo S.C., Cerro del Vigilante 166, Col. Romero de Terrenos, 04310 Mexico DF, Mexico. TEL 915-5-54-14-03. (Subscr. to: Gral. Lazaro Cardenas 24, Fracc. La Paz, San Sebastian, Apdo. Postal 314, Texacoco, Mexico. TEL 91-595-4-70-11) Ed. Jose Fco. Burguete Hernanez. adv.; bk.rev.; abstr.; bibl.; charts; illus.; stat.; circ. 1,500 (controlled). (back issues avail.) **Document type:** academic/scholarly publication.
Supersedes in part (in 1990): Agrociencia (ISSN 0185-0288)

338.1 XO
AGROEKONOMIKA. 1962. m. $18. Ministerstvo Podmospodarstva a Vyzivy, Dobrovicova 12, 800 00 Bratislava, Slovakia.
Former titles (until 1992): Ekonomika Polnohospodarstva (ISSN 0323-2670); (until 1976): Ekonomika Zemedelstvi (ISSN 0013-3124)

338.1 301.35 YU ISSN 0350-5928
AGROEKONOMIKA. (Text in Serbo-Croatian; summaries in English) 1972. a. 10000 din.($2) Institute of Agricultural Economics and Rural Sociology, Veljka Vlahovica 2, 21000 Novi Sad, Yugoslavia. TEL 58-366. Ed. Bronislav S. Djurdjev. adv.; bk.rev. circ. 1,000. (back issues avail.)
Description: Covers theoretical and empirical contributions from the areas of agricultural economics and rural sociology.

338 US
AGROINDUSTRY: LATIN AMERICAN INDUSTRIAL REPORT. (Avail. for each of 22 Latin American countries) 1985. a. $435 per country report. Aquino Productions, Box 125, Rochester, VT 05767. Ed. Andres C. Aquino.

338.1 MX
AGRONEGOCIOS EN MEXICO. 1992. m. Mex.$150. 3A Coa. Bahamas 31, Col. Lomas Estrella, Iztapalapa, 09890 Mexico DF, Mexico. TEL 656-59-18. Ed. Alfredo Saenz Colin; Pub. Salvador Sosa Fuentes. circ. 3,000. **Document type:** trade publication.
Description: Covers cattle, finance, forestry, poultry and industry.

AGRONOMIE; sciences des productions vegetales et de l'environnement. see AGRICULTURE — Crop Production And Soil

338.1 FR ISSN 0989-2648
AGROPERFORMANCES. 1987. 6/yr. 300 F. S E P C O, Departement de Communication, 83-85 av. de la Grande-Armee, 75782 Paris Cedex 16, France. TEL 40-66-21-71. FAX 1-45-01-82-87. TELEX 642020F. Ed. Franck Martin. adv.: color page 13200 F. circ. 3,500.

338.1 PL ISSN 0239-927X
AKADEMIA ROLNICZA IM. HUGONA KOLLATAJA W KRAKOWIE. ZESZYTY NAUKOWE. SERIA: EKONOMIKA. (Text in Polish; summaries in English) 1959. a. price varies. Akademia Rolnicza im. Hugona Kollataja w Krakowie, c/o Ligia Hayto, Biblioteka Glowna AR, Al. Mickiewicza 24-28, 30-059 Krakow, Poland. TEL 48-12-119144. FAX 48-12-336245. TELEX 322469 PL. E-mail: hayto.victoria@uci.agh.edu.pl. Ed. Zdzislaw Piskornik. circ. 120 (paid). **Indexed:** AgroLibrex. **Document type:** academic/scholarly publication.
Former titles (until 1979): Akademia Rolnicza w Krakowie. Zeszyty Naukowe. Ekonomika (ISSN 0137-1827); (until 1972): Wyzsza Szkola Rolnicza w Krakowie. Zeszyty Naukowe. Ekonomika (ISSN 0137-2041)

AGRICULTURE — AGRICULTURAL ECONOMICS

338.1   PL   ISSN 0137-1711
AKADEMIA ROLNICZA, POZNAN. ROCZNIKI. EKONOMIKA I ORGANIZACJA ROLNICTWA. (Text and summaries in English, Polish) 1974. irreg. price varies. Wydawnictwo Akademii Rolniczej w Poznaniu, Ul. Witosa 45, 60-667 Poznan, Poland. TEL 48-61-487809. FAX 48-61-487802. E-mail: wgolob@owl.au.poznan.pl; URL: http://swan.au.poznan.pl/bib/bghome.html. R&P contact: Elzbieta Zagorska. TEL 48-61-487806. **Indexed:** AgroLibrex, Bibl.Agri. **Document type:** academic/scholarly publication.
    Description: Methodology of economics and agricultural research, macroeconomics of agriculture, management and organization on the farm, cumulative energy consumption of agricultural production, village sociology, organization of technical services for agriculture.

338.1   NE   ISSN 0923-7143
AKKERBOUW (THE HAGUE). 1971. quinquennial. fl.47. Landbouw-Economisch Instituut, Burg. Patijnlaan 19, 2585 BE The Hague, Netherlands. TEL 31-70-3308330. FAX 31-70-3615624. E-mail: postmaster@lei.dlo.nl; URL: http://www.lei.dlo.nl/lei. Ed. J.H. Jager.
    Description: Industrial economic reflections on arable farming over the past five years.

381.41 633.31   US
ALFALFA HAY, CALIFORNIA MARKET SUMMARY. a. $20. (Department of Food and Agriculture) Federal-State Market News Service (Sacramento), 1220 N St., Rm. A-247, Box 942871, Sacramento, CA 94271-0001. TEL 916-654-0298. FAX 916-654-1046. **Document type:** government publication.

338.1   US
AMERICAN AGRICULTURAL ECONOMICS ASSOCIATION. HANDBOOK-DIRECTORY. biennial. $20. American Agricultural Economics Association, 1110 Buckeye Ave., Ames, IA 50010-8063. TEL 515-233-3202. FAX 515-233-3101. **Document type:** directory.
    Formerly: American Agricultural Economics Association. Handbook.

338.1   US   ISSN 1065-3775
HF1416.5
AMERICAN FOOD AND AG EXPORTER DIRECTORY. 1989. a. $120 to libraries. American Dream Network Inc., Box 810391, Boca Raton, FL 33481-0391. TEL 407-447-0810. FAX 407-368-9125. Ed. James E. Prevor. circ. 16,000.
    Formerly: American Agricultural Exporter Directory.
    Description: Lists export firms, agents, brokers, manufacturers, growers, processors, freight forwarders, and others involved in exporting America's agricultural commodities; also lists contact names, addresses, phone and fax numbers.

338.1   US
AMERICAN FOOD AND AG EXPORTER MAGAZINE. 1989. q. American Dream Network Inc., Box 810391, Boca Raton, FL 33481-0391. TEL 407-447-0810. FAX 407-368-9125. Ed. James Prevor. circ. 16,000.
    Formerly: American Agricultural Exporter Magazine; Incorporates: California Agricultural Exporter.
    Description: Covers information for importers of America's food and agricultural export products. Includes agricultural news and stories about growers, handlers, services and export businesses.

338.1   US   ISSN 0002-9092
S560   CODEN: AJAEBA
AMERICAN JOURNAL OF AGRICULTURAL ECONOMICS. 1919. 5/yr. $90 to non-members (foreign $105) (effective 1997). American Agricultural Economics Association, 1110 Buckeye Ave., Ames, IA 50010-8063. TEL 515-233-3202. FAX 515-233-3101. Ed. Michael Wohlgenant. adv.; bk.rev.; bibl.; charts; illus.; stat.; index. circ. 7,000. (also avail. in microfilm from PMC; microfiche from PMC; back issues avail.) **Indexed:** Apic.Abstr., ASCA, Asian-Pac.Econ.Lit., B.P.I., Bibl.Ind., Biol.& Agr.Ind., Biostat., BPIA, Bus.Ind., C.R.E.J., Cott.& Trop.Fibr.Abstr., Curr.Cont., Dairy Sci.Abstr., Ecol.Abstr., Energy Info.Abstr., Environ.Abstr., Excerp.Med., Field Crop Abstr., Food Sci.& Tech.Abstr., Geo.Abstr.H.G., Herb.Abstr., IDA, Ind.Sci.Rev., INIS Atomind., Int.Abstr.Oper.Res., Int.Lab.Doc., Irr.& Drain.Abstr., J.of Econ.Lit., Maize Abstr., Mid.East: Abstr.& Ind., Nutr.Abstr., Oper.Res.Manage.Sci., P.A.I.S., Pig News & Info., Potato Abstr., Qual.Contr.Appl.Stat., Rice Abstr., Risk Abstr., Rural Devel.Abstr., Rural Ext.Educ.& Tr.Abstr., Sci.Cit.Ind., Sel.Water Res.Abstr., Soils & Fert., Soyabean Abstr., SSCI, Tr.& Indus.Ind., Triticale Abstr., World Agri.Econ.& Rural Sociol.Abstr. **Document type:** academic/scholarly publication.
    ●Also available online. Vendor(s): Information Access Co., UMI.
    —BLDSC (0820.950000); CISTI; Ei; KR SourceOne; Linda Hall; SWETS; UMI; UnCover. **CCC.**
    Formerly: Journal of Farm Economics.

338.1   MX   ISSN 0185-6944
ANALISIS DE LA AGRICULTURA SINALOENSE. 1963. q. $40. Confederacion de Asociaciones Agricolas del Estado de Sinaloa, Juan Carrasco 787 Nte., 80000 Culiacan, Sinaloa, Mexico. TEL 31097. FAX 671-30108. TELEX 665822 CAAC ME. circ. 500.
    Formerly: Analisis de la Situacion Agricola de Sinaloa (ISSN 0517-6956)

338.1   SP   ISSN 0210-637X
ANUARIO HORTOFRUTICOLA ESPANOL. 1968. a. 14000 ptas. Sucro, S.A., Hernan Cortes, 5-1, 46004 Valencia, Spain. TEL 34-6-351-5301. FAX 34-6-352-57-52. adv. contact: Jose Maria Server Martinez. circ. 5,000. **Document type:** directory.

338 630   UK   ISSN 0305-0920
T1
APPROPRIATE TECHNOLOGY. 1974. q. £15($28) to individuals; institutions £20 ($37) (effective 1996). Intermediate Technology Publications Ltd., 103-105 Southampton Row, London WC1B 4HH, England. TEL 44-171-436-9761. FAX 44-171-436-2013. E-mail: itpubs@gn.apc.org; URL: http://www.oneworld.org/itdg/publications.html. Ed. Kimberly Clarke. adv.; bk.rev.; illus.; index. circ. 3,500. **Indexed:** Abstr.Rural Dev.Trop., Agri.Eng.Abstr., AIT Reports, Apic.Abstr., ASCA, Br.Tech.Ind., CLOSS, Curr.Cont., Educ.Tech.Abstr., Energy Info.Abstr., Energy Rev., Environ.Abstr., Environ.Per.Bibl. (1989-), Excerp.Med., Field Crop.Abstr., Fluidex, Forest.Abstr., Forest Prod.Abstr., Geo.Abstr.H.G., Herb.Abstr., IDA, J.of Ferroc., Repindex, Rural Recreat.Tour.Abstr., So.Pac.Per.Ind., Soils & Fert., Soyabean Abstr., Stud.Wom.Abstr., W.R.C.Inf., World Agri.Econ.& Rural Sociol.Abstr. **Document type:** academic/scholarly publication.
    —BLDSC (1580.700000); CISTI; Ei; Genuine Article; Linda Hall; SWETS; UnCover. **CCC.**
    Formerly: Intermediate Technology Development Group. Bulletin (ISSN 0538-4028)
    Description: Discusses less technologically advanced but more environmentally sustainable solutions to problems in developing nations.
    Refereed Serial

ARAB WORLD AGRIBUSINESS/AL-ZIRA'AH FI-L-ALAM AL-ARABI. see *AGRICULTURE*

ARUSHA CHAMBER OF COMMERCE AND AGRICULTURE. BULLETIN TO MEMBERS. see *BUSINESS AND ECONOMICS — Chamber Of Commerce Publications*

338.1   CC
ASIA - PACIFIC AGRIBUSINESS REPORT. (Text in English) 1988. m. $240. Asia Letter Group, G.P.O. Box 10874, Hong Kong, People's Republic of China. TEL 852-526-2950. FAX 852-526-7131. TELEX HX-61166-HKNW. (US subscr. to: 88189, Los Angeles, CA 90009-8189) bk.rev. **Document type:** newsletter.
    Description: Covers trends and developments in the region's biggest business sector, agribusiness. Includes two special report sections in each issue.

333.76   BG   ISSN 1018-5291
ASIA - PACIFIC JOURNAL OF RURAL DEVELOPMENT. (Text in English) 1991. s-a. Tk.300 (Asia-Pacific $12; elsewhere $24). Centre on Integrated Rural Development for Asia and the Pacific, Chameli House, 17 Topkhana Rd., G.P.O. Box 2883, Dhaka 1000, Bangladesh. Ed. Leelangi Wanasundera. adv.: page $100; adv. contact: D.P. Mazumder. **Indexed:** Geo.Abstr.H.G. **Document type:** academic/scholarly publication.
    —BLDSC (1742.260940).

338.1   AT   ISSN 1321-7844
HD2151
AUSTRALIAN BUREAU OF AGRICULTURAL AND RESOURCE ECONOMICS. AUSTRALIAN COMMODITIES. 1948. q. Aus.$135 (effective 1997). Australian Bureau of Agricultural and Resource Economics, G.P.O. Box 1563, Canberra, A.C.T. 2601, Australia. TEL 61-6-2722211. FAX 61-6-2722330. E-mail: deniseflamia@abare.gov.au. Ed. Andrew Wright. charts; mkt.; stat.; index. **Indexed:** Aus.P.A.I.S., Dairy Sci.Abstr., Geo.Abstr., Rural Recreat.Tour.Abstr., World Agri.Econ.& Rural Sociol.Abstr. **Document type:** government publication.
    —BLDSC (1798.184000); UnCover.
    Former titles: Australia. Australian Bureau of Agricultural and Resource Economics. Agriculture and Resources Quarterly (ISSN 1032-9722); (until Mar. 1989): Australia. Australian Bureau of Agricultural and Resource Economics. Quarterly Review of the Rural Economy; Australia. Bureau of Agricultural Economics. Quarterly Review of the Rural Economy (ISSN 0156-7446); Supersedes (in 1978): Quarterly Review of Agricultural Economics (ISSN 0033-5754)
    Description: Features short-term outlook for agriculture, forestry and fisheries.

350 631   AT   ISSN 1325-8931
AUSTRALIAN BUREAU OF AGRICULTURAL AND RESOURCE ECONOMICS. AUSTRALIAN CROP REPORT. 1980. bi-m. Aus.$99 (effective 1997). Australian Bureau of Agricultural and Resource Economics, G.P.O. Box 1563, Canberra, A.C.T. 2601, Australia. TEL 61-6-2722211. FAX 61-6-2722330. E-mail: deniseflamia@abare.gov.au. (Subscr. to: A B A R E Publications, G.P.O. Box 1563, Canberra, A.C.T. 2601, Australia) Ed. Andrew Wright. circ. 800. **Document type:** government publication.
    Former titles: Australia Bureau of Agricultural and Resource Economics. Crop Report (ISSN 1038-4235); Australian Bureau of Agricultural Economics. Crop Report.
    Description: Forecasts of crop areas, yield, and production by state.

AUSTRALIAN FARM JOURNAL. see *AGRICULTURE*

AGRICULTURE — AGRICULTURAL ECONOMICS

338.1   UK   ISSN 1364-985X
HD1401
AUSTRALIAN JOURNAL OF AGRICULTURAL & RESOURCE ECONOMICS. 1997. 3/yr. £60 in Europe; N. America $95; elsewhere £66 (effective 1997). (Australian Agricultural and Resource Economics Society, AT) Blackwell Publishers Ltd., 108 Cowley Rd., Oxford OX4 1JF, England. TEL 44-1865-791100. FAX 44-1865-791347. E-mail: jnlinfo@blackwellpublishers.co.uk; URL: http://www.blackwellpublishers.co.uk. Eds. D. Maclaren, L. Malcolm. adv.; bk.rev.; charts; cum.index every 3 yrs. circ. 1,400. (reprint service avail. from ISI) Indexed: ASCA, Aus.P.A.I.S., C.R.E.J., Curr.Cont., Dairy Sci.Abstr., Field Crop.Abstr., Geo.Abstr.H.G., Herb.Abstr., IDA, Ind.Sci.Rev., Irr.& Drain.Abstr., J.of Econ.Lit., Rural Recreat.Tour.Abstr., Sci.Cit.Ind., SSCI, World Agri.Econ.& Rural Sociol.Abstr. **Document type:** academic/scholarly publication.
— BLDSC (7791.500000); UnCover. CCC.
Formed by the merger of (1957-1997): Australian Journal of Agricultural Economics (ISSN 0004-9395); (1945-1997): Review of Marketing and Agricultural Economics (ISSN 0034-6616); Which superseded (1937-1945): New South Wales Pastoral Conditions (ISSN 0047-9926)
Description: Covers economic analysis of Australian agriculture. Includes theoretical and methodological material.

338.1   GW   ISSN 0179-5066
B N - BETRIEBSWIRTSCHAFTLICHE NACHRICHTEN FUER DIE LANDWIRTSCHAFT. 1940. m. DM.41. Verlag Pflug und Feder GmbH, Koelnstr. 202, 53757 Sankt Augustin, Germany. TEL 02241-204085.

338.1   PE
BANCO AGRARIO DEL PERU. MEMORIA. no.45, 1976. a. Banco Agrario del Peru, c/o Axel Pflucker Otoya, Augusto Wiese 543-547, Lima, Peru.

338.1   BG   ISSN 0070-8143
BANGLADESH. DIRECTORATE OF AGRICULTURAL MARKETING. AGRICULTURAL MARKETING SERIES. * (Text in English) irreg. Directorate of Agricultural Marketing, Ministry of Agriculture, Bangladesh Secretariat, Bhaban 4, Dhaka, Bangladesh.

BAY OF PLENTY FARMER. see AGRICULTURE

381.41 635.53   US   ISSN 1066-0607
BEAN MARKET NEWS. 1965. w. (plus a. summary). $55 (Canada and Mexico $60; elsewhere $90). U.S. Department of Agriculture, Agricultural Marketing Service (Greely), Livestock & Seed Division, 711 O St., Greely, CO 80631. TEL 970-353-9750. FAX 970-353-9790. (Subscr. to: U.S.D.A. Agricultural Marketing Service, Livestock & Seed Division, Rm., 2623-S, Box 96456, Washington, DC 20090-6456. FAX 202-245-4732) (looseleaf format; also avail. in microfiche from CIS; back issues avail.; reprint service avail. from CIS) Indexed: Amer.Stat.Ind. (1984-). **Document type:** government publication.

BEDRIJFSUITKOMSTEN EN FINANCIELE POSITIE; samenvattend overzicht van landbouwbedrijven tot en met boekjaar. see AGRICULTURE

338.1   NE   ISSN 0921-4097
BEDRIJFSUITKOMSTEN IN DE LANDBOUW. 1970. a. fl.58. Landbouw-Economisch Instituut, Burg. Patijnlaan 19, 2585 BE The Hague, Netherlands. TEL 31-70-3308330. FAX 31-70-3615624. E-mail: postmaster@lei.dlo.nl; URL: http://www.lei.dlo.nl/lei. Ed.Bd. stat. **Document type:** government publication.
Description: Extended data on income and profitability of Dutch agriculture.

BEDRIJFSUITKOMSTEN IN DE TUINBOUW. see AGRICULTURE — Abstracting, Bibliographies, Statistics

338.1 634   US
BENTON HARBOR FRUIT & VEGETABLE REPORT. 3/wk. (Jul.-Sep.) $20. U.S. Department of Agriculture (Benton Harbor), Box 1204, 175 Territorial Rd., Benton Harbor, MI 49022. TEL 616-925-3270. FAX 616-925-3272. (back issues avail.) **Document type:** newsletter, government publication.
Description: Provides Benton Harbor fruit market prices, as well as those for the Chicago and Detroit terminal markets.

338.1 581 575.1   YU   ISSN 0351-9430
BILTEN ZA HMELJ, SIRAK I LEKOVITO BILJE. (Text in Serbo-Croatian; summaries in English) 1969. q. exchange basis. Institut za Ratarstvo i Povrtarstvo, Poljoprivredni Fakultet, Lenjinova 5, Backi Petrovac, Vojvodina, Yugoslavia. TELEX 15059 IFVCNS YU. Ed. Jan Kisgeci. adv.; bk.rev. circ. 600. (back issues avail.) **Indexed:** Biol.Abstr., Hort.Abstr.

338.1 631   BS
BOTSWANA. MINISTRY OF AGRICULTURE. FARM MANAGEMENT SURVEY RESULTS. 1980. a. free. Ministry of Agriculture, Division of Planning and Statistics, Private Bag 003, Gaborone, Botswana. FAX 267-356027. TELEX 2543 VET BD. Ed. Henry G. Jobeta. R&P contact: Dan B. Gombalume. bibl.; stat. circ. 400. (back issues avail.) **Document type:** government publication.
Formerly: Botswana. Ministry of Commerce and Industry. Farm Management Survey Results.

338.1   US
BROCK REPORT. 1976. w. $355. Brock & Associates, 2050 W. Good Hope Rd., Milwaukee, WI 53209. TEL 414-351-5500. FAX 414-351-3140. Ed. Jeffrey J. Wilson; Pub. Richard A. Brock. **Document type:** newsletter.
Incorporates (in 1989): Top Farmer Market Insight (ISSN 0730-6326)

BUSINESS TIMES. see BUSINESS AND ECONOMICS

338.1 330.1   UV   ISSN 1021-3236
C E D R E S. REVUE ECONOMIQUE ET SOCIALE. (Text in French) 1977. q. 40000 Fr.CFA. Centre d'Etudes, de Recherche Economique et Social, Universite de Ouagadougou, B.P. 7021, Ouagadougou, Burkina Faso. TEL 31-19-67. FAX 31-26-86. Ed. Soulama Souleymane. circ. 500.

338.1 613.1   FR
C E M A G R E F MONTAGNE. ETUDES. irreg. Centre National de Machinisme Agricole du Gerie Rural, des Eaux et des Forets, Domaine de Laluas, 63200 Riom, France. TEL 33-4-73382052. FAX 33-4-73387641. Ed. Philippe Coussot.

338.1 613.1   FR
C E M A G R E F PRODUCTION ET ECONOMIE AGRICOLES. ETUDES. irreg. Centre National de Machinisme Agricole du Gerie Rural, des Eaux et des Forets, Domaine de Laluas, 63200 Riom, France. TEL 33-4-73382052. FAX 33-4-73387641. Ed.Bd.

C R B FUTURES PERSPECTIVE - AGRICULTURAL EDITION. (Commodity Research Bureau) see BUSINESS AND ECONOMICS — Investments

338.1   CK
CADERNOS DE DESARROLLO RURAL. 1979. s-a. Col.$7000($8) (effective 1997). Pontificia Universidad Javeriana, Facultad de Ciencias Economicas y Administrativas, Calle 40 No. 6-23, Piso 7, Santafe de Bogota, Colombia. TEL 57-1-2870388. FAX 57-1-2857289. E-mail: jrey@javercol.javeriana.edu.co. abstr.; bibl.
Formerly (until 1993): Cadernos de Agroindustria y Economia Rural (ISSN 0120-3606)

338.1   FR   ISSN 0755-9208
HN49.C6
CAHIERS D'ECONOMIE ET SOCIOLOGIE RURALES. (Text in English, French) 1984. 4/yr. 400 F. (foreign 490 F.) (effective 1997); newsstand price: 140 F. Institut National de la Recherche Agronomique, Departement d'Economie et de Sociologie Rurales, 63-65 bd. de Brandebourg, 94205 Ivry Cedex, France. TEL 33-1-49596900. FAX 33-1-46704113. E-mail: seurat@ivry.inra.fr; URL: http://www.dijon.inra.fr/esr/publications/cesr/index.html. Ed. Jean-Pierre Amigues. R&P contact: Elena Rivkine. TEL 33-1-49596976. bk.rev. circ. 500. Indexed: ELLIS, World Agri.Econ.& Rural Sociol.Abstr. **Document type:** academic/scholarly publication.
Description: Focuses on agriculture and related activities, the way they function from an economic point of view, their social characteristics and their relations with the national and international economy.

630 338.1   VE   ISSN 0798-6270
CALENDARIO AGRICOLA. 1970. irreg., latest 1987. free. Ministerio de Agricultura y Cria, Direccion de Planificacion y Estadistica, Division de Estadistica, Centro Simon Bolivar, Torre Norte 16o, Caracas 1010, Venezuela. TEL 2-509-0111. stat.

381.41 635.53   US
CALIFORNIA. DEPARTMENT OF FOOD AND AGRICULTURE. LIVESTOCK. w. $75. Federal-State Market News Service (Sacramento), 1220 N St., Rm. A-247, Box 942871, Sacramento, CA 94271-0001. TEL 916-654-0298. FAX 916-654-1046. **Document type:** government publication.
Description: Covers California auctions, direct sales, midwest markets - cattle, hogs and sheep.

338.1   US   ISSN 0891-9097
HD9007.C2
CALIFORNIA AGRICULTURAL EXPORT DIRECTORY. 1982. biennial. $50 (diskette $195) (effective 1996). (California Department of Food and Agriculture, Agricultural Export Program) Database Publishing Company, 1590 S. Lewis St., Anaheim, CA 92805-6423. TEL 714-778-6400. FAX 714-778-6811. (Subscr. to: Box 70024, Anaheim, CA 92825-0024. TEL 800-888-8434) Ed. Ken Gregory. circ. 3,000. (also avail. in diskette format) **Document type:** directory.
Description: Provides key facts on California companies involved in exporting agricultural products, both fresh and processed; includes growers, packers, processors, and brokers. Companies are listed alphabetically and by products; includes company name, address, telephone and fax numbers, contact name and title, number of fulltime and seasonal employees, year established, products, packaging and brand names.

381.41 653.53   US
CALIFORNIA FRUIT REPORT. d. and w. $90 (foreign $180) per mo.; for weekly $17 (foreign $34) per mo. (Department of Food and Agriculture) Federal-State Market News Service (Sacramento), 1220 N St., Rm. A-247, Box 942871, Sacramento, CA 94271-0001. TEL 916-654-0298. FAX 916-654-1046. **Document type:** government publication.
Description: California fruit shipping point prices, volume, market situation and selected wholesale markets.

381.41 635.53   US
CALIFORNIA GRAIN AND FEEDERS REPORT. w. $99. (Department of Food and Agriculture) Federal-State Market News Service (Sacramento), 1220 N St., Rm. A-247, Box 942871, Sacramento. TEL 916-654-0298. FAX 916-654-1046. **Document type:** government publication.
Description: Covers grain, foodstuffs, hay, livestock, poultry and egg prices; grain market situation, futures, and exports.

CANADA. GRAIN COMMISSION. CORPORATE SERVICES. VISIBLE GRAIN SUPPLIES AND DISPOSITION. see AGRICULTURE — Feed, Flour And Grain

338.1   CN   ISSN 1190-8408
HD9014.C2
CANADA. NATIONAL FARM PRODUCTS COUNCIL. ANNUAL REVIEW. (Text in English and French) 1973. a. free. National Farm Products Council, P.O. Box 3430, Stn. D, Ottawa, ON K1P 6L4, Canada. FAX 613-995-2097. Ed. Carola McWade. circ. 2,000. **Document type:** government publication.
Former titles (until 1994): Canada. National Farm Products Council. Annual Report (ISSN 1190-8394); (until 1993): Canada. National Farm Products Marketing Council. Annual Report (ISSN 0383-414X)

338.1   CN   ISSN 0317-7483
HD9014.C2
CANADA'S TRADE IN AGRICULTURAL PRODUCTS. (Issued as subseries of Economics Branch Bulletin) a. free. Agriculture Canada, Policy Branch, Ottawa, ON K1A 0C7, Canada. TEL 613-995-5222. **Document type:** government publication.
Formerly: Canada. Agriculture Canada. Policy Branch. Trade in Agricultural Products (ISSN 0068-7286)

338.1   IS
CENTER FOR AGRICULTURAL ECONOMIC RESEARCH, REHOVOT. WORKING PAPERS. 1969. irreg. Center for Agricultural Economic Research, P.O. Box 12, Rehovot, Israel. FAX 972-8-466267. **Document type:** monographic series.
Description: Preliminary reports of research findings in agricultural economics.

CENTRAL PLANTATION CROPS RESEARCH INSTITUTE. ANNUAL REPORT. see AGRICULTURE

AGRICULTURE — AGRICULTURAL ECONOMICS

CERES; the F A O review on agriculture and development. see *AGRICULTURE*

338.1 631.3   US
CHANGING HORIZONS. m. $7. Montgomery County Cooperative Extension, Co. Annex Bldg., Box 1500, NY 12068. TEL 518-853-3471. Ed. Susan Maloney. adv. circ. 450. (back issues avail.) **Document type:** newsletter.
    Formerly: Montgomery County Agricultural News.

338.1   CC
CHINA AGRIBUSINESS REPORT. (Text in English) 1987. s-m. $595. Asia Letter Group, G.P.O. Box 10874, Hong Kong, People's Republic of China. TEL 852-526-2950. FAX 852-526-7131. TELEX HX-61166-HKNW. (US subscr. to: Box 92619, Los Angeles, CA 90009) bk.rev.
    Description: Covers China's biggest and most important business sector - agribusiness.

338.1   US   ISSN 0886-5558
CHOICES: THE MAGAZINE OF FOOD, FARM AND RESOURCE ISSUES. 1988. q. $20 to individuals; institutions $32.50 (effective 1997). American Agricultural Economics Association, 1110 Buckeye Ave., Ames, IA 50010-8063. TEL 515-233-3202. FAX 515-233-3101. For export contact: sclarke@iastate.edu. circ. 6,000. **Document type:** consumer publication. —UnCover. **CCC.**
    Description: For people interested in food, farm and resource issues and the policies that affect them.

338.1   CU   ISSN 0138-8584
CIENCIA Y TECNICA EN LA AGRICULTURA. SERIE: ECONOMIA AGROPECUARIA. (Table of contents and abstracts in English) 1978. 2/yr. $14 in N. and S. America; Europe $16; elsewhere $17; or exchange basis. Centro de Informacion y Documentacion Agropecuario, Gaveta Postal 4149, Havana 4, Cuba. (Dist. by: Ediciones Cubanas, Obispo No. 527, Apdo. 605, Havana, Cuba) **Indexed:** Agrindex.

338.1 636 330.9   US   ISSN 0732-7226
HD1775.C6
COLORADO AGRIBUSINESS ROUNDUP. 1967. a. $5. Colorado State University, Department of Agricultural Economics, B-326 Clark Bldg., CO 80523. TEL 303-491-6133. FAX 303-491-6441. Ed. J. Hugh Winn. circ. 2,500.

338.1   AT   ISSN 0314-0164
COMPLAN HANDBOOK. 1977. a. University of New England, Agricultural Business Research Institute, Armidale, N.S.W. 2351, Australia. TEL 067-733555. FAX 067-725376.

338.1 301.35   BL   ISSN 0102-2253
HD1871
CONGRESSO BRASILEIRO DE ECONOMIA E SOCIOLOGIA RURAL. ANAIS. 1962. a. $90 (effective Jan. 1993). Sociedade Brasileira de Economia Rural, Edificio Brasilia Radio Center, Av. W-3 Norte - Quadra 702, Salas 1049-50, 70710 Brasilia, D.F., Brazil. TEL 061-225-6144. bk.rev. clrc. 1,000.
    Formerly: Sociedade Brasileira de Economistas Rurais. Anais da Reuniao.

338.1   US   ISSN 0093-6553
SB369.2.F6
COST OF PICKING AND HAULING FLORIDA CITRUS FRUITS. (Subseries of Agricultural Economics Report) a. University of Florida, Institute of Food and Agricultural Sciences, Food and Resource Economics Department, Box 110240, Gainesville, FL 32611-0240. TEL 904-392-6015. stat.

338.7   II   ISSN 0304-6907
HD9086.I4
COTTON CORPORATION OF INDIA. ANNUAL REPORT. Key Title: Annual Report - Cotton Corporation of India. (Text in English) a. Cotton Corporation of India, Air India Building, 12th Floor, Nariman Point, Bombay 400 021, India. **Document type:** corporate report.

338.1 664   FR   ISSN 1161-8043
COURRIER DE LA PLANETE; agriculture, environnement, alimentation, trois defis pour un monde solidaire. (Supplements avail.) 1981. bi-m. 285 F. to individuals (outside EC 335 F.); institutions 500 F. (outside EC 550 F.) (effective 1995). Solidarites Agro-Alimentaires, BP 5056, 3191 route de Mende, 34033 Montpellier Cedex 1, France. TEL 67-54-47-23. FAX 67-54-25-27. Ed.Bd. adv.; bk.rev.; charts; illus.; stat.; index. circ. 5,000. (back issues avail.) **Document type:** newspaper.
    Formerly (until 1991): Lettre de Solagral (ISSN 0293-3055)

332 630   FR   ISSN 1243-9193
CREDIT AGRICOLE PARIS. 1968. bi-m. 220 F. (Federation Nationale du Credit Agricole) F N C A, 48 rue la Boetie, 75008 Paris, France. TEL 45-63-03-00. FAX 49-53-44-81. TELEX FENAGRI 650 718. adv.; bk.rev.; illus.; stat. circ. 36,000.
    Formerly (until 1993): Administrateur du Credit Agriculture (ISSN 0988-9183)

338.1 368   US
CROP INSURANCE INSIDER. 1984. q. membership. American Association of Crop Insurers, 1 Massachusetts Ave., N.W., No. 800, Washington, DC 20001-1431. TEL 202-789-4100. E-mail: aac:@erols.com; URL: http://www.erols.com/aac: Ed. Michael R. McLeod. Publisher: Bonnie Goff. charts; illus.; stat.; tr.lit. circ. 4,500. (looseleaf format) **Document type:** newsletter.
    Formed by the merger of: American Association of Crop Insurers. Washington Update & American Association of Crop Insurers. Agent Newsletter.
    Description: Covers crop insurance.

338.1   CU
CUBA. CENTRO DE INFORMACION Y DOCUMENTACION AGROPECUARIO. BOLETIN DE RESENAS. SERIE: ECONOMIA AGROPECUARIA. (Abstracts in English) 1986. irreg. exchange basis. Centro de Informacion y Documentacion Agropecuario, Gaveta Postal 4149, Havana 4, Cuba. (Dist. by: Ediciones Cubanas, Obispo No. 461, Apdo. 605, Havana, Cuba) **Indexed:** Agrindex.

338.1   CY   ISSN 0379-0827
HD2057
CYPRUS. AGRICULTURAL RESEARCH INSTITUTE. AGRICULTURAL ECONOMICS REPORT. 1973. irreg., no.34, 1993. free. Ministry of Agriculture, Natural Resources and the Environment, Agricultural Research Institute, P.O. Box 2016, 1516 Nicosia, Cyprus. TEL 357-2-305101. FAX 357-2-316770. E-mail: library@arinet.ar.gov.cy; URL: http://www.ari.gov.cy. Ed. S. Papachristodoulou. circ. 400. **Indexed:** Food Sci.& Tech.Abstr. **Document type:** monographic series, government publication.
    —BLDSC (0745.746000).
    Description: Contains input-output analytical data on the crop and animal market.

338.1   BL   ISSN 0100-9605
DADOS SOBRE A SITUACAO DA AGROPECUARIA MUNICIPAL NO ESTADO DO PARANA. 1977. a. Associacao de Credito e Assistencia Rural, Caixa Postal 900, Belo Horizonte 30000, Minas Gerais, Brazil.

338.109489   DK   ISSN 1395-5705
HD2001
DENMARK. STATENS JORDBRUGS- OG FISKERIOEKONOMISKE INSTITUT. RAPPORT/DENMARK. INSTITUTE OF AGRICULTURAL AND FISHERIES ECONOMICS. REPORT. irreg. (5-7/yr.). price varies. Statens Jordbrugs- og Fiskerioekonomiske Institut - Danish Institute of Agricultural and Fisheries Economics, Toftegaards Plads, Gammel Koege Landevej 1-3, DK-2500 Valby (Copenhagen), Denmark. TEL 45-36-44-20-80. FAX 45-36-44-11-10.
    —BLDSC (7269.250000).
    Former titles (until 1995): Denmark. Statens Jordbrugsoekonomiske Institut. Rapport (ISSN 0108-7398); (until 1983): Denmark. Jordbrugsoekonomisk Institut. Rapport (ISSN 0107-5357)

338.1309489   DK   ISSN 0107-5675
HD2001
DENMARK. STATENS JORDBRUGS- OG FISKERIOEKONOMISKE INSTITUT. SERIE A: LANDBRUGSREGNSKABSSTATISTIK/AGRICULTURAL ACCOUNTS STATISTICS. Key Title: Landbrugsregnskabsstatistik. (Text in Danish; summaries in English) 1917. a. price varies. Statens Jordbrugs- og Fiskerioekonomiske Institut - Danish Institute of Agricultural and Fisheries Economics, Toftegaards Plads, Gammel Koege Landevej 1-3, DK-2500 Valby (Copenhagen), Denmark. TEL 45-36-44-20-80. FAX 45-36-44-11-10.
    —BLDSC (8442.005000).

338.1309489   DK   ISSN 0107-5691
DENMARK. STATENS JORDBRUGS- OG FISKERIOEKONOMISKE INSTITUT. SERIE C: LANDBRUGETS PRISFORHOLD/AGRICULTURAL PRICE STATISTICS. Key Title: Landbrugets Prisforhold. 1967. a. price varies. Statens Jordbrugs- og Fiskerioekonomiske Institut - Danish Institute of Agricultural and Fisheries Economics, Toftegaards Plads, Gammel Koege Landevej 1-3, DK-2500 Valby (Copenhagen), Denmark. TEL 45-36-44-20-80. FAX 45-36-44-11-10. Ed. Arne Larsen.

338.1309489   DK   ISSN 0107-5705
SB319.3.D4
DENMARK. STATENS- JORDBRUGS OG FISKERIOEKONOMISKE INSTITUT. SERIE D: GARTNERI-REGNSKABSSTATISTIK/HORTICULTURAL ACCOUNTS STATISTICS. Key Title: Gartneriregnskabsstatistik. (Text in Danish; summaries in English) 1980. a. price varies. Statens Jordbrugs- og Fiskerioekonomiske Institut - Danish Institute of Agricultural and Fisheries Economics, Toftegaards Plads, Glammel Koege Landevej 1-3, DK-2500 Valby (Copenhagen), Denmark. TEL 45-36-44-20-80. FAX 45-36-44-11-10.

338.1 631.1   NE   ISSN 0926-5589
DEVELOPMENTS IN AGRICULTURAL ECONOMICS. 1983. irreg., vol.9, 1991. price varies. Elsevier Science B.V., Books Division, P.O. Box 211, 1000 AE Amsterdam, Netherlands. TEL 31-20-4853911. FAX 31-20-4853705. TELEX 18582 ESPA NL. E-mail: nlinfo-f@elsevier.nl; usinfo-f@elsevier.com; forinfo-kyf04035@niftyserve.or.jp; URL: http://www.elsevier.nl/. (Subscr. in the Americas to: Elsevier Science, Regional Sales Office, Box 945, New York, NY 10159-0945. TEL 212-633-3730. FAX 212-633-3680; Subscr. in Australasia and the Far East to: Elsevier Science (Singapore) Pte Ltd, No.1 Temasek Ave., No.17-01 Millenia Tower, Singapore 039192, Singapore. TEL 65-434-3727. FAX 65-337-2230; Subscr. in Japan to: Elsevier Science Japan, 9-15 Higashi-Azabu 1-chome, Minato-ku, Tokyo 106, Japan. TEL 81-3-5561-5033. FAX 81-3-5561-5047) (back issues avail.) **Document type:** monographic series.
    —BLDSC (3579.061150).
    Refereed Serial

630 338   UK   ISSN 1359-9232
DIRECTORY OF AGRICULTURAL CO-OPERATIVES IN THE UNITED KINGDOM. 1970. a. £40. Plunkett Foundation, 23 Hanborough Business Park, Long Hanborough, Oxford OX8 8LH, England. TEL 44-1993-883636. FAX 44-1993-883576. E-mail: plunkett@gn.apc.org. stat. circ. 1,060. **Document type:** directory.
    —BLDSC (9082.656184).
    Former titles: Directory of Agricultural, Horticultural and Fishery Co-Operatives in the United Kingdom (ISSN 0265-7155); Directory of Agricultural Co-Operatives in the United Kingdom (ISSN 0307-689X)
    Description: Covers 700 agricultural, horticultural and fishery co-operatives in the U.K. Provides name and address, names of chairman and secretary, telephone and telex numbers, registration number, activities, membership and turnover figure.

338.1   CN   ISSN 0708-3017
DIRECTORY OF ALBERTA'S AGRICULTURAL PROCESSING INDUSTRY. 1975. a. free. Alberta Agriculture, Food & Rural Development, Industry Development Branch, 7000-113 St., 3rd Fl., Rm. 304, Edmonton, AB T6H 5T6, Canada. TEL 403-427-7325. FAX 403-422-3655. E-mail: pelleti@agric.gov.ab.ca. Ed. Allan Pelletier. R&P contact: Allan Pelletier. charts; illus. circ. 2,000. **Document type:** directory, government publication.
    Formerly: Agricultural Processing and Manufacturing Guide (ISSN 0708-3025)

AGRICULTURE — AGRICULTURAL ECONOMICS

E U FOOD LAW. (European Union) see *LAW — International Law*

---

338 **630** **UG**
EASTERN AFRICA JOURNAL OF RURAL DEVELOPMENT. 1968. s-a. Makerere University, Department of Agricultural Economics, P.O. Box 7062, Kampala, Uganda. (Co-sponsor: Eastern Africa Economic Society) Ed. J.R. Bibangambah. adv.; bk.rev.; bibl.; charts; stat. circ. 800. (also avail. in microform from UMI; reprint service avail. from UMI) **Indexed:** P.L.E.S.A., Soc.Sci.Ind.
Formerly: East Africa Journal of Rural Development (ISSN 0012-8233)

338.1 633.73 **CK** **ISSN 0046-1148**
HD9199.A1
ECONOMIA CAFETERA. 1966. m. free. Federacion Nacional de Cafeteros de Colombia, Estudios y Proyectos Basicos Cafeteros, Calle 73 No. 8-13, piso 10 B, Bogota D.E., Colombia. TEL 57-1-3451088. FAX 57-1-2171021. TELEX 44655. charts; stat.; circ. 8,000. (controlled) **Document type:** bulletin.
Description: Provides Colombian coffee statistics.
Refereed Serial

338.1 **CN** **ISSN 1191-3576**
ECONOMIC PLANNING IN FREE SOCIETIES; journal for agriculture and related industries. 1965. bi-m. Can.$24 (US $24, elsewhere $28) (effective 1998). Academic Publishing Co., P.O. Box 145, Mont Royal, PQ H3P 3B9, Canada. TEL 514-738-5255. Ed. Peter Harsany. adv. contact: A. Graul. bk.rev.; stat.; index. circ. 5,200. (tabloid format) **Indexed:** BPIA, Cadscan, Curr.Cont., Dairy Sci.Abstr., Lead Abstr., P.A.I.S., Rural Devel.Abstr., Rural Recreat.Tour.Abstr., Soyabean Abstr., World Agri.Econ.& Rural Sociol.Abstr., Zincscan. **Document type:** academic/scholarly publication.
—BLDSC (3654.090500).
Formerly (until 1992): Economic Planning (ISSN 0013-0222).
Description: Examines economic planning, agricultural policy and the world's food supply.

338.1 **UK** **ISSN 0262-9135**
ECONOMIC REPORT ON SCOTTISH AGRICULTURE. 1981. a. price varies. Scottish Office, Agriculture and Fisheries Department, Pentland House, 47 Robb's Loan, Edinburgh EH14 1TY, Scotland. (Avail. from: The Scottish Office Library, Rm. 1-44 New St. Andrews House, Edinburgh EH1 3TG, Scotland) **Indexed:** Anim.Breed.Abstr., Dairy Sci.Abstr., Geo.Abstr., Nutr.Abstr., World Agri.Econ.& Rural Sociol.Abstr. **Document type:** government publication.
—BLDSC (3654.449000); Linda Hall.
Incorporates: Scottish Agricultural Economics; Some Studies of Current Economic Conditions in Scottish Farming (ISSN 0080-7966); Agricultural Statistics, Scotland (ISSN 0065-4582)

338.1 **KE**
ECONOMIC REVIEW OF AGRICULTURE. 1963. a. free. Ministry of Agriculture, Development Planning Division, P.O. Box 30028, Nairobi, Kenya. TEL 254-2-718870. TELEX 22766. Ed. Protus Sigei. circ. 1,500. (back issues avail.) **Indexed:** Rural Recreat.Tour.Abstr., World Agri.Econ.& Rural Sociol.Abstr. **Document type:** academic/scholarly publication, government publication.
Description: Provides a review over a period of one year or the agricultural activities of Kenya, from production to marketing. Also reviews government policy concerning food and agriculture.
Refereed Serial

338.1 **FR** **ISSN 0070-8798**
ECONOMIE ET FINANCES AGRICOLES/AGRICULTURAL ECONOMICS AND FINANCE. (Includes supplement) 1971. 10/yr. 186 F. Caisse Nationale de Credit Agricole, 91-93 Bd. Pasteur, 75015 Paris, France. Ed. Jacques Lenormand. bk.rev. circ. 8,000. **Indexed:** Food Sci.& Tech.Abstr., P.A.I.S.For.Lang.Ind., Soyabean Abstr., World Agri.Econ.& Rural Sociol.Abstr.
—BLDSC (3657.506000).

338.1 330.9 **FR** **ISSN 0013-0559**
ECONOMIE RURALE. 1949. bi-m. 690 F. (outside EU 720 F.) (effective 1997). Societe Francaise d'Economie Rurale, 16 rue Claude Bernard, 75231 Paris Cedex 05, France. TEL 33-1-47074786. FAX 33-1-44081842. Ed. Philippe Lacombe. adv.; bk.rev.; bibl.; charts; index; circ. 1,000. (paid). **Indexed:** Excerp.Med., IBR, Int.Lab.Doc., P.A.I.S.For.Lang.Ind., Rural Ext.Educ.& Tr.Abstr. **Document type:** academic/scholarly publication, bibliography.
—BLDSC (3658.400000); SWETS.
Description: Academic journal dealing with French and European agricultural policy, geography, trade, agricultural development, and methodology.
Refereed Serial

338.1 **FR** **ISSN 0068-4899**
ECONOMIES ET SOCIETES. SERIE AG. PROGRES ET AGRICULTURE. 1962. irreg. 350 F. Presses Universitaires de Grenoble, B.P. 47, 38040 Grenoble Cedex 9, France. Ed.Bd. circ. 1,600. **Indexed:** World Agri.Econ.& Rural Sociol.Abstr.
—SWETS.

338.1 **YU** **ISSN 0352-3462**
EKONOMIKA POLJOPRIVREDA. (Text in Serbo-Croatian; summaries in English and Russian) 1954. m. 1500 din. Savez Poljoprivrednih Inzenjera i Tehnicara Jugoslavije - Society of Agricultural Engineers and Technicians, Kneza Milosa 9, Belgrade, Yugoslavia. Ed. Vucic Jovanovic. adv.; bk.rev. circ. 1,100. **Indexed:** Rural Recreat.Tour.Abstr., World Agri.Econ.& Rural Sociol.Abstr.
—BLDSC (3669.055000).
Former titles (until 1979): Ekonomika Proizvodnje Hrane (ISSN 0352-3454); (until 1977): Ekonomika Poljoprivreda (ISSN 0013-306X)

338.1 **RU**
EKONOMIKA SEL'SKOGO KHOZYAISTVA ROSSII. (Text in Russian; content page in English and Russian) 1921. m. $1268 (effective 1998). AgriPress, Sadovaya-Spasskaya, 18, 107807 Moscow, Russia. TEL 7-095-2071662. (Dist. by: Mezhdunarodnaya Kniga, B. Yakimanka 39, 117049 Moscow, Russia. TEL 7-095-2384967. FAX 7-095-2384634) Ed. Marlen M. Makeenko. adv.; bk.rev.; bibl.; charts; illus.; stat. circ. 50,000. **Indexed:** Agri.Eng.Abstr., Chem.Abstr., Curr.Dig.Sov.Press, Dairy Sci.Abstr., Geo.Abstr., Maize Abstr., Rural Recreat.Tour.Abstr., Triticale Abstr., World Agri.Econ.& Rural Sociol.Abstr.
Formerly (until 1994): Ekonomika Sel'skogo Khozyaistva (ISSN 0013-3094)
Refereed Serial

338.1 **FR** **ISSN 0396-0102**
ELEVEUR DE FRANCE. 6/yr. Societe Neolait Codislait, B.P. 1, 22120 Yffiniac, France. TEL 96-72-61-81. Ed. Jean-Jacques Bree. circ. 40,000.

630 338.1 **VE** **ISSN 0798-6351**
ENCUESTA AGROPECUARIA. 1969. a. free. Ministerio de Agricultura y Cria, Direccion de Planificacion y Estadistica, Division de Estadistica, Centro Simon Bolivar, Torre Norte 16o, Caracas 1010, Venezuela. stat.

338.1 633.73 **CK**
ENSAYOS SOBRE ECONOMIA CAFETERA. 1987. s-a. Federacion Nacional de Cafeteros de Colombia, Calle 73 No. 8-13, piso 10 B, Bogota D.E., Colombia.

ETUDES RURALES; revue trimestrielle d'histoire, geographie, sociologie et economie des campagnes. see *SOCIOLOGY*

338.1 **UK** **ISSN 1360-4392**
▼**EUROPEAN POTATO MARKETS MONTHLY.** 1995. m. £265 (rest of Europe £275; elsewhere £320) (effective 1997). Agra Europe (London) Ltd., 25 Frant Rd., Tunbridge Wells, Kent TN2 5JT, England. TEL 44-1892-533813. FAX 44-1892-544895. E-mail: 100637.3460@compuserve.com.

338.1 **GW** **ISSN 0165-1587**
CODEN: ERAEDA
EUROPEAN REVIEW OF AGRICULTURAL ECONOMICS. 1973. q. DM.159 (foreign DM.165) to individuals; institutions DM.361 (foreign DM.367) (effective 1998). Walter de Gruyter und Co., Genthiner Str. 13, 10785 Berlin, Germany. TEL 49-30-260050. FAX 49-30-26005251. E-mail: wdg-info@degruyter.de; URL: http://www.degruyter.de. Ed. Arie Oskam. adv.; bk.rev.; cum.index. circ. 800. **Indexed:** Agrindex, ASCA, Biostat., C.R.E.J., Curr.Cont., Dairy Sci.Abstr., Fam.Ind., Food Sci.& Tech.Abstr., Geo.Abstr.H.G., Helminthol.Abstr., IDA, Int.Lab.Doc., J.of Econ.Lit., Lang.& Lang.Behav.Abstr., Maize Abstr., Soyabean Abstr., SSCI, Triticale Abstr., World Agri.Econ.& Rural Sociol.Abstr. **Document type:** trade publication.
—BLDSC (3829.940000); Genuine Article; SWETS; UnCover. CCC.

338.1 **UN** **ISSN 1010-1365**
CODEN: ASBFDF
F A O AGRICULTURAL SERVICES BULLETIN. French edition: Bulletin des Services Agricoles (ISSN 1014-4218); Spanish edition: Boletin de Servicios Agricolas (ISSN 1014-4226) (Text in English) 1968. irreg., latest no.111. price varies. Food and Agriculture Organization of the United Nations, Bernan Associates, 4611-F Assembly Dr., Lanham, MD 20706-4391. TEL 301-459-7666. FAX 301-459-0056. circ. 3,800 (2,000 English edition; 1,000 French edition; 800 Spanish edition). **Indexed:** Biodet.Abstr., Food Sci.& Tech.Abstr., Nutr.Abstr., Rice Abstr., Rural Recreat.Tour.Abstr., World Agri.Econ.& Rural Sociol.Abstr. **Document type:** monographic series.
—BLDSC (3865.591500); CASDDS; CISTI; Linda Hall.
Formerly: Agricultural Services Bulletin (ISSN 0378-2182)

338.1 **UN** **ISSN 0071-7002**
HD1401
F A O COMMODITY REVIEW AND OUTLOOK. French edition: F A O Rapport et Perspectives sur les Produits (ISSN 0251-1509); Spanish edition: F A O Situacion y Perspectivas de los Productos Basicos (ISSN 0251-1517) (Text in English) 1961. a. $50. Food and Agriculture Organization of the United Nations, Bernan Associates, 4611-F Assembly Dr., Lanham, MD 20706-4391. TEL 301-459-7666. FAX 301-459-0056. (also avail. in microfiche from CIS) **Indexed:** IIS, Nutr.Abstr.
—CISTI; Linda Hall.
Formerly (until 1968): F A O Commodity Review (ISSN 1014-384X)

338.1 **UN** **ISSN 0259-2495**
F A O FERTILIZER AND PLANT NUTRITION BULLETIN. Spanish edition: Boletin F A O, Fertilizantes y Nutricion Vegetal (ISSN 1014-4072); French edition: Bulletin F A O, Engrais et Nutrition Vegetale (ISSN 0259-6180) irreg., no.11, 1988. price varies. Food and Agriculture Organization of the United Nations, Bernan Associates, 4611-F Assembly Dr., Lanham, MD 20706-4391. TEL 301-459-7666. FAX 301-459-0056. **Indexed:** Geo.Abstr., Soils & Fert., Weed Abstr. **Document type:** monographic series.
Formerly (until 1981): F A O Fertilizer Bulletin (ISSN 0254-5764)

338.1 338.91 **UN** **ISSN 1011-5366**
F A O INVESTMENT CENTRE TECHNICAL PAPER. French edition: F A O Document Technique du Centre d'Investissement (ISSN 0259-627X); Spanish edition: F A O Documento Tecnico del Centro de Inversiones (ISSN 1014-3084) (Text in English) 1985. irreg. Food and Agriculture Organization of the United Nations (Rome), Via delle Terme di Caracalla, 00100 Rome, Italy. TEL 5794350. FAX 57974608.
—BLDSC (3865.683300).

338.1 **UN** **ISSN 0071-7118**
HD1421
F A O PRODUCTION YEARBOOK. (Text in English, French and Spanish) 1958. a. $50. Food and Agriculture Organization of the United Nations, Bernan Associates, 4611-F Assembly Dr., Lanham, MD 20706-4391. TEL 301-459-7666. FAX 301-459-0056. (also avail. in microfiche from CIS) **Indexed:** Dairy Sci.Abstr., Food Sci.& Tech.Abstr., Hort.Abstr., IIS, Nutr.Abstr., Soils & Fert.
Formerly (until 1958): Food and Agriculture Organization of the United Nations. Production Yearbook (ISSN 0378-0775)

AGRICULTURE — AGRICULTURAL ECONOMICS

338.1 382 UN ISSN 1014-7632
HD9000.4
F A O YEARBOOK, TRADE. (Text in English, French and Spanish) 1947. a. $45. Food and Agriculture Organization of the United Nations, Bernan Associates, 4611-F Assembly Dr., Lanham, MD 20706-4391. TEL 301-459-7666. FAX 301-459-0056. (also avail. in microfiche from CIS) **Indexed:** Anim.Breed.Abstr., Dairy Sci.Abstr., Hort.Abstr., IIS.
—BLDSC (3865.749350).
Former titles: Food and Agriculture Organization of the United Nations. Trade Yearbook (ISSN 0071-7126); Yearbook of Food and Agricultural Statistics (ISSN 0378-3898)

338.1 US
F C A BULLETIN. 1986. m. free. Farm Credit Administration, Office of Congressional & Public Affairs, 1501 Farm Credit Dr., McLean, VA 22102-5090. TEL 703-883-4056. FAX 703-883-4066. Ed. Christine Quinn. circ. 3,000. **Document type:** government publication.
Description: Presents news and information on regulatory matters and legislation pertaining to the activities of the Farm Credit Administration, which examines and regulates Farm Credit System institutions.

338.1 US ISSN 1076-3856
F M R A NEWS. 1955. bi-m. $24. American Society of Farm Managers and Rural Appraisers, 950 S. Cherry St., Ste. 508, Denver, CO 80222-2664. TEL 303-758-3513. FAX 303-758-0190. E-mail: asfmra@aol.com. Ed. Alan L. Yoder. circ. 3,500.
Description: Contains articles of interest to agricultural consultants, farm managers, rural appraisers, and other agricultural professionals.
Refereed Serial

338.1 US
FARM BUSINESS MANAGEMENT ANALYSIS REPORT; annual report for North East and East Central Minnesota. 1955. a. $5. Central Lakes College, 1830 Airport Rd., Staples, MN 56479. TEL 218-894-1053. Ed. DelRay D. Lecy. charts; index. circ. 1,200. **Document type:** academic/scholarly publication.
Formerly: Farm Business Management.
Description: Record summary of farmers enrolled in farm business management education programs.

332.71 338.1 334 US
FARM CREDIT ADMINISTRATION. ANNUAL REPORT. 1933. a. free. Farm Credit Administration, Office of Congressional & Public Affairs, 1501 Farm Credit Dr., McLean, VA 22102-5090. TEL 703-883-4056. FAX 703-883-4066. Ed. Christine Quinn. circ. 5,000. **Document type:** government publication.
Former titles (until 1984): U.S. Farm Credit Administration. Annual Report of the Farm Credit Administration and the Cooperative Farm Credit System; U.S. Farm Credit Administration. Annual Report of the Farm Credit Administration on the Work of the Cooperative Farm Credit System (ISSN 0083-0542)
Description: Provides statistical information on and analysis of the yearly activities of the FCA and the financial condition of the Farm Credit System institutions, which are examined and regulated by the FCA.

338.1 US
FARM INCOME. a. free. Agricultural Statistics Service, Box 27767, 2 W. Edenton St., Raleigh, NC 27611. TEL 919-755-4394. Ed. Becky Meadows. circ. 1,500. **Document type:** government publication, bulletin.

338.1 336.1 US ISSN 1053-6086
KF6369.8.F3
FARM INCOME TAX MANUAL. 1954. a. $90 (effective 1995). Michie Company, Box 7587, Charlottesville, VA 22906-7587. TEL 804-972-7600.

338.1 UN ISSN 0430-084X
FARM MANAGEMENT NOTES FOR ASIA AND THE FAR EAST. 1965. biennial. free. Food and Agriculture Organization of the United Nations, Regional Office for Asia and the Pacific, Commission on Farm Management for Asia and the Far East, Maliwan Mansion, Phra Atit Rd., Bangkok 2, Thailand. circ. 300.

338.1 UK
FARM MANAGEMENT POCKETBOOK. a. £8. University of London, Wye College, Department of Agricultural Economics, Ashford, Kent TN25 5AH, England. TEL 44-1233-812401. **Document type:** academic/scholarly publication, monographic series.

FARM TAX BRIEF; practical guidance on effective tax planning and the law relating to agricultural land. *see* BUSINESS AND ECONOMICS — Public Finance, Taxation

338.1 US
FARM TAX SAVER. 1975. m. $50. Farm Progress Companies (Subsidiary of: A B C Publishing, Inc.), 191 S. Gary Ave., Carol Stream, IL 60188. TEL 708-690-5600. FAX 708-462-2869. Ed. Trenna Grabowski; Pub. Allan Johnson. circ. 3,200. (back issues avail.) **Document type:** newsletter.
Description: Informs on new and existing tax laws of interest to farmers and agriculturists.

338.1 US ISSN 1049-393X
FARMING. 1957. bi-m. free to qualified personnel. Farming Magazine, 43 So. Water St. E., Fort Atkinson, WI 53508. TEL 414-563-9500. adv.; circ. 600,000 (controlled).
Description: Provides farm operators with financial management information.

338.1 UK
FARMING IN THE EAST MIDLANDS. FINANCIAL RESULTS. 1948. a. University of Nottingham, Rural Business Research Unit, Sutton Bonington Campus, Loughborough LE12 5RD, England. TEL 44-115-951-6070. FAX 44-115-951-6089. E-mail: sazmfs@szni.nottingham.ac.uk. Ed. Martin Seabrook. circ. 600. **Document type:** bulletin.

FEDERAL RESERVE BANK OF MINNEAPOLIS. AGRICULTURAL CREDIT CONDITIONS SURVEY. *see* BUSINESS AND ECONOMICS — Banking And Finance

FEED INDUSTRY REVIEW; a structural and financial analysis of the UK and European animal feed industries. *see* AGRICULTURE — Feed, Flour And Grain

338.1 631.8 US
FERTILIZER FINANCIAL FACTS & PRODUCTION COST SURVEY; industry production costs, financial data. a. $400 (effective 1997). Fertilizer Institute, 501 Second St., N.E., Washington, DC 20002. TEL 202-675-8250. FAX 202-544-8123. circ. 600. **Document type:** trade publication.
Description: Provides financial data and production cost estimates for the fertilizer industry.

338.1 631.8 US
FERTILIZER RECORD. m. $500 (effective 1997). Fertilizer Institute, 501 Second Ave., N.E., Washington, DC 20002. TEL 202-675-8250. FAX 202-544-8123. circ. 700. **Document type:** trade publication.
Description: Monthly production inventory package.

FINANCIELE POSITIE VAN DE LANDBOUW; boekjaar en vergelijkingen met voorgaande jaren. *see* AGRICULTURE

DE FINANCIELE POSITIE VAN DE TUINBOUW. *see* AGRICULTURE — Abstracting, Bibliographies, Statistics

FOOD AID NEEDS ASSESSMENT REPORT. *see* BUSINESS AND ECONOMICS — International Development And Assistance

338.1 382 US ISSN 0083-0976
FOOD AND AGRICULTURAL EXPORT DIRECTORY. 1972. biennial. free. U.S. Department of Agriculture, Foreign Agricultural Service, Information Division, Rm. 5920-S, Washington, DC 20250-1000. TEL 202-720-7937. (Avail. from Supt. of Documents, U.S. Government Printing Office, Washington, DC 20402. TEL 202-783-3238. FAX 202-512-2233) adv.; bk.rev.; circ. 10,000 (controlled). **Document type:** government publication, directory.

338.1 PH
FOOD BALANCE SHEET OF THE PHILIPPINES. a., latest 1993. $22 in Asia (Australia & New Zealand $28; US & Canada $32; Europe $36; Latin America $42; elsewhere $45). National Statistical Coordination Board, c/o National Statistical Information Center, Midland-Buendia Bldg., 403 Sen. Gil Puyat Ave., Makati City, Philippines. TEL 63-2-890-9405. FAX 63-2-890-9408. E-mail: nscb___nsic@mozcom.com. stat. (processed) **Document type:** government publication.
Former titles: Philippine Food Balance Sheet; Philippines. National Economic and Development Authority. Food Balance Series.
Description: Provides quantitative information on the national food supply situation. Shows trends in food production, changing patterns, flows, and the net supply of food in the country.

338.1 US ISSN 1047-0441
HD1751
FOOD COST REVIEW. 1983. a. U.S. Department of Agriculture, Economic Research Service, c/o Debbie Haugan, Rm. 110, 1301 New York Ave., N.W., Washington, DC 20005-4788. TEL 202-219-0515. (Dist. by: ERS-NASS, 341 Victory Dr., Herndon, VA 22070. TEL 800-999-6779) **Document type:** government publication.
Formerly: Developments in Farm to Retail Price Spreads for Food Products (ISSN 0741-0174)

338.1 UK ISSN 0306-9192
HD9000.1
FOOD POLICY. 1976. bi-m. fl.1022($588) (effective 1998). Elsevier Science Ltd., Pergamon, P.O. Box 800, Kidlington, Oxford OX5 1DX, England. TEL 44-1865-843000. FAX 44-1865-843010. TELEX 83111 BHPOXF G. E-mail: nlinfo-f@elsevier.nl; usinfo-f@elsevier.com; forinfo-kyf04035@niftyserve.or.jp; URL: http://www.elsevier.nl/. (Subscr. to: Elsevier Science, Regional Sales Office, P.O. Box 211, 1000 AE Amsterdam, Netherlands. TEL 31-20-4853757. FAX 31-20-4853432; Subscr. in the Americas to: Elsevier Science, Regional Sales Office, Box 945, New York, NY 10159-0945. TEL 212-633-3730. FAX 212-633-3680; Subscr. in Australasia and the Far East to: Elsevier Science (Singapore) Pte Ltd, No.1 Temasek, No.17-01 Millenia Tower, Singapore 039192, Singapore. TEL 65-434-3727. FAX 65-337-2230) Ed. Penny Street. adv.; bk.rev.; index. (also avail. in microform from UMI; back issues avail.) **Indexed:** Abstr.Rural Dev.Trop., ASCA, Asian-Pac.Econ.Lit., Asian-Pac.Econ.Lit., Bibl.Agri., Biol.& Agr.Ind., C.R.E.J., Curr.Cont., Dairy Sci.Abstr., Documentatieblad, E.I., Energy Ind., Energy Info.Abstr., Environ.Abstr., Environ.Per.Bibl. (1978-), Food Sci.& Tech.Abstr., Fut.Surv., Geo.Abstr.H.G., IDA, Ind.Sci.Rev., Key to Econ.Sci., Maize Abstr., Nutr.Abstr., P.A.I.S., Rice Abstr., Risk Abstr., Rural Devel.Abstr., Rural Ext.Educ.& Tr.Abstr., Sci.Cit.Ind., Soils & Fert., Sorghum & Millets Abstr., Soyabean Abstr., SSCI, Triticale Abstr., Trop.Oil Seeds Abstr., World Agri.Econ.& Rural Sociol.Abstr. **Document type:** academic/scholarly publication.
—BLDSC (3981.780000); CIS; Genuine Article; KR SourceOne; SWETS; UMI; UnCover. **CCC**.
Description: Focuses on the politics, economics and planning aspects of food, agriculture and nutrition. International in scope.
Refereed Serial

338.1 341 UK ISSN 0778-7065
FOOD POLICY INTERNATIONAL. m. £247 (rest of Europe £252; elsewhere £275) (effective 1997). Agra Europe (London) Ltd., 25 Frant Rd., Tunbridge Wells, Kent TN2 5JT, England. TEL 44-1892-533813. FAX 44-1892-544895. TELEX 95114 AGRATW G. E-mail: 100637.340@compuserve.com. **Document type:** trade publication.
Description: Contains strategic briefings on European and international policy developments for senior agribusiness executives.

AGRICULTURE — AGRICULTURAL ECONOMICS

382.41 338.1   US   ISSN 0046-4546
HD9001
FOREIGN AGRICULTURAL TRADE OF THE UNITED STATES. s-a. $30 (foreign $37.50) (subscr. includes fiscal and calendar year supplement). U.S. Department of Agriculture, Economic Research Service, c/o Debbie Haugan, Rm. 110, 1301 New York Ave., N.W., Washington, DC 20005-4788. TEL 202-219-0512; 800-999-6779. (Dist. by: ERS-NASS, 341 Victory Dr., Herndon, VA 22070. TEL 202-512-1800. FAX 202-512-2250) Ed. Thomas Warden. stat. circ. 1,700. (also avail. in microfiche from UPD,CIS; reprint service avail. from CIS) **Indexed:** Amer.Stat.Ind. (1974-), Mid.East: Abstr.& Ind., PROMT, World Agri.Econ.& Rural Sociol.Abstr. **Document type:** government publication.
   Description: Contains quantity and value of U.S. farm exports and imports, plus price trends.

FRANCE. CAISSE NATIONALE DE CREDIT AGRICOLE. RAPPORT SUR LE CREDIT AGRICOLE MUTUEL. see BUSINESS AND ECONOMICS — Banking And Finance

338.1   FR
HD9323.1
FRANCE. MINISTERE DE L'AGRICULTURE, DE LA PECHE ET DE L'ALIMENTATION. AGRESTE PRIMEUR. 1974. irreg. 200 F. (foreign 230 F.) (effective 1997). Ministere de l'Agriculture, de la Peche et de l'Alimentation, Service Central des Enquetes et Etudes Statistiques, 4 av. de Saint Mande, 75570 Paris Cedex 12, France. TEL 33-1-49558585. FAX 33-1-49558503. (Subscr. to: B.P. 88, 31326 Castanet Tolosan Cedex, France) **Document type:** government publication.
   Formerly: France. Ministere de l'Agriculture et de la Foret. Donnees; Incorporates in part: France. Ministere de l'Agriculture. Series "S". Industries Agricoles et Alimentaires (ISSN 0243-6647); France. Ministere de l'Agriculture. Note de Conjoncture Production Vegetale (ISSN 0243-6248)

338.1   FR   ISSN 1274-1086
FRANCE. MINISTERE DE L'AGRICULTURE, DE LA PECHE ET DE L'ALIMENTATION. CONJONCTURE. 1979. m. 440 F. (foreign 520 F.) (effective 1997). Ministere de l'Agriculture, de la Peche et de l'Alimentation, Service Central des Enquetes et Etudes Statistiques, 4 av. Saint Mande, 75570 Paris Cedex 12, France. TEL 33-1-49558585. FAX 33-1-49558503. (Subscr. to: B.P. 88, 31326 Castanet Tolosan Cedex, France) **Document type:** government publication.
   Former titles (until 1995): France. Ministere de l'Agriculture et de la Foret. Conjoncture Generale (ISSN 0998-416X); (until 1990): France. Ministere de l'Agriculture. Situation Agricole en France. Conjoncture Generale (ISSN 0222-5220)

338.1   FR
FRANCE. MINISTERE DE L'AGRICULTURE, DE LA PECHE ET DE L'ALIMENTATION. CONJONCTURE AVICULTURE. 1990. m. 370 F. (foreign 390 F.) (effective 1997). Ministere de l'Agriculture, de la Peche et de l'Alimentation, Service Central des Enquetes et Etudes Statistiques, 14 av. de Saint Mande, 75570 Paris Cedex 12, France. TEL 33-1-49558585. FAX 33-1-49558503. (Subscr. to: B.P. 88, 31326 Castanet Tolosan Cedex, France) **Document type:** government publication.
   Formerly: France. Ministere de l'Agriculture et de la Foret. Agreste. La Statistique Agricole. Series Aviculture (ISSN 1150-1529); Which was formed by the merger of (1980-1990): France. Ministere de l'Agriculture. Informations Rapides. Secteur Avicole (ISSN 0223-4920); Which was formerly (1977-1980): France. Ministere de l'Agriculture. Note Mensuelle. Secteur Avicole (ISSN 0243-6205); (1976-1990): France. Ministere de l'Agriculture. Situation Agricole en France. Note de Conjoncture Production Avicole (ISSN 0243-6183); Which was formerly (1973-1976): France. Ministere de l'Agriculture. Note Trimestrielle de Conjoncture Avicole (ISSN 0243-6191)

338.1   FR
FRANCE. MINISTERE DE L'AGRICULTURE, DE LA PECHE ET DE L'ALIMENTATION. CONJONCTURE ANIMAUX HEBDO. 1974. w. 717 F. (foreign 1025 F.) (effective 1997). Ministere de l'Agriculture, de la Peche et de l'Alimentation, Service Central des Enquetes et Etudes Statistiques, 4 av. de Saint Mande, 75570 Paris Cedex 12, France. TEL 33-1-49558585. FAX 33-1-49558503. (Subscr. by fax only. FAX 33-5-61288366) **Document type:** government publication.
   Incorporates: France. Ministere de l'Agriculture. Situation Agricole en France. Note de Conjoncture Production Bovine (ISSN 0243-6280) & France. Ministere de l'Agriculture. Situation Agricole en France. Note de Conjoncture Production Porcine (ISSN 0243-6175)

FRANCE. MINISTERE DE L'AGRICULTURE, DE LA PECHE ET DE L'ALIMENTATION. CONJONCTURE EXTERIEUR AGRO-ALIMENTAIRE. see BUSINESS AND ECONOMICS — International Commerce

338.1   FR
FRANCE. MINISTERE DE L'AGRICULTURE, DE LA PECHE ET DE L'ALIMENTATION. CONJONCTURE FRUITS. 1977. 7/yr. (m. May-Nov.). 184 F. (foreign 210 F.) (effective 1997). Ministere de l'Agriculture, de la Peche et de l'Alimentation, Service Central des Enquetes et Etudes Statistiques, 4 av. de Saint Mande, 75570 Paris Cedex 12, France. TEL 33-1-49558585. FAX 33-1-49558503. (Subscr. to: B.P. 88, 31326 Castanet Tolosan Cedex, France) **Document type:** government publication.
   Formerly: France. Ministere de l'Agriculture et de la Foret. Conjoncture Fruits; Incorporates in part: France. Ministere de l'Agriculture. Note de Conjoncture Production Vegetale (ISSN 0243-6248); **Formerly:** France. Ministere de l'Agriculture. Informations Rapides. Fruits (ISSN 0243-6108)

338.1   FR   ISSN 0242-2085
HD1941
FRANCE. MINISTERE DE L'AGRICULTURE, DE LA PECHE ET DE L'ALIMENTATION. CONJONCTURE GRAPH-AGRI; annuaire de graphiques agricoles. 1979. a. 130 F. (foreign 150 F.). Ministere de l'Agriculture, de la Peche et de l'Alimentation, Service Central des Enquetes et Etudes Statistiques, 4 av. de Saint Mande, 75570 Paris Cedex 12, France. TEL 33-1-49558585. FAX 33-1-49558503. **Document type:** government publication.

338.1   FR
FRANCE. MINISTERE DE L'AGRICULTURE, DE LA PECHE ET DE L'ALIMENTATION. CONJONCTURE GRANDES CULTURES. 1975. m. 148 F. (foreign 170 F.) (effective 1997). Ministere de l'Agriculture, de la Peche et de l'Alimentation, Service Central des Enquetes et Etudes Statistiques, 4 av. de Saint Mande, 75570 Paris Cedex 12, France. TEL 33-1-49558585. FAX 33-1-49558503. (Subscr. to: B.P. 88, 31326 Castanet Tolosan Cedex, France) **Document type:** government publication.
   Formerly: France. Ministere de l'Agriculture et de la Foret. Conjoncture Grandes Cultures; Incorporates in part: France. Ministere de l'Agriculture. Note de Conjoncture Production Vegetale (ISSN 0243-6248)
   Description: Contains statistics on agricultural production in France.

338.1   FR
FRANCE. MINISTERE DE L'AGRICULTURE, DE LA PECHE ET DE L'ALIMENTATION. CONJONCTURE LEGUMES. 1977. m. 316 F. (foreign 340 F.) (effective 1997). Ministere de l'Agriculture, de la Peche et de l'Alimentation, Service Central des Enquetes et Etudes Statistiques, 4 av. de Saint Mande, 75570 Paris Cedex 12, France. TEL 33-1-49558585. FAX 33-1-45558503. (Subscr. to: B.P. 88, 31326 Castanet Tolosan Cedex, France) **Document type:** government publication.
   Formerly: France. Ministere de l'Agriculture et de la Foret. Conjoncture Legumes; Incorporates in part: France. Ministere de l'Agriculture. Note de Conjoncture Production Vegetale (ISSN 0243-6248); **Formerly:** France. Ministere de l'Agriculture. Informations Rapides. Legumes (ISSN 0243-6140)

FRANCE. MINISTERE DE L'AGRICULTURE, DE LA PECHE ET DE L'ALIMENTATION. CONJONCTURE LAIT ET PRODUITS LAITIERS. see AGRICULTURE — Abstracting, Bibliographies, Statistics

338.1   FR
FRANCE. MINISTERE DE L'AGRICULTURE, DE LA PECHE ET DE L'ALIMENTATION. CONJONCTURE PRODUCTIONS ANIMALES. 1977. irreg. 148 F. (foreign 165 F.) for 10 nos. (effective 1997). Ministere de l'Agriculture, de la Peche et de l'Alimentation, Service Central des Enquetes et Etudes Statistiques, 4 av. de Saint Mande, 75570 Paris Cedex 12, France. TEL 33-1-49558585. FAX 33-1-49558503. (Subscr. to: B.P. 88, 31326 Castanet Tolosan Cedex, France) **Document type:** government publication.
   Former titles: France. Ministere de l'Agriculture et de la Foret. Conjoncture Productions Animales; France. Ministere de l'Agriculture. Informations Rapides. Production Animale (ISSN 0223-4912)

338.1   FR
FRANCE. MINISTERE DE L'AGRICULTURE, DE LA PECHE ET DE L'ALIMENTATION. CONJONCTURE VITICULTURE. 1978. 5/yr. (m. July-Nov.). 74 F. (foreign 77 F.) (effective 1997). Ministere de l'Agriculture, de la Peche et de l'Alimentation, Service Central des Enquetes et Etudes Statistiques, 4 av. de Saint Mande, 75570 Paris Cedex 12, France. TEL 33-1-49558585. FAX 33-1-49558503. (Subscr. to: B.P. 88, 31326 Castanet Tolosan Cedex, France) **Document type:** government publication.
   Former titles: France. Ministere de l'Agriculture et de la Foret. Conjoncture Viticulture; France. Ministere de l'Agriculture. Informations Rapides. Viticulture.

FRANCE. MINISTERE DE L'AGRICULTURE, DE LA PECHE ET DE L'ALIMENTATION. DONNEES CHIFFRES AGRICULTURE. see AGRICULTURE — Abstracting, Bibliographies, Statistics

FRANCE. MINISTERE DE L'AGRICULTURE, DE LA PECHE ET DE L'ALIMENTATION. DONNEES CHIFFRES. I A A. see AGRICULTURE — Abstracting, Bibliographies, Statistics

338.1   FR
FRANCE. MINISTERE DE L'AGRICULTURE, DE LA PECHE ET DE L'ALIMENTATION. SERIE COMMERCE EXTERIEUR BOIS ET DERIVES. 1981. q. 108 F. (foreign 134 F.) (effective 1997). Ministere de l'Agriculture, de la Peche et de l'Alimentation, Service Central des Enquetes et Etudes Statistiques, 4 av. de Saint Mande, 75570 Paris Cedex 12, France. TEL 33-1-49558585. FAX 33-1-49558503. (Subscr. to: B.P. 88, 31326 Castanet Tolosan Cedex, France) **Document type:** government publication.
   Former titles: France. Ministere de l'Agriculture et de la Foret. Serie Commerce Exterieur Bois et Derives; France. Ministere de l'Agriculture. Serie Commerce Exterieur Bois et Derives; France. Ministere de l'Agriculture. Situation Agricole en France. Commerce Exterieur Bois et Derives (ISSN 0243-8283)

338.1 633   US
FRESH FRUIT AND VEGETABLE MARKET NEWS: WEEKLY SUMMARY, SHIPMENTS - ARRIVALS. w. $8 (foreign $16). U.S. Department of Agriculture, Agricultural Marketing Division, Fruit and Vegetable Division, Washington, DC 20250. TEL 202-720-2175.
   Formerly: Fresh Fruit and Vegetable Market News: Weekly Summary, Shipments, Unloads (ISSN 0094-4858)

338.1 634   US
FRUIT AND VEGETABLE TRUCK RATE AND COST SUMMARY. 1975. a. $10. Federal-State Market News Service, 630 Sansome St., Rm. 727, San Francisco, CA 94111. TEL 415-705-1300. FAX 415-705-1301. (looseleaf format; back issues avail.) **Document type:** government publication, newsletter.
   Former titles: Fruit and Vegetable Truck Rate; Fruit and Vegetable Truck Rate and Cost Summary.
   Description: Presents lists of price ranges for, and the cost components and availability of, truck transportation for hauling produce, for all areas of the United States.

AGRICULTURE — AGRICULTURAL ECONOMICS

388.1 634   US
FRUIT AND VEGETABLE TRUCK RATE REPORT.
(Supplement included: Truck Cost Report) 1978. w. (plus m. supplement). $96 (foreign $132) (includes supplement). (U.S. Department of Agriculture) Federal-State Market News Service, 630 Sansome St., Rm. 727, San Francisco, CA 94111. TEL 415-705-1300. FAX 415-705-1301. circ. 120. (also avail. in microfiche from CIS; back issues avail.; reprint service avail. from CIS) **Indexed:** Amer.Stat.Ind. (1979-). **Document type:** government publication.
Description: Provides information on rates for shipping loads of selected produce items to various U.S. cities. Also includes a section on the volume of shipments in the U.S., as compared to the previous week and the previous year.

338.1   GM   ISSN 0301-8423
GAMBIA. PRODUCE MARKETING BOARD. ANNUAL REPORT. 1971. a. free. Produce Marketing Board, P.O. Box 284, Marina Foreshore, Banjul, Gambia. illus. **Document type:** corporate report, government publication.
Formerly: Gambia. Oilseeds Marketing Board. Report.

338.1   US
GIANNINI FOUNDATION OF AGRICULTURAL ECONOMICS. INFORMATION SERIES. 1964. irreg., no.96-1, 1996. free. University of California at Berkeley, Giannini Foundation of Agricultural Economics, 207 Giannini Hall, Ste. 3310, Berkeley, CA 94720-3310. TEL 510-642-7121. (Subscr. to: University of California, Agriculture and Natural Resources Publications, 6701 San Pablo Ave., Oakland, CA 94608) Ed. Peter Berck. R&P contact: Robert SAms. TEL 916-754-8539. **Document type:** monographic series.
Formerly: Information Series on Agricultural Economics (ISSN 0073-7887)

338.1   US   ISSN 0575-4208
GIANNINI FOUNDATION OF AGRICULTURAL ECONOMICS. MONOGRAPH. no.10, 1961. irreg., no.42, 1995. free. University of California at Berkeley, Giannini Foundation of Agricultural Economics, 207 Giannini Hall, Ste. 3310, Berkeley, CA 94720-3310. TEL 510-642-7121. (Subscr. to: University of California, Agriculture and Natural Resources Publications, 6701 San Pablo Ave., Oakland, CA 94608) Ed. Peter Berck. R&P contact: Robert Sams. TEL 916-754-8539. **Indexed:** Soils & Fert., Triticale Abstr., World Agri.Econ.& Rural Sociol.Abstr. **Document type:** monographic series.
—BLDSC (4169.300000).

338.1   US   ISSN 0072-4459
HD1759
GIANNINI FOUNDATION OF AGRICULTURAL ECONOMICS. RESEARCH REPORT. 1930. irreg., no.343, 1995. free. University of California at Berkeley, Giannini Foundation of Agricultural Economics, 207 Giannini Hall, Ste. 3310, Berkeley, CA 94720-3310. TEL 510-642-7121. (Subscr. to: University of California, Agriculture and Natural Resources Publications, 6701 San Pablo Ave., Oakland CA 94608) Ed. Peter Berck. R&P contact: Robert Sams. TEL 916-754-8539. **Indexed:** World Agri.Econ.& Rural Sociol.Abstr. **Document type:** monographic series.

338.1 600   CN   ISSN 0834-2660
GLOBAL LINK. (Text in English and French) 1979. 3/yr. Canadian Hunger Foundation, 323 Chapel St., Ottawa, ON K1N 7Z2, Canada. TEL 613-237-0180. FAX 613-237-5969. Ed. Ariella Hostetter. bk.rev. circ. 10,000. (tabloid format) **Document type:** newsletter.
Formerly (until 1986): Thought for Food (ISSN 0715-7320).

338.1   SP   ISSN 0211-867X
GONDOLA; revista tecnica del comercio, distribucion y consumo. 1980. m. 7000 ptas. Editorial de Medios Tecnicos de Expresion, S.A., Comercio, 4, Estrella San Roma, 28007 Madrid, Spain. TEL 1-433-67-50. FAX 1-433-88-74. Ed. Javier Perez Serna.

338.1   UK
▼**GOOD PRACTICE IN RURAL DEVELOPMENT.** 1997. irreg. Stationery Office Bookstore, 21 S. Gyle Crescent, Edinburgh, Scotland. TEL 44-131-479-3141. FAX 44-131-479-3142. **Document type:** monographic series.

630 658.8   UK   ISSN 0963-1682
GREEN PAGES; the directory of agriculture in the U.K. 1990. a. £16 (foreign £24). Geraldine Flower Publications, 192 Acton Ln., London W4 5DL, England. TEL 0181-747-8028. FAX 0181-747-8054. Ed. Geraldine Flower. R&P contact: Geraldine Flower. adv. contact: Geraldine Flower. circ. 20,000 (paid). **Document type:** directory.
●Also available on CD-ROM.
Description: Lists manufacturers and suppliers of agricultural equipment and supplies.

338.1   AU
GRUENER BERICHT. 1959. a. free. Bundesministerium fuer Land- und Forstwirtschaft, Stubenring 1, A-1010 Vienna, Austria. TEL 43-1-711006753. FAX 43-1-711002127. circ. 3,100. **Indexed:** Nutr.Abstr. **Document type:** government publication.
Formerly: Bericht ueber die Lage der Oesterreichischen Landwirtschaft.

338.1   GT
GUATEMALA. BANCO NACIONAL DE DESARROLLO AGRICOLA. MEMORIA. Abbreviated title: Banadesa. 1971. a. Banco Nacional de Desarrollo Agricola, 9 Calle No. 9-47, Zona 1, Guatemala, Guatemala. stat.

338.1 636   GW   ISSN 0723-7383
HANDBUCH DER TIERISCHEN VEREDLUNG. 1974. a. DM.39.50. Kamlage Verlag GmbH, Iburgerstr. 112, 49082 Osnabrueck, Germany. TEL 49-541-52371. FAX 49-541-54879. Ed. Barbara Kamlage. R&P contact: Barbara Kamlage. adv.: page DM.3985; trim 95 x 150; adv. contact: Barbara Kamlage. circ. 40,000 (paid). (back issues avail.) **Document type:** trade publication.
—BLDSC (4254.539500).

HAY & FORAGE GROWER. see AGRICULTURE — Feed, Flour And Grain

381.41 635.53   US   ISSN 0744-1517
HAY MARKET NEWS. w. $99. (Department of Food and Agriculture) Federal-State Market News Service (Sacramento), 1220 N St., Rm. A-247, Box 942871, Sacramento, CA 94271-0001. TEL 916-654-0298. FAX 916-654-1046. (also avail. in microfiche from CIS; reprint service avail. from CIS) **Indexed:** Amer.Stat.Ind. (1984-). **Document type:** government publication.
Description: Covers California, Arizona, Utah, Nevada and Washington hay prices and market situation.

381.41 635.53   US
HAY MARKET NEWS - NATIONAL. w. $70 (Canada and Mexico $75; elsewhere $105). (U.S. Department of Agriculture, Agricultural Marketing Service, Livestock & Seed Division) Market News, 210 Walnut St., Rm. 767, Des Moines, IA 50309. **Document type:** government publication.

HELADERIA INTERNACIONAL; revista profesional de heladeria y afines. see FOOD AND FOOD INDUSTRIES — Bakers And Confectioners

338.1 638.1   US   ISSN 0364-2054
HONEY MARKET NEWS. m. $36 (foreign $72) (effective 1997). U.S. Department of Agriculture, Agricultural Marketing Service (Yakima), Honey Market News, Fruit and Vegetable Division, 2015 S. First St., Rm. 4, Yakima, WA 98903. TEL 509-575-2494. FAX 509-457-7132. Pub. Linda Verstrate. **Indexed:** Amer.Stat.Ind. (1974-). **Document type:** government publication, newsletter.
Description: Covers bee culture.

338.1   US   ISSN 1075-9255
HORIZONS (BLACKSBURG). 1931. bi-m. free. Rural Economic Analysis Program, Department of Agricultural and Applied Economics, Virginia Tech, Blacksburg, VA 24061-0401. TEL 540-231-9443. FAX 540-231-7417. Ed. Karen Mundy. R&P contact: Karen Mundy. stat. circ. 3,000. **Indexed:** Energy Ind., Energy Info.Abstr. (until 1994). **Document type:** newsletter.
—Linda Hall.
Former titles (until 1989): Virginia Agricultural Economics (ISSN 0042-6466); Virginia Farm Economics.
Description: Covers a broad range of topics related to rural and agricultural economies and communities and to the natural resource base of rural and agricultural areas.

I C A S A NEWS. (International Consortium for Agricultural Systems Applications (ICASA)) see AGRICULTURE — Crop Production And Soil

I C C O QUARTERLY BULLETIN OF COCOA STATISTICS. (International Cocoa Organization) see FOOD AND FOOD INDUSTRIES

I C C O WORLD COCOA DIRECTORY. (International Cocoa Organization) see FOOD AND FOOD INDUSTRIES

338.1   GW   ISSN 0081-7198
I F O STUDIEN ZUR AGRARWIRTSCHAFT. 1967. irreg., no.31, 1995. price varies. I F O Institut fuer Wirtschaftsforschung, Poschingerstr. 5, 81679 Munich, Germany. TEL 49-89-9224-0. FAX 49-89-985369. circ. 400. **Indexed:** Rural Recreat.Tour.Abstr., World Agri.Econ.& Rural Sociol.Abstr. **Document type:** monographic series.
—Linda Hall.
Description: Presents research results of the Department of Agriculture.

338.1   US
I F P R I REPORT. (Text in English, French, Spanish) 1979. q. free. International Food Policy Research Institute, 1200 17th St., N.W., Washington, DC 20036. TEL 202-862-5600. FAX 202-467-4439. TELEX 440054. Ed. Barbara Rose. circ. 7,000. (back issues avail.) **Document type:** newsletter.

338.1 664   US
I F P R I RESEARCH REPORT. (Abstracts in English, French, Spanish) 1976. irreg. (approx. 7/yr.). free. International Food Policy Research Institute, 1200 17th St., N.W., Washington, DC 20036. TEL 202-862-5600. FAX 202-467-4439. TELEX 440054. Ed. Barbara Rose. bibl.; charts; illus.; stat. circ. 3,000. (also avail. in microfiche from NTI; back issues avail.) **Indexed:** Abstr.Rural Dev.Trop., Dairy Sci.Abstr., Geo.Abstr.P.G., IDA, Rural Devel.Abstr., World Agri.Econ.& Rural Sociol.Abstr. **Document type:** academic/scholarly publication.
Description: Research on food policy for developing countries.

338.1 300   FR   ISSN 0988-3266
I N R A SCIENCES SOCIALES. 1988. bi-m. 140 F. (foreign 170 F.) (effective 1996 & 1997); newsstand price: 30 F. Institut National de la Recherche Agronomique, Departement d'Economie et Sociologie Rurales, 63-65 bvd. de Brandebourg, 94205 Ivry Cedex, France. TEL 49-59-69-00. FAX 46-70-41-13. E-mail: velt3@ivry.inra.fr. (Subscr. to: INRA Editions, Route de St. Cyr, 78026 Versailles Cedex, France) Ed. Gerard Buttoud. stat. circ. 1,500. **Document type:** newsletter.
Description: Publishes the essentials of the department's research results for professionals in farming, the agro-food industries, teaching, research and technical journalism.

338.1   II   ISSN 0019-5014
HD101
INDIAN JOURNAL OF AGRICULTURAL ECONOMICS. (Supplement avail.: Conference Annual) (Text in English) 1940. q. Rs.125($50) to individuals; institutions Rs.250($80). Indian Society of Agricultural Economics, 46-48 Esplanade Mansion, Mahatma Gandhi Road, Fort, Mumbai 400 001, India. TEL 91-22-2842542. Ed. N.A. Mujumdar. R&P contact: Tara Shukla. adv.; bk.rev.; charts; stat.; index. circ. 1,800. **Indexed:** Abstr.Rural Dev.Trop., Agroforest Abstr., Cott.& Trop.Fibr.Abstr., Curr.Cont., Dairy Sci.Abstr., Food Sci.& Tech.Abstr., Geo.Abstr.H.G., IDA, Int.Lab.Doc., Irr.& Drain.Abstr., Pub.Admin.Abstr., Rice Abstr., Rural Devel.Abstr., Rural Recreat.Tour.Abstr., Soils & Fert., Triticale Abstr., Trop.Oil Seeds Abstr., World Agri.Econ.& Rural Sociol.Abstr. **Document type:** academic/scholarly publication.
—BLDSC (4409.950000); SWETS; UnCover.
Description: Features agricultural and rural development, growth rates in agriculture, dry farming, poverty and income, forestry, livestock, fisheries, and agricultural price policy.

338.1   CU   ISSN 0138-7480
INFORMACION EXPRESS. SERIE: ECONOMIA Y ORGANIZACION DEL TRABAJO AGROPECUARIO. 1977. 2/yr. $5 in N. America; S. America and Europe $6; elsewhere $9; or exchange basis. Centro de Informacion y Documentacion Agropecuario, Gaveta Postal 4149, Havana 4, Cuba. (Dist. by: Ediciones Cubanas, Obispo No. 527, Apdo. 605, Havana, Cuba) **Indexed:** Agrindex.

AGRICULTURE — AGRICULTURAL ECONOMICS

338.1   EI   ISSN 0073-7895
INFORMATION SERVICE OF THE EUROPEAN COMMUNITIES. NEWSLETTER ON THE COMMON AGRICULTURAL POLICY. irreg. (approx. 20/yr.). Press and Information Service of the European Communities, 200 rue de la Loi, B-1049 Brussels, Belgium. **Document type:** newsletter.

338.1 338.9   CM
INSTITUT PANAFRICAIN POUR LE DEVELOPPEMENT. TRAVAUX MANUSCRITS. 1972. irreg. price varies. Institut Panafricain pour le Developpement, Centre de Documentation, B.P. 4078, Douala, Cameroon. circ. 200.

338.1 636.932   FR   ISSN 0398-8287
INSTITUT TECHNIQUE DE L'AVICULTURE. TENDANCES DES MARCHES. 1962. s-m. 1600 F. Institut Technique de l'Aviculture, 28 rue du Rocher, 75008 Paris, France. TEL 33-1-45226240. FAX 33-1-43874613. bk.rev. circ. 400. (looseleaf format; back issues avail.)

338.1   BL
INSTITUTO DE ECONOMIA AGRICOLA. INFORMACOES ECONOMICAS. 1966. m. $7. Instituto de Economia Agricola, Av. Miguel Stefano, 3900, Caixa Postal 6802, 04301-903 Sao Paulo, SP, Brazil. FAX 55-11-2764062. TELEX 011-56730. charts; stat.; circ. controlled. **Indexed:** Cott.& Trop.Fibr.Abstr., Field Crop Abstr., Hort.Abstr., Maize Abstr., Potato Abstr., Rural Recreat.Tour.Abstr., Soyabean Abstr., Triticale Abstr., World Agri.Econ.& Rural Sociol.Abstr.
—BLDSC (4481.130000).
Former titles: Mercados Agricolas; Instituto de Economia Agricola. Informacoes Economicas (ISSN 0100-4409)

338.1   NE   ISSN 0927-9113
INTERCAMBIO; cooperacion agraria mundial. (Text in Spanish) 1984. q. fl.20. Paulo Freire Stichting, Willemsplein 44-3, 6811 KD Arnhem, Netherlands. TEL 31-26-4455445. FAX 31-26-4455978. E-mail: pfs@antenna.nl. Ed. Jur Schuurman. adv.: page fl.500; trim 148 x 223; adv. contact: Jur Schuurman. bk.rev.
Description: Includes articles on rural development policy, to promote discussion, exchanges, and cooperation between peasants' organizations in industrialized and developing countries.

338.1   SZ   ISSN 0074-2856
INTERNATIONAL CONFEDERATION FOR AGRICULTURAL CREDIT. ASSEMBLY AND CONGRESS REPORTS.* 1951. irreg., 1973, 7th Congress, St. Louis, U.S.A. International Confederation for Agricultural Credit, Birmendorferstr. 67, CH-8004 Zurich, Switzerland. circ. 500.

338.13   UK   ISSN 0074-2902
HD1405
INTERNATIONAL CONFERENCE OF AGRICULTURAL ECONOMISTS. PROCEEDINGS. 1929. triennial, 18th, 1982, Jakarta, Indonesia. £55.95. (International Association of Agricultural Economists) Dartmouth Publishing Co. Ltd., Gower House, Croft Rd., Aldershot, Hants. GU11 3HR, England. Eds. John Irwin. R&P contact: Margaret O'Reilley. adv. contact: Jason Aldous. **Indexed:** World Agri.Econ.& Rural Sociol.Abstr. **Document type:** proceedings, academic/scholarly publication.
—SWETS.

338.1   US
▼**INTERNATIONAL FOOD AND AGRIBUSINESS MANAGEMENT REVIEW.** Announced for publication in 1998. q. $80 (foreign $100) to individuals; institutions $175 (foreign $195) (effective 1998). J A I Press Inc., 55 Old Post Rd., No. 2, Box 1678, Greenwich, CT 06830-1678. TEL 203-661-7602. FAX 203-661-0792. E-mail: jai@jaipress.com. (Subscr. in the UK and Europe to: JAI Press Ltd., 38 Tavistock St., Covent Garden, London WC2E 7PB, England. TEL 44-171-379-8834. FAX 44-171-379-8835) **Document type:** trade publication.

338.1 633   UK
INTERNATIONAL GRAINS COUNCIL. GRAIN MARKET REPORT. (Editions in English, French, Russian, Spanish) 1972. m. (11/yr.) £250($400) (effective Jul. 1996). International Grains Council, One Canada Sq., Canary Wharf, London E14 5AE, England. TEL 44-171-513-1122. FAX 44-171-513-0630. E-mail: igc-fac@int-grains-council.org.uk. charts; stat. **Indexed:** IIS, Maize Abstr., Rice Abstr., Rural Recreat.Tour.Abstr., Triticale Abstr., World Agri.Econ.& Rural Sociol.Abstr. **Document type:** trade publication.
Formerly: International Wheat Council. Grain Market Report.
Description: Contains comprehensive facts and figures on the current world market situation for wheat and coarse grains. Supplemented by analyses on matters of topical interest.

338.1   SP   ISSN 0213-635X
HD2021
INVESTIGACION AGRARIA. ECONOMIA. 1971. s-a. 6000 ptas. (foreign 9800 ptas.) (effective 1996). Ministerio de Agricultura, Pesca y Alimentacion, Instituto Nacional de Investigacion y Tecnologia Agraria y Alimentaria, Centro de Publicaciones, Paseo de la Infanta Isabel 1, 28071 Madrid, Spain. TEL 34-1-3475551. FAX 34-1-3475722. TELEX 48989 INIA E. (I.N.I.T.A.A. addr.: Jose Abascal, 56, 28003 Madrid, Spain) Ed. Luis M. Albisu. R&P contact: Juan carlos Palacios Lopez. **Indexed:** Food Sci.& Tech.Abstr., Ind.SST. **Document type:** academic/scholarly publication.
—BLDSC (4557.715500); CINDOC.
Formerly (until 1985): Spain. Instituto Nacional de Investigaciones Agrarias. Anales. Serie: Economia y Sociologia Agrarias (ISSN 0373-5796)

J D JOURNAL. (John Deere) see *AGRICULTURE — Agricultural Equipment*

JAPAN. HOKURIKU NATIONAL AGRICULTURAL EXPERIMENT STATION. BULLETIN. see *AGRICULTURE — Crop Production And Soil*

338.18   SW   ISSN 0021-7441
HD2016
JORDBRUKSEKONOMISKA MEDDELANDEN/JOURNAL OF AGRICULTURAL ECONOMICS. Abbreviated title: J E M. (Text in Swedish; titles and summaries in English) 1939. m. SEK 450. Statens Jordbruksverk, S-551 82 Joenkoeping, Sweden. TEL 46-36-15-50-00. FAX 46-36-71-51-14. Eds. Christer Wallinder, Eva Loefdahl. adv. contact: Eva Loefdahl. charts; mkt.; stat.; index. circ. 800. **Indexed:** Agri.Eng.Abstr., Arts & Hum.Cit.Ind., Curr.Cont., Dairy Sci.Abstr., Maize Abstr., Pig News & Info., Potato Abstr., Poult.Abstr., Rural Recreat.Tour.Abstr., SSCI, World Agri.Econ.& Rural Sociol.Abstr. **Document type:** consumer publication.
—BLDSC (4673.900000).
Formerly (until vol.7, 1950): Jordbruksekonomiska Uppgifter.

338.1   US   ISSN 1068-5502
HD1401
JOURNAL OF AGRICULTURAL & RESOURCE ECONOMICS. 1976. s-a. $40 (outside N. America $44) (effective 1998). Western Agricultural Economics Association, Utah State Univ., Economics Dept., Logan, UT 84322-3530. TEL 801-797-2294. FAX 801-797-2701. E-mail: bruceg@ext.usu.edu. Ed. Wade Brorsen. R&P contact: E. Bruce Godfrey. bk.rev. circ. 1,100. (back issues avail.) **Indexed:** ASCA, Curr.Cont., Curr.Cont., J.of Econ.Lit., Rural Recreat.Tour.Abstr., Soc.Sci.Ind., SSCI, World Agri.Econ.& Rural Sociol.Abstr. **Document type:** academic/scholarly publication.
—BLDSC (4920.150000); Genuine Article; UnCover.
Formerly (until 1992): Western Journal of Agricultural Economics (ISSN 0162-1912); Which superseded: Western Agricultural Economics Association. Proceedings.
Refereed Serial

338.1   UK   ISSN 0021-857X
HD1401   CODEN: JAGEA7
JOURNAL OF AGRICULTURAL ECONOMICS. 1928. 3/yr. £6. University of London, Wye College, Agricultural Economics Society, c/o Department of Agricultural Economics, Ashford, Kent TN25 5AH, England. TEL 44-1233-812401. Ed. D.I. Buteman. adv.; bk.rev.; bibl.; charts. **Indexed:** Agroforest.Abstr., Arts & Hum.Cit.Ind., Biol.& Agr.Ind., BPIA, C.R.E.J., Cott.& Trop.Fibr.Abstr., Curr.Cont., Dairy Sci.Abstr., Environ.Abstr., Food Sci.& Tech.Abstr., Geo.Abstr.P.G., IDA, Ind.Sci.Rev., J.of Econ.Lit., Maize Abstr., Nutr.Abstr., P.A.I.S., Potato Abstr., Poult.Abstr., RICS, Risk Abstr., Rural Devel.Abstr., Rural Recreat.Tour.Abstr., Sci.Cit.Ind., Soils & Fert., SSCI, Triticale Abstr., Trop.Oil Seeds Abstr., World Agri.Econ.& Rural Sociol.Abstr. **Document type:** academic/scholarly publication.
—BLDSC (4920.700000); KR SourceOne; SWETS; UnCover.

338.1   US   ISSN 1074-0708
HD1401   CODEN: JAIAE9
JOURNAL OF APPLIED AGRICULTURAL ECONOMICS. 1969. s-a. $20 (foreign $30) (effective 1997 & 1998). Southern Agricultural Economics Association, c/o Phil Kenkel, Department of Agricultural Economics, Oklahoma State University, Stillwater, OK 74078-0505. TEL 405-794-6157. FAX 405-794-8210. E-mail: JAAE@agecon.uga.edu; URL: http://www.agecon.uga.edu/~jaae/jaae.htm. (Subscr. to: H.A. Clonts, W.E. Hardy, Department of Agricultural Economics, Auburn University, Auburn, AL 36849) Eds. C. Huang, M. Wetzstein. R&P contact: M. Wetzstein. TEL 706-542-0758. circ. 1,100. (also avail. in microform from UMI; reprint service avail. from UMI) **Indexed:** BPIA, Cott.& Trop.Fibr.Abstr., Dairy Sci.Abstr., Energy Ind., Energy Info.Abstr. (until 1994), Geo.Abstr., IDA, Ind.Vet., J.of Econ.Lit., Maize Abstr., Pig News & Info., Poult.Abstr., Rice Abstr., Rural Ext.Educ.& Tr.Abstr., Soils & Fert., Soyabean Abstr., Triticale Abstr., World Agri.Econ.& Rural Sociol.Abstr. **Document type:** academic/scholarly publication.
—BLDSC (4919.999400); UMI; UnCover.
Formerly (until 1992): Southern Journal of Agricultural Economics (ISSN 0081-3052)
Description: Provides a forum for creative and scholarly work in agricultural economics and related areas. Contributions on methodology and applications in business, research, and teaching phases of agricultural and applied economics are equally encouraged.
Refereed Serial

630   JA   ISSN 0913-6134
JOURNAL OF COMMUNICATION BETWEEN RURAL COMMUNITIES AND TOWNS/NOSON TO TOSHI O MUSUBU. (Text in Japanese) 1951. m. 3300 Yen. Agriculture, Forestry and Fisheries Ministry Workers Union, 2-1, 1-chome, Kasumigaseki, Chiyoda-ku, Tokyo 100, Japan. TEL 03-3508-1395. FAX 03-5512-7555. Ed. Yasuo Kondo. adv. circ. 11,000. **Document type:** academic/scholarly publication.

JOURNAL OF CROP PRODUCTION; innovations in practice, theory & research. see *AGRICULTURE — Crop Production And Soil*

630 658.8   US   ISSN 0897-4438
HD9000.1   CODEN: JIFMEI
JOURNAL OF INTERNATIONAL FOOD & AGRIBUSINESS MARKETING. 1989. q. $45.50 to individuals (Canada $58.50; elsewhere $63); institutions $75 (Canada $97.50; elsewhere $105); libraries $150 (Canada $195; elsewhere $210) (effective 1996-1997). Haworth Press, Inc., 10 Alice St., Binghamton, NY 13904. TEL 607-722-5857; 800-342-9678. FAX 607-722-1424. Ed. Erdener Kaynak. adv.; bk.rev (also avail. in microfiche from UMI; microform from HAW; reprint service avail. from HAW) **Indexed:** B.P.I., Bibl.Agri., Curr.Cont., Documentatieblad, Food Sci.& Tech.Abstr.
—BLDSC (5007.661500); Haworth; KR SourceOne; SWETS; UnCover.
Description: Presents current and insightful information - descriptive and analytical - on the international food and agribusiness marketing theory and practice.
Refereed Serial

JOURNAL OF PHILIPPINE DEVELOPMENT. see *BUSINESS AND ECONOMICS — Public Finance, Taxation*

JOURNAL OF RURAL COOPERATION. see *BUSINESS AND ECONOMICS — Cooperatives*

AGRICULTURE — AGRICULTURAL ECONOMICS

JOURNAL OF VEGETABLE CROP PRODUCTION. see *AGRICULTURE — Crop Production And Soil*

338.1   KE
KENYA. MINISTRY OF AGRICULTURE. DEVELOPMENT PLANNING DIVISION. YIELDS, COSTS, PRICES. a. Ministry of Agriculture, Development Planning Division, P.O. Box 30028, Nairobi, Kenya. TEL 254-2-718870. Ed. Protus Sigei. **Document type:** government publication.
    Formerly: Kenya. Central Development and Marketing Unit. Yields, Costs, Prices.

338 630   II   ISSN 0023-1029
HD2346.I5
KHADI GRAMODYOG; journal of rural economy. (Editions in English and Hindi) 1954. m. Rs.60. Khadi and Village Industries Commission, Directorate of Publicity, Gramodaya, Irla Rd., Vile Parle (West), Bombay 400056, India. Ed. Kamal Taori; Pub. S.R. Fulmali. bk.rev.; stat. **Indexed:** Agri.Eng.Abstr., Int.Lab.Doc.

338.1   JA
KONNYAKU NEWS. (Text in Japanese) 1948. 3/m. 9000 Yen. Konnyaku Shinbunsha, 12-9, Igusa 5-chome, Suginami-ku, Tokyo 167, Japan. TEL 03-399-0425. Ed. Teiichi Murakami. adv. circ. 2,000. (back issues avail.)
    Description: Contains information about price and exchange rate of konnyaku (paste made from the arum root) for the konnyaku industry.

338.1   RU
KREST'YANSKIE VEDOMOSTI. 1990. w. 7 Rub. per no. Igor' Abakumov, Ed. & Pub., Ul. Gilyarovskogo 57, 129110 Moscow, Russia. TEL 095-284-0446. FAX 095-284-5673. (Co-sponsor: Agroprombank) Ed. Igor' Abakumov. adv.; bk.rev. circ. 97,000. **Document type:** newspaper.
    Description: Covers agricultural information.

333 300   US   ISSN 0023-7639
HB1   CODEN: LAECAD
LAND ECONOMICS; a quarterly journal devoted to the study of economic and social institutions. 1925. q. $40 to individuals; institutions $83. (University of Wisconsin at Madison, Land Tenure Center) University of Wisconsin Press, Journal Division, 114 N. Murray St., Madison, WI 53715. TEL 608-262-4952. FAX 608-262-7560. Ed. Daniel Bromley. adv.; bk.rev.; bibl.; index. circ. 2,700. (also avail. in microform from UMI; back issues avail.; reprint service avail. from KTO,UMI) **Indexed:** ABI Inform., Acid Rain Abstr., Acid Rain Ind., Amer.Hist.& Life (1964-1995), ASCA, Asian-Pac.Econ.Lit., Avery Ind.Archit.Per., B.P.I., BPIA, Bus.Ind., C.R.E.J., Compumath, Curr.Adv.Ecol.Sci., Curr.Cont., Deep Sea Res.& Oceanogr.Abstr., E.I., Energy Info.Abstr., Environ.Abstr., Excerp.Med., Farm & Garden Ind., Forest Prod.Abstr., Geo.Abstr.P.G., GeoRef, Hist.Abstr. (1964-1995), IBR, IDA, Ind.Per.Art.Relat.Law, INIS Atomind., Int.Lab.Doc., Irr.& Drain.Abstr. , J.of Econ.Lit., Manage.Cont., Mid.East: Abstr.& Ind., P.A.I.S., Pub.Admin.Abstr., RICS, Risk Abstr., Rural Recreat.Tour.Abstr., Sage Pub.Admin.Abstr., Sage Urb.Stud.Abstr., Sel.Water Res.Abstr., Soc.Sci.Ind., SSCI, Tr.& Indus.Ind., World Agri.Econ.& Rural Sociol.Abstr. **Document type:** academic/scholarly publication.
    ●Also available online. Vendor(s): Information Access Co.
    —BLDSC (5146.800000); CIS; Genuine Article; KR SourceOne; SWETS; UMI; UnCover. **CCC.**
    Formerly: Journal of Land and Public Utility Economics.

333   US   ISSN 0075-7837
LAND ECONOMICS MONOGRAPHS. 1966. irreg. (University of Wisconsin at Madison, Land Tenure Center) University of Wisconsin Press, Journal Division, 114 N. Murray St., Madison, WI 53715. TEL 608-262-4952. FAX 608-262-7560. (reprint service avail. from UMI) **Document type:** monographic series, academic/scholarly publication.

301   UN   ISSN 0251-1894
HD101
LAND REFORM, LAND SETTLEMENT AND COOPERATIVES. Spanish edition: Reforma Agraria, Colonizacion y Cooperativas (ISSN 0251-1886); French edition: Reforme Agraire, Colonisation et Cooperatives (ISSN 0251-1878) (Text in English) 1963. a. $12. Food and Agriculture Organization of the United Nations, Rural Institutions Division, Bernan Associates, 4611-F Assembly Dr., Lanham, MD 20706-4391. TEL 301-459-7666. FAX 301-459-0056. Ed. H. Meliczek. bk.rev.; bibl.; charts; illus.; cum.index. **Indexed:** Geo.Abstr.P.G., IDA, Int.Lab.Doc., Irr.& Drain.Abstr., P.A.I.S., Protozool.Abstr., Rural Devel.Abstr., Rural Recreat.Tour.Abstr., World Agri.Econ.& Rural Sociol.Abstr. **Document type:** government publication.
    —BLDSC (5146.880000); SWETS.

333 630   US   ISSN 0084-0793
LAND TENURE CENTER. PAPER. Short title: L T C Paper. (Text mainly in English, occasionally in other languages) 1965. irreg., no.150, 1993. price varies in North America and Western Europe; free elsewhere. University of Wisconsin at Madison, Land Tenure Center, 1357 University Ave., Madison, WI 53715. TEL 608-262-3657. FAX 608-262-2141. TELEX 3797422 LAND TENURE. Ed. Steven G. Smith. **Document type:** monographic series.
    Description: Promotes research and education on social structure, rural institutions, resource use and development.

333   US   ISSN 0084-0815
HD107
LAND TENURE CENTER. RESEARCH PAPER. (Text mainly in English; occasionally in other languages) 1964. irreg., no.120, 1993. price varies in N. America and Western Europe; elsewhere free. University of Wisconsin at Madison, Land Tenure Center, 1357 University Ave., Madison, WI 53715. TEL 608-262-3657. FAX 608-262-2141. TELEX 3797422 LAND TENURE. Ed. Steven G. Smith. **Indexed:** Abstr.Rural Dev.Trop. **Document type:** monographic series.
    Description: Promotes research and education on social structure, rural institutions, resource use and development.

338.1   NE   ISSN 0169-3255
LANDBOUW-ECONOMISCH BERICHT. (Text in Dutch; summaries in English) 1972. a. fl.69. Landbouw-Economisch Instituut, Burg. Patijnlaan 19, 2585 BE The Hague, Netherlands. TEL 31-70-3308330. FAX 31-70-3615624. E-mail: postmaster@lei.dlo.nl; URL: http://www.lei.dlo.nl/lei. Ed.Bd. **Indexed:** Dairy Sci.Abstr. **Document type:** government publication.
    Description: Overview of economic situation in agriculture of the Netherlands and the European Community.

338.1   NE   ISSN 0166-8072
LANDBOUW-ECONOMISCH INSTITUUT. MAANDBLAD PRIJSSTATISTIEK. 1952. m. price varies. Landbouw-Economisch Instituut, Burg. Patijnlaan 19, 2585 BE The Hague, Netherlands. TEL 31-70-3308330. FAX 31-70-3615624. E-mail: postmaster@lei.dlo.nl; URL: http://www.lei.dlo.nl/lei. **Document type:** government publication.
    Formerly: Landbouw-Economisch Instituut. Prijsstatistiek (ISSN 0032-8219)

338.1   NO   ISSN 0800-5974
LANDBRUKSOEKONOMISK FORUM; tidsskrift for landbruk, miljoe og samfunn. (Text in Norwegian) 1983. q. NOK 400 in Nordic countries; elsewhere $79 (effective 1997). Scandinavian University Press, P.O. Box 2959 Toeyen, N-0608 Oslo, Norway. TEL 47-22-57-54-00. FAX 47-22-57-53-53. E-mail: mail@scup.no; URL: http://www.scup.no. (US addr.: 875 Massachusetts Ave., Ste. 82, Cambridge, MA 02139. TEL 617-497-6515. FAX 617-354-6875) Ed.Bd. **Document type:** academic/scholarly publication.
    Description: Covers agriculture in a wide sense, with economic, environmental and social issues.

338.1   GW
LANDFRAUEN TASCHENKALENDER. 1987. a. DM.9.50. Landwirtschaftsverlag GmbH, Huelsebrockstr. 2, 48165 Muenster, Germany. TEL 49-2501-8010. FAX 49-2051-801-215. (Subscr. to: Postfach 480249, 48079 Muenster, Germany) **Document type:** bulletin.

338.1   GW   ISSN 0341-8278
LANDWIRTSCHAFTLICHER TASCHENKALENDER. a. DM.8.50. Landwirtschaftsverlag GmbH, Huelsebrockstr. 2, 48165 Muenster, Germany. TEL 49-2501-801-0. FAX 49-2501-801-215. (Subscr. to: Postfach 480249, 48079 Muenster, Germany) **Document type:** bulletin.

338.1   SP
LATIENDA; organo informativo de los comerciantes detallistas de la alimentacion. 1980. m. 6000 ptas. (effective 1994). Asociacion Madrilena de Empresarios Minoristas de Alimentacion "La Unica", Jorge Juan, 19-2o, 28001 Madrid, Spain. TEL 91-575-38-89. FAX 91-577-96-86. Ed. Primitivo Sanz Martin. adv.: B&W page 110000 ptas., color page 150000 ptas.; 210 x 197; adv. contact: Emilio Agreda Marchante. circ. 10,000. **Document type:** trade publication.

338.1   BL   ISSN 0103-443X
SB87.B8
LEVANTAMENTO SISTEMATICO DA PRODUCAO AGRICOLA/SYSTEMATIC SURVEY OF AGRICULTURAL PRODUCTION. 1975. m. $360. Fundacao Instituto Brasileiro de Geografia e Estatistica, Centro de Documentacao e Disseminacao de Informacoes, Rua General Canabarro 706, 2o andar, Maracana 20271-201 Rio de Janeiro, Brazil. TEL 55-21-2645424. FAX 55-21-2841959. bk.rev.; stat. circ. 700. (back issues avail.)
    Description: Presents the results of the survey investigating the total cultivated area, the expected production and productivity of 35 agricultural products.

338.1   NZ   ISSN 1170-7607
LINCOLN UNIVERSITY. AGRIBUSINESS AND ECONOMICS RESEARCH UNIT. DISCUSSION PAPER. 1968. irreg. $20 per no; also avail. on exchange. Lincoln University, Agribusiness and Economics Research Unit, P.O. Box 84, Canterbury, New Zealand. TEL 64-3-32528111. FAX 64-3-352099. **Indexed:** Herb.Abstr., Poult.Abstr., World Agri.Econ.& Rural Sociol.Abstr. **Document type:** academic/scholarly publication.
    —BLDSC (3597.385100).
    Formerly: Lincoln College. Agricultural Economics Research Unit. Discussion Paper (ISSN 0110-7720)

338.1   NZ   ISSN 1170-7682
HD1407
LINCOLN UNIVERSITY. AGRIBUSINESS AND ECONOMICS RESEARCH UNIT. RESEARCH REPORT. 1964. irreg. $30 per no.; also avail. on exchange. Lincoln University, Agribusiness and Economics Research Unit, P.O. Box 84, Canterbury, New Zealand. TEL 64-3-252811. FAX 64-3-252099. **Indexed:** Bibl.Agri., Rural Recreat.Tour.Abstr., World Agri.Econ.& Rural Sociol.Abstr. **Document type:** academic/scholarly publication.
    —BLDSC (7762.452820).
    Former titles (until 1990): Lincoln College. Agribusiness and Economics Research Unit. Research Report (ISSN 0113-4485); (until 1987): Agricultural Economics Research Unit. Research Report (ISSN 0069-3790); (until 1968): Agricultural Economics Research Unit. Publication (ISSN 0069-3847)

381.41 636   US
LIVESTOCK AND MEAT PRICES AND RECEIPTS AT CERTAIN CALIFORNIA AND WESTERN AREA MARKETS. a. $30. Federal-State Market News Service (Sacramento), 1220 N St., Rm. A-247, Box 942871, Sacramento, CA 94271-0001. TEL 916-654-0298. FAX 916-654-1046. **Document type:** government publication.
    Description: Includes a market review, graphs and prices for cattle, calves, hogs, sheep, and lambs.

LIVESTOCK, DAIRY AND POULTRY SITUATION & OUTLOOK. see *AGRICULTURE — Poultry And Livestock*

338.1   US
LOS ANGELES WHOLESALE FRUIT & VEGETABLE REPORT. d. $180. U.S. Department of Agriculture, Agricultural Marketing Service (Los Angeles), 1320 E. Olympic Blvd., Ste. 212, Los Angeles, CA 90021-1907. TEL 213-894-3077. FAX 213-894-2898. **Document type:** government publication.

AGRICULTURE — AGRICULTURAL ECONOMICS

338.7 II ISSN 0304-7245
HD2346.I52
MADHYA PRADESH STATE AGRO-INDUSTRIES DEVELOPMENT CORPORATION LTD. ANNUAL REPORT. Key Title: Annual Report - Madhya Pradesh State Agro-Industries Development Corporation Ltd. (Text in English) a. Madhya Pradesh State Agro-Industries Development Corporation Ltd., New Market, T. T. Nagar, Bhopal, India.

338.1 634 US
MARKET MICHIGAN FRUIT. a. $20. U.S. Department of Agriculture (Benton Harbor), Box 1204, 175 Territorial Rd., Ste. 201, Benton Harbor, MI 49022. TEL 616-925-3270. FAX 616-925-3272. (back issues avail.) **Document type:** government publication.
Description: Lists fruit shipments, Michigan F.O.B. prices, and wholesale terminal market prices.

630 658.8 AT
MARKET NOTES FOR LIVESTOCK AND MEAT. w. free. Australian Meat and Livestock Corporation, Market Intelligence Unit, G.P.O. Box 4129, Sydney, N.S.W. 2001, Australia. TEL 61-2-2603275. FAX 61-2-2603208. circ. 4,500.
Description: Market information for livestock, meat production and exports.

381.41 634.21 US
MARKETING CALIFORNIA APRICOTS. a. $20. (Department of Food and Agriculture) Federal-State Market News Service (Sacramento), 1220 N St., Rm. A-247, Box 942871, Sacramento, CA 94271-0001. TEL 916-654-0298. FAX 916-654-1046. **Document type:** government publication.

381.41 635.31 US
MARKETING CALIFORNIA ASPARAGUS. a. $20. (Department of Food and Agriculture) Federal-State Market News Service (Sacramento), 1220 N St., Rm. A-247, Box 942871, Sacramento, CA 94271-0001. TEL 916-654-0298. FAX 916-654-1046. **Document type:** government publication.

381.41 635.35 US ISSN 0148-4966
HD9235.B762
MARKETING CALIFORNIA BROCCOLI. a. $20. (Department of Food and Agriculture) Federal-State Market News Service (Sacramento), 1220 N St., Rm. A-247, Box 942871, Sacramento, CA 94271-0001. TEL 916-654-0298. FAX 916-654-1046. **Document type:** government publication.

381.41 635.13 US ISSN 0146-0676
HD9235.C342
MARKETING CALIFORNIA CARROTS. a. $20. (Department of Food and Agriculture) Federal-State Market News Service (Sacramento), 1220 N St., Rm. A-247, Box 942871, Sacramento, CA 94271-0001. TEL 916-654-0298. FAX 916-654-1046. **Document type:** government publication.

381.41 635.35 US ISSN 0098-4493
HD9235.C372
MARKETING CALIFORNIA CAULIFLOWER. a. $20. (Department of Food and Agriculture) Federal-State Market News Service (Sacramento), 1220 N St., Rm. A-247, Box 942871, Sacramento, CA 94271-0001. TEL 916-654-0298. FAX 916-654-1046. **Document type:** government publication.

381.41 635.53 US ISSN 0148-4974
HD9235.C442
MARKETING CALIFORNIA CELERY. a. $20. (Department of Food and Agriculture) Federal-State Market News Service (Sacramento), 1220 N St., Rm. A-247, Box 942871, Sacramento, CA 94271-0001. TEL 916-654-0298. FAX 916-654-1046. **Document type:** government publication.

381.41 634.23 US
MARKETING CALIFORNIA CHERRIES. a. $20. (Department of Food and Agriculture) Federal-State Market News Service (Sacramento), 1220 N St., Rm. A-247, Box 942871, Sacramento, CA 94271-0001. TEL 916-654-0298. FAX 916-654-1046. **Document type:** government publication.

381.41 634.88 US
MARKETING CALIFORNIA GRAPES FOR FRESH USE; table and juice grapes. a. $20. (Department of Food and Agriculture) Federal-State Market News Service (Sacramento), 1220 N St., Rm. A-247, Box 942871, Sacramento, CA 94271-0001. TEL 916-654-0298. FAX 916-654-1046. **Document type:** government publication.

381.41 634.2 US
MARKETING CALIFORNIA NECTARINES, PEACHES, AND PLUMS. a. $30. (Department of Food and Agriculture) Federal-State Market News Service (Sacramento), 1220 N St., Rm. A-247, Box 942871, Sacramento, CA 94271-0001. TEL 916-654-0298. FAX 916-654-1046. **Document type:** government publication.

381.41 US ISSN 0190-7492
MARKETING CALIFORNIA ORNAMENTAL CROPS. 1968. a. $10. (U.S. Department of Agriculture) Federal-State Market News Service, 630 Sansome St., Rm. 727, San Francisco, CA 94111. TEL 415-556-5587. FAX 415-705-1301. (looseleaf format; back issues avail.) **Document type:** government publication, newsletter.

381.41 634.13 US ISSN 0277-1489
HD9259.P333
MARKETING CALIFORNIA PEARS. a. $20. (Department of Food and Agriculture) Federal-State Market News Service (Sacramento), 1220 N St., Rm. A-247, Box 942871, Sacramento, CA 94271-0001. TEL 916-654-0298. FAX 916-654-1046. **Document type:** government publication.
Formerly: Marketing California Pears for Fresh Market (ISSN 0098-8928)

381.41 634.11 US
MARKETING CALIFORNIA SELECTED FRUITS; including apples, kiwifruit, avocados. a. $20. (Department of Food and Agriculture) Federal-State Market News Service (Sacramento), 1220 N St., Rm. A-247, Box 942871, Sacramento, CA 94271-0001. TEL 916-654-0298. FAX 916-654-1046. **Document type:** government publication.

381.41 634.75 US
MARKETING CALIFORNIA STRAWBERRIES. 1950. a. $10. Federal-State Market News Service, 630 Sansome St., Rm. 727, San Francisco, CA 94111. TEL 415-705-1300. FAX 415-705-1301. **Document type:** government publication, newsletter.

381.41 635.642 US
MARKETING CALIFORNIA TOMATOES. a. $20. (Department of Food and Agriculture) Federal-State Market News Service (Sacramento), 1220 N St., Rm. A-247, Box 942871, Sacramento, CA 94271-0001. TEL 916-654-0298. FAX 916-654-1046. **Document type:** government publication.

381.41 635.53 US ISSN 0732-7625
HD9235.L42
MARKETING LETTUCE FROM SALINAS-WATSONVILLE, OTHER CENTRAL CALIFORNIA DISTRICTS, AND COLORADO. a. $20. (Department of Food and Agriculture) Federal-State Market News Service (Sacramento), 1220 N St., Rm. A-247, Box 942871, Sacramento, CA 94271-0001. TEL 916-654-0298. FAX 916-654-1046. **Document type:** government publication.

338.1 NZ ISSN 0112-0603
MASSEY UNIVERSITY. CENTRE FOR APPLIED ECONOMICS AND POLICY STUDIES. AGRICULTURAL POLICY DISCUSSION PAPER. Key Title: Agricultural Policy Discussion Paper. 1976. irreg., no.13, 1993. price varies. Massey University, Centre for Applied Economics and Policy Studies, Palmerston North, New Zealand. TEL 64-6-356-9099. FAX 64-6-350-5642. E-mail: J.Fisher@massey.ac.nz. **Indexed:** Dairy Sci.Abstr. **Document type:** academic/scholarly publication.
Former titles: Massey University. Centre for Agricultural Policy Studies. Agricultural Policy Discussion Paper; (until 1982): Massey University. Department of Agricultural Economics and Farm Management. Technical Discussion Paper.

338.1 NZ ISSN 0111-6339
MASSEY UNIVERSITY. CENTRE FOR APPLIED ECONOMICS AND POLICY STUDIES. AGRICULTURAL POLICY PROCEEDINGS. Key Title: Agricultural Policy Proceedings. 1976. irreg., no.19, 1997. price varies. Massey University, Centre for Applied Economics and Policy Studies, Palmerston North, New Zealand. TEL 64-6-356-9099. FAX 64-6-350-5642. E-mail: J.Fisher@massey.ac.nz. circ. 200. **Indexed:** Poult.Abstr., Soyabean Abstr. **Document type:** proceedings.
Formerly: Massey University. Centre for Agricultural Policy Studies. Agricultural Policy Proceedings.

338.1 NZ ISSN 0110-5558
MASSEY UNIVERSITY. CENTRE FOR APPLIED ECONOMICS AND POLICY STUDIES. AGRICULTURAL POLICY PAPER. Key Title: Agricultural Policy Paper. 1976. irreg., no.19, 1996. price varies. Massey University, Centre for Applied Economics and Policy Studies, Palmerston North, New Zealand. TEL 64-6-356-9099. FAX 64-6-350-5642. E-mail: J.Fisher@massey.ac.nz. circ. 200. **Document type:** academic/scholarly publication.
Formerly: Massey University. Centre for Agricultural Policy Studies. Agricultural Policy Paper.

338.1 NZ ISSN 0110-2044
MASSEY UNIVERSITY. CENTRE FOR APPLIED ECONOMICS AND POLICY STUDIES. NATURAL RESOURCE DISCUSSION PAPER. Key Title: Discussion Paper in Natural Resource Economics. 1977. irreg., no.18, 1995. price varies. Massey University, Centre for Applied Economics and Policy Studies, Palmerston N., New Zealand. TEL 64-6-3569099. FAX 64-6-3505660. **Document type:** monographic series.

338.1 631.3 RU ISSN 0202-6325
MESTNYI PROIZVODSTVENNYI OPYT V SEL'SKOM KHOZYAISTVE/LOCAL LEVEL EXPERIENCE IN AGRICULTURAL DEVELOPMENT; nauchno-tekhnicheskii referativnyi sbornik. 1971. m. 7.20 Rub. Moskovskii Gorodskoi Territorial'nyi Tsentr Nauchno-Tekhnicheskoi Informatsii i Propagandy, Pr. Serova 5, 101958 Moscow, Russia. TEL 921-67-05. (Co-sponsor: State Planning Committee of the R.S.F.S.R.) Ed. Galina P. Bogachev. circ. 2,200. (back issues avail.)
Description: Covers agrotechnics, livestock improvement techniques, planning and management methods, agricultural equipment and technology developments.

338.1 634 US
MICHIGAN APPLE REPORT. w. $25. U.S. Department of Agriculture (Benton Harbor), Box 1204, 175 Territorial Rd., Ste. 201, Benton Harbor, MI 49022. TEL 616-925-3270. FAX 616-925-3272. (back issues avail.) **Document type:** newsletter, government publication.
Description: Provides data on Michigan apple shipments, including F.O.B. and terminal market prices.

338.1 634 US
MICHIGAN FRUIT & VEGETABLE REPORT. 2/w. $165. U.S. Department of Agriculture (Benton Harbor), Box 1204, 175 Territorial Rd., Ste. 201, Benton Harbor, MI 49022. TEL 616-925-3270. FAX 616-925-3272. (back issues avail.) **Document type:** government publication.

338.1 US ISSN 0065-4442
HD1407
MICHIGAN STATE UNIVERSITY. AGRICULTURAL ECONOMICS REPORT. 1965. irreg. (approx. 8/yr.). free. Michigan State University, Department of Agricultural Economics, Reference Rm., East Lansing, MI 48824-1039. TEL 517-355-6650. FAX 517-432-1800. E-mail: agecon@www2.lib.msu.edu. circ. 90 (controlled). (processed) **Indexed:** Dairy Sci.Abstr., GeoRef, Rural Recreat.Tour.Abstr., Soyabean Abstr., World Agri.Econ.& Rural Sociol.Abstr. **Document type:** academic/scholarly publication.
Description: Focuses on farm management and the economics of agriculture for researchers in the field.
Refereed Serial

AGRICULTURE — AGRICULTURAL ECONOMICS

338.1 US ISSN 1074-357X
MID-SOUTH FARMER. 1994. m. Farm Progress Companies (Subsidiary of A B C Publishing Companies), 191 S. Gary Ave., Carol Stream, IL 69177. TEL 630-462-2900. FAX 630-462-2869. (Edit. addr.: 235 Germantown Bend Cove, Ste. 5, Cordova, TN 38018. TEL 901-753-5112. FAX 901-753-5972) Ed. Ken Bretches. adv.: B&W page $5200, color page $5980; trim 7 X 10. circ. 30,386 (paid). **Document type:** trade publication.

MIDWEST DAIRYBUSINESS. see *AGRICULTURE — Dairying And Dairy Products*

338.1 US ISSN 0885-4874
HD101
MINNESOTA AGRICULTURAL ECONOMIST. 1914. free. University of Minnesota, Department of Applied Economics, 1994 Buford Ave., St. Paul, MN 55108. TEL 612-625-1705. FAX 612-625-6245. Ed. Steven Taff. charts; illus.; circ. 4,000 (controlled). (back issues avail.) **Indexed:** P.A.I.S. **Document type:** newsletter.
  Description: Reports information flowing from the research and educational efforts of the Department of Applied Economics.

633.5 US ISSN 0027-0318
HD9093.U4
MONTHLY COTTON LINTERS REVIEW.* 1930. m. free. U.S. Agricultural Marketing Service, Cotton Division, 302 Annex Bldg., 12th and C Sts., S.W., Washington, DC 20250. stat. (processed; also avail. in microfiche from CIS; reprint service avail. from CIS) **Indexed:** Amer.Stat.Ind. (1973-).

338.1 581 BE ISSN 0773-4123
MUSEE ROYAL DE L'AFRIQUE CENTRALE. ANNALES - SCIENCES ECONOMIQUES. SERIE IN 8/KONINKLIJK MUSEUM VOOR MIDDEN-AFRIKA. ANNALEN - ECONOMISCHE WETENSCHAPPEN. REEKS IN 8. 1947. irreg., no.23, 1993. price varies. Musee Royal de l'Afrique Centrale - Koninklijk Museum voor Midden-Afrika, 13 Steenweg op Leuven, B-3080 Tervuren, Belgium. TEL 32-2-7695299. FAX 32-2-7670242. charts; illus. (back issues avail.) **Indexed:** Forest.Abstr., Forest Prod.Abstr. **Document type:** monographic series.
  —BLDSC (0933.970000).
  Supersedes (in 1964): Musee Royal du Congo Belge. Annales - Sciences Historiques et Economiques (ISSN 0773-4115)

N A C T A JOURNAL. (National Association of Colleges and Teachers of Agriculture) see *AGRICULTURE*

338.1 KO
N A F NEWS. 1989. q. National Agricultural Cooperative Federation, 75, 1-Ka, Chungjeong-Ro, Jung-Ku, Seoul, S. Korea. FAX 02-737-7815. TELEX NACOF-K27421.

338.1 338 US
HD1401
N C STATE ECONOMIST. 1952. bi-m. free. North Carolina State University, North Carolina Cooperative Extension Service, Box 8109, Raleigh, NC 27695. TEL 919-515-4553. FAX 919-515-6268. Ed. Edmunnd A. Estes. R&P contact: Edmund A. Estes. charts; illus. circ. 9,500. **Document type:** newsletter.
  Former titles: Tar Heel Economist (ISSN 0039-9612); Tarheel Farm Economist.

338.1 SP
NEKAZAL SEKTOREAREN EKONOMI KONTUAK/CUENTAS ECONOMICAS DEL SECTOR AGRARIO. (Text in Basque, English) a. 1000 ptas. (Nekazaritza eta Arrantza Saila - Departamento de Agricultura y Pesca) Eusko Jaurlaritzaren Argitalpen-Zerbitzu Nagusia - Servicio Central de Publicaciones del Gobierno Vasco, C. Duque de Wellington 2, 01010 Vitoria Gasteiz, Spain. TEL 34-45-188000. FAX 34-45-189702. circ. 1,500. **Document type:** government publication.

338.1 US
NEW MEXICO STATE UNIVERSITY. AGRICULTURAL EXPERIMENT STATION. BULLETIN. irreg. (5-10/yr.), latest no.766, 1992. New Mexico State University, Agricultural Experiment Station, Drawer 3Al, Las Cruces, NM 88003. TEL 505-646-2701. Ed. Terry Canup. **Indexed:** Anim.Breed.Abstr., Field Crop Abstr., Herb.Abstr., Rural Recreat.Tour.Abstr., Soils & Fert., Sport Fish.Abstr., Wild.Rev., World Agri.Econ.& Rural Sociol.Abstr. **Document type:** bulletin.

338.1 AT ISSN 0310-186X
NEW SOUTH WALES. DEPARTMENT OF AGRICULTURE. COMMODITY BULLETIN. 1972. 4/yr. Department of Agriculture, Locked Bag 21, Orange, N.S.W. 2800, Australia. TEL 61-63-913433. **Document type:** bulletin.
  Description: Applied economic analysis of descriptive material relevant to all segments of the domestic and export sectors of Australian agricultural and fishing industries.

338.1 JA ISSN 0387-3234
NOGYO KEIZAI KENKYU/JOURNAL OF AGRICULTURAL ECONOMICS. (Text in Japanese) 1925. q. 5000 Yen. (Nihon Nogyo Keizai Gakkai - Agricultural Economic Society of Japan) Iwanami Shoten Publishers, 5-5 Hitotsubashi 2-chome, Chiyoda-ku, Tokyo 101-02, Japan. FAX 03-239-9618. (Dist. overseas by: Japan Publications Trading Co., Ltd., Box 5030, Tokyo International, Tokyo 100-31, Japan; Or: 1255 Howard St., San Francisco, CA 94103) bk.rev. **Indexed:** Amer.Hist.& Life (1959-1961), Asian-Pac.Econ.Lit., Geo.Abstr., Hist.Abstr. (1959-1961), Rural Recreat.Tour.Abstr., World Agri.Econ.& Rural Sociol.Abstr.
  —BLDSC (5052.128000); UnCover.

338.1 JA ISSN 0387-3242
NOGYO SOGO KENKYU. Variant title: Quarterly Journal of Agricultural Economy. (Text in Japanese) 1947. q. Norinsuisan-sho, Nogyo Sogo Kenkyujo - Ministry of Agriculture, Forestry, and Fisheries, National Research Institute of Agricultural Economics, 2-1 Nishi-gahara 2-chome, Kita-ku, Tokyo 114, Japan. FAX 81-3-3910-3946. E-mail: www@nriae.affrc.go.jp. Ed. Kazuo Nonaka. bk.rev. **Indexed:** Amer.Hist.& Life (1958-1966), Excerp.Med., Forest.Abstr., Hist.Abstr. (1958-1966), Int.Abstr.Oper.Res. **Document type:** government publication.
  —BLDSC (7187.750000).

338.1 JA ISSN 0029-0912
NOGYO TO KEIZAI/AGRICULTURE AND ECONOMY. (Text in Japanese) 1934. m. Fumin Kyokai, Shuppan-bu - Better Farming Association, Publishing Division, c/o Mainichi Shinbunsha, 1-Dojima, Kita-ku, Osaka 530, Japan. Ed. Masamitsu Duchi.

338.1 CC ISSN 1003-7470
HD2096
NONGCUN JINGJI/RURAL ECONOMY. (Text in Chinese) 1983. m. Y9 (effective 1994). Sichuan Shehui Kexueyuan, Nongcun Jingji Yanjiusuo - Sichuan Academy of Social Sciences, Rural Economy Research Institute, Shehui Kexueyuan, Qingyang Gong, Chengdu, Sichuan 610072, People's Republic of China. TEL 769347-353. (Co-sponsor: Sichuan Agricultural Economy Society) Ed. Guo Zhongzhen. adv.; bk.rev. **Document type:** academic/scholarly publication.

338.1 CC ISSN 1002-5596
NONGYE HEZUO JINGJI JINGYING GUANLI/MANAGEMENT AND ADMINISTRATION IN RURAL ECONOMY. (Text in Chinese) m. Y19.20. Nongye Bu, Hezuo Jingji Jingying Guanli Zongzhan, 11, Nongzhanguan Nanli, Beijing 100026, People's Republic of China. TEL 5005773. Ed. Huian Li.
  Formerly (until 1991): Nongye Jingying Guanli yu Kuaiji Yanjiu.

338.1 CC ISSN 1001-3059
NONGYE JINGJI/AGRICULTURAL ECONOMICS. (Subseries of: Fuyin Baokan Ziliao) (Text in Chinese) 1978. m. $136.25. Zhongguo Renmin Daxue, Shubao Ziliao Zhongxin - China People's University, Book & Newspaper Information Center, 3 Zhang Zizhong Rd., P.O. Box 1122, Beijing 100007, People's Republic of China. TEL 86-10-4015080. (Dist. in US by: China Publications Service, Box 49614, Chicago, IL 60649. TEL 312-288-3291. FAX 312-288-8570) pp./issue: 208.

338.1 CC ISSN 1000-6389
HD1401
NONGYE JINGJI WENTI/PROBLEMS OF AGRICULTURAL ECONOMICS. (Text in Chinese) 1980. m. $54. Zhongguo Nongye Kexueyuan - Chinese Academy of Agricultural Science, 30 Baishiqiao Lu, Beijing 100081, People's Republic of China. TEL 8314433. (Dist. in US by: China Books & Periodicals, Inc., 2929 24th St., San Francisco, CA 94110. TEL 415-282-2994) Ed. Liu Zhicheng.
  —BLDSC (6617.875950); UnCover.

338.1 CC ISSN 1000-6370
NONGYE JISHU JINGJI/ECONOMICS FOR AGRICULTURAL TECHNOLOGY. (Text in Chinese) 1982. 6/yr. $24. Zhongguo Nongye Jishu Jingji Yanjiuhui - Chinese Society for Agricultural Technology Economics, 30 Baishiqiao Lu, Beijing 100081, People's Republic of China. TEL 86-10-6217-6213. FAX 86-10-6218-7545. TELEX 222720 CAAS CN. (Dist. in U.S. by: China Books & Periodicals, Inc., 2929 24th St., San Francisco, CA 94110. TEL 415-282-2994) (Co-sponsor: Zhongguo Nongye Kexueyuan Nongye Jingji Yanjiusuo - C A A S, Institute of Agricultural Economics) Ed. Xigang Zhu; Pub. Chen Liangbiao. adv.; bk.rev. circ. 3,000. **Document type:** academic/scholarly publication.
  Description: Contains research articles, reports, notes and reviews on all aspects of agricultural economics and technologies.
  Refereed Serial

333 NO ISSN 0801-2334
NORGES LANDBRUKSHOEGSKOLE. INSTITUTT FOR JORDSKIFTE OG AREALPLANLEGGING. MELDING/AGRICULTURAL UNIVERSITY OF NORWAY. DEPARTMENT OF LAND USE PLANNING. SERIE. 1956. irreg. (2-4/yr.). price varies. Norges Landbrukshoegskole, Institutt for Jordskifte og Arealplanlegging - Agricultural University of Norway, P.O. Box 29, N-1432 Aas-NLH, Norway. **Indexed:** Biol.Abstr., Nutr.Abstr., Seed Abstr.
  Formerly: Norges Landbrukshoegskole. Institutt for Jordskifte og Eiendomsutforming. Melding (ISSN 0065-0242)

338.1 NO ISSN 0333-2500
S249
NORSK INSTITUTT FOR LANDBRUKSOEKONOMISK FORSKNING. DRIFTSGRANSKINGER I JORD- OG SKOGBRUK. 1912. a. NOK 100. Norsk Institutt for Landbruksoekonomisk Forskning (NILF), P.O. Box 8024 Dep., N-0030 Oslo, Norway. TEL 47-22-17-35-40. FAX 47-22-17-35-38. E-mail: synnovekjos.frank@nilf.nlh.no. Ed. Synnove Kjos Frank. circ. 2,900. **Indexed:** Potato Abstr. **Document type:** government publication.
  —BLDSC (3625.300000).
  Formerly: Norges Landbruksoekonomiske Institutt. Driftsgranskinger i Jordbruket (ISSN 0078-1223)
  Description: Reports results of the annual Norwegian Farm Management survey.

338.1 639.2 AT
NORTHERN TERRITORY. DEPARTMENT OF PRIMARY INDUSTRY AND FISHERIES. AGNOTE. irreg. free. Department of Primary Industry and Fisheries, P.O. Box 79, Berrimah, N.T. 0828, Australia. FAX 61-89-992307. E-mail: graham.calley@nt.gov.au. Ed. G. Calley. R&P contact: Graham Calley. (back issues avail.) **Document type:** government publication, monographic series.
  Former titles: Northern Territory. Department of Industries and Development. Agnote; Northern Territory. Department of Primary Production. Agnote (ISSN 0157-8243)

NORTHWEST REPORT. see *BUSINESS AND ECONOMICS — Economic Situation And Conditions*

338.1 AU ISSN 0026-9220
OESTERREICHISCHE LANDWIRTSCHAFT. MONATSBERICHTE. vol.17, 1970. m. S.900 (foreign S.1050). (Bundesministerium fuer Land- und Forstwirtschaft, Agrarwirtschaftliches Institut) Oesterreichischer Agrarverlag GmbH, Inkustr. 1-7, A-3400 Klosterneuburg, Austria. TEL 02243-333006. FAX 02243-3330056. Ed. Werner Pevetz. charts; mkt.; stat.; index. circ. 680. **Indexed:** P.A.I.S.For.Lang.Ind., Rural Recreat.Tour.Abstr., World Agri.Econ.& Rural Sociol.Abstr.

338.1 GW
OIL WORLD ANNUAL. 1987. a. DM.128.60 (Europe DM.164; elsewhere DM.181) (effective 1997). I S T A Mielke GmbH, Langenberg 25, 21077 Hamburg, Germany. TEL 49-40-7610500. FAX 49-40-76105090. E-mail: 100611.3253@compuserve.com. Ed. Thomas Mielke. **Document type:** corporate report.

AGRICULTURE — AGRICULTURAL ECONOMICS

664.3   GW   ISSN 0029-8700
OIL WORLD WEEKLY; the weekly forecasting and information service for oilseeds, oilmeals, oils and fats. (Text in English) 1958. w. DM.734.40 (Europe DM.990; elsewhere DM.1047) (effective 1997). I S T A Mielke GmbH, Langenberg 25, 21077 Hamburg, Germany. TEL 49-40-7610500. FAX 49-40-76105090. E-mail: 100611.3253@compuserve.com. Ed. Thomas Mielke. adv.; index. (looseleaf format) **Document type:** trade publication.
—CCC.

338.1   US   ISSN 0030-1701
HD1775.O5
OKLAHOMA CURRENT FARM ECONOMICS. 1927. q. free. Oklahoma Agricultural Experiment Station, Stillwater, OK 74078. TEL 405-744-6161. FAX 405-744-8210. Ed. David M. Henneberry. charts; illus.; mkt.; index. circ. 1,600. (also avail. in microfilm from UMI; reprint service avail. from UMI) **Indexed:** Curr.Cont., Dairy Sci.Abstr., Field Crop Abstr., Herb.Abstr., Maize Abstr., Soils & Fert., Soyabean Abstr., Triticale Abstr., World Agri.Econ.& Rural Sociol.Abstr. **Document type:** monographic series.
—UMI.
    Description: Covers current agricultural issues, including policy analysis, market strategies and production alternatives, as well as related concerns such as rural development, environmental quality and natural resources.

338.1   US
OUTLOOK (YEAR) PROCEEDINGS. Variant title: Annual Agricultural Outlook Conference Proceedings. (Conference is held in Nov.) 1982. a. $20 (foreign $25). U.S. Department of Agriculture, World Agricultural Outlook Board, 14th St. and Independence Ave., S.W., Rm. 5143-S, Washington, DC 20250-3900. TEL 202-447-5447. (Dist. by: In Focus, 341 Victory Ln., Herndon, VA 22070. TEL 800-999-6779; Avail. from: Supt. of Documents, U.S. Government Printing Office, Washington, DC 20402. TEL 202-783-3238. FAX 202-512-2233) Ed. Raymond L. Bridge. index. circ. 1,000. **Indexed:** Bibl.Agri. **Document type:** government publication, proceedings.
●Also available online. Vendor(s): Ovid Technologies, Inc., Knight-Ridder Information, Inc.
    Description: Proceedings of speeches and statements submitted by Annual Agricultural Outlook Conference participants.

OXFORD DEVELOPMENT STUDIES. see *BUSINESS AND ECONOMICS — International Development And Assistance*

338.1 633   US
PEANUT NEWS. m. $75. (National Peanut Council) Lettercom, Inc., 310 Swann Ave., Alexandria, VA 22314. TEL 703-683-3105. (Subscr. to: 1500 King St., Ste. 301, Alexandria, VA 22314) Ed. C. Edward Ashdown. circ. 650.

338.1 633   US
PEANUT REPORT. w. $8 per mo. (foreign $16). U.S. Department of Agriculture, Agricultural Marketing Division, Fruit and Vegetable Division, Washington, Washington, DC 20250. TEL 202-720-2175. (also avail. in microfiche from CIS; reprint service avail. from CIS) **Indexed:** Amer.Stat.Ind. (1973-).
    Formerly (until 1982): Peanut Market News, Weekly Report.

338.1   BL
PERNAMBUCO. SECRETARIA DA AGRICULTURA. PLANO ANUAL DE TRABALHO. a. Secretaria da Agricultura, Recife, Brazil.
    Formerly: Brazil. Departamento de Agricultura e Abastecimento. Plano Anual de Trabalho do D A A.

630 338.1   PH
PHILIPPINES. DEPARTMENT OF AGRARIAN REFORM. PLANNING SERVICE. ANNUAL REPORT. (Text in English) 1973. a. Department of Agrarian Reform, Planning Service, Manila, Philippines. **Document type:** government publication.

PLENTY BULLETIN. see *BUSINESS AND ECONOMICS — International Development And Assistance*

POLICY IMPACT ANALYSIS. see *LAW — International Law*

338.1 633   UK   ISSN 0079-4309
POTATO MARKETING BOARD, OXFORD. ANNUAL REPORT AND ACCOUNTS. a. Potato Marketing Board, Broad Field House, 4 Between Towns Rd., Cowley, Oxford OX4 3NA, England. TEL 44-1865-714455. FAX 44-1865-716418. Ed. P. Oldfield. **Indexed:** Field Crop Abstr., Herb.Abstr. **Document type:** corporate report.

POTATO NEWS. see *AGRICULTURE — Crop Production And Soil*

338.1   IT   ISSN 0478-1805
PREVIDENZA SOCIALE NELL'AGRICOLTURA. 1950. bi-m. Via Barberini 95, Rome, Italy. bibl.; stat.

PRICE PERCEPTIONS. see *BUSINESS AND ECONOMICS — Investments*

338.1 330.8   UN
PRICES OF AGRICULTURAL PRODUCTS AND SELECTED INPUTS IN EUROPE AND NORTH AMERICA. 1950. biennial. $36 (effective 1997). (Economic Commission for Europe (ECE)) United Nations Publications, Sales and Marketing Section, Room DC2-0853, New York, NY 10017. TEL 212-963-8302; 800-253-9646. FAX 212-963-3489. E-mail: publications@un.org; URL: http://www.un.org/publications. (Or: Distribution and Sales Section, Palais des Nations, 1211 Geneva 10, Switzerland) (also avail. in microfiche from CIS) **Indexed:** IIS.

338.1 630   AT   ISSN 0155-9222
PRIMARY INDUSTRY NEWSLETTER. 1966. w. Aus.$295. Australian Press Services Pty. Ltd., P.O. Box E 160, Queen Victoria Terrace, A.C.T. 2600, Australia. Ed. David Barnett. **Document type:** newsletter.

338.1   CN   ISSN 0830-1654
PRO-FARM. 1984. 6/yr. membership. Western Canadian Wheat Growers Association, 1836 Victoria Ave., E., Regina, SK S4N 7K3, Canada. TEL 306-586-5866. FAX 306-586-2707. Ed. Alanna Koch; Pub. Chris Dodd. R&P contact: Chris Dodd. adv. contact: Chris Dodd. charts; illus.; stat. circ. 9,000. **Document type:** academic/scholarly publication.
    Description: Dedicated to the professional farmer in western Canada. Deals with increasing the productivity and awareness of these large scale farmers.

338.1 631   ZA
PRODUCTIVE FARMING. (Text in English) 1973. K.36000 (Africa K.90000; Europe K.132000; N. America K.150000). Zambia National Farmers Union, Taz House, Cha Cha Cha Rd., P.O. Box 30395, Lusaka, Zambia. TEL 260-1-222797. FAX 260-1-222736. TELEX ZA 40164. Ed. George Gray. adv. contact: E. Hara. bk.rev.; index. circ. 1,850. (back issues avail.) **Document type:** trade publication.
    Description: Covers all aspects of commercial agriculture in Zambia.

630 338.1   DK   ISSN 0108-5883
PRODUKTION. 1960. 5/yr. $150. Dansk Landbrugs Grovvareselskab a.m.b.a., Axelborg, DK-1503 Copenhagen V, Denmark. TEL 45-33-15-11-13. FAX 45-33-15-13-56. Ed. Christian Pedersen. adv.; circ. 126,000 (controlled). **Document type:** trade publication.
    Description: Features articles on grain, feeds, fertilizers, seeds, and plant protection, as well as on farm management in general.

338.1   AT   ISSN 0312-889X
PROFESSIONAL FARM MANAGEMENT GUIDEBOOK. 1967. irreg. (approx. 1/yr.). Aus.$3. University of New England, Agricultural Business Research Institute, Armidale, N.S.W. 2351, Australia. circ. 4,000.

338.1   IT
PROPRIETA FONDIARIA. 1947. m. L.2000. Proprieta Fondiaria Agricola, Via S. Tecla 5, 20122 Milan, Italy. TEL 2-805-71-25. Ed. Franco Albertini. adv. circ. 25,000.

338.1   IT
Q A. (Questione Agraria) 1981. 4/yr. L.90000 (foreign L.130000) (effective 1993). Franco Angeli Editore, Viale Monza 106, 20127 Milan, Italy. TEL 02-2827651. **Indexed:** Agri.Eng.Abstr., Maize Abstr., Soyabean Abstr., Triticale Abstr., World Agri.Econ.& Rural Sociol.Abstr.

338.1   SP   ISSN 0213-0319
QUADERNS AGRARIS. 1980. a. free to qualified personnel. Institucion Catalana d'Estudis Agraris, Calle del Carme, 47, 08001 Barcelona, Spain. TEL 93-318 55 16. Ed. Juanta de Govern. **Indexed:** Ind.SST.
—CINDOC.

332.6   CH   ISSN 0033-5665
QUARTERLY JOURNAL OF TAIWAN LAND CREDIT.* 1964. q. Land Bank of Taiwan, Credit Investigation & Research Department, 46 Kuan Chien Rd., Taipei, Taiwan, Republic of China. TEL 02-3613020. FAX 02-3115782. Ed. Lu Nien-Tsing. bk.rev.; charts; mkt.; stat.; circ. 500 (controlled).

338.1   US
QUARTERLY SURVEY OF AGRICULTURAL CREDIT CONDITIONS. 1976. q. free. Federal Reserve Bank of Dallas, Sta. K, Dallas, TX 75222. TEL 214-651-6289. circ. 1,200. (also avail. in microfiche from CIS; back issues avail.; reprint service avail. from CIS) **Indexed:** Amer.Stat.Ind. (1982-).

630 658.8   DK
RAADSNYT. w. free to qualified personnel. Landbrugsraadet, Axeltorv 3, 1609 Copenhagen V, Denmark. FAX 33-145072. adv. circ. 685. **Document type:** newsletter.
    Formerly (until 1982): Landsbrugsraadets Meddelelser.

RABOBANK. see *BUSINESS AND ECONOMICS — Banking And Finance*

338.1   II
RAJASTHAN AGRICULTURALIST. (Text in English) 1961. a. S.K.N. College of Agriculture, University of Udaipur, Jobner 303 329, Rajasthan, India. Ed. K.K. Vyas. **Indexed:** Biol.Abstr.

338.1   SP   ISSN 0213-5140
RED CONTABLE AGRARIA NACIONAL. irreg., latest 1988. 3300 ptas. Ministerio de Agricultura, Pesca y Alimentacon, Secretaria General Tecnica, Centro de Publicaciones, Paseo de la Infanta Isabel 1, 28071 Madrid, Spain. TEL 34-1-3475551. R&P contact: Juan Carlos Palacios Lopez. charts; stat.

338.1   DK   ISSN 0903-2037
REGNSKABSSTATISTIK-LANDBRUG. a. free. Danske Landboforenings Landsudvalg for Driftsoekonomi, Udkaersvej 15, DK-8200 Aarhus N, Denmark. illus. circ. 12,000.
    Formerly: Landboforeningernes Driftsoekonomiske Virksomhed, Regnskabsresultater, Kalenderaar (ISSN 0107-1300).

633.7 380.1   II
REPORT ON THE MARKETING OF TOBACCO IN ANDHRA PRADESH. a. Rs.9.90. Directorate of Marketing, Hyderabad, Andhra Pradesh, India. charts; stat.

338.1   US   ISSN 0276-1653
HD9000.1
RESEARCH IN DOMESTIC AND INTERNATIONAL AGRIBUSINESS MANAGEMENT. 1980. irreg., vol.12, 1996. $73.25. J A I Press Inc., 55 Old Post Rd., No. 2, Box 1678, Greenwich, CT 06830-1678. TEL 203-661-7602. FAX 203-661-0792. E-mail: jai@jaipress.com. (Subscr. in the UK and Europe to: JAI Press Ltd., 38 Tavistock St., Covent Garden, London WC2E 7PB, England. TEL 44-171-379-8834. FAX 44-171-379-8835) Ed. Ray A. Goldberg. **Indexed:** Int.Lab.Doc. **Document type:** monographic series.
—BLDSC (7738.898000).

338.1   HU   ISSN 0541-9417
RESEARCH INSTITUTE FOR AGRICULTURAL ECONOMICS. BULLETIN. (Text in English) 1962. irreg. exchange basis. Agrargazdasagi Kutato es Informatikai Intezet - Research and Information Institute for Agricultural Economics, Zsil u. 3-5, P.O. Box 5, 1355 Budapest, Hungary. TEL 217-10-11. FAX 361-217-7037. TELEX 22-6923. Ed. Adam Bisztray. **Indexed:** Maize Abstr., Rural Recreat.Tour.Abstr., World Agri.Econ.& Rural Sociol.Abstr. **Document type:** bulletin.
    Formerly: Hungarian Academy of Sciences. Research Institute for Agricultural Economics. Bulletin.

RESOURCES (WASHINGTON). see *CONSERVATION*

AGRICULTURE — AGRICULTURAL ECONOMICS

338.1 US ISSN 1058-7195
HD1401
REVIEW OF AGRICULTURAL ECONOMICS. 1979. s-a. $20 (foreign $25) (effective 1996). American Agricultural Economics Association, 1110 Buckeye Ave., Ames, IA 50010-8063. TEL 515-233-3234. FAX 515-233-3101. E-mail: sclarke@iastate.edu; URL: http://www.aaea.org. Eds. David Debertin, Angelos Pagoulatos. R&P contact: David Debertin. adv.: page $500. index. circ. 4,200. (back issues avail.) **Indexed:** Biostat., Geo.Abstr., Oper.Res.Manage.Sci., Qual.Contr.Appl.Stat., Rural Recreat.Tour.Abstr., World Agri.Econ.& Rural Sociol.Abstr. **Document type:** academic/scholarly publication.
—SWETS; UnCover.
Former titles (until 1991): North Central Journal of Agricultural Economics (ISSN 0191-9016); Ohio State University Agricultural Economics; Purdue University Agricultural Economics.
Description: Provides a forum for exchange of ideas and empirical findings in agricultural economics, particularly in the areas of extension education, applied economic and policy analysis, and decision support analysis.
Refereed Serial

338.1 NQ
REVISTA DE ECONOMIA AGRICOLA. q. $9 (Central America and Caribbean $15; N. & S. America $18; Europe $22; elsewhere $24). Universidad Nacional Autonoma de Nicaragua, Departamento de Economia Agricola, Apdo. 763, Zona 5, Correo Central, Managua, Nicaragua. TEL 505-2-23311. Ed.Bd.

338.1 301.35 BL ISSN 0103-2003
REVISTA DE ECONOMIA E SOCIOLOGIA RURAL. (Text in Portuguese, abstracts in English, Portuguese) 1962. q. Cr.$75000($80) (effective 1992). Sociedade Brasileira de Economia e Sociologia Rural, Edificio Brasilia Radio Center, Av. W3 Norte - Quadra 702, Salas 1049-1050, 70719-900 Brasilia DF, Brazil. TEL 061-225-6144. bibl. **Indexed:** Hisp.Amer.Per.Ind. (1984-).
Formerly (until 1988): Revista de Economia Rural.

338.1 SP ISSN 1135-6138
HD101
REVISTA ESPANOLA DE ECONOMIA AGRARIA. (Text in Spanish; summaries in English, French, Spanish) 1952. q. 7200 ptas. to individuals; students 5000 ptas.; foreign 9500 ptas. (effective 1997). Ministerio de Agricultura, Pesca y Alimentacion, Secretaria General Tecnica, Centro de Publicaciones, Paseo de la Infanta Isabel 1, 28071 Madrid, Spain. TEL 34-1-3475551. FAX 34-1-3475722. Ed. Jose Maria Sumpsi Vinas. R&P contact: Juan Carlos Palacios Lopez. adv.; bk.rev.; abstr.; bibl.; index, cum.index. circ. 2,500. **Indexed:** Dairy Sci.Abstr., ELLIS, Food Sci.& Tech.Abstr., Geo.Abstr., Ind.SST, Irr.& Drain.Abstr., Maize Abstr., P.A.I.S.For.Lang.Ind., Pig News & Info., Poult.Abstr., Rural Recreat.Tour.Abstr., Soils & Fert., Triticale Abstr., World Agri.Econ.& Rural Sociol.Abstr. **Document type:** academic/scholarly publication.
●Also available on CD-ROM.
—BLDSC (7853.948000); CINDOC.
Formerly (until no.4, 1994): Revista de Estudios Agro-Sociales (ISSN 0034-8155)
Description: Analyzes the procedures and politics of the agrarian sector.
Refereed Serial

RHEINLAND AKTUELL; Analysen - Daten - Informationen. see *AGRICULTURE — Abstracting, Bibliographies, Statistics*

338.1 IT ISSN 0035-6190
HD1401
RIVISTA DI ECONOMIA AGRARIA. (Text in Italian; summaries in English) 1946. q. Lit.140000 (effective 1997). (Istituto Nazionale di Economia Agraria) Societa Editrice II Mulino, Strada Maggiore, 37, 40125 Bologna, Italy. TEL 39-51-256011. FAX 39-51-256034. E-mail: riviste@mulino.it. (Co-sponsor: Istituto Nazionale di Economia Agraria) Ed. Francesco Bellia. adv. contact: M. Luisa Vezzali. bk.rev.; index, cum.index. circ. 1954-1964. circ. 1,600. (tabloid format; back issues avail.) **Indexed:** Curr.Cont., Dairy Sci.Abstr., Food Sci.& Tech.Abstr., Forest Prod.Abstr., Hort.Abstr., Int.Lab.Doc., P.A.I.S.For.Lang.Ind., Rural Recreat.Tour.Abstr., Trop.Oil Seeds Abstr., World Agri.Econ.& Rural Sociol.Abstr.
—BLDSC (7985.200000); SWETS.

338.1 IS
RIVON KUTNA. 1986. q. IS.125. Heshev, P.O. Box 40021, Tel Aviv 61 400, Israel. FAX 266233. circ. 150.

338.1 PL ISSN 0080-3715
ROCZNIKI NAUK ROLNICZYCH. SERIA G. EKONOMIKA ROLNICTWA. (Text in Polish; summaries in English, Polish or Russian) 1903. irreg., vol.86, 1994. price varies. (Polska Akademia Nauk, Komitet Organizacji Produkcji Rolnej i Wyzywienia Kraju) Wydawnictwo Naukowe P W N, Ul. Miodowa 10, 00-251 Warsaw, Poland. TEL 48-22-312738. FAX 48-22-6954288. Ed. Z. Wojtaszek. bibl.; charts. circ. 430. **Indexed:** AgroLibrex.

630.994 AT ISSN 1039-3897
RURAL BUSINESS. 1982. m. Aus.$52 (effective Feb. 1997). Richard Milne Pty. Ltd., P.O. Box 163, Drummoyne, N.S.W. 2047, Australia. TEL 61-2-8197322. FAX 61-2-8197650. E-mail: milnepublications@ibm.net. Ed. Michael O'Donnell. R&P contact: Andrew Nicholls. adv. contact: Greyson Maling. bk.rev. circ. 3,836. (back issues avail.)
Former titles (until 1992): Milne's Rural Business (ISSN 1037-387X); (until 1991): Rural Business (ISSN 1032-3872); (until 1989): Rural Business Magazine (ISSN 1031-3079); (until 1988): Rural Merchant Magazine (ISSN 0729-5588)
Description: News and information for the farm service industry.

338.1 352 CN ISSN 0036-0007
JS1721.S3
THE RURAL COUNCILLOR. 1966. m. (except Jan. & Aug.). Can.$30 to non-members (effective 1997). Saskatchewan Association of Rural Municipalities, c/o Leeann Minogue, Ed., 2075 Hamilton St., Regina, SK S4P 2E1, Canada. TEL 306-757-3577. FAX 306-565-2141. E-mail: sarm_mg@sk.sympatico.ca. adv. contact: Leeann Minogue. bk.rev. circ. 3,000. (back issues avail.) **Document type:** newsletter.
Description: Provides information to local rural governments in Saskatchewan.

338.1 US ISSN 0886-8611
HC501
RURAL DEVELOPMENT NEWS. 1974. 4/yr. free. North Central Regional Center for Rural Development, 404 East Hall, Iowa State University, Ames, IA 50011. TEL 515-294-8321. FAX 515-294-2303. E-mail: jstewart@iastate.edu; URL: http://www.ag.iastate.edu/centers/rdev/ruraldev.html. Ed. Julie Stewart. bk.rev. circ. 3,500. **Indexed:** Environ.Abstr. **Document type:** newsletter.
Formerly: North Central Regional Center for Rural Development. Research Report.
Description: Provides information on research projects, publications, conferences and extension services of interest to readers in the 12 state North Central region.

630 UG ISSN 0080-4851
RURAL DEVELOPMENT RESEARCH PAPER. 1965. irreg. price varies. Department of Rural Economy, P.O. Box 7062, Kampala, Uganda.

338.1 381 II ISSN 0036-0058
HN681
RURAL INDIA. (Text in English and Hindi) 1938. m. Rs.75 (foreign $22 or £11). Adarsh Seva Sangha, Gopal Sadan, Hospital Rd., Gwalior, India. TEL 91-71-267-4466. FAX 91-71-482-2293. adv.: page Rs.1000; trim 5 1/2 x 8. bk.rev.; illus.; mkt.; stat.; index. circ. 1,800. (back issues avail.) **Indexed:** Rural Recreat.Tour.Abstr., World Agri.Econ.& Rural Sociol.Abstr.
Description: Devoted to issues relating to Indian agricultural development and management.

338.1 PE
RURALTER. 1986. s-a. $20. Centro Internacional de Cooperacion para el Desarrollo Agricola (CICDA), Casilla 3720, Lima 100, Peru. TEL 639545. Ed. Juan Damonte. bk.rev. circ. 2,000.
Description: Covers rural development in underdeveloped countries, especially the Andean area.

338.1 634 US
SAN FRANCISCO FRESH FRUIT AND VEGETABLE WHOLESALE MARKET PRICES. 1932. a. $10. (U.S. Department of Agriculture) Federal-State Market News Service, 630 Sansome St., Rm. 727, San Francisco, CA 94111-0001. TEL 415-705-1300. FAX 415-705-1301. **Document type:** government publication, newsletter.

338.1 US
SAN FRANCISCO WHOLESALE FRUIT AND VEGETABLE REPORT. 1932. d. $180 (foreign $360). (U.S. Department of Agriculture) Federal-State Market News Service, 630 Sansome St., Rm. 727, San Francisco, CA 94111. TEL 415-705-1300. FAX 415-705-1301. circ. 280. (back issues avail.) **Document type:** government publication.
Description: Presents lists of price ranges, offerings, and status of the produce market; region-by-region market briefs on produce exportation in California.

SCANDINAVIAN INSTITUTE OF AFRICAN STUDIES. RURAL DEVELOPMENT. see *ANTHROPOLOGY*

630 AU ISSN 0036-6986
DAS SCHRIFTTUM DER AGRARWIRTSCHAFT. 1961. 6/yr. S.885 (foreign S.930). (Bundesministerium fuer Land- und Forstwirtschaft, Agrarwirtschaftliches Institut) Oesterreichischer Agrarverlag GmbH, Inkustr. 1-7, A-3400 Klosterneuburg, Austria. TEL 02243-333006. FAX 02243-3330056. Ed. Hans Alfons. bk.rev.; abstr.; bibl.; index. **Indexed:** Soils & Fert., World Agri.Econ.& Rural Sociol.Abstr.
—Linda Hall.

SCHWEIZER LANDTECHNIK. see *AGRICULTURE*

SHEEP & GOAT RESEARCH JOURNAL. see *AGRICULTURE — Poultry And Livestock*

338.1 382 US
HD9001
SITUATION & OUTLOOK REPORT. AGRICULTURAL EXPORTS. q. $17. U.S. Department of Agriculture, Economic Research Service, c/o Debbie Haugan, Rm. 110, 1301 New York Ave., N.W., Washington, DC 20005. TEL 202-219-0515. URL: http://www.mannlib.cornell.edu/reports/erssor/trade/aes-bb/. (Dist. by: ERS-NASS, 341 Victory Dr., Herndon, VA 22070. TEL 800-999-6779) (Co-sponsor: U.S. Foreign Agricultural Service) (also avail. in microfiche from CIS; back issues avail.; reprint service avail. from CIS) **Indexed:** Amer.Stat.Ind. (1974-). **Document type:** government publication.
●Also available online. Vendor(s): Information Access Co.
Formerly: Outlook for U.S. Agricultural Exports (ISSN 0148-9526)

338.1 US
SITUATION & OUTLOOK REPORT. AGRICULTURAL INCOME & FINANCE. 1961. q. $18. U.S. Department of Agriculture, Economic Research Service, c/o Debbie Haugan, Rm. 110, 1301 New York Ave., N.W., Washington, DC 20005-4788. TEL 202-219-0515. (Dist. by: ERS-NASS, 341 Victory Dr., Herndon, VA 22070. TEL 800-999-6779) (also avail. in microfiche from CIS; reprint service avail. from CIS) **Indexed:** Amer.Stat.Ind. (1988-). **Document type:** government publication.
●Also available online. Vendor(s): Knight-Ridder Information, Inc.
Former titles: U.S. Department of Agriculture. Agricultural Finance Outlook and Situation; U.S. Department of Agriculture. Agricultural Income and Finance Outlook and Situation; (until 1980): Agricultural Finance Outlook (ISSN 0501-9117)

AGRICULTURE — AGRICULTURAL ECONOMICS

338.1 664.1   US   ISSN 0896-0240
HD9101
SITUATION & OUTLOOK REPORT. SUGAR & SWEETENER. 1975. q. $22. U.S. Department of Agriculture, Economic Research Service, c/o Debbie Haugan, Rm. 110, 1301 New York Ave., N.W., Washington, DC 20005-4788. TEL 202-219-0515. E-mail: rlord@econ.ag.gov; URL: http://usda.mannlib.cornell.edu/reports/erssor/specialty/sss-bb/. (Dist. by: ERS-NASS, 341 Victory Dr., Herndon, VA 22070. TEL 800-999-6779) (also avail. in microfiche from CIS; back issues avail.; reprint service avail. from CIS) **Indexed:** Amer.Stat.Ind. (1975-), Potato Abstr. **Document type:** government publication.
●Also available online. Vendor(s): Information Access Co., Knight-Ridder Information, Inc.
Former titles (until 1986): U.S. Department of Agriculture. Outlook and Situation Report. Sugar and Sweetener (ISSN 8755-8548); U.S. Department of Agriculture. Sugar and Sweetener Outlook and Situation (ISSN 0362-9511); U.S. Department of Agriculture. Economics Management Staff. Sugar and Sweetener Report; Which was formed by merger of: U.S. Department of Agriculture. Economic Research Service. Sugar and Sweetener Situation (ISSN 0360-0521); U.S. Agricultural Marketing Service. Sugar Market News.

633.71 338.1   US   ISSN 0893-8946
HD9131
SITUATION & OUTLOOK REPORT. TOBACCO. (Supplement avail.: U.S. Department of Agriculture. Situtation and Outlook Yearbook. Tobacco) 1937. q. $19. U.S. Department of Agriculture, Economic Research Service, c/o Debbie Haugan, Rm. 110, 1301 New York Ave., N.W., DC 20005-4789. TEL 202-219-4060. (Dist. by: ERS-NASS, 341 Victory Dr., Herndon, VA 22070. TEL 800-999-6779) bk.rev.; charts; mkt.; stat.; index. circ. 3,000. (processed; also avail. in microfiche from CIS; back issues avail.; reprint service avail. from CIS) **Indexed:** Amer.Stat.Ind. (1974-), Tob.Abstr. **Document type:** government publication.
●Also available online. Vendor(s): Information Access Co., Knight-Ridder Information, Inc.
Former titles (until 1986): U.S. Department of Agriculture. Outlook and Situation Report. Tobacco (ISSN 0889-7948); (until 1981): U.S. Department of Agriculture. Tobacco Situation (ISSN 0040-8344)

635 338.1   US   ISSN 1049-3352
HD9220.U5   CODEN: VSSRES
SITUATION & OUTLOOK REPORT. VEGETABLES & SPECIALTIES. 1955. s-a. $18 (effective 1996). U.S. Department of Agriculture, Economic Research Service, c/o Debbie Haugan, Rm. 110, 1301 New York Ave., N.W., Washington, DC 20005-4788. TEL 202-219-0515. (Dist. by: ERS-NASS, 341 Victory Dr., Herndon, VA 22070. TEL 800-999-6779) mkt.; stat. (processed; also avail. in microfiche from CIS; back issues avail.; reprint service avail. from CIS) **Indexed:** Amer.Stat.Ind. (1974-). **Document type:** government publication.
●Also available online. Vendor(s): Information Access Co., Knight-Ridder Information, Inc.
Former titles: U.S. Department of Agriculture. Situation and Outlook Report. Vegetables (ISSN 0893-8938); U.S. Department of Agriculture. Vegetable Outlook and Situation (ISSN 0277-9900); U.S. Department of Agriculture. Economics Management Staff. Vegetable Situation.

338.1   SA
SOUTH AFRICA. DEPARTMENT OF AGRICULTURE. DIRECTORATE OF AGRICULTURAL STATISTICS. TRENDS IN THE AGRICULTURAL SECTOR. 1968. s-a. free. Department of Agriculture, Directorate of Agricultural Statistics, Private Bag X144, Pretoria 0001, South Africa. stat.; circ. controlled.
Former titles: South Africa. Department of Agriculture and Fisheries. Division of Economic Services. Trends in the Agricultural Sector; South Africa. Department of Agricultural Economics and Marketing. Division of Agricultural Marketing and Research. Trends in the Agricultural Sector.

338   US
SOUTHERN RURAL DEVELOPMENT CENTER. CAPSULES. 1981. m. free. Southern Rural Development Center, Box 9656, Mississippi State, MS 39762. TEL 601-325-3207. FAX 601-325-8915. Ed. Jacqueline F. Tisdale. bk.rev. circ. 3,000. **Document type:** newsletter.

338.1   UK   ISSN 0958-9732
S562.G6
SPECIAL STUDIES IN AGRICULTURAL ECONOMICS. 1970. irreg., no.103, 1988. University of Reading, Department of Agricultural Economics & Management, 4 Earley Gate, Whiteknights Rd., P.O. Box 237, Reading RG6 2AR, England. TEL 44-1734-875123. FAX 44-1734-756467. TELEX 847813-RULIB-G. **Indexed:** Anim.Breed.Abstr. **Document type:** monographic series.
Formerly: Agricultural Enterprise Studies in England and Wales.
Description: Reports on the results of economic research on crops and livestock.

338.1 630   SJ
SUDAN YEARBOOK OF AGRICULTURAL STATISTICS. (Text in English) 1974. a. Department of Agricultural Economics, Statistics Division, P.O. Box 1246, Khartoum, Sudan.
Supersedes: Bulletin of Agricultural Statistics of the Sudan.

SURVEY OF HOUSEHOLD ECONOMIC ACTIVITIES (YEAR). see BUSINESS AND ECONOMICS — Economic Situation And Conditions

633   UK   ISSN 0309-2968
SUTTON BRIDGE ANNUAL REVIEW. 1970. a. Potato Marketing Board, Broad Field House, 4 Between Towns Rd., Cowley, Oxford OX4 3NA, England. TEL 44-1865-714455. FAX 44-1865-716418. Ed. A.C. Cunnington. **Document type:** trade publication.

SZABAD FOLDMUVES. see AGRICULTURE

338.1   GW   ISSN 0177-6673
TECHNISCHE UNIVERSITAET BERLIN. INSTITUT FUER SOZIALOEKONOMIE DER AGRARENTWICKLUNG. SCHRIFTENREIHE DES FACHBEREICHS. 1960. irreg. (5-8/yr.). free. Technische Universitaet Berlin, Fachbereich Internationale Agrarentwicklung, Hellriegelstr. 6, 14195 Berlin, Germany. TEL 030-314-71312. FAX 030-314-23222. TELEX 184262-TUBLN-D. circ. 150. (processed) **Indexed:** Abstr.Rural Dev.Trop.
Formerly: Technische Universitaet Berlin. Institut fuer Sozialoekonomie der Agrarentwicklung. Jahresbericht (ISSN 0170-8376); Incorporates: Technische Universitaet Berlin. Institut fuer Sozialoekonomie der Agrarentwicklung. Annual Report (Abridged Edition) (ISSN 0170-8309); (until 1976): Technische Universitaet. Institut fuer Sozialoekonomie der Agrarentwicklung. Taetigkeitsbericht (ISSN 0067-6039)
Description: Reports on the activities of the institute's faculty; research programs of study, proceedings, and papers focused on the problem of agricultural development in developing countries.

338.1   NE   ISSN 0921-481X
TIJDSCHRIFT VOOR SOCIAAL WETENSCHAPPELIJK ONDERZOEK VAN DE LANDBOUW. Short title: T S L. (Text in Dutch and English) 1986. q. $35 to individuals; institutions $50 (effective 1996). Landbouw-Economisch Instituut - Agricultural Economics Institute, P.B. 29703, 2502 LS The Hague, Netherlands. TEL 31-70-3614161. FAX 31-70-3615624. E-mail: postmaster@lei.dlo.nl; URL: http://www.lei.dlo.nl/lei. (Editorial addr.: Universiteit Gent, Vakgroep voor Landbouwecomie, Coupure Links 653, 9000 Ghent, Belgium) Ed. Guido van Huylenbroeck. bk.rev.; index. circ. 350. (back issues avail.)
—BLDSC (8844.460000).

TURF NEWS. see AGRICULTURE — Crop Production And Soil

338.1 600   CN   ISSN 0715-6650
TWO THIRDS. 1982. q. Can.$3 per copy. Canadian Hunger Foundation, 323 Chapel St., Ottawa, ON K1N 722, Canada. TEL 613-237-0180. FAX 613-237-5969. Ed. Tom Taylor. circ. 1,100. **Indexed:** HR Rep. **Document type:** newsletter.

338.1   MY   ISSN 0304-8349
HD1471.M34
UNITED PLANTING ASSOCIATION OF MALAYSIA. ANNUAL REPORT. (Text in English) 1968. a. M.$10. United Planting Association of Malaysia, Box 10272, 50708 Kuala Lumpur, Malaysia. TEL 603-2485622. FAX 603-2415449. circ. 1,100. **Document type:** corporate report.

338.1   US   ISSN 0083-0445
HD1751
U.S. DEPARTMENT OF AGRICULTURE. AGRICULTURAL ECONOMIC REPORTS. 1961. irreg. price varies. U.S. Department of Agriculture, Economic Research Service, c/o Debbie Haugan, Rm. 110, 1301 New York Ave., N.W., Washington, DC 20005-4788. TEL 202-219-0515. (Subscr. to: ERS-NASS, 341 Victory Dr., Herndon, VA 22072. TEL 800-999-6799) **Indexed:** Cott.& Trop.Fibr.Abstr., Dairy Sci.Abstr., Field Crop Abstr., Geo.Abstr., Rural Recreat.Tour.Abstr., Soils & Fert., Triticale Abstr., Trop.Oil Seeds Abstr., World Agri.Econ.& Rural Sociol.Abstr. **Document type:** government publication.
Reports 1-233 (1916-1972) issued as: U.S. Department of Agriculture. Economic Research Service. Agricultural Economics Report.

338.1   US   ISSN 0099-1066
HD1751   CODEN: AGOUD7
U.S. DEPARTMENT OF AGRICULTURE. AGRICULTURAL OUTLOOK. 1975. m. (11/yr.). $39 (foreign $48.75) (effective 1996). U.S. Department of Agriculture, Economic Research Service, c/o Debbie Haugan, Rm. 110, 1301 New York Ave., N.W., Washington, DC 20005-4788. TEL 202-219-0515. (Dist. by: ERS-NASS, 341 Victory Dr., Herndon, VA 22070. TEL 800-999-6779) Ed. M. Reardon. stat. circ. 10,000. (also avail. in microfiche from CIS; back issues avail.; reprint service avail. from CIS) **Indexed:** Amer.Stat.Ind. (1975-), Biol.& Agr.Ind., BPIA, Farm & Garden Ind., Food Sci.& Tech.Abstr., Ind.U.S.Gov.Per., Intl.Polym.Sci.& Tech., P.A.I.S., PROMT, Ref.Pt.Food Indus.Abstr., Rural Recreat.Tour.Abstr. **Document type:** government publication.
●Also available online. Vendor(s): Knight-Ridder Information, Inc.
—BLDSC (0750.760000); KR SourceOne; SWETS; UMI; UnCover.
Former titles: U.S. Department of Agriculture. Economic Research Service. Farm Income Situation (ISSN 0014-7974); U.S. Department of Agriculture. Economic Research Service. Marketing and Transport Situation (ISSN 0025-3677); U.S. Department of Agriculture. Economic Research Service. Agricultural Outlook Digest; U.S. Department of Agriculture. Economic Research Service. Demand and Price Situation; Incorporates: U.S. Department of Agriculture. Economic Research Service. Checklist of New Reports.
Description: Presents the U.S.D.A. farm income and food price forecasts. Emphasizes the short-term outlook as well as issues that range from international trade to U.S. land use.

U.S. DEPARTMENT OF AGRICULTURE. AGRICULTURAL STATISTICS BOARD REPORT: AGRICULTURAL PRICES. see AGRICULTURE — Abstracting, Bibliographies, Statistics

664 338.19   US   ISSN 1056-327X
HD9001   CODEN: FORVEZ
U.S. DEPARTMENT OF AGRICULTURE. ECONOMIC RESEARCH SERVICE. FOOD REVIEW. 1942. q. $8.50 (foreign $10.65). U.S. Department of Agriculture, Economic Research Service, c/o Debbie Haugan, Rm. 110, 1301 New York Ave., N.W., Washington, DC 20005-4788. TEL 202-219-0515. (Dist. by: ERS-NASS, 341 Victory Dr., Herndon, VA 22070. TEL 800-999-6779) Ed. Mary Maher. charts; mkt.; stat. circ. 4,000. (also avail. in microform from UMI; microfiche from CIS; back issues avail.; reprint service avail. from CIS,UMI) **Indexed:** Amer.Stat.Ind. (1974-1975, 1978-), B.P.I, BPIA, Bus.Ind., Curr.Pack.Abstr., Food Sci.& Tech.Ind., Hlth.Ind., Ind.U.S.Gov.Per., MEDOC, P.A.I.S., PROMT, Ref.Pt.Food Indus.Abstr., Tr.& Indus.Ind. **Document type:** government publication.
●Also available online. Vendor(s): Lexis-Nexis.
—BLDSC (3982.610000); KR SourceOne; SWETS; UMI; UnCover.
Formerly (until 1990): National Food Review (ISSN 0164-3428); Supersedes (in 1978): U.S. Department of Agriculture. Economic Research Service. National Food Situation (ISSN 0027-9277)
Description: Offers the latest developments in food prices, product safety, nutrition programs, consumption patterns, and marketing.

AGRICULTURE — AGRICULTURAL ECONOMICS

338.14 US ISSN 0082-9781
HD1751 CODEN: XAGMAF
U.S. DEPARTMENT OF AGRICULTURE. MARKETING RESEARCH REPORT. 1952. irреg. U.S. Department of Agriculture, Office of Public Affairs, 14th St. & Independence Ave, S.W., Washington, DC 20250-1300. TEL 202-720-2791. (also avail. in microfiche from UPD) **Indexed:** Rural Recreat.Tour.Abstr., World Agri.Econ.& Rural Sociol.Abstr. **Document type:** government publication. —CASDDS; CISTI.

338.1 US ISSN 0082-979X
S21 CODEN: XAPRA7
U.S. DEPARTMENT OF AGRICULTURE. PRODUCTION RESEARCH REPORTS. 1956. irreg. U.S. Department of Agriculture, Office of Public Affairs, 14th St. & Independence Ave., S.W., Washington, DC 20250-1300. TEL 202-720-2791. (also avail. in microfiche from UPD) **Indexed:** Biol.Abstr., Pollut.Abstr. **Document type:** government publication. —CASDDS.

338.1 US ISSN 0742-9509
U.S. DEPARTMENT OF AGRICULTURE. RURAL BUSINESS - COOPERATIVE SERVICE. RESEARCH REPORTS. (Former name of issuing body: U.S.D.A. Agricultural Cooperative Service) irreg. price varies. U.S. Department of Agriculture, Rural Business - Cooperative Service, AG Box 3285, Washington, DC 20250-3255. TEL 202-720-6483. FAX 202-720-4641. charts; stat. **Document type:** government publication, monographic series.
Description: Presents the results of U.S.D.A. Cooperative Service studies.

630 338.1 US
U.S. DEPARTMENT OF AGRICULTURE. SITUATION & OUTLOOK REPORT. AGRICULTURE AND TRADE: FORMER U S S R. a. $9 per no. U.S. Department of Agriculture, Economic Research Service, c/o Debbie Haugan, Rm. 110, 1301 New York Ave., N.W., Washington, DC 20005-4788. TEL 202-219-0515. (Dist. by: ERS-NASS, 341 Victory Dr., Herndon, VA 22070. TEL 800-999-6779) **Document type:** government publication.
●Also available online. Vendor(s): Information Access Co., Knight-Ridder Information, Inc.
Former titles (until May 1992): U.S. Department of Agriculture. Situation and Outlook Series. Agriculture and Trade: U S S R (ISSN 1045-6848); World Agriculture Regional Supplement: U S S R; World Agriculture Regional Supplement: Soviet Union; Agricultural Situation in the Soviet Union (ISSN 0360-4098)

630 US ISSN 0093-4429
UNITED STATES: COTTON QUALITY REPORTS FOR GINNINGS.* Title varies. 1928. m. free. U.S. Agricultural Marketing Service, Cotton Division, 302 Annex Bldg., 12th and C Sts., S.W., Washington, DC 20250. TEL 202-447-3193. stat. (processed; also avail. in microfiche from CIS; reprint service avail. from CIS) **Indexed:** Amer.Stat.Ind. (1973-).

338.1 IT
UNIVERSITA DEGLI STUDI DI TRIESTE. ISTITUTO DI RICERCHE ECONOMICO AGRARIE. PUBBLICAZIONE. 1971. irreg. Universita degli Studi di Trieste, Istituto di Ricerche Economico-Agrarie, Trieste, Italy. **Indexed:** Geo.Abstr.

338.1 US ISSN 0886-4845
UNIVERSITY OF FLORIDA. FOOD AND RESOURCE ECONOMICS DEPARTMENT. ECONOMIC INFORMATION REPORT. Key Title: Economic Information Report. 1969. irreg., no.123, 1979. free. University of Florida, Institute of Food and Agricultural Sciences, c/o Dr. Lawrence Libby, Chairman, Food and Resource Economics Department, Box 110240, Gainesville, FL 32611-6015. TEL 904-392-1733. Ed. Richard Bellock. circ. 2,500.
Former titles: University of Florida. Food and Resource Economics Department. Economics Report; University of Florida. Institute of Food and Agricultural Sciences. Agricultural Economics Series.

338.1 US ISSN 0073-5213
UNIVERSITY OF ILLINOIS AT URBANA-CHAMPAIGN. DEPARTMENT OF AGRICULTURAL ECONOMICS. AGRICULTURAL FINANCE PROGRAM REPORT. 1970. irreg., latest 1970. price varies. University of Illinois at Urbana-Champaign, Department of Agricultural Economics, Urbana, IL 61801. TEL 217-333-7425.

338.1 US
HD1511.U6
UNIVERSITY OF ILLINOIS AT URBANA-CHAMPAIGN. DEPARTMENT OF AGRICULTURAL ECONOMICS. LEASE SHARES AND FARM RETURNS. 1961. a. $3. University of Illinois at Urbana-Champaign, Department of Agricultural Economics, Urbana, IL 61801. TEL 217-333-2638. Ed. John T. Scott. stat.; circ. controlled.
Formerly: University of Illinois at Urbana-Champaign. Department of Agricultural Economics. Landlord and Tenant Shares (ISSN 0160-3027)

338.1 UK
UNIVERSITY OF LONDON. WYE COLLEGE. AGRARIAN DEVELOPMENT UNIT. OCCASIONAL PAPER. 1974. irreg. price varies. University of London, Wye College, Department of Agricultural Economics, Ashford, Kent TN25 5AH, England. TEL 44-1233-812401. **Indexed:** Geo.Abstr., Rural Recreat.Tour.Abstr., World Agri.Econ.& Rural Sociol.Abstr. **Document type:** academic/scholarly publication, monographic series.

338.1 631 UK
UNIVERSITY OF LONDON. WYE COLLEGE. DEPARTMENT OF AGRICULTURAL ECONOMICS. FARM BUSINESS UNIT. OCCASIONAL PAPER. 1978. irreg. price varies. University of London, Wye College, Department of Agricultural Economics, Farm Business Unit, Ashford, Kent TN25 5AH, England. TEL 44-1233-812401. **Indexed:** Rural Recreat.Tour.Abstr., World Agri.Econ.& Rural Sociol.Abstr. **Document type:** academic/scholarly publication, monographic series.
Formerly: Wye College (University of London). School of Rural Economics and Related Studies. Farm Business Unit. Occasional Paper.

338.1 UK
UNIVERSITY OF MANCHESTER. SCHOOL OF ECONOMIC STUDIES. FARM BUSINESS UNIT. BULLETIN. irreg., no.231, 1995. £10.50. University of Manchester, School of Economic Studies, Farm Business Unit, Oxford Rd., Manchester M13 9PL, England. **Document type:** bulletin.
Formerly (until 1995): University of Manchester. Faculty of Economic and Social Studies. Department of Agricultural Economics. Bulletin.

338.1 UK ISSN 0557-6911
UNIVERSITY OF READING. DEPARTMENT OF AGRICULTURAL ECONOMICS & MANAGEMENT. FARM BUSINESS DATA. 1974. a. £8. University of Reading, Department of Agricultural Economics & Management, 4 Earley Gate, Whiteknights Rd., P.O. Box 237, Reading RG6 2AR, England. TEL 44-1734-875123. FAX 44-1734-756467. Ed. A.J. Errington. bibl.; charts; stat. **Document type:** bulletin.
Description: Explores business ratios for account analysis, research reports and forward planning.

338.1 UK
UNIVERSITY OF READING. DEPARTMENT OF AGRICULTURAL ECONOMICS & MANAGEMENT. OCCASIONAL PAPERS. 1993. irreg., no.3, 1994. £8. 4 Earley Gate, Whiteknights Rd., P.O. Box 237, Reading RG6 2AR, England. TEL 44-1734-875123. FAX 44-1734-756467. **Document type:** monographic series.

338.1 AT ISSN 0817-8771
UNIVERSITY OF SYDNEY. DEPARTMENT OF AGRICULTURAL ECONOMICS. RESEARCH REPORT.. 1957. irreg., no.13, 1989. price varies. University of Sydney, Department of Agricultural Economics, Sydney, N.S.W. 2006, Australia. TEL 02-692-2574. FAX 02-692-2945. TELEX AA26169 UNISYD. circ. 400. (processed) **Document type:** academic/scholarly publication.
Formerly: University of Sydney. Department of Agricultural Economics. Mimeographed Report. (ISSN 0082-0555)
Description: Contains results of detailed analyses of problems in both agricultural and applied economics.

338.1 639.2 UY ISSN 0797-3357
URUGUAY. MINISTERIO DE AGRICULTURA Y PESCA. PRECIOS DE PRODUCTOS E INSUMOS AGROPECUARIOS. 1974. m. Ministerio de Agricultura y Pesca, Direccion de Investigaciones Economicas Agropecuarias, Rincon 22, Montevideo, Uruguay. adv.

338.1 SP
VALENCIA - FRUITS; semanario europeo de informacion economica. 1962. w. 21000 ptas. Sucro, S.A., Hernan Cortes, 5-1, 46004 Valencia, Spain. TEL 34-6-3510295. FAX 34-6-3525752. Ed. Amparo Vallier Pino. adv. contact: Jose Maria Server Martinez. **Document type:** newspaper.

338.1 US ISSN 1064-4075
VIRGINIA FRUIT AND VEGETABLE BULLETIN. s-w. Virginia Department of Agriculture & Consumer Services, 1100 Bank St., Ste. 805, Richmond, VA 23219-3638. TEL 804-786-3947. FAX 804-371-7787. Ed. J.P. Welch. circ. 500. (back issues avail.) **Document type:** government publication.
Description: Provides fruit and vegetable market prices since the last issue, to Virginia farmers, agribusinesses and other readers.

338.1 301.35 PL
WARSAW AGRICULTURAL UNIVERSITY. S G G W. ANNALS. AGRICULTURAL ECONOMICS AND RURAL SOCIOLOGY. (Text mainly in English; occasionally in French, German or Russian; summaries in Polish) 1957. irreg. $10 per no. Szkola Glowna Gospodarstwa Wiejskiego (SGGW) - Warsaw Agricultural University, Ul. Nowoursynowska 166, 02-766 Warsaw, Poland. Ed. M. Adamowicz. **Indexed:** AgroLibrex, Forest Prod.Abstr. **Document type:** academic/scholarly publication.
—BLDSC (1035.013000).
Formerly: Warsaw Agricultural University. S G G W - A R. Annals. Agricultural Economics and Rural Sociology (ISSN 0208-5720)

338.1 US
WEEKLY COTTON TRADE REPORT. 1920? w. $100. New York Cotton Exchange, 4 World Trade Center, New York, NY 10048. TEL 212-938-7909. Ed. Tom Bertolini. charts; illus.; stat. circ. 250. (looseleaf format; back issues avail.)
Description: Weekly economic analysis of the futures and cash cotton markets. Includes commentary on the week's events.

630 338.1 US ISSN 0043-1850
WEEKLY MARKET BULLETIN. 1918. w. $20. Department of Agriculture, Markets & Food, Box 2042, Concord, NH 03302-2042. Ed. Stephen H. Taylor. adv. circ. 9,400. (back issues avail.) **Document type:** government publication, bulletin.
Description: Provides news and information for New Hampshire farmers and rural residents.

338.1 634 US
WEEKLY MICHIGAN POTATO REPORT. w. $25. U.S. Department of Agriculture (Benton Harbor), Box 1204, 175 Territorial Rd., Ste. 201, Benton Harbor, MI 49022. TEL 616-925-3270. FAX 616-925-3272. (back issues avail.) **Document type:** newsletter, government publication.
Description: Lists Michigan potato shipments, F.O.B. prices, and terminal market wholesale prices.

WELSH AGRICULTURAL STATISTICS. see *AGRICULTURE — Abstracting, Bibliographies, Statistics*

338.1 US
WESTERN CITRUS REPORT. s-w. $132. U.S. Department of Agriculture, Agricultural Marketing Service (Los Angeles), 1320 E. Olympic Blvd., Ste. 212, Los Angeles, CA 90021-1907. TEL 213-894-3077. FAX 213-894-2898. **Document type:** government publication.

338.1 US
WESTERN MELON AND VEGETABLE REPORT.* d. $180. U.S. Department of Agriculture, Agricultural Marketing Service (Phoenix), 522 N. Central, No. 245, Phoenix, AZ 85007. TEL 602-252-0966. FAX 602-252-0623. **Document type:** government publication.

338.1 US
WESTERN POTATO AND ONION REPORT. d. $180. U.S. Department of Agriculture, Agricultural Marketing Service (Idaho Falls), 1820 E. 17th St., Ste. 130, Idaho Falls, ID 83404. TEL 208-526-0740. FAX 208-526-9433. **Document type:** government publication.

WHEATGROWER. see *AGRICULTURE — Crop Production And Soil*

AGRICULTURE — AGRICULTURAL EQUIPMENT

338.1   PL   ISSN 1230-0659
WIES I PANSTWO. 1990. q. Spoldzielnia Wydawnictwo Ludowe, Ul. Grzybowska 4, P.O. Box 71, 00-950 Warsaw, Poland. TEL 48-22-208741. Ed. Ryszard Miazek. **Indexed:** AgroLibrex.
—BLDSC (9316.370000).

338.1   PL   ISSN 0137-1673
WIES I ROLNICTWO. (English version avail. on request) (Text in Polish; summaries in English) 1973. q. 15 Zl. (foreign 30 Zl.) (efective 1998). Polska Akademia Nauk, Instytut Rozwoju Wsi i Rolnictwa, Ul. Nowy Swiat 72, 00-330 Warsaw, Poland. TEL 48-22-8266371. FAX 48-22-8266371. E-mail: irwir@irwirpan.waw.pl. (Dist. by: RUCH S.A., Oddzial Warszawa, Ul. Towarowa 28, 00-958 Warsaw, Poland) Ed. Maria Wieruszewska. R&P contact: Mariusz Safin. adv. contact: Mariusz Safin. bk.rev. circ. 460. **Indexed:** AgroLibrex. **Document type:** academic/scholarly publication.
    Description: Presents the changes in the rural community and agriculture in Poland and other Central and Eastern European countries in the period of transformation of the political and economic system, and in a perspective of an accession to the European Union.
    Refereed Serial

338.1 382   US
WOOD PRODUCTS: INTERNATIONAL TRADE AND FOREIGN MARKETS. 1985. 5/yr. $21. U.S. Department of Agriculture, Foreign Agricultural Service, Information Division, Rm. 5920-S, Washington, DC 20250-1000. TEL 202-720-7937. (Subscr. to: Supt. of Documents, U.S. Government Printing Office, Washington, DC 20402. TEL 202-783-3238. FAX 202-512-2233) charts; stat. circ. 360. (also avail. in microfiche from CIS; reprint service avail. from CIS) **Indexed:** Amer.Stat.Ind. (1984-1986, 1988-). **Document type:** government publication.

WOOL MARKET REVIEW. see *TEXTILE INDUSTRIES AND FABRICS*

338.1   US   ISSN 0162-5586
HD9001
WORLD AGRICULTURAL SUPPLY AND DEMAND ESTIMATES. 1977. m. $30 (foreign $37.50). U.S. Department of Agriculture, World Agricultural Outlook Board, 14th St. and Independence Ave., S.W., Rm. 5143-S, Washington, DC 20250-3800. TEL 202-250-3800. (Dist. by: In Focus, 341 Victory Dr., Herndon, VA 22070. TEL 800-999-6779; Avail. from: Supt. of Documents, U.S. Government Printing Office, Washington, DC 20402. TEL 202-783-3238. FAX 202-512-2233) Ed. Raymond L. Bridge. stat. circ. 1,300. (also avail. in microfiche from CIS; reprint service avail. from CIS) **Indexed:** Amer.Stat.Ind. (1980-). **Document type:** government publication.
    ● Also available online. Vendor(s): Knight-Ridder Information, Inc.
    Description: Provides monthly forecasts of production, domestic use, stocks, and exports for major crops of the U.S. and the world, as well as for U.S. livestock and sugar production.

WORLD COTTON SITUATION. see *AGRICULTURE — Crop Production And Soil*

YELLOW SHEET (TOMS RIVER). see *AGRICULTURE — Poultry And Livestock*

338.1   PL   ISSN 0044-1600
HD1995.7
ZAGADNIENIA EKONOMIKI ROLNEJ. (Text in Polish; summaries in English) 1953. bi-m. 24 Zl.($15) (effective 1997). Instytut Ekonomiki Rolnictwa i Gospodarki Zywnosciowej, Ul. Swietokrzyska 20, 00-002 Warsaw, Poland. TEL 48-22-8266117. FAX 48-22-8271960. (Dist. by: RUCH S.A., Towarowa 28, Warsaw, Poland) (Co-sponsors: Polska Akademia Nauk; Ministerstwo Rolnictwa i Gospodarki Zywnosciowej) Ed W. Jozwiak. adv. contact: Wojciech Jozwiak. bk.rev.; bibl.; charts; index. circ. 400. **Indexed:** AgroLibrex, Geo.Abstr., IDA, Rural Recreat.Tour.Abstr., World Agri.Econ.& Rural Sociol.Abstr. **Document type:** academic/scholarly publication.
—BLDSC (9425.500000).
    Refereed Serial

338.1   XR   ISSN 0139-570X
HD101
ZEMEDELSKA EKONOMIKA/AGRICULTURAL ECONOMY; vedecky casopis. (Text and summaries in Czech or Slovak and English) 1954. m. $170 in Europe; elsewhere $177 (effective 1997). Ustav Zemedelskych a Potravinarskych Informaci, Slezska 7, 120 56 Prague 2, Czech Republic. TEL 420-2-24257939. FAX 420-2-24253938. E-mail: uzlk@uzpi.cz. Ed. Alena Rottova. adv.; bk.rev.; abstr.; stat.; index. circ. 500. **Indexed:** Agri.Eng.Abstr., Dairy Sci.Abstr., Geo.Abstr., Maize Abstr., Rural Ext.Educ.& Tr.Abstr., Rural Recreat.Tour.Abstr., Seed Abstr., Soils & Fert., World Agri.Econ.& Rural Sociol.Abstr. **Document type:** academic/scholarly publication.
—BLDSC (9499.550000).
    Incorporates (in 1993): Sociologie Venkova a Zemedelstvi; Which was formerly: U V T I Z Sbornik - Sociologie Zemedelstvi (ISSN 0231-5688); U V T I Z Sbornik - Sociologie a Historie Zemedelstvi (ISSN 0231-5572).

338.1   CC   ISSN 1006-4583
ZHONGGUO NONGCUN GUANCHA/CHINA RURAL SURVEY. (Text in Chinese) 1988. bi-m. $48 (effective 1997 & 1998). Zhongguo Shehui Kexueyuan, Nongcun Fazhan Yanjiusuo - Chinese Academy of Social Science, Institute of Rural Development, No.5, Jianguomennei Dajie, Beijing 100732, People's Republic of China. TEL 86-10-6513-7744. Ed. Jiyuan Chen. adv. contact: Jinsong Chen. **Document type:** academic/scholarly publication.
    Formerly (until 1995): Nongcun Jingji yu Shehui - Rural Economy and Society (ISSN 1002-8889)

338.1   CC   ISSN 1002-8870
ZHONGGUO NONGCUN JINGJI/CHINESE RURAL ECONOMY. (Text in Chinese) m. $96 (effective 1997 & 1998). Zhongguo Shehui Kexueyuan, Nongcun Fazhan Yanjiusuo - Chinese Academy of Social Sciences, Institute of Rural Development, No. 5, Jianguomennei Dajie, Beijing 100732, People's Republic of China. TEL 86-10-6513-7744. (Dist. in US by: China Books & Periodicals, Inc., 2929 24th St., San Francisco, CA 94110. TEL 415-282-2994) Ed. Jiyuan Chen. adv. contact: Jinsong Chen.
—BLDSC (3181.075000); UnCover.

AGRICULTURE — Agricultural Equipment

631.3   AT   ISSN 1036-4242
A F D J. (Australian Farmers' Dealers' Journal) 1984. 4/yr. Aus.$30 (foreign Aus.$70) (effective 1997). Norley Pty. Ltd., 3 Lygon St., S. Caulfield, Vic. 3162, Australia. TEL 61-3-95789122.
FAX 61-3-95782784. E-mail: norley@werple.net.au; URL: http://www.infoweb.com.au/agmachinery/. Ed. Peter Levy. adv.; B&W page $1450, color page $2050; trim 275 x 210; adv. contact: Garry Kennedy. bk.rev.; tr.lit. circ. 18,500.
    Formerly (until 1990): Australian Farm Dealers Journal (ISSN 0818-2183)
    Description: Covers Australian farm machinery market.

631.3   JA   ISSN 0084-5841
S671   CODEN: AMAADL
A M A - AGRICULTURAL MECHANIZATION IN ASIA, AFRICA AND LATIN AMERICA. (Text in English) 1971. q. 6000 Yen($56) (Shin-Norinsha Co., Ltd.) Shin-Norinsha Co., Ltd. - Farm Machinery Industrial Research Corp., 7, 2-chome, Kanda Nishiki-cho, Chiyoda-ku, Tokyo 101, Japan. TEL 03-3291-3674. FAX 03-3291-5717. Ed. Yoshisuke Kishida. adv. contact: K. Ikeda. bk.rev.; film rev.; bibl.; charts; illus.; stat.; circ. 15,000 (controlled). (back issues avail.) **Indexed:** AIT Reports, Cott.& Trop.Fibr.Abstr., Dairy Sci.Abstr., Field Crop Abstr., Herb.Abstr., Int.Abstr.Oper.Res., Irr.& Drain.Abstr., Potato Abstr., Rice Abstr., Rural Recreat.Tour.Abstr., Seed Abstr., Sorghum & Millets Abstr., Sugar Ind.Abstr., Triticale Abstr., World Agri.Econ.& Rural Sociol.Abstr. **Document type:** academic/scholarly publication.
—BLDSC (0750.421000); Ei; Linda Hall; SWETS; UnCover.
    Former titles: A M A - Agricultural Mechanization in Southeast Asia; A M A - Agricultural Mechanization in Asia.
    Description: Covers agricultural equipment and mechanical engineering.

A S A E TRANSACTIONS. INFORMATION AND ELECTRICAL TECHNOLOGIES - EMERGING TECHNOLOGIES. (American Society of Agricultural Engineers) see *ENGINEERING — Electrical Engineering*

631.3 620   US
A S A E TRANSACTIONS. POWER & MACHINERY. 1970. a. $66.50 to non-members; members $34 (effective 1997). American Society of Agricultural Engineers, 2950 Niles Rd., St. Joseph, MI 49085-9659. TEL 616-429-0300.
FAX 616-429-3852. E-mail: hq@asae.org; URL: http://asae.org/. Ed. Pamela DeVore-Hansen. circ. 150. **Document type:** trade publication.
    Description: Addresses tractors and other field equipment, fuels, conveyors, fruit and vegetable harvesting, greenhouse mechanization and more.
    Refereed Serial

631.3   US
AG EQUIPMENT POWER. 1977. m. $12. Clintron Publishers, Inc., 102 N. 6th Ave., Box 547, Yakima, WA 98907. TEL 509-575-6774.
FAX 509-457-3885. Ed. John Dahlin; Pub. Clint Withers. R&P contact: John Dahlin. adv. contact: Karen L. Punch. circ. 13,000. (back issues avail.) **Document type:** newspaper.
    Formed by the merger of (1988-1993): Fruit Country & Agri-Equipment and Chemical; Which was formerly: Agri-Equipment Today (ISSN 0192-9526)
    Description: Contains new and used machinery guide and news of interest for growers in Northwestern agriculture.

AGRAR-UEBERSICHT; das active Magazin fuer active Landwirte. see *AGRICULTURE*

631.3   GW
AGRARGEWERBLICHE WIRTSCHAFT. fortn. DM.200. V d A W Beratungs- und Servicegesellschaft mbH, Wollgrasweg 31, 70599 Stuttgart, Germany. TEL 0711-167790. FAX 0711-451093. **Document type:** trade publication.

631.3   SA   ISSN 0379-6604
AGRICULTURAL ENGINEERING IN SOUTH AFRICA. (Text and summaries in Afrikaans, English) 1967. biennial. R.60($20) South African Institute of Agricultural Engineers, P.O. Box 912 719, Silverton 0127, South Africa. TEL 27-12-8041540. FAX 27-12-8040753. Ed. A.J. Heyns. adv.; circ. 600 (controlled). (back issues avail.) **Indexed:** Agri.Eng.Abstr., Ind.S.A.Per.
    Description: Features scientific and semi-scientific papers on applied engineering in South African agriculture. Covers agricultural equipment, irrigation, soil and water engineering, animal housing, processing.

631.3   SA
AGRICULTURAL MACHINERY DEALERS' GUIDE. 1966. bi-m. R.409.72. Mead & McGrouther (Pty) Ltd., P.O. Box 1240, Randburg 2125, South Africa. TEL 27-11-7893213. FAX 27-11-7895218. adv.; B&W page R.550, color page R.900. circ. 464. **Document type:** trade publication.
    Formerly: Agricultural Machinery Dealers' Digest (ISSN 0378-5246)
    Description: Reports trade and retail prices of used agricultural machinery in South Africa

631.3   YU
AGROOPREMA; list. 1975. bi-m.? Abrooprema, Balkanska 44, Belgrade, Yugoslavia. Ed. Gordana Petronijevic.

631.3   PL   ISSN 1234-0677
AKADEMIA ROLNICZA IM. HUGONA KOLLATAJA W KRAKOWIE. ZESZYTY NAUKOWE. SERIA: TECHNIKA ROLNICZA. (Text in Polish; summaries in English) 1984. a. price varies. Akademia Rolnicza im. Hugona Kollataja w Krakowie, c/o Ligia Hayto, Biblioteka Glowna AR, Al. Mickiewicza 24-28, 30-059 Krakow, Poland. TEL 48-12-119144. FAX 48-12-336245. TELEX 322469 PL. Ed. Zdzislaw Piskornik. circ. 120 (paid). **Indexed:** AgroLibrex. **Document type:** academic/scholarly publication.
    Formerly (until 1993): Akademia Rolnicza im. Hugona Kollataja w Krakowie. Zeszyty Naukowe. Seria: Mechanizacja i Energetyka Rolnictwa (ISSN 0239-9083)

AKADEMIA ROLNICZA WE WROCLAWIU. ZESZYTY NAUKOWE. GEODEZJA I URZADZENIA ROLNE. see *GEOGRAPHY*

AGRICULTURE — AGRICULTURAL EQUIPMENT

631.3 621   PL   ISSN 0867-3756
AKADEMIA ROLNICZA WE WROCLAWIU. ZESZYTY NAUKOWE. MECHANIZACJA ROLNICTWA. (Subseries of: Akademia Rolnicza we Wroclawiu. Zeszyty Naukowe (ISSN 0867-7964)) (Text in Polish; summaries in English) 1990. irreg. price varies. Akademia Rolnicza we Wroclawiu, Ul. Norwida 25, 50-375 Wroclaw, Poland. FAX 48-71-229576. (Subscr. to: Wydawnictwo Akademii Rolniczej, ul. Sopocka 23, 50-344 Wroclaw, Poland. TEL 48-71-211277) circ. 270. **Indexed:** AgroLibrex. **Document type:** academic/scholarly publication.

631.3   CN
ALBERTA FARM LIFE. 1980. s-w. Can.$155($155) (effective 1997). Murray McMaster, 225 5438 11th St. N.E., Calgary, AB T2E 7E9, Canada. TEL 403-274-4002. FAX 403-274-4116. E-mail: farmlife@cadvision.com. Ed. M. Larie. adv.; bk.rev. circ. 69,000.
    Former titles: Giant Farm Life; Giant.

631   FR
ANNUAIRE DE L'EQUIPEMENT VINICOLE: MATERIELS - FOURNITURES - PRESTATIONS. 1992. biennial. Vigne et Vin Publications Internationales, 42 rue Marsan, 33300 Bordeaux, France. TEL 33-5-57876869. FAX 33-5-57876848. E-mail: vvpi@inlandsys.com. Ed. Michael Paetzold. adv. circ. 1,000.

631.3   US   ISSN 1042-7392
ANTIQUE POWER; the tractor collector's magazine. 1988. bi-m. $22 (Canada $32; elsewhere $36). Antique Power Inc., Box 838, Yellow Springs, OH 45387. TEL 513-767-1433. FAX 513-767-2726. E-mail: auntpow@aol.com. (Subscr. addr.: Box 562, Yellow Springs, OH 45387) Ed. Patrick W. Ertel. adv.: page $490; adv. contact: Arlene Goldstein. illus.; circ. 22,000 (paid). **Document type:** consumer publication.
    Description: Devoted to the interests of antique tractor enthusiasts. Covers all makes of antique tractors. Contains historical research, recollections of their use, restoration tips, show information, toys, literature.

AUSTRALIAN SEED INDUSTRY MAGAZINE. see AGRICULTURE — Crop Production And Soil

631.3   II
AUTOMOBILE, TRACTOR, SCOOTER REPORT. 1967. w. Rs.615($75) International Press Cutting Service, P.O. Box 121, Allahabad 211001, India. Ed. N. Khanna. bk.rev.; index. circ. 1,200. (looseleaf format) **Document type:** newsletter.
    Formerly: Automobile and Tractor (ISSN 0045-1053)

THE BELT PULLEY. see HOBBIES

631.3 362.4   US
BREAKING NEW GROUND; cultivating independence for farmers and ranchers with disabilities. 1982. q. free. Breaking New Ground Resource Center, Purdue University, 1146 Agricultural and Biological Engineering Bldg., West Lafayette, IN 47907-1146. TEL 765-494-5088; 800-825-4264. FAX 765-496-1356. E-mail: delks@ecn.purdue.edu; URL: http://www.ecn.purdue.edu/ABE/extension/BNG/index.html. Ed. Bill Field. circ. 11,000. **Document type:** newsletter.
    Description: Discusses events that benefit farmers and ranchers with physical disabilities.

631.3   CN   ISSN 0045-432X
    CODEN: CAEOAI
CANADIAN AGRICULTURAL ENGINEERING. (Text in English, French) 1959. q. Can.$50 (foreign $50) (effective 1997). Canadian Society of Agricultural Engineering, Box 381, R P O University, Saskatoon, SK S7N 4J8, Canada. TEL 306-966-5335. FAX 306-966-5334. E-mail: norum@engr.usask.ca; URL: http://www.engr.usask.ca/societies/csae/. (Outside Canada subscr. to: ASAE, 2950 Niles Rd., St. Joseph, MI 49085-9659) Ed. John Feddes; Pub. Donald I. Norum. bk.rev. circ. 1,050. (also avail. in microfilm from UMI) **Indexed:** Agri.Eng.Abstr., ASCA, Biol.Abstr., Curr.Adv.Ecol.Sci., Curr.Cont., Eng.Ind., Excerp.Med., Field Crop Abstr., Food Sci.& Tech.Abstr., Herb.Abstr., Hort.Abstr., Ind.Vet., Int.Abstr.Oper.Res., Irr.& Drain.Abstr., Maize Abstr., Ornam.Hort., Pig News & Info., Potato Abstr., Sci.Cit.Ind., Sel.Water Res.Abstr., Soils & Fert., Soyabean Abstr., Triticale Abstr., Vet.Bull., World Agri.Econ.& Rural Sociol.Abstr. **Document type:** academic/scholarly publication.
    —BLDSC (3016.700000); CASDDS; CISTI; Ei; Genuine Article; Linda Hall; UnCover. **CCC.**
    Refereed Serial

631.3 636   US
CENTRAL OREGON RANCHER. 1953. m. $18 (effective 1995). Central Oregon Rancher, 9263 S. Copley Rd., Box 1, Powell Butte, OR 97753-0001. TEL 503-548-8700. Ed. Rod S. Johnson. adv. contact: Scott Johnson. circ. 13,200. **Document type:** consumer publication.

CHANGING HORIZONS. see AGRICULTURE — Agricultural Economics

631.3   CU   ISSN 0138-8681
CIENCIA Y TECNICA EN LA AGRICULTURA. SERIE: MECANIZACION DE LA AGRICULTURA. (Table of contents and abstracts in English) 1978. s-a. $14 in N. and S. America; Europe $16; elsewhere $17; or exchange basis. Centro de Informacion y Documentacion Agropecuario, Gaveta Postal 4149, Havana 4, Cuba. (Dist. by: Ediciones Cubanas, Obispo No. 527, Apdo. 605, Havana, Cuba) **Indexed:** Agrindex, Rice Abstr.

CIENCIAS DEL SUELO, RIEGO Y MECANIZACION. see AGRICULTURE — Crop Production And Soil

631.3   CU   ISSN 1016-9512
CUBA. CENTRO DE INFORMACION Y DOCUMENTACION AGROPECUARIO. BOLETIN DE RESENAS. SERIE: MECANIZACION DE LA AGRICULTURA. (Abstracts in English) 1974. irreg. exchange basis. Centro de Informacion y Documentacion Agropecuario, Gaveta Postal 4149, Havana 4, Cuba. (Dist. by: Ediciones Cubanas, Obispo No. 461, Apdo. 605, Havana, Cuba) **Indexed:** Agrindex.
    Formerly: Cuba. Centro de Informacion y Divulgacion Agropecuario. Boletin de Resenas. Serie: Mecanizacion.

631.3   BL   ISSN 0012-3374
DIRIGENTE RURAL. 1961. m. $70. Editora Visao Ltda., Rua Alvaro de Carvalho, 350, 2o andar, C.P. 3082, 01050 Sao Paulo, Brazil. TEL 256-5011. FAX 258-1919. TELEX 1121436. Ed. Hamilton Lucas de Oliveira. adv.; bk.rev.; abstr.; bibl.; charts; illus. circ. 61,000.

631.1   GW
EILBOTE. 1952. w. DM.130. Eilbote Boomgaarden Verlag GmbH, Winsener Landstr. 7, OT Luhdorf, 21423 Winsen-Luhe, Germany. TEL 49-4171-76074. FAX 49-4171-74984. Ed. Juergen Boomgaarden. adv.; bk.rev./ circ. 8,500 (controlled). **Document type:** newspaper.

631.3 621.9   US
EQUIPMENT MANUFACTURERS INSTITUTE. FIRST OF THE WEEK NEWSLETTER. irreg. membership. Equipment Manufacturers Institute, 10 S. Riverside Plaza, Ste. 1220, Chicago, IL 60606-3710. TEL 312-321-1470. **Document type:** newsletter.
    Formerly: Farm and Industrial Equipment Institute. First of the Week Newsletter.

631.3 621.9   US
EQUIPMENT MANUFACTURERS INSTITUTE. RETAIL SALES REPORTS. m. $200. Equipment Manufacturers Institute, 10 S. Riverside Plaza, Ste. 1220, Chicago, IL 60606-3710. TEL 312-321-1470.
    Formerly: Farm and Industrial Equipment Institute. Retail Sales Reports.

631.3 621.9   US
EQUIPMENT MANUFACTURERS INSTITUTE. STATE OF THE INDUSTRY. s-a. $25. Equipment Manufacturers Institute, 10 S. Riverside Plaza, Ste. 1220, Chicago, IL 60606-3710. TEL 312-321-1470.
    Formerly: Farm and Industrial Equipment Institute. State of the Industry.

631.3   US
F E W A TIPS. m. membership. Farm Equipment Wholesalers Association, Box 1347, Iowa City, IA 52240. TEL 319-354-5156. FAX 319-354-5157. Ed. Patricia Collins. **Document type:** newsletter.

631.3 664.1   GW
F.O. LICHT'S GUIDE TO EQUIPMENT PRODUCTS AND SERVICES FOR THE SUGAR AND ALLIED INDUSTRIES. (Text in English, German) a. DM.75 in US & Canada. F.O. Licht GmbH, Am Muehlengraben 22, 23902 Ratzeburg, Germany. FAX 49-4541-82145. **Document type:** trade publication.

631.3   UK
FARM AND HORTICULTURAL EQUIPMENT COLLECTOR. bi-m. £12.50 (Europe £14; rest of world £16.50) (effective 1997). Kelsey Publishing Ltd., Kelsey House, 77 High St., Beckenham, Kent BR3 1AN, England. TEL 44-181-658-3531. FAX 44-181-650-8035. adv. **Document type:** consumer publication.

631.3   US   ISSN 0014-7958
FARM EQUIPMENT. 1969. 7/yr. $40 (Canada and Mexico $55; elsewhere $120) (effective 1997). Johnson Hill Press, Inc. (Subsidiary of: Cygnus Publishing), 1233 Janesville Ave., Ft. Atkinson, WI 53538. TEL 920-563-6388. FAX 920-563-1701. Ed. Curt Bennick; Pub. Phil Merrick. adv.; illus.; index; circ. 13,500 (controlled). **Document type:** trade publication.
    Formerly: Agricultural Equipment Dealer.
    Description: Provides business management information to owners and managers of farm equipment dealerships.

631.3   US
FARM EQUIPMENT CATALOG. 1989. s-a. Johnson Hill Press, Inc. (Subsidiary of: Cygnus PublishingCorp.), 1233 Janesville Ave., Fort Atkinson, WI 53538. TEL 920-563-6388. FAX 920-563-1699. adv. circ. 85,000. **Document type:** catalog.
    Description: Lists farm equipment in ten categories for upper class 1A farm operations in the U.S.

631.3   CN
FARM MACHINERY CUSTOM AND RENTAL RATE GUIDE. 1975. a. free. Saskatchewan Agriculture and Food Library, B5 Walter Scott Bldg., 3085 Albert St., Regina, SK S4S 0B1, Canada. TEL 306-787-6933. FAX 306-787-0216. E-mail: pdc@agr.gov.sk.ca; URL: http://www.gov.sk.ca/agfood. stat. circ. 6,000. (also avail. in microfiche) **Document type:** government publication.

631.3   US   ISSN 0163-4518
FARM SHOW MAGAZINE. 1977. bi-m. $15.95. Farm Show Publishing Inc., Box 1029, 20088 Kenwood Trail, Lakeville, MN 55044. TEL 612-469-5572. FAX 612-469-5575. Ed. Mark Newhall. R&P contact: Mark Newhall. circ. 175,000. (tabloid format) **Document type:** trade publication.

631.3   US
FASTLINE: DAKOTA EDITION. 1993. m. $8 (effective 1997). Fastline Publications, Inc., 4900 Fox Run Rd., Buckner, KY 40010. TEL 502-222-0146; 800-332-7854. FAX 502-222-0615. E-mail: fastpub@aol.com. Ed. William G. Howard; Pub. William G. Howard. R&P contact: William G. Howard. circ. 22,000. **Document type:** catalog.
    Description: Designed for the farming industry.

631.3   US
FASTLINE: ILLINOIS EDITION. 1988. m. $8 (effective 1997). Fastline Publications, Inc., 4900 Fox Run Rd., Buckner, KY 40010. TEL 502-222-0146; 800-332-7854. FAX 502-222-0615. E-mail: fastpub@aol.com. Ed. William G. Howard; William G. Howard. R&P contact: William G. Howard. circ. 22,000. **Document type:** catalog.
    Formerly: Farmers Fastline: Illinois Edition.
    Description: Designed for the farming industry.

AGRICULTURE — AGRICULTURAL EQUIPMENT

631.3　　　　　US
FASTLINE: INDIANA EDITION. 1981. m. $8 (effective 1997). Fastline Publications, Inc., 4900 Fox Run Rd., Buckner, KY 40010. TEL 502-222-0146; 800-332-7854. FAX 502-222-0615. E-mail: fastpub@aol.com. Ed. William G. Howard; Pub. William G. Howard. R&P contact: William G. Howard. adv. circ. 22,000. **Document type:** catalog.
　　Former titles: Farmers Fastline: Indiana Edition & Indiana Farmers Fastline.
　　Description: Designed for the farming industry.

631.3　　　　　US
FASTLINE: IOWA EDITION. 1988. m. $8 (effective 1997). Fastline Publications, Inc., 4900 Fox Run Rd., Buckner, KY 40010. TEL 502-222-0146; 800-332-7854. FAX 502-222-0615. Ed. William G. Howard; Pub. William G. Howard. R&P contact: William G. Howard. circ. 22,000. **Document type:** catalog.
　　Former titles: Farmers Fastline: Iowa Edition & Iowa Farmers Fastline.
　　Description: Designed for the farming industry.

631.3　　　　　US
FASTLINE: KANSAS EDITION. 1991. m. $8. Fastline Publications, Inc., 4900 Fox Run Rd., Buckner, KY 40010. TEL 502-222-0146; 800-332-7854. FAX 502-222-0615. E-mail: fastpub@aol.com. circ. 22,000. **Document type:** catalog.
　　Formerly: Farmers Fastline: Kansas Edition.
　　Description: Designed for the farming industry.

631.3　　　　　US
FASTLINE: KENTUCKY EDITION. 1987. m. $8 (effective 1997). Fastline Publications, Inc., 4900 Fox Run Rd., Buckner, KY 40010. TEL 502-222-0146; 800-332-7852. FAX 502-222-9874. E-mail: fastpub@aol.com. Ed. William G. Howard; Pub. William G. Howard. R&P contact: William G. Howard. circ. 22,000. **Document type:** catalog.
　　Former titles: Farmers Fastline: Kentucky Edition & Kentucky Farmers Fastline.
　　Description: Design for the farming industry.

631.3　　　　　US
FASTLINE: MID-ATLANTIC EDITION. 1990. m. $8 (effective 1997). Fastline Publications, Inc., 4900 Fox Run Rd., Buckner, KY 40010. TEL 502-222-0146; 800-332-7854. FAX 502-222-0615. E-mail: fastpub@aol.com. Ed. William G. Howard; Pub. William G. Howard. R&P contact: William G. Howard. circ. 22,000. **Document type:** catalog.
　　Formerly: Farmers Fastline: North Carolina Edition.
　　Description: Designed for the farming industry.

631.3　　　　　US
▼**FASTLINE: MID-WEST EDITION**. 1996. m. $8 (effective 1997). Fastline Publications, Inc., 4900 Fox Run Rd., Buckner, KY 40010. TEL 502-222-0146; 800-332-7854. FAX 502-222-0615. E-mail: fastpub@aol.com. Ed. William G. Howard; Pub. William G. Howard. R&P contact: William G. Howard. circ. 22,000. **Document type:** catalog.
　　Description: Designed for the farming industry.

631.3　　　　　US
FASTLINE: MIDSOUTH EDITION. 1992. m. $8 (effective 1997). Fastline Publications, Inc., 4900 Fox Run Rd., Buckner, KY 40010. TEL 502-222-0146; 800-332-7852. FAX 502-222-0615. E-mail: fastpub@aol.com. Ed. William G. Howard; Pub. William G. Howard. R&P contact: William G. Howard. circ. 22,000. **Document type:** catalog.
　　Formerly: Farmers Fastline: Arkansas Edition.
　　Description: Designed for the farming industry.

631.3　　　　　US
FASTLINE: MINNESOTA EDITION. 1988. m. $8 (effective 1997). Fastline Publications, Inc., Box 248, Buckner, KY 40010. TEL 502-222-0146; 800-332-7854. FAX 502-222-0615. E-mail: fastpub@aol.com. Ed. William G. Howard; Pub. William G. Howard. R&P contact: William G. Howard. circ. 22,000. **Document type:** catalog.
　　Former titles: Farmers Fastline: Minnesota Edition & Midwest Farm Exchange - Minnesota.
　　Description: Design for the farming industry.

631.3　　　　　US
FASTLINE: MISSOURI EDITION. 1989. m. $8 (effective 1997). Fastline Publications, Inc., 4900 Fox Run Rd., Buckner, KY 40010. TEL 502-222-0146; 800-332-7854. FAX 502-222-0146. E-mail: fastpub@aol.com. Ed. William G. Howard; Pub. William G. Howard. R&P contact: William G. Howard. circ. 22,000. **Document type:** catalog.
　　Formerly: Farmers Fastline: Missouri Edition.
　　Description: Designed for the farming industry.

631.3　　　　　US
FASTLINE: NEBRASKA EDITION. 1991. m. $8 (effective 1997). Fastline Publications, Inc., 4900 Fox Run Rd., Buckner, KY 40010. TEL 502-222-0146; 800-332-7854. FAX 502-222-0615. E-mail: fastpub@aol.com. Ed. William G. Howard; Pub. William G. Howard. R&P contact: William G. Howard. circ. 22,000. **Document type:** catalog.
　　Formerly: Farmers Fastline: Nebraska Edition.
　　Description: Designed for the farming industry.

631.3　　　　　US
▼**FASTLINE: NORTHEAST EDITION**. 1996. m. $8 (effective 1997). Fastline Publications, Inc., 4900 Fox Run Rd., Buckner, KY 40010. TEL 502-222-0146; 502-222-0615; 800-332-7854. E-mail: fastpubl@aol.com. Ed. William G. Howard; Pub. William G. Howard. R&P contact: William G. Howard. circ. 22,000. **Document type:** catalog.
　　Description: Designed for the farming industry.

631.3　　　　　US
▼**FASTLINE: NORTHLAND EDITION**. 1997. m. $8 (effective 1997). Fastline Publications, Inc., 4900 Fox Run Rd., Buckner, KY 40010. TEL 502-222-0146; 800-332-7854. FAX 502-222-0615. Ed. William G. Howard; Pub. William G. Howard. R&P contact: William G. Howard. circ. 22,000.
　　Description: Designed for the farming industry.

631.3　　　　　US
FASTLINE: OHIO EDITION. 1981. m. $8 (effective 1997). Fastline Publications, Inc., 4900 Fox Run Rd., Buckner, KY 40010. TEL 502-222-0146; 800-332-7854. FAX 502-222-0615. E-mail: fastpub@aol.com. adv. circ. 22,000. **Document type:** catalog.
　　Former titles: Farmers Fastline: Ohio Edition & Ohio Farmers Fastline.
　　Description: Designed for the farming industry.

631.3　　　　　US
FASTLINE: OKLAHOMA EDITION. 1992. m. $8 (effective 1997). Fastline Publications, Inc., 4900 Fox Run Rd., Buckner, KY 40010. TEL 502-222-0146; 502-222-0615; 800-332-7854. E-mail: fastpub@aol.com. Ed. William G. Howard. circ. 22,000. **Document type:** catalog.
　　Description: Designed for the farming industry.

631.3　　　　　US
▼**FASTLINE: ROCKY MOUNTAIN EDITION**. 1995. m. $8 (effective 1997). Fastline Publications, Inc., 4900 Fox Run Rd., Buckner, KY 40010. TEL 502-222-0146; 800-332-7854. FAX 502-222-0615. E-mail: fastpub@aol.com. Ed. William G. Howard; Pub. William G. Howard. R&P contact: William G. Howard. circ. 22,000.
　　Description: Designed for the farming industry.

631.3　　　　　US
FASTLINE: SOUTHEAST EDITION. 1990. m. $8 (effective 1997). Fastline Publications, Inc., 4900 Fox Run Rd., Buckner, KY 40010. TEL 502-222-0146; 800-332-7854. FAX 502-222-0615. E-mail: fastpub@aol.com. Ed. William G. Howard; Pub. William G. Howard. R&P contact: William G. Howard. circ. 22,000. **Document type:** catalog.
　　Formerly: Farmers Fastline: Georgia Edition.
　　Description: Designed for the farming industry.

631.3　　　　　US
▼**FASTLINE: SOUTHWEST EDITION**. 1997. m. $8 (effective 1997). Fastline Publications, Inc., 4900 Fox Run Rd., Buckner, KY 40010. TEL 502-222-7852; 800-332-7854. FAX 502-222-0615. E-mail: fastpub@aol.com. Ed. William G. Howard; Pub. William G. Howard. R&P contact: William G. Howard. circ. 22,000. **Document type:** catalog.
　　Description: Designed for the farming industry.

631.3　　　　　US
FASTLINE: TENNESSEE EDITION. 1990. m. $8 (effective 1997). Fastline Publications, Inc., 4900 Fox Run Rd., Buckner, KY 40010. TEL 502-222-0146; 800-332-7854. FAX 502-222-0615. E-mail: fastpub@aol.com. circ. 22,000. **Document type:** catalog.
　　Formerly: Farmers Fastline: Tennessee Edition.
　　Description: Designed for the farming industry.

631.3　　　　　US
FASTLINE: TEXAS EDITION. 1993. m. $8. Fastline Publications, Inc., 4900 Fox Run Rd., Buckner, KY 40010. TEL 502-222-0146; 800-332-7854. FAX 502-222-0615. E-mail: fastpub@aol.com. Ed. William G. Howard; Pub. William G. Howard. R&P contact: William G. Howard. adv.: B&W page $585, color page $810; trim 7 1/2 X 10 3/4. illus. circ. 22,000. **Document type:** consumer publication.
　　Formerly: Farmers Fastline: Texas Edition.
　　Description: Buyer's guide to farm equipment.

631.3　　　　　US
▼**FASTLINE: TRI-STATE EDITION**. 1995. m. $8 (effective 1997). Fastline Publications, Inc., 4900 Fox Run Rd., Buckner, KY 40010. TEL 502-222-0146; 800-332-7854. FAX 502-222-0615. E-mail: fastpub@aol.com. Ed. William G. Howard; Pub. William G. Howard. R&P contact: William G. Howard. circ. 22,000. **Document type:** catalog.
　　Description: Designed for the trucking industry.

631.3　　　　　FR
FICHES TECHNIQUES R T D APPLICATIONS AGRICOLES. (Revue Technique Diesel) irreg. price varies. Editions Techniques pour l'Automobile et l'Industrie (ETAI), 20-22 rue de la Saussiere, 92100 Boulogne-Billancourt, France. charts; illus. (looseleaf format)

631.3　　　　　GW　　ISSN 0931-6264
FORSCHUNGSBERICHT AGRARTECHNIK. irreg. Max-Eyth-Gesellschaft Agrartechnik im V D I, Graf-Recke-Str. 84, 40239 Duesseldorf, Germany. TEL 0211-62140. **Document type:** monographic series.

635　　　　　BU
GRADINARSTVO.* 1959. m. 2.50 lv.($6) (Ministerstvo na Zemedelieto i Khranitelna Promishlenost) Izdatelstvo Profizdat, Dondukov Blvd., 32, Sofia, Bulgaria. (Dist. by: Hemus, 6, Rouski Blvd., 1000 Sofia, Bulgaria) Ed. A. Mikhov. circ. 4,575. **Indexed:** Chem.Abstr.

631.3　　　　　UK　　ISSN 0017-3932
GREEN BOOK; the authority on tractors and farm equipment. 1951. a. £100. Argus Business Publications Ltd. (Subsidiary of: Argus Press Group), Queensway House, 2 Queensway, Redhill, Surrey RH1 1QS, England. Ed. H. Catling. adv.; illus. circ. 4,000. (reprint service avail. from UMI)
　　Formerly (until 1971): British Tractors and Farm Machinery (ISSN 0521-1824)

631.3　　　　　II
HANDBOOK OF INDIAN PUMPS FOR IRRIGATION; salient features and performances. 1988. a. Rs.300($60) Indian Society of Agricultural Engineers, Satya Mansion, Flats No.305-306, Community Centre, Ranjit Nagar, New Delhi 100 008, India. TEL 11-5709003.

631.3　　　　　US　　ISSN 1047-725X
HOT LINE FARM EQUIPMENT GUIDE. 1981. a. (plus m. updates). $69.95. Heartland Ag-Business Group, Inc., 1003 Central Ave., Fort Dodge, IA 50501. TEL 515-955-1600; 800-247-2000. FAX 515-955-1600. Ed. Lisa Ziems; Pub. Lisa Ziems. R&P contact: Lisa Ziems. adv. contact: Lisa Ziems. circ. 15,000. **Document type:** trade publication.
　　Formerly: Farm Equipment Guide.
　　Description: Informs customers about fluctuating farm equipment prices.

AGRICULTURE — AGRICULTURAL EQUIPMENT

631.3 US ISSN 0019-2953
IMPLEMENT & TRACTOR; the business magazine of the farm and industrial equipment industry. 1886. 6/yr. $25. Freiberg Publishing Company, Inc., 2302 W. First St., Box 7, Cedar Falls, IA 50613. TEL 319-277-3599. FAX 319-277-3783. URL: http://www.agimplement.com. Ed. Bill Freiberg. adv.; bk.rev.; charts; illus.; mkt.; pat.; stat.; tr.lit.; index. circ. 11,000. (back issues avail.) **Indexed:** Agri.Eng.Abstr., Bus.Ind., Farm & Garden Ind., PROMT, SRI, Tr.& Indus.Ind. **Document type:** trade publication.
●Also available online. Vendor(s): Information Access Co.
—CISTI.

631.372 US ISSN 0073-5566
IMPLEMENT & TRACTOR PRODUCT FILE. (Supplement to: Implement and Tractor) a. $29.95 (or included with Implement & Tractor). Farm Press, Division on Intertec Publishing, Box 1420, Clarksdale, MS 38614. TEL 601-624-8503. FAX 601-627-1977. Ed. Scott McClure; Pub. John L. Montandon. R&P contact: Teresa Casburn. adv. contact: Teresa Casburn. **Document type:** directory.

631.3 US ISSN 0073-5574
IMPLEMENT & TRACTOR RED BOOK. a. $29.95 (or included with Implement & Tractor). Farm Press, Division of Intertec Publishing, Box 1420, Clarksdale, MS 38614. TEL 601-624-8503. FAX 601-627-1977. Ed. Scott McClure; Pub. John L. Montandon. R&P contact: Teresa Casburn. adv. contact: Teresa Casburn. **Document type:** directory.

631.3 CU ISSN 0138-7332
INFORMACION EXPRESS. SERIE: MECANIZACION AGROPECUARIA. 1977. 3/yr. $6 in N. America; S. America $9; Europe $10; elsewhere $14. Centro de Informacion y Documentacion Agropecuario, Gaveta Postal 4149, Havana 4, Cuba. (Dist. by: Ediciones Cubanas, Obispo No. 527, Apdo. 605, Havana, Cuba) **Indexed:** Agrindex.

631.3 IS
INSTITUTE OF AGRICULTURAL ENGINEERING, BET DAGAN. SCIENTIFIC ACTIVITIES. (Text in English) 1971. triennial. $25 (effective 1996). Agricultural Research Organization, Institute of Agricultural Engineering, Volcani Center, P.O. Box 6, Bet Dagan 50250, Israel. TEL 972-3-9683111. FAX 972-3-993998. TELEX 381476. illus. circ. 300. **Indexed:** Biol.Abstr. **Document type:** government publication, academic/scholarly publication.

631.3 NG ISSN 0534-4794
INTER-AFRICAN CONFERENCE OF THE MECHANISATION OF AGRICULTURE MEETING.* 1955. irreg. (Commission for Technical Co-Operation in Africa South of the Sahara) Maison de l'Afrique, B.P. 878, Niamey, Niger.

INTERNATIONAL GRAINS COUNCIL. REPORT FOR FISCAL YEAR. see *AGRICULTURE — Feed, Flour And Grain*

631.3 NE ISSN 0168-6291
CODEN: IDRSEG
IRRIGATION AND DRAINAGE SYSTEMS; an international journal. 1986. q. fl.496 to institutions; $254.50 to institutions in U.S. (effective 1998). Kluwer Academic Publishers, Postbus 17, 3300 AA Dordrecht, Netherlands. TEL 31-78-6392392. FAX 31-78-6392254. TELEX 29245 KAPG NL. E-mail: services@wkap.nl; URL: http://www.wkap.nl. (Dist. by: Kluwer Academic Publishers Group, P.O. Box 322, 3300 AH Dordrecht, Netherlands. TEL 31-78-6392392. FAX 31-78-6546474; N. America dist. addr.: Box 358, Accord Sta., Hingham, MA 02018-0358. TEL 617-871-6600. FAX 617-871-6528) Ed. Marinus G. Bos. adv. (also avail. in microform from UMI; back issues avail.; reprint service avail. from SWZ) **Indexed:** Agri.Eng.Abstr., Biol.Abstr., Ecol.Abstr., Environ.Per.Bibl. (1992-), Geo.Abstr.H.G., Geo.Abstr.P.G., Hort.Abstr., IDA, Irr.& Drain.Abstr., Soils & Fert., Sport Fish.Abstr., Wild.Rev., World Agri.Econ.& Rural Sociol.Abstr. **Document type:** academic/scholarly publication.
—BLDSC (4580.948000); Ei; EMDOCS; KR SourceOne; Linda Hall; SWETS; UMI; UnCover. CCC.
Description: Publishes general research and review articles on all aspects of irrigation, including water supply, drainage systems and design, efficiency and management, as well as public health and disease prevention issues.
Refereed Serial

631.3 380 US ISSN 0277-6529
HD1720
IRRIGATION ASSOCIATION. MEMBERSHIP DIRECTORY AND BUYERS' GUIDE. a. $25 to non-members (effective 1997). Irrigation Association, 8260 Willow Oaks Corp. Dr., Ste. 120, Fairfax, VA 22031. TEL 703-573-3551. FAX 703-573-1913. URL: http://www.irrigation.org. adv. circ. 2,000. **Document type:** directory.
Description: Features a listing of irrigation companies that are members of the association.

IRRIGATION BUSINESS & TECHNOLOGY. see *AGRICULTURE — Crop Production And Soil*

631.3 US
IRRIGATION ENGINEERING. 1985. s-a. $48 to non-members (foreign $53); members $30.75 (foreign $35.75) (effective 1997). American Society of Agricultural Engineers, 2950 Niles Rd., St. Joseph, MI 49085-9659. TEL 616-429-0300. FAX 616-429-3852. E-mail: hq@asae.org; URL: http://asae.org/. Ed. Pamela DeVore-Hansen. **Document type:** trade publication.
Description: Includes over 30 technical articles on drip, surface, sprinkler, trickle, and other irrigation methods and practices.

631.3 338.1 US
J D JOURNAL. (John Deere) 1972. 3/yr. Deere & Company, John Deere Rd., Moline, IL 61265. TEL 309-765-4974. Ed. John Gerstner. circ. 76,000.
Description: Company-wide employee magazine to tie various units and divisions together and keep J.D. people informed of company goals, policies, accomplishments and trends.

631.3 620 JA ISSN 0386-5126
JAPAN. MINISTRY OF AGRICULTURE, FORESTRY AND FISHERIES. NATIONAL RESEARCH INSTITUTE OF AGRICULTURAL ENGINEERING. ABSTRACTS FROM RESEARCH REPORTS. (Text in Japanese) 1974. a. free. Ministry of Agriculture, Forestry and Fisheries, National Research Institute of Agricultural Engineering, 2-1-2, Kannondai, Tsukuba, Ibaraki 305, Japan. TEL 81-298-38-7505. Ed. Hiroshi Sato. **Document type:** government publication.

631.3 620 JA ISSN 0549-5725
S671
JAPAN. MINISTRY OF AGRICULTURE, FORESTRY AND FISHERIES. NATIONAL RESEARCH INSTITUTE OF AGRICULTURAL ENGINEERING. BULLETIN. (Text in Japanese; summaries in English) 1963. a. Ministry of Agriculture, Forestry and Fisheries, National Research Institute of Agricultural Engineering, 2-1-2, Kannondai, Tsukuba, Ibaraki 305, Japan. TEL 81-298-38-7505. **Document type:** government publication, bulletin.
—BLDSC (2643.200000).

631.3 620 JA ISSN 0287-0029
TC1
JAPAN. MINISTRY OF AGRICULTURE, FORESTRY AND FISHERIES. NATIONAL RESEARCH INSTITUTE OF AGRICULTURAL ENGINEERING. TECHNICAL REPORT. (Text in Japanese) irreg. free. Ministry of Agriculture, Forestry and Fisheries, National Research Institute of Agricultural Engineering, 2-1-2, Kannondai, Tsukuba, Ibaraki 305, Japan. TEL 81-298-38-7505. Ed. Hiroshi Sato. **Document type:** government publication.

JARMUVEK, EPITOIPARI ES MEZOGAZDASAGI GEPEK; motorok, vasuti jarmuvek, kozuti jarmuvek, hajok, mezogazdasagi gepek, epitoipari gepek, repulogepek. see *ENGINEERING — Mechanical Engineering*

631.3 GW
K T B L ARBEITSBLAETTER BAULICH-TECHNISCHE SELBSTHILFE. irreg., no.2058, 1992. DM.3. Kuratorium fuer Technik und Bauwesen in der Landwirtschaft e.V., Bartningstr. 49, 64289 Darmstadt, Germany. TEL 06151-7001-0. FAX 06151-7001123. **Document type:** monographic series.

631.3 UK
KEY NOTE MARKET REPORT: AGRICULTURAL MACHINERY. Variant title: Agricultural Machinery. 1981. irreg., no.10, 1994. £205. Key Note Ltd., Field House, 72 Oldfield Rd., Hampton, Middlesex TW12 2HQ, England. TEL 44-181-783-0755. FAX 44-181-783-0049. **Document type:** trade publication.
●Also available online.
Also available on CD-ROM.
Formerly: Key Note Report: Agricultural Machinery (ISSN 0951-6697)

631.3 JA ISSN 0023-1371
KIKAIKA NOGYO/FARMING MECHANIZATION. (Text in Japanese; table of contents in English) 1940. m. 8500 Yen. Shin-Norinsha Co., Ltd. - Farm Machinery Industrial Research Corp., Shin-Norin Bldg., 7, 2-chome, Kanda Nishiki-cho, Chiyoda-ku, Tokyo 101, Japan. TEL 03-3291-3674. FAX 03-3291-5717. Ed. Yoshisuke Kishida. adv. contact: K. Ikeda. bk.rev.; bibl.; charts; illus.; stat.; index. circ. 100,000. **Indexed:** Field Crop Abstr., Hort.Abstr., Maize Abstr., Potato Abstr., Seed Abstr., Sorghum & Millets Abstr., Soyabean Abstr., Triticale Abstr.

631.3 GW ISSN 0179-4744
L U JOURNAL; Fachzeitschrift fuer Landwirtschaftliche Lohnunternehmer und Agrardienstleistungen. 1985. m. DM.109.20($70) A S R Verlag GmbH, Eichendorffweg 51, 53359 Rheinbach, Germany. TEL 02226-3197. Ed. Erich Johannluekens. index. circ. 39,500.

631.3 SP ISSN 0210-1718
LABOREO; revista de la nueva agricultura espanola. 1969. m. 6700 ptas.($212) Laboreo S.L., C. Orellana, 10, 28004 Madrid, Spain. TEL 34-1-3081898. FAX 34-1-3192006. Ed. Antonio Ahijado Gallardo. adv.: B&W page 150000 ptas., color page 200000 ptas.; 195 x 260; adv. contact: Victoria Ramos Sanz. bk.rev.; illus.; stat. circ. 25,000. **Indexed:** Ind.SST. **Document type:** trade publication.

631.3 NE ISSN 0023-7795
LANDBOUWMECHANISATIE. (Text in Dutch, summaries in English) 1950. m. fl.97 (foreign fl.144.50. Wageningen Pers, Postbus 42, 6700 AA Wageningen, Netherlands. TEL 31-317-476508. FAX 31-317-426044. E-mail: wageningenpers@company.diva.nl. Ed. J. Heeres. adv.; bk.rev.; charts; illus.; stat.; tr.lit.; tr.mk.; index. circ. 15,000. **Indexed:** Agri.Eng.Abstr., C.I.S. Abstr., Chem.Abstr., Dairy Sci.Abstr., Excerp.Med., Field Crop Abstr., Herb.Abstr., Nutr.Abstr., Rural Recreat.Tour.Abstr., Seed Abstr., Soils & Fert., Triticale Abstr., World Agri.Econ.& Rural Sociol.Abstr. **Document type:** trade publication.
—SWETS.

631.302 DK ISSN 0107-461X
LANDBRUGETS MASKINOVERSIGT. 1972. a. DKK 350 (effective 1997). Landskontoret for Bygninger og Maskiner, Udkaersvej 15, Skejby, DK-8200 Aarhus N., Denmark. TEL 45-86-10-90-88. FAX 45-86-10-97-00. Ed. Jens J. Hoy. circ. 400. **Document type:** catalog.

631.3 AU ISSN 0023-7973
LANDMASCHINEN - HANDWERK - HANDEL. 1964. m. S.760 (effective 1997). (Bundesberufsgruppen des Landmaschinenhandels und Landmaschinenhandwerks Oesterreichs) Verlag Lorenz, Ebendorferstr. 10, A-1010 Vienna, Austria. TEL 43-1-4056695. FAX 43-1-4068693. adv.: B&W page S.15300, color page S.29400. bk.rev.; illus.; pat.; stat. circ. 3,500. (tabloid format) **Document type:** trade publication.

631.3 GW ISSN 0047-3995
LANDMASCHINEN RUNDSCHAU; Agrartechnik Report. 1949. bi-m. DM.27. Verlag Otto Gengenbach GmbH, Sachsenstr. 4, 75177 Pforzheim, Germany. adv.; bk.rev.; charts; illus.; stat. circ. 5,900.

631.3 GW ISSN 0341-261X
LOHNUNTERNEHMEN IN LAND- UND FORSTWIRTSCHAFT; Zeitschrift fuer ueberbetrieblichen Maschineneinsatz. 1945. m. DM.129. Verlag Eduard F. Beckmann KG, Postfach 1120, 31251 Lehrte, Germany. TEL 49-5132-8591-0. FAX 49-5132-859125. Ed. Heiner Behre. adv. contact: Jan-Klaus Beckmann. bk.rev.; illus. circ. 4,000. **Document type:** trade publication.

AGRICULTURE — AGRICULTURAL EQUIPMENT

631.3   IT
MACCHINE E MOTORI AGRICOLI; rivista mensile di meccanizzazione agricola. Short title: M & M A. 1942. m. (11/yr.). L.80000 (effective 1996). Edagricole S.p.A., Via Emilia Levante 31, 40139 Bologna, Italy. TEL 39-51-492211. FAX 39-51-493660. Ed. Enzo Manfredi. adv.: B&W page L.1030000, color page L.1550000; trim 185 x 247. bk.rev.; bibl.; charts; mkt.; pat.; stat.; index. circ. 16,700. **Indexed:** Agri.Eng.Abstr., Maize Abstr., Rice Abstr., Seed Abstr., Triticale Abstr.
    Formerly: Macchine e Motori Agricoli - I M A il Trattorista; Which was formed by the merger of: Macchine e Motori Agricoli (ISSN 0024-8967); I M A Trattorista (ISSN 0041-1841)

631.3   DK   ISSN 0109-0291
MASKINSTATIONEN OG LANDBRUGSLEDEREN. 1962. m. DKK 350 (effective 1997). (Landsforeningen Danske Maskinstationer - National Association of Agricultural Contractors) I-S Moeller, L.P. Bechs Vej 29, DK-8240 Risskov, Denmark. TEL 45-86-17-77-58. FAX 45-86-17-46-80. (Co-sponsors: Foreningen Landbrugslederen; Foereningen Skaanes Maskinstationer) Eds. Anne Kristine Jaegerum Moeller, Vagn Moeller. adv.: B&W page DKK 4975, color page DKK 8600; trim 247 x 172. bk.rev.; abstr.; charts; illus.; mkt.; stat.; circ. 4,200 (controlled). **Document type:** trade publication.
    Formerly (until 1973): Maskinstationen (ISSN 0025-4630)

630   RU   ISSN 0206-572X
S671
MEKHANIZATSIYA I ELEKTRIFIKATSIYA SEL'SKOGO KHOZYAISTVA. 1930. m. $182 (effective 1998). Sadovaya-Spasskaya, 18, 107807 Moscow, Russia. TEL 7-095-2072127. FAX 7-095-2072870. (Dist. by: Mezhdunarodnaya Kniga, B. Yakimanka 39, 117049 Moscow, Russia. TEL 7-095-2384967. FAX 7-095-2384634) Ed. Ivan E. Chesnokov. bibl.; illus.; index. circ. 7,090. **Indexed:** Agri.Eng.Abstr., Dairy Sci.Abstr., Field Crop Abstr., Herb.Abstr., Maize Abstr., Seed Abstr.
    —BLDSC (0111.915000); CISTI.
    Formerly (until 1980): Mekhanizatsiya i Elektrifikatsiya Sotsialisticheskogo Sel'skogo Khozyaistva (ISSN 0130-8076)

MESTNYI PROIZVODSTVENNYI OPYT V SEL'SKOM KHOZYAISTVE/LOCAL LEVEL EXPERIENCE IN AGRICULTURAL DEVELOPMENT; nauchno-tekhnicheskii referativnyi sbornik. see
AGRICULTURE — Agricultural Economics

631.3   IS   ISSN 0792-9080
MIKUN VEHANDASA BECHAKLAUT/AGRICULTURAL MACHINERY & ENGINEERING. (Text in Hebrew) 1956. bi-m. IS.110 (effective 1995). Israel Field Crop Growers Association, Saul Hamelech Blvd. 8, Tel Aviv 64733, Israel. TEL 972-3-6966256. FAX 972-3-6953809. (Co-sponsors: Ministry of Agriculture, Department of Mechanization and Engineering; Institute of Agricultural Engineering; Israel Association for Agricultural Engineering) Ed. Dan Meir. adv. circ. 1,000.

631.3   FR   ISSN 0027-2272
MOTORISATION AGRICOLE;* la premiere revue technique de l'agriculture moderne. 1947. m. 60 F. 8 Cite Paradis, 75010 Paris, France. TEL 40-22-79-47. FAX 48-24-03-15. TELEX 660 067. adv.; illus. circ. 19,000. **Indexed:** Agri.Eng.Abstr.
    Incorporates: Moniteur des Travaux Agricoles et des Battages (ISSN 0026-9697)

631.3   US
NEAL'S CATALOG FILE.* 1981. a. A C I Advertising, Inc., 1717 Folkstone Dr., St. Louis, MO 63131-3949. TEL 314-966-2580. adv. circ. 5,400.

631.3 643   NR   ISSN 0794-6414
NIGERIAN STORED PRODUCTS RESEARCH INSTITUTE. ANNUAL REPORT. 1956. a. Federal Ministry of Science & Technology, P.M.B. 1489, Ilorin, Kwara State, Nigeria. Ed. J.O. Oyeniran. charts; illus.; stat.; index. circ. 3,000. (back issues avail.) **Document type:** corporate report, government publication.

631.3   JA   ISSN 0071-3937
NOGYO KIKAI NENKAN/FARM MACHINERY YEARBOOK. (Text in Japanese; summary, contents and statistical section in English) 1943. a. 10300 Yen. Shin-Norinsha Co., Ltd. - Farm Machinery Industrial Research Corp., Shin-Norin Bldg., 7, 2-chome, Kanda Nishiki-cho, Chiyoda-ku, Tokyo 101, Japan. TEL 03-3291-3674. FAX 03-3291-5717. Ed. Yoshisuke Kishida. adv. contact: K. Ikeda. circ. 10,000.
    Description: Contains latest comments, statistics and useful addresses pertaining to agricultural mechanization in Japan. Commentaries focus on trends in Japan's agricultural development, in agricultural machinery industry and production, and on results of farm machinery research efforts.

631.3   JA   ISSN 0029-0971
NOKI SHINBUN/AGRICULTURAL MACHINERY NEWS. (Text in Japanese; summaries in English) 1933. w. 15000 Yen. Shin-Norinsha Co., Ltd. - Farm Machinery Industrial Research Corp., Shin-Norin Bldg., 7, 2-chome, Kanda Nishiki-cho, Chiyoda-ku, Tokyo 101, Japan. TEL 03-3291-3674. FAX 03-3291-5717. Ed. Yoshisuke Kishida. adv.; bk.rev.; bibl.; charts; illus.; pat.; stat. circ. 50,000. (tabloid format)

631.3   CC   ISSN 1002-5294
NONGCUN JIXIEHUA/MECHANIZATION IN RURAL AREAS. (Text in Chinese) 1986. bi-m. Zhongguo Nongye Jixiehua Kexue Yanjiuyuan - Chinese Institute of Agricultural Mechanization, 1 Bei Shatan, Dewai, Beijing 100083, People's Republic of China. TEL 2017082. Ed. Liang Qijun. **Document type:** academic/scholarly publication.

631.3   CC
NONGJI SHIYAN YU TUIGUANG/AGRICULTURAL MACHINERY EXPERIMENT AND POPULARIZATION. (Text in Chinese) bi-m. Nongye Bu, Nongji Shiyan Jianding Zongzhan - Ministry of Agriculture, Appraisal Station of Agricultural Machinery Experiments, Shilihe, Dongsanhuan Nanlu, Beijing 100021, People's Republic of China. TEL 784361. Ed. Ding Guizhi.

631.3   CC   ISSN 0546-9538
NONGYE JIXIE/AGRICULTURAL MACHINERY. (Text in Chinese) m. 1 Bei Shatan, Dewai, Beijing 100083, People's Republic of China. TEL 2017082. adv. circ. 120,000.

631.3   CC   ISSN 1000-1298
NONGYE JIXIE XUEBAO/CHINESE SOCIETY OF AGRICULTURAL MACHINERY. TRANSACTIONS. (Text in Chinese) 1957. q. $6.40 per no. Zhongguo Nongye Jixie Xuehui - Chinese Society of Agricultural Machinery, 1 Bei Shatan, Dewai, Beijing 100083, People's Republic of China. TEL 86-10-6201-7131. FAX 86-10-6204-3686. (Subscr. to: China International Book Trading Corp., P.O. Box 399, Beijing, P.R. China) Ed. Bingyuan Feng; Pub. Ruiwen Liu. R&P contact: Bingyuan Feng. circ. 1,500. **Indexed:** Agri.Eng.Abstr., Cott.&Trop.Fibr.Abstr., Ind.Vet., Pig News & Info., Rice Abstr., Seed Abstr., Soyabean Abstr., Trop.Oil Seeds Abstr. **Document type:** academic/scholarly publication.
    ●Also available on CD-ROM.
    —Ei.
    Description: Contains studies and researches on theories, designing and manufacturing, and technologies of agricultural machinery.
    Refereed Serial

631.3   CC
NONGYE JIXIE ZAZHI/JOURNAL OF AGRICULTURAL MACHINERY. (Text in Chinese) m. Zhongguo Nongye Jixiehua Kexue Yanjiuyuan - Chinese Institute of Agricultural Mechanization, 1 Bei Shatan, Dewai, Beijing 100083, People's Republic of China. TEL 2017082. Ed. Shi Yu-Wen. adv. circ. 120,000.

631.3   US
NORTH AMERICAN FARM EQUIPMENT JOURNAL. 1887. m. $36 (foreign $72). G J P Enterprises Inc., 101 W. 29th St., Ste. 102, Box 1210, Marshfield, WI 54449. TEL 715-389-2234. FAX 715-389-2380. Ed. Gerald J. Petcher; Pub. Gerald J. Petcher. adv.; illus.; pat.; tr.lit.; index; circ. 6,050 (controlled). **Document type:** trade publication, newspaper.
    Formerly (until 1994): Northwest Farm Equipment Journal (ISSN 0029-3350)
    Description: Sent to implement dealers across the USA and Canada.

631.3   UK
O E M NEWS. bi-m. £12. Richard Lee Magazines, 88 Main Rd., Gidea Park, Romford, Essex RM2 5JB, England. TEL 44-1708-743626. FAX 44-1708-743626. Ed. Richard Lee. adv. contact: Steve Bradshaw. circ. 1,200. **Document type:** trade publication.
    Formerly: O E M Newsletter (ISSN 0267-307X); Which incorporates: Workshop Equipment News (ISSN 0260-6887)

631.3   US   ISSN 1048-3039
O E M OFF-HIGHWAY. (Original Equipment Manufacturers) 8/yr. Johnson Hill Press, Inc. (Subsidiary of: Cygnus Publishing), 1233 Janesville Ave., Ft. Atkinson, WI 53538-2738. TEL 920-563-6388. FAX 920-563-1699. Ed. Iris Poliski; Pub. Phil Merrick. adv. contact: Phil Merrick. circ. 17,500. **Document type:** trade publication.
    Former titles (until 1990): O E M (ISSN 0893-5890); (until 1987): Farm Equipment O E M (ISSN 0886-1366)
    Description: Resource for component and general productivity information to engineering, purchasing, manufacturing, marketing and company management.

631.3 658   US   ISSN 0889-3950
OFFICIAL INDUSTRIAL EQUIPMENT GUIDE. s-a. price varies. North American Equipment Dealers Association, 10877 Watson Rd., St. Louis, MO 63127. TEL 314-821-7220. FAX 314-821-0674. **Document type:** trade publication.
    Description: For evaluation of previously owned machinery. Includes rental information.

631.3   FR
L'OFFICIEL DE L'ARTISAN RURAL.* 6/yr. 31, cite d'Antin, 75009 Paris, France. TEL 48-78-55-05. Ed. Agnes Objois. adv. circ. 14,000.

631.3 977   US   ISSN 0896-4955
OLD ABE'S NEWS. 1985. q. $20. (J.I. Case Collectors Association, Inc.) Crooked Hollow Farm, 400 Carriage Dr., Plain City, OH 43064-2101. TEL 614-873-3896. Ed. David T. Erb. adv. contact: David T. Erb. bibl.; illus.; stat.; tr.lit. circ. 2,000. (back issues avail.) **Document type:** newsletter.
    Description: Includes restoration tips, techniques, articles, people stories, club news, and convention news.

631.3   US   ISSN 0897-2540
OLD ALLIS NEWS. 1983. q. $20 in U.S. and Canada; elsewhere $25 (effective 1997). Nan Jones, Ed. & Pub., 10925 Love Rd., Bellevue, MI 49021. TEL 616-763-9770. FAX 616-763-9770. circ. 3,000. (back issues avail.) **Document type:** newsletter.
    Description: For the collector and enthusiast of Allis-Chalmers tractors and equipment.

631.3 658   US   ISSN 0735-6676
S713
OUTDOOR POWER EQUIPMENT OFFICIAL GUIDE. a. price varies. North American Equipment Dealers Association, 10877 Watson Rd., St. Louis, MO 63127. TEL 314-821-7220. FAX 314-821-0674. **Document type:** trade publication.
    Description: Provides values and serial number information on used lawn and garden machinery.

631.3 634.9   AT   ISSN 0817-6043
POWER EQUIPMENT AUSTRALASIA. 1979. bi-m. Aus.$36. Glenvale Publications Pty. Ltd., 4 Palmer Court, Mount Waverley, Vic. 3149, Australia. TEL 61-3-544-2233. FAX 61-3-543-1150. Ed. Steve Symmons. adv.; bk.rev. circ. 7,500. (back issues avail.) **Document type:** trade publication.
    Formerly (until 1985): Power Equipment Australia (ISSN 0817-6035)

631.3   AT   ISSN 0311-1911
POWER FARMING. 1892. bi-m. Aus.$24 (foreign Aus.$42) (effective 1997). Diverse Publishing Co. Pty. Ltd., P.O. Box 370, North Melbourne, Vic. 3051, Australia. TEL 61-3-93296040. FAX 61-3-93281116. Ed. John Howell. adv.; charts; illus.; stat.; index. circ. 16,000. **Indexed:** Agri.Eng.Abstr., Aus.Sci.Ind., Cott.&Trop.Fibr.Abstr., Field Crop Abstr., Herb.Abstr., Hort.Abstr.
    Formerly: Power Farming and Better Farming Digest (ISSN 0032-5996)

AGRICULTURE — AGRICULTURAL EQUIPMENT

631.3   AT   ISSN 1030-0325
POWER FARMING ANNUAL. 1937. a. Aus.$23.95 (foreign Aus.$28.95). Diverse Publishing Co. Pty. Ltd., P.O. Box 370, North Melbourne, Vic. 3051, Australia. TEL 61-3-93296040. FAX 61-3-92381116. adv.
    Formerly: Power Farming Technical Annual (ISSN 0079-4422)

631.3   CN   ISSN 0831-2338
PRAIRIE FARMERS CATALOGUE. 1979. a. free. Prairie Publishing Co., P.O. Box 100, Oakville, Man. R0H 0Y0, Canada. TEL 204-267-2102. FAX 204-267-2585. Ed. Dale H. Crampton. adv. circ. 150,000.

631.3 745.1   US   ISSN 0896-5617
PRAIRIE GOLD RUSH; quarterly newsletter for all Twin City, Minneapolis and Moline enthusiasts. 1980. q. $16 (foreign $20). Prairie Gold Rush (PGR), Rte. 1, Box 119, Francesville, IN 47946. Ed. Paul Lowry; Pub. Paul Lowry. adv. contact: Paul Lowry. circ. 900. (back issues avail.) **Document type:** newsletter.

631.3   PL   ISSN 0867-8243
PRZEGLAD TECHNIKI ROLNICZEJ I LESNEJ. 1953. m. $50. (Stowarzyszenie Inzynierow i Technikow Mechanikow Polskich, Sekcja Maszyn i Ciagnikow Rolniczych) Oficyna Wydawnicza SIMP Press, Ltd., Ul. Swietokrzyska 14A, 00-950 Warsaw, Poland. TEL 40-38-02. Ed. Czeslaw Waszkiewicz. adv. circ. 1,500. **Indexed:** Agri.Eng.Abstr., Field Crop Abstr., Seed Abstr., Triticale Abstr.
    Former titles (until 1992): Maszyny i Ciagniki Rolnicze i Lesne; (until 1990): Maszyny i Ciagniki Rolnicze (ISSN 0465-2592); (until 1963): Maszyny Rolnicze.

631.3   UK
RED MACHINERY GUIDE. 1960. m. £52.70($80) Red Machinery Guide Ltd., 15 N. Audley St., London W1Y 2LR, England. TEL 0171-629-9619. Ed. W.D.A. Fuller. adv. (back issues avail.)

631.3 658 S677   US   ISSN 0162-6809
REGIONAL OFFICIAL GUIDES: TRACTORS AND FARM EQUIPMENT. 1969. q. price varies. North American Equipment Dealers Association, 10877 Watson Rd., St. Louis, MO 63127. TEL 314-821-7220. FAX 314-821-0674. Ed. John A. Wallace. **Document type:** trade publication.
    Formerly: Official Guide: Tractors and Farm Equipment.
    Description: Provides evaluations of used machinery, with serial numbers and rental information.

631.3   IT
REPERTORIO DELLE MACCHINE AGRICOLE. 1971. s-a. free to M M & A subscribers. Edagricole S.p.A., Via Emilia Levante 31, 40139 Bologna, Italy. TEL 39-51-492211. FAX 39-51-493660. adv.: B&W page L.1250000, color page L.1850000; trim 185 x 247. circ. 21,300.
    Supersedes (in 1981): Catalogo e Repertorio delle Macchine Agricole.
    Description: Reviews all farm machinery presently available on the domestic market.

631.3   GW
REPORT FUER DIE MITARBEITER IN DEUTSCHLAND. 1969. q. Deere & Company, Postfach 100862, 68008 Mannheim, Germany. TEL 49-621-8104418. FAX 49-621-8104-300. TELEX 63056-DCEOD. Ed. Rainer Mache. bk.rev. circ. 9,700. **Document type:** trade publication.

631.3 621.9   US
REPRESENTATIVE. m. Agricultural and Industrial Manufacturers Representatives Association, 5818 Reeds Rd., Mission, KS 66202-2740. TEL 913-262-4511. FAX 913-262-0174.

631.3   FR   ISSN 0223-0135
REVUE TECHNIQUE MACHINISME AGRICOLE. 1979. 7/yr. 515 F. (foreign 565 F.). Editions Techniques pour l'Automobile et l'Industrie (ETAI), 20 rue de la Saussiere, 92100 Boulogne Billancourt, France. TEL 46-04-81-13. FAX 48-25-56-92. TELEX ETAIRTA 204850 F. Ed. Christian Rey. charts; illus. circ. 17,000.
—CCC.
    Description: Explains how to dismantle, repair and reassemble farm tractors, combine harvesters and related machines.

631.3   UK   ISSN 1362-7376
RURAL DESIGN AND BUILDING. 1968. s-a. £10 (Europe & Ireland £25; overseas £33) (effective 1997). Rural Design and Building Association, Harper Adams, Newport, Shropshire TF10 8NB, England. TEL 44-1952-814555. FAX 44-1952-814777. Ed. Fiona Grice. R&P contact: Fiona Grice. adv. contact: Fiona Grice. bk.rev.; abstr.; bibl.; charts; illus.; stat. circ. 1,500. **Indexed:** Agri.Eng.Abstr., Br.Ceram.Abstr., Ind.Vet., Pig News & Info., RICS, Vet.Bull. **Document type:** academic/scholarly publication.
—CISTI.
    Former titles: Farm Buildings and Engineering (ISSN 0265-5373); (until 1984): Farm Buildings Digest (ISSN 0014-7877)
    Refereed Serial

631.3   FR
SEDIMAGAZINE. 4/yr. C D E F G, 6 bd. Jourdan, 75014 Paris, France. TEL 45-89-11-99. FAX 45-88-42-18. TELEX 204 264. Ed. Regis Elies. circ. 2,500.

631.3   RU   ISSN 0131-7393
SEL'SKII MEKHANIZATOR. 1958. m. $65 (effective 1998). Sadovaya-Spasskaya, 18, 107807 Moscow, Russia. TEL 7-095-2072300. FAX 7-095-2072870. (Dist. by: Mezhdunarodnaya Kniga, B. Yakimanka 39, 117049 Moscow, Russia) Ed. Aleksandr I. Kolpakov. charts; illus.; index. circ. 58,000.
—BLDSC (0162.800000).

631.3   BU   ISSN 0037-1718
CODEN: STFMBL
SELSKOSTOPANSKA TEKHNIKA. (Summaries in German and Russian) 1964. 8/yr. 1.30 lv. per no. (Akademiia na Selskostopanskite Nauki) Publishing House of the Bulgarian Academy of Sciences, Acad. G. Bonchev St., Bldg. 6, 1113 Sofia, Bulgaria. (Dist. by: Hemus, 6, Rouski Blvd., 1000 Sofia, Bulgaria) Ed. Nikola Gaidarov. circ. 1,690. (reprint service avail. from IRC) **Indexed:** Agri.Eng.Abstr., Chem.Abstr., Dairy Sci.Abstr., Excerp.Med., Field Crop Abstr., Hort.Abstr., Maize Abstr., Ornam.Hort., Rural Recreat.Tour.Abstr., Seed Abstr., Soyabean Abstr., World Agri.Econ.& Rural Sociol.Abstr.
—BLDSC (0163.135000); CASDDS.

631.3   JA   ISSN 0371-3385
CODEN: STDZAF
SHIGA-KENRITSU TANKI DAIGAKU GAKUJUTSU ZASSHI/SHIGA PREFECTURAL JUNIOR COLLEGE. SCIENTIFIC REPORTS. (Text in Japanese; summaries in English) 1951. s-a. Shiga-kenritsu Tanki Daigaku - Shiga Prefectural Junior College, Hassaka-cho, Hikone-shi, Shiga-ken 522, Japan. circ. 1,200. **Indexed:** Agrindex, Chem.Abstr., Jap.Per.Ind.
—CASDDS.

631.3   US
SHORTLINER.* 1951. fortn. qualified personnel only. Farm Equipment Manufacturers Association, 1000 Executive Pky. Dr., No. 100, St. Louis, MO 63141-6369. TEL 314-991-0702. FAX 314-991-5732. Ed. Robert Schnell. circ. 1,000. (back issues avail.)

631.3   US
SOUTHERN FARM EQUIPMENT MANUFACTURERS. NEWSLETTER.* q. Southern Farm Equipment Manufacturers, c/o Marlon H. Cohn & Associates, 5000 Royal Marco Way, Apt. 334, Marco Island, FL 34145-1897. **Document type:** newsletter.

SPUDMAN; voice of the potato industry. see *AGRICULTURE — Crop Production And Soil*

SUSTAINABLE FARMING; resource efficient agricultural production. see *AGRICULTURE — Crop Production And Soil*

631.3   RU   ISSN 0131-7105
TEKHNIKA V SEL'SKOM KHOZYAISTVE. (Contents page in English, French, German) 1941. bi-m. $77 (effective 1998). Sadovaya-Spasskaya, 18, 107807 Moscow, Russia. TEL 7-095-2073762. FAX 7-095-2072870. (Dist. by: Mezhdunarodnaya Kniga, B. Yakimanka 39, 117049 Moscow, Russia. TEL 7-095-2384967. FAX 7-095-2384634) Ed. Petr S. Popov. adv.; illus. circ. 3,650. **Indexed:** Agri.Eng.Abstr., Field Crop Abstr., Maize Abstr., Ornam.Hort., Seed Abstr., Triticale Abstr.
—BLDSC (0180.330000).

631.3   FR   ISSN 0754-121X
TRACTEURS ET MACHINES AGRICOLES; l'officiel de l'agro-equipement. Abbreviated title: T M A. 1925. m. (11/yr.). 375 F. (foreign 525 F.). Societe d'Edition de la Press Agricole (SEPA), B.P. 107, 95170 Deuil la Barre, France. TEL 34285867. FAX 39842787. Ed. Pierre Lafon. adv. circ. 8,000. **Indexed:** Agri.Eng.Abstr. **Document type:** trade publication.
    Formerly: Farmes Modernes.
    Description: Information for those involved in agriculture. Aimed mainly at professionals interested in management and the latest equipment and technology.

631.3   UK   ISSN 0262-8090
TRACTOR & FARM MACHINERY TRADER. m. £30 (foreign £45). Richard Lee Magazines, 88 Main Rd., Gidea Park, Romford, Essex RM2 5JB, England. TEL 44-1708-743626. FAX 44-1708-743626. Ed. Richard Lee. adv. contact: Steve Bradshaw. circ. 2,000. **Document type:** trade publication.
    Incorporates: Outdoor Power Equipment News.

631.3   UK   ISSN 1357-3101
TRACTOR MAGAZINE. 1994. m. £22 (rest of Europe £28; elsewhere £33). Kelsey Publishing Ltd., Kelsey House, 77 High St., Beckenham, Kent BR3 1AN, England. TEL 44-181-658-3531. FAX 44-181-650-8035. **Document type:** consumer publication.

631.372   AU   ISSN 0041-0985
TRAKTOR AKTUELL. 1966. q. S.60. Agrar Post Verlag Dr. Bruno Mueller GmbH, Schulstr. 80, A-2103 Langenzersdorf, Austria. TEL 02244-4647. FAX 02244-422323. Ed. Franz Schachinger. adv.: color page S.38880; trim 210 x 270. charts; illus. circ. 145,000. (tabloid format)

631.3   RU   ISSN 0235-8573
TRAKTORY I SEL'SKOHOZYAISTVENNYE MASHINY. 1930. m. $231 (effective 1998). (Glavsel'khozmash Komitet Rossiiskoi Federatsii po Mashinostroeniyu) Izdatel'stvo Mashinostroenie, 4, Stromynsky per., 107076 Moscow, Russia. TEL 7-095-2697141. FAX 7-095-2694897. Ed. A.A. Shandybo. adv.: page DM.800. circ. 1,000. **Document type:** academic/scholarly publication.
—Linda Hall.
    Description: Covers tests conducted in construction, design, production, exploitation of tractors and farming machinery.

631.3   IT
▼**TRATTORI E MACCHINE AGRICOLE.** 1997. 10/yr. L.42000 (foreign $80). Vado e Torno Edizioni s.r.l., Via Lattanzio 77, 20139 Milan, Italy. TEL 39-2-55193629. FAX 39-2-55193660. Ed. Maurizio Cervetto; Pub. Gianni Sacedotti. adv.: B&W page L.5800000, color page L.10500000; adv. contact: Ornella Cavalli. circ. 26,000. **Document type:** trade publication.

631.3   NE   ISSN 1380-8559
TREKKER & WERKTUIG. m. (11/yr.). fl.95 (1800 BEF). Misset (Subsidiary of: Reed Elsevier plc), Postbus 4, 7000 BA Doetinchem, Netherlands. TEL 31-314-349371. FAX 31-314-363638. adv.: B&W page fl.2473, color page fl.3973; trim 215 x 285; adv. contact: Cor van Nek. illus. circ. 12,490. **Document type:** trade publication.
    Formerly (until 1992): Trekker.
    Description: Covers all aspects of tractors.

TURF NEWS. see *AGRICULTURE — Crop Production And Soil*

631.3   FR
UNETAR. 6/yr. 200 F. (foreign 300 F.). Etar 2000, 71 bd. des Rochers, 35500 Vitre, France. TEL 99-75-37-20. FAX 99-75-10-21. Ed. Annie Boulmer. adv. circ. 4,000.

631.3 669   RM   ISSN 1224-6077
UNIVERSITATEA POLITEHNICA DIN TIMISOARA. BULETINUL STIINTIFIC. SERIA MECANICA AGRICOLA, METALURGIE. (Text in English, French, German, Rumanian) 1970. a. $20 (effective 1997). Universitatea Politehnica din Timisoara, Piata Victoriei 2, 1900 Timisoara, Rumania. TEL 40-56-200333. FAX 40-56-190321. bk.rev. circ. 500. **Document type:** bulletin.

AGRICULTURE — COMPUTER APPLICATIONS

631.3 SP ISSN 1133-8938
VIDA RURAL. 1990. 21/yr. 10000 ptas. (foreign 15000 ptas.) (effective 1997). Edagricole Espana S.A., Castello 32 Dcha. 3o, 28001 Madrid, Spain. TEL 34-1-5780534. FAX 34-1-5753297. Ed. Jaime Lamo. adv.: B&W page 128000 ptas., color page 190000 ptas.; 23 x 30 1/2; adv. contact: Julia Dominguez. circ. 28,000. **Indexed:** Ind.SST.
Formerly (1990-1993): M T - Maquinas y Tractores Agricolas (ISSN 0214-9206)
Description: For large farm managers, machinery distributors, agricultural experts and technicians.

631 UK ISSN 0263-7529
VINTAGE TRACTOR. 1980. q. $20. Allan T. Condie Publications, Merrivale, Main St., Carlton, Nuneaton, Warks. CV13 0BZ, England. TEL 01455-290389. Ed. A.T. Condie. adv.; bk.rev.; illus. circ. 2,000.
Document type: consumer publication.
Incorporates: Fordson and Old Tractor Magazine; Which incorporated: Ford Fergie Farmer; Which was formerly: Small Farmer.

631.3 US ISSN 1044-7768
WESTERN RETAILER. 1889. m. $12. Western Retail Implement & Hardware Association, Box 19264, Kansas City, MO 64141. TEL 816-561-5323. FAX 816-561-1249. Ed. Mike Griffith; Pub. Jeff Flora. adv. contact: Mike Griffith. charts; illus.; stat. circ. 2,000. **Document type:** trade publication.
Formerly (until May 1989): Hardware and Farm Equipment (ISSN 0017-7679)

WISCONSIN R E C NEWS. see GENERAL INTEREST PERIODICALS — United States

631.3 DK
WORLD PLOUGHING CONTEST. OFFICIAL HANDBOOK. (Text in English and in language of country in which the contest is held) 1954. a. price varies. World Ploughing Organization, Sokildevej 17, DK-5270 Odense N, Denmark. TEL 045-65978006. Ed. Carl Alleso. adv./ index. circ. 10,000. **Document type:** catalog.
Description: Devoted to news and information about contests, competitors and champions. Also covers technical, historical and international information about ploughing. Includes list of exhibitions and demonstrations.

ZEMEDELSKA TECHNIKA/AGRICULTURAL TECHNOLOGY; vedecky casopis. see AGRICULTURE

631.3 621.9 US
9N - 2N - 8N - NAA NEWSLETTER. 1986. q. $14 (Canada $17; elsewhere $20). Gerard W. Rinaldi, Ed. & Pub., Box 235, Chelsea, VT 05038-0235. bk.rev.; circ. 6,000 (paid). (back issues avail.)
Document type: newsletter.
Formerly: 9N - 2N - 8N Newsletter (ISSN 0896-5641)
Description: Directed to enthusiasts of the Ford Model N and other Ford "gray line" tractors and related equipment.

AGRICULTURE — Computer Applications

630 NE ISSN 0925-4455
AGRO INFORMATICA. 1987. 5/yr. fl.45($32) (Vereniging voor Informatici in de Agrarische Sector) Wageningen Pers, Postbus 42, 6700 AA Wageningen, Netherlands. TEL 31-317-476506. FAX 31-317-426044. E-mail: wageningenpers@company.diva.nl. Ed. J. Heeres. circ. 600 (paid).
Document type: academic/scholarly publication.

AGROCIENCIA. MATEMATICAS APLICADAS, ESTADISTICA Y COMPUTACION. see AGRICULTURE — Agricultural Economics

C A SELECTS. PESTICIDE ANALYSIS. see BIOLOGY — Abstracting, Bibliographies, Statistics

630 NE ISSN 0168-1699
CODEN: CEAGE6
COMPUTERS AND ELECTRONICS IN AGRICULTURE; an international journal. 1984. 9/yr. fl.1320($759) (effective 1998). Elsevier Science B.V., P.O. Box 211, 1000 AE Amsterdam, Netherlands. TEL 31-20-4853911. FAX 31-20-4853598. TELEX 18582 ESPA NL. E-mail: nlinfo-f@elsevier.nl; usinfo-f@elsevier.com; forinfo-kyf04035@niftyserve.or.jp; URL: http://www.elsevier.nl:80/inca/publications/store/5/0/3/3/6/4/503304.pub.shtml. (Subscr. in the Americas to: Elsevier Science, Regional Sales Office, Box 945, New York, NY 10159-0945. TEL 212-633-3730. FAX 212-633-3680; Subscr. in Australasia and the Far East to: Elsevier Science (Singapore) Pte Ltd, No.1 Temasek Ave., No.17-01 Millenia Tower, Singapore 039192, Singapore. TEL 65-434-3727. FAX 65-337-2230; Subscr. in Japan to: Elsevier Science Japan, 9-15 Higashi-Azabu 1-chome, Minato-ku, Tokyo 106, Japan. TEL 81-3-5561-5033. FAX 81-3-5561-5047) Ed. S.W.R. Cox. (also avail. in microform from UMI; back issues avail.) **Indexed:** Agri.Eng.Abstr., Anim.Breed.Abstr., ASCA, Bibl.Agri., Biol.Abstr., Compumath, Comput.& Info.Sys., Curr.Cont., Ecol.Abstr., Eng.Ind., Field Crop Abstr., Food Sci.& Tech.Abstr., Geo.Abstr.H.G., Geo.Abstr.P.G., Hort.Abstr., IDA, Ind.Vet., INSPEC (1985-), Maize Abstr., Rice Abstr., Soils & Fert., Sorghum & Millets Abstr., Vet.Bull., World Agri.Econ.& Rural Sociol.Abstr. **Document type:** academic/scholarly publication.
—BLDSC (3394.682000); AskIEEE; CISTI; Ei; Genuine Article; KR SourceOne; Linda Hall; SWETS; UnCover. **CCC.**
Description: Provides international coverage of advances in the application of computers and electronic instrumentation and control systems to agriculture and related industries.
Refereed Serial

630 005.3 AT ISSN 1036-9821
FARM COMPUTING. 1991. q. Aus.$20. Seaqus Publications, 2 Larne Ave., Donvale, Vic. 3111, Australia. TEL 61-3-98425311. FAX 61-3-98429392. Ed. Leslie Dale; Pub. Leslie Dale. adv.: page Aus.$400; adv. contact: Leslie Dale. bk.rev.; software rev.; illus.; mkt.; circ. 300 (paid). (back issues avail.) **Document type:** consumer publication.
Description: Aimed at helping farmers to become computer literate by using their own computers for keeping farm management records.

630 US
FARM SMART; the journal of computerized farm management. 1981. q. $18 (foreign $25). F B S System, Inc., 1855 55th Ave., Aledo, IL 61231-8610. TEL 800-437-7638. Ed. Wesley Prosser; Pub. Norman Brown. R&P contact: Norman Brown. adv. contact: Wesley Prosser. bk.rev. circ. 5,000. (looseleaf format) **Document type:** newsletter.
Formerly (until 1984): Friendly Farm Computer Newsletter.
Description: For farmers interested in computerized farm management. Articles cover finance, budgeting, and management.

630 US
TECAGRI NEWS. 1987. irreg. Clark Consulting International, Inc., Box 600, Dundee, IL 60118-0600. TEL 847-836-5100. FAX 847-836-5140. E-mail: ag-pr@agpc.com; URL: http://www.agpr.com/consulting/. Ed. Warren Clark; Pub. Warren Clark. R&P contact: Warren Clark. adv. contact: Warren Clark. circ. 90,000 (controlled).
Document type: newsletter.
Formerly: TechAgra News.
Description: For large, innovative farmers and ranchers who use computerized farm management to increase profitability.

630 GW ISSN 0942-6620
ZEITSCHRIFT FUER AGRARINFORMATIK. bi-m. DM.114 (foreign DM.123.60) (effective 1997). (Gesellschaft fuer Informatik in der Land-, Forst- und Ernaehrungswirtschaft) Landwirtschaftsverlag GmbH, Huelsebrockstr. 2, 48165 Muenster, Germany. TEL 49-2501-801-0. FAX 49-2501-801-204. (Subscr. to: Postfach 480249, 48079 Muenster, Germany) **Document type:** trade publication.

AGRICULTURE — Crop Production And Soil

see also Agriculture–Feed, Flour and Grain; Gardening and Horticulture; Rubber; Tobacco

631 US ISSN 0197-8748
CODEN: PPESD9
A P R E S PROCEEDINGS. a. membership. American Peanut Research and Education Society, c/o Dr. James R. Sholar, 376 Ag Hall, Oklahoma State University, Stillwater, OK 74078. TEL 405-744-9634. FAX 405-744-5269. circ. 750. **Indexed:** Bio-Contr.News & Info., Biol.Abstr., Chem.Abstr., Cott.&Trop.Fibr.Abstr., Crop Physiol.Abstr., Field Crop Abstr., Plant Grow.Reg.Abstr., Seed Abstr., Sorghum & Millets Abstr., Trop.Oil Seeds Abstr., Weed Abstr. **Document type:** proceedings.
—BLDSC (6627.801000); CASDDS; Linda Hall.
Former titles: American Peanut Research and Education Association. Proceedings (ISSN 0160-6719); American Peanut Research and Education Association. Journal (ISSN 0587-503X)

631 US ISSN 8755-1187
S671 CODEN: ASEPER
A S A E STANDARDS. 1954. a. $140 to non-members (foreign $154); members $46 (foreign $50.60) (effective 1997). American Society of Agricultural Engineers, 2950 Niles Rd., St. Joseph, MI 49085-9659. TEL 616-429-0300. FAX 616-429-3852. E-mail: hq@asae.org; URL: http://asae.org/. Ed. Russell Hahn. (also avail. in microfilm) **Indexed:** Agri.Eng.Abstr. **Document type:** trade publication.
—Ei. **CCC.**
Supersedes: Agricultural Engineers Yearbook of Standards (ISSN 0065-4477)
Description: Contains over 210 current ASAE Standards, Engineering Practice and Data. Presents performance criteria for products, materials, and systems.

631 US
A S A E TRANSACTIONS. SOIL & WATER. 1970. a. $77.50 to non-members; members $43 (effective 1997). American Society of Agricultural Engineers, 2950 Niles Rd., St. Joseph, MI 49085-9659. TEL 616-429-0300. FAX 616-429-3852. E-mail: hq@asae.org; URL: http://asea.org/. Ed. Pamela DeVore-Hansen. circ. 300. **Indexed:** Geo.Abstr. **Document type:** trade publication.
Description: Addresses irrigation, hydrology, drainage, erosion and soil science.
Refereed Serial

631.091 CU ISSN 1010-3732
A T A C. q. $24 in S. America; N. America $26; elsewhere $30. (Asociacion de Tecnicos Azucareros de Cuba, Departamento de Exportacion) Ediciones Cubanas, Obispo No. 527, Apdo. 605, Havana, Cuba. charts; illus. **Indexed:** Agri.Eng.Abstr., Biol.Abstr., Food Sci.& Tech.Abstr., Plant Breed.Abstr., Rural Recreat.Tour.Abstr., Soils & Fert., Sugar Ind.Abstr., World Agri.Econ.& Rural Sociol.Abstr.

AGRICULTURE — CROP PRODUCTION AND SOIL

613 PL ISSN 0860-2832
CODEN: ATOAE5
ACTA ACADEMIAE AGRICULTURAE AC TECHNICAE OLSTENENSIS. AGRICULTURA/AGRICULTURAL AND TECHNICAL ACADEMY IN OLSZTYN. AGRICULTURE. (Supplement avail.: Agricultura; English, Polish) 1956. s-a. price varies. (Akademia Rolniczo-Techniczna im. M. Oczapowskiego) Wydawnictwo A R T Olsztyn, Blok 12, 10-957 Olsztyn-Kortowo, Poland. TEL 48-89-5273310. TELEX 0526419. E-mail: artbib@moskit.art.olsztyn.pl. (Dist. by: Ars Polona-Ruch, Krakowskie Przedmiescie 7, Warsaw, Poland. TEL 48-22-265334) Ed. Barbara Grudniewska. R&P contact: Jolanta Mieszkalska. adv. contact: Maciej Gajecki. bibl.; charts; illus.; circ. 180 (controlled). **Indexed:** Agri.Eng.Abstr., AgroLibrex, Chem.Abstr., Excerpt.Med., Fababean Abstr., Field Crop Abstr., Forest.Abstr., Geo.Abstr., Herb.Abstr., Hort.Abstr., Maize Abstr., Potato Abstr., Ref.Zh., Seed Abstr., Triticale Abstr., Weed Abstr. **Document type:** academic/scholarly publication.
—CASDDS.
Former titles: Akademia Rolniczo-Techniczna. Zeszyty Naukowe. Rolnictwo (ISSN 0324-9204); Wyzsza Szkola Rolnicza, Olsztyn. Zeszyty Naukowe (ISSN 0078-4583)

630 PL ISSN 0065-0919
CODEN: AASABP
ACTA AGRARIA ET SILVESTRIA. SERIES AGRARIA. (Text in Polish; summaries in English and Russian) 1961. irreg. (1-2/yr.) price varies. (Polska Akademia Nauk, Oddzial w Krakowie, Komisja Nauk Rolniczych i Lesnych) Ossolineum, Publishing House of the Polish Academy of Sciences, Pl. Solny 14a, 50-062 Wroclaw, Poland. TEL 48-71-343-6961. FAX 48-71-448-103. TELEX 0712771 OSS PL. Ed. Eugeniusz Gorlach. **Indexed:** AgroLibrex, Biol.Abstr., Chem.Abstr., Excerpt.Med., Field Crop Abstr., Herb.Abstr., Hort.Abstr., Plant Breed.Abstr., Plant Grow.Reg.Abstr., Potato Abstr., Seed Abstr., Soils & Fert., Triticale Abstr., Weed Abstr. **Document type:** academic/scholarly publication.
—BLDSC (0588.620000); CASDDS; KNAW.
Formerly (until 1965): Acta Agraria et Silvestria. Seria Rolnicza (ISSN 0515-2690)
Description: Occurrence and control of diseases and pests of plants. Effect of fertilization and cultivation measures.

631 NO ISSN 0906-4710
SB13 CODEN: AASBEV
ACTA AGRICULTURAE SCANDINAVICA. SECTION B, SOIL AND PLANT SCIENCE. (Supplement avail.: Acta Agriculturae Scandinavica. Supplementum) (Text in English) 1950. q. NOK 925 in Nordic countries; elsewhere $159 (effective 1997). (Kungliga Skogs-och Lantbruksakademien - Royal Swedish Academy of Agriculture and Forestry) Scandinavian University Press, P.O. Box 2959 Toeyen, N-0608 Oslo, Norway. TEL 47-22-57-53-53. FAX 47-22-57-53-53. E-mail: mail@scup.no; URL: http://www.scup.no. (U.S. addr.: 875 Massachusetts Ave., Ste. 84, Cambridge, MA 02139. TEL 617-497-6515. FAX 617-354-6875) (Co-sponsor: Nordiska Jordbruksforskares Foerening) Ed. Sven-Uno Skarp. bibl.; charts; illus. circ. 1,000. (back issues avail.; reprint service avail.) **Indexed:** ASCA, Curr.Cont., Food Sci.& Tech.Abstr., Ind.Sci.Rev. **Document type:** academic/scholarly publication.
—BLDSC (0589.010000); CASDDS; Genuine Article; Linda Hall; SWETS; UnCover. **CCC.**
Supersedes in part (in 1992): Acta Agriculturae Scandinavica (ISSN 0001-5121)
Refereed Serial

631 CK ISSN 0120-2812
CODEN: CAGAY
ACTA AGRONOMICA. (Text in Spanish; summaries in English and Spanish) 1951. q. Col.$1200($40) or exchange basis. Universidad Nacional de Colombia, Facultad de Ciencias Agropecuarias Palmira, Apdo. 237, Palmira, Colombia. FAX 931-32477. Ed. Heimar Quintero. bibl.; charts; circ. 1,000. **Indexed:** Bio-Contr.News & Info., Biol.Abstr., Chem.Abstr., Curr.Adv.Ecol.Sci., Dairy Sci.Abstr., Field Crop Abstr., Herb.Abstr., Hort.Abstr., Nutr.Abstr., Plant Breed.Abstr., Plant Grow.Reg.Abstr., Rev.Plant Path., Soils & Fert., Sorghum & Millets Abstr., Soyabean Abstr.
—BLDSC (0589.900000).

ACTA BOTANICA MALACITANA. see *BIOLOGY — Botany*

ACTUALIZACION DE LAS INVERSIONES AZUCARERAS.
see *BUSINESS AND ECONOMICS — Investments*

630 GW ISSN 0301-2727
SB123 CODEN: FSPZAR
ADVANCES IN PLANT BREEDING/FORTSCHRITTE DER PFLANZENZUECHTUNG. (Supplement to: Zeitschrift fuer Pflanzenzuechtung) (Text in English or German; summaries in English, French, German) 1971. irreg., no.16, 1994. price varies. Verlag Paul Parey (Berlin), Seelbuschring 9-17, 12105 Berlin, Germany. TEL 030-70784-0. FAX 030-70784199. **Indexed:** Biol.Abstr., Curr.Cont., Plant Breed.Abstr. **Document type:** academic/scholarly publication.
—BLDSC (0710.150000); CISTI.

ADVANCES IN SOIL SCIENCES. see *EARTH SCIENCES*

631 UK
THE ADVISOR. 1994. q. £20 (foreign £30). Carter Spencer Publishing Ltd., Chancery Ct., Lincoln Rd., High Wycombe, Bucks. HP12 3RE, England. TEL 44-1494-442424. FAX 44-1494-472790. Ed. Nick Carter; Pub. David Spencer. R&P contact: David Spencer. adv.: page £1550; trim 297 x 210; adv. contact: David Spencer. charts; illus.; pat., stat.; tr.lit.; circ. 3,500. (back issues avail.) **Document type:** trade publication.
Description: Discusses cultivation of crops and the use of fertilizers and disease-control agents, along with their economic and environmental implications.

633 UG ISSN 1021-9730
SB95.A338
AFRICAN CROP SCIENCE JOURNAL; a journal of tropical crop science and production. 1993. q. $80 to individuals; institutions $180 (effective 1997 & 1998). African Crop Science Society, Faculty of Agriculture and Forestry, Makerere University, P.O. Box 7062, Kampala, Uganda. TEL 256-41-540464. FAX 256-41-531641. E-mail: acss@starcom.co.ug. Ed. Adipala Ekwamu. adv.; bk.rev. circ. 300. **Indexed:** Food Sci.& Tech.Abstr. **Document type:** academic/scholarly publication.
Description: Presents a forum for new research in tropical crop science and agricultural development.
Refereed Serial

632 CM ISSN 0379-6930
AFRICAN JOURNAL OF PLANT PROTECTION/REVUE AFRICAINE DE LA PROTECTION DES VEGETAUX. (Text in English, French) 1980. s-a. Inter-African Phyto-Sanitary Council, B.P. 4170, Yaounde, Cameroon. bibl. **Indexed:** Rev.Plant Path.
Formerly: Inter-African Phyto-Sanitary Bulletin.

633 SA ISSN 1022-0119
CODEN: GSPCB4
AFRICAN JOURNAL OF RANGE & FORAGE SCIENCE. (Text and summaries in Afrikaans or English) 1966; N.S. 1984. q. R.150. Grassland Society of Southern Africa, P.O. Box 100327, Scottsville 3209, South Africa. Ed. C.R. Hurt. adv.; bk.rev.; cum.index. circ. 800. (back issues avail.) **Indexed:** Agroforest.Abstr., Bibl.Agri., Biol.Abstr., Biol.& Agr.Ind., Chem.Abstr., Field Crop Abstr., Geo.Abstr., Herb.Abstr., Ind.S.A.Per., Soils & Fert., Sorghum & Millets Abstr., Sport Fish.Abstr., Weed Abstr., Wild.Rev., World Agri.Econ.& Rural Sociol.Abstr. **Document type:** academic/scholarly publication.
—CASDDS; Linda Hall; UnCover.
Formerly (until vol.10, 1993): Grassland Society of Southern Africa. Journal (ISSN 0256-6702); **Supersedes** (in 1984): Grassland Society of Southern Africa. Proceedings of the Annual Congresses (ISSN 0072-5560)
Description: Studies of range and forage science, grasslands, natural vegetation, planted pastures and animal populations.

630.24 US ISSN 1072-7361
HD9660.P3
AG CHEM NEW COMPOUND REVIEW; an annual review covering the latest new product developments in the world's crop production industry. 1983. a. $350 (effective 1997). Ag Chem Information Services, 6705 E. 71st St., Indianapolis, IN 46220. TEL 317-845-0681. FAX 317-841-1210. Pub. William L. Hoplins. **Document type:** catalog.
Former titles (until 1992): Ag Chem New Product Review; (until 1988): Agricultural Chemical New Product Development Review.
Description: Identifies over 250 experimental compounds in some phase of public testing. Updates status of previously listed compounds.

631.8 US ISSN 1072-9267
HD9483.U5
AG RETAILER MAGAZINE. 1956. 9/yr. free in N. America; elsewhere $40. Doane Agricultural Service Co., 11701 Borman Dr., Ste. 100, Saint Louis, MO 63146-4199. TEL 314-569-2700. FAX 314-569-1083. Ed. Den Gardner; Pub. John Appleton. R&P contact: John Appleton. adv. contact: Jack Tower. charts; illus.; stat.; circ. 21,966 (controlled). **Indexed:** Alloys Ind., Chem.Abstr., Eng.Mat.Abstr., Excerpt.Med., INSPEC, Met.Abstr., Met.Abstr.Ind., Nonfer.Met.Alert, PCC Alert, Soils & Fert., Steels Alert, World Alum.Abstr. **Document type:** trade publication.
—Linda Hall; UMI.
Former titles: Solutions (ISSN 0199-9869); (until 1980): Fertilizer Solutions (ISSN 0015-0312)

631 GW ISSN 0176-0955
AGRAR-PRAXIS.* 1882. m. DM.85.20. Verlag Kouradin, Ernst-Mey-Str. 8, Postfach 100252, D-7022 Leinfelden-Echterdingen, Germany. TEL 0711-7594-0. Ed. Helmut von Bockelmann. adv.; bk.rev.; charts; illus.; mkt.; stat. circ. 60,264. **Indexed:** INIS Atomind.
Formerly (until 1984): Feld und Wald (ISSN 0014-9748)

631 GW ISSN 0941-1186
AGRARMETEOROLOGISCHER WOCHENBERICHT SCHLESWIG-HOLSTEIN, HAMBURG, NIEDERSACHSEN UND BREMEN. 1977. w. DM.100 (effective 1996 & 1997). Deutscher Wetterdienst, Aussenstelle Schleswig, Regenpfeiferweg 9, 24837 Schleswig, Germany. TEL 49-4621-5073. FAX 494621-52777. circ. 200. **Document type:** government publication.
Formerly: Agrarmeteorologischer Wochenbericht fuer Norddeutschland (ISSN 0344-0397)
Description: Contains a brief description of the weather conditions of the previous week and its effects on the development of agriculture and crops.

631.8 US
AGRIBUSINESS FIELDMAN.* 1972. m. $19.95 (overseas $195). Western Agricultural Publishing Co. Inc., 4969 E. Clinton Way, Ste. 119, Fresno, CA 93727-1549. TEL 209-252-7000. FAX 209-252-7387. Ed. Mark Arcamonte. adv.; bk.rev. circ. 7,000. **Document type:** trade publication.

634 US
AGRIBUSINESS FRESH FRUIT AND RAISIN NEWS. m. $10 (foreign $25) (effective 1997). Agribusiness Publications, 612 N St., Sanger, CA 93657. TEL 209-875-4585. FAX 209-875-4587. Ed. John C. Stubbs; Pubs. John C. Stubbs, John Van Nortwick. adv.: B&W page $880, color page $1280; trim 10 3/4 x 14; adv. contact: Bob Werbiskis. circ. 10,000 (controlled). (tabloid format) **Document type:** trade publication.

631 634 SP ISSN 0211-2728
AGRICOLA VERGEL; fruticultura, horticultura, floricultura, citricultura, vid, arroz. 1982. m. 8500 ptas. (foreign 12675 ptas.) (effective 1997). Ediciones y Promociones Lav, S.L., Apdo. 473, 46080 Valencia, Spain. TEL 34-6-3720261. FAX 34-6-3710516. Ed. Francisco Salvador Planes Planes. **Indexed:** Ind.SST.
Description: Dedicated to floriculture, fruit culture, and horticulture.

668.6 630 UK ISSN 0140-0657
AGRICULTURAL & VETERINARY CHEMICALS. 1960. bi-m. £25($70) (overseas £35) (effective 1997). Chandler Publications Ltd., 10 South St., Totnes, Devon TQ9 5DZ, England. TEL 44-1803-864668. FAX 44-1803-865649. Ed. Jack R.D. Heming; Pub. Jack R.D. Heming. adv.; bk.rev.; charts; illus. circ. 2,000. **Indexed:** Chem.Abstr. **Document type:** newsletter.
—BLDSC (0743.200000).
Formerly (until no.26): Agricultural and Veterinary Chemicals and Agricultural Engineering (ISSN 0002-1377)
Description: Covers news of interest to research chemists, managers of research stations, and converters and formulators of agricultural and veterinary chemicals.

AGRICULTURAL ENGINEERING IN SOUTH AFRICA. see *AGRICULTURE — Agricultural Equipment*

AGRICULTURE — CROP PRODUCTION AND SOIL

631 636 660   US   ISSN 0002-161X
S1   CODEN: AGREA5
AGRICULTURAL RESEARCH. 1953. m. $29 (foreign $36.50). U.S. Department of Agriculture, Agricultural Research Service, Rm. 408, 6303 Ivy Ln., Greenbelt, MD 20770. TEL 301-344-2514. FAX 301-344-2325. E-mail: lmclaugh@asrr.arsusda.gov; URL: http://www.ars.usda.gov/is/AR. (Dist. by: Superintendent of Documents, U.S. Government Printing Office, Box 371954, Pittsburgh, PA 15250-7954. TEL 202-512-1800. FAX 202-512-2250) Ed. Lloyd M. McLaughlin. illus.; index. circ. 39,000. (also avail. in microform from UMI; back issues avail.) **Indexed:** Bio-Contr.News & Info., Biog.Ind., Biol.Abstr., Biol.Dig., Biotech.Abstr., Chem.Abstr., Cott.& Trop.Fibr.Abstr., Curr.Adv.Ecol.Sci., Curr.Cont., Dairy Sci.Abstr., Environ.Abstr., Excerp.Med., Gard.Lit. (1992-), Helminthol.Abstr., Ind.Vet., INIS Atomind., Intl.Mgmt.Info., Maize Abstr., Pig News & Info., Pollut.Abstr., Potato Abstr., PROMT, Rev.Appl.Entomol., Sugar Ind.Abstr., Triticale Abstr., Vet.Bull., Weed Abstr. **Document type:** government publication, consumer publication.
●Also available online. Vendor(s): Information Access Co., UMI.
—BLDSC (0751.950000); CIS; CISTI; Genuine Article; Linda Hall; SWETS; UMI; UnCover.
   Description: Presents in nontechnical language information about government research on food, feed, and natural fiber production and use; human nutrition; renewable energy; natural resource conservation; and other agricultural programs.

631 333.91   NE   ISSN 0924-3062
AGRICULTURAL RESEARCH DEPARTMENT. WINAND STARING CENTRE FOR INTEGRATED LAND, SOIL AND WATER RESEARCH. REPORTS. (Text in English) 1981. irreg., no.48, 1991. free to qualified personnel. Dienst Landbouwkundig Onderzoek - Agricultural Research Department, Winand Staring Centre for Integrated Land, Soil and Water Research, P.O. Box 125, 6700 AC Wageningen, Netherlands. TEL 31-8370-74200. FAX 31-8370-24812. Eds. J.C. van Top. abstr. circ. 250. (back issues avail.)
●Also available online.
   Formerly (until no.26, 1989): Instituut voor Cultuurtechniek en Waterhuishouding. Reports.
   Description: Reports the results of agricultural, environmental, hydrological and related research projects conducted under the auspices of the Center.

AGRICULTURAL SCIENCE DIGEST. see *AGRICULTURE*

631   NE   ISSN 0378-3774
S494.5.W3   CODEN: AWMADF
AGRICULTURAL WATER MANAGEMENT; an international journal. (Text in English) 1976. 9/yr. fl.1362($783) (effective 1998). Elsevier Science B.V., P.O. Box 211, 1000 AE Amsterdam, Netherlands. TEL 31-20-4853911. FAX 31-20-4853598. TELEX 18582 ESPA NL. E-mail: nlinfo-f@elsevier.nl; usinfo-f@elsevier.com; forinfo-kyf04035@niftyserve.or.jp; URL: http://www.elsevier.nl/. (Subscr. in the Americas to: Elsevier Science, Regional Sales Office, Box 945, New York, NY 10159-0945. TEL 212-633-3730. FAX 212-633-3680; Subscr. in Australasia and the Far East to: Elsevier Science (Singapore) Pte Ltd, No.1 Temasek Ave., No.17-01 Millenia Tower, Singapore 039192, Singapore. TEL 65-434-3727. FAX 65-337-2230; Subscr. in Japan to: Elsevier Science Japan, 9-15 Higashi-Azabu 1-chome, Minato-ku, Tokyo 106, Japan. TEL 81-3-5561-5033. FAX 81-3-5561-5047) Ed. J. van Schilfgaarde. adv.; bk.rev.; bibl.; illus.; index. (also avail. in microform from UMI) **Indexed:** Agri.Eng.Abstr., Agroforest.Abstr., ASCA, Biol.Abstr., Biol.& Agr.Ind., Cott.& Trop.Fibr.Abstr., Curr.Adv.Ecol.Sci., Curr.Cont., Ecol.Abstr., Energy Ind., Energy Info.Abstr., Environ.Per.Bibl. (1990-), Field Crop Abstr., Geo.Abstr.H.G., Geo.Abstr.P.G., GeoRef., Hort.Abstr., IDA, Ind.Sci.Rev., Int.Abstr.Oper.Res., Irr.& Drain.Abstr., Maize Abstr., Meteor.& Geoastrophys.Abstr., Potato Abstr., Rice Abstr., Sci.Cit.Ind., Sel.J.Water, Sel.Water Res.Abstr., Soils & Fert., Sorghum & Millets Abstr., Sugar Ind.Abstr., Triticale Abstr., W.R.C.Inf. **Document type:** academic/scholarly publication.
—BLDSC (0757.540000); CISTI; EMDOCS; Genuine Article; KR SourceOne; Linda Hall; SWETS; UnCover. CCC.
   Description: Presents scientific papers of international significance to the management of agricultural water resources.
Refereed Serial

631 638.1   UN   ISSN 0257-5035
AGRO-CHEMICALS NEWS IN BRIEF. (Includes 2 special issues) (Text in English) 1978. q. $100. United Nations Economic and Social Commission for Asia and the Pacific (ESCAP), Fertilizer Advisory, Development and Information Network for Asia and the Pacific (FADINAP), United Nations Bldg., Rajadamnern Ave., Bangkok 10200, Thailand. TEL 2-282-9161. (Co-sponsors: FAO; UNIDO) Ed. Ivy Rodricks. R&P contact: Ivy Rodricks. TEL 662-288-1348. bk.rev.; bibl.; charts; illus.; mkt. circ. 1,000. (also avail. in microfiche from CIS; back issues avail.) **Indexed:** IIS, Soils & Fert.
—BLDSC (0764.587000).
   Description: Deals with trade, handling, distribution and use of fertilizers and pesticides in Asia and the Pacific. Also covers environmental and safety aspects.

632.9   JA   ISSN 0919-5505
SB950.3.J3   CODEN: AGJAEP
AGROCHEMICALS JAPAN. (Text in English) 1969. s-a. $115. Japan Plant Protection Association - Nihon Shokubutsu Boeki Kyokai, 1-43-11 Komagome, Toshima-ku, Tokyo 170, Japan. (Subscr. to: Sun Publications Service Ltd., Ishii Bldg. 3-37, Sakumacho, Kanda, Chiyoda-Ku, Tokyo 101, Japan. TEL 81-3-3866-9897. FAX 81-3-3861-7715) Ed. Kazuo Fukunaga. cum.index every 10 vols. **Indexed:** Bio-Contr.News & Info., Biol.Abstr., Biotech.Abstr., Chem.Abstr., Helminthol.Abstr., Hort.Abstr., Maize Abstr., Potato Abstr., Rev.Appl.Entomol., Rev.Plant Path., Rice Abstr., Soils & Fert., Weed Abstr.
—BLDSC (0764.586700); CASDDS; SWETS; UnCover.
   Formerly (until 1992): Japan Pesticide Information (ISSN 0368-265X)
   Description: Covers the development of pesticides, their uses, pesticide registration and other related matters. Assists readers engaged in pesticide science and industry as well as pest control techniques in improving their professional work.

631   MX   ISSN 0188-3046
SB605.M6
AGROCIENCIA. PROTECCION VEGETAL. 1966. 3/yr. Mex.$45($20) (effective 1992). Colegio de Postgraduados, Instituto de Estudios, Investigaciones y Servicio Agripefor Chapingo S.C., Cerro del Vigilante 166, Col. Romero de Terrenos, 04310 Mexico DF, Mexico. TEL 915-5-54-14-03. Ed. Gabriel Otero Colina. adv.; bk.rev.; abstr.; bibl.; charts; illus.; stat.; circ. 1,500 (controlled). (back issues avail.) **Document type:** academic/scholarly publication.
   Supersedes in part (in 1990): Agrociencia (ISSN 0185-0288)

631   PO   ISSN 0002-1911
S15   CODEN: AGLUAN
AGRONOMIA LUSITANA. (Text in Portuguese; summaries in English, French, Portuguese) 1939-19??; resumed 1988. q. Esc.2000 (foreign Esc.2500) (effective 1995). Estacao Agronomica Nacional, 2780 Oeiras, Portugal. TEL 351-1-4416855. FAX 351-1-4416011. TELEX 63698 EAN P. Ed. Fernando Ilharco. bibl.; charts; illus.; index, cum.index; vols.1-20. circ. 1,200. **Indexed:** Anim.Breed Abstr., Bibl.Agri., Biol.Abstr., Chem.Abstr., Curr.Adv.Ecol.Sci., Field Crop Abstr., Food Sci.& Tech.Abstr., Forest.Abstr., Helminthol.Abstr., Herb.Abstr., Hort.Abstr., Nutr.Abstr., Plant Breed.Abstr., Rev.Appl.Entomol., Rev.Plant Path., Rural Recreat.Tour.Abstr., Soils & Fert., VITIS, Water Resour.Abstr., World Agri.Econ.& Rural Sociol.Abstr.
—BLDSC (0768.000000); CASDDS; Linda Hall. CCC.

631.4   VE   ISSN 0002-192X
                                 CODEN: ATMVAK
AGRONOMIA TROPICAL. (Text in Spanish; summaries in English and Spanish) 1951. q. Bs.1200 or exchange basis. Fondo Nacional de Investigaciones Agropecuarias, Apdo. 2103, Maracay 2105, Venezuela. FAX 58-43-831423. Ed. Aydee Cabrera de Green. bk.rev.; bibl.; charts; illus.; maps; index, cum.index: 1951-1962, 1963-1967, 1968-1990. circ. 4,653. **Indexed:** Agri.Eng.Abstr., Agroforest.Abstr., Anim.Breed Abstr., Biol.Abstr., Chem.Abstr., Cott.& Trop.Fibr.Abstr., Curr.Cont., Excerp.Med., Fababean Abstr., Field Crop Abstr., Helminthol.Abstr., Hort.Abstr., Ind.Vet., Irr.& Drain.Abstr., Maize Abstr., Nutr.Abstr., Ornam.Hort., Plant Breed.Abstr., Potato Abstr., Rev.Plant Path., Seed Abstr., Soils & Fert., Trop.Abstr., Trop.Oil Seeds Abstr., Vet.Bull., Weed Abstr.
—CASDDS.

338.1 631   FR   ISSN 0249-5627
SB7   CODEN: AGRNDZ
AGRONOMIE; sciences des productions vegetales et de l'environnement. (Text in English or French; summaries in English, French) 1981. 10/yr. 2262 F. (institutions in the Americas $433; elsewhere 2740F.) (effective 1998). (Institut National de la Recherche Agronomique (INRA)) Editions Scientifiques et Medicales Elsevier, 141 rue de Javel, 75747 Paris, France. TEL 33-1-45589022. FAX 33-1-45589421. URL: http://www.elsevier.nl/. (Subscr. in U.S. and Canada to: Elsevier Science Inc., Box 945, Madison Sq. Sta., New York, NY 10159-0945. TEL 212-633-3730. FAX 212-633-3680) Ed. Max Rives. bk.rev.; bibl.; illus.; index. circ. 2,500. (also avail. in microform from UMI) **Indexed:** Agri.Eng.Abstr., Apic.Abstr., ASCA, Bio-Contr.News & Info., Biol.Abstr., Biotech.Abstr., Cadscan, Crop Physiol.Abstr., Curr.Adv.Ecol.Sci., Curr.Cont., Ecol.Abstr., Entomol.Abstr., Excerp.Med., Field Crop Abstr., Forest.Abstr., Geo.Abstr.P.G., Helminthol.Abstr., Herb.Abstr., Hort.Abstr., IDA, INIS Atomind., Irr.& Drain.Abstr., Lead Abstr., Maize Abstr., Ornam.Hort., Plant Breed.Abstr., Plant Grow.Reg.Abstr., Potato Abstr., Rev.Appl.Entomol., Rev.Plant Path., Rice Abstr., Sci.Cit.Ind., Seed Abstr., Soils & Fert., Sorghum & Millets Abstr., Soyabean Abstr., SSCI, Triticale Abstr., Trop.Oil Seeds Abstr., VITIS, World Agri.Econ.& Rural Sociol.Abstr., Zincscan. **Document type:** academic/scholarly publication.
—BLDSC (0769.750000); CASDDS; CISTI; EMDOCS; Genuine Article; Linda Hall; SWETS. **CCC.**
   Description: Publishes scientific articles on both fundamental and applied approaches to plant production and agrarian systems covering biological, physiological, genetic, ecological and economic aspects.
Refereed Serial

631   NZ   ISSN 0110-6589
AGRONOMY SOCIETY OF NEW ZEALAND. PROCEEDINGS. 1971. a. NZ.$30($15) Agronomy Society of New Zealand, Private Bag 4704, Christchurch, New Zealand. TEL 64-3-3256400. FAX 64-3-3252074. E-mail: deruiterj@crop.cri.nz. Ed. J.G. Hampton. R&P contact: B.A. McKenzie. TEL 64-3-3252811. bk.rev. circ. 400. (back issues avail.) **Indexed:** Agri.Eng.Abstr., Biol.Abstr., Field Crop Abstr., Herb.Abstr., Hort.Abstr., Nutr.Abstr., Seed Abstr., Soils & Fert. **Document type:** proceedings.
—BLDSC (6840.228500).
   Description: Publishes original research on the agronomy of crops and forages as well as progress reports, reviews and new techniques.

631   NZ   ISSN 0111-9184
AGRONOMY SOCIETY OF NEW ZEALAND. SPECIAL PUBLICATION.. 1982. irreg. Agronomy Society of New Zealand, Private Bag 4704, Christchurch, New Zealand. TEL 6-3-3256400. FAX 64-3-3252074. E-mail: deruiterj@crop.cri.nz. Ed. J.G. Hampton. R&P contact: B.A. McKenzie. TEL 64-3-3252811.
—BLDSC (8371.850000); CISTI.

631.4   NR   ISSN 0065-4728
AHMADU BELLO UNIVERSITY. INSTITUTE FOR AGRICULTURAL RESEARCH. SOIL SURVEY BULLETIN. 1956. irreg., no.46, 1990. $20. Ahmadu Bello University, Institute for Agricultural Research, P.M.B. 1044, Samaru-Zaria, Kaduna State, Nigeria. FAX 234-69-50563. **Document type:** academic/scholarly publication.
   Description: Records soil survey work done in Nigeria.

AGRICULTURE — CROP PRODUCTION AND SOIL

AKADEMIA ROLNICZA IM. HUGONA KOLLATAJA W KRAKOWIE. ZESZYTY NAUKOWE. SERIA: INZYNIERIA SRODOWISKA. see *ENVIRONMENTAL STUDIES*

631.7   PL   ISSN 1230-7394
AKADEMIA ROLNICZA, POZNAN. ROCZNIKI. MELIORACJE I INZYNIERIA SRODOWISKA. (Text in Polish; summaries in English) 1972. irreg. price varies. Wydawnictwo Akademii Rolniczej w Poznaniu, Ul. Witosa 45, 60-667 Poznan, Poland. TEL 48-61-487809. FAX 48-61-487802. E-mail: wgolob@owl.au.poznan.pl; URL: http://swan.au.poznan.pl/bib/bghome.html. R&P contact: Elzbieta Zagorska. TEL 48-61-487806. **Indexed:** AgroLibrex, Bibl.Agri., Forest.Abstr. **Document type:** academic/scholarly publication.
Former titles: Akademia Rolnicza, Poznan. Roczniki. Melioracje; Akademia Rolnicza, Poznan. Roczniki. Melioracje Wodne (ISSN 0208-8932)
Description: Series on natural and technical basis for land reclamation, irrigation, drainage, hydro-reclamation structures, and environmental engineering.

631   PL   ISSN 0137-1924
AKADEMIA ROLNICZA W SZCZECINIE. ZESZYTY NAUKOWE. ROLNICTWO. (Text in Polish; abstract in English) 1958. a. price varies. Akademia Rolnicza w Szczecinie, Dzial Wydawnictw, Ul. Doktora Judyma 22, 71-460 Szczecin, Poland. TEL 48-91-541639. FAX 48-91-541642. TELEX 0425494 AR. Ed. Antoni Furowicz. bk.rev. **Indexed:** AgroLibrex, Chem.Abstr., Crop Physiol.Abstr., Field Crop Abstr., Herb.Abstr., Nutr.Abstr., Potato Abstr., Soils & Fert., Triticale Abstr., Weed Abstr. **Document type:** academic/scholarly publication.
Refereed Serial

631.7   PL   ISSN 0137-1967
        CODEN: ZNAMDX
AKADEMIA ROLNICZA WE WROCLAWIU. ZESZYTY NAUKOWE. MELIORACJA. (Subseries of: Akademia Rolnicza we Wroclawiu. Zeszyty Naukowe (ISSN 0867-7964)) (Text in Polish; summaries in English) 1956. irreg. price varies. Akademia Rolnicza we Wroclawiu, Ul. Norwida 25, 50-375 Wroclaw, Poland. FAX 48-71-229576. (Subscr. to: Wydawnictwo Akademii Rolniczej, ul. Sopocka 23, 50-344 Wroclaw, Poland. TEL 48-71-211277) circ. 350. **Indexed:** AgroLibrex. **Document type:** academic/scholarly publication.
—CASDDS.
Formerly (until 1973): Wyzsza Szkola Rolnicza we Wroclawiu. Zeszyty Naukowe. Melioracja (ISSN 0520-9293)

ALBERTA FARM AND RANCH MAGAZINE. see *AGRICULTURE*

631.5 368   CN   ISSN 0319-3535
HG9968.H35
ALBERTA HAIL AND CROP INSURANCE CORPORATION. ANNUAL REPORT. 1970. a. Alberta Hail and Crop Insurance Corporation, Bag Service no.16, 5718 56th St., Lacombe, Alta. T0C 1S0, Canada.

631   IS   ISSN 0333-8886
SB354.6.I75
ALON HANOTEA. 1945. m. $60. Israel Fruit Growers Association, P.O. Box 40007, Tel Aviv 61400, Israel. TEL 972-3-6966267. FAX 972-3-6917625. Ed. J. Kovetz. circ. 5,000. **Indexed:** Bio-Contr.News & Info., Biodet.Abstr., Crop Physiol.Abstr., Hort.Abstr., Plant Grow.Reg.Abstr. **Document type:** bulletin.

635   US   ISSN 0883-0142
AMARANTH TODAY. q. $15. Rodale Press, Inc., 33 E. Minor St., Emmaus, PA 18049. TEL 610-967-5171. FAX 610-967-7725. **Document type:** consumer publication.
Description: Focuses on developing amaranth as a commercial crop.

AMATEUR DE BORDEAUX. see *BEVERAGES*

AMERICAN JOURNAL OF ENOLOGY AND VITICULTURE. see *BEVERAGES*

633.491   US   ISSN 0003-0589
        CODEN: APOJAY
AMERICAN POTATO JOURNAL. 1913. bi-m. $40 to individuals; libraries $65 (foreign $70) (effective 1996 & 1997). Potato Association of America, 157 Park St., Ste. 23, Bangor, ME 04401. TEL 207-942-9732. FAX 207-942-9733. Ed. Hugh J. Murphy. R&P contact: Hugh J. Murphy. bk.rev.; abstr.; bibl.; charts; illus.; index. circ. 1,200. (also avail. in microfilm from UMI) **Indexed:** Agri.Eng.Abstr., ASCA, Bibl.Agri., Biol.Abstr., Chem.Abstr., Crop Physiol.Abstr., Curr.Adv.Ecol.Sci., Curr.Cont., Excerp.Med., Field Crop Abstr., Food Sci.& Tech.Abstr., Helminthol.Abstr., Herb.Abstr., Ind.Sci.Rev., Irr.& Drain.Abstr., Nutr.Abstr., Plant Breed.Abstr., Plant Grow.Reg.Abstr., Potato Abstr., Rev.Plant Path., Sci.Cit.Ind., Seed Abstr., Soils & Fert., Weed Abstr. **Document type:** academic/scholarly publication.
—BLDSC (0852.000000); CASDDS; CISTI; EMDOCS; Genuine Article; Linda Hall; SWETS; UMI; UnCover.
Refereed Serial

633   US   ISSN 0741-9848
        CODEN: AMVGA5
AMERICAN VEGETABLE GROWER. 1953. m. $15.95 (effective 1997). Meister Publishing Co., 37733 Euclid Ave., Willoughby, OH 44094. TEL 216-942-2000. FAX 216-942-2000. E-mail: aug-circ@meisterpubl.com. Ed. Rick Melnick. adv.; bk.rev.; charts; illus.; mkt.; tr.lit. circ. 29,000. (also avail. in microfilm from UMI) **Indexed:** Agri.Eng.Abstr., Biol.& Agr.Ind., Farm & Garden Ind., Food Sci.& Tech.Abstr., Hort.Abstr., Soils & Fert. **Document type:** trade publication.
—KR SourceOne; Linda Hall; SWETS; UMI; UnCover. **CCC.**
Former titles (until 1983): American Vegetable Grower and Greenhouse Grower (ISSN 0161-8946); (until 1977): American Vegetable Grower (ISSN 0003-1461)

630   BE   ISSN 0303-9099
        CODEN: AGEMAW
ANNALES DE GEMBLOUX. 1894. q. 1800 BEF. Association des Ingenieurs Issus de la Faculte des Sciences Agronomiques de Gembloux, B-5030 Gembloux, Belgium. FAX 32-81-614544. Ed. C. Verstraeten. adv.; bk.rev.; bibl.; illus.; index. circ. 1,500. (back issues avail.) **Indexed:** Agri.Eng.Abstr., Biol.Abstr., Chem.Abstr., Curr.Adv.Ecol.Sci., Excerp.Med., Field Crop Abstr., Forest.Abstr., Forest Prod.Abstr., Geo.Abstr., GeoRef., Hort.Abstr., INIS Atomind., Nutr.Abstr., Plant Breed.Abstr., Rural Recreat.Tour.Abstr., Soils & Fert., Weed Abstr., World Agri.Econ.& Rural Sociol.Abstr. **Document type:** academic/scholarly publication.
—BLDSC (0975.000000); CASDDS; Linda Hall.
Description: Examines agricultural engineering.

631 550   II   ISSN 0570-1791
S341   CODEN: ANAZBX
ANNALS OF ARID ZONE. (Text in English) 1962. q. Rs.900($70) (Arid Zone Research Association of India) Scientific Publishers, P.O. Box 91, 5A, New Pali Rd., Jodhpur 342 001, India. TEL 91-291-33323. (Dist. overseas by: HPC Publishers' Distributors Pvt Ltd., 4805-24, 1st Fl., Bharat Ram Rd., Darya Ganj, New Delhi 110 002, India. TEL 91-11-3254401. FAX 91-11-6863511) Ed. Vinod Shankar. adv.; bk.rev.; bibl.; charts; illus. circ. 800. (back issues avail.) **Indexed:** Anim.Breed.Abstr., ASCA, Biol.Abstr., Chem.Abstr., Curr.Adv.Ecol.Sci., Curr.Cont., Field Crop Abstr., Forest.Abstr., Forest Prod.Abstr., Geo.Abstr., Herb.Abstr., Hort.Abstr., Irr.& Drain.Abstr., Lang.& Lang.Behav.Abstr., Nutr.Abstr., Risk Abstr., Rural Recreat.Tour.Abstr., Sociol.Abstr., Soils & Fert., Sorghum & Millets Abstr., Sport Fish.Abstr., SSCI, Wild.Rev., World Agri.Econ.& Rural Sociol.Abstr., Zoo.Rec. **Document type:** academic/scholarly publication.
—BLDSC (1038.500000); CASDDS; Genuine Article; Linda Hall; SWETS; UnCover.

ANNUAIRE DE L'EQUIPEMENT VINICOLE: MATERIELS - FOURNITURES - PRESTATIONS. see *AGRICULTURE — Agricultural Equipment*

634 338.1   FR   ISSN 0066-3131
ANNUAIRE FRUCTIDOR; annuaire international des fruits, legumes, primeurs, derives et industries annexes. 1935. a. 900 F. (foreign 950 F.). Helios International, 14 bd. Montmartre, 75009 Paris, France. TEL 33-1-42469294. FAX 33-4-90882849. TELEX 432845. **Document type:** directory.

ANNUAL BOOK OF A S T M STANDARDS. VOLUME 04.08. SOIL AND ROCK; DIMENSION STONE; GEOSYNTHETICS. see *ENGINEERING — Engineering Mechanics And Materials*

631   AG   ISSN 0066-5207
ANUARIO F.H.I. ARGENTINA: FRUTAS Y HORTALIZAS INDUSTRIALIZADAS Y FRESCAS/F.H.I. ANNUAL: FRESH AND INDUSTRIALIZED FRUITS AND VEGETABLES. (Text in Spanish; summaries in English) 1935. irreg. $10. Riccardo Luchini, Ed. & Pub., 2455 Canning, 1425 Buenos Aires, Argentina. adv.; bk.rev. circ. 1,500.

631.4   NE   ISSN 0929-1393
QH541.5.S6
APPLIED SOIL ECOLOGY. (Section of: Agriculture, Ecosystems & Environment (ISSN 0167-8809)) (Text in English) 1994. 9/yr. fl.1440($828) (effective 1997). Elsevier Science B.V., P.O. Box 211, 1000 AE Amsterdam, Netherlands. TEL 31-20-4853911. FAX 31-20-4853598. TELEX 18582 ESPA NL. E-mail: nlinfo-f@elsevier.nl; usinfo-f@elsevier.com; forinfo-kyf04035@niftyserve.or.jp; URL: http://www.elsevier.nl/. (Subscr. in the Americas to: Elsevier Science, Regional Sales Office, Box 945, New York, NY 10159-0945; Subscr. in Australasia and the Far East to: Elsevier Science (Singapore) Pte Ltd, No.1 Temasek Ave., No.17-01 Millenia Tower, Singapore 039192, Singapore; Subscr. in Japan to: Elsevier Science Japan, 9-15 Higashi-Azabu 1-chome, Minato-ku, Tokyo 106, Japan. TEL 212-989-5800. FAX 212-633-3990) Eds. C.A. Edwards, L. Brussaard. abstr.; bibl.; charts; stat.; index. (also avail. in microfilm from UMI; back issues avail.) **Indexed:** ASCA, Curr.Cont. **Document type:** academic/scholarly publication.
—BLDSC (1578.400000); EMDOCS; Genuine Article; KR SourceOne; SWETS. **CCC.**
Description: Publishes original research into the role of soil organisms and their interactions in relation to agricultural productivity, nutrient cycling and other soil processes.
Refereed Serial

631   UK   ISSN 0300-2829
ARABLE FARMING. 1974. m. £33($86) (Eire £45) (effective 1996). Miller Freeman Professional Ltd. (Subsidiary of: Miller Freeman plc), 2 Wharfedale Rd., Ipswich, Suffolk IP14 4LG, England. TEL 44-1473-241122. FAX 44-1473-240501. Ed. John Blackbeard. R&P contact: John Blackbeard. adv. contact: David Bentley. illus. circ. 35,674. **Indexed:** Agri.Eng.Abstr., Curr.Adv.Ecol.Sci., Field Crop Abstr., Hort.Abstr., Soils & Fert., Weed Abstr. **Document type:** trade publication.
—BLDSC (1583.460000).
Formerly: Arable Farmer (ISSN 0003-7524)
Description: Geared to farmers and farm managers in Great Britain who grow cereals, sugarbeets, potatoes and other vegetables.

634   FR   ISSN 0003-794X
        CODEN: AFRUAC
ARBORICULTURE FRUITIERE. 1954. m. 345 F. (foreign 476 F.) (effective 1997). Editions du Chastaing, 4 bis, rue de Clery, 75002 Paris, France. TEL 33-1-44823040. FAX 33-1-44823001. Ed. Dominique Brochet. R&P contact: Dominique Brochet. adv. contact: Hubert de Serval. bk.rev.; illus.; index. circ. 6,500. **Indexed:** Agri.Eng.Abstr., Bio-Contr.News & Info., Biol.Abstr., Chem.Abstr., Crop Physiol.Abstr., Forest.Abstr., Hort.Abstr., Plant Grow.Reg.Abstr., Rural Recreat.Tour.Abstr., Soils & Fert., World Agri.Econ.& Rural Sociol.Abstr. **Document type:** newspaper.
—SWETS.

AGRICULTURE — CROP PRODUCTION AND SOIL

630 NE ISSN 0365-0340
CODEN: AAPBCE
ARCHIV FUER ACKER- UND PFLANZENBAU UND BODENKUNDE/ARCHIVES OF AGRONOMY AND SOIL SCIENCE. (Text in German; summaries in English, German and Russian) 1956. m. (in 2 vols.) $147 (effective 1998). (Akademie der Landwirtschaftswissenschaften) Gordon and Breach - Harwood Academic, Amsteldisk 166, 1st Fl., 1079 LH Amsterdam, Netherlands. (Subscr. to: International Publishers Distributor, Box 32160, Newark, NJ 07102. TEL 800-545-8398. FAX 215-750-6343) Ed. P. Kundler. bk.rev.; charts; stat.; index. **Indexed:** Biol.Abstr., Chem.Abstr., Crop Physiol.Abstr., Curr.Adv.Ecol.Sci., Curr.Cont., Excerp.Med., Fababean Abstr., Field Crop Abstr., Food Sci.& Tech.Abstr., Forest.Abstr., Geo.Abstr., Helminthol.Abstr., Herb.Abstr., INIS Atomind., Irr.& Drain.Abstr., Maize Abstr., Plant Breed.Abstr., Plant Grow.Reg.Abstr., Rural Recreat.Tour.Abstr., Sci.Cit.Ind., Seed Abstr., Soils & Fert., Triticale Abstr., VITIS, Weed Abstr., World Agri.Econ.& Rural Sociol.Abstr.
—BLDSC (1630.923000); CASDDS; Linda Hall; SWETS. **CCC.**
Formerly (until 1970): Albrecht-Thaer-Archiv (ISSN 0002-4929)

631.5 II
AREA AND PRODUCTION OF PRINCIPAL CROPS IN INDIA. SUMMARY TABLES. (Text in English, Hindi) 1951. a. Rs.427.50($25.65) Ministry of Agriculture, Department of Agriculture and Cooperation, Directorate of Economics and Statistics, A-2E-3 Kasturba Gandhi Marg Barracks, New Delhi 110 001, India. TEL 11-381523. Ed. Brajesh Kumar Gautam. circ. 650. **Document type:** government publication.
Formerly: Estimates of Area and Production of Principal Crops in India. Summary Tables (ISSN 0085-0314)

631.4 574 UK ISSN 0890-3069
S592.17.A73 CODEN: ASRREU
ARID SOIL RESEARCH AND REHABILITATION. q. £136($225) to institutions (effective 1998). Taylor & Francis Ltd., 1 Gunpowder Sq., London EC4A 3DE, England. TEL 44-171-583-0490.
FAX 44-171-583-0585. E-mail: info@tandf.co.uk; URL: http://www.tandf.co.uk/. (Subscr. in N. America to: Taylor & Francis Inc., 1900 Frost Rd., Ste. 101, Bristol, PA 19007-1598. TEL 800-821-8312. FAX 215-785-5515) Ed. J. Skujins. **Indexed:** Agri.Eng.Abstr., Agroforest.Abstr., ASCA, Bibl.Agri., Crop Physiol.Abstr., Curr.Cont., Ecol.Abstr., Environ.Per.Bibl. (1990-), Fababean Abstr., Field Crop Abstr., Forest.Abstr., Geo.Abstr.P.G., Herb.Abstr., Hort.Abstr., IDA, Plant Grow.Reg.Abstr., Rice Abstr., Seed Abstr., Soils & Fert., Sorghum & Millets Abstr., Triticale Abstr. **Document type:** academic/scholarly publication.
—BLDSC (1668.290000); CASDDS; Ei; EMDOCS; Genuine Article; Linda Hall; SWETS; UnCover. **CCC.**
Description: Provides a forum for articles on basic and applied aspects of arid and semi-arid soils.
Refereed Serial

ARKANSAS. AGRICULTURAL EXPERIMENT STATION. RESEARCH BULLETIN. see *AGRICULTURE — Abstracting, Bibliographies, Statistics*

ARKANSAS. AGRICULTURAL EXPERIMENT STATION. RESEARCH SERIES. see *AGRICULTURE — Abstracting, Bibliographies, Statistics*

ASIAN AND PACIFIC COCONUT COMMUNITY. BIBLIOGRAPHY SERIES. see *AGRICULTURE — Abstracting, Bibliographies, Statistics*

631 IO
ASIAN AND PACIFIC COCONUT COMMUNITY. TECHNICAL MEETINGS. PROCEEDINGS. a. price varies. Asian and Pacific Coconut Community, Wisma Bakrie, 3rd Fl., Jl. H.R. Rasuna Said, Kuningan, Jakarta 12920, Indonesia. TEL 62-21-520-5160.
FAX 62-21-520-5160. TELEX 62863 APCCIA. **Document type:** proceedings.
Description: Contains original papers on coconut production & productivity, coconut based farming systems, and small scale processing of coconut products.

631 IO
ASSESSMENT OF EXPERIENCES WITH NEW VARIETIES OF COCONUT. a.? $10. Asian and Pacific Coconut Community, Wisma Bakrie, 3rd Fl., Jl. H.R. Rasuna Said, Kuningan, Jakarta 12920, Indonesia. TEL 62-21-510-073. FAX 62-21-520-5160. TELEX 62863 APCCIA. **Document type:** monographic series.
Description: Incorporates the findings of the field studies done by national experts from India, Indonesia, Papua New Guinea, Philippines, Sri Lanka, Thailand, Vanuatu and Western Samoa and assess their experience with new high yielding varieties of coconut.

632 US ISSN 0066-9431
ASSOCIATION OF AMERICAN PESTICIDE CONTROL OFFICIALS. OFFICIAL PUBLICATION. 1964. a. $30 (effective 1997). Association of American Pesticide Control Officials, c/o IN State Chemist, Purdue Univ., Biochem Dept., West Lafayette, IN 47907. (Subscr. to: Philip M. Gray, Secy., P.O. Box 1249, Hadwick, VT 05843. TEL 802-472-6956. FAX 802-472-6957) Ed. Ed White. circ. 200. **Document type:** directory.

631.8 US ISSN 0094-8764
S641 CODEN: OPAAAN
ASSOCIATION OF AMERICAN PLANT FOOD CONTROL OFFICIALS. OFFICIAL PUBLICATION. 1947. a. $25. Association of American Plant Food Control Officials, Inc., Division of Regulatory Services, University of Kentucky, Lexington, KY 40546.
TEL 606-257-2668. FAX 606-257-7351. E-mail: dterry@c.uky.edu; URL: http://www.uky.edu/agriculture/regulatorservices/aapfco.htm. Ed. D.L. Terry. circ. 400 (paid). **Document type:** directory.
—Linda Hall.
Formerly: Association of American Fertilizer Control Officials. Official Publication.
Description: Model legislation, definitions, and enforcement policies for regulation of fertilizers.

631.5 US
ASSOCIATION OF OFFICIAL SEED CERTIFYING AGENCIES. REPORT OF ACRES APPLIED FOR CERTIFICATION BY SEED CERTIFYING AGENCIES. 1959. a. $25. Association of Official Seed Certifying Agencies, Box 9812, Mississippi State, MS 39762.
TEL 601-325-4567. FAX 601-325-8118. Ed. Vance H. Watson. circ. 500.
Former titles: Association of Official Seed Certifying Agencies. Production Publication; International Crop Improvement Association. Production Publication (ISSN 0538-7043)
Description: Covers the seed varieties and acreage being certified by each state, Canada, and New Zealand.

ATTENDERINGSBULLETIN BIBLIOTHEEK STARING-GEBOUW: LAND, BODEM, WATER. see *ENVIRONMENTAL STUDIES — Abstracting, Bibliographies, Statistics*

634 AT
AUSTRALASIAN TREE CROPS SOURCEBOOK. (Print edition ceased 1997) irreg. price varies. Tree Crops Centre, P.O. Box 27, Subiaco, W.A. 6008, Australia. TEL 61-8-03991065. FAX 61-8-92881852. E-mail: treecrop@AOl.com.au; URL: http://www.AOl.com.au/atcros/.
●Available only online.

633 AT
AUSTRALIA. DEPARTMENT OF PRIMARY INDUSTRIES AND ENERGY. COTTON MARKET NEWS. 1972. m. Department of Primary Industries and Energy, G.P.O. Box 858, Canberra, A.C.T. 2600, Australia. stat.
Former titles: Australia. Department of Primary Industry. Cotton Market News; Australia. Department of Agriculture. Marketing Division. Cotton Market News (ISSN 0310-2084)

631 633.5 AT
AUSTRALIA. DEPARTMENT OF PRIMARY INDUSTRIES AND ENERGY. RAW COTTON MARKETING ADVISORY COMMITTEE. ANNUAL REPORT. 1968. a. free. Department of Primary Industries and Energy, Crops Division, Edmund Barton Bldg., Broughton St., Barton, A.C.T. 2600, Australia.
FAX 61-6-272-5672.
Formerly: Australia. Department of Primary Industry. Raw Cotton Marketing Advisory Committee. Annual Report.

AUSTRALIAN BUREAU OF AGRICULTURAL AND RESOURCE ECONOMICS. AUSTRALIAN CROP REPORT. see *AGRICULTURE — Agricultural Economics*

631 AT ISSN 0159-1290
CODEN: AUCOFT
AUSTRALIAN COTTONGROWER. 1980. bi-m. Aus.$25 (foreign $30) (effective 1997). Berekua Pty. Ltd., P.O. Box 766, Toowoomba, Qld. 4350, Australia. TEL 61-76-971199. FAX 61-76-971184. Ed. D.G. Dowling. adv. contact: Brian O'Connell. bk.rev. circ. 1,600. (back issues avail.) **Indexed:** Text.Tech.Dig. **Document type:** consumer publication.

634.8 AT ISSN 0727-3606
CODEN: AGWIEC
AUSTRALIAN GRAPEGROWER & WINEMAKER. 1963. m. Aus.$55 (foreign Aus.$58) (effective 1997). Ryan Publications, 95 Currie St., Adelaide, S.A., Australia. TEL 61-8-82316082. FAX 61-8-82127504. Ed. Justin Brady; Pub. John Ryan. R&P contact: Justin Brady. adv. contact: Justin Brady. bk.rev.; circ. 4,655 (paid). **Indexed:** Food Sci.& Tech.Abstr., VITIS. **Document type:** trade publication.
—BLDSC (1801.160000); UnCover.
Formerly: Australian Grapegrower (ISSN 0004-9239)
Description: Covers various aspects of viticulture oenology.

631 AT ISSN 0816-1089
CODEN: AJEAEL
AUSTRALIAN JOURNAL OF EXPERIMENTAL AGRICULTURE. 1961. 8/yr. Aus.$340($340) (effective 1998). (C.S.I.R.O. Australia) C.S.I.R.O. Publishing, 150 Oxford St., Collingwood, Vic. 3066, Australia. TEL 61-3-96627614.
FAX 61-3-96627611. E-mail: chris.anderson@publish.csiro.au; URL: http://www.publish.csiro.au/journals/ajea/online__journal.html. (Co-sponsor: Australian Agricultural Council) Eds. C.A. Anderson, L. Muir. R&P contact: C.A. Anderson. adv.; index. circ. 1,000. (also avail. in microform from UMI; back issues avail.) **Indexed:** Agroforest.Abstr., Anim.Breed.Abstr., Apic.Abstr., ASCA, Biol.Abstr., Biol.& Agr.Ind., Biotech.Abstr., Cadscan, Chem.Abstr., Crop Physiol.Abstr., Curr.Adv.Ecol.Sci., Curr.Cont., Dairy Sci.Abstr., Ecol.Abstr., Excerp.Med., Fababean Abstr., Field Crop Abstr., Food Sci.& Tech.Abstr., Forest Abstr., Forest Prod.Abstr., Geo.Abstr.H.G., Geo.Abstr.P.G., Helminthol.Abstr., Herb.Abstr., Hort.Abstr., Ind.Sci.Rev., Ind.Vet., Irr.& Drain.Abstr., Lead Abstr., Maize Abstr., Nutr.Abstr., Ornam.Hort., Pig News & Info., Plant Breed.Abstr., Plant Grow.Reg.Abstr., Rev.Appl.Entomol., Rev.Med.& Vet.Mycol., Rev.Plant Path., Rice Abstr., Rural Recreat.Tour.Abstr., Sci.Cit.Ind., Seed Abstr., Sel.Water Res.Abstr., Soils & Fert., Sorghum & Millets Abstr., Soyabean Abstr., Sugar Ind.Abstr., Triticale Abstr., Trop.Oil Seeds Abstr., Vet.Bull., Weed Abstr., World Agri.Econ.& Rural Sociol.Abstr., Zincscan. **Document type:** academic/scholarly publication.
●Also available online.
—BLDSC (1807.695000); CASDDS; CISTI; EMDOCS; Genuine Article; KR SourceOne; Linda Hall; SWETS; UMI; UnCover. **CCC.**
Formerly: Australian Journal of Experimental Agriculture and Animal Husbandry (ISSN 0045-060X)
Description: Publishes original research into applied agriculture, papers in animal production, animal-plant interactions, pasture and fodder crops, field crops, agroforestry, extension methodology and horticulture.

631.4 AT ISSN 1032-2426
S622 CODEN: JSCWEZ
AUSTRALIAN JOURNAL OF SOIL AND WATER CONSERVATION. 1945. a. Aus.$58 (foreign Aus.$70) (effective 1997 & 1998). c/o Geoff Cunningham, 9 The Crest, Killara, N.S.W. 2071, Australia. TEL 61-2-94161995.
FAX 61-2-94166626. Ed. P.E.V. Charman. R&P contact: Geoff Cunningham. adv. contact: Geoff Cunningham. bk.rev.; charts; illus.; index. circ. 3,000. (back issues avail.) **Indexed:** Agroforest.Abstr., Biol.Abstr., Herb.Abstr., INIS Atomind., Seed Abstr., Soils & Fert. **Document type:** academic/scholarly publication, consumer publication.
—BLDSC (1812.590000); Linda Hall; UnCover.
Supersedes (in 1988): Journal of Soil Conservation (ISSN 0028-6818)
Description: The journal's feature, technical and research articles aim to promote the conservation of soil and water resources and sustainable systems of land use.
Refereed Serial

AGRICULTURE — CROP PRODUCTION AND SOIL

631.4   AT   ISSN 0004-9573
S590   CODEN: ASORAB
AUSTRALIAN JOURNAL OF SOIL RESEARCH. 1963. bi-m. Aus.$320($320) (effective 1998). (C.S.I.R.O. Australia) C.S.I.R.O. Publishing, 150 Oxford St., Collingwood, Vic. 3066, Australia. TEL 61-3-96627628. FAX 61-3-96627611. E-mail: jenny.fegent@publish.csiro.au; URL: http://www.publish.csiro.au/journals/ajsr/electronic.html. Ed. J.C. Fegent. adv.; bibl.; charts; illus.; stat.; index. circ. 750. (also avail. in microform from UMI; back issues avail.) **Indexed:** AESIS, ASCA, Aus.Rd.Ind., Biol.Abstr., Biol.& Agr.Ind., Chem.Abstr., Curr.Adv.Ecol.Sci., Curr.Cont., Ecol.Abstr., Environ.Abstr., Environ.Per.Bibl. (1972-1994), Excerp.Med., Field Crop.Abstr., Forest.Abstr., Forest Prod.Abstr., Geo.Abstr.P.G., Geol.Abstr., GeoRef., Herb.Abstr., Hort.Abstr., Ind.Sci.Rev., INIS Atomind., Irr.& Drain.Abstr., Maize Abstr., Mineral.Abstr., Rice Abstr., Sci.Cit.Ind., Sel.Water Res.Abstr., So.Pac.Per.Ind., Soils & Fert., Triticale Abstr. **Document type:** academic/scholarly publication.
● Also available online.
— BLDSC (1812.600000); CASDDS; CIS; CISTI; Ei; EMDOCS; Genuine Article; KR SourceOne; Linda Hall; SWETS; UMI; UnCover. **CCC.**
Description: Covers all aspects of soil science: genesis, morphology and classification; physics and hydrology; chemistry and mineralogy; biology and biochemistry; soil fertility and plant nutrition; soil and water management and conservation.

634   AT   ISSN 0811-3475
AUSTRALIAN MACADAMIA SOCIETY. NEWS BULLETIN. 1974. bi-m. Aus.$150 (foreign $250). Australian Macadamia Society, 5-76 Woodlark St., Lismore, N.S.W. 2480, Australia. TEL 61-66-224933. FAX 61-66-224932. E-mail: macadamiajon@msr.com; URL: http://www.nor.com.au/agriculture/ans/Macadami.htm. Ed. Beverly Atkinson. R&P contact: Beverly Atkinson. adv.: page Aus.$320; adv. contact: Beverly Atkinson. circ. 600. (also avail. in diskette format) **Document type:** bulletin.
Description: Provides research, development and marketing information relating to macadamia.

633   AT   ISSN 0313-3192
AUSTRALIAN PLANT INTRODUCTION REVIEW. 1975. s-a. free. C.S.I.R.O., Division of Plant Industry, G.P.O. Box 1600, Canberra, A.C.T. 2601, Australia. TEL 61-6-2465483. FAX 61-6-2465255. E-mail: g.orr@pi.csiro.au. Ed. Gary Orr. R&P contact: Gary Orr. circ. 450. **Indexed:** Field Crop Abstr., Herb.Abstr., Plant Breed.Abstr., Rice Abstr., Sorghum & Millets Abstr. **Document type:** government publication.
Supersedes: Commonwealth Scientific and Industrial Research Organization. Division of Plant Industry. Plant Introduction Review.

633   AT   ISSN 0813-5231
AUSTRALIAN SEED INDUSTRY MAGAZINE. 1983. q. Aus.$16 (New Zealand Aus.$24; elsewhere Aus.$36) (effective 1997-98). Downs Media Services, P.O. Box 270, Toowoomba, Qld. 4350, Australia. TEL 61-7-46391622. FAX 61-7-46392832. Ed. Chris R. Warmington. adv.: B&W page Aus.$750, color page Aus.$1500. bk.rev. circ. 2,700. (back issues avail.) **Document type:** trade publication.
Description: Provides specific business, management and topical information, the latest Australian and overseas trends and technology, as well agronomic, technical and legislative information for trade and seed growers.

632   AT   ISSN 0310-0405
AUSTRALIAN WEED CONTROL HANDBOOK. 1973. biennial. price varies. Butterworth - Heinemann Australia, 22 Salmon St., Port Melbourne, Vic. 3207, Australia. TEL 61-3-92457111. FAX 61-3-92457577. Ed. Jonathan Glasspool. R&P contact: Jonathan Glasspool. adv. circ. 3,000.

663.2 634   AU
TP544   CODEN: MIKLD4
AUSTRIA. HOEHERE BUNDESLEHRANSTALT UND BUNDESAMT FUER WEIN- UND OBSTBAU. MITTEILUNGEN KLOSTERNEUBURG; Rebe und Wein, Obstbau und Fruechteverwertung. (Text in German; summaries in English, French) 1951. bi-m. S.950 (effective 1997 & 1998). Hoehere Bundeslehranstalt und Bundesamt fuer Wein- und Obstbau, Wienerstr. 74, A-3400 Klosterneuburg, Austria. FAX 43-2243-26705. Ed. Karl Vogl. adv.; bk.rev.; abstr.; illus.; index. **Indexed:** Chem.Abstr., Food Sci.& Tech.Abstr., Hort.Abstr., Plant Grow.Reg.Abstr., Sugar Ind.Abstr. **Document type:** academic/scholarly publication.
— CASDDS.
Formerly: Austria. Hoehere Bundeslehr- und Versuchsanstalt fuer Wein- und Obstbau. Mitteilungen Klosterneuburg (ISSN 0007-5922)
Description: Viticulture, fruit growing, wine and fruit processing.

631   FR   ISSN 0300-2942
AVENIR AGRICOLE ET VITICOLE AQUITAIN. 1972. 24/yr. 17 cours Xavier-Arnozan, 33082 Bordeaux, France. TEL 96-88-00. Ed. Mme. Artigue. circ. 23,500.

634.772   AT
B G F BULLETIN. 1936. m. Aus.$30 (foreign Aus.$35) (effective 1997). Banana Growers Federation Co-operative Ltd., P.O. Box 31, Murwillumbah, N.S.W. 2484, Australia. TEL 066-722488. FAX 066-724868. Ed. Michael Lines-Kelly. adv.; circ. 2,000 (controlled). (also avail. in microfilm from UMI) **Indexed:** Hort.Abstr., Plant Breed.Abstr. **Document type:** bulletin.
Formerly: Banana Bulletin (ISSN 0045-1398)

631   US   ISSN 0271-5864
BADGER COMMON'TATER. 1948. m. $18 (foreign $50). Wisconsin Potato & Vegetable Growers Association, 700 Fifth Ave., Box 327, Antigo, WI 54409. TEL 715-623-7683. FAX 715-623-3176. E-mail: wpvga@newnorth.net. Ed. Tamas Houlihan. R&P contact: Tamas Houlihan. adv. contact: Tamas Houlihan. circ. 3,850. **Document type:** trade publication.
Description: News and events of the Wisconsin potato industry and agribusiness in general.

631.5   BG   ISSN 0070-8151
BANGLADESH. DIRECTORATE OF AGRICULTURE. SEASON AND CROP REPORT.* (Text in English) a. Ministry of Agriculture, Bangladesh Secretariat, Bhaban 4, Dhaka, Bangladesh.

631.4 570   BG   ISSN 0253-5440
S590   CODEN: BJSSDJ
BANGLADESH JOURNAL OF SOIL SCIENCE. (Text in English) vol.7, 1971. s-a. Tk.10($1.25) Soil Science Society of Bangladesh, c/o Dept. of Soil Science, University of Dhaka, Ramna, Dhaka 2, Bangladesh. Ed. A. Karim. charts; illus.; stat. circ. 350. **Indexed:** Field Crop Abstr., Herb.Abstr.
— CASDDS.
Formerly: Pakistan Journal of Soil Science (ISSN 0030-9893)

633.18   BG
BANGLADESH RICE RESEARCH INSTITUTE. ANNUAL REPORT. (Text in English) 1976. a. Tk.30. Bangladesh Rice Research Institute, Publications and Public Relations Division, Joydebpur, Dhaka, Bangladesh. Ed. Mohammad H.R. Talukdar. stat. circ. 1,000.

631   CN   ISSN 1188-8911
BARLEY COUNTRY. 1992. q. Can.$10 (foreign Can.$15). Alberta Barley Commission, 237, 2116-27 Ave. N.E., Calgary, AB T2E 7A6, Canada. TEL 403-291-9111. FAX 403-291-0190. Ed. Shannon Park. adv.: B&W page Can.$2500, color page Can.$3000; trim 11 3/8 x 17. circ. 40,000. (tabloid format) **Document type:** newsletter.

630.24   GW
BAYER AGROCHEM COURIER. 1956. s-a. Bayer AG, Abteilung Publikationen, 51368 Leverkusen, Germany. TEL 49-217-3383133. FAX 49-217-3383045. Eds. Bernhard Grupp, Georg Priestel. circ. 1,200,000. **Document type:** newsletter.

630   US   ISSN 0084-7747
SB327
BEAN IMPROVEMENT COOPERATIVE. ANNUAL REPORT. 1959. a. $12 (Canada & Mexico $15; elsewhere $20). Colorado State University, Department of Bioagricultural Sciences & Pest Management, Ft. Collins, CO 80523-1177. TEL 970-491-6987. FAX 970-491-3862. E-mail: hfspp@lamar.colostate.edu. Ed. Dr. H.F. Schwartz. bk.rev. circ. 350. **Indexed:** Plant Breed.Abstr. **Document type:** proceedings.
— BLDSC (1113.184000).

631   CC   ISSN 1001-5698
BEIFANG GUOSHU/NORTHERN FRUIT TREES. (Text in Chinese) 1978. q. $2.5. Liaoning Sheng Guoshu Yanjiusuo - Liaoning Research Institute of Fruit Trees, Tiedong Jie, Wenquan Lu, Xiongyue Cheng, Gai Xian, Liaoning 115214, People's Republic of China. TEL 0417-742192. (Co-sponsor: Shenyang University of Agriculture, Department of Horticulture) Ed. Xiao Yunqin. adv. **Document type:** academic/scholarly publication.
Description: Contains fruit tree experimental studies, and production and management experience.

BENTON HARBOR FRUIT & VEGETABLE REPORT. see AGRICULTURE — Agricultural Economics

631   IO   ISSN 0852-0321
BERITA - PUSAT PENELITIAN PERKEBUNAN GULA INDONESIA/INDONESIAN SUGAR RESEARCH CENTER. NEWS. (Text in Indonesian; summaries in English) irreg. $6 per no. Pusat Penelitian Perkebunan Gula Indonesia, Jl. Pahlawan 25, Pasurnan 67126, Indonesia. TEL 0343-21086. FAX 0343-21178. TELEX 31008 SUGEXS IA. Ed. Ir. Hermono Budhisantoso. circ. 650.
— BLDSC (1940.010000).

631   NE   ISSN 0168-7484
BESCHRIJVENDE RASSENLIJST VOOR LANDBOUWGEWASSEN. Short title: Landbouwgewassen. 1924. a. fl.19.50. (Centrum voor Plantenveredelings- en Reproduktieonderzoek) Roto Smeets de Boer n.v., Postbus 507, 1200 AM Hilversum, Netherlands. TEL 31-35-258611. FAX 31-35-238978. Ed. J.E. Parleviet.
Description: Descriptive list of recommended strains and varieties of field crops.

630   NE   ISSN 0922-8829
BESCHRIJVENDE RASSENLIJST VOOR SIERGEWASSEN (YEAR); bloemisterijgewassen. 1987. biennial, 3rd., 1992. fl.29.50. (Centrum voor Plantenveredelings- en Reproduktieonderzoek, Commissie voor de Samenstelling van de Rassenlijst voor Siergewassen) Roto Smeets de Boer n.v., Postbus 507, 1200 AM Hilversum, Netherlands. TEL 31-35-258611. FAX 31-43-238978. Ed. J.J. Bakker. circ. 3,000.
Description: Descriptive list of recommended varieties of cut flowers and bulbs.

631.8   US   ISSN 0006-0089
BETTER CROPS WITH PLANT FOOD. 1923. q. $8. Potash & Phosphate Institute, 655 Engineering Dr., Ste. 110, Norcross, GA 30092-2843. TEL 770-447-0335. FAX 770-448-0439. Ed. Donald L. Armstrong. R&P contact: Donald L. Armstrong. adv.; bibl.; charts; illus.; stat.; tr.lit. (also avail. in microform from UMI; reprint service avail. from UMI) **Indexed:** Biol.Abstr., Chem.Abstr., Cott.& Trop.Fibr.Abstr., Farm & Garden Ind., Field Crop Abstr., Helminthol.Abstr., Herb.Abstr., Hort.Abstr., Plant Breed.Abstr., Sorghum & Millets Abstr., Soyabean Abstr., Triticale Abstr. **Document type:** trade publication.
— BLDSC (1947.000000); Linda Hall; UMI; UnCover.
Description: Discusses innovations in the fertilizer industry.

631   BE
BETTERAVIER. Flemish edition: Bietplanter. 1967. 11/yr. 350 BEF (foreign 600 BEF). Confederation des Betteraviers Belges - Confederatie van de Belgische Bietplanters, Boite 10, 111 Bd. Anspachlaan, B-1000 Brussels, Belgium. TEL 32-2-5136898. FAX 32-2-5121988. Dir. Jean-Francois Sneessens. adv.; bk.rev. circ. 23,000. **Indexed:** Food Sci.& Tech.Abstr., Sugar Ind.Abstr. **Document type:** newsletter.

AGRICULTURE — CROP PRODUCTION AND SOIL

631   **FR**   ISSN 0405-6701
LE BETTERAVIER FRANCAIS. 1946. bi-m. 200 F. (foreign 260 F.) (effective 1997). Societe d'Edition et de Documentation Agricole (SEDA), 25 rue de Madrid, 75008 Paris, France. TEL 33-1-44707494. FAX 33-1-44707499. Ed. Jacques Baret. adv. contact: Pierre Tailliardat. illus.; tr.lit. (tabloid format)
Supersedes: Planteurs Betteraves.

631.4   **GW**   ISSN 0178-4765
BIO NACHRICHTEN. 1979. 4/yr. membership. Biokreis Ostbayern e.V., Theresienstr. 36, 94032 Passau, Germany. TEL 0851-31696. FAX 0851-32332. Ed. Wolfgang Denk. adv. contact: Wolfgang Denk. bk.rev. circ. 750. **Document type**: newsletter.

631 595.7   **UK**   ISSN 0958-3157
SB975   CODEN: BSTCE6
BIOCONTROL SCIENCE AND TECHNOLOGY. Online edition (UK ISSN 1360-0478) 1991. q. £92($158) to individuals; institutions £298 ($548) (effective 1997). Carfax Publishing Co., P.O. Box 25, Abingdon, Oxon. OX14 3UE, England. TEL 44-1235-401000. FAX 44-1235-401550. E-mail: enquiries@carfax.co.uk. (Subscr. in N. America to: Carfax Publishing Co., 875-81 Massachusetts Ave., Cambridge, MA 02139) Ed. C.C. Payne. adv.; bk.rev.; index. (also avail. in microfiche; back issues avail.) **Indexed**: ASCA, Curr.Cont., Ecol.Abstr., IDA. **Document type**: academic/scholarly publication.
• Also available online.
—BLDSC (2071.150000); EMDOCS; Genuine Article; SWETS; UMI. **CCC.**
Description: Presents original research and reviews in the fields of biological pest, disease, and weed control, including basic research and applications of new techniques.
Refereed Serial

631.4   **US**   ISSN 0006-2863
S1
BIODYNAMICS; a periodical furthering soil conservation and increased fertility in order to improve nutrition and health. 1941. bi-m. $35 (foreign $45). Bio-Dynamic Farming and Gardening Association, Inc., c/o Charles Beedy, Box 550, Kimberton, PA 19442. TEL 215-935-7797. FAX 610-983-3196. Ed. Alan York. adv.; bk.rev.; illus.; index, cum.index. circ. 1,200. (also avail. in microform from UMI; reprint service avail. from UMI) **Indexed**: Biol.Abstr., Chem.Abstr., Environ.Per.Bibl. (1981-1993).
—BLDSC (2072.005000); Linda Hall; UMI; UnCover.

631 577   **GW**   ISSN 0178-2762
CODEN: BFSOEE
BIOLOGY AND FERTILITY OF SOILS. Online edition (GW ISSN 1432-0789) (Text in English) 1985. 8/yr. DM.2020 (foreign DM.2039.60) (effective 1998). (International Society of Soil Science) Springer-Verlag, Heidelberger Platz 3, 14197 Berlin, Germany. TEL 49-30-82787-0. FAX 49-30-82787448. E-mail: subscriptions@springer.de; URL: http://link.springer.de. (Subscr. in N. America to: Springer-Verlag New York, Inc., 333 Meadowlands Pkwy., Secaucus, NJ 07094. TEL 212-460-1500. FAX 212-473-6272) Ed. J.C.G. Ottow. (also avail. in microform from UMI; back issues avail.; reprint service avail. from ISI) **Indexed**: Agroforest.Abstr., ASCA, Biol.Abstr., Curr.Adv.Ecol.Sci., Curr.Cont., Ecol.Abstr., Excerp.Med., Fababean Abstr., Field Crop Abstr., Forest.Abstr., Geo.Abstr.P.G., Herb.Abstr., Hort.Abstr., Ind.Sci.Rev., Irr.& Drain.Abstr., Maize Abstr., Rice Abstr., Sci.Cit.Ind., Sel.Water Res.Abstr., Soils & Fert., Soyabean Abstr., Triticale Abstr., Weed Abstr. **Document type**: academic/scholarly publication.
• Also available online.
—BLDSC (2086.998000); CASDDS; EMDOCS; Genuine Article; Linda Hall; SWETS; UMI; UnCover. **CCC.**
Description: Covers fundamental and applied aspects of biology and productivity of soils.

631   **BE**   ISSN 1370-6233
CODEN: BRAGBF
BIOTECHNOLOGIE, AGRONOMIE, SOCIETE ET ENVIRONNEMENT. (Text and summaries in English, French) 1932-1995 (vol.30); N.S. 1997. q. 2000 BEF (foreign 2400 BEF($70)) (effective 1997 & 1998). Faculte des Sciences Agronomiques de Gembloux, Comite d'Edition - Bibliotheque, Passage des Deportes, 2, B-5030 Gembloux, Belgium. TEL 32-81-622103. FAX 32-81-614544. E-mail: BASE@fsagx.ac.be; URL: http://www.bib.fsagx.ac.be/base/. Ed. J.P. Baudoin; Pub. B. Pochet. R&P contact: J.P. Baudoin. bk.rev. circ. 900. (back issues avail.) **Indexed**: Agri.Eng.Abstr., Agrindex, Biol.Abstr., Chem.Abstr., Curr.Adv.Ecol.Sci., Excerp.Med., Field Crop Abstr., Food Sci.& Tech.Abstr., Forest.Abstr., Forest Prod.Abstr., Herb.Abstr., Hort.Abstr., Ind.Vet., Irr.& Drain.Abstr., Nutr.Abstr., Plant Grow.Reg.Abstr., Potato Abstr., Poult.Abstr., Protozool.Abstr., Rice Abstr., Seed Abstr., Soils & Fert., Soyabean Abstr., Sugar Ind.Abstr., Triticale Abstr., VITIS. **Document type**: academic/scholarly publication.
—BLDSC (2089.823000); CASDDS.
Formerly (until 1997): Bulletin des Recherches Agronomiques de Gembloux (ISSN 0435-2033); (until 1965): Bulletin de l'Institut Agronomique et des Stations de Recherches de Gembloux.
Description: Offers original papers, research notes, review articles, and summaries of books and theses as well as reviews of workshops and conferences in the fields of crop and animal production sciences, forestry, soil and earth sciences, rural engineering, environment, bioindustries, food technologies, economy and sociology.

631   **TU**   ISSN 0406-3597
SB599
BITKI KORUMA BULTENI/PLANT PROTECTION BULLETIN. (Text in Turkish; contents page, summaries in English) 1959. q. free. (Tarim ve Koyisleri Bakanligi, Tarimsal Arastirmalar Genel Mudurlugu - Ministry of Agriculture and Rurla Affairs, General Directorate of Agricultural Research) Ankara Zirai Mucadele Arastirma Enstitusu - Ankara Plant Protection Research Institute, Bagdat Caddesi No. 250, P.K. 49, Yenimahalle - Ankara 06172, Turkey. TEL 3445993. FAX 3151531. Ed. Baki Tastan. bibl.; charts; illus.; index. circ. 1,500. **Indexed**: Agri.Eng.Abstr., Bio-Contr.News & Info., Biol.Abstr., Field Crop Abstr., Forest.Abstr., Helminthol.Abstr., Herb.Abstr., Hort.Abstr., Nutr.Abstr., Potato Abstr., Rev.Appl.Entomol., Rev.Plant Path., Weed Abstr. **Document type**: academic/scholarly publication.
—BLDSC (2096.100000).
Description: Publishes original research on plant protection in Turkey.

635   **PL**   ISSN 0509-6839
CODEN: BIWAA9
BIULETYN WARZYWNICZY/BULLETIN OF VEGETABLE CROPS RESEARCH WORK. (Text and summaries in English or Polish) 1953. irreg., no.45, 1996. 12 ZI.($4) Instytut Warzywnictwa - Research Institute of Vegetable Crops, Ul. Konstytucji 3 Maja 1-3, 96-100 Skierniewice, Poland. E-mail: iwarz@linux.iwarz.skierniewice.pl. Ed. A. Dobrzanski. charts; illus.; cum.index. circ. 400. (tabloid format; also avail. in cards) **Indexed**: Agri.Eng.Abstr., Biol.Abstr., Field Crop Abstr., Herb.Abstr., Hort.Abstr., Ornam.Hort., Plant Breed.Abstr., Ref.Zh., Seed Abstr., Soils & Fert., Weed Abstr. **Document type**: academic/scholarly publication, bulletin.
—BLDSC (2105.700000); CASDDS; Linda Hall.
Description: Examines various aspects of vegetable crop research and developments such as crop and soil cultivation, plant breeding, plant protection, weed science, plant nutrition, storage.

631 641.1   **US**   ISSN 1081-5228
BLUEBOOK UPDATE. (Supplement to: Soya Bluebook Plus (ISSN 1081-3063)) 1994. q. Soyatech, Inc., 318 Main St., Box 84, Bar Harbor, ME 04609. TEL 207-288-4969; 800-424-SOYA. FAX 207-288-5264. Ed. Keri Hayes; Pub. Peter Golbitz. R&P contact: Peter Golbitz. adv. contact: Joy Froding. circ. 4,600. **Document type**: newsletter.

631   **SZ**
BODENKUNDLICHE GESELLSCHAFT DER SCHWEIZ. BULLETIN. 1977. a. Bodenkundliche Gesellschaft der Schweiz, Eidg. Forschungsanstalt fuer Landwirtschaftlichen Pflanzenbau, CH-8046 Zurich, Switzerland. TEL 01-3777111. Ed. Moritz Mueller. **Document type**: government publication, academic/scholarly publication.

634.63   **SP**
BOLETIN DE INFORMACION NOTICIAS DEL OLIVAR. 12/yr. M.S. Torres Acosta 10D, 23001 Jaen, Spain. TEL 53-22-51-62. Ed. Jose Bautista.

633 663.93   **GT**   ISSN 1010-1527
BOLETIN DE PROMECAFE. 1978. q. free. Instituto Interamericano de Cooperacion para la Agricultura - O E A, Programa Cooperativo Regional para al Desarrollo Tecnologico y Modernizacion de la Caficultura en Mexico, Centroamerica, Republica Dominicana y Jamaica, Apdo. Postal 1815, Guatemala, Guatemala. TEL 502-2347602. FAX 502-2326795. Ed. Jose Roberto Hernandez Molina. bk.rev.; bibl.; stat. circ. 1,300. (also avail. in microfilm) **Indexed**: Hort.Abstr. **Document type**: bulletin.

631 635   **SP**
BOLETIN DEL REGISTRO DE VARIEDADES. 4/yr. 2420 ptas. (effective 1996). Ministerio de Agricultura, Pesca y Alimentacion, Instituto Nacional de Semillas y Plantas de Vivero, Centro de Publicaciones, Paseo de la Infanta Isabel 1, 28071 Madrid, Spain. TEL 34-1-3475551. FAX 34-1-3475722. (Subscr. to: I.N.S.P.V., Jose Abascal 56, 28003 Madrid, Spain) Ed. Guillermo Artolachipi Esteban. R&P contact: Juan Carlos Palacios Lopez. **Document type**: bulletin.

631.4   **US**
BOOKS IN SOILS PLANTS AND THE ENVIRONMENT SERIES. 1967. irreg., vol.53, 1997. price varies. Marcel Dekker, Inc., 270 Madison Ave., New York, NY 10016. TEL 212-696-9000. FAX 212-685-4540. TELEX 421419. Ed. Russell Dekker; Pub. Graham Garratt. R&P contact: Julia Mulligan. **Document type**: monographic series.
Former titles: Books in Soil and the Environment Series (ISSN 0081-1890); Soil Science Library.
Refereed Serial

631   **BS**
BOTSWANA. MINISTRY OF AGRICULTURE. DIVISION OF ARABLE CROPS RESEARCH. ANNUAL REPORT. a. free. Ministry of Agriculture, Division of Arable Crop Research, Agricultural Research Station, Private Bag 0033, Gaborone, Botswana. TEL 267-328780. FAX 267-328847. TELEX 2752 SACCAR BD. Ed. Henry G. Jobeta. R&P contact: Dan B. Gombalume. charts; illus.; stat. circ. 250. (tabloid format; back issues avail.) **Indexed**: Biol.Abstr. **Document type**: government publication, academic/scholarly publication.
Supersedes (1947-1959): Bechuanaland Protectorate. Ministry of Agriculture. Review of Crop Experiments.
Description: Covers experimental work on variety, spacing, fertilizer, and cultivation trials on maize.

BOTSWANA. MINISTRY OF AGRICULTURE. FARM MANAGEMENT SURVEY RESULTS. see
AGRICULTURE — Agricultural Economics

BOVILOGISK TIDSSKRIFT KVAEGET. see
AGRICULTURE — Dairying And Dairy Products

633   **BL**
BRAZIL. CENTRO NACIONAL DE PESQUISA DE MILHO E SORGO. BOLETIM DE PESQUISA. 1995. irreg., latest no.2. Centro Nacional de Pesquisa de Milho e Sorgo, Km 65 da Rodovia 424, Caixa Postal 151, 35701-970 Sete Lagoas MG, Brazil. TEL 55-31-7735466. FAX 55-31-7739252. E-ma ainfo@cnpms.embrapa.br. bibl.; charts. circ. 1,000.

633   **BL**   ISSN 0100-8013
BRAZIL. CENTRO NACIONAL DE PESQUISA DE MILHO E SORGO. CIRCULAR TECNICA. 1980. irreg., latest no.21. Centro Nacional de Pesquisa de Milho e Sorgo, Km 65 da Rodovia 424, Caixa Postal 151, 35701-970 Sete Lagoas MG, Brazil. TEL 55-31-7735644. FAX 55-31-7739252. E-ma ainfo@cnpms.embrapa.br. bibl.charts. circ. 1,000.
—BLDSC (3265.129500).

633   **BL**   ISSN 0101-9864
BRAZIL. CENTRO NACIONAL DE PESQUISA DE MILHO E SORGO. DOCUMENTOS. 1982. irreg., latest no.8. Centro Nacional de Pesquisa de Milho e Sorgo, Km 65 da Rodovia 424, Caixa Postal 151, 35701-97 Sete Lagoas, MG, Brazil. TEL 55-31-7735466. FAX 55-31-7739252. E-mail: ainfo@cnpms.embrapa.br. Ed.Bd. circ. 1,000. **Document type**: monographic series.
—BLDSC (3612.112080).

AGRICULTURE — CROP PRODUCTION AND SOIL

633   BL   ISSN 0101-1251
BRAZIL. CENTRO NACIONAL DE PESQUISA DE MILHO E SORGO. RELATORIO TECNICO ANUAL. 1979. irreg., vol.6, 1994. Centro Nacional de Pesquisa de Milho e Sorgo, Km 65 da Rodovia 424, Caixa Postal 151, 35701-970 Sete Lagoas, MG, Brazil. TEL 55-31-7735466. FAX 55-31-7739252. E-mail: ainfo@cnpms.embrapa.br. charts. circ. 1,500. **Document type:** academic/scholarly publication.

631   BL   ISSN 0101-3122
BRAZILIAN SEED JOURNAL/REVISTA BRASILEIRA DE SEMENTES. (Text in Portuguese; summaries in English) 1979. 2/yr. Cr.$50000($15) Associacao Brasileira de Tecnologia de Sementes - Brazilian Association of Seed Technology, P.O. Box 02372, 70849 Brasilia, DF, Brazil. TEL 61-347-6324. FAX 61-274-3212. TELEX 61-1622. Ed. Mirian T.S. Eira. adv. circ. 2,000. (back issues avail.) **Indexed:** Field Crop Abstr., Herb.Abstr., Trop.Oil Seeds Abstr. **Document type:** newsletter.

631.5   CN   ISSN 0706-4306
BRITISH COLUMBIA. MINISTRY OF AGRICULTURE FISHERIES AND FOOD. BERRY PRODUCTION GUIDE. Key Title: Berry Production Guide. 1970. a. Can.$10. Ministry of Agriculture Fisheries and Food, Extension Systems Branch, Parliament Bldgs., Victoria, BC V8W 2Z7, Canada. (Orders to: W A I R, 742 Vanalman Ave., Victoria, BC V8V 1X4, Canada) **Document type:** government publication.
Formerly: Ministry of Agriculture. Berry Production Recommendations (ISSN 0706-4314)

631.5   CN   ISSN 1183-5710
BRITISH COLUMBIA. MINISTRY OF AGRICULTURE FISHERIES AND FOOD. GREENHOUSE FLORICULTURE PRODUCTION GUIDE FOR COMMERCIAL GROWERS. a. Can.$10. Ministry of Agriculture Fisheries and Food, Extension Systems Branch, Parliament Bldgs., Victoria, BC V8W 2Z7, Canada. (Orders to: W A I R, 742 Vanalman Ave., Victoria, BC V8V 1X4, Canada) circ. 1,200. **Document type:** government publication.
Supersedes in part: British Columbia. Ministry of Agriculture Fisheries and Food. Nursery, Greenhouse Vegetable and Ornamental Production Guide for Commercial Growers (ISSN 0840-8068); Which was formed by the merger of: British Columbia. Ministry of Agriculture and Food. Greenhouse Vegetable Production Guide (ISSN 0835-0760); British Columbia. Ministry of Agriculture. Nursery Production Guide (ISSN 0705-5757)

631.5   CN   ISSN 1192-9197
BRITISH COLUMBIA. MINISTRY OF AGRICULTURE FISHERIES AND FOOD. GREENHOUSE VEGETABLE PRODUCTION GUIDE FOR COMMERCIAL GROWERS. 1972. a. Can.$10. Ministry of Agriculture Fisheries and Food, Extension Systems Branch, Parliament Bldgs., Victoria, BC V8W 2Z7, Canada. (Orders to: W A I R, 742 Vanalman Ave., Victoria, BC V8V 1X4, Canada) **Indexed:** Geo.Abstr. **Document type:** government publication.
Supersedes in part: British Columbia. Ministry of Agriculture Fisheries and Food. Nursery, Greenhouse Vegetable and Ornamental Production Guide for Commercial Growers (ISSN 0840-8068); Which was formed the merger of: British Columbia. Ministry of Agriculture. Nursery Production Guide (ISSN 0705-5757); British Columbia. Ministry of Agriculture Fisheries and Food. Greenhouse Vegetable Production Guide (ISSN 0835-0760)

631.5   CN   ISSN 1198-001X
BRITISH COLUMBIA. MINISTRY OF AGRICULTURE FISHERIES AND FOOD. MANAGEMENT GUIDE FOR GRAPES. a. Can.$10. Ministry of Agriculture Fisheries and Food, Extension Systems Branch, Parliament Bldgs., Victoria, BC V8W 2Z7, Canada. (Orders to: W A I R, 742 Vanalman Ave., Victoria, BC V8V 1X4, Canada) bibl. circ. 600. **Document type:** government publication.
Former titles: British Columbia. Ministry of Agriculture Fisheries and Food. Grape Production Guide; British Columbia. Ministry of Agriculture and Food. Grape Production Guide; British Columbia. Ministry of Agriculture. Grape Production Guide (ISSN 0701-9858)

631.5   CN   ISSN 0705-470X
BRITISH COLUMBIA. MINISTRY OF AGRICULTURE FISHERIES AND FOOD. TREE FRUIT PRODUCTION GUIDE FOR INTERIOR DISTRICTS. Key Title: Tree-Fruit Production Guide for Interior Districts. 1978. a. Can.$10. Ministry of Agriculture Fisheries and Food, Extension Systems Branch, Parliament Bldgs., Victoria, BC V8W 2Z7, Canada. (Orders to: W A I R, 742 Vanalman Ave., Victoria, BC V8V 1X4, Canada) circ. 3,400. **Document type:** government publication.
Former titles: British Columbia. Ministry of Agriculture and Food. Tree Fruit; British Columbia. Ministry of Agriculture. Tree Fruit Production Guide for Interior Districts.

631.5   CN   ISSN 0318-3661
BRITISH COLUMBIA. MINISTRY OF AGRICULTURE FISHERIES AND FOOD. VEGETABLE PRODUCTION GUIDE. Key Title: Vegetable Production Guide. a. Can.$10. Ministry of Agriculture Fisheries and Food, Extension Systems Branch, Parliament Bldgs., Victoria, BC V8W 2Z7, Canada. (Orders to: W A I R, 742 Vanalman Ave., Victoria, BC V8V 1X4, Canada) circ. 3,000. **Document type:** government publication.
Former titles: British Columbia. Ministry of Agriculture and Food. Vegetable Production Guide; British Colombia. Ministry of Agriculture. Vegetable Production REcommendations (ISSN 0318-367X)

631   UK   CODEN: MBCCDO
BRITISH CROP PROTECTION COUNCIL. SYMPOSIUM PROCEEDINGS. 1970. irreg., no.63, 1995. British Crop Protection Council, Bear Farm, Binfield, Bracknell, Berkshire RG12 5QE, England. TEL 44-1734-342727. FAX 44-1734-341998. **Document type:** proceedings.
—CASDDS; CISTI.
Formerly: British Crop Protection Council. Monograph (ISSN 0306-3941)

631 581   UK   ISSN 1351-6566
CODEN: MBSREE
BRITISH SOCIETY FOR PLANT GROWTH REGULATION. MONOGRAPHS. 1978. s-a. £10($20) British Society for Plant Growth Regulation, University of Bristol, Department of Agricultural Science, Long Ashton Research Station, Bristol BS18 9AF, England. FAX 0275-394007. Ed. M.B. Jackson. circ. 500. (back issues avail.) **Indexed:** Chem.Abstr., Crop Physiol.Abstr., Curr.Adv.Plant.Sci., Field Crop Abstr., Herb.Abstr., Hort.Abstr., Plant Grow.Reg.Abstr., Potato Abstr., Seed Abstr., Triticale Abstr.
—CASDDS; CISTI; UMI.
Formerly (until 1990): British Plant Growth Regulator Group. Monographs (ISSN 0952-6463)

633.63   UK   ISSN 0007-1854
BRITISH SUGAR BEET REVIEW. 1927. q. free. British Sugar plc., Box 26, Oundle Rd., Peterborough, Cambs. PE2 9QU, England. TEL 01733-422904. FAX 01733-422487. Ed. Bill Hollowell. adv.; bk.rev.; charts; illus.; stat.; tr.lit. circ. 15,000 (controlled). **Indexed:** Agri.Eng.Abstr., Biol.Abstr., Chem.Abstr., Curr.Adv.Ecol.Sci., Curr.Cont., Field Crop Abstr., Helminthol.Abstr., Herb.Abstr., Irr.& Drain.Abstr., Plant Breed.Abstr., Rural Recreat.Tour.Abstr., Seed Abstr., Soils & Fert., Sugar Ind.Abstr., Weed Abstr., World Agri.Econ.& Rural Sociol.Abstr. **Document type:** trade publication.
—BLDSC (2345.000000); UnCover.

BUG BULLETIN; integrated pest management for ornamental plants. see *GARDENING AND HORTICULTURE*

BULLETIN DE L'O I V; revue internationale. see *BEVERAGES*

631 636   GW   ISSN 0723-5321
BUNDESFORSCHUNGSANSTALT FUER LANDWIRTSCHAFT. MITTEILUNGEN UND INFORMATIONEN. 1981. q. free. Bundesforschungsanstalt fuer Landwirtschaft Braunschweig-Voelkenrode, Bundesallee 50, 38116 Braunschweig, Germany. TEL 49-531-596-1. FAX 49-531-596-814. Ed.Bd. circ. 1,400. (back issues avail.) **Document type:** government publication.

BURKINA FASO. DIRECTION DE L'HYDRAULIQUE ET DE L'EQUIPEMENT RURAL. SERVICE I.R.H. RAPPORT D'ACTIVITES. see *WATER RESOURCES*

BUSINESS RATIO REPORT: FERTILISERS & AGROCHEMICALS. see *ENGINEERING — Chemical Engineering*

633 330   US
BUYERS GUIDE TO U.S. COTTON. 1969. a. free to qualified. Cotton Council International, 1521 New Hampshire Ave., N.W., Washington, DC 20036-1205. TEL 202-745-7805. FAX 202-483-4040. URL: http://www.cottonusa.org/CCI/. Dir. Allen A. Terhaar. circ. 4,000.
Description: Covers U.S. cotton production, varieties, classifications and exporters.

C M B NEWSLETTER. (Ghana Cocoa Marketing Board) see *BUSINESS AND ECONOMICS — Marketing And Purchasing*

633   SP
C O I HOJA DE INFORMACION. French edition: C O I Feuille d'Information. 1962. s-m. 6000 ptas. (Europe $70; America $115) (effective 1996). Consejo Oleicola Internacional - International Olive Oil Council - Conseil Oleicole International, Calle Principe de Vergara 154, 28002 Madrid, Spain. TEL 34-1-5630071. FAX 34-1-5631263. Ed. Fausto Luchetti. bk.rev.; stat.; index. circ. 480. (back issues avail.)

631   UK
C R U INTERNATIONAL METALS DATABOOK. irreg., latest 1997. £260($399) C R U Publishing Ltd., 31 Mount Pleasant, London WC1X 0AD, England. TEL 44-171-837-5600. FAX 44-171-837-0292. TELEX 918918 SULFEX G. Pub. John French. R&P contact: John French. **Document type:** directory.
Formerly (until 1997): C R U World Metals Capacity Databook and Atlas.

633.63   NE   ISSN 0165-9375
C S M INFORMATIE. 1946. m. (7/yr.). free to qualified personnel. C S M Suiker B.V., Postbus 349, 1000 AH Amsterdam, Netherlands. TEL 31-20-5906911. FAX 31-20-5906395. circ. 11,000. **Document type:** trade publication.
—BLDSC (3490.293500).
Formerly (until 1973): Centrale Suiker Maatschappij. Voorlichtingsblad (ISSN 0027-710X)
Description: Covers news and topics relating to sugar-beet cultivation and processing.

634.653
THE CALAVO NEWS. 1927. q. free. Calavo Growers of California, Box 26081, Santa Ana, CA 92799-6081. TEL 714-259-1166. FAX 714-259-1973. Ed. Bob Duke. R&P contact: Robert A. Duke. circ. 2,500. **Document type:** newsletter.
Former titles (until 1994): Calavo Newsletter; Together: Calavo Newsletter; Calavo Newsletter (ISSN 0008-0578)
Description: News and announcements pertaining to marketing and development in the avocado industry in California.

CALIFORNIA. AGRICULTURAL STATISTICS SERVICE. CROP WEATHER REPORT. see *AGRICULTURE — Abstracting, Bibliographies, Statistics*

CALIFORNIA. AGRICULTURAL STATISTICS SERVICE. FIELD CROP REVIEW. see *AGRICULTURE — Abstracting, Bibliographies, Statistics*

CALIFORNIA. AGRICULTURAL STATISTICS SERVICE. FRUIT AND NUT REVIEW. see *AGRICULTURE — Abstracting, Bibliographies, Statistics*

CALIFORNIA. AGRICULTURAL STATISTICS SERVICE. GRAPE ACREAGE. see *AGRICULTURE — Abstracting, Bibliographies, Statistics*

CALIFORNIA. AGRICULTURAL STATISTICS SERVICE. GRAPE CRUSH REPORT. see *AGRICULTURE — Abstracting, Bibliographies, Statistics*

CALIFORNIA. AGRICULTURAL STATISTICS SERVICE. VEGETABLE REVIEW. see *AGRICULTURE — Abstracting, Bibliographies, Statistics*

CALIFORNIA. AGRICULTURAL STATISTICS SERVICE. WALNUTS, RAISINS AND PRUNES (PRICE REPORT). see *AGRICULTURE — Abstracting, Bibliographies, Statistics*

633.51   US   ISSN 0008-090X
CALIFORNIA - ARIZONA COTTON.* 1965. 9/yr. $19.95 (overseas $195). Western Agricultural Publishing Co. Inc., 4969 E. Clinton Way, Ste. 119, Fresno, CA 93727-1549. TEL 209-252-7000. FAX 209-252-7387. Ed. Mark Arcamonte. adv.; illus. circ. 7,000. **Document type:** trade publication.

AGRICULTURE — CROP PRODUCTION AND SOIL

631 US ISSN 0888-1715
CALIFORNIA GROWER; avocados, citrus, grapes, apples & pears, stonefruit, specialty crops. 1977. m. $22 (foreign $47) (effective 1996). Rincon Information Management Corp., Box 370, Carpinteria, CA 93014. TEL 805-684-6581. FAX 805-684-1535. E-mail: cgeditor@west.net. Ed. Christine Jutzi; Pub. Willard Thompson. R&P contact: Willard Thompson. adv.: B&W page $1945, color page $2860; adv. contact: James Heath. bk.rev.; cum.index. circ. 10,000. **Indexed:** Bibl.Agri. **Document type:** trade publication.
Formerly: Avocado Grower.

634 US ISSN 0068-5720
CALIFORNIA MACADAMIA SOCIETY. YEARBOOK. 1955. a. $17.50 membership. California Macadamia Society, Box 1298, Fallbrook, CA 92088. TEL 619-728-8081. Ed. Jim Russell. adv.; cum.index: 1955-1962, 1963-68, 1959-1974, 1975-1980, 1981-85, 1986-1990. circ. 600. **Document type:** academic/scholarly publication.

631 US
CALIFORNIA PRUNE NEWS. irreg. free. California Prune Board, 5990 Stoneridge Dr., Ste. 101, Pleasanton, CA 94588-3234. TEL 510-734-0150. FAX 510-734-0525. Ed. Richard Peterson. circ. 1,750 (controlled). **Document type:** newsletter.
Description: California prune industry information.

631 US ISSN 0527-3277
CALIFORNIA TOMATO GROWER. 1958. m. (9/yr.) $30 (foreign $45; air mail $80). California Tomato Growers Association, Inc., 10730 Siskiyou Ln., Box 7398, Stockton, CA 95209. TEL 209-478-1761. FAX 209-478-9460. Ed. John C. Welty. R&P contact: John C. Welty. adv. contact: Tom Fielding. illus.; stat. circ. 2,200. **Document type:** trade publication.

CANADA. ENVIRONMENT CANADA. ENVIRONMENTAL PROTECTION SERIES REPORTS. see *ENVIRONMENTAL STUDIES*

631.4 CN ISSN 0008-4271
CODEN: CJSSAR
CANADIAN JOURNAL OF SOIL SCIENCE. (Text in English or French) 1921. q. Can.$58 (foreign Can.$62) (effective 1997). Agricultural Institute of Canada, 141 Laurier Ave. W., Ste 1112, Ottawa, ON K1P 5J3, Canada. TEL 613-232-9459. FAX 613-594-5190. E-mail: journals@aic.ca; URL: http://www.aic.ca. Ed. A. Mermut. bibl.; charts; illus.; stat.; index. circ. 1,200. (also avail. in microform from UMI,PMC; reprint service avail. from UMI) **Indexed:** Acid Pre.Dig., Acid Rain Abstr., Acid Rain Ind., Agri.Eng.Abstr., ASCA, Bibl.Agri., Biol.Abstr., Biol.& Agr.Ind., Chem.Abstr., Curr.Adv.Ecol.Sci., Curr.Adv.Physiol., Curr.Cont., Ecol.Abstr., Environ.Abstr., Environ.Per.Bibl. (1972-1993), Excerp.Med., Fababean Abstr., Field Crop Abstr., Forest Abstr., Forest Prod.Abstr., Geo.Abstr.P.G., GeoRef., Helminthol.Abstr., Herb.Abstr., Hort.Abstr., Ind.Sci.Rev., INIS Atomind., Irr.& Drain.Abstr., Maize Abstr., Plant Breed.Abstr., Pollut.Abstr., Potato Abstr., Sci.Cit.Ind., Seed Abstr., Sel.Water Res.Abstr., Soils & Fert., Soyabean Abstr., Triticale Abstr., Weed Abstr. **Document type:** academic/scholarly publication.
—BLDSC (3035.700000); CASDDS; CIS; CISTI; EMDOCS; Genuine Article; KR SourceOne; Linda Hall; SWETS; UMI; UnCover. **CCC.**
Description: Publishes pure and applied research on the use, management, structure and development of soils.
Refereed Serial

631.5 CN ISSN 0068-9610
CANADIAN SEED GROWERS ASSOCIATION. ANNUAL REPORT. 1903. a. Canadian Seed Growers Association, Box 8455, Ottawa, ON K1G 3T1, Canada. TEL 613-236-0497. circ. 6,000. **Document type:** corporate report.
—CISTI.

631 CN ISSN 0715-3651
CANOLA DIGEST. 1967. 8/yr. Can.$32.10 (foreign $30). Canola Council of Canada - Conseil de Canola du Canada, 400-167 Lombard Ave., Winnipeg, MB R3B 0T6, Canada. TEL 204-982-2100. FAX 204-942-1841. adv. contact: Wendy Miller. circ. 1,100. **Document type:** newsletter, academic/scholarly publication, bulletin.

631.5 US
CARGILL BULLETIN. 1925. m. $12 (foreign $13). Cargill, Inc., Box 5625, Minneapolis, MN 55440-5625. TEL 612-742-6202. FAX 612-475-6208. TELEX 290625 CARGILL MPS. Ed. Linda Thrane. R&P contact: Wendy Tai. charts; stat. circ. 8,000. **Document type:** bulletin.
—Linda Hall.
Formerly: Cargill Crop Bulletin (ISSN 0008-641X)
Description: Reviews current domestic and international market conditions and public policy questions involving agriculture and world trade.

631 US ISSN 1071-6653
CARROT COUNTRY. 1993. q. $8 (Canada & Mexico $14; elsewhere $18). Columbia Publishing and Design, 2520 W. Washington, Ste. 2, Box 9036, Yakima, WA 98909-0036. TEL 509-248-2452; 800-900-2452. FAX 509-248-4056. E-mail: dede@freshcut.com. Ed. D. Brent Clement; Pub. J. Mike Stoker. R&P contact: J. Mike Stoker. adv. contact: J. Mike Stoker. circ. 2,430. (back issues avail.) **Document type:** trade publication.
Description: Covers carrot production and marketing.

634.573 II ISSN 0970-2423
THE CASHEW. (Text in English) 1967. q. Rs.120. Ministry of Agriculture, Department of Agriculture and Co-operation, Directorate of Cashewnut Development, Karimpalta Cross Rd., Ernakulam, Cochin 682 016, Kerala, India. TEL 0484-373239. FAX 0484-373239. Ed. P.P. Balasubramanian. adv.; bk.rev. circ. 400. **Document type:** bulletin.
Formerly (until 1987): Cashew Causerie (ISSN 0970-1818); **Supersedes:** Cashew News Teller (ISSN 0045-5911)
Description: Articles on cashew cultivation, processing, exports, imports and utilisation of by-products.

633 NE
CENTRE FOR PLANT BREEDING AND REPRODUCTION RESEARCH. ANNUAL REPORT. Short title: C P R O - D L O Annual Report. 1955; N.S. 1991. a. free. C P R O - D L O, Postbus 16, 6700 AA Wageningen, Netherlands. TEL 31-317-477017. FAX 31-317-418094. E-mail: info@cpro.dlo.nl; URL: http://www.bib.wau.nl/cpro/. Ed. H.A.J.M. Toussaint. R&P contact: H.A.J.M. Toussaint. charts; illus.; index; circ. 3,100 (controlled). **Document type:** corporate report.
●Also available online.
Supersedes (in 1992): Centrum voor Rassenonderzoek en Zaadtechnologie. Jaarverslag; **Former titles** (until Jan. 1990): Rijksuniversiteit voor het Rassenonderzoek van Cultuurgewassen. Jaarverslag (ISSN 0168-9843); Instituut voor Rassenonderzoek van Landbouwgewassen. Jaarverslag.
Description: Covers recent developments in research, with lists of personnel and publications. Includes articles covering actual developments in genetic research

632.9 581 US
CEREAL RUST BULLETIN. 1963. irreg. free. U.S. Department of Agriculture, Agricultural Research Service (St. Paul), Cereal Rust Laboratory, 1551 Lindig St., St. Paul, MN 55108. TEL 612-625-6299. FAX 612-649-5054. E-mail: davidl@puccini.crl.umn.edu; URL: http://www.umn.edu/rustlab/. Ed. David L. Long. R&P contact: David L. Long. circ. 500 (controlled). (looseleaf format) **Indexed:** Field Crop Abstr., Herb.Abstr., Maize Abstr., Plant Breed.Abstr., Rev.Plant Path., Triticale Abstr. **Document type:** bulletin.
Description: Studies the development of the small-grain cereal rusts in the U.S.

632 GW ISSN 0009-1308
CODEN: CHMPDB
DER CHAMPIGNON; Zeitschrift fuer den Pilzenbau. 1961. bi-m. DM.190 (foreign DM.221) (effective 1996). Bund Deutscher Champignonzuechter e.V., Godesberger Allee 142-148, 53175 Bonn, Germany. TEL 49-228-8100226. FAX 49-228-8100247. Ed. Eberhard Peters. adv.: B&W page DM.1000, color page DM.2170; trim 270 x 185; adv. contact: Liane Wilden. bk.rev.; charts; illus.; stat. circ. 1,000. **Indexed:** Biodet.Abstr., Food Sci.& Tech.Abstr., Forest Prod.Abstr., Hort.Abstr., Maize Abstr., Soyabean Abstr. **Document type:** consumer publication.
—BLDSC (3129.580000).

632 NE ISSN 0009-1316
DE CHAMPIGNONCULTUUR. (Text in Dutch, summaries in English) 1957. 10/yr. fl.145 (airmail fl.180) (effective 1995). Bromyc B.V., Postbus 6042, 5960 AA Horst, Netherlands. TEL 31-77-4647523. FAX 31-77-4641567. E-mail: mushex@via.nl; URL: http://www.agro.nl/appliedresearch/pc.ht, Ed.Bd. adv.: B&W page fl.650. bk.rev. circ. 625. **Indexed:** Biodet.Abstr., Food Sci.& Tech.Abstr., Hort.Abstr., Soils & Fert.

CHANGING HORIZONS. see *AGRICULTURE — Agricultural Economics*

633.72 CC
CHAYE KEXUE JIANBAO/SCIENTIFIC BULLETIN OF TEA. (Text in Chinese) q. Y1.50. Fujian Sheng Nongye Kexueyuan - Fujian Academy of Agricultural Science, She Kou, Fu'an, Fujian 355015, People's Republic of China. TEL 05031. (Dist. overseas by: Jiangsu Publications Import & Export Corp., 56 Gao Ying Ling, Nanjing, Jiangsu, P.R.C.) Ed. Lin Xinjiong.
Description: Discusses cultivation and propagation of tea shrubs as well as tea processing. Also includes trade information and scientific research on tea in other countries.

632.9 660 NE ISSN 0927-0094
CODEN: CHEAET
CHEMICALS IN AGRICULTURE. (Text in English) 1988. irreg., vol.2, 1991. price varies. Elsevier Science B.V., Books Division, P.O. Box 211, 1000 AE Amsterdam, Netherlands. TEL 31-20-4853911. FAX 31-20-4853705. TELEX 18582 ESPA NL. E-mail: nlinfo-f@elsevier.nl; usinfo-f@elsevier.com; forinfo-kyf04035@niftyserve.or.jp; URL: http://www.elsevier.nl/. (Subscr. in the Americas to: Elsevier Science, Regional Sales Office, Box 945, New York, NY 10159-0945. TEL 212-633-3730. FAX 212-633-3680; Subscr. in Australasia and the Far East to: Elsevier Science (Singapore) Pte Ltd, No.1 Temasek Ave., No.17-01 Millenia Tower, Singapore 039192, Singapore. TEL 65-434-3727. FAX 65-337-2230; Subscr. in Japan to: Elsevier Science Japan, 9-15 Higashi-Azabu 1-chome, Minato-ku, Tokyo 106, Japan. TEL 81-3-5561-5033. FAX 81-3-5561-5047) (back issues avail.) **Document type:** monographic series.
—CASDDS.
Refereed Serial

631 RH
CHEMISTRY AND SOIL RESEARCH INSTITUTE. ANNUAL REPORT. (Text in English) 1964. a. free. Ministry of Lands, Agriculture and Rural Resettlement, Research and Specialist Services, Chemistry and Soil Research Institute, P.O. Box CY594, Causeway, Harare, Zimbabwe. circ. 300. (back issues avail.)

631.4 AG ISSN 0326-3169
CODEN: CISUDT
CIENCIA DEL SUELO/ARGENTINE SOCIETY OF SOIL SCIENCE. JOURNAL. (Text in English, Spanish; summaries in English) 1983. s-a. $40 (effective 1996 & 1997). Asociacion Argentina de la Ciencia del Suelo, J. Ramirez de Velasco 847, 1414 Buenos Aires, Argentina. TEL 54-1-7718968. E-mail: radio@ferlav.agro.uba.ar. (Subscr. to: AACS, c/o R. Alvarez, Laboratorio de Radioisotopos, Fac. de Agronomia, Univ. de B.A., Av. San Martin 4453, 1417 Buenos Aires, Argentina. FAX 54-1-522-1687) Ed. Roberto Alvarez. adv.; index. circ. 800. **Indexed:** Chem.Abstr., Curr.Adv.Ecol.Sci., Field Crop Abstr., Geo.Abstr.P.G., Irr.& Drain.Abstr., Maize Abstr., Soils & Fert., Soyabean Abstr., Triticale Abstr. **Document type:** academic/scholarly publication.
—CASDDS.
Description: Covers original papers from Argentinian and foreign researchers. Includes all areas of soil science; physics, chemistry, biology, biochemistry, fertility, and management.
Refereed Serial

631 CU ISSN 1013-9834
CODEN: CTACEV
CIENCIA Y TECNICA EN LA AGRICULTURA. SERIE: CAFE CACAO. (Table of contents and abstracts in English) 1978. s-a. $14 in N. and S. America; Europe $16; elsewhere $17; or exchange basis. Centro de Informacion y Documentacion Agropecuario, Gaveta Postal 4149, Havana 4, Cuba. (Dist. by: Ediciones Cubanas, Obispo No. 527, Apdo. 605, Havana, Cuba) **Indexed:** Agrindex, Agroforest.Abstr., Soils & Fert., Weed Abstr.

AGRICULTURE — CROP PRODUCTION AND SOIL

631 CU ISSN 0138-7014
CIENCIA Y TECNICA EN LA AGRICULTURA. SERIE: CANERA. 3/yr. Centro de Informacion y Documentacion Agropecuario, Gaveta Postal 4149, Havana 4, Cuba. (Dist. by: Ediciones Cubanas, Obispo No.527, Apdo. 605, Havana, Cuba) (Co-sponsor: Cuba. Ministerio de Azucar)

634 CU ISSN 0138-8835
CIENCIA Y TECNICA EN LA AGRICULTURA. SERIE: CITRICOS Y OTROS FRUTALES. (Table of contents and abstracts in English) 1978. q. $17 in N. America; S. America $19; Europe $21; elsewhere $24; or exchange basis. Centro de Informacion y Documentacion Agropecuario, Gaveta Postal 4149, Havana 4, Cuba. (Dist. by: Ediciones Cubanas, Obispo No. 527, Apdo. 605, Havana, Cuba) **Indexed:** Agrindex.
Formerly: Ciencia y Tecnica en la Agricultura. Serie: Citricos.

631 CU ISSN 0138-8630
CIENCIA Y TECNICA EN LA AGRICULTURA. SERIE: HORTALIZAS, PAPAS, GRANOS Y FIBRAS. (Table of contents and abstracts in English) 1982. s-a. $14 in N. and S. America; Europe $16; elsewhere $17; or exchange basis. Centro de Informacion y Documentacion Agropecuario, Gaveta Postal 4149, Havana 4, Cuba. (Dist. by: Ediciones Cubanas, Obispo No. 527, Apdo. 605, Havana, Cuba) **Indexed:** Agrindex, Maize Abstr.
Formerly (until 1983): Ciencia y Tecnica en la Agricultura. Serie: Viandas, Hortalizas y Granos.

631 CU ISSN 0138-8932
CIENCIA Y TECNICA EN LA AGRICULTURA. SERIE: PROTECCION DE PLANTAS. (Table of contents and abstracts in English) 1978. q. $17 in N. America; S. America $19; Europe $21; elsewhere $24; or exchange basis. Centro de Informacion y Documentacion Agropecuario, Gaveta Postal 4149, Havana 4, Cuba. (Dist. by: Ediciones Cubanas, Obispo No. 527, Apdo 605, Havana, Cuba) **Indexed:** Agrindex, Field Crop Abstr., Herb.Abstr., Sugar Ind.Abstr., Weed Abstr.

631.7 CU ISSN 0138-8487
CIENCIA Y TECNICA EN LA AGRICULTURA. SERIE: RIEGO Y DRENAJE. (Table of contents and abstracts in English) 1978. s-a. $14 in N. and S. America; Europe $16; elsewhere $17; or exchange basis. Centro de Informacion y Documentacion Agropecuario, Gaveta Postal 4149, Havana 4, Cuba. (Dist. by: Ediciones Cubanas, Obispo No. 527, Aptdo. 605, Havana, Cuba) **Indexed:** Agrindex, Field Crop Abstr., Geo.Abstr., Herb.Abstr., Soils & Fert.

631.7 CU ISSN 0138-8983
CIENCIA Y TECNICA EN LA AGRICULTURA. SERIE: SUELOS Y AGROQUIMICA. (Table of contents and abstracts in English) 1978. 3/yr. $17 in N. America; S. America $19; Europe $20; elsewhere $22; or exchange basis. Centro de Informacion y Documentacion Agropecuario, Gaveta Postal 4149, Havana 4, Cuba. (Dist. by: Ediciones Cubanas, Obispo No. 527, Apdo. 605, Havana, Cuba) **Indexed:** Agrindex, Field Crop Abstr., Herb.Abstr., Hort.Abstr., Rice Abstr.

631 CU ISSN 0138-8886
CIENCIA Y TECNICA EN LA AGRICULTURA. SERIE: VIANDAS TROPICALES. (Table of contents and abstracts in English) 1983. s-a. $14 in N. and S. America; Europe $16; elsewhere $17; or exchange basis. Centro de Informacion y Documentacion Agropecuario, Gaveta Postal 4149, Havana 4, Cuba. (Dist. by: Ediciones Cubanas, Obispo No. 527, Apdo. 605, Havana, Cuba) **Indexed:** Agri.Eng.Abstr., Agrindex, Field Crop Abstr., Herb.Abstr.
Formerly (until 1983): Ciencia y Tecnica en la Agricultura. Serie: Viandas, Hortalizas y Granos.

631 CU
CIENCIAS DEL SUELO, RIEGO Y MECANIZACION. 3/yr. $22 in S. America; N. America $24; elsewhere $28. Ediciones Cubanas, Obispo No. 527, Apdo. 605, Havana, Cuba.

631 BL ISSN 0100-0039
SF641 CODEN: CNTFBM
CIENTIFICA; revista de agronomia. (Text in Portuguese; summaries in English and Portuguese) 1974. s-a. $30 or exchange basis. Universidade Estadual Paulista, Av. Vicente Ferreira, 1278, Caixa Postal 71, 17515-901 Marilia SP, Brazil. TEL 55-144-222504. FAX 55-144-222504. E-mail: uespre@brfapesp.bitnet. bibl.; charts; stat. circ. 1,000. **Indexed:** Abstr.Trop.Agri., Agri.Eng.Abstr., Agrindex, Anim.Breed Abstr., Aqua.Sci.& Fish.Abstr., Curr.Adv.Ecol.Sci., Field Crop Abstr., Food Sci.& Tech.Abstr., Forest.Abstr., Helminthol.Abstr., Herb.Abstr., Hort.Abstr., INIS Atomind., Irr.& Drain.Abstr., Maize Abstr., Meteor.& Geoastrophys.Abstr., Nutr.Abstr., Plant Breed.Abstr., Rev.Appl.Entomol., Rice Abstr., Soils & Fert., Sorghum & Millets Abstr., Sugar Ind.Abstr., Triticale Abstr., Trop.Oil Seeds Abstr., Weed Abstr. **Document type:** academic/scholarly publication.
—BLDSC (3198.207000); CASDDS; Linda Hall.

631 FR ISSN 0751-6037
CIRCUITS CULTURE. 1973. m. 395 F. (foreign 489 F.) (effective 1997). Groupe Liaisons S.A., 1 av. Edouard Belin, 92856 Rueil Malmaison, France. TEL 33-1-41299999. FAX 33-1-41299838. Ed. Fabrice Deschamps. adv.: B&W page 16000 F., color page 20000 F.; adv. contact: Martine Pinel. circ. 5,500.

634.3 US ISSN 0009-7578
CITROGRAPH;* magazine of the citrus industry. 1915. m. $19.95 (overseas $195). Western Agricultural Publishing Co. Inc., 4969 E. Clinton Way, Ste. 119, Fresno, CA 93727-1549. TEL 209-252-7000. FAX 209-252-7387. adv.: bk.rev.; charts; illus.; stat.; tr.lit. circ. 7,500. **Indexed:** Bio-Contr.News & Info., Biol.Abstr., Chem.Abstr., Food Sci.& Tech.Abstr., Hort.Abstr., Rev.Appl.Entomol., Rev.Plant Path. **Document type:** trade publication.
—Linda Hall; SWETS; UnCover.
Formerly (until 1969): California Citrograph (ISSN 1054-7177)
Description: Gives tips on growing produce.

634 633 US ISSN 0009-7586
CODEN: CVGMAX
CITRUS & VEGETABLE. 1938. m. $25 (foreign $70) (effective 1997). Vance Publishing Corporation (Lenexa), 10901 W. 84th Terr., Lenexa, KS 66214-1631. TEL 913-438-8700. FAX 913-438-0695. Ed. Gordon Smith. adv.; bk.rev.; illus. circ. 12,500. **Indexed:** Biol.Abstr., Curr.Adv.Ecol.Sci., Curr.Adv.Genetics & Molec.Biol., Farm & Garden Ind., Food Sci.& Tech.Abstr., Helminthol.Abstr., Hort.Abstr. **Document type:** trade publication.
—BLDSC (3267.800000); SWETS; UnCover.

634 SA ISSN 1018-953X
CITRUS JOURNAL. Afrikaans title: Sitrus Joernaal. (Text in English, Afrikaans) 1991. bi-m. Outspan International, P.O. Box 7733, 0046 Hennopsmeer, South Africa. TEL 27-11-492-1232. (Alt. addr.: 1006 Lenchen Ave. N., 0157 Centurion, South Africa) Ed. Jan Branders; Pub. Penelope Palmer. adv. **Document type:** trade publication.
—BLDSC (3267.950000).
Description: Covers the trade and marketing of citrus fruits in South Africa.

633.74 UK ISSN 0045-7256
COCOA GROWERS BULLETIN. 1963. s-a. free. Cadbury Ltd., Bournville, Birmingham B30 2LU, England. Ed. Tony Lass. bk.rev.; abstr.; illus.; stat.; index; circ. 1,500 (controlled). **Indexed:** Hort.Abstr., Plant Breed.Abstr., Rev.Appl.Entomol., Soils & Fert., Trop.Abstr. **Document type:** bulletin.
—BLDSC (3292.738000).
Description: Provides an information service to cocoa growers, plantation staff, extension officers and research workers.

634 IO ISSN 0854-235X
COCONUT STATISTICAL YEARBOOK. (Text in English) a. $50 in Asia & Pacific; elsewhere $60. Asian and Pacific Coconut Community, Wisma Bakrie, 3rd Fl., Jl. H.R. Rasuna Said Kav. B-7, Kuningan, Jakarta 12920, Indonesia. TEL 62-21-5221712. FAX 62-21-5221714. TELEX 62209 APCC IA. E-mail: apcc@indo.net.id; URL: http://www.idrc.org.sg/pan/apcc.
Description: Presents the latest statistical data on world's coconut industry, including production, volume & value of exports, import destinations, processing capacities and coconut conversion tables.

631 IO
COCONUT WOOD UTILIZATION; proceedings of the workshop for policy makers. a.? $10. Asian and Pacific Coconut Community, Wisma Bakrie, 3rd Fl., Jl. H.R. Rasuna Said, Kuningan, Jakarta 12920, Indonesia. TEL 62-21-510-073. FAX 62-21-520-5160. TELEX 62863 APCCIA. **Document type:** proceedings.
Description: Covers products, sawmills and equipment, marketing prospects in Europe, profitability of coconut wood utilization and its integration with national replanting programs.

COFFEE ANNUAL. see *FOOD AND FOOD INDUSTRIES*

COFFEE INTELLIGENCE. see *FOOD AND FOOD INDUSTRIES*

631 RH
COFFEE RESEARCH INSTITUTE. ANNUAL REPORT. COFFEE RESEARCH STATION. 1976. a. free. Ministry of Agriculture, Coffee Research Institute, P.O. Box 61, Chipinge, Zimbabwe. (Subscr. to: P.O. Box 8108, Causeway, Zimbabwe) Ed. D. Kumah. circ. 300. **Document type:** government publication.
Formerly: Horticulture and Coffee Research Institute. Annual Report. Part 2. Coffee Research Station.

633 FR
COMMERCE FRANCAIS DE LA POMME DE TERRE. 6/yr. 40 F. Secopot, 220 Bourse du Commerce, 75040 Paris Cedex 1, France. adv.

631.4 AT ISSN 1032-5441
S599.7.A1
COMMONWEALTH SCIENTIFIC AND INDUSTRIAL RESEARCH ORGANIZATION. DIVISION OF SOILS. ANNUAL REPORT. 1949. a. free. C S I R O, Division of Soils, Private Bag No. 2, Glen Osmond, S.A. 5064, Australia. TEL 61-8-3038400. FAX 61-8-3038550. E-mail: library@adl.soils.csiro.au. R&P contact: Kathy Heinze. circ. 1,500. **Indexed:** Biol.Abstr., Soils & Fert. **Document type:** corporate report.
—CISTI.
Former titles (until 1986): Commonwealth Scientific and Industrial Research Organization. Division of Soils. Research Report (ISSN 0729-4336); (1972-1975): Commonwealth Scientific and Industrial Research Organization. Division of Soils. Biennial Report (ISSN 0069-7583)
Description: Outlines the research programs of the division.

631.4 AT ISSN 0725-8526
COMMONWEALTH SCIENTIFIC AND INDUSTRIAL RESEARCH ORGANIZATION. DIVISION OF SOILS. DIVISIONAL REPORT. 1975. irrog. Aus.$10 per no. C S I R O, Division of Soils, Private Bag 2, Glen Osmond, S.A. 5064, Australia. E-mail: library@adl.soils.csiro.au. (Subscr. to: CSIRO Publications, P.O. Box 89, E. Melbourne, Vic. 3002, Australia. TEL 61-3-4187333. FAX 61-3-4190459) R&P contact: Kathy Heinze. **Indexed:** Field Crop Abstr., Herb.Abstr., Soils & Fert., Triticale Abstr. **Document type:** academic/scholarly publication.
—BLDSC (3604.924750); CISTI.
Description: Papers on soil-related matters.

631 581 AT ISSN 1036-0220
S381
COMMONWEALTH SCIENTIFIC AND INDUSTRIAL RESEARCH ORGANIZATION. DIVISION OF TROPICAL CROPS AND PASTURES. BIENNIAL RESEARCH REPORT. 1988. biennial. free. C.S.I.R.O., Division of Tropical Crops and Pastures, St. Lucia, Brisbane, Qld. 4067, Australia. FAX 61-7-33713946. E-mail: library@tcp.csiro.au. R&P contact: Roger K. Jones. **Document type:** corporate report.

AGRICULTURE — CROP PRODUCTION AND SOIL

631 636   AT   ISSN 0159-6071
COMMONWEALTH SCIENTIFIC AND INDUSTRIAL RESEARCH ORGANIZATION. DIVISION OF TROPICAL CROPS AND PASTURES. GENETIC RESOURCES COMMUNICATION. 1980. irreg. free. C.S.I.R.O., Division of Tropical Crops and Pastures, St. Lucia, Brisbane, Qld. 4067, Australia.
TEL 61-7-33770209. FAX 61-7-33713946. E-mail: library@tcp.csiro.au. R&P contact: Roger K. Jones. **Document type:** monographic series.
—BLDSC (4111.910000).

631.5 581   AT   ISSN 0155-4077
                    CODEN: DTCADB
COMMONWEALTH SCIENTIFIC AND INDUSTRIAL RESEARCH ORGANIZATION. DIVISION OF TROPICAL CROPS AND PASTURES. TECHNICAL PAPER. 1961. irreg. Aus.$7 per issue. C.S.I.R.O., Division of Tropical Crops and Pastures, St. Lucia, Brisbane, Qld. 4067, Australia. TEL 61-7-33770209. FAX 61-7-33713946. E-mail: library@tcp.csiro.au. R&P contact: Roger K. Jones. circ. 900. **Indexed:** Aus.Sci.Ind., Biol.Abstr., Herb.Abstr., Soils & Fert. **Document type:** monographic series.
—CASDDS; CISTI; Linda Hall.
Supersedes (in 1977): C.S.I.R.O. Division of Tropical Agronomy. Technical Paper (ISSN 0155-4069); Which was formerly (until 1975): C.S.I.R.O. Division of Tropical Tropical Pastures Technical Paper (ISSN 0069-7613)

631.4   US   ISSN 0010-3624
S590   CODEN: CSOSA2
COMMUNICATIONS IN SOIL SCIENCE AND PLANT ANALYSIS. 1970. 20/yr. $1450 (foreign $1525) (effective 1998). Marcel Dekker Journals, 270 Madison Ave., New York, NY 10016.
TEL 212-696-9000. FAX 212-685-4540. TELEX 421419. (Subscr. to: Box 5017, Monticello, NY 12701) Ed. J. Benton Jones, Jr. adv. (also avail. in microform from RPI) **Indexed:** Agri.Eng.Abstr., Anal.Abstr., ASCA, Biol.Abstr., Biol.& Agr.Ind., Chem.Abstr., Chem.Cit.Ind., Cott.& Trop.Fibr.Abstr., Curr.Adv.Ecol.Sci., Curr.Cont., Ecol.Abstr., Energy Ind., Energy Info.Abstr., Environ.Per.Bibl. (1973-1994), Excerp.Med., Farm & Garden Ind., Field Crop.Abstr., Forest.Abstr., Forest Prod.Abstr., Geo.Abstr.H.G., Geo.Abstr.P.G., GeoRef., Herb.Abstr., Hort.Abstr., IDA, Ind.Sci.Rev., INIS Atomind., Irr.& Drain.Abstr., Maize Abstr., Ornam.Hort., Plant Grow.Reg.Abstr., Potato Abstr., Rice Abstr., Sci.Cit.Ind., Seed Abstr., Sel.Water Res.Abstr., Soils & Fert., Sorghum & Millets Abstr., Triticale Abstr., Weed Abstr. **Document type:** academic/scholarly publication.
—BLDSC (3363.420000); CASDDS; CISTI; EMDOCS; Genuine Article; Linda Hall; SWETS; UMI; UnCover. **CCC.**
Refereed Serial

631   US
COMPENDIUM OF PLANT DISEASE SERIES. irreg., no.22, 1991. $35 (foreign $44). (American Phytopathological Society) A P S Press, 3340 Pilot Knob Rd., St. Paul, MN 55121-2079.
TEL 612-454-7250; 800-328-7560.
FAX 612-454-0766. E-mail: aps@scisoc.org; URL: http://www.scisoc.org.

COMPOST SCIENCE & UTILIZATION. see
ENVIRONMENTAL STUDIES — Waste Management

CONNECTICUT GREENHOUSE NEWSLETTER. see
GARDENING AND HORTICULTURE

634   IO
CORD. (Text in English) s-a. $20 in Asia & Pacific; elsewhere $25. Asian and Pacific Coconut Community, Wisma Bakrie, 3rd Fl., Jl. H.R. Rasuna Said, Kuningan, Jakarta 12920, Indonesia.
FAX 0062-21-5205160. TELEX 62863 APCC IA.
Description: Devoted to original articles on coconut research and development.

633   US   ISSN 0069-9993
CORN ANNUAL. 1970. a. free. Corn Refiners Association, Inc., 1701 Pennsylvania Ave., N.W., Ste. 950, Washington, DC 20006. TEL 202-331-1634. FAX 202-331-2054. Ed. Deborah Schwartz. circ. 10,000. **Indexed:** SRI. **Document type:** trade publication.
—Linda Hall.

633.15   US
CORN FARMER. 1991. a. Meredith Corporation, 1716 Locust St., Des Moines, IA 50336.
TEL 515-284-2700. circ. 68,000 (controlled).
Description: For the Mid-Western farmer raising more than 250 acres of corn.

631
CORNELL FIELD CROPS AND SOILS HANDBOOK. every 10 yrs. $7.50. Cornell University, Media Services, 7-8 Business and Technology Park, Ithaca, NY 14850. TEL 607-255-2080. FAX 607-255-9946. **Document type:** bulletin.

632.9   US
CORNELL RECOMMENDATIONS FOR COMMERCIAL TURFGRASS MANAGEMENT. a. price varies. Cornell University, Media Services, 7-8 Business and Technology Park, Ithaca, NY 14850.
TEL 607-255-2080. FAX 607-255-9946. **Document type:** bulletin.

631   US
CORNELL RECOMMENDATIONS FOR FIELD CROPS. a. price varies. Cornell University, Media Services, 7-8 Business and Technology Park, Ithaca, NY 14850.
TEL 607-255-2080. FAX 607-255-9946. **Document type:** bulletin.

632.9   US
CORNELL RECOMMENDATIONS FOR PEST CONTROL FOR COMMERCIAL PRODUCTION AND MAINTENANCE OF TREES & SHRUBS. irreg. price varies. Cornell University, Media Services, 7-8 Business and Technology Park, Ithaca, NY 14850.
TEL 607-255-2080. FAX 607-255-9946. **Document type:** bulletin.

630.24   BL   ISSN 0100-3909
CORREIO AGRICOLA. 1961. s-a. free. Bayer do Brasil Industrias Quimicas S.A., C.P. 22-523, 04779-900 Sao Paulo SP, Brazil. TEL 011-525-5284.
FAX 011-525-5251. TELEX 011-57629. Ed. Sergio Malta Cardoso. adv.; bk.rev.; charts; illus. circ. 57,500 (controlled). **Document type:** trade publication.
Formerly (until 1969): Correio Agro-pecuario (ISSN 0010-9061)
Description: Contains information about cultivation and provides phytosanitary techniques.

630.24   PO
CORREIO AGRICOLA. Portuguese translation of: Pflanzenschutz Kurier. 1964. irreg. free. Bayer Portugal S A R L, Apdo. 3306, 1308 Lisbon, Portugal. TEL 417-21-21. FAX 417-20-64. (Main Office: Bayer Pflanzenschutz, Leverkusen, Germany) charts; illus.; circ. controlled.

633 330   US
COTTON ECONOMIC REVIEW. m. $50. National Cotton Council, 1918 N. Pkwy., Shelby County, Memphis, TN 38112. TEL 901-274-9030.
FAX 901-725-0510. TELEX 650-263-2485 MCI. Ed. Mark Lange. circ. 4,000.
Description: Covers U.S. cotton production, supply and exports.

633.51   US   ISSN 0194-9772
COTTON GROWER. 1964. 9/yr. $16.95 (effective 1997). Meister Publishing Co., 37733 Euclid Ave., Willoughby, OH 44094. TEL 216-942-2000. Ed. William Spencer. adv.; bk.rev.; charts; illus. circ. 57,000. **Indexed:** Text.Tech.Dig. **Document type:** trade publication.
—CCC.
Formerly: American Cotton Grower (ISSN 0044-765X)

633   KE
COTTON LINT AND SEED MARKETING BOARD. ANNUAL REPORT AND ACCOUNTS. (Text in English) a. Cotton Lint and Seed Marketing Board, P.O. Box 30477, Nairobi, Kenya. **Document type:** corporate report.

633   US
QK1   CODEN: CRPSD3
CRITICAL REVIEWS IN PLANT SCIENCES. 1983. bi-m. $495 (effective 1998). C R C Press, Inc., 2000 Corporate Blvd., N.W., Boca Raton, FL 33431.
TEL 561-994-0555; 800-272-7737.
FAX 561-998-9784. TELEX 568689-CRC PRESS. Ed. B.V. Conger. **Indexed:** Agri.Eng.Abstr., ASCA, Chem.Abstr., Cott.& Trop.Fibr.Abstr., Crop Physiol.Abstr., Curr.Adv.Ecol.Sci., Curr.Cont., Field Crop Abstr., Food Sci.& Tech.Abstr., Forest.Abstr., Herb.Abstr., Hort.Abstr., Ind.Sci.Rev., Maize Abstr., Plant Grow.Reg.Abstr., Potato Abstr., Sci.Cit.Ind., Soyabean Abstr., Triticale Abstr., Weed Abstr. **Document type:** academic/scholarly publication.
—BLDSC (3487.480000); CASDDS; CISTI; Genuine Article; Linda Hall; SWETS; UnCover. **CCC.**
Formerly: C R C Critical Reviews in Plant Sciences (ISSN 0735-2689)
Description: Presents current reviews on subjects in areas such as shortages in world food supply, energy resources, the role of research in increasing crop productivity; also basic research areas in photosynthesis, nitrogen fixation, gene regulation, and genetic engineering.
Refereed Serial

631   RH
CROP BREEDING INSTITUTE. ANNUAL REPORT. 1975. a. free. Ministry of Lands, Agriculture and Rural Resettlement, Research and Specialist Services, Information Services, P.O. Box 8108, Causeway, Harare, Zimbabwe. circ. 250. (back issues avail.)

CROP PRODUCTION HALF-YEARLY STATISTICS. see
AGRICULTURE — Abstracting, Bibliographies, Statistics

CROP PROTECTION; an international journal of pest, disease & weed control. see *ENGINEERING — Chemical Engineering*

630.24   GW   ISSN 0590-1243
CROP PROTECTION COURIER (INTERNATIONAL). German edition: Pflanzenschutz-Kurier (ISSN 0722-0510) Spanish edition: Correo Fitosanitario (International). 1960. 3/yr. free. Bayer AG, Abteilung Publikationen, 51368 Leverkusen, Germany.
TEL 49-214-3062875. FAX 49-214-3071985. Ed. Bernhard Grupp. charts; illus.; circ. 33,500 (controlled). **Document type:** bulletin.

631   UK   ISSN 0953-2463
THE CROP PROTECTION DIRECTORY. 1988. a. £110. Elaine Warrell Associates, 105 Lee Rd., London SE3 9DZ, England. TEL 0181-852-6158.
FAX 0181-297-0789. Ed. Elaine Warrell. **Document type:** directory.
—BLDSC (3488.370000).

631   II   ISSN 0970-4884
                CODEN: CROREU
CROP RESEARCH; an international journal. (Text in English) 1988. 3/yr. Rs.100($40) membership. Agricultural Research Information Centre, 1314 HIG-II (GF), Housing Board Colony, Sec. 15A, Hisar 125 001, India. Ed. Vedpal Singh. adv.: page Rs.1600 or $160. (back issues avail.) **Indexed:** Biol.Abstr., Field Crop Abstr., Forest.Abstr., Herb.Abstr., Hort.Abstr., Plant Breed Abstr., Protozool.Abstr., Rev.Plant Path., Sorghum & Millets Abstr., Weed Abstr., World Agri.Econ.& Rural Sociol.Abstr. **Document type:** academic/scholarly publication.
—BLDSC (3488.472000).
Description: Contains original research on crops relating to basic and applied aspects of agriculture botany, crop physiology, entomology, horticulture, soil sciences and vegetable crops.

AGRICULTURE — CROP PRODUCTION AND SOIL

631 US ISSN 0011-183X
SB183 CODEN: CRPSAY
CROP SCIENCE. 1961. bi-m. $118. Crop Science Society of America, 677 S. Segoe Rd., Madison, WI 53711. TEL 608-273-8080. FAX 608-273-2021. URL: http://www.agronomy.org/journals/cs.html. Ed. John Radin. adv. contact: Keith R. Schlesinger. charts; illus.; index. circ. 7,300. **Indexed:** Agri.Eng.Abstr., Apic.Abstr., ASCA, Bibl.Agri., Biol.Abstr., Biol.& Agr.Ind., Biol.Dig., Biotech.Abstr., Chem.Abstr., Cott.& Trop.Fibr.Abstr., Crop Physiol.Abstr., Curr.Adv.Ecol.Sci., Curr.Adv.Genetics & Molec.Biol., Curr.Cont., Excerp.Med., Farm & Garden Ind., Field Crop Abstr., Food Sci.& Tech.Abstr., Helminthol.Abstr., Herb.Abstr., Hort.Abstr., Ind.Sci.Rev., Irr.& Drain.Abstr., Maize Abstr., Nutr.Abstr., Ornam.Hort., Plant Breed Abstr., Plant Grow.Reg.Abstr., Rev.Appl.Entomol., Rev.Med.& Vet.Mycol., Rev.Plant Path., Sci.Cit.Ind., Seed Abstr., Sel.Water Res.Abstr., Soils & Fert., Sorghum & Millets Abstr., Soyabean Abstr., THA, Triticale Abstr., Trop.Oil Seeds Abstr., VITIS, Weed Abstr. **Document type:** academic/scholarly publication.
—BLDSC (3488.500000); CASDDS; CISTI; EMDOCS; Genuine Article; KR SourceOne; Linda Hall; SWETS; UnCover. **CCC.**
Description: Reports on recent developments in crop breeding and genetics, crop physiology and biochemistry, ecology, cytology, crop and seed production, statistics, and weed control.

631 UK ISSN 0266-5174
CROPS; the practical management journal for arable farmers. 1984. fortn. £55 (effective 1996). Reed Business Publishing Ltd., Farmers Publishing Group (Subsidiary of: Reed Elsevier group), Quadrant House, The Quadrant, Sutton, Surrey SM2 5AS, England. TEL 44-181-652-4081. FAX 44-181-652-8928. TELEX 892084-REEDBP-G. Ed. Debbie Beaton. R&P contact: Debbie Beaton. adv. contact: Vic Bunby. circ. 32,800. (tabloid format; back issues avail.) **Document type:** trade publication.
—BLDSC (3488.645500).
Description: Directed at arable farmers. Focuses on agronomy and business management.

631 CN
CROSSROADS. 1973. w. Wenger Bros. Ltd., Box 390, Wingham, Ont., Canada. Ed. Barry Wenger. adv.; bk.rev. circ. 20,000. (also avail. in microfilm)

634 CU ISSN 0138-8339
CUBA. CENTRO DE INFORMACION Y DOCUMENTACION AGROPECUARIO. BOLETIN DE RESENAS. SERIE: CITRICOS. (Abstracts in English) 1974. irreg. exchange basis. Centro de Informacion y Documentacion Agropecuario, Gaveta Postal 4149, Havana 4, Cuba. TEL 292227. (Dist. by: Ediciones Cubanas, Obispo No. 461, Apdo. 605, Havana, Cuba) abstr.; charts; stat. **Indexed:** Agrindex.
Formerly: Cuba. Centro de Informacion y Divulgacion Agropecuario. Boletin de Resenas. Serie: Citricos y Otras Frutales.

631 CU ISSN 0138-8436
CUBA. CENTRO DE INFORMACION Y DOCUMENTACION AGROPECUARIO. BOLETIN DE RESENAS. SERIE: CAFE Y CACAO. (Abstracts in English) 1980. irreg. exchange basis. Centro de Informacion y Documentacion Agropecuario, Gaveta Postal 4149, Havana 4, Cuba. TEL 301672. (Dist. by: Ediciones Cubanas, Obispo No. 461, Apdo. 605, Havana, Cuba) stat. **Indexed:** Agrindex.
Formerly: Cuba. Centro de Informacion y Divulgacion Agropecuario. Boletin de Resenas. Serie: Cafe y Cacao.

631 CU ISSN 0138-8231
CUBA. CENTRO DE INFORMACION Y DOCUMENTACION AGROPECUARIO. BOLETIN DE RESENAS. SERIE: HORTALIZAS, PAPAS, GRANOS Y FIBRAS. (Abstracts in English) 1984. irreg. exchange basis. Centro de Informacion y Documentacion Agropecuario, Gaveta Postal 4149, Havana 4, Cuba. (Dist. by: Ediciones Cubanas, Obispo No. 461, Apdo. 605, Havana, Cuba) **Indexed:** Agrindex.
Supersedes in part: Cuba. Centro de Informacion y Divulgacion Agropecuario. Boletin de Resenas. Serie: Viandas, Hortalizas y Granos.

631 CU ISSN 0138-8088
CUBA. CENTRO DE INFORMACION Y DOCUMENTACION AGROPECUARIO. BOLETIN DE RESENAS. SERIE: PROTECCION DE PLANTAS. (Abstracts in English) 1974. s-a. exchange basis. Centro de Informacion y Documentacion Agropecuario, Gaveta Postal 4149, Havana 4, Cuba. TEL 301672. TELEX 051-1007. (Dist. by: Ediciones Cubanas, Obispo No. 461, Apdo. 605, Havana, Cuba) **Indexed:** Agrindex.
Formerly: Cuba. Centro de Informacion y Divulgacion Agropecuario. Boletin de Resenas. Serie: Proteccion de Plantas.

631.7 CU ISSN 0138-788X
CUBA. CENTRO DE INFORMACION Y DOCUMENTACION AGROPECUARIO. BOLETIN DE RESENAS. SERIE: RIEGO Y DRENAJE. (Abstracts in English) 1974. irreg. exchange basis. Centro de Informacion y Documentacion Agropecuario, Gaveta Postal 4149, Havana 4, Cuba. (Dist. by: Ediciones Cubanas, Obispo No. 461, Apdo. 605, Havana, Cuba) **Indexed:** Agrindex, Field Crop Abstr., Herb.Abstr., Hort.Abstr.
Formerly: Cuba. Centro de Informacion y Divulgacion Agropecuario. Boletin de Resenas. Serie: Riego y Drenaje.

631.7 CU ISSN 0138-7936
CUBA. CENTRO DE INFORMACION Y DOCUMENTACION AGROPECUARIO. BOLETIN DE RESENAS. SERIE: SUELOS Y AGROQUIMICA. (Abstracts in English) 1974. irreg. exchange basis. Centro de Informacion y Documentacion Agropecuario, Gaveta Postal 4149, Havana 4, Cuba. (Dist. by: Ediciones Cubanas, Obispo No. 461, Apdo. 605, Havana, Cuba) **Indexed:** Agrindex.
Formerly: Cuba. Centro de Informacion y Divulgacion Agropecuario. Boletin de Resenas. Serie: Suelos y Agroquimica.

631 CU ISSN 0253-5777
SB215 CODEN: CEAZDS
CUBA. MINISTERIO DE EDUCACION SUPERIOR. CENTRO AZUCAR. 3/yr. $20 in N. and S. America; Europe $24. Ediciones Cubanas, Obispo No. 527, Apdo. 605, Havana, Cuba. **Indexed:** Sugar Ind.Abstr.
—BLDSC (3113.170220); CASDDS.

631 CU
CUBA. MINISTERIO DEL AZUCAR. INSTITUTO DE INVESTIGACIONES DE LA CANA DE AZUCAR. BOLETIN. 3/yr. Ministerio del Azucar, Instituto de Investigaciones de la Cana de Azucar, Ave. Vantroi No. 17 203, Boyeros, Havana, Cuba. **Indexed:** Irr.& Drain.Abstr.

633.6 CU ISSN 0590-2916
HD9114.C88C78 CODEN: CUAZAZ
CUBA AZUCAR. (Text in Spanish; summaries in English, French) 1966. q. $20 in N. and S. America; Europe $24. (Ministerio de la Azucarera) Ediciones Cubanas, Obispo No. 527, Apdo. 605, Havana, Cuba. Dir. Rodolfo Escriva. abstr.; charts; bibl.; illus.; stat. **Indexed:** Food Sci.& Tech.Abstr., Sugar Ind.Abstr.
—CASDDS.

631 CU ISSN 0258-5936
SB111.A2
CULTIVOS TROPICALES. (Text in English or Spanish; summaries in English and Spanish) 1979. 3/yr. $30 (effective Jan. 1997). Instituto Nacional de Ciencias Agricolas, Gaveta Postal No. 1, San Jose de las Lajas, Havana 32700, Cuba. TEL 537-64-63290. FAX 537-64-63867. E-mail: inca@redunix.edu.cu. Ed. Maria Mariana Perez Jorge. adv. contact: Walfredo Torres de la Moral. circ. 350. **Indexed:** Abstr.Trop.Agri., Agrindex, Hort.Abstr., Plant Grow.Reg.Abstr., Ref.Zh., Rice Abstr., Soyabean Abstr., Weed Abstr. **Document type:** academic/scholarly publication.
●Also available online.
Also available on CD-ROM.
Description: Includes scientific resuls of agricultural reseaches.
Refereed Serial

CURRENT AGRO-TECHNOLOGY FOR POTATO PRODUCTION. see AGRICULTURE

CURRENT PLANT SCIENCE AND BIOTECHNOLOGY IN AGRICULTURE. see BIOLOGY — Biotechnology

631.7 627 BL
D N O C S - FINS E ATIVIDADES. irreg. Departamento Nacional de Obras Contra as Secas, Fortaleza, Ceara, Brazil. illus.

DAIRY AND FIELD CROP DIGEST. see AGRICULTURE — Dairying And Dairy Products

631 DK ISSN 0106-3863
DANSK FROEAVL. (Supplements avail.: Samvirkende Danske Froeavlerforeninger. Temhaefte (ISSN 0901-7461), Dansk Froeavl Info (ISSN 0907-5704)) (Text in Danish) 1918. fortn. DKK 550($30) Samvirkende Danske Froeavlerforeninger - Federation of Danish Seedgrowers Association, Ledreborg Alle 104, DK-4000 Roskilde, Denmark. TEL 46-32-33-33. FAX 46-32-08-11. Ed. Niels Vestergaard Olsen. adv.; index. circ. 3,000. (back issues avail.) **Indexed:** Field Crop Abstr., Herb.Abstr., Soils & Fert.
—BLDSC (3526.050000).
Incorporates (1946-1973): Dansk Havefroeavl (ISSN 0106-3855)

631.8 US ISSN 1043-3104
HD9483.U5 CODEN: DEPREN
DEALER PROGRESS. 1970. bi-m. $40 (foreign $80). Clear Window, Inc., 15444 Clayton Rd., Ballwin, MO 63011. TEL 314-527-4001. FAX 314-527-4010. Ed. K. Elliott Nowels. adv. circ. 26,000 (controlled). **Document type:** trade publication.
—BLDSC (3535.960105); CISTI.
Former titles (until 1988): Progress (ISSN 0895-1616); (until 1987): Fertilizer Progress (ISSN 0002-1598)
Description: For the commercial fertilizer and agricultural chemical retail dealer.

632.95 DK
DENMARK. BEKAEMPELSESMIDDELFORSKNING FRA MILJOESTYRELSEN. 1990. irreg. price varies. Miljoestyrelsen - Danish Environmental Protection Agency, Strandgade 29, DK-1401 Copenhagen K, Denmark. TEL 45-32-66-01-00. Ed.Bd. circ. 500.

631 DK ISSN 0905-8478
DENMARK. KGL. VETERINAER- OG LANDBOHOEJSKOLE. FORSKNINGSRAPPORT/RESEARCH REPORT. irreg. free. Kgl. Veterinaer- og Landbohoejskole, Institut for Jordbrugsvidenskab, Sektion for Kulturteknik og Planteernaering, Thorvaldsens vej 40, DK-1871 Frederiksberg C, Denmark. TEL 45-35-28-34-96. FAX 45-35-28-34-60.
Formerly: Denmark. Kgl. Veterinaer- og Landbohoejskole. Meddelelser (ISSN 0105-2543)

632.9 ET ISSN 0418-761X
DESERT LOCUST CONTROL ORGANIZATION FOR EASTERN AFRICA. ANNUAL REPORT. 1962. a. free. Desert Locust Control Organization for Eastern Africa, P.O. Box 4255, Addis Ababa, Ethiopia. TEL 251-1-611475. FAX 251-1-611648. TELEX 21510 DLCO ET. **Indexed:** Rev.Appl.Entomol.
Supersedes: East Africa High Commissions Desert Locust Survey. Report.

634.8 GW ISSN 0943-089X
DAS DEUTSCHE WEINMAGAZIN. 1946. 2/mo. DM.131.40 (foreign DM.167.40) (effective 1997). Fachverlag Dr. Fraund GmbH, Postfach 1329, 61364 Friedrichsdorf, Germany. TEL 49-6172-7106-0. FAX 49-6172-710610. adv.; bk.rev. circ. 9,400. **Indexed:** Biol.Abstr., Chem.Abstr., Excerp.Med., Food Sci.& Tech.Abstr., Rural Recreat.Tour.Abstr., VITIS, World Agri.Econ.& Rural Sociol.Abstr. **Document type:** trade publication.
Formerly (until 1992): Deutsche Weinbau (ISSN 0012-0979)

630 NE ISSN 0167-4137
CODEN: DAENDT
DEVELOPMENTS IN AGRICULTURAL ENGINEERING. 1980. irreg., vol.10, 1989. price varies. Elsevier Science B.V., Books Division, P.O. Box 211, 1000 AE Amsterdam, Netherlands. TEL 31-20-4853911. FAX 31-20-4853705. TELEX 18582 ESPA NL. E-mail: nlinfo-f@elsevier.nl; usinfo-f@elsevier.com; forinfo-kyf04035@niftyserve.or.jp; URL: http://www.elsevier.nl/. (Subscr. in the Americas to: Elsevier Science, Regional Sales Office, Box 945, New York, NY 10159-0945. TEL 212-633-3730. FAX 212-633-3680; Subscr. in Australasia and the Far East to: Elsevier Science (Singapore) Pte Ltd, No.1 Temasek Ave., No.17-01 Millenia Tower, Singapore 039192, Singapore. TEL 65-434-3727. FAX 65-337-2230; Subscr. in Japan to: Elsevier Science Japan, 9-15 Higashi-Azabu 1-chome, Minato-ku, Tokyo 106, Japan. TEL 81-3-5561-5033. FAX 81-3-5561-5047) (back issues avail.) **Document type:** monographic series.
—BLDSC (3579.061200); CASDDS; CISTI.
Refereed Serial

AGRICULTURE — CROP PRODUCTION AND SOIL

631   NE   ISSN 0378-519X
CODEN: DCSCDC
DEVELOPMENTS IN CROP SCIENCE. (Text in English) 1975. irreg., vol.22, 1992. price varies. Elsevier Science B.V., Books Division, P.O. Box 211, 1000 AE Amsterdam, Netherlands. TEL 31-20-4853911. FAX 31-20-4853705. TELEX 18582 ESPA NL. E-mail: nlinfo-f@elsevier.nl; usinfo-f@elsevier.com; forinfo-kyf04035@niftyserve.or.jp; URL: http://www.elsevier.nl/. (Subscr. in the Americas to: Elsevier Science, Regional Sales Office, Box 945, New York, NY 10159-0945. TEL 212-633-3730. FAX 212-633-3680; Subscr. in Australasia and the Far East to: Elsevier Science (Singapore) Pte Ltd, No.1 Temasek Ave., No.17-01 Millenia Tower, Singapore 039192, Singapore. TEL 65-434-3727. FAX 65-337-2230; Subscr. in Japan to: Elsevier Science Japan, 9-15 Higashi-Azabu 1-chome, Minato-ku, Tokyo 106, Japan. TEL 81-3-5561-5033. FAX 81-3-5561-5047) (back issues avail.) **Document type:** monographic series.
—BLDSC (3579.070100); CASDDS; CISTI.
Refereed Serial

631   NE   ISSN 0167-840X
CODEN: DVPSD8
DEVELOPMENTS IN PLANT AND SOIL SCIENCES. 1981. irreg., vol.51, 1993. Kluwer Academic Publishers, Postbus 17, 3300 AA Dordrecht, Netherlands. TEL 31-78-6392392. FAX 31-78-6392254. TELEX 29245 KAPG NL. E-mail: services@wkap.nl; URL: http://www.wkap.nl. (Dist. by: Kluwer Academic Publishers Group, P.O. Box 322, 3300 AH Dordrecht, Netherlands. TEL 31-78-6392392. FAX 31-78-6546474; N. America dist. addr.: Box 358, Accord Sta., Hingham, MA 02018-0358. TEL 617-871-6600. FAX 617-871-6528) **Indexed:** Chem.Abstr., Soils & Fert. **Document type:** monographic series.
—BLDSC (3579.086080); CASDDS; CISTI.
Refereed Serial

631.4   NE   ISSN 0166-0918
CODEN: DSSCDM
DEVELOPMENTS IN SOIL SCIENCE. 1972. irreg., vol.21, 1993. price varies. Elsevier Science B.V., Books Division, P.O. Box 211, 1000 AE Amsterdam, Netherlands. TEL 31-20-4853911. FAX 31-20-4853705. TELEX 18582 ESPA NL. E-mail: nlinfo-f@elsevier.nl; usinfo-f@elsevier.com; forinfo-kyf04035@niftyserve.or.jp; URL: http://www.elsevier.nl/. (Subscr. in the Americas to: Elsevier Science, Regional Sales Office, Box 945, New York, NY 10159-0945. TEL 212-633-3730. FAX 212-633-3680; Subscr. in Australasia and the Far East to: Elsevier Science (Singapore) Pte Ltd, No.1 Temasek Ave., No.17-01 Millenia Tower, Singapore 039192, Singapore. TEL 65-434-3727. FAX 65-337-2230; Subscr. in Japan to: Elsevier Science Japan, 9-15 Higashi-Azabu 1-chome, Minato-ku, Tokyo 106, Japan. TEL 81-3-5561-5033. FAX 81-3-5561-5047) (back issues avail.) **Indexed:** Biol.Abstr., GeoRef. **Document type:** monographic series.
—BLDSC (3579.090000); CASDDS; CISTI. CCC.
Refereed Serial

DIENST LANDBOUWKUNDIG ONDERZOEK. STARING CENTRUM, INSTITUUT VOOR ONDERZOEK VAN HET LANDELIJK GEBIED. JAARBOEK. see *ENVIRONMENTAL STUDIES*

DIENST LANDBOUWKUNDIG ONDERZOEK. STARING CENTRUM, INSTITUUT VOOR ONDERZOEK VAN HET LANDELIJK GEBIED. RAPPORT. see *ENVIRONMENTAL STUDIES*

631   IT   ISSN 0391-4119
LA DIFESA DELLE PIANTE; rivista trimestrale di fitoiatria fitofarmacia e diserbo. 1978. q. L.29. Cooperativa Libraria Universitaria Editrice Bologna, Via Marsala 24, 40126 Bologna, Italy. TEL 051-220736. FAX 051-237758. Ed. Roberta Robert. adv.; bk.rev.; index. circ. 900. (back issues avail.) **Indexed:** Bio-Contr.News & Info., Entomol.Abstr., Hort.Abstr., Seed Abstr., Soils & Fert., Triticale Abstr., Weed Abstr.

     VE
DIRECTORIO INDUSTRIAL AZUCARERO. 1972. a. Bs.50. Distribuidora Venezolana de Azucares, Departamento de Promocion Industrial, Edificio Torre Europa, Av. de Miranda, Caracas 106, Venezuela. adv.; charts; stat.

631.4   FR   ISSN 0180-9555
CODEN: DOPEDJ
DOCUMENTS PEDOZOOLOGIQUES. (Text in French; summaries in English) 1979. irreg. free to qualified personnel. Institut National de la Recherche Agronomique, Laboratoire de Zooecologie du Sol, CEPE, B.P. 5051, F-34033 Montpellier Cedex, France. Ed. M.B. Bouche. circ. 300. **Indexed:** Biol.Abstr., Chem.Abstr., Zoo.Rec.
—CASDDS.

DOJO BISEIBUTSU KENKYUKAI KOEN YOSHUSHU/SOIL MICROBIOLOGICAL SOCIETY OF JAPAN. ABSTRACTS OF THE MEETING. see *BIOLOGY — Abstracting, Bibliographies, Statistics*

631   IO
DOMESTIC MARKETING OF COCONUT PRODUCTS. a.? $15. Asian and Pacific Coconut Community, Wisma Bakrie, 3rd Fl., Jl. H.R. Rasuna Said, Kuningan, Jakarta 12920, Indonesia. TEL 62-21-510-073. FAX 62-21-520-5160. TELEX 62863 APCCIA. **Document type:** monographic series.
Description: Analyzes the current status of Indonesian marketing of coconut products in relation to its share in the export market.

DROUGHT NETWORK NEWS. see *WATER RESOURCES*

633.491   NE   ISSN 0376-4729
CODEN: ACEPDG
E A P R ABSTRACTS OF CONFERENCE PAPERS. (Text in English, French, German) 1961 (1st Conference in 1960). triennial. fl.65($38) European Association for Potato Research, Postbus 20, 6700 AA Wageningen, Netherlands. TEL 31-317-483041. FAX 31-317-484575. URL: http://www.agro.wau.nl.eapr. circ. 700. **Indexed:** Field Crop Abstr., Herb.Abstr. **Document type:** proceedings.
—BLDSC (9050.458000).
Formerly (until 1975): European Association for Potato Research. Proceedings of the Triennial Conference (ISSN 0071-2507)

632   UK   ISSN 0250-8052
CODEN: OEPBAO
E P P O BULLETIN. Variant title: Bulletin O E P P. (Text in English and French) 1951; N.S. 1971. q. £198($362) (foreign £218) (effective 1998). (European and Mediterranean Plant Protection Organization - Organisation Europeenne et Mediterraneenne pour la Protection des Plantes) Blackwell Science Ltd., Osney Mead, Oxford OX2 0EL, England. TEL 44-1865-206206. FAX 44-1865-721205. E-mail: journals.cs@blacksci.co.uk; URL: http://www.black.co.uk. Ed. I.M. Smith; Pub. Allen Stevens. R&P contact: Sarah Pollard. adv. contact: Martine Cariou-Keen. bk.rev.; abstr.; bibl.; charts; illus. circ. 8QO. (also avail. in microform from UMI; back issues avail.) **Indexed:** Agri.Eng.Abstr., Biodet.Abstr., Fababean Abstr., Field Crop Abstr., Forest.Abstr., Hort.Abstr., Maize Abstr., Plant Breed.Abstr., Potato Abstr., Rev.Plant Path., Seed Abstr., Soils & Fert., Weed Abstr. **Document type:** academic/scholarly publication.
—BLDSC (3794.370000); CASDDS; UMI. CCC.
Former titles: European and Mediterranean Plant Protection Organization. Publications. Series A: Reports of Technical Meetings; European and Mediterranean Plant Protection Organization. Publications. Series C: Reports of Working Parties (ISSN 0071-240X)
Refereed Serial

EARTH GARDEN. see *NEW AGE PUBLICATIONS*

634   BE   ISSN 0775-6771
L'ECHO DE NOS VERGERS. (Text in French) 1987. m. membership. Ligues Pomologiques Wallonnes, Rue de la Resistance 11, 5100 Wepion, Belgium. TEL 32-81-625620. FAX 32-81-611202. Ed. A. Sansdrap.
Description: Covers technical and economic aspects of fruit production.

ECONOMIA CAFETERA. see *AGRICULTURE — Agricultural Economics*

630.24 668.6   EC
ECUADOR. INSTITUTO NACIONAL DE INVESTIGACIONES AGROPECUARIAS. INFORME TECNICO. irreg. Instituto Nacional de Investigaciones Agropecuarias, Departamento de Comunicacion, Casilla 2600, Quito, Ecuador.

631.7   UA   ISSN 0302-6701
S590   CODEN: EJSSAF
EGYPTIAN JOURNAL OF SOIL SCIENCE. Key Title: Al-Magallat al-Misriyyat li-'Ulum al-Aradi. (Text in English; summaries in English and Arabic) 1961. 4/yr. $107 (effective 1997). (Society of Soil Science, Research Department) National Information and Documentation Centre (NIDOC), Tahrir St., Dokki, Awqaf P.O., Cairo, Egypt. TEL 20-2-3371696. Ed. H.M. Hamdi. abstr.; bibl.; charts. circ. 1,500. (reprint service avail. from IRC) **Indexed:** Biol.Abstr., Chem.Abstr., Curr.Adv.Ecol.Sci., Excerp.Med., Field Crop Abstr., GeoRef., Herb.Abstr., Hort.Abstr., Soils & Fert. **Document type:** academic/scholarly publication.
—BLDSC (3664.420000); CASDDS; CISTI; Linda Hall; UnCover.
Supersedes (in 1972): Magallat 'Ulum al-Aradi lil-Gumhuriyyat al-'Arabiyyat al-Muttahidah (ISSN 0449-3176)

633.851   MY   ISSN 0128-1828
CODEN: ELAEE3
ELAEIS; the international journal of oil palm research and development. (Text in English) 1989. s-a. M.$40($30) Palm Oil Research Institute of Malaysia, P.O. Box 10620, 50720 Kuala Lumpur, Malaysia. TEL 03-8259155. FAX 03-8259446. URL: http://porim.gov.my. Ed. Yusof Basiron. bk.rev. circ. 500. (back issues avail.) **Indexed:** Chem.Abstr., Food Sci.& Tech.Abstr. **Document type:** academic/scholarly publication.
—BLDSC (3670.110000); CASDDS.

ENSAYOS SOBRE ECONOMIA CAFETERA. see *AGRICULTURE — Agricultural Economics*

631.7   IT   ISSN 0014-1100
EST SESIA. 1954. q. free. Associazione Irrigazione Est Sesia, Via Negroni 7, Novara, Italy. Ed. Sergio Baratti. charts; illus. circ. 10,000.
Description: Focuses on irrigation and land reclamation.

631 581   SP   ISSN 0365-1800
S15
ESTACION EXPERIMENTAL DE AULA DEI. ANALES. (Text and summaries in English and Spanish) 1948. a. 3800 ptas. (effective 1995). Estacion Experimental de Aula Dei, Apdo. de Correos 202, C. Montanana 177, 50081 Zaragoza, Spain. TEL 34-76-576511. FAX 34-76-575620. E-mail: martinez@mizar.csic.es. Ed.J. Abadia Bayona. circ. 1,000. (back issues avail.) **Indexed:** Biol.Abstr., Bull.Signal., Chem.Abstr., Crop Physiol.Abstr., Hort.Abstr., Ind.SST, Plant Breed.Abstr., Plant Grow.Reg.Abstr., Soils & Fert., VITIS, Zoo.Rec.
Description: Original research in agriculture and related subjects.
Refereed Serial

631.4   FR   ISSN 1252-6851
CODEN: BUFSAS
ETUDES ET GESTION DES SOLS. (Supplement avail.: Lettre de l'Association (ISSN 0295-1347)) (Text and summaries in English, French) 1963. q. 300 F. Association Francaise pour l'Etude du Sol, 2 rue Le Notre, 49045 Angers Cedex 01, France. TEL 33-2-41225421. FAX 33-2-41731557. E-mail rossignol@angers.inra.fr. Ed. Jean-Pierre Rossignol. bk.rev.; charts; index; circ. 1,300 (controlled). **Indexed:** Biol.Abstr., Chem.Abstr., Excerp.Med., GeoRef., Soils & Fert.
—CASDDS.
Supersedes in part (in 1993): Science du Sol (ISSN 0767-2853); Which was formerly (until 1983): Association Francaise pour l'Etude du Sol. Bulletin (ISSN 0335-1653); Which was formed by the merger of (1963-1973): Science du Sol (ISSN 0036-8318); And (1957-1973): Association Francaise pour l'Etude du Sol. Bulletin (ISSN 0519-0800).

AGRICULTURE — CROP PRODUCTION AND SOIL

631.53   NE   ISSN 0014-2336
CODEN: EUPHAA
EUPHYTICA; international journal on plant breeding. (Text in English) 1952. 18/yr. fl.2910 to institutions; $1494 to institutions in U.S. (effective 1998). (Stichting Euphytica - Foundation Euphytica) Kluwer Academic Publishers, Postbus 17, 3300 AA Dordrecht, Netherlands. TEL 31-78-6392392. FAX 31-78-6392254. TELEX 29245 KAPG NL. E-mail: services@wkap.nl; URL: http://www.wkap.nl. (Dist. by: Kluwer Academic Publishers Group, P.O. Box 322, 3300 AH Dordrecht, Netherlands. TEL 31-78-6392392. FAX 31-78-6546474; N. America dist. addr.: Box 358, Accord Sta., Hingham, MA 02018-0358. TEL 617-871-6600. FAX 617-871-6528) Ed. A.C. Zeven. adv.; bk.rev.; bibl.; charts; illus.; index. (also avail. in microform from UMI; reprint service avail. from SWZ) **Indexed:** Apic.Abstr., ASCA, Biol.Abstr., Chem.Abstr., Compumath, Cott.& Trop.Fibr.Abstr., Crop Physiol.Abstr., Curr.Adv.Ecol.Sci., Curr.Cont., Field Crop Abstr., Food Sci.& Tech.Abstr., Forest.Abstr., Helminthol.Abstr., Herb.Abstr., Ind.Sci.Rev., Irr.& Drain.Abstr., Maize Abstr., Ornam.Hort., Plant Breed.Abstr., Plant Grow.Reg.Abstr., Potato Abstr., Rev.Plant Path., Rice Abstr., Sci.Cit.Ind., Seed Abstr., Soils & Fert., Sorghum & Millets Abstr., Triticale Abstr., Trop.Oil Seeds Abstr., VITIS, Weed Abstr. **Document type:** academic/scholarly publication.
—BLDSC (3828.000000); CASDDS; CISTI; EMDOCS; Genuine Article; Linda Hall; SWETS; UMI; UnCover. **CCC.**
   Description: Publishes original research results, critical reviews and short communications on all aspects of plant breeding research.
Refereed Serial

631.4   RU   ISSN 1064-2293
S590   CODEN: ESSCEY
EURASIAN SOIL SCIENCE. English translation of: Pochvovedenie (RU ISSN 0032-180X) 1958. m. $1575 (foreign $1761) (effective 1997). (Russian Academy of Sciences, RU) Maik Nauka - Interperiodica, Mezhdunarodnyi Otdel, Ul. Profsoyuznaya, 90, 117864 Moscow, Russia. (Dist. by: Maik Nauka - Interperiodica, Subscription Office, Box 1831, Birmingham, AL 35201-1831, U.S.A. TEL 205-995-1567. FAX 205-995-1588) Ed. Andrew P. Mazurak. adv.; bk.rev.; abstr.; bibl.; charts; illus.; index. circ. 500. (also avail. in microform from UMI) **Indexed:** Agri.Eng.Abstr., Agroforest.Abstr., ASCA, Biol.Abstr., Curr.Adv.Ecol.Sci., Curr.Cont., Field Crop Abstr., Forest.Abstr., Geo.Abstr.P.G., Geotech.Abstr., IBR, IDA, Irr.& Drain.Abstr., Potato Abstr., Rice Abstr., Sci.Cit.Ind., Sel.Water Res.Abstr., Soils & Fert., Triticale Abstr., Weed Abstr. **Document type:** academic/scholarly publication.
—BLDSC (0411.747000); EMDOCS; Genuine Article; KR SourceOne; Linda Hall; SWETS; UMI. **CCC.**
   Formerly (until 1992): Soviet Soil Science (ISSN 0038-5832)
   Description: Covers current Russian literature on all aspects of the soil sciences, including mineralogy and physical properties of soils, as well as soil melioration, irrigation and drainage, forest and range soils, soil pollution and management. Also includes selected relevant articles from periodicals in related fields such as agricultural engineering.

EUROFRUIT MAGAZINE. see *FOOD AND FOOD INDUSTRIES — Grocery Trade*

633   BE   ISSN 0071-2825
EUROPEAN GRASSLAND FEDERATION. PROCEEDINGS OF THE GENERAL MEETING. 1965. irreg. 48 Fr. European Grassland Federation, c/o Rijksstation voor Plantenveredeling, Burg. Van Gansberghelaan 109, 9220 Merelbeke, Belgium. (Inquiries to: J.W. Minderhoud, Department of Field Crops and Grassland Husbandry, State Agricultural University, Haarweg 33, Wageningen, Netherlands) circ. 340.

631.4   UK   ISSN 1351-0754
S590   CODEN: ESOSES
EUROPEAN JOURNAL OF SOIL SCIENCE. q. £156($285.50) (foreign £172) (effective 1998). (British Society of Soil Science) Blackwell Science Ltd., Osney Mead, Oxford OX2 OEL, England. TEL 44-1865-206206. FAX 44-1865-721205. E-mail: journals.cs@blacksci.co.uk; URL: http://www.black.co.uk. (Co-sponsor: National Societies of Soil Science in Europe) Ed. R. Webster; Pub. Allen Stevens. R&P contact: Sarah Pollard. adv. contact: Martine Cariou-Keen. bk.rev.; bibl.; charts; illus.; index. circ. 2,165. (also avail. in microform from UMI; back issues avail) **Indexed:** Acid Pre.Dig., Agri.Eng.Abstr., Appl.Mech.Rev., ASCA, Ash.G.Bot.Per., Biol.Abstr., Biol.& Agr.Ind., Br.Archaeol.Abstr., Br.Ceram.Abstr., Cadscan, Chem.Abstr., Curr.Adv.Ecol.Sci., Curr.Cont., Ecol.Abstr., Ecol.Abstr., Field Crop Abstr., Forest.Abstr., Forest Prod.Abstr., Geo.Abstr.P.G., Geol.Abstr., Geotech.Abstr., Hort.Abstr., HRIS, Ind.Sci.Rev., Irr.& Drain.Abstr., Lead Abstr., Maize Abstr., Mat.Sci.Cit.Ind., Mineral.Abstr., Petrol.Abstr., Plant Breed.Abstr., Sci.Cit.Ind., Seed Abstr., Sel.Water Res.Abstr., Soils & Fert., Triticale Abstr., Weed Abstr., Zincscan. **Document type:** academic/scholarly publication.
—BLDSC (3829.741700); CASDDS; CISTI; Ei; EMDOCS; Genuine Article; KR SourceOne; Linda Hall; SWETS; UMI; UnCover. **CCC.**
   Formerly (until 1993): Journal of Soil Science (ISSN 0022-4588); Supersedes in part (in 1993): Pedologie (ISSN 0079-0419); And (in 1993): Science du Sol (ISSN 0767-2853); Which was formerly: Association Francaise pour l'Etude du Sol. Bulletin (ISSN 0335-1653); Which was formed by the merger of (1963-1973): Science du Sol (ISSN 0036-8318); And (1957-1973): Association Francaise pour l'Etude du Sol. Bulletin (ISSN 0519-0800).
Refereed Serial

631.8   II
F A I ANNUAL REVIEW OF FERTILISER PRODUCTION AND CONSUMPTION. (Text in English) a. $10. Fertiliser Association of India, 10 Shaheed Jit Singh Marg, New Delhi 110 067, India. TEL 91-11-667144. FAX 91-11-696-0052. TELEX 031-83056.

631.8   UN   ISSN 0251-1525
HD9483.A1
F A O FERTILIZER YEARBOOK. (Tables in English and French with Spanish glossary; text in English, French and Spanish) 1951. a. $40. Food and Agriculture Organization of the United Nations, Bernan Associates, 4611-F Assembly Dr., Lanham, MD 20706-4391. TEL 301-459-7666. FAX 301-459-0056. (also avail. in microfiche from CIS) **Indexed:** IIS.
—Linda Hall.
   Former titles: Annual Fertilizer Review (ISSN 0084-6546); Fertilizers: An Annual Review of World Production, Consumption and Trade (ISSN 0071-464X); Annual Review of World Production, Consumption and Trade of Fertilizers.

631.4   UN   ISSN 0253-2050
CODEN: FSBUDD
F A O SOILS BULLETIN. (Editions in English, French, Spanish) 1965. irreg., no.70, 1994. price varies. Food and Agriculture Organization of the United Nations, Bernan Associates, 4611-F Assembly Dr., Lanham, MD 20706-4391. TEL 301-459-7666. FAX 301-459-0056. bibl. **Document type:** monographic series.
—BLDSC (3865.742000); CASDDS; Linda Hall.
   Formerly (until 1977): Food and Agriculture Organization of the United Nations. Soils Bulletin (ISSN 0532-0437)

634 635   FR   ISSN 0758-8526
F E L ACTUALITES. 1961. w. 1500 F. (rest of EU 1250 F.; elsewhere 2000 F.) (effective 1996-1997). (Association Interprofessionelle des Fruits et Legumes Paris) Editions Interfel, 115 rue du Faubourg Poissonniere, 75009 Paris, France. TEL 33-01-44537510. FAX 33-01-44537539. Ed. Remy Leprette. adv. contact: Bernard-Loic Calleja. bk.rev.; stat. circ. 7,500. **Document type:** trade publication.
   Former titles: Fruits et Legumes Actualites; (until 1984): Marches Europeens des Fruits et Legumes (ISSN 0395-5494)

F.O. LICHT'S DAILY SUGAR INFORMATION SERVICE. see *FOOD AND FOOD INDUSTRIES*

F.O. LICHT'S WORLD SUGAR AND SWEETENER YEARBOOK. see *FOOD AND FOOD INDUSTRIES*

631   UK
F O S F A INTERNATIONAL. NEWSLETTER. 1985. q. Federation of Oils, Seeds and Fats Associations Ltd., 20 St. Dunstan's Hill, London EC3R 8HL, England. TEL 44-171-283-5511. FAX 44-171-623-1310. Ed. William King. R&P contact: William King. circ. 1,000. **Document type:** trade publication.

630.24 668.6   US   ISSN 0092-0053
HD9483.U5   CODEN: FARCAC
FARM CHEMICALS. 1894. m. $23 (effective 1997). Meister Publishing Co., 37733 Euclid Ave., Willoughby, OH 44094. TEL 216-942-2000. Ed. James C. Sulecki. adv.; bk.rev.; charts; illus.; mkt.; tr.lit. circ. 29,000. (also avail. in microform from UMI; reprint service avail. from UMI) **Indexed:** Biol.& Agr.Ind., Chem.Abstr., Farm & Garden Ind., Ind.Vet., PROMT, Vet.Bull., Weed Abstr. **Document type:** trade publication.
—BLDSC (3872.000000); CASDDS; Linda Hall; SWETS; UMI; UnCover. **CCC.**
   Formed by the merger of: Ag Chem and Commercial Fertilizer (ISSN 0092-0037); Farm Chemicals and Croplife (ISSN 0014-7885)
   Description: Addresses fertilizer and pesticide manufacturing processes.

630.24 668.6   US   ISSN 0430-0750
S633   CODEN: FMCHA2
FARM CHEMICALS HANDBOOK. 1914. a. $89 (effective 1997). Meister Publishing Co., 37733 Euclid Ave., Willoughby, OH 44094. TEL 216-942-2000; 800-572-7740. FAX 216-942-0662. E-mail: fehb-circ@meisterpubl.com. Ed. Richard T. Meister. adv. contact: William J. Miller. circ. 13,000. **Document type:** trade publication.
●Also available on CD-ROM.
—CASDDS; CISTI. **CCC.**
   Supersedes: American Fertilizer Handbook.

630.24 668.6   US   ISSN 1043-8858
FARM CHEMICALS INTERNATIONAL. q. $29 (foreign $35) (effective 1997). Meister Publishing Co., 37733 Euclid Ave., Willoughby, OH 44094. TEL 216-942-2000. Ed. Cathy Hoehn. adv. contact: Ann Markey. circ. 9,000. **Document type:** trade publication.
—BLDSC (3873.100000). **CCC.**
   Description: Serves manufacturers, formulators, mixers, dealers, and commercial applicators of fertilizers and pesticides.

631.7   AT   ISSN 0014-844X
FARMERS NEWSLETTER. (Large Area Edition; Horticultural Edition avail.) 1948. q. Aus.$20 (free to qualified personnel). Irrigation Research & Extension Committee, c/o C.S.I.R.O., Division of Water Resources, Private Bag, Griffith, N.S.W. 2680, Australia. TEL 61-69-601550. FAX 61-69-601600. Ed. Michall Murray. adv.; bk.rev.; illus. circ. 4,200. **Indexed:** Hort.Abstr., Rural Recreat.Tour.Abstr., World Agri.Econ.& Rural Sociol.Abstr. **Document type:** newsletter.

631   IO
FARMERS RECEPTIVITY TO NEW TECHNOLOGIES IN COCONUT. a. $10. Asian and Pacific Coconut Community, Wisma Bakrie, 3rd Fl., Jl. H.R. Rasuna Said, Kuningan, Jakarta 12920, Indonesia. TEL 62-21-510-073. FAX 62-21-520-5160. TELEX 62863 APCCIA.
   Description: Covers the new technologies in the form of new high yielding varieties, use of organic and inorganic fertilizer, pest and disease control, intercropping and intergrazing in coconut land.

631   US   ISSN 0744-7876
FARMER'S REPORT. 1979. w. $7.50. Rochelle Newspapers Inc., 401 N. Main, Rochelle, IL 61068. TEL 815-562-4174. Ed. Ken Wise. adv. circ. 10,500.

631   UK   ISSN 0071-3961
FARMING IN THE EAST MIDLANDS. a. £7. University of Nottingham, Rural Business Research Unit, Sutton Bonington Campus, Loughborough LE12 5RD, England. TEL 44-115-951-6070. FAX 44-115-951-6089. E-mail: sazmfs@szni.nottingham.ac.uk. Ed. Martin Seabrook. **Indexed:** IDA. **Document type:** bulletin.
   Formerly: Farm Management Notes.

AGRICULTURE — CROP PRODUCTION AND SOIL

FEDERACION NACIONAL DE CAFETEROS DE COLOMBIA. INFORME DE LABORES DE LOS COMITES DEPARTAMENTALES DE CAFETEROS. see *FOOD AND FOOD INDUSTRIES*

631 US
FEDERAL MARKETING ORDERS FOR AVOCADOS; grown in Florida. a. Florida Avocado Administrative Committee, 18710 S.W. 288th St., Homestead, FL 33030. TEL 305-247-0848. FAX 305-245-1315. (Subscr. to: Box 900188, Homestead, FL 33090-0188)
Description: Covers grade, size, maturity and pack requirements for avocados grown in Florida, and import regulations.

631.8
FERTILISER DIGEST. 1962. bi-m. Rs.3. Fertiliser Corporation of India Ltd., Madhuban, 55 Nehru Place, New Delhi 110019, India. Ed. R.S. Mathur. circ. 4,000.

631.8 II ISSN 0257-8034
FERTILISER MARKETING NEWS. (Text in English) 1970. m. $35. Fertiliser Association of India, 10 Shaheed Jit Singh Marg, New Delhi 110067, India. TEL 91-11-667144. FAX 91-11-696-0052. TELEX 031-73056. Ed. T.M. Alexander. adv.; charts; illus. circ. 2,500.

631.8 II ISSN 0015-0266
S631 CODEN: FENEAQ
FERTILISER NEWS. (Text in English) 1956. m. $60. Fertiliser Association of India, 10 Shaheed Jit Singh Marg, New Delhi 110 067, India. TEL 91-11-667144. FAX 91-11-696-0052. TELEX 031-73056. Ed. K.P. Sundaram. adv.; bk.rev.; abstr.; bibl.; charts; illus.; pat.; index. circ. 4,000. **Indexed:** Chem.Abstr., Excerp.Med., Field Crop Abstr., Herb.Abstr., Hort.Abstr., IDA, Irr.& Drain.Abstr., Potato Abstr., Rice Abstr., Rural Recreat.Tour.Abstr., Seed Abstr., Soils & Fert., Soyabean Abstr., Trop.Oil Seeds Abstr., World Agri.Econ.& Rural Sociol.Abstr.
—BLDSC (3909.620000); CASDDS; Linda Hall.
Incorporates: Fertiliser Association of India. Annual Review of Fertiliser. Consumption and Production (ISSN 0430-3288)
Description: Features academic and practical research on the productivity and safety of fertilizers in India.

630.24 661 US ISSN 1067-1986
THE FERTILIZER & AG-CHEMICAL DIGEST. 1978. q. $20 (effective Jan. 1996). Anderson Management Services, Inc., 1111 Lincoln Mall, Ste. 308, Lincoln, NE 68508-2882. TEL 402-476-1528. FAX 402-476-1259. Ed. Robert L. Anderson. adv. contact: Rebecca Barker. circ. 800 (paid). **Document type:** trade publication.
Formerly: Nebraska Fertilizer and Ag-Chemical Digest (ISSN 0199-672X)

FERTILIZER FINANCIAL FACTS & PRODUCTION COST SURVEY; industry production costs, financial data. see *AGRICULTURE — Agricultural Economics*

631.8 UK ISSN 0951-1490
FERTILIZER FOCUS. 1984. 10/yr. £160. FMB House, 6 Windmill Rd., Hampton Hill, Middx. TW12 1RH, England. TEL 44-181-979-7866. FAX 44-181-979-4573. TELEX 296022-FMBCON-G. Ed. Mike Smith; Pub. Andrew Osborne. adv. contact: Andrew Osborne. bk.rev. circ. 2,890. **Document type:** trade publication.
—BLDSC (3910.150000).

631.8 UK ISSN 0015-0304
HD9483. CODEN: FRZIAJ
FERTILIZER INTERNATIONAL. 1967. bi-m. £190($290) (effective May 1997). British Sulphur Publishing (Subsidiary of: C R U Publishing Ltd.), 31 Mount Pleasant, London WC1X 0AD, England. TEL 44-171-837-5600. FAX 44-171-837-0292. TELEX 918918 SULFEX G. Pub. John French. R&P contact: John French. adv. contact: Tina Firman. abstr.; charts; pat.; stat. circ. 791. (tabloid format; avail. on records; reprint service avail. from UMI) **Indexed:** Chem.Abstr., Excerp.Med., Key to Econ.Sci., PROMT, Soils & Fert., World Agri.Econ.& Rural Sociol.Abstr. **Document type:** trade publication.
●Also available online. Vendor(s): Information Access Co.
—BLDSC (3910.300000); CASDDS; Ei; Linda Hall; SWETS.
Formerly: World of N P K S.
Description: Deals with all aspects of the world market for fertilizers.

FERTILIZER RECORD. see *AGRICULTURE — Agricultural Economics*

631.8 US ISSN 0071-4623
CODEN: FZSTA5
FERTILIZER SCIENCE AND TECHNOLOGY SERIES. 1968. irreg., vol.7, 1991. price varies. Marcel Dekker, Inc., 270 Madison Ave., New York, NY 10016. TEL 212-696-9000. FAX 212-658-4540. TELEX 421419. Ed. T.P. Hignett; Pub. Graham Garratt. R&P contact: Julia Mulligan. (also avail. in microform from RPI) **Indexed:** Chem.Abstr., I.M.M.Abstr. **Document type:** monographic series.
—BLDSC (3910.450000); CASDDS; CISTI. **CCC**.
Refereed Serial

631.8 UK
FERTILIZER TECHNOLOGY DATABANK. irreg., 4th edition, 1994. £150. British Sulphur Publishing (Subsidiary of: C R U Publishing Ltd.), 31 Mount Pleasant, London WC1X 0AD, England. TEL 44-171-837-5600. FAX 44-171-837-0292. TELEX 918918 SULFEX G. Pub. John French. R&P contact: John French. (reprint service avail. from UMI) **Document type:** directory.
Former titles: N P K S Processes and Plant Suppliers. World Directory; World Guide to Fertilizer Processes and Plant Suppliers; World Guide to Fertilizer Processes and Constructors.

631.8 382 UN
FERTILIZER TRADE INFORMATION MONTHLY BULLETIN. (Text in English) 1982. m. $110. United Nations Economic and Social Commission for Asia and the Pacific (ESCAP), Fertilizer Advisory, Development and Information Network for Asia and the Pacific (FADINAP), Agriculture and Rural Development Division, United Nations Bldg., Rajadamnern Ave., Bangkok 10200, Thailand. TEL 2-282-9161. TELEX 82392-ESCAP-TH. (Co-sponsors: FAO; UNIDO) Ed. Naripone Sivanunwong. circ. 300. **Document type:** bulletin.
Description: Provides fertilizer prices, amounts traded, and countries buying and selling, for transactions involving Asia - Pacific countries.

631.8 UK ISSN 0951-7472
FERTILIZER WEEK. 1987. 50/yr. £835. C P U International Ltd., 31 Mount Pleasant, London WC1X 0AD, England. TEL 0171-837-5600. FAX 0171-837-0292. TELEX 918918-SULFEX-G. Ed. Stephen Mitchell. **Document type:** newsletter.

631.5 NE ISSN 0378-4290
CODEN: FCREDZ
FIELD CROPS RESEARCH; an international journal. 1978. 15/yr. fl.2345($1348) (effective 1998). Elsevier Science B.V., P.O. Box 211, 1000 AE Amsterdam, Netherlands. TEL 31-20-4853911. FAX 31-20-4853598. TELEX 18582 ESPA NL. E-mail: nlinfo-f@elsevier.nl; usinfo-f@elsevier.com; forinfo-kyf04035@niftyserve.or.jp; URL: http://www.elsevier.nl/. (Subscr. in the Americas to: Elsevier Science, Regional Sales Office, Box 945, New York, NY 10159-0945. TEL 212-633-3730. FAX 212-633-3680; Subscr. in Australasia and the Far East to: Elsevier Science (Singapore) Pte Ltd, No.1 Temasek Ave., No.17-01 Millenia Tower, Singapore 039192, Singapore. TEL 65-434-3727. FAX 65-737-2230; Subscr. in Japan to: Elsevier Science Japan, 9-15 Higashi-Azabu 1-chome, Minato-ku, Tokyo 106, Japan. TEL 81-3-5561-5033. FAX 81-3-5561-5047) Eds. R.H. Brown, G.L. Wilson. (also avail. in microform from UMI; reprint service avail. from SWZ) **Indexed:** Agroforest.Abstr., ASCA, Biol.Abstr., Biol.& Agr.Ind., Biotech.Abstr., Crop Physiol.Abstr., Curr.Adv.Ecol.Sci., Curr.Cont., Ecol.Abstr., Environ.Abstr., Environ.Per.Bibl. (1987-1993), Field Crop Abstr., Forest.Abstr., Geo.Abstr., Helminthol.Abstr., Herb.Abstr., Ind.Sci.Rev., Irr.& Drain.Abstr., Maize Abstr., Nutr.Abstr., Plant Grow.Reg.Abstr., Potato Abstr., Rice Abstr., Sci.Cit.Ind., Seed Abstr., Soils & Fert., Sorghum & Millets Abstr., Soyabean Abstr., Triticale Abstr., Trop.Oil Seeds Abstr., Weed Abstr. **Document type:** academic/scholarly publication.
—BLDSC (3920.057000); EMDOCS; Genuine Article; KR SourceOne; Linda Hall; SWETS; UnCover. **CCC**.
Description: Publishes research results of international relevance arising from the scientific study of crops and farming systems.
Refereed Serial

FIJI SUGAR YEAR BOOK. see *FOOD AND FOOD INDUSTRIES*

631 576 BL ISSN 0100-4158
CODEN: FIBRD2
FITOPATOLOGIA BRASILEIRA. (Text in Portuguese; occasionally in English, French and Spanish; summaries in English and Portuguese) 1976. q. Cr.$5000($60) Sociedade Brasileira Fitopatologia, Caixa Postal 04482, 70919-970 Brasilia DF, Brazil. TEL 61-3482424. FAX 61-2741065. Ed. E.W. Kitajima. adv.; bk.rev.; index. circ. 1,000. (back issues avail.) **Indexed:** Biodet.Abstr., Biol.Abstr., Chem.Abstr., Excerp.Med., Field Crop Abstr., Forest.Abstr., Hort.Abstr., INIS Atomind., Maize Abstr., Plant Grow.Reg.Abstr., Potato Abstr., Rev.Med.& Vet.Mycol., Rev.Plant Path., Seed Abstr., Sorghum & Millets Abstr., Triticale Abstr., Trop.Oil Seeds Abstr., Weed Abstr. **Document type:** academic/scholarly publication.
—BLDSC (3948.235500); CASDDS; Linda Hall.

631 US
FLORIDA AVOCADO ADMINISTRATIVE COMMITTEE. ANNUAL REPORT. 1954. a. Florida Avocado Administrative Committee, 18710 S.W. 288th St., Homestead, FL 33030. TEL 305-247-0848. FAX 305-245-1315. (Subscr. to: Box 900188, Homestead, FL 33090-0188) circ. 500. (back issues avail.)
Description: Summary of year's events, shipment totals, research, weather, statistics, and financial report.

631 US
FLORIDA AVOCADO ADMINISTRATIVE COMMITTEE. MEETING MINUTES. 1954. m. Florida Avocado Administrative Committee, 18710 S.W 288th St., Homestead, FL 33030. TEL 305-247-0848. FAX 305-245-1315. (Subscr. to: Box 900188, Homestead, FL 33090-0188) circ. 400. (back issues avail.)
Description: Special guest articles and reports from the administrator pertaining to items received in the Committee office.

631 US
FLORIDA LIME ADMINISTRATIVE COMMITTEE. ANNUAL REPORT. 1955. a. Florida Lime Administrative Committee, 18710 S.W. 288th St., Homestead, FL 33030. TEL 305-247-0848. FAX 305-245-1315. (Subscr. to: Box 900188, Homestead, FL 33090-0188) circ. 500. (back issues avail.)
Description: Summary of year's events, shipment totals, research, weather, statistics, and financial report.

631 US
FLORIDA LIME ADMINISTRATIVE COMMITTEE. MEETING MINUTES. 1955. m. Florida Lime Administrative Committee, 18710 S.W. 288th St., Homestead, FL 33030. TEL 305-247-0848. FAX 305-245-1315. (Subscr. to: Box 900188, Homestead, FL 33090-0188) circ. 400. (back issues avail.)
Description: Special guest articles and reports from the administrator regarding items received in the Committee office.

631 GW ISSN 0015-4733
FLUR UND FURCHE; Landwirtschaftsmagazin. English edition: Furrow (ISSN 0016-3112) 1964. q. free. Deere & Company, Postfach 100862, 68008 Mannheim, Germany. FAX 49-621-8104-300. TELEX 463056-DCEOD. (U.S. addr.: John Deere Rd., Moline, IL 61265) Ed. Rainer Mache. adv.; illus.; index. circ. 163,500. **Document type:** trade publication.

632.97 573.8 UK ISSN 1360-5860
▼**FOCUS ON BIOPESTICIDES PLUS.** 1996. m. £245($450) (effective 1997). The Royal Society of Chemistry, Thomas Graham House, Science Park, Milton Rd., Cambridge CB4 4WF, England. TEL 44-1223-420066. FAX 44-1223-423623. E-mail: sales@rsc.org; URL: http://chemistry.rsc.org/rsc/. (Subscr. to: Turpin Distribution Services Ltd., Blackhorse Rd., Letchworth, Herts SG6 1HN, England. TEL 44-1462-672555. FAX 44-1462-480947) Ed. Len Copping. **Document type:** newsletter.
Description: Reports on all uses of natural organisms, their genes and their secondary metabolites in crop protection.

AGRICULTURE — CROP PRODUCTION AND SOIL

632 UN
FOOD AND AGRICULTURE ORGANIZATION OF THE UNITED NATIONS. ASIA AND PACIFIC PLANT PROTECTION COMMISSION. QUARTERLY NEWSLETTER. (Text and summaries in English) 1958. q. free. Food and Agriculture Organization of the United Nations, Regional Office for Asia and the Pacific, Maliwan Mansion, Phra Atit Road, Bangkok 10200, Thailand. circ. 500. (back issues avail.) **Indexed:** Soyabean Abstr. **Document type:** newsletter.
Formerly: Food and Agricultural Organization of the United Nations. Plant Protection Committee for Southeast Asia and Pacific Region. Quarterly Newsletter (ISSN 0428-9749)
Description: Disseminates information on plant quarantine and protection in these regions.

631 UN ISSN 1014-3351
FOOD AND AGRICULTURE ORGANIZATION OF THE UNITED NATIONS. ASIA AND PACIFIC PLANT PROTECTION COMMISSION. TECHNICAL DOCUMENT. (Text and summaries in English) 1958. irreg. (6-8/yr.). free. Food and Agriculture Organization of the United Nations, Regional Office for Asia and the Pacific, Maliwan Mansion, Phra Atit Rd., Bangkok 10200, Thailand. circ. 500 (controlled). **Indexed:** Rev.Appl.Entomol., Rev.Plant Path., Weed Abstr.
Formerly: Food and Agricultural Organization of the United Nations. Plant Protection Committee for Southeast Asia and Pacific Region. Technical Document (ISSN 0428-9765)
Description: Aimed at professionals and technical field personnel. Contains agricultural research results.

631.4 UN ISSN 0532-0488
CODEN: WSRRDX
FOOD AND AGRICULTURE ORGANIZATION OF THE UNITED NATIONS. WORLD SOIL RESOURCES REPORTS. irreg., no.80, 1995. price varies. Food and Agriculture Organization of the United Nations, Bernan Associates, 4611-F Assembly Dr., Lanham, MD 20706-4391. TEL 301-459-7666. FAX 301-459-0056. **Indexed:** Rural Recreat.Tour.Abstr., Soils & Fert., World Agri.Econ.& Rural Sociol.Abstr. **Document type:** monographic series.
—BLDSC (9360.035000); Linda Hall.

FOOD BIOTECHNOLOGY. see BIOLOGY — Biotechnology

633.4 CN ISSN 0384-7322
FRASER'S POTATO NEWSLETTER. 1967. w. Can.$90($85) (effective 1997). Harry Fraser, Ed. & Pub., Charlottetown, R.R.1, Hazelbrook, PE C1A 7J6, Canada. adv. circ. 2,100. **Document type:** newsletter.

631 US
FRESH FRUIT AND VEGETABLE MARKET NEWS. 1936. 3/wk. free. Department of Agriculture, Box 22159, Honolulu, HI 96822. TEL 808-548-2211. Ed. James Omori. stat. circ. 1,000. (processed)

FRESH FRUIT AND VEGETABLE MARKET NEWS: WEEKLY SUMMARY, SHIPMENTS - ARRIVALS. see AGRICULTURE — Agricultural Economics

FRESH PRODUCE JOURNAL. see FOOD AND FOOD INDUSTRIES

FRIENDS OF THE TREES SOCIETY NEWSLETTER. see FORESTS AND FORESTRY

FRUCHTHANDEL; internationale Fachzeitschrift fuer den Handel mit Fruechten und Gemuese. see FOOD AND FOOD INDUSTRIES — Grocery Trade

380.1 FR
FRUCTIDOR INTERNATIONAL. 1935. a. 940 F. Helios International, 14 bd Montmartre, 75009 Paris, France. TEL 33-1-42469294. FAX 33-4-90882849. TELEX 432845. adv. circ. 6,000. **Document type:** directory.

630 SZ ISSN 0016-2221
FRUECHTE UND GEMUESE/FRUITS ET LEGUMES. (Text in French, German) 1933. 25/yr. 85 SFr. (foreign 150 SFr.). Schweizerischer Obstverband, Baarerstr. 88, CH-6302 Zug, Switzerland. TEL 41-41-7286868. FAX 41-41-7286800. E-mail: fruit.swiss@interconnect.ch. (Co-sponsor: Schweizerischer Gemuese-Union) Ed. Christian Hilbrand. adv.; bk.rev.; mkt.; stat. circ. 2,500. **Document type:** trade publication.
Description: Focuses on fruit and vegetable production, processing and marketing.

634 DK ISSN 0906-1738
FRUGT OG BAER. 1934. m. DKK 550. Dansk Erhvervsfrugtavl, Lavsenvaenget 20, 5200 Odense V, Denmark. TEL 45-61-12-63-32. FAX 45-66-12-63-35. Ed. Evald Burgaard. adv. contact: Anne Lise Mikkelsen. bk.rev. circ. 1,300. **Indexed:** Agri.Eng.Abstr., Hort.Abstr., Plant Grow.Reg.Abstr., World Agri.Econ.& Rural Sociol.Abstr. **Document type:** trade publication.
—BLDSC (4042.568000).
Former titles: Frugtavleren (ISSN 0106-004X); Erhvervsfrugtavleren.

634 UK ISSN 0961-0464
FRUIT AND VEGETABLE MARKETS. m. £275 (rest of Europe £310; elsewhere £345) (effective 1997). Agra Europe (London) Ltd., 25 Frant Rd., Tunbridge Wells, Kent TN2 5JT, England. TEL 44-1892-533813. FAX 44-1892-544895. TELEX 95114 AGRATW G. E-mail: 100637.3460@compuserve.com. **Document type:** trade publication.
Formerly: Agrafile: Fruit and Vegetables (ISSN 0950-4931)
Description: Presents a pan-European view of fresh and processed fruit and vegetables. Includes crop reports, market and trade news, EU report, legislation and the latest price production and trade statistics.

FRUIT AND VEGETABLE TRUCK RATE AND COST SUMMARY. see AGRICULTURE — Agricultural Economics

FRUIT AND VEGETABLE TRUCK RATE REPORT. see AGRICULTURE — Agricultural Economics

634 BE ISSN 0016-2248
CODEN: FRUBA7
FRUIT BELGE. 1933. bi-m. 1400 BEF in Europe (elsewhere 1800 BEF) (effective 1996). Ligues Pomologiques Wallonnes, Rue de la Resistance 11, 5100 Wepion, Belgium. TEL 32-81-625620. FAX 32-81-611202. Ed. A. Sansdrap. adv.; bk.rev.; abstr.; illus.; index. circ. 1,500. **Indexed:** Chem.Abstr., Curr.Adv.Ecol.Sci., Food Sci.& Tech.Abstr., Hort.Abstr.
—BLDSC (4042.700000); CASDDS; SWETS.
Description: Information on all aspects of the Belgian fruit industry.

FRUIT STATISTICAL YEARBOOK. see AGRICULTURE — Abstracting, Bibliographies, Statistics

634 FR ISSN 0754-0698
FRUITS ET LEGUMES. 1983. m (except July-Aug. combined). 275 F. (Europe 355 F.; elsewhere 425 F.) (effective 1997). Publications Agricoles, Batiment Alphagro, B.P. 200, 47931 Agen Cedex 9, France. TEL 33-5-53772130. FAX 33-5-53772131. Ed. Jean-Bernard Pouey. adv. contact: Louis Uminski. circ. 8,500.

634 BE ISSN 1370-0235
FRUITTEELT NIEUWS. (Text in Dutch) 1988. fortn. 2000 BEF (effective 1998). Brede Akker 3, 3800 Sint-Truiden, Belgium. FAX 32-11-674318. (Co-sponsors: Koninlijk Opzoekingsstation van Gorsem Sint-Truiden; Nationale Vakgroep Fruit van de Belgische Boerenbond Leuven; Studiekring Guvelingen Sint-Truiden) Ed. R. Geerdens; Pub. Luc Dirix. R&P contact: J. Mathijs. adv. circ. 2,700. **Document type:** trade publication.
Formerly (until 1993): Fruitteelt (ISSN 0775-5678)
Description: For fruitgrowers: apples, pears, strawberries, berries, plums.

631 SP ISSN 1131-5660
FRUTICULTURA PROFESIONAL; revista especializada del sector. 1986. bi-m. (plus 1 monograph). 7400 ptas. (foreign 8100 ptas.) (effective 1997). Agro Latino, S.L., Apdo. 20151, 08080 Barcelona, Spain. TEL 34-3-4568563. FAX 34-3-4359104. Ed. L. Daniel Aradas Llorens. adv. **Indexed:** Ind.SST. **Document type:** trade publication.

633.72 CC ISSN 1005-2291
FUJIAN CHAYE/TEA IN FUJIAN. (Text in Chinese) q. Y4.80. Fujian Sheng Chaye Xiehui - Fujian Provincial Tea Association, Waimao Zhongxin - Foreign Trade Center, Wusi Lu, Fuzhou, Fujian 350001, People's Republic of China. TEL 86-591-756-5272. (Dist. overseas by: Jiangsu Publications Import & Export Corp., 56 Gao Yun Ling, Nanjing, Jiangsu, P.R.C.) Ed. Xinjiong Lin.
Description: Addresses the need of professionals engaged in tea production and research to acquire modern techniques of production and processing and to exchange their experience.

634.6 CC ISSN 1004-6089
FUJIAN GUOSHU/FUJIAN FRUIT TREES. (Text in Chinese) 1973. q. Y12 (effective 1997); Y12 (effective 1998). Fujian Sheng Nongye Kexueyuan, Guoshu Yanjiusuo - Fujian Academy of Agricultural Science, Fruit Tree Research Institute, Pudang, Fuzhou Shijiao (Suburb), Fuzhou, Fujian 350013, People's Republic of China. TEL 7596409. (Dist. overseas by: Jiangsu Publications Import & Export Corp., 56 Gao Yun Ling, Nanjing, Jiangsu, P.R.C.) Ed. Huang Jinsong. **Document type:** academic/scholarly publication.
Description: Covers the cultivation of subtropical fruit trees and related research.

FUJIAN NONGYE DAXUE XUEBAO/FUJIAN AGRICULTURAL UNIVERSITY. JOURNAL. see AGRICULTURE

632.9 US ISSN 0148-9038
CODEN: FNETDO
FUNGICIDE AND NEMATICIDE TESTS. (Text in English, Spanish) a. $22.50. (American Phytopathological Society) A P S Press, 3340 Pilot Knob Rd., St. Paul, MN 55121-2097. TEL 612-454-7250; 800-328-7560. FAX 612-454-0766. TELEX 6502439657 (MCI UW). E-mail: aps@scisoc.org; URL: http://www.scisoc.org. index. circ. 1,000. (back issues avail.) **Indexed:** Field Crop Abstr., Helminthol.Abstr., Maize Abstr., Ornam.Hort., Rev.Plant Path., Soils & Fert.
—Linda Hall.
Description: Highlights pest control methods.

631 IS
GAN SADEH VEMESHEK. m. Israel Vegetable Growers Association, 8 Shaul Hamelech Blvd., Tel Aviv 64 733, Israel. Ed. Yaacov Shlish.

630 IT ISSN 0016-6863
GENIO RURALE. Short title: G R. 1937. m. (11/yr.). L.76000 (effective 1996). Edagricole S.p.A., Via Emilia Levante 31, 40139 Bologna, Italy. TEL 39-51-492211. FAX 39-51-493660. Ed. Paolo de Castro. adv.: B&W page L.1200000, color page L.1900000; trim 185 x 247. bk.rev.; charts; illus.; index. circ. 25,300. **Indexed:** Agri.Eng.Abstr., Apic.Abstr., Dairy Sci.Abstr., Field Crop Abstr., Forest.Abstr., Forest Prod.Abstr., Geo.Abstr., Herb.Abstr., Hort.Abstr., Irr.& Drain.Abstr., Maize Abstr., Ornam.Hort., P.A.I.S.For.Lang.Ind., Pig News & Info., Soils & Fert., Soyabean Abstr., Triticale Abstr.
Description: Covers agricultural engineering.

AGRICULTURE — CROP PRODUCTION AND SOIL

631.4 550   NE   ISSN 0016-7061
CODEN: GEDMAB
GEODERMA; an international journal of soil science. (Text in English, French and German) 1967. 24/yr. fl.2970($1707) (effective 1998). Elsevier Science B.V., P.O. Box 211, 1000 AE Amsterdam, Netherlands. TEL 31-20-4853911. FAX 31-20-4853598. TELEX 18582 ESPA NL. E-mail: nlinfo-f@elsevier.nl; usinfo-f@elsevier.com; forinfo-kyf04035@niftyserve.or.jp; URL: http://www.elsevier.nl/. (Subscr. in the Americas to: Elsevier Science, Regional Sales Office, Box 945, New York, NY 10159-0945. TEL 212-633-3730. FAX 212-633-3680; Subscr. in Australasia and the Far East to: Elsevier Science (Singapore) Pte Ltd, No.1 Temasek Ave., No.17-01 Millenia Tower, Singapore 039192, Singapore. TEL 65-434-3727. FAX 65-337-2230; Subscr. in Japan to: Elsevier Science Japan, 9-15 Higashi-Azabu 1-chome, Minato-ku, Tokyo 106, Japan. TEL 81-3-5561-5033. FAX 81-3-5561-5047) Eds. J. Bouman, J.A. McKeague. adv.; bk.rev.; abstr.; charts; illus.; index. (also avail. in microform from UMI; reprint service avail. from SWZ) **Indexed:** AESIS, ASCA, Biol.Abstr., Bull.Signal., Cadscan, Chem.Abstr., Curr.Adv.Ecol.Sci., Curr.Cont., Ecol.Abstr., Energy Ind., Energy Info.Abstr., Environ.Per.Bibl. (1987-), Excerp.Med., Field Crop Abstr., Forest.Abstr., Geo.Abstr.P.G., Geol.Abstr., GeoRef., Herb.Abstr., IDA, Ind.Sci.Rev., Irr.& Drain.Abstr., Lead Abstr., Sci.Cit.Ind., Sel.Water Res.Abstr., So.Pac.Per.Ind., Soils & Fert., Weed Abstr., Zincscan. **Document type:** academic/scholarly publication.
—BLDSC (4118.050000); CASDDS; CISTI; EMDOCS; Genuine Article; KR SourceOne; Linda Hall; SWETS; UnCover. **CCC.**
Description: Interdisciplinary papers from the different fields of pedology, focusing on the occurrence and dynamic characterization in space and time of soils in the field.
Refereed Serial

GERMINATIONS; newsletter of the Butterbrooke Farm seed co-op. see *GARDENING AND HORTICULTURE*

631.7   IT   ISSN 1122-603X
GIORNALE DELL'IRRIGAZIONE. 1994. m. L.42000 (foreign L.62000) (effective 1995). Edagricole S.p.A., Via Emilia Levante 31, 40139 Bologna, Italy. TEL 39-51-492211. FAX 39-51-493660. Ed. Giorgio Amadei. adv. contact: Giuliano Avoni. circ. 12,900. **Document type:** trade publication.

631   IT   ISSN 0393-9200
GIORNALE DELLA SOIA. 1985. 5/yr. Via Savorgnana 26, 33100 Udine, Italy. TEL 432-26-972. FAX 432-507013. Ed. Enos Costantini. circ. 20,000.

632.97   US   ISSN 1091-1375
▼**GLOBAL FUNGICIDE DIRECTORY.** 1996. every 30 mos. $125 commercial; academic $90. Ag Chem Information Services, 6705 E. 71st St., Indianapolis, IN 46220. TEL 317-845-0681. FAX 317-841-1210. **Document type:** directory.
Description: Covers all existing and experimental fungicide products and compounds in the global crop protection industry, plus a brief overview of the global market for all fungicide compounds.

632.97   US   ISSN 1079-3275
SB951.4
GLOBAL HERBICIDE DIRECTORY. 1994. every 30 mos. $150. Ag Chem Information Services, 6705 E. 71st St., Indianapolis, IN 46220. TEL 317-845-0681. FAX 317-841-1210. Pub. William L. Hopkins. **Document type:** catalog.
Description: Covers all existing and new herbicide product development in the world's crop protection industry, and a brief overview of the global herbicide market in dollar value.

632.97   US   ISSN 1088-8497
▼**GLOBAL INSECTICIDE DIRECTORY.** 1996. every 30 mos. $125 commercial; academic $90. Ag Chem Information Services, 6705 E. 71st St., Indianapolis, IN 46220. TEL 317-845-0681. FAX 317-841-1210. **Document type:** directory.
Description: Covers all existing and experimental insecticide products and compounds in the global crop protection industry, plus a brief overview of the global market for all insecticide compounds.

GLOBAL PESTICIDE CAMPAIGNER. see *ENVIRONMENTAL STUDIES — Toxicology And Environmental Safety*

796   AT
GOLF AND SPORTS TURF. 1993. bi-m. Aus.$40 (foreign $74). Glenvale Publications Pty. Ltd., 4 Palmer Court, Mount Waverley, Vic. 3149, Australia. TEL 61-3-95442233. FAX 61-3-95431150. circ. 5,014. **Document type:** trade publication.

631   AT
GRAINS RESEARCH AND DEVELOPMENT CORPORATION. ANNUAL REPORT. a. free. Australian Government Publishing Service, G.P.O. Box 84, Canberra, A.C.T. 2601, Australia. TEL 61-6-295-4411. FAX 61-6-295-4455. TELEX AA62013.
Formed by the merger of: Barley Research Council. Annual Report & Grain Legumes Research Council. Annual Report & Oilseeds Research Council. Annual Report & Wheat Research Council. Annual Report (ISSN 0819-5854)

634.8   US   ISSN 1049-670X
GRAPE GROWER.* 1969. m. $19.95 (overseas $195). Western Agricultural Publishing Co. Inc., 4969 E. Clinton Ave., Ste. 119, Fresno, CA 93727-1549. TEL 209-252-7000. FAX 209-252-7387. Ed. Mark Arcamonte. adv. circ. 11,000. **Document type:** trade publication.
Formerly: California and Western States Grape Grower (ISSN 0092-2145)

633.2   JA
CODEN: NPSGAI
GRASSLAND SCIENCE/NIPPON SOCHI GAKKAI-SHI. (Text in English, Japanese) 1955. q. 8000 Yen to individual members; institutions 11000 Yen. Japanese Society of Grassland Science, c/o National Grassland Research Institute, 768 Senbonmatsu, Nishinasuno-cho, Nasu-gun, Tochigi-ken 329-27, Japan. TEL 81-287-36-0111.
FAX 81-287-36-6629. (Non-members subscr. to: Maruzen Co. Ltd., P.O. Box 5050, Tokyo International, 100-31, Japan) (Co-sponsor: Ministry of Education, Science and Culture) Ed. Tohoru Shimada. adv.; bk.rev. circ. 1,400. **Indexed:** Agri.Eng.Abstr., Biol.Abstr., Chem.Abstr., Curr.Cont., Field Crop Abstr., Herb.Abstr., Plant Grow.Reg.Abstr., Seed Abstr., Soils & Fert., Sorghum & Millets Abstr., Triticale Abstr., Trop.Oil Seeds Abstr., Weed Abstr. **Document type:** academic/scholarly publication.
—CASDDS.
Former titles (until vol.41, 1995): Japanese Society of Grassland Science. Journal (ISSN 0447-5933); (until 1961): Japanese Society of Herbage Crops and Grassland Farming - Nippon Sochi Kenkyukaishi (ISSN 0447-5941)
Description: Aims to develop methods of production and utilization of grass and forage crops, and to advance education and research in grassland management.

631.4   UK   ISSN 0072-7164
S599.4.G72   CODEN: GBSEA7
GREAT BRITAIN. SOIL SURVEY OF ENGLAND AND WALES. BULLETIN. 1964. irreg., no.15, 1984. price varies. Soil Survey and Land Research Centre, Silsoe Campus, Silsoe, Bedford MK45 4DT, England. TEL 44-1525-60428. FAX 44-1525-61147. **Document type:** government publication.
—Linda Hall.
Description: Soil surveys at varied scales.

631.4   UK   ISSN 0072-7202
CODEN: SSSWD9
GREAT BRITAIN. SOIL SURVEY OF ENGLAND AND WALES. SPECIAL SURVEYS. 1969. irreg., no.15, 1988. price varies. Soil Survey and Land Research Centre, Silsoe Campus, Silsoe, Bedford MK45 4DT, England. TEL 44-1525-863242.
FAX 44-1525-863253. **Indexed:** Geo.Abstr., Soils & Fert. **Document type:** government publication.
—Linda Hall.
Description: Soil surveys of problem areas of land.

631.4   UK   ISSN 0072-7210
CODEN: SSTMDI
GREAT BRITAIN. SOIL SURVEY OF ENGLAND AND WALES. TECHNICAL MONOGRAPHS. 1969. irreg., no.18, 1987. price varies. Soil Survey and Land Research Centre, Silsoe Campus, Silsoe, Bedford MK45 4DT, England. TEL 44-1525-863242. FAX 44-1525-863253. **Indexed:** Geo.Abstr., Soils & Fert. **Document type:** government publication.
—Linda Hall.

634   US
GREAT LAKES FRUIT GROWERS NEWS. 1961. m. $7. Great Lakes Publishing Co., 343 S. Union St., Box 128, Sparta, MI 49345. TEL 616-887-9008. Ed. Matt McCallum. R&P contact: Matt McCallum. adv. contact: Dee Rau. circ. 13,157. **Document type:** newsletter, trade publication.
Description: Covers growing and marketing techniques, business management ideas, events, meetings, and developments important to the industry.

635   US   ISSN 1049-8494
CODEN: GLVNEL
GREAT LAKES VEGETABLE GROWERS NEWS. 1966. m. $7. Great Lakes Publishing Co., 343 S. Union St., Box 128, Sparta, MI 49345. TEL 616-887-9008. Ed. Matt McCallum. R&P contact: Matt McCallum. adv. contact: Dee Rau. circ. 13,260. **Document type:** trade publication, newsletter.
Description: Covers growing and marketing techniques, business management ideas, events, meetings and developments for vegetable and potato growers, bedding plant and greenhouse operators and farm and roadside market operators.

GREEN MARKETS WORLD DIRECTORY OF THE FERTILIZER INDUSTRY. see *BUSINESS AND ECONOMICS — Trade And Industrial Directories*

634.772   GD
GRENADA BANANA CO-OPERATIVE SOCIETY. ANNUAL REPORT AND FINANCIAL STATEMENTS. a. Grenada Banana Co-operative Society, Scott St., St. George's, Grenada, W.I. **Document type:** corporate report.

GROUND WATER CANADA. see *WATER RESOURCES*

634   CN   ISSN 0017-4777
THE GROWER. 1879. m. $30 (foreign $40). Ontario Fruit and Vegetable Growers Association, 355 Elmira Rd., No. 103, Guelph, ON N1K 1S5, Canada. TEL 519-763-8728. FAX 519-763-6604. Ed. Gayle Anderson; Pub. Michael Mazur. R&P contact: Gayle Anderson. adv.: B&W page Can.$1995, color page Can.$2939; trim 1 3/8 x 16; adv. contact: Nancy Nemeth. bk.rev.; charts; illus.; mkt.; stat. circ. 10,000. (tabloid format) **Indexed:** Agri.Eng.Abstr., PROMT. **Document type:** newspaper, trade publication.
Description: Presents information on new products, services, systems, labor, research, market events and upcoming trends. Provides a forum and insight into the broader infrastructure of national and international horticultural industries.

633   US   ISSN 0745-1784
THE GROWER. 1966. m. $25 (foreign $40) (effective 1997). Vance Publishing Corporation (Lenexa), 10901 W. 84th Terr., Lenexa, KS 66214-1631. TEL 913-438-8700. FAX 913-938-0695. adv.; charts; illus.; stat. circ. 28,050. (also avail. in microfilm from UMI) **Document type:** trade publication.
—**CCC.**

632.9540968   SA
GUIDE TO THE USE OF HERBICIDES. (Text in English) 14th ed., 1993. irreg. R.15. (Department of Agriculture) Department of Agricultural Development, Private Bag X144, Pretoria 0001, South Africa. TEL 27-12-206-2181. FAX 27-21-323-2516. (Affiliate: Directorate of Livestock Improvement and Agricultural Production Resources) **Document type:** government publication.

632.95   SA
GUIDE TO THE USE OF PESTICIDES AND FUNGICIDES IN THE REPUBLIC OF SOUTH AFRICA. (Text in English) 1961. a., 36th ed., 1993. price varies. (Department of Agriculture) Department of Agricultural Development, Private Bag X144, Pretoria 0001, South Africa. TEL 27-12-206-2181.
FAX 27-12-323-2516. (Affiliate: Directorate of Livestock Improvement and Agricultural Production Resources) Ed.Bd. circ. 6,000. **Document type:** government publication.
Formerly: Guide to the Use of Insecticides and Fungicides in South Africa.

AGRICULTURE — CROP PRODUCTION AND SOIL

633.6   GY
GUYANA SUGAR CORPORATION. ANNUAL REPORTS AND ACCOUNTS. 1976. a. Guyana Sugar Corporation Ltd., 22 Church St., Georgetown, Guyana. TEL 592-2-62918. FAX 592-2-57274. illus. circ. 1,000. **Document type:** corporate report.
  Description: Outlines the activities and achievements of the year. Includes a chairman's statement, directors' report, review of operations and financial-statistical statements.

H D R A NEWS. (Henry Doubleday Research Association) see *GARDENING AND HORTICULTURE*

630   US
H O M E VOICE. 1994. q. $25. Hoosier Organic Marketing Education, 8364 S. State Rd. 39, Clayton, IN 46118-9178. Ed. Cissy Bowman. adv.; bk.rev. **Document type:** newsletter, consumer publication, trade publication.

HANDBOOK OF INDIAN PUMPS FOR IRRIGATION; salient features and performances. see *AGRICULTURE — Agricultural Equipment*

631 540 660   KO   ISSN 0368-2897
                        CODEN: JKACA7
HANGUK NONGHWAHAKHOECHI/AGRICULTURAL CHEMISTRY AND BIOTECHNOLOGY. (Text in Korean; abstracts in English) 1960. bi-m. Korean Agricultural Chemical Society, c/o Dept. of Agricultural Chemistry, College of Agriculture & Life Sciences, Seoul National University, Suwon 441-744, S. Korea. TEL 0331-290-2415. FAX 0331-294-3929. Ed. Jin Jung.
  —BLDSC (0745.013000); CASDDS.

631   PP   ISSN 0378-8865
                   CODEN: HARVDQ
HARVEST. (Text in English) 1971. 3/yr. K.13.05 to Australia, Asia, Pacific; other countries K.18. Department of Agriculture and Livestock, Publication Section, P.O. Box 417, Konedobu, Papua New Guinea. TEL 214699. Ed. Ray Kumar. adv.; bk.rev.; illus. circ. 2,000. **Indexed:** So.Pac.Per.Ind. **Document type:** academic/scholarly publication.
  —BLDSC (4270.872500).
  Description: Information on projects, research and new recommendations in agriculture, livestock, soil in Papua New Guinea. For DAL officers, research workers, schools and institutions.

HAWAII WEEKLY WEATHER & CROP BULLETIN. see *METEOROLOGY*

633.6   US
             CODEN: HSEAAL
HAWAIIAN SUGAR PLANTERS' ASSOCIATION. ANNUAL REPORT. 1947. a. exchange basis only. Hawaiian Agriculture Research Center, 99-193 Aiea Heights Dr., Aiea, HI 96701. TEL 808-486-5335. FAX 808-486-5335. **Indexed:** Biol.Abstr., Rev.Appl.Entomol., Weed Abstr.
  Formerly: Hawaiian Sugar Planters' Association Experiment Station. Annual Report (ISSN 0073-1366)

631   US
HAY & FEEDSTUFFS. w. $70 (Canada & Mexico $75; elsewhere $105). U.S. Department of Agriculture, Agricultural Marketing Service (Greely), Livestock & Seed Division, 711 O St., Greely, CO 80631. TEL 303-353-9750. FAX 303-353-9790. (Subscr. to: U.S.D.A. Agricultural Marketing Service, Livestock & Seed Division, Rm. 2623-S, Box 96456, Washington DC 20090-6456. FAX 202-245-4732) **Document type:** government publication.

631   US
HAY THERE. 1972. m. $260 membership only. National Hay Association, 102 Treasure Isle Causeway, Ste. 201, St. Petersburg, FL 33706. TEL 813-367-9702. FAX 813-367-9608. Ed. Donald Kieffer. adv. circ. 500. **Document type:** trade publication.
  Description: Covers agricultural marketing concerns for hay producers.

633.491   US   ISSN 0018-1986
HINTS TO POTATO GROWERS. 1920. irreg. (2-4/yr.). $10 to non-members. New Jersey State Potato Association, Box 231 Blake Hall, Cook College, Rutgers University, New Brunswick, NJ 08903. Ed. Dr. Melvin Henninger. charts; stat. circ. 150. (processed)

630 581.1   UK
HOME-GROWN CEREALS AUTHORITY. CEREALS R & D CONFERENCE. PROCEEDINGS. 1991. a. Home-Grown Cereals Authority, Research and Development Advisory Committee, Hamlyn House, Highgate Hill, London N19 5PR, England. TEL 0171-263-3391. TELEX 27615. **Document type:** proceedings.

633.82   GW   ISSN 0018-4845
HOPFEN - RUNDSCHAU. 1950. m. DM.65 (foreign DM.75). Verband Deutscher Hopfenpflanzer e.V., Postfach 1229, 85280 Wolnzach, Germany. TEL 49-8442-9250-0. FAX 49-8442-4270. Ed. O. Weingarten. adv.: B&W page DM.1445; trim 189 x 255. bk.rev.; charts; illus.; mkt.; stat.; tr.mk. circ. 4,000. (processed; also avail. in cards) **Indexed:** Food Sci.& Tech.Abstr., Hort.Abstr. **Document type:** trade publication.
  —BLDSC (4326.650000).
  Description: Reviews all aspects of hops.

633   US   ISSN 0889-0463
HOPS MARKET NEWS. m. $18 (Canada & Mexico $20; elsewhere $25). U.S. Department of Agriculture, Agricultural Marketing Service (Portland), Livestock & Seed Division, 1220 S.W. Third Ave., Rm. 1772, Portland, OR 97204. (Subscr. to: U.S.D.A. Agricultural Marketing Service, Livestock & Seed Division, Rm. 2623, Box 96456, Washington, DC 20090-6456. FAX 202-245-4732) Ed. Lowell Serfling. (tabloid format; also avail. in microfiche from CIS; back issues avail.; reprint service avail. from CIS) **Indexed:** Amer.Stat.Ind. (1984-). **Document type:** government publication.
  Description: Provides information about prices and data for national hops production.

634   US
HORT EXPO NORTHWEST. 1990. a. Columbia Publishing and Design, 2520 W. Washington, Ste. 2, Box 9036, Yakima, WA 98909-0036. TEL 509-248-2452; 800-900-2452. FAX 509-248-4056. E-mail: dede@freshcut.com. Ed. Ken Hodge. adv. contact: Lynn Schuchardt. circ. 10,796 (controlled). **Document type:** trade publication.
  Description: Focuses on the northwest fruit industry with emphasis on trade shows in Oregon and Washington.

631   RH
HORTICULTURE RESEARCH INSTITUTE. ANNUAL REPORT. PART 1. HORTICULTURAL RESEARCH CENTRE. (Text in English) 1976. a. free. Ministry of Agriculture, Horticulture Research Institute, P.O. Box 3748, Marondera, Zimbabwe. (Subscr. to: P.O. Box 8108, Causeway, Harare, Zimbabwe) Ed. J.E. Jackson. circ. 300. **Document type:** government publication.
  Formerly: Horticulture and Coffee Research Institute. Annual Report. Part 1. Horticultural Research Centre.

631 635   UK   ISSN 0963-3235
HORTICULTURE RESEARCH INTERNATIONAL. 1914. a. £10. Horticulture Research International, West Malling, Kent ME19 6BJ, England. TEL 44-1732-843833. FAX 44-1732-849067. circ. 3,000. **Indexed:** Apic.Abstr., Biol.Abstr., Field Crop Abstr., Helminthol.Abstr., Herb.Abstr., Hort.Abstr., Rev.Appl.Entomol., Rev.Plant Path., Weed Abstr. **Document type:** academic/scholarly publication.
  —BLDSC (1290.310000). **CCC**.
  Former titles: B S H R Institute of Horticultural Research. Annual Report (ISSN 0953-2455); A F R C Institute of Horticultural Research Annual Report; (until 1989): East Malling Research Station. Annual Report (ISSN 0306-6398)

631   CN   ISSN 0319-6038
HURON SOIL AND CROP NEWS. 1956. a. Exeter Times-Advocate, 424 Main St., Exeter, ON, Canada. TEL 519-235-1331. Ed. Ross Haugh. adv. circ. 7,000.
  Former titles (until 1964): Huron County Soil and Crop News (ISSN 0319-602X); (until 1961): Huron Soil and Crop News (ISSN 0319-6011)

631   US
I C A S A NEWS. a. free. International Consortium for Agricultural Systems Applications (ICASA), 2500 Dole St., Krauss 22, Honolulu, HI 96822. TEL 808-956-8858. FAX 808-956-3421. E-mail: icasa@agrss-sherman.hawaii.edu; URL: http://agrss.sherman.hawaii.edu/icasa. Ed. Gordon Y. Tsuji. adv. contact: Agnes Shimamura. circ. 300 (controlled). (back issues avail.) **Document type:** newsletter.
  Former titles (until 1995): I B S N A T Views (ISSN 0883-8631); (until 1993): Agrotechnology Transfer.
  Description: Updates on applications, reports on advances in technology and information on program status.
  Refereed Serial

I C C O COCOA NEWSLETTER. (International Cocoa Organization) see *FOOD AND FOOD INDUSTRIES*

631.8   FR
I F A TECHNICAL CONFERENCE. PROCEEDINGS. (Former publisher: International Superphosphate Manufacturers Association, Ltd.) biennial. International Fertilizer Industry Association, 28 rue Marbeuf, 75008 Paris, France. TEL 33-1-53930500. FAX 33-1-53930547. TELEX 640481F. E-mail: ifamail@worldnet.fr; URL: htpp://www.worldnet.net/~ifamail/. **Document type:** proceedings.
  Formerly: I S M A Technical Conference. Proceedings.

633.2   UK   ISSN 1358-5991
I G E R TECHNICAL REVIEW. 1994. irreg. Institute of Grassland and Environmental Research, Aberystwyth Research Centre, Plas Gogerddan, Aberystwyth, Dyfed SY23 3EB, Wales. TEL 44-1970-828255. FAX 44-1970-828357. (Alt. addr.: North Wyke Research Station, Okehampton, Devon EX20 2SB, England. TEL 44-1837-82558) **Document type:** monographic series.

631   SZ
I P I BULLETIN. (Text mainly in English; occasionally in Spanish) 1974. irreg., no. 15, 1996. price varies. International Potash Institute, P.O. Box 1609, CH-4001 Basel, Switzerland. TEL 41-61-2612922. FAX 41-61-2612925. **Indexed:** Biol.Abstr., Field Crop Abstr., Herb.Abstr., Soils & Fert. **Document type:** bulletin.

631   SZ   ISSN 0379-0495
                       CODEN: IRTOD9
I P I RESEARCH TOPICS. (Text in English) 1976. irreg., no. 20, 1996. price varies. International Potash Institute, P.O. Box 1609, CH-4001 Basel, Switzerland. TEL 41-61-2612922. FAX 41-61-2612925. **Indexed:** Biol.Abstr., Field Crop Abstr., Herb.Abstr., Soils & Fert. **Document type:** monographic series.
  —CASDDS; Linda Hall.

I S O S C PROCEEDINGS. (International Society for Soilless Culture) see *GARDENING AND HORTICULTURE*

630   SZ   ISSN 0019-0713
I S T A NEWS BULLETIN. (Text in English, French, Spanish) 1959. 3/yr. free. International Seed Testing Association, P.O. Box 412, CH-8046 Zurich, Switzerland. TEL 41-1-3713133. FAX 41-1-3713427. E-mail: istach@iprolink.ch. Ed. H. Schmid. (processed) **Indexed:** Hort.Abstr., Plant Breed.Abstr. **Document type:** newsletter.
  Description: Includes seed testing results, reports and announcements of meetings, courses and seminars and association news.

631   SP   ISSN 1130-6017
I T E A PRODUCCION VEGETAL. (Text in Spanish; summaries in English) 1986. 3/yr. 3500 ptas. (effective 1996). Asociacion Interprofesional para el Desarrollo Agrario, Montanana 177, Apdo. 727, 50080 Zaragoza, Spain. TEL 34-76-576311. FAX 34-76-575501. E-mail: alberti@mizar.csic.es. Ed. C. Zaragoza. R&P contact: Leonardo Plana. adv. contact: Joaquin Uriarte. circ. 600. **Indexed:** Ind.SST. **Document type:** academic/scholarly publication.
  Supersedes in part (in 1990): Informacion Tecnica Economica Agraria (ISSN 0212-2731)
  Refereed Serial

AGRICULTURE — CROP PRODUCTION AND SOIL

633.6 DR ISSN 1013-980X
INAZUCAR. bi-m. RD.$3. Instituto Azucarero Dominicano, Centro de los Heroes, Apdo. de Correos 667, Santo Domingo, Dominican Republic. Ed. Quirilio Vilorio Sanchez. illus.; stat.

631 II
INDIA. CARDAMOM BOARD. ANNUAL REPORT. (Text in English) a. Spices Board, K.C. Ave., St. Vincent Cross Rd., P.B. No. 1909, Ernakulam, Kochi 682 018, India. TEL 353837. FAX 484-364429. TELEX 0885-6534 SEPC IN.

631.8 II
INDIAN FERTILISER INDUSTRY DESKBOOK. (Text in English) 1977. biennial. Rs.175($55) Technical Press Publications, 5-1 Convent St., Colaba, Mumbai 400 039, India. TEL 91-22-2021446. FAX 91-22-2871499. TELEX 011-83479 CHEM IN. Ed. J.P. de Sousa. adv.; bk.rev.; adver.; charts; illus. circ. 6,400. (also avail. in microform from UMI) **Document type:** trade publication.

INDIAN FERTILISER STATISTICS. see AGRICULTURE — Abstracting, Bibliographies, Statistics

633 II ISSN 0073-649X
SB229.I4
INDIAN INSTITUTE OF SUGARCANE RESEARCH, LUCKNOW. ANNUAL REPORT. (Text in English) 1954. a. exchange basis. Indian Institute of Sugarcane Research, Indian Council of Agricultural Research, Lucknow 2, Uttar Pradesh, India. **Indexed:** Rev.Plant Path.

630.24 668.6 II ISSN 0367-8229
CODEN: IJACBO
INDIAN JOURNAL OF AGRICULTURAL CHEMISTRY. (Text in English) 1968. 3/yr. Rs.250. Indian Society of Agricultural Chemists, c/o Sheila Dhar Institute of Soil Science, University of Allahabad, 5 - Lajpat Rai Rd., Allahabad 211002, India. (Co-sponsor: Indian Council of Agricultural Research) Ed. Samarendra Kumar De. adv.; bk.rev. circ. 400. (back issues avail.) **Indexed:** Biol.Abstr., Biol.& Agr.Ind., Chem.Abstr., Crop Physiol.Abstr., Curr.Adv.Ecol.Sci., Excerp.Med., Field Crop Abstr., Herb.Abstr., Hort.Abstr., Irr.& Drain.Abstr., Seed Abstr., Soils & Fert., Triticale Abstr., Trop.Oil Seeds Abstr., Weed Abstr.
—CASDDS; CISTI; Linda Hall; UMI; UnCover.

631.4 II ISSN 0970-3349
INDIAN JOURNAL OF SOIL CONSERVATION. (Text in English) 1972. bi-m. $60. Central Soil and Water Conservation Research and Training Institute, 218 Kaulagarh Rd., Dehradun 248195, India. TEL 91-135-758564. FAX 91-135-624213. TELEX 585-237 SCRI IN. E-mail: cswcrti@x400.nicgw.nic. in. (Dist. by: HPC Publishers' Distributors (Pvt.) Ltd., 4805-24, 1st Fl., Bharat Ram Rd., Darya Ganj, New Delhi 110 002, India. TEL 91-11-3254402. FAX 91-11-6863511) (Co-sponsor: Association of Soil and Water Conservationists and Trainees) Ed. K.S. Dadhwal. bk.rev. **Indexed:** Geo.Abstr., Soils & Fert.
—BLDSC (4421.230000).
Formerly (until 1978): Soil Conservation Digest (ISSN 0377-5402)

631 II ISSN 0970-8235
INDIAN POTATO ASSOCIATION. JOURNAL. (Text and summaries in English) 1974. q. Rs.400($40) Indian Potato Association, Central Potato Research Institute, Simla 171 001, India. TEL 0177-72182. FAX 0177-5016. TELEX 0391-240 MOOL IN. E-mail: spri@hub.nic.in. Ed. S.M. Paul Khurana. adv.; bk.rev.; circ. 700 (paid). (back issues avail.) **Indexed:** Biol.Abstr., Curr.Adv.Ecol.Sci., Field Crop Abstr., Herb.Abstr., Soils & Fert. **Document type:** academic/scholarly publication.
Description: Disseminates the research work, development and technology on potato production to researchers, growers and potato industry.
Refereed Serial

INDIAN SPICES. see BUSINESS AND ECONOMICS — International Commerce

633 II ISSN 0019-6428
CODEN: ISUGAS
INDIAN SUGAR; complete sugar journal. (Text in English) 1950. m. Rs.120. Indian Sugar Mills Association, Sugar House, 39, Nehru Place, New Delhi 110 019, India. TEL 6416601. Ed. S.L. Jain. adv.; bk.rev.; charts; stat.; index. circ. 1,100. **Indexed:** Chem.Abstr., Field Crop Abstr., Food Sci.& Tech.Abstr., Herb.Abstr., Hort.Abstr., Soils & Fert., Sugar Ind.Abstr.
—BLDSC (4429.800000); CASDDS; CISTI.

631 575.1 NE ISSN 0926-6690
CODEN: ICRDEW
INDUSTRIAL CROPS AND PRODUCTS. (Text in English) 1992. q. fl.880($506) (effective 1998). (Association for the Advancement of Industrial Crops) Elsevier Science B.V., P.O. Box 211, 1000 AE Amsterdam, Netherlands. TEL 31-20-4853911. FAX 31-20-4853598. TELEX 18582 ESPA NL. E-mail: nlinfo-f@elsevier.nl; usinfo-f@elsevier.com; forinfo-kyf04035@niftyserve.or.jp; URL: http://www.elsevier.nl/. (Subscr. in the Americas to: Elsevier Science, Regional Sales Office, Box 945, New York, NY 10159-0945. TEL 212-633-3730. FAX 212-633-3680; Subscr. in Australasia and the Far East to: Elsevier Science (Singapore) Pte Ltd, No.1 Temasek Ave., No.17-01 Millenia Tower, Singapore 039192, Singapore. TEL 65-434-3727. FAX 65-337-2230; Subscr. in Japan to: Elsevier Science Japan, 9-15 Higashi-Azabu 1-chome, Minato-ku, Tokyo 106, Japan. TEL 81-3-5561-5033. FAX 81-3-5561-5047) Eds. F.S. Nakayama, W.M.J. van Gelder. bk.rev. (also avail. in microform from UMI; back issues avail.) **Indexed:** ASCA, Curr.Cont., Ecol.Abstr., Food Sci.& Tech.Abstr., IDA. **Document type:** academic/scholarly publication.
—BLDSC (4448.357000); CASDDS; CISTI; EMDOCS; Genuine Article; KR SourceOne; SWETS; UnCover. **CCC.**
Description: Covers advances in the development, production, harvesting, storage and processing of nonfood crops for industrial uses, including applications of pharmaceuticals, lubricants, fuels, fibers, essential oils, biologically active materials, and uses for industrial crop by-products.
Refereed Serial

634 GW ISSN 0367-939X
CODEN: INOGAV
INDUSTRIELLE OBST- UND GEMUESEVERWERTUNG. 1914. m. DM.189. Verlag Guenter Hempel, Postfach 100706, 38407 Wolfsburg, Germany. TEL 05361-12042. **Indexed:** Food Sci.& Tech.Abstr., INIS Atomind., Packag.Sci.Tech.
—CASDDS.

631 CU ISSN 0138-7634
INFORMACION EXPRESS. SERIE: CAFE Y CACAO. 1977. 3/yr. $6 in N. America; S. America $9; Europe $10; others $14; or exchange basis. Centro de Informacion y Documentacion Agropecuario, Gaveta Postal 4149, Havana 4, Cuba. TEL 301672. TELEX 0511007. (Dist. by: Ediciones Cubanas, Obispo No. 527, Apdo. 605, Havana, Cuba) stat. **Indexed:** Agrindex.

631 CU ISSN 0138-743X
INFORMACION EXPRESS. SERIE: CITRICOS Y OTROS FRUTALES. 1977. 3/yr. C.$0.90($6) in N. America; S. America $9; Europe $10; others $14; or exchange basis. Centro de Informacion y Documentacion Agropecuario, Gaveta Postal 4149, Havana 4, Cuba. TEL 301672. TELEX 0511007. (Dist. by: Ediciones Cubanas, Obispo No. 527, Apdo. 605, Havana, Cuba) stat. **Indexed:** Agrindex.

631 CU ISSN 0138-7286
INFORMACION EXPRESS. SERIE: PROTECCION DE PLANTAS. 1977. 4/yr. C.$1.20($9) in N. America; S. America $11; Europe $13; others $18; or exchange basis. Centro de Informacion y Documentacion Agropecuario, Gaveta Postal 4149, Havana 4, Cuba. TEL 3016272. (Dist. by: Ediciones Cubanas, Obispo No. 527, Apdo. 605, Havana, Cuba) **Indexed:** Agrindex.

631 CU
INFORMACION EXPRESS. SERIE: RIEGO Y DRENAJE. 1978. 3/yr. $6 in N. America; S. America $9; Europe $10; others $14; or exchange basis. Centro de Informacion y Documentacion Agropecuario, Gaveta Postal 4149, Havana 4, Cuba. (Dist. by: Ediciones Cubanas, Obispo No. 527, Apdo. 605, Havana, Cuba) **Indexed:** Agrindex.

631 CU ISSN 0138-7030
INFORMACION EXPRESS. SERIE: SUELOS Y AGROQUIMICA. 1977. 4/yr. $9 in N. America; S. America $11; Europe $13; others $18; or exchange basis. Centro de Informacion y Documentacion Agropecuario, Gaveta Postal 4149, Havana 4, Cuba. (Dist. by: Ediciones Cubanas, Obispo No. 527, Apdo. 695, Havana, Cuba) **Indexed:** Agrindex.

631 CU ISSN 0138-7138
INFORMACION EXPRESS. SERIE: TABACO. 1977. 2/yr. C.$0.60($5) in N. America; S. America and Europe $6; others $9; or exchange basis. Centro de Informacion y Documentacion Agropecuario, Gaveta Postal 4149, Havana 4, Cuba. (Dist. by: Ediciones Cubanas, Obispo No. 527, Apdo. 605, Havana, Cuba) stat. **Indexed:** Agrindex.

631 CU ISSN 0138-7189
INFORMACION EXPRESS. SERIE: VIANDAS, HORTALIZAS Y GRANOS. 1977. 5/yr. $10 in N. America; S. America $14; Europe $15; others $21; or exchange basis. Centro de Informacion y Documentacion Agropecuario, Gaveta Postal 4149, Havana 4, Cuba. (Dist. by: Ediciones Cubanas, Obispo No. 527, Apdo. 605, Havana, Cuba) **Indexed:** Agrindex.

630 664 FR ISSN 1242-1626
INGENIEURS DE LA VIE. 1945. q. 200 F. Amicale des Anciens de l'Agro, 5 Quai Voltaire, 75007 Paris, France. FAX 33-1-42614850. Ed. Georges Darret. adv.; bk.rev.; charts; illus.; stat. circ. 5,000. **Indexed:** Excerp.Med., GeoRef.
—BLDSC (4510.045000).
Formerly: Cahiers des Ingenieurs Agronomes (ISSN 0035-2179)

INSTITUT PHYTOPATHOLOGIQUE BENAKI. ANNALES. NOUVELLE SERIE. see AGRICULTURE

633 SA
INSTITUTE FOR TROPICAL AND SUBTROPICAL CROPS. BULLETIN. no.426, 1994. irreg. Agricultural Research Council, Institute for Tropical and Subtropical Crops, P.O. Box 8783, Pretoria 0001, South Africa. illus. **Document type:** monographic series, bulletin.

631 UK ISSN 0955-9051
INSTITUTE OF ARABLE CROPS RESEARCH. REPORT. 1903. a. free. Institute of Arable Crops Research, Harpenden, Herts. AL5 2JQ, England. TEL 44-1582-763133. FAX 44-1582-760981. Ed. S.E. Allsopp. index. circ. 3,000. **Indexed:** Biol.Abstr., Cott.&Trop.Fibr.Abstr., Fababean Abstr., Field Crop Abstr., Herb.Abstr., Hort.Abstr., Maize Abstr., Ornam.Hort., Rev.Appl.Entomol., Rev.Plant Path., Rice Abstr., VITIS, Weed Abstr. **Document type:** corporate report.
—CISTI; Linda Hall.
Supersedes (in 1988): Rothamsted Experimental Station Report (ISSN 0262-1215); Which was formerly: Long Ashton Research Station Report (ISSN 0954-4968); (until 1985): Long Ashton Research Station Annual Report (ISSN 0368-7708)

633 IS
INSTITUTE OF FIELD AND GARDEN CROPS. SCIENTIFIC ACTIVITIES. (Text in English) triennial. $25 (effective 1996). Agricultural Research Organization, Institute of Field and Garden Crops, Volcani Centre, P.O. Box 6, Bet Dagan 50250, Israel. TEL 972-3-980205. FAX 972-3-993998. **Indexed:** Biol.Abstr. **Document type:** government publication.

633.2 UK ISSN 0961-6071
S542.G72
INSTITUTE OF GRASSLAND AND ENVIRONMENTAL RESEARCH (UK). ANNUAL REPORT. 1965. a. price varies. Institute of Grassland and Environmental Research, Plas Gogerddan, Aberystwyth, Dyfed SY23 3EB, Wales. TEL 44-1970-828255. FAX 44-1970-828357. Ed. Caroline Moss-Gibbons. circ. 2,000. **Indexed:** Anim.Breed.Abstr., Biol.Abstr., Field Crop Abstr., Herb.Abstr., Soils & Fert., Weed Abstr. **Document type:** corporate report.
—BLDSC (7369.273700); Linda Hall.
Former titles (until 1990): Institute for Grassland and Animal Production, England (Berkshire) (ISSN 0953-7295); Animal and Grassland Research Institute, Hurley, England (Berkshire) Technical Reports; Grassland Research Institute, Hurley, England (Berkshire) Technical Reports (ISSN 0072-5552)

AGRICULTURE — CROP PRODUCTION AND SOIL

633.2   UK
▼**INSTITUTE OF GRASSLAND AND ENVIRONMENTAL RESEARCH (UK). TECHNICAL ADVISORY REPORT.** 1996. irreg. price varies. Institute of Grassland and Environmental Research, Aberystwyth Research Centre, Plas Gogerddan, Aberystwyth, Dyfed SY23 3EB, Wales. TEL 44-1970-828255. FAX 44-1970-828357. **Document type:** monographic series.

630   IS
INSTITUTE OF PLANT PROTECTION. SCIENTIFIC ACTIVITIES. (Text in English) triennial. $25 (effective 1996). Agricultural Research Organization, Institute of Plant Protection, Volcani Center, P.O. Box 6, Bet Dagan 50250, Israel. TEL 972-3-9683216. FAX 972-3-993998. Ed. V.R. Priel. circ. 200. **Document type:** government publication.

631.4   IS
INSTITUTE OF SOILS & WATER. SCIENTIFIC ACTIVITIES. (Text in English) triennial. $25. Agricultural Research Organization, Institute of Soils & Water, Volcani Center, P.O. Box 6, Bet Dagan 50250, Israel. TEL 972-3-9683216. FAX 972-3-993998. **Document type:** government publication.

631 630   II   ISSN 0257-3431
S671
INSTITUTION OF ENGINEERS (INDIA). AGRICULTURAL ENGINEERING DIVISION. JOURNAL. (Text in English) 1983. s-a. Rs.60($20) Institution of Engineers (India), Agricultural Engineering Division, 8 Gokhale Rd., Calcutta 700 020, India. TEL 91-33-2238334. FAX 91-33-2238345. TELEX 021-7855 IEIC IN. Ed. S.P. Misra. adv. circ. 2,000. **Indexed:** Met.Abstr. **Document type:** academic/scholarly publication.
—CISTI; Ei; Linda Hall.
   Refereed Serial

633.491   RM   ISSN 1016-4839
INSTITUTUL DE CERCETARE SI PRODUCTIE PENTRU CULTURA SI INDUSTRIALIZAREA SFECLEI DE ZAHAR SI A SUBSTANTELOR DULCI-FUNDULEA. LUCRARI STIINTIFICE. SFECLA SI ZAHAR. (Text in Rumanian; summaries in English, French, German, Russian) 1969. a. 615 lei. Institutul de Cercetare si Productie pentru Cultura si Industrializarea Sfeclei de Zahar si a Substantelor Dulci-Fundulea, Judetul Calarasi, 8264 Fundulea, Rumania. **Indexed:** Biol.Abstr., Field Crop Abstr., Herb.Abstr., Plant Breed.Abstr., Sugar Ind.Abstr.
   Former titles: Institutul de Cercetari si Productie a Cartofului, Brasov. Anale. Lucrari Stiintifice; Institutul de Cercetari pentru Cultura Cartofului si Sfeclei de Zahar, Brasov. Anale. Cartoful (ISSN 0074-0373)

633.41   RM
INSTITUTUL DE CERCETARI PENTRU CEREALE SI PLANTE TEHNICE. LABORATOR SFECLA DE ZAHAR. ANALE. LUCRARI STIINTIFICE. (Text in Rumanian; summaries in English, German, Russian) 1968. a. 15000 lei. Institutul de Cercetari pentru Cereale si Plante Tehnice, 8264 Fundulea-Calarasi, Rumania. Ed. Aurel Florentin Badiu. **Indexed:** Biol.Abstr., Irr.& Drain.Abstr., Weed Abstr. **Document type:** academic/scholarly publication.
   Formerly: Institutul de Cercetari pentru Cultura Cartofului si Sfeclei de Zahar, Brasov. Anale. Sflecla de Zahar (ISSN 0074-0381)

632 581   NE   ISSN 0074-0446
SB599
INSTITUUT VOOR PLANTEZIEKTENKUNDIG ONDERZOEK. JAARVERSLAG/RESEARCH INSTITUTE FOR PLANT PROTECTION. ANNUAL REPORT. (Text in Dutch, English) 1950. a. price varies. Instituut voor Planteziektenkundig Onderzoek, P.O. Box 9060, 6700 GW Wageningen, Netherlands. FAX 08370-10113. TELEX 65888 INTAS.

631   PL   ISSN 0373-7837
INSTYTUT HODOWLI I AKLIMATYZACJI ROSLIN. BIULETYN/INSTITUTE OF PLANT BREEDING AND ACCLIMATIZATION. BULLETIN. (Text in Polish; summaries in English) 1951. q. $160. Instytut Hodowli i Aklimatyzacji Roslin, Radzikow, 05-870 Blonie, Poland. TEL 725-3611. FAX 725-4714. TELEX 812914 IHAR PL. (Dist. by: Centrala Kolportazu Prasy i Wydawnictw, ul. Towarowa 28, Warsaw, Poland) Ed. Henryk J. Czembor. R&P contact: Roman Osinski. adv. contact: Roman Osinski. bk.rev. (reprint service avail.) **Indexed:** AgroLibrex, Biol.Abstr., Crop Physiol.Abstr., Field Crop Abstr., Herb.Abstr., Hort.Abstr., Plant Breed.Abstr., Plant Grow.Reg.Abstr., Rev.Plant Path., Seed Abstr., Triticale Abstr. **Document type:** academic/scholarly publication.
—BLDSC (2099.300000).
   Description: Contains publications of plant breeding and genetics, physiology, biochemistry, phytopathology - important for practical plant breeding and seed production, as well as publications on the value of collected germ plasm for creation of new plant genotypes.

632.97   UK   ISSN 1353-5226
SB950.9
▼**INTEGRATED PEST MANAGEMENT REVIEWS.** Abbreviated title: I P M R. 1995. q. £65 (foreign $110) to individuals; institutions £195 (foreign $325) (effective 1998). Thomson Science (Subsidiary of: International Thomson Publishing Group), 2-6 Boundary Row, London SE1 8HN, England. TEL 44-171-8650066. FAX 44-171-5229623. TELEX 290164 CHAPMA G. E-mail: jhelp@chall.co.uk; URL: http://www.thomsonscience.com. (Subscr. to: International Thomson Publishing Services Ltd., Cheriton House, North Way, Andover, Hants. SP10 5BE, England. TEL 44-1264-342713. FAX 44-1264-342807; Subscr. in N. America to: Chapman & Hall, Journals Promotion Department, One Penn Plaza, 41st Fl., New York, NY 10119. TEL 800-552-5866) Ed. David Dent. adv.; bk.rev. (reprint service avail.) **Document type:** academic/scholarly publication.
●Also available online.
—BLDSC (4531.816103).
   Description: Publishes papers and reviews on all aspects of integrated pest management from a broad range of disciplines.
   Refereed Serial

630 574.191   PL   ISSN 0236-8722
                                        CODEN: INAGEX
INTERNATIONAL AGROPHYSICS; a quarterly journal on physical properties and processes affecting plant production. (Former name of issuing body: Akademiai Kiado, Publishing House of the Hungarian Academy of Sciences) (Text in English) 1985-1989 (vol.5); resumed vol.6, 1992. q. $140 (effective 1997 & 1998). Polska Akademia Nauk, Instytut Agrofizyki - Polish Academy of Sciences, Institute of Agrophysics, Ul. Doswiadczalna 4, P.O. Box 121, 20-236 Lublin, Poland. TEL 48-81-7445061. FAX 48-81-7445067. TELEX 643733 IAF PL. E-mail: fundacja@demeter.ipan.lublin.pl. (Dist. by: Foundation for Development of Agrophysical Research, ul. Doswiadczalna 4, P.O. Box 121, 20-236 Lublin, Poland) (Co-sponsor: State Committee for Scientific Research) Ed. Jan Glinski. adv.: page $25; adv. contact: Ewa Sikora. (reprint service avail.) **Indexed:** AgroAgen, Chem.Abstr., Ecol.Abstr., Geo.Abstr.P.G. **Document type:** trade publication.
—BLDSC (4535.654000); CASDDS; EMDOCS; KR SourceOne; Linda Hall. **CCC.**
   Refereed Serial

631.8   UK
INTERNATIONAL CONFERENCE ON FERTILIZERS. PROCEEDINGS. 8th, 1985. irreg. £95. British Sulphur Publishing (Subsidiary of: C R U Publishing Ltd.), 31 Mount Pleasant, London WC1X 0AD, England. TEL 44-171-837-5600. FAX 44-171-837-0292. TELEX 918918 SULFEX G. Pub. John French. R&P contact: John French. **Document type:** proceedings.

631.8   SZ   ISSN 1012-103X
INTERNATIONAL FERTILIZER CORRESPONDENT. (Text in English) 1960. 3/yr. 18 SFr.($14) International Potash Institute, P.O. Box 1609, CH-4001 Basel, Switzerland. TEL 41-61-2612922. FAX 41-61-2612925. Ed.Bd. **Document type:** newsletter.
   Description: Provides short informations on achievements in the fields of fertilizers and crop fertilization.

INTERNATIONAL FRUIT WORLD; review of the international fruit and vegetable wholesale trade. see *FOOD AND FOOD INDUSTRIES*

633   RU   ISSN 0074-6185
INTERNATIONAL GRASSLAND CONGRESS. PROCEEDINGS. 1927. irreg., 12th, 1974, Moscow. $50. International Grassland Congress, All-Union Research Forage Institute, c/o Dr. V.G. Iglovikov, Ed., Moscow Region, 141740 Lugovaya, Russia. **Indexed:** Field Crop Abstr., Herb.Abstr., Weed Abstr.

633.6   BE
INTERNATIONAL INSTITUTE FOR BEET RESEARCH. CONGRESS PROCEEDINGS. Short title: I I R B Congress Proceedings. (Text and summaries in English, French, German) 21st, 1958. a. 2200 BEF (effective 1996). International Institute for Beet Research, 47 rue Montoyer, 1000 Brussels, Belgium. TEL 32-2-5091531. FAX 32-2-5126506. Ed.Bd. adv. circ. 710. (back issues avail.) **Indexed:** Food Sci.& Tech.Abstr., Weed Abstr. **Document type:** proceedings.
   Former titles: International Institute for Beet Research. Journal; International Institute for Sugar Beet Research. Reports of the Winter Congress (ISSN 0074-6460)

631.6   NE   ISSN 0165-1803
S605   CODEN: AILRAS
INTERNATIONAL INSTITUTE FOR LAND RECLAMATION AND IMPROVEMENT. ANNUAL REPORT. (Text in English) 1960. a. free. International Institute for Land Reclamation and Improvement, P.O. Box 45, 6700 AA Wageningen, Netherlands. TEL 31-317-490144. FAX 31-317-417187. TELEX 45888 INTAS NL. E-mail: ilri@ilri.nl. Ed. M.G. Bos. R&P contact: E.A. Rylhsen. adv. contact: E.A. Rylhsen. charts; illus.; stat. **Indexed:** Documentatieblad, Field Crop Abstr., Herb.Abstr., Soils & Fert., Weed Abstr. **Document type:** corporate report.
—BLDSC (1311.500000); CISTI.
   Description: Collects and disseminates research on land and water management throughout the world. Also covers consultancy, training, as well as activities and publications of the Institute.

631.6   NE   ISSN 0074-6452
                                   CODEN: PILIAU
INTERNATIONAL INSTITUTE FOR LAND RECLAMATION AND IMPROVEMENT. PUBLICATION. (Some nos. include diskette) (Text in English) 1958. irreg., no.55, 1994. price varies. International Institute for Land Reclamation and Improvement, P.O. Box 45, 6700 AA Wageningen, Netherlands. TEL 31-317-490144. FAX 31-317-417187. TELEX 45888 INTAS NL. E-mail: ilri@ilri.nl. Ed. M.G. Bos. R&P contact: E.A. Rylhsen. adv. contact: E.A. Rylhsen. (back issues avail.) **Indexed:** Forest.Abstr., Forest Prod.Abstr., Irr.& Drain.Abstr., Soils & Fert. **Document type:** government publication, monographic series.
   Description: Publishes research studies dealing with topics and issues in land and water use, including agricultural development, irrigation, water quality, and related concerns. Also publishes specialized computer programs for applications in the field.

AGRICULTURE — CROP PRODUCTION AND SOIL

632.9 UK ISSN 0967-0874
SB950.A1 CODEN: IPEMEH
INTERNATIONAL JOURNAL OF PEST MANAGEMENT. Online edition (UK ISSN 1366-5863) vol.17, 1971. q. £198($327) to institutions (£238($392) with online ed.) (effective 1998). Taylor & Francis Ltd., 1 Gunpowder Sq., London EC4A 3DE, England. TEL 44-171-583-0490. FAX 44-171-583-0585. TELEX 858540. E-mail: info@tandf.co.uk; URL: http://www.tandf.co.uk/. (Subscr. to: Taylor & Francis Inc., 1900 Frost Rd., Ste. 101, Bristol, PA 19007-1598. TEL 800-821-8312. FAX 215-785-5515) Eds. Neil Kidd, Mark Jervis. bk.rev.; charts; illus.; stat.; index. circ. 3,000. **Indexed:** Apic.Abstr., ASCA, Bio-Contr.News & Info., Biodet.Abstr., Biol.Abstr., Biotech.Abstr., Chem.Abstr., Cott.& Trop.Fibr.Abstr., Curr.Adv.Ecol.Sci., Curr.Cont., Ecol.Abstr., Ecol.Abstr., Environ.Per.Bibl. (1990-), Field Crop Abstr., Food Sci.& Tech.Abstr., Forest.Abstr., Forest Prod.Abstr., Geo.Abstr.H.G., Helminthol.Abstr., Hort.Abstr., IDA, Ind.Vet., Irr.& Drain.Abstr., Maize Abstr., Plant Breed.Abstr., Plant Grow.Reg.Abstr., Rev.Appl.Entomol., Rev.Plant Path., Rice Abstr., Seed Abstr., So.Pac.Per.Ind., Soils & Fert., Sorghum & Millets Abstr., Trop.Oil Seeds Abstr., Vet.Bull., Weed Abstr. **Document type:** trade publication.
●Also available online.
—BLDSC (4542.452800); CASDDS; Genuine Article; Linda Hall; SWETS; UnCover. **CCC**.
Former titles: Tropical Pest Management (ISSN 0143-6147); P A N S (ISSN 0030-7793)
Description: Covers all spheres of pre- and postharvest pest management, vector-borne diseases and public health, and the relationship of pest management to the wider aspects of farming systems and rural developments.
Refereed Serial

INTERNATIONAL PEST CONTROL; crop protection, public health, wood preservation. see BIOLOGY — *Entomology*

632.97 UK ISSN 1351-346X
SB951
INTERNATIONAL PESTICIDE DIRECTORY. 1981. a. £30($60) (effective 1997). Research Information Ltd., 222 Maylands Ave., Hemel Hempstead, Herts. HP2 7TD, England. TEL 44-1442-213222. FAX 44-1442-259395. E-mail: resinf@globalnet.co.uk. adv.: B&W page £960; adv. contact: J. Kumar Patel. circ. 6,400. **Document type:** directory.
—BLDSC (4544.911000).
Description: Directory on trade named pesticides, their active ingredients and the companies that manufacture and market them.

631.8 SZ ISSN 0074-7491
CODEN: PCPIA8
INTERNATIONAL POTASH INSTITUTE. COLLOQUIUM. PROCEEDINGS. (Text in English) 1963. irreg., 24th, 1995. price varies. International Potash Institute, P.O. Box 1609, CH-4001 Basel, Switzerland. TEL 41-61-2612922. FAX 41-61-2612925. **Indexed:** Biol.Abstr., Chem.Abstr. **Document type:** proceedings.
—CASDDS.

631.8 SZ
CODEN: PCIIDA
INTERNATIONAL POTASH INSTITUTE. CONGRESS PROCEEDINGS. (Text in English) irreg., 1994, Sri Lanka. price varies. International Potash Institute, P.O. Box 1609, CH-4001 Basel, Switzerland. TEL 41-61-2612922. FAX 41-61-2612925. **Document type:** proceedings.
—BLDSC (6842.890000); CASDDS.
Formerly: International Potash Institute. Congress Report (ISSN 0074-7505)

633 338.1 UN ISSN 0538-9550
CODEN: IRCNAK
INTERNATIONAL RICE COMMISSION. NEWSLETTER. 1952. a. free. Food and Agriculture Organization of the United Nations, Agriculture Department, Via delle Terme di Caracalla, 00100 Rome, Italy. TEL 5225155769. FAX 52253152. TELEX 625842 FAO I. Ed. Dat Van Tran. bk.rev. circ. 1,200. (also avail. in microfiche from CIS) **Indexed:** Agri.Eng.Abstr., Bio-Contr.News & Info., Biol.Abstr., Field Crop Abstr., Herb.Abstr., IIS, Plant Breed.Abstr., Rev.Plant Path., Rice Abstr., Seed Abstr., Weed Abstr., World Agri.Econ.& Rural Sociol.Abstr. **Document type:** newsletter.
—BLDSC (4548.120000).
Description: Provides member countries and other rice research and development institutions with reviews and relevant information on the world rice situation and outlook, new breakthroughs in research, national rice programs and FAO-supported activities.

631.4 AU ISSN 0374-0447
INTERNATIONAL SOCIETY OF SOIL SCIENCE. BULLETIN. (Text in English, French, German, Spanish) 1952. s-a. $50 to non-members; free to members. International Society of Soil Science, c/o Institute of Soil Science, University of Agriculture, Gregor-Mendel-Str. 33, A-1180 Vienna, Austria. TEL 43-1-310-6026. FAX 43-1-3106027. TELEX 111010 TZSTA. E-mail: isss@edu1.boku.ac.at. (Subscr. to: Dr. P. Luescher, Forschungsanstalt W S L, Zuercherstr. 111, CH-8903 Birmensdorf bei Zurich, Switzerland) Ed. Winfried Blum. R&P contact: Winfried Blum. adv. contact: Peter Luescher. bk.rev. circ. 7,000. **Document type:** bulletin.
Description: Provides society news and reports of events and activities, both nationally and internationally. Includes announcements of meetings, conferences and symposia.

631.5 BE
S5
INTERNATIONAL SYMPOSIUM ON CROP PROTECTION. PROCEEDINGS. (Included in: Universiteit Gent. Faculteit van de Landbouwkundige en Toegepaste Biologische Wetenschappen. Mededelingen) (Text and summaries in English, French, German) 1948. a. 2700 BEF. Universiteit Gent, Faculteit van de Landbouwkundige en Toegepaste Biologische Wetenschappen, Coupure Links 653, 9000 Ghent, Belgium. TEL 32-9-2646011. FAX 32-9-2646239. **Indexed:** Agri.Ind., Chem.Abstr., Helminthol.Abstr., Herb.Abstr. **Document type:** proceedings.
Supersedes: International Symposium on Crop Protection. Communications (ISSN 0074-8803)

632 SP ISSN 0213-5000
SB87.S64 CODEN: IAPVES
INVESTIGACION AGRARIA. PRODUCCION Y PROTECCION VEGETALES. (Text in Spanish; summaries in English, Spanish) 1952. 3/yr. 6000 ptas. (foreign 9800 ptas.) (effective 1996). Ministerio de Agricultura, Pesca y Alimentacion, Instituto Nacional de Investigacion y Tecnologia Agraria y Alimentaria, Centro de Publicaciones, Paseo de la Infanta Isabel 1, 28071 Madrid, Spain. TEL 34-1-3475551. FAX 34-1-3475722. (I.N.I.T.A.A. addr.: Jose Abascal 56, 28003 Madrid, Spain) Ed. Joaquin Berengena Herrera. R&P contact: Juan Carlos Palacios Lopez. bibl.; charts; illus. circ. 1,500. **Indexed:** Bio-Contr.News & Info., Biol.Abstr., Field Crop Abstr., Herb.Abstr., Hort.Abstr., Ind.SST, Irr.& Drain.Abstr., Plant Breed.Abstr., Rev.Appl.Entomol., Soils & Fert., Triticale Abstr., Weed Abstr. **Document type:** academic/scholarly publication.
—CASDDS.
Formerly (until 1985): Spain. Instituto Nacional de Investigaciones Agrarias. Anales. Serie: Agricola (ISSN 0211-4682); Which was formed by the 1980 merger of: Spain. Instituto Nacional de Investigaciones Agrarias. Anales. Serie: Produccion Vegetal (ISSN 0376-1851); Spain. Instituto Nacional de Investigaciones Agrarias. Anales. Serie: Proteccion Vegetal (ISSN 0210-2501); Which both superseded in part (in 1971): Spain. Instituto Nacional de Investigaciones Agronomicas. Anales (ISSN 0020-4129); Which was formerly: Spain. Instituto Nacional de Investigacion Agronomica. Boletin (0020-4137); And incorporated (1927-1969): Boletin de Patologia Vegetal y Entomologia Agricola (0366-2381); Which was formerly: Estacion de Patologia Vegetal. Boletin (0210-3273).

631 US
IOWA SEED NEWS. 1947. q. membership. Iowa Crop Improvement Association, Iowa State University, 2023 Agronomy Hall, Ames, IA 50011. TEL 515-294-6921. FAX 515-294-1897. Ed. Eileen M. Feilmeier. **Document type:** newsletter.
Formerly: Seed News.

631.5 US ISSN 0160-7499
S612.2 CODEN: TCPADV
IRRIGATION ASSOCIATION. TECHNICAL CONFERENCE PROCEEDINGS. Key Title: Technical Conference Proceedings - Irrigation Association. 1977. a. $15 (effective 1996). Irrigation Association, 8260 Willow Oaks Corp. Dr., Ste. 120, Fairfax, VA 22031-4513. TEL 703-573-3551. FAX 703-573-7913. URL: http://www.irrigation.org. circ. 2,000. **Indexed:** Biol.Abstr. **Document type:** proceedings.
—CASDDS; Linda Hall.
Formerly: Sprinkler Irrigation Association. Technical Conference Proceedings.

631.7 US
IRRIGATION BUSINESS & TECHNOLOGY. bi-m. $15 to non-members (foreign $25); free to members. Irrigation Association, 8260 Willow Oaks Corp. Dr., Ste. 120, Fairfax, VA 22031-4513. TEL 703-573-3551. FAX 703-573-7913. URL: http://www.irrigation.org. adv. circ. 12,500.
Formerly: Irrigation News.
Description: Features association and industry developments, new products, and people in the news. Includes special calendar issues.

631.7 627 US ISSN 0047-1518
IRRIGATION JOURNAL. 1951. 7/yr. $40 (foreign $65) (effective 1997). Hunter Publishing Limited Partnership, 2101 S. Arlington Heights Rd., Ste. 150, Arlington Heights, IL 60005. TEL 847-427-9512. FAX 847-427-2097. URL: http://www.aip.com. Ed. Robert Reaves; Pub. Colleen Long. adv. contact: Desmond Abicair. bk.rev.; tr.lit. circ. 15,000. (also avail. in microform from UMI; reprint service avail. from UMI) **Indexed:** Sel.Water Res.Abstr. **Document type:** trade publication.
—BLDSC (4580.967000); Linda Hall; SWETS; UMI; UnCover.
Former titles: Irrigation Engineering and Maintenance; (until 1970): World Irrigation (ISSN 0043-8588)
Description: Directed to farmers/growers, irrigation specialists and irrigation contractors and services.

630 631 IT ISSN 0304-0615
ISTITUTO SPERIMENTALE AGRONOMICO. ANNALI. 1970. a. exchange basis. Istituto Sperimentale Agronomico, Via C. Ulpiani 5, 70125 Bari, Italy. TEL 39-80-5475011. FAX 39-80-5475023. Ed. Dr. V. Rizzo. circ. 1,000. (back issues avail.) **Indexed:** Agri.Eng.Abstr., Field Crop Abstr., Herb.Abstr., Soils & Fert., Triticale Abstr. **Document type:** corporate report, proceedings.

631 630 JA ISSN 0388-4449
IWATE HORTICULTURE EXPERIMENT STATION. BULLETIN. (Summaries in English) 1971. irreg., no.6, 1985. Iwate Horticulture Experiment Station, 20-1 Narita, Kitakami-shi 024, Japan. TEL 0197-68-2331. Ed. Akiharu Itoh. circ. 500. **Document type:** bulletin.

633.61 JM
JAMAICAN ASSOCIATION OF SUGAR TECHNOLOGISTS. PROCEEDINGS. 1937. a. membership. Jamaican Association of Sugar Technologists, c/o Sugar Industry Research Institute, Agricultural Division, Mandeville, Jamaica, W.I. Ed. Trevor Falloon. circ. 500. **Indexed:** Sugar Ind.Abstr.

631 338.1 JA ISSN 0439-3600
CODEN: HNGSAG
JAPAN. HOKURIKU NATIONAL AGRICULTURAL EXPERIMENT STATION. BULLETIN. (Text in Japanese; summaries in English) 1960. a. Hokuriku National Agricultural Experiment Station - Hokuriku Kokuritsu Nogyo Shikenjo, Inada Joetsu, Niigata 943-01, Japan. TEL 0255-23-4131. FAX 0255-24-8578. Ed. Akira Nakane. circ. 950. **Indexed:** Rice Abstr.
—BLDSC (2555.302000); CASDDS.
Description: Agricultural research in field crops, environment, farm management and land utilization.

AGRICULTURE — CROP PRODUCTION AND SOIL

631 JA
CODEN: NISAAJ
JAPANESE JOURNAL OF CROP SCIENCE/NIHON SAKUMOTSU GAKKAI KIJI. (Text in English or Japanese) 1927. q. 7000 Yen (membership). Crop Science Society of Japan - Nihon Sakumotsu Gakkai, c/o Faculty of Agriculture, University of Tokyo, 1-1-1 Yayoi, Bunkyo-ku, Tokyo 113, Japan. FAX 03-3815-5851. Ed. T. Horie; Pub. R. Ishii. R&P contact: M. Kokubun. adv. contact: R. Ohsugi. bk.rev. circ. 2,000. **Indexed:** ASCA, Biol.Abstr., Chem.Abstr., Cott.& Trop.Fibr.Abstr., Crop Physiol.Abstr., Curr.Adv.Genetics & Molec.Biol., Curr.Cont., Excerp.Med., Fababean Abstr., Field Crop Abstr., Food Sci.& Tech.Abstr., Helminthol.Abstr., Herb.Abstr., Hort.Abstr., Irr.& Drain.Abstr., Plant Breed.Abstr., Plant Grow.Reg.Abstr., Potato Abstr., Rev.Plant Path., Rice Abstr., Seed Abstr., Soils & Fert., Soyabean Abstr., Sugar Ind.Abstr., Triticale Abstr., Trop.Oil Seeds Abstr., Weed Abstr. **Document type:** academic/scholarly publication.
—CASDDS; EMDOCS; Genuine Article; Linda Hall; SWETS.
Formerly (until 1977): Crop Science Society of Japan. Proceedings (ISSN 0011-1848)

633 JA
CODEN: TKKADS
JAPANESE SOCIETY OF SUGAR BEET TECHNOLOGISTS. PROCEEDINGS. (Text in Japanese; summaries in English) 1963. a. free. Sugar Crop Development Fund, Upland Agriculture Research Center, Hokkaido National Agricultural Experiment Sta., Shinsei, Memuro, Hokkaido 082, Japan. TEL 81-155-62-2721. FAX 81-155-61-2127. Ed. Masakatsu Tanaka. circ. 450. **Indexed:** Food Sci.& Tech.Abstr., Sugar Ind.Abstr. **Document type:** proceedings.
—BLDSC (6742.499000); CASDDS.
Former titles: Sugar Beet Research Association. Proceedings (ISSN 0912-1048); (until 1974): Bulletin of Sugar Beet Research. Supplement (ISSN 0068-4090)
Description: Covers research in all fields of sugar beet technology.
Refereed Serial

634.8 FR ISSN 1151-0285
CODEN: JISVE8
JOURNAL INTERNATIONAL DES SCIENCES DE LA VIGNE ET DU VIN. (Text in French or English) 1967. q. 390 F. (foreign 490 F.) (effective 1997). (Association des Anciens Eleves de l'Institut d'Oenologie de Bordeaux) Vigne et Vin Publications Internationales, 42 rue Marsan, 33300 Bordeaux, France. TEL 33-5-57876869. FAX 33-5-57876848. E-mail: vvpi@inlandsys.com. Eds. M. Guimberteau, M. Sapis. adv.; bk.rev. circ. 1,500. (tabloid format) **Indexed:** Anal.Abstr., Biol.Abstr., Chem.Abstr., Crop Physiol.Abstr., Food Sci.& Tech.Abstr., Forest.Abstr., Forest Prod.Abstr., Hort.Abstr., Seed Abstr., VITIS.
—BLDSC (5007.686250); CASDDS.
Formerly: Connaissance de la Vigne et du Vin (ISSN 0010-597X)
Description: Discusses viticulture and enology.

668.6 US ISSN 0021-8561
S583 CODEN: JAFCAU
JOURNAL OF AGRICULTURAL AND FOOD CHEMISTRY. 1953. m. $513 to institutional non-members; members $39 (effective 1997). American Chemical Society, 1155 16th St., N.W., Washington, DC 20036. TEL 800-333-9511. FAX 614-447-3671. E-mail: jafe@gold.tc.umn.edu; URL: http://pubs.acs.org/journals/jafcau/index.html. (Subscr. to: Membership and Subscription Services, Box 3337, Columbus, OH 43210. TEL 614-447-3776) Ed. Irvin E. Liener. adv.; bibl.; charts; illus.; index. circ. 4,300. (also avail. in microform; back issues avail.) **Indexed:** A.S.& T.Ind., Anal.Abstr., Apic.Abstr., ASCA, Biol.Abstr., Biol.& Agr.Ind., Biotech.Abstr., Chem.Abstr., Chem.Cit.Ind., Cott.& Trop.Fibr.Abstr., Crop Physiol.Abstr., Curr.Biotech.Abstr., Curr.Chem.React., Curr.Cont., Dairy Sci.Abstr., Dok.Arbeitsmed., Energy Info.Abstr., Environ.Abstr., Environ.Per.Bibl., Excerp.Med., Field Crop Abstr., Food Sci.& Tech.Abstr., Forest Prod.Abstr., Helminthol.Abstr., Herb.Abstr., Hort.Abstr., Ind.Chem., Ind.Sci.Rev., Ind.Vet., INIS Atomind., Irr.& Drain.Abstr., Maize Abstr., Mass Spectr.Bull., Nutr.Abstr., Ocean.Abstr., Pig News & Info., Plant Breed.Abstr., Plant Grow.Reg.Abstr., Pollut.Abstr., Potato Abstr., Poult.Abstr., Rev.Appl.Entomol., Rev.Med.& Vet.Mycol., Rev.Plant Path., Rice Abstr., Sci.Cit.Ind., Seed Abstr., Sel.Water Res.Abstr., Soils & Fert., Sorghum & Millets Abstr., Soyabean Abstr., Telegen, Triticale Abstr., Trop.Oil Seeds Abstr., Vet.Bull., W.R.C.Inf., Weed Abstr. **Document type:** academic/scholarly publication.
●Also available online. Vendor(s): STN International (CJACS).
—BLDSC (4920.000000); CASDDS; CISTI; Genuine Article; KR SourceOne; Linda Hall; SWETS; UMI; UnCover. **CCC.**
Description: Contains documentation of significant advances in the science of agriculture and food chemistry.
Refereed Serial

630 UK ISSN 0021-8634
S671 CODEN: JAERA2
JOURNAL OF AGRICULTURAL ENGINEERING RESEARCH. 1956. m. £364 (effective 1998). (British Society for Research in Agricultural Engineering) Academic Press Ltd. (Subsidiary of: Harcourt Brace & Company Ltd.), 24-28 Oval Rd., London NW1 7DX, England. TEL 44-171-267-4466. FAX 44-171-482-2293. TELEX 25775 ACPRES G. E-mail: apsubs@acad.com; URL: http://www.hbuk.co.uk/ap/jaer; http://www.europe.idealibrary.com/. (Subscr. to: Harcourt Brace & Company Ltd., Foots Cray High St., Sidcup, Kent DA14 5HP, England. TEL 44-181-300-3322. FAX 44 181 309-0807) Ed. D.J. White. R&P contact: Catherine John. adv. contact: Nik Screen. bk.rev.; bibl.; charts; illus.; index. (reprint service avail. from SWZ) **Indexed:** Agri.Eng.Abstr., ASCA, Biol.Abstr., Biol.& Agr.Ind., Curr.Cont., Dairy Sci.Abstr., Energy Ind., Energy Info.Abstr., Excerp.Med., Field Crop Abstr., Food Sci.& Tech.Abstr., Geotech.Abstr., Herb.Abstr., Hort.Abstr., Ind.Sci.Rev., Ind.Vet., Int.Abstr.Oper.Res., Irr.& Drain.Abstr., Maize Abstr., Nutr.Abstr., Ornam.Hort., Pig News & Info., Rice Abstr., Risk Abstr., Sci.Cit.Ind., Seed Abstr., Soils & Fert., Triticale Abstr., Vet.Bull., Weed Abstr. **Document type:** academic/scholarly publication.
●Also available online.
—BLDSC (4921.000000); CISTI; Genuine Article; KR SourceOne; Linda Hall; SWETS; UnCover. **CCC.**
Description: Reflects the spectrum of interdisciplinary interests inherent in this field, including tractor and vehicle design, cultivation systems, soil drainage and irrigation, crop production, farm buildings, waste engineering, and livestock feeding.

630 GW ISSN 0931-2250
CODEN: ZAPFAR
JOURNAL OF AGRONOMY AND CROP SCIENCE/ZEITSCHRIFT FUER ACKER- UND PFLANZENBAU. (Text in English, German) 1853. 8/yr. DM.1634 in Europe; rest of world DM.1641 (effective 1998). Blackwell Wissenschaft, Kurfuerstendamm 57, 10707 Berlin, Germany. TEL 49-30-32790634. FAX 49-30-32790610. E-mail: aboverwalt@blackwis.de; URL: http://www.blackwis.com. Ed.Bd. adv.: B&W page DM.560; trim 190 x 122. bk.rev.; bibl.; illus.; stat.; index. circ. 450. (back issues avail.) **Indexed:** Agri.Eng.Abstr., ASCA, Bio-Contr.News & Info., Biol.Abstr., Chem.Abstr., Cott.& Trop.Fibr.Abstr., Crop Physiol.Abstr., Curr.Adv.Ecol.Sci., Curr.Adv.Genetics & Molec.Biol., Curr.Cont., Environ.Per.Bibl. (1972-1994), Excerp.Med., Fababean Abstr., Field Crop Abstr., Food Sci.& Tech.Abstr., Forest.Abstr., Helminthol.Abstr., Herb.Abstr., Hort.Abstr., Irr.& Drain.Abstr., Nutr.Abstr., Plant Breed.Abstr., Plant Grow.Reg.Abstr., Potato Abstr., Rev.Appl.Entomol., Rev.Plant Path., Rice Abstr., Seed Abstr., Soils & Fert., Sorghum & Millets Abstr., Soyabean Abstr., Triticale Abstr., Trop.Oil Seeds Abstr., Weed Abstr. **Document type:** academic/scholarly publication.
—BLDSC (4926.300000); CASDDS; EMDOCS; Genuine Article; SWETS. **CCC.**
Description: Publishes original papers in the fields of general and special plant production.

632.9 II ISSN 0970-3810
JOURNAL OF APHIDOLOGY. 1987. s-a. Rs.250($40) (effective 1997). Aphidological Society, India, Aphid Biocontrol Laboratory, Department of Zoology, University of Gorakhpur, Gorakhpur 273 009, U.P., India. TEL 91-551-333944. FAX 91-551-336797. Ed. Rajendra Singh. R&P contact: Rajendra Singh. adv.: page Rs.500. bk.rev. circ. 500. **Document type:** academic/scholarly publication.
Description: Contains original research and reviews in the fields of aphid research, including evolution, biosystematics, cytogenetics, bioecology, population dynamics of aphids and their predators and parasitoids, trophic interactions and aphid control.
Refereed Serial

632.9 II ISSN 0970-5732
CODEN: JBCOES
JOURNAL OF BIOLOGICAL CONTROL. (Text in English) 1987. s-a. Rs.40 to individuals; institutions Rs.100; foreign $15. Tamilnadu Agricultural University, Indian Society for Biocontrol Advancement, c/o R.J. Rabindra, Department of Entomology, TNAU, Coimbatore -641003, India. Ed. S. Jayaraj. **Indexed:** Biol.Abstr. (1988-).
—BLDSC (4953.030000); Linda Hall; UnCover.
Description: Covers all aspects relating to the biological control of pests, pathogens and weeds of crop plants.

634 US
▼**JOURNAL OF CITRICULTURE.** 1997. s-a. $36 to individuals; institutions $48; libraries $60 (effective 1998-1999). Haworth Press, Inc., 10 Alice St., Binghamton, NY 13094. TEL 607-722-5857; 800-342-9676. FAX 607-722-6362. E-mail: getinfo@haworth.com; URL: http://www.haworth.com. Ed. Robert J. McNeil; Pub. Bill Cohen. R&P contact: Ruthann Heath. adv.: B&W page $300; trim 4 3/8 x 7 1/8; adv. contact: Jackie Blakeslee. bk.rev. (also avail. in microfiche from UMI; reprint service avail. from HAW) **Document type:** academic/scholarly publication.
—Haworth.
Description: Provides worldwide applied research information to citrus growers, citrus extension workers, applied citrus researchers and all others involved with the commercial citrus industry.
Refereed Serial

AGRICULTURE — CROP PRODUCTION AND SOIL

631 338.1 US ISSN 1092-678X
▼**JOURNAL OF CROP PRODUCTION**; innovations in practice, theory & research. 1998. s-a. $45 to individuals; institutions $60; libraries $90. Haworth Press, Inc., 10 Alice St., Binghamton, NY 13904. TEL 607-722-5857; 800-342-9676. FAX 607-722-6362. E-mail: getinfo@haworth.com; URL: http://www.haworth.com. (Editorial addr.: Department of Botany, Punjab Agricultural University, Ludhiana 141 004, India. TEL 91-161-401961. FAX 91-161-400945) Ed. Amarjit S. Basra; Pub. Bill Cohen. R&P contact: Ruthann Heath. adv.: B&W page $300; trim 4 3/8 x 7 1/8; adv. contact: Jackie Blakeslee. (also avail. in microform from HAW)
—Haworth.
Description: Provides an international forum for both scientists and practitioners to discuss the latest advancements in basic and applied aspects of crop production.

JOURNAL OF ENVIRONMENTAL QUALITY. see ENVIRONMENTAL STUDIES

631 US ISSN 1059-9053
S530 CODEN: JRLEEJ
JOURNAL OF NATURAL RESOURCES AND LIFE SCIENCES EDUCATION. 1972. s-a. $18. American Society of Agronomy, Inc., 677 S. Segoe Rd., Madison, WI 53711. TEL 608-273-8080. FAX 608-273-2021. Ed. John Graveel. R&P contact: David M. Kral. adv. contact: Keith R. Schlesinger. bk.rev.; software rev.; video rev.; charts; illus. circ. 1,000. (back issues avail.) **Indexed:** Bibl.Agri., Bibl.Agri., C.I.J.E., Energy Abstr., Environ.Abstr. **Document type:** academic/scholarly publication.
—BLDSC (5021.227000); CASDDS; Ei; SWETS; UnCover. **CCC.**
Formerly (until 1992): Journal of Agronomic Education (ISSN 0094-2391)
Description: Designed for educators in universities, extension, and industry. Presents innovative concepts and techniques for improving education programs.
Refereed Serial

630 570 II ISSN 0379-5489
S589.5 CODEN: JNABDS
JOURNAL OF NUCLEAR AGRICULTURE AND BIOLOGY. 1972. q. Rs.200($65) (effective 1991). Indian Society for Nuclear Techniques in Agriculture and Biology, Nuclear Research Laboratory, Indian Agricultural Research Institute, New Delhi 110012, India. Ed. M.S. Chatrath. R&P contact: M.S. Chatrath. adv. contact: M.S. Sachdey. bk.rev.; circ. 400 (controlled). (back issues avail.) **Indexed:** Biol.Abstr., Chem.Abstr., Curr.Cont., Excerp.Med., Field Crop Abstr., Herb.Abstr., Hort.Abstr., Ind.Vet., INIS Atomind., Irr.& Drain.Abstr., Nutr.Abstr., Plant Breed.Abstr., Rev.Appl.Entomol., Rev.Plant Path., Rice Abstr., Seed Abstr., Soils & Fert., Soyabean Abstr., Sugar Ind.Abstr., Triticale Abstr., Vet.Bull., Weed Abstr. **Document type:** academic/scholarly publication.
—BLDSC (5022.848000); CASDDS; CISTI; Linda Hall; UnCover.
Formerly: I S N A Newsletter.

630 II ISSN 0970-2776
CODEN: JOREES
JOURNAL OF OILSEEDS RESEARCH. (Text in English) 1984. s-a. $100. Indian Society of Oilseeds Research, Rajendranagar, Hyderabad 500 030, India. TEL 48331. (Dist. overseas by: HPC Publishers' Distributors Pvt. Ltd., 4805-24, 1st Fl., Bhara Ram Rd., Darya Ganj, New Delhi 110 002, India. TEL 91-11-3254401. FAX 91-11-6863511) Ed. Satyabrata Maiti. index. circ. 350. (back issues avail.) **Indexed:** Field Crop Abstr., INIS Atomind., Irr.& Drain.Abstr., Seed Abstr., Soils & Fert., Sorghum & Millets Abstr., Soyabean Abstr., Trop.Oil Seeds Abstr.
—BLDSC (5026.305000); CASDDS; Ei.

JOURNAL OF PESTICIDE SCIENCE (INTERNATIONAL EDITION). see ENGINEERING — Chemical Engineering

631 II ISSN 0304-5242
SB111.A2 CODEN: JPCRDW
JOURNAL OF PLANTATION CROPS. (Text in English) 1972. s-a. $75. Indian Society for Plantation Crops, Central Plantation Crops Research Institute, Kasaragod - 671 124, Kerala, India. TEL 91-499-530894. FAX 91-499-530322. TELEX 0800 1202 PALM IN. E-mail: cpcri@x400.nicgw. nic.in. Ed. V. Rajagopal; Pub. A.S. Sukumaran. adv.; bk.rev.; film rev.; software rev.; bibl.; illus. circ. 600. **Indexed:** Bio-Contr.News & Info., Biol.Abstr., Chem.Abstr., Curr.Adv.Ecol.Sci., Curr.Cont., Food Sci.& Tech.Abstr., Helminthol.Abstr., Hort.Abstr., Plant Breed.Abstr., Rev.Appl.Entomol., Rev.Plant Path., Rural Recreat.Tour.Abstr., Soils & Fert., Trop.Abstr., Trop.Oil Seeds Abstr., World Agri.Econ.& Rural Sociol.Abstr. **Document type:** academic/scholarly publication.
—BLDSC (5040.540000); CASDDS; Linda Hall; UMI; UnCover.
Refereed Serial

631.5 II ISSN 0378-2409
CODEN: JRCRDC
JOURNAL OF ROOT CROPS. (Text in English) 1975. s-a. Rs.200($70) (effective 1992). Indian Society for Root Crops, c/o Central Tuber Crops Research Institute, Trivandrum 695017, India. TEL 91-471-448551. FAX 91-471-448431. TELEX 0435-247 ROOT IN. Ed. M.S. Palaniswami; Pub. Santha V. Pillai. circ. 300. **Indexed:** Bio-Contr.News & Info., Biol.Abstr., Chem.Abstr., Excerp.Med., Field Crop Abstr., Food Sci.& Tech.Abstr., Herb.Abstr., Irr.& Drain.Abstr., Plant Breed.Abstr., Rev.Plant Path., Soils & Fert. **Document type:** academic/scholarly publication.
—CASDDS; CISTI.

631 US ISSN 1052-0015
SB381 CODEN: JSFVED
JOURNAL OF SMALL FRUIT & VITICULTURE. 1992. q. $36 to individuals (Canada $46.80; elsewhere $50.40); institutions $48 (Canada $62.40; elsewhere $67.20); libraries $125 (Canada $162.50; elsewhere $175) (effective 1997-1998). Haworth Press, Inc., 10 Alice St., Binghamton, NY 13904. TEL 607-722-5857; 800-342-9676. FAX 607-722-6362. TELEX 4932599. E-mail: getinfo@haworth.com; URL: http://www.haworth. com. Ed. Robert E. Gough; Pub. Bill Cohen. R&P contact: Ruthann Heath. adv.: B&W page $300; trim 4 3/8 x 7 1/8; adv. contact: Jackie Blakeslee. bk.rev. (also avail. in microfiche from UMI; microform from HAW; reprint service avail. from HAW) **Indexed:** Ecol.Abstr., Food Sci.& Tech.Abstr., Geo.Abstr.P.G., Ref.Zh. **Document type:** academic/scholarly publication.
—BLDSC (5064.710700); Haworth.
Description: Contains current applicable research for the grower. Focuses on new technologies and innovative approaches to the management and marketing of small fruit.
Refereed Serial

631.4 333.91 US ISSN 0022-4561
S622 CODEN: JSWCA3
JOURNAL OF SOIL AND WATER CONSERVATION. 1946. bi-m. $39 (outside N. America $45). Soil and Water Conservation Society, 7515 N.E. Ankeny Rd., Ankeny, IA 50021. TEL 515-289-2331. FAX 515-289-1227. E-mail: sueb@swcs.org; URL: http://www.swcs.org/JSWCwelcom.htm. Ed. Sue Ballantine. adv. contact: Karen Howe. bk.rev.; film rev.; abstr.; bibl.; charts; illus.; maps; tr.lit.; index, cum.index: vols.1-20; vols.21-25; vols.26-30. circ. 13,800. (also avail. in microform from UMI; back issues avail.; reprint service avail. from UMI,ISI) **Indexed:** Acid Pre.Dig., Agri.Eng.Abstr., Agroforest.Abstr., Bibl.Agri., Biol.Abstr., Biol.& Agr.Ind., Biol.Dig., CAD CAM Abstr., Chem.Abstr., Curr.Adv.Ecol.Sci., Curr.Cont., Dairy Sci.Abstr., Ecol.Abstr., Energy Info.Abstr., Environ.Abstr., Environ.Ind., Environ.Per.Bibl. (1972-), Excerp.Med., Farm & Garden Ind., Field Crop Abstr., Forest.Abstr., Forest Prod.Abstr., Geo.Abstr.H.G., GeoRef., Herb.Abstr., IDA, Ind.Sci.Rev., Int.Abstr.Oper.Res., Irr.& Drain.Abstr., Maize Abstr., Ocean.Abstr., Pollut.Abstr., Risk Abstr., Rural Ext.Educ.& Tr.Abstr., Rural Recreat.Tour.Abstr., Sci.Cit.Ind., Sel.Water Res.Abstr., Soils & Fert., Sorghum & Millets Abstr., Soyabean Abstr., Sport Fish.Abstr., Triticale Abstr., Urb.Aff.Abstr., W.R.C.Inf., Weed Abstr., Wild.Rev., World Agri.Econ.& Rural Sociol.Abstr., Zoo.Rec. **Document type:** academic/scholarly publication.
●Also available online. Vendor(s): Information Access Co., UMI.
—BLDSC (5064.940000); CIS; CISTI; Ei; EMDOCS; Genuine Article; KR SourceOne; Linda Hall; SWETS; UMI; UnCover.
Refereed Serial

JOURNAL OF SOIL CONTAMINATION. see ENVIRONMENTAL STUDIES — Pollution

631 II ISSN 0971-3328
JOURNAL OF SPICES AND AROMATIC CROPS. (Text in English) 1992. s-a. Rs.150($40) Indian Society for Spices, c/o Indian Institute of Spices Research, P.O. Box 1701, Marikunnu P.O., Calicut 673 012, Kerala, India. TEL 91-495-370294. FAX 91-495-370294. E-mail: iisyspices@x400. nicgw.nic.in. Ed. P.N. Ravindran. adv.: B&W page Rs. 2000. bk.rev.; bibl.; circ. 500 (paid). **Indexed:** Food Sci.& Tech.Abstr. **Document type:** academic/scholarly publication.
—BLDSC (5066.181000).
Description: Devoted to the advancement of research on spices, aromatic crops, medicinal and related plants.
Refereed Serial

632 641 UK ISSN 0022-474X
TX599 CODEN: JSTPAR
JOURNAL OF STORED PRODUCTS RESEARCH. 1965. q. fl.1207($694) (effective 1998). Elsevier Science Ltd., Pergamon, P.O. Box 800, Kidlington, Oxford OX5 1DX, England. TEL 44-1865-843000. FAX 44-1865-843010. E-mail: nlinfo-f@elsevier.nl; usinfo-f@elsevier.com; forinfo-kyf04035@niftyserve. or.jp; URL: http://www.elsevier.nl/. (Subscr. to: Elsevier Science, Regional Sales Office, P.O. Box 211, 1000 AE Amsterdam, Netherlands. TEL 31-20-4853757. FAX 31-20-4853432; Subscr. in the Americas to: Elsevier Science, Regional Sales Office, Box 945, New York, NY 10159-0945. TEL 212-633-3730. FAX 212-633-3680; Subscr. in Australasia and the Far East to: Elsevier Science (Singapore) Pte Ltd, No.1 Temasek Ave., No.17-01 Millenia Tower, Singapore 039192, Singapore. TEL 65-434-3727. FAX 65-337-2230) Ed. P. Credland. adv.; bk.rev.; charts; illus.; stat. circ. 1,000. (also avail. in microfilm from UMI; back issues avail.) **Indexed:** Agri.Eng.Abstr., ASCA, Bio-Contr.News & Info., Biol.Abstr., Biotech.Abstr., Chem.Abstr., Curr.Adv.Ecol.Sci., Curr.Cont., Dairy Sci.Abstr., Excerp.Med., Field Crop Abstr., Food Sci.& Tech.Abstr., Forest Prod.Abstr., Herb.Abstr., Ind.Sci.Rev., Nutr.Abstr., Rev.Appl.Entomol., Rev.Plant Path., Rice Abstr., Sci.Cit.Ind., Sorghum & Millets Abstr., Triticale Abstr., Weed Abstr. **Document type:** academic/scholarly publication.
—BLDSC (5066.871000); CASDDS; Ei; EMDOCS; Genuine Article; Linda Hall; SWETS; UMI; UnCover. **CCC.**
Description: Covers research dealing with the biology, ecology, physiology, behavior, taxonomy, genetics or control of the insects and organisms associated with stored products.
Refereed Serial

AGRICULTURE — CROP PRODUCTION AND SOIL

634 US ISSN 1055-1387
CODEN: JTFPF3
JOURNAL OF TREE FRUIT PRODUCTION. 1994. s-a. $36 to individuals (Canada $46.80; elsewhere $50.40); institutions $60 (Canada $78; elsewhere $84); libraries $95 (Canada $123.50; elsewhere $133) (effective 1997-1998). Haworth Press, Inc., 10 Alice St., Binghamton, NY 13904. TEL 607-722-5857; 800-342-9676. FAX 607-722-6362. TELEX 4932599. E-mail: getinfo@haworth.com; URL: http://www.haworth.com. Ed. Wesley R. Autio; Pub. Bill Cohen. R&P contact: Ruthann Heath. adv.: B&W page $300; trim 4 3/8 x 7 1/8; adv. contact: Jackie Blakeslee. bk.rev. (also avail. in microfiche from UMI; reprint service avail. from HAW) **Indexed:** Food Sci.& Tech.Abstr.
—Haworth.
Description: Focuses on the innovative approaches to tree fruit production and the marketing of apples, pears, peaches, plums, cherries, citrus fruits and olives.
Refereed Serial

632.9 US ISSN 1070-437X
CODEN: JTUMEY
▼**JOURNAL OF TURFGRASS MANAGEMENT.** 1995. q. $45 to individuals (Canada $58.50; elsewhere $63); institutions $80 (Canada $104; elsewhere $112); libraries $90 (Canada $117; elsewhere $126) (effective 1997-1998). Haworth Press, Inc., Food Products Press, 10 Alice St., Binghamton, NY 13904. TEL 607-722-5857; 800-342-9676. FAX 607-722-6362. E-mail: getinfo@haworth.com; URL: http://www.haworth.com. Ed. William A. Torello; Pub. Bill Cohen. R&P contact: Ruthann Heath. adv.: B&W page $300; trim 4 3/8 x 7 1/8; adv. contact: Jackie Blakeslee. (also avail. in microform from HAW,UMI; reprint service avail. from HAW) **Indexed:** Geo.Abstr.H.G., Per.Islam. (1995-). **Document type:** academic/scholarly publication, trade publication.
—CASDDS; Haworth.
Description: Reports on all the facets of turfgrass research and management. Disseminates current advances in basic, as well as applied turfgrass research for the benefit of the turfgrass scientist, as well as the practicing turfgrass manager.
Refereed Serial

631 US ISSN 1049-6467
JOURNAL OF VEGETABLE CROP PRODUCTION. 1993. s-a. $36 to individuals; institutions $60; libraries $90 (effective 1997). Haworth Press, Inc., 10 Alice St., Binghamton, NY 13904. TEL 607-722-5857; 800-342-9676. FAX 607-722-6362. E-mail: getinfo@haworth.com; URL: http://www.haworth.com. (Editorial addr.: Box 539, Calhoun, LA 71225. TEL 318-644-2662. FAX 318-644-7244) Ed. M. Leron Robbins; Pub. Bill Cohen. R&P contact: Ruthann Heath. adv.: B&W page $300; trim 4 3/8 x 7 1/8; adv. contact: Jackie Blakeslee. bk.rev. (also avail. in microfilm from UMI; microform from HAW; reprint service avail. from HAW) **Indexed:** Food Sci.& Tech.Abstr.
—BLDSC (5072.276000); Haworth; SWETS.
Description: For specialists and professionals who labor with the problems of vegetable crop management - from land preparation to seeding and consumption. Articles cover the wide spectrum of the vegetable industry, including field-related problems like harvesting, shipping, and final consumption; and scientific input about vegetables.
Refereed Serial

634.8 663.2 UK ISSN 0957-1264
JOURNAL OF WINE RESEARCH. 1990. 3/yr. £72($142) to individuals; institutions £238 ($418) (effective 1997). (Institute of Masters of Wine) Carfax Publishing Co., P.O Box 25, Abingdon, Oxon. OX14 3UE, England. TEL 44-1235-401000. FAX 44-1235-401550. E-mail: enquiries@carfax.co.uk. (U.S. subscr. to: Carfax Publishing Co., 875-81 Massachusetts Ave., Cambridge, MA 02139) Eds. Tim Unwin, Jasper Morris. adv.; bk.rev.; index. (also avail. in microfiche; back issues avail.) **Indexed:** Food Sci.& Tech.Abstr. **Document type:** academic/scholarly publication.
—BLDSC (5072.632200). **CCC.**
Description: Publishes the results of recent research an all aspects of viticulture, oenology, and the wine trade.
Refereed Serial

631.4 RU ISSN 0022-9148
CODEN: KAOVA7
KARTOFEL' I OVOSHCHI. 1956. bi-m. $51 (effective 1998). Sadovaya-Spasskaya, 18, kom.702, 107807 Moscow, Russia. TEL 7-095-2071711. FAX 7-095-2072870. Ed. Svetlana I. Sanina. bk.rev. circ. 17,400. **Indexed:** Agri.Eng.Abstr., Biol.Abstr., Chem.Abstr., Field Crop Abstr., Food Sci.& Tech.Abstr., Herb.Abstr., Hort.Abstr., Plant Breed.Abstr., Potato Abstr., Seed Abstr.
—BLDSC (0088.340000).

633.491 GW ISSN 0022-9156
DER KARTOFFELBAU. 1949. m. DM.90 (foreign DM.132) (effective 1996). (Vorstand der Foerderungsgemeinschaft der Kartoffelwirtschaft e.V.) Verlag Th. Mann, Nordring 10, 45894 Gelsenkirchen, Germany. TEL 49-209-9304184. FAX 49-209-9304185. (Subscr. to: Postfach 200254, 45837 Gelsenkirchen, Germany) Eds. Heinz-Peter Puetz, Guenter Weiss. adv.: B&W page DM.2560, color page DM.4550; trim 186 x 270; adv. contact: Richard Heineke. bk.rev.; charts; illus.; stat.; circ. 5,491 (controlled). **Indexed:** Agri.Eng.Abstr., Field Crop Abstr., Food Sci.& Tech.Abstr., Herb.Abstr., Nutr.Abstr., Plant Breed.Abstr., Potato Abstr., Soils & Fert., Weed Abstr. **Document type:** trade publication.
—BLDSC (5086.450000); SWETS.
Description: News about potatoes.

631 US
KENTUCKY PRAIRIE FARMER. (Supplement avail.: Dairy Producer) 1989. 15/yr. free to qualified personnel. Farm Progress Companies (Subsidiary of: A B C Publishing Companies), 191 S. Gary Ave., Carol Stream, IL 60188. TEL 630-690-5600. FAX 630-462-2869. (Edit. addr.: 10303 Vantage Rd., Jeffersontown, KT 40299. TEL 502-266-9556) Ed. Tim Sickman. adv.: B&W page $1775, color page $2040; trim 7 X 10; adv. contact: Charles Roth. circ. 9,958 (paid). **Document type:** trade publication.
Description: Covers production, marketing and management of corn, soybeans and tobacco.

631 KE
KENYA. NATIONAL CEREALS AND PRODUCE BOARD. ANNUAL REPORT. a. National Cereals and Produce Board, Nairobi, Kenya. **Document type:** government publication.
Former titles: Kenya. Maize and Produce Board. Report; Kenya. Wheat Board. Report.

631.7 KE ISSN 0075-5915
KENYA. NATIONAL IRRIGATION BOARD. REPORTS AND ACCOUNTS. 1967. irreg; latest 1973. free to recognized institutions. National Irrigation Board, Lenana Rd., P.O. Box 30372, Nairobi, Kenya. **Document type:** government publication.

KENYA COFFEE; monthly bulletin. see *FOOD AND FOOD INDUSTRIES*

631 UK
KEY NOTE MARKET REPORT: AGROCHEMICALS & FERTILIZERS. Variant title: Agrochemicals & Fertilizers. 1993. irreg. £205. Key Note Ltd., Field House, 72 Oldfield Rd., Hampton, Middlesex TW12 2HQ, England. TEL 44-181-783-0755. FAX 44-181-783-0049. **Document type:** trade publication.
●Also available online.
Also available on CD-ROM.
Formerly: Key Note Report: Agrochemicals and Fertilizers (ISSN 1352-657X)

631.8 II ISSN 0023-1010
KHAD PATRIKA. (Text in Hindi) 1960. m. Rs.20. Fertiliser Association of India, Near Jawaharlal Nehru University, New Delhi 110067, India. Ed. P.C. Pathak. circ. 2,400.

630 KR ISSN 0023-1223
KHLIBOROB UKRAINY. (Text in Ukrainian) m. $13.20. Vydavnitstvo Urozhai, Yaroslavov val 10, 242034 Kiev, Ukraine. TEL 044-220-1626. charts; illus.; index.

633.51 RU ISSN 0023-1231
SB245 CODEN: KHLOAK
KHLOPKOVODSTVO. 1922. m. $11.40. Izdatel'stvo Kolos, Sadovaya-Spasskaya, 18, 107807 Moscow, Russia. (Co-sponsor: Ministerstvo Sel'skogo Khozyaistva) Ed. I.D. Blinov. adv.; bk.rev.; charts; illus.; stat.; index. circ. 13,500. **Indexed:** Biol.Abstr., Biotech.Abstr., Chem.Abstr., Cott.& Trop.Fibr.Abstr., Field Crop Abstr., Herb.Abstr., Plant Grow.Reg.Abstr., Rev.Plant Path., Seed Abstr., Weed Abstr., World Text.Abstr.
—CASDDS.

632 JA ISSN 0368-623X
CODEN: KNBKAY
KITA NIHON BYOGAICHU KENKYU KAIHO/SOCIETY OF PLANT PROTECTION OF NORTH JAPAN. ANNUAL REPORT. Key Title: Kita Nippon Byogaichu Kenkyukai Ho. (Text in Japanese; summaries in English or Japanese) 1950. a. 3000 Yen($1.50) Kita Nihon Byogaichu Kenkyukai - Society of Plant Protection of North Japan, c/o Tohoku National Agricultural Experiment Station, 3 Shimofurumichi, Yotsuya, Omagari-shi, Akita-ken 014-01, Japan. TEL 0187-66-1221. Ed. Haruo Miura. adv.; cum.index 1950-1959; 1960-1969. **Indexed:** Chem.Abstr., Helminthol.Abstr., Rev.Plant Path. **Document type:** academic/scholarly publication.
—CASDDS. **CCC.**

632 JA ISSN 0023-2521
KOBE PLANT PROTECTION AND PLANT QUARANTINE INFORMATION/KOBE SHOKUBUTSU BOEKI JOHO.* (Text in Japanese) 1954. m. $1. Kobe Plant Protection Station - Kobe-shi Shokubutsu Boekisho, 1-1 Hatoba-cho Chuo-ku, Kobe-shi, Hyogo-ken 650, Japan. Ed. Bd. charts; illus.; stat.; index. circ. 1,500.

630.24 668.6 NE ISSN 0169-7625
KOERIER AGRO CHEMIE. Dutch translation of: Pflanzenschutz Kurier. 1959. irreg. (2-3/yr.). free. Bayer Nederland B.V., Postbus 80, 3640 AB Mijdrecht, Netherlands. TEL 02979-80666. FAX 02979-84165. (Main office: Bayer Pflanzenschutz, Leverkusen, Germany) charts; illus. circ. 25,000.
Former titles (until 1978): Agro Chemie-Koerier (ISSN 0166-2252); Agro Chemie-Koerier Voor Plantenziektenbestrijding.
Description: Covers chemical research in pesticides and treatment of diseases in various domestic crops by the Bayer Company in the Netherlands.

632 JA ISSN 0023-334X
KONGETSU NO NOGYO/AGRICULTURAL CHEMICALS MONTHLY. (Text in Japanese) 1957. m. 865 Yen per no. Chemical Daily Co., Ltd., International Affairs, 3-16-8, Nihonbashi Hamacho, Chuo-Ku, Tokyo 103, Japan. TEL 81-3-3663-7932. FAX 81-3-3663-7275. TELEX 2422362 NIPPO J. Ed. Isao Imanaka. adv.; bk.rev.; charts; illus. circ. 40,000. **Indexed:** Chem.Abstr.
Description: Examines pesticides and their uses.

632 KO ISSN 1225-0171
KOREAN JOURNAL OF APPLIED ENTOMOLOGY. (Text in Korean; summaries in English) 1962. q. 15000 Won($30) (effective 1991). Korean Society of Applied Entomology, c/o Dept. of Entomology, Agricultural Sciences Institute, Rural Development Administration, Suwon 441-707, S. Korea. TEL 0331-291-3681. FAX 0331-291-5830. (Alt. addr.: c/o Department of Agricultural Biology, College of Agriculture, Seoul National University, Suwon 440-707, S. Korea) Ed. Seung Chan Lee. index. circ. 600. (back issues avail.) **Indexed:** Bio-Contr.News & Info., Biol.Abstr., Forest.Abstr., Plant Breed.Abstr., Rev.Appl.Entomol., Rev.Plant Path., Rice Abstr., Triticale Abstr. **Document type:** academic/scholarly publication.
—BLDSC (5113.513500).
Formerly (until 1988): Korean Journal of Plant Protection.

KOREAN JOURNAL OF BREEDING. see *AGRICULTURE — Poultry And Livestock*

AGRICULTURE — CROP PRODUCTION AND SOIL

633.2 GW ISSN 0023-4427
CODEN: KFFUAS
KRAFTFUTTER/FEED MAGAZINE; Zeitschrift fuer die Futtermittel- und Getreidewirtschaft. (Text in English, German) 1953. m. DM.213 (Europe DM.234.33; elsewhere DM.225) (effective 1997). Verlag Alfred Strothe, Mainzer Landstr. 251, 60326 Frankfurt a.M., Germany. TEL 49-69-759501. FAX 49-69-75951260. adv.; bk.rev.; charts; illus.; stat.; index. circ. 2,300. **Indexed:** Biodet.Abstr., Biotech.Abstr., Chem.Abstr., Excerp.Med. **Document type:** trade publication.
—CASDDS; SWETS. **CCC.**

634 II
KRISHI CHAYANIKA. (Text in Hindi) 1979. q. Rs.32($12) Indian Council of Agricultural Research, Krishi Anusandhan Bhavan, Pusa, New Delhi 110012, India. Ed. Kuldeep Sharma. adv.; bk.rev.; charts; illus.; index. circ. 3,000. (back issues avail.)
Description: A digest of the specialized knowledge on agricultural research conducted in India and abroad.

633.15 RU ISSN 0233-7770
KUKURUZA I SORGO. (Text in Russian) 1956. bi-m. $50 (effective 1998). A.O. Agro, Sadovaya-Spasskaya, 18, 107807 Moscow, Russia. TEL 7-095-2072381. FAX 7-095-2072381. Ed. Ekaterina A. Safonova. adv. contact: Ekateriana A. Safonova. bk.rev.; bibl.; index. circ. 1,420. **Indexed:** Biol.Abstr., Chem.Abstr., Field Crop Abstr., Herb.Abstr., Plant Breed.Abstr. **Document type:** trade publication.
—BLDSC (0094.100000).
Formerly: Kukuruza (ISSN 0023-5040)

631 GW ISSN 0458-6859
CODEN: LVOEAC
LANDBAUFORSCHUNG VOELKENRODE; wissenschaftliche Mitteilungen der Bundesforschungsanstalt fuer Landwirtschaft Braunschweig-Voelkenrode. (Text in German; summaries in English) 1950. q. DM.60. Bundesforschungsanstalt fuer Landwirtschaft Braunschweig-Voelkenrode, Bundesallee 50, 38116 Braunschweig, Germany. TEL 49-531-596-1. FAX 49-531-596-814. index. circ. 900. (back issues avail.) **Indexed:** Agri.Eng.Abstr., Anim.Breed.Abstr., ASCA, Curr.Adv.Ecol.Sci., Curr.Cont., Dairy Sci.Abstr., Fababean Abstr., Field Crop Abstr., Herb.Abstr., IBR, Ind.Vet., Maize Abstr., Pig News & Info., Potato Abstr., Poult.Abstr., Seed Abstr., Sorghum & Millets Abstr., Soyabean Abstr., SSCI, Triticale Abstr., Trop.Oil Seeds Abstr., Vet.Bull., VITIS, World Agri.Econ.& Rural Sociol.Abstr. **Document type:** government publication.
—BLDSC (5147.000000); CASDDS; Genuine Article. **CCC.**

631.7 627 US ISSN 0745-3795
SB472.53
LANDSCAPE & IRRIGATION. 1977. m. $40 (foreign $65) (effective 1997). Hunter Publishing Limited Partnership, 2101 S. Arlington Heights Rd., Ste. 150, Arlington Heights, IL 60005. TEL 847-427-9512. FAX 847-427-2097. Ed. Helen Stone. adv.; bk.rev.; charts; stat.; tr.lit.; index. circ. 37,000. (back issues avail.) **Document type:** trade publication.
—UnCover.
Incorporates (in 1985): Western Landscape News; Former titles: Landscape West and Irrigation News (ISSN 0191-8745); Landscape West.

632 US ISSN 0894-1254
SB610
LANDSCAPE MANAGEMENT; commercial turf magazine for turf and ornamental care and control. 1962. m. $39 (Canada $66; elsewhere $130) (effective 1996). Advanstar Communications, Inc., 7500 Old Oak Blvd., Cleveland, OH 44130. TEL 216-826-2855. FAX 216-891-2675. (Subscr. to: 131 W. First St., Duluth, MN 55802. TEL 800-346-0085) Ed. Gerald Roche. adv.; bk.rev.; charts; illus.; index. circ. 45,103. (also avail. in microform from UMI) **Indexed:** Excerp.Med., Farm & Garden Ind., Soils & Fert., Weed Abstr. **Document type:** trade publication.
—UMI. **CCC.**
Incorporates (in 1992): Landscape Management Golf Daily; (1977-1992): Lawn Care Industry (ISSN 0160-6042); Former titles (until 1987): Weeds, Trees and Turf (ISSN 0043-1753); (until 1987): Weeds, Trees and Golf Daily.
Description: Covers weed control, insect control and turf management.

631 GW
LANDTECHNIK (MUENSTER); Fachzeitschrift fuer Agrartechnik und laendliches Bauen. (Text in German; summaries in English and German) 1950. bi-m. DM.196 (foreign DM.206.40) (effective 1997). (Verein Deutscher Ingenieure) Landwirtschaftsverlag GmbH, Huelsebrockstr. 2, 48165 Muenster, Germany. TEL 49-2501-801-0. FAX 49-2501-801-204. Ed. R. Metzner. bk.rev.; charts; illus.; index. circ. 1,725. **Indexed:** Agri.Eng.Abstr., Excerp.Med., Hort.Abstr., Nutr.Abstr., Pig News & Info., Soils & Fert., Sugar Ind.Abstr., World Agri.Econ.& Rural Sociol.Abstr. **Document type:** trade publication.
—Linda Hall. **CCC.**
Formerly: Grundlagen der Landtechnik (ISSN 0017-4920)

630 II ISSN 0250-5371
CODEN: LRESDD
LEGUME RESEARCH; journal of legume physiology, genetics, breeding, bacterial activity, product quality and technological aspects of cultivation, processing and evaluation. (Text in English) 1978. q. $60 (effective 1997). Agricultural Research Communication Centre, 1130 Sadar, Karnal 132001, Haryana, India. TEL 91-184-255080. Ed. V.P. Singh. bk.rev. circ. 3,000. **Indexed:** Biol.Abstr., Chem.Abstr., Crop Physiol.Abstr., Field Crop Abstr., Food Sci.& Tech.Abstr., Irr.& Drain.Abstr., Plant Breed.Abstr., Plant Grow.Reg.Abstr., Rev.Appl.Entomol., Rev.Plant Path., Seed Abstr., Soils & Fert., Soyabean Abstr., Trop.Oil Seeds Abstr., Weed Abstr.
—CASDDS; Linda Hall; UMI; UnCover.

631 SP ISSN 0457-6039
LEVANTE AGRICOLA; revista internacional de citricos. 1962. q. (plus special issue). 6500 ptas. (foreign 7800 ptas.) (effective 1997). Ediciones y Promociones Lav, S.L., Apdo. 473, 46080 Valencia, Spain. TEL 34-6-3720261. FAX 34-6-3710516. Ed. Francisco Salvador Planes Planes. adv.; abstr.; illus.; charts; stat. **Indexed:** Ind.SST.

631 SA
LINK; information bulletin for the sugar industry. 1992. q. free. South African Sugar Association Experiment Station, Private Bag X02, Mount Edgecombe 4300, South Africa. TEL 27-31-593205. FAX 27-31-595406. TELEX 6-23020. illus. circ. 3,000. **Indexed:** Per.Islam. (1990-). **Document type:** newsletter.

631 NE ISSN 0169-0396
LISSE. LABORATORIUM VOOR BLOEMBOLLENONDERZOEK. JAARVERSLAG. (Text in Dutch; summaries in English) 1953. a. Laboratorium voor Bloembollenonderzoek, Vennestraat 22, Postbus 85, 2160 AB Lisse, Netherlands. TEL 31-252-462121. FAX 31-252-417762. E-mail: postbox@lbo.agro.nl; URL: http://www.agro.nl/ appliedresearch. Ed. Mrs. M.J. Zwart. circ. 2,000. **Indexed:** Biol.Abstr. **Document type:** corporate report.
—BLDSC (4610.300000).

631.4 UK
S605.5
LIVING EARTH & THE FOOD MAGAZINE. 1947. q. £18 (effective 1997). Soil Association, 86 Colston St., Bristol BS1 5BB, England. TEL 44-117-929-0661. FAX 44-117-925-2504. E-mail: soilassoc@gn.apc.org. Ed. Charlotte Russell. R&P contact: Paul Adams. adv. contact: Paul Adams. bk.rev.; charts; illus. circ. 9,000. **Indexed:** Environ.Per.Bibl., Soils & Fert. **Document type:** consumer publication.
—BLDSC (5282.610000); CISTI; UnCover.
Formed by the 1993 merger of: Food Magazine & Living Earth (ISSN 0954-1098); Which was formerly (until 1988): Soil Association. Review (ISSN 0951-2381); (until 1985): Soil Association. Quarterly Review (ISSN 0307-2576); (until 1975): Soil Association. Journal (ISSN 0038-0709)
Description: Supports organic food and sustainable farming.

632.9 ML ISSN 0459-6803
LOCUSTA. (Text in English or French) 1954. irreg. Organisation Internationale Contre le Criquet Migrateur Africain - International African Migratory Locust Organization, B.P. 136, Bamako, Mali.

633.15 UK ISSN 0024-6026
LONDON CORN CIRCULAR. 1843. w. £75. Nene House, London Rd., Peterborough, Cambs. PE2 8AH, England. TEL 01733-555079. FAX 01733-896046. Ed. John V. Bird. adv.; bk.rev.; stat. circ. 1,000. (back issues avail.) **Document type:** trade publication.

LOS ANGELES WHOLESALE FRUIT & VEGETABLE REPORT. see AGRICULTURE — Agricultural Economics

634.8 HU ISSN 0866-6083
TP559.H9 CODEN: BORGBB
MAGYAR SZOLO- ES BORGAZDASAG/HUNGARIAN JOURNAL OF VITICULTURE AND ENOLOGY. (Text in Hungarian; table of contents, summaries in English) 1991. bi-m. 1800 Ft.($20) (Wine Producer's Council) Dinasztia Kiado, Erzsebet Kiralyne u. 36-b, 1142 Budapest, Hungary. TEL 36-1-252-4772. FAX 36-1-252-6758. (Subscr. to: Kultura, Box 149, 1389 Budapest, Hungary) Ed. Eva Herpay. adv.; bk.rev. **Indexed:** Food Sci.& Tech.Abstr., VITIS. **Document type:** academic/scholarly publication.
—CASDDS.
Formed by the merger of (1953-1990): Borgazdasag (ISSN 0006-7741); Which was formerly (until 1954): Borgazdasagi Ertesito (ISSN 0200-2892); (1971-1990): Szolo-bor Inform (ISSN 0133-5286); (1981-1990): Szolotermesztes es Boraszat (ISSN 0230-2241); Which was formerly: Szolotermesztes (ISSN 0139-4660).
Description: Covers research, production, management, economics, and news of the association.

630 US ISSN 1070-1494
S69 CODEN: MLSBBX
MAINE AGRICULTURAL AND FOREST EXPERIMENT STATION. BULLETIN. irreg. Maine Agricultural and Forest Experiment Station, University of Maine, 5782 Winslow Hall, Rm. 1, Orono, ME 04469. TEL 207-891-3277. **Document type:** bulletin.
—BLDSC (2789.152900); CASDDS; Linda Hall.
Former titles (until 1993): Maine Agricultural Experiment Station. Bulletin (ISSN 0734-9548); (until 1983): Maine Life Sciences and Agricultural Experiment Station. Bulletin (ISSN 0099-4448)

633.4 US
MAINE POTATO NEWS. 1955. m. free. (Maine Potato Board) Northeast Publishing Company, Box 510, Presque Isle, ME 04769. TEL 207-764-7033. FAX 207-764-4499. Ed. Martha M. Lostrom. adv. contact: Martha M. Lostrom. illus.; circ. 6,000 (controlled). (tabloid format) **Document type:** trade publication, newspaper.
Formerly (until Jun. 1987): Potato Councillor (ISSN 0032-5570)
Description: Official voice of the Maine potato industry.

633 GW ISSN 0341-5155
MAIS; Zeitschrift ueber Forschung, Produktionstechnik, Verwertung und Oekonomik. 1973. q. DM.34 (foreign DM.43) (effective 1997). (Deutsches Maiskomitee e.V.) Verlag Th. Mann, Nordring 10, 45894 Gelsenkirchen, Germany. TEL 49-209-9304184. FAX 49-209-9304185. Ed. Helmut Messner. adv.: B&W page DM.3070, color page DM.5380; trim 186 x 270; adv. contact: Richard Heineke. circ. 6,223. **Document type:** trade publication.
—BLDSC (5352.690000). **CCC.**

633 CC ISSN 1001-0092
MALINGSHU ZAZHI/JOURNAL OF POTATOES. (Text in Chinese) q. Dongbei Nongxueyuan – Northeast Institute of Agriculture, Xiangfang-qu, Harbin, Heilongjiang 150030, People's Republic of China. TEL 55981. Ed. Tang Hongfen.

MANITOBA CROP INSURANCE CORPORATION. ANNUAL REPORT. see INSURANCE

MARKET MICHIGAN FRUIT. see AGRICULTURE — Agricultural Economics

631 MR ISSN 0851-1667
MAROC FRUITS. (Text in French) 1958. w. 22 rue Al Messaoudi, Casablanca 02, Morocco. Ed. Ahmed Mansour Nejjai. adv.

AGRICULTURE — CROP PRODUCTION AND SOIL

631   RU   ISSN 0207-2165
MASLICHNYE KUL'TURY. 1981. bi-m. 40 Kop. per issue. Izdatel'stvo Kolos, Sadovo-Spasskaya, 18, 107807 Moscow, Russia. Ed. E.A. Glazunov. circ. 2,000. **Indexed:** Field Crop Abstr., Seed Abstr., Soyabean Abstr., Trop.Oil Seeds Abstr.

633.1   IT   ISSN 0025-6153
CODEN: MYDCAH
MAYDICA; a journal devoted to maize and allied species. (Text in English) 1956. q. L.250000 (effective 1995). Istituto Sperimentale per la Cerealicoltura, Sezione di Bergamo, Via Stezzano 24, 24126 Bergamo, Italy. TEL 39-35-313132. FAX 39-35-316054. Eds. Angelo Bianchi, P.A. Peterson. adv.; bk.rev.; charts; illus.; index. circ. 1,000. **Indexed:** ASCA, Biol.Abstr., Chem.Abstr., Curr.Adv.Ecol.Sci., Curr.Cont., Field Crop Abstr., Herb.Abstr., Ind.Sci.Rev., Maize Abstr., Plant Breed.Abstr., Plant Grow.Reg.Abstr., Rice Abstr., Sci.Cit.Ind., Seed Abstr., Soils & Fert., Sorghum & Millets Abstr.
—BLDSC (5413.340000); CASDDS; EMDOCS; Genuine Article; SWETS; UnCover.
Description: Publishes original papers in the field of genetics, molecular biology, biochemistry, physiology, breeding and agronomy of corn and allied species.
Refereed Serial

631   IO
MEETING OF COCONUT PRODUCTS EXPORTERS (YEAR). PROCEEDINGS. a. price varies. Asian and Pacific Coconut Community, Wisma Bakrie, 3rd Fl., Jl. H.R. Rasuna Said, Kuningan, Jakarta 12920, Indonesia. TEL 62-21-510-073. FAX 62-21-520-5160. TELEX 62863 APCCIA. **Document type:** proceedings.
Description: Contains assessments of the market situation during the year as well as outlook for the following year with data on production, export of coconuts and other oilseeds, oils and fats.

MEGADRILOGICA. see *BIOLOGY — Zoology*

MESTNYI PROIZVODSTVENNYI OPYT V SEL'SKOM KHOZYAISTVE/LOCAL LEVEL EXPERIENCE IN AGRICULTURAL DEVELOPMENT; nauchno-tekhnicheskii referativnyi sbornik. see *AGRICULTURE — Agricultural Economics*

MICHIGAN APPLE REPORT. see *AGRICULTURE — Agricultural Economics*

MICHIGAN FRUIT & VEGETABLE REPORT. see *AGRICULTURE — Agricultural Economics*

631   UK   ISSN 0957-4360
MICRONUTRIENT NEWS AND INFORMATION. 1980. 4/yr. £113 (U.S. and Canada $213; rest of world £115). Micronutrient Bureau, M.B. House, Wigginton, Tring, Herts. HP23 6ED, England. TEL 0442-822720. Ed. Victor Shorrocks. bk.rev.; illus. (back issues avail.) **Indexed:** Copper Abstr. **Document type:** academic/scholarly publication, newsletter.
Formerly (until 1990): Micronutrient News (ISSN 0261-5002); **Incorporates:** (from 1980-??) Zinc in Agriculture (ISSN 0261-5452); Boron in Agriculture (0261-5444); Copper in Agriculture (0261-5436); Iron in Agriculture (0264-5998); Manganese in Agriculture (0261-5010); Molybdenum in Agriculture (0261-5045).
Description: Contains the latest information on worldwide use of and research into micronutrients in agriculture.

632.9   UN   ISSN 1014-2193
MIGRANT PEST NEWSLETTER. (Editions in English and French) 1961. a. free. Food and Agriculture Organization of the United Nations, Sales & Distribution Section, Via delle Terme di Caracalla, 00100 Rome, Italy. TEL 57971. FAX 6799563. TELEX 610181 FAO. E-mail: publications-sales@fao.org. **Document type:** newsletter.
Former titles: Locust Newsletter (ISSN 1014-2207); Desert Locust Newsletter (ISSN 0417-0946)

MONITEUR VINICOLE. see *BEVERAGES*

631   IO
MONOGRAPHS ON COCONUT INDUSTRY. a.? price varies. Asian and Pacific Coconut Community, Wisma Bakrie, 3rd Fl., Jl. H.R. Rasuna Said, Kuningan, Jakarta 12920, Indonesia. TEL 62-21-510-073. FAX 62-21-520-5160. TELEX 62863 APCCIA. **Document type:** monographic series.
Description: Studies the coconut industry in member countries. Deals with the current state of development of the crop as an economic resource, development plans, economic aspects and a range of other topics.

333.7   UK
MONOGRAPHS ON SOIL AND RESOURCES SURVEY. irreg. price varies. Oxford University Press, Walton St., Oxford OX2 6DP, England. TEL 44-1865-56767. FAX 44-1865-56646. (Subscr. in US to: Oxford University Press Inc., 2001 Evans Rd., Cary, NC 27513. TEL 919-677-0977. FAX 9191-677-1714) Ed.Bd. **Indexed:** I.M.M.Abstr. **Document type:** monographic series.
Supersedes: Monographs on Soil Survey.
Refereed Serial

631.4   US   ISSN 0147-6874
S590   CODEN: MUSBDU
MOSCOW UNIVERSITY SOIL SCIENCE BULLETIN. English translation in part of: Moskovskii Universitet. Vestnik. Seriya 16: Biologiya (UR ISSN 0137-0952) 1974. q. $970 (effective 1998). (Moskovskii Universitet, RU) Allerton Press, Inc., 150 Fifth Ave., New York, NY 10011. TEL 212-924-3950. FAX 212-463-9684. Ed. A.D. Voronin. charts; illus.; index. **Indexed:** Agroforest.Abstr., Biol.Abstr., Environ.Per.Bibl., Excerp.Med., Field Crop Abstr., Forest.Abstr., GeoRef., Herb.Abstr., Hort.Abstr., Irr.& Drain.Abstr., Maize Abstr., Potato Abstr., Soils & Fert., Triticale Abstr., Weed Abstr. **Document type:** academic/scholarly publication.
—BLDSC (0416.245000); Linda Hall; UnCover. CCC.
Description: Covers soil genesis, soil chemistry, soil reclamation and physics, plant productivity, soil biology, ecology.

MOSKOVSKII UNIVERSITET. VESTNIK. SERIYA 16: BIOLOGIYA. see *BIOLOGY*

631   US   ISSN 0541-3869
MUSHROOM NEWS. (Includes insert: News Flash) 1955. m. $275. American Mushroom Institute, One Massachusetts Ave., N.W., Ste. 800, Washington, DC 20001-1401. TEL 202-842-4344. FAX 202-408-7763. adv.: B&W page $558, color page $947; adv. contact: Dave King. bk.rev.; index. circ. 1,000. (back issues avail.) **Document type:** trade publication.
—BLDSC (5990.160000).
Description: Covers information on mushroom growing and the US mushroom industry.
Refereed Serial

631   UN   ISSN 1011-260X
MUTATION BREEDING NEWSLETTER. (Text in English) 1972. irreg. free. International Atomic Energy Agency, Wagramerstr. 5, P.O. Box 100, A-1400 Vienna, Austria. TEL 43-1-20600. FAX 43-1-20607. E-mail: Maluszyn@ripo1.iaea.or.at. (Co-sponsor: Food and Agriculture Organization) circ. 1,300. **Indexed:** Cott.& Trop.Fibr.Abstr., Field Crop Abstr., Ornam.Hort., Plant Breed.Abstr., Plant Grow.Reg.Abstr., Rice Abstr., Seed Abstr., Sorghum & Millets Abstr., Triticale Abstr., Trop.Oil Seeds Abstr. **Document type:** newsletter.
—BLDSC (5991.898000).

631   UN   ISSN 1011-2618
MUTATION BREEDING REVIEW. (Text in English) 1982. a. free. International Atomic Energy Agency, Wagramerstr. 5, P.O. Box 100, A-1400 Vienna, Austria. TEL 43-1-20600. FAX 43-1-20607. E-mail: maluszn@ripo1.iaea.or.at. (Co-sponsor: Food and Agriculture Organization) circ. 500. **Document type:** monographic series.

MYCORRHIZA. see *BIOLOGY — Botany*

632.9   PH
N C P C ANNUAL REPORT. 1969. a. free. National Crop Protection Center, College, Laguna 3720, Philippines. Eds. Aurora M. Baltazar, Pablo P. Ocampo. circ. 2,000. **Indexed:** Biol.Abstr.
Formerly: University of the Philippines at Los Banos. Rodent Research Center. Annual Report.

631   UK   ISSN 1361-8822
N I A B OILSEEDS VARIETY HANDBOOK. a. £10.50 (foreign £15.50). National Institute of Agricultural Botany, Huntington Rd., Cambridge CB3 0LE, England. TEL 44-1223-276381. FAX 44-1223-277602. Ed. Paul Nelson. **Indexed:** Field Crop Abstr., Herb.Abstr., Plant Breed.Abstr. **Document type:** bulletin.
—BLDSC (6252.610500).
Former titles: N I A B Recommended Varieties of Oilseed Crops (ISSN 1354-1382); (until 1994): Farmers Leaflet (ISSN 0305-1277)

631   UK   ISSN 1361-8857
N I A B PULSE VARIETY HANDBOOK. a. £10.50. National Institute of Agricultural Botany, Huntingdon Rd., Cambridge CB3 0LE, England. TEL 44-1223-276381. FAX 44-1223-277602. Ed. Paul Nelson. **Document type:** bulletin.
Formerly: N I A B Recommended Varieties of Field Peas and Field Beans.

NABOR CARRILLO LECTURE SERIES. PROCEEDINGS. see *ENGINEERING — Civil Engineering*

630   GW   ISSN 0027-7479
CODEN: NDPBA6
NACHRICHTENBLATT DES DEUTSCHEN PFLANZENSCHUTZDIENSTES. (Text in German; summaries in English, German) 1949. m. DM.202.20. (Biologische Bundesanstalt fuer Land- und Forstwirtschaft) Verlag Eugen Ulmer GmbH, Wollgrasweg 41, 70599 Stuttgart, Germany. TEL 49-711-4507-0. FAX 49-711-4507-120. (Subscr. to: Postfach 700561, 70574 Stuttgart, Germany) Ed. Prof. Dr. F. Klingauf. R&P contact: G. Friedrich. adv. contact: F. Signore. bk.rev.; illus.; index. circ. 1,200. (tabloid format) **Indexed:** Agri.Eng.Abstr., Bio-Contr.News & Info., Biol.Abstr., Chem.Abstr., Excerp.Med., Field Crop Abstr., Forest.Abstr., Helminthol.Abstr., Herb.Abstr., Hort.Abstr., Irr.& Drain.Abstr., Plant Breed.Abstr., Plant Grow.Reg.Abstr., Potato Abstr., Rev.Appl.Entomol., Rev.Med.& Vet.Mycol., Rev.Plant Path., Seed Abstr., Soils & Fert., VITIS, Weed Abstr. **Document type:** newsletter.
—BLDSC (6007.500000); CASDDS; SWETS. **CCC.**
Incorporates: Nachrichtenblatt fuer den Pflanzenschutzdienst in der DDR (ISSN 0323-5912)

638   UK
NATIONAL INSTITUTE OF AGRICULTURAL BOTANY, CAMBRIDGE, ENGLAND. ANNUAL REPORT AND ACCOUNTS. 1919. a. £10. National Institute of Agricultural Botany, Huntingdon Rd., Cambridge CB3 0LE, England. TEL 44-1223-276381. FAX 44-1223-277602. Ed. Paul Nelson. circ. 7,000. **Indexed:** Biol.Abstr., Field Crop Abstr., Herb.Abstr., Weed Abstr. **Document type:** corporate report.
Formerly: National Institute of Agricultural Botany, Cambridge, England. Annual Report of the Council and Accounts (ISSN 0077-4782)

634   US   ISSN 0092-2633
NATIONAL PEACH COUNCIL. PROCEEDINGS. Also called: Proceedings, Annual Convention. a. National Peach Council, Box 11280, Columbia, SC 29211. TEL 803-799-7923. Ed. Martin Eubanks. adv.; illus.
Description: Technical papers and presentations on peach growing and marketing.

631   US
NATIONAL POTATO COUNCIL. YEARBOOK. a. $25. National Potato Council, 5690 D T C Blvd., Ste. 230-E, Englewood, CO 80111. TEL 303-773-9295. FAX 303-773-9296.

631.4 635   US
NATURAL SOLUTIONS. 1981. a. free. Necessary Trading Co., 1 Nature's Way, New Castle, VA 24127. TEL 703-864-5103. FAX 703-864-5186. bk.rev.; index. circ. 100,000. **Document type:** catalog.
Formerly (until 1991): Necessary Catalogue.
Description: Lists products for organic and sustainable agriculture, for farm, home and garden.

AGRICULTURE — CROP PRODUCTION AND SOIL

668.6   FR
NEGOCE ET AGRICULTURE. 1886. bi-m. 200 F. Federation Nationale du Commerce des Engrais et Produits Connexes, Secograins, 216 Bourse du Commerce, 75040 Paris Cedex 01, France. Ed. Pierre Neuviale. adv.; charts; illus. circ. 4,000. **Indexed:** Chem.Abstr. **Document type:** trade publication.
   Incorporates: Grains (ISSN 0046-6263); Formerly: Engrais.
   Description: Covers agricultural chemistry.

631   IT   ISSN 0391-9749
NEMATOLOGIA MEDITERRANEA. (Text in English, French, Italian, Portuguese, Spanish) 1973. s-a. L.100000 (effective 1995). Istituto di Nematologia Agraria, Via G. Amendola, 165-A, 70126 Bari, Italy. TEL 39-80-5484186. FAX 39-80-5484165. E-mail: f.elia@area.ba.cnr.it; URL: http://www.ba.cnr.it/nemmed.html. Eds. F. Lamberti, C.E. Taylor. bk.rev.; bibl.; charts; illus.; index; circ. 300 (controlled). (back issues avail.) **Indexed:** Agroforest.Abstr., Bio-Contr.News & Info., Cott.& Trop.Fibr.Abstr., Helminthol.Abstr., Hort.Abstr., Potato Abstr., Seed Abstr., Soils & Fert., Triticale Abstr., Weed Abstr. **Document type:** academic/scholarly publication.
   —BLDSC (6075.497000); SWETS.
   Refereed Serial

338.1   US   ISSN 0098-9541
SB354.6.U5
NEW JERSEY ORCHARD AND VINEYARD SURVEY. irreg., approx. quinquennial. Crop Reporting Service, Rm. 204, Health and Agriculture Bldg., Trenton, NJ 08625. TEL 609-292-6385. illus.

631   AT   ISSN 0727-9078
NEW SOUTH WALES. DEPARTMENT OF AGRICULTURE. SOIL SURVEY BULLETIN. 1954. irreg. price varies. Department of Agriculture, Soil Survey Unit, PMB 10, Rydalmere, N.S.W. 2116, Australia. TEL 02-683-9777. FAX 02-630-4475. circ. 500. **Document type:** bulletin.
   Formerly: New South Wales. Department of Agriculture. Soil Survey Unit. Bulletin (ISSN 0545-3631)
   Description: Results of soil and land resources surveys. Often includes maps and microfiche.

632.9   NZ
NEW ZEALAND AGRICHEMICAL MANUAL. 1984. a. $85. W H A M Chemsafe, P.O. Box 11-092, Wellington, New Zealand. TEL 64-4-4739243. FAX 64-4-4734530. E-mail: 100406.2225@compuserve.com. Ed. Trevor Walton; Pubs. Angela Fussell, Trevor Walton. R&P contact: Trevor Walton. adv. contact: Angela Fussell. circ. 7,000. **Document type:** directory.
   Former titles: New Zealand Agrichemical and Plant Protection Manual (ISSN 0114-4022); (until 1990): New Zealand Agricultural Manual (ISSN 0112-2290)
   Description: Listings of all agrichemicals used in New Zealand, their properties, active ingredients and how to use them.

631   NZ   ISSN 0113-8723
NEW ZEALAND KIWIFRUIT. 1983. bi-m. NZ.$58.72 (effective 1997). Kiwifruit New Zealand, P.O. Box 9906, Auckland, New Zealand. TEL 64-9-3677500. FAX 64-9-3670220. E-mail: elainefgraham@xta.co.na. Ed. Elaine Fisher. R&P contact: Elaine Fisher. adv.: B&W page NZ.$800, color page NZ.$1400; trim 297 x 210. circ. 4,000. **Document type:** trade publication.
   Refereed Serial

631.4   NZ   ISSN 0545-7904
S599.75.A1
NEW ZEALAND SOIL NEWS. 1953. bi-m. membership. New Zealand Society of Soil Science, c/o Dept. of Soil Science, P.O. Box 84, Lincoln University, Canterbury 8150, New Zealand. TEL 64-3-3252811. FAX 64-3-3252607. E-mail: Campbell@lincoln.ac.nz. Ed. A.S. Campbell. R&P contact: A.S. Campbell. adv. contact: A.S. Campbell. bk.rev. circ. 550. **Document type:** newsletter.
   —CCC.
   Description: Covers all aspects of soil science.

631   JA   ISSN 0029-0610
CODEN: NIDHAX
NIPPON DOJO HIRYOGAKU ZASSHI/JAPANESE JOURNAL OF SOIL SCIENCE AND PLANT NUTRITION. (Text in Japanese) 1927. bi-m. 20000 Yen. Nippon Dojo Hiryo Gakkai - Japanese Society of Soil Science and Plant Nutrition, Hongo New Housing, Rm. 202, 26-10 Hongo 6-chome, Bunkyo-ku, Tokyo 113, Japan. TEL 81-3-3815-2085. FAX 81-3-3815-6018. Ed. Satoshi Matsumoto. adv.; bk.rev.; abstr.; charts; illus. circ. 3,300. **Indexed:** Chem.Abstr., Field Crop Abstr. **Document type:** academic/scholarly publication.
   —CASDDS; Linda Hall; UnCover.
   Formerly (until 1934): Dojo Hiryogaku Zasshi - Society of the Science of Soil and Manure of Japan. Journal (ISSN 0911-9973)

NIPPON NOGEIKAGAKU KAISHI/JAPAN SOCIETY FOR BIOSCIENCE, BIOTECHNOLOGY, AND AGROCHEMISTRY. JOURNAL. see *BIOLOGY — Biotechnology*

NIPPON NOYAKU GAKKAISHI. see *ENGINEERING — Chemical Engineering*

631.8   UK   ISSN 0029-0777
TP245.N8   CODEN: NNNNAY
NITROGEN; covers all aspects of world ammonia and nitrogen fertilizer industry. 1959. bi-m. £340($495) (effective May 1997). British Sulphur Publishing (Subsidiary of: C R U Publishing Ltd.), 31 Mount Pleasant, London WC1X OAD, England. TEL 44-171-837-5600. FAX 44-171-837-0292. TELEX 918918 SULFEX G. Ed. Richard Hands; Pub. John French. R&P contact: John French. adv. contact: Tina Firman. bk.rev.; charts; illus.; mkt.; stat.; index. circ. 597. (also avail. in microform from UMI; reprint service avail. from UMI) **Indexed:** Chem.Abstr., PROMT, Soils & Fert. **Document type:** trade publication.
   ●Also available online. Vendor(s): Information Access Co.
   —BLDSC (6113.700000); CASDDS; Ei; Linda Hall; SWETS; UMI.

631   JA   ISSN 0029-0882
NOGYO FUMIN/AGRICULTURE AND BETTER FARMING. (Text in Japanese) 1929. m. 1560 Yen. Fumin Kyokai, Shuppan-bu - Better Farming Association, Publishing Division, c/o Mainichi Shinbunsha, Dojima, Kita-ku, Osaka 530, Japan. Ed. Yasuji Miyata. adv.; abstr.; charts; illus.; stat.; index. circ. 190,000. (processed)

632.9   CC   ISSN 1002-5480
CODEN: NKYGEH
NONGYAO KEXUE YU GUANLI/PESTICIDE SCIENCE AND MANAGEMENT. (Text in Chinese) 1989. $80. Nongye Bu, Nongyao Jiandingsuo - Ministry of Agriculture, Institute for the Control of Agrochemicals, Liangmaqiao, Beijing 100026, People's Republic of China. TEL 10-5025929. Ed. Jing Zhiyuan. **Document type:** academic/scholarly publication, government publication.
   —BLDSC (6428.449000); CASDDS.
   Description: Covers the policies and regulations of pesticide, use of pesticide, product analytical methods, and pesticide toxicology.

630.24 668.6   US   ISSN 0065-4418
NORTH CAROLINA AGRICULTURAL CHEMICALS MANUAL. 1948. a. $15. North Carolina State University, School of Agriculture-Life Sciences, Box 7603, Raleigh, NC 27695. TEL 919-737-3173. FAX 919-737-7191. index. circ. 5,000. **Document type:** academic/scholarly publication, bulletin.

631   CK
NOTICIAS COMALFI. 3/yr. Sociedad Colombiana de Control de Malezas y Fisiologia Vegetal, Ciudad Universitaria, Carrera 50 No. 27-70, Bloque C, Modulo 3 Nivel 8, Bogota DF, Colombia. TEL 2219643. Ed. Jaime Soriano.

634   CN   ISSN 0078-2386
NOVA SCOTIA FRUIT GROWERS ASSOCIATION. ANNUAL REPORT AND PROCEEDINGS. 1874. a. Can.$15 membership. Nova Scotia Fruit Growers Association, Kentville, N.S. B4N 1J5, Canada. TEL 902-678-1093. FAX 902-679-1567. adv. circ. 300. **Indexed:** Chem.Abstr., Hort.Abstr. **Document type:** corporate report, proceedings.

631   US   ISSN 0745-3469
NUT GROWER.* 1982. m. $19.95 (foreign $195). Western Agricultural Publishing Co. Inc., 4969 E. Clinton Ave., Ste. 119, Fresno, CA 93727-1549. TEL 209-252-7000. FAX 209-252-7387. Ed. Mark Arcamonte. circ. 11,000. **Document type:** trade publication.

631.8   NE   ISSN 1385-1314
S631   CODEN: NCAGFC
NUTRIENT CYCLING IN AGROECOSYSTEMS. (Text in English) 1980. 9/yr. fl.1614 to institutions; $828 to institutions in U.S. (effective 1998). Kluwer Academic Publishers, Postbus 17, 3300 AA Dordrecht, Netherlands. TEL 31-78-6392392. FAX 31-78-6392254. TELEX 29245 KAPG NL. E-mail: services@wkap.nl; URL: http://www.wkap.nl. (Dist. by: Kluwer Academic Publishers Group, P.O. Box 322, 3300 AH Dordrecht, Netherlands. TEL 31-78-6392392. FAX 31-78-6546474; N. America dist. addr.: Box 358, Accord Sta., Hingham, MA 02018-0358. TEL 617-871-6600. FAX 617-871-6528) Ed. Paul L.G. Vlek. adv.; bk.rev. (also avail. in microform from UMI; back issues avail.; reprint service avail. from SWZ) **Indexed:** ASCA, Biol.Abstr., Bull.Signal., Chem.Abstr., Cott.& Trop.Fibr.Abstr., Crop Physiol.Abstr., Curr.Adv.Ecol.Sci., Curr.Cont., Ecol.Abstr., Fababean Abstr., Field Crop Abstr., Forest.Abstr., Geo.Abstr., Geo.Abstr.H.G., Geo.Abstr.P.G., Herb.Abstr., Hort.Abstr., IDA, Int.Abstr.Biol.Sci., Irr.& Drain.Abstr., Maize Abstr., Ornam.Hort., Potato Abstr., Rice Abstr., Seed Abstr., Soils & Fert., Sorghum & Millets Abstr., Soyabean Abstr., Sugar Ind.Abstr., Triticale Abstr., Trop.Oil.Seeds Abstr., Weed Abstr. **Document type:** academic/scholarly publication.
   —BLDSC (6187.690000); CASDDS; EMDOCS; Genuine Article; KR SourceOne; Linda Hall; SWETS; UMI; UnCover. CCC.
   Formerly (until vol.48, 1997): Fertilizer Research (ISSN 0167-1731)
   Refereed Serial

NUTSHELL (NEW CARLISLE). see *GARDENING AND HORTICULTURE*

O A N DIRECTORY & BUYER'S GUIDE. (Oregon Association of Nurserymen) see *BUSINESS AND ECONOMICS — Trade And Industrial Directories*

O C L. (Oleagineux Corps gras Lipides) see *CHEMISTRY — Organic Chemistry*

OBST - WEIN - GARTEN. see *GARDENING AND HORTICULTURE*

630   XR   ISSN 0862-8645
CODEN: SUSRD8
OCHRANA ROSTLIN/PLANT PROTECTION; vedecky casopis. (Text and summaries in Czech or Slovak and English) 1965. q. $51 in Europe; elsewhere $53 (effective 1997). Ustav Zemedelskych a Potravinarskych Informaci, Slezska 7, 120 56 Prague 2, Czech Republic. TEL 420-24257939. FAX 420-24253938. E-mail: uzlk@uzpi.cz. Ed. Marcela Braunova. bk.rev. circ. 600. (back issues avail.) **Indexed:** Apic.Abstr., Bibl.Agri., Bio-Contr.News & Info., Biol.Abstr., Field Crop Abstr., Helminthol.Abstr., Herb.Abstr., Hort.Abstr., Landwirt.Zentralbl., Maize Abstr., Potato Abstr., Ref.Zh., Rev.Plant Path., Seed Abstr., Soils & Fert., Triticale Abstr., VITIS. **Document type:** academic/scholarly publication.
   —BLDSC (6234.900000).
   Formerly (until 1989): U V T I Z Sbornik - Ochrana Rostlin (ISSN 0036-5394)

631   US
OHIO ECOLOGICAL FOOD AND FARM ASSOCIATION NEWS. 1979. bi-m. $15. Ohio Ecological Food and Farm Association, Box 82234, Columbus, OH 43202. Ed. Holly Harman Fackler. adv.; bk.rev.; illus.; stat. circ. 1,200. (processed) **Document type:** newsletter.
   Description: Covers news and information on alternative food systems.

OIKO: THE ALTERNATIVE ENVIRONMENTAL DIGEST. see *AGRICULTURE — Abstracting, Bibliographies, Statistics*

AGRICULTURE — CROP PRODUCTION AND SOIL

631 US ISSN 0145-9392
OKLAHOMA FARMER-STOCKMAN. 1911. m. $19.95. Farm Progress Companies (Subsidiary of: A B C Publishing Companies), 191 S. Gary Ave., Carol Stream, IL 60188. TEL 630-690-5600. FAX 630-462-2869. (Edit. addr.: 408 S. Main, Ste. 3, Stillwater, OK 74074. TEL 405-377-5565. FAX 405-377-5595) Ed. Dan Crummett. adv.: B&W page $3400, color page $3910; trim 7 X 10. circ. 24,650 (paid).

633 SP ISSN 0255-996X
OLIVAE. French edition (ISSN 0255-9978); Italian edition (ISSN 0255-9986); English edition (ISSN 0255-9994) 1984. 5/yr. 3000 ptas. (Europe $31; America $38) (effective 1996). Consejo Oleicola Internacional - International Olive Oil Council, Calle Principe de Vergara 154, 28002 Madrid, Spain. TEL 34-1-5630071. FAX 34-1-5631263. Ed. Fausto Luchetti. adv.: bk.rev.; charts; illus.; stat. circ. 4,000. Indexed: Agri.Eng.Abstr., Field Crop Abstr., Hort.Abstr., Plant Grow.Reg.Abstr., Soyabean Abstr., World Agri.Econ.& Rural Sociol.Abstr.

ON YOUR MARK. see NUTRITION AND DIETETICS

631 US ISSN 0892-578X
ONION WORLD. 1985. 8/yr. $15 (Canada and Mexico $27; elsewhere $45). Columbia Publishing and Design, 2520 W. Washington, Ste. 2, Box 9036, Yakima, WA 98909-0036. TEL 509-248-2452; 800-900-2452. FAX 509-248-4056. E-mail: dede@freshcut.com. Ed. Ken Hodge; Pub. J. Mike Stoker. R&P contact: J. Mike Stoker. adv. contact: Lynn Schuchardt. circ. 6,552. (back issues avail.) **Document type:** trade publication.
Description: Covers onion research, production, and marketing.

ONTARIO. MINISTRY OF AGRICULTURE, FOOD AND RURAL ANALYSIS. MONTHLY CROP AND LIVESTOCK REPORT. see AGRICULTURE — Poultry And Livestock

633 CN ISSN 0008-7297
ONTARIO CORN PRODUCER. 1938. 10/yr. (Ontario Corn Producers' Association) N C C Publishing, 222 Argyle Ave., Delhi, ON N4B 2Y2, Canada. TEL 519-582-2510. FAX 519-582-4040. (Subscr. to: 190 Nicklin Rd., Guelph, ON N1H 7L5, Canada) Ed. Terry Boland. adv.: B&W page Can.$2123; trim 8 x 11; adv. contact: Jim Countryman. illus. circ. 29,819. **Document type:** trade publication.
Formerly (until 1985): Cash Crop Farming (ISSN 1193-7440)

634.8 663.1 CN ISSN 0380-6057
ONTARIO GRAPE GROWER. 1968. q. free. Ontario Grape Growers' Marketing Board, Box 100, Vineland, ON L0R 2E0, Canada. TEL 905-688-0990. FAX 905-688-3211. Ed. Brian Leyden. circ. 8,000 (controlled). (tabloid format; back issues avail.) **Document type:** newsletter.

631 634 NZ
ORCHARDIST. 1928. m. (except Jan.). NZ.$72 (foreign NZ.$130($88)). New Zealand Fruitgrowers Federation, P.O. Box 2175, Wellington, New Zealand. TEL 64-4-4726559. FAX 64-4-4726409. E-mail: hans@pims.co.nz. Ed. Hans Kuiper. R&P contact: Hans Kuiper. adv. contact: Ann Quinlan. bk.rev.; index. circ. 6,000. (back issues avail.) **Indexed:** Agri.Eng.Abstr., Bio-Contr.News & Info., Biol.Abstr., Hort.Abstr., Rev.Plant Path. **Document type:** trade publication.
—UnCover. CCC.
Formerly: Orchardist of New Zealand (ISSN 0110-6260)
Description: Provides news and practical growing information to all New Zealand fruitgrowers. Includes previously unpublished research findings that may be of use to growers and also acts as a communication device for the scientific community.

ORCHIDEEEN. see BIOLOGY — Botany

OREGON WHEAT. see AGRICULTURE — Feed, Flour And Grain

ORGANIC GROWER. see GARDENING AND HORTICULTURE

633.007 DK ISSN 0900-5293
OVERSIGT OVER LANDSFORSOEGENE; forsoeg og undersoegelser i de landoekonomiske foreninger. 1971. a. DKK 75 (effective 1997). Landsudvalget for Planteavl - Danish Agricultural Advisory Centre, Udkaersvej 15, DK-8200 Aarhus N., Denmark. TEL 45-87-40-50-00. FAX 45-87-40-50-10. E-mail: cap@lr.dk. Ed. Carl Aage Pedersen. circ. 21,000.
Description: Contains computerized results of field experiments commented on by specialists in crop husbandry.

633.851 MY ISSN 0127-0249
P O R I M BULLETIN. 1980. s-a. M.10 per no. Palm Oil Research Institute of Malaysia, P.O. Box 10620, 50720 Kuala Lumpur, Malaysia. TEL 03-8259155. FAX 03-8259446. URL: http://porim.gov.my.
—BLDSC (6554.510000).

633.851 MY ISSN 0127-2209
P O R I M OCCASIONAL PAPER. (Text in English) 1982. irreg., no.35, 1995. M.$10 per no. Palm Oil Research Institute of Malaysia - Institiut Penyelidikan Minyak Kelapa Sawit Malaysia, P.O. Box 10620, 50720 Kuala Lumpur, Malaysia. TEL 03-8259155. FAX 03-8259446. URL: http://porim.gov.my.

633.851 MY ISSN 0127-0257
P O R I M TECHNOLOGY. (Text in English) 1981. irreg., no.19, 1996. M.$10 per no. Palm Oil Research Institute of Malaysia - Institiut Penyelidikan Minyak Kelapa Sawit, P.O. Box 10620, 50720 Kuala Lumpur, Malaysia. TEL 03-8259155. FAX 03-8259446. URL: http://porim.gov.my.
—BLDSC (6554.518000).

633.851 MY
P O R I M WORKSHOP PROCEEDINGS. (Text in English) 1986. irreg., no.42, 1996. price varies. Palm Oil Research Institute of Malaysia - Institiut Penyelidikan Minyak Kelapa Sawit, P.O. Box 10620, 50720 Kuala Lumpur, Malaysia. TEL 03-8259155. FAX 03-8250446. URL: http://porim.gov.my.

PACKER - SHIPPER. see PACKAGING

631.5 PK ISSN 0078-7930
PAKISTAN CENTRAL COTTON COMMITTEE. AGRICULTURAL SURVEY REPORT. (Text in English) no.2, 1960. irreg. Pakistan Central Cotton Committee, Secretary, Moulvi Tamizuddin Khan Rd., Karachi 1, Pakistan. TEL 524104-6.

633.51 PK ISSN 0027-0334
HD9086.P3
PAKISTAN CENTRAL COTTON COMMITTEE. MONTHLY COTTON REVIEW. (Text in English) 1968. m. free. Pakistan Central Cotton Committee, Secretary, Moulvi Tamizuddin Khan Rd., Karachi 1, Pakistan. TEL 524104-6.

631.5 PK ISSN 0078-7949
PAKISTAN CENTRAL COTTON COMMITTEE. TECHNOLOGICAL BULLETIN. SERIES A. (Head of title: Pakistan Institute of Cotton Research and Technology) (Text in English) 1960. irreg. Pakistan Central Cotton Committee, Secretary, Moulvi Tamizuddin Khan Rd., Karachi 1, Pakistan. TEL 524104-6.

631.5 PK ISSN 0078-7957
PAKISTAN CENTRAL COTTON COMMITTEE. TECHNOLOGICAL BULLETIN. SERIES B. (Head of Title: Pakistan Institute of Cotton Research and Technology) (Text in English) 1959. irreg. Pakistan Central Cotton Committee, Secretary, Moulvi Tamizuddin Khan Rd., Karachi 1, Pakistan. TEL 524104-6.

633.851 MY ISSN 0127-3329
PALM OIL DEVELOPMENTS. 1984. s-a. M.10 per no. Palm Oil Research Institute of Malaysia, P.O. Box 10620, 50720 Kuala Lumpur, Malaysia. TEL 03-8259155. FAX 03-8259446. URL: http://porim.gov.my. **Document type:** academic/scholarly publication.
—BLDSC (6345.562095).

634.8 FR ISSN 0249-8286
PAYS DE COGNAC. 1972. m. 250 F. Societe d'Editions Viticoles, 25 rue de Cagouillet, B.P. 87, 16103 Cognac Cedex, France. TEL 33-5-45363408. FAX 33-5-45363409. Ed. Philippe Guelin. adv. contact: Marie-Renee Mesnard. circ. 8,000.
Formerly (until 1981): Champagne de Cognac.

634.8 FR ISSN 0997-7759
PAYSAN FRANCAIS. 1978. 12/yr. 10 rue de Bellefonds, 16106 Cognac Cedex, France. TEL 45-35-28-17. FAX 45-35-22-58. Eds. L. Ducom, C. Mausnier. circ. 17,165.
Formerly (until 1988): Revue le Paysan (ISSN 0184-9638); Which was formed by the merger of (1977-1978): Revue le Paysan (Armagnac, Libournais) (ISSN 0154-4586); (1972-1978): Revue le Paysan (Edition Charentes) (ISSN 0154-4578); Which was formerly (1925-1972): Paysan (ISSN 0996-3359)

634 US ISSN 0031-3610
PEACH - TIMES. 1956. q. $20 membership. National Peach Council, Box 11280, Columbia, SC 29211. TEL 803-253-4036. Ed. Charles Walker. adv.; illus.; stat. circ. 1,500. (tabloid format) **Document type:** newsletter.
Description: For peach growers, packers, horticulturalists; topics include council activities, orchard operation, peach horticulture, research, marketing.

633.368 US ISSN 0031-3653
THE PEANUT FARMER; for commercial growers of peanuts and related agribusiness. 1965. m. (Jan.-July). $12 (foreign $40). SpecComm International, Inc., 3000 Highwoods Blvd., Ste. 300, Raleigh, NC 27604-1029. TEL 919-872-5040. FAX 919-876-6531. Ed. Renee Ganna; Pub. Dayton Matlick. adv. contact: Ken Hayes. charts; illus.; mkt.; pat.; tr.mk.; circ. 20,000 (controlled). **Document type:** trade publication.

633.368 US ISSN 1042-9379
THE PEANUT GROWER. 1989. m. (Jan.-July). $20 (foreign $50) (effective 1996). Vance Publishing Corporation, Box 83, Tifton, GA 31793. TEL 912-386-8591. FAX 912-386-9772. Ed. Catherine C. Andrews; Pub. Sonia Tighe. adv.; circ. 22,500 (controlled). **Document type:** trade publication.
Description: Covers peanut production practices, marketing, legislation, research and news important to peanut growers.

PEANUT NEWS. see AGRICULTURE — Agricultural Economics

PEANUT REPORT. see AGRICULTURE — Agricultural Economics

633 US
PEANUT RESEARCH. q. membership. American Peanut Research and Education Society, c/o Dr. James R. Sholar, 376 Ag Hall, Oklahoma State University, Stillwater, OK 74078. TEL 405-744-9634. FAX 405-744-5269. Ed. Corley Holbrook. **Document type:** newsletter.

633.368 US ISSN 0095-3679
SB351.P3 CODEN: PNTSBY
PEANUT SCIENCE. 1974. s-a. $17 per issue. American Peanut Research and Education Society (Raleigh), c/o Dr. Thomas Stakler, Ed., North Carolina State Univ., Raleigh, NC 27695. illus. circ. 800. **Indexed:** Biol.Abstr., Chem.Abstr., Field Crop Abstr., Food Sci.& Tech.Abstr., Herb.Abstr., Seed Abstr., Soils & Fert., Trop.Oil Seeds Abstr., Weed Abstr. **Document type:** trade publication.
—BLDSC (6413.810000); CASDDS; Linda Hall; UnCover.

641.345 US ISSN 1044-9639
PECAN GROWER.* 1989. q. $8 (foreign $20) (effective 1996). Georgia Pecan Growers Association, 4807 Woodland Dr., Tifton, GA 31794-9389. TEL 912-759-2187. FAX 912-759-2187. Ed. Jane Crocker; Pub. Jane Crocker. circ. 3,300.

634.52 US
PECAN SOUTH. 1984. m. $18 (foreign $30) (effective 1997). Texas Pecan Growers Association, Inc., P.O. Drawer CC, College Sta., TX 77841. TEL 409-846-3285. FAX 409-846-1752. Ed. Rebecca Abernathy. adv.: page $700; adv. contact: Jacqueline LeRond. bk.rev.; charts; illus.; index. circ. 4,900. (also avail. in microfilm from UMI; back issues avail.) **Indexed:** Hort.Abstr. **Document type:** trade publication.
Formerly (until 1993): Pecan South Including Pecan Quarterly (ISSN 8750-5797); Incorporates: Pecan Press (ISSN 0892-2942); Which was formerly: Texas Pecan Press; Formed by the merger of (1974-1984): Pecan South (ISSN 0192-0863); (1967-1984): Pecan Quarterly (ISSN 0048-3117)

AGRICULTURE — CROP PRODUCTION AND SOIL

631.4 GW ISSN 0031-4056
CODEN: PDBLAM
PEDOBIOLOGIA. (Text in English, French, German) 1961. 6/yr. DM.536 (foreign DM.548) (effective 1996). Gustav Fischer Verlag Jena, Villengang 2, 07745 Jena, Germany. TEL 49-3641-626444. FAX 49-3641-626500. (Subscr. to: Postfach 100537, 07705 Jena, Germany) Ed. M. Schaefer. adv.: page DM.660; trim 170 x 240. bk.rev.; bibl.; charts; illus.; index. circ. 450. (reprint service avail. from ISI) **Indexed:** Acid Rain Abstr., Acid Rain Ind., ASCA, Biol.Abstr., Chem.Abstr., Curr.Adv.Biochem., Curr.Adv.Ecol.Sci., Curr.Cont., Ecol.Abstr., Excerp.Med., Forest.Abstr., Forest Prod.Abstr., Geo.Abstr.H.G., Helminthol.Abstr., IBR, Ind.Sci.Rev., Irr.& Drain.Abstr., Protozool.Abstr., Ref.Zh., Rice Abstr., Sci.Cit.Ind., Soils & Fert., Sugar Ind.Abstr., Triticale Abstr., Weed Abstr. **Document type:** academic/scholarly publication.
—BLDSC (6417.750000); CASDDS; CISTI; EMDOCS; Genuine Article; SWETS; UnCover. **CCC.**

631.4 BE ISSN 0378-181X
PEDOFAUNA. (Text in English, French, and German) 1964 N.S. irreg., vols.49-50, 1991. 1200 BEF for 3 yrs. International Society of Soil Science, Sub-commission D, Rue Vautier 29, B-1040 Brussells, Belgium. Ed. George Wauthy. bk.rev. circ. 500. **Indexed:** Soils & Fert. **Document type:** academic/scholarly publication.
—CISTI; Linda Hall.
Formerly (until vol.23, 1976): Biologie du Sol (ISSN 0067-8805)

631.4 JA ISSN 0031-4064
CODEN: PDRJAS
PEDOLOGIST/PEDOROJISUTO. (Text in English, Japanese) 1957. s-a. 5000 Yen. Japanese Society of Pedology - Nippon Pedorogi Gakkai, c/o National Institute of Agro-Environmental Sciences, 3-1-1 Kannondai, Tsukuba, Ibaraki 305, Japan. TEL 81-298-38-8275. FAX 81-298-38-8199. Ed. Nobufumi Miyauchi. adv.; bk.rev.; abstr.; bibl.; charts; index; circ. 700 (controlled). **Indexed:** Chem.Abstr., Herb.Abstr., Hort.Abstr., Soils & Fert. **Document type:** academic/scholarly publication.
—CASDDS. **CCC.**
Description: Covers soil science, soil survey and classification.
Refereed Serial

338.1 US ISSN 0079-046X
PENNSYLVANIA. AGRICULTURAL STATISTICS SERVICE. CROP AND LIVESTOCK ANNUAL SUMMARY. Also called: Annual Bulletin. a. $5. Agricultural Statistics Service, 2301 N. Cameron St., Harrisburg, PA 17110-9408. TEL 717-787-3904. (Dist. by: Agricultural Statistics Board Publications, S. Bldg., Rm. 5829, U.S. Department of Agriculture, Washington, DC 20250) circ. 5,000. **Document type:** government publication.
Formerly: Pennsylvania Crop Reporting Service. C.R.S. (ISSN 0079-0478); Incorporates: Pennsylvania's Machinery Custom Rates.

631 US
PEOPLE, FOOD & LAND. 1974. a. $15 (includes monthly bulletin). People, Food & Land Foundation, 35751 Oak Spring Dr., Tollhouse, CA 93677. TEL 209-855-3710. Ed. George Ballis. bk.rev. circ. 1,150.

632.9 NL ISSN 1017-6276
PEST ADVISORY LEAFLET. French edition: Commission de Pacifique Sud. Fiche Technique (ISSN 1017-6284) (Text in English) 1976. irreg., no.24, 1991. South Pacific Commission, B.P. D5, 98848 Noumea Cedex, New Caledonia. TEL 687-262000. FAX 687-263818. E-mail: spc@spc.org.nc. **Document type:** monographic series.
—BLDSC (6428.270000).
Formerly (until 1989): Advisory Leaflet.

632.9 US ISSN 0031-6121
TX325 CODEN: PCONAI
PEST CONTROL. 1933. m. $39 (effective 1996). Advanstar Communications, Inc., 7500 Old Oak Blvd., Cleveland, OH 44130. TEL 216-243-8100. FAX 216-891-2675. (Subscr. to: 131 W. First St., Duluth, MN 55802. TEL 800-346-0085) Ed. Jerry Mix. adv.; bk.rev.; charts; illus.; stat.; tr.lit.; index. circ. 16,466. (also avail. in microform from UMI) **Indexed:** Biol.Abstr., Biol.& Agr.Ind., Biotech.Abstr., Chem.Abstr., Energy Info.Abstr., Excerp.Med., Farm & Garden Ind., Forest Prod.Abstr., Ind.Vet., Rev.Appl.Entomol., Small Anim.Abstr., Sport Fish.Abstr., Wild.Rev., Zoo.Rec. **Document type:** trade publication.
●Also available online. Vendor(s): Information Access Co.
—BLDSC (6428.300000); CASDDS; CISTI; Linda Hall; SWETS; UMI; UnCover. **CCC.**
Description: Emphasis is on continued technological and educational advancement in pest detection, treatment and control methods.
Refereed Serial

PEST CONTROL TECHNOLOGY. see *ENGINEERING — Chemical Engineering*

632.97 UK
PEST MANAGEMENT FOCUS. 10/yr. £165($297) (effective 1997). Research Information Ltd., 222 Maylands Ave., Hemel Hempstead, Herts. HP2 7TD, England. TEL 44-1442-213222. FAX 44-1442-259395. E-mail: resinf@globalnet.co.uk. Ed.Bd. **Document type:** academic/scholarly publication.
Formerly: Research Trends in Pest Management.
Description: Reports on international crop protection developments.

632.9 US
PEST MANAGEMENT RECOMMENDATIONS FOR COMMERCIAL TREE-FRUIT PRODUCTION. 1950. a. price varies. (New York State College of Agriculture and Life Sciences) Cornell University, Media Services, 7-8 Business and Technology Park, Ithaca, NY 14850. TEL 607-255-2080. FAX 607-255-9946. circ. 4,000. **Document type:** bulletin.
Former titles (until 1990): Cornell Recommendations for Commercial Tree-Fruit Production; Tree-Fruit Production Recommendations (ISSN 0070-0118)

631 US
PEST MANAGEMENT RECOMMENDATIONS FOR COMMERCIAL VEGETABLE AND POTATO PRODUCTION. a. price varies. Cornell University, Media Services, 7-8 Business and Technology Park, Ithaca, NY 14850. TEL 607-255-2080. FAX 607-255-9946. **Document type:** bulletin.
Formerly (until 1990): Cornell Recommendations for Commercial Potato Production; Incorporates (in 1990): Cornell Recommendations for Commercial Vegetable Production; Which was formerly: Vegetable Production Recommendations.

632.9 US
PEST MANAGEMENT RECOMMENDATIONS FOR SMALL FRUIT CROPS. a. price varies. Cornell University, Media Services, 7-8 Business and Technology Park, Ithaca, NY 14850. TEL 607-255-2080. FAX 607-255-9946. **Document type:** bulletin.
Formerly (until 1990): Small Fruit Pest Control and Culture Guide.

668.65 US ISSN 0048-3575
SB951 CODEN: PCBPBS
PESTICIDE BIOCHEMISTRY AND PHYSIOLOGY; an international journal. 1971. 9/yr. $585 (foreign $695) (effective 1997). Academic Press, Inc., Journal Division, 525 B St., Ste. 1900, San Diego, CA 92101-4495. TEL 619-230-1840. FAX 619-699-6800. E-mail: apsubs@acad.com; URL: http://www.apnet.com/www/journal/pb/htm; http://www.idealibrary.com/. (Subscr. to: Box 620000, Orlando, FL 32891-8340. TEL 407-347-4040. FAX 407-363-9661) Ed. Fumio Matsumura. adv.; index. (back issues avail.) **Indexed:** Abstr.Hyg., ASCA, Bibl.Agri., Bio-Contr.News & Info., Biodet.Abstr., Biol.Abstr., Biol.& Agr.Ind., Biotech.Abstr., Chem.Abstr., Cott.& Trop.Fibr.Abstr., Crop Physiol.Abstr., Curr.Adv.Ecol.Sci., Curr.Cont., Curr.Ref.Fish Res., Dairy Sci.Abstr., Energy Ind., Energy Info.Abstr., Environ.Per.Bibl., Excerp.Med., Field Crop Abstr., Helminthol.Abstr., Hort.Abstr., Ind.Sci.Rev., Ind.Vet., Maize Abstr., Plant Breed.Abstr., Plant Grow.Reg.Abstr., Poult.Abstr., Rev.Appl.Entomol., Rev.Plant Path., Rice Abstr., Sel.Water Res.Abstr., Soils & Fert., Soyabean Abstr., Sport Fish.Abstr., Triticale Abstr., Trop.Dis.Bull., Vet.Bull., Weed Abstr., Wild.Rev., Zoo.Rec. **Document type:** academic/scholarly publication.
●Also available online.
—BLDSC (6428.370000); ADONIS; CASDDS; CISTI; EMDOCS; Genuine Article; KR SourceOne; Linda Hall; SWETS; UnCover. **CCC.**
Description: Discusses the modes of action of plant protection agents such as insecticides, fungicides, herbicides, and similar compounds including nonlethal pest control agents, biosynthesis of pheromones, hormones, and plant resistance agents.
Refereed Serial

PESTICIDE INDEX. see *AGRICULTURE — Abstracting, Bibliographies, Statistics*

632.9 UK ISSN 0956-1250
CODEN: PEOUEN
PESTICIDE OUTLOOK. 1989. bi-m. £299 to institutions (US $553) (effective 1997). The Royal Society of Chemistry, Thomas Graham House, Science Park, Milton Rd., Cambridge CB4 4WF, England. TEL 44-1223-420066. FAX 44-1223-423429. E-mail: sales@rsc.org; URL: http://chemistry.rsc.org/rsc/. (Dist. by: Turpin Distribution Services Ltd., Blackhorse Rd., Letchworth, Herts. SG6 1HN, England. TEL 44-1462-672555. FAX 44-1462-480947) **Indexed:** W.R.C.Inf. **Document type:** academic/scholarly publication.
—BLDSC (6428.410000); CASDDS; SWETS; UnCover. **CCC.**
Description: Presents news and reviews on pesticides in crop protection, animal and human health, and wood preservation.

AGRICULTURE — CROP PRODUCTION AND SOIL

632   UK   ISSN 0031-613X
CODEN: PSSCBG
PESTICIDE SCIENCE. 1970. m. $995 (foreign $995) (effective 1998). (Society of Chemical Industry) John Wiley & Sons Ltd., Journals, Baffins Ln., Chichester, W. Sussex PO19 1UD, England. TEL 44-1243-779777. FAX 44-1243-775878. E-mail: info-assets@wiley.co.uk; URL: http://www.wiley.co.uk. (Subscr. in the Americas to: John Wiley & Sons, Inc., 605 Third Ave., New York, NY 10158. TEL 212-850-6645. FAX 212-850-6021) Eds. G.T. Brooks, L.G. Copping. adv.: B&W page £595, color page £1495; trim 297 x 210; adv. contact: Bob Kern. charts; illus.; index. circ. 706. (also avail. in microform from UMI; back issues avail.; reprint service avail. from ISI) **Indexed:** Agri.Eng.Abstr., Anal.Abstr., Apic.Abstr., ASCA, Bio-Contr.News & Info., Biol.Abstr., Biol.& Agr.Ind., Biotech.Abstr., Br.Tech.Ind., Chem.Abstr., Chem.Cit.Ind., Compumath, Cott.& Trop.Fibr.Abstr., Crop Physiol.Abstr., Curr.Adv.Ecol.Sci., Curr.Cont., Curr.Ref.Fish Res., Dairy Sci.Abstr., Ecol.Abstr., Environ.Abstr., Environ.Per.Bibl. (1990-), Excerp.Med., Field Crop Abstr., Food Sci.& Tech.Abstr., Forest.Abstr., Geo.Abstr.H.G., Geo.Abstr., Helminthol.Abstr., Herb.Abstr., Hort.Abstr., Ind.Sci.Rev., Ind.Vet., Irr.& Drain.Abstr., Maize Abstr., Mass Spectr.Bull., Nutr.Abstr., Plant Breed.Abstr., Plant Grow.Reg.Abstr., Pollut.Abstr., Rev.Appl.Entomol., Rev.Plant Path., Rice Abstr., Sci.Cit.Ind., Seed Abstr., Sel.Water Res.Abstr., Soils & Fert., Sport Fish.Abstr., Triticale Abstr., Vet.Bull., W.R.C.Inf., Weed Abstr., Wild.Rev., Zoo.Rec. **Document type:** academic/scholarly publication.
—BLDSC (6428.440000); ADONIS; CASDDS; CISTI; EMDOCS; Genuine Article; KR SourceOne; Linda Hall; SWETS; UnCover. **CCC.**
Description: Devoted to research, development and effect of products designed for pest control and crop protection.
Refereed Serial

630.24   UK
PESTICIDE USAGE SURVEY REPORTS ON AGRICULTURE AND HORTICULTURE. 1965. a. M A F F Publications, London SE99 7TP, England. TEL 44-1645-556000. (back issues avail.) **Document type:** bulletin.
Refereed Serial

632.9 628.96   US   ISSN 0896-7253
PESTICIDES AND YOU. 1981. q. $25 to individuals; institutions $100. National Coalition Against the Misuse of Pesticides, 701 E St., S.E., Ste. 200, Washington, DC 20003. TEL 202-543-5450. Ed. Jay Feldman. abstr.; illus.; cum.index 1981-1989. circ. 4,500. (back issues avail.) **Indexed:** Environ.Abstr. **Document type:** newsletter.

632.9   PK
PESTICIDES BULLETIN. (Text in English) 1988. q. $3 per no. Press Corporation of Pakistan, P.O. Box 3138, Karachi 75400, Pakistan. TEL 21-455-3703. FAX 21-7736198. Ed. Saeed Hafeez. circ. 3,000.

630.24   YU   ISSN 0352-9029
CODEN: PSTIE9
PESTICIDI; casopis za pitanja proizvodnje, prometa i primene pesticida. q.? 30000 din. (foreign 60000 din.). Privredni Pregled, Marsala Birjuzova 3-5, 11000 Belgrade, Yugoslavia. TEL 011-628-477. Ed. Nesko Neskovic.
—BLDSC (6428.777000); CASDDS.
Description: Covers production, distribution and application of pesticides.

363.783409   DK   ISSN 0108-2086
TX571.P4
PESTICIDRESTER I DANSKE LEVNEDSMIDLER/PESTICIDE RESIDUES IN DANISH FOOD. (Text in Danish, English) 1983. biennial. DKK 130. Sundhedsministeriet, Levnedsmiddelstyrelsen, Moerkhoej Bygade 19, DK-2860 Soeborg, Denmark. (Dist. by: Gyldendals Forlag, Lindgrens Alle 12, DK-2300 Copenhagen S, Denmark) circ. 550. **Indexed:** Chem.Abstr.
Formerly: Rapport over Pesticidrester i Danske Levnedsmidler.

634.8   GW   ISSN 0031-6660
PFAELZER BAUER;* Wochenblatt fuer Landwirtschaft und Weinbau. 1949. w. DM.36. (Pfaelzische Bauern- und Winzerschaft e.V.) Pfaelzer Bauernverlag GmbH, Roechlingstr. 1, Postfach 3027, 6750 Kaiserslautern, Germany. Ed. Heinz-Peter Diehl. adv.; bk.rev. circ. 10,300.

630.24   GW   ISSN 0405-0738
PFLANZENSCHUTZ KURIER. English edition: Crop Protection Courier (International) (ISSN 0590-1243) Spanish edition: Correo Fitosanitario (International). 1956. 2/yr. free. Bayer AG, Geschaeftsbereich Pflanzenschutz, 51368 Leverkusen, Germany. Ed. Bernhard Grupp. R&P contact: Bernhard Grupp. charts; illus.; circ. 168,000 (controlled). **Document type:** bulletin.

630.24   GW   ISSN 0340-1723
CODEN: PNBYAT
PFLANZENSCHUTZ-NACHRICHTEN BAYER. English edition (ISSN 0170-0405) (Editions in English and German) 1948. 3/yr. free. Bayer AG, Geschaeftsbereich Pflanzenschutz, 51368 Leverkusen, Germany. Ed. Maria Esters. **Indexed:** Abstr.Hyg., Anal.Abstr., Biol.Abstr., Biotech.Abstr., Curr.Adv.Ecol.Sci., Excerp.Med., Food Sci.& Tech.Abstr., Helminthol.Abstr., Herb.Abstr., Hort.Abstr., Plant Breed.Abstr., Rev.Appl.Entomol., Rev.Appl.Mycol., Rev.Plant Path., Seed Abstr., Soils & Fert., Triticale Abstr., VITIS, Weed Abstr. **Document type:** bulletin.
—CASDDS. **CCC.**
Formerly: Hoefchen-Briefe.

354.599   PH
PHILIPPINE COCONUT AUTHORITY. AGRICULTURAL RESEARCH ANNUAL REPORT. (Text in English) 1974. a. Philippine Coconut Authority, Agricultural Research and Development Branch, Diliman, Quezon City, Philippines. illus.; stat. circ. 200. **Document type:** government publication.
Formerly: Philippine Coconut Authority. Agricultural Research Department. Annual Report.

630   PH   ISSN 0048-3826
PHILIPPINE JOURNAL OF PLANT INDUSTRY. 1908. q. P.300($20) Bureau of Plant Industry, 692 San Andres St., Malate, Manila, Philippines 1004. TEL 632-521-76-48. FAX 632-521-76-50. Ed. Nerius I. Roperod. **Indexed:** Biol.Abstr., Chem.Abstr., Field Crop Abstr., Herb.Abstr., Plant Breed.Abstr., Rice Abstr.
Formerly: Philippine Journal of Agriculture.

632.4   SP
PHYTOMA ESPANA; revista de proteccion vegetal. 1988. m. 9000 ptas. Agropubli S.L., Blasco Ibanez 24, 2a, 46010 Valencia, Spain. TEL 6-393-39-49. FAX 6-360-57-79. Ed. Joan Benlloch. adv. contact: Loca Ortega. index. circ. 7,000. (back issues avail.) **Indexed:** Ind.SST.
Description: Presents research and development in vegetable protection in Spain.
Refereed Serial

630   FR   ISSN 1164-6993
CODEN: PYTOAU
PHYTOMA, LA DEFENSE DES VEGETAUX. 1948. m. 360 F. (foreign 425 F.) (effective 1997). Ruralia, 1 rue Gambetta, 92100 Boulogne, France. TEL 33-1-42615142. FAX 33-1-49279190. (Subscr. to: Service Abonnement, 78 rue de la Condamine, 75017 Paris, France. TEL 33-1-44907041) Ed. M. Decoin. adv. contact: M.F. Delannoy. bk.rev. circ. 9,000. **Indexed:** Bio-Contr.News & Info., Biol.Abstr., Biotech.Abstr., Chem.Abstr., Cott.& Trop.Fibr.Abstr., Excerp.Med., Field Crop Abstr., Forest.Abstr., Hort.Abstr., Ornam.Hort., Plant Grow.Reg.Abstr., Potato Abstr., Rev.Appl.Entomol., Rev.Plant Path., Seed Abstr., Triticale Abstr., VITIS.
—BLDSC (6491.000000); CASDDS; SWETS.
Formed by the merger of (1948-1990): Phytoma (ISSN 0048-4091); (1946-1990): Defense des Vegetaux (ISSN 0011-7579)

631   IS   ISSN 0334-2123
CODEN: PHPRA2
PHYTOPARASITICA: ISRAEL JOURNAL OF PLANT PROTECTION SCIENCES. 1973. 4/yr. £90 (effective 1997). Priel Publishers, P.O. Box 2385, Rehovot 76123, Israel. TEL 972-8-9365757. FAX 972-8-9365858. E-mail: apriel@netvision.net.il. Ed. V.R. Priel. index. **Indexed:** Agroforest.Abstr., ASCA, Bio-Contr.News & Info., Biodet.Abstr., Biol.Abstr., Biotech.Abstr., Chem.Abstr., Cott.& Trop.Fibr.Abstr., Curr.Adv.Ecol.Sci., Curr.Cont., Excerp.Med., Field Crop Abstr., Forest.Abstr., Forest Prod.Abstr., Helminthol.Abstr., Herb.Abstr., Hort.Abstr., Maize Abstr., Potato Abstr., Rev.Appl.Entomol., Rev.Plant Path., Sci.Cit.Ind., Seed Abstr., Soils & Fert., VITIS, Weed Abstr. **Document type:** academic/scholarly publication, proceedings.
—BLDSC (6494.550000); CASDDS; EMDOCS; Genuine Article; Linda Hall; SWETS; UnCover.
Refereed Serial

PHYTOPATHOLOGIA POLONICA. see *BIOLOGY — Botany*

632   IT   ISSN 0393-8131
PHYTOPHAGA. (Text in Italian; summaries in English) 1955. biennial. exchange only. Universita degli Studi di Palermo, Istituto di Entomologia Agraria, Viale delle Scienze, 90128 Palermo, Italy. TEL 39-91-423130. FAX 39-91-423410.
Formerly (until 1983): Universita degli Studi di Palermo. Istituto di Entomologia Agraria. Bollettino (ISSN 0078-8619)

631 581.2   CN   ISSN 0031-9511
CODEN: PYTPAX
PHYTOPROTECTION. (Text and summaries in English, French) 1963. 3/yr. Can.$25 to individuals (foreign Can.$30); institutions Can.$45 (foreign Can.$55). Societe de Protection des Plantes du Quebec - Quebec Society for the Protection of Plants, 430 bvd. Gouin, St-Jean-sur-Richelieu, PQ J3B 3E6, Canada. TEL 514-346-4494. FAX 514-346-7740. Ed. Anne Legere. adv. contact: Jean-Charles Cote. charts; illus.; index, cum.index. circ. 400. (back issues avail.) **Indexed:** ASCA, Bibl.Agri., Biol.Abstr., Chem.Abstr., Curr.Adv.Ecol.Sci., Curr.Cont., Environ.Per.Bibl., Field Crop Abstr., Forest.Abstr., Forest Prod.Abstr., Helminthol.Abstr., Herb.Abstr., Hort.Abstr., Maize Abstr., Ornam.Hort., Plant Breed.Abstr., Rev.Appl.Entomol., Rev.Plant Path., Sci.Cit.Ind., Seed Abstr., Soils & Fert., Triticale Abstr., Weed Abstr. **Document type:** academic/scholarly publication.
—BLDSC (6497.050000); CASDDS; CIS; Genuine Article; Linda Hall; UMI; UnCover. **CCC.**
Description: Presents original scientific research papers or notes dealing with all aspects of plant protection; includes abstracts of papers presented at the annual meeting of the Society.
Refereed Serial

631 581   NE
PLANT ANALYSIS MANUAL. (Text in English) base vol. (plus irreg. supplements). Kluwer Academic Publishers, Postbus 17, 3300 AA Dordrecht, Netherlands. TEL 31-78-6392392. FAX 31-78-6392254. E-mail: services@wkap.nl; URL: http://www.wkap.nl. (Dist. by: Kluwer Academic Publishers Group, P.O. Box 322, 3300 AH Dordrecht, Netherlands. TEL 31-78-6392392. FAX 31-78-6546474; N. America dist. addr.: Box 358, Accord Sta., Hingham, MA 02018-0358. TEL 617-871-6600. FAX 617-871-6528) (looseleaf format) **Document type:** academic/scholarly publication.
Description: Covers manual and automated digestion and determination methods, and procedures for agricultural chemists.

PLANT BREEDING/ZEITSCHRIFT FUER PFLANZENZUECHTUNG. see *BIOLOGY — Botany*

631   US   ISSN 0730-2207
SB123   CODEN: PBREE3
PLANT BREEDING REVIEWS. 1983. a. price varies. (American Society for Horticultural Science) John Wiley & Sons, Inc., 605 Third Ave., New York, NY 10158. TEL 212-850-6000. FAX 212-850-6088. (Co-sponsors: Crop Science Society of America; Society of American Foresters; National Council of Plant Breeders) Ed. Jules Janick. cum.index 1982-1986. circ. 1,200. **Indexed:** Rice Abstr. **Document type:** monographic series.
—BLDSC (6514.140000); CASDDS; CISTI; UnCover.

AGRICULTURE — CROP PRODUCTION AND SOIL

631 581   UK
▼**PLANT BREEDING SERIES.** 1995. irreg. Chapman & Hall, 2-6 Boundary Row, London SE1 8HN, England. TEL 44-171-856-0066. FAX 44-171-522-9623. TELEX 449149 INSTP G. E-mail: chsub@itps.co.uk. Ed. P.D.S. Caligari. **Document type:** monographic series.

632   US   ISSN 0191-2917
SB599   CODEN: PLDIDE
PLANT DISEASE; an international journal of applied plant pathology. 1917. m. $270 (foreign $320) (effective 1996 & 1997). (American Phytopathological Society) A P S Press, 3340 Pilot Knob Rd., St. Paul, MN 55121-2097. TEL 612-454-7250; 800-328-7560. FAX 612-454-0766. TELEX 6502439657 (MCI UW). Ed. Michael R. McLaughlin; Pub. Steven C. Nelson. adv. contact: Kayleen Larson. bk.rev.; bibl.; charts; illus.; stat.; index. circ. 3,700. (also avail. in microform from MIM,UMI,PMC; back issues avail.; reprint service avail. from UMI) **Indexed:** Abstr.Bull.Inst.Pap.Chem., Bibl.Agri., Bio-Contr.News & Info., Biodet.Abstr., Biol.Abstr., Biol.& Agr.Ind., Biol.Dig., Biotech.Abstr., Chem.Abstr., Cott.& Trop.Fibr.Abstr., Crop Physiol.Abstr., Curr.Adv.Ecol.Sci., Curr.Cont., Excerp.Med., Fababean Abstr., Field Crop Abstr., Food Sci.& Tech.Abstr., Forest.Abstr., Forest Prod.Abstr., Helminthol.Abstr., Herb.Abstr., Hort.Abstr., Ind.Sci.Rev., Ind.U.S.Gov.Per., Ind.Vet., Irr.& Drain.Abstr., Maize Abstr., Plant Breed.Abstr., Plant Grow.Reg.Abstr., Potato Abstr., Rev.Med.& Vet.Mycol., Rev.Plant Path., Rice Abstr., Sci.Cit.Ind., Seed Abstr., So.Pac.Per.Ind., Soils & Fert., Sorghum & Millets Abstr., Soyabean Abstr., Triticale Abstr., Trop.Oil Seeds Abstr., VITIS, Weed Abstr.
—BLDSC (6514.943000); CASDDS; EMDOCS; Genuine Article; KR SourceOne; Linda Hall; SWETS; UMI; UnCover. **CCC.**
     Formerly (until vol.63, Dec. 1979): Plant Disease Reporter (ISSN 0032-0811)
     Description: Reports on plant diseases with news about new products and equipment.
     Refereed Serial

PLANT FOODS FOR HUMAN NUTRITION. see *NUTRITION AND DIETETICS*

631   CH   ISSN 0577-750X
     CODEN: PLPBBH
PLANT PROTECTION BULLETIN (TAIWAN). (Text in Chinese or English; summaries in Chinese and English) 1959. q. NT.$1200 (foreign NT.$2000). Plant Protection Society of the Republic of China, 189 Chung Cheng Rd., Wufeng, Taichung Hsien, Taiwan 431, Republic of China. TEL 04-3302301. FAX 04-3338162. Ed. J.S. Hwang; Pub. T.Y. Lin. R&P contact: W.H. Tsai. adv. contact: H.R. Yang. circ. 500. **Indexed:** Bio-Contr.News & Info., Biol.Abstr., Curr.Adv.Ecol.Sci., Food Sci.& Tech.Abstr., Hort.Abstr., Maize Abstr., Potato Abstr., Rev.Appl.Entomol., Rice Abstr., Seed Abstr., Soils & Fert., Soyabean Abstr., Weed Abstr. **Document type:** academic/scholarly publication.
—BLDSC (6523.080000); CASDDS.

631   AT   ISSN 0815-2195
     CODEN: PPQUE8
PLANT PROTECTION QUARTERLY. 1981. q. Aus.$50 to individuals; institutions Aus.$80 (effective 1997 & 1998). R.G. & F.J. Richardson, Ed. & Pub., P.O. Box 42, Meredith, Vic. 3333, Australia. TEL 61-3-52861533. FAX 61-3-52861533. E-mail: robfiona@iaccess.com.au. R&P contact: R.G. Richardson. adv. contact: F.J. Richardson. bk.rev.; circ. 500 (paid). (back issues avail.) **Indexed:** Agri.Eng.Abstr., Bio-Contr.News & Info., Biol.Abstr., Chem.Abstr., Curr.Adv.Ecol.Sci., Field Crop Abstr., Forest.Abstr., Maize Abstr., Seed Abstr., Triticale Abstr., Weed Abstr., World Agri.Econ.& Rural Sociol.Abstr. **Document type:** academic/scholarly publication.
—BLDSC (6523.280000); CASDDS; UnCover.
     Formerly: Australian Weeds (ISSN 0725-0150)
     Description: Covers all aspects of the protection of economic plants and desirable vegetations from weeds, pests and diseases.
     Refereed Serial

631 595.7   RH
PLANT PROTECTION RESEARCH INSTITUTE. ANNUAL REPORT. a. free. Ministry of Lands, Agriculture and Rural Resettlement, Research and Specialist Services, Information Services, Box 8108, Causeway, Harare, Zimbabwe. circ. 250. (back issues avail.) **Indexed:** Biol.Abstr.

PLANT RESOURCES OF SOUTH-EAST ASIA. see *BIOLOGY — Botany*

630   UK   ISSN 0952-3863
SB113.2   CODEN: PVSEEC
PLANT VARIETIES AND SEEDS. 1922. 3/yr. £50 (Europe £51; rest of world £57) (effective 1997). National Institute of Agricultural Botany, Huntingdon Rd., Cambridge CB3 0LE, England. TEL 44-1223-276381. FAX 44-1223-277602. Ed. V. Silvey. bk.rev.; index. circ. 1,000. **Indexed:** Agri.Eng.Abstr., ASCA, Chem.Abstr., Curr.Adv.Ecol.Sci., Curr.Cont., Field Crop Abstr., Food Sci.& Tech.Abstr., Herb.Abstr., Hort.Abstr., Ornam.Hort., Plant Breed.Abstr., Rev.Plant Path., Soils & Fert., Weed Abstr. **Document type:** academic/scholarly publication.
—BLDSC (6523.695000); CASDDS; EMDOCS; Linda Hall; SWETS; UMI; UnCover.
     Formerly (until vol.17, no.3): National Institute of Agricultural Botany, Cambridge, England. Journal (ISSN 0077-4790)
     Refereed Serial

631   UK   ISSN 0048-4342
PLANT VARIETIES AND SEEDS GAZETTE. 1965. m. £35 (effective 1996). Ministry of Agriculture, Fisheries and Food, Whitehouse Ln., Huntingdon Rd., Cambridge CB3 0LF, England. TEL 44-1223-342350. FAX 44-1223-342386. (Dist. by: HMSO London Print Services, Sovereign Press, 11 Steedman St., London SE17 3AF, England) Ed. Margaret Vaughan. stat. circ. 330. (back issues avail.) **Document type:** government publication.
—**CCC.**

632.9 581   UN   ISSN 0257-9030
PLANT VARIETY PROTECTION. 1975. irreg. (3-4/yr.) free. International Union for the Protection of New Varieties of Plants (UPOV), 34 Chemin des Colombettes, CH-1211 Geneva 20, Switzerland. TEL 022-730-9111. FAX 022-733-5428. TELEX 412912 OMPI CH. bk.rev.; charts; index. circ. 1,500. **Document type:** bulletin, newsletter.
     Description: Events on plant variety protection legislation and events of general interest in the UPOV member states.

354.489   DK   ISSN 0909-1378
SB114.D4
PLANTEDIREKTORATET. BERETNING. (Supplement avail.) (Text in Danish; summaries in English) 1886. a. free. Landbrugs- og Fiskeriministeriet, Plantedirektoratet - Ministry of Agriculture and Fisheries, Danish Plant Directorate, Skovbrynet 20, DK-2800 Lyngby, Denmark. TEL 45-45-96-66-00. FAX 45-45-96-66-10. Ed. Anne Buelow-Olsen. stat. circ. 1,250. (back issues avail.) **Indexed:** Field Crop Abstr. **Document type:** government publication, corporate report.
     Formed by the 1994 merger of: Plantedirektorats Beretning (ISSN 0906-6217) & Plantedirektorats Beretning. Foder, Goedning, Voksemedier, EF-Stoetteordninger (ISSN 0906-6195) & Plantedirektoratets Beretning. Frugt og Groent, Plantesundhed, Miljoeforanstaltninger, Kartofler, Forstligt, Formeringsmateriale (ISSN 0906-6209)

631.6   RU   ISSN 0032-180X
S590   CODEN: PVDEAZ
POCHVOVEDENIE. English translation: Eurasian Soil Science (US ISSN 1064-2293) (Text in Russian; contents page and summaries in English) 1899. m. 6 Rub. (Rossiiskaya Akademiya Nauk) Izdatel'stvo Nauka, 90 Profsoyuznaya ul., 117864 Moscow, Russia. (Dist. by: Mezhdunarodnaya Kniga, ul. Dimitrova D.39, 113095 Moscow, Russia) Ed. V. Volobuev. bk.rev.; bibl.; charts; illus.; stat.; index. circ. 4,635. **Indexed:** Biol.Abstr., Chem.Abstr., Excerp.Med., Field Crop Abstr., Forest.Abstr., Herb.Abstr., Plant Breed.Abstr. **Document type:** academic/scholarly publication.
—BLDSC (0131.000000); CASDDS; Ei; KNAW; Linda Hall. **CCC.**

631.4   BU   ISSN 0861-9425
     CODEN: PAEKEH
POCHVOZNANIE, AGROKHIMIIA I EKOLOGIIA.* (Text in Bulgarian; summaries in Bulgarian, English, Russian) 1966. bi-m. 1.40 lv. per no. Selskostopanska Akademiya, Bul. Tsarugradsko Shose 25, 1113 Sofia, Bulgaria. (Dist. by: Hemus, 6, Rouskii Blvd., 1000 Sofia, Bulgaria) Ed. Petko Ivanov. circ. 1,228. (reprint service avail. from IRC) **Indexed:** Agri.Eng.Abstr., Biol.Abstr., Chem.Abstr., Curr.Adv.Ecol.Sci., Field Crop Abstr., Forest.Abstr., Forest Prod.Abstr., Herb.Abstr., Hort.Abstr., Irr.& Drain.Abstr., Maize Abstr., Plant Breed.Abstr., Plant Grow.Reg.Abstr., Rev.Plant Path., Rice Abstr., Seed Abstr., Soils & Fert., Triticale Abstr., Trop.Oil Seeds Abstr., Weed Abstr.
—BLDSC (0131.005000); CASDDS; Linda Hall.
     Formerly (until 1992): Pochvoznanie i Agrokhimiia (ISSN 0554-341X)

631.4   PL   ISSN 0079-2985
S590   CODEN: PJSOBN
POLISH JOURNAL OF SOIL SCIENCE. (Text in English; summaries in Polish and Russian) 1968. s-a. $21. (Polska Akademia Nauk, Komitet Gleboznawstwa i Chemii Rolnej - Polish Academy of Sciences, Committee of Soil Science and Agricultural Chemistry) Ossolineum, Publishing House of the Polish Academy of Sciences, Pl. Solny 14a, 50-062 Wroclaw, Poland. TEL 48-71-3436961. FAX 48-71-448103. TELEX 0712771 OSS PL. Ed. Stanislaw Uzial. bibl.; charts; illus. **Indexed:** Agri.Eng.Abstr., AgroAgen, Biol.Abstr., Chem.Abstr., Ecol.Abstr., Excerp.Med., Field Crop Abstr., Forest.Abstr., Geo.Abstr., Geol.Abstr., Herb.Abstr., Soils & Fert., Weed Abstr. **Document type:** academic/scholarly publication.
—BLDSC (6543.672000); CASDDS; Linda Hall.
     Description: Theoretical and practical works on soil physics, chemistry and fertilizing.

POLISH PHYTOPATHOLOGICAL SOCIETY. PROCEEDINGS. see *BIOLOGY — Botany*

633.491   FR   ISSN 0032-4159
POMME DE TERRE FRANCAISE. 1938. bi-m. 225 F. Editions du Billon, 7 rue Sainte Anne, 72320 Saint-Maixent, France. FAX 33-2-43717677. Ed. Dorothee Bourget; Pub. Sylvain Cousin. adv.; bk.rev.; charts; illus.; stat.; index. circ. 6,500. **Indexed:** Biol.Abstr., Field Crop Abstr., Food Sci.& Tech.Abstr., Herb.Abstr., Plant Breed.Abstr., Potato Abstr., Rural Recreat.Tour.Abstr., Soils & Fert., World Agri.Econ.& Rural Sociol.Abstr.

POMONA. see *GARDENING AND HORTICULTURE*

POSTHARVEST NEWS AND INFORMATION. see *AGRICULTURE — Abstracting, Bibliographies, Statistics*

658.8 634   US   ISSN 0886-4780
POTATO COUNTRY. 1973. 9/yr. $15 (Canada and Mexico $30; elsewhere $45). Columbia Publishing and Design, 2520 W. Washington, Ste. 2, Box 9036, Yakima, WA 98909-0036. TEL 509-248-2452; 800-900-2452. FAX 509-248-4056. E-mail: dede@freshcut.com. Ed. D. Brent Clement; Pub. J. Mike Stoker. R&P contact: J. Mike Stoker. adv. contact: J. Mike Stoker. circ. 7,400. (back issues avail.) **Document type:** trade publication.
     Former titles (until 1985): Ag-Marketer; Agrow-Marketer (ISSN 0193-7901)
     Description: Covers potato research, production, and marketing.

631   US   ISSN 0146-499X
POTATO GROWER OF IDAHO. 1972. m. $19.95. (Potato Growers of Idaho, Inc.) Harris Publishing, Inc. (Idaho Falls), 520 Park Ave., Idaho Falls, ID 83402. TEL 208-524-7000. FAX 208-522-5241. adv.; illus. circ. 16,000.

POTATO MARKETING BOARD, OXFORD. ANNUAL REPORT AND ACCOUNTS. see *AGRICULTURE — Agricultural Economics*

631   UK   ISSN 0963-6641
POTATO NEWS. m. £13. Potato Marketing Board, Broad Field House, 4 Between Towns Rd., Cowley, Oxford OX4 3NA, England. TEL 44-1865-714455. FAX 44-1865-716418. Ed. P. Oldfield. **Document type:** newsletter.

AGRICULTURE — CROP PRODUCTION AND SOIL

631 CN
POTATO NEWSLETTER. (Text in English, French) 1979. bi-m. free. Department of Agriculture, Plant Industry Branch, Box 6000, Fredericton, NB E3B 5H1, Canada. TEL 506-457-7244. FAX 506-457-7267. E-mail: mmacdonald@gov.nb.ca. Ed. Robert P. Hinds. circ. 1,000 (controlled). (looseleaf format; also avail. in diskette format; back issues avail.) **Document type:** government publication, newsletter. ●Also available online.
Description: Covers cost of production, market reports, producer's budgeting, extension specialists.

633.4 NE ISSN 0014-3065
CODEN: PORHBW
POTATO RESEARCH. (Text in English, French, German) 1958. q. fl.250 (effective 1996). European Association for Potato Research, Postbus 20, 6700 AA Wageningen, Netherlands. TEL 31-317-483041. FAX 31-317-484575. URL: http://www.agro.wau.nl/eapr. Ed.Bd. bk.rev. circ. 1,000. **Indexed:** ASCA, Biodet.Abstr., Biol.Abstr., Biotech.Abstr., Chem.Abstr., Crop Physiol.Abstr., Curr.Adv.Ecol.Sci., Curr.Adv.Genetics & Molec.Biol., Curr.Cont., Excerp.Med., Field Crop Abstr., Food Sci.& Tech.Abstr., Helminthol.Abstr., Herb.Abstr., Irr.& Drain.Abstr., Plant Breed.Abstr., Plant Grow.Reg.Abstr., Potato Abstr., Rev.Plant Path., Sci.Cit.Ind., Soils & Fert., Weed Abstr., World Agri.Econ.& Rural Sociol.Abstr. **Document type:** academic/scholarly publication.
—BLDSC (6565.450000); CASDDS; EMDOCS; Genuine Article; SWETS; UnCover.
Formerly: European Potato Journal.

632 GW ISSN 0032-6801
DER PRAKTISCHE SCHAEDLINGSBEKAEMPFER. 1949. m. DM.180. (Deutscher Schaedlingsbekaempfer-Verband) Verlag Eduard F. Beckmann KG, Postfach 1120, 31251 Lehrte, Germany. TEL 49-5132-8591-0. FAX 49-5132-859125. Ed. Heiner Behre. adv.; bk.rev.; charts; illus.; stat.; index. circ. 1,600. **Indexed:** Biotech.Abstr. **Document type:** trade publication.
—BLDSC (6601.140000); SWETS.

631 RU ISSN 0207-2173
PRIUSADEBNOE KHOZYAISTVO.* 1981. m. $74 (effective 1998). Sel'skaya Nov', Ul. Sadovaya-Spasskaya 20, 107807 GSP-6 Moscow, B-78, Russia. TEL 7-095-9301039. FAX 7-095-9754976. (Dist. by: Mezhdunarodnaya Kniga, B. Yakimanka 39, 117049 Moscow, Russia. TEL 7-095-2384967. FAX 7-095-2384634) Ed. A.I. Rebel'skii. circ. 25,000.
—BLDSC (0133.100200).

PRO-FARM. see AGRICULTURE — Agricultural Economics

631.7 DK ISSN 0906-9658
PRODUCENTER OG IMPORTOERER AF GOEDNINGER OG JORDFORBEDRINGSMIDLER. 1964. a. free. Plantedirektoratet, Skovbrynet 20, DK-2800 Lyngby, Denmark. TEL 45-45-96-66-00. FAX 45-45-96-66-10. Ed. M. Brink. circ. 800. **Document type:** government publication, catalog.
Former titles: Fortegnelse over Fabrikanter og Importoerer af Goedninger og Jordforbedringsmidler; Fortegnelse over Fabrikanter og Importoerer af Goedninger og Grundforbedringsmidler (ISSN 0109-5498); Fortegnelse over Fabrikanter og Importoerer af Goedningsstoffer og Grundforbedringsmidler.

PRODUCTIVE FARMING. see AGRICULTURE — Agricultural Economics

635 US
PRODUCTORES DE HORTALIZAS. (Text in Spanish) 1992. m. $70 (effective 1997). Meister Publishing Co., 37733 Euclid Ave., Willoughby, OH 44094. TEL 216-942-2000. FAX 216-975-3447. Ed. Jim Moore. adv.: B&W page $1350, color page $1750; trim 8 x 10 3/4. circ. 10,000. **Document type:** trade publication.

635 BE ISSN 0777-9844
PROEFTUIN NIEUWS. (Text in Dutch) 1990. fortn. 3500 BEF (effective 1997). Binnenweg 6, 2860 Sint-Ka telijine-Waver, Belgium. TEL 32-15-552771. FAX 32-15-553061. URL: http://www.agris.be. Ed. D. Huygens; Pub. J. Lauwers. R&P contact: D. Huygens. adv. contact: F. Peeters. circ. 4,023 (controlled). **Document type:** trade publication.
Description: For greenhouse nurseries in Flanders. Refereed Serial

632.97 AT
▼**PROFESSIONAL PEST MANAGER.** 1996. bi-m. Aus.$30. Richard Milne Pty. Ltd., P.O. Box 163, Drummoyne, N.S.W. 2047, Australia. TEL 61-2-98197322. FAX 61-2-98197650. E-mail: milnepublications@ibm.net.

631 BL ISSN 0100-526X
PROGNOSTICO. (Text in Portuguese) 1972. a. Instituto de Economia Agricola, Av. Miguel Stefano 3900, Caixa Postal 6802, 04301-9031 Sao Paulo SP, Brazil. FAX 55-11-2764062. TELEX 011-56730. stat.; circ. controlled.
Formerly: Prognostico da Agricultura Paulista.
Description: Agricultural analysis indicating perspectives in future harvest techniques.

634.8 FR ISSN 0369-8173
PROGRES AGRICOLE ET VITICOLE. 1884. bi-m. 500 F. (foreign 740 F.). Societe du Progres Agricole et Viticole, 1 bis rue de Verdun, 3400 Montpellier, France. adv.; bk.rev. circ. 18,000. **Indexed:** Agri.Eng.Abstr., Crop Physiol.Abstr., Hort.Abstr., Hort.Abstr., Plant Breed.Abstr., Plant Grow.Reg.Abstr., Rev.Plant Path., Soils & Fert., VITIS, Weed Abstr., World Agri.Econ.& Rural Sociol.Abstr.
—Linda Hall.

PROGRESS IN PESTICIDE BIOCHEMISTRY AND TOXICOLOGY. see ENGINEERING — Chemical Engineering

630.24 668.6 MX
PRONTUARIO AGROQUIMICO. 1984. a. Ediciones P L M, S.A. de C.V., San Bernadino 17, Col. del Valle, 03100 Mexico, D.F., Mexico. TEL 684-1311. TELEX 01772912 EPLM ME. Ed. Emilio Rosenstein. circ. 40,000.

630 PL ISSN 0079-7154
PRZEGLAD NAUKOWEJ LITERATURY ROLNICZEJ I LESNEJ; gleboznawstwo, chemia rolna, ogolna uprawa roli i roslin i siedliska lesne. 1955. a. price varies. Polskie Towarzystwo Gleboznawcze, Ul. Wisniowa 61, 02-520 Warsaw, Poland. (Dist. by: Ars Polona, Krakowskie Przedmiescie 7, 00-068 Warsaw, Poland) Ed. W. Trzcinski. circ. 1,210.

631 IO ISSN 0216-9967
PUSAT PENELITIAN PERKEBUNAN GULA INDONESIA. ANNUAL REPORT/INDONESIAN SUGAR RESEARCH CENTER. ANNUAL REPORT. a. $15. Pusat Penelitian Perkebunan Gula Indonesia, Jl. Pahlawan 25, Pasurnan 67126, Indonesia. TEL 0343-21086. FAX 0343-21178. TELEX 31008 SUGEXS IA. Ed. H. Untung Murdiyatmo. circ. 650.

631 IO ISSN 0125-9997
PUSAT PENELITIAN PERKEBUNAN GULA INDONESIA. BULLETIN/INDONESIAN SUGAR RESEARCH CENTER. BULLETIN. (Text in Indonesian; summaries in English) irreg. $6 per no. Pusat Penelitian Perkebunan Gula Indonesia - Indonesian Sugar Research Institute, Jl. Pahlawan 25, Pasurnan 67126, Indonesia. TEL 0343-21086. FAX 0343-21178. TELEX 31008 SUGEXS IA. circ. 650.
—BLDSC (2564.285000).

631 IO ISSN 0216-0021
PUSAT PENELITIAN PERKEBUNAN GULA INDONESIA. PROSIDING/INDONESIAN SUGAR RESEARCH CENTER. PROSIDING. irreg. prices vary. Pusat Penelitian Perkebunan Gula Indonesia, Jl. Pahlawan 25, Pasurnan 67126, Indonesia. TEL 0343-21086. FAX 0343-21178. TELEX 31008 SUGEXS IA. Ed. Soeprayitnd Lamadji. circ. 650.

634 AT ISSN 0312-8989
QUANDONG. q. Aus.$40 includes WANATCA Yearbook. West Australian Nut & Tree Crop Association (Inc.), P.O. Box 565, Subiaco, W.A. 6008, Australia. FAX 61-9-3881852. E-mail: wanatca@AOl.com.au; URL: http://www.AOl.com.au. adv.; bk.rev. circ. 600.
—BLDSC (7168.186000).

632.9 NL ISSN 1017-6268
QUARANTINE ADVISORY LEAFLET. 1984. irreg., no.21, 1988. South Pacific Commission, B.P. D5, 98848 Noumea Cedex, New Caledonia. TEL 687-262000. FAX 687-263817. E-mail: spc@spc.org.nc. **Document type:** monographic series.

631 GW ISSN 0724-4606
RAPS; Fachzeitschrift fuer Oel- und Eiweisspflanzen. 1983. q. DM.34 (foreign DM.43) (effective 1997). Verlag Th. Mann, Nordring 10, 45894 Gelsenkirchen, Germany. TEL 49-209-9304184. FAX 49-209-9304185. (Subscr. to: Postfach 200254, 45837 Gelsenkirchen, Germany) Eds. Dr. Heinz-Peter Puetz, Guenter Weiss. adv.: B&W page DM.3580, color page DM.6205; trim 186 x 270; adv. contact: Richard Heineke. circ. 18,812. (back issues avail.) **Document type:** trade publication.
—SWETS.

634.9 NE ISSN 0924-929X
RASSENLIJST VOOR BOMEN. 1990. a. fl.24.50. (Centrum voor Plantenveredelings- en Reproduktieonderzoek) Roto Smeets de Boer N.V., Postbus 507, 1200 AM Hilversum, Netherlands. TEL 31-35-258611. FAX 31-35-238978.
Description: Recommendations for improved strains and varieties of trees for commercial production.

631 NE ISSN 0169-6750
RASSENLIJST VOOR FRUITGEWASSEN. 1933. quinquennial, 18th ed., 1992. fl.24.50. (Centrum voor Plantenveredelings- en Reproduktieonderzoek) Roto Smeets de Boer n.v., Postbus 507, 1200 AM Hilversum, Netherlands. TEL 31-35-258611. FAX 31-35-238978. Ed.Bd.
Description: Descriptive list of recommended strains and varieties of fruit for commercial cultivation.

631 NE ISSN 0169-6319
RASSENLIJST VOOR GROENTEGEWASSEN: GLASGROENTEN. vol.32, 1983. a. fl.27.50. (Centrum voor Plantenveredelings- en Reproduktieonderzoek) Roto Smeets de Boer n.v., Postbus 507, 1200 AM Hilversum, Netherlands. TEL 31-35-258611. FAX 31-35-238978. Ed.Bd.

631 NE ISSN 0169-636X
RASSENLIJST VOOR GROENTEGEWASSEN: VOLLEGRONDSGROENTEN. 1943. a., 37th, 1992. fl.29.50. (Centrum voor Plantenveredelings- en Reproduktieonderzoek) Roto Smeets de Boer n.v., Postbus 507, 1200 AM Hilversum, Netherlands. TEL 31-35-258611. FAX 31-35-238978. Ed.Bd.
Description: Descriptive list of recommended varieties of vegetables.

633 BU ISSN 0568-465X
CODEN: RSTNA7
RASTENIEVADNI NAUKI. (Text in Bulgarian; summaries in Russian and English) 1964. 10/yr. 1.40 lv.($24) per no. (Akademiia na Selskostopanskite Nauki) Publishing House of the Bulgarian Academy of Sciences, Acad. G. Bonchev St., Bldg. 6, 1113 Sofia, Bulgaria. (Dist. by: Hemus, 6, Rouski Blvd., 1000 Sofia, Bulgaria) Ed. Pavel Popov. circ. 1,300. (reprint service avail. from IRC) **Indexed:** Agri.Eng.Abstr., Apic Ahstr., Biol.Abstr., BSL Biol., Chem.Abstr., Cott.& Trop.Fibr.Abstr., Curr.Adv.Ecol.Sci., Field Crop Abstr., Food Sci.& Tech.Abstr., Herb.Abstr., Hort.Abstr., Maize Abstr., Ornam.Hort., Plant Breed.Abstr., Plant Grow.Reg.Abstr., Potato Abstr., Rev.Appl.Entomol., Rev.Plant Path., Seed Abstr., Soils & Fert., Sorghum & Millets Abstr., Soyabean Abstr., Triticale Abstr., Trop.Oil Seeds Abstr., VITIS, Weed Abstr.
—BLDSC (0140.266000); CASDDS; Linda Hall.

632.9 BU
RASTITELNA ZASHTITA.* 1952. m. $11. (Ministerstvo na Zemedelieto i Khranitelna Promishlenost) Izdatelstvo Profizdat, Dondukov Blvd., 32, Sofia, Bulgaria. (Dist. by: Hemus, 6, Rouski Blvd., 1000 Sofia, Bulgaria) Ed. Georgi Polianov. circ. 7,550. **Indexed:** Hort.Abstr., Rev.Appl.Entomol., Rev.Plant Path.

REBE UND WEIN. see BEVERAGES

AGRICULTURE — CROP PRODUCTION AND SOIL

631 628.4   IO
REGIONAL WORKSHOP ON WASTE HEAT RECOVERY TECHNOLOGY IN COCONUT PROCESSING. a.? $10. Asian and Pacific Coconut Community, Wisma Bakrie, 3rd Fl., Jl. H.R. Rasuna Said, Kuningan, Jakarta 12920, Indonesia. TEL 62-21-510-073. FAX 62-21-520-5160. TELEX 62863 APCCIA. **Document type:** proceedings.
    Description: Contains reports and technical papers that deal with the basis of the technology, financial and economic appraisal of application of waste heat technology in coconut processing and the transfer strategy for the process.

631.4   US   ISSN 1066-4106
REMINERALIZE THE EARTH. 1985. 3/yr. $25 (foreign $30) (effective 1996 & 1997). 152 South St., Northampton, MA 01060-4021. TEL 413-586-4429. FAX 413-586-6064. E-mail: reminearth@aol.com. Ed. Joanna Campe; Pub. Joanna Campe. R&P contact: Joanna Campe. adv. contact: Joanna Campe. bk.rev. circ. 1,500. **Document type:** newsletter.
    Formerly: Soil Remineralization Newsletter.
    Description: Forum for the exchange of ideas, experiences and research of those concerned with the networking and implementation of soil and forest remineralization through the use of finely ground gravel and rock dust.

631.8   II   ISSN 0257-3245
RESEARCH AND DEVELOPMENT REPORTER. (Text in English) 1984. s-a. Rs.10. Rajasthan Fertilizers Trading Corporation, 18-9 Trikuta Nagar, Jammu (J&K) 180 004, India. TEL 531124. Ed. R.S. Sharma. circ. 500. **Indexed:** Sugar Ind.Abstr.
—BLDSC (7714.796150).

631   NE
    CODEN: IBJAA6
RESEARCH INSTITUTE FOR AGROBIOLOGY AND SOIL FERTILITY. ANNUAL REPORT. Variant title: Jaarverslag A B - D L O. (Text and summaries in Dutch) 1916. a. free. Research Institute for Agrobiology and Soil Fertility, Postbus 14, 7600 AA Wageningen, Netherlands. TEL 31-317-475700. FAX 31-317-423110. Ed. H. Terburg. circ. 1,500. (back issues avail.) **Indexed:** Biol.Abstr., Field Crop Abstr., Herb.Abstr., Hort.Abstr., Soils & Fert. **Document type:** corporate report.
    Formerly: Instituut voor Bodemvruchtbaarheid. Jaarverslag (ISSN 0434-6785)
    Description: Covers research done in the various departments of the Institute, as well as information on organization, events, activities, tests and more.

630   US   ISSN 1076-3333
S671   CODEN: AGENAZ
RESOURCE (ST. JOSEPH); engineering & technology for a sustainable world. bi-m. $51.50 to non-members (foreign $71.50); members $24 (foreign $44) (effective 1997). American Society of Agricultural Engineers, 2950 Niles Rd., St. Joseph, MI 49085-9659. TEL 616-429-0300. FAX 616-429-3852. E-mail: hq@asae.org; URL: http://asae.org/resource. Ed. Jackie Elowsky. adv.; bk.rev.; bibl.; charts; illus.; tr.lit.; index. circ. 8,000. (also avail. in microfilm from UMI) **Indexed:** Agri.Eng.Abstr., Biodet.Abstr., Biol.Abstr., Biol.& Agr.Ind., CAD CAM Abstr., Chem.Abstr., Dairy Sci.Abstr., Eng.Ind., Environ.Abstr., Environ.Per.Bibl. (1989-1995), Excerp.Med., Farm & Garden Ind., Field Crop Abstr., Geotech.Abstr., Helminthol.Abstr., Herb.Abstr., Hort.Abstr., INIS Atomind., Intl.Polym.Sci.& Tech., Nutr.Abstr., Risk Abstr., Sel.Water Res.Abstr., Soyabean Abstr., SSCI, W.R.C.Inf. **Document type:** trade publication, academic/scholarly publication.
●Also available online. Vendor(s): Information Access Co.
—CIS; CISTI; Ei; Genuine Article; KR SourceOne; Linda Hall; SWETS; UMI; UnCover. CCC.
    Formed by the merger of (1920-1994): Agricultural Engineering (ISSN 0002-1458); (1983-1994): Within A S A E (ISSN 0741-0387)
    Description: Focuses on trends in technology. Broad interest articles and continuing departments spotlight engineering progress in agriculture, food, biotechnology, aquaculture, forestry, machinery, and soil and water.

631   FR   ISSN 0996-858X
REUSSIR CEREALES - GRANDES CULTURES. 1987. 11/yr. 190 F. (foreign 230 F.) (effective 1997); newsstand price: 25 F. G I E Reussir, 19 quai du Juillet, B.P. 18, 14005 Caen Cedex, France. TEL 33-2-31357704. FAX 33-2-31822963. Ed. Marie-Hombeline Vincent; Pub. Henri Lefebvre. R&P contact: Marc Jourdan. adv. contact: Jean-Pierre Dumas. circ. 86,000. **Document type:** newspaper.
    Description: Technical and economical informations about crop production.

633   FR   ISSN 1261-8160
REUSSIR FRUITS ET LEGUMES. 1994. 10/yr. 190 F. (foreign 230 F.) (effective 1997); newsstand price: 25 F. G I E Reussir, 19 quai de Juillet, B.P. 18, 14005 Caen Cedex, France. TEL 33-2-31357704. FAX 33-2-31822963. Ed. Antoine Herve; Pub. Henri Lefebvre. R&P contact: Marc Jourdan. adv. contact: Jean-Pierre Dumas. circ. 15,000.
    Description: Technical and economical information about fruit and vegetable production.

634.8   FR   ISSN 1261-0208
REUSSIR VIGNE. 1994. 10/yr. 190 F. (foreign 230 F.) (effective 1997); newsstand price: 25 F. G I E Reussir, 19 quai de Juillet, B.P. 18, 14005 Caen Cedex, France. TEL 33-2-31357704. FAX 33-2-31822963. Ed. Marie-Annick Carre; Pub. Henri Lefebvre. R&P contact: Marc Jourdan. adv. contact: Jean-Pierre Dumas. circ. 20,000.
    Description: Technical and economical information about wine production.

635   SP
REVISTA A C O R. 1971. q. free. (Azucarera Cooperativa "Onesimo Redondo") Sociedad Cooperativa Azucarera, Paseo Isabel la Catolica, 1, 47001 Valladolid, Spain. TEL 35 04 00. TELEX 26474 SCAZ. adv.; illus.; tr.lit. circ. 7,500.

633   AG   ISSN 0327-151X
    CODEN: RAMAEF
REVISTA AGROPECUARIO DE MANFREDI Y MARCOS JUAREZ. Abbreviated title: R A M. (Text mainly in Spanish, occasionally in English; abstracts in English, Spanish) 1985. s-a. Arg.$6($8) Estacion Experimental Agropecuaria Manfredi, 5988 Manfredi, Cordoba, Argentina. TEL 0572-93053. FAX 0572-93061. Ed. Carlos Alberto Villata. bibl.; charts; illus. circ. 1,200. **Indexed:** Field Crop Abstr. **Document type:** academic/scholarly publication.
    Formerly (until 1987): Revista Agronomica de Manfredi (ISSN 0326-7296)

631   CK   ISSN 0120-0682
    CODEN: RECODY
REVISTA COMALFI. (Text in Spanish; summaries in English) 1974. 3/yr. Col.$10000 to individuals (foreign $20); students Col.$5000 (foreign $15). Sociedad Colombiana de Control de Malezas y Fisiologia Vegetal, Ciudad Universitaria, Carrera 50 No. 27-70, Bloque C, Modulo 3 Nivel 8, Bogota DF, Colombia. TEL 57-2219643. FAX 57-2217458. Ed. Jaime Soriano. adv.; bk.rev.; charts; illus.; stat. circ. 1,000. **Indexed:** Weed Abstr.
    Description: Covers articles on tropical weeds, vegetation and plant physiology. Includes original results of research done in the field of the science of tropical weeds as well as in vegetation.

631   CU   ISSN 1010-2752
REVISTA DE PROTECCION VEGETAL. 3/yr. $20 in N. and S. America; Europe $24. (Instituto de Ciencias Agropecuarias de La Habana, Centro Nacional de Semillas Agropecuaria) Ediciones Cubanas, Obispo No. 527, Apdo. 605, Havana, Cuba. TEL 32-5556-60. **Indexed:** Bio-Contr.News & Info., Hort.Abstr.

631   MX   ISSN 0185-3309
REVISTA MEXICANA DE FITOPATOLOGIA. (Text and summaries in English, Spanish) 1981. 2/yr. $60 to individuals; institutions $100 (effective 1996). Sociedad Mexicana de Fitopatologia, Apdo. Postal 128-F., Ciudad Universitaria, 66450 San Nicolas de los Garza, NL, Mexico. TEL 52-8-3766320. E-mail: mrocha@ccr.dsi.uanl.mx. Ed. Mario Rocha-Pena. adv.; B&W page $1000; adv. contact: Gustavo Frias. bk.rev.; abstr.; charts; illus. circ. 700. **Document type:** academic/scholarly publication.
    Description: Publishes original research articles dealing with fundamental and applied aspects of plant pathology.
    Refereed Serial

631   MF   ISSN 0370-3576
    CODEN: RASMA9
REVUE AGRICOLE ET SUCRIERE DE MAURICE/AGRICULTURAL AND SUGAR REVIEW OF MAURITIUS. (Text in English and French) 1922. 3/yr. Rs.300($18) Societe de Technologie Agricole et Sucriere de l'Ile Maurice, c/o M.S.I.R.I., Reduit, Mauritius. TEL 230-4541061. FAX 230-4541971. Eds. Guy McIntyre, Clency Barbe. adv. circ. 600. **Indexed:** Bio-Contr.News & Info., Biol.Abstr., Cott.& Trop.Fibr.Abstr., Excerp.Med., Field Crop Abstr., Food Sci.& Tech.Abstr., Herb.Abstr., Hort.Abstr., Maize Abstr., P.L.E.S.A., Plant Breed Abstr., Rev.Appl.Entomol., Rev.Plant Path., Soils & Fert. **Document type:** proceedings.
—BLDSC (7883.100000); CASDDS.
    Refereed Serial

634.8   FR
REVUE D'INFORMATION DES TECHNIQUES VITICOLES. 1987. a. 190 F. (foreign 220 F.). Vigne et Vin Publications Internationales, Bordeaux Technopolis, Site Montesquieu, 33651 Martillac Cedex, France. TEL 56-64-82-30. FAX 56-64-82-28. TELEX 550 415 F.

REVUE D'OENOLOGUES ET DES TECHNIQUES VITI-VINICOLES ET OENOLOGIQUES. see *BEVERAGES*

634.8   FR   ISSN 0395-899X
    CODEN: RFOEE4
REVUE FRANCAISE D'OENOLOGIE. (Supplement avail.: Union Francaise des Oenologues. Annuaire (ISSN 1161-3580)) 1956. 5/yr. 415 F. (foreign 485 F.) (effective 1996). Revue Francaise des Oenologues, Maison des Agriculteurs, Mas de Saporta, 34970 Lattes, France. TEL 67-20-88-76. FAX 67-58-68-91. Ed. Dominique Traxel. adv. contact: Elise Galabert. circ. 14,000. **Document type:** academic/scholarly publication, proceedings.
—BLDSC (7904.211000); CASDDS.

REVUE SUISSE DE VITICULTURE, ARBORICULTURE ET HORTICULTURE. see *GARDENING AND HORTICULTURE*

631 633.18   US   ISSN 0035-4961
RICE JOURNAL; for commercial growers of rice and related agribusiness. 1897. 5/yr. $12 (foreign $40). Specialized Agricultural Publications, Inc., 3000 Highwoods Blvd., Ste. 300, Raleigh, NC 27604-1029. TEL 919-872-5040. FAX 919-872-6531. Ed. Dayton Matlick; Pub. Dayton Matlick. adv. contact: Dorothy Kuffler. bk.rev.; charts; illus.; mkt.; index. circ. 12,000. **Indexed:** Biol.Abstr., Chem.Abstr., Curr.Adv.Ecol.Sci., Curr.Cont., Field Crop Abstr., Food Sci.& Tech.Abstr., Helminthol.Abstr., Herb.Abstr., Rice Abstr., Soils & Fert., Weed Abstr. **Document type:** trade publication.
—BLDSC (7963.850000); Linda Hall; SWETS; UnCover.

633.18   PH   ISSN 0117-0090
RICE LITERATURE UPDATE. (Text in English) 1989. 3/yr. $24. International Rice Research Institute, P.O. Box 933, Manila, Philippines. TEL 63-2-818-1926. FAX 63-2-891-1292.

631   UK
RICE MARKET CIRCULAR. m. London Rice Brokers' Association, Prince Rupert House, 9-10 College Hill, London EC4, England.

631   US
RICE WORLD. 1981. m. $24 (effective 1997). John Hart, Ed. & Pub., 3100 Weslayan, Ste. 200, Houston, TX 77027. TEL 713-621-8807. FAX 713-621-8817. adv. contact: John Hart. bk.rev. circ. 4,500. (also avail. in microform) **Document type:** trade publication.
    Formerly: Rice World and Soybean News (ISSN 0738-5943)

631   SP   ISSN 0213-3660
RIEGOS Y DRENAJES XXI; revista de la tecnologia del riego drenajes, suelos, fertilizantes, invernaderos y agricultura intensiva. 1985. 6/yr. 10500 ptas.($98) (effective 1996). Elsevier Prensa S.A., Avda Parallel, 180, 08015 Barcelona, Spain. TEL 34-3-3255350. FAX 34-3-4252880. Ed. Marcel Lleal; Pub. Manuel Masip. adv. contact: Manuel Fernandez de Liencres. illus. circ. 3,000. **Indexed:** Ind.SST. **Document type:** trade publication.
    Description: Covers irrigation technologies, draining, soil, fertilization, greenhouses and intensive agricultural techniques.

AGRICULTURE — CROP PRODUCTION AND SOIL

631.4   IT   ISSN 0035-6034
CODEN: RAGOAN
RIVISTA DI AGRONOMIA. (Text in Italian; summaries in English) 1967. q. L.69000 (effective 1996). (Societa Italiana di Agronomia) Edagricole S.p.A., Via Emilia Levante 31, 40139 Bologna, Italy. TEL 39-51-492211. FAX 39-51-493660. Ed. Paolo Talamucci. adv.: B&W page L.1200000. bk.rev.; index. circ. 2,600. **Indexed:** Biol.Abstr., Chem.Abstr., Excerp.Med., Field Crop Abstr., Herb.Abstr., Hort.Abstr., Maize Abstr., Ornam.Hort., Plant Breed.Abstr., Soils & Fert., Triticale Abstr., Weed Abstr.
—BLDSC (7980.400000); CASDDS; Linda Hall; UMI.
   Description: Contains concise descriptions of technical and analytical procedures, instruments and equipments to solve problems inherent in agricultural research.

634   IT   ISSN 0016-2310
RIVISTA DI FRUTTICOLTURA E DI ORTOFLORICOLTURA. (Text in Italian; summaries in English) 1937. m. (11/yr.). L.76000 (effective 1996). Edagricole S.p.A., Via Emilia Levante 31, 40139 Bologna, Italy. TEL 39-51-492211. FAX 39-51-493660. Ed. Silviero Sansavini. adv.: B&W page L.1050000, color page L.1480000; 185 x 247. bk.rev.; charts; illus.; index. circ. 22,600. **Indexed:** Biol.Abstr., Chem.Abstr., Food Sci.& Tech.Abstr., Hort.Abstr., Plant Breed.Abstr., Rural Recreat.Tour.Abstr., World Agri.Econ.& Rural Sociol.Abstr.
   Description: For industrial producers of fruits, vegetables, grapes and flowers.

630   IT   ISSN 0304-0593
RIVISTA DI INGEGNERIA AGRARIA. 1970. q. L.75000 (effective 1996). (Associazione Italiana di Genio Rurale) Edagricole S.p.A., Via Emilia Levante 31, 40139 Bologna, Italy. TEL 39-51-492211. FAX 39-51-493660. Ed. Ettore Gasparetto. adv.: B&W page L.1200000; trim 170 x 245. bk.rev.; charts; illus.; stat.; index. circ. 4,800. **Indexed:** Agri.Eng.Abstr., Dairy Sci.Abstr., Food Sci.& Tech.Abstr., Hort.Abstr., Maize Abstr., Ornam.Hort., Rice Abstr., Soils & Fert., Triticale Abstr., World Agri.Econ.& Rural Sociol.Abstr.
—BLDSC (7987.010000).
   Description: For technicians, researchers and designers of farm machinery.

634.8 663.2   IT   ISSN 0370-7865
CODEN: RVENAL
RIVISTA DI VITICOLTURA E DI ENOLOGIA. 1948. q. Lit.90000 (foreign Lit.120000) (effective 1998). Via XXVIII Aprile, 26, 31015 Conegliano (TV), Italy. TEL 39-438-456711. FAX 39-438-64779. **Indexed:** Food Sci.& Tech.Abstr.
—BLDSC (7993.600000); CASDDS; CISTI.

631.4   PL   ISSN 0080-3642
S590   CODEN: ROGLAA
ROCZNIKI GLEBOZNAWCZE. (Text mainly in Polish, occasionally in English; summaries in English, Russian) 1950. q. $40. Polskie Towarzystwo Gleboznawcze, Ul. Wisniowa 61, 02-520 Warsaw, Poland. (Dist. by: Ars Polona, Krakowskie Przedmiescie 7, 00-068 Warsaw, Poland) Ed. Wladyslaw Trzcinski. circ. 1,470. **Indexed:** Agroforest.Abstr., AgroLibrex, Field Crop Abstr., Herb.Abstr., Hort.Abstr., Irr.& Drain.Abstr., Potato Abstr., Soils & Fert., Weed Abstr.
—BLDSC (8010.000000); CASDDS.
   Description: Publishes original papers in soil science, chemistry, mineralogy, soil biology, water supply.

633 635   PL   ISSN 0080-3650
SB13   CODEN: RNRAAP
ROCZNIKI NAUK ROLNICZYCH. SERIA A. PRODUKCJA ROSLINNA. (Text in Polish; summaries in English, Polish, Russian) 1903. irreg., vol.111, 1995. price varies. (Polska Akademia Nauk, Komitet Uprawy Roslin) Wydawnictwo Naukowe P W N, Ul. Miodowa 10, 00-251 Warsaw, Poland. TEL 48-22-312738. FAX 48-22-6954288. Ed. W. Roszak. bibl.; charts. circ. 750. **Indexed:** AgroLibrex, Biol.Abstr., Chem.Abstr., Excerp.Med., Field Crop Abstr., Helminthol.Abstr., Herb.Abstr., Hort.Abstr., Nutr.Abstr., Potato Abstr., Rev.Appl.Entomol., Rev.Plant Path., Seed Abstr., Soils & Fert., Triticale Abstr., Weed Abstr.
—CASDDS.

632.9   PL   ISSN 0080-3693
SB599   CODEN: RNORAR
ROCZNIKI NAUK ROLNICZYCH. SERIA E. OCHRONA ROSLIN. (Text mainly in Polish, occasionally in English; summaries in English and Russian) 1970. irreg., vol.17, 1988. price varies. Instytut Ochrony Roslin, Ul. Miczurina 20, 60-318 Poznan, Poland. (Dist. by: Ars Polona, Krakowskie Przedmiescie 7, 00-068 Warsaw, Poland) (Co-sponsor: Polska Akademia Nauk, Komitet Ochrony Roslin) Ed. Wladyslaw Wegorek. bibl.; charts; illus. circ. 610. **Indexed:** Helminthol.Abstr., Plant Breed.Abstr., Rev.Appl.Entomol., Soils & Fert., Triticale Abstr.
—BLDSC (8014.900000); CASDDS.

631.7   SA   ISSN 0258-5081
S A IRRIGATION/S A BESPROEIING. Title varies slightly: South African Irrigation. (Text in Afrikaans and English) 1979. bi-m. R.13.50. S.A. Irrigation (Pty) Ltd., 403 SASBO House, 97-99 Simmonds St., Braamfontein, P.O. Box 3387, Johannesburg 2000, South Africa. Ed. S.R. Shorten. adv. circ. 2,835. **Indexed:** Ind.S.A.Per.

631.4   US   ISSN 0081-1904
CODEN: SSAPAV
S S S A SPECIAL PUBLICATION SERIES. 1967. irreg., no.24, 1989. price varies. Soil Science Society of America, 677 S. Segoe Rd., Madison, WI 53711. TEL 608-273-8080. FAX 608-273-2021. (Affiliate: American Society of Agronomy) Ed. Jerry Bigham. R&P contact: David Kral. adv. contact: Keith R. Schlesinger. **Indexed:** Abstr.Anthropol., Agri.Eng.Abstr., Bibl.Agri., Biol.Abstr., GeoRef., Soils & Fert. **Document type:** monographic series.
—CASDDS; CISTI; Ei. **CCC.**

SAFETY NEWS (DENVER). see *WATER RESOURCES*

633.63   RU   ISSN 0036-3359
SAKHARNAYA SVEKLA; proizvodstvo i pererabotka. 1956. m. $51 (effective 1998). Beta, Sadovaya-Spasskaya, 18, 107807 Moscow, Russia. TEL 7-095-2076408. FAX 7-095-2072870. (Dist. by: Mezhdunarodnaya Kniga, B. Yakimanka 39, 117049 Moscow, Russia. TEL 7-095-2384967. FAX 7-095-2384634) Ed. Valentina G. Zharkova. bk.rev.; bibl.; stat.; index. circ. 9,000. **Indexed:** Biol.Abstr., Chem.Abstr., Field Crop Abstr., Food Sci.& Tech.Abstr., Herb.Abstr., Plant Breed.Abstr., Seed Abstr., Sugar Ind.Abstr., Weed Abstr.
—BLDSC (0154.600000).

SAN FRANCISCO FRESH FRUIT AND VEGETABLE WHOLESALE MARKET PRICES. see *AGRICULTURE — Agricultural Economics*

SAN FRANCISCO WHOLESALE FRUIT AND VEGETABLE REPORT. see *AGRICULTURE — Agricultural Economics*

631 627   NE   ISSN 0925-1413
SCAN. (Text in English) 1990. a. free. Dienst Landbouwkundig Onderzoek, Staring Centrum, Instituut voor Onderzoek van het Landelijk Gebied - D L O Winand Staring Centre for Integrated Land, Soil and Water Research, P.O. Box 125, 6700 AC Wageningen, Netherlands. TEL 31-317-474200. FAX 31-317-424812. TELEX 75230 VISI NL. E-mail: postkamer@sc.dlo.nl. Ed. E.C.W.M. Ruyten. abstr.; bibl.; illus.; stat.; circ. 2,000 (controlled). **Indexed:** Geo.Abstr.H.G., Geo.Abstr.P.G. **Document type:** corporate report.
—BLDSC (8087.463900).
   Description: Covers the center's activities in soil, hydrological, environmental, ecological and planning research, including related disciplines, as well as joint projects conducted outside the Netherlands

631.4   GW   ISSN 1432-9492
▼**SCIENCES OF SOIL.** (Text in English) 1996. a. (with irreg. updates). free. Kurfurstenstr. 13, 54295 Trier, Germany. TEL 49-651-47163. FAX 49-651-47163. E-mail: sos@hintze-online.com; URL: http://hintze-online.com/sos/. Ed. Thomas Hintze. abstr.; charts; illus. (back issues avail.) **Document type:** academic/scholarly publication.
●Available only online.
   Description: Focuses on scholarly research and methodology on all aspects of soil science. *Refereed Serial*

SCOOP. see *ENVIRONMENTAL STUDIES — Abstracting, Bibliographies, Statistics*

631   FR   ISSN 1140-5066
SEED AND AG'CHEM BUSINESS. 1983. 2/yr. Groupe Liaisons S.A., 1 av. Edouard Belin, 92856 Rueil Malmaison, France. TEL 33-1-41299999. FAX 33-1-41299838. Ed. Blandine Cailliez. adv. contact: Martine Pinel. circ. 10,000.
Formed by the merger of: Seed Business & Ag'Chem Business.
   Description: Covers the agrichemical and fertilizer industry.

631   US
SEED AND CROPS DIGEST; the business magazine for agriculture. (Supplement avail.: Buyers' Desk Reference) 1950. 9/yr. $35 (foreign $40). Freiberg Publishing Company, Inc., 2302 W. First St., Box 7, Cedar Falls, IA 50613. TEL 319-277-3599. FAX 319-277-3783. Ed. Bill Freiberg. adv. contact: Kathy Freiberg. circ. 6,000. (back issues avail.) **Document type:** trade publication.
—SWETS.
   Former titles: Seed and Crops Industry (ISSN 1065-5980); Seed Industry Journal (ISSN 1041-0678); Seedmen's Digest.

631   II   ISSN 0379-5594
CODEN: SEREDM
SEED RESEARCH. (Text in English) 1973. s-a. $15 to individuals; institutions $50. Indian Society of Seed Technology, Indian Agricultural Research Institute, Division of Seed Science & Technology, New Delhi 110 012, India. TEL 91-11-5784869. FAX 91-11-5752006. TELEX 3177161 IARI IN. Ed. S.P. Sharma. circ. 700. **Indexed:** Biol.Abstr., Chem.Abstr., Cott.& Trop.Fibr.Abstr., Crop Physiol.Abstr., Curr.Adv.Ecol.Sci., Field Crop Abstr., Forest.Abstr., Herb.Abstr., Hort.Abstr., Plant Grow.Reg.Abstr., Rev.Med.& Vet.Mycol., Rice Abstr., Seed Abstr., Soils & Fert., Sorghum & Millets Abstr., Soyabean Abstr., Triticale Abstr., Trop.Oil Seeds Abstr. **Document type:** academic/scholarly publication.
—BLDSC (8218.130000); CASDDS; CISTI; Linda Hall.
   Description: Aims to promote the research and development of seed science and technology.

631.5   CN   ISSN 0049-0040
SEED SCOOP. French edition: Actualite Semence (ISSN 0715-4844) 1955. 3/yr. Canadian Seed Growers Association, Box 8455, Ottawa, ON K1G 3T1, Canada. TEL 613-236-0497. circ. 10,500. **Document type:** bulletin.

631   US
SEED TECHNOLOGIST NEWS. Spine title: S C S T Newsletter. (Aug. issue represents Annual Conference Proceedings) vol.68, 1994. 3/yr. plus a. proceedings. $35. Society of Commercial Seed Technologists, c/o Cathy Weidmaier, Sec.-Treas., Box 1393, 225 Florence Rd., St. Joseph, MO 64502. TEL 816-238-7333. Ed. DaNell Jamieson. **Document type:** newsletter.
   Description: Contains membership news and testing information, along with testing research proposals.

631.5   US   ISSN 0080-8504
SEED TRADE BUYER'S GUIDE. (Supplement to: Seed World (ISSN 0037-0797)) 1917. a. $35. Scranton Gillette Communications, Inc., 380 E. Northwest Hwy., Des Plaines, IL 60016-2282. TEL 847-391-1000. FAX 847-390-0408. Ed. Mindy Haff. adv. circ. 5,000. (also avail. in microform from UMI) **Document type:** trade publication.
   Description: Contains a compilation of revised state-by-state seed laws, as well as company and supplier listings.

AGRICULTURE — CROP PRODUCTION AND SOIL

631.5   US   ISSN 0037-0797
CODEN: SWORAX
SEED WORLD. (Supplement avail.: Seed Trade Buyer's Guide) 1915. m. $30. Scranton Gillette Communications, Inc., 380 E. Northwest Hwy., Des Plaines, IL 60016-2282. TEL 847-391-1000. FAX 847-390-0408. URL: http://www.sgcpubs.com/seedworld.html. Ed. Mindy Haff; Pub. Ed Glllette. R&P contact: Ed Gillette. TEL 847-391-1021. adv. contact: Mary Tharp. illus.; mkt. circ. 5,000. (also avail. in microform from UMI; reprint service avail. from UMI) **Indexed:** Biol.Abstr., Chem.Abstr., Farm & Garden Ind., Field Crop Abstr., Herb.Abstr., Soils & Fert. **Document type:** trade publication.
—Linda Hall; SWETS; UMI; UnCover. **CCC.**
Incorporates: Florist and Nursery Exchange (ISSN 0015-4407)
Description: Articles on the latest developments in the production and marketing of crop, vegetable, and fruit seeds, with an ad index, industry announcements and legislative updates.

633   US
▼**SEEDSMAN N W.** 1996. q. $12 in US and Canada (Mexico & elsewhere $18). Columbia Publishing and Design, 2520 W. Washington, Ste. 2, Box 9036, Yakima, WA 98909-0036. TEL 509-248-2452; 800-900-2452. FAX 509-248-4056. E-mail: dede@freshcut.com. Ed. Jennifer Hager; Pub. J. Mike Stoker. adv. contact: Loren Queen. circ. 8,800. (back issues avail.) **Document type:** trade publication.
Description: Covers seed production, research, and marketing.

SELEKTSIYA I NASINNITSTVO; respublikanskyi mizhvidomchyi tematichnyi naukovyi zbirnik. see BIOLOGY — Botany

631.5   RU   ISSN 0037-1459
SELEKTSIYA I SEMENOVODSTVO. 1929. q. $80 (effective 1998). Sadovaya-Spasskaya, 18, 107807 Moscow, Russia. TEL 7-095-9232771. FAX 7-095-2072870. (Dist. by: Mezhdunarodnaya Kniga, B. Yakimanka 39, 117049 Moscow, Russia. TEL 7-095-2384967. FAX 7-095-2384634) Ed. Lidiya A. Tumanova. adv.; bk.rev.; bibl.; index. circ. 4,000. **Indexed:** Biol.Abstr., Chem.Abstr., Field Crop Abstr., Herb.Abstr., Hort.Abstr., Irr.& Drain.Abstr., Maize Abstr., Plant Breed.Abstr., Potato Abstr., Rev.Plant Path., Rice Abstr., Seed Abstr., Soyabean Abstr., Triticale Abstr., Weed Abstr.
—BLDSC (0162.000000); CISTI.

631   RU   ISSN 0582-5164
SEL'SKAYA NOV'. 1966. m. $60 (effective 1998). Molodezhnaya ul., 4, 117296 Moscow, Russia. TEL 7-095-9302898. (Dist. by: Mezhdunarodnaya Kniga, B. Yakimanka 39, 117049 Moscow, Russia. TEL 7-095-2384967. FAX 7-095-2384634; Dist. in U.S. by: Victor Kamkin Inc., 4956 Boiling Brook Pkwy., Rockville, MD 20852. TEL 301-881-5973. FAX 301-881-1637) (Co-sponsor: Ministerstvo Sel'skogo Khozyaistva) Ed. A.A. Kulikov. illus. circ. 238,600. **Indexed:** Plant Breed.Abstr.

634.8   SP   ISSN 0037-184X
CODEN: SEVIAH
SEMANA VITIVINICOLA; al servicio de la vid y el vino. 1945. w. 22000 ptas. Apartado de Correos, 642, 46080 Valencia, Spain. TEL 34-6-3749500. FAX 34-6-3749561. Ed. Salvador Manjon Estela; Pub. Fernando Manjon Estela. adv.; bk.rev.; advpt.; bibl.; illus.; stat.; tr.lit.; index. circ. 14,000. **Indexed:** Chem.Abstr., Food Sci.& Tech.Abstr., Ind.SST.
—BLDSC (8237.820000); CASDDS.

631.5   IT   ISSN 0037-1890
CODEN: SEELBA
SEMENTI ELETTE. Short title: S E. 1955. bi-m. L.69000 (effective 1996). Edagricole S.p.A., Via Emilia Levante 31, 40139 Bologna, Italy. TEL 39-51-492211. FAX 39-51-493660. Ed. Roberto Anderlini. adv.: B&W page L.1000000; 185 x 247. bk.rev.; charts; illus.; index. circ. 4,700. **Indexed:** Chem.Abstr., Fababean Abstr., Field Crop Abstr., Herb.Abstr., Hort.Abstr., Ornam.Hort., Plant Breed.Abstr., Plant Grow.Reg.Abstr., Seed Abstr., Soils & Fert., Soyabean Abstr., Triticale Abstr.
—BLDSC (8237.850000); UMI.
Description: Deals with seed problems of any field, horticultural or garden crop.

632   JA   ISSN 0037-4091
CODEN: SHBOAO
SHOKUBUTSU BOEKI/PLANT PROTECTION. (Text in Japanese) 1947. m. 8060 Yen. Japan Plant Protection Association - Nihon Shokubutsu Boeki Kyokai, 1-43-11 Komagome, Toshima-ku, Tokyo 170, Japan. TEL 03-3866-9897. FAX 03-3861-7715. (Subscr. to: Sun Publications, Ishi Bldg., 3-37, Sakuma-cho, Tokyo 101, Japan) Ed. Takeo Endo. **Indexed:** Cott.& Trop.Fibr.Abstr., Field Crop Abstr., Protozool.Abstr., Seed Abstr.
—BLDSC (6523.000000).

631.4 333.7   CC   ISSN 1000-288X
SHUITU BAOCHI TONGBAO/BULLETIN OF SOIL AND WATER CONSERVATION. (Text in Chinese; abstracts in Chinese, English) 1981. bi-m. Y24 (foreign $60). Zhongguo Kexueyuan, Xibei Shuitu Baochi Yanjiusuo, Yangling Qu, Xi'an, Shaanxi 712100, People's Republic of China. TEL 86-910-7012412. FAX 86-910-7012210. E-mail: libinfo@ms.iswc.ac.cn. (Dist. overseas by: China International Book Trading Corp., P.O. Box 399, Beijing 100044, P.R. China) Ed. Tian Junliang. R&P contact: Wang Xiu. **Document type:** academic/scholarly publication.
●Also available on CD-ROM.

631.4 333.7   CC   ISSN 1005-3409
SHUITU BAOCHI YANJIU/RESEARCH OF SOIL AND WATER CONSERVATION. (Text in Chinese; abstracts in Chinese, English) 1994. q. Y20 (foreign $50). Zhongguo Kexueyuan, Xibei Shuitu Baochi Yanjiusuo, Yangling Qu, Xi'an, Shaanxi 712100, People's Republic of China. TEL 86-910-7012412. FAX 86-910-7012210. E-mail: Libinfo@ms.iswc.ac.cn. Ed. Li Rui. **Document type:** academic/scholarly publication.

338.1   US   ISSN 1051-7901
HD9241
SITUATION & OUTLOOK REPORT. FRUIT & TREE NUTS. 1937. q. $18. U.S. Department of Agriculture, Economic Research Service, c/o Debbie Haugan, Rm. 110, 1301 New York Ave., N.W., DC 20005-4788. TEL 202-219-0515. (Dist. by: ERS-NASS, 341 Victory Dr., Herndon, VA 22070. TEL 800-999-6779) Ed.Bd. (also avail. in microfiche from CIS; back issues avail.; reprint service avail. from CIS) **Indexed:** Amer.Stat.Ind. (1974-), Rural Recreat.Tour.Abstr., World Agri.Econ.& Rural Sociol.Abstr. **Document type:** government publication.
●Also available online. Vendor(s): Information Access Co., Knight-Ridder Information, Inc.
Former titles (until 1988): U.S. Department of Agriculture. Situation and Outlook Report. Fruit; (until 1986): U.S. Department of Agriculture. Outlook and Situation Report. Fruit (ISSN 8756-9914)

633.6   CU   ISSN 0049-0849
TP375   CODEN: SDCAAR
SOBRE LOS DERIVADOS DE LA CANA DE AZUCAR. (Text in Spanish; summaries in English) 1967. 3/yr. $26 in S. America; N. America $28; elsewhere $34. (Instituto Cubano de Investigaciones de los Derivados de la Cana de Azucar) Ediciones Cubanas, Obispo No. 527, Apdo. 605, Havana, Cuba. Eds. Gladys Blanco Carracedo, Rainerio Garcia Carmenates. charts; illus.; circ. 1,500 (controlled). **Indexed:** Abstr.Bull.Inst.Pap.Chem., Biol.Abstr., Chem.Abstr., Food Sci.& Tech.Abstr., Sugar Ind.Abstr.
—CASDDS.

631.4   US   ISSN 0096-4522
S590   CODEN: SCSFAD
SOIL AND CROP SCIENCE SOCIETY OF FLORIDA. ANNUAL PROCEEDINGS. a. University of Florida, Institute of Food and Agricultural Sciences, Soil and Crop Science Society of Florida, 304 Newell Hall, Gainesville, FL 32611-0602. Ed. E.S. Horner. **Indexed:** ASCA, Bibl.Agri., Biol.Abstr., Chem.Abstr., Curr.Adv.Ecol.Sci., Curr.Cont., Excerp.Med., Geo.Abstr., GeoRef., Helminthol.Abstr., Irr.& Drain.Abstr., Maize Abstr., Rice Abstr., Soils & Fert., Sorghum & Millets Abstr., SSCI, Trop.Oil Seeds Abstr., Weed Abstr.
—BLDSC (6818.800000); CASDDS; CISTI; Genuine Article.

SOIL & ENVIRONMENT. see ENVIRONMENTAL STUDIES

635 631.4   NZ   ISSN 0038-0687
SOIL & HEALTH JOURNAL. 1941. bi-m. NZ.$38. Soil & Health Association of New Zealand, P.O. Box 36-170, Northcote, Auckland 9, New Zealand. FAX 09-443-8436. Ed. Chris Wheeler. adv.; bk.rev. circ. 5,000.
—BLDSC (8321.620000). **CCC.**
Formerly: Compost Journal.
Description: Covers organic agriculture and holistic health issues.

631.4   US
SOIL - PLANT ANALYST. 1983. q. $40. Soil and Plant Analysis Council, Georgia University Sta., Box 2007, Athens, GA 30612-0007. TEL 706-546-0425. FAX 706-548-4891. Ed. J. Benton Jones. adv.: page $1,200; circ. 350. (looseleaf format; back issues avail.) **Document type:** newsletter.
Description: For operators of soil and plant analysis laboratories. Covers methods for analyzing nutrients in soils, plants, animal wastes, and water. Explores the use of diagnostic techniques that improve nutrient management in crop production and the environment.

631.4   US   ISSN 0038-075X
S590   CODEN: SOSCAK
SOIL SCIENCE; an interdisciplinary approach to soils research. 1916. m. $108 to individuals (foreign $153); institutions $195 (foreign $240) (effective 1998). (Rutgers University) Williams & Wilkins (Subsidiary of: Waverly International), 351 W. Camden St., Baltimore, MD 21201-2436. TEL 410-528-4068; 800-222-3790. FAX 410-528-4452. TELEX 87669. E-mail: lgibson@wwilkins.com; URL: http://www.wwilkins.com. Ed. Dr. Robert L. Tate III. adv. contact: Lynn Gibson. bk.rev.; bibl.; charts; illus.; stat. circ. 1,784. (also avail. in microfilm from WWS; reprint service avail.) **Indexed:** Abstr.Bull.Inst.Pap.Chem., Agri.Eng.Abstr., Apic.Abstr., ASCA, Bibl.Agri., Biol.Abstr., Biol.& Agr.Ind., Biotech.Abstr., Chem.Abstr., Curr.Adv.Ecol.Sci., Curr.Cont., Deep Sea Res.& Oceanogr.Abstr., Ecol.Abstr., Environ.Abstr., Environ.Per.Bibl. (1982-1994), Excerp.Med., Farm & Garden Ind., Field Crop Abstr., Forest.Abstr., Forest Prod.Abstr., Geo.Abstr.H.G., Geol.Abstr., Geotech.Abstr., Helminthol.Abstr., Herb Abstr., Hort.Abstr., IBR, IDA, Irr.& Drain.Abstr., Maize Abstr., Petrol.Abstr., Plant Breed.Abstr., Rev.Plant Path., Rice Abstr., Sci.Cit.Ind., Sel.Water Res.Abstr., Soils & Fert., Soyabean Abstr., Triticale Abstr., W.R.C.Inf., Weed Abstr. **Document type:** academic/scholarly publication.
●Also available online. Vendor(s): Ovid Technologies, Inc.
—BLDSC (8324.000000); CASDDS; CISTI; Ei; EMDOCS; Genuine Article; KR SourceOne; Linda Hall; SWETS; UnCover. **CCC.**
Description: Research articles of interest to soil testing bureaus, soil scientists, agronomists and environmentalists.
Refereed Serial

SOIL SCIENCE ALERT; an alerting service covering current articles in Elsevier soil science journals. see EARTH SCIENCES — Abstracting, Bibliographies, Statistics

631.4   JA   ISSN 0038-0768
CODEN: SSPNAW
SOIL SCIENCE AND PLANT NUTRITION. (Text in English) 1955. q. $100. (Japan Society of Soil Science and Plant Nutrition) Business Center for Academic Societies Japan, 5-16-9 Honkomagome, Bunkyo-ku, Tokyo 113, Japan. TEL 03-5814-5811. FAX 03-5814-5822. TELEX 2722268 BCJSP J. **Indexed:** Agri.Eng.Abstr., ASCA, Biol.Abstr., Chem.Abstr., Crop Physiol.Abstr., Curr.Adv.Ecol.Sci., Curr.Cont., Energy Ind., Energy Info.Abstr., Excerp.Med., Field Crop Abstr., Forest.Abstr., Herb.Abstr., Hort.Abstr., Irr.& Drain.Abstr., Maize Abstr., Ornam.Hort., Plant Breed.Abstr., Rice Abstr., Sci.Cit.Ind., Sel.Water Res.Abstr., Soils & Fert., Sorghum & Millets Abstr., Soyabean Abstr., Sugar Ind.Abstr., Triticale Abstr., Weed Abstr. **Document type:** academic/scholarly publication.
—BLDSC (8324.100000); CASDDS; EMDOCS; Genuine Article; Linda Hall; SWETS; UnCover.

AGRICULTURE — CROP PRODUCTION AND SOIL

631.4 US ISSN 0361-5995
S590.S64 CODEN: SSSJD4
SOIL SCIENCE SOCIETY OF AMERICA. JOURNAL. 1936. bi-m. $108. Soil Science Society of America, 677 S. Segoe Rd., Madison, WI 53711.
TEL 608-273-8080. FAX 608-273-2021. URL: http://www.soils.org/journals/ss.html. Ed. Lloyd Hossner. R&P contact: David Kral. adv. contact: Keith R. Schlesinger. bk.rev.; bibl.; charts; illus.; index. circ. 6,000. (also avail. in microform from PMC) **Indexed:** Abstr.Bull.Inst.Pap.Chem., Acid Rain Abstr., Acid Rain Ind., Agri.Eng.Abstr., ASCA, Bibl.Agri., Biodet.Abstr., Biol.Abstr., Biol.& Agr.Ind., Chem.Abstr., Chem.Cit.Ind., Cott.& Trop.Fibr.Abstr., Curr.Adv.Ecol.Sci., Curr.Cont., Deep Sea Res.& Oceanogr.Abstr., Ecol.Abstr., Energy Ind., Energy Info.Abstr., Eng.Ind., Environ.Abstr., Environ.Per.Bibl. (1972-), Excerpt.Med., Field Crop Abstr., Forest.Abstr., Forest Prod.Abstr., Geo.Abstr.H.G., Geol.Abstr., GeoRef., Geotech.Abstr., Herb.Abstr., Hort.Abstr., IDA, Ind.Sci.Rev., Irr.& Drain.Abstr., Maize Abstr., Mat.Sci.Cit.Ind., Ocean.Abstr., Petrol.Abstr., Plant Breed.Abstr., Pollut.Abstr., Potato Abstr., Rice Abstr., Sci.Cit.Ind., Sel.Water Res.Abstr., Sel.Water Res.Abstr., Soils & Fert., Sorghum & Millets Abstr., Soyabean Abstr., Triticale Abstr., W.R.C.Inf., Weed Abstr. **Document type:** academic/scholarly publication.
—BLDSC (8324.300000); CASDDS; CISTI; Ei; EMDOCS; Genuine Article; KR SourceOne; Linda Hall; SWETS; UnCover. **CCC.**
Formerly (until 1976): Soil Science Society of America. Proceedings (ISSN 0038-0776)
Description: Contains papers on new developments in soil physics, mineralogy, chemistry, microbiology, fertility and plant nutrition, soil genesis and classification, soil and water management, forest and range soils, and fertilizer use and technology.
Refereed Serial

631.4 US ISSN 1047-4986
CODEN: SABSEP
SOIL SCIENCE SOCIETY OF AMERICA BOOK SERIES. 1989. irreg. Soil Science Society of America, 677 S. Segoe Rd., Madison, WI 53711.
TEL 608-273-8080. FAX 608-273-2021. R&P contact: David Kral. **Document type:** monographic series.
—BLDSC (8324.280000); CASDDS. **CCC.**

631.4 CE ISSN 1015-0803
SOIL SCIENCE SOCIETY OF SRI LANKA. JOURNAL. (Text in English) 1970. a. Rs.100($4) Soil Science Society of Sri Lanka, c/o Faculty of Agriculture, University of Sri Lanka, Peradeniya, Sri Lanka. Ed. R.B. Mapa. adv.; bk.rev. circ. 150. **Indexed:** Sri Lanka Sci.Ind.
Formerly: Soil Science Society of Ceylon. Journal.

631.4 333.7 US ISSN 0584-0554
S592.14
SOIL SURVEY HORIZONS. 1975. q. $13. Soil Science Society of America, 677 S. Segoe Rd., Madison, WI 53711. TEL 608-273-8080. FAX 608-273-2021. Ed, Gerald Miller. R&P contact: David Kral. bk.rev. circ. 1,200. (back issues avail.) **Indexed:** Agri.Eng.Abstr., Hort.Abstr., Soils & Fert.
—BLDSC (8324.790000). **CCC.**
Description: Expresses ideas, problems, and philosophies concerning the study of soils in the field.

631.4 UK ISSN 0951-3485
SOIL SURVEY RECORD. 1970. irreg., no.115, 1990. price varies. Soil Survey and Land Research Centre, Silsoe Campus, Silsoe, Bedford MK45 4DT, England. TEL 44-1525-863242. FAX 44-1525-863253. **Indexed:** Geo.Abstr., Soils & Fert. **Document type:** government publication.
—Linda Hall.
Supersedes: Great Britain. Soil Survey of England and Wales. Records (ISSN 0072-7180)
Description: Information about land use and soil content of selected 100 square kilometer areas of England and Wales.

631.4 NE ISSN 0933-3630
CODEN: SOTEEZ
SOIL TECHNOLOGY. (Text and summaries in English) 1988. bi-m. fl.792($489) (effective 1997). Elsevier Science B.V., P.O. Box 211, 1000 AE Amsterdam, Netherlands. TEL 31-20-4853911.
FAX 31-20-4853598. TELEX 18582 ESPA NL. E-mail: nlinfo-f@elsevier.nl; usinfo-f@elsevier.com; forinfo-kyf04035@niftyserve.or.jp; URL: http://www.elsevier.nl/. (Subscr. in the Americas to: Elsevier Science, Regional Sales Office, Box 945, New York, NY 10159-0945. TEL 212-633-3730. FAX 212-633-3680; Subscr. in Australasia and the Far East to: Elsevier Science (Singapore) Pte Ltd, No.1 Temasek Ave., No.17-01 Millenia Tower, Singapore 039192, Singapore. TEL 65-434-3727. FAX 65-337-2230; Subscr. in Japan to: Elsevier Science Japan, 9-15 Higashi-Azabu 1-chome, Minato-ku, Tokyo 106, Japan. TEL 81-3-5561-5033. FAX 81-3-5561-5047) Ed.Bd. (also avail. in microform from UMI; back issues avail.; reprint service avail. from SWZ) **Indexed:** Agroforest.Abstr., ASCA, Curr.Cont., Ecol.Abstr., Environ.Abstr., Geo.Abstr.H.G., Geo.Abstr.P.G., IDA, Irr.& Drain.Abstr., Sugar Ind.Abstr. **Document type:** academic/scholarly publication.
—BLDSC (8326.050000); EMDOCS; Genuine Article; Linda Hall; SWETS; UnCover. **CCC.**
Description: Publishes applied research and field applications on soil physics, soil mechanics, soil erosion and conservation, drainage and irrigation and soil restoration.
Refereed Serial

631.4 NE ISSN 0936-2568
SOIL TECHNOLOGY SERIES. (Text and summaries in English) 1989. a. price varies. Elsevier Science B.V., P.O. Box 211, 1000 AE Amsterdam, Netherlands. TEL 31-20-4853911. FAX 31-20-4853598. E-mail: nlinfo-f@elsevier.nl; usinfo-f@elsevier.com; forinfo-kyf04035@niftyserve.or.jp; URL: http://www.elsevier.nl/. (Subscr. in the Americas to: Elsevier Science, Regional Sales Office, Box 945, New York, NY 10159-0945. TEL 212-633-3730. FAX 212-633-3680; Subscr. in Australasia and the Far East to: Elsevier Science (Singapore) Pte Ltd, No.1 Temasek Ave., No.17-01 Millenia Tower, Singapore 039192, Singapore. TEL 65-434-3727. FAX 65-337-2230; Subscr. in Japan to: Elsevier Science Japan, 9-15 Higashi-Azabu 1-chome, Minato-ku, Tokyo 106, Japan. TEL 81-3-5561-5033. FAX 81-3-5561-5047) circ. 1,000. (back issues avail.) **Indexed:** Curr.Cont., Geo.Abstr. **Document type:** proceedings.

631.4 UK ISSN 0266-0032
S590 CODEN: SUMAEU
SOIL USE AND MANAGEMENT. 1985. q. £110($195) (effective 1997). (British Society of Soil Science) CAB International, Wallingford, Oxon. OX10 8DE, England. TEL 01491-832111.
FAX 44-1491-826090. TELEX 847964 COMAGG G. E-mail: cabi@cabi.org; URL: http://www.cabi.org. (U.S. subscr. to: CAB International, N. American Office, 198 Madison Ave., New York, NY 10016. TEL 212-726-6490. FAX 212-686-7993) Ed. John D. Allen. adv.; bk.rev.; charts; illus. (back issues avail.) **Indexed:** Agri.Eng.Abstr., ASCA, Bibl.Agri., Curr.Adv.Ecol.Sci., Curr.Cont., Ecol.Abstr., Environ.Per.Bibl. (1989-), Fababean Abstr., Field Crop Abstr., Forest.Abstr., Geo.Abstr.H.G., Geo.Abstr.P.G., Hort.Abstr., IDA, Irr.& Drain.Abstr., Seed Abstr., Soils & Fert., W.R.C.Inf. **Document type:** academic/scholarly publication.
—BLDSC (8326.150000); CASDDS; Ei; EMDOCS; Genuine Article; Linda Hall; SWETS; UMI; UnCover.
Refereed Serial

SOILS AND GROUNDWATER CLEANUP. see
ENVIRONMENTAL STUDIES — Waste Management

631.4 AT ISSN 0081-1912
S599.A8 CODEN: AOSLAJ
SOILS AND LAND USE SERIES. 1949. irreg. Aus.$12 per no. C S I R O, Division of Soils, Private Bag No. 2, Glen Osmond, S.A. 5064, Australia. E-mail: library@adl.sols.csiro.au. (Subscr. to: CSIRO Publications, P.O. Box 89, E. Melbourne, Vic. 3002, Australia. TEL 61-3-4187333. FAX 61-3-4190459) R&P contact: Kathy Heinze. circ. 700. **Indexed:** Biol.Abstr., Soils & Fert. **Document type:** academic/scholarly publication, monographic series.
—Linda Hall.
Description: Describes the soils and land use of various areas of Australia.

631.4 AT ISSN 0812-017X
SOILS NEWS. 1957? q. Australian Society of Soil Science, Federal Council, c/o CSIRO Division of Soils, P.M.B. 2, Glen Osmond, S.A. 5064, Australia. TEL 61-8-274-9311. FAX 61-8-338-1636. TELEX AA 82406. Ed. Clive Kirkby. bk.rev. circ. 700.
Description: Published to inform members about decisions by the council, the activities of the different branches, and events of interest.

631 UN ISSN 1011-2650
SOILS NEWSLETTER. (Text in English) 1978. 2/yr. free. International Atomic Energy Agency, Wagramerstr. 5, P.O. Box 100, A-1400 Vienna, Austria. TEL 43-1-20600. FAX 43-1-2060-29302. E-mail: hera@ripo1.iaea.or.at. (Co-sponsor: Food and Agriculture Organization) circ. 450. **Document type:** newsletter.

631.4 NR ISSN 0038-1209
S590 CODEN: SOLAAD
SOLS AFRICAINS/AFRICAN SOILS. (Text in English and French) 1951. 3/yr. $25. Organization of African Unity, Inter-African Bureau for Soils - Organisation de l'Unite Africaine, NPA Bldg., 4th Fl., 26-28 Marina, P.M.B. 2359, Lagos, Nigeria. TEL 234-1-2633430. FAX 234-1-2636093. TELEX 22199 TECOAU NG. charts; illus.; tr.lit.; cum.index every 2 yrs. circ. 2,000. (back issues avail.) **Indexed:** Biol.Abstr., Chem.Abstr., GeoRef., Geotech.Abstr. **Document type:** academic/scholarly publication.

631 SA ISSN 0257-1862
CODEN: SAJSEV
SOUTH AFRICAN JOURNAL OF PLANT AND SOIL. 1983. q. R.118 to individuals; institutions R.138 (foreign $45) (effective 1997). (South African Society for Crop Production) Foundation for Education, Science & Technology, P.O. Box 1758, Pretoria 0001, South Africa. TEL 27-12-3226404. FAX 27-12-3207803. E-mail: buro@shuttle.up.ac.za. (Co-sponsors: Southern African Weed Science Society; Soil Science Society of Southern Africa) Ed. M.V. Fey. adv. contact: M.V. Fey. circ. 1,200. **Indexed:** Chem.Abstr., Cott.& Trop.Fibr.Abstr., Crop Physiol.Abstr., Curr.Adv.Ecol.Sci., Field Crop Abstr., Food Sci.& Tech.Abstr., Geo.Abstr.H.G., Herb.Abstr., Hort.Abstr., Ind.S.A.Per., Irr.& Drain.Abstr., Maize Abstr., Plant Breed.Abstr., Plant Grow.Reg.Abstr., Soils & Fert., Sorghum & Millets Abstr., Soyabean Abstr., Triticale Abstr., Weed Abstr. **Document type:** academic/scholarly publication.
—BLDSC (8339.710000); CASDDS; CISTI. **CCC.**
Refereed Serial

631 SA ISSN 0375-2682
SOUTH AFRICAN SUGAR ASSOCIATION EXPERIMENT STATION. ANNUAL REPORT. (Text in English) a. R.20 (free to registered growers and research organizations). South African Sugar Association Experiment Station, Private Bag X02, Mount Edgecombe 4300, South Africa.
TEL 27-31-593205. FAX 27-31-595406. TELEX 6-23020. illus. circ. 3,200. **Document type:** corporate report.
—BLDSC (1245.800000).
Description: Includes information on sugarcane breeding, pest and disease control, soil research, biotechnology, farm planning, irrigation, extension, and agronomy research.

SOUTH AFRICAN SUGAR ASSOCIATION EXPERIMENT STATION. BIOTECHNOLOGY DEPARTMENT. ANNUAL REVIEW. see *BIOLOGY — Biotechnology*

631 SA
SOUTH AFRICAN SUGAR ASSOCIATION EXPERIMENT STATION. BULLETIN. (Text in English) irreg. R.15. South African Sugar Association Experiment Station, Private Bag X02, Mount Edgecombe 4300, South Africa. TEL 27-31-593205. FAX 27-31-595406. TELEX 6-23020. charts; illus. circ. 3,000. (back issues avail.) **Document type:** bulletin.
Description: Includes information on breeding, pest and disease control, irrigation and soil conservation.

SOUTH AFRICAN SUGAR JOURNAL. see *FOOD AND FOOD INDUSTRIES*

AGRICULTURE — CROP PRODUCTION AND SOIL

631 SA ISSN 0373-045X
CODEN: PSATAA
SOUTH AFRICAN SUGAR TECHNOLOGISTS' ASSOCIATION. PROCEEDINGS. (Text in English) 1927. a. R.60. South African Sugar Technologists' Association, Private Bag X02, Mount Edgecombe 4300, South Africa. TEL 27-31-593205. FAX 27-31-595406. TELEX 6-23020. illus. **Document type:** proceedings.
—BLDSC (6840.560000); CASDDS.
Description: Contains information on sugarcane agriculture, breeding, pests, diseases, manufacturing, milling, soil research, biotechnology, irrigation, agronomy, and extension.

633.368 US ISSN 0038-3694
SOUTHEASTERN PEANUT FARMER. 1961. m. (except Oct. & Dec.). $5 (effective 1997). Georgia Peanut Commission, Box 706, Tifton, GA 31794. TEL 912-386-3470. FAX 912-386-3501. (Co-sponsor: Alabama Peanut Producers Association; Florida Peanut Producers Association) Ed. Don Koehler. adv. contact: Joan Underwood. circ. 11,200. (tabloid format) **Document type:** newspaper.
Description: News articles on the legislative, financial, and policy issues affecting this agricultural industry in this region of the country.

630.24 US ISSN 0362-4463
SB610.2 CODEN: SWSPBE
SOUTHERN WEED SCIENCE SOCIETY. PROCEEDINGS. a. $25. Southern Weed Science Society, c/o Robert A. Schmidt, 1508 W. University, Champaign, IL 61821-3133. TEL 217-352-4212. FAX 217-352-4241. **Indexed:** Biol.Abstr., Hort.Abstr., Soils & Fert., Weed Abstr. **Document type:** proceedings.
—BLDSC (6841.945000); CASDDS.

633 664 US ISSN 1081-3063
HD9235.S62
SOYA BLUEBOOK PLUS. 1947. a. $60 in N. America; elsewhere $75 (includes q. Bluebook Update) (effective 1997). Soyatech, Inc., 318 Main St., Box 84, Bar Harbor, ME 04609. TEL 207-288-4969; 800-424-SOYA. FAX 207-288-5264. Ed. Keri Hayes; Pub. Peter Golbitz. R&P contact: Peter Golbitz. adv. contact: Joy Froding. charts; stat. circ. 2,500. (also avail. in microfilm; back issues avail.) **Indexed:** SRI. **Document type:** directory.
—Linda Hall.
Former titles (until 1996): Soya Bluebook (ISSN 0275-4509); (until 1980): Soybean Digest Blue Book (ISSN 0081-3222)
Description: Lists key players in the global oilseed processing industry. Includes company information, product listings, and reference material for the soybean, corn, cottonseed, canola, rapeseed, sunflower, palm and palm kernel industries.

633.34 US ISSN 0038-6014
SB205.S7
SOYBEAN DIGEST. 1940. m. (11/yr.). $20 (foreign $25). (American Soybean Association) Intertec Publishing Corp., Webb Division, 7900 International Dr., Ste. 300, Minneapolis, MN 55425. TEL 612-851-4678. FAX 612-351-4601. E-mail: soybeandigest@intertec.com. Ed. Syl Markins. adv.; charts; illus.; mkt.; stat.; tr.lit.; index. circ. 218,300. **Indexed:** Biol.Abstr., Chem.Abstr., Farm & Garden Ind. **Document type:** trade publication.
—Linda Hall; UMI. **CCC.**

633 SP
SPAIN. DIRECCION GENERAL DE LA PRODUCCION AGRARIA. CAMPANA ALGODONERA. irreg. Ministerio de Agricultura, Direccion General de la Produccion Agraria, Madrid, Spain.

632.9 581 616.9 SP ISSN 0213-6910
SPAIN. MINISTERIO DE AGRICULTURA, PESCA Y ALIMENTACION. BOLETIN DE SANIDAD VEGETAL: PLAGAS. 1975. q. 3500 ptas. (foreign 4500 ptas.) (effective 1992). Ministerio de Agricultura, Pesca y Alimentacion, Subdireccion General de Sanidad Vegetal, Centro de Publicaciones, Paseo de la Infanta Isabel 1, 28071 Madrid, Spain. TEL 34-1-3475551. (Edit. addr.: Subdireccion General de Sanidad Vegetal, C. Velazquez 147, 28002 Madrid, Spain) Ed. Ramon Vazquez Hombrados. R&P contact: Juan Carlos Palacios Lopez. **Indexed:** Biodet.Abstr. **Document type:** academic/scholarly publication.
Formerly (until 1985): Spain. Ministerio de Agricultura, Pesca y Alimentacion. Servicio de Defensa Contra Plagas e Inspeccion Fitopatologica. Boletin (ISSN 0210-8038)

633 CN ISSN 0828-3737
SPECIALTY CROP REPORT. 1982. a. free. Saskatchewan Agriculture and Food Library, B5 Walter Scott Bldg., 3085 Albert St., Regina, SK S4S 0B1, Canada. TEL 306-787-6933. FAX 306-787-0216. E-mail: pdc@agr.gov.sk.ca; URL: http://www.gov.sk.ca/agfood. circ. 7,000. (back issues avail.) **Document type:** government publication.
Description: Reports the production of lentils, beans, peas, mustard, sunflowers, caraway seed, buckwheat, triticale and fababeans grown in Saskatchewan.

SPORTSTURF. see *SPORTS AND GAMES — Ball Games*

631 US ISSN 0739-022X
SPUDLETTER. bi-m. National Potato Council, 5690 D T C Blvd., Ste. 230-E, Englewood, CO 80111-3200. TEL 303-773-9295. FAX 303-773-9296. Ed. Carol Reseigh. circ. 10,500. **Document type:** newsletter.

633.491 631.3 US ISSN 0038-8661
SPUDMAN; voice of the potato industry. 1963. 8/yr. $30 (effective 1997). Box 1752, Monterey, CA 93942. TEL 408-373-7991. FAX 408-373-2923. Pub. Donald D. Miller. R&P contact: Donald D. Miller. adv.: B&W page $2382, color page $3658; trim 8 1/2 x 11. bk.rev. circ. 17,519. (back issues avail.) **Document type:** trade publication.
Description: For growers and decision-makers involved with the shipping, packing, buying and processing of potatoes.

633.51 US ISSN 0279-3148
STAPLREVIEW. 1921. m. $1. Staple Cotton Cooperative Association, 210-214 W. Market St., Greenwood, MS 38930. TEL 601-453-6231. Ed. R.L. Clarke. adv.; charts; stat. (tabloid format; also avail. in microfiche from CIS; reprint service avail. from CIS) **Indexed:** Amer.Stat.Ind. (1973-), Text.Tech.Dig.
—Linda Hall.
Formerly: Staple Cotton Review (ISSN 0038-9838)

631 BE ISSN 0770-9404
CODEN: SUBEAH
SUCRERIE BELGE. (Text in French) 1872. a. free. Societe Generale des Fabricants de Sucre de Belgique, 182 av. Tervuren, B-1150 Brussels, Belgium. FAX 32-2-7710154. TELEX 24523 RAFT B. (Co-sponsor: Societe Technique et Chimique de Sucrerie de Belgique) Ed. Marc Rosiers. adv. contact: Christine Sneppe. circ. 1,000. **Indexed:** Chem.Abstr., Excerp.Med., Field Crop Abstr., Food Sci.& Tech.Abstr., Herb.Abstr., Nutr.Abstr., Sugar Ind.Abstr. **Document type:** bulletin.
—BLDSC (8506.000000).

631 SJ ISSN 0562-5068
SUDAN COTTON REVIEW. (Text in English) 1958. a. Cotton Public Corporation, Box 1672, Khartoum, Sudan.

SUGAR MILLING RESEARCH INSTITUTE. ANNUAL REPORT. see *FOOD AND FOOD INDUSTRIES*

631 US ISSN 0039-4750
SUGARBEET GROWER. 1963. bi-m. $9 (foreign $15) (effective 1997 & 1998). Sugar Publications, 503 Broadway, Fargo, ND 58102. TEL 701-237-5747. FAX 701-235-0140. Ed. Don Lilleboe. R&P contact: Don Lilleboe. adv. contact: Don Lilleboe. illus.; circ. 12,800. (controlled). **Document type:** trade publication.

633.63 NE
SUIKER UNIE. 1966. m. free. Cooperatie Suiker Unie, Postbus 3411, 4800 MG Breda, Netherlands. TEL 31-76-279000. FAX 31-76-279279. TELEX 54370. Ed. W.H. Dijkstra. charts; illus.; mkt.; stat. circ. 25,000. **Document type:** trade publication.
Formerly (until 1995): Maandblad Suiker Unie (ISSN 0024-8606)
Description: Agricultural publication devoted to sugar beet production. Covers crop research, diseases, quality control, marketing prices, and association news.

SUN-DIAMOND GROWER. see *FOOD AND FOOD INDUSTRIES*

631.5 664 US ISSN 0192-8988
SUNFLOWER (BISMARCK). vol.5, 1979. 6/yr. $9 (foreign $36). National Sunflower Association, 4023 State St., Bismarck, ND 58501. TEL 701-328-5100. FAX 701-328-5101. E-mail: klngrtner@sunflowerusa.com. Ed. Larry Kleingartner. R&P contact: Ruth Isaak. adv. contact: Ruth Isaak. circ. 21,500. **Document type:** trade publication.
—CISTI.
Description: Aimed at sunflower producers and those involved in the sunflower industry. Includes production techniques, marketing updates, legislative and industry related news.

630 CN ISSN 1180-1506
SUSTAINABLE FARMING; resource efficient agricultural production. 1987. q. Can.$20 (foreign $20) (effective 1997-1998). Resource Efficient Agricultural Production - Canada, Glenaladale House, Box 125, Ste. Anne de Bellevue, PQ H9X 3V9, Canada. TEL 514-398-7743. FAX 514-398-7972. E-mail: reap@interlink.net. Ed. Rod MacRae; Pub. Roger Samson. R&P contact: Roger Samson. adv. contact: Tomas Nimmo. bk.rev. circ. 800. (back issues avail.) **Document type:** newspaper.
Formerly (until 1990): R E A P (ISSN 0847-477X)
Description: Describe sustainable farming systems, biomass crops for fibre and energy, permaculture systems

631.5 SW ISSN 0346-2099
SVENSK FROETIDNING. 1932. m. (10/yr.). SEK 150. Sveriges Froe- och Oljevoextodlana, P.O. Box 271, S-701 45 Oerebro, Sweden. FAX 019-10-21-33. Ed. Ann-Charlotte Wallenhammer. adv. circ. 19,500. **Indexed:** Field Crop Abstr., Herb.Abstr., Seed Abstr. **Document type:** academic/scholarly publication.

631.5 SW ISSN 0039-6990
CODEN: SUTTAG
SVERIGES UTSAEDESFOERENINGS TIDSKRIFT; organ foer svensk vaextforaedling. (Text in English, Swedish; summaries in English) 1891. q. SEK 80 (effective 1997). Sveriges Utsaedesfoerening - Swedish Seed Association, S-268 81 Svaloev, Sweden. TEL 418-67000. FAX 418-67100. Ed. R. von Bothmer. adv.; bk.rev.; bibl.; charts; illus.; index. circ. 1,300. **Indexed:** Biol.Abstr., Chem.Abstr., Field Crop Abstr., Helminthol.Abstr., Potato Abstr., Seed Abstr., Triticale Abstr., Weed Abstr.
—CASDDS.
Formerly (until 1894): Allmaenna Svenska Utsaedesfoereningens Tidskrift.

630 PL ISSN 0082-1276
CODEN: STNRDA
SZCZECINSKIE TOWARZYSTWO NAUKOWE. WYDZIAL NAUK PRZYRODNICZO-ROLNICZYCH. PRACE. (Text in Polish; summaries in English, German and Russian) 1959. irreg. price varies. Szczecinskie Towarzystwo Naukowe, Wydzial Nauk Przyrodniczo-Rolniczych, Ul. Wojska Polskiego 96, 70-481 Szczecin, Poland. TEL 48-91-231862. (Dist. by: Ars Polona-Ruch, Krakowskie Przedmiescie 7, Warsaw, Poland) **Indexed:** Biol.Abstr.

661.8 US
T F I ACTION. 1968. m. The Fertilizer Institute, 501 Second St., N.E., Washington, DC 20002. TEL 202-675-8250. FAX 202-544-8123. circ. 3,000.
Description: Informs members of the institute's activities.

633.007 DK ISSN 0908-0813
TABELBILAG TIL LANDSFORSOEGENE; forsoeg i de landoekonomiske foreninger. 1971. a. DKK 176 (effective 1997). Landsudvalget for Planteavl - Danish Agricultural Advisory Centre, Udkaersvej 15, DK-8200 Aarhus N, Denmark. TEL 45-87-40-50-00. FAX 45-87-40-50-10. Ed. Carl Aage Pedersen. circ. 900.
Description: Contains results of field experiments collected and calculated in experimental series, conducted by local agricultural advisors and members of the farmers union.

AGRICULTURE — CROP PRODUCTION AND SOIL

633 CH ISSN 0255-5581
SB215.T33
TAIWAN SUGAR RESEARCH INSTITUTE. ANNUAL REPORT/TAI-WAN TANG YEH YEN CHIU SO NIEN PAO. (Text in English) 1967. a. free. Taiwan Sugar Research Institute, 54 Sheng Chan Rd., Tainan, Taiwan, Republic of China. TEL 06-2671911. FAX 06-2685425. E-mail: tsri@mail.ncku.edu.tw. Ed. Long-Hue Wang. R&P contact: Long-Huei Wang. adv. contact: Long-Hue Wang. illus. circ. 850. **Indexed:** Biol.Abstr., Excerpt.Med., Field Crop Abstr., Herb.Abstr., Hort.Abstr., Plant Breed Abstr., Potato Abstr., Rev.Plant Path., Sugar Ind.Abstr. **Document type:** academic/scholarly publication.
—BLDSC (1464.600000).
Description: Annual report on the progress and achievements of research on sugar cane breeding, cultivation, pest control, sugar manufacturing, by-products utilization, and improvement of Phalaenopsis orchids.

631.7 JA ISSN 0915-6550
TAMEIKE NO SHIZEN/NATURE OF IRRIGATION POND. (Text in Japanese) 1983. 2/yr. membership. Temeike no Shizen Kenkyukai - Nature Study of Irrigation Pond Society, Japan, c/o Mr. Murakami, Nagoyashi Kogai Kenkyujo, 1-14 Chudocho, Minami-ku, Nagoya-shi, Aichi-ken 457, Japan.

TAMIL NADU. DEPARTMENT OF STATISTICS. SEASON AND CROP REPORT. see AGRICULTURE — Abstracting, Bibliographies, Statistics

631 TZ
TANZANIA. NATIONAL AGRICULTURAL RESEARCH PROGRAMME. PROJECT REPORT. (Text in English) a. Ministry of Agriculture, Crop Development Division, P.O. Box 9071, Dar es Salaam, Tanzania. **Document type:** government publication.
Formerly: Tanzania. National Agricultural Research Programme. Summary of Programmes.

631.5 GW ISSN 0082-1799
TASCHENBUCH DER PFLANZENARZTES. 1951. a. DM.39. Landwirtschaftsverlag GmbH, Huelsebrockstr. 2, 48165 Muenster, Germany. TEL 49-2501-801-0. FAX 49-2501-801-215. TELEX 892665-LANDV-D. (Subscr. to: Postfach 480249, 48079 Muenster, Germany) Ed. Hellmut Thiede. **Document type:** bulletin.

631 US
TATER NEWS.* m. free. National Potato Promotion Board, 7555 E. Hampden Ave., No. 412, Denver, CO 80231-4835. TEL 303-758-7783. FAX 303-756-9256. Ed. Holly Hull. bk.rev.; circ. 17,000 (controlled). **Document type:** newsletter.
Formerly (until May 1990): Spotlight (Denver).
Description: Provides information to the potato-agriculture industry on the board and its programs.

TEA RESEARCH ASSOCIATION. MEMORANDUM. see BEVERAGES

TEA RESEARCH ASSOCIATION. OCCASIONAL SCIENTIFIC PAPERS. see BEVERAGES

TEA RESEARCH ASSOCIATION. TOCKLAI EXPERIMENTAL STATION. SCIENTIFIC ANNUAL REPORT. see BEVERAGES

631 636.2 MX
TECNICA EN AGRICULTURA Y GANADERIA. 1970. bi-m. (Asociacion Mexicana de Periodistas) Publicaciones y Promociones Impresas, Melchor Ocampo 156 1 Piso, A.P. 30-526, Mexico 4, D.F., Mexico. adv. circ. 5,000.

633.5 RU ISSN 0235-2559
CODEN: TABKA8
TEKHNICHESKIE KUL'TURY. 1988. q. $43 (effective 1997). Sadovaya-Spasskaya, 18, 107807 Moscow, Russia. TEL 7-095-2071655. (Dist. by: Mezhdunarodnaya Kniga, B. Yakimanka 39, 117049 Moscow, Russia. TEL 7-095-2384967. FAX 7-095-2384634) **Indexed:** Agri.Eng.Abstr., Biol.Abstr., Chem.Abstr., Field Crop Abstr., Herb.Abstr., Plant Breed.Abstr., Seed Abstr.
—BLDSC (0180.382000); CASDDS.
Former by the merger of (1924-1988): Len i Konoplya (ISSN 0024-418X); (1937-1988): Tabak (ISSN 0039-873X)

631 MG ISSN 0563-1637
HD2135.M26
TERRE MALGACHE/TANY MALAGASY. (Text in French) 1967. irreg., no.20, 1980. FMG.2000. Universite de Madagascar, Etablissement d'Enseignement Superieur des Sciences Agronomiques, B.P. 175, Antananarivo, Madagascar. charts; illus.; stat. circ. 1,500. **Indexed:** Curr.Cont.Africa.

634.8 FR
TERRES DE BOURGOGNE. Cote d'Or edition: Terres de Bourgogne (Edition Cote d'Or) (ISSN 1145-1572); Nievre edition: Terres de Bourgogne (Edition Nievre) (ISSN 1145-1564); Yonne edition: Terres de Bourgogne (Edition Yonne) (ISSN 1146-2140) 50/yr. 15 rue de Colmar, 21000 Dijon, France. TEL 80-70-06-30. Ed. Jean-Luc Berthome. circ. 20,000.

631 US ISSN 0279-165X
TEXAS FARMER-STOCKMAN. 1911. m. $12. Farm Progress Companies (Subsidiary of: A B C Publishing Companies), 191 S. Gary Ave., Carol Stream, IL 60188. TEL 630-690-5600. FAX 630-462-2869. (Edit. addr.: 301 Hesters Crossing, Ste. 130, Round Rock, TX 78681. TEL 512-310-9940. FAX 512-310-9942) adv.: B&W color page $3850, color page $4430; trim 7 X 10. circ. 59,876 (paid).

631.8 TH ISSN 0085-7246
THAILAND. DIVISION OF AGRICULTURAL CHEMISTRY. REPORT ON FERTILIZER EXPERIMENTS AND SOIL FERTILITY RESEARCH.* (Text in English) 1966. irreg. Ministry of Agriculture, Division of Agricultural Chemistry, Rajadamnern Ave., Bangkok 9, Thailand.

631 NE ISSN 0922-6419
TIJDSCHRIFT LANDINRICHTING. 1961. 8/yr. fl.62.50 to individuals (foreign fl.67.50); institutions fl.80 (foreign fl.85) (effective 1995 & 1996). Stichting Tijdschrift Landinrichting, P.O. Box 20021, 3502 LA Utrecht, Netherlands. TEL 31-30-858722. FAX 31-30-858999. Ed. P.C. van Zijst. adv.; bk.rev.; bibl.; charts; illus. circ. 1,600. **Document type:** trade publication.
—SWETS.
Formerly (until 1988): Cultuurtechnisch Tijdschrift (ISSN 0045-9267)
Refereed Serial

AL-TIKNULUJIA AL-MULA'IMAH/MIDDLE EAST APPROPRIATE TECHNOLOGY NEWS. see TECHNOLOGY: COMPREHENSIVE WORKS

631 IE
THE TILLAGE FARMER - INCORPORATING BIATAS. 1947. bi-m. I£28.98. Irish Sugar plc, Athy Rd., Carlow, Ireland. TEL 0503-31487. FAX 0503-43087. Ed. Michael Grimes. adv.: B&W page I£850, color page I£1050; trim 186 x 252. bk.rev. circ. 7,000. **Indexed:** Field Crop Abstr., Herb.Abstr., Plant Breed.Abstr. **Document type:** trade publication.
Former titles (until 1993): Biatas (ISSN 0332-3153); (until 1956): Beetgrower (ISSN 0332-1614).

630.24 668.6 JA ISSN 0040-8719
S19 CODEN: TJARAJ
TOHOKU JOURNAL OF AGRICULTURAL RESEARCH. (Text in English) 1950. q. exchange basis only. Tohoku Daigaku, Nogakubu - Tohoku University, Faculty of Agriculture, 1-1 Tsutsumi-dori Amamiya-cho, Sendai-shi, Miyagi-ken 981, Japan. charts; illus. circ. 1,000. **Indexed:** Anim.Breed.Abstr., Biol.Abstr., Chem.Abstr., Dairy Sci.Abstr., Field Crop Abstr., Food Sci.& Tech.Abstr., Herb.Abstr., Hort.Abstr., Ind.Vet., Nutr.Abstr., Plant Breed.Abstr., Poult.Abstr., Soils & Fert., Sport Fish.Abstr., Vet.Bull., Weed Abstr., Wild.Rev., Zoo.Rec. **Document type:** academic/scholarly publication.
—BLDSC (8860.000000); CASDDS; CISTI; Linda Hall; UnCover.

620.24 668.6 JA ISSN 0563-8313
TOKYO UNIVERSITY OF AGRICULTURE AND TECHNOLOGY. ANNUAL REPORT/TOKYO NOKO DAIGAKU NENPO. (Text in Japanese; summaries in English) 1949. biennial. exchange basis. Tokyo University of Agriculture and Technology - Tokyo Noko Daigaku, Fuchu-shi, Tokyo, Japan. FAX 0423-60-9140. bk.rev. circ. 2,000. **Indexed:** Text.Tech.Dig.
—BLDSC (1471.750000).

633 US
▼**TOMATO MAGAZINE.** 1997. bi-m. Columbia Publishing and Design, 2520 W. Washington, Ste. 2, Box 9036, Yakima, WA 98909-0036. TEL 509-248-2452; 800-900-2452. FAX 509-248-4056. E-mail: dede@freshcut.com. Ed. D. Brent Clement. adv. contact: Lynn Schuchardt. circ. 4,000 (controlled). **Document type:** trade publication.
Description: Focuses on the tomato industry with emphasis on fresh and greenhouse tomatoes.

634 US
TREE FRUIT.* bi-m. $19.95 (overseas $195). Western Agricultural Publishing Co. Inc., 4969 E. Clinton Way, Ste. 119, Fresno, CA 93727-1549. TEL 209-252-7000. FAX 209-252-7387. Ed. Mark Arcanmonte. adv.: B&W page $1676, color page $2406; trim 8 3/8 x 10 7/8. circ. 7,600. **Document type:** trade publication.
Description: Covers improving production practices, economics of production and marketing, on-farm feature stories, and research and legislative developments.

631 MW
TREE NUT AUTHORITY. REPORT. (Text in English) 1970. a. Tree Nut Authority, P.O. Box 2134, Blantyre, Malawi. TEL 265-670007. stat. **Document type:** corporate report.
Supersedes: Tung Board. Annual Report.

634.3 US ISSN 0041-2570
TRIANGLE (LAKELAND). 1950. w. (except July). membership. Florida Citrus Mutual, Box 89, Lakeland, FL 33802. TEL 941-682-1111. FAX 941-682-1074. Ed. Shannon Ross. R&P contact: Shannon Ross. charts; stat.; mkt. circ. 12,000. (tabloid format) **Indexed:** Chem.Abstr. **Document type:** newsletter.

633.2 AT ISSN 0049-4763
SB202.A8 CODEN: TRGRB4
TROPICAL GRASSLANDS. 1967. 4/yr. Aus.$110 to non-members. Tropical Grassland Society of Australia Inc., 306 Carmody Rd., St. Lucia, Qld. 4067, Australia. TEL 61-73-3713946. E-mail: tgs@tep.csiro.au. Ed. Lyle Winks. R&P contact: Lyle Winks. adv.; bk.rev.; charts; index. circ. 626. (also avail. in microfilm from UMI) **Indexed:** Agroforest.Abstr., ASCA, Biol.Abstr., Curr.Adv.Ecol.Sci., Curr.Cont., Dairy Sci.Abstr., Field Crop Abstr., Forest.Abstr., Helminthol.Abstr., Herb.Abstr., Herb.Abstr., Ind.Sci.Rev., Ind.Vet., Nutr.Abstr., Rural Recreat.Tour.Abstr., Sci.Cit.Ind., Seed Abstr., So.Pac.Per.Ind., Soils & Fert., Sorghum & Millets Abstr., Trop.Abstr., Vet.Bull., Weed Abstr., World Agri.Econ. & Rural Sociol.Abstr. **Document type:** academic/scholarly publication.
—BLDSC (9056.200000); Genuine Article; SWETS; UMI; UnCover.
Description: Publishes the results of research and development in the evaluation, management and utilization of pastures and fodder crops in tropical and sub-tropical agriculture, descriptions of farming systems and review articles.

632 TZ ISSN 0082-6642
TROPICAL PESTICIDES RESEARCH INSTITUTE. ANNUAL REPORT. 1957. a. available on exchange basis. Tropical Pesticides Research Institute, P.O. Box 3024, Arusha, Tanzania. **Indexed:** Biol.Abstr., Hort.Abstr., Rev.Appl.Entomol., Rev.Plant Path.

630.13 BE ISSN 0771-3312
CODEN: TRPIEP
TROPICULTURA. (Text in English, French, Spanish; contents page in English) 1983. 4/yr. free. A G C D - A B O S, Rue du Trone 4, Bte. 605, 1000 Brussels, Belgium. TEL 32-2-5190447. Ed. J. Gijsen. bk.rev. circ. 2,200. **Document type:** academic/scholarly publication.
—BLDSC (9057.040000); UnCover.
Refereed Serial

TSUCHI TO BISEIBUTSU/SOIL MICROORGANISMS. see BIOLOGY — Microbiology

TURANG/PEDOLOGY. see EARTH SCIENCES

AGRICULTURE — CROP PRODUCTION AND SOIL

631.8   CC   ISSN 1002-0616
TURANG FEILIAO/SOIL FERTILIZER. (Text in Chinese) bi-m. Zhongguo Nongye Kexueyuan, Turang Feiliao Yanjiusuo - Chinese Academy of Agricultural Sciences, Institute of Soil Fertilizer, 30 Baishiqiao Lu, Beijing 100081, People's Republic of China. TEL 896531. Ed. Lin Bao.

631.4 333.7   CC   ISSN 1007-2209
TURANG QINSHI YU SHUITU BAOCHI XUEBAO/JOURNAL OF SOIL EROSION AND SOIL AND WATER CONSERVATION. (Text in Chinese) 1987. q. Y16 (foreign $44). Zhongguo Kexueyuan, Xibei Shuitu Baochi Yanjiusuo, Yangling Qu, Xi'an, Shaanxi 712100, People's Republic of China. TEL 86-910-7012412. FAX 86-910-7012210. E-mail: libinfo@ms.iswc.ac.cn. bk.rev. **Indexed:** ASCA. **Document type:** academic/scholarly publication.
● Also available on CD-ROM.
Formerly (until vol.9, no.4, 1995): Shuitu Baochi Xuebao - Journal of Soil and Water Conservation.

TURANG XUE JINZHAN/ADVANCES IN PEDOLOGY. see EARTH SCIENCES

631 631.3 338.1   US   ISSN 0899-417X
TURF NEWS. 1977. bi-m. membership. Turfgrass Producers International, 1855-A Hicks Rd., Rolling Meadows, IL 60008. TEL 847-705-9898. FAX 847-705-8347. Ed. Wendell Mathews. R&P contact: Douglas Fender. adv.: B&W page $1080; trim 8 1/8 x 10 7/8; adv. contact: Terri Berkowitz. bk.rev.; circ. 1,450 (paid). (back issues avail.) **Document type:** trade publication.
Description: Sent to turfgrass sod farm operations, suppliers, educators, students, and industry associates. Topic include seed, equipment, business, marketing, and agronomics for turfgrass sod farmers.

632.9 635   UK   ISSN 0952-7788
SB950.3.G7
U K PESTICIDE GUIDE. a. £18.95($35) CAB International, Wallingford, Oxon. OX10 8DE, England. TEL 44-1491-832111. FAX 44-1491-826090. TELEX 847964 COMAGG G. E-mail: cabi@cabi.org; URL: http://www.cabi.org. (U.S. subscr. to: CAB International, North American Office, 198 Madison Ave., New York, NY 10016. TEL 212-726-6490. FAX 212-686-7993) (back issues avail.) **Indexed:** Rev.Plant Path., Weed Abstr. **Document type:** trade publication.
—BLDSC (9082.665470); CISTI.
Description: Lists all agrochemical products registered and marketed for use in the UK, with guidance on uses, efficacy, precautions, and environmental safety.

631   US
U S A RICE QUARTERLY. 1989. q. free to qualified personnel. U S A Rice Federation, 6699 Rookin, Box 740123, Houston, TX 77274. TEL 713-270-6699; 800-888-RICE. FAX 713-270-9021. (Alt. addr.: 4301 N. Fairfax Dr., Ste. 305, Arlington, VA 22203-1616. TEL 703-351-1861. FAX 703-351-8162) (Co-sponsors: U S Rice Producers' Group; Rice Millers' Association; U S A Rice Council) Pub. Patricia Alderson. circ. 16,000 (controlled). **Document type:** newsletter.
Former titles (until 1997): U S A Rice Council Review; U S A Rice Council. Newsletter; Rice Council for Market Development. Newsletter.

634.8   FR   ISSN 0242-6706
UNION GIRONDINE DES VINS DE BORDEAUX. 11/yr. Federation des Syndicats des Grands Vins de Bordeaux, 1 cours du 30 Juillet, 33000 Bordeaux, France. TEL 56-48-19-95. FAX 56-48-53-79. Ed. M. Dando. circ. 9,000.

U.S. DEPARTMENT OF AGRICULTURE. AGRICULTURAL STATISTICS BOARD REPORT: CROP PRODUCTION. see AGRICULTURE — Abstracting, Bibliographies, Statistics

U.S. DEPARTMENT OF AGRICULTURE. AGRICULTURAL STATISTICS BOARD REPORT: NONCITRUS FRUITS AND NUTS. see AGRICULTURE — Abstracting, Bibliographies, Statistics

U.S. DEPARTMENT OF AGRICULTURE. AGRICULTURAL STATISTICS BOARD REPORT: POTATOES AND POTATO STOCKS. see AGRICULTURE — Abstracting, Bibliographies, Statistics

U.S. DEPARTMENT OF AGRICULTURE. AGRICULTURAL STATISTICS BOARD REPORT: PEANUT STOCKS AND PROCESSING. see AGRICULTURE — Abstracting, Bibliographies, Statistics

U.S. DEPARTMENT OF AGRICULTURE. AGRICULTURAL STATISTICS BOARD REPORT: VEGETABLES. see AGRICULTURE — Abstracting, Bibliographies, Statistics

632   US   ISSN 0083-0518
U.S. ENVIRONMENTAL PROTECTION AGENCY. PESTICIDES ENFORCEMENT DIVISION. NOTICES OF JUDGMENT UNDER FEDERAL INSECTICIDE, FUNGICIDE, AND RODENTICIDE ACT. Variant title: Pesticide Enforcement. irreg. free. U.S. Environmental Protection Agency, 401 M St., S.W., Washington, DC 20460. (Orders to: National Technical Information Service, 5285 Port Royal Rd., Springfield, VA 22161. TEL 703-487-4650. FAX 703-321-8547) **Document type:** government publication.

631.4   US   ISSN 0083-3304
U.S. NATURAL RESOURCES CONSERVATION SERVICE. NATIONAL ENGINEERING HANDBOOK SECTIONS. irreg. U.S. Natural Resources Conservation Service, Box 2890, Washington, DC 20013. TEL 202-720-2472. FAX 202-720-4593. (Orders to: National Technical Information Service, 5285 Port Royal Rd., Springfield, VA 22161. TEL 703-487-4650. FAX 703-321-8547) (also avail. in microfiche) **Document type:** government publication.

631.4   US   ISSN 0083-3320
S599.A1   CODEN: SSIRA9
U.S. NATURAL RESOURCES CONSERVATION SERVICE. SOIL SURVEY INVESTIGATION REPORTS. 1967. irreg. U.S. Natural Resources Conservation Service, Box 2890, Washington, DC 20013. TEL 202-720-2472. FAX 202-720-4593. (Orders to: National Technical Information Service, 5285 Port Royal Rd., Springfield, VA 22161. TEL 703-487-4650. FAX 703-321-8547; And: National Soil Survey Center, Midwest NTC, Federal Bldg., Rm.152, 100 Centennial Mall N., Lincoln, NE 68508-3866. TEL 402-437-5363. FAX 402-437-5336) **Indexed:** GeoRef. **Document type:** government publication.
Description: Presents soil characterization data and discusses the chemical, physical, and morphological aspects of important soils for a given region.

631.4   US   ISSN 0083-3339
U.S. NATURAL RESOURCES CONSERVATION SERVICE. TECHNICAL PUBLICATIONS. irreg. price varies. U.S. Natural Resources Conservation Service, Box 2890, Washington, DC 20013. TEL 202-720-2472. FAX 202-720-4593. (Orders to: National Technical Information Service, 5285 Port Royal Rd., Springfield, VA 22161. TEL 703-487-4650. FAX 703-321-8547) **Indexed:** GeoRef. **Document type:** government publication, monographic series.

631   PE
UNIVERSIDAD NACIONAL DE AGRARIA. TALLER DE ESTUDIOS ANDINOS. SERIE COSTA CENTRAL. 1978. irreg. Universidad Nacional Agraria "La Molina", Taller de Estudios Andinos, Departamento de Ciencias Humanas, Apdo. 456, Lima, Peru.

631.6   RM
UNIVERSITATEA DE STIINTE AGRONOMICE. LUCRARI STIINTIFICE. SERIA E, IMBUNATATIRI FUNCIARE. (Text in Rumanian; summaries in English) 1973. a. exchange basis only. Universitatea de Stiinte Agronomice si Medicina Veterinaria, Bdul. Marasti, 59, Bucharest, Sec. 1, Rumania. **Document type:** academic/scholarly publication.
Formerly (until 1992): Institutul Agronomic Nicolae Balcescu. Lucrari Stiintifice. Seria E, Imbunatatiri Funciare (ISSN 1015-2172)

632   BE   ISSN 0435-950X
UNIVERSITEIT GENT. CENTRUM VOOR ONKRUIDONDERZOEK. MEDEDELING. (Text in Dutch or English; summaries in English) 1965. s-a. 300 BEF per no. (free to research institutions). Universiteit Gent, Centrum voor Onkruidonderzoek, Coupure Links 653, B-9000 Ghent, Belgium. FAX 32-9-2646224. TELEX 12754 RUGENT B. Dirs. T. Behaeghe, Robert Bulcke. circ. 250. **Indexed:** Herb.Abstr., Weed Abstr. **Document type:** academic/scholarly publication.

UNIVERSITEIT GENT. FACULTEIT VAN DE LANDBOUWKUNDIGE EN TOEGEPASTE BIOLOGISCHE WETENSCHAPPEN. MEDEDELINGEN. see BIOLOGY — Biotechnology

631   XV
UNIVERSITY IN LJUBLJANA. BIOTECHNICAL FACULTY. RESEARCH REPORTS; crop production and soil. (Text in English or Slovenian) 1957. s-a. $30. University in Ljubljana, Biotechnical Faculty, P.O. Box 486, Jamnikarjeva 101, 61001 Ljubljana, Slovenia. FAX 38-61-261-073. Ed. Joze Macek. circ. 450. (back issues avail.) **Indexed:** Biol.Abstr., Sport Fish.Abstr., Wild.Rev., Zoo.Rec.
—BLDSC (9428.470000).
Formerly: University E. Kardelja in Ljubljana. Biotechnical Faculty. Research Reports (ISSN 0459-6404)

631   US   ISSN 0096-8498
S445
UNIVERSITY OF GEORGIA. AGRICULTURAL EXPERIMENT STATIONS. SOUTHERN COOPERATIVE SERIES BULLETIN. irreg., latest 1983. University of Georgia, Agricultural Experiment Stations, Athens, GA 30602. Ed. Kathleen Sheridan. **Indexed:** Hort.Abstr.
—Linda Hall.

631.4   CN   ISSN 0085-1329
UNIVERSITY OF GUELPH. DEPARTMENT OF LAND RESOURCE SCIENCE. PROGRESS REPORT. 1954. a. free. University of Guelph, Department of Land Resource Science, Guelph, ON N1G 2W1, Canada. TEL 519-824-4120. FAX 519-824-5730. URL: http://www.uoguelph.ca. Ed. T. McGonigle. R&P contact: T.J. Gillespie. bibl.; charts; illus. circ. 1,500. (processed) **Document type:** academic/scholarly publication.
Description: Provides details of personnel and programs within the department, as well as brief articles on current research activities.

UNIVERSITY OF LONDON. WYE COLLEGE. DEPARTMENT OF AGRICULTURAL ECONOMICS. FARM BUSINESS UNIT. OCCASIONAL PAPER. see AGRICULTURE — Agricultural Economics

633   TR
UNIVERSITY OF THE WEST INDIES. ANNUAL REPORT ON COCOA RESEARCH. 1930. a. free. University of the West Indies, St. Augustine, Trinidad & Tobago, W.I. Ed. A.J. Kennedy. bibl.; illus. circ. 200. **Indexed:** Biol.Abstr.

630.24   SW   ISSN 0346-4997
VAEXTSKYDDSKURIREN. 1960. s-a. free. Bayer (Sverige) AB, Agro-Kemi, P.O. Box 50113, S-202 11 Malmoe, Sweden. Ed. Gunnar Holma. charts; illus.; circ. 40,000 (controlled).

631   US   ISSN 0889-4787
VALLEY POTATO GROWER. 1946. m. free to qualified personnel (foreign $25) (effective 1995). Red River Valley Potato Growers Association, Box 301, 420 Business Hwy. 2, E. Grand Forks, MN 56721. TEL 218-773-3633. FAX 218-773-6227. Ed. Coreen Haux. R&P contact: Coreen Haux. adv.: B&W page $1560, color page $2480; trim 8 1/2 x 10 7/8; adv. contact: Gary Shields. circ. 11,814. **Document type:** trade publication.
Description: For potato farmers thoughout the U.S. and the world. Covers current events, innovations, industry problems and solutions, marketing and production information, research results, safety and governmental issues, and pest-weed control.

635   US
VEGETABLE.* 1991. bi-m. Western Agricultural Publishing Co. Inc., 4969 E. Clinton Way, Ste. 119, Fresno, CA 93727-1549. TEL 209-252-7000. FAX 209-252-7387. Ed. Mark Arcamonte. adv.: B&W page $1100, color page $1600; trim 8 3/8 x 10 7/8. circ. 6,200.
Description: Covers improving production practices, economics of production and marketing, on-farm feature stories, and research and legislative developments.

631   UK   ISSN 1361-2069
VEGETABLE VARIETY HANDBOOK. a. £15 (foreign £20.50). National Institute of Agricultural Botany, Huntingdon Rd., Cambridge CB3 0LE, England. TEL 44-1223-276381. FAX 44-1223-277602. Ed. Paul Nelson. **Document type:** bulletin.
Formerly: Vegetable Growers Leaflets (ISSN 0470-1321)

AGRICULTURE — CROP PRODUCTION AND SOIL

632.9   DK   ISSN 0907-4066
VEJLEDNING I PLANTEVAERN. 1984. a. DKK 80 (effective 1997). Landbrugets Informationskontor, Udkaervej 15, DK-8200 Aarhus N, Denmark. TEL 45-86-10-90-11. FAX 45-86-10-90-22. Eds. Jan Sepstrup. Georg Nielsen. R&P contact: Georg Nielsen. circ. 8,000. **Document type:** academic/scholarly publication.
  Formed by the 1992 merger of: Plantevaern i Landbruget (ISSN 0109-3312); Vejledning i Plantebeskyttelse i Landbrugs- og Specialafgoeder (ISSN 0905-4359)

632   US   ISSN 0507-6773
                   CODEN: PVPCBM
VERTEBRATE PEST CONFERENCE. PROCEEDINGS. 1962. biennial. $25. Vertebrate Pest Council, c/o DANR - North Region, University of California at Davis, Davis, CA 95616. TEL 916-754-8491. FAX 916-754-8499. E-mail: vpc@davis.com. Ed. R.E. Marsh. circ. 1,000. **Indexed:** Biol.Abstr., Biotech.Abstr., Sport Fish.Abstr., Wild.Rev., Zoo.Rec. **Document type:** proceedings.
—BLDSC (6849.815000); CASDDS; Linda Hall.

VESITALOUS; Finnish journal of water economy, hydraulic and agricultural engineering. see *WATER RESOURCES*

631   CU
VIANDAS TROPICALES. BOLETIN DE RESENAS. 1974. irreg. exchange basis. Centro de Informacion y Documentacion Agropecuario, Instituto Nacional de Investigaciones en Viandas Tropicales, Gaveta Postal 4149, Havana 4, Cuba. (Dist. by: Ediciones Cubanas, Obispo No. 461, Apdo. 605, Havana, Cuba) bibl.; charts; stat.
  Supersedes in part: Cuba. Centro de Informacion y Divulgacion Agropecuario. Boletin de Resenas. Serie: Viandas, Hortalizas y Granos; Which was formerly: Cuba. Centro de Informacion y Documentacion Agropecuario. Boletin de Resenas. Serie: Viandas, Hortalizas y Granos.
  Description: Covers recent advances in science and technology while examining the various tendencies and developments in these areas.

634.8   FR   ISSN 1145-5799
VIGNE. 11/yr. 511 F. C E P Groupe France Agricole, 8 Cite Paradis, 75493 Paris Cedex 10, France. TEL 33-1-40227900. FAX 33-1-48240315. Ed. Cesar Compadre. circ. 30,000.

634.8   FR   ISSN 0049-643X
VIGNERON CHAMPENOIS; organe de la vigne et du vin de champagne. 1873. m. (11/yr.). 370 F. (effective 1997). Association Viticole Champenoise, 5 rue Henri-Martin, B.P. 135, 51204 Epernay Cedex, France. TEL 33-3-26511930. FAX 33-3-26511957. Ed. D. Moncomble. adv. contact: Xavier Rinville. stat. circ. 5,500. **Indexed:** VITIS. **Document type:** bulletin.

634.8   FR   ISSN 0995-7944
VIGNERON DES COTES DU RHONE ET DU SUD EST. 1946. 24/yr. 130 F. 6 rue des Trois Faulons, 84000 Avignon, France. TEL 90-27-24-24. FAX 90-85-26-83. Eds. F. Fabre, Sylvie Reboul. adv.: B&W page 11245 F., color page 16875 F.; trim 340 x 255. circ. 10,000. **Document type:** newspaper.

634.8   FR
VIGNES LANGUEDOC-ROUSILLON. m. B.P. 249, 34434 St. Jean de Vedas, France. TEL 33-04-67070371. FAX 33-04-67070371. Ed. M. Ponce Andre. circ. 21,000. **Document type:** newspaper.
  Formerly: Vignes Provence Languedoc-Rousillon.

634.8 663.2   IT   ISSN 0390-0479
SB387   CODEN: VIGNDL
VIGNEVINI. Short title: V V. 1974. m. (10/yr.). L.80000 (effective 1996). Edagricole S.p.A., Via Emilia Levante 31, 40139 Bologna, Italy. TEL 39-51-492211. FAX 39-51-493660. Ed. Mario Fregoni. adv.: B&W page L.115000, color page L.1750000; 185 x 247. circ. 26,200. **Indexed:** Agri.Eng.Abstr., Chem.Abstr., Food Sci.& Tech.Abstr., Hort.Abstr., Plant Breed.Abstr., Soils & Fert., VITIS.
—BLDSC (9236.110000); CASDDS.
  Description: Covers wine and vineyards.

631 663   US   ISSN 1047-4951
TP544   CODEN: VWMAE9
VINEYARD AND WINERY MANAGEMENT; the bottom line resource for grower and vintner. 1975. bi-m. $25. Vineyard & Winery Services, Inc., 103 Third St., Box 231, Watkins Glen, NY 14891. TEL 607-535-7133. FAX 607-535-2998. Ed. J. William Moffett. R&P contact: J. William Moffett. adv. contact: Hope Merletti. bk.rev. circ. 3,600. **Indexed:** VITIS. **Document type:** trade publication.
  Formerly: Eastern Grape Grower and Winery News (ISSN 0194-5254)

VINS D'ALSACE; revue viticole et vinicole mensuelle. see *BEVERAGES*

634 635   US   ISSN 1064-4083
VIRGINIA FRUIT AND VEGETABLE MARKET INFORMATION. m. Department of Agriculture and Consumer Services, 1100 Bank St., Ste. 805, Richmond, VA 23219-3638. TEL 804-786-3947. FAX 804-371-7787. Ed. J.P. Welch. circ. 500. (back issues avail.) **Document type:** government publication.
  Description: Provides fruit and vegetable crop and market conditions for Virginia and competing areas, to Virginia farmers and agribusinesses only

634.8   FR   ISSN 0757-4673
VITI. 11/yr. 260 F. Groupe Liaisons S.A., 1 av. Edouard Belin, 92856 Rueil Malmaison, France. TEL 33-1-40051818. FAX 33-1-40051007. Ed. Denis Le Chatelier. adv. circ. 32,513.
  Formerly (until 1982): Vititechnique (ISSN 0399-3558)

634.8   FR   ISSN 0244-4860
VITI VINICOLE. w. B.P. 57, 34140 Mauguio Cedex, France. TEL 67-29-36-29. FAX 67-29-59-20. TELEX 485 807. Ed. Alain Gosse. circ. 19,683.

634.8   SP   ISSN 1131-5679
VITICULTURA ENOLOGIA PROFESIONAL. 1989. bi-m. 5550 ptas. (foreign 6100 ptas.) (effective 1997). Agro Latino, S.L., Apdo. 20151, 08080 Barcelona, Spain. TEL 34-3-4568563. FAX 34-3-4359104. adv. **Indexed:** Ind.SST. **Document type:** trade publication.

634.8   FR   ISSN 1151-1109
VITICULTURE EN VAL DE LOIRE. 8/yr. 150 F. 11 Impasse Ambroise-Croizat, B.P. 136, 37701 Saint-Pierre-des-Corps, France. TEL 47-44-21-85. FAX 47-32-02-55. Ed. M. Aubard. circ. 3,200.

630   RU   ISSN 0372-3283
S13   CODEN: TVZKA3
VSESOYUZNYI NAUCHNO-ISSLEDOVATEL'SKII INSTITUT ZERNOVOGO KHOZYAISTVA. TRUDY.* 1964. irreg. price varies. Rossiiskaya Akademiya Sel'skokhozyaistvennykh Nauk, c/o Tsentral'naya Nauchnaya Sel'skokhozyaistvennaya Biblioteka, Orlikov per. 3, 107804 Moscow, Russia. bibl.; illus. circ. 3,500. **Indexed:** Chem.Abstr.
—CASDDS.

631.7   PL
             CODEN: AWARD6
WARSAW AGRICULTURAL UNIVERSITY. S G G W. ANNALS. LAND RECLAMATION. (Text mainly in English; occasionally in French, German or Russian; summaries in Polish) 1957. irreg. $10 per no. Szkola Glowna Gospodarstwa Wiejskiego (SGGW) - Warsaw Agricultural University, Ul. Nowoursynowska 166, 02-/66 Warsaw, Poland. Ed. C. Somorowski. **Indexed:** Chem.Abstr. **Document type:** academic/scholarly publication.
—BLDSC (1035.045000); CASDDS; Linda Hall.
  Former titles: Warsaw Agricultural University. S G G W - A R. Annals. Land Reclamation (ISSN 0208-5771); (until 1980): Akademia Rolnicza, Warsaw. Zeszyty Naukowe. Melioracje Rolne (ISSN 0373-0034)

WASEDA SEIBUTSU/WASEDA BIOLOGY. see *BIOLOGY*

631   UK
WATER RESOURCES NETWORK. irreg., no.10, 1992. Overseas Development Institute, Regent's College, Inner Circle, Regent's Park, London NW1 4NS, England. TEL 0171-487-7413. FAX 0171-487-7590. TELEX 94082191 ODI G. E-mail: odi@gn.apc.org. Ed. Hugh Turral. **Indexed:** Abstr.Rural Dev.Trop. **Document type:** monographic series.
  Formerly: Irrigation Management Network Paper (ISSN 0951-189X)

632   US   ISSN 0741-9856
WEED CONTROL MANUAL. a. $54 (effective 1997). Meister Publishing Co., 37733 Euclid Ave., Willoughby, OH 44094. TEL 800-572-7742. FAX 216-942-0662. E-mail: wem-circ@meisterpubl.com. Ed. Stella Naegely. adv. contact: William J. Miller. circ. 8,000. **Document type:** trade publication.
—CCC.
  Formerly: Weed Control Manual and Herbicide Guide (ISSN 0511-411X)

632   UK   ISSN 0043-1737
SB611   CODEN: WEREAT
WEED RESEARCH. (Text in English, French, or German) 1961. bi-m. £210($383.50) (foreign £231) (effective 1998). (European Weed Research Society) Blackwell Science Ltd., Osney Mead, Oxford OX2 OEL, England. TEL 44-1865-206206. FAX 44-1865-721205. E-mail: journals.cs@blacksci.co.uk; URL: http://www.black.co.uk. Ed. H. Lawson; Pub. Allen Stevens. R&P contact: Sarah Pollard. adv. contact: Martine Cariou-Keen. bibl.; charts; illus.; index. circ. 1,350. (also avail. in microform from UMI; back issues avail; reprint service avail. from ISI) **Indexed:** Agroforest.Abstr., ASCA, Bio-Contr.News & Info., Biol.Abstr., Biol.& Agr.Ind., Biotech.Abstr., Chem.Abstr., Crop Physiol.Abstr., Curr.Adv.Ecol.Sci., Curr.Cont., Ecol.Abstr., Environ.Per.Bibl. (1989-1994), Excerp.Med., Fababean Abstr., Field Crop Abstr., Forest.Abstr., Geo.Abstr.H.G., Herb.Abstr., Hort.Abstr., Maize Abstr., Plant Grow.Reg.Abstr., Potato Abstr., Rice Abstr., Rural Recreat.Tour.Abstr., Sci.Cit.Ind., Seed Abstr., Soils & Fert., Sorghum & Millets Abstr., Soyabean Abstr., Triticale Abstr., Trop.Oil Seeds Abstr., Weed Abstr., World Agri.Econ.& Rural Sociol.Abstr. **Document type:** academic/scholarly publication.
—BLDSC (9284.400000); CASDDS; EMDOCS; Genuine Article; KR SourceOne; Linda Hall; SWETS; UMI; UnCover. **CCC.**
  Refereed Serial

632   US   ISSN 0043-1745
SB611   CODEN: WEESA6
WEED SCIENCE. 1952. q. $125. Weed Science Society of America, 1508 W. University, Champaign, IL 61821-3133. TEL 217-352-4212. FAX 217-352-4241. Ed. R.J. Aldrich. abstr.; bibl.; charts; illus.; index. circ. 3,000. (also avail. in microform from UMI,PMC; reprint service avail. from UMI,ISI) **Indexed:** Agri.Eng.Abstr., ASCA, Bibl.Agri., Bio-Contr.News & Info., Biol.Abstr., Biol.& Agr.Ind., Biotech.Abstr., Chem.Abstr., Cott.& Trop.Fibr.Abstr., Crop Physiol.Abstr., Curr.Adv.Ecol.Sci., Curr.Cont., Environ.Per.Bibl. (1990-1993), Excerp.Med., Farm & Garden Ind., Field Crop Abstr., Forest.Abstr., Geo.Abstr., Helminthol.Abstr., Herb.Abstr., Hort.Abstr., Ind.Sci.Rev., Ind.Vet., Irr.& Drain.Abstr., Maize Abstr., Ocean.Abstr., Plant Breed.Abstr., Plant Grow.Reg.Abstr., Pollut.Abstr., Potato Abstr., Poult.Abstr., Rice Abstr., Sci.Cit.Ind., Seed Abstr., Sel.Water Res.Abstr., Soils & Fert., Sorghum & Millets Abstr., Soyabean Abstr., Triticale Abstr., Trop.Oil Seeds Abstr., Vet.Bull., Weed Abstr., World Agri.Econ.& Rural Sociol.Abstr. **Document type:** academic/scholarly publication.
—BLDSC (9284.450000); CASDDS; CISTI; EMDOCS; Genuine Article; KR SourceOne; Linda Hall; SWETS; UMI; UnCover.
  Formerly: Weeds.
  Description: Covers the science of weeds and other topics related to this science.
  Refereed Serial

WEEKLY MICHIGAN POTATO REPORT. see *AGRICULTURE — Agricultural Economics*

631.4   UK   ISSN 0083-7938
WELSH SOILS DISCUSSION GROUP. REPORT. 1960. a. price varies. Welsh Soils Discussion Group, c/o Dr. D.A. Jenkins, Dept. of Biochemistry and Soil Science, University College of North Wales, Bangor, Gwynedd LL57 2UW, Wales. circ. 250. **Indexed:** Chem.Abstr., Soils & Fert.

633.18   IV
WEST AFRICA RICE DEVELOPMENT ASSOCIATION. ANNUAL REPORT. a. West Africa Rice Development Association, 01 B.P. 2551, Bouake 01, Ivory Coast. TEL 225-634514. FAX 225-634714. E-mail: warda@cgnet.con. **Document type:** corporate report.

AGRICULTURE — CROP PRODUCTION AND SOIL

634 641.345   AT   ISSN 0810-6681
WEST AUSTRALIAN NUT AND TREE CROP ASSOCIATION YEARBOOK. Short title: W A N A T C A Yearbook. 1975. a. Aus.$40 includes Quandong (effective 1997). West Australian Nut & Tree Crop Association (Inc.), P.O. Box 565, Subiaco, W.A. 6008, Australia. FAX 61-9-3881852. E-mail: wanatca@AOl.com.au; URL: http://www.AOl.com.au. circ. 500. **Indexed:** Biol.Abstr., Hort.Abstr.
   Formerly (until 1980): West Australian Nutgrowing Society Yearbook (ISSN 0312-8997)

WESTERN CITRUS REPORT. see *AGRICULTURE — Agricultural Economics*

634   US   ISSN 0043-3764
WESTERN FRUIT GROWER. 1954. m. $15.95. Meister Publishing Co., 37733 Euclid Ave., Willoughby, OH 44094. TEL 216-942-2000; 800-572-7740. FAX 216-942-0662. E-mail: afg-circ@meisterpubl.com. Ed. Gary Acuff. adv. contact: William J. Miller. bk.rev.; illus.; mkt.; stat. circ. 26,000. (reprint service avail. from UMI) **Document type:** trade publication.

630 658   US   ISSN 0043-3799
WESTERN GROWER AND SHIPPER; the business magazine of the Western produce industry. Short title: W G & S. 1929. m. $18 (effective 1997). (Western Growers Association) Western Grower and Shipper Publishing Co., Box 2130, Newport Beach, CA 92658. TEL 714-863-1000. FAX 714-863-9028. Ed. Heather Flower. adv. contact: Tom Fielding. charts; illus. circ. 5,000. **Document type:** trade publication.
   ●Also available online. Vendor(s): Knight-Ridder Information, Inc.
   —Linda Hall.

WESTERN MELON AND VEGETABLE REPORT. see *AGRICULTURE — Agricultural Economics*

WESTERN POTATO AND ONION REPORT. see *AGRICULTURE — Agricultural Economics*

634.11   US   ISSN 0043-4701
WHEAT LIFE. 1956. m. (11/yr.). $12. Washington Association of Wheat Growers, 109 E. First Ave., Ritzville, WA 99169-2394. TEL 509-659-0610. Ed. David A. Andersen. adv.; mkt. circ. 14,100. (tabloid format)

338.1   CN   ISSN 0829-4763
WHEATGROWER. 1974. 2/yr. membership. Western Canadian Wheat Growers Association, 1836 Victoria Ave., E., Regina, SK S4N 7K3, Canada. TEL 306-586-5866. FAX 306-586-2707. Ed. Alanna Koch. adv.; bk.rev.; illus.; tr.lit. circ. 7,000. **Document type:** newsletter.
   Former titles (until 1985): Palliser Wheatgrower; Palliser Wheat Growers Association. Newsletter (ISSN 0704-1349)
   Description: Informs members of policy developments in the western Canadian grain industry.

630   US
WILEY SERIES IN GEOTECHNICAL ENGINEERING. 1951. irreg., latest 1993. price varies. John Wiley & Sons, Inc., 605 Third Ave., New York, NY 10158. TEL 212-850-6000. FAX 212-850-6088. TELEX 12-7063. Eds. T. William Lambe, Robert V. Whitman. **Document type:** monographic series.
   Former titles: Series in Geotechnical Engineering; Soil Engineering Series.
   Refereed Serial

WINES AND VINES; the authoritative voice of the grape and wine industry. see *BEVERAGES*

634.8   AU   ISSN 0043-5953
DER WINZER. 1945. m. S.590 (foreign S.730). (Bundesverband der Weinbautreibenden Oesterreichs) Oesterreichischer Agrarverlag GmbH, Inkustr. 1-7, A-3400 Klosterneuburg, Austria. TEL 02243-333006. FAX 02243-3330056. Ed. Hans Weiss. adv.; bk.rev.; illus. circ. 23,000.

**631.4   GW   ISSN 0049-7711
CODEN: WIFUAB**
DAS WIRTSCHAFTSEIGENE FUTTER; Erzeugung-Konservierung-Verwertung. (Text in German; summaries in English, French, German) 1955. 3/yr. DM.148 (foreign DM.151) (effective 1996). (Deutsche Landwirtschafts-Gesellschaft e.V.) D L G Verlags GmbH, Eschborner Landstr. 122, 60489 Frankfurt a.M., Germany. TEL 069-24788-0. FAX 069-24788480. Ed. Dr. Staudacher. adv.; bk.rev.; charts; illus. circ. 800. **Indexed:** Biol.Abstr., Chem.Abstr., Dairy Sci.Abstr., Excerp.Med., Field Crop Abstr., Herb.Abstr., Maize Abstr., Nutr.Abstr., Plant Breed.Abstr., Seed Abstr., Soils & Fert., Soyabean Abstr., Triticale Abstr., Weed Abstr. **Document type:** trade publication.
   —BLDSC (9325.553000); CASDDS. **CCC.**

633 338.1   US
WORLD COTTON SITUATION. m. $30. U.S. Department of Agriculture, Foreign Agricultural Service, Information Division, Rm. 5920-S, Washington, DC 20250-1000. TEL 202-720-7937. index. (also avail. in microfiche from CIS; back issues avail.; reprint service avail. from CIS) **Indexed:** Amer.Stat.Ind. (1981-). **Document type:** government publication.
   ●Also available online. Vendor(s): Information Access Co.

631 595.7   NE
WORLD CROP PESTS. (Text in English) 1985. irreg., vol.5, 1991. price varies. Elsevier Science B.V., Books Division, P.O. Box 211, 1000 AE Amsterdam, Netherlands. TEL 31-20-4853911. FAX 31-20-4853705. TELEX 18582 ESPA NL. E-mail: nlinfo-f@elsevier.nl; usinfo-f@elsevier.com; forinfo-kyf04035@niftyserve.or.jp; URL: http://www.elsevier.nl/. (Subscr. in the Americas to: Elsevier Science, Regional Sales Office, Box 945, New York, NY 10159-0945. TEL 212-633-3730. FAX 212-633-3680; Subscr. in Australasia and the Far East to: Elsevier Science (Singapore) Pte Ltd, No.1 Temasek Ave., No.17-01 Millenia Tower, Singapore 039192, Singapore. TEL 65-434-3727. FAX 65-337-2230; Subscr. in Japan to: Elsevier Science Japan, 9-15 Higashi-Azabu 1-chome, Minato-ku, Tokyo 106, Japan. TEL 81-3-5561-5033. FAX 81-3-5561-5047) (back issues avail.) **Document type:** monographic series.
   Refereed Serial

WORLD DIRECTORY OF AGROBIOLOGICALS. see *CHEMISTRY — Organic Chemistry*

661   UK
WORLD DIRECTORY OF FERTILIZER MANUFACTURERS. irreg., 9th ed., 1996. £260($400) (effective May 1997). British Sulphur Publishing (Subsidiary of: C R U Publishing Ltd.), 31 Mount Pleasant, London WC1X 0AD, England. TEL 44-171-837-5600. FAX 44-171-837-0292. TELEX 918918 SULFEX G. Pub. John French. R&P contact: John French. **Document type:** directory.

661   UK
WORLD DIRECTORY OF FERTILIZER PRODUCTS. irreg., 10th edition, 1997. £250($400) British Sulphur Publishing (Subsidiary of: C R U Publishing Ltd.), 31 Mount Pleasant, London WC1X 0AD, England. TEL 44-171-837-5600. FAX 44-171-837-0292. TELEX 918918 SULFEX G. Pub. John French. R&P contact: John French. **Document type:** directory.

632.97 628.96   UK
WORLD DIRECTORY OF PESTICIDE CONTROL ORGANISATIONS. irreg 3rd ed., 1996. £49.50. The Royal Society of Chemistry, Thomas Graham House, Science Park, Milton Rd., Cambridge CB4 4WF, England. TEL 44-1223-420066. FAX 44-1223-423623. E-mail: sales@rsc.org; URL: http://chemistry.rsc.org/rsc/. (Dist. by: Turpin Distribution Services Ltd., Blackhorse Rd., Letchworth, Herts SG6 1HN, England. TEL 44-1462-672555. FAX 44-1462-480947; Subscr. in N. America to: ACS, 1155 Sixteenth St., N.W., Washington, DC 22036, USA. TEL 202-776-8100. FAX 202-872-6067) Ed. George Ekstroem. **Document type:** directory.
   Description: Lists groups and government agencies worldwide involved in the control of pesticides.

631.8   UK   ISSN 0512-2953
WORLD FERTILIZER PLANT LIST AND ATLAS. 1964. irreg., 11th ed. 1997. £260($400) British Sulphur Publishing (Subsidiary of: C R U Publishing Ltd.), 31 Mount Pleasant, London WC1X 0AD, England. TEL 44-171-837-5600. FAX 44-171-837-0292. TELEX 918918 SULFEX G. Pub. John French. R&P contact: John French. **Document type:** directory.

631   UK   ISSN 0142-5757
WORLD SUGAR JOURNAL.* 1978. m. $280. NG Osman & Assoc. Ltd., Sugerama, One Murdoch Rd., Wokingham, Berks. RG 11 2DL, England. Ed. N.G. Osman. adv.; bk.rev.

633.6 664.1   JA   ISSN 0049-8149
WORLD SUGAR NEWS/KAIGAI SATO JOHO. (Text in Japanese) 1962. bi-m. membership. Japan Sugar Refiners' Association - Seito Kogyokai, 5-5 Sanbancho, Chiyoda-ku, Tokyo 102, Japan. stat. circ. 600.

631   UK
WORLD SULPHUR & SULPHURIC ACID PLANT LIST & ATLAS. irreg., 7th ed., 1995. £250($395) British Sulphur Publishing (Subsidiary of: C R U Publishing Ltd.), 31 Mount Pleasant, London WC1X 0AD, England. TEL 44-171-837-5600. FAX 44-171-837-0292. TELEX 918918 SULFEX G. Ed. Kevin Cunningham; Pub. John French. R&P contact: John French. (back issues avail.) **Document type:** directory.
   Description: Contains essential data for the sulfur and sulfuric acid industries.

634.8   SA   ISSN 0043-9657
WYNBOER; a magazine for wine-lovers, wine-growers and those interested in good living - tydskrif vir wynliefhebbers, wynboere en almal geinteresseerd in wellewendheid. (Text in Afrikaans, English) 1931. m. R.130. Kooperatieve Wijnbouwers Vereniging van S.A. Bpk. (KWV), Main St., P.O. Box 528, Suider Paarl 7624, South Africa. TEL 27-21-8073304. FAX 27-21-8631562. E-mail: ridderd@kwv.co.za. Ed. Henry C.K. Hopkins. R&P contact: Henry C.K. Hopkins. adv. contact: Sue Smith. bk.rev.; illus.; mkt.; stat.; index. circ. 7,663. **Indexed:** Food Sci.& Tech.Abstr., Ind.S.A.Per., VITIS. **Document type:** trade publication.

632   JA   ISSN 0049-8335
YOKOHAMA PLANT PROTECTION NEWS/YOKOHAMA SHOKUBUTSU BOEKI NYUSU. (Text in Japanese) 1952. s-m. free. Yokohama Plant Protection Station - Norin-sho Yokohama Shokubutsu Boekisho, 5-57 Kita-Naka-dori, Naka-ku, Yokohama 231, Japan. Ed. Keiji Sawada. charts; illus.; stat.; index. circ. 2,000. (looseleaf format)

631   ZA
ZAMBIA. DEPARTMENT OF AGRICULTURE. RESEARCH AND SPECIALIST SERVICES. ANNUAL REPORT. a. free. Department of Agriculture, Research Branch, Principal Research Officer, Mount Makulu Research Sta., Private Bag 7, Chilanga, Zambia. circ. 2,000. **Document type:** government publication.

631.4   ZA
ZAMBIA. MINISTRY OF AGRICULTURE AND WATER DEVELOPMENT. LAND USE BRANCH. SOIL SURVEY REPORT. (Text in English) 1967. irreg. exchange basis. Ministry of Agriculture and Water Development, Land Use Branch, c/o Soil Survey Unit, Mount Makulu Research Station, Private Bag 7, Chilanga, Zambia. TEL 260-1-278087. (Co-sponsor: Norwegian Agency for International Development) circ. controlled. **Document type:** government publication.
   Formerly: Zambia. Ministry of Lands and Agriculture. Land Use Branch. Soil Survey Report.

AGRICULTURE — DAIRYING AND DAIRY PRODUCTS

632   RU   ISSN 0044-1864
CODEN: ZSRSBX
ZASHCHITA RASTENII. 1932. m. $94 (effective 1998). Izdatel'stvo Kolos, Sadovaya-Spasskaya, 18, 107807 Moscow, Russia. TEL 7-095-2072130. FAX 7-095-2072140. (Dist. by: Mezhdunarodnaya Kniga, B. Yakimanka 39, 117049 Moscow, Russia. TEL 7-095-2384967. FAX 7-095-2384634) Ed. V.E. Savzdarg. index. circ. 64,000. **Indexed:** Apic.Abstr., Bio-Contr.News & Info., Biodet.Abstr., Biol.Abstr., Biotech.Abstr., Chem.Abstr., Cott.& Trop.Fibr.Abstr., Field Crop Abstr., Forest.Abstr., Herb.Abstr., Hort.Abstr., Maize Abstr., Ornam.Hort., Plant Grow.Reg.Abstr., Potato Abstr., Rev.Appl.Entomol., Rev.Plant Path., Rice Abstr., Seed Abstr., Triticale Abstr., Weed Abstr.
—CASDDS.

631.7   GW   ISSN 0049-8602
S612   CODEN: ZBEWDX
ZEITSCHRIFT FUER BEWAESSERUNGSWIRTSCHAFT. (Text and summaries in English, German) 1966. s-a. DM.9 (members DM.7.20) (effective 1996). D L G Verlags GmbH, Eschborner Landstr. 122, 60489 Frankfurt a.M., Germany. TEL 069-24788-0. FAX 069-24788480. Ed. Dr. Wolff. adv.; bk.rev.; bibl.; illus.; index. circ. 600. **Document type:** trade publication.
—CCC.

ZEITSCHRIFT FUER KULTURTECHNIK UND LANDENTWICKLUNG/JOURNAL OF RURAL ENGINEERING AND DEVELOPMENT. see *ENGINEERING — Civil Engineering*

633   RU   ISSN 0235-2532
S13   CODEN: ZRKZAB
ZERNOVYE KUL'TURY. 1963. q. $53 (effective 1998). Sadovaya-Spasskaya, 18, 107807 Moscow, Russia. (Dist. by: Mazhdunarodnaya Kniga, B. Yakimanka 39, 117049 Moscow, Russia. TEL 7-095-2384967. FAX 7-095-2384634; Dist. in U.S. by: Victor Kamkin Inc., 4956 Boiling Pkwy., Rockville, MD 20852. TEL 301-881-5973. FAX 301-881-1637) Ed. Viktor V. Kasatkin. index. **Indexed:** Field Crop Abstr., Triticale Abstr.
—BLDSC (0072.141000); CASDDS.
Formerly (until 1988): Zernovoe Khozyaistvo (ISSN 0372-9893)

632.9   CC   ISSN 1004-7255
ZHIBAO JISHU YU TUIGUANG. (Text in Chinese) 1981. q. Quanguo Zhiwu Baohu Zongzhan - National Plant Protection Station, 11 Nongzhanguan Nanli, Beijing 100026, People's Republic of China. TEL 5003579. FAX 01-5025146. TELEX 210086 CPPGS CN. Ed. Feng Guichun. adv. **Document type:** academic/scholarly publication.
Formerly (until 1993): Bingchong Cebao (ISSN 1002-4948)

633   CC   ISSN 1000-6346
ZHONGGUO SHUCAI/CHINESE VEGETABLES. (Text in Chinese) 1981. bi-m. $18 (effective 1994). Zhongguo Nongye Kexueyuan, Shucai Huahui Yanjiusuo - Chinese Academy of Agricultural Sciences, Institute of Vegetables and Flowers, 30 Baishiqiao Rd., Beijing 100081, People's Republic of China. TEL 8314433. FAX 8316374. TELEX 222720 CAAS CN. Ed. Li Shude. adv.: color page $3000; adv. contact: Mo Qing. **Document type:** academic/scholarly publication.

631.4   CC   ISSN 1000-0941
ZHONGGUO SHUITU BAOCHI. (Text in Chinese) m. Shuili Bu, Huang He Shuili Weiyuanhui, 11 Jinshui Lu, Zhengzhou, Henan 450003, People's Republic of China. TEL 22971. Ed. Hao Zhifeng.

633   CC   ISSN 1000-8071
ZHONGZI SHIJIE/WORLD OF SEEDS. (Text in Chinese) m. Heilongjiang Sheng Zhongzi Xiehui, 43, Wenchang Jie, Harbin, Heilongjiang 150001, People's Republic of China. TEL 224517. Ed. Guan Xun.

631   RH
ZIMBABWE. COFFEE RESEARCH INSTITUTE. ANNUAL REPORT. PART 2. NYANGA EXPERIMENTAL STATION. 1976. a. free. Ministry of Agriculture, Coffee Research Institute, Marondera, B.P. 3748, Marondera, Zimbabwe. (Subscr. to: P.O. Box 8108, Causeway, Zimbabwe) circ. 300. **Document type:** government publication.
Formerly: Horticultural and Coffee Research Institute. Annual Report. Part 3. Rhodes Experimental Station.

633.51   RH
ZIMBABWE. COTTON RESEARCH INSTITUTE. ANNUAL REPORT. (Text in English) 1969. a. free. Ministry of Lands, Agriculture and Rural Resettlement, Research and Specialist Services, Information Services, P.O. Box 8108, Causeway, Zimbabwe. circ. 300 (controlled). (back issues avail.) **Indexed:** Field Crop Abstr., Herb.Abstr. **Document type:** government publication.

631   RH
ZIMBABWE. MINISTRY OF AGRICULTURE. SEED SERVICES. ANNUAL REPORT. a. free. Ministry of Lands, Agriculture and Rural Resettlement, Research and Specialist Services, Information Services, P.O. Box 8108, Causeway, Harare, Zimbabwe. circ. 250. (back issues avail.) **Indexed:** Biol.Abstr. **Document type:** government publication.

633.6   GW   ISSN 0044-5398
DIE ZUCKERRUEBE. 1952. bi-m. DM.43.80 (foreign DM.55.20) (effective 1997). Verlag Th. Mann, Nordring 10, 45894 Gelsenkirchen, Germany. TEL 49-209-9304184. FAX 49-209-9304185. (Subscr. to: Postfach 200254, 45837 Gelsenkirchen, Germany) Ed. W.C. von Kessel. adv.: B&W page DM.4060, color page DM.7410; trim 186 x 270; adv. contact: Richard Heineke. charts; illus. circ. 22,603. **Indexed:** Field Crop Abstr., Helminthol.Abstr., Herb.Abstr., Soils & Fert., Sugar Ind.Abstr. **Document type:** trade publication.

637   GW
DIE ZUCKERRUEBEN ZEITUNG. 1965. 6/yr. DM.20. Verband Sueddeutscher Zueckerruebenanbauer e.V., Simon-Breu-Str. 52, 97074 Wuerzburg, Germany. TEL 49-931-796950. Ed. Henning Wiedenroth. circ. 37,000. **Document type:** newsletter.
Formerly: Deutsche Zuckerruebenzeitung.

633   CC   ISSN 1000-6435
SB123.3
ZUOWU PINZHONG ZIYUAN/CROP GENETIC RESOURCES. (Text in Chinese) 1982. q. Y10($10) (foreign $10) (effective 1997). Zhongguo Nongye Kexueyuan, Zuowu Pinzhong Ziyuan Yanjiusuo - Chinese Academy of Agricultural Science, Institute of Crop Genetic Resources, 30 Baishiqiao Lu, Beijing 100081, People's Republic of China. TEL 86-10-6218-6657. FAX 86-10-6218-6629. Ed. Li Shenglin. adv. **Document type:** academic/scholarly publication.
—BLDSC (3488.130000).

633   CC   ISSN 0496-3490
CODEN: TSHPA9
ZUOWU XUEBAO/ACTA AGRONOMICA SINICA. (Text in Chinese; summaries in English) 1975. bi-m. (Zhongguo Zuowu Xuehui) Science Press, Marketing and Sales Department, 16 Donghuangchenggen North St., Beijing 100717, People's Republic of China. TEL 86-1-4010642. FAX 86-1-4019810. (Editorial addr.: 30 Baishi Qiao Rd., Beijing 100081, P.R. China; Dist. overseas by: China International Book Trading Corp., P.O. Box 399, Beijing, P.R. China) Ed. Qiaosheng Zhuang. adv. circ. 11,000. **Indexed:** Cott.& Trop.Fibr.Abstr., Crop Physiol.Abstr., Field Crop Abstr., Herb.Abstr., Irr.& Drain.Abstr., Maize Abstr., Plant Grow.Reg.Abstr., Rice Abstr., Seed Abstr., Sorghum & Millets Abstr., Soyabean Abstr., Triticale Abstr., Weed Abstr. **Document type:** academic/scholarly publication.
—BLDSC (0590.400000); Linda Hall.
Description: Publishes research in all areas of crop science.
Refereed Serial

AGRICULTURE — Dairying And Dairy Products

see also Agriculture–Poultry and Livestock

ACTA ACADEMIAE AGRICULTURAE AC TECHNICAE OLSTENENSIS. TECHNOLOGIA ALIMENTORUM/AGRICULTURAL AND TECHNICAL ACADEMY IN OLSZTYN. FOOD TECHNOLOGY. see *FOOD AND FOOD INDUSTRIES*

637   US   ISSN 1056-9537
AGRI-MARK, INC. JOURNAL. 1973. 4/yr. $15. Agri-Mark, Inc., 100 Milk St., Office Park, Methuen, MA 01844. TEL 617-689-4442. (Alt. addr.: Box 5800, Lawrence, MA 01842)
Former titles (until 1986): Agri-Mark Journal (ISSN 0274-9270); (until 1980): Yankeemilk News (ISSN 0161-3537)
Description: Concerned with Northeast and national dairy industries with emphasis on the cooperative members of Agri-Mark. Covers dairy policy legislation and practices with feature stories on Northeast dairy farmers.

637   US
AGRI-MARK MONTHLY. 1980. m. $15. Agri-Mark, Inc., 100 Milk St., Office Park, Methuen, MA 01844. TEL 508-689-4442. (Alt. addr.: Box 5800, Lawrence, MA 01842) Ed. Douglas DiMento. circ. 4,500. **Document type:** newsletter.
Description: Newsletter on Northeast dairying published for the members of the Agri-Mark dairy cooperative. Covers national and regional dairy industry events, legislation, and pricing.

637   US
AGRIBUSINESS DAIRYMAN. 1983. m. $36 (foreign $60) (effective 1997); newsstand price: $4.50. Agribusiness Publications, 612 N St., Sanger, CA 93657. TEL 309-875-4585. FAX 309-875-4587. Ed. John C. Stubbs; Pubs. John C. Stubbs, John Van Nortwick. adv.: B&W page $1270, color page $1930; trim 8 1/4 x 10 3/4. circ. 10,000 (controlled). (back issues avail.) **Document type:** trade publication.
Description: Focuses monthly on different editorial subjects. Coves all the major dairy fairs and expositions.

637.1   US   ISSN 0065-7263
AMERICAN ASSOCIATION OF MEDICAL MILK COMMISSIONS. METHODS AND STANDARDS FOR THE PRODUCTION OF CERTIFIED MILK.* 1909. a. free. American Association of Medical Milk Commissions, Inc., c/o Hopping, Box 1063, Roswell, GA 30077.

637   FR   ISSN 1163-9849
ANNUAIRE DES INDUSTRIES LAITIERES. 1950. a. 980 F. Editions Comindus, 1 rue Descombes, 75017 Paris, France. TEL 1-43-80-79-16. FAX 1-40-53-91-92.
Former titles (until 1991): Annuaire du Lait (ISSN 1154-4538); (until 1990): Annuaire National du Lait (ISSN 0084-6538)

ARCHIVOS DE ZOOTECNIA. see *AGRICULTURE — Poultry And Livestock*

637.1 664.028   SP
ARTE HELADERO. 6/yr. Carmen 4 y 6, 08190 Sant Cugat del Valles (Barcelona), Spain. TEL 3-675-08-11. FAX 3-675-38-61. Ed. Ignacio Corbero. circ. 6,000.

637   AT
AUSTRALIAN DAIRY FARMER. 1977. bi-m. Aus.$24 to individuals; free to members. (Australian Dairy Industry Council) Rural Press Magazines, P.O. Box 160, Port Melbourne, Vic. 3207, Australia. TEL 61-3-92870900. FAX 61-3-92870800. E-mail: adic@dairy.com.au. Ed. Alastair Dowie; Pub. Tim Mannes. R&P contact: Alastair Dowie. adv. contact: Peter Roach. bk.rev. circ. 18,500. **Document type:** trade publication.

636   AT
THE AUSTRALIAN HOLSTEIN JOURNAL. 1906. m. Aus.$60 (foreign Aus.$65) (effective 1996). (Holstein Friesian Association of Australia) Australian Holstein Journal, P.O. Box 6759, Shepparton, Vic. 3632, Australia. TEL 61-58-315205. FAX 61-58-311747. (Subscr. to: HFAA, Private Bag 14, Flemington, Vic. 3031, Australia. TEL 61-3-93761811. FAX 61-3-9372-1394) Ed. Jackie Ekers. adv.: B&W page Aus.$500, color page Aus.$700; adv. contact: June Clark. illus. circ. 3,500. (back issues avail.) **Indexed:** Farm & Garden Ind. **Document type:** trade publication.
Former titles (until 1994): Australian Holstein Dairyman (ISSN 1038-8923); (until 1992): Australian Holstein-Friesian Dairyman (ISSN 1035-0004); Supersedes in part (in 1989): Dairyman (ISSN 0311-9653); Which was formerly: Australian Dairy Journal; Livestock Bulletin (ISSN 0024-5186).
Description: Contains dairy industry information.

AGRICULTURE — DAIRYING AND DAIRY PRODUCTS

637   AT   ISSN 0004-9433
CODEN: AJDTAZ
AUSTRALIAN JOURNAL OF DAIRY TECHNOLOGY. 1945. 2/yr. Aus.$55 (foreign Aus.$75) (effective 1997). Dairy Industry Association of Australia, P.O. Box 8000, Glen Iris, Vic. 3146, Australia, Australia. FAX 61-3-92526555. Ed. H. Deeth. R&P contact: L. Muller. adv. contact: G.E. Bell. bk.rev.; abstr.; charts; illus.; index, cum.index every 10 yrs. circ. 2,000. (also avail. in microfilm from PMC) **Indexed:** Anim.Breed.Abstr., ASCA, Biodet.Abstr., Biol.Abstr., Chem.Abstr., Curr.Adv.Ecol.Sci., Curr.Cont., Curr.Pack.Abstr., Dairy Sci.Abstr., Excerp.Med., Food Sci.& Tech.Abstr., Ind.Sci.Rev., Ind.Vet., Nutr.Abstr., Rural Recreat.Tour.Abstr., Sugar Ind.Abstr., Vet.Bull., World Agri.Econ.& Rural Sociol.Abstr. **Document type:** academic/scholarly publication.
●Also available online. Vendor(s): Knight-Ridder Information, Inc.
—BLDSC (1807.000000); CASDDS; CISTI; Genuine Article; Linda Hall; SWETS; UMI; UnCover.
Refereed Serial

636.234   UK   ISSN 0005-2442
AYRSHIRE CATTLE SOCIETY'S JOURNAL. 1929. s-a. £30 to non-members for 3 yrs. Ayrshire Cattle Society of Great Britain & Ireland, 1 Racecourse Rd., Ayr, Ayrshire KA7 2DE, Scotland. TEL 0292-267123. FAX 01292-611973. Ed. Stuart Thomson. adv.; bk.rev.; illus.; mkt. circ. 4,000. **Indexed:** Dairy Sci.Abstr. **Document type:** trade publication.
Description: Relates to all activities of Ayrshire dairy cow, including genetic improvement, promotion, show and sales.

637   UK
AYRSHIRE DAIRYMAN. 1985. s-a. £10. Ayrshire Cattle Society of Great Britain & Ireland, 1 Racecourse Rd., Ayr, Ayrshire KA7 2DE, Scotland. TEL 01292-267123. FAX 01292-611973. Ed. Stuart Thompson. circ. 2,600. (back issues avail.) **Document type:** newsletter.
Description: Presents farm features, show and sales reports, and other dairy-related information for dairy farmers, advisors, and colleges.

637   US   ISSN 0005-2450
AYRSHIRE DIGEST. 1912. bi-m. $14 (Canada $20). Ayrshire Breeders' Association, Box 1608, Brattleboro, VT 05302-1608. TEL 802-247-7460. FAX 802-254-8251. Ed. Joanie Richardson; Pub. Becky Payne. adv. contact: Bonnie Wentworth. bk.rev.; illus.; stat. circ. 2,000. **Document type:** trade publication.
Description: Details cattle breeding.

637   UK
THE AYRSHIRE JOURNAL. 1928. s-a. £10. Ayrshire Society of Great Britain & Ireland, 1 Racecourse Rd., Ayr KA7 2DE, Scotland. TEL 0292-267123. FAX 0292-611973. circ. 2,500.
Description: Covers information about the Ayrshire breed of dairy cow.

630   BL   ISSN 0005-4275
BALDE BRANCO. 1964. m. Cr.$10200. Cooperativa Central de Laticinios do Estado de Sao Paulo, Rua Gomes Cardim 532, 03050 Sao Paulo, SP, Brazil. Ed. Luiza Roxo Pimentel. adv.; bk.rev.; illus.; circ. 30,000 (controlled).

636   CN
BELL/CLOCHE. (Text in English and French) 1983. q. Can.$16 (foreign Can.$28). Canadian Brown Swiss and Braunvieh Association, 9-350 Speedvale Ave. W., Guelph, ON M1H 7M7, Canada. TEL 519-821-2811. FAX 519-821-2273. adv. circ. 500. **Document type:** newsletter.
Description: Covers the dairy industry, genetics, artificial insemination, embryo transfer, dairy products.

637   DK
BOVILOGISK TIDSSKRIFT KVAEGET. 1987. m. DKK 425 (effective 1997). Dansk Agrar Forlag A-S, Tagtaekkervej 8, DK-523- Odense M, Denmark. TEL 45-66-15-60-87. FAX 45-66-60-37. Ed. Knud E. Madsen. circ. 3,500.
Description: Covers subjects of interest to dairy farmers.

637   AT   ISSN 0815-9777
BRITISH ALPINE BREEDERS GROUP OF AUSTRALIA. NEWSLETTER. 1972. q. Aus.$6. British Alpine Breeders Group of Australia, RMB 8680, Bannockburn, Vic. 3331, Australia. Ed. P.C. Keays. adv.; bk.rev. circ. 50. (back issues avail.) **Document type:** newsletter.

637   UK   ISSN 0955-3614
BRITISH HOLSTEIN SOCIETY JOURNAL. 1975. 5/yr. £18 (foreign £25). British Holstein Society, Foley House, 28 Worcester Rd., Malvern, Worcs. WR14 4YY, England. TEL 44-1684-565477. FAX 44-1684-893290. Ed. Martin Hall. R&P contact: Martin Hall. adv. contact: Martin Hall. circ. 3,500. **Document type:** trade publication.
Description: Contains news and information on the society and its activities of interest to members. Publishes articles related to the breeding of Holstein cattle, along with their management and feeding. Announces awards.

637   US   ISSN 0007-2516
BROWN SWISS BULLETIN. 1922. m. $15 (foreign $30). Brown Swiss Cattle Breeders Association of U.S.A., 800 Pleasant St., Box 1038, Beloit, WI 53512-1038. TEL 608-365-4474. FAX 608-365-5577. Ed. Connie Gritton. adv. circ. 3,000. **Document type:** trade publication.
—Linda Hall; UnCover.
Description: Contains stories and information on Brown Swiss breed, breeders, meetings, shows and sales reports.

BROWSE. see *AGRICULTURE — Poultry And Livestock*

637 658.8   UK   ISSN 0269-0861
BUSINESS RATIO REPORT: DAIRY PRODUCE; an industry sector analysis. 1986. a. I C C Business Ratios Ltd., Freepost, Field House, Hampton, Mddx. TW12 1BR, England. TEL 081-783-0977. FAX 081-783-1940. charts; stat. **Document type:** trade publication.

637.12   CN   ISSN 0007-7275
BUTTER-FAT. 1923. 4/yr. Can.$8 to non-members; members Can.$5. Agrifoods International Cooperative Ltd., P.O. Box 9100, Vancouver, BC V6B 4G4, Canada. TEL 604-420-6611. FAX 604-520-1626. Ed. G.M. Chadsey. adv.; bk.rev.; charts; illus.; stat. circ. 1,750. **Indexed:** Dairy Sci.Abstr. **Document type:** trade publication.
Description: Informs members of activities in the co-op and dairy industries.

CALIFORNIA DAIRY INFORMATION BULLETIN. see *AGRICULTURE — Abstracting, Bibliographies, Statistics*

637   CN   ISSN 1205-0040
CODEN: MDRYA6
CANADIAN DAIRY; Canada's business magazine for dairy processors & distributors. (Includes Annual Buyers Guide) 1923. 5/yr. Can.$30 (U.S. & U.K. Can.$40; elsewhere Can.$50) (effective 1997-1998). Maccan Publishing Company Ltd., 3269 Bloor St. W., Ste. 205, Toronto, ON M8X 1E2, Canada. TEL 416-239-8423. URL: http://www.inforamp.net/~dbattler. Ed. Iain Macnab; Pub. Iain Macnab. R&P contact: Iain Macnab. TEL 416-239-8423. adv.: B&W page Can.$1290, color page Can.$2065; adv. contact: Iain Macnab. illus.; tr.lit. circ. 2,023. (back issues avail.) **Indexed:** Biol.Abstr., Curr.Pack.Abstr., Dairy Sci.Abstr., Food Sci.& Tech.Abstr. **Document type:** trade publication.
—CISTI. CCC.
Former titles (until 1995): Modern Dairy (ISSN 0026-7651); (until 1968): Canadian Dairy and Ice Cream Journal (ISSN 0366-5658)

637   BL   ISSN 0100-7904
CENTRO NACIONAL DE PESQUISA DE GADO DE LEITE. RELATORIO TECNICO. 1978. irreg. Centro Nacional de Pesquisa de Gado de Leite, Rodovia MG 133, km 42, 36155 Coronel Pacheco MG, Brazil. TEL 55-32-2158550. FAX 55-32-2158550. circ. 3,000.
—BLDSC (7354.106300).

CHANGING HORIZONS. see *AGRICULTURE — Agricultural Economics*

338.1   US   ISSN 0891-1509
CODEN: CHMNE6
CHEESE MARKET NEWS. 1981. w. $78 (Canada $120; elsewhere $285) (effective Oct. 1996). Cahners Publishing Company (Middleton), Division of Reed Elsevier Inc., Box 620244, Middleton, WI 53562. TEL 608-831-6002. FAX 608-831-1004. E-mail: chmarknews@aol.com; URL: http://www.cahners.com/mainmag/cmn.htm. Ed. Heather Lee Schroeder; Pub. Susan K. Quarne. R&P contact: Susan K. Quarne. adv. contact: Susan K. Quarne. bk.rev.; tr.lit.; illus.; circ. 2,500 (paid). (tabloid format; back issues avail.) **Document type:** trade publication.
—CCC.
Supersedes (1981-1986): National Dairy News (ISSN 0279-2508)
Description: Covers vital decision-making information for the cheese and dairy/deli business.

637.3   US   ISSN 0009-2142
CODEN: CHERA8
CHEESE REPORTER. 1876. w. $75 (foreign air mail $200) (effective 1997). Cheese Reporter Publishing Co., Inc., 4210 E. Washington Ave., Madison, WI 53704-3742. TEL 608-246-8430. FAX 608-246-8431. E-mail: cheesreprt@aol.com; URL: http://www.cheesereporter.com. Ed. Richard Groves; Pub. Richard Groves. R&P contact: Kevin Thome. adv. contact: Kevin Thome. bk.rev.; illus.; circ. 2,250 (paid). (tabloid format) **Indexed:** Food Sci.& Tech.Abstr. **Document type:** trade publication.
Description: Key price and production trends, indicators and analysis; legislation and regulatory initiatives affecting the dairy industry; analysis of current events; consumer trends and industry response; industry events and company and personnel transitions.

637.4   US
CHIMES (SUDBURY). q. International Association of Ice Cream Vendors, 1900 Arch St., Philadelphia, PA 19103-1498. Ed. Dale Zeigler. circ. 250 (paid). **Document type:** newsletter.

COATES'S HERD BOOK (BEEF). see *AGRICULTURE — Poultry And Livestock*

637   UK   ISSN 0069-4932
COATES'S HERD BOOK (DAIRY). 1822. a. £10($20) Shorthorn Society of Great Britain and Ireland, 4th St. National Agricultural Centre, Stoneleigh Park, Kenilworth, Warwickshire CV8 2LG, England. TEL 44-1203-696549. FAX 44-1203-696729. Ed. J. Wood Roberts. circ. 700. **Document type:** trade publication.

637   US
CREAM SEPARATOR AND DAIRY NEWSLETTER. bi-m. $15. Cream and Dairy Collector Association, Rte. 3, Arcadia, WI 54612. TEL 608-323-7470. Ed. Paul Dettloff Dum. adv.; circ. 250 (paid). (back issues avail.) **Document type:** newsletter.

637   FR   ISSN 1141-7730
CREMIER FROMAGER. 1989. 9/yr. 300 F. E P R I M, 60 bis, rue de l'Hermitage, 95300 Pontoise, France. TEL 30-38-30-77. FAX 30-73-05-97. Ed. Samy Kerkeny; Pub. Jacques Boursier. R&P contact: Yves Roux. adv. contact: Marjorie Leveque. bk.rev. circ. 6,000.

637   US   ISSN 0045-9259
CODEN: CDPJDE
CULTURED DAIRY PRODUCTS JOURNAL.* 1966. q. $10. American Cultured Dairy Products Institute, c/o Mississippi State Univ., Food Science Dept., P.O. Drawer NH, Mississippi State, MS 39762. adv.; bk.rev.; abstr.; charts; illus. circ. 1,500. **Indexed:** Biodet.Abstr., Chem.Abstr., Curr.Pack.Abstr., Dairy Sci.Abstr., Food Sci.& Tech.Abstr., Ind.Vet., Rural Recreat.Tour.Abstr., World Agri.Econ. & Rural Sociol.Abstr.
—CASDDS; Linda Hall; UnCover.

636.234   UK
D A I S Y - THE DAIRY INFORMATION SYSTEM. no.2, 1994. irreg. University of Reading, Department of Agriculture, Earley Gate, Reading, Berks. RG6 6AT, England. Ed. R.J. Esslemont. adv. contact: R.J. Esslemont. **Document type:** academic/scholarly publication.
Description: Covers the veterinary and economic aspects of raising dairy cows.

AGRICULTURE — DAIRYING AND DAIRY PRODUCTS

637 GW ISSN 0938-9369
CODEN: DMZEAI
D M Z - LEBENSMITTELINDUSTRIE UND MILCHWIRTSCHAFT; magazine for food and dairy industry. 1878. w. DM.355 (foreign DM.386) (effective 1997). Volkswirtschaftlicher Verlag (VV GmbH), Kederbacherstr. 50, 81377 Munich, Germany. TEL 49-89-7141013. FAX 49-89-7192753. Ed. Simone Ostertag. adv. contact: Inge Seifert. circ. 3,470. (back issues avail.) **Indexed:** Anim.Breed.Abstr., Dairy Sci.Abstr., Food Sci.& Tech.Abstr., Ind.Vet., INIS Atomind., Packag.Sci.Tech., Vet.Bull., World Agri.Econ.& Rural Sociol.Abstr. **Document type:** trade publication.
—BLDSC (3605.718100); CASDDS. **CCC**.
Formerly: Deutsche Molkerei-Zeitung (ISSN 0366-9424)

338.1 631 US
DAIRY AND FIELD CROP DIGEST. 1970. bi-m. Regional Cooperative Extension Dairy Program, 208 Broadway, Montour Falls, NY 14865. TEL 607-535-7161. Ed. William J. Menzi, Jr.

637 IE ISSN 0790-732X
DAIRY EXECUTIVE. 1903. bi-m. I£15. Dairy Executives' Association, 33 Kildare St., Dublin 2, Ireland. Ed. Kyran Lynch. adv.; stat. circ. 2,000. **Document type:** trade publication.
Formerly: Irish Agricultural and Creamery Review (ISSN 0021-1036)

637 IE
DAIRY EXECUTIVE. DIRECTORY AND DIARY. 1906. a. I£50 per issue. Dairy Executives' Association, 33 Kildare St., Dublin 2, Ireland. Ed. Kyran Lynch. adv.; bk.rev. circ. 2,000. **Document type:** directory.
Former titles: Irish Creamery Managers' Association. Creamery Directory and Diary; Irish Creamery Managers' Association. Creamery Yearbook and Diary (ISSN 0075-0751)

637 UK ISSN 0011-5576
DAIRY FARMER. (Supplement avail.: S W Dairy Farmer) 1929. m. £30($100) (Eire £42) (effective 1996). Miller Freeman Professional Ltd. (Subsidiary of: Miller Freeman plc), 2 Wharfedale Rd., Ipswich, Suffolk IP1 4LG, England. TEL 44-1473-241122. FAX 44-1473-240501. Ed. Graeme Kirk. adv. contact: John M. Welford. bk.rev.; charts; illus.; mkt.; pat.; tr.lit.; tr.mk. circ. 25,732. **Indexed:** Agri.Eng.Abstr., Dairy Sci.Abstr., Ind.Vet. **Document type:** trade publication.
—BLDSC (3514.695000).
Description: Topics of interest to farmers and farm managers who raise dairy cows in Great Britain.

637 US ISSN 1055-0607
TX795.A1 CODEN: DAFIEK
DAIRY FIELD; the how-to magazine for dairy processor growth. (Annual Buyers Guide avail.) 1905. m. $55 (foreign $110); free to qualified personnel (effective 1996). Stagnito Publishing Company, 1935 Shermer Rd., Ste. 100, Northbrook, IL 60062. TEL 847-205-5660. FAX 847-205-5680. Ed. Susan Ruland; Pub. Harry Stagnito. R&P contact: Susan Ruland. adv. contact: Sophia Giannakopoulos. illus.; tr.lit.; circ. 18,000 (controlled). **Indexed:** Biol.Abstr., Chem.Abstr., Curr.Pack.Abstr., Dairy Sci.Abstr., Food Sci.& Tech.Abstr., Rural Recreat.Tour.Abstr., World Agri.Econ.& Rural Sociol.Abstr. **Document type:** trade publication.
—BLDSC (3514.710000); Linda Hall; UMI; UnCover.
Former titles (until 1991): Dairy Field Today (ISSN 1053-9425); (until 1990): Dairy Field (ISSN 0198-9995); (until 1979): Dairy and Ice Cream Field (ISSN 0011-555X); (until 1967): Ice Cream Field and Ice Cream Trade Journal (ISSN 0536-2598); Which was formed by the merger of (1922-1965): Ice Cream Field (ISSN 0096-2546); And (1905-1965): Ice Cream Trade Journal (ISSN 0096-2031); Incorporates (1917-1968): Ice Cream Review (ISSN 0096-2023) & (1911-1968): Milk Dealer (ISSN 0097-3289); Which incorporated (in 1967): Manufactured Milk Products Journal (ISSN 0099-5258); Which had former titles (until 1962): Milk Products Journal (ISSN 0099-7099); (until 1953): Butter, Cheese and Milk Products Journal (ISSN 0099-510X); (until 1950): National Butter and Cheese Journal (ISSN 0099-5320); (until 1936): National Butter Journal (ISSN 0099-7625); (until 1930): Butter and Cheese Journal (ISSN 0099-7412); (until 1928): Butter Cheese and Egg Journal (ISSN 0735-0902).
Description: Contains articles of interest to executives and department heads in the dairy processing industry.

DAIRY, FOOD AND ENVIRONMENTAL SANITATION; a publication for sanitarians and fieldmen. see *PUBLIC HEALTH AND SAFETY*

DAIRY FOODS; innovative ideas and technologies for dairy processors. see *FOOD AND FOOD INDUSTRIES*

637 US
DAIRY FOODS NEWSLETTER. 1959-19??; resumed 1985. w. $279 (foreign $329.90). Cahners Publishing Company (Des Plaines), Division of Reed Elsevier Inc., 1350 E. Touhy Ave., Box 5080, Des Plaines, IL 60018-5080. TEL 847-635-8800. FAX 847-390-2445. Ed. Peggy Anderson. circ. 800. (also avail. in microform from UMI; reprint service avail. from UMI) **Indexed:** BPIA. **Document type:** newsletter, trade publication.
—CCC.
Former titles (until 1989): Dairy Industry Newsletter; (until 1975): Dairy, Natural and Dietary Food Industry Newsletter (ISSN 0011-5657)
Description: Covers mergers and acquisitions, company earnings, new products, marketing strategy, dairy market statistics and government regulations.

637 CN ISSN 0011-5606
DAIRY GUIDE. Bound with: Country Guide (ISSN 0383-7114) 1970. 10/yr. Farm Business Communications, Box 6600, Winnipeg, MB R3C 3A7, Canada. TEL 204-944-5761. FAX 204-942-8463. Ed. Gren Winslon. adv. contact: Tom Mumby. bk.rev. circ. 18,333. (also avail. in microfilm) **Document type:** trade publication.

637 II ISSN 0970-3438
DAIRY GUIDE. (Text in English) 1978. q. Rs.200. C. P. Narang (Pvt.) Ltd., 1700-IV, Urban Estate, Gurgaon 122 001, India. TEL 91-124-320728. FAX 91-124-327400. Ed. Ricky Thaper. adv.; page Rs.1000; trim 140 x 190. bk.rev. circ. 7,300. **Document type:** trade publication.

636.234 US ISSN 0011-5614
DAIRY HERD MANAGEMENT; the business magazine for top dairy farmers. 1965. m. $25 (foreign $50) (effective 1997). Vance Publishing Corporation (Lenexa), 10901 W. 84th Terr., Ste. 200, Lenexa, KS 66214-1631. TEL 913-438-8700. FAX 913-438-0695. adv.; abstr.; charts; illus.; stat. circ. 96,007. (also avail. in microform from UMI; reprint service avail. from UMI) **Indexed:** Biol. & Agr.Ind., Dairy Sci.Abstr., Farm & Garden Ind., Ind.Vet. **Document type:** trade publication.
—UMI; UnCover. **CCC.**

637 II ISSN 0970-9932
DAIRY INDIA YEARBOOK. (Text in English) 1983. irreg. $295. P.R. Gupta, Pub., A-25 Priyadarshini Vihar, Delhi 110 092, India. TEL 91-11-2243326. FAX 91-11-2243039. E-mail: yearbook@giasdl01.vsnl.net.in. Ed. Sharad Gupta. adv.; circ. 2,500 (paid). **Indexed:** Anim.Breed.Abstr., Dairy Sci.Abstr.
—BLDSC (3514.950000).
Description: Sourcebook on trade technical and economic aspects of dairying. 7000 specialists and organizations are listed by business name and geographic location.

637 AT ISSN 0810-4115
DAIRY INDUSTRY LEADER. 1972. bi-m. free. New South Wales Dairy Corporation, P.O. Box A2613, Sydney S., N.S.W. 1235, Australia. FAX 61-2-92612434. adv. circ. 5,000. **Indexed:** Dairy Sci.Abstr. **Document type:** trade publication.
Formerly (until 1982): New South Wales Dairyman (ISSN 0310-3714)

637 US
DAIRY: LATIN AMERICAN INDUSTRIAL REPORT. (Avail. for each of 22 Latin American countries) 1985. a. $435 per country report. Aquino Productions, Box 125, Rochester, VT 05767. Ed. Andres C. Aquino.

637.1 SA
DAIRY MAIL. (Text in Afrikaans, English) 1964. m. Milk Board - Melkraad, P.O. Box 1284, Pretoria 0001, South Africa. TEL 27-12-8044800. FAX 27-12-8044811. Ed. Hennie Basson. adv. contact: Gerhard van der Merwe. charts; illus.; stat.; index. circ. 10,000. **Indexed:** Dairy Sci.Abstr. **Document type:** newsletter.
Formerly (until 1994): Milk Producer (ISSN 0026-4199)

637 UK ISSN 0957-8625
DAIRY MARKETS WEEKLY. w. £435 (rest of Europe £470; elsewhere £525) (by fax: £560; rest of Europe £635; elsewhere £800) (effective 1997). Agra Europe (London) Ltd., 25 Frant Rd., Tunbridge Wells, Kent TN2 5JT, England. TEL 44-1892-533813. FAX 44-1892-544895. TELEX 95114 AGRATW G. E-mail: 100637.3460@compuserve.com. (also avail. by fax) **Document type:** trade publication.
●Also available online. Vendor(s): Information Access Co.
Description: Reports the latest figures on European dairy prices and production and the important trade and company news of the week.

637 IE
DAIRY NEWS. 4/yr. Bord Bainne, Grattan House, Mount St., Dublin 2, Ireland. TEL 619599. FAX 612788. TELEX 93615. Ed. Aidan McCarthy.

330 CN ISSN 0318-2967
DAIRY POLICY. (Text in English and French) a. free. Dairy Farmers of Canada, 75 Albert St., Ste. 1101, Ottawa, ON K1P 5E7, Canada.
Description: Policy statement of Dairy Farmers of Canada, developed by Canadian milk producers as basis for future lobbying activity.

637 US
DAIRY PRODUCER. (Supplement to several Farm Progress Publications titles) 1990. 10/yr. $17.95. Farm Progress Companies (Subsidiary of: A B C Publishing Companies), 191 S. Gary Ave., Carol Stream, IL 60188. TEL 708-690-5600. FAX 708-462-2869. Ed. Stevie Kenyon; Pub. Allan Johnson. adv. circ. 101,248. **Document type:** trade publication.
Description: Covers dairy practices and marketing. Features successful producers in the Great Lakes, Northeast and West dairy regions.

637 US
DAIRY PRODUCER HIGHLIGHTS. 1950. a. $1. National Milk Producers Federation, 1840 Wilson Blvd., Arlington, VA 22201. TEL 703-243-6111. FAX 703-841-9328. Ed. Michael Brown. charts; stat. circ. 5,000.
Description: Includes statistics on the dairy industry from farm to consumer, covering production, processing and consumption of milk, with information on Federal programs affecting the industry.

AGRICULTURE — DAIRYING AND DAIRY PRODUCTS

637.1   664   658.8   UK
DAIRY PRODUCTS: THE INTERNATIONAL MARKET. (Subseries of: Market Direction reports) a. £2500($5000) (effective 1997). Euromonitor, 60-61 Britton St., London EC1M 5NA, England. TEL 44-171-251-8024. FAX 44-171-608-3149. E-mail: info@euromonitor.com; URL: http://www.euromonitor.com. (Addr. in N. America: Euromonitor International, 122 S. Michigan Ave., Ste. 1200, Chicago, IL 60603. TEL 800-577-3876. FAX 312-922-1157) (looseleaf format) **Document type:** trade publication.
●Also available online. Vendor(s): Data-Star, Knight-Ridder Information, Inc.
   Description: Analyzes the markets for dairy products for France, Germany, Italy, Spain, the U.K., the U.S., Japan, and Canada.

637   US
DAIRY ROUNDUP. 1973. a. free. Kent Feeds, Inc., 1600 Oregon St., Muscatine, IA 52761. TEL 319-264-4211. (tabloid format)

637   US   ISSN 1056-1382
DAIRY TODAY. 1985. 10/yr. Farm Journal, Inc., 1500 Market St., Philadelphia, PA 19102-2181. TEL 612-271-3363. Ed. Jim Dickrell. adv. circ. 128,021. **Document type:** trade publication.
   Formerly: Dairy Extra.
   Description: Contains information on changes in federal regulations, marketing data and insight related to the industry.

637   US   ISSN 0736-4962
DAIRY WORLD. 1967. bi-m. $12. Independent Buyers Association Inc., 27 Providence Rd., Millbury, MA 01527. TEL 508-865-2507. Ed. Peter Bianca. adv.; bk.rev.; circ. 41,250 (controlled). (also avail. in microfilm from UMI) **Indexed:** Farm & Garden Ind.
—UMI.

637   NZ   ISSN 0301-8830
DAIRYFARMING ANNUAL. 1948. a. NZ.$8. Massey University, Animal Science Department, Palmerston North, New Zealand. Ed. G.F. Wilson. adv. circ. 800. (back issues avail.) **Indexed:** Anim.Breed.Abstr., Biol.Abstr., Dairy Sci.Abstr., Field Crop Abstr., Herb.Abstr.

637   US   ISSN 0745-9033
DAIRYMEN'S DIGEST: NORTH CENTRAL REGION EDITION. 1969. m. $10 (effective 1997). Associated Milk Producers, Inc. (New Ulm), Box 455, New Ulm, MN 56073. TEL 507-354-8295. FAX 507-359-8608. Ed. Sheryl Doering Meshke. R&P contact: Sheryl Doering Meshke. adv.: B&W page $817.29; trim 8 1/4 x 10 3/4; adv. contact: Julie Nelson. circ. 13,500. (also avail. in microfiche; back issues avail.) **Document type:** trade publication.
   Description: Provides information on dairying issues, including methods, products and manufacturing, and lobbying activities.

637   US   ISSN 0164-6486
DAIRYMEN'S DIGEST: SOUTHERN REGION EDITION. 1969. m. free. Associated Milk Producers, Inc., Box 5040, Arlington, TX 76005. TEL 817-461-2674. Ed. Raymond Crouch. adv.; bk.rev. circ. 9,400. (back issues avail.)

637   US   ISSN 0011-5738
DAIRYNEWS. 1917. 6/yr. $8. Dairylea Cooperative, Inc., Box 4844, Syracuse, NY 13221-4844. TEL 315-433-0100. FAX 315-433-2345. Ed. Wayne A. Westervelt. adv. contact: Edward L. Byrnes. bk.rev.; illus.; mkt. circ. 5,300. **Document type:** newsletter.
   Formerly: Dairymen's League News.

637   DK   ISSN 0904-4310
DANISH DAIRY & FOOD INDUSTRY-WORLDWIDE. (Text in English) 1976. biennial. free. Association of Dairy Engineers, P.O. Box 421, DK-5220 Odense S OE, Denmark. FAX 66144026. (Co-sponsor: Association of Danish Dairy Managers) Ed. K. Mark Christensen. adv.; charts; illus.; mkt.stat.; index. circ. 20,000. **Indexed:** Chem.Abstr., Dairy Sci.Abstr., Food Sci.& Tech.Abstr., Rural Recreat.Tour.Abstr., World Agri.Econ.& Rural Sociol.Abstr.
—BLDSC (3519.127000).
   Formerly (until 1988): Danish Dairy Industry-Worldwide (ISSN 0105-1210)

DEPARTMENT OF ANIMAL BREEDING AND GENETICS. REPORT. see AGRICULTURE — Poultry And Livestock

637   GW   ISSN 0012-0480
DEUTSCHE MILCHWIRTSCHAFT. 1887. fortn. DM.38.40 (foreign DM.41.60) (effective 1996). (Zentralverband Deutscher Milchwirtschaftler e.V.) Verlag Th. Mann, Nordring 10, 45894 Gelsenkirchen, Germany. TEL 49-209-9304184. FAX 49-209-9304185. (Subscr. to: Postfach 200254, 45837 Gelsenkirchen, Germany) Ed. Roland Sossna. adv.: B&W page DM.2946, color page DM.4731; trim 186 x 270. bk.rev.; bibl.; pat.; stat.; tr.lit.; index, cum.index; circ. 3,481. (processed) **Indexed:** Agri.Eng.Abstr., Biol.Abstr., Dairy Sci.Abstr., Food Sci.& Tech.Abstr., Ind.Vet., Int.Packag.Abstr., Packag.Sci.Tech., Rural Recreat.Tour.Abstr., Soyabean Abstr., World Agri.Econ.& Rural Sociol.Abstr. **Document type:** trade publication.
—BLDSC (3573.030000).

DIRECTORIO DE LACTEOS MEXICANOS. see BUSINESS AND ECONOMICS — Trade And Industrial Directories

338.1   UK
E C DAIRY FACTS AND FIGURES. (European Community) a. £20. Residuary Milk Marketing Board, Thames Ditton, Surrey KT7 0EL, England. TEL 0181-398-4101. FAX 0181-398-8485. circ. 1,800. **Indexed:** Dairy Sci.Abstr. **Document type:** trade publication.
   Formerly: E E C Dairy Facts and Figures.

338.1   FR
E N I L REVUE. 1975. 9/yr. (Ecoles Nationales d'Industrie Laitiere des Organismes Associes) Promotion Presse Internationale, 7 ter, Cour des Petites-Ecuries, 75010 Paris, France. TEL 33-1-42471205. adv. circ. 5,000.

637   FR   ISSN 1143-4376
ECHO DE LA CREMERIE. 1989. 4/yr. 29 rue Violet, 75015 Paris, France. TEL 45-75-05-60. FAX 45-79-98-34. Ed. Jacques Aroud. circ. 10,000.

637   CN   ISSN 0226-3947   SF227.C2
ECONOMICS OF MILK PRODUCTION IN ALBERTA. a. Alberta Agriculture, Production Economics Branch, Food & Rural Development, 7000-113 St., 3rd Fl., Rm. 303, Edmonton, AB T6H 5T6, Canada. TEL 403-427-4005. FAX 403-427-5220. **Document type:** government publication.

637   UA   ISSN 0378-2700   CODEN: EJDSDB
EGYPTIAN JOURNAL OF DAIRY SCIENCE. (Text in English; summaries in Arabic, English) 1973. s-a. $45 (effective 1996 & 1997). Egyptian Society of Dairy Science, National Research Centre, Sharia Tahrir, Dokki, Cairo, Egypt. TEL 20-2-701211. FAX 20-2-700931. Ed. A.A. Hofi. R&P contact: M.H. Abd El-Salam. adv. contact: M.H. Abd El-Salam. bk.rev.; abstr. circ. 1,000. (back issues avail.) **Indexed:** Biodet.Abstr., Chem.Abstr., Curr.Pack.Abstr., Dairy Sci.Abstr., Excerp.Med., Food Sci.& Tech.Abstr., Nutr.Abstr. **Document type:** academic/scholarly publication.
—BLDSC (3664.370000); CASDDS.
   Description: Publishes original research findings in the field of dairy science.
   Refereed Serial

EIER-WILD-GEFLUEGEL-MARKT. see FOOD AND FOOD INDUSTRIES

EMPIRE STATE FARMER. see AGRICULTURE

637   GW   ISSN 0724-3219
EUROPAEISCHER MOLKEREI UND KAESEREI ADRESSKALENDER; Vormerk-, Auskunfts- und Fachanschriftenbuch fuer die gesamte Milchwirtschaft. 1976. a. DM.62 (effective 1997). Volkswirtschaftlicher Verlag (VV GmbH), Kederbacherstr. 50, 81377 Munich, Germany. TEL 49-89-7141013. FAX 49-89-7192753. Eds. Hilde Walter, Rosemarie von Funcke. adv. contact: Inge Seifert. (back issues avail.) **Document type:** trade publication.

637   GW
EUROPEAN DAIRY DIRECTORY. 1965. a. DM.46. V V GmbH - Volkswirtschaftlicher Verlag, Kederbacherstr. 50, 81377 Munich, Germany. TEL 089-7141013. FAX 089-7192753. Ed. Hilde Walter. adv.: page DM.1520; trim 127 x 86; adv. contact: Inge Seifert. circ. 1,500 (paid). **Document type:** directory.

637   GW   ISSN 0936-6318
EUROPEAN DAIRY MAGAZINE. (Text in English, French, German) 1989. bi-m. DM.82.50 (effective 1997). Verlag Th. Mann, Nordring 10, 45894 Gelsenkirchen, Germany. TEL 49-209-9304184. FAX 49-209-9304185. (Subscr. to: Postfach 200254, 45837 Gelsenkirchen, Germany) Ed. Roland Sossna. adv.: B&W page DM.3820, color page DM.5530; trim 186 x 270. circ. 5,376. (back issues avail.) **Indexed:** Biodet.Abstr., Dairy Sci.Abstr., Food Sci.& Tech.Abstr. **Document type:** trade publication.
—BLDSC (3829.688830). CCC.

637   US   ISSN 0014-7826
FARM AND DAIRY; the auction guide & the rural marketplace. 1914. w. $25 (effective 1997); newsstand price: $1.25. Lyle Printing and Publishing Co., 185 East State St., Box 38, Salem, OH 44460. TEL 330-337-3419. FAX 330-337-9550. Ed. Susan M. Crowell; Pub. W.T. Darling. adv.: B&W page $552, color page $1027; adv. contact: Scot Darling. bk.rev.; bibl.; illus.; circ. 23,000. circ. 27,500 (paid). **Document type:** newspaper.
   Description: Serves as a key to reaching the rural audience in Ohio, western Pennsylvania and the panhandle of West Virginia.

637   658   UK   ISSN 0968-0128
FARMING BUSINESS. 1966. bi-m. membership. Genus Ltd., Westmere Dr., Crewe, Ches. CW1 1ZY, England. TEL 44-1270-536536. FAX 44-1270-536601. Ed. Jane Craigie. charts; illus.; circ. 40,000 (controlled). **Indexed:** Dairy Sci.Abstr., Herb.Abstr., Maize Abstr., Rural Recreat.Tour.Abstr., World Agri.Econ.& Rural Sociol.Abstr. **Document type:** trade publication.
   Supersedes (in 1992): Better Breeding (ISSN 0006-0046); Formerly: Better Management (ISSN 0006-0186)
   Description: Covers farm management, cattle breeding, and animal health.

637   US   ISSN 1056-3210
FARMLIFE. 1921. m. $2.50. Eastern Milk Producers Cooperative Association, 2401 Burnet Ave., Box 6966, Syracuse, NY 13217-6966. TEL 315-463-0781. Ed. Anthony G. Schlesier. adv.; stat. circ. 11,000. (back issues avail.)
   Formerly (until 1991): Eastern Milk Producer (ISSN 8755-9544)

637   US   ISSN 0745-7553
FARMSHINE. 1979. w. $15 (effective 1997). Dieter Krieg, Ed. & Pub., Box 219, Brownstown, PA 17508-0219. TEL 717-656-8050. FAX 717-656-8188. Ed. Dieter Krieg. adv. circ. 13,540.
   Description: Provides news, features, and market reports to dairy farmers in Pennsylvania and surrounding states.

637   FI   ISSN 0367-2387   CODEN: FJDSAJ
FINNISH JOURNAL OF DAIRY SCIENCE. (Text in English, Finnish and German; summaries in English) 1939. a. FIM 50. Finnish Society of Dairy Science - Meijeritieteellinen Seura r.y., Elintarviketeknologian Laitos, PL 27, FIN-00014 Helsingin Yliopisto, Finland. FAX 90-708-5212. Eds. Eeva-Liisa Ryhanen, Sade Mantere-Alhonen. adv. circ. 600. (back issues avail.) **Indexed:** Biol.Abstr., Chem.Abstr., Dairy Sci.Abstr., Food Sci.& Tech.Abstr., Ind.Vet., Vet.Bull., World Agri.Econ.& Rural Sociol.Abstr.
—CASDDS.
   Formerly (until 1990): Meijeritieteellinen Aikakauskirja.

GELATO ARTIGIANALE. see FOOD AND FOOD INDUSTRIES

637   UK
GOLD TOP NEWS. 3/yr. Quality Milk Producers Ltd., The Bury Farm, Pednor Rd., Chesham, Bucks HP5 2JY, England. TEL 0494-784572. FAX 0494-791700. Ed. S.R. Baker. circ. 1,200.

637   636.2   US   ISSN 0017-5110
GUERNSEY BREEDERS' JOURNAL. 1910. 10/yr. $15 (foreign $18). American Guernsey Association, 7614 Slate Ridge Blvd., Box 666, Reynoldsburg, OH 43068. TEL 614-864-2409. FAX 614-864-5614. Ed. Becky Payne. adv.; stat.; illus.; s-a. index. circ. 2,000. (also avail. in microform from UMI; reprint service avail. from UMI) **Document type:** trade publication.
—Linda Hall; UMI; UnCover.

AGRICULTURE — DAIRYING AND DAIRY PRODUCTS

H R I - BUYERS GUIDE. (Hotels, Restaurants, Institutions) see FOOD AND FOOD INDUSTRIES

637 636   JA   ISSN 0387-7647
S18   CODEN: HDSKDJ
HIROSHIMA DAIGAKU SEIBUTSU SEISAN GAKUBU KIYO/HIROSHIMA UNIVERSITY. FACULTY OF APPLIED BIOLOGICAL SCIENCE. JOURNAL. (Text in English and Japanese) 1955. s-a. free. Hiroshima University, Faculty of Applied Biological Science, Saijo, Higashi-Hiroshima, Japan. circ. 1,000. **Indexed:** Anim.Breed.Abstr., Biol.Abstr., Dairy Sci.Abstr., Food Sci.& Tech.Abstr., INIS Atomind., Sport Fish.Abstr., Wild.Rev., Zoo.Rec. **Document type:** academic/scholarly publication.
—BLDSC (4743.410000); Linda Hall.
    Formerly (until 1978): Hiroshima Daigaku Suichikusan Gakubu Kiyo.

637   US   ISSN 0018-2885
HOARD'S DAIRYMAN; the national dairy farm magazine. 1885. s-m. (20/yr.) $14 (foreign $25) (effective 1997). W.D. Hoard and Sons Co., 28 Milwaukee Ave. W., Ft. Atkinson, WI 53538. TEL 414-563-5551. FAX 414-563-7298. E-mail: hoards@aol.com; URL: http://www.n-s.com/hoards.html. Ed. W.D. Knox; Pub. W.D. Knox. R&P contact: Ewing Row. adv.: B&W page $10517, color page $13017; adv. contact: Gary Vorpahl. charts; illus.; stat.; index; circ. 113,638 (paid). (also avail. in microfilm from UMI; reprint service avail. from UMI) **Indexed:** Biol.& Agr.Ind., Dairy Sci.Abstr., Farm & Garden Ind., Food Sci.& Tech.Abstr., Rural Recreat.Tour.Abstr., World Agri.Econ.& Rural Sociol.Abstr. **Document type:** trade publication.
—Linda Hall; SWETS; UMI.
    Description: Offers dairy farm news and information in the U.S. and Canada.

637 664   JA   ISSN 0285-1806
HOKKAIDO EIYO SYOKURYO GAKKAISHI/HOKKAIDO SOCIETY OF FOOD AND NUTRITION. JOURNAL. (Text and summaries in Japanese) 1954. a. 1300 Yen($6.50) Hokkaido Society of Food and Nutrition, c/o Department of Biochemistry, Hokkaido University School of Medicine, N-15 W-7, Kita-ku, Sapporo 060, Japan. Ed. Yoh Imai. adv. circ. 1,000.

637   UK   ISSN 0954-6219
HOLSTEIN FRIESIAN JOURNAL. 1919. bi-m. £18 (foreign £30) (effective 1996). Holstein Friesian Society of Great Britain & Ireland, Scotsbridge House, Rickmansworth, Herts. WD3 3BB, England. TEL 44-1923-494600. FAX 44-1923-770003. E-mail: 101322,1347@compuserve.com.uk. Ed. Ann Hardy. adv. contact: Jennifer Alderman. bk.rev.; illus.; circ. 14,500. **Indexed:** Anim.Breed.Abstr. **Document type:** trade publication.
    Formerly: British Friesian Journal (ISSN 0007-0726)
    Description: Provides information on cattle breeding and genetic improvement with herd, show, sale, research, new product and regional features.
    Refereed Serial

626.234   NE   ISSN 1380-2879
HOLSTEIN INTERNATIONAL; maandblad voor de moderne Holsteinfokker. English edition (ISSN 1380-2887); German edition (ISSN 1380-2895) 1994. m. fl.65 (U.K. $35; Canada Can.$50; U.K. and Ireland £20; Germany DM.65; elsewhere $40). Holstein International BV, Witewei 2, 9051 TB Stiens, Netherlands. TEL 31-5109-4100. FAX 31-1833-3967. (Addr. in N. America: H.F.W., Inc., Box 299, Sandy Creek, NY 13145. TEL 315-387-3441. FAX 315-387-3655) Eds. Jan Bierma, Han Hopman. adv.: B&W page $905, color page $1200; trim 8 1/4 x 11 5/8. illus. circ. 10,000. (back issues avail) **Document type:** trade publication.
    Description: Contains articles of interest to breeders and marketers of top-quality Holstein cattle.

636.4   CN   ISSN 0710-1309
HOLSTEIN JOURNAL. (Text mainly in English; occasionally in French) 1938. m. Can.$30 (foreign Can.$70). Holstein Journal Group Inc., 9120 Leslie St., Unit 105, Richmond Hill, ON L4B 3J9, Canada. TEL 905-886-4222. FAX 905-886-0037. Ed. Bonnie E. Cooper; Pub. G. Peter English. adv. contact: G. Peter English. bk.rev.; charts; illus.; index; circ. 9,577 (paid). **Document type:** trade publication.
—Linda Hall.
    Formerly: Holstein-Friesian Journal (ISSN 0018-3687)
    Description: Provides news and information on Holstein dairy cattle breeding.

636.234   US   ISSN 0199-4239
HOLSTEIN WORLD. (Supplements annual.) 1904. m. $29.95 (foreign $80). Holstein-Friesian World, Inc., 8036 Lake St., Box 299, Sandy Creek, NY 13145. TEL 315-387-3441. FAX 315-387-3655. Ed. Joel Hastings. adv.; bk.rev.; charts; illus.; mkt.; stat.; index. circ. 20,000. (also avail. in microfilm from UMI; reprint service avail. from UMI)
—Linda Hall; UMI; UnCover.
    Formerly: Holstein-Friesian World (ISSN 0018-3695)
    Description: For high-income milk producers who own or manage genetically superior Holstein dairy cattle.

HUSDJUR. see AGRICULTURE — Poultry And Livestock

637   SP   ISSN 0210-0037
I L E. (Industrias Lacteas Espanolas) 1978. m. 13000 ptas. (Europe 18500 ptas; elsewhere 20500 ptas.) (effective 1996). Publicaciones Tecnicas Alimentarias, S.A., Po. Imperial, 8 2o, 28005 Madrid, Spain. TEL 34-1-3665207. FAX 34-1-3640774. Ed. Alfredo Val. R&P contact: Carlos Ayala. adv. contact: Paloma del Olmo. bk.rev. circ. 4,000. (reprint service avail.) **Indexed:** Ind.SST. **Document type:** trade publication.
    Description: Covers all areas of the dairy trade.

637   II   ISSN 0019-4603
SF221
INDIAN DAIRYMAN. (Text in English) 1949. m. Indian Dairy Association, I D A House, Sector IV, R.K. Puram, New Delhi 110 022, India. TEL 91-11-6165340. Ed. A. Banerjee. adv. contact: S. Harikaran. charts; illus.; tr.lit. circ. 2,000. **Indexed:** Anim.Breed.Abstr., Chem.Abstr., Dairy Sci.Abstr., Food Sci.& Tech.Abstr., Ind.Vet., Rural Devel.Abstr., Rural Recreat.Tour.Abstr., World Agri.Econ. & Rural Sociol.Abstr. **Document type:** government publication.
—BLDSC (4396.100000).

637   II   ISSN 0019-5146
SF221   CODEN: IJDSAI
INDIAN JOURNAL OF DAIRY SCIENCE. (Text in English) 1948. m. (q. before Apr. 1991). Indian Dairy Association, I D A House, Sector IV, R.K. Puram, New Delhi 110 022, India. Ed. A. Banerjee. adv. contact: S. Harikaran. bk.rev.; bibl.; charts; stat.; index. **Indexed:** Anim.Breed.Abstr., Biol.Abstr., Chem.Abstr., Curr.Pack.Abstr., Dairy Sci.Abstr., Field Crop Abstr., Food Sci.& Tech.Abstr., Herb.Abstr., Ind.Vet., Maize Abstr., Nutr.Abstr., Rice Abstr., Rural Devel.Abstr., Rural Recreat.Tour.Abstr., Sugar Ind.Abstr., Vet.Bull., World Agri.Econ. & Rural Sociol.Abstr. **Document type:** academic/scholarly publication.
—BLDSC (4411.000000); CASDDS; CISTI; SWETS.

637   AG   ISSN 0046-9181
INDUSTRIA LECHERA. 1919. bi-m. Arg.$15($5) Centro de la Industria Lechera, Mediano 281, Buenos Aires 1178, Argentina. adv.; play rev.; bibl.; illus.; stat. circ. 3,000. **Indexed:** Chem.Abstr., Dairy Sci.Abstr., Food Sci.& Tech.Abstr.

637   FR   ISSN 0046-9432
INFORMATIONS LAITIERES. 1950. 42/yr. 800 F. (foreign 1000 F.) (effective 1997). Editions Caracter's, 8 rue de la Bergere, 25000 Besancon, France. TEL 33-3-81527453. FAX 33-3-81520805. Ed. Katia David. adv.; bk.rev. circ. 12,500.

637   BL   ISSN 0100-3674
    CODEN: RILCAY
INSTITUTO DE LATICINIOS CANDIDO TOSTES. REVISTA. 1946. bi-m. Instituto de Laticinios Candido Tostes, Caixa Postal 183, 36045-560 Juiz de Fora, MG, Brazil. TEL 55-32-2243116. FAX 55-32-2243113. Ed. Geraldo Magela Carozzi de Miranda.
—BLDSC (7819.700000); CASDDS.
    Formerly (until 1957): Felctiano (ISSN 0102-2237)

637.1   US   ISSN 0074-1671
INTERNATIONAL ASSOCIATION OF MILK CONTROL AGENCIES. PROCEEDINGS OF ANNUAL MEETINGS. 1937. a. $10. International Association of Milk Control Agencies, c/o Lyle Newcomb, New York Int'l Dept. of Agriculture and Markets, 1 Winners Circle, Albany, NY 12235. TEL 518-457-5731. FAX 518-485-5816. circ. controlled. **Document type:** proceedings.

637   BE   ISSN 0259-8434
SF221   CODEN: BIDFDY
INTERNATIONAL DAIRY FEDERATION. BULLETIN/FEDERATION INTERNATIONALE DE LAITERIE. BULLETIN. (Text in English, French) 1960. m. 13500 BEF. International Dairy Federation - Federation Internationale de Laiterie, Square Vergote 41, 1030 Brussels, Belgium. TEL 32-2-7339888. FAX 32-2-7330413. index, cum.index. circ. 1,500. **Indexed:** Agri.Eng.Abstr., Anim.Breed.Abstr., Biol.Abstr., Chem.Abstr., Curr.Pack.Abstr., Dairy Sci.Abstr., Food Sci.& Tech.Abstr., Herb.Abstr., Ind.Vet., Nutr.Abstr., Rural Ext.Educ.& Tr.Abstr., Rural Recreat.Tour.Abstr., Vet.Bull., World Agri.Econ.& Rural Sociol.Abstr. **Document type:** bulletin.
—BLDSC (2587.550000); CASDDS; SWETS.
    Former titles (until 1985): Federation Internationale de Laiterie. Bulletin Annuel (ISSN 0250-5118); International Dairy Federation. Annual Bulletin (ISSN 0074-4484)

637   BE   ISSN 0538-7094
INTERNATIONAL DAIRY FEDERATION. INTERNATIONAL STANDARD/FEDERATION INTERNATIONALE DE LAITERIE. NORME INTERNATIONALE. 1955. irreg. price varies. International Dairy Federation - Federation Internationale de Laiterie, Square Vergote 41, 1030 Brussels, Belgium. TEL 32-2-7339888. FAX 32-2-7330413. circ. 3,000. **Indexed:** Biol.Abstr., Dairy Sci.Abstr.

637   UK   ISSN 0958-6946
    CODEN: IDAJE6
INTERNATIONAL DAIRY JOURNAL. 1991. m. fl.1846($1061) (effective 1998). Elsevier Science Ltd., P.O. Box 800, Kidlington, Oxford OX5 1DX, England. TEL 44-1865-843000. FAX 44-1865-843010. E-mail: nlinfo-f@elsevier.nl; usinfo-f@elsevier.com; forinfo-kyf04035@niftyserve.or.jp; URL: http://www.elsevier.nl/. (Subscr. to: Elsevier Science, Regional Sales Office, P.O. Box 211, 1000 AE Amsterdam, Netherlands. TEL 31-20-4853757. FAX 31-20-4853432; Subscr. in the Americas to: Elsevier Science, Regional Sales Office, Box 945, New York, NY 10159-0945. TEL 212-633-3730. FAX 212-633-3680; Subscr. in Australasia and the Far East to: Elsevier Science (Singapore) Pte Ltd, No.1 Temasek Ave., No.17-01 Millenia Tower, Singapore 039192, Singapore. TEL 65-434-3727. FAX 65-337-2230) Ed.Bd. adv. (also avail. in microform from UMI; back issues avail.) **Indexed:** ASCA, Curr.Cont., Food Sci.& Tech.Abstr. **Document type:** academic/scholarly publication.
—BLDSC (4539.501800); CASDDS; EMDOCS; Genuine Article; Linda Hall; SWETS; UnCover. **CCC**.
    Incorporates (as of Jan. 1997): Netherlands Milk and Dairy Journal (ISSN 0028-209X)
    Description: Publishes original papers and critical reviews on all aspects of dairy science and technology.
    Refereed Serial

AGRICULTURE — DAIRYING AND DAIRY PRODUCTS

637   UK   ISSN 1364-727X
SF221   CODEN: IJDTFQ
INTERNATIONAL JOURNAL OF DAIRY TECHNOLOGY. 1947. q. £95($165) (effective 1997). Society of Dairy Technology, 72 Ermine St., Huntingdon, Cambs. PE18 6EZ, England. TEL 44-1480-450741. FAX 44-1480-431800. Ed. S. Burkhart. adv.; bk.rev.; bibl.; charts; illus.; stat.; index. circ. 1,400. (back issues avail.) **Indexed:** Anim.Breed.Abstr., ASCA, Biol.Abstr., Chem.Abstr., Curr.Cont., Dairy Sci.Abstr., Excerp.Med., Food Sci.& Tech.Abstr., Ind.Vet., Int.Packag.Abstr., Nutr.Abstr., Packag.Sci.Tech., Rural Recreat.Tour.Abstr., Soyabean Abstr., SSCI, Sugar Ind.Abstr., Vet.Bull., World Agri.Econ.& Rural Sociol.Abstr. **Document type:** trade publication, academic/scholarly publication.
—BLDSC (4542.182500); CASDDS; Genuine Article; Linda Hall; SWETS; UncOver.
Formerly (until 1997): Society of Dairy Technology. Journal (ISSN 0037-9840)

637.1   GW
JAHRBUCH DER EUROPAEISCHEN MILCHWIRTSCHAFT. 1950. a. DM.89 (effective 1997). (Zentralverband Deutscher Milchwirtschaftler e.V.) Verlag Th. Mann, Nordring 10, 45894 Gelsenkirchen, Germany. TEL 49-209-9304-0. FAX 49-209-9304165. (Subscr. to: Postfach 200254, 45837 Gelsenkirchen, Germany) Ed. Roland Sossna. adv.: B&W page DM.1815, color page DM.3075; trim 81 x 122. circ. 4,500. **Document type:** trade publication.
Formerly: Jahrbuch der Milchwirtschaft (ISSN 0721-4332)
Description: Reports on dairy farming in Germany and Europe.

636 637   UI   ISSN 0446-7310
JERSEY AT HOME. 1951. bi-a. £21 for 3 yrs. Royal Jersey Agricultural and Horticultural Society, Springfield, St. Helier, Jersey JE2 4LF, Channel Islands. TEL 44-1534-866555. FAX 44-1534-865619. Ed. J.W. Godfrey. adv.; bk.rev.; stat.; tr:lit.; circ. 2,000 (controlled). **Document type:** newsletter, proceedings.
Description: Official publication of the R.J.A.H.S. covering activities of the society, Jersey cattle, agriculture, and country issues on the island of Jersey.
Refereed Serial

637   UK   ISSN 0022-0299
CODEN: JDRSAN
JOURNAL OF DAIRY RESEARCH. 1929. q. £207($364) (effective 1998). (Institute of Food Research) Cambridge University Press, Edinburgh Bldg., Shaftesbury Rd., Cambridge CB2 2RU, England. TEL 44-1223-312393. FAX 44-1223-315052. TELEX 851817256. E-mail: information@cup.cam.ac.uk; URL: http://www.cup.cam.ac.uk. (N. American addr.: Cambridge University Press, 40 W. 20th St., New York, NY 10011. TEL 212-924-3900. FAX 212-691-3239) (Hannah Research Institute) Eds. B.A. Rolls, M.L. Green. R&P contact: Linda Nicol. adv. contact: Rebecca Symons. bibl.; charts; illus.; index. (also avail. in microform from UMI; back issues avail.; reprint service avail. from SWZ,UMI) **Indexed:** Agri.Eng.Abstr., Anal.Abstr., Anim.Breed.Abstr., ASCA, Biol.Abstr., Biol.& Agr.Ind., Biotech.Abstr., Chem.Abstr., Curr.Cont., Curr.Pack.Abstr., Dairy Sci.Abstr., Excerp.Med., Field Crop Abstr., Food Sci.& Tech.Abstr., Herb.Abstr., Ind.Med., Ind.Sci.Rev., Ind.Vet., NRN, Nutr.Abstr., Sci.Cit.Ind., Vet.Bull.
—BLDSC (4966.000000); CASDDS; Genuine Article; Linda Hall; SWETS; UMI; UncOver. **CCC**.
Description: Research on all aspects of milk production and preservation, and fundamental effects of processing. Includes the composition of milk for several animal species.

637   US   ISSN 0022-0302
SF221   CODEN: JDSCAE
JOURNAL OF DAIRY SCIENCE. 1917. m. $155 in N. America; elsewhere $160 (effective 1997). American Dairy Science Association, 1111 N. Dunlap Ave., Savoy, IL 61874. TEL 217-356-3182. FAX 217-398-4119. E-mail: adsa@adsa.org; URL: http://orion.adsa.uiuc.edu/. Ed. John W. Fuquay. R&P contact: John W. Fuquay. TEL 601-325-2802. adv. contact: C.K. Nimz. abstr.; bibl.; charts; illus.; index. circ. 5,400. (also avail. in microform from UMI,PMC; reprint service avail.) **Indexed:** Anal.Abstr., Anim.Breed.Abstr., ASCA, Bibl.Agri., Biol.Abstr., Biol.& Agr.Ind., Biotech.Abstr., Chem.Abstr., Curr.Cont., Curr.Pack.Abstr., Dairy Sci.Abstr., Dent.Ind., Environ.Abstr., Excerp.Med., Field Crop Abstr., Food Sci.& Tech.Abstr., Helminthol.Abstr., Herb.Abstr., Ind.Med., Ind.Sci.Rev., Ind.Vet., INIS Atomind., Maize Abstr., Nutr.Abstr., Ocean.Abstr., Pig News & Info., Pollut.Abstr., Protozool.Abstr., Rev.Plant Path., Rice Abstr., Rural Recreat.Tour.Abstr., Sci.Cit.Ind., Soyabean Abstr., SSCI, Sugar Ind.Abstr., Telegen, Triticale Abstr., Trop.Oil Seeds Abstr., Vet.Bull., W.R.C.Inf., World Agri.Econ.& Rural Sociol.Abstr. **Document type:** academic/scholarly publication.
●Also available online.
—BLDSC (4967.000000); CASDDS; CISTI; Genuine Article; KR SourceOne; Linda Hall; SWETS; UMI; UncOver. **CCC**.
Description: Provides current technical and scientific information for all segments of the dairy industry.
Refereed Serial

637   II   ISSN 0971-4456
CODEN: JFHSEP
JOURNAL OF DAIRYING, FOOD & HOME SCIENCES. 1982. q. $60 (effective 1997). Agricultural Research Communication Centre, 1130 Sadar, Karnal 132001, Haryana, India. TEL 91-184-255080. Ed. V.D. Mudgal. **Indexed:** Anim.Breed.Abstr., Biodet.Abstr., Biol.Abstr., Chem.Abstr., Dairy Sci.Abstr., Food Sci.& Tech.Abstr., Indian Sci.Abstr., Packag.Sci.Tech.
—BLDSC (4967.101000); CASDDS; UMI.
Formerly (until 1992): Asian Journal of Dairy Research (ISSN 0253-6595)
Description: Features original research articles on all aspects of dairying, foods and home sciences by eminent research workers.

JOURNAL OF FOOD PROTECTION. see *PUBLIC HEALTH AND SAFETY*

KANSAS FOOD DEALERS BULLETIN. see *FOOD AND FOOD INDUSTRIES — Grocery Trade*

637   UK
KEY NOTE MARKET REPORT: MILK & DAIRY PRODUCTS. Variant title: Milk & Dairy Products. irreg., no.12, 1996. £205. Key Note Ltd., Field House, 72 Oldfield Rd., Hampton, Middlesex TW12 2HQ, England. TEL 44-181-783-0755. FAX 44-181-783-0049. **Document type:** trade publication.
●Also available online.
Also available on CD-ROM.
Formerly: Key Note Report: Milk and Dairy Products (ISSN 0954-4275)

637 338.1   TH   ISSN 0023-1053
KHAO SETTHAKIT KAN-KASET/AGRICULTURAL ECONOMIC NEWS. 1955. m. free. (Ministry of Agriculture and Cooperatives, Office of Agricultural Economics) Chuan Pim Partnership Ltd., 469 Phra Su Maen Rd., Bangkok, Thailand. Ed. Nipont Dilokkunanant. circ. 120,000.

637   GW   ISSN 0023-1347
SF227.G3   CODEN: KMWFAF
KIELER MILCHWIRTSCHAFTLICHE FORSCHUNGSBERICHTE. 1949. 4/yr. DM.144 (foreign DM.154) (effective 1997). (Bundesanstalt fuer Milchforschung) Verlag Th. Mann, Nordring 10, 45894 Gelsenkirchen, Germany. TEL 49-209-9304184. FAX 49-209-9304185. (Subscr. to: Postfach 200254, 45837 Gelsenkirchen, Germany) Ed. E. Schlimme. adv.: B&W page DM.937, color page DM.2240; trim 126 x 190; adv. contact: Richard Heineke. bk.rev. circ. 825. **Indexed:** Agri.Eng.Abstr., Anim.Breed.Abstr., ASCA, Biol.Abstr., Chem.Abstr., Curr.Cont., Dairy Sci.Abstr., Excerp.Med., Food Sci.& Tech.Abstr., INIS Atomind., INSPEC, Pig News & Info., Soyabean Abstr., Vet.Bull., World Agri.Econ.& Rural Sociol.Abstr. **Document type:** trade publication.
—BLDSC (5095.025000); CASDDS; Genuine Article; Linda Hall; UMI.

KOREAN JOURNAL OF ANIMAL SCIENCES. see *AGRICULTURE — Poultry And Livestock*

LACTEOS Y CARNICOS MEXICANOS. see *FOOD AND FOOD INDUSTRIES*

LACTIC ACID BACTERIA. see *BIOLOGY — Microbiology*

637.1 576   FR   ISSN 0023-7302
CODEN: LAITAG
LE LAIT. (Text mainly in French; summaries in English, French) 1921. bi-m. 1410 F. (institutions in the Americas $270; elsewhere 1750 F.) (effective 1998). (Institut National de la Recherche Agronomique) Editions Scientifiques et Medicales Elsevier, 141 rue de Javel, 75747 Paris, France. TEL 33-1-45589022. FAX 33-1-45589421. URL: http://www.elsevier.nl/. (Subscr. in U.S. and Canada to: Elsevier Science Inc., Box 945, Madison Sq. Sta., New York, NY 10159-0945. TEL 212-633-3730. FAX 212-633-3680) Ed. J.L. Maubois. adv. circ. 2,500. (also avail. in microform from PMC) **Indexed:** ASCA, Biol.Abstr., Chem.Abstr., Curr.Cont., Dairy Sci.Abstr., Excerp.Med., Food Sci.& Tech.Abstr., Sci.Cit.Ind. **Document type:** academic/scholarly publication.
—BLDSC (5143.800000); CASDDS; Genuine Article; Linda Hall; SWETS. **CCC**.
Description: Includes scientific articles on the microbiology, biochemistry and physiochemistry of milk and its derivatives, or on transformation procedures.
Refereed Serial

637   IT   ISSN 0392-6060
LATTE; rivista tecnica per l'industria lattiero-casearia. 1976. m. (12/yr.) L.75000 (Europe L.140000; elsewhere L.185000) (effective 1997). Tecniche Nuove s.p.a., Via Menotti 14, 20129 Milan, Italy. TEL 39-2-75701. FAX 39-2-7610351. E-mail: abbonamenti@tecnet.it; URL: http://www.tecnet.it. Ed. Guiseppe Nardella. adv.: B&W page L.2020000, color page L.3232000; trim 210 x 297. bk.rev.; abstr.; bibl.; charts; illus.; stat.; index. circ. 7,000. **Indexed:** Chem.Abstr., Curr.Cont., Dairy Sci.Abstr., Food Sci.& Tech.Abstr., Herb.Abstr., Ind.Vet., Rural Recreat.Tour.Abstr., World Agri.Econ.& Rural Sociol.Abstr.
—BLDSC (5160.400000).
Description: Information concerning plants, production techniques and methods of analysis used in the dairy and cheese industry.

637   US   ISSN 1073-3019
LECHERO LATINO. Mexico & Puerto Rico edition (ISSN 1073-5542) 1987. 4/yr. $20 (foreign $30). Holstein-Friesian World, Inc., 2078 Lake St., Box 299, Sandy Creek, NY 13145. TEL 315-387-3441. FAX 315-387-3655. Ed. Ludwig M. Johonnsen. adv.: B&W page $1635, color page $2180; trim 8 x 10 7/8. circ. 19,000. (back issues avail.)
Supersedes (in 1990): Lechero Latinoamericano; Which was formerly: Holstein Latinoamericano.
Description: For larger, progressive dairymen in Mexico, Central and South America, Spain and Portugal.

637   NZ
LIVESTOCK IMPROVEMENT ANNUAL REVIEW. 1992. a. Livestock Improvement Corporation Ltd., Cnr. Ruakura & Morrinsville Rds., Pravate Bag 3016, Hamilton, New Zealand. TEL 64-7-8560700. FAX 64-7-8562428. Ed. Robyn Sherson. charts; illus. circ. 17,000. (back issues avail.) **Document type:** consumer publication.

LOUISIANA CATTLEMAN. see *AGRICULTURE — Poultry And Livestock*

637.1   DK   ISSN 0107-7988
MAELKEPRODUCENTEN. 1981. q. membership. Landsforeningen af Danske Maelkproducenter, Oesteranden 15, Hornborg, 8762 Flemming, Denmark. illus.

AGRICULTURE — DAIRYING AND DAIRY PRODUCTS

637   DK   ISSN 0024-9645
MAELKERITIDENDE. 1888. bi-w. DKK 816 (foreign DKK 732) (effective 1997). Danish Dairy Engineers Association, Det Gamle Mejeri, Landbrugsvej 65, DK-5620 Odense S, Denmark. TEL 45-66-12-40-25. FAX 45-66-14-40-26. Ed. K. Mark Christensen. adv.: B&W page DKK 6225, color page DKK 13400; trim 278 x 188; adv. contact: K. Mark Christensen. circ. 2,100. **Indexed:** Dairy Sci.Abstr., Food Sci.& Tech.Abstr.
    Description: Focuses on the latest developments within dairy production, processing and related fields.

637   NO   ISSN 0025-8776
MEIERIPOSTEN. (Text in Norwegian; summaries in English) 1912. m. NOK 360 (foreign NOK 480) (effective 1997). Norske Mejerifolks Landsforening - Norwegian Association of Dairy Managers, P.O. Boks 398 Sentrum, N-0103 Oslo, Norway. TEL 47-22-42-25-20. FAX 47-22-41-38-01. Ed. Steinar Husby. adv.: B&W page NOK 4000, color page NOK 7840; trim 185 x 260. bk.rev. circ. 2,263. **Indexed:** Chem.Abstr., Dairy Sci.Abstr., Food Sci.& Tech.Abstr., Ind.Vet., Nutr.Abstr., Packag.Sci.Tech., Rural Recreat.Tour.Abstr., Sugar Ind.Abstr., World Agri.Econ.& Rural Sociol.Abstr. **Document type:** trade publication.
—BLDSC (5536.350000).
    Description: Focuses on development in technology and economy in the dairy and ice cream industry, as well as related food industries locally and abroad.

637   DK   ISSN 0107-7635
MEJERISTEN. 1932. 10/yr. Dansk Mejeristforbund, Rosenvangsalle 235, DK-8270 Hojbjerg, Denmark. adv. circ. 3,100.

637   IS
MESHEK HA-BAKAR VE HA-CHALAV. (Text in Hebrew) 1953. bi-m. IS.30. Association of Cattle Growers in Israel, 25 Arlozorov St., Tel Aviv 62 148, Israel. TEL 03-240112. FAX 03-248109. Ed. Mordechai Mal'an. adv.; bk.rev. circ. 2,200.

637   MX
MEXICO HOLSTEIN. 1969. m. (Mexican Holstein Breeders Association) Editorial Ano Dos Mil, S.A., Indianapolis 70, 03810 Mexico, D.F., Mexico. TEL 543-0710. (In U.S.: Box 299, 8036 Lake St., Sandy Creek, NY 13145. TEL 315-387-3441) Eds. Raul Campos, Leonardo Martinez. adv.: B&W page $780, color page $1115; trim 8 1/4 x 10 5/8. circ. 6,500.

637   US
MICHIGAN DAIRY LINE. 1987. q. free. Michigan Dairy Council, 2163 Jolly Rd., Okemos, MI 48864-3961. TEL 517-349-8480. FAX 517-349-6218. Ed. Kimberley Stapelfeldt. circ. 5,000. **Document type:** newsletter.

631.12   US   ISSN 0026-2315
MICHIGAN MILK MESSENGER. 1919. m. $5 to non-members (effective 1997). Michigan Milk Producers Association, Box 8002, Novi, MI 48375-8002. TEL 810-474-6672. FAX 810-474-0924. Ed. Laura Moser. adv. contact: Laura Moser. illus.; mkt.; stat. circ. 6,200. **Document type:** trade publication.

637.1   US   ISSN 0195-5624
MID-AM REPORTER. 1968. m. $12 (foreign $14) (effective 1997). Mid-America Dairymen, Inc., 3253 E. Chestnut Expy., Springfield, MO 65802-2584. TEL 417-865-7100. FAX 417-865-9176. E-mail: Midamdairy@AOL/com. Ed. Dan Reuwee. adv. contact: Jack Stubbs. circ. 26,000. **Document type:** newspaper.
    Description: Covers cooperative, legislative developments, dairy industry news, health, economic events and human interest stories.

637   US   ISSN 1087-7096
MIDWEST DAIRYBUSINESS. 1996. bi-m. $20 (effective 1997). H F W Communications Inc., 5923 S. Main St., Box 299, Sandy Creek, NY 13145. TEL 315-387-3441. FAX 315-387-3655. E-mail: cbryant@hfw.com. (Subscr. to: Box 850948, Braintree, MA 02185-0948. TEL 800-439-3990. FAX 617-356-8577) Ed. Carrie J. Bryant; Pub. Joel P. Hastings. circ. 32,000. **Document type:** trade publication.
    Description: Provides midwestern milk producers with business and management information to enhance profitability.

MILCH - FETTWAREN - EIER - HANDEL. see *FOOD AND FOOD INDUSTRIES*

637.1   GW   ISSN 0176-5124
MILCH-MARKETING. 1984. m. DM.132 (foreign DM.162) (effective 1997). Milchwirtschaftlicher Fachverlag GmbH, Rheintalstr. 6, 53498 Bad Breisig, Germany. TEL 49-2633-454000. FAX 49-2633-97415. Ed. Stephan Camphausen. circ. 13,000. (back issues avail.) **Document type:** trade publication.

637   GW
MILCH POST. 1978. m. Agrar Verlag Allgaeu, Porschestr. 2, 87437 Kempten, Germany. TEL 0831-7495. (looseleaf format)

637   GW   ISSN 0343-0200
DIE MILCHPRAXIS UND RINDERMAST. 1964. q. DM.34 (foreign DM.43) (effective 1997). Verlag Th. Mann, Nordring 10, 45894 Gelsenkirchen, Germany. TEL 49-209-9304184. FAX 49-209-9304185. (Subscr. to: Postfach 200254, 45837 Gelsenkirchen, Germany) Eds. Heinz-Peter Puetz, Guenter Weiss. adv.: B&W page DM.4120, color page DM.6520; trim 186 x 270; adv. contact: Richard Heineke. bk.rev.; charts; illus. circ. 51,089. **Indexed:** Agri.Eng.Abstr., Anim.Breed.Abstr., Dairy Sci.Abstr., Ind.Vet., Vet.Bull. **Document type:** trade publication.
—BLDSC (5766.450000).
    Formerly: Milch-Praxis (ISSN 0026-3753)

631 658.8   UK   ISSN 0309-0809
MILK BULLETIN. 1954. m. £9.25. Scottish Milk Marketing Board, Underwood Rd., Paisley, Renfrewshire PA3 1TJ, Scotland. FAX 041-889-1225. adv.; charts; mkt.; stat.; circ. 3,200 (controlled). (tabloid format) **Indexed:** Dairy Sci.Abstr. **Document type:** bulletin.
    Formerly: S.M.M.B. Bulletin (ISSN 0036-1666)

637.1   US   ISSN 0740-9222
HD9275.U8
MILK FACTS. 1938. a. $35 (effective 1997). Milk Industry Foundation, 1250 H St., N.W., Washington, DC 20005. FAX 202-331-7820. Ed. Martin Veeger. **Document type:** trade publication.
    Description: Reference data on the production and consumption of dairy products, and on the economics of the dairy industry.

637   UK
HD9282.G69   CODEN: MIINAV
MILK INDUSTRY INTERNATIONAL; the journal for manufacturers, processors and retailers. 1920. m. £50 (foreign £65). National Dairymen's Association, 19 Cornwall Terrace, London NW1 4QP, England. TEL 0171-935-4562. FAX 0171-486-7244. Ed. Ron Jeffries. adv.; bk.rev.; charts; illus.; stat. circ. 5,100. (also avail. in microform from UMI) **Indexed:** Curr.Cont., Curr.Pack.Abstr., Dairy Sci.Abstr., Food Sci.& Tech.Abstr., Int.Packag.Abstr., Packag.Sci.Tech., Rural Recreat.Tour.Abstr., World Agri.Econ.& Rural Sociol.Abstr. **Document type:** trade publication.
—UMI.
    Formerly (until 1995): Milk Industry (ISSN 0026-4172)

637   US   ISSN 0162-2781
MILK MARKETER. 1916. m. (combined July-Aug. & Dec.-Jan.). $5 to non-members. Milk Marketing Inc., 8257 Dow Circle, Box 36050, Strongsville, OH 44136. TEL 216-826-4730. FAX 216-826-1971. Ed. D. Schriver. adv.; mkt.; stat. circ. 11,500.
    Formerly: Milk Reporter (ISSN 0011-5746); Supersedes in part: Cincinnati Gazette & Ft. Wayne Newsletter & Central Ohio Digest & Miami Valley Dairyman (ISSN 0026-1955)
    Description: Describes dairy cooperative marketing for MMI members.

637.1   UK   ISSN 0950-3730
MILK PRODUCTS. irreg. approx. 10/yr. £310 (rest of Europe £325; elsewhere £355) (effective 1997). Agra Europe (London) Ltd., 25 Frant Rd., Tunbridge Wells, Kent TN2 5JT, England. TEL 44-1892-533813. FAX 44-1892-544895. TELEX 95114 AGRATW G. E-mail: 100637.3460@compuserve.com. charts; stat. **Document type:** trade publication.
    Description: Covers the butter, cheese, and milk markets in European and major milk-producing countries. Reports the current market situation with tables and graphs for each product.

338.4   US
MINNESOTA DAIRY PLANTS. 1910. a. free. Department of Agriculture, Dairy and Food Inspection Division, 90 W. Plato Blvd., St. Paul, MN 55107. TEL 612-296-3647. FAX 612-297-5176. Ed. Sandra Dunn. circ. 400. **Document type:** government publication.

637   CI   ISSN 0026-704X
    CODEN: MLJEAU
MLJEKARSTVO; list za unapredenje mljekarstva. (Text in Croatian) 1950. m. 120 HRK. Udruzenje Mlekarskih Radnika Republike Hrvatske - Association of Dairyman of SR Croatia, Ilica 31-III, Zagreb, Croatia. TEL 424-420. Ed. Ljerka Krsev. adv.; bk.rev.; film rev.; software rev.; index. circ. 1,000. **Indexed:** Chem.Abstr., Dairy Sci.Abstr., Food Sci.& Tech.Abstr., Rural Recreat.Tour.Abstr., World Agri.Econ.& Rural Sociol.Abstr.
—BLDSC (5879.740000); CASDDS.

637   GW   ISSN 0043-2512
DIE MOLKEREI-ZEITUNG WELT DER MILCH. 1946. fortn. DM.714. Heinrichs Verlag GmbH and Co. KG, Postfach 100550, 31105 Hildesheim, Germany. TEL 49-5121-53279. Ed. J. Heiber. adv.; illus. **Indexed:** Agri.Eng.Abstr., Dairy Sci.Abstr., Food Sci.& Tech.Abstr., Nutr.Abstr., Rural Recreat.Tour.Abstr., World Agri.Econ.& Rural Sociol.Abstr. **Document type:** trade publication.

637   RU   ISSN 1019-8946
    CODEN: MOPRAI
MOLOCHNAYA PROMYSHLENNOST'. 1988. bi-m. $100 (effective 1998). Sadovaya-Spasskaya , 18, 107807 Moscow, Russia. TEL 7-95-2072050. FAX 7-95-2072870. E-mail: noreditor@rosnet.rosmailcom. (Dist. by: Mezhdunarodnaya Kniga, B. Yakimanka 39, 117049 Moscow, Russia. TEL 7-095-2384967. FAX 7-095-2384634) Ed. Tat'yana A. Kuznetsova. bk.rev.; bibl.; illus.; index. **Indexed:** Biol.Abstr., Chem.Abstr., Dairy Sci.Abstr., Food Sci.& Tech.Abstr., Nutr.Abstr., Packag.Sci.Tech., Rural Recreat.Tour.Abstr., World Agri.Econ.& Rural Sociol.Abstr.
—BLDSC (0116.000000); CASDDS; CISTI; Linda Hall.
    Supersedes in part (in 1992): Molochnaya i Myasnaya Promyshlennost' (ISSN 0235-2575); Formed by the merger of (1934-1988): Molochnaya Promyshlennost' (ISSN 0026-9026); (1940-1988): Myasnaya Industriya S.S.S.R. (ISSN 0027-5492)
    Refereed Serial

591   KR   ISSN 0544-7453
MOLOCHNO-M'YASNE SKOTARSTVO; mizhvidomchyi temetichnyi naukovyi zbirnik. (Text in Ukrainian; summaries in English, Russian) 1965. s-a. $3.18 6 grivnas. Akademiya Nauk Ukrainy, Institut Tvarinnitstva, P-v Kulinichi, 312120 Kharkov, Ukraine. TEL 38-572-953181. FAX 38-572-953066. Ed. A.M. Mamenko. R&P contact: V.S. Linnik. circ. 1,000 (paid). (back issues avail.) **Indexed:** Anim.Breed.Abstr. **Document type:** academic/scholarly publication.
    Description: Presents results of research in the fields of dairy and beef cattle breeding, nutrition, feeding and housing, for animal scientists.
    Refereed Serial

MONTHLY PRICE REVIEW. see *FOOD AND FOOD INDUSTRIES*

THE MOOSLETTER. see *HOBBIES*

NAS CHOV; casopis pro zivocisnou vyrobu. see *AGRICULTURE — Poultry And Livestock*

636   US   ISSN 0077-3255
NATIONAL ASSOCIATION OF ANIMAL BREEDERS. ANNUAL PROCEEDINGS. 1952. a. $5. National Association of Animal Breeders, 401 Bernadette St., Box 1033, Columbia, MO 65205. TEL 573-445-4406. FAX 573-446-2279. Ed. Gordon A. Doak. **Document type:** proceedings.

637   CN
NATIONAL DAIRY COUNCIL OF CANADA. DIRECTION. (Text in English, French) 1973. bi-m. free. National Dairy Council of Canada, 221 Laurier Ave., E., Ottawa, ON K1N 6P1, Canada. TEL 613-238-4116. FAX 613-238-6247. circ. 1,500 (controlled). **Document type:** bulletin.
    Former titles: National Dairy Council of Canada. Resume; (until 1973): National Dairy Council of Canada. Bulletin.

AGRICULTURE — DAIRYING AND DAIRY PRODUCTS

637   II   ISSN 0301-8407
NATIONAL DAIRY RESEARCH INSTITUTE. ANNUAL REPORT. (Text in English) 1923. a. free. Indian Council of Agricultural Research, National Dairy Research Institute, Karnal 132 001, Haryana, India. TEL 91-184-252800. TELEX 0396-204-NDRI. E-mail: ndri@x400.nicgw.nic.in. Ed. O.S. Tomer. circ. 1,500. **Indexed:** Anim.Breed.Abstr., Biol.Abstr., Dairy Sci.Abstr., Field Crop Abstr., Food Sci.& Tech.Abstr., Herb.Abstr. **Document type:** academic/scholarly publication.

636.2   FI   ISSN 0028-131X
NAUTAKARJA/CATTLE. (Text in Finnish; summaries in Swedish) 1971. 4/yr. FIM 190. Suomen Kotielainjalostusosuuskunta - Finnish Animal Breeding Cooperative, P.O. Box 40, FIN-01301 Vantaa, Finland. TEL 358-0-857061. FAX 358-0-833949. TELEX 125 890 FABA SF. Ed. Jouko Syvaerjaervi. adv.; bk.rev.; charts; illus.; stat. circ. 19,000.
    Supersedes: Finlands Ayrshireboskap.
    Description: Covers cattle breeding and care.

NETHERLANDS. CENTRAAL BUREAU VOOR DE STATISTIEK. PRODUCTIE STATISTIEK VAN DE ZUIVELINDUSTRIE/NETHERLANDS. CENTRAL BUREAU OF STATISTICS. PRODUCTION STATISTICS OF THE DAIRY INDUSTRY. see *AGRICULTURE — Abstracting, Bibliographies, Statistics*

637   AT
NEW SOUTH WALES DAIRY DIGEST. 1919. m. Aus.$35 (foreign Aus.$45) (effective 1995). (New South Wales Dairy Farmers Association Limited) D F A Newspapers Ltd., 491 Elizabeth St., Surry Hills, N.S.W. 2010, Australia. TEL 61-2-3180688. FAX 61-2-3193349. Ed. Margaret Konemann. adv.: page Aus.$1744. stat. circ. 2,500. (back issues avail.) **Document type:** newspaper, trade publication.
    Formerly: New South Wales Dairymen's Digest (ISSN 0310-3722)
    Description: Contains industry news and advertising aimed at every dairy farmer in State of NSW, Australia.

637   US   ISSN 0279-8611
NEW YORK HOLSTEIN NEWS. 1946. m. $15 (foreign $30). New York Holstein Association, Box 190, Ithaca, NY 14851. TEL 607-273-7591. FAX 607-273-7612. Ed. Kelly A. Driver. adv. contact: Kelly A. Driver. index; circ. 4,300 (controlled). (reprint service avail. from UMI) **Document type:** trade publication.
    Formerly: New York Holstein Friesian News (ISSN 0028-727X)
    Description: Provides milk production records, cattle show results, and merchandising information for the top cows and best managed herds in New York state.

637   US   ISSN 0732-9121
SF232.N7
NEW YORK STATE DAIRY STATISTICS. a. free. Department of Agriculture and Markets, Division of Dairy Industry Services, 1 Winner's Cir., Albany, NY 12235. circ. 1,800. **Document type:** government publication, bulletin.
    Former titles: New York Dairy Statistics; New York Crop Reporting Service. Statistics Relative to the Dairy Industry in New York State (ISSN 0077-8974)

354   NZ
NEW ZEALAND DAIRY BOARD. ANNUAL REPORT AND STATEMENT OF ACCOUNTS. 1935. a. NZ.$10. New Zealand Dairy Board, P.O. Box 417, Wellington, New Zealand. FAX 64-4-4723691. Ed. N.H. Martin. illus.; stat.; circ. 50,000 (controlled). **Document type:** corporate report.
    Former titles (until 1987): New Zealand Dairy Board. Report for the Year Ended (Year) (ISSN 0112-7268); (until 1977): New Zealand Dairy Board. Annual Report and Statement of Accounts (ISSN 0112-725X); Which superseded (in 1966): New Zealand Dairy Production and Marketing Board. Annual Report and Statement of Account (ISSN 0545-7041); Which was formerly (until 1962): New Zealand Dairy Board. Annual Report and Statement of Accounts (ISSN 0112-2363).

637   NZ   ISSN 0111-915X
NEW ZEALAND DAIRY EXPORTER. 1925. m. NZ.$25 (foreign NZ.$90). New Zealand Dairy Exporter Ltd., P.O. Box 299, Wellington, New Zealand. TEL 64-4-990300. FAX 64-4-4990330. Ed. Lance McEldowney. adv. contact: Corrie Cook. bk.rev.; index. circ. 23,464. **Indexed:** Dairy Sci.Abstr. **Document type:** trade publication.
    —CCC.
    Description: Spans the industry with stories on dairy farm production, research, manufacturing, and marketing.
    Refereed Serial

637   GW   ISSN 0724-3227
NORDDEUTSCHER MOLKEREI UND KAESEREI ADRESSKALENDER; Vormerk-, Auskunfts- und Fachanschriftenbuch fuer die gesamte Milchwirtschaft. 1936. a. DM.49 (effective 1996). Volkswirtschaftlicher Verlag (VV GmbH), Kederbacherstr. 50, 81377 Munich, Germany. TEL 49-89-7141013. FAX 49-89-7141013. Eds. Hilde Walter, Rosemarie von Funche. (back issues avail.) **Document type:** trade publication.

353.9   US   ISSN 0091-9446
HD9282.U5
NORTH DAKOTA. MILK STABILIZATION BOARD. ANNUAL REPORT OF ADMINISTRATIVE ACTIVITIES. (Report year ends June 30) 1968. a. North Dakota Milk Stabilization Board, 206 1-2 N. 6th St., Rm. 5, Bismarck, ND 58501. TEL 701-224-2988. circ. 300.

637   JA   ISSN 0910-7878
NYUGIKYO SHIRYO/JAPAN DAIRY TECHNICAL ASSOCIATION. BULLETIN. (Text in Japanese) 1951. bi-m. Nihon Nyugyo Gijutsu Kyokai, 14-19, Kudan Kita 1-chome, Chiyoda-ku, Tokyo 102, Japan. TEL 03-264-1921. circ. 750. (back issues avail.)
    Formerly (until 1967): Gikyo Shiryo - Japan Dairy Products Technical Association. Bulletin (ISSN 0910-786X)

636 637.1   AU   ISSN 0369-786X
DIE OESTERREICHISCHE MILCHWIRTSCHAFT. 1946. s-m. S.1550 (foreign S.1895). (Milchwirtschaftsfonds) Oesterreichischer Agrarverlag GmbH, Inkustr. 1-7, A-3400 Klosterneuburg, Austria. TEL 02243-33006. FAX 02243-3330056. Ed. Wilhelm Sadofsky. circ. 2,000. **Indexed:** Dairy Sci.Abstr., Food Sci.& Tech.Abstr., Nutr.Abstr., Pig News & Info., Rural Recreat.Tour.Abstr., Soyabean Abstr., World Agri.Econ.& Rural Sociol.Abstr.

636   US   ISSN 0899-4862
OHIO NEWS. Masthead title: Holstein News. 1925. bi-m. $15 (effective 1997). Ohio Holstein-Friesian Association, Inc., 1375 Heyl Rd., Box 479, Wooster, OH 44691. TEL 330-264-9088. FAX 330-263-1653. Ed. Esther Welch. R&P contact: Esther Welch. adv.: B&W page $190, color page $540; adv. contact: Esther Welch. bk.rev. circ. 3,000. **Document type:** trade publication.
    —Linda Hall.
    Formerly: Ohio Holstein News (ISSN 0199-7580)

637   CN   ISSN 1192-800X
ONTARIO DAIRY FARMER MAGAZINE. 6/yr. Bowes Publishers Ltd., P.O. Box 7400, London, ON N5Y 4X3, Canada. TEL 519-473-0010. FAX 519-473-2256. Ed. Paul Mahon; Pub. M.J. Hawkins. **Document type:** trade publication.
    Former titles: Dairy Farmer Quarterly Magazine (ISSN 1182-8900); Ontario Dairy Farmer (ISSN 0832-5162)
    Description: Dairy farming business news for Ontario.

637   CN   ISSN 0030-3038
ONTARIO MILK PRODUCER. (Text and summaries in English and French) 1925. m. Can.$25.68 (foreign Can.$36). Ontario Milk Marketing Board, 6780 Campobello Rd., Mississauga, ON L5N 2L8, Canada. TEL 905-821-8970. FAX 905-821-3160. Ed. Bill Dimmick. adv. contact: Bob Mercer. mkt. circ. 14,000.
    —Linda Hall.

P L M. (Production Laitiere Moderne) see *AGRICULTURE — Poultry And Livestock*

637   IT
PARMIGIANO-REGGIANO. 1971. s-a. free. Consorzio Formaggio Parmigiano-Reggiano, Via Kennedy, 18, 42100 Reggio Emilia, Italy. Ed. Luigi Verrini. adv. circ. 13,000.

338.1   FR
POT A LAIT. m. Syndicat de l'Industrie Laitiere de l'Est, rue Giradet, B.P. 433, 54001 Nancy, France. Ed. Roger Hardy. adv. circ. 10,000.

POTRAVINARSKE AKTUALITY. MLEKARENSKY PRUMYSL see *FOOD AND FOOD INDUSTRIES*

POULTRY AND EGG MARKETING; the bi-monthly news magazine of the poultry marketing industry. see *AGRICULTURE — Poultry And Livestock*

637.1   UK   ISSN 0141-223X
PRESERVED MILK. 1964. irreg., approx. 10/yr. £325 (rest of Europe £345; elsewhere £376) (effective 1997). Agra Europe (London) Ltd., 25 Frant Rd., Tunbridge Wells, Kent TN2 5JT, England. TEL 44-1892-533813. FAX 44-1892-544895. TELEX 95114 AGRATW G. E-mail: 100637.3460@compuserve.com. Ed. Guy Faulkner. (back issues avail.) **Document type:** trade publication.
    —BLDSC (6609.790000).
    Description: Covers stocks, exports, imports, and prices in the preserved-milk world market.

636.234   FR   ISSN 1161-2665
LA PRIM HOLSTEIN. 1946. q. 104.37 F. Unite Nationale de Selection et de Promotion de la Race Bovine Prim Holstein, Le Montsoreau, 49480 St. Sylvain d'Anjou, France. FAX 33-2-41432396. Ed. Jacques Boully. adv.; stat. circ. 15,000.
    Former titles (until 1990): Francaise Frisonne (ISSN 0240-0154); Francaise Frisonne Pied Noire (ISSN 0046-4872)

637   FR   ISSN 0998-6650
PROCESS MAGAZINE; le mensuel des techniques laitieres et alimentaires. 1945. m. 498 F. (foreign 598 F.). Editions du Boisbaudry, Rue des Landelles, ZI Rennes Sud-Est, B.P. 6359, 35063 Rennes cedex, France. TEL 99-32-21-21. FAX 99-32-14-17. TELEX 730619F. Ed. Francois Morel. adv.; bibl.; illus.; tr.lit.; index. circ. 6,000. **Indexed:** Biol.Abstr., Dairy Sci.Abstr., Food Sci.& Tech.Abstr., Nutr.Abstr., Rural Recreat.Tour.Abstr., World Agri.Econ.& Rural Sociol.Abstr.
    —BLDSC (6849.983150).
    Former titles (until 1989): Process; Technique Laitiere et Marketing; Technique Laitiere (ISSN 0040-1242)
    Description: Deals with the dairy industry and the various branches technically or economically connected to it.

637   CN   ISSN 0228-1686
PRODUCTEUR DE LAIT QUEBECOIS. (Text in French) 1980. m. Can.$15. Federation des Producteurs de Lait du Quebec, 555 bd. Roland Therrien, Longueuil PQ J4H 3Y9, Canada. TEL 514-679-0530. FAX 514-679-5436. Ed. Hugues Belzile. circ. 18,000. (back issues avail.) **Document type:** trade publication.

637   AT   ISSN 0033-6106
QUEENSLAND DAIRYFARMER. 1946. m. Aus.$35 (free to Queensland dairyfarmers) (foreign Aus.$45). Queensland Dairyfarmers Organization, P.O. Box 61 Brisbane Roma St., Brisbane, Qld. 4003, Australia. TEL 07-236-2955. FAX 07-236-2956. Ed. Anne Chamberlain. R&P contact: Anne Chamberlain. TEL 61-7-38930359. adv. contact: Marris Lake. bk.rev. illus. circ. 2,500. (tabloid format) **Document type:** newspaper.
    Description: Latest developments in Queensland and Australian dairy industry and tropical dairy farming techniques.

AGRICULTURE — DAIRYING AND DAIRY PRODUCTS

637   **JA**   ISSN 0388-001X
CODEN: JCDSDH
RAKUNO GAKUEN DAIGAKU KIYO. SHIZEN KAGAKU HEN/RAKUNO GAKUEN UNIVERSITY. JOURNAL: NATURAL SCIENCE. (Text mainly in Japanese; occasionally in English and German; summaries mainly in English) 1961. a. exchange basis. Rakuno Gakuen Daigaku - Rakuno Gakuen University, 582-1 Bunkyodai Midori-cho, Ebetsu-shi, Hokkaido 069, Japan. Ed. Kazuo Horiuchi. abstr. circ. 1,000. **Indexed:** Agrindex, Biol.Abstr., Chem.Abstr., Curr.Cont., Dairy Sci.Abstr., Herb.Abstr., Jap.Per.Ind., Rev.Med.& Vet.Mycol., Sport Fish.Abstr., Vet.Bull., Wild.Rev., Zoo.Rec. **Document type:** academic/scholarly publication.
—CASDDS.
    Supersedes in part: College of Dairy Agriculture, Hokkaido. Journal (ISSN 0069-570X)

637   **US**
RECAP OF MILK RECEIPTS AND UTILIZATION IN MONTANA. s-a. free. Milk Control Bureau, 1520 E. Sixth Ave., Rm. 50, Box 200512, Helena, MT 59620-0512. TEL 406-444-2875. FAX 406-444-4186. Ed. Marlys Koontz. circ. 560. **Document type:** trade publication.
    Formerly: Report of Milk Utilization in Montana (ISSN 0080-1267)

637.1   **FR**   ISSN 0995-6492
REUSSIR LAIT - ELEVAGE. 1987. 11/yr. 190 F. (foreign 230 F.) (effective 1997); newsstand price: 25 F. 19 quai du Juillet, B.P. 18, 14005 Caen Cedex, France. TEL 33-2-31357704. FAX 33-2-31822963. TELEX 632 322 F. Ed. Annick Conte; Pub. Henri Lefebvre. R&P contact: Marc Jourdan. adv. contact: Jean-Pierre Dumas. circ. 67,000. **Document type:** newspaper.
    Description: Technical and economical information about milk production.

637.1   **AG**   ISSN 0327-5418
REVISTA ARGENTINA DE LACTOLOGIA. 1988. s-a. Universidad Nacional del Litoral Santa Fe, Facultad de Ingenieria Quimica, Instituto de Lactologia Industrial, Santiago del Estero 2829, 3000 Santa Fe, Argentina. TEL 54-42-530302. FAX 54-42-571162. E-mail: azalazar@fiqus.unl.edu.ar. (Co-sponsor: Centro Regional de Investigacion y Desarrollo de Santa Fe) Ed. Carlos A. Zalazar. **Indexed:** Dairy Sci.Abstr. **Document type:** academic/scholarly publication.
—BLDSC (7841.260000).

REVISTA BRASILEIRA DE ZOOTECNIA. see *VETERINARY SCIENCE*

637   **CU**
REVISTA PASTOS Y FORRAJES. (Text in Spanish; summaries in English) 3/yr. $18 in N. and S. America; Europe $20. (Centro Universitario de Matanzas, Estacion Experimental de Pastos y Forrajes "Indio Hatuey") Ediciones Cubanas, Obispo No. 527, Apdo. 605, Havana, Cuba. TEL 32-5556-60. **Indexed:** Agroforest.Abstr., Sugar Ind.Abstr.

637   **FR**   ISSN 0035-3590
SF221   CODEN: RLAFA9
REVUE LAITIERE FRANCAISE. 1876. 10/yr. 440 F.($60) (effective 1997). Societe des Editions Laitieres Francaises, 19 quai de Juillet, 14000 Caen, France. TEL 33-2-31708818. FAX 33-2-31822963. Ed. Rita Lemoine; Pub. Marc Jourdan. adv. contact: Jean-Pierre Dumas. bk.rev.; bibl.; charts; illus.; stat.; index. circ. 4,500. **Indexed:** Dairy Sci.Abstr., Food Sci.& Tech.Abstr. **Document type:** newspaper.
    Incorporating: Industrie Laitiere.
    Description: Focuses on the dairy industry: process, research, companies, economy, milk products and their market.

637   **IT**   ISSN 0392-3827
CODEN: RILAAS
RIVISTA DEL LATTE. 1946. q. L.4500. Associazione Licenziati Istituto Sperimentale di Caseificio, Via Novara 89, 20153 Milan, Italy. TEL 2-404-79-41. FAX 2-400-900-10. Ed. Elio Ligugnana. adv. circ. 1,000. **Indexed:** Dairy Sci.Abstr., Food Sci.& Tech.Abstr.
—CASDDS.

637   **SW**   ISSN 1101-2706
CODEN: SDINEW
S D I - SCANDINAVIAN DAIRY INFORMATION. (Text in English) 1935. q. $38. (Scandinavian Dairy Industry) Tidskrifts AB Nordisk Mejeriindustri, S-105 46 Stockholm, Sweden. TEL 46-8-700-28400. FAX 46-8-700-2842. Ed. Henning Mortensen; Pub. Ulf Borgstroem. adv.: B&W page DKK 9950, color page DKK 16070; trim 190 x 267; adv. contact: Marianne Kalriis. bk.rev.; charts; illus.; tr.lit.; index. circ. 6,000. **Indexed:** Dairy Sci.Abstr., Excerp.Med., Food Sci.& Tech.Abstr., Int.Packag.Abstr., Nutr.Abstr., Rural Recreat.Tour.Abstr., Soyabean Abstr., World Agri.Econ.& Rural Sociol.Abstr. **Document type:** trade publication.
—BLDSC (8087.474700).
    Former titles (until 1987): North European Food and Dairy Journal (ISSN 0903-9759); North European Dairy Journal (ISSN 0109-3207); Nordeuropaeisk Mejeri-Tidsskrift (ISSN 0106-7265); Nordisk Mejeri-Tidsskrift (ISSN 0029-1439)
    Description: Focuses on current issues in the dairy industry, such as technology, products, research and tests.

338.1 637   **UK**
S W DAIRY FARMER. (Supplement to: Dairy Farmer (ISSN 0011-5576)) a. £22($33) (includes Dairy Farmer magazine). Morgan-Grampian (Farming Press) Ltd. (Subsidiary of: Morgan-Grampian plc), Morgan-Grampian House, 30 Calderwood St., London SE18 6QH, England. TEL 01473-241122. FAX 01473-240501. Ed. Shirley Macmillan. adv. contact: John M. Welford. bk.rev. (back issues avail.) **Document type:** trade publication.
    Description: Covers all aspects of dairy farming.

SAM. see *AGRICULTURE — Poultry And Livestock*

637   **SZ**   ISSN 0370-9108
SCHWEIZERISCHE MILCHZEITUNG. (Text in French, German) 1874. 52/yr. 146 SFr. (effective 1997). Publi-Lactis AG, Gurtengasse 6, CH-3001 Bern, Switzerland. TEL 41-31-3122431. FAX 41-31-212185. Ed. Ulrich Wenger. R&P contact: Stephanie Mermoz. adv. contact: Kurt Flueckiger. circ. 5,300. **Indexed:** Dairy Sci.Abstr., Food Sci.& Tech.Abstr., Nutr.Abstr. **Document type:** trade publication.
—BLDSC (8118.800000).

637   **IT**   ISSN 0036-889X
CODEN: SLCAAF
SCIENZA E TECNICA LATTIERO-CASEARIA. (Text in English, Italian) 1949. bi-m. L.100000($63) (Associazione Italiana Tecnici del Latte - Italian Dairy Science Association) AITec, Via Torelli 17, 43100 Parma, Italy. TEL 39-51-489428. FAX 39-521-484512. Ed. Luigi Zannoni. adv.: B&W page L.500000; trim 170 x 240; adv. contact: Claudio Rizzi. bk.rev.; abstr.; bibl.; charts; illus.; cum.index. circ. 1,700. (tabloid format) **Indexed:** Anim.Breed.Abstr., Chem.Abstr., Dairy Sci.Abstr., Food Sci.& Tech.Abstr., Ind.Vet., Rural Recreat.Tour.Abstr., Vet.Bull., World Agri.Econ.& Rural Sociol.Abstr. **Document type:** bulletin.
    Description: Contributes to the difusion of the studies and techniques related to the production, preservation, transportation and utilization of milk and its by-products.

SICAMOB INFORMATION. see *AGRICULTURE — Poultry And Livestock*

SMALLHOLDER; the practical monthly guide for the small farmer. see *AGRICULTURE*

637   **JA**   ISSN 1340-2773
CODEN: SBRRE7
SNOW BRAND R & D REPORTS/YUKIJIRUSHI NYUGYO KENKYU HOKOKU. (Text in Japanese; summaries in English, Japanese) 1950. irreg. (approx. a.). free. Snow Brand Milk Products Co. Ltd. - Yukijirushi Nyugyo K.K., R&D Planning Department, 1-1-2 Minami-dai, Kawagoe, Saitama 350-11, Japan. TEL 0492-42-8111. FAX 0492-46-5649. Ed. Masayoshi Fukushima; Pub. Kazuo Ido. R&P contact: Masayoshi Fukushima. circ. 400. **Indexed:** Chem.Abstr., Dairy Sci.Abstr., Food Sci.& Tech.Abstr., Soyabean Abstr., Triticale Abstr. **Document type:** academic/scholarly publication.
—BLDSC (8313.990000); CASDDS.
    Formerly: Snow Brand Milk Products Company. Research Laboratory. Reports - Yukijirushi Nyugyo Kenkyujo Hokoku (ISSN 0082-4763)

354.68   **SA**
SOUTH AFRICA. MILK BOARD. ANNUAL REPORT. (Text in Afrikaans, English) 1946. a. free. Milk Board - Melkraad, P.O. Box 1284, Pretoria 0001, South Africa. TEL 27-12-8044800. FAX 21-12-8044811. Ed. J. Hanekom. circ. 1,000. **Document type:** government publication.
    Former titles (until 1995): South Africa. Dairy Board. Annual Report; South Africa. Dairy Control Board. Annual Report; South Africa. Milk Board. Annual Report.

637   **US**
SOUTHEAST DAIRY OUTLOOK.* 1966. bi-m. $6. Dairy Farmers Inc., 166 Lookout Pl., Ste. 101, Maitland, FL 32751-4496. TEL 305-647-8899. FAX 407-647-0606. Ed. Sandra Fabing Schuman. adv.; bk.rev. circ. 1,762.
    Formerly: Southeastern Dairy Review (ISSN 0038-3643)

637   **US**
SOUTHERN DAIRY. 1992. bi-m. free. Rural Press U S A, 7701 Six Forks Rd., Ste. 132, Raleigh, NC 27615. TEL 919-676-3276; 800-477-1737. FAX 919-676-9803. (Subscr. to: Box 150001, Raleigh, NC 27624) Ed. Amy Leslie; Pub. Jeff Tennant. adv.: B&W page $1954. circ. 16,000. **Document type:** newspaper.

637   **GW**   ISSN 0724-3235
SUEDDEUTSCHER MOLKEREI UND KAESEREI ADRESSKALENDER; Vormerk-, Auskunfts- und Fachanschriftenbuch fuer die gesamte Milchwirtschaft. 1924. a. DM.49 (effective 1996). Volkswirtschaftlicher Verlag (VV GmbH), Kederbacherstr. 50, 81377 Munich, Germany. TEL 49-89-7141013. FAX 49-89-7192753. Eds. Hilde Walter, Rosemarie von Funcke. (back issues avail.) **Document type:** trade publication.

SUIZO CARNE Y LECHE. see *AGRICULTURE — Poultry And Livestock*

636   **US**
TECHNICAL CONFERENCE ON ARTIFICIAL INSEMINATION AND REPRODUCTION. 1966. biennial. $15. National Association of Animal Breeders, 401 Bernadette St., Box 1033, Columbia, MO 65205. TEL 573-445-4406. FAX 573-446-2279. Ed. Gordon A. Doak. **Indexed:** Anim.Breed.Abstr. **Document type:** academic/scholarly publication, proceedings.

637.1   **FR**   ISSN 1167-8550
TELEX LAITERIE -BOISSONS. 11/yr. Groupe Alain Thirion, 58 rue d'Alsace, 88000 Epinal, France. TEL 33-3-29291226. FAX 33-3-29354154. Ed. Alain Thirion. R&P contact: Nathalie Berthier. circ. 10,000. **Document type:** trade publication.

637   **JA**   ISSN 0289-3096
TOCHIGI PREFECTURAL DAIRY EXPERIMENTAL INSTITUTE. BULLETIN. (Text in Japanese) a. free. Tochigi Prefectural Dairy Experimental Institute, 298 Senbonmatu, Nishinasuno-machi, Nasu-gun, Tochigi 329-27, Japan. Ed. Michihiro Sogama. adv. contact: Michihiro Sugama. circ. 300. (back issues avail.) **Document type:** bulletin.

TYPEX MAGAZINE; the international business magazine for dairy pedigree breeders. see *AGRICULTURE — Poultry And Livestock*

637.1   **UK**
U K DAIRY FACTS AND FIGURES. 1956. a. £22. Residuary Milk Marketing Board, Thames Ditton, Surrey KT7 OEL, England. TEL 0181-398-4101. FAX 0181-398-8485. Ed. Lynn Pickett. circ. 1,900. (back issues avail.) **Document type:** trade publication.

338.177   **DK**
UGENYT FRA MEJERIFORENINGEN. 1973. w. DKK 375 (foreign DKK 325) (effective 1997). Mejeriforeningen - Danish Dairy Board, Frederiks Alle 22, DK-8000 Aarhus C, Denmark. TEL 45-87-31-20-00. FAX 45-87-31-20-01. E-mail: ddb@mejeri.dk- Eds. Henning Mortensen, Eivind Hougaard. bk.rev. circ. 3,800. **Document type:** trade publication.
    Formerly: Mejeribrugets Uge-Nyt (ISSN 0302-833X)
    Description: Information from the Danish Dairy Board for member dairy companies.

UNITED CAPRINE NEWS. see *AGRICULTURE — Poultry And Livestock*

AGRICULTURE — FEED, FLOUR AND GRAIN

637.1 UK
UNITED NEWS. 1963. m. free. United Dairy Farmers Ltd., 456 Antrim Rd., Belfast, N. Ireland. FAX 0232-372222. TELEX 747136. Ed. Norman Murray. adv. contact: Malcom Bridges. bk.rev. circ. 8,000. **Document type:** trade publication.
Formerly (until 1995): Topics.

U.S. DEPARTMENT OF AGRICULTURE. AGRICULTURAL STATISTICS BOARD REPORT: DAIRY PRODUCTS. see *AGRICULTURE — Abstracting, Bibliographies, Statistics*

U.S. DEPARTMENT OF AGRICULTURE. AGRICULTURAL STATISTICS BOARD REPORT: MILK PRODUCTION. see *AGRICULTURE — Abstracting, Bibliographies, Statistics*

WEEKLY INSIDERS DAIRY & EGG LETTER. see *FOOD AND FOOD INDUSTRIES*

637 CN ISSN 1194-9511
WESTERN DAIRY FARMER QUARTERLY MAGAZINE. 1991. q. Can.$16($30) (foreign $30) (effective 1997). Bowes Publishers Ltd. (Alberta), 4504-61 Ave., Leduc, AB T9E 2Y1, Canada. TEL 403-986-2271. FAX 403-986-6397. E-mail: wdfarmer@ccinet.ab.ca. Ed. Ken Nelson; Pub. Neil Sutcliffe. adv.: B&W page Can.$795, color page Can.$1170; trim 8 1/8 x 10 3/4; adv. contact: Neil Sutcliffe. circ. 6,982. **Document type:** trade publication.

637 US ISSN 1079-0578
SF232.W47
WESTERN DAIRYMAN. 1922. m. $35 (foreign $95). Holstein-Friesian World, Inc., 8036 Lake Rd., Box 299, Sandy Creek, NY 13145. TEL 315-387-3441. FAX 315-387-3655. Ed. Dennis J. Halladay; Pub. Stanley E. Bird. adv.: B&W page $2305, color page $3130; trim 8 x 10 7/8. bk.rev.; illus.; mkt.; stat.; index. circ. 18,000. (back issues avail.)
—UnCover.
Formerly: Dairyman (ISSN 0011-572X)
Description: For the large herd dairy farmer. Emphasizes news about dairy farmers and dairy farming, and related dairy industries. Covers state and national legislation, scientific and technical advances in milk production and marketing, feeding, and breeding.

637 NE
ZELFKAZER. 1947. m. fl.31 (effective Jan. 1991). Centraal Orgaan Zuivelcontrole, Afd Boerenkaas, P.O. Box 250, 3830 EG Leusden, Netherlands. FAX 033-940674. TELEX 79386. circ. 1,700.

637 CC ISSN 1001-2230
ZHONGGUO RUPIN GONGYE/CHINA DAIRY INDUSTRY. (Text in Chinese) bi-m. Heilongjiang Rupin Gongye Jishu Kaifa Zhongxin, 113, Xuefu Lu, Nangang-qu, Harbin, Heilongjiang 150086, People's Republic of China. TEL 62740. Ed. Wu Songcheng. **Indexed:** Food Sci.& Tech.Abstr.

637 NE
ZUIVELKOERIER. 1948. 11/yr. fl.80 (effective 1995). (Stichting Promotion Detailhandel) Uitgeverij Adrem B.V., Randway 3-B, 4104 AC Culemborg, Netherlands. TEL 31-345-533011. FAX 31-345-533166. (Subscr. to: Stichting Promotie Detailhandel, Postbus 2005, 6900 CA Zevenaar, Netherlands. TEL 31-316-527101. FAX 31-316-333669) Ed. J.Th. Puttman. adv. contact: Andre Schappen. charts; illus.; pat.; stat.; tr.lit. circ. 7,000. **Document type:** trade publication.
Former titles (until 1977): Melk en Zuivel (ISSN 0025-8970); Melk en Zuivelhandel.

637 NE ISSN 0044-5436
ZUIVELNIEUWS. 1968. w. fl.120. GemZu, Patrijsweg 58, 2289 EX Rijswijk, Netherlands. TEL 31-70-3369450. FAX 31-70-3369454. Ed. M.P.J. Poot. adv.; bk.rev.; charts. circ. 950. **Document type:** bulletin, newsletter.
Formerly: Kaas.

637 NE ISSN 0165-8573
ZUIVELZICHT. 1906. bi-m. fl.400. Dutch Dairy Association, Bleiswijkseweg 35, 2712 PB Zoetermeer, Netherlands. TEL 31-79-430312. FAX 31-79-412572. Ed. T. Brouwers. adv.; bk.rev. circ. 3,500. **Indexed:** Dairy Sci.Abstr., Food Sci.& Tech.Abstr., Geo.Abstr., Key to Econ.Sci., World Agri.Econ.& Rural Sociol.Abstr.
—SWETS.

AGRICULTURE — Feed, Flour And Grain

A F I A SAFETYGRAM. (American Feed Industry Association) see *AGRICULTURE — Poultry And Livestock*

664.7 PL ISSN 0860-2603
CODEN: AATZE6
ACTA ACADEMIAE AGRICULTURAE AC TECHNICAE OLSTENENSIS. ZOOTECHNICA/AGRICULTURAL AND TECHNICAL ACADEMY IN OLSZTYN. ANIMAL HUSBANDRY. (Supplement avail.: Zootechnics) (Text in Polish; summaries in English, Polish) 1956. s-a. price varies. (Akademia Rolniczo-Techniczna im. M. Oczapowskiego) Wydawnictwo A R T Olsztyn, Blok 12, 10-957 Olsztyn-Kortowo, Poland. TEL 48-89-5273310. TELEX 0526419. E-mail: artbib@moskit.art.olsztyn.pl. (Dist. by: Ars Polona-Ruch, Krakowskie Przedmiescie 7, 00-901 Warsaw, Poland. TEL 48-22-265334) Ed. Barbara Grudniewska. R&P contact: Jolanta Mieszkalska. adv. contact: Maciej Gajecki. bibl.; charts; illus.; circ. 130 (controlled). **Indexed:** AgroLibrex, Anim.Breed.Abstr., Chem.Abstr., Dairy Sci.Abstr., Herb.Abstr., Maize Abstr., Pig News & Info., Potato Abstr., Poult.Abstr., Ref.Zh., Sport Fish.Abstr., Wild.Rev. **Document type:** academic/scholarly publication.
—CASDDS.
Formerly: Akademia Rolniczo-Techniczna. Zeszyty Naukowe. Zootechnika (ISSN 0324-9239)

THE ADVISOR. see *AGRICULTURE — Crop Production And Soil*

AGRARISCH WEEKOVERZICHT. see *AGRICULTURE — Abstracting, Bibliographies, Statistics*

933 936 US ISSN 1075-0487
ALIMENTOS BALANCEADOS PARA ANIMALES. (Text in Spanish) 1994. bi-m. $30 (foreign $54). Watt Publishing Co., 122 S. Wesley Ave., Mt. Morris, IL 61054. TEL 815-734-4171. FAX 815-734-4201. Ed. Clayton Gill; Pub. Clay Schreiber. R&P contact: Clay Schreiber. adv.: B&W page $2785, color page $3785; trim 8 x 10 3/4; adv. contact: Donna Carlson. circ. 9,000 (controlled). **Document type:** trade publication.
Description: For professionals in the Latin American poultry and livestock feed industry.

664.7 AU ISSN 0002-5992
ALLGEMEINER MUEHLEN-MARKT; Fach- und Ankuendigungsblatt fuer die Getreide-, Muehlen- und Futtermittelwirtschaft. 1900. m. S.480. Victoria Druck- und Verlag Poech und Co. GmbH, Millergasse 20, A-1060 Vienna, Austria. TEL 01-5976570. FAX 01-5976428. TELEX 111912. Ed. Hannes Ametsreiter. adv.; bk.rev.; bibl.; charts; illus.; mkt.; stat. **Indexed:** Food Sci.& Tech.Abstr.

AMERICAN FEED INDUSTRY ASSOCIATION. ANNUAL AND SEMIANNUAL MEETINGS OF THE NUTRITION COUNCIL. PROCEEDINGS. see *AGRICULTURE — Poultry And Livestock*

AMERICAN FEED INDUSTRY ASSOCIATION. PRODUCTION SCHOOL PROCEEDINGS. see *AGRICULTURE — Poultry And Livestock*

633.2 US ISSN 0886-6899
AMERICAN FORAGE AND GRASSLAND COUNCIL. PROCEEDINGS OF THE ANNUAL CONFERENCE. 1968. a. $30. American Forage and Grassland Council, Box 891, Georgetown, TX 78627. TEL 512-283-0747. FAX 512-238-0703. **Document type:** proceedings.
Formerly (until 1978): American Forage and Grassland Council. Proceedings of the Research Industry Conference (ISSN 0196-0326)

633.2 NE ISSN 0377-8401
CODEN: AFSTDH
ANIMAL FEED SCIENCE AND TECHNOLOGY; an international scientific journal. (Text in English) 1976. 28/yr. fl.2835($1629) (effective 1998). Elsevier Science B.V., P.O. Box 211, 1000 AE Amsterdam, Netherlands. TEL 31-20-4853911. FAX 31-20-4853598. TELEX 18582 ESPA NL. E-mail: nlinfo-f@elsevier.nl; usinfo-f@elsevier.com; forinfo-kyf04035@niftyserve.or.jp; URL: http://www.elsevier.nl/. (Subscr. in the Americas to: Elsevier Science, Regional Sales Office, Box 945, New York, NY 10159-0945. TEL 212-633-3730. FAX 212-633-3680; Subscr. in Australasia and the Far East to: Elsevier Science (Singapore) Pte Ltd, No.1 Temasek Ave., No.17-01 Millenia Tower, Singapore 039192, Singapore. TEL 65-434-3727. FAX 65-337-2230; Subscr. in Japan to: Elsevier Science Japan, 9-15 Higashi-Azabu 1-chome, Minato-ku, Tokyo 106, Japan. TEL 81-3-5561-5033. FAX 81-3-5561-5047) Eds. J.F.D. Greenhalgh, P.J. van Soest. adv.; bk.rev.; illus.; bibl.; index. (also avail. in microform from UMI) **Indexed:** ASCA, Biodet.Abstr., Biol.Abstr., Chem.Abstr., Curr.Cont., Dairy Sci.Abstr., Field Crop.Abstr., Food Sci.& Tech.Abstr., Herb.Abstr., Ind.Sci.Rev., Ind.Vet., Maize Abstr., Nutr.Abstr., Pig News & Info., Poult.Abstr., Ref.Zh., Rice Abstr., Sci.Cit.Ind., Soils & Fert., Sorghum & Millets Abstr., Soyabean Abstr., Sport Fish.Abstr., Sugar Ind.Abstr., Triticale Abstr., Trop.Oil Seeds Abstr., Vet.Bull., Wild.Rev. **Document type:** academic/scholarly publication.
—BLDSC (0903.550000); CASDDS; CISTI; Genuine Article; Linda Hall; SWETS; UnCover. **CCC**.
Description: Publishes scientific papers dealing with the production, composition and nutritive value of feeds for animals.
Refereed Serial

633.2 FR ISSN 0752-7535
ANNUAIRE DE L'ALIMENTATION ANIMALE. English edition: European Feed Directory. a. 535 F. (foreign 585 F.) (effective 1997-98). (Groupe pour la Croissance et le Developpement International des Industries de l'Agro-Alimentaire, du Commerce et de l'Habitat) Gedeon Marketing Eurl, B.P. 16, 29560 Telgruc-sur-Mer, France. TEL 33-2-98273766. FAX 33-2-98273765. Ed. Jacques Fitamant; Pub. Jacques Fitamant. adv. contact: Jacques Fitamant. circ. 2,500 (controlled).

664.72 FR ISSN 0295-7868
ANNUAIRE DE LA MEUNERIE FRANCAISE. a. 400 F. (effective 1997). Arts Graphiques de Perche Edition (AGP), 1 rue du Coq-Heron, 75001 Paris, France. TEL 33-1-40265708. FAX 33-1-40263440.

ARCHIVOS DE ZOOTECNIA. see *AGRICULTURE — Poultry And Livestock*

633.18 CK ISSN 0120-2634
ARROZ EN LAS AMERICAS. 1979. s-a. free to qualified personnel. Centro Internacional de Agricultura Tropical, Unidad de Comunicaciones - International Center for Tropical Agriculture, Communications Unit, Apdo. Aereo 6713, Cali, Colombia. TEL 57-2-4450000. FAX 57-2-4450073. E-mail: ciat@cgnet.com. Ed. Luis R. Saniut. circ. 1,000 (controlled). **Document type:** newsletter.
Description: Provides progress reports from rice researchers and developers in tropical countries, interchange of technical notes, and other news.

633.2 US
ASSOCIATION OF AMERICAN FEED CONTROL OFFICIALS. OFFICIAL PUBLICATION. 1942. a. $25 (effective 1997 & 1998). (Association of American Feed Control Officials, Inc.) American Feed Control Officials, c/o Georgia Dept. of Agriculture, Capitol Sq., Atlanta, GA 30334. TEL 404-656-3637. FAX 404-656-9380. Ed. Paul Bachman; Pub. Paul Bachman. R&P contact: Paul Bachman. TEL 612-297-7176. adv. contact: Paul Bachman. circ. 2,500. (back issues avail.) **Document type:** trade publication.

633.1 US
ASSOCIATION OF OPERATIVE MILLERS. BULLETIN. 1918. m. membership only. Association of Operative Millers, 5001 College Blvd., Ste. 104, Shawnee Mission, KS 66211-1618. TEL 913-338-3377. FAX 913-338-3553. Ed. Harvey McCray. index. circ. 1,800. (looseleaf format; back issues avail.) **Indexed:** Food Sci.& Tech.Abstr. **Document type:** bulletin.

AGRICULTURE — FEED, FLOUR AND GRAIN

664.752   US
BAKING, SNACK DIRECTORY & BUYERS GUIDE. a. $90. Sosland Publishing Company, 4800 Main St., Ste. 100, Kansas City, MO 64112-2513. TEL 816-756-1000. FAX 816-756-0494. E-mail: bakesnack@sosland.com. Ed. Laurie Gorton. **Document type**: directory.
  Formerly: Baking Directory - Buyers Guide.

633.1   GW
BESCHREIBENDE SORTENLISTE GETREIDE, MAIS, OELFRUECHTE, LEGUMINOSEN UND HACKFRUECHTE. a. DM.3.90. (Bundessortenamt) Buchedition Agrimedia Hils OHG, Nienhoefenerstr. 29-37, 25421 Pinneberg, Germany. TEL 04101-62023. FAX 04101-68047. circ. 6,000. **Document type**: directory.

633.1   GW
BESCHREIBENDE SORTENLISTE KARTOFFELN. a. DM.3.90. (Bundessortenamt) Buchedition Agrimedia Hils OHG, Nienhoefenerstr. 29-37, 25421 Pinneberg, Germany. TEL 04101-62023. FAX 04101-68047. circ. 2,500. **Document type**: directory.

633.2   PL   ISSN 1231-8337
BIULETYN NAUKOWY PRZEMYSLU PASZOWEGO/BULLETIN SCIENTIFIC OF FEED INDUSTRY. 1962. q. Centralne Laboratorium Przemyslu Paszowego, Branzowy Osrodek Informacji Naukowej, Technicznej i Ekonomicznej, Ul. Chmielna 2, 20-079 Lublin, Poland. TEL 48-81-24716. FAX 48-81-22564. Ed. Jadwiga Najda. **Indexed**: AgroLibrex.
  —BLDSC (2105.429000).
  Former titles (until 1994): Biuletyn Informacyjny Przemyslu Paszowego (ISSN 0137-1568); (until 1966): Centrane Laboratorium Przemyslu Paszowego. Biuletyn Informacyjny (ISSN 1230-4735)

BOVILOGISK TIDSSKRIFT KVAEGET. see AGRICULTURE — Dairying And Dairy Products

BULLETIN OF GRAIN TECHNOLOGY. see AGRICULTURE

633 658.8   UK   ISSN 0261-7692
BUSINESS RATIO REPORT: COMPOUND ANIMAL FEEDSTUFFS; an industry sector analysis. 1980. a. l C C Business Ratios Ltd., Freepost, Field House, Hampton, Mddx. TW12 1BR, England. TEL 081-783-0977. FAX 081-783-1940. charts; stat. **Document type**: trade publication.

CANADA. GRAIN COMMISSION. CORPORATE SERVICES. CANADIAN GRAIN EXPORTS. see AGRICULTURE — Abstracting, Bibliographies, Statistics

CANADA. GRAIN COMMISSION. CORPORATE SERVICES. EXPORTS OF CANADIAN GRAIN AND WHEAT FLOUR. see AGRICULTURE — Abstracting, Bibliographies, Statistics

633.1 338.14   CN   ISSN 0380-8718
HD9044.C2
CANADA. GRAIN COMMISSION. CORPORATE SERVICES. VISIBLE GRAIN SUPPLIES AND DISPOSITION. Key Title: Visible Grain Supplies and Disposition. 1952. a. Can.$14. Grain Commission, Corporate Services, 700-303 Main St., Winnipeg, MB R3C 3G8, Canada. TEL 204-983-2793. R&P contact: Peter Kuzyk. circ. 350. **Document type**: government publication.
  Former titles: Canada. Grain Commission. Economics and Statistics Division. Visible Grain Supplies and Disposition; Canada. Grain Commission. Marketings, Distribution and Visible Carry-over of Canadian Grain in and Through Licensed Elevators (ISSN 0068-7065)
  Description: Marketings, distribution and visible carry-over of Canadian grain in and through licensed elevators.

CANADA GRAINS COUNCIL. STATISTICAL HANDBOOK. see AGRICULTURE — Abstracting, Bibliographies, Statistics

633.1   CN   ISSN 1200-7331
SB189   CODEN: CGLRA2
CANADIAN GRAIN COMMISSION GRAIN RESEARCH LABORATORY. ACTIVITY HIGHLIGHTS. (Editions in English, French) 58th report, 1984. a. free. Canadian Grain Commission, Grain Research Laboratory, 1404-303 Main St., Winnipeg, MB R3C 3G8, Canada. TEL 204-949-4626. FAX 204-983-0724. URL: http://www.cgc.ca. Ed. Louise Cooke. circ. 1,150.
  —CISTI.
  Formerly: Canadian Grain Commission Grain Research Laboratory. Annual Report (ISSN 0317-1892)

CANADIAN GRAINS INDUSTRY STATISTICAL HANDBOOK. see AGRICULTURE — Abstracting, Bibliographies, Statistics

664   US   ISSN 0146-6283
TS2120   CODEN: CFWODA
CEREAL FOODS WORLD. 1956. m. (except Nov.-Dec. combined). $95 (foreign $130) (effective 1996 & 1997). American Association of Cereal Chemists, Inc., 3340 Pilot Knob Rd., St. Paul, MN 55121-2097. TEL 800-328-7560. FAX 612-454-0766. TELEX 6502439657 (MCI UW). URL: http://www.scisoc.org/aacc/pubs/journ/cfw/cfwinfo.html. Ed. Jody Grider; Pub. Steven C. Nelson. R&P contact: Ina Pfefer. adv. contact: Amy Hope. bk.rev.; bibl.; charts; illus.; index. circ. 4,700. (also avail. in microfilm from UMI; back issues avail.) **Indexed**: Anal.Abstr., ASCA, Bibl.Agri., Biol.Abstr., Chem.Abstr., Curr.Adv.Ecol.Sci., Curr.Cont., Curr.Pack.Abstr., Dairy Sci.Abstr., Field Crop Abstr., Food Sci.& Tech.Abstr., Helminthol.Abstr., Herb.Abstr., Ind.Sci.Rev., Int.Packag.Abstr., Plant Breed.Abstr., Sci.Cit.Ind., Seed Abstr., Soils & Fert., Sorghum & Millets Abstr., Sugar Ind.Abstr., Triticale Abstr. **Document type**: academic/scholarly publication.
  —BLDSC (3120.002000); CASDDS; CISTI; Genuine Article; Linda Hall; SWETS; UMI; UnCover. **CCC**.
  Formerly: Cereal Science Today (ISSN 0009-0360)
  Description: Discussions of new and continuing developments in cereal-based industry and research.

633 664   UN
CEREAL POLICIES REVIEW. 1991. a. Food and Agriculture Organization of the United Nations (Rome), Commodities and Trade Division, Via delle Terme di Caracalla, 00100 Rome, Italy.

633.1   HU   ISSN 0133-3720
CODEN: CRCMCL
CEREAL RESEARCH COMMUNICATIONS. (Text and summaries in English and Russian) 1973. q. $100 or exchange basis. Cereal Research Institute, P.O. Box 391, 6701 Szeged, Hungary. TEL 36-62-435-235. FAX 36-62-434-163. TELEX 82450. E-mail: H9865KER@ella.hu. Ed. Zoltan Kertesz. adv. contact: J. Frank. bk.rev. circ. 700. (back issues avail.) **Indexed**: ASCA, Biol.Abstr., Chem.Abstr., Crop Physiol.Abstr., Curr.Adv.Ecol.Sci., Curr.Cont., Fung Crop Abstr., Food Sci.& Tech.Abstr., Herb.Abstr., INIS Atomind., Maize Abstr., Plant Breed.Abstr., Plant Grow.Reg.Abstr., Rice Abstr., Seed Abstr., Soils & Fert., Triticale Abstr. **Document type**: newspaper.
  —BLDSC (3120.008000); CASDDS; EMDOCS; Genuine Article; UnCover.

CHILE. INSTITUTO NACIONAL DE ESTADISTICAS. INDUSTRIA MOLINERA. TRIGO. see AGRICULTURE — Abstracting, Bibliographies, Statistics

633.1   CC   ISSN 1005-4111
CHINESE RICE RESEARCH NEWSLETTER/ZHONGGUO SHUIDAO YANJIU TONGBAO. (Text in English) 1990. q. $20. Zhongguo Shuidao Yanjiusuo, 359 Tiyuchang Lu, Hangzhou, Zhejiang 310006, People's Republic of China. TEL 86-571-33715711. FAX 86-571-3371-5745. Ed. Cunshan Ying. R&P contact: Nantian Li. adv. contact: Nantian Li. **Document type**: newsletter.
  —BLDSC (3181.072000).
  Description: Provides information on Chinese rice in such areas as genetics, breeding methods, yield potential, grain quality, nutrition, farm machinery, and soils and fertilizer management.

633.18   CU   ISSN 0138-8789
CIENCIA Y TECNICA EN LA AGRICULTURA. SERIE: ARROZ. (Table of contents and abstracts in English) 1978. s-a. $14 in N. and S. America; Europe $16; others $17; or exchange basis. Centro de Informacion y Documentacion Agropecuario, Gaveta Postal 4149, Havana 4, Cuba. (Dist. by: Ediciones Cubanas, Obispo No. 527, Apdo. 605, Havana, Cuba) **Indexed**: Agrindex, Field Crop Abstr., Herb.Abstr., Rice Abstr.

633.18   CU   ISSN 0138-8533
CIENCIA Y TECNICA EN LA AGRICULTURA. SERIE: PASTOS Y FORRAJES. (Text in Spanish; table of contents and abstracts in English) 1978. 2/yr. $14 in N. and S. America; Europe $16; elsewhere $17; or exchange basis. Centro de Informacion y Documentacion Agropecuario, Gaveta Postal 4149, Havana 4, Cuba. (Dist. by: Ediciones Cubanas, Obispo No. 527, Apdo. 605, Havana, Cuba) **Indexed**: Agrindex, Dairy Sci.Abstr., Field Crop Abstr., Herb.Abstr., Hort.Abstr., Nutr.Abstr., Seed Abstr., Soils & Fert., Soyabean Abstr.

CIENCIA Y TECNICA EN LA AGRICULTURA. SERIE: VIANDAS TROPICALES. see AGRICULTURE — Crop Production And Soil

636.1   US   ISSN 0010-3101
COMMERCIAL REVIEW. 1890. w. $30. (Oregon Feed and Grain Association) Commercial Review, Inc., 2380 N.W. Roosevelt St., Portland, OR 97210-2323. TEL 503-226-2758. FAX 503-244-0947. Ed. Dennis Hays. adv.; illus. circ. 1,500. **Document type**: trade publication.
  Formerly: Oregon Feed, Seed and Suppliers Association. Commercial Review.

633   CN   ISSN 1181-7771
COST OF PRODUCING GRAIN CROPS IN SASKATCHEWAN. 1987. a. free. Saskatchewan Agriculture and Food Library, B5 Walter Scott Bldg., 3085 Albert St., Regina, SK S4S 0B1, Canada. TEL 306-787-6933. FAX 306-787-0216. E-mail: pdc@agr.gov.sk.ca; URL: http://www.gov.sk.ca/agfood. bk.rev.; charts; stat. circ. 2,000. (also avail. in microfiche) **Document type**: government publication.
  Formerly (until 1988): Top Management Program Cost of Producing Grain Crops in Saskatchewan (ISSN 1185-233X)

633.18   CU   ISSN 0138-838X
CUBA. CENTRO DE INFORMACION Y DOCUMENTACION AGROPECUARIO. BOLETIN DE RESENAS. SERIE: ARROZ. (Abstracts in English) 1974. irreg. exchange basis. Centro de Informacion y Documentacion Agropecuario, Gaveta Postal 4149, Havana 4, Cuba. TEL 301672. (Dist. by: Ediciones Cubanas, Obispo No. 461, Aptdo. 605, Havana, Cuba) abstr.; stat. **Indexed**: Agrindex.
  Formerly: Cuba. Centro de Informacion y Divulgacion Agropecuario. Boletin de Resenas. Serie: Arroz.

633.2   CU   ISSN 0138-7839
CUBA. CENTRO DE INFORMACION Y DOCUMENTACION AGROPECUARIO. BOLETIN DE RESENAS. SERIE: PASTOS Y FORRAJES. (Text in Spanish; abstracts in English) 1974. irreg. C.$1000 or exchange basis. Centro de Informacion y Documentacion Agropecuario, Gaveta Postal 4149, Havana 4, Cuba. TEL 292227. (Dist. by: Ediciones Cubanas, Obispo No. 461, Aptdo. 605, Havana, Cuba) charts; illus.; stat. **Indexed**: Agrindex.
  Formerly: Cuba. Centro de Informacion y Divulgacion Agropecuario. Boletin de Resenas. Serie: Pastos.

633.2   US
DIRECT-FED MICROBIAL, ENZYME & FORAGE ADDITIVE COMPENDIUM. 1992. a. $99. Miller Publishing Co., 12400 Whitewater Dr., Ste. 160, Minnetonka, MN 55343. TEL 612-931-0211. FAX 612-938-1832. Ed. Sarah Muirhead. adv.: B&W page $1940, color page $3180; trim 8 1/4 x 11. circ. 1,200.

633.1   US
DURAM WHEAT REPORT. q. $8 (Canada & Mexico $9; elsewhere $11). U.S. Department of Agriculture, Agricultural Marketing Service (Greely), Livestock & Seed Division, 711 O St., Greely, CO 80631. TEL 303-353-9750. FAX 303-353-9790. (Subscr. to: U.S.D.A. Agricultural Marketing Service, Livestock & Seed Division, Rm. 2623-S, Boox 96456, Washington, DC 20090-6456. FAX 202-245-4732) **Document type**: government publication.

AGRICULTURE — FEED, FLOUR AND GRAIN

633.11   US
DURUM KERNELS. bi-m. $20. U S Durum Growers Association, 824 Thompson St., Bottineu, ND 58318. TEL 701-228-3057.

633.1   US
DURUM WHEAT REPORT. q. $8 (Canada & Mexico $9; elsewhere $11). U.S. Department of Agriculture, Agricultural Marketing Service (St. Paul), Livestock & Seed Division, 208 New Livestock Exchange Bldg., South St. Paul, MN 55675. (Subscr. to: U.S.D.A. Agricultural Marketing Service, Livestock & Seed Division, Rm. 2623-S, Box 96456, Washington, DC 20090-6456. FAX 202-245-4732) circ. 90. (also avail. in microfiche from CIS; reprint service avail. from CIS) **Indexed:** Amer.Stat.Ind. (1984-). **Document type:** government publication.
Description: Presents national information about the prices and supply of durum wheat.

338.1   GW   ISSN 0014-0228
ERNAEHRUNGSDIENST; Handels- und Boersenzeitung fuer die Agrarmaerkte. 1946. 2/wk. DM.624.60 (Europe DM.692.24; elsewhere DM.698.95) (effective 1997). Verlag Alfred Strothe, Mainzer Landstr. 251, 60326 Frankfurt a.M., Germany. TEL 49-69-759501. FAX 49-69-75951260. adv.; bk.rev.; charts; stat. circ. 5,900. **Indexed:** Rural Recreat.Tour.Abstr., World Agri.Econ.& Rural Sociol.Abstr. **Document type:** trade publication.

EUROPEAN ASSOCIATION FOR ANIMAL PRODUCTION. ANNUAL MEETING. BOOK OF ABSTRACTS. see *AGRICULTURE — Poultry And Livestock*

EUROPEAN ASSOCIATION FOR ANIMAL PRODUCTION. PUBLICATIONS. see *AGRICULTURE — Poultry And Livestock*

633   US   ISSN 1072-9038
FARM SUPPLY RETAILING. 1993. 6/yr. $40 (effective 1996). Pro Group, Inc., Box 6585, Englewood, CO 80155. TEL 303-792-3000. FAX 303-792-5589. Ed. Liz Gowins. bk.rev.; circ. 22,000. (controlled). **Document type:** trade publication.
Description: Focuses on the distribution of feed, crop chemicals, animal health and other general farm supplies. Includes case histories, merchandising techniques, new products and industry news.

635 636   AT
FARMERS & STOCKOWNERS. 1976. fortn. Aus.$35. South Australian Farmers' Federation, 122 Frome St., Adelaide, S.A. 5000, Australia. TEL 08-231-5544. FAX 2315340. Ed. Anita Poddar. adv.; bk.rev. circ. 25,870.
Formerly: Farmer and Grazier.

633.1   US   ISSN 0071-450X
FEED ADDITIVE COMPENDIUM. 1963. a. (with 11 supplements). $199. Miller Publishing Co., 12400 Whitewater Dr., Ste. 160, Box 2400, Minnetonka, MN 55343. TEL 612-931-0211. FAX 612-938-1832. Ed. Sarah Muirhead. adv.: B&W page $2825, color page $4065. circ. 2,900. (reprint service avail. from UMI)
—CCC.

633.2   US   ISSN 0886-5884
FEED AND FEEDING DIGEST. vol.24, 1972 m. membership. National Grain and Feed Association, 1201 New York Ave., N.W., Ste. 830, Washington, DC 20005. TEL 202-289-0873. circ. 2,800. **Document type:** trade publication.

633.2 631.3   US   ISSN 1055-3223
FEED AND GRAIN. 1969. 7/yr. $40 (Canada and Mexico $55; elsewhere $120). Johnson Hill Press, Inc. (Subsidiary of: Cygnus Publishing), 1233 Janesville Ave., Ft. Atkinson, WI 53538. TEL 920-563-6388. FAX 920-563-1702. Ed. Becky Schultz. adv.: B&W page $3680; trim 7 7/8 x 10 3/4. illus.; index; circ. 19,000 (controlled). **Indexed:** Nutr.Abstr.
Former titles: Feed and Grain Times (ISSN 0163-4119) & Feed - Grain Equipment Times (ISSN 0014-9551)
Description: Provides owners and operators of feed and allied grain-handling and processing industries with business management, industry and equipment information.

664.76 338.76   US
FEED & GRAIN PARA AMERICA LATINA. 1992. q. $25 (effective 1997). Johnson Hill Press, Inc. (Subsidiary of: Cygnus Publishing), Box 803, Fort Atkinson, WI 53538-0803. TEL 920-563-6388. FAX 920-563-1702. Ed. Becky L. Schultz; Pub. Michael Martin. adv.: B&W page $2615; trim 7 7/8 x 10 3/4; adv. contact: Arlette Sambs. circ. 6,400. (back issues avail.) **Document type:** trade publication.
Former titles: Feed & Grain de Mexico.

636   ISSN 0014-9543
FEED BULLETIN. d. $340 (foreign $520) (effective 1996). Jacobsen Publishing Co., 300 W. Adams St., Chicago, IL 60606. TEL 312-726-6600; 312-726-6654. TELEX 190053. Ed. Al Collins. adv.; mkt.; stat. (processed) **Document type:** bulletin.
Description: Daily comparative price guides and editorial market update.

633.2   UK   ISSN 0950-771X
FEED COMPOUNDER. 1980. m. (except June-July combined). £45 (rest of Europe £75; elsewhere £106). H.G.M. Publications, Abney House, Baslow, Bakewell, Derbys. DE45 1RZ, England. TEL 01246-582470. FAX 01246-582425. Ed. Andrew D. Mounsey; Pub. Howard Mounsey. adv. contact: Simon P. Mounsey. bk.rev.; circ. 3,200. (back issues avail.) **Indexed:** Dairy Sci.Abstr., Food Sci.& Tech.Abstr., Pig News & Info., Rev.Med.& Vet.Mycol. **Document type:** trade publication.
—BLDSC (3902.118000).
Description: Technical journal for manufacturers of animal feedingstuffs covering nutrition, animal health, mill machinery, economics, legislation.

633.2   US
FEED CONTROL COMMENT. m. membership only. American Feed Industry Association, 1501 Wilson Blvd., Ste. 1100, Arlington, VA 22209. TEL 703-524-0810. FAX 703-524-1921. URL: www.afia.org. **Document type:** newsletter.
Description: Provides current information on happenings in the area of regulatory compliance and nutrition. Reports news of FDA, USDA and feed control matters nationwide.

630   UK   ISSN 0965-2558
FEED FACTS QUARTERLY. q. £57 (rest of Europe £74; elsewhere £91). H.G.M. Publications, Abney House, Baslow, Bakewell, Derbys. DE45 1RZ, England. TEL 44-1246-582470. FAX 44-1246-582425. Ed. Simon P. Mounsey; Pub. Howard Mounsey. adv. contact: Simon P. Mounsey. bk.rev.; charts; illus.; stat.; tr.lit. circ. 1,200. **Document type:** trade publication.
Formerly (until 1990): Digest of Feed Facts and Figures.
Description: Provides reports and analysis of British and European Community feed production and ration formulation data.

633.1   US   ISSN 0071-4518
FEED INDUSTRY RED BOOK; reference manual for the feed industry. 1938. a. $40 (Canada $45; elsewhere $62). Z M A G Publishing, Inc., 500 Pine St., Ste. 202, Chaoka, MN 55318. TEL 612-448-5402. FAX 612-448-6935. Ed. Frank Zaworski. **Document type:** trade publication.
Formerly: Feed Bag Red Book.

633.2 338.1   UK
FEED INDUSTRY REVIEW; a structural and financial analysis of the UK and European animal feed industries. 1988. triennial. £395. H G M Publications, Abney House, School Ln., Baslow, Bakewell, Derbys. DE45 1RZ, England. TEL 44-1246-582470. FAX 44-1246-582425. Ed. Roger W. Dean. adv.: B&W page £435, color page £870; trim 297 x 210; adv. contact: Simon P. Mounsey. circ. 400. **Document type:** trade publication.
Description: Supplies an extensive structural and financial analysis of the U.K. and European compound animal feeding stuffs industries. Aimed at senior personnel in the industry and to suppliers and advisors to the industry.

636   US   ISSN 0274-5771
                      CODEN: FEINEW
FEED INTERNATIONAL. m. $36 (foreign $72) (effective 1997). Watt Publishing Co., 122 S. Wesley Ave., Mt. Morris, IL 61054. TEL 815-734-4171. FAX 815-734-4201. Ed. Clayton Gill; Pub. Clay Schreiber. adv.: B&W page $4450, color page $6050; trim 8 x 10 3/4; adv. contact: Laura Orsted. circ. 20,605 (controlled). **Indexed:** Sugar Ind.Abstr. **Document type:** trade publication.
—BLDSC (3902.122700). CCC.
Description: For the feed industry worldwide, except North America and Latin America.

633 340   UK   ISSN 0969-0735
KD2376.F4
FEED LEGISLATION. 1993. biennial. £38 (U.S. $70). H G M Publications, Abney House, Schl. Ln., Baslow, Bakewell, Derbyshire DE45 1RZ, England. TEL 44-1246-582470. FAX 44-1246-582425. Ed. David Williams. adv. contact: Simon P. Mounsey. charts; illus.; circ. 600. **Document type:** trade publication.
Description: Comprehensive guide to U.K. and European legislation concerning the manufacture, storage and distribution of feedstuffs for livestock.

636   US   ISSN 0014-956X
                      CODEN: FEMAA9
FEED MANAGEMENT; the magazine for manufacturers of animal feed in North America. 1950. m. $48. Watt Publishing Co., 122 S. Wesley Ave., Mt. Morris, IL 61054. TEL 815-734-4171. FAX 815-734-4201. Ed. Domenick Castaldo; Pub. Clay Schreiber. R&P contact: Clay Schreiber. adv.: B&W page $4200, color page $5710; trim 8 x 10 3/4; adv. contact: Nancy Wagner. charts; illus.; stat.; tr.lit.; index; circ. 20,182 (controlled). (also avail. in microfiche from UMI; reprint service avail.) **Indexed:** Biol.Abstr., Excerp.Med., Farm & Garden Ind., Sport Fish.Abstr., Wild.Rev. **Document type:** trade publication.
—Linda Hall; UMI; UnCover. CCC.
Incorporates: Feed Age.
Description: Serves feed manufacturers and mixers.

633.1   UK
                      CODEN: MFFED5
FEED MILLING INTERNATIONAL. 1891. m. £97 (foreign £114) (effective 1996). Turret Group Plc., Turret House, 171 High St., Rickmansworth, Herts WD3 1SN, England. TEL 44-1923-777000. FAX 44-1923-771297. (Subscr. to: 177 Hagden Ln., Watford, Herts WD1 8SN, England. TEL 44-1923-228577. FAX 44-1923-221346) Ed. Susan Fraser. adv.: B&W page £845, color page £1333; trim 297 x 210; adv. contact: Andrew West. bk.rev.; illus.; mkt.; stat. circ. 10,000. **Indexed:** Biol.Abstr., Br.Tech.Ind., Curr.Cont., Dairy Sci.Abstr., Food Sci.& Tech.Abstr., Nutr.Abstr., PROMT. **Document type:** trade publication.
—CISTI; Linda Hall; UMI.
Former titles: International Milling Flour and Feed (ISSN 0954-4860); Milling Feed and Farm Supplies; Milling Feed and Fertiliser (ISSN 0140-4059); (until 1977): Journal of Flour and Animal Feed Milling (ISSN 0305-716X); **Incorporates:** Feed and Farm Supplies (ISSN 0015-0258); Milling (ISSN 0026-4296).

633.2   NE   ISSN 0928-124X
FEED MIX. bi-m. $125. Misset International (Subsidiary of: Reed Elsevier plc), Postbus 4, 7000 BA Doetinchem, Netherlands. TEL 31-314-349562. FAX 31-314-340515. Ed. Naheeda Kahn. adv. contact: Miguel Mendes de Leon. circ. 7,000.
—BLDSC (3902.123800).

633.11   NE
▼**FEED TECH.** 1997. 8/yr. $95. Misset International (Subsidiary of: Reed Elsevier plc), Postbus 4, 7000 BA Doetinchem, Netherlands. TEL 31-314-349562. FAX 31-314-340515. Eds. Naheeda Kahn, Roger Gilbert. adv. contact: Miguel Mendes de Leon. circ. 12,000.
Description: Focuses on worldwide developments in feed milling technology and animal feed including ingredients, pet food, aquaculture, and nutrition.

636 338.1   JA   ISSN 0014-9586
FEED TRADE. (Text in Japanese) 1965. 6/yr. 3000 Yen (foreign $200). Japan Feed Trade Association - Shiryo Yushutsunyu Kyogikai, c/o Koizumi Bldg., 4-3-13 Ginza, Chuo-ku, Tokyo 104, Japan. TEL 03-3563-6441. FAX 03-3567-2297. Ed. Morio Morisaki. illus. circ. 2,000.

AGRICULTURE — FEED, FLOUR AND GRAIN

633.2 US
FEEDGRAM. m. membership only. American Feed Industry Association, 1501 Wilson Blvd., Ste. 1100, Arlington, VA 22209. TEL 703-524-0810. FAX 703-524-1921. URL: www.afia.org.
 Description: Provides current news on industry developments and the association's activities. Features legislative, regulatory and feed control updates; committee news, membership items, meeting reports, and USDA briefs.

633.1 636 US ISSN 0014-9624
HD9052.U5 CODEN: FDSTAL
FEEDSTUFFS; the weekly newspaper for agribusiness. 1929. w. $109. A B C, Inc., 12400 Whitewater Dr., Ste. 160, Box 2400, Minnetonka, MN 55343. TEL 612-931-0211. FAX 612-938-1832. URL: http://www.feedstuffs.com. Ed. Sarah Muirhead. adv.; bk.rev.; charts; illus.; mkt.; stat.; tr.lit. circ. 17,275. (tabloid format; also avail. in microform from UMI; reprint service avail. from UMI) **Indexed:** Anim.Breed.Abstr., Biodet.Abstr., Biol.Abstr., Biotech.Abstr., Bus.Ind., Chem.Abstr., Dairy Sci.Abstr., Farm & Garden Ind., Field Crop Abstr., Geo.Abstr., Herb.Abstr., Hlth.Ind., Ind.Vet., Maize Abstr., Manage.Cont., Nutr.Abstr., Poult.Abstr., PROMT, Rural Recreat.Tour.Abstr., Sorghum & Millets Abstr., Soyabean Abstr., Tr.& Indus.Ind., Triticale Abstr., Trop.Oil Seeds Abstr., Vet.Bull., World Agri.Econ.& Rural Sociol.Abstr. **Document type:** newspaper, trade publication.
 ●Also available online.
 —BLDSC (3902.200000); CASDDS; UMI. **CCC.**

FOOD SCIENCE CATALOG. see *FOOD AND FOOD INDUSTRIES*

630 CN ISSN 0383-3356
FORAGE CROP RECOMMENDATIONS. 1972. biennial. free. Saskatchewan Agriculture and Food Library, B5 Walter Scott Bldg., 3085 Albert St., Regina, SK S4S 0B1, Canada. TEL 306-787-6933. FAX 306-787-0216. E-mail: pdc@agr.gov.sk.ca; URL: http://www.gov.sk.ca/agfood. Ed. Michel Tremblay. circ. 20,000. (back issues avail.) **Document type:** government publication.
 Description: Forage crops, grasses and legumes recommended for Saskatchewan's farmers, seeding rates, herbicides used in grasses and legumes.

664.75 GW ISSN 0367-4177
TX761 CODEN: GEMBAN
GETREIDE, MEHL UND BROT. 1947. bi-m. DM.369 (effective 1996). (Arbeitsgemeinschaft Getreideforschung) Deutscher Baecker Verlag GmbH, Postfach 102050, 44791 Bochum, Germany. TEL 49-234-90199-0. FAX 49-234-9019928. Ed. W. Seibel. adv. contact: Kirsten Lehmann. bk.rev.; charts; illus.; index. circ. 3,000. **Indexed:** Biol.Abstr., Chem.Abstr., Excerp.Med., Field Crop Abstr., Food Sci.& Tech.Abstr., Herb.Abstr., Maize Abstr., Soils & Fert. **Document type:** academic/scholarly publication, trade publication.
 —BLDSC (4165.165000); CASDDS; Linda Hall; SWETS. **CCC.**
 Formed by the merger of: Getreide und Mehl (ISSN 0046-5879); Brot und Gebaeck (ISSN 0007-2419)

633 PH
GINTONG BUTIL/GOLDEN GRAINS. (Text in English, Pilipino) 1973. m. free. National Food Authority, E. Rodriguez Sr. Ave., Quezon City, Philippines. FAX 7121364. Ed. Rebecca C. Olarte. illus.; circ. 10,000 (controlled).

633 636 338.1 US
GRAIN AND FEED MARKET NEWS; weekly summary and statistics. 1953. w. $85 (Canada & Mexico $90; elsewhere $120). U.S. Department of Agriculture, Agricultural Marketing Service, Livestock & Seed Division, South Bldg., Rm. 2623, Box 96456, Washington, DC 20090-6456. TEL 202-720-6231. FAX 202-690-3732. (Subscr. to: U.S.D.A. Agricultural Marketing Service, Livestock and Seed Division, Rm. 2623-S, Box 96456, Washington, DC 20090-6456. TEL 202-720-7316. FAX 202-245-4732) Ed. Kim Harmon. stat. (also avail. in microfiche from CIS; reprint service avail. from CIS) **Indexed:** Amer.Stat.Ind. (1974-). **Document type:** government publication.
 Formed by the 1982 merger of: Grain Market News (ISSN 0364-099X); Feed Market News (ISSN 0364-2046); Which superseded in part: Grain Market News and Feed Market News (ISSN 0017-3061)

658.8 US ISSN 1047-4978
 CODEN: GFEMER
GRAIN & FEED MARKETING. q. K.R. Publishing, Box 1036, Mercer Island, WA 98040. TEL 206-236-2353. Ed. Donald W. Kinnan. adv. circ. 15,000. **Indexed:** BPIA. **Document type:** trade publication.

633.1 UK ISSN 1356-9155
GRAIN AND OILSEEDS. m. £242 (rest of Europe £260; elsewhere £275) (effective 1997). Agra Europe (London) Ltd., 25 Frant Rd., Tunbridge Wells, Kent TN2 5JT, England. TEL 44-1892-533813. FAX 44-1892-544895. TELEX 95114 AGRATW G. E-mail: 100637.3460@compuserve.com. **Document type:** trade publication.
 Formerly (until 1994): Agrafile: Grain and Oilseeds (ISSN 0950-494X)
 Description: Contains E.U. and national policy, trade, and markets reports.

338.1 US ISSN 0274-7138
GRAIN JOURNAL. 1972. bi-m. $40. Country Journal Publishing Company, 2490 N. Water St., Decatur, IL 62526. TEL 217-877-9660. FAX 217-877-6647. Ed. Ed Zdroueski; Pub. Mark Avery. adv. contact: Deb Coontz. circ. 10,600. (back issues avail.) **Document type:** trade publication.

338.1 CN ISSN 0383-4417
HD9044.C3
GRAIN MATTERS. 1976. bi-m. free. Canadian Wheat Board, 423 Main St., Winnipeg, MB R3B 1B3, Canada. TEL 204-983-3421. FAX 204-983-4678. TELEX 07-57801. URL: http://www.cwb.ca. Ed. Brian Stacey. R&P contact: Brian Stacey. circ. 120,000 (118,000 English edition, 2,000 French edition). (back issues avail.) **Document type:** newsletter.

633 US
GRAIN STOCKS REPORT. w. $65 (Canada & Mexico $70; elsewhere $105) (effective 1997). U.S. Department of Agriculture, Agricultural Marketing Service (Portland), Livestock & Seed Division, 1220 S.W. Third Ave., Rm. 1772, Portland, OR 97204. (Subscr. to: U.S.D.A. Agricultural Marketing Service, Livestock & Seed Division, Rm. 2623-S, Box 96456, Washington, DC 20090-6456. FAX 202-245-4732) Ed. Lowell Serfling. (tabloid format; also avail. in microfiche from CIS; back issues avail.; reprint service avail. from CIS) **Indexed:** Amer.Stat.Ind. (1975-). **Document type:** government publication.

GRAIN TRANSPORTATION SITUATION. see *TRANSPORTATION*

633.1 CN ISSN 0229-8060
GRAINEWS; cattleman's corner. 1975. 16/yr. Can.$29.50. United Grain Growers Ltd., Box 6600, 201 Portage Ave., Winnipeg, MB R3C 3A7, Canada. TEL 800-665-0502. FAX 204-944-5416. URL: http:www.fbc.unitedgrain.ca. Ed. Andy Sirski; Pub. Palmer Anderson. R&P contact: Andy Sirski. adv. contact: Tom Mumby. illus.; index; circ. 52,000 (paid). (tabloid format) **Document type:** newspaper, trade publication.
 Description: Agricultural newspaper for farm families. Provides information on grain and oilseed production and marketing, financial management, machinery management, livestock production and marketing. Includes cartoons, jokes, and articles on everyday life.

633 AT
GRAINLINE. 1967. a. free. GrainCorp Operations Ltd., Level 10, 51 Druitt St., Sydney, N.S.W. 2000, Australia. FAX 61-2-3259180. Ed. Bill O'Connor; Pub. Bill O'Connor. R&P contact: Bill O'Connor. adv. circ. 7,000. **Document type:** newsletter.
 Former titles: Bulk Grain (ISSN 1032-5824); (until 1988): Bulk Wheat Year Book (ISSN 0813-3735)

633 US
GRASS & GRAIN. 1955. w. $28. Ag Press, Inc., 1531 Yuma, Box 1009, Manhattan, KS 66502. TEL 913-539-7558. Ed. Beth Gaines; Pub. Dean Cougenhour. adv. contact: Peggy Giles. circ. 16,500. **Document type:** newspaper.

GROVVARELEDEREN. see *BUSINESS AND ECONOMICS — Domestic Commerce*

HANDBOOK OF MEDICINAL FEED ADDITIVES. see *AGRICULTURE — Poultry And Livestock*

633 338.1 US ISSN 0891-5946
HAY & FORAGE GROWER. 1986. 4/yr. $11.95 (foreign $25). Intertec Publishing Corp., Webb Division, 7900 International Dr., Ste. 300, Minneapolis, MN 55425. TEL 612-851-4677. FAX 612-851-4601. E-mail: hay&foragegrower@intertec.com. Ed. Neil Tietz. circ. 90,000. (back issues avail.) **Document type:** trade publication.
 —CCC.

HOME-GROWN CEREALS AUTHORITY. CEREALS STATISTICS. see *AGRICULTURE — Abstracting, Bibliographies, Statistics*

633.1 338.1 UK ISSN 0951-0958
HOME-GROWN CEREALS AUTHORITY. PROGRESS REPORTS ON RESEARCH AND DEVELOPMENT. 1968? irreg. Home-Grown Cereals Authority, Research and Development Advisory Committee, Hamlyn House, Highgate Hill, London N19 5PR, England. TEL 0171-263-3391. TELEX 27615. **Document type:** monographic series.

633 PH
SB191.R5
I R R I CORPORATE REPORT. 1974. a. price varies. International Rice Research Institute, P.O. Box 933, Manila, Philippines. TEL 63-2-818-1926. FAX 63-2-891-1292. adv. contact: R.D. Huggan. **Indexed:** Field Crop Abstr., Herb.Abstr., Rev.Appl.Entomol., Rev.Plant Path. **Document type:** corporate report.
 —BLDSC (4580.665000).
 Formerly: I R R I Research Highlights (ISSN 0115-1142)

633 PH ISSN 0117-0880
SB191.R5
I R R I PROGRAM REPORT. (Text in English) 1963. a. price varies. International Rice Research Institute, P.O. Box 933, Manila, Philippines. TEL 63-2-818-1926. FAX 63-2-891-1292. index. circ. 5,000. (also avail. in microfiche) **Indexed:** B.R.I., Bibl.Agri., Biol.Abstr., Field Crop Abstr., Herb.Abstr., Plant Breed.Abstr., Rev.Appl.Entomol., Rev.Plant Path., Trop.Abstr., Weed Abstr., World Agri.Econ.& Rural Sociol.Abstr., Zoo.Rec. (until 19??).
 —BLDSC (6864.495000).
 Formerly: I R R I Annual Report (ISSN 0074-7793)

633 PH ISSN 0115-2467
I R R I REPORTER. 3. $5. International Rice Research Institute, P.O. Box 933, Manila, Philippines. TEL 63-2-818-1926. FAX 63-2-891-1292. **Indexed:** Ind.Phil.Per., Plant Breed.Abstr., Rev.Appl.Entomol., Rev.Plant Path., Soils & Fert., Weed Abstr.

338.1 US ISSN 0897-5019
IDAHO GRAIN. bi-m. $50. Idaho Grain Producers Association, 1109 Main St., Ste. 315, Boise, ID 83702. TEL 208-345-0706. (Co-sponsors: Idaho Wheat Commission, Idaho Barley Commission) Ed. Steve C. Johnson. adv. circ. 20,000. (back issues avail.) **Document type:** trade publication.
 Formerly: Idaho Wheat.
 Description: Provides information growers need to keep aware of the issues that can and do affect their farming operations.

INDUSTRIES DES CEREALES. see *FOOD AND FOOD INDUSTRIES*

633.18 CU ISSN 0138-7731
INFORMACION EXPRESS. SERIE: ARROZ. 1977. 3/yr. C.$0.90($6) in N. America; S. America $9; Europe $10; others $14; or exchange basis. Centro de Informacion y Documentacion Agropecuario, Gaveta Postal 4149, Havana 4, Cuba. TEL 301672. (Dist. by: Ediciones Cubanas, Obispo No. 527, Apdo. 605, Havana, Cuba) stat. **Indexed:** Agrindex.

633.2 CU ISSN 0138-6786
INFORMACION EXPRESS. SERIE: PASTOS Y FORRAJES. 1977. 4/yr. $9 in N. America; S. America $11; Europe $13; elsewhere $18; or exchange basis. Centro de Informacion y Documentacion Agropecuario, Gaveta Postal 4149, Havana 4, Cuba. (Dist. by: Ediciones Cubanas, Obispo No. 527, Apdo. 605, Havana, Cuba) **Indexed:** Agrindex.

INTERNATIONAL GRAINS COUNCIL. GRAIN MARKET REPORT. see *AGRICULTURE — Agricultural Economics*

AGRICULTURE — FEED, FLOUR AND GRAIN

338.1   UK
INTERNATIONAL GRAINS COUNCIL. REPORT FOR FISCAL YEAR. (Editions in English, French, Russian, Spanish) 1949. a. £30($50) to non-members (effective 1997). International Grains Council, One Canada Sq., Canary Wharf, London E14 5AE, England. TEL 44-171-513-1122. FAX 44-171-513-0630. E-mail: igc-fac@int-grains-council.org.uk. charts; stat. **Document type:** proceedings.
   Formerly: International Wheat Council. Report for Fiscal Year; Which formed by the 1986 merger of: Review of the World Wheat Situtation; Which was formerly: International Wheat Council. Review of the World Grains Situation (ISSN 0539-1318); And: International Wheat Council Annual Report; Which was formerly: International Wheat Council. Report for Crop Year (ISSN 0539-1296)
   Description: Provides a detailed review of the activities of the IGC and FAC and its committees.

633 338.1   UK
INTERNATIONAL GRAINS COUNCIL. WHEAT AND COARSE GRAIN SHIPMENTS. a. £75($120) (effective 1997). International Grains Council, One Canada Sq., Canary Wharf, London E14 5AE, England. TEL 44-171-513-1122. FAX 44-171-513-0630. E-mail: igc-fac@int-grains-council.org.uk. charts; stat. **Document type:** trade publication.
   Formerly: International Wheat Council. Record of Coarse Grains Shipments.
   Description: Covers commercial and noncommercial shipments of wheat and coarse grains by origin and destination.

633.8   XV   ISSN 0074-6223
INTERNATIONAL HOP GROWERS CONVENTION. REPORT OF CONGRESS.* (Supplement to: Hopfenrundschau) a. International Hop Growers Convention, Titova 19, Ljubljana, Slovenia.

633   PH
INTERNATIONAL RICE RESEARCH NOTES. 1976. 3/yr. International Rice Research Institute, P.O. Box 933, Manila, Philippines. TEL 63-2-818-1926. FAX 63-2-891-1292. **Indexed:** Agroforest.Abstr., Bio-Contr.News & Info., Crop Physiol.Abstr., Field Crop Abstr., Forest Prod.Abstr., Helminthol.Abstr., Herb.Abstr., Ind.Phil.Per., Irr.& Drain.Abstr., Maize Abstr., Plant Breed.Abstr., Plant Grow.Reg.Abstr., Potato Abstr., Rev.Appl.Entomol., Rev.Plant Path., Rice Abstr., Seed Abstr., Sorghum & Millets Abstr., Triticale Abstr., Weed Abstr. **Document type:** newsletter.
—Linda Hall.
   Formerly: International Rice Research Newsletter (ISSN 0115-0944)

633.1   IT   ISSN 0374-535X
ISTITUTO SPERIMENTALE PER LA CEREALICOLTURA. ANNALI. (Text and summaries in English, Italian) 1970. a. L.180000($116) (effective Jan. 1993). Istituto Sperimentale per la Cerealicoltura, Via Cassia 176, 00191 Rome, Italy. TEL 06-32957705. FAX 06-36306022. Ed. Angelo Bianchi. **Indexed:** Biol.Abstr., Field Crop.Abstr., Herb.Abstr., Seed Abstr., Soils & Fert., Sorghum & Millets Abstr., Triticale Abstr.

633.1   UK   ISSN 0733-5210
                             CODEN: JCSCDA
JOURNAL OF CEREAL SCIENCE. 1983. bi-m. £68($113) to individuals; institutions £278 (effective 1998). Academic Press Ltd. (Subsidiary of: Harcourt Brace & Company Ltd.), 24-28 Oval Rd., London NW1 7DX, England. TEL 44-171-267-4466. FAX 44-171-482-2293. TELEX 25775 ACPRES G. E-mail: apsubs@acad.com; URL: http://www.hbuk.co.uk/ap/jcs; http://www.europe.idealibrary.com/. (Subscr. to: Harcourt Brace & Company Ltd., Foots Cray High St., Sidcup, Kent DA14 5HP, England. TEL 44-181-300-3322. FAX 44-181-309-0807) Ed. J.D. Schofield. R&P contact: Catherine John. adv. contact: Nik Screen. (reprint service avail. from SWZ) **Indexed:** Agri.Eng.Abstr., ASCA, Chem.Abstr., Curr.Cont., Field Crop Abstr., Food Sci.& Tech.Abstr., Ind.Sci.Rev., Rice Abstr., Sci.Cit.Ind., Seed Abstr., Soils & Fert., Sorghum & Millets Abstr., Triticale Abstr. **Document type:** academic/scholarly publication.
●Also available online.
—BLDSC (4955.105000); CASDDS; CISTI; Ei; Genuine Article; Linda Hall; SWETS; UnCover. **CCC**.
   Description: Provides an international forum for the publication of original research papers covering all aspects of cereal science related to the functional and nutritional quality of cereal grains and their products.

633 338.1   US
KANSAS CITY BOARD OF TRADE REVIEW. 1916. d. $120 (effective 1997). Kansas City Board of Trade, 4800 Main St., No.303, Kansas City, MO 64112. TEL 816-753-7500. FAX 816-753-3944. E-mail: kcbt@kcbt.com; URL: http://www.kcbt.com. Ed. Sheila Summers. **Document type:** newsletter.
●Also available online.
   Formerly: Kansas City Grain Market Review (ISSN 0738-7296)
   Description: Contains commentary on KCBT futures trading, futures prices and open interest, Kansas City Spot Basis, nominal ranges for corn, sorghum and soybeans, Kansas City truck bids, regional truck bids, gulf grain bids.

633   US
KANSAS CORN PERFORMANCE TESTS. (Subseries of its: Report of Progress) 1939. a. free. Kansas State University, Agricultural Experiment Station, Manhattan, KS 66506. TEL 913-532-7251. Ed. Kraig Roozeboom. stat. circ. 7,500.

633   US
KANSAS SORGHUM PERFORMANCE TESTS. GRAIN & FORAGE. (Subseries of its: Report of Progress) 1958. a. free. Kansas State University, Agricultural Experiment Station, Manhattan, KS 66506. TEL 913-532-7251. Ed. Kraig Roozeboom. stat. circ. 12,000.
   Formerly: Kansas Grain Sorghum Performance Tests.

633   US
KANSAS STATE UNIVERSITY. FOOD AND FEED GRAIN INSTITUTE. TECHNICAL ASSISTANCE IN GRAIN STORAGE, PROCESSING AND MARKETING, AND AGRIBUSINESS DEVELOPMENT. (In 4 subseries: Technical Assistance Reports (US ISSN 0453-2481); Manuals; Special Reports; Research Reports) 1968. irreg. Kansas State University, Food and Feed Grain Institute, Shellenberger Hall, Manhattan, KS 66506. TEL 913-532-6161. (Co-sponsor: U.S. Agency for International Development) circ. 150. (also avail. in microform)
   Formerly (until 1974): Kansas State University. Food and Feed Grain Institute. Technical Assistance in Food Grain Drying, Storage, Handling and Transportation (ISSN 0071-7150)

633   UK
KEY NOTE MARKET REPORT: ANIMAL FEEDSTUFFS. Variant title: Animal Feedstuffs. irreg., no.8, 1995. £205. Key Note Ltd., Field House, 72 Oldfield Rd., Hampton, Middlesex TW12 2HQ, England. TEL 44-181-783-0755. FAX 44-181-783-0049. Ed. Anthony Doyle. **Document type:** trade publication.
●Also available online.
Also available on CD-ROM.
   Formerly: Key Note Report: Animal Feedstuffs.

633.1 664.752   RU   ISSN 0235-2508
S13   CODEN: KHLEES
KHLEBOPRODUKTY. 1927. m. $192 (effective 1998). 1-i Shchipovskii per., d.20, 113093 Moscow, Russia. TEL 7-095-2377432. Ed. Aleksei I. Dushkin. index. circ. 3,000. **Indexed:** Biol.Abstr., Chem.Abstr., Dairy Sci.Abstr., Food Sci.& Tech.Abstr., Rice Abstr., Sugar Ind.Abstr.
—BLDSC (0394.810000); CASDDS; Linda Hall.
   Former titles (until 1988): Khlebopekarnaya i Konditerskaya Promyshlennost' (ISSN 0023-1215); Zakupki Sel'skokhozyaistvennykh Produktov; Mukomolno-elevatornaya i Kombikormovaya Promyshlennost' (ISSN 0131-2413)

633.1   US   ISSN 0885-5811
KING'S GULF GRAIN GUIDE. 1985. w. $687. King Publishing Co., Box 52210, Knoxville, TN 37950. TEL 615-584-6294. (back issues avail.)

633   RU   ISSN 0235-2605
KOMBIKORMOVAYA PROMYSHLENNOST'. 1972. 8/yr. $90 (effective 1998). Sadovaya-Spasskaya, 18, 107807 Moscow, Russia. TEL 7-095-2071645. FAX 7-095-9755452. (Dist. by: Mezhdunarodnaya Kniga, B. Yakimanka 39, 117049 Moscow, Russia. TEL 7-095-2384967. FAX 7-095-2384634) Ed. Nataliya V. Olevskaya. adv: B&W page $800, color page $2000. circ. 1,800. **Indexed:** Food Sci.& Tech.Abstr.

KOREAN JOURNAL OF ANIMAL SCIENCES. see AGRICULTURE — Poultry And Livestock

633   RU
KORMOPROIZVODSTVO. 1966. q. $45 (effective 1996). Sadovaya-Spasskaya, 18, 107807 Moscow, Russia. TEL 7-095-9753255. FAX 7-095-2072870. (Dist. by: Mezhdunarodnaya Kniga, B. Yakimanka 39, 117049 Moscow, Russia. TEL 7-095-2384967. FAX 7-095-2384634) Ed. Gennadii M. Chemodanov. circ. 5,270.
   Former titles: Kormovye Kul'tury (ISSN 0235-2540); (until 1988): Kormoproizvodstvo (ISSN 0206-538X)

636   CI   ISSN 0023-4850
                             CODEN: KRMIA9
KRMIVA; mjesecnik za pitanje ishrane stoke i proizvodnje stocne hrane. (Text in Croatian; summaries in English) 1959. m. Hrvatsko Agronomsko Drustvo, Gunduliceva 45, 41000 Zagreb, Croatia. Ed. Hrvoje Zlatic. adv.; bk.rev. circ. 1,000. **Indexed:** Chem.Abstr., Dairy Sci.Abstr., Food Sci.& Tech.Abstr., Ind.Vet., Maize Abstr., Nutr.Abstr., Pig News & Info., Poult.Abstr., Soyabean Abstr., Triticale Abstr., Vet.Bull.
—BLDSC (5118.400000); CASDDS.

633.18   BL   ISSN 0023-9143
                             CODEN: LARRAL
LAVOURA ARROZEIRA. 1947. bi-m. $50. Instituto Rio Grandense do Arroz, Missoes Av. 342, 90230-100 Porto Alegre RS, Brazil. TEL 051-226-51-44. FAX 051-226-15-67. Ed. Maria da Graca Coelho de Souza. adv.; bk.rev.; charts; illus.; mkt.; stat.; index. circ. 19,200. **Indexed:** Abstr.Trop.Agri., Chem.Abstr., Crop Physiol.Abstr., Field Crop Abstr., Herb.Abstr., Ind.Agri.Am.Lat.Caribe, Irr.& Drain.Abstr., Maize Abstr., P.A.I.S.For.Lang.Ind., Rice Abstr., Seed Abstr., Soils & Fert., Soyabean Abstr., Weed Abstr.
—BLDSC (5161.000000); CASDDS.

633.1   CN   ISSN 0831-9421
LE MEUNIER; au service du producteur agricole. 1965. 4/yr. Can.$10 (effective 1996). Association Quebecoise des Industris de Nutrition Animale et Cerealiere, 2323, boul. Versant Nord, local 115, Ste-Foy, PQ G1N 4P4, Canada. TEL 418-688-9221. FAX 418-688-3575. Ed. Andre J. Pilon. adv: B&W page Can.$995, color page Can.$1620. circ. 16,000. **Document type:** trade publication.
   Formerly (until 1986): Meunier Quebecois (ISSN 0831-9413)

MILLING & BAKING NEWS. see FOOD AND FOOD INDUSTRIES — Bakers And Confectioners

633   UK
MILLING INTERNATIONAL DIRECTORY AND BUYERS' GUIDE. 1991. a. £85 (foreign £90) (effective 1996). Turret Group Plc., Turret House, 171 High St., Rickmansworth, Herts WD3 1SN, England. TEL 44-1923-777000. FAX 44-1923-771297. (Subscr. to: P.O. Box 77, Watford, Herts WD1 8UT, England. TEL 44-1923-228577. FAX 44-1923-221346) Ed. Susan Fraser; Pub. Susan Fraser. **Document type:** directory.
   Formerly: Milling European Directory and Buyers' Guide (Year).

664.7   US
MILLING JOURNAL. 1993. q. $40. Country Journal Publishing Company, 2490 N. Water St., Decatur, Il 62526. TEL 217-877-9660. FAX 217-877-6647. Ed. Ed Zdrouewski; Pub. Mark Avery. adv: B&W page $450; trim 8 1/2 x 11; adv. contact: Deb Coontz. circ. 1,550. **Document type:** trade publication.
   Description: Provides technical and equipment information for the milling industry.

621.210 664.72   DK   ISSN 0026-8852
MOELLEN. 1884. 6/yr. DKK 200 membership. Dansk Moellerforening, Eranthisvej 20, DK-5000 Odense C, Denmark. TEL 45-66-12-30-67. Ed. Otto Rasmussen. adv.; bk.rev. circ. 800. (tabloid format)
   Formerly (until 1895): Tidsskrift for Skandinavisk Moelleindustri (ISSN 0909-3222)
   Description: Features articles on the history and preservation of wind and water mills, and the milling of flour and grain.

AGRICULTURE — FEED, FLOUR AND GRAIN

664.7   IT   ISSN 0026-9018
MOLINI D'ITALIA; rassegna mensile dei cereali e derivati. 1950. m. L.60000 (foreign L.100000) (effective 1992). (Associazione degli Industriali Mugnai e Pastai d'Italia) Avenue Media, Via Riva Reno, 61, 40122 Bologna, Italy. TEL 39-51-227597. FAX 39-51-262203. Ed. Luigi Costato. adv.; charts; illus.; stat.; index. circ. 3,000. **Indexed**: Chem.Abstr.
—Linda Hall.

664.7   GW   ISSN 0027-2949
TS2150
DIE MUEHLE UND MISCHFUTTERTECHNIK; internationale Fachzeitschrift fuer Getreideverarbeitung, Mischfutterherstellung und verwandte Gebiete. 1863. fortn. DM.264. Verlag Moritz Schaefer, Postfach 2254, 32712 Detmold, Germany. TEL 49-5231-24637. FAX 49-5231-35896. Ed. Klaus Kurt Kunis. adv.; bk.rev.; charts; illus.; pat.; stat.; t..lit.; index. circ. 3,800. **Indexed**: Agri.Eng.Abstr., C.I.S. Abstr., Fababean Abstr., Food Sci.& Tech.Abstr., Maize Abstr., Nutr.Abstr., Pig News & Info., Poult.Abstr., Seed Abstr., Soyabean Abstr., Sugar Ind.Abstr., Triticale Abstr., Trop.Oil Seeds Abstr. **Document type**: trade publication.
—CCC.

633   US
N C P A NEWSLETTER. fortn. membership. National Cottonseed Products Association, Box 172267, Memphis, TN 38187-2267. TEL 901-682-0800. FAX 901-682-2856. Ed. Ben Morgan. **Document type**: newsletter.

633   UK
N I A B CEREAL VARIETY HANDBOOK. a. £15 (foreign £20.50). National Institute of Agricultural Botany, Huntingdon Rd., Cambridge CB3 0LE, England. TEL 44-1223-276381. FAX 44-1223-277602. Ed. Paul Nelson. **Document type**: bulletin.
—BLDSC (3120.025200).
Formerly: N I A B Recommended Lists of Cereal (ISSN 1357-1400).

665   US   ISSN 0077-4022
NATIONAL COTTONSEED PRODUCTS ASSOCIATION. TRADING RULES. 1897. a. $10 to non-members. National Cottonseed Products Association, Box 1772267, Memphis, TN 38187-2267. TEL 901-682-0800. FAX 901-682-2856. TELEX WUI 650-274-5680. Ed. Ben Morgan. circ. 1,000.

633   US
NATIONAL OILSEED PROCESSORS ASSOCIATION. YEARBOOK AND TRADING RULES. 1936. a. $50. National Oilseed Processors Association, 1255 23rd St. N.W., Ste. 850, Washington, DC 20037. TEL 202-452-8040. FAX 202-835-0400. circ. 2,500. **Document type**: directory.
Former titles: National Oilseed Processors Association. Yearbook; (until Aug. 1989): National Soybean Processors Association. Yearbook (ISSN 0077-5789).

NETHERLANDS. CENTRAAL BUREAU VOOR DE STATISTIEK. PRODUKTIESTATISTIEKEN: VEEVOEDERINDUSTRIE. see AGRICULTURE — Abstracting, Bibliographies, Statistics

664.752   US
HD9056.U4
NORTH AMERICAN GRAIN & MILLING ANNUAL. Variant title: Grain & Milling Annual. 1995. a. $90. Sosland Publishing Company, 4800 Main St., Ste. 100, Kansas City, MO 64112-2513. TEL 816-756-1000. FAX 816-756-0494. E-mail: worldgrain@sosland.com. Ed. Melissa Cordonier. adv.; stat. circ. 9,200. **Document type**: directory.
Formed by the merger of (1987-1995): Milling Directory - Buyer's Guide (ISSN 1045-9030); (1987-1995): Grain Digest - North American Yearbook (ISSN 1049-4073); **Which superseded**: Grain Directory - Buyer's Guide.

L MILL GAZETTEER. see ENGINEERING — Chemical Engineering

633.1   CN
ONTARIO. MINISTRY OF AGRICULTURE, FOOD AND RURAL ANALYSIS. GRAIN LETTER. m. Ministry of Agriculture, Food and Rural Analysis, Policy Analysis Branch, Legislative Bldgs., Queen's Park, Toronto, ON M7A 2B2, Canada. TEL 519-674-1561. FAX 519-674-1570. Ed. George McCaw. charts. **Document type**: newsletter.
Formerly: Ontario. Ministry of Agriculture and Food. Grain Letter (ISSN 0843-6533)

633.11 338.1   US
OREGON WHEAT. 1954. m. $15 to non-members. Oregon Wheat Growers League, 202 S.E. Dorion, Box 400, Pendleton, OR 97801. TEL 503-276-7330. FAX 503-276-1723. Ed. J. Scott Hutchinson. adv. contact: Bill Johnson. circ. 6,050 (controlled). **Document type**: trade publication.

633   US
PACIFIC NORTHWEST GRAIN MARKET NEWS. w. $45 (Canada & Mexico $70; elsewhere $100) (effective 1997). U.S. Department of Agriculture, Agricultural Marketing Service (Portland), Livestock & Seed Division, 1220 S.W. Third Ave., Rm. 1772, Portland, OR 97204. (Subscr. to: U.S.D.A. Agricultural Marketing Service, Livestock & Seed Division, Rm. 2623-S, Box 96456, Washington, DC 20090-6456. FAX 202-245-4732) Ed. Lowell Serfling. (tabloid format; back issues avail.) **Document type**: government publication.
Description: Provides prices and data on a regional basis of grains.

PANORAMA PANADERO. see FOOD AND FOOD INDUSTRIES — Bakers And Confectioners

633   US   ISSN 0740-2996
SB114.U7
PENNSYLVANIA. DEPARTMENT OF AGRICULTURE. SEED REPORT. 1927. a. free. Department of Agriculture, Bureau of Plant Industry, 2301 N. Cameron St., Harrisburg, PA 17110-9408. TEL 717-787-4843. FAX 717-787-2387. Ed. Joe D. Garvey. circ. 550. **Document type**: government publication.

633   BL   ISSN 0101-5559
PESQUISA EM ANDAMENTO - MILHO E SORGO. 1982. irreg., no.14, 1996. price varies. Centro Nacional de Pesquisa de Milho e Sorgo, Km 65 da Rodovia 424, Caixa Postal 151, 35701-970 Sete Lagos, MG, Brazil. TEL 55-31-7735466. FAX 55-31-7739252. E-mail: ainfo@cnpms.embrapa.br. bibl.
—BLDSC (6428.237700).

664.7   PL   ISSN 0033-2461
SB189
PRZEGLAD ZBOZOWO - MLYNARSKI. (Includes q. supplement) 1946. m. $81.50. Wydawnictwo Czasopism i Ksiazek Technicznych SIGMA - NOT, Ul. Ratuszowa 11, P.O. Box 1004, 00-950 Warsaw, Poland. TEL 48-22-180918. FAX 48-22-192187. TELEX 814550 SIGMA PL. (Dist. by: SIGMA NOT Ltd., Ul. Bartycka 20, 00-716 Warsaw, Poland) Ed. Magdalena Mart. adv.: B&W page $1000. bk.rev.; abstr.; bibl.; charts; illus.; pat.; stat.; index. circ. 1,650. **Indexed**: AgroLibrex, Chem.Abstr., Food Sci.& Tech.Abstr., Nutr.Abstr.

633.1   AT   ISSN 1321-1986
QUEENSLAND GRAINGROWER. 1959. w. Aus.$50. (Queensland Graingrowers' Association) Western Publishers Pty. Ltd., P.O. Box 188, 10 Joseph St., Toowoomba, Qld. 4350, Australia. TEL 076-32444. FAX 076-382118. Ed. Stephen Darracott. adv. circ. 10,000. (back issues avail.)

636.085   AT   ISSN 0819-4823
RECENT ADVANCES IN ANIMAL NUTRITION IN AUSTRALIA (YEAR). 1981. biennial. price varies. University of New England, Department of Biochemistry, Microbiology and Nutrition, Armidale, N.S.W. 2351, Australia. TEL 61-67-732270. FAX 61-67-728235. Ed. D.J. Farrell. **Document type**: proceedings.

633.1   BL   ISSN 0101-9708
REUNIAO GERAL DE CULTURA DO ARROZ. ANAIS. 1976. a. Centro de Pesquisa Agropecuaria de Terras Baixas de Clima Temperado, Setor de Difusao de Tecnologia, Caixa Postal 553, 96001 Pelotas, Brazil. charts; stat. circ. 600. **Indexed**: Field Crop Abstr., Herb.Abstr., Weed Abstr.
Description: Covers Brazilian rice cultivation, includes the technology used, the various forms of cultivation, and discusses the various events held for organizations involved with rice cultivation.

633   SP   ISSN 0210-1270
REVISTA DE PASTOS. 1971. s-a. 3000 ptas. Sociedad Espanola para el Estudio de los Pastos, Apdo. 8.111, 28080 Madrid, Spain. **Indexed**: Ind.SST.

636   FR   ISSN 0242-6595
CODEN: REAADG
REVUE DE L'ALIMENTATION ANIMALE; mensuel des industries de la nutrition animale. 1950. m. (10/yr.). 690 F. (foreign 770 F.) (effective 1997). Gedeon Marketing Eurl, B.P. 16, 29560 Telgruc-sur-Mer, France. TEL 33-2-98273766. FAX 33-2-98273765. Ed. Jacques Fitamant; Pub. Jacques Fitamant. adv. contact: Jacques Fitamant. index; circ. 3,000 (controlled). (back issues avail.) **Indexed**: Chem.Abstr., Nutr.Abstr. **Document type**: trade publication, directory.
—CASDDS.
Formerly (until 1981): Industries de l'Alimentation Animale (ISSN 0046-9300)
Description: Covers stratety, buying, formulating, processing and marketing feed for any kind of animals.

633.1   US
RICE FARMING. 1967. 6/yr. $25. Vance Publishing, Inc., 6263 Poplar Ave., Ste. 540, Memphis, TN 38119. TEL 901-767-4020. Ed. Marci Deshaies; Pub. John Sowell. R&P contact: Bob Wiley. adv. contact: Vince Angeletti. charts; illus.; tr.lit. circ. 13,000. **Document type**: trade publication.
Formerly: Rice Farming and Rice Industry News (ISSN 0194-0929)

633.1   US   ISSN 0364-8087
RICE MARKET NEWS. w. $80 (Canada and Mexico $85; elsewhere $110); $130 by fax. U.S. Department of Agriculture, Agricultural Marketing Service (Little Rock), Livestock & Seed Division, Box 391, Little Rock, AR 72203. (Subscr. to: U.S.D.A. Agricultural Marketing Service, Livestock & Feed Division, Rm. 2623-S, Box 96456, Washington, DC 20090-6456. FAX 202-245-4732) Ed. Steve Cheney. (also avail. in microfiche from CIS; back issues avail.; also avail. by fax; reprint service avail. from CIS) **Indexed**: Amer.Stat.Ind. (1984-). **Document type**: government publication.

ROCKY MOUNTAIN LIVESTOCK JOURNAL. see AGRICULTURE — Poultry And Livestock

633.1   SZ
SCHWEIZER HANDELS-BOERSE. 1919. w. 138 SFr. (foreign 180 SFr.). Schweizerische Handelsboerse, Bahnhofquai 7, Postfach 7075, CH-8023 Zurich, Switzerland. TEL 01-2112870. FAX 01-2112872. circ. 2,600.

664.7   SZ
SCHWEIZERISCHER MUEHLEN - ANZEIGER; Fachblatt fuer die Muehlenindustrie. 1890. s-m. 103 SFr. (foreign 170 SFr.). Schweizerische Handelsboerse, Bahnhofquai 7, Postfach 7075, CH-8023 Zurich, Switzerland. TEL 01-2112870. FAX 01-2112872. circ. 800. **Document type**: trade publication.

633   FR   ISSN 0395-8930
SEMENCES ET PROGRES. 1974. q. 160 F. to individuals (foreign 350 F.); libraries 144 F. (foreign 315 F.) (effective 1997-98). 44 rue du Louvre, 75001 Paris, France. TEL 33-1-42363960. FAX 33-1-42361617. Ed. Francois Haquin. R&P contact: Francois Haquin. adv. contact: Mireille Dorothee. circ. 9,000 (paid). **Document type**: newspaper.

633.2   CC   ISSN 1001-0084
SILIAO BOLAN/FEED PANORAMA. (Text in Chinese; abstracts in English) 1988. bi-m. $30. Dongbei Nongxueyuan - Northeast Agricultural University, Xiangfang-qu, Harbin, Heilongjiang 150030, People's Republic of China. TEL 0451-5665886. FAX 0451-5665886. Ed. Wang Qinggao. circ. 5,000.

633.11   SA
SOUTH AFRICA. WHEAT BOARD. ANNUAL REPORT. (Report year ends Oct. 31st) 1939. a. free. Wheat Board - Koringraad, P.O. Box 908, Pretoria 0001, South Africa. TEL 27-12-3251970. FAX 27-12-216448. illus.; stat. circ. 510.

266 AGRICULTURE — POULTRY AND LIVESTOCK

664.7   IT   ISSN 0040-1862
TS2120   CODEN: TEMOAZ
TECNICA MOLITORIA. (Text in Italian; summaries in English) 1950. m. L.140000($90) (effective 1997). Chiriotti Editori, Viale Rimembranza 60, Box 66, 10064 Pinerolo, Italy. TEL 39-121-393127. FAX 39-121-794480. Ed. Chiriotti Giovanni. adv.: B&W page L.1100000, color page L.1300000; adv. contact: Giuseppe Chiriotti. bk.rev.; abstr.; bibl.; charts; illus.; pat.; index. circ. 4,000. Indexed: Agri.Eng.Abstr., Chem.Abstr., Dairy Sci.Abstr., Field Crop Abstr., Food Sci.& Tech.Abstr., Herb.Abstr., Nutr.Abstr., Seed Abstr., Triticale Abstr. **Document type:** trade publication.
—BLDSC (8762.510000); CASDDS; Linda Hall; UMI. **CCC.**
   Description: Covers pasta making, wheat milling, feed mills, silos and cereal chemistry. Includes technical and scientific articles by Italian and foreign experts. Supplies descriptions of machines.

633.2 636.2   AT   ISSN 1034-6147
TODAY'S FEED LOTTING. 1988. q. Aus.$45. Peter Buffey Media Pty. Ltd., P.O. Box 6337, Toowoomba West, Qld. 4350, Australia. TEL 61-76-333262. FAX 61-76-333285. Ed. Peter Buffey. R&P contact: Peter Buffey. adv.: B&W page Aus.$640, color page Aus.$880; adv. contact: Lyn Buffey. circ. 1,700. **Document type:** consumer publication, trade publication.
   Incorporates (1987-1996): Prime Beef (ISSN 1030-1992)

U.S. DEPARTMENT OF AGRICULTURE. AGRICULTURAL STATISTICS BOARD REPORT: GRAIN STOCKS. see AGRICULTURE — Abstracting, Bibliographies, Statistics

U.S. DEPARTMENT OF AGRICULTURE. AGRICULTURAL STATISTICS BOARD REPORT: RICE STOCKS. see AGRICULTURE — Abstracting, Bibliographies, Statistics

V W D - GETREIDE, FUTTERMITTEL, OELE. see BUSINESS AND ECONOMICS — Investments

633   CN   ISSN 0382-3601
VARIETIES OF GRAIN CROPS FOR SASKATCHEWAN. 1972. a. free. Saskatchewan Agriculture and Food Library, B5 Walter Scott Bldg., 3085 Albert St., Regina, SK S4S 0B1, Canada. TEL 306-787-6933. FAX 306-787-0216. E-mail: pdc@agr.gov.sk.ca; URL: http://www.gov.sk.ca/agfood. stat. circ. 100,000. (also avail. in microfiche) **Document type:** government publication.

663.2   US   ISSN 1065-5948
VIRGINIA HAY CLEARING HOUSE. m. Department of Agriculture and Consumer Services, 1100 Bank St., Ste. 805, Richmond, VA 23219-3638. TEL 804-786-3947. FAX 804-371-7787. Ed. J.P. Welch. circ. 800. (back issues avail.) **Document type:** government publication.
   Description: Serves as a clearing house between buyers and sellers of Virginia hay. Lists buyers, sellers and descriptions of hay.

633.2   US
WASHINGTON FEEDLINE. irreg. (3-5/yr.). membership. American Feed Industry Association, 1501 Wilson Blvd., Ste. 1100, Arlington, VA 22209. TEL 703-524-0810. FAX 703-524-1921. URL: www.afia.org.
   Description: Provides designated recipients of member companies with news of legislation important to the feed industry. Gives accounts of actions taken in response to specific bills and alerts members to the potential effect of certain legislative proposals.

633.2   US
WAYN-E-GRAM MAGAZINE. 1966. q. Continental Grain Company, Wayne Feed Division, 10 S. Riverside Plaza, Chicago, IL 60606-3708. TEL 312-930-1050. FAX 312-466-6614. Ed. Barbara K. Becker. adv. contact: Meg Arbetman. circ. 2,500. (controlled). **Document type:** newsletter.
   Description: For dealers who market Wayne feed products.

633.1   US   ISSN 0745-8991
HD9030.1   CODEN: WOGREJ
WORLD GRAIN. 10/yr. $24. Sosland Publishing Company, 4800 Main St., Ste. 100, Kansas City, MO 64112-2513. TEL 816-756-1000. FAX 816-756-0494. E-mail: worldgrain@sosland.com. Ed. Melissa Cordonier. adv. circ. 8,700. Indexed: Food Sci.& Tech.Abstr. **Document type:** trade publication.
—BLDSC (9356.029700); Linda Hall.

633.1 664.7   CC   ISSN 1001-6899
    CODEN: WLGXEG
WUHAN LIANGSHI GONGYE XUEYUAN XUEBAO/WUHAN FOOD INDUSTRY COLLEGE. JOURNAL. (Text in English) 1982. q. Y10($10) (effective till 1997). Wuhan Liangshi Gongye Xueyuan, 129 Shundao St., Wuhan, Hubei 430022, People's Republic of China. TEL 027-5866971. FAX 027-5834951. Eds. Fu Lumin, Xu Xianghua. adv.: page $250; adv. contact: Xu Xianghua. circ. 6,000 (paid). Indexed: Food Sci.& Tech.Abstr. **Document type:** academic/scholarly publication.
   Description: Publishes academic papers on food technology, grain lipid engineering, animal breeding, grain and oil processing machinery, economics, management and computer application.

633.2   GW   ISSN 0941-9098
Z M P BILANZ GETREIDE, OELSAATEN, FUTTERMITTEL. 1975. a. DM.65 (foreign DM.150) (effective 1997). Zentrale Markt und Preisberichtstelle GmbH, Rochusstr. 2, 53123 Bonn, Germany. TEL 49-228-9777173. FAX 49-228-9777179. adv. **Document type:** trade publication.
   Formerly: Z M P Bilanz Getreide-Futtermittel (ISSN 0170-7809)

338.1   GW
Z V INFORMATIONEN. m. DM.60. Zentralverband des Deutschen Getreide-, Futter- und Duengemittelhandels e.V., Buschstr. 2, 53113 Bonn, Germany. TEL 0228-215058. circ. 1,500. (back issues avail.)

633.1   CC   ISSN 1001-7216
ZHONGGUO SHUIDAO KEXUE/CHINESE JOURNAL OF RICE SCIENCE. (Text in Chinese, English) 1986. q. $30. Zhongguo Shuidao Yanjiusuo - China National Rice Research Institute, 359 Tiyuchang Lu, Hangzhou, Zhejiang 310006, People's Republic of China. TEL 86-571-33715711. FAX 86-571-3371-5745. Ed. Shaokai Min. R&P contact: Li Jian. adv. contact: Li Jian. **Document type:** academic/scholarly publication.
—BLDSC (3180.674500).

633   YU   ISSN 0351-0999
    CODEN: ZIHLDU
ZITO HLEB; casopis za tehnologiju zita i brasna. 1974. bi-m. DM.70. Jugoslovenski Institut Prehrambenog Inzenierstva, Tehnoloski Fakultet, Bulevar Avnoja 1, Novi Sad, Vojvodina, Yugoslavia. TEL 0038 21-350-120. FAX 21-216-332. TELEX YU 14466. Ed. Rozika Vukobratovic. adv.; bk.rev. circ. 550. Indexed: Chem.Abstr., Food Sci.& Tech.Abstr., Ref.Zh.
—CASDDS.

AGRICULTURE — Poultry And Livestock

see also Agriculture–Dairying and Dairy Products; Leather and Fur Industries; Veterinary Science

636 346.066   US
A A M P LIFIER. s-m. $50 to non-members. American Association of Meat Processors, Box 269, Elizabethtown, PA 17022. TEL 717-367-1168. FAX 717-367-9096. E-mail: aamp@aamp.com. Ed. Anne B. Tantum. circ. 2,200. (back issues avail.) **Document type:** newsletter.
   Description: Provides information for the meat industry on trends, education and developments. Includes news for members and an update.

636   CU
A C P A. s-a. $18 in S. America; N. America $20; elsewhere $22. (Asociacion Cubana de Produccion Animal) Ediciones Cubanas, Obispo No. 527, Apdo. 605, Havana, Cuba.

636   US
A F I A SAFETYGRAM. m. $65 to non-members; members $32.50. American Feed Industry Association, 1501 Wilson Blvd., Ste. 1100, Arlington, VA 22209. TEL 703-524-0810. FAX 703-524-1921. URL: www.afia.org.
   Description: Features the latest in safety practices, prevention, and regulations.

636.2   BL
A GRANJA. 1944. m. Editora Centaurus Ltda., Av. Getulio Vargas 1556 e 1558, Caixa Postal 2890, 90000 Porto Alegre RS, Brazil. TEL 0512-33-18-22. FAX 0512-33-24-56. TELEX 051-23-33. Ed. Hugo F. Hoffmann. circ. 106,000.

636 179   US
A I F NEWSLETTER. 1987. m. $25 donation (effective 1997 & 1998). Animal Industry Foundation, 1501 Wilson Blvd., Ste. 1100, Arlington, VA 22209. TEL 703-524-0810. FAX 703-524-1921. E-mail: aif@aif.org; URL: http://www.aif.org. Ed. Steve Kopperud. R&P contact: Kay Johnson. circ. 3,500. (looseleaf format; back issues avail.) **Document type:** newsletter.
   Description: Serves as an information source for what is happening in the animal rights movement and activist groups' activities. Also provides updates on achievements in animal agriculture research and education, new educational materials, and future products and materials to benefit producers and the industry.

636   UN
A L P A N NETWORK PAPER. (African Livestock Policy Analysis Network) 1985. 2/yr. International Livestock Centre for Africa, P.O. Box 5689, Addis Ababa, Ethiopia. TEL 251-1-61-31-15. FAX 251-1-61-18-92. TELEX 21207 ILCA ET. E-mail: ILCA@CGNET.COM.
   Description: Information network for policy makers, analysts and implementors involved in livestock research and development in Africa.

636   UN
A L P A N NEWSLETTER. (African Livestock Policy Analysis Network) 1985. 2/yr. International Livestock Centre for Africa, P.O. Box 5689, Addis Ababa, Ethiopia. TEL 251-1-61-32-15. FAX 251-1-61-18-92. TELEX 21207 ILCA ET. E-mail: ILCA@CGNET.COM. **Document type:** newsletter.
   Description: Provides information on developments in the livestock field and introduces Network Papers authored by ALPAN members.

636.6   US
A P A NEWS AND VIEWS. q. $10 membership (foreign $25) (effective 1997 & 1998). American Poultry Association, 133 Millville Rd., Mendon, MA 01756-1210. **Document type:** newsletter.
   Former titles: Fancy Feather. A P A News and Views; (until 1987): American Poultry Association. News and Views.
   Description: Covers purebred poultry as a hobby and exhibition poultry.

636.2   UK
ABERDEEN - ANGUS HERD BOOK. 1884. a. £30. Aberdeen-Angus Cattle Society, Pedigree House, 6 King's Pl., Perth PH2 8AD, Scotland. TEL 44-1738-22477. FAX 44-1738-36436. circ. 350. (back issues avail.) **Document type:** trade publication.

636.2   UK   ISSN 0001-317X
ABERDEEN - ANGUS REVIEW. 1919. a. £5. Aberdeen-Angus Cattle Society, Pedigree House, 6 King's Pl., Perth PH2 8AD, Scotland. TEL 44-1738-622477. FAX 44-1738-636436. Ed. E.J. Gillanders. adv.; illus.; mkt. circ. 2,600. **Document type:** trade publication.

ACTA ACADEMIAE AGRICULTURAE AC TECHNICAE OLSTENENSIS. ZOOTECHNICA/AGRICULTURAL AND TECHNICAL ACADEMY IN OLSZTYN. ANIMAL HUSBANDRY. see AGRICULTURE — Feed, Flour And Grain

AGRICULTURE — POULTRY AND LIVESTOCK

636   PL   ISSN 0065-0935
SF1   CODEN: AASZBW
ACTA AGRARIA ET SILVESTRIA. SERIES ZOOTECHNICA. (Text in Polish; summaries in English and Russian) 1961. irreg. (1-2/yr.). price varies. (Polska Akademia Nauk, Oddzial w Krakowie, Komisja Nauk Rolniczych i Lesnych) Ossolineum, Publishing House of the Polish Academy of Sciences, Pl. Solny 14a, 50-062 Wroclaw, Poland. TEL 48-71-343-6961. FAX 48-71-448-103. TELEX 0712771 OSS PL. Ed. Thomas M. Janowski. bibl.; charts. **Indexed:** Agri.Eng.Abstr., AgroLibrex, Anim.Breed.Abstr., Biol.Abstr., Chem.Abstr., Excerp.Med., Field Crop Abstr., Herb.Abstr., Ind.Vet., Irr.& Drain.Abstr., Maize Abstr., Nutr.Abstr., Pig News & Info., Poult.Abstr., Soils & Fert., Triticale Abstr., Vet.Bull. **Document type:** academic/scholarly publication.
—BLDSC (0588.640000); CASDDS; KNAW.
    Formerly (until 1965): Acta Agraria et Silvestria. Seria Zootechniczna (ISSN 0376-1568)
    Description: Experimental studies on farm animal breeding, physiology, animal hygiene and environment as well as animal reproduction.

636   NO   ISSN 0906-4702
SF1   CODEN: ASSAEI
ACTA AGRICULTURAE SCANDINAVICA. SECTION A, ANIMAL SCIENCE. (Supplement avail.: Acta Agriculturae Scandinavica. Supplementum (ISSN 0065-0943)) (Text in English) 1950. q. NOK 925 in Nordic countries; elsewhere $159 (effective 1997). (Kungliga Skogs- och Lantbruksakademien - Royal Swedish Academy of Agriculture and Forestry) Scandinavian University Press, P.O. Box 2959 Toeyen, N-0608 Oslo, Norway. TEL 47-22-57-54-00. FAX 47-22-57-53-53. E-mail: mail@scup.no; URL: http://www.scup.no. (U.S. addr.: 875 Massachusetts Ave., Ste. 84, Cambridge, MA 02139. TEL 617-497-6515. FAX 617-354-6875) (Co-sponsor: Scandinavian Association of Agricultural Scientists) Ed.Bd. bibl.; charts; illus. circ. 1,000. (back issues avail; reprint service avail.) **Indexed:** Acid Rain Abstr., Acid Rain Ind., Agri.Eng.Abstr., Anim.Breed.Abstr., ASCA, Biodet.Abstr., Biol.Abstr., Cadscan, Chem.Abstr., Crop Physiol.Abstr., Curr.Adv.Ecol.Sci., Curr.Cont., Dairy Sci.Abstr., Excerp.Med., Field Crop Abstr., Food Sci.& Tech.Abstr., Helminthol.Abstr., Herb.Abstr., Hort.Abstr., Ind.Sci.Rev., Ind.Vet., Lead Abstr., Nutr.Abstr., Pig News & Info., Plant Breed.Abstr., Poult.Abstr., Rev.Med.& Vet.Mycol., Rev.Plant Path., Rural Ext.Educ.& Tr.Abstr., Rural Recreat.Tour.Abstr., Sci.Cit.Ind., Seed Abstr., Sel.Water Res.Abstr., Soyabean Abstr., Sport Fish.Abstr., Sugar Ind.Abstr., Triticale Abstr., Vet.Bull., Wild.Rev., World Agri.Econ.& Rural Sociol.Abstr., Zincscan, Zoo.Rec. **Document type:** academic/scholarly publication.
—BLDSC (0589.005000); CASDDS; Genuine Article; Linda Hall; SWETS; UnCover. **CCC.**
    Supersedes in part (in 1992): Acta Agriculturae Scandinavica (ISSN 0001-5121)
    Refereed Serial

636   US
ACTIONGRAM. 1976. m. membership. Livestock Publications Council, 2631 Garland St., Eureka, CA 95501. TEL 707-445-3124. FAX 707-445-3124. Ed. Bill Shepard. circ. 500. **Document type:** newsletter.

636   UK
ADVANCES IN MEAT RESEARCH SERIES. 1985. irreg., vol.7, 1991. price varies. Elsevier Science Ltd., Books Division, P.O. Box 800, Kidlington, Oxford OX5 1DX, England. TEL 44-1865-843000. FAX 44-1865-843010. E-mail: nlinfo-f@elsevier.nl; usinfo-f@elsevier.com; forinfo-kyf04035@niftyserve.or.jp; URL: http://www.elsevier.nl/. (Subscr. to: Elsevier Science, Regional Sales Office, P.O. Box 211, 1000 AE Amsterdam, Netherlands. TEL 31-20-4853757. FAX 31-20-4853432; Subscr. in the Americas to: Elsevier Science, Regional Sales Office, Box 945, New York, NY 10159-0945. TEL 212-633-3730. FAX 212-633-3680; Subscr. in Australasia and the Far East to: Elsevier Science (Singapore) Pte Ltd, No.1 Temasek Ave., No.17-01 Millenia Tower, Singapore 039192, Singapore. TEL 65-434-3727. FAX 65-337-2230) Eds. A.M. Pearson, T.R. Dutson. **Document type:** monographic series.

636   UN   ISSN 1013-7750
AFRICAN LIVESTOCK RESEARCH. (Text in English, French) 1978-1989 (no.35); resumed N.S. 1992. q. $75 to individuals; institutions $120 or exchange basis; free to agricultural research services in Africa. International Livestock Centre for Africa - Centre International pour l'Elevage en Afrique, P.O. Box 5689, Addis Ababa, Ethiopia. E-mail: ILCA@CGNET.COM. Ed. Michael Smalley. circ. 3,431. (also avail. in microfiche) **Indexed:** Agri.Eng.Abstr., Agroforest.Abstr., Anim.Breed.Abstr., Field Crop Abstr., Herb.Abstr., Maize Abstr., P.L.E.S.A., Rural Devel.Abstr., Soils & Fert., Sorghum & Millets Abstr., Soyabean Abstr., Triticale Abstr., World Agri.Econ.& Rural Sociol.Abstr. **Document type:** academic/scholarly publication.
    Supersedes: I L C A Bulletin (ISSN 0255-0008); Bulletin du C I P E A (ISSN 0255-0016)
    Description: Disseminates the results of strategic, basic and applied research that relates to livestock and mixed crop-livestock systems in Africa.
    Refereed Serial

636.2   SA   ISSN 0515-6203
AFRIKANER BEESJOERNAAL. (Text in Afrikaans and English) 1953. q. (Afrikaner Cattle Breeders' Association) Dreyer Printers & Publishers, 21 Krause St., Box 286, Bloemfontein 9300, South Africa. adv.

AGRI-PRACTICE; the journal of medicine and surgery for the food animal practitioner. see *VETERINARY SCIENCE*

636   SP   ISSN 0213-196X
AGRICULTOR PRACTICO GANADERO. 1972. bi-m. 5000 ptas. (foreign 7000 ptas. ($70)) (effective 1995). Editorial Serie Dos, S.A., Modesto Lafuente, 16, bajo A., 28010 Madrid, Spain. TEL 34-1-4455550. FAX 34-1-4455162. Ed. Javier/Goyoaga. adv.: B&W page 72500 ptas., color page 119000 ptas.; trim 185 x 265. **Document type:** trade publication.
    Description: Contains news, reports, interviews, and background articles.

AGRICULTURA; revista agropecuaria. see *AGRICULTURE*

AGRICULTURAL RESEARCH. see *AGRICULTURE — Crop Production And Soil*

AGRICULTURAL SCIENCE DIGEST. see *AGRICULTURE*

636   PL   ISSN 0239-9350
    CODEN: ZARZDW
AKADEMIA ROLNICZA IM. HUGONA KOLLATAJA W KRAKOWIE. ZESZYTY NAUKOWE. SERIA: ZOOTECHNIKA. (Text in Polish; summaries in English) 1957. a. price varies. Akademia Rolnicza im. Hugona Kollataja w Krakowie, c/o Ligia Hayto, Biblioteka Glowna AR, Al. Mickiewicza 24-28, 30-059 Krakow, Poland. TEL 48-12-119144. FAX 48-12-336245. TELEX 322469 PL. Ed. Zdzislaw Piskornik. circ. 120 (paid). **Indexed:** AgroLibrex. **Document type:** academic/scholarly publication.
—CASDDS.
    Former titles (until 1979): Akademia Rolnicza w Krakowie. Zeszyty Naukowe. Zootechnika (ISSN 0137-1916); (until 1972): Wyzsza Szkola Rolnicza w Krakowie. Zeszyty Naukowe. Zootechnika (ISSN 0452-6716)
    Description: Covers animal breeding and nutrition, animal genetics and reproduction, zoology.

AKADEMIA ROLNICZA, POZNAN. ROCZNIKI. ZOOTECHNIKA. see *BIOLOGY — Zoology*

636   PL   ISSN 0137-1940
SF1
AKADEMIA ROLNICZA W SZCZECINIE. ZESZYTY NAUKOWE. ZOOTECHNIKA. (Includes: Teratologica Scripta) (Text in Polish; abstract in English) 1966. a. price varies. Akademia Rolnicza w Szczecinie, Dzial Wydawnictw, Ul. Doktora Judyma 22, 71-460 Szczecin, Poland. TEL 48-91-541639. FAX 48-91-541642. TELEX 0425494 AR. Ed. Antoni Furowicz. bk.rev. **Indexed:** Chem.Abstr., Field Crop Abstr., Nutr.Abstr. **Document type:** academic/scholarly publication.
    Refereed Serial

636   PL   ISSN 0137-2017
    CODEN: ZNAZD4
AKADEMIA ROLNICZA WE WROCLAWIU. ZESZYTY NAUKOWE. ZOOTECHNIKA. (Subseries of: Akademia Rolnicza we Wroclawiu. Zeszyty Naukowe (ISSN 0867-7964)) (Text in Polish; summaries in English) 1956. irreg. price varies. Akademia Rolnicza we Wroclawiu, Ul. Norwida 25, 50-375 Wroclaw, Poland. FAX 48-71-229576. (Subscr. to: Wydawnictwo Akademii Rolniczej, ul. Sopocka 23, 50-344 Wroclaw, Poland. TEL 48-71-211277) circ. 320. **Indexed:** AgroLibrex. **Document type:** academic/scholarly publication.
—CASDDS.
    Formerly (until 1973): Wyzsza Szkola Rolnicza we Wroclawiu. Zeszyty Naukowe. Zootechnika (ISSN 0520-9323)

636.2   US   ISSN 0516-3889
ALABAMA CATTLEMAN. 1958. m. $29 membership only. Alabama Cattleman's Association, 201 S. Bainbridge St., Box 2499, Montgomery, AL 36102-2499. FAX 334-834-6326. Ed. William E. Powell. adv.; circ. 17,000 (controlled).

636.2   CN   ISSN 1187-0761
ALBERTA BEEF. 1976. m. Can.$20 (foreign $35). Creative Motion Publishing, 202-2915 19th St., N.E., Calgary, AB T2E 7A2, Canada. TEL 403-250-1090. FAX 403-291-9546. Ed. Cindy McCreath. adv. contact: Lee Gunderson. bk.rev. circ. 14,000. **Document type:** trade publication.
    Former titles (until 1991): World of Beef (ISSN 0848-8142); World of Beef and Feedlot Management; World of Beef and Stockmans Record; World of Beef.
    Description: Targets Alberta's commercial beef producers.

ALIMENTOS BALANCEADOS PARA ANIMALES. see *AGRICULTURE — Feed, Flour And Grain*

636   HU   ISSN 0230-1814
    CODEN: ATAKDW
ALLATTENYESZTES ES TAKARMANYOZAS/HUNGARIAN JOURNAL OF ANIMAL PRODUCTION. 1951. bi-m. 2000 Ft. (Ministry of Agriculture) Allattenyesztesi es Takarmanyozasi Kutato-Intezet, 2053 Hercegahalom, Hungary. TEL 36-1-23-319133. FAX 36-1-23-319133. TELEX 226664. Ed. Janos Gundel. bk.rev. circ. 1,000. **Document type:** newsletter.
—BLDSC (0789.760000); CASDDS.
    Formerly (until 1980): Allattenyesztes - Animal Breeding (ISSN 0365-4052)
    Description: Covers research and development in animal production and nutrition in Hungary.

636.3   IT
ALLEVATORE DI OVINI E CAPRINI. 1983. m. L.20000 (effective 1995). Associazione Nazionale della Pastorizia, Viale di Villa Massimo 39, 00161 Rome, Italy. TEL 39-6-44291756. FAX 39-6-44241459. Ed. Ennio Giuliani. adv.: B&W page L.1100000, color page L.1320000; adv. contact: Costantino Finocchi. bk.rev. circ. 18,000. (tabloid format) **Document type:** trade publication.
    Description: Provides sheep and goat livestock genetic improvement program and technical information for breeders.

636   FR
ALLIANCE PASTORALE. BULLETIN. 1932. m. 60 F. (foreign 160 F.) (effective 1995). Syndicat de l'Alliance Pastorale, 86500 Montmorillon, France. TEL 49-83-30-30. FAX 49-83-30-50. TELEX 130 960 CODE 7704. Ed. Nicolas Decazes. adv. contact: Mme Marlaud. **Document type:** bulletin.

636.587   US   ISSN 0065-745X
SF489.B2
AMERICAN BANTAM ASSOCIATION. YEARBOOK. 1917. a. $10. American Bantam Association, Box 127, Augusta, NJ 07822. Ed. Eleanor Vinhage. adv. circ. 3,000. **Document type:** directory.

664.9   US   ISSN 1042-5233
AMERICAN CATTLEWOMAN. 1972. bi-m. $25. American National CattleWomen, Inc., Box 3881, Englewood, CO 80155. TEL 303-694-0313. FAX 303-694-2390. Ed. Patricia Sherwood; Pub. Patricia Sherwood. R&P contact: Patricia Sherwood. bk.rev. circ. 7,000. **Document type:** newsletter.
    Former titles: American National CattleWomen Newsletter (ISSN 0744-4389); American National CowBelles Newsletter.
    Description: Profiles women in the cattle industry.

AGRICULTURE — POULTRY AND LIVESTOCK

636.2 US
AMERICAN DEXTER CATTLE ASSOCIATION. BULLETIN.
bi-m. $10. American Dexter Cattle Association, R.R. 1, Box 378, Concordia, MO 64020-9233. TEL 816-463-7704. **Document type:** bulletin.

636.2 US ISSN 0065-8081
AMERICAN DEXTER CATTLE ASSOCIATION. HERD BOOK. 1920. a. $10. American Dexter Cattle Association, R.R. 1, Box 378, Concordia, MO 64020-9233. TEL 816-463-7704. Ed. Rosemary Fleharty. cum.index: 1960-1987. **Document type:** directory.

AMERICAN FARRIER'S ASSOCIATION NEWSLETTER. see SPORTS AND GAMES — Horses And Horsemanship

AMERICAN FARRIERS JOURNAL. see SPORTS AND GAMES — Horses And Horsemanship

636 US ISSN 1057-6649
CODEN: PMACEN
AMERICAN FEED INDUSTRY ASSOCIATION. ANNUAL AND SEMIANNUAL MEETINGS OF THE NUTRITION COUNCIL. PROCEEDINGS. 1944. a. $40 to non-members; members $20 (effective 1996). American Feed Industry Association, Nutrition Council, 1501 Wilson Blvd., Ste. 1100, Arlington, VA 22209. TEL 703-524-0810. FAX 703-524-1921. URL: www.afia.org. Ed.Bd. circ. 1,500. (back issues avail.) **Indexed:** Biol.Abstr. **Document type:** proceedings.
Formerly: American Feed Manufacturers Association. Annual Meeting of the Nutrition Council. Proceedings.
Description: Presentations given during the national and regional production schools. Subjects vary widely. Covers truck operations, workers' compensation, energy management, OSHA regulations, FDA updates, safety, pelleting, etc.

636 US
AMERICAN FEED INDUSTRY ASSOCIATION. PRODUCTION SCHOOL PROCEEDINGS. a. $50 to non-members; members $25. American Feed Industry Association, Production School, 1501 Wilson Blvd., Ste. 1100, Arlington, VA 22209. TEL 703-524-0810. FAX 703-524-1921. URL: www.afia.org. **Document type:** proceedings.

636.39 US ISSN 0065-8456
AMERICAN GOAT SOCIETY. YEAR BOOK. (Includes: A G S Dairy Goat Yearbook) 1935. a. membership. American Goat Society, Inc., R.R. 1, Box 56, Esperance, NY 12066. TEL 518-875-6708. Ed. Valerie Ciesnynki. adv.; index. circ. 3,500. **Document type:** bulletin.

636.3 US
AMERICAN GOAT SOCIETY BUYERS GUIDE. a. $15 to non-members. American Goat Society, R.R. 1, Box 56, Esperance, NY 12066-9704. TEL 518-875-6708. circ. 600. (looseleaf format) **Document type:** directory, trade publication.

AMERICAN MEAT SCIENCE ASSOCIATION. RECIPROCAL MEAT CONFERENCE. PROCEEDINGS. see FOOD AND FOOD INDUSTRIES

636.3 US
AMERICAN POLYPAY SHEEP NEWS. m. $50 membership. American Polypay Sheep Association, 609 S. Central Ave., Ste. 9, Sidney, MT 59210. TEL 406-482-7768. FAX 406-482-7768. circ. 250. **Document type:** newsletter.
Description: Covers all areas of interest concerning the polypay sheep - sales, production, health; inquiries and their breeders.

636.3 US
AMERICAN RAMBOUILLET SHEEP BREEDERS ASSOCIATION. NEWSLETTER. q. American Rambouillet Sheep Breeders Association, 2709 Sherwood Way, San Angelo, TX 76901. TEL 915-949-4414. **Document type:** newsletter.

636 US ISSN 0886-4357
AMERICAN RED ANGUS. 1954. 10/yr. $15. Red Angus Association of America, 4201 I-35 North, Denton, TX 76207. TEL 817-387-3502. FAX 817-383-4036. adv.; charts; illus.; stat.; circ. 8,000 (controlled). **Document type:** trade publication.
—UnCover.

636 US ISSN 0569-7832
CODEN: PMWSA7
AMERICAN SOCIETY OF ANIMAL SCIENCE. WESTERN SECTION PROCEEDINGS. 1949. a. $18. American Society of Animal Science, 1111 N. Dunlap Ave., Savoy, IL 61874. TEL 217-356-3182. FAX 217-398-4119. E-mail: joannw@assochq.org. R&P contact: John Edwards. circ. 600. **Indexed:** Food Sci.& Tech.Abstr. **Document type:** academic/scholarly publication, proceedings.
—BLDSC (6631.870000); Linda Hall.

AMERICAN STANDARD CHINCHILLA RABBIT ASSOCIATION. NEWSLETTER. see PETS

636.39 SA ISSN 0003-3464
ANGORA GOAT & MOHAIR JOURNAL/ANGORABOK- EN SYBOKHAARBLAD. (Text in Afrikaans, English) 1959. s-a. R.40 (effective 1996). S.A. Mohair Grower's Association, P.O. Box 50, Jansenville 6265, South Africa. TEL 27-24-4932-140. (Co-sponsors: Angora Goat Stud Breeders' Association of S.A.; Mohair Board) Ed.Bd. adv. circ. 3,500. **Indexed:** Anim.Breed.Abstr., Ind.S.A.Per.
Description: Covers mohair matters and agricultural concerns.
Refereed Serial

636.39 US
ANGORA GOAT EXCHANGE. bi-m. $9. 2458 Morrice Rd., Owosso, MI 48867.
Description: For angora goat raisers.

636.2 US
ANGUS; the magazine. 1987. m. $15. James Danekas & Associates, Inc., Box 613, Fair Oaks, CA 95628. TEL 916-965-6122. FAX 916-965-1128. Ed. James A. Danekas. adv. circ. 4,600. **Document type:** consumer publication.
Description: Keeps members of the Western State Angus Association abreast of trends and changes in the Angus industry in the West and beyond.

636.2 NZ ISSN 0300-3345
ANGUS HERD BOOK OF NEW ZEALAND. 1919. a. NZ.$25 membership. New Zealand Angus Association Inc., P.O. Box 1241, Hastings, New Zealand. TEL 64-6-8766122. FAX 64-6-8760856. Ed. David Ousley. circ. 350. **Document type:** trade publication.
Description: Lists pedigree Angus cattle registered in New Zealand.

636.2 US ISSN 0194-9543
ANGUS JOURNAL. 1979. m. $30 (Canada $50; elsewhere $125). American Angus Association, 3021 Frederick Blvd., St. Joseph, MO 64506. TEL 816-233-0508. FAX 816-233-6575-112. E-mail: journal@ngus.org. Ed. Jerilyn Johnson. R&P contact: Jerilyn Johnson. adv. contact: Cheyl Okley. bk.rev.; illus.; mkt. circ. 22,000. (also avail. in microform from UMI) **Document type:** trade publication.
—Linda Hall; UMI; UnCover.
Supersedes (as of vol.60, 1979): Aberdeen-Angus Journal (ISSN 0001-3161)
Description: Discusses the Angus cattle industry in the United States.

636.2 US ISSN 0402-4265
ANGUS TOPICS. 1955. m. $12 (foreign $24). Angus Topics, Inc., Box 397, Carmi, IL 62821. TEL 618-382-8553. FAX 618-382-3436. Ed. Judy M. Bingman. adv. contact: E.R. Bingman. circ. 10,000. **Document type:** trade publication.
Description: Provides informative articles and sale opportunities relative to breeding and raising registered Angus cattle.

ANIMAL BIOTECHNOLOGY. see BIOLOGY — Biotechnology

636 US
ANIMAL FINDERS' GUIDE. 1984. 18/yr. $25 (effective $35). Box 99, Prairie Creek, IN 47869. TEL 812-898-2678. FAX 812-898-2013. Ed. Patrick D. Hoctor; Pub. Patrick D. Hoctor. R&P contact: Patrick D. Hoctor. adv. contact: Sharon K. Hoctor. circ. 5,000 (paid). **Document type:** trade publication.
Description: Devoted to the exotic animal owner.

636 636.089 GR
ANIMAL HUSBANDRY AND BREEDING. (Text in Greek) 1986. q. Agrotechnical Publications S.A., 24-26 Favierou, 104 38 Athens, Greece. TEL 30-1-5222-054. FAX 30-1-5246-628. TELEX 222264 STIM GR. Ed. Costas Colotouros. circ. 8,000. (back issues avail.) **Document type:** academic/scholarly publication.
Description: Covers livestock production and provides marketing information on new methods, technology and techniques, breeders, scientists and traders.

636 AT ISSN 0728-5965
ANIMAL PRODUCTION IN AUSTRALIA. 1956. biennial. Aus.$80 (effective 1998). (Australian Society of Animal Production) A.S.A.P. Publications, c/o Mrs. Lyn Yates, A.B.R.I., University of New England, Armidale, N.S.W. 2351, Australia. TEL 61-67-733773. FAX 61-67-733773. Ed. C.J. Thwaites. circ. 2,485 (paid). (back issues avail.) **Indexed:** Agri.Eng.Abstr., Agroforest.Abstr., Anim.Breed.Abstr., Biol.Abstr., Chem.Abstr., Dairy Sci.Abstr., Field Crop Abstr., Food Sci.& Tech.Abstr., Helminthol.Abstr., Herb.Abstr., Ind.Vet., Nutr.Abstr., Rural Recreat.Tour.Abstr., Sugar Ind.Abstr., Vet.Bull., World Agri.Econ.& Rural Sociol.Abstr. **Document type:** proceedings.
—BLDSC (6656.400000); Linda Hall.
Former titles: Australian Society of Animal Production. Proceedings (ISSN 0067-2149); Animal Production in Australia.
Refereed Serial

636 NE ISSN 0378-4320
CODEN: ANRSDV
ANIMAL REPRODUCTION SCIENCE. 1977. 20/yr. fl.2175($1250) (effective 1998). Elsevier Science B.V., P.O. Box 211, 1000 AE Amsterdam, Netherlands. TEL 31-20-4853911. FAX 31-20-4853598. TELEX 18582 ESPA NL. E-mail: nlinfo-f@elsevier.nl; usinfo-f@elsevier.com; forinfo-kyf04035@niftyserve.or.jp; URL: http://www.elsevier.nl/. (Subscr. in the Americas to: Elsevier Science, Regional Sales Office, Box 945, New York, NY 10159-0945. TEL 212-633-3730. FAX 212-633-3680; Subscr. in Australasia and the Far East to: Elsevier Science (Singapore) Pte Ltd, No.1 Temasek Ave., No.17-01 Millenia Tower, Singapore 039192, Singapore. TEL 65-434-3727. FAX 65-337-2230; Subscr. in Japan to: Elsevier Science Japan, 9-15 Higashi-Azabu 1-chome, Minato-ku, Tokyo 106, Japan. TEL 81-3-5561-5033. FAX 81-3-5561-5047) Ed. T.J. Robertson. (also avail. in microform from UMI) **Indexed:** Anim.Breed.Abstr., ASCA, Bibl.Repro., Chem.Abstr., Curr.Adv.Ecol.Sci., Curr.Cont., Dairy Sci.Abstr., Excerpt.Med., Ind.Sci.Rev., Ind.Vet., Pig News & Info., Poult.Abstr., Ref.Zh., Sci.Cit.Ind., Sport Fish.Abstr., Vet.Bull., Wild.Rev., Zoo.Rec. **Document type:** academic/scholarly publication.
—BLDSC (0905.076000); CASDDS; EMDOCS; Genuine Article; Linda Hall; SWETS; UnCover. CCC.
Description: Publishes scientific papers dealing with the study of reproduction of all animals which could be regarded as being useful to man.
Refereed Serial

636 JA ISSN 0017-7520
ANIMAL REPRODUCTION TECHNIQUES/HANSHOKU GIJUTSU. (Text in Japanese) 1950. q. 1000 Yen($15.) Hokkaido Artificial Insemination Technician Association - Hokkaido Kachiku Jinko Juseishi Kyokai, c/o Hokunoren, Nishi-1-chome, Kita-4-jo, Sapporo 060, Japan. Ed. Michiro Wakabayashi. adv.; bk.review. circ. 2,000.

AGRICULTURE — POULTRY AND LIVESTOCK

636   UK   ISSN 1357-7298
SF1
ANIMAL SCIENCE. 1944. bi-m. £165($295) (effective 1997). (British Society of Animal Science) Durrant Periodicals, Winton Lea, Pencaitland, E. Lothian EH34 5AY, Scotland. TEL 01875-340354. FAX 01875-340354. Ed. T.L.J. Lawrence; Pub. S.L. Fraser. bibl.; charts; illus.; stat.; index; circ. 2,150 (paid). (back issues avail.) **Indexed:** Anim.Breed.Abstr., ASCA, Biol.& Agr.Ind., Biotech.Abstr., Chem.Abstr., Curr.Adv.Ecol.Sci., Curr.Cont., Dairy Sci.Abstr., EC Ind., Field Crop.Abstr., Food Sci.& Tech.Abstr., Helminthol.Abstr., Herb.Abstr., Ind.Sci.Rev., Ind.Vet., Nutr.Abstr., Pig News & Info., Poult.Abstr., Rural Recreat.Tour.Abstr., Sci.Cit.Ind., Soils & Fert., Soyabean Abstr., Sport Fish.Abstr., Sugar Ind.Abstr., Triticale Abstr., Vet.Bull., Wild.Rev., World Agri.Econ.& Rural Sociol.Abstr., Zoo.Rec. **Document type:** academic/scholarly publication.
—BLDSC (0905.101800); CASDDS; Genuine Article; KR SourceOne; Linda Hall; SWETS; UnCover. **CCC.**
    Former titles (until 1995): Animal Production (ISSN 0003-3561); (until 1959): British Society of Animal Production. Proceedings (ISSN 0369-8521)
    Description: Papers deal with genetics, nutrition, husbandry, physiology, biochemical variation and the interrelationships of the animal environment.
Refereed Serial

636   JA   ISSN 0918-2365
CODEN: ALSTEQ
ANIMAL SCIENCE AND TECHNOLOGY. (Text in English, Japanese; summaries in English) 1924. m. 15000 Yen to non-members; members 8000 Yen. Japanese Society of Zootechnical Science - Nihon Chikusan Gakkai, 201 Nagatani Corporas, Ikenohata 2-9-4, Taito-ku, Tokyo 110, Japan. TEL 03-3828-8409. FAX 03-3828-7649. Ed. Hiroaki Shishido. adv.; bk.rev.; charts. circ. 3,000. **Indexed:** Anim.Breed.Abstr., Biol.Abstr., Chem.Abstr., Dairy Sci.Abstr., Food Sci.& Tech.Abstr., Herb.Abstr., Ind.Vet., Maize Abstr., Nutr.Abstr., Pig News & Info., Poult.Abstr., Protozool.Abstr., Rice Abstr., Soyabean Abstr., Sport Fish.Abstr., Triticale Abstr., Vet.Bull., Wild.Rev., Zoo.Rec. **Document type:** academic/scholarly publication.
—BLDSC (0905.105500); CASDDS; CISTI; UnCover.
    Formerly (until 1991): Japanese Journal of Zootechnical Science (ISSN 0021-5309)

ANNALES DE ZOOTECHNIE. see *BIOLOGY — Zoology*

636   FR   ISSN 1161-9635
ANNUAIRE DES INDUSTRIES AVICOLES. 1956. a. 640 F. Editions Comindus, 1 rue Descombes, 75017 Paris, France. TEL 1-43-80-79-16. FAX 1-40-53-91-92.
    Formerly (until 1991): Annuaire National de l'Aviculture (ISSN 0066-3328)

636   FR   ISSN 1166-1011
ANNUAIRE DES INDUSTRIES CHARCUTIERES. a. 920 F. Editions Comindus, 1 rue Descombes, 75017 Paris, France. TEL 1-43-80-79-16. FAX 1-40-53-91-92.
    Former titles (until 1991): Annuaire de la Charcuterie (ISSN 1154-452X); (until 1990): Annuaire Officiel de la Charcuterie (ISSN 0293-9967)

636.5   BL
ANUARIO AVICOLA & SUINICOLA. 1912. a. $80. Gessulli Editores Ltda., Caixa Postal, 198, 18540-000 Porto Feliz SP, Brazil. TEL 55-152-623133. FAX 55-152-623919. Ed. Osvaldo Penha Gessulli. adv.; bk.rev. circ. 15,000.
    Former titles (until 1989): Anuario Avicola e Anuario Suincola; Anuario Agricola e Avicola.

APIS; the international journal bulletin for specialty livestock and pet-animal product development. see *VETERINARY SCIENCE*

636   SP
APLAUSOS. 52/yr. Av. Baron de Carcer 48, 46001 Valencia, Spain. TEL 6-351-81-76. FAX 6-351-48-80. circ. 16,908.

636.5   GW   ISSN 0003-9098
CODEN: AGEFAB
ARCHIV FUER GEFLUEGELKUNDE/ARCHIVES OF POULTRY SCIENCE/ARCHIVES DE SCIENCE AVICOLE. (Text in German; summaries in English, French and Russian) 1927. bi-m. DM.688.20. (Deutsche Vereinigung fuer Gefluegelwissenschaft e.V) Verlag Eugen Ulmer GmbH, Wollgrasweg 41, 70599 Stuttgart, Germany. TEL 49-711-4507-0. FAX 49-711-4507-120. (Subscr. to: Postfach 700561, 70574 Stuttgart, Germany) Ed. Prof. Dr. S. Scholtyssek. R&P contact: G. Friedrich. adv. contact: F. Signore. bk.rev.; charts; illus.; stat.; index. circ. 550. (also avail. in microfilm from PMC) **Indexed:** Anim.Breed.Abstr., ASCA, Biol.Abstr., Biotech.Abstr., Chem.Abstr., Curr.Adv.Ecol.Sci., Curr.Cont., Food Sci.& Tech.Abstr., Helminthol.Abstr., Ind.Vet., Maize Abstr., Nutr.Abstr., Poult.Abstr., Protozool.Abstr., Rev.Med.& Vet:Mycol., Sci.Cit.Ind., Soyabean Abstr., Vet.Bull. **Document type:** academic/scholarly publication.
—BLDSC (1610.950000); CASDDS; Genuine Article; SWETS. **CCC.**

ARCHIVES OF ANIMAL NUTRITION/ARCHIV FUER TIERERNAEHRUNG. see *VETERINARY SCIENCE*

636 633.2 637   SP   ISSN 0004-0592
SF1   CODEN: AZOTAW
ARCHIVOS DE ZOOTECNIA. (Text and summaries in English, French, Spanish) 1952. 4/yr. 5000 ptas. (foreign 7000 ptas.($70) or exchange basis (effective 1997 & 1998). Instituto de Zootecnia, Facultad de Veterinaria, Avda. de Medina Azahara, 9, 14005 Cordoba, Spain. TEL 34-57-218743. FAX 34-57-218666. E-mail: pa1gocag@lucano.uco.es. Ed. Dr. A.G. Gomez Castro. bk.rev.; abstr.; bibl.; charts; illus.; index, cum.index: 1952-1996. circ. 600. (back issues avail.) **Indexed:** Anim.Breed.Abstr., Bibl.Agri., Biol.Abstr., Bull.Signal., Chem.Abstr., Curr.Adv.Ecol.Sci., Dairy Sci.Abstr., Excerp.Med., Fababean Abstr., Field Crop Abstr., Food Sci.& Tech.Abstr., Helminthol.Abstr., Herb.Abstr., Ind.SST, Ind.Vet., Maize Abstr., Nutr.Abstr., Poult.Abstr., Soyabean Abstr., Sport Fish.Abstr., Triticale Abstr., Vet.Bull., Virol.Abstr., Wild.Rev., Zoo.Rec. **Document type:** academic/scholarly publication.
—BLDSC (1658.000000); CASDDS; Linda Hall. **CCC.**
    Description: Publishes experimental and research work on forage and pasture production, animal feeding, genetics, ethnology and reproduction and the optimization of systems in animal production. Its main emphasis is on the Mediterranean regions.
Refereed Serial

636.2   AG
ARGENTINA. JUNTA NACIONAL DE CARNES. BOLETIN DIARO DE INFORMACIONES. d. Arg.$40000 (for 6 mos.). Junta Nacional de Carnes, San Martin 459, Buenos Aires, Argentina.

636.2   AG
ARGENTINA. JUNTA NACIONAL DE CARNES. BOLETIN SEMANAL SOBRE GANADOS, CARNES Y SUBPRODUCTOS. w. Arg.$25000 (for 6 mos.). Junta Nacional de Carnes, San Martin 459, Buenos Aires, Argentina.

636 382   AG
ARGENTINA. JUNTA NACIONAL DE CARNES. EXPORTACIONES DE PRODUCTOS GANADEROS. 1968. m. Arg.$8700, Junta Nacional de Carnes, San Martin 459, Buenos Aires, Argentina. stat. circ. 300.

338.1   AG
ARGENTINA. MERCADO NACIONAL DE HACIENDA. ANUARIO. a. Mercado Nacional de Hacienda, Tellier 2406, Buenos Aires 1440, Argentina. illus.; stat.
    Formerly: Argentine Republic. Mercado Nacional de Hacienda. Memoria (ISSN 0570-8621)

ARGENTINA. SECRETARIA DE AGRICULTURA GANADERIA Y PESCA. SITUACION DEL MERCADO DE CARNES. see *AGRICULTURE — Abstracting, Bibliographies, Statistics*

636.2   US   ISSN 8750-8281
ARIZONA CATTLELOG. 1945. m. $9. (Arizona Cattlemen's Association) Charles R. Stocks, Co., Box 7127, Albuquerque, NM 87194. TEL 505-243-9515. FAX 505-243-9598. R&P contact: Sandy Eastlake. adv. circ. 1,800. (back issues avail.) **Document type:** trade publication.
    Description: Covers all aspects of cattle production.

636.2   US   ISSN 0004-1750
ARKANSAS CATTLE BUSINESS. 1965. m. $20 (foreign $75). Arkansas Cattlemen's Association, 310 Executive Ct., Little Rock, AR 72205-4550. TEL 501-244-2114. FAX 501-224-5377. E-mail: acacattlemen@worldnet.att.net. Ed. Jim Clower. R&P contact: Jodi Shull. adv. contact: Jo Ann Hall. bk.rev.; circ. 14,500 (paid). **Document type:** trade publication.
    Description: Contains articles and features of interest to cattle ranchers in Arkansas.

636 660   KO   ISSN 1011-2367
CODEN: AJASEL
ASIAN - AUSTRALASIAN JOURNAL OF ANIMAL SCIENCES. (Text in English) 1988. bi-m. $50 to nonmembers; members $40; institutions $60 (effective 1996). Asian - Australasian Association of Animal Production Societies, c/o Dept. of Animal Science & Technology, College of Agriculture & Life Sciences, Seoul National University, Suweon 441-744, S. Korea. TEL 82-331-292-0898. FAX 82-331-294-6543. Ed. D.A. Kim. R&P contact: Dong A. Kim. **Indexed:** Anim.Breed.Abstr., ASCA, Bibl.Agri., Biol.Abstr., Food Sci.& Tech.Abstr., SSCI. **Document type:** academic/scholarly publication.
—BLDSC (1742.389000); CASDDS; Genuine Article; UnCover.
    Description: Disseminates research on the zoology of domestic farm animals, including diseases and environmental issues.
Refereed Serial

636.4   AG   ISSN 0004-4741
ASOCIACION ARGENTINA CRIADORES DE CERDOS. REVISTA. 1922. 3/yr. membership or exchange basis. Asociacion Argentina Criadores de Cerdos, Florida 520, 1005 Buenos Aires, Argentina. Ed. Carlos M. Vieites. adv.; bk.rev.; mkt.; stat. circ. 5,000.

636   VE
ASOCIACION LATINOAMERICANA DE PRODUCCION ANIMAL. MEMORIA. (Text in Spanish; summaries in English, Portuguese, Spanish) 1966. a. $15. Asociacion Latinoamericana de Produccion Animal, Apartado Postal 4653, Maracay 2101-A, Venezuela. Ed. Claudio F. Chicco. abstr.; cum.index: vols. 1-10. circ. 1,500. (back issues avail.) **Indexed:** Anim.Breed.Abstr., Biol.Abstr., Dairy Sci.Abstr., Nutr.Abstr., Rural Recreat.Tour.Abstr., World Agri.Econ.& Rural Sociol.Abstr.

636.2   CN   ISSN 1184-0021
ATLANTIC BEEF QUARTERLY. 1990. q. Can.$12 (foreign $14) (effective 1997); newsstand price: Can.$3. D v L Publishing, P.O. Box 1509, Liverpool, NS B0T 1K0, Canada. TEL 902-354-3321. E-mail: dvl@atcon.com. Ed. Dirk van Loon; Pub. Dirk van Loon. R&P contact: Anne Gray. adv. contact: Anne Gray. bk.rev. circ. 4,500. **Document type:** consumer publication.
    Description: For and about beef producers in the four provinces of Atlantic Canada.

AUSTRALIA. BUREAU OF STATISTICS. LIVESTOCK PRODUCTS, AUSTRALIA. see *AGRICULTURE — Abstracting, Bibliographies, Statistics*

AUSTRALIA. BUREAU OF STATISTICS. QUEENSLAND OFFICE. CATTLE BREEDS, QUEENSLAND. see *AGRICULTURE — Abstracting, Bibliographies, Statistics*

AUSTRALIA. BUREAU OF STATISTICS. SHEEP AND WOOL, AUSTRALIA, PRELIMINARY. see *AGRICULTURE — Abstracting, Bibliographies, Statistics*

AUSTRALIA. BUREAU OF STATISTICS. VICTORIAN OFFICE. LIVESTOCK AND LIVESTOCK PRODUCTS, VICTORIA. see *AGRICULTURE — Abstracting, Bibliographies, Statistics*

636 330   AT   ISSN 0157-0005
AUSTRALIAN CHICKEN FARMER. 1968. bi-m. Aus.$15. Australian Chicken Growers Council, P.O. Box 187, Ingleburn, N.S.W. 2565, Australia. TEL 61-2-6058672. Ed. R. Swinfield. adv. circ. 950. **Document type:** newsletter.

636.39   AT   ISSN 0045-0472
AUSTRALIAN GOAT WORLD. 1945. bi-m. Aus.$18. Dairy Goat Society of Australia, P.O. Box 189, Kiama, N.S.W. 2533, Australia. Ed. R. Heston; Pub. R./Heston. circ. 900. **Document type:** newsletter.

AGRICULTURE — POULTRY AND LIVESTOCK

636   AT   ISSN 0814-7663
AUSTRALIAN HEREFORD QUARTERLY. 1961. q. Aus.$35. Australian Hereford Society Ltd., P.O. Box 246, Roma St., Brisbane, Qld. 4003, Australia. TEL 61-7-854-1360. FAX 61-7-252-7954. Ed. Bruce Mills. R&P contact: Bruce Mills. adv. contact: Tony Lamberth. bk.rev. circ. 10,000. **Document type**: trade publication.
—UnCover.
Former titles: Australian Hereford Annual (ISSN 0067-1886); Hereford Quarterly (ISSN 0311-2144)

636.2   AT
AUSTRALIAN POLL DORSET JOURNAL. 1970. 3/yr. Aus.$20. (Australian Poll Dorset Association Inc.) Weston Studstock Advertising Pty. Ltd., G.P.O. Box 75 B, Melbourne, Vic. 3001, Australia. FAX 61-3-98176711. Ed. P.C. Mills. adv.; bk.rev. circ. 1,600.

636   AT   ISSN 1034-6260
AUSTRALIAN POULTRY SCIENCE SYMPOSIUM. 1989. a. Aus.$25 (effective 1996 & 1997). University of Sydney, Poultry Research Foundation, Sydney, N.S.W. 2006, Australia. TEL 61-46-550277. FAX 61-46-551331. R&P contact: D. Balnave. circ. 200. (back issues avail.) **Indexed**: Food Sci.& Tech.Abstr. **Document type**: proceedings.
—BLDSC (6842.496400).
Formerly (until 1989): Poultry Husbandry Research Foundation Symposium.
Description: Covers nutrition, disease control and production of poultry. Includes research, education, industry and government services.
Refereed Serial

636.4   AT
AUSTRALIAN PUREBRED PIG HERD BOOK. 1911. a. Aus.$5. Australian Pig Breeders' Association, P.O. Box 189, Kiama, N.S.W. 2533, Australia. FAX 61-42-323350. Ed. Mrs. C. Brown. adv. circ. 200. **Document type**: directory.
Formerly (until 1990): Australian Stud Pig Herd Book.

636   SP   ISSN 0005-1896
AVANCES EN ALIMENTACION Y MEJORA ANIMAL. 1960. bi-m. 4264 ptas. (foreign $50) (effective 1997). Juan Vigon 3, 2o D., 28003 Madrid, Spain. Ed. Amalio de Juana Sardon. adv.; bk.rev.; bibl.; charts; illus.; mkt.; pat.; stat.; index. circ. 2,000. **Indexed**: Anim.Breed.Abstr., Biol.Abstr., Chem.Abstr., Dairy Sci.Abstr., Fababean Abstr., Ind.SST, Nutr.Abstr., Pig News & Info., Potato Abstr., Poult.Abstr., Soyabean Abstr., Triticale Abstr., World Agri.Econ.& Rural Sociol.Abstr.
Incorporates (in 1976-198?): Suplemento Ganado Porcino.
Refereed Serial

636   CL   ISSN 0378-4509
    CODEN: APANDD
AVANCES EN PRODUCCION ANIMAL. (Text in Spanish; summaries in English) 1976. s.a. Esc.200($4) Universidad de Chile, Facultad de Ciencias Agrarias, Veterinarias y Forestales, Casilla 1004, Santiago, Chile. TEL 56-2-5417703. FAX 56-2-5417055. Ed. Mario Silva G. R&P contact: Alberto Mansilla. bk.rev.; charts; illus.; abstr.; index, cum.index. circ. 1,000. **Indexed**: Anim.Behav.Abstr., Anim.Breed.Abstr., Biol.Abstr., Bull.Signal., Chem.Abstr., Dairy Sci.Abstr., Food Sci.& Tech.Abstr., Genet.Abstr., Herb.Abstr., Nutr.Abstr. **Document type**: newspaper.
—CASDDS.

636.5   FR   ISSN 0150-939X
AVICULTEUR. m. 415 F. (foreign 515 F.). Editions du Boisbaudry, B.P. 6359, 35063 Rennes Cedex, France. TEL 99-32-21-21. FAX 99-32-14-17. TELEX 730619F. adv.; illus. circ. 6,500. **Indexed**: Helminthol.Abstr.

636.5   CK
AVICULTURA COLOMBIANA. 1980. m. Apdo. Aereo 24215, Bogota, Colombia. adv. circ. 10,000.

636.5   BL   ISSN 0009-0905
AVICULTURA INDUSTRIAL. 1910. m. Cr.$90. Gessulli Editores Ltda., Caixa Postal 198, 18540-000 Porto Feliz SP, Brazil. TEL 55-152-623133. FAX 55-152-623919. Ed. Osvaldo Penha Gessulli. adv.; B&W page $2580, color page $3600; 215 x 290. illus.; index. circ. 20,000.
Formerly: Chacaras e Quintais - Agricultura e Pecuaria.

636.5   US   ISSN 0736-2056
AVICULTURA PROFESIONAL.* (Text in Spanish) 1983. q. free to qualified personnel. Avicultura Profesional, Inc., 184 Hickory Poin Dr., Athens, GA 30605. TEL 706-549-4092. FAX 706-543-1854. Ed. Nick Dale. adv.; bk.rev.; circ. 7,500 (controlled).
Description: Source of current technology for the Latin American poultry industry.

636.5   NE
AVICULTURA PROFESSIONAL. 10/yr. $60. Misset International (Subsidiary of: Reed Elsevier plc), Postbus 4, 7000 BA Doetinchem, Netherlands. TEL 31-314-349562. FAX 31-314-340515. Ed. Soledad Urrutia. adv. contact: Tomas Domic. circ. 10,000.
Description: Addresses the specific needs of the commercial poultry sector in Latin America.

636.4   DK   ISSN 0907-0567
AVLS-INFORMATION. 1989. q. Avlscentret Mulstrup, Boers-Mark, c/o Gitte Boersing, Sparsborgvej 12, DK-7600 Struer, Denmark. TEL 45-97-84-13-80. FAX 45-97-84-13-70. adv.; B&W page DKK 6200, color page DKK 11420. circ. 4,000.

636 591.15   FR   ISSN 0153-6281
B T I A. (Bulletin Technique de l'Insemination Artificielle); la revue francaise de la genetique et de la reproduction. 1976. q. 191 F. in France; (foreign 260 F.) (effective 1996). (Association pour l'Information en Insemination Artificielle) Societe de Diffusion de la Presse Agricole, B.P. 47, 63370 Lempdes, France. TEL 73-42-17-17. FAX 73-91-35-60. TELEX 397-467. Ed. Maurice Lacroix. adv.; bk.rev. **Document type**: bulletin.
—BLDSC (2354.590000).
Description: For specialists in the reproduction and insemination of cattle, including veterinarians and owners of livestock.

630   US
THE BAGPIPE. 1983. q. $16. American Highland Cattle Association, 4701 Marion St., Ste. 200, Denver, CO 80216-2134. TEL 303-292-9102. FAX 303-292-9171. Pub. Colin Davidson. R&P contact: Ginnah Moses. adv. contact: Ginnah Moses. circ. 1,000. **Document type**: trade publication.
Description: Highland cattle information.

636   BG   ISSN 0379-430X
BANGLADESH JOURNAL OF ANIMAL SCIENCE. (Text in English) 1968. s.a. Tk.100($15) Bangladesh Husbandry Association, Bangladesh Agricultural University, Department of Animal Nutrition, Mymensingh 2202, Bangladesh. Ed. Abidur Reza. adv.; bk.rev.; charts; stat. circ. 1,000. **Indexed**: Anim.Breed.Abstr., Biol.Abstr., Chem.Abstr.
—BLDSC (1861.640000).
Formerly: Animal Science Journal of Pakistan (ISSN 0003-3588)

338.1   US
BANTAM STANDARD. irreg. $30. American Bantam Association, Box 127, Augusta, NJ 07822. **Document type**: directory.
Description: Descriptions of Bantam chickens with complete variety listings.

636.2   US   ISSN 0005-7738
BEEF. 1964. 13/yr. $25 (foreign $35). Intertec Publishing Corp., Webb Division, 7900 Int'l Dr., Ste. 300, Minneapolis, MN 55425. TEL 612-851-4710. FAX 612-851-4601. E-mail: beef@intertec.com; URL: beef@intmin.ccmail.compuserve.com. Ed. Joe Roybal. adv.; illus. circ. 101,946. **Indexed**: Farm & Garden Ind. **Document type**: trade publication.
—UMI; UnCover. **CCC**.
Description: Focuses on beef cattle industry.

636.2   US
BEEF BULLETIN.* q. Illinois Beef Council, 2060 W. Iles Ave., No.B, Springfield, IL 62704-4174. TEL 217-787-4280. Ed. Patricia Merna Petska.

636.085   US   ISSN 0744-253X
BEEF BUSINESS BULLETIN. 1977. w. membership. National Cattlemen's Beef Association, 5420 S. Quebec St., Englewood, CO 80155. TEL 303-694-0305. Ed. Curt Olson. R&P contact: Curt Olson. adv. contact: Brett Erickson. stat. circ. 38,794. **Document type**: trade publication, bulletin.
Formerly: N C A Weekly Bulletin; **Supersedes**: N L F A Feed-Lines (ISSN 0047-8938)
Description: Focuses on the cattle industry.

636.2   AT   ISSN 1324-5309
BEEF IMPROVEMENT NEWS. 1988. 11/yr. Aus.$55 (effective July 1995). (Beef Improvement Association of Australia) Livestock Publications, 5B Lion St., Hawthorn, Vic. 3122, Australia. TEL 61-3-98188600. FAX 61-3-998188611. Ed. Athol Economou; Pub. Athol Economou. R&P contact: Athol Economou. adv.: B&W page Aus.$2250, color page Aus.$2850; 340 x 240; adv. contact: Athol Economou. charts; illus.; mkt.; maps; stat.; tr.lit.; circ. 15,000 (paid). (tabloid format) **Document type**: newspaper.
Description: Provides technical, commercial and marketing information for progressive beef producers and service providers to the beef industry.

636.2   CN   ISSN 0846-0043
BEEF IN B C. 1986. 7/yr. Can.$24. 10145 Durango Rd. 4, Kamloops, BC V2C 6T4, Canada. TEL 604-573-3611. FAX 604-573-5155. Ed. A.L. Leach. adv.; bk.rev. circ. 3,200.

636.2   US
BEEF ROUNDUP. 1973. a. free. Kent Feeds, Inc., 1600 Oregon St., Muscatine, IA 52761. TEL 319-264-4211. (tabloid format)
Description: Focuses on the cattle breeding industry.

636.2   US
BEEF TIMES. 1993. 10/yr. $15 (effective 1996). Farm Times, 504 Sixth St., Rupert, ID 83350. TEL 208-436-1111. FAX 208-436-9455. Ed. Eric Goodell; Pub. Steven R. Ward. adv. contact: Steven R. Ward. circ. 5,500. **Document type**: newspaper.
Description: Conveys current information to beef producers on economic, political, and technical trends in the industry.

636   US   ISSN 1056-1390
BEEF TODAY. 1985. m. (10/yr.). Farm Journal, Inc., 1500 Market St., Philadelphia, PA 19102-2181. TEL 316-767-7041. Ed. Bill Miller. adv. contact: 224,840. **Document type**: trade publication.
—UnCover.
Formerly (until 1987): Beef Extra.
Description: Focuses on the cattle breeding industry.

636   US   ISSN 0747-010X
BEEFALO NICKEL. 1979. bi-m. $15 (foreign $25) (effective 1996 & 1997). (American Beefalo World Registry) Olvis Publishing Co., Box 178, Lexington, OK 73051. TEL 405-527-9252. FAX 405-527-9266. Ed. Mike Edwards. adv. contact: O.L. Edwards. circ. 1,500 (paid). **Document type**: trade publication.
Formerly (until 1984): Beefalo Journal (ISSN 0199-3542)
Description: Information on all aspects of Beefalo cattle breeding.

636.2   US   ISSN 0194-4282
BEEFMASTER COWMAN. 1979. m. $20. (Beefmaster Breeders Universal) Gulf Coast Publishing, 11201 Morning Court, San Antonio, TX 78213. TEL 210-344-8300. Ed. Gretchen Reuwer. adv. contact: Patrick Murphy. circ. 8,200. **Document type**: trade publication.
Formerly: Beefmaster Bull-Etin.
Description: Focuses on the Beefmaster cattle breeding industry.

BELL/CLOCHE. see AGRICULTURE — *Dairying And Dairy Products*

636   IT
BIANCO NERO. 11/yr. National Association of Frisian Cattle Farmers and Breeders, Via Bergamo 292, 26100 Cremona, Italy. TEL 372-412-521. FAX 372-296-70. TELEX 316608 ANAFI I. Ed. Bruno Biseo. circ. 11,000.

BIRD KEEPING IN AUSTRALIA. see BIOLOGY — *Ornithology*

636   US   ISSN 1056-2400
BISON WORLD. 1975. q. $50. National Bison Association, 4701 Marion St., Ste. 100, Denver, CO 80216. TEL 303-292-2833. FAX 303-292-2564. Ed. Sam Albrecht. R&P contact: Sam Albrecht. adv.: B&W page $350, color page $425; adv. contact: Oranna Wood. bk.rev.; circ. 2,500 (paid). **Document type**: trade publication.
Description: Contains articles for people involved in the bison industry.
Refereed Serial

AGRICULTURE — POULTRY AND LIVESTOCK

677.3 636.3 US
BLACK SHEEP NEWSLETTER. 1974. q. $14 (foreign $18). Black Sheep Press, 25455 N.W. Dixie Mtn. Rd., Scappose, OR 97056. TEL 503-621-3063. Ed. Peggy Lundquist; Pub. Peggy Lundquist. adv. contact: Peggy Lundquist. bk.rev. circ. 2,500.
    Description: For growers, spinners and textile artists interested in colored and white sheep wool and other animal fibers.

636.3 UK
BLACK WELSH MOUNTAIN SHEEP BREEDERS' ASSOCIATION. ANNUAL FLOCK BOOK. 1922. a. £20 (effective 1998). Black Welsh Mountain Sheep Breeders' Association, Brierley House, Summer Ln., Combe Down, Bath BA2 5LE. TEL 44-1225-837904. R&P contact: David Child. circ. 400. **Document type:** directory.
    Description: Lists breeders with details of their flocks.

636.3 UK
BLACKFACE SHEEP BREEDERS' ASSOCIATION JOURNAL. 1948. a. £12. Blackface Sheep Breeders' Association, c/o A.M. Fenton, 26 York Pl., Perth PH2 8EH, Scotland. TEL 44-1738-623780. FAX 44-1738-621206. adv.; bk.rev. circ. 200. (processed) **Document type:** trade publication.

BLOODSTOCK BREEDERS' REVIEW. see SPORTS AND GAMES — Horses And Horsemanship

636 BL ISSN 0067-9615 CODEN: BOIPAQ
BOLETIM DE INDUSTRIA ANIMAL. (Text in Portuguese; summaries in English) 1929. s-a. $41. Instituto de Zootecnia, Rua Heitor Penteado 56, Caixa Postal 60, 13460 Nova Odessa, SP, Brazil. FAX 0194-661415. TELEX 192274 IZNO BR. E-mail: izooctf@turing.unicamp.br. Ed. Valdinei Tadeu Paulino. R&P contact: Mario Augusto Brajao. adv.; bk.rev.; index. circ. 1,200. (back issues avail.) **Indexed:** Abstr.Trop.Agri., Anim.Breed.Abstr., Biol.Abstr., Dairy Sci.Abstr., Field Crop Abstr., Food Sci.& Tech.Abstr., Herb.Abstr., Maize Abstr., Nutr.Abstr., Pig News & Info., Plant Breed.Abstr., Poult.Abstr., Soyabean Abstr., Sugar Ind.Abstr., Trop.Oil Seeds Abstr. **Document type:** bulletin.
    —BLDSC (2153.500000); CASDDS; CISTI.
    Formerly: Revista de Industria Animal.

636 SP ISSN 0213-8980
BOLETIN VERDE; informacion agraria y lactea. 1972. q. free. Nestle - Espana, Avda. Paises Catalanes, 25-54, 08950 Espugas de Llobregat (Barcelona), Spain. TEL 34-93-3717100. Ed. Jose Pablo Semur Decha. **Indexed:** Ind.Vet.

636.3 SA
BONSMARA BRIEF. (Text in Afrikaans, English) 1994. a. Bonsmara Beestelersgenootskap van S.A. - Bonsmara Cattle Breeders' Society of S.A., P.O. Box 912790, Silverton 0127, South Africa. illus. **Indexed:** Ind.S.A.Per. **Document type:** newsletter.

636.587 US ISSN 0068-0117
BOOK OF BANTAMS. 1963. irreg. $8.50. American Bantam Association, Box 127, Augusta, NJ 07822. Ed. George Fitterer. circ. 10,000. **Document type:** directory.

636 SA
BORDER AGRICULTURAL SHOW PRIZE LIST. (Text in Afrikaans and English) a. Border Agricultural Society, Komani St., P.O. Box 159, Queenstown, South Africa. adv. circ. 7,000.

636.3 UK
BORDER LEICESTER FLOCK BOOK. 1896. a. £15 to non-members. Society of Border Leicester Sheep Breeders, 4 Alexander Dr., Edinburgh EH11 2RH, Scotland. TEL 44-131-313-5037. Ed. Colin E. Douglas. circ. 400. **Document type:** directory.

636 BS
BOTSWANA. MINISTRY OF AGRICULTURE. LIVESTOCK MANAGEMENT SURVEY RESULTS. 1983. a. free. Ministry of Agriculture, Division of Planning and Statistics, Private Bag 003, Gaborone, Botswana. FAX 267-356027. TELEX 2543 VET BD. Ed. Henry G. Jobeta. R&P contact: Dan B. Gombalume. **Document type:** government publication.

636.2 FR ISSN 0985-150X
BOVINS LIMOUSINS. 1964. 5/yr. 250 F. (effective 1997). France Limousin Selection, UPRA, Lanaud, 87220 Boisseuil, France. TEL 33-5-55064631. FAX 33-5-55064630. URL: http://www.limousine.org. Ed. Dominique Favier; Pub. Bernard Roux. R&P contact: Dominique Favier. adv. contact: Marie-Christine de Corgnol. circ. 3,500.

636.2 US ISSN 0192-6764
BRAHMAN JOURNAL. 1970. m. $15. (American Brahman Breeders Association) Sagebrush Publishing Co., Inc., Box 220, Eddy, TX 76524. TEL 817-859-5507. FAX 817-859-5451. Ed. Joe Brockett. R&P contact: Joe Brockett. TEL 817-859-5507. adv. contact: Joe Brockett. bk.rev.; circ. 4,755 (paid). **Document type:** trade publication.

636 AT
BRAHMAN NEWS. 1972. q. Aus.$25 (foreign Aus.$50) (effective 1997). Australian Brahman Breeders' Association, Ltd., P.O. Box 796, Rockhampton, Qld. 4700, Australia. TEL 079-277799. FAX 079-225805. Ed. J. Croaker. adv. contact: paula Driscoll. circ. 2,500.

636.2 US ISSN 0006-9132
BRANGUS JOURNAL. 1952. m. $20 (foreign $40). (International Brangus Breeders Association) Brangus Publications, Inc., 5750 Epsilon, San Antonio, TX 78249. TEL 210-696-4343. Ed. Lea Weinheimer. adv.; charts; illus. circ. 3,000. **Document type:** trade publication.
    Description: Covers news about the beef cattle industry and how it affects Brangus breeders.

636.2 GW ISSN 0930-3650
BRAUNVIEHZUECHTER. 1921. a. Braunviehzuchtverband Baden-Wuerttemberg e.V., Waldseerstr. 13, 88400 Biberach, Germany. TEL 49-7351-159110. FAX 49-7351-159122. **Document type:** trade publication.

636.2 US
BREEDERS JOURNAL. q. free. American Breeders Service, 2016 Simsbury Court, Fort Collins, CO 80524-1979. TEL 303-482-8918. FAX 303-482-8916. Ed. Kathleen Bee. adv. contact: Ed Peck. circ. 126,000. **Document type:** trade publication.

636.39 UK ISSN 0068-2039
BRITISH GOAT SOCIETY. HERD BOOK. 1886. a. £15. British Goat Society, 34-36 Fore St., Bovey Tracey, Newton Abbot, Devon TQ13 9AD, England. TEL 44-1626-833168. **Document type:** directory.
    Description: Contains details of all milk-producing goats registered in the previous year in England.

636.39 UK ISSN 0953-8070
BRITISH GOAT SOCIETY. MONTHLY JOURNAL. 1879. m. (11/yr.). £15. British Goat Society, 34-36 Fore St., Bovey Tracey, Newton Abbot, Devon TQ13 9AD, England. TEL 44-1626-833168. Ed. Patricia Oddie. adv.; illus. (tabloid format) **Document type:** trade publication.
    —SWETS.
    Description: Contains articles on goatkeeping, reports of society meetings, letters, announcements, show results, and milk yields.

636.39 UK ISSN 0068-2047
BRITISH GOAT SOCIETY. YEAR BOOK. 1921. a. £7. British Goat Society, 34-36 Fore St., Bovey Tracey, Newton Abbot, Devon TQ13 9AD, England. TEL 44-1626-833168. **Indexed:** Anim.Breed.Abstr. **Document type:** trade publication.
    Description: Contains review articles on a wide range of subjects concerning goat keeping.

636.5 UK ISSN 0007-1668
BRITISH POULTRY SCIENCE. 1960. 5/yr. £78($136) to individuals; institutions £156 ($278) (effective 1997). Carfax Publishing Co., P.O. Box 25, Abingdon, Oxon. OX14 3UE, England. TEL 44-1235-401000. FAX 44-1235-401550. E-mail: enquiries@carfax.co.uk. (Subscr. in N. America to: Carfax Publishing Co., 875-81 Massachusetts Ave., Cambridge, MA 02139) Ed. Dr. B.O. Hughes. adv.; bk.rev.; charts; illus.; mkt.; index. (also avail. in microfiche; back issues avail.) **Indexed:** Anim.Breed.Abstr., ASCA, Biol.Abstr., Biotech.Abstr., Chem.Abstr., Curr.Adv.Biochem., Curr.Adv.Cell & Devel.Biol., Curr.Adv.Ecol.Sci., Curr.Adv.Genetics & Molec.Biol., Curr.Cont., Curr.Pack.Abstr., Food Sci.& Tech.Abstr., Helminthol.Abstr., Ind.Med., Ind.Sci.Rev., Ind.Vet., Maize Abstr., Nutr.Abstr., Poult.Abstr., Protozool.Abstr., Rural Recreat.Tour.Abstr., Sci.Cit.Ind., Soyabean Abstr., Sport Fish.Abstr., Triticale Abstr., Trop.Oil Seeds Abstr., Vet.Bull., Wild.Rev., World Agri.Econ.& Rural Sociol.Abstr., Zoo.Rec. **Document type:** academic/scholarly publication.
    —BLDSC (2339.300000); CASDDS; Genuine Article; Linda Hall; SWETS; UMI; UnCover. CCC.
    Refereed Serial

636.932 UK ISSN 0068-2411
BRITISH RABBIT COUNCIL YEAR BOOK. 19. a. £8 membership. British Rabbit Council, 7 Kirkgate, Newark, Notts. NG24 1AD, England. TEL 44-1636-76042. FAX 44-1636-611683. Ed. J. Jalland. circ. 9,000.
    Formerly (until 1969): British Rabbits.

636.5 US ISSN 0007-2176
BROILER INDUSTRY. 1938. m. $54 (free to qualified personnel). Watt Publishing Co., 122 S. Wesley Ave., Mt. Morris, IL 61054. TEL 815-734-4171. FAX 815-734-4201. Ed. Gary Thornton; Pub. Charles Olentine. adv.: B&W page $3040, color page $4065; adv. contact: Corinne Riehle. charts; illus. circ. 17,000. (reprint service avail. from UMI) **Indexed:** Biotech.Abstr., Curr.Pack.Abstr. **Document type:** trade publication.
    —BLDSC (2349.400000); UMI; UnCover. CCC.
    Incorporating: Poultry Processing and Marketing; Which was formerly (until 1977): Broiler Business; (until 1975): Poultry Meat (ISSN 0048-4970)
    Description: Covers the commercial broiler industry in the United States, with information on the processing and marketing of broiler chickens.

637 636.39 CN
BROWSE. 1952. bi-m. Can.$20. Ontario Goat Breeders' Association, Box 2776, Sta. "A", Sudbury, ON P3A 5J3, Canada. TEL 705-866-2770. Ed. Pat Marcotte. adv. contact: Manon Whitman. circ. 300. (back issues avail.) **Document type:** newsletter.

636.293 TH ISSN 0857-1554
BUFFALO JOURNAL; an international journal of buffalo science. (Text in English) 1985. 3/yr. $60 in S.E. Asia; elsewhere $65. Chulalongkorn University, Research Centre for Bioscience in Animal Production, Faculty of Veterinary Science, Henri Dunant St., Bangkok 10330, Thailand. TEL 662-2518936. FAX 662-2553910. E-mail: fvetmkm@chulkn.car.chula.ac.th. Ed. M. Kamonpatana. **Indexed:** Food Sci.& Tech.Abstr. **Document type:** academic/scholarly publication.
    —BLDSC (2357.595000).
    Description: Publishes research paper, reviews and comments on buffalo anatomy, breeding, diseases, genetics, management, nutrition, physiology, reproduction, and socio-economic problem.

AGRICULTURE — POULTRY AND LIVESTOCK

636.089   KE   ISSN 0378-9721
CODEN: BAHADH
BULLETIN OF ANIMAL HEALTH AND PRODUCTION IN AFRICA/BULLETIN DES SANTE ET PRODUCTION ANIMALES EN AFRIQUE. (Supplement avail.: Weekly Information Leaflets) (Text and summaries in English and French) 1953. q. $15 (foreign $20) (effective 1994). Organization of African Unity, Inter-African Bureau of Animal Resources - Organisation de l'Unite Africaine, Bureau Interafricain des Resources Animales, P.O. Box 30786, Nairobi, Kenya. TEL 254-2-338544. FAX 254-2-332046. TELEX 22983. Ed. W.N. Masiga. abstr.; bibl.; charts; illus.; index. (back issues avail.) Indexed: Agri.Eng.Abstr., Anim.Breed.Abstr., Biol.Abstr., Curr.Cont., Helminthol.Abstr., Ind.Vet., Pig News & Info., Poult.Abstr., Rev.Med.& Vet.Mycol., Sport Fish.Abstr., Vet.Bull., Wild.Rev., Zoo.Rec. **Document type:** academic/scholarly publication.
—CASDDS; SWETS.
Formerly: Bulletin of Epizootic Diseases of Africa (ISSN 0525-1443)
Description: Publishes articles on original research relevant to animal health and production activities that may lead to improvement of the livestock industry in Africa and better utilization of her animal resources.

636   JA   ISSN 0386-8419
BULLETIN OF BEEF CATTLE SCIENCE. (Text in Japanese) 1964. s-a. 3000 Yen. (Society of Beef Cattle Science) Sakura Print, c/o Department of Animal Science, College of Agriculture, Kyoto University, Kyoto 606, Japan. TEL 81-75-753-6054. FAX 81-75-753-6344. Ed. Shinobu Ozawa. adv. contact: Hideo Yano. circ. 750. (back issues avail.) **Document type:** academic/scholarly publication.
Description: Research on nutrition, feeding management and breeding in beef cattle.
Refereed Serial

636.2   CN   ISSN 1041-3669
NC1763.P66
BULL'S EYE. 1992. 2/yr. Maine - Anjou International, 3016 19th St. N.E., Ste. 110, Calgary, Alta. T2E 6V9, Canada. TEL 403-291-7077. FAX 403-291-0274. Ed. Jeff Owen. adv. circ. 15,000. (tabloid format) **Document type:** trade publication.
Description: Dedicated to the promotion of Maine-Anjou cattle breed to commercial cattle producers.

BUNADARRIT. see *AGRICULTURE*

BUNDESFORSCHUNGSANSTALT FUER LANDWIRTSCHAFT. MITTEILUNGEN UND INFORMATIONEN. see *AGRICULTURE — Crop Production And Soil*

636 330.9   UK   ISSN 1354-540X
BUSINESS RATIO PLUS: MEAT PROCESSORS. 1975. a. £249. I C C Business Publications Ltd., Field House, 72 Oldfield Rd., Hampton, Mddx. TW12 2HQ, England. TEL 44-181-783-0922. FAX 44-181-783-1940. charts; stat. **Document type:** trade publication.
Formerly: Business Ratio Report: Meat Processors (ISSN 0267-6699); Which supersedes in part (in 1985): Business Ratio Report: Meat and Poultry Processors (ISSN 0261-9032)
Description: Analyses and compares the financial performances of leading companies. Provides industry performance summaries, trends, and forecasts.

636 330.9   UK   ISSN 1354-3431
BUSINESS RATIO PLUS: MEAT WHOLESALERS. 1975. a. £249. I C C Business Publications Ltd., Field House, 72 Oldfield Rd., Hampton, Mddx. TW12 2HQ, England. TEL 44-181-783-0922. FAX 44-181-783-1940. charts; stat. **Document type:** trade publication.
Formerly: Business Ratio Report: Meat Wholesalers (ISSN 0261-9040)
Description: Analyses and compares the financial performance of leading companies. Provides industry performance summaries, trends, and forecasts.

636 658   UK   ISSN 0267-730X
BUSINESS RATIO REPORT: POULTRY PROCESSORS; an industry sector analysis. 1975. a. I C C Business Ratios Ltd., Freepost, Field House, Hampton, Mddx. TW12 1BR, England. TEL 081-783-0977. FAX 081-783-1940. charts; stat. **Document type:** trade publication.
Supersedes in part (in 1985): Business Ratio Report: Meat and Poultry Processors (ISSN 0261-9032)

636   NO   ISSN 0807-5069
BUSKAP. 1949. q. NOK 125 (effective 1997). (N R F Norwegian Cattle) Norsk Roedt Fe, P.O. Box 4123, N-2301 Hamar, Norway. TEL 47-62-52-60-28. FAX 47-62-53-36-80. E-mail: mari.bjarke@nrf.no. Ed. Mari Bjaerke. adv. contact: Hans A. Hals. circ. 32,000. **Indexed:** Anim.Breed.Abstr., Dairy Sci.Abstr., Field Crop Abstr., Herb.Abstr.
—BLDSC (2934.965000). **CCC.**
Formerly (until 1996): Buskap og Avdraatt (ISSN 0007-7194); Incorporates (1962-1964): Avslaget for Norsk Roedt FE - Medlemsblad (ISSN 0806-2781)

636   US
C A L F NEWS CATTLE FEEDER. 1963. m. $29 (foreign $33). (Concerning America's Livestock Feeders) C A L F News Magazine Inc., Box 88312, Colorado Springs, CO 80908-8312. TEL 719-495-0303. Ed. Steve Dittmer. adv.; bk.rev.; illus.; stat. circ. 4,800. **Document type:** trade publication.
Formerly: C A L F News (ISSN 0007-7798)

636   UV
C E B V. no.7, 1974. irreg. Communaute Economique du Betail et de la Viande, Secretariat, Ouagadougou, Burkina Faso.

CALIFORNIA. AGRICULTURAL STATISTICS SERVICE. LIVESTOCK REVIEW. see *AGRICULTURE — Abstracting, Bibliographies, Statistics*

CALIFORNIA. AGRICULTURAL STATISTICS SERVICE. POULTRY REPORT. see *AGRICULTURE — Abstracting, Bibliographies, Statistics*

636.2   US   ISSN 0008-0942
CALIFORNIA CATTLEMAN. 1917. m. $20. (California Cattlemen's Association) James Danekas & Associates, Inc., Box 613, Fair Oaks, CA 95628-0613. TEL 916-965-6122. FAX 916-965-1128. Ed. Kimberly Bradley. adv.; illus. circ. 4,836. **Indexed:** Cal.Per.Ind. (1980-). **Document type:** consumer publication.
Description: Keeps members current on Association activities, policies and legislation, both state and national, that affect the California beef industry and ranching industry.

636   US
CALIFORNIA WOOL GROWERS NEWSLETTER. m. membership. California Wool Growers Association, 1225 H St., Ste. 101, Sacramento, CA 95814. TEL 916-444-8122. Ed. Jay B. Wilson. R&P contact: Jay Wilson. adv. circ. 1,000. **Document type:** newsletter.
Formerly: California Wool Growers Association. Bi-Weekly Newsletter.

636.2   BL   ISSN 0008-2465
CAMPO;* revista mensal de temas agropecuarios. vol.4, 1969. m. Cr.$6.50. Rua Sao Pedro 733, 3 Andar, Porto Alegre, Brazil. Ed. Oscar Santos. adv.; charts; illus.; stat.

636.5   CN   ISSN 1182-638X
CANADA. AGRICULTURE CANADA. HATCHERY REVIEW. 1960. q. free. Agriculture Canada, Sir John Carling Bldg., 930 Carling Ave., Ottawa, ON K1A 0C7, Canada. TEL 819-994-0246. FAX 819-953-0969. **Document type:** government publication.
Formerly: Canada. Agriculture Canada. Hatchery Outlook.
Description: Coverage of hatchery operations in Canada, by province and month, with comparative figures.

636   CN   ISSN 0068-7324
CANADA. AGRICULTURE CANADA. LIVESTOCK MARKET REVIEW. a. free. Agriculture Canada, Red Meat Division, Sir John Carling Bldg., 930 Carling Ave., Ottawa, ON K1A 0C7, Canada. TEL 819-994-0246. FAX 819-953-0969. **Document type:** government publication.
Description: Annual market situation commentary, numbers of animals marketed, average prices, preliminary imports and exports on a monthly and annual comparison base.

636   CN   ISSN 0705-9981
CANADA LIVESTOCK MEAT TRADE REPORT. (Includes 2 monthly supplements) 1949. w. free. Agriculture Canada, Red Meat Division, Sir John Carling Bldg., 930 Carling Ave., Ottawa, ON K1A 0C7, Canada. TEL 819-994-0246. FAX 819-953-0969. **Document type:** government publication.
Formerly (until 1973): Live Stock and Meat Trade Report (ISSN 0706-0009)
Description: Comprehensive summary of livestock prices, numbers, slaughterings, carcass weights and movements at various locations within the provinces of Canada.

636.5   CN   ISSN 0008-2732
CANADA POULTRYMAN. (Text in English, French) 1912. m. Can.$20.35 (foreign Can.$28). Annex Publishing, 222 Argyle Ave., Delhi, ON N4B 2Y2, Canada. TEL 519-582-2513. FAX 519-582-4040. Ed. Anthony Greaves. adv.; charts; illus.; stat. circ. 8,387. (back issues avail.) **Document type:** trade publication.
Incorporating: Aviculteur Canadien.
Description: Provides information on poultry and the poultry industry, designed primarily for Canadian commercial poultry producers.

636.5   CN   ISSN 0068-8134
CANADA WHO'S WHO OF THE POULTRY INDUSTRY. 1955. a. Can.$23.54. Annex Publishing, 222 Argyle Ave., Delhi, ON N4B 2Y2, Canada. TEL 519-582-2513. FAX 519-582-4040. Ed. Anthony Greaves. adv.; illus.; stat.; index. circ. 5,076. **Document type:** trade publication.

636.2   CN   ISSN 0008-2961
CANADIAN AYRSHIRE REVIEW. (Text in English, French) 1920. m. Can.$32.10 (Quebec Can.$34.19; U.S. $25; elsewhere $30) (effective 1997). Ayrshire Breeders' Association of Canada, P.O. Box 188, Ste. Anne de Bellevue, PQ H9X 3V9, Canada. TEL 514-398-7970. FAX 514-398-7972. Ed. Linda Ness. R&P contact: Linda Ness. adv. contact: Linda Ness. circ. 1,700. (back issues avail.) **Document type:** trade publication.
—Linda Hall.

636.2   CN   ISSN 0843-9613
CANADIAN CATTLE BUYER; business news of the cattle and beef packing industry. fortn. Ministry of Agriculture, Food and Rural Affairs, Policy Analysis Branch, Legislative Bldg., Queen's Park, Toronto, ON M7A 2B2, Canada. TEL 416-326-3246. FAX 416-326-9892. Ed. Lorrie Mackinnon. charts. **Document type:** newsletter.

636.3   CN   ISSN 0829-075X
HD9904.C2
CANADIAN CO-OPERATIVE WOOL GROWERS MAGAZINE. 1958. a. Can.$3 to non-members. Canadian Cooperative Wool Growers Ltd., Box 130, Carleton Place, ON K7C 3P3, Canada. FAX 613-257-8896. Ed. Eric Bjergso. adv. circ. 12,000. **Document type:** trade publication.
Former titles: Canadian Wool Grower; Canadian Wool Grower and Sheep Breeder (ISSN 0045-5598)

636   CN   ISSN 1203-8881
CANADIAN FEED INDUSTRY ASSOCIATION. EASTERN NUTRITION CONFERENCE. PROCEEDINGS. (Text in English; abstracts in French) 1996. a. Can.$40 to non-members; members Can.$30 (effective 1997). Canadian Feed Industry Association, 325 Dalhousie St., Ste. 625, Ottawa, ON K1N 7G2, Canada. TEL 613-241-6421. FAX 613-241-7970. E-mail: cfia@magma.ca. (back issues avail.) **Document type:** proceedings.
Description: Discusses animal nutrition research.

AGRICULTURE — POULTRY AND LIVESTOCK

636.2   CN   ISSN 0831-3008
CANADIAN GUERNSEY JOURNAL. 1927. 6/yr. Can.$35 (foreign Can.$50). Canadian Guernsey Association, 368 Woolwich St., Guelph, ON N1H 3W6, Canada. TEL 519-836-2141. Ed. V.M. Macdonald. adv.; bk.rev. circ. 1,000. **Document type:** trade publication. —Linda Hall.
    Formerly: Canadian Guernsey Breeders' Journal (ISSN 0045-4907)

636.2   CN   ISSN 0008-3739
CANADIAN HEREFORD DIGEST. (Text mainly in English; occasionally in French) 1956. 9/yr. Can.$53.50($50) (foreign Can.$60) (effective 1997). Gilmore Publications (1980) Ltd., 5160 Skyline Way N.E., Calgary, AB T2E 6V1, Canada. TEL 403-274-1734. FAX 403-275-4999. Ed. Kurt Gilmore. adv. contact: Janice McCurdie. circ. 3,500.

636.2   CN   ISSN 0008-3909
CANADIAN JERSEY BREEDER. (Includes a French section) 1946. 10/yr. Can.$25. Jersey Cattle Association of Canada, 350 Speedvale Ave. W., Unit 9, Guelph, ON N1H 7M7, Canada. TEL 519-821-9150. FAX 519-821-2723. Ed. Betty Clements. adv.; charts; illus.; index. circ. 1,800. —Linda Hall

636   CN   ISSN 0382-6406
CANADIAN JERSEY HERD RECORD. vol.38, 1978. irreg. 1986. Jersey Cattle Association of Canada, 350 Speedvale Ave. W., Unit 9, Guelph, ON N1H 7M7, Canada. TEL 519-821-1020. FAX 519-821-2723.
    Formerly: Jersey Cattle Association of Canada. Record (ISSN 0382-6414)

591   CN   ISSN 0008-3984
                      CODEN: CNJNAT
CANADIAN JOURNAL OF ANIMAL SCIENCE. (Text in English or French) 1921. q. Can.$58 (foreign Can.$62) (effective 1997). (Canadian Society of Animal Science) Agricultural Institute of Canada, 141 Laurier Ave., W. Ste. 1112, Ottawa, ON K1P 5J3, Canada. TEL 613-232-9459. FAX 613-594-5190. E-mail: journals@aic.ca; URL: http://www.aic.ca. Ed. A. Schaefer. R&P contact: T. Fenton. adv. contact: T. Fenton. bibl.; charts; illus.; stat.; index. circ. 1,300. (also avail. in microform from UMI,PMC; back issues avail.) **Indexed:** Agri.Eng.Abstr., Anim.Breed.Abstr., ASCA, Biodet.Abstr., Biol.Abstr., Biol.& Agr.Ind., Biotech.Abstr., Cadscan, Chem.Abstr., Curr.Adv.Ecol.Sci., Curr.Cont., Dairy Sci.Abstr., Environ.Abstr., Environ.Per.Bibl., Food Sci.& Tech.Abstr., Helminthol.Abstr., Herb.Abstr., Ind.Sci.Rev., Ind.Vet., INIS Atomind., Lead Abstr., Maize Abstr., Nutr.Abstr., Pig News & Info., Pollut.Abstr., Potato Abstr., Poult.Abstr., Rev.Appl.Entomol., Rev.Med.& Vet.Mycol., Sci.Cit.Ind., Sorghum & Millets Abstr., Soyabean Abstr., Sport Fish.Abstr., SSCI, Triticale Abstr., Vet.Bull., Wild.Rev., Zincscan, Zoo.Rec. **Document type:** academic/scholarly publication.
—BLDSC (3028.500000); CASDDS; CIS; CISTI; Genuine Article; KR SourceOne; Linda Hall; SWETS; UMI; UnCover. **CCC.**
    Description: Research on all aspects of farm animals and their products.
    Refereed Serial

636   CN   ISSN 0008-4344
CANADIAN LACOMBE BREEDERS ASSOCIATION. NEWSLETTER. 1958. irreg. (3-4/yr.). Dr. H.T. Fredeen, Ed. & Pub., 2320-41 Ave. N.E., Calgary, Alta. T2E 6W8, Canada. mkt. circ. 300. (processed) **Document type:** newsletter.
    Formerly: Lacombe News.

636.6   CN
CANADIAN OSTRICH. 6/yr. Can.$42($45) Pawn Press, P.O. Box 355, Stn. H, Montreal, PQ H3G 2L1, Canada. TEL 514-483-5970. FAX 514-483-6152. circ. 3,000. **Document type:** trade publication.
    Description: Full color glossy magazine directed to ostrich producers and those involved in the business.

636.5   CN
CANADIAN PERCHERON BROADCASTER. bi-m. Canadian Percheron Association, Bag 200, Crossfield, Alta. TOM 0S0, Canada. TEL 403-946-5425.

636.4   CN   ISSN 0045-5423
CANADIAN SWINE.* 1939. q. Can.$12. Canadian Swine Breeders' Association, 2417 Holly La., Ottawa, ON K1V 7P2, Canada. TEL 613-731-5531. Ed. Karen Sample. adv.; bk.rev. circ. 3,000.
    Description: Information on the Canadian purebred swine industry.

636 346.066   US
CAPITOL LINE-UP. s-m. $50 (includes A A M P Lifier). American Association of Meat Processors, Box 269, Elizabethtown, PA 17022. TEL 717-367-1168. FAX 717-367-9096. E-mail: aamp@aamp.com. Eds. Stephen Krut, Bernard Shine. circ. 2,300. **Document type:** newsletter.
    Description: Updates on regulatory and legislative matters.

630   SP   ISSN 0214-249X
CARNE; revista profesional. 1943. m. (10/yr.). 200 ptas. Federacion Madrilena de las Industrias de Carnes, Canos del Peral, 1, 28013 Madrid, Spain. TEL 1-274-13-24. FAX 1-542-77-85. Ed. Eugenio Cano Hernandez. circ. 10,000.

636   SP   ISSN 0210-5543
CARNICA 2000; revista de las industrias carnicas espanolas. 1973. m. 13000 ptas. (Europe 20500 ptas.; elsewhere 24000 ptas.) (effective 1996). Publicaciones Tecnicas Alimentarias, S.A., Po. Imperial 8, 2o, 28005 Madrid, Spain. TEL 34-1-3665207. FAX 34-1-3640774. Ed. Alfredo Val. R&P contact: Carlos Ayala. adv. contact: Paloma Del Olmo. bk.rev. circ. 6,500. (reprint service avail.) **Indexed:** Ind.SST. **Document type:** trade publication.
    Description: Covers all topics of the meat trade, from production to consumption.

636.2   US   ISSN 1058-0484
CASCADE CATTLEMAN. 1988. m. $10. Klamath Publishing, Box 788, Klamath Falls, OR 97601. TEL 503-883-4000. Ed. Becky Hatfield-Hyde; Pub. Dwight Tracy. R&P contact: Dennis Taylor. adv. contact: Maureen Thomas. circ. 5,200. **Document type:** trade publication.

636   SP
CATALOGO DE INSTALACIONES, EQUIPOS Y UTENSILIOS PARA GANADERIA. a. 4900 ptas. (foreign 6200 ptas.) (effective 1997). Tecnipublicaciones, S.A., C. Albacete 5, 28027 Madrid, Spain. TEL 34-1-3261440. FAX 34-1-3262407. **Document type:** catalog.

636.2   US   ISSN 0897-2737
CATTLE BUSINESS. Key Title: Cattle Business in Mississippi. 1958. m. membership. Mississippi Cattlemen's Association, 680 Monroe St., Ste. A, Jackson, MS 39202-3422. TEL 601-354-8951. FAX 601-355-7128. Ed. Jim Newsome. adv.; B&W page $605, color page $1005; trim 8 1/2 x 11; adv. contact: Amanda Bray. bk.rev.; illus.; stat. circ. 6,000. (reprint service avail.) **Document type:** trade publication.

636   US   ISSN 0411-289X
CATTLE GUARD. 1954. m. $20. Colorado Cattlemen's Association, 8833 Ralston Rd., Arvada, CO 80002-2239. TEL 303-431-6422. FAX 303-431-6446. URL: http://www.yampa.com/cca. Ed. Todd Inglee; Pub. Todd Inglee. R&P contact: Todd Inglee. adv. contact: Todd Inglee. circ. 3,000. **Document type:** trade publication.
—UnCover.
    Description: Features stories about Colorado cattlemen; regular columns from association president, association executive vice president, Colorado Cattle Women's president, and Colorado State University; stories on the cattle industry economics, trends, and business management; and reports on association conventions, meetings, and policy statements.

636.2   US   ISSN 0008-8552
CATTLEMAN. 1914. m. (foreign $40) (effective 1997). Texas and Southwestern Cattle Raisers Association Inc., 1301 W. Seventh St., Fort Worth, TX 76102. TEL 817-332-7155. Ed. Lionel Chambers. adv.; illus.; stat.; index; circ. 22,000. circ. 22,000 (paid). (also avail. in microfilm from UMI; reprint service avail. from UMI)
—UMI; UnCover.

636.2   AT   ISSN 0313-9158
CATTLEMAN. m. $12. Western Publishers Pty. Ltd., 10 Joseph St., P.O. Box 188, Toowoomba, Qld.4350, Australia. TEL 076-324444. FAX 076-382118. Ed. Stephen Darracott. adv. circ. 5,200.

636   RH
CATTLEMAN OF THE YEAR. (Supplement to: The Farmer (ISSN 1011-0488)) a. Modern Farming Publications Trust, P.O. Box 1622, Harare, Zimbabwe. TEL 263-4-753278. FAX 263-4-750754. TELEX 22084 CFU ZW. Ed. Felicity Wood. adv.: B&W page Z.$3806, color page Z.5006; bleed 280 x 216; adv. contact: Michael Rook. illus. **Document type:** trade publication.

636.2   CN   ISSN 0008-3143
CATTLEMEN; the beef magazine. 1938. m. Can.$24. Farm Business Communications, P.O. Box 6600, Winnipeg, MB R3C 3A7, Canada. TEL 204-944-5761. FAX 204-942-8463. Ed. Gren Winslow. adv. contact: Tom Mumby. charts; illus.; mkt.; pat.; stat. circ. 28,700. (also avail. in microform from UMI) **Document type:** trade publication.
    Formerly: Canadian Cattlemen.

636.2   MX
CEBU. 1976. m. $20. (Asociacion Mexicana de Criadores de Cebu) Editorial Ano Dos Mil, S.A., Indianapolis 70, 03810 Mexico, D.F., Mexico. Ed. Juan Francisco Gonzalez Inigo. adv. circ. 7,500.

CENTRAL OREGON RANCHER. see **AGRICULTURE — Agricultural Equipment**

636.932   US   ISSN 0009-1294
CHAMPAGNE NEWS.* m. $3. (Champagne d'Argent Rabbit Federation) Wayne Cleer, Ed. & Pub., 1704 Heisel, Pekin, IL 61554. adv.; charts; stat. circ. 385. (processed)

636   FR   ISSN 0395-8183
CHAROLAIS. 1966. q. 150 F. (Europe 180 F.; elsewhere 200 F.) (effective 1997). Herd Book Charolais, 8 rue de Lourdes, B.P. 222, 58002 Nevers Cedex, France. TEL 33-3-86597700. FAX 33-3-86597719. Ed. David Jouys; Pub. David Jouys. adv. contact: Roger Laurisson. circ. 8,250. **Document type:** bulletin.

636.2   CN   ISSN 0824-1767
CHAROLAIS BANNER; official publication of the Canadian purebred Charolais cattle industry. 1966. 10/yr. Can.$32.10($35) (effective 1996). Charolais Banner Ltd., South Airways Bldg., Ste. 205, 3016-19th St., N.E., Calgary, AB T2E 6Y9, Canada. TEL 403-291-1420. FAX 403-291-0081. Ed. Robert L. Pek. adv.; illus. circ. 2,500.
    Formerly: Canadian Charolais Banner (ISSN 0008-5499)

636.2   CN   ISSN 0828-7600
CHAROLAIS CONNECTION; official publication of the Canadian commercial Charolais industry. 1984. 2/yr. included with Charolais Banner. Charolais Banner Ltd., South Airway Bldg., Ste. 205, 3016-19th St., N.E., Calgary, AB T2E 6Y9, Canada. TEL 403-291-1420. FAX 403-291-0081. Ed. Robert L. Pek. adv.; charts; illus.; stat.; tr.lit. circ. 18,000. (back issues avail.)

636   US   ISSN 0191-5444
CHAROLAIS JOURNAL. 1977. m. $20. Charolais Publications, Inc., Box 20247, Kansas City, MO 64195. TEL 816-464-5977. FAX 816-464-5959. Ed. Julie Olson; Pub. Bill Able. R&P contact: David Hobbs. adv. contact: David Hobbs. circ. 5,000. **Document type:** trade publication.

AGRICULTURE — POULTRY AND LIVESTOCK

636.4 US ISSN 1082-6920
SF393.C5
CHESTER WHITE JOURNAL - POLAND CHINA ADVANTAGE - SPOTTED NEWS. 1994. bi-m. $10. Poland China Record Association, Box 9758, Peoria, IL 61612-9758. TEL 309-691-6301. FAX 309-691-0168. (Co-sponsor: Chester White Swine Record Association; Spotted Swine Association) Ed. Daniel Parrish. adv.; illus.; stat. circ. 2,500. **Document type:** trade publication.
—Linda Hall; UnCover.
Formerly (until 1995): Chester White Journal - Spotted News; Which was formed by the merger of (1910-1994): Chester White Journal (ISSN 0009-3386); (1961-1994): Spotted News (ISSN 0038-8432); (1984-1994): Purebred Picture (ISSN 8750-1880); Which was formed by the merger of: Poland China World (ISSN 0032-2466); And: American Landrace - Berkshire News; Which was formed by the merger of (1953-1982): American Landrace (ISSN 0002-970X) & (1935-1982): Berkshire News (ISSN 0005-9196).
Description: Contains tips on raising hogs.

636.39 FR ISSN 0045-6608
CHEVRE; revue des eleveurs de chevres. 1958. 6/yr. 220 F. (foreign 330 F.) (effective 1997); newsstand price: 40 F. (Institut Technique de l'Elevage Ovin et Caprin) Societe de Presse et d'Edition Ovine et Caprine (S.P.E.O.C.), 19 quai de Juillet, B.P. 18, 14005 Caen Cedex, France. TEL 33-2-31357704. FAX 33-2-31822963. Ed. Jean-Claude Lejaouen; Pub. Andre Zawadzki. R&P contact: Marc Jourdan. adv. contact: Jean-Pierre Dumas. circ. 4,500 (controlled). **Indexed:** Anim.Breed.Abstr., Dairy Sci.Abstr., Rural Recreat.Tour.Abstr., World Agri.Econ.& Rural Sociol.Abstr.
Description: Technical and economical information about goat breeding.

CHICAGO DAILY HIDE AND TALLOW BULLETIN; the first daily hide market service established in America. see *LEATHER AND FUR INDUSTRIES*

338.1 US
CHICKEN DISEASES. 1980. a. $6. American Bantam Association, Box 127, Augusta, NJ 07822. Ed. F.P. Jeffrey.

636 JA ISSN 0009-3874
CHIKUSAN NO KENKYU/ANIMAL HUSBANDRY. (Text in Japanese) 1947. m. 16000 Yen. Yokendo Co., Ltd., 30-15 Hongo 5-chome, Bunkyo-ku, Tokyo 113, Japan. TEL 03-3814-0911. FAX 03-3812-2615. Ed. Kiyoshi Oikawa. adv.; bk.rev.; index. circ. 20,000. **Indexed:** Agri.Ind., Dairy Sci.Abstr., Food Sci.& Tech.Abstr., Rural Recreat.Tour.Abstr., World Agri.Econ.& Rural Sociol.Abstr. **Document type:** academic/scholarly publication.

CHILE. INSTITUTO NACIONAL DE ESTADISTICAS. ESTADISTICAS PECUARIAS. see *AGRICULTURE — Abstracting, Bibliographies, Statistics*

636 XR ISSN 0323-1534
CHOVATEL. 1966. m. $21.10. Cesky Svaz Chovatelu, Makova 3, 182 53 Prague 8, Czech Republic. (Subscr. to: Artia, Ve Smeckach 30, 111 27 Prague 1, Czech Republic) Ed. Hana Zvolska. **Indexed:** Anim.Breed.Abstr.
Formerly: Drobne Hospodarske Zvirectvo.

636.4 CU ISSN 0138-8738
CODEN: CAGPDY
CIENCIA Y TECNICA EN LA AGRICULTURA. SERIE: GANADO PORCINO. (Table of contents and abstracts in English) 1978. 4/yr. $17 in N. America; S. America $19; Europe $21; elsewhere $24; or exchange basis. Centro de Informacion y Documentacion Agropecuario, Gaveta Postal 4149, Havana 4, Cuba. (Dist. by: Ediciones Cubanas, Obispo No. 527, Aptdo 605, Havana, Cuba) **Indexed:** Agrindex, Anim.Breed.Abstr., Nutr.Abstr., Pig News & Info.

636 US
CLYDESDALE NEWS. 1970. a. $12. Clydesdale Breeders of the U.S.A., 17346 Kelley Rd., Pecatonica, IL 61063. TEL 815-247-8780. FAX 815-247-8337. E-mail: clydesusa@aol.com. circ. 1,500. (back issues avail.) **Document type:** trade publication.

636.2 UK ISSN 0069-4924
COATES'S HERD BOOK (BEEF). 1882. a. £10 to members. Shorthorn Society of Great Britain and Ireland, 4th St. National Agricultural Centre, Stoneleigh Park, Kenilworth, Warwickshire CV8 2LG, England. TEL 44-1203-696549. FAX 44-1203-696729. Ed. J.H. Wood Roberts. adv. circ. 800. **Document type:** trade publication.

COLORADO AGRIBUSINESS ROUNDUP. see *AGRICULTURE — Agricultural Economics*

COMMONWEALTH SCIENTIFIC AND INDUSTRIAL RESEARCH ORGANISATION. DIVISION OF ANIMAL PRODUCTION. DIVISIONAL INFORMATION SHEETS. see *BIOLOGY — Physiology*

COMMONWEALTH SCIENTIFIC AND INDUSTRIAL RESEARCH ORGANIZATION. DIVISION OF ANIMAL PRODUCTION. DIVISIONAL INFORMATION. see *BIOLOGY — Physiology*

COMMONWEALTH SCIENTIFIC AND INDUSTRIAL RESEARCH ORGANIZATION. DIVISION OF TROPICAL CROPS AND PASTURES. GENETIC RESOURCES COMMUNICATION. see *AGRICULTURE — Crop Production And Soil*

636.932 SP
CONILLS. (Text in Catalan) 1991. q. 1000 ptas. (Federacio d'Associacions de Cuniculturs de Catalunya) Edicions la Terra, S.L., Avda. Francesc Cambo 14, 3-B, 08003 Barcelona, Spain. TEL 34-3-2680900. FAX 34-3-2684893. Ed. Dolors Aixala. adv. contact: Josep M. Escola. circ. 1,500. **Document type:** trade publication.

CONSUMO PECUARIO NACIONAL. see *AGRICULTURE — Abstracting, Bibliographies, Statistics*

636.2 US ISSN 0279-8204
COW COUNTRY. 1950. m. $20. Wyoming Stock Growers Association, Box 206, Cheyenne, WY 82003. TEL 307-638-3942. FAX 307-635-2524. Ed. Jeannie W. Mitchell. adv. contact: Renee Goetz. circ. 1,520. (back issues avail.) **Document type:** trade publication.
Description: Discusses cattle breeding.

636 382 US
COW NEWS & BULL VIEWS. 1987. bi-m. $5. American Breed International Association, Inc., 1530 S. Ave. E, Portales, NM 88130. TEL 505-359-1496. Ed. Jewell W. Jones. adv. circ. 500. (looseleaf format) **Document type:** newsletter.
Formerly: News and Views (Portales).
Description: News and information on recording, registering and promoting American Breed cattle which are approximately 1/2 Brahman, 1/4 Charolais, 1/8 Bison, 1/16 Hereford, 1/16 Shorthorn.

636.2 US
COWBOYS DIGEST. 1974. bi-m. $15. Box 1196, Kalispell, MT 59903. TEL 406-752-7525. FAX 406-752-7520. Ed. Jeanne Carpenter; Pub. Jeanne Carpenter. R&P contact: Jeanne Carpenter. adv. contact: Jeanne Carpenter. circ. 2,000. (tabloid format) **Document type:** newspaper.

636.5 CU
CUBA. CENTRO DE INFORMACION Y DOCUMENTACION AGROPECUARIO. BOLETIN DE RESENAS. SERIE: AVICULTURA. 1974. irreg. exchange basis. Centro de Informacion y Documentacion Agropecuario, Gaveta Postal 4149, Havana 4, Cuba.
Formerly: Cuba. Centro de Informacion y Divulgacion Agropecuario. Boletin de Resenas. Serie: Avicultura.

636.4 CU ISSN 1011-968X
CUBA. CENTRO DE INFORMACION Y DOCUMENTACION AGROPECUARIO. BOLETIN DE RESENAS. SERIE: GANADO PORCINO. (Text in Spanish; abstracts in English) 1974. irreg. exchange basis. Centro de Informacion y Documentacion Agropecuario, Gaveta Postal 4149, Havana 4, Cuba. (Dist. by: Ediciones Cubanas, Obispo No. 461, Apdo. 605, Havana, Cuba) **Indexed:** Agrindex.
Formerly: Cuba. Centro de Informacion y Divulgacion Agropecuario. Boletin de Resenas. Serie: Ganado Porcino.

636.932 SP ISSN 0210-1912
CUNICULTURA. 1976. bi-m. 6600 ptas.($58) Real Escuela de Avicultura, Plana del Paraiso, 14, 08350 Arenys de Mar (Barcelona), Spain. TEL 34-3-7921137. FAX 34-3-7921537. Ed. Jose A. Castello; Pub. Jose A. Castello. adv. contact: Conchita Luque. bk.rev.; illus.; stat.; index. circ. 2,950. **Document type:** academic/scholarly publication.
Description: For rabbit growers.

636.932 FR ISSN 0152-3058
CUNICULTURE; la revue de l'eleveur de lapins. 1974. bi-m. 242 F. (foreign 348 F.) (effective 1997). Association Francaise de Cuniculture, B.P. 50, 63370 Lempdes, France. TEL 33-4-73920152. FAX 33-4-73928680.
—BLDSC (3492.481400).

CYPRUS. DEPARTMENT OF STATISTICS AND RESEARCH. CENSUS OF POULTRY. see *AGRICULTURE — Abstracting, Bibliographies, Statistics*

636.5 636.4 GW ISSN 0340-3858
CODEN: DDGSE8
D G S. (Deutsche Gefluegelwirtschaft und Schweineproduktion) 1948. w. DM.315.60. (Zentralverband der Deutschen Gefluegelwirtschaft) Verlag Eugen Ulmer GmbH, Wollgrasweg 41, 70599 Stuttgart, Germany. TEL 49-711-4507-0. FAX 49-711-4507-120. (Subscr. to: Postfach 700561, 70574 Stuttgart, Germany) Ed. F. Sundermann. R&P contact: G. Friedrich. adv. contact: A. Purwing. bk.rev.; charts; illus.; stat.; index. circ. 5,000. **Indexed:** Rural Recreat.Tour.Abstr., World Agri.Econ.& Rural Sociol.Abstr. **Document type:** trade publication.
—CCC.
Formerly: Deutsche Gefluegelwirtschaft (ISSN 0012-0162)

636 BL
D N P A. irreg. Ministerio da Agricultura, Departamento Nacional de Producao Animal, Brasilia, Brazil. stat. **Document type:** government publication.

636.39 US ISSN 0011-5592
DAIRY GOAT JOURNAL. 1916. m. $20 (foreign $30). Duck Creek Publications, Box 10, 128 E. Lake St., Lake Mills, WI 53551. TEL 414-648-8285. FAX 414-648-3770. Ed. Dave Thompson. adv.; bk.rev.; illus. circ. 8,000. **Indexed:** Biol.Abstr.
—Linda Hall; SWETS; UMI; UnCover.
Description: Provides current information on the dairy goat, including milking and cheese-making techniques.

636.39 AT ISSN 0815-9769
DAIRY GOAT SOCIETY OF AUSTRALIA. VICTORIAN BRANCH NEWSLETTER. q. Aus.$20. Dairy Goat Society of Australia, Victorian Branch, RMB 8680, Bannockburn, Vic. 3331, Australia. TEL 61-52-711254. Ed. G. Keays. R&P contact: G. Keays. adv.; bk.rev. circ. 400. (back issues avail.) **Document type:** newsletter.

DAIRY INDIA YEARBOOK. see *AGRICULTURE — Dairying And Dairy Products*

636 CC
DANGDAI XUMU/MODERN ANIMAL HUSBANDRY. (Text in Chinese) q. Beijing Shi Xumu Ju - Beijing Bureau of Animal Husbandry, 75 Bingjiaokou, Dewai, Beijing 100088, People's Republic of China. TEL 2014549. Ed. Yu Shuangmuo.

636.5 DK ISSN 0045-9607
DANSK ERHVERVSFJERKRAE. 1879. m. DKK 825. Dansk Erhvervsfjerkrae - Danish Poultry and Egg Producers Association, Oester Finderupsvej 2, Finderup, DK-6900 Skjern, Denmark. TEL 45-97-36-10-50. FAX 45-93-36-12-50. Ed. L. Yding Soerensen. adv.; bk.rev.; charts; illus.; index. circ. 1,400. **Document type:** trade publication.
Supersedes in part (in 1971): Tidsskrift for Fjerkraeavl (ISSN 0040-7046); Which incorporates (1964-1965): Erhvervsfjerkrae (ISSN 0425-1954)

636.3 UK
DARTMOOR SHEEP BREEDERS' ASSOCIATION. ANNUAL FLOCK BOOK. 1909. a. £10. Dartmoor Sheep Breeders' Association, Aish Park House, Fore St., South Brent, Devon TQ10 9BQ, England. TEL 03647-3657. Ed. J.A. Hanney.

AGRICULTURE — POULTRY AND LIVESTOCK

636.2   UK   ISSN 0070-2986
DAVY'S DEVON HERD BOOK. 1851. a. £15. Devon Cattle Breeders' Society, Barn Lane Farm, Stoke Rivers, Barnstaple, Devon EX32 7LD, England. TEL 44-1958-710836. FAX 44-1598-710836. Ed. Albert E. Beer; Pub. Albert E. Beer. R&P contact: Albert E. Beer. adv. contact: Albert E. Beer. circ. 85.
   Description: Carries the registrations of cattle for the Devon breed in the UK.

636   NZ   ISSN 0110-7992
DEER FARMER. 1979. 10/yr. NZ.$78.75 (Australia Aus.$96.90; Canada Can.$142.50; elsewhere $102.60). Deer Farmer Publications Ltd., P.O. Box 11092, Wellington, New Zealand. TEL 64-4-4739243. FAX 64-4-4734530. E-mail: 100406.2225@compuserve.com; URL: http://www.ourworld.compuserve.com/homepages/deerfarmer. Ed. Brendan Hutching; Pub. Trevor Walton. adv. contact: Angel Fussell. bk.rev. circ. 4,000. **Document type**: trade publication.
—BLDSC (3541.205000).

351.823 636   DK   ISSN 0106-8547
DENMARK. STATENS HUSDYRBRUGSFORSOEG. AARSRAPPORT/DENMARK. DANISH INSTITUTE OF ANIMAL SCIENCE. ANNUAL REPORT. 1974. a. free. Statens Husdyrbrugsforsoeg - Danish Institute of Animal Science, Research Center Foulum, P.O. Box 39, DK-8830 Tjele, Denmark. TEL 45-89-99-19-00. FAX 45-89-99-19-19.

636   DK   ISSN 0105-6883
              CODEN: BSHUDX
DENMARK. STATENS HUSDYRBRUGSFORSOEG. BERETNING/DENMARK. DANISH INSTITUTE OF ANIMAL SCIENCE. REPORT. (Text in Danish; summaries in English) 1883. irreg. price varies. Statens Husdyrbrugsforsoeg - Danish Institute of Animal Science, Research Center Foulum, P.O. Box 39, DK-8830 Tjele, Denmark. circ. 1,300. **Indexed**: Anim.Breed.Abstr., Dairy Sci.Abstr., Field Crop Abstr., Food Sci.& Tech.Abstr., Herb.Abstr., Ind.Vet., Nutr.Abstr., Rural Recreat.Tour.Abstr., Soyabean Abstr., Sugar Ind.Abstr., Triticale Abstr., World Agri.Econ.& Rural Sociol.Abstr.
—BLDSC (1904.500000).
   Former titles (until 1975): Denmark. Forsoegslaboratoriet. Beretning (ISSN 0005-8904); (until 1915): Denmark. Den Kongelige Veterinaer- og Landbohoejskoles Laboratorium for Landoekonomiske Forsoeg. Beretning (ISSN 0105-2314).

636   DK   ISSN 0908-021X
DENMARK. STATENS HUSDYRBRUGSFORSOEG. FORSKNINGSRAPPORT/DENMARK. DANISH INSTITUTE OF ANIMAL SCIENCE. RESEARCH REPORT. 1993. irreg. price varies. Statens Husdyrbrugsforsoeg - Danish Institute of Animal Science, Research Center Foulum, P.O. Box 39, DK-8330 Tjele, Denmark. TEL 45-89-99-19-00. FAX 45-89-99-19-19. (back issues avail.)

636   DK   ISSN 0908-0368
DENMARK. STATENS HUSDYRBRUGSFORSOEG. HUSDYRSFORSKNING/DENMARK. DANISH INSTITUTE OF ANIMAL SCIENCE. SCIENTIFIC REPORT. 1974. 6/yr. DKK 125 (effective 1997). Statens Husdyrbrugsforsoeg - National Institute of Animal Science, Research Center Foulum, P.O. Box 39, DK-8830 Tjele, Denmark. (back issues avail.)
   Formerly (until 1992): Denmark. Statens Husdyrbrugsforsoeg. Meddelelse (ISSN 0106-8857).

636 637   SW   ISSN 0347-9706
SF41.R37   CODEN: RSLSDJ
DEPARTMENT OF ANIMAL BREEDING AND GENETICS. REPORT. (Text in English and Swedish; summaries in English) 1973. irreg., no.62 1984. free. Swedish University of Agricultural Sciences, Department of Animal Breeding and Genetics, P.O. Box 7023, S-750 07 Uppsala, Sweden. FAX 018-672848. **Document type**: academic/scholarly publication.
—BLDSC (7273.207500).

636.3   GW   ISSN 0720-0862
DEUTSCHE SCHAFZUCHT. 1908. fortn. DM.157.80. (Vereinigung Deutscher Landesschafzuchtverbaender) Verlag Eugen Ulmer GmbH, Wollgrasweg 41, 70599 Stuttgart, Germany. TEL 49-711-4507-0. FAX 49-711-4507120. (Subscr. to: Postfach 700561, 70574 Stuttgart, Germany) Ed. G. Dierichs. R&P contact: G. Friedrich. adv. contact: A. Purwing. illus.; mkt.; stat. circ. 8,700. **Document type**: trade publication.
—CCC.
   Formerly (until 1980): Deutsche Schaefereizeitung (ISSN 0012-0677)

636.3   UK
DORSET DOWN FLOCK BOOK. 1906. a. £5 to non-members. Dorset Down Sheep Breeders' Association, c/o June Pither, Sec., Greenway Farm, Bishop's Lydeard, Taunton, Somerset, England. TEL 44-1823-432301. FAX 44-1823-432301. R&P contact: June Pither. adv. circ. 150. **Document type**: directory.

636.3   UK
DORSET HORN AND POLL DORSET SHEEP BREEDERS' ASSOCIATION. FLOCK BOOK. a. £30. Dorset Horn and Poll Dorset Sheep Breeders' Association, Agriculture House, Acland Rd., Dorchester, Dorset DT1 1EF, England. TEL 44-1305-262126. circ. 350.

636   US   ISSN 0012-5865
DRAFT HORSE JOURNAL. 1964. q. $20 (foreign $25). Draft Horse Journal, Inc., Box 670, 2700 Fifth Ave., N.W., Waverly, IA 50677. TEL 319-352-4046. FAX 319-352-2232. URL: http://www.horseshoes.com. Ed. Lynn Telleen; Pubs. Maurice & Jeannine Telleen. adv. contact: Pat Hillard. bk.rev.; illus. circ. 24,000. **Document type**: trade publication.
   Description: Covers trade news of the draft horse industry, including all draft horse breeds and draft mules.

636   US   ISSN 0012-6454
DROVERS JOURNAL. 1873. m. $25 (foreign $50) (effective 1997). Vance Publishing Corporation (Lenexa), 10901 W. 84th Terr., Ste. 200, Lenexa, KS 66214-1631. TEL 913-438-8700. FAX 913-438-0695. Ed. Greg Henderson. adv.; illus.; circ. 90,965 (controlled). **Document type**: trade publication.
—UMI; UnCover. CCC.

636.5 637.5   US   ISSN 0896-2804
EGG INDUSTRY; covering egg production, processing & marketing. 1895. m. $24. Watt Publishing Co., 122 S. Wesley Ave., Mt. Morris, IL 61054. TEL 815-734-4171. FAX 815-734-4201. Ed. Virginia Lazar; Pub. Clay Schreiber. adv.: B&W page $1925, color page $2615. illus.; mkt. circ. 8,000. (also avail. in microfilm from UMI) **Indexed**: Biol.Abstr., Curr.Pack.Abstr.
Document type: newsletter.
—Linda Hall; UMI. **CCC**.
   Formerly (until Oct. 1987): Poultry Tribune (ISSN 0032-5805)
   Description: Publishes articles on the production of eggs, processing and marketing; for the U.S. commercial egg industry.

637.5   US
EGG PRODUCTION TESTS: UNITED STATES AND CANADA.* 1959. a. free. U.S. Animal and Plant Health Inspection Service, 4700 River Rd., Unit 6, Riverdale, MD 20737. TEL 301-734-5240. Ed. R.D. Schar. circ. 15,000.

636   UA   ISSN 0302-4520
              CODEN: EGAPBW
EGYPTIAN JOURNAL OF ANIMAL PRODUCTION. (Text in English; summaries in Arabic, English) 1961. s-a. $57 (effective 1997). (Egyptian Society of Animal Production, Research Department) National Information and Documentation Centre (NIDOC), Tahrir St., Dokki, Awqaf P.O., Cairo, Egypt. TEL 20-2-3371696. Ed. M. El-Shafie. charts; illus.; stat. circ. 1,000. (reprint service avail. from IRC) **Indexed**: Anim.Breed Abstr., Biol.Abstr., Chem.Abstr., Curr.Adv.Ecol.Sci., Dairy Sci.Abstr., Food Sci.& Tech.Abstr., Herb.Abstr., Ind.Vet., Nutr.Abstr., Poult.Abstr., Sorghum & Millets Abstr., Vet.Bull. **Document type**: academic/scholarly publication.
—BLDSC (3664.270000); CASDDS; Linda Hall.

636   JA   ISSN 0286-4754
EIYO SEIRI KENKYUKAIHO/JAPANESE SOCIETY FOR ANIMAL NUTRITION AND METABOLISM. PROCEEDINGS. (Text in Japanese) 1956. s-a. membership. Kachiku Eiyo Seiri Kenkyukai - Japanese Society for Animal Nutrition and Metabolism, Kyoto University, Faculty of Agriculture, Dept. of Animal Science, Sakyo-ku, Kyoto 606-01, Japan. TEL 81-75-753-6055. Ed. Hideo Yono. adv. **Document type**: proceedings.
—BLDSC (6742.485500).

636.932   FR   ISSN 0220-5149
ELEVEUR DE LAPINS. 1978. 5/yr. 200 F. (foreign 300 F.). Editions du Boisbaudry, B.P. 6359, 35063 Rennes Cedex, France. TEL 99-32-21-21. FAX 99-32-14-17. TELEX 730619F. adv. circ. 4,200.

636   FR   ISSN 0046-1822
ELEVEUR MAINE ANJOU. 1952. q. free. U P R A Maine Anjou, 36-38 rue de Razilly, B.P. 52, 53200 Chateau Gontier, France. Ed. E. Labit. bk.rev.

636.5   ES
ENCUESTA AVICOLA.* irreg. exchange. Ministerio de Agricultura y Ganaderia, Direccion General de Economia Agropecuaria, c/o Ospa 31, Avda. del Sur, 627, San Salvador, El Salvador. TEL 23-2598. Dir. Rene Aguilar Giron. stat.

636.2   UK   ISSN 0071-0571
ENGLISH GUERNSEY HERD BOOK. 1885. a. £15. English Guernsey Cattle Society, The Bury Farm, Pednor Rd., Chesham, Bucks. HP5 2LA, England. index.
   Description: Details cattle breeding.

636   SP   ISSN 0213-3792
ESPANA AGRICOLA Y GANADERA. 1962. m. (11/yr.). 4000 ptas. Prensa Hispanoamericana, S.A., C. Gascuena 21, 28022 Madrid, Spain. TEL 1-747-80-00. FAX 1-747-9056. Ed. J. Luis Hernandez. adv.; charts; illus.; mkt.; index. circ. 165,000. **Indexed**: Ind.SST.
   Former titles (until 1985): Espana Agricola (ISSN 0210-8992); (until 1978): Espana Agraria (ISSN 0014-049X)

ETHNOZOOTECHNIE. see ANTHROPOLOGY

ETHOLOGY. see BIOLOGY — Zoology

636   NE   ISSN 1382-6077
▼**EUROPEAN ASSOCIATION FOR ANIMAL PRODUCTION. ANNUAL MEETING. BOOK OF ABSTRACTS**. Short title: E A A P Book of Abstracts Series. 1995. a. price varies. Wageningen Pers, Postbus 42, 6700 AA Wageningen, Netherlands. TEL 31-317-476515. FAX 31-317-426044. E-mail: wageningenpers@company.diva.nl. Ed. J.A.M. van Arendonk. R&P contact: Koen Bakkers. **Document type**: proceedings, academic/scholarly publication.

636   NE   ISSN 0071-2477
SF1   CODEN: EAAPAN
EUROPEAN ASSOCIATION FOR ANIMAL PRODUCTION. PUBLICATIONS. (Text in English, occasionally in French or other European languages) 1950. irreg., no.90, 1996. price varies. (European Association for Animal Production) Wageningen Pers, Postbus 42, 6700 AA Wageningen, Netherlands. TEL 31-317-476515. FAX 31-317-426044. E-mail: wageningenpers@company.diva.nl; URL: http://www.zod.wau.nl/WegPers. R&P contact: Koen Bakkers. circ. 1,000. (back issues avail.) **Indexed**: Biol.Abstr., Chem.Abstr., Food Sci.& Tech.Abstr. **Document type**: monographic series, proceedings.
—BLDSC (7059.750000); CISTI. **CCC**.

636   UN   ISSN 0254-6019
              CODEN: FAPPDA
F A O ANIMAL PRODUCTION AND HEALTH PAPERS. Spanish edition: Estudio F A O, Produccion y Sanidad Animal (ISSN 1014-1200); French edition: Etude F A O, Production et Sante Animales (ISSN 1014-1197) (Text in English) irreg., no.119, 1994. price varies. Food and Agriculture Organization of the United Nations, Bernan Associates, 4611-F Assembly Dr., Lanham, MD 20706-4391. TEL 301-459-7666. FAX 301-459-0056. **Indexed**: Food Sci.& Tech.Abstr., Nutr.Abstr., Rev.Appl.Entomol. **Document type**: monographic series.
—BLDSC (3865.593800); CISTI; Linda Hall.
   Formerly: F A O Animal Production and Health Series (ISSN 1010-9021)

AGRICULTURE — POULTRY AND LIVESTOCK

636 SP
F A S A G A - ANDALUCIA; la revista del campo andaluz. 1985. m. free. Federacion del Agricultores y Ganaderos de Andalucia, Edificio Jerez-74, planta 2, Jerez de la Frontera, Cadiz, Spain. TEL (956)30 79 00. TELEX 75083 ASAJ E. Ed. Cristobal Cantos Ruiz.

636.3 SW ISSN 0014-8598
FAARSKOETSEL. 1921. 10/yr. SEK 390 to members (effective 1995). Svenska Faaravelsfoerbundet - Swedish Sheep Breeders Association, Brogaarden, Jaella, 755 94 Uppsala, Sweden. TEL 46-18-31-75-74. FAX 46-18-31-70-86. Ed. Inger Wennbom. adv.; bk.rev.; abstr.; charts; illus.; mkt.; stat.; tr.lit.; index. circ. 5,983. **Indexed:** Anim.Breed.Abstr., Dairy Sci.Abstr.
  Former titles (until 1961): Svenska Faaravelsfoereningens Tidskrift; (until 1928): Svenska Faaravelsfoereningens Maanadsblad.

636.932 DK ISSN 0900-288X
FAELLESUDVALGET TIL KANINAVLENS FREMME. BERETNING. 1965. biennial. DKK 45. Faellesudvalget til Kaninavlens Fremme, Birkevaenget 74, DK-6600 Vejen, Denmark. illus.

635.5 UK ISSN 0262-3846
FANCY FOWL. 1981. m. $40. Fancy Fowl Publications Ltd., Andover Rd., Highclere, Newbury, Berks., England. TEL 44-1635-253239. FAX 44-1635-254146. Ed. Shirley Murdoch. R&P contact: Shirley Murdoch. adv. contact: Rosalind Wilson. bk.rev. circ. 3,000. **Document type:** trade publication.
  Description: Journal for those interested in breeding, conserving and exhibiting poultry, including waterfowl and pigeons.

636 UK ISSN 0144-6169
FARM ANIMAL WELFARE CO-ORDINATING EXECUTIVE. NEWSLETTER. 1979. a. free. Farm Animal Welfare Co-ordinating Executive, c/o Miss D. Hayman, Springhill House, 280 London Rd., Cheltenham GL52 6HS, England. Ed. Robin Corbett. circ. 3,000. **Document type:** newsletter.

FARM SCIENTIST. see *VETERINARY SCIENCE*

FARMER STOCKMAN OF THE MIDWEST. see *AGRICULTURE*

FARMERS & STOCKOWNERS. see *AGRICULTURE — Feed, Flour And Grain*

636 CN ISSN 0380-352X
FEATHER FANCIER. 1945. m. Can.$18($20) (foreign $20) (effective 1997). Jim Gryner, Ed. & Pub., 4094 Ross St., R.R. 5, Forest, ON N0N 1J0, Canada. TEL 519-899-2364. FAX 519-899-2364. E-mail: ffancier@xulco.on.ca; URL: http://www.farmshow.net/feather. Pub. Jim Gryner. adv. contact: Linda Gryner. bk.rev./; circ. 28,000. (paid).
  Description: Devoted to the improvement of standard-bred poultry, pigeons, waterfowl, pheasants and other avian species.

FEED CONTROL COMMENT. see *AGRICULTURE — Feed, Flour And Grain*

636.2 US ISSN 1083-5385
FEED-LOT. 1993. 6/yr. $15 (foreign $30). Feed-Lot Magazine, Box 850, Dighton, KS 67839-0850. TEL 316-397-2838. FAX 316-397-2839. Ed. Robert Strong. R&P contact: Robert Strong. adv.: B&W page $2164, color page $2612; trim 8 x 10 3/4; adv. contact: Greg Strong. circ. 9,042 (controlled). **Document type:** trade publication.
  Description: For large feedlots and their related cow and calf operations and large 500 plus cow - calf, stocker operations. Covers all phases of production from breeding, genetics, animal health, nutrition, equipment design, research through finishing fat cattle.

FEEDBACK. see *FOOD AND FOOD INDUSTRIES*

FEEDGRAM. see *AGRICULTURE — Feed, Flour And Grain*

636.4 JA ISSN 0289-7237
FEEDING. m. 1400 Yen per no. Chikusan Publishing Co., Ltd. (Subsidiary of: Midori Group), Ikebukuro Nishiguchi Sky Bldg., 2-14-4 Ikebukuro, Toshima-ku, Tokyo 171, Japan. TEL 03-3590-9454. circ. 15,000. **Document type:** trade publication.
  Description: Covers nutrition, marketing, and technical information of farm management for farmers, manufacturers and distributors.

FEEDSTUFFS; the weekly newspaper for agribusiness. see *AGRICULTURE — Feed, Flour And Grain*

FINANCIAL SURVEY. MEAT AND POULTRY. SCOTLAND; company data for success. see *BUSINESS AND ECONOMICS — Trade And Industrial Directories*

636.3 US
FINNSHEEP SHORT TALES. 1980. s-a. Finnsheep Breeders Association, 107 Morning Glory Ln., Aurora, NC 27806-9466. TEL 317-297-3670. Ed. Claire H. Carter. **Document type:** newsletter, directory.

636.5 SW ISSN 0015-3338
FJAEDERFAE. 1908. m. SEK 250 (effective 1997). S F S - Svenska Aegg, Mullbacken, Irsta, S-725 97 Vaesteraas, Sweden. TEL 46-21-29632. FAX 46-21-20670. E-mail: journalistgruppen@secker.pp.se. Ed. Sven Secher. adv. contact: Jon Axel Roslund. bk.rev.; illus.; stat. circ. 1,900. **Document type:** newspaper.

636.5 NO ISSN 0015-3354
FJOERFE. 1884. m. NOK 300 (effective 1997). Norsk Fjoerfelag, P.O. Box 73, 1430 Aas, Norway. TEL 64-943366. FAX 64-943370. Ed. Dagfinn Valland. adv.; bk.rev.; charts; illus.; mkt.stat. circ. 1,912.
  —CCC

636.3 AT ISSN 0314-7312
FLEECE AND FLOCK; a guide for hand spinners, weavers and coloured sheep breeders. 1974. a. membership. South Australian Coloured Sheep Owners' Society Inc. (SACSOS), P.O. Box 110, Eastwood, S.A. 5063, Australia. Ed. Verle Wood. circ. 250. (back issues avail.) **Document type:** catalog.

636.2 GW ISSN 0946-2902
FLEISCHRINDER JOURNAL. 1994. q. DM.42 (foreign DM.46.80) (effective 1997). Landwirtschaftsverlag GmbH, Huelsebrockstr. 2, 48165 Muenster, Germany. TEL 49-2501-801-0. FAX 49-2501-801-204. circ. 11,303. **Document type:** trade publication.

636.3 UK
FLOCK BOOK OF DEVON CORNWALL LONGWOOL SHEEP. 1977. a. £10. Devon and Cornwall Longwool Flockbook Association, Cherbourne, West Lane, Dolton, Winkleigh, Devon EX19 8QU. circ. 100.

636.3 UK
FLOCK BOOK OF OXFORD DOWN SHEEP. 1889. a. £7 (foreign £8.50). Oxford Down Sheep Breeder's Association, 4 Brookfield, Hampsthwaite, Harrogate, N. Yorkshire HG3 2EF, England. TEL 44-1423-770736. Ed. Jeffrey Stephenson. adv. contact: Ann Knott. circ. 150. **Document type:** directory.

636.2 US ISSN 0015-3958
FLORIDA CATTLEMAN AND LIVESTOCK JOURNAL. 1936. m. $35.35 membership. Florida Cattlemen's Association, Box 421403, Kissimmee, FL 34742-1403. TEL 407-846-8025. FAX 407-933-8209. Ed. Beverly Buckler. adv.: B&W page $540, color page $840; trim 8 1/4 x 11. bk.rev.; illus. circ. 6,872. **Document type:** trade publication.

636 SP ISSN 0211-3767
FRISONA ESPANOLA. 1981. bi-m. 7000 ptas. (Europe 10000 ptas.; elsewhere 12000 ptas.) (effective Jan. 1995). Confederacion de Asociaciones de Frisona Espanola, Apdo. de Correos 31, 28340 Valdemoro (Madrid), Spain. TEL 34-1-8952412. FAX 34-1-8951471. Ed. Domnino Garrote Manso. adv. contact: Baldomero Fernandez. **Indexed:** Ind.SST.
  Description: Technical coverage of the Holstein Freisian breed.

636 UK ISSN 0950-7701
GALLOWAY HERD BOOK. 1878. a. £8. Galloway Cattle Society, 15 New Market St., Castle Douglas, Kirkcudbrightshire DG7 1HY, Scotland. Ed. A.J. McDonald. **Document type:** trade publication.

636.2 UK ISSN 0430-9928
GALLOWAY JOURNAL. a. free. Galloway Cattle Society, 15 New Market St., Castle Douglas, Kirkcudbrightshire DG7 1HY, Scotland. Ed. A.J. McDonald. adv. circ. 2,000. **Document type:** trade publication.

636.2 US ISSN 1078-8654
GALLOWAY PRESS. 1992. q. $10 (Canada & Mexico $15; elsewhere $25) (effective Sep. 1994). (American Galloway Breeders' Association) Galloway Press, 647 Fouth St., Berthoud, CO 80513. TEL 970-532-0797. FAX 970-532-0797. Ed. Eric Grant. adv.: B&W page $100. circ. 800. (looseleaf format) **Document type:** trade publication, directory.
  Description: Contains show & sale reports, breeder profiles, reports on the Galloway industry worldwide educational columns, management and breeding practices, historical information, and a schedule of events.
  Refereed Serial

636.2 MX
GANADERO/RANCHER. (Text in English, Spanish) 1975 bi-m. Mex.$150($72) Editorial Ocampo S.A. de C.V, Zaragoza No. 11, San Juan Tepepan, 16020 Mexico DF, Mexico. TEL 52-5-5901445. (Subscr. to: Estafetas No.5 Col. Postal, 03410 Mexico DF, Mexico) Dir. Jorge Ruben Ocampo Trujillo. adv.: B&W page $835, color page $1170; adv. contact: Ana Cristina Miranda. circ. 7,000. **Document type:** consumer publication.
  Description: Covers the livestock industry in Mexico and other countries.

636.4 MX
GANADO PORCINO. 1978. s-a. Vivero de la Floresta No 116 Tlanepantla, Eno. de Mexico, Mexico. Dir. J. Filberto Ruiz Valerio. adv. circ. 20,000. **Indexed:** Ind.SST, Nutr.Abstr.

636.39 NE ISSN 0165-9812
GEITENHOUDERIJ. 1906. bi-m. fl.35. Stichting Vakblaad De Geitenhouderij, Postbus 59381, 1040 KJ Amsterdam, Netherlands. TEL 31-20-6161436. FAX 31-20-6161436. Ed.Bd. **Document type:** newsletter.
  Description: Covers the care and breeding of goats, and commercial enterprises.

636.2 US ISSN 1084-5100
GELBVIEH WORLD. 1987. m. $25 (effective 1995). American Gelbvieh Association, 10900 Dover St., Westminster, CO 80021. TEL 303-465-2333. FAX 303-46-2339. E-mail: epoldwest@aol.com. Ed. Troy Applehans. adv.: page $550; trim 8 1/2 x 11; adv. contact: Troy Applehans. charts; illus.; mkt.; maps; tr.lit. circ. 3,900. (back issues avail.) **Document type:** trade publication.
  Description: Designed to educate association members and promote the Gelbvieh breed of cattle in North America.

GENETICS, SELECTION, EVOLUTION. see *BIOLOGY — Genetics*

636.2 US
GEORGIA CATTLEMAN. 1972. m. $15 to members; non-members $20. Georgia Cattlemen's Association Box 11307, Macon, GA 31212-1307. TEL 912-474-6560. Ed. Glenn Smith. adv. circ. 6,700.

636 US
GEORGIA LIVESTOCK. w. $40 (Canada and Mexico $45; elsewhere $75). U.S. Department of Agriculture, Agricultural Marketing Service (Greely), Livestock & Seed Division, 711 O St., Greely, CO 80631. (Subscr. to: U.S.D.A. Agricultural Marketing Service, Livestock & Seed Division, Rm. 2623-S, Box 96456, Washington, DC 20090-6456. FAX 202-245-4732) Ed. Ernie Morgan. (tabloid format; back issues avail.) **Document type:** government publication.

636.952 US ISSN 0017-1506
GOBBLES. 1945. m. $25. Minnesota Turkey Growers Association, 2380 Wycliff St., Saint Paul, MN 55114-1257. TEL 612-646-4553. FAX 612-646-4554. Ed. Lara Ginsburg. R&P contact: Lara Ginsburg. adv.: B&W page $450, color page $1230; adv. contact: Lara Ginsburg. circ. 1,025. **Document type:** trade publication.
  Description: Reaches an audience involved in all aspects of the turkey industry: hatchery, grower, processor and breedman. Covers research and current industry events.

AGRICULTURE — POULTRY AND LIVESTOCK

636.3   SA   ISSN 0257-2044
GOLDEN FLEECE/GOUE VAG. (Text in Afrikaans, English) 1970. m. R.18. Wolex, 18 Grahamstown Rd., P.O. Box 2191, Port Elizabeth 6056, South Africa. TEL 041-544301. FAX 041-546760. Ed. Jan Bezuidenhout. adv. circ. 31,763. (back issues avail.) **Indexed:** Anim.Breed.Abstr., Ind.S.A.Per., INIS Atomind., Text.Tech.Dig., World Text.Abstr.
   Description: Provides sheep breeding information.

636 664.9   PL   ISSN 0367-4916
CODEN: GOMIAC
GOSPODARKA MIESNA. 1949. m. $41. Wydawnictwo Czasopism i Ksiazek Technicznych SIGMA - NOT, Ul. Ratuszowa 11, P.O. Box 1004, 00-950 Warsaw, Poland. TEL 48-22-180918. FAX 48-22-192187. TELEX 814550 SIGMA PL. (Dist. by: SIGMA NOT Ltd., Ul. Bartycka 20, 00-716 Warsaw, Poland) Ed. Krzysztof Lekawski. adv.: page $1000. circ. 1,300. **Indexed:** AgroLibrex, Chem.Abstr., Food Sci.& Tech.Abstr., Nutr.Abstr.
—CASDDS.

GRAIN AND FEED MARKET NEWS; weekly summary and statistics. see *AGRICULTURE — Feed, Flour And Grain*

636.5   BL   ISSN 0101-255X
GRANJA AVICOLA. 1944. m. Av. Getulio Vargas 1556, Caixa Postal 2890, CEP 90.000 Porto Alegre, RS, Brazil. Ed. Carlos M. Wallace. adv. circ. 36,000.

GUERNSEY BREEDERS' JOURNAL. see *AGRICULTURE — Dairying And Dairy Products*

636.2   UK
GUERNSEY BREEDERS' JOURNAL. s-a. £1 per no. English Guernsey Cattle Society, The Bury Farm, Pednor Rd., Chesham, Bucks. HP5 2LA, England. (also avail. in microform from UMI)

636.2   US   ISSN 0017-5552
GULF COAST CATTLEMAN. 1935. m. $15. Gulf Coast Publishing, 11201 Morning Ct., San Antonio, TX 78213. TEL 210-344-8300. Ed. E.C. Larkin, Jr. adv. contact: Patrick Murphy. circ. 16,100. **Document type:** trade publication.
—Linda Hall; UnCover.
   Description: Covers the production of commercial beef cattle in the Gulf Coast states.

636   CC   ISSN 1002-6746
GUOWAI XUMU KEJI/FOREIGN ANIMAL HUSBANDRY SCIENCE AND TECHNOLOGY. (Text in Chinese) 1974. bi-m. Y18 (effective 1997). Zhongguo Nongye Kexueyuan, Xumu Yanjiusuo - Chinese Academy of Agricultural Science, Institute of Animal Husbandry, Yuanminyuan Lu, Haidian-qu, Beijing 100094, People's Republic of China. TEL 86-10-6258-1177. FAX 86-10-6258-2594. Ed. Nianfan Guo. **Document type:** academic/scholarly publication.

H R I - BUYERS GUIDE. (Hotels, Restaurants, Institutions) see *FOOD AND FOOD INDUSTRIES*

636   GW   ISSN 0945-2117
HAFLINGER MAGAZIN. bi-m. DM.58.20 (foreign DM.67.20) (effective 1997). Landwirtschaftsverlag GmbH, Huelsebrockstr. 2, 48165 Muenster, Germany. TEL 49-2501-801-0. FAX 49-2501-801-204. **Document type:** trade publication.

636.2   DK   ISSN 0900-8012
HANDBOG FOR KVAEGHOLD. 1958. a. DKK 48. Landbrugets Informationskontor, Udkaersvej 15, DK-8200 Aarhus N, Denmark. TEL 45-86-10-10-11. FAX 45-86-10-90-22. Eds. Georg Nielsen, Jan Sepstrup. R&P contact: Georg Nielsen. adv. contact: Georg Nielsen. circ. 3,200. **Document type:** academic/scholarly publication.

636.085   UK   ISSN 0956-8220
HANDBOOK OF MEDICINAL FEED ADDITIVES. 1982. a. £34 (rest of Europe £37; elsewhere £42). H G M Publications, Abney House, School Ln., Baslow, Bakewell, Derbys. DE45 1RZ, England. TEL 44-1246-582470. FAX 44-1246-582425. Ed. Andrew D. Mounsey; Pub. Howard Mounsey. adv. contact: Simon P. Mounsey. circ. 3,000. **Document type:** directory.
   Description: Compendium of data sheets for medicinal products licensed for use in livestock feeds and drinking waters. Publication is used by animal feed manufacturers, veterinary surgeons and livestock farmers.

HANDBUCH DER TIERISCHEN VEREDLUNG. see *AGRICULTURE — Agricultural Economics*

HANDBUCH MEDIKAMENTE. see *PHARMACY AND PHARMACOLOGY*

636.5   US   ISSN 0082-9722
HATCHERIES AND DEALERS PARTICIPATING IN THE NATIONAL POULTRY IMPROVEMENT PLAN.* 1937. a. free. U.S. Animal and Plant Health Inspection Service, Animal Physiology and Genetics Institute, 4700 River Rd., Unit 6, Riverdale, MD 20737. TEL 301-734-5240. Ed. R.D. Schar. circ. 6,500.
   Formerly: U.S. Department of Agriculture. Animal Science Research Branch. Hatcheries and Dealers Participating in the National Improvement Plan.

636.2   UK   ISSN 0073-1943
HERD BOOK OF HEREFORD CATTLE. 1846. a. £30. Hereford Cattle Society, Hereford House, Three Offa St., Hereford HR1 2LL, England. TEL 44-1432-272057. FAX 44-1432-350608. Ed. David Prothero.
   Description: Records all pedigree Hereford cattle born in the U.K.

636.2   UK   ISSN 0073-1951
HEREFORD BREED JOURNAL. 1932. a. £20 (foreign £25). Hereford Cattle Society, Hereford House, Three Offa St., Hereford HR1 2LL, England. TEL 44-1432-272057. FAX 44-1432-350608.
   Description: Contains current information on pedigree Hereford cattle in the U.K. and worldwide.

636.2   US
HEREFORD WORLD. 1995. m. (11/yr.). $20 (foreign $40). (American Polled Hereford Association) Hereford Publications, Inc., Box 014059, Kansas City, MO 64101-0059. TEL 816-842-3757. FAX 816-842-6931. Ed. Ed Bible. adv.; bk.rev.; illus. circ. 10,000. **Document type:** trade publication.
—Linda Hall; UnCover.
   Formed by the merger of (1947-1995): Polled Hereford World (ISSN 0162-7953); (1910-1995): American Hereford Journal (ISSN 0002-872X)
   Description: Contains news, information, and acts as a marketing medium for breeders of Hereford cattle, horned and polled.

HIROSHIMA DAIGAKU SEIBUTSU SEISAN GAKUBU KIYO/HIROSHIMA UNIVERSITY. FACULTY OF APPLIED BIOLOGICAL SCIENCE. JOURNAL. see *AGRICULTURE — Dairying And Dairy Products*

636.4   US
HOG PRODUCER. 10/yr. Farm Progress Companies (Subsidiary of: A B C Publishing, Inc.), 191 S. Gary Ave., Carol Stream, IL 60188. TEL 708-690-5600. FAX 708-462-2869. Ed. JoAnn Alumbaugh. adv. contact: Charles Roth. circ. 115,287. **Document type:** trade publication.

636   US   ISSN 1056-1374
HOGS TODAY. 1985. m. (10/yr.). Farm Journal, Inc., 1500 Market St., Philadelphia, PA 19102-2148. TEL 816-586-5641. Ed. Dean Houghton. circ. 121,697. **Document type:** trade publication.
   Formerly: Hog Extra.

HORSE CONNECTION. see *SPORTS AND GAMES — Horses And Horsemanship*

636 637.1   SW   ISSN 0046-8339
HUSDJUR. 1945. m. SEK 280 (effective 1996). Svensk Husdjursskoetsel, Haallsta, S-631 84 Eskilstuna, Sweden. TEL 016-163400. FAX 016-21216. Ed. Britt-Marie Jafner. R&P contact: Britt-Marie Jafner. adv. contact: Sten Larsson. bk.rev. circ. 29,000. **Indexed:** Anim.Breed.Abstr., Dairy Sci.Abstr. **Document type:** newspaper.
   Former titles (until 1968): Svensk Husdjursskoetsel; (until 1958): Ladugaarden.

636.4   DK   ISSN 0906-0995
HYOLOGISK. 1979. m. DKK 415 (effective 1997). Dansk Agrar Forlag AS, Tagtaekkervej 8, P.O. Box 762, DK-5230 Odense, Denmark. TEL 45-66-15-60-87. FAX 45-66-15-60-37. Ed. Knud Erik Madsen. R&P contact: Nels Kenne. adv. contact: Kirsten Mette Andersen. circ. 5,600. **Document type:** consumer publication.
   Formerly (until 1990): Hyologisk Tidsskrift Svinet (ISSN 0106-1933)

636.006   UN   ISSN 1014-9015
SF83.A35
I L C A ANNUAL REPORT AND PROGRAMME HIGHLIGHTS. (Editions in English, French) a. International Livestock Centre for Africa, P.O. Box 5689, Addis Ababa, Ethiopia. TEL 251-1-61-32-15. FAX 251-1-61-18-92. TELEX 21207 ILCA ET. E-mail: ILCA@CGNET.COM. charts; illus. **Indexed:** Seed Abstr.
—BLDSC (4364.102500).
   Former title: I L C A Annual Report (ISSN 0255-0040)
   Description: Highlights ILCA's research at the head-quarters and its field research programmes in Ethiopia, Niger, Nigeria, Mali, and Kenya, as well as work on livestock economics and politics, trypanotolerance, forage agronomy, small ruminants, soils and plant nutrition, and support services.

636   UN   ISSN 0255-0024
I L C A NEWSLETTER. French edition (ISSN 0255-0032) (Editions in English and French) 1982. q. International Livestock Centre for Africa, P.O. Box 5689, Addis Ababa, Ethiopia. TEL 251-1-61-32-15. FAX 251-1-61-18-92. TELEX 21207 ILCA ET. E-mail: ILCA@CGNET.COM. **Indexed:** Food Sci.& Tech.Abstr. **Document type:** newsletter.
   Description: Describes ILCA's research and collaboration with agricultural research services, along with news of workshops and conferences, all in the context of African livestock research and development.

636   UN
I L C A PROCEEDINGS. 1980. irreg. International Livestock Centre for Africa, P.O. Box 5689, Addis Ababa, Ethiopia. TEL 251-1-61-32-15. FAX 251-1-61-18-92. TELEX 21207 ILCA ET. E-mail: ILCA@CGNET.COM. **Document type:** proceedings.

636   UN   ISSN 0257-8409
I L C A RESEARCH REPORT. (Editions in English and French) 1982. irreg., no.16, 1987. International Livestock Centre for Africa, P.O. Box 5689, Addis Ababa, Ethiopia. TEL 251-1-61-32-15. FAX 251-1-61-18-92. TELEX 21207 ILCA ET. E-mail: ILCA@CGNET.COM.
   Formerly: International Livestock Centre for Africa. Research Report.

636   SP   ISSN 1130-6009
I T E A PRODUCCION ANIMAL. (Text in Spanish; summaries in English) 1970. 3/yr. 3500 ptas. (effective 1996). Asociacion Interprofesional para el Desarrollo Agrario, Montanana 177, Apdo. 727, 50080 Zaragoza, Spain. TEL 34-76-576311. FAX 34-76-575501. Ed. C. Zaragoza. R&P contact: Leonardo Plana. adv. contact: Joaquin Uriarte. circ. 600. **Indexed:** Ind.SST. **Document type:** academic/scholarly publication.
   Supersedes in part (in 1990): Informacion Tecnica Economica Agraria (ISSN 0212-2731)
   Refereed Serial

IDAHO FARMER. see *AGRICULTURE*

636.3 677.31   US
IDAHO WOOL GROWERS BULLETIN. 1928. m. $20. Idaho Wool Growers Association, 802 W. Bannock, No. 205, Box 2596, Boise, ID 83701. TEL 208-344-2271. FAX 208-336-9447. Ed. Billie Jean Siddoway; Pub. Mike Guerry. R&P contact: Billie Jean Siddoway. adv.: page $285; trim 7 1/2 x 9 3/4; adv. contact: Bilie Jean Siddoway. charts; illus.; mkt.; stat.; tr.lit. circ. 800. (also avail. in diskette format; back issues avail.) **Document type:** bulletin, newsletter, trade publication.
●Also available on CD-ROM.

636.2   US
ILLINOIS BEEF.* 1987. bi-m. $30. Illinois Beef Association, 2060 W. Iles Ave., No.B, Springfield, IL 62704-4174. TEL 217-787-4280. FAX 217-793-3605. Ed. Maralee M. Johnson. adv. circ. 3,757.
   Description: Contains association news, information and educational articles about the beef industry.

INDIA. MINISTRY OF AGRICULTURE. BULLETIN ON FOOD STATISTICS. see *AGRICULTURE — Abstracting, Bibliographies, Statistics*

AGRICULTURE — POULTRY AND LIVESTOCK

636.084 ‖ ISSN 0970-3209
CODEN: IJNUEA
INDIAN JOURNAL OF ANIMAL NUTRITION. (Text in English) 1984. q. $70. Animal Nutrition Society of India, National Dairy Research Institute, Karnal 132 001 (Haryana), India. TEL 91-21832. TELEX 0396-204 NDRI IN. E-mail: ndri@x400.nigw.nic.in. Ed. K.K. Singhal. adv.; bk.rev.; circ. 650. (back issues avail.) **Indexed:** Dairy Sci.Abstr., Food Sci.& Tech.Abstr., Herb.Abstr., Ind.Vet., Maize Abstr., Nutr.Abstr., Pig News & Info., Poult.Abstr., Rev.Med.& Vet.Mycol., Rice Abstr., Sorghum & Millets Abstr., Soyabean Abstr., Sugar Ind.Abstr., Triticale Abstr., Trop.Oil Seeds Abstr. **Document type:** academic/scholarly publication.
—Linda Hall.
Description: Animal nutrition research in ruminants, poultry and other monogastric animals.
Refereed Serial

636 ‖ ISSN 0970-1524
INDIAN JOURNAL OF ANIMAL PRODUCTION AND MANAGEMENT. (Text in English) 1970. q. Rs.300($50) (effective 1997). Indian Society of Animal Production and Management, Dept. of Livestock Production & Management, Haryana Agricultural University, Hisar 125 004, India. (Dist. by: HPC Publisher's Distributors (Pvt.) Ltd., 4805-24, 1st Fl., Bharat Ram Rd., Darya Ganj, New Delhi 110 002, India. TEL 91-11-3254402. FAX 91-11-6863511) Ed. C.K. Aggarwal. adv.; bk.rev.; bibl.; charts; stat. circ. 450. **Indexed:** Anim.Breed.Abstr., Sugar Ind.Abstr., Vet.Bull. **Document type:** academic/scholarly publication.
—BLDSC (4410.192200).
Formerly (until 1985): Indian Journal of Animal Production.

636 ‖ ISSN 0367-6722
SF1 CODEN: IALRBR
INDIAN JOURNAL OF ANIMAL RESEARCH; half-yearly research journal of animal, food and zoological sciences. (Text in English) 1967. s-a. $40 (effective 1997). Agricultural Research Communication Centre, 1130 Sadar, Karnal 132 001, Haryana, India. TEL 91-184-255080. Ed. Dr. D.D. Sharma. **Indexed:** Anim.Breed.Abstr., Biol.Abstr., Chem.Abstr., Dairy Sci.Abstr., Food Sci.& Tech.Abstr., Helminthol.Abstr., Herb.Abstr., Ind.Vet, Nutr.Abstr., Poult.Abstr., Protozool.Abstr., Rev.Med.& Vet.Mycol., Small Anim.Abstr., Vet.Bull.
—CASDDS; CISTI; Linda Hall; UMI; UnCover.
Formerly: Indian Journal of Science and Industry. Section B. Animal Sciences (ISSN 0367-830X); **Supersedes in part:** Indian Journal of Science and Industry (ISSN 0019-5618)

636.5 ‖ ISSN 0019-5529
CODEN: IJPOAW
INDIAN JOURNAL OF POULTRY SCIENCE.* (Text in English) 1966. q. $75. Indian Poultry Science Association, c/o Prints India, 11 Darya Ganj, New Dalhi 110002, India. TEL 91-11-268645. TELEX BG 845-2671 PRI IN. Ed. P. N. Verman. adv.; bk.rev.; bibl.; charts; stat. circ. 500. **Indexed:** Anim.Breed.Abstr., Biol.Abstr., Chem.Abstr., Food Sci.& Tech.Abstr., Ind.Vet., Nutr.Abstr., Poult.Abstr., Protozool.Abstr., Rev.Med.& Vet.Mycol., Rural Recreat.Tour.Abstr., Vet.Bull., World Agri.Econ.& Rural Sociol.Abstr.
—BLDSC (4420.190000); CASDDS; Linda Hall; SWETS; UnCover.
Incorporates (1982-1984): Avian Research (ISSN 0970-1273); **Which was formerly** (1913-1981): Indian Poultry Gazette (ISSN 0019-6142)

636.5 ‖ ISSN 0970-9738
INDIAN POULTRY INDUSTRY YEARBOOK. 1974. a. $250. S.P. Gupta, Pub., A-25 Priyadarshini Vihar, Patparganj Rd., Delhi 110 092, India. TEL 91-11-224-3326. FAX 91-11-2243039. Ed. Sharad Gupta. adv.: B&W page $800; trim 20 x 15. bk.rev.; circ. 2,500 (paid). **Indexed:** Anim.Breed.Abstr., Nutr.Abstr.
Description: Sourcebook on trade, technical and economic aspects of poultry. Lists 7,000 specialists and organizations by business and geographic locations.

636.5 ‖ ISSN 0019-6150
CODEN: IPRWD9
INDIAN POULTRY REVIEW. 1969. m. $70 (effective 1995). Indian Poultry Lovers Association, 57-B Townshend Rd., Calcutta 700 025, India. TEL 4750838. Ed. G.N. Ghosh. adv.; bk.rev.; abstr.; illus. circ. 18,000. (looseleaf format) **Indexed:** Chem.Abstr., Indian.Sci.Abstr.
—BLDSC (4427.850000); CASDDS.

636.2 US
INDIANA BEEF. 1981. bi-m. free. Indiana Beef Cattle Association, 8770 Guion Rd., Ste. A, Indianapolis, IN 46268-3043. TEL 317-872-2333. FAX 812-872-2364. Ed. Debbie Shoufler. adv. contact: Debbie Shoufler. circ. 7,600. **Document type:** trade publication, directory, catalog.
Description: Includes articles on management, marketing and beef industry activities for beef cattle feeders, producers and supporters.

636.5 ISSN 0019-7467
INDUSTRIA AVICOLA. (Includes annual buyers guide) (Text in Spanish) 1952. m. $54 (dist. only in Pan-American countries) (effective Jan.). Watt Publishing Co., 122 S. Wesley, Mt. Morris, IL 61054. TEL 815-734-4171. FAX 815-734-4201. Ed. Chris Wright; Pub. Charles Olentine. adv.: B&W page $3810, color page $5105; trim 8 x 10 3/4; adv. contact: Elsie Hackbarth. charts; illus.; stat. circ. 16,000. **Document type:** trade publication.
—SWETS. **CCC.**
Description: For the commercial poultry industry in Latin America; covers all aspects of growing, processing and marketing of poultry and eggs.

636.4 US ISSN 0279-7771
INDUSTRIA PORCINA. (Includes annual buyers guide) (Text in Spanish) 1981. q. $25 (foreign $45) (effective 1997). Watt Publishing Co., 122 S. Wesley Ave., Mt. Morris, IL 61054. TEL 815-734-4171. FAX 815-734-4201. Ed. Peter Best; Pub. Clay Schreiber. R&P contact: Clay Schreiber. adv.: B&W page $2800, color page $3910; trim 8 x 10 3/4; adv. contact: Donna Carlson. circ. 8,842 (controlled). **Document type:** trade publication.
—SWETS.
Description: For distribution to swine industry leaders in Latin American countries.

636 SP
INFORMACION AGROPECUARIA. 1975. w. free. Consorcio para el Fomento de la Riqueza Ganadera, Diputacion y Caja de Ahorros, Delegacion Agricultura J. de C.L., Delegacion Territorial de Agricultura, G. y M. Santa Catalina, 15, 40003 Segovia, Spain. TEL (911) 43 14 14.

636 CU ISSN 0138-7685
INFORMACION EXPRESS. SERIE: APICULTURA. 1977. 2/yr. $5 in America and Europe; elsewhere $9; or exchange basis. Centro de Informacion y Documentacion Agropecuario, Gaveta Postal 4149, Havana 4, Cuba. (Dist. by: Ediciones Cubanas, Obispo No. 527, Aptdo. 605, Havana, Cuba) **Indexed:** Agrindex.

636 CU ISSN 0138-7383
INFORMACION EXPRESS. SERIE: AVICULTURA. 1977. 3/yr. C.$1.50($10) in N. America; S. America $14; Europe $15; others $21; or exchange basis. Centro de Informacion y Documentacion Agropecuario, Gaveta Postal 4149, Havana 4, Cuba. TEL 301672. (Dist. by: Ediciones Cubanas, Obispo No. 527, Apdo. 605, Havana, Cuba) charts; illus.; stat. **Indexed:** Agrindex, Chem.Abstr.

636 CU ISSN 0138-7537
INFORMACION EXPRESS. SERIE: GANADO EQUINO. 1977. a. $3 in N. America; S. America and Europe $4; others $5; or exchange basis. Centro de Informacion y Documentacion Agropecuario, Gaveta Postal 4149, Havana 4, Cuba. (Dist. by: Ediciones Cubanas, Obispo No. 527, Apdo. 605, Havana, Cuba) **Indexed:** Agrindex.

636 CU ISSN 0138-7588
INFORMACION EXPRESS. SERIE: GANADO PORCINO. 1977. 4/yr. $9 in N. America; S. America $11; Europe $13; others $18; or exchange basis. Centro de Informacion y Documentacion Agropecuario, Gaveta Postal 4149, Havana 4, Cuba. (Dist. by: Ediciones Cubanas, Obispo No. 527, Apdo. 605, Havana, Cuba) **Indexed:** Agrindex.

636 CU ISSN 0138-7081
INFORMACION EXPRESS. SERIE: RUMIANTES. 1977. 4/yr. $9 in N. America; S. America $11; Europe $13; others $18; or exchange basis. Centro de Informacion y Documentacion Agropecuario, Gaveta Postal 4149, Havana 4, Cuba. (Dist. by: Ediciones Cubanas, Obispo No. 527, Apdo. 605, Havana, Cuba) **Indexed:** Agrindex.

636 IT ISSN 0020-0778
INFORMATORE ZOOTECNICO. Short title: I Z. 1954. fortn. L.69000 (effective 1996). Edagricole S.p.A., Via Emilia Levante 31, 40139 Bologna, Italy. TEL 39-51-492211. FAX 39-51-493660. Ed. Angelo Gamberini. adv.: B&W page L.1850000, color page L.2800000; trim 212 x 287. bk.rev.; charts; illus.; index. circ. 53,700. **Indexed:** Nutr.Abstr.
—BLDSC (4496.900000).
Description: Provides up-to-date information on animal husbandry. Includes articles on breeding and reproduction methods.

636 US ISSN 1073-144X
INLAND FARMER. 1891. m. $19.95. Western Farmer-Stockman Magazines (Subsidiary of: Cowles Publishing Co.), Box 2160, Spokane, WA 99210-1615. TEL 509-459-5361. FAX 509-459-5102. E.W. Ramsey, Pub. Dir. adv. contact: Richard C. Brantley. bk.rev.; stat.; circ. 14,750 (paid). **Document type:** trade publication.
Formerly (until 1993): Inland Farmer - Stockman (ISSN 1062-290X); **Supersedes** (in 1992): Oregon Farmer - Stockman (ISSN 1041-2719); **Formerly** (until 1971): Oregon Farmer; Oregon Agriculturist; Rural Northwest; **Which supersedes in part:** Western Farmer and Agricultural Age.

636.2 BL
INSEMINACAO ARTIFICIAL. irreg. Ministerio da Agricultura, Departamento Nacional de Producao Animal, Divisao de Fisiopatologia da Inseminacao Artificial, Brasilia, Brazil.

636 RW
INSTITUT DES SCIENCES AGRONOMIQUES DU RWANDA. DEPARTEMENT DES PRODUCTIONS ANIMALES. COMPTE RENDU DES TRAVAUX. a. Institut des Sciences Agronomiques, Departement des Productions Animales, B.P. 138, Butare, Rwanda.

INSTITUT TECHNIQUE DE L'AVICULTURE. TENDANCES DES MARCHES. see *AGRICULTURE — Agricultural Economics*

636.2 636.5 US
INTERNATIONAL CONFERENCE ON LIVESTOCK IN THE TROPICS. (Text in English, Spanish) 1967. a. $10. University of Florida, Animal Science Department, 125 Tropical Animal Science, 459 Shealy Dr., Box 110910, Gainesville, FL 32611-0910. TEL 904-392-2186. FAX 904-3922-7652. TELEX 568757. (Co-sponsors: Institute of Food and Agricultural Sciences, Florida Cooperative Extension Service) Eds. J.H. Conrad, V. Carbia. circ. 500. **Document type:** proceedings.
Former titles: International Conference on Livestock and Poultry in the Tropics (Proceedings); Livestock and Poultry in Latin America. Annual Conference (ISSN 0085-2805)

636 UK ISSN 0959-9363
INTERNATIONAL HATCHERY PRACTICE. 1985. 8/yr. £55. Positive Action Publications Ltd., P.O. Box 4, Driffield, N. Humberside YO25 9DJ, England. TEL 44-1377-241724. FAX 44-1377-241910. Ed. Nigel Horrox; Pub. Nigel Horrox. adv. contact: Geoff Hall. bk.rev. circ. 13,500. **Indexed:** Rev.Med.& Vet.Mycol. **Document type:** trade publication.
—BLDSC (4540.702000).
Description: Technical publication for poultry breeders and hatcheries worldwide.

AGRICULTURE — POULTRY AND LIVESTOCK

636 179 660   II   ISSN 0970-2857
CODEN: IASCEK
INTERNATIONAL JOURNAL OF ANIMAL SCIENCES. (Text in English) 1986. s-a. $100. Nitasha Publications, 921, Sector 14, Sonepat, 131001 Haryana, India. TEL 91-1662-32703. Ed. Sadhana Jindai. adv.; bk.rev.; bibl.; charts; illus. **Indexed:** Biol.Abstr., Chem.Abstr., Dairy Sci.Abstr., Ind.Vet., Nutr.Abstr. **Document type:** academic/scholarly publication.
—BLDSC (4542.082000); SWETS. CCC.
Formerly: Farm Animals.
Description: Publishes research and review articles in the field of animal health, animal biology, animal production, dairy science and biotechnology.
Refereed Serial

636   UN   ISSN 0259-8183
HD9433.A1
INTERNATIONAL MARKETS FOR MEAT. French edition: Marches Internationaux de la Viande (ISSN 0259-8191); Spanish edition: Mercados Internacionales de la Carne (ISSN 0259-8205) 1981. a. 25 SFr. General Agreement on Tariffs and Trade, Centre William Rappard, 154 rue de Lausanne, CH-1211 Geneva 21, Switzerland. TEL 022-739-5208. FAX 022-739-5458. (also avail. in microfiche from CIS) **Indexed:** IIS. **Document type:** trade publication.
Former titles (until 1985): Arrangement Regarding Bovine Meat (ISSN 1014-031X); World Market for Bovine Meat (ISSN 1011-4645)
Description: Reports on main trends in international trade of bovine meat.

636   SP   ISSN 0074-6959
INTERNATIONAL MEETING OF ANIMAL NUTRITION EXPERTS. PROCEEDINGS. (Text in English, French, Italian and Spanish) 1958. irreg. $8. Ritena, P.O.B. 466, 08080 Barcelona, Spain. FAX 34-3-2370771. Ed. J. Amich-Gali. bk.rev.; cum.index every 6 yrs. circ. 1,200. **Document type:** proceedings.

636   US
INTERNATIONAL NUBIAN BREEDERS ASSOCIATION NEWSLETTER. q. $10 (foreign $14) (effective 1996). International Nubian Breeder Association, 773 Cherokee Rd., Inman, KS 67546-8931. Ed. Sue Laswell. circ. 400. (tabloid format) **Document type:** newsletter.
Description: Anyone interested in the Nubian breed of dairy goats.

636.4   UK   ISSN 0963-5866
INTERNATIONAL PIG TOPICS. 1985. 8/yr. £55. Positive Action Publications Ltd., P.O. Box 4, Driffield, N. Humberside YO25 9DJ, England. TEL 44-1377-241724. FAX 44-1377-241910. Ed. Nigel Horrox; Pub. Nigel Horrox. adv. contact: Colin Foster. circ. 18,500. **Indexed:** Food Sci.& Tech.Abstr. **Document type:** trade publication.
—BLDSC (4544.935200).
Description: Technical publication for progressive pig producers around the world.

636.5   US
INTERNATIONAL POULTRY EXPOSITION GUIDE. 1984. a. $5. Watt Publishing Co., Sandstone Bldg., 122 S. Wesley Ave., St. Morris, IL 61054. TEL 815-734-4171. FAX 815-734-4201. Ed. Lisa Thornton; Pub. Charles Olentine. adv.: B&W page $3255, color page $4380; trim 8 x 10 3/4; adv. contact: Anita Martin. circ. 24,000. (back issues avail.) **Document type:** trade publication.
—CCC.
Formerly: International Poultry Trade Show Guide (ISSN 1044-551X)
Description: Provides a preview of the Southeastern International Poultry Trade Show.

636   UK
INTERNATIONAL POULTRY PRODUCTION. 6/yr. £55. Positive Action Publications Ltd., P.O. Box 4, Driffield, N. Humberside YO25 9DJ, England. TEL 44-1377-241724. FAX 44-1377-241910. Ed. Nigel Horrox; Pub. Nigel Horrox. R&P contact: Nigel Horrox. adv. contact: Geoff Hall. bk.rev. circ. 18,000. **Document type:** trade publication.
Description: Technical publication for poultry growers, egg producers and processors worldwide.

636   SP   ISSN 0213-5035
CODEN: IAPAEX
INVESTIGACION AGRARIA. PRODUCCION Y SANIDAD ANIMALES. (Text in Spanish; summaries in English, Spanish) 1952. 3/yr. 6000 ptas. (foreign 9800 ptas.) (effective 1996). Ministerio de Agricultura Pesca y Alimentacion, Instituto Nacional de Investigacion y Tecnologia Agraria y Alimentaria, Centro de Publicaciones, Paseo de la Infanta Isabel 1, 28071 Madrid, Spain. TEL 34-1-3475551. FAX 34-1-3475722. (I.N.I.T.A.A. addr.: Jose Abascal 56, 28003 Madrid, Spain) Ed. Juan Jose Jurado Garcia. R&P contact: Juan Carlos Palacios Lopez. charts. circ. 1,500. **Indexed:** Anim.Breed.Abstr., Biol.Abstr., Chem.Abstr., Dairy Sci.Abstr., Field Crop Abstr., Food Sci.& Tech.Abstr., Herb.Abstr., Ind.SST, Ind.Vet., Maize.Abstr., Nutr.Abstr. **Document type:** academic/scholarly publication.
—BLDSC (4557.716000); CASDDS.
Formerly (until 1985): Spain. Instituto Nacional de Investigaciones Agrarias. Anales. Series: Ganaderia (ISSN 0211-4674); Which was formed by the 1981 merger of: Spain. Instituto Nacional de Investigaciones Agrarias. Anales. Serie: Higiene y Sanidad Animal (ISSN 0210-2498); Spain. Instituto Nacional de Investigaciones Agrarias. Anales. Serie: Produccion Animal (ISSN 0376-1843); Which superseded in part (in 1971): Spain. Instituto Nacional de Investigaciones Agronomicas. Anales (ISSN 0020-4129)

636   US   ISSN 0279-4608
IOWA CATTLEMAN. 1972. 10/yr. $40 membership. Iowa Cattlemen's Association, Box 1490, Ames, IA 50014-1490. TEL 515-233-3270. FAX 515-233-5531. Ed. Carol Balvanz; Pub. Carol Balvanz. R&P contact: Carol Balvanz. TEL 515-296-2266. adv. contact: Ward McCleary. circ. 14,000. **Document type:** trade publication.
Description: Covers developments in beef production with information and services to members of the Iowa Cattlemen's Association.

636.4   US
IOWA PORK PRODUCER. 1970. m. membership. Iowa Pork Producers Association, Box 71009, Clive, IA 50325-0009. TEL 515-225-7675; 800-372-7675. FAX 515-225-0563. Ed. Peter H. Theodore; Pub. Peter H. Theodore. adv.: B&W page $1400, color page $2150; trim 8 x 10 3/4; adv. contact: Mary Lea Hampton. bk.rev. circ. 25,000. **Document type:** newsletter, trade publication, proceedings.
Description: Presents information on swine production, marketing, and animal health, as well as state and national legislative issues of importance to the swine industry in Iowa.

636.4 664.9   US   ISSN 1043-9676
IOWA PORK TODAY. 1987. 10/yr. $16. Gazette Company, Box 5279, Cedar Rapids, IA 52406. TEL 319-398-8461. E-mail: IFT@FYIowa.infi.net. Ed. Lori Leonard. adv. contact: Terry Reilly. circ. 31,000. **Document type:** trade publication.
Description: Covers the pork industry in Iowa. Contains production, and animal and herd health information.

IRELAND. CENTRAL STATISTICS OFFICE. AGRICULTURE - JUNE SURVEY - FINAL ESTIMATES. see AGRICULTURE — Abstracting, Bibliographies, Statistics

636   IE   ISSN 0791-3133
IRELAND. CENTRAL STATISTICS OFFICE. DECEMBER LIVESTOCK SURVEY. a. I£2. Central Statistics Office, Skehard Rd., Cork, Ireland. TEL 353-21-359000. FAX 353-21-359090. E-mail: information@cso.ie; URL: http://www.cso.ie. (processed) **Document type:** government publication.
Former titles: Ireland Central Statistics Office. Livestock Enumeration; (until 1984): Ireland Central Statistics Office. Livestock Numbers (ISSN 0075-059X)

636   JA   ISSN 0289-4238
JAPAN. IBARAKI NATIONAL INSTITUTE OF ANIMAL INDUSTRY. ANNUAL REPORT/NIPPON IBARAKI CHIKUSAN SHIKENJO NENPO. (Text in Japanese) a. Ibaraki National Institute of Animal Industry - Ibaraki Chikusan Shikenjo, Tsukuba Norindanchi, P.O. Box 5, Ibaraki 305, Japan. **Indexed:** Agri.Eng.Abstr. **Document type:** government publication.
Formerly: Japan. Chiba National Institute of Animal Industry. Annual Report.

636   JA   ISSN 0077-488X
CODEN: CSKKAQ
JAPAN. IBARAKI NATIONAL INSTITUTE OF ANIMAL INDUSTRY. BULLETIN/NIPPON IBARAKI CHIKUSAN SHIKENJO. CHIKUSAN SHIKENJO KENKYU HOKOKU. (Text in Japanese; summaries in English) 1963. irreg. Ibaraki National Institute of Animal Industry - Ibaraki Chikusan Shikenjo, Tsukuba Norindanchi, P.O. Box 5, Ibaraki 305, Japan. Ed.Bd. adv.; charts; illus. circ. 1,100. **Indexed:** Anim.Breed.Abstr., Bibl.Agri., Biol.Abstr., Chem.Abstr., Dairy Sci.Abstr., Field Crop Abstr., Food Sci.& Tech.Abstr., Herb.Abstr., Ind.Vet., Nutr.Abstr., Pig News & Info., Plant Breed.Abstr. **Document type:** bulletin, government publication.
—BLDSC (2640.050000); CASDDS.
Formerly: Japan. Chiba National Institute of Animal Industry. Bulletin.
Description: Presents summaries of articles published on animal industry research.

636.2   UK   ISSN 0021-5929
THE JERSEY. no.107, 1971. 2/yr. £10 (effective 1993). Jersey Cattle Society of the United Kingdom, Scotsbridge House, Scots Hill, Rickmannsworth, Herts WD3 3BB, England. TEL 44-1923-897063. FAX 44-1923-897691. Ed. C. Barnes. adv.; circ. 1,000 (controlled). (back issues avail.) **Indexed:** Dairy Sci.Abstr. **Document type:** trade publication.
Formerly: Jersey Cow.
Description: Keeps those interested up to date with all matters pertaining to Jersey cattle.

JERSEY AT HOME. see AGRICULTURE — Dairying And Dairy Products

636   UK
JERSEY HERD BOOK AND MEMBERS DIRECTORY. 1958. a. £25. Jersey Cattle Society of the United Kingdom, Scotsbridge House, Scots Hill, Rickmannsworth, Herts WD3 3BB, England. TEL 44-1923-897063. FAX 44-1923-897691. (microfiche) **Document type:** directory.
Former titles: Combined Jersey Herd Book, Directory and Elite Register of the U.K; Jersey Herd Book and Directory of the U.K. (ISSN 0075-3629); Jersey Herd Book of the U.K.

636.2   US   ISSN 0021-5953
JERSEY JOURNAL. 1953. m. $20 (foreign $30) (effective 1997). American Jersey Cattle Association, 6486 E. Main St., Reynoldsburg, OH 43068-2362. TEL 614-861-3636. FAX 614-861-8040. E-mail: usjersey@iwaynet.net. Ed. Sara L. Gaetz. R&P contact: Sara L. Gaetz. adv. contact: Sara L. Gaetz. bk.rev.; illus. circ. 3,983. **Document type:** trade publication.
—Linda Hall; UnCover.
Description: Contains news and advertising of interest to Jersey cattle owners. Reflects policies and positions of the AJCA Board of Directors.

636   PL   ISSN 1230-1388
CODEN: JFESEA
JOURNAL OF ANIMAL AND FEED SCIENCES. (Text in English; summaries in English, Polish) 1903; N.S. 1992. q. 30 Zl. (foreign $50). Polska Akademia Nauk, Instytut Fizjologii i Zywienia Zwierzat im. Jana Kielanowskiego - Polish Academy of Science, Kielanowski Institute of Animal Physiology and Nutrition, 00-110 Jablonna, Poland, Poland. TEL 48-22-7824175. FAX 48-22-7742038. E-mail: infiz@atos.warman.com.pl. (Dist. by: ORWN PAN, Palac Kultury i Nauki, 00-901 Warsaw, Poland) Ed. Jan Kowalczyk. bibl.; charts. circ. 300. **Indexed:** AgroLibrex, Anim.Breed.Abstr., Biol.Abstr., Chem.Abstr., Dairy Sci.Abstr., Field Crop Abstr., Food Sci.& Tech.Abstr., Herb.Abstr., Ind.Vet., Nutr.Abstr., Pig News & Info., Poult.Abstr., Soyabean Abstr., Triticale Abstr., Vet.Bull., 048547922tr. **Document type:** academic/scholarly publication, monographic series.
—BLDSC (4935.375000); CASDDS.
Formerly (until 1992): Roczniki Nauk Rolniczych. Seria B - Zootechniczna (ISSN 0080-3669)
Description: Publishes original papers on basic and applied research in the field of animal breeding and genetics, physiology of nutrition, animal feeding, feed technology and food preservation.
Refereed Serial

AGRICULTURE — POULTRY AND LIVESTOCK

636 GW ISSN 0931-2668
SF1 CODEN: JABAE8
JOURNAL OF ANIMAL BREEDING AND GENETICS/ZEITSCHRIFT FUER TIERZUECHTUNG UND ZUECHTUNGSBIOLOGIE. (Text in English, French or German; summaries in English, French, German, Spanish) 1924. 6/yr. DM.1120 in Europe; rest of world DM.1128 (effective 1998). Blackwell Wissenschaft, Kurfuerstendamm 57, 10707 Berlin, Germany. TEL 49-30-32790679. FAX 49-30-32790610. E-mail: aboverwalt@blackwis.de; URL: http://www.blackwis.com. Ed. F. Pirchner. adv.: B&W page DM.560; trim 192 x 122. bk.rev.; illus.; stat.; index. circ. 400. (reprint service avail. from ISI; back issues avail.) **Indexed:** Anim.Breed.Abstr., ASCA, Biol.Abstr., Chem.Abstr., Curr.Adv.Ecol.Sci., Curr.Cont., Dairy Sci.Abstr., Food Sci.& Tech.Abstr., Ind.Vet., Nutr.Abstr., Pig News & Info., Poult.Abstr., Small Anim.Abstr., Sport Fish.Abstr., Vet.Bull., Wild.Rev., World Agri.Econ.& Rural Sociol.Abstr., Zoo.Rec. **Document type:** academic/scholarly publication.
—BLDSC (4935.450000); CASDDS; Genuine Article; SWETS; UnCover. **CCC.**
Formerly (until 1987): Zeitschrift fuer Tierzuechtung und Zuechtungsbiologie (ISSN 0044-3581)
Description: Reports on the progress of research in animal production, quantitative genetics, biology, and evolution of domestic animals.

636 US ISSN 0021-8812
SF1 CODEN: JANSAG
JOURNAL OF ANIMAL SCIENCE. 1942. m. (1 vol./yr.). $135 to individuals in N. America (elsewhere $160); institutions in N. America $190 (elsewhere $215); online version to individuals $90. American Society of Animal Science, 1111 N. Dunlap Ave., Savoy, IL 61874. TEL 217-356-3182. FAX 217-398-4119. E-mail: asas@assachq.org; URL: http://www.asas.org/jas.html. Ed. Gregory Lewis. R&P contact: 540-231-9482. adv. contact: John W. Edwards. bibl.; charts; illus.; stat.; index, cum.index 1942-1996. circ. 7,000. (also avail. in microform from UMI,PMC; reprint service avail. from KTO) **Indexed:** Anim.Breed.Abstr., ASCA, Biol.Abstr., Biol.& Agr.Ind., Biotech.Abstr., Chem.Abstr., Curr.Adv.Biochem., Curr.Adv.Genetics & Molec.Biol., Curr.Cont., Curr.Pack.Abstr., Dairy Sci.Abstr., Environ.Per.Bibl., Excerp.Med., Farm & Garden Ind., Field Crop Abstr., Food Sci.& Tech.Abstr., Helminthol.Abstr., Herb.Abstr., Ind.Med., Ind.Sci.Rev., Ind.Vet., INIS Atomind., Maize Abstr., NRN, Nutr.Abstr., Pig News & Info., Plant Grow.Reg.Abstr., Poult.Abstr., Protozool.Abstr., Rev.Med.& Vet.Mycol., Rice Abstr., Rural Recreat.Tour.Abstr., Sci.Cit.Ind., Soils & Fert., Sorghum & Millets Abstr., Soyabean Abstr., Sport Fish.Abstr., SSCI, Sugar Ind.Abstr., Triticale Abstr., Trop.Oil Seeds Abstr., Vet.Bull., Wild.Rev., World Agri.Econ.& Rural Sociol.Abstr., Zoo.Rec. **Document type:** academic/scholarly publication.
●Also available online.
—BLDSC (4937.000000); CASDDS; Genuine Article; KR SourceOne; Linda Hall; SWETS; UMI; UnCover.
Refereed Serial

636 US
JOURNAL OF ANIMAL SCIENCE. SUPPLEMENT. BIENNIAL SYMPOSIUM ON ANIMAL REPRODUCTION. biennial. $10. American Society of Animal Science, 1111 N. Dunlap Ave., Savoy, IL 61874. TEL 217-356-3192. FAX 217-398-4119. E-mail: asas@assachq.org. **Indexed:** Ind.Med. **Document type:** monographic series.
Formerly: Journal of Animal Science. Supplement (ISSN 0075-4129)
Refereed Serial

JOURNAL OF APPLIED ANIMAL WELFARE SCIENCE. see ANIMAL WELFARE

636 US
JUMPING POUCH NEWSLETTER. 6/yr. $12. RR 9, Box 47, Bloomfield, IA 52537. TEL 515-772-3374. (back issues avail.)
Description: Provides current news and information on wallabies, kangaroos, and wallaroos.

636.2 DK ISSN 0109-3800
KALVEPRODUCENTEN. 1983. bi-m. membership. Landsforeningen af Danske Slagtekalveproducenter, c/o Eilif Bigum, Binderupvej 17, Gislum, DK-9600 Aars, Denmark. adv.; illus. circ. 200.

KANSAS CITY BOARD OF TRADE REVIEW. see AGRICULTURE — Feed, Flour And Grain

636.2 US
KANSAS FARMER. 1864. 15/yr. $19.95. Farm Progress Companies (Subsidiary of: A B C Publishing Companies), 191 S. Gary Ave., Carol Stream, IL 60188. TEL 630-690-5600. FAX 630-462-2869. (Edit. addr.: 2714 N.W. Topeka Blvd., Topeka, KS 66617. TEL 913-232-3276. FAX 913-232-3124) Ed. Hank Ernst. adv.: B&W page $3400, color page $3910; trim 7 X 10. bk.rev.; charts; illus.; stat.; tr.lit.; circ. 39,269 (paid).
—Linda Hall.
Former titles: Kansas Farmer-Stockman (ISSN 0451-4041); Kansas Farmer (ISSN 0022-8583)

636 US ISSN 0022-8826
KANSAS STOCKMAN. 1916. 10/yr. $100 (effective 1997). Kansas Livestock Association, 6031 SW 37th St., Topeka, KS 66614-5128. TEL 913-273-5115. Ed. Todd Domer. adv.; bk.rev.; charts; illus.; stat. circ. 7,500. **Document type:** trade publication.

636 SX
KARAKUL. 1958. a. Board of Karakul Breeders Society of South Africa, Head Office, P.O. Box 128, Windhoek 9100, Namibia. Ed. B. Von Kunow. adv. circ. 2,000.

636.3 UK
KERRY HILL FLOCK BOOK SOCIETY. FLOCK BOOK. a. Kerry Hill Flock Book Society, Cilmaenowydd, Llandegley, Llandrindod Wells, Powys LD1 5UH, Wales. TEL 059-787495.

636 US ISSN 0889-2857
KETCH PEN. 1983. m. membership. Washington Cattlemen's Association, 1720 Canyon Rd., Box 96, Ellensburg, WA 98926. TEL 509-925-9871. FAX 509-925-3004. adv. circ. 1,500.

636.3 SZ
KLEINVIEHZUECHTER. 1955. bi-w. 37 SFr. (foreign 57 SFr.). Schweizerische Zentralstelle fuer Kleinviehzucht, Belpstr. 16, CH-3000 Bern 14, Switzerland. TEL 031-3886111. FAX 031-3819044. Ed. Josef Schmidlin. adv.; bk.rev. circ. 6,687. **Indexed:** Dairy Sci.Abstr., Ind.Vet. **Document type:** bulletin.

KOETTBRANSCHEN. see FOOD AND FOOD INDUSTRIES

636 637 633.2 KO ISSN 0367-5807
SF1 CODEN: HGCHAG
KOREAN JOURNAL OF ANIMAL SCIENCES. (Text mainly in Korean; summaries in English) 1958. bi-m. $40 (effective Jan. 1991). Korean Society of Animal Sciences, c/o Dept. of Animal Science and Technology, College of Agriculture and Life Sciences, Seoul National University, Suwon 441-744, S. Korea. TEL 0331-292-5616. FAX 0331-292-5616. Ed. S.W. Lee. adv.; bk.rev. circ. 1,500. **Indexed:** Anim.Breed.Abstr., Biol.Abstr., Chem.Abstr., Dairy Sci.Abstr., Field Crop Abstr., Food Sci.& Tech.Abstr., Herb.Abstr., Ind.Vet., Maize Abstr., Packag.Sci.Tech., Pig News & Info., Poult.Abstr., Soils & Fert., Sorghum & Millets Abstr., Soyabean Abstr., Sugar Ind.Abstr., Triticale Abstr., Vet.Bull., World Agri.Econ.& Rural Sociol.Abstr. **Document type:** academic/scholarly publication.
—BLDSC (5113.510000); CASDDS; UMI. **CCC.**

636 631 634.9 635 KO ISSN 0250-3360
CODEN: KJBRDU
KOREAN JOURNAL OF BREEDING. (Text in Korean or English; abstracts in English) 1969. 4/yr. 30000 Won($40) Korean Breeding Society, College of Agriculture and Life Sciences, Seoul National University, Suwon 441-744, S. Korea. TEL 0331-290-6641. FAX 0331-292-4560. E-mail: heejkoh@alliant.snu.ac.kr. Ed. Hae-Chun Choi. adv. contact: Seok-Dong Kim. circ. 700. (back issues avail.) **Indexed:** Biol.Abstr., INIS Atomind., Plant Breed.Abstr. **Document type:** academic/scholarly publication.
—BLDSC (5113.523000); CASDDS.
Refereed Serial

636 RU ISSN 0023-4885
KROLIKOVODSTVO I ZVEROVODSTVO. 1910. bi-m. $44 (effective 1998). Izdatel'stvo Kolos, Sadovaya-Spasskaya, 18, 107807 Moscow, Russia. TEL 7-095-2072110. FAX 7-095-2072870. Ed. A.T. Erin. bk.rev.; index. circ. 38,400. **Indexed:** Anim.Breed.Abstr., Biol.Abstr., Chem.Abstr., Ind.Vet., Nutr.Abstr., Protozool.Abstr., Rev.Med.& Vet.Mycol., Vet.Bull.

636.2 CN
KYLOE CRY. a. membership. Canadian Highland Cattle Society, 307 Spicer, Knowlton, PQ J0E 1V0, Canada. TEL 514-243-1150. FAX 514-243-5543. URL: http://www.okstate.edu/osu-ag/ansci.html. Ed. Margaret Badger; Pub. Margaret Badger. R&P contact: Margaret Badger. circ. 500. **Document type:** trade publication.

636 SP
LABRANZA; publicacion de formacion e informacion para el agricultor y ganadero. 1982. bi-m. 1200 ptas. Pollo Martin, 34 1oC, 37005 Salamanca, Spain. TEL 923-25-64-80. Ed. Jorge Avenas Rodriguez. circ. 25,000.

636 SW ISSN 0023-7159
LADUGAARDSFOERMANNEN. 1929. m. (11/yr.). SEK 50. Ladugaardsfoermannens Riksfoerfund, PL 2409, 311 00 Falkenberg, Sweden. Ed. Leif Lindwall.

LANDBAUFORSCHUNG VOELKENRODE; wissenschaftliche Mitteilungen der Bundesforschungsanstalt fuer Landwirtschaft Braunschweig-Voelkenrode. see AGRICULTURE — Crop Production And Soil

636.5 DK ISSN 0105-9882
LANDSUDVALGET FOR FJERKRAE. MEDDELELSE.* irreg. (Landsudvalget for Fjerkrae) Danske Fjerkraeraad Landbrugets, Raadgivningscenter, Velkaersvej 15, 8200 Aarhus, Denmark. **Document type:** trade publication.

636 US
LEAN TRIMMINGS. (Former name of issuing body: Western States Meat Association) 1980. w. membership. National Meat Association, 1970 Broadway, Ste. 825, Oakland, CA 94612. TEL 510-763-1533. FAX 510-763-6186. E-mail: nma@hooked.net; URL: http://www.hooked.net/users/nma/. Ed. Erica Smith. adv.; circ. 1,400 (controlled). (looseleaf format; back issues avail.) **Document type:** newsletter.
Formerly: W S M A Bulletin.
Description: Covers regulatory stipulations, news, technology and other developments in the meat industry.

LEBENSMITTEL- UND BIOTECHNOLOGIE. see FOOD AND FOOD INDUSTRIES

636.3 UK
LEICESTER LONGWOOL SHEEPBREEDERS' ASSOCIATION. FLOCK BOOK. biennial. £5 associate; £15 member. Leicester Longwool Sheepbreeders' Association, Street House Farm, Loftus, Saltburn, Cleveland TS13 4UX, England. TEL 0287-640541.

338.1 636.088 FI ISSN 1236-1895
LIHATALOUS. (Text in Finnish; summaries in English, German) 1948. 8/yr. FIM 200. Finnish Meat Research Institute, P.O. Box 56, FIN-13101 Hameenlinna, Finland. TEL 358-17-6821551. FAX 358-17-6533051. Ed. Veikko Siltala. adv. contact: Christian Soederstroem. circ. 45,000. **Document type:** consumer publication, bulletin.
Former titles (until 1993): Lihantuottaja (ISSN 0355-046X); (until 1971): Osuusteurastamo (ISSN 0472-2116)

636.2 CN ISSN 0381-5552
LIMOUSIN LEADER. m. Can.$25. Bollum Marketing Inc., 1935 32nd Ave., N.E., Ste. 253, Calgary, AB T2E 7C8, Canada. TEL 403-291-6770. Ed. Randy Bollum; Pub. Randy Bollum. R&P contact: Randy Bollum. adv. contact: Randy Bollum. **Document type:** trade publication.
Description: Edited for breeders of Limousin cattle. Works with farmers and ranchers to take the Limousin story to purebred breeders and commercial cattlemen.

AGRICULTURE — POULTRY AND LIVESTOCK

636.2 US ISSN 8750-2127
LIMOUSIN WORLD. 1983. m. $22 (effective 1997). Limousin World, Inc., Box 850870, Yukon, OK 73085. FAX 405-350-0054. Ed. Kyle Haleysch; Pub. Dan Wedman. adv. contact: Lisa Garza. circ. 10,000. (reprint service avail.)
Description: Features news and educational material of interest and use to Limousin cattle breeders.

636.2 DK ISSN 0900-050X
LIMOUSINE NYT. 1979. 4/yr. membership. Dansk Limousine Forening, Udkaersvej 15, 8200 Aarhus N, Denmark. TEL 86-106088. FAX 86-10-94-24. Ed. Jacob Dan Nielsen. adv. circ. 1,600.

636.3 UK
LINCOLN LONGWOOL SHEEP BREEDERS' ASSOCIATION. ANNUAL FLOCK BOOK. a. £28. Lincoln Longwool Sheep Breeders' Association, Lincolnshire Showground, Grange-de-Lings, Lincoln LN2 2NA, England. TEL 44-1522-511395. circ. 120.
Document type: bulletin.

636 UK
LINCOLN RED CATTLE SOCIETY ANNUAL HERD BOOK. 1896. a. £40. Lincoln Red Cattle Society, Lincolnshire Showground, Grange-de-Lings, Lincoln LN2 2NA, England. TEL 44-1522-511395. Ed. J.P. Skehel. adv. circ. 120. **Document type:** bulletin.
Description: Examines Lincoln Red Cattle registration, rules, and regulations as they pertain to the Pedigree Cattle Society.

636.2 US
LINE RIDER. 1965. bi-m. membership. Idaho Cattle Association, Box 15397, Boise, ID 83715. TEL 208-343-1615. FAX 208-344-6695. Ed. Sharon Olsen. adv. contact: David Britton. illus.
Formerly: Idaho Cattleman.

636 FR ISSN 0981-4183
LINEAIRES. 11/yr. 270 F. (foreign 370 F.). Editions du Boisbaudry, B.P. 6359, 35063 Rennes Cedex, France. TEL 99-32-21-21. FAX 99-32-14-17. TELEX 730619 F.

636 II ISSN 0970-3004
LIVESTOCK ADVISER; an English monthly dedicated to improve the animal wealth of India. (Text in English) 1976. m. Rs.300 (foreign $50 or £30)(effective 1996). 97 St. John's Church Rd., Bangalore 560 005, India. TEL 91-80-561627. Ed. R.S. Rafiuddin. adv.; bk.rev. circ. 3,400. (back issues avail.) **Indexed:** Anim.Breed.Abstr., Dairy Sci.Abstr., Food Sci.& Tech.Abstr., Ind.Vet., Pig News & Info., Poult.Abstr., Protozool.Abstr., Rev.Med.& Vet.Mycol., Small Anim.Abstr., Trop.Oil Seeds Abstr., Vet.Bull., World Agri.Econ.& Rural Sociol.Abstr. **Document type:** trade publication.
—BLDSC (5281.340000).
Description: Covers scientific, as well as practical aspects of raising a variety of livestock in India.

636 UK ISSN 1356-9139
LIVESTOCK AND MEAT. 1986. m. £245 (rest of Europe £265; elsewhere £285) (effective 1997). Agra Europe (London) Ltd., 25 Frant Rd., Tunbridge Wells, Kent TN2 5JT, England. TEL 44-1892-533813. FAX 44-1892-544895. TELEX 95114 AGRATW G. E-mail: 100637.3460@compuserve.com. **Document type:** trade publication.
Formerly: Agrafile: Livestock and Meat (ISSN 0950-4958)
Description: Contains EC and national policy, trade, and markets reports.

338.1 636 US ISSN 1076-2183
HD9411
LIVESTOCK, DAIRY AND POULTRY SITUATION & OUTLOOK. 1937. 34/yr. $66. U.S. Department of Agriculture, Economic Research Service, c/o Debbie Haugan, Rm. 110, 1301 New York Ave., N.W., Washington, DC 20005-4788. TEL 202-219-4060. (Dist. by: ERS-NASS, 341 Victory Dr., Herndon, VA 22070. TEL 800-999-6779) Ed. Leland Southard. charts; mkt.; stat.; index. circ. 9,000. (processed; also avail. in microfiche from CIS; reprint service avail. from CIS) **Indexed:** Amer.Stat.Ind. (1974-).
Document type: government publication.
●Also available online. Vendor(s): Information Access Co., Knight-Ridder Information, Inc.
Formed by the 1994 merger of: Livestock and Poultry Update (ISSN 1048-1605) & Situation and Outlook Report. Dairy (ISSN 1050-9151) & Situation and Outlook Report. Livestock and Poultry (ISSN 1054-0849); Former titles of Situation and Outlook Report. Dairy (until 1986): Outlook and Situation Report. Dairy (ISSN 0889-9835); (until 1984): Dairy Outlook and Situation (0734-9505); (until 1981): Dairy Situation (ISSN 0011-5703); Former titles of Situation and Outlook Report. Livestock & Poultry (until 1986): Livestock and Poultry Outlook and Situation; Livestock and Poultry Situation; Livestock and Meat Outlook and Situation (ISSN 0278-923X); Livestock and Meat Situation (ISSN 0024-516X); Poultry and Egg Outlook and Situation (ISSN 0277-0814); Poultry and Egg Situation (ISSN 0032-5708).

636 US
LIVESTOCK: LATIN AMERICAN INDUSTRIAL REPORT. (Avail. for each of 22 Latin American countries) 1985. a. $435 per country report. Aquino Productions, Box 125, Rochester, VT 05767. Ed. Andres C. Aquino.

636 658.8 US ISSN 0024-5208
LIVESTOCK MARKET DIGEST. 1953. w. $20. Livestock Market Digest, Inc, Box 7458, Albuquerque, NM 87194. Ed. Emil Reutzel, Jr. adv.; charts; mkt. circ. 45,000. (tabloid format) **Indexed:** BPIA.

636 US
LIVESTOCK MARKET NEWS. w. $75. (Department of Food & Agriculture) Federal-State Market News Service (Sacramento), 1220 N. St., Rm. A-247, Sacramento, CA 94271. TEL 916-654-0298. FAX 916-654-1046. (looseleaf format; back issues avail.) **Document type:** government publication.
Description: Contains California livestock auction prices, and direct livestock sale prices.

636 677.3 US
LIVESTOCK, MEAT AND WOOL MARKET NEWS. w. $70 (Canada and Mexico $75; elsewhere $105). U.S. Department of Agriculture, Agricultural Marketing Service (Washington), Livestock & Seed Division, South Bldg., Rm. 2623, Box 96456, Washington, DC 20090-6456. TEL 202-720-6231. FAX 202-690-3732. (Subscr. to: U.S.D.A. Agricultural Marketing Service, Livestock & Seed Division, Rm. 2623-S, Box 96456, Washington, DC 20090-6456. FAX 202-245-4732) Ed. Kim R. Harmon. (also avail. in microfiche from CIS; reprint service avail. from CIS) **Indexed:** Amer.Stat.Ind. (1974-). **Document type:** government publication.

636 NE ISSN 0301-6226
CODEN: LPSCDL
LIVESTOCK PRODUCTION SCIENCE. (Text in English) 1974. m. fl.1700($977) (effective 1998). (European Association for Animal Production) Elsevier Science B.V., P.O. Box 211, 1000 AE Amsterdam, Netherlands. TEL 31-20-4853911. FAX 31-20-4853598. TELEX 18582 ESPA NL. E-mail: nlinfo-f@elsevier.nl; usinfo-f@elsevier.com; forinfo-kyf04035@niftyserve.or.jp; URL: http://www.elsevier.nl/. (Subscr. in the Americas to: Elsevier Science, Regional Sales Office, Box 945, New York, NY 10159-0945. TEL 212-633-3730. FAX 212-633-3680; Subscr. in Australasia and the Far East to: Elsevier Science (Singapore) Pte Ltd, No.1 Temasek Ave., No.17-01 Millenia Tower, Singapore 039192, Singapore. TEL 65-434-3727. FAX 65-337-2230; Subscr. in Japan to: Elsevier Science Japan, 9-15 Higashi-Azabu 1-chome, Minato-ku, Tokyo 106, Japan. TEL 81-3-5561-5033. FAX 81-3-5561-5047) Ed. R.D. Politiek. adv.; bk.rev.; abstr.; bibl.; illus.; index. (also avail. in microform from UMI) **Indexed:** Anim.Breed.Abstr., ASCA, Biol.Abstr., Curr.Adv.Ecol.Sci., Curr.Adv.Genetics & Molec.Biol., Curr.Cont., Dairy Sci.Abstr., Field Crop Abstr., Food Sci.& Tech.Abstr., Geo.Abstr.P.G., Helminthol.Abstr., Herb.Abstr., Ind.Sci.Rev., Ind.Vet., Landwirt.Zentralbl., Maize Abstr., Nutr.Abstr., Pig News & Info., Ref.Zh., Sci.Cit.Ind., Sport Fish.Abstr., SSCI, Sugar Ind.Abstr., Triticale Abstr., Vet.Bull., Wild.Rev., World Agri.Econ.& Rural Sociol.Abstr. **Document type:** academic/scholarly publication.
—BLDSC (5282.350000); CASDDS; Genuine Article; Linda Hall; SWETS; UnCover. **CCC.**
Description: Publishes original research papers and comprehensive reviews in the field of livestock production.
Refereed Serial

636 US ISSN 0162-5047
LIVESTOCK WEEKLY. 1949. w. $25 (effective Mar. 1995). Southwest Publishers, Inc., Box 3306, San Angelo, TX 76902. TEL 915-949-4611. FAX 915-949-4614. Ed. Steve Kelton; Pub. Robert S. Frank. adv. contact: Paula Rankin. illus.; circ. 18,000 (paid). **Document type:** newspaper.
Formerly: West Texas Livestock Weekly (ISSN 0049-724X)

636.2 US
LOUISIANA CATTLEMAN. 1967. m. $25 membership. Louisiana Cattlemen's Association, 4921 I-10 Frontage Rd., Port Allen, LA 70767. TEL 504-343-3491. FAX 504-336-0002. Ed. Sharon Lytle Hoffeld. adv.: B&W page $490, color page $1150; trim 7 1/4 x 10; adv. contact: Bob Felknor. circ. 5,500. **Document type:** trade publication.
Formerly: Louisiana Cattleman - Louisiana Dairyman.
Description: Provides information on current activities, research and programs related to the cattle industry both nationally and locally.

636.7 US ISSN 0146-9436
M A S K C KOMONDOR NEWS. 1973. bi-m. $22 (foreign $25) (effective 1996). Middle Atlantic States Komondor Club, Inc., 102 Russell Rd., Princeton, NJ 08540. TEL 609-924-0199. Ed. Gail Sheddy. adv. contact: Joy C. Levy. bk.rev. circ. 350. (back issues avail.) **Document type:** newsletter.
Description: Reports on the Hungarian Komondor, a rare and endangered breed of livestock guard dog.

MAGAZYN - DROBIARSTWO. see *VETERINARY SCIENCE*

636 CN ISSN 0823-4604
MAINE - ANJOU INTERNATIONAL. 1981. bi-m. Can.$25($25) (effective Jan. 1991). Maine - Anjou International, 3016 19th St. N.E., Ste. 110, Calgary, Alta. T2E 6V9, Canada. TEL 403-291-7077. FAX 403-291-0274. Ed. Jeff Owen. adv.: B&W page Can.$450. circ. 4,500. **Document type:** trade publication.

636 US
MARCHIGIANA NEWS. 1984. bi-m. $10. American International Marchigiana Society, Marky Cattle Association, Box 198, Walton, KS 67151-0198. TEL 316-837-3303. Ed. Martie Knudsen. (back issues avail.) **Document type:** newsletter.
Description: For Marchigiana cattle breeders - information on the breed, upcoming events, latest happenings.

MARKET NOTES FOR LIVESTOCK AND MEAT. see *AGRICULTURE — Agricultural Economics*

MEAT/VLEIS. see FOOD AND FOOD INDUSTRIES

636.008 338.4 UK
MEAT AND LIVESTOCK COMMISSION. ECONOMICS SERVICES. MEAT DEMAND TRENDS. 1976. 4/yr. £105 (foreign £125) (effective 1997). Meat and Livestock Commission, Economic Services, P.O. Box 44, Winterhill House, Snowdon Dr., Milton Keynes, Bucks. MK6 1AX, England. TEL 44-1908-677577. FAX 44-1908-609221. Ed. Jenny Spencer. **Indexed:** Food Sci.& Tech.Abstr. **Document type:** trade publication.
 Formerly (until 1993): Meat and Livestock Commission. Economic Information Service. Meat Demand Trends (ISSN 0140-6388)
 Description: Provides analysis and articles on all aspects of consumption and demand for meat and meat products in Europe.

636 UK ISSN 0263-2217
MEAT AND LIVESTOCK COMMISSION. INTERNATIONAL MEAT MARKET REVIEW. 1968. s-a. £83. Meat and Livestock Commission, P.O. Box 44, Winterhill House, Snowdon Dr., Milton Keynes, Bucks. MK6 1AX, England. TEL 44-1908-677577. FAX 44-1908-609221. charts; stat. circ. 1,000. **Indexed:** Poult.Abstr. **Document type:** trade publication.
 Formerly: Meat and Livestock Commission, Bucks, England. International Market Survey (ISSN 0047-634X)

636 US ISSN 0738-6745
HD9413
MEAT & POULTRY DIRECTORY. 1984. biennial. $950. Urner Barry Publications, Inc., Box 389, Toms River, NJ 08754-0389. TEL 908-240-5330. FAX 908-341-0891. E-mail: mail@urnerbarry.com; URL: http://www.urnerbary.com. Ed. Paul Brown, Jr. R&P contact: Paul Brown. adv. contact: Angela Cuccinello. circ. 2,000 (paid). **Document type:** directory.
 Description: Contains 8,000 listings of meat and poultry producers, processors, brokers, distributors, renderers, and slaughterers.

636 353 664.9 US
MEAT AND POULTRY INSPECTION REGULATIONS; meat inspection, poultry inspection, rabbit inspection, voluntary inspection and certificate service of meat and poultry, humane slaughter of livestock. 1990. base vol. (plus m. updates). $232 (foreign $290) (effective 1995). U.S. Department of Agriculture, Food Safety and Inspection Service, Administration Bldg., Rm. 311 E, Independence Ave. between 12th and 14th Sts., S.W., Washington, DC 20250. TEL 202-720-7025. (Subscr. to: Superintendent of Documents, U.S. Government Printing Office, Box 371954, Pittsburgh, PA 15250-7954. TEL 202-512-1800. FAX 202-512-2250) (looseleaf format)
 Description: Publishes the regulations for slaughter and processing of livestock and poultry, as well as certain voluntary services for more humane slaughter.

636 338.1 NZ ISSN 0112-739X
MEAT AND WOOL BOARDS' ECONOMIC SERVICE. ANNUAL REVIEW OF THE NEW ZEALAND SHEEP & BEEF INDUSTRY; review of physical and economic conditions in sheepfarming in New Zealand. 1952. a. NZ.$50 or on exchange basis. Meat and Wool Boards' Economic Service, P.O. Box 5179, Wellington, New Zealand. FAX 64-4-4712-173. circ. 2,500. **Indexed:** Anim.Breed.Abstr.
 Formerly: Meat and Wool Boards' Economic Service. Annual Review of the Sheep Industry (ISSN 0078-0138)

MEAT BOARD REPORTS. see FOOD AND FOOD INDUSTRIES

636 NE ISSN 0924-7068
MEAT INTERNATIONAL. (Text in English) 1991. 10/yr. $69. Misset International (Subsidiary of: Reed Elsevier plc), Postbus 4, 7000 BA Doetinchem, Netherlands. TEL 31-314-349562. FAX 31-314-340515. adv.: B&W page $4595; trim 204 x 276; adv. contact: Ramon Portocarrero. illus. circ. 21,000. **Document type:** trade publication.
 —BLDSC (5413.735500).
 Description: Covers all aspects of the international meat industry.

636 330.9 US ISSN 0889-3608
MEAT SHEET. 1974. d. $400 (effective 1997). Box 124, Westmont, IL 60559-0124. TEL 630-963-2252. FAX 630-963-2980. Ed. Deborah A. Ash; Pub. Tiffany M. Albanos. adv. contact: William Albanos. circ. 2,000. (looseleaf format; back issues avail.) **Document type:** newsletter.
 Description: Gives prices of wholesale beef, pork, and poultry cuts used by meat packers, processors, and retailers.

636 IS ISSN 0539-421X
MESHEK HAOFOTE. 1950. m. IS.25. 8 Shaul Hamelech Blvd., 16th Fl., Tel Aviv, Israel. TEL 03-257265. Ed. A. Simone.

MESTNYI PROIZVODSTVENNYI OPYT V SEL'SKOM KHOZYAISTVE/LOCAL LEVEL EXPERIENCE IN AGRICULTURAL DEVELOPMENT; nauchno-tekhnicheskii referativnyi sbornik. see AGRICULTURE — Agricultural Economics

636 US
▼**MID-SOUTH LIVESTOCK REVIEW.** 1995. m. $18 (effective Apr. 1996). Don Dowdle, Box 519, Somerville, TN 38068. TEL 901-465-4042. FAX 901-465-5493. E-mail: fcreview@bellsouth.com. Ed. Sharon Keith. adv. contact: Karen Gurkin. bk.rev. circ. 12,000. (tabloid format) **Document type:** trade publication, consumer publication.

MILCH - FETTWAREN - EIER - HANDEL. see FOOD AND FOOD INDUSTRIES

636.2 GW ISSN 0941-1348
MILCHRIND; Journal fuer Zuechtung, Biotechnologie und Leistungspruefung. 1977. q. DM.42.60 (foreign DM.48) (effective 1997). (Deutscher Holstein Verband e.V.) Landwirtschaftsverlag GmbH, Huelsebrockstr. 2, 48165 Muenster, Germany. TEL 49-2501-801-0. FAX 49-2051-801-204. (Subscr. to: Postfach 480249, 48079 Muenster, Germany) circ. 44,892. **Document type:** trade publication.
 Formerly: Deutsche Schwarzbunte.

636.234 US ISSN 1073-9394
SF199.S56
MILKING SHORTHORN JOURNAL. 1919. bi-m. $15 (foreign $20). American Milking Shorthorn Society, Box 449, Beloit, WI 53512-0449. TEL 608-365-3332. FAX 608-365-6644. Ed. Debbie Little. R&P contact: Debbie Little. adv.: B&W page $265; adv. contact: Debbie Little. bk.rev.; charts; illus. circ. 1,000. **Document type:** trade publication.
 —Linda Hall; UnCover.
 Former titles (until 1992): Journal of the Milking Shorthorn and Illawarra Breeds (ISSN 0145-8264); (until 1975): Milking Shorthorn Journal (ISSN 0026-4229)
 Description: Discusses cattle breeding, society programs, articles relating to dairying, production achievements and state association news.

636 US ISSN 1058-7063
MINIATURE DONKEY TALK. 1987. bi-m. $32 (foreign $55). Pheasant Meadow Farm, 1338 Hughes Shop Rd., Westminster, MD 21158. TEL 410-875-0118. FAX 410-857-9145. E-mail: minidonk@qis.net; URL: http://users.aol.com/minidonk/private/donktext.htm. Ed. Bonnie Gross; Pub. Bonnie Gross. R&P contact: Bonnie Gross. adv.; bk.rev. circ. 5,500. **Document type:** trade publication.
 Description: Covers health and training topics.

636 SP
MIRADOR AVICOLA. 1967. q. free to qualified personnel. Cooperativa Comarcal de Avicultura, Apdo. do correos, 64, Reus (Tarragona), Spain. TEL (977)31 75 11. TELEX 56858 COAV. Ed. Ricardo Artiga Esplugas.

636 NE
MISSET PIGS; international magazine on pig keeping. (Text in English) 1984. 8/yr. $78. Misset International (Subsidiary of: Reed Elsevier plc), Postbus 4, 7000 BA Doetinchem, Netherlands. TEL 31-314-349562. FAX 31-314-340515. Ed. Anabel Evans. adv.: B&W page fl.4950; unit 204 x 276; adv. contact: Miguel Mendes de Leon. circ. 15,000. **Indexed:** Food Sci.& Tech.Abstr., Ind.Vet., Pig News & Info., Soyabean Abstr. **Document type:** trade publication.
 —UnCover.
 Formerly: Pigs (ISSN 0168-9533)
 Description: Covers breeding techniques, diet and health care, housing and pigsty equipment.

636 NE
MISSET VLEESVEE. m. Misset (Subsidiary of: Reed Elsevier plc), Postbus 4, 7000 BA Doetinchem, Netherlands. TEL 31-314-349371. FAX 31-314-363638. TELEX 45481 MSSETNL. adv.: B&W page fl.2334, color page fl.3394; trim 230 x 290; adv. contact: Cor van Nek. illus. circ. 4,810. **Document type:** trade publication.
 Description: Contains practical information on all aspects of beef farming.

636.5 NE ISSN 0926-924X
MISSET WORLD POULTRY. 1990. m. $97. Misset International (Subsidiary of: Reed Elsevier plc), Postbus 4, 7000 BA Doetinchem, Netherlands. TEL 31-314-349562. FAX 31-314-340515. Ed. Wicbe van der Sluis. adv.: B&W page fl.7250; 204 x 276; adv. contact: Miguel Mendes de Leon. illus. circ. 25,395. **Indexed:** Agri.Eng.Abstr., Food Sci.& Tech.Abstr., Ind.Vet., Poult.Abstr., Vet.Bull. **Document type:** trade publication.
 —BLDSC (5828.698100); Linda Hall; SWETS.
 Formed by the merger of (1984-1990): Poultry (ISSN 0169-4405) & World Poultry (ISSN 0960-1694); Which was formerly titled (until 1984): World Poultry Industry (ISSN 0260-387X); (1936-1980): Poultry Industry (ISSN 0032-5759)
 Description: Covers breeding techniques, feeding and veterinary care of poultry.

MISSOURI. DEPARTMENT OF AGRICULTURE. DAILY MARKET SUMMARY. see AGRICULTURE

MISSOURI. DEPARTMENT OF AGRICULTURE. WEEKLY MARKET SUMMARY. see AGRICULTURE

636.2 US ISSN 0192-3056
MISSOURI BEEF CATTLEMAN.* 1971. m. $37 membership. (Missouri Cattlemen's Association) Missouri Beef Cattleman, Inc., Box 025727, Kansas City, MO 64102-5727. TEL 913-384-1918. FAX 913-384-2455. Ed. Larry Atzenweiler. adv. circ. 6,300. **Document type:** trade publication.

MOLOCHNO-M'YASNE SKOTARSTVO; mizhvidomchyi temetichnyi naukovyi zbirnik. see AGRICULTURE — Dairying And Dairy Products

630 RU ISSN 0026-9034
MOLOCHNOE I MYASNOE SKOTOVODSTVO. 1956. bi-m. $113 (effective 1998). Sadovaya-Spasskaya, 18, 107807 Moscow, Russia. TEL 7-095-2071946. FAX 7-095-2072870. (Dist. by: Mezhdunarodnaya Kniga, B. Yakimanka 39, 117049 Moscow, Russia. TEL 7-095-2384967. FAX 7-095-2384634) Ed. Vadim V. Korzhenevskii. bk.rev.; bibl.; illus.; stat.; index. circ. 4,000. (tabloid format) **Indexed:** Anim.Breed.Abstr., Chem.Abstr., Dairy Sci.Abstr., Food Sci.& Tech.Abstr., Nutr.Abstr.
 —BLDSC (0117.100000).

636 US ISSN 1073-1458
MONTANA FARMER. 1913. m. $15. Western Farmer-Stockman Magazines (Subsidiary of: Cowles Publishing Co.), Box 2160, Spokane, WA 99210-1615. TEL 509-459-5361. FAX 509-459-5102. E.W. Ramsey, Pub. Dir. adv. contact: Richard C. Brantley. bk.rev.; stat.; circ. 16,458 (paid). **Document type:** trade publication.
 Formerly (until 1993): Montana Farmer - Stockman (ISSN 1041-1674)

AGRICULTURE — POULTRY AND LIVESTOCK

636 US ISSN 0047-7990
MONTANA STOCKGROWER. 1910. 2/yr. membership. Montana Stockgrowers Association, Box 1679, Helena, MT 59624. TEL 406-442-3420. FAX 406-449-5105. E-mail: msgahelena@aol.com. Ed. Beth Almond. adv.: B&W page $400, color page $800; trim 8.5 x 11; adv. contact: Jerry Gliko. bk.rev. circ. 3,700.
  Description: Contains market information, industry issues and regulatory information, and general background of Montana's beef cattle industry.

636.3 US ISSN 0027-0024
CODEN: MWOGA
MONTANA WOOL GROWER. 1928. bi-m. $35. Montana Wool Growers Association, Box 1693, Helena, MT 59624. FAX 406-449-8606. Ed. Robert N. Gilbert. R&P contact: Robert N. Gilbert. adv.; stat.; tr.lit.; index; circ. 2,100 (paid). (tabloid format) **Indexed**: Biol.Abstr. **Document type**: trade publication.
  Description: Provides information relating to the sheep industry, especially in Montana.

MONTHLY PRICE REVIEW. see *FOOD AND FOOD INDUSTRIES*

THE MOOSLETTER. see *HOBBIES*

636 US
MULES AND MORE. 1990. m. $18 (foreign $30) (effective Nov. 1997). Mules and More, Box 460, Bland, MO 65014. TEL 573-646-3934. FAX 573-646-3407. E-mail: mules@i1net; URL: http://www.mules.com. Ed. Sue Cole. R&P contact: Sue Cole. adv. contact: Leona Reid. bk.rev. circ. 6,600. **Document type**: trade publication.
  Description: For mule, wagon and harness enthusiasts. Carries mule show results, training, calendar of events, sales, etc.

636 SP ISSN 0214-9192
MUNDO GANADERO. 11/yr. 7400 ptas. (foreign 12500 ptas.) (effective 1997). Edagricole Espana S.A., Castello 32, Dcha. 3o, 28001 Madrid, Spain. TEL 34-1-5780534. FAX 34-1-5753297. Ed. Carlos Buxade Carbo. adv.: B&W page 97000 ptas., color page 126000 ptas.; 23 x 30 1/5; adv. contact: Julia Dominquez. circ. 14,500. **Indexed**: Ind.SST.
  Description: For stock breeders, distributors of zoosanitary products, veterinarians, and agricultural experts.

636.2 AT ISSN 0310-9666
MURRAY GREY WORLD.* 1972. bi-m. Aus.$20. Holstein Friesian Association of Australia, 504 Race Course Rd., Flemington, Vic. 3031, Australia. TEL 61-3-3761811. FAX 61-3-3721394. Ed. Geoffrey J. Phillips. adv. circ. 2,650.
  Description: Provides cattle breeding tips.

MYASNAYA INDUSTRIYA. see *FOOD AND FOOD INDUSTRIES*

636.3 AT ISSN 1033-3029
N.S.W. FARMERS NEWS. (New South Wales) vol.18, 1969. m. membership only. N.S.W. Farmers Association, G.P.O. Box 1068, Sydney, N.S.W. 2001, Australia. TEL 61-2-2511700. FAX 61-2-2315249. Ed. Donna Gersbach. R&P contact: Donna Gersbach. adv.: B&W page Aus.$2500; adv. contact: Donna Gersbach. charts; illus. circ. 20,000. **Document type**: trade publication, newsletter.
  Formerly (until Jan. 1990): Livestock and Grain Producers; Incorporates: Muster (ISSN 0027-4925); United Farmer.
  Description: Focuses on agriculture, including sheep, cattle, pigs, goats, grains, horticulture and agricultural economics.

636 XR ISSN 0027-8068
NAS CHOV; casopis pro zivocisnou vyrobu. (Supplement avail.: Plemenarstvi (ISSN 0231-6293)) (Text in Czech; summaries in English, German, Russian) 1940. m. 48 Kc.($25.20) Strategie, spol. s r.o., Nas Chov, Elisky Peskove 13, 150 00 Prague 5, Czech Republic. (Subscr. to: Artia, Ve Smeckach 30, 111 27 Prague 1, Czech Republic) Ed. Jiri Matous. **Indexed**: Anim.Breed.Abstr., Dairy Sci.Abstr., Nutr.Abstr.
  —BLDSC (6015.360000).
  Incorporates: Chov Hospodarskych Zvierat (ISSN 0323-1488)

NATIONAL AGRICULTURAL STATISTICS SERVICE. CATTLE ON FEED. see *AGRICULTURE — Abstracting, Bibliographies, Statistics*

NATIONAL ASSOCIATION OF ANIMAL BREEDERS. ANNUAL PROCEEDINGS. see *AGRICULTURE — Dairying And Dairy Products*

636 US
NATIONAL CARLOT MEAT TRADE REPORT. d. $290 (Canada and Mexico $315; elsewhere $460). U.S. Department of Agriculture, Agricultural Marketing Service (Greely), Livestock & Seed Division, 711 O St., Greely, CO 80631. (Subscr. to: U.S.D.A. Agricultural Marketing Service, Livestock & Seed Division, Rm. 2623-S, Box 96456, Washington, DC 20090-6456. FAX 202-245-4732) Ed. Mike Erwin. **Document type**: government publication.
  Description: Contains carcass information and data on livestock species.

636 US ISSN 0885-7679
NATIONAL CATTLEMEN. 1985. m. membership. National Cattlemen's Beef Association, 5420 S. Quebec St., Englewood, CO 80155. TEL 303-694-0305. Ed. Heather Draper. R&P contact: Heather Draper. adv. contact: Brett Erickson. circ. 41,604. **Document type**: trade publication.
  —UnCover.

636.932 US
NATIONAL FEDERATION OF FLEMISH GIANT RABBIT BREEDERS. QUARTERLY NEWSLETTER. q. $10 membership. National Federation of Flemish Giant Rabbit Breeders, 233 Aultman Ave., N.W., Canton, OH 44708. TEL 330-477-1382. Ed. Roger E. Dent; Pub. Roger E. Dent. circ. 500. **Document type**: newsletter.

636 US
NATIONAL HEREFORD HOG ANNUAL NEWSLETTER. 1942. a. free. National Hereford Hog Record Association, Rte. 1, Box 37, Flandreau, SD 57028. TEL 605-997-2116. FAX 605-997-2116. Ed. Ruby Schrecengost. adv. circ. 300. (looseleaf format) back issues avail.) **Document type**: newsletter.

636.4 US ISSN 0027-9447
CODEN: NAHFAP
NATIONAL HOG FARMER. 1956. m. $25 (foreign $35). Intertec Publishing Corp., Webb Division, 7900 International Dr., Ste. 300, Minneapolis, MN 55425. TEL 612-851-4710. FAX 612-851-4601. E-mail: nhf@intertec.com; jmartinsen@usinternet.com; URL: http://www.homefarm.com. Ed. Dale Miller. adv.; bk.rev.; illus.; circ. 88,373. **Indexed**: Farm & Garden Ind. **Document type**: trade publication.
  —UMI; UnCover. **CCC**.

636.5 US
NATIONAL POULTRY NEWS. 1980. q. $10 (foreign $40). National Poultry News, Dept. UIPD, Box 1647, Easley, SC 29641. TEL 803-855-0140. Ed. Glenda L. Heyward. adv. (back issues avail.) **Document type**: newspaper.
  Formerly (until 1988): Hen House Herald.
  Description: Promotes poultry, exotic fowl and exotic animals.

630 677.3 US ISSN 1066-0593
NATIONAL WOOL MARKET REVIEW. Variant title: Wool Market News. 33/yr. $40 (Canada & Mexico $45; elsewhere $75). U.S. Department of Agriculture, Agricultural Marketing Service (Greely), Livestock & Seed Division, 711 O St., Greely, CO 80631. TEL 970-353-9750. FAX 970-353-9790. (Subscr. to: U.S.D.A. Agricultural Marketing Service, Livestock & Seed Division, Rm. 2623-S, Box 96456, Washington, DC 20090-6456. FAX 202-245-4732) (also avail. in microfiche from CIS; back issues avail.; reprint service avail. from CIS) **Indexed**: Amer.Stat.Ind. (1974-). **Document type**: government publication.

NAUTAKARJA/CATTLE. see *AGRICULTURE — Dairying And Dairy Products*

636 SP ISSN 0214-6401
NAVARRA AGRARIA; revista tecnica de agricultura, ganaderia y montes. 1985. m. (10/yr.). 2650 ptas. (Departamento de Agricultura, Ganaderia y Montes) Gobierno de Navarra, Fondo de Publicaciones, Navas de Tolosa, 21, 31002 Pamplona, Spain. TEL 34-48-107121. FAX 34-48-227673. circ. 165,000. **Indexed**: Ind.SST.

636.2 US ISSN 1062-8274
NEBRASKA CATTLEMAN. 1944. m. $50 (effective 1997). Nebraska Cattlemen, Inc., 1335 H St., Lincoln, NE 68508-3748. TEL 402-475-2333. Ed. Mike Fitzgerald. adv. contact: Steve Ditmer. circ. 9,040. **Document type**: trade publication.
  —UnCover.
  Description: Covers production and marketing of beef cattle, legislative action affecting the industry, and activities sponsored by the organization.

636 340 US
NEBRASKA LIVESTOCK BRAND BOOK. 1908. quadrennial. $40.20. Nebraska Brand Committee, Box 1, Alliance, NE 69301. TEL 308-763-2930. FAX 308-763-2934. circ. 500.

636.2 US ISSN 0047-9489
THE NEVADA RANCHER. 1971. m. $10.75. Jay Publishing, Box 1523, Sparks, NV 89432. TEL 702-358-2681. FAX 702-358-2686. Ed. Carolyn Hansen. adv. contact: Carolyn Hansen. bk.rev.; illus. circ. 3,700. (tabloid format; also avail. in microfilm from LIB) **Document type**: newspaper.
  Description: For the agricultural community of Nevada and neighboring states.

636.2 US
NEW MEXICO STOCKMAN. 1935. m. $9. (New Mexico Cattle Growers Association) Charles R. Stocks Co., 2231 Rio Grande Blvd. N.W., Box 7127, Albuquerque, NM 87194. TEL 505-243-9515. FAX 505-243-9598. (Co-sponsors: New Mexico Wool Growers; New Mexico Horse Council) adv.; bk.rev. circ. 10,799.

636.2 NZ ISSN 1170-2915
THE NEW ZEALAND ANGUS CATTLEMAN. 1990. q. NZ.$15 membership. New Zealand Angus Association Inc., P.O. Box 1241, Hastings, New Zealand. TEL 64-6-8766122. FAX 64-6-8760856. Ed. Anna Mackenzie. adv.: B&W page NZ.$695, color page NZ.$895. **Document type**: trade publication.
  Description: Covers beef industry in general.

636 NZ ISSN 0111-3976
NEW ZEALAND SOCIETY OF ANIMAL PRODUCTION. OCCASIONAL PUBLICATION. 1972. irreg. price varies. New Zealand Society of Animal Production, c/o AgResearch Ruakura, Private Bag 3123, Hamilton, New Zealand. TEL 64-7-8569157. FAX 64-7-8569150.

636 NZ ISSN 0370-2731
CODEN: PZAPAD
NEW ZEALAND SOCIETY OF ANIMAL PRODUCTION. PROCEEDINGS. 1941. a. price varies. New Zealand Society of Animal Production, c/o AgResearch Ruakura, Private Bag 3123, Hamilton, New Zealand. TEL 64-7-8569157. FAX 64-7-8569150. circ. 1,000. **Indexed**: Anim.Breed.Abstr., Biol.Abstr., Dairy Sci.Abstr., Food Sci.& Tech.Abstr., Herb.Abstr., Ind.Vet., Nutr.Abstr., Rev.Med.& Vet.Mycol., Sport Fish.Abstr., Triticale Abstr., Vet.Bull., Wild.Rev., World Agri.Econ.& Rural Sociol.Abstr., Zoo.Rec. **Document type**: proceedings.
  —BLDSC (6774.300000); CASDDS; Linda Hall.

636 CN ISSN 0228-1023
NIAGARA FARMERS' MONTHLY. 1972. 11/yr. $15. 131 College St., Box 52, Smithville, ON L0R 2A0, Canada. TEL 416-957-3751. FAX 416-957-0088. Ed. Ivan G. Carruthers. circ. 15,200.
  Description: Covers the Niagara peninsula; editorial content provides information on new and up-to-date methods in poultry, beef, pork, fruit farming, local interest stories, and information on new machinery.

636 NR ISSN 0189-0514
NIGERIA. NATIONAL ANIMAL PRODUCTION RESEARCH INSTITUTE. JOURNAL. Abbreviated title: N A P R I Journal. (Text in English) 1981. s-a. $60 per no. (effective 1994). National Animal Production Research Institute, Ahmadu Bello University, P.M.B. 1096, Zaria, Kaduna State, Nigeria. Ed. O.A. Osinowo. adv.; bk.rev.; cum.index. circ. 1,000. (back issues avail.) **Indexed**: Poult.Abstr. **Document type**: academic/scholarly publication.

AGRICULTURE — POULTRY AND LIVESTOCK

636　　　　　NR
NIGERIAN JOURNAL OF ANIMAL PRODUCTION. s-a. £N2050 to individuals (foreign $85); institutions £N5050 (foreign $125); students £N1000 (effective 1997). University of Agriculture, Department of Animal Nutrition, P.M.B. 2240, Abeokuta, Ogun State, Nigeria. TEL 234-3924-5170. FAX 234-3924-3045.

636.5　　　JA　　ISSN 0029-0254
CODEN: NKKGAB
NIHON KAKIN GAKKAISHI/JAPANESE POULTRY SCIENCE. (Text in English, Japanese) 1964. bi-m. 9000 Yen. Nihon Kakin Gakkai - Japan Poultry Science Association, c/o National Institute of Animal Industry, Tsukuba Norin-danchi Box 5, Ibaraki 305, Japan. FAX 81-298-38-8606. Ed. Y. Akiba. adv. contact: M. Takemasa. bibl.; charts; index, cum.index. circ. 1,300. **Indexed:** Anim.Breed.Abstr., Biol.Abstr., Biotech.Abstr., Food Sci.& Tech.Abstr., Ind.Vet., Nutr.Abstr., Poult.Abstr., Soyabean Abstr., Triticale Abstr., Vet.Bull. **Document type:** academic/scholarly publication.
—BLDSC (4660.750000); CASDDS; Linda Hall. CCC.

636.3　　　UK
NORTH COUNTRY CHEVIOT SHEEP SOCIETY. FLOCK BOOK. 1946. a. £5 (foreign £7.50). North Country Cheviot Sheep Society, 16 St. Vincent Rd., Tain, Ross-shire IV19 1JR, Scotland. TEL 44-1862-894014. FAX 44-1862-894014. E-mail: ncc.w.morrison@compuserve.com. Ed. W. Morrison. R&P contact: W. Morrison. circ. 500. **Document type:** trade publication.

636　　　SP　　ISSN 0210-5659
NUESTRA CABAÑA; revista de la nueva ganaderia espanola. 1972. m. 5900 ptas. (foreign 10800 ptas.) (effective 1997). Tecnipublicaciones, S.A., C. Albacete, 5, 28027 Madrid, Spain. TEL 34-1-3261440. FAX 34-1-3262407. adv.; bk.rev.; illus.; stat. circ. 11,000. **Indexed:** Ind.SST.
Description: Contains information on new products and technology for the feeding, health, sanitation, commercialization and management of livestock.

636　　　AU
OESTERREICHISCHE FLEISCHER-ZEITUNG. w. S.1040. Oesterreichischer Wirtschaftsverlag, Nikolsdorfergasse 7-11, A-1051 Vienna, Austria. TEL 0222-555585. TELEX 1-11669. Ed. Gottfried Rajchl. adv.; bk.rev. circ. 3,600.
Formerly: Viehhandel (ISSN 0049-6308)

636.2　　　AU　　ISSN 0029-9111
OESTERREICHISCHE GEFLUEGELWIRTSCHAFT. 1962. m. S.620 (foreign S.720). (Arbeitsgemeinschaft des Landwirtschaftlichen Gefluegelwirtschaft Oesterreichs) Hugo H. Hitschmann Verlag GmbH, Inkustr. 1-7, A-3400 Klosterneuburg, Austria. TEL 02243-88686. FAX 02243-8868656. Ed. Hermann Rebernig. adv.; bk.rev.; bibl.; charts; illus.; mkt.; stat. circ. 2,500. **Document type:** trade publication.

636.2　　　US　　ISSN 0048-1556
OHIO JERSEY NEWS. 1936. m. $5. Ohio Jersey Breeders Association Inc., Box 532, Prospect, OH 43342. TEL 614-262-1452. Ed. A. Bud Baird. adv. circ. 1,200.

OHIO NEWS. see AGRICULTURE — Dairying And Dairy Products

636　　　JA　　ISSN 0915-4728
OKAYAMA-KEN SOGO CHIKUSAN SENTA KENKYU HOHKOKU/OKAYAMA PREFECTURAL CENTER FOR ANIMAL HUSBANDRY AND RESEARCH. BULLETIN. (Text in Japanese; summaries in English, Japanese) 1990. a. Okayama-ken Sogo Chikusan Senta - Okayama Prefectural Center for Animal Husbandry and Research, 2272, Asahi-cho Kita, Kume-gun, Okayama-ken 709-34, Japan. TEL 086727-3321. Ed. Seigo Amano; Pub. Mitsuo Akagi. **Document type:** bulletin.
—BLDSC (2668.447000).

636.2　　　US　　ISSN 0030-1698
OKLAHOMA COWMAN. 1961. m. $50 membership. Oklahoma Cattlemen's Association, Box 82395, Oklahoma City, OK 73148. TEL 405-235-4391. FAX 405-235-3608. Ed. A.J. Smith. R&P contact: A.J. Smith. adv.; bk.rev.; illus.; circ. 5,600 (paid). **Document type:** trade publication.
Description: Provides cattle breeding tips.

636.2　　　NE　　ISSN 0030-2775
ONS VEE;* maandblad voor de veehouderij. vol.18, 1967. m. fl.15.15. Past. van Akenstraat 8, Roosendaal, Netherlands. adv.; illus.

630　　　CN
ONTARIO. MINISTRY OF AGRICULTURE, FOOD AND RURAL ANALYSIS. MONTHLY CROP AND LIVESTOCK REPORT. 1882. 8/yr. free. Ministry of Agriculture, Food and Rural Analysis, Policy Analysis Branch, Legislative Bldg., Queen's Park, Toronto, ON M7A 2B2, Canada. TEL 416-326-3214. FAX 416-326-9892. Ed. Mafat Patel. circ. 1,500. **Document type:** government publication.
Formerly: Ontario. Ministry of Agriculture and Food. Monthly Crop and Livestock Report (ISSN 0027-0342)
Description: Statistical report containing estimates of field crop area production, farm prices, cash receipts, operating expenses, and livestock inventories.

636　　　CN
ONTARIO BEEF. 1963. 5/yr. membership. Ontario Cattlemen's Association, 130 Malcolm Rd., Guelph, ON N1K 1B1, Canada. TEL 519-824-0334. FAX 519-824-9101. E-mail: ontbeef@cattle.guelph.on.ca; URL: http://www.cattle.guelph.on.ca. Ed. Sandra Beirnes. R&P contact: Sandra Beirnes. adv. contact: Cathy Lasby. circ. 20,931 (controlled). (back issues avail.) **Document type:** trade publication.
Formerly (until 1994): Breeder & Feeder (ISSN 0712-5291)
Description: Provides information to Ontario beef cattle producers, cow-calf, backgrounder, feed lot and seed stock operators.

636　　　CN　　ISSN 1195-5457
ONTARIO BEEF FARMER MAGAZINE. 1993. 4/yr. Can.$16.05 (US Can.$20, elsewhere Can.$25). Bowes Publishers Ltd., P.O. Box 7400, London, ON N5Y 4X3, Canada. TEL 519-473-0010. FAX 519-473-2256. Ed. Paul Mahon; Pub. Mervyn J. Hawkins. adv.: B&W page Can.$1150, color page Can.$1645; trim 8 1/8 x 10 3/4. circ. 13,499.

636.4　　　CN
ONTARIO HOG FARMER MAGAZINE. 1988. 6/yr. Bowes Publishers Ltd., P.O. Box 7400, London, ON N5Y 4X3, Canada. TEL 519-473-0010. FAX 519-473-2256. Ed. Paul Mahon; Pub. M.J. Hawkins. adv. circ. 8,498. **Document type:** trade publication.
Former titles: Ontario Hog Farmer Quarterly (ISSN 0847-7752); (until 1989): Ontario Hog Farmer (ISSN 0847-7760)

636.3　　　CN　　ISSN 0844-5303
ONTARIO SHEEP NEWS. 1987. bi-m. Can.$12.84. 130 Malcolm Rd., Guelph, ON N1K 1B1, Canada. TEL 519-836-0043. FAX 519-824-9101. Ed. Kelly Maloney. R&P contact: Kelly Maloney. adv. contact: Kelly Maloney. circ. 5,800. **Document type:** trade publication.

636.2　　　US
OREGON BEEF PRODUCER. 1952. m. membership. Oregon Cattlemen's Association, 1200 N.W. Front St., Ste. 290, Portland, OR 97209-2829. TEL 503-229-6830. FAX 503-229-5232. E-mail: wrangler@teleport.com. Ed. Rod Dowse. adv.; bk.rev. circ. 2,500. **Document type:** trade publication.
Formerly: Oregon Cattleman (ISSN 0471-9174)

636.6 598.2　　　US　　ISSN 1067-7712
OSTRICH NEWS. 1987. m. $48. Ostrich News, Inc., Box 860, Cache, OK 73527-0860. URL: http://www.ostrichnews.com. Ed. Melodye Crawford. **Document type:** trade publication.

636.6 598.2　　　US　　ISSN 1068-5774
OSTRICH NEWS RATITE DIRECTORY. 1987. a. Ostrich News, Inc., Box 860, Cache, OK 73527-0860. adv.; illus.
Former titles (until 1992): National Ostrich - Ratite Directory (ISSN 1050-981X); National Ostrich - Exotics Directory (ISSN 1050-9801)

636　　　SP　　ISSN 1130-4863
OVIS. 1979. bi-m. 4770 ptas. Luzan 5 S.A. de Ediciones, Virgen de la Alegria 9, 28027 Madrid, Spain. **Indexed:** Ind.SST.

636.3　　　UK
OXFORD DOWN SHEEP BREEDER'S ASSOCIATION MAGAZINE. 3/yr. £10 (effective 1997). Oxford Down Sheep Breeder's Association, 4 Brookfield, Hampsthwaite, Harrogate, N. Yorkshire HG3 2EF, England. TEL 44-1423-770736. Ed. Jeffrey Stephenson. adv.: color page £130; adv. contact: Ann Knott. circ. 350 (paid). **Document type:** newsletter.

636 637　　　FR　　ISSN 1143-5852
P L M. (Production Laitiere Moderne) m. 352 F. (foreign 452 F.). Editions du Boisdoubry, B.P. 6359, 35063 Rennes Cedex, France. TEL 99-32-21-21. FAX 99-32-14-17. TELEX 730619F. adv.; illus. circ. 32,000. **Indexed:** Agri.Eng.Abstr., Anim.Breed.Abstr., Dairy Sci.Abstr., Maize Abstr.
Formerly: Eleveur de Bovins - P L M.

636　　　PK　　ISSN 0083-8292
PAKISTAN. DIRECTORATE OF LIVESTOCK FARMS. REPORT. (Text in English) 1962-63. a. Directorate of Livestock Farms, 16 Cooper Rd., Lahore, Pakistan. circ. 100.

636　　　PK
PAKISTAN JOURNAL OF ANIMAL SCIENCES. (Text in English) q. Rs.10($1.25) Society for the Advancement of Animal Sciences, c/o Veterinary Research Institute, Ghazi Rd., Lahore 13, Pakistan. adv.; bibl.; charts.

636.2　　　MX　　ISSN 0304-2502
PASTIZALES. (Text in Spanish; summaries in English) 1970. s-a. free. Instituto Nacional de Investigaciones Forestales, Agricolas y Pecuarias, Campo Experimental "La Campana", Apdo. Postal 1204, Chihuahua, Chih., Mexico. TEL 52-14-810769. FAX 52-14-810257. Eds. Esteban Gutierrez Ronquillo, Raul Escobar Tolentino. bibl.; charts; illus. circ. 1,500. (back issues avail.) **Document type:** bulletin.
Description: Provides results of research in range management, cattle production and other topics.

636.6　　　SP
PASTORS. (Text in Catalan) 1993. q. 1000 ptas. Edicions la Terra, S.L., Avda. Francesc Cambo 14, 3-B, 08003 Barcelona, Spain. TEL 34-3-2680900. Ed. Dolors Aixala i Mateu. adv. contact: Josep M. Escola. circ. 1,000. **Document type:** trade publication.
Description: Covers the raising of sheep and goats.

636　　　FR　　ISSN 0475-9141
PATRE. 1953. m. (10/yr.). 260 F. (foreign 390 F.) (effective 1997); newsstand price: 30 F. (Institut Technique de l'Elevage Ovin et Caprin) Societe de Presse et d'Edition Ovine et Caprine (S.P.E.O.C.), 19 quai de Juillet, B.P. 18, 14005 Caen Cedex, France. TEL 33-2-31357704. FAX 33-2-31822963. Ed. Jean-Claude Lejaouen; Pub. Andre Zawadzki. R&P contact: Marc Jourdan. adv. contact: Jean-Pierre Dumas. charts; illus.; stat.; circ. 5,300 (controlled). **Indexed:** Anim.Breed.Abstr.
Description: Technical and economical information about sheep breeding.

636.5　　　US
PEAFOWL REPORT. 1991. bi-m. $20 (Canada $35; elsewhere $45). Iowa Peacock Farm Publications, Peacocks - UR, Minden, IA 51553. TEL 712-483-2473. FAX 712-483-2155. URL: http://www.peafowl.com. Eds. Dennis Fett, Debra Buck. R&P contact: Dennis Fett. circ. 1,000 (paid). **Document type:** newsletter.
Formerly: Wacky World of Peafowl Report (ISSN 1056-6759)
Description: Provides current news and information on the raising and care of peafowl (peacocks and peahens).

636.5　　　YU　　ISSN 0031-6792
PERADARSTVO; casopis za problematiku peradarske proizvodnje. 1966. m. 300 din. Savez Zivinara SR Srbije, Bulevar JNA 18, Belgrade, Yugoslavia. Ed. M. Gancic. adv.; bk.rev. **Indexed:** Anim.Breed.Abstr., Ind.Vet., Poult.Abstr., Vet.Bull.
—BLDSC (6422.980000).

636.5　　　CN
PERCHERON PROGRESS NEWSLETTER. q. Canadian Percheron Association, Bag 200, Crossfield, Alta. TOM 0S0, Canada. TEL 403-946-5425. **Document type:** newsletter.

AGRICULTURE — POULTRY AND LIVESTOCK

636.5   PK
PIA-SHAVER/POULTRY. (Text in English and Urdu) 1971. m. $2 per no. Press Corporation of Pakistan, P.O. Box 3138, Karachi 75400, Pakistan. TEL 21-455-3703. FAX 21-7736198. Ed. Saeed Hafeez. circ. 3,000.

636.4   UK   ISSN 0031-9759
PIG FARMING. 1954. m. £25($66) (Eire £35) (effective 1996). Miller Freeman Professional Ltd. (Subsidiary of: Miller Freeman plc), 2 Wharfedale Rd., Ipswich, Suffolk IP1 4LG, England. TEL 44-1473-241122. FAX 44-1473-240501. Ed. Brian Kelly. R&P contact: Brian Kelly. adv. contact: Ces Kerridge. bk.rev.; charts; illus.; tr.lit. circ. 9,000. **Indexed:** Agri.Eng.Abstr., Biotech.Abstr., Dairy Sci.Abstr., Excerp.Med., Ind.Vet. **Document type:** trade publication.
—BLDSC (6500.000000).
Description: News and articles of interest to farmers and farm managers in Great Britain and Northern Ireland who raise sows or pigs.

636.4   US
PIG INTERNATIONAL; covering the pig industry in Europe, Asia-Pacific, North America and Africa. (Annual Buyer's Guide issue avail.) 1971. m. $48 (foreign $84). Watt Publishing Co., 122 S. Wesley Ave., Mt. Morris, IL 61054. TEL 815-734-4171. FAX 815-734-4201. Ed. Peter Best; Pub. Clay Schreiber. adv.: B&W page $4200, color page $5710; trim 8 x 10 3/4; adv. contact: Nancy Wagner. circ. 20,000 (controlled). **Document type:** trade publication.
—BLDSC (6500.027000); UMI. **CCC.**
Former titles: Pig International. Europe, Africa and Asia - Pacific (ISSN 0191-8834); Pig International. Europe, Asia, Africa, Latin America and Oceania Edition.
Description: Features all aspects of pig production and marketing for pig businessmen in Europe, Asia, Africa, and North America.

THE PIG JOURNAL. see *VETERINARY SCIENCE*

636.4   JA   ISSN 0915-9622
PIG MAGAZINE/YOTONKAI. (Text in Japanese) m. 800 Yen per no. Chikusan Publishing Co., Ltd. (Subsidiary of: Midori Group), Ikebukuro Nishiguchi Sky Bldg., 2-14-4 Ikebukuro, Toshima-ku, Tokyo 171, Japan. TEL 03-3590-9454. circ. 32,000. **Document type:** trade publication.
Description: Covers pig breeding, fattening, and pig farm management for pig farmers, researchers, students and government.

636.4   UK   ISSN 0143-9014
                         CODEN: PNINEZ
PIG NEWS & INFORMATION. 1980. q. £130($230) (effective 1997). CAB International, Wallingford, Oxon. OX10 8DE, England. TEL 44-1491-832111. FAX 44-1491-826090. TELEX 847964 COMAGG G. E-mail: cabi@cabi.org; URL: http://www.cabi.org. (U.S. subscr. to: CAB International, North American Office, 198 Madison Ave., New York, NY 10016. TEL 212-726-6490. FAX 212-686-7933) (also avail. in microfiche) **Indexed:** Anim.Breed.Abstr., Dairy Sci.Abstr., Food Sci.& Tech.Abstr., Ind.Vet., Nutr.Abstr., Pig News & Info., Sugar Ind.Abstr., Vet.Bull. **Document type:** trade publication.
●Also available online. Vendor(s): DIMDI, European Space Agency, Knight-Ridder Information, Inc., STN International.
—SWETS; UnCover.

636   UK   ISSN 0966-3592
PIG WORLD. 1987. m. £20 (foreign £30). P.O. Box 181, Benniworth, Lincoln LN3 6LE, England. FAX 44-1507-313798. Ed. S. Walton. adv.; circ. 8,000 (paid). **Document type:** trade publication.
Description: All aspects of indoor and outdoor pig husbandry in the UK and other EC countries.

636   UK
PIGPLAN MANAGEMENT SERVICES. QUARTERLY DATA SHEET. q. £6.50 per no. Meat and Livestock Commission, P.O. Box 44, Winterhill House, Snowdon Dr., Milton Keynes, Bucks. MK6 1AX, England. TEL 44-1908-677577.
FAX 44-1908-609221. **Document type:** bulletin.
Formerly (until 1992): Pig Improvement Services. Quarterly Data Sheet.

636.5   BE   ISSN 0771-3908
PLUIMVEE. 1965. m. 1000 BEF (foreign 1200 BEF). Opworp 13, B-3560 Lummen, Belgium. TEL 32-13-521715. FAX 32-13-52-19-55. E-mail: clem.reynders@ping.be. Ed. Clem Reynders; Pub. Clem Reynders. R&P contact: Clem Reynders. adv. contact: Clem Reynders. circ. 4,000. (reprint service avail.) **Document type:** trade publication.

636.5   NE   ISSN 0166-8250
PLUIMVEEHOUDERIJ. 1923. w. fl.139.50. (Nederlandse Organisatie van Pluimveehouders - Dutch Organization of Poultry-Keepers) Misset (Subsidiary of: Reed Elsevier plc), Postbus 4, 7000 BA Doetinchem, Netherlands. TEL 31-314-349371. FAX 31-314-363638. TELEX 45481. Ed. Wim Wisman. adv.: B&W page fl.2809, color page fl.4309; trim 215 x 285; adv. contact: Cor van Nek. bk.rev.; charts; illus.; mkt. circ. 6,730. **Indexed:** Key to Econ.Sci. **Document type:** trade publication.
Formerly: Bedrijfspluimveehouder (ISSN 0005-7649)
Description: Trade news for the entire poultry industry.

636.7 799.2   US   ISSN 1067-0947
THE POINTING DOG JOURNAL. 1993. bi-m. $21.95. Wildwood Press, L.C., Box 38, Adel, IA 50003-0038. TEL 515-993-4345. FAX 515-993-4930. (Subscr. to: Box 968, Traverse City, MI 49685. TEL 800-333-7646) Ed. David G. Meisner; Pub. David G. Meisner. adv. contact: John Shoemaker. bk.rev.; circ. 30,000 (paid). (back issues avail.) **Document type:** consumer publication.
Description: Caters to outdoor sports enthusiasts who hunt upland game birds with pointers.

POLSKA AKADEMIA NAUK. INSTYTUT GENETYKI I HODOWLI ZWIERZAT. PRACE I MATERIALY ZOOTECHNICZNE. see *BIOLOGY — Zoology*

POLSKA AKADEMIA NAUK. INSTYTUT GENETYKI I HODOWLI ZWIERZAT. PRACE I MATERIALY ZOOTECHNICZNE. ZESZYT SPECIALNY. see *BIOLOGY — Zoology*

636.4 664.9   FR   ISSN 0296-9076
PORC MAGAZINE. 1968. m. 348 F. (foreign 448 F.). Editions du Boisbaudry, B.P. 6359, 35063 Rennes Cedex, France. TEL 99-32-21-21. FAX 99-32-14-17. TELEX 730619F. adv.; illus. circ. 12,000. **Indexed:** Ind.Vet., Vet.Bull.
—BLDSC (6554.050000).
Formerly (until 1985): Eleveurs de Porcs (ISSN 0395-8353)

636   AT   ISSN 1032-3759
SF391
PORK JOURNAL. (Monthly Newsletter avail.) 1978. bi-m. Aus.$45 including Newsletter (effective Feb. 1997). Richard Milne Pty. Ltd., P.O. Box 163, Drummoyne, N.S.W. 2047, Australia. TEL 61-2-98197322. FAX 61-2-98197650. E-mail: milnepublications@ibm.net. Ed. Brian McErlane. R&P contact: Brian McErlane. adv. contact: Liz Rafferty. circ. 3,517. (back issues avail.)
Incorporates: Pig Farmer (ISSN 0031-9740);
Formerly: Australian Pork Journal (ISSN 0156-5907)
Description: News and management hints for pig farmers.

636.4   CN   ISSN 1197-1363
PORK PRODUCER; serving Canada's leading hog farmers. 1970. q. Can.$12 (foreign Can.$15.50). Agricultural Publishing Co. Ltd., 1 Yonge St. Ste. 1504, Toronto, ON M5E 1E5, Canada. TEL 416-364-5324. FAX 416-364-5857. E-mail: agpub@inforamp.net; URL: http://www.agpub.on.ca. Ed. John M. Muggeridge. adv. contact: James Shaw. illus. circ. 10,442. **Document type:** trade publication.
Former titles (until 1993): Hog Marketplace Quarterly (ISSN 0380-3651); Market Place Quarterly.

636.4   AT
THE PORK PRODUCER. 1980? m. Aus.$24. (Queensland Pork Producers Organisation) Collins Speciality Media, P.O. Box 387, Cleveland, Qld. 4163, Australia. TEL 61-7-32861833. FAX 61-7-38212637. Ed. Ron Collins. adv.: B&W page Aus.$840; color Aus.$1150; 400 x 250; adv. contact: Margaret Darvall. bk.rev. circ. 3,100. (tabloid format) **Document type:** newspaper.
Description: Covers industry news, research, products.

636.4   US
PORK PRODUCER NEWS. 1973. q. free. Kent Feeds Inc., Advertising Department, 1600 Oregon St., Muscatine, IA 52761. TEL 319-264-4211. (tabloid format)
Formerly (until 197?): Pork Roundup.

636.4   US
PORK REPORT. 1982. 6/yr. membership. National Pork Producers Council, Box 10383, Des Moines, IA 50306. TEL 515-223-2600. FAX 513-223-2646. E-mail: porkreport@nppc.org. Ed. Jan Tayloe. adv.: B&W page $3400, color page $4500; trim 8 1/4 x 10 7/8. circ. 109,000 (controlled).

636.4   CN
PORK REPORT. w. free. S P I Marketing Group, 502 45th St. W., 2nd Fl., Saskatoon, SK S7L 6H2, Canada. TEL 306-653-3014; 800-667-2003. FAX 306-244-2918. E-mail: spi@sk.sympatio.ca; URL: http://agri-infolink.com/spi. Ed. Rob Brown. R&P contact: Rob Brown. adv.; circ. 2,100 (controlled). **Document type:** newsletter.
Description: Include information on the production and marketing of pork and related matters.

POTRAVINARSKE AKTUALITY. DRUBEZARSKY PRUMYSL. see *FOOD AND FOOD INDUSTRIES*

636   UK   ISSN 1357-048X
SF481
POULTRY AND AVIAN BIOLOGY REVIEWS. 1987. 4/yr. £182($305) (effective 1998). Science and Technology Letters, P.O. Box 81, Northwood, Middlesex HA6 3DY, England. TEL 44-1923-823586. FAX 44-1923-825066. E-mail: scilet@scilet.com; URL: http://www.scilet.com/scilet.htm. (Subscr. in U.S. and Canada to: Henchek and Associates, 155 N. Michigan Ave., Ste. 500, Chicago, IL 60601. FAX 312-913-1404) adv. **Indexed:** Food Sci.& Tech.Abstr. **Document type:** academic/scholarly publication.
—BLDSC (6568.828000); Genuine Article; Linda Hall; SWETS. **CCC.**
Former titles (until vol.6, 1995): Poultry Science Reviews (ISSN 0964-6604); (until 1992): Critical Reviews in Poultry Biology (ISSN 0889-4434)
Description: Covers the entire scope of scientific enquiries pertaining to avian species, including fundamental biological research.
Refereed Serial

636.5 637.5 338.1   US   ISSN 0032-5716
POULTRY AND EGG MARKETING; the bi-monthly news magazine of the poultry marketing industry. 1921. 6/yr. $12 (free to qualified personnel). Poultry and Egg News, 345 Green St., N.W., Box 1338, Gainesville, GA 30503. TEL 404-536-2476. FAX 404-532-4894. Ed. Jim Mathis; Pub. Sandra Bailey. R&P contact: Randall Smallwood. adv.: B&W page $1425, color page $1825; trim 11 x 13 1/4; adv. contact: Charles McEachern. charts; illus.; stat. circ. 10,400. **Document type:** trade publication.
Formerly: Poultry and Eggs Weekly.

636.5   US   ISSN 0032-5724
POULTRY DIGEST. 1939. m. $54 (effective Jan.). Watt Publishing Co., 122 S. Wesley Ave., Mt. Morris, IL 61054. TEL 815-734-4171. FAX 815-734-4201. Ed. Charles Perry; Pub. Charles Olentine. adv.: B&W page $3625, color page $4900; trim 8 x 10 3/4; adv. contact: Elsie Hachbarth. charts; illus.; stat.; index. circ. 18,000. (also avail. in microform from UMI; reprint service avail.) **Indexed:** Biol.Abstr., Biol.& Agr.Ind., Ind.Vet., Poult.Abstr., Protozool.Abstr., Rev.Med.& Vet.Mycol., Vet.Bull. **Document type:** trade publication.
—BLDSC (6570.120000); Linda Hall; UMI; UnCover. **CCC.**
Description: How-to husbandry magazine with information on commercial egg, broiler and turkey production in the U.S.

636   AT   ISSN 1032-3767
POULTRY DIGEST. 1985. bi-m. Aus.$29 (effective Feb. 1997). Richard Milne Pty. Ltd., P.O. Box 163, Drummoyne, N.S.W. 2047, Australia. TEL 61-2-98197322. FAX 61-2-98197650. E-mail: milnepublications@ibm.net. Ed. Brian McErlane. R&P contact: Brian McErlane. adv. contact: Liz Rafferty. circ. 2,429. (back issues avail.) **Indexed:** Poult.Abstr.
Formerly: Australian Poultry Digest (ISSN 0815-9297)
Description: Information for egg and broiler farmers.

AGRICULTURE — POULTRY AND LIVESTOCK

636   UK   ISSN 1354-2591
POULTRY FORUM. 8/yr. National Farmers' Union, Agriculture House, 164 Shaftesbury Ave., London WC2H 8HL, England. TEL 44-171-331-7200. FAX 44-171-331-7406. Ed. Judy Rockliffe. circ. 4,500. **Document type:** trade publication.

636.5   II   ISSN 0032-5740
POULTRY GUIDE. (Editions in English, Hindi) 1964. bi-m. Rs.300. C.P. Narang (Pvt.) Ltd., 1700-IV, Urban Estate, Gurgaon 122 001, India. TEL 91-124-320728. FAX 91-124-327400. Ed. Ricky Thaper. adv.: page Rs.1000; trim 140 x 190. bk.rev.; charts; illus.; mkt.; stat.; tr.lit. circ. 7,000. **Indexed:** Food Sci.& Tech.Abstr., Nutr.Abstr. **Document type:** trade publication.
—BLDSC (6570.250000).
Description: Provides technical and other useful information for efficient and profitable production in the trade.

636.5   US   ISSN 0032-5767
CODEN: POINE8
POULTRY INTERNATIONAL. (Dist. only in Europe, Middle East, Africa, Asia & the Pacific) (Text in English) 1962. 14/yr. $63. Watt Publishing Co., 122 S. Wesley Ave., Mt. Morris, IL 61054. TEL 815-734-4171. FAX 815-734-4201. Ed. David Martin; Pub. Charles Olentine. adv.: B&W page $4500, color page $6025; trim 8 x 10 3/4; adv. contact: Barb Burke. charts; stat. circ. 23,000. **Indexed:** Agri.Eng.Abstr., Anim.Breed.Abstr., Biotech.Abstr., Food Sci.& Tech.Abstr., Ind.Vet., Maize Abstr., Poult.Abstr., Protozool.Abstr., Rev.Med.& Vet.Mycol. **Document type:** trade publication.
—BLDSC (6570.310000); SWETS; UMI. **CCC.**
Description: International commercial focus on production, processing and marketing of eggs, broilers and turkeys.

636.5 338.1   CN   ISSN 0032-5775
POULTRY MARKET REVIEW. 1950. a. free. Agriculture Canada, Poultry Development Division, Sir John Carling Bldg., 930 Carling Ave., Ottawa, ON K1A 0C7, Canada. TEL 819-994-0246. FAX 819-953-0969. circ. 2,000. **Document type:** government publication.
Description: Provides annual poultry market statistics, number of birds slaughtered, hatched, set, table eggs graded, processed egg production, imports, exports and interprovincial movement on a monthly, provincial and annual basis.

POULTRY MARKET STATISTICS. see AGRICULTURE — Abstracting, Bibliographies, Statistics

636.5   LE
POULTRY MIDDLE EAST & NORTH AFRICA. (Text in Arabic) 1979. 6/yr. £L25000($15) (effective 1998). Middle East Agriculture Publishers (M E A P), Zalka, Cite Moussa, Block A, P.O. Box 90, 1170 Beirut, Lebanon. TEL 961-1-896478. FAX 961-1-897259. (Alternate addr.: P.O. Box 1825, Limassol, Cyprus. FAX 327-5-339345) Ed. Ghassan Sayegh; Pub. Antoine Sayegh. adv. contact: Mary Beyrouty. circ. 22,000. **Document type:** trade publication.

636.5   US   ISSN 0032-5783
POULTRY PRESS. 1914. m. $16. Box 542, Connersville, IN 47331-0542. TEL 317-827-0932. FAX 317-827-4186. Ed. William F. Wulff. R&P contact: William F. Wulff. adv.: bk.rev.; illus. circ. 5,800. (tabloid format) **Document type:** trade publication.

636.2   US
POULTRY ROUNDUP. 1973. a. free. Kent Feeds, Inc., 1600 Oregon St., Muscatine, IA 52761. TEL 319-264-4211.

636.5   US   ISSN 0032-5791
SF481   CODEN: POSCAL
POULTRY SCIENCE. 1908. m. $125. Poultry Science Association Inc., 1111 N. Dunlap Ave., Savoy, IL 61874. TEL 217-356-3182. FAX 217-398-4119. E-mail: psa@adsa.org; URL: http://gallus.tamu.edu/psa/psa.html; http://www.psa.uiuv.edu/toc.html. Ed. H.S. Siegel. adv. contact: Janet Brown. bk.rev.; bibl.; index. circ. 3,700. (also avail. in microform from UMI; reprint service avail. from UMI) **Indexed:** Agri.Eng.Abstr., Anim.Breed.Abstr., ASCA, Bibl.Agri., Bio-Contr.News & Info., Biol.Abstr., Biol.& Agr.Ind., Chem.Abstr., Curr.Adv.Ecol.Sci., Curr.Cont., Curr.Pack.Abstr., Dairy Sci.Abstr., Dent.Ind., Excerp.Med., Food Sci.& Tech.Abstr., Helminthol.Abstr., Ind.Med., Ind.Sci.Rev., Ind.Vet., Maize Abstr., Nutr.Abstr., Packag.Sci.Tech., Poult.Abstr., Protozool.Abstr., Rev.Med.& Vet.Mycol., Rev.Plant Path., Rural Recreat.Tour.Abstr., Sci.Cit.Ind., Sorghum & Millets Abstr., Soyabean Abstr., Sport Fish.Abstr., Triticale Abstr., Trop.Oil Seeds Abstr., Vet.Bull., Wild.Rev., World Agri.Econ. & Rural Sociol.Abstr., Zoo.Rec. **Document type:** academic/scholarly publication.
—BLDSC (6571.000000); CASDDS; KR SourceOne; Linda Hall; SWETS; UMI; UnCover.

636.5   UK   ISSN 0966-7318
POULTRY SCIENCE SYMPOSIUM SERIES. a. £49($78) to individuals; institutions £98 ($156) (effective 1997). Carfax Publishing Co., P.O. Box 25, Abingdon, Oxon. OX14 3UE, England. TEL 44-1235-401000. FAX 44-1235-401550. E-mail: enquiries@carfax.co.uk. (Subscr. in N. America to: Carfax Publishing Co., 875-81 Massachusetts Ave., Cambridge, MA 02139) **Document type:** academic/scholarly publication.
—UMI. **CCC.**
Refereed Serial

636.5   US   ISSN 0885-3371
POULTRY TIMES. 1954. bi-w. $9 (effective Jan. 1992). Poultry and Egg News, 345 Green St., N.W., Box 1338, Gainesville, GA 30503. TEL 404-536-2476. FAX 404-532-4894. Ed. Jim Mathis; Pub. Sandra Bailey. R&P contact: Randall Smallwood. adv.: B&W page $3000, color page $3475; trim 11 x 13 1/4; adv. contact: Charles McEahern. illus. circ. 13,400. **Document type:** newspaper, trade publication.
Formed by the merger of: Poultryman (ISSN 0278-5595); Southeastern Poultry Times (ISSN 0038-3708); Texas Poultry and Egg News (ISSN 0040-4608); Incorporates: Georgia Poultry Times.

636.5   UK   ISSN 0032-5813
POULTRY WORLD. 1874. m. £20 in UK; elswewhere £40. Reed Business Information (Subsidiary of: Reed Elsevier group), Quadrant House, The Quadrant, Sutton, Surrey SM2 5AS, England. TEL 44-181-652-4021. FAX 44-181-652-4748. Ed. J. Farrant; Pub. Jerry Gosney. adv. contact: Chris Joslin. charts; illus.; stat. circ. 5,862. (reprint service avail. from RBP) **Indexed:** Agri.Eng.Abstr. **Document type:** trade publication.
—BLDSC (6571.150000).

636   NE   ISSN 0928-2076
PRAKTIJKONDERZOEK. Key Title: P P Uitgave. 1990. 4/yr. fl.50 (foreign fl.65) includes Jaarverslag (effective 1997). Praktijkonderzoek Pluimveehouderij, Postbus 31, 7360 AA Beekbergen, Netherlands. TEL 31-55-5066500. FAX 31-55-5066500. Ed. F.G. Vink. circ. 700. **Document type:** corporate report.
Former titles: Praktijkonderzoek Pluimveehouderij; Praktijkonderzoek voor de Pluimveehouderij (ISSN 0924-9087)

PRODUCAO DA PECUARIA MUNICIPAL. see AGRICULTURE — Abstracting, Bibliographies, Statistics

636   IT   ISSN 0033-0000
PRODUZIONE ANIMALE. (Text in English, French, German, Italian) 1962. q. L.7000($13.) Istituto della Produzione Animale, Facolta di Agraria, 80055 Portici, Naples, Italy. Ed. Manlio Bettini. adv.; abstr.; charts; illus.; index. circ. 500. **Indexed:** Anim.Breed.Abstr., Biol.Abstr., Chem.Abstr., Dairy Sci.Abstr., Nutr.Abstr.

636 664   IT
PROFESSIONEALLEVATORE. 1984. 14/yr. L.50000 (foreign L.100000). S.E.M.IN.A. s.r.l., Piazza S. Camillo de Lellis 1, 20124 Milan, Italy. TEL 02-66984966. FAX 02-66984980. adv. circ. 32,000.

636.5   RU   ISSN 0033-3239
PTITSEVODSTVO/POULTRY. 1951. bi-m. $66 (effective 1998). Sadovaya-Spasskaya, 18, 107807 Moscow, Russia. TEL 7-095-2071660. FAX 7-095-2072870. (Dist. by: Mezhdunarodnaya Kniga, B. Yakimanka 39, 117049, Moscow, Russia. TEL 7-095-2384967. FAX 7-095-2384634) Ed. Mikhail G. Petrash. bk.rev.; illus.; index. **Indexed:** Anim.Breed.Abstr., Biol.Abstr., Chem.Abstr., Nutr.Abstr., Poult.Abstr., Soyabean Abstr., Triticale Abstr.
—BLDSC (0135.000000).

636.2   GW
R U W REPORT. 1969. 4/yr. free. Rinder-Union-West, Postfach 6680, 48035 Muenster, Germany. TEL 49-251-92880. FAX 49-251-9288236. Ed. Stefan Rensing. adv.: B&W page DM.2500, color page DM.4375; trim 191 x 260. bk.rev.; film rev.; play rev.; bibl.; illus.; stat. circ. 45,000. (processed) **Document type:** newsletter.
Formerly (until 1993): Mitteilungen aus der Rheinischen Rinderzucht (ISSN 0026-6868)

626.932   US   ISSN 0894-7791
SF451
RABBIT GAZETTE. 1979. bi-m. $12. R G Publishing, 1725 S.W. Blvd., Kansas City, KS 66103. TEL 913-722-2229. Ed. Charlie Clarke. circ. 2,400.
Formerly: Rabbits (ISSN 0277-3171)

636.932   CN   ISSN 0033-7242
RABBITS IN CANADA. 1970. bi-m. $9. Clay Publishing Co. Ltd., One Oak St., Bewdley, Ont. K0L 1E0, Canada. TEL 416-797-2281. Ed. Charlotte F. Clay. bk.rev.; stat. circ. 1,000.

636.5   DK   ISSN 0909-1904
RACEFJERKRAE. m. DKK 260. Danmarks Fjerkraeavlerforening for Raceavl, Noerreportcentret, P.O. Box 1327, DK-7500 Holsterbro, Denmark. TEL 45-07-42-23-74. FAX 45-97-40-18-65. Ed. Willy Littau. adv. circ. 5,500.
Formerly (until 1994): Tidsskrift for Racefjerkraeavl (ISSN 0106-438X); Which supersedes in part (in 1971): Tidsskrift for Fjerkraeavl (ISSN 0040-7046); Which incorporates (1964-1965): Erhvervsfjerkrae (ISSN 0425-1954)

636   US   ISSN 1084-5402
SF371
RANCH & RURAL LIVING MAGAZINE. 1920. m. $22 (foreign $33) (includes Breeder Directory, Wool & Mohair Warehouse Directory). Ranch & Rural Living Magazine, Box 2678, San Angelo, TX 76902. TEL 915-655-4434. FAX 915-658-8250. URL: http://www.biz2.iadfw.net/ranchmag/. Ed. Scott Campbell; Pub. Scott Campbell. R&P contact: Scott Campbell. adv.: B&W page $475; adv. contact: Becky Williams. circ. 7,000. (also avail. in microfiche) **Indexed:** Sport Fish.Abstr., Wild.Rev. **Document type:** trade publication.
—Linda Hall; UnCover.
Former titles (until 1991): Ranch Magazine (ISSN 0145-8515); (until 1971): Sheep and Goat Raiser (ISSN 0037-3397)
Description: Covers sheep, goats and cattle of the livestock industry.

RANCH DOG TRAINER. see PETS

636.4   US   ISSN 0190-0528
CODEN: RNGLE7
RANGELANDS. (Text in English; occasional notes in Spanish) 1974. bi-m. $50 (foreign $67); with Journal of Range Management $140 (foreign $158) (effective 1995-1997). Society for Range Management, 1839 York St., Denver, CO 80206-1213. TEL 303-355-7070. Ed. Gary Frasier. adv. contact: Patty Rich. bk.rev.; bibl. circ. 5,100. (also avail. in microfilm from UMI; microfiche from UMI; reprint service avail. from UMI) **Indexed:** Ecol.Abstr., Geo.Abstr.H.G., Geo.Abstr.P.G., IDA, Sport Fish.Abstr., Wild.Rev., Zoo.Rec. **Document type:** trade publication.
—BLDSC (7254.417300); UMI; UnCover.
Former titles (until 1979): Rangeman's Journal (ISSN 0095-6236); (until 1974): Rangeman's News.
Description: Offers non-technical advice for land users and land managers.

RARE BREEDS JOURNAL. see PETS

AGRICULTURE — POULTRY AND LIVESTOCK

636   IT   ISSN 0300-3477
RAZZA BOVINA PIEMONTESE. (Text in Italian, English) 1970. q. free. Associazione Nazionale Allevatori Bovini di Razza Piemontese, Via Valeggio 22, 10128 Turin, Italy. TEL 39-173-750791. FAX 39-173-750915. Ed. Vittorio Faroppa. illus.; index; circ. 4,000 (controlled). **Document type:** newspaper.
   Description: Contains information on the results of genetic selection, development and promotion of the Piedmontese breed worldwide.

636   US   ISSN 0034-1614
RECORD STOCKMAN. 1889. w. $35. R S Livestock Publishers, Box 1209, 4800 Wadsworth, Ste. 320, Wheat Ridge, CO 80034-1209. TEL 303-425-5777. FAX 303-431-7545. Ed. Dan Green; Pub. Harry Green Jr. adv. contact: Ann Meyers. bk.rev.; illus.; mkt. circ. 18,500. **Document type:** newspaper.

636.2   US
RED POLL BEEF JOURNAL.* 1937. 4/yr. $15. American Red Poll Association, Box 014096, Kansas City, MO 64101-0096. Ed.Bd. adv.; illus.; mkt. circ. 3,400.
   Formerly: Red Poll News (ISSN 0034-2033)

636.2   UK
RED POLL HERD BOOK. 1874. a. £20. Red Poll Cattle Society, Market Hill, Woodbridge, Suffolk IP12 4LU, England. TEL 44-1394-380643. Ed. Philip Ryder-Davies. R&P contact: Philip Ryder-Davies. adv. circ. 200. **Document type:** directory.

636.5   FR   ISSN 1261-4319
REUSSIR AVICULTURE. 1994. 10/yr. 190 F. (foreign 230 F.) (effective 1997); newsstand price: 25 F. G I E Reussir, 19 quai de Juillet, B.P. 18, 14005 Caen Cedex, France. TEL 33-2-31357704. FAX 33-2-31822963. Ed. Pascal Le Douarin; Pub. Henri Lefebvre. R&P contact: Marc Jourdan. adv. contact: Jean-Pierre Dumas. circ. 8,000.
   Description: Technical and economical information about poultry and egg production.

636.2   FR
REUSSIR BOVINS. 11/yr. 230 F. G I E Reussir, 19 quai du Juillet, B.P. 18, 14005 Caen Cedex, France. TEL 33-1-31357704. FAX 33-2-31822963. Ed. Francois d'Alteroche. R&P contact: Marc Jourdan. adv. contact: Jean-Pierre Dumas. circ. 55,000. **Document type:** newspaper.

636.2   FR   ISSN 1260-1799
REUSSIR BOVINS - VIANDE. 1994. 11/yr. 190 F. (foreign 230 F.) (effective 1997); newsstand price: 25 F. G I E Reussir, 19 quai de Juillet, B.P. 18, 14005 Caen Cedex, France. TEL 33-2-31357704. FAX 33-2-31822963. Ed. Francois d'Alteroche; Pub. Henri Lefebvre. R&P contact: Marc Jourdan. adv. contact: Jean-Pierre Dumas.
   Description: Technical and economical information about beef production.

636.4   FR   ISSN 1261-4327
REUSSIR PORCS. 1994. 11/yr. 190 F. (foreign 230 F.) (effective 1997); newsstand price: 25 F. G I E Reussir, 19 quai de Juillet, B.P. 18, 14005 Caen Cedex, France. TEL 33-2-31357704. FAX 33-2-31822963. Ed. Francoise Fourn; Pub. Henri Lefebvre. R&P contact: Marc Jourdan. adv. contact: Jean-Pierre Dumas. circ. 14,000.
   Description: Technical and economical information about pig production.

636.5   CU   ISSN 0138-6352
REVISTA CUBANA DE CIENCIA AVICOLA. (Text in Spanish; summaries in English, Spanish) 3/yr. $28 in S. America; N. America $30; elsewhere $34 (effective 1998). Instituto de Investigaciones Avicolas, Biblioteca, Gaveta Postal No. 1, Santiago de las Vegas, CP 17200 Havana, Cuba. (Dist. by: Empresa Ediciones Cubanas, Apdo. 605, Havana 1, Cuba) Ed. Elena Trujillo Gil; Pub. Ramon Elias Laurent. R&P contact: Ramon Elias Laurent. adv. contact: Alberto Ramirez Moreno. bibl.; charts; cum.index: 1972-1979. **Indexed:** Anim.Breed.Abstr., Biol.Abstr., Chem.Abstr., Ind.Med., Ind.Vet., Nutr.Abstr., Poult.Abstr., Protozool.Abstr., Rev.Med.& Vet.Mycol., Soyabean Abstr., Vet.Bull. **Document type:** academic/scholarly publication.
  —BLDSC (7852.097300).

636   CU   ISSN 0258-6010
REVISTA DE PRODUCCION ANIMAL. 1985. 3/yr. $20 in N. and S. America; Europe $24. (Ministerio de Educacion Superior) Ediciones Cubanas, Obispo No. 527, Apdo. 605, Havana, Cuba.

636   VE
REVISTA PECUARIA/RANCHING REVIEW. 1938. bi-m. Federation Nacional de Ganaderos de Venezuela, Edf. Casa de Italia, Piso 7, Ofc. 16-19, Ave. La Industria San Bernardino, Caracas 101, Venezuela. Ed. Adolfo Alvarez Perera.

636.5   FR   ISSN 0048-7902
REVUE AVICOLE. 1891. 6/yr. 140 F. (foreign 150 F.). Societe Centrale d'Aviculture de France, 34 rue de Lille, 75007 Paris, France. TEL 42-61-26-44. Ed. Jean-Claude Periquet. adv.; bk.rev.; illus.; stat.
   Description: Concerned with the breeding of poultry, rabbits, and pigeons.

REVUE D'ELEVAGE ET DE MEDECINE VETERINAIRE DES PAYS TROPICAUX. see *VETERINARY SCIENCE*

REVUE DE L'ALIMENTATION ANIMALE; mensuel des industries de la nutrition animale. see *AGRICULTURE — Feed, Flour And Grain*

636   FR   ISSN 1266-5975
REVUE DE L'ELEVEUR LAITIER. 11/yr. 439 F. (effective 1997). C E P Groupe France Agricole, 8 Cite Paradis, 75010 Paris, France. TEL 33-1-40227900. FAX 33-1-48240315. Ed. Bruno Patenotre. circ. 40,000.
   Formerly (until 1995): Revue de l'Eleveur (ISSN 1254-2768)

636   GW
RIND IM BILD. 1922. q. DM.40 to non-members. (Rinderzucht Schleswig-Holstein eG) Rind im Bild Selbstverlag, Rendsburgerstr. 178, 24537 Neumuenster, Germany. FAX 49-4321-905395. (Co-sponsors: Landeskontrollverband Schleswig-Holstein e.V.; Verband Schleswig-Holsteiner Fleischrinderzuechter e.V.) Ed. H. Ruediger Wolf. adv.; B&W page DM.1800, color page DM.2500. bk.rev.; abstr.; charts; illus.; mkt.; stat. **Document type:** trade publication.
   Former titles: Bullen (ISSN 0942-282X); (until 1992) Angler Rinderzucht (ISSN 0171-7383); (until 1977): Angler Tierzucht (ISSN 0003-3227)

636.2   GW   ISSN 0948-9118
▼**RINDERZUCHT BRAUNVIEH.** Variant title: Braunvieh. 1995. q. DM.36 (foreign DM.39) (effective 1997); newsstand price: DM.9.50. B L V Verlagsgesellschaft mbH, Lothstr. 29, 80797 Munich, Germany. TEL 49-89-12705-0. FAX 49-89-12705354. **Document type:** trade publication.

636.2   GW   ISSN 0948-7247
RINDERZUCHT FLECKVIEH. Variant title: Fleckvieh. q. DM.32 (foreign DM.39) (effective 1997); newsstand price: DM.9.30. B L V Verlagsgesellschaft mbH, Lothstr. 29, 80797 Munich, Germany. TEL 49-89-12705-0. FAX 49-89-12705354. **Document type:** trade publication.

636.5   IT   ISSN 0005-2213
RIVISTA DI AVICOLTURA. Short title: A V. 1931. m. (11/yr.). L.59000 (effective 1996). Edagricole S.p.A., Via Emilia Levante 31, 40139 Bologna, Italy. TEL 39-51-492211. FAX 39-51-493660. Ed. Giulio Zucchi. adv.; B&W page L.760000, color page L.1200000; trim 185 x 247. bk.rev.; bibl.; charts; illus.; mkt.; stat.; tr.lit.; tr.mk.; index. circ. 5,100. **Indexed:** Anim.Breed.Abstr., Ind.Vet., Nutr.Abstr., Poult.Abstr., Protozool.Abstr., Rev.Med.& Vet.Mycol., Soyabean Abstr., Vet.Bull., World Agri.Econ.& Rural Sociol.Abstr.
  —BLDSC (7981.620000).
   Description: Shows the problems of Italian poultry breeding in a worldwide context.

636.932   IT   ISSN 0010-5929
RIVISTA DI CONIGLICOLTURA. Short title: C N. 1963; N.S. m. (11/yr.). L.62000 (effective 1996). Edagricole S.p.A., Via Emilia Levante 31, 40139 Bologna, Italy. TEL 39-51-492211. FAX 39-51-493660. Ed. Angelo Gamberini. adv.: B&W page L.760000, color page L.1200000; trim 185 x 247. bk.rev.; charts; illus.; index. circ. 8,600. **Indexed:** Anim,Breed.Abstr., Ind.Vet., Nutr.Abstr., Rev.Med.& Vet.Mycol., Triticale Abstr., Vet.Bull., World Agri.Econ.& Rural Sociol.Abstr.
  —BLDSC (7984.200000).
   Description: For breeders of rabbits and fur animals.

636.4   IT   ISSN 0035-662X
RIVISTA DI SUINICOLTURA; rivista tecnico-economica per gli allevatori di suini. Short title: S N. 1960. m. L.62000 (effective 1996). Edagricole S.p.A., Via Emilia Levante 31, 40139 Bologna, Italy. TEL 39-51-492211. FAX 39-51-493660. Ed. Giulio Zucchi. adv.: B&W page L.790000, color page L.1260000; trim 185 x 247. circ. 15,500. **Indexed:** Agri.Eng.Abstr., Anim.Breed.Abstr., Ind.Vet., Nutr.Abstr., Pig News & Info., Soyabean Abstr., Sugar Ind.Abstr., Vet.Bull.
  —BLDSC (7993.220000).
   Description: Deals with all economic problems of pig breeding, feeding, processing and marketing.

636   IT   ISSN 0304-0607
                                                      CODEN: RZOVBM
RIVISTA DI ZOOTECNIA E VETERINARIA;* rassegna di informazione e aggiornamento. (Text in Italian; summaries in English, German, French) 1924. bi-m. L.5000. (Societa Farmaceutici Italia) Centralvet, Via Colleoni 15, 20041 Agrate Brianza, Italy. Ed. Remo Faustini. adv.; bk.rev.; abstr.; bibl.; charts; illus.; stat.; index, cum.index. **Indexed:** Anim.Breed.Abstr., Biol.Abstr., Biotech.Abstr., Chem.Abstr., Dairy Sci.Abstr., Field Crop Abstr., Food Sci.& Tech.Abstr., Helminthol.Abstr., Herb.Abstr., Ind.Vet., Nutr.Abstr., Pig News & Info., Sport Fish.Abstr., Vet.Bull., Wild.Rev.
  —BLDSC (7993.705000); CASDDS; Linda Hall.
   Formerly (until 1973): Rivista di Zootecnia (ISSN 0035-6646)

636 633   US   ISSN 1072-5636
ROCKY MOUNTAIN LIVESTOCK JOURNAL. 1991. m. $24. Twin Publishing Co., Inc., 425 W. Griggs, Las Cruces, NM 88005. TEL 505-524-1012; 800-524-0070. FAX 505-524-1702. Ed. Stephanie Taylor. adv.; page $1160. circ. 18,000. (tabloid format; back issues avail.) **Document type:** trade publication.
   Formerly: Rocky Mountain Feed and Livestock Journal.
   Description: Covers traditional and alternative livestock industries with related activities and equipment and examines legislation affecting these industries.

636 575.1   PL   ISSN 0137-1657
                                                      CODEN: RNZOD8
ROCZNIKI NAUKOWE ZOOTECHNIKI/ANNALS OF ANIMAL SCIENCE. (Text in English, Polish; summaries in English, German, Polish, Russian) 1974. s-a. 88000 Zl. (effective 1991). Instytut Zootechniki - Institute of Animal Production, Ul. Sarego 2, 31-047 Krakow, Poland. TEL 48-12-227333. FAX 48-12-228065. TELEX PL 0322304 ZOOT. Ed. Andrzej Laszczka. circ. 800. (back issues avail.) **Indexed:** AgroLibrex, Anim.Breed.Abstr., Biol.Abstr., Food Sci.& Tech.Abstr., Nutr.Abstr., Poult.Abstr., Soyabean Abstr., Sport Fish.Abstr., Wild.Rev. **Document type:** academic/scholarly publication.
● Also available online.
Also available on CD-ROM.
  —BLDSC (8015.703000); CASDDS.
   Description: Covers breeding, feeding and feed science, technology, ethology and animal production economics.

636.3   UK
ROMNEY SHEEP BREEDERS' SOCIETY. HANDBOOK. 1895. a. free. Romney Sheep Breeders' Society, Geneva, School Rd., St. Mary in the Marsh, Romney Marsh, Kent TN29 0DG, England. TEL 44-1494-363839. FAX 44-1494-363839. Ed. David Roberts. adv. circ. 2,000. **Document type:** trade publication.
   Formerly: Romney Sheep Breeders' Society. Flock Book (ISSN 0305-5965)

AGRICULTURE — POULTRY AND LIVESTOCK

636 US ISSN 0889-2970
RURAL HERITAGE. 1975. bi-m. $22 (Canada $23.20; elsewhere $27). 281 Dean Ridge Ln., Gainesboro, TN 38562-5039. TEL 615-268-0655. Ed. Gail Damerow; Pub. Allan Damerow. R&P contact: Gail Damerow. adv. contact: Allan Damerow. bk.rev.; illus.; circ. 3,000 (paid). (back issues avail.) reprint service avail. **Document type:** consumer publication.
 Formerly: Evener (ISSN 0164-6613)
 Description: In support of modern farming and logging with horses, mules and oxen.

636.085 US ISSN 0036-0104
RURAL ROUNDUP. 1950. a. free. Kent Feeds Inc., 1600 Oregon St., Muscatine, IA 52761. TEL 319-264-4211. charts; illus. (tabloid format)

RWANDA. MINISTERE DE L'AGRICULTURE ET DE L'ELEVAGE. RAPPORT ANNUEL. see *AGRICULTURE*

636.3 AT
S A C S O S NEWSLETTER. 1974. m. Aus.$12.50. South Australian Coloured Sheep Owners' Society Inc., P.O. Box 110, Eastwood, S.A. 5063, Australia. Ed. Verle Wood. (back issues avail.) **Document type:** newsletter.
 Description: For breeders of colored sheep and users of natural colored wool.

636.2 SA ISSN 1018-6492
S A HOLSTEIN FRIESLAND JOURNAL. (Text and summaries in Afrikaans, English) 1912. a. S A Holstein Friesland Society, P.O. Box 544, Bloemfontein 9300, South Africa. TEL 27-51-479123. FAX 27-51-304224. Ed. Magda Auld. adv.: B&W page R.500, color page R.850; adv. contact: Magda Auld. illus. circ. 2,000. **Indexed:** Dairy Sci.Abstr., Ind.S.A.Per.
 Formerly: South African Friesland Journal (ISSN 0036-0724)
 Description: For breeding of pure Holstein Friesland cattle in South Africa.

636.2 SA ISSN 1018-6506
S A HOLSTEIN FRIESLAND MINI JOURNAL. (Text in Afrikaans, English) 1991. 10/yr. S A Holstein Friesland Society, P.O. Box 544, 9300 Bloemfontein, South Africa. TEL 27-51-479123. FAX 27-51-304224. Ed. Magda Auld. adv.: B&W page R.500. illus. circ. 2,000.

636 US
SALT AND TRACE MINERALS NEWSLETTER. 1966. s-a. free. Salt Institute, 700 N. Fairfax St., Ste. 600, Alexandria, VA 22314-2040. TEL 703-549-4648. FAX 703-548-2194. E-mail: info@saltinstitute.org; URL: http://www.saltinstitute.org. Ed. Judy Freeman. circ. 2,500. **Document type:** newsletter.
 Formerly: Agricultural Digest (ISSN 0568-2622)

636 SP
SAM. 1952. q. free. Cooperativa Lechera S A M, Barrio de San Antonio, s-n, 39470 Renedo de Pielagos (Cantabria), Spain. TEL 42-57-03-43. FAX 42-57-07-86. Ed. Juan Ignacio de Sebastian Palomares. circ. 12,000.

636.2 US ISSN 0036-455X
SANTA GERTRUDIS JOURNAL. 1959. m. $15. Box 938, Keller, TX 76244. adv.; illus.; stat.; index. circ. 3,600. (reprint service avail.) **Document type:** trade publication.

636.3 NO ISSN 0036-5009
SAU OG GEIT. 1947. bi-m. NOK 320 (effective 1997). Norsk Sau- og Geitalslag - Norwegian Sheep and Goatbreeders Association, P.O. Box 2323 Solli, 0201 Oslo 2, Norway. TEL 47-02-444288. FAX 47-2-43-16-60. Ed. Arne Maurtvedt. adv.; bk.rev.; illus. circ. 21,000. (tabloid format) **Indexed:** Anim.Breed.Abstr., Nutr.Abstr.
 —CCC.
 Description: Provides articles and information on animal husbandry, particularly that of sheep and goat breeding.

636.3 NE ISSN 0165-3156
HET SCHAAP. 1956. 10/yr. fl.72.50. (Nederlands Texels Schapenstamboek en Noord Hollands Schapenstamboek - Studbook Organisations for Sheepbreeding in the Netherlands) Misset (Subsidiary of: Reed Elsevier plc), Postbus 4, 7000 BA Doetinchem, Netherlands. TEL 31-314-349371. FAX 31-314-363638. TELEX 45481. Ed. Wim Wisman. adv.: B&W page fl.1842, color page fl.3367; trim 215 x 285; adv. contact: Cor van Nek. bk.rev.; charts; illus.; stat. circ. 10,390. **Document type:** trade publication.
 Description: Specialist trade news about sheep farming in the Netherlands.

636.3 AU
SCHAFE AKTUELL. 1991. q. S.118. Leopold Stocker Verlag, Hofgasse 5, A-8011 Graz, Austria. TEL 43-316-821636. FAX 43-316-835612. Ed. Ferdinand Ringdorfer. adv.: B&W page S.11490, color page S.24700; trim 195 x 260; adv. contact: Thomas Muehlbacher. circ. 7,000. **Document type:** trade publication.

636.4 GW ISSN 0036-7176
SCHWEINEZUCHT UND SCHWEINEMAST. 1953. 6/yr. DM.52.80 (foreign DM.62.40) (effective 1997). (Zentralverband der Deutschen Schweineproduktion e.V.) Landwirtschaftsverlag GmbH, Huelsebrockstr. 2, 48165 Muenster, Germany. TEL 49-2501-801-0. FAX 49-2501-801-204. (Subscr. to: Postfach 480249, 48079 Muenster, Germany) adv.; bk.rev.; early.; bibl.; charts; illus.; index. circ. 15,293. **Indexed:** Anim.Breed.Abstr., Dairy Sci.Abstr., Food Sci.& Tech.Abstr., Ind.Vet., Nutr.Abstr., Vet.Bull. **Document type:** trade publication.
 —CCC.

636 SZ
SCHWEIZER FLECKVIEH. (Text in French, German) 8/yr. Schweizerische Fleckviehzuchtverband, CH-3052 Zollikofen, Switzerland. TEL 031-9106111. FAX 031-9106199. Ed. Niklaus Flueckiger. circ. 14,500. **Document type:** trade publication.
 Formerly: Simmentaler Fleckvieh (ISSN 0258-6509)

636.5 SZ ISSN 1420-9217
SCHWEIZERISCHE GEFLUEGELZEITUNG. 1939. m. 39 SFr. Verlag Schweizerische Gefluegelzeitung, Burgerweg 24, CH-3052 Zollikofen, Switzerland. TEL 41-31-9110127. FAX 41-31-9116460. Ed. H.-R. Meier. R&P contact: Manuel Strasser. adv. contact: Manuel Strasser. bk.rev.; charts; illus. circ. 1,300. **Document type:** newspaper.
 Former titles: Geflugel und Kleinvieh (ISSN 0016-5832); Gefluegelhof.

636 SZ
SCHWEIZERISCHE VIEHAENDLER ZEITUNG. (Text in French, German, Italian) q. Postfach 53, CH-9413 Oberegg, Switzerland. TEL 01-2563209. Ed. A. Schuler. circ. 1,779.

636.4 US ISSN 1079-7963
SEEDSTOCK EDGE. 1994. m. (10/yr.). $15. National Swine Registry, 1769 U.S. Hwy. 52, W., Box 2417, West Lafayette, IN 47906. TEL 765-463-3594. FAX 765-497-2959. Ed. Darrell D. Anderson. adv. contact: Elaine Hughes. illus.; mkt.; circ. 5,000 (paid). **Document type:** trade publication.
 —Linda Hall; UnCover.
 Formed by the 1994 merger of: Duroc News (ISSN 0012-7299) & Yorkshire Journal (ISSN 0044-0612)
 Description: Includes swine-based articles, specializing in genetics and the sale of breeding stock.

636 JA ISSN 0386-8362
SEKAI NO CHIKUSAN/WORLD LIVESTOCK INDUSTRY. (Text in Japanese) 1976. bi-m. 3600 Yen (foreign 6600 Yen). Japan F A O Association - Kokusai Shokuryo Nogyo Kyokai, Bajichikusan-Kaikan, 1-2 Kanda Surugadai, Chiyoda-ku, Tokyo 101, Japan. TEL 81-3-3294-2425. FAX 81-3-3294-2427. Ed. Yutaka Furuya. adv. contact: Toyo Sekikawa. circ. 1,300. **Document type:** bulletin.

338.1 637.5 SP ISSN 0210-0541
SELECCIONES AVICOLAS. 1959. m. 9200 ptas.($80) Real Escuela de Avicultura, Plana del Paraiso, 14, 08350 Arenys de Mar (Barcelona), Spain. TEL 34-3-7921137. FAX 34-3-7921537. Ed. Jose A. Castello; Pub. Jose A. Castello. adv. contact: Conchita Luque. bk.rev.; abstr.; illus.; stat.; index. circ. 3,100. (back issues avail.)
 Description: Serves the poultry industry in Spain and Latin American countries.

636 FR
SELECTIONS AVICOLES; aviculture, colombiculture, cuniculture. 1962. m. (10/yr.). 50 F. Editions H. Artese, B.P. 245, 47006 Agen Cedex, France. TEL 53-66-51-13. FAX 53-66-67-33. adv. circ. 16,000.

636.5 CN ISSN 0315-6915
SHAVER FOCUS. 1964. 2/yr. free. Shaver Poultry Breeding Farms, Ltd., Box 400, Cambridge, ON N1R 5V9, Canada. TEL 519-621-5191. FAX 519-621-9407. TELEX 069-59337. Ed. Dr. Peter Hunton. charts; illus. circ. 10,000. **Document type:** newsletter.
 Description: Contains technical information relating to the production of eggs and meat chickens. Includes nutrition, disease control, breeding and genetics, management and husbandry, economics, processing and marketing.

636.3 338.1 US
SHEEP & GOAT RESEARCH JOURNAL. 1984. 3/yr. $30 (foreign $95) (effective 1997). American Sheep Industry Association, 6911 S. Yosemite St., Englewood, CO 80112-1414. TEL 303-771-3500. FAX 303-771-8200. Ed. Maurice Shelton; Pub. Paul Rogers. **Document type:** academic/scholarly publication.
 Description: Reports on research on the keeping of sheep and goats in agriculture.

636.3 UN
SHEEP AND GOATS IN HUMID WEST AFRICA. irreg. International Livestock Centre for Africa, P.O. Box 5689, Addis Ababa, Ethiopia.

636.3 US ISSN 0037-3400
SHEEP BREEDER AND SHEEPMAN. 1880. m. $18. Mead Livestock Services, Box 796, Columbia, MO 65205. TEL 314-442-8257. Ed. Larry E. Mead. adv.; bk.rev.; charts. circ. 10,000.
 —Linda Hall; SWETS; UnCover.

636.3 UK ISSN 0141-2434
THE SHEEP FARMER. 1974. m. £20 (foreign £30). National Sheep Association, c/o John Kendall, Ed., 132 Ebury St., London SW1W 922, England. TEL 0171-824-8681. FAX 0171-730-1390. adv. contact: Mandy Burgess. bk.rev. circ. 11,000. **Document type:** trade publication.
 Description: Studies all aspects of the production and marketing of sheep and wool.

636.3 677.3 US ISSN 0279-9200
SHEEP! MAGAZINE; published for practical sheep farmers and ranchers. 1979. m. $19 (foreign $25). Duck Creek Publications, Box 10, 128 E. Lake St., Lake Mills, WI 53551. TEL 414-648-8285. FAX 414-648-3770. Ed. Dave Thompson. adv.: page $649; trim 9 3/4 x 12 3/4; adv. contact: Dave Thompson. bk.rev.; illus. circ. 15,000. (tabloid format; back issues avail.) **Document type:** trade publication.

636.3 US ISSN 8750-7897
SHEPHERD; a guide for sheep and farm life. 1956. m. $20. Sheep and Farm Life, Inc., 5696 Johnston Rd., New Washington, OH 44854. TEL 419-492-2364. (Ed. addr.: Box 97, Cardington, OH 43315-0097. TEL 419-947-9289) Ed. Guy Flora. R&P contact: Pat Flora. adv. contact: Ken Kark. bk.rev.; illus.; index; circ. 6,000 (paid). **Document type:** trade publication.
 —SWETS; UnCover.
 Sheep Tales; Lamb Producers Journal; Lamb and Wool Production.

AGRICULTURE — POULTRY AND LIVESTOCK

636 US ISSN 0149-9319
SHORTHORN COUNTRY. 1976. m. (except Jun.). $24. Durham Management Co., 8288 Hascall St., Omaha, NE 68124. TEL 402-393-7051. FAX 402-393-7080. Ed. Debbie Hostert. circ. 3,200 (paid). (back issues avail.) **Document type:** trade publication.
—UnCover.
Description: Presents articles on management and the beef industry for producers of Shorthorn beef cattle.

636.234 UK ISSN 0141-4895
SHORTHORN JOURNAL. 1932. s-a. £6($10) Shorthorn Society of Great Britain and Ireland, 4th St. National Agricultural Centre, Stoneleigh Park, Kenilworth, Warwickshire CV8 2LG, England. TEL 44-1203-696549. FAX 44-1203-696729. Ed. J. Wood Roberts. adv.; bk.rev.; illus. circ. 1,000. **Document type:** trade publication.
Formerly (until 1978): Dairy Shorthorn Journal (ISSN 0011-569X)

636.2 CN ISSN 0037-427X
SHORTHORN NEWS. 1940. 8/yr. Can.$20. Progress Typesetting, Box 63, Qu'Appelle, Sask. S0G 4A0, Canada. TEL 306-699-7110. FAX 306-699-7111. Ed. Craig Andrew. adv.; illus. circ. 11,800.

636 637 FR
SICAMOB INFORMATION. 6/yr. Rue Morice-du-Parc, 29248 Guerlesquin, France. TELEX 940 603. Ed. Roger Eon. circ. 11,700.
Description: For breeders of cattle, pigs, poultry, rabbits and producers of milk and eggs.

636.4 FI ISSN 0037-5101
SIKA/PIG. (Text in Finnish; summaries in Swedish) 1910. 5/yr. FIM 170. Suomen Kotielainjalostusosuuskunta - Finnish Animal Breeding Cooperative, P.O. Box 40, FIN-01301 Vantaa, Finland. TEL 358-0-831736. FAX 358-0-833949. TELEX 125890. Ed. Jouko Syvaerjaervi. adv.; illus.; stat. circ. 8,000.

636.2 630 AT
SIMBEEF. 1974. 4/yr. Aus.$30. Australian Simmental Breeders Association Ltd., G.P.O. Box 5219, Sydney, N.S.W. 2001, Australia. TEL 61-2-93322114. FAX 61-2-93323617. E-mail: simmental@magnet.com.au. Ed. P. Speers. adv.; charts; illus.; tr.lit. circ. 2,000. **Indexed:** Anim.Breed.Abstr., Dairy Sci.Abstr., Ind.Vet. **Document type:** newsletter, trade publication.
Formerly (until 1995): Simmental News (ISSN 0815-6077)
Description: Covers news relating to Australian Simmental, Simbeef and Simbrah cattle.

636.2 SA
SIMMBULLETIN. (Text in Afrikaans, English) 1986. irreg., latest 1994. Simmental Cattle Breeders' Society of S.A. - Simmentaler Beestelersgenootskap van S.A., P.O. Box 3868, Bloemfontein 9300, South Africa. TEL 27-51-477696. FAX 27-51-471529. (tabloid format) **Document type:** bulletin.
Formerly (until 1993): Kliente Bulletin - Clients Bulletin.

636 UK
SIMMENTAL ANNUAL REVIEW. 1972. a. £20. British Simmental Cattle Society, National Agricultural Centre, Kenilworth, Warks. CV8 2LR, England. TEL 01203-696513. FAX 01203-696724. TELEX 31697 RASE G. Ed. David S. Gaunt. adv. contact: David S. Gaunt. circ. 2,750. **Document type:** bulletin.

636 US ISSN 0192-3072
SIMMENTAL SHIELD. 1972. m. $18. (American Simmental Association) Shield Publishing Co. Inc., Box 71, Lindsborg, KS 67456-0071. adv. circ. 7,000. (back issues avail.; reprint service avail.)

636.2 SA
SIMMENTALER JOURNAL. (Text in Afrikaans, English) 1976. a. $30. Simmentaler Cattle Breeders' Society of S.A. - Simmentaler Beestelersgenootskap van S.A., P.O. Box 3868, Bloemfontein 9300, South Africa. TEL 27-51-477696. FAX 27-51-471529. Ed. C.P. Massmann. adv.; circ. 1,200 (controlled). **Document type:** trade publication.

636.5 MX
SINTESIS-AVICOLA. m. Mex.$940. Editorial Ano Dos Mil, S.A., Indianapolis 70, 03810 Mexico D.F., Mexico. Ed. Juan Francisco Gonzalez Inigo.

636.4 MX
SINTESIS-PORCINA. m. Mex.$940. Editorial Ano Dos Mil, S.A., Indianapolis 70, 03810 Mexico D.F., Mexico. Ed. J. Mario Montanez.

636.3 NE ISSN 0921-4488
SF380 CODEN: SRUREW
SMALL RUMINANT RESEARCH. (Text in English; summaries in French, German and Spanish) 1980-1984; resumed N.S. 1988. m. fl.1880($1080) (effective 1998). (International Goat Association) Elsevier Science B.V., P.O. Box 211, 1000 AE Amsterdam, Netherlands. TEL 31-20-4853911. FAX 31-20-4853598. TELEX 18582 ESPA NL. E-mail: nlinfo-f@elsevier.nl; usinfo-f@elsevier.com; forinfo-kyf04035@niftyserve.or.jp; URL: http://www.elsevier.nl/. (Subscr. in the Americas to: Elsevier Science, Regional Sales Office, Box 945, New York, NY 10159-0945. TEL 212-633-3730. FAX 212-633-3680; Subscr. in Australasia and the Far East to: Elsevier Science (Singapore) Pte Ltd, No.1 Temasek Ave., No.17-01 Millenia Tower, Singapore 039192, Singapore. TEL 65-434-3727. FAX 65-337-2230; Subscr. in Japan to: Elsevier Science Japan, 9-15 Higashi-Azabu 1-chome, Minato-ku, Tokyo 106, Japan. TEL 81-3-5561-5033. FAX 81-3-5561-5047) Ed. G.F.W. Haenline. bk.rev. circ. 500. (also avail. in microform from UMI; back issues avail.) **Indexed:** Anim.Breed.Abstr., ASCA, Biol.Abstr., Chem.Abstr., Curr.Cont., Food Sci.& Tech.Abstr., Ind.Vet., Nutr.Abstr., Rural Recreat.Tour.Abstr., Vet.Bull., World Agri.Econ.& Rural Sociol.Abstr. **Document type:** academic/scholarly publication.
—BLDSC (8310.140000); CASDDS; Genuine Article; Linda Hall; SWETS; UnCover. **CCC.**
Formerly (until 1984): International Goat and Sheep Research (ISSN 0197-7393)
Description: Covers nutrition, physiology, anatomy, genetics, microbiology, ethology, product technology, socio-economics, management, veterinary medicine and husbandry engineering.
Refereed Serial

636 UN
SMALL RUMINANT RESEARCH NETWORK NEWSLETTER. 1984. 3/yr. free. International Livestock Center for Africa, P.O. Box 46847, Nairobi, Kenya. FAX 254-2-631481. TELEX 25747 ILCA KE. Ed. S.H.B. Lebbie. bk.rev. circ. 1,400. **Document type:** newsletter.
Formerly: Small Ruminant and Camel Group Newsletter.

630 AG ISSN 0037-8631
S15
SOCIEDAD RURAL ARGENTINA. ANALES. 1866. 10/yr. Arg.$22000. Sociedad Rural Argentina, Florida 460, Buenos Aires, Argentina. adv. circ. 15,000. **Indexed:** Biol.Abstr., Chem.Abstr., IBR.

338.1 AG ISSN 0081-0630
SOCIEDAD RURAL ARGENTINA. MEMORIA. (Supplements its Anales) 1887. a. free. Sociedad Rural Argentina, Florida 460, Buenos Aires, Argentina. circ. 15,000.

SOCIETY FOR RANGE MANAGEMENT. INTERNATIONAL RANGELAND CONGRESS. ABSTRACTS OF PAPERS. see *AGRICULTURE — Abstracting, Bibliographies, Statistics*

636 SA ISSN 0375-1589
CODEN: SAJAC9
SOUTH AFRICAN JOURNAL OF ANIMAL SCIENCE. (Text in English) 1971. q. R.145 to individuals; institutions R.165 (foreign $55) (effective 1997). (South African Society of Animal Production) Foundation for Education, Science & Technology, P.O. Box 1758, Pretoria 0001, South Africa. TEL 27-12-3226404. FAX 27-12-3207803. E-mail: buro@shuttle.up.ac.za. Ed. J.G. van der Walt. adv. contact: J.G. van der Walt. circ. 1,100. **Indexed:** Anim.Breed.Abstr., ASCA, Biol.Abstr., Chem.Abstr., Curr.Adv.Ecol.Sci., Curr.Cont., Dairy Sci.Abstr., Field Crop Abstr., Food Sci.& Tech.Abstr., Helminthol.Abstr., Herb.Abstr., Ind.S.A.Per., Ind.Vet., Maize Abstr., Nutr.Abstr., Pig News & Info., Poult.Abstr., Rural Devel.Abstr., Rural Recreat.Tour.Abstr., Soils & Fert., Sorghum & Millets Abstr., Sport Fish.Abstr., Sugar Ind.Abstr., Triticale Abstr., Vet.Bull., Wild.Rev., World Agri.Econ.& Rural Sociol.Abstr., Zoo.Rec. **Document type:** academic/scholarly publication.
—BLDSC (8338.650000); CASDDS; Genuine Article; Linda Hall; UMI; UnCover. **CCC.**
Incorporates: South African Society of Animal Production. Proceedings. Handelinge (ISSN 0081-2536)
Description: Publishes original contributions in animal science research.
Refereed Serial

636.5 SA ISSN 0257-201X
SOUTH AFRICAN POULTRY BULLETIN. (Text in Afrikaans, English) 1906. m. R.85.50 to non-members (foreign R.200; airmail R.300) (effective 1995). (South African Poultry Association) Promass (Pty) Ltd., P.O. Box 1192, Honeydew 2040, South Africa. TEL 27-11-795-2051. FAX 27-11-795-3180. Ed. Zach Coetzee. adv.: B&W page R.1050; trim 300 x 210. bk.rev. circ. 2,250. (back issues avail.) **Document type:** bulletin.

636 US ISSN 0038-3384
SOUTH DAKOTA STOCKGROWER. 1930. m. $5. South Dakota Stock Growers Association, 426 St. Joe St., Rapid City, SD 57701. TEL 605-342-0429. Ed. Darlene Huettl. adv.; illus. circ. 15,000. **Document type:** trade publication.
—Linda Hall.

636.2 US
SOUTHERN CATTLE. 1992. q. free. Rural Press U S A, 7701 Six Forks Rd., Ste. 132, Raleigh, NC 27615. TEL 919-676-3276; 800-477-1737. FAX 919-676-9803. (Subscr. to: Box 150001, Raleigh, NC 27624) Ed. Amy Leslie; Pub. Jeff Tennant. adv.: B&W page $1954. circ. 15,000. **Document type:** newspaper.

636.4 US
SOUTHERN HOGS. 1992. m. free. Rural Press U S A, 7701 Six Forks Rd., Ste. 132, Raleigh, NC 27615. TEL 919-676-3276; 800-477-1737. FAX 919-676-9803. (Subscr. to: Box 150001, Raleigh, NC 27624) Ed. Amy Leslie; Pub. Jeff Tennant. adv.: B&W page $1954. circ. 15,000. **Document type:** newspaper.

636.5 US
SOUTHERN POULTRY. 1992. q. free. Rural Press U S A, 7701 Six Forks Rd., Ste. 132, Raleigh, NC 27615. TEL 919-676-3276. FAX 919-676-9803. (Subscr. to: Box 150001, Raleigh, NC 27624) Ed. Amy Leslie; Pub. Jeff Tennant. circ. 12,000. **Document type:** newspaper.

636 US ISSN 1050-9526
SOUTHWEST STOCKMAN. w. $30. R S Livestock Publishers, 4800 Wadsworth, Box 1209, Wheat Ridge, CO 80034-1209. TEL 303-425-5777. FAX 303-431-7545. Ed. Dan Green; Pub. Harry Green Jr. adv. contact: Ann Meyers. circ. 16,000. (tabloid format) **Document type:** newspaper.

636.3 US ISSN 0038-6626
SPEAKING OF "COLUMBIAS". 1960. m. membership. Columbia Sheep Breeders Association of America, Box 272, Upper Sandusky, OH 43351. TEL 419-482-2608. Ed. Richard L. Gerber. adv. circ. 3,000.

STATISTICAL OFFICE OF THE EUROPEAN COMMUNITIES. AGRICULTURAL PRICES; selected series - chronos data bank. see *AGRICULTURE — Abstracting, Bibliographies, Statistics*

AGRICULTURE — POULTRY AND LIVESTOCK

636 NE ISSN 0926-485X
STICHTING PRAKTIJKONDERZOEK PLUIMVEEHOUDERIJ. JAARVERSLAG. 1977. a. Stichting Praktijkonderzoek Pluimveehouderij, Postbus 31, 7360 AA Beekbergen, Netherlands. TEL 31-55-5066500. FAX 31-55-5064858. **Document type:** corporate report.
 Supersedes (in 1991): Stichting Pluimveeteeltproefbedrijven. Jaarverslag (ISSN 0927-0442)

636 NE ISSN 0927-0213
STICHTING PRAKTIJKONDERZOEK PLUIMVEEHOUDERIJ. ONDERZOEKVERSLAG. 1990. irreg. (3-4/yr.) fl.50 (foreign fl.65) (effective 1994). Stichting Praktijkonderzoek Pluimveehouderij, Postbus 15, 7360 AA Beekbergen, Netherlands. TEL 31-5766-6500. FAX 31-5766-4858. **Document type:** academic/scholarly publication.
 Supersedes (in 1991): Stichting Pluimveeteeltproefbedrijven. Onderzoekverslag (ISSN 0924-9362)

636.2 NE
STIERENBOEK. 2/yr. Misset (Subsidiary of: Reed Elsevier plc), Postbus 4, 7000 BA Doetinchem, Netherlands. TEL 31-8340-49911. FAX 31-8340-43839. TELEX 45481. circ. 2,000. **Document type:** trade publication.
 Former titles: Boerderij Stierenboek; Stierenboek.
 Description: Current genetic information on all available breeding bulls.

636 AT ISSN 0039-162X
STOCK JOURNAL. 1904. w. Aus.$98.50. Stock Journal Publishers Pty. Ltd., 123 Greenhill Rd., Unley, S.A. 5061, Australia. TEL 61-8-3725222. FAX 61-8-3725272. Ed. Sharon Watt; Pub. Neil Holthouse. adv. contact: Dan Eime. bk.rev.; abstr.; stat. circ. 18,926. (tabloid format) **Document type:** newspaper.
 Formerly: Adelaide Stock and Station Journal.

636 CN ISSN 0820-4683
STOCKGROWER DIGEST. 1972. m. Can.$2($3) Maple Creek News Ltd., P.O. Box 1360, Maple Creek, SK S0N 1N0, Canada. TEL 306-667-2133. Ed. Jack Migowsky. adv.; illus. circ. 6,000. (tabloid format)
 Former titles (until 1987): Saskatchewan Stockgrower Magazine (ISSN 0820-4675); (until 1984): Saskatchewan Stockgrower (ISSN 0315-6117)

636 US ISSN 0899-1057
STOCKMAN - GRASS FARMER. 1945. m. $15. Mid-South Stockman-Farmer, Box 9607-MF, Jackson, MS 39206. Ed. H. Allan Nation. adv.; illus. circ. 10,632.
 Former titles: Stockman Farmer (ISSN 0192-7140); Mid-South Stockman Farmer; Mississippi Valley Stockman-Farmer (ISSN 0026-6434)
 Description: Devoted to the art and science of turning grass into beef, lamb, or milk.

636.3 UK
SUFFOLK SHEEP SOCIETY FLOCK BOOK. 1887. a. £18. Suffolk Sheep Society, Sheep Centre, Malvern, Worcs WR13 6PH, England. Ed. Penny Lawrence. circ. 1,400. **Document type:** trade publication.
 Description: Pedigrees of registered Suffolk sheep.

SUFFOLK STUD BOOK. see SPORTS AND GAMES — Horses And Horsemanship

636.4 BL ISSN 0100-9125
SUINOCULTURA INDUSTRIAL. 1979. m. Cr.$60. Gessulli Editores Ltda., Caixa Postal 198, 18540-000 Porto Feliz SP, Brazil. TEL 55-152-623133. FAX 55-152-623919. Ed. Osvaldo Penha Gessulli. adv.: B&W page $2340, color page $3265; 215 x 290. illus.; index. circ. 13,000.

636.2 MX ISSN 1025-2568
SUIZO CARNE Y LECHE. (Text in English, Spanish) 1989. bi-m. Mex.$150($72) (effective 1995). Editorial Ocampo, S.A. de C.V., Zaragoza No. 11, San Juan Tepepan, 16020 Mexico DF, Mexico. TEL 525-590-1445. (Subscr. to: Estafetas No. 5 Col. Postal, 03410 Mexico DF, Mexico) Ed. Ruben Ocampo Trujillo. adv.: B&W page $835, color page $1170; adv. contact: Ana Cristina Miranda. circ. 3,000. **Document type:** consumer publication.
 Description: Covers Brown Swiss and Braunvieh cattle.

636.5 FI ISSN 1238-9889
SUOMEN SIIPIKARJA. 1919. 4/yr. FIM 200 (effective 1997). Suomen Siipikarjaliitto ry - Poultry Federation of Finland - Finlands Fjaederfaefoerbund, Keskuskatu 21, FIN-31600 Jokioinen, Finland. TEL 02-4384-737. FAX 02-84738. Ed. Jarmo Sipila. adv.: color page FIM 11800; adv. contact: Anneli Raitanen. charts; illus.; stat.; index. circ. 3,000. **Document type:** trade publication.
 Formed by the 1995 merger of Siipikarja (ISSN 0037-5098) & Kanatalous (ISSN 0356-2743)

SURINAAMSE LANDBOUW/SURINAM AGRICULTURE. see AGRICULTURE

636.294 SW ISSN 1101-198X
SVENSK HJORTAVEL. 1971. bi-m. SEK 300 membership (effective 1993). Riksfoerbundet foer Svensk Hjortavel, c/o E. Johansson, Hjortaroed, S-282 00 Tyringe, Sweden.

636.4 DK ISSN 0904-3640
SVINEAVL OG PRODUKTION I DANMARK. AARSBERETNING/NATIONAL COMMITTEE FOR PIG BREEDING, HEALTH AND PRODUCTION. ANNUAL REPORT. 1973. a. free. Landsudvalget for Svin - National Committee for Pig Breeding, Health and Production, Axelborg, Axeltorv 3, DK-1609 Copenhagen V, Denmark. FAX 45-33-11-68-14. TELEX 22975. E-mail: LU@ds-data.dk. Ed. Martin E. Andersson. illus. circ. 30,000. **Document type:** corporate report.
 Formerly (until 1988): Svineavl og Produktion i Danmark (ISSN 0106-7338)
 Refereed Serial

636.4 NO ISSN 0332-7566
SVINEAVLSNYTT. 1965. 8/yr. NOK 400 to members; others NOK 500 (effective 1997). (Norsk Svineavlslag) Norsk Svineavlslag, Norsvinsenteret, Box 504, N-2301 Hamar, Norway. TEL 47-62-51-01-00. FAX 47-62-51-01-01. Ed. Arnulf Jensen. adv.: B&W page NOK 10200, color page NOK 13800; trim 188 x 265; adv. contact: Bjoern Erik haug. circ. 5,196. **Document type:** trade publication, consumer publication.

636.4 RU ISSN 0039-713X
CODEN: SVINAI
SVINOVODSTVO. 1930. q. $40. Sadovaya-Spasskaya, 18, 107807 Moscow, Russia. TEL 7-095-975133. FAX 7-095-2072870. (Dist. by: Mezhdunarodnaya Kniga, B. Yakimanka 39, 117049 Moscow, Russia. TEL 7-095-2384967. FAX 7-095-2384634) Ed. Kim D. Baev. bk.rev.; illus.; index. circ. 5,700. (tabloid format) **Indexed:** Anim.Breed.Abstr., Biol.Abstr., Chem.Abstr., Dairy Sci.Abstr., Maize Abstr., Nutr.Abstr., Pig News & Info., Soyabean Abstr., Sugar Ind.Abstr., Triticale Abstr.
 —CASDDS.

636.4 SW ISSN 0346-2471
SVINSKOETSEL/PIG FARMING. 1910. m. (10/yr.). SEK 450. (Svenska Grisproducenter) Agrar Press AB, Pl. 6479, S-692 93 Kumla, Sweden. TEL 46-19 576090. FAX 46-19-580050. E-mail: lg.lannhard@agrar.se. Ed. Lars-Gunnar Lannhard. adv.; index. circ. 4,900. **Indexed:** Anim.Breed.Abstr., Pig News & Info. **Document type:** newspaper.
 Formerly (until vol.8, 1962): Svenska Svinavelsfoereningens tidskrift.

636 635 II
SWARAJYA SANDESH. (Text in Hindi) 1964. w. Rs.120; newsstand price: Rs.3. R.K. Sharma, Ed. & Pub., 2-8, Ansari Rd., Daryaganj, New Delhi 110 002, India. TEL 326-6178. circ. 51,030. cols./p.: 5.
 Description: Covers rural development, poultry, animal husbandry, horticulture, and co-operatives.

636.5 US ISSN 0082-8661
TABLES ON HATCHERY AND FLOCK PARTICIPATION IN THE NATIONAL POULTRY IMPROVEMENT PLAN.* 1937. a. free. U.S. Animal and Plant Health Inspection Service, 4700 River Rd., Unit 6, Riverdale, MD 20737. TEL 301-734-5240. Ed. R.D. Scher. circ. 4,000.
 Incorporates: U.S. Agricultural Research Service. Animal Science Research Division. Tables on Hatchery and Flock Participation in the National Turkey Improvement Plan (ISSN 0082-867X)

636.4 US ISSN 0082-1608
TAMWORTH ANNUAL. 1965. irreg. single copy free; additional copies $0.25 ea. Tamworth Swine Association, 414 Van Deman St., Washington Court House, OH 43160. Ed. Robert Highfield. bk.rev. circ. 1,500.

TECHNICAL CONFERENCE ON ARTIFICIAL INSEMINATION AND REPRODUCTION. see AGRICULTURE — Dairying And Dairy Products

TECNICA EN AGRICULTURA Y GANADERIA. see AGRICULTURA — Crop Production And Soil

636.2 MX ISSN 0040-1889
CODEN: TPMXA3
TECNICA PECUARIA EN MEXICO. (Text in Spanish; summaries in English) 1963. s-a. Mex.$80($4) Instituto Nacional de Investigaciones Pecuarias, Departamento de Divulgacion Tecnica, KM 15.5 Carretera Mexico-Toluca, Apdo. Postal 41-652, Cuajimalpa 05110 Mexico DF, Mexico. (Co-sponsor: Secretaria de Agricultura y Recursos Hidraulicos) Ed.Bd. bibl.; charts; illus.; stat. circ. 2,000. **Indexed:** Anim.Breed.Abstr., Biol.Abstr., Chem.Abstr., Dairy Sci.Abstr., Field Crop Abstr., Herb.Abstr., Ind.Vet., Nutr.Abstr., Protozool.Abstr., Rural Recreat.Tour.Abstr., Small Anim.Abstr., Soils & Fert., Vet.Bull., World Agri.Econ.& Rural Sociol.Abstr.
 —CASDDS.

636.6 UK
TEESWATER SHEEP BREEDERS' ASSOCIATION. ANNUAL FLOCK BOOK. 1949. a. £10 large breeders; £7 small breeders. Teeswater Sheep Breeders' Association, 1 The Mount, Leyburn, N. Yorks DL8 5JA, England. TEL 44-1969-23432. adv.; circ. 140 (controlled). **Document type:** directory.
 Description: Records pedigree registered lambs and breeders' names and addresses.

636 664.9 628 YU ISSN 0494-9846
TS1950 CODEN: TEMEA5
TEHNOLOGIJA MESA/MEAT TECHNOLOGY: casopis industrije mesa Jugoslavije. (Text in English and Serbo-Croatian) 1960. m. 7500 din.($50) Yugoslav Institute of Meat Technology, Kacanskog 13, P.O. Box 548, 11000 Belgrade, Yugoslavia. TEL 011 650-655. Ed. Zivka Tadic. circ. 1,000. **Indexed:** Food Sci.& Tech.Abstr.
 —BLDSC (8763.920000); CASDDS.

636 US
TEXAS BRANGUS. m. Texas Brangus Breeders Association, Box 690750, San Antonio, TX 78269-0750. TEL 409-846-5733.

636.2 US ISSN 0744-4761
TEXAS HEREFORD. 1951. m. $10. Texas Hereford Association, 4609 Airport Frwy., Ft. Worth, TX 76117. TEL 817-831-3161. FAX 817-831-3162. Ed. Jack Chastain; Pub. Jack Chastain. R&P contact: Jack Chastain. adv. contact: Jack Chastain. circ. 2,200 (paid). **Document type:** trade publication.
 Description: Contains information for members and others interested in Hereford cattle. Informs readers of news, sales, shows, and other events.

636.309489 DK ISSN 0906-1746
TIDSSKRIFT FOR DANSK FAAREAVL. 1936. 10/yr. DKK 575. Dansk Faareavl, Landbrugets Raadgivningscenter, Udkaersvej 15, DK-8200 Aarhus N, Denmark. TEL 45-86-10-90-88. FAX 45-86-10-97-00. Ed. Peter Busch. adv. contact: Peter Busch. charts; illus.; mkt.; stat. circ. 2,500. **Indexed:** Anim.Breed.Abstr., Dairy Sci.Abstr. **Document type:** newsletter.
 —BLDSC (8822.650000).
 Formerly (until 1991): Tidsskrift for Faareavl (ISSN 0040-7038)

636.9322 DK ISSN 0900-3401
TIDSSKRIFT FOR KANINAVL. 1895. m. DKK 200($35) Danmarks Kaninavlerforening, Kirkevej 6, Blistrup, DK-3230 Graested, Denmark. TEL 45-48-71-58-88. FAX 45-48-71-74-26. Ed. Frederik Andersen. circ. 2,500.

TODAY'S FEED LOTTING. see AGRICULTURE — Feed, Flour And Grain

AGRICULTURE — POULTRY AND LIVESTOCK

636 **US**
TRI-STATE LIVESTOCK NEWS. 1963. w. $25. 1022 Main St., Box 129, Sturgis, SD 57785. TEL 605-347-2585. FAX 605-347-2525. Ed. Frances Severson. adv. circ. 12,000.
Description: Agricultural news serving cattle, sheep and horse producers and crop producers in South Dakota, North Dakota, Montana, Wyoming and Nebraska.

TROPICAL ANIMAL HEALTH AND PRODUCTION. see *VETERINARY SCIENCE*

TURK VETERINERLIK VE HAYVANCILIK DERGISI/TURKISH JOURNAL OF VETERINARY AND ANIMAL SCIENCES. see *VETERINARY SCIENCE*

636.592 016 **US** **ISSN 0041-4271**
TURKEY WORLD. 1926. bi-m. $28. Watt Publishing Co., 122 S. Wesley Ave., Mt. Morris, IL 61054. TEL 815-734-4171. FAX 815-734-4201. Ed. Bernard E. Heffernan; Pub. Charles Olentine. adv.: B&W page $2325, color page $3025; trim 8 x 10 3/4; adv. contact: Corinne Riehle. charts; illus.; stat.; tr.lit. circ. 7,190. **Indexed:** Ind.Vet. **Document type:** trade publication.
—Linda Hall; UnCover. **CCC.**
Description: An international turkey magazine dealing with the production, processing and marketing of turkeys.

636.5 **UK**
TURKEYS. 1951. bi-m. $31. Fancy Fowl Publications Ltd., Andover Rd., Highclere, Newbury, Berks., England. TEL 44-1635-253239. FAX 44-1635-254146. Ed. Shirley Murdoch. R&P contact: Shirley Murdoch. adv. contact: Shirley Murdoch. bk.rev. circ. 2,000. **Document type:** trade publication.
Description: For all sectors of turkey growing: breeding, processing and marketing. Includes papers from technical conferences.

636 **FR** **ISSN 1142-2149**
TYPEX MAGAZINE. English edition (ISSN 1357-6798) (Editions in English, French, German and Spanish) 1989. m. Editions du Boisbaudry, B.P. 6359, 35063 Rennes Cedex, France. TEL 99-32-21-21. FAX 99-32-14-17. TELEX 730619F.

636 **UK** **ISSN 1357-6798**
TYPEX MAGAZINE; the international business magazine for dairy pedigree breeders. French edition (ISSN 1142-2149) (Editions in English, French, German, and Spanish) 1989. 11/yr. £38. Asbury Publications Ltd., Stoke Road, Bishop's Cleeve, Gloucestershire GL52 4RW, England. TEL 44-1242-676645. FAX 44-1242-674032. E-mail: 10544.2147@compuserve.com. Ed. Roger Gilbert; Pub. Roger Gilbert.
Description: Sections include bull proofs, colour breeds, farm visits, Holsteins Europe, specific sires, and features on genetics and other topics.

636 **AT**
U G A GRAZIER. m. Aus.$18. United Graziers Association of Queensland, P.O. Box 167, Brisbane Roma St., Qld. 4003, Australia. Ed. Mark Phelps. adv.: page Aus.$900; adv. contact: Mark Phelps. circ. 3,000. (tabloid format; back issues avail.) **Document type:** newspaper.
Description: Provides news and information for Queensland graziers.

637.5 **US**
U S D A EGG MARKET NEWS REPORT. s-w. $125 (Mexico and Canada $140; elsewhere $175); by fax in the U.S. $250. U.S. Department of Agriculture, Agricultural Marketing Service (Des Moines), Poultry Division, Market News Branch, 210 Walnut St., Rm. 951, Des Moines, IA 50309. TEL 515-284-4471. FAX 515-284-4468. URL: http://www.ams.usda.gov/marketnews.htm. (also avail. by fax; back issues avail.) **Document type:** government publication.
Formerly: Egg Report.

636 **US**
U S D A POULTRY & EGG WEEKLY REVIEW. w. $100 (Mexico and Canada $110; elsewhere $125); by fax in the U.S. $150. U.S. Department of Agriculture, Agricultural Marketing Service (Des Moines), Poultry Division, Market News Branch, 210 Walnut St., Rm. 951, Des Moines, IL 50309. TEL 515-284-4471. FAX 515-284-4468. URL: http://www.ams.usda.gov/marketnews.htm. (also avail. by fax) **Document type:** government publication.
Formerly: Poultry and Egg Weekly Review.

636.5 **US**
U S D A POULTRY MARKET NEWS. ANNUAL SUMMARY. a. $15 (outside N. America $20). U.S. Department of Agriculture, Agricultural Marketing Service (Des Moines), Poultry Division, Market News Branch, 210 Walnut St., Rm. 951, Des Moines, IA 50309. TEL 515-284-4471. FAX 515-284-4468. URL: http://www.ams.usda.gov/marketnews.htm. **Document type:** government publication.
Formerly: Poultry Market News. Annual Summary.

636.5 **US**
U S D A POULTRY MARKET NEWS. MONTHLY SUMMARY. m. $100 (Mexico and Canada $110; elsewhere $130); by fax in the U.S. $225. U.S. Department of Agriculture, Agricultural Marketing Service (Des Moines), Poultry Division, Market News Branch, 210 Walnut St., Rm. 951, Des Moines, IA 50309. TEL 515-284-4471. FAX 515-284-4468. URL: http://www.ams.usda.gov/marketnews.htm. (also avail. in microfiche from CIS; also avail. by fax; reprint service avail. from CIS) **Indexed:** Amer.Stat.Ind. (1973-). **Document type:** government publication.
Former titles: Poultry Maket News. Monthly Summary; Cold Storage Report Monthly Summary; Cold Storage Report Monthly.

338.1 **US**
U S D A POULTRY REPORT. s-w. $285 (Mexico and Canada $320; elsewhere $410); by fax in the U.S. $625. U.S. Department of Agriculture, Agricultural Marketing Service (Des Moines), Poultry Division, Market News Branch, 210 Walnut St., Rm. 951, Des Moines, IA 50309. TEL 515-284-4471. FAX 515-284-4468. URL: http://www.ams.usda.gov/marketnews.htm. (also avail. by fax; back issues avail.) **Document type:** government publication.
Formerly: Poultry Report.

636.5 **IT**
UNAVICOLTURA. 1965. q. L.20000 (foreign L.30000) (effective 1995). Unione Nazionale dell'Avicoltura - Servizi s.r.l., Via Piemonte 117, 00187 Rome, Italy. TEL 39-6-33254015. FAX 39-6-463811. Dir. Rino Celadon. adv. contact: Rita Pasquarelli. bk.rev.; abstr.; charts; illus.; stat. circ. 9,800.
Former titles (until 1986): U N A Notizie di Avicoltura; U N A Informazione Avicole.

636.39 **US** **ISSN 0164-9353**
UNITED CAPRINE NEWS. m. $17. Box 365, Granbury, TX 76048-0365. TEL 817-579-5211. FAX 817-579-2606. Pub. Jeff Klein. adv. **Document type:** trade publication.

636 **US**
U.S. BELTIE NEWS. 1980. m. $25 membership. Belted Galloway Society, Inc., 174 Spore Rd., Potts Camp, MS 38659. TEL 601-333-4453. Ed. Jane Faul. **Document type:** newsletter.
Description: Covers cattle breeds.

U.S. DEPARTMENT OF AGRICULTURE. AGRICULTURAL STATISTICS BOARD REPORT: CATTLE. see *AGRICULTURE — Abstracting, Bibliographies, Statistics*

U.S. DEPARTMENT OF AGRICULTURE. AGRICULTURAL STATISTICS BOARD REPORT: CHICKENS AND EGGS. see *AGRICULTURE — Abstracting, Bibliographies, Statistics*

U.S. DEPARTMENT OF AGRICULTURE. AGRICULTURAL STATISTICS BOARD REPORT: EGG PRODUCTS. see *AGRICULTURE — Abstracting, Bibliographies, Statistics*

U.S. DEPARTMENT OF AGRICULTURE. AGRICULTURAL STATISTICS BOARD REPORT: HOGS AND PIGS. see *AGRICULTURE — Abstracting, Bibliographies, Statistics*

U.S. DEPARTMENT OF AGRICULTURE. AGRICULTURAL STATISTICS BOARD REPORT: LIVESTOCK SLAUGHTER. see *AGRICULTURE — Abstracting, Bibliographies, Statistics*

U.S. DEPARTMENT OF AGRICULTURE. AGRICULTURAL STATISTICS BOARD REPORT: POULTRY SLAUGHTER. see *AGRICULTURE — Abstracting, Bibliographies, Statistics*

636 **RM** **CODEN: LSIVDF**
UNIVERSITATEA AGRONOMICA ION IONESCU DE LA BRAD. LUCRARI STIINTIFICE. SERIA ZOOTEHNIE - MEDICINA VETERINARIA. 1957. a. Universitatea Agronomica "Ion Ionescu de la Brad", Aleea M. Sadoveanu, Nr. 3, Jassy, Rumania. **Indexed:** Anim.Breed.Abstr., Biol.Abstr., Ind.Vet., Nutr.Abstr., Rev.Med.& Vet.Mycol., Vet.Bull.
—BLDSC (5303.406000); CASDDS.
Formerly: Institutul Agronomic Ion Ionescu de la Brad. Lucrari Stiintifice. Seria Zootehnie - Medicina Veterinaria (ISSN 0075-3513)

636 636.089 **RM** **ISSN 1221-3594** **CODEN: BIAVDX**
UNIVERSITATEA DE STIINTE AGRICOLE CLUJ-NAPOCA. BULETINUL. SERIA ZOOTEHNIE SI MEDICINA VETERINARA. (Text in Rumanian; summaries in English, French) 1975. a. Universitatea de Stiinte Agricole Cluj-Napoca, Str. Manastur No. 3, 3400 Cluj-Napoca, Rumania. Ed. Alexandru Salontai. circ. 500. (back issues avail.) **Indexed:** Biodet.Abstr., Biol.Abstr., Ind.Vet., Landwirt.Zentralbl., Poult.Abstr., Soyabean Abstr., Sport Fish.Abstr., Vet.Bull., Wild.Rev., Zoo.Rec.
—CASDDS.
Formerly (until 1992): Institutul Agronomic Cluj-Napoca. Buletinul. Seria Zootehnie si Medicina Veterinara (ISSN 0557-4668); Supersedes in part (in 1977): Institutul Agronomic Cluj-Napoca. Buletinul (ISSN 0378-0554).

636 **RM**
UNIVERSITATEA DE STIINTE AGRONOMICE. LUCRARI STIINTIFICE. SERIA D, ZOOTEHNIE. (Text in Rumanian; summaries in English) 1960. a. exchange basis only. Universitatea de Stiinte Agronomice si Medicina Veterinaria, Bdul. Marasti, 59, Bucharest, Sec. 1, Rumania. **Document type:** academic/scholarly publication.
Formerly (until 1992): Institutul Agronomic Nicolae Balcescu. Lucrari Stiintifice. Seria D, Zootehnie (ISSN 0374-8898); Which supersedes in part (in 1970): Institutul Agronomic Nicolae Balcescu. Lucrari Stiintifice. Seria C, Zootehnie si Medicina Veterinara (ISSN 0524-8108); Which supersedes in part: Institutul Agronomic Nicolae Balcescu. Anuarul Lucrarilor Stiintifice (ISSN 1120-1987).

UNIVERSITIES FEDERATION FOR ANIMAL WELFARE. SYMPOSIUM ON POULTRY WELFARE. PROCEEDINGS. see *ANIMAL WELFARE*

338.19 664 **US** **ISSN 0273-9992**
URNER BARRY'S PRICE-CURRENT. 1858. d. (Mon.-Fri.). $415 (by fax $360/q.; e-mail $120/m.). Urner Barry Publications, Inc., Box 389, Toms River, NJ 08754. TEL 908-240-5330. FAX 908-341-0891. E-mail: mail@urnerbarry.com; URL: http://www.urnerbarry.com. Ed. Paul B. Brown. adv. contact: Angela Cuccinello. mkt.; stat. circ. 3,000. **Document type:** newspaper, trade publication.
•Also available online.
Formerly: Producers' Price-Current (ISSN 0032-9711)
Description: Eight page market price report serving the poultry and egg industries.

338.19 664 **US** **ISSN 0273-5016**
URNER BARRY'S PRICE CURRENT (WEST COAST EDITION). 1858. s-w. $147. Urner Barry Publications, Inc., P.O. Box 389, Toms River, NJ 08754. TEL 908-240-5330. FAX 908-341-0891. E-mail: mail@urnerbarry.com; URL: http://www.urnerbarry.com. Ed. Richard A. Brown. adv. contact: Angela Cuccinello. circ. 150. (back issues avail.) **Document type:** newspaper, trade publication.
Formerly: Producer's Price Current (West Coast Edition) (ISSN 0270-420X)

636 382 **UY** **ISSN 0797-5716**
HD9424.U79
URUGUAY. INSTITUTO NACIONAL DE CARNES. ANUARIO ESTADISTICO DE EXISTENCIAS, FAENA Y EXPORTACION. 1970. a. free. Instituto Nacional de Carnes, Montevideo, Uruguay. FAX 59-82-962933. TELEX INACUY 22076. circ. 700.
Formerly: Uruguay. Instituto Nacional de Carnes. Anuario Estadistico de Faena y Exportacion (ISSN 0797-132X); Which was formed by the merger of: Uruguay. Instituto Nacional de Carnes. Departamento de Exportaciones. Exportacion de Carnes. Estadisticas; Uruguay. Instituto Nacional de Carnes. Departamento de Exportaciones. Anuario.

AGRICULTURE — POULTRY AND LIVESTOCK

636.2   GW   ISSN 0722-3668
V F Z. (Vieh und Fleisch Handelszeitung) 1900. w. DM.98. Deutsche Viehhandelsgessellschaft mbH Fachverlag, c/o Dr. Hans-Joachim Bauer, Adenauerallee 176, 53113 Bonn, Germany. TEL 0228-213081. adv.; bk.rev.; abstr.; tr.lit. circ. 5,000. **Document type:** newspaper, trade publication.
  Formerly: Vieh und Fleische.

V W D - VIEH UND FLEISCH. see *BUSINESS AND ECONOMICS — Investments*

636.4   NE   ISSN 0166-5952
VARKENS; vakblad voor devarkenshouderij. 1937. 16/yr. fl.84($99) Nederlands Varkensstamboek, Postbus 43, 6640 AA Beuningen, Netherlands. TEL 31-24-6779999. FAX 31-24-6779800. E-mail: nvs@euroneb.nl. Ed. Bianca Domhof. adv. circ. 17,550. **Document type:** trade publication.
—BLDSC (9146.670000).
  Former titles: Maandblad Varkens; (until 1987): Mandblad voor de Varkensfokkeren en -Mesterij (ISSN 0923-0122); (until 1982): Varkensfokkerij-Mesterij (ISSN 0923-015/); (until 1976): Varkensfokkerij (ISSN 0923-0149); (until 1975): Maandblad voor de Varkensfokkerij (ISSN 0024-8649)

636.4   NE   ISSN 0169-0167
VARKENSHOUDERIJ. (Supplement to: Boerderij (ISSN 0006-5617)) 1972. bi-w. fl.217.50 (includes Boerderij). Misset (Subsidiary of: Reed Elsevier plc), Postbus 4, 7000 BA Doetinchem, Netherlands. TEL 31-314-349371. FAX 31-314-363638. TELEX 45481. Ed. Henk E.P. Dokter. adv.: B&W page fl.3396, color page fl.5496; trim 230 x 295; adv. contact: Cor van Nek. bk.rev.; charts; illus. circ. 15,670. **Document type:** trade publication.
  Description: Covers all aspects of pig husbandry: management, health care, housing and feeding.

636.2   NE   ISSN 0168-6585
VEEHOUDEN NU; kritisch voorlichtingsblad voor veehouderij en veredelingslandbouw. 1951. 9/yr. fl.20. Agrio, Postbus 5881, 7030 AB Wehl, Netherlands. TEL 31-314-68448. FAX 31-314-682008. (Editorial addr.: Haarbrinksweg 19, 7678 RS Geesteren Ov., Netherlands. TEL 31-5492-31314. FAX 31-5492-31802) Ed. Steven G. Berendsen. adv. contact: E. Voortman. bk.rev. circ. 20,000. **Document type:** bulletin.
  Formerly: Veevoeding (ISSN 0042-3041)

636   NE   ISSN 0169-0213
VEEHOUDERIJ. (Supplement to: Boerderij (ISSN 0006-5617)) 1972. bi-w. fl.217.50 (includes Boerderij). Misset (Subsidiary of: Reed Elsevier plc), Postbus 4, 7000 BA Doetinchem, Netherlands. TEL 31-314-349371. FAX 31-314-363638. TELEX 45481. Eds. P. Bos, Henk E.P. Dokter. adv.: B&W page fl.5001, color page fl.7081; trim 230 x 295; adv. contact: Cor van Nek. bk.rev.; charts; illus. circ. 36,940. **Document type:** trade publication.
  Description: Information on all aspects of dairy farming: breeding policy, health care of cattle, stall accomodation, milk production and mechanization of labor.

636   NE   ISSN 0168-7565
VEETEELT. 1972. fortn. fl.76. Koninklijk Nederlands Rundvee Syndicaat, Postbus 454, 6800 AL Arnhem, Netherlands. TEL 31-85-861111. FAX 31-85-861462. TELEX 45541 NRS NL. Ed. R. Strikwerda. adv.: page fl.4520; adv. contact: Willem Gemmink. bk.rev.; charts; illus. circ. 52,400. **Document type:** trade publication.
  Former titles (until 1984): Friese Veefokkerij; Friesch Rundvee-Stamboek. Mededelingen (ISSN 0016-1381)

639   VE
VENEZUELA. MINISTERIO DE AGRICULTURA Y CRIA. DIVISION DE ESTADISTICA. ENCUESTA AVICOLA NACIONAL. 1962. a. free. Ministerio de Agricultura y Cria, Direccion de Planificacion y Estadistica, Division de Estadistica, Centro Simon Bolicar, Torre Norte 16o, Caracas 1010, Venezuela. illus. **Document type:** government publication.

639   VE
VENEZUELA. MINISTERIO DE AGRICULTURA Y CRIA. DIVISION DE ESTADISTICA. ENCUESTA DE GANADO PORCINO. a. Ministerio de Agricultura y Cria, Direccion de Planificacion y Estadistica, Division de Estadistica, Centro Simon bolivar, Torre Norte 16o, Caracas 1010, Venezuela. **Document type:** government publication.

VETERINARIA E ZOOTECNIA. see *VETERINARY SCIENCE*

636   FR   ISSN 0241-0389
VIANDES ET PRODUITS CARNES. 1979. bi-m. 560 F. (foreign 590 F.) (effective 1996). Association pour le Developpement de l'Institut de la Viande, 2 rue Chappe, 63039 Clermont-Ferrand Cedex 2, France. TEL 33-4-73907297. FAX 33-4-73921777. Ed. Roger Boccard; Pub. Michel Saudan. R&P contact: Xavier Vigneron. adv.: B&W page 1800 F.; adv. contact: Xavier Vigneron. circ. 550. **Indexed:** Food Sci.& Tech.Abstr. **Document type:** bulletin.
—BLDSC (9232.040000).
  Description: A technical review for meat processors and traders, technical schools and advisory services. *Refereed Serial*

636.2   US
VIRGINIA CATTLEMAN; the monthly voice of Virginia's cattle industry. m. membership. Virginia Cattlemen's Association, Box 176, Daleville, VA 24083. TEL 540-992-1009. (Co-sponsor: National Cattlemen's Association) Ed. Reginald B. Reynolds. R&P contact: H. Suzanne Heflin. adv.: page $420; 10 x 13; adv. contact: Frances Via. circ. 10,000. **Document type:** newspaper, trade publication.

VIRGINIA HORSE COUNCIL NEWS. see *SPORTS AND GAMES — Horses And Horsemanship*

636.39   US   ISSN 0042-8078
VOICE OF A G S. 1936. q. membership. American Goat Society, Inc., RD 1, Box 56, Esperance, NY 12066-9704. TEL 518-875-6708. adv. circ. 600. **Document type:** bulletin.

636   PL
CODEN: AAASEQ
WARSAW AGRICULTURAL UNIVERSITY. S G G W. ANNALS. ANIMAL SCIENCE. (Text mainly in English; occasionally in French, German or Russian; summaries in Polish) 1957. irreg. $6 per no. Szkola Glowna Gospodarstwa Wiejskiego (SGGW) - Warsaw Agricultural University, Ul. Nowoursynowska 166, 02-766 Warsaw, Poland. (Dist. by: Ars Polona-Ruch, Krakowskie Przedmiescie 7, 00-608 Warsaw, Poland) Ed. W. Empel. **Indexed:** AgroLibrex, Food Sci.& Tech.Abstr.
—BLDSC (1035.015000); CASDDS; Linda Hall.
  Former titles: Warsaw Agricultural University. S G G W - A R. Annals. Animal Science (ISSN 0208-5739); (until 1980): Akademia Rolnicza, Warsaw. Zeszyty Naukowe. Zootechnika; Szkola Glowna Gospodarstwa Wiejskiego. Zeszyty Naukowe. Zootechnika (ISSN 0509-7134)

WASHINGTON FEEDLINE. see *AGRICULTURE — Feed, Flour And Grain*

WEEKLY INSIDERS POULTRY REPORT. see *FOOD AND FOOD INDUSTRIES*

WEEKLY INSIDERS TURKEY REPORT AND WEEKLY HATCH REPORT. see *AGRICULTURE — Abstracting, Bibliographies, Statistics*

636   US   ISSN 0043-1842
WEEKLY LIVESTOCK REPORTER. 1897. w. $18 (effective 1996); newsstand price: $1. Livestock Service, Inc., 120 N. Rayner St., Box 7655, Fort Worth, TX 76111-0655. TEL 817-831-3147. FAX 817-831-3117. Ed. Phil Stoll. adv.: B&W page $800, color page $1200; trim 13 1/2 x 10 1/4. bk.rev. circ. 14,000. **Document type:** newsletter.
  Incorporates: Texas Livestock Journal; **Formerly:** Daily Livestock Reporter.
  Description: For commercial cowmen, purebred breeders and buyers, feedlot operators and agribusiness people.

636.2   UK
WELSH BLACK CATTLE SOCIETY HERD BOOK. 1904. a. £10. Welsh Black Cattle Society, 13 Bangor St., Caernarfon, Gwynedd LL55 1AP, Wales. TEL 44-1286-672391. Ed. S. Evelyn Jones. circ. 1,000. (back issues avail.) **Document type:** catalog.

636.2   UK
WELSH BLACK CATTLE SOCIETY JOURNAL. (Text in English and Welsh) 1976. a. £2. Welsh Black Cattle Society, 13 Bangor St., Caernarfon, Gwynedd LL55 1AP, Wales. TEL 44-1286-672391. Ed. S. Evelyn Jones. adv. circ. 1,000. **Document type:** newsletter.

636   639.2   GW   ISSN 0170-7353
WER UND WAS IN DER DEUTSCHEN FLEISCH- FISCH- UND FEINKOST-INDUSTRIE. 1976. biennial. DM.245 (effective 1997). B. Behr's Verlag GmbH, Averhoffstr. 10, 22085 Hamburg, Germany. TEL 49-40-2270080. FAX 49-40-2201091. E-mail: behrs@behrs.de; URL: http://www.behrs.de. **Document type:** directory.

637   AT   ISSN 0729-3445
WESTERN AUSTRALIAN EGG MARKETING BOARD. NEWSLETTER. 1949. m. free. Western Australian Egg Marketing Board, 43-45 McGregor Rd., Palmyra, Australia. adv.; stat. circ. 500.

636.2   US   ISSN 1074-0031
WESTERN BEEF PRODUCER. 1993. 16/yr. Western Farmer-Stockman Magazines (Subsidiary of: Cowles Publishing Co.), Box 2160, Spokane, WA 99210-1615. TEL 509-459-5361. FAX 509-459-5102. E.W. Ramsey, Pub. Dir. adv. contact: Richard C. Brantley. circ. 34,404 (controlled). **Document type:** trade publication.

636.4   CN   ISSN 0225-3488
WESTERN HOG JOURNAL. 1972. q. free to hog breeders. Alberta Pork Producers Development Corp., 10319 Princess Elizabeth Ave., Edmonton, AB T5G 0Y5, Canada. TEL 403 474-8288. FAX 403-471-8065. TELEX 03-73367. Ed. Ward W. Toma. adv. contact: Ward W. Toma. bk.rev.; charts; illus.; stat.; circ. 9,559 (controlled). **Document type:** trade publication.
  Formerly (until vol. 8, 1979): Alberta Hog Journal (ISSN 0315-3800)

636   US   ISSN 0094-6710
WESTERN LIVESTOCK JOURNAL WEEKLY. w. $27. Crow Publications, Inc. (Denver), 650 S. Lipan, Denver, CO 80223. TEL 303-722-7600. (Or: Drawer 17F, Denver, CO 80217) adv.; illus. (tabloid format)

636   US
WESTERN LIVESTOCK REPORTER. 1940. w. $28. Western Livestock Reporter, Inc., Box 30758, Billings, MT 59107. TEL 406-259-4589. FAX 406-259-6888. Ed. Chuck Rightmire; Pub. Pat Goggins. adv.; bk.rev.; illus.; stat. circ. 12,000. (tabloid format) **Document type:** newspaper.
  Description: Provides in-depth national, state, and local news for livestock producers, cattlemen, and sheep growers in the Northwest.

636.5   US
WHO'S WHO INTERNATIONAL IN THE EGG & POULTRY INDUSTRY. 1970. a. $15. Watt Publishing Co., 122 S. Wesley Ave., Mt. Morris, IL 61054-1497. TEL 815-734-4171. FAX 815-734-4201. Ed. David Martin; Pub. Charles Olentine. adv.: B&W page $4500, color page $6025; trim 8 x 10 3/4; adv. contact: Anita Martin. circ. 23,000. **Document type:** directory.

636   US
WINGS & HOOVES. 1989. m. $16 (Canada and Mexico $30; elsewhere $45) (effective 1997). J. Haid, Ed. & Pub., Rt. 1, Box 32, Forestburg, TX 76239-9706. TEL 817-964-2314. FAX 817-964-2314. R&P contact: J. Haid. adv. contact: J. Haid. bk.rev. circ. 5,000. **Document type:** newsletter.
  Description: Looks at the exotic animal marketplace and provides husbandry information. Devoted to profitable agriculture and livestock. Includes the Bookrack: over 1600 animal titles for sale.

636.3 677.3   NZ   ISSN 0043-7875
WOOL TECHNOLOGY AND SHEEP BREEDING. 1954. q. NZ.$75 (libraries NZ.$115) (effective 1997). Wool Research Organisation of New Zealand Inc., Private Bag 4749, Christchurch, New Zealand. TEL 64-3-3252421. FAX 64-3-3242717. E-mail: cottle@wronz.org.nz; URL: http://www.wronz.org.nz. Ed. David J. Cottle. R&P contact: David J. Cottle. adv. contact: David J. Cottle. bk.rev. circ. 510. **Indexed:** Anim.Breed.Abstr., ASCA, Biol.Abstr., Chem.Abstr., Curr.Cont., Helminthol.Abstr., Ind.Vet., Soils & Fert., SSCI, Text.Tech.Dig., Vet.Bull., World Agri.Econ. & Rural Sociol.Abstr., World Text.Abstr. **Document type:** academic/scholarly publication.
—SWETS; UnCover.
  Description: Contains articles about on-farm production, handling, transport, early-stage processing and marketing of wool, and all aspects of sheep breeding and husbandry.
Refereed Serial

AGRICULTURE — POULTRY AND LIVESTOCK

THE WORKING BORDER COLLIE. see *PETS*

636   UN   ISSN 0049-8025
SF1   CODEN: WARVAI
WORLD ANIMAL REVIEW. Spanish edition: Revista Mundial de Zootecnia (ISSN 0252-0184); French edition: Revue Mondiale de Zootechnie (ISSN 0252-0176) 1972. q. $24. Food and Agriculture Organization of the United Nations (Rome), Via delle Terme de Caracalla, 00100 Rome, Italy. TEL 57974350. FAX 57975155. **Indexed:** Agri.Eng.Abstr., Anim.Breed.Abstr., Apic.Abstr., ASCA, Biol.Abstr., Curr.Adv.Ecol.Sci., Curr.Cont., Dairy Sci.Abstr., Field Crop Abstr., Food Sci.& Tech.Abstr., Helminthol.Abstr., Herb.Abstr., Ind.Vet., Nutr.Abstr., Pig News & Info., Rural Recreat.Tour.Abstr., So.Pac.Per.Ind., Soyabean Abstr., Vet.Bull., World Agri.Econ.& Rural Sociol.Abstr.
—CASDDS; Linda Hall; SWETS.
Description: Brings into focus the various aspects of animal production, animal health and animal products. Designed for those concerned with livestock and their related food by-products industries.

WORLD BUIATRICS CONGRESS. see *VETERINARY SCIENCE*

636   UY   ISSN 0084-1552
WORLD CONFERENCE ON ANIMAL PRODUCTION. PROCEEDINGS. (Proceedings published by organizing committee) (Text in English, French, German or Spanish) 1963. irreg., 1973, 3rd, Melbourne. World Association for Animal Production, c/o Dr. Hernan Caballero, Secretary General, Casilla de Correos 1217, Montevideo, Uruguay. **Document type:** proceedings.

WORLD RABBIT SCIENCE. see *BIOLOGY — Zoology*

636.5   NE
WORLD'S POULTRY SCIENCE ASSOCIATION. PROCEEDINGS OF WORLD'S POULTRY CONGRESS. (Proceedings published and distributed by host country.) quadrennial; 20th, 1996, New Delhi. World's Poultry Science Association, c/o Dr. Piet Simons, Sec., P.O. Box 31, 7360 AA Beekbergen, Netherlands. TEL 31-55-5064858. adv.; bk.rev.
Indexed: Curr.Cont. **Document type:** proceedings.
Formerly: World's Poultry Science Association. Report of the Proceedings of International Congress (ISSN 0084-2532)

636.5   UK   ISSN 0043-9339
SF481   CODEN: WPSJAO
WORLD'S POULTRY SCIENCE JOURNAL. 1944. 3/yr. £85. (World's Poultry Science Association) Butterworth - Heinemann, Part of the Reed Elsevier group, Linacre House, Jordan Hill, Oxford OX2 8DP, England. TEL 44-1865-310366. FAX 44-1865-310898. TELEX 83111 BHPOXF G. (Subscr. to: Turpin Transactions Ltd., Distribution Centre, Blackhorse Rd., Letchworth, Herts. SG6 1HN, England. TEL 44-1462-672555) Ed. C.M. Hann. adv.; bk.rev.; bibl.; charts; illus.; stat. (also avail. in microform from UMI; reprint service avail.; back issues avail.) **Indexed:** Anim.Breed.Abstr., ASCA, Biol.Abstr., Biol.& Agr.Ind., Biotech.Abstr., Chem.Abstr., Curr.Adv.Ecol.Sci., Curr.Pack.Abstr., Food Sci.& Tech.Abstr., Helminthol.Abstr., Ind.Sci.Rev., Ind.Vet., Nutr.Abstr., Poult.Abstr., Rural Recreat.Tour.Abstr., Sci.Cit.Ind., Sport Fish.Abstr., Vet.Bull., Wild.Rev., World Agri.Econ.& Rural Sociol.Abstr. **Document type:** academic/scholarly publication.
—BLDSC (9364.000000); CASDDS; Genuine Article; Linda Hall; SWETS; UMI; UnCover.
Description: Recent developments in poultry science and industry.
Refereed Serial

636   US   ISSN 0043-9800
WYOMING STOCKMAN FARMER. 1895. m. $12. Wyoming Stockman-Farmer, Inc., 702 W. Lincolnway, Cheyenne, WY 82001-4397. TEL 307-634-7964. FAX 307-778-7163. Ed. Janet L. Jedrzejewski. adv.; bk.rev.; charts; illus. circ. 6,672. **Document type:** trade publication.

636.3   US   ISSN 0043-9827
WYOMING WOOL GROWER. 1927. a. $40 membership. Wyoming Wool Growers Association, 811 N. Glenn, Box 115, Casper, WY 82602. TEL 307-265-5250. FAX 307-234-9701. Ed. Bryce Reece. adv. contact: Darlene Neeff. bk.rev.; illus. circ. 1,200. **Document type:** trade publication.

636.3   US
WYOMING WOOL GROWERS PRODUCER'S BULLETIN. m. $40 (effective 1994). Wyoming Wool Growers Association, 811 N. Glenn, Box 115, Casper, WY 82602. TEL 307-265-5250. FAX 307-234-9701. Ed. Bryce Reece. adv.: page $185; 7 1/2 x 7; adv. contact: Darlene Neeff. charts; illus.; stat. circ. 1,100. (tabloid format; back issues avail.) **Document type:** bulletin, newsletter.
Description: Informs members of changing issues in local, state, and federal politics; upgrades and changes in animal or land stewardship; other items that affect wool production and marketing efforts.

XUMU SHOUYI XUEBAO/ACTA VETERINARIA ET ZOOTECHNICA SINICA. see *VETERINARY SCIENCE*

636 338.1   US   ISSN 1066-8195
YELLOW SHEET (TOMS RIVER). 1892. d. $389 for print ed.; by fax and e-mail, price varies. Urner Barry Publications, Inc., Box 389, Toms River, NJ 08754-0389. TEL 908-240-5330. FAX 908-240-0891. E-mail: mail@urnerbarry.com; URL: http://www.urnerbarry.com. Ed. Joseph Muldowney. adv. contact: Angela Cuccinello. circ. 1,500 (paid). (also avail. by fax; back issues avail.) **Document type:** bulletin.
Description: Provides eight pages of unbiased meat quotes to help pinpoint the latest trading levels of beef, pork, lamb, veal, meat by-products, carcasses and boxed cuts.

636   RU   ISSN 0235-246X
ZHIVOTNOVOD. 1987. m. $96 (effective 1996). Sadovaya-Spasskaya, 20, 107807 Moscow, Russia. TEL 7-095-2075069. FAX 7-095-2072870. (Dist. by: Mezhdunarodnaya Kniga, B. Yakimanka 39, 117049 Moscow, Russia. TEL 7-095-2384967. FAX 7-095-2384634) Ed. Lyudmila A. Pervova. illus. circ. 62,500.

ZHONGGUO NONGYE KEXUE/CHINESE AGRICULTURAL SCIENCES. see *AGRICULTURE*

636.0855   CC   ISSN 1004-3314
ZHONGGUO SILIAO/CHINA FEED. (Text in Chinese) 1990. s-m. Zhongguo Siliao Gongye Xiehui, 33 Dongdan Santiao, Beijing 100005, People's Republic of China. TEL 86-10-5136541. (Dist. overseas by: China International Book Trading Corp., P.O. Box 399, Beijing 100044, P.R. China) adv.

636   RH
ZIMBABWE. MINISTRY OF AGRICULTURE. DIVISION OF LIVESTOCK AND PASTURES. ANNUAL REPORT. 1973. a. free. Ministry of Lands, Agriculture and Rural Resettlement, Research and Specialist Services, Information Services, Box 8108, Causeway, Harare, Zimbabwe. circ. 800. (back issues avail.) **Document type:** government publication.

636   XR   ISSN 0044-4847
                       CODEN: ZIVYAY
ZIVOCISNA VYROBA/ANIMAL PRODUCTION; vedecky casopis. (Text in Czech, English, Slovak; summaries in English) 1954. m. $170 in Europe; elsewhere $177 (effective 1997). Ustav Zemedelskych a Potravinarskych Informaci, Slezska 7, 120 56 Prague 2, Czech Republic. TEL 420-2-24253489. FAX 420-2-24253938. E-mail: uzlk@uzpi.cz. Ed. Marie Cerna. bk.rev.; bibl.; charts. circ. 600. **Indexed:** Anim.Breed.Abstr., ASCA, Biol.Abstr., Chem.Abstr., Curr.Cont., Dairy Sci.Abstr., Food Sci.& Tech.Abstr., Herb.Abstr., Ind.Vet., Maize Abstr., Nutr.Abstr., Pig News & Info., Poult.Abstr., Rev.Med.& Vet.Mycol., Soyabean Abstr., SSCI, Vet.Bull.
—BLDSC (9514.830000); CASDDS; Genuine Article; Linda Hall.

636   BU   ISSN 0514-7441
SF1   CODEN: ZHVNAS
ZIVOTNOVADNI NAUKI. (Summaries in English, German and Russian) 1964. 8/yr. 1.50 lv. per no. (Akademiia na Selskostopanskite Nauki) Publishing House of the Bulgarian Academy of Sciences, Acad. G. Bonchev St., Bldg. 6, 1113 Sofia, Bulgaria. (Dist. by: Hemus, 6, Rouski Blvd., 1000 Sofia, Bulgaria) Ed. Zahari Zahariev. bk.rev.; bibl.; illus. circ. 1,000. (reprint service avail. from IRC) **Indexed:** Biol.Abstr., Chem.Abstr., Ind.Vet., Vet.Bull.
—BLDSC (0058.010000); CASDDS;

636   BL   ISSN 0044-5320
ZOOTECNIA. (Text in Portuguese; summaries in English) 1961. q. $43. Instituto de Zootecnia, Rua Heitor Penteado 56, Caixa Postal 60, 13460 Nova Odessa, SP, Brazil. FAX 0194-661415. TELEX 192274 IZNO BR. E-mail: izooctl@turing.unicamp.br. Ed. Valdinei Tadeu Paulino. R&P contact: Mario Augusto Brajao. **Indexed:** Abstr.Trop.Agri., Herb.Abstr., Nutr.Abstr.
—BLDSC (9532.150000).

636   CU
ZOOTECNIA DE CUBA. 1991. 4/yr. $14 ($30 in S. America; N. America $32; elsewhere $36). Centro de Informacion y Documentacion Agropecuario, Gaveta Postal 4149, Havana 4, Cuba. TEL 29-2227. (International dist. by: Ediciones Cubanas, Obispo No. 527, Apdo. 605, Havana, Cuba; Subscr. to: Dpto. de Ediciones y Extension Agropecuarias, Comercializacion y Dist., Omoa-Este No. 12-B entre Pila y Matadero, Cerro, Havana, Cuba) Ed. Juan Manuel Castro Morejon. circ. 2,000.
Description: Contains articles on the results of scientific and technical research about the species of greatest economic importance to Cuban agriculture.

636   VE   ISSN 0798-7269
ZOOTECNIA TROPICAL. (Text in English, Spanish) 1982. s-a. exchange basis. Fondo Nacional de Investigaciones Agropecuarias, Apdo. 2103, Maracay 2105, Venezuela. FAX 58-43-831423. Ed. Alberto Valle. bibl.; charts; illus. circ. 600.

633.2 636   IT   ISSN 0390-0487
                       CODEN: ZNAND2
ZOOTECNICA E NUTRIZIONE ANIMALE. (Text and summaries in English and Italian) 1975. bi-m. L.75000 (effective 1996). (Associazione Scientifica di Produzione Animale) Edagricole S.p.A., Via Emilia Levante 31, 40139 Bologna, Italy. TEL 39-51-492211. FAX 39-51-493660. Ed.Bd. adv.: B&W page L.700000, color page L.1100000; 140 x 215. bk.rev.; index. circ. 4,500. **Indexed:** Agroforest.Abstr., Anim.Breed.Abstr., Biol.Abstr., Chem.Abstr., Curr.Cont., Dairy Sci.Abstr., Field Crop Abstr., Herb.Abstr., Ind.Vet., Maize Abstr., Nutr.Abstr., Pig News & Info., Poult.Abstr., Rev.Med.& Vet.Mycol., Soyabean Abstr., Sugar Ind.Abstr., Vet.Bull.
—BLDSC (9532.195000); CASDDS; Linda Hall; UMI.
Formerly: Alimentazione Animale (ISSN 0002-5429)
Description: For livestock breeders and feed producers.

636   RU   ISSN 0235-2478
                       CODEN: ZHIVAL
ZOOTEKHNIIA. 1928. m. $159 (effective 1998). Sadovaya-Spasskaya, 18, 107807 Moscow, Russia. TEL 7-095-2072080. (Dist. by: Mezhdunarodnaya Kniga, B. Yakimanka 39, 117049 Moscow, Russia. TEL 7-095-2384967. FAX 7-095-2384634) Ed. Andrei T. Mysik. bk.rev.; illus.; index. circ. 10,070. **Indexed:** Anim.Breed.Abstr., Biol.Abstr., Chem.Abstr., Dairy Sci.Abstr., Field Crop Abstr., Food Sci.& Tech.Abstr., Herb.Abstr., Ind.Vet., Maize Abstr., Nutr.Abstr., Pig News & Info., Potato Abstr., Poult.Abstr., Sorghum & Millets Abstr., Soyabean Abstr., Triticale Abstr., Vet.Bull.
—CASDDS; Linda Hall.
Formerly: Zhivotnovodstvo (ISSN 0044-4480)

636   GW
ZUCHTWAHL UND BESAMUNG. 1955. 2/yr. DM.2.60. Besamungsverein Neustadt an der Aisch e.V., Karl-Eibl-Str. 17-27, 31535 Neustadt a.d. Aisch, Germany. TEL 09161-78770. FAX 09161-78763. TELEX 624013-BVNEA-D. Ed. W. Breuer. circ. 25,000. (back issues avail.) **Indexed:** Agri.Eng.Abstr., Anim.Breed.Abstr., Ind.Vet.

636 GW ISSN 0044-5401
CODEN: ZUECAZ
ZUECHTUNGSKUNDE. (Summaries in English, French and Russian) 1926. bi-m. DM.723.60. (Deutsche Gesellschaft fuer Zuechtungskunde e.V.) Verlag Eugen Ulmer GmbH, Wollgrasweg 41, 70599 Stuttgart, Germany. TEL 49-711-4507-0. FAX 49-711-4507-120. (Subscr. to: Postfach 700561, 70574 Stuttgart, Germany) Ed. F. Schmitten. R&P contact: G. Friedrich. adv. contact: F. Laucher. bk.rev.; abstr.; bibl.; charts; illus. circ. 1,200. **Indexed:** Anim.Breed.Abstr., Biol.Abstr., Chem.Abstr., Curr.Adv.Ecol.Sci., Curr.Adv.Genetics & Molec.Biol., Dairy Sci.Abstr., Food Sci.& Tech.Abstr., Helminthol.Abstr., IBR, Ind.Vet., Nutr.Abstr., Pig News & Info., Rural Recreat.Tour.Abstr., Sci.Cit.Ind., Vet.Bull., World Agri.Econ. & Rural Sociol.Abstr. **Document type:** academic/scholarly publication.
—BLDSC (9537.000000); CASDDS; Genuine Article; Linda Hall. **CCC.**

AIR TRANSPORT

see Transportation–Air Transport

AIRLINE INFLIGHT AND HOTEL INROOM

see Travel and Tourism–Airline Inflight and Hotel Inroom

ALLERGOLOGY AND IMMUNOLOGY

see Medical Sciences–Allergology and Immunology

ALTERNATIVE MEDICINE

see also Medical Sciences

A A M TERRA NUOVA; rivista ecoalternativa. (Agricoltura Alimentazione Medicina) *see ENVIRONMENTAL STUDIES*

615.892 615.845 US ISSN 0360-1293
RM184 CODEN: AEREDS
ACUPUNCTURE AND ELECTRO-THERAPEUTICS RESEARCH; the international journal. 1976. q. $205 (foreign $225) (effective 1998). (International College of Acupuncture and Electro-Therapeutics) Cognizant Communication Corporation, 3 Hartsdale Rd., Elmsford, NY 10523-3701. TEL 914-592-7720. FAX 914-592-8981. Ed. Dr. Yoshiaki Omura; Pub. Robert N. Miranda. R&P contact: Robert N. Miranda. adv. contact: Lori Miranda. bk.rev.; abstr.; bibl.; charts; illus.; stat.; index. circ. 1,000. (also avail. in microform) **Indexed:** ASCA, Bioeng.Abstr., Biol.Abstr., Chem.Abstr., CINAHL, Curr.Adv.Ecol.Sci., Curr.Cont., Dent.Ind., Excerp.Med., Ind.Med., Psychol.Abstr., Sci.Cit.Ind. **Document type:** academic/scholarly publication.
—BLDSC (0677.930000); CASDDS; CISTI; Ei; EMDOCS; Genuine Article; KNAW; SWETS; UMI; UnCover. **CCC.**
Description: Covers developments in basic and clinical research in acupuncture, electro-therapeutics and related fields. Fosters efforts to understand and improve these treatments and their use in diagnosis, prognosis, treatment and prevention of diseases in both Western and Oriental medicine.
Refereed Serial

615.89 UK ISSN 0964-5284
CODEN: ACMEF
ACUPUNCTURE IN MEDICINE. 1982. s-a. British Medical Acupuncture Society, Newton House, Newton Lane, Lower Whitley, Warrington, Cheshire WA4 4JA, England. TEL 44-1925-730727. FAX 44-1925-730492. E-mail: Bmasadmin@aol.com. Ed. Dr. Simon Hayhoe. adv.: page £205. bk.rev. circ. 2,000. (back issues avail.) **Indexed:** Excerp.Med. (1996-). **Document type:** academic/scholarly publication.
—BLDSC (0677.935000); EMDOCS.
Description: Covers medical acupuncture and related subjects. Includes controlled trials, research and clinical review, neurophysiology and other topics in science.
Refereed Serial

610.95 615.892 NE ISSN 1382-6883
▼**ADVANCED TRADITIONAL CHINESE MEDICINE SERIES.** (Text in English, occasionally in Chinese) 1996. irreg., vol.4, 1996. price varies. I O S Press, Van Diemonstraat 94, 1013 CN Amsterdam, Netherlands. TEL 31-20-638189. FAX 31-20-6203419. E-mail: market@iospress.nl; URL: http://www.iospress.nl/iospress. (In N. America: Box 10558, Burke, VA 22009-0558. TEL 703-323-5554. FAX 703-250-4705) (back issues avail.) **Document type:** monographic series.
Description: Publishes studies on the theory and practice of traditional Chinese medicine, including discussions of herbs, techniques, and clinical applications. Volumes include glossary of terminology in Pinyin and Chinese characters.

ADVERSE EFFECTS OF HERBAL DRUGS. *see PHARMACY AND PHARMACOLOGY*

615.89 GW ISSN 0720-6003
AERZTEZEITSCHRIFT FUER NATURHEILVERFAHREN. (Text mainly in German; summaries in English and French) 1963. m. DM.118 (students DM.88.50). (Zentralverband der Aerzte fuer Naturheilverfahren e.V.) Medizinisch-Literarische Verlagsgesellschaft mbH, Postfach 1151-1152, 29501 Uelzen, Germany. TEL 0581-808151. FAX 0581-808158. TELEX 91326-AZ-D. Ed. K.C. Schimmel. adv.; bk.rev.; charts; illus.; index, cum.index. circ. 9,800. (tabloid format; back issues avail.) **Indexed:** Excerp.Med. **Document type:** academic/scholarly publication.
—BLDSC (1738.250000); KNAW. **CCC.**
Formerly: Physikalische Medizin und Rehabilitation (ISSN 0031-9287)

615.892 GW ISSN 0340-3130
CODEN: AKUPE
AKUPUNKTUR: THEORIE UND PRAXIS. 1973. q. DM.72 (students DM.54). (Deutsche Aerztegesellschaft fuer Akupunktur e.V.) Medizinisch-Literarische Verlagsgesellschaft mbH, Postfach 1151-1152, 29501 Uelzen, Germany. TEL 0581-808151. FAX 0581-808158. TELEX 91326-AZD. Ed. Dr. R. Beck. adv.; bk.rev. circ. 7,400. (back issues avail.) **Indexed:** Excerp.Med. **Document type:** academic/scholarly publication.
—**CCC.**
Description: Articles on scientific research in acupuncture. Includes lists of courses and events.

615.53 SW ISSN 1100-7079
ALTERNATIV MEDICIN.* 1989. q. Svenska Naturmedicinska Saellskapet, Storgatan 17, S-352 31 Vaexjoe, Sweden.

615.89 US ISSN 1076-2809
R733 CODEN: ACTHFZ
▼**ALTERNATIVE & COMPLEMENTARY THERAPIES;** a bimonthly publication for health care practitioners. 1995. bi-m. $61 to individuals (foreign $122); institutions $154 (foreign $176) (effective 1998). Mary Ann Liebert, Inc. Publishers, 2 Madison Ave., Larchmont, NY 10538. TEL 914-834-3100. FAX 914-834-3688. E-mail: liebert@pipeline.com. Ed. Anne Coulter.
—BLDSC (0803.581470); CISTI.
Description: Covers latest trends in the field of alternative medicine. Topics covered include a variety of nontraditional holistic health specialties.

615.89 US ISSN 1076-1675
▼**ALTERNATIVE HEALTH PRACTITIONER;** the journal of complementary and natural care. 1995. 3/yr. $36 to individuals (foreign $40); institutions $70 (foreign $79) (effective 1997). Springer Publishing Company, 536 Broadway, New York, NY 10012-3955. TEL 212-431-4370. FAX 212-941-7842. E-mail: springer@thron.net; URL: http://www.liberty.com/springer.html. Ed. Carolyn Chambers Clark. adv.: B&W page $300; adv. contact: Rafael Ortiz. bk.rev.; abstr. **Document type:** trade publication.
—BLDSC (0803.584500); CISTI. **CCC.**
Description: Serves as a forum for alternative health care practitioners and traditional health care professionals who incorporate alternative methods into their practices (e.g. homeopathy, meditation, hypnotherapy, acupressure and acupuncture, chiropractic medicine, art therapy, and related disciplines and procedures). Includes news from NIH - OAM, and a calendar.
Refereed Serial

615.89 US ISSN 1081-4000
ALTERNATIVE MEDICINE DIGEST. 1994. bi-m. $20 (foreign $45) (effective 1997). Future Medicine Publishing, Inc., 1640 Tiburon Blvd., Ste. 2, Tiburon, CA 94920. TEL 415-435-1779; 800-333-4325. FAX 415-435-9448. URL: http://www.alternativemedicine.com. Ed. Richard Leviton; Pub. Burton Goldberg. R&P contact: Ron Curtis. adv. contact: Jay Eisenberg. bk.rev.; illus. circ. 170,000. **Document type:** consumer publication.
Description: Offers feature articles, departments, and digest summaries of information from doctor's journals, research, conferences and newsletters, covering the entire field of alternative medicine.

610 US
ALTERNATIVE THERAPIES IN CLINICAL PRACTICE. 1994. bi-m. $91 to individuals (Canada $107; elsewhere $119); institutions $128 (Canada $167; elsewhere $215) (effective 1997). Prime National Corp., 470 Boston Post Rd., Weston, MA 02193. TEL 617-899-2702. FAX 617-899-4900. Ed. R. Patrick Gates; Pub. Richard A. DeVito. adv.; bk.rev.; index. (back issues avail.; reprint service avail.) **Document type:** academic/scholarly publication.
—**CCC.**
Former titles (until 1996): Complementary Medicine International (ISSN 1086-5934); (until vol.3, 1996): Alternative Medicine Journal (ISSN 1075-3893)
Refereed Serial

615.89 US
▼**ALTERNATIVE THERAPIES IN HEALTH AND MEDICINE.** 1995. bi-m. $51 to individuals (foreign $69); institutions $127 (foreign $146) (effective 1998). American Association of Critical Care Nurses, InnoVision Communications, 101 Columbia, Aliso Viejo, CA 92656. TEL 714-362-2000. E-mail: alttherapy@aol.com. (Subscr. addr.: Box 6627, Holmes, PA 19043. TEL 800-345-8112) circ. 20,000. (paid). **Document type:** academic/scholarly publication.
Description: Explores the integration of alternative therapies with conventional medical practices.
Refereed Serial

615.892 US ISSN 0091-3960
CODEN: AJAPB9
AMERICAN JOURNAL OF ACUPUNCTURE. 1972. q. $60 to individuals; institutions $90 (effective 1997). 1840 41st Ave., Ste. 102, Box 610, Capitola, CA 95010. TEL 408-475-1700. FAX 408-475-1439. Ed. W.G. Grace; Pub. Deborah Salisbury. adv. contact: P. Scarborough. bk.rev.; abstr.; charts; illus. circ. 4,800. (back issues avail.; reprint service avail. from ISI) **Indexed:** ASCA, Biol.Abstr., Curr.Cont., Dent.Abstr., Excerp.Med., Ind.Vet., Med. Care Rev., Oral Res.Abstr., Pig News & Info., Sci.Cit.Ind., Vet.Bull. **Document type:** academic/scholarly publication.
—BLDSC (0820.945000); CISTI; EMDOCS; Genuine Article; KNAW; SWETS; UnCover. **CCC.**
Description: Publishes papers spanning the full spectrum of acupuncture modalities from classical to modern variations plus correlations and combinations with Western medicine. Includes instruction on methods and treatment, research, case studies.
Refereed Serial

AMERICAN JOURNAL OF CHINESE MEDICINE. *see MEDICAL SCIENCES — Abstracting, Bibliographies, Statistics*

ALTERNATIVE MEDICINE

615.53 II ISSN 0257-7941
R605
ANCIENT SCIENCE OF LIFE. (Text in English) 1981. q. Rs.140($37) International Institute of Ayurveda, P.B. No. 7102, Ramanathapuram, Coimbatore 641 045, India. TEL 213188. FAX 214953. Ed. S. Vijayan; Pub. Suresh Kunar. R&P contact: P.R. Krishna Kumar. adv.: B&W page Rs.2500; 220 x 165. bk.rev. circ. 2,000. **Indexed:** Forest.Abstr., Forest Prod.Abstr., Hort.Abstr., Rev.Med.& Vet.Mycol. **Document type:** academic/scholarly publication.
—BLDSC (0900.325500).
Description: Publishes research papers on Ayurveda, the Indian system of medicine, and allied disciplines. Also acts as an interdisciplinary medium on all aspects of medical health care.

615.3 AT ISSN 1033-8330
AUSTRALIAN JOURNAL OF MEDICAL HERBALISM. 1989. q. Aus.$75 (effective July 1997). National Herbalists Association of Australia, Ste. 305, 3 Smail St., Broadway, N.S.W. 2007, Australia. TEL 61-2-92116437. FAX 61-2-92116452. E-mail: nhaa@nhaa.org.au. Ed. Anne Cowper. R&P contact: Anne Cowper. TEL 049734107. adv.: page Aus.$250; adv. contact: Anne Cowper. bk.rev.; abstr.; index. circ. 1,600. **Document type:** academic/scholarly publication.
—BLDSC (1810.230000).
Description: Publishes material on all aspects of medical herbalism with emphasis on phytochemistry, pharmacology and clinical applications of medicinal plants.
Refereed Serial

615.53 II
AYURVEDA SAUKHYAM SERIES. (Text in English, Sanskrit) 1980. irreg. price varies. Concept Publishing Company, A 15-16, Commercial Block, Mohan Garden, New Delhi 110 059, India. TEL 91-11-550-4042. index. **Document type:** monographic series.
Description: Includes fundamental principles of Ayurveda, anatomy, physiology, hygiene, various aspects of public health, and the treatment of diseases.

615.89 CC ISSN 0476-0247
BEIJING ZHONGYI/BEIJING TRADITIONAL CHINESE MEDICINE. (Text in Chinese) bi-m. (Beijing Zhongyi Xuehui) Beijing Zhongyi Zazhishe, A-7 Dongdan Santiao, Beijing 100005, People's Republic of China. TEL 6127766.

615.892 UK ISSN 0260-5996
BRITISH ACUPUNCTURE ASSOCIATION. NEWSLETTER.*
1965. 2/yr. British Acupuncture Association & Register, 34 Alderney St., London SW1V 4EW, England. **Document type:** newsletter.
Formerly (until 1976): Acupuncture Association. Newsletter (ISSN 0307-4994)

615.89 UK ISSN 0959-6879
BRITISH JOURNAL OF PHYTOTHERAPY. 1990. 2/yr. £38 to individuals; institutions £45 for 4 nos. School of Phytotherapy, Bucksteep Manor, Bodle St. Green, Near Hailsham, E. Sussex BN27 4RJ, England. TEL 44-1323-833812. FAX 44-1323-833869. E-mail: medherb@pavilion.co.uk. Ed. Colin Nicholls. R&P contact: Colin Nicholls. adv. contact: Colin Nicholls. bk.rev. circ. 600. **Document type:** academic/scholarly publication.
—BLDSC (2319.300000); KNAW.
Refereed Serial

615.89 581 II ISSN 0253-6889
CODEN: BMERDZ
BULLETIN OF MEDICO-ETHNO-BOTANICAL RESEARCH.*
(Text in English; summaries in Hindi) 1980. q. Rs.60. Central Council for Research in Ayurveda and Siddha, c/o Sahitya Akademi - National Academy of Letters, Rabindra Bhavan, 35 Ferozshah Rd., New Delhi 110 001, India. TEL 11-669315. Ed. V.N. Pandey. adv.; bk.rev.; bibl.; charts; illus. circ. 300. **Indexed:** Hort.Abstr.
—CASDDS; CISTI.
Description: Covers folk medicine, pharmacognosy, and phytochemistry. Examines the correlation between ancient insights and modern scientific thought.

615.89 FR ISSN 1243-7042
CAHIERS PRATIQUES DE MEDECINE. 1993. m. Editions 109, B.P. 2, 14130 Blangy-le-Chateau, France. TEL 16-31-64-88-88.

615.321 CN ISSN 0848-9629
CANADIAN JOURNAL OF HERBALISM. 1979. q. Can.$25 membership. Ontario Herbalists Association, 11 Winthrop Pl., Stoney Creek, ON L8G 3M3, Canada. TEL 416-664-6715. Ed. Keith Stelling. adv. contact: Carol Wilcox. bk.rev. circ. 2,500. (reprint service avail.) **Document type:** consumer publication.
—BLDSC (3031.610000).
Formerly (until 1988): Ontario Herbalists Association. Journal.
Description: Covers herbal medicine, complementary health care. Includes botanical and pharmacological profiles on specific plants, therapeutics and updates on legislation and quality control as well as environmental issues relating to health.

615.89 GW ISSN 0930-2786
CHINESISCHE MEDIZIN; theoretische Grundlagen, Diagnostik, Akupunktur, Arzneimittel, Taiji, Qigong. 1986. q. DM.184 (foreign DM.190) (effective 1998). (Societas Medicinae) Urban and Vogel, Lindwurmstr. 95, 80337 Munich, Germany. TEL 49-89-53292-0. FAX 49-89-53292-100. (Subscr. to: Postfach 152209, 80052 Munich, Germany) Eds. E. Stueder-Wobmann, C.H. Hempen. circ. 1,500. **Document type:** academic/scholarly publication.
—CISTI

CHOJUGAKU KENKYU/RESEARCH OF LONGEVITY SCIENCE. see *GERONTOLOGY AND GERIATRICS*

615.89 JA ISSN 0389-4843
CHUI RINSHO/CLINICAL JOURNAL OF TRADITIONAL CHINESE MEDICINE. (Text in Japanese) 1980. q. 1600 Yen per no. Toyo Gakujutsu Shuppansha, 1-5, Miyakubo 3-chome, Ichikawa-shi, Chiba-ken 272, Japan.

700 535.84 UK ISSN 1351-1696
COLOURAMA; colour-light-art research. 1970. s-a (Mar., Sept.). £2.50 per no. International Association for Colour Therapy (IACT), P.O. Box 3, Potter's Bar, Herts. EN6 3ET, England. TEL 44-1223-563463. Ed. Michael R. Grevis. R&P contact: Michael R. Grevis. adv.; bk.rev. circ. 122. **Document type:** consumer publication.
Formerly: Colour Circle.
Description: Concerns the power of color and vibrational healing, and related topics in complimentary medicine.

COMMON GROUND HAWAII. see *PSYCHOLOGY*

COMPLEMENTARY MEDICINE FOR THE PHYSICIAN. see *MEDICAL SCIENCES*

COMPLEMENTARY THERAPIES IN MEDICINE. see *MEDICAL SCIENCES — Chiropractic, Homeopathy, Osteopathy*

COMPLEMENTARY THERAPIES IN NURSING & MIDWIFERY. see *MEDICAL SCIENCES — Nurses And Nursing*

615.89 US
THE COUNTRY DOCTOR. 1994. m. free. E-mail: naturapath@sc.net. **Document type:** newsletter.
●Available only online.
Formerly: Health and Longevity.
Description: Deals wtih alternative treatment modalities.

615.89 II ISSN 0970-3381
DEERGHAYU INTERNATIONAL. (Text in English) 1984. q. Institute of Indian Medicine, 36 Kothrud, Pune 411 029, India. TEL 442233. Ed. P.H. Kulkarni. adv. contact: Pavan Kulkarni.
—BLDSC (3541.230000).
Description: Contains case reports, research results and reviews on Indian medicine.

DELICIOUS!; guide to natural living. see *NUTRITION AND DIETETICS*

615.89 US
DINSHAH HEALTH SOCIETY NEWSLETTER. 1980. q. $3. Dinshah Health Society, Box 707, Malaga, NJ 08328. TEL 609-692-4686. Ed. Darius Dinshah. circ. 3,000. (back issues avail.) **Document type:** newsletter.
Description: Covers general health topics, including unorthodox methods of healing (primarily chromopathy).

615.89 PL ISSN 1230-9370
DOMOWY DOKTOR; miesiecznik medycyny naturalnej. 1993. m. newsstand price: 2.60 Zl. Faktor Sp. z o.o., Ul. Ksiecia Wladyslawa Opolskiego 3a, 32-650 Kety, Poland. TEL 48-33-453888. Ed. Jozef Gaweda. circ. 17,500. (back issues avail.)
Description: Covers natural medicine.

615.53 US ISSN 1069-6253
THE DOOR OPENER; Connecticut's holistic health and metaphysical networking magazine. 1986. q. $10 (effective 1990); newsstand price: $2.50. An Open Door, 70 Valley Falls Rd., Vernon, CT 06066. TEL 860-875-4101. FAX 860-875-4101. E-mail: anopendoor@aol.com; URL: www.anopendoor.com. Ed. Jon Roe; Pub. Jon Roe. adv.: page $290; trim 8 1/2 x 11; adv. contact: Jon Roe. circ. 2,200 (paid). (back issues avail.) **Document type:** consumer publication.
Description: Includes articles, calendar of events, and lists of resources covering holistic health and metaphysics in Connecticut.

615.8 US ISSN 1085-0880
▼**DR. ANDREW WEIL'S SELF HEALING.** 1995. m. $29. Thorne Communications, Inc., 42 Pleasant St., Watertown, MA 02172. TEL 617-926-0200. FAX 617-926-5021. URL: http://www.drweil.com. (Subscr. to: Box 788, Mt. Morris, IL 61054) Ed. Dr. Andrew Weil; Pub. David Thorne. circ. 13,000 (paid). **Document type:** newsletter.
Description: Covers natural health and well-being.

ESALEN CATALOG. see *PSYCHOLOGY*

ETHNOBOTANY. see *BIOLOGY — Botany*

EUROPEAN JOURNAL OF HERBAL MEDICINE. see *PHARMACY AND PHARMACOLOGY*

610.95 UK ISSN 1351-6647
EUROPEAN JOURNAL OF ORIENTAL MEDICINE. 1977; N.S. 1993. 2/yr. £14 (Europe £15; elsewhere £20). 19 Trinity Rd., London N2 8JJ, England. adv.; bk.rev. circ. 700. (back issues avail.) **Document type:** academic/scholarly publication.
—BLDSC (3829.733260).
Former titles (until 1993): British Journal of Acupuncture (ISSN 0143-4977); (until 1979): British Acupuncture Association. Journal (ISSN 0142-2340)
Description: Stimulates debate and scholarship in Chinese medicine and other traditions of Oriental medicine.

615.89 619 CC ISSN 1000-338X
FUJIAN ZHONGYI YAO/FUJIAN JOURNAL OF TRADITIONAL CHINESE MEDICINE. (Text in Chinese) 1956-1966; resumed 1981. bi-m. $1.20 per no. Fujian Zhongyi Xueyuan - Fujian Institute of Traditional Chinese Medicine, 282 Wusi Lu, Fuzhou, Fujian 350003, People's Republic of China. TEL 0591-7841296. FAX 0591-7842524. (Dist. overseas by: China International Book Trading Corporation, Chegongzhuang Xilu 35, P.O. Box 399, Beijing, P.R.C.) (Co-sponsor: Zhonghua Quanguo Zhongyi Xuehui Fujian Fenhui) Ed. Yu Changrong. adv.; bk.rev. circ. 16,000. **Indexed:** ExtraMED.
●Also available on CD-ROM.

615.89 JA
FUKUOKA ISHI KANPO KENKYUKAI KAIHO/FUKUOKA MEDICAL ASSOCIATION FOR KAMPO MEDICINE. (Text in Japanese) 1980. m. Fukuoka Ishi Kanpo Kenkyukai, 6-1, Wakahisa 2-chome, Minami-ku, Fukuoka-shi, Fukuoka-ken 815, Japan.

615.89 JA ISSN 0388-6719
CODEN: GTIGDO
GENDAI TOYO IGAKU/JOURNAL OF TRADITIONAL SINO-JAPANESE MEDICINE. (Text in Japanese) 1980. q. 1800 Yen per no. Igaku Shuppan Senta - Medical Publication Center Inc., 25-2, Asakusabashi 1-chome, Taito-ku, Tokyo 111, Japan.
—CASDDS.

GINSHENG REVIEW. see *PHARMACY AND PHARMACOLOGY*

615.89 CC
GUANGXI ZHONGYI YAO/GUANGXI TRADITIONAL CHINESE MEDICINE. (Text in Chinese) bi-m. Guangxi Zhongyi Xueyuan - Guangxi Institute of Traditional Chinese Medicine, 21 Mingxiu Donglu, Nanning, Guangxi 530001, People's Republic of China. TEL 32101. (Co-sponsor: Zhonghua Quanguo Zhongyi Xuehui, Guangxi Fenhui) Ed. Ban Qiuwen.

ALTERNATIVE MEDICINE

615.89 US
H L Q THREE RIVERS RESOURCE GUIDE FOR HOLISTIC LIVING. 1980. a. $7 (foreign $9) (effective 1997). H L Q Associates, Box 86054, Pittsburgh, PA 15221-0054. TEL 412-242-9355. E-mail: hlq@ttrfn.clpgh.org; URL: http://trfn.clpgh.org/hlq. Ed. Allen Goodman; Pub. Priscilla Brown. adv. contact: Marlene Linden. bk.rev.; index; circ. 10,000 (paid). **Document type:** directory.
Former titles: Three Rivers Wellness Directory (ISSN 1060-006X); **Former titles:** H L Q Wellness Calendar; H L Q Magazine; Holistic Learning Quarterly.
Description: Focuses on personal health, social responsibility, global awareness, and self sufficiency.
Refereed Serial

HEALING AND WHOLENESS. see *RELIGIONS AND THEOLOGY*

615.89 AT
HEALTH & HEALING; journal of complementary medicine. 1981. q. Aus.$21.80 (foreign $41.90) (effective 1996). Trim-Keg Party Ltd, 29 Terrace St., P.O. Box 206, Kingscliff, N.S.W. 2487, Australia. TEL 61-66-742407. FAX 61-66-743633. Ed. Maurice Finkel. R&P contact: Maurice Finkel. adv. contact: Maurice Finkel. bk.rev.; abstr.; circ. 12,000 (paid). (back issues avail.) **Document type:** consumer publication.
Formerly: Australasian Health and Healing (ISSN 0812-3896)

615.89 US ISSN 0895-9986
HEALTH CONSCIOUSNESS; the international holistic magazine. 1980. bi-m. $18 (foreign $32). Dr. Roy B. Kupsinel, Ed. & Pub., Shangri-La Ln., Box 550, Oviedo, FL 32765. TEL 407-365-6681. FAX 407-365-1834. adv.; bk.rev.; illus. circ. 2,500. (back issues avail.)
—BLDSC (4274.959800).
Formerly: Kup's Komments.
Description: Contains health news for both the lay and professional reader. Includes viewpoints from pioneers in alternative medicine.

615 US ISSN 0888-7330
HEALTH WORLD. Variant title: New Editions, Health World. 1982. q. $12 (foreign $30) (effective 1997). Health World, Inc., Box 4157, Burlingame, CA 94010. TEL 510-784-2318. FAX 510-781-0248. E-mail: nehealth@dsp.com. Ed. Dr. Kumar Pati; Pub. Kumar Pati. R&P contact: Kumar Pati. adv. contact: Kumar Pati. bk.rev. circ. 110,000. (also avail. in microform from UMI; back issues avail.) **Document type:** consumer publication.
—UMI.
Former titles (until 1986): Holistic Health (ISSN 0882-8148); (until 1985): International Journal of Holistic Health and Medicine (ISSN 0737-9560)
Description: Provides information on different health therapies, remedies, and practices around the world with emphasis on homeopathy, Chinese medicine, herbs, acupuncture and chiropractic.

615.89 US ISSN 1082-6734
▼**HEALTHINFORM**; essential information on alternative health care. 1995. s-w. $60 (fax $75). Infolink, Box 306, 31 Albany Post Rd., Montrose, NY 10548. TEL 914-736-1565; 800-743-LINK. FAX 914-736-3806. Ed. Katherine Mason-Page; Pub. Janet Gotkin. R&P contact: Katherine Mason-Page. bk.rev.; index. (also avail. by fax; back issues avail.) **Document type:** newsletter, abstracting/indexing, academic/scholarly publication.
Description: Covers alternative and complementary medicine for health care professionals. Includes information on research conferences, proceedings, and grants.
Refereed Serial

615.8 613.7 US ISSN 1079-4530
HEALTHY & NATURAL JOURNAL. 1994. bi-m. $17.50. Measurements & Data Corporation, 100 Wallace Ave., Ste. 100, Sarasota, FL 34237. TEL 941-366-1153. FAX 941-366-5743. E-mail: hnnmag@gate.net; URL: http://www.healthyandnatural.com. Ed. Michael L. Keenan; Pub. Robert S. Aronson. adv.: color page $4370; trim 8 x 10 7/8; adv. contact: Laura Baily. bk.rev.; illus. circ. 215,000. (back issues avail.) **Document type:** consumer publication.
Description: Provides information on the latest developments in natural health, natural and organic foods, consumer activism, and the environment.

615.89 CC ISSN 1002-2619
HEBEI ZHONGYI/HEBEI TRADITIONAL MEDICINE. (Text in Chinese) 1979. bi-m. Y3.20 per no. Hebei Yixue Kexueyuan, Qingbao Yanjiusuo, Zhongyi Fenhui - Hebei Academy of Medical Sciences, Information Institute, Department of Traditional Medicine, 241 Qingyuan St., Shijiazhuang, Hebei 050021, People's Republic of China. TEL 86-311-5812687. FAX 86-311-5809161. E-mail: mazhi@public.sj.hj.cn. Ed. Jintang Xia; Pub. Dingwen Shi. R&P contact: Zhi Ma. adv. contact: Weiguo Liu. bk.rev. circ. 500. **Document type:** academic/scholarly publication.
Refereed Serial

615.89 GW
HEILMITTEL AUS DER NATUR. a. Otto Hoffmanns Verlag GmbH, Arnulfstr. 10, 80335 Munich, Germany. TEL 49-89-545845-0. FAX 49-89-54584520. adv.: B&W page DM.32500, color page DM.44200; trim 112 x 175. circ. 2,100,000. **Document type:** bulletin, consumer publication.

615.5 IC
HEILSUHRINGURINN; timarit um hollefni og heilsuraekt. 1978. s-a. ISK 1000. Heilsuhringurinn, Sidumula 27, IS-108 Reykjavik, Iceland. TEL 354-568-9933. Ed.Bd. circ. 2,000. (also avail. in magnetic tape; back issues avail.)
Description: Deals with issues in alternative medicine, orthomolecular medicine and natural hygiene.

HERBALGRAM. see *BIOLOGY — Botany*

615.89 UK ISSN 1353-5307
HOLISTIC GUIDE. 1994. a. City X Media Ltd., Lonsdale House, 52 Blucher St., Birmingham B1 1QU, England. TEL 44-121-687-8181. FAX 44-121-687-8883. **Document type:** directory.

HOLISTIC HEALTH DIRECTORY. see *NEW AGE PUBLICATIONS*

HOLISTIC HEALTH SOURCEBOOK. see *NEW AGE PUBLICATIONS*

615.89 US ISSN 1060-2615
HOLISTIC LIFE/VIDA HOLISTICA; take control of your own health/ponga el control de su salud en usted mismo. (Text in English, Spanish) 1991. s-a. $32.95. New York Institute for Holistic Life, Box 302, Bronx, NY 10458. TEL 718-364-2202. FAX 718-364-2202. E-mail: holisticlife@msn.com; URL: http://www.dorsai.org/~holistic. Ed. Dr. Francisco Monegro. R&P contact: Alberto Monegro. adv. contact: Mario Cabrera. bk.rev. circ. 6,000. **Document type:** newsletter.
Refereed Serial

615.89 US
HOLISTIC LIVING; a celebration of life. 1983. bi-m. $18 (effective 1997). Holistic Health Association of the Princeton Area, 360 Nassau St., Princeton, NJ 08540. TEL 609-924-8711. FAX 609-924-3836. E-mail: mandala@ix.netcom.com; URL: http://www.holisticliving.org. Ed. David Nemitz. R&P contact: David Nemitz. adv. contact: David Nemitz. bk.rev. circ. 250,000. **Document type:** consumer publication.
Description: Explores healing processes, environmental legislation and common health problems, spirituality, and methods of stress-management.

615.53 US ISSN 0898-6029
HOLISTIC MEDICINE. 1978. bi-m. $30. American Holistic Medical Association, 4101 Lake Boone Trl., Ste. 201, Raleigh, NC 27607-6518. TEL 919-787-5181. FAX 919-787-4916. Ed. Missy Turk. R&P contact: Missy Turk. adv. contact: Lucille Cavalla. bk.rev. circ. 1,500. **Indexed:** Excerp.Med. **Document type:** trade publication.
Description: Essays on holistic medicine.

615.89 157.61 US
HOLY SMOKE; for people who need good medicine. q. $20. Sweetlight Books, 16625 Heitman Rd., Cottonwood, CA 96022. TEL 916-529-5392. E-mail: swtlight@snowcrest.net; URL: http://www.snowcrest.net/swtlight. Ed. Guy Mount. R&P contact: Guy Mount. adv.: page $80; 5 1/2 x 8 1/2. bk.rev.; film rev.; illus.; circ. 350 (paid). **Document type:** newsletter.
Description: Contains commentaries, stories, poems, testimonials, scientific and medical research that deals with the medical, spiritual, and agricultural benefits of marijuana.

362 US ISSN 1081-5570
R726.8   CODEN: HOSPFB
HOSPICE. 1990. 4/yr. $22.50 (foreign $30). National Hospice Organization, 1901 N. Moore St., Ste. 901, Arlington, VA 22209. TEL 703-243-5900. FAX 703-525-5762. Ed. Joseph Cerquone. R&P contact: David Schneider. adv. contact: Catherine Marlowe. **Document type:** trade publication.
Description: For professionals and volunteers involved in hospice care for terminally ill people.

615.892 JA ISSN 0287-6760
IDO NO NIPPON/JOURNAL OF JAPANESE ACUPUNCTURE & MOXIBUSTION. (Text in Japanese) 1938. m. 450 Yen per no. Ido no Nipponsha, 1-45, Oppama Honcho, Yokosuka-shi, Kanagawa-ken 237, Japan.
—BLDSC (5008.610000).

651.89 CN
▼**IN TOUCH (CALGARY)**; a magazine of people & possibilities. 1990. 5/yr. 7620 Elbow Dr. S.W., Calgary, AB T2V 1K2, Canada. E-mail: hayv@intouchmag.com; URL: http://www.intouchmag.com. Ed. Veronica M. Hay.
●Also available online.
Description: Seeks to connect people and explore possibilities in a rich exchange of vital information about health, ecology, personal growth, professional development, creativity, and wellness.

INCANTESIMO. see *ASTROLOGY*

INDIAN INSTITUTE OF HISTORY OF MEDICINE. BULLETIN (NEW DELHI). see *MEDICAL SCIENCES*

615.89 II ISSN 0971-314X
INDIAN MEDICINE/INDIYAN MEDISIN. (Text in English and Telegu) vol.20, 1971. m. Rs.50. Indian Medicine Industries, Dubagunta Nivas, Vijayawada 520 002, India. Ed. Dr. D.L. Narayana. adv.; bk.rev.; charts. circ. 2,000.
Description: Covers alternative medicine with special emphasis on Ayurveda.

615.89 US
INTERNATIONAL CONFERENCE ON THE STUDY OF SHAMANISM AND ALTERNATE MODES OF HEALING. PROCEEDINGS. 1984. a. $25. Independent Scholars of Asia, Inc., 2321 Russell St., No. 3C, Berkeley, CA 94705-1959. TEL 510-849-3791. FAX 510-849-3791. Ed. Ruth-Inge Heinze. index; circ. 300 (paid). (back issues avail.) **Document type:** proceedings.
Description: Essay and discussions of interdisciplinary approaches to alternative healing techniques.

615.89 US ISSN 1047-1979
RM184
INTERNATIONAL JOURNAL OF CLINICAL ACUPUNCTURE. 1990. q. $110 (foreign $145) to individuals; institutions $250 (foreign $285) (effective 1998). Allerton Press, Inc., 150 Fifth Ave., New York, NY 10011. TEL 212-924-3950. FAX 212-463-9684. Ed. Dr. Quan Ruxian. **Document type:** academic/scholarly publication.
—BLDSC (4542.169500); KNAW; SWETS. **CCC.**
Description: Emphasizes clinical results.

615.89 US ISSN 1044-0003
INTERNATIONAL JOURNAL OF ORIENTAL MEDICINE/GUOJI HANFANG YIYAO ZAZHI. (Text in Chinese, English) 1976. q. $60 (foreign $80) (effective 1996). Oriental Healing Arts Institute, 1945 Palo Verde Ave., Ste. 208, Long Beach, CA 90815. TEL 310-431-3544. FAX 310-594-6513. Ed. Dr. Qing-fu Hu. bibl.; index. circ. 500. (back issues avail.)
—BLDSC (4542.435400); UnCover.
Former titles (until 1989): Oriental Healing Arts International Bulletin (ISSN 0888-9341); (until 1986): Oriental Healing Arts Institute of U S A. Bulletin (ISSN 0278-5315)

ALTERNATIVE MEDICINE

615.89   CC   ISSN 1001-9537
CODEN: CIYCD5
JIANGSU ZHONGYI/JIANGSU TRADITIONAL CHINESE MEDICINE. (Text in Chinese) 1956. m. Jiangsu Sheng Weisheng Ting - Jiangsu Provincial Bureau of Public Health, 42 Zhongyang Lu, Nanjing, Jiangsu 210008, People's Republic of China. TEL 643684. (Dist. overseas by: China International Book Trading Corp., P.O. Box 399, Beijing, P.R. China) Ed. Zhang Huaqiang. adv.: B&W page Y.2500, color page Y.5000; adv. contact: Yabo Huang. bk.rev. circ. 100,000. Document type: academic/scholarly publication.
    Description: Covers Chinese herbal medicine, acupuncture, massage, qigong, and health care issues.

615.89   CC
JILIN ZHONGYIYAO/JILIN TRADITIONAL CHINESE MEDICINE. (Text in Chinese) bi-m. Changchun Zhongyiyuan - Changchun Institute of Traditional Chinese Medicine, 15, Gongnong Dalu, Changchun, Jilin 130021, People's Republic of China. Ed. Gao Guangzhen.

615.8 615.5   US   ISSN 1075-5535
R733   CODEN: JACPFP
JOURNAL OF ALTERNATIVE & COMPLEMENTARY MEDICINE; research on paradigm, practice, and policy. (Supplement avail.) 1993. q. $81 to individuals (foreign $122); institutions $167 (foreign $188) (effective through 1998). Mary Ann Liebert, Inc. Publishers, 2 Madison Ave., Larchmont, NY 10538. TEL 914-834-3100. FAX 914-834-3688. E-mail: liebert@pipeline.com. Eds. Kim Jobst, Fredi Kronenberg, Jackie Wootton. Document type: academic/scholarly publication.
—BLDSC (4927.202300); CISTI
    Description: Acts as an interdisciplinary source for research in alternative medical therapies. The primary goal is the establishment of rigorous research methodologies.

JOURNAL OF ANTHROPOSOPHICAL MEDICINE. see MEDICAL SCIENCES

JOURNAL OF BODYWORK & MOVEMENT THERAPIES. see MEDICAL SCIENCES — Physical Medicine And Rehabilitation

615.89   UK   ISSN 0143-8042
JOURNAL OF CHINESE MEDICINE. 1979. 3/yr. £21 (foreign £22) (effective 1997). 22 Cromwell Rd., Hove, E. Sussex BN3 3EB, England. TEL 44-1273-777760. FAX 44-1273-7485888. E-mail: jcm@pavilion.co.uk; URL: http://www.pavilion.co.uk/jcm/. (Dist. in US by: Eastland Press, 1240 Activity Dr., Ste. D, Vista, CA 92083. TEL 800-453-3278) Ed. Peter Deadman. R&P contact: Peter Deadman. adv.; bk.rev. circ. 2,000. (back issues avail.) Document type: academic/scholarly publication.
—BLDSC (4958.110000).
    Description: Covers the entire field of traditional Chinese medicine.

JOURNAL OF INTERPROFESSIONAL CARE. see MEDICAL SCIENCES

JOURNAL OF NATURAL HYGIENE; the science and philosophy of natural hygiene. see PUBLIC HEALTH AND SAFETY

615.535   US   ISSN 1047-7837
JOURNAL OF NATUROPATHIC MEDICINE. 1990. q. $65 to individuals (foreign $90); institutions $90 (foreign $110); students $35 (foreign $60). Journal Management Group, Inc., 10 Morgan Ave., Norwalk, CT 06851. Ed. Peter J. D'Adamo; Pub. Martha Mosko. adv.; bk.rev. circ. 3,500. Document type: academic/scholarly publication.
—BLDSC (5021.308000).

615.89   II   ISSN 0254-3478
R605
JOURNAL OF RESEARCH IN AYURVEDA AND SIDDHA.* (Text in English; summaries in Hindi) 1966. q. Rs.60($4) Central Council for Research in Ayurveda and Siddha, Dharma Bhawan, S-10, Green Park Extn. Market, New Delhi 110 016, India. TEL 11-669315. Ed. Dr. V.N. Pandey. adv.; bk.rev.; abstr.; bibl.; charts; illus.; stat.; index. circ. 300. (processed) Indexed: Biol.Abstr., Chem.Abstr.
—BLDSC (5052.003000); CISTI
    Formerly (until 1980): Journal of Research in Indian Medicine (ISSN 0022-4286)
    Description: Covers work on fundamental anthropological and behavioral details referred to in clinical and literary studies of medicinal systems.

615.89 200   US   ISSN 1079-8390
JOURNAL OF SPIRITUAL BODYWORK. 1995. q. $25 (effective 1997). (Church for Spiritual Healing and Health) Spiritual Massage healing Ministry, 6907 Sherman St., Philadelphia, PA 19119. TEL 215-842-0265. FAX 215-842-0265. E-mail: maryella@tiac.net. Ed. Albert Schatz; Pub. Albert Schatz. R&P contact: Albert Schatz. bk.rev.; index. circ. 325. (back issues avail.) Document type: academic/scholarly publication.
—CCC
    Description: Provides information about different kinds of spiritual healing (including massage) to laymen, clergymen, and members of licensed professions concerned with the healing arts.
    Refereed Serial

615.89   JA   ISSN 0288-2485
KANPO IGAKU/CHINESE MEDICINE. (Text in Japanese) 1977. m. 450 Yen per no. Kanpo Igakusha - Kanpo Medicine Publications, 12-7, Nibancho, Chiyoda-ku, Tokyo 102, Japan.

615.89   JA   ISSN 0385-6526
KANPO KENKYU/STUDY ON CHINESE MEDICINE. (Text in Japanese) 1975. m. 400 Yen per no. Gekkan Kanpo Kenkyu, 5-23, Nakatsu 2-chome, Kita-ku, Osaka 531, Japan.

615.89   JA   ISSN 0451-307X
KANPO NO RINSHO/JOURNAL OF KAMPO MEDICINE. (Text in Japanese) 1954. m. 600 Yen per no. Toa Igaku Kyokai - Association of East Asian Medicine, 1-5, Misakicho 2-chome, Chiyoda-ku, Tokyo 101, Japan.
—CCC

615.89   JA   ISSN 0288-3643
KANPO SHINRYO/JOURNAL OF JAPANESE KANPO HERBAL MEDICINE. (Text in Japanese) 1982. bi-m. 980 Yen per no. (Rinsho Joho Senta - Clinical Information Center, Inc.) Kyowa Kikaku Ltd., 4-7, Koraibashi 2-chome, Chuo-ku, Osaka 541, Japan.

615.89   JA   ISSN 0914-6407
KANPO TO MEN'EKI ARERUGI/KAMPO AND IMMUNO-ALLERGY. (Text in Japanese; summaries in English, Japanese) 1988. a. 4500 Yen. Fama Intanashonaru - Pharma International, Inc., 14-29, Takada 3-chome, Toshima-ku, Tokyo 171, Japan.

615.89   JA   ISSN 0912-9545
KANSAI SHINKYU TANKI DAIGAKU NENPO/KANSAI COLLEGE OF ACUPUNCTURE MEDICINE. ANNUAL REPORT. (Text in English, Japanese) 1985. a. Kansai Shinkyu Tanki Daigaku, 990, Ogaito, Kumatoricho, Sennan-gun, Osaka 590-04, Japan.

615.89   JA   ISSN 0912-0718
KATSU/JAPAN INSTITUTE OF TRADITIONAL MEDICINE. NEWS. (Text in Japanese) 1959. m. 400 Yen per no. Nihon Kanpo Igaku Kenkyujo, 2-20, Nihonbashi 2-chome, Chuo-ku, Tokyo 103, Japan.

615.89   JA
KEIRAKU CHIRYO/JAPANESE SOCIETY OF ACUPUNCTURE. JOURNAL. (Text in Japanese) 1965. q. 7000 Yen. Keiraku Chiryo Gakkai, 14-9, Jinan 1-chome, Shibuya-ku, Tokyo 150, Japan. TEL 81-3-3461-2426. FAX 81-3-3770-1675. Ed. Okabe Somei. R&P contact: Okabe Somei. adv. contact: Okabe Somei. bk.rev.
    Refereed Serial

KRAUT UND RUEBEN; das Magazin fuer biologischen Gaertnern und naturgemaesses Leben. see GARDENING AND HORTICULTURE

615.88   PL   ISSN 1233-9253
▼**LEKARZ DOMOWY MEDYCYNY LUDOWEJ**; miesiecznik lekarski. 1995. bi-m. newsstand price: 2.50. Faktor Sp. z o.o., Ul. Ksiecia Wladyslawa Opolskiego 3a, 32-650 Kety, Poland. TEL 48-33-453888. Ed. Jozef Gaweda. circ. 8,000. (back issues avail.)
    Description: Covers folk herbal medicine.

615.89 615.328   CC   ISSN 1000-1719
R97.7.C5   CODEN: LZZAEJ
LIAONING ZHONGYI ZAZHI/LIAONING JOURNAL OF TRADITIONAL CHINESE MEDICINE. (Text in Chinese) 1979. m. $0.70 per no. Liaoning Zhongyi Xueyuan - Liaoning College of Traditional Chinese Medicine, 79 Congshan Donglu, Shenyang, Liaoning 110032a, People's Republic of China. (Dist. outside China by: China International Book Trading Corporation, P.O. Box 399, Beijing, P.R.C.) (Co-sponsor: Zhonghua Quanguo Zhongyi Xuehui Liaoning Fenhui) Indexed: Dent.Ind., Ind.Med.

LONGEVITY REPORT. see GERONTOLOGY AND GERIATRICS

MACROBIOTICS TODAY. see NUTRITION AND DIETETICS

615.89   FR
MEDECINES NOUVELLES. 1985. q. 230 F. Societe J A G, B.P. 2, 14130 Blangy-le-Chateau, France. TEL 33-2-31646300. adv. Document type: consumer publication.

MEDICINA NATURALE. see MEDICAL SCIENCES — Chiropractic, Homeopathy, Osteopathy

615.89   JA   ISSN 0912-2419
MEIJI SHINKYU IGAKU/MEIJI COLLEGE OF ORIENTAL MEDICINE. BULLETIN. (Text in English, Japanese) 1985. a. Meiji Shinkyu Daigaku, Hiyoshicho, Funai-gun, Kyoto 629-03, Japan.

615.89   FR   ISSN 0301-6366
MENSUEL DU MEDECIN ACUPUNCTEUR. 1973. m. 400 F. Nguyen Van Nghi, Ed. & Pub., 27 bd. d'Athenes, 13001 Marseille, France. adv.; bibl.; illus.

615.892   US
MERIDIANS; redefining health. s-a. $35 membership. Traditional Acupuncture Institute, 10227 Wincopin Circle, Ste. 100, Columbia, MD 21044. TEL 301-596-6006. Ed. Mary Ellen Zorbaugh. R&P contact: Barbara Tansill. TEL 410-997-4888. bk.rev.; illus. circ. 2,000.
    Formerly (until 1992): Journal of Traditional Acupuncture (ISSN 0270-661X)
    Description: Contains detailed articles and information regarding acupuncture and related health care issues.

615.89   GW   ISSN 0340-577X
MODERNES LEBEN - NATUERLICHES HEILEN; Monatsblaetter fuer naturgemaesse Lebenspflege, Homoeopathie und Naturheilkunde. 1875. m. Verlag Helmut Preussler, Dagmarstr. 8, 90482 Nuernberg, Germany. Document type: consumer publication.

N A P S A C NEWS. (National Association of Parents and Professionals for Safe Alternatives in Childbirth, International) see MEDICAL SCIENCES — Obstetrics And Gynecology

N C A H F NEWSLETTER; quality in the health marketplace. (National Council Against Health Fraud, Inc.) see PUBLIC HEALTH AND SAFETY

362   US   ISSN 1081-5678
N H O NEWSLINE. 1984. 24/yr. membership only. National Hospice Organization, 1901 N. Moore St., Ste. 901, Arlington, VA 22209. TEL 703-243-5900. FAX 703-525-5762. Ed. Jennifer Morales. R&P contact: David Schneider. adv. contact: Catherine Marlowe. circ. 2,800. Document type: newsletter.
    Former titles (until 1991): N H O Hospice News; N H O President's Letter.
    Description: Provides brief updates of regulatory and educational news and information of relevance to hospice administrators.

N O H A NEWS. (Nutrition for Optimal Health Association) see NUTRITION AND DIETETICS

ALTERNATIVE MEDICINE

615.89 JA ISSN 0911-9760
NAGAKURA KANPO DAIJESUTO/NAGAKURA KANPO DIGEST. (Text in Japanese) 1970. a. Nagakura Seiyaku K.K. - Nagakura Pharmaceutical Co., Ltd., 7-16, Shotenshita 1-chome, Nishinari-ku, Osaka 557, Japan.

613.7 US ISSN 1060-7846
RA773
NATURAL HEALING & NUTRITION ANNUAL. a. $19.95. Rodale Press, Inc., Prevention Magazine, 33 E. Minor St., Emmaus, PA 18049. TEL 610-967-5171; 800-441-7761. FAX 610-967-7725. Eds. Mark Bricklin, Sharon Stocker Ferguson. **Document type:** consumer publication.

613.7 US ISSN 1067-9588
AP2
NATURAL HEALTH; the guide to well-being. 1971. bi-m. $24 (Canada $27; elsewhere $36) (effective 1994). Natural Health L.P., 17 Station St., Box 1200, Brookline, MA 02147. TEL 617-232-1000. FAX 617-232-1572. (Subscr. to: Box 7440, Red Oak, IA 51591-0440) Ed. Anne Alexander; Pub. Christopher Kimball. adv. contact: Ann D'Alesandro. bk.rev.; circ. 200,000 (paid). (also avail. in microform from UMI; back issues avail.; reprint service avail. from UMI) **Indexed:** Alt.Press Ind., CHNI, New Per.Ind., Per.Islam. (1991-). **Document type:** consumer publication.
●Also available online. Vendor(s): Information Access Co.
—BLDSC (6037.930000); UMI; UnCover.
Former titles (until Nov. 1992): EastWest Natural Health (ISSN 1061-4664); (until Jan. 1992): EastWest (ISSN 0888-1375); (until 1986): East West Journal (ISSN 0191-3700); (until 1978): EastWest (ISSN 0149-0362); (until 1977): East West Journal (ISSN 0149-7839)
Description: Covers all aspects of natural health and self-care, including naturopathy, holistic health and alternative health care and prevention options.

613.7 658.8 US
NATURAL HEALTH HANDBOOK; the retailer's guide to natural products. 1994. a. $9.95 (effective 1994). Natural Health L.P., 17 Station St., Box 1200, Brookline, MA 02147. TEL 617-232-1000. Ed. Anne Alexander. adv. contact: Ann D'Alesandro. tr.lit. **Document type:** trade publication, directory.
Description: Provides health products retailers with information on natural foods, herbal and natural remedies, natural cosmetics and other products of interest.

NATURAL PHARMACY. see PHARMACY AND PHARMACOLOGY

615.89 GW ISSN 0028-081X
DER NATURARZT; Zeitschrift fuer naturgemaesse Lebens- und Heilweisen. 1861. m. DM.70. Access Marketing GmbH, Alt Falkenstein 379, 61462 Koenigstein, Germany. TEL 06174-9263-0. FAX 06174-926329. adv.; bk.rev.; charts; illus.; index. circ. 70,000. **Document type:** consumer publication.

615.89 110 AT ISSN 0815-7006
NATURE AND HEALTH. 1977. bi-m. Aus.$35.70 (foreign Aus.$100) (effective Aug. 1996). Yaffa Publishing Group, 17-21 Bellevue St., Surry Hills, N.S.W. 2010, Australia. TEL 61-2-92812333. FAX 61-2-92812750. Ed. Pamela Allardice; Pub. Tracy Yaffa. adv.: B&W page Aus.$1880, color page Aus.$2895; 273 x 210; adv. contact: Carol Roselli. bk.rev.
—UnCover.
Former titles (until 1984): Nature and Health Australia (ISSN 0815-6999); (until 1980): Nature and Health Quarterly (ISSN 0158-9911)
Description: Covers a wide spectrum of topics - natural health, self improvement body care, relationships, organic gardening, natural beauty and fitness, oriental herbs, whole foods, science, social change and spirituality.

615.89 GW ISSN 0177-6754
NATURHEILPRAXIS MIT NATURMEDIZIN; Fachzeitschrift fuer Naturheilkunde, Erfahrungsheilkunde und biologische Heilverfahren. 1947. m. DM.153.60 (Europe DM.177). Richard Pflaum Verlag GmbH und Co. KG, Lazarettstr. 4, 80636 Munich, Germany. TEL 49-89-12607-0. FAX 49-89-12607333. Ed. K.F. Liebau. adv. contact: Roland de la Rosee. bk.rev.; illus.; index. circ. 17,000. **Document type:** academic/scholarly publication.
—CCC.
Former titles (until 1984): N. Naturheilpraxis (ISSN 0177-6746); (until 1983): Naturheilpraxis (ISSN 0028-0941)

615.89 US ISSN 0028-100X
NATUROPATH.* 1961. m. $7.50. Naturopath Publishing Co., 141 N. Steelhammer Dr., Silverton, OR 97381-1821. TEL 206-695-0213. Ed. Robert W. Noble. adv.; bk.rev.; stat.; tr.lit. circ. 3,600.

NEW AGE JOURNAL SOURCEBOOK. see NEW AGE PUBLICATIONS

615.89 158 US
NEXUS (BOULDER); Colorado's holistic journal. 1980. bi-m. $21. 1680 Sixth St., Ste. 6, Boulder, CO 80302. TEL 303-442-6662. FAX 303-442-7596. E-mail: nexuspub@aol.com. Ed. Barbralu Cohen; Pub. Ravi Dykema. R&P contact: Margo Pedrick. adv. contact: Margo Pedrick. bk.rev.; illus.; circ. 54,000 (controlled). (tabloid format) **Document type:** newspaper.
Description: Publishes news and commentary pertaining to all aspects of holistic and alternative health care and related issues.

NUTRITION FORUM. see NUTRITION AND DIETETICS

ONKRUID; goed voor aarde, lichaam en geest. see NEW AGE PUBLICATIONS

ORGANICA; a magazine of arts & activism. see LITERATURE

615.89 JA
ORIENTAL MEDICINE. m. 1408 Yen per no. Midori - Shobo Co., Ltd. (Subsidiary of: Midori Group), Ikebukuro Nishiguchi Sky Bldg., 2-14-4 Ikebukuro, Toshima-ku, Tokyo 171, Japan. TEL 03-35990-4441. FAX 03-3590-4446. Ed. Toshikazu Nakamura. circ. 18,000. **Document type:** trade publication.
Description: Covers kampo medicine, acupuncture, moxibustion, manipulative therapeutics for physicians, herbal pharmacists, and manufacturers.

DE ORTHOMOLECULAIRE KOERIER; Nederlands - Vlaams tijdschrift voor nutritieve geneeskunde. see NUTRITION AND DIETETICS

THE PANIC RELIEF NEWS. see PSYCHOLOGY

615.8 SA ISSN 1022-2170
PATHWAYS TO HEALTH. (Text in English) 1993. bi-m. R.45. F A S Publications, P.O. Box 41632, Craighall 2024, South Africa. TEL 27-11-7893740. FAX 27-11-7876316. Ed. Monica Fairall; Pub. Ian Hughes. R&P contact: Ian Hughes. adv. contact: Joanne Lawrie. **Document type:** consumer publication.
Description: Covers complementary and alternative therapies.

POTPOURRI FROM HERBAL ACRES. see GARDENING AND HORTICULTURE

615.89 PL ISSN 1231-6652
PRZEPISY MEDYCYNY LUDOWEJ; miesiecznik zdrowia. 1994. bi-m. newsstand price: 2.50 Zl. Gawenda Sp. z o.o., Ul. Kiecia Wladyslawa Opolskiego 3a, 32-650 Kety, Poland. TEL 48-33-453888. Ed. Jozef Gaweda. circ. 22,500. (back issues avail.)
Description: Covers folk medicine.

615.892 US
QUINTESSENCE. 4/yr. $35 membership. Traditional Acupuncture Institute, 10227 Wincopin Circle, Ste. 100, Columbia, MD 21044. TEL 301-596-6006. FAX 410-944-3544. Ed. Barbara Tansill. R&P contact: Barbara Tansill. TEL 410-997-4888. bk.rev. circ. 5,000. **Document type:** newsletter.
Description: Informs acupuncture patients and the general public about acupuncture, self-health care and the development of Oriental medicine in America.

615.89 US
THE RADIANCE TECHNIQUE NEWSLETTER. 1980. 2/yr. $10. The Radiance Technique Association International, Inc., Box 40570, St. Petersburg, FL 33743-0570. TEL 813-595-5004. FAX 813-595-5004. Ed. Fred W. Wright, Jr. R&P contact: Fred W. Wright, Jr. TEL 813-347-2106. adv.; bk.rev.; circ. 1,000 (paid). (back issues avail.) **Document type:** newsletter.
Former titles: Radiance Technique Journal (ISSN 1040-5836); Reiki Journal.
Description: Features alumni sharing news of their use of The Radiance Technique; includes the latest articles on the subject.

REFLECTIONS MAGAZINE - DIRECTORY. see NEW AGE PUBLICATIONS

615.89 FR ISSN 0337-6877
REVUE FRANCAISE D'ACUPUNCTURE. (Text in French; summaries in English) 1975. q. 330 (foreign 380 F.) (effective 1997). Association Francaise d'Acupuncture, Tour CIT, 3 rue de l'Arrivee, 75749 Paris Cedex 15, France. TEL 33-1-43202626. FAX 33-1-43205446. URL: http://members.aol.com:/lishishen/acupuncture. Ed. Gilles Andres. adv. contact: Denis Arlet. bk.rev.; cum.index: 1975-1977; 1978-1991; 1982-1984; 1985-1988; 1989-1993. (also avail. in diskette format; back issues avail.) **Document type:** academic/scholarly publication.
Description: Covers techniques in acupuncture medicine.
Refereed Serial

291.144 HU ISSN 1216-7827
BL2370.S5
SHAMAN. (Text in English) 1993. s-a. $40 (effective 1997 & 1998). Molnar & Kelemen Oriental Publishers, P.O. Box 1195, 6701 Szeged, Hungary. TEL 36-1-3310007. FAX 36-1-3025009. Eds. Mihaly Hoppal, Adam Molnar. R&P contact: Adam Molnar. adv.: page $99. bk.rev. **Document type:** academic/scholarly publication.
Description: Covers shamanism, cultural anthropology, religious history, alternative medicine, ethnomusicology.
Refereed Serial

615.89 615.328 CC ISSN 0559-7269
SHANGHAI ZHONGYIYAO ZAZHI/SHANGHAI JOURNAL OF TRADITIONAL CHINESE MEDICINE/REVUE DE MEDECINE TRADITIONNELLE CHINOISE/REVISTA DE MEDICINA TRADICIONAL CHINA DE SHANGHAI. (Text in Chinese) m. $0.80 per no. Guoji Shudian, Qikan Bu - China International Book Trading Corp., Chegongzhuang Xilu 21, P.O. Box 399, Beijing 100044, People's Republic of China. **Document type:** academic/scholarly publication.

615.89 CC ISSN 1000-7156
SHANXI ZHONGYI/SHANXI TRADITIONAL MEDICINE. (Text in Chinese) bi-m. (Shanxi Sheng Weisheng Ting) Shanxi Zhongyi Bianjibu, 23 Donghua Men, Taiyuan, Shanxi 030013, People's Republic of China. TEL 382791. Ed. Cui Tianyue. pp./issue: 56. **Document type:** academic/scholarly publication.
Description: Covers the latest development, trends, theories and applications of traditional Chinese medicine.

615.89 US
SHARE GUIDE. 1989. q.; on-line ed. w. $8 (foreign $12). 11540 Los Amigos Rd., Healdsburg, CA 95448. TEL 707-433-4044. FAX 707-433-1073. E-mail: share@shareguide.com; URL: http://www.shareguide.com. Ed. Janice Hughes.
●Also available online.
Description: A holistic health magazine focusing on alternative medicine, personal growth, and environmental awareness.

SHIZHEN GUOYAO YANJIU/SHIZHEN JOURNAL OF TRADITIONAL CHINESE MEDICINE RESEARCH. see PHARMACY AND PHARMACOLOGY

615.89 CC ISSN 1000-3649
SICHUAN ZHONGYI/SICHUAN JOURNAL OF TRADITIONAL CHINESE MEDICINE. (Text in Chinese) m. Zhonghua Quanguo ZhongYi Xuehui, Sichuan Fenhui - Chinese National Society for Traditional Chinese Medicine, Sichuan Branch, 80, Wenmiao Xijie, Chengdu, Sichuan 610041, People's Republic of China. TEL 26595. Ed. Jin Jiajun.

SPECTRUM - THE WHOLISTIC NEWS MAGAZINE. see NEW AGE PUBLICATIONS

ALTERNATIVE MEDICINE — ABSTRACTING, BIBLIOGRAPHIES, STATISTICS

615.852 291.31   US   ISSN 1080-3262
▼SPIRITUAL MASSAGE MINISTRY NEWSLETTER. 1995. q. $15 (foreign $20) (effective 1997 & 1998). Church for Spiritual Healing and Health, Spiritual Massage Healing Ministry, 6907 Sherman St., Philadelphia, PA 19119. TEL 215-842-0265. FAX 215-842-0265. E-mail: maryella@tiac.net. Ed. Rev. Albert Schatz; Pub. Rev. Albert Schatz. R&P contact: Rev. Albert Schatz. bk.rev.; index. circ. 250. (looseleaf format; back issues avail.) Document type: newsletter.
 Description: Provides information about different types of spiritual healing to laymen, clergymen, and other professionals who are concerned with health and the healing arts.

615.89 110   US   ISSN 1084-2209
SUBTLE ENERGIES; an interdisciplinary journal of energetic and informational interactions. 1991. 3/yr. $50 per volume (effective 1997). International Society for the Study of Subtle Energies and Energy Medicine, 356 Goldco Circle, Golden, CO 80403-1347. TEL 303-278-2228. FAX 303-279-3539. TELEX 159294488. E-mail: 74040.12730@compuserve.com; URL: http://vitalenergy.com/issseem/. Ed. Steven L. Fahrion. R&P contact: C. Penny Hiernu. bk.rev. circ. 1,200. Document type: academic/scholarly publication.
 —BLDSC (8503.535000).
 Description: Concerned with the study of informational systems and energies that interact with the human psyche and physiology, either enhancing or perturbing healthy homeostasis.
 Refereed Serial

615.537   IT
TERAPIE NATURALI E ERBE. 1984. m. L.70000($70) (effective Jan. 1997). Stampa Natura Solidarieta s.p.a., Via Bazzini 40, 20131 Milan, Italy. TEL 39-2-26680654. FAX 39-2-26680664. adv. circ. 40,000. Document type: academic/scholarly publication.
 Former titles: Erbe e Terapie Naturali; Erbe Secondo Natura.

615.82   NE   ISSN 0928-0065
TIJDSCHRIFT VOOR INTEGRALE GENEESKUNDE. (Text in Dutch; summaries in Dutch, English) 1984. bi-m. fl.95 (effective 1995). Stichting Tijdschrift voor Integrale Geneeskunde, Tooropstraat 181, 6521 NM Nijmegen, Netherlands. TEL 31-80-601688. (Editorial addr.: c/o Utrecht University, Postbus 80046, 3508 TA Utrecht, Netherlands) Ed. Dr. C.W. Kramers. adv.; bk.rev. (back issues avail.) Document type: academic/scholarly publication.
 —BLDSC (8841.850000); SWETS.
 Description: Publishes studies of fundamental and applied research relating to complementary medicine, alternative medicine, homeopathy, health policy and developments in diagnosis and other branches of the medical sciences.
 Refereed Serial

TIJDSCHRIFT VOOR KREATIEVE THERAPIE. see PSYCHOLOGY

615.89   US
TOWNSEND LETTER FOR DOCTORS & PATIENTS. 1983. m. (10/yr.) $53 ($49 in WA state; Canada & Mexico $79;elsewhere $117) (effective 1997). 911 Tyler St., Port Townsend, WA 98368-6541. TEL 360-385-6021. FAX 360-385-0699. E-mail: info@tldp.com; URL: http://www.tldp.com. Ed. Dr. Jonathan Collin; Pub. Dr. Jonathan Collin. R&P contact: Barbara Smith. adv. contact: Jonathan Collin. bk.rev./ circ. 5,500 (paid). Document type: consumer publication.
 Formerly (until 1995): Townsend Letter for Doctors (ISSN 1059-5864)

TRAGER INSTITUTE NEWSLETTER. see MEDICAL SCIENCES — Physical Medicine And Rehabilitation

615.89 133   US   ISSN 1076-4437
VISIONS (MOORPARK). 1975. 6/yr. free. 4388 Amberwick Ln., Moorpark, CA 93021. TEL 805-523-1483. FAX 805-523-1405. E-mail: mmeade@vc.net; URL: http://www.vcnet.com/mmeade. Ed. Mark Meade; Pub. Antonia L. Rodriguez. R&P contact: Antonia L. Rodriguez. adv. contact: Antonia L. Rodriguez. bk.rev. circ. 1,000. Document type: consumer publication.
 Description: Covers herbs, nutrition, metaphysics and parapsychology.

613.7 613.2   CN   ISSN 1180-0291
VITALITY MAGAZINE; Toronto's monthly wellness journal. 1989. m. (10/yr.). Can.$30. 356 Dupont St., Toronto, ON M5R 1V9, Canada. TEL 416-964-0528. Ed. Julia Woodford. adv. contact: Jody Hatt. circ. 40,000 (controlled). Document type: consumer publication.
 Description: Covers holistic health, nutritional medicine, self development, news and reviews of events and services in Toronto.

615.89   US
VOICE OF NAPRAPATHY. 1955. irreg., vol.82, 1988. American Naprapathic Association, 5321 N. Central Ave., Chicago, IL 60630. TEL 312-685-6020. (Subscr. to: 5913 W. Montrose Ave., Chicago, IL 60634) (Co-sponsor: Illinois Naprapathic Association) Ed. Ray Webster. circ. 5,000. (back issues avail.)
 Description: A forum for practitioners of naprapathy, a system of manipulation administered by the hands.

615.89   US   ISSN 1352-1241
WHAT DOCTORS DON'T TELL YOU. 1989. m. $39.95 to individuals; institutions $79.95. Wallace Press, 4364 44th St. S., St. Petersburg, FL 33711-4426. Ed. Lynne McTaggart; Pub. Bryan Hubbard. bk.rev.; abstr. (back issues avail.) Document type: academic/scholarly publication.
 —BLDSC (9309.679050).
 Description: Criticizes conventional medicine and shows its failings through scientific evidence.

615.89 615.328   CC   ISSN 0256-7415
XINZHONGYI/NEW JOURNAL OF TRADITIONAL CHINESE MEDICINE. (Text in Chinese) 1969. m. $24. Guangzhou Zhongyi Xueyuan, Xinzhongyi Bianjibu - Guangzhou College of Traditional Chinese Medicine, Xinzhongyi Editorial Department, Sanyuanli, Guangzhou, Guangdong 510407, People's Republic of China. TEL 6661233. FAX 6594735. (Dist. by: China International Book Trading Corporation, P.O. Box 339, Beijing, P.R.C.) Ed. Cheng Fang. adv.: B&W page $5000. circ. 80,000. Document type: academic/scholarly publication.
 Description: Covers theory and clinical practice of traditional Chinese medicine.

615.89 615.328   CC   ISSN 0255-2914
R97.7.C5
YUNNAN ZHONGYI ZAZHI/YUNNAN JOURNAL OF TRADITIONAL CHINESE MEDICINE. (Text in Chinese) 1980. m. $0.80 per no. Yunnan Sheng Zhongyi Zhongyao Yanjiusuo - Yunnan Research Institute of Traditional Chinese Medicine and Material Medica, Lianhua Chi, Kunming, Yunnan 650223, People's Republic of China. TEL 5154494. (Dist. overseas by: Guoji Shudian - China International Book Trading Corp., P.O. Box 399, Beijing, People's Republic of China) Ed. Zhang Zhen. adv. contact: Zhao Hua. Indexed: ExtraMED. Document type: academic/scholarly publication.
 ●Also available on CD-ROM.
 Description: Covers scientific researches, theories and clinical practices in traditional Chinese medicine, medical materials, acupuncture, and moxibustion.

615.89   GW   ISSN 0044-3182
ZEITSCHRIFT FUER NATURHEILKUNDE. 1949. m. DM.54. Berufsverband der Heilpraktiker Nordrhein-Westfalen e.V., Koernerstr. 59, 42659 Solingen, Germany. adv.; bk.rev. circ. 4,700. Document type: consumer publication.

615.89 615.328   CC   ISSN 0411-8421
ZHEJIANG ZHONGYI ZAZHI/ZHEJIANG JOURNAL OF TRADITIONAL CHINESE MEDICINE. (Text in Chinese) m. $1.90 per no. Zhejiang Sheng Zhongyiyao Yanjiusuo - Zhejiang Provincial Institute of Traditional Chinese Medicine, 26 Tianmushan Lu, Hangzhou, Zhejiang 310007, People's Republic of China. (Dist. overseas by: Guoji Shudian - China International Book Trading Corporation, P.O. Box 399, Beijing, P.R.C.) Indexed: ExtraMED. Document type: academic/scholarly publication.
 ●Also available on CD-ROM.

615.892   CC
ZHONGGUO ZHENJIU/CHINESE ACUPUNCTURE AND MOXIBUSTION. (Text mostly in Chinese, partly in English) 1981. bi-m. $2.40 per no. (China Academy of Traditional Chinese Medicine) Zhongguo Zhenjiu Zazhishe, Dongzhimennei, Beijing 100700, People's Republic of China. TEL 01-4014411. TELEX 210340. (Dist. overseas by: Zhongguo Guoji Shudian - China International Book Trading Corporation, P.O. Box 2820, Beijing, P.R.C.) (Co-sponsor: Chinese Society of Acupuncture and Moxibustion)

ZHONGGUO ZHONGYAO ZAZHI/CHINA JOURNAL OF CHINESE MATERIA MEDICA. see PHARMACY AND PHARMACOLOGY

615.89 370   CC   ISSN 1003-305X
ZHONGYI JIAOYU/EDUCATION OF TRADITIONAL CHINESE MEDICINE. (Text in Chinese) 1982. bi-m. (Beijing Zhongyi Daxue) Zhongyi Jiaoyu Bianjibu, 11 Beisanhuan Donglu, Beijing 100029, People's Republic of China. TEL 86-10-4225566. FAX 86-10-4220890. (Dist. overseas by: China International Book Trading Corp., P.O. Box 399, Beijing 100044, P.R. China) Ed. Liu Zhenmin. Document type: academic/scholarly publication.
 Description: Covers all aspects of education of traditional Chinese medicine.

615.89 615.328   CC
ZHONGYI ZAZHI/JOURNAL OF TRADITIONAL CHINESE MEDICINE. (Text in Chinese) m. $1.10 per no. (All-China Association of Workers of Traditional Chinese Medicine) Guoji Shudian, Qikan Bu - China International Book Trading Corp., Chegongzhuang Xilu 21, P.O. Box 399, Beijing, People's Republic of China. Indexed: Helminthol.Abstr.

ZHONGYI ZHENGGUY/JOURNAL OF TRADITIONAL CHINESE ORTHOPEDICS AND TRAUMATOLOGY. see MEDICAL SCIENCES — Orthopedics And Traumatology

ALTERNATIVE MEDICINE —
Abstracting, Bibliographies, Statistics

016.61 615.89   UK   ISSN 0950-6667
COMPLEMENTARY MEDICINE INDEX. m. £53 (outside Europe £69) (effective 1995). British Library, Medical Information Centre, Boston Spa, Wetherby, W. Yorks. LS23 7BQ, England. TEL 44-1937-546039. FAX 44-1937-546458. E-mail: maggie.taylor@bl.uk. Pub. Maggie Taylor. Document type: abstracting/indexing.
 ●Also available online.
 —BLDSC (3364.203720).
 Description: Lists current index of literature for alternative medicine.

615.89 633.88   HU   ISSN 1219-2155
▼FITOTERAPIA. (Text in Hungarian; table of contents in English, Hungarian) 1995. irreg. 250 Ft. Magyar Fitoterapias Tarsasag, Zrinyi u. 3, 1051 Budapest V, Hungary. TEL 1171488. Ed. Zoltan Hanko.
 —BLDSC (3948.249000).

016.615   CC   ISSN 1003-3521
ZHONGGUO YAOXUE WENZHAI/CHINESE PHARMACEUTICAL ABSTRACTS. (Text in Chinese; a. index in English and Latin) 1982. m. $220 (effective 1997); $250 (effective 1998). Guojia Yiyao Guanli-ju, Keji Qingbao Yanjiusuo - State Pharmaceutical Administration of China, Science and Technology Information Research Institute, A-38 Beilishilu, Beijing 100810, People's Republic of China. TEL 86-10-6831-3344. FAX 86-10-6831-1978. Ed. Fengwen Guo. adv. Document type: abstracting/indexing, academic/scholarly publication.
 Description: Published on the basis of the Traditional Chinese Medicines (TCMs) Contemporary Literature Database, as well as abstracts in modern drugs in China. Covers 420 current domestic medical journals.
 Refereed Serial

ANAESTHESIOLOGY

see Medical Sciences—Anaesthesiology

ANALYTICAL CHEMISTRY

see Chemistry—Analytical Chemistry

ANIMAL WELFARE

see also Pets

A I F NEWSLETTER. (Animal Industry Foundation) see AGRICULTURE — Poultry And Livestock

179.3 US
A S P C A ANIMAL WATCH. 1947. q. $20 to members. American Society for the Prevention of Cruelty to Animals, 424 E. 92nd St., New York, NY 10128. TEL 212-876-7700. Ed. Cindy A. Adams; Pub. Roger A. Caras. bk.rev.; illus.; stat. circ. 190,000. (back issues avail.)
 Formerly (until 1992): A S P C A Report; Supersedes (in 1981): A S P C A Bulletin; Which superseded (in 1977): Animal Protection (ISSN 0003-357X)
 Description: Animal welfare issues and features on care of companion animals, as well as wild animals.

179.3 179.4 US ISSN 0274-7774
HV4701
THE A V MAGAZINE. 1892. q. $20 membership (effective 1997). American Anti-Vivisection Society, Noble Plaza, Ste. 204, 801 Old York Rd., Jenkintown, PA 19046. TEL 215-887-0816. FAX 215-887-2088. E-mail: aavsonline@aol.com; URL: http://www.aavs.org/. Ed. Tina Nelson. bk.rev. circ. 8,500. **Document type:** academic/scholarly publication, consumer publication.
 —UnCover.
 Formerly: A-V (ISSN 0001-2831)

179.3 179.4 US ISSN 1071-1384
HV4701
A W I QUARTERLY. 1951. q. $25 (free to qualified personnel). Animal Welfare Institute, Box 3650, Washington, DC 20007. TEL 202-337-2332. FAX 202-338-9478. E-mail: awi@igc. anicmalwelfare.com; URL: http://www.animalwelfare.com. bk.rev. circ. 20,000. **Document type:** newsletter.
 Former titles (until 1992): Animal Welfare Institute Quarterly (ISSN 0743-0841); (until 1981): Animal Welfare Institute Information Report (ISSN 0003-3596)
 Description: Reports on current animal welfare issues, including treatment of captive animals in laboratories, commercial trade, factory farms, and traplines, laws and treaties affecting animals.

179.3 179.4 AT
ACTION (ELWOOD); the animals' voice. 1980. q. Aus.$15. Animal Liberation, P.O. Box 15, Elwood, Vic. 3184, Australia. TEL 61-3-95314367. FAX 61-3-95314257. Ed. Patty Mark. R&P contact: Patty Mark. TEL 61-3-93292511. adv.; bk.rev. circ. 3,000. **Document type:** consumer publication.
 Former titles: Animal Liberation Action & Animal Liberation Magazine (ISSN 0816-486X); (until 1985): Outcry (ISSN 0725-9700)

179.3 US
ACTION ALERT (NEW YORK). 1973. 3/yr. $15 membership. Beauty Without Cruelty U S A, 175 W. 12th St., Ste. 16G, New York, NY 10011-8275. TEL 212-989-8073. FAX 212-989-8073. Ed. Ethel Thurston. bk.rev. circ. 7,000. **Document type:** newsletter.
 Description: Consists of instructions to individuals on how and where to write letters protesting fur promotions; also encourages and assists the finding of clothing and cosmetics produced in ways that do not involve suffering, confinement or death of animals.

179.3 333.7 US ISSN 1072-2068
ACT!ONLINE. Variant title: Action Line (Darien). 1977. 4/yr. $25. Friends of Animals, Inc., 777 Post Rd., Ste. 205, Darien, CT 06820-4721. TEL 203-656-1522. FAX 203-656-0267. E-mail: foa@igc.apc.org; URL: http://www.envirolink.org/arrs/foa/home.htm. Ed. Priscilla Feral. adv.; bk.rev. circ. 150,000.
 Former titles: Friends of Animals Reports; Animals (New York); Actionline.
 Description: Works to protect animals from cruelty, abuse and institutionalized exploitation.

179.3 US ISSN 1040-2225
ADVOCATE (ENGLEWOOD). 1952. q. $15. American Humane Association, Animal Protection Division, 63 Inverness Dr. E., Englewood, CO 80112-5117. TEL 303-792-9900. FAX 303-792-5333. URL: http://www.amerhumane.org. Ed. Jane Ehrhardt. illus.; stat. circ. 48,000. **Document type:** newsletter.
 Former titles (until 1983): National Animal Protection Newsletter; Animal Protection News; Which was formed by the merger of: National Humane Review (ISSN 0027-948X); Animal Shelter Shoptalk (ISSN 0027-9471); National Humane Newsletter; National Humane Shoptalk (ISSN 0027-9498); American Humane Association Annual Report; American Humane Association. National Humane Report (ISSN 0065-8596).
 Description: Informs readers of the Association's progress in protecting animals.

179.3 179.4 UK
ADVOCATES FOR ANIMALS. ANNUAL PICTORIAL REVIEW. (Former name of issuing body: Scottish Society for Prevention of Vivisection) 1912. a. free. Advocates for Animals, 10 Queensferry St., Edinburgh EH2 4PG, Scotland. TEL 44-131-225-6039. FAX 44-131-220-6377. Dir. Les Ward; Pub. Les Ward. R&P contact: Les Ward. adv. contact: Les Ward. bk.rev. circ. 10,000.
 Formerly (until 1990): Scottish Society for Prevention of Vivisection. Annual Pictorial Review (ISSN 0080-8210)

ALCES; a journal devoted to the biology and management of moose. see BIOLOGY — Zoology

ALTEX. see MEDICAL SCIENCES — Experimental Medicine, Laboratory Technique

179.3 UK
ANIMAL ACTION. 1975. bi-m. £5.50. Royal Society for the Prevention of Cruelty to Animals, Causeway, Horsham, W. Sussex RH12 1HG, England. TEL 44-1403-264181. FAX 44-1403-241048. Ed. Michaela Miller. circ. 70,000.
 Former titles (until 1994): Animal World (ISSN 0968-2147); (until 1981): Animal Ways.
 Description: Covers all aspects of animal welfare and the work of the Royal Society for young people.

179.3 US ISSN 1045-9979
ANIMAL ACTIVIST ALERT. 1983. q. $10 minimum donation; free to members. Humane Society of the United States, 2100 L St., N.W., Washington, DC 20037. TEL 202-452-1100. Ed. Ann Stockho. circ. 10,000. (tabloid format; back issues avail.) **Document type:** newsletter.
 Description: Provides information on how readers can act (write letters, make calls) on behalf of animals in emergency situations.

179.3 SA ISSN 0379-654X
ANIMAL ANTI-CRUELTY LEAGUE. CHAIRMAN'S REPORT. 1972. a. R.10. Animal Anti-Cruelty League, P.O. Box 7, Rosettenville 2130, Transvaal, South Africa. TEL 27-11-435-0672. FAX 27-11-435-0693. **Document type:** corporate report.

179.4 179.3 UK
ANIMAL CONCERN. ANNUAL REPORT; for the total abolition of animal exploitation. a. £10 (unwaged £5; under 16 £2) (effective 1997). Animal Concern Ltd., 62 Old Dumbarton Rd., Glasgow G3 8RE, Scotland. TEL 44-141-334-6014. FAX 44-141-445-6470. Ed. John F. Robins. R&P contact: John F. Robins. adv. contact: John F. Robins. **Document type:** corporate report.
 Formerly: Scottish Anti-Vivisection Society. Annual Report.
 Description: Advocates the total abolition of live animal research and the promotion of animal rights.

179.4 179.3 UK
ANIMAL CONCERN NEWS; campaigning for the exploited. 1981. q. £10 (unwaged £5; under 16 £2) (effective 1997); newsstand price: 20p. Animal Concern Ltd., 62 Old Dumbarton Rd., Glasgow G3 8RE, Scotland. TEL 44-141-334-6014. FAX 44-141-445-6470. Ed. John F. Robins. R&P contact: John F. Robins. adv. contact: John F. Robins. bk.rev. circ. 1,200. **Document type:** newsletter.
 Former titles (until 1988): S A V S News; Scottish Anti-Vivisection Society. Newsletter (ISSN 0261-2089)
 Description: Reports on the welfare of animals in zoos, parks, and laboratories and the action the organization is taking on their behalf. Advises the public on action they should take.

179.4 UK
ANIMAL CONCERN NEWS UPDATE. 1994. q. £10 (unwaged £5; under 16 £2) (effective 1997). Animal Concern Ltd., 62 Old Dumbarton Rd., Glasgow G3 8RE, Scotland. TEL 44-141-334-6014. FAX 44-141-445-6470. Ed. John F. Robins; Pub. John F. Robins. R&P contact: John F. Robins. adv. contact: John F. Robins. illus. **Document type:** bulletin.
 Description: Alerts persons concerned with animal welfare to important events and political action steps they can take.

179.3 CN ISSN 0044-829X
ANIMAL DEFENCE LEAGUE OF CANADA. NEWS BULLETIN. 1957. 2/yr. free. Animal Defense League of Canada, Box 3880, Sta. C, Ottawa, ON K1Y 4M5, Canada. TEL 613-233-6117. bk.rev. circ. 3,500. **Document type:** bulletin.
 Description: Promotes animal welfare - rights, increases public awareness, offers suggestions the public can use to help end animal exploitation, cruelty and suffering.

ANIMAL LAW REPORT. see LAW

179.3 UK ISSN 0964-4628
ANIMAL LIFE. 1971. 4/yr. £6. Royal Society for the Prevention of Cruelty to Animals, Causeway, Horsham, W. Sussex RH12 1HG, England. TEL 44-1403-264181. FAX 44-1403-241048. Ed. Martin O'Halloran. adv.; bk.rev.; charts; illus. circ. 35,000. **Document type:** bulletin.
 Formerly (until 1990): R S P C A Today (ISSN 0048-8720)
 Description: Covers all aspects of animal welfare and cruelty.

179 636 US ISSN 1071-0035
ANIMAL PEOPLE. 1992. 10/yr. $22. Box 960, Clinton, WA 98236-0960. TEL 360-589-2505. Ed. Merritt Clifton; Pub. Kim Bartlett. adv.: B&W page $1000. bk.rev. circ. 15,000. (tabloid format) **Document type:** newspaper.
 Description: Hard news coverage and informed opinion pertaining to all aspects of animal protection, including conservation of endangered species, animal control and rescue, animal rights, etc.

179.3 US
HV4762.A56
ANIMAL SHELTERING; the community animal care, control, and protection resource. 1978. bi-m. $8 (effective 1996). Humane Society of the United States, 2100 L St., N.W., Washington, DC 20037. TEL 202-452-1100. FAX 202-258-3081. E-mail: asm@ix.netcom.com. Ed. Geoffrey L. Handy. adv. circ. 3,000. **Document type:** trade publication.
 Formerly (until 1996): Shelter Sense (ISSN 0734-3078)
 Description: Covers animal control and sheltering.

179 UK ISSN 0962-7286
 CODEN: ANWEEF
ANIMAL WELFARE. 1992. q. £40($80) to members; non-members £50($100); member institutions £50($100); non-member institutions £70($140) (effective 1997). Universities Federation for Animal Welfare, 8 Hamilton Close, S. Mimms, Potters Bar, Herts. EN6 3QD, England. TEL 44-1707-658202. FAX 44-1707-649279. Ed. James Kirkwood. bk.rev.; video rev. (back issues avail.) **Indexed:** ASCA, InterActions Bibl. (1992-), SSCI. **Document type:** academic/scholarly publication.
 —BLDSC (0905.132000); Genuine Article; UnCover. **CCC.**
 Description: Publishes research on the well-being of wild and domesticated animals.

ANIMAL WELFARE

179.309 CN ISSN 1186-6071
ANIMAL WELFARE IN FOCUS. 1986. s-a. free. Canadian Federation of Humane Societies, 30 Concourse Gate, Ste. 102, Nepean, ON K2E 7V7, Canada. TEL 613-224-8072. FAX 613-723-0252. E-mail: cfhs@magi.com. Ed. Frances Rodenburg. circ. 4,500. (looseleaf format; back issues avail.) **Document type:** newsletter.

179.3 US
ANIMAL WELFARE INFORMATION CENTER BULLETIN. 1990. q. free. U.S. Animal Welfare Information Center, National Agricultural Library, U.S. Department of Agriculture, 10301 Baltimore Blvd., 5th Fl., Beltsville, MD 20705-2351. TEL 301-504-6212. FAX 301-504-7125. E-mail: tallen@nal.usda.gov; URL: http://netvet.wustl.edu/awic.htm. Ed. Tim Allen. R&P contact: Tim Allen. TEL 301-504-5174. circ. 6,200. **Document type:** bulletin, government publication.
● Also available online.
— BLDSC (0905.136500).
Formerly: Animal Welfare Information Center Newsletter (ISSN 1050-561X)
Description: Publishes articles on animal-welfare issues, along with other information of use to persons conducting biomedical research. Lists funding opportunities for related research.

179.3 US
ANIMALIFE. 1989. s-a. $1.50 (foreign $2.50) per issue. Cornell Students for the Ethical Treatment of Animals, Cornell University, Willard Straight Hall, Box 39, Ithaca, NY 14853. TEL 607-256-5600. URL: http://www.envirolink.org/arrs/AnimaLife. adv.; illus. circ. 2,000.

179.3 US ISSN 0030-6835
HV4701
ANIMALS. 1868. bi-m. $19.94 (effective 1997). Massachusetts Society for the Prevention of Cruelty to Animals, 350 S. Huntington Ave., Boston, MA 02130. TEL 617-541-5065. FAX 617-522-4885. E-mail: animals@enews.com; URL: http://www.americast.com; http://www.mspca.org/. (Co-sponsor: American Humane Education Society) Ed. Joni Praded. adv. contact: Joseph Kaknes. bk.rev.; illus. circ. 92,000. (also avail. in microfilm from UMI; reprint service avail. from UMI) **Document type:** consumer publication.
● Also available online.
— UMI.
Formerly: Our Dumb Animals.
Description: News, articles, and photography on domesticated and wild creatures throughout the world, focusing on their protection and environmental conditions.

179.3 179.4 US
ANIMAL'S ADVOCATE. 1982. 4/yr. (effective 1997 & 1998). Animal Legal Defense Fund (ALDF), 127 Fourth St., Petaluma, CA 94952-3005. TEL 707-769-7771. FAX 707-769-0785. E-mail: info@aldf.org; URL: http://www.aldf.org. Ed. Laura Wilensky. R&P contact: Laura Wilensky. circ. 50,000. (looseleaf format; back issues avail.) **Document type:** newsletter.
Formerly: Animal Legal Defense Fund. Newsletter.
Description: Animal protection litigation reviews.

179.3 US ISSN 0892-8819
ANIMALS' AGENDA; helping people help animals. 1981. bi-m. $24 (Canada, Mexico $30; elsewhere $37). Animal Rights Network, Inc., Box 25881, Baltimore, MD 21224. TEL 410-675-4566; 800-426-6884. FAX 410-675-0066. E-mail: 75543.3331@compuserve.com; office@animalsagenda.org; URL: http://www.envirolink.org/arrs/aa/. (Subscr. to: Box 3083, Langhore, PA 19047-9183. TEL 215-788-5500) Ed. Kim W. Stallwood. R&P contact: Kirsten Rosenberg. adv. contact: Jessica Petaccia. bk.rev.; illus. circ. 30,000. (also avail. in microfilm from UMI; back issues avail.; reprint service avail.) **Indexed:** Abstr.Engl.Stud., Alt.Press Ind. **Document type:** consumer publication.
— UMI; UnCover.
Formerly (until 1985): Agenda (Westport) (ISSN 0741-5044)
Description: Provides a broad range of information about animal rights issues, providing a forum for discussion of problems and ideas.
Refereed Serial

179 UK
ANIMALS DEFENDER. 1879. s-a. £17 (foreign £30) (effective 1997). Animal Defenders, 261-263 Goldhawk Rd., London W12 9PE, England. TEL 44-181-846-9777. FAX 44-181-846-9712. Ed. Jan Creamer. adv.
Supersedes in part (in 1990): Campaigner and Animal's Defender; Which incorporated (in 1986): Campaigner; Formerly: Animals: Defender and Anti-Vivisection News.
Description: Details the activities of the organisation, an animal welfare and conservation group specialising in animal rescues and anti-circus campaigning.

179.3 UK ISSN 0254-3923
HV4701
ANIMALS INTERNATIONAL. 1974. 2/yr. £12.50($20) World Society for the Protection of Animals, 2 Langley Ln., London SW8 1TJ, England. TEL 44-171-793-0540. FAX 44-171-793-0208. E-mail: wspa@wspa.org.uk; URL: http://www.way.net.wspa/. Ed. Jonathan Pearce. bk.rev.; illus.; stat. circ. 35,000. **Indexed:** Curr.Adv.Ecol.Sci. **Document type:** newsletter.
Formerly: Animalia; Which supersedes: W F P A News (ISSN 0049-8068)

179.2 AT ISSN 1320-2464
ANIMALS TODAY. 1993. q. Aus.$20 (foreign Aus.$35). Australian and New Zealand Federation of Animal Societies Inc., P.O. Box 1023, Collingwood, Vic. 3066, Australia. TEL 61-3-93296333. FAX 61-3-93296441. E-mail: animals@malbpc.org.au; URL: http://melbourne.net/animals_australia/today.html. Eds. Keith & Heather Edwards. R&P contact: Glerys Oogjes. adv. contact: Glerys Oogjes. bk.rev. circ. 3,000. **Document type:** bulletin, consumer publication.
Description: Focuses on the plight of exploited animals in society and reports on what is being done to help them.

179.3 CN ISSN 0700-8392
ANIMALS' VOICE. 1957. q. Can.$15. Ontario S P C A, 16640 Yonge St., Newmarket, ON L3Y 4V8, Canada. TEL 905-898-7122. FAX 905-853-8643. E-mail: jingham@hockup.net. Ed. Joe Ingham. R&P contact: Joe Ingham. adv.: B&W page $850. bk.rev.; circ. 50,000 (controlled).
Description: Deals with the issues affecting animal welfare and the environment. Aims to increase people's awareness and knowledge of important issues concerning both animals and the environment.
Refereed Serial

179 CN ISSN 1192-4861
ANIMALTALK. Key Title: Animal Talk. 1974. 3/yr. donation. Toronto Humane Society, 11 River St., Toronto, ON M5A 4C2, Canada. TEL 416-392-2273. FAX 416-392-9978. E-mail: ths@io.org; URL: http://www.io.org/~ths/index.html. Ed. Sandra Evan-Jones. R&P contact: Sandra Evan-Jones. adv. contact: Sandra Evan-Jones. bk.rev. circ. 50,000. **Document type:** newsletter.
Former titles (until 1990): Toronto Humane Society. Society News (ISSN 0845-5082); (until 1987): Humane Viewpoint (ISSN 0316-9014)
Description: News, features and reviews of the Society, and animal welfare, pet care and animal behavior issues.

179.3 FR ISSN 0986-3354
ANIMAUX MAGAZINE. 1982. m 198 F. (effective 1997). Societe Protectrice des Animaux, 39 bd. Berthier, 75017 Paris, France. TEL 33-1-43804066. FAX 33-1-47637476. E-mail: infos@spa.asso.fr; URL: http://www.spa.asso.fr. Ed. Evelyne Stawicki. R&P contact: Maryline Brisson. adv. contact: Maryline Brisson.
Formerly (until 1982): S.P.A. (ISSN 0180-6564)
Description: News on animal welfare and on SPA actions, wildlife subjects.

APIS; the international journal bulletin for specialty livestock and pet-animal product development. see VETERINARY SCIENCE

179.3 UK ISSN 0004-167X
ARK. 1937. 3/yr. £5($10) Catholic Study Circle for Animal Welfare, c/o Hon. Secretary, 39 Onslow Gardens, S. Woodford, London E18 1ND, England. Ed. Fr. Fr. Leon Ostaszewski. bk.rev.; illus. circ. 2,000. **Indexed:** Anim.Breed.Abstr., Br.Archaeol.Abstr.
Description: Promotes concern and respect for animals.

ASIAN PRIMATES. see CONSERVATION

ASKO; dwumiesiecznik kynologiczny. see PETS

AUSTRALIAN PRIMATOLOGY. see BIOLOGY — Zoology

613.1 333.7 US
THE BEAVER DEFENDERS; they shall never be trapped anymore. 1970. q. $10 membership. Unexpected Wildlife Refuge, Box 765, Newfield, NJ 08344. TEL 609-697-3541. Ed. Hope S. Buyukmihci. bk.rev.; illus. circ. 200. (back issues avail.) **Document type:** newsletter.
Description: Examines the natural history of beavers, the happenings at the wildlife refuge, solving beaver problems, and humane education.

179 GW ISSN 0936-3815
BERLINER TIERFREUND. 1989. bi-m. DM.30. Tierschutzverein fuer Berlin, Dessauerstr. 21, 12249 Berlin, Germany. TEL 49-30-76888114. FAX 49-30-7721066. Ed. Carola Ruff. R&P contact: Carola Ruff. adv.: B&W page DM.1200; adv. contact: Carola Ruff. bk.rev. (back issues avail.) **Document type:** newsletter.

179.3 UK
BLUE CROSS ILLUSTRATED. 3/yr. £3. Blue Cross, 1-5 Hugh St., Victoria, London SW1 1QQ, England. Ed. James Combe. illus. circ. 9,000. (back issues avail.)
Description: Illustrates the many aspects of Blue Cross work and shows supporters how their money is spent. Includes features, news and reviews.

BUSTARD STUDIES. see CONSERVATION

C B S G NEWS. (Captive Breeding Specialist Group) see CONSERVATION

179.3 US
C H A I LIGHTS. 1984. a. $18. Concern for Helping Animals in Israel, Box 3341, Alexandria, VA 22302. TEL 703-658-9650. FAX 703-941-6132. E-mail: 74754,654.compuserve.com; URL: http://envirolink.org/arrs/CHAI/CHAIhome.html. Ed. Nina Natelson. R&P contact: Nina Natelson. circ. 3,000 (controlled). (back issues avail.) **Document type:** newsletter, proceedings.
Description: Relates problems for animals in Israel and CHAI's effort to help.

179.4 SZ
C I V I S: INTERNATIONAL FOUNDATION REPORT; for the abolition of vivisection. (Text in English) 1988. q. 20 SFr.($15) (Centro Informazione Vivisezionista Internazionale Scientifica) Fondazione Hans Ruesch, P.O. Box 152, Via Motta 51, CH-6900 Massagno, Switzerland. TEL 83-41166. (US addr.: Box 26, Swain, NY 14884) Ed. Hans Ruesch. (back issues avail.; reprint service avail.)
Description: Aims to demonstrate that animal experimentation does not promote human health, and therefore should be abolished.

C - PAPER. see CONSERVATION

179 UK
CAMPAIGNER. 1879. s-a. £17 (foreign £23) (effective 1997). National Anti-Vivisection Society, Ravenside, 261-263 Goldhawk Rd., London W12 9PE, England. TEL 44-181-846-9777. FAX 44-181-846-9712. Ed. Jan Creamer. adv.; bk.rev.; illus.; index. circ. 16,000. **Document type:** bulletin.
Supersedes in part (in 1990): Campaigner and Animal's Defender; Which incorporated (in 1986): Campaigner; Formerly: Animals: Defender and Anti-Vivisection News (ISSN 0954-321X)
Description: Gives reports on the dangers and futility of using animals in medical research; news on drugs, health and animal experiments.

ANIMAL WELFARE

179   CN
CAN - AG - FAX. 3/yr. free. Canfact, Ste. 808, Unit 6, 367 Woodlawn Rd., W., Guelph, ON N1H 7K9, Canada. TEL 519-836-6590. **Document type:** newsletter.
   Description: Provides information on animal welfare issues.

CAPRINAE NEWS. see CONSERVATION

179   CN   ISSN 0825-1711
CARING FOR ANIMALS. 1984. s-a. free. Canadian Federation of Humane Societies, Experimental Animals Committee, 30 Concourse Gate, Ste. 102, Nepean, ON K2E 7V7, Canada. TEL 613-224-8072. FAX 613-723-0252. E-mail: cfhs@magi.com. Ed. Stephanie Brown. circ. 2,800. (looseleaf format; back issues avail.) **Document type:** newsletter.
   Description: For members of animal care communities.

CARTA NOTICIAS. see CONSERVATION

CAT NEWS. see CONSERVATION

179.3 798   IT
CAVALLO MAGAZINE; mensile di natura, politica e cultura. 1986. m. L.76000. Solitaire S.p.A., Via Enrico Mattei 106, 40138 Bologna, Italy. TEL 39-51-536496. FAX 39-51-536497. Ed. Roberto Pignoni. R&P contact: Roberto Pignoni. adv. contact: Cinzia Romano. bk.rev.; circ. 26,322 (controlled). (back issues avail.) **Document type:** consumer publication.

179   BE
CHAINE/KETEN. (Text in Dutch, French) 1962. q. 250 BEF. Chaine Bleue Mondiale a.s.b.l., Ave. de Vise, 39, 1170 Brussels, Belgium. TEL 32-2-6735230. **Document type:** bulletin.
   Description: Promotes worldwide education to protect animals from cruelty, and to protect nature and the environment.

CHELONIAN CONSERVATION BIOLOGY. see CONSERVATION

CHILDREN'S WHALEWATCH. see CHILDREN AND YOUTH — For

THE CIVIL ABOLITIONIST. see MEDICAL SCIENCES

CLUMBER SPANIEL CORRESPONDENCE. see PETS

179.3   US
COMPASSIONATE SHOPPER. 1973. 3/yr. $15 membership. Beauty Without Cruelty U S A, 175 W. 12th St., Ste. 16G, New York, NY 10011-8275. TEL 212-989-8073. Ed. Ethel Thurston. circ. 7,000. (back issues avail.) **Document type:** consumer publication, newsletter.
   Description: Informs the public about the massive suffering imposed on animals by the fashion, cosmetic and household product industries.

179.3   NE
D A R - GELUIDEN. bi-m. fl.2.75 per no. for non-members. (Vereniging Dierenambulance Rotterdam) De Groene Lijn, Essendijkweg 1, 4693 SC Poortvliet, Netherlands. adv. circ. 4,500.

DEUTSCHER JAGDTERRIERCLUB. NACHRICHTENBLATT. see PETS

179   NE   ISSN 0165-3172
DIER. 1920. bi-m. membership. Nederlandse Vereniging tot Bescherming van Dieren, Postbus 85980, 2508 CR The Hague, Netherlands. TEL 31-70-3142700. FAX 31-70-3142777. Ed. J.B. Dobbe. R&P contact: J.B. Dobbe. adv.; bk.rev.; illus. circ. 175,000. **Document type:** consumer publication.
   Formerly (until 1978): Dierenbescherming (ISSN 0012-2599)

179.1 179.3   SW   ISSN 0345-2409
DJURENS RAETT; med Djurfront. 1906. 5/yr. SEK 75 (foreign SEK 105)(effective 1997); newsstand price: SEK 15. Nordiska Samfundet Mot Plaagsamma Djurfoersoek - Swedish Society Against Painful Experiments on Animals, Box 2005, SE-125 Aelvsjoe, Sweden. TEL 46-8-749-20-40. FAX 46-8-749-20-02. E-mail: nsmpd@educate.se; URL: http://www.educate.se/nsmpd. Ed. Ingegerd Erlandsson; Pub. Kristina Mattsson. adv. contact: Ingegerd Erlandsson. bk.rev. circ. 48,000. cols./p.: 5. (also avail. in audio cassette) **Document type:** newspaper.
   Incorporates (1974-1988): Djurfront (ISSN 0345-2417)
   Description: Focuses on issues concerned with anti-vivisection and rights of animals.

179.3   SW   ISSN 1101-4423
DJURTIDNINGEN DJURSKYDDET. 1890. q. SEK 85. Sveriges Djurskyddsfoereningars Riksfoerbund - Swedish Association for Animal Welfare, Markvardsgatan 10, 4 Tr., S-113 53 Stockholm, Sweden. TEL 46-8-6733511. FAX 46-8-6733666. Ed. John Erik Trollsten. adv.; bk.rev.; illus. circ. 12,000.
   Former titles (until vol.3, 1989): Djurskyddet; (until vol.4, 1970): Djurvaennernas Tidning Djurskyddet; (until 1938): Djurskyddet (ISSN 0012-4346)

179.3 636.1   AT   ISSN 1031-6280
DONKEY DIGEST. 1972. q. Aus.$20 (effective 1996). Affiliated Donkey Societies of Australia, 5 Doyle Rd., Dagun, Qld. 4570, Australia. TEL 61-07-54843749. FAX 61-07-54843771. Eds. Stephen Burgess, Elaine Bradley. R&P contact: Stephen Burgess. adv. contact: Stephen Burgess. bk.rev.; illus. circ. 600. (back issues avail.) **Document type:** bulletin.
   Description: All aspects of donkey welfare and training.

179 628   UK
ENVIRONMENTAL ENRICHMENT REPORTS. 1988. irreg., no.4, 1991. £0.50($1.50) per no. Universities Federation for Animal Welfare, 8 Hamilton Close, S. Mimms, Potters Bar, Herts. EN6 3QD, England. TEL 44-1707-658202. FAX 44-1707-649279. (back issues avail.) **Document type:** monographic series.

179.3   UK   ISSN 0268-4306
F R A M E NEWS. 1979. 3-4/yr. £15($25) (free to qualified personnel). Fund for the Replacement of Animals in Medical Experiments, Russel & Burch House, 96-98 N. Sherwood St., Nottingham NG1 4EE, England. TEL 44-115-958-4740. FAX 44-115-950-3570. E-mail: atla@frake-uk.demon.co.uk. Ed. Vivienne Hunter. illus. **Document type:** newsletter.
   Formerly (until 1984): F R A M E Technical News (ISSN 0143-8352)
   Description: Discusses the organization's efforts to abolish the use of animals in laboratory testing. Reports general news in the area.

179.3   US
FEMINISTS FOR ANIMAL RIGHTS. SEMIANNUAL PUBLICATION. vol.5, 1990. s-a. $25 membership. Feminists for Animal Rights, Box 694, Cathedral Sta., New York, NY 10025. TEL 212-866-6422. Ed. Batya Bauman. bk.rev. **Document type:** newsletter.

FISH. see CONSERVATION

FLAMINGO RESEARCH. see CONSERVATION

179.3   UK   ISSN 0016-1276
FRIEND OF ANIMALS. 1916. q. £2. Humane Education Society, The Council for Protection of Animals, Animals' Convalescent Home, Newgate, Wilmslow, Ches. SK9 5LN, England. TEL 44-1625-520802. Ed. Arthur Thompson. bk.rev.; illus.; index. circ. 1,500. **Document type:** newsletter.
   Formerly: Little Animal's Friend.
   Description: Contains articles and stories of interest to animal lovers.

FRIENDS IN DANGER. see CHILDREN AND YOUTH — For

179.3   UK
FRIENDS OF F R A M E. m. Fund for the Replacement of Animals in Medical Experiments, Russel & Burch House, 96-98 N. Sherwood St., Nottingham NG1 4EE, England. TEL 44-115-958-4740. FAX 44-115-950-3570. E-mail: atla@frame-uk.demon.co.uk. Ed. Vivienne P. Hunter. illus. **Document type:** newsletter.
   Description: Covers organization news and events for donors.

FROGLOG. see CONSERVATION

GAJAH. see CONSERVATION

GAN NO SHINPOJUMU/SYMPOSIUM ON WILD GEESE. see CONSERVATION

GNUSLETTER. see CONSERVATION

GOOSE STUDY. see CONSERVATION

179.3   US   ISSN 1078-6244
GRRR!; the zine that bites back. 1994. $15 membership. People for the Ethical Treatment of Animals, Inc., 501 Front St., Norfolk, VA 23510. TEL 757-622-PETA. FAX 757-622-0457. E-mail: peta@norfolk.infi.net; URL: http://envirolink.org/arrs/peta. Ed. Ingrid Newkirk. R&P contact: Muriel Ducloy. bk.rev.; illus. circ. 3,000.

179.3   US   ISSN 1059-1621
HV4702
H S U S NEWS. 1954. q. $10 membership. Humane Society of the United States, 2100 L St., N.W., Washington, DC 20037. TEL 202-452-1100. URL: http://www.hsus.org/pubs.html. Ed. Deborah Salem. circ. 450,000.
—UnCover.
   Former titles: Humane Society News; Humane Society of the United States. News (ISSN 0018-733X)

179 636   NE   ISSN 0922-520X
HART VOOR DIEREN. 1988. m. fl.49.50 (920 BEF) (effective 1997). Vipmedia Publishing en Services, Willemstraat 23, 3811 AJ Breda, Netherlands. TEL 31-76-5301713. FAX 31-76-5144531. (Subscr. to: Postbus 7040, 4800 GA Breda, Netherlands; Subscr. in Belgium to: Vipmedia, Bredabaan 852, 2170, Merksem, Belgium. TEL 32-3-6453751) adv.: B&W page fl.4300, color page fl.6000; trim 216 x 276. illus. circ. 111,000. **Document type:** consumer publication.

HAUSTIER; die Zeitschrift fuer den Tierfreund. see PETS

179.3   US
HERON CONSERVATION NEWSLETTER. 1988. s-a. free. Department of Biology, University of Mississippi, University, MS 38677. TEL 601-232-7203. Ed. James Kushlan. bk.rev. circ. 300. **Document type:** newsletter.

179   US
HUMANE NEWS. 1970. m. $10. Associated Humane Societies, Inc., 124 Evergreen Ave., Newark, NJ 07114. TEL 201-824-7080. FAX 201-824-2720. Ed. Roseann Trezza. R&P contact: Roseann Trezza. adv. contact: Roseann Trezza. bk.rev. circ. 75,000. **Document type:** newsletter, newspaper.
   Description: Covers animal rights, legislation and animal welfare.

179.3 179.4   UK   ISSN 0263-1407
HUMANE SLAUGHTER ASSOCIATION NEWSLETTER. 1979. a. £10. Humane Slaughter Association and Council of Justice to Animals, 34 Blanche Ln., South Mimms, Potters Bar, Herts. EN6 3PA, England. TEL 01707-659040. FAX 01707-649279. circ. 1,000. (back issues avail.) **Document type:** newsletter.

179.3   UK   ISSN 0264-8741
HUMANE SLAUGHTER ASSOCIATION REPORT AND ACCOUNTS. 1922. a. £10. Humane Slaughter Association and Council of Justice to Animals, 34 Blanche Ln., South Mimms, Potters Bar, Herts. EN6 3PA, England. TEL 01707-659040. FAX 01707-649279. circ. 1,000. (back issues avail.) **Document type:** corporate report.

ANIMAL WELFARE 303

179.3 AT
IMPACT. 1980. bi-m. Aus.$25 membership (foreign Aus.$31). Animal Liberation (Qld.) Ltd., P.O. Box 5785, West End, Qld. 4101, Australia. TEL 61-7-8445533. FAX 61-7-8441658. Ed. Jeannie Sheppard. R&P contact: Jeannie Sheppard. bk.rev. circ. 1,200. **Document type:** newsletter.
  Formerly: Qualm (ISSN 0813-6440)
  Description: Covers aspects of cruelty to animals. Includes president's report, thank you's to volunteers and supporters, compassionate shop news, and information on current campaigns.

179.3 US
IN DEFENSE OF ANIMALS. q. 131 Camino Alto, Ste. E, Mill Valley, CA 94941. TEL 415-388-9641. FAX 415-388-0388. E-mail: ida@idausa.org; URL: http://www.idausa.org. Ed. Laura Moretti. circ. 70,000. **Document type:** newsletter.

INTERNATIONAL BEAR NEWS. see *CONSERVATION*

INTERNATIONAL JOURNAL OF ANIMAL SCIENCES. see *AGRICULTURE — Poultry And Livestock*

179.3 US ISSN 1051-8827
INTERNATIONAL SOCIETY FOR ANIMAL RIGHTS REPORT. 1959. q. $15. International Society for Animal Rights, Inc., 421 S. State St., Clarks Summit, PA 18411. TEL 717-586-2200. FAX 717-586-9580. E-mail: isar@aol.com. Ed. Susan Altieri. bk.rev. circ. 50,000. **Document type:** newsletter.
  Former titles (until Aug. 1983): Society for Animal Rights Report; N C S A W Report (ISSN 0027-6340)

INTERNATIONAL UNION FOR CONSERVATION OF NATURE AND NATURAL RESOURCES. SPECIES SURVIVAL COMMISSION - CACTI AND SUCCULENT SPECIALIST GROUP NEWSLETTER. see *CONSERVATION*

INTERNATIONAL UNION FOR CONSERVATION OF NATURE AND NATURAL RESOURCES. SPECIES SURVIVAL COMMISSION - CROCODILE SPECIALIST GROUP NEWSLETTER. see *CONSERVATION*

INTERNATIONAL UNION FOR CONSERVATION OF NATURE AND NATURAL RESOURCES. SPECIES SURVIVAL COMMISSION - CANID SPECIALIST GROUP. NEWSLETTER. see *CONSERVATION*

INTERNATIONAL UNION FOR CONSERVATION OF NATURE AND NATURAL RESOURCES. SPECIES SURVIVAL COMMISSION - DEER SPECIALIST GROUP. NEWSLETTER. see *CONSERVATION*

INTERNATIONAL UNION FOR CONSERVATION OF NATURE AND NATURAL RESOURCES. SPECIES SURVIVAL COMMISSION - HYAENA SPECIALIST GROUP BULLETIN. see *CONSERVATION*

INTERNATIONAL UNION FOR CONSERVATION OF NATURE AND NATURAL RESOURCES. SPECIES SURVIVAL COMMISSION - OTTER SPECIALIST GROUP BULLETIN. see *CONSERVATION*

INTERNATIONAL UNION FOR CONSERVATION OF NATURE AND NATURAL RESOURCES. SPECIES SURVIVAL COMMISSION - SPECIALIST GROUP ON STORKS, IBISES, AND SPOONBILLS NEWSLETTER. see *CONSERVATION*

INTERNATIONAL UNION FOR CONSERVATION OF NATURE AND NATURAL RESOURCES. SPECIES SURVIVAL COMMISSION - VETERINARY SPECIALIST GROUP. NEWSLETTER. see *CONSERVATION*

179 US QL55
JOURNAL OF APPLIED ANIMAL WELFARE SCIENCE. Short title: J A A W S. 1989. q. $50 to non-members; members $40. American Society for the Prevention of Cruelty to Animals, 424 E. 92nd St., New York, NY 10128. E-mail: jaaws.aspca.org; URL: http://www.aspca.org/calendar/jaaws.html. (Co-sponsor: Psychologists for the Ethical Treatment of Animals) Eds. Stephen Zawistowski, Kenneth Shapiro. cum.index. (back issues avail.) **Indexed:** InterActions Bibl. (1992-). **Document type:** academic/scholarly publication.
  Supersedes (in 1995): Humane Innovations and Alternatives (ISSN 1062-4805); Which was formerly (until 1991): Humane Innovations and Alternatives in Animal Experimentation (ISSN 0893-9535)
  Description: Publishes reports and articles on methods of experimentation, husbandry and care that demonstrably enhance the welfare of farm, laboratory, companion and wild animals.
  Refereed Serial

179.3 GW
KATZENSCHUTZ KORRESPONDENZ. 1976. q. DM.15. Dortmunder Katzenschutzverein e.V., Postfach 102124, 44021 Dortmund, Germany. adv.; bk.rev. circ. 2,300. (back issues avail.)

179.3 614.7 028.5 US ISSN 1050-821X
KIND NEWS JR. (Kids in Nature's Defense) 1983. 9/yr. $20 (foreign $32). Humane Society of the United States, National Association for Humane and Environmental Education, Box 362, East Haddam, CT 06423-0362. TEL 860-434-8666. FAX 860-434-9579. Ed. Bill DeRosa. R&P contact: Bill DeRosa. illus. (tabloid format)
  Formerly: Kind News 1.
  Description: For schoolchildren in grades 3-4. Teaches children kindness to people, animals, and the Earth.

179.3 028.5 US ISSN 1069-4544
KIND NEWS PRIMARY. 1993. 9/yr. $20 (foreign $32). Humane Society of the United States, National Association for Humane and Environmental Education, Box 362, East Haddam, CT 06423-0362. TEL 860-434-8666. FAX 860-434-9579. Ed. Bill DeRosa. R&P contact: Bill DeRosa. illus. **Document type:** newspaper.
  Description: For kindergarteners and first- and second-graders. Teaches children kindness to people, animals, and the Earth.

179.3 614.7 028.5 US ISSN 1050-9542
KIND NEWS SR. 1983. 9/yr. $20 (foreign $32). Humane Society of the United States, National Association for Humane and Environmental Education, Box 362, East Haddam, CT 06423-0362. TEL 860-434-8666. FAX 860-434-9579. Ed. Bill DeRosa. R&P contact: Bill DeRosa. illus. (tabloid format)
  Formerly: Kind News 2.
  Description: For schoolchildren in grades 5-6. Teaches children kindness to people, animals, and the Earth.

LAGOMORPH NEWSLETTER. see *CONSERVATION*

LATHAM LETTER. see *SOCIAL SERVICES AND WELFARE*

179 100 US
LIVE AND LET LIVE. 1992. irreg. $3 for 4 issues. James N. Dawson, Ed. & Pub., Box 613, Redwood Valley, CA 95470. TEL 707-485-7092. bk.rev. circ. 250. (back issues avail.) **Document type:** newsletter.
  Description: Seeks to explore and develop a theory and strategy of fetal and animal rights from a libertarian - individualist framework; provides a forum for libertarian and other animal-rights advocates outside the political, religious and philosophical mainstream of the animal-rights movement.

179.4 363.7 641.5 UK
LIVING WITHOUT CRUELTY DIARY (YEAR). 1989. a. £5. Jon Carpenter Publishing, P.O. Box 129, Oxford OX1 4PH, England. TEL 01865-790715. Ed. Mark Gold; Pub. Jon Carpenter. **Document type:** directory.
  Description: Provides recipes, news features, and other information for vegetarians and persons concerned with the environment. Contains a directory of environmental organizations.

179.3 179.4 UK
LORD DOWDING FUND FOR HUMANE RESEARCH. BULLETIN. no.14, 1980. s-a. contributions. National Anti-Vivisection Society, Ravenside, 261-263 Goldhawk Rd., London W12 9PE, England. TEL 44-181-846-9777. FAX 44-181-846-9712. Ed. Jan Creamer. illus. circ. 10,000. **Document type:** bulletin.
  Description: Gives scientific reports on projects that will replace the use of live animals in medical research.

179.3 US ISSN 0891-088X
MAINSTREAM (SACRAMENTO). 1969. q. $25 includes membership. Animal Protection Institute, Box 22505, Sacramento, CA 95822. TEL 916-731-5521; 800-348-7387. FAX 916-731-4467. E-mail: onlineapi@aol.com; URL: http://www.g-net.com/api.htm. Ed. Gil Lamont; Pub. Alan Berger. R&P contact: Gil Lamont. adv. contact: Barbara Tugaeff. bk.rev.; illus. circ. 50,000. **Document type:** academic/scholarly publication.
  Description: Covers animal-related issues on the plight of wild and domesticated animals.

MEAT AND POULTRY INSPECTION REGULATIONS; meat inspection, poultry inspection, rabbit inspection, voluntary inspection and certificate service of meat and poultry, humane slaughter of livestock. see *AGRICULTURE — Poultry And Livestock*

179.4 US ISSN 0270-8132
N A V S BULLETIN. 1930. q. $25 membership. National Anti-Vivisection Society, 53 W. Jackson Blvd., Ste. 1552, Chicago, IL 60604-3795. TEL 312-427-6065. FAX 312-427-6524. E-mail: navs@navs.org; URL: http://www.navs.org; http://www.cygnet.co.uk/NAVS. Ed. Marcia Kramer. R&P contact: Marcia Kramer. adv. contact: Clare Haggerty. bk.rev. circ. 30,000. (back issues avail.) **Document type:** bulletin, newsletter.
  Description: Publishes news and commentary on issues pertaining to vivisection and animal research, and reports the society's activities to foster public awareness and protest the continued existence of these practices.

179 US
N E A V S UPDATE. 1921. q. membership. New England Anti-Vivisection Society, 333 Washington St., Ste. 850, Boston, MA 02108-5100. TEL 617-523-6020. FAX 617-523-7923. E-mail: info@ma-neavs.com; URL: http://www.neavs.org. Ed. Karin Zupko. circ. 3,000. **Document type:** newsletter.
  Former titles: N E A V S Members Quarterly (ISSN 1052-6978); (until 1990): Reverence for Life (ISSN 0279-0513)

179.3 US
N Y T T S NEWSNOTES. 1970. q. $15. New York Turtle and Tortoise Society, 163 Amsterdam Ave., Ste. 365, New York, NY 10023. TEL 212-459-4803. Ed. Jim Van Abbema. adv. circ. 1,500.
  Description: Covers the care, breeding and conservation of the turtles and tortoises of the world.

179.3 UK ISSN 0077-4448
NATIONAL EQUINE (AND SMALLER ANIMALS) DEFENCE LEAGUE. ANNUAL REPORT. 1909. a. £3. National Equine Defence League, Oak Tree Farm, Wetheral Shields, Carlisle CA4 8JA, England. TEL 44-1228-560082. FAX 44-1228-560985. Ed. Frank E. Tebbutt. R&P contact: Frank Tebbutt. circ. 3,000. **Document type:** newsletter, corporate report.

NATURFREUNDE - KINDERPOST. see *CHILDREN AND YOUTH — For*

NEW ZEALAND BEEKEEPER. see *BIOLOGY — Entomology*

NORTHEAST CANINE COMPANION. see *PETS*

OTTER RAFT. see *CONSERVATION*

ANIMAL WELFARE

179.3 US ISSN 0030-6789
OUR ANIMALS. 1906. q. $25 membership (effective 1997-1998). San Francisco Society for the Prevention of Cruelty to Animals, 2500 16th St., San Francisco, CA 94103. TEL 415-554-3009. FAX 415-431-6641. E-mail: public_info@sfspca.org; URL: http://www.sfspca.org. Ed. Paul M. Glassner; Pub. Paul Glassner. R&P contact: Paul Glassner. adv. contact: Paul Glassner. bk.rev.; charts; illus. circ. 50,000. **Document type:** consumer publication.
Description: Publishes upbeat stories and articles about the services of the San Francisco S.P.C.A. Also includes pet care tips.

179.3 US
HV4763
P E T A'S ANIMAL TIMES (ENGLISH EDITION). 1980. q. $15 membership. People for the Ethical Treatment of Animals, Inc., 501 Front St., Norfolk, VA 23510. TEL 757-622-PETA. FAX 757-622-0457. E-mail: peta@norfolk.infi.net; URL: http://envirolink.org/arrs/peta/. Ed. Ingrid Newkirk. R&P contact: Muriel Ducloy. bk.rev. circ. 250,000. (back issues avail.) **Document type:** newsletter.
—UnCover.
Formerly (until 1994): P E T A News (ISSN 0899-9708)
Description: Examines issues of animal abuse and animal rights.

179.3 GW ISSN 0947-8507
P E T A'S ANIMAL TIMES (GERMAN EDITION). 1994. q. DM.50 membership. People for the Ethical Treatment of Animals, Inc., Postfach 311503, 70475 Stuttgart, Germany. TEL 49-711-8666165. FAX 49-711-8666166. Ed. Ingrid Newkirk. illus.; tr.lit.; circ. 20,000 (paid). (back issues avail.) **Document type:** bulletin.

PACHYDERM. see CONSERVATION

PARADE OF ROYALTY (YEAR). see PETS

PETSPECTIVES. see PETS

PRIMATE CONSERVATION. see CONSERVATION

179 IS ISSN 0793-0070
PROANIMAL; independent non-profit bulletin for animal welfare and rights in Israel. (Text in English) 1992. 4/yr. $5 per issue. P.O. Box 2039, Rehovot 76120, Israel. FAX 972-8-9467632. Eds. Suzanne Trauffer, Karin Zupko. adv.; bk.rev.; illus. circ. 3,000. (back issues avail) **Document type:** bulletin.
Description: Publishes articles, reviews and news relating to animal welfare and animal rights issues in Israel.

179.3 FR
PROTECTION DES ANIMAUX. q. (Societe Protectrice des Animaux) Publications Periodiques Specialisees, 17, place Bellencour, 69002 Lyon, France. adv. circ. 28,000.

RE-INTRODUCTION NEWS. see CONSERVATION

179.3 US
RESCUE (WOODSTOCK). 1990. bi-m. $25. National Dog Registry, Rescue Fund, Box 116, Woodstock, NY 12498. TEL 914-679-2355. FAX 914-679-4538. Ed. Gregory R. Becker. adv.; bk.rev. circ. 45,000.
Description: Dedicated to the security, health and safety of pets.

179 628 NZ ISSN 1171-6320
SAFEGUARD; the magazine safeguarding animals and the environment. 1983. s-a. NZ.$15. S A F E Inc. (Save Animals from Exploitation), P.O. Box 13366, Christchurch, New Zealand. TEL 64-3-3799711. E-mail: safe@chch.planet.co.nz. Ed. Anthony Terry. circ. 2,500. (back issues avail.)
Description: Provides current news and information of issues relating to animal rights and the environment.

179.3 US ISSN 0149-9084
SANCTUARY NEWS. 1986. q. $15 membership. Farm Sanctuary, Box 150, Watkins Glen, NY 14891. TEL 607-583-2225. FAX 607-583-2041. Ed. Lorri Bauston. adv. circ. 50,000. **Document type:** newsletter.
Description: Provides news, issues and updates on animal agriculture issues and campaigns.

SANS LAISSE. see PETS

179 CN
SASKATCHEWAN HUMANITARIAN. q. Saskatchewan Society for Prevention of Cruelty to Animals, P.O. Box 37, Saskatoon, SK S7K 3K1, Canada. TEL 306-382-7722. FAX 306-384-3425. Ed. Susan McCune. **Document type:** newsletter.

SATYA; magazine of vegetarianism, environmentalism, and animal advocacy. see NUTRITION AND DIETETICS

179 NZ
SAVE ANIMALS FROM EXPLOITATION. CAMPAIGN REPORT. s-a. S A F E Inc. (Save Animals from Exploitation), P.O. Box 13366, Christchurch, New Zealand. TEL 64-3-3799711. E-mail: safe@chch.planet.co.nz. Ed. Anthony Terry.
Description: Provides a comprehensive insight and focus on particular issues relating to animal rights in New Zealand and how to help.

179.3 SZ
SCHWEIZER TIERSCHUTZ; du und die Natur. 1874. 4/yr. 12.80 SFr. Schweizer Tierschutz STS, Dornacherstr. 101, CH-4008 Basel, Switzerland. TEL 41-61-3611515. FAX 41-61-3611516. Ed. H.P. Haering. adv.; bk.rev. circ. 60,000. **Document type:** bulletin.
Formerly: Tierfreund (ISSN 0040-7313)
Description: Covers laws and regulations concerning protection of animals, research in behavior and habits, zoology, hunting, etc. Includes association news, reports of events, and new publications.

179.3 US ISSN 0742-5260
SCIENTISTS CENTER FOR ANIMAL WELFARE. NEWSLETTER. 1978. q. $40. Scientists Center for Animal Welfare, 7833 Walker Dr., No. 340, Greenbelt, MD 20770-3211. TEL 301-354-3500. FAX 301-345-3503. Ed. Lee Krulisch. R&P contact: Lee Krulisch. bk.rev.; index. circ. 5,000. (back issues avail.) **Document type:** newsletter.
Description: Directed to scientists, administrators, and regulatory agencies interested in current issues of animal welfare in research, testing, and education.

179.3 US ISSN 1066-4890
SHOPTALK (ENGLEWOOD). q. $10. American Humane Association, Animal Protection Division, 63 Inverness Dr. E., Englewood, CO 80112-5117. TEL 303-792-9900. FAX 303-792-5333. Ed. Jane Ehrhardt. adv. contact: Jane Ehrhardt. stat.; circ. 9,300 (controlled). (back issues avail.) **Document type:** trade publication.
Description: Publishes practical information on animal shelter management for the animal care and control professional.

SIRENEWS. see CONSERVATION

SMALL CARNIVORE CONSERVATION. see CONSERVATION

179.3 156 UK ISSN 1063-1119
QL85 CODEN: SANIEL
SOCIETY & ANIMALS; social scientific studies of the human experience of other animals. 1983. N.S. 1993. 3/yr. £24($40) to individuals; institutions £48($80); students £16($30) (effective 1998). (Psychologists for the Ethical Treatment of Animals, US) White Horse Press, 10 High St., Knapwell, Cambridge CB3 8NR, England. TEL 44-1954-267527. FAX 44-1954-267527. E-mail: aj@erica.demon.co.uk; URL: http://www.erica.demon.co.uk/psyeta/sa. (Subscr. to: White Horse Press, 1 Strond, Isle of Harris, Western Isles HS5 3UD, Scotland. TEL 44-1859-520204. FAX 44-1859-520204; U.S. subscr. to: PSYETA, Box 1297, Washington Grove, MD 20880-1297) Ed. Kenneth J. Shapiro. cum.index. circ. 750. (back issues avail.) **Indexed:** ASCA, InterActions Bibl., SSCI. **Document type:** academic/scholarly publication.
—BLDSC (8319.187500); Genuine Article; UnCover. **CCC.**
Former titles (until 1993): P S Y E T A Bulletin; (until 1986): P S Y E T A Newsletter.
Description: Publishes original research studies describing and analyzing the ways in which animals figure in human life, in particular examining applied uses of animals in research, medicine, science and agriculture, animals in the popular culture, including animal symbolism and cultic rituals, wildlife and environmental issues, as well as sociopolitical and legal concerns.
Refereed Serial

156 179 UK ISSN 1363-464X
SOCIETY FOR COMPANION ANIMAL STUDIES. JOURNAL. 1988. 3/yr. £15 membership. Society for Companion Animal Studies, 10B Leny Rd., Callander FK17 8BA, Scotland. TEL 44-1877-330996. FAX 44-1877-330996. URL: http://www.vetweb.co.uk/sites/scas/scashome.htm. Ed. Anne Docherty. R&P contact: Anne Docherty. adv. contact: Anne Docherty. circ. 450. **Indexed:** InterActions Bibl. (1989-). **Document type:** newsletter.

TAPIR CONSERVATION. see CONSERVATION

TENTACLE. see CONSERVATION

THERAPY DOGS INTERNATIONAL. MINI-NEWSLETTER. see PETS

636 NE ISSN 1384-6795
▼**TOMMY;** het dierenblad voor iedereen. 1996. m. fl.58.50 (1500 BEF) (foreign fl.110). Uitgeverij Scala bv, Postbus 28009, 3828 ZG Hoogland, Netherlands. TEL 31-33-4806896. FAX 31-33-4802281. E-mail: bluegras@worldacces.nl. Ed. Gerrit Band. adv.; illus. **Document type:** consumer publication.
Description: Articles on animal welfare issues, pets and companion animals, and reports on wild animals around the world.

179.3 179.4 UK
U A C T A. (United Against Cruelty to Animals) 1965. bi-m. £3 to non-members. Animals' Vigilantes, James Mason House, 24 Salisbury St., Fordingbridge, Hants. SP6 1AF, England. TEL 44-425-653663. Ed. Ted Cox. bk.rev. circ. 10,000.

179 UK
U F A W ANIMAL WELFARE RESEARCH REPORT. no.2, 1988. irreg., no.9, 1996. price varies. Universities Federation for Animal Welfare, 8 Hamilton Close, S. Mimms, Potters Bar, Herts. EN6 3QD, England. TEL 44-1707-658202. FAX 44-1707-649279. **Document type:** monographic series.

179.3 UK ISSN 0263-4600
U F A W ANNUAL REPORT AND ACCOUNTS. 1926. a. membership (includes U F A W News-Sheet). Universities Federation for Animal Welfare, 8 Hamilton Close, S. Mimms, Potters Bar, Herts. EN6 3QD, England. TEL 44-1707-58202. FAX 44-1707-49279. Ed.Bd. bk.rev. circ. 2,000. **Document type:** corporate report.
Description: Discusses animal welfare and scientific research into the needs of animals.

179 UK
U F A W HANDBOOK ON THE CARE AND MANAGEMENT OF LABORATORY ANIMALS. 6th edition, 1993. base vol. (plus irreg. supplements). £91($185) Universities Federation for Animal Welfare, 8 Hamilton Close, S. Mimms, Potters Bar, Herts. EN6 3QD, England. TEL 44-1707-658202. FAX 44-1707-649279. **Document type:** trade publication.
Description: Provides guidance on practical animal husbandry, breeding, laboratory procedures and disease control for a wide variety of vertebrates.

179.3 UK ISSN 0566-8700
U F A W NEWS-SHEET. 1965. a. (free with Annual Report and Accounts). Universities Federation for Animal Welfare, 8 Hamilton Close, S. Mimms, Potters Bar, Herts. EN6 3QD, England. TEL 44-1707-58202. FAX 44-1707-49279. bk.rev. circ. 2,000. **Document type:** newsletter.

179 636.5 UK
UNIVERSITIES FEDERATION FOR ANIMAL WELFARE. SYMPOSIUM ON POULTRY WELFARE. PROCEEDINGS. 1993. a. £10($25) Universities Federation for Animal Welfare, 8 Hamilton Close, S. Mimms, Potters Bar, Herts. EN6 3QD, England. TEL 44-1707-658202. FAX 44-1707-649279. Eds. C.J. Savory, B.O. Hughes. **Document type:** proceedings.

THE VEGAN. see NUTRITION AND DIETETICS

THE VEGAN NEWS. see NUTRITION AND DIETETICS

179 636 GW ISSN 0176-2206
VORTRAEGE ZUM THEMA MENSCH UND TIER. Key Title: Studium Generale (Hannover). 1984. irreg. price varies. (Tieraerztliche Hochschule Hannover) Verlag M. und H. Schaper GmbH, Kalandstr. 4, 31061 Alfeld, Germany. TEL 05181-8009-0. FAX 05181-800933. (Subscr. to: Postfach 1642, 31046 Alfeld, Germany) **Indexed:** InterActions Bibl. (1987-). **Document type:** monographic series.

VYSKUMNY USTAV ZIVOCISNEJ VYROBY V NITRE. VEDECKE PRACE/JOURNAL OF FARM ANIMAL SCIENCE. see AGRICULTURE

179.3 UK ISSN 0143-9138
WAIFARERS.* 1979. 6/yr. Cats' Protection League, Derby & District Branch, 17 King's Rd., Horsham, W. Sussex RH13 5PP, England.
 Formerly: Cats' Protection League. Derby and District Branch. Newsletter.

179.3 333.7 US
WHALEWATCH. q. $17 membership. International Wildlife Coalition, 70 E. Falmouth Hwy., East Falmouth, MA 02536. TEL 508-548-8328. Ed. James Kinney. (back issues avail.)
 Description: Describes the IWC's whale protection and whale advocacy activities for members who have adopted whales.

179 333.95 US
WILD HORSE AND BURRO DIARY. 1960. q. membership. International Society for the Protection of Mustangs and Burros, 6212 E. Sweetwater Ave., Scotsdale, AZ 85254. TEL 602-991-0273. FAX 602-991-2920. E-mail: 103053,1112@compuserve.com. Ed. Karen Sussman. bk.rev. circ. 2,000. (back issues avail.) **Document type:** newsletter.
 Description: Brings readers in touch with current issues pertaining to the protection of wild horses and burros and their habitat in the United States and worldwide.

179.3 UK
WILDLIFE GUARDIAN. 1924. q. £2. League Against Cruel Sports Ltd., Sparling House, 83-87 Union St., London SE1 1SG, England. FAX 44-171-357-6749. E-mail: 100647.3311@compuserve.com; URL: http://www.lightman.co.uk/lacs. Ed. John Bryant. R&P contact: John Bryant. adv. contact: Kevin Flack. bk.rev. circ. 40,000. **Document type:** bulletin.
 Formerly: Cruel Sports.
 Description: Presents news about cruelty to animals through sporting activities. Features protection efforts and personal profiles.
 Refereed Serial

179.3 AT ISSN 0312-3480
WORKING KELPIE COUNCIL. NATIONAL STUD BOOK. 1967. irreg. Aus.$7 to non members. Working Kelpie Council, P.O. Box 306, Castle Hill, N.S.W. 2154, Australia. FAX 61-2-8999224. Ed. B.M. Cooper. circ. 620.

179 639.9 US ISSN 0276-3303
QL76
ZOO VIEW. q. $7. Greater Los Angeles Zoo Association, 5333 Zoo Dr., Los Angeles, CA 90027-1498. TEL 213-664-1100. FAX 213-662-6879. Ed. Claire Peeler. R&P contact: Claire Peeler. circ. 47,648 (paid). (back issues avail.)
 Description: Educates on exotic animals and promotes interest in the Los Angeles Zoo.

179.3 RU
...OV. 1990. w. Vsesoyuznoe Obshchestvo Zashchity Zhivotnykh, 2-oi Neopalimovskii per. 3, 119121 Moscow, Russia. TEL 247-17-04. Ed. I. Minushov. circ. 200,000.

ANIMAL WELFARE — Abstracting, Bibliographies, Statistics

...ANDBOOK OF LIVE ANIMAL TRANSPORT. see TRANSPORTATION — Abstracting, Bibliographies, Statistics

...UMANS & OTHER SPECIES; the quarterly journal of resources on their relationship. see PSYCHOLOGY — Abstracting, Bibliographies, Statistics

ANTHROPOLOGY

see also Folklore

572 US ISSN 0090-9939
GN43.A2
A A A GUIDE (YEAR). 1968. a. $50 to non-members; members $35 (effective 1996). American Anthropological Association, 4350 N. Fairfax Dr., Ste. 640, Arlington, VA 22203-1621. TEL 703-528-1902. Ed. Frederick T. Custer. R&P contact: Terry Clifford. index. circ. 4,000. (reprint service avail.) **Document type:** trade publication.
 Formerly: Guide to Departments of Anthropology (Year).
 Description: Lists academic, museum and research departments of anthropology; faculties and their specialties; student enrollment figures; PhD dissertations in anthropology.

305.8 IT
A E S; materiali, studi e argomenti di etnografia e storia sociale. 1993. s-a. L.60000 membership (effective 1993). Associazione di Etnografia e Storia Sociale, c/o Diakronia, Via Albini 4-b, 27029 Vigevano, Italy.

A G S QUARTERLY. (Association for Gravestone Studies) see ART

572 US ISSN 0738-064X
A M S STUDIES IN ANTHROPOLOGY. 1983. irreg., no.11, 1993. price varies. (Abrahams Magazine Service) A M S Press, Inc., 56 E. 13th St., New York, NY 10003. TEL 212-777-4700. FAX 212-995-5413. (back issues avail.) **Document type:** monographic series.
 Description: Monographs of specific ethnographic studies in anthropology.
 Refereed Serial

A P U PRESS ALASKANA BOOK SERIES. (Alaska Pacific University Press) see HISTORY — History Of North And South America

572 US
A S A RESEARCH METHODS IN SOCIAL ANTHROPOLOGY. 1976. irreg., vol.2, 1987. price varies. (Association of Social Anthropologists of the Commonwealth) Academic Press, Inc., 525 B St., Ste. 1900, San Diego, CA 92101-4495. TEL 619-231-0926. FAX 619-699-6715. (Subscr. to: Order Dept., 6277 Sea Harbor Dr., 4th Fl., Orlando, FL 32887. TEL 800-321-5068) index. (reprint service avail. from ISI) **Document type:** monographic series.
 —CISTI.
 Formerly: A S A Monographs (San Diego) (ISSN 0066-9679)

ABORIGINAL HISTORY. see HISTORY — History Of Australasia And Other Areas

572 CH ISSN 0001-3935
ACADEMIA SINICA. INSTITUTE OF ETHNOLOGY. BULLETIN. Key Title: Minxuxue Yanjiusuo Jikan, Zhongyang Yanjiuyuan. (Text in Chinese and English) 1956. s-a. NT.$400($40) Academia Sinica, Institute of Ethnology - Chung Yang Yen Chiu Yuan Min Tsu Hsueh Yen Chiu So, Nankang, Taipei, Taiwan 11529, Republic of China. FAX 866-2-652-3378. E-mail: Lexis@ms6.hinet.net. (Subscr. to: Lexis Book Co., Ltd., 10F-1 No. 138, Sec.2, Chin-Shan South Rd., Taipei, Taiwan, R.O. China. TEL 886-2-3219033. FAX 866-2-356-8068) Ed. Cheng-Kuang Hsu. illus. circ. 1,500. **Indexed:** A.I.C.P., Anthropol.Lit., Lang.& Lang.Behav.Abstr. **Document type:** bulletin.
 —CISTI; UnCover.

ACADEMIE POLONAISE DES SCIENCES. CENTRE D'ARCHEOLOGIE MEDITERRANEENE. TRAVAUX. see ARCHAEOLOGY

ACTA ANATOMICA NIPPONICA/KAIBOGAKU ZASSHI. see BIOLOGY

ACTA ANTHROPOGENETICA; international journal of research in human genetics. see BIOLOGY — Genetics

305.8 HU ISSN 1216-9803
GN1
ACTA ETHNOGRAPHICA HUNGARICA; an international journal of ethnography. (Text in English, French, German, Russian) 1950. q. $136 (effective 1998). (Magyar Tudomanyos Akademia) Akademiai Kiado Rt., P.O. Box 245, H-1519 Budapest, Hungary. TEL 36-1-2043976. FAX 36-1-2045600. Ed. Bertalan Andrasfalvy. adv./ bk.rev.; bibl.; charts; illus.; index. **Indexed:** Anthropol.Lit., Arts & Hum.Cit.Ind., Biol.Abstr., Curr.Adv.Ecol.Sci., Curr.Cont., IBR, M.L.A., RILM, SSCI. **Document type:** academic/scholarly publication.
 —CISTI. **CCC.**
 Formerly (until 1991): Academiae Scientiarum Hungaricae. Acta Ethnografica (ISSN 0001-5628)
 Description: Publishes contributions describing recent scientific advances in ethnography, folklore and cultural and social anthropology.

572 GW
ACTA HUMBOLDTIANA. irreg., vol.14, 1993. price varies. (Deutsche Ibero-Amerika-Stiftung) Franz Steiner Verlag Wiesbaden GmbH, Birkenwaldstr. 44, 70191 Stuttgart, Germany. TEL 49-711-2582-0. FAX 49-711-2582390. (Subscr. to: Postfach 101061, 70009 Stuttgart, Germany) Ed. Wolfgang Haberland. R&P contact: Sabine Koerner. **Document type:** monographic series.
 Formerly: Acta Humboldtiana. Series Geographica et Ethnographica (ISSN 0400-4043)

301.2 XR ISSN 0862-1209
ACTA MUSEI MORAVIAE. SUPPLEMENTUM: FOLIA ETHNOGRAPHICA. (Supplement to: Moravske Zemske Muzeum. Casopis. Vedy Spolecenske (ISSN 0323-0570)) (Text in Czech, English and German) 1959. a. $17. Moravske Zemske Muzeum, Zelny trh 6, 659 37 Brno, Czech Republic. TEL 420-5-42321205. FAX 420-5-42212792. E-mail: mzm@mzm.anet.cz. Ed. Eva Vecerkova. **Indexed:** A.I.C.P. **Document type:** academic/scholarly publication.
 Formerly (until 1986): Ethnographica (ISSN 0425-4570)

572 370 PL ISSN 0208-6042
ACTA UNIVERSITATIS LODZIENSIS: FOLIA ETHNOLOGICA. (Text in Polish; summaries in various languages) irreg. Wydawnictwo Uniwersytetu Lodzkiego, Ul. Jaracza 34, Lodz, Poland. TEL 331671. (Dist. by: Ars Polona-Ruch, Krakowskie Przedmiescie 7, Warsaw, Poland) **Document type:** academic/scholarly publication.
 —BLDSC (0585.206300); KNAW.
 Formerly (until 1982): Acta Universitatis Lodziensis: Folia Ethnographica.
 Description: Covers all aspects of ethnology.

ACTA UNIVERSITATIS LODZIENSIS: FOLIA ZOOLOGICA. see BIOLOGY — Zoology

572 PL
ACTA UNIVERSITATIS WRATISLAVIENSIS. ETHNOLOGICA. (Text in Polish; summaries in English or German) 1993. irreg. price varies. (Uniwersytet Wroclawski) Wydawnictwo Uniwersytetu Wroclawskiego, Spolska z o.o., Pl. Uniwersytecki 9-13, 50-137 Wroclaw, Poland. TEL 48-71-441006. FAX 48-71-402735. Ed. Edward Pietraszek. circ. 300. **Document type:** academic/scholarly publication.

572 PL
ACTA UNIVERSITATIS WRATISLAVIENSIS. STUDIA ANTROPOLOGICZNE. 1994. irreg. price varies. (Uniwersytet Wroclawski) Wydawnictwo Uniwersytetu Wroclawskiego, Spolka z o.o., Pl. Uniwersytecki 9-13, 50-137 Wroclaw, Poland. TEL 48-71-441006. FAX 48-71-402735. Ed. Tadeusz Krupinski. **Document type:** academic/scholarly publication.

ACTION AFRICA. see RELIGIONS AND THEOLOGY

305.8 US ISSN 1069-0573
ADVANCES IN HUMAN ECOLOGY. 1992. irreg., vol.6, 1997. $78.50. (Society for Human Ecology) J A I Press Inc., 55 Old Post Rd., No. 2, Box 1678, Greenwich, CT 06830-1678. TEL 203-661-7602. FAX 203-661-0792. E-mail: jai@jaipress.com. (Addr. in Europe: J A I Press Ltd., 38 Tavistock St., Covent Garden, London WC2E 7PB, England. TEL 44-171-379-8834. FAX 44-171-379-8835) Ed. Lee Freese. **Document type:** academic/scholarly publication.
 —BLDSC (0709.066000). **CCC.**

ANTHROPOLOGY

AFRICA. see HISTORY — History Of Africa

AFRICA TERVUREN. see HISTORY — History Of Africa

572 960   CN   ISSN 0832-8277
AFRICAN OCCASIONAL PAPERS SERIES. irreg. price varies. University of Calgary Press, 2500 University Dr. N.W., Calgary, AB T2N 1N4, Canada. TEL 403-220-7578. FAX 403-282-0085. URL: http://www.ucalgary.ca/ucpress. (Subscr. to: UBC Press, 6344 Memorial Rd., Vancouver, BC V6T 1Z2, Canada. TEL 604-822-5959. FAX 604-822-6083) Dir. Shirley A. Onn. R&P contact: Sharon Boyle. TEL 403-220-5284. adv. contact: Sharon Boyle. **Document type:** academic/scholarly publication.
   Description: Provides information on topics relevant to African archaeology and anthropology; most material is taken from edited theses submitted for higher degrees at various African universities.

960   SA   ISSN 0002-0184
DT751
AFRICAN STUDIES; a biannual journal devoted to the study of African anthropology, history, sociology, literature and languages. 1921. s-a. R.55 (foreign $38 or £24) (effective 1997). Witwatersrand University Press, Wits 2050, South Africa. FAX 27-11-4845971. E-mail: wup@iafrica.com; 099afrst@cosmos.wits.ac.za; URL: http://sunsite.wits.ac.za/wits/wits__university__press/african-studies/homepage.html. Ed. Deborah A. James. adv.; bk.rev.; charts; index. circ. 600. (reprint service avail. from KTO) **Indexed:** A.I.C.P., Abstr.Anthropol., Amer.Hist.& Life (1963-1978), Anthropol.Lit., Bibl.Ling., Curr.Cont., Curr.Cont.Africa, Documentatieblad, Geo.Abstr., Hist.Abstr. (1963-1978), IBR, IDA, Ind.S.A.Per., Int.Pol.Sci.Abstr., Lang.& Lang.Behav.Abstr., M.L.A., Mid.East: Abstr.& Ind., MLA Intl.Bibl., Rural Devel.Abstr., Soc.Sci.Ind., SSCI, World Agri.Econ.& Rural Sociol.Abstr. **Document type:** academic/scholarly publication.
—BLDSC (0734.000000); Genuine Article; SWETS; UnCover.
   Description: Scholarly articles on topics relevant to African anthropology, history, politics, linguistics, literature, sociology and related studies.

572 630   JA   ISSN 0285-1601
DT1
AFRICAN STUDY MONOGRAPHS. (Supplement avail. (ISSN 0286-9667)) (Text and summaries in English and French) 1981. q. Kyoto University, Center for African Area Studies, 46 Shimoadachi-cho, Yoshida, Sakyo-ku, Kyoto 606-01, Japan. TEL 81-75-753-7800. FAX 81-75-753-7810. Ed. Yasuo Takamura. circ. 1,200. (back issues avail.) **Indexed:** Abstr.Rural Dev.Trop., Anthropol.Lit., Bibl.Ling., Documentatieblad. **Document type:** monographic series.
—BLDSC (0734.920000).
   Description: Research on the nature of Africa, and the people and cultures there.

572 630   JA   ISSN 0286-9667
DT1
AFRICAN STUDY MONOGRAPHS. SUPPLEMENTARY ISSUE. (Text in English, French) 1982. irreg. Kyoto University, Center for African Area Studies, 46 Shimoadachi-cho, Yoshida, Sakyo-ku, Kyoto 606-01, Japan. TEL 81-753-7800. FAX 81-753-7810. Ed. Naoki Koyama. circ. 1,200. (back issues avail.) **Indexed:** Anthropol.Lit., Documentatieblad. **Document type:** monographic series.
—BLDSC (0734.921000).
   Description: Research on the nature of Africa, and the people and cultures there.

572   BE   ISSN 0776-7323
AFRICANA GANDENSIA. 1976. irreg. Rijksuniversiteit te Ghent, Seminarie voor Afrikaanse Cultuurgeschiedenis, St. Pietersplein 4, B-9000 Ghent, Belgium. **Indexed:** Bibl.Ling., Curr.Cont.Africa.

301.2 572   PH   ISSN 0117-6595
AGHAMTAO. 1978. a. P.150($15) Ugnayang Pang-Aghamtao, Inc. - Anthropological Association of the Philippines, Rm. 208, Philippine Social Science Center, Commonwealth Ave., Diliman, Quezon City, Philippines. TEL 922-9621. Ed.Bd. bk.rev. circ. 1,000. **Document type:** academic/scholarly publication.
   Description: Publishes anthropological papers by Filipino authors.
Refereed Serial

ALASKA HISTORY. see HISTORY — History Of North And South America

ALASKA NATIVE LANGUAGE CENTER RESEARCH PAPERS. see LINGUISTICS

ALBERTA ARCHAEOLOGICAL REVIEW. see ARCHAEOLOGY

572 913   CN   ISSN 0831-5671
ALGONQUIAN CONFERENCE. PAPERS. (Text in English, French) 1976. a. Can.$48 (effective 1996). Algonquian Conference, Department of Linguistics, University of Manitoba, Winnipeg, MB R3T 2N2, Canada. TEL 204-474-9596. Ed. David H. Pentland. R&P contact: David Pentland. circ. 300. **Indexed:** Anthropol.Lit., Bibl.Ling. **Document type:** proceedings, academic/scholarly publication.
—BLDSC (6393.600000).
Refereed Serial

ALTAIR. see TRAVEL AND TOURISM

ALTERNATE ROUTES; a journal of critical social research. see SOCIAL SCIENCES: COMPREHENSIVE WORKS

301.2 918.503   PE   ISSN 0252-886X
F3429
AMAZONIA PERUANA. 1977. s-a. $40 in Latin America; elsewhere $50. Centro Amazonico de Antropologia y Aplicacion Practica, Programa de Difusion, Gonzales Prada 626, Madgalena del Mar, Apdo. 14-0166, Lima 17, Peru. FAX 638846. Ed. Jaime Regan. adv. contact: Manuel Cornejo. bk.rev.; bibl.; charts; illus. circ. 1,000. (back issues avail.) **Indexed:** Anthropol.Lit., Hisp.Amer.Per.Ind. (1981-), IBR, Sel.Water Res.Abstr., W.R.C.Inf., Weed Abstr. **Document type:** academic/scholarly publication.

301 570 970   MX   ISSN 0185-1179
E51
AMERICA INDIGENA. (Supplement avail.: Anuario Indigenista) (Text in English, Spanish, Portuguese; summaries in English) 1941. q. $75 in Latin America; N. America $80; elsewhere $85. Instituto Indigenista Interamericano, Apdo. Postal 20315, 01001 Mexico DF, Mexico. TEL 525-5680819. FAX 525-6521274. bk.rev.; bibl.; charts; illus.; stat.; cum.index: 1940-1980, 1980-1990. (reprint service avail. from SWZ) **Indexed:** A.I.C.P., Amer.Hist.& Life, Anthropol.Lit., Bibl.Ling., Geo.Abstr.H.G., Hisp.Amer.Per.Ind. (1970-), Hist.Abstr., IBR, IDA, Int.Lab.Doc.
—BLDSC (0809.750000); KR SourceOne; SWETS.
   Description: Covers anthropology and history of the Indian culture in Latin America. Explores all the natural, social and human disciplines.

301.2   US   ISSN 0160-1873
GN3
AMERICAN ANTHROPOLOGICAL ASSOCIATION. ABSTRACTS OF MEETINGS. a. $15 (effective 1996). American Anthropological Association, 4350 N. Fairfax Dr., Ste. 640, Arlington, VA 22203-1621. TEL 703-528-1902. Ed. Frederick T. Custer. R&P contact: Terry Clifford. adv.: page $385; trim 8 1/2 x 11; adv. contact: Terry Clifford. (reprint service avail.) **Indexed:** A.I.C.P. **Document type:** abstracting/indexing, proceedings.
—BLDSC (0553.842500).
   Description: Publishes the abstracts of papers to be presented at the annual meeting.

572   US   ISSN 0002-7294
GN1   CODEN: AMATA7
AMERICAN ANTHROPOLOGIST. (Supplement avail.) 1899. q. $50 to individuals; institutions $105 (effective 1996). American Anthropological Association, 4350 N. Fairfax Dr., Ste. 640, Arlington, VA 22203-1621. TEL 703-528-1902. URL: http://www.ameranthassn.org/ameranth.htm. Eds. Barbara Tedlock, Dennis Tedlock. R&P contact: Terry Clifford. adv.: page $700; trim 8 1/2 x 11; adv. contact: Terry Clifford. bk.rev.; bibl.; charts; index. circ. 12,000. (also avail. in microform (ISSN 0364-9873) from MIM,UMI; reprint service avail. from KTO) **Indexed:** A.I.C.P., Abstr.Anthropol., Acad.Ind., Amer.Bibl.Slavic & E.Eur.Stud., Amer.Hist.& Life (1963-1972), (1982-), Anthropol.Lit., Arts & Hum.Cit.Ind., ASCA, ASSIA, Bibl.& Ind.Geol., Bibl.Engl.Lang.& Lit., Bibl.Engl.Lang.& Lit., Bibl.Ind., Bibl.Ling., Biol.Abstr., Biol.& Agr.Ind., Bk.Rev.Dig., Bk.Rev.Ind. (1965-), Br.Archaeol.Abstr., Chic.Per.Ind., Child.Bk.Rev.Ind. (1965-), Child.Lit.Abstr., Commun.Abstr., Curr.Adv.Ecol.Sci., Curr.Cont., E.I., Ecol.Abstr., Excerp.Med., Film Lit.Ind. (1977-), Gen.Sci.Ind., Geo.Abstr., Geol.Abstr., Hist.Abstr. (1963-1972), (1982-), Int.Polit.Sci.Abstr., Lang.& Lang.Behav.Abstr., M.L.A., Maize Abstr., Mid.East: Abstr.& Ind., MLA Intl.Bibl., Popul.Ind., Psychol.Abstr. (1928-), Ref.Sour., So.Pac.Per.Ind., Soc.Sci.Ind., SSCI, SSSI, Stud.Wom.Abstr., Triticale Abstr., World Agri.Econ.& Rural Sociol.Abstr. **Document type:** academic/scholarly publication.
—BLDSC (0810.290000); Genuine Article; KR SourceOne; SWETS; UMI; UnCover. **CCC.**
   Description: Covers cultural, physical, linguistic and applied anthropology. Includes information on archaeology.
Refereed Serial

572   US   ISSN 0065-6941
AMERICAN ANTHROPOLOGIST. SPECIAL PUBLICATION. 1964. q. American Anthropological Association, 4350 N. Fairfax Dr., Ste. 640, Arlington, VA 22203-1621. TEL 703-538-1902. R&P contact: Terry Clifford. adv. contact: Terry Clifford. (reprint service avail.) **Indexed:** Anthropol.Lit. **Document type:** academic/scholarly publication.
Refereed Serial

572 301.205   US   ISSN 0094-0496
GN1
AMERICAN ETHNOLOGIST. 1974. q. $50 to individuals; institutions $70 (effective 1996). (American Ethnological Society) American Anthropological Association, 4350 N. Fairfax Dr., Ste. 640, Arlington, VA 22203-1621. TEL 703-528-1902. URL: http://www.ameranthassn.org/aespubs.htm. Ed. Michael Herzfeld. R&P contact: Terry Clifford. adv.: page $330; trim 6 3/4 x 10; adv. contact: Terry Clifford. bk.rev.; bibl.; illus. circ. 3,000. (also avail. in microform from UMI; reprint service avail.) **Indexed:** A.I.C.P., Anthropol.Lit., Arts & Hum.Cit.Ind., ASCA, ASSIA, Bibl.Ind., Bibl.Ling., Bk.Rev.Ind. (1989-), CERDIC, Child.Bk.Rev.Ind. (1989-), Commun.Abstr., Curr.Cont., E.I., Mid.East: Abstr.& Ind., Psychol.Abstr. (1974-), RILM, So.Pac.Per.Ind., Soc.Sci.Ind., SSCI. **Document type:** academic/scholarly publication.
—BLDSC (0814.200000); Genuine Article; KR SourceOne; SWETS; UMI; UnCover. **CCC.**
   Description: Presents topical papers, review articles, comments and reflections, and reviews in areas such as ecology, economy, social organization, ethnicity, politics, and ideology.

ANTHROPOLOGY

572 970 398   US   ISSN 0095-182X
E75   CODEN: AIQUEW
AMERICAN INDIAN QUARTERLY. 1974. q. $25 to individuals (foreign $32); institutions $45 (foreign $47). University of Nebraska Press, 312 N. 14th St., Box 880484, Lincoln, NE 68588-0484. TEL 402-472-3581. FAX 402-472-6214. Ed. Gary Dunham. R&P contact: Elaine Maruhn. adv. contact: Mary Cadwallader. bk.rev.; bibl.; index. circ. 1,000. (also avail. in microform from UMI; back issues avail.) **Indexed:** Abstr.Anthropol., Abstr.Folk.Stud., Amer.Hist.& Life (1974-), Anthropol.Lit., Bibl.Ind., Bk.Rev.Ind. (1974-1979), C.I.J.E., Child.Bk.Rev.Ind. (1974-1979), Child.Lit.Abstr., Hist.Abstr. (1974-), Hum.Ind., M.L.A., MLA Intl.Bibl. **Document type:** academic/scholarly publication.
●Also available online. Vendor(s): Information Access Co.
—BLDSC (0819.800000); KR SourceOne; SWETS; UMI; UnCover.
Description: Provides an interdisciplinary approach to American Indian studies. Covers history, anthropology, folklore and literature.

573   US   ISSN 0002-9483
GN1   CODEN: AJPNA9
AMERICAN JOURNAL OF PHYSICAL ANTHROPOLOGY. 1918. 14/yr. $1895 (foreign $2140) (effective 1998). (American Association of Physical Anthropologists) John Wiley & Sons, Inc., Journals, 605 Third Ave., New York, NY 10158. TEL 212-850-6645. FAX 212-850-6021. TELEX 12-7063. E-mail: SUBINFO@JWILEY.COM; URL: http://www.wiley.com/0002-9483/. (Subscr. outside the Americas to: John Wiley & Sons Ltd., Baffins Ln., Chichester, W. Sussex PO19 1UD, England. TEL 44-1243-779777. FAX 44-1243-446128) Ed. Emoke J.E. Szathmary. adv.: B&W page £640, color page £1515; trim 254 x 174. bk.rev.; bibl.; charts; illus.; index. circ. 2,550. (also avail. in microform from UMI; back issues avail.; reprint service avail. from SWZ) **Indexed:** A.I.C.P., Abstr.Anthropol., Anthropol.Lit., Arts & Hum.Cit.Ind., ASCA, Behav.Med.Abstr., Bibl.Dev.Med.& Child Neur., Bibl.Ind., Biol.Abstr., Chic.Per.Ind., Curr.Adv.Ecol.Sci., Curr.Adv.Genetics & Molec.Biol., Curr.Cont., Curr.Tit.Dent., Dent.Ind., Fam.Ind., Helminthol.Abstr., Ind.Med., Ind.Sci.Rev., Mid.East: Abstr.& Ind., Nutr.Abstr., Risk Abstr., Sci.Cit.Ind., Soc.Sci.Ind., SSCI, Stud.Wom.Abstr.
—BLDSC (0832.000000); CISTI; EMDOCS; Genuine Article; KNAW, KR SourceOne; Linda Hall; SWETS; UnCover. **CCC.**
Description: Publishes information on human evolution and variation, including primate morphology, physiology, genetics, adaptation, growth, development, and behavior past and present.
Refereed Serial

AMERICAN JOURNAL OF PRIMATOLOGY. see
BIOLOGY — Zoology

572   US   ISSN 0065-9452
GN2   CODEN: APNHAN
AMERICAN MUSEUM OF NATURAL HISTORY. ANTHROPOLOGICAL PAPERS. 1907. irreg. price varies. American Museum of Natural History, Central Park W. at 79th St., New York, NY 10024-5192. TEL 212-769-5545. FAX 212-769-5009. E-mail: scipubs@amnh.org. Ed. Brenda Jones. circ. 1,000. **Indexed:** Amer.Hist.& Life (1963-1970), Biol.Abstr., Bull.Signal., Hist.Abstr.(1963-1970), SSCI, Zoo.Rec. **Document type:** monographic series.
—BLDSC (1542.900000); Linda Hall; UMI.
Description: Professional basic research papers in anthropology.
Refereed Serial

AMERICAN UNIVERSITY STUDIES. SERIES 11. ANTHROPOLOGY AND SOCIOLOGY. see *SOCIAL SCIENCES: COMPREHENSIVE WORKS*

572   UY
AMERINDIA; revista de prehistoria y etnologia de America. 1962. biennial. Centro de Estudios Arqueologicos y Antropologicos Americanos, Zuballaga 1117, Montevideo, Uruguay. bk.rev. **Indexed:** A.I.C.P., Bibl.Ling., IBR, M.L.A.

572   MX   ISSN 0185-1225
GN560.M6
ANALES DE ANTROPOLOGIA. 1964; N.S. 1992. a. Mex.$60. Universidad Nacional Autonoma de Mexico, Instituto de Investigaciones Antropologicas, Circuito Exterior, Ciudad Universitaria, 04510 Mexico, D.F., Mexico. TEL 52-5-6229531. FAX 52-5-6229651. E-mail: ugartech@servidor.unam.mx. Ed. Jose Luiz Orozco. bibl. **Indexed:** A.I.C.P., Amer.Hist.& Life (1967-1971), Anthropol.Lit., Bibl.& Ind.Geol., Hisp.Amer.Per.Ind. (1970-), Hist.Abstr. (1967-1971). **Document type:** academic/scholarly publication.

ANALES DE ARQUEOLOGIA Y ETNOLOGIA. see *ARCHAEOLOGY*

572 410   CG   ISSN 0254-4296
DT641
ANNALES AEQUATORIA. (Text in English, French) 1980. a. $25. Centre Aequatoria, B.P. 276, Mbandaka, Democratic Republic of the Congo. (Subscr. to: Aequatoria, Te Boelaerlei, 11, B-2140 Borgerhout, Belgium) Ed. Honore Vinck. bk.rev.; cum.index: 1938-1962; 1980-1989. circ. 500. **Indexed:** A.I.C.P., Anthropol.Lit., Bibl.Ling., Bull.Signal., Documentatieblad, P.L.E.S.A. (1987-). **Document type:** academic/scholarly publication.
Supersedes (1938-1962): Aequatoria.
Description: Research into Central African cultures, history and languages, with particular emphasis on Zaire.

301 069   SA   ISSN 0256-6699
GN1   CODEN: ACMSEW
ANNALS OF THE CAPE PROVINCIAL MUSEUMS: HUMAN SCIENCES. (Text in English) 1979. irreg. price varies. Albany Museum, Somerset St., Grahamstown 6140, South Africa. TEL 27-461-22397. FAX 27-461-22398. E-mail: amfg@giraffe.ru.ac.za. (Co-sponsors: East London Museum; Kaffraria Museum, King William's Town; Port Elizabeth Museum) Ed. F.W. Gess. (back issues avail.) **Indexed:** Ind.S.A.Per., Zoo.Rec. **Document type:** monographic series.

572   RM   ISSN 0570-2259
GN1   CODEN: ARNAAG
ANNUAIRE ROUMAIN D'ANTHROPOLOGIE. vol.17, 1980. a. (Academia Romana) Editura Academiei Romane, Calea 13 Septiembrie 13, 76117 Bucharest, Rumania. (Dist. by: Rodipet SA, Piata Presei Libere 1, Sec. 1, Bucharest, Rumania. TEL 401-6185103. FAX 401-2226407) Ed. Olga Necrasov. **Indexed:** A.I.C.P., Anthropol.Lit., Biol.Abstr., Excerp.Med.
—BLDSC (1073.420000); KNAW.

301.2   US
ANNUAL EDITIONS: ANTHROPOLOGY. 1974. a. $12.95. Dushkin Publishing Group, Sluice Dock, Guilford, CT 06437-9989. TEL 203-453-4351. FAX 203-453-6000. Ed. Elvio Angeloni; Pub. Ian Nielsen. illus. **Document type:** academic/scholarly publication.
Formerly: Annual Editions: Readings in Anthropology (ISSN 0095-5582)
Refereed Serial

573   US
ANNUAL EDITIONS: PHYSICAL ANTHROPOLOGY. 1992. a. $12.95. Dushkin Publishing Group, Sluice Dock, Guilford, CT 06437-9989. TEL 203-453-4351. FAX 203-453-6000. Ed. Elvio Angeloni; Pub. Ian Nielsen. **Document type:** academic/scholarly publication.

301   US   ISSN 0084-6570
GN1   CODEN: ARAPCW
ANNUAL REVIEW OF ANTHROPOLOGY. 1972. a. $55 to individuals (foreign $60); institutions $110 (foreign $120) (effective 1998). Annual Reviews Inc., 4139 El Camino Way, Box 10139, Palo Alto, CA 94303-0139. TEL 650-493-4400; 800-523-8635. FAX 650-424-0910. E-mail: service@annurev.org; URL: http://www.AnnualReviews.org/. Ed. William H. Durham; Pub. John S. McNeil. R&P contact: Jeanne Kunz. bibl.; charts; index, cum.index. (also avail. in microfilm from UMI; back issues avail.; reprint service avail.) **Indexed:** A.I.C.P., Anthropol.Lit., ASCA, Bibl.& Ind.Geol., Bibl.Ling., Biol.Abstr., Br.Archaeol.Abstr., Chem.Abstr., Curr.Adv.Ecol.Sci., Curr.Cont.Africa, Curr.Cont., IBR, Int.Polit.Sci.Abstr., Lang.& Lang.Behav.Abstr., M.M.R.I., Psychol.Abstr. (1976-), Soc.Sci.Ind. (1994-), SSCI. **Document type:** academic/scholarly publication.
—BLDSC (1520.474000); CASDDS; Genuine Article; KR SourceOne; SWETS; UMI; UnCover. **CCC.**
Description: Original critical reviews of the significant primary literature and current developments in anthropology.

301.2   HU   ISSN 0574-3842
ANTHROPOLOGIA HUNGARICA. (Text in English) 1956. s-a. $24 (effective 1998). Magyar Termeszettudomanyi Muzeum - Hungarian Natural History Museum, Baross u. 13, 1088 Budapest, Hungary. TEL 36-1-3130035. FAX 36-1-11171669. Ed. I. Pap. adv. contact: Ildiko Pap. illus. circ. 250. (back issues avail.) **Indexed:** Anthropol.Lit. **Document type:** academic/scholarly publication.
Formerly (until 1970): Crania Hungarica.
Description: Contains papers written by museum staff members or based on materials deposited there.

572   HU   ISSN 0003-5440
GN1
ANTHROPOLOGIAI KOZLEMENYEK; a Magyar Biologiai Tarsasag embertani szakosztalyanak folyoirata. (Text in English, Hungarian; summaries in English) 1957. s-a. $25 per vol. Magyar Biologiai Tarsasag - Hungarian Biological Society, c/o Eotvos Lorand University, Dept. Anthropology, Puskin u. 3, 1088 Budapest, Hungary. TEL 36-1-2667857. Ed. Otto G. Eiben. adv.; bk.rev. circ. 400. (back issues avail.) **Indexed:** A.I.C.P., Biol.Abstr., Curr.Cont., SSCI. **Document type:** academic/scholarly publication.
—KNAW.
Refereed Serial

572 570   CN   ISSN 0003-5459
E78.C2   CODEN: ATRPBS
ANTHROPOLOGICA. (Text in English, French) 1955; N.S. 1959. s-a. Can.$40 (foreign $40) (effective 1997). (Wilfrid Laurier University) Wilfrid Laurier University Press, 75 University Ave. W., Waterloo, ON N2L 3C5, Canada. TEL 519-884-0710. FAX 519-725-1399. E-mail: press@mach1.wlu.ca; URL: http://info.wlu.ca/~wwwpress/. Ed. Andrew Lyons. adv.; bk.rev.; charts; illus.; index. circ. 380. (also avail. in microform from MIM,MML,SWZ,UMI) **Indexed:** A.I.C.P., Abstr.Anthropol., Amer.Hist.& Life (1978-), Anthropol.Lit., Biol.Abstr., Can.B.P.I., CMI, E.I., Hist.Abstr. (1978-), IBR, Lang.& Lang.Behav.Abstr., Psychol.Abstr. (1968-), Pt.de Rep., RADAR, SSCI. **Document type:** academic/scholarly publication.
—BLDSC (1542.860000); KR SourceOne; UnCover. **CCC.**
Description: Presents articles on social-cultural anthropology and related fields.
Refereed Serial

572   SP   ISSN 0301-6587
BD450
ANTHROPOLOGICA; revista de etnopsicologia y etnopsiquiatria. (Text in Spanish; summaries in English, French, German) 1973. s-a. 2000 ptas.($15) Instituto de Antropologia de Barcelona, Melchor de Palau, 145, T-4, 08014 Barcelona, Spain. FAX 34-3-2610570. Ed. Angel Aguirre Baztan. bk.rev.; bibl. circ. 5,000. **Indexed:** Abstr.Anthropol., Anthropol.Lit., M.L.A. **Document type:** academic/scholarly publication.
—CINDOC.

ANTHROPOLOGY

572   PE   ISSN 0254-9212
F3429
ANTHROPOLOGICA. Key Title: Anthropologica del Departamento de Ciencias Sociales. 1983. a. $19.40. Pontificia Universidad Catolica del Peru, Departamento de Ciencias Sociales, Fondo Editorial, Apdo. 1761, Lima 32, Peru. TEL 51-14-626390. FAX 51-14-611785. E-mail: editorial@pucp.edu.pe; URL: http://www.pucp.edu.pe. Ed. Alejandro Ortiz Rescaniere. **Indexed:** Abstr.Anthropol., Anthropol.Lit. **Document type:** academic/scholarly publication.
     Incorporates: Revista de Debates: Debates en Antropologia; Which supersedes in part: Debates en Antropologia.
     Refereed Serial

572   AT   ISSN 0066-4677
GN1
ANTHROPOLOGICAL FORUM; an international journal of social and cultural anthropology and comparative sociology. 1963. a. Aus.$20 (effective Jan. 1996). University of Western Australia, Department of Anthropology, Nedlands, W.A. 6007, Australia. TEL 61-9-3802851. FAX 61-9-3801062. TELEX AA 92992. E-mail: jgordon@uniwa.uwa.edu.au; URL: http://www.arts.uwa.edu.au/anthropwww/overview.htm. (Dist. by: University Co-operative Bookshop, Library and Professional Branch, P.O. Box 54, Broadway, N.S.W. 2007, Australia. TEL 61-2-2359722. FAX 61-2-2359701) Ed. John L. Gordon. adv.; bk.rev.; circ. 600 (paid). **Indexed:** A.I.C.P., Anthropol.Lit., E.I. **Document type:** academic/scholarly publication.
—BLDSC (1542.870000).
     Refereed Serial

301   SZ   ISSN 0960-0604
GN1   CODEN: AJECER
ANTHROPOLOGICAL JOURNAL ON EUROPEAN CULTURES. 1990. s-a. 37 SFr. to individuals; institutions 55 SFr.; students 21 SFr. (effective 1997). Universite de Fribourg, Seminaire d'Ethnologie, 11 Rte. des Bonnesfontaines, CH-1700 Fribourg, Switzerland. TEL 41-37-219207. FAX 41-37-219729. Eds. Christian Giordano, Ina-Maria Greverus. **Document type:** academic/scholarly publication.
—BLDSC (1542.878000).

ANTHROPOLOGICAL LINGUISTICS. see *LINGUISTICS*

ANTHROPOLOGICAL LITERATURE; an index to periodical articles and essays. see *ANTHROPOLOGY — Abstracting, Bibliographies, Statistics*

570   US   ISSN 0003-5491
GN1
ANTHROPOLOGICAL QUARTERLY. 1928. q. $28 to individuals; institutions $45 (effective 1998). Catholic University of America Press, 620 Michigan Ave., N.E., Washington, DC 20064. TEL 202-319-5052. FAX 202-319-4985. E-mail: cua-press@cua.edu; URL: http://www.press.uchicago.edu/cgi-bin/hfs.cgi/66/catholic/aqu.ch. Ed. Phyllis Chock. adv.; bk.rev.; abstr.; charts; illus.; index, cum.index. circ. 913. (also avail. in microform from MIM,UMI; reprint service avail. from UMI) **Indexed:** A.I.C.P., Abstr.Anthropol., Amer.Bibl.Slavic & E.Eur.Stud., Anthropol.Lit., Arts & Hum.Cit.Ind., ASCA, Cath.Ind., Curr.Cont., Curr.Lit.Fam.Plan., E.I., Fam.Ind., Geo.Abstr.H.G., IDA, IMFL, Lang.& Lang.Behav.Abstr., Mid.East: Abstr.& Ind., MLA Intl.Bibl., Mult.Ed.Abstr., Rural Devel.Abstr., Rural Ext.Educ.& Tr.Abstr., So.Pac.Per.Ind., Soc.Sci.Ind., Sociol.Educ.Abstr., Sp.Ed.Needs Abstr., SSCI, Stud.Wom.Abstr., World Agri.Econ.& Rural Sociol.Abstr. **Document type:** academic/scholarly publication.
—BLDSC (1544.400000); Genuine Article; KR SourceOne; SWETS; UMI; UnCover. **CCC.**
     Description: Covers all areas of social and cultural anthropology.

572   JA   ISSN 0918-7960
GN1
ANTHROPOLOGICAL SCIENCE. (Text in English, Japanese) 1884. 5/yr. $150. (Anthropological Society of Nippon) Business Center for Academic Societies Japan, 5-16-9 Honkomagome, Bunkyo-ku, Tokyo 113, Japan. TEL 03-5814-5811. FAX 03-5814-5822. TELEX 2722268 BCJSP J. adv.; bk.rev.; index. circ. 1,300. **Indexed:** A.I.C.P., Anthropol.Lit., Arts & Hum.Cit.Ind., ASCA, Biol.Abstr., Curr.Cont., Excerp.Med., SSCI. **Document type:** academic/scholarly publication.
—BLDSC (1545.200000); Genuine Article; UnCover.
     Formerly: Anthropological Society of Nippon. Journal (ISSN 0003-5505)

572   UK   ISSN 0044-8370
GN1
ANTHROPOLOGICAL SOCIETY OF OXFORD. JOURNAL. Short title: J A S O. 1970. 3/yr. £14($28) to individuals; institutions £25 ($50) (effective 1995-1996). Anthropological Society of Oxford, 51 Banbury Rd., Oxford OX2 6PE, England. TEL 44-1865-274682. Ed. Jonathan Webber. adv.; bk.rev.; cum.index every 10 yrs. circ. 700. **Indexed:** A.I.C.P., Anthropol.Lit., E.I. **Document type:** academic/scholarly publication.
—BLDSC (4698.150000); UnCover.
     Description: Provides a forum for current research in social anthropology.

301   UK
ANTHROPOLOGICAL SOCIETY OF OXFORD. OCCASIONAL PAPERS SERIES. a. price varies. Anthropological Society of Oxford, 51 Banbury Rd., Oxford OX2 6PE, England. TEL 44-1865-274682. **Document type:** academic/scholarly publication.

572   FR   ISSN 0003-5521
                              CODEN: ATRPAR
L'ANTHROPOLOGIE. 1890. 4/yr. 1260 F. (foreign 1665 F.) (effective 1997). Masson - Periodiques, 120 bd. St. Germain, 75006 Paris, France. TEL 33-1-40466200. FAX 33-1-40466201. (Subscr. to: Societe de Periodiques Specialises, B.P. 22-F, 41354 Vineuil Cedex, France. TEL 33-2-54504612. FAX 33-2-54504611) Ed. H. de Lumley. bk.rev.; abstr.; illus.; index. circ. 825. (also avail. in microform from UMI; reprint service avail. from ISI) **Indexed:** A.I.C.P., Abstr.Anthropol., Anthropol.Lit., Bibl.& Ind.Geol., Biol.Abstr., Curr.Cont.Africa, Excerp.Med., SSCI. **Document type:** academic/scholarly publication.
—BLDSC (1546.000000); Genuine Article; KR SourceOne; Linda Hall; SWETS; UMI. **CCC.**
     Description: Contains original articles from all anthropological sciences.

572 301.2   XR   ISSN 0323-1119
ANTHROPOLOGIE/ANTHROPOLOGY. (Editions in English, French, German) 1962. 3/yr. price varies. Moravske Zemske Muzeum, Zelny trh 6, 659 37 Brno, Czech Republic. TEL 420-5-52321205. FAX 420-5-42219511. E-mail: mzm@mzm.anet.cz. (Subscr. to: Karger Libri AG, Petersgraben 31 CH-4011 Basel, Switzerland.) (Co-sponsor: Anthropos Institute) Ed. Marta Dockalova. illus.; maps. circ. 500. **Indexed:** A.I.C.P., Anthropol.Lit., Curr.Cont., IBR, SSCI. **Document type:** academic/scholarly publication.
—BLDSC (1545.800000).

572 301.2   GW   ISSN 0066-4685
ANTHROPOLOGIE. (Text in Czech and German) 1962. irreg., vol.33, 1995. DM.72. (Moravske Museum, Brno, CS) Dr. Rudolf Habelt GmbH, Am Buchenhang 1, 53115 Bonn, Germany. TEL 49-228-9238322. FAX 49-228-923836. Ed. J. Jelinek. **Indexed:** Arts & Hum.Cit.Ind., ASCA. **Document type:** monographic series.

301.2 930.1   BE
GN4
ANTHROPOLOGIE ET PREHISTOIRE. (Text in English, Flemish, French; summaries in English, French) 1882. a. 1200 BEF. Societe Royale Belge d'Anthropologie et de Prehistoire, 29 rue Vautier, 1040 Brussels, Belgium. TEL 32-2-6274381. FAX 32-2-6464433. bk.rev.; illus. circ. 350. **Indexed:** A.I.C.P., Anthropol.Lit., Br.Archaeol.Abstr., Excerp.Med., GeoRef., Zoo.Rec. **Document type:** bulletin.
—BLDSC (2748.800000).
     Formerly (until vol.101, 1990): Societe Royale Belge d'Anthropologie et de Prehistoire. Bulletin (ISSN 0304-1425)

572 917.106   CN   ISSN 0702-8997
GN301   CODEN: ANSOFQ
ANTHROPOLOGIE ET SOCIETES. (Text in French; summaries in English, French) 1977. 3/yr. Can.$38 to individuals (US Can.$45); institutions Can.$70 (US Can.$82; elsewhere Can.$95) (effective 1997). Universite Laval, Department d'Anthropologie, Ste.-Foy, PQ G1K 7P4, Canada. TEL 418-656-3027. FAX 418-656-3284. E-mail: proanth@ant.ulaval.ca; URL: http://www.fss.ulaval.ca/ant/ant.html. Ed. Marie-Andree Couillard. adv.; bk.rev.; index, cum.index. circ. 1,200. (back issues avail.) **Indexed:** A.I.C.P., Abstr.Anthropol., Anthropol.Lit., Curr.Cont., IBR, Pt.de Rep., SSCI. **Document type:** academic/scholarly publication.
—SWETS.
     Description: Open to all theoretical perspectives and cultures of the contemporary world or past societies. Devoted to actual debates in and the contemporary practice of the discipline.
     Refereed Serial

ANTHROPOLOGIE - MARITIME. see *BIOLOGY — Zoology*

572 960   FR   ISSN 0993-4871
ANTHROPOLOGIE VISUELLE. 1988. irreg., no.3, 1992. Editions de l' Ecole des Hautes Etudes en Sciences Sociales, 131 bd. St-Michel, 75005 Paris, France. TEL 33-1-40467080. FAX 33-1-44070889. E-mail: editions@ehess.fr; URL: http://www.ehess.fr/editions. (Dist. by: Centre Interinstitutionnel pour la Diffusion de Publications en Sciences Humaines, 131 bd. St-Michel, 75005 Paris, France. TEL 33-1-43544715. FAX 33-1-43548073)

301.2   AU   ISSN 0066-4693
ANTHROPOLOGISCHE GESELLSCHAFT, VIENNA. MITTEILUNGEN. 1870. a. price varies. Verlag Ferdinand Berger und Soehne GmbH, Wienerstr. 21-23, A-3580 Horn, Austria. TEL 43-2982-4161232. FAX 43-2982-2317235. **Indexed:** A.I.C.P., Amer.Hist.& Life (1960-1973), Anthropol.Lit., Biol.Abstr., Br.Archaeol.Abstr., Hist.Abstr. **Document type:** proceedings.
—Linda Hall.

572   II   ISSN 0003-5556
ANTHROPOLOGIST.* (Text in English) 1954. irreg. $5. University of Delhi, Department of Anthropology, Delhi 110007, India. Ed. P.C. Biswas. **Indexed:** A.I.C.P., Anthropol.Lit.

570   US   ISSN 1061-1959
GN1
ANTHROPOLOGY AND ARCHEOLOGY OF EURASIA; a journal of translations from Soviet sources. 1962. q. $110 to individuals (foreign $160); institutions $460 (foreign $520) (effective 1997). M.E. Sharpe, Inc., 80 Business Park Dr., Armonk, NY 10504. TEL 914-273-1800; 800-541-6563. FAX 914-273-2106. Ed. Marjorie M. Balzer. R&P contact: Ginny Chandoha. adv.: page $300; 5 x 8; adv. contact: Barbara Ladd. index. (back issues avail.) **Indexed:** A.I.C.P., Abstr.Anthropol., Anthropol.Lit., ASCA, Curr.Cont., SSCI. **Document type:** academic/scholarly publication.
—BLDSC (1546.502670); Genuine Article; SWETS; UMI; UnCover. **CCC.**
     Formerly: Soviet Anthropology and Archeology (ISSN 0038-528X)
     Refereed Serial

ANTHROPOLOGY

572 370   US   ISSN 0161-7761
ANTHROPOLOGY & EDUCATION QUARTERLY. 1970. q. $40 to individuals; institutions $60 (effective 1996). (Council on Anthropology and Education) American Anthropological Association, 4350 N. Fairfax Dr., Ste. 640, Arlington, VA 22203-1621. TEL 703-528-1902. URL: http://www.ameranthassn.org/caepubs.htm. Ed. Kathryn Anderson-Levitt. R&P contact: Terry Clifford. adv.: $220; trim 6 x 9; adv. contact: Terry Clifford. bk.rev. circ. 1,000. (also avail. in microform from UMI; reprint service avail. from UMI) **Indexed:** A.I.C.P., Anthropol.Lit., Arts & Hum.Cit.Ind., ASCA, C.I.J.E., Child.Lit.Abstr., Cont.Pg.Educ., Curr.Cont., Educ.Ind., Educ.Tech.Abstr., Lang.& Lang.Behav.Abstr., Mid.East: Abstr.& Ind., Mult.Ed.Abstr., Psychol.Abstr. (1985-), Sociol.Abstr., Sociol.Educ.Abstr., SOMA, Sp.Ed.Needs Abstr., SSCI, Stud.Wom.Abstr., Tech.Educ.Abstr. **Document type:** academic/scholarly publication.
—BLDSC (1546.502700); Genuine Article; KR SourceOne; SWETS; UMI; UnCover.
  Former titles: Council on Anthropology and Education Quarterly (ISSN 0098-2881); C A E Newsletter.
  Description: Publishes anthropological research in education, as well as discussions of educational development and the teaching of anthropology.

572   US
GN1
ANTHROPOLOGY AND HUMANISM. 1974. s-a. $35 to non-members and institutions; members $20 (effective 1996). American Anthropological Association, 4350 N. Fairfax Dr., Ste. 640, Arlington, VA 22203-1621. TEL 703-528-1902. URL: http://www.ameranthass.org/shapubs.htm. Ed. Edith Turner. R&P contact: Terry Clifford. adv. contact: Terry Clifford. bk.rev. circ. 455. (back issues avail.) **Indexed:** Abstr.Anthropol., Anthropol.Lit., E.I., Mid.East: Abstr.& Ind. **Document type:** academic/scholarly publication.
—SWETS; UMI; UnCover.
  Formerly (until 1992): Anthropology and Humanism Quarterly (ISSN 0193-5615)
  Description: Scholarly journal concerned with what it is to be human; contributions from all major fields of anthropology, including physical anthropology, archaeology, linguistics and ethnology.

306.461   UK   ISSN 1364-8470
ANTHROPOLOGY & MEDICINE. vol.4, 1997. 3/yr. £48 to individuals; institutions £98 (effective 1997). Carfax Publishing Co., P.O. Box 25, Abingdon, Oxon OX14 3UE, England. TEL 44-1235-401000. FAX 44-1235-401550. E-mail: enquiries@carfax.co.uk. (N. American subscr. to: Carfax Publishing Co., 875-81 Massachusetts Ave., Cambridge, MA 02139. FAX 617-354-6875) Ed. Sushrut Jadhav. **Document type:** academic/scholarly publication.
—CCC.
  Description: Publishes original papers within the broad framework of medical anthropology and now addresses a world-wide audience.

572   US   ISSN 0098-1605
GN2
ANTHROPOLOGY NEWSLETTER. (Includes: Research Reports) 1947. m. (except June, July and Aug.). $55 to individuals; institutions $75 (effective 1996). American Anthropological Association, 4350 N. Fairfax Dr., Ste. 640, Arlington, VA 22203-1621. TEL 703-528-1902. Ed. Susan Skomal. R&P contact: Terry Clifford. adv.: page $1650; trim 11 1/2 x 15; adv. contact: Terry Clifford. bibl.; illus. circ. 10,000. (tabloid format; also avail. in microfiche; reprint service avail.) **Document type:** newsletter.
  Formerly: American Anthropological Association. Newsletter (ISSN 0002-7286)
  Description: News of interest to anthropologists; association affairs, departments and people, jobs, grants and support, brief research reports, and announcements.

572 153   US   ISSN 1053-4202
                  CODEN: ATCNEI
ANTHROPOLOGY OF CONSCIOUSNESS. 1985. q. $42 to individuals; institutions $56 (effective 1997). American Anthropological Association, Society for the Anthropology of Consciousness, 4350 N. Fairfax Dr., Ste. 640, Arlington, VA 22203-1621. TEL 703-528-1902. E-mail: 71554.1033@compuserve.com; URL: http://www.ameranthassn.org/sacpubs.htm. Ed. Lisa Ann Mertz. R&P contact: Rick Custer. bk.rev.; circ. 250 (paid). (back issues avail.) **Indexed:** Abstr.Anthropol., Anthropol.Lit. **Document type:** academic/scholarly publication.
—BLDSC (1546.502770).
  Former titles (until vol.5, 1989): A A S C Quarterly (ISSN 1045-4330); A A S C Newsletter (ISSN 0897-2672)
  Description: Interdisciplinary forum addressing the cross-cultural dimension of human consciousness from empirical, experimental, and theoretical perspectives.
Refereed Serial

301   US   ISSN 0883-024X
                  CODEN: AWORE9
ANTHROPOLOGY OF WORK REVIEW. 1983. q. $18 (effective 1996). (Society for the Anthropology of Work) American Anthropological Association, 4350 N. Fairfax Dr., Ste. 640, Arlington, VA 22203-1621. TEL 703-528-1902. FAX 703-528-3546. Ed. Rose-Marie Chierici. R&P contact: Terry Clifford. **Document type:** academic/scholarly publication.
—BLDSC (1546.515000).
  Description: Presents articles, reviews and notes from the perspectives of sociocultural, biological, archeological, linguistic, and/or applied anthropology.

301.2   II
ANTHROPOLOGY RESEARCH ASSOCIATION. RESEARCH BULLETIN. (Text in English) 1973. q. $5. University of Lucknow, Anthropology Research Association, Department of Anthropology, Badshaw Bagh, Lucknow, Uttar Pradesh, India. Ed. S.M. Mujtaba. adv. circ. 200. **Document type:** bulletin.

306.05   UK   ISSN 0268-540X
GN1
ANTHROPOLOGY TODAY. 1974. bi-m. £31($49) (effective 1997). Royal Anthropological Institute of Great Britain and Ireland, 50 Fitzroy St., London W1P 5HS, England. TEL 44-171-387-0455. FAX 44-171-383-4235. (Subscr. to: Turpin Distribution Services Ltd., Blackhorse Rd., Letchworth, Herts. SG6 1HN, England. TEL 44-1462-672555. FAX 44-1462-480947) Ed. Jonathan Benthall. R&P contact: Jonathan Benthall. adv. contact: Jonathan Benthall. bk.rev.; bibl.; film rev.; illus. circ. 2,800. (also avail. in microform from UMI; reprint service avail. from UMI) **Indexed:** A.I.C.P., Anthropol.Lit., Br.Archaeol.Abstr., Per.Islam. (1991-). **Document type:** academic/scholarly publication.
●Also available on CD-ROM.
—BLDSC (1546.512600); SWETS; UMI; UnCover.
  Incorporates (in 1985): R A I N: Royal Anthropological Institute News (ISSN 0307-6776)
  Description: Discusses a wide range of topical, anthropological and ethnographic subjects worldwide.

570   US   ISSN 0003-5564
ANTHROPOLOGY U C L A. 1969. a. $10 to individuals; institutions $15. University of California at Los Angeles, Department of Anthropology, 405 Hilgard Ave., Los Angeles, CA 90024. TEL 310-825-2055. Ed. Whitney White. adv.; bk.rev.; charts; circ. 250 (paid). (reprint service avail. from ISI) **Indexed:** Abstr.Anthropol., Anthropol.Lit., Curr.Cont., Mid.East: Abstr.& Ind., SSCI. **Document type:** academic/scholarly publication.
—BLDSC (1546.514000); UnCover.
  Description: Publishes articles in all fields and subfields of anthropology.
Refereed Serial

572 410   SZ   ISSN 0257-9774
GN1
ANTHROPOS; revue internationale d'ethnologie et de linguistique. (Text in English, French, German) 1906. 2/yr. 180 SFr. (effective 1996). (Anthropos Institut) Editions Saint-Paul, Perolles 42, CH-1700 Fribourg, Switzerland. TEL 41-37-864331. FAX 41-37-864330. bk.rev.; abstr.; bibl.; charts; illus.; index, cum.index. circ. 1,000. **Indexed:** A.I.C.P., Bibl.Ling., Curr.Cont., IBR, M.L.A., Mid.East: Abstr.& Ind., Psychol.Abstr., RILM, So.Pac.Per.Ind., Soc.Sci.Ind. **Document type:** academic/scholarly publication.
—BLDSC (1546.519300); Genuine Article; KR SourceOne; SWETS; UMI.
  Description: Discusses ethnological issues.

ANTHROPOS; studies in paleontology and geomorphology. see *PALEONTOLOGY*

572   IT   ISSN 0391-3163
ANTHROPOS. 1979. irreg., no.30, 1996. price varies. Liguori Editore s.r.l., Via Posillipo 394, 80123 Naples, Italy. TEL 39-81-7206111. FAX 39-81-7206244. Ed. Vittorio Lanternari; Pub. Guido Liguori. adv. contact: Maria Liguori. **Document type:** monographic series.

572   VE   ISSN 0254-1629
ANTHROPOS. 1980. 2/yr. Bs.60($10) Instituto Superior Salesiano de Filosofia y Educacion, Avda. El Liceo-Apdo. 43, 1201 A-Los Teques, Venezuela. bk.rev. **Indexed:** ASSIA.

573   GR   ISSN 1105-2155
ANTHROPOS: YEARBOOK IN ANTHROPOLOGY. 1974. a. $50. Anthropological Association of Greece, 5 Daphnomili St., 114 71 Athens, Greece. TEL 30-1-3610-251. Ed. Aris N. Poulianos. bk.rev. circ. 1,000. **Indexed:** A.I.C.P., Bibl.& Ind.Geol. **Document type:** academic/scholarly publication.
  Description: Covers physical anthropology, prehistory, and ethnology.

ANTHROPOZOOLOGICA. see *BIOLOGY — Zoology*

ANTHROPOZOOLOGICA NUMERO SPECIAL. see *BIOLOGY — Zoology*

156 591   US   ISSN 0892-7936
QL85
ANTHROZOOS; a multidisciplinary journal on the interactions of people and animals. 1987. q. $40 to individuals (foreign $50). Delta Society, 289 Perimeter Rd. E., Renton, WA 98055-1329. TEL 206-226-7357. FAX 206-235-1076. Ed. Andrew Rowan. adv.; bk.rev.; abstr.; index. circ. 1,200. (back issues avail.) **Indexed:** Anim.Behav.Abstr., Arts & Hum.Cit.Ind., ASCA, Bibl.Agri., Curr.Cont., Environ.Abstr., Environ.Per.Bibl. (1989-), Ind.Vet., InterActions Bibl. (1989-), Key Word Ind.Wildl.Res., Psychol.Abstr. (1987-), Rural Devel.Abstr., Sci.Cit.Ind., Small Anim.Abstr., Sociol.Abstr., Sport Fish.Abstr., SSCI, Wild.Rev. **Document type:** academic/scholarly publication.
—BLDSC (1546.670000); CIS; Genuine Article; UnCover. **CCC.**
  Description: Explore impact of animals on human health and culture.
Refereed Serial

301   DK   ISSN 0906-3021
ANTROPOLOGI. Variant title: Tidsskriftet Antropologi. (Text in Danish, Norwegian and Swedish; summaries in English) 1977. 2/yr. $42 to individuals; institutions $52. Foreningen Stofskifte, Koebenhavns Universitet, Institut for Antropologi, Frederiksholms Kanal 4, DK-1220 Copenhagen K, Denmark. TEL 45-35-32-34-72. FAX 45-35-32-34-65. E-mail: tidsskrift.antropologi@anthro.ku.dk. Ed. Kennet Pedersen. adv.; bk.rev.; illus. circ. 750. **Indexed:** Anthropol.Lit. **Document type:** academic/scholarly publication.
  Former titles: Tidskrift for Antropologi; (until Mar. 1990): Stofskifte (ISSN 0108-1012)

572   BO
ANTROPOLOGIA. 1979. s-a. Bol.$180($8) Instituto Nacional de Antropologia, Centro de Documentacion Antropologica, Casilla 20898, La Paz, Bolivia. Ed.Bd. bk.rev. (looseleaf format; also avail. in microfilm; back issues avail.)

ANTHROPOLOGY

572   PE
ANTROPOLOGIA ANDINA. 1976. a. $10. Centro de Estudios Andinos Cuzco, Apartado 582, Cuzco, Peru. Ed. J. Flores Ochoa. adv.; bk.rev. circ. 1,000. **Indexed:** A.I.C.P.

572   IT   ISSN 0392-9035
ANTROPOLOGIA CONTEMPORANEA. q. L.100000 (foreign L.150000). Editrice Sedicesimo, Via Mannelli 29r, 50136 Florence, Italy. TEL 055-2476781. FAX 055-2478568. **Indexed:** Anthropol.Lit.

572 972   MX
F1219
ANTROPOLOGIA E HISTORIA.* 1960. irreg. price varies. Instituto Nacional de Antropologia e Historia, Cordoba 45, 06700 Mexico 7, D.F., Mexico. Ed. Jorge Gurria Lacroix. illus. **Indexed:** A.I.C.P., Hisp.Amer.Per.Ind. (1970-1980).
     Formerly (until 1976): Instituto Nacional de Antropologia e Historia. Boletin (ISSN 0020-4102)

301.2   EC   ISSN 1018-7537
ANTROPOLOGIA ECUATORIANA.* 1978. irreg. S/50 per no. Casa de la Cultura Ecuatoriana, Seccion Academica de Antropologia y Arqueologia, Av. 6 de Diciembre 794, Casilla 67, Quito, Ecuador.

572   PO   ISSN 0870-0990
GN1
ANTROPOLOGIA PORTUGUESA. (Text in Portuguese; summaries in English or French) 1983. a. $11.50 (effective 1995). Universidade de Coimbra, Museu e Laboratorio Antropologico, 3000 Coimbra, Portugal. TEL 351-39-23491. FAX 351-39-23491. E-mail: bicker@gemini.ci.uc.ft. Dir. Manuel Laranjeira Rodrigues de Areia. Pub. Joao Manuel Bicker. R&P contact: M.L. Rodrigues Areia. bk.rev. circ. 1,000. **Indexed:** Anthropol.Lit. **Document type:** academic/scholarly publication.
     Refereed Serial

301   MX   ISSN 0186-9787
ANTROPOLOGIA Y TECNICA. 1988? s-a.? Universidad Nacional Autonoma de Mexico, Instituto de Investigaciones Antropologicas, Circuito Exterior, Ciudad Universitaria, 04510 Mexico, D.F., Mexico. TEL 52-5-6229531. FAX 52-5-6229651. Ed. Luis Torres M.

572   VE   ISSN 0003-6110
F2229
ANTROPOLOGICA. (Text in Spanish; occasionally in English.) 1956. 2/yr. Bs.180($25) to individuals; institutions Bs.200($28). Fundacion la Salle de Ciencias Naturales, Instituto Caribe de Antropologia y Sociologia, Av. Boyaca-Mariperez, Apdo. 1930, Carcacas 1010A, Venezuela. FAX 781-5732. TELEX 21-553 FLASA. Ed. Werner Wilbert. adv.; bk.rev.; charts; illus.; cum.index: nos.1-62. circ. 1,000. **Indexed:** A.I.C.P., Abstr.Anthropol., Anthropol.Lit., Hisp.Amer.Per.Ind. (1970-), IBR, SSCI.
     Description: Covers original research in anthropology and related disciplines conducted in the Caribbean and South America north of the equator.

572   MX
ANTROPOLOGICAS. 1964; N.S. 1992. s-a. Mex.$30. Universidad Nacional Autonoma de Mexico, Instituto de Investigaciones Antropologicas, Circuito Exterior, Ciudad Universitaria, 04510 Mexico, D.F., Mexico. TEL 52-5-6229531. FAX 52-5-6229651. Ed. Lorenzo Ochoa S. bibl. **Document type:** academic/scholarly publication.

301 599.9   SW   ISSN 0345-0902
GN301
ANTROPOLOGISKA STUDIER. (Text in English, Swedish) 1971. q. SEK 175 to individuals; institutions SEK 250 (foreign individual SEK 195; institutions SEK 270) (effective through 1998). Antropologfoereningen vid Stockholms Universitet, Socialantropologiska Institutionen, S-106 91 Stockholm, Sweden. TEL 46-8-16-33-71. FAX 46-8-15-88-94. E-mail: anna.hallselstrom@ socant.su.se. Eds. Anna Hasselstroem, Per Staahlberg. bk.rev.; charts; illus.; index, cum.index. circ. 500. **Indexed:** Anthropol.Lit. **Document type:** academic/scholarly publication.
     Formerly (until 1971): Antropolognytt (ISSN 0003-6129)
     Refereed Serial

572   MX
ANUARIO (YEAR) LABORATORIO DE ANTROPOLOGIA. a. Universidad de Guadalajara, Direccion de Publicaciones, Apdo. Postal 4-010, 44430 Guadalajara, Jalisco, Mexico. circ. 1,000.

572   BL   ISSN 0102-4302
ANUARIO ANTROPOLOGICO. 1976. a. $20. Edicoes Tempo Brasileiro Ltda, Rua Gago Coutinho 61, C.P. 16099, ZC-01 Laranjeiras, Rio de Janeiro, Brazil. Dir. Roberto Cardosa de Oliveira. **Indexed:** Anthropol.Lit.

ANUARIO DE ESTUDIOS AMERICANOS. see *HISTORY — History Of North And South America*

572 917.206   MX
F1219
ANUARIO DE ESTUDIOS INDIGENAS. 1986. a. Mex.$18($8) or exchange basis. Instituto de Estudios Indigenas, Dr. Felipe Flores 14, San Cristobal de las Casas, 29200 Chiapas, Mexico. FAX 83534. E-mail: risoch@montebello.unach.mx. (back issues avail.) **Document type:** academic/scholarly publication.
     Formerly: Centro de Estudios Indigenas. Anuario (ISSN 0188-4239)
     Description: Regional studies about Chiapas.
     Refereed Serial

572   MX   ISSN 0304-2596
E51
ANUARIO INDIGENISTA/INDIANIST YEARBOOK. (Supplement to: America Indigena) (Text in Spanish; summaries in English) 1962. a. $20 (or included in subscr. to America Indigena). Instituto Indigenista Interamericano, Apdo. Postal 20315, 01001 Mexico DF, Mexico. TEL 525-5680819. FAX 525-6521274. bk.rev.; circ. controlled. (processed; reprint service avail. from SWZ) **Indexed:** A.I.C.P., Amer.Hist.& Life (1963-1990), (1992-), Anthropol.Lit., Hisp.Amer.Per.Ind. (1970), Hist.Abstr. (1963-1990), (1992-), Int.Lab.Doc.
     Formerly: Boletin Indigenista.
     Description: Provides news about the indians and reports on the institution's activities.

APPLICATIONS ET TRANSFERTS DE LA S E L A F. see *LINGUISTICS*

APPLIED HUMAN SCIENCE; journal of physiological anthropology. see *BIOLOGY — Physiology*

ARCHAEOLOGIA AUSTRIACA; Beitraege zur Palaeantologie, Ur- und Fruehgeschichte Oesterreichs. see *ARCHAEOLOGY*

ARCHAEOLOGICAL SOCIETY OF NEW JERSEY. NEWSLETTER. see *ARCHAEOLOGY*

ARCHAEOLOGIE OESTERREICHS. see *ARCHAEOLOGY*

ARCHAEOLOGY IN MONTANA. see *ARCHAEOLOGY*

ARCHAEOLOGY IN OCEANIA. see *ARCHAEOLOGY*

301.2   AU   ISSN 0066-6513
GR1
ARCHIV FUER VOELKERKUNDE. 1946. a. S.415. Verein Freunde der Voelkerkunde, Neue Burg, A-1014 Vienna 1, Austria. TEL 43-1-53430-0. FAX 43-1-5355320. Eds. Gerard Van Bussel, Axel Steinmann. bk.rev. circ. 800. (reprint service avail. from KTO) **Indexed:** A.I.C.P., Anthropol.Lit., Bibl.Ling., Curr.Cont., E.I., IBR. **Document type:** academic/scholarly publication.

572   IT   ISSN 0373-3009
GN1
ARCHIVIO PER L'ANTROPOLOGIA E LA ETNOLOGIA. (Text in English, French and Italian) 1871. a. L.180000 (foreign L.200000) (effective 1997). Societa Italiana di Antropologia e Etnologia, Palazzo Nonfinito, Via del Proconsolo, 12, 50122 Florence, Italy. TEL 39-55-2396449. FAX 39-55-219438. Pub. Cieto Corrain. **Indexed:** A.I.C.P., Anthropol.Lit. **Document type:** academic/scholarly publication.
     —Linda Hall.

ARCHIVO HISTORICO DIOCESANO DE SAN CRISTOBAL DE LAS CASAS. BOLETIN. see *HISTORY — History Of North And South America*

572 998   US   ISSN 0066-6939
G600   CODEN: ARANBP
ARCTIC ANTHROPOLOGY. 1962. s-a. $33 to individuals; institutions $96 (effective 1997). (University of Wisconsin at Madison) University of Wisconsin Press, Journal Division, 114 N. Murray St., Madison, WI 53715. TEL 608-262-4952. FAX 608-262-7560. URL: http://www.wisc.edu/wisconsinpress/journals.html; http://www.press.uchicago.uede/cgi-bi/hfs.cgi/66/wisconsin/arct.html. Ed. Allen McCartney. index. circ. 800. (also avail. in microform from UMI; back issues avail.; reprint service avail. from UMI,KTO) **Indexed:** A.I.C.P., Abstr.Anthropol., Amer.Bibl.Slavic & E.Eur.Stud., Amer.Hist.& Life (1970-1972), (1982-), Anthropol.Lit., Arts & Hum.Cit.Ind., ASCA, Bibl.& Ind.Geol., Bibl.Ling., Biol.Abstr., Curr.Cont., Geo.Abstr.H.G., Hist.Abstr. (1970-1972), (1982-), IDA, NAA, SSCI. **Document type:** academic/scholarly publication.
     —BLDSC (1663.070000); Genuine Article; KR SourceOne; SWETS; UMI; UnCover. **CCC.**
     Description: Covers arctic and subarctic anthropology, archaeology, ethnology and ethnohistory, linguistics, human biology and related fields, with emphasis on circumpolar anthropology.
     Refereed Serial

ARCTIQUE. see *LINGUISTICS*

913   US   ISSN 0271-0641
ARIZONA STATE UNIVERSITY ANTHROPOLOGICAL RESEARCH PAPERS. 1969. irreg. (2-5/yr.), no.47, 1995. price varies. Arizona State University, Department of Anthropology, Tempe, AZ 85287-2402. TEL 602-965-7596. FAX 602-965-7671. E-mail: atgac@asuvm.inre.asu.edu. Ed. G.A. Clark. R&P contact: G.A. Clark. circ. 750 (controlled). **Indexed:** Anthropol.Lit. **Document type:** monographic series.
     Description: Publishes original research in archaeology, physical anthropology, social and cultural anthropology and linguistics.

ARKANSAS AMATEUR. see *ARCHAEOLOGY*

ASCLEPIO; archivo iberoamericano de historia de la medicina. see *MEDICAL SCIENCES*

ASIE ET MONDE INSULINDIEN. see *LINGUISTICS*

570   US   ISSN 0066-9172
ASSOCIATION FOR SOCIAL ANTHROPOLOGY IN OCEANIA. MONOGRAPH SERIES. 1970. irreg. price varies. University of Pittsburgh Press, 3347 Forbes Ave., Pittsburgh, PA 15261. TEL 800-666-2211. FAX 800-688-2877. (Also avail. from: UMI, 300 N. Zeeb Rd., Ann Arbor, MI 48106) Ed. Andrew Strathern; Pub. Cynthia Miller. R&P contact: Margie Bachman. **Indexed:** Sociol.Abstr. **Document type:** monographic series.

572   US   ISSN 1095-3000
ASSOCIATION FOR SOCIAL ANTHROPOLOGY IN OCEANIA NEWSLETTER. 1967. 3/yr. $35 to members; students $20; institutions $115. Association of Social Anthropology in Oceania, 2499 Kapiolani Blvd. No. 2403, Honolulu, HI 96826. TEL 808-943-0836. FAX 808-956-4893. E-mail: rensel@hawaii.edu; URL: http://www.soc.hawaii.edu/asao/padific/hawaiki.html. Ed. Jan Rensel. R&P contact: Jan Rensel. bk.rev. circ. 400. (looseleaf format; back issues avail.) **Document type:** academic/scholarly publication, newsletter.

ASSOCIATION FOR THE STUDY OF PLAY NEWSLETTER. see *PSYCHOLOGY*

572   US
ASSOCIATION OF SOCIAL ANTHROPOLOGISTS OF THE COMMONWEALTH. STUDIES. 1975. irreg. (Association of Social Anthropologists of the Commonwealth) John Wiley & Sons, Inc., Journals, 605 Third Ave., New York, NY 10158-0012. TEL 212-850-6000. FAX 212-850-6088. TELEX 12-7063. Ed.Bd. **Document type:** monographic series.

| 572 | DK | ISSN 1024-3275 |

ASUNTOS INDIGENAS. English edition: Indigenous Affairs (ISSN 1024-3283) (Supplement avail.: I W G I A Documento (ISSN 0108-9927)) (Text in Spanish) 1979. q. DKK 125($20) to individuals; institutions DKK 225($35) (includes IWGIA Documento). International Work Group for Indigenous Affairs - Grupo Internacional de Trabajo sobre Asuntos Indigenas, Fiolstraede 10, DK-1171 Copenhagen K, Denmark. TEL 45-33-12-47-24. FAX 45-33-14-77-49. Ed.Bd. cum.index. **Indexed:** HR Rep.
 Formerly (until 1994): Grupo Internacional de Trabajo sobre Asuntos Indigenas. Boletin (ISSN 0107-556X)
 Description: Discusses efforts in supporting indigenous peoples worldwide in their struggle against oppression.

| 572 950 | FR | ISSN 0993-538X |

ATELIER A S E M I. 1988. irreg., no.2, 1992. Editions de l' Ecole des Hautes Etudes en Sciences Sociales, 131 bd. St-Michel, 75005 Paris, France. TEL 33-1-40467080. FAX 33-1-44070889. E-mail: editions@ehess.fr; URL: http://www.ehess.fr/editions. (Dist. by: Centre Interinstitutionnel pour la Diffusion de Publications en Sciences Humaines, 131 bd. St-Michel, 75005 Paris, France. TEL 33-1-43544715. FAX 33-1-43548073)

| 301.2 390 | PL | ISSN 0067-0316 |

ATLAS POLSKICH STROJOW LUDOWYCH. (Text in Polish; summaries in English) 1949. irreg. price varies. Polskie Towarzystwo Ludoznawcze, Ul. Szewska 36, 50-139 Wroclaw, Poland. (Dist. by Ars Polona, Krakowskie Przedmiescie 7, Warsaw, Poland) Ed. Barbara Bazielich. circ. 1,500.

| 572 DU120 | AT | ISSN 0729-4352 |

AUSTRALIAN ABORIGINAL STUDIES. 1963. s-a. Aus.$35 (effective 1997). Australian Institute of Aboriginal and Torres Strait Islander Studies, P.O. Box 553, Canberra, A.C.T. 2601, Australia. TEL 61-6-2461111. FAX 61-6-2497310. Ed. Mary Edmunds. adv.; bk.rev.; film rev.; index; circ. controlled. **Indexed:** Abstr.Anthropol., Anthropol.Lit., Bibl.Ling., RILM. **Document type:** academic/scholarly publication.
 —UnCover.
 Formerly (until 1983): A I A S Newsletter (ISSN 0004-9344)

| 572 | GW | ISSN 0005-3856 |

BAESSLER ARCHIV; Beitraege zur Voelkerkunde. (Text in English, German) 1952. s-a. DM.158. (Museum fuer Voelkerkunde, Berlin) Dietrich Reimer Verlag, Unter den Eichen 57, 12203 Berlin, Germany. TEL 030-8314081. FAX 030-83163123. Eds. D. Eisleb, K. Helfrich. charts; illus.; maps. (also avail. in microfiche from IDC) **Indexed:** A.I.C.P., Anthropol.Lit., E.I., IBR. **Document type:** academic/scholarly publication.
 —CCC.

| 572 301.2 | US | |

BALLENA PRESS ANTHROPOLOGICAL PAPERS. 1973. irreg., no.46, 1997. price varies. Ballena Press, 823 Valparaiso Ave., Menlo Park, CA 94025. TEL 415-323-9261. FAX 415-883-4280. (Subscr. to: Box 2510, Novato, CA 94948) Ed. Sylvia Brakke Vane. R&P contact: Sylvia Brakke Vane. circ. 2,000. **Document type:** academic/scholarly publication.
 Description: Information on the Indians of California and the west.
 Refereed Serial

| 572 | SZ | ISSN 0067-4478 |

BASLER BEITRAEGE ZUR ETHNOLOGIE. (Text in German; summaries in French and English) 1965. irreg. 55 SFr. (Museum der Kulturen) Verlag Wepf und Co., Eisengasse 5, CH-4001 Basel, Switzerland. TEL 41-61-3119576. FAX 41-61-3119576. Ed. Alfred Buehler. **Indexed:** Bibl.& Ind.Geol. **Document type:** monographic series.
 Formerly (until 1966): Basler Beitraege zur Geographie und Ethnologie. Ethnologische Reihe.

| 305.89 | YU | ISSN 0353-9008 |

BASTINA; glasnik. Variant title: Glasnik Bastina. 1991. irreg. Institut za Proucavanje Kulture Srba, Crnogoraca, Hrvata i Muslimana, Valjevska 2, Pristina, Yugoslavia. Ed. Milenko Jevtovic.

AUERNHAEUSER AUS MITTELEUROPA; Aufmasse und Publikationen von Gerhard Eitzen. see *ARCHITECTURE*

BEAD FORUM. see *ARCHAEOLOGY*

| 739.27 301 NK3650 | CN | ISSN 0843-5499 |

BEADS. 1989. a. $20 (foreign $30) (effective 1997). Society of Bead Researchers, 1600 Liverpool Ct., Ottawa, ON K1A 0M5, Canada. TEL 613-990-4814. FAX 613-952-1756. E-mail: karlis-karklins@pch.gc.ca; URL: http://www.spiretech.com/~lester/sbr/index.htm. Ed. Karlis Karklins. adv.; bk.rev.; illus. circ. 1,200. (back issues avail.) **Document type:** academic/scholarly publication.
 Description: Fosters serious research on beads of all materials and periods.
 Refereed Serial

BEITRAEGE ZUR AFRIKAKUNDE. see *HISTORY — History Of Africa*

| 301.2 | GW | ISSN 0408-8514 |

BEITRAEGE ZUR MITTELAMERIKANISCHEN VOELKERKUNDE. 1953. irreg., no.14, 1977. price varies. (Hamburgisches Museum fuer Voelkerkunde) Klaus Renner Verlag, Am Hohenhang 8, 82069 Hohenschaeftlarn, Germany.

BEITRAEGE ZUR RHEINISCHEN VOLKSKUNDE. see *FOLKLORE*

BERNICE PAUAHI BISHOP MUSEUM, HONOLULU. OCCASIONAL PAPERS. see *SCIENCES: COMPREHENSIVE WORKS*

BERNICE PAUAHI BISHOP MUSEUM, HONOLULU. SPECIAL PUBLICATIONS. see *SCIENCES: COMPREHENSIVE WORKS*

| 301.2 | PY | |

BIBLIOTECA PARAGUAYA DE ANTROPOLOGIA. 1980. irreg., vol.20, 1993. price varies. Universidad Catolica Nuestra Senora de la Asuncion, Centro de Estudios Antropologicos, Casilla de Correo 1718, Asuncion, Paraguay. TEL 595-21-446251. FAX 595-21-445245. circ. 1,000. (back issues avail.)

| 572 305.8 | NE | ISSN 0067-8023 |

BIBLIOTHECA INDONESICA. (Text in English and various Indonesian languages) 1968. irreg., no. 26, 1986. price varies. (Koninklijk Instituut voor Taal-, Land- en Volkenkunde) K I T L V Press, P.O. Box 9515, 2300 RA Leiden, Netherlands. TEL 31-71-5272372. FAX 31-71-5272638. E-mail: kitlvpress@rullet.leidenuniv.nl. (back issues avail.) **Document type:** monographic series.
 —KNAW.
 Description: Details literature and poetry of numerous cultures in Indonesia. Aimed at anthropologists, linguists, historians and other scholars interested in Southeast Asia.

| 572 410 DS611 | NE | ISSN 0006-2294 CODEN: BTTVE2 |

BIJDRAGEN TOT DE TAAL-, LAND- EN VOLKENKUNDE. Short title: B K I. (Text in Dutch, English) 1853. 4/yr. fl.135 (effective 1996). (Koninklijk Instituut voor Taal-, Land- en Volkenkunde) K I T L V Press, P.O. Box 9515, 2300 RA Leiden, Netherlands. TEL 31-71-5272372. FAX 31-71-5272638. E-mail: kitlvpress@rullet.leidenuniv.nl. Ed. Dr. B. Arps. bk.rev.; illus.; index, cum.index. (back issues avail.; reprint service avail. from SWZ) **Indexed:** A.I.C.P., Amer.Hist.& Life, Anthropol.Lit., Arts & Hum.Cit.Ind., ASCA, Bibl.Ling., Curr.Cont., E.I., Hist.Abstr., M.L.A., MLA Intl.Bibl., Per.Islam. (1991-), SSCI. **Document type:** academic/scholarly publication.
 —Genuine Article; KR SourceOne; Linda Hall; SWETS; UnCover.
 Description: Focuses on the linguistics, anthropology and history of Southeast Asia, with particular emphasis on Indonesia.

| 572 | US | ISSN 0893-3111 |

BISHOP MUSEUM BULLETINS IN ANTHROPOLOGY. 1922. irreg., no.6, 1996. price varies. (Bernice Pauahi Bishop Museum) Bishop Museum Press, 1525 Bernice St., Box 19000-A, Honolulu, HI 96817. TEL 808-847-3511. FAX 808-841-8968. circ. 300. (reprint service avail.) **Indexed:** Biol.Abstr., Deep Sea Res.& Oceanogr.Abstr. **Document type:** bulletin.
 —BLDSC (2094.263030); CISTI; Linda Hall.
 Supersedes in part (in 1987): Bernice P. Bishop Museum Bulletin (ISSN 0005-9439)
 Description: Contains original and analytical materials on anthropology and archaeology of Hawaii and the Pacific Basin.

| 572 DS646.3 | US | ISSN 0006-7806 |

BORNEO RESEARCH BULLETIN.* 1969. s-a. $10. Borneo Research Council, Dept. of Anthropology, College of William & Mary, Box 8795, Williamsburg, VA 23187. Ed. V.H. Sutlive. bk.rev.; bibl. circ. 600. **Indexed:** A.I.C.P., Anthropol.Lit., Bibl.Ling., E.I., Herb.Abstr., IBR, Rural Devel.Abstr., World Agri.Econ.& Rural Sociol.Abstr. **Document type:** bulletin.
 —UnCover.

| 572 410 918.106 | BL | ISSN 0101-0484 |

BRAZIL. MUSEU DO INDIO. BOLETIM. DOCUMENTACAO. 1976. irreg., no.5, Dec. 1996. free. Museu do Indio, Biblioteca Marechal Rondon, Rua das Palmeiras 55, Botafogo, CEP 22270-070 Rio de Janeiro, RJ, Brazil. TEL 55-21-2868899. FAX 55-21-2868899. E-mail: museudoindio@ax.apc.org.br. **Document type:** monographic series.
 Incorporates (1974-1992): Brazil. Museu do Indio. Boletim. Antropologia (ISSN 0101-0433); (1979-1992): Brazil. Museu do Indio. Boletim. Etno-Historia (ISSN 0100-7475); (1980-1992): Brazil. Museu do Indio. Boletim. Linguistica (ISSN 0101-0530)

BRITISH CENTRE FOR DURKHEIMIAN STUDIES. OCCASIONAL PAPERS. see *SOCIOLOGY*

BRITISH FORUM FOR ETHNOMUSICOLOGY. NEWSLETTER. see *MUSIC*

BRITISH JOURNAL OF ETHNOMUSICOLOGY. see *MUSIC*

| 301.2 GN301 | BU | ISSN 0323-9268 |

BULGARSKA ETNOGRAFIIA. (Text in Bulgarian; summaries in English, Russian) 1975. s-a. price varies. (Bulgarska Akademiia na Naukite) Publishing House of the Bulgarian Academy of Sciences, Acad. G. Bonchev St., Bldg. 6, 1113 Sofia, Bulgaria. (Dist. by: Hemus, 6, Rouski Blvd., 1000 Sofia, Bulgaria) Ed. V. Hadzhinikolov. illus. circ. 580. (reprint service avail. from IRC) **Indexed:** A.I.C.P.

BULLETIN OF TIBETOLOGY. see *HISTORY — History Of Asia*

C I H M E C H. (Centro de Investigaciones Humanisticas de Mesoamerica y el Estado de Chiapas) see *ARCHAEOLOGY*

| 572 | BL | ISSN 0104-5679 |

CADERNOS DE CAMPO; revista dos alunos de pos-graduacao em antropologia. 1991. a. $9. Universidade de Sao Paulo, Programa de Pos-Graduacao em Antropologia Social, Dept. de Antropologia - USP, Caixa Postal 8105, 05508-900 Sao Paulo SP, Brazil. TEL 55-11-8183779. FAX 55-11-8183163. E-mail: mrufino@cat.cce.usp.br. Ed. Piero de Camargo Leirner. adv.; bk.rev.; abstr.bibl. **Document type:** academic/scholarly publication.
 Description: Covers ethnology, urban anthropology, anthropology of peasantry, anthropological theory, Brazilian anthropology. Articles and reviews written by students and teachers.

CAESARAUGUSTA. see *ARCHAEOLOGY*

ANTHROPOLOGY

301   FR   ISSN 0758-2714
GN51
CAHIERS D'ANTHROPOLOGIE ET BIOMETRIE HUMAINE. (Text in French; summaries in English, French) 1932. 2/yr. 230 F. Societe de Biometrie Humaine, 28 rue de Charenton, 75012 Paris, France. TEL 33-1-46330596. FAX 33-1-43408785. Ed. E.A. Cabanis. R&P contact: Ms. Pineau. adv. contact: Ms. Pineau. bk.rev.; bibl.; charts; illus.; index. circ. 600. Indexed: Anthropol.Lit., Biol.Abstr., Chem.Abstr., Excerp.Med., Nutr.Abstr., Psychol.Abstr., Ref.Zh. **Document type:** proceedings.
—CISTI; Linda Hall.
    Former titles (until 1983): Societe de Biometrie Humaine. Revue (ISSN 0183-5688); Biometrie Humaine (ISSN 0006-3428); Biotypologie.

305.896 960   FR   ISSN 0008-0055
DT1
CAHIERS D'ETUDES AFRICAINES. (Text in English, French) 1960. q. 270 F. to individuals; institutions 420 F. (foreign 480 F.) (effective 1998). Editions de l' Ecole des Hautes Etudes en Sciences Sociales, 131 bd. St-Michel, 75005 Paris, France. TEL 33-1-40467080. FAX 33-1-44070889. E-mail: editions@ehess.fr; URL: http://www.ehess.fr/editions. (Dist. by: Centre Interinstitutionnel pour la Diffusion de Publications en Sciences Humaines, 131 bd. St-Michel, 75005 Paris, France. TEL 33-1-43544715. FAX 33-1-43548073; Subscr. to: EHESS Service Abonnements, 55 route de Longjumeau, F-91387 Chilly-Mazarin Cedex, France. TEL 33-1-64547695. FAX 33-1-64547665) Ed. J.L. Amselle. adv.; bk.rev.; charts; illus. circ. 760. (also avail. in microfiche from IDC) Indexed: A.B.C.Pol.Sci., A.I.C.P., Amer.Hist.& Life (1966-), Anthropol.Lit., Arts & Hum.Cit.Ind., Bibl.Ling., Curr.Cont., Curr.Cont.Africa, Documentatieblad, Geo.Abstr.H.G., Hist.Abstr. (1966-), IBR, IDA, Int.Polit.Sci.Abstr., Lang.& Lang.Behav.Abstr., M.L.A., MLA Intl.Bibl., Rural Devel.Abstr., SSCI, World Agri.Econ.& Rural Sociol.Abstr. **Document type:** academic/scholarly publication.
—BLDSC (2948.868000); KR SourceOne; SWETS; UnCover.

572   FR   ISSN 0068-5046
CAHIERS DE L'HOMME. 1961. irreg., no.33, 1995. price varies. Editions de l' Ecole des Hautes Etudes en Sciences Sociales, 131 bd. St-Michel, 75005 Paris, France. TEL 33-1-40467080. FAX 33-1-44070889. E-mail: editions@ehess.fr; URL: http://www.ehess.fr/editions. (Dist. by: Centre Interinstitutionnel pour la Diffusion de Publications en Sciences Humaines, 131 bd. St-Michel, 75005 Paris, France. TEL 33-1-43544715. FAX 33-1-43548073)

CAHIERS DE PALEOANTHROPOLOGIE. see *PALEONTOLOGY*

CAHIERS DE SOCIOLOGIE ECONOMIQUE ET CULTURELLE. see *SOCIOLOGY*

CAHIERS DES EXPLORATEURS. see *GEOGRAPHY*

572 301   UK   ISSN 0068-6719
CAMBRIDGE PAPERS IN SOCIAL ANTHROPOLOGY. 1958. irreg. price varies. Cambridge University Press, Edinburgh Bldg., Shaftesbury Rd., Cambridge CB2 2RU, England. TEL 44-1223-312393. FAX 44-1223-315052. TELEX 851817256. E-mail: information@cup.cam.ac.uk; URL: http://www.cup.cam.ac.uk. (N. American addr.: Cambridge University Press, Journals Dept., 40 W. 20th St., New York, NY 10011. TEL 212-924-3900. FAX 212-691-3239) Ed. Jack Goody. R&P contact: Linda Nicol. **Document type:** monographic series.

599.9   UK   ISSN 0957-0306
                        CODEN: CSBAEN
CAMBRIDGE STUDIES IN BIOLOGICAL ANTHROPOLOGY. 1958. irreg. Cambridge University Press, Edinburgh Bldg., Shaftesbury Rd., Cambridge CB2 2RU, England. TEL 44-1223-312393. FAX 44-1223-315052. TELEX 817256. E-mail: information@cup.cam.ac.uk; URL: http://www.cup.cam.ac.uk. (N. American addr.: Cambridge University Press, 40 W. 20th St., New York, NY 10011. TEL 212-924-3900. FAX 212-691-3239) R&P contact: Linda Nicol. **Document type:** monographic series.
—BLDSC (3015.992400); KNAW.

572   UK
CAMBRIDGE STUDIES IN CULTURAL SYSTEMS. 1977. irreg. price varies. Cambridge University Press, Edinburgh Bldg., Shaftesbury Rd., Cambridge CB2 2RU, England. TEL 44-1223-312393. FAX 44-1223-315052. TELEX 851817256. E-mail: information@cup.cam.ac.uk; URL: http://www.cup.cam.ac.uk. (N. American addr.: Cambridge University Press, 40 W. 20th St., New York, NY 10011. TEL 212-924-3900. FAX 212-691-3239) Ed. Clifford Geertz. R&P contact: Linda Nicol. **Document type:** monographic series.

572   UK   ISSN 0955-2405
CAMBRIDGE STUDIES IN ORAL AND LITERATE CULTURE. 1981. irreg. price varies. Cambridge University Press, Edinburgh Bldg., Shaftesbury Rd., Cambridge CB2 2RU, England. TEL 44-1223-312393. FAX 44-1223-315052. TELEX 851817256. E-mail: information@cup.cam.ac.uk; URL: http://www.cup.cam.ac.uk. (N. American addr.: Cambridge University Press, Journals Dept., 40 W. 20th St., New York, NY 10011. TEL 212-924-3900. FAX 212-691-3239) Eds. P. Burke, R. Finnegan. R&P contact: Linda Nicol. **Document type:** monographic series.
—BLDSC (3015.995520).

572   UK   ISSN 0068-6794
CAMBRIDGE STUDIES IN SOCIAL ANTHROPOLOGY. 1967. irreg. price varies. Cambridge University Press, Edinburgh Bldg., Shaftesbury Rd., Cambridge CB2 2RU, England. TEL 44-1223-312393. FAX 44-1223-315052. TELEX 851817256. E-mail: information@cup.cam.ac.uk; URL: http://www.cup.cam.ac.uk. (N. Amer. addr.: Cambridge University Press, Journals Dept., 40 W. 20th St., New York, NY 10011. TEL 212-924-3900. FAX 212-691-3239) Ed. Jack Goody. R&P contact: Linda Nicol. Indexed: Math.R. **Document type:** monographic series.

305.8   CN   ISSN 0315-8705
F1035.A1
CANADIAN ETHNIC STUDIES ASSOCIATION. BULLETIN/SOCIETE CANADIENNE D'ETUDES ETHNIQUES. BULLETIN. (Text in English, French) 1974. irreg., vol.21, no.1, 1995. Can.$45 membership; institutions Can.$55; students Can.$15 (effective 1997). Canadian Ethnic Studies Association, Centre d'Etudes Ethniques, University of Montreal, P.O. Box 6128, Succ. Centre-Ville, Montreal, PQ H3C 3J7, Canada. TEL 514-343-6111. FAX 514-343-7078. E-mail: scee@ere.umontreal.ca. Ed. James Frideres. R&P contact: Michel Ledoux. bk.rev.; bibl. circ. 1,000. Indexed: Can.Rev.Comp.Lit., M.L.A., Mult.Ed.Abstr., Sp.Ed.Needs Abstr. **Document type:** academic/scholarly publication.
    Description: Provides information on the Association, current developments in ethnic studies, research projects, forthcoming meetings, conferences and publications.

301   CN   ISSN 0316-1897
CANADIAN MUSEUM OF CIVILIZATION. MERCURY SERIES. CANADIAN CENTRE FOR FOLK CULTURE STUDIES. PAPER (NO.)/MUSEE CANADIEN DES CIVILISATIONS. COLLECTION MERCURE. CENTRE CANADIEN D'ETUDES SUR LA CULTURE TRADITIONNELLE. DOSSIER. (Text in English, French) 1972. irreg. price varies. Canadian Museum of Civilization, 100 Laurier St., P.O. Box 3100, Stn. B, Hull, PQ J8X 4H2, Canada. E-mail: publications@cmcc.muse.digital.ca. Ed. Jean-Francois Blanchette. R&P contact: Nicole Chamberland. adv. contact: Pam Coulas. **Document type:** academic/scholarly publication, monographic series, government publication.

572   CN   ISSN 0316-1862
CANADIAN MUSEUM OF CIVILIZATION. MERCURY SERIES. CANADIAN ETHNOLOGY SERVICE. PAPER (NO.)/MUSEE CANADIEN DES CIVILISATIONS. COLLECTION MERCURE. SERVICE CANADIEN D'ETHNOLOGIE. DOSSIER. (Text in English, French) 1972. irreg. price varies. Canadian Museum of Civilization, 100 Laurier St., P.O. Box 3100, Stn. B, Hull, PQ J8X 4H2, Canada. E-mail: publications@cmcc.muse.digital.ca. Ed. Jean-Francois Blanchette. R&P contact: Nicole Chamberland. adv. contact: Pam Coulas. Indexed: Anthropol.Lit. **Document type:** academic/scholarly publication, monographic series, government publication.
    Description: Designed to permit the rapid dissemination of information pertaining to the disciplines in which the museum is active.

THE CANADIAN REVIEW OF SOCIOLOGY AND ANTHROPOLOGY/REVUE CANADIENNE DE SOCIOLOGIE ET D'ANTHROPOLOGIE. see *SOCIOLOGY*

572   AT   ISSN 0314-9099
GN1
CANBERRA ANTHROPOLOGY; an Australian journal of anthropology. 1977. 2/yr. Aus.$24 (foreign Aus.$30). Australian National University, Research School of Pacific and Asian Studies, Department of Anthropology, Canberra, A.C.T. 0200, Australia. TEL 61-6-2490769. FAX 61-6-2494896. Ed. Michael Young. (back issues avail.) Indexed: Anthropol.Lit., E.I., So.Pac.Per.Ind. **Document type:** academic/scholarly publication.
—UnCover.
    Refereed Serial

572   VI
CARIBBEAN ETHNOLOGY. 1992. q. Caribbean Anthropological Foundation, Inc., P.O. Box 1848, Frederiksted, St. Croix, VI 00841. Ed. A.E. Figueredo.

572 972.9   NE   ISSN 0921-9781
CARIBBEAN SERIES. (Text in Dutch, English) 1985. irreg., vol.16, 1995. price varies. (Koninklijk Instituut voor Taal-, Land- en Volkenkunde) K I T L V Press, P.O. Box 9515, 2300 RA Leiden, Netherlands. TEL 31-71-5272372. FAX 31-71-5272638. E-mail: ktlvpress@rullet.leidenuniv.nl. (back issues avail.) **Document type:** monographic series.
—KNAW.

CARNEGIE MUSEUM OF NATURAL HISTORY. ANNALS. see *SCIENCES: COMPREHENSIVE WORKS*

CARNEGIE MUSEUM OF NATURAL HISTORY. BULLETIN. see *SCIENCES: COMPREHENSIVE WORKS*

CARNIVORE; interfacing biology, anthropology and environmental studies. see *BIOLOGY*

301.2   US
CASE STUDIES IN CULTURAL ANTHROPOLOGY.* irreg. price varies. Holt, Rinehart and Winston, Inc., c/o Harcourt Brace Jovanovich, Orlando, FL 32887. TEL 407-345-2500.

572   UK   ISSN 0069-0880
CASS LIBRARY OF AFRICAN STUDIES. AFRICANA MODERN LIBRARY. 1967. irreg., no.18, 1972. price varies. Frank Cass, Newbury House, 890-900 Eastern Ave., Newbury Park, Ilford, Essex IG2 7HH, England. TEL 44-181-599-8866. FAX 44-181-599-0984. E-mail: sales@frankcass.com; URL: http://www.frankcass.com. (Dist. in the U.S. by: I.S.B.S., 5804 N.E. Hassalo St., Portland, OR 97213-3644. TEL 800-944-6190. FAX 503-280-8832) **Document type:** academic/scholarly publication.

305.8 494   FI   ISSN 0355-0141
CASTRENIANUMIN TOIMITTEITA. (Text in various languages) 1971. irreg. price varies. Suomalais-Ugrilainen Seura, PL 320, FIN-00171 Helsinki, Finland. (Dist. by: Tiedekirja - Vetenskapsbokhandeln, Kirkkokatu 14, FIN-00170 Helsinki, Finland) **Document type:** academic/scholarly publication.

572 930.1   US
CENTER FOR ANTHROPOLOGICAL STUDIES. CONTRIBUTIONS TO ANTHROPOLOGICAL STUDIES. 1978. irreg., no.4, 1987. price varies. Center for Anthropological Studies, Box 14576, Albuquerque, NM 87191-4576. TEL 505-296-6336. Dir. Albert E. Ward. R&P contact: Albert E. Ward. adv. contact: Albert E. Ward. circ. 1,000. **Document type:** monographic series.

572 913   US
CENTER FOR ANTHROPOLOGICAL STUDIES. ETHNOHISTORICAL REPORT SERIES. 1980. irreg., no.2, 1987. price varies. Center for Anthropological Studies, Box 14576, Albuquerque, NM 87191-4576. TEL 505-296-6336. Ed. Albert E. Ward. R&P contact: Albert E. Ward. adv. contact: Albert E. Ward. **Document type:** monographic series.

ANTHROPOLOGY

572 913 US
CENTER FOR ANTHROPOLOGICAL STUDIES. SPANISH BORDERLANDS RESEARCH. 1980. irreg. price varies. Center for Anthropological Studies, Box 14576, Albuquerque, NM 87191. TEL 505-296-6336. Ed. Albert E. Ward. R&P contact: Albert E. Ward. adv. contact: Albert E. Ward. **Document type**: monographic series.
Description: Studies from the Spanish Colonial period in the southern US.

301 US ISSN 0577-0963
CENTRAL STATES ANTHROPOLOGICAL SOCIETY. BULLETIN. 1966. s-a. $15 (effective 1996). American Anthropological Association, 4350 N. Fairfax Dr., Ste. 640, Arlington, VA 22203-1621. TEL 703-528-1902. FAX 703-528-3546. **Document type**: bulletin.

572 301 CG
CENTRE D'ETUDES ETHNOLOGIQUES. PUBLICATIONS. SERIE 2: MEMOIRES ET MONOGRAPHIES. 1970. irreg., no.103, 1989. C E E B A Publications, B.P. 246, Bandundu, Democratic Republic of the Congo. bibl.; charts; illus.

572 960 CG
CENTRE D'ETUDES ETHNOLOGIQUES BANDUNDU. PUBLICATIONS. 1966. irreg., latest no.100, 1988. price varies. C E E B A Publications, B.P. 246, Bandundu, Democratic Republic of the Congo. Ed. Hermann Hochegger. bibl.; charts. circ. 700.
Formerly: Centre d'Etudes Ethnologiques. Publications (ISSN 0577-1331)
Description: Discusses anthropology, arts and handicrafts, folklore, linguistics, nutrition, history of Africa, religion, rites and mythology, sociology and theater, development and human promotion.

572 913 BE ISSN 0777-5466
CENTRE GENEVOIS D'ANTHROPOLOGIE. BULLETIN. (Text in French) 1988. a., vol.4, 1993. 45 SFr. (1500 BEF) (effective 1994). (Universite de Geneve, Departement d'Anthropologie, Centre Genevois d'Anthropologie, SZ) Editions Peeters s.p.r.l., Bondgenotenlaan 153, 3000 Leuven, Belgium. TEL 32-16-235170. FAX 32-16-228500. URL: http://www.peeters-leuven.be. (Subscr. to: BCGA, Universite de Geneve, Departement d'Anthropologie, 12, rue de Gustave-Revilliod, CH-1227 Carouge - Geneva, Switzerland. TEL 41-22-436930. FAX 41-22-3000351) (Co-sponsor: Musee d'Ethnographie) Eds. Alain Gallay, Louis Necker. bk.rev.; bibl.; illus.; stat. **Indexed**: Anthropol.Lit. **Document type**: academic/scholarly publication, bulletin.

301.2 913 PO
CENTRO DE ESTUDOS REGIONAIS. BOLETIM CULTURAL. 1984. s-a. $5. Centro de Estudos Regionais, Largo do Instituto Historico do Minho, 20-22, 4900 Viana do Castelo, Portugal. TEL 828192. Pub. Antonio A. Parente Pereira. circ. 1,000. **Document type**: bulletin, monographic series.

572 BL ISSN 0104-2262
CENTRO DE MEMORIA REGIONAL. CADERNO. 1993. s-a. Universidade Sao Francisco, Centro de Memoria Regional, Av. Sao Francisco de Assis 218, 12900-00 Braganca Paulista, Brazil. TEL 55-11-4041500 ext. 218. E-mail: usfbib@eu.ansp.br. Ed. Marcos Cezar de Freitas. **Document type**: bulletin.

572 XR ISSN 0009-0794
DB191
CESKY LID/CZECH PEOPLE;* narodni casopis. (Text in Czech; summaries in English, French, German) 1892. q. DM.152. Ceska Akademie Ved, Ustav pro Etnografii a Folkloristiku, Narodni tr. 3, 111 42 Prague, Czech Republic. (Dist. in Western countries by: Kubon und Sagner GmbH, Hessstr. 39-41, 80328 Munich, Germany. TEL 49-89-54218130. FAX 49-89-54218218) Ed. Antonin Robek. bk.rev.; bibl.; illus.; index. circ. 1,000. **Indexed**: A.I.C.P., Amer.Hist.& Life (1969-1973), Bibl.Ling., Hist.Abstr. (1969-1973), IBR, M.L.A., MLA Intl.Bibl., Numis.Lit., RILM.
Description: Devoted to European ethnology and social anthropology, especially the ethnology of the Czech people and of Czech minorities in foreign countries.

CHESOPIEAN. see ARCHAEOLOGY

CHINESE SOCIOLOGY AND ANTHROPOLOGY; a journal of translations. see SOCIOLOGY

572 US ISSN 0893-0465
HT101 CODEN: CISOEC
CITY & SOCIETY (WASHINGTON). 1987-1992 (Dec.); resumed. s-a. $30 (effective 1996). (Society for Urban Anthropology) American Anthropological Association, 4350 N. Fairfax Dr., Ste. 640, Arlington, VA 22203. TEL 703-528-1902. FAX 703-528-3546. Ed. Jack Kugelmass. R&P contact: Terry Clifford. circ. 1,000. (reprint service avail.) **Indexed**: Abstr.Anthropol., Amer.Hist.& Life (1987-1992), (1994-), Anthropol.Lit., Hist.Abstr. (1987-1992), (1994-). **Document type**: academic/scholarly publication.
—UMI; UnCover.
Description: Presents articles concerned with urban communities and complex societies.

CODEX FILATELICA. see PHILATELY

301.2 ES ISSN 0256-7202
COLECCION ANTROPOLOGIA E HISTORIA. 1973. irreg. Ministerio de Educacion, Direccion de Patrimonio Cultural, Biblioteca del Museo Nacional, Avda. Revolucion, Colonia San Benito, San Salvador, El Salvador. TEL 23-6246. bibl.; charts; illus.

572 913.031 IT
COLLANA DI STUDI PALEONTOLOGICI. 1977. irreg. price varies. (Universita degli Studi di Pisa, Istituto di Antropologia e Paleontologia Umana) Giardini Editori e Stampatori, Via Santa Bibbiana 28, 56100 Pisa, Italy. TEL 050-502531. **Document type**: monographic series.

572 GW
COLLECTANEA INSTITUTI ANTHROPOS. 1967. irreg., no.41, 1994. price varies. (Anthropos Institut) Academia Verlag GmbH, Postfach 1663, 53734 Sankt Augustin, Germany. TEL 49-2241-345210. FAX 49-2241-345316. E-mail: 100325.3207@compuserve.com; URL: http://www.raps.com/academia. Ed.Bd. illus. **Document type**: monographic series.

572 CI ISSN 0350-6134
CODEN: COANDS
COLLEGIUM ANTROPOLOGICUM. (Text in English; summaries in English and Croatian) 1977. s-a. $10 to individuals; institutions $50. Croatian Anthropological Society, Institute for Medical Research and Occupational Health, Mose Pijade 158, P.O. Box 291, 41001 Zagreb, Croatia. TEL 41-432-186. FAX 41-274-572. (Co-sponsor: School of Biological Anthropology) Eds. Hubert Maver, Pavao Rudan. adv.; bk.rev.; charts; illus.; stat. circ. 1,000. (back issues avail.) **Indexed**: Abstr.Anthropol., Anthropol.Lit., ASCA, Curr.Cont., Per.Islam. (1991-), SSCI. **Document type**: academic/scholarly publication.
—BLDSC (3311.355000); CASDDS; Genuine Article; UnCover.

573 US
COMMUNICATOR (WASHINGTON). s-a. $6 (effective 1996). American Anthropological Association, 4350 N. Fairfax Dr., Ste. 640, Arlington, VA 22203-1621. TEL 703-528-1902. FAX 703-528-3546. Ed. Miriam Chaiken. R&P contact: Terry Clifford. bk.rev. **Document type**: academic/scholarly publication.
Description: Publishes notices and reports of domestic and international meetings, curriculum guides, and other information for professionals in academic and applied careers with interests in anthropological study of food and nutrition.

COMPARATIVE CIVILIZATIONS REVIEW. see SOCIAL SCIENCES: COMPREHENSIVE WORKS

301.2 398 PE ISSN 1022-1514
COMUNIDADES Y CULTURAS PERUANAS. 1973. irreg., no.26, 1995. price varies. Instituto Linguistico de Verano, Casilla 2492, Lima 100, Peru. FAX 5114-629-629. (Subscr. to: E. Iturriaga y Cia., Jiron Ica 441, Ofc. 202-203, Casilla 4640, Lima 100, Peru) Ed. Mary Ruth Wise. R&P contact: Mary Ruth Wise. (also avail. in microfiche; back issues avail.) **Document type**: academic/scholarly publication.

CONFLICT RESOLUTION NOTES. see LAW

572 301 MX ISSN 0074-0810
CONGRESOS INDIGENISTAS INTERAMERICANOS. ACTAS. every 4 yrs.; 11th, 1993, Managua, Nicaragua. Instituto Indigenista Interamericano, Apdo. Postal 20315, 01001 Mexico DF, Mexico. TEL 525-5680819. FAX 525-6521274. circ. controlled. **Document type**: proceedings.
Formerly: Inter-American Conference on Indian Life. Acts - Congresos Indigenistas Interamericanos. Acta.

572 FJ ISSN 0217-2992
CONTRIBUTIONS TO SOUTHEAST ASIAN ETHNOGRAPHY. 1982. irreg., no.11, 1997. price varies. Institute of Pacific Studies, University of the South Pacific, Suva, Fiji. TEL 679-212015. FAX 679-301594. E-mail: walker__a@usp.ac.fj. Ed. A.R. Walker; Pub. A.R. Walker. R&P contact: A.R. Walker. circ. 500. (back issues avail.) **Indexed**: Anthropol.Lit., E.I. **Document type**: academic/scholarly publication.

572 US ISSN 0890-9377
CONTRIBUTIONS TO THE STUDY OF ANTHROPOLOGY. 1987. irreg. price varies. Greenwood Press, Inc. (Subsidiary of: Greenwood Publishing Group Inc.), 88 Post Rd. W., Box 5007, Westport, CT 06881-5007. TEL 203-226-3571. FAX 203-22-1502.
—BLDSC (3461.453400).

572 301.2 US ISSN 0198-9871
CONTRIBUTIONS TO THE STUDY OF POPULAR CULTURE. 1981. irreg. price varies. Greenwood Press, Inc. (Subsidiary of: Greenwood Publishing Group Inc.), 88 Post Rd. W., Box 5007, Westport, CT 06881-5007. TEL 203-226-3571. FAX 203-222-1502.
—BLDSC (3461.454200).

301.2 909 UN ISSN 0304-3134
IL CORRIERE UNESCO. 1947. m. Lit.48000 to individuals (foreign Lit.80000); institutions Lit.40800 (foreign Lit.68000) (effective 1998). Giunti Gruppo Editoriale S.p.A., Via Bolognese 165, 50139 Florence, Italy. TEL 39-55-6679267. FAX 39-55-6679298. URL: http://www.giunti.it; http://www.unesco.org/publications.

572 301 UK ISSN 0308-275X
GN1
CRITIQUE OF ANTHROPOLOGY; a journal for the critical reconstruction of anthropology. 1974. q. £34($54) to individuals; institutions £135($216) (effective 1998). Sage Publications Ltd., 6 Bonhill St., London EC2A 4PU, England. TEL 44-171-374-0645. FAX 44-171-374-8741. E-mail: market@sagepub.co.uk; URL: http://www.sagepub.co.uk/. Eds. Steven Nugent, John Gledhill. adv. contact: Bernie Folan. bk.rev. (back issues avail.) **Indexed**: A.I.C.P., Abstr.Anthropol., Abstr.Anthropol., Alt.Press Ind., Alt.Press Ind., Anthropol.Lit., Arts & Hum.Cit.Ind., ASCA, ASSIA, Curr.Cont., Human Resour.Abstr., IBZ, Int.Bibl.Soc.Sci., Lang.& Lang.Behav.Abstr., Left Ind. (1986-), Mid.East: Abstr.& Ind., Sage Fam.Stud.Abstr., Sociol.Abstr., SSCI. **Document type**: academic/scholarly publication.
—BLDSC (3487.490300); SWETS; UnCover.
Description: Dedicated to the development of anthropology as a discipline that subjects social reality to critical analysis.
Refereed Serial

CROSS-CULTURAL RESEARCH METHODS. see PSYCHOLOGY

301.2 GT ISSN 0590-160X
CUADERNOS DE ANTROPOLOGIA. 1962. q. Universidad de San Carlos de Guatemala, Facultad de Humanidades, Departamento de Publicaciones, 9a Avenida 13-39, Zona 1, Guatemala, Guatemala. **Indexed**: A.I.C.P., Amer.Hist.& Life (1965-1966), Hist.Abstr. (1965-1966).

572 573 SP ISSN 0590-1871
GN585.S7
CUADERNOS DE ETNOLOGIA Y ETNOGRAFIA DE NAVARRA. 1969. 2/yr. 2000 ptas. (effective 1997). Gobierno de Navarra, Fondo de Publicaciones, Departamento de Educacion y Cultura, Navas de Tolosa, 21, 31002 Pamplona, Spain. TEL 34-48-427123. charts; illus.; index. (back issues avail.) **Indexed**: Anthropol.Lit. **Document type**: government publication.
—CINDOC.

ANTHROPOLOGY

572 972   MX   ISSN 0185-1659
GN1
CUICUILCO. 1980. q. $15. Instituto Nacional de Antropologia e Historia, Cordoba 45, 06700 Mexico 7, D.F., Mexico. TEL 582-56-02. FAX 915-2087282. Ed. Arturo Arias Fernandez. adv.; bk.rev. circ. 2,000.

301.2   PE   ISSN 1017-9542
CULTURA PERUANA.* 1941. q. Instituto Nacional de Cultura, Departamental Ancash, Oficio Numero 363, Huaras, Peru.

301.2   US   ISSN 0886-7356
GN301
CULTURAL ANTHROPOLOGY. 1986. q. $40 to individuals; institutions $50 (effective 1996). American Anthropological Association, 4350 N. Fairfax Dr., Ste. 640, Arlington, VA 22203-1621. TEL 703-528-1902. E-mail: cultanth@email.pitzer.edu; URL: http://www.pitzer.edu/~cultanth/. Ed. Daniel Segal. R&P contact: Terry Clifford. adv.: page $220; trim 6 x 9; adv. contact: Terry Clifford. circ. 1,000. (reprint service avail. from UMI) **Indexed:** Abstr.Anthropol., Amer.Hist.& Life (1996-), Anthropol.Lit., Arts & Hum.Cit.Ind., ASCA, Curr.Cont., Hist.Abstr. (1996-), Soc.Sci.Ind. (1994-), SSCI. **Document type:** academic/scholarly publication.
—BLDSC (3491.661000); Genuine Article; KR SourceOne; SWETS; UMI; UnCover.
    Description: Examines the relationship between anthropology and social and cultural history, hermeneutics, phenomenology and all fields of cultural studies. Includes literary criticism and theory.

CULTURAL DYNAMICS. see *PHILOSOPHY*

301   US
CULTURAL SURVIVAL. OCCASIONAL PAPERS. 1980. irreg., no.16, 1985. Cultural Survival, Inc., 96 Mt. Auburn St., Cambridge, MA 02138-5017. TEL 617-441-5400. FAX 617-441-5417. E-mail: csinc@cs.org. Ed. Amy Stall. R&P contact: Sofia Flynn. adv. contact: Sofia Flynn. **Indexed:** Anthropol.Lit. **Document type:** academic/scholarly publication, bulletin.

301   US   ISSN 0740-3291
GN380
CULTURAL SURVIVAL QUARTERLY. 1976. q. $45 to individuals; institutions $60. Cultural Survival, Inc., 96 Mt. Auburn St., Cambridge, MA 02138-5017. TEL 617-441-5400. FAX 617-441-5417. E-mail: csinc@cs.org; URL: http://www.cs.org. Ed. Amy Stall. R&P contact: Sofia Flynn. adv. circ. 10,000. (back issues avail.) **Indexed:** Alt.Press Ind., Anthropol.Lit., Environ.Per.Bibl. (1991-), Geo.Abstr.H.G., Geo.Abstr.P.G., HR Rep. (1984-1990), IDA, Polit.Sci.Abstr. **Document type:** academic/scholarly publication, bulletin.
—BLDSC (3491.668450); UnCover.
    Formerly (until 1982): Cultural Survival Newsletter.

301   US
CULTURAL SURVIVAL REPORT. irreg. no.22, 1987. Cultural Survival, Inc., 96 Mt. Auburn St., Cambridge, MA 02138-5017. TEL 617-441-5400. FAX 617-441-5417. E-mail: csinc@cs.org. R&P contact: Sofia Flynn. adv. contact: Sofia Flynn. **Indexed:** Anthropol.Lit. **Document type:** academic/scholarly publication.

301.2   NO   ISSN 0902-7521
GN301
CULTURE & HISTORY. (Text in English) 1987. irreg. NOK 210 (effective 1997). Scandinavian University Press, P.O. Box 2959 Toeyen, N-0608 Oslo, Norway. TEL 47-22-57-54-00. FAX 47-22-57-53-53. E-mail: mail@scup.no; URL: http://www.scup.no. (US addr.: 875 Massachusetts Ave., Ste. 84, Cambridge, MA 02139. TEL 617-497-6515. FAX 617-354-6875) Eds. Michael Harbsmeier, M.T. Larsen, U. Oestergaard. **Indexed:** Amer.Hist.& Life (1990-), Anthropol.Lit., Hist.Abstr. (1990-). **Document type:** academic/scholarly publication.
—BLDSC (3491.668590); KR SourceOne; SWETS.
    Description: Interdisciplinary journal of historical anthropology, functioning as an international forum for debate in the general field of cultural historical studies.

CULTURE & PSYCHOLOGY. see *PSYCHOLOGY*

572   NE   ISSN 0167-4447
                           CODEN: CIHEET
CULTURE, ILLNESS AND HEALING; studies in comparative cross-cultural research. (Text in English) 1980. irreg. price varies. Kluwer Academic Publishers, Postbus 17, 3300 AA Dordrecht, Netherlands. TEL 31-78-6392392. FAX 31-78-6392254. TELEX 29245 KAPG NL. E-mail: services@wkap.nl; URL: http://www.wkap.nl. (Dist. by: Kluwer Academic Publishers Group, P.O. Box 322, 3300 AH Dordrecht, Netherlands. TEL 31-78-6392392. FAX 31-78-6546474; N. America dist. addr.: Box 358, Accord Sta., Hingham, MA 02018-0358. TEL 617-871-6600. FAX 617-871-6528) Eds. Allan Young, Margaret Lock. **Document type:** monographic series.
    Refereed Serial

301.2 616.89   NE   ISSN 0165-005X
RC455.4.E8   CODEN: CMPSD2
CULTURE, MEDICINE AND PSYCHIATRY; an international journal of comparative cross-cultural research. (Text in English) 1977. q. fl.480 to institutions; $246.50 to institutions in U.S. (effective 1998). Kluwer Academic Publishers, Postbus 17, 3300 AA Dordrecht, Netherlands. TEL 31-78-6392392. FAX 31-78-6392254. TELEX 29245 KAPG NL. E-mail: services@wkap.nl; URL: http://www.wkap.nl. (Dist. by: Kluwer Academic Publishers Group, P.O. Box 322, 3300 AH Dordrecht, Netherlands. TEL 31-78-6392392. FAX 31-78-6546474; N. America dist. addr.: Box 358, Accord Sta., Hingham, MA 02018-0358. TEL 617-871-6600. FAX 617-871-6528) Ed. Byron J. Good. adv.; bk.rev.; illus. (also avail. in microform from UMI; reprint service avail. from SWZ) **Indexed:** Abstr.Anthropol., Anthropol.Lit., Arts & Hum.Cit.Ind., ASCA, Biol.Abstr., Bull.Signal., Curr.Cont., E.I., Excerp.Med., Ind.Med., Lang.& Lang.Behav.Abstr., Mid.East: Abstr.& Ind., Phil.Ind., Psychol.Abstr. (1977-), Risk Abstr., Sociol.Abstr., SSCI. **Document type:** academic/scholarly publication.
—BLDSC (3491.669100); CISTI; Genuine Article; KR SourceOne; SWETS; UMI; UnCover. **CCC**.
    Description: Provides an international and interdisciplinary forum for the discussion of medical and psychiatric anthropology, cross-cultural psychiatry, and related cross-societal clinical and epidemiological studies.
    Refereed Serial

CULTURES AU ZAIRE ET EN AFRIQUE. see *SOCIAL SCIENCES: COMPREHENSIVE WORKS*

572   GW   ISSN 0344-8622
RC455.4.E8
CURARE; Zeitschrift fuer Ethnomedizin - journal for ethnomedicine. (Text in English, French, German) 1978. s-a. DM.92 (foreign DM.94) (effective 1998). (Arbeitsgemeinschaft Ethnomedizin e.V.) V W B - Verlag fuer Wissenschaft und Bildung, Markgrafenstr. 67, 10969 Berlin, Germany. TEL 49-30-2510415. FAX 49-30-2510412. E-mail: 100615.1565@compuserve.com. circ. 1,000. (back issues avail.) **Indexed:** Abstr.Hyg., E.I., Lang.& Lang.Behav.Abstr., Trop.Dis.Bull. **Document type:** academic/scholarly publication.
—BLDSC (3493.435000); KNAW. **CCC**.
    Description: Forum of exchange and discussion concerning traditional medical systems, medical aid programs, health planning, and related issues.

572   US   ISSN 0011-3204
GN1   CODEN: CUANAX
CURRENT ANTHROPOLOGY. 1960. 5/yr. $45 to individuals (developing nations $25); institutions $120 (developing nations $55); students $25 (effective 1998). (Wenner-Gren Foundation for Anthropological Research) University of Chicago Press, Journals Division, Box 37005, Chicago, IL 60637. TEL 773-753-3347. FAX 773-753-0811. TELEX 25-4603. E-mail: subscriptions@journals.uchicago.edu; URL: http://www.journals.uchicago.edu/CA/home.html. Ed. Richard G. Fox. adv.: page $385 (8 1/2 x 11). bk.rev.; charts; illus.; index, cum.index: 1960-1974. circ. 5,300. (also avail. in microform from UMI; reprint service avail. from UMI,ISI) **Indexed:** A.I.C.P., Abstr.Anthropol., Abstr.Pop.Cult., Acad.Ind., Amer.Hist.& Life (1971-1974), (1980-1990), Anthropol.Lit., Arts & Hum.Cit.Ind., ASCA, ASSIA, Bibl.& Ind.Geol., Bibl.Ling., Biol.Abstr., Commun.Abstr., Curr.Cont., Curr.Tit.Dent., E.I., Fam.Ind., Geo.Abstr., Hist.Abstr. (1971-1974), (1980-1990), IBR, IDA, Int.Polit.Sci.Abstr., Lang.& Lang.Behav.Abstr., M.L.A., Mid.East: Abstr.& Ind., MLA Intl.Bibl., Psychol.Abstr. (1971-), RILM, Sci.Cit.Ind., So.Pac.Per.Ind., Soc.Sci.Ind., Sociol.Abstr., SSCI, Stud.Wom.Abstr. **Document type:** academic/scholarly publication.
—BLDSC (3494.200000); Genuine Article; KR SourceOne; SWETS; UMI; UnCover. **CCC**.
    Description: Contains research articles and commentary throughout social, cultural, and physical anthropology; ethnology; folklore; and more.
    Refereed Serial

DAGESTANSKII ETNOGRAFICHESKII SBORNIK. see *SOCIOLOGY*

572   SA
DART. (Text in English) irreg. membership. Institute for the Study of Man in Africa, University of the Witwatersrand Medical School, Rm. 2B17, York Rd., Parktown 2193, South Africa. TEL 27-11-6472203. FAX 27-11-6434318. E-mail: isma@chiron.wits.ac.za. Ed. Kevin Kuykendall. **Document type:** academic/scholarly publication, newsletter.
    Description: News and activities of the institute.

572   US   ISSN 1087-9900
DEVELOPMENT ANTHROPOLOGIST. 1981. s-a. $20. Institute For Development Anthropology, 99 Collier St., Box 2207, Binghamton, NY 13902-2207. TEL 607-772-6244. FAX 607-773-8993. Ed. Michael Horowitz. bibl.; charts; illus. circ. 1,500. **Indexed:** Abstr.Rural Dev.Trop., Irr.& Drain.Abstr. **Document type:** bulletin.
—BLDSC (3579.004900).
    Formerly: Development Anthropology Network (ISSN 8756-0488)
    Description: Applications of anthropology to development, with emphasis on socioeconomic and ecological impacts.

572 320.531   NE   ISSN 0304-4092
HX550.A56   CODEN: DIAAER
DIALECTICAL ANTHROPOLOGY; an independent international journal in the critical tradition committed to the transformation of our society and the humane union of theory and practice. (Text in English) 1975. q. fl.460 to institutions; $236 to institutions in U.S. (effective 1998). Kluwer Academic Publishers, Postbus 17, 3300 AA Dordrecht, Netherlands. TEL 31-78-6392392. FAX 31-78-6392254. TELEX 29245 KAPG NL. E-mail: services@wkap.nl; URL: http://www.wkap.nl/kapis/CGI-BIN/WORLD/journalhome.htm?0304-4092. (Dist. by: Kluwer Academic Publishers Group, P.O. Box 322, 3300 AH Dordrecht, Netherlands. TEL 31-78-6392392. FAX 31-78-6546474; N. America dist. addr.: Box 358, Accord Sta., Hingham, MA 02018-0358. TEL 617-871-6600. FAX 617-871-6528) Ed.Bd. adv.; bk.rev.; index. (also avail. in microform from UMI; reprint service avail. from SWZ) **Indexed:** Anthropol.Lit., Arts & Hum.Cit.Ind., ASCA, Curr.Cont., Lang.& Lang.Behav.Abstr., Left Ind. (1982-), Mid.East: Abstr.& Ind., Phil.Ind., Sociol.Abstr., SSCI.
—BLDSC (3579.704000); Genuine Article; SWETS; UMI; UnCover. **CCC**.
    Description: Social critique of all aspects of contemporary civilization.
    Refereed Serial

DIGGING STICK. see *ARCHAEOLOGY*

DISCOVERY (NEW HAVEN). see *SCIENCES: COMPREHENSIVE WORKS*

572 · · · · · · · · · · · · CK · · ISSN 0120-050X
DIVULGACIONES ETNOLOGICAS. 1952. s-a. Universidad del Atlantico, Instituto de Investigacion Etnologica, Carrera 43, No. 50-53, Apdo. Aereo 1890, Barranquilla, Colombia. bk.rev. circ. 2,000. **Indexed:** A.I.C.P.

572 · · · · · · · · · · · · GW
DOBRUDSCHABOTE. 1976. q. free. Landsmannschaft der Dobrudschadeutschen, Oraniensteiner Weg 8, 65549 Limburg-Lahn, Germany. circ. 850.

DONGNAN WENHUA/CULTURE OF SOUTHEAST CHINA. see ARCHAEOLOGY

301.2 572 · · · · · · · NO · · ISSN 0332-5784
DUGNAD; tidsskrift for etnologi. 1975. 4/yr. NOK 190 to individuals; institutions NOK 340 (effective 1997). Novus Forlag, P.O. Box 748 Sentrum, N-0106 Oslo, Norway. TEL 47-22-71-74-50. FAX 47-22-71-81-07. E-mail: novus@novus.no; URL: http://www.sn.no/novus. Ed. Arne Lie Christensen. bk.rev. circ. 700. **Indexed:** Anthropol.Lit. **Document type:** academic/scholarly publication.
   Description: Explores the different living conditions and styles in various parts of Norway.

EARLY MAN NEWS; newsletter for human palecology. see ARCHAEOLOGY

572 390 · · · · · · · · · II · · ISSN 0012-8686
GN1 · · · · · · · · · · · · · · · CODEN: EAANAH
EASTERN ANTHROPOLOGIST. (Text in English) 1947. q. $125. Ethnographic & Folk Culture Society, Box 209, L-II-31, Sector B, Aliganj Housing Scheme, Lucknow 226 024, India. TEL 91-522-372362. (Dist. by: Scientific Distribution Service, 5-A, Bhagat-ki-kothi Box No. 33, Jodhpur, Rajasthan 342 001, India) Ed.Bd. R&P contact: P.K. Tewari. bk.rev.; bibl.; charts; index. circ. 1,000. **Indexed:** A.I.C.P., Anthropol.Lit., Biol.Abstr., Curr.Cont., E.I., IBR, Int.Polit.Sci.Abstr., Lang.& Lang.Behav.Abstr., Mid.East: Abstr.& Ind., Per.Islam. (1991-), Pub.Admin.Abstr., Rural Devel.Abstr., Sociol.Abstr., SSCI, World Agri.Econ.& Rural Sociol.Abstr. **Document type:** academic/scholarly publication.
   —SWETS; UnCover.

572 913 · · · · · · · · · US · · ISSN 0070-8232
EASTERN NEW MEXICO UNIVERSITY. CONTRIBUTIONS IN ANTHROPOLOGY. 1968. irreg., vol.11, 1984. price varies. Eastern New Mexico University, Department of Social and Behavioral Sciences, Station No.3, Portales, NM 88130. Ed. Phillip Shelley. circ. 750. **Indexed:** Abstr.Anthropol.

572 · · · · · · · · · · · · · · · · US
ECONOMIC ANTHROPOLOGY. 1983. irreg. (Society for Economic Anthropology) University Press of America, 4720 Boston Way, Ste. A, Lanham, MD 20706. TEL 301-459-3366. Ed. Sutti Ortiz. **Document type:** monographic series.
   Formerly: Monographs in Economic Anthropology.

ESPACIO ABIERTO; cuaderno venezolano de sociologia. see SOCIOLOGY

572 972 · · · · · · · · · · GT
ESTUDIOS; revista de antropologia, arqueologia e historia. N.S. 1993. s-a.? Universidad de San Carlos de Guatemala, Instituto de Investigaciones Historicas, Antropologicas y Arqueologicas, Edf. S-1, Ciudad Universitaria, Zona 12, Guatemala, Guatemala. Ed. Oscar R. Gutierrez.

599.9 · · · · · · · · · · · · · MX
ESTUDIOS DE ANTROPOLOGIA BIOLOGICA. 1982. biennial. Mex.$40 per no. (effective 1997). Universidad Nacional Autonoma de Mexico, Instituto de Investigaciones Antropologicas, Circuito Exterior, Ciudad Universitaria, 04510 Mexico, D.F., Mexico. TEL 52-5-6229531. FAX 52-5-6229651. Ed. Luis Alberto Vargas.
   Description: Includes lectures and conferences given at the Physical Anthropology Congress "Juan Comas".

ESTUDIOS DE CULTURA MAYA. see HISTORY — History Of North And South America

ESTUDIOS ETNOHISTORICOS DEL ECUADOR. see HISTORY — History Of North And South America

ESTUDIOS MICHOACANOS. see HISTORY — History Of North And South America

301.2 · · · · · · · · · · PO · · ISSN 0870-4457
ESTUDOS DE ANTROPOLOGIA CULTURAL E SOCIAL. 1965. irrreg. price varies. Instituto de Investigacao Cientifica Tropical, Centro de Antropologia Cultural e Social, Rua da Junqueira 30, 1300 Lisbon, Portugal. TEL 351-1-3622621. FAX 351-1-3631460. E-mail: cdi@iict.pt; URL: http/www.iict.pt. (Subscr. to: Centro de Documentacao e Informacao, Rua Jau 47, 1300 Lisbon, Portugal) circ. 1,000. **Document type:** monographic series.
   Formerly: Estudos de Antropologia Cultural (ISSN 0870-6891)

ETHNOARTS INDEX. see ART — Abstracting, Bibliographies, Statistics

301.2 · · · · · · · · · · HU · · ISSN 0014-1798
ETHNOGRAPHIA. (Text in Hungarian; summaries in four languages) 1890. q. $16 (effective 1993). Kultura, P.O. Box 149, 1389 Budapest 62, Hungary. TEL 361-250-01-94. FAX 361-250-02-33. TELEX 20-2855 KULT H. Ed. Dr. Laszlo Keszi-Kovacs. bk.rev.; abstr.; bibl.; charts; illus.; maps; cum.index. circ. 900. **Indexed:** A.I.C.P., Anthropol.Lit., MLA Intl.Bibl.

572 · · · · · · · · · · · · BE · · ISSN 0336-1438
L'ETHNOGRAPHIE. 1859. a. 1500 BEF (effective 1994). (Societe d'Ethnographie de Paris, FR) Editions Peeters s.p.r.l., Bondgenotenlaan 153, 3000 Leuven, Belgium. TEL 32-16-235170. FAX 32-16-228500. URL: http://www.peeters-leuven.be. Eds. Andre-Marcel d'Ans, Robert Lacombe. adv.; bk.rev.; cum.index. circ. 1,000. (back issues avail.) **Indexed:** A.I.C.P., Anthropol.Lit., IBR. **Document type:** academic/scholarly publication.
   —SWETS.

572 900 390 · · · · · US · · ISSN 0014-1801
E51
ETHNOHISTORY; a quarterly journal relating to the past of culture and societies in all areas of the world, emphasizing the use of documentary and field materials and historiographic and anthropological approaches. 1954. q. $25 to individuals; institutions $45 (effective 1997). Duke University Press, Box 90660, Durham, NC 27708-0660. TEL 919-687-3600. FAX 919-688-4574. E-mail: amylee@acpub.acpub.duke.edu; URL: http://www.duke.edu/web/dupress/. Ed. Ross Hassig. R&P contact: Kay Robin Alexander. adv. contact: Amy Hartzler. bk.rev.; bibl.; charts; illus. circ. 1,500. (also avail. in microform from UMI; reprint service avail. from SCH) **Indexed:** A.I.C.P., Abstr.Anthropol., Amer.Bibl.Slavic & E.Eur.Stud., Amer.Hist.& Life (1963-), Anthropol.Lit., Arts & Hum.Cit.Ind., ASCA, Curr.Cont., Fam.Ind., Hist.Abstr. (1963-), Hum.Ind., Mid.East: Abstr.& Ind., Soc.Sci.Ind., SSCI.
   —BLDSC (3815.115000); Genuine Article; KR SourceOne; SWETS; UMI; UnCover. **CCC.**
   Refereed Serial

305.8 599.97 · · · · · DK · · ISSN 0425-4597
ETHNOLOGIA EUROPAEA/JOURNAL OF EUROPEAN ETHNOLOGY. 1967. s-a. DKK 200($35) to individuals; institutions DKK 280 ($50) (effective 1997). Museum Tusculanum Press, University of Copenhagen, Njalsgade 92, DK-2300 Copenhagen S, Denmark. TEL 45-35-32-91-09. FAX 45-35-32-91-13. Ed. Bjarne Stoklund. **Indexed:** A.I.C.P., Anthropol.Lit., M.L.A., MLA Intl.Bibl. **Document type:** academic/scholarly publication.
   —BLDSC (3815.118000); SWETS.

572 · · · · · · · · · · · · PL · · ISSN 0137-4079
GN1
ETHNOLOGIA POLONA. (Text in English) vol.2, 1976. a. price varies. Polska Akademia Nauk, Instytut Historii Kultury Materialnej, Al. Solidarnosci 105, 00-140 Warsaw, Poland. Ed. Maria Frankowska. bk.rev.; bibl.; illus. circ. 450. **Indexed:** Anthropol.Lit.
   Description: Provides theoretical articles and results of detailed studies on ethnology of various countries.

572 · · · · · · · · · · · · FR · · ISSN 0046-2616
ETHNOLOGIE FRANCAISE/FRENCH ETHNOLOGY. (Summaries in English, French) 1971. q. 86 ECU($105) Armand Colin (Subsidiary of: Masson), 103 bd. Saint Michel, 75005 Paris cedex 05, France. TEL 1-46-34-19-12. FAX 1-43-26-96-38. TELEX 201 269 F. Ed. Gerard Collomb. circ. 1,500. (also avail. in microform from UMI) **Indexed:** A.I.C.P., Anthropol.Lit., MLA Intl.Bibl., RILM.
   —KR SourceOne; SWETS.
   Former titles: Archives d'Ethnologie Francaise (ISSN 0066-6580); Arts et Traditions Populaires.

572 390 · · · · · · · · · US · · ISSN 0014-1828
GN1 · · · · · · · · · · · · · · CODEN: ETNLB6
ETHNOLOGY; an international journal of cultural and social anthropology. 1962. q. $21 to individuals; institutions $40 (effective 1997 & 1998). University of Pittsburgh, Department of Anthropology, Pittsburgh, PA 15260. TEL 412-648-7503. FAX 412-648-7535. E-mail: ethnolog@vms.cis.pitt.edu; URL: http://www.pitt.edu/~caswww/cdesc/index.html. Ed. Leonard Plotnicov. R&P contact: Stacy Hoffman. charts; circ. 2,000 (paid). (also avail. in microform from UMI; reprint service avail. from UMI; back issues avail.) **Indexed:** A.I.C.P., Amer.Bibl.Slavic & E.Eur.Stud., Amer.Hist.& Life (1969-1972), (1983-), Anthropol.Lit., Arts & Hum.Cit.Ind., ASCA, ASSIA, Biol.Abstr., Curr.Cont., E.I., Fam.Ind., Geo.Abstr.H.G., Hist.Abstr. (1969-1972), (1983-), IBR, IDA, IDA, Ind.Sci.Rev., Key Word Ind.Wildl.Res., M.L.A., Mid.East: Abstr.& Ind., MLA Intl.Bibl., Per.Islam. (1993-), Poult.Abstr., Sage Urb.Stud.Abstr., So.Pac.Per.Ind., Soc.Sci.Ind., Soc.Work Res.& Abstr., SSCI, World Agri.Econ.& Rural Sociol.Abstr. **Document type:** academic/scholarly publication.
   ●Also available online. Vendor(s): Information Access Co., UMI.
   —BLDSC (3815.120000); Genuine Article; KR SourceOne; SWETS; UMI; UnCover.
   Refereed Serial

572 · · · · · · · · · · · · · · · · II
ETHNOLOGY. (Text in English) a. $50. Hindustan Publishing Corp., 4805-24, 1st Fl., Bharat Ram Rd., Darya Ganj, New Delhi 110 002, India. TEL 91-11-3254401. FAX 91-11-6863511. E-mail: hpcpd@giasdl01.vsnl.net.in.

ETHNOMUSICOLOGIE. see MUSIC

ETHNOMUSICOLOGY. see MUSIC

ETHNOMUSICOLOGY ONLINE. see MUSIC

572 930.1 · · · · · · · SW · · ISSN 0014-1844
GN1 · · · · · · · · · · · · · · CODEN: ESEMBP
ETHNOS. (Text in English) 1936. q. NOK 450 in Nordic countries; elsewhere $79 (effective 1997). Folkens Museum Etnografiska - National Museum of Ethnography, P.O. Box 27140, 102 52 Stockholm, Sweden. FAX 46-8-666-50-70. URL: http://www.teelemuseum.se/museer/Folkmus/Ie.html. (Dist. by: Scandinavian University Press, P.O. Box 2959 Toeyen, N-0608 Oslo, Norway. TEL 47-22-57-54-00. FAX 47-22-57-53-53; US addr.: 875 Massachusetts Ave., Cambridge, MA 02139. TEL 617-497-6515. FAX 617-354-6875) Eds. Don Kulick, Wilhelm Oestberg. bk.rev.; bibl.; illus.; cum.index every 10 yrs. circ. 1,000. (reprint service avail. from SWZ) **Indexed:** A.I.C.P., Abstr.Anthropol., Amer.Hist.& Life, Anthropol.Lit., Bibl.Ling., Biol.Abstr., Curr.Cont.Africa, E.I., Geo.Abstr.H.G., Hisp.Amer.Per.Ind. (1977-1978), Hist.Abstr., IBR, IDA, Mid.East: Abstr.& Ind., SSCI. **Document type:** academic/scholarly publication.
   —BLDSC (3815.200000); SWETS; UnCover. **CCC.**
   Description: Presents articles on social and cultural anthropology, ethnography and non-Western archaeology.
   Refereed Serial

572 401 · · · · · · · · · BE · · ISSN 0299-1098
ETHNOSCIENCES. (Subseries of: Bibliotheque de la S E L A F) 1985. irreg., vol.10, 1995. price varies. (Societe d'Etudes Linguistiques et Anthropologiques de France (SELAF), Laboratoire de Langues et Civilisations a Tradition Orale) Editions Peeters s.p.r.l., Bondgenotenlaan 153, 3000 Leuven, Belgium. TEL 32-16-235170. FAX 32-16-228500. URL: http://www.peeters-leuven.be. (back issues avail.) **Document type:** monographic series.

ANTHROPOLOGY

573 636   FR   ISSN 0397-6572
CODEN: ETHNEJ
ETHNOZOOTECHNIE. 1962. s-a. 160 F. membership (effective 1995 & 1996). Societe d'Ethnozootechnie, 25 bd Arago, 75013 Paris, France. (back issues avail.) **Indexed:** InterActions Bibl. (1989; 1991-), Zoo.Rec. **Document type:** monographic series, proceedings.
—BLDSC (3815.210000).
Description: Studies relations among humans, animals and environment in ancient and modern societies. Considers the history and future of the raising of domesticated animals.

572   301.2   US   ISSN 0091-2131
GN270   CODEN: ETHSAU
ETHOS (WASHINGTON). 1973. q. $44 to individuals; institutions $60 (effective 1996). (Society for Psychological Anthropology) American Anthropological Association, 4350 N. Fairfax Dr., Ste. 640, Arlington, VA 22203-1621. TEL 703-528-1902. E-mail: ethos@po.cwru.edu; URL: http://www.cwru.edu/orgs/spa/ethos.html. Ed. Robert A. Paul. R&P contact: Terry Clifford. adv.: page $220; trim 6 x 9; adv. contact: Terry Clifford. bk.rev.; charts. circ. 1,100. (also avail. in microform from UMI; reprint service avail. from UMI) **Indexed:** Abstr.Anthropol., Anthropol.Lit., Lang.& Lang.Behav.Abstr., Psychol.Abstr. (1973-). **Document type:** academic/scholarly publication.
—BLDSC (3815.300000); CINDOC; Genuine Article; SWETS; UMI; UnCover. **CCC.**
Description: Research in psychological anthropology and cross-cultural psychology, including studies on cultural cognition, transcultural psychiatry, ethnopsychiatry, socialization, psychoanalytic anthropology and other psychocultural topics.

572   SP   ISSN 1132-0729
ETNIKER BIZKAIA. 1985. a. Instituto Labayru, Departamento de Etnografia, Calle Aretxabaleta, 1, 1o, 48010 Bilbao, Spain. TEL 34-4-4541571. E-mail: labayr01@sarenet.es. Ed. Gurutzi Arregi. bk.rev. **Document type:** bulletin.
—CINDOC.
Supersedes (1975-1982): Etniker (ISSN 1132-0737)

305.8   IT
ETNOANTROPOLOGIA. 1993. s-a. L.45000 (Europe L.55000; elsewhere L.80000). Rosenberg & Sellier, Via Andrea Doria 14, 10123 Turin, Italy. TEL 39-11-8127820. FAX 39-11-8127744. (Edit. addr.: AISEA, c/o Museo delle Arti e Tradizioni Popolari, Piazza Marconi 8, 00185 Rome, Italy. FAX 39-16-8443598) Ed. Tullio Tentori.

572 398   BO
ETNOFOLK. 1992. 3/yr. Comite Departamental de Etnografia y Folklore, Oruro, Bolivia. Ed. Alberto Guerra Gutierrez.

301.2   PL   ISSN 0071-1861
GN585.P6
ETNOGRAFIA POLSKA. (Text in Polish; summaries in English, occasionally in French or Russian) 1958. s-a. $40. Polska Akademia Nauk, Instytut Historii Kultury Materialnej, Al. Solidarnosci 105, 00-140 Warsaw, Poland. Ed. W. Paprocka. circ. 650. **Indexed:** A.I.C.P., Amer.Hist.& Life (1959-), Hist.Abstr. (1959-), IBR, Numis.Lit.
Description: Dissertations on ethnological research from Polish scholars about Poland and the world.

572   RU   ISSN 0869-5415
GN1
ETNOGRAFICHESKOE OBOZRENIE. (Text in Russian; summaries in English, French) 1926. bi-m. $222 (effective 1998). (Rossiiskaya Akademiya Nauk, Institut Etnologii i Antropologii im. N.N. Miklukho-Maklaya) Izdatel'stvo Nauka, 90 Profsoyuznaya ul., 117864 Moscow, Russia. (Dist. by: Mezhdunarodnaya Kniga, ul. B. Yakimanka 39, 117049 Moscow, Russia; Dist. in U.S by: Victor Kamkin Inc., 4956 Boiling Brook Pkwy, Rockville, MD 20852. TEL 301-881-5973) Ed. K.V. Chistov. bk.rev.; charts; illus.; index, cum.index every 5 yrs. (also avail. in microform) **Indexed:** A.I.C.P., Amer.Hist.& Life (1968-), Biol.Abstr., E.I., Hist.Abstr. (1968-), IBR, Lang.& Lang.Behav.Abstr. —KNAW.
Former titles (until 1991): Sovetskaya Etnografiya (ISSN 0038-5050); (until 1931): Etnografiya (ISSN 0257-988X)

572   YU
ETNOGRAFSKI MUZEJ NA CETINJU. GLASNIK. 1961. irreg. Etnografski Muzej na Cetinju, Trg Revolucije, Cetinje, Montenegro, Yugoslavia.

572   YU   ISSN 0350-0322
DR314.A1
ETNOGRAFSKI MUZEJ U BEOGRADU. GLASNIK. 1926. a. Etnografski Muzej u Beogradu, Studentski trg 13, Belgrade, Yugoslavia. **Indexed:** Anthropol.Lit., RILM.
Description: Articles and essays about national culture and museological researches.

ETNOLOGIA I ANTROPOLOGIA KULTUROWA. see FOLKLORE

572 398   CU
ETNOLOGIA Y FOLKLORE. 1966. 2/yr. Academia de Ciencias de Cuba, Instituto de Etnologia y Folklore, Havana, Cuba. **Indexed:** A.I.C.P.

572   SW   ISSN 0374-7530
ETNOLOGISKA STUDIER. 1935. irreg. price varies. Etnografiska Museet Goeteborg, Aavaegen 24, P.O. Box 5303, S-402 27 Goeteborg, Sweden. TEL 46-31-612776. FAX 46-317730920. Ed. Sven-Erik Isacsson. R&P contact: Jan Slavik. circ. 1,600. **Document type:** directory, monographic series.

572 398   CI   ISSN 0351-1944
DR1523
ETNOLOSKA TRIBINA. (Text in Croatian; summaries in English, German, French) 1970. a. $8. Institut za Etnologiju i Folkloristiku, Ul. Kralja Zvonimira 17, 41000 Zagreb, Croatia. TEL 385-41-440880. E-mail: capo@maief.ief.hr. Ed. Jasna Capo. bk.rev.; charts; illus. circ. 300. (back issues avail.)
Description: Publishes scientific and professional papers covering all areas of ethnology and anthropology.
Refereed Serial

390 572   YU   ISSN 0423-5509
GN1
ETNOLOSKI PREGLED/REVUE D'ETHNOLOGIE. 1962. s-a. (Etnolosko Drustvo Jugoslavije) Etnografski muzej u Beogradu, Studentski trg 13, Belgrade, Yugoslavia. Ed. Milovan Gavazzi. illus. **Indexed:** A.I.C.P.

305.8   IT   ISSN 1122-6234
GN301
ETNOSISTEMI; processi e dinamiche culturali. 1994. a. L.30000($50) Centro Informazione e Stampa Universitaria, Viale Ippocrate 97, 00161 Rome, Italy. TEL 39-6-491474. FAX 39-6-4450613. Ed. Mariano Pavanello. **Document type:** monographic series.

572 410   CG
ETUDES AEQUATORIA. 1982. irreg., no.12, 1993. price varies. Centre Aequatoria, B.P. 276, Mbandaka, Democratic Republic of the Congo. Ed. Honore Vinck. circ. 250. **Document type:** monographic series.
Description: Monographs on the peoples of Zaire: their history, culture, language and literature.

572   IV   ISSN 0423-5673
ETUDES EBURNEENNES.* 1951. a. Ministry of National Education and Scientific Research, B.P. V120, Abidjan, Ivory Coast. bibl.; illus. **Indexed:** A.I.C.P.

ETUDES ETHNO-LINGUISTIQUES MAGHREB-SAHARA. see LINGUISTICS

572 960   SG
ETUDES MAURITANIENNES.* 1948. irreg. Institut Fondamental d'Afrique Noire, Centre de Mauritanie, B.P. 206, Dakar, Senegal. **Document type:** monographic series.

572   MX   ISSN 0378-5726
ETUDES MESOAMERICAINES. (Text in French; summaries in Spanish) 1972 (series 1). s-a. price varies. (Ministere des Affaires Etrangeres, FR) Centre d'Etudes Mexicaines et Centramericaines, Sierra Leone 330, Apdo. 41-879, 11000 Mexico, D.F., Mexico. TEL 5405921. Ed. Joelle Gaillac. adv.; bk.rev.; abstr.; bibl.; charts; illus.; pat.; tr.lit. circ. 750. **Indexed:** Anthropol.Lit.

951.7   FR   ISSN 0766-5075
DS798.A2
ETUDES MONGOLES ET SIBERIENNES. 1970. a. 100 F. (effective 1997). Laboratoire d'Ethnologie et de Sociologie Comparative, Universite de Paris X, 200 av. de la Republique, 92001 Nanterre, France. TEL 33-2-40977522. FAX 33-2-40977117. E-mail: socethno@u-paris10.fr. Ed. Marie-Lise Beffa. bk.rev.; bibl. circ. 500. (back issues avail.) **Indexed:** Amer.Hist.& Life (1974-), Anthropol.Lit., Bibl.Ling., Hist.Abstr. (1974-), M.L.A. **Document type:** academic/scholarly publication.
Formerly: Etudes Mongoles (ISSN 0150-3014)
Refereed Serial

572   NG   ISSN 0373-6296
ETUDES NIGERIENNES. 1953. irreg. Institut de Recherches en Sciences Humaines (IRSH), Service de Documentation, B.P. 318, Niamey, Niger. TELEX 5258 UNINIM. illus.

ETUDES OCEAN INDIEN. see LINGUISTICS

ETUDES RWANDAISES. see HISTORY — History Of Africa

572   TG   ISSN 0531-2051
DT582.A2
ETUDES TOGOLAISES; revue togolaise des sciences. 1965; N.S. 1971. q. Institut National de la Recherche Scientifique, B.P. 2240, Lome, Togo. illus. (reprint service avail.) **Indexed:** Curr.Cont.Africa.

EUROPE DE TRADITION ORALE. see LINGUISTICS

572   US   ISSN 1060-1538
GN281   CODEN: EVANEW
EVOLUTIONARY ANTHROPOLOGY; issues, news, and reviews. 1992. bi-m. $235 (foreign $340) (effective 1998). John Wiley & Sons, Inc., Journals, 605 Third Ave., New York, NY 10158-0012. TEL 212-850-6000. FAX 212-850-6088. TELEX 12-7063. URL: http://www.wiley.co.uk. (Subscr. to: John Wiley & Sons, Inc., Box 2575, Secaucus, NJ 07096-2575) Ed. John Fleagle. adv.: B&W page $640, color page £1515; trim 279 x 210. (also avail. in microform from UMI; back issues avail.) **Indexed:** A.I.C.P., Abstr.Anthropol., Anthropol.Lit., Ecol.Abstr. **Document type:** academic/scholarly publication.
—BLDSC (3834.390000); UnCover. **CCC.**
Description: Focuses on all aspects of biological anthropology, paleoanthropology, archaeology, as well as social biology, genetics, and ecology.
Refereed Serial

EVOLUTIONARY MONOGRAPHS. see BIOLOGY

069 930.1   US   ISSN 0014-4738
GN1
EXPEDITION. 1958. 3/yr. $24 (foreign $28); newsstand price: $9.50. University of Pennsylvania Museum, 33rd & Spruce Sts., Philadelphia, PA 19104-6324. TEL 215-898-0023. FAX 215-898-0657. E-mail: expedition@sas.upenn.edu; URL: http://www.upenn.edu/museum_pubs/intro.html. Ed. Helen Schenck. R&P contact: Jennifer Quick. TEL 215-898-4119. charts; illus.; index. circ. 6,000. (also avail. in microform from UMI; reprint service avail. from UMI) **Indexed:** Abstr.Anthropol., Anthropol.Lit., Art & Archaeol.Tech.Abstr., Avery Ind.Archit.Per., Br.Archaeol.Abstr., Mid.East: Abstr.& Ind., Numis.Lit. **Document type:** academic/scholarly publication.
—BLDSC (3836.470000); KR SourceOne; SWETS; UMI; UnCover.
Description: Presents articles on current research in archaeology and anthropology to an audience composed of scholars, students, and the lay public.
Refereed Serial

F I P L V WORLD NEWS. (Federation Internationale des Professeurs de Langues Vivantes) see EDUCATION

FACES; the magazine about people. see CHILDREN AND YOUTH — For

572   SW   ISSN 0348-971X
DL1
FATABUREN; Nordiska Museets och Skansen Aarsbok. (Text in Swedish; summaries in English) 1906. a. SEK 275. Nordiska Museet, P.O. Box 27820, S-115 93 Stockholm, Sweden. TEL 46-08-666-46-00. FAX 46-08-666-47-67. circ. 5,000. **Indexed:** A.I.C.P., IBR, M.L.A., MLA Intl.Bibl., Numis.Lit.
Supersedes: Meddelanden fraan Nordiska Museet

ANTHROPOLOGY

572　　　　　　　US　　ISSN 0071-4739
GN2　　　　　　　　　　CODEN: FIEAAV
ELDIANA: ANTHROPOLOGY. 1895. irreg. (Field Museum of Natural History, Library - Publications Division) Field Museum Press, Roosevelt Rd. at Lake Shore Dr., Chicago, IL 60605-2498. TEL 312-922-9410. FAX 312-427-7269. bibl.; charts; illus.; index. circ. 450. (back issues avail.; reprint service avail. from UMI) **Indexed:** Biol.Abstr., E.I., Geo.Abstr.H.G.
—Linda Hall.
Description: Studies, descriptions and catalogues based on Field Museum collections and research in the field.
Refereed Serial

LM AUSTRALIA EDUCATION CATALOGUE. see *MOTION PICTURES*

572　　　　　　　US　　ISSN 0891-1835
NDING THE SOURCE. 1987. irreg. price varies. Greenwood Press, Inc. (Subsidiary of: Greenwood Publishing Group Inc.), 88 Post Rd. W., Box 5007, Westport, CT 06881-5007. TEL 203-226-3571. FAX 203-22-1502.
—BLDSC (3927.734130).

NISTERRA; revista portuguesa de geografia. see *GEOGRAPHY*

NNISCH-UGRISCHE FORSCHUNGEN; Zeitschrift fuer Finnisch-Ugrische Sprach- und Volkskunde. see *LINGUISTICS*

NSKT MUSEUM. see *ARCHAEOLOGY*

572　　　　　　　US　　ISSN 0015-3893
E78.F6　　　　　　　　　CODEN: FANTA9
LORIDA ANTHROPOLOGIST. 1948. q. $25 membership; foreign $35. Florida Anthropological Society, Inc., Box 82255, Tampa, FL 33682-2255. TEL 813-821-7600. FAX 813-822-2368. E-mail: janusres@ix.netcom.com. (Back issues from: Graves Museum of Archaeology and Natural History, 481 S. Federal Hwy., Dania, FL 33004) Ed. Robert J. Austin. R&P contact: Robert J. Austin. bk.rev.; charts; illus.; cum.index: vols.1-36, vols.37-40; circ. 900 (paid). **Indexed:** A.I.C.P., Abstr.Anthropol., Anthropol.Lit., Biol.Abstr. **Document type:** academic/scholarly publication.
—Linda Hall; UnCover.
Incorporates: Florida Anthropological Society Publications.
Description: Covers archaeology, ethnology, physical anthropology, cultural anthropology and associated topics with a focus on Florida and surrounding areas in the Southeastern U.S. and Caribbean.
Refereed Serial

572　　　　　　　US　　ISSN 0164-1662
GN1　　　　　　　　　　CODEN: FJANER
LORIDA JOURNAL OF ANTHROPOLOGY. 1976. a. $15 to individuals; institutions $19 (effective 1995). University of Florida, Department of Anthropology, 1350 GPA, Gainesville, FL 32611. TEL 904-392-2031. FAX 904-392-6929. E-mail: rshtul@ufcc.ufl.edu. Ed. Robin Shtulman. adv.; bk.rev.; circ. 125 (paid). **Indexed:** Anthropol.Lit., SSCI. **Document type:** academic/scholarly publication.
—BLDSC (3956.058000).
Refereed Serial

390　　　　　　　　DK　　ISSN 0085-0756
OLK; journal of the Danish Ethnographic Society. (Text in English) 1959. a. DKK 250. Dansk Etnografisk Forening - Danish Ethnographic Society, Institute of Anthropology, University of Copenhagen, Frederiksholms Kanal 4, DK-1220 Copenhagen K, Denmark. TEL 45-35-32-34-67. FAX 45-35-32-34-65. E-mail: journal.folk@anthro.ku.dk. Ed.Bd. bk.rev.; bibl.; illus. circ. 1,000. **Indexed:** A.I.C.P., Anthropol.Lit., IBR, Lang.& Lang.Behav.Abstr., Numis.Lit., Sociol.Abstr.
—BLDSC (3974.570000); UnCover.
Description: Presents articles on social and cultural anthropology to an international audience.

572　　　　　　　UK　　ISSN 0430-8778
GR140
FOLK LIFE: JOURNAL OF ETHNOLOGICAL STUDIES. 1963. a. $30. Society for Folk Life Studies, Museum of English Rural Life, University of Reading, Whiteknights Park, Reading, England. TEL 44-118-931-8663. FAX 44-118-975-1264. E-mail: r.d.brigden@reading.ac.uk. Ed. Roy Brigden. adv.; bk.rev.; illus.; index. circ. 500. **Indexed:** A.I.C.P., Arts & Hum.Cit.Ind., ASCA, Br.Archaeol.Abstr., Curr.Cont., Forest Prod.Abstr., M.L.A., MLA Intl.Bibl., RILA. **Document type:** academic/scholarly publication.
—BLDSC (3974.571500); Genuine Article; UnCover.
Description: Devoted to the study of traditional ways of life in Great Britain and Ireland.

301.2　　　　　　　SW　　ISSN 1102-6502
FOLKENS MUSEUM - NATIONAL MUSEUM OF ETHNOGRAPHY. 1953. irreg. price varies. Folkens Museum - Etnografiska, P.O. Box 27140, S-102 52, Stockholm, Sweden. FAX 46-8-666-50-7- Ed. Ulla Wagner. circ. 1,000. **Document type:** monographic series.
Formerly: Ethnographical Museum of Sweden. Monograph Series (ISSN 0081-5632)

572　　　　　　　FI　　ISSN 0085-0764
GR200
FOLKLIVSSTUDIER. (Subseries of: Svenska Litteratursaellskapet i Finland. Skrifter) (Text in Swedish; summaries in English and German) 1945. irreg., no.19, 1993. FIM 150. Svenska Litteratursaellskapet i Finland, Marieg. 8, 00170 Helsinki 17, Finland. FAX 358-0-632820. Ed. Magnus Pettersson. circ. controlled. **Document type:** academic/scholarly publication, monographic series.

FOLKLORE FORUM. see *FOLKLORE*

FOLLETOS DE DIVULGACION. see *ARCHAEOLOGY*

FOOD AND FOODWAYS; explorations in the history and culture of human nutrition. see *NUTRITION AND DIETETICS*

572　　　　　　　NE　　ISSN 0275-5769
FOOD AND NUTRITION IN HISTORY AND ANTHROPOLOGY. 1980. irreg., latest vol.11. Gordon and Breach - Harwood Academic, Amsteldisk 166, 1st Fl., 1079 LH Amsterdam, Netherlands. (Subscr. to: International Publishers Distributor, Box 32160, Newark, NJ 07102. TEL 800-545-8398. FAX 215-750-6343) Ed. J. Robson. **Document type:** monographic series.
—BLDSC (3977.043500).
Refereed Serial

FORSCHUNGSBERICHTE ZUR UR- UND FRUEHGESCHICHTE. see *ARCHAEOLOGY*

FRONTIERES; les vivants et les morts. see *PSYCHOLOGY*

FRONTLINE REPORT. see *RELIGIONS AND THEOLOGY — Roman Catholic*

572　　　　　　　BO
FUENTES PRIMARIAS. 1983. irreg. $20. Museo Nacional de Etnografia y Folklore, Calle Ingavi 916, Casilla 5817, La Paz, Bolivia. circ. 1,000.

GALA; revista d'arqueologia i antropologia. see *ARCHAEOLOGY*

572　　　　　　　FR
GALAXIE ANTHROPOLOGIQUE. 1992. q? Association Nouvelles Etudes Anthropologiques, c/o Jean-Marie Brohm, 28 av. Herbillon, 94160 Saint-Mande, France. TEL 1-43-74-01-02. (Subscr. to: 30 rue Duperre, 75009 Paris, France. TEL 1-42-82-12-54) Ed. Louis-Vincent Thomas.

572 570　　　　　　PO　　ISSN 0870-0168
GARCIA DE ORTA: SERIE DE ANTROPOBIOLOGIA. (Text in English, French, Italian, Portuguese and Spanish) 1982. 2/yr. price varies. Instituto de Investigacao Cientifica Tropical, Rua da Junqueira 30, 1300 Lisbon, Portugal. TEL 351-1-3622621. FAX 351-1-3631460. E-mail: cdi@iict.pt; URL: http://www.iict.pt. (Subscr. to: Centro de Documentacao e Informacao, Rua Jau 47, 1300 Lisbon, Portugal) circ. 1,000. **Indexed:** Anthropol.Lit., Documentatieblad. **Document type:** academic/scholarly publication.

572　　　　　　　UK　　ISSN 0435-3684
　　　　　　　　　　　　　CODEN: GAHGAJ
GEOGRAFISKA ANNALER. SERIES B. HUMAN GEOGRAPHY. (Text in English) q. £85($134) (foreign £85) (effective 1997). (Svenska Saellskapet foer Antropologi och Geografi - Swedish Society of Anthropology and Geography) Blackwell Publishers Ltd., 108 Cowley Rd., Oxford OX4 1JF, England. TEL 44-1865-791100. FAX 44-1865-791347. E-mail: jnlinfo@blackwellpublishers.co.uk; URL: http://www.blackwellpublishers.co.uk. Ed. Claes Alvstam. **Indexed:** Anthropol.Lit., Bibl.Cart., Biol.Abstr., Deep Sea Res.& Oceanogr.Abstr., Geo.Abstr.H.G., IDA, Rural Devel.Abstr., SSCI, World Agri.Econ.& Rural Sociol.Abstr. **Document type:** academic/scholarly publication.
—BLDSC (4124.060000); Linda Hall; SWETS; UnCover. **CCC.**
Supersedes in part: Geografiska Annaler (ISSN 0016-7231)

GEOGRAPHICA HELVETICA; Schweizerische Zeitschrift fuer Laender- und Voelkerkunde. see *GEOGRAPHY*

572　　　　　　　AT　　ISSN 0072-1190
GEORGE ERNEST MORRISON LECTURES IN ETHNOLOGY. 1932. irreg. Aus.$5. Australian National University, Department of Anthropology, Canberra, A.C.T. 0200, Australia. TEL 06-2494150. (back issues avail.) **Document type:** academic/scholarly publication.

GERMANIA. see *ARCHAEOLOGY*

572　　　　　　　SW　　ISSN 0280-3887
GN301
GOETEBORGS ETNOGRAFISKA MUSEUM. AARSTRYCK/ETHNOGRAPHICAL MUSEUM, GOTHENBURG, SWEDEN. ANNUAL REPORT. (Text in English, Spanish and Swedish) 1956. biennial. Etnografiska Museet Goeteborg, Aavaegen 24, P.O. Box 5303, S-402 27 Goeteborg, Sweden. TEL 46-31-612776. FAX 46-317730920. Ed. Sven-Erik Isacsson. R&P contact: Jan Slavik. **Indexed:** A.I.C.P. **Document type:** corporate report.
Formerly: (until 1970): Etnografiska Museet, Goeteborg. Aarstyck (ISSN 0436-2020)

301.2　　　　　　　SW　　ISSN 0348-4076
GOTHENBURG STUDIES IN SOCIAL ANTHROPOLOGY. (Subseries of: Acta Universitatis Gothoburgensis) 1978. irreg., no.12, 1990. price varies; also exchange basis. Goeteborg University Library, P.O. Box 5096, S-402 22 Goeteborg, Sweden. TEL 46-31-7731733. FAX 46-31-163797. E-mail: jan.ahman@ub.gu.se. Ed. Kaj Aarhem. **Indexed:** Anthropol.Lit. **Document type:** monographic series.

572　　　　　　　FR　　ISSN 0764-8928
GN1
GRADHIVA; revue d'histoire et d'archives de l'anthropologie. 2/yr. 230 F. (foreign 280 F.) (effective 1996). (Musee de l'Homme, Departement d'Archives de l'Ethnologie) Editions Jean Michel Place, 12 rue Pierre et Marie Curie, 75005 Paris, France. TEL 46-33-05-11. FAX 47-05-66-74. (also avail. in microfiche) **Indexed:** Curr.Cont.

GRASSROOTS DEVELOPMENT. see *BUSINESS AND ECONOMICS — International Development And Assistance*

GUIZHOU MINZU YANJIU/STUDY OF GUIZHOU NATIONALITIES. see *ORIENTAL STUDIES*

572　　　　　　　US　　ISSN 0017-6087
DX101　　　　　　　　　CODEN: GYLJAC
GYPSY LORE SOCIETY. JOURNAL. 1888-1982; N.S. 1991. s-a. $35 in US & Canada; elsewhere $40 (includes the Newsletter) (effective 1996). Gypsy Lore Society, 5607 Greenleaf Rd., Cheverly, MD 20785. TEL 301-341-1261. FAX 301-341-1261. E-mail: ssalo@capaccess.org; URL: http://metro.turnpike.net/R/rtracy/index.html. Ed. Sheila Salo. adv.; bk.rev.; illus. circ. 300. (back issues avail. for new series) **Indexed:** A.I.C.P., Amer.Hist.& Life (1991-), Bibl.Ling., Br.Hum.Ind., Hist.Abstr. (1991-). **Document type:** academic/scholarly publication.
—CCC.
Description: Publishes original research in Gypsy studies, including articles in anthropology, history, linguistics, music and folklore.
Refereed Serial

ANTHROPOLOGY

572 300 398   US   ISSN 1070-4604
DX101
GN1
GYPSY LORE SOCIETY. NEWSLETTER. 1978. q. $35 with the Journal. Gypsy Lore Society, 5607 Greenleaf Rd., Cheverly, MD 20785. TEL 301-341-1261. E-mail: ssalo@capaccess.org; URL: http://metro.turnpike.net/R/rtracy/index.html. Ed. Homer W. Cates. bibl. circ. 300. (back issues avail.) **Document type:** newsletter.
—CCC.
    Formerly: Gypsy Lore Society. North American Chapter. Newsletter (ISSN 0731-4841)
    Description: Resource on current research in Gypsy studies.

HALKBILIMI. see *FOLKLORE*

301.2   GW   ISSN 0072-9469
GN2
HAMBURGISCHES MUSEUM FUER VOELKERKUNDE. MITTEILUNGEN. (Text in German, occasionally in English or French) 1971; N.S. a. price varies. Rothenbaumchaussee 64, 20148 Hamburg, Germany. TEL 49-40-44195505. Ed. Wulf Koepke. R&P contact: Bernd Schmelz. adv. contact: Bernd Schmelz. circ. 600. (back issues avail.) **Indexed:** Anthropol.Lit. **Document type:** newsletter.

HEIMDAL; revue d'heritage Norois. see *HISTORY — History Of Europe*

HESSISCHE BLAETTER FUER VOLKS- UND KULTURFORSCHUNG. see *ETHNIC INTERESTS*

HIIDENKIVI. see *HISTORY*

HISTORIA, ANTROPOLOGIA Y FUENTES ORALES. see *HISTORY*

HISTORICAL BIOLOGY; an international journal of paleobiology. see *PALEONTOLOGY*

572 900   NE   ISSN 0275-7206
GN1   CODEN: HIAND7
HISTORY AND ANTHROPOLOGY. 4/yr. $105 (effective 1998). Gordon and Breach - Harwood Academic, Amsteldisk 166, 1st Fl., 1079 LH Amsterdam, Netherlands. (Subscr. to: International Publishers Distributor, Box 32160, Newark, NJ 07102. TEL 800-545-8398. FAX 215-750-6343) Ed.Bd. adv. (also avail. in microform) **Indexed:** A.I.C.P., Amer.Hist.& Life (1984-), Hist.Abstr. (1984-). **Document type:** academic/scholarly publication.
—BLDSC (4317.778600); SWETS; UnCover. CCC.
    Refereed Serial

572   US   ISSN 0891-9348
                   CODEN: HIANE8
HISTORY OF ANTHROPOLOGY (SERIES). 1983. irreg. price varies. (University of Wisconsin at Madison) University of Wisconsin Press, 114 N. Murray St., Madison, WI 53715. TEL 800-829-9559. FAX 800-473-8310. TELEX 26-5452. Ed. George W. Stocking. bibl.; index. **Document type:** monographic series.
—BLDSC (4317.855000).
    Description: Covers the history and present practice of anthropological inquiry.

572   US   ISSN 0362-9074
HISTORY OF ANTHROPOLOGY NEWSLETTER. 1974. s-a. $5 to individuals; institutions $7 (effective 1997-1998). c/o George W. Stocking, 1126 E. 59th St., University of Chicago, Dept. of Anthropology, Chicago, IL 60637. TEL 312-702-7702. FAX 312-702-4503. Ed.Bd. bk.rev.; bibl.; circ. 300 (controlled). **Indexed:** A.I.C.P., Amer.Hist.& Life, Anthropol.Lit., Hist.Abstr. **Document type:** newsletter, academic/scholarly publication.

572   NZ   ISSN 1172-2541
HOCKEN LECTURE. 1969. a. price varies. University of Otago, Hocken Library, P.O. Box 56, Dunedin, New Zealand. FAX 64-3-4795078. E-mail: hocken@library.otago.ac.nz. Ed. S.R. Strachan. R&P contact: S.R. Strachan. circ. 250.

301 930.1   PN   ISSN 0439-397X
GN1
HOMBRE Y CULTURA. 1962; N.S. 1991. s-a. Universidad de Panama, Centro de Investigaciones Antropologicas, Estafeta Universitaria 10826, Panama, Panama. Dir. Francoise Guionneau-Sinclair. **Document type:** academic/scholarly publication.
    Description: Publishes works in anthropology and archaeology.

572 390   FR   ISSN 0439-4216
GN1
HOMME; revue francaise d'anthropologie. 1961. q. 300 F. to individuals; institutions 420 F. (foreign 480 F.) (effective 1998). (Laboratoire d'Anthropologie Sociale) Editions de l' Ecole des Hautes Etudes en Sciences Sociales, 131 bd. St.Michel, 75005 Paris, France. TEL 33-1-40467080. FAX 33-1-44070889. E-mail: editions@ehess.fr; URL: http://www.ehess.fr/editions. (Dist. by: Centre Interinstitutionnel pour la Diffusion de Publications en Sciences Humaines, 131 bd. St-Michel, 75005 Paris, France. TEL 33-1-43544715. FAX 33-1-43548073; Subscr. to: EHESS Service Abonnements, 55 route Longjumeau, F-91387 Chilly-Mazarin Cedex, France. TEL 33-1-64547695. FAX 33-1-64547665) Ed. Jean Jamin. adv.; bk.rev.; illus.; index. circ. 1,000. **Indexed:** A.I.C.P., Anthropol.Lit., Arts & Hum.Cit.Ind., ASCA, Bibl.Ling., Curr.Cont., E.I., IBR, Int.Polit.Sci.Abstr., Sociol.Abstr. (1971-), SSCI. **Document type:** academic/scholarly publication.
—BLDSC (4326.180000); Genuine Article; KR SourceOne; SWETS.

572   GW   ISSN 0018-442X
GN1   CODEN: HOMOA7
HOMO; Zeitschrift fuer die vergleichende Forschung am Menschen. 1950. q. DM.504 (foreign £222) (effective 1997). (Deutsche Gesellschaft fuer Anthropologie) Gustav Fischer Verlag, Villengang 2, 07745 Jena, Germany. TEL 49-3641-626430. FAX 49-3641-626421. E-mail: office.j@gfischer.de. (Subscr. to: Stockton Press, Subscriptions Dept., Houndmills, Basingstoke, Hants RG21 6XS, England) Ed.Bd. adv.; bk.rev.; abstr.; bibl.; charts; illus.; index. circ. 600. **Indexed:** A.I.C.P., Abstr.Anthropol., Anthropol.Lit., Arts & Hum.Cit.Ind., Biol.Abstr., Curr.Cont., NAA, SSCI. **Document type:** academic/scholarly publication.
—Genuine Article; SWETS; UnCover. CCC.

301   BL   ISSN 0103-7706
HORIZONTES; review of social ideas, history. 1990. s-a. Universidade de Sao Francisco, Instituto Franciscano de Antropologia, Av. Sao Francisco de Assis 218, 12900-00 Braganca Paulista, Brazil. TEL 55-11-78448300. FAX 55-11-78441825. E-mail: usfbib@eu.ansp.br. Ed. Marcos Cezar de Freitas. **Document type:** academic/scholarly publication.

304.2   US   ISSN 0300-7839
GF1   CODEN: HMECAJ
HUMAN ECOLOGY (NEW YORK); an interdisciplinary journal. 1972. q. $355 (foreign $415) (effective 1998). Plenum Publishing Corp., 233 Spring St., New York, NY 10013-1578. TEL 212-620-8000. FAX 212-463-0742. TELEX 23-421139. (Editorial addr.: Dr. Daniel Bates, Rm. HN723, Hunter College, 695 Park Ave., New York, NY 10021) Ed. Daniel G. Bates. adv.; bk.rev. (back issues avail.) **Indexed:** A.I.C.P., Abstr.Anthropol., Agroforest.Abstr., Anthropol.Lit., Biol.Abstr., Curr.Adv.Ecol.Sci., Curr.Cont., Deep Sea Res.& Oceanogr.Abstr., E.I., Ecol.Abstr., Energy Ind., Energy Info.Abstr., Energy Rev., Eng.Ind., Environ.Per.Bibl. (1972-), Excerp.Med., Geo.Abstr.H.G., Geo.Abstr.P.G., IDA, IMFL, Lang.& Lang.Behav.Abstr., Mid.East: Abstr.& Ind., Mult.Ed.Abstr., NAA, Peace Res.Abstr., Pollut.Abstr., Protozool.Abstr., Psychol.Abstr., Rural Devel.Abstr., Soc.Sci.Ind., Sociol.Abstr., Sport Fish.Abstr., SSCI, Stud.Wom.Abstr., Wild.Rev., Zoo.Rec. **Document type:** academic/scholarly publication.
    ●Also available online. Vendor(s): Information Access Co.
—BLDSC (4336.055000); Ei; Genuine Article; KR SourceOne; Linda Hall; SWETS; UMI; UnCover. CCC.
    Description: Discusses the quality of the environment and the role of social and cultural factors and population density in the maintenance of ecosystems.
    Refereed Serial

156 591.5   US
HUMAN ETHOLOGY BULLETIN. 1974. q. $25 (effective 1997 & 1998). International Society for Human Ethology, Wayne State University, Department of Psychology, Detroit, MI 48202. TEL 313-577-2835. FAX 313-577-7636. E-mail: barbara/fuller@uchsc.edu; URL: http://evolution.humb.univie.ac.at. Ed. Glenn Weisfeld. R&P contact: Glenn Weisfeld. adv.; bk.rev.; circ. 400 (paid). **Document type:** academic/scholarly publication.
    Formerly: Human Ethology Newsletter (ISSN 0739-2036)
    Description: Publishes essays, brief research reports, listings of current literature, announcements.

599.938   IT   ISSN 0393-9375
GN281
HUMAN EVOLUTION; international journal. (Text in English; summaries in English and French) 1986. q. L.150000 to individuals; institutions L.200000 (effective 1995). (International Institute for the Study of Man) Angelo Pontecorboli Editore, c/o Inst.d'Antropologia, Universita di Firenze, Via del Proconsolo 12, 50122 Florence, Italy. TEL 39-55-2398065. FAX 39-55-283358. E-mail: antropos@cesit1.unifi.it. Ed. A.B. Chiarelli. adv.; bk.rev. circ. 700. (magnetic tape; back issues avail.) **Indexed:** Anthropol.Lit., Curr.Cont., Excerp.Med.
—BLDSC (4336.071200); Linda Hall; SWETS; UnCover.
    Description: Multi-disciplinary forum on the study of human evolution. Reflects current interests in molecular evolution, genetics, palaeontology and biological variability considered in social, cultural and physical contexts.

572 913   US   ISSN 0018-7240
GN1
HUMAN MOSAIC; a journal of the social sciences. 1966. a. $9. Tulane University, Department of Anthropology, c/o Graduate Students of the Social Sciences, New Orleans, LA 70118. TEL 504-865-5336. FAX 504-865-5332. Ed. Shannon K. Chappell. adv.; bk.rev.; bibl.; charts; illus. circ. 120. (tabloid format; also avail. in microform from UMI; reprint service avail. from UMI; back issues avail.) **Indexed:** Abstr.Anthropol., Anthropol.Lit., Lang.& Lang.Behav.Abstr., Mid.East: Abstr.& Ind. **Document type:** academic/scholarly publication.
—UMI; UnCover.
    Formerly: Mosaic (New Orleans).
    Description: Provides articles in archaeology, linguistics, cultural and physical anthropology, and all social science disciplines.

572   US   ISSN 0018-7259
GN1   CODEN: HUORAY
HUMAN ORGANIZATION. 1941. q. $60. Society for Applied Anthropology, Box 24083, Oklahoma City, OK 73124-0084. TEL 405-843-5113. E-mail: sfaa@telepath.com; URL: http://www.telepath/sfaa; http://www.smu.edu/~anthrop/humanorg.html. Ed. Robert Van Kemper. adv.; index, cum.index. circ. 4,000. (also avail. in microform; back issues avail.; reprint service avail. from SCH) **Indexed:** A.I.C.P., Abstr.Anthropol., Acad.Ind., Adol.Ment.Hlth.Abstr., Agroforest.Abstr., Amer.Hist.& Life (1963-), Anthropol.Lit., ASCA, ASSIA, C.I.J.E., Commun.Abstr., Curr.Cont., Curr.Lit.Fam.Plan., E.I., Forest.Abstr., Geo.Abstr.H.G., Hist.Abstr. (1963-), IBR, IDA, Int.Polit.Sci.Abstr., Irr.& Drain.Abstr., Lang.& Lang.Behav.Abstr., Maize Abstr., Med.Care Rev., Mult.Ed.Abstr., Potato Abstr., Psychol.Abstr. (1987- Pub.Admin.Abstr., Rice Abstr., Rural Devel.Abstr., Rural Ext.Educ.& Tr.Abstr., Sage Urb.Stud.Abstr., So.Pac.Per.Ind., Soc.Sci.Ind., Soc.Work Res.& Abstr., Sociol.Abstr., Soils & Fert., SSCI, World Agri.Econ.& Rural Sociol.Abstr. **Document type:** academic/scholarly publication.
—BLDSC (4336.250000); KR SourceOne; Linda Hall; SWETS; UMI; UnCover. CCC.
    Formerly: Applied Anthropology (ISSN 0093-2914)
    Description: Applies the concepts of social and behavioral science to issues and problems in the contemporary world.
    Refereed Serial

ANTHROPOLOGY

572 954 II ISSN 0970-3411
DS430
HUMAN SCIENCE. (Text in English) 1954. q. Rs.340($106) Anthropological Survey of India, 27 Jawaharlal Nehru Marg, Calcutta 700 016, India. Ed. A.K. Danda. bk.rev.; abstr.; bibl.; charts; illus.; stat.; index. circ. 1,500. **Indexed:** A.I.C.P., Anthropol.Lit., IBR.
    Formerly: Anthropological Survey of India. Bulletin (ISSN 0003-5513)

572 US ISSN 1059-8316
GN397
I D A WORKING PAPERS. (Text in English, French, Spanish) 1976. irreg. Institute for Development Anthropology, 99 Collier St., Box 2207, Binghamton, NY 13902-2207. TEL 607-772-6244. FAX 607-773-8993. bibl.; charts; illus.; stat. (back issues avail.) **Indexed:** Sport Fish.Abstr., Wild.Rev. **Document type:** academic/scholarly publication.
    Description: Presents recent work on specific areas of Third World development, focusing on applications of anthropology to rural change and environment.

I P C REPRINTS. (Institute of Philippine Culture) see *SOCIOLOGY*

572 SA ISSN 0073-893X
I S M A OCCASIONAL PAPERS. (Text in English) 1964. irreg., latest 1978. R.3 per no. Institute for the Study of Man in Africa, University of the Witwatersrand Medical School, Rm. 2B17, York Rd., Parktown 2193, South Africa. TEL 27-11-647-2203. Ed. Noam J. Pines. circ. 800. **Document type:** monographic series.

572 SA ISSN 0073-8921
I S M A PAPERS. (Text in English) 1961. irreg., no.41, 1987. R.2 per no. Institute for the Study of Man in Africa, University of the Witwatersrand Medical School, Rm. 2B10, York Rd., Parktown 2193, South Africa. TEL 27-11-647-2203. Ed. Noam J. Pines. circ. 800. **Document type:** monographic series.
    Description: Promotes the scientific and social study of man and man's ancestors in Africa from an academic perspective.

572 AU
I U A E S COMMISSION ON URGENT ANTHROPOLOGICAL RESEARCH. NEWSLETTER. (Text in English) 1976. irreg., no.6, 1984. (International Committee on Urgent Anthropological and Ethnological Research) Verlag Stiglmayr, Wienerstr. 141, 2822 Foehrenau, Austria. Ed. Anna Hohenwart-Gerlachstein. index. circ. 800.

572 323.4 DK ISSN 0105-4503
I W G I A DOCUMENTS; documentation of oppression of ethnic groups in various countries. Spanish edition: I W G I A Documento (ISSN 0108-9927) (Editions in English, Spanish) 1971. irreg. (approx. 4/yr.). $25 to individuals; institutions $40. International Work Group for Indigenous Affairs, Fiolstraede 10, DK-1171 Copenhagen K, Denmark. TEL 45-33-12-47-24. FAX 45-33-14-77-49. cum.index. **Indexed:** HR Rep., Refug.Abstr., Rural Devel.Abstr.
    Description: Each issue deals with one subject or one group or tribe, providing documentation on the human rights situation of indigenous peoples throughout the world.

572 323.4 DK ISSN 1011-6087
GN380
I W G I A YEARBOOK. 1988. a. International Work Group for Indigenous Affairs, Fiolstraede 10, DK-1171 Copenhagen K, Denmark. TEL 45-33-12-47-24. FAX 45-33-14-77-49. Ed.Bd. **Indexed:** HR Rep. (1989-), Refug.Abstr.
    Description: Covers the challenges and threats to indigenous peoples in the past year. Includes a report of the organization's activites.

572 NR
IGBO PHILOSOPHY.* 1971. a. £N0.2 per no. Igbo Philosophical Association, Bigard Memorial Seminary, P.M.B. 921, Enugu, East Central State, Nigeria. Ed. Rev. Fr. C. E. Ohaeri.

ILLINOIS STEWARD. see *CONSERVATION*

572 US ISSN 0073-5167
CODEN: ISANBI
ILLINOIS STUDIES IN ANTHROPOLOGY. 1961. irreg. University of Illinois Press, 1325 S. Oak St., Champaign, IL 61820. TEL 217-333-0950. FAX 217-244-8082. (reprint service avail. from UMI) **Indexed:** Biol.Abstr. **Document type:** academic/scholarly publication.
    —CCC.
    Refereed Serial

572 PH
DS688.M2
IMMACULATE CONCEPTION COLLEGE. LA SALLE JOURNAL. (Text in Bisayan, Filipino, or English) 1974. a. P.125 (foreign $15). Immaculate Conception College, La Salle Graduate School Department, 7200 Ozamiz City, Philippines. TEL 65-521-10-10. FAX 65-521-10-10. Ed. Emma Villaseran. bk.rev. circ. 300. **Indexed:** Ind.Phil.Per. **Document type:** academic/scholarly publication.
    Formerly (until 1994): Northwestern Mindanao Research Journal (ISSN 0115-2009)
    Description: Publishes original articles on topics regarding humanities, social science, education, business, and local history.

IMMIGRANT COMMUNITIES & ETHNIC MINORITIES IN THE UNITED STATES & CANADA. see *POPULATION STUDIES*

572 II ISSN 0019-4387
GN1 CODEN: JIASDA
INDIAN ANTHROPOLOGICAL SOCIETY. JOURNAL. (Text in English) 1966. 3/yr. Rs.250($50) Indian Anthropological Society, 27 Jawaharlal Nehru Marg, Calcutta 700016, India. Eds. A.K. Danda, Arabinda Basu. adv.; bk.rev.; charts; illus.; stat.; index. circ. 700. (looseleaf format) **Indexed:** A.I.C.P., Anthropol.Lit., Biol.Abstr., Forest.Abstr., IDA, Rural Devel.Abstr., Sociol.Abstr. **Document type:** academic/scholarly publication.
    —BLDSC (4761.950000); UnCover.
    Description: Publishes articles in all branches of anthropology including medical anthropology.

572 II ISSN 0970-0927
INDIAN ANTHROPOLOGIST. (Text in English) 1971. s-a. Rs.600($150) (effective 1996). Indian Anthropological Association, Department of Anthropology, University of Delhi, Delhi 110 007, India. Ed. J.S. Bhandari. adv.; bk.rev. circ. 500. (back issues avail.) **Indexed:** A.I.C.P., Anthropol.Lit. **Document type:** academic/scholarly publication.

573 II ISSN 0378-8156
GN49 CODEN: IJPGDB
INDIAN JOURNAL OF PHYSICAL ANTHROPOLOGY AND HUMAN GENETICS. 1975-1994; resumed 1997. s-a. Rs.200($30) (Ethnographic and Folk Culture Society) Palaka Prakashan, Box 209, L-II-31, Sec. B, Aliganj Housing Scheme, Aliganj Lucknow 226024, India. Ed. B.R.K. Shukla. adv.: page Rs.1000; 145 x 195. bk.rev.; bibl.; charts; cum.index every 10 yrs. **Indexed:** A.I.C.P., Anthropol.Lit., Biol.Abstr., Curr.Adv.Ecol.Sci. **Document type:** academic/scholarly publication.
    —KNAW; Linda Hall.
    Description: Serves as a medium for scholarly studies devoted to biological aspects of human populations including genetics, evolution, ecology, dermography, growth, physiology, biochemistry, pharmacology, disease patterns and behaviour of individuals comprising them.

301.2 974 573 GW ISSN 0341-8642
INDIANA; contributions to ethnology and linguistics, archaeology and physical anthropology of Indian America. (Text in English, German or Spanish) 1973. irreg. price varies. (Ibero-Amerikanisches Institut Preussischer Kulturbesitz Berlin) Gebr. Mann Verlag GmbH, Charlottenstr. 13, 10969 Berlin, Germany. TEL 49-30-2591-3589. FAX 49-30-2591-3537. (reprint service avail.) **Indexed:** Anthropol.Lit., Bibl.Ling., IBR. **Document type:** academic/scholarly publication.
    Description: Covers research in the archaeology, ethnology, physical anthropology, and linguistics of the Indian peoples of the Americas.

572 323.4 DK ISSN 1024-3283
GN380
INDIGENOUS AFFAIRS. Spanish edition: Asuntos Indigenas (ISSN 1024-3275) (Supplement avail.: I W G I A Documents Series (ISSN 0105-4503)) (Text in English) q. $20 to individuals; institutions $35. International Work Group for Indigenous Affairs, Fiolstraede 10, DK-1171 Copenhagen K, Denmark. TEL 45-33-12-47-24. FAX 45-33-14-77-49. Ed.Bd. **Indexed:** A.I.C.P., Anthropol.Lit., HR Rep. (1985-), Refug.Abstr., Rural Devel.Abstr., World Agri.Econ.& Rural Sociol.Abstr.
    —BLDSC (4437.083000).
    Formerly (until Jan. 1994): I W G I A Newsletter (ISSN 0105-6387)
    Description: Discusses efforts in supporting indigenous peoples worldwide in their struggle against oppression.

573 570 IO ISSN 0216-7204
GN49
INDONESIAN JOURNAL OF BIOANTHROPOLOGY/BERKALA BIOANTROPOLOGI INDONESIA. (Text and summaries in English and Indonesian) 1980. irreg., latest vol.4, no.3, 1984. Rps.7500($20) Gadjah Mada University, College of Medicine, Department of Physical Anthropology - Universitas Gadjah Mada, Fakultas Kedokteran, Sekip, Yogyakarta, Indonesia. Ed. Teuku Jacob. adv.; bk.rev.; charts; illus.; stat. circ. 1,000. (back issues avail.)
    —CCC.

572 CK ISSN 0121-2079
INFORMES ANTROPOLOGICOS. 1985. irreg. exchange basis. Instituto Colombiano de Cultura, Instituto Colombiano de Antropologia, Apdo. Aereo 407, Calle 8 No. 8-87, Bogota, D.F., Colombia. TEL 3330548. FAX 2330960. E-mail: scolican@col1.telecom.com.co. Ed. Margarita Reyes. circ. 1,000. **Document type:** monographic series.
    Description: Publishes preliminary or provisional reports on Colombian archaeology, anthropology and related topics.

572 FR ISSN 0248-3912
Z5111
INSTITUT D'ETHNOLOGIE. ARCHIVES ET DOCUMENTS, MICRO EDITION. SCIENCES HUMAINES. a. Musee de l'Homme, Institut d'Ethnologie, Palais de Chaillot, Place du Tracadero, 75116 Paris, France.

572 RU
INSTITUT ETNOGRAFII. POLEVYE ISSLEDOVANIYA. 1975. irreg. price varies. (Rossiiskaya Akademiya Nauk, Institut Etnografii) Izdatel'stvo Nauka, 90 Profsoyuznaya ul., 117864 Moscow, Russia. TEL 095-336-0266. (Dist. by: Mezhdunarodnaya Kniga, B. Yakimanka 39, 117049 Moscow, Russia) illus.

572 II ISSN 0541-7562
AS472.M13
INSTITUTE OF TRADITIONAL CULTURES, MADRAS. BULLETIN. (Text in English) s-a. University of Madras, Institute of Traditional Cultures of South & South East Asia, c/o Director, Publications Division, Madras 600 005, India. TEL 91-44-568778. FAX 91-44-566693. **Document type:** bulletin.
    —BLDSC (2585.172000).

572 CK
INSTITUTO COLOMBIANO DE ANTROPOLOGIA. NOTICIAS. 1993. q. free. Instituto Colombiano de Antropologia, Apdo. Aereo 407, Calle 8 No. 8-87, Bogota D.F., Colombia. TEL 3330548. FAX 2330960. E-mail: scolican@col1.telecom.com.co. Ed. Margarita Reyes. circ. 1,000.
    Description: Contains information on research and other activities carried out by ICAN and other institutions in anthropology.

572 PE
INSTITUTO DE ESTUDIOS PERUANOS. MISCELANEA. 1981. irreg., no.9, 1995. price varies. (Instituto de Estudios Peruanos) I E P Ediciones, Horacio Urteaga 694, Lima 11, Peru. TEL 51-14-323070. FAX 51-14-324981. E-mail: libreria@iep.org.pe. (back issues avail.) **Document type:** academic/scholarly publication.

ANTHROPOLOGY

572   PE   ISSN 1019-4525
INSTITUTO DE ESTUDIOS PERUANOS. PROYECTO DE ESTUDIOS ETNOLOGICOS DEL VALLE DE CHANCAY. MONOGRAFIA. 1968. irreg., no.7, 1983. price varies. I E P Ediciones, Horacio Urteaga 694, Lima 11, Peru. TEL 51-14-323070. FAX 51-14-324981. E-mail: libreria@iep.org.pe. **Indexed:** Geo.Abstr. **Document type:** academic/scholarly publication.

301   BL   ISSN 0104-2300
INSTITUTO FRANCISCANO DE ANTROPOLOGIA. CADERNOS. 3/yr. Universidade de Sao Francisco, Instituto Franciscano de Antropologia, Av. Sao Francisco de Assis 218, 12900-00 Braganca Paulista, Brazil. TEL 55-11-78448300. FAX 55-11-78441825. E-mail: usfbib@eu.ansp.br. Ed. Alberto da Silva Moreira. **Document type:** academic/scholarly publication.

INSTITUTO GOIANO DE PRE-HISTORIA E ANTROPOLOGIA. CADERNOS DE PESQUISA. see *ARCHAEOLOGY*

572   HO
INSTITUTO HONDURENO DE ANTROPOLOGIA E HISTORIA. ESTUDIOS ANTROPOLOGICOS. 1978. irreg., latest no.9. $6 in N. America; Europe $9 (effective 1993). Instituto Hondureno de Antropologia e Historia, Departamento de Investigaciones, Apartado 1518, Tegucigalpa D.C., Honduras. TEL 504-223470. FAX 504-222552. circ. 1,000. **Document type:** monographic series.

570   MX   ISSN 0076-7611
INSTITUTO NACIONAL DE ANTROPOLOGIA E HISTORIA. COLECCION CIENTIFICA. 1967. irreg., latest no.148. Instituto Nacional de Antropologia e Historia, Cordoba 45, 06700 Mexico 7, D.F., Mexico. **Indexed:** Anthropol.Lit.
    Formerly: Instituto Nacional de Antropologia e Historia. Series Cientifica.

572 913   AG
INSTITUTO NACIONAL DE ANTROPOLOGIA Y PENSAMIENTO LATINOAMERICANO. CUADERNOS. 1960. irreg. exchange basis. Instituto Nacional de Antropologia y Pensamiento Latinoamericano, Av. 3 de Febrero 1370, 1426 Buenos Aires, Argentina. TEL 54-1-7843371. FAX 54-1-7836554. E-mail: postmaster@bibapl.edu.ar. bk.rev.; bibl. **Document type:** academic/scholarly publication.
    Former titles (until 1991): Instituto Nacional de Antropologia. Cuadernos (ISSN 0570-8346); (until 1962): Instituto Nacional de Investigaciones Folkloricas. Cuadernos.

INSTITUTUM CANARIUM YEARBOOK. ALMOGAREN. see *ARCHAEOLOGY*

572   AU   ISSN 0538-5865
INTERNATIONAL COMMITTEE ON URGENT ANTHROPOLOGICAL AND ETHNOLOGICAL RESEARCH. BULLETIN. (Text in English, French, German) 1958. a. S.140. Verlag Stiglmayr, Wienerstr. 141, 2822 Foehrenau, Austria. Ed. Dr. Anna Hohenwart-Gerlachstein. charts; illus.; stat. circ 600. (back issues avail.) **Indexed:** A.I.C.P., Abstr.Anthropol., Anthropol.Lit., Bibl.Ling., Curr.Cont.Africa, Documentatieblad, E.I. **Document type:** bulletin.
—BLDSC (2587.450000).

572 972.9   CN   ISSN 0538-6381
F2001
INTERNATIONAL CONGRESS FOR THE STUDY OF PRE-COLUMBIAN CULTURES OF THE LESSER ANTILLES. PROCEEDINGS. 1963. irreg., vol.9, 1982. price varies. International Congress for the Study of Pre-Columbian Cultures of the Lesser Antilles, University of Manitoba, Department of Anthropology, Winnipeg, Man., Canada. Ed. Louis Allaire. **Document type:** proceedings.

572 591   GW   ISSN 0074-3895
INTERNATIONAL CONGRESS OF PRIMATOLOGY. PROCEEDINGS. 1967. biennial; 11th, 1986, Goettingen. International Primatological Society, c/o Dr. H.-J. Kuhn, German Primate Center, Kellnerweg 4, 37077 Goettingen, Germany. Ed.Bd. **Indexed:** Biol.Abstr. **Document type:** proceedings.

INTERNATIONAL DIRECTORY OF PRIMATOLOGY. see *BIOLOGY — Zoology*

INTERNATIONAL DOCUMENTARY. see *MOTION PICTURES*

572   IT   ISSN 0393-9383
INTERNATIONAL JOURNAL OF ANTHROPOLOGY. (Text in English) 1986. q. Lit.120000 to individuals; institutions Lit.150000 (effective 1997). (European Anthropological Association) Angelo Pontecorboli Editore, Via S. Slataper 10, 50134 Florence, Italy. TEL 39-55-496502. FAX 39-55-473164. E-mail: antropos@cesit1.unifi.it; URL: http://www.unifi.it/unifi/anthop/. Ed. Brunetto Chiarelli. adv.; bk.rev.; index. circ. 500. (back issues avail.) **Indexed:** Anthropol.Lit., Excerp.Med. **Document type:** academic/scholarly publication.
—BLDSC (4542.083000); UnCover.
    Description: Covers anthropological topics outside the scope of human evolution such as auxology, nutrition, paleopathology, applied anthropology, and population biology. Also covers all sectors of contemporary physical anthropology.

INTERNATIONAL JOURNAL OF COMPARATIVE SOCIOLOGY AND ANTHROPOLOGY. see *SOCIOLOGY*

572   UK   ISSN 1047-482X
                            CODEN: IJOHEA
INTERNATIONAL JOURNAL OF OSTEOARCHAEOLOGY. 1991. bi-m. $435 (foreign $435) (effective 1998). John Wiley & Sons Ltd., Journals, Baffins Ln., Chichester, W. Sussex PO19 1UD, England. TEL 44-1243-779777. FAX 44-1243-775878. E-mail: info-assets@wiley.co.uk; URL: http://www.wiley.co.uk. (Subscr. in the Americas to: John Wiley & Sons, Inc., 605 Third Ave., New York, NY 10158. TEL 212-850-6645. FAX 212-850-6021) Eds. Ann Stirland, Tony Waldron; Pub. Helen Bailey. adv.: B&W page £595, color page £1495; trim 260 x 200; adv. contact: Bob Kern. bk.rev. circ. 179. (also avail. in microfilm from UMI; microfiche; back issues avail.; reprint service avail. from SWZ) **Indexed:** Anthropol.Lit., ASCA, Curr.Cont. **Document type:** academic/scholarly publication.
—BLDSC (4542.440500); Genuine Article; SWETS; UMI; UnCover. CCC.
    Description: Deals with all aspects of the study of animal and human bones.
    Refereed Serial

410 572   US   ISSN 0895-9897
INTERNATIONAL MUSEUM OF CULTURES. PUBLICATION. (Text in English; occasionally in Spanish or Portuguese) 1976. irreg. Summer Institute of Linguistics, Inc., Academic Publications, 7500 W. Camp Wisdom Rd., Dallas, TX 75236. TEL 972-708-7403. FAX 972-708-7387. E-mail: academic_books@sil.org; URL: http://www.sil.org. Ed. Barbara Moore. (also avail. in microfiche; back issues avail.) **Indexed:** Lang.& Lang.Behav.Abstr. **Document type:** monographic series.
—BLDSC (7086.530000).
    Formerly: Summer Institute of Linguistics. Museum of Anthropology Publication (ISSN 0197-3746)

572   UK   ISSN 0074-3496
INTERNATIONAL UNION OF ANTHROPOLOGICAL AND ETHNOLOGICAL SCIENCES NEWSLETTER. 1981. 3/yr. $15 to individuals; institutions $50; students $10. International Union of Anthropological and Ethnological Sciences, c/o Eric Sunderland, Ed., University of Wales, Bangor, Gwynedd LL57 2DG, Wales. TEL 44-1248-354036. FAX 44-1248-355830. R&P contact: Eric Sunderland. adv. contact: Eric Sunderland. circ. 300. **Document type:** newsletter.
    Description: Covers anthropology, ethnology, archaeology, linguistics, and news of the Union's activities.

571   IT   ISSN 1025-4080
INTERNATIONAL UNION OF PREHISTORIC AND PROTOHISTORIC SCIENCES. CONGRESS. BULLETIN. (Text in English) 1958. s-a. free. International Union of Prehistoric and Protohistoric Sciences, Via S. Marchesi 12, 47100 Forli, Italy. TEL 39-543-35725. FAX 39-543-35805. Ed. Ubaldo Marra. **Indexed:** Abstr.Anthropol.
    Formerly (until 1994): International Union of Prehistoric and Protohistoric Sciences. Congress Proceedings (ISSN 0074-9478)

572 420   IO   ISSN 0304-2189
GN635.I65
IRIAN: BULLETIN OF IRIAN JAYA. (Text and summaries in English, Indonesian) 1972. a. Rps.20000($20) University of Cendarawasih, Box 1800, Jayapura 99018, Irian Jaya, Indonesia. FAX 62-967-81302. Ed. Philip Kosho. charts. circ. 350. (also avail. in microfiche; back issues avail.) **Indexed:** A.I.C.P., Bibl.Ling., E.I., M.L.A., MLA Intl.Bibl. **Document type:** bulletin.
    Description: An anthropological journal focusing specifically on the indigenous cultures of Irian Jaya.

ITALIAN HISTORY & CULTURE. see *HISTORY — History Of Europe*

570 990   NZ   ISSN 0032-4000
GN2
J P S. (Journal of the Polynesian Society) 1892. q. NZ.$40 to non-member individuals; institutions & libraries NZ.$70. Polynesian Society, Inc., c/o Maori Dept., University of Auckland, Auckland, New Zealand. Ed. Ray Harlow. adv.; bk.rev.; bibl.; charts; illus.; index, cum.index: 1892-1991. circ. 1,000. (also avail. in microform from UMI; microfilm from BHP) **Indexed:** Amer.Hist.& Life (1955-1960), (1964-), Anthropol.Lit., Arts & Hum.Cit.Ind., ASCA, Curr.Cont., Hist.Abstr. (1955-1960), (1964-), IBR, Ind.N.Z.Per., MLA Intl.Bibl., RILM, So.Pac.Per.Ind., SSCI. **Document type:** academic/scholarly publication.
—Genuine Article; KR SourceOne; UMI; UnCover.
    Refereed Serial

JAHRBUCH FUER OSTDEUTSCHE VOLKSKUNDE. see *FOLKLORE*

JAHRBUCH FUER RELIGIOESE ANTHROPOLOGIE/YEARBOOK FOR RELIGIOUS ANTHROPOLOGY. see *RELIGIONS AND THEOLOGY*

572   JA   ISSN 0021-5023
JAPANESE JOURNAL OF ETHNOLOGY/MINZOKUGAKU KENKYU. (Text in Japanese; summaries in English) 1935. q. $108.50 to non-members; members $50. Japanese Society of Ethnology - Nihon Minzoku Gakkai, 3-1-17 Higashi-cho, Hoya-shi, Tokyo 202, Japan. TEL 0424-23-5645. Ed. Yamashita Shinji. bk.rev.; charts; illus. **Indexed:** A.I.C.P., Anthropol.Lit., Curr.Cont., E.I., Jap.Per.Ind. **Document type:** academic/scholarly publication.
—UnCover.

572   JA
JINRUI DOTAI GAKKAI PUROGURAMU YOKOSHU/HUMAN ERGOLOGY SOCIETY. PROGRAM AND PREPRINTS OF THE CONFERENCE. Jinrui Dotai Gakkai, Rodo Kagaku Kenkyujo, 8-14, Sugao 2-chome, Miyamae-ku, Kawasaki-shi, Kanagawa-ken 213, Japan.

572   JA   ISSN 0289-5293
JINRUIGAKU SHUHO/ANTHROPOLOGICAL REPORTS. (Text in English, Japanese) 1948. irreg. Jinruigaku Shuho Hakkojo - Publishing Office of Anthropological Reports, Osaka Shiritsu Daigaku, Igakubu Kaibogaku Kyoshitsu, 4-54 Asahicho 1-chome, Abeno-ku, Osaka 545, Japan.

800   BO
JISUNU. 1974. irreg. Bol.$40($2) (Academia de la Culturas Nativas de Oriente Boliviano) Editorial los Huerfanos, Casilla 2225, Santa Cruz de la Sierra, Bolivia. Ed.Bd. adv.; bibl.; tr.lit. circ. 1,000.

960   FR   ISSN 0399-0346
DT1
JOURNAL DES AFRICANISTES. (Text in English and French) 1931. s-a. 300 F. (foreign 400 F.). Societe des Africanistes, Musee de l'Homme, Pl. du Trocadero, 75116 Paris, France. TEL 47-27-72-55. Ed. Marc Piault. adv. contact: Marie-Paule Ferry. bk.rev.; bibl. circ. 1,500. (back issues avail.) **Indexed:** A.I.C.P., Anthropol.Lit., Bibl.Ling., Curr.Cont.Africa, Documentatieblad. **Document type:** academic/scholarly publication.
    Formerly: Societe des Africanistes. Journal (ISSN 0037-9166)
    Description: Studies the ethnography, ethnology, sociology, physical anthropology, history, linguistics, archeology and geography of Africa.

ANTHROPOLOGY

572 936 960　　US　　ISSN 0270-2495
DT14
JOURNAL OF AFRICAN CIVILIZATIONS. 1979. a., vol.12, 1994. $20. (Rutgers University, Douglass College, African Studies Department) Transaction Publishers, Transaction Periodicals Consortium, Department 3092, New Brunswick, NJ 08903.
TEL 908-445-2280. FAX 908-445-3138. Ed. Ivan Van Sertima. adv.; bk.rev.; illus. circ. 1,500. (back issues avail.) **Document type:** academic/scholarly publication.
—BLDSC (4919.988000); UMI; UnCover. **CCC.**
　Description: Covers recent archaeological and anthropological studies. Explores contributions by African people to the advancement of world civilization.

JOURNAL OF AFRICAN HISTORY. see *HISTORY — History Of Africa*

572 930.1　　US　　ISSN 0278-4165
CC79.E85
JOURNAL OF ANTHROPOLOGICAL ARCHAEOLOGY. 1982. q. $151 (foreign $189) (effective 1997). Academic Press, Inc., Journal Division, 525 B St., Ste. 1900, San Diego, CA 92101-4495.
TEL 619-230-1840. FAX 619-699-6859. E-mail: apsubs@acad.com; URL: http://www.apnet.com/www/journal/aa.html. (Subscr. to: Box 8612123 Orlando, FL 32886-1213. TEL 407-347-4040. FAX 407-363-9661) Ed. John M. O'Shea. (back issues avail.) **Indexed:** Anthropol.Lit., Arts & Hum.Cit.Ind., ASCA, Br.Archaeol.Abstr., Curr.Cont., Hum.Ind., SSCI, SSRI. **Document type:** academic/scholarly publication.
●Also available online.
—BLDSC (4937.600000); Genuine Article; KR SourceOne; SWETS; UnCover. **CCC.**
　Description: Devoted to the development of theory, and methodology for the systematic and rigorous understanding of the organization, operation, and evolution of human societies.
Refereed Serial

572　　US　　ISSN 0091-7710
GN1　　　CODEN: JAPRCP
JOURNAL OF ANTHROPOLOGICAL RESEARCH. 1945. q. $30 to individuals; institutions $50. University of New Mexico, Department of Anthropology, Albuquerque, NM 87131. TEL 505-277-4544.
FAX 505-277-0874. E-mail: LSTRAUS@UNM.EDU; jar45@unm.edu; URL: http://www.unm.edu/~jar. Ed. Lawrence G. Straus. bk.rev.; bibl.; charts; illus.; stat.; index, cum.index: 1945-1964, 1965-1991; circ. 1,395 (paid). (also avail. in microfilm from UMI; reprint service avail. from UMI,KTO) **Indexed:** A.I.C.P., Abstr.Anthropol., Amer.Bibl.Slavic & E.Eur.Stud., Amer.Hist.& Life (1963-1969), (1984-), Anthropol.Lit., Arts & Hum.Cit.Ind., ASCA, Bibl.Ling., Biol.Abstr., Br.Archaeol.Abstr., Chic.Per.Ind., Commun.Abstr., Curr.Cont., Curr.Cont.Africa, E.I., Fam.Ind., Hist.Abstr. (1963-1969), (1984-), Hist.Abstr., IBR, Lang.& Lang.Behav.Abstr., M.L.A., MLA Intl.Bibl., Rural Devel.Abstr., Soc.Sci.Ind., Sociol.Abstr., SSCI, World Agri.Econ.& Rural Sociol.Abstr. **Document type:** academic/scholarly publication.
—BLDSC (4937.700000); Genuine Article; KR SourceOne; SWETS; UMI; UnCover.
　Formerly: Southwestern Journal of Anthropology (ISSN 0038-4801)
　Description: Problem-oriented articles on recent research findings in ethnology, archaeology, biological anthropology, and linguistic anthropology.
Refereed Serial

JOURNAL OF ASIAN AND AFRICAN STUDIES. see *SOCIOLOGY*

572　　US　　ISSN 0191-3557
E78.C15　　　CODEN: JGBAEG
JOURNAL OF CALIFORNIA AND GREAT BASIN ANTHROPOLOGY. 1974. s-a. $25 per vol. California State University, Bakersfield, Department of Sociology - Anthropology, 9001 Stockdale Hwy., Bakersfield, CA 93311. TEL 805-664-3153. Ed. Mark Q. Sutton. R&P contact: Mark Q. Sutton. adv. contact: Jill Gardner. bk.rev.; illus.; charts; illus. circ. 500. **Indexed:** A.I.C.P., Abstr.Anthropol., Amer.Hist.& Life (1974-), Anthropol.Lit., Hist.Abstr. (1974-). **Document type:** academic/scholarly publication.
—BLDSC (4954.740500); UnCover.
　Formerly (until 1979): Journal of California Anthropology (ISSN 0361-7181)
　Description: Original manuscripts on the ethnography, ethnohistory, languages, arts, archaeology, and prehistory of the native peoples of Alta and Baja California and the Great Basin.
Refereed Serial

JOURNAL OF CENTRAL ASIA. see *ARCHAEOLOGY*

JOURNAL OF CONTEMPORARY ETHNOGRAPHY; a journal of ethnographic research. see *SOCIOLOGY*

JOURNAL OF CROSS-CULTURAL GERONTOLOGY. see *GERONTOLOGY AND GERIATRICS*

JOURNAL OF CULTURAL GEOGRAPHY. see *GEOGRAPHY*

JOURNAL OF ETHNOBIOLOGY. see *BIOLOGY*

JOURNAL OF HUMAN ECOLOGY; international, interdisciplinary journal of man-environment relationship. see *ENVIRONMENTAL STUDIES*

572　　CN　　ISSN 0838-4711
JOURNAL OF INDIGENOUS STUDIES. 1989. s-a. Can.$20 to individuals; institutions Can.$30. Gabriel Dumont Institute of Native Studies and Applied Research, 505 - 23rd St., E., Saskatoon, SK S7K 4K7, Canada. TEL 306-934-4941.
FAX 306-934-4941. Ed. Karla Williamson. bk.rev. circ. 200. (back issues avail.) **Document type:** academic/scholarly publication, abstracting/indexing, bibliography.
●Also available online.
　Description: Provides an open forum for the dissemination of scholarly research, discussion and ideas.
Refereed Serial

301　　JA　　ISSN 0388-0508
CB251
JOURNAL OF INTERCULTURAL STUDIES. (Text mainly in English) 1974. a. 2500 Yen($25) Kansai Gaidai University, Intercultural Research Institute, 16-1 Kitakatahoko-cho, Hirakata-shi, Osaka 573, Japan. TEL 81-70-56-1721. FAX 81-720-55-5552. (Dist. by: Maruzen Co., Ltd., P.O. Box 5050 Tokyo International 100-31, Japan. TEL 81-3-3273-3234. FAX 81-3-3271-6076) Ed. Michiharu Ito. adv.; bk.rev.; charts; illus. circ. 800. **Indexed:** Bibl.Ling., Lang.& Lang.Behav.Abstr., Mid.East: Abstr.& Ind. **Document type:** academic/scholarly publication.
　Description: Explores the anthropological aspects of any culture.

JOURNAL OF ISLAMIC STUDIES. see *RELIGIONS AND THEOLOGY — Islamic*

301　　US
JOURNAL OF LATIN AMERICAN ANTHROPOLOGY. s-a. $25 to individuals; institutions $40 (effective 1996). American Anthropological Association, 4350 N. Fairfax Dr., Ste. 640, Arlington, VA 22203-1621. TEL 703-528-1902. FAX 703-528-3546. R&P contact: Terry Clifford. **Indexed:** Abstr.Anthropol. **Document type:** academic/scholarly publication.
　Description: Contains feature articles, research reports, and news briefs concerning Latin American current affairs, activities, academic programs and more.

JOURNAL OF LATIN AMERICAN LORE. see *FOLKLORE*

306 410　　US　　ISSN 1055-1360
P35　　　CODEN: JLIAEI
JOURNAL OF LINGUISTIC ANTHROPOLOGY. 1991. s-a. $38 to individuals; institutions $40 (effective 1996). American Anthropological Association, 4350 N. Fairfax Dr., Ste. 640, Arlington, VA 22203.
TEL 703-528-1902. URL: http://www.ameranthassn.org/slapnbs.html. Ed. Judith T. Irvine. R&P contact: Terry Clifford. adv. contact: Terry Clifford. **Indexed:** Abstr.Anthropol., Anthropol.Lit., Curr.Cont., MLA Intl.Bibl. **Document type:** academic/scholarly publication.
—BLDSC (5010.474900); UMI; UnCover.

JOURNAL OF MATERIAL CULTURE. see *SOCIOLOGY*

JOURNAL OF MEDITERRANEAN STUDIES; history, culture and society in the Mediterranean world. see *HUMANITIES: COMPREHENSIVE WORKS*

069.9306 069　　UK　　ISSN 0954-7169
GN301
JOURNAL OF MUSEUM ETHNOGRAPHY. 1976. a. £20. Museum Ethnographers Group, c/o Margret Carey, 2 Frank Dixon Way, London SE21 7BB, England. Ed. Linda Mowat. R&P contact: Linda Mowat. bk.rev.; illus. (back issues avail.) **Document type:** academic/scholarly publication.
—BLDSC (5021.128000).
　Formerly (until 1989): Museum Ethnographers Group. Newsletter (ISSN 0260-0366)

JOURNAL OF NORTHERN LUZON; a semi-annual research forum. see *SOCIOLOGY*

572 930.1　　NE　　ISSN 0922-2995
GN33　　　CODEN: JQANEI
JOURNAL OF QUANTITATIVE ANTHROPOLOGY. (Text in English) 1989. q. fl.284 to institutions; $169 to institutions in U.S. (effective 1997). Kluwer Academic Publishers, Postbus 17, 3300 AA Dordrecht, Netherlands. TEL 31-78-6392392.
FAX 31-78-6392254. TELEX 29245 KAPG NL. E-mail: services@wkap.nl; URL: http://www.wkap.nl. (Dist. by: Kluwer Academic Publishers, P.O. Box 322, 3300 AH Dordrecht, Netherlands. TEL 31-78-6392392. FAX 31-78-6546474; N. America dist. addr.: Box 358, Accord Sta., Hingham, MA 02018-0358. TEL 617-871-6600. FAX 617-871-6528) Ed. Jeffrey C. Johnson. (also avail. in microform from UMI; back issues avail.; reprint service avail. from SWZ) **Indexed:** Anthropol.Lit., Ind.Med., Sociol.Abstr. **Document type:** academic/scholarly publication.
—SWETS; UMI; UnCover. **CCC.**
　Description: Provides a forum for scientific research, methodological developments, computer application and other subjects of interest to anthropologists.
Refereed Serial

JOURNAL OF RESEARCH IN AYURVEDA AND SIDDHA. see *ALTERNATIVE MEDICINE*

301.2　　II　　ISSN 0449-315X
GN1
JOURNAL OF SOCIAL RESEARCH. (Text in English) 1958. s-a. Rs.14($4) Ranchi University, Department of Anthropology, Ranchi 834001, Bihar, India. (Co-sponsor: Council of Social and Cultural Research) Ed. L.P. Vidyarth. bk.rev. circ. 150. **Indexed:** A.I.C.P., Anthropol.Lit., ASSIA, IBR, Lang.& Lang.Behav.Abstr., Mid.East: Abstr.& Ind., Rural Devel.Abstr, Rural Ext.Educ.& Tr.Abstr.

JOURNAL OF THE SOUTHWEST. see *HISTORY — History Of North And South America*

JOURNAL OF WORLD PREHISTORY. see *ARCHAEOLOGY*

JUDAICA IBEROAMERICANA. see *ETHNIC INTERESTS*

JURNAL ANTROPOLOGI DAN SOSIOLOGI. see *SOCIOLOGY*

KALULU; bulletin of Malawian oral literature and cultural studies. see *LITERATURE*

ANTHROPOLOGY

572 913   US   ISSN 1069-0360
KANSAS ANTHROPOLOGICAL ASSOCIATION NEWSLETTER. 1955-1979; N.S. 1989. bi-m. $22 to individuals; institutions $25 (effective 1997). Kansas Anthropological Association, 6425 S.W. Sixth Ave., Topeka, KS 66615-1099. TEL 913-272-8681. FAX 913-272-8682. Ed. Virginia A. Wulfkuhle. (back issues avail.) **Document type:** newsletter.
    Description: Contains short articles of interest to Kansas and region; includes association news and announcements.

572 913   US   ISSN 1069-0379
THE KANSAS ANTHROPOLOGIST. 1989. s-a. $22 to individuals; institutions $25 (effective 1997). Kansas Anthropological Association, c/o Kansas State Historical Society, 6425 S.W. Sixth Ave., Topeka, KS 66615-1099. TEL 913-272-8681. FAX 913-272-8682. Ed. Virginia A. Wulfkuhle. bk.rev.; charts; illus. circ. 450. (back issues avail.) **Document type:** academic/scholarly publication.
    Former titles (until 1989): Kansas Anthropological Association. Journal; (until 1979): Kansas Anthropological Association. Newsletter (ISSN 0022-8451)

573 301   FI   ISSN 0355-1830
DK445
KANSATIETEELLINEN ARKISTO. (Text in English, Finnish, German and Swedish) 1934. irreg., latest vol.41, 1996. price varies. Suomen Muinaismuistoyhdistys - Finnish Antiquarian Society, P.O. Box 913, Nervanderinkatu 13, FIN-00101 Helsinki 10, Finland. Ed. Leena Sammallahti. illus. **Indexed:** M.L.A., MLA Intl.Bibl. **Document type:** academic/scholarly publication.

KAYA TAO. see SOCIOLOGY

301.2 572   SP   ISSN 0214-7939
KOBIE, REVISTA DE BELLAS ARTES Y CIENCIAS: SERIE ANTROPOLOGIA CULTURAL. Key Title: Kobie. Antropologia Cultural. (Text in Basque, French, Spanish; summaries in Basque, English, French, German, Spanish) 1969. a. 2500 ptas. Diputacion Foral de Bizkaia, Departamento de Cultura, P.O. Box 97, Bilbao, Spain. TEL 34-4-4157217. FAX 34-4-4162981. (back issues avail.)
—CINDOC.
    Formerly (until 1984): Kobie. Etnografia (ISSN 0214-7920); Which supersedes in part (in 1984): Kobie (ISSN 0211-1942)

572 930.1   SP   ISSN 0214-7971
KOBIE, REVISTA DE BELLAS ARTES Y CIENCIAS: SERIE PALEOANTROPOLOGIA. Key Title: Kobie. Paleoantropologia. (Text in English, French, Spanish; summaries in Basque, English, French, German) 1969. a. 2500 ptas. Diputacion Foral de Bizkaia, Departamento de Cultura, P.O. Box 97, Bilbao, Spain. TEL 34-4-4157217. FAX 34-4-4162981. (back issues avail.)
—CINDOC.
    Supersedes in part (in 1985): Kobie. Paleoantropologia y Ciencias Naturales (ISSN 0214-7963); Which supersedes in part (in 1984): Kobie (ISSN 0211-1942)

572   NE
KONINKLIJK INSTITUUT VOOR TAAL-, LAND- EN VOLKENKUNDE. PROCEEDINGS. (Text in English) 1994. irreg., vol.2, 1995. K I T L V Press, P.O. Box 9515, 2300 RA Leiden, Netherlands. TEL 31-71-5272372. FAX 31-71-5272638. E-mail: kitlvpress@rullet.leidenuniv.nl. (back issues avail.) **Document type:** proceedings.

572   NE   ISSN 0074-0470
KONINKLIJK INSTITUUT VOOR TAAL-, LAND- EN VOLKENKUNDE. TRANSLATION SERIES. (Text in English) 1956. irreg., no.25, 1995. price varies. K I T L V Press, P.O. Box 9515, 2300 RA Leiden, Netherlands. TEL 31-71-5272638. E-mail: kitlvpress@rullet.leidenuniv.nl. (back issues avail.) **Document type:** academic/scholarly publication, monographic series.
—BLDSC (9024.912100).

572   NE
KONINKLIJK INSTITUUT VOOR TAAL-, LAND- EN VOLKENKUNDE. VERHANDELINGEN. (Text in English) 1938. irreg., no.170, 1995. price varies. K I T L V Press, P.O. Box 9515, 2300 RA Leiden, Netherlands. TEL 31-71-5272372. FAX 31-71-5272638. E-mail: kitlvpress@rullet.leidenuniv.nl. **Indexed:** Anthropol.Lit., Bibl.Ling., Rural Devel.Abstr. **Document type:** academic/scholarly publication, monographic series.
    Description: Scholarly monographs on historical, cultural, social and linguistic aspects of Indonesian cultures in pre-colonial, colonial and modern times.

KONTEKSTY; polska sztuka ludowa. see ART

572   US   ISSN 0023-4869
GN2
KROEBER ANTHROPOLOGICAL SOCIETY. PAPERS. 1950. irreg. (approx. a.). $22 (foreign $28) (effective 1998). Kroeber Anthropological Society, Dept. of Anthropology, Univ. of California, Berkeley, CA 94720-3710. TEL 415-642-6932. E-mail: <kas@zal.berkeley.edu> Ed.Bd. bk.rev.; charts; illus.; cum.index. circ. 500. **Indexed:** A.I.C.P., Amer.Hist.& Life (1963-1974), (1986-), Anthropol.Lit., Art & Archaeol.Tech.Abstr., Hist.Abstr. (1963-1974), (1986-), So.Pac.Per.Ind. **Document type:** academic/scholarly publication.
—BLDSC (5118.450000).

305.8   SW   ISSN 1102-7908
KULTURELLA PERSPEKTIV; svensk etnologisk tidskrift. 1992. q. SEK 175 (effective 1996). (Carlsson Bokfoerlag) Foereningen Kulturella Perspektiv, Etnologiska Institutionen, S-901 87 Umeaa, Sweden. TEL 46-90-16-56-95. FAX 46-90-16-77-70.

572 570   JA   ISSN 0286-4568
KYOTO DAIGAKU. REICHORUI KENKYUJO NENPO/KYOTO UNIVERSITY. PRIMATE RESEARCH INSTITUTE. ANNUAL REPORT. (Text in Japanese) 1971. a. free. Kyoto University, Primate Research Institute - Kyoto Daigaku Reichorui Kenkyujo, Kanrin, Inuyama-shi, Aichi-ken 484, Japan. TEL 81-568-63-0567. FAX 81-568-63-0085. E-mail: Shomu@smtp.pri.kyoto-u.ac.jp; URL: http://www.pri.kyoto-u.ac.jp/. Ed.Bd. circ. 1,000. (back issues avail.) **Indexed:** Jap.Per.Ind. **Document type:** academic/scholarly publication.

L A C I T O DOCUMENTS AFRIQUE. (Laboratoire de Langues et Civilisations a Tradition Orale) see LINGUISTICS

L A C I T O DOCUMENTS ASIE - AUSTRONESIE. (Laboratoire de Langues et Civilisations a Tradition Orale) see LINGUISTICS

L A C I T O DOCUMENTS EURASIE. (Laboratoire de Langues et Civilisations a Tradition Orale) see LINGUISTICS

572   US
LAMBDA ALPHA JOURNAL. 1969. s-a. $10 (effective 1997). Lambda Alpha Anthropology Honors Society, Wichita State University, Department of Anthropology, Wichita, KS 67260-0052. TEL 316-689-3195. Ed. Peer Moore-Jansen. circ. 175. **Indexed:** Anthropol.Lit. **Document type:** academic/scholarly publication.
    Formerly: Lambda Alpha Journal of Man (ISSN 0047-3928)

LANGUAGE AND CULTURE. see LINGUISTICS

LANGUES ET CIVILISATIONS A TRADITION ORALE. see LINGUISTICS

LANGUES ET CULTURES AFRICAINES. see LINGUISTICS

LANGUES ET CULTURES DU PACIFIQUE. see LINGUISTICS

LANGUES ET SOCIETES D'AMERIQUE TRADITIONNELLE. see LINGUISTICS

LAW & ANTHROPOLOGY; internationales Jahrbuch fuer Rechtsanthropologie. see LAW

572   US   ISSN 0141-1012
LIBRARY OF ANTHROPOLOGY. 1971. irreg., latest vol.11. price varies. Gordon & Breach Science Publishers, c/o International Publishers Distributor, P.O. Box 3054, Langhorne, PA 19047-3054. TEL 215-750-2642. FAX 215-750-6343. (Subscr. to: International Publishers Directory, P.O. Box 90, Reading, Berkshire RG1 8JL, England. TEL 44-173-456-8316) Ed. Anthony L. LaRuffa. **Document type:** monographic series.
—BLDSC (5188.846000).
    Refereed Serial

LITHIQUES. see ARCHITECTURE

306.14   UK
LIVERPOOL STUDIES IN EUROPEAN REGIONAL CULTURES. irreg., vol.5, 1997. £15. Liverpool University Press, Senate House, Abercromby Sq., Liverpool L69 3BX, England. TEL 44-151-794-2237. FAX 44-151-794-2235. Eds. Ullrich Kockel, Mairead Nic Craith. **Document type:** monographic series.

572 301   UK   ISSN 0077-1074
LONDON SCHOOL OF ECONOMICS MONOGRAPHS ON SOCIAL ANTHROPOLOGY. 1940. irreg., no. 65, 1994. price varies. Athlone Press Ltd., 1 Park Dr., London NW11 7SG, England. TEL 44-181-548-0888. FAX 44-181-201-8115. (Dist. in the U.S. by: Athlone Press, 165 First Ave., Atlantic Highlands, NJ 07781. TEL 908-872-1441) (reprint service avail. from UMI) **Document type:** monographic series.
    Description: Covers various aspects of social anthropology, including field studies and studies of anthropological theory.

LORE AND LANGUAGE. see LINGUISTICS

LUD. see SOCIOLOGY

MAGAZIN FUER AMERIKANISTIK; Zeitschrift fuer amerikanische Geschichte. see HISTORY — History Of North And South America

572 913   CK   ISSN 0120-3045
GN1
MAGUARE. 1987. irreg. exchange basis. Universidad Nacional de Colombia, Facultad de Ciencias Humanas, Cuidad Universitaria, Bogota D.E., Colombia. Dir. Alvaro Roman Saavedra.

572 560 913.031   II   ISSN 0258-0446
GN855.I4
MAN & ENVIRONMENT. (Text in English) 1976. s-a. Rs.1000 in S. Asia; elsewhere $150. Indian Society for Prehistoric and Quaternary Studies, c/o Department of Archaeology, Deccan College, Pune - 411 006, India. TEL 0212-662982. FAX 0212-660104. Ed. V.N. Misra. bk.rev. circ. 500. **Indexed:** Anthropol.Lit., Biol.Abstr. **Document type:** academic/scholarly publication.
—Linda Hall; UnCover.

301   II
MAN AND LIFE. (Text in English) 1975. s-a. Rs.60($18) Institute of Social Research and Applied Anthropology, 727 Lake Town, Calcutta 700 089, West Bengal, India. Eds. P.K. Bhowmick, R.K. Gupta. adv.; bk.rev. circ. 600. **Indexed:** Anthropol.Lit.

572   II   ISSN 0025-1569
GN1   CODEN: MANIAJ
MAN IN INDIA. (Text in English) 1921. q. $32 (effective 1998). 18 Church Rd., Ranchi-834 001, Bihar, India. (Dist. by: HPC Publishers' Distributors Pvt. Ltd., 4805-24, 1st Fl., Bharat Ram Rd., Darya Ganj, New Delhi 110 002, India. TEL 91-11-3254401. FAX 91-11-6863511) Ed. Surajit Sinha. bk.rev.; bibl.; charts; illus.; index. circ. 800. (back issues avail.; reprint service avail. from SWZ) **Indexed:** A.I.C.P., Amer.Hist.& Life (1971-1972), Anthropol.Lit., Arts & Hum.Cit.Ind., ASCA, Biol.Abstr. Curr.Cont., Fam.Ind., Forest.Abstr., Forest Prod.Abstr., Hist.Abstr. (1971-1972), IBR, Lang.& Lang.Behav.Abstr., Pub.Admin.Abstr., Rural Devel.Abstr., Rural Recreat.Tour.Abstr., SSCI, World Agri.Econ.& Rural Sociol.Abstr. **Document type:** academic/scholarly publication.
—BLDSC (5358.020000); UnCover.
    Description: Focuses on ethnology, culture and customs.

ANTHROPOLOGY

301 BL ISSN 0104-9313
▼**MANA**; estudos de antropologia social. (Text in Portuguese; summaries in English, Portuguese) 1995. s-a. $29 to individuals (foreign $48); institutions $44 (foreign $69) (effective 1998). Universidade Federal do Rio de Janeiro, Departamento de Antropologia, Programa de Pos-Graduacao em Antropologia Social, Quinta da Boa Vista s-n, Sao Cristovao, 20940-040 Rio de Janeiro RJ, Brazil. TEL 55-21-5689642. FAX 55-21-2546695. E-mail: ppgas@ax.apc.org. (Subscr. to: Contra Capa Libraria Limitada, Rua Barata Ribeiro 370, Loja 208. 22040-000 Rio de Janeiro, Brazil. TEL 55-21-2361999. FAX 55-21-2560526) Ed.Bd. adv. circ. 1,000. **Document type:** academic/scholarly publication.
  Description: Presents research projects on social and cultural issues. Seeks to acquaint readers with current issues and up-to-date questions carried out by anthropological research.
  Refereed Serial

572 US ISSN 0025-2344
GN1 CODEN: MKQUA4
MANKIND QUARTERLY; an international quarterly journal dealing with both physical and cultural anthropology including related subjects such as psychology, demography, genetics, linguistics and mythology. 1960. q. $40 to individuals; libraries and institutions $90. Scott - Townsend Publishers, Box 34070, N.W., Washington, DC 20043. TEL 202-371-2700. FAX 202-371-1523. URL: http://www.manking.org/mqartlst.htm. Ed. Richard Lynn. adv. contact: James Johnson. bk.rev.; charts; illus.; index. circ. 1,025. **Indexed:** A.I.C.P., Abstr.Anthropol., Amer.Hist.& Life (1921-1977), Anthropol.Lit., Arts & Hum.Cit.Ind., ASCA, ASSIA, Bibl.Ling., Biol.Abstr., Curr.Cont., E.I., Fam.Ind., Hist.Abstr. (1972-1977), IBR, Lang.& Lang.Behav.Abstr., M.L.A., Mid.East: Abstr.& Ind., MLA Intl.Bibl., Polit.Sci.Abstr., Psychol.Abstr., Sociol.Abstr., SSCI. **Document type:** academic/scholarly publication.
  —BLDSC (5360.900000); Genuine Article; SWETS; UMI; UnCover.
  Description: Articles on anthropology, anthropological linguistics, mythology and religion, psychology, demography and genetics.
  Refereed Serial

572 US ISSN 0076-4116
MANKIND QUARTERLY MONOGRAPH SERIES. 1961. irreg., latest no.5. price varies. Institute for the Study of Man, 1133 13th St., N.W., No. C-2, Washington, DC 20005. TEL 202-371-2700. FAX 202-371-1523. **Indexed:** Biol.Abstr. **Document type:** academic/scholarly publication, monographic series.
  Description: Monographs presenting in-depth studies in the areas of anthropology, psychology and evolution.

301.29 MY ISSN 0126-8678
GN635.M4
MANUSIA DAN MASYARAKAT/MAN AND SOCIETY. Title varies slightly. (Text in English or Malay) 1972. a. $4. (University of Malaya, Anthropology and Sociology Department - Universiti Malaya, Jabatan Antropologi dan Sosiologi) University of Malaya Press, c/o University Library, Pantai Valley, 59100 Kuala Lumpur, Malaysia. TEL 03-7555266. FAX 603-7573661. TELEX UNIMAL-MA-39845. adv.; bk.rev. circ. 1,000. **Document type:** academic/scholarly publication.

MANYU YANJIU/JOURNAL OF MANCHU STUDIES. see *ORIENTAL STUDIES*

MARGARET SHAW LECTURES. see *ARCHAEOLOGY*

MARGARETOLOGIST. see *JEWELRY, CLOCKS AND WATCHES*

MARKA INSTITUTO DE HISTORIA Y ANTROPOLOGIA ANDINA. MEMORIA. see *HISTORY — History Of North And South America*

MBYA GUARANI. see *ETHNIC INTERESTS*

998.2 DK ISSN 0106-1062
E99.E7
MEDDELELSER OM GROENLAND, MAN & SOCIETY. 1878. irreg. price varies. (Kommissionen for Videnskabelige Undersoegelser i Groenland, GL - Commission for Scientific Research in Greenland) Geografforlaget ApS, Fruerhoejvej 43, DK-5464 Brenderup, Denmark. Ed.Bd. charts; illus. **Indexed:** Biol.Abstr. **Document type:** academic/scholarly publication.
  —BLDSC (5487.300000); CISTI; Linda Hall.
  Formerly: Greenland, Man and Society; Supersedes in part (in 1979): Meddelelser om Groenland (ISSN 0025-6676)

301.2 610 NE ISSN 0145-9740
GN296 CODEN: MDANES
MEDICAL ANTHROPOLOGY; cross-cultural studies in health and illness. 1977. 4/yr. (in 1 vol., 4 nos./vol.) $98 (effective 1998). Gordon and Breach - Harwood Academic, Amsteldisk 166, 1st Fl., 1079 LH Amsterdam, Netherlands. (Subscr. to: International Publishers Distributor, Box 32160, Newark, NJ 07102. TEL 800-545-8398. FAX 215-750-6343) Ed. Peter Brown. cum.index. (also avail. in microform; reprint service avail. from ISI and UMI) **Indexed:** A.I.C.P., Abstr.Anthropol., Anthropol.Lit., Behav.Med.Abstr., Chic.Per.Ind., Psychol.Abstr. (1985-), So.Pac.Per.Ind. **Document type:** academic/scholarly publication.
  —BLDSC (5526.220000); SWETS; UnCover. **CCC.**
  Refereed Serial

572 610 US ISSN 0745-5194
GN296 CODEN: MAQUD5
MEDICAL ANTHROPOLOGY QUARTERLY; international journal for the cultural and social analysis of health. 1970. q. $75 to individuals; institutions $80 (effective 1996). (Society for Medical Anthropology) American Anthropological Association, 4350 N. Fairfax Dr., Ste. 640, Arlington, VA 22203-1621. TEL 703-528-1902. URL: http://www. ameranthassn.org/smapubs.htm. Ed. Gay Backer. R&P contact: Terry Clifford. adv.: page $275; trim 6 x 9; adv. contact: Terry Clifford. bk.rev. circ. 2,000. (reprint service avail. from UMI,ISI) **Indexed:** A.I.C.P., Abstr.Anthropol., Anthropol.Lit., Arts & Hum.Cit.Ind., ASCA, Curr.Cont., E.I., Fam.Ind., Ind.Med. (1995-), Lang.& Lang.Behav.Abstr., So.Pac.Per.Ind., SSCI. **Document type:** academic/scholarly publication.
  —BLDSC (5526.231000); Genuine Article; SWETS; UMI; UnCover.
  Former titles: Medical Anthropology Newsletter (ISSN 0543-2499); Medical Anthropology.
  Description: Review articles and brief research reports on health, disease and illness from a biological, cultural, linguistic, and historical perspective.

572 AG ISSN 0327-5752
MEMORIA AMERICANA; * cuadernos de etnohistoria. 1991. s-a. Universidad de Buenos Aires, Instituto de Ciencias Antropologicas, Facultad de Filosofia y Letras, Calle Viamonte 430-444, 1053 Buenos Aires, Argentina. TEL 54-1-334-7512. FAX 54-1-432-2292. Ed. Ana Maria Lorandi. **Document type:** academic/scholarly publication.

MESCALITO - SPRUNG IN DIE UNMOEGLICHKEIT; Magazin fuer Magie und Schamanismus. see *PARAPSYCHOLOGY AND OCCULTISM*

301.2 398 MX
MEXICO. DEPARTAMENTO DE INVESTIGACION DE LAS TRADICIONES POPULARES. BOLETIN. 1975. irreg. Departamento de Investigacion de las Tradiciones Populares, Direccion General de Arte Popular, Apdo. Postal 1856, Mexico, D.F., Mexico.

572 917 GW ISSN 0720-5988
F1219
MEXICON; aktuelle Informationen und Studien zu Mesoamerika. (Text in English, German and Spanish) 1979. bi-m. DM.35($20) Mexicon Verlag Karl Friedrich von Flemming, Katharinenstr. 20, D-1000 Berlin 37, Germany. bibl.; charts; illus.; cum.index every 5 yrs. circ. 800. (back issues avail.) **Indexed:** Anthropol.Lit., IBR.
  —CCC.

572 US
MICHIGAN STATE UNIVERSITY. MUSEUM PUBLICATIONS. ANTHROPOLOGICAL SERIES.. 1971. irreg. price varies. Michigan State University, Museum, East Lansing, MI 48824. TEL 517-355-2370. Ed.Bd. charts; illus. circ. 1,500. **Document type:** academic/scholarly publication, monographic series.
  Refereed Serial

570 996 GU ISSN 0026-279X
QH198.M48 CODEN: MCNSBU
MICRONESICA. (Irreg. supplements avail.) (Text and summaries in English) 1964. s-a. $20 to individuals; institutions $30 (effective 1997 & 1998). (University of Guam, Graduate School and Research) University of Guam Press, UOG Station, Mangilao, Guam 96923. TEL 671-735-2787. FAX 671-734-1299. Ed. C.S. Lobban. R&P contact: C.S. Lobban. bk.rev.; bibl.; charts; illus.; index. circ. 350. **Indexed:** A.I.C.P., Abstr.Anthropol., Biol.Abstr., Deep Sea Res.& Oceanogr.Abstr., Geo.Abstr., GeoRef., So.Pac.Per.Ind., Sport Fish.Abstr., Wild.Rev., Zoo.Rec. **Document type:** academic/scholarly publication.
  —BLDSC (5759.340000); UnCover.
  Description: Original research on anthropology, biology and related fields of the tropical Pacific.
  Refereed Serial

MINSU/FOLKLORE. see *FOLKLORE*

MINZU HUABAO/NATIONALITY PICTORIAL. see *ETHNIC INTERESTS*

MINZU YANJIU (BEIJING, 1979)/STUDY IN NATIONALITIES. see *ORIENTAL STUDIES*

572 266 US ISSN 0091-8296
BV2000
MISSIOLOGY; an international review. 1953. q. $18 to individuals; institutions $25; students $13. American Society of Missiology, Asbury Theological Seminary, E. Stanley Jones School of World Mission and Evangelism, Wilmore, KY 40390. TEL 606-858-2215. FAX 606-858-2375. (Subscr. to: American Missiology Society, 616 Walnut Ave., Scottdale, PA 15683-1999) Ed. Darrell L. Whiteman. R&P contact: Darrell L. Whiteman. adv. contact: Steve Shenk. bk.rev.; index; circ. 3,200 (paid). (also avail. in microform from UMI; reprint service avail. from UMI) **Indexed:** A.I.C.P., Amer.Hist.& Life, CERDIC, Chr.Per.Ind., Chr.Per.Ind., E.I., Hist.Abstr., Per.Islam. (1993-), Rel.& Theol.Abstr. (1973-), Rel.Ind.One, Rel.Per., So.Pac.Per.Ind. **Document type:** academic/scholarly publication.
  —BLDSC (5828.912600); SWETS; UMI; UnCover.
  Formerly: Practical Anthropology (ISSN 0032-633X)
  Description: Multi-disciplinary journal for missionaries and professors of mission studies.

MITEKUFAT HAEVEN. see *ARCHAEOLOGY*

572 UY ISSN 0076-9770
MOANA: ESTUDIOS DE ANTROPOLOGIA OCEANICA. 1966. 3/yr. price varies. Olaf Blixen, Ed. & Pub., P.O. Box 495, Montevideo, Uruguay. **Indexed:** Anthropol.Lit., So.Pac.Per.Ind.

572 FR ISSN 0758-4431
MONDE ALPIN ET RHODANIEN; revue regionale d'ethnologie. 1973. q. 230 F. (foreign 250 F.) (effective 1997). Centre Alpin et Rhodanien d'Ethnologie, Musee Dauphinois, 30 rue Maurice Gignoux, 38031 Grenoble Cedex, France. TEL 33-4-76851913. FAX 33-4-76876022. E-mail: abry@icp.grenet.fr. (Co-sponsor: Conseil General de l'Isere) Ed. Christian Abry. adv. contact: Jeannine Collovati. bk.rev.; bibl.; illus. circ. 1,500. **Indexed:** A.I.C.P., RILM. **Document type:** academic/scholarly publication.
  Description: Publishes in-depth studies and articles on ethnology, history and linguistics of southeast France, as well as Switzerland and Italy.
  Refereed Serial

MONOGRAPHS AND THEORETICAL STUDIES IN SOCIOLOGY AND ANTHROPOLOGY IN HONOUR OF NELS ANDERSON. see *SOCIOLOGY*

ANTHROPOLOGY

572 US
MONOGRAPHS IN DEVELOPMENT ANTHROPOLOGY. irreg. Institute for Development Anthropology, 99 Collier St., Box 2207, Binghamton, NY 13902-2207. TEL 607-772-6244. FAX 607-773-8993. (Subscr. to: Westview Press, 5500 Central Ave., Boulder, CO 80301. TEL 303-444-3541) Ed.Bd. bibl.; charts; illus. (back issues avail.) **Document type:** monographic series.
Description: Covers anthropology and development in West Africa, East Africa, North Africa and the Middle East.

MONTALBAN. see *HUMANITIES: COMPREHENSIVE WORKS*

301.2 AA ISSN 0253-1607
MONUMENTET/MONUMENTS.* (Text in Albanian; summaries in French) 1971. s-a. $10.25. Instituti i Monumenteve te Kultures - Institute des Monuments de Culture, Rruga Seremedin Seid Toptani Nr. 7, Tirana, Albania. Ed. Valter Shtylla.

301 930.1 SP ISSN 1132-2217
QH7 CODEN: MNBEA4
MUNIBE ANTROPOLOGIA - ARKEOLOGIA. (Monographic supplements avail.) (Text mainly in Spanish; occasionally in English & French) 1949. a. 5000 ptas. (foreign 6000 ptas.). Sociedad de Ciencias Aranzadi, Plaza de I. Zuloaga (Museo), 20003 Donostia-San Sebastian, Spain. TEL 943-42-29-45. FAX 943-42-13-16. Ed.Bd. bk.rev.; index, cum.index: 1949-1972, 1973-1977, 1978-1982, 1983-1987. circ. 2,500. **Indexed:** A.I.C.P., Amer.Hist.& Life, Biol.Abstr., Chem.Abstr., GeoRef., Hist.Abstr., Ind.SST.
—BLDSC (5983.915005); CINDOC.
Formerly (until 1986): Munibe. Antropologia y Arqueologia (ISSN 0214-767X); **Supersedes in part** (in 1984): Munibe (ISSN 0027-3414)

MUSEE ROYAL DE L'AFRIQUE CENTRALE. ANNALES - SCIENCES HUMAINES. SERIE IN 8/KONINKLIJK MUSEUM VOOR MIDDEN-AFRIKA. ANNALEN - MENSELIJKE WETENSCHAPPEN. SERIE IN 8. see *HUMANITIES: COMPREHENSIVE WORKS*

572 BE
MUSEE ROYAL DE L'AFRIQUE CENTRALE. ARCHIVES D'ANTHROPOLOGIE/KONINKLIJK MUSEUM VOOR MIDDEN-AFRIKA. ARCHIEF VOOR ANTROPOLOGIE. Short title: Archives d'Anthropologie. 1960. irreg., no.31, 1991. price varies. Musee Royal de l'Afrique Centrale - Koninklijk Museum voor Midden-Afrika, 13 Steenweg op Leuven, B-3080 Tervuren, Belgium. TEL 32-2-7695299. FAX 32-2-7670242. (back issues avail.) **Indexed:** Lang.& Lang.Behav.Abstr. **Document type:** monographic series.
Supersedes: Archives d'Ethnographie (ISSN 0563-1742)
Description: Discussions of anthropological, ethnographic, historical and linguistic subjects pertaining to Central Africa.

MUSEO CHILENO DE ARTE PRECOLOMBINO. BOLETIN. see *ART*

572 913 DR ISSN 0252-8614
MUSEO DEL HOMBRE DOMINICANO. BOLETIN. 1972. q. $25. Museo del Hombre Dominicano, Calle Pedro Henriquez Urena, Plaza de la Cultura, Santo Domingo, Dominican Republic. circ. 1,000. **Indexed:** Anthropol.Lit. **Document type:** bulletin.

572 301.2 DR
MUSEO DEL HOMBRE DOMINICANO. PAPELES OCASIONALES. 1973. irreg, no.7, 1981. price varies. Museo del Hombre Dominicano, Calle Pedro Henriquez Urena, Plaza de la Cultura, Santo Domingo, Dominican Republic.

MUSEO DEL HOMBRE DOMINICANO. SERIE CATALOGOS Y MEMORIAS. see *MUSEUMS AND ART GALLERIES*

301.2 DR
MUSEO DEL HOMBRE DOMINICANO. SERIE INVESTIGACIONES ANTROPOLOGICAS. 1975. irreg. no.24, 1982. price varies. Museo del Hombre Dominicano, Calle Pedro Henriquez Urena, Plaza de la Cultura, Santo Domingo, Dominican Republic. charts; illus.

MUSEO DEL HOMBRE DOMINICANO. SERIE MESA REDONDA CONFERENCIAS. see *MUSEUMS AND ART GALLERIES*

572 CK ISSN 0120-7296
MUSEO DEL ORO. BOLETIN. 1978. 3/yr. Col.$3600($15) Banco de la Republica, Departamento Editorial, Calle 13 No. 35-51, Bogota, Colombia. Eds. Dario Jaramillo Agudelo, Clemencia Plazas. bk.rev. circ. 2,000. **Indexed:** Anthropol.Lit.

MUSEO MUNICIPAL DE HISTORIA NATURAL DE SAN RAFAEL. INSTITUTO DE CIENCIAS NATURALES. NOTAS. see *EARTH SCIENCES — Geology*

573 PE
MUSEO NACIONAL DE ANTROPOLOGIA Y ARQUEOLOGIA. SERIE: ANTROPOLOGIA FISICA. 1976. irreg. Museo Nacional de Antropologia y Arqueologia, Plaza Bolivar, Pueblo Libre, Lima 21, Peru.

MUSEO NACIONAL DE HISTORIA NATURAL. BOLETIN. see *SCIENCES: COMPREHENSIVE WORKS*

572 UY ISSN 0077-1244
MUSEO NACIONAL DE HISTORIA NATURAL. COMUNICACIONES ANTROPOLOGICAS. 1956. irreg. free on exchange. Museo Nacional de Historia Natural, Casilla de Correos 399, 11000 Montevideo, Uruguay. illus. circ. 1,200.

MUSEO NACIONAL DE HISTORIA NATURAL. NOTICIARIO MENSUAL. see *SCIENCES: COMPREHENSIVE WORKS*

572 591 PO ISSN 0871-4843
QL1 CODEN: AMBOEZ
MUSEU BOCAGE. ARQUIVOS. (Text in English, French, Portuguese, Spanish; summaries in English, French) 1930; N.S. 1965; N.S. 1987. irreg. exchange basis only. Museu Bocage, Rua da Escola Politechnica 58, Lisbon 1200, Portugal. Ed. G.F. Sacarrao. charts; illus.; index. **Indexed:** Biol.Abstr., Sport Fish.Abstr., Wild.Rev., Zoo.Rec. **Document type:** academic/scholarly publication.
—CISTI.
Formed by the 1987 merger of: Museu Bocage. Arquivos. Serie A (ISSN 0254-0444); Museu Bocage. Arquivos. Series B, Notas (ISSN 0254-0452); Museu Bocage. Arquivos. Serie C, Supplementos (ISSN 0254-0460); Museu Bocage. Arquivos. Serie D, Extensao Cultural e Ensino (ISSN 0870-0540); Which supersedes (in 1981): Museu Bocage. Arquivos (ISSN 0027-3988); Which was formerly titled (until 1965): Revista Portuguesa de Zoologia e Biologia Geral (ISSN 0484-8136); (until 1957): Museu Bocage. Arquivos (ISSN 0374-1087).

572 BL
MUSEU PARAENSE EMILIO GOELDI. BOLETIM. SERIE ANTROPOLOGIA. (Text mainly in Portuguese; occasionally in French, English) 1957. s-a. Conselho Nacional de Desenvolvimento Cientifico e Tecnologico, Museu Paraense Emilio Goeldi, Caixa Postal 399, 66017-970 Belem, Para, Brazil. TEL 091-228-2341. FAX 091-229-1412. TELEX 091-1419. bibl.; maps. circ. 1,000. **Indexed:** Anthropol.Lit., Bibl.& Ind.Geol., Biol.Abstr., Curr.Adv.Ecol.Sci., IDA.
—BLDSC (2143.400000).
Formerly (until 1983, no.84): Museu Paraense Emilio Goeldi. Boletim. Nova Serie: Antropologia (ISSN 0522-7291)
Description: Publishes original papers in anthropology.

301 069 US
MUSEUM ANTHROPOLOGY. vol.20, 1996. 3/yr. $30 to individuals; institutions $45 (effective 1996). (Council for Museum Anthropology) American Anthropological Association, 4350 N. Fairfax Dr., Ste. 640, Arlington, VA 22203-1621. TEL 703-528-1902. FAX 703-528-3546. R&P contact: Terry Clifford.
Formerly (until 1986): Council for Museum Anthropology Newsletter (ISSN 0199-1450)

069.930605 572 UK ISSN 0264-1704
MUSEUM ETHNOGRAPHERS GROUP. OCCASIONAL PAPER. 1982. irreg., no.4, 1995. £11.50 (foreign £12.50). Museum Ethnographers Group, c/o Margret Carey, 2 Frank Dixon Way, London SE21 7BB, England. Ed. Linda Mowat. R&P contact: Linda Mowat. **Document type:** academic/scholarly publication.
—BLDSC (6217.888200).

301.2 960 GW ISSN 0067-5962
MUSEUM FUER VOELKERKUNDE, BERLIN. VEROEFFENTLICHUNGEN. NEUE FOLGE. ABTEILUNG: AFRIKA. 1960. irreg., vol.12, 1992. price varies. Staatliche Museen zu Berlin - Preussischer Kulturbesitz, Generalverwaltung, Stauffenbergstr. 41, 10785 Berlin, Germany. FAX 030-2662612. TELEX 183160. **Document type:** monographic series.

301.2 970 980 GW
MUSEUM FUER VOELKERKUNDE, BERLIN. VEROEFFENTLICHUNGEN. NEUE FOLGE. ABTEILUNG: AMERIKANISCHE NATURVOELKER. 1967. irreg., vol.8, 1990. price varies. Staatliche Museen zu Berlin - Preussischer Kulturbesitz, Generalverwaltung, Stauffenbergstr. 41, 10785 Berlin, Germany. FAX 030-2662612. TELEX 183160. **Document type:** monographic series.

MUSEUM FUER VOELKERKUNDE, BERLIN. VEROEFFENTLICHUNGEN. NEUE FOLGE. ABTEILUNG: MUSIKETHNOLOGIE. see *MUSIC*

301.2 990 GW ISSN 0067-5989
MUSEUM FUER VOELKERKUNDE, BERLIN. VEROEFFENTLICHUNGEN. NEUE FOLGE. ABTEILUNG: SUEDSEE. 1961. irreg., vol.12, 1993. price varies. Staatliche Museen zu Berlin - Preussischer Kulturbesitz, Generalverwaltung, Stauffenbergstr. 41, 10785 Berlin, Germany. FAX 030-2662612. TELEX 183160. **Document type:** monographic series.

301.2 PL ISSN 0076-0315
GN585.P6
MUZEUM ARCHEOLOGICZNE I ETNOGRAFICZNE, LODZ. PRACE I MATERIALY. SERIA ETNOGRAFICZNA. (Text in Polish; summaries in English, French) 1957. irreg., no.30, 1995. price varies. Muzeum Archeologiczne i Etnograficzne w Lodzi, Pl. Wolnosci 14, 91-415 Lodz, Poland. TEL 48-42-328480. FAX 48-42-329714. Ed. Elzbieta Krolikowska. circ. 300. **Indexed:** Anthropol.Lit.

301.2 PL ISSN 0068-4643
MUZEUM GORNOSLASKIE W BYTOMIU. ROCZNIK. SERIA ETNOGRAFIA. (Text in Polish; summaries in English or German and Russian) 1966. irreg. $15. Muzeum Gornoslaskie, Pl. Sobieskiego 2, 41-902 Bytom, Poland. TEL 48-32-81-34-01.

MYTHIC SOCIETY. QUARTERLY JOURNAL. see *FOLKLORE*

301 US
N A S A BULLETIN. s-a. $12 (effective 1996). (National Association of Student Anthropologists) American Anthropological Association, 4350 N. Fairfax Dr., Ste. 640, Arlington, VA 22203-1621. TEL 703-528-1902. FAX 703-528-3546. Ed. Donald D. Wesolowski. R&P contact: Terry Clifford. **Document type:** bulletin.

NAMIBIA SCIENTIFIC SOCIETY. NEWSLETTER/NAMIBIA WISSENSCHAFTLICHE GESELLSCHAFT. MITTEILUNGEN. see *SCIENCES: COMPREHENSIVE WORKS*

NAMIBIANA. see *HISTORY — History Of Africa*

301 JA
NANZAN ANTHROPOLOGICAL INSTITUTE NEWSLETTER. (Text in Japanese) 1992. a. free. Nanzan University, Nanzan Anthropological Institute, 18 Yamazato-cho, Showa-ku, Nagoya 466, Japan. TEL 052-832-3111. FAX 052-833-6157. **Document type:** newsletter.

306 JA
NANZAN STUDIES IN CULTURAL ANTHROPOLOGY. (Text in Japanese; summaries in English) 1982. every 3 yrs. $20. Nanzan University, Nanzan Anthropological Institute, 18 Yamazato-cho, Showa-ku, Nagoya 466, Japan. TEL 052-832-3111. FAX 052-833-6157. **Document type:** academic/scholarly publication.

ANTHROPOLOGY

301.2 398   XR   ISSN 0231-844X
DS1
NAPRSTKOVO MUZEUM ASIJSKYCH, AFRICKYCH A AMERICKYCH KULTUR. ANNALS. Key Title: Annals of the Naprstek Museum. (Text in English, French, German, Spanish) 1962-1992; resumed 1997. a. $15 (effective 1997). (Narodni Muzeum v Praze) Naprstkovo Muzeum Asijskych, Africkych a Americkych Kultur - Naprstek Museum of Asian, African and American Culture, Betlemske nam. 1, 110 00 Prague 1, Czech Republic. TEL 42-2-24214537. FAX 42-2-24226488. Ed. Sylva Pavlasova. bk.rev. circ. 500. **Indexed:** A.I.C.P., Anthropol.Lit., Documentatieblad. **Document type:** academic/scholarly publication.
 Description: Covers Oriental and non-European studies.
 Refereed Serial

572   KR   ISSN 0130-6936
NK976.U5
NARODNA TVORCHIST' TA ETNOGRAFIYA; naukovo-populyarny zhurnal. (Text in Ukrainian) 1925. m. $65 (effective 1998). (Akademiya Nauk Ukrainy, Institut Mystetsvo-znavstva, Folkloru ta Etnografii) Vidavnitstvo Naukova Dumka, Vul. Tereshchenkivska 3, 252601 Kiev, Ukraine. TEL 044-224-4068. FAX 044-224-7060. Ed. S.D. Zubko. bk.rev.; dance rev.; film rev.; play rev.; illus.; index. circ. 5,000. (also avail. in microfiche from IDC) **Indexed:** A.I.C.P., M.L.A., MLA Intl.Bibl.
 —BLDSC (0119.190000).

NATIONAL MUSEUM OF NATURAL HISTORY QUEST. see *SCIENCES: COMPREHENSIVE WORKS*

572   JA   ISSN 0385-3039
GN1   CODEN: BNSADR
NATIONAL SCIENCE MUSEUM. BULLETIN. SERIES D: ANTHROPOLOGY/KOKURITSU KAGAKU HAKUBUTSUKAN KENKYU HOKOKU. D RUI: JINRUIGAKU. (Text in English) 1957. a. exchange basis. Monbusho, Kokuritsu Kagaku Hakubutsukan - Ministry of Education, Science and Culture, National Science Museum, 7-20 Ueno Koen, Taito-ku, Tokyo 110, Japan. **Indexed:** A.I.C.P., Anthropol.Lit., Biol.Abstr., INIS Atomind.
 —BLDSC (2644.050000).

913   CH
NATIONAL TAIWAN UNIVERSITY. DEPARTMENT OF ANTHROPOLOGY. BULLETIN. (Text in Chinese and English) 1953. irreg. $10 per no. National Taiwan University, Department of Anthropology, Taipei, Taiwan, Republic of China. FAX 02-363-1658. Ed.Bd. bk.rev. circ. 1,000. **Indexed:** A.I.C.P.
 Formerly (until 1981): National Taiwan University. Department of Archaeology and Anthropology. Bulletin (ISSN 0077-5843)

NATURHISTORISCHES MUSEUM IN WIEN. ANNALEN. SERIE A, MINERALOGIE UND PETROGRAPHIE, GEOLOGIE UND PALEONTOLOGIE, ANTHROPOLOGIE UND PRAEHISTORIE. see *SCIENCES: COMPREHENSIVE WORKS*

570   HU   ISSN 0077-6599
NEPRAJZI ERTESITO/ETHNOGRAPHIC REVIEW. (Text in Hungarian; summaries in English, French, German, Russian) 1900. a. exchange basis. Neprajzi Muzeum - Ethnographical Museum, Kossuth Lajos ter 12, 1055 Budapest, Hungary. TEL 1-326-340. FAX 2-692-419. Ed. Attila Selmeczi-Kovacs. **Indexed:** A.I.C.P. **Document type:** bulletin.
 —BLDSC (6075.697000).

390   HU   ISSN 0028-2774
NEPRAJZI KOZLEMENYEK. (Text in Hungarian; summaries in English, Russian) 1956. a. exchange basis. Neprajzi Muzeum - Ethnographical Museum, Kossuth Lajos ter 12, 1055 Budapest, Hungary. TEL 1-326-340. FAX 2-692-419. E-mail: kili@post.nem.hu. Ed. Ibolya Forrai. bk.rev. **Document type:** monographic series.

305.5   HU   ISSN 0077-6602
NEPRAJZI TANULMANYOK/ETHNOGRAPHICAL STUDIES. 1968. irreg., latest 1997. price varies. (Magyar Tudomanyos Akademia, Neprajzi Kutato Csoport) Akademiai Kiado Rt., P.O. Box 245, H-1519 Budapest, Hungary. TEL 36-1-20439765. FAX 36-1-2043973. **Document type:** monographic series.

572   US   ISSN 0077-7897
E78.N4
NEVADA. STATE MUSEUM, CARSON CITY. ANTHROPOLOGICAL PAPERS. 1959. irreg., no.23, 1990. price varies. Nevada State Museum, Department of Anthropology, Publications Office, Capitol Complex, Carson City, NV 89710. TEL 702-687-4810. **Indexed:** Abstr.Anthropol.

NEW ENGLAND ANTIQUITIES RESEARCH ASSOCIATION JOURNAL. see *ARCHAEOLOGY*

572   CN   ISSN 0711-5342
NEXUS (HAMILTON); the Canadian student journal of anthropology. 1980. a. Can.$10 to individuals; institutions Can.$20. c/o Department of Anthropology, McMaster University, Hamilton, ON L8S 4L9, Canada. TEL 416-525-9140. Ed. Jasmin Habib. adv. contact: Clare McVeigh. bk.rev. circ. 65. (also avail. in microfilm from UMI; reprint service avail. from UMI) **Indexed:** Anthropol.Lit., Mult.Ed.Abstr. **Document type:** academic/scholarly publication.
 ●Available only online.
 —BLDSC (6109.058000).
 Supersedes (1975-1980): Journal of Anthropology at McMaster.
 Description: Publishes papers of anthropological interest written by graduates and senior undergraduates at both Canadian and foreign universities.
 Refereed Serial

305.8 457   IT
R NI D'AIGURA/NIDO D'AQUILA; rivista etno-antropologica e linguistica-letteraria delle culture e delle Alpi Liguri-Marittime. (Text in Brigascan, French, Italian, Ligurian dialects, Provencal; summaries in French, English) 1983. s-a. Lit.20000($30) (effective 1997). Ni d'Aigura, Center for Studies, Via F.D. Guerrazzi 14-14, 16146 Genova, Italy. TEL 39-10-3621829. Ed. Pierleone Massajoli. adv.: page Lit.400000; trim 190 x 280. bk.rev.; bibl.; charts; illus.; maps; cum.index. circ. 1,000. (back issues avail.) **Document type:** academic/scholarly publication.
 Description: Research in the field of ethno-anthropological matters and linguistic and dialectological matters.

NIHON SEIRI JINRUI GAKKAI TAIKAI SHORKUSHU/JAPAN SOCIETY OF PHYSIOLOGICAL ANTHROPOLOGY. ABSTRACTS OF THE MEETING. see *BIOLOGY — Abstracting, Bibliographies, Statistics*

572   JA
NIPPON JINRUI GAKKAI KINESHIROJI BUNKAKAI NYUSURETA/ANTHROPOLOGICAL SOCIETY OF NIPPON. DIVISION OF KINESIOLOGY. NEWSLETTER. (Text in Japanese) 1989. s-a. membership. Nippon Jinrui Gakkai, Kineshioroji Bunkakai - Anthropological Society of Nippon, Division of Kinesiology, Kyoto Daigaku Reichorui Kenkyujo, Kanrin, Inuyama-shi, Aichi-ken 484, Japan.

305.9   SW   ISSN 0822-7942
GN387   CODEN: NOPEES
NOMADIC PEOPLES. Variant title: Newsletter - Commission on Nomadic Peoples, International Union of Anthropological and Ethnological Sciences. (Text in English and French) 1978-1988; resumed 1990. s-a. $35 (effective 1993). International Union of Anthropological and Ethnological Sciences, Commission on Nomadic Peoples, c/o EPOS, Stureg. 9, S-753 14 Uppsala, Sweden. Ed. Philip Carl Salzman. bk.rev. (back issues avail.) **Indexed:** Anthropol.Lit., Ecol.Abstr., Geo.Abstr.P.G., IDA, Per.Islam. (1992-), Rural Devel.Abstr.
 —BLDSC (6116.706000); UnCover.
 Formerly (until vol.5, 1980): Newsletter of the Commission on Nomadic Peoples, International Union of Anthropological and Ethnological Sciences.
 Description: Studies nomadic peoples from a multidisciplinary standpoint.

500.9   CN   ISSN 0078-1053
                              CODEN: CNORE2
NORDICANA. (Text and summaries in English and French) 1964. irreg. (3-5/yr.). price varies. Universite Laval, Centre d'Etudes Nordiques, Quebec, PQ G1K 7P4, Canada. TEL 418-656-3340. (back issues avail.) **Document type:** monographic series, proceedings.
 Formerly (until no.49 1986): Quebec (City) Universite Laval. Centre d'Etudes Nordiques. Travaux Divers.

301   MX
NOROESTE DE MEXICO. 1976. irreg., no.11, 1990. $6. Centro I N A H Sonora, Apdo. Postal 1664, 83080 Hermosillo, Sonora, Mexico. TEL 52-62-131234. FAX 52-62-172580. E-mail: inahson@rtn.unison.mx. Ed. Maria Elisa Villalpondo Canchola. adv.; bk.rev. **Indexed:** A.I.C.P. **Document type:** academic/scholarly publication, monographic series.
 Description: Papers concerning recent studies in archaeology, history, linguistics and social anthropology of northwest Mexico.
 Refereed Serial

301 306   NO   ISSN 0802-7285
NORSK ANTROPOLOGISK TIDSSKRIFT. (Text in Norwegian; summaries in English) 1990. q. NOK 410 in Nordic countries; elsewhere $83 (effective 1997). (Sosialantropologisk Forening) Scandinavian University Press, P.O. Box 2959 Toeyen, N-0608 Oslo, Norway. TEL 47-22-57-54-00. FAX 47-22-57-53-53. E-mail: mail@scup.no; URL: http://www.scup.no. (US addr.: 875 Massachusetts Ave., Ste. 84, Cambridge, MA 02139. TEL 617-497-6515. FAX 617-354-6875) Ed. Edvard Hviding. **Document type:** academic/scholarly publication.
 Description: Presents research by Norwegian anthropologists.

301.2   US   ISSN 1068-9982
E78.E2   CODEN: MNOREA
NORTHEAST ANTHROPOLOGY. 1971. s-a. $20 to individuals (foreign $25); institutions $55 (foreign $60) (effective 1997). State University of New York at Albany, c/o Department of Anthropology, Social Science Bldg. 263, Albany, NY 12222. TEL 518-442-4721. FAX 518-442-5710. E-mail: neanth@cnsvax.albany.edu. Ed. Richard Wilkinson. R&P contact: Richard Wilkinson. adv.; bk.rev.; bibl.; illus.; circ. 300 (paid). (back issues avail.) **Indexed:** A.I.C.P., Abstr.Anthropol., Anthropol.Lit., Geo.Abstr. **Document type:** academic/scholarly publication.
 —UnCover.
 Formerly (until 1993): Man in the Northeast (ISSN 0191-4138)
 Description: Research-based articles and book reviews focusing on past and present populations of the Northeastern U.S. and adjacent provinces of Canada.
 Refereed Serial

570 390   US   ISSN 0029-3296
E78.N77   CODEN: NARNAV
NORTHWEST ANTHROPOLOGICAL RESEARCH NOTES. 1967. s-a. $40. University of Idaho, Laboratory of Anthropology, Moscow, ID 83844-1111. TEL 208-885-6123. FAX 208-885-2034. E-mail: rsprague@uidaho.edu. Ed. Roderick Sprague. abstr.; bibl.; charts; illus. circ. 300. (back issues avail.) **Indexed:** A.I.C.P., Abstr.Anthropol., Amer.Hist.& Life (1970-1971), Anthropol.Lit., Art & Archaeol.Tech.Abstr., Biol.Abstr., Hist.Abstr. (1970-1971). **Document type:** academic/scholarly publication.
 —KR SourceOne; UnCover.
 Refereed Serial

572 913   MX
NOTAS MESOAMERICANAS. (Text in English, Spanish) 1950. a. $10. Universidad de las Americas, Puebla, Departamento de Antropologia, Apdo. Postal 100, Santa Catarina Martir, 72820 Puebla, Pue., Mexico. TEL 52-22-470000. Ed. Gabriela Urunuela. adv. circ. 950. **Indexed:** A.I.C.P. **Document type:** academic/scholarly publication.
 Former titles: Notas Americanas; Mesoamerican Notes.

572   MX   ISSN 0185-0636
NUEVA ANTROPOLOGIA; revista de ciencias sociales. 1975. 3/yr. $35 in N., S., Central America and Europe; elsewhere $45 (effective 1998 & 1999). (Escuela Nacional de Antropologia e Historia) Nueva Antropologia A.C., Av. Popocatepetl 510, 03330 Mexico, D.F., Mexico. TEL 52-5-6889831. FAX 52-5-6889965. E-mail: sgomez@colmex.mx. Ed. Silvia Gomez Tagle; Pub. Silvia Gomez Tagle. R&P contact: Silvia Gomez Tagle. adv. contact: Silvia Gomez Tagle. bk.rev.; charts; illus.; stat.; cum.index every 2 yrs. circ. 1,000. **Indexed:** A.I.C.P., Anthropol.Lit., Hisp.Amer.Per.Ind. (1975-), IBR. **Document type:** academic/scholarly publication.
 Description: Publishes articles on anthropology and social sciences.

ANTHROPOLOGY

572 300 PH
NUEVA CACERES REVIEW. 1979? s-a. University of Nueva Caceres, School of Graduate Studies and Research, Jaime Hernandez Ave., Naga City 4400, Philippines. **Indexed:** Ind.Phil.Per.
   Description: Contains interdisciplinary coverage of the Bicol region of southern Luzon.

NYT FRA NATIONALMUSEET. see *ARCHAEOLOGY*

572 US ISSN 0078-3005
OCCASIONAL PAPERS IN ANTHROPOLOGY. 1968. irreg., no.14, 1992. $16. Pennsylvania State University, Department of Anthropology, 409 Carpenter Bldg., University Park, PA 16802. TEL 814-865-2509. FAX 814-863-1474. circ. 500. **Indexed:** SSCI. **Document type:** monographic series.
   Refereed Serial

572 AT ISSN 0029-8077
DU28 CODEN: OCEADN
OCEANIA; devoted to the study of the indigenous peoples of Australia, Melanesia, Micronesia, Indonesia, Polynesia and Insular Southeast Asia. 1930. q. $50 to individuals, institutions $60 (effective 1997). University of Sydney, Sydney, N.S.W. 2006, Australia. TEL 61-2-93512666. FAX 61-2-93517488. E-mail: dlcoller@oceania. usyd.edu.au. Ed.Bd. adv.; bk.rev.; illus.; index. circ. 900. (also avail. in microform from UMI; microfilm; back issues avail.; reprint service avail. from UMI,KTO) **Indexed:** A.I.C.P., Anthropol.Lit., Arts & Hum.Cit.Ind., ASCA, ASSIA, Aus.P.A.I.S., Bibl.Ling., Curr.Cont., E.I., Energy Ind., Energy Info.Abstr., MLA Intl.Bibl., So.Pac.Per.Ind., Soc.Sci.Ind., Sport Fish.Abstr., SSCI, Wild.Rev., Zoo.Rec. **Document type:** academic/scholarly publication.
   ●Also available online. Vendor(s): Information Access Co., UMI.
   —BLDSC (6231.400000); CISTI; Genuine Article; KR SourceOne; SWETS; UMI; UnCover. CCC.

OCEANIC LINGUISTICS. see *LINGUISTICS*

OESTERREICHISCHE GESELLSCHAFT FUER UR- UND FRUEHGESCHICHTE. VEROEFFENTLICHUNGEN. see *ARCHAEOLOGY*

OESTERREICHISCHES MUSEUM FUER VOLKSKUNDE. VEROEFFENTLICHUNGEN. see *FOLKLORE*

572 US ISSN 0078-432X
E78.045
OKLAHOMA ANTHROPOLOGICAL SOCIETY. BULLETIN. 1952. a. membership. Oklahoma Anthropological Society, c/o Pete Thurmond, Sec.-Treas., Rte. 1, Box 62B, Cheyenne, OK 73628. TEL 405-497-2662. Ed. Richard R. Drass. circ. 625. **Indexed:** Abstr.Anthropol., Anthropol.Lit.

572 US ISSN 0474-0696
OKLAHOMA ANTHROPOLOGICAL SOCIETY. MEMOIR. 1964. irreg. price varies. Oklahoma Anthropological Society, c/o Pete Thurmond, Sec.-Treas., Rte. 1, Box 62B, Cheyenne, OK 73628. TEL 405-497-2662. Ed. Don G. Wyckoff. circ. 350. **Indexed:** Abstr.Anthropol., Anthropol.Lit.

572 US ISSN 0078-4338
OKLAHOMA ANTHROPOLOGICAL SOCIETY. NEWSLETTER. 1952. m. (9/yr.). membership. Oklahoma Anthropological Society, c/o Pete Thurmond, Sec.-Treas., Rte. 1 Box 62B, Cheyenne, OK 73628. TEL 405-487-2662. Ed. Frieda U. Odell. bk.rev. circ. 625. **Indexed:** Abstr.Anthropol., Anthropol.Lit. **Document type:** newsletter.

ORAL HISTORY. see *HISTORY — History Of Europe*

ORALITE - DOCUMENTS. see *LINGUISTICS*

988.36 301 NE ISSN 0167-4099
OSO; tijdschrift voor Surinaamse taalkunde, letterkunde, culture en geschiedenis. (Text in Dutch, occasionally in English) 1982. 2/yr. fl.39($25) Stichting Instituut ter Bevordering van de Surinamistiek, Koperslagershoek 13, 3981 SB Bunnik, Netherlands. TEL 31-30-6567543. FAX 31-30-2534666. E-mail: whoogbergen@fsw. ruu.nl. Ed. W. Hoogbergen. adv.; B&W page fl.275. bk.rev.; bibl.; illus.; maps; index. (back issues avail.) **Document type:** academic/scholarly publication.
   Description: Publishes articles on the anthropology, archaeology, linguistics, literature, culture and history of Surinam.
   Refereed Serial

572 IT ISSN 1122-2581
OSSIMORI; periodico di antropologia e scienze umane. 1992. s-a. Lit.50000 to individuals; institutions Lit.90000; foreign Lit.120000 (effective 1997 &1997). Protagon Editori Toscani, Strada di Ficareto, 53100 Siena, Italy. TEL 39-577-55359. FAX 39-577-56117. Ed. Paolo de Simonis. R&P contact: Paolo de Simonis. TEL 39-577-56117. bk.rev. circ. 1,000. **Document type:** academic/scholarly publication.

572 US ISSN 0742-1184
OTHER REALITIES; descriptive, methodological and theoretical texts. 1979. irreg., no.7, 1986. price varies. (University of California at Los Angeles, Department of Anthropology) Undena Publications, Box 97, Malibu, CA 90265. TEL 805-746-5870. FAX 805-746-2728. (Dist. by: Crescent Academic Services, 29528 Madera Ave., Shafter, CA 93263) Ed. Jacques Maquet. (back issues avail.) **Document type:** monographic series.
   Refereed Serial

301.2 UK
OXFORD MONOGRAPHS ON SOCIAL ANTHROPOLOGY. irreg. price varies. Oxford University Press, Walton St., Oxford OX2 6DP, England. TEL 44-1865-56767. FAX 44-1865-56646. (Subscr. in US to: Oford University Press Inc., 2001 Evans Rd., Cary, NC 27513. TEL 919-677-0977. FAX 919-677-1714) Ed.Bd. **Document type:** monographic series.

572 US ISSN 0078-740X
PACIFIC ANTHROPOLOGICAL RECORDS. 1968. irreg. price varies. (Bishop Museum, Department of Anthropology) Bishop Museum Press, 1525 Bernice St., Box 19000-A, Honolulu, HI 96817. TEL 808-848-4135. (reprint service avail. from UMI)

PACIFIC ISLAND FOCUS; occasional journal of student research. see *HISTORY — History Of Australasia And Other Areas*

572 990 JA ISSN 0387-4745
PACIFIC SOCIETY. JOURNAL/TAIHEIYO GAKKAI SHI. (Text in English and Japanese) 1979. q. 5000 Yen($20) Pacific Society - Taiheiyo Gakkai, 4-15-29-3F, Mita, Minato-ku, Tokyo 108, Japan. TEL 81-3-5442-2706. FAX 81-3-5442-2716. E-mail: pacsoc@po.iijnet.or.jp. Ed. Hiroshi Nakajima. R&P contact: Hiroshi Nakajima. bk.rev. circ. 1,500. (back issues avail.) **Document type:** academic/scholarly publication.
   Refereed Serial

PACIFIC STUDIES; an interdisciplinary journal devoted to the study of the Pacific - its islands and adjacent countries. see *SOCIAL SCIENCES: COMPREHENSIVE WORKS*

572 GW ISSN 0078-7809
PAIDEUMA; Mitteilungen zur Kulturkunde. (Text in English, French, German) 1938. a. DM.80 (effective 1997). (Universitaet Frankfurt, Frobenius Institut) Franz Steiner Verlag Wiesbaden GmbH, Birkenwaldstr. 44, 70191 Stuttgart, Germany. TEL 49-711-2582-0. FAX 49-711-2582390. (Subscr. to: Postfach 101061, 70009 Stuttgart, Germany) Ed. Beatrix Heintze. R&P contact: Sabine Koerner. illus. circ. 860. (back issues avail.) **Indexed:** A.I.C.P., Amer.Hist.& Life (1977-1978), (1991-), Amer.Hum.Ind., Anthropol.Lit., Bibl.Ling., Curr.Cont.Africa, Curr.Cont., Documentatieblad, E.I., Hist.Abstr. (1977-1978), (1991-), IBR, MLA Intl.Bibl. **Document type:** academic/scholarly publication.

PAPUA NEW GUINEA NATIONAL BIBLIOGRAPHY. see *BIBLIOGRAPHIES*

301 GW ISSN 0938-0116
PARAGRANA; internationale Zeitschrift fuer historische Anthropologie. (Text in English, French, German) 1992. s-a. DM.54 (foreign DM.64) (effective 1997). (Freie Universitaet Berlin, Forschungszentrum fuer Historische Anthropologie) Akademie Verlag GmbH, Muehlenstr. 33-34, 13187 Berlin, Germany. TEL 49-30-47889348. FAX 49-30-47889357. E-mail: info@akademie-verlag.de. (Subscr. in the Americas to: John Wiley & Sons, Inc., 605 Third Ave., New York, NY 10158. TEL 212-850-6645. FAX 212-850-6021) **Document type:** academic/scholarly publication.
   Description: Covers current efforts in the continuing study of phenomena and structure of mankind following the collapse of a binding abstract anthropological norm.

570 US
PENNSYLVANIA. HISTORICAL AND MUSEUM COMMISSION. ANTHROPOLOGICAL SERIES. 1971. irreg., latest no.7. price varies. Historical and Museum Commission, William Penn Memorial Museum and Archives Bldg., Box 1026, Harrisburg, PA 17108-1026. TEL 717-783-2618. R&P contact: Diane B. Reed. **Document type:** academic/scholarly publication, monographic series.
   Description: Scholarly monographs on the subjects of Indian archeology, anthropology and history focused on Pennsylvania.

PENNSYLVANIA ETHNIC STUDIES NEWSLETTER. see *ETHNIC INTERESTS*

PEOPLES OF EAST AFRICA. see *HISTORY — History Of Africa*

573 US
PEOPLES OF THE WORLD. (Regional volumes each updated quinquennially) 1993. irreg. $39.95 per vol. Gale Research, 835 Penobscot Bldg., 645 Griswold St., Detroit, MI 48226-4094. TEL 313-961-2242; 800-877-4253. FAX 800-414-5043. E-mail: daniel__snyder@gale. com.
   Description: Studies the culture, geographical setting and historical background of the various peoples of the world in regional editions.

PERIPHERIE; Zeitschrift fuer Politik und Oekonomie in der dritten Welt. see *BUSINESS AND ECONOMICS — International Development And Assistance*

PERSPECTIVES IN HUMAN BIOLOGY. see *BIOLOGY*

572 PE
PERU INDIGENA. 1948-1961; resumed 1967. s-a. $40. Instituto Indigenista Peruano, Avda. Salaverry, Lima, Peru. Ed. David Alvarado. **Indexed:** A.I.C.P.
   Description: Looks at the socio-economic problems and culture of the native and farmer communities of Peru.

572 BL ISSN 0553-8467
F2519.1.R6
PESQUISAS: PUBLICACOES DE ANTROPOLOGIA. Key Title: Pesquisas. Antropologia. (Numbering continues those of articles published in Pesquisas) 1957. irreg. price varies or exchange basis. (Universidade do Vale do Rio dos Sinos, Instituto Anchietano de Pesquisas) Unisinos, Av. Unisinos, 950, 93022-000 Sao Leopoldo RS, Brazil. TEL 55-51-5903333 ext. 1951. FAX 55-51-5921035. **Indexed:** Anthropol.Lit. **Document type:** academic/scholarly publication.
   —CISTI.
   Supersedes in part (in 1960): Instituto Anchietano de Pesquisas. Pesquisas (ISSN 0480-1873)

PHILIPPINE SOCIOLOGICAL REVIEW. see *SOCIOLOGY*

PIEMME. see *RELIGIONS AND THEOLOGY*

PILIPINAS; an interdisciplinary scholarly journal of Philippine studies. see *HISTORY — History Of Asia*

ANTHROPOLOGY

572 970.1   US   ISSN 0032-0447
E78.G73   CODEN: PLNAA3
PLAINS ANTHROPOLOGIST; a medium for the anthropological interpretation of the Plains area in the United States. 1954. q. $20 individual membership (foreign $25); institutions $35 (foreign $40) (effective 1996 & 1997). Plains Anthropological Society, c/o Lawrence Tomsyck, 410 Wedgewood Dr., Lincoln, NE 68510. TEL 402-488-3813. bk.rev.; bibl.; charts; illus.; index. circ. 850. (also avail. in microfilm from UMI; back issues avail.; reprint service avail. from UMI) **Indexed:** Abstr.Anthropol., Amer.Hist.& Life (1963-), Anthropol.Lit., Arts & Hum.Cit.Ind., ASCA, Biol.Abstr., Br.Archaeol.Abstr., Curr.Cont., Geo.Abstr., Hist.Abstr. (1963-), SSCI. **Document type:** academic/scholarly publication.
—BLDSC (6507.100000); KR SourceOne; UMI; UnCover.
Refereed Serial

305.8 708.1 910.02   US   ISSN 1081-4523
▼**PLATEAU JOURNAL;** land and peoples of the Colorado Plateau. 1995. s-a. $17 to non-members (effective 1997). Museum of Northern Arizona, 3101 N. Fort Valley Rd., Flagstaff, AZ 86001. TEL 520-774-5211. E-mail: canyonpub@aol.com. (Co-sponsor: Grand Canyon Association) Eds. Carol Haralson, Pamela Frazier. **Document type:** consumer publication.
Formerly: Canon Journal.
Description: Explores the historical, natural, scientific and environmental issues that have affected and are still impacting the Colorado Plateau.

POINT SERIES. see *ORIENTAL STUDIES*

301 320 340   US   ISSN 1081-6976
GN492
POLITICAL AND LEGAL ANTHROPOLOGY REVIEW. Short title: Po L A R. 1993. 3/yr. $20 to individuals; institutions $30 (effective 1996). (Association for Political and Legal Anthropology) American Anthropological Association, 4350 N. Fairfax Dr., Ste. 640, Arlington, VA 22203-1621. TEL 703-528-1902. FAX 703-528-3546. Ed. Bill Maurer. R&P contact: Terry Clifford. bk.rev.; bibl. **Indexed:** Amer.Hist.& Life (1986-1988), (1990-), Hist.Abstr. (1986-1988), (1990-). **Document type:** academic/scholarly publication.
Description: Includes articles, correspondence, and syllabi encompassing current theories and research in the intersection of law, political science, anthropology and sociology.

301   US   ISSN 1060-2720
GN492
POLITICAL AND LEGAL ANTHROPOLOGY SERIES. 1980. a., latest vol.9. $34.95 cloth; paper $21.95. (Association for Political and Legal Anthropology) Transaction Publishers, Transaction Periodicals Consortium, Department 3092, Rutgers University, New Brunswick, NJ 08903. TEL 908-445-2280. FAX 908-445-3138. Ed. Myron J. Aronoff. **Document type:** academic/scholarly publication.
—BLDSC (6543.870580). **CCC.**
Formerly (until 1991): Political Anthropology (ISSN 0732-1228)
Description: Contains original analyses of political man. Articles cover a wide range of theoretical, conceptual, and methodological approaches to interrelationships among socioeconomic, cultural, and political phenomena.

572   US   ISSN 0888-4552
GN397
PRACTICING ANTHROPOLOGY. q. $30. Society for Applied Anthropology, Box 24083, Oklahoma City, OK 73124-0084. TEL 405-843-5113. E-mail: sfaa@telepath.com; URL: http://www.zoom1.telepath.com/sfaa/sfaapubs.html. adv. (back issues avail.) **Indexed:** Abstr.Anthropol., Anthropol.Lit. **Document type:** academic/scholarly publication.
—UnCover. **CCC.**
Description: Source of career information for applied social and behavioral scientists.

PRETENTAINE. see *SOCIOLOGY*

573 599.8   GW   ISSN 0343-3528
PRIMATE REPORT. irreg. DM.18 price varies. Verlag Erich Goltze GmbH und Co. KG, Hans-Boeckler-Str. 7, 37079 Goettingen, Germany. TEL 49-551-506760. FAX 49-551-5067622. Ed. A. Spiegel. **Document type:** academic/scholarly publication, monographic series.
—BLDSC (6612.923300).

PRIMATES; journal of primatology. see *BIOLOGY — Zoology*

572 900 730   IT
PRIMEVAL SCULPTURE. (Text in English, German, Spanish) 1984. 3/yr. L.27000($22) Primigenia Editrice, Piazza Paolo da Novi 3-7, I-16129 Genoa, Italy. Ed. Pietro Gaietto. abstr.; bibl.; illus. circ. 1,000. (back issues avail.)

572 949.7   CI   ISSN 0351-8825
PROBLEMI SJEVERNOG JADRANA. (Text in Croatian; summaries in Italian) 1963. irreg. Hrvatska Akademija Znanosti i Umjetnosti, Zrinski trg 11, 41000 Zagreb, Croatia. TEL 38-41-433-611. FAX 38-41-433-383. (Subscr. to: Zavod za Povijesne i Drustvene Znanosti J.A.Z.U., Brace Supak 5, 51000 Rijeka, Croatia) circ. 700. (back issues avail.)

570   PL   ISSN 0033-2003
GN2   CODEN: PZANA7
PRZEGLAD ANTROPOLOGICZNY. (Text in Polish and English; summaries in English) 1926. s-a. price varies. Polskie Towarzystwo Antropologiczne, Ul. Marymoncka 34, 01-813 Warsaw, Poland. E-mail: strzalko@vm.amu.edu.pl. (Dist. by: Ars Polona, Krakowskie Przedmiescie 7, 00-068 Warsaw, Poland) Ed. Jan Strzalko. R&P contact: Jan Strzalko. adv. contact: Jan Strzalko. bk.rev.; bibl.; illus.; circ. 500 (controlled). **Indexed:** A.I.C.P., Anthropol.Lit., Biol.Abstr. **Document type:** academic/scholarly publication, proceedings.
—BLDSC (6938.800000).
Refereed Serial

572 300   AG   ISSN 0327-6627
PUBLICAR EN ANTROPOLOGIA Y CIENCIAS SOCIALES. 1992. m.? Colegio de Graduados en Antropologia, 25 de Mayo 217, 4o piso, 1002 Buenos Aires, Argentina. Ed. Marcelo Alvarez.

PUBLIKATIONEN ZU WISSENSCHAFTLICHEN FILMEN. SEKTION ETHNOLOGIE. see *MOTION PICTURES*

572   BO
PUMAPUNKU. N.S. 1991. s-a.? Centro de Investigaciones Antropologicas Tiwanaku, Avda. 6 de Agosto 2607 (altos), Casilla de Correo 2325, La Paz, Bolivia. TEL 340107. **Document type:** academic/scholarly publication.

PURUSHARTHA. see *HISTORY — History Of Asia*

QINGHAI MINZU XUEYUAN XUEBAO/QINGHAI INSTITUTE OF NATIONALITIES. JOURNAL. see *ORIENTAL STUDIES*

572   IT
QUADERNI DI ANTROPOLOGIA E SEMIOTICA. 1983. irreg., no.6, 1990. L.6000 per no. Edizioni Quattroventi, Via Dini 16, Casella Postale 156, 61029 Urbino, Italy. TEL 0722-2588. FAX 0722-320998. Ed. Maurizio Del Ninno.

572   IT   ISSN 0391-7312
QUADERNI TERZO MONDO. 1973. q. L.60000($60) (effective 1997 & 1998). Centro Studi Terzo Mondo, Via G. B. Morgagni 39, 20129 Milan, Italy. TEL 39-2-29409041. Ed. Dr. Umberto Melotti. R&P contact: Elena Sala. adv. contact: Elena Sala. circ. 3,000. **Document type:** monographic series.
Description: Covers various problems of the Third World in anthropological, sociological, historical and political perspective.

QUALITATIVE INQUIRY. see *SOCIAL SCIENCES: COMPREHENSIVE WORKS*

301.2 282   BD
QUE VOUS EN SEMBLE?. (Text in French, Kirundi) 1968. irreg. (approx. q.) 500 Fr.CFA($20) Cercle Saint Paul, Grand Seminaire Jean-Paul II, B.P. 254 Gitega, Burundi. TEL 040-21-62. Ed. Damien Rwasa. adv. circ. 350.
Description: Examines the customs, literature and music of traditional Burundi culture in a Christian perspective.

572   AU   ISSN 0048-6507
R E. (Review of Ethnology) 1968. s-m. $10 per volume. Institut fuer Voelkerkunde, Universitatstr. 7, A-1010 Vienna, Austria. Ed. E. Stiglmayr. bk.rev.; charts. **Indexed:** A.I.C.P., Anthropol.Lit.

573 996.1   US   ISSN 1040-1385
F3169   CODEN: RNJOFW
RAPA NUI JOURNAL. 1987. 4/yr. $25 (foreign $35) (effective 1997); $30 (foreign $40) (effective 1998). Easter Island Foundation, Box 6774, Los Osos, CA 93412-6774. TEL 805-528-6279. FAX 805-534-9301. E-mail: 74221.2046@compuserve.com. Ed. Georgia Lee. R&P contact: Georgia Lee. adv.; bk.rev. circ. 500. **Document type:** academic/scholarly publication.
—BLDSC (7254.434550).
Formerly: Rapa Nui Notes (ISSN 0890-2097)
Description: Source for current Easter Island and East Polynesian scientific studies and events.
Refereed Serial

RASSEGNA DELLE TRADIZIONI POPOLARI; rivista trimestrale di ricerca scientifica demologica folklorica antropologica. see *FOLKLORE*

572 918   CN   ISSN 0318-4137
E78.Q3
RECHERCHES AMERINDIENNES AU QUEBEC. (Text mainly in French; occasionally in English) 1971. 4/yr. Can.$42 to individuals; institutions Can.$52; students Can.$35 (effective 1993-94). Societe de Recherches Amerindiennes au Quebec, 6742 rue St.-Denis, Montreal, PQ H2S 2S2, Canada. TEL 514-277-6178. Ed.Bd. adv.; bk.rev.; bibl.; index. circ. 1,000. (back issues avail.) **Indexed:** A.I.C.P., Abstr.Anthropol., Amer.Hist.& Life (1985-), Anthropol.Lit., Bibl.Ling., Bull.Signal., Hist.Abstr. (1985-), Pt.de Rep. (1986-). **Document type:** academic/scholarly publication.
Description: Devoted to the ethnology and archeology of the Inuit and American Indian populations. Covers problems they face in lodging, health, territorial rights.

RECHERCHES PHILOSOPHIQUES AFRICAINES. see *PHILOSOPHY*

572   CC   ISSN 1000-3193
GN1
RENLEIXUE XUEBAO/ACTA ANTHROPOLOGICA SINICA. (Text in Chinese; summaries in English) 1982. q. $64.80. (Chinese Academy of Sciences, Institute of Vertebrata Palasiatica - Academia Sinica, Institute of Vertebrata Palasiatica) Science Press, Marketing and Sales Department, 16 Donghuangchenggen North St., Beijing 100717, People's Republic of China. TEL 86-10-4010642. FAX 86-10-4019810. adv. circ. 11,000. **Indexed:** Abstr.Anthropol., Anthropol.Lit. **Document type:** academic/scholarly publication.
Description: Includes theses on paleoanthropology, modern physical anthropology, applied anthropology, paleolithic culture, and articles on natural environments of ancient man.
Refereed Serial

301.51 572   US   ISSN 0190-1281
GN448   CODEN: REANEM
RESEARCH IN ECONOMIC ANTHROPOLOGY. 1978. irreg., vol.18, 1997. $73.25. J A I Press Inc., 55 Old Post Rd., No. 2, Box 1678, Greenwich, CT 06830-1678. TEL 203-661-7602. FAX 203-661-0792. E-mail: jai@jaipress.com. (Subscr. in the UK and Europe to: JAI Press Ltd., 38 Tavistock St., Covent Garden, London WC2E 7PB, England. TEL 44-171-379-8834. FAX 44-171-379-8835) Ed. Barry Isaac. **Indexed:** Anthropol.Lit. **Document type:** monographic series.
—BLDSC (7738.910000); UnCover. **CCC.**

572 995 300   PP   ISSN 0254-0665
GN671.N5
RESEARCH IN MELANESIA; a newsletter of anthropological and sociological research in Papua New Guinea. (Text and summaries in English) 1968. s-a. K.10 pacific-Oceania (elsewhere K.15). University of Papua New Guinea, Department of Anthropology & Sociology, Box 320 University, Papua New Guinea. FAX 267187. TELEX 22366. E-mail: 100254.3541@compuserve.com. Ed. Colin S. Filer. bk.rev.; bibl. circ. 400. (processed; back issues avail.) **Indexed:** A.I.C.P., Anthropol.Lit. **Document type:** academic/scholarly publication.
Formerly: Man in New Guinea (ISSN 0025-1577)

ANTHROPOLOGY

301 US
RESEARCH IN YORUBA LANGUAGE AND LITERATURE SERIES. 1991. s-a. $20 per no. to individuals; institutions $30. Technicians of the Sacred, 1317 N. San Fernando Blvd., Ste. 310, Burbank, CA 91504. **Document type:** monographic series.

301.2 US
RESOURCES FOR THE STUDY OF ANTHROPOLOGY.* irreg. price varies. Houghton Mifflin Co., 222 Berkeley St., Boston, MA 02116-3764. TEL 617-725-5000. FAX 617-227-5409.

572 NE ISSN 0093-8157
Z5111 CODEN: REVAEK
REVIEWS IN ANTHROPOLOGY. 1974. 8/yr. (in 2 vols., 4 nos./vol.) $79 (effective 1998). Gordon and Breach - Harwood Academic, Amsteldisk 166, 1st Fl., 1079 LH Amsterdam, Netherlands. URL: http://www.gbhap.us.com/journals/176/176-top.htm. (Subscr. to: International Publishers Distributor, Box 32160, Newark, NJ 07102. TEL 800-545-8398. FAX 215-750-6343) Ed. Nina L. Etkin. adv.; bk.rev. (also avail. in microform from UMI; reprint service avail. from UMI) **Indexed:** Amer.Bibl.Slavic & E.Eur.Stud., Bk.Rev.Ind. (1975-1989), Child.Bk.Rev.Ind. (1975-1989), Per.Islam. (1992-). **Document type:** academic/scholarly publication.
—BLDSC (7786.980000); SWETS. **CCC.**
Description: Presents review commentary from the professional literature of anthropology, including the sub-disciplines of human biology, sociocultural anthropology, archaeology and comparative linguistics.
Refereed Serial

572 CL ISSN 0716-3312
F3069
REVISTA CHILENA DE ANTROPOLOGIA. 1962. a. $25 (effective 1996). Universidad de Chile, Departamento de Antropologia, Casilla 10115, Santiago, Chile. FAX 56-2-6787756. Ed. Manuel Dannemann. bk.rev. circ. 500. **Indexed:** Anthropol.Lit. **Document type:** academic/scholarly publication.
Former titles (until 1978): Boletin de Prehistoria de Chile; Antropologia.
Description: Devoted to all areas of anthropology.

572 CK ISSN 0486-6525
GN1
REVISTA COLOMBIANA DE ANTROPOLOGIA. 1943. a. exchange basis. Instituto Colombiano de Cultura, Instituto Colombiano de Antropologia, Apdo. Aereo 407, Calle 8 No. 8-87, Bogota, D.F., Colombia. TEL 3330548. FAX 2330960. E-mail: scolican@col1.telecom.com.co. Ed. Leonor Herrera Angel. bk.rev. circ. 1,000. **Indexed:** A.I.C.P., Anthropol.Lit., Hisp.Amer.Per.Ind. (1966-), IBR. **Document type:** academic/scholarly publication.
—Linda Hall.
Description: Publishes scientific papers in archaeology, anthropology, ethnohistory, and ethnobotany.

572 SP ISSN 1132-6581
REVISTA D'ETNOLOGIA DE CATALUNYA. (Text in Catalan) 1992. s-a. 3500 ptas. Departament de Cultura, Centre de Promocio de la Cultura Popular i Tradicional Catalana, Portal de Santa Madrona, 6-8, 08001 Barcelona, Spain. Ed. Antoni Anguela; Pub. Lluis Calvo. bk.rev. **Indexed:** A.I.C.P.

572 EC ISSN 0557-8507
REVISTA DE ANTROPOLOGIA. 1973. q. Casa de la Cultura Ecuatoriana, Avda. 6 de Diciembre 794, Casilla 67, Quito, Ecuador. Ed. Manuel A. Landivar U. bk.rev.; bibl.; charts; illus. **Indexed:** Anthropol.Lit.

570 BL ISSN 0034-7701
GN1
REVISTA DE ANTROPOLOGIA. 1953. s-a. $30. Universidade de Sao Paulo, Faculdade de Filosofia, Letras e Ciencias Humanas, C.P. 8105, 01065-970 Sao Paulo SP, Brazil. TEL 55-11-8183726. FAX 55-11-8183163. Dir. Paula Montero. bk.rev. circ. 1,000. **Indexed:** A.I.C.P., Anthropol.Lit., Biol.Abstr., Hisp.Amer.Per.Ind. (1981-), IBR.
Refereed Serial

301 PE
REVISTA DE ANTROPOLOGIA. 1994. a. S/20 (foreign $15). Universidad Nacional Mayor de San Marcos, Escuela Academico Profesional de Antropologia, Ciudad Universitaria, Av. Venezuela s-n, Lima 1, Peru. TEL 51-14-527630. Ed. Jorge Casanova Velasquez. **Document type:** academic/scholarly publication.

301 SP ISSN 1131-558X
REVISTA DE ANTROPOLOGIA SOCIAL. 1991. a. 2000 ptas.($22) (effective 1997). Universidad Complutense, Facultad de Ciencias Politicas y Sociologia. Departamento de Antropologia Social, Servicio de Publicaciones, Calle Isaac Peral s-n, Ciudad Universitaria, 28040 Madrid, Spain. TEL 34-1-3946934. FAX 34-1-3946954. (back issues avail.)
—CINDOC.
Description: Presents advanced studies on social anthropology and ethnography in Spain.

572 CK
REVISTA DE ANTROPOLOGIA Y ARQUEOLOGIA. 1985. s-a. $20. Universidad de Los Andes, Departamento de Antropologia, Apdo. Aereo 4976, Bogota, Colombia. TEL 282-40-66. FAX 2841890. TELEX 42343 UNAND CO. Ed. Felipe Cardenas. adv.; bk.rev. circ. 1,000. (back issues avail.) **Indexed:** Amer.Hist.& Life (1956-1966), Anthropol.Lit., Hist.Abstr. (1956-1966).
Formerly: Revista de Antropologia (ISSN 0120-6613)

572 RM ISSN 0034-8198
GR257
REVISTA DE ETNOGRAFIE SI FOLCLOR. (Text in Rumanian; summaries in French) 1956. 6/yr. (Academia Romana, Institutul de Etnografie si Folclor C. Brailoiu) Editura Academiei Romane, Calea 13 Septembrie 13, 76117 Bucharest, Rumania. (Dist. by: Rodipet SA, Piata presei Libere 1, Sec. 1, Box 33-57, Bucharest, Rumania. TEL 401-618-5103. FAX 401-2226407) Ed. Alex Dobre. bk.rev.; bibl.; charts; illus. circ. 1,630. (tabloid format) **Indexed:** Bibl.Ling., M.L.A., MLA Intl.Bibl., RILM.

REVISTA DE HISTORIA. see HISTORY

572 980 DR
REVISTA DOMINICANA DE ANTROPOLOGIA E HISTORIA. 1972. s-a. $5. Universidad Autonoma de Santo Domingo, Departamento de Historia y Antropologia, Biblioteca Central, Ciudad Universitaria, Santo Domingo, Dominican Republic. circ. 1,000. **Indexed:** Hisp.Amer.Per.Ind. (1972-1974).

301 SP ISSN 0556-6533
E51
REVISTA ESPANOLA DE ANTROPOLOGIA AMERICANA. (Text in French, English, Spanish) 1952-1961; resumed 1969. a. 2000 ptas.($22) (effective 1997). Universidad Complutense, Facultad de Geografia e Historia. Departamento de Historia de America II, Servicio de Publicaciones, Calle Isaac Peral s-n, Ciudad Universitaria, 28040 Madrid, Spain. TEL 34-1-3946934. FAX 31-4-3946954. Ed. Emma Sanchez Montanes. bk.rev. (back issues avail.) **Indexed:** Amer.Hist.& Life (1969-1972), Hisp.Amer.Per.Ind. (1981-), Hist.Abstr. (1969-1972), IBR. **Document type:** academic/scholarly publication.
—CINDOC.
Supersedes (1952-1961): Seminario de Estudios Americanistas. Trabajos y Conferencias (ISSN 0541-8658)
Description: Focuses on american antropology and ethnology.

573 SP ISSN 1134-7368
GN49
REVISTA ESPANOLA DE ANTROPOLOGIA BIOLOGICA. 1980. a. 1500 ptas. Sociedad Espanola de Antropologia Biologica, Fac. de Biologia, Dpto. Biologia Animal I, Univ. Complutense, 28040 Madrid, Spain. TEL 34-1-3944936. FAX 34-1-3944947. E-mail: vfuster@eucmax.sim.ucm.es. Ed. Vicente Fuster. bk.rev. circ. 210. **Indexed:** Abstr.Anthropol., Ind.SST. **Document type:** academic/scholarly publication.
Formerly (until 1994): Sociedad Espanola de Antropologia Biologica. Boletin (ISSN 0213-179X)
Description: Covers physical and biological anthropology.
Refereed Serial

570 PO ISSN 0870-0206
REVISTA LUSITANA. (Text in English, French, Italian, Spanish) 1887; N.S. 1981. irreg. Cr.$600 per no. Universidade de Lisboa, Centro de Estudos Geograficos, Centro de Tradicoes Populares Portuguesas, Cidade Universitaria, 1699 Lisbon Codex, Portugal. TEL 351-1-796-5162. FAX 351-1-796-0063. bk.rev. circ. 1,000. **Document type:** academic/scholarly publication.
Description: Contains articles about anthropology and ethnology.

301 SP ISSN 1135-691X
REVISTA MURCIANA DE ANTROPOLOGIA. 1994. irreg. 2000 ptas. (effective 1997). Universidad de Murcia, Servicio de Publicaciones, Santo Cristo 1, 30080 Murcia, Spain. TEL 34-68-363014. FAX 34-68-363414. E-mail: vgm@pas.um.es; URL: http://www.um.es/~spumweb. Ed. Antonino Gonzalez Blanco. circ. 500. (back issues avail.) **Document type:** academic/scholarly publication.

REVUE D'ETHNOLINGUISTIQUE; cahiers du L A C I T O. see LINGUISTICS

RHEINISCH-WESTFAELISCHE ZEITSCHRIFT FUER VOLKSKUNDE. see HISTORY — History Of Europe

572 SW ISSN 0035-5267
DL601
RIG. (Text in Swedish; summaries in English or German) 1918. q. SEK 100. Foereningen foer Svensk Kulturhistoria, Finngatan 8, S-223 62 Lund, Sweden. TEL 46-46-222-7665. FAX 46-46-222-4205. E-mail: birgitta.svensson@etn.lu.se. (Co-sponsors: Etnologiskainstitutionen med Folksarkivet) adv.; bk.rev.; illus.; index, cum.index. **Indexed:** Amer.Hist.& Life (1963-), Hist.Abstr. (1963-).

572 IT ISSN 0085-5723
RIVISTA DI ANTROPOLOGIA. (Text in Italian; summaries in English and French) 1893. a. L.180000 (effective 1991). Istituto Italiano di Antropologia, Via di Tor di Nona, 89, 00186 Rome, Italy. (Dist. by: Libreria gia Nardecchia, s.r.l., Via Tor di Nona 39, 00186 Rome, Italy. FAX 396-68300010) Ed. Pietro Passarello. bk.rev. (back issues avail.) **Indexed:** A.I.C.P., Anthropol.Lit. **Document type:** academic/scholarly publication.
Formerly (until vol.15): Societa Romana di Antropologia. Atti.
Description: Publishes memoirs, communications and reports about scientific subjects concerning the anthropological sciences.

512 IT
LA RIVOLTA. s-a. L.15000. Vittorio Baccelli, Ed. & Pub., C.P. 132, 55100 Lucca, Italy. circ. 3,000. (looseleaf format)

301.2 913.031 AT ISSN 0813-0426
ROCK ART RESEARCH. (Text in English; summaries in French, German, Spanish) 1984. s-a. Aus.$20. (Australian Rock Art Research Association) Archaeological Publications, P.O. Box 216, Caulfield South, Vic. 3162, Australia. TEL 61-3-95230549. FAX 61-3-95230549. E-mail: aurawww@sli.unimelb.edu.au; URL: http://sunspot.sli.unimelb.edu.a/aura/Welcome.html. Ed. Robert G. Bednarik; Pub. Robert G. Bednarik. R&P contact: Robert G. Bednarik. adv. contact: Robert G. Bednarik. bk.rev.; abstr.; bibl.; charts; illus.; index. circ. 1,000. (back issues avail.) **Indexed:** Anthropol.Lit. **Document type:** academic/scholarly publication.
—BLDSC (8001.445000); UnCover.
Description: Devoted to developing theory and methodology for a scientific understanding of prehistoric art forms worldwide.
Refereed Serial

ANTHROPOLOGY

572   UK   ISSN 1359-0987
GN1
ROYAL ANTHROPOLOGICAL INSTITUTE. JOURNAL. N.S. 1966. q. £95($147) (effective 1997). Royal Anthropological Institute of Great Britain and Ireland, 50 Fitzroy St., London W1P 5HS, England. TEL 44-171-3870455. FAX 44-171-3834235. (Subscr. to: Turpin Distribution Services Ltd., Blackhorse Rd., Letchworth, Herts. SG6 1HN, England. TEL 44-1462-672555. FAX 44-1462-480947) Ed. Simon Harrison. R&P contact: Jonathan Benthall. adv. contact: Valerie Phillips. bk.rev.; charts; illus.; index. circ. 3,200. (also avail. in microform from UMI,BHP; microfilm from BHP; back issues avail.; reprint service avail. from UMI) **Indexed:** A.I.C.P., Abstr.Anthropol., Abstr.Crim.& Pen., Amer.Hist.& Life, Anthropol.Lit., ASCA, Biol.Abstr., Br.Archaeol.Abstr., Br.Hum.Ind., Curr.Cont., Curr.Cont.Africa, E.I., Excerp.Med., Geo.Abstr.P.G., Hist.Abstr., IDA, Lang.& Lang.Behav.Abstr., Mid.East: Abstr.& Ind., Soc.Sci.Ind., SSCI, Stud.Wom.Abstr. **Document type:** academic/scholarly publication.
●Also available online. Vendor(s): UMI.
Also available on CD-ROM.
—BLDSC (4851.900000); KR SourceOne; Linda Hall; SWETS; UMI; UnCover.
    Formerly (until 1995): Man (ISSN 0025-1496); Incorporates: Royal Anthropological Institute of Great Britain and Ireland. Journal (ISSN 0307-3114)
    Description: Covers all areas of anthropology: physical, social, cultural. Includes information on archaeology and linguistics.

352.7   NE   ISSN 0922-7911
S481
ROYAL TROPICAL INSTITUTE. BULLETIN. Key Title: Bulletin - Royal Tropical Institute. irreg. (4-6/yr.) fl.15 per no. (effective 1996). Koninklijk Instituut voor de Tropen - Royal Tropical Institute, Mauritskade 63, 1092 AD Amsterdam, Netherlands. TEL 31-20-5688272. FAX 31-20-5688286. TELEX 15080 KIT NL. illus. **Document type:** bulletin.
—BLDSC (2701.250000); KNAW.
    Former titles (until 1988): Koninklijk Instituut voor de Tropen. A O Bulletin; Koninklijk Instituut voor de Tropen. Afdeling Plattelandsontwikkeling. Communications and Bulletins; Formed by the merger of (1914-19??): Koninklijk Instituut voor de Tropen. Afdeling Agrarisch Onderzoek. Bulletin; Koninklijk Instituut voor de Tropen. Afdeling Agrarisch Onderzoek. Communication (ISSN 0370-1670)
    Description: Publishes basic and applied multidisciplinary research in the fields of rural development, health and development, tropical hygiene, culture, history and anthropology.

305.898   AG   ISSN 0325-1217
GN1
RUNA. 1948. irreg., no.10, 1992. $13. Universidad de Buenos Aires, Facultad de Filosofia y Letras, Instituto de Ciencias Antropologicas, Museo Etnografico Juan B. Ambrosetti, Moreno 350, 1091 Buenos Aires, Argentina. TEL 54-1-331-7788. Eds. Carlos Herran, Jose Antonio Perez Gollan. **Indexed:** Hisp.Amer.Per.Ind. (1986-), IBR. **Document type:** academic/scholarly publication.
    Refereed Serial

301 917.306   US   ISSN 1066-0127
RUSSIA AND HER NEIGHBORS; facts and views on daily life. 1985. irreg. $25 to individuals; institutions $30 (foreign $35). Highgate Road Social Science Research Station, Inc., 32 Highgate Rd., Berkeley, CA 94707. TEL 510-525-3248. FAX 510-525-3313. E-mail: edunn@well.com. Ed. Eugenia Miller. bk.rev.; bibl.; illus. circ. 250. (back issues avail.) **Document type:** newsletter.
    Formerly: Station Relay (ISSN 0887-8935)
    Refereed Serial

301   US   ISSN 1077-5714
S A C C NOTES - TEACHING ANTHROPOLOGY. s-a. $15 (effective 1996). (Society for Teaching Anthropology in Community Colleges) American Anthropological Association, 4350 N. Fairfax Dr., Ste. 640, Arlington, VA 22203-1621. TEL 703-528-1902. FAX 703-528-3546. R&P contact: Terry Clifford.

S E M NEWSLETTER. (Society for Ethnomusicology) see *MUSIC*

S I L - A A I B OCCASIONAL PAPERS. (Summer Institute of Linguistics, Australian Aborigines and Islanders Branch) see *LINGUISTICS*

306 948   NO   ISSN 0581-4480
SAMISKE SAMLINGER. (Numbers not issued in consecutive order) 1938. irreg., latest 1992. price varies. Norsk Folkemuseum, N-0287-Oslo, Norway. TEL 47-22-12-37-00. FAX 47-22-12-37-77.
    Formerly (until 1948): Nordnorske Samlinger (ISSN 0801-1060)

572   US   ISSN 0080-5890
SAN DIEGO MUSEUM OF MAN. ETHNIC TECHNOLOGY NOTES. 1967. irreg., no.24, 1996. price varies. San Diego Museum of Man, 1350 El Prado, Balboa Park, San Diego, CA 92101. TEL 619-239-2001. Ed. Ken Hedges. R&P contact: Ken Hedges. **Document type:** monographic series.
    Description: Contains studies on specific topics in all areas of New World anthropology and archaeology.

572   US   ISSN 0080-5904
SAN DIEGO MUSEUM OF MAN. PAPERS. 1929. irreg., no.33, 1995. price varies. San Diego Museum of Man, 1350 El Prado, Balboa Park, San Diego, CA 92101. TEL 619-239-2001. Ed. Ken Hedges. index. **Document type:** monographic series.
—BLDSC (8072.880000).
    Description: Contains in-depth studies in all areas of New World anthropology and archaeology.

SAN YUE SAN. see *LITERATURE*

SANAKIRJOJA - LEXICA SOCIETATIS FENNO-UGRICAE. see *LINGUISTICS*

572   EC   ISSN 0252-8630
SARANCE. 1975. 3/yr. exchange basis. Instituto Otavaleno de Antropologia, Centro de Documentacion, Seccion Canje, Casilla 10-02-1478, Otavalo, Ecuador. TEL 593-6-920321. FAX 593-6-920461. circ. 500. **Indexed:** IBR.

301.2 338.1   SW
SCANDINAVIAN INSTITUTE OF AFRICAN STUDIES. RURAL DEVELOPMENT. Short title: Rural Development Series. irreg. (Nordiska Afrikainstitutet - Scandinavian Institute of African Studies) A W I International AB, P.O. Box 4627, S-116 91 Stockholm, Sweden. TEL 46-8-7282500. FAX 46-8-338707. (back issues avail.) **Document type:** monographic series.

SCOTTISH STUDIES. see *HISTORY — History Of Europe*

SCRIPTA MEDITERRANEA. see *HISTORY — History Of The Near East*

572 914.606   SP
SEMANA INTERNACIONAL DE ANTROPOLOGIA VASCA. ACTAS. irreg. Gran Enciclopedia Vasca, Apdo. 1510, Calzadas de Mallona 8, Bilbao 6, Spain.

572   IT   ISSN 0392-9094
SEMINARIO DI SCIENZE ANTROPOLOGICHE. (Text in English and Italian; summaries in English, French, Italian) 1979. a. L.50000. Centro di Documentazione per le Scienze Antropologiche, Via del Proconsolo No. 12, 50122 Florence, Italy. (Co-sponsor: Societa Italiana di Ecologia Umana) Ed. Quinzio Milanesi. adv.; bk.rev. circ. 1,000. (back issues avail.)

SERIE DE VOCABULARIOS Y DICCIONARIOS INDIGENAS "MARIANO SILVA Y ACEVES". see *LINGUISTICS*

572   JA   ISSN 0387-2483
SHAKAI JINRUIGAKU NENPO. (Text in Japanese) 1975. a. 3800 Yen. (Tokyo-toritsu Daigaku, Shakai Jinrui Gakkai - Tokyo Metropolitan University, Society for Social Anthropology) Kobundo, 1-7-13 Kanda Surugadai, Chiyoda-ku, Tokyo, Japan. TEL 03-3294-7542. Ed.Bd. adv. circ. 2,000. **Document type:** academic/scholarly publication.

SHAMAN. see *ALTERNATIVE MEDICINE*

572 281.9   US   ISSN 0887-8897
BL2370.S5
SHAMAN'S DRUM; a journal of experiential Shamanism. 1985. q. $16 (foreign $20). Cross-Cultural Shamanism Network, Shaman's Drum, Box 97, Ashland, OR 97520. TEL 541-552-0839. FAX 707-459-1006. Ed. Timothy White. R&P contact: Roberta Louis. adv. contact: Judy Wells. bk.rev.; circ. 17,000 (paid). **Document type:** consumer publication.
    Description: Discusses cross-cultural shamanism, Native American healing and ethnic spirituality.

SIGN LANGUAGE STUDIES. see *LINGUISTICS*

SLOVACI V ZAHRANICI. see *HISTORY — History Of Europe*

572   XV   ISSN 0350-0330
GN1
SLOVENSKI ETNOGRAF. (Text in Slovenian; summaries in English, French, German) 1926. a. $25. Slovenski Etnografski Muzej, Presernova cesta 20, 61000 Ljubljana, Slovenia. FAX 061-218844. bk.rev. circ. 1,000. **Indexed:** A.I.C.P., M.L.A.
    Formerly (until 1945): Etnolog (ISSN 0353-4855)

SLOVENSKO ETNOLOSKO DRUSTVO. GLASNIK. see *HISTORY — History Of Europe*

SLOVENSKY NARODOPIS/SLOVAK ETHNOGRAPHY. see *ETHNIC INTERESTS*

572   US   ISSN 0081-0223
GN1   CODEN: SMCAAM
SMITHSONIAN CONTRIBUTIONS TO ANTHROPOLOGY. 1965. irreg., no.36, 1992. Smithsonian Institution Press, 470 L'Enfant Plaza, Ste. 7100, Washington, DC 20560. TEL 202-287-3738. FAX 202-287-3637. Ed. Don Fisher. circ. 2,100. (reprint service avail. from UMI) **Indexed:** Anthropol.Lit., Biol.Abstr., GeoRef. **Document type:** academic/scholarly publication.
—BLDSC (8311.490000); Linda Hall.

572   II
SNENG KHASI. (Text in Khasi) 1977. m. Rs.9($9) Hipshon Roy, Ed. & Pub., Riatsamthiah, Shillong 793001, India. adv.; bk.rev. circ. 600.

572 301   AT   ISSN 0155-977X
HM1
SOCIAL ANALYSIS; journal of cultural and social practice. 1979. 3/yr. Aus.$34 to individuals; institutions Aus.$53 (effective 1998). University of Adelaide, Department of Anthroplogy, Social Analysis, Adelaide, S.A. 5005, Australia. TEL 61-8-83706806. FAX 61-8-83035733. TELEX UNIVAD AA 89141. E-mail: ggarbett@arts.adelaide.edu.com. Ed. K. Garbett, J. Weiner. adv. circ. 300. (back issues avail.) **Indexed:** Anthropol.Lit., Aus.P.A.I.S., E.I., So.Pac.Per.Ind. **Document type:** academic/scholarly publication.
—BLDSC (8318.041600); SWETS; UnCover.

301.1   UK   ISSN 0964-0282
GN575   CODEN: SNTHE3
SOCIAL ANTHROPOLOGY. 1992. 3/yr. £62($102) (effective 1998). (European Association of Social Anthropologists) Cambridge University Press, Edinburgh Bldg., Shaftesbury Rd., Cambridge CB2 2RU, England. TEL 44-1223-312393. FAX 44-1223-315052. TELEX 851817256. E-mail: information@cup.cam.ac.uk; URL: http://www.cup.cam.ac.uk. (N. American addr.: Cambridge University Press, Journals Dept., 40 W. 20th St., New York, NY 10011. TEL 212-924-3900. FAX 212-691-3239) Ed. Jean-Claude Galey. R&P contact: Linda Nicol. adv. contact: Rebecca Symons. bk.rev. (back issues avail.) **Indexed:** A.I.C.P. **Document type:** academic/scholarly publication.
—BLDSC (8318.053750); SWETS; UMI; UnCover. CCC.
    Description: Covers all aspects of anthropology and social anthropology.
    Refereed Serial

SOCIAL SCIENCE INFORMATION. see *SOCIAL SCIENCES: COMPREHENSIVE WORKS*

572   FR   ISSN 0037-8984
    CODEN: BSANA8
SOCIETE D'ANTHROPOLOGIE DE PARIS. BULLETINS & MEMOIRES. 1860. 4/yr. 396.90 F. (outside the EU 440 F.) (effective 1997). Societe d'Anthropologie de Paris, Musee de l'Homme, 17 Place du Trocadero, 75116 Paris, France. TEL 33-1-44057255. FAX 33-1-44057241. E-mail: jakobi@mnhn.fr; peyre@mnhn.fr. Ed. Pierre Darli; Pub. Alain Froment. R&P contact: Evelyne Peyre. adv. contact: Lucienne Jakobi. bk.rev. **Indexed:** Anthropol.Lit., Biol.Abstr., Bull.Signal., Excerp.Med., GeoRef., SSCI. **Document type:** academic/scholarly publication.
—Linda Hall; SWETS.

SOCIETE D'ETUDES LINGUISTIQUES ET ANTHROPOLOGIQUES DE FRANCE. NUMERO SPECIAL. see *LINGUISTICS*

ANTHROPOLOGY

570 970   FR   ISSN 0037-9174
E51
SOCIETE DES AMERICANISTES. JOURNAL. (Text in English, French, Portuguese, Spanish) 1896; N.S. 1903. s-a. 250 F. (effective 1997-1998). Societe des Americanistes, Musee de l'Homme, 17 Place du Trocadero, 75116 Paris, France.
TEL 33-1-47046311. (Affiliate: Centre National de la Recherche Scientifique) Ed. Doiminique Michelet. R&P contact: Martine Bercovici. adv. contact: Martine Bercovici. bk.rev.; bibl.; charts; illus.; cum.index. circ. 1,000. (also avail. in microfiche) **Indexed:** A.I.C.P., Amer.Hist.& Life (1963-), Anthropol.Lit., Bibl.Ling., Hisp.Amer.Per.Ind. (1968-), Hist.Abstr. (1963-), IBR, SSCI. **Document type:** academic/scholarly publication.
—SWETS.
    Refereed Serial

SOCIETE DES EXPLORATEURS ET DES VOYAGEURS FRANCAIS. ANNUAIRE GENERAL. see *GEOGRAPHY*

917 572 918   SZ   ISSN 0582-1592
E51
SOCIETE SUISSE DES AMERICANISTES. BULLETIN/SCHWEIZERISCHE AMERIKANISTEN-GESELLSCHAFT. BULLETIN. (Text in English, French, German, Portuguese, Spanish) 1950; N.S. 1980. a. 35 SFr. membership. Societe Suisse des Americanistes - Schweizerische Amerikanisten-Gesellschaft, 65-67, Boulevard Carl-Vogt, CH-1205 Geneva, Switzerland.
TEL 41-22-4184544. FAX 41-22-4184551. Ed. Gerhard Baer. R&P contact: Cendrine Hostettler. adv. contact: Cendrine Hostettler. bibl.; charts; illus. circ. 750. **Indexed:** A.I.C.P., Anthropol.Lit. **Document type:** academic/scholarly publication.
—BLDSC (2756.700000).

SOCIETY/SOCIETE. see *SOCIOLOGY*

572   US
SOCIETY FOR APPLIED ANTHROPOLOGY. NEWSLETTER. 1990. q. membership. Society for Applied Anthropology, Box 24083, Oklahoma City, OK 73124-0083. TEL 405-843-5113.
FAX 405-843-8553. E-mail: sfaa@telepath.com; URL: http://www.telepath.com/sfaa. Ed. Michael Whiteford. circ. 2,000 (paid). **Document type:** newsletter.
    Description: Includes news and items of current interest for members and others interested in the application of the social and behavioral sciences to contemporary issues.

SOCIOLINGUISTIQUE; systemes de langues et interactions sociales et culturelles. see *LINGUISTICS*

SOCIOLOGICAL OBSERVATIONS. see *SOCIOLOGY*

SOCIOLOGY WORKING PAPERS. see *SOCIOLOGY*

SOJOURN; social issues in Southeast Asia. see *SOCIOLOGY*

SOLOMON ISLANDS MUSEUM ASSOCIATION. JOURNAL. see *MUSEUMS AND ART GALLERIES*

572 960   SA   ISSN 0379-8860
GN301   CODEN: SAJEEN
SOUTH AFRICAN JOURNAL OF ETHNOLOGY/SUID-AFRIKAANSE TYDSKRIF VIR ETNOLOGIE. (Text in English; summaries in Afrikaans, English) 1978. q. R.118 to individuals; institutions R.138 (foreign $45) (effective 1997). (Association of Afrikaans Ethnologists) Foundation for Education, Science & Technology, P.O. Box 1758, Pretoria 0001, South Africa.
TEL 27-12-3226404. FAX 27-12-3207803. E-mail: buro@shuttle.up.ac.za. Ed. J.D. Kriel. adv. contact: J.D. Kriel. index. circ. 500. **Indexed:** Abstr.Anthropol., Documentatieblad, Ind.S.A.Per., Mult.Ed.Abstr., Sp.Ed.Needs Abstr., Stud.Wom.Abstr. **Document type:** academic/scholarly publication.
—CCC.
    Description: Publishes original articles of research, updates and comments in the fields of anthropology, ethnology and archaeology.
    Refereed Serial

SOUTH AFRICAN MUSEUM. ANNALS/SUID-AFRIKAANSE MUSEUM. ANNALE. see *BIOLOGY*

SOUTH ASIA: JOURNAL OF SOUTH ASIAN STUDIES. see *HISTORY — History Of Asia*

572   II   ISSN 0257-7348
GN1
SOUTH ASIAN ANTHROPOLOGIST. 1980. s-a. $25 (effective 1997 & 1998). Sarat Chandra Roy Institute of Anthropological Studies, House No. H 1-98, Harmu Housing Colony, Harmu, Ranchi 834 012, Bihar, India. TEL 91-651-307824. Ed. P. Dash Sharma. adv.; bk.rev.; cum.index: 1980-1993 in vol.15. circ. 300. (back issues avail.) **Indexed:** A.I.C.P., Anthropol.Lit., IBR, Rice Abstr. **Document type:** academic/scholarly publication.
—BLDSC (8348.621000); UnCover.
    Description: Publishes articles on any field of anthropology relevant to South Asia, including biological, genetical, environmental and developmental studies in South Asia.
    Refereed Serial

572   US   ISSN 0081-2994
GN2
SOUTHERN ANTHROPOLOGICAL SOCIETY. PROCEEDINGS. 1968. a. price varies. University of Georgia Press, 330 Research Dr., Athens, GA 30602-4901. TEL 706-369-6130.
FAX 706-369-6131. **Indexed:** Anthropol.Lit. **Document type:** proceedings.
—BLDSC (8352.700000).

572   US
SOUTHWESTERN ANTHROPOLOGICAL ASSOCIATION NEWSLETTER. 1959. a. $20. Southwestern Anthropological Association, Box 660831, Sacramento, CA 95866-0831. TEL 213-343-2239. E-mail: donoghue@ix.netcom.com; wainani7@aol.com. (Alt. addr.: Anthropology Dept., California State Univ. L.A., 5151 State University Dr., L.A., CA 90032. FAX 213-343-2446) Ed. Jim Bell. bk.rev. **Document type:** academic/scholarly publication, newsletter.
    Description: Includes information on association meetings and members.

SOUTHWESTERN LORE. see *ARCHAEOLOGY*

572   II
SPECTRA OF ANTHROPOLOGICAL PROGRESS. (Text in English) 1978. irreg. Rs.25($6) University of Delhi, Department of Anthropology, Delhi 110007, India. **Indexed:** Anthropol.Lit.

572   YU   ISSN 0374-082X
AS346
SRPSKA AKADEMIJA NAUKA I UMETNOSTI. ETNOGRAFSKI INSTITUT. GLASNIK. (Text in Serbo-Croatian; summaries in English) 1894. irreg. Srpska Akademija Nauka i Umetnosti, Etnografski Institut, Knez Mihailova 35, 11001 Belgrade, Serbia, Yugoslavia. bk.rev.; bibl. **Indexed:** Anthropol.Lit.

572   YU
SRPSKA AKADEMIJA NAUKA I UMETNOSTI. ETNOGRAFSKI INSTITUT. ZBORNIK RADOVA. (Text in Serbo-Croatian; summaries in French) 1950. irreg. Srpska Akademija Nauka i Umetnosti, Etnografski Institut, Knez Mihailova 35, 11001 Belgrade, Serbia, Yugoslavia. **Indexed:** Anthropol.Lit.

572 301.2   YU   ISSN 0081-4067
SRPSKI ETNOGRAFSKI ZBORNIK. NASELJA I POREKLO STANOVNISTVA. (Text in Serbo-Croatian; summaries in English, French, German or Russian) 1902. irreg. price varies. Srpska Akademija Nauka i Umetnosti, Knez Mihailova 35, 11001 Belgrade, Serbia, Yugoslavia. FAX 38-11-182-825. TELEX 72593 SANU YU. (Dist. by: Prosveta, Terazije 16, Belgrade, Serbia, Yugoslavia) circ. 1,000.

572 301.2 390   YU   ISSN 0081-4075
SRPSKI ETNOGRAFSKI ZBORNIK. RASPRAVE I GRADJA. (Text in Serbo-Croatian; summaries in English, French, German or Russian) 1934. irreg. price varies. Srpska Akademija Nauka i Umetnosti, Knez Mihailova 35, 11001 Belgrade, Serbia, Yugoslavia. FAX 38-11-182-825. TELEX 72593 SANU YU. (Dist. by: Prosveta, Terazije 16, Belgrade, Serbia, Yugoslavia) circ. 1,000.

572 301.2 390   YU   ISSN 0081-4083
SRPSKI ETNOGRAFSKI ZBORNIK. SRPSKE NARODNE UMOTVORINE. (Text in Serbo-Croatian; summaries in English, French, German or Russian) 1927. irreg. price varies. Srpska Akademija Nauka i Umetnosti, Knez Mihailova 35, 11001 Belgrade, Serbia, Yugoslavia. FAX 38-11-182-825. TELEX 72593 SANU YU. (Dist. by: Prosveta, Terazije 16, Belgrade, Serbia, Yugoslavia) circ. 1,000.

572 390   YU   ISSN 0081-4091
SRPSKI ETNOGRAFSKI ZBORNIK. ZIVOT I OBICAJI NARODNI. (Text in Serbo-Croatian; summaries in English, French, German or Russian) 1894. irreg. price varies. Srpska Akademija Nauka i Umetnosti, Knez Mihailova 35, 11001 Belgrade, Serbia, Yugoslavia. FAX 38-11-182-825. TELEX 72593 SANU YU. (Dist. by: Prosveta, Terazije 16, Belgrade, Serbia, Yugoslavia) circ. 1,000.

STAATLICHE MUSEUMS FUER VOELKERKUNDE DRESDEN. ABHANDLUNGEN UND BERICHTE. see *MUSEUMS AND ART GALLERIES*

572   US
STATE UNIVERSITY OF NEW YORK AT ALBANY. INSTITUTE FOR MESOAMERICAN STUDIES. MONOGRAPHS. 1977. irreg., no.10.1985. State University of New York at Albany, Institute for Mesoamerican Studies, Albany, NY 12222.
TEL 518-442-4722. Dir. Michael E. Smith. **Document type:** monographic series.

572 913   US   ISSN 0039-1344
GN2
STEWARD ANTHROPOLOGICAL SOCIETY. JOURNAL. 1969. s-a. $18 to individuals; institutions $25 (effective 1997). J S A S, Department of Anthropology, University of Illinois, 109 Davenport Hall, 607 S. Matthews St., Urbana, IL 61801.
TEL 217-244-0183. FAX 217-244-3490. Ed. Rossana de la Noval. bk.rev.; charts; illus. circ. 300. (processed) **Indexed:** A.I.C.P., Abstr.Anthropol., Anthropol.Lit., M.L.A., Mid.East: Abstr.& Ind. **Document type:** academic/scholarly publication.
—KR SourceOne; UnCover.

301.2   IT   ISSN 0394-7963
STORIA, ANTROPOLOGIA E SCIENZE DEL LINGUAGGIO. 1986. 3/yr. L.38000. Bulzoni Editore, Via dei Liburni 14, 000185 Rome, Italy. TEL 06-4455207. FAX 06-4450355.

572   IT
STUDI ETNO-ANTROPOLOGICI E SOCIOLOGICI. 1946. a. L.35000. Atena 2000 s.a.s., Corso Vitt. Emanuele, 110, 80121 Naples, Italy. (Edit. addr.: Viale A. Gramsci 20, 80122 Naples, Italy) Ed.Bd. adv.; bk.rev. circ. 2,000. **Indexed:** A.I.C.P., Anthropol.Lit., IBR.
    Former titles: Etnologia - Antropologia Culturale (ISSN 0392-7008); (until 1973): Rivista di Etnografia (ISSN 0085-5731)

572 560   IT   ISSN 0392-6788
STUDI PER L'ECOLOGIA DEL QUATERNARIO. 1979. a. L.45000 (effective 1994). Laboratorio di Ecologia del Quaternario, Via del Proconsolo, 12, 50122 Florence, Italy. TEL 055-293028.
FAX 055-293028. Ed. E. Borzatti von Loewenstern. bk.rev. circ. 800. **Indexed:** Anthropol.Lit. **Document type:** academic/scholarly publication.
    Description: Contains previously unpublished works concerning ecology of the Quaternary era, prehistoric ecology, palaeoethnology, Quaternary geology, human paleontology and anthropology.

572   BE
STUDIA ANTHROPOLOGICA. 1987. irreg., vol.3, 1996. price varies. Leuven University Press, Blijde Inkomststraat 5, 3000 Leuven, Belgium.
TEL 32-16-325345. FAX 32-16-325352. E-mail: university.press@upers.kuleuven.ac.be; URL: http://www.kuleuven.ac.be/upers. Ed.Bd. (back issues avail.) **Document type:** monographic series.

572   SW   ISSN 0491-2705
STUDIA ETHNOGRAPHICA UPSALIENSIA. 1956. a. (Uppsala Universitet, Institutionen foer Allmaem och Jaemfoerande Etnografi) A W I International AB, P.O. Box 4627, S-116 91 Stockholm, Sweden.
TEL 46-8-7282500. FAX 46-8-338707. (back issues avail.) **Document type:** academic/scholarly publication.

572   SW   ISSN 0346-900X
STUDIA ETHNOLOGICA UPSALIENSIA. 1976. irreg. price varies. (Universitet i Uppsala) A W I International AB, P.O. Box 4627, S-116 91 Stockholm, Sweden.
TEL 46-8-7282500. FAX 46-8-338707. (back issues avail.) **Document type:** academic/scholarly publication.

ANTHROPOLOGY

305.89 894   FI   ISSN 1235-1954
GN585.F53
STUDIA FENNICA. ETHNOLOGICA. 1933. irreg. Suomalaisen Kirjallisuuden Seura - Finnish Literature Society, Hallituskatu 1, P.O. Box 259, FIN-00170 Helsinki, Finland. TEL 358-0-131231. FAX 358-0-13123220. Ed.Bd. **Indexed:** A.I.C.P., MLA Intl.Bibl.
    Supersedes in part (in 1992): Studia Fennica (ISSN 0085-6835)

572   SZ   ISSN 0570-3085
STUDIA INSTITUTI ANTHROPOS. (Text in Dutch, English, French, and German) 1950. irreg., no.46, 1992. price varies. (Anthropos Institut) Universitaetsverlag Freiburg, Perolles 42, CH-1705 Fribourg, Switzerland. TEL 41-26-4264311. FAX 41-26-4264300. illus. **Document type:** monographic series.

572   US   ISSN 0585-5578
STUDIA SUMIRO-HUNGARICA. (Text in English and Hungarian) 1968. irreg., vol.3, 1974. Gilgamesh Publishing Co., 6050 Boulevard East, 20-A, W. New York, NJ 07093. Ed. Miklos Erdy. bibl.; charts; illus. circ. 2,000.

572   GW   ISSN 0170-3544
STUDIEN ZUR KULTURKUNDE. (Text in English, French and German) irreg., vol.103, 1992. price varies. (Universitaet Frankfurt, Frobenius-Institut) Lit Verlag, Dieckstr. 56, 48145 Muenster, Germany. TEL 0251-231972. Ed. Eike Haberland. **Document type:** monographic series.

STUDIES IN ANTHROPOLOGICAL LINGUISTICS. see *LINGUISTICS*

STUDIES IN ANTHROPOLOGY AND HISTORY. see *HISTORY*

572   US   ISSN 0733-5776
STUDIES IN MAYAN LINGUISTICS. (Subseries of: University of Missouri at Columbia. Museum of Anthropology. Miscellaneous Publications in Anthropology) 1975. irreg. price varies. University of Missouri at Columbia, Department of Anthropology, Columbia, MO 65201. TEL 314-882-3573. **Document type:** monographic series.

306.08 995   US
STUDIES IN MELANESIAN ANTHROPOLOGY. 1983. irreg., no.13, 1995. University of California Press, 2120 Berkeley Way, Berkeley, CA 94720. TEL 510-642-4247. FAX 510-643-7127. (Orders to: California-Princeton Fulfillment Services, 1445 Lower Ferry Rd., Ewing, NJ 08618. TEL 800-777-4726. FAX 800-999-1958) Ed.Bd. (back issues avail.) **Document type:** monographic series.
    Description: Studies the ways and culture of Melanesian peoples.
    Refereed Serial

573.05   PL   ISSN 0324-8291
GN49
STUDIES IN PHYSICAL ANTHROPOLOGY. (Text in English; summaries in Polish) irreg. price varies. Polska Akademia Nauk, Zaklad Antropologii, Ul. Kuznicza 35, 50-951 Wroclaw, Poland. (Dist. by: Ars Polona, Krakowskie Przedmiescie 7, 00-068 Warsaw, Poland) Ed. T. Bielicki. bibl. circ. 360. **Indexed:** A.I.C.P., Anthropol.Lit., Biol.Abstr., Excerp.Med.
—Linda Hall.

301   US   ISSN 1040-9548
STUDIES ON CULTURE AND SOCIETY. 1986. irreg., vol.6, 1994. price varies. State University of New York, Institute for Mesoamerican Studies, Albany, NY 12222. TEL 518-442-4722. E-mail: ims@csc.albany.edu; URL: http://www.albany.edu/anthro/imspage.html. Ed. Louise Burkhart. R&P contact: Louise Bukhart. **Document type:** monographic series.
—BLDSC (8490.319500).

STUDIES ON RELIGION IN AFRICA. see *RELIGIONS AND THEOLOGY*

570   RM   ISSN 0039-3886
GN58.R8   CODEN: SCANCH
STUDII SI CERCETARI DE ANTROPOLOGIE. (Text in Rumanian; summaries in English and French) 1964. a. (Academia Romana, Centrul de Cercetari Antropologice din Bucuresti) Editura Academiei Romane, Calea 13 Septembrie 13, 76117 Bucharest, Rumania. (Dist. by: Rodipet SA, Piata Presei Libere 1, Sec. 1, PO Box 33-57, Bucharest, Rumania. TEL 401-6185103. FAX 401-2226407) Ed. Olga Necrasov. bk.rev.; charts; illus.; index. **Indexed:** A.I.C.P., Anthropol.Lit., Biol.Abstr.
—BLDSC (8492.295000).
    Formerly: Probleme de Antropologie.

301.2 572   SJ   ISSN 0562-5130
SUDAN SOCIETY/MUJTAMA. (Text in Arabic and English) 1962. a. University of Khartoum, Social Studies Society, Faculty of Economic and Social Studies, Box 321, Khartoum, Sudan. **Indexed:** A.I.C.P.

305.8 494   FI   ISSN 0355-0214
SUOMALAIS-UGRILAISEN SEURAN AIKAKAUSKIRJA/SOCIETE FINNO-OUGRIENNE. JOURNAL. (Text in English, Finnish, French and Russian) 1885. a. FIM 140 to non-members. Suomalais-Ugrilainen Seura, PL 320, FIN-00171 Helsinki, Finland. (Dist. by: Tiedekirja - Vetenskapsbokhandeln, Kirkkokatu 14, FIN-00170 Helsinki, Finland) Ed. Riho Gruenthal. circ. 600. **Indexed:** Bibl.Ling., MLA Intl.Bibl. **Document type:** academic/scholarly publication, proceedings.

305.8 494   FI   ISSN 0359-7679
SUOMALAIS-UGRILAISEN SEURAN KANSATIETEELLISIA JULKAISUJA/TRAVAUX ETHNOGRAPHIQUES DE LA SOCIETE FINNO-OUGRIENNE. (Text in various languages) 1899. price varies. Suomalais-Ugrilainen Seura, PL 320, FIN-00171 Helsinki, Finland. (Dist. by: Tiedekirja - Vetenskapsbokhandeln, Kirkkokatu 14, FIN-00170 Helsinki, Finland) **Document type:** academic/scholarly publication.

305.8 494   FI   ISSN 0355-0230
PH1
SUOMALAIS-UGRILAISEN SEURAN TOIMITUKSIA/SOCIETE FINNO-OUGRIENNE. MEMOIRES. (Text in various languages) 1890. irreg. price varies. Suomalais-Ugrilainen Seura, PL 320, FIN-00171 Helsinki, Finland. (Dist. by: Tiedekirja, Kirkkokatu 14, FIN-00170 Helsinki, Finland) **Document type:** academic/scholarly publication.

301.2   FI   ISSN 0355-3930
SUOMEN ANTROPOLOGI/ANTROPOLOGI I FINLAND/FINNISH ANTHROPOLOGICAL SOCIETY. JOURNAL. (Text in English, Finnish, Swedish) 1976. q. FIM 130 in Nordic countries; elsewhere FIM 160 (effective 1998). Suomen Antropologinen Seura - Finnish Anthropological Society, P.O. Box 13, SF-00014 University of Helsinki, Finland. TEL 358-9-191-7828. FAX 358-9-191-7829. E-mail: panttone@cc.helsinki.fi. Eds. Matti Sarmela, Pertti Anttonen. bk.rev. circ. 600. **Indexed:** A.I.C.P., Anthropol.Lit., M.L.A., MLA Intl.Bibl. **Document type:** academic/scholarly publication.
    Description: Contains scholarly articles concerning research and study in anthropology and related fields in the study of cultures.
    Refereed Serial

SUOMEN MUSEO. see *ARCHAEOLOGY*

SURVIVAL (LONDON, 1993). see *POLITICAL SCIENCE — Civil Rights*

572 323.4   UK   ISSN 0308-2857
GN380
SURVIVAL INTERNATIONAL REVIEW. 1976. s-a. £15($30) membership. Survival International, 11-15 Emerald St., London WC1N 3QL, England. TEL 44-171-242-1441. FAX 44-171-242-1771. Ed. Alison Sanders. adv.; bk.rev. circ. 15,000. (also avail. in microfiche) **Indexed:** Anthropol.Lit., HR Rep., IDA. **Document type:** newsletter.
    Description: Works for the rights of threatened tribal people.

301   AT   ISSN 1035-8811
GN1   CODEN: AJANE6
T A J A. (The Australian Journal of Anthropology) 1931. 3/yr. Aus.$50 to individuals; institutions Aus.$87 (effective 1997). Australian Anthropological Society, c/o Dept. of Anthropology, Univ. of Sydney, Sydney, N.S.W. 2006, Australia. TEL 61-2-93515489. FAX 61-2-93515489. E-mail: john__ovenshine@iacnet.com. Ed. Michael Allen. R&P contact: Michael Allen. TEL 61-2-98105006. adv. contact: Robyn Wood. bk.rev.; bibl.; charts; illus.; index; circ. 450 (paid). (back issues avail.) **Indexed:** A.I.C.P., Abstr.Anthropol., Anthropol.Lit., Aus.P.A.I.S, Br.Archaeol.Abstr., Curr.Cont., E.I., IBR, Ref.Zh., Soc.Sci.Ind. (until 1994), Sociol.Abstr., SSCI. **Document type:** academic/scholarly publication.
●Also available online. Vendor(s): Information Access Co.
—KR SourceOne; SWETS; UMI; UnCover.
    Formerly (until 1990): Mankind (ISSN 0025-2328)
    Description: Publishes scholarly papers in anthropology and related disciplines, particularly concerning Australia and neighboring countries, including Asia.

918 972.606   MX   ISSN 0185-6286
F1219
T R A C E. (Travaux et Recherches dans les Ameriques du Centre) (Text in French and Spanish) 1978. s-a. varies. (Ministere des Affaires Etrangeres, FR) Centre d'Etudes Mexicaines et Centramericaines - Centro de Estudios Mexicanos y Centroamericanos, Sierra Leona 330, Apdo. 41-879, 11000 Mexico, D.F., Mexico. TEL 540-59-21. FAX 540-59-23. Ed. Joelle Gaillac. adv.; bk.rev. circ. 2,000. **Indexed:** Anthropol.Lit., IBR.
    Former titles (until 1984): Centre d'Etudes Mexicaines et Centramericaines. Bulletin; Mission Archeologique et Ethnologique Francaise au Mexique.
    Description: Contains social science articles about Central America and the West Indies.

301 572   PH   ISSN 0117-6323
TAMBARA; Ateneo de Davao University journal. (Text in English) 1984. a. P.250($13) Ateneo de Davao University, P.O. Box 13, Davao City 8000, Philippines. TEL 221-2411. Ed. Heidi K. Gloria. R&P contact: Heidi K. Gloria. circ. 1,000 (paid). **Indexed:** Ind.Phil.Per. **Document type:** academic/scholarly publication.
    Description: Covers community studies on socio-cultural, historical, and theological issues in Mindanao.

572   US   CODEN: TEBIDX
TEBIWA. 1958. irreg. $10. Idaho Museum of Natural History, Idaho State University, Box 8096, Pocatello, ID 83209. TEL 208-236-2262. Ed. E.S. Lohse. abstr.; 10-yr. cum.index in vol. 11. circ. 500. (also avail. in microform from UMI; reprint service avail. from UMI) **Indexed:** A.I.C.P., Abstr.Anthropol., Anthropol.Lit., Biol.Abstr., Geo.Abstr., GeoRef., Sport Fish.Abstr., Wild.Rev., Zoo.Rec. **Document type:** monographic series, academic/scholarly publication.
—Linda Hall; UMI; UnCover.
    Former titles: Tebiwa Miscellaneous Papers; (until vol.19): Tebiwa (ISSN 0040-0823)

572   AT
TEMPUS. (In 2 vols.) 1973; N.S. 1989. irreg., vol.6, 1996. price varies. University of Queensland, Anthropology Museum, St. Lucia, Qld. 4072, Australia. TEL 61-7-33652674. FAX 61-7-33654696. E-mail: j.hall@mailbox.uq.edu.au. Ed.Bd. R&P contact: Jay Hall. circ. 900 (paid). **Indexed:** A.I.C.P. **Document type:** academic/scholarly publication, monographic series.
    Supersedes (in 1989): Occasional Papers in Anthropology.
    Description: Provides a forum for communicating anthropologically oriented studies in archaeology and material culture.
    Refereed Serial

TENDENZEN (YEAR). see *FOLKLORE*

ANTHROPOLOGY

572 930.1   US
TENNESSEE ANTHROPOLOGICAL ASSOCIATION. MISCELLANEOUS PAPER. 1976. irreg. $10 membership (foreign $20) (effective 1997) (includes Association Newsletter and Tennessee Anthropologist). Tennessee Anthropological Association, Department of Anthropology, University of Tennessee, Knoxville, TN 37996-0720. TEL 615-974-4408. Ed. Charles H. Faulkner. R&P contact: Charles H. Faulkner. circ. 300. **Document type:** monographic series.

572 930.1   US   ISSN 0196-0377
TENNESSEE ANTHROPOLOGICAL ASSOCIATION. NEWSLETTER. 1976. bi-m. $10 membership (foreign £20) (effective 1997) (includes Miscellaneous Papers and Teexas Anthropologist). Tennessee Anthropological Association, Department of Anthropology, University of Tennessee, Knoxville, TN 37996-0720. TEL 615-974-4408. Ed. Charles H. Faulkner. **Indexed:** A.I.C.P., Anthropol.Lit. **Document type:** newsletter.

572 930.1   US   ISSN 0892-7979
GN1   CODEN: TEANEA
TENNESSEE ANTHROPOLOGIST. 1976. s-a. $10 membership (foreign $20) (effective 1997) (includes Miscellaneous Papers and Newsletter). Tennessee Anthropological Association, Department of Anthropology, University of Tennessee, Knoxville, TN 37996-0720. TEL 615-974-4408. Ed. Charles H. Faulkner. R&P contact: Charles H. Faulkner. **Indexed:** A.I.C.P., Abstr.Anthropol., Anthropol.Lit. **Document type:** academic/scholarly publication, newsletter.
—BLDSC (8790.550000).

TERRA. see *MUSEUMS AND ART GALLERIES*

572 917 970   IT   ISSN 0040-375X
E51
TERRA AMERIGA. (Text in English, French, German, Italian, Portuguese and Spanish) 1965. q. $10. Associazione Italiana Studi Americanistici, Villa De Mari-Gruber, Corso Solferino 29, Salita S. Maria della Sanita 43, 16122 Genoa, Italy. Dir. Ernesto Lunardi. adv.; bk.rev.; film rev.; rec.rev.; charts; illus.; stat.; tr.lit.; cum.index every 2 yrs. circ. 2,000. **Indexed:** Anthropol.Lit., Hisp.Amer.Per.Ind. (1970-1986).

572   FR   ISSN 0760-5668
DC34   CODEN: TERRF6
TERRAIN; carnets du patrimoine ethnologique. 1983. s-a. 360 F. for 2 yrs. Ministere de la Culture, 65 rue de Richelieu, 75002 Paris, France. TEL 33-1-40158527. FAX 33-1-40158733. (Subscr. to: CNMHS, 62 rue Saint-Antoine, 75004 Paris, France) Ed. Christine Langlois. R&P contact: Christine Langlois. adv. contact: Dorine Bertrand. bk.rev.; illus. **Document type:** academic/scholarly publication.
—BLDSC (8794.768000).
  Description: Studies European social anthropology and history.
  Refereed Serial

THEM DAYS. see *FOLKLORE*

THESIS ELEVEN; rethinking social and political theory. see *SOCIOLOGY — Abstracting, Bibliographies, Statistics*

THRACO-DACICA. see *HISTORY — History Of Europe*

572   RM
TIBISCUS. SERIA ETNOGRAFIE. (Text in Rumanian; summaries in German) a. Muzeul Banatului, Piata Huniade Nr. 1, Timisoara, Rumania.

390 970.1   MX   ISSN 0040-8239
TLALOCAN; revista de fuentes para el conocimiento de las culturas indigenas de Mexico. (Text in English, Mexican aboriginal languages, Spanish) 1942. irreg., vol.11, 1989. $17. Universidad Nacional Autonoma de Mexico, Instituto de Investigaciones Filologicas, Circuito Mario de la Cueva, Zona Cultural, Ciudad Universitaria, 04510 Mexico, D.F., Mexico. TEL 52-5-6227489. FAX 52-5-6657874. Ed. Karen Dakin. illus. circ. 2,000. **Indexed:** Anthropol.Lit., Hisp.Amer.Per.Ind. (1985), M.L.A., MLA Intl.Bibl.

301   SP   ISSN 0210-1483
TRABAJOS DE ANTROPOLOGIA. 1970. irreg. 800 ptas. Universidad de Barcelona, Facultad de Biologia, Seccion de Antropologia, Avda. Diagonal 645, 08017 Barcelona, Spain.

572   PO   ISSN 0304-243X
TRABALHOS DE ANTROPOLOGIA E ETNOLOGIA. (Text occasionally in English, French, German, Portuguese, Spanish) 1919. 2/yr. (4 nos./vol.). $17. Sociedade Portuguesa de Antropologia e Etnologia, Faculdade de Ciencias, Universidade do Porto, 4000 Porto, Portugal. Ed. Vitor Oliveira Jorge. adv.; bk.rev.; illus. circ. 1,500. **Indexed:** A.I.C.P., Anthropol.Lit. **Document type:** academic/scholarly publication.
  Formerly: Sociedade Portuguesa de Antropologia e Etnologia. Trabalhos.
  Description: Covers current research in archaeology and anthropology. Includes papers mainly on Portuguese and Spanish subjects.

572   XV   ISSN 0352-0447
DR381.S64
TRADITIONES. (Text in Slovenian; summaries in English, French, German and Italian) 1972. irreg. price varies. Slovenska Akademija Znanosti in Umetnosti, Razred za Filoloske in Literarne Vede, Novi Trg 5-1, Ljubljana, Slovenia. FAX 3861-155-232. (Dist. by: Biblioteka Slovenske Akademije Znanosti in Umetnosti, Novi Trg 3, 61000 Ljubljana, Slovenia) Ed. Mojca Ravnik. bk.rev.; illus.; bibl. circ. 1,000. **Indexed:** M.L.A., MLA Intl.Bibl.
—BLDSC (8881.080000).

TRANSCULTURAL PSYCHIATRY. see *MEDICAL SCIENCES — Psychiatry And Neurology*

572   US   ISSN 1051-0559
GN1
TRANSFORMING ANTHROPOLOGY. 1990. s-a. $25 (effective 1996). Association of Black Anthropologists, 4350 N. Fairfax Dr., Ste. 640, Arlington, VA 22203. TEL 703-528-1902. Ed. Arthur Spears. R&P contact: Terry Clifford. adv. contact: Rick Custer. circ. 250. **Indexed:** A.I.C.P., Anthropol.Lit. **Document type:** academic/scholarly publication.
  Description: Seeks to advance the understanding of all forms of human diversity and commonality. Addresses social inequities based on race, gender, ethnicity, and class.

572   US   ISSN 0890-1562
TRANSWORLD IDENTITY SERIES. 1982. irreg., vol.3, 1984. Eurolingua, Box 101, Bloomington, IN 47402-0101. TEL 812-332-8918. **Document type:** monographic series.
  Description: Monographs on integrative processes in global ramification from political and anthropological points of view.

911   GW   ISSN 0082-6413
TRIBUS; Jahrbuch des Linden-Museums Stuttgart. (Text in German; occasionally in English, French, Spanish) 1951. a. DM.39. Linden-Museum Stuttgart-Staatliches Museum fuer Voelkerkunde, Hegelplatz 1, 70174 Stuttgart, Germany. TEL 49-711-2022400. FAX 49-711-2022590. Ed. Peter Thiele. adv. contact: Peter Thiele. bk.rev.; circ. 800 (controlled). **Indexed:** A.I.C.P., Anthropol.Lit., IBR. **Document type:** academic/scholarly publication.

301.451   TU   ISSN 0082-6898
TURK ETNOGRAFYA DERGISI/TURKISH REVIEW OF ETHNOGRAPHY. 1956. a. exchange basis. Ministry of Culture, General Directorate of Monuments and Museums - Kultur Bakanligi, Anitlar ve Muzeler Genel Mudurlugu, 06100 Ulus - Ankara, Turkey. TEL 90-312-3104960. FAX 90-312-3111417. (Orders to: Kultur Bakanligi, Doner Sermaye Isletmesi Merkez Mudurlugu, Akdale Sok. No. 18-1, Yenisehir - Ankara, Turkey) **Document type:** academic/scholarly publication.
  Formerly: Turk Tarih-Arkeologya ve Etnografya Dergisi.

301 930.1   GT
U TZ'IB. 1991. s-a. Asociacion Tikal, Edif. Galerias Reforma, Of. 322, Avda. Reforma 8-60, Zona 9, Guatemala 01009, Guatemala. TEL 311176. **Document type:** academic/scholarly publication.
  Description: Publishes research results, educational material and findings related to the archaeology, anthropology and history of Guatemala.

572   GW   ISSN 0341-9274
UEBERSEE-MUSEUM, BREMEN. VEROEFFENTLICHUNGEN. REIHE D: VOELKERKUNDLICHE MONOGRAPHIEN. 1976. irreg., vol.16, 1988. price varies. Uebersee-Museum Bremen, Bahnhofsplatz 13, 28195 Bremen, Germany. Ed. Herbert Ganslmayr. **Document type:** monographic series.

301.2   PY   ISSN 0378-9896
F2679
UNIVERSIDAD CATOLICA NUESTRA SENORA DE LA ASUNCION. CENTRO DE ESTUDIOS ANTROPOLOGICOS. SUPLEMENTO ANTROPOLOGICO. 1965. 2/yr. (in 1 vol.). 18000 g.($30) (effective 1995). Universidad Catolica Nuestra Senora de la Asuncion, Centro de Estudios Antropologicos, Casilla de Correo 1718, Asuncion, Paraguay. TEL 595-21-446251. FAX 595-21-445245. Ed. Adriano Irala-Burgos. adv.; bk.rev.; cum.index. circ. 1,000. **Indexed:** A.I.C.P., Anthropol.Lit., IBR. **Document type:** academic/scholarly publication.
—BLDSC (8547.158000).

572   CK   ISSN 0120-2510
GN2
UNIVERSIDAD DE ANTIOQUIA. DEPARTAMENTO DE ANTROPOLOGIA. BOLETIN DE ANTROPOLOGIA. 1954. s-a. $20 or on exchange basis. Universidad de Antioquia, Departamento de Antropologia, Apdo. Aereo 1226, Medellin, Colombia. TEL 2630011 ext. 5778. FAX 2638282. E-mail: bolant@catios.udea.edu.co. Ed. Sofia Boten Paez. bk.rev.; bibl. circ. 1,920. **Indexed:** A.I.C.P., Anthropol.Lit. **Document type:** academic/scholarly publication, bulletin.
  Formerly: Universidad de Antioquia. Instituto de Antropologia. Boletin de Antropologia (ISSN 0041-8323)
  Description: Publishes the department's anthropological research related to Colombia and America.

572   UY   ISSN 0250-6564
UNIVERSIDAD DE LA REPUBLICA. FACULTAD DE HUMANIDADES Y CIENCIAS. REVISTA. SERIE CIENCIAS ANTROPOLOGICAS. N.S. 1979. irreg. exchange basis. Universidad de la Republica, Facultad de Humanidades y Ciencias, Seccion Revista, Tristan Narvaja 1674, Montevideo, Uruguay. Dir. Beatriz Martinez Osorio.
  Supersedes in part: Universidad de la Republica. Facultad de Humanidades. Revista.

572   SP   ISSN 0080-9101
UNIVERSIDAD DE SEVILLA. SEMINARIO DE ANTROPOLOGIA AMERICANA. PUBLICACIONES. 1960. irreg., latest no.17. Universidad de Sevilla, Servicio de Publicaciones, Calle Porvenir 27, 41013 Seville, Spain. TEL 34-5-4221958. FAX 34-5-4-232245. Ed. Alfredo Jimenez-Nunez.

301.2   PE
UNIVERSIDAD NACIONAL DEL CENTRO DEL PERU. CUADERNOS UNIVERSITARIOS. SERIE: ESTUDIOS ANDINOS DEL CENTRO. (Numbers not issued consecutively) irreg., no.4, 1978. Universidad Nacional del Centro del Peru, Departamento de Publicaciones, Calle Real 160, Huancayo, Peru.

572   BL
UNIVERSIDADE DE SAO PAULO. MUSEU PAULISTA. COLECAO. SERIE DE ETNOLOGIA. 1975. a. Universidade de Sao Paulo, Museu Paulista, Caixa Postal 42.503, Parque da Independencia, 04263 Sao Paulo, Brazil. Ed. Setembrino Petri. **Indexed:** Anthropol.Lit.
  Supersedes in part (in 1975): Museu Paulista. Colecao (ISSN 0080-6382)

572   BL   ISSN 0581-6076
UNIVERSIDADE FEDERAL DE SANTA CATARINA. MUSEU DE ANTROPOLOGIA. ANAIS. Continues the publication with the same title issued by the museum under its earlier name, Instituto de Antropologia. 1968. irreg. free or exchange basis. Universidade Federal de Santa Catarina, Museu de Antropologia, Cx. Postal 476, Campus Universitario, Trindade, 88000 Florianopolis, S.C., Brazil. Ed. Neusa Maria Bloemer. bk.rev.; bibl.; charts; illus. **Indexed:** Anthropol.Lit., IBR.

572 301   FR   ISSN 0249-5635
UNIVERSITE DE BORDEAUX II. CAHIERS ETHNOLOGIQUES. (Supplement avail.: Memoires) 1972. s-a. 180 F. (effective 1996). (Universite de Bordeaux II, Departement d'Anthropologie Sociale - Ethnologie) Presses Universitaires de Bordeaux, 3 place de la Victoire, 33000 Bordeaux, France. TEL 54-31-33-14. FAX 56314694. TELEX UNIBX II 572 237 F. Ed. Christian Meriot. R&P contact: Christian Meriot. abstr.; bibl.; illus.; cum.index: 1973-1992. circ. 250. **Indexed:** A.I.C.P., Anthropol.Lit. **Document type:** academic/scholarly publication.
  Formerly: Universite de Bordeaux II. Centre d'Etudes et de Recherches Ethnologiques. Cahiers.
  Refereed Serial

ANTHROPOLOGY

301   IV   ISSN 1010-674X
UNIVERSITE NATIONALE DE COTE D'IVOIRE. ANNALES. SERIE F: ETHNOSOCIOLOGIE. 1969. irreg., vol.8, 1979. price varies. Universite Nationale de Cote d'Ivoire, Institut d'Ethnosociologie, B.P. 865, Abidjan 08, Ivory Coast. TEL 43-90-00. bk.rev.; bibl.; charts; illus. circ. 1,000. Indexed: A.I.C.P., Anthropol.Lit., P.A.I.S.For.Lang.Ind.
    Formerly: Universite d'Abidjan. Annales. Serie F: Ethnosociologie.

572   US   ISSN 0041-9354
F906
UNIVERSITY OF ALASKA. ANTHROPOLOGICAL PAPERS. Cover title: Anthropological Papers of the University of Alaska. 1952. s-a. $20 (effective 1992). University of Alaska Fairbanks, Department of Anthropology, Box 757720, 310 Eielson Bldg., Fairbanks, AK 99775-7720. TEL 907-474-7288. FAX 907-474-7453. Ed. Linda J. Ellanna. adv.; bk.rev.; bibl.; charts; illus.; index. circ. 375. (back issues avail.) Indexed: Anthropol.Lit. Document type: monographic series.
    —BLDSC (1543.700000); Linda Hall.
    Refereed Serial

572   US   ISSN 0066-7501
UNIVERSITY OF ARIZONA. ANTHROPOLOGICAL PAPERS. 1959. irreg., no. 60, 1996. price varies. (University of Arizona, Department of Anthropology) University of Arizona Press, 1230 N. Park Ave., Tucson, AZ 85719. TEL 602-621-1441. (Co-sponsor: Arizona State Museum) Ed. Carol A. Gifford. (back issues avail.) Indexed: Anthropol.Lit. Document type: monographic series.
    Description: Publishes original studies in archaeology and anthropology, with particular emphasis on Arizona, the Southwest, and Mexico.
    Refereed Serial

572   US   ISSN 0068-6336
E51   CODEN: APREC2
UNIVERSITY OF CALIFORNIA PUBLICATIONS. ANTHROPOLOGICAL RECORDS. 1937. irreg., vol.31, 1995. price varies. University of California Press, 2120 Berkeley Way, Berkeley, CA 94720. TEL 510-642-4247. FAX 510-643-7127. (Orders to: California-Princeton Fulfillment Services, 1445 Lower Ferry Rd., Ewing, NJ 08618. TEL 800-777-4726. FAX 800-999-1958) Ed.Bd. (also avail. in microform from BHP; back issues avail.) Indexed: Biol.Abstr.
    —Linda Hall.
    Refereed Serial

572   US   ISSN 0068-6379
UNIVERSITY OF CALIFORNIA PUBLICATIONS IN ANTHROPOLOGY. 1937. irreg., vol.21, 1996. price varies. University of California Press, 2120 Berkeley Way, Berkeley, CA 94720. TEL 510-642-4247. FAX 510-643-7127. (Orders to: California-Princeton Fulfillment Services, 1445 Lower Ferry Rd., Ewing, NJ 08618. TEL 800-777-4726. FAX 800-999-1958) Ed.Bd. (back issues avail.) Document type: monographic series.
    Description: Explores the cultures of prehistoric and indigenous peoples.
    Refereed Serial

572   US
UNIVERSITY OF CHICAGO STUDIES IN ANTHROPOLOGY. SERIES IN SOCIAL, CULTURAL, AND LINGUISTIC ANTHROPOLOGY. 1975. irreg. $7.50. University of Chicago, Department of Anthropology, 1126 E. 59th St., Chicago, IL 60637. TEL 312-947-1000. FAX 312-702-4503.

301.2   GH   ISSN 0533-8646
UNIVERSITY OF GHANA. INSTITUTE OF AFRICAN STUDIES. LOCAL STUDIES SERIES. irreg., no.5, 1972. price varies. University of Ghana, Institute of African Studies, P.O. Box 73, Legon, Ghana. Document type: monographic series.

UNIVERSITY OF HULL. DEPARTMENT OF SOCIOLOGY AND SOCIAL ANTHROPOLOGY. OCCASIONAL PAPERS. see *SOCIOLOGY*

572   US   ISSN 0085-2457
UNIVERSITY OF KANSAS. DEPARTMENT OF ANTHROPOLOGY. PUBLICATIONS IN ANTHROPOLOGY. Key Title: University of Kansas Publications in Anthropology. 1969. irreg., no.19, 1991. price varies. University of Kansas Libraries, Exchange & Gifts Department, Level 2W Watson Library, Lawrence, KS 66045. TEL 913-864-3746. Ed. John M. Janzen. circ. 1,000. Indexed: Anthropol.Lit. Document type: academic/scholarly publication.
    Refereed Serial

572 913.031 410   CN   ISSN 0227-0072
UNIVERSITY OF MANITOBA ANTHROPOLOGY PAPERS. 1973. irreg., no.32, 1992. price varies. University of Manitoba, Department of Anthropology, U M A P Committee, 432 Fletcher Argue Building, Winnipeg, MB R3T 2N2, Canada. TEL 204-474-9423. Ed. David Stymeist. circ. 100. (back issues avail.) Document type: academic/scholarly publication.

572   US   ISSN 0564-8602
UNIVERSITY OF MEMPHIS. ANTHROPOLOGICAL RESEARCH CENTER. OCCASIONAL PAPERS. (Former name of issuing body: Memphis State University) 1967. irreg., no.16, 1991. price varies. University of Memphis, Anthropological Research Center, Memphis, TN 38152. TEL 901-678-2618. FAX 901-678-2069. E-mail: mcnuttch@cc.memphis.edu. Ed. Charles H. McNutt. circ. 200. Document type: monographic series, academic/scholarly publication.
    Refereed Serial

572   US   ISSN 0076-8367
GN2
UNIVERSITY OF MICHIGAN. MUSEUM OF ANTHROPOLOGY. ANTHROPOLOGICAL PAPERS. 1949. irreg., no.90, 1996. price varies. University of Michigan, Museum of Anthropology, University Museums Bldg., Ann Arbor, MI 48109. TEL 313-764-0482. FAX 313-763-7783. E-mail: shorv@umich.edu; URL: http://www.umma.lsa.umich.edu. Ed. Sally Horvath. R&P contact: Sally Horvath. TEL 313-764-0452. (also avail. in microform from UMI) Indexed: Anthropol.Lit., Biol.Abstr. Document type: monographic series, academic/scholarly publication.

572   US   ISSN 0076-8375
UNIVERSITY OF MICHIGAN. MUSEUM OF ANTHROPOLOGY. MEMOIRS. 1969. irreg., no.30, 1997. price varies. University of Michigan, Museum of Anthropology, University Museums Bldg., Ann Arbor, MI 48109. TEL 313-764-0482. FAX 313-763-7783. E-mail: shorv@umich.edu; URL: http://www.umma.lsa.umich.edu. Ed. Sally Horvath. R&P contact: Sally Horvath. TEL 313-764-0452. (reprint service avail. from UMI) Indexed: Anthropol.Lit. Document type: monographic series, academic/scholarly publication.

572   US   ISSN 0196-8297
UNIVERSITY OF MICHIGAN. MUSEUM OF ANTHROPOLOGY. TECHNICAL REPORTS. 1971. irreg., no.26, 1994. price varies. University of Michigan, Museum of Anthropology, University Museums Bldg., Ann Arbor, MI 48109. TEL 313-764-0482. FAX 313-763-7783. E-mail: shorv@umich.edu; URL: http://www.umma.lsa.umich.edu. Ed. Sally Horvath. R&P contact: Sally Horvath. TEL 313-764-0452. (reprint service avail. from UMI) Indexed: Biol.Abstr. Document type: monographic series.
    —BLDSC (8717.245000).

572   US
UNIVERSITY OF MISSOURI AT COLUMBIA. MUSEUM OF ANTHROPOLOGY. MISCELLANEOUS PUBLICATIONS IN ANTHROPOLOGY. 1972. irreg., price varies. University of Missouri at Columbia, Museum of Anthropology, 104 Swallow Hall, Columbia, MO 65211. TEL 314-882-3573. Document type: monographic series.
    Refereed Serial

572   US   ISSN 0362-1235
GN1
UNIVERSITY OF MISSOURI AT COLUMBIA. MUSEUM OF ANTHROPOLOGY. MUSEUM BRIEFS. 1969. irreg., no.26, 1982. irreg. price varies. University of Missouri at Columbia, Museum of Anthropology, 104 Swallow Hall, Columbia, MO 65211. TEL 314-882-3573. Document type: monographic series.

572 917   US
UNIVERSITY OF MISSOURI MONOGRAPHS IN ANTHROPOLOGY. 1974. irreg., no.10, 1991. price varies. University of Missouri at Columbia, Museum of Anthropology, 104 Swallow Hall, Columbia, MO 65211. TEL 314-882-3573. Ed.Bd. Document type: monographic series.
    Refereed Serial

572   US   ISSN 0078-6071
UNIVERSITY OF OREGON ANTHROPOLOGICAL PAPERS. 1971. irreg., vol.53, 1996. price varies. University of Oregon, Department of Anthropology, Eugene, OR 97403-1218. TEL 541-346-5102. FAX 541-346-0668. (Co-sponsor: Oregon State Museum of Anthropology) Ed. C. Melvin Aikens. R&P contact: C. Melvin Aikens. circ. 500. Document type: academic/scholarly publication, monographic series.
    —BLDSC (9116.245000).
    Refereed Serial

UNIVERSITY OF SOUTH CAROLINA. INSTITUTE OF ARCHEOLOGY AND ANTHROPOLOGY. ANNUAL REPORT. see *ARCHAEOLOGY*

572   US   ISSN 0083-4947
E51
UNIVERSITY OF UTAH ANTHROPOLOGICAL PAPERS. 1950. irreg., no.117, 1992. price varies. University of Utah Press, 101 University Services Bldg., Salt Lake City, UT 84112. TEL 801-581-6771. Indexed: Biol.Abstr. Document type: monographic series.
    Refereed Serial

301.2   PL   ISSN 0137-1460
UNIWERSYTET IM. ADAMA MICKIEWICZA. ANTROPOLOGIA. (Text in Polish; summaries in English) 1971. irreg., latest no.20. price varies. Adam Mickiewicz University Press, Nowowiejskiego 55, 61-734 Poznan, Poland. TEL 48-61-527380. FAX 48-61-527701. TELEX 413260 UAM PL. Pub. Maria Jankowska. R&P contact: Malgorzata Bis. Document type: academic/scholarly publication, monographic series.
    —BLDSC (9120.420000).
    Formerly: Uniwersytet im. Adama Mickiewicza w Poznaniu. Wydzial Biologii i Nauk o Ziemi. Prace. Seria Antropologia.

572 301.2   PL   ISSN 0083-4327
GN2
UNIWERSYTET JAGIELLONSKI. ZESZYTY NAUKOWE. PRACE ETNOGRAFICZNE. 1963. irreg., no.697, 1983. price varies. Uniwersytet Jagiellonski, Ul. Golegia 24, 31-007 Krakow, Poland. (Dist. by: Ars Polona, Krakowskie Przedmiescie 7, 00-068 Warsaw, Poland) Ed. Jadwiga Klimaszewska. index. circ. 600.

572   IT
UOMO & CULTURA; rivista di studi antropologici. 1967. biennial. price varies. S.F. Flaccovio Editore, Via Ruggero Settimo 37, 90139 Palermo, Italy. FAX 091-6112750. Ed. Silvana Miceli. bk.rev. Indexed: Anthropol.Lit.

301.2   SW   ISSN 0348-5099
UPPSALA STUDIES IN CULTURAL ANTHROPOLOGY. (Subseries of Acta Universitatis Upsaliensis) irreg. (Uppsala Universitet) A W I International AB, P.O. Box 4627, S-116 91 Stockholm, Sweden. TEL 46-8-7282500. FAX 46-8-338707. Ed. Anita Jacobson-Widding. Indexed: Rural Devel.Abstr., World Agri.Econ.& Rural Sociol.Abstr. Document type: academic/scholarly publication.
    —KNAW.

572 301   US   ISSN 0894-6019
URBAN ANTHROPOLOGY AND STUDIES OF CULTURAL SYSTEMS AND WORLD ECONOMIC DEVELOPMENT. 1972. q. $15 to individuals; institutions $80 (effective 1998). The Institute, Inc., 56 Centennial Ave., Brockport, NY 14420. TEL 716-637-6531. E-mail: jrollwag@acspr1.acs.brockport.edu. Ed. Jack R. Rollwagen. R&P contact: Jack R. Rollwagen. circ. 500. Indexed: Abstr.Anthropol., C.I.J.E., Curr.Cont., Sage Urb.Stud.Abstr., Soc.Sci.Ind., Sociol.Abstr., SSCI. Document type: academic/scholarly publication.
    —BLDSC (9123.320000); KR SourceOne; SWETS; UnCover. **CCC**.
    Formerly (until 1984): Urban Anthropology (ISSN 0363-2024)
    Description: Articles on urban anthropology and the impact of world economic development on the world's cultural systems.
    Refereed Serial

ANTHROPOLOGY

301.2 301   PE   ISSN 0586-5913
URBANIZACION, MIGRACIONES Y CAMBIOS EN LA SOCIEDAD PERUANA. 1968. irreg., no.12, 1991. price varies. (Instituto de Estudios Peruanos) I E P Ediciones, Horacio Urteaga 694, Lima 11, Peru. TEL 51-14-323070. FAX 51-14-324981. E-mail: libreria@iep.org.pe. (back issues avail.) **Document type:** academic/scholarly publication.

URGENT ACTION BULLETIN. see *POLITICAL SCIENCE — Civil Rights*

572   US
VANDERBILT UNIVERSITY PUBLICATIONS IN ANTHROPOLOGY. (Text in English or Spanish) 1972. s-a. price varies. (Vanderbilt University, Department of Anthropology) Vanderbilt University Publications in Anthropology, Box 1532, Sta. B, Nashville, TN 37235. TEL 615-322-7522. FAX 615-343-0230. Ed. John Monaghan. R&P contact: John Monaghan. circ. 500. **Document type:** monographic series.
   Description: Covers the archaeology, ethnology, and ethnohistory of indigenous cultures in Oaxaca and elsewhere in Mexico.
Refereed Serial

572   II   ISSN 0042-2622
VANYAJATI. (Text in English and Hindi) 1953. q. Rs.60. Bharatiya Adimjati Sevak Sangh, New Link Rd. (Dr. Ambedkar Road), Jhandewalan, New Delhi 55, India. TEL 7525492. Ed. J.H. Chinchalkar. adv.; bk.rev.; illus.; index. circ. 1,000. (also avail. in microform) **Indexed:** A.I.C.P. **Document type:** academic/scholarly publication.
   Description: Designed for the Indian tribal communities. Promotes their social, cultural and economic progress and safeguards their constitutional rights.

VEREIN FUER VOLKSKUNDE IN WIEN. SONDERSCHRIFTEN.. see *FOLKLORE*

572   CR   ISSN 0304-3703
F1545
VINCULOS. (Text and abstracts in English, Spanish) 1975. 2/yr. $20 or exchange basis. Museo Nacional de Costa Rica, Departamento de Antropologia e Historia, Apdo. 749, 1000 San Jose, Costa Rica. TEL 506-57-1433. FAX 506-33-74-27. Ed.Bd. charts; illus. circ. 1,000. **Indexed:** A.I.C.P., Anthropol.Lit., Avery Ind.Archit.Per., Hisp.Amer.Per.Ind. (1975-), IBR.

572   NE   ISSN 0894-9468
GN347   CODEN: VIANEQ
VISUAL ANTHROPOLOGY. 1987. 4/yr. $117 (effective 1998). (Commission on Visual Anthropology) Gordon and Breach - Harwood Academic, Amsteldisk 166, 1st Fl., 1079 LH Amsterdam, Netherlands. URL: http://www.gbhap.co.com/journals/176/176-sub.htm. (Subscr. to: International Publishers Distributor, Box 32160, Newark, NJ 07102. TEL 800-545-8398. FAX 215-750-6343) Ed. Paul Hockings. bk.rev.; film rev. (also avail. in microform) **Indexed:** Abstr.Anthropol., Anthropol.Lit. **Document type:** academic/scholarly publication.
—BLDSC (9241.227300); UnCover. **CCC.**
Refereed Serial

572   US   ISSN 1058-7187
GN347
VISUAL ANTHROPOLOGY REVIEW. 1985. s-a. $25 (effective 1996). American Anthropological Association, 4350 N. Fairfax Dr., Ste. 640, Arlington, VA 22203. TEL 703-528-1902. Ed. Nancy Lutkehaus. R&P contact: Terry Clifford. bk.rev.; film rev. **Indexed:** Film Lit.Ind. (1989-). **Document type:** academic/scholarly publication. **Former titles** (until 1991): Society for Visual Anthropology Review (ISSN 1053-7147); (until 1990): S V A Review (ISSN 1053-6779); (until 1989): S V A Newsletter (ISSN 1046-7688)
   Description: Includes commentary, articles and thematic analyses of visual anthropology topics.

301.2   GW   ISSN 0073-0270
VOELKERKUNDLICHE ABHANDLUNGEN. 1964. irreg. price varies. (Niedersaechsisches Landesmuseum, Hannover) Dietrich Reimer Verlag, Unter den Eichen 57, 12203 Berlin, Germany. TEL 030-8314081. FAX 030-8316323. circ. 500. **Document type:** monographic series.

572   AU
VOELKERKUNDLICHE VEROEFFENTLICHUNGEN. irreg. price varies. (Anthropologische Gesellschaft in Wien) Verlag Ferdinand Berger und Soehne GmbH, Wienerstr. 21-23, A-3580 Horn, Austria. TEL 43-2982-4161232. FAX 43-2982-2317235. Ed. Paul Spindler. **Document type:** academic/scholarly publication.

572 398 949.2   NE   ISSN 0166-0667
VOLKSKUNDIG BULLETIN; tijdschrift voor Nederlandse cultuurwetenschap. (Text in Dutch; summaries in English) 1975. 3/yr. fl.35. (Koninklijke Nederlandse Akademie van Wetenschappen, P.J. Meertens-Instituut, Volkskunde Department) Uitgeverij S U N, Postbus 1609, 6501 BP Nijmegen, Netherlands. TEL 31-24-3221700. FAX 31-24-3235493. Ed. H.W. Roodenburg. bk.rev.; abstr.; index, cum.index. circ. 500. (back issues avail.) **Document type:** academic/scholarly publication.
—KNAW; SWETS.
Refereed Serial

572   GY   ISSN 0256-4653
F2379
WALTER ROTH MUSEUM OF ANTHROPOLOGY. JOURNAL. 1978. s-a. $20 per no. Walter Roth Museum of Anthropology, 61 Main St., P.O. Box 10187, Georgetown, Guyana. TEL 592-2-58486. FAX 592-2-58511. Ed. Denis Williams. R&P contact: Jennifer Wishart. bk.rev. circ. 300. **Indexed:** Anthropol.Lit. **Document type:** academic/scholarly publication.
   Formerly: Walter Roth Museum of Archaeology and Anthropology. Journal.

WEIMARER MONOGRAPHIEN ZUR UR- UND FRUEHGESCHICHTE. see *ARCHAEOLOGY*

301   AU
WIENER BEITRAEGE ZUR ETHNOLOGIE UND ANTHROPOLOGIE. 1979. irreg., vol.5, 1988. S.280. Verlag Ferdinand Berger und Soehne GmbH, Wienerstr. 21-23, A-3580 Horn, Austria. TEL 43-2982-4161232. FAX 43-2982-2317235. **Document type:** monographic series.

572   AU   ISSN 0084-0068
GN1
WIENER VOELKERKUNDLICHE MITTEILUNGEN. 1953. a. S.150($15) (foreign S.200). Oesterreichische Ethnologische Gesellschaft, c/o Museum fuer Voelkerkunde, Neue Hofburg, A-1014 Vienna, Austria. TEL 43-1-53430519. FAX 43-1-5355320. E-mail: voelkerkundemuseum@magnet.at. Ed. Armand Duchateau. R&P contact: Armand Duchateau. adv.; bk.rev. circ. 500. **Indexed:** A.I.C.P., Anthropol.Lit., E.I., IBR. **Document type:** academic/scholarly publication.

301   GW   ISSN 0930-1992
WISSENSCHAFT UND LOGOS; Jahresschrift fuer Anthropologie, Medizin und Religionswissenschaft. (Text in German; summaries in English, German) 1986. a. DM.59. Glaser Verlag und Versandbuchhandlung, Bahnhofstr. 41, 65185 Wiesbaden, Germany. TEL 49-611-3082096. FAX 49-611-3082096. (back issues avail.) **Document type:** academic/scholarly publication.

WORLD COUNCIL OF INDIGENOUS PEOPLES. NEWSLETTER. see *POLITICAL SCIENCE — Civil Rights*

XIBEI MINZU YANJIU/NORTHWEST MINORITIES STUDIES. see *ORIENTAL STUDIES*

XIZANG YANJIU/TIBETAN STUDIES. see *ORIENTAL STUDIES*

572   US
YALE UNIVERSITY. DEPARTMENT OF ANTHROPOLOGY. PUBLICATIONS IN ANTHROPOLOGY. 1936. irreg., latest no.80. price varies. Yale University, Department of Anthropology, Box 208277, New Haven, CT 06520. TEL 203-432-3670. FAX 203-432-3669. Ed. Leopold Pospisil. R&P contact: Leopold Pospisil. **Document type:** monographic series.
Refereed Serial

972.83 572   HO   ISSN 0254-7627
YAXKIN. 1975. s-a. L.25 ($14 to individuals in N. America; Europe $22; institutions in N. America $18; Europe $26). Instituto Hondureno de Antropologia e Historia, Departamento de Investigaciones, Apdo. 1518, Tegucigalpa D.C., Honduras. TEL 504-223470. FAX 504-222552. Ed. Kevin Ruben Avalos. adv. contact: Olga Joya. bk.rev.; illus.; index. circ. 1,000. **Indexed:** Anthropol.Lit. **Document type:** academic/scholarly publication.
   Description: Covers anthropology, history and cultural geography, usually based on field research carried out in Honduras.

573   US   ISSN 0096-848X
    CODEN: YANTAE
YEARBOOK OF PHYSICAL ANTHROPOLOGY. (Supplement to: American Journal of Physical Anthropology) 1945. a. (American Association of Physical Anthropologists) John Wiley & Sons, Inc., Journals, 605 Third Ave., New York, NY 10158. TEL 212-850-8800. (Subscr. to: Joyce E. Sirianni, Sec.-Treas., Department of Anthropology, 380 MFAC, SUNY-Buffalo, Buffalo, NY 14261. TEL 716-636-2414) Ed. Francis E. Johnston. **Indexed:** A.I.C.P., Abstr.Anthropol., Anthropol.Lit., ASCA, Biol.Abstr., Curr.Adv.Ecol.Sci., Deep Sea Res.& Oceanogr.Abstr., SSCI.
—BLDSC (9415.000000); CISTI; Linda Hall; UnCover. **CCC.**

301.2 572   CN   ISSN 0140-2226
YEARBOOK OF SYMBOLIC ANTHROPOLOGY.* 1975. a. Universite Laval, Department de l'Anthropologie, 5980 Durocher, Outremont, Montreal H2V 3Y4, Canada. Ed. Erik Schulmmer.

YMER. see *GEOGRAPHY*

YUNNAN MINZU XUEYUAN XUEBAO/YUNNAN INSTITUTE OF NATIONALITIES. JOURNAL. see *ORIENTAL STUDIES*

572 410   ZA
ZAMBIA MUSEUMS JOURNAL. 1965. irreg., vol.7, 1989. K.20($20) Livingstone Museum, Box 60498, Livingstone, Zambia. Ed. F.B. Musonda. adv.; bk.rev.; illus. circ. 2,000. **Indexed:** Anthropol.Lit., P.L.E.S.A.
   Formerly: Zambia Journal; Supersedes (1959-1964): Northern Rhodesia Journal.

572   GW   ISSN 0044-2666
ZEITSCHRIFT FUER ETHNOLOGIE. 1869. s-a. DM.140. (Deutsche Gesellschaft fuer Voelkerkunde) Dietrich Reimer Verlag, Unter den Eichen 57, 12203 Berlin, Germany. TEL 030-8314081. FAX 030-8316323. (Co-sponsor: Berliner Gesellschaft fuer Anthropologie, Ethnologie und Urgeschichte) Eds. Ulla Johansen, Claudius Mueller. bk.rev.; abstr.; bibl.; illus.; stat.; index. (reprint service avail. from SWZ) **Indexed:** A.I.C.P., Anthropol.Lit., Bibl.Ling., Curr.Cont.Africa, E.I., IBR, SSCI. **Document type:** academic/scholarly publication.
—SWETS. **CCC.**

572.8   GW   ISSN 0044-314X
QM1   CODEN: ZMOAAN
ZEITSCHRIFT FUER MORPHOLOGIE UND ANTHROPOLOGIE. (Text in English, French, German) 1899. 3/yr. price varies. E. Schweizerbart'sche Verlagsbuchhandlung, Johannesstr. 3A, 70176 Stuttgart, Germany. TEL 49-711-625001. FAX 49-711-625005. Eds. H.W. Juergens, Chr. Vogel. **Indexed:** A.I.C.P., Anthropol.Lit., Biol.Abstr., IBR, Ind.Med. **Document type:** academic/scholarly publication.
—BLDSC (9473.250000); CISTI; KNAW; SWETS. **CCC.**

ZEITSCHRIFT FUER VOLKSKUNDE. see *FOLKLORE*

ZESZYTY TARNOGORSKIE. see *HISTORY — History Of Europe*

ZHONGGUO ZANGXUE/STUDY - TIBETAN NATIONALITIES see *ORIENTAL STUDIES*

ANTHROPOLOGY — Abstracting, Bibliographies, Statistics

572 016   US   ISSN 0001-3455
GN1
ABSTRACTS IN ANTHROPOLOGY. 1970. 8/yr. (in 2 vols., 4 nos./vol.). $291 (effective 1997). Baywood Publishing Co., Inc., 26 Austin Ave., Box 337, Amityville, NY 11701. TEL 516-691-1270. FAX 516-691-1770. E-mail: baywood@baywood.com; URL: http://baywood.com. Eds. Roger W. Moeller, Jay F. Custer. R&P contact: Julie Krempa. adv. contact: Michelle Satchell. abstr.; index. (back issues avail.) **Indexed:** A.I.C.P., Br.Archaeol.Abstr., E.I. **Document type:** abstracting/indexing.
—CCC.
Description: Covers the fields of archaeology, physical anthropology, linguistics, and cultural anthropology.
Refereed Serial

572   GW   ISSN 0173-2986
GN1
ABSTRACTS IN GERMAN ANTHROPOLOGY. (Text in English) 1980. s-a. DM.96($58) Edition Re, Wolfgang-Doering-Str. 4, 37077 Goettingen, Germany. FAX 49-511-6478673. E-mail: elias@by-mediaart.com. Eds. U. Oberdick, M.K. Ramaswamy. adv.; bk.rev. circ. 750. (back issues avail.) **Indexed:** Br.Archaeol.Abstr., E.I. **Document type:** abstracting/indexing.

572 016   UK   ISSN 0960-1651
ANTHROPOLOGICAL INDEX TO CURRENT PERIODICALS IN THE LIBRARY OF THE MUSEUM OF MANKIND LIBRARY. Short title: Anthropological Index. 1963. q. £84($132) (effective 1997). Royal Anthropological Institute of Great Britain and Ireland, 50 Fitzroy St., London W1P 5HS, England. TEL 44-171-387-0455. FAX 44-171-383-4235. (Dist. by: Turpin Distribution Services Ltd., Blackhorse Rd., Letchworth, Herts. SG6 1HN, England. TEL 44-1462-672555. FAX 44-1462-480947) Eds. Janice Archer, Damaris Dodds. bibl. (back issues avail.) R&P contact: Jonathan Benthall. **Indexed:** A.I.C.P., E.I. **Document type:** abstracting/indexing.
—BLDSC (1542.873000); CISTI.
Former titles (until 1977): Royal Anthropological Institute of Great Britain and Ireland. Library. Anthropological Index (ISSN 0003-5467); Royal Anthropological Institute of Great Britain and Ireland. Library. Index to Current Periodicals Received in the Library.
Description: Each issue contains about 2,000 titles of articles published in current journals worldwide that cover all aspects of anthropology, archaeology, ethnography and linguistics.

572   US   ISSN 0190-3373
Z5112
ANTHROPOLOGICAL LITERATURE; an index to periodical articles and essays. 1979. q. $225 (effective 1997). Harvard University, Tozzer Library, 21 Divinity Ave., Cambridge, MA 02138. TEL 617-495-2253. FAX 617-496-2741. Ed. Emily Moss. bk.rev.; bibl. circ. 600. (back issues avail.) **Document type:** abstracting/indexing, academic/scholarly publication.
●Also available online. Vendor(s): Research Libraries Group Information Network.
Also available on CD-ROM.
Description: Author and subject index to 8000 articles in approximately 800 serials and edited works each year. Articles are focused on the fields of archaeology, biological and physical anthropology, cultural and social anthropology and linguistics.

572 016   GW   ISSN 0003-5548
GN1
ANTHROPOLOGISCHER ANZEIGER. (Text in English and German; occasionally in French, Italian) 1924. q. DM.364($255.50) (foreign $262.30) (effective 1997). E. Schweizerbart'sche Verlagsbuchhandlung, Johannesstr. 3A, 70176 Stuttgart, Germany. TEL 49-711-625001. FAX 49-711-625005. Eds. G. Hauser, H. Walter. adv.; bk.rev.; illus. **Indexed:** A.I.C.P., Anthropol.Lit., Biol.Abstr., Dent.Ind., Excerp.Med., IBR, Ind.Med. **Document type:** academic/scholarly publication.
—BLDSC (1546.500000); Linda Hall; SWETS; UMI; UnCover. CCC.

ARCHIVO HISTORICO DIOCESANO DE SAN CRISTOBAL DE LAS CASAS. SERIE TECNICA. see PUBLIC ADMINISTRATION — Abstracting, Bibliographies, Statistics

572   AT   ISSN 1320-1158
AUSTRALIAN INSTITUTE OF ABORIGINAL AND TORRES STRAIT ISLANDER STUDIES. ANNUAL BIBLIOGRAPHY.
a. Aus.$12. Australian Institute of Aboriginal and Torres Strait Islander Studies, P.O. Box 553, Canberra, A.C.T. 2601, Australia. TEL 06-246-1111. FAX 06-249-7310. Ed. V. Chapman. **Document type:** bibliography.
Former titles: Australian Institute of Aboriginal Studies. Annual Bibliography (ISSN 0156-1553); Australian Institute of Aboriginal Studies. Current Bibliography and Partial Accessions List.
Description: Contains articles, research notes and reviews on all aspects of Australian Aboriginal studies.

572 913   US   ISSN 0896-8101
Z5111
BIBLIOGRAPHIC GUIDE TO ANTHROPOLOGY AND ARCHAEOLOGY. 1987. a. $270 (effective 1997). G.K. Hall & Co., MacMillan Library Reference USA, Box 159, Thorndike, ME 04986. TEL 212-654-8452; 800-223-6121. FAX 207-9482863. URL: http://www.mir.com/thorndike. (Subscr. to: Simon & Schuster, Library Reference Order Processing, 200 Old Tappan Rd., Old Tappan, NJ 07675. TEL 800-223-2336) **Document type:** bibliography, abstracting/indexing.
Description: Includes comprehensive subject bibliographies providing complete Library of Congress cataloging and ISBN information for each title.

291 301.2   GW   ISSN 0067-706X
Z7836
BIBLIOGRAPHIE ZUR SYMBOLIK, IKONOGRAPHIE UND MYTHOLOGIE. 1968. a. DM.48. Verlag Valentin Koerner GmbH, Postfach 100164, 76482 Baden-Baden, Germany. TEL 49-7221-22425. FAX 49-7221-38697. Ed. Hermann Jung. adv.; bk.rev. circ. 1,000. **Document type:** bibliography.
Description: List of books on symbolics, iconography and mythological studies published worldwide.

572   US   ISSN 0742-6844
BIBLIOGRAPHIES AND INDEXES IN ANTHROPOLOGY.
1984. irreg. price varies. Greenwood Press, Inc. (Subsidiary of: Greenwood Publishing Group Inc.), 88 Post Rd. W., Box 5007, Westport, CT 06881-5007. TEL 203-226-3571. FAX 203-222-1502. **Document type:** bibliography.
—BLDSC (1993.097200).

572 016   MX   ISSN 0252-841X
E51
BOLETIN DE ANTROPOLOGIA AMERICANA. (Text in English, French, Portuguese, Spanish) 1937. s-a. $38 in N. & C. America; S. America & Europe $43; Asia $48 (effective 1997). Instituto Panamericano de Geografia e Historia, Ex-Arzobispado 29, Col. Observatorio, Deleg. Miguel Hidalgo, 11860 Mexico D.F., Mexico. TEL 52-5-2775888. FAX 52-5-2716172. E-mail: ipgh@laneta.apc.org. (Subscr. to: IPGH, Depto. de Distribucion y Ventas, Apdo. 18879, 11870 Mexico DF, Mexico) Ed. Luis F. Bate. cum.index: 1937-1980. (also avail. in microform from UMI; reprint service avail. from UMI) **Indexed:** A.I.C.P., Amer.Hist.& Life (1982-1986), Anthropol.Lit., Geo.Abstr.H.G., Hisp.Amer.Per.Ind. (1980-), Hist.Abstr. (1982-1986), IBR. **Document type:** academic/scholarly publication.
—KR SourceOne.
Formerly (until 1979): Boletin Bibliografico de Antropologia Americana.

016.9729   NE   ISSN 0925-8507
CARIBBEAN ABSTRACTS. (Text in English) 1990. a. fl.40 (effective 1996). (Koninklijk Instituut voor Taal-, Land- en Volkenkunde) K I T L V Press, P.O. Box 9515, 2300 RA Leiden, Netherlands. TEL 31-71-5272372. FAX 31-71-5272638. E-mail: kitlvpress@rullet.leidenuniv.nl. Ed.Bd. **Document type:** abstracting/indexing.
Description: Publishes abstracts of selected books and articles in the humanities and social sciences acquired by the Institute's Department of Caribbean Studies.

301.2 890 410 959   NE   ISSN 0046-0885
Z3273
E I. (Excerpta Indonesica) (Text in English) 1970. 2/yr. fl.45 (effective 1996). (Koninklijk Instituut voor Taal-, Land-, en Volkenkunde, Afdeling Documentatie Modern Indonesie - Royal Institute of Linguistics and Anthropology, Documentation Centre for Modern Indonesia) K I T L V Press, P.O. Box 9515, 2300 RA Leiden, Netherlands. TEL 31-71-5272372. FAX 31-71-5272638. E-mail: kitlvpress@rullet.leidenuniv.nl. Eds. S. Karni. adv.; bk.rev.; abstr.; bibl.; cum.index every 5 yrs. circ. 1,000. (also avail. in microfiche from IDC) **Indexed:** Key to Econ.Sci. **Document type:** abstracting/indexing.
Description: Abstracts recently published articles and books in all fields of the social sciences and humanities pertaining to Indonesia.

EXCERPTA MEDICA. SECTION 1: ANATOMY, ANTHROPOLOGY, EMBRYOLOGY & HISTOLOGY. see MEDICAL SCIENCES — Abstracting, Bibliographies, Statistics

F R A N C I S. 521: SOCIOLOGIE. see SOCIOLOGY — Abstracting, Bibliographies, Statistics

572   FR   ISSN 1157-3791
GN301
F R A N C I S. 529: ETHNOLOGIE. (Printed format ceased Jan. 1995) (Text in English, French) 1947. q. Centre National de la Recherche Scientifique, Institut de l'Information Scientifique et Technique, 2 allee du Parc de Brabois, 54514 Vandoeuvre-les-Nancy Cedex, France. TEL 83-50-46-00. FAX 83-50-46-50. adv. contact: Veronique Guinvarc'h. index, cum.index. **Document type:** bibliography.
●Also available online. Vendor(s): Telesystemes - Questel.
Also available on CD-ROM.
Formerly: Bulletin Signaletique. Part 529: Ethnologie (ISSN 0765-1473); Supersedes in part: Bulletin Signaletique. Part 521: Sociologie - Ethnologie (ISSN 0007-5566).

573   US
FILMS: THE VISUALIZATION OF ANTHROPOLOGY. 1972. irreg. (every 2-3 yrs.), latest 1988. Pennsylvania State University, Audio-Visual Services, University Park, PA 16802. TEL 800-826-0132. FAX 814-863-2574. **Document type:** catalog.

016 300.7   II
I C S S R JOURNAL OF ABSTRACTS AND REVIEWS: SOCIOLOGY & SOCIAL ANTHROPOLOGY. (Text in English) 1972. s-a. Rs.30 to individuals; institutions Rs.50. Indian Council of Social Science Research, 35 Ferozshah Rd., New Delhi 110 001, India. TEL 91-11-338-3091. FAX 91-11-338-8037. TELEX 31-61083-ISSR-IN. Ed. Karuna Ahmed. index. circ. 450. (back issues avail.) **Indexed:** IBR. **Document type:** abstracting/indexing.
Formerly: I C S S R Journal of Abstracts and Reviews (ISSN 0302-7546).
Description: Selected reviews of publications in the fields of sociology and social anthropology. Includes works in criminology.

016.30608   AT
INDIGENOUS KNOWLEDGE INDEX. 1994. a. Aus.$150 (effective 1997 & 1998). Noyce Publishing, G.P.O. Box 2222T, Melbourne, Vic. 3001, Australia. (back issues avail.)

572 016   UK   ISSN 0085-2074
Z7161
INTERNATIONAL BIBLIOGRAPHY OF THE SOCIAL SCIENCES. SOCIAL AND CULTURAL ANTHROPOLOGY. Title page also reads: International Bibliography of Social and Cultural Anthropology. 1955. a. £125($230) in U.K. and Europe. (British Library of Political and Economic Science) Routledge, 11 New Fetter Lane, London EC4P 4EE, England. TEL 44-171-583-9855. FAX 44-171-583-0701. TELEX 263398-ROUT-G. URL: http://www.routledge.com/routledge/journal/journals.html. Ed. Lynne J. Brindley. adv. circ. 2,000. **Indexed:** A.I.C.P. **Document type:** academic/scholarly publication, abstracting/indexing, bibliography.
●Also available online. Vendor(s): QL Systems Ltd.
—BLDSC (4537.107000).
Description: Covers monographs and the contents of over 2000 journals in the social sciences from a selective bibliography indexed by subject, geographical term, and author.

ANTIQUES

960 016   US   ISSN 0021-731X
Z3509
JOINT ACQUISITIONS LIST OF AFRICANA. Short title: J A L A. (Text in English, French, German, Russian) 1962. bi-m. $30. Northwestern University, Melville J. Herskovits Library of African Studies, Africana Department, 1935 Sheridan Rd., Evanston, IL 60201. TEL 708-491-7684. Ed. Daniel Britz. bibl. circ. 350. (also avail. in microfiche) **Document type:** bibliography.

KONINKLIJK INSTITUUT VOOR TAAL-, LAND- EN VOLKENKUNDE. BIBLIOGRAPHICAL SERIES. see *LINGUISTICS — Abstracting, Bibliographies, Statistics*

016.3058   NE   ISSN 1380-6610
Z3273
KONINKLIJK INSTITUUT VOOR TAAL-, LAND- EN VOLKENKUNDE. LIBRARY. ACCESSIONS LIST. Cover title: Accessions List K I T L V Library. 1994. m. fl.90 (airmail fl.118) (effective 1996). (Koninklijk Instituut voor Taal-, Land- en Volkenkunde, Library) K I T L V Press, P.O. Box 9515, 2300 RA Leiden, Netherlands. TEL 31-71-5272372. FAX 31-71-5272638. E-mail: kitlvpress@rullet.leidenuniv.nl. **Document type:** bibliography.
Description: Offers a complete overview of all publications acquired by the Library in the fields of Indonesian studies, Caribbean studies, and social sciences and humanities.

572   BO
LURATHA. 1978. bi-m. Bol.$60($5) Instituto Nacional de Antropologia, Centro de Documentacion Antropologica, Casilla 20898, La Paz, Bolivia. Ed.Bd. adv.; bk.rev.; index. (looseleaf format; back issues avail.)

NOVAYA LITERATURA PO SOTSIAL'NYM I GUMANITARNYM NAUKAM. ISTORIYA - ARKHEOLOGIYA - ETNOGRAFIYA; bibliograficheskii ukazatel' see *HISTORY — Abstracting, Bibliographies, Statistics*

OESTERREICHISCHE VOLKSKUNDLICHE BIBLIOGRAPHIE. see *FOLKLORE — Abstracting, Bibliographies, Statistics*

301.2   SW   ISSN 0282-3519
DL631
SWEDEN. STATISTISKA CENTRALBYRAAN. STATISTISKA MEDDELANDEN. SERIE KU, KULTUR. (Text in Swedish; summaries in English) 1985. irreg. SEK 375 (effective 1992). Statistiska Centralbyraan, Publishing Unit, S-701 89 Oerebro, Sweden. TEL 019-176594.

ANTIQUES

see also Art

745.1   US
A A D A NEWS. bi-m. Associated Antique Dealers of America, Box 320, Corte Madera, CA 94925. TEL 415-924-2171.
Description: Describes membership activities. Includes new members list.

629.222 388.3   US
A M G B A OCTAGON. 1976. bi-m. $25 (foreign $35). American M G B Association, Box 11401, Chicago, IL 60611. TEL 773-878-5055; 800-723-MGMG. FAX 773-769-3240. E-mail: amgba@aol.com; URL: http://www.mgcars. Ed. Frank Ochal. R&P contact: Frank Ochal. adv. contact: Frank Ochal. bk.rev. circ. 2,500. (back issues avail.) **Document type:** newsletter.
Incorporates: A M G B A Quarterly (ISSN 0199-6797)
Description: Provides news for enthusiasts of MG automobiles, in particular the following MG models: MGB, MGB-GT, and MG Midget.

745.1 387.7   US   ISSN 0048-2358
A P M BULLETIN. 1972. q. $36 membership (includes AAA News and International Antique Airplane Digest). (Air Power Museum) Antique Airplane Association, Inc., 22001 Bluegrass Rd., Ottumwa, IA 52501-8569. TEL 515-938-2773. Ed. Robert L. Taylor; Pub. Robert L. Taylor. R&P contact: Robert L. Taylor. adv. contact: Robert L. Taylor. bk.rev.; bibl.; illus. circ. 5,000. **Document type:** bulletin.
Description: Covers donations to APM, news, photos, and activities of other aviation museums worldwide.

A P M MONOGRAPH SERIES. (Antique Phonograph Monthly) see *MUSIC*

A T H S SHOW TIME. (American Truck Historical Society) see *TRANSPORTATION — Trucks And Trucking*

629.222 338.476   US
ACCELERATOR. 1974. q. $35 membership. Auburn - Cord - Duesenberg Museum, 1600 S. Wayne St., Box 271, Auburn, IN 46706. TEL 219-925-1444. FAX 219-925-6266. Ed. Gregg Buttermore. bk.rev. circ. 1,650. **Document type:** newsletter.
Description: Contains current museum event notices and historic automotive feature articles.

ACTA UNIVERSITATIS WRATISLAVIENSIS. ANTIQUITAS. see *CLASSICAL STUDIES*

629.222   US   ISSN 0044-6092
ACTION ERA VEHICLE.* vol.5, 1971. bi-m. $11. Contemporary Historical Vehicle Association, P.O. Box 994485, Redding, CA 96099-4485. TEL 818-893-6531. Ed. Charles R. Smith. adv.; bk.rev.; illus. circ. 2,000.
Description: Presents brief histories of vintage automobiles.

745.1 705   FR   ISSN 0981-1389
ALADIN; antiques - arts - brocante - collections - encheres. 1987. m. 225 F.($80) per no. 28F. Editions Aladin, 7 rue Jean-Mermoz, 78000 Versailles, France. TEL 39-50-72-10. FAX 39-53-86-10. Ed. Jean-Stephane Vincent; Pub. Bruno Delaine. adv. contact: Bruno Delaine. circ. 55,000. **Document type:** consumer publication.
Description: Covers antiques fairs, auctions and collections, art showing and expositions, art news and analysis.

629.222   US   ISSN 1072-2548
BL2747.3
AMERICAN AUSTIN BANTAM CLUB NEWS. 1961. bi-m. $6. American Austin-Bantam Club, 516 W. Washington, Washington, IA 52353. Ed. James Peterson. adv. circ. 300.

666   US   ISSN 0739-6546
AMERICAN CLAY EXCHANGE.* 1980. 18/yr. $21. Page One Publications, 800 Murray Dr., El Cajon, CA 92020. Ed. Susan N. Cox. cum.index: 1980-1985. (back issues avail.)

790.132   US
NK1125
AMERICAN COLLECTOR (NORTHPORT). 1990. 8/yr. $25. Collector Publishing, 225 Main St., Ste. 300, Northport, NY 11768. TEL 516-261-8337. FAX 516-261-8235. URL: http://www.tias.com. Ed. Donna C. Kaonis. adv.: B&W page $550, color page $850; trim 8 3/8 x 10 7/8. bk.rev. circ. 15,000. **Document type:** consumer publication.
Formerly: Inside Collector (ISSN 1052-861X)
Description: Covers Americana, folk art, furniture and high quality collectibles.

745.1   US
AMERICANA FLEA MARKET DIRECTORY.* a. $10.95. 1205 Cranbrook Dr., Saginaw, MI 48603-5440. **Document type:** directory.
Formerly: Flea Market Directory.

745.1   NE   ISSN 0003-5653
NK1125
ANTIEK; tijdschrift voor liefhebbers en kenners van oude kunst en kunstnijverheid. 1966. 10/yr. fl.89 (foreign fl.128.50) (effective 1997). Waanders Uitgevers, Postbus 1129, 8001 BC Zwolle, Netherlands. TEL 31-38-4658628. FAX 31-38-4655989. Ed. Mrs. C. Thunissen. adv.; bk.rev.; illus.; index. circ. 5,200. **Indexed:** Artbibl, Artbibl.Mod., RILA. **Document type:** consumer publication.
—SWETS.

745.1   BE
ANTIEK & CURIOSA; verzamelhobby. (Text in Dutch) 1987. m. 750 BEF (Europe 1000 BEF). P.R.C. Claes, Nielsestraat 181, B-2850 Boom, Belgium. TEL 32-3-888-7461. Ed. Marc Claes. adv.; bk.rev.; index. circ. 14,000. (back issues avail.) **Document type:** bulletin.
Formerly: Verzamelhobby Magazine (ISSN 0776-2852)
Description: News and articles on antiques, collectibles, memorabilia, auctions, flea markets and more.

745.1   SW   ISSN 0282-8200
ANTIK & AUKTION. 1975. m. SEK 390 (effective 1996). Aller Specialtidningar AB, Landskronavaegen 23, S-251 85 Helsingborg, Sweden. TEL 46-42-173500. FAX 46-42-173600. Ed. Stina Norling. adv.: page SEK 21000; trim 190 x 258; adv. contact: Jan Gerland. bk.rev.; illus.; circ. 50,600 (controlled).
Former titles (until 1985): Nya Antik och Auktion (ISSN 0346-9212); (until 1978): Antik och Auktion.
Description: Focuses on antiques, art, auctions, and interior decoration.

ANTIKE KUNST. see *ARCHAEOLOGY*

ANTIKE KUNST. BEIHEFTE. see *ARCHAEOLOGY*

ANTIQUARIAN. see *HISTORY — History Of North And South America*

745.1   IT
ANTIQUARIATO. 1978. 12/yr. L.80000 (foreign L.140000) (effective 1997). Editoriale Giorgio Mondadori S.p.A., Via A. Ponti, 10, 20143 Milan, Italy. TEL 02-891661. FAX 02-89125888. Ed. Daniela Clerici. adv.; bk.rev.; charts, illus. circ. 40,000.
Formerly: BolaffiArte Antiquariato.

ANTIQUE AIRPLANE ASSOCIATION NEWS. see *AERONAUTICS AND SPACE FLIGHT*

ANTIQUE ANGLER; a quarterly newsletter-history of fishing-collectible tackle, etc. see *SPORTS AND GAMES — Outdoor Life*

745.1   US
ANTIQUE APPRAISAL ASSOCIATION OF AMERICA. NEWSLETTER. m. Antique Appraisal Association of America, 11361 Garden Grove Blvd., Garden Grove, CA 92643. TEL 714-530-7090. **Document type:** newsletter.

629.222   US   ISSN 0003-5831
TL1
ANTIQUE AUTOMOBILE. 1937. bi-m. $24 membership (effective 1997). Antique Automobile Club of America, 501 W. Governor Rd., Hershey, PA 17033. TEL 717-534-1910. Ed. William H. Smith. adv.; bk.rev.; charts; illus.; index, cum.index: 1935-1978. circ. 40,000. (also avail. in microform from UMI; back issues avail.; reprint service avail. from UMI) —UMI; UnCover.
Description: Focuses on car collecting and collectors.

745.1   US   ISSN 8750-1481
ANTIQUE BOTTLE AND GLASS COLLECTOR. 1984. m. $21 (Canada $24). Antique Bottle and Glass Collector, 102 Jefferson St., Box 180, E. Greenville, PA 18041. TEL 215-679-5849. FAX 215-679-3068. Ed. James Hagenbuch. adv. contact: James Hagenbuch. bk.rev.; circ. 4,100 (paid). (back issues avail.; reprint service avail.) **Document type:** trade publication.
Description: Feature articles on antique bottles; includes calendar of events.

629.222   US   ISSN 0164-7237
ANTIQUE CAR TIMES. bi-m. $15. William F. Gardner, Ed. & Pub., P.O. Box 2995, Jackson, TN 38302-2995. **Document type:** newsletter.
Description: Features articles on antique cars.

ANTIQUES

745.1 UK ISSN 0003-584X
ANTIQUE COLLECTING. 1965. m. (except Aug. & Jan.). $40. Antique Collectors Club, 5 Church St., Woodbridge, Suffolk IP12 1DS, England. TEL 44-1394-385501. FAX 44-1394-384434. URL: http://www.antiquece.com/mag/. Ed. Susan Wilson. adv.; bk.rev.; illus.; index. circ. 20,000. **Indexed:** Artbibl.Mod., Br.Hum.Ind. **Document type:** consumer publication.
—BLDSC (1550.230000).
Incorporating: Antique Finder (ISSN 0003-5874)

745.1 US ISSN 0892-7162
NK4890.C63
ANTIQUE COMB COLLECTOR. 1985. bi-m. $25 includes membership (foreign $24-$27) (effective Oct. 1995). (Antique Comb Collectors Club International) Belva Green, Ed. & Pub.; 3748 Sunray Dr., Holiday, FL 34691-3239. TEL 813-942-7354. (Subscr. to: c/o Linda Shapiro, 8712 Pleasant View Rd., Bangor, PA 18013) R&P contact: Belva Green. adv.; bk.rev.; illus.; stat.; tr.lit.; circ. 100 (paid). (back issues avail.) **Document type:** newsletter.
Description: Research on the current cost, history, dating, manufacturing, materials, design and styles and care of head jewelry. Includes profiles of members.

745.1 UK ISSN 0003-5866
NK1125
ANTIQUE DEALER AND COLLECTOR'S GUIDE. 1946. m. £33 (overseas £44) (effective 1997). Statuscourt Ltd., P.O. Box 805, London SE10 8TD, England. TEL 44-181-691-4820. FAX 44-181-691-2489. E-mail: antiquedealercollectorsguide@ukbusiness.com; URL: http://www.ukbusiness.com/antiquedealercollectorsguide. Ed. Philip Bartlam. R&P contact: Philip Bartlam. adv.; B&W page £650, color page £905; trim 229 x 295; adv. contact: Janet Pruce. bk.rev. circ. 12,000. **Indexed:** Artbibl.Mod. **Document type:** consumer publication.
—CCC.
Incorporating: Art and Antiques.
Description: Contains complete trade, auction, antiques fair and dealer news.

745.1 US ISSN 1069-5141
ANTIQUE DOLL WORLD. 1993. 7/yr. $22.50. I C Holdings Inc., 225 Main St., Ste. 300, Northport, NY 11768. TEL 516-261-8337. FAX 516-261-8235. URL: http://www.tias.com/mags/IC/AntiqueDollWorld. Ed. Donna C. Kaonis; Pub. Keith Kaonis. R&P contact: Keith Kaonis. adv.; B&W page $550; adv. contact: Keith Kaonis. circ. 9,000 (paid). **Document type:** consumer publication.
Description: Covers antique dolls (made prior to 1940), doll accessories and soft toys, with articles on subjects such as paper dolls, children's tea sets, ethnic dolls and costumes.

974 **745.1** US ISSN 1070-8421
GA197.3
ANTIQUE MAP PRICE RECORD & HANDBOOK. * 1983. a. $31.05. David C. Jolly, Ed.& Pub.; 1310 N. Mitchell Ave., Arlington Heights, IL 60004-4650. TEL 617-232-6222. bk.rev.
Formerly: Antique Maps, Sea Charts, City Views, Celestial Charts and Battle Plans, Price Record and Handbook for (Year) (ISSN 0749-4971)
Description: Contains reference information, international dealer directory, and compilation of prices from dealer catalogs.

796.95 US
ANTIQUE OUTBOARD MOTOR CLUB NEWSLETTER. (Supplement to: Antique Outboarder) vol.9, 1976. 8/yr. membership. Antique Outboard Motor Club, Inc., Box 09293, Milwaukee, WI 53209-0293. Ed. Larry Ross. R&P contact: Larry Ross. adv.; tr.lit. circ. 1,799. **Document type:** newsletter.
Description: Provides current information on club and member activities as well as tips, leads on where to find motors, and new ideas.

ANTIQUE OUTBOARDER. see SPORTS AND GAMES — Boats And Boating

ANTIQUE PHONOGRAPH MONTHLY. see MUSIC

ANTIQUE RADIO CLASSIFIED. see COMMUNICATIONS — Radio

745.1 US ISSN 0883-833X
ANTIQUE REVIEW. 1975. m. $20. Ohio Antique Review, Inc., 12 E. Stafford Ave., Box 538, Worthington, OH 43085. TEL 614-885-9757. FAX 614-885-9762. Ed. Charles Muller; Pub. James E. Loeffler. adv. contact: Julie Cecutti. bk.rev.; illus.; index, cum.index; circ. 10,000 (paid). (tabloid format; back issues avail.) **Document type:** trade publication.
Formerly: Ohio Antique Review (ISSN 0192-6721)

745.1 CN ISSN 0713-6315
ANTIQUE SHOWCASE; the magazine for antique collectors. 1963. 9/yr. Can.$28.95($28.95) (foreign Can.$38.95) (effective 1997). Trajan Publishing Corp., 202-103 Lakeshore Rd., St-Catherine, ON L2N 2T6, Canada. TEL 905-646-7744. FAX 905-646-0995. URL: http://www.cmpa.ca/h2.html. Ed. Barbara Sutton-Smith; Pub. Paul Fiocca. adv.; B&W page Can.$450; trim 8 1/8 x 10 3/4; adv. contact: Paul Starrs. bk.rev.; illus. circ. 8,000.
Formerly (until vol.17, Nov. 1981): Ontario Showcase (ISSN 0030-3119)
Description: Aimed at antique lovers and collectors. Articles focus on factual and helpful information for seasoned and beginner collectors.

745.1 696 US
ANTIQUE STOVE ASSOCIATION. YEARBOOK. 1984. a. $15 membership. Antique Stove Association, 2617 Riverside Dr., Houston, TX 77004-7610. TEL 713-528-2990. FAX 713-529-2122. Ed. Macy Stern. circ. 700 (paid). (looseleaf format; back issues avail.) **Document type:** monographic series.
Description: Reference book on antique stoves.

745.1 696 697 US
ANTIQUE STOVE ASSOCIATION QUARTERLY. 1983. q. $15 membership. Antique Stove Association, 2617 Riverside Dr., Houston, TX 77004-7610. TEL 713-528-2990. FAX 713-529-2122. Ed. Macy Stern. adv. circ. 700. (back issues avail.) **Document type:** newsletter.
Formerly: Stove Parts Needed.
Description: Antique stove restoration, maintenance and technology. Includes historical notes.

ANTIQUE TOY WORLD. see HOBBIES

745.1 US ISSN 0161-8342
ANTIQUE TRADER WEEKLY. 1957. w. $35 (foreign $58). Antique Trader Publications, Box 1050, 100 Bryant St., Dubuque, IA 52004-1050. TEL 319-588-2073. FAX 319-588-0888. URL: http://www.csmonline.com/antiquetrader. adv.; bk.rev.; illus. circ. 65,000. **Document type:** newspaper, trade publication.
Formerly: Antique Trader (ISSN 0003-5912)

745.1 US
ANTIQUES AND ART AROUND FLORIDA. 1985. s-a. $10 for 2 yrs. (effective Mar. 1996). Antiques and Art Around Publishing, Inc., Box 2481, Fort Lauderdale, FL 33303-2481. TEL 954-768-9430; 800-248-9430. FAX 954-768-0621. Ed. Joan Bryant; Pub. Joan Bryant. adv.: page $1058; trim 5 3/8 x 8 3/8; adv. contact: Michele Anderson. illus.; maps; tr.lit.; circ. 60,000 (controlled). (back issues avail.) **Document type:** consumer publication.
●Also available online.
Description: Includes maps to the Florida antiques, art, and collectibles market; related feature articles; antiques show schedule; and museum schedules.

745.1 US
ANTIQUES AND AUCTION NEWS; the most widely read collector's newspaper in the East. 1969. w. $15. Engle Publishing Company, Rte. 230 W., Box 500, Mount Joy, PA 17552. TEL 717-653-4300; 800-482-2886. FAX 717-653-6165. Ed. Denise M. Sater. adv. contact: Marty Wilcox. bk.rev.; illus.; index. circ. 30,000. (tabloid format) **Document type:** newspaper, consumer publication.
Formerly: Joel Sater's Antiques and Auction News.
Description: For antiquers, collectors, auctioneers, and show promoters.

745.1 US ISSN 0274-6085
ANTIQUES & COLLECTIBLES MAGAZINE. 1980. m. $18 (foreign $18). Antiques & Collectibles, Inc., Box 33, Westbury, NY 11590. TEL 516-334-9650. FAX 516-334-5740. Ed. Rich Branciforte. adv.; bk.rev.; circ. 5,000 (controlled). (tabloid format) **Document type:** consumer publication.
Description: For dealers and serious collectors.

745.1 790.023 US ISSN 1084-0818
ANTIQUES & COLLECTING MAGAZINE. 1931. m. $28. Lightner Publishing Corporation, 1006 S. Michigan Ave., Chicago, IL 60605. TEL 312-939-4767. FAX 312-939-0053. E-mail: antiquewk@aol.com; URL: http://www.antiqueweek.com. Ed. Frances L. Graham. adv.; bk.rev.; illus. circ. 18,000. (also avail. in microfilm from UMI; reprint service avail. from UMI) **Indexed:** Bk.Rev.Ind. (1965-), Child.Bk.Rev.Ind. (1965-), Mag.Ind., Music Ind., PMR, R.G.Abstr., R.G. **Document type:** consumer publication.
—KR SourceOne; UMI; UnCover.
Former titles (until Oct. 1993): Antiques and Collecting Hobbies (ISSN 0884-6294); (until 1985): Hobbies, the Magazine for Collectors (ISSN 0018-2907)

745.1 UK ISSN 1351-1661
ANTIQUES BULLETIN. 1982. w. £39.50/$140) H.P. Publishing, Two Hampton Ct., Harborne, Birmingham B17 2AE, England. TEL 021-426-3300. FAX 021-428-1214. Ed. John Hubbard. adv.; bk.rev. circ. 8,000. (back issues avail.)
Description: A weekly preview of auctions and antiques fairs, sales reports, prices, calendars and news.

749.1 745.1 NE ISSN 1383-6595
▼**ANTIQUES CALENDAR INTERNATIONAL.** 1996. bi-m. fl.55($45) (effective 1997-1998). L & H Publishers v.o.f., Postbus 141, 9640 AC Veendam, Netherlands. TEL 31-598-631748. FAX 31-598-616688. E-mail: aci@pi.net. Ed. Henk van der Heide; Pub. C. Luten. adv.: B&W page fl.1890; trim 186 x 268; adv. contact: Henk van der Heide. circ. 40,000. **Document type:** trade publication.
Description: Reports on the European antiques market, including fairs and auctions.

745.1 US
THE ANTIQUES DIRECTORY. 1991. m. $1.50. Brimfield Publishing, Box 273, Brimfield, MA 01010. TEL 413-267-3813. Ed. Alan J. Morin. illus. circ. 500.

745.1 UK
ANTIQUES FAIRS & MARKETS DIARY: CENTRAL, SOUTH & SOUTH-WEST. 1983. bi-m. £8 (foreign £16). P.O. Box 30, Twyford, Reading, Berks. RG10 8DQ, England. TEL 44-1734-402165. FAX 44-1734-403541. Ed. Peter E. Allwright. adv. circ. 5,000.

745.1 UK
ANTIQUES FAIRS & MARKETS DIARY: LONDON. 1983. bi-m. £8 (foreign £16). P.O. Box 30, Twyford, Reading, Berks. RG10 8DQ, England. TEL 44-1734-402165. FAX 44-1734-403541. Ed. Peter Allwright. adv. circ. 8,000.

745.1 UK
ANTIQUES FAIRS & MARKETS DIARY: NORTH & MIDLANDS. 1983. bi-m. £8 (foreign £16). P.O. Box 30, Twyford, Reading, Berks. RG10 8DQ, England. TEL 44-1734-402165. FAX 44-1734-403541. Ed. Peter W. Allwright. adv. circ. 9,000.

745.1 UK
ANTIQUES FOLIO. 1963. q. $15. Antiques & General Advertising, 24 Comely Bank, Edinburgh EH14 1AL, Scotland. TEL 44-131-332-4481. Ed. Maria Rayska. circ. 5,000 (controlled). **Document type:** newsletter.
Incorporating: Antiques in Britain (ISSN 0003-5955)
Description: Calendar of leading provincial antiques shows in the U.K., with general news of the antiques world.

745.1 UK ISSN 0306-1051
ANTIQUES TRADE GAZETTE. 1971. w. £230. Metropress Ltd., 17 Whitcomb St., London WC2H 7PL, England. TEL 44-171-930-7192. FAX 44-171-930-6391. Ed. Mark Bridge; Pub. Mark Bridge. adv. contact: Melanie Hewes. bk.rev. circ. 19,958. **Indexed:** RICS. **Document type:** trade publication.
Description: For the professional in the art and antiques market. Lists and reports on auctions and shows.

745.1 US
ANTIQUES WEST. m. $18. Monka Publishing Inc., 3315 Sacramento St., Ste. 618, San Francisco, CA 94118. Ed. Linda S. Monka. adv.; illus. **Document type:** newspaper, trade publication, consumer publication.

ANTIQUES

745.1 US
ANTIQUEWEEK - CENTRAL. 1968. w. $27.45. Mayhill Publications, Inc., Attn.: Gary Thoe, Pres., 27 N. Jefferson St., Box 90, Knightstown, IN 46148. TEL 317-345-5133. Ed. Tom Hoepf. adv.; bk.rev.; charts; illus.; mkt. circ. 46,000. (tabloid format; also avail. in microfilm; back issues avail.) **Document type:** newspaper.
Former titles: AntiqueWeek (ISSN 0888-5451); AntiqueWeek - Tri-State Trader (ISSN 0746-4118); Tri-State Trader (ISSN 0041-2503)

745.1 US
ANTIQUEWEEK - EASTERN EDITION; weekly antique, auction & collectors' newspaper. 1986. w. $23.95. Mayhill Publications, Inc., Attn.: Gary Thoe, Pres., 27 N. Jefferson St., Box 90, Knightstown, IN 46148. TEL 317-345-5133. FAX 800-876-5133. Ed. Connie Swain. adv.; bk.rev.; charts; illus.; mkt. circ. 24,268. (tabloid format; also avail. in microfilm; back issues avail.) **Document type:** newspaper.

745.1 US
ANTIQUING DIRECTORY AND TRAVELER'S GUIDE.* 1985. a. $8.95. August Enterprises, c/o Kate Broughton, Ed., 12 Sandborn Ter., Amesbury, MA 01913-1618. TEL 617-665-9181. FAX 617-662-4256. Ed. Kate Broughton. adv. circ. 12,500. **Document type:** directory.
Former titles (until 1991): Antiques and Art Directory and Traveler's Guide; (until 1990): Antiques and Art Directory; Antiques Directory.
Description: Guide to the location and specialties of approximately 2,500 New England and Hudson Valley antiques shops, shows and auctions, flea markets, geographically arranged with maps, indexed to specialties and services; includes 13-month calendar of antiques shows in the Northeast.

745.1 GW
ANTIQUITAETEN-ZEITUNG. 1972. bi-w. DM.104. Antiquitaeten-Zeitung Verlag GmbH, Nymphenburgerstr. 84, 80636 Munich, Germany. TEL 49-89-126990-0. FAX 49-89-12699048. Ed. Jonathan Franks. R&P contact: Juergen Kleidt. adv. contact: Constanze Schmachtenberger. bk.rev.; index. circ. 10,000. (tabloid format; back issues avail.) **Document type:** newspaper.

APOLLO; the international magazine of the arts. see ART

APPRAISERS STANDARD; for collectors, auctioneers, dealers, etc. see ART

629.288
ARC & SPARK. 1966. m. membership. Kalamazoo Antique Auto Restorers Club, Box 532, Oshtemo, MI 49007. TEL 616-624-6757. FAX 616-387-3999. E-mail: David.Lyon@wmich.edu. Ed. David O. Lyon. bk.rev. circ. 225. (looseleaf format) **Document type:** newsletter.
Description: News, information and history of antique automobiles.

ARCHAEOLOGIA. see ARCHAEOLOGY

739.7 UK ISSN 0004-2439
U799
ARMS AND ARMOUR SOCIETY JOURNAL. 1953. s-a. £15 membership (overseas £20) (effective 1997). Arms and Armour Society, c/o Anthony Dove, P.O. Box 10232, London SW19 2ZD, England. TELEX 87323 FSI G. (Subscr. to: The Arms and Armour Society, 135 Peterborough Rd., Leyton, London E10 6EL, England) Ed. C.J. Gravett. adv. contact: M.J. Sarche. bk.rev.; circ. 500 (paid). **Indexed:** Amer.Hist.& Life (1956-1963), Br.Archaeol.Abstr., Hist.Abstr. (1956-1963). **Document type:** academic/scholarly publication.
Description: Presents historical research on arms and armor: swords, daggers, guns, and rifles.

739.7 US ISSN 0380-982X
ARMS COLLECTING. 1963. q. $22 (effective 1997). Museum Restoration Service, Box 70, Alexandria Bay, NY 13607. TEL 613-393-2980. FAX 613-393-3378. Ed. S.J. Gooding. adv.; bk.rev.; charts; illus.; pat.; index. circ. 2,100.
Formerly: Canadian Journal of Arms Collecting (ISSN 0008-3992)

745.1 666 US ISSN 1043-3317
ARS CERAMICA. 1983. a. $27.50 to individuals; US family $32.50; institutions & foreign $35 (effective 1996 & 1997). Wedgwood Society of New York, 5 Dogwood Ct., Glen Head, NY 11545. TEL 516-626-3427. FAX 516-626-3430. Ed. Harwood Johnson. R&P contact: Barnard Starr. adv.: page $400; trim 8 1/2 x 11; adv. contact: Michelle Weinstein. bk.rev.; 10-yr. index; circ. 550 (paid). (back issues avail.) **Document type:** academic/scholarly publication, newsletter.
Description: Contains general articles on ceramics, pottery, glass, and archaeology.

745.1 751.6 US ISSN 0195-8208
N6505
ART & ANTIQUES. 1978. m. (11/yr.). $35 (Canada $50; elsewhere $55). Trans World Publishing, Inc., 2100 Powers Ferry Rd., Ste. 300, Atlanta, GA 30339. TEL 770-955-5656. FAX 770-952-0669. E-mail: service@www.iiyama.com; URL: http://www.artantqmag.com. Dir. Monte Clott. R&P contact: JoAnn Miller. adv. contact: JoAnn Miller. bk.rev.; charts; illus.; circ. 188,735 (paid). (back issues avail.) **Indexed:** Access (1981-), Amer.Hist.& Life (1979-1988), Art Ind., Artbibl.Mod., Avery Ind.Archit.Per., Hist.Abstr. (1979-1988), PMR. **Document type:** consumer publication.
—BLDSC (1733.346500); KR SourceOne; UMI; UnCover.
Incorporates (1967-Jan. 1994): Antique Monthly (ISSN 0003-5882); **Formerly** (until 1980): American Art and Antiques (ISSN 0148-9100)
Description: Includes stories of artists, art movements and periods, and collections.

ART - ANTIQUES INVESTMENT REPORT. see ART

ARTS, ANTIQUES ET AUCTIONS. see ART

ASHTRAY COLLECTORS' CONNECTIONS. see HOBBIES

629.222 US
AUBURN - CORD - DUESENBERG CLUB NEWSLETTER. 1953. 10/yr. $25. Auburn - Cord - Duesenberg Club, 983 County Road 413, Killen, IL 35645. TEL 205-757-8755. (Subscr. to: c/o Matt Bogart, 18 Poplar Rd., Ringoes, NJ 08551) Ed. James Corbin. adv. circ. 2,000. (back issues avail.) **Document type:** newsletter.
Description: For members who have an interest in Auburn - Cord - Duesenberg automobiles (manufactured 1903-1937).

AUSTIN - HEALEY MAGAZINE. see TRANSPORTATION — Automobiles

745.1 AT ISSN 0004-8704
AUSTRALIAN ANTIQUE COLLECTOR. 1966. s-a. Aus.$8. Reed Business Publishing Pty. Ltd. (Subsidiary of: Reed International PLC), P.O. Box 5487, W. Chatswood, N.S.W. 2057, Australia. TEL 61-2-3725222. FAX 61-2-4197064. Ed. R. McGuire. adv.; bk.rev.; illus.; index. circ. 6,000.

629.222 NE
AUTOMOBIEL KLASSIEK. m. fl.99.50 (effective 1997). Wegener Tijdschriften Groep B.V., Postbus 1860, 1110 CD Diemen, Netherlands. TEL 31-418-634443. FAX 31-418-634278. Ed. G. te Lintelo. adv. **Document type:** consumer publication.
Description: Covers old timers and classic cars, their maintenance and renovation, auctions and events, club news and road tests.

AUTOMOTIVE INVESTOR. see TRANSPORTATION — Automobiles

745.1 UK ISSN 0968-1485
B B C HOMES AND ANTIQUES. 1993. m. £23.40 (Europe & Ireland £38.80; rest of world £58.20) (effective 1996). (British Broadcasting Corporation) B B C Worldwide Publishing, Broadcasting House, Whiteladies Rd., Bristol GS8 2LR, England. TEL 44-181-576-2000. FAX 44-181-576-2931. (Subscr. to: P.O. Box 425, Woking, Surrey GU21 1GP, England. TEL 44-1483-733716. FAX 44-1483-756792) **Document type:** consumer publication.

745.1 IT ISSN 0006-6745
BOLLETTINO DI LIBRI ANTICHI E MODERNI DI VARIA CULTURA ESAURITI E RARI. s-a. Libreria Guida, Via Port'Alba 20-23, 80134 Naples, Italy. TEL 081-446377. FAX 081-451883. Ed. Mario Guida. adv.; bk.rev.; bibl.

629.222 US
BORGWARD - OWNERS' CLUB. NEWSLETTER; open to owners of Borgward products and enthusiasts. 1974. q. $20. Borgward - Owners' Club, 77 New Hampshire Ave., Bay Shore, NY 11706. TEL 516-273-0458. Ed. Dyck Livant. adv. circ. 100. (back issues avail.; reprint service avail.) **Document type:** newsletter.
Description: Deals with the preservation and enjoyment of Borgward automobiles and products.

745.1 UK
BRITISH ANTIQUE DEALERS' ASSOCIATION YEARBOOK. 1986. a. £7.50. British Antique Dealers' Association (B.A.D.A.), 20 Rutland Gate, London SW7 1BD, England. TEL 44-171-589-4128. FAX 44-171-581-9083. adv. contact: Michael Sakali. circ. 7,000. **Document type:** directory, consumer publication.
Formerly: British Antique Dealers' Association Handbook.
Description: Illustrated guide to members' shops. Includes information on buying antiques.

629.222 US ISSN 0194-8415
TL215.B84
BUICK BUGLE.* m. membership. Buick Club of America, Box 401927, Hesperia, CA 92340-1927.
Description: For car enthusiasts sharing an interest in the restoration and preservation of old Buicks.

745.1 FR
BULLETIN DE L'ANTIQUAIRE ET DU BROCANTEUR. 1948. m. (10/yr.). 85 F. (effective 1991). Syndicat National du Commerce de l'Antiquite et de l'Occasion (SNCAO), 18 rue de Provence, 75009 Paris, France. adv. circ. 5,500.

745.1 JA
DS820.8 CODEN: KNKAAF
BUNKAZAI HOZON SYUHUKU GAKKAISI. (Text in English and Japanese; summaries in English) 1951. a. 8000 Yen membership. Japan Society for the Conservation of Cultural Property, Tokyo Kokuritsu Bunkazai Kenkyujo, 13-27 Ueno Koen, Taito-ku, Tokyo 110, Japan. TEL 81-3-3823-2241. FAX 81-3-3828-2434. Ed. Sadatoshi Miura. adv. circ. 600. **Document type:** academic/scholarly publication, newsletter.
—CASDDS. **CCC.**
Formerly (until vol.40, 1996): Kobunkazai no Kagaku - Scientific Papers on Japanese Antiques and Art Crafts (ISSN 0368-6272)
Description: Contains articles on conservation of artistic, archaeological and historical objects mainly of Japan, China and Korea.

745.1 IT
BUSINESS ART. 1989. 6/yr. L.50000($90) Antea Edizioni, Via F. Petrarca 4, 20123 Milan, Italy. TEL 2-48-00-63-57. FAX 2-48-00-75-65. Ed. Alessandro Tirelli. adv.: B&W page L.7000000, color page L.8500000. circ. 16,000.

745.1 UK ISSN 0269-8994
BUSINESS RATIO REPORT: ANTIQUES & FINE ART; an industry sector analysis. 1986. a. I C C Business Ratios Ltd., Freepost, Field House, Hampton, Mddx. TW12 1BR, England. TEL 081-783-0977. FAX 081-783-1940. charts; stat. **Document type:** trade publication.

C.A.L. - N-X-211 COLLECTORS SOCIETY. NEWSLETTER. see AERONAUTICS AND SPACE FLIGHT

796.77 629.222 US ISSN 1072-3277
CAMARO ENTHUSIAST. 1984. bi-m. $30. United States Camaro Club, Inc., Box 608167, Orlando, FL 32860-8167. TEL 407-880-1967. FAX 407-880-1972. Ed. Ken Moorhead. adv.; bk.rev.; charts; illus.; stat. circ. 15,000. (back issues avail.) **Document type:** consumer publication.
Formerly: Camaro Corral (ISSN 1058-739X)
Description: For the collector, restorer, driver and enthusiast of the Chevrolet Camaro car.

CAR COLLECTOR AND CAR CLASSICS. see TRANSPORTATION — Automobiles

ANTIQUES

745.1 US ISSN 0892-9769
CAROUSEL NEWS & TRADER. 1985. m. $29 (Canada $35; elsewhere $45) (effective 1997). Walter Loucks, Ed. & Pub., 87 Park Ave. W., No. 206, Mansfield, OH 44902. TEL 419-529-4999. FAX 419-529-2321. adv.: B&W page $450, color page $800; trim 8 1/2 x 11; adv. contact: Walter Loucks. bk.rev.; video rev. circ. 5,500. (back issues avail.) **Document type:** trade publication.
Formerly (until 1987): Carousel Trader (ISSN 0892-9750)
Description: Covers all aspects of collecting carousel art.

CARS & PARTS; the magazine serving the car hobbyist. see TRANSPORTATION — Automobiles

745.1 AT ISSN 1320-5560
CARTER'S ANTIQUES & COLLECTABLES MAGAZINE. 1981. m. Aus.$60 (foreign Aus.$145). Carter's Promotions Pty. Ltd., Unit 9, 26-30 Tepko Rd., Terrey Hills, N.S.W. 2084, Australia. TEL 61-2-450-0011. (Subscr. to: Locked Bag 3, Terrey Hills, N.S.W. 2084, Australia) Ed. Julie McGaw. adv. contact: Christine Carter. circ. 15,000. (back issues avail.) **Document type:** consumer publication.
Formerly: Australian Antique Trader.

745.1 747 AT ISSN 0815-7065
CARTER'S PRICE GUIDE TO ANTIQUES IN AUSTRALIA. 1985. a. Aus.$78. Carter's Promotions Pty. Ltd., Unit 9, 26-30 Tepko Rd., Terrey Hills, N.S.W. 2084, Australia. TEL 61-2-450-0011. (Subscr. to: Locked Bag 3, Terrey Hills, N.S.W. 2084, Australia) Ed. Alan Carter. adv. circ. 10,000. **Document type:** consumer publication.
Description: Guide to prices of antiques and collectibles of every kind.

"CHECK THE OIL!" MAGAZINE; the publication devoted exclusively to Petroliana. see HOBBIES

629.288 US
CHRYSLER 300 CLUB NEWS. 1970. q. $20 (effective Jan. 1991). Chrysler 300 Club International, Inc., 4900 Jonesville Rd., Jonesville, MI 49250. TEL 517-849-2783. FAX 517-849-7445. Ed. Eleanor Riehl. R&P contact: George Riehl. adv.; charts; illus.; stat. circ. 900. (back issues avail.) **Document type:** newsletter.
Description: Provides technical statistics on automobiles represented by the Club, restoration information, and member stories.

745 355 US ISSN 0094-1182
NK1127
CIVIL WAR COLLECTORS' DEALER DIRECTORY.* 1974. irreg., latest 1987-88. $4.95. Essential Electronics, 409 Jesse Lee Ln., Hampstead, NC 28443. Ed. C.L. Batson. adv. circ. 1,000.

745.1 US
CLARK'S FLEA MARKET U S A; a national directory of flea markets & swap meets. 1977. q. $30. Clark Publications, 419 Gracon Point Rd., Milton, FL 32583. TEL 904-623-0794. Ed. Dorothy Clark; Pub. Charles E. Clark. adv.: B&W page $300; adv. contact: Dorothy Clark. circ. 9,000. **Document type:** consumer publication, directory.
Description: Lists names, locations, days, cost of space, facilities such as restrooms, showers, camping and food concessions, as well as phone numbers.

629.2 UK ISSN 0957-2406
CLASSIC AMERICAN. 1988. m. £35.40. Myatt McFarlane plc, Trident House, Heath Rd., Hale, Altrincham, Cheshire WA14 2UJ, England. TEL 44-161-928-3480. FAX 44-161-941-6897. Ed. Paul Guiness; Pub. Steven Myatt. R&P contact: Alastair McFarlane. adv. contact: James Gibbon. bk.rev. circ. 30,000. (back issues avail.) **Document type:** consumer publication.
Incorporates (in 1992): Vee Magazine.
Description: Examines cars and motorcycles from the 50's and 60's, plus other "Americana" collectables.

CLASSIC & SPORTSCAR. see TRANSPORTATION — Automobiles

629.288 US ISSN 1042-5683
CLASSIC AUTO RESTORER. 1989. m. $27.97 (Canada $38.47; elsewhere $43.97) (effective 1996). Fancy Publications, Inc., 3 Burroughs, Irvine, CA 92618-2804. TEL 714-855-8822. FAX 714-855-3045. (Subscr. to: Neodata, Box 58025, Boulder, CO 80322. TEL 800-365-4221. FAX 303-604-7455) Ed. Dan Burger. bk.rev. circ. 37,659. **Document type:** consumer publication.
Description: Features old cars, restoration information, parts sources, auto club listings and auctions and events.

CLASSIC BIKE. see SPORTS AND GAMES — Bicycles And Motorcycles

629.222 US ISSN 0009-8310
TL7
CLASSIC CAR. 1953. q. Classic Car Club of America, Inc., 1645 S. River Rd., Ste. 7, Des Plaines, IL 60018-2206. TEL 847-390-0443. FAX 847-390-7118. (Editorial Office: 215 E. 80th St., New York, NY 10021) Ed. Beverly Rae Kimes; Pub. Warren Gordon. adv.; bk.rev.; illus.; index, cum.index. circ. 5,000. **Document type:** consumer publication.
Description: Articles on the history and contemporary restoration and preservation of distinctive automobiles produced from 1925 to 1948.

CLASSIC CAR MART. see TRANSPORTATION — Automobiles

629.222 796.77 UK ISSN 0959-9738
CLASSIC CAR WEEKLY. 1990. w. £57.20 (effective 1997). E M A P - National Publications, Bushfield House, Orton Centre, Peterborough, Cambs. PE2 0UW, England. TEL 44-1733-237111. FAX 44-1733-239527. (Dist. by: Frontline, Park House, 117 Park Rd., Peterborough, Cambs. PE2, England; Subscr. to: Classic Car Weekly Subscriptions, Sovereign Park, Leicester LE87 4PA, England) Ed. Geoff Browne; Pub. Rob Croxall. adv.: B&W page £1470, color page £1960; trim 340 x 271; adv. contact: Helen Morkel. bk.rev.; circ. 26,000. (paid). pp./issue: 36. (tabloid format; back issues avail.) **Document type:** newspaper.
Description: Covers all aspects of driving and owning classic automobiles.

CLASSIC FORD X. see TRANSPORTATION — Automobiles

THE CLASSIC MOTORCYCLE. see SPORTS AND GAMES — Bicycles And Motorcycles

CLOCKS. see JEWELRY, CLOCKS AND WATCHES

COLLECTIBLE AUTOMOBILE. see TRANSPORTATION — Automobiles

745.1 US ISSN 1086-1602
COLLECTIBLES, FLEA MARKET FINDS. 1993. q. $18.97 (foreign $23.97). G C R Publishing Group, Inc., 1700 Broadway, 34th Fl., New York, NY 10019. TEL 212-541-7100. FAX 212-245-1241. URL: http://www.mediafinder.com/magazine/mo412002.htm. (Subscr. to: Box 336, Mt. Morris, IL 61054) Ed. Cathy Cook; Pub. Jason Goodman. R&P contact: Sandy Kosherick. adv. contact: Dana Linden. circ. 200,000. **Document type:** consumer publication.
Formerly: Collectibles, Country and Americana (ISSN 1073-8142)
Description: Covers vintage collectibles from the 1940's through the 1970's. Includes stories on flea market and garage sale finds.

745.1 UK ISSN 0963-7451
COLLECTING DOULTON; the international magazine for collectors of Royal Doulton & Beswick both old & new. 1987. bi-m. £17.80 (N. America $45). Francis Joseph, 15 St. Swithuns Rd., London SE13 6RW, England. Ed. Frank Salmon. R&P contact: 44-181-318-9580. adv. contact: Frank Salmon. **Document type:** consumer publication.
Description: Contains articles of interest to persons collecting, buying and selling Royal Doulton and Beswick fine china.

745 UK ISSN 0955-0356
THE COLLECTOR. 1987. bi-m. £12($70) (rest of Europe £24; elsewhere £30). Barrington Publications, 54 Uxbridge Rd., London W12 8LP, England. adv.; circ. 18,500 (controlled). (back issues avail.)
Description: Contains information about antiques and collectibles.

COLLECTOR CAR & TRUCK PRICES. see TRANSPORTATION — Automobiles

745.1 US ISSN 1077-2774
NK1133
COLLECTOR MAGAZINE & PRICE GUIDE. 1970. m. $17.95 (foreign $26.95). Antique Trader Publications, Box 1050, 100 Bryant St., Dubuque, IA 52004-1050. TEL 319-588-2073. FAX 319-588-0888. URL: http://www.csmonline.com/collectormag. Ed. Kyle Husfloen. adv.; illus.; stat. circ. 25,000. (back issues avail.) **Document type:** trade publication.
Formerly (until 1994): Antique Trader Price Guide to Antiques and Collectors' Items (ISSN 0556-5367)
Description: Covers all categories of antiques and collectibles and their current market values.

745.1 US
THE COLLECTOR NEWSMAGAZINE. (Print edition ceased 1996) q. free. D R S Internet Publishing Group, Box 488, Matthews, NC 28106. E-mail: gourmetfare@ceo-online.com; URL: http://www.ceo-online.com/thecollector. Ed. Diana F. Savastano; Pub. Diana F. Savastano. adv.
●Available only online.
Description: Publishes news on collectibles, antiques and giftware.

745 UK ISSN 0957-6304
COLLECTOR'S GAZETTE. 1978. m. (10/yr.). £22 (rest of Europe £27; elsewhere £35) (effective Jan. 1996); newsstand price: £1.50. Kirkby-in-Ashfield, Nottingham NG17 9AG, England. TEL 44-1623-752080. FAX 44-1623-720443. E-mail: clt.vrr@pop3.hiway.co.uk; URL: http://www.hiway.co.uk/icn/cg.html. Ed. Martin R. Weiss. R&P contact: Martin Weiss. adv.: page £907.20. bk.rev. circ. 20,000. **Document type:** newspaper.
Description: Highlights modern replicas, auctions, news reports, and events and shows concerning miniature auto, toy, and train collections.

745.1 US ISSN 1066-551X
COLLECTORS MART MAGAZINE. 1976. bi-m. $23.95 (effective 1997). Krause Publications, Inc., 700 E. State St., Iola, WI 54990. TEL 715-445-2214. FAX 715-445-4087. TELEX 556461 KRAUSE PUB UD. URL: http://www.krause.com/subs/html/cl.html. Ed. Mary Sieber; Pub. Greg Smith. adv. contact: Greg Smith. bk.rev.; illus. circ. 115,610. **Indexed:** Artbibl. **Document type:** consumer publication.
—UMI.
Former titles: Collectors Mart (ISSN 0744-9879); Antique and Collectors Mart (ISSN 0194-5890)
Description: Written for the collector who buys limited-edition plates, prints, dolls, figurines and other collectibles.

790.023 US ISSN 0162-1033
COLLECTORS NEWS & THE ANTIQUE REPORTER. Cover title: Collectors News. 1959. m. $48. Collectors News Company, Box 156, Grundy Center, IA 50638. TEL 319-824-6981; 800-352-8039. FAX 319-824-3414. E-mail: collect@collectors-news.com; URL: http://www.collectors-news.com. Ed. Linda Kruger; Pub. Cherie Souhrada. R&P contact: Linda Krueger. adv. contact: Ronda Jans. bk.rev.; illus. circ. 13,000. **Document type:** consumer publication.
Description: Everything for some collectors and something for every collector.

745.1 737 US ISSN 0744-5989
NK805
COLLECTORS' SHOWCASE. 1981. bi-m. $19.95. C S C, Inc., 4099 McEwen, Ste. 350, Dallas, TX 75244. Ed. Brian Walker; Pub. Robert Bennett. R&P contact: Mistie Smailer. adv. contact: Cheg Reynolds. bk.rev.; illus.; circ. 14,000 (paid). (also avail. in microform; reprint service avail. from UMI) **Document type:** consumer publication.
—UnCover.
Description: Contains articles for collectors of animation art, characters and entertainment collectibles and memorabilia.

ANTIQUES

COMBAT HANDGUNS. see SPORTS AND GAMES

629.222 745.1   US   ISSN 0045-8554
CORMORANT NEWS BULLETIN. 1953. m. membership. Packard Automobile Classics, 420 S. Ludlow St., Dayton, OH 45402. Ed. Stuart Blond. adv.; charts; illus. circ. 3,300. (looseleaf format)

745.1   IT   ISSN 1122-2395
COSE ANTICHE. 1992. m. (11/yr.). L.88000. Edimarketing, Via Pacini 41, 20131 Milan, Italy. TEL 39-2-70632494. Ed. Paola Lazzaretto. adv.: B&W page L.3800000, color page L.5800000. circ. 30,000. **Document type:** consumer publication.

COUNTRY HOMES & INTERIORS. see INTERIOR DESIGN AND DECORATION

745.1   US
DISCOVER MID-AMERICA. 1971. m. $18. Discovery Publications, Inc., 400 Grand Ave., Kansas City, MO 64106. TEL 800-899-9730. FAX 816-474-1427. E-mail: busmgr@discoverypub.com; URL: http://discoverypub.com/kc. Ed. Kenneth C. Weyand. adv. circ. 40,000. **Document type:** newspaper.
  Former titles: Discover K C; Discover (Kansas City); Discover North.
  Description: Guide to unique shops in the Midwest, with articles pertaining to antiques and collectibles, events, events calendar and historical sites.

DISCOVERIES (PORT TOWNSEND); magazine for collectible records & CD's. see MUSIC

THE DOUBLE GUN JOURNAL. see SPORTS AND GAMES — Outdoor Life

E T CETERA. (Early Typewriter Collectors Association) see BUSINESS AND ECONOMICS — Office Equipment And Services

EDITION WEISS-BLAU; das Magazin der BMW-Freunde. see TRANSPORTATION — Automobiles

ENJINE!-ENJINE!. see FIRE PREVENTION

745.1 700   US   ISSN 8756-775X
EVALUATOR.* 1979. q. membership. International Society of Fine Arts Appraisers, Ltd., 701S Euclid Ave., Oak Park, IL 60304. TEL 312-848-3340. Ed. Elizabeth Carr. bk.rev. circ. 500. (back issues avail.)

745.1 630   US
FARM ANTIQUES NEWS. 1991. bi-m. $16. 812 N. Third St., Tarkio, MO 64491. TEL 816-736-4528. Ed. Gary Van Hoozer; Pub. Gary Van Hoozer. adv.; bk.rev.; circ. 2,000 (paid). **Document type:** consumer publication.
  Description: Covers anything old from the farm: collecting and pricing.

FILOMATA. see HISTORY

621   US   ISSN 0745-6824
FINE TOOL JOURNAL. 1970. q. $27 (foreign $45) (effective 1997 & 1998). Antique & Collectible Tools, Inc., 27 Fickett Rd., Pownal, ME 04069. TEL 207-688-4962. FAX 207-688-4152. E-mail: ftjceb@aol.com; URL: http://www.wowpages.com/FTJ/. Ed. Clearence Blanchard. adv.; bk.rev.; circ. 2,000 (paid). **Document type:** catalog, consumer publication.
  Description: Covers tools, tool collecting, tool history, and tools for sale.

666 973   US   ISSN 1078-5647
FLASH POINT. 1988. q. membership only. Tile Heritage Foundation, Box 1850, Healdsburg, CA 95448. TEL 707-431-8453. FAX 707-431-8455. Ed. Joseph A. Taylor. R&P contact: Joseph A. Taylor. adv.; bk.rev.; circ. (controlled). **Document type:** bulletin, newsletter.
  Description: Discusses the history of the tile industry in America and provides an interactive network for tile makers and collectors today.

FLEETLINE. see TRANSPORTATION

629.222   US
GALAXIE GAZETTE. 1983. bi-m. $25 in N. America; elsewhere $30. Ford Galaxie Club of America, 1469 Williams Lake Rd., Evans, WA 99126-9714. TEL 509-685-0798. E-mail: galaxieclub@collector.org; URL: http://www.galaxieclub.com. Ed. Mark Reynolds. adv.; circ. 725 (paid). **Document type:** newsletter.
  Description: Contains articles and technical information pertaining to Ford Galaxies built by Ford Motor Company 1959 to 1974.

745.1   SP   ISSN 1130-2747
N7101
GALERIA ANTIQUARIA. 12/yr. Nunez de Balboa 118, 3o C, 28006 Madrid, Spain. TEL 1-563-40-04. FAX 1-261-01-65. Ed. Manuel Merchan Diaz. circ. 10,000.
—CINDOC.
  Formed by the 1989 merger of: Galeria (ISSN 1130-2755); Antiquaria (ISSN 0212-8810).

794   US   ISSN 1050-6608
GV1225.U6
GAME RESEARCHER'S NOTES. 1987. 3/yr. $25 membership. American Game Collectors Association, Box 44, Dresher, PA 19025. Ed. David Galt.

794   US   ISSN 1050-6594
GV1312
GAME TIMES. 1985. 3/yr. $25 membership. American Game Collectors Association, Box 44, Dresher, PA 19025. Ed. Jim Polczynski. adv.; B&W page $80. bk.rev. circ. 450. **Document type:** newsletter.
  Description: Covers history, preservation and collecting of games.

739.7 355   SP   ISSN 0436-029X
GLADIUS;* etudes sur les armes anciennes, l'armement, l'art militaire et la vie culturelle en Orient et Occident. (Text in English, French, German and Spanish) 1961. a. price varies. Consejo Superior de Investigaciones Cientificas (C.S.I.C.), Instituto de Estudios sobre Armas Antiguas, Apdo. 4, Jarandilla (Caceres), Spain. Ed. Ada Bruhn Dehoffmeyer. bk.rev.; bibl.; illus.; index, cum.index. circ. 625. **Indexed:** Br.Archaeol.Abstr., Numis.Lit.

GLASS COLLECTOR'S DIGEST. see CERAMICS, GLASS AND POTTERY

GOLD BOOK CLASSICS & ANTIQUES. see TRANSPORTATION — Automobiles

745.1   UK   ISSN 0262-8902
GOSS AND CRESTED CHINA. m. £18 (overseas £30). Milestone Publications, 62 Murray Rd., Horndean, Waterlooville, Hants PO8 9JL, England. TEL 44-1705-597440. FAX 44-1705-591975. Ed. L. Pine. R&P contact: N. Pine. circ. 1,000. circ. 1,000. **Document type:** bulletin.

745.1
GUIDE TO THE ANTIQUE SHOPS OF BRITAIN (YEAR). a. $29.50. Antique Collectors Club, 5 Church St., Woodbridge, Suffolk IP12 IDS, England. TEL 44-1394-385501. FAX 44-1394-384434. **Document type:** directory.

623.4   US   ISSN 0894-8119
GUN LIST. 1984. bi-w. $29.95 (effective 1997). Krause Publications, Inc., 700 E. State St., Iola, WI 54990. TEL 715-445-2214. FAX 715-445-4087. TELEX 55 6461 KRAUSE PUB UD. Pub. David Kowalski. adv. contact: John Kronschnabi. circ. 70,322. (tabloid format)
  Description: Covers the marketplace for buying and selling collectible firearms.

739.7   US   ISSN 0896-6001
GUN SHOW CALENDAR. 1979. q. $14.95 (effective 1997). Krause Publications, Inc., 700 E. State St., Iola, WI 54990. TEL 715-445-2214. FAX 715-445-4087. TELEX 55 6461 KRAUSE PUB UD. Pub. David Kowalski. adv. contact: John Kronschnabi. circ. 10,701.
  Description: Contains chronological listing of gun shows cross-referenced by state and month. Listings are updated quarterly. Intended as a guide for anyone who attends or displays at gun shows.

745.1 355   UK   ISSN 0262-4915
H B S A NEWSLETTER. 1981. q. membership. Historical Breechloading Smallarms Association, P.O. Box 12778, London SE1 6XB, England. Ed. B. Bergman-Field. bk.rev. (looseleaf format; back issues avail.) **Document type:** newsletter.
  Formerly: H B S A Occasional Papers.

HALI; the international magazine of antique carpet and textile art. see ARTS AND HANDICRAFTS

745.1 700   US
HAWAII ANTIQUES, ART, & COLLECTIBLES QUARTERLY. 1991. q. $6. Service Publications, Inc. (Honolulu), Box 853, Honolulu, HI 96808. TEL 808-591-0049. FAX 808-591-0038. Ed. Campbell Mansfield; Pub. Campbell Mansfield. adv.: page $415; trim 10 1/4 x 12; adv. contact: Lorraine Walters. circ. 8,000. (tabloid format) **Document type:** consumer publication, newspaper.
  Description: Contains articles and information on events, art, antiques and collectibles for the consumer and dealer.

HEARTHSTONE COLLECTION OF FOLKLORE, NOSTALGIA AND HISTORY. see FOLKLORE

666   US   ISSN 0731-8014
NK5198.A23
HEISEY NEWS. 1972. m. $22 membership (effective 1997). Heisey Collectors of America, Inc., 169 W. Church St., Newark, OH 43055. TEL 614-345-2932. FAX 614-345-9638. E-mail: heisey@infinet.com; URL: http://www.ahheisey.com. Ed. Molly Kaspar. adv. contact: Molly Kaspar. bk.rev.; illus.; tr.lit.; index, cum.index: 1972-1981, 1982-1992. circ. 2,700. (back issues avail.) **Document type:** newsletter.
  Description: Promotes the education and study of A.H. Heisey and Co. glassware produced in Newark, OH from 1896-1957.

HEMMINGS MOTOR NEWS. see TRANSPORTATION — Automobiles

629.222   US   ISSN 0363-4639
TL12
HEMMING'S VINTAGE AUTO ALMANAC. 1976. biennial. $12.95. Watering, Inc., Box 256, Bennington, VT 05201. TEL 802-442-3101; 800-277-4373. URL: http://www.hmn.com. (Subscr. to: Box 945, Bennington, VT 05201. FAX 802-447-1561) Ed. David Brownell. R&P contact: Heather Hamilton. adv. contact: Randy Shannon. illus. circ. 25,000. —CISTI.
  Formerly: Vintage Auto Almanac.

745.1   GW
HENRY'S AUKTIONEN. 1984. m. DM.80 (Europe DM.160; overseas DM.320) (effective 1996). Henry's Auktionshaus GmbH, An der Fohlenweide 12-14, 67112 Mutterstadt, Germany. TEL 49-6234-80110. Ed. Heinrich Haege. circ. 100,000. **Document type:** catalog.

745.1   UK   ISSN 0018-1846
HILLANDALE NEWS. 1960. bi-m. City of London Phonograph & Gramophone Society, 2 Kirklands Park, Cupar, Fife KY15 4EP, Scotland. TEL 44-1334-54390. Ed. Christopher Hamilton. adv.; bk.rev.; rec.rev.; illus.; index. circ. 600. (processed) **Document type:** newsletter.
—BLDSC (4314.830000).

HISTORIC MORRIS EMPORIUM; fine wares for fine shoppers. see LEISURE AND RECREATION

739.7   US   ISSN 0440-9221
HISTORICAL ARMS SERIES. 1963. irreg. price varies. Museum Restoration Service, Box 70, Alexandria Bay, NY 13607. Ed. S. James Gooding. circ. 5,000.

629.22   UK
HISTORICAL COMMERCIAL NEWS. 1962. every 6 weeks. £15. Historic Commercial Vehicle Society, Iden Grange, Cranbrook Rd., Staplehurst, Tonbridge, Kent TN12 0ET, England. FAX 580-893227. adv.; bk.rev.; bibl.; illus. circ. 4,250. **Document type:** newsletter.
  Formerly: H C V C Newsletter.
  Description: Concerns antique automobiles.

ANTIQUES   341

739.7 799.202   SA   ISSN 0018-2451
HISTORICAL FIREARMS SOCIETY OF SOUTH AFRICA. JOURNAL/HISTORIESE VUURWAPENVERENIGING VAN SUID-AFRIKA. TYDSKRIF. (Text in English; title in Afrikaans, English) 1958. s-a. R.45 membership. Historical Firearms Society of South Africa, Box 145, Newlands 7725, Cape Province, South Africa. TEL 27-21-642294. Ed. B.M. Berkovitch. adv. circ. 450. **Indexed:** Ind.S.A.Per. **Document type:** newsletter.
Formerly (until 1962): South African Muzzle Loaders Association. Journal.
Description: Covers antique and historical firearms used in South Africa.

739.23 666.1   US
HOBSTAR. 1978. m. (10/yr.). $30 (effective through June 1996). American Cut Glass Association, Box 482, Ramona, CA 92065-0482. TEL 714-831-2566. Ed. Nicholas J. Boonstra. adv. circ. 1,400. (tabloid format; back issues avail.) **Document type:** newsletter.
Description: Studies American cut and engraved glass of the period of 1850-1920, emphasizing the "brilliant" period, 1880-1920.

HORN & WHISTLE. see ARCHAEOLOGY

790.13 384.5   US   ISSN 0898-6959
HORN SPEAKER; the newspaper for the hobbyist of vintage electronics and sound. 1972. m. (10/yr.). $15. Jim Cranshaw, Ed. & Pub., Box 1193, Mabank, TX 75147. TEL 903-848-0304. E-mail: cranshaw@e-tex.com; URL: http://home.navisoft.com/horn/ths2.htm. R&P contact: Jim Cranshaw. adv. contact: Jim Cranshaw. bk.rev.; bibl.; illus.; tr.lit.; circ. 1,500 (paid). **Document type:** newspaper, consumer publication.
Description: Discusses radios and phonographs for historical and collecting purposes.

629.221 790.023   US   ISSN 0018-5213
TL1
HORSELESS CARRIAGE GAZETTE. 1937. bi-m. $35. Horseless Carriage Club of America, 128 S. Cypress St., Orange, CA 91266-1314. TEL 714-538-4222. FAX 714-538-5764. Ed. John C. Meyer III. adv.; bk.rev.; illus.; cum.index. circ. 5,500. (also avail. in microform from UMI; reprint service avail. from UMI)
Description: Highlights cars built before January 1st, 1916.

745.1   US
THE HUDSON VALLEY ANTIQUER. 1992. m. $18.95. Antiquer Publications, Box 561, Rhinebeck, NY 12572. TEL 914-876-8766. Ed. Ted Fox; Pub. Ted Fox. R&P contact: Ted Fox. adv. contact: Gina Walker Fox. bk.rev. circ. 22,500. **Document type:** newspaper, consumer publication, trade publication.
Description: For antiques enthusiasts. Features include centerfold pullout Antiquer's Map.

745.1 780   US
IN THE GROOVE. 1976. m. $22 membership (Canada $24; elsewhere $37) (effective 1996). Michigan Antique Phonograph Society, 2609 Devonshire, Lansing, MI 48910. TEL 517-482-7996. Eds. John Whitacre, Duane Wilkie. R&P contact: John Whitacre. adv.: B&W page $35: trim 8 1/4 x 11. bk.rev. circ. 900. **Document type:** newsletter.
Description: Provides news and articles of interest to collectors of antique phonographs and other mechanical music instruments and their records or discs.

INDIAN ILLUSTRATED. see SPORTS AND GAMES — Bicycles And Motorcycles

INTERNATIONAL ANTIQUE AIRPLANE DIGEST. see AERONAUTICS AND SPACE FLIGHT

745.1 790.132   UK   ISSN 1350-8849
INTERNATIONAL BOND & SHARE SOCIETY JOURNAL. 1979. q. £10($20) International Bond & Share Society, 68 Viney Bank, Croydon CR0 9JT, England. TEL 081-657-7721. FAX 081-657-0744. (Subscr. to: c/o M. Veissis, Collectors Gallery, 6 Castle Gates, Shrewsbury SY1 2AE, England) Ed. H.J. Shakespeare. adv.; bk.rev.; index. circ. 700. (back issues avail.) **Document type:** newsletter.

701.18   US   ISSN 0734-5534
NK9507
INTERNATIONAL CHINESE SNUFF BOTTLE SOCIETY. JOURNAL. 1974. q. $95 membership (effective 1996). International Chinese Snuff Bottle Society, 2601 N. Charles St., Baltimore, MD 21218. TEL 410-467-9400. FAX 410-243-3451. Ed. Berthe H. Ford. R&P contact: Berthe Ford. adv.: B&W page $475, color page $1050; adv. contact: John Ford. bk.rev. circ. 700. **Document type:** academic/scholarly publication.

INTERNATIONAL PRESERVATION NEWS. see LIBRARY AND INFORMATION SCIENCES

745.1 796.95   US
IRON DOG TRACKS. 1976. bi-m. membership. (Antique Snowmobile Club of America) Weber & Sons, Park Falls, WI 54552. TEL 715-762-2678. (back issues avail.) **Document type:** newsletter.
Description: Contains information on summer and winter meetings, shows, parades and competitive events.

739.7 952 723   US   ISSN 1043-1640
JAPANESE SWORD SOCIETY OF THE U S BULLETIN. 1959. a. $30 in N. America; foreign $40. Japanese Sword Society of the U.S., Inc., c/o Dr. T.C. Ford, Box 712, Breckenridge, TX 76424. Ed. T.C. Ford. adv.; bk.rev. circ. 1,100. **Document type:** bulletin.

739.7
JAPANESE SWORD SOCIETY OF THE U S NEWSLETTER. 1969. bi-m. $30 in N. America; foreign $40. Japanese Sword Society of the U.S., Inc., c/o Dr. T.C. Ford, Box 712, Breckenridge, TX 76424. Ed. T.C. Ford. circ. 1,100. **Document type:** newsletter.

745.1   US   ISSN 0098-9266
N6520
JOURNAL OF EARLY SOUTHERN DECORATIVE ARTS. 1975. s-a. $30 to individuals; institutions $25 (foreign $40). Museum of Early Southern Decorative Arts, P.O. Box 10310, Winston-Salem, NC 27108-0310. TEL 910-721-7360. FAX 910-721-7367. Ed. B.L. Rauschenberg. bk.rev. circ. 1,500. **Indexed:** Amer.Hist.& Life (1988-), Hist.Abstr. (1988-), RILA. **Document type:** academic/scholarly publication.
Description: Features articles on Southern decorative arts from 1670 to 1820; includes furniture, paintings, ceramics, textiles and metalwork.
Refereed Serial

745.1   US   ISSN 0738-9736
KANHISTIQUE; Kansas history and antiques. 1975. m. $18 (effective 1996). Ellsworth Reporter, Box 7, 220 Court St., Ellsworth, KS 67439. TEL 913-472-3103. FAX 913-472-3268. Ed. Edna Marie Lee; Pub. Karl K. Gaston. adv.; bk.rev. **Document type:** newspaper.

625.1   US   ISSN 0271-3241
TF347
KEY, LOCK AND LANTERN. 1966. q. $21. Key, Lock and Lantern, Inc., Box 65, Demrest, NJ 07627. TEL 201-767-9311. adv.; bk.rev. circ. 1,000. (back issues avail.)
Description: Promotes the hobby of antique railroad hardware collecting.

745.1 737 789.56   PL   ISSN 1427-3039
KOLEKCJONER LOMZYNSKI. 1991. a. 3 Zl. Polskie Towarzystwo Numizmatyczne, Oddzial w Lomzy, Ul. Krzywe Kolo 1, 18-400 Lomza, Poland. TEL 162937. (Co-sponsor: Urzad Wojewodzki w Lomzy) R&P contact: Sylwester Banaskiewicz. adv.: page 250 Zl.; adv. contact: Sylwester Banaskiewicz. mkt. circ. 1,000. (back issues avail.) **Document type:** bulletin.
Description: Deals with collecting in general prefering the subjects connected with the region of Lomza.
Refereed Serial

745.1   US   ISSN 0738-2405
NK1125
KOVEL'S ANTIQUES AND COLLECTIBLES PRICE LIST. a. $9.95. Crown Publishers, Inc., 201 E. 50th St., New York, NY 10022. TEL 212-254-1600. Eds. Ralph & Terry Kovel.
Formerly: Kovel's Antiques Price List.

745.1   US   ISSN 0741-6091
NK1125
KOVELS ON ANTIQUES AND COLLECTIBLES; the newsletter for dealers, collectors and investors. 1974. m. $36. Antiques, Inc., 30799 Pinetree Rd., Ste. 127, Pepper Pike, OH 44124. TEL 800-829-9158. (Subscr. to: Box 420347, Palm Coast, FL 32142-0347) Ed. Nancy Saada. R&P contact: Terry Kovel. bk.rev.; bibl.; illus.; stat.; index. (looseleaf format; back issues avail.) **Document type:** newsletter.

745.1   NE   ISSN 0165-3687
KUNST & ANTIEKREVUE. 1975. bi-m. fl.95 (foreign fl.115). Antiekrevue B.V., Postbus 85994, 2508 CR The Hague, Netherlands. TEL 31-70-3648800. FAX 31-78-3633322. Ed. Richard Wagner. adv.; bk.rev. circ. 7,000.
Formerly: Antiekrevue.

KUNSTPREIS-JAHRBUCH. see ART

745.1   US
F96
THE LANDMARK (HARTFORD).* 1949. 3/yr. $25 to individuals; institutions $16.50. Antiquarian and Landmarks Society, Inc., 66 Forest St., Hartford, CT 06105-3204. TEL 860-247-8996. FAX 860-249-4907. Ed. Trudy K. Jones. R&P contact: Trudy K. Jones. adv.; bk.rev.; bibl.; illus.; circ. 2,000 (paid). **Indexed:** Amer.Hist.& Life (1978-1990), Hist.Abstr. (1978-1990). **Document type:** newsletter.
Formerly (until 1991): Connecticut Antiquarian (ISSN 0010-6054)

LOOSE CHANGE. see SPORTS AND GAMES

745.1   US
LYLE OFFICIAL REVIEW ANTIQUES PRICE GUIDE. 1971. a. Berkley Publishing, 200 Madison Ave., New York, NY 10016. TEL 800-223-0510. Ed. Tony Curtis. adv.; illus.; index. circ. 30,000.
Formerly: Lyle Official Antiques Review.
Description: Details of thousands of antiques.

745.1   US   ISSN 0161-9284
NK1125
THE MAGAZINE ANTIQUES. 1922. m. $39.95. Brant Publications, Inc., 575 Broadway, 5th Fl., New York, NY 10012. TEL 212-941-2800. (Subscr. to: Box 10547, Des Moines, IA 50340. TEL 800-925-9271) Ed. Allison Ledes; Pub. Sandra Brant. R&P contact: Stephanie Rosenfeld. adv. contact: Diege McLaughlin. bk.rev.; illus.; cum.index. circ. 63,300. (also avail. in microfilm from UMI) **Indexed:** Amer.Hist.& Life (1983-1987), Art Ind., Arts & Hum.Cit.Ind., Arts & Hum.Cit.Ind., ASCA, Bk.Rev.Ind., Curr.Cont., Hist.Abstr. (1983-1987), Mag.Ind., PMR, R.G., R.G.Abstr. **Document type:** consumer publication.
●Also available online. Vendor(s): Information Access Co.
—BLDSC (5332.807000); KR SourceOne; UMI; UnCover.
Formerly: Antiques (ISSN 0003-5939)
Description: Emphasizes antique furniture, but also covers paintings, architecture, glass, and textiles.

745.1   US   ISSN 0147-0639
MAINE ANTIQUE DIGEST. 1973. m. $37 (foreign $49) (effective 1997). Maine Antique Digest, Inc., Box 1429, Waldoboro, ME 04572. TEL 207-832-7534. FAX 207-832-7341. E-mail: mad@maine.com; URL: http://www.maineantiquedigest.com. Ed. Sally C. Pennington. adv.; bk.rev.; charts; illus. circ. 30,000. (tabloid format; also avail. in microform from UMI) **Document type:** newspaper.
—UMI.
Description: Covers the market for art and antiques in Maine and the U.S. in general.

739.7   US   ISSN 0191-3522
NK6900
MAN AT ARMS; the magazine of arms collecting-investing. 1979. bi-m. $27 (foreign 35) (effective 1997). Stuart C. Mowbray, Box 460, Lincoln, RI 02865. TEL 401-726-8011. E-mail: smowbray@aol.com. Ed. Stuart C. Mowbray. adv. contact: Joanne Langlois. bk.rev.; charts; illus.; index. circ. 20,000. (back issues avail.) **Document type:** consumer publication.
Description: Devoted to history of arms and armour; contains articles on gun and sword collecting.

ANTIQUES

799.202 US ISSN 0883-6949
MANNLICHER COLLECTOR. 1985. q. $20 (effective 1997). Mannlicher Collectors Association, Box 7144, Salem, OR 97303. TEL 503-472-7710. FAX 503-472-1440. Ed. Don L. Henry. adv.; bk.rev. circ. 650. **Document type**: academic/scholarly publication.

MARKETPLACE. see TRANSPORTATION — Automobiles

745.1 US ISSN 0279-8344
MASSBAY ANTIQUES.* 1980. m. $15. Northshore Weeklies, Inc., Box 293, Danvers, MA 01923-0493. FAX 508-685-3782. Ed. Shannon Aaron. adv.; bk.rev. circ. 22,000.
Description: For antiques dealers and collectors in the New England area.

631.3 745.1 US ISSN 0897-215X
MASSEY COLLECTORS NEWS - WILD HARVEST. 1984. bi-m. $20 (Canada $24; elsewhere $32) (effective 1997). Massey Collectors News, Box 529, Denver, IA 50622. TEL 319-984-5292. FAX 319-984-6408. Ed. Keith Oltrogge. adv. circ. 1,100. (tabloid format; back issues avail.) **Document type**: newsletter.
Description: For collectors of Massey Harris and MF tractors and equipment.

MECHANICAL MUSIC. see MUSIC

912 US ISSN 1086-6728
GA101
MERCATOR'S WORLD; the magazine of maps, globes and charts. bi-m. $39.95 (N. America $49.95; elsewhere £39.95) (effective 1997). Aster Publishing Corp., 845 Willamette St., Eugene, OR 97401. TEL 541-345-3800. FAX 541-345-0000. E-mail: jlindsey@mercatormag.com; URL: http://www.mercatormag.com. (In Americas subscr. to: Box 10603, Eugene, OR 97440; Elsewhere subscr. to: Ste. B31, Grosvenor House, Central Park, Telford, Shropshire, TF2 9TW, England. TEL 44-1-952-200207) Ed. Jennifer Lindsey; Pub. Kim Welsh. R&P contact: Jennifer Lindsey. adv. contact: Beverlee McNett. **Document type**: consumer publication.
—BLDSC (5678.818800).
Description: For people who are interested in exploring the world of maps, atlases, globes and charts. It's topics range from antiquarian maps and digital technologies, to exploration and discovery.

745.1 US
MERRY-GO-ROUNDUP. 1973. q. $36 (foreign $36). National Carousel Association, c/o Cynthia L. Hennig, Ed., 128 Courtshire Ln., Penfield, NY 14526. TEL 716-377-6762. E-mail: chennig@frontiernet.net. adv.; bk.rev. circ. 1,450. (back issues avail.) **Document type**: consumer publication.
Former titles: National Carousel Association. Carousel Archives; National Carousel Association. Carousel Census.
Description: Articles on the history and preservation of carousels and news related to the subject.

745.1 US
MID-AM ANTIQUE APPRAISERS ASSOCIATION. NEWSLETTER. a. Karen Hall Publishing Co., Box 9681, Springfield, MO 65801. TEL 417-865-7269. Ed. Suzanne De Vol. **Document type**: newsletter.

745.1 US ISSN 1042-2501
MIDATLANTIC ANTIQUES MAGAZINE; monthly guide to antiques, auctions, art & collectibles. 1983. m. $18; newsstand price: $3. Henderson Newspapers Inc., 304 S. Chestnut St., Box 908, Henderson, NC 27536. TEL 919-492-4001; 800-326-3894. FAX 919-430-0125. (Dist. by: Ingram Periodicals, LaVergne, TN 37086-7000. TEL 615-793-5000. FAX 615-783-6043) Ed. Lydia A. Stainback; Pub. Richard Bean. R&P contact: Lydia A. Stainback. adv.; bk.rev. circ. 14,500. (tabloid format; also avail. in microfilm from UMI; back issues avail.) **Document type**: trade publication.
Description: Provides auctions and antique show reports listing prices; compares regional prices.

739.7 US ISSN 0026-3966
UC463
MILITARY COLLECTOR & HISTORIAN. 1951. q. $30 to non-members. Company of Military Historians HQ and Museum, N. Main St., Westbrook, CT 06498. TEL 203-399-9460. Ed. Fred Gaede. adv.; bk.rev. circ. 4,200. (also avail. in microform from UMI)
Indexed: Amer.Hist.& Life (1963-1990), Hist.Abstr. (1963-1990).
—UMI; UnCover.
Description: Historical articles on the material, culture, and traditions of members of the U.S. Armed Forces worldwide and of other nations that serve the Western Hemisphere.

745.1 UK ISSN 0262-1851
MILLER'S ANTIQUES PRICE GUIDE. 1980. a. £22.50($35) Reed Consumer Books Ltd., Part of the Reed Elsevier group, Michelin House, 81 Fulham Rd., London SW3 6RB, England. TEL 44-171-581-9393. FAX 44-171-589-8419. (Dist. in US by: Antique Collectors' Club, Market Street Industrial Park, Wappinger's Falls, NY 12590. TEL 914-297-0003) Ed. Alison Starling. R&P contact: Alison Starling. adv. contact: Elizabeth Smith. illus. circ. 181,000. **Document type**: consumer publication.
—BLDSC (5773.960000).
Description: Contains price values and text descriptions of antiques and collectibles.

745.1 UK
MILLER'S COLLECTABLES PRICE GUIDE. a. £16.99($25) (effective 1996). Reed Consumer Books Ltd., Part of the Reed Elsevier group, Michelin House, 81 Fulham Rd., London SW3 6RB, England. TEL 44-171-581-9393. FAX 44-171-589-8419. (Dist. in US by: Antique Collectors' Club, Market Street Industrial Park, Wappinger's Falls, NY 12590. TEL 914-297-0003) Ed. Alison Starling. adv. contact: Elizabeth Smith. circ. 50,000. **Document type**: directory.

MINIATURA. see PUBLISHING AND BOOK TRADE

MINUTIA. see TRANSPORTATION — Automobiles

629.222 US ISSN 1074-3510
MISS INFORMATION'S AUTOMOTIVE CALENDAR OF EVENTS. 1985. m. $15. Bobbie'dine Rodda, Ed. & Pub., 1232 Highland Ave., Glendale, CA 91202. TEL 818-887-1646. FAX 818-888-2648. adv. circ. 4,000. **Document type**: newsletter.
Description: Lists more than 700 shows, swap meets, auctions, and tours of interest to automotive enthusiasts.

MOTO LEGENDE. see SPORTS AND GAMES — Bicycles And Motorcycles

629.222 US ISSN 0894-5179
MUSTANG & FORDS. 1980. bi-m. $15.95. Petersen Publishing Co., 6420 Wilshire Blvd., Los Angeles, CA 90048. TEL 213-782-2000. Ed. Jerry Pittwell. adv.; illus. circ. 100,000. (also avail. in microfiche from UMI) **Document type**: consumer publication.
Formerly: Mustang.

745.1 US ISSN 0741-2673
MYSTIC LIGHT OF THE ALADDIN KNIGHTS. 1973. bi-m. $25. J.W. Courter, Ed. & Pub., 3935 Kelley Rd., Kevil, KY 42053-9431. TEL 502-488-2116. URL: http://www.alladinknights.org. circ. 1,500. (looseleaf format) **Document type**: newsletter.
Description: Covers antique oil and electric lighting.

NASH TIMES. see TRANSPORTATION — Automobiles

745.1 US
NATIONAL ASSOCIATION OF DEALERS IN ANTIQUES. BULLETIN. m. membership only. National Association of Dealers in Antiques, Inc., Box 421, Barrington, IL 60011. TEL 312-381-7096. bk.rev. **Document type**: bulletin.
Description: Educational and association news. Includes obituaries and membership profiles.

745.1 US ISSN 0899-6172
AM303
NATIONAL DIRECTORY OF ART & ANTIQUES BUYERS & SPECIALISTS.* 1991. biennial. $75. Merit Agencies, Inc., c/o William D'Angelo, 10417 Fair Oaks, Columbia, MD 21044-4148. Ed. Bill D'Angelo. circ. 1,000. **Document type**: directory.
Description: Contains over 6,000 specialists from over 800 categories of art, antiques and collectables.

623.4 US ISSN 1051-4600
NATIONAL KNIFE MAGAZINE. 1976. m. $35 membership. National Knife Collector Association, Box 21070, Chattanooga, TN 37424. TEL 423-892-5007. Ed. Lisa Broyles. adv. contact: Lisa Broyles. bk.rev.; illus. circ. 10,000. (back issues avail.) **Document type**: consumer publication.
Formerly: National Knife Collector (ISSN 0164-7547).

745.1 US ISSN 0897-5795
NEW ENGLAND ANTIQUES JOURNAL. 1983. m. $19.95 (Canada $30) (effective 1997). Turley Publications, Box 120, Ware, MA 01082-0120. TEL 413-967-3505; 800-432-3505. FAX 413-967-6009. E-mail: 76710.2327@compuserve.com. Ed. Jamie Mercier; Pub. Pat Turley. R&P contact: Jamie Mercier. adv.: B&W page $595; 10 x 15 3/4; adv. contact: Jody Young. bk.rev. circ. 20,000. (tabloid format; back issues avail.) **Document type**: trade publication.
Description: For antiques dealers and collectors: educational articles, auction and antiques show reviews, news and commentary.

NEW GLEANINGS. see MUSEUMS AND ART GALLERIES

745.1 US ISSN 0738-8365
NEW YORK ANTIQUE ALMANAC. 1975. 9/yr. $10 (Canada $22; elsewhere $24). New York Eye Publishing Co., Inc., Box 2400, New York, NY 10021. TEL 212-988-2700. FAX 212-988-5255. Ed. Carol Nadel; Pub. Carol Nadel. adv. contact: Enid Van Raalte. bk.rev.; illus.; stat. circ. 69,000. (tabloid format; back issues avail.) **Document type**: trade publication.
Description: Focuses on the current market in art, antiques and collectibles.

745.1 US
NEW YORK - PENNSYLVANIA COLLECTOR; antiques, art & Americana. 1976. m. $21. Messenger-Wolfe Publications, Inc., Box C, Fishers, NY 14453. TEL 716-924-4040. FAX 716-924-7734. E-mail: WolfePub@frontiernet.net. Ed. Ellen Coller; Pub. George M. Ewing Jr. adv. contact: Ros Parrish. bk.rev. circ. 7,000. **Document type**: newspaper, trade publication.
Description: Contains articles on antiques and collectibles, a special series on antique furniture restoration and identification, and calendars of coming shows and auctions.

629.288 US
NEWS-FLITE. 1977. q. $20 (effective Jan. 1991). Chrysler 300 Club International, Inc., 4900 Jonesville Rd., Jonesville, MI 49250. TEL 517-849-2783. FAX 517-849-7447. Ed. Eleanor Riehl. R&P contact: George Riehl. adv.; charts; illus.; stat. circ. 900. (back issues avail.) **Document type**: newsletter.
Description: Provides technical information, restoration information, and reprinted articles.

NINETEENTH CENTURY (WESTFIELD). see HISTORY — History Of North And South America

745.5 US
NORTHEAST - JOURNAL OF ANTIQUES & ART; antiques - art - historic homes - country life - preservation & restoration. Cover title: Art & Antiques Northeast. m. $9.95 (single copies free). 354 Warren St., Hudson, NY 12534. TEL 518-828-1616; 800-836-4069. FAX 518-828-9437. Ed. Harold M. Hanson; Pub. William C. Lundquest. adv.; illus. cols./p.: 5; pp./issue: 32. (tabloid format) **Document type**: newspaper.
Description: Covers upstate New York art and antique shows in detail.

629.222 388.3 SW ISSN 1103-7334
NOSTALGIA MOTOR MAGAZINE. 1993. bi-m. SEK 225 (foreign SEK 261) (effective 1997); newsstand price: SEK 42. Albinsson & Sjoeberg, P.O. Box 529, S-371 23 Karlskrona, Sweden. TEL 46-455-335325. FAX 46-455-311715. E-mail: fabas@fabas.se. Ed. Goeran Ambell; Pub. Stig L. Sjoeberg. adv.: B&W page SEK 8000, color page SEK 12000; trim 190 x 275; adv. contact: Susanne Zec. circ. 18,700 (controlled). cols./p.: 4; pp./issue: 100. **Document type**: consumer publication.

OLD AUTOS. see TRANSPORTATION — Automobiles

OLD CARS; weekly news and marketplace. see TRANSPORTATION — Automobiles

ANTIQUES

629.222 US ISSN 0194-6404
OLD CARS PRICE GUIDE. 1978. bi-m. $18.95 (effective 1997). Krause Publications, Inc., 700 E. State St., Iola, WI 54990. TEL 715-445-2214. FAX 715-445-4087. TELEX 55 6461 KRAUSE PUB UD. URL: http://www.krause.com/subs/html/pg.html. Ed. Kenneth Buttolph; Pub. Greg Smith. adv. contact: Richard Hare. charts; stat. circ. 95,121. (also avail. in microform from UMI)
  Description: Market value news featuring over 130,000 individual prices, vehicle conditions in six grades, list of all American-made automobiles from 1901 to 1986, and identification photos of models.

745.1 US ISSN 1064-4164
OLD TOY SOLDIER; the journal for collectors. 1976. q. $25 (Canada $35; foreign $42 by air mail). O T S N, Inc., 209 N. Lombard, Oak Park, IL 60302. TEL 708-383-6525. FAX 708-383-2182. Ed. Steve Sommers. R&P contact: Jo Sommers. adv.: B&W page $150; adv. contact: Jo Sommers. bk.rev.; illus.; cum.index: vols.1-10, 11-15; circ. 1,800 (paid). (back issues avail.) **Document type:** academic/scholarly publication.
  Formerly: Old Toy Soldier Newsletter (ISSN 8756-7652)
  Description: Publishes articles and information of interest to collectors of military and civilian toy figures.

745.1 US ISSN 0164-3398
THE ORIENTALIA JOURNAL. bi-m. $15 (foreign $24). Box 94, Little Neck, NY 11363.
  Description: For collectors and investors of antiques.

745.1 NE ISSN 0929-1032
ORIGINE; art, antiques & interior. 1992. bi-m. fl.52.50. Origine, P.O. Box 5220, 2000 GE Haarlem, Netherlands. TEL 31-23-5324233. FAX 31-23-5324518. circ. 13,800.
  Description: Includes original articles concerning 500 years of art and antiques documented by original private interiors, exhibitions, news, restoration, and interviews.

745.1 US
P A C: PAPER AND ADVERTISING COLLECTOR. 1979. m. membership. (National Association of Paper and Advertising Collectors) Engle Publishing Company, Rte. 230 W., Box 500, Mount Joy, PA 17552. TEL 717-653-4300; 800-482-2886. FAX 717-653-6165. Ed. Denise M. Sater. adv.; index. **Document type:** newspaper.

629.222 US ISSN 0362-9368
TL215.P25
PACKARD CORMORANT. 1953. q. membership. Packard Automobile Classics, 420 S. Ludlow St., Dayton, OH 45402. Ed. Richard M. Langworth. charts; illus.; tr.lit.
  Formerly: Cormorant (ISSN 0045-8546)

745.1 790.13 US ISSN 0741-4927
PN4877
PAPER COLLECTOR'S MARKETPLACE. 1983. m. $19.95. Watson Graphic Designs, 470 Main St., Box 128, Scandinavia, WI 54977. TEL 715-467-2379. FAX 715-467-2243. E-mail: pcmpaper@gglbbs.com. Ed. Doug Watson; Pub. Doug Watson. adv.; bk.rev. circ. 4,000. (back issues avail.) **Document type:** consumer publication.
  Description: For collectors of paper memorabilia, including magazines, newspapers, advertising, postcards, posters and more.

745 US
PATINAGRAM. 1977. bi-m. membership. Potomac Antique Tools and Industries Association, 13004 Clarion Rd., Ft. Washington, MD 20744. TEL 301-292-1606. Ed. Dale Bultman. bk.rev.; circ. 360 (controlled). (back issues avail.) **Document type:** newsletter.

745.1 US ISSN 0031-6644
PEWTER COLLECTORS' CLUB OF AMERICA. BULLETIN. 1934. s-a. membership. Pewter Collectors' Club of America, c/o Webster Goodwin, 730 Commonwealth Ave., Warwick, RI 02886. Ed.Bd. bk.rev.; illus.; cum.index every 10 nos. circ. 600. (looseleaf format) **Document type:** bulletin.

629.222 US ISSN 0032-1737
PLYMOUTH BULLETIN. 1959. bi-m. $18 (foreign $45). Plymouth Owners Club, Inc., Box 416, Cavalier, ND 58220. TEL 701-549-3746. FAX 701-549-3744. Ed. Lanny Knutson. adv.; bk.rev.; illus. circ. 3,500. (back issues avail.) **Document type:** newsletter.
  Description: Covers automotive history relating to the Plymouth automoblie.

POSTCARD ART - POSTCARD FICTION. see *ART*

PRACTICAL CLASSICS. see *TRANSPORTATION — Automobiles*

PRAIRIE GOLD RUSH; quarterly newsletter for all Twin City, Minneapolis and Moline enthusiasts. see *AGRICULTURE — Agricultural Equipment*

745.1 US
PRICE GUIDE (DUBUQUE). m. $14.95. Antique Trader Publications, Box 1050, 100 Bryant St., Dubuque, IA 52004-1050. TEL 319-588-2073. FAX 319-588-2073. circ. 65,000. **Document type:** consumer publication.

745.1 UK
PRICE GUIDE TO CRESTED CHINA. a. Milestone Publications, 62 Murray Rd., Horndean, Waterlooville, Hants PO8 9JL, England. TEL 44-1705-597440. FAX 44-1705-591975. Ed.Bd. **Document type:** catalog.

REFLECT. see *LITERATURE*

745.1 US
RENNINGER'S ANTIQUE GUIDE; to shows, shops, antique - flea markets and auctions. 1975. 25/yr. $15 (effective 1997). Box 495, Lafayette Hill, PA 19444-0495. TEL 610-828-4614. FAX 610-834-1599. Ed. Harriett Ackerman; Pub. Herbert Kratchman. R&P contact: Herbert Kratchman. adv.: B&W page $440; adv. contact: Herbert Kratchman. bk.rev. circ. 60,000. **Document type:** newspaper, trade publication.

RETROVISEUR. see *TRANSPORTATION — Automobiles*

ROCKIN' RECORDS; buyers - sellers reference book and price guide. see *MUSIC*

ROUGH RIDER. see *TRANSPORTATION — Automobiles*

629.222 IT ISSN 1121-5321
RUOTECLASSICHE. 1987. m. (11/yr.). L.81000($105) Editoriale Internazionale Milano, Via Achille Grandi, 5-7, 20089 Rozzano (MI), Italy. TEL 39-2-824721. FAX 39-2-26863123. TELEX 316822 EDIDOM I. Ed. Marco Centenari; Pub. Giovanna Mazzocchi. adv.: color page L.11500000; adv. contact: Giuseppe Bolandrina. circ. 32,000. **Document type:** newspaper.
  Description: Covers antique automobiles, their history, technology, restoration, and culture.

796.77 US
SACRED OCTAGON. 1964. bi-m. $35. New England M G 'T' Register, Drawer 220, Oneonta, NY 13820. FAX 607-432-3342. Ed. Richard L. Knudsen. R&P contact: Richard L. Knudsen. adv.; bk.rev.; illus.; circ. 5,000 (paid).
  Description: Contains information of interest to vintage sports car enthusiasts.

745.1 790.132 SW ISSN 1102-5212
SAMLARBOKEN. 1991. a. SEK 98 (effective 1993). Tonkin AB, Box 99, S-582 20 Linkoeping, Sweden. Ed. Archie Tonkin.
  Incorporates (1989-1991): Tallriksboken (ISSN 0347-3228)

745.1 GW ISSN 0342-7684
SAMMLER JOURNAL. 1972. m. DM.22 (foreign DM.115.60) (effective 1997). Journal Verlag Schwend GmbH, Schmollerstr. 31, 74523 Schwaebisch Hall, Germany. TEL 49-791-404550. FAX 49-791-404555. Ed. Agnes Schwend. adv.; B&W page DM.2703, color page DM.3816; trim 197 x 265; adv. contact: Uwe Turtschau. bk.rev. circ. 38,000. (back issues avail.) **Indexed:** IBR. **Document type:** consumer publication.

745.1 US
HF5482
SCHROEDER'S ANTIQUES PRICE GUIDE. 1977. a. $12.95. Collector Books, Box 3009, Paducah, KY 42002-3009. TEL 502-898-6211; 800-626-5420. Eds. Sharon & Bob Huxford, Lisa Stroup; Pub. Bill Schroeder. illus. **Document type:** catalog.
  Formerly (until 1983): Flea Market Trader (ISSN 0364-023X)
  Description: Offers prices and information on more than 50,000 items.

739.23 US ISSN 0899-6105
NK7100
SILVER. 1969. bi-m. $35 (foreign $45). Silver Magazine Inc., Box 9690, Rancho Santa Fe, CA 92067. TEL 619-756-1054. FAX 619-756-9928. E-mail: silver@silvermag.com; URL: http://www.silvermag.com. Ed. Connie McNally; Pub. William McNally. R&P contact: Connie McNally. adv. contact: William McNally. bk.rev.; index; circ. 2,500 (paid). (back issues avail.) **Document type:** academic/scholarly publication.
  Former titles (until 1985): Silver Magazine (ISSN 0747-4482); Silver-Rama (ISSN 0037-5357)
  Description: Covers all aspects of silver collecting: American, English and other flatware, hollow ware and novelties.
  Refereed Serial

SLANT 6 NEWS. see *TRANSPORTATION — Automobiles*

745.1 917.404 US ISSN 1051-6719
NK1127
SLOAN'S GREEN GUIDE TO ANTIQUING IN NEW ENGLAND. 1989. 2/yr. $20. Antique Press, 66 Charles St., No. 140, Boston, MA 02114. TEL 617-723-3001; 800-552-5632. FAX 617-248-0185. Ed. Susan P. Sloan. adv. contact: Susan P. Sloan. circ. 10,000 (paid). **Document type:** trade publication.
  Formerly (until 1992): Sloan's Green Guide to Antiques Dealers (New England) (ISSN 0898-090X)
  Description: Lists over 2800 antiques shops, antiquarian booksellers, period restoration specialists, weekend markets in six New England and eastern New York states.

745.1 UK
N8640
SOTHEBY'S ART AT AUCTION: THE ART MARKET REVIEW (YEAR). 1967. a. $80. (Sotheby's Publications) Conran Octopus, 37 Shelton St., London WC2H 9HN, England. (Dist. in U.S. by: Rizzoli International Publications, Inc., 300 Park Ave. S., New York, NY 10010. TEL 212-982-2300) Ed. Sandy Mallet. illus.; index. **Document type:** corporate report. —BLDSC (8328.787050).
  Supersedes: Art at Auction: the Year at Sotheby's and Parke-Bernet (ISSN 0084-6783)

SOTHEBY'S NEWSLETTER. see *ART*

SPECIAL INTEREST AUTOS. see *TRANSPORTATION — Automobiles*

629.222 745.1 US ISSN 0279-0998
SPORTING CLASSICS. 1981. bi-m. $28.95 (effective 1997). Live Oak Press, Inc., Box 23707, Columbia, SC 29224-3707. TEL 803-736-2424; 800-849-1004. Ed. Charles Wechsler. adv. contact: Art Carter. bk.rev. circ. 30,000. (back issues avail.) **Indexed:** Amer.Hist.& Life (1984-1987), Hist.Abstr. (1984-1987). **Document type:** consumer publication.
  Description: Features on-location hunting and fishing adventures around the world; articles on fine-quality sporting equipment, collectibles and wildlife artists.

STUDIES IN THE DECORATIVE ARTS. see *ART*

745.1 US ISSN 1080-451X
STYLE 1900; the quarterly journal of the arts and crafts movement. 1986. q. $25 (foreign $35); newsstand price: $4.95. 17 S. Main St., Lambertville, NJ 08530. TEL 609-397-4104. FAX 609-397-9377. E-mail: style1900@aol.com. Ed. David Rago; Pub. Steven Becker. adv. contact: Miriam Assion. bk.rev. circ. 5,500. (back issues avail.) **Document type:** consumer publication.
  Formerly: Arts and Crafts Quarterly (ISSN 1074-4568)
  Description: Devoted to exploring the art, artists, and philosophers within the arts and crafts movement of the turn of the century.

TABLEAU. see *ART*

THIMBLELETTER; an informal newsletter for thimble collectors. see *HOBBIES*

THRIFT SCORE. see *HOBBIES*

THUNDERBIRD SCOOP. see *TRANSPORTATION — Automobiles*

745.1 US
TOBACCIANA REPORTS; collectable items related to tobacco and its use. 1993. q. $2.95 per no. Chuck Thompson & Associates, 10802 Greencreek Dr., Ste. 703, Houston, TX 77070-5367. TEL 713-442-7200. Ed. Chuck Thompson. bk.rev.; illus. (back issues avail.) **Document type:** consumer publication.
   Description: Includes history and money-saving tips for collectors and others interested in specific tobacco-related subjects.

745.1 US ISSN 1066-7423
TODAY'S COLLECTOR; the nation's antiques & collectibles marketplace. 1993. m. $21.95 (effective 1997). Krause Publications, Inc., 700 E. State St., Iola, WI 54990. TEL 715-445-2214. FAX 715-445-4087. Ed. Steve Ellingboe; Pub. Greg Smith. adv.: B&W page $595, color page $820; trim 10 x 11; adv. contact: Richard Hare. circ. 73,149. **Document type:** consumer publication.

TRASTIENDA; revista del mercado de arte y antiguedades. see *ART*

745.1 US ISSN 0897-814X
TREASURE CHEST; the information source & marketplace for collectors & dealers. 1988. m. $25 (effective 1996). Treasure Chest Publishing, Inc., Box 245, North Scituate, RI 02857-0245. TEL 401-647-0050. FAX 401-647-0051. Pub. Howard E. Fischer; Pubs. David F. Donnelly, Constance Lee Donnelly. adv.; bk.rev.; illus. circ. 50,000. (tabloid format; back issues avail.) **Document type:** newspaper.
   Description: Includes information on antiques and collectibles. Includes calendar of events on auctions, shows, flea markets, and recent sales, features articles, cartoons.

745.1 GW ISSN 0944-3134
TROEDLER- UND MAGAZIN SAMMELN. 1979. m. DM.54 (foreign DM.66). Gemi Verlags GmbH, Pfaffenhofener Str. 3, 85293 Reichertshausen, Germany. TEL 08441-4018. FAX 08441-71846. Ed. Karl Ruisinger. circ. 50,000. **Document type:** consumer publication.
   Formed by 1992 merger of: Troedler- und Antiquitaetenmagazin (ISSN 0944-3126) & Magazin Sammeln (ISSN 1010-3686)
   Description: Information about antique collecting, flea markets and fairs.

TROUVAILLES. see *ART*

THE TRUMPET (NEW YORK). see *ART*

TUCKER TOPICS. see *TRANSPORTATION — Automobiles*

U S TOY COLLECTOR MAGAZINE. see *GIFTWARE AND TOYS*

745.1 US ISSN 0049-5174
UNDERGROUND LAMP POST. 1967. 2/yr. free. Henry A. Pohs, Ed. & Pub., 4537 Quitman St., Denver, CO 80212. TEL 303-455-3922. bk.rev.; charts; illus.; pat.; circ. 450 (controlled). (processed) **Document type:** newsletter.
   Description: Discusses antique non-electric mine lights.

745.1 CN ISSN 0711-0081
THE UPPER CANADIAN; current trends in antiques and collectibles. 1980. bi-m. Can.$26($27) (foreign $36) (effective 1997); newsstand price: Can.$4.50. 710198 Ontario Inc., P.O. Box 653, Smiths Falls, ON K7A 4T6, Canada. TEL 613-283-1168. FAX 613-283-1345. Ed. Bill Dobson; Pub. Bill Dobson. adv.: page Can.$440; trim 10 1/4 x 15 1/2; adv. contact: Bill Dobson. bk.rev.; illus, tr.lit. circ. 5,000. cols./p.: 4; pp./issue: 62. (tabloid format; also avail. in microfiche; back issues avail.) **Document type:** newspaper.
   Description: Caters to the business and passion of antiques and collectibles for collectors and dealers, novice and expert alike. Articles, columns, show and auction coverage and commentary encompass a broad range of issues and topics. Emphasis on price reporting and pictorials.

629.222 US ISSN 0274-5003
V-EIGHT TIMES. 1969. bi-m. $25. Early Ford V-8 Club of America, Box 2122, San Leandro, CA 94577. Ed. Robert McCoppin. adv.; bk.rev.; charts; illus. circ. 8,000.

V M R STANDARD USED CAR PRICES. see *TRANSPORTATION — Automobiles*

629.222 US
V V W C A NEWSLETTER. 1976. m. $20. Vintage Volkswagen Club of America, 818 Main St., Portage, PA 15946. TEL 814-736-4343. Ed. Terry Shuler. adv.; bk.rev. (back issues avail.)

739.7 DK ISSN 0108-707X
VAABENHISTORISKE AARBOEGER. (Text in Danish; summaries in English and German) 1934. a. DKK 400 (effective 1997). Vaabenhistorisk Selskab - Danish Arms and Armour Society, Aavangen 8, Skt. Klemens, DK-5360 Odense, Denmark. E-mail: o.skott@winsloew.ou.dk. Ed. Ole SKoett. bk.rev.; cum.index: vols.1-10 in vol.10; vols.11-20 in vol.20. **Document type:** academic/scholarly publication.

629.222 GW
VETERAN. 1975. bi-m. DM.30. Citroen Veteranen Club, c/o Klaus Schaefer, Goschmeersweg 21, 26605 Aurich, Germany. TEL 49-4941-62433. FAX 49-4941-66433. Ed. Helmut Kloos. adv. contact: Klaus Schaefer. bk.rev. circ. 750. **Document type:** newsletter.

629.222 796.7 FR ISSN 0151-2188
VIE DE L'AUTO. 1976. w. 350 F.($97) (foreign 520 F.) (effective 1997). Elvea - La Vie de l'Auto, B.P. 88, 77303 Fontainbleau Cedex, France. TEL 33-1-60715555. FAX 33-1-60722237. adv. contact: Emmanuelle Wurtz. bk.rev.; circ. 68,500 (controlled). (tabloid format; back issues avail.) **Document type:** newspaper.
   Description: Covers classic cars as well as old tractors and trucks.

629 796.7 FR ISSN 0989-0009
VIE DE LA MOTO. 1989. s-m. 200 F. (foreign 275 F.) (effective 1997). Elvea - La Vie de l'Auto, B.P. 88, 77303 Fontainbleau Cedex, France. TEL 33-1-60715555. FAX 33-1-60722237. adv. contact: Emmanuelle Wurtz. index; circ. 43,000 (controlled). (tabloid format; back issues avail.)

VINTAGE AIRPLANE. see *AERONAUTICS AND SPACE FLIGHT*

629.222 US ISSN 0042-6350
TL215.F7
VINTAGE FORD. 1966. bi-m. $22 (Canada $27; elsewhere $28). Model T Ford Club of America, Box 743936, Dallas, TX 75374-3936. TEL 972-783-7531. FAX 972-783-0575. E-mail: JAYFTFC@@AIRMAIL@net; URL: http://www.MTFCA.COM. Ed. Jay G. Klehfoth. R&P contact: Jay G. Klehfoth. adv. contact: Barbara L. Klehfoth. bk.rev.; charts; illus.; stat. circ. 7,800. (processed) **Document type:** academic/scholarly publication.

VINTAGE TRACTOR. see *AGRICULTURE — Agricultural Equipment*

745.13 GW ISSN 0043-261X
WELTKUNST; the world art review. 1930. s-m. DM.250.20 (foreign DM.260.40). Weltkunst Verlag GmbH, Nymphenburgerstr. 84, 80636 Munich, Germany. TEL 49-89-126990-0. FAX 49-89-12699011. Ed. Gloria Ehret. adv.; bk.rev.; charts; illus. circ. 14,000. **Indexed:** Art & Archaeol.Tech.Abstr., Artbibl.Mod., IBR, RILA. **Document type:** consumer publication.
   Description: Information on art exhibitions, auctions, art fairs and other events.

745.1 US
WEST COAST LOCK COLLECTORS. 1978. q. $15. West Coast Lock Collectors, 1427 Lincoln Blvd., Santa Monica, CA 90401. TEL 310-454-7295. Ed. Don Jackson; Pub. Don Jackson. R&P contact: Bob Heilemann. adv. contact: Bob Heilemann. circ. 215 (paid). **Document type:** newsletter.
   Description: Reports on the history and research of antique locks, keys, and related items.

745.1 US ISSN 0199-3356
WEST COAST PEDDLER; oldest journal of antiques, art & collectibles in the Pacific states. 1971. m. $24 (effective 1996). Box 5134, Whittier, CA 90607. TEL 310-698-1718. FAX 310-698-1500. Ed. Robert M. Dannenbaum. bk.rev.; circ. 18,975 (paid); controlled. (tabloid format) **Document type:** consumer publication, newspaper.
   Description: Directed to West Coast antique collectors of antiques, fine art, and other investment-grade collectibles.

745.1 US
▼**WESTERN CONNECTICUT - WESTERN MASSACHUSETTS ANTIQUER.** 1995. m. $18.95 (effective 1997). Antiquer Publications, Box 561, Rhinebeck, NY 12572. TEL 914-876-8766. Ed. Ted Fox; Pub. Ted Fox. adv. contact: Gina Walker Fox. bk.rev. **Document type:** newspaper, consumer publication, trade publication.
   Description: For antiques enthusiasts. Features include centerfold pullout Antiquer's Map.

WHEELS OF TIME. see *TRANSPORTATION — Trucks And Trucking*

WORLD FINE ART. see *ART*

745.1 US ISSN 0194-9349
YESTERYEAR. 1975. m. $17 (effective 1994). Yesteryear Publications, Inc., Box 2, Princeton, WI 54968. TEL 414-787-4808. FAX 414-787-7381. Ed. Michael Jacobi. adv.; bk.rev. circ. 8,000 (paid). (tabloid format; back issues avail.) **Document type:** newspaper.

YOUR CLASSIC. see *TRANSPORTATION — Automobiles*

9N - 2N - 8N - NAA NEWSLETTER. see *AGRICULTURE — Agricultural Equipment*

78 QUARTERLY. see *MUSIC*

629.222 US
1932 BUICK REGISTRY. 1974. s-a. free. 1932 Buick Registry, 3000 Warren Rd., Indiana, PA 15701. TEL 412-463-3372. Ed. M.G. Blair. adv. (looseleaf format; back issues avail.) **Document type:** newsletter.
   Description: For owners of 1925-1935 Buicks. Provides lists of parts for sale, literature, and restoration tips.

ARCHAEOLOGY

see also Paleontology

930.1 NO ISSN 0802-4936
A M S - RAPPORT. (Text in Norwegian; summaries in English) 1988. irreg. price varies. Arkeologisk Museum i Stavanger, P.O. Box 478, N-4001 Stavanger, Norway. TEL 47-51-84-60-00. FAX 47-51-84-61-99. E-mail: bjornm@ark.museum.no. Ed.Bd. (back issues avail.) **Document type:** monographic series.
   Formerly (until 1989): Arkeologisk Museum i Stavanger. Oppdragsrapport (ISSN 0802-2615)
   Description: Presents reports on excavations and projects.

ARCHAEOLOGY

913 NO ISSN 0800-0816
A M S - SKRIFTER. (Text in English, Norwegian; summaries in English or German) 1976. irreg. price varies. Arkeologisk Museum i Stavanger, P.O. Box 478, N-4001 Stavanger, Norway.
TEL 47-51-84-60-00. FAX 47-51-84-61-99. E-mail: bjornm@ark.museum.no. Ed.Bd. (back issues avail.) **Indexed:** NAA. **Document type:** monographic series.
—CCC.
Formerly: Arkeologisk Museum i Stavanger. Skrifter.
Description: Research papers dealing with prehistoric man and his environment, with emphasis on southwest Norway.

913 NO ISSN 0332-6411
A M S - SMAATRYKK. (Text in English, French, German and Norwegian) 1978. irreg. price varies. Arkeologisk Museum i Stavanger, P.O. Box 478, N-4001 Stavanger, Norway. TEL 47-51-84-60-00. FAX 47-51-84-61-99. E-mail: bjornm@ark.museum.no. (back issues avail.) **Indexed:** NAA. **Document type:** academic/scholarly publication, catalog.
—CCC.
Description: Popular information on archaeology in Rogaland, S.W. Norway, along with museum catalogues.

930.1 NO ISSN 0803-5903
A M S - TILVEKST. 1991. irreg. price varies. Arkeologisk Museum i Stavanger, P.O. Box 478, N-4001 Stavanger, Norway. TEL 47-51-84-60-00. FAX 47-51-84-61-99. E-mail: bjornm@ark.museum.no. Ed.Bd. (back issues avail.) **Document type:** catalog.
Description: Catalogue of the museum's acquisitions.

913 NO ISSN 0332-6306
A M S - VARIA. (Text in Norwegian; summaries in English) 1978. irreg. price varies. Arkeologisk Museum i Stavanger, P.O. Box 478, N-4001 Stavanger, Norway. TEL 47-51-84-60-00. FAX 47-51-84-61-99. E-mail: bjornm@ark.museum.no. (back issues avail.) **Indexed:** NAA. **Document type:** monographic series.
—CCC.
Description: Research papers and reports dealing with prehistoric man and his environment in southwest Norway.

A P V A NEWSLETTER. (Association for the Preservation of Virginia Antiquities) see HISTORY — History Of North And South America

917 US
A S M, INK.* 1964. m. $10. Archaeological Society of Maryland, c/o Ethel Eaton, Ed., 138 The Maine, Williamsburg, VA 23185-1423. bk.rev. circ. 360.
Formerly: Archaeological Society of Maryland. Newsletter.

ACADEMIA ROMANA. SECTIA DE STIINTE ISTORICE SI ARHEOLOGIE. MEMORIILE. see HISTORY — History Of Europe

ACADEMIA SINICA. INSTITUTE OF HISTORY AND PHILOLOGY. BULLETIN. see HISTORY — History Of Asia

913 HU ISSN 0001-5210
DB920 CODEN: ACGCBJ
ACADEMIAE SCIENTIARUM HUNGARICAE. ACTA ARCHAEOLOGICA. (Text mainly in English, German, occasionally in French, Italian, Russian) 1951. q. $188 (effective 1998). (Magyar Tudomanyos Akademia) Akademiai Kiado Rt., P.O. Box 245, H-1519 Budapest, Hungary. TEL 36-1-2043976. FAX 36-1-2043973. Ed. Denes Gabler. adv.; bk.rev.; bibl.; charts; illus.; index. **Indexed:** Anthropol.Lit., Arts & Hum.Cit.Ind., ASCA, Biol.Abstr., Br.Archaeol.Abstr., Curr.Cont., GeoRef., IBR, Numis.Lit., RILA, SSCI. **Document type:** academic/scholarly publication.
—BLDSC (0596.320000); SWETS. CCC.
Description: Covers studies of the most important excavations, finds and problems of the period from the Paleolothic to the Middle Ages. Includes short papers on individual finds.

913 PL ISSN 0079-3566
ACADEMIE POLONAISE DES SCIENCES. CENTRE D'ARCHEOLOGIE MEDITERRANEENNE. ETUDES ET TRAVAUX. (Text in English, French, Gemran, Italian) 1966. irreg., no.17, 1995. $35 per issue. Polska Akademia Nauk, Zaklad Archeologii Srodziemnomorskiej, Palac Kultury i Nauki, p. 2105, 00-901 Warsaw, Poland. TEL 48-22-6248593. FAX 48-22-6207651. (Dist. by: Osrodek Rozpowszechniania Wydawnictw Naukowych PAN - Export, Palac Kultury i Nauki, 00-901 Warsaw, Poland. FAX 48-22-8268670) (Co-sponsor: State Committee for Scientific Research) Ed. Barbara Lichocka. illus. circ. 185. **Document type:** bulletin.
Description: Covers archaeology of the Mediterranean, particularly Egypt, Syria, Cyprus, Nubia.
Refereed Serial

930.1 PL ISSN 0554-5927
ACADEMIE POLONAISE DES SCIENCES. CENTRE D'ARCHEOLOGIE MEDITERRANEENNE. TRAVAUX. (Text in English or French) 1959. irreg., no.33, 1995. $50 per issue. Polska Akademia Nauk, Zaklad Archeologii Srodziemnomorskiej, Palac Kultury i Nauki, p. 2105, 00-901 Warsaw, Poland. TEL 48-22-6248593. FAX 48-22-6207651. (Dist. by: Osrodek Rozpowszechniania Wydawnictw Naukowych PAN - Export, Palac Kultury i Nauki, 00-901 Warsaw, Poland. FAX 48-22-8268670) Ed. Barbara Lichocka. **Document type:** monographic series.
Description: Studies in the archaeology, anthropology and ancient art of the Mediterranean.
Refereed Serial

930.1 UK
ACCORDIA SPECIALIST STUDIES ON ITALY. irreg., no.5, 1996. University of London, Accordia Research Centre, 31-34 Gordon Sq., London WC1H 0PY, England.

913 IT ISSN 0333-1512
ACTA AD ARCHAEOLOGIAM ET ARTIUM HISTORIAM PERTINENTIA (MISCELLANEOUS). (Text in language of contributor) 1981. irreg., vol.8, 1992. price varies. (Istituto di Norvegia in Roma) Giorgio Bretschneider, Via Crescenzo 43, 00193 Rome, Italy. E-mail: bretschneider@euronet.it. **Indexed:** Art & Archaeol.Tech.Abstr., Avery Ind.Archit.Per., RILA. **Document type:** academic/scholarly publication.

913 IT ISSN 0065-0900
N1.A1
ACTA AD ARCHAEOLOGIAM ET ARTIUM HISTORIAM PERTINENTIA (MONOGRAPH). (Text in language of contributor) 1962. irreg., vol.11, 1995. price varies. (Istituto di Norvegia in Roma) Giorgio Bretschneider, Via Crescenzio 43, 00193 Rome, Italy. E-mail: bretschneider@euronet.it. circ. 700. **Indexed:** Art & Archaeol.Tech.Abstr., RILA. **Document type:** monographic series, academic/scholarly publication.

913 SW ISSN 0065-1001
ACTA ARCHAELOGICA LUNDENSIA: MONOGRAPHS OF LUNDS UNIVERSITETS HISTORISKA MUSEUM. SERIES IN 4. (Text in English and German) 1954. irreg. price varies. A W I International AB, P.O. Box 4627, S-116 91 Stockholm, Sweden. TEL 46-8-7282500. FAX 46-8-338707. bk.rev. (back issues avail.) **Indexed:** Anthropol.Lit. **Document type:** monographic series.

571 SW ISSN 0065-0994
ACTA ARCHAEOLOGICA LUNDENSIA: MONOGRAPHS OF LUNDS UNIVERSITETS HISTORISKA MUSEUM. SERIES IN 8. (Text in English, German, Swedish) 1957. irreg. price varies. A W I International AB, P.O. Box 4627, S-116 91 Stockholm, Sweden. TEL 46-8-7282500. FAX 46-8-338707. Ed. Berta Stjernquist. bk.rev. (back issues avail.) **Indexed:** Anthropol.Lit., NAA. **Document type:** monographic series.

930.1 DK ISSN 0065-101X
CC1
ACTA ARCHAEOLOGICA. (Text in English, German) a. DKK 490 in Europe (US, Canada and Japan DKK 510) (effective 1997). Munksgaard International Publishers Ltd., 35 Noerre Soegade, P.O. Box 2148, DK-1016 Copenhagen K, Denmark.
TEL 45-33-127030. FAX 45-33-129387. TELEX 19431-MUNKS-DK. E-mail: fsub@mail.munksgaard.dk. (In N. America: Commerce Place, 350 Main St., Malden, MA 02148-5018. TEL 617-388-8273. FAX 617-388-8274) Ed. Klavs Randsborg. adv.; bk.rev. circ. 650. (reprint service avail. from ISI) **Indexed:** A.I.C.P., Anthropol.Lit., Arts.& Hum.Cit.Ind., Br.Archaeol.Abstr., Curr.Cont., NAA, Numis.Lit., SSCI. **Document type:** academic/scholarly publication.
—CCC.
Refereed Serial

913 PL ISSN 0001-5229
DB350
ACTA ARCHAEOLOGICA CARPATHICA. (Text in English, German, Polish and Russian; summaries in English, French, German and Polish) 1958. a. price varies. Polska Akademia Nauk, Oddzial w Krakowie, Komisja Archeologiczna, Ul. Slawkowska 17, 31-016 Krakow, Poland. TEL 48-12-224853. FAX 48-12-222791. Ed. Zenon Wozniak. bk.rev. **Indexed:** Anthropol.Lit., Br.Archaeol.Abstr., GeoRef., IBR, Numis.Lit. **Document type:** academic/scholarly publication.
—KNAW.
Description: Prehistory and Early Middle Ages of the Carpathian countries, transcarpathian cultural relations, problems of mountain archaeology.

913 PL ISSN 0065-0986
ACTA ARCHAEOLOGICA LODZIENSIA. (Text in Polish; summaries in English and French) 1937. a. $59 (effective 1996 & 1997). Lodzkie Towarzystwo Naukowe - Lodz Scientific Society, Ul. Piotrkowska 179, 90-447 Lodz, Poland. TEL 48-42-361026. FAX 48-42-361995. (Dist. by: Ars Polona, Krakowskie Przedmiescie 7, 00-068 Warsaw, Poland) Ed. Andrzej Abramowicz. bk.rev. **Indexed:** Numis.Lit. **Document type:** monographic series.
—BLDSC (0596.350000); KNAW.

930.1 BE
ACTA ARCHAEOLOGICA LOVANIENSIA - MONOGRAPHIAE. 1962; N.S. 1989. irreg., vol.8, 1996. (Katholieke Universiteit Leuven, Afdeling Archeologie en Kunstwetenschap) Leuven University Press, Blijde Inkomststraat 5, 3000 Leuven, Belgium.
TEL 32-16-325345. FAX 32-16-325352. E-mail: university.press@upers.kuleuven.ac.be; URL: http://www.kuleuven.ac.be/upers. Ed. A. Provoost. bk.rev. circ. 450. (back issues avail.) **Indexed:** Anthropol.Lit., Br.Archaeol.Abstr., Numis.Lit. **Document type:** monographic series.
Formerly: Acta Archaeologica Lovaniensia (ISSN 0776-2984)

913 SZ ISSN 0065-1052
ACTA BERNENSIA: BEITRAEGE ZUR PRAEHISTORISCHEN, KLASSISCHEN UND JUENGEREN ARCHAEOLOGIE. 1963. irreg. price varies. Staempfli AG, Hallerstr. 7-9, CH-3012 Bern, Switzerland.
TEL 41-31-3006666. FAX 41-31-3006688. Eds. H.G. Bandi, H. Mueller-Beck. **Indexed:** Br.Archaeol.Abstr. **Document type:** academic/scholarly publication.
—CCC.

913 940 SP ISSN 0212-2960
ACTA HISTORICA ET ARCHAEOLOGICA MEDIAEVALIA. 1980. a. 2500 ptas. Universidad de Barcelona, Departamento de Historia Medieval, Paleografia y Diplomatica, Facultad de Geografia e Historia, Torre B, Planta 6a, 08028 Barcelona, Spain.
TEL 318-42-66. FAX 449-85-10. (Subscr. to: Universidad de Barcelona, Edificio Central, Avenida Cortes Catalanas, 585, 08007 Barcelona, Spain) Eds. Manuel Riu, Salvador Claramunt. adv.; bk.rev. circ. 1,000.
—CINDOC.

ARCHAEOLOGY

937   DK   ISSN 0904-2067
DE1
ACTA HYPERBOREA. (Text in English) 1988. irreg. $35 (effective 1997). (Collegium Hyperboreum) Museum Tusculanum Press, University of Copenhagen, Njalsgade 92, DK-2300, Copenhagen S, Denmark. TEL 45-35-32-9109. FAX 45-35-32-9113. (Dist. in U.S. and Canada by: Paul & Co., c/o P C S Data Processing, Inc., 360 W. 31st St., New York, NY 10001. TEL 212-564-3730. FAX 212-971-7200) Ed.Bd. illus. **Indexed:** IBR. **Document type:** academic/scholarly publication.
Description: Covers, in thematic issues, important aspects of classical archaeology.

ACTA IRANICA; encyclopedie permanente des etudes iraniennes. see HISTORY — History Of The Near East

913   900 400   SW   ISSN 0347-5123
ACTA REGIAE SOCIETATITIS HUMANIORUM LITTERARUM LUNDENSIS. (Text in English, French, German and Swedish) 1960. irreg. price varies. A W I International AB, P.O. Box 4627, S-116 91 Stockholm, Sweden. TEL 46-8-7282500. FAX 46-8-338707. Ed. Berta Stjernquist.

913   SZ
ACTA REI CRETARIAE ROMANAE FAUTORUM. SUPPLEMENTA. 1974. irreg., vol.7, 1990. 15 SFr. Rei Cretariae Romanae Fautorum, c/o Katrin Roth-Rubi, Lorrainestr. 32, CH-3013 Bern, Switzerland. **Document type:** monographic series.

ACTA UNIVERSITATIS DE ATTILA JOZSEF NOMINATAE. ACTA ANTIQUA ET ARCHAEOLOGICA. see CLASSICAL STUDIES

913 370   PL   ISSN 0208-6034
DK4088
ACTA UNIVERSITATIS LODZIENSIS: FOLIA ARCHAEOLOGICA. (Text in Polish; summaries in various languages) 1955-1974; N.S. 1980. irreg. Wydawnictwo Uniwersytetu Lodzkiego, Ul. Jaracza 34, Lodz, Poland. TEL 336541. (Dist. by: Ars Polona-Ruch, Krakowskie Przedmiescie 7, Warsaw, Poland) Ed.Bd. **Indexed:** Anthropol.Lit. **Document type:** academic/scholarly publication.
—BLDSC (0585.205000); KNAW.
Supersedes in part: Uniwersytet Lodzki. Zeszyty Naukowe. Seria 1: Nauki Humanistyczno-Spoleczne (ISSN 0076-0358)
Description: Presents articles concerning studies on settlement, culture, and the environmental background of settlement development. Studies cover prehistoric times and the Middle Ages, mainly in northern Poland.

913   PL   ISSN 0137-6616
ACTA UNIVERSITATIS NICOLAI COPERNICI. NAUKI HUMANISTYCZNO-SPOLECZNE. ARCHEOLOGIA. 1968. irreg. price varies. Uniwersytet Mikolaja Kopernika, Wydawnictwo, Ul. Gagarina 11, 87-100 Torun, Poland. TEL 48-56-14295. TELEX 21224. (Dist. by Osrodek Rozpowszechniania Wydanictw Naukowych PAN, Palac Kultury i Nauki, 00-901 Warsaw, Poland) **Indexed:** Anthropol.Lit. **Document type:** academic/scholarly publication.
Formerly (until 1973): Uniwersytet Mikolaja Kopernika w Torun. Nauki Humanistyczno-Spoleczne. Zeszyty Naukowe. Archeologia (ISSN 0083-4467)

913   PL   ISSN 0081-6302
GN705
ACTA UNIVERSITATIS WRATISLAVIENSIS. STUDIA ARCHAEOLOGICZNE. (Text in Polish; summaries in English) irreg. price varies. (Uniwersytet Wroclawski) Wydawnictwo Uniwersytetu Wroclawskiego, Spolka z o.o., Pl. Uniwersytecki 9-13, 50-137 Wroclaw, Poland. TEL 48-71-441076. FAX 48-71-402735. Ed. Wlodzimierz Wojciechowski. charts; illus. circ. 300. **Indexed:** Numis.Lit. **Document type:** academic/scholarly publication.
Formerly (until 1965): Uniwersytet Wroclawski im. Boleslawa Bieruta. Zeszyty Naukowe. Seria A: Nauki Humanistyczne (ISSN 0520-9234)

903 930.1   SW   ISSN 0349-8808
ADORANTEN. 1978. a. SEK 40 (effective 1997). Scandinavian Society for Prehistoric Art, Tanums Haellristningsmseum, Underskoes, S-457 91 Tanumshede, Sweden. TEL 46-525-295-55. FAX 46-525-295-55. E-mail: adorant@post5.tele.dk; URL: http://www.ssfpa.se. Ed. Gerard Milstreu. adv.; bk.rev.
Description: Presents articles and information on pre-historic rock carvings, primarily in Scandinavia.

930.1 560   US
ADVANCES IN ARCHAEOLOGICAL AND MUSEUM SCIENCE. 1992. irreg. price varies. (Society for Archaeological Sciences) Plenum Publishing Corp., 233 Spring St., New York, NY 10013-1578. TEL 212-620-8000. FAX 212-463-0742. TELEX 23-421139. E-mail: books@plenum.com. Ed.Bd. (back issues avail.) **Document type:** monographic series.

913   AU   ISSN 1015-5104
DT57
AEGYPTEN UND LEVANTE/EGYPT AND THE LEVANT. 1990. a. S.756. (Universitaet Wien, Institut fuer Aegyptologie) Verlag der Oesterreichischen Akademie der Wissenschaften, Dr. Ignaz-Seipel-Platz 2, A-1010 Vienna, Austria. TEL 43-1-51581401. FAX 43-1-51581400. E-mail: verlag@oeaw.ac.at; URL: http://www.ac.at/einheiten/verlag. (Co-sponsor: Oesterreichisches Archaeologisches Institut Kairo) **Indexed:** IBR. **Document type:** academic/scholarly publication.
Description: Covers archaeological research in Egypt and the Levant.

913   SZ   ISSN 1017-5474
AEGYPTICA HELVETICA. 1974. irreg., latest no.10. price varies. (Universite Geneve, Faculte des Lettres) Editions Medecine et Hygiene, Case Postale 456, CH-1211 Geneva 4, Switzerland. TEL 41-22-7029311. FAX 41-22-7029355. E-mail: abonnements@medecinehygiene.ch. (Co-sponsor: Universitaet Basel) Ed. Robert Hari. circ. 600. **Document type:** monographic series.

AEGYPTOLOGISCHE FORSCHUNGEN. see HISTORY — History Of The Near East

932   IT   ISSN 0001-9046
PA3339
AEGYPTUS; rivista italiana di egittologia e di papirologia. (Text in English, French and German) 1920. s-a. Lit.183000 (foreign Lit.257000($186)) (effective 1997); newsstand price: Lit.113000. (Universita Cattolica del Sacro Cuore) Vita e Pensiero, Largo Gemelli 1, 20123 Milan, Italy. TEL 39-2-72342370. FAX 39-2-72342974. TELEX 321033 UCATMI 1. Ed. Orsolina Montevecchi. adv.; bk.rev.; bibl.; charts; illus.; stat.; cum.index: vols.1-50 (1920-1970). circ. 850. **Indexed:** Bibl.Ling., IBR, M.L.A., New Test.Abstr., Numis.Lit., Old Test.Abstr. **Document type:** academic/scholarly publication.
—KR SourceOne.
Description: Publishes scientific articles on the study of ancient Egypt; its culture, people, history and other related areas.

930.1 770   UK   ISSN 0140-9220
DA670.E13
AERIAL ARCHAEOLOGY. (Text in English; summaries in English, French and German) 1977. irreg. price varies. Aerial Archaeology Publications, Lansdown, 3 Breton Close, Toftwood, E. Dereham, Norfolk NR19 1JH, England. Ed. Derek A. Edwards. bk.rev. **Indexed:** Br.Archaeol.Abstr., Geo.Abstr. **Document type:** academic/scholarly publication.

930.1 526.982   US
▼**THE AERIAL ARCHAEOLOGY NEWSLETTER.** 1996. q. E-mail: jaybird@nmia.com; URL: http://www.nmia.com/~jaybird/AAnewsletter/. Ed. Tom Baker. **Document type:** newsletter.
●Available only online.
Description: Contains discussions of archaeological data gathered from aircraft, satellites, or remote sensors on the ground.

AEVUM ANTIQUUM. see CLASSICAL STUDIES

930.1 960   US   ISSN 0263-0338
DT13   CODEN: AAREF2
AFRICAN ARCHAEOLOGICAL REVIEW. 1983-1994; resumed with vol.13, 1996. q. $125 (foreign $145) (effective 1998). Plenum Publishing Corp., 233 Spring St., New York, NY 10013-1578. TEL 212-620-8000; 800-221-9369. FAX 212-463-0742. TELEX 23-421139. E-mail: info@plenum.com; URL: http://www.infor.com. Ed. Fekri A. Hassan. adv.; bk.rev. (also avail. in microform from UMI; back issues avail.) **Indexed:** Abstr.Anthropol., Anthropol.Lit., Documentatieblad, Ecol.Abstr., Geo.Abstr.H.G. **Document type:** academic/scholarly publication.
—BLDSC (0732.314000); SWETS; UMI; UnCover.
Description: Publishes articles on all aspects of the archaeology of Africa and neighboring islands, including new field data and discussions of interregional processes, cultural transitions, and Africa's place in world archaeology.
Refereed Serial

AFRICAN OCCASIONAL PAPERS SERIES. see ANTHROPOLOGY

AKADEMIYA NAUK GRUZII. IZVESTIYA. SERIYA ISTORII, ETNOGRAFII I ISTORII ISKUSSTVA. see HISTORY — History Of Europe

935.03   BE   ISSN 0772-1331
AKKADICA. (Supplements avail.) (Text in English, Flemish, French) 1977. 5/yr. 1200 BEF (foreign 2250 BEF; N. America $65) (effective 1996). Fondation Assyriologique Georges Dossin - Assyriological Foundation Georges Dossin, Parc du Cinquantenaire 10, 1000 Brussels, Belgium. TEL 32-2-7417373. FAX 32-2-7337735. E-mail: homes@kmkg-mrah.be. (Subscr. in N. America to: Akkadica: David I. Owen, Near Eastern Studies, Rockefeller Hall 360, Cornell University, Ithaca, NY 14853-2502) Ed. L. De Meyer. bk.rev. **Indexed:** Bibl.Ling., IBR. **Document type:** academic/scholarly publication, bulletin, bibliography.

935.03   BE   ISSN 0779-7842
AKKADICA SUPPLEMENTUM. Key Title: Akkadica Plus. (Text in English, French, German) 1984. irreg., vol.9, 1993. price varies. Fondation Assyriologique Georges Dossin - Assyriological Foundation Georges Dossin, Parc du Cinquantenaire 10, 1000 Brussels, Belgium. TEL 32-2-7417373. FAX 32-2-7337735. E-mail: homes@kmkg-mrah.be. (Dist. by: Editions Peeters s.p.r.l., Bondgenotenlaan 153, 3000 Leuven, Belgium. TEL 32-16-235170. FAX 32-16-228500) (back issues avail.) **Document type:** monographic series.

917   US
ALABAMA ARCHAEOLOGICAL SOCIETY. SPECIAL PUBLICATION. 1974. irreg. Alabama Archaeological Society, 13075 Moundville Archaeological Park, Moundville, AL 35474. TEL 205-371-2266. FAX 205-371-2494. Ed. Bart Hanson. circ. 500. (also avail. in microform from UMI; reprint service avail. from UMI) **Document type:** academic/scholarly publication.

913   IT   ISSN 0394-9427
ALBA POMPEIA; rivista semestrale di studi storici artistici e naturalistici per Alba e territori connessi. (Text in Italian; summaries in English, French) 1908. s-a. L.35000($35) (effective 1997). Comune di Alba, Museo Civico "Federico Eusebio", Via Paruzza 1-a, 12051 Alba, Italy. TEL 39-173-290092. FAX 39-173-362075. E-mail: bibto046@itocsivm.csi.it. Ed. Gianfranco Maggi. bk.rev.; bibl.; cum.index: 1908-1989; circ. 500 (controlled). (back issues avail.) **Document type:** bulletin.

913 572   CN   ISSN 0701-1776
F1076.9
ALBERTA ARCHAEOLOGICAL REVIEW. 1977. s-a. Can.$12. Archaeological Society of Alberta, c/o Department of Geography, University of Lethbridge, 4401 University Drive, Lethbridge, Alta. T1K 3M4, Canada. TEL 403-329-2524. Ed. M.C. Wilson. adv.; bk.rev. circ. 400. **Indexed:** A.I.C.P., Amer.Hist.& Life (1985-1988), Anthropol.Lit., Hist.Abstr. (1985-1988).
Supersedes: Archaeological Society of Alberta. Newsletter.

ARCHAEOLOGY 347

913 US ISSN 0002-4953
ALBUQUERQUE ARCHAEOLOGICAL SOCIETY NEWSLETTER. 1966. m. $15 to individuals; institutions $18; families $20. Albuquerque Archaeological Society, Box 4029, Albuquerque, NM 87196. Ed. Kay Adams. bk.rev.; bibl.; illus. circ. 275. (processed) **Document type:** newsletter.
  Description: Covers current activities of AAS and feature articles of interest.

917 US ISSN 0894-2625
ALEXANDRIA ARCHAEOLOGY VOLUNTEER NEWS. 1982. m. $20. Friends of Alexandria Archeology, 105 N. Union St., Alexandria, VA 22314. TEL 703-838-4399. (Subscr. to: Box 21475, Alexandria, VA 22320) bk.rev.; illus. circ. 500. **Document type:** newsletter.
  Description: Covers the urban archaeology program of Alexandria, VA, including volunteer opportunities, current digs, local seminars and field trips, and local history.

932 PL ISSN 0138-0486
ALEXANDRIE. (Text in English, French) 1976. irreg., no.6, 1992. $39 per issue. Polska Akademia Nauk, Zaklad Archeologii Srodziemnomorskiej, Palac Kultury i Nauki, p. 2105, 00-901 Warsaw, Poland. TEL 48-22-6248593. FAX 48-22-6207651. (Dist. by: Osrodek Rozpowszechniania Wydawnictw Naukowych PAN - Export, Palac Kultury i Nauki, 00-901 Warsaw, Poland. FAX 48-22-8268670) (Co-sponsor: State Committee for Scientific Research) Ed. Zsolt Kiss. illus. circ. 100. (back issues avail.) **Document type:** monographic series.
  Description: Presents excavation results of the Polish Archaeological Mission at Alexandria, Egypt.
  Refereed Serial

ALGONQUIAN CONFERENCE. PAPERS. see *ANTHROPOLOGY*

ALLE TIDERS ODSHERRED. see *HISTORY — History Of Europe*

AMALTHEIA. see *HISTORY — History Of Europe*

913 US ISSN 0002-7316
E51 CODEN: AANTAM
AMERICAN ANTIQUITY. 1935. q. $175 (includes: S A A Bulletin) (effective 1997-1998). Society for American Archaeology, 900 Second St., N.W., No. 12, Washington, DC 20002-3557. TEL 202-789-8200. FAX 202-789-0284. E-mail: publications@saa.org; URL: http://www.saa.org/Publications/AmAntiq/amantiq.html. Ed. Lynne Goldstein. adv.; bk.rev.; charts; illus.; index, cum.index. circ. 5,700. (also avail. in microform; back issues avail.; reprint service avail. from KTO, UMI) **Indexed:** A.I.C.P., Abstr.Anthropol., Amer.Hist.& Life (1969-1971), (1982-), Anthropol.Lit., Art Ind., Arts & Hum.Cit.Ind., ASCA, Bk.Rev.Ind. (1980-), Br.Archaeol.Abstr., Ceram.Abstr., Chem.Abstr., Child.Bk.Rev.Ind. (1980-), Curr.Cont., GeoRef., Hisp.Amer.Per.Ind. (1970-1992), Hist.Abstr. (1969-1971), (1982-), Hist.Abstr., Hum.Ind., Hum.Ind., IBR, Intl.Bibl.S.S.Soc.Cult.Anthro., Mid.East: Abstr.& Ind., Sportsearch, SSCI. **Document type:** academic/scholarly publication.
  ●Also available online. Vendor(s): Information Access Co.
  —BLDSC (0810.300000); Genuine Article; KR SourceOne; SWETS; UMI; UnCover. CCC.
  Description: Publishes original articles on the archaeology of the New World and related topics, along with research reports and commentary.
  Refereed Serial

930.1 US ISSN 1093-8400
AMERICAN ARCHAEOLOGY. 1980. q. $25. Archaeological Conservancy, 5301 Central Ave., N.E., Ste. 1218, Albuquerque, NM 87108-1517. TEL 505-266-1540. FAX 505-266-0311. E-mail: 104017.3526@compuserve.com. Ed. Rob Crisell. R&P contact: Erika Olsson. TEL 505-266-9668. adv. contact: Carrie Baikie. bk.rev. circ. 13,000. (back issues avail.) **Document type:** consumer publication.
  Formerly (until 1997): Archaeological Conservancy Newsletter.
  Description: Devoted to presenting the rich diversity of archaeology in the Americas. Helps readers understand and appreciate the achaeological wonders available to them.
  Refereed Serial

913 US
AMERICAN BOTTOM ARCHAEOLOGY. irreg. University of Illinois Press, 1325 S. Oak St., Champaign, IL 61820. TEL 217-333-0950. FAX 217-244-8082. **Indexed:** Anthropol.Lit. **Document type:** academic/scholarly publication.
  Refereed Serial

913 US ISSN 0002-9114
CC1
AMERICAN JOURNAL OF ARCHAEOLOGY. 1885. q. $60 to individuals (foreign $80); institutions $120 (foreign $140). Archaeological Institute of America (Boston), c/o Fred S. Kleiner, Ed., 656 Beacon St., Boston, MA 02215. TEL 617-353-9364. FAX 617-353-6550. E-mail: AJA@BU.EDU; URL: http://classics.lsa.umich.edu/AJA.html. bk.rev.; charts; illus.; index. circ. 3,600. (also avail. in microfilm from UMI,PMC; back issues avail.) **Indexed:** A.I.C.P., Amer.Bibl.Slavic & E.Eur.Stud., Anthropol.Lit., Art Ind., Arts & Hum.Cit.Ind., ASCA, Avery Ind.Archit.Per., Bibl.Ling., Bk.Rev.Dig., Bk.Rev.Ind. (1965-), Br.Archaeol.Abstr., Chem.Abstr., Child.Bk.Rev.Ind. (1965-), Curr.Cont., Hum.Ind., IBR, Mid.East: Abstr.& Ind., New Test.Abstr., Numis.Lit., Old Test.Abstr., Rel.Ind.One, SSCI. **Document type:** academic/scholarly publication.
  —BLDSC (0821.200000); KR SourceOne; SWETS; UMI; UnCover.
  Description: Scholarly essays on archaeology of ancient Europe and the Mediterranean from prehistoric times to the Late Antique.

916 706 US ISSN 0065-9991
DT57
AMERICAN RESEARCH CENTER IN EGYPT. JOURNAL. 1962. a. $20. J.J. Augustin, Inc., Box 311, Locust Valley, NY 11560. TEL 516-676-1510. Ed. Gerald E. Kadish. bk.rev. circ. 800. **Indexed:** Art & Archaeol.Tech.Abstr., Bibl.Ling. **Document type:** academic/scholarly publication.
  —BLDSC (4692.200000); SWETS; UnCover.

913 US ISSN 0732-6432
AMERICAN RESEARCH CENTER IN EGYPT. REPORTS. 1980. irreg., no.12, 1990. price varies. (American Research Center in Egypt, Inc.) Eisenbrauns, Box 275, Winona Lake, IN 46590. TEL 219-269-2011. FAX 219-269-6788. URL: http://www.cisenbrauns.com. Ed. John L. Foster. bk.rev.; bibl.; illus.; charts. (back issues avail.) **Indexed:** Math.R. **Document type:** academic/scholarly publication.
  —BLDSC (7373.285000).
  Refereed Serial

930.1 572 US ISSN 0066-0027
GN700
AMERICAN SCHOOL OF PREHISTORIC RESEARCH. BULLETINS. (Vols. not issued consecutively) 1936. irreg., no.43, 1997. price varies. Peabody Museum of Archaeology and Ethnology, Harvard University, 11 Divinity Ave., Cambridge, MA 02138. TEL 617-495-3938. FAX 617-495-7535. (Dist. by: University Museum Publications, University of Pennsylvania, 33rd & Spruce Sts. Philadelphia, PA 19104. TEL 215-898-4124) Ed. Margaret R. Courtney. R&P contact: Donna M. Dickerson. **Indexed:** Biol.Abstr., Mid.East: Abstr.& Ind. **Document type:** bulletin, monographic series.

AMERICAN SCHOOLS OF ORIENTAL RESEARCH. ANNUAL. see *HISTORY — History Of The Near East*

AMERICAN SCHOOLS OF ORIENTAL RESEARCH. NEWSLETTER. see *ORIENTAL STUDIES*

917 US
AMERICAN SOCIETY FOR CONSERVATION ARCHAEOLOGY. PROCEEDINGS.* 1976. a. $10. American Society for Conservation Archaeology, c/o Joel I. Klein, Ed., 118 Old Post Rd. N., Croton on Hudson, NY 10520-1934. bk.rev. circ. 450. **Indexed:** Anthropol.Lit. **Document type:** proceedings.

913 US ISSN 0748-5107
AMERICAN SOCIETY FOR CONSERVATION ARCHAEOLOGY REPORT. 1974. s-a. $20 to individuals; institutions $25. American Society for Conservation Archaeology, A C A Sta. No. 9, Eastern New Mexico University, Portales, NM 88130. FAX 505-562-2578. Ed. John Montgomery. bk.rev. circ. 450. **Indexed:** Anthropol.Lit.
  Formerly: American Society for Conservation Archaeology Newsletter.

913 US ISSN 0003-1186
AS36.A497
AMERICAN SOCIETY OF PAPYROLOGISTS. BULLETIN. q. $35 (foreign $40) (effective 1998). Scholars Press, Box 15399, Atlanta, GA 30333-0399. TEL 404-727-2320; 888-747-2354. FAX 404-727-2348. E-mail: scholars@emory.edu. Ed. J.G. Keenen. R&P contact: Dennis Ford. (back issues avail.) **Indexed:** Art & Archaeol.Tech.Abstr., Arts & Hum.Cit.Ind., ASCA, Bibl.Ling., Curr.Cont. **Document type:** bulletin.
  —SWETS; UnCover.
  Description: Papers on the study of papyrology.

AMSTERDAM STUDIES IN CLASSICAL PHILOLOGY. see *LINGUISTICS*

930.1 FR
▼**AMURRU.** 1996. irreg. price varies. Editions Recherche sur les Civilisations, 28 rue de Bourgogne, 75007 Paris, France. TEL 33-1-40628062. FAX 33-1-40628071. Ed. Hina Descat; Pub. Hina Descat. circ. 600. **Document type:** monographic series.

918 572 AG ISSN 0325-0288
ANALES DE ARQUEOLOGIA Y ETNOLOGIA. 1940. a. exchange basis. Universidad Nacional de Cuyo, Instituto de Arqueologia y Etnologia, Casilla Correo 345, Mendoza, Argentina. TEL 54-61-253010. FAX 54-61-380457. Ed. Olga Rodriguez de Moyano. bk.rev. circ. 500. **Indexed:** A.I.C.P., Amer.Hist.& Life, Anthropol.Lit., Hist.Abstr. **Document type:** academic/scholarly publication.
  Former titles (until 1946): Anales del Instituto de Etnologia Americana; (until 1944): Anales del Instituto de Etnografia Americana.

939.561 UK ISSN 1362-3567
DR431
ANATOLIAN ARCHAEOLOGY. (Related title: Anatolian Archaeology (ISSN 0066-1546)) 1996. a. £37 (includes subscr. to Anatolian Studies). British Institute of Archaeology at Ankara, 31-34 Gordon Sq., London WCiH OPY, England. TEL 44-171-388-2361. FAX 44-1171-388-2361. Ed. Gina Coulthard.
  Description: Reports on recent British archaeological research in Turkey.

939.561 UK ISSN 0066-1546
DS56
ANATOLIAN STUDIES. (Related title: Anatolian Archaeology (ISSN 1362-3567)) 1951. a. £27.75 (includes subscr. to Anatolian Archaeology) (effective 1997). British Institute of Archaeology at Ankara, TU , 31-34 Gordon Sq., London WC1H 0PY, England. TEL 44-171-388-2361. FAX 44-171-388-2361. Ed. Prof. O.R. Gurney. index; circ. 900 (paid). **Indexed:** Anthropol.Lit., Art & Archaeol.Tech.Abstr., Avery Ind.Archit.Per., Bibl.Ling., Br.Hum.Ind., IBR, Numis.Lit. **Document type:** academic/scholarly publication.
  ●Also available online.
  —UnCover.
  Description: Contains academic archaeological studies.

ANATOLICA; annuaire internationale pour les civilisations de l'Asie anterieure. see *HISTORY — History Of Asia*

915.49 CE ISSN 0258-9257
ANCIENT CEYLON. (Text in English) 1971. irreg. price varies. Archaeological Survey Department, Sir Marcus Fernando Rd., Colombo 7, Sri Lanka. FAX 0094-1-696250. bk.rev.; illus. **Indexed:** A.I.C.P.

ANCIENT MONUMENTS SOCIETY TRANSACTIONS. see *ARCHITECTURE*

ANCIENT NEPAL. see *ORIENTAL STUDIES*

913 FR ISSN 0735-1348
ANCIENT T L. 1979. 3/yr. 130 F. to individuals; institutions 180 F. (includes a. supplement) (effective 1997). Laboratoire de Physique Copusculaire, 63177 Aubiere Cedex, France. TEL 33-4-73407289. FAX 33-4-73264598. E-mail: anctl@admin.in2p3.fr. Ed. Didier Miallier. adv. circ. 120. **Document type:** academic/scholarly publication.
  —BLDSC (0900.326100).
  Description: Covers research and information on the application of luminescence and electron spin resonance techniques to dating archaeological and geological materials.
  Refereed Serial

ARCHAEOLOGY

ANCIENT WORLD; a scholarly journal for the study of antiquity. see HISTORY

930.1   US   ISSN 1055-8756
F2229
ANDEAN PAST. 1987. a. $22.50 (foreign $24). Cornell University, Latin American Studies Program, Ithaca, NY 14853. TEL 607-255-2245. FAX 607-255-8919. E-mail: daniels@maine.maine.edu. (Edit. addr.: Daniel H. Sandweiss, Dept. of Anthropology, Univ. of Maine, S. Stevens Hall, Orono, ME 04469-5773. TEL 207-581-1889. FAX 207-581-1203) Eds. Daniel H. Sandweiss, Monica Barnes. circ. 250 (paid); 50 (controlled). **Indexed:** Anthropol.Lit., IBR. **Document type:** academic/scholarly publication.
   Description: Publishes original research on the prehistory and ethnohistory of South America.
   Refereed Serial

913   II
ANDHRA PRADESH, INDIA. DEPARTMENT OF ARCHAEOLOGY AND MUSEUMS. ANNUAL REPORT. (Text in English) irreg. price varies. Department of Archaeology and Museums, Hyderabad, 500 001, Andhra Pradesh, India.

700 913   II
ANDHRA PRADESH, INDIA. DEPARTMENT OF ARCHAEOLOGY AND MUSEUMS. ARCHAEOLOGICAL SERIES. (Text in English) irreg. price varies. Department of Archaeology and Museums, Hyderabad 500001, Andhra Pradesh, India. (Or: Publications Bureau, Directorate of Government Printing, Chanchalguda, Hyderabad, Andhra Pradesh, India) **Document type:** monographic series.
   Formerly: Andhra Pradesh, India. Department of Archaeology and Museums. Art and Architectural Series.

913   II
ANDHRA PRADESH, INDIA. DEPARTMENT OF ARCHAEOLOGY AND MUSEUMS. ARCHAEOLOGICAL SERIES: A.P. JOURNAL OF ARCHAEOLOGY. (Text in English) 1978. irreg. price varies. Department of Archaeology and Museums, Gunfoundry, Hyderabad 500 001, Andhra Pradesh, India. circ. 500. **Indexed:** Anthropol.Lit.

571 954   II
ANDHRA PRADESH, INDIA. DEPARTMENT OF ARCHAEOLOGY AND MUSEUMS. EPIGRAPHY SERIES. (Text in English) 1967. irreg., no.11, 1976. price varies. Department of Archaeology and Museums, Hyderabad 500001, Andhra Pradesh, India. (Or: Publication Bureau, Directorate of Government Printing, Chanchalguda, Hyderabad, Andhra Pradesh, India) **Document type:** monographic series.
   Formerly: Andhra Pradesh, India. Department of Archaeology. Epigraphy Series (ISSN 0066-1651)

914   SP   ISSN 0561-3663
ANEJOS DE ARCHIVO ESPANOL DE ARQUEOLOGIA. 1951. irreg. price varies. Consejo Superior de Investigaciones Cientificas (C.S.I.C.), Instituto Espanol de Arqueologia, Vitruvio, 8, 28006 Madrid, Spain. illus.

914.2   UK   ISSN 0306-5790
DA740.A5
ANGLESEY ANTIQUARIAN SOCIETY TRANSACTIONS. (Text in English and Welsh) 1913. a. £4. Anglesey Antiquarian Society and Field Club, c/o Hon. Secretary, 1 Fronheulog, Tregarth, Bangor, Gwynedd, Wales. Ed. A.D. Carr. bk.rev.; charts; illus. circ. 1,000. (tabloid format) **Indexed:** Br.Archaeol.Abstr.
—BLDSC (8899.900000).

913   FR   ISSN 0003-4398
DC607.1
ANNALES DU MIDI; revue de la France Meridionale. 1889. q. 500 F. (effective 1997). Editions Edouard Privat, 14 rue des Arts, B.P. 828, 31080 Toulouse Cedex, France. TEL 33-5-61110320. FAX 33-5-61137441. (Subscr. to: Interconnexion Annales du Midi - Service Abonnements, B.P. 44, 31150 Fenouillet, France. TEL 33-5-61371666) Dirs. Jean-Bernard Marquette, Michel Taillefert. bk.rev.; ibid.; charts; illus.; index, cum.index: 1919-1958. (tabloid format; back issues avail.) **Indexed:** Amer.Hist.& Life (1967-), Hist.Abstr., IBR, M.L.A., MLA Intl.Bibl.
—SWETS.

913   IT
ANNALI BENACENSI; rassegna di studi paletnologici ed archeologici. 1974. a. L.30000($28) Gruppo Archeologico Cavriana, Museo Archeologico dell'Alto Mantovano, Piazza Castello N.5, 46040 Cavriana (MN), Italy. Ed. Adalberto Piccoli. **Document type:** academic/scholarly publication.

913   HU   ISSN 0238-0218
DB920
ANTAEUS; communicationes ex Instituto Archaeologico Academiae Scientiarum. (Text in English, German) 1970. a. exchange basis. Magyar Tudomanyos Akademia, Regeszeti Intezet - Hungarian Academy of Sciences, Archaeological Institute, Uri utca 49, 1250 Budapest, Hungary. FAX 36-1-1564567. Ed. Laszlo Torok. **Indexed:** A.I.C.P., Hum.Ind. **Document type:** academic/scholarly publication, monographic series.
   Formerly (until 1986): Ungarische Akademie der Wissenschaften. Archaelogisches Institut. Mitteilungen (ISSN 0133-6924)

ANTHROPOLOGICA. see ANTHROPOLOGY

ANTHROPOLOGIE ET PREHISTOIRE. see ANTHROPOLOGY

913   GR   ISSN 0253-5092
ANTHROPOLOGIKA. 1980. 3/yr. $150. Paratiritis S.A., 15, Al. Stavrou Str., 54644 Thessaloniki, Greece. Ed. G. Hourmouziades. adv.; bk.rev. circ. 1,500.

ANTHROPOLOGY AND ARCHEOLOGY OF EURASIA; a journal of translations from Soviet sources. see ANTHROPOLOGY

709   SZ   ISSN 0003-5688
N5320
ANTIKE KUNST. (Text in English, French, German, Italian) 1958. s-a. 88 SFr. Vereinigung der Freunde Antiker Kunst, c/o Archaeologisches Seminar der Universitaet, Schoenbeinstr. 20, CH-4056 Basel, Switzerland. Ed.Bd. adv.; illus.; index. circ. 1,150. **Indexed:** Art Ind., Avery Ind.Archit.Per., IBR, Numis.Lit. **Document type:** academic/scholarly publication.
—KR SourceOne; SWETS; UnCover.

700   SZ   ISSN 0066-4782
ANTIKE KUNST. BEIHEFTE. (Text in English, French or German) 1963. irreg., vol.17, 1993. price varies. Vereinigung der Freunde Antiker Kunst, c/o Archaeologisches Seminar der Universitaet, Schoenbeinstr. 20, CH-4056 Basel, Switzerland. Ed. Kristine Gex. circ. 550. **Document type:** academic/scholarly publication.

905   GW   ISSN 0003-570X
CB311
ANTIKE WELT; Zeitschrift fuer Archaeologie und Kulturgeschichte. (Supplement avail.: Antike Welt. Sondernummer (ISSN 1015-9274)) 1970. 6/yr. DM.106. Verlag Philipp von Zabern GmbH, Philipp-von-Zabern-Platz 1-3, 55116 Mainz, Germany. TEL 06131-28747-0. FAX 06131-223710. Ed. Arthur Golfetto. adv.; bk.rev. circ. 11,000. **Indexed:** Art & Archaeol.Tech.Abstr., Art Ind., Br.Archaeol.Abstr., IBR. **Document type:** academic/scholarly publication.
—KR SourceOne.

913   UK   ISSN 0003-5815
DA20
ANTIQUARIES JOURNAL. 1921. a. £48($84) Society of Antiquaries of London, Burlington House, London WC1V 0HS, England. bk.rev.; bibl.; illus.; maps; index. (also avail. in microform from UMI; microfiche from IDC) **Indexed:** A.I.C.P., Abstr.Anthropol., Amer.Hist.& Life (1990-1996), Anthropol.Lit., Art & Archaeol.Tech.Abstr., Avery Ind.Archit.Per., Bk.Rev.Ind. (1967-), Br.Archaeol.Abstr., Br.Hum.Ind., Curr.Cont., Geo.Abstr., Hist.Abstr. (1990-1996), IBR, NAA, Numis.Lit., RILA, SSCI. **Document type:** academic/scholarly publication.
—BLDSC (1550.000000); SWETS; UMI; UnCover. CCC.
   Formerly: Society of Antiquaries. Proceedings.
   Description: International journal of record within archaeology, reporting specialist work to the wider readership and larger issues that concern every archaeologist.

ANTIQUITAS. REIHE 3. ABHANDLUNGEN ZUR VOR- UND FRUEHGESCHICHTE, ZUR KLASSISCHEN UND PROVINZIAL-ROEMISCHEN ARCHAEOLOGIE UND ZUR GESCHICHTE DES ALTERTUMS. see HISTORY

940.1   BE   ISSN 1250-7334
ANTIQUITE TARDIVE; revue internationale d'histoire et d'archeologie. (Text in French) 1993. a. 2000 BEF (effective 1998). (Association pour l'Antiquite Tardive) N.V. Brepols, Steenweg op Tielen 68, 2300 Turnhout, Belgium. TEL 32-14-402500. FAX 32-14-428919. (In France: Editions Brepols, 23 rue des Grands Augustins, 75006, Paris, France. TEL 1-44412000. FAX 1-43262377) (back issues avail.) **Document type:** academic/scholarly publication.
   Description: Publishes original multidisciplinary contributions on the arts, history, archaeology, epigraphy, law and philosophy of late antiquity, covering the 4th through 8th centuries.

ANTIQUITES AFRICAINES. see HISTORY — History Of Africa

913   UK   ISSN 0003-598X
CC1   CODEN: ATQYAF
ANTIQUITY; a periodical review of archaeology. 1927. q. £58($106) (effective 1996). (Antiquity Trust) Company of Biologists Ltd., Bidder Bldg., 140 Cowley Rd., Cambridge CB4 4DL. TEL 44-1223-426164. FAX 44-1223-423353. E-mail: cob@cambridge.cityscape.co.uk; URL: http://www.cityscape.co.uk/users/ag64; http://intarch.ac.uk/antiquity. Ed. Christopher Chippindale. adv.; bk.rev.; bibl.; charts; illus.; maps; index, cum.index: vols.1-50. (also avail. in microform from UMI,MIM; microfiche from IDC) **Indexed:** A.I.C.P., Abstr.Anthropol., Acad.Ind., Anthropol.Lit., Art & Archaeol.Tech.Abstr., Art Ind., Arts & Hum.Cit.Ind., ASCA, Avery Ind.Archit.Per., Bibl.Ling., Br.Hum.Ind., Curr.Cont., Ecol.Abstr., Geo.Abstr.H.G., Geol.Abstr., GeoRef., Hum.Ind., IBR, M.L.A., Mid.East: Abstr.& Ind., NAA, Numis.Lit., SSCI. **Document type:** academic/scholarly publication.
● Also available online. Vendor(s): Information Access Co.
—BLDSC (1551.000000); Genuine Article; KR SourceOne; SWETS; UMI; UnCover. **CCC.**
   Description: Reports on specialist work in archaeology.

ANZEIGER FUER DIE ALTERTUMSWISSENSCHAFT. see CLASSICAL STUDIES

930.1   GT
APUNTES ARQUEOLOGICOS. 1991. s-a.? Universidad de San Carlos de Guatemala, Escuela de Historia, Area de Arqueologia, Ciudad Universitaria, zona 12, Edificio de Rectoria, Of. 307, Guatemala, Guatemala. **Document type:** academic/scholarly publication.

913   IT   ISSN 0391-7304
AQUILEIA NOSTRA. 1930. a. L.50000. Associazione Nazionale per Aquileia, Casa Bertoli, Via Popone 6, 33051 Aquileia (UD), Italy. TEL 39-431-91113. index. circ. 750. (back issues avail.)

930.1   DK   ISSN 0905-7196
DS211   CODEN: AAEPE3
ARABIAN ARCHAEOLOGY AND EPIGRAPHY. (Text in English) 1990. s-a. DKK 790 to individuals in Europe (US, Canada and Japan DKK 820); institutions DKK 1790 (US, Canada and Japan DKK 1820) (effective 1997). Munksgaard International Publishers Ltd., 35 Noerre Soegade, P.O. Box 2148, DK-1016 Copenhagen K, Denmark. TEL 45-33-127030. FAX 45-33-129387. E-mail: fsub@mail.munksgaard.dk; URL: http://www.munksgaard.dk/. (In N. America: Commerce Place, 350 Main St., Malden, MA 02148-5018. TEL 617-388-8273. FAX 617-388-8274) Ed. Daniel T. Potts. adv.; charts; illus. circ. 300. (reprint service avail.) **Indexed:** Anthropol.Lit., Arts & Hum.Cit.Ind., ASCA, ASCA, Bibl.Ling., Curr.Cont., Geo.Abstr.H.G., Geo.Abstr.P.G., Per.Islam. (1994-), SSCI. **Document type:** academic/scholarly publication.
—Genuine Article. **CCC.**
   Refereed Serial

930.1   TU   ISSN 1017-7663
ARASTIRMA SONUCLARI TOPLANTISI. (Text in Turkish, occasionally in English, German) 198. a. exchange basis. Ministry of Culture, General Directorate of Monuments and Museums - Kultur Bakanligi, Anitlar ve Muzeler Genel Mudurlugu, 06100 Ulus - Ankara, Turkey. TEL 90-312-3104960. FAX 90-312-3111417. **Document type:** academic/scholarly publication.
   Description: Publishes papers on archaeological and epigraphical research at sites in Turkey.

ARCHAEOLOGY 349

913 730 GW ISSN 0066-5738
N8555
ARBEITSBLAETTER FUER RESTAURATOREN. 1968. 2/yr. DM.44 (foreign DM.45.50) (effective 1997 & 1998). Roemisch-Germanisches Zentralmuseum, Forschungsinstitut fuer Vor- und Fruehgeschichte, Ernst-Ludwig-Platz 2, 55116 Mainz, Germany. TEL 49-6131-9124-0. FAX 49-6131-9124199. Indexed: Art & Archaeol.Tech.Abstr., RILM. Document type: academic/scholarly publication.

913.031 GW ISSN 0177-4840
CC5
ARCHAEOLOGICA VENATORIA. MITTEILUNGSBLATT. 1981. irreg. (1-2/yr.). membership. Archaeologica Venatoria e.V., c/o Institut fuer Urgeschichte, 72074 Tuebingen, Germany. TEL 07071-292416. FAX 07071-294995. bk.rev. circ. 350. (back issues avail.)
Description: Reports on the activities of the Institute for Prehistory.

913 GW ISSN 0066-5886
ARCHAEO-PHYSIKA. 1965. irreg., vol.13, 1993. price varies. Rheinland Verlag GmbH, Abtei Brauweiler, Postfach 2140, 50250 Pulheim, Germany. TEL 49-2234-9854265. FAX 49-2234-82503. (Dist. by: Dr. Rudolf Habelt GmbH, Am Buchenhang 1, 53115 Bonn, Germany) Indexed: Br.Archaeol.Abstr., Geo.Abstr., NAA. Document type: monographic series.
—BLDSC (1595.151000).

913 520 US ISSN 0190-9940
E59.A8
ARCHAEOASTRONOMY. 1977. a. (plus q. newsletter). $36 to individuals (foreign $42); institutions and libraries $60 (foreign $66) includes subscr. to Archaeoastronomy & Ethnoastronomy News. Center for Archaeoastronomy, Box X, College Park, MD 20740-1024. TEL 301-864-6637. Ed. John B. Carlson. adv.; bk.rev. circ. 1,300. (back issues avail.) Indexed: Anthropol.Lit., Br.Archaeol.Abstr., Math.R.
—CISTI; Linda Hall.
Formerly (until 1982): Archaeoastronomy Bulletin (ISSN 0272-5436)
Refereed Serial

ARCHAEOASTRONOMY. see ASTRONOMY

913 520 US ISSN 1062-189X
E59.A8
ARCHAEOASTRONOMY & ETHNOASTRONOMY NEWS. q. $36 to individuals (foreign $42); institutions $60 (foreign $66) includes subscr. to Archaeoastronomy. University of Maryland, Center for Archaeoastronomy, Box X, College Park, MD 20740. TEL 301-864-6637. Document type: newsletter.

913 709 929 745.1 UK ISSN 0261-3409
DA20
ARCHAEOLOGIA. 1770. irreg. £25. Society of Antiquaries of London, Burlington House, London W1V OHS, England. FAX 44-171-287-6967. Ed. Elizabeth Nichols. circ. 2,000. (also avail. in microfilm from UMI; microfiche from IDC; reprint service avail. from UMI) Indexed: A.I.C.P., Art & Archaeol.Tech.Abstr., Br.Archaeol.Abstr., Br.Hum.Ind., Numis.Lit., RILA. Document type: academic/scholarly publication.
—KR SourceOne; UMI.
Description: Articles concerned with antiquarian interests.
Refereed Serial

ARCHAEOLOGIA AELIANA. see HISTORY — History Of Europe

913 943.6 571 AU ISSN 0003-8008
DB1
ARCHAEOLOGIA AUSTRIACA; Beitraege zur Palaeontologie, Ur- und Fruehgeschichte Oesterreichs. (Supplements avail.) 1947. a. (Universitaet Wien, Institut fuer Ur- und Fruehgeschichte) Franz Deuticke Verlag GmbH, Schwarzenbergstr. 5, A-1010 Vienna, Austria. TEL 0222-51405-0. Ed Herwig Friesinger. bk.rev.; bibl.; charts; illus.; cum.index circ. 400. (back issues avail.) Indexed: A.I.C.P., Anthropol.Lit., Br.Archaeol.Abstr., Chem.Abstr., IBR. Document type: academic/scholarly publication.

571 UK ISSN 0066-5894
DA670.K2
ARCHAEOLOGIA CANTIANA. 1858. a. £15 to individuals; institutions £25. Kent Archaeological Society, Dunelm House, Main Rd., Icklesham, Winchelsea, E. Sussex TN36 4AR, England. Ed. A.P. Detsicas. adv.; bk.rev.; index, cum.index. circ. 1,750. Indexed: Avery Ind.Archit.Per., Br.Archaeol.Abstr., Br.Hum.Ind., Numis.Lit. Document type: academic/scholarly publication.
—BLDSC (1594.630000).
Description: Covers archeology and history of Kent.

913 XR ISSN 0231-5823
ARCHAEOLOGIA HISTORICA. 1976. a. Muzejni a Vlastivedna Solecnost, Koblizna 1, 659 37 Brno, Czech Republic. (Subscr. to: Buchexport-Import, Kubon u. Sagner, Box 340108, D-8000 Munich, Germany) Ed. Vladimir Nekuda. bk.rev.; illus. circ. 1,500. Indexed: A.I.C.P. Document type: academic/scholarly publication.

560 JA ISSN 0402-852X
ARCHAEOLOGIA JAPONICA. (Text in Japanese; summaries in English) 1948. a. 6180 Yen. Japanese Archaeological Association - Nihon Kokogaku Kyokai, 5-15-5 Hirai, Edogawa-ku, Tokyo J-132, Japan. TEL 81-3-3618-6608. FAX 81-3-3618-6625. Ed. Iwasaki Takuya. circ. 3,850. Document type: academic/scholarly publication.
Refereed Serial

930.1 BE ISSN 0775-3314
ARCHAEOLOGIA TRANSATLANTICA. 1981. irreg., no.14, 1996. price varies. Association des Diplomes Histoire Art et Archeologie, Centre d'Archeologie Grecque, College Erasme, Place Blaise Pascal 1, 1348 Louvain-la-Neuve, Belgium. FAX 32-10-472579. E-mail: hackens@arka.ucl.ac.be. (U.S. addr.: Box 1837, Providence, RI 02912) (Co-sponsor: Brown University, Center for Old World Archaeology and Art) Ed. Tony Hackens. Document type: monographic series.

930.1 ZA ISSN 0570-6068
ARCHAEOLOGIA ZAMBIANA. (Text in English) no.14, 1971. irreg., latest no.23. National Heritage Conservation Commission, P.O. Box 60124, Livingstone, Zambia. TEL 260-320354. FAX 260-324509. Ed. Maxwell Zulu. R&P contact: Maxwell Zulu. adv. contact: Maxwell Zulu. Indexed: Anthropol.Lit. Document type: academic/scholarly publication.

913 HU ISSN 0003-8032
DB920
ARCHAEOLOGIAI ERTESITO/ARCHAEOLOGICAL BULLETIN. (Text in Hungarian; summaries in English, French, German or Russian) 1869. s-a. $48 (effective 1998). (Magyar Tudomanyos Akademia) Akademiai Kiado Rt., P.O. Box 245, H-1519 Budapest, Hungary. TEL 36-1-2043976. FAX 36-1-2043973. Ed. Istvan Fodor. adv.; bk.rev.; illus.; index. Indexed: A.I.C.P., Anthropol.Lit., Avery Ind.Archit.Per., IBR. Document type: academic/scholarly publication.

ARCHAEOLOGICAL COMPLETION REPORT SERIES. see HISTORY — History Of North And South America

930.1 NE ISSN 1380-2038
ARCHAEOLOGICAL DIALOGUES; Dutch perspectives on current issues in archaeology. (Text in English) 1994. s-a. fl.100 (effective 1994). (Archaeological Dialogues Foundation) Van Gorcum en Co. B.V., P.O. Box 43, 9400 AA Assen, Netherlands. TEL 31-5920-46846. FAX 31-5920-72064. Ed.Bd. (back issues avail.) Document type: academic/scholarly publication.
—BLDSC (1594.715000).
Description: Promotes theoretically oriented approaches which go beyond traditional archaeological issues and consider historical, social and philosophical perspectives.

930.1 AT
ARCHAEOLOGICAL DIGGINGS. bi-m. Aus.$30 (foreign Aus.$33). D.K. Down, Ed. & Pub., 2 Neridah Ave., Mount Colah, N.S.W. 2079, Australia. TEL 61-2-94773595. FAX 61-2-94871659. R&P contact: D.K. Down. adv. contact: D.K. Down. circ. 5,000. (paid). Document type: academic/scholarly publication.

913 US ISSN 0066-5975
ARCHAEOLOGICAL EXPLORATION OF SARDIS. MONOGRAPHS. 1971. irreg., vol.9, 1991. Harvard University Art Museums, Sardis Exploration Office, 7 Sumner Rd., Cambridge, MA 02138. TEL 617-495-3940. Ed. Andrew Ramage. R&P contact: Michael O'Grady. Document type: monographic series, academic/scholarly publication.
Refereed Serial

930.1 US ISSN 1061-8961
CC76
ARCHAEOLOGICAL FIELDWORK OPPORTUNITIES BULLETIN. 1975. a. $11 to non-members; members $9 (effective 1997). (Archaeological Institute of America) Kendall - Hunt Publishing Co., 4050 Westmark Dr., Dubuque, IA 52002. TEL 319-589-1000. Ed. Susanna Burns. circ. 2,500 (paid). Document type: bulletin, directory.
Description: Comprehensive guide to excavations, field schools and special programs with openings for volunteers, students and staff throughout the world.

930.1 UK ISSN 0066-5983
DA20
ARCHAEOLOGICAL JOURNAL. 1844. a. £28. Royal Archaeological Institute, c/o Society of Antiquaries, Burlington House, Picadilly, London W1V OHS, England. Ed. B.E. Vyner. bk.rev.; index, cum.index every 25 yrs. circ. 2,100. Indexed: A.I.C.P., Anthropol.Lit., Art Ind., Avery Ind.Archit.Per., Br.Archaeol.Abstr., Br.Hum.Ind., Br.Tech.Ind., IBR, Numis.Lit., RILA. Document type: academic/scholarly publication.
—BLDSC (1594.750000); KR SourceOne; SWETS; UnCover.
Refereed Serial

913 572 US ISSN 0194-3413
ARCHAEOLOGICAL NEWS. 1972. a. $15 to individuals (Canada & Mexico $17.50; elsewhere $19); institutions $22.50 (Canada & Mexico $25; elsewhere $26.50) (effective 1997). University of Georgia, Department of Classics, Park Hall, Athens, GA 30602. TEL 404-542-2187. Ed. Naomi J. Norman. adv. contact: Amanda Mastrovita. bk.rev.; bibl.; illus. circ. 317. (back issues avail.) Indexed: Avery Ind.Archit.Per., IBR. Document type: academic/scholarly publication.

913 CN ISSN 0563-9239
CC1
ARCHAEOLOGICAL NEWSLETTER. 1965; N.S. 1981. 6/yr. free. Royal Ontario Museum, Committee for Field Archaeology, 100 Queen's Park, Toronto, ON M5S 2C6, Canada. TEL 416-586-5698. FAX 416-586-5863. E-mail: imogenef@rom.on.ca; mimak@rom.on.ca; URL: http://www.rom.on.ca/ebuff/aboutarc.htm. Ed. Mima Kapchesast. circ. 4,800. (looseleaf format; also avail. in microfilm from MML; back issues avail.) Indexed: Anthropol.Lit. Document type: newsletter.
•Also available online.
Description: Each newsletter is a first-hand, often from-the-field account of a dig or other project conducted by ROM archaeologists and associates.

930.1 UK ISSN 1075-2196
CODEN: ARPOE4
ARCHAEOLOGICAL PROSPECTION. 1994. q. $345 (foreign $345) (effective 1997). John Wiley & Sons Ltd., Journals, Baffins Ln., Chichester, W. Sussex PO19 1UD, England. TEL 44-1243-779777. FAX 44-1243-775878. E-mail: cs-journals@wiley.co.uk; URL: http://www.wiley.co.uk. (Subscr. in the Americas to: John Wiley & Sons, Inc., 605 Third Ave., New York, NY 10158. TEL 212-850-6645. FAX 212-850-6021) Eds. A.M. Pollard, A. Aspinall; Pub. Helen Bailey. adv.: B&W page £595, color page £1495; trim 260 x 200; adv. contact: Bob Kern. circ. 500. (also avail. in microform from UMI; back issues avail.) Document type: academic/scholarly publication.
—BLDSC (1594.795000). CCC.
Refereed Serial

913 UK ISSN 0141-8971
ARCHAEOLOGICAL REPORTS (DURHAM). 1977. a. £4 (effective 1996). University of Durham, Department of Archaeology, South Rd., Durham DH1 3LE, England. FAX 44-191-374-3719. (Co-sponsor: University of Newcastle-upon-Tyne) Ed. S. Lucy. R&P contact: S. Lucy. circ. 200. Indexed: Br.Hum.Ind. Document type: academic/scholarly publication.
Description: Brief reports on archaeological fieldwork undertaken by the universities.

ARCHAEOLOGY

938 UK ISSN 0570-6084
ARCHAEOLOGICAL REPORTS (LONDON). (Supplement to: Journal of Hellenic Studies (ISSN 0075-4269)) 1954. a. £40 (foreign £41($90)) (effective 1998). Society for the Promotion of Hellenic Studies, Senate House, London WC1E 7HU, England. TEL 44-171-232-9590. FAX 44-171-232-9591. E-mail: hellenic@sas.ac.uk. **Document type:** academic/scholarly publication.
—BLDSC (1594.810000).
Description: Summarizes recent archaeological work in Greece and other lands touched by Hellenic civilizations.

913 US
ARCHAEOLOGICAL RESEARCH TOOLS. 1981. irreg., vol.5, 1989. price varies. University of California at Los Angeles, Institute of Archaeology, 405 Hilgard Ave., Los Angeles, CA 90024-1510. TEL 213-825-7411. FAX 213-206-4723. **Indexed:** Anthropol.Lit. **Document type:** academic/scholarly publication.
Description: Describes practical methods, tools, and techniques used in archaeology.

913 UK ISSN 0261-4332
ARCHAEOLOGICAL REVIEW FROM CAMBRIDGE. 1981. s-a. £12 to individuals (foreign £14); institutions £16 (foreign £18) (effective 1996). c/o Department of Archaeology, Downing St., Cambridge CB2 3D2, England. TEL 44-1223-333520. FAX 44-1223-333503. Ed. Dorian Fuller. R&P contact: Dorian Fuller. adv. contact: Nick Hanson-James. bk.rev.; illus.; charts; circ. 200 (controlled). (back issues avail.) **Indexed:** Anthropol.Lit., Br.Archaeol.Abstr. **Document type:** academic/scholarly publication.
—BLDSC (1594.920000); KR SourceOne.

913 US ISSN 0739-5612
F96
ARCHAEOLOGICAL SOCIETY OF CONNECTICUT. BULLETIN. 1936. a. $15 membership (effective 1996). Archaeological Society of Connecticut, Archaeological Research Specialists, 437 Broad St., Meriden St., CT 06450. TEL 203-237-4777. FAX 203-237-4667. Ed. Lucianne Lavin. R&P contact: Reger Mueller. bk.rev.; film rev.; abstr.; bibl.; charts; illus.; index. circ. 250. (back issues avail.) **Indexed:** Abstr.Anthropol., Anthropol.Lit. **Document type:** bulletin.

917 US
ARCHAEOLOGICAL SOCIETY OF CONNECTICUT. NEWSLETTER. 3/yr. membership. Archaeological Society of Connecticut, Archaeological Research Specialists, 437 Broad St., Meriden, CT 06450. TEL 203-237-4777. FAX 203-237-4667. Ed. Tom Harris. R&P contact: Roger W. Mueller. **Document type:** newsletter.

913 US ISSN 0003-8067
F161
ARCHAEOLOGICAL SOCIETY OF DELAWARE. BULLETIN. 1933. a. $10 to individuals; institutions $15. Archaeological Society of Delaware, Box 12483, Wilmington, DE 19850-2483. TEL 302-831-6590. Ed. Keith R. Doms. charts. (also avail. in microform from UMI) **Indexed:** Abstr.Anthropol. **Document type:** bulletin.
—UMI.

917 US
ARCHAEOLOGICAL SOCIETY OF DELAWARE. MONOGRAPH. 1976. irreg. Archaeological Society of Delaware, Box 12483, Wilmington, DE 19850-2483. TEL 302-831-6590. Ed. Keith Doms. **Document type:** monographic series.

913 JA ISSN 0003-8075
DS11
ARCHAEOLOGICAL SOCIETY OF JAPAN. JOURNAL/KOKOGAKU ZASSHI. (Text in Japanese; summaries in English) 1910. q. 4000 Yen. Archaeological Society of Japan - Nihon Koko Gakkai, c/o Tokyo National Museum, 13-9 Ueno Park, Daito-ku, Tokyo 110, Japan. bk.rev.; illus.; index. circ. 2,800. **Indexed:** Amer.Hist.& Life, Anthropol.Lit., Hist.Abstr.
—UnCover.

913 US ISSN 0196-8319
E78.N6 CODEN: BASJEW
ARCHAEOLOGICAL SOCIETY OF NEW JERSEY. BULLETIN. 1948. a. $15 individual membership; institutional $20. Archaeological Society of New Jersey, Humanities Bldg., Seton Hall University, South Orange, NJ 07079. Ed. Charles A. Bello. R&P contact: Charles A. Bello. bibl.; charts; illus. circ. 300. **Indexed:** Abstr.Anthropol. **Document type:** academic/scholarly publication, bulletin.
Description: Contains articles and reports of historic and prehistoric archaeological sites by a variety of scholars and other profesionals.

913 305.8 US ISSN 0195-6337
ARCHAEOLOGICAL SOCIETY OF NEW JERSEY. NEWSLETTER. a. $15 individual membership; institutional $20. Archaeological Society of New Jersey, Humanities Bldg., Seton Hall University, South Orange, NJ 07079. Ed. Charles A. Bello. R&P contact: Charles A. Bello. **Document type:** newsletter.
Description: Deals with notes of current interest to society members.

917 US ISSN 0587-1719
E78.N65
ARCHAEOLOGICAL SOCIETY OF NEW MEXICO. PAPERS. 1968. a. $25 (includes newsletter). Archaeological Society of New Mexico, Box 3485, Albuquerque, NM 87190-3485. TEL 505-599-6146. Ed. David Kirkpatrick. circ. 400. **Document type:** academic/scholarly publication.
Description: Publication in honor of a noted scholar, on the latest archaeological scholarship in New Mexico and the Southwest.

933 IS
ARCHAEOLOGICAL SURVEY OF ISRAEL. SURVEY MAP SERIES. (Text in Hebrew, summaries in English) 1972. irreg., no.23, 1996. price varies. Israel Antiquities Authority, P.O. Box 586, Jerusalem 91004, Israel. TEL 972-2-5602607. FAX 972-2-5602628. E-mail: harriet@israntique.org.il. **Document type:** academic/scholarly publication.
Description: Annotated maps pertaining to archaeological sites in Israel.

913 SZ ISSN 0255-9005
ARCHAEOLOGIE DER SCHWEIZ/ARCHEOLOGIE SUISSE/ARCHEOLOGIA SVIZZERA. (Text in French, German and Italian) 1978. q. 45 SFr. Schweizerische Gesellschaft fuer Ur- und Fruehgeschichte, Petersgraben 9-11, CH-4001 Basel, Switzerland. TEL 41-61-2613078. Ed. Genevieve Luescher. adv.; charts; illus. circ. 3,700. **Indexed:** Anthropol.Lit., Br.Archaeol.Abstr. **Document type:** academic/scholarly publication.
Supersedes (1970-1977): Schweizerische Gesellschaft fuer Ur- und Fruehgeschichte. Mitteilungsblatt; Helvetia Archaeologica (ISSN 0018-0173)

913 GW ISSN 0176-8522
ARCHAEOLOGIE IN DEUTSCHLAND. 1984. q. DM.64 (effective 1998). (Verband der Landesarchaeologen in der Bundesrepublik Deutschland) Konrad Theiss Verlag GmbH, Moenchhaldenstr. 28, 70191 Stuttgart, Germany. TEL 49-711-2552714. FAX 49-711-2552717. adv.; bk.rev. circ. 11,000. **Indexed:** IBR. **Document type:** academic/scholarly publication.
—CCC.

913 943.6 AU ISSN 1018-1857
ARCHAEOLOGIE OESTERREICHS. 1950. s-a. S.250 membership. Oesterreichische Gesellschaft fuer Ur- und Fruehgeschichte, Franz-Klein-Gasse 1, A-1190 Vienna, Austria. TEL 43-1-31352373. FAX 43-1-31352350. Ed. Alexandra Krenn-Leeb. bk.rev. **Document type:** academic/scholarly publication.
Formerly: Oesterreichische Arbeitsgemeinschaft fuer Ur- und Fruehgeschichte. Mitteilungen (ISSN 0029-9693)

930.1 GW
ARCHAEOLOGISCHE FORSCHUNGEN. 1975. irreg. (Deutsches Archaeologisches Institut Berlin) Gebr. Mann Verlag GmbH, Charlottenstr. 13, 10969 Berlin, Germany. TEL 49-30-2591-3589. FAX 49-30-2591-3537. (back issues avail.) **Document type:** monographic series.

913 AU
ARCHAEOLOGISCHE GESELLSCHAFT STEIERMARK. MITTEILUNGEN. (Text in English, French, German, Italian) 1987. irreg., no.5, 1991. price varies. Archaeologische Gesellschaft Steiermark, Institut fuer Klassische Archaeologie, Universitaet Graz, Universitaetsplatz 3, A-8010 Graz, Austria. TEL 43-316-3802386. FAX 43-316-3802386. E-mail: erwin.pochmarski@kfunigraz.ac.at. Ed. Erwin Pochmarski. bk.rev. **Document type:** monographic series.
Formerly: Archaeologische Gesellschaft Graz. Mitteilungen.

913 GW ISSN 0341-2873
ARCHAEOLOGISCHE INFORMATIONEN. MITTEILUNGEN ZUR UR- UND FRUEHGESCHICHTE. 1972. irreg., vol.19, 1996. DM.70. (Deutsche Gesellschaft fuer Ur- und Fruehgeschichte) Dr. Rudolf Habelt GmbH, Am Buchenhang 1, 53115 Bonn, Germany. TEL 49-228-9238322. FAX 49-228-923836. **Indexed:** Anthropol.Lit., Br.Archaeol.Abstr., IBR. **Document type:** monographic series.

913.5 GW ISSN 0066-6033
DS261
ARCHAEOLOGISCHE MITTEILUNGEN AUS IRAN. NEUE FOLGE. 1968. a. price varies. (Deutsches Archaeologisches Institut, Abteilung Teheran) Dietrich Reimer Verlag, Unter den Eichen 57, 12203 Berlin, Germany. TEL 49-30-8314081. FAX 49-30-8316323. **Indexed:** Anthropol.Lit., Art & Archaeol.Tech.Abstr., Bibl.Ling., IBR. **Document type:** academic/scholarly publication, monographic series.
—CCC.
Description: Reports on archaeological excavations and research in Iran conducted by the German Archaeological Institute.

913 GW ISSN 0170-5776
ARCHAEOLOGISCHE MITTEILUNGEN AUS NORDWESTDEUTSCHLAND. 1978. a. DM.25. (Staatliches Museum fuer Naturkunde und Vorgeschichte Oldenburg) Verlag Isensee, Haarenstr. 20, 26122 Oldenburg, Germany. TEL 49-441-25388. FAX 49-441-17872. circ. 1,200. **Document type:** academic/scholarly publication.

930.1 GW
ARCHAEOLOGISCHE PARK XANTEN. FUEHRER UND SCHRIFTEN. 1977. irreg., no.17, 1995. (Archaeologische Park Xanten) Rheinland Verlag GmbH, Abtei Brauweiler, Postfach 2140, 50250 Pulheim, Germany. TEL 49-2234-9854265. FAX 49-2234-82503. (Dist. by: Dr. Rudolf Habelt GmbH, Am Buchenhang 1, 53115 Bonn, Germany. TEL 49-228-232016. FAX 49-228-9238322) (Co-sponsor: Landschaftsverband Rheinland) **Document type:** monographic series.

913 GW ISSN 0003-8105
CC5
ARCHAEOLOGISCHER ANZEIGER. (Supplement to: Deutsches Archaeologisches Institut. Jahrbuch) q. DM.240 (foreign DM.252; students DM.171) (effective 1998). (Deutsches Archaeologisches Institut) Walter de Gruyter und Co., Genthiner Str. 13, 10785 Berlin, Germany. TEL 49-30-26005-0. FAX 49-30-26005251. E-mail: wdg-info@degruyter.de; URL: http://www.degruyter.de. (U.S. addr.: Walter de Gruyter, Inc., 200 Saw Mill River Rd., Hawthorne, NY 10532. TEL 914-747-0110) bk.rev.; index. **Indexed:** Art Ind., Br.Archaeol.Abstr., IBR, Numis.Lit. **Document type:** academic/scholarly publication.
—KR SourceOne; SWETS. CCC.

913.363 GW ISSN 0342-734X
DD51
ARCHAEOLOGISCHES KORRESPONDENZBLATT. 1971. 4/yr. DM.46.80 (foreign DM.57) (effective 1997 & 1998). Roemisch-Germanisches Zentralmuseum, Forschungsinstitut fuer Vor- und Fruehgeschichte, Ernst-Ludwig-Platz 2, 55116 Mainz, Germany. TEL 49-6131-9124-0. FAX 49-6131-9124199. illus.; index. circ. 2,500. (back issues avail.) **Indexed:** Avery Ind.Archit.Per., Br.Archaeol.Abstr., IBR, NAA. **Document type:** academic/scholarly publication.
—BLDSC (1595.156000).

ARCHAEOLOGY

913 GW ISSN 0948-8359
CC1
ARCHAEOLOGISCHES NACHRICHTENBLATT. 1956. q. DM.65 (foreign DM.85); students DM.30 (foreign DM.38) (effective 1997). Akademie Verlag GmbH, Muehlenstr. 33-34, 13187 Berlin, Germany. TEL 49-30-47889348. FAX 49-30-47889357. E-mail: info@akademie-verlag.de. (Subscr. in the Americas to: John Wiley & Sons, Inc., 605 Third Ave., New York, NY 10158. TEL 212-850-6645. FAX 212-850-6021) Ed.Bd. abstr.; bibl.; charts; illus.; maps. **Indexed:** A.I.C.P., Anthropol.Lit., Arts & Hum.Cit.Ind., ASCA, Br.Archaeol.Abstr., Curr.Cont., IBR, Numis.Lit., SSCI. **Document type:** academic/scholarly publication.
—BLDSC (1595.156612); Genuine Article.
Formerly (until 1995): Ausgrabungen und Funde (ISSN 0004-8127)
Description: Publishes papers on the organizational, legal, structural and methodological issues concerning the preservation of historical buildings and monuments.

913 US ISSN 0003-8113
GN700
ARCHAEOLOGY. 1948. bi-m. $20; newsstand price: $4.95. Archaeological Institute of America, 135 William St., New York, NY 10038. TEL 212-732-5154. FAX 212-732-5707. E-mail: edit1@archaeology.org; URL: http://www.he.net/~archaeol/. Ed. Peter Young. adv.; bk.rev.; charts; illus.; maps; cum.index: vols.1-10, 11-26; circ. 200,000 (paid). (also avail. in microform from UMI; back issues avail.) **Indexed:** Abstr.Anthropol., Amer.Bibl.Slavic & E.Eur.Stud., Amer.Hist.& Life, Art & Archaeol.Tech.Abstr., Art Ind., Arts & Hum.Cit.Ind., Avery Ind.Archit.Per., Bk.Rev.Dig., Bk.Rev.Ind. (1977-), Child.Bk.Rev.Ind. (1977-), Curr.Cont., GeoRef., Hist.Abstr., Hum.Ind., IBR, INIS Atomind., Mid.East: Abstr.& Ind., NAA, Numis.Lit., PMR, R.G.Abstr., Ref.Sour., Rel.Ind.One., So.Pac.Per.Ind., SSCI. **Document type:** consumer publication, academic/scholarly publication.
—BLDSC (1595.050000); KR SourceOne; SWETS; UMI; UnCover.
Description: Reports on archaeological news at sites and museums throughout the world.
Refereed Serial

913 IS
ARCHAEOLOGY. (Text in Hebrew) 1986. q. (Israel Association of Archaeologists) Ariel Publishing, P.O. Box 3328, Jerusalem, Israel. **Indexed:** Art Ind., Bk.Rev.Dig., Curr.Cont., Hum.Ind., R.G.Abstr.

913 UK ISSN 0140-7880
ARCHAEOLOGY ABROAD BULLETIN. 1972. 3/yr. £10($25) to individuals overseas; institutions overseas £15 ($35) (effective 1997). Archaeology Abroad, 31-34 Gordon Sq., London WC1H 0PY, England. TEL 44-0171-387-7050. FAX 44-0171-383-2572. E-mail: arch.abroad@ucl.ac.uk. Ed. Wendy Rix Morton. circ. 600. **Document type:** bulletin.
Description: Provides information about opportunities for archaeological fieldwork and excavation outside the U.K., listing both volunteer and staff requirements for approximately 400 sites annually.

930.1 500 SW ISSN 1104-3121
ARCHAEOLOGY AND NATURAL SCIENCE. (Text in English) 1993. irreg. (Council for Research in the Humanities and Social Sciences) Paul Aastroems Foerlag, William Gibsons vaeg 11, S-433 76 Jonsered, Sweden. Ed. Peter M. Fischer. **Document type:** academic/scholarly publication, proceedings.

930.1 UK
ARCHAEOLOGY IN LINCOLN SERIES. irreg. price varies. Council for British Archaeology, Bowes Morrell House, 111 Walmgate, York YO1 2UA, England. TEL 44-1904-671417. FAX 44-1904-671384. Ed. Christine Pietrowski. R&P contact: Christine Pietrowski. (back issues avail.) **Document type:** monographic series, academic/scholarly publication.
Description: Reports on archaeological research at prehistoric, Roman, Saxon, and medieval sites in and around Lincoln.

917 US ISSN 0044-8591
ARCHAEOLOGY IN MONTANA. 1958. 3/yr. $10 to individuals; institutions $15. Montana Archaeological Society, Dept. of Sociology, Montana State Univ., Bozeman, MT 59717. TEL 406-994-0211. Ed. Dr. Leslie B. Davis. adv.; bk.rev.; bibl.; charts; illus.; stat.; index, cum.index: 1958-1969. circ. 250. (processed) **Indexed:** Abstr.Anthropol., Amer.Hist.& Life (1983-), Anthropol.Lit., Hist.Abstr. (1983-).
—UnCover.

913 NZ ISSN 0113-7832
DU416
ARCHAEOLOGY IN NEW ZEALAND. 1957. q. NZ.$45 (foreign NZ.$60) (effective 1997). New Zealand Archaeological Association, P.O. Box 6337, Dunedin North, New Zealand. TEL 64-9-3737599. E-mail: j.lawrence.@auckland.ac.nz. Ed. J. Lawrence. bk.rev.; charts; illus.; maps; cum.index: vols.1-30 (1957-1987). circ. 500. **Indexed:** A.I.C.P., Anthropol.Lit., So.Pac.Per.Ind.
—UnCover.
Formerly: New Zealand Archaeological Association. Newsletter (ISSN 0028-7962)
Description: Provides an outlet for shorter papers on any topic connected with the study of the prehistory and archaeology.

940 570 AT ISSN 0003-8121
DU1
ARCHAEOLOGY IN OCEANIA. 1966. 3/yr. $45 (foreign $45) (effective 1997). University of Sydney, Sydney, N.S.W. 2006, Australia. TEL 61-2-93512666. FAX 61-2-93517488. E-mail: dlcoller@oceania.usyd.edu.au. Ed. Dr. J.P. White. adv.; bk.rev.; bibl.; charts; illus.; stat.; index. circ. 600. (also avail. in microfiche; microfilm; reprint service avail. from UMI,KTO) **Indexed:** A.I.C.P., Abstr.Anthropol., Anthropol.Lit., Bibl.& Ind.Geol., Biol.Abstr., IBR, So.Pac.Per.Ind. **Document type:** academic/scholarly publication.
—KR SourceOne; Linda Hall; UMI; UnCover. **CCC.**
Formerly: Archaeology and Physical Anthropology in Oceania (ISSN 0728-4896)

220.9 US ISSN 1058-2673
ARCHAEOLOGY IN THE BIBLICAL WORLD.* 1991. a. $25 includes society Bulletin and Newsletter. Near East Archaeological Society, 1325 Remington Rd., Ste. H, Schaumberg, IL 60173-4815. TEL 847-869-4919. Ed. Steve Reimer. R&P contact: Bill Berry. **Indexed:** Rel.& Theol.Abstr. **Document type:** academic/scholarly publication.

913 IE ISSN 0790-892X
DA920
ARCHAEOLOGY IRELAND. 1987. q. $35. P.O. Box 69, Bray, Co. Wicklow, Ireland. TEL 353-1-2862649. FAX 353-1-2864215. E-mail: wordwell@internet-eirann.ie. **Document type:** consumer publication.
—BLDSC (1595.090500).

917 US ISSN 0360-1021
E77.8 CODEN: AENAEV
ARCHAEOLOGY OF EASTERN NORTH AMERICA. 1973. a. $30. Eastern States Archeological Federation, Box 386, Bethlehem, CT 06751. TEL 203-266-7741. Ed. Arthur Spiess. R&P contact: Roger W. Mueller. illus. circ. 500. **Indexed:** Anthropol.Lit. **Document type:** academic/scholarly publication.
—KR SourceOne.

936.2843 UK ISSN 0963-0937
ARCHAEOLOGY OF YORK SERIES. irreg. price varies. Council for British Archaeology, Bowes Morrell House, 111 Walmgate, York YO1 2UA, England. TEL 44-1904-671417. FAX 44-1904-671384. Ed. Christine Pietrowski. R&P contact: Christine Pietrowski. (back issues avail.) **Document type:** monographic series, academic/scholarly publication.
Description: Reports on archaeological research at prehistoric, Roman, Viking, Saxon, and medieval sites in and around York.

919 US ISSN 0191-7730
DU628.K3
ARCHAEOLOGY ON KAUA'I. (Print edition ceased in 1996) (Text in English and Hawaiian) 1972. s-a. Anthropology Club of Kaua'i, 3-1901 Kaumualii Hwy., Lihue, HI 96766. TEL 808-245-8311. FAX 808-245-8220. Ed. William K. Kikuchi. circ. 450. **Document type:** newsletter.
●Available only online.

913 700 UK ISSN 0003-813X
CC75 CODEN: ARCHAG
ARCHAEOMETRY. 1958. s-a. £21 (foreign $46) to individuals; institutions £46 (foreign $100) (effective 1998). University of Oxford, Research Laboratory for Archaeology, 6 Keble Rd., Oxford OX1 3QJ, England. TEL 44-1865-515211. FAX 44-1865-273932. Ed. M.S. Tite. adv.; bk.rev.; bibl.; charts; illus. circ. 1,500. (reprint service avail. from ISI) **Indexed:** A.I.C.P., Abstr.Anthropol., Anthropol.Lit., Art & Archaeol.Tech.Abstr., Arts & Hum.Cit.Ind., ASCA, Br.Archaeol.Abstr., Chem.Abstr., Curr.Cont., IBR, INIS Atomind., INSPEC (1973-), Mid.East: Abstr.& Ind., Numis.Lit., Plant Breed.Abstr., SSCI. **Document type:** academic/scholarly publication.
—BLDSC (1595.150000); AskIEEE; CASDDS; Genuine Article; KR SourceOne; SWETS; UMI; UnCover.
Description: Discusses the involvement of the physical sciences in archaeology and art history, with state-of-the-art specialist reports covering current research.

913 551.46 FR ISSN 0154-1854
ARCHAEONAUTICA. 1977. a. price varies. (Centre National de la Recherche Scientifique) C N R S Editions, 20-22 rue St. Amand, 75105 Paris, France. TEL 45-33-16-00. FAX 45-33-92-13. TELEX 200 356 F. Ed. Bernard Liou. adv.; bk.rev.; index; circ. 1,250 (controlled). **Indexed:** Br.Archaeol.Abstr.
Description: Reports concerning oceanic sedimentology.

930.1 560 FR ISSN 0299-3600
CC79.5.A5 CODEN: ARZOEK
ARCHAEOZOOLOGIA; revue international d'archeozoologie. (Text mainly in English; occasionally in French; summaries in English, French) 1987. 2/yr. 400 F. to individuals (foreign 420 F.); institutions 540 F. (foreign 560 F.). Pensee Sauvage, B.P. 141, F-38002 Grenoble Cedex, France. TEL 76-87-13-03. FAX 76-46-27-25. **Indexed:** Anthropol.Lit., InterActions Bibl., Zoo.Rec. **Document type:** proceedings.
—BLDSC (1595.151500).
Description: Devoted to the publication of papers presented at the International Congress of Archaeozoology. Of interest to archaeozoologists, and other archaeological scientists and zoologists.

937 NE
▼**ARCHAIA HELLAS**; monographs on ancient Greek History and archaeology. (Text in English) 1995. irreg. price varies. J.C. Gieben, Nieuwe Heregracht 35, 1011 RM Amsterdam, Netherlands. TEL 31-20-6275170. FAX 31-20-6275170. (Dist. in N. America by: John Benjamins Publishing Co., Box 27519, Philadelphia, PA 19118-0519. TEL 215-836-1200. FAX 215-836-1204) Ed. Sara B. Aleshire. **Document type:** monographic series.

913 GR ISSN 1105-0969
ARCHAILOGIKE HETAIREIA EN ATHENAIS. PRAKTIKA. (Text in Greek) 1837. a. price varies. Archaeological Society at Athens - Archaiologike Hetaireia en Athenais, Panepistimiou 22, 106 72 Athens, Greece. TEL 30-1-3626-043. FAX 30-1-3644-996. illus. circ. 500. (back issues avail.) **Indexed:** Numis.Lit. **Document type:** proceedings.
Description: Publishes full-text reports on the excavations being carried out by the Archaeological Society.

930.1 GR
ARCHAIOLOGIA. (Text in Greek; summaries in English) 1981. q. Dr.3500($27) Lambrakis Press S.A., 10 Karytsi Sq., 102 33 Athens, Greece. TEL 30-1-325-3246. (Subscr. to: 3 Christou Lada, 102 37 Athens, Greece. TEL 30-1-333-3810) Ed. Anna Lambraki. bk.rev.; cum.index. circ. 7,000. **Indexed:** Numis.Lit. **Document type:** academic/scholarly publication, newsletter.

ARCHAEOLOGY

930.1   **GR**   **ISSN 1105-0950**
DF10
ARCHAIOLOGIKE EPHEMERIS. (Text mainly in Greek; occasionally in English, French, German) 1837. a. Archaeological Society at Athens - Archaiologike Hetaireia en Athenais, Panepistimiou 22, 106 72 Athens, Greece. TEL 30-1-3646-043. FAX 30-1-3644-996. bibl.; cum.index: vols.1-21 (1837-1874), vols.22-62 (1883-1923), vols.63-133 (1924-1994). circ. 500. (back issues avail.) Indexed: A.I.C.P., IBR, Numis.Lit. **Document type:** academic/scholarly publication.
—BLDSC (1595.153300).
Formerly (until 1909): Ephemeris Archaiolokike (ISSN 1105-0942)
Description: Publishes excavation reports and papers on various archaeological subjects.

913   **GR**   **ISSN 0570-6211**
ARCHAIOLOGIKE HETAIREIA. TO ERGON KATA TO (YEAR). Key Title: To Ergon Tes Archaeologikes Etaireias kata to ... (Text in Greek) 1954. a. $21. Archaeological Society at Athens - Archaiologike Hetaireia en Athenais, Panepistimiou 22, 106 72 Athens, Greece. TEL 30-1-3646-043. FAX 30-1-3644-996. illus. (back issues avail.) **Document type:** academic/scholarly publication.
Description: Provides a summary of the Archaeological Society's excavations and scientific work.

913   **GR**   **ISSN 0570-622X**
ARCHAIOLOGIKON DELTION. (In 2 parts: Meletes, Chronika) (Text in English, French, German, Greek, Italian) 1915. irreg. (2-3/yr.). price varies. Ministry of Culture, Archaeological Receipts Fund (TAP Service), 57, Panepistimiou Ave., Athens 105 64, Greece. TEL 30-1-325-3901-6. FAX 30-1-324-2684. TELEX 225932 TAP GR. (Dist. by: Wasmuth, K.G., Hardenbergstr. 9A, 1000 Berlin 12, Germany) charts; illus. **Indexed:** Avery Ind.Archit.Per., Numis.Lit. **Document type:** academic/scholarly publication, government publication.
Description: Publishes studies on Greek archaeology of all periods, and reports of archaeological activities in Greece.

ARCHEION EUVOIKON MELETON/ARCHIVES OF EUBOEAN STUDIES; Braveio Akademias Athenon. see HISTORY — History Of Europe

ARCHEION THESSALIKON MELETON. see HISTORY — History Of Europe

913   **IT**   **ISSN 1120-4559**
ARCHEO. 1985. m. L.86400. (Istituto Geografico de Agostini) Rizzoli Editore, Via Gaspare Gozzi 5, 20129 Milan, Italy. TEL 39-2-700231. FAX 39-2-70100336. Ed. Federico Curti. adv. contact: Bruno Pasini. circ. 58,000.

913   **IT**   **ISSN 0392-0038**
ARCHEOGRAFO TRIESTINO; raccolta di opuscoli e notizie per Trieste e per l'Istria. 1829. a. L.40000 (effective 1996). Societa di Minerva, c/o Biblioteca Civica "Attilio Hortis", Piazza Attilio Hortis 4, 34123 Trieste, Italy. TEL 39-40-301214. bk.rev.; abstr.; index. circ. 500. **Indexed:** Numis.Lit. **Document type:** academic/scholarly publication.
Description: Contains articles on archaeology, architecture, history, linguistics, numismatics, and art, mainly concerning Trieste and its region.
Refereed Serial

930.1   **FR**   **ISSN 0570-6270**
CC3
ARCHEOLOGIA. 1964. m. (11/yr.). 340 F. (foreign 395 F.) (effective 1997). Editions Faton S.A., 25 rue Berbisey, 21000 Dijon, France. TEL 33-3-80404104. (Subscr. to: 1 rue des Artisans, B.P. 90, 21803 Quetigny Cedex, France. TEL 33-3-80489848. FAX 33-3-80489846) adv. circ. 55,000. **Indexed:** A.I.C.P., Br.Archaeol.Abstr., Br.Tech.Ind., Geo.Abstr., INIS Atomind.
—BLDSC (1595.400000); SWETS.

930.1   **PL**   **ISSN 0066-605X**
CC13.P6
ARCHEOLOGIA. (Text in English, French, German and Polish; summaries in French and Russian) 1950. a. $28. Polska Akademia Nauk, Instytut Historii Kultury Materialnej, Al. Solidarnosci 105, 00-190 Warsaw, Poland. Ed. Z. Nowicka. **Indexed:** IBR, Numis.Lit.
Description: Archaeological research in Poland and throughout the world.

913   **IT**   **ISSN 0391-8165**
DE1
ARCHEOLOGIA CLASSICA. 1949. a., latest no.47, 1995(1996). L.350000 (effective 1997). (Universita degli Studi di Roma, Istituti di Archeologia e Storia dell'Arte Greca e Romana e di Etruscologia e Antichita Italiche) L'Erma di Bretschneider, Via Cassiodoro 19, 00193 Rome, Italy. TEL 39-6-6874127. FAX 39-6-6874129. Dir. Giovanni Colonna. bk.rev.; charts; illus.; index. **Indexed:** Avery Ind.Archit.Per., Br.Archaeol.Abstr., M.L.A., Numis.Lit.

930.1   **IT**   **ISSN 0390-0592**
ARCHEOLOGIA MEDIEVALE. (Supplement avail.: Archeologia dell'Architettura) a. L.90000 (effective 1997). Edizioni all'Insegna del Giglio s.a.s., Via R. Giuliani 152r., Florence, Italy. TEL 39-55-451593. FAX 39-55-450030.

913   **PL**   **ISSN 0003-8180**
ARCHEOLOGIA POLSKI. (Summaries in English, French and German) 1957. s-a. price varies. Polska Akademia Nauk, Instytut Historii Kultury Materialnej, Al. Solidarnosci 105, 00-190 Warsaw, Poland. (Dist. by: Ars Polona-Ruch, Krakowskie Przedmiescie 7, Warsaw, Poland) Ed. Z. Bukowski. bk.rev.; abstr.; bibl.; charts; illus.; index. circ. 600. (cards) **Indexed:** A.I.C.P., Br.Archaeol.Abstr., IBR, Numis.Lit.
—BLDSC (1595.450000).
Description: Studies on archaeological elements and methodology; discussions, chronicles.

913   **IT**   **ISSN 0392-9485**
ARCHEOLOGIA VIVA. 1982. bi-m. Lit.34000 (foreign Lit.49000) (effective 1997). Giunti Gruppo Editoriale S.p.A., Via Bolognese 165, 50139 Florence, Italy. TEL 39-55-6679267. FAX 39-55-6679298. URL: http://www.giunti.it. Ed. Piero Pruneti. adv.: B&W page Lit.3750000, color page Lit.6000000. circ. 17,600. **Indexed:** Numis.Lit.

913   **US**
ARCHEOLOGICAL SOCIETY OF SOUTH CAROLINA. OCCASIONAL PAPERS. 1979. irreg. price varies. Archeological Society of South Carolina, Inc., Institute of Archeology and Anthropology, University of South Carolina, Columbia, SC 29208. TEL 803-777-8170. Ed. Kenneth Sassaman. bk.rev. circ. 500. **Document type:** academic/scholarly publication.

917   **US**   **ISSN 0003-8202**
F221
ARCHEOLOGICAL SOCIETY OF VIRGINIA. QUARTERLY BULLETIN. 1946. q. $20 (foreign $30) membership (effective 1997). A S V Press, Box 70395, Richmond, VA 23255-0395. TEL 804-273-9291. FAX 804-273-0885. Ed. William (Jack) Hranicky. R&P contact: Harry A. Waeger. circ. 1,000 (paid). **Indexed:** Amer.Hist.& Life (until 1990), Hist.Abstr. (until 1990), IBR. **Document type:** academic/scholarly publication, bulletin, proceedings.
Description: Publishes technical papers on archeology and historical preservation in Virginia and nearby areas, as well as results of recent research, excavation and preservation activities and programs.
Refereed Serial

913.031   **XR**   **ISSN 0323-1267**
ARCHEOLOGICKE ROZHLEDY/ARCHAEOLOGICAL REVIEW. (Text mainly in Czech or Slovak; occasionally in English, French or German) 1949. bi-m. DM.236. Ceska Akademie Ved, Archeologicky Ustav, Letenska 4, 118 01 Prague 1, Czech Republic. TEL 42-2-539351. (Dist. in Western countries by: Kubon & Sagner, P.O. Box 341018, 80328 Munich, Germany) Ed. Jiri Hrala. bk.rev.; charts; illus. circ. 1,450. **Indexed:** A.I.C.P., Anthropol.Lit., Br.Archaeol.Abstr., IBR, Numis.Lit.
Description: Articles and reports on new research, studies in problems of European prehistory and new methods of investigation, anthropological papers, international bibliography of iron metallurgy.

930.1 943.7   **XO**   **ISSN 0231-925X**
ARCHEOLOGICKE VYSKUMY A NALEZY NA SLOVENSKU. 1974. irreg. (Slovenska Akademia Vied, Archeologicky Ustav) Veda, Publishing House of the Slovak Academy of Sciences, Bradacova 7, 852 86 Bratislava, Slovakia. Ed. Bohuslav Chropovsky. circ. 500.

930.1   **NE**   **ISSN 1384-7538**
ARCHEOLOGIE IN LIMBURG. 1977. q. fl.42($54) Limburgs Geschied- en Oudheidkundig Genootschap, Sectie Archeologie, Postbus 83, 6200 AB Maastricht, Netherlands. TEL 31-43-3212586. FAX 31-43-3218572. (Co-sponsor: Archeologische Vereniging Limburg) Ed. W. Dijkman. bk.rev. circ. 500.
Description: Publishes articles on archaeology, with particular emphasis on the province of Limburg.
Refereed Serial

930.1   **BE**   **ISSN 0778-2837**
ARCHEOLOGIE IN VLAANDEREN; Flanders archeological bulletin. (Supplement avail. (ISSN 1370-5768)) (Text in Dutch, occasionally in English or French; summaries in English) 1938-1988; N.S. 1991. a. 1580 BEF. Instituut voor het Archeologisch Patrimonium, Doornveld 1 bus 30, 1731 Asse (Zellik), Belgium. TEL 32-2-4631333. FAX 32-2-4631951. Ed. Guy De Boe. bk.rev.; abstr.; bibl.; illus.; maps. circ. 1,000. **Indexed:** Br.Archaeol.Abstr., Numis.Lit. **Document type:** academic/scholarly publication.
Supersedes (in 1991): Archeologie (ISSN 0003-8210)
Description: Publishes excavation reports and studies on archaeology in Flanders (Belgium).

930.1   **BE**   **ISSN 1370-5768**
ARCHEOLOGIE IN VLAANDEREN. MONOGRAFIEEN. (Text in Dutch) 1994. irreg. price varies. Instituut voor het Archeologisch Patrimonium, Doornveld 1 bus 30, 1731 Asse (Zellik), Belgium. TEL 32-2-4631333. FAX 32-2-4631951. **Document type:** monographic series.
Description: Publishes in-depth studies on the archaeology of Flanders (Belgium).

930.1 297   **FR**   **ISSN 1156-7198**
ARCHEOLOGIE ISLAMIQUE. 1990. a. 220 F. Editions Maisonneuve et Larose, 15 rue Victor-Cousin, 75005 Paris, France. TEL 33-1-44414935. FAX 33-1-43257741. Ed. Alain Jauson. adv. contact: Laurence De Coninck. circ. 1,000. **Document type:** academic/scholarly publication.
—BLDSC (1595.729000).

930.1   **NE**   **ISSN 0928-1444**
ARCHEOLOGISCHE ROUTES IN NEDERLAND; op zoek naar de geschiedenis in het landschap. 1993. q. fl.6 (effective 1996). Rijksdienst voor het Oudheidkundig Bodemonderzoek te Amersfoort, Kerkstraat 1, 3811 CV Amersfoort, Netherlands. TEL 31-33-4634233. FAX 31-33-4653235. E-mail: arne.haytsma@archis.nl; URL: http://www.archis.nl/. Ed. A. Haytsma. illus.; maps. **Document type:** consumer publication.
Description: Discusses archaeology, history and environmental education in the Netherlands. Provides information for recreational tours, walking and bicycling.

ARCHIV FUER PAPYRUSFORSCHUNG UND VERWANDTE GEBIETE. see HISTORY

930.1   **FR**   **ISSN 0768-3537**
ARCHIVES ROYALES DE MARI. 1983. irreg. price varies. Editions Recherche sur les Civilisations, 28 rue de Bourgogne, 75007 Paris, France. TEL 33-1-40628062. FAX 33-1-40628071. Ed. Hina Descat; Pub. Hina Descat. circ. 600. (also avail. in microfilm) **Document type:** monographic series.

ARCHIVIO STORICO TICINESE. see HISTORY — History Of Europe

931   **SP**   **ISSN 0066-6742**
DP44
ARCHIVO ESPANOL DE ARQUEOLOGIA. (Text in English, French, German, Italian, Spanish) 1925. s-a. 6300 ptas. (foreign 9900 ptas.) (effective 1997). Consejo Superior de Investigaciones Cientificas (C.S.I.C.), Instituto Espanol de Arqueologia, Vitruvio 8, 28006 Madrid, Spain. TEL 34-1-5612833. FAX 34-1-5629634. Ed. Luis Caballero. bk.rev. circ. 850. (reprint service avail. from SCH) **Indexed:** A.I.C.P., Art Ind., Br.Archaeol.Abstr., Numis.Lit.
—BLDSC (1654.947000); CINDOC. **CCC.**
Supersedes in part (in 1940): Archivo Espanol de Arte y Arqueologia (ISSN 0210-4180)
Description: Covers new developments and historical articles of Spanish arqueology.

ARETHUSA. see CLASSICAL STUDIES

ARHEOLOGIA MOLDOVEI/ARCHEOLOGIE DE LA MOLDAVIE. see HISTORY — History Of Europe

ARCHAEOLOGY

913   CI   ISSN 0350-7165
DB361
ARHEOLOSKI MUZEJ U ZAGREBU. VJESNIK. (Text in Croatian; summaries in English, French, German) 1870. a. Arheoloski Muzej u Zagrebu, Trg. N. Zrinskog 19, 41000 Zagreb, Croatia. bk.rev.; illus. circ. 600. **Indexed:** Bibl.Ling.
—BLDSC (9245.130000).

913   XV   ISSN 0570-8966
ARHEOLOSKI VESTNIK/ACTA ARCHAEOLOGICA. (Text in English, French, German, Italian, Serbo-Croatian, Slovenian) 1950. a. $50. Slovenska Akademija Znanosti in Umetnosti, Znanstvenoraziskovalni Center, Institut za Arheologijo, Gosposka 13, 61000 Ljubljana, Slovenia. TEL 38-61-1256068. FAX 38-61-1255253. Ed. Slavko Ciglenecki. bk.rev. circ. 1,200. **Indexed:** A.I.C.P., Anthropol.Lit., Curr.Cont., IBR, Numis.Lit. **Document type:** academic/scholarly publication.
—BLDSC (1664.470000); KNAW.
   Description: Provides studies and articles by Yugoslav and foreign scientists on prehistory, Roman provincial archaeology, and archaeology of the Migration Period and the early Middle Ages of the eastern Alpine and western Balkan region.

913   US
ARIZONA ARCHAEOLOGIST. 1965. irreg., no.27, 1994. price varies. Arizona Archaeological Society, Inc., Box 9665, Phoenix, AZ 85068. TEL 602-488-9589. Ed. Alan Ferg. (back issues avail.) **Document type:** academic/scholarly publication.
   Refereed Serial

917 572   US   ISSN 0518-6617
ARKANSAS AMATEUR. 1962. bi-m. $15 includes subscr. to Central States Archaeological Journal. Northwest Arkansas Archaeological Society, Inc., Box 1154, Fayetteville, AR 72702. TEL 501-855-1970. Ed. Larry Swaim; Pub. Larry Swaim. bk.rev.; charts; illus. circ. 450. (looseleaf format; back issues avail.) **Document type:** newsletter.

913   US   ISSN 0015-0711
ARKANSAS ARCHEOLOGICAL SOCIETY. FIELD NOTES. 1965. 6/yr. $25 to institutions (foreign $30) includes Arkansas Archeologist. Arkansas Archeological Society, Box 1222, Fayetteville, AR 72702-1222. TEL 501-575-3556. FAX 501-575-5453. Ed. Hester A. Davis. R&P contact: Hester A. Davis. bk.rev.; charts; illus. circ. 750. **Document type:** newsletter.
   Description: News from surrounding area research and membership information.

917   US   ISSN 0587-3533
ARKANSAS ARCHEOLOGICAL SURVEY. PUBLICATIONS ON ARCHEOLOGY. POPULAR SERIES. 1969. irreg., no.3, 1992. price varies. Arkansas Archeological Survey Publications, Box 1249, Fayetteville, AR 72702-1249. TEL 501-575-3556. FAX 501-575-5453. E-mail: mkennedy@comp.uark. edu. Ed. Mary Lynn Kennedy. R&P contact: Hester Davis. charts; illus.

917   US   ISSN 0277-6308
ARKANSAS ARCHEOLOGICAL SURVEY. PUBLICATIONS ON ARCHEOLOGY. RESEARCH REPORTS. 1975. irreg., no.27, 1990. price varies. Arkansas Archeological Survey Publications, Box 1249, Fayetteville, AR 72702-1249. TEL 501-575-3556. FAX 501-575-5453. E-mail: mkennedy@comp.uark. edu. Ed. Mary Lynn Kennedy. **Document type:** monographic series.

917   US   ISSN 0882-5491
E78.A8
ARKANSAS ARCHEOLOGICAL SURVEY. PUBLICATIONS ON ARCHEOLOGY. RESEARCH SERIES. 1967. irreg., no.48, 1997. price varies. Arkansas Archeological Survey Publications, Box 1249, Fayetteville, AR 72702-1249. TEL 501-575-3556. FAX 501-575-5453. E-mail: mkennedy@comp.uark. edu. Ed. Mary Lynn Kennedy. charts; illus. **Indexed:** Anthropol.Lit., GeoRef.

913   US
ARKANSAS ARCHEOLOGICAL SURVEY. PUBLICATIONS ON ARCHEOLOGY. TECHNICAL PAPERS. 1981. irreg., no.9, 1990. price varies. Arkansas Archeological Survey Publications, Box 1249, Fayetteville, AR 72702-1249. TEL 501-575-3556. FAX 501-575-5453. E-mail: mkennedy@comp.uark. edu. Ed. Mary Lynn Kennedy.

913   US   ISSN 0004-1718
E78.A8
ARKANSAS ARCHEOLOGIST. 1960. a. $25 to institutions (foreign $30) includes Field Notes. Arkansas Archeological Society, Box 1222, Fayetteville, AR 72702-1222. TEL 501-575-3556. Ed. Hester A. Davis. R&P contact: Hester A. Davis. illus.; maps. circ. 750. **Indexed:** Amer.Hist.& Life, Anthropol.Lit., Hist.Abstr. **Document type:** monographic series.

930.1   FR
ARKEO JUNIOR. 11/yr. 260 F. (foreign 310 F.) (effective 1997). Editions Faton S.A., 25 rue Berbisey, 21000 Dijon, France. TEL 33-3-80404120. (Subscr. to: 1 rue des Artisans, B.P. 90, 21803 Quetigny Cedex, France. TEL 33-3-80489848. FAX 33-3-80489846)

930.1   SP   ISSN 0213-8921
ARKEOIKUSKA; arkeologi aldizkaria. (Text in Basque, Spanish) 1981. a. (Kultura Saila - Departamento de Cultura) Eusko Jaurlaritzaren Argitalpen-Zerbitzu Nagusia - Servicio Central de Publicaciones del Gobierno Vasco, Duque de Wellington 2, 01010 Vitoria-Gasteiz, Spain. TEL 34-45-188000. FAX 34-45-189535. circ. 2,500.
   Description: Presents all archeological activities conducted in the Basque region.

930.1   SW   ISSN 0284-5407
ARKEOLOGI I SVERIGE. 1958. a. SEK 300 (effective 1993). Riksantikvarieaembetet, Fornminnesavdelingen, P.O. Box 5405, S-114 84 Stockholm, Sweden.

914   DK   ISSN 0901-0815
ARKEOLOGISKE UDGRAVNINGER I DANMARK. 1985. a. free. Danmark National Museet, Museumstjenesten, Sjoerupvej 1, DK-8800 Lysgaard, Denmark.

930.1 560   TU   ISSN 1017-7671
ARKEOMETRI SONUCLARI TOPLANTISI. (Text and summaries in Turkish, occasionally in English) 1985. a. Ministry of Culture, General Directorate of Monuments and Museums - Kultur Bakanligi, Anitlar ve Muzeler Genel Mudurlugu, 06100 Ulus - Ankara, Turkey. TEL 90-312-3104960. FAX 90-312-3111417. abstr.; bibl.; illus.; maps; stat. **Document type:** academic/scholarly publication.
   Description: Publishes reports of archaeometric evaluations of archaeological finds and prehistoric sites and artifacts, including dendrochronological studies in the Mediterranean basin.

ARKHEOGRAFICHESKII EZHEGODNIK. see *HISTORY*

913   TA   ISSN 0201-7539
ARKHEOLOGICHESKIE RABOTY V TADZHIKISTANE. vol.11, 1971. irreg. 1.45 Rub. Akademiya Nauk Tajikistana, Institut Istorii, Arkheologii i Etnografii im. A. Donisha, Pr. Rudaki 33, 734025 Dushanbe, Tajikistan. Ed. B. Litvinskii.

913   BU   ISSN 0324-1203
CC13.R9   CODEN: ARKHDP
ARKHEOLOGIIA. (Text in Bulgarian; summaries in French) 1959. q. 1.80 lv. per issue. (Bulgarska Akademiia na Naukite, Arkheologicheski Institut i Muzei) Publishing House of the Bulgarian Academy of Sciences, Acad. G. Bonchev St., Bldg. 6, 1113 Sofia, Bulgaria. (Dist. by: Hemus, 6, Rouski Blvd., 1000 Sofia, Bulgaria) Ed. D. Dimitrov. bk.rev.; bibl.; charts; illus. circ. 1,800. (reprint service avail. from IRC) **Indexed:** Anthropol.Lit., Avery Ind.Archit.Per., IBR, Numis.Lit., SSCI.
—BLDSC (0009.200000); CASDDS.

913   KR   ISSN 0320-9407
DK508.3   CODEN: ARKLAY
ARKHEOLOGIYA; respublikanskyi mizhvidomchyi zbirnik naukovykh prac. (Text in Ukrainian; summaries in English, Russian) 1971. 4/yr. $33 (effective 1998). Akademiya Nauk Ukrainy, Institut Arkheologii, Vul. Volodimirs'ka, 3, 252039 Kiev, Ukraine. TEL 38-44-2284405. (Dist. by: Mezhdunarodnaya Kniga, B. Yakimanka 39, 117049 Moscow, Russia. TEL 7-095-2384967. FAX 7-095-2384634) (Co-sponsor: Ukrajins'ke Tovarystvo Okhorony Pam'jaytnkiv Istoriji ta Kultury) Ed. P.P. Tolochko. **Indexed:** A.I.C.P., Djerelo, GeoRef., Numis.Lit.

930.1   RU   ISSN 0320-9431
ARKHEOLOGIYA I ETNOGRAFIYA UDMURTII. 1975. irreg. 1 Rub. per issue. Udmurdskii Institut Istorii, Ekonomiki, Literatury, Sovetskaya, 14, 426020 Izhevsk, Udmurt A.R., Russia. circ. 500.

930.1   SP
ARQUENAS; investigacion y ciencias de la naturaleza. irreg. Edita Impresion, C. Magallanes 34, 39007 Santnader, Spain. Ed. Carlos Gonzalez Luque.

930.1   PO   ISSN 0870-2306
CC13.P8
ARQUEOLOGIA. 1980. s-a. Esc.900. Grupo de Estudos Arqueologicos do Porto, R. Antonio Cardoso, 175, 4100 Porto, Portugal. Ed. Vitor Oliveira Jorge. adv. circ. 1,000. **Indexed:** Anthropol.Lit. **Document type:** academic/scholarly publication.

913   MX   ISSN 0187-6074
CC13.S66
ARQUEOLOGIA. 1987, N.S. 1989. s-a. $20. Instituto Nacional de Antropologia e Historia, Consejo de Monumentos Prehispanicos, Moneda 16, 06060 Mexico D.F., Mexico. TEL 522-7404. FAX 522-2847. Ed. Alba Guadalupe Mastache F. circ. 2,000. **Indexed:** Anthropol.Lit.
   Description: Covers the archaeology of Mesoamerica and northern Mexico.

930.1   AG   ISSN 0327-5159
F2821
ARQUEOLOGIA.* 1991. a.? Universidad de Buenos Aires, Instituto de Ciencias Antropologicas, Seccion Prehistoria, Calle Viamonte 430-444, 1053 Buenos Aires, Argentina. TEL 541-334-7512. FAX 541-432-2292. **Document type:** academic/scholarly publication.

930.1   PE
ARQUEOLOGIA DE CERRO SECHIN. 1992. irreg., latest 1996. Pontificia Universidad Catolica del Peru, Direccion Academica de Investigacion, Av. Universitaria, cuadra 18, San Miguel, Peru. TEL 622540. **Document type:** academic/scholarly publication.
   Supersedes (1980-1985): Arqueologia de Sechin.

918 600   PO   ISSN 0870-8355
ARQUEOLOGIA INDUSTRIAL. 1987. a. Esc.2500($15) Mueu da Ciencia e Industria, Adpo. 4204, 4003 Porto codex, Portugal. TEL 351-2-2003146. FAX 351-2-2003146. E-mail: cordeiro@ci.uminho. pt. Ed. Jose M. Lopes Cordeiro. adv.; bk.rev. circ. 500. **Document type:** academic/scholarly publication.
   Description: Covers industrial archaeology in Portugal, with emphasis on architecture and economic history.

930.1   PO   ISSN 0872-2250
ARQUEOLOGIA MEDIEVAL. 1992. a. Esc.3800. (Campo Arqueologico de Mertola) Edicoes Afrontamento, Lda., Rua de Costa Cabral, 859, Apdo. 2009, 4201 Porto Codex, Portugal. TEL 351-2-529271. FAX 351-2-591777.

913 700   US   ISSN 0004-2986
ART AND ARCHAEOLOGY NEWSLETTER.* (Text in English; occasionally in Ancient Egyptian, Greek and Latin) 1965. q. $7. Otto F. Reiss, Ed. & Pub., c/o H.L. Brill., 5939 Parsons Blvd., Flushing, NY 11365. adv.; bk.rev.; illus.; index. circ. 1,800. (also avail. in microform from UMI)
—UMI.

L-ART IMQADDSA; rivista biblika. see *RELIGIONS AND THEOLOGY — Roman Catholic*

ARTE E ARCHEOLOGIA; studi e documenti. see *ART*

ARTE Y ARQUEOLOGIA. see *ART*

913   AT   ISSN 0044-9075
ARTEFACT. 1965. a. Aus.$20 (foreign Aus.$25) (effective 1997 & 1998). Archaeological and Anthropological Society of Victoria, G.P.O. 328C, Melbourne, Vic. 3001, Australia. TEL 61-3-95230549. URL: http://www.vicnet. au/~aasv/aasvhom.htm. Ed. R.G. Bednarik; Pub. R.G. Bednarik. R&P contact: James F. Evans. TEL 61-3-94994343. adv.; bk.rev.; circ. 450 (controlled). **Indexed:** Abstr.Anthropol., Anthropol.Lit., Aus.P.A.I.S. **Document type:** academic/scholarly publication.
—BLDSC (1733.490000); UnCover.
   Description: Covers archaeology, ethnohistory and anthropology of the Pacific region.
   Refereed Serial

ARTIBUS ASIAE; quarterly of Asian art and archaeology for scholars and connoisseurs. see *ART*

ARCHAEOLOGY

ARTIBUS ASIAE SUPPLEMENTA. see *ART*

913   US   ISSN 0004-3680
E78.S7
ARTIFACT. 1964. q. $25. El Paso Archaeological Society, Inc., Box 4345, El Paso, TX 79914-4345. TEL 915-751-3295. Ed. Carrol Hederick. bk.rev. circ. 300. **Indexed:** Abstr.Anthropol., Anthropol.Lit. **Document type:** academic/scholarly publication.

950   US   ISSN 0066-8435
DS514
ASIAN PERSPECTIVES; the journal of archaeology for Asia and the Pacific. 1957. s-a. $27 to individuals (foreign $28); institutions $34 (foreign $36) (effective 1997). (University of Hawaii) University of Hawaii Press, Journals Department, 2840 Kolowalu St., Honolulu, HI 96822. TEL 808-956-8833. FAX 808-988-6052. E-mail: uhpjourn@hawaii.edu; URL: http://ww2.hawaii.edu/uhpress/Journals/AP/APHome.html. Ed. Michael W. Graves. R&P contact: S. Samuelson. TEL 808-956-6809. adv. contact: Ann Ludeman. bk.rev.; index. circ. 430. (also avail. in microform from UMI; back issues avail.; reprint service avail. from UMI,ISI,KTO) **Indexed:** A.I.C.P., Abstr.Anthropol., Abstr.Mil.Bibl., Anthropol.Lit., Geo.Abstr.H.G., Hum.Ind., IBR, Per.Islam. (1991-), Polit.Sci.Abstr., Rice Abstr., So.Pac.Per.Ind., SSCI. **Document type:** academic/scholarly publication.
—BLDSC (1742.710000); KR SourceOne; SWETS; UMI; UnCover.
    Description: Presents papers on prehistory and archaeology of Asia and the Pacific.
    Refereed Serial

932   BE
ASSASIF. (Text in German) 1990. irreg. price varies. Fondation Egyptologique Reine Elisabeth, Parc du Cinquantenaire 10, 1000 Brussels, Belgium. TEL 32-2-7417364. **Document type:** monographic series.

930.1   UK   ISSN 1365-3881
▼**ASSEMBLAGE;** the Sheffield graduate journal of archaeology. 1996. 2/yr. University of Sheffield, Research School of Archaeology, 2 Mappin St., Sheffield S1 4DT, England. TEL 44-114-222-5102. FAX 44-114-272-7347. E-mail: assemblage@sheffield.ac.uk; URL: http://www.shef.ac.uk/uni/union/susoc/assem/. Ed. Kathryn Denning. bk.rev. **Document type:** academic/scholarly publication.
●Available only online.
    Refereed Serial

914 720   IT
ASSOCIAZIONE PER IMOLA STORICO ARTISTICA. ATTI. 1980. irreg., latest no.13. price varies. University Press Bologna, Santerno Edizioni, Via 4 Novembre, 7, 40026 Imola (Bo), Italy. TEL 39-542-20908. FAX 39-546-55082. bk.rev.; bibl. circ. 2,000. **Document type:** monographic series.
    Supersedes: Realta Regionale. Fonti e Studi.

953.57   TS
AL-ATHAR FI DAWLAT AL-IMARAT AL-ARABIYYAH AL-MUTTAHIDAH/ARCHAEOLOGY IN THE UNITED ARAB EMIRATES. (Text in Arabic, English) 1976. irreg. exchange basis. Department of Antiquities and Tourism, P.O. Box 15715, Al-Ain, United Arab Emirates. TEL 641595. Ed. Saif bin Ali al-Darmaki.
    Description: Publishes the results of archaeological investigations in the U.A.E.

913   GR   ISSN 0004-6604
DF10
ATHENS ANNALS OF ARCHAEOLOGY. (Text in English, French, German, Greek, and Italian) 1968. irreg. (1-3/yr.). price varies. Ministry of Culture, Archaeological Receipts Fund (TAP Service), 57, Panepistimiou St., Athens 105 64, Greece. TEL 30-1-325-3901-6. FAX 30-1-324-2684. TELEX 225932 TAP GR. (Dist. by: Wasmuth K.G., Hardenbergstrasse 9A, 1000 Berlin 12, Germany) charts; illus. **Indexed:** RILA. **Document type:** academic/scholarly publication, government publication.
    Description: Covers archaeological news from Greece.

930.1 956   UK
▼**ATHLONE PUBLICATIONS IN EGYPTOLOGY AND ANCIENT NEAR EASTERN STUDIES.** 1996. irreg. Athlone Press, 1 Park Dr., London NW11 7SG, England. TEL 44-181-458-0888. FAX 44-181-201-8115. Ed. J.R. Baines. illus. **Document type:** academic/scholarly publication, monographic series.
    Description: Aims to contribute across a broad front to an understanding of ancient history, the social sciences, art history and allied disciplines.

571   IS   ISSN 0792-8424
DS111.A1
ATIQOT. Variant title: Archaeological Reports. (Text in English) 1955. irreg., vol.29, 1996. price varies. Israel Antiquities Authority, P.O. Box 586, Jerusalem 91004, Israel. TEL 972-2-5602607. FAX 972-2-5602628. E-mail: harriet@israntique.org.il. Ed. Ayala Sussmann. circ. 1,500. (back issues avail.) **Indexed:** New Test.Abstr., Numis.Lit., Zoo.Rec. **Document type:** academic/scholarly publication.
    Formed by the 1991 merger of: Atiqot (Hebrew Series) (ISSN 0067-0138); Atiqot (English Series) (ISSN 0066-488X)

ATLAS POLSKICH STROJOW LUDOWYCH. see *ANTHROPOLOGY*

936   GW   ISSN 0172-7540
AUSGRABUNGEN UND FUNDE IN OBERFRANKEN. 1979. biennial. DM.20. Dr. Rudolf Habelt GmbH, Am Buchenhang 1, 53115 Bonn, Germany. TEL 49-228-9238322. FAX 49-228-923836. **Document type:** monographic series.

913   AT   ISSN 1322-9214
DU106
AUSTRALASIAN HISTORICAL ARCHAEOLOGY. a. Aus.$25 to individuals; corporate members Aus.$30 (includes Newsletter). Australasian Society for Historical Archaeology, Box 220 Holme Bldg., University of Sydney, Sydney, N.S.W., 2006, Australia. bk.rev. circ. 400. (also avail. in microform; back issues avail.) **Indexed:** Abstr.Anthropol., Anthropol.Lit. **Document type:** academic/scholarly publication.
    Formerly: Australian Journal of Historical Archaeology (ISSN 0810-1868); Supersedes (in 1983): Australian Society for Historical Archeology. (Annual Publication); Which was formerly (until 1973): Studies in Historical Archeology.

913   AT
AUSTRALASIAN SOCIETY FOR HISTORICAL ARCHAEOLOGY. NEWSLETTER. 1970. q. Aus.$25 to individuals; corporate members Aus.$30 (includes Journal). Australasian Society for Historical Archaeology, Box 220 Holme Bldg., University of Sydney, Sydney, N.S.W. 2001, Australia. TEL 61-2-3512763. FAX 61-2-3514889. Ed. I. Powell. circ. 750. (back issues avail.) **Document type:** newsletter.
    Formerly: Australian Society for Historical Archaeology. Research Bulletin (ISSN 0819-4076)
    Description: Promotes the study of historical archaeology both in Australia and overseas.
    Refereed Serial

AUSTRALIAN ABORIGINAL STUDIES. see *ANTHROPOLOGY*

914.2   AT   ISSN 0312-2417
AUSTRALIAN ARCHAEOLOGY. 1974. 2/yr. Aus.$42 to individuals (foreign Aus.$50); institutions Aus.$50; students Aus.$25. Australian Archaeological Association Inc., c/o Division of Archaeology & Natural History, Research School of Pacific & Asian Studies, Australian National University, Canberra, A.C.T. 0200, Australia. TEL 61-6-2495111. FAX 61-6-2571893. Eds. M. Smith, S. Feary. R&P contact: M. Smith. bk.rev.; cum.index: vols.1-20. circ. 500. (back issues avail.) **Indexed:** Anthropol.Lit. **Document type:** academic/scholarly publication.
—BLDSC (1797.378500); UnCover.
    Description: Articles on Australian historic and prehistoric archaeology.

917   US   ISSN 0749-1816
AWANYU. 1973. q. $25. Archaeological Society of New Mexico, Box 3485, Albuquerque, NM 87190-3485. TEL 505-881-1675. Eds. Nancy Olsen, Karl Olsen. bk.rev.; charts; illus.; index. circ. 350. (back issues avail.) **Document type:** newsletter.
    Superseded by: A S N M Newsletter.

913   UK
DA880.A9
AYRSHIRE MONOGRAPHS. 1877; N.S. 1950. s-a. price varies. Ayrshire Archaeological & Natural History Society, c/o Ronald W. Brash, Publication Mgr., 10 Robsland Ave., Ayr KA7 2RW, Scotland. TEL 44-1292-266745. Ed. J. Strawhorn. bibl.; charts; illus.; index. circ. 900. (back issues avail.) **Indexed:** Br.Archaeol.Abstr. **Document type:** monographic series.
    Formerly (until 1987): Ayrshire Collections (ISSN 0302-3176)

930.1   UK
AYRSHIRE NOTES. s-a. £0.50. Ayrshire Archaeological & Natural History Society, c/o Ronald W. Brash, Publication Mgr., 10 Robsland Ave., Ayr KA7 2RW, Scotland. TEL 44-1292-266745. Ed. John Strawhorn. bibl.; charts; illus. **Document type:** monographic series.

AZANIA. see *HISTORY — History Of Africa*

930.1   UK
B A A S BULLETIN. no.4, 1981. s-a. membership. Bristol and Avon Archaeological Society, Bristol City Museum, Queen's Rd., Bristol BS8 1RL, England. **Document type:** newsletter.
    Formerly: B A A R G Bulletin (ISSN 0262-9828)
    Description: Lists future group events and news of local archaeology.

913 930   FR
B E F A R. PUBLICATION. 1878. irreg., (1-2/yr.). price varies. (Bibliotheque des Ecoles Francaises d'Athenes et de Rome) De Boccard Edition, 11 rue de Medicis, 75006 Paris, France. Ed.Bd. bibl. (also avail. in microform from BHP)

930.1   US
BACKDIRT. a. University of California at Los Angeles, Institute of Archaeology, 405 Hilgard Ave., Los Angeles, CA 90024-1510. TEL 310-206-8934. FAX 310-206-4723. illus. **Document type:** academic/scholarly publication.
    Description: Contains information regarding the activities of the Institute of Archaeology.

930.1   GW   ISSN 0939-0022
BAGHDADER FORSCHUNGEN. 1979. irreg., vol.18, 1995. DM.148. (Deutsches Archaeologisches Institut, Abteilung Baghdad) Verlag Philipp von Zabern GmbH, Philipp-von-Zabern-Platz 1-3, 55116 Mainz, Germany. TEL 06131-28747-0. FAX 06131-223710. Ed. Stephan Maul. **Document type:** monographic series.

913   GW   ISSN 0418-9698
DS69.5
BAGHDADER MITTEILUNGEN. 1960. a. (Deutsches Archaeologisches Institut) Verlag Philipp von Zabern GmbH, Philipp-von-Zabern-Platz 1-3, 55116 Mainz, Germany. TEL 49-6131-28747-0. FAX 49-6131-223710. (back issues avail.) **Indexed:** Bibl.Ling., IBR. **Document type:** academic/scholarly publication.

BANGLADESH LALIT KALA. see *MUSEUMS AND ART GALLERIES*

BAUTENSCHUTZ UND BAUSANIERUNG; Zeitschrift fuer Bauinstandhaltung und Denkmalpflege. see *BUILDING AND CONSTRUCTION*

739.27 301   CN   ISSN 0829-8726
BEAD FORUM. 1981. s-a. $20 (foreign $30) (effective 1997). Society of Bead Researchers, 1600 Liverpool Ct., Ottawa, ON K1A 0M5, Canada. TEL 613-990-4814. FAX 613-952-1756. E-mail: karlis-karklins@pch.gc.ca; URL: http://www.spiretech.com/~lester/sbr/index.htm. Ed. Karlis Karklins. bibl.; illus. circ. 400. (back issues avail.) **Document type:** newsletter.
    Description: Intended to disseminate timely information related to bead research worldwide.
    Refereed Serial

BEADS. see *ANTHROPOLOGY*

ARCHAEOLOGY

220.93 939.4   IS   ISSN 0334-2255
BS1178.H4
BEER-SHEVA. (Text mostly in English, occasionally in Hebrew; summaries in English) 1973. a. price varies. (Ben Gurion University of the Negev) Ben Gurion University of the Negev Press, P.O. Box 653, Beersheva, Israel. FAX 972-7-6472913. (Dist. by: Bialik Institute, P.O. Box 92, Jerusalem 91290, Israel. TEL 972-2-6783554. FAX 972-2-6783706) Ed.Bd. illus. circ. 1,000. **Document type:** academic/scholarly publication, monographic series.
   Description: Scholarly monographs on topics pertaining to Biblical archaeology and the ancient Near East.
   Refereed Serial

915   CC   ISSN 1001-0483
DS793.H4
BEIFANG WENWU/NORTHERN CULTURAL RELICS. (Text in Chinese) 1985. q. $22.50. (Heilongjiang Wenwu Guanli Weiyuanhui - Heilongjiang Provincial Cultural Relics Management Committee) Beifang Wenwu Bianjibu, 50 Hongjun Jie, Dangang District, Harbin, Heilongjiang 150001, People's Republic of China. TEL 3635089. (Dist. in US by: China Books & Periodicals, Inc., 2929 24th St., San Francisco, CA 94110. TEL 415-282-2994) Ed. Wu Wenjie. bk.rev.

930.1   GW   ISSN 0067-4893
BEIHEFTE DER BONNER JAHRBUECHER. 1950. irreg., no.50, 1994. price varies. (Landschaftsverband Rheinland) Rheinland Verlag GmbH, Abtei Brauweiler, Postfach 2140, 50250 Pulheim, Germany. TEL 49-2234-9854265. FAX 49-2234-82503. (Dist. by: Dr. Rudolf Habelt GmbH, Am Buchenhang 1, 53115 Bonn, Germany. TEL 49-228-232016. FAX 49-228-9238322) (Co-sponsors: Rheinisches Landesmuseum, Verein von Altertumsfreunden in Rheinland) **Indexed:** RILA. **Document type:** monographic series.

BEITRAEGE ZUR RHEINISCHEN VOLKSKUNDE. see *FOLKLORE*

913   GW   ISSN 0067-5245
BEITRAEGE ZUR UR- UND FRUEHGESCHICHTLICHEN ARCHAEOLOGIE DES MITTELMEERKULTURRAUMES. 1965. irreg., vol.31, 1992. price varies. Dr. Rudolf Habelt GmbH, Am Buchenhang 1, 53115 Bonn, Germany. TEL 49-228-9238322. FAX 49-228-923836. Ed. H. Hauptmann. **Document type:** monographic series.

914   UK   ISSN 0309-3093
BERKSHIRE ARCHAEOLOGICAL JOURNAL. 1871. a. £2. Berkshire Archaeological Society, 28 Holmes Rd., Reading, Berks, England. Ed C.F. Slade. bk.rev.; bibl.; illus.; index. circ. 200. **Indexed:** Avery Ind.Archit.Per., Br.Archaeol.Abstr., Numis.Lit.
  —BLDSC (1940.700000).
   Description: Covers archaeology and history of Berkshire.
   Refereed Serial

913   GW   ISSN 0344-5089
CC79.C5
BERLINER BEITRAEGE ZUR ARCHAEOMETRIE. (Text in English and German) 1976. a. DM.60. Staatliche Museen, Preussischer Kulturbesitz, Schlossstr. 1a, 14059 Berlin, Germany. TEL 49-30-32091297. FAX 49-30-3221614. Ed. Josef Riederer. bk.rev. circ. 800. **Indexed:** Anthropol.Lit. **Document type:** academic/scholarly publication.
   Description: Information about the scientific analysis and conservation of works of art.

914   SZ
BERN UNIVERSITAET. SEMINAR FUER KLASSISCHE ARCHAEOLOGIE. HEFTE. (Text in French, German and Italian) 1975. a. price varies. Universitaet Bern, Institut fuer Klassische Archaeologie, Laenggassstr. 10, CH-3012 Bern, Switzerland. TEL 41-31-6318991. FAX 41-31-6314905. E-mail: dwillers@arch.unibe.ch. Ed. Dietrich Willers. illus. circ. 20. **Document type:** academic/scholarly publication.
   Formerly: Bern Universitaet. Archaeologisches Seminar. Hefte.

930.1   LE   ISSN 0067-6195
DS41
BERYTUS ARCHEOLOGICAL STUDIES. (Text in English, French, German) 1934. a. $15 (foreign $20) (effective 1996). American University of Beirut, Faculty of Arts and Sciences, A U B Post Hall 106, Beirut, Lebanon. FAX 873-1450231. TELEX 20801 LE AMUNOB. E-mail: hseeden@aub.edu.lb; URL: http://www.aub.edu.lb/. Ed. Helga Seeden. adv.; bk.rev. circ. 400. (back issues avail.) **Indexed:** A.I.C.P., Bibl.Ling., IBR, Mid.East: Abstr.& Ind., Numis.Lit. **Document type:** academic/scholarly publication.
  —EMDOCS; KR SourceOne.
   Description: Devoted to historical and archaeological studies on Syria and Lebanon from prehistoric to Islamic times.
   Refereed Serial

BIBBIA E ORIENTE; rivista per la conoscenza della Bibbia. see *RELIGIONS AND THEOLOGY*

220 913   US   ISSN 1079-6959
BIBLE AND SPADE. 1972-1983; resumed 1987. q. $30 to libraries; individuals $35 includes newsletter. Associates for Biblical Research, Box 125, Ephrata, PA 17522. TEL 717-733-3585; 800-430-0008. FAX 717-733-3585. E-mail: abrofc@msn.com; URL: http://www.christiananswers.net/abr/abrhome.html. Ed. Bryant G. Wood. R&P contact: Bryant G. Wood. adv. contact: Gary A. Byers. bk.rev.; charts; illus.; index; circ. 800 (paid). **Indexed:** Chr.Per.Ind. **Document type:** newsletter.
   Former titles (until 1993): Archaeology and Biblical Research (ISSN 1071-0507); (until 1983): Bible and Spade (ISSN 0162-9301)

913   US   ISSN 0098-9444
BS620.A1
BIBLICAL ARCHAEOLOGY REVIEW. 1975. 6/yr. $27 (foreign $33). Biblical Archaeology Society, 4710 41st St., N.W., Washington, DC 20016. TEL 202-364-3300. FAX 202-364-2636. URL: http://www.tradepub.com/paid/TITLES/paid.Biblical__Archae_Revi.html. (Subscr. to: Box 4966, Des Moines, IA 50340) Ed. Hershel Shanks. R&P contact: Lisa Straus. adv.; bk.rev.; illus. circ. 200,000. **Indexed:** Avery Ind.Archit.Per., Chr.Per.Ind., G.Soc.Sci.& Rel.Per.Lit., Jewish Abstr., Mid.East: Abstr.& Ind., New Test.Abstr., Old Test.Abstr., Per.Islam. (1991-), Rel.& Theol.Abstr. (1978-), Rel.Ind.One. **Document type:** consumer publication.
  —BLDSC (1947.851000); SWETS; UnCover.

913   RM   ISSN 0067-7388
BIBLIOTECA DE ARHEOLOGIE. (Text in Rumanian; summaries in French) 1957. irreg., vol.49, 1988. (Institutul de Arheologie) Editura Academiei Romane, Calea 13 Septembrie 13, 76117 Bucharest, Rumania. (Dist. by: Rodipet SA, Piata Presei Libere 1, Sec. 1 Bucharest, Rumania. TEL 401-6185103. FAX 401-2226407)

913   BE   ISSN 0067-7817
BIBLIOTHECA AEGYPTIACA. 1932. irreg., no.18, 1991. price varies. Fondation Egyptologique Reine Elisabeth, Parc du Cinquantenaire 10, 1000 Brussels, Belgium. TEL 32-2-7417364. **Document type:** monographic series.

913   IT
BIBLIOTHECA ARCHAEOLOGICA. 1980. irreg., no.19, 1996. price varies. L'Erma di Bretschneider, Via Cassiodoro 19, 00193 Rome, Italy. TEL 39-6-6874127. FAX 39-6-6874129.

BIBLIOTHECA LATINA MEDII ET RECENTIORIS AEVI. see *HISTORY — History Of Europe*

930.1   GR   ISSN 1105-7785
BIBLIOTHEKE TES EN ATHENAIS ARCHAILOGIKES HETAIREIAS/ARCHAEOLOGICAL SOCIETY AT ATHENS LIBRARY. (Text in Greek, English, French, German) 1851. irreg., no.160, 1996. price varies. Archaeological Society at Athens - Archaiologike Hetaireia en Athenais - Archaiologike Hetaireia en Athenais, Panepistimiou 22, 106 72 Athens, Greece. TEL 30-1-3646-043. FAX 60-1-3644-996. illus. (back issues avail.) **Document type:** monographic series.
   Description: Each publication covers a topic concerning the archaeology, art, history, or culture of Greek antiquity.

BIBLIOTHEQUE D'ETUDES COPTES. see *RELIGIONS AND THEOLOGY*

913   UK   ISSN 0140-4202
BIRMINGHAM & WARWICKSHIRE ARCHAEOLOGICAL SOCIETY. TRANSACTIONS. 1871. a. £15 to non-members (effective 1996-1967). Birmingham & Warwickshire Archaeological Society, Birmingham & Midland Institute, Margaret Street, Birmingham B3 3BS, England. Ed. D. Hooke. R&P contact: D. Hooke. bk.rev.; charts; illus.; circ. 350 (controlled). **Indexed:** Br.Archaeol.Abstr., Br.Hum.Ind., Numis.Lit. **Document type:** academic/scholarly publication.
   Description: Contains papers on the archaeology of Birmingham and Warwickshire, including excavation reports.

914   SP   ISSN 0213-6090
DP44
BOLETIN DE ARQUEOLOGIA MEDIEVAL. 1987. a. price varies. Asociacion Espanola de Arqueologia Medieval, Apdo. Postal 50449, Breton de los Herreros 59, 30 Izq., 28003 Madrid, Spain. Ed.Bd. R&P contact: Juan Zozaya. bk.rev.; circ. 613 (controlled). **Document type:** academic/scholarly publication.
  —CINDOC.
   Description: Covers medieval archaeology, Christian and Islam, preferably relating to Spain.

913   GW   ISSN 0344-810X
CC5
BOREAS; Muenstersche Beitraege zur Archaeologie. (Supplement avail: Boreas. Beiheft (ISSN 0722-768X)) 1978. a. DM.80. (Westfaelische Wilhelms Universitaet, Archaeologisches Seminar und Museum) Wasmuth GmbH und Co. KG, Hardenbergstr. 9A, 10623 Berlin, Germany. TEL 49-30-3131920. FAX 49-30-3126370. bk.rev. **Indexed:** Avery Ind.Archit.Per., Numis.Lit., Sci.Cit.Ind. **Document type:** academic/scholarly publication.

913   GW   ISSN 0722-768X
BOREAS. BEIHEFT. (Supplement to: Boreas (ISSN 0344-810X)) 1980. irreg. (Westfaelische Wilhelms Universitaet, Archaeologisches Seminar und Museum) Wasmuth GmbH und Co. KG, Hardenbergstr. 9A, 10623 Berlin, Germany. TEL 49-30-3131920. FAX 49-30-3126370. **Document type:** monographic series.

BRACARA AUGUSTA; revista cultural de regionalismo e historia. see *HISTORY — History Of Europe*

930.1   BE
BRAIVES. 1981. irreg., no.5, 1993. 2500 BEF. Association des Diplomes Histoire Art et Archeologie, College Erasme, Place Blaise Pascal 1, 1348 Louvain-la-Neuve, Belgium. FAX 32-10-472579. E-mail: hackens@arka.ucl.ac.be. Ed. Tony Hackens. **Document type:** monographic series.

913   XO
BRATISLAVA-STUDIA. 1975. irreg. price varies. (Archiv) Obzor, Spitalska 35, 815 85 Bratislava, Slovakia.

BREIFNE; journal of Cumann Seanchais Bhreifne. see *HISTORY — History Of Europe*

914.2   UK   ISSN 0263-1091
BRISTOL AND AVON ARCHAEOLOGY. 1982. a. £7. Bristol and Avon Archaeological Society, Bristol City Museum, Queen's Rd., Bristol BS8 1RL, England. Ed. R. Birchall. bk.rev.; charts; illus.; index. circ. 350. **Indexed:** Br.Archaeol.Abstr. **Document type:** proceedings.
  —BLDSC (2284.640000).
   Supersedes: B A R G Review (ISSN 0144-6576); **Formerly** (until 1980): B A R G Bulletin.
   Description: Contains articles relevant to Avon County.

930.1   UK   ISSN 0068-1032
BRISTOL AND GLOUCESTERSHIRE ARCHAEOLOGICAL SOCIETY, BRISTOL, ENGLAND. TRANSACTIONS. 1876. a. £13 to individuals and institutions. Bristol and Gloucestershire Archaeological Society, 22 Beaumont Rd., Gloucester GL2 0EJ, England. TEL 01452-302610. Ed. John Jurica. bk.rev.; cum.index every 10 yrs. (vol.79-90 in 1974, vol.91-100 in 1987). circ. 1,050. **Indexed:** Br.Archaeol.Abstr., Br.Hum.Ind., IBR, Numis.Lit., RILA. **Document type:** academic/scholarly publication.
  —BLDSC (8905.700000).
   Description: Covers archaeological and historical research in the city of Bristol and in Gloucestershire.

ARCHAEOLOGY

930.1   UK   ISSN 0953-542X
BRITANNIA MONOGRAPH SERIES. 1981. irreg., no.12, 1997. Society for the Promotion of Roman Studies, Senate House, Malet House, London WC1E 7HU, England. TEL 44-171-323-9583. FAX 44-171-323-9584. E-mail: romansoc@sas.ac.uk. **Indexed**: Br.Archaeol.Abstr. **Document type**: monographic series.
   Description: Archeological studies of Romano-British sites and general studies related to Roman Britain.

930.1 940   UK   ISSN 0068-1202
AS122
BRITISH ACADEMY. PROCEEDINGS. 1903. a., vol.86, 1995. Oxford University Press, Walton St., Oxford OX2 6DP, England. TEL 01865-267907. FAX 01865-267773. TELEX 837330-OXPRES-G. E-mail: jnlorders@oup.co.uk. (U.S. subscr. to: Oxford University Press Inc., 200 Madison Ave., New York, NY 10016. TEL 212-679-7300) cum.index: vols.1-63. (reprint service avail. from KTO) **Indexed**: Amer.Hist.& Life (1953-), ASCA, Bibl.Ling., Br.Archaeol.Abstr., Br.Hum.Ind., Hist.Abstr. (1953-), RILA. **Document type**: academic/scholarly publication.
  —BLDSC (6665.200000); UnCover. **CCC**.

930.1   UK
BRITISH ACADEMY MONOGRAPHS IN ARCHAEOLOGY. vol.3, 1992. irreg., vol.7, 1995. price varies. Oxford University Press, Walton St., Oxford OX2 6DP, England. TEL 44-1865-56767. FAX 44-1865-56646. (Subscr. in U.S. to: Oxford University Press Inc., 2001 Evans Rd., Cary, NC 27513. TEL 919-677-0977. FAX 919-677-1714) (back issues avail.) **Document type**: monographic series.

913 709 723   UK   ISSN 0144-0179
BRITISH ARCHAEOLOGICAL ASSOCIATION. CONFERENCE TRANSACTIONS. 1980. a. W.S. Maney & Son Ltd., Hudson Rd., Leeds LS9 7DL, England. TEL 01532-497481. FAX 01532-486983. **Indexed**: Br.Archaeol.Abstr. **Document type**: academic/scholarly publication.
  —BLDSC (3410.268000).

571 913   UK   ISSN 0068-1288
DA20
BRITISH ARCHAEOLOGICAL ASSOCIATION. JOURNAL. 1843. a. £17.50. W.S. Maney & Son Ltd., Hudson Rd., Leeds LS9 7DL, England. TEL 01532-497481. FAX 01532-486983. (Alt. addr.: c/o Institute of Archaeology, 36 Beaumont St., Oxford OX1 2PG, England. TEL 01532-497481. FAX 01532-486983) Ed. Martin Henig. bk.rev.; cum.index every 5 yrs. circ. 1,000. (back issues avail.) **Indexed**: Avery Ind.Archit.Per., Br.Archaeol.Abstr., Br.Hum.Ind., IBR, Numis.Lit., RILA. **Document type**: academic/scholarly publication.
  —BLDSC (4712.600000).
  Refereed Serial

930.1   UK   ISSN 1357-4442
BRITISH ARCHAEOLOGY. Abbreviated title: B A. (Consists of two sections: Magazine and Briefing) 10/yr. £17($50) to non-members (rest of Europe £22). Council for British Archaeology, Bowes Morrell House, 111 Walmgate, York YO1 2UA, England. TEL 44-1904-671417. FAX 44-1904-671384. E-mail: 100271.456@compuserve.com; URL: http://britac3.britac.ac.uk/cba/ba/ba.html. Ed. Simon Denison. R&P contact: Christine Pietrowski. adv.; bk.rev.; illus. circ. 3,500. (processed) **Document type**: academic/scholarly publication, bulletin.
  —BLDSC (2289.151400).
  Former titles: British Archaeological News (ISSN 0269-1906); Council for British Archaeology. Newsletter and Calendar of Excavations (ISSN 0309-3204); Which incorporated (in 1981): Current Archaeological Offprints and Reports (ISSN 0305-5280); Which was formerly: Current and Forthcoming Offprints on Archaeology in Great Britain and Ireland (ISSN 0526-4375)
  Description: Combines the latest British archaeological news with a calendar of conferences, volunteer opportunities at excavations, and study tours.

700 949.5   UK   ISSN 0068-2454
DF11
BRITISH SCHOOL AT ATHENS. ANNUAL. (Text in English; abstracts in English, Greek) 1894. a. £35 (effective Mar. 1993). British School at Athens, 31-34 Gordon Sq., London WC1H 0PY, England. TEL 44-171-387-8029. FAX 44-171-383-0781. Ed. Graham J. Shipley. index. circ. 938. (also avail. in microfilm from BHP; microfiche from IDC; reprint service avail. from KTO) **Indexed**: A.I.C.P., Art & Archaeol.Tech.Abstr., Avery Ind.Archit.Per., Bibl.Ling., Br.Archaeol.Abstr., Br.Hum.Ind., Br.Tech.Ind., Numis.Lit. **Document type**: academic/scholarly publication.
  —BLDSC (1073.675000).
  Description: Includes the work of B.S.A. members on cultural, historical, artistic, or geographic aspects of Greece in classical, medieval, and modern times.
  Refereed Serial

930.1   UK
BRITISH SCHOOL AT ROME. ARCHAEOLOGICAL MONOGRAPHS. irreg., no.9. British School at Rome, c/o The British Academy, 20-21 Cornwall Terr., London NW1 4QP, England. TEL 44-1396-323-0743. (Dist. by: Oxbow Books, Park End Pl., Oxford OX1 1HN, England) Pub. Gillian Clark. **Document type**: academic/scholarly publication.

913   UK
DG12
BRITISH SCHOOL AT ROME. PAPERS. ARCHAEOLOGY, HISTORY, HISTORY OF ART. 1902. a. £31. British School at Rome, c/o The British Academy, 20-21 Cornwall Terr., London NW1 4QP, England. TEL 44-1396-323-0743. (Vols. 1-24 dist. in U.S. by: Johnson Reprint Corporation, Dept. S L, 111 Fifth Ave., New York, NY 10003) Hon. Ed. B. Ward-Perkins. circ. 750. (reprint service avail. from SCH) **Indexed**: Avery Ind.Archit.Per., Br.Archaeol.Abstr., Br.Hum.Ind., IBR, RILA. **Document type**: academic/scholarly publication.
  Formerly: British School at Rome. Papers. Archeology (ISSN 0068-2462)

930   BE   ISSN 0165-9367
DE2
BULLETIN ANTIEKE BESCHAVING; annual papers on classical archaeology. Short title: Babesch. (Supplements avail.) (Text in English, French, German, Italian) 1926. a. 3000 BEF (effective 1996). (Stichting Babesch) Editions Peeters s.p.r.l., Bondgenotenlaan 153, 3000 Leuven, Belgium. TEL 32-16-235170. FAX 32-16-228500. URL: http://www.peeters-leuven.be. Ed. M.H. Wijnen. adv.; bk.rev. **Indexed**: Avery Ind.Archit.Per. **Document type**: academic/scholarly publication.
  —SWETS.
  Supersedes: Vereniging tot Bevordering der Kennis van de Antieke Beschaving. Bulletin.
  Description: Publishes original research papers and short communications of broad archaeological significance.

930.1   MR   ISSN 0068-4015
DT311
BULLETIN D'ARCHEOLOGIE MAROCAINE. 1956. a. Institut National des Sciences, de l'Archeologie et du Patrimoine, Av. John Kennedy - Route des Zaers, Rabat-Souissi, Morocco. **Indexed**: A.I.C.P., Anthropol.Lit., Numis.Lit. **Document type**: academic/scholarly publication, bulletin.

932   UA   ISSN 1110-2489
DT57
BULLETIN D'INFORMATION ARCHEOLOGIQUE. 1990. a., latest vol.7. £25 (overseas 40 F.). Institut Francais d'Archeologie Orientale du Caire, P.O. Box 11562 Kasr el-Aini, 37 Sharia Sheikh Aly Youssef, Mounira, Cairo, Egypt. TEL 20-2-3571622. FAX 20-2-3544635. E-mail: bph@ritsec3.com.eg. (Dist. by: Boustany's Publishing House, 29 Faggalah St., 11271 Cairo, Egypt. TEL 20-2-5915315. FAX 20-2-4177915; In France: Imprimerie Nationale - D A C F, 27 rue de la Convention, 75732 Paris Cedex 15, France. TEL 33-1-40583105. FAX 33-1-40583064) (back issues avail.) **Document type**: bulletin.

BULLETIN DE CORRESPONDANCE HELLENIQUE. see *CLASSICAL STUDIES*

BULLETIN DU MUSEE HONGROIS DES BEAUX-ARTS. see *ART*

913   FR   ISSN 0007-473X
N2
BULLETIN MONUMENTAL. 1834. q. 485 F. (foreign 1998). Societe Francaise d'Archeologie, Musee National des Monuments Francais, Palais de Chaillot, 1 Place du Trocadero, 75116 Paris, France. TEL 33-1-47047896. FAX 33-1-44059425. bk.rev.; bibl.; illus.; cum.index: 1834-1925, 1926-1954, 1955-1975, 1976-1990. circ. 2,300. (also avail. in microfiche from IDC) **Indexed**: Art Ind., Arts & Hum.Cit.Ind., ASCA, Avery Ind.Archit.Per., Br.Archaeol.Abstr., Curr.Cont., IBR, RILA, SSCI. **Document type**: bulletin.
  —KR SourceOne; SWETS.

930.1   UK   ISSN 0307-1650
BULLETIN SUBTERRANEA BRITANNICA. 1975. a. £12. Subterranea Britannica, 96A Brighton Rd., S. Croydon, Surrey CR2 6AD, England. TEL 44-1737-823456. FAX 44-181-654-8507. Ed. P.W. Sowan. (back issues avail.) **Document type**: academic/scholarly publication, bulletin.
  Description: Features the archeology and history of excavating, and the primary and secondary uses of underground space.
  Refereed Serial

913 200   AT   ISSN 0007-6260
BS620.A1
BURIED HISTORY. 1964. q. Aus.$25 (New Zealand Aus.$30; elsewhere Aus.$32) (effective 1998). Australian Institute of Archaeology, Level 2, Centreway Arcade, 259 Collins St., Melbourne, Vic. 3000, Australia. TEL 61-3-96503477. FAX 61-3-96542774. Ed. Piers Crocker. R&P contact: Piers Crocker. adv. contact: Piers Crocker. bk.rev.; illus. circ. 550. (also avail. in microform) **Indexed**: Chr.Per.Ind., Old Test.Abstr. **Document type**: academic/scholarly publication.
  —BLDSC (2931.633000).
  Description: Recent discoveries in biblical and Near Eastern archaeology.
  Refereed Serial

914 949.7   CI   ISSN 0350-6088
BUZETSKI ZBORNIK. 1976. a. Opcinska Konferencija S.S.R.N. Buzet, 51 420 Buzet, Croatia. FAX 053-61-413. adv. circ. 1,000.

917   US
C A A SCIENTIFIC PAPERS. (Center for American Archeology) 1976. irreg., vol.6, 1991. price varies. Center for American Archeology Press, Box 22, Kampsville, IL 62053-0022. TEL 618-653-4688.

917   US
C A A TECHNICAL REPORTS. (Center for American Archeology) irreg., vol.5, 1994. price varies. Center for American Archeology Press, Box 22, Kampsville, IL 62053-0022. TEL 618-653-4688.

913   ISSN 0589-9028
C B A ANNUAL REPORT. a. £10 to non-members. Council for British Archaeology, Bowes Morrell House, 111 Walmgate, York YO1 2UA, England. TEL 44-1904-671417. FAX 44-1904-671384. Ed. Christine Pieterowski. R&P contact: Christine Pietrowski. **Document type**: corporate report.
  Description: Contains reports of the C B A and its constituent committees and regional groups and on the annual accounts, membership lists, the annual Beatrice de Cardi Lecture, and presidential addresses.

930.1 UK ISSN 0589-9036
CODEN: RRCADF
C B A RESEARCH REPORTS. 1955. irreg. price varies. Council for British Archaeology, Bowes Morrell House, 111 Walmgate, York YO1 2UA, England. TEL 44-1904-671417. FAX 44-1904-671384. Ed. Christine Pietrowski. R&P contact: Christine Pietrowski. (back issues avail.) **Document type:** monographic series, academic/scholarly publication. —BLDSC (3095.120000); CASDDS.
   Description: Covers archaeological and scholarly research throughout Great Britain.

930.1097275 MX ISSN 0187-652X
C I H M E C H. 1988. s-a. Mex.$30 per no. (effective 1997). Universidad Nacional Autonoma de Mexico, Centro de Investigaciones Humanisticas de Mesoamerica y el Estado de Chiapas, 28 de Abril No. 11, San Cristobal de las Casas, 029200 Chiapas, Mexico. TEL 52-967-82944. FAX 52-967-82997. E-mail: cihmech@servidor.unam.mx. Ed. Pablo Gonzalez Casanova Henriquez.
   Description: Includes articles, notes and essays on archaeology, anthropology, history and ethnology of Chiapas, Mexico.

930.1 551.46 IS ISSN 0792-6073
C M S NEWS. (Text in English) 1978. s-a. free. Haifa University, Center for Maritime Studies, Ha-Carmel, Haifa 31905, Israel. FAX 972-4-8240493. TELEX 46660-UNIHA-IL. E-mail: maritime@research.haifa.ac.il. Ed. Nira Karmon. bk.rev. circ. 1,000. **Document type:** newsletter.
   Description: Covers topics in underwater and marine archaeology, marine resources and geology.

913 737 SP ISSN 0007-9502
CC37
CAESARAUGUSTA. 1951. a. 2500 ptas. per no. (effective 1997). Institucion Fernando el Catolico, Plaza de Espana 2, 50071 Zaragoza, Spain. TEL 34-976-288878. FAX 34-976-288846. E-mail: ifc@mail.sendanet.es. Ed. Miguel Beltran Lloris. R&P contact: Felix Sanchez. adv. contact: Maria-Luz Cortes. bk.rev.; bibl.; charts; illus.; index, cum.index. circ. 1,000. **Indexed:** Amer.Hist.& Life (1957-1970), Br.Archaeol.Abstr., Hist.Abstr. (1957-1970), Numis.Lit. **Document type:** academic/scholarly publication.
   —CINDOC.
   Refereed Serial

914 700 FR ISSN 0575-0385
DC648.6
CAHIERS ALSACIENS D'ARCHEOLOGIE D'ART ET D'HISTOIRE. 1909. a. 165 F. (effective 1996-1997). Societe pour la Conservation des Monuments Historiques d'Alsace, 2 place du Chateau, 67000 Strasbourg, France. TEL 88-52-50-00. Ed. B. Schnitzler. bk.rev. circ. 1,000. **Document type:** monographic series, academic/scholarly publication.
   Incorporating (1857-1956): Societe pour la Conservation des Monuments Historiques d'Alsace. Bulletin.

913 FR ISSN 0068-4945
CC3
CAHIERS ARCHEOLOGIQUES. 1966. a. price varies. Editions A. et J. Picard, 82 rue Bonaparte, 75006 Paris, France. FAX 43-26-42-64. **Indexed:** Art Ind., IBR. **Document type:** academic/scholarly publication, monographic series.
   —BLDSC (2948.624000); KR SourceOne.
   Formerly: Bibliotheque des Cahiers Archeologiques (ISSN 0067-8309)

913 900 FR ISSN 0007-9693
CAHIERS D'ARCHEOLOGIE ET D'HISTOIRE DU BERRY. 1965. q. 200 F. (foreign 230 F.). Societe d'Archeologie et d'Histoire du Berry, 8 Pl. des 4 Piliers, B.P. 69, 18002 Bourges Cedex, France. TEL 33-2-48243340. bk.rev.; bibl.; illus. circ. 600. (tabloid format) **Indexed:** IBR, Numis.Lit. **Document type:** bulletin.

930.1 FR
CAHIERS DE KARNAK. (Text in English, French; summaries in Arabic) 1982. irreg. price varies. Editions Recherche sur les Civilisations, 28 rue de Bourgogne, 75007 Paris, France. TEL 33-1-40628062. FAX 33-1-40628071. Ed. Hina Descat; Pub. Hina Descat. circ. 600. **Document type:** monographic series.

930.1 FR ISSN 0291-2694
CAHIERS DE L'EUPHRATE. (Text in English, French) 1985. irreg. price varies. Editions Recherche sur les Civilisations, 28 rue de Bourgogne, 75007 Paris, France. TEL 33-1-40628062. FAX 33-1-40628071. Ed. Hina Descat; Pub. Hina Descat. circ. 600. **Document type:** monographic series.

932 666 UA ISSN 0259-7381
DT62.P72
CAHIERS DE LA CERAMIQUE EGYPTIENNE. 1987. irreg., vol.5, 1997. price varies. Institut Francais d'Archeologie Orientale du Caire, P.O. Box 11562 Kasr el-Aini, 37 Sharia Sheikh Aly Youssef, Mounira, Cairo, Egypt. TEL 20-2-3571622. FAX 20-2-3544635. E-mail: mcmichael@fao.eg-net.net. (Dist. by: Boustany's Publishing House, 29 Faggalah St., 11271 Cairo, Egypt. TEL 20-2-5915315. FAX 20-2-4177915; In France: Imprimerie Nationale - D A C F, 27 rue de la Convention, 75732 Paris Cedex 15, France. TEL 33-1-40583105. FAX 33-1-40583064) (back issues avail.) **Document type:** academic/scholarly publication, proceedings.
   Description: Publishes studies of Egyptian ceramics from prehistoric, Pharaonic, Classical, medieval and modern times, including technical, economic and cultural aspects.

930.1 FR
CAHIERS DE TANIS. 1988. irreg. price varies. Editions Recherches sur les Civilisations, 28 rue de Bourgogne, 75007 Paris, France. TEL 33-1-40628062. FAX 33-1-40628071. Ed. Hina Descat; Pub. Hina Descat. circ. 600. **Document type:** monographic series.

913.38 CN ISSN 0317-5065
CB311
CAHIERS DES ETUDES ANCIENNES. 1972. irreg. price varies. Universite du Quebec a Trois Rivieres, C.P. 500, Trois-Rivieres. PQ G9A 5H7, Canada. TEL 514-671-3888. FAX 514-671-2121. (Dist. by: Exportlivre, C.P. 305, Saint Lambert, Que. J4P 3P8, Canada) Ed. Pierre Senay. illus. circ. 700.

913 FR ISSN 0180-9261
CAHIERS DU MEMONTOIS. 1973. irreg., latest no.65. price varies. Groupe Archeologique du Memontois, Malain, 21410 Pont-de-Pany, France. Ed.Bd.; Pub. Louis Roussel. bk.rev.; charts; illus. circ. 1,000. (back issues avail.) **Document type:** monographic series.
   Description: Covers local archeological and historical facts.

CAHIERS DU VITREZAIS. see *HISTORY — History Of Europe*

CAHIERS LEOPOLD DELISLE. see *HISTORY*

571 IT ISSN 1012-0238
CAHIERS LIGURES DE PREHISTOIRE ET DE PROTOHISTOIRE. (Text in French) 1952-1988; resumed 199? a. Lit.40000 (effective 1997). Istituto Internazionale di Studi Liguri - International Institute of Ligurian Studies, Museo Bicknell, Via Romana, 39, 18012 Bordighera, Italy. TEL 39-184-263601. FAX 39-184-266421. circ. 1,000. **Indexed:** A.I.C.P. **Document type:** academic/scholarly publication.
   Formerly (until 1984): Cahiers Ligures de Prehistoire et d'Archeologie (ISSN 0575-108X); **Supersedes** (1931-1949): Cahiers d'Histoire et d'Archeologie.
   Description: Provides prehistoric and archeological articles on mediterranean France.

CAHIERS LORRAINS. see *HISTORY — History Of Europe*

913 979.4 US
CALIFORNIA ARCHEOLOGICAL REPORTS. 1961. irreg., latest no. 24. price varies. Department of Parks and Recreation, 1405 Resources Bldg., 1416 9th St., Box 2390, Sacramento, CA 95811. TEL 916-445-6477. Ed. Peter D. Schulz. circ. 800.
   Formerly: California. Department of Parks and Recreation. Archaeological Report (ISSN 0068-5550)

942 UK ISSN 0068-659X
CAMBRIDGE AIR SURVEYS. 1952. irreg., latest 1990. price varies. Cambridge University Press, Edinburgh Bldg., Shaftesbury Rd., Cambridge CB2 2RU, England. TEL 44-1223-312393. FAX 44-1223-315052. TELEX 851817256. E-mail: information@cup.cam.ac.uk; URL: http://www.cup.cam.ac.uk. (N. American addr.: Cambridge University Press, Journals Dept., 40 W. 20th St., New York, NY 10011. TEL 212-924-3900. FAX 212-691-3239) R&P contact: Linda Nicol. **Document type:** academic/scholarly publication.

CAMBRIDGE ANTIQUARIAN SOCIETY. PROCEEDINGS. see *HISTORY — History Of Europe*

930.1 UK ISSN 0959-7743
CC1
CAMBRIDGE ARCHAEOLOGICAL JOURNAL. 1991. s-a. £48($75) (effective 1998). (University of Cambridge, McDonald Institute for Archaeological Research) Cambridge University Press, Edinburgh Bldg., Shaftesbury Rd., Cambridge CB2 2RU, England. TEL 44-1223-312393. FAX 44-1223-315052. TELEX 851817256. E-mail: information@cup.cam.ac.uk; URL: http://www.cup.org/Journals/CUPJNLS.html. (N. American addr.: Cambridge University Press, Journals Dept., 40 W. 20th St., New York, NY 10011. TEL 212-924-3900. FAX 212-691-3239) Ed. Chris Scarre. R&P contact: Rebecca Symons. adv. contact: Rebecca Symons. (back issues avail.) **Indexed:** Anthropol.Lit. **Document type:** academic/scholarly publication.
   —BLDSC (3015.941330); UMI; UnCover. **CCC.**
   Description: Features theoretical and descriptive research articles, ranging widely in time and covering general topics of archaeology.
   Refereed Serial

971.01 CN ISSN 0705-2006
F1019
CANADIAN JOURNAL OF ARCHAEOLOGY. (Text in English and French) 1977. a. Can.$50 to individuals; students Can.$35; institutions Can.$65. Canadian Archaeological Association, c/o Bjorn Simonsen, Secy.-Treas., 352 Viaduct Ave. W., R.R. 3, Victoria, BC V8X 3X1, Canada. TEL 604-479-1147. FAX 604-381-3890. URL: http://www.canadianarchaeology.com/caa.files/caabiblio/cja1.htm. Ed. Mima Kapches. adv.; bk.rev.; illus. circ. 500. **Indexed:** Anthropol.Lit., Br.Archaeol.Abstr. **Document type:** academic/scholarly publication.
   —CCC.
   Formerly: Canadian Archaeological Association. Bulletin (ISSN 0315-761X)
   Refereed Serial

917 CN ISSN 0317-2244
CANADIAN MUSEUM OF CIVILIZATION. MERCURY SERIES. ARCHAEOLOGICAL SURVEY OF CANADA. PAPER (NO.)/MUSEE CANADIEN DES CIVILISATIONS. COLLECTION MERCURE. COMMISSION ARCHEOLOGIQUE DU CANADA. DOSSIER. (Text in English, French) 1972. irreg. price varies. Canadian Museum of Civilization, 100 Laurier St., P.O. Box 3100, Stn. B, Hull, PQ J8X 4H2, Canada. E-mail: publications@cmcc.muse.digital.ca. Ed. Jean-Francois Blanchette. R&P contact: Nicole Chamberland. adv. contact: Pam Coulas. charts; illus.; cum.index. **Document type:** academic/scholarly publication, monographic series, government publication.
   Description: Designed to permit the rapid dissemination of information pertaining to the disciplines in which the museum is active.

930.1 AU ISSN 1025-2320
▼**CARNUNTUM JAHRBUCH.** 1995. a. Verlag der Oesterreichischen Akademie der Wissenschaften, Dr. Ignaz-Seipel-Platz 2, A-1010 Vienna, Austria. TEL 43-1-51581401. FAX 43-1-51581400. E-mail: verlag@oeaw.ac.at; URL: http://www.oeaw.ac.at/einheiten/verlag. **Document type:** academic/scholarly publication, monographic series.

CASA DE VELASQUEZ, MADRID. MELANGES/CASA DE VELASQUEZ, MADRID. MISCELLANIES. see *ART*

CELESTINESCA. see *LITERATURE*

CENTER FOR ANTHROPOLOGICAL STUDIES. CONTRIBUTIONS TO ANTHROPOLOGICAL STUDIES. see *ANTHROPOLOGY*

ARCHAEOLOGY

CENTER FOR ANTHROPOLOGICAL STUDIES. ETHNOHISTORICAL REPORT SERIES. see *ANTHROPOLOGY*

CENTER FOR ANTHROPOLOGICAL STUDIES. SPANISH BORDERLANDS RESEARCH. see *ANTHROPOLOGY*

913   US   ISSN 0008-9559
E75
CENTRAL STATES ARCHAEOLOGICAL JOURNAL. 1954. q. $15 (effective 1995). Central States Archaeological Societies, Inc., 646 Knierim Pl., Kirkwood, MO 63122. TEL 314-821-7675. Ed. Alan L. Banks; Pub. Richard A. Watts. bk.rev.; charts; illus.; stat.; index, cum.index. circ. 4,000. **Indexed:** Abstr.Anthropol., Anthropol.Lit. **Document type:** academic/scholarly publication.
    Refereed Serial

917 560   US   ISSN 0882-3693
F388
CENTRAL TEXAS ARCHEOLOGIST. 1935. irreg. $12. Baylor University, Geology Department, Box 97363, Waco, TX 76798-7363. TEL 817-755-3164. Ed. John W. Fox. bibl.; charts; illus. circ. 500. **Indexed:** Anthropol.Lit.

CENTRE FOR THE STUDY OF THE CIVILIZATIONS OF CENTRAL ASIA. PUBLICATIONS. see *HISTORY — History Of Asia*

913   IT
CENTRE JEAN BERARD. CAHIER. 1974. irreg., no.16, 1986. price varies. L'Erma di Bretschneider, Via Cassiodoro 19, 00193 Rome, Italy. TEL 39-6-6874127. FAX 39-6-6874129.

CENTRE NATIONAL D'ARCHEOLOGIE ET D'HISTOIRE DU LIVRE. PUBLICATION. see *PUBLISHING AND BOOK TRADE*

913.031 709   IT
CENTRO CAMUNO DI STUDI PREISTORICI. ARCHIVI. (Text in various languages) 1968. irreg., vol.9, 1987. L.70000 per no. Centro Camuno di Studi Preistorici, Edizioni del Centro, Capo di Ponte, 25044 Brescia, Italy. TEL 364-42091. FAX 364-42572. E-mail: ccsp@globalnet.it; URL: http://ccsp.lo.it. Ed. Emmanuel Anati. bibl.; index. **Document type:** monographic series.
    Description: Includes topics concerned with prehistoric art and other manifestations of intellectual life of prehistoric and primitive man.

913 709   IT   ISSN 0577-2168
GN818.C3
CENTRO CAMUNO DI STUDI PREISTORICI. BOLLETTINO. (Text in various languages) 1968. a. L.45000. Centro Camuno di Studi Preistorici, Edizioni del Centro, Capo di Ponte, 25044 Brescia, Italy. TEL 39-364-42091. FAX 39-364-42572. E-mail: ccsp@globalnet.it; URL: http://ccsp.lo.it. Ed. Emmanuel Anati. bk.rev.; bibl.; charts; illus. (back issues avail.) **Indexed:** A.I.C.P., Anthropol.Lit., Br.Archaeol.Abstr.
    Description: Contains articles, research reports and surveys on recent discoveries throughout the world. Each published in its original language.

913.031 709   IT
CENTRO CAMUNO DI STUDI PREISTORICI. STUDI CAMUNI. (Text in various languages) irreg., vol.16, 1995. L.40000 per no. Centro Camuno di Studi Preistorici, Edizioni del Centro, Capo di Ponte, 25044 Brescia, Italy. TEL 39-364-42091. FAX 39-364-42572. E-mail: ccsp@globalnet.it; URL: http://ccsp.lo.it. illus.
    Description: Essays on prehistoric art and archaeology. Includes topics on ancient people, their art, history and evolution.

CENTRO CAMUNO DI STUDI PREISTORICI. SYMPOSIA. see *ART*

CENTRO DE ESTUDIOS AVANZADOS DE PUERTO RICO Y EL CARIBE. REVISTA. see *HISTORY — History Of North And South America*

CENTRO DE ESTUDOS REGIONAIS. BOLETIM CULTURAL. see *ANTHROPOLOGY*

913   IT   ISSN 0069-2204
CENTRO STUDI PER LA MAGNA GRECIA, NAPLES. PUBBLICAZIONI PROPRIE.* 1959. irreg., no.6, 1969. price varies. Centro Studi per la Magna Grecia, Istituto di Archeologia, Via Porta di Massa 1, 80133 Naples, Italy.

CERCLE D'HISTOIRE ET D'ARCHEOLOGIE DE SAINT-GHISLAIN ET DE LA REGION. ANALES. see *HISTORY — History Of Europe*

CERCLE HISTORIQUE ET FOLKLORIQUE DE BRAINE-LE-CHATEAU DE TUBIZE ET DES REGIONS VOISINES. ANNALES. see *HISTORY — History Of Europe*

914   BE   ISSN 0775-4671
CERCLE ROYAL D'HISTOIRE ET D'ARCHEOLOGIE D'ATH ET DE LA REGION. BULLETIN. 1967. bi-m. 800 BEF includes Annales. Cercle Royal d'Histoire et d'Archeologie d'Ath et de la Region et Musees Athois, 13, rue de la Poterne, 7800 Ath, Belgium. **Document type:** bulletin.

914   BE
CERCLE ROYAL D'HISTOIRE ET D'ARCHEOLOGIE D'ATH ET DE LA REGION ET MUSEES ATHOIS. ANNALES. 1913. biennial. 800 BEF includes Bulletin. Cercle Royal d'Histoire et d'Archeologie d'Ath et de la Region et Musees Athois, 13, rue de la Poterne, 7800 Ath, Belgium. **Document type:** monographic series.

914   BE   ISSN 0771-5692
CERCLE ROYAL D'HISTOIRE ET D'ARCHEOLOGIE D'ATH ET DE LA REGION ET MUSEES ATHOIS. ETUDES ET DOCUMENTS. 1969. a. Cercle Royal d'Histoire et d'Archeologie d'Ath et de la Region et Musees Athois, 13, rue de la Poterne, 7800 Ath, Belgium. **Document type:** academic/scholarly publication.

914   XR
CESKA ARCHEOLOGICKA SPOLECNOST. ZPRAVY/CZECH ARCHAEOLOGICAL SOCIETY. NEWS. (Text in Czech; summaries in German) 1957. irreg. exchange basis only. Ceska Archeologicka Spolecnost, Letenska 4, 118 01 Prague 1, Czech Republic. Ed. Karel Sklenar. adv. contact: Supplement avail. illus. circ. 1,000. **Indexed:** Anthropol.Lit. **Document type:** bulletin.
    Formerly (until 1992): Ceskoslovenska Spolecnost Archeologicka. Zpravy.

913   UK   ISSN 0307-6628
CHESHIRE ARCHAEOLOGICAL BULLETIN. 1973. a. £2.50. 11 Wold Court, Hawarden, Clwyd CH5 3LN, Wales. Ed. Janet A. Rutter. adv.; bk.rev. circ. 250. **Indexed:** Br.Archaeol.Abstr. **Document type:** bulletin.

913   US   ISSN 0009-3300
E77.8
CHESOPIEAN. 1963. q. $15 (Canada $16; elsewhere $17) (effective 1996 & 1997). Institute for Human History, Box 648, Gloucester, VA 23061-0648. TEL 804-642-2851. Ed. Christine W. Dragoo. bk.rev.; charts; illus.; cum.index every 5 yrs. circ. 500. **Indexed:** Abstr.Anthropol., Amer.Hist.& Life (1979-1988), Anthropol.Lit., Hist.Abstr (1979-1988). **Document type:** academic/scholarly publication.

930.1   UK
CHESTER ARCHAEOLOGY. EXCAVATION AND SURVEY REPORTS. 1978. irreg., latest no.10. price varies. Chester City Council, Archaeological Service, Chester, England. TEL 44-1244-402028. E-mail: p.carrington@chestercc.gov.uk; URL: http://www.chestercc.gov.uk/chestercc.htmls/archpub.htm. (Subscr. to: Grosvenor Museum Shop, 27 Grosvenor St., Chester CH1 2DD, England. TEL 44-1244-402029. FAX 44-1244-347587) Ed. Peter Carrington. R&P contact: Peter Carrington. illus. **Document type:** monographic series.
    Former titles (until 1994, no.8): Chester City Council. Archaeological Service Excavation and Survey Reports; (until 1991, no.6): Grosvenor Museum Archaeological and Survey Reports.
    Description: Reports on the preliminary and final findings at archaeological excavations taking place in and around Chester, England.

930.1   UK
CHESTER ARCHAEOLOGY. OCCASIONAL PAPERS. 1993. irreg., no.3. TEL 44-1244-402028. E-mail: p.carrington@chestercc.gov.uk. (Subscr. to: Grosvenor Museum Shop, 27 Grosvenor St., Chester CH1 2DD, England. TEL 44-1244-402029. FAX 44-1244-347587) Ed. Peter Carrington. R&P contact: Peter Carrington. **Document type:** monographic series.
    Formerly (until 1994, no.2): Chester City Council. Archaeological Service Occasional Papers.
    Description: Contains conference proceedings and miscellaneous publications on the archaeology of the Chester region of England.

913   GW   ISSN 0069-3715
CHIRON. 1971. a. DM.98. (Deutsches Archaologisches Institut, Kommission fuer Alte Geschichte und Epigraphik) C.H. Beck'sche Verlagsbuchhandlung, Wilhelmstr. 9, 80801 Munich, Germany. TEL 089-38189-338. FAX 089-38189-398. circ. 600. (back issues avail.) **Indexed:** Bibl.Ling., Numis.Lit., Psychol.Abstr. **Document type:** academic/scholarly publication. —BLDSC (3181.129500); SWETS.

CHRONIKA TES CHALKIDIKES. see *HISTORY — History Of Europe*

CHRONIQUE D'EGYPTE. see *ORIENTAL STUDIES*

CIMBEBASIA. see *SCIENCES: COMPREHENSIVE WORKS*

914.5 300   IT   ISSN 0392-9884
CIRCOLO CULTURALE B.G. DUNS SCOTO DI ROCCARAINOLA. ATTI. (Text in Italian; summaries in English) 1975. irreg. free. Domenico Capolongo, Ed. & Pub., Via Roma 8, 80030 Roccarainola, Italy. cum.index: 1975-1991.

913 940   UK
CIRENCESTER EXCAVATIONS. 1981. irreg., latest Jun. 1994. price varies. Cotswold Archaeological Trust, Cirencester Excavation Committee, Corinium Museum, Park St., Cirencester, Glos. GL7 2BX, England. TEL 01285-643625. FAX 01285-644641. circ. 1,000. **Indexed:** Br.Archaeol.Abstr. **Document type:** academic/scholarly publication, monographic series.
    Description: Discusses the archaeology of Cirencester (Roman Corinium) and the preservation of the city's and region's historical and archaeological heritage.
    Refereed Serial

913 945   IT   ISSN 0393-4977
CITTANOVA; mensile indipendente per Nocera, il suo agro e un po piu oltre. 1979. m. L.10000($5) Antonio Pecoraro, Ed. & Pub., Via Giovanni Nicotera, 37, 84014 Nocera Inferiore (SA), Italy. (Subscr. to: Casella Postale 2, 84014 Nocera Inferiore (SA), Italy) adv.; bk.rev. circ. 1,000. (tabloid format; back issues avail.) **Document type:** newspaper.

CLASSICAL AND BYZANTINE MONOGRAPHS. see *CLASSICAL STUDIES*

917 978   US   ISSN 0887-6282
F791
COAS: NEW MEXICO ARCHAEOLOGY AND HISTORY. 1983. q. $10. Coas Publishing and Research, 535 S. Melendres, Las Cruces, NM 88005. TEL 505-524-0301. Ed. Patrick H. Beckett. circ. 300. (back issues avail.)

CODEX FILATELICA. see *PHILATELY*

918   IT
COLLANA CORPUS ANTIQUITATUM AMERICANENSIUM ITALIA. 1981. irreg. L.50000. (Unione Accademica Nazionale) Bonsignori Editore s.r.l., Viale dei Quattro Venti, 47, 00152 Rome, Italy. TEL 06-5881496. FAX 06-5882839. **Document type:** monographic series.

914   IT
COLLANA CORPUS VASORUM ANTIQUORUM ITALIA. 1950. irreg. L.220000. (Unione Accademica Nazionale) Bonsignori Editore s.r.l., Viale dei Quattro Venti, 47, 00152 Rome, Italy. TEL 06-5881496. FAX 06-5882839. (back issues avail.) **Document type:** monographic series.

COLLANA DI STUDI PALEONTOLOGICI. see *ANTHROPOLOGY*

914   IT   ISSN 0392-0879
COLLEZIONI E MUSEI ARCHEOLOGICI DEL VENETO. 1973. irreg., vol.39, 1995. price varies. Giorgio Bretschneider, Via Crescenzo 43, 00193 Rome, Italy. E-mail: bretschneider@euronet.it. Ed. Gustavo Traversari. (back issues avail.) **Document type:** academic/scholarly publication.

975 917.55   US   ISSN 0069-5971
COLONIAL WILLIAMSBURG ARCHAEOLOGICAL SERIES. 1960. irreg., no.10, 1983. price varies. Colonial Williamsburg Foundation, Box 1776, Williamsburg, VA 23187-1776. TEL 757-220-7342. Ed. Ivor Noe Hume. **Document type:** monographic series.

ARCHAEOLOGY

913 US
COLORADO ARCHAEOLOGICAL SOCIETY MEMOIR SERIES. irreg., no.5, 1992. price varies. Colorado Archaeological Society, Inc., c/o Audrey Merritt, Membership Chairman, 4215 Balsam St., Wheatridge, CO 80033. TEL 303-431-9060. **Document type:** academic/scholarly publication.

913 IT
COMMISSIONE ARCHEOLOGICA COMUNALE DI ROMA. BULLETTINO/ARCHAEOLOGICAL COMMISSION OF ROME. BULLETIN. 1872. a., latest no. 96, 1994(1996). price varies. L'Erma di Bretschneider, Via Cassiodoro 19, 00193 Rome, Italy. TEL 39-6-6874127. FAX 39-6-687412. circ. 1,500. **Indexed:** Numis.Lit. **Document type:** bulletin.

CONDUIT. see HISTORY — History Of Europe

913 720 FR ISSN 0069-8881
DC30
CONGRES ARCHEOLOGIQUE DE FRANCE (PUBLICATION). 1834. a. 485 F. (effective 1998). Societe Francaise d'Archeologie, Musee National des Monuments Francais, Palais de Chaillot, 1 Place du Trocadero, 75116 Paris, France. TEL 33-1-47047896. FAX 33-1-44059425. cum.index: 1834-1925, 1926-1954, 1955-1975, 1976-1990. circ. 2,500. **Indexed:** Avery Ind.Archit.Per. **Document type:** proceedings.
—BLDSC (3410.935000); KR SourceOne.

930.1 FR
DC30
CONGRES NATIONAL DES SOCIETES HISTORIQUES ET SCIENTIFIQUES. ACTES. SECTION D'ARCHEOLOGIE. 1957 (congress of 1954). a. price varies. Comite des Travaux Historiques et Scientifiques, Section d'Archeologie, 1 rue Descartes, 75231 Paris Cedex 05, France. (Affiliate: Ministerie de l'Education Nationale) Ed. Martine Francois. index. circ. 650. **Document type:** proceedings.
Formerly: Congres National des Societes Savantes. Actes. Section d'Archeologie (ISSN 0071-8416)

913 PO ISSN 0084-9189
CONIMBRIGA. (Text in English, French, Portuguese, Spanish) 1959. a. Esc.4000. Universidade de Coimbra, Instituto de Arqueologia - University of Coimbra, Institute of Archaeology, 3049 Coimbra, Portugal. TEL 351-39-4191600. Ed. Jorge de Alarcao. bk.rev. circ. 450. **Document type:** academic/scholarly publication.

913 MX
CONSEJO DE ARQUEOLOGIA. BOLETIN. 1989. a. Instituto Nacional de Antropologia e Historia, Consejo de Arqueologia, Moneda 16, 06060 Mexico D.F., Mexico. TEL 522-28-47. FAX 522-58-86. illus.
Description: Informs readers about projects of archaeological research carried out in Mexico.

930.1 UK ISSN 1350-5033
CC135
▶ **CONSERVATION AND MANAGEMENT OF ARCHAEOLOGICAL SITES.** 1995. q. £40($60) to individuals; institutions £75($110). James & James (Science Publishers) Ltd., 35-37 William Rd., London NW1 3ER, England. TEL 44-171-387-8558. FAX 44-171-387-8998. E-mail: james@jxj.com; URL: http://www.jxj.com/. Ed.Bd.; Pub. Edward Milford. **Document type:** academic/scholarly publication.
—BLDSC (3417.967000).
Description: Reports on new approaches to the long-term preservation and presentation of archeological sites worldwide.
Refereed Serial

915.4 II ISSN 0376-7965
N9051
CONSERVATION OF CULTURAL PROPERTY IN INDIA. (Text in English) 1966. a. Rs.100($16) Indian Association for the Study of Conservation of Cultural Property, c/o National Museum, Janpath, New Delhi 110 011, India. TEL 11-3016098. Ed. Shri N. Harinarayana. adv.; bibl. circ. 500. **Indexed:** Art & Archaeol.Tech.Abstr. **Document type:** academic/scholarly publication.
—UnCover.

CONTINUITY AND CHANGE; a journal of social structure, law and demography in past societies. see POPULATION STUDIES

913 UK ISSN 0307-5087
CONTREBIS. 1974. a. £5 (foreign £8) (effective 1997). Lancaster Archaeological and Historical Society, c/o P.J. Hudson, Proctor House, Kirkgate, Settle, N. Yorks BD24, England. TEL 44-1524-33649. Ed. W.T.W. Potts. bk.rev.; bibl.; charts; illus. circ. 200. **Indexed:** Br.Archaeol.Abstr., Numis.Lit. **Document type:** academic/scholarly publication.
—BLDSC (3426.440000).

914.2 IE ISSN 0010-8731
CORK HISTORICAL AND ARCHAEOLOGICAL SOCIETY. JOURNAL. 1892. a. I£15 (Europe I£18; elsewhere I£20). Cork Historical and Archaeological Society, Drominn, Crosshaven, Co. Cork, Ireland. TEL 353-21-831322. Ed. Diarmuid O. Murchadha. bk.rev.; charts; illus.; index, cum. index: 1892-1940; 1941-1960; 1961-1970; 1971-1985; 1986-1995. circ. 600. (back issues avail.) **Indexed:** Amer.Hist.& Life (1955-1957), Br.Archaeol.Abstr., Hist.Abstr. (1955-1957). **Document type:** academic/scholarly publication.
—BLDSC (4732.250000).

913 UK ISSN 0070-024X
CORNISH ARCHAEOLOGY. 1962. a. £10. Cornwall Archaeological Society, c/o Royal Institution of Cornwall, River St., Truro, Cornwall, England. (Subscr. to: Mr. D.S. Donohue, 115 Longfield, Falmouth, Cornwall, England) Ed. C. Dunn. bk.rev. circ. 700. **Indexed:** Anthropol.Lit., Br.Archaeol.Abstr., Numis.Lit. **Document type:** academic/scholarly publication.
—BLDSC (3471.430000).
Refereed Serial

913 SP
CORPUS DE MOSAICOS ROMANOS DE ESPANA. 1978. irreg. price varies. Consejo Superior de Investigaciones Cientificas (C.S.I.C.), Instituto Espanol de Arqueologia, Vitruvio, 8, 28006 Madrid, Spain. TEL 5854846. illus.

CORPUS OF MAYA HIEROGLYPHIC INSCRIPTIONS. see HISTORY — History Of North And South America

CORSI INTERNAZIONALI DI CULTURA SULL'ARTE RAVENNATE E BIZANTINA. ATTI. see ART

913 IE
COUNTY KILDARE ARCHAEOLOGICAL SOCIETY. JOURNAL. 1891. a. I£10 to non-members. County Kildare Archaeological Society, St. Patricks College, Dept. of Modern History, Maynooth, Co. Kildare, Ireland. E-mail: gillespie@vaxi.may.ie. Ed. Raymond Gillespie. bk.rev.; charts; illus. circ. 600. (back issues avail.) **Indexed:** Br.Archaeol.Abstr., Br.Hum.Ind., RILA. **Document type:** academic/scholarly publication.

571 913 IE ISSN 0070-1327
DA990.L89
COUNTY LOUTH ARCHAEOLOGICAL AND HISTORICAL JOURNAL. 1904. a. I£7. County Louth Archaeological and Historical Society, 5, Oliver Plunkett Park, Dundalk, Ireland. Ed. Noel Ross. bk.rev. circ. 650. **Indexed:** Br.Archaeol.Abstr., RILA.
Formerly: County Louth Archaeological Journal.

938 IT
CRETAN STUDIES. 1988. irreg., vol.5, 1995. price varies. A.M. Hakkert, C. Parroco Fr. Rodriguez Rodriguez 26, 35010 Las Palmas de Gran Canaria, Spain. TEL 34-28-277350. FAX 34-28-761619. E-mail: willem@dial.ecunet.es. (Dist. in N. America by: John Benjamins Publishing Co., Box 27519, Philadelphia, PA 19118-0519. TEL 215-836-1200. FAX 215-836-1204) (back issues avail.) **Document type:** academic/scholarly publication.

913 707 IT
CRONACHE DI ARCHEOLOGIA. (Text in English, French, German and Italian) 1962. s-a. $70. (Universita di Catania, Istituto di Archeologia e Storia dell'Arte) L'Erma di Bretschneider, Via Cassiodoro 19, 00193 Rome, Italy. Ed.Bd. illus. circ. 300.
Formerly: Cronache di Archeologia e di Storia dell'Arte (ISSN 0011-1767)

913.031 SP ISSN 0211-3228
CUADERNOS DE PREHISTORIA. 1976. a. 4000 ptas. Universidad de Granada, Servicio de Publicaciones, Antiguo Colegio Maximo, Campus de Cartuja, 18071 Granada, Spain. TEL 34-58-243930. FAX 34-58-242827. Ed. Fernando Molina Gonzalez. **Document type:** monographic series.
—CINDOC.

913 UK ISSN 0143-1625
CUMBERLAND AND WESTMORLAND ANTIQUARIAN AND ARCHAEOLOGICAL SOCIETY. RESEARCH SERIES. 1979. irreg. £18 for paper; hardback £23. Cumberland and Westmorland Antiquarian and Archaeological Society (Carlisle), 10 Peter St., Carlisle, Cumbria CA3 8QP, England. TEL 44-1228-544120. Eds. B.C. Jones, W.G. Wiseman. R&P contact: R. Hall. TEL 44-1539-773432. **Document type:** monographic series.
—BLDSC (3491.785000).

913 929 UK ISSN 0309-7986
CUMBERLAND AND WESTMORLAND ANTIQUARIAN AND ARCHAEOLOGICAL SOCIETY. TRANSACTIONS. 1866. a. £15 paper; cloth £20 (effective 1997 & 1998). Cumberland and Westmorland Antiquarian and Archaeological Society (Kendal), 2 High Tenterfell, Kendal, Cumbria LA9 4PG, England. TEL 44-1539-773542. Ed. W.G. Wiseman. R&P contact: W.G. Wiseman. TEL 44-1539-726816. circ. 750. **Indexed:** Apic.Abstr. **Document type:** proceedings.
—BLDSC (8929.240000).

417.7 930.1 NE ISSN 0929-0052
CUNEIFORM MONOGRAPHS. (Text in English) 1992. irreg., vol.6, 1996. price varies. Styx Publications, Postbus 2659, 9704 CR Groningen, Netherlands. TEL 31-50-717502. FAX 31-50-733325. (back issues avail.) **Document type:** monographic series.

913 UK ISSN 0011-3212
DA90
CURRENT ARCHAEOLOGY. 1967. bi-m. £15($36) (foreign £18) (effective 1996). A.R.L. Selkirk, 9 Nassington Rd., London NW3 2TX, England. TEL 44-171-435-7517. FAX 44-171-916-2405. E-mail: subs@archaeology.co.uk; URL: http://www.archaeology.co.uk. Eds. Andrew & Wendy Selkirk. bk.rev.; charts; illus.; biennial index. circ. 14,000. (back issues avail.) **Indexed:** Abstr.Anthropol., Anthropol.Lit., Art & Archaeol.Tech.Abstr., Br.Archaeol.Abstr. **Document type:** academic/scholarly publication.
—BLDSC (3494.250000).
Supersedes (in 1965): Archaeological Newsletter.
Description: Presents latest news of British archaeology on a semipopular level.

930.1 560 US ISSN 8755-898X
E61
CURRENT RESEARCH IN THE PLEISTOCENE. 1984. a. $20. Oregon State University, Center for the Study of First Americans, Weniger 355, Corvalis, OR 97331-6510. TEL 541-737-4595. E-mail: halla@cla.orst.edu. Ed. Brad Lepper; Pub. Robson Bonnichsen. circ. 500. **Indexed:** Anthropol.Lit., Geo.Abstr. **Document type:** academic/scholarly publication.
—BLDSC (3501.972500).
Formerly: Center for the Study of Early Man. Current Research.
Description: Note-length reports on research on the earliest peopling of the Americas.
Refereed Serial

930.1 SW ISSN 1102-7355
DL621
CURRENT SWEDISH ARCHAEOLOGY. 1943. a. SEK 150 (effective through 1998). Svenska Arkeologiska Samfundet - Swedish Archaeological Society, Stockholm University, S-106 91 Stockholm, Sweden. TEL 46-8-783-90-00. Eds. Anders Carlsson, Mats Burstroem. circ. 500. **Indexed:** Br.Archaeol.Abstr. **Document type:** academic/scholarly publication.
Former titles (until 1993): Swedish Archaeology (ISSN 0282-0803); (until 1983): Swedish Archaeological Bibliography (ISSN 0586-2000)

913 937 CY ISSN 1010-1136
DS54.3
CYPRUS. DEPARTMENT OF ANTIQUITIES. ANNUAL REPORT. (Editions in English, Greek) 1934-1991; resumed 1995. a. £C30($6) Department of Antiquities, Ministry of Communications and Works, Nicosia, Cyprus. TEL 357-2-302189. FAX 357-2-303148. Ed. Hadjissavas Yiannis. **Indexed:** A.I.C.P., Anthropol.Lit. **Document type:** academic/scholarly publication, corporate report, government publication.
Description: Contains summary accounts of archaeological research and discoveries during the year; also features an illustrated record of conservation works carried out at sites in Cyprus.

ARCHAEOLOGY

913 937　　　　　CY　ISSN 0070-2374
DS54.3
CYPRUS. DEPARTMENT OF ANTIQUITIES. REPORT. (Text in English) 1934. a. price varies. Department of Antiquities, Ministry of Communications and Works, Nicosia, Cyprus. TEL 357-2-302189. FAX 357-2-303148. Ed. Hadjissavas Yiannis. **Document type:** academic/scholarly publication, monographic series.
　Description: Contains fully illustrated excavation reports and articles by archaeologists on Cypriote archaeology, culture, and art.

913　　　　　　RM　ISSN 0070-251X
DR211
DACIA; REVUE D'ARCHEOLOGIE ET D'HISTOIRE ANCIENNE. (Text in English, French, German and Russian) 2/yr. Editura Academiei Romane, Calea 13 Septembrie 13, 76117 Bucharest, Rumania. (Dist. by: Rodipet SA, Piata Presei Libere 1, Sec. 1, PO Box 33-57, Bucharest, Rumania. TEL 401-6185103. FAX 401-2226407) Ed. Petre Alexandrescu. **Indexed:** A.I.C.P., Anthropol.Lit., Numis.Lit.

914　　　　　　CH　ISSN 0496-6724
DALU ZAZHI/CONTINENT MAGAZINE. (Text in Chinese) 1950. m. $50. 11-6 Foochow St., Taipei, Taiwan, Republic of China. TEL 02-351-3810. FAX 02-392-3820. Ed. Chen-Shen Tu; Pub. Chou-Yun Shu. R&P contact: Chen-Hwa Lee. adv. contact: Chen-Hwa Lee. **Indexed:** Amer.Hist.& Life (1955-1957), Hist.Abstr. **Document type:** academic/scholarly publication.

DEAD SEA DISCOVERIES; a journal of current research on the scrolls and related literature. see *RELIGIONS AND THEOLOGY*

913　　　　　UK　ISSN 0954-8874
DEAN ARCHAEOLOGY. 1988. a. £4.95. Dean Archaeological Group, 5 Park Court, Bathurst Park Rd., Lydney, Glos. GL15 5HG, England. TEL 44-1594-843548. (U.S. subscr. to: B.H. Blackwell Ltd., Periodicals Dir., P.O. Box 40, Hythe Bridge St., Oxford OX1 2EU England) Ed. Alf Webb. R&P contact: Alf Webb. circ. 500. (back issues avail.) **Document type:** academic/scholarly publication, proceedings.

932　　　　　　PL　ISSN 0137-6446
DEIR EL-BAHARI. (Text in English or French) 1974. irreg., no.5, 1986. $35 per issue. Polska Akademia Nauk, Zaklad Archeologii Srodziemnomorskiej, Palac Kultury i Nauki, p. 2105, 00-901 Warsaw, Poland. TEL 48-22-6248593. FAX 48-22-6207651. (Dist. by: Osrodek Rozpowszechniania Wydawnictw Naukowych PAN - Export, Palac Kultury i Nauki, 00-901 Warsaw, Poland. FAX 48-22-8268670) Ed. Jadwiga Lipinska. illus. (back issues avail.) **Document type:** monographic series.
　Description: Presents excavation results of Polish Archaeological Missions at Deir el-Bahari, Egypt.
　Refereed Serial

935　　　　　　IR　ISSN 0765-104X
DS261
DELEGATION ARCHEOLOGIQUE FRANCAISE EN IRAN. CAHIERS. Key Title: Cahiers de la D A F I. 1971. a. price varies. Institut Francais de Recherche en Iran, Ave. Shahid Nizari, 52 Adib St., P.O. Box 15815-3495, Tehran, Iran. TEL 98-21-6401192. FAX 98-21-6405501. Ed. Remy Boucharlat. illus. circ. 500. **Indexed:** Anthropol.Lit. **Document type:** academic/scholarly publication.

914　　　　　GW　ISSN 0720-9835
DENKMALPFLEGE IN NIEDERSACHSEN. BERICHTE. 1981. q. DM.25.20. (Niedersaechsisches Landesverwaltungsamt, Institut fuer Denkmalpflege) Verlag C.W. Niemeyer, Osterstr. 19, 31785 Hameln, Germany. FAX 05151-200319. Ed. Christiane Segers-Glocke. adv.; bk.rev.; charts; illus.; index. circ. 2,860. (back issues avail.) **Indexed:** IBR. **Document type:** bulletin.

900　　　　　DK　ISSN 0902-2961
DENMARK. NATIONALMUSEET. PUBLICATIONS: ARCHAEOLOGICAL HISTORICAL SERIES. (Text in Danish, English, French and German) 1943. irreg. price varies. Nationalmuseet, Frederiksholms Kanal 12, DK-1220 Copenhagen K, Denmark. TEL 45-33-13-44-11. FAX 45-33-47-33-30. (Dist. in the U.S. by: Humanities Press, 171 First Ave., Atlantic City, NJ 07716)
　Formerly (until 1969): Denmark. Nationalmuseet. Nationalmuseets Skrifter (ISSN 0902-2953)

571 913　　　　UK　ISSN 0070-3788
DERBYSHIRE ARCHAEOLOGICAL JOURNAL. 1879. a. £12. Derbyshire Archaeological Society, 12 Longbow Close, Stretton, Burton-on-Trent, Derbys. DE13 OXY, England. TEL 01283-530218. Ed. D.V. Fowkes. bk.rev. circ. 650. **Indexed:** Br.Archaeol.Abstr., Br.Hum.Ind., Numis.Lit. **Document type:** academic/scholarly publication.
　—BLDSC (3554.900000).
　Refereed Serial

913　　　　　　GW
DEUTSCHE ORIENT-GESELLSCHAFT. ABHANDLUNG. 1913. irreg., vol.22, 1993. price varies. Deutsche Orient-Gesellschaft e.V., Bitterstr. 8-12, 14195 Berlin, Germany. TEL 49-30-8383347. FAX 49-30-8314252. Ed. Helmut Freydank. (reprint service avail.) **Document type:** monographic series.
　Formerly: Uruk-Warka: Abhandlungen der Deutsche Orient-Gesellschaft (ISSN 0083-4793)

DEUTSCHE ORIENT-GESELLSCHAFT. MITTEILUNGEN. see *HISTORY — History Of The Near East*

DEUTSCHE ORIENT-GESELLSCHAFT. WISSENSCHAFTLICHE VEROEFFENTLICHUNGEN. see *HISTORY — History Of The Near East*

DEUTSCHER PALAESTINA-VEREIN. ZEITSCHRIFT. see *ORIENTAL STUDIES*

913　　　　　GW　ISSN 0342-1295
DE2
DEUTSCHES ARCHAEOLOGISCHES INSTITUT. ATHENISCHE ABTEILUNG. MITTEILUNGEN - ATHENISCHE MITTEILUNGEN. (Text in English, German and Greek) 1885. a. (Deutsches Archaeologisches Institut, Abteilung Athen) Gebr. Mann Verlag GmbH, Charlottenstr. 13, 10969 Berlin, Germany. TEL 49-30-2591-3589. FAX 49-30-2591-3537. circ. 600. (reprint service avail.) **Indexed:** Art Ind., IBR, Numis.Lit. **Document type:** academic/scholarly publication.
　—KR SourceOne.
　Description: Covers developments in archaeological research carried out at the German Archaeological Institute in Athens.

913　　　　　GW　ISSN 0070-4415
DE2
DEUTSCHES ARCHAEOLOGISCHES INSTITUT. JAHRBUCH. (Text in English, French, German, Italian) 1886. a. DM.165. Walter de Gruyter und Co., Genthiner Str. 13, 10785 Berlin, Germany. TEL 49-30-26005-0. FAX 49-30-26005-251. E-mail: wdg-info@degruyter.de; URL: http://www.degruyter.de. (U.S. addr.: Walter de Gruyter, Inc., 200 Saw Mill River Rd., Hawthorne, NY 10532. TEL 914-747-0110) **Indexed:** Avery Ind.Archit.Per., Br.Archaeol.Abstr., IBR, Numis.Lit. **Document type:** academic/scholarly publication.
　—KR SourceOne.

913　　　　　　UK
DEVON ARCHAEOLOGICAL SOCIETY. NEWSLETTER. no.21, 1982. 3/yr. £9 membership (students £3). Devon Archaeological Society, R.A.M. Museum, Queen St., Exeter EX4 3RX, England. Ed. Robert Wilson-North. **Indexed:** Br.Archaeol.Abstr. **Document type:** newsletter.
　Description: Covers future events, current excavations, and topics of debate in Devon archaeology.

913　　　　　UK　ISSN 0305-5795
DEVON ARCHAEOLOGICAL SOCIETY. PROCEEDINGS. 1929. a. £9 membership (students £3). Devon Archaeological Society, R.A.M. Museum, Queen St., Exeter EX4 3RX, England. circ. 1,000. **Indexed:** Br.Archaeol.Abstr., Br.Hum.Ind., Numis.Lit. **Document type:** proceedings.
　—BLDSC (6689.800000).
　Description: Includes academic reports on archaeological projects, artefacts and standing buildings in Devon.

913　　　　　UK　ISSN 0264-7540
DEVON ARCHAEOLOGY. 1983. irreg. £1 to non-members. Devon Archaeological Society, Royal Albert Museum, Queen St., Exeter EX4 3RX, England. circ. 2,000.
　—BLDSC (3579.105200).
　Description: Summary reports on current Devon archaeology.

DIALOGOS; Hellenic studies review. see *CLASSICAL STUDIES*

913 572　　　　SA　ISSN 1013-7521
DIGGING STICK. (Text in English) 1984. 3/yr. to institutions (includes Bulletin); Africa R.140; elsewhere R.210 ($50) (£32) (DM.76) (effective 1997). South African Archaeological Society, P.O. Box 15700, Vlaeberg 8018, South Africa. TEL 27-21-243330. FAX 27-21-246716. Ed. David Morris. bk.rev.; charts; illus. circ. 1,300. (back issues avail.) **Indexed:** Ind.S.A.Per. **Document type:** academic/scholarly publication.
　Description: Popular articles on archaeology-related subjects, with an emphasis on Southern Africa.

220.93　　　　AT　ISSN 1320-4424
DIGGINGS. 1985. m. Aus.$20($24) (effective 1996). D.K. Down, Ed. & Pub., 2 Neridah Ave., Mount Colah, N.S.W. 2079, Australia. TEL 61-2-94773595. FAX 61-2-94871659. (Subscr. to: P.O. Box 341, Hornsby 2077, Australia) R&P contact: D.K. Down. adv. contact: D.K. Down. bk.rev.; circ. 1,500 (paid). **Document type:** academic/scholarly publication.
　Description: Archaeological news that keeps readers informed on latest discoveries on the land of the Bible.

915　　　　　　BA
DILMUN. (Text in Arabic, English) 1973. 2/yr. Bahrain Historical and Archaeological Society, P.O. Box 5087, Manama, Bahrain. TEL 727895. Ed. Muhammad Khozai. circ. 2,000.

933 296.155　　UK　ISSN 0070-668X
DISCOVERIES IN THE JUDAEAN DESERT OF JORDAN. irreg., vol.10, 1994. price varies. Oxford University Press, Walton St., Oxford OX2 6DP, England. TEL 44-1865-56767. FAX 44-1865-56646. E-mail: jnlorders@oup.co.uk. (US subscr. to: Oxford University Press Inc., 2001 Evans Rd., Cary, NC 27513. TEL 919-677-0977. FAX 919-677-1714) **Document type:** monographic series.

DOCUMENTA ET MONUMENTA ORIENTIS ANTIQUI. see *HISTORY — History Of The Near East*

709.0113 936.3　SW　ISSN 1400-6235
DOCUMENTATION AND REGISTRATION OF ROCK ART IN TANUM. (Text in English) 1997. a. SEK 150 (effective through 1999). Scandinavian Society for Prehistoric Art, Tanums Haellristningsmuseum, Undersloes, S-457 91 Tanumshede, Sweden. TEL 46-46-525-295-55. FAX 46-525-295-55. E-mail: adorant@post5.tele.dk; URL: http://www.ssfpa.se. Ed. Gerhard Milstreu.
　Description: Presents the result of the Documentation-project on pre-historic rock art and the database HELIOS.

930.1　　　　　IT
DOCUMENTI E RICERCHE D'ARTE ALESSANDRINA. 1946. irreg., latest vol.6. price varies. L'Erma di Bretschneider, Via Cassiodoro 19, 00193 Rome, Italy. TEL 39-6-6874127. FAX 39-6-6874129. Dirs. Nicola Bonacasa, Antonino Di Vita.

930 572　　　　CC　ISSN 1001-179X
DONGNAN WENHUA/CULTURE OF SOUTHEAST CHINA. (Text in Chinese) 1985. bi-m. Y8($6) per no. Nanjing Bowuguan - Nanjing Museum, 321 Zhongshan Donglu, Nanjing, Jiangsu 210016, People's Republic of China. TEL 025-645349. Ed. Bao Wei-Dong. adv.; bk.rev. circ. 3,000. **Document type:** academic/scholarly publication.
　Description: Covers archaeology, history, religion, technology, architecture, ethnography and folklore.

913　　　　　　UK
DORSET NATURAL HISTORY & ARCHAEOLOGICAL SOCIETY. MONOGRAPH SERIES. 1980. irreg., no. 14, 1993. price varies. Dorset County Museum, Dorchester, Dorset, England. TEL 44-1305-26273 Ed. Jo Draper. R&P contact: R. de Peyer. **Document type:** monographic series.

DORSET NATURAL HISTORY AND ARCHAEOLOGICAL SOCIETY. PROCEEDINGS. see *SCIENCES: COMPREHENSIVE WORKS*

ARCHAEOLOGY

930.1   FR   ISSN 1141-7137
DOSSIERS D'ARCHEOLOGIE. m. (10/yr.). 415 F. (foreign 465 F.) (effective 1997). Editions Faton S.A., 25 rue Berbisey, 21000 Dijon, France. TEL 33-1-80404104. (Subscr. to: 1 rue des Artisans, B.P. 90, 21803 Quetigny Cedex, France. TEL 33-3-80489848. FAX 33-3-80489846)
Indexed: Anthropol.Lit., Pt.de Rep. (1989-).
Former titles (until 1989): Dossiers Histoire et Archeologie (ISSN 0299-7339); (until 1985): Histoire et Archeologie (ISSN 0294-6017)

914 947   RU
DREVNEISHIE GOSUDARSTVA NA TERRITORII S.S.S.R/ANCIENT STATES IN THE TERRITORY OF THE U.S.S.R.; materialy i issledovaniya. (Text in Russian; summaries in English) 1976. irreg., (approx. a.). price varies. (Rossiiskaya Akademiya Nauk, Institut Istorii) Izdatel'stvo Nauka, 90 Profsoyuznaya ul., 117864 Moscow, Russia. TEL 234-05-84. (Subscr. to: Akademkniga, Michurinskii pr. 12, 117485 Moscow, Russia) Ed. A.P. Novosel'tsev. bk.rev. circ. 4,250.

DRUSTVO KONZERVATORA SRBIJE. GLASNIK. see *CONSERVATION*

913   US
DUMBARTON OAKS CONFERENCE PROCEEDINGS. 1968. irreg., latest 1995. price varies. Dumbarton Oaks, Publications Office, 1703 32nd St., N.W., Washington, DC 20007. TEL 202-339-6431. Ed. Veffrey Quilter. bibl.; charts; illus. circ. 1,000. (back issues avail.) Document type: proceedings.
Description: Contains papers of the annual conference; covers pre-Columbian art and archaeology.

709   US   ISSN 0070-7546
DF503
DUMBARTON OAKS PAPERS. 1940. irreg., no.34, 1980. price varies. (Dumbarton Oaks Center for Byzantine Studies) J.J. Augustin, Inc., Box 311, Locust Valley, NY 11560. TEL 516-676-1510.
Indexed: Amer.Bibl.Slavic & E.Eur.Stud., Art & Archaeol.Tech.Abstr., Avery Ind.Archit.Per., Numis.Lit., RILA.
—BLDSC (3631.050000).

940   US   ISSN 0070-7554
DUMBARTON OAKS STUDIES. 1950. irreg. price varies. (Dumbarton Oaks Center for Byzantine Studies) J.J. Augustin, Inc., Box 311, Locust Valley, NY 11560. TEL 516-676-1510.
—BLDSC (3631.054000).

930.1 294.3   CC   ISSN 1000-4106
DS793.T8
DUNHUANG YANJIU/DUNHUANG STUDIES. (Text in Chinese) 1983. q. $10 (effective 1995 & 1996). Dunhuang Yanjiu Yuan - Dunhuang Research Institute, Dunhuang, Gansu 736200, People's Republic of China. TEL 86-9473-69009. FAX 86-9473-23007. (Dist. overseas by: Jiangsu Publications Import & Export Corp., 56 Gao Yun Ling, Nanjing, P.R.C.) Ed. Duan Wenjie. bk.rev.; circ. 4,000 (paid). Document type: academic/scholarly publication.
Description: Presents Chinese and foreign academic essays on the Dunhuang (Tun Huang) frescoes, including archaeological, religious and literary findings about the Dunhuang Caves.

942.8   UK   ISSN 0265-8038
DURHAM ARCHAEOLOGICAL JOURNAL. 1862. a. £15 to individuals; institutions £20. Architectural and Archaeological Society of Durham and Northumberland, c/o Department of Archaeology, South Rd., Durham DH1 3LE, England. Ed. Anthony Harding. bk.rev. circ. 450. (back issues avail.)
Indexed: Br.Archaeol.Abstr., Br.Hum.Ind. Document type: academic/scholarly publication.
—BLDSC (3632.321000).
Formerly (until 1984): Architectural and Archaeological Society of Durham and Northumberland. Transactions. New Series (ISSN 0066-6203)

930.1 949.2   NE   ISSN 0169-8060
DUTCH ARCHAEOLOGICAL AND HISTORICAL SOCIETY. STUDIES. Key Title: Studies of the Dutch Archaeological and Historical Society. 1969. irreg., vol.11, 1985. price varies. E.J. Brill, P.O. Box 9000, 2300 PA Leiden, Netherlands. TEL 31-71-5353500. FAX 31-71-5317532. TELEX 39296 BRILL NL. E-mail: ejbrill@brill.nl. (In N. America: E.J. Brill, 24 Hudson St., Kinderhook, NY 12106. TEL 800-962-4406. FAX 518-758-1959) R&P contact: Elizabeth Vennekamp. Document type: monographic series.

930.1   NE   ISSN 0924-3550
DUTCH MONOGRAPHS ON ANCIENT HISTORY AND ARCHAEOLOGY. (Text in English) 1985. irreg., vol.14, 1996. price varies. J.C. Gieben, Nieuwe Herengracht 35, 1011 RM Amsterdam, Netherlands. TEL 31-20-6275170. FAX 31-20-6275170. (Dist. in N. America by: John Benjamins Publishing Co., Box 27519, Philadelphia, PA 19118-0519. TEL 215-836-1200. FAX 215-836-1204) Eds. F.J.A.M. Meijer, H.W. Pleket. (back issues avail.) Document type: monographic series.
Description: Publishes scholarly studies of topics in ancient history and archaeology, with particular focus on the Roman Empire.

931 951 952   UK   ISSN 0961-7345
E A A N NOUNCEMENTS. (East Asian Archaeology Network) Key Title: EAANnouncements. 1990. 3/yr. £15 to institutions. University of Durham, Department of East Asian Studies, Centre for Research in East Asian Archaeology, Durham DH1 3TH, England. TEL 44-191-374-7319. FAX 44-191-374-3242. (Co-sponsor: Society for East Asian Archaeology) adv.; bk.rev.; bibl. circ. 300. (back issues avail.) Document type: newsletter.
Description: Provides current information on the archaeology and early history and art history of China, Japan, and Korea. Includes SEAA membership news and news of the society's activities, field and research reports, dissertation abstracts, conference calendar and reports, job and grant opportunities, and museum and exhibition news.

913   GW   ISSN 0174-4224
GN700
EARLY MAN NEWS; newsletter for human palecology. (Text in English) 1976. irreg. (approx. 1/yr). Archaeologica Venatoria e.V., c/o Institut fuer Urgeschichte, 72074 Tuebingen, Germany. TEL 07071-292416. FAX 07071-294995. bk.rev. circ. 300. (back issues avail.) Indexed: Anthropol.Lit. Document type: newsletter, academic/scholarly publication.

913   UK   ISSN 0307-2460
EAST ANGLIAN ARCHAEOLOGY. REPORT. 1975. irreg., no.79, 1996. price varies. Norfolk Field Archaeology Division, Union House, Gressenhall, Dereham, Norfolk NR20 4DR, England. TEL 44-1362-860528. FAX 44-1362-860951. (Dist. by: Kate Skipper, Centre of East Anglian Studies, University of East Anglia, Norwich NR4 7TJ, England. FAX 44-1603-58553) (Co-sponsors: Scole Archaeological Committee, Norwich Survey, Suffolk Archaeological Unit, Essex Archaeological Unit, Lincolnshire Archaeological Unit, Fenland Project) Ed. Jenny Glazebrook. R&P contact: Jenny Glazebrook. circ. 400. Indexed: Anthropol.Lit., Br.Archaeol.Abstr. Document type: monographic series.
—BLDSC (3645.790000).
Description: Reports on archaeological excavations and surveys in region of East Anglia.
Refereed Serial

913   UK   ISSN 0012-852X
DA670.Y59
EAST RIDING ARCHAEOLOGIST.* 1968. irreg. £15 to institutions. East Riding Archaeological Society, 35 Queensway, Cottingham, N. Humberside HU16 4EJ, England. Ed.Bd. charts; illus. circ. 400. Document type: monographic series.
—BLDSC (3646.520000).

EASTERN NEW MEXICO UNIVERSITY. CONTRIBUTIONS IN ANTHROPOLOGY. see *ANTHROPOLOGY*

913   US
EASTERN STATES ARCHEOLOGICAL FEDERATION. BULLETIN. 1941. a. Eastern States Archeological Federation, c/o Edmond Dlutowski, 105 Woodlawn Rd., Butler, PA 16001. circ. 500. Document type: bulletin.

ECHOS DU MONDE CLASSIQUE/CLASSICAL VIEWS. see *CLASSICAL STUDIES*

913 900   FR
ECOLE FRANCAISE DE ROME. COLLECTION. 1976. irreg., (4-5/yr.). price varies. De Boccard Edition, 11 rue de Medicis, 75006 Paris, France.
Supersedes: Ecole Francaise de Rome. Melanges: Supplement.

913   FR   ISSN 0223-5102
D111
ECOLE FRANCAISE DE ROME. MELANGES: ANTIQUITE. (In 3 series: Antiquite, Moyen Age, Italie et Mediterranee) (Text in French, German, Italian) 1881. a. (in 2 vols.). 700 F. De Boccard Edition, 11 rue de Medicis, 75006 Paris, France. TEL 1-43260037. FAX 1-43548585. cum.index: vols.1-82 (1881-1975). (back issues avail.)
Indexed: Bibl.Ling., Br.Archaeol.Abstr., Numis.Lit. Document type: academic/scholarly publication.
—SWETS.
Formerly (until 1971): Melanges d'Archeologie et d'Histoire (ISSN 0223-4874)
Description: Contains archaeology and chemical studies relating to Italy and western Mediterranean from prehistoric times to the end of the Roman Empire.

962 932   UA   ISSN 0082-7835
EGYPT. SERVICE DES ANTIQUITES. ANNALES. (Text in language of author) 1900. irreg. price varies. Service des Antiquites, Museums Sector, c/o Egyptian National Museum, Midan al-Tahrir, Kasr el-Nil, Cairo, Egypt. Dir. Mohammed Mohsen. bk.rev.; cum.index: vols.1-30, vols.31-40. (also avail. in microfiche from IDC) Indexed: A.I.C.P.

932   BE
▼**EGYPTIAN PREHISTORY MONOGRAPHS.** 1995. irreg. price varies. Leuven University Press, Blijde Inkomststraat 5, 3000 Leuven, Belgium. TEL 32-16-325345. FAX 32-16-325352. E-mail: university.press@upers.kuleuven.ac.be; URL: http://kuleuven.ac.be/upers. Ed.Bd. Document type: monographic series.

EIRENE; studia graeca et latina. see *CLASSICAL STUDIES*

571   US   ISSN 0070-9573
EL PASO ARCHAEOLOGICAL SOCIETY. SPECIAL REPORTS. 1963. a. price varies. El Paso Archaeological Society, Inc., Box 4345, El Paso, TX 79914-4345. TEL 915-751-3295. Ed. Carrol Hedrick. bk.rev. circ. 300. (also avail. in microform) Document type: academic/scholarly publication.

913   US   ISSN 0013-4023
EL PASO ARCHAEOLOGY. 1968. m. $25 includes Artifact & Newsletter. El Paso Archaeological Society, Inc., Box 4345, El Paso, TX 79914-4345. TEL 915-751-3295. Ed. Meliha Duran. bk.rev.; charts; illus.; index. circ. 300. Document type: newsletter.

932   BE
ELKAB. 1971. irreg., no.5, 1990. price varies. Fondation Egyptologique Reine Elisabeth, Comite des Fouilles Belges en Egypte, Parc du Cinquantenaire 10, 1000 Brussels, Belgium. TEL 32-2-7339610. Document type: monographic series.

341   SP   ISSN 0213-9278
DP44
EMPURIES; revista de prehistoria, arqueologia y etnologia. 1939. a. 6000 ptas. or exchange basis (effective 1997). Departament de Cultura, Museu d'Arqueologia de Catalunya, Passeig de Santa Madrona, 39-41, Parque de Montjuich, 08038 Barcelona, Spain. TEL 34-3-4232149. FAX 34-3-4254244. E-mail: biblio@arsweb.com. bibl.; illus.; circ. controlled. Indexed: A.I.C.P., Amer.Hist.& Life (1964-1968), Anthropol.Lit., Br.Archaeol.Abstr., Hist.Abstr. (1964-1968), Numis.Lit. Document type: academic/scholarly publication.
—CINDOC. **CCC.**
Formerly (until 1982): Ampurias (ISSN 0212-0909)

930.1   RM   ISSN 1220-5249
EPHEMERIS NAPOCENSIS. (Text in Rumanian; summaries in English, French, German) 1990. a. (Academia Romana, Institutul de Istorie si Arheologie Cluj-Napoca) Editura Academiei Romane, Calea 13 Septembrie 13, 76117 Bucharest, Rumania. (Dist. by: Rodipet SA, Piata Presei Libere 1, Sec.1, PO Box 33-57, Bucharest, Rumania. TEL 401-6185103. FAX 401-2226407) Ed. Nicolae Gudea.

913   II   ISSN 0013-9564
EPIGRAPHIA INDICA. (Text in English) 1888. irreg. Rs.64 per vol. (8 nos./vol.). Archaeological Survey of India, Old University Office Bldg., Mysore 570005, India. (Subscr. to: Controller of Publications, Government of India, Civil Lines, Delhi 110054, India) Ed. K.G. Krishnan. bk.rev.; charts; illus.; biennial index. circ. 740. **Indexed:** E.I.

913 410   US   ISSN 1061-5938
CN1
EPIGRAPHIC SOCIETY. OCCASIONAL PAPERS. Short title: E S O P. 1974. a. $32.50 (foreign $34.50) includes membership. Epigraphic Society, Inc., 6625 Bamburgh Dr., San Diego, CA 92117. TEL 619-571-1344. FAX 619-571-1124. Ed. Bill Rudersdorf. adv.; bk.rev.; cum.index: vols.1-10 in 1984, vols.1-15 in 1987. circ. 1,100. (back issues avail.) **Indexed:** Anthropol.Lit., Lang.& Lang.Behav.Abstr. **Document type:** academic/scholarly publication.
Formerly (until 1990): Epigraphic Society. Occasional Publications (ISSN 0192-5148)
Description: Contains articles and photographs of discoveries and decipherment of ancient inscriptions in current research.

913   IT   ISSN 0013-9572
DS417
EPIGRAPHICA; rivista italiana di epigrafia. 1939. s-a. L.85000($90) Fratelli Lega Editori, Corso Mazzini 33, 48018 Faenza, Italy. TEL 0546-21060. bk.rev.; illus.
—SWETS.

938 417.7   NE
EPIGRAPHICA BOEOTICA. (Text in English) 1991. irreg. price varies. J.C. Gieben, Nieuwe Herengracht 35, 1011 RM Amsterdam, Netherlands. TEL 31-20-6275170. FAX 31-20-6275170. (Dist. in N. America by: John Benjamins Publishing Co., Box 27519, Philadelphia, PA 19118-0519. TEL 215-836-1200. FAX 215-836-1204) Ed. John M. Fossey. (back issues avail.) **Document type:** monographic series.
Description: Publishes scholarly studies of the ancient inscriptions in Boiotia.

913   GW   ISSN 0343-6500
ERDSTALL. 1975. a. DM.20. Arbeitskreis fuer Erdstallforschung, Tulpenweg 11, 93426 Roding, Germany. TEL 49-9461-2831. Ed. Regine Glatthaar. adv. contact: Hannelore Schulz. **Document type:** academic/scholarly publication.

913 933   IS   ISSN 0071-108X
DS111.A2
ERETZ-ISRAEL. ARCHAEOLOGICAL, HISTORICAL AND GEOGRAPHICAL STUDIES. (Text in English and Hebrew) 1951. irreg. vol.26, 1998. price varies. Israel Exploration Society, P.O. Box 7041, Jerusalem 91070, Israel. TEL 972-2-6257991. FAX 972-2-6247772. E-mail: ies@vms.huji.ac.il. circ. 1,200. (back issues avail.) **Indexed:** Ind.Heb.Per., Rel.& Theol.Abstr. (1982-). **Document type:** academic/scholarly publication, monographic series.
Description: Festschrifts on Israeli archaeology, ancient history and geography.

ERETZ MAGAZINE. see CONSERVATION

ERFGOED VAN INDUSTRIE EN TECHNIEK. see TECHNOLOGY: COMPREHENSIVE WORKS

ERRANT NEWS. see ART

914.2 942   UK   ISSN 0014-0961
ESSEX JOURNAL; a review of Essex archaeology and local history. 1966. 3/yr. £10. c/o Michael Beale, The Laurels, The Street, Great Waltham, Chelmsford, Essex CMJ 1DE, England. TEL 0245-360344. adv.; bk.rev.; charts; illus.; index. circ. 600. (back issues avail.) **Document type:** academic/scholarly publication.
—BLDSC (3811.980000).
Incorporates: Essex Review.

918   CL   ISSN 0716-0925
ESTUDIOS ATACAMENOS. 1973. irreg. exchange basis. Universidad Catolica del Norte, Instituto de Investigaciones Arqueologicas, R.P. Gustavo le Paige S.J., San Pedro de Atacama, Chile. FAX 241724. TELEX 225097 UNORTE CL. Ed. Agustin Llagostera Martinez. circ. 1,000. **Indexed:** A.I.C.P. **Document type:** academic/scholarly publication.
Description: Andean archaeology studies in the north of Chile, with emphasis on the Atacamena region.

ETHNOS. see ANTHROPOLOGY

ETRUSCAN STUDIES. see CLASSICAL STUDIES

ETUDES DE PHILOLOGIE, D'ARCHEOLOGIE ET D'HISTOIRE ANCIENNE. see LINGUISTICS

930.1   MR   ISSN 0071-2027
ETUDES ET TRAVAUX D'ARCHEOLOGIE MAROCAINE. 1965. irreg. vol.9, 1981. Institut National des Sciences, de l'Archeologie et du Patrimoine, Av. John Kennedy - Route des Zaers, Rabat-Souissi, Morocco. **Document type:** academic/scholarly publication, monographic series.

ETUDES OCEAN INDIEN. see LINGUISTICS

913.031   FR
ETUDES PREHISTORIQUES; revue du Sud-Est Rhodanien et Mediterraneen. 1971. irreg. 70 F. Societe "Etudes Prehistoriques", c/o Secretariat: Jean Combier, 71570 Romaneche-Thorins, France. TEL 85-35-50-36. Ed. Jean Combier. bk.rev.;'bibl.; illus. circ. 1,000. **Indexed:** Br.Archaeol.Abstr., Bull.Signal.

930.1   GW   ISSN 0949-0434
▼**EURASIA ANTIQUA.** 1996. irreg. (Deutsches Archaeologisches Institut) Verlag Philipp von Zabern GmbH, Philipp-von-Zabern-Platz 1-3, 55116 Mainz, Germany. TEL 49-6131-28747-0. FAX 49-6131-223710. **Document type:** monographic series.

EUROPEAN STUDIES JOURNAL. see HISTORY — History Of Europe

913   SP   ISSN 0071-3279
EXCAVACIONES ARQUEOLOGICAS EN ESPANA. 1962. irreg. 1600 ptas. Instituto del Patrimonio Historico Espanol, C. El Greco, 4, Ciudad Universitaria, 28040 Madrid, Spain. (Subscr. to: C. Abdon Terradas 7, 28015 Madrid, Spain. TEL 34-1-5439366) **Indexed:** Anthropol.Lit. **Document type:** monographic series. *Refereed Serial*

933   IS   ISSN 0334-1607
DS111.A1
EXCAVATIONS AND SURVEYS IN ISRAEL. English translation of: Hadashot Arkheologiyot (IS ISSN 0047-1569) 1982. s-a. $36. Israel Antiquities Authority, P.O. Box 586, Jerusalem 91004, Israel. TEL 972-2-5602607. FAX 972-2-5602628. E-mail: harriet@israntiques.org.il. (Co-sponsors: Israel Exploration Society, W.F. Albright Institute of Archaeological Research, Nelson Glueck School of Biblical Archaeology) Ed. Ayala Sussman. illus. (back issues avail.) **Indexed:** Anthropol.Lit. **Document type:** academic/scholarly publication.
—BLDSC (3835.038000).
Description: Overview of archaeological activity in Israel, with preliminary excavation reports.

913   US   ISSN 0071-3287
EXCAVATIONS AT DURA-EUROPOS. irreg. price varies. (Yale University) Yale University Press, Box 209040, New Haven, CT 06520. TEL 203-432-0940. (Co-sponsor: French Academy of Inscriptions and Letters)

EXCERITUS; bulletin for practical research into the Roman army. see CLASSICAL STUDIES

EXPEDITION. see ANTHROPOLOGY

EXPLORING THE ROMAN WORLD. see CLASSICAL STUDIES

913   PL   ISSN 0860-0007
DK4088
FASCISCULI ARCHAEOLOGIAE HISTORICAE. (Text in English, French, German and Russian) 1987. a. price varies. Polska Akademiya Nauk, Oddzial w Lodzi - Polish Academy of Sciences, Lodz Section, Ul. Piotrkowska 179, 90-447 Lodz, Poland. TEL 48-42-368018. FAX 48-42-362-415. Ed. Andrzej Nadolski. **Indexed:** Amer.Hist.& Life (until 1990), Hist.Abstr. (until 1990), IBR. **Document type:** academic/scholarly publication.
Description: Different papers and reports on archaeological research.

913 350   US
FEDERAL ARCHEOLOGICAL PROGRAMS AND ACTIVITIES: THE SECRETARY OF THE INTERIOR'S REPORT TO CONGRESS. 1974. a. free. U.S. National Park Service, c/o Departmental Consulting Archaeologist, Archaeological Assistance, Box 37127, Ste. 210, Washington, DC 20013-7127. TEL 202-343-4101. FAX 202-523-1547. circ. 2,000. (back issues avail.) **Document type:** government publication.
Former titles: U.S. National Park Service. Federal Archeology: The Current Program; U.S. National Park Service. Annual Report to Congress on the Federal Archeological Program.
Description: Reports on the archaeological activites of federal agencies. Concerned with helping preserve America's archaeological and cultural heritage.

FELIX RAVENNA; RIVISTA DI ANTICHITA RAVENNATI, CRISTIANE E BIZANTINE. see ART

LA FENICE. see HISTORY

913 709   CI   ISSN 0352-6712
DR1521   CODEN: RSPZER
FILOZOFSKI FAKULTET - ZADAR. RAZDIO POVIJESNIH ZNANOSTI. RADOVI. (Text in Croatian; summaries in English) 1963. a. $20 (effective 1989). Filozofski Fakultet u Zadru, Obala Marsala Tita, 2, 57000 Zadar, Croatia. TEL 057-436-623. (Co-sponsor: Samoupravna Interesna Zajednica Znanosti SR Hrvatske) Ed. Janko Belosevic. index, cum.index no.1-12. circ. 800. (back issues avail.)

709 305.8   FI   ISSN 0355-1814
DK445
FINSKT MUSEUM. (Text in English, German, Swedish) 1894. a. FIM 100. Suomen Muinaismuistoyhdistys - Finnish Antiquarian Society, P.O. Box 213, Nervanderinkatu 13, FIN-00101 Helsinki, Finland. Ed. Marianne Schauman-Loenqvist. illus.; cum.index: 1894-1943. **Indexed:** A.I.C.P., Amer.Hist.& Life (1967-), Anthropol.Lit., Br.Archaeol.Abstr., Hist.Abstr. (1967-), IBR, NAA, Numis.Lit. **Document type:** academic/scholarly publication.
Description: Publishes contributions in archaeology, anthropology, art history, and cultural history.

930.1   SW   ISSN 0281-3386
FJOELNIR; medlemstidning foer arkeologiska foereningen Fjoelnir. 1982. q. SEK 75 (members only) (effective 1990). Fjoelnir, Institutionen foer Arkeologi, Gustavianum, S-753 10 Uppsala, Sweden.

FLINTSHIRE HISTORICAL SOCIETY. PUBLICATIONS, JOURNAL AND RECORD SERIES. see HISTORY — History Of Europe

FLORIDA ANTHROPOLOGIST. see ANTHROPOLOGY

913.031 943.8   PL   ISSN 0239-8524
DK4088
FOLIA PRAEHISTORICA POSNANIENSIA. (Text in English and German; summaries in English) 1985. a., vol.6, 1994. price varies. (Adam Mickiewicz University, Institute of Prehistory) Adam Mickiewicz University Press, Nowowiejskiego 55, 61-734 Poznan, Poland. TEL 48-61-527380. FAX 48-61-527701. Ed. Jan Zak; Pub. Maria Jankowska. R&P contact: Malgorzata Bis. bk.rev.; abstr.; illus. circ. 600. (back issues avail.) **Indexed:** Anthropol.Lit. **Document type:** academic/scholarly publication, monographic series.

918 572   UY
FOLLETOS DE DIVULGACION. 1969. irreg. Centro de Estudios Arqueologicos, Casilla de Correos 6436, Montevideo, Uruguay. Ed. Jorge Baeza. adv.
Formerly: Congreso Nacional de Arqueologia. Actas.

943.8 913   PL   ISSN 0071-6863
FONTES ARCHAEOLOGICI POSNANIENSES/ANNALES MUSEI ARCHAEOLOGICI POSNANIENSIS. (Text in Polish; summaries in English, French and German) 1950. irreg. price varies. Muzeum Archeologiczne, Ul. Wodna 27, Palac Gorkow, 61-781 Poznan, Poland. FAX 48-61-525306. Ed. Lech Krzyzaniak. R&P contact: Wojciech Smigielski. bk.rev. circ. 800. Indexed: A.I.C.P., Anthropol.Lit., Br.Archaeol.Abstr. Document type: academic/scholarly publication.
—BLDSC (3976.700000).
Formerly: Fontes Praehistorici (ISSN 0867-1184)

913   XR   ISSN 0015-6183
GN705
FONTES ARCHAEOLOGICI PRAGENSES. (Text in English, French, German, Russian) 1958. irreg. price varies. Narodni Muzeum, Historicke Muzeum, Vaclavske nam. 68, 115 79 Prague 1, Czech Republic. FAX 42-2-24226488. Ed. Milan Licka. charts; illus.; stat.; cum.index. circ. 700. (tabloid format) Document type: academic/scholarly publication.

914   IT
FORMA ITALIAE. SERIE I. 1926. irreg., no.37, 1996. price varies. Casa Editrice Leo S. Olschki, Casella Postale 66, 50100 Florence, Italy. TEL 39-55-6530684. FAX 39-55-6530214. E-mail: celso@olschki.it. Document type: monographic series.
Supersedes in part (in 1977): Forma Italia (ISSN 0392-0119)

914   IT
FORMA ITALIAE. SERIE II. DOCUMENTI. 1926. irreg., no.2, 1981. price varies. Casa Editrice Leo S. Olschki, Casella Postale 66, 50100 Florence, Italy. TEL 39-55-6530684. FAX 39-55-6530214. E-mail: celso@olschki.it. circ. 1,000. Document type: monographic series.
Supersedes in part (in 1972): Forma Italia (ISSN 0392-0119)

937   IT
FORMIANUM. Represents: Convegno di Studi sull'Antico Territorio di Formia. Atti. 1993. a. (Archeoclub d'Italia) Armando Caramanica Editore, Via Appia 762, 04020 Marina di Minturno (LT), Italy. TEL 39-771-680838.

609 936.3   SW   ISSN 0283-3301
FORNTIDA TEKNIK. 1979. s.-a. SEK 120. Stiftelsen Institutet foer Forntida Teknik, Bergsgatan 30, S-832 00 Froesoen, Sweden. TEL 46-63-13-77-56.
Formerly (until 1986): Institutet foer Foerhistorisk Teknologi - Medlemsblad.

913   SW   ISSN 0015-7813
DL601
FORNVAENNEN; tidskrift foer svensk antikvarisk forskning/journal of Swedish antiquarian research. (Text in Danish, English, German, Norwegian, Swedish; summaries in English) 1906. 4/yr. SEK 160 (foreign SEK 200) (effective 1997). Kungliga Vitterhets, Historie- och Antikvitets Akademien - Royal Academy of Letters, History and Antiquities, P.O. Box 5622, S-114 86 Stockholm, Sweden. TEL 46-8-200936. FAX 46-8-200981. Ed. G. Trotzig. bk.rev.; charts; illus. circ. 2,000. Indexed: A.I.C.P., Anthropol.Lit., Art & Archaeol.Tech.Abstr., Bibl.Ling., Br.Archaeol.Abstr., IBR, NAA, Numis.Lit.
—KNAW.

FORSCHUNGEN ZUR KUNSTGESCHICHTE UND CHRISTLICHEN ARCHAEOLOGIE. see ART

913   AU
FORSCHUNGSBERICHTE ZUR UR- UND FRUEHGESCHICHTE. 1959. biennial. price varies. Oesterreichische Gesellschaft fuer Ur- und Fruehgeschichte, Franz-Klein-Gasse 1, A-1190 Vienna, Austria. TEL 4321-31352373. FAX 43-1-31352350. Ed. Dr. J-W. Neugebauer. Document type: academic/scholarly publication.

913   FR
FOUILLES DE DELPHES: COLLECTION. irreg. De Boccard Edition, 11 rue de Medicis, 75006 Paris, France.

930.1   FR
FOUILLES RECENTES A KHIROKITIA. (Text in English, French) 1985. irreg. price varies. Editions Recherche sur les Civilisations, 28 rue de Bourgogne, 75007 Paris, France. TEL 33-1-40628062. FAX 33-1-40628071. Ed. Hina Descat; Pub. Hina Descat. circ. 600. Document type: monographic series.

917   US   ISSN 1070-7549
PS508.I5
FOUR DIRECTIONS; American Indian literary quarterly. 1972. q. membership. (Institute for American Indian Studies) Snowbird Publishing Company, Box 729, Tellico Plains, TN 37385. TEL 615-253-3680. (Subscr. to: Institute for American Indian Studies, Box 1260, Washington, CT 06793. TEL 203-868-0518. FAX 203-868-1649) Ed. Joanna Meyer; Pub. William H. Meyer. adv. contact: William H. Meyer. bk.rev.; film rev.; index. circ. 1,600. Document type: academic/scholarly publication.
Formerly (until 1992): Artifacts (Washington).
Description: Seeks to further awareness of the American Indian spirit in all areas among both American Indian and non-Indian audiences.

913   NO   ISSN 0015-9255
FRA HAUG OG HEIDNI. 1960. q. NOK 75. (Rogalands Arkeologiske Forening) Arkeologisk Museum i Stavanger, P.O. Box 478, N-4001 Stavanger, Norway. TEL 47-51-84-60-00. FAX 47-51-84-61-99. E-mail: bjornm@ark.museum.no. Ed.Bd. (back issues avail.) Indexed: IBR, NAA.
—CCC.
Description: Presents archaeology in southwest Norway.

FRA HOLBAECK AMT: HISTORISKE AARBOEGER. see HISTORY — History Of Europe

914   FR   ISSN 0399-6662
DC801.S235
FRANCE. CENTRE REGIONAL ARCHEOLOGIQUE D'ALET. DOSSIERS. 1973. s.-a. 190 F. (effective 1997). Centre Regional Archeologique d'Alet, Rue de Gaspe, B.P. 60, 35413 Saint Malo Cedex, France. TEL 33-2-99826373. Ed. Loic Langouet. adv.; bk.rev. (back issues avail.) Document type: bulletin.
Description: Studies the archaeology of Brittany.

913   FR   ISSN 0071-8394
DC2
FRANCE. COMITE DES TRAVAUX HISTORIQUES ET SCIENTIFIQUES. BULLETIN ARCHEOLOGIQUE. (In two fascicules: Antiquites Nationales; Afrique du Nord) 1883. a. price varies. Ministere de l'Education Nationale, Comite des Travaux Historiques et Scientifiques, 1 rue Descartes, 75005 Paris, France. cum.index: 1883-1940. circ. 750. Indexed: Avery Ind.Archit.Per., GeoRef.

709   GW   ISSN 0071-9757
FUEHRER ZU ARCHAEOLOGISCHEN DENKMAELERN IN DEUTSCHLAND. 1983. irreg., vol.124, 1992. price varies. (Nordwestdeutscher und West- und Sueddeutscher Verband fuer Altertumsforschung) Konrad Theiss Verlag GmbH, Moenchhaldenstr. 28, 70191 Stuttgart, Germany. TEL 49-711-25527-0. FAX 49-711-2552717. index. Document type: monographic series.

915 069   CC
FUJIAN WENBO/FUJIAN RELICS AND MUSEUM. (Text in Chinese) 1979. s-a. Y3. Fujian Kaogu Bowuguan Xuehui - Fujian Archaeological Museum Society, Fujian Sheng Bowuguan, Xihu, Fuzhou, Fujian 350001, People's Republic of China. TEL 554244. (Dist. overseas by: Jiangsu Publications Import & Export Corp., 56 Gao Yun Ling, Nanjing, Jiangsu, P.R.C.) Ed. Chen Cunxi.
Description: Presents archaeological findings and research results.

930.1   US
▼**FUNDAMENTAL ISSUES IN ARCHAEOLOGY.** 1995. irreg. price varies. Plenum Publishing Corp., 233 Spring St., New York, NY 10013-1578. TEL 212-620-8000. FAX 212-463-0742. TELEX 23-421139. E-mail: books@plenum.com. Eds. Gary M. Feinman, T. Douglas Price. Document type: monographic series.
Description: Examines current critical issues of broad relevance to anthropological archaeology.
Refereed Serial

913   GW   ISSN 0071-9889
FUNDBERICHTE AUS HESSEN. 1961. irreg. price varies. Dr. Rudolf Habelt GmbH, Am Buchenhang 1, 53115 Bonn, Germany. TEL 49-228-9238322. FAX 49-228-923836. Indexed: Br.Archaeol.Abstr., Numis.Lit. Document type: monographic series.
—BLDSC (4056.097500).

914 709   GW   ISSN 0723-8630
FUNDE UND AUSGRABUNGEN IM BEZIRK TRIER. 1969. a. DM.10. Rheinisches Landesmuseum Trier, Weimarer Allee 1, 54290 Trier, Germany. TEL 49-651-9774-0. FAX 49-651-9774222. Ed.Bd. circ. 2,000. (back issues avail.) Indexed: Anthropol.Lit., IBR. Document type: academic/scholarly publication.

930.102809   DK   ISSN 0109-1441
FYNBOER OG ARKAEOLOGI. 1979. 3/yr. free. Odense Bys Museer, Publikumsafdeling, Bangs Boder 5, DK-5000 Odense C, Denmark. TEL 45-66-13-13-72. FAX 45-65-95-84-90. Ed. Jytte Raun. R&P contact: Nils M. Jensen. bk.rev.; illus. circ. 800. Document type: newsletter.

FYND. see MUSEUMS AND ART GALLERIES

FYNSKE MINDER. see HISTORY — History Of Europe

913   PE   ISSN 0254-8240
F2229
GACETA ARQUEOLOGICA ANDINA. 1982. bi-m. Instituto Andino de Estudios Arqueologicos, Apartado 11279, Lima 14, Peru. bk.rev.; abstr.; bibl.; charts; illus. (tabloid format; back issues avail.) Indexed: Anthropol.Lit., IBR.

930.1 301   SP   ISSN 1132-2470
GALA; revista d'arqueologia i antropologia. 1992. a. Museu Arqueologia i Antropologia, Can Xifreda, C. Dr. Reig, 08182 St. Feliu de Codines (Barcelona), Spain. Eds. M. Garriga, J. Rovira.

GALLAECIA. see HISTORY — History Of Europe

913   FR   ISSN 0016-4119
DC30
GALLIA; fouilles et monuments archeologiques en France metropolitaine. (Includes supplements) 1943. s.-a. price varies. (Centre National de la Recherche Scientifique) C N R S Editions, 20-22 rue St. Amand, 75015 Paris, France. TEL 45-33-16-00. FAX 45-33-92-13. TELEX 200 356 F. adv.; bk.rev.; charts; illus.; index. circ. 1,500. Indexed: Avery Ind.Archit.Per., Br.Archaeol.Abstr., IBR.

913   FR   ISSN 0072-0119
GALLIA. SUPPLEMENT. 1943. irreg. price varies. (Centre National de la Recherche Scientifique) C N R S Editions, 20-22 rue St. Amand, 75015 Paris, France. TEL 45-33-16-00. FAX 45-33-92-13. TELEX 200 356 F. adv.; bk.rev.; index; circ. 1,500 (controlled). Indexed: Avery Ind.Archit.Per.

913   FR   ISSN 0016-4127
GN811.A1
GALLIA PREHISTOIRE; fouilles et monuments archeologiques en France metropolitaine. (Includes supplements) 1958. s.-a. price varies. (Centre National de la Recherche Scientifique) C N R S Editions, 20-22 rue St. Amand, 75015 Paris, France. TEL 45-33-16-00. FAX 45-33-92-13. TELEX 200 356 F. Ed. Leroi-Gourhan. charts; illus.; index. Indexed: Anthropol.Lit., Br.Archaeol.Abstr., GeoRef.

913   FR   ISSN 0072-0100
GALLIA PREHISTOIRE. SUPPLEMENT. 1958. irreg. price varies. (Centre National de la Recherche Scientifique) C N R S Editions, 20-22 rue St. Amand, 75015 Paris, France. TEL 45-33-16-00. FAX 45-33-92-13. TELEX 200 356 F. adv.; bk.rev.; index; circ. 1,500 (controlled). Indexed: GeoRef.

GAYA. see HISTORY — History Of Europe

GDANSKIE TOWARZYSTWO NAUKOWE. WYDZIAL 1 - NAUK SPOLECZNYCH I HUMANISTYCZNYCH. KOMISJA ARCHEOLOGICZNA. PRACE. see HISTORY — History Of Europe

GELDERS ERFGOED. see HISTORY — History Of Europe

913 709   SZ   ISSN 0072-0585
GENAVA; revue d'archeologie et d'histoire de l'art. 1923. a. 50 SFr. Musee d'Art et d'Histoire, Geneva, Rue Charles Galland 2, CH-1211 Geneva 3, Switzerland. TEL 41-22-4182600. FAX 41-22-4182601. Ed. Danielle Buyssens. Indexed: A.I.C.P., Avery Ind.Archit.Per., IBR, Numis.Lit., RILA. Document type: academic/scholarly publication.

ARCHAEOLOGY

913   IT   ISSN 0390-2196
GEO - ARCHEOLOGIA. 1982. s-a. L.85000. Herder Editrice e Libreria s.r.l., Piazza Montecitorio, 117-120, 00186 Rome, Italy. TEL 6794628. FAX 6784751. Ed. Claudio Saporetti. **Indexed:** IBR. **Document type:** academic/scholarly publication.
    Description: Covers the culture of the geological sciences, includes research and study of various topics in these fields.

913   US   ISSN 0883-6353
CC77.5   CODEN: GEOAEY
GEOARCHAEOLOGY; an international journal. 1986. 8/yr. $656 (foreign $796) (effective 1998). John Wiley & Sons, Inc., Journals, 605 Third Ave., New York, NY 10158-0012. TEL 212-850-6645. FAX 212-850-6021. TELEX 12-7063. E-mail: SUBINFO@JWILEY.COM. (Subscr. outside the Americas to: John Wiley & Sons Ltd., Baffins Ln., Chichester, W. Sussex PO19 1UD, England. TEL 44-1243-779777. FAX 44-1243-776128) Ed. Jack Donahue. bk.rev. (also avail. in microform from UMI; back issues avail.) **Indexed:** Abstr.Anthropol., Anthropol.Lit., Geo.Abstr.H.G. **Document type:** academic/scholarly publication.
    —BLDSC (4116.841000); Linda Hall; SWETS; UMI; UnCover. **CCC.**
    Description: Publishes original reports on the environmental settings of archaeological sites, materials analysis of artifacts, and process papers describing new techniques and equipment. Serves as an interface between geology and archaeology.
    Refereed Serial

930.1   GW   ISSN 1381-0472
GEOGRAPHICA HISTORICA. 1976. irreg., vol.9, 1997. price varies. Franz Steiner Verlag Wiesbaden GmbH, Birkenwaldstr. 44, 70191 Stuttgart, Germany. TEL 49-711-2582-0. FAX 49-711-2582390. Ed. Eckart Olshausen. **Document type:** monographic series, proceedings.

GERION. see HISTORY

913   GW   ISSN 0016-8874
GERMANIA. 1917. a. DM.60. (Deutsches Archaeologisches Institut, Roemisch-Germanische Kommission) Verlag Philipp von Zabern GmbH, Philipp-von-Zabern-Platz 1-3, 55116 Mainz, Germany. TEL 06131-287470. FAX 06131-223710. Ed.Bd. bk.rev.; abstr.; bibl.; charts; illus.; index, cum.index 1917-1958. (reprint service avail. from KTO) **Indexed:** A.I.C.P., Anthropol.Lit., Br.Archaeol.Abstr., IBR, Numis.Lit., SSCI. **Document type:** academic/scholarly publication.
    —EMDOCS; KR SourceOne.

913   GW   ISSN 0418-9779
GERMANISCHE DENKMAELER DER VOELKERWANDERUNGSZEIT. SERIES B. irreg., vol.17, 1996. price varies. (Roemisch-Germanische Kommission des Deutschen Archaeologischen Instituts) Franz Steiner Verlag Wiesbaden GmbH, Birkenwaldstr. 44, 70191 Stuttgart, Germany. TEL 49-711-2582-0. FAX 49-711-2582390. (Subscr. to: Postfach 101061, 70009 Stuttgart, Germany) Ed. Kurt Boehner. R&P contact: Sabine Koerner. **Document type:** monographic series.

913   SZ   ISSN 0072-4270
GESELLSCHAFT PRO VINDONISSA. JAHRESBERICHT. 1907. a. price varies. Gesellschaft pro Vindonissa, Vindonissa Museum, CH-5200 Brugg, Switzerland. TEL 41-56-4112184. **Indexed:** Br.Archaeol.Abstr., Numis.Lit. **Document type:** academic/scholarly publication.

708   SZ   ISSN 0072-4289
GESELLSCHAFT PRO VINDONISSA. VEROEFFENTLICHUNGEN. (Supplements avail.) 1942. irreg., latest no.13, 1996. price varies. Gesellschaft pro Vindonissa, Vindonissa Museum, CH-5200 Brugg, Switzerland. TEL 41-56-4411284. charts; illus.; stat. **Document type:** monographic series.

GIORNALE STORICO DELLA LUNIGIANA E DEL TERRITORIO LUCENSE. see HISTORY — History Of Europe

913   UK   ISSN 0305-8980
GLASGOW ARCHAEOLOGICAL JOURNAL. 1969. a. £15. Glasgow Archaeological Society, c/o Department of Archaeology, University of Glasgow G12 8QQ, Scotland. TEL 041-9654156. FAX 041-943-0106. (Alt. addr.: c/o Miss Elaine K. Hyland, Publications Officer, 8 The Cottages, Craighton Village, Milngavie, Glasgow G62 7HQ, Scotland) Eds. A. Morrison, E. Mackie. bk.rev. circ. 400. (back issues avail.) **Indexed:** Anthropol.Lit., Br.Archaeol.Abstr., Numis.Lit.
    —BLDSC (4183.050000).

GOETTINGISCHE GELEHRTE ANZEIGEN. see LINGUISTICS

930.1   SA   ISSN 0304-3460
               CODEN: GSSSDZ
GOODWIN SERIES. OCCASIONAL PAPERS. (Text in English) 1972. irreg., no.7, 1993. membership. South African Archaeological Society, P.O. Box 15700, Vlaeberg 8018, South Africa. TEL 27-21-243330. FAX 27-21-246716. Ed.Bd. circ. 1,300. **Document type:** monographic series.

930.1 390   BE
GRAAFSCHAP JETTE. JAARBOEK/COMTE DE JETTE. ANNALES. (Text in Dutch and French) q. 400 BEF per no. Cercle d'Histoire, d'Archeologie et de Folklore du Comte de Jette et des Environs, 35 Avenue de Brouckere, 1083 Brussels, Belgium. Ed. F. Van Bellingen. bk.rev.; charts; illus. **Document type:** bulletin.
    Formerly: Comte de Jette. Bulletin (ISSN 0010-4914)

913   AU   ISSN 0376-5253
PA1.A1
GRAEZER BEITRAEGE; Zeitschrift fuer klassische Altertumswissenschaft. (Text in English, French, German, Italian) 1973. s-a. S.890($60) per vol. Verlag Ferdinand Berger und Soehne GmbH, Wienerstr. 21-23, A-3580 Horn, Austria. TEL 43-2982-4161232. FAX 43-2982-2317235. Ed.Bd. adv.; bk.rev. circ. 200. (back issues avail.) **Indexed:** Bibl.Ling., IBR. **Document type:** academic/scholarly publication.
    —BLDSC (4214.340000).

GREAT BRITAIN. ROYAL COMMISSION ON ANCIENT AND HISTORICAL MONUMENTS IN WALES. INTERIM REPORT. see HISTORY — History Of Europe

571 720   UK   ISSN 1350-407X
DA655
GREAT BRITAIN. ROYAL COMMISSION ON THE HISTORICAL MONUMENTS OF ENGLAND. ANNUAL REPORT. 1910. a. free. Royal Commission on the Historical Monuments of England, National Monuments Record Centre, Kemble Dr., Swindon SN2 2GZ, England. TEL 44-1793-414700. FAX 44-1793-414707. URL: http://www.rchme.gov.uk. Eds. Jon Cannon, Andrew Sargeant. R&P contact: DonMackay. TEL 44-1793-414626. adv. contact: Jon Cannon. **Document type:** newsletter, government publication.
    —BLDSC (1417.880000).
    Former titles: Great Britain. Royal Commission on the Historical Monuments of England. Interim Report; Great Britain. Royal Commission on the Ancient and Historical Monuments and Constructions of England. Interim Report (ISSN 0072-7067)
    Description: Surveys the discovery and preservation of historical monuments throughout the UK. Includes a financial statement and a list of books and articles published by the RCHME staff.

914.2 942   UK   ISSN 0957-0241
GREAT BRITAIN. ROYAL COMMISSION ON THE HISTORICAL MONUMENTS OF ENGLAND. NEWSLETTER. 2/yr. free. Royal Commission on the Historical Monuments of England, National Monuments Record Centre, Kemble Dr., Swindon SN2 2GZ, England. TEL 44-1793-414700. FAX 44-1793-414707. E-mail: pubs@rchme.gov.uk; URL: http://www.rchme.gov.uk. Ed. Jon Cannon. R&P contact: Donnie Mackay. TEL 44-1793-414626. adv. contact: Jon Cannon. **Document type:** newsletter, government publication.

932 666   UA   ISSN 0255-0903
GROUPE INTERNATIONAL D'ETUDE DE LA CERAMIQUE EGYPTIENNE. BULLETIN DE LIAISON. Key Title: Bulletin de Liaison du Groupe International d'Etude de la Ceramique Egyptienne. (Text in English, French, German) 1975. a. £35 (overseas 53 F.) (effective 1997). Institut Francais d'Archeologie Orientale du Caire, P.O. Box 11562 Kasr el-Aini, 37 Sharia Sheikh Aly Youssef, Mounira, Cairo, Egypt. TEL 20-2-3571622. FAX 20-2-3544635. E-mail: mcmichael@fao.eg-net.net. (Dist. by: Boustany's Publishing House, 29 Faggalah St., 11271 Cairo, Egypt. TEL 20-2-5915315. FAX 20-2-4177915; In France: Imprimerie Nationale - D A C F, 27 rue de la Convention, 75732 Paris Cedex 15, France. TEL 33-1-40583064. FAX 33-1-40583105) Ed. Helen Jacquet-Gordon. circ. 200. (back issues avail.) **Document type:** academic/scholarly publication.
    Description: Recent discoveries in Egypt and news about ceramological studies in Egyptology.

913   PO
GRUPO DE INVESTIGACAO ARQUEOLOGICA DO NORTE. TRABALHOS. 1982. irreg. Grupo de Investigacao Arqueologica do Norte, Rua de Santiage 237-4450, S. da Hora (Matosinhos), Porto, Portugal. circ. 1,000.

913   IT   ISSN 1121-3949
GRUPPO ARCHEOLOGICO OSTIGLIESE. QUADERNI. 1991. a. L.15000. Gruppo Archeologico Ostigliese, Via Piave n. 5, 46035 Ostiglia (MN), Italy. Dir. Mauro Calzolari.
    Description: Publishes research works related to the province of Mantova, especially the eastern region.

918   GT
GUATEMALA. CONSEJO NACIONAL PARA LA PROTECCION DE LA ANTIGUA GUATEMALA. CARTA INFORMATIVA. (Supplements avail.; Annual avail.: Memoria de Labores) bi-m. Consejo Nacional para la Proteccion de la Antigua Guatemala, Convento de Capuchinas, 03001 La Antigua Guatemala, Guatemala. circ. 500.

915   CC   ISSN 0452-7402
GUGONG BOWUYUAN YUANKAN/PALACE MUSEUM. JOURNAL. (Text in Chinese) q. $30. Gugong Bowuyuan - Palace Museum, Beijing 100009, People's Republic of China. TEL 5132255. (Dist. in U.S. by: China Books & Periodicals, Inc., 2929 24th St., San Francisco, CA 94110. TEL 415-282-2992) Ed. Liu Beisi.
    —UnCover.

930.1   US
GUIDE TO HISTORICAL ARCHAEOLOGICAL LITERATURE. 1990. irreg. price varies. Society for Historical Archaeology, Box 30446, Tucson, AZ 85751. TEL 520-886-8006. FAX 520-886-0182. E-mail: sha@azstarnet.com; sha__editor@cup.edu. **Document type:** bibliography, academic/scholarly publication.
    Description: Bibliographic essays and compiled references on ethnic group experiences in the New World.

933   IS
GUIDES TO ANTIQUITY SITES. (Editions in English, Hebrew) 1992. a. price varies. Israel Antiquities Authority, P.O. Box 586, Jerusalem 91004, Israel. TEL 972-2-5602607. FAX 972-2-5602628. E-mail: harriet@israntique.org.il. (back issues avail.) **Document type:** monographic series.

070.5 590   NO   ISSN 0332-8554
QH168   CODEN: KNVGDN
GUNNERIA. (Text and summaries in English, German, Norwegian) 1971. irreg., no.38, 1981. Norges Teknisk-Naturvitenskapelige Universitet, Vitenskapmuseet - Norwegian University of Science and Technology, Museum of Natural History and Archaeology, N-7004 Trondheim, Norway. TEL 47-73-59-21-45. FAX 47-73-59-22-23. Ed. Astrid Langvath. circ. 500. **Indexed:** Biol.Abstr., Chem.Abstr., Curr.Adv.Ecol.Sci., Deep Sea Res.& Oceanogr.Abstr., NAA. **Document type:** academic/scholarly publication.
    —CCC.
    Formerly (until no.26, 1977): Kongelige Norske Videnskabers Selskab. Museet. Miscellanea (ISSN 0332-8430)
    Refereed Serial

ARCHAEOLOGY

913 GW ISSN 0072-9183
HABELTS DISSERTATIONSDRUCKE. REIHE KLASSISCHE ARCHAEOLOGIE. 1969. irreg., no. 27, 1988. price varies. Dr. Rudolf Habelt GmbH, Am Buchenhang 1, 53115 Bonn, Germany. TEL 49-228-9238322. FAX 49-228-923836. **Document type:** monographic series.

933 IS ISSN 0047-1569
HADASHOT ARKHEOLOGIYOT. English translation: Excavations and Surveys in Israel (IS ISSN 0334-1607) (Text in Hebrew) 1961. s-a. $36. Israel Antiquities Authority, P.O. Box 586, Jerusalem 91004, Israel. TEL 972-2-5602607. FAX 972-2-5602628. E-mail: harriet@israntiques.org.il. Ed. Ayala Sussmann. illus.; index. circ. 1,500. **Indexed:** Ind.Heb.Per., Numis.Lit. **Document type:** academic/scholarly publication.
  Former titles: Israel. Department of Antiquities and Museums. Archaeological Newsletter - Hadashot Arkheologiyot; Israel. Department of Antiquities and Museums. Archaeological News.

HALLAND; aarsbok foer kulturhistoria och hembygdsvaard i Hallands laen. see HISTORY — History Of Europe

913 GW ISSN 0341-3152
HAMBURGER BEITRAEGE ZUR ARCHAEOLOGIE. 1971. irreg., vol.21, 1994. price varies. Verlag Philipp von Zabern GmbH, Philipp-von-Zabern-Platz 1-3, 55116 Mainz, Germany. TEL 06131-28747-0. FAX 06131-223710. Ed.Bd. **Indexed:** Br.Archaeol.Abstr. **Document type:** monographic series.

940 UK
HAMPSHIRE STUDIES (YEAR). 1885. a. £12. Hampshire Field Club, c/o A.C. King, King Alfred's College, Winchester SO22 4NR, England. TEL 44-1962-841515. Ed. A.C. King. bk.rev.; charts; illus. circ. 900. (back issues avail.) **Indexed:** Br.Archaeol.Abstr., Br.Geol.Lit., Geo.Abstr., Numis.Lit., RILA. **Document type:** academic/scholarly publication.
  —BLDSC (6706.600000).
  Formerly (until 1996): Hampshire Field Club and Archaeological Society. Proceedings (ISSN 0142-8950); (until 1958): Hampshire Field Club and Archaeological Society. Papers and Proceedings.
  Refereed Serial

HANDBUCH DER ORIENTALISTIK. see ORIENTAL STUDIES

HANDBUCH DER ORIENTALISTIK. 1. ABTEILUNG. DER NAHE UND DER MITTLERE OSTEN. see ORIENTAL STUDIES

936.3 DK ISSN 0105-1660
HARJA. 1976-1985; resumed 199? irreg. (approx. a.). DKK 25. Harja Arkaeologisk Forening, c/o Jane Kjaergaard Andresen, Maagebakken 166, DK-5250 Odense SV, Denmark. TEL 45-66-17-50-20. Ed. Jane Kjaergaard Anddresen. illus.

HEIMATJAHRBUCH KREIS AHRWEILER. see LITERATURE

913 BE ISSN 0018-0009
HELINIUM; revue consacree a l'archeologie des Pays-Bas, de la Belgique et du Grand Duche de Luxembourg. 1961. 2/yr. 1000 Fr. Universa - Wetteren, Rue Hoender 24, 9200 Wetteren, Belgium. Ed.Bd. bk.rev.; charts; illus. **Indexed:** A.I.C.P., Anthropol.Lit., Br.Archaeol.Abstr., IBR, NAA, Numis.Lit.
  —BLDSC (4285.280000).

HELLENIKA. see CLASSICAL STUDIES

HERITAGE NEWS. see ARCHITECTURE

930.1 BE ISSN 0779-6080
HERLEVEND VERLEDEN - ARCHEOLOGISCHE GIDSEN. 1993. irreg., no.2, 1994. price varies. Instituut voor het Archeologisch Patrimonium, Doorneveld 1 bus 30, 1731 Asse (Sellik), Belgium. TEL 32-2-4631333. FAX 32-2-4631951. (back issues avail.) **Document type:** monographic series.
  Description: Publishes guides on topics in the archaeology of Flanders (Belgium).

913 US ISSN 0018-098X
DF10
HESPERIA. (Irregular supplement avail.) (Text in ancient Greek and English) 1932. q. $60 (foreign $69.50) to individuals; institutions $65 (foreign $74.50) (effective 1997). American School of Classical Studies at Athens, GR , 6-8 Charlton St., Princeton, NJ 08540-5232. TEL 609-683-0800. FAX 609-924-0578. E-mail: kak@ascsa.org; URL: http://www.cornell.edu/. Ed. Kathleen Krattenmaker. R&P contact: Kathleen Krattenmaker. charts; illus.; cum.index. circ. 1,000. (back issues avail.; reprint service avail. from SWZ) **Indexed:** Art Ind., Arts & Hum.Cit.Ind., Bibl.Ling., Curr.Cont., IBR, Numis.Lit., SSCI, SSCI. **Document type:** academic/scholarly publication.
  —BLDSC (4300.860000); Genuine Article; KR SourceOne; SWETS; UnCover.
  Description: Scholarly research on historical, archaeological and epigraphical topics concerning ancient Greece.
  Refereed Serial

HIAKA KHRONIKA. see HISTORY — History Of Europe

HIKUIN. see HISTORY — History Of Europe

HIMAVANTA; India's only mountaineering monthly. see SPORTS AND GAMES — Outdoor Life

HISTOIRE ET ARCHEOLOGIE. see HISTORY — History Of Europe

913 940 CI
HISTORIA ARCHAEOLOGICA. (Text in Croatian; summaries in English, German, Italian) 1970. a. Arheoloski Muzej Istre, Pula, M. Balote 3, 52000 Pula, Croatia. FAX 52-42-415. Ed. Robert Matijacic. bibl.; charts; illus. circ. 1,000.

HISTORIC ILLINOIS. see ARCHITECTURE

913 US ISSN 0440-9213
E11
HISTORICAL ARCHAEOLOGY. 1967. q. $75 to individuals; institutions $110; students $45 (includes S H A Newsletter) (effective 1998). Society for Historical Archaeology, Box 30446, Tucson, AZ 85751. TEL 520-886-8006. FAX 520-886-0182. E-mail: sha@azstarnet.com; sha_editor@cup.edu; URL: http://www.sha.org. Ed. Ronald L. Michael. R&P contact: Ronald L. Michael. bk.rev.; circ. 2,500. (paid). (back issues avail.) **Indexed:** Abstr.Anthropol., Amer.Hist.& Life (1973-), Anthropol.Lit., Art & Archaeol.Tech.Abstr., ASCA, Br.Archaeol.Abstr., Curr.Cont., Geo.Abstr., Hist.Abstr. (1973-), Hum.Ind. **Document type:** academic/scholarly publication, newsletter.
  —BLDSC (4316.117000); Genuine Article; KR SourceOne; UnCover.
  Description: Presents theoretical perspectives, comparative studies and artifact and site analysis.
  Refereed Serial

THE HISTORICAL REVIEW. see HISTORY — History Of Asia

HISTORISCHER VEREIN FUER DAS FUERSTENTUM LIECHTENSTEIN. JAHRBUCH. see HISTORY — History Of Europe

HOMBRE Y CULTURA. see ANTHROPOLOGY

609 US
HORN & WHISTLE. 1982. q. $14 membership (outside N. America $20) (effective 1997). Horn and Whistle Enthusiasts Group, 275 Windswept Dr., North East, PA 16428. TEL 814-725-8150. Ed. Harry Barry; Pub. Edward Fagen. R&P contact: Edward Fagen. TEL 802-388-2374. adv. contact: Larry Spreckelmeier. bk.rev.; circ. 175 (paid). (back issues avail.) **Document type:** newsletter.
  Description: Covers the preservation and the increase and dissemination of knowledge about horns, whistles, sirens, bells, and related devices used in industrial, marine, railroad, and other signaling and warning applications.

938 NE
HOROS. 1983. a., latest vol.10. price varies. J.C. Gieben, Nieuwe Herengracht 35, 1011 RM Amsterdam, Netherlands. TEL 31-20-6275170. FAX 31-20-6275170. (Dist. in N. America by: John Benjamins Publishing Co., Box 27519, Philadelphia, PA 19118-0519. TEL 315-836-1200. FAX 215-836-1204) (back issues avail.) **Document type:** academic/scholarly publication.
  Description: Devoted to epigraphical studies, museology and archaeological research in Greece.

915 CC ISSN 1001-9928
HUAXIA KAOGU/HUAXIA ARCHAEOLOGY. (Text in Chinese) 1987. q. $3 per no. Henan Sheng Wenwu Yanjiusuo - Henan Cultural Relics Research Institute, No. 9, Longhai Bei 3 Jie, Zhengzhou, Henan 450004, People's Republic of China. TEL 6252066. Ed. Hao Benxing. adv.; bk.rev.; circ. 5,000 (controlled). **Document type:** academic/scholarly publication.

HUMAN MOSAIC; a journal of the social sciences. see ANTHROPOLOGY

I A. (Industrial Archeology) see TECHNOLOGY: COMPREHENSIVE WORKS

933 IS
▼**I A A REPORTS.** (Text in English) 1996. price varies. Israel Antiquities Authority, P.O. Box 586, Jerusalem 91004, Israel. TEL 972-2-5602607. FAX 972-2-5602628. E-mail: harriet@israntiques.org.il. **Document type:** academic/scholarly publication.
  Description: Publishes reports and monographs on large-scale archaeological excavations in Israel.

913 UK ISSN 0261-068X
I A M S NEWSLETTER. (Institute for Archaeo-Metallurgical Studies) 1980. s-a. £5. University College London, Institute of Archaeology, 31-34 Gordon Sq., London WC1H OPY, England. TEL 0171-380-7532. FAX 0171-383-2572. Ed. Peter A. Clayton. illus. circ. 1,000. **Indexed:** CERDIC, I.M.M.Abstr. **Document type:** newsletter.
  Description: Reports of I A M S.

913 AU
I.C. NACHRICHTEN. 1969. 2/yr. S.120($12) Instituttum Canarium, Wagrainerstr. 9, A-4840 Voecklabruck, Austria. Ed. Werner Pichler. bk.rev.; charts; illus. circ. 400. **Document type:** academic/scholarly publication.

I C S NEWSLETTER. (International Catacomb Society) see ART

930.1 US
I N A QUARTERLY. 1979. q. $30 individual membership; students $20 (effective 1998). Institute of Nautical Archaeology, Drawer HG, College Station, TX 77841-5137. TEL 409-845-6694. FAX 409-847-9260. URL: http://nautarch.tamu.edu. Ed. Christine Powell. R&P contact: Christine Powell. bk.rev. circ. 1,350. **Document type:** academic/scholarly publication, newsletter.
  Formerly (until 1991): I N A Newsletter (ISSN 0738-4505)

ICONOLOGICAL STUDIES IN ROMAN ART. see ART

ILLINOIS. STATE MUSEUM. SCIENTIFIC PAPERS SERIES. see SCIENCES: COMPREHENSIVE WORKS

913 US ISSN 8756-0070
ILLINOIS ANTIQUITY. QUARTERLY NEWSLETTER. 1969. q. membership. Illinois Association for Advancement of Archaeology, c/o Ellis J. Neiburger, Ed., 1000 North Ave., Waukegan, IL 60085. (Subscr. to: Richard Ade, 641 Crest Ln., Lisle, IL 60532) R&P contact: Pub. E. Neiburger. bk.rev.; illus. circ. 400. (tabloid format; back issues avail.) **Document type:** academic/scholarly publication.
  Formerly: Illinois Association for Advancement of Archaeology. Quarterly Newsletter.

930.1 US ISSN 1050-8244
E78.I3
ILLINOIS ARCHAEOLOGY. 1989. s-a. $20 to individuals; institutions £30. University of Illinois, Illinois Archaeology Survey, Urbana, IL 61801. TEL 618-653-4688. FAX 618-653-4232. Ed. Thomas E. Emerson. R&P contact: Thomas E. Emerson. TEL 217-244-7476. adv. contact: Thomas E. Emerson. bk.rev.; circ. 200 (paid).

ARCHAEOLOGY

930.1 398   US   ISSN 0736-265X
INDIAN - ARTIFACT MAGAZINE. Short title: IAM. 1982. q. $20 (foreign $24) (effective 1997). Fogelman Publishing Co., RD 1, Box 240, Turbotville, PA 17772-9599. TEL 717-437-3698. FAX 717-437-3411. E-mail: iam@mail.csrlink.net. Ed. Gary L. Fogelman. Pub. Gary L. Fogelman. R&P contact: Gary L. Fogelman. adv. contact: Joanne Fogelman. bk.rev.; circ. 4,000 (paid). **Indexed:** Amer.Hist.& Life, Hist.Abstr. **Document type:** consumer publication.
   Description: Presents American Indian prehistory, artifacts, tools, life-styles, customs, tribes and archaeology presented in an easy-to-read format.

INDIANA; contributions to ethnology and linguistics, archaeology and physical anthropology of Indian America. see *ANTHROPOLOGY*

990 930.1   AT   ISSN 0156-1316
INDO-PACIFIC PREHISTORY ASSOCIATION BULLETIN. 1978. irreg. Aus.$25. Indo-Pacific Prehistory Association, c/o Dept. of Archaeology and Anthropology, Australian National University, Canberra, A.C.T. 0200, Australia. TEL 61-6-2492711. Ed. P. Bellwood. **Document type:** academic/scholarly publication.
   —BLDSC (2564.290000).

609   UK   ISSN 0019-7971
T37
INDUSTRIAL ARCHAEOLOGY; the journal of the history of industry and technology. 1964. a. £24($48) (foreign £26 ($52)). Graphmitre Ltd., 1 West St., Tavistock, Devon PL19 8DS, England. adv.; bk.rev.; illus.; cum.index: vols.1-16. circ. 1,000. (back issues avail.) **Indexed:** Amer.Hist.& Life (1977-1984), Avery Ind.Archit.Per., Br.Archaeol.Abstr., Br.Hum.Ind., Br.Tech.Ind., Geo.Abstr., Hist.Abstr. (1977-1984), Mid.East: Abstr.& Ind., RILA. **Document type:** academic/scholarly publication.
   —SWETS.
   Formerly: Journal of Industrial History.

609   UK   ISSN 1354-1455
INDUSTRIAL ARCHAEOLOGY NEWS. 1974. q. membership. Association for Industrial Archaeology, The Wharfage, Ironbridge, Telford, Shrops. TF8 7AW, England. TEL 44-1952-432141. FAX 44-1952-4322377. Ed. Peter Stanier. **Document type:** newsletter, academic/scholarly publication.
   Formerly (until 1994): A I A Bulletin (ISSN 0309-0051)
   Description: Covers news and issues in the archaeology of commercial and residential buildings built during the Industrial Revolution.

609   UK   ISSN 0309-0728
T37
INDUSTRIAL ARCHAEOLOGY REVIEW. 1976. a. Association for Industrial Archaeology, The Wharfage, Ironbridge, Telford, Shrops. TF8 7AW, England. TEL 44-1952-432141. FAX 44-1952-432237. Eds. M. Palmer, Peter Neaverson. adv.; bk.rev.; bibl.; illus.; index. **Indexed:** Abstr.Anthropol., Amer.Hist.& Life (1976-), Archit.Per.Ind., Br.Archaeol.Abstr., Geo.Abstr.H.G., Hist.Abstr. (1976-), IBR, RILA. **Document type:** academic/scholarly publication.
   —BLDSC (4445.330000); CISTI; Ei; SWETS.

930.1 943   GW   ISSN 0937-0994
INFORMATIONEN UND BERICHTE. 1987. q. DM.8. Braunschweigisches Landesmuseum, Burgplatz 1, 38100 Braunschweig, Germany. TEL 49-531-4842602. FAX 49-531-4842607. Ed. Gerd Biegel. circ. 1,000. **Document type:** bulletin.

913   PL   ISSN 0085-1876
INFORMATOR ARCHEOLOGICZNY. 1968. a. latest 1993 (for the year 1990). free. Osrodek Dokumentacji Zabytkow, Al. Ujazdowskie 6, 00-461 Warsaw, Poland. TEL 48-22-212573. Ed. Marek Konopka.

913   US
INKSHERDS. 1955. 4/yr. Archaeological Society of Delaware, Box 12483, Wilmington, DE 19850-2483. TEL 302-831-6590. Ed. Ronald Thomas. bk.rev. circ. 110. **Indexed:** Abstr.Anthropol. **Document type:** newsletter.

913   GW
INSCHRIFTEN GRIECHISCHER STAEDTE AUS KLEINASIEN. 1972. irreg. no.53, 1997. price varies. (Oesterreichischen Akademie der Wissenschaften, AU) Dr. Rudolf Habelt GmbH, Am Buchenhang 1, 53115 Bonn, Germany. TEL 49-228-9238322. FAX 49-228-923836. (Co-sponsor: Nordrhein-Westfaelische Akademie der Wissenschaften) **Document type:** monographic series.

930.1   BE   ISSN 0776-1244
INSTITUT ARCHEOLOGIQUE DU LUXEMBOURG. ANNALES. 1847. biennial. 750 BEF (includes Bulletins) (effective 1992). Institut Archeologique du Luxembourg, Bibliotheque, 13 rue des Martyrs, 6700 Arlon, Belgium. TEL 32-63-221236. Ed. Louis Lefebvre. **Document type:** bulletin.

913   BE   ISSN 0020-2177
INSTITUT ARCHEOLOGIQUE DU LUXEMBOURG. BULLETINS; archeologie-art-histoire-folklore. 1925. q. 750 BEF (includes Annales) (effective 1992). Institut Archeologique du Luxembourg, Bibliotheque, 13 rue des Martyrs, 6700 Arlon, Belgium. TEL 32-63-221236. Ed. Louis Lefebvre. bk.rev.; bibl.; illus. **Document type:** bulletin.

913   BE
INSTITUT ARCHEOLOGIQUE LIEGEOIS. BULLETIN. 1852. a. 1000 BEF. (Ministere de l'Education Nationale et de la Culture Francaise) Institut Archeologique Liegeois, Quai de Maastricht 13, 4000 Liege, Belgium. TEL 32-41-219404. FAX 32-41-219432. **Indexed:** Numis.Lit. **Document type:** academic/scholarly publication, bulletin.

932   UA   ISSN 0259-3823
INSTITUT FRANCAIS D'ARCHEOLOGIE ORIENTALE DU CAIRE. BIBLIOTHEQUE D'ETUDE. Key Title: Bibliotheque d'Etude - Institut Francais d'Archeologie Orientale. (Text mainly in French, occasionally in English) 1908. irreg., vol.115, 1996. price varies. Institut Francais d'Archeologie Orientale du Caire, P.O. Box 11562 Kaser-el-Aini, 37 Sharia Sheikh Aly Youssef, Mounira, Cairo, Egypt. TEL 20-2-3571622. FAX 20-2-3544635. E-mail: mcmichael@fao.eg-net.net. (Dist. by: Boustany's Publishing House, 29 Faggalah St., 11271 Cairo, Egypt. TEL 20-2-5195315. FAX 20-2-4177915) (back issues avail.) **Document type:** monographic series.
   Description: Scholarly studies of topics relating to the history, archaeology, art and culture of Egypt from Pharaonic times to the present day.

932   UA
INSTITUT FRANCAIS D'ARCHEOLOGIE ORIENTALE DU CAIRE. BIBLIOTHEQUE GENERALE. (Text in French, occasionally in Arabic) 1959. irreg., vol.17, 1997. price varies. Institut Francais d'Archeologie Orientale du Caire, P.O. Box 11562 Kasr-el-Aini, 37 Sharia Sheikh Aly Youssef, Mounira, Cairo, Egypt. TEL 20-2-3571622. FAX 20-2-3544635. E-mail: mcmichael@fao.eg-net.net. (Dist. by: Boustany's Publishing House, 29 Faggalah St., 11271 Cairo, Egypt. TEL 20-2-5195315. FAX 20-2-4177915) (back issues avail.) **Document type:** monographic series.
   Description: Publishes archaeological studies, guides, historical and linguistic studies.

932   UA   ISSN 0255-0962
INSTITUT FRANCAIS D'ARCHEOLOGIE ORIENTALE DU CAIRE. BULLETIN. Key Title: Bulletin de l'Institut Francais d'Archeologie Orientale. Short title: B I F A O. (Text in English, French, German) 1901. a. £E200 (overseas 300 F.) (effective 1997). Institut Francais d'Archeologie Orientale du Caire, P.O. Box 11562 Kasr el-Aini, 37 Sharia Sheikh Aly Youssef, Mounira, Cairo, Egypt. TEL 20-2-3571622. FAX 20-2-3544635. E-mail: mcmichael@fao.eg-net.net. (Dist. by: Boustany's Publishing House, 29 Faggalah St., 11271 Cairo, Egypt. TEL 20-2-5195315. FAX 20-2-4177915) circ. 800. (also avail. in microfiche from IDC; back issues avail.) **Indexed:** Bibl.Ling., IBR. **Document type:** academic/scholarly publication, bulletin.
   Description: Research on Egyptology (history, archaeology, linguistics).

932   UA   ISSN 0768-2964
INSTITUT FRANCAIS D'ARCHEOLOGIE ORIENTALE DU CAIRE. DOCUMENTS DE FOUILLES. Key Title: Documents de Fouilles. (Text in French) 1934. irreg., vol.32, 1997. price varies. Institut Francais d'Archeologie Orientale du Caire, P.O. Box 11562 Kasr-el-Aini, 37 Sharia Sheikh Aly Youssef, Mounira, Cairo, Egypt. TEL 20-2-3571622. FAX 20-2-3544635. E-mail: mcmichael@fao.eg-net.net. (Dist. by: Boustany's Publishing House, 29 Faggalah St., 11271 Cairo, Egypt. TEL 20-2-5195315. FAX 20-2-4177915) (back issues avail.) **Document type:** monographic series.
   Description: Publishes reports of archaeological studies conducted in Egypt, including catalogues of ostraca and papyrii.

932   UA   ISSN 0768-4703
INSTITUT FRANCAIS D'ARCHEOLOGIE ORIENTALE DU CAIRE. FOUILLES. Short title: F I F A O. (Text in French) 1924. irreg., vol.37, 1995. price varies. Institut Francais d'Archeologie Orientale du Caire, P.O. Box 11562 Kasr-el-Aini, 37 Sharia Sheikh Aly Youssef, Mounira, Cairo, Egypt. TEL 20-2-3571622. FAX 20-2-3544635. E-mail: mcmichael@fao.eg-net.net. (Dist. by: Boustany's Publishing House, 29 Faggalah St., 11271 Cairo, Egypt. TEL 20-2-5195315. FAX 20-2-4177915) (back issues avail.) **Document type:** monographic series.
   Description: Publishes preliminary reports and detailed reports of archaeological excavations conducted in Egypt.

932   UA   ISSN 0257-411X
INSTITUT FRANCAIS D'ARCHEOLOGIE ORIENTALE DU CAIRE. MEMOIRES. Key Title: Memoires Publies par les Membres de l'Institut Francais d'Archeologie Orientale. (Text in French) 1902. irreg., vol.112, 1995. price varies. Institut Francais d'Archeologie Orientale du Caire, P.O. Box 11562 Kasr-el-Aini, 37 Sharia Sheikh Aly Youssef, Mounira, Cairo, Egypt. TEL 20-2-3571622. FAX 20-2-3544635. E-mail: mcmichael@fao.eg-net.net. (Dist. by: Boustany's Publishing House, 29 Faggalah St., 11271 Cairo, Egypt. TEL 20-2-5195315. FAX 20-2-4177915) (back issues avail.) **Document type:** monographic series.
   Incorporates (1883-1934): Memoires Publies par les Membres de la Mission Archeologique Francaise au Caire (ISSN 0257-4128)

970.1   US
INSTITUTE FOR AMERICAN INDIAN STUDIES. OCCASIONAL PAPER AND BOOKS. 1974. irreg. Institute for American Indian Studies, 38 Curtis Rd., Box 1260, Washington, CT 06793. TEL 860-868-0518. FAX 203-868-1649. Ed. Alberto C. Meloni. R&P contact: Alberto C. Meloni. adv. contact: Mary L. Fletcher. circ. 2,000. **Indexed:** Anthropol.Lit. **Document type:** newsletter, academic/scholarly publication, bibliography.
   Formerly: American Indian Archaeological Institute. Occasional Paper.

913 333.79 550
560   US
INSTITUTE FOR THE STUDY OF EARTH AND MAN NEWSLETTER. 1974. a. free. Southern Methodist University, Institute for the Study of Earth and Man, c/o Heroy Science Hall, Dallas, TX 75275-0274. TEL 214-768-2425. FAX 214-768-4289. Ed. Susan J. Liepins. bibl.; illus. circ. 2,500. **Document type:** newsletter.

930.1 301   BL
INSTITUTO GOIANO DE PRE-HISTORIA E ANTROPOLOGIA. CADERNOS DE PESQUISA. irreg., no.9, 1995. Universidad Catolica de Goias, Instituto Goiano de Pre-historia e Antropologia, Praca Universitaria 1440, 74605-010 Goiania GO, Brazil. TEL 55-62-2271221. FAX 55-62-2243617. **Document type:** monographic series.

INSTITUTO NACIONAL DE ANTROPOLOGIA Y PENSAMIENTO LATINOAMERICANO. CUADERNOS. se *ANTHROPOLOGY*

ARCHAEOLOGY

914 949.8   RM
INSTITUTUL DE ARHEOLOGIE - CLUJ-NAPOCA. ANUARUL. vol.23, 1980. a. $38. Editura Academiei Romane, Calea 13 Septembrie 13, 76117 Bucharest, Rumania. (Dist. by: Rodipet SA, Piata Presei Libere 1, Sec. 1, P.O. Box 33-57, Bucharest, Rumania. TEL 401-6185103. FAX 401-2226407) Ed. Aurel Radutiu.
Supersedes in part: Institutul de Istorie si Arheologie - Cluj-Napoca. Anuarul (ISSN 0065-048X)

913 949.8   RM   ISSN 1221-3705
DR201
INSTITUTUL DE ISTORIE "A.D. XENOPOL". ANUARUL. 1963. a. Editura Academiei Romane, Calea 13 Septembrie 13, 76117 Bucharest, Rumania. (Subscr. to: Rodipet SA, Piata Presei Libere 1, Sec. 1, P.O. Box 33-57, Bucharest, Rumania. TEL 401-6185103. FAX 401-2226407) Ed. Leon Simanschi. **Indexed:** Amer.Hist.& Life, Hist.Abstr., IBR. —BLDSC (1565.308000).
Formerly (until 1990): Institutul de Istorie si Arheologie "A.D. Xenopol" - Iasi. Anuarul (ISSN 0074-039X)

913 400   AU
INSTITUTUM CANARIUM YEARBOOK. ALMOGAREN. (Text in English, French, German, Spanish) 1970. a. S.770($77) Institutum Canarium, Wagrainerstr. 9, A-4840 Voecklabruck, Austria. Ed. Hans-Joachim Ulbrich. bk.rev. circ. 500. **Indexed:** Anthropol.Lit., Curr.Cont.Africa. **Document type:** academic/scholarly publication.
Formerly: Almogaren.

INSTYTUT BALTYCKI GDANSK. KOMUNIKATY. see HISTORY — History Of Europe

930.1   US
INTERDISCIPLINARY CONTRIBUTIONS TO ARCHAEOLOGY. 1987. irreg., latest 1997. price varies. Plenum Publishing Corp., 233 Spring St., New York, NY 10013-1578. TEL 212-620-8000; 800-221-9369. FAX 212-463-0742. TELEX 23-421139. E-mail: books@plenum.com. Ed. Michael Jochim. (back issues avail.) **Document type:** monographic series.
Refereed Serial

571 930   IT   ISSN 0074-1469
INTERNATIONAL ASSOCIATION FOR CLASSICAL ARCHAEOLOGY. PROCEEDINGS OF CONGRESS. (Proceedings published by host country) irreg., 1978, 11th, London. International Association for Classical Archaeology, 49 Piazza San Marco, 00186 Rome, Italy.

571   UK   ISSN 0074-3429
INTERNATIONAL CONGRESS FOR PAPYROLOGY. PROCEEDINGS. triennial, 15th Congress 1977, Brussels. DM.120. International Association of Papyrologists, c/o Dr. R.A. Coles, Papyrology Rooms, Ashmolean Museum, Oxford, England.

INTERNATIONAL JOURNAL OF CULTURAL PROPERTY. see ART

930.1   US   ISSN 1092-7697
▼**INTERNATIONAL JOURNAL OF HISTORICAL ARCHAEOLOGY.** 1997. q. $100 to institutions (foreign $115) (effective 1997). Plenum Publishing Corp., 233 Spring St., New York, NY 10013-1578. TEL 212-620-8000; 800-221-9369. FAX 212-463-0742. E-mail: info@plenum.com; URL: http://www.plenum.com. Ed. Charles E. Orser, Jr. **Indexed:** Amer.Hist.& Life (1997-), Hist.Abstr. (1997-). **Document type:** academic/scholarly publication.
Description: Publishes theoretical, methodological, site-specific and descriptive articles on all topics of interest to historical archaeologists.
Refereed Serial

913   UK   ISSN 1057-2414
CC77
INTERNATIONAL JOURNAL OF NAUTICAL ARCHAEOLOGY. 1972. q. £132 (effective 1998). (Nautical Archeology Society) Academic Press Ltd. (Subsidiary of: Harcourt Brace & Company Ltd.), 24-28 Oval Rd., London NW1 7DX, England. TEL 44-171-267-4466. FAX 44-171-482-2293. TELEX 25775 ACPRES G. E-mail: apsubs@acad.com; URL: http://www.hbuk.co.uk/ap/ijna; http://europe.idealibrary.com/. (Subscr. to: Harcourt Brace & Company Ltd., Foots Cray High St., Sidcup, Kent DA14 5HP, England. TEL 44-181-300-3322. FAX 44-181-309-0807) Ed. V. Fenwick. R&P contact: Catherine John. adv. contact: Nik Screen. bk.rev.; index. (reprint service avail. from SWZ) **Indexed:** Abstr.Anthropol., Anthropol.Lit., Arts & Hum.Cit.Ind., ASCA, Br.Archaeol.Abstr., Curr.Cont., Mid.East: Abstr.& Ind., SSCI. **Document type:** academic/scholarly publication.
●Also available online.
—Genuine Article; KR SourceOne; SWETS; UnCover. CCC.
Formerly: International Journal of Nautical Archaeology and Underwater Exploration (ISSN 0305-7445)
Description: Covers all aspects of nautical archaeological research.

INTERNATIONAL UNION OF PREHISTORIC AND PROTOHISTORIC SCIENCES. CONGRESS. BULLETIN. see ANTHROPOLOGY

930.1   UK   ISSN 1363-5387
CC1
▼**INTERNET ARCHAEOLOGY.** 1996. s-a. free. Council for British Archaeology, Internet Archaeology Office, Dept. of Archaeology, University of York, The King's Manor, York YO1 2EP, England. TEL 44-1904-433955. FAX 44-1904-433939. E-mail: editor@intarch.ac.uk; URL: http://intarch.ac.uk. Ed. Alan Vince. R&P contact: Sandra Garsde-Neville. software rev. **Document type:** academic/scholarly publication.
●Available only online.
Description: Publishes the results of archaeological research, including excavation reports, analyses of large datasets, programs used to analyze data, and applications of information technology.
Refereed Serial

931   US
INTERPRETING THE PAST. 1990. irreg., no.7, 1994. price varies. University of California Press, 2120 Berkeley Way, Berkeley, CA 94720. TEL 510-642-4247. FAX 510-643-7127. (Orders to: California-Princeton Fulfillment Services, 1445 Lower Ferry Rd., Ewing, NJ 08618. TEL 800-777-4726. FAX 800-999-1958) (back issues avail.) **Document type:** monographic series.
Description: Examines classical and Near Eastern history and culture by analyzing art objects and other material remains.
Refereed Serial

917   US   ISSN 0535-5729
E78.I6
IOWA ARCHAEOLOGICAL SOCIETY. JOURNAL. 1951. a. $15 individual membership; institutions $20 (effective 1997). Iowa Archeological Society, c/o Office of the State Archaeologist, University of Iowa, Iowa City, IA 52242. TEL 319-335-2389. FAX 319-335-2776. E-mail: kris-hirst@uiowa.edu. Ed. Kris Hirst. R&P contact: Kris Hirst. bk.rev. circ. 500. **Indexed:** Anthropol.Lit. **Document type:** academic/scholarly publication.
—UnCover.
Description: Publishes articles, discussions of current issues, biographies, and abstracts of current research of permanent scientific value to archaeology.

917.7   US   ISSN 0578-655X
E78.I6
IOWA ARCHEOLOGICAL SOCIETY. NEWSLETTER. 1951. q. $15 individual membership; institutions $20 (effective 1997). Iowa Archeological Society, c/o Office of the State Archaeologist, University of Iowa, Iowa City, IA 52242. TEL 319-335-2394. FAX 319-335-2776. E-mail: kris-hirst@uiowa.edu. Ed. Sheila Hainlin. R&P contact: Kris Hirst. bk.rev.; bibl.; charts; illus. circ. 500. (also avail. in microform) **Indexed:** Anthropol.Lit. **Document type:** newsletter.
Description: Contains short articles and announcements pertinent to members of the society.

571   US   ISSN 0085-2252
IOWA STATE ARCHAEOLOGIST. REPORT. 1970. irreg., no.20, 1995043908300. price varies. Office of State Archaeologist, Eastlawn Bldg., University of Iowa, Iowa City, IA 52242. TEL 319-335-2389. Ed. William Green. bibl.; charts; illus. circ. 750. (reprint service avail. from UMI) **Document type:** academic/scholarly publication.

935   BE   ISSN 0021-0870
DS251
IRANICA ANTIQUA. (Supplement avail.) (Text in English, French) 1961. irreg., vol.30, 1995. 3200 BEF (effective 1996). (Gent University, Seminar for Near Eastern Art and Archaeology) Editions Peeters s.p.r.l., Bondgenotenlaan 153, 3000 Leuven, Belgium. TEL 32-16-235170. FAX 32-16-228500. URL: http://www.peeters-leuven.be. Eds. L. Vanden Berghe, A. Tourovets. illus.; maps. (back issues avail.) **Indexed:** Avery Ind.Archit.Per., Bibl.Ling., IBR, Numis.Lit. **Document type:** academic/scholarly publication.
—KR SourceOne.
Description: Publishes studies in the art, archaeology, ancient history and culture of the Iranian region.
Refereed Serial

935   BE   ISSN 0169-877X
IRANICA ANTIQUA SUPPLEMENTA. (Supplement to: Iranica Antiqua (ISSN 0021-0870)) 1962. irreg., vol.6, 1993. price varies. Editions Peeters s.p.r.l., Bondgenotenlaan 153, 3000 Leuven, Belgium. TEL 32-16-235170. FAX 32-16-228500. URL: http://www.peeters-leuven.be. (back issues avail.) **Document type:** monographic series.

913   UK   ISSN 0021-0889
DS78.A2
IRAQ. 1934. a. £25($45) British School of Archaeology in Iraq, Gertrude Bell Memorial, 31-34 Gordon Sq., London WC1H OPY, England. TEL 44-171-733-8912. Eds. A.R. George, D. Collon. charts; illus.; index, cum.index vols.1-50. circ. 750. (reprint service avail. from SWZ) **Indexed:** A.I.C.P., Anthropol.Lit., Avery Ind.Archit.Per., Bibl.Ling., Br.Hum.Ind., IBR, Mid.East: Abstr.& Ind., Old Test.Abstr., Rel.Ind.One. **Document type:** academic/scholarly publication.
—SWETS.

930.1   FI   ISSN 0355-3108
ISKOS. (Text in English, Finnish and Swedish) 1976. irreg., latest vol.10, 1990. price varies. Suomen Muinaismuistoyhdistys - Finnish Antiquarian Society, P.O. Box 913, Nervanderinkatu 13, FIN-00101 Helsinki 10, Finland. E-mail: Torsten.Edgren@NBA.fi. (Dist. by: Bookstore Tiedekirja, Kirkkokatu 14, FIN-00170, Helsinki, Finland. TEL 358-0-635-177) Ed. Torsten Edgren. **Document type:** academic/scholarly publication.

HID ISLENZKA FORNLEIFAFELAG. ARBOK. see HISTORY — History Of Europe

933   IS   ISSN 0021-2059
DS111.A1   CODEN: IEXJAM
ISRAEL EXPLORATION JOURNAL. (Text in English) 1951. 3/yr. $54 (effective 1998). Israel Exploration Society, P.O. Box 7041, Jerusalem 91070, Israel. TEL 972-2-6257991. FAX 972-2-6247772. E-mail: ies@vms.huji.ac.il. Eds. B.A. Levine, Miriam Tadmor. bk.rev.; charts; illus.; maps; cum.index every 10 yrs. circ. 2,500. (also avail. in microform from UMI; back issues avail.; reprint service avail. from UMI) **Indexed:** Anthropol.Lit., Arts & Hum.Cit.Ind., ASCA, Bibl.Ling., Chem.Abstr., Curr.Cont., IBR, Ind.Jew.Per., Mid.East: Abstr.& Ind., New Test.Abstr., Numis.Lit., Old Test.Abstr., Rel.& Theol.Abstr. (1971-), Rel.Ind.One, Rel.Per., RILA, SSCI. **Document type:** academic/scholarly publication.
—BLDSC (4583.700000); Genuine Article; Linda Hall; SWETS; UMI; UnCover.
Description: Includes articles on biblical archaeology, ancient history, and archaeology of later periods, preliminary excavation reports, special discoveries and finds.

ARCHAEOLOGY

913 950   GW   ISSN 0341-9142
DS41
ISTANBULER MITTEILUNGEN. 1950. a. price varies. (Deutsches Archaeologisches Institut, Abteilung Istanbul) Ernst Wasmuth Verlag GmbH, Fuerststr. 133, 72072 Tuebingen, Germany. TEL 49-7071-33658. FAX 49-7071-35776. Ed. Sigrid Hauser. R&P contact: Sigrid Hauser. circ. 500. **Indexed:** Bibl.Ling., IBR. **Document type:** academic/scholarly publication.
   Description: Explores the pre-history, archaeology, history and art history of Asia Minor up until the Ottomanic period.

ISTANBULER MITTEILUNGEN. BEIHEFTE. see HISTORY — History Of The Near East

571   IT   ISSN 0530-9867
ISTITUTO INTERNAZIONALE DI STUDI LIGURI. COLLEZIONE DI MONOGRAFIE PREISTORICHE E ARCHEOLOGICHE. (Text in Italian, French and Spanish) 1946. irreg. price varies. Istituto Internazionale di Studi Liguri - International Institute of Ligurian Studies, Via Romana, 39, 18012 Bordighera, Italy. TEL 39-184-263601. FAX 39-184266421. circ. 1,000. **Document type:** proceedings, monographic series.
   Description: Provides research and scholarly articles in prehistoric, Roman and medieval Liguria (a coastal region of northwestern Italy).

930.1 700   IT
ISTITUTO NAZIONALE DI ARCHEOLOGIA E STORIA DELL'ARTE. RIVISTA. 1929. a. L.150000. Istituto Nazionale di Archeologia e Storia dell'Arte, Piazza S. Marco 49, 00186 Rome, Italy. Ed. Paolo Pellegrino. circ. 800. (back issues avail.) **Indexed:** Avery Ind.Archit.Per., RILA.

913 945   IT   ISSN 0392-7601
ITALICA. 1910. a. avail. on exchange basis. Consejo Superior de Investigaciones Cientificas (C.S.I.C.), Escuela Espanola de Historia y Arqueologia en Roma, Via di Villa Albani 16, 00198 Rome, Italy. **Indexed:** RILM.
  —CINDOC.
  Formerly (until 1981): Escuela Espanola de Historia y Arqueologia en Roma. Cuadernos de Trabajos (ISSN 0392-0801)

913 947   BU   ISSN 0204-403X
IZVESTIYA NA MUZEITE OT IUGOIZTOCHNA BULGARIYA. 1976. a. Dargavno Izdatelstvo Christo G. Danov, Ul. Petko Karavelov 17, 4000 Plodiv, Bulgaria. (Dist. by: Hemus Foreign Trade Co., 6 Ruski Blvd., 1000 Sofia, Bulgaria)

913 947   BU   ISSN 0204-4072
IZVESTIYA NA MUZEITE OT IUZHNA BULGARIYA. 1975. a. Dargavno Izdatelstvo Christo G. Danov, Ul. Petko Karavelov 17, 4000 Plodiv, Bulgaria. (Dist. by: Hemus Foreign Trade Co., 6 Ruski Blvd., 1000 Sofia, Bulgaria) **Indexed:** BSL Biol.

J P S. (Journal of the Polynesian Society) see ANTHROPOLOGY

930.1   US   ISSN 1063-4304
J R A - THE SUPPLEMENTARY SERIES. (Journal of Roman Archaeology) 1990. irreg. (2-6/yr.) price varies. 95 Peleg Rd. Rd., Portsmouth, RI 02871. TEL 401-683-1955. FAX 401-683-1975. E-mail: jra@wsii.com; URL: http://www.personal.umich.edu/ ~pfoss/jra/jra_home.html. Ed. John H. Humphrey. bibl.; illus. **Document type:** academic/scholarly publication, monographic series.
  —BLDSC (5052.118100).
  Description: Covers the history, culture, and archaeology of the Roman world.
  Refereed Serial

930.1   CC   ISSN 1001-0327
JIANGHAN KAOGU/JIANGHAN ARCHAEOLOGY. (Text in Chinese) 1980. q. Y16($16) (foreign $16) (effective 1997). Archaeological Institute of Hubei Province - Hubei Provincial Museum, Tian'e Cun, Donghu Lu, Wuchang-qu, Wuhan, Hubei 430077, People's Republic of China. TEL 86-10-27-6813122. (Dist. in U.S. by: China Books & Periodicals, Inc., 2929 24th St., San Francisco, CA 94110. TEL 415-282-2994) Ed. Tianyuan Li; Pub. Kaogu Jiang. adv. contact: Xiuzhen Fang. bk.rev. circ. 2,000. **Document type:** monographic series.
  ●Also available on CD-ROM.
  Description: Monographic series on archaeology, palaeoanthropology and paleontology.

JOURNAL DES AFRICANISTES. see ANTHROPOLOGY

JOURNAL OF AFRICAN CIVILIZATIONS. see ANTHROPOLOGY

JOURNAL OF AFRICAN HISTORY. see HISTORY — History Of Africa

913   US   ISSN 0449-2153
E78.A28
JOURNAL OF ALABAMA ARCHAEOLOGY. 1955. s-a. $12 to individuals; institutions $17 (includes Stones and Bones Newsletter). Alabama Archaeological Society, 13075 Moundville Archaeological Park, Moundville, AL 35474. TEL 205-371-2266. FAX 205-371-2494. Ed. Eugene M. Futato. bibl.; charts; illus. circ. 500. (also avail. in microform from UMI; back issues avail.; reprint service avail. from UMI) **Indexed:** Abstr.Anthropol., Amer.Hist.& Life (1989-), Anthropol.Lit., Hist.Abstr. (1989-). **Document type:** academic/scholarly publication.
  —UMI; UnCover.

JOURNAL OF ANTHROPOLOGICAL ARCHAEOLOGY. see ANTHROPOLOGY

930.1   US   ISSN 1072-5369
CC75   CODEN: JAMTEI
JOURNAL OF ARCHAEOLOGICAL METHOD AND THEORY. 1994. q. $165 (foreign $195) (effective 1998). Plenum Publishing Corp., 233 Spring St., New York, NY 10013-1578. TEL 212-620-8000. FAX 212-463-0742. TELEX 23-421139. Ed. Michael Brian Schiffer. adv. **Indexed:** A.I.C.P. **Document type:** academic/scholarly publication.
  —BLDSC (4947.177300); SWETS; UnCover. **CCC.**
  Description: Presents original articles that critically assess and integrate research on a specific subject in archaeological method and theory, including topics in the history of archaeology, significant explorations, and relevant case studies.
  Refereed Serial

930.1   US   ISSN 1059-0161
CC1   CODEN: JARRE3
JOURNAL OF ARCHAEOLOGICAL RESEARCH. 1993. q. $175 (foreign $204.75) (effective 1998). Plenum Publishing Corp., 233 Spring St., New York, NY 10013-1578. TEL 212-620-8000. FAX 212-463-0742. TELEX 23-421139. Eds. Gary M. Feinman, T. Douglas Price. bibl. (also avail. in microfilm from UMI) **Indexed:** A.I.C.P., Geo.Abstr.P.G. **Document type:** academic/scholarly publication.
  —BLDSC (4947.177500); SWETS; UnCover. **CCC.**
  Description: Presents state of the art research on specific scholarly issues or themes in archaeology, and reviews current discoveries, field work and excavations.
  Refereed Serial

913   UK   ISSN 0305-4403
CC1   CODEN: JASCDU
JOURNAL OF ARCHAEOLOGICAL SCIENCE. 1974. m. £385 (effective 1998). (Society for Archaeological Sciences, US) Academic Press Ltd. (Subsidiary of: Harcourt Brace & Company Ltd.), 24-28 Oval Rd., London NW1 7DX, England. TEL 44-171-267-4466. FAX 44-171-482-2293. TELEX 25775 ACPRES G. E-mail: asubs@acad.com; URL: http://www.hbuk.co.uk/ap/jas/; http://www.europe.idealibrary.com. (Subscr. to: Harcourt Brace & Co. Ltd., Foots Cray High St., Sidcup, Kent DA14 5HP, England. TEL 44-181-300-3322. FAX 44-181-309-0807) Ed.Bd. R&P contact: Catherine John. adv. contact: Nik Screen. bk.rev.; bibl.; index. (reprint service avail. from SWZ) **Indexed:** A.I.C.P., Abstr.Anthropol., Anthropol.Lit., Art & Archaeol.Tech.Abstr., Arts & Hum.Cit.Ind., ASCA, Biol.Abstr., Br.Archaeol.Abstr., Ceram.Abstr., Curr.Cont., Ecol.Abstr., Food Sci.& Tech.Abstr., Geo.Abstr.P.G., Geol.Abstr., GeoRef., Mid.East: Abstr.& Ind., NAA, SSCI, Zoo.Rec. **Document type:** academic/scholarly publication.
  ●Also available online.
  —BLDSC (4947.178000); Genuine Article; SWETS; UnCover. **CCC.**
  Description: Directed to archaeologists and scientists with particular interests in advances in the application of the scientific techniques and methodologies to all areas of archeology.

913   II
JOURNAL OF ARCHAEOLOGY IN ANDHRA PRADESH. (Text in English) 1979. irreg. price varies. Department of Archaeology and Museums, Hyderabad 500 001, Andhra Pradesh, India. Ed. V.V. Krishna Sastry. bk.rev. circ. 500. **Document type:** academic/scholarly publication.

301.2 915   PK   ISSN 1016-0701
JOURNAL OF CENTRAL ASIA. (Text in English) 1978. s-a. Rs.200($20) per no. (effective 1996 & 1997). (International Association for the Study of the Cultures of Central Asia) Quaid-i-Azam University, Centre for the Study of the Civilizations of Central Asia, Islamabad 45320, Pakistan. (Co-sponsor: Unesco) Ed. Dr. Ahmad Hasan Dani. bk.rev. circ. 500. (back issues avail.) **Indexed:** IBR, Per.Islam. (1989-). **Document type:** academic/scholarly publication.

417.7 935   US   ISSN 0022-0256
PJ3102   CODEN: JCUSAV
JOURNAL OF CUNEIFORM STUDIES. (Text in English, French and German) 1947-1991; resumed 1994. a. $42.75 to individuals (foreign $47.75); institutions $52.25 (foreign $57.25) (effective 1998). (American Schools of Oriental Research) Scholars Press, Box 15399, Atlanta, GA 30333-0399. TEL 404-727-2320; 888-747-2354. FAX 404-727-2348. E-mail: scholars@emory.edu. Ed. Piotr Michalowski. R&P contact: Dennis Ford. bk.rev.; bibl.; illus.; index. circ. 625. (also avail. in microform from UMI; back issues avail.; reprint service avail. from SWZ,UMI) **Indexed:** Anthropol.Lit., IBR, Math.R., MLA Intl.Bibl., Old Test.Abstr., Rel.& Theol.Abstr. (1980-1993), Rel.Ind.One. **Document type:** academic/scholarly publication.
  —SWETS; UMI.
  Description: Presents technical articles on the history and languages of the ancient Mesopotamian and Anatolian literate cultures.

948.901   DK   ISSN 0108-464X
DL121
JOURNAL OF DANISH ARCHAEOLOGY. 1982. a. DKK 200 (effective 1997). Odense University Press, Campusvej 55, DK-5230 Odense M, Denmark. TEL 66-157999. FAX 66-158126. E-mail: press@forlag.ou.dk. illus. **Indexed:** Anthropol.Lit., Br.Archaeol.Abstr., NAA. **Document type:** academic/scholarly publication.
  —BLDSC (4967.380000).

932   UK   ISSN 0307-5133
DT57
JOURNAL OF EGYPTIAN ARCHAEOLOGY. (Text in English; occasionally in French and German) 1914. a. £40 to non-members; membership £30 (effective 1997). Egypt Exploration Society, 3 Doughty Mews, London WC1N 2PG, England. TEL 44-171-242-1880. FAX 44-171-404-6118. E-mail: eeslondon@compuserve.com; URL: http://britac3.brita.ac.uk/institutes/egypt/pubs.html. Ed. Lisa M. Leahy. R&P contact: Patricia Spencer. bk.rev.; cum.index every 5 yrs. circ. 3,500. (also avail. in microfiche from IDC; back issues avail.) **Indexed:** A.I.C.P., Art Ind., Arts & Hum.Cit.Ind., ASCA, Avery Ind.Archit.Per., Bibl.Ling., Br.Hum.Ind., Curr.Cont., IBR, Mid.East: Abstr.& Ind., Old Test.Abstr. **Document type:** academic/scholarly publication.
  —SWETS.
  Refereed Serial

JOURNAL OF ETHNOBIOLOGY. see BIOLOGY

JOURNAL OF EUROPEAN STUDIES. see HISTORY — History Of Europe

ARCHAEOLOGY

913   US   ISSN 0093-4690
CC1
JOURNAL OF FIELD ARCHAEOLOGY. 1974. q. $48 to individuals (foreign $54); institutions $60 (foreign $66); students $25. Boston University, Journal of Field Archaeology, 675 Commonwealth Ave., Boston, MA 02215. TEL 617-353-2357.
FAX 617-353-6800. E-mail: jfa@crsa.bu.edu; URL: http://jfa.web.bu.edu. (Subscr. to: Boston University Scholarly Publications, 985 Commonwealth Ave., Boston, MA 02215. TEL 617-353-4106) Ed. Ricardo Elia. R&P contact: Al B. Wesolowsky. adv. contact: Al B. Wesolowsky. bk.rev.; charts; illus.; circ. 1,400 (paid). (also avail. in microfilm from UMI) **Indexed:** Abstr.Anthropol., Anthropol.Lit., Art & Archaeol.Tech.Abstr., Art Ind., Arts & Hum.Cit.Ind., ASCA, Avery Ind.Archit.Per., Br.Archaeol.Abstr., Curr.Cont., Geo.Abstr., GeoRef., Hum.Ind., IBR, Mid.East: Abstr.& Ind., NAA, Old Test.Abstr., RILA, So.Pac.Per.Ind., SSCI. **Document type:** academic/scholarly publication.
—BLDSC (4984.100000); Genuine Article; KR SourceOne; SWETS; UMI; UnCover.
    Description: Publishes articles that deal with reports of field excavation and survey the world over as well as studies of methodological and technical matters, scientific advances in archaeology, and larger interpretive studies.
    Refereed Serial

913   IE   ISSN 0268-537X
JOURNAL OF IRISH ARCHAEOLOGY. 1983. a. I£8 to individuals; institutions I£10. National Museum of Ireland, Irish Antiquities Division, Kildare St., Dublin 2, Ireland. TEL 01-6618811. FAX 01-6766116. (Subscr. to: c/o Dr. John Waddell, Dept. of Archaeology, University College, Galway, Ireland. TEL 091-24411. FAX 091-25700) Ed. Raghnall O'Floinn. bk.rev. circ. 600. **Indexed:** Anthropol.Lit. **Document type:** academic/scholarly publication.
—BLDSC (5008.080000).
    Description: Review articles on Irish archaeology, excavation reports and papers on Irish archaeology from prehistory to the later middle ages.

930.1 340   PL   ISSN 0075-4277
THE JOURNAL OF JURISTIC PAPYROLOGY. (Text in English, French, German, Italian) 1946. a. price varies. (Uniwersytet Warszawski, Instytut Papirologii i Prawa Antycznego - Warsaw University, Institute of Papyrology and Ancient Laws) Wydawnictwa Uniwersytetu Warszawskiego, Ul. Nowy Swiat 4, 00-497 Warsaw, Poland. TEL 48-22-6253044. FAX 48-22-6253044. (Dist. by: Ars Polona, Krakowskie Przedmiescie 7, 00-068 Warsaw, Poland) Eds. Henryk Kupiszewski, Ewa Wipszycka. R&P contact: Jolanta Okonska. bk.rev. circ. 400. **Document type:** academic/scholarly publication.
—BLDSC (5009.700000).

930.09   UK   ISSN 0952-7648
DE1
JOURNAL OF MEDITERRANEAN ARCHAEOLOGY. 1988. 2/yr. £20($30) to individuals; institutions £60($90) (effective 1997). Sheffield Academic Press Ltd., Mansion House, 19 Kingfield Rd., Sheffield S11 9AS, England.
TEL 44-114-255-4433. FAX 44-114-255-4626. E-mail: admin@sheffac.demon.co.uk; URL: http://www.shef-ac-press.co.uk. Eds. A. Bernard Knapp, John Cherry. adv.; bk.rev. **Indexed:** Anthropol.Lit., Geo.Abstr.P.G. **Document type:** academic/scholarly publication.
—BLDSC (5017.582000); SWETS; UnCover.

913   US   ISSN 0883-9697
E78.M65   CODEN: JMAAEJ
JOURNAL OF MIDDLE ATLANTIC ARCHAEOLOGY. 1985. a. $25 (effective 1997 & 1998). Archaeological Services, 68 Sunny Ridge Rd., Box 386, Bethlehem, CT 06751. TEL 203-266-7741. Ed. Roger W. Moeller; Pub. Roger W. Moeller. R&P contact: Roger W. Moeller. bk.rev.; illus. circ. 200. **Indexed:** Abstr.Anthropol., Anthropol.Lit. **Document type:** academic/scholarly publication.
—BLDSC (5019.850000); UnCover.

913   US   ISSN 0022-2968
DS41   CODEN: JNESBT
JOURNAL OF NEAR EASTERN STUDIES. 1884. q. $42 to individuals; (Canada $49.94; elsewhere $47); institutions $109 (Canada $121.63; elsewhere $114) (effective 1998). University of Chicago Press, Journals Division, Box 37005, Chicago, IL 60637. TEL 773-753-3347. FAX 773-753-0811. TELEX 25-4603. E-mail: subscriptions@journals.uchicago.edu; URL: http://www.journals.uchicago.edu/JNES/. Ed. Robert D. Biggs. adv.: page $355; trim 6 5/8 x 9 1/2. bk.rev.; illus.; index. circ. 1,900. (also avail. in microform from MIM,UMI,PMC; reprint service avail. from UMI,ISI,SCH) **Indexed:** Abstr.Anthropol., Abstr.Folk.Stud., Anthropol.Lit., Art & Archaeol.Tech.Abstr., Arts & Hum.Cit.Ind., ASCA, Bibl.Ling., Curr.Cont., Hum.Ind., IBR, Int.Z.Bibelwiss., Lang.& Lang.Behav.Abstr., M.L.A., Mid.East: Abstr.& Ind., MLA Intl.Bibl., New Test.Abstr., Old Test.Abstr., Per.Islam. (1992-), Rel.& Theol.Abstr. (1968-), Rel.Ind.One, SSCI. **Document type:** academic/scholarly publication.
● Also available online. Vendor(s): Knight-Ridder Information, Inc.
—BLDSC (5021.393000); Genuine Article; KR SourceOne; SWETS; UMI; UnCover. **CCC.**
    Description: Covers a broad scope of examinations into the ancient and medieval civilizations of the area, including archaeology, history, literature, religion, linguistics, and law.
    Refereed Serial

913 291.042   SW   ISSN 0283-8486
    CODEN: JPRGE7
JOURNAL OF PREHISTORIC RELIGION. (Text in English, French and German) 1987. a. $15. Paul Aastroems Foerlag, William Gibsons Vaeg 11, S-433 76 Jonsered, Sweden. TEL 46-31-7956600. FAX 46-31-7956710. Ed. Paul Aastroem. adv.; bk.rev. circ. 1,000. **Indexed:** Anthropol.Lit. **Document type:** academic/scholarly publication.
—SWETS.

JOURNAL OF QUATERNARY SCIENCE. see *EARTH SCIENCES — Geology*

930.1   US   ISSN 1047-7594
DG11
JOURNAL OF ROMAN ARCHAEOLOGY. (Supplements avail.) 1988. a. $45 to individuals (foreign $47); libraries $79 (foreign $87) (effective 1997). 95 Peleg Rd., Portsmouth, RI 02871.
TEL 401-683-1955. FAX 313-662-3240. E-mail: jra@wsii.com; URL: http://www-personal.umich.edu/-pfoss/jra/JRA__Home.html. Ed. John H. Humphrey; Pub. John H. Humphrey. R&P contact: John H. Humphrey. bk.rev. circ. 1,050. **Indexed:** Art Ind., New Test.Abstr. **Document type:** academic/scholarly publication.
—BLDSC (5052.118000); KR SourceOne; SWETS.
    Description: Concerned with all aspects of archaeology in every part of the Roman Empire.

913 551   AU
JOURNAL OF SALT HISTORY/JAHRBUCH FUER SALZGESCHICHTE; Annales d'Histoire du Sel. (Text in English, French, German, Italian, Spanish) 1993. a. (International Commission for the History of Salt) Berenkamp Verlag, Salvatorgasse 15, A-6060 Hall, Austria. TEL 43-5223-57667.
FAX 43-5223-576674. (Subscr. to: Rudolf Palme, Institut fuer Rechtsgeschichte, Christoph-Probst-Platz, A-6020 Innsbruck, Austria. TEL 43-512-5078058. FAX 43-512-5072831) Ed. Rudolf Palme; Pub. Wolfgang Ingenhaeff. R&P contact: Rudolf Palme. circ. 500. **Document type:** bulletin.

913   US
THE JOURNAL OF VERMONT ARCHAEOLOGY.* 1994. biennial. $21.95. (Vermont Archaeological Society) Mountain Publications, 214 Jefferson Ave., Bennington, VT 05201-2325. Ed. David Starbuck. bibl.; charts; illus. (back issues avail.) **Document type:** academic/scholarly publication.
    Description: Publishes papers by Vermont archaeologists on prehistoric, historic, military, industrial, and underwater archaeology.

913 572   US   ISSN 0892-7537
GN700   CODEN: JWPREB
JOURNAL OF WORLD PREHISTORY. 1987. q. $275 (foreign $320) (effective 1998). Plenum Publishing Corp., 233 Spring St., New York, NY 10013-1578. TEL 212-620-8000. FAX 212-463-0742. TELEX 23-421139. Ed. A.E. Close. adv. (also avail. in microfilm from UMI; back issues avail.) **Indexed:** Anthropol.Lit., Arts & Hum.Cit.Ind., ASCA, Curr.Cont., Geo.Abstr.P.G., Geol.Abstr., SSCI. **Document type:** academic/scholarly publication.
—BLDSC (5072.685000); Genuine Article; KR SourceOne; SWETS; UMI; UnCover. **CCC.**
    Refereed Serial

933 296.155   IS   ISSN 0075-4501
JUDEAN DESERT STUDIES. (Text in English) 1963. irreg., no.11, 1992. price varies. Israel Exploration Society, P.O. Box 7041, Jerusalem 91070, Israel. TEL 972-2-6257991. FAX 972-2-6247772. E-mail: ies@vms.huji.ac.il. **Document type:** academic/scholarly publication, monographic series.
    Description: Monographs on Israeli archaeological discoveries and excavations at prehistoric sites.

JYSK ARKAEOLOGISK SELSKABS. SKRIFTER/JUTLAND ARCHAEOLOGICAL SOCIETY. PUBLICATIONS. see *HISTORY — History Of Europe*

917   US   ISSN 1047-742X
K A C RESEARCH SERIES. irreg. (Center for American Archeology, Kampsville Archaeological Center) Center for American Archeology Press, Box 22, Kampsville, IL 62053-0022. TEL 618-653-4316.
    Formerly: C A A Research Series; Superseded (1982-1984): Northwestern University. Center for American Archeology. Research Series.

932   US   ISSN 1053-0827
DT57
K M T;* a modern journal of ancient Egypt. 1990. q. $32 (Canada $36; elsewhere $38) (effective 1996). K M T Communications, 18 Lucero Rd., Santa Fe, NM 87505-8845. Ed. Dennis Forbes; Pub. M. Kuhlmann. adv.; bk.rev.; illus. circ. 10,000. (back issues avail.) **Document type:** academic/scholarly publication.
—BLDSC (5099.800000).
    Description: Presents research on ancient Egyptian civilization.

913   IS   ISSN 0033-4839
DS111.A1
KADMONIOT; journal for the antiquities of Eretz-Israel and Biblical lands. Variant spelling of title: Qadmoniot. (Text in Hebrew; contents page in English) 1968. q. $30 (effective 1998). Israel Exploration Society, P.O. Box 7041, Jerusalem 91070, Israel. TEL 972-2-6257991.
FAX 972-2-6247772. E-mail: ies@vms.huli.ac.il. Ed. A. Mazar. bk.rev.; illus.; index. circ. 4,000. (back issues avail.) **Indexed:** IBR, Ind.Heb.Per., New Test.Abstr., Numis.Lit., Rel.& Theol.Abstr. (1971-). **Document type:** academic/scholarly publication.
    Supersedes: Israel Exploration Society. Bulletin; Which was formerly (until 1933): Jewish Palestine Exploration Society. Yediot - Bulletin.
    Description: Includes articles on biblical archaeology, ancient history, history and archaeology of later periods, and preliminary excavation reports.

938 481.7   GW   ISSN 0022-7498
CN1
KADMOS; Zeitschrift fuer vor- und fruehgriechische Epigraphik. (Supplement avail. (ISSN 0453-0586)) (Text in English, French or German) 1962. 2/yr. DM.232 (foreign DM.235) (effective 1998). Walter de Gruyter und Co., Genthiner Str. 13, 10785 Berlin, Germany. TEL 49-30-26005-0.
FAX 49-30-26005251. E-mail: wdg-info@degruyter.de; URL: http://www.degruyter.de. (U.S. addr.: Walter de Gruyter, Inc., 200 Saw Mill River Rd., Hawthorne, NY 10532. TEL 914-747-0110. FAX 914-747-1326) Ed. Wolfgang Bluemel. adv.; bk.rev. **Indexed:** Bibl.Ling., M.L.A., MLA Intl.Bibl., Numis.Lit. **Document type:** academic/scholarly publication.
—BLDSC (5079.600000); SWETS. **CCC.**

938 481.7   GW   ISSN 0453-0586
KADMOS. SUPPLEMENT. (Text in Greek, German) 1967. irreg., vol.3, 1992. price varies. Walter de Gruyter und Co., Genthiner Str. 13, 10785 Berlin, Germany. TEL 49-30-26005-0. FAX 49-30-26005251. E-mail: wdg-info@degruyter.de; URL: http://www.degruyter.de. (U.S. addr.: Walter de Gruyter, Inc., 200 Saw Mill River Rd., Hawthorne, NY 10532. TEL 914-747-0110. FAX 914-747-1326) Ed. William C. Brice. (back issues avail.) **Document type:** monographic series.

917   US
KAMPSVILLE SEMINARS IN ARCHEOLOGY. 1982. irreg., vol.2, 1986. price varies. (Northwestern University, Center for American Archeology) Center for American Archeology Press, Box 22, Kampsville, IL 62053-0022. Ed. Jodie O'Gorman. R&P contact: Jodie O'Gorman.

917   US
KAMPSVILLE STUDIES IN ARCHEOLOGY AND HISTORY. irreg., no.4, 1997. price varies. Center for American Archeology Press, Box 22, Kampsville, IL 62053-0022. TEL 618-653-4688.

KANSAS ANTHROPOLOGICAL ASSOCIATION NEWSLETTER. see ANTHROPOLOGY

THE KANSAS ANTHROPOLOGIST. see ANTHROPOLOGY

913   CC   ISSN 0453-2899
KAOGU/ARCHAEOLOGY. (Text in Chinese; table of contents in English) m. $185.40. (Chinese Academy of Sciences, Institute of Archaeology) Science Press, Marketing and Sales Department, 16 Donghuangchenggen North St., Beijing 100717, People's Republic of China. TEL 4010642. FAX 4019810. (Dist. outside China by: China International Book Trading Corp., P.O. Box 2820, Beijing, P.R.C.) Eds. Xu Pingfang, Lu Zhaoyin. adv.; bk.rev.; charts; illus. circ. 25,000. **Document type:** academic/scholarly publication.
—UnCover.
Description: For popular reading. Contains field reports and short sketches of excavations, discussions about major issues in archeology, and comprehensive reports of excavated materials.
Refereed Serial

913   CC   ISSN 0453-2902
DS715   CODEN: KKHPAO
KAOGU XUEBAO/ACTA ARCHAEOLOGICA SINICA. (Text in Chinese; table of contents in English) 1936. q. $79.60. (Chinese Academy of Sciences, Institute of Archaeology) Science Press, Marketing and Sales Department, 16 Donghuangchenggen North St., Beijing 100717, People's Republic of China. TEL 4010642. FAX 4019810. (Dist. outside China by: China International Book Trading Corp., P.O. Box 2820, Beijing, P.R.C.) Eds. Xu Pingfang, Huang Zhanyue. adv.; maps; illus.; charts. circ. 15,000. **Indexed:** IBR. **Document type:** academic/scholarly publication.
—BLDSC (0596.200000); UnCover.
Description: Includes reports on field excavations, articles on archeological theory, research articles on ancient history and on identifying ancient constructions, anthropology and paleontology.
Refereed Serial

930.1   CC   ISSN 1000-7830
KAOGU YU WENWU/ARCHAEOLOGY AND CULTURAL RELICS. (Text in Chinese; table of contents in English) 1980. bi-m. Y33($81) Shaanxi Sheng Kaogu Yanjiusuo - Shaanxi Institute of Archaeology, No. 3, Leyou Lu, Xi'an, Shaanxi 710054, People's Republic of China. FAX 86-29-5526892. (Dist. outside China by: China International Book Trading Corp., P.O. Box 399, Beijing, P.R.C.; Dist. in U.S. by: China Books & Periodicals, Inc., 2929 24th St., San Francisco, CA 94110. TEL 415-282-2994) Ed. Gong Qiming. charts; illus. circ. 8,000. **Document type:** academic/scholarly publication.

913   FR   ISSN 0453-3429
DT269.C3
KARTHAGO; revue d'archeologie mediterraneenne. 1950. irreg., vol.23, 1996. 350 F. Universite de Paris IV (Paris-Sorbonne), Centre d'Etudes Archeologiques de la Mediterranee, c/o Institut d'Art, 3 rue Michelet, 75006, France. TEL 33-1-40463217. (Dist. by: Editions Peeters s.p.r.l., Bondgenotenlaan 153, B-3000 Leuven, Belgium. TEL 016-235170) Ed. Andre Laronde; Pub. Andre Laronde. adv.; bk.rev. circ. 750. **Indexed:** Numis.Lit. **Document type:** academic/scholarly publication.
Formerly: Karthago. Collection Epigraphique (ISSN 0075-5184)
Description: Covers archaeology and history of ancient North Africa and Mediterranean.
Refereed Serial

930.1 560   TU   ISSN 1017-7655
KAZI SONUCLARI TOPLANTISI. (Text in Turkish, occasionally in English, German) 1980. a. exchange basis. Ministry of Culture, General Directorate of Monuments and Museums - Kultur Bakanligi, Anitlar ve Muzeler Genel Mudurlugu, 06100 Ulus - Ankara, Turkey. TEL 90-312-3104960. FAX 90-312-3111417. **Indexed:** Anthropol.Lit. **Document type:** academic/scholarly publication.
Description: Reports of explorations, excavations, archaeological and palaeontological research undertaken at sites throughout Turkey.

913   GW
KEILSCHRIFTTEXTE AUS BOGHAZKOI. 1939. irreg., vol.38, 1996. price varies. (Academie der Wissenschaften und der Literatur Mainz) Gebr. Mann Verlag GmbH, Charlottenstr. 13, 10969 Berlin, Germany. TEL 49-30-2591-3589. FAX 49-30-2591-3537. Ed. Heinrich Otten. (reprint service avail.) **Document type:** monographic series.

KEILSCHRIFTURKUNDEN AUS BOGHAZKOEI. see HISTORY — History Of Asia

914.2   UK   ISSN 1365-4055
KENT ARCHAEOLOGICAL RESCUE UNIT. SPECIAL SUBJECT SERIES. 1983. irreg., no.9, 1997. £3. Kent Archaeological Rescue Unit, 5 Harvest Bank Rd., W. Wickham, Kent BR4 9DL, England. TEL 44-181-462-4737. FAX 44-181-462-4737. Ed. Brian Philp. R&P contact: Brian Philp. **Document type:** monographic series.
Description: Series of publications on excavations and research in Kent and southeast London.

913   UK   ISSN 0023-0014
DA670.K2
KENT ARCHAEOLOGICAL REVIEW. 1965. q. £3. Council for Kentish Archaeology, c/o Dover Roman Painted House, New St., Dover, Kent, England. TEL 44-1304-203279. FAX 44-181-462-4737. Ed. Audrey Button. adv.; bk.rev.; charts; illus.; cum.index. circ. 900. (back issues avail.) **Indexed:** Br.Archaeol.Abstr. **Document type:** newsletter.
—BLDSC (5089.588000).

930.1   UK
KENT ARCHAEOLOGICAL SOCIETY. NEWSLETTER. 1982. q. membership. Kent Archaeological Society, Dunelm House, Main Rd., Icklesham, Winchelsea, E. Sussex TN36 4AR, England. **Document type:** newsletter.
Description: Archeology and history of Kent.

914.2   UK   ISSN 0141-2264
KENT MONOGRAPH SERIES. 1968. irreg., vol. 7, 1996. £12. Kent Archaeological Rescue Unit, 5 Harvest Bank Rd., W. Wickham, Kent BR4 9DL, England. TEL 44-181-462-4737. FAX 44-181-462-4737. Ed. Brian Philp. R&P contact: Brian Philp. charts; illus. circ. 1,000. (back issues avail.) **Document type:** monographic series.
Description: Series of publications on excavations within Kent since 1965.

930.1   US
KENT STATE RESEARCH PAPERS IN ARCHAEOLOGY. 1981. irreg. Kent State University Press, Box 5190, 307 Lowry Hall, Kent, OH 44242. TEL 330-672-7913. FAX 330-672-3104. Ed. Mark F. Seeman. (reprint service avail. from UMI) **Document type:** monographic series, academic/scholarly publication.

941.5   IE   ISSN 0085-2503
KERRY ARCHAEOLOGICAL AND HISTORICAL SOCIETY. JOURNAL. 1968. a. I£15($30) to individuals; I£25($50) to institutions; family I£20($40); students I£5($10); free to members. Kerry Archaeological and Historical Society, County Library, Tralee, Co. Kerry, Ireland. TEL 066-21200. Ed. Rev. Kieran O'Shea. circ. 450. **Indexed:** Br.Archaeol.Abstr.

914.2   IE   ISSN 0791-2846
KERRY MAGAZINE. a. I£2. Kerry Archaeological and Historical Society, County Library, Tralee, Co. Kerry, Ireland. TEL 066-21200. Ed. Kieran O'Shea. circ. 500.

930.1   FR
KITION-BAMBOULA. 1982. irreg. price varies. Editions Recherche sur les Civilisations, 28 rue de Bourgogne, 75007 Paris, France. TEL 33-1-40628062. FAX 33-1-40628071. Ed. Hina Descat; Pub. Hina Descat. circ. 600. **Document type:** monographic series.

913 970.1   US   ISSN 0023-1940
F786
KIVA. 1935. q. $40. Arizona Archaeological and Historical Society, Arizona State Museum, University of Arizona, Tucson, AZ 85721. TEL 520-621-3656. Ed. Tobi Taylor. R&P contact: Tobi Taylor. adv. contact: Tobi aylor. bk.rev.; charts; illus.; index, cum.index: vols.1-30, 31-40, 41-50. circ. 1,100. **Indexed:** Abstr.Anthropol., Amer.Hist.& Life (1963-), Anthropol.Lit., Hist.Abstr. (1963-), IBR. **Document type:** academic/scholarly publication.
—BLDSC (5098.345000); UnCover.

KOBIE, REVISTA DE BELLAS ARTES Y CIENCIAS: SERIE PALEOANTROPOLOGIA. see ANTHROPOLOGY

913   GW
DD901.C745
KOELNER JAHRBUCH. 1955. irreg., vol.28, 1995. price varies. (Roemisch-Germanisches Museum) Gebr. Mann Verlag GmbH, Charlottenstr. 13, 10969 Berlin, Germany. TEL 49-30-2591-3589. FAX 49-30-2591-3537. (Co-sponsor: Archaeologische Gesellschaft, Cologne) (reprint service avail. from SCH) **Indexed:** Anthropol.Lit., IBR, Numis.Lit. **Document type:** monographic series.
Formerly (until 1993): Koelner Jahrbuch fuer Vor- und Fruehgeschichte (ISSN 0075-6512)
Description: Discusses the art and archaeological artifacts in the collection of the Roemisch-Germanischen Museum.

913 930   IT   ISSN 0392-0887
KOKALOS. (Text in various languages) 1964. irreg., vol.40, 1994. price varies. (Universita degli Studi di Palermo, Istituto di Storia Antica) Giorgio Bretschneider, Via Crescenzo 43, 00193 Rome, Italy. E-mail: bretschneider@euronet.it. **Indexed:** Bibl.Ling., Numis.Lit. **Document type:** academic/scholarly publication.

930.1   GW
▼**KOLLOQUIEN ZUR VOR- UND FRUEHGESCHICHTE.** 1997. irreg. price varies. (Deutsches Archaeologisches Institut, Roemisch-Germanische Kommission) Dr. Rudolf Habelt GmbH, Am Buchenhang 1, 53115 Bonn, Germany. TEL 49-228-9238322. FAX 49-228-923836. **Document type:** academic/scholarly publication, monographic series.

913   GW   ISSN 0941-6013
KOMMISSION FUER ARCHAEOLOGISCHE LANDESFORSCHUNG IN HESSEN. BERICHTE. 1992. a. price varies. (Kommission fuer Archaeologische Landesforschung in Hessen) Dr. Rudolf Habelt GmbH, Am Buchenhang 1, 53115 Bonn, Germany. TEL 49-228-9238322. FAX 49-228-923836. Ed. Margarete Dohrn. **Document type:** corporate report.

KONINKLIJKE KRING VOOR OUDHEIDKUNDE LETTEREN EN KUNST VAN MECHELEN. HANDELINGEN. see HISTORY — History Of Europe

ARCHAEOLOGY

930.1 949 NE ISSN 0166-0470
KONINKLIJKE NEDERLANDSE OUDHEIDKUNDIGE BOND. BULLETIN. Cover title: Bulletin K N O B. (Text in Dutch; summaries in English) 1899. 6/yr. fl.75 to individuals; institutions fl.125. Koninklijke Nederlandse Oudheidkundige Bond - Royal Netherlands Archeological Society, Mariaplaats 51, 3511 LM Utrecht, Netherlands. TEL 31-30-2321756. FAX 31-30-2312951. adv.; bk.rev.; bibl. circ. 2,500. **Indexed:** RILA. **Document type:** academic/scholarly publication, bulletin. —SWETS.

913 BE
KONINKLIJKE OUDHEIDKUNDIGE KRING VAN ANTWERPEN. JAARBOEK. (Text in Dutch) 1910. a. Koninklijke Oudheidkundige Kring van Antwerpen, Leopoldstr. 57, 2000 Antwerp, Belgium.
Formerly: Antwerpens Oudheidkundige Kring. Jaarboek.

930.1 948.5 SW ISSN 0345-6498
KONTAKTSTENCIL. 1970. s-a. Goeteborg Universitet, Institutionen foer Arkeologi, P.O. Box 2133, S-403 13 Goeteborg, Sweden.

KRONIKA; casopis za Slovensko krajevno zgodovino. see HISTORY — History Of Europe

KRONOS; journal of Cape history. see HISTORY — History Of Africa

930.1 948.5 708.8 SW ISSN 1100-4800
KULTURMILJOEVAARD; information. 1967. bi-m. SEK 175 (effective 1993). Riksantikvarieaembetet, P.O. Box 5405, S-114 84 Stockholm, Sweden.
Former titles (until 1989): Kulturminnesvaard; (until 1976): Meddelanden fraan Riksantikvarieaembetet.

948.901 DK ISSN 0454-6245
KUML. (Text in Danish; summaries in English) 1951. irreg., latest 1993-94. price varies. (Jysk Arkaeologisk Selskab - Jutland Archeological Society) Aarhus University Press, Aarhus University, Bldg. 170, DK-8000 Aarhus C, Denmark. TEL 45-86-19-70-33. FAX 45-86-19-84-33. illus. **Indexed:** Anthropol.Lit., Br.Archaeol.Abstr. **Document type:** academic/scholarly publication. —BLDSC (5123.300000).

914 GW ISSN 0342-0736
DIE KUNDE; Zeitschrift fuer Ur- und Fruehgeschichte. 1933. a. DM.60. Niedersaechsischer Landesverein fuer Urgeschichte, Willy-Brandt-Allee 5, 30169 Hannover, Germany. TEL 49-511-9807715. FAX 49-511-9807710. Ed. Guenter Wegner. bk.rev.; bibl. circ. 800. (back issues avail.) **Indexed:** Anthropol.Lit., IBR, NAA. **Document type:** academic/scholarly publication.
Description: Archaeology of Lower Saxony and neighboring regions.

KUNGLIGA VITTERHETS HISTORIE OCH ANTIKVITETS AKADEMIEN. AARSBOK. see HISTORY — History Of Europe

KUNGLIGA VITTERHETS HISTORIE OCH ANTIKVITETS AKADEMIEN. ANTIKVARISKT ARKIV. see ART

KUNGLIGA VITTERHETS HISTORIE OCH ANTIKVITETS AKADEMIEN. HANDLINGAR. ANTIKVARISKA SERIEN/ROYAL ACADEMY OF LETTERS, HISTORY AND ANTIQUITIES. PROCEEDINGS. ANTIQUARIAN SERIES. see ART — Abstracting, Bibliographies, Statistics

KUNGLIGA VITTERHETS HISTORIE OCH ANTIKVITETS AKADEMIEN. KONFERENSER. see MEETINGS AND CONGRESSES

913 GW ISSN 0075-725X
KUNST UND ALTERTUM AM RHEIN. 1956. irreg., vol.141, 1996. price varies. (Landschaftsverband Rheinland, Rheinisches Landesmuseum) Rheinland Verlag GmbH, Abtei Brauweiler, Postfach 2140, 50250 Pulheim, Germany. TEL 49-2234-9854265. FAX 49-2234-82503. (Dist. by: Dr. Rudolf Habelt GmbH, Am Buchenhang 1, 53115 Bonn, Germany. TEL 49-228-9238322. FAX 49-228-232017) (Co-sponsors: Rheinisches Landesmuseum Bonn; Rheinisches Amt fuer Bodendenkmalpflege) **Document type:** monographic series.

KWARTALNIK HISTORII KULTURY MATERIALNEJ. see HISTORY — History Of Europe

913 200 US ISSN 1053-931X
LANDMARK STUDIES. 1990. bi-m. $7. Sally Goodspeed, Ed. & Pub., 2318 N. Charles St., Baltimore, MD 21218. bk.rev.; illus.; cum.index. circ. 500. (looseleaf format; back issues avail.)
Description: Discussions about ancient sites and religions, especially as relating to subterranean water and cattleways.

914 SP ISSN 1130-989X
LAROUCO; revista da historia primitiva, tradicions orais e patrimonio cultural de Galicia. 1991. irreg. 1700 ptas. (Grupo Arqueoloxico Larouco) Edicios do Castro, O Castro, s-n, 15168 Sada, Coruna, Spain. TEL 34-81-620200. FAX 34-81-623804.

918 US ISSN 1045-6635
F1219
LATIN AMERICAN ANTIQUITY. (Text in English, Spanish) 1990. q. $115 in the U.S.; Latin America $28 (effective 1997 & 1998). Society for American Archaeology, 900 Second St., N.W., No. 12, Washington, DC 20002-3557. TEL 202-789-8200. FAX 202-789-0284. E-mail: publications@saa.org; URL: http://www.saa.org/Publications/LatAmAnt/latamant.html. Ed. Gary Feinman. adv.; bk.rev. circ. 1,400. **Indexed:** Acad.Ind., Anthropol.Lit., Hisp.Amer.Per.Ind. (1990-). **Document type:** academic/scholarly publication. —BLDSC (5157.799000); UMI; UnCover. **CCC.**
Description: Publishes articles dealing with the archaeology, prehistory, and ethnohistory of Mesoamerica, Central America, South America, and culturally related areas. Promotes communication between English- and Spanish-speaking archaeologists working in Latin America.
Refereed Serial

930.1 945 IT
LE MARCHE ARCHEOLOGIA, STORIA, TERRITORIO. 1987. s-a. L.30000 (foreign L.60000). Istituto Regionale per la Pre-Protostoria nelle Marche Arcevia - Sassoferrato, Vicolo Lazzarini 2, 60041 Sassoferrato (AN), Italy. TEL 0732-9465. Ed. Perseo Trojani.

913 PO ISSN 0870-0044
CC13.P67
LEBA; estudos de quaternario, pre-historia e arqueologia. 1978. irreg. price varies. Instituto de Investigacao Cientifica Tropical, Centro de Pre-Historia e Arqueologia, Rua da Junqueira 30, 1300 Lisbon, Portugal. TEL 351-1-3622621. FAX 351-1-3631460. E-mail: cdi@iict.pt; URL: http://www.iict.pt. (Subscr. to: Centro de Documentacao e Informacao, Rua Jau 47, 1300 Lisbon, Portugal) bk.rev. circ. 1,000. **Indexed:** A.I.C.P., Anthropol.Lit., Documentatieblad. **Document type:** academic/scholarly publication. —BLDSC (5179.569000).
Description: Covers pre-historical studies and archeology.

930.1 UK
LEICESTER ARCHAEOLOGY MONOGRAPH. irreg., no.3, 1995. University of Leicester, School of Archaeological Studies, Leicester LE1 7RH, England. TEL 44-116-252-2611. FAX 44-116-252-5005. E-mail: adm3@leicester.ac.uk. Eds. Jane Webster, Nicholas Cooper. **Document type:** academic/scholarly publication, monographic series.

913 940 UK ISSN 0140-3990
LEICESTERSHIRE ARCHAEOLOGICAL AND HISTORICAL SOCIETY. TRANSACTIONS. 1866. a. £12. Leicestershire Archaeological and Historical Society, The Guildhall, Guildhall Lane, Leicester LE1 5FQ, England. adv.; bk.rev. circ. 600. **Indexed:** Br.Archaeol.Abstr., Br.Hum.Ind., Geo.Abstr. **Document type:** academic/scholarly publication. —BLDSC (8978.350000).
Description: Archaeological and historical articles covering local material and annual notes of work carried out in the field.
Refereed Serial

913 956.9 UK ISSN 0075-8914
DS56
LEVANT. 1969. a. £30($55) (effective 1997). British School of Archaeology in Jerusalem, c/o British Academy, 20-21 Cornwall Terrace, London NW1 4QP, England. URL: http://www.man.ac.uk/arts/archaeology/levant.html. (Co-publisher: British Institute at Amman for Archaeology and History) Ed. Kay Prag. bk.rev. circ. 800. (back issues avail.) **Indexed:** Abstr.Anthropol., Anthropol.Lit., IBR, Mid.East: Abstr.& Ind., New Test.Abstr., Old Test.Abstr., Rel.& Theol.Abstr. (1969-), Rel.Ind.One. **Document type:** academic/scholarly publication. —BLDSC (5185.460000).
Refereed Serial

930.1 UK ISSN 0263-7189
LIBYAN STUDIES. 1969. a. £16 (effective 1996 & 1997). Society for Libyan Studies, c/o Institute of Archaeology, 31-34 Gordon Sq., London WC1H 0PY, England. TEL 44-171-323-8557. FAX 44-171-323-8355. Ed. D.M. Bailey. R&P contact: Shirley Strong. adv. contact: Shirley Strong. bk.rev. circ. 350. **Indexed:** Bibl.Ling., Documentatieblad, IBR. **Document type:** academic/scholarly publication. —BLDSC (5207.547400).

LINCOLNSHIRE HISTORY AND ARCHAEOLOGY. see HISTORY — History Of Europe

LINCOLNSHIRE PAST AND PRESENT. see HISTORY — History Of Europe

913 AA
LLIRIA. (Text in Albanian; summaries in French) 1971. s-a. $7.50 (foreign $25). Akademia e Shkencave e RPSSH, Instituti Arkeologjik - Academy of Sciences, Institute of Archaeology, Tirana, Albania. TEL 42-26501. Ed. M. Korkuti. bk.rev. circ. 700. **Document type:** academic/scholarly publication.
Description: Publishes the results of research, scientific activity and excavations in Albania.

571 913 UK ISSN 0076-0501
DA675
LONDON AND MIDDLESEX ARCHAEOLOGICAL SOCIETY. TRANSACTIONS. 1855. a. £15 for individual membership; institutions £19.50. London and Middlesex Archaeological Society, Museum of London, London Wall, London EC2Y 5HN, England. circ. 900. **Indexed:** Br.Archaeol.Abstr., Br.Hum.Ind., Numis.Lit. **Document type:** academic/scholarly publication.

913 UK
LONDON AND MIDDLESEX ARCHAEOLOGICAL SOCIETY & SURREY ARCHAEOLOGICAL SOCIETY. JOINT PUBLICATION. 1978. irreg. £25 (foreign £35) membership. Surrey Archaeological Society, Castle Arch, Guildford, Surrey GU1 3SX, England. TEL 44-1483-32454. FAX 44-1483-32454. (Co-sponsor: London and Middlesex Archaeological Society) Ed. Glenys Crocker. R&P contact: Glenys Crocker. (back issues avail.) **Document type:** academic/scholarly publication.

913 UK ISSN 0024-5984
DA677.1
LONDON ARCHAEOLOGIST. 1968. q. £7($15) London Archaeologist Association, 7 Coalecroft Rd., London SW15 6LW, England. TEL 0181-788-0015. (Subscr. to: Sheila Broomfield, 8 Woodview Cresc., Hildenborough, Tonbridge, Kent TN11 9HD, England) Ed. Clive Orton. adv.; bk.rev.; charts; illus.; index. circ. 1,500. (back issues avail.) **Indexed:** Art & Archaeol.Tech.Abstr., Avery Ind.Archit.Per., Br.Archaeol.Abstr, IBR. **Document type:** academic/scholarly publication. —BLDSC (5292.950000).
Description: Covers recent excavations, archaeological research, synthesis reports, related historical articles.

913 SW ISSN 0458-4767
LUND UNIVERSITET. HISTORISKA MUSEUM. MEDDELANDEN. 1930. biennial. (Historiska Museet) A W I International AB, P.O. Box 4627, S-116 91 Stockholm, Sweden. TEL 46-8-7282500. FAX 46-8-338707. (back issues avail.) **Indexed:** A.I.C.P., Anthropol.Lit., Br.Archaeol.Abstr. **Document type:** academic/scholarly publication.
Formerly (until 1975): Lund Universitet. Historiska Museet Samt Mynt-och Medaljkabinettet. Meddelanden.

ARCHAEOLOGY

913   US   ISSN 1048-5325
CC1   CODEN: MRPAEQ
M A S C A RESEARCH PAPERS IN SCIENCE AND ARCHAEOLOGY. 1965. a. $20 (effective 1997). (Applied Science Center for Archaeology) Museum Applied Science Center for Archaeology, University of Pennsylvania Museum, 33rd & Spruce Sts., Philadelphia, PA 19104. TEL 215-898-4060. FAX 215-898-0657. Ed. Kathleen Ryan. adv. contact: Tony DeAnsuntis. bk.rev. circ. 1,000. (back issues avail.) **Indexed:** Abstr.Anthropol., Anthropol.Lit., Art & Archaeol.Tech.Abstr., Br.Archaeol.Abstr., Ceram.Abstr., Chem.Abstr., Geo.Abstr., GeoRef. **Document type:** academic/scholarly publication.
— BLDSC (5383.685000); CASDDS.
    Former titles (until 1988): M A S C A Journal (ISSN 0198-0106); A S C A Newsletter (ISSN 0024-791X)
    Description: Information on scientific archaeological techniques.

913   US   ISSN 1062-1504
M A S NEWSLETTER. 1987. irreg. $15 membership. Maine Archaeological Society, Inc., P.O. Box 982, Augusta, ME 04332-0982. Ed. John Mother. **Document type:** newsletter.

MACEDONIAN STUDIES. see HISTORY — History Of Europe

930.1   NE   ISSN 0926-4639
MCGILL UNIVERSITY MONOGRAPHS IN CLASSICAL ARCHAEOLOGY AND HISTORY. Key Title: Monographies en Archeologie et Histoire Classiques de l'Universite McGill. (Includes subseries: Boeotia Antiqua) 1981. irreg., vol.16, 1995. price varies. J.C. Gieben, Nieuwe Herengracht 35, 1011 RM Amsterdam, Netherlands. TEL 31-20-6275170. FAX 31-20-6275170. (Dist. in N. America by: John Benjamins Publishing Co., Box 27519, Philadelphia, PA 19118-0519. TEL 215-836-1200. FAX 215-836-1204) Ed. J.M. Fossey. (back issues avail.) **Document type:** monographic series, proceedings.

913   PO
MADAN. s-a. Centro de Arqueologia de Almada, Apdo. 103 (Torcatas), 2801 Almada Codex, Portugal. Ed. Luis Manuel Boaventura de Barrios. circ. 1,500.

913   GW   ISSN 0418-9744
DP44
MADRIDER MITTEILUNGEN. 1960. a. DM.198. (Deutsches Archaeologisches Institut, Abteilung Madrid) Verlag Philipp von Zabern GmbH, Philipp-von-Zabern-Platz 1-3, 55116 Mainz, Germany. TEL 06131-28747-0. FAX 06131-223710. **Indexed:** Amer.Hist.& Life, Hist.Abstr., IBR, Numis.Lit. **Document type:** academic/scholarly publication.

913   IT   ISSN 0024-9955
MAGNA GRAECIA; rassegna di archeologia storia arte attualita. 1966. bi-m. L.40000 to individuals (foreign L.70000); institutions L.50000. Editoriale Magna Graecia, Viale della Repubblica 293-C, 87100 Cosenza, Italy. TEL 0984-71858. Ed. Tanino De Santis. adv.; bk.rev.; charts; illus.; stat.; tr.lit. circ. 2,000. (also avail. in microfilm)

MAGUARE. see ANTHROPOLOGY

913   HU   ISSN 0076-2504
MAGYARORSZAG REGESZETI TOPOGRAFIAJA. (Text in Hungarian) 1967. irreg., vol.9, 1993. price varies. (Magyar Tudomanyos Akademia) Akademiai Kiado Rt., P.O. Box 245, H-1519 Budapest, Hungary. TEL 36-1-2043976. FAX 36-1-2043973. **Document type:** academic/scholarly publication.

571   II   ISSN 0076-2520
MAHARAJA SAYAJIRAO UNIVERSITY OF BARODA. DEPARTMENT OF ARCHAEOLOGY AND ANCIENT HISTORY. ARCHAEOLOGY SERIES. (Text in English) 1953. irreg. (approx. 1/yr.). price varies. Maharaja Sayajirao University of Baroda, Department of Archaeology and Ancient History, Baroda 390002, Gujarat, India. Ed. K.T.M. Hegde. circ. 500. **Document type:** academic/scholarly publication.

MAIHAUGEN. see HISTORY — History Of Europe

913   US   ISSN 0542-1292
F21
MAINE ARCHEOLOGICAL SOCIETY BULLETIN. 1960. s-a. $15 to non-members and institutions. Maine Archaeological Society, Inc., Box 982, Augusta, ME 04332-0982. Ed. David Cook. bk.rev. circ. 350. **Indexed:** Abstr.Anthropol., Anthropol.Lit. **Document type:** academic/scholarly publication.

MAINZER ZEITSCHRIFT; Mittelrheinisches Jahrbuch fuer Archaeologie, Geschichte und Kunst. see ART

935   IR   ISSN 1015-2830
DS261
MAJALLAH-I BASTANSHINASI VA TARIKH/IRANIAN JOURNAL OF ARCHAEOLOGY AND HISTORY. (Text in Persian) 1986. s-a. IRl.3000 per no. (Middle East £16; Europe £18; elsewhere £21). Markaz-i Nashr-i Danishgahi - Iran University Press, 85 Park Ave., Dr. Bihishti Ave., P.O. Box 15875-4748, Tehran, Iran. TEL 98-21-8713232. FAX 98-21-8861749. TELEX 213636-8-D5300. Ed. Ahmad H.A. Moojani. illus.; maps. circ. 3,000. **Document type:** academic/scholarly publication.
    Description: Publishes articles related to history and archaeology in general, and archaeological and historical topics directly related to Iran in particular.

MAKEDONIKA. see HISTORY — History Of Europe

930.1 948.5   SW   ISSN 0349-697X
MALMOEYA. 1970. irreg. (free to qualified personnel). Malmoe Museer, Stadsantikvariska Avdelingen, P.O. Box 406, S-201 24 Malmoe, Sweden. TEL 46-40-34-44-34. FAX 46-40-34-42-45.

930.1 560   US   ISSN 8755-6898
E61
MAMMOTH TRUMPET. 1984. q. $20 (effective 1997). Oregon State University, Center for the Study of First Americans, Weniger 355, Corvallis, OR 97331-6510. TEL 541-737-4595. FAX 541-737-3651. E-mail: halla@cla.orst.edu; URL: http://www.peak.org/csfa/csfa.html. Ed. Don Alan Hall; Pub. Robson Bonnichsen. circ. 1,500. (back issues avail.) **Indexed:** Anthropol.Lit. **Document type:** newspaper.
    Description: News of discoveries and theories relevant to the earliest peopling of the Americas.

MAN & ENVIRONMENT. see ANTHROPOLOGY

913   CN   ISSN 1188-5424
F1062.9
MANITOBA ARCHAEOLOGICAL JOURNAL. (Supplement avail. q.: Manitoba Archaeological Newsletter (ISSN 0844-5958)) 1964. 2/yr. Can.$20 to individuals; students Can.$12; institutions Can.$30. Manitoba Archaeological Society, Inc., Box 1171, Winnipeg, MB R3C 2Y4, Canada. TEL 204-942-7243. FAX 204-942-3749. Ed. Leo Pettipas. R&P contact: Leo Pettipas. adv. contact: Leo Pettipas. bk.rev.; bibl.; charts; illus.; index, cum.index every 5 yrs. circ. 200. **Indexed:** Abstr.Anthropol., Amer.Hist.& Life (1988-), Anthropol.Lit., Hist.Abstr. (1988-). **Document type:** newsletter, academic/scholarly publication.
— BLDSC (5360.348000).
    Formerly (until 1991): Manitoba Archaeological Quarterly.
    Description: Contains research articles on archaeology in Manitoba.

930.1 900   FR
MAR NERO; annales d'archeologie et d'histoire. (Text in English, French, German, Italian) 1994. a. 167 F. Editions de la Maison des Sciences de l'Homme, 54 bd. Raspail, 75270 Paris Cedex 06, France. TEL 33-1-49542030. FAX 33-1-45488353. (Co-publisher: Edizioni Quasar di Severino Tognon) Ed. Maurice Aymard; Pub. Francoise Kahn. R&P contact: Francoise Kahn. adv. **Document type:** academic/scholarly publication.

930.1   IT   ISSN 1125-3878
IL MAR NERO. 1994. a. Lit.50000 in Europe; elsewhere Lit.60000 (effective 1997). Edizioni Quasar, Via di Monte del Gallo 26a, 00165 Roma, Italy. TEL 39-6-634944. FAX 39-6-634618. E-mail: quasar@mail.xplore.it. (Co-publisher: Editions de la Maison des Sciences de l'Homme) Eds. Petre Alexandrescu, Serban Papacostea. **Document type:** academic/scholarly publication.

930.1 572   SA
MARGARET SHAW LECTURES. 1984. biennial, vol.4, 1994. price varies. South African Museum, P.O. Box 61, Cape Town 8000, South Africa. TEL 27-21-243330. FAX 27-21-246716. E-mail: elouw@nv1.samuseum.ac.za. circ. 450 (controlled). **Document type:** academic/scholarly publication, monographic series.
    Description: Publishes lectures delivered by invited speakers. Honors Margaret Shaw and her contribution to ethnography of southern Africa.

MARGARETOLOGIST. see JEWELRY, CLOCKS AND WATCHES

913 440   FR
MARI ANNALES DE RECHERCHES INTERDISCIPLINAIRES. 1982. irreg. price varies. Editions Recherche sur les Civilisations, 28 rue de Bourgogne, 75007 Paris, France. TEL 33-1-40628062. FAX 33-1-40628071. Ed. Hina Descat; Pub. Hina Descat. R&P contact: Hina Descat. circ. 600. **Indexed:** Anthropol.Lit. **Document type:** bulletin.

930.102804   SW   ISSN 1100-9632
MARINARKEOLOGISK TIDSKRIFT; meddelanden fraan Marinarkeologiska Saellskapet. 1978. q. SEK 200 membership (effective 1997). Marinarkeologiska Saellskapet, c/o Marcus Lindstroem, Oesthammarsgatan 75, S-115 28 Stockholm, Sweden. TEL 46-8-661-71-17. Ed. Karin Virgin. **Document type:** academic/scholarly publication.
    Formerly (until 1989): Meddelanden fraan Marinarkeologiska Saellskapet.

930.14372   XR   ISSN 1211-6327
MASARYKOVA UNIVERZITA. FILOZOFICKA FAKULTA. SBORNIK PRACI. M: RADA ARCHEOLOGICKA. (Text in Czech; summaries in various languages) 1956. a. price varies. Masarykova Univerzita, Filozoficka Fakulta, A. Novaka 1, 660 88 Brno, Czech Republic. TEL 420-5-41121102. FAX 420-5-41121406. E-mail: exchange@phil.muni.cz. R&P contact: Ivan Seidl. TEL 420-5-41121337. bk.rev. **Document type:** academic/scholarly publication.
    Supersedes in part (in 1996): Masarykova Univerzita. Filozoficka Fakulta. Sbornik Praci. E: Rada Archeologicko - Klasicka; Which was formerly: Univerzita J.E. Purkyne. Filozoficka Fakulta. Sbornik Praci. E: Rada Archeologicko - Klasicka (ISSN 0231-7915)
    Description: Presents studies in archaeology, especially in the Slavonic prehistory of southern Moravia.

913   US   ISSN 0148-1886
F66
MASSACHUSETTS ARCHAEOLOGICAL SOCIETY. BULLETIN. 1939. 2/yr. $18 to individuals (foreign $20); institutions $30 (foreign $35) (effective 1997). Massachusetts Archaeological Society, Inc., Robbins Museum of Archaeology, Box 700, Middleboro, MA 02346. TEL 508-947-9005. Ed. Shirley Blancke. R&P contact: Elizabeth Little. bk.rev.; index, cum.index: vols.1-38, vols.39-48 (1978-1987). circ. 800. **Indexed:** Abstr.Anthropol., Anthropol.Lit. **Document type:** academic/scholarly publication, bulletin.

970.1   US
MASSACHUSETTS ARCHAEOLOGICAL SOCIETY. NEWSLETTER. N.S. 1974. 3/yr. free to members. Massachusetts Archaeological Society, Inc., Robbins Museum of Archaeology, Box 700, Middleboro, MA 02346. TEL 508-947-9005. Ed. Thomas E. Lux. R&P contact: Thomas E. Lux. adv.: page $90; 7 1/4 x 9 1/4. circ. 800. **Document type:** newsletter.
    Description: News, announcements and items of interest to members of the society.

913   RM   ISSN 1220-5222
MATERIALE SI CERCETARI ARHEOLOGICE. (Text in Rumanian; summaries in French, Rumanian) 1955-19??; resumed 1992. a. (Academia Romana, Comisia Nationala de Arheologie) Editura Academiei Romane, Calea 13 Septembrie 13, 76117 Bucharest, Romania. (Dist. by: Rodipet SA, Piata Presei Libere 1, Sec. 1, PO Box 33-57, Bucharest, Rumania. TEL 401-6185103. FAX 401-2226407) Ed. Nicolae Conovici. **Indexed:** A.I.C.P., Numis.Lit.

918   PE
MATERIALES PARA LA ARQUEOLOGIA DEL PERU.* 1981. irreg. Instituto Nacional de Cultura, Proyecto Especial de Irrigacion Jequetepeque-Zana, Casilla 5247, Ancash 390, Lima, Peru.

ARCHAEOLOGY

930.1   GW
MATERIALHEFTE ZUR ARCHAEOLOGIE IN BADEN-WUERTTEMBERG. 1982. irreg., vol.30, 1995. (Landesdenkmalamt Baden-Wuerttemberg) Konrad Theiss Verlag GmbH und Co., Villastr. 11, 70190 Stuttgart, Germany. TEL 49-711-2686101. FAX 49-711-2686115. Ed. Gerhard Wesselkamp. **Document type:** academic/scholarly publication, monographic series.
    Formerly: Materialhefte zur Vor- und Fruehgeschichte in Baden-Wuerttemberg (ISSN 0938-6769)

930.1   GW
MATERIALHEFTE ZUR BAYERISCHEN VORGESCHICHTE. 1953. irreg. price varies. (Bayerisches Landesamt fuer Denkmalpflege, Abteilung Bodendenkmalpflege) Verlag Michael Lassleben, Lange Gasse 19, 93183 Kallmuenz, Germany. **Document type:** monographic series.

MATERIALI E DOCUMENTI TICINESI. see *HISTORY — History Of Europe*

MATERIALIEN ZUR ROEMISCH-GERMANISCHEN KERAMIK. see *CERAMICS, GLASS AND POTTERY*

MAYAQUEST NEWS. see *EDUCATION — Computer Applications*

930.1   SW   ISSN 0585-3214
MEDELHAVSMUSEET. BULLETIN. 1961. a. SEK 150 (effective 1992). Medelhavsmuseet - Museum of Mediterranean and Near Eastern Antiquities, Fredsgatan 2, P.O. Box 5405, S-114 84 Stockholm, Sweden. TEL 46-8-783-94-00. FAX 46-8-783-92-80. Ed. Eva Rystedt. circ. 1,600. **Document type:** bulletin.

913   UK   ISSN 0076-6097
D111
MEDIEVAL ARCHAEOLOGY. 1957. a. £18 to individuals; institutions £25. Society for Medieval Archaeology, Department of Archaeology, University of York, York YO1 1JZ, England. TEL 44-1904-636731. FAX 44-1904-433433. TELEX 57933-YORKUL. (Subscr. to: Medieval Archaeology, P.O. Box YR7, Leeds LS9 7UU, England. TEL 44-1532-497481) Ed. H. Mytum. bk.rev. circ. 1,500. Indexed: Art & Archaeol.Tech.Abstr., Avery Ind.Archit.Per., Bibl.Engl.Lang.& Lit., Br.Archaeol.Abstr., Br.Hum.Ind., Hum.Ind., IBR, Numis.Lit., RILA. **Document type:** academic/scholarly publication.
   —BLDSC (5534.265000); KR SourceOne; UnCover.
   Refereed Serial

930.1 936   SW   ISSN 0349-456X
MEDUSA. 1980. q. SEK 150 (effective 1996). Foereningen Foer en Svensk Antiktidskrift, Roedabergsbrinken 14, S-113 30 Stockholm, Sweden. TEL 46-8-32-20-56. FAX 46-8-643-70-89. Ed. Charlotte Scheffer. bk.rev.
   Description: Contains articles of a popular nature on archaeology and ancient history.

935   IR   ISSN 1148-6198
MEMOIRES DE LA DELEGATION ARCHEOLOGIQUE FRANCAISE EN IRAN. (Former name of issuing body: Delegation Archeologique Francaise en Iran) 1900. irreg. price varies. Institut Francais de Recherche en Iran, Ave. Shahid Nizari, 52 Adib St., P.O. Box 15815-3495, Tehran. TEL 98-21-6401192. FAX 98-21-6405501. Ed. Remy Boucharlat. **Document type:** academic/scholarly publication.
   Supersedes: Delegation Archeologique Francaise en Iran. Memoires (ISSN 0169-880X)

913   GR   ISSN 1105-7181
O MENTOR. (Text in Greek) 1988. q. Archaeological Society at Athens - Archaiologike Hetaireia en Athenais, Panepistimiou 22, 106 72 Athens, Greece. TEL 30-1-364-6043. FAX 30-1-364-4996. illus. (back issues avail.) **Document type:** academic/scholarly publication.
   Formerly (until 1991): Archaiologike en Athenais Hetaireia. Enemerotiko Deltio (ISSN 1105-1205)
   Description: Contains Archaeological Society news and short articles on subjects of archaeological or antiquarian interest, along with notes on the current state and condition of Greek antiquities.

913   IT   ISSN 0076-6615
MESOPOTAMIA; rivista di archeologia, epigrafia e storia orientale antica. (Text in English and Italian) 1966. a., latest vol.31, 1996. L.260000 (foreign L.320000). Centro Ricerche Archeologiche e Scavi di Torino, Via Gaudenzio Ferrari 1, 10124 Torino, Italy. TEL 39-11-8125023. FAX 39-11-8126190. (Co-sponsor: Universita degli Studi di Torino, Dipartimento S.A.A.S.T.) Ed. Antonio Invernizzi. circ. 1,000. Indexed: Anthropol.Lit., Bibl.Ling., IBR, Numis.Lit. **Document type:** academic/scholarly publication.

930.1   SW   ISSN 0348-7903
META; medeltidsarkeologisk tidskrift. 1979. q. SEK 100 membership (effective 1993). Medeltidsarkeologiska Foereningen (Meta), Lunds Universitets Historiska Museum, Krafts torg 1, S-223 50 Lund, Sweden.

MEXICON; aktuelle Informationen und Studien zu Mesoamerika. see *ANTHROPOLOGY*

930.1   IS   ISSN 0334-7311
DS111.A1
MICHMANIM. (Text and summaries in English, Hebrew) 1985. s-a. $10. Reuben and Edith Hecht Museum, Haifa University, Mt. Carmel, Haifa 31905, Israel. TEL 972-4-8257773. FAX 972-4-8240724. E-mail: mushecht@research.haip.ac.il. Ed. Moshe Dothan. R&P contact: Ofra Rimon. circ. 500. **Document type:** academic/scholarly publication, bulletin.
   Description: Publishes articles concerning artifacts in the museum's collections, conferences and archaeological activities in the north of Israel.
   Refereed Serial

973.92605   US   ISSN 0146-1109
E77.8
MIDCONTINENTAL JOURNAL OF ARCHAEOLOGY. Cover title: M C J A. 1976. s-a. $19 to individuals; institutions $28 (effective 1997 & 1998). University of Iowa, Office of State Archaeologist, 303 Eastlawn, Iowa City, IA 52242-1411. TEL 319-335-2389. FAX 319-335-2776. URL: http://www.uiowa.edu/~osa/publica/mcja/mcja.htm. Eds. William Green, David S. Brose. adv.; bk.rev.; charts; illus. circ. 600. (back issues avail.; reprint service avail. from UMI) Indexed: Abstr.Anthropol., Amer.Hist.& Life (1986-), Anthropol.Lit., Br.Archaeol.Abstr., Hist.Abstr. (1986-), IBR. **Document type:** academic/scholarly publication.
   —BLDSC (5761.314900); UMI; UnCover. **CCC.**

917   CN   ISSN 0047-7222
THE MIDDEN. 1969. 5/yr. Can.$14.50 (foreign Can.$17). Archaeological Society of British Columbia, Box 520, Sta. A, Vancouver, BC V6C 2N3, Canada. TEL 604-822-2567. Ed. Joyce Johnson. bk.rev.; index. circ. 350. Indexed: Abstr.Anthropol. **Document type:** academic/scholarly publication.
   Formerly: Archaeological Society of British Columbia. Newsletter.

917   US   ISSN 0026-5403
F608
MINNESOTA ARCHAEOLOGIST. 1934. 2/yr. $20 (Canada $22). Minnesota Archaeological Society, Fort Snelling History Center, St. Paul, MN 55111. TEL 612-726-1171. Ed. Ted Lofstrom. bk.rev.; illus. circ. 400. (also avail. in microfilm from UMI,BHP; back issues avail.) Indexed: Anthropol.Lit. **Document type:** academic/scholarly publication.
   —UMI; UnCover.

930.1 955   IR
MIRAS-E FARHANGI. vol.11, 1990. m. Rs.800 per no. Sazman-i Miras-i Farhangi-i Kishvar - Iranian Cultural Heritage Organization, Azadi Ave., Zanjan St., P.O. Box 13445-719, Tehran 13345, Iran. TEL 98-21-6013527. FAX 98-21-6013498. circ. 10,000.
   Description: Serves as a platform for the publications of articles concerning archaeology, ethnology, traditional arts, architecture, museology and the restoration of artifacts.

913   US   ISSN 0743-7641
F468
MISSOURI ARCHAEOLOGICAL SOCIETY. QUARTERLY. 1984. q. membership. Missouri Archaeological Society, 101 A Museum Support Center, Rock Quarry Rd. at Hinkson Creek, Columbia, MO 65211. TEL 573-882-3544. FAX 573-882-9410. (Subscr. to: Box 958, Columbia, MO 65205) Ed. Michael J. O'Brien. circ. 1,500 (paid). (back issues avail.) Indexed: Anthropol.Lit. **Document type:** newsletter.
   —UnCover.
   Formerly (until 1983): Missouri Archaeological Society. Newsletter (ISSN 0076-955X)

913   US   ISSN 0076-9576
F468
MISSOURI ARCHAEOLOGIST. 1935. a. $15 membership. Missouri Archaeological Society, 101 A Museum Support Center, Rock Quarry Rd. at Hinkson Creek, Columbia, MO 65211. TEL 573-882-3544. FAX 573-882-9410. (Subscr. to: Box 958, Columbia, MO 65205) Ed. W. Raymond Wood. charts; illus. circ. 1,500. (back issues avail.) Indexed: Abstr.Anthropol., Anthropol.Lit. **Document type:** monographic series.
   —UnCover.

930.1   IS   ISSN 0334-3839
MITEKUFAT HAEVEN. (Text in English; summaries in Hebrew) 1985. a. IS.30($25) Israel Prehistoric Society, P.O. Box 1502, Jerusalem 910014, Israel. TEL 972-2-882434. FAX 972-2-825548. Eds. Erella Hovers, Uri Baruch. bk.rev. circ. 400. Indexed: Anthropol.Lit. **Document type:** academic/scholarly publication.

MITTEILUNGEN ZUR CHRISTLICHEN ARCHAEOLOGIE. see *ART*

MNEMOSYNE. see *HISTORY — History Of Europe*

913 200   FR   ISSN 0154-9049
MONDE DE LA BIBLE; archeologie & histoire. 1957. 4/yr. 260 F. (outside EC 300 F.). Bayard Presse, 3 rue Bayard, 75393 Paris Cedex 08, France. TEL 33-1-44356060. FAX 33-1-44356091. TELEX 648 094 F. (Subscr. to: Bayard Presse International, B.P. 12, 99505 Paris Entreprises, France. TEL 33-1-44216000. FAX 33-3-20274192) Ed. Frederic Boyer. adv.; bk.rev. circ. 18,000. Indexed: Old Test.Abstr.
   —BLDSC (5906.890000).
   Supersedes: Bible et Terre Sainte (ISSN 0006-0712)
   Description: Provides an archeological perspective of Biblical times.

913   SP   ISSN 0544-7941
MONOGRAFIAS ARQUEOLOGICAS.* 1982. irreg. Universidad Autonoma de Madrid, Departamento de Prehistoria y Arqueologia, Carretera de Colmenar, km 15000, Canto Blanco, 28049 Madrid, Spain.
   —CINDOC.

913   IT   ISSN 0077-0493
MONOGRAFIE DI ARCHEOLOGIA LIBICA. 1948. irreg., vol.23, 1989. price varies. L'Erma di Bretschneider, Via Cassiodoro 19, 00193 Rome, Italy. TEL 39-6-6874127. FAX 39-6-6874129. **Document type:** monographic series.

932   BE
MONOGRAPHIES REINE ELISABETH. 1971. irreg., latest vol.6, 1989. price varies. Fondation Egyptologique Reine Elisabeth, Parc du Cinquantenaire 10, 1000 Brussels, Belgium. TEL 32-2-7417364. **Document type:** monographic series.

932   BE   ISSN 0077-1376
MONUMENTA AEGYPTIACA. 1968. irreg., latest no.6, 1994. price varies. Fondation Egyptologique Reine Elisabeth, Parc du Cinquantenaire 10, 1000 Brussels, Belgium. TEL 32-2-7417364. **Document type:** monographic series.

913   GW   ISSN 0077-1384
MONUMENTA AMERICANA. (Text in German; occasionally also in English or Spanish) 1965. irreg., vol.5, 1997. price varies. (Ibero-Amerikanisches Institut Preussischer Kulturbesitz Berlin) Gebr. Mann Verlag GmbH, Charlottenstr. 13, 10969 Berlin, Germany. TEL 49-30-2591-3589. FAX 49-30-2591-3537. Ed. Gerdt Kutscher. (reprint service avail.) **Document type:** monographic series.

ARCHAEOLOGY

913 　　　　　 IT
MONUMENTA ANTIQUA ETRURIAE. 1993. irreg. price varies. L'Erma di Bretschneider, Via Cassiodoro 19, 00193 Rome, Italy. TEL 39-6-6874127. FAX 39-6-6874129.

913 　　　　　 US 　　ISSN 0363-7565
MONUMENTA ARCHAEOLOGICA. 1976. irreg., vol.15, 1990. University of California at Los Angeles, Institute of Archaeology, 405 Hilgard Ave., Los Angeles, CA 90024-1510. TEL 213-825-7411. FAX 213-206-4723. Ed. Ernestine S. Elster. **Document type:** academic/scholarly publication.
　Description: Publishes reports and analyses of worldwide archaeological data.

913 709 　　　 GW 　　ISSN 0077-1406
MONUMENTA ARTIS ROMANAE. 1959. irreg., vol.24, 1995. DM.168. Verlag Philipp von Zabern GmbH, Philipp-von-Zabern-Platz 1-3, 55116 Mainz, Germany. TEL 06131-28747-0. FAX 06131-223710. Eds. F. Sinn, K.S. Freyberger. (back issues avail.) **Document type:** monographic series.

MORAVSKE ZEMSKE MUZEUM. CASOPIS. VEDY SPOLECENSKE/ACTA MUSEI MORAVIAE - SCIENTIAE SOCIALES. see HISTORY — History Of Europe

930.1 　　　　　 GW 　　ISSN 0178-0492
MUENCHNER ARCHAEOLOGISCHE STUDIEN. 1970. irreg., vol.8. DM.36. Wilhelm Fink Verlag, Ohmstr. 5, 80802 Munich, Germany. TEL 49-89-348017. FAX 49-89-341378. URL: http://www.fink.de. R&P contact: Marlene Braun. **Document type:** monographic series.

MUENSTERSCHE BEITRAEGE ZUR ANTIKEN HANDELSGESCHICHTE. see CLASSICAL STUDIES

MUNIBE ANTROPOLOGIA - ARKEOLOGIA. see ANTHROPOLOGY

MUSE (COLUMBIA). see ART

MUSEO ARCHEOLOGICO DI TARQUINIA. MATERIALI. see MUSEUMS AND ART GALLERIES

913 　　　　　 SP
MUSEO ARQUEOLOGICO NACIONAL. CATALOGOS CIENTIFICOS. 1980. irreg. price varies. Ministerio de Cultura, Museo Arqueologico Nacional, Serrano 13, 28001 Madrid, Spain. TEL 5577912. FAX 4316840. circ. 700. **Document type:** bulletin.

MUSEO CHILENO DE ARTE PRECOLOMBINO. BOLETIN. see ART

MUSEO CIVICO ARCHEOLOGICO UGO GRANAFEI DI MESAGNE. TESTI E MONUMENTI. see MUSEUMS AND ART GALLERIES

MUSEO DEL HOMBRE DOMINICANO. BOLETIN. see ANTHROPOLOGY

MUSEO MUNICIPAL DE HISTORIA NATURAL DE SAN RAFAEL. REVISTA. see SCIENCES: COMPREHENSIVE WORKS

913 700 　　　 BL 　　ISSN 0103-9709
F2519
MUSEU DE ARQUEOLOGIA E ETNOLOGIA. REVISTA. 1991. a. $15 to individuals; institutions $25; foreign $30. Universidade de Sao Paulo, Museu de Arqueologia e Etnologia, Av. Prof. Almeida Prado, 1466, Cidade Universitaria, 05508-900 Sao Paulo SP, Brazil. TEL 55-11-8184978. FAX 55-11-8185042. Eds. Maria Cristina Mineiro Scatamacchia, Maria Isabel D'Agostino Fleming. bk.rev.; bibl.; charts; illus. circ. 2,000. **Indexed:** A.I.C.P., Anthropol.Lit., IBR. **Document type:** academic/scholarly publication.
　Supersedes (1965-1974): Dedalo (ISSN 0011-7455); (1979-1989): Revista de Prehistoria (ISSN 0100-7726)
　Refereed Serial

917 　　　　　 GW
MUSEUM FUER VOELKERKUNDE, BERLIN. VEROEFFENTLICHUNGEN. NEUE FOLGE. ABTEILUNG: AMERIKANISCHE ARCHAEOLOGIE. 1970. irreg., vol.9, 1994. price varies. Staatliche Museen zu Berlin - Preussischer Kulturbesitz, Generalverwaltung, Stauffenbergstr. 41, 10785 Berlin, Germany. FAX 030-2662612. **Document type:** monographic series.

MUSEUM HELVETICUM; Schweizerische Zeitschrift fuer klassische Altertumswissenschaft. see CLASSICAL STUDIES

913 　　　　　 IS 　　ISSN 0082-2620
MUSEUM OF ANTIQUITIES OF TEL-AVIV-YAFO. PUBLICATIONS. 1964. irreg. $1. Museum of Antiquites of Tel-Aviv-Yafo, Box 8406, Tel Aviv-Jaffa, Israel.

MUZE/MUSEUM. see MUSEUMS AND ART GALLERIES

914 069 　　　 CI 　　ISSN 0350-9370
MUZEJSKI VJESNIK/MUSEUM NEWS MAGAZINE. (Text in Croatian; summaries in German) 1978. a. free. North-West Croatian Museums, Muzejsko Drustvo Sjeverozapadne Hrvatske, 42000 Varazdin, Croatia. Ed. Darko Sacic. bk.rev. circ. 800. (back issues avail.)

930.1 　　　　　 RM 　　ISSN 0255-6812
MUZEUL NATIONAL DE ISTORIE A ROMANIEI. CERCETARI ARHEOLOGICE. Key Title: Cercetari Arheologice. (Text in Rumanian; summaries in English, French) 1975. a. Muzeul National de Istorie a Romaniei, Calea Victoriei, 12, Bucharest, Rumania. TEL 40-1-6149070. Ed.Bd. **Indexed:** Numis.Lit. **Document type:** academic/scholarly publication.
　Formerly: Muzeul de Istorie al Republici Socialiste Romania. Cercetari Arheologice.

MUZEUL NATIONAL DE ISTORIE A ROMANIEI. CERCETARI NUMISMATICE. see NUMISMATICS

913 943.8 　　　 PL 　　ISSN 0458-1520
MUZEUM ARCHEOLOGICZNE I ETNOGRAFICZNE, LODZ. PRACE I MATERIALY. SERIA ARCHEOLOGICZNA. (Text in Polish; summaries in English) 1956. irreg., no.37-38, 1991-92. price varies. Muzeum Archeologiczne i Etnograficzne w Lodzi, Pl. Wonosci 14, 91-415 Lodz, Poland. TEL 48-42-328440. FAX 48-42-329740. Ed. Ryszard Grygiel. circ. 500. **Indexed:** Anthropol.Lit. **Document type:** academic/scholarly publication.

930.1 　　　　　 PL 　　ISSN 0075-7039
MUZEUM ARCHEOLOGICZNE, KRAKOW. MATERIALY ARCHEOLOGICZNE. 1959. irreg., vol.27, 1993. $20. Muzeum Archeologiczne, Krakow, Senacka 3, 31-002 Krakow, Poland. TEL 48-12-227560. circ. 450. **Indexed:** Anthropol.Lit. **Document type:** academic/scholarly publication.
　—BLDSC (5396.724000).
　Description: Covers prehistory and medieval ages in Poland as well as Mediterranean (Greek, Hellenistic, Roman) and Egyptian archaeology.

930.1 　　　　　 PL 　　ISSN 0581-1112
MUZEUM ARCHEOLOGICZNE, KRAKOW. ODDZIAL W NOWEJ HUCIE. MATERIALY ARCHEOLOGICZNE NOWEJ HUTY. 1968. a. $20. Muzeum Archeologiczne, Krakow, Senacka 3, 31-002 Krakow, Poland. TEL 48-12-227560. FAX 48-12-227761. circ. 450. **Document type:** academic/scholarly publication.
　Description: Covers prehistory and medieval ages in the territory of Krakow - Nowa Huta.

913 　　　　　 PL 　　ISSN 0068-4635
MUZEUM GORNOSLASKIE W BYTOMIU. ROCZNIK. SERIA ARCHEOLOGIA. (Text in Polish; summaries in German and Russian) 1962. irreg. $15. Muzeum Gornoslaskie, Pl. Sobieskiego 2, 41-902 Bytom, Poland. TEL 48-32-81-34-01. **Document type:** proceedings.

MUZEUM MESTA BLANSKA. SBORNIK. see HISTORY — History Of Europe

930.1 　　　　　 US
N E A R A TRANSIT NEWSLETTER. s-a. New England Antiquities Research Association, 94 Cross Point Rd., Edgecomb, ME 04556. TEL 207-882-8155. FAX 207-882-8162. E-mail: krosspt@lincoln.midcoast.com. (Subscr. to: 788 Whalley Rd., Charlotte, VT 05445) Ed. Roslyn Strong. R&P contact: Suzanne Carlson. circ. 500. **Document type:** newsletter.

930.1 　　　　　 US
N E A S NEWSLETTER.* q. (Near East Archaeological Society) Berry Publishing Services, 1325 Remmington Rd., Ste. H, Schaumberg, IL 60173-4815. TEL 800-274-9447. FAX 708-869-4825. E-mail: 76105.3503@compuserve.com. Pub. Bill Berry. **Document type:** newsletter.

930.1 900 　　　 GW 　　ISSN 1432-0282
▼**NACHRICHTEN AUS DEM MARTIN-VON-WAGNER-MUSEUM.** 1996. irreg. Ergon Verlag, Grombuehlstr. 7, 97080 Wuerzburg, Germany. TEL 49-931-280084. FAX 49-931-282872. E-mail: ergon-verlag@t-online.de. Eds. S. Kummer, U. Sinn. **Document type:** academic/scholarly publication.

001.3 　　　　　 SA 　　ISSN 1015-0935
AZ188.S6
NATAL MUSEUM JOURNAL OF HUMANITIES. (Text in English, French, German; summaries in English) 1989. a. price varies. Natal Museum, Private Bag 9070, Pietermaritzburg 3200, South Africa. TEL 27-331-451404. FAX 27-331-450561. Ed. D. Barraclough. R&P contact: D. Barraclough. cum.index. circ. 200. (back issues avail.) **Indexed:** IBR, Ind.S.A.Per. **Document type:** academic/scholarly publication.
　Description: Research articles on archaeology, anthropology, rock art, shipwrecks, cultural and historical studies.
　Refereed Serial

930.1 　　　　　 IE
NATIONAL MUSEUM OF IRELAND. MEDIEVAL DUBLIN EXCAVATIONS. SERIES A. 1992. irreg. Royal Irish Academy, 19 Dawson St., Dublin 2, Ireland. TEL 353-1-6762570. FAX 353-1-6762346. (Co-sponsor: National Museum of Ireland) Ed. Patrick Wallace. **Document type:** monographic series.

930.1 　　　　　 IE
NATIONAL MUSEUM OF IRELAND. MEDIEVAL DUBLIN EXCAVATIONS. SERIES B. irreg., vol.3, 1993. Royal Irish Academy, 19 Dawson St., Dublin 2, Ireland. TEL 353-1-6762570. FAX 353-1-6762346. (Co-sponsor: National Museum of Ireland) Ed. Sean McGrail. **Document type:** monographic series.

NATIONAL TAIWAN UNIVERSITY. DEPARTMENT OF ANTHROPOLOGY. BULLETIN. see ANTHROPOLOGY

NATUR UND MENSCH: JAHRESMITTEILUNGEN DER NATURHISTORISCHEN GESELLSCHAFT NUERNBERG. see BIOLOGY

NATURAL HISTORY MUSEUM AND INSTITUTE, CHIBA. BULLETIN. HUMANITIES. see HISTORY — History Of Asia

913 570 　　　 GW 　　ISSN 0077-6149
NATURHISTORISCHE GESELLSCHAFT NUERNBERG. ABHANDLUNGEN. 1851. irreg. price varies. Naturhistorische Gesellschaft Nuernberg e.V., Gewerbemuseumsplatz 4, Luitpoldhaus, 90403 Nuernberg, Germany. TEL 0911-227970. circ. 2,500. **Indexed:** Biol.Abstr. **Document type:** monographic series.

913 980 　　　 US 　　ISSN 0077-6297
F2229
NAWPA PACHA. (Text in English, French, Inca, Spanish; contributions in other languages accepted) 1963. a. $15 to individuals; institutions $20. Institute of Andean Studies, Box 9307, Berkeley, CA 94709. TEL 510-525-7816. Eds. John H. Rowe, Patricia J. Lyon. circ. 550 (controlled). **Indexed:** A.I.C.P., Anthropol.Lit., Hisp.Amer.Per.Ind. (1969-), IBR.
　Description: Scholarly journal dealing with Andean archaeology and related topics.

913 　　　　　 PL 　　ISSN 0137-608X
NEA PAPHOS. (Text English or French) 1976. irreg., vol.4, 1991. $26 per issue. Polska Akademia Nauk, Zaklad Archeologii Srodziemnomorskiej, Palac Kultury i Nauki, p. 2105, 00-901 Warsaw, Poland. TEL 48-22-6248593. FAX 48-22-6207651. (Dist. by: Osrodek Rozpowszechniania Wydawnictw Naukowych PAN - Export, Palac Kultury i Nauki, 00-901 Warsaw, Poland. FAX 48-22-8268670) (Co-sponsor: State Committee for Scientific Research) Ed. W.A. Daszewski. bibl.; illus. circ. 105. (back issues avail.) **Document type:** monographic series.
　Description: Presents excavation results of Polish Archaeological Mission at Kato Paphos, Cyprus.
　Refereed Serial

ARCHAEOLOGY

930.1 US ISSN 0739-0068
DS56
NEAR EAST ARCHAEOLOGICAL SOCIETY. BULLETIN.*
1971. irreg., approx a., no.38, 1994. $25 includes all society publications (effective 1995 & 1996). Near East Archaeological Society, 1325 Remington Rd., Ste. H, Schaumberg, IL 60173-4815. TEL 847-869-4919. Ed. John Wineland. R&P contact: Bill Berry. bk.rev.; charts; illus. circ. 350. **Document type:** academic/scholarly publication, bulletin, trade publication.

930.1 US
NEAR EAST ARCHAEOLOGICAL SOCIETY. NEWSLETTER.*
s-a. $25 includes all society publications. Near East Archaeological Society, 1325 Remington Rd., Ste. H, Schaumberg, IL 60173-4815. Ed. Reuben Bullard. R&P contact: Bill Berry. **Document type:** newsletter.

930.1 US ISSN 1094-2076
BS620.A1
NEAR EASTERN ARCHAEOLOGY. 1938. q. $33.25 to individuals (foreign $38.25); institutions $42.75 (foreign $47.75) (effective 1998). (American Schools of Oriental Research) Scholars Press, Box 15399, Atlanta, GA 30333-0399. TEL 301-727-2320; 888-747-2354. FAX 301-727-2348. E-mail: scholars@emory.edu; URL: http://scholar.cc.emory.edu/scripts/publications/journals/BA.html. Ed. David Hopkins. R&P contact: Dennis Ford. adv.; bk.rev.; bibl.; charts; illus.; index. circ. 5,500. (also avail. in microform from UMI; back issues avail.; reprint service avail. from UMI) **Indexed:** A.I.C.P., Abstr.Anthropol., Anthropol.Lit., Art & Archaeol.Tech.Abstr., Art Ind., Arts & Hum.Cit.Ind., ASCA, Cath.Ind., Chr.Per.Ind., Curr.Cont., Hum.Ind., IBR, M.L.A., Mid.East: Abstr.& Ind., MLA Intl.Bibl., Old Test.Abstr., Rel.& Theol.Abstr. (1971-), Rel.Ind.One, Rel.Per., SSCI, Oumis.Lit. **Document type:** academic/scholarly publication.
—BLDSC (0856.455000); KR SourceOne; SWETS; UMI; UnCover.
Formerly (until 1998): Biblical Archaeologist (ISSN 0006-0895)
Description: Presents articles that illustrate Old and New Testament scriptures and history, interpret the meaning of archaeological finds, and trace the evolution of Western culture and traditions.

NEDERLANDS INSTITUUT TE ROME. MEDEDELINGEN.
see HISTORY — History Of Europe

930.1 NE ISSN 0167-9783
NEDERLANDSE OUDHEDEN. (Text in English, German) 1955. irreg., vol.15, 1993. price varies. Rijksdienst voor het Oudheidkundig Bodemonderzoek te Amersfoort, Kerkstraat 1, 3811 CV Amersfoort, Netherlands. TEL 31-33-4634233. FAX 31-33-4653235. E-mail: arne.haytsma@archis.nl; URL: http://www.archis.nl/. Ed. A. Haytsma. abstr.; bibl.; illus.; maps. **Document type:** monographic series, government publication.
Description: Covers archaeology in the Netherlands, from prehistoric times through the post-Medieval period.
Refereed Serial

938 720 NE
NETHERLANDS INSTITUTE AT ATHENS. PUBLICATIONS. (Text in English) 1990. irreg., vol.2, 1995. J.C. Gieben, Nieuwe Herengracht 35, 1011 RM Amsterdam, Netherlands. TEL 31-20-6275170. FAX 31-20-6275170. (Dist. in N. America by: John Benjamins Publishing Co., Box 27519, Philadelphia, PA 19118-0519. TEL 215-836-1200. FAX 215-8236-1204) Ed. J.A.K.E. de Waele. illus. (back issues avail.) **Document type:** monographic series, proceedings.

932 962 NE ISSN 0922-5234
NETHERLANDS INSTITUTE OF ARCHAEOLOGY AND ARABIC STUDIES IN CAIRO. PUBLICATIONS. 1973. irreg., vol.5, 1988. price varies. E.J. Brill, P.O. Box 9000, 2300 PA Leiden, Netherlands. TEL 31-71-5353500. FAX 31-71-5317532. TELEX 39296 BRILL NL. E-mail: ejbrill@brill.nl. (In N. America: E.J. Brill, 24 Hudson St., Kinderhook, NY 12106. TEL 800-962-4406. FAX 518-758-1959) R&P contact: Elizabeth Vennekamp. **Document type:** monographic series.
Refereed Serial

NEVADA. STATE MUSEUM, CARSON CITY. ANTHROPOLOGICAL PAPERS. see ANTHROPOLOGY

930.1 US ISSN 0149-2551
F6
NEW ENGLAND ANTIQUITIES RESEARCH ASSOCIATION JOURNAL. 1964. q. $25 (foreign $30). New England Antiquities Research Association, 94 Cross Point Rd., Edgecomb, ME 04556. TEL 207-882-8155. FAX 207-882-8162. E-mail: krosspt@lincoln.midsoast.com. (Subscr. to: 78 Whalley Rd., Charlotte, VT 05445) Ed. Suzanne Carlson; Pub. Suzanne Carlson. R&P contact: Suzanne Carlson. bk.rev. circ. 500. (back issues avail.) **Indexed:** Abstr.Anthropol., Anthropol.Lit. **Document type:** academic/scholarly publication.
Formerly: New England Antiquities Research Association Newsletter.
Description: Examines an expanding range of associated disciplines and explores their interrelationships, contributing to a clearer understanding of the origins and purposes of American lithic sites.

930.1 US ISSN 0545-1604
NEW HAMPSHIRE ARCHEOLOGICAL SOCIETY NEWSLETTER. 1950. q. free with subscription to New Hampshire Archeologist. New Hampshire Archeological Society, c/o Phillips Exeter Academy, 20 Main St., MSC 81337, Department of Anthropology, Exeter, NH 03833-2460. TEL 603-778-3452. Ed. V. Bunker. bk.rev.; bibl.; illus. circ. 250. (processed) **Indexed:** Anthropol.Lit. **Document type:** newsletter.

930.1 US ISSN 0077-8346
F36
NEW HAMPSHIRE ARCHEOLOGIST. 1950. a. $15 to individuals; institutions $18; includes Newsletter. New Hampshire Archeological Society, c/o Phillips Exeter Academy, 20 Main St. MSC 81337, Department of Anthropology, Exeter, NH 03833-2460. TEL 603-772-4311. Ed. V. Bunker. illus. circ. 250. **Indexed:** Anthropol.Lit. **Document type:** academic/scholarly publication.

913 UK
NEW STUDIES IN ARCHAEOLOGY. 1976. irreg. price varies. Cambridge University Press, Edinburgh Bldg., Shaftesbury Rd., Cambridge CB2 2RU, England. TEL 44-1223-312393. FAX 44-1223-315052. TELEX 851817256. E-mail: information@cup.cam.ac.uk; URL: http://www.cup.cam.ac.uk. (N. American addr.: Cambridge University Press, Journals Dept., 40 W. 20th St., New York, NY 10011. TEL 212-924-3900. FAX 212-691-3239) Ed.Bd. R&P contact: Linda Nicol. **Document type:** academic/scholarly publication.

913 US ISSN 0077-8915
NEW WORLD ARCHAEOLOGICAL FOUNDATION. PAPERS. 1959. irreg. price varies. Brigham Young University, New World Archaeological Foundation, Provo, UT 84602. TEL 801-378-4971. Ed. John E. Clark. R&P contact: John E. Clark. circ. 1,000. **Document type:** academic/scholarly publication.
—UnCover.

913 US ISSN 1046-2368
F121 CODEN: BJNAE9
NEW YORK STATE ARCHAEOLOGICAL ASSOCIATION. BULLETIN. Key Title: Bulletin - New York State Archaeological Association (1987). 1954. 2/yr. $9 to individuals; institutions $15. Rochester Museum and Science Center, 657 East Ave., Box 1480, Rochester, NY 14603-1480. TEL 716-271-4552. FAX 716-271-5935. Ed. Charles F. Hayes III. charts; illus. circ. 750. (back issues avail.; reprint service avail. from KTO) **Indexed:** Amer.Hist.& Life (1986-1988), Anthropol.Lit., Hist.Abstr. (1986-1988). **Document type:** academic/scholarly publication, bulletin.
—BLDSC (2652.080000).
Former titles (until 1987): New York State Archaeological Association. Bulletin and Journal (ISSN 0730-5710); New York State Archaeological Association. Bulletin (ISSN 0028-7512)
Description: Publishes papers in the prehistoric and historical archaeology of New York State sites, including Native American and colonial era settlements.

NEW ZEALAND HISTORIC PLACES. see HISTORY — History Of Australasia And Other Areas

913 NZ ISSN 0110-540X
DU416
NEW ZEALAND JOURNAL OF ARCHAEOLOGY. 1979. a. NZ.$25 (foreign NZ.$35) (effective 1997). New Zealand Archaeological Association, P.O. Box 6337, Dunedin North, New Zealand. TEL 64-9-3737599. E-mail: anth33@rivendell.otago.ac.nz. (Subscr. to: Business Manager, NZ Journal of Archaeology, P.O. Box 6133, Dunedin North, New Zealand) (Co-sponsor: University of Otago) Ed. J. Davidson. charts; illus. circ. 350. **Indexed:** Anthropol.Lit., So.Pac.Per.Ind. **Document type:** academic/scholarly publication.
—BLDSC (6093.100000).
Description: Publishes articles on all aspects of prehistoric and historic archaeology in New Zealand and the Pacific.

NEWCOMEN SOCIETY FOR THE STUDY OF THE HISTORY OF ENGINEERING AND TECHNOLOGY. TRANSACTIONS.
see ENGINEERING

NEWSLETTER EAST ASIAN ART & ARCHAEOLOGY. see ART

913 630 US
NONGYE KAOGU/AGRICULTURAL ARCHAEOLOGY. (Text in Chinese) q. $38.40. China Books & Periodicals, Inc., 2929 24th St., San Francisco, CA 94110. TEL 415-282-2994. FAX 415-282-0994.

NORSK SJOEFARTSMUSEUM. AARSBERETNING. see HISTORY — History Of Europe

913 US ISSN 0197-6931
E43 CODEN: NAAREU
NORTH AMERICAN ARCHAEOLOGIST. 1979. q. $136 (effective 1997). Baywood Publishing Co., Inc., 26 Austin Ave., Box 337, Amityville, NY 11701. TEL 516-691-1270. FAX 516-691-1770. E-mail: baywood@baywood.com; URL: http://Literaty.COM/baywood/pages/NA/index.html. Ed. Dr. Roger W. Moeller. (back issues avail.) **Indexed:** Abstr.Anthropol., Amer.Hist.& Life (1986-), Anthropol.Lit., Br.Archaeol.Abstr., Hist.Abstr. (1986-), IBR. **Document type:** academic/scholarly publication.
—BLDSC (6147.958000); UnCover. **CCC.**
Description: Covers all aspects of prehistoric and historic archaeology from Paleo-Indian studies to industrial sites; also features the results of resource management and contract archaeology.
Refereed Serial

913 US
NORTH CAROLINA ARCHAEOLOGICAL SOCIETY. NEWSLETTER. 1938. a. $10 to individuals; institutions $25 (includes Southern Indian Studies). North Carolina Archaeological Society, 109 E. Jones St., Raleigh, NC 27601-2807. TEL 919-733-7342. FAX 919-733-8653. Ed. Mark A. Mathis. circ. 500. **Document type:** newsletter.
Formerly: Archaeological Society of North Carolina. Newsletter.
Description: North Carolina archaeological news for society members.

913 UK ISSN 0305-4659
NORTHAMPTONSHIRE ARCHAEOLOGY. 1966. a. £10 to individuals; institutions £28; students £8. Northamptonshire Archaeological Society, Nene College, History Department, Moulton Park, Northampton NN2 7AL, England. TEL 44-1604-735500. E-mail: liz.musgrave@nene.ac.uk. Eds. E. Musgrave, M. Tingle; Pub. Alan Sutton. adv.; bk.rev.; illus. circ. 500. **Indexed:** Br.Archaeol.Abstr., Geo.Abstr. **Document type:** academic/scholarly publication.
Formerly (until 1973): Northamptonshire Federation of Archaeological Societies. Bulletin.
Description: Reports on individual archaeological sites and subjects in the English Midlands region.

914 GW ISSN 0936-8345
NORTHEIMER JAHRBUCH. 1925. a. DM.30 (effective 1997 & 1998). Heimat- und Museumsverein Northeim, Vennigerholzstr. 23, 37154 Northeim, Germany. TEL 49-5551-3348. Ed. Guenter Merl. bk.rev.; illus.; index. circ. 650. **Document type:** proceedings.
Formerly: Northeimer Heimatblaetter (ISSN 0721-4863)

ARCHAEOLOGY

930.1   NO   ISSN 0029-3652
DL421   CODEN: NRACBX
NORWEGIAN ARCHAEOLOGICAL REVIEW. (Text in English) 1968. s-a. NOK 305 in Nordic countries; elsewhere $49 (effective 1997). Scandinavian University Press, P.O. Box 2959 Toeyen, N-0608 Oslo, Norway. TEL 47-22-57-54-00. FAX 47-22-57-53-53. E-mail: mail@scup.no; URL: http://www.scup.no. (US addr.: 875 Massachusetts Ave., Ste. 84, Cambridge, MA 02139. TEL 617-497-6515. FAX 617-354-6875) Ed. Ericka Engelstad. adv.; bk.rev.; charts; illus.; index. circ. 750. (also avail. in microform from UMI; back issues avail.; reprint service avail. from ISI) **Indexed:** Abstr.Anthropol., Anthropol.Lit., Br.Archaeol.Abstr., Chem.Abstr., Geo.Abstr.P.G., GeoRef., IBR, NAA, Numis.Lit. **Document type:** academic/scholarly publication.
—BLDSC (6152.105000); UnCover. **CCC**.
    Description: Focuses on methodological and theoretical aspects of archaeology, especially Scandinavian.

NOTAS MESOAMERICANAS. see *ANTHROPOLOGY*

NOTRE COMTE/ONS GRAAFSCHAP. see *HISTORY — History Of Europe*

930.1   UK   ISSN 0143-0297
NOTTINGHAMSHIRE INDUSTRIAL ARCHAEOLOGICAL SOCIETY JOURNAL. 1979. 2/yr. £2.50. Nottinghamshire Industrial Archaeological Society, c/o Howard Rees, Ed., 47 St. Mary's Close, Attenborough, Beeston, Nottingham NG9 6AT, England. TEL 44-115-9253226. R&P contact: Howard Rees. adv. contact: Don Morley. bk.rev.; illus. circ. 80. **Document type:** bulletin.
    Formerly: Nottinghamshire Industrial Archaeological Society. Newsletter.

913   PL   ISSN 0860-5777
NOVENSIA. Key Title: Novaensia. (Text in Polish; summaries in English, Russian) 1987. irreg., no.8, 1995. price varies. (Uniwersytet Warszawski, Zaklad Archeologii Srodziemnomorskiej) Wydawnictwa Uniwersytetu Warszawskiego, Ul. Nowy Swiat 4, 00-497 Warsaw, Poland. TEL 48-22-6253044. FAX 48-22-6253044. (Dist. by: Ars Polona, Krakowskie Przedmiescie 7, 00-068 Warsaw, Poland) Ed. Ludwika Press. R&P contact: Jolanta Okonska. circ. 350. **Document type:** academic/scholarly publication.

932   PL   ISSN 0860-7923
NUBIA; Dongola. (Text in English) 1990. irreg. $45 per issue. Polska Akademia Nauk, Zaklad Archeologii Srodziemnomorskiej, Palac Kultury i Nauki, p. 2105, 00-901 Warsaw, Poland. TEL 48-22-6248593. FAX 48-22-6207651. (Dist. by: Osrodek Rozpowszechniania Wydawnictw Naukowych PAN - Export, Palac Kultury i Nauki, 00-901 Warsaw, Poland. FAX 48-22-8268670) Ed. Stefan Jakobielski. illus. **Document type:** monographic series.
    Description: Presents excavation results of Polish Archaeological Mission at Old Dangola, Sudan.
    Refereed Serial

930.1   GW   ISSN 0938-9539
NUERNBERGER BLAETTER ZUR ARCHAEOLOGIE. 1990. a. DM.20. Stadt Nuernberg, Bildungszentrum, Postfach, 90317 Nuernberg, Germany. TEL 49-911-2312461. FAX 49-911-2315497. E-mail: klaus__dornisch@bz.stadt.nuernberg.de; URL: http://www.nuernberg.de/rer/bz. Ed. Klaus Dornisch. **Document type:** academic/scholarly publication.

NUMISMATICA E ANTICHITA CLASSICHE. see *NUMISMATICS*

914 945   IT
NUOVO BULLETTINO ARCHEOLOGICO SARDO. 1984. a. L.70000 (foreign L.85000). Carlo Delfino Editore, Piazza D' Italia, 11, 07100 Sassari (Sardegna), Italy. TEL 079-235691. Ed. Giovanni Lilliu. bk.rev.; index. circ. 1,000. (back issues avail.) **Document type:** academic/scholarly publication.

913 700   DK   ISSN 0085-3208
N9
NY CARLSBERG GLYPTOTEK. MEDDELELSER. (Text in Danish; summaries in English) 1944. a. DKK 120. Ny Carlsberg Glyptotek, Dantes Plads 1556, Copenhagen V, Denmark. TEL 45-33-41-81-41. FAX 45-33-91-20-58. Ed.Bd. circ. 1,000. **Indexed:** RILA. **Document type:** bulletin.

069.094891   DK   ISSN 0105-8819
NYT FRA NATIONALMUSEET. 1979. q. DKK 50. Nationalmuseet - National Museum of Denmark, Frederiksholms Kanal 12, DK-1220 Copenhagen K, Denmark. Eds. Helle Damsgaard, Jette Sandahl. R&P contact: Helle Damsgaard. adv. contact: Helle Damsgard. circ. 25,000. **Indexed:** NAA. **Document type:** academic/scholarly publication.

OBEROESTERREICHISCHER MUSEALVEREIN. JAHRBUCH. see *HISTORY — History Of Europe*

930.1   NE   ISSN 0924-0381
OBOLOS. 1989. irreg. Styx Publications, Postbus 2659, 9704 CR Groningen, Netherlands. TEL 31-50-717502. FAX 31-50-733325. **Document type:** monographic series.

930.1   IT   ISSN 1122-6315
OCNUS. 1993. a. L.73000 (foreign L.130000) (effective 1996). (Universita degli Studi di Bologna, Scuola di Specializzazione in Archeologia) Cooperativa Libraria-Universitaria Editrice Bologna, Via Marsala 24, 40126 Bologna, Italy. TEL 39-51-220736. FAX 39-51-237758. **Document type:** academic/scholarly publication.
    Description: Covers prehistorical, oriental, classical, late-antique and medieval archaeology.

ODENSE UNIVERSITY CLASSICAL STUDIES. see *CLASSICAL STUDIES*

913 943.6   AU
OESTERREICHISCHE GESELLSCHAFT FUER UR- UND FRUEHGESCHICHTE. VEROEFFENTLICHUNGEN. irreg. price varies. Oesterreichische Gesellschaft fuer Ur- und Fruehgeschichte, Franz-Klein-Gasse 1, A-1190 Vienna, Austria. TEL 43-1-31352373. FAX 43-1-31352350. **Document type:** proceedings.

OESTERREICHISCHE ZEITSCHRIFT FUER KUNST UND DENKMALPFLEGE. see *ART*

913   AU
OESTERREICHISCHES ARCHAEOLOGISCHES INSTITUT. JAHRESHEFTE. 1898. 2/yr. (Oesterreichisches Archaeologisches Institut) Verlag R.M. Rohrer GmbH, Wassergasse 1, A-2500 Baden, Austria. TEL 43-2252-88600-0. Ed. Elma Heinzel. circ. 450. **Indexed:** Avery Ind.Archit.Per., IBR. **Document type:** academic/scholarly publication.
    Superseded: Oesterreichisches Archaeologisches Institut. Jahreshefte: Grabungen (ISSN 0078-3579)

OGAM; tradition Celtique. see *HISTORY — History Of Europe*

917   US   ISSN 0048-153X
OHIO ARCHAEOLOGIST. 1950. q. $17.50. Archaeological Society of Ohio, Box 61, Plain City, OH 43064-0061. TEL 614-873-5471. Ed. Robert N. Converse. bk.rev.; charts; illus. circ. 3,000. (tabloid format) **Indexed:** Anthropol.Lit. **Document type:** academic/scholarly publication.

938   GW   ISSN 0474-1242
OLYMPISCHE FORSCHUNGEN. 1944. irreg., vol.26, 1997. price varies. (Deutsches Archaeologisches Institut) Walter de Gruyter und Co., Genthiner Str. 13, 10785 Berlin, Germany. TEL 49-30-26005-0. FAX 49-30-26005251. E-mail: wdg-info@degruyter.de; URL: http://www.degruyter.de. (U.S. addr.: Walter de Gruyter, Inc., 200 Saw Mill River Rd., Hawthorne, NY 10532. TEL 914-747-0110. FAX 914-747-1326) (back issues avail.) **Document type:** monographic series.
    Description: Publishes results of German archaeological research relating to Olympus and Ancient Greece.

917   CN   ISSN 0048-1742
ONTARIO ARCHAEOLOGICAL SOCIETY. ARCH NOTES. (Subscr. includes: Ontario Archaeology) bi-m. Can.$40 to individuals; institutions Can.$60 (effective 1998). Ontario Archaeological Society, 126 Willowdale Ave., North York, ON M2N 4Y2, Canada. TEL 416-730-0797. FAX 416-730-0797. Ed. Suzanne Need-Howarth. R&P contact: Ellen Blaubergs. adv. contact: Ellen Blaubergs. circ. 800. **Indexed:** Anthropol.Lit. **Document type:** newsletter.
    Description: Contains news and information of the Society and of interest to members.

917   CN   ISSN 0078-4672
                         CODEN: ONAREU
ONTARIO ARCHAEOLOGY. (Subscr. includes: Arch Notes) 1956. 2/yr. Can.$40 to individuals; institutions Can.$60 (effective 1998). Ontario Archaeological Society, 126 Willowdale Ave., North York, ON M2N 4Y2, Canada. Ed. Alexander von Gernet. R&P contact: Ellen Blaubergs. circ. 800. (back issues avail.) **Indexed:** Amer.Hist.& Life (1986-), Anthropol.Lit., Hist.Abstr. (1986-). **Document type:** academic/scholarly publication.
    Refereed Serial

OPUSCULA ATHENIENSIA. see *CLASSICAL STUDIES*

ORIENT EXPRESS; notes et nouvelles d'archeologie orientale. see *ORIENTAL STUDIES*

935   US   ISSN 0146-678X
PJ2
ORIENTAL INSTITUTE COMMUNICATIONS. 1922. irreg., vol.27, 1995. price varies. University of Chicago, Oriental Institute, 1155 E. 58th St., Chicago, IL 60637. TEL 312-702-9508. FAX 312-702-9853. illus. (back issues avail.) **Document type:** academic/scholarly publication.
    Description: Reports the progress and results of institute activities for the general reader, including archaeological expeditions and excavations.

ORIENTAL INSTITUTE MUSEUM PUBLICATIONS. see *MUSEUMS AND ART GALLERIES*

932 961   US
ORIENTAL INSTITUTE NUBIAN EXPEDITION. 1967. irreg., vol.10, 1992. price varies. University of Chicago, Oriental Institute, 1155 E. 58th St., Chicago, IL 60637. TEL 312-702-9508. FAX 312-702-9853. (back issues avail.) **Document type:** monographic series.
    Description: Presents information on archaeological materials excavated in Nubia.

ORIENTALIA. see *ORIENTAL STUDIES*

930   CN   ISSN 0702-7974
OTTAWA ARCHAEOLOGIST. 1971. 5/yr. Can.$15. Ontario Archaeological Society, Ottawa Chapter, P.O. Box 4939, Sta. E, Ottawa, Ont. K1S 5J1, Canada. TEL 819-776-8503. Eds. Helen Kriemadis, Jeff Campbell. bk.rev.; illus. circ. 80. (processed) **Document type:** newsletter.
    Formerly (until Feb. 1976): Archaic Notes (ISSN 0381-8357)
    Description: Archaeological news for members of the Society.

930.1   NE
OUDHEIDKUNDIG GENOOTSCHAP NIFTARLAKE. JAARBOEKJE. a. price varies. Uitgeverij Verloren, Larenseweg 123, 1221 CL Hilversum, Netherlands. TEL 31-35-6859856. FAX 31-35-6836557. **Document type:** academic/scholarly publication.

930.1 417.7   UK   ISSN 0309-0701
OXFORD EDITIONS OF CUNEIFORM TEXTS. 1923. irreg. price varies. Oxford University Press, Walton St., Oxford OX2 6DP, England. TEL 44-1865-56767. FAX 44-1865-56646. (Subscr. in US to: Oxford University Press Inc., 2001 Evans Rd., Cary, NC 27513. TEL 919-677-0977. FAX 919-677-1714) **Document type:** monographic series.
    Formerly: Oxford Editions of Cuneiform Inscriptions.

913   UK   ISSN 0262-5253
CC1   CODEN: OJARE2
OXFORD JOURNAL OF ARCHAEOLOGY. 1982. 3/yr. £131($275) (foreign £174) (effective 1997). Blackwell Publishers Ltd., 108 Cowley Rd., Oxford OX4 1JF, England. TEL 44-1865-791100. FAX 44-1865-791347. E-mail: jnlinfo@blackwellpublishers.co.uk; URL: http://www.blackwellpublishers.co.uk/scripts/webjrn1.idc. Ed.Bd. adv. circ. 550. (reprint service avail. from SWZ) **Indexed:** Anthropol.Lit., Art & Archaeol.Tech.Abstr., Avery Ind.Archit.Per., Br.Archaeol.Abstr., Geo.Abstr.P.G. **Document type:** academic/scholarly publication.
—BLDSC (6321.005840); SWETS; UMI; UnCover. **CCC**.
    Refereed Serial

ARCHAEOLOGY

930.1   UK
OXFORD MONOGRAPHS ON CLASSICAL ARCHAEOLOGY. irreg. price varies. Oxford University Press, Walton St., Oxford OX2 6DP, England. TEL 44-1865-56767. FAX 44-1865-56646. (Subscr. in US to: Oxford University Press Inc., 2001 Evans Rd., Cary, NC 27513. TEL 919-677-0977. FAX 919-677-1714) Ed.Bd. **Document type:** monographic series.

913 940   UK   ISSN 0308-5562
OXONIENSIA. 1936. a. £12. Oxfordshire Architectural and Historical Society, c/o Kellogg College, Rewley House, 1 Wellington Sq., Oxford OX1 2JA, England. Ed. Adrienne Rosen. R&P contact: Adrienne Rosen. bk.rev.; bibl.; charts; illus.; index. circ. 650. **Indexed:** Br.Archaeol.Abstr., Br.Hum.Ind., Geo.Abstr., Numis.Lit. **Document type:** academic/scholarly publication.

930.1   US   ISSN 0270-6776
P C A S NEWSLETTER. 1961. m. $10 (foreign $14) (effective June 1997). Pacific Coast Archaeological Society, Inc., Box 10926, Costa Mesa, CA 92627-0926. circ. 200. **Indexed:** Abstr.Anthropol. **Document type:** newsletter.
   Formerly (until Feb. 1978): Smoke Signals.

930.1   US   ISSN 0552-7252
E78.C15
PACIFIC COAST ARCHAEOLOGICAL SOCIETY QUARTERLY. 1965. q. $32 (foreign $41) (effective 1996 & 1997). Pacific Coast Archaeological Society, Inc., Box 10926, Costa Mesa, CA 92627-0926. bibl.; circ. 200 (paid). **Indexed:** Abstr.Anthropol., Amer.Hist.& Life (1986-1996), Anthropol.Lit., Cal.Per.Ind. (1978-), Hist.Abstr. (1986-1996). **Document type:** academic/scholarly publication.

913 500   BE   ISSN 0779-5661
PACT. 1977. irreg. (4-5/yr.), vol.45, 1995. price varies. European Study Group on Physical, Chemical and Mathematical Techniques Applied to Archaeology, c/o Tony Hackens, Ed., 28a Av. Leopold, B-1330 Rixensart, Belgium. TEL 32-10-474880. FAX 32-2-6530015. E-mail: hackens@arka.ucl/ac.be. Ed. Tony Hackens. bk.rev. circ. 1,000. **Indexed:** Anthropol.Lit., Chem.Abstr., GeoRef. **Document type:** academic/scholarly publication, proceedings.
   Description: Promotes the use of science and the development of scientific techniques in the study of cultural heritage.

930.1   IT   ISSN 0393-0149
PADUSA. (Text in English, Italian) 1965. a. L.50000($30.40) (effective 1997). Centro Polesano di Studi Storici, Archeologici ed Etnografici, Casella Postale 106, Piazza S. Bortolo 18, 45100 Rovigo, Italy. TEL 39-425-21021. Ed. Paolo Bellintani. abstr.; bibl. circ. 2,000. **Document type:** academic/scholarly publication.

571   PK   ISSN 0078-7868
DS378
PAKISTAN ARCHAEOLOGY. (Text in English) 1964. a. price varies. Department of Archaeology and Museums, 27-A Central Union Commercial Area, Shaheed-e-Millat Rd., Karachi 8, Pakistan. **Indexed:** Anthropol.Lit. **Document type:** academic/scholarly publication.

930.1 570   NE   ISSN 0552-9344
CC1   CODEN: PLHIAV
PALAEOHISTORIA; acta et communicationes instituti bioarchaeologici universitatis groningianae. (Text in Dutch, English) 1951. a., vol.35-36, 1995 (for the years 1993-1994). price varies. (Rijksuniversiteit Groningen, Biologisch- Archaeologisch Instituut) A.A. Balkema, P.O. Box 1675, 3000 BR Rotterdam, Netherlands. TEL 31-10-4145822. FAX 31-10-4135947. E-mail: sales@balkema.nl; URL: http://www.jcn.nl/ima/balkema/. (Dist. in U.S. by: Ashgate Publishing Co., Old Post Rd., Brookfield, VT 05036. TEL 800-535-9544. FAX 802-276-3837) (back issues avail.) **Indexed:** IBR, Zoo.Rec. **Document type:** academic/scholarly publication.
   —BLDSC (6343.460000). **CCC.**

220.9 933   NE   ISSN 0920-7422
PALAESTINA ANTIQUA. (Text in English, German) 1982. irreg., vol.8, 1994. price varies. Kok Pharos Publishing House, Postbus 5016, 8260 GA Kampen, Netherlands. TEL 31-38-3392565. FAX 31-38-3328912. E-mail: jhkok@pi.net; URL: http://www.kokkampen.com. illus.; maps. (back issues avail.) **Document type:** monographic series.
   Description: Scholarly studies of topics in the history and archaeology of ancient Palestine and neighboring areas.

913 956   UK   ISSN 0031-0328
PALESTINE EXPLORATION QUARTERLY. 1869. s-a. £25($50) to individuals; institutions £30($60). Palestine Exploration Fund, 2 Hinde Mews, London W1M 5RR, England. Ed. Dr. G.I. Davies. adv.; bk.rev.; illus.; index, cum.index every 2 yrs. circ. 900. (back issues avail.) **Indexed:** A.I.C.P., Abstr.Anthropol., Art Ind., Bibl.Ling., Br.Hum.Ind., IBR, Mid.East: Abstr.& Ind., New Test.Abstr., Numis.Lit., Old Test.Abstr., Rel.& Theol.Abstr. (1968-), Rel.Ind.One, Rel.Per. **Document type:** academic/scholarly publication.
   —BLDSC (6345.360000); KR SourceOne; SWETS; UnCover.

939.39   PL   ISSN 0209-0015
PALMYRE. (Text in French) 1960. irreg., no.8, 1984. $42 per issue. Polska Akademia Nauk, Zaklad Archeologii Srodziemnomorskiej, Palac Kultury i Nauki, p. 2105, 00-901 Warsaw, Poland. TEL 48-22-6248593. FAX 48-22-6207651. (Dist. by: Osrodek Rozpowszechniania Wydawnictw Naukowych PAN - Export, Palac Kultury i Nauki, 00-901 Warsaw, Poland. FAX 48-22-8268670) Ed. Michal Gawlikowski. illus. (back issues avail.) **Document type:** monographic series.
   Description: Presents excavation results of Polish Archaeological Mission at Palmyra, Syria.
   Refereed Serial

913   XR   ISSN 0031-0506
PAMATKY ARCHEOLOGICKE/ARCHAEOLOGICAL MONUMENTS. (Supplement avail.) (Text in Czech and German; summaries in English, French, German, Russian, Spanish) 1854. s-a. DM.300. Ceska Akademie Ved, Archeologicky Ustav, Letenska 4, 118 01 Prague 1, Czech Republic. TEL 42-2-539351. (Dist. in Western countries by: Kubon & Sagner, P.O. Box 341018, 80328 Munich, Germany) Ed. Jan Fridrich. bk.rev.; charts; illus.; maps. **Indexed:** A.I.C.P., Anthropol.Lit. **Document type:** academic/scholarly publication.
   Description: Basic studies of evolution in the prehistorical and earlier historical era; methodical articles of a general nature; studies dealing with recent research as well as museum collections.

PAM'IYATKY UKRAINY. see *HISTORY — History Of Europe*

PAMYATNIKI KUL'TURY. NOVYE OTKRYTIYA/MONUMENTS OF CULTURE. NEW DISCOVERIES. see *ART*

930.26   PL   ISSN 0137-2831
PANSTWOWE MUZEUM ARCHEOLOGICZNE. MATERIALY STAROZYTNE I WCZESNOSREDNIOWIECZNE. 1971. irreg. Wydawnictwa Akcydensowe, Ul. Dluga 52, 00-241 Warsaw, Poland. TEL 48-22-313221. FAX 48-22-315195. adv. contact: Wojciech Brzezinski. (back issues avail.) **Indexed:** A.I.C.P. **Document type:** academic/scholarly publication.
   Formed by the merger of (1949-1971): Panstwowe Muzeum Archeologiczne. Materialy Wczesnosredniowieczne (ISSN 0465-3580); (1956-1971): Panstwowe Muzeum Archeologiczne. Materialy Starozytne (ISSN 0543-0739)

932   BE   ISSN 0078-9402
PAPYROLOGICA BRUXELLENSIA. 1962. irreg., no.28, 1997. Fondation Egyptologique Reine Elisabeth, Parc du Cinquantenaire 10, 1000 Brussels, Belgium. TEL 32-2-7417364. **Document type:** monographic series.

913   VC
PAPYROLOGICA CASTROCTAVIANA. 1967. irreg., no.12, 1988. price varies. (Pontificio Istituto Biblico) Biblical Institute Press, Piazza della Pilotta 35, 00187 Rome, Italy. TEL 39-6-678-15-67. FAX 39-6-678-05-88. **Document type:** academic/scholarly publication.
   Description: Publishes previously unedited papyri and research on related subjects.

PAPYROLOGY AND HISTORICAL PERSPECTIVES. see *HISTORY*

PAS-DU-CALAIS. COMMISSION DEPARTEMENTALE D'HISTOIRE ET D'ARCHEOLOGIE. MEMOIRES. see *HISTORY — History Of Europe*

PATMA-BANASIRAKAN ANDES. see *HISTORY — History Of Europe*

PAYS BAS-NORMAND. see *HISTORY — History Of Europe*

PAYS LORRAIN. see *HISTORY — History Of Europe*

930.1   US
PEABODY MUSEUM BULLETINS. 1976. irreg., no.5, 1996. price varies. Peabody Museum of Archaeology and Ethnology, Harvard University, 11 Divinity Ave., Cambridge, MA 02138. TEL 617-495-3938. FAX 617-495-7535. (Dist. by: University Museum Publications, University of Pennsylvania, 33rd & Spruce Sts., Philadelphia, PA 19104. TEL 215-898-4124) **Document type:** bulletin.

930.1 572   US   ISSN 0079-029X
PEABODY MUSEUM OF ARCHAEOLOGY AND ETHNOLOGY. MEMOIRS. (Vols. not issued consecutively) 1896. irreg., vol.17, 1990. price varies. Peabody Museum of Archaeology and Ethnology, Harvard University, 11 Divinity Ave., Cambridge, MA 02138. TEL 617-495-3938. FAX 617-495-7535. (Dist. by: University Museum Publications, University of Pennsylvania, 33rd & Spruce Sts., Philadelphia, PA 19104. TEL 215-898-4124) **Document type:** monographic series.

930.1   US
PEABODY MUSEUM OF ARCHAEOLOGY AND ETHNOLOGY. MONOGRAPHS. 1974. irreg., vol.7, 1983. price varies. Peabody Museum of Archaeology and Ethnology, Harvard University, 11 Divinity Ave., Cambridge, MA 02138. TEL 617-495-3938. FAX 617-495-7535. (Dist. by: University Museum Publications, University of Pennsylvania, 33rd & Spruce Sts., Philadelphia, PA 19104. TEL 215-898-4124) **Document type:** monographic series.

930.1 572   US   ISSN 0079-0303
E51   CODEN: HPAEAQ
PEABODY MUSEUM OF ARCHAEOLOGY AND ETHNOLOGY. PAPERS. (Vols. not issued consecutively) 1891. irreg., vol.82, 1995. price varies. Peabody Museum of Archaeology and Ethnology, Harvard University, 11 Divinity Ave., Cambridge, MA 02138. TEL 617-495-3938. FAX 617-495-7535. (Dist. by: University Museum Publications, University of Pennsylvania, 33rd & Spruce Sts., Philadelphia, PA 19104. TEL 215-898-4124) **Indexed:** Anthropol.Lit., Biol.Abstr., GeoRef. **Document type:** monographic series.
—Linda Hall.

PERITIA. see *HISTORY — History Of Europe*

PERSICA. see *HISTORY — History Of Asia*

917   US
PERSPECTIVES IN CALIFORNIA ARCHAEOLOGY. 1991. irreg. price varies. University of California at Los Angeles, Institute of Archaeology, 405 Hilgard Ave., Los Angeles, CA 90024-1510. TEL 213-825-7411. FAX 213-206-4723. Ed. Jeanne E. Arnold. **Document type:** academic/scholarly publication.
   Description: Covers the prehistoric and historic archaeology of California, including theoretical contributions, methodological or technical studies, regional or chronological themes, and interpretation of excavation data.

ARCHAEOLOGY

938 720   NE   ISSN 1380-2240
DF10
PHAROS. (Text in English, French) N.S. 1993. a. fl.75 (effective 1994). (Netherlands Institute at Athens) J.C. Gieben, Nieuwe Herengracht 35, 1011 RM Amsterdam, Netherlands. TEL 31-20-6275170. FAX 31-20-6275170. (Dist. in N. America by: John Benjamins Publishing Co., Box 27519, Philadelphia, PA 19118-0519. TEL 215-836-1200. FAX 215-836-1204) Eds. J.J. Feije, J.J. Hekman. (back issues avail.) Document type: academic/scholarly publication.
   Formerly (until 1993): Netherlands Institute at Athens. Newsletter.
   Description: Publishes reports of Dutch archaeological and other researches in Greece.

913 950   NE   ISSN 0031-8329
PHOENIX. (Text in Dutch and English) 1955. s-a. price varies. Vooraziatisch-Egyptisch Genootschap "Ex Oriente Lux", Postbus 9515, 2300 RA Leiden, Netherlands. Ed. L.M.J. Zonhoven. adv.; illus. circ. 1,400. Indexed: IBR, Phil.Ind.
—SWETS.
   Description: Focuses on recent discoveries in the Ancient Near East and Egypt.

PIRRADAZISH: BULLETIN OF ACHAEMENIAN STUDIES.
see HISTORY — History Of The Near East

PLAINS ANTHROPOLOGIST; a medium for the anthropological interpretation of the Plains area in the United States. see ANTHROPOLOGY

PLATON. see CLASSICAL STUDIES

943.8 913   PL   ISSN 0079-3256
GN705.P6
POLSKA AKADEMIA NAUK. ODDZIAL W KRAKOWIE. KOMISJA ARCHEOLOGICZNA. PRACE. (Text in English, German and Polish; summaries in English, German and Russian) 1960. irreg., no.28, 1990. price varies. Polska Akademia Nauk, Oddzial w Krakowie, Komisja Archeologiczna, Ul. Slawkowska 17, 31-016 Krakow, Poland. TEL 48-12-224853. FAX 48-12-222791. Document type: monographic series.
—KNAW.

930.1   SW   ISSN 0281-014X
POPULAER ARKEOLOGI. 1983. q. SEK 185 in Sweden; other Nordic countries SEK 200; elsewhere SEK 225 (effective 1997). F H T Norrgaarde AB, Norrgaarde Hellvi, S-620 34 Laerbro, Sweden. TEL 46-8-651-28-29. E-mail: birgitta_gustafson@gotlandica.se. Ed. Birgitta Gustafson. adv.; bk.rev. circ. 4,000. (also avail. in audio cassette)

913   US   ISSN 1046-3437
CC1
POPULAR ARCHAEOLOGY. bi-m. $16.75 includes American Archaeologist. Life & Lettres Publishers, Inc., Box 11256, Alexandria, VA 22312. Ed. W. Jack Hranicky. adv.; illus. circ. 7,700. (also avail. in microfilm from UMI; reprint service avail. from UMI) Indexed: Br.Archaeol.Abstr.

POSITIONS FOR CLASSICISTS & ARCHAEOLOGISTS. see OCCUPATIONS AND CAREERS

913   UK   ISSN 0079-4236
DA90
POST-MEDIEVAL ARCHAEOLOGY. 1967. a. (plus 2 updates). £15($30) to individuals; institutions £24($48). Society for Post-Medieval Archaeology, c/o Dr. Paul Courtney, 20 Lytton Rd., Leicester LE2 1WJ, England. TEL 44-1533-707999. Ed. John Kenyon. bk.rev.; cum.index: vols. 1-5, 6-10. circ. 650. (back issues avail.) Indexed: Abstr.Anthropol., Br.Archaeol.Abstr., Numis.Lit., RILA. Document type: academic/scholarly publication.
—BLDSC (6558.900000); UnCover.
   Refereed Serial

913   US   ISSN 0738-8020
POTTERY SOUTHWEST; news, queries & views on archaeological ceramics by Southwesternists. 1974. q. $4 in US & Canada (elsewhere $5). Albuquerque Archaeological Society, 6207 Mossman Place, N.E., Albuquerque, NM 87110. Ed. Eric Blinman. illus. Indexed: Anthropol.Lit. Document type: academic/scholarly publication.

POWER PLACES OF CALIFORNIA. see EARTH SCIENCES — Geophysics

913   PL   ISSN 0137-3250
POZNANSKIE TOWARZYSTWO PRZYJACIOL NAUK. KOMISJA ARCHEOLOGICZNA. PRACE. (Text in Polish; summaries in English, German) 1922. irreg., vol. 13, 1995. Poznanskie Towarzystwo Przyjaciol Nauk, Komisja Archeologiczna, Ul. Mielzynskiego 27-29, 61-725 Poznan, Poland. (Dist. by Ars Polona, Krakowskie Przedmiescie 7, 00-068 Warsaw, Poland) Ed.Bd. circ. 420. Indexed: Chem.Abstr. Document type: monographic series.

913   GW   ISSN 0079-4848
PRAEHISTORISCHE ZEITSCHRIFT. 1909. a. DM.279 (foreign DM.282) (effective 1998). Walter De Gruyter und Co., Genthiner Str. 13, 10785 Berlin, Germany. TEL 49-30-26005-0. FAX 49-30-26005251. E-mail: wdg-info@degruyter.de; URL: http://www.degruyter.de. (U.S. addr.: 200 Saw Mill River Rd., Hawthorne, NY 10532. TEL 914-747-0110) Ed.Bd. adv.; bk.rev.; cum.index: vols.1-55 in 1985. circ. 550. Indexed: A.I.C.P., Anthropol.Lit., Br.Archaeol.Abstr., IBR. Document type: academic/scholarly publication.
—BLDSC (6598.300000); SWETS. **CCC.**

930.1   BE   ISSN 0779-8024
PREHISTOIRE EUROPEENNE/EUROPEAN PREHISTORY. (Text in English, French, German) 1992. s-a. 1100 BEF. Universite de Liege, Service de Prehistoire, Place du 20 Aout, 7, bat. A1, 4000 Liege, Belgium. TEL 32-4-3665341. FAX 32-4-3665551. E-mail: prehist@ulg.ac.be; URL: http://www.ulg.ac.be/prehist/. Ed. Marcel Otte; Pub. Marcel Otte. adv. contact: Sylvia Menendez. bk.rev.; illus. Document type: bulletin, newsletter.
—BLDSC (6605.167300).
   Description: Provides rapid publication of information on prehistoric civilizations on the European continent, including supra-regional comparisons and historical and anthropological interpretations.

930.1   US   ISSN 1075-4288
PREHISTORIC ANTIQUITIES & ARCHAEOLOGICAL NEWS QUARTERLY. 1981. q. $16 (effective 1996); newsstand price: $6. Prehistoric Antiquities, 7045 E. Rte. 245, Box 296, North Lewisburg, OH 43060. TEL 513-747-2225. Ed. B. Ballinger. adv.: page $130; trim 8 1/2 x 11. bk.rev.; circ. 3,000 (paid). (back issues avail.) Document type: consumer publication.
   Description: Includes calendar of events, sources, books, and articles.

913   UK   ISSN 0079-497X
GN700
PREHISTORIC SOCIETY, LONDON. PROCEEDINGS. 1911. a. £25 to individuals; institutions £38 (effective 1997). Prehistoric Society, Institute of Archaeology, 31-34 Gordon Sq., London WC1H 0PY, England. Ed. Julie Gardiner. R&P contact: T. Gingell. adv.; bk.rev. circ. 2,000. Indexed: A.I.C.P., Anthropol.Lit., Art & Archaeol.Tech.Abstr., Br.Archaeol.Abstr., Br.Hum.Ind., Ecol.Abstr., Geo.Abstr., NAA, Numis.Lit., SSCI. Document type: proceedings.
—BLDSC (6787.760000).
   Refereed Serial

PRESERVATION NOTES. see ARCHITECTURE

914 330.1 949.7   BN   ISSN 0350-1159
PRILOZI/CONTRIBUTIONS. 1965. a. 2000 din.($5) Institut za Istoriju Sarajevo - Institute of History in Sarajevo, Djure Djakovica 9, 71000 Sarajevo, Bosnia Hercegovina. TEL 038 71-38899. bk.rev. circ. 500. (also avail. in microfilm; back issues avail.) Indexed: Bibl.Ling.

PRINCETON MONOGRAPHS IN ART AND ARCHAEOLOGY.
see ART

PRINCETON UNIVERSITY. ART MUSEUM. RECORD. see MUSEUMS AND ART GALLERIES

913   AU   ISSN 0478-3166
PRO AUSTRIA ROMANA. 1951. 4/yr. S.100 (foreign S.150) (effective 1997). Oesterreichisches Archaeologisches Institut, Institut fuer Klassische Archaeologie, Universitaet Graz, Universitaetsplatz 3, A-8010 Graz, Austria. TEL 43-316-3802386. FAX 43-316-3809026. E-mail: erwin.pochmarski@kfunigraz.ac.at. (Co-sponsor: Oesterreichische Gesellschaft fuer Ur- und Fruehgeschichte) Ed. Erwin Pochmarski. bibl.; illus. Document type: newsletter.
   Description: Contains reports on recent excavations of Roman times in the territory of Austria.

913   RU   ISSN 0135-8316
PROBLEMY ARKHEOLOGII I ETNOGRAFII. 1977. irreg. 0.73 Rub. per no. Sankt-Peterburgskii Universitet, Universitetskaya Nab. 7-9, St. Petersburg V-164, Russia. circ. 1,185. Document type: academic/scholarly publication.

PROSPETTIVA; rivista di storia dell'arte antica e moderna. see ART

572   IT   ISSN 0079-7022
CC75
PROSPEZIONI ARCHEOLOGICHE/ARCHAEOLOGICAL PROSPECTION. (Text and summaries mainly in English and Italian) 1966-1977; resumed N.S. 1990. a. Fondazione Carlo M. Lerici, Via V. Veneto 108, 00187 Rome, Italy. (Subscr. to: Edizioni Et, Corso Indipendenza 12, 20129 Milan, Italy, FAX: 392-70100137) Eds. L. Cavagnaro Vanoni, M. Cucarzi. adv.; bk.rev. circ. 400. (back issues avail.) Indexed: Anthropol.Lit., Br.Archaeol.Abstr.

913   PL   ISSN 0079-7138
PRZEGLAD ARCHEOLOGICZNY. (Text in English and Polish; summaries in English and German) 1919. a. price varies. Polska Akademia Nauk, Instytut Historii Kultury Materialnej, Al. Solidarnosci 105, 00-140 Warsaw, Poland. (Dist. by: Ars Polona-Ruch, Krakowskie Przedmiescie 7, Warsaw, Poland) Ed. Tadeusz Wislanski. bk.rev. circ. 500. Indexed: A.I.C.P., Anthropol.Lit., Br.Archaeol.Abstr.
—BLDSC (6938.820000).
   Description: Papers on material culture in Poland and Europe.

PURABHILEKH - PURATATVA/ARCHIVES - ARCHAEOLOGY. see HISTORY — History Of Asia

PUTEOLI; studi di storia antica. see HISTORY — History Of Europe

571   SP   ISSN 0079-8215
PYRENAE: CRONICA ARQUEOLOGICA; annual scientific journal. 1965. a. 2000 ptas.($6) (effective 1993). Universidad de Barcelona, Facultad de Geografia y Historia, Instituto de Arqueologia, Avenido de Jose Antonio 585, Barcelona 7, Spain. TEL 3-333-34-66. FAX 3-449-85-10. Ed. Juan Maluquer de Motes. bk.rev. circ. 600. Indexed: Amer.Hist.& Life, Anthropol.Lit., Hist.Abstr., Numis.Lit. Document type: academic/scholarly publication.
—CINDOC.

933   IS   ISSN 0333-5844
QEDEM. (Text in English) 1970. irreg., vol.34, 1993. price varies. Hebrew University of Jerusalem, Institute of Archaeology, Jerusalem, Israel. (Subscr. to: Israel Exploration Society, P.O. Box 7041, Jerusalem 91070, Israel. TEL 972-2-257991. FAX 972-2-247772) Ed. Sue Gorodetsky. circ. 1,550. (back issues avail.) Document type: academic/scholarly publication, monographic series.
   Description: Scholarly studies and excavation reports on the archaeology of Israel, and related topics pertaining to the Middle East, including numismatics, architecture and prehistoric sites.

913   IT   ISSN 0079-8258
QUADERNI DI ARCHEOLOGIA DELLA LIBIA. 1950. irreg., vol.17, 1994. price varies. L'Erma di Bretschneider, Via Cassiodoro, 19, 00193 Rome, Italy. TEL 39-6-6874127. FAX 39-6-6874129. Indexed: Avery Ind.Archit.Per.

913 526   IT   ISSN 1122-0953
QUADERNI DI TOPOGRAFIA ANTICA. irreg., no.10, 1988. price varies. (Universita degli Studi di Roma La Sapienza) Casa Editrice Leo S. Olschki, Casella Postale 66, 50100 Florence, Italy. TEL 39-55-6530684. FAX 39-55-6530214. E-mail: celso@olschki.it. Document type: monographic series.

930.1   IT   ISSN 1122-7133
QUADERNI FRIULANI DI ARCHEOLOGIA. 1991. a. $15 (foreign $20). Societa Friulana di Archeologia, c/o Civici Musei, 33100 Castello di Udine, Italy. TEL 39-432-26560. E-mail: saccavini@udprvx.fisica.univa.it. Ed. Maurizio Buora; Pub. Massimo Lavarone. R&P contact: Andrea Pessina. bk.rev. circ. 1,100. Document type: academic/scholarly publication.
   Description: Covers archaeology in north-east Italy and Alpine region.
   Refereed Serial

ARCHAEOLOGY

914 946   SP   ISSN 0211-142X
QUADERNS D'HISTORIA TARRACONENSE. 1977. irreg. price varies. Institut d'Estudis Tarraconenses Ramon Berenguer IV, Seccio d'Arqueologia i Historia, Santa Anna, 8, Tarragona, Spain. TEL 235032. Ed. F. Xavier Ricoma. **Document type:** bulletin.
—CINDOC.

913.031   GW   ISSN 0375-7471
QE696   CODEN: QURTBJ
QUARTAER; Jahrbuch fuer Erforschung des Eiszeitalters und der Steinzeit. (Text in English, French and German) 1946. a. price varies. (Hugo-Obermaier-Gesellschaft) Saarbruecker Druckerei und Verlag GmbH, Halbergstr. 3, 66121 Saarbruecken, Germany. TEL 49-681-66501-0. FAX 49-681-6650110. Ed.Bd. bk.rev. circ. 2,000. (reprint service avail. from UMI) **Indexed:** A.I.C.P., Anthropol.Lit., Br.Archaeol.Abstr., GeoRef. **Document type:** academic/scholarly publication.
—BLDSC (7169.500000).

913 930   GW   ISSN 0079-9149
QUELLENSCHRIFTEN ZUR WESTDEUTSCHEN VOR- UND FRUEHGESCHICHTE. 1939. irreg., no.10, 1982. price varies. Dr. Rudolf Habelt GmbH, Am Buchenhang 1, 53115 Bonn, Germany. TEL 49-228-9238322. FAX 49-228-923836. Ed. R. Stampfuss. **Document type:** monographic series.

930.1   FR
RAS SHAMRA-OUGARIT. (Text in English, French) 1983. irreg. price varies. Editions Recherche sur les Civilisations, 28 rue de Bourgogne, 75007 Paris, France. TEL 33-1-40628062. FAX 33-1-40628071. Ed. Hina Descat; Pub. Hina Descat. circ. 600. **Document type:** monographic series.

930.1   IT
RASSEGNA DI ARCHEOLOGIA. a. L.50000 (effective 1997). Edizioni all'Insegna del Giglio s.a.s., Via R. Giuliani 152r., Florence, Italy. TEL 39-55-451593. FAX 39-55-450030.

RAYDAN; journal of ancient Yemeni antiquities and epigraphy. see *HISTORY — History Of The Near East*

READING THE PAST. see *LINGUISTICS*

900   IS   ISSN 0792-4224
READINGS IN GLASS HISTORY. (Text in English) 1973. irreg., vol.24, 1994. price varies. Phoenix Publications Jerusalem, P.O. Box 8190, Jerusalem, Israel. TEL 972-2-633266. FAX 972-2-690460. Ed. Anita Engle. illus.; maps; index. cum.index: vols.1-8 in vol.9. circ. 1,000. (back issues avail.) **Document type:** monographic series.
—BLDSC (7302.125000).
Description: Scholarly monographs on topics in the history of glass vessels and beads, and the glass industries, with a focus on the ancient, medieval and pre-modern Middle East up to the rise of the Venetian glass industries.

913   US
READINGS IN LONG ISLAND ARCHAEOLOGY AND ETHNOHISTORY SERIES. 1977. a. price varies. Suffolk County Archaeological Association, Box 1542, Stony Brook, NY 11790-0910. TEL 516-929-8725. Ed. Gaynell Stone. illus. circ. 1,000. (back issues avail.) **Document type:** academic/scholarly publication.

913   SP   ISSN 0034-0863
REAL SOCIEDAD ARQUEOLOGICA. BOLETIN ARQUEOLOGICO. (Text mainly in Spanish) 1901. a. $10. Real Sociedad Arqueologica Tarraconense, Museo Nacional Arqueologico, Tarragona, Spain. (Subscr. to: Apartado 573, Tarragona, Spain) Ed. Rodolfo Cortes. bk.rev.; abstr.; illus.; circ. 1,000 (controlled).
—CINDOC.

RECHERCHES AMERINDIENNES AU QUEBEC. see *ANTHROPOLOGY*

914   BE
RECHERCHES ARCHEOLOGIQUES EN HAINAUT OCCIDENTAL. BILAN. (Text in French) 1972. every 5 yrs. Cercle Royal d'Histoire et d'Archeologie d'Ath et de la Region et Musees Athois, 13, rue de la Poterne, 7800 Ath, Belgium. **Document type:** catalog.

932 892.7   UA   ISSN 1011-1883
RECHERCHES D'ARCHEOLOGIE, DE PHILOLOGIE ET D'HISTOIRE. (Text in French) 1930. irreg., vol.31, 1986. price varies. Institut Francais d'Archeologie Orientale du Caire, P.O. Box 11562 Kasr-el-Aini, 37 Sharia Sheikh Aly Youssef, Mounira, Cairo, Egypt. TEL 20-2-3571622. FAX 20-2-3544635. E-mail: mcmichael@fao.eg-net.net. (Dist. by: Boustany's Publishing House, 29 Faggalah St., 11271 Cairo, Egypt. TEL 20-2-5915315. FAX 20-2-4177915) (back issues avail.) **Document type:** monographic series.
Description: Scholarly studies of topics relating to the history, archaeology and linguistics of Egypt from Pharaonic to modern time, and other parts of the Islamic world.

913   US
REDISCOVERY; journal of archaeology. 1968. a. $4.95. Illinois Association for Advancement of Archaeology, c/o Ellis J. Neiburger, Ed., 1000 North Ave., Waukegan, IL 60085. adv.; bk.rev. circ. 750.

915   CC   ISSN 1004-6275
DS715
RELICS FROM SOUTH. (Text in Chinese) q. $12. Jiangxi Sheng Bowuguan - Jiangxi Provincial Museum, No. 95, Bayi Dadao, Nanchang, Jiangxi 330003, People's Republic of China. TEL 0791-63531. Peng Shifan. adv.; bk.rev. circ. 2,500. **Document type:** academic/scholarly publication, government publication.
Formerly (until 1992): Jiangxi Cultural Relics.

RELIGIONS IN THE GRAECO-ROMAN WORLD. see *RELIGIONS AND THEOLOGY*

REPORTS IN MACKINAC HISTORY AND ARCHAEOLOGY. see *HISTORY — History Of North And South America*

913.031   UK   ISSN 0950-5830
RESCUE NEWS. 1972. 3/yr. £12 to individuals; libraries £15 (effective 1996-1997). Rescue British Archaeological Trust, 15a Bull Plain, Hertford, Herts SG14 1DX, England. TEL 44-1992-553377. Ed. N. Crummy. adv.; bk.rev.; bibl.; illus. circ. 1,500. (tabloid format) **Indexed:** Br.Archaeol.Abstr. **Document type:** newspaper.
Description: Comment and opinion on archaeological issues.

RESTAURACION HOY. see *ART*

913   GW   ISSN 0232-2609
RESTAURIERUNG UND MUSEUMSTECHNIK. 1976. irreg. price varies. Museum fuer Ur- und Fruehgeschichte Thueringens, Humboldtstr. 11, 99423 Weimar, Germany. Ed. R. Feustel.

930.1   US   ISSN 1050-4877
THE REVIEW OF ARCHAEOLOGY. 1980. s-a. $18 (effective Fall 1995). Review of Archaeology, Inc., 10 Liberty St., Salem, MA 01970. TEL 508-745-1876. FAX 508-745-8303. Ed. Frederick Hadleigh West. R&P contact: Margaret A. Dorsey. bk.rev. **Document type:** academic/scholarly publication.
—UnCover.
Formerly (until 1989): Quarterly Review of Archaeology (ISSN 0278-9825)
Description: Review of archaeological literature providing a critical evaluation of the many kinds of records that affect the conduct of archaeology and the interpretation of prehistory.
Refereed Serial

REVIEW OF SCOTTISH CULTURE. see *ETHNIC INTERESTS*

913   BL   ISSN 0102-0420
REVISTA DE ARQUEOLOGIA. 1983. s-a. $10. Museu Paraense Emilio Goeldi, Setor de Difusao Cientifica e Cultural, C.P. 339, 66.000 Belem, Para, Brazil.

930.1   SP   ISSN 0212-0062
CC13.S66
REVISTA DE ARQUEOLOGIA. 1980. m. 8500 ptas. (Europe $125; America & Africa $145). Zugarto Ediciones, S.A., Pablo Aranda, 3, 28006 Madrid, Spain. TEL 411-42-64. FAX 562-26-77. Ed. Rafael Tauler Fesser.
—CINDOC.

918   MX   ISSN 0188-3631
E61
REVISTA DE ARQUEOLOGIA MEXICANA. (Text in English, French, Portuguese, Spanish) 1990. s-a. n. & C. America $38; S. America & Europe $43; Asia $48 (effective 1997). Instituto Panamericano de Geografia e Historia - Pan American Institute of Geography and History, Ex-Arzobispado 29, Col. Observatorio, Deleg. Miguel Hidalgo, 11860 Mexico, D.F., Mexico. TEL 52-5-2775888. FAX 52-5-2716271. E-mail: ipgh@laneta.apc.org. (Subscr. to: IPGH, Depto. de Distribucion y Ventas, Apdo. 18879, 11870 Mexico DF, Mexico) Ed. Oscar Fonseca. circ. 700. (also avail. in microfilm from UMI; reprint service avail. from UMI) **Document type:** academic/scholarly publication.

REVISTA DE HISTORIA. see *HISTORY*

913   FR   ISSN 0035-0737
CC3
REVUE ARCHEOLOGIQUE. 1844. s-a. 490 F. to individuals (foreign 580 F.); agencies 441 F. (foreign 522 F.) (effective 1998). Presses Universitaires de France, Departement des Revues, 14 av. du Bois-de-l'Epine, 91003 Evry Cedex, France. TEL 33-1-60778205. FAX 33-1-60792045. TELEX PUF 600 474 F. Dir. Christian le Roy. bk.rev.; charts; illus.; index. (also avail. in microform from UMI; reprint service avail. from KTO,UMI) **Indexed:** Art Ind., Avery Ind.Archit.Per., Biol.Abstr., RILA, SSCI. **Document type:** academic/scholarly publication.
—KR SourceOne; SWETS; UMI. **CCC.**
Description: Publishes recent studies on the Greco-Roman times, the Bronze Age, and the start of the Middle Ages.

930.1   FR   ISSN 1154-1342
REVUE ARCHEOLOGIQUE DE BORDEAUX. 1894. a. 145 F. to individuals; students 100 F. Societe Archeologique de Bordeaux, Hotel des Societes Savantes, 1, place Bardineau, 33000 Bordeaux, France. TEL 56-44-48-18. **Indexed:** Numis.Lit.
Former titles (until 1989): Societe Archeologique de Bordeaux (ISSN 0995-0761); (until 1985): Societe Archeologique de Bordeaux. Bulletin et Memoires (ISSN 0755-7051); (until 1917): Societe Archeologique de Bordeaux (ISSN 1155-6471)

913   FR   ISSN 0035-0745
DC30
REVUE ARCHEOLOGIQUE DE L'EST ET DU CENTRE-EST. (Supplement avail. (ISSN 0220-7796)) 1950. biennial. price varies. (Centre National de la Recherche Scientifique) C N R S Editions, 20-22 rue St. Amand, 75015 Paris, France. TEL 45-33-16-00. FAX 45-33-92-13. TELEX 200 356 F. Ed. Claude Rolley. adv.; bk.rev.; bibl.; illus.; index; circ. 1,500 (controlled). (also avail. in microform) **Indexed:** Anthropol.Lit., Arts & Hum.Cit.Ind., Avery Ind.Archit.Per., Br.Archaeol.Abstr., Curr.Cont., Numis.Lit., SSCI. **Document type:** academic/scholarly publication.

913   FR
REVUE ARCHEOLOGIQUE DE L'EST ET DU CENTRE-EST. SUPPLEMENT. (Supplement to: Revue Archeologique de l'Est et du Centre-Est (ISSN 0035-0737)) a. price varies. (Centre National de la Recherche Scientifique) C N R S Editions, 20-22 rue St. Amand, 75015 Paris, France. TEL 45-33-16-00. FAX 45-33-92-13. TELEX 200 356 F. adv.; bk.rev.; index. circ. 1,250. **Document type:** academic/scholarly publication.

914   FR   ISSN 0767-709X
DC609.4
REVUE ARCHEOLOGIQUE DE L'OUEST. 1984. a. 172 F. (effective 1997). Association R.A.O., c/o Laboratoire d'Archeometrie, Universite de Rennes, 35042 Rennes Cedex, France. TEL 33-2-99286070. FAX 33-2-99286934. Ed. Laurent Monnier; Pub. Loic Langouet. R&P contact: Loic Langouet. adv. contact: Loic Langouet. bk.rev. (back issues avail.) **Indexed:** Anthropol.Lit. **Document type:** bulletin.
Description: Studies the archeology of the west of France: Brittany, Normandy and the Loire country.

930.1   FR   ISSN 0752-5656
WMLC 93-4387   CODEN: RAPCE2
REVUE ARCHEOLOGIQUE DE PICARDIE. 1982. q. Societe des Antiquites Historiques de Picardie, 5 rue H. Daussy, 80000 Amiens, France.
—BLDSC (7891.121000).

ARCHAEOLOGY

913   DC30   FR   ISSN 0220-6617
REVUE ARCHEOLOGIQUE DU CENTRE DE LA FRANCE. 1961. a. 290 F. (foreign 320 F.)(effective 1997). (Ministere de la Culture) Editions la Simarre, Z.I. No. 2 - rue Joseph-Cugnot, 37300 Joue-les-Tours, France. TEL 33-2-47535366. FAX 33-2-47674505. Ed. Henri Galinie. bk.rev.; abstr.; bibl.; charts; illus.; index, cum.index every 10 yrs.
—BLDSC (7891.105000).
Formerly: Revue Archeologique du Centre (ISSN 0035-0753)

913   DC801.N24   FR   ISSN 0557-7705
REVUE ARCHEOLOGIQUE NARBONNAISE. 1968. a. price varies. C N R S Editions, 20-22 rue St. Amand, 75015 Paris, France. TEL 45-33-16-00. FAX 45-33-92-13. TELEX 200 356 F. adv.; bk.rev.; circ. 1,500 (controlled). **Indexed:** Avery Ind.Archit.Per., Numis.Lit.
—BLDSC (7891.119000).
Description: Publishes leading articles, notes and documents on archaeological discoveries and monuments.

REVUE BELGE D'ARCHEOLOGIE ET D'HISTOIRE DE L'ART/BELGISCH TIJDSCHRIFT VOOR OUDHEIDKUNDE EN KUNSTGESHIEDENIS. see *ART*

REVUE BELGE DE NUMISMATIQUE ET DE SIGILLOGRAPHIE. see *NUMISMATICS*

REVUE BIBLIQUE. see *RELIGIONS AND THEOLOGY*

923   PJ1003   BE   ISSN 0035-1849
REVUE D'EGYPTOLOGIE. (Supplement avail.: Societe d'Egyptologie Francaise. Bulletin (ISSN 0037-9379)) (Text in English, French, German) 1935. irreg., approx. a., vol.46, 1995. 3000 BEF (effective 1996). (Societe Francaise d'Egyptologie, FR) Editions Peeters s.p.r.l., Bondgenotenlaan 153, 3000 Leuven, Belgium. TEL 32-16-235170. FAX 32-16-228500. URL: http://www.peeters-leuven.be. bk.rev.; illus.; cum.index: vols.1-20. (back issues avail.) **Indexed:** Bibl.Ling., IBR. **Document type:** academic/scholarly publication.
—SWETS.

REVUE DE COMMINGES. see *HISTORY — History Of Europe*

913   FR   ISSN 0035-1342
REVUE DE L'AVRANCHIN ET DU PAYS DE GRANVILLE. 1882. q. 16 F. Societe d'Archeologie, de Litterature, Sciences et Arts d'Avranches, Mortain et Granville, 26 rue d'Auditoire, Avranches (Manche), France. adv.; charts; illus.; index.

913 940   D756.5.S2   FR   ISSN 1161-7721
REVUE DE LA MANCHE. 1959. q. 180 F. (foreign 200 F.). Societe d'Archeologie et d'Histoire de la Manche, B.P. 540, 50010 St-Lo Cedex, France. TEL 02-33-57-15-17. FAX 02-33-57-04-86. Ed.Bd. adv.; bk.rev.; bibl.; illus. circ. 1,500. **Document type:** academic/scholarly publication, bibliography, bulletin.
Formerly: (until 1991): Societe d'Archeologie et d'Histoire de la Manche. Departement de la Manche. Revue (ISSN 0996-3642)

REVUE DE QUMRAN. see *RELIGIONS AND THEOLOGY*

REVUE DES ARCHEOLOGUES ET HISTORIENS D'ART DE LOUVAIN. see *ART*

REVUE DES ETUDES GRECQUES. see *CLASSICAL STUDIES*

913 310   FR   ISSN 0398-0022
REVUE DROMOISE. 1866. q. 130 F. Societe d'Archeologie de la Drome, Archives Departementales, 14 rue de la Manutention, 26000 Valence, France. Ed.Bd. adv.; bk.rev.; index. circ. 500. **Document type:** academic/scholarly publication.
Formerly: Bulletin d'Archeologie et de Statistique de la Drome (ISSN 0037-8992)

REVUE DU NORD. see *HISTORY — History Of Europe*

913 944   FR   ISSN 0035-3272
REVUE HISTORIQUE ARDENNAISE. 1969. a. 160 F. (effective 1997). Societe d'Etudes Ardennaises, B.P. 831, 08011 Charleville-Mezieres Cedex, France. Ed. Odile Jurbert. adv.; bk.rev.; charts; illus. circ. 1,275. (back issues avail.) **Document type:** bulletin.
—SWETS.
Formerly: Etudes Ardennaises (ISSN 0014-1968)

913 940   FR   ISSN 1158-3371
REVUE HISTORIQUE ET ARCHEOLOGIQUE DU MAINE. 1876. a. 170 F. Societe Historique et Archeologique du Maine, 17 rue de la Reine Berengere 1, Le Mans, France. bibl. circ. 450.

913 943   SZ   ISSN 1013-6924
REVUE HISTORIQUE VAUDOISE. 1893. a. 40 SFr. Societe Vaudoise d'Histoire et d'Archeologie, Rue de la Mouline 32, CH-1002 Chavannes-pres-Renens, Switzerland. TEL 41-21-3233497. Ed. Felix Stuerner. R&P contact: Ruth Liniger. adv. contact: Ruth Liniger. charts; illus. **Document type:** academic/scholarly publication.

913   GW   ISSN 0557-7853
RHEINISCHE AUSGRABUNGEN. 1968. irreg., no.39, 1995. price varies. (Landschaftsverband Rheinland) Rheinland Verlag GmbH, Abtei Brauweiler, Postfach 2140, 50250 Pulheim, Germany. TEL 49-2234-9854265. FAX 49-2234-82503. (Distr. by: Dr. Rudolf Habelt GmbH, Am Buchenhang 1, 53115 Bonn, Germany. TEL 49-228-9238322. FAX 49-228-232017) (Co-sponsor: Rheinisches Amt fuer Bodendenkmalpflege) **Indexed:** Br.Archaeol.Abstr. **Document type:** monographic series.

913   GW
RHEINISCHES LANDESMUSEUM BONN. KATALOGE. 1994. irreg., no.4, 1995. price varies. Rheinland Verlag GmbH, Abtei Brauweiler, Postfach 2140, 50250 Pulheim, Germany. TEL 49-2234-9854265. FAX 49-2234-82503. (Distr. by: Dr. Rudolf Habelt GmbH, Am Buchenhang 1, 53115 Bonn, Germany. TEL 49-228-9238322. FAX 49-228-232017) **Document type:** monographic series.

914   DJ51   NE   ISSN 0167-5443
RIJKSDIENST VOOR HET OUDHEIDKUNDIG BODEMONDERZOEK TE AMERSFOORT. BERICHTEN. (Text in Dutch, English and German) 1950. a. fl.120. Rijksdienst voor het Oudheidkundig Bodemonderzoek te Amersfoort, Kerkstraat 1, 3811 CV Amersfoort, Netherlands. TEL 31-33-4634233. FAX 31-33-4653235. E-mail: arne.haytsma@archis.nl; URL: http://www.archis.nl/. Ed. A. Haytsma. abstr.; bibl.; illus.; maps. circ. 1,000. **Indexed:** Anthropol.Lit. **Document type:** academic/scholarly publication, government publication.
Description: Covers the archaeology and archaeological heritage of the Netherlands from prehistoric times to the post-Medieval period.

930.1   NE   ISSN 0924-2767
RIJKSDIENST VOOR HET OUDHEIDKUNDIG BODEMONDERZOEK TE AMERSFOORT. JAARVERSLAG. 1947. a. free. Rijksdienst voor het Oudheidkundig Bodemonderzoek te Amersfoort, Kerkstraat 1, 3811 CV Amersfoort, Netherlands. TEL 31-33-4634233. FAX 31-33-4653235. URL: http://www.archis.nl/. Ed. G. Scheepstra. bibl.; illus. **Document type:** corporate report.
Description: Publishes information on the archaeological activities of the Service, including investigation reports, reports from provincial and regional archaeologists, and from the Department of Nautical Archaeology.

913   NE   ISSN 0920-4776
RIJKSMUSEUM VAN OUDHEDEN, LEIDEN. OUDHEIDKUNDIGE MEDEDELINGEN. (Text in Dutch, English, French, German) 1907. a. price varies. Rijksmuseum van Oudheden, Postbus 11114, 2301 EC Leiden, Netherlands. TEL 31-71-5163163. FAX 31-71-5149941. Ed. M.J. Raven. R&P contact: Marijke Brower. circ. 300. **Indexed:** A.I.C.P. **Document type:** academic/scholarly publication.
—SWETS.
Refereed Serial

913 975   US   ISSN 0271-6925
RIPLEY P. BULLEN MONOGRAPHS IN ANTHROPOLOGY AND HISTORY. 1978. irreg., no.14, 1993. price varies. (Florida Museum of Natural History) University Press of Florida, 15 N.W. 15th St., Gainesville, FL 32611. TEL 904-392-1351. FAX 904-392-7302. Ed. Jerald T. Milanich. (back issues avail.) **Document type:** monographic series.

932   BE
RITES EGYPTIENS. (Text in French or German) vol.2, 1975. irreg., vol.8, 1995. price varies. Fondation Egyptologique Reine Elisabeth, Parc du Cinquantenaire 10, 1000 Brussels, Belgium. TEL 32-2-7417364. (back issues avail.) **Document type:** monographic series.

913 709   IT   ISSN 0080-3235
RIVISTA ARCHEOLOGICA DELL'ANTICA PROVINCIA E DIOCESI DI COMO; periodico di antichita ed arte. 1872. a. L.50000 (foreign $50) (effective 1997). Societa Archeologica Comense, Piazza Medaglie d'Oro 6, 22100 Como, Italy. TEL 39-31-269022. FAX 39-31-269022. Ed. Giorgio Luraschi. adv. contact: Giorgio Luraschi. bk.rev. circ. 1,200. (back issues avail.) **Indexed:** Numis.Lit. **Document type:** bulletin.
Formerly: Rivista Archeologica della Provincia di Como.

RIVISTA DEGLI STUDI ORIENTALI. see *ORIENTAL STUDIES*

913   CC9   IT   ISSN 0392-0895
RIVISTA DI ARCHEOLOGIA. 1977. a. price varies. Giorgio Bretschneider, Via Crescenzo 43, 00193 Rome, Italy. E-mail: bretschneider@euronet.it. Ed. Gustavo Traversari. (back issues avail.) **Indexed:** Avery Ind.Archit.Per. **Document type:** academic/scholarly publication.

913   BR130   VC   ISSN 0035-6042
RIVISTA DI ARCHEOLOGIA CRISTIANA. 1924. s-a. L.80000 (foreign L.100000). Pontificio Istituto di Archeologia Cristiana, Pontificia Commissione di Archeologia Sacra, Via Napoleone III no.1, 00185 Rome, Italy. TEL 39-6-4465574. FAX 39-6-4469197. Ed. Mons. Patrick Saint Roch. bk.rev.; bibl.; illus.; index. **Indexed:** Avery Ind.Archit.Per., Br.Archaeol.Abstr., IBR, New Test.Abstr., RILA.

572   GN700   IT   ISSN 0035-6514
RIVISTA DI SCIENZE PREISTORICHE. (Text in Italian; summaries in English and French) 1946. a. L.70000 (effective 1997). Istituto Italiano di Preistoria e Protostoria, Via S. Egidio 21, 50122 Florence, Italy. TEL 39-55-2340765. FAX 39-55-2340765. Dir. A. Vigliardi. bk.rev.; abstr.; bibl.; illus.; index. circ. 550. **Indexed:** A.I.C.P., Anthropol.Lit., Br.Archaeol.Abstr., IBR. **Document type:** bulletin.

913   IT   ISSN 0390-3877
RIVISTA DI STUDI FENICI. (Text in English, French, German, Italian and Spanish) 1973. s-a. $135. (C.N.R. Istituto di Studi Fenici-Punici) Courier Distribuzione Libri, P.O. Box 67, 50145 Florence, Italy. FAX 39-55-300036. Ed. Enrico Acquaro. bk.rev. circ. 1,000. (back issues avail.) **Indexed:** Bibl.Ling., IBR, Numis.Lit. **Document type:** academic/scholarly publication.

914.5   IT   ISSN 1120-3579
RIVISTA DI STUDI POMPEIANI. 1987. irreg., vol.6, 1993-94. price varies. (Associazione Internazionale Amici di Pompei) L'Erma di Bretschneider, Via Cassiodoro 19, 00193 Rome, Italy. TEL 39-6-6874127. FAX 39-6-6874129.

RIVISTA INGALINA E INTEMELIA. see *ART*

RIVISTA STORICA DELL'ANTICHITA. see *HISTORY*

ARCHAEOLOGY

930.1 970.1   US   ISSN 0888-6482
ROCHESTER MUSEUM AND SCIENCE CENTER. RESEARCH DIVISION. RESEARCH RECORDS. Key Title: Research Records - Rochester Museum and Science Center. Research Division. Variant series title: Charles F. Wray Series in Seneca Archaeology. no.12, 1965. irreg., no.23, 1995. $15. Rochester Museum and Science Center, Research Division, 657 East Ave., Box 1480, Rochester, NY 14603-1480. TEL 716-271-4321. Ed. Charles F. Hayes III. illus. **Indexed:** Anthropol.Lit. **Document type:** academic/scholarly publication, monographic series, proceedings.
  Description: Scholarly studies and conference proceedings on topics pertaining to the archaeology and history of New York State Native American tribes.

ROCK ART RESEARCH. see *ANTHROPOLOGY*

913   709   GW   ISSN 0080-3782
ROEMISCHE BRONZEN AUS DEUTSCHLAND. 1960. irreg. price varies. Verlag Philipp von Zabern GmbH, Philipp-von-Zabern-Platz 1-3, 55116 Mainz, Germany. TEL 06131-28747-0. FAX 06131-223710. Ed. Heinz Menzel. index. **Document type:** monographic series.

ROMHORISONT. see *HISTORY — History Of Europe*

914   GW   ISSN 0341-9312
ROMISCH-GERMANISCHEN KOMMISSION. BERICHTE. 1910. a. DM.50. Verlag Philipp von Zabern GmbH, Philipp-von-Zabern-Platz 1-3, 55116 Mainz, Germany. TEL 06131-28747-0. FAX 06131-223710. **Indexed:** IBR. **Document type:** academic/scholarly publication.

913   RU
ROSSIISKAYA AKADEMIYA NAUK. INSTITUT ARKHEOLOGII. KRATKIE SOOBSHCHENIYA. 1939. irreg. price varies. Izdatel'stvo Nauka, 90 Profsoyuznaya ul., 117864 Moscow, Russia. (Dist. by: Mezhdunarodnaya Kniga, ul. Dimitrova D.39, 113095 Moscow, Russia) Ed. I.T. Kruglikova. circ. 2,150. **Indexed:** Numis.Lit.
  Formerly (until 1993): Akademiya Nauk S.S.S.R. Institut Arkheologii. Kratkie Soobshcheniya (ISSN 0130-2620)

913   RU   ISSN 0869-6063
DK30
ROSSIISKAYA ARKHEOLOGIYA. (Text in Russian; contents page and summaries in French) 1957. q. $215 (effective 1998). (Rossiiskaya Akademiya Nauk, Institut Arkheologii) Izdatel'stvo Nauka, 90 Profsoyuznaya ul., 117864 Moscow, Russia. TEL 095-336-0266. FAX 095-420-2220. (Dist. by: Mezhdunarodnaya Kniga, B. Yakimanka 39, 117049 Moscow, Russia; Distr. in U.S. by: Victor Kamkin Inc., 4956 Boiling Brook Pkwy., Rockville, MD 20852. TEL 301-881-5973. FAX 301-881-1637) bk.rev.; bibl.; illus.; maps. circ. 1,957. (also avail. in microform) **Indexed:** A.I.C.P., Biol.Abstr., IBR, Numis.Lit. **Document type:** academic/scholarly publication.
  Formerly: Sovetskaya Arkheologiya (ISSN 0038-5034)

ROTUNDA. see *ART*

930.1   US
ROUND ROBBINS NEWSLETTER. 1993. 3/yr. free to qualified personnel. Massachusetts Archaeological Society, Inc., Robbins Museum of Archaeology, Box 700, Middleboro, MA 02346. TEL 508-947-9005. Ed. Ruth Warfield. R&P contact: Ruth Warfield. **Document type:** newsletter.

930.1   IE
ROYAL IRISH ACADEMY. DISCOVERY PROGRAMME. REPORTS. irreg., no.2, 1995. Royal Irish Academy, Discovery Programme, 19 Dawson St., Dublin 2, Ireland. **Document type:** academic/scholarly publication, monographic series.

914.2 820   IE   ISSN 0035-8991
ROYAL IRISH ACADEMY. PROCEEDINGS. SECTION C: ARCHAEOLOGY, CELTIC STUDIES, HISTORY, LINGUISTICS AND LITERATURE. 1836. irreg. price varies. Royal Irish Academy, 19 Dawson St., Dublin 2, Ireland. TEL 353-1-6762570. FAX 353-1-6762346. Eds. T. Barry, M. O'Dowd. charts; illus.; index, cum.index. circ. 600. (also avail. in microform from PMC) **Indexed:** A.I.C.P., Amer.Hist.& Life (1954-1967), (1970-1989), Arts & Hum.Cit.Ind., Br.Archaeol.Abstr., Curr.Cont., Hist.Abstr. (1954-1967), (1970-1989), IBR, Numis.Lit. **Document type:** proceedings.
  —BLDSC (6799.058000); KNAW.

913   CN   ISSN 0316-1285
ROYAL ONTARIO MUSEUM. ARCHAEOLOGY MONOGRAPHS. 1973. irreg., latest 1986. price varies. Royal Ontario Museum, Publications, 100 Queen's Park, Toronto, ON M5S 2C6, Canada. TEL 416-586-5581. FAX 416-586-5887. E-mail: sandras@rom.on.ca. (Subscr. to: University of Toronto Press, Order Fulfilment Division, 5201 Dufferin St., Downsview, ON M3H 5T8, Canada. TEL 416-667-7791) Ed. Sandra Shaul. R&P contact: Glen Ellis. TEL 416-586-5582. bibl.; illus. **Document type:** monographic series, academic/scholarly publication.

913   IE   ISSN 0035-9106
DA900
ROYAL SOCIETY OF ANTIQUARIES OF IRELAND. JOURNAL. 1849. a. I£26 (effective 1997). Royal Society of Antiquaries of Ireland, 63 Merrion Square, Dublin 2, Ireland. TEL 353-1-6761749. FAX 353-1-6761749. Ed. Michael Herity. bk.rev.; illus.; index, cum.index: 1849-1930. circ. 1,200. **Indexed:** A.I.C.P., Br.Archaeol.Abstr., Br.Hum.Ind., IBR, Numis.Lit., RILA. **Document type:** academic/scholarly publication.
  —BLDSC (4863.800000).
  Description: Publishes contributions to knowledge in the fields of Irish archaeology, architecture, history, genealogy, sociology, folklore and many kindred subjects.

930.1 970.01   US
E51
S A A BULLETIN. 1983. 5/yr. membership. Society for American Archaeology, 900 Second St., N.W., No. 12, Washington, DC 20002-3557. TEL 202-789-8200. FAX 202-789-0284. E-mail: publications@saa.org.; saanews@alishaw.ucsb.edu; URL: http://www.sscf.ucsb.edu/saabulletin. adv. **Document type:** academic/scholarly publication, bulletin, newsletter.
  —BLDSC (2758.260000). CCC.
  Formerly (until 1990): Society for American Archaeology. Bulletin (ISSN 0741-5672)

913   US   ISSN 0899-8922
                            CODEN: SARTE6
S A S BULLETIN. 1977. q. $75 to individuals (includes Journal of Archaeological Science); libraries $30 (S A S Bulletin only) (effective 1995-1996). Society for Archaeological Sciences, Radiocarbon Laboratory, Department of Anthropology, University of California at Riverside, Riverside, CA 92521. TEL 909-787-5521. FAX 909-787-5409. E-mail: cprior@ucrac1.ucr.edu. Ed. Christopher Nagle. R&P contact: R.E. Taylor. adv. contact: R.E. Taylor. bk.rev.; circ. 600 (paid). **Indexed:** Anthropol.Lit. **Document type:** newsletter.
  Formerly (until 1988): S A S Newsletter (ISSN 0739-0637)
  Description: Contains cooperative and interdisciplinary research between archaeology and the natural and physical sciences.

913   US   ISSN 0888-9570
S O P A NEWSLETTER. 1977. m. membership. Society of Professional Archeologists, c/o Institute for the Study of Earth and Man, Southern Methodist University, Dallas, TX 75275-0336. TEL 214-768-2938. FAX 214-768-2906. E-mail: slinder@sun.cis.smu.edu; URL: http://www.smu.edu/~anthrop/sopa.html. Ed. Sue Linder-Linsley. adv.; bk.rev. circ. 800. **Document type:** newsletter.
  Formerly: Society of Professional Archeologists Newsletter.
  Description: Covers cultural resource management issues, ethical problems, contract archeology and society news.

SABAZIA. see *HISTORY*

SAGA OCH SED. see *FOLKLORE*

913   GW   ISSN 0080-5866
DF221.S3
SAMOS. 1961. irreg., vol.19, 1995. price varies. (Deutsches Archaeologisches Institut) Dr. Rudolf Habelt GmbH, Am Buchenhang 1, 53115 Bonn, Germany. TEL 49-228-9238322. FAX 49-228-923836. **Document type:** monographic series.

SAN DIEGO MUSEUM OF MAN. ETHNIC TECHNOLOGY NOTES. see *ANTHROPOLOGY*

SAN DIEGO MUSEUM OF MAN. PAPERS. see *ANTHROPOLOGY*

SASKATCHEWAN. DEPARTMENT OF CULTURE AND RECREATION. ANNUAL REPORT. see *ART*

913   CN   ISSN 0227-7514
SASKATCHEWAN ARCHAEOLOGICAL SOCIETY NEWSLETTER. 1963. bi-m. membership. Saskatchewan Archaeological Society, 5 - 816 First Ave. N., Saskatoon, SK S7K 1Y3, Canada. TEL 306-664-4124. Ed. J. Finnigan. bk.rev.; cum.index. circ. 650. (processed) **Indexed:** Anthropol.Lit., GeoRef. **Document type:** newsletter.
  Formerly: Saskatchewan Archaeology Newsletter (ISSN 0036-4878)

917   CN   ISSN 0227-5872
F1071.9
SASKATCHEWAN ARCHAEOLOGY. 1980. a. Can.$15. Saskatchewan Archaeological Society, 5 - 816 First Ave. N., Saskatoon, SK S7K 1Y3, Canada. Ed. Terry Gibson. circ. 650. (back issues avail.) **Indexed:** Anthropol.Lit.

SCHOLIA; Natal studies in classical antiquity. see *CLASSICAL STUDIES*

914   SZ
SCHWEIZER BEITRAEGE ZUR KULTURGESCHICHTE UND ARCHAEOLOGIE DES MITTELALTERS. 1974. a. Walter-Verlag AG, Amthausquai 21, CH-4600 Olten, Switzerland. FAX 62321184. TELEX 981690. illus. circ. 1,000.

913   SZ   ISSN 0252-1881
GN841
SCHWEIZERISCHE GESELLSCHAFT FUER UR- UND FRUEHGESCHICHTE. JAHRBUCH. (Text in French, German, Italian) 1908. a. 150 SFr. Petersgraben 9-11, CH-4001 Basel, Switzerland. TEL 41-61-2613078. Ed. Urs Niffeler. bk.rev.; index. **Indexed:** A.I.C.P., Br.Archaeol.Abstr., IBR, Numis.Lit. **Document type:** academic/scholarly publication.

913   UK   ISSN 0262-4389
SCOTTISH ARCHAEOLOGICAL REVIEW. 1982. a. £20. Archaeological Review, c/o Department of Archaeology, Glasgow G12 8QQ, Scotland. (Subscr. to: Martinus Nijhoff, P.O.B. 269, 2501 AX The Hague, Netherlands) Eds. J.B. Stevenson, J.C. Barrett. bk.rev. **Indexed:** Anthropol.Lit., Br.Archaeol.Abstr.
  —BLDSC (8206.042000).

917   US   ISSN 0048-9832
E78.O6
SCREENINGS. 1951. m. $4 to non-members. Oregon Archaeological Society, Box 13293, Portland, OR 97213. Ed. Harvey Steele. bk.rev.; charts; illus. circ. 1,000. (back issues avail.)

930.1   NE
SCRINIUM. irreg., vol.11, 1996. Thesis Publishers, P.O. Box 14791, 1001 LG Amsterdam, Netherlands. TEL 31-20-6255429. FAX 31-20-6203395. E-mail: thesis@thesis.antenna.nl. Ed. A. Leewis. **Document type:** monographic series.

SCRIPTA MEDITERRANEA. see *HISTORY — History Of The Near East*

913   SW   ISSN 0439-8912
SCRIPTA MINORE. REGIAE SOCIETATIS HUMANIORUM LITTERARUM LUNDENSIS. (Text in English) 1957. a. price varies. A W I International AB, P.O. Box 4627, S-116 91 Stockholm, Sweden. TEL 46-8-7282500. FAX 46-8-338707. Ed. Berta Stjernquist. (back issues avail.) **Indexed:** NAA. **Document type:** academic/scholarly publication.

ARCHAEOLOGY

913 IT ISSN 0067-009X
SCUOLA ARCHEOLOGICA DI ATENE E DELLE MISSIONI ITALIANE IN ORIENTE. MONOGRAFIE. 1964. irreg., no.6, 1993. price varies. L'Erma di Bretschneider, Via Cassiodoro 19, 00193 Rome, Italy. TEL 39-6-6874127. FAX 39-6-6874129. R&P contact: Roberto Marcucci. circ. 750. **Document type:** monographic series.

387 IS ISSN 0077-5193
SEFUNIM. (Text in English, Hebrew) 1966. irreg., vol.8, 1995. $10. Friends of the National Maritime Museum Haifa, 198 Allenby Rd., P.O. Box 44855, Haifa 31447, Israel. TEL 972-4-8536622. FAX 972-4-8539286. Ed. Joseph Ringel. adv.; bk.rev. circ. 1,000. **Indexed:** Numis.Lit. **Document type:** academic/scholarly publication.
Description: Publishes scholarly research on maritime archaeology and history conducted by international scholars affiliated with the museum.

930.1 305.8927 UK ISSN 0308-8421
SEMINAR FOR ARABIAN STUDIES. PROCEEDINGS. 1971. a. £25 (effective 1997). Seminar for Arabian Studies, c/o The Institute of Archaeology, 31-34 Gordon Sq., London WC1H 0PY, England. bk.rev. circ. 200. **Indexed:** Anthropol.Lit., Bibl.Ling., IBR. **Document type:** proceedings.
—BLDSC (6849.117500).

931 CC
SICHUAN WENWU/RELICS OF SICHUAN. (Text in Chinese) bi-m. $18.50. Sichuan Wenwu Guanli Weiyuanhui - Sichuan Relics Management Commission, 5 Renmin Nanlu Siduan (Sec. 4), Chengdu, Sichuan 610041, People's Republic of China. TEL 553110. (Dist. in US by: China Books & Periodicals, Inc., 2929 24th St., San Francisco, CA 94110. TEL 415-282-2994)

913 IT ISSN 0037-4571
DG865
SICILIA ARCHEOLOGICA; rassegna periodica di studi, notizie e documentazione. 1968. 3/yr. L.25000. Azienda Provinciale per il Turismo di Trapani, Via Vito Sorba 15, 91100 Trapani, Sicily, Italy. FAX 0923-29430. adv.; bk.rev.; bibl.; charts; illus. circ. 1,000. **Indexed:** Numis.Lit.

913 930 IT ISSN 0392-0909
SIKELIKA. SERIE ARCHEOLOGICA. 1979. irreg., vol.4, 1992. price varies. (Centro Siciliano di Studi Storico-Archeologici "Biagio Pace") Giorgio Bretschneider, Via Crescenzo 43, 00193 Rome, Italy. E-mail: bretschneider@euronet.it. (back issues avail.) **Document type:** academic/scholarly publication.

SIKELIKA. SERIE STORICA. see HISTORY

913 PL ISSN 0080-9594
SILESIA ANTIQUA. (Text in Polish; summaries in English, French and German) 1959. a. price varies. Muzeum Archeologiczne, Wroclaw, Ul. Kazimierza Wielkiego 34, 50-077 Wroclaw, Poland. (Dist. by: Ars Polona-Ruch, Krakowskie Przedmiescie 7, Warsaw, Poland) Ed. J. Lodowski. **Indexed:** A.I.C.P., Br.Archaeol.Abstr., IBR. **Document type:** academic/scholarly publication.
Description: Devoted to the actual research and excavations in the area of Upper and Lower Silesia and of Opole region.

SKALK; nyt om gammelt. see HISTORY — History Of Europe

930.1 PL ISSN 0520-9250
SLASKIE SPRAWOZDANIA ARCHEOLOGICZNE. 1958. irreg., vol.33, 1993. price varies. (Uniwersytet Wroclawski, Katedra Archeologii) Wydawnictwo Uniwersytetu Wroclawskiego, Spolka z o.o., Pl. Uniwerstytecki 9-13, 50-137 Wroclaw, Poland. TEL 48-71-441006. FAX 48-71-402735. charts; illus. circ. 300. **Document type:** academic/scholarly publication.

913 XO ISSN 0037-6949
SLOVENSKA ARCHEOLOGIA/SLOVAK ARCHEOLOGY. (Text and summaries in German and Slovak) 1953. s-a. $180 in US (effective 1996). (Slovenska Akademia Vied, Archeologicky Ustav) Vydavatel'stvo S A P, s.r.o. - Slovak Academic Press Ltd., P.O. Box 57, Nam. Slobody 6, 810 05 Bratislava, Slovakia. TEL 42-7-211728. Ed. Bohuslav Chropovsky. bk.rev.; charts; illus. (tabloid format) **Indexed:** A.I.C.P., Anthropol.Lit., Numis.Lit. **Document type:** academic/scholarly publication.
Description: Publishes studies and papers on archaeological research results and theoretical questions concerning Central Europe, especially the Carpathian basin. Presents information on the latest archaeological research in Slovakia.

913 700 IT
SOCIETA PER GLI STUDI STORICI, ARCHEOLOGICI ED ARTISTICI DELLA PROVINCIA DI CUNEO. BOLLETTINO. 1929. s-a. L.60000 (effective 1993). Societa per gli Studi Storici, Archeologici ed Artistici della Provincia di Cuneo, c/o Biblioteca Civica, Via Cacciatori delle Alpi 9, Casella Postale 91, 12100 Cuneo, Italy. TEL 0171-634367. bk.rev. circ. 1,000.

930.1 700 IT ISSN 1121-9319
SOCIETA PIEMONTESE DI ARCHEOLOGIA E BELLE ARTI. BOLLETTINO. 1874. a. Lit.50000($35) (effective 1997). Societa Piemontese di Archeologia e Belle Arti, Via Napione 2, 10124 Turin, Italy. TEL 39-11-8177178. Ed. Bruno Signorelli. cum.index: 1874-1990. circ. 600. (back issues avail.) **Document type:** academic/scholarly publication.
Description: Covers archeology from the Stone Age to medieval times, architecture and all types of art of the Piedmont region.

SOCIETA SAVONESE DI STORIA PATRIA. ATTI E MEMORIE. see HISTORY — History Of Europe

913 IT ISSN 0394-1663
SOCIETA TIBURTINA DI STORIA E D'ARTE. ATTI E MEMORIE. 1921. a. Societa Tiburtina di Storia e d'Arte, Villa d'Este, 00019 Tivoli, Italy. **Indexed:** Numis.Lit.
Formerly (until 1929): Societa Tiburtina di Storia e d'Arte. Atti e Memorie (ISSN 0392-0348).

914 FR
SOCIETE ARCHEOLOGIQUE DE TARN ET GARONNE. BULLETIN ARCHEOLOGIQUE, HISTORIQUE ET ARTISTIQUE. 1869. a. 100 F. (effective 1997). Societe Archeologique de Tarn et Garonne, Rue des Soubirous-Bas, Tarn et Garonne, Montauban, France. (Co-sponsors: Conseil General du Tarn et Garonne; Ville de Montauban) Ed. Jean Boutonnet. R&P contact: Jean Boutonnet. bk.rev. **Document type:** bulletin.

914 FR ISSN 1153-2521
SOCIETE ARCHEOLOGIQUE DE TOURAINE. BULLETIN. 1868. a. Societe Archeologique de Touraine, B.P. 1105, 37011 Tours Cedex, France. Pub. Jean Moreau. adv. contact: Jean Moreau. **Document type:** bulletin.

913 FR ISSN 1149-4670
SOCIETE ARCHEOLOGIQUE DE TOURAINE. MEMOIRES. 1842. a. Societe Archeologique de Touraine, B.P. 1105, 37011 Tours Cedex, France. Ed.Bd.; Pub. Jean Moreau. adv. contact: Jean Moreau. charts; illus. **Document type:** monographic series.

913 944 FR ISSN 0037-8895
SOCIETE ARCHEOLOGIQUE, HISTORIQUE, LITTERAIRE & SCIENTIFIQUE DU GERS. BULLETIN. 1900. q. 180 F. (foreign 260 F.) (effective 1997). Societe Archeologique, Historique, Litteraire & Scientifique du Gers, c/o Andre Dieulafait, Tres., 13 Place Saluste-du-Bartas, B.P. 16, 32001 Auch Cedex, France. Pub. Georges Courtes. R&P contact: Georges Courtes. bk.rev.; charts; illus.; index, cum.index every 10 yrs. circ. 1,550. **Document type:** academic/scholarly publication, bulletin.

932.023 281.7 UA ISSN 0068-5283
SOCIETE D'ARCEOLOGIE COPTE. BIBLIOTHEQUE DE MANUSCRITS. 1934; N.S. 1967. irreg., latest no.3, 1977. £E30($8) per no. Society for Coptic Archaeology - Societe d'Archeologie Copte, 222 rue Ramses, Cairo, Egypt. TEL 824252. bk.rev. **Document type:** monographic series, bibliography.

932.023 281.7 UA ISSN 0068-5291
SOCIETE D'ARCHEOLOGIE COPTE. BULLETIN. (Text in English, French, German, Italian) 1935. irreg., approx. a. vol.36, 1997. £E70($20) per no. Society for Coptic Archaeology - Societe d'Archeologie Copte, 222 rue Ramses, Cairo, Egypt. TEL 20-2-4824252. bk.rev.; cum.index: vols.1-20 in vol.20. (reprint service avail. from KTO) **Document type:** academic/scholarly publication, bulletin.

932.023 281.7 UA ISSN 0068-5305
SOCIETE D'ARCHEOLOGIE COPTE. TEXTES ET DOCUMENTS. 1942. irreg., latest no.17, 1985. price varies. Society for Coptic Archaeology - Societe d'Archeologie Copte, 222 rue Ramses, Cairo, Egypt. TEL 20-2-4824252. bk.rev. (back issues avail.) **Document type:** monographic series.
Description: Scholarly bibliographies, translations and editions of historical texts documents and manuscripts relating to the Coptic church in Egypt.

949.33 BE
SOCIETE D'ARCHEOLOGIE, D'HISTOIRE ET DE FOLKLORE DE NIVELLES ET DU BRABANT WALLON. ANNALES. 1879. irreg, latest vol.26, 1989. 850 BEF. Societe d'Archeologie d'Histoire et de Folklore de Nivelles et du Brabant Wallon, Musee de Nivelles, 27 rue de Bruxelles, 1400 Nivelles, Belgium. TEL 32-67-212161. Ed. J.L. Delattre. bk.rev.; illus. circ. 500.

914 FR ISSN 0753-4825
SOCIETE D'ARCHEOLOGIE ET D'HISTOIRE DE LA CHARENTE MARITIME. BULLETIN DE LIAISON. 1966. a. 70 F. Societe d'Archeologie et d'Histoire de la Charente Maritime, 9, rue Mauny, 17100 Saintes, France. TEL 46-74-67-75. **Document type:** bulletin.
Formerly (until 1976): Societe d'Archeologie et d'Histoire de la Charente Maritime et Section Archeologique de Saintes. Bulletin de Liaison (ISSN 0753-4817); Supersedes in part (in 1974): Societe d'Archeologie et d'Histoire de la Charente Maritime et Groupe de Recherches Archeologiques de Saintes. Recueil (ISSN 0753-4809); Which was formerly (until 1973): Societe d'Archeologie et d'Histoire de la Cherente Maritime. Recueil (ISSN 0753-4795).

913 FR ISSN 0037-9158
SOCIETE D'EMULATION DU BOURBONNAIS. BULLETIN; lettres, sciences et arts. 1846. q. 180 F. Societe d'Emulation du Bourbonnais, 4 Place de l'Ancien Palais, 03000 Moulins, France. TEL 70-44-39-03. adv.; bk.rev.; illus.; index. (back issues avail.)

913 940 900 SZ ISSN 1017-849X
DQ441
SOCIETE D'HISTOIRE ET D'ARCHAEOLOGIE DE GENEVE. BULLETIN. 1892. a. 25 SFr. Societe d'Histoire et d'Archeologie de Geneve, c/o Bibliotheque Publique et Universitaire de Geneve, Promenade des Bastions, CH-1211 Geneva 4, Switzerland. TEL 41-22-3466666. FAX 41-22-3472391. (Subscr. to: Librairie Droz S.A., 11, rue Massot, CH-1211 Geneva 12, Switzerland.) index. circ. 500. **Document type:** academic/scholarly publication, bulletin.
Description: Details of research, events and developments in history and archaeology in relation to the society.

914 SZ
SOCIETE D'HISTOIRE ET D'ARCHEOLOGIE. MEMOIRES ET DOCUMENTS. SERIE IN 4. (Text in French) irreg., vol.10, 1988. price varies. Librairie Droz S.A., 11, rue Massot, CH-1211 Geneva 12, Switzerland. TEL 41-22-3466666. FAX 41-22-3472391. E-mail: drozsa@dial.eunet.ch; URL: http://www.eunet.ch/customers/droz. (Subscr. to: Case Postale 389, CH-1211 Geneva 12, Switzerland) Ed.Bd. **Document type:** monographic series.

914 SZ
SOCIETE D'HISTOIRE ET D'ARCHEOLOGIE. MEMOIRES ET DOCUMENTS. SERIE IN 8. (Text in French) irreg., vol.58, 1997. price varies. Librairie Droz S.A., 11 rue Massot, CH-1211 Geneva 12, Switzerland. TEL 41-22-3466666. FAX 41-22-3472391. E-mail drozsa@dial.eunet.ch; URL: http://www.eunet.ch/customers/droz. (Subscr. to: Base Postale 389, CH-1211 Geneva 12, Switzerland) Ed.Bd. **Document type:** monographic series.

ARCHAEOLOGY

913   FR   ISSN 0081-0967
SOCIETE D'HISTOIRE ET D'ARCHEOLOGIE DE LA GOELE. BULLETIN D'INFORMATION. 1968. a. 100 F. (effective 1996 & 1997). Societe d'Histoire et d'Archeologie de la Goele, Mairie, 77230 Dammartin-en-Goele, France. Ed. Jean Golinelli. R&P contact: Jean Golinelli. adv.; bk.rev. circ. 1,000. **Document type:** academic/scholarly publication.

913 944   FR   ISSN 1153-3277
SOCIETE D'HISTOIRE ET D'ARCHEOLOGIE DE VICHY ET DES ENVIRONS. BULLETIN. 1937. s-a. 200 F. Societe d'Histoire et d'Archeologie de Vichy, Centre Culturel Valery Larbaud, 15 rue M. Foch, 03200 Vichy, France. Ed. George Tixier. bk.rev.; bibl.; charts; illus. circ. 350. **Document type:** bulletin.

SOCIETE DES ANTIQUAIRES DE L'OUEST. BULLETIN. see HISTORY — History Of Europe

930.1 944   FR   ISSN 0037-9204
SOCIETE DES ANTIQUAIRES DE PICARDIE. BULLETIN TRIMESTRIEL. 1836. q. 210 F. (foreign 230 F.). Societe des Antiquaires de Picardie, Musee de Picardie, 48 rue de la Republique, 80000 Amiens, France. bk.rev.; illus.; cum.index every 3 yrs. **Document type:** bulletin.
   Description: Features archaeology, history for the whole province of Picardie.

930.1 944   FR   ISSN 0399-1717
SOCIETE DES ANTIQUAIRES DE PICARDIE. MEMOIRES. SERIES IN 4. 1838. irreg. price varies. Societe des Antiquaires de Picardie, Memoires, Musee de Picardie, 48 rue de la Republique, 80000 Amiens, France. Ed. Geoffroy Asselin. **Indexed:** Numis.Lit. **Document type:** bulletin.
   Formerly (until 1971): Societe des Antiquaires de Picardie. Memoires (ISSN 1140-8863); **Incorporates** (1845-1934): Societe des Antiquaires de Picardie. Memoires. Documents Inedits Concernant la Province (ISSN 0399-1709)

SOCIETE DES OCEANISTES. JOURNAL. see SOCIAL SCIENCES: COMPREHENSIVE WORKS

SOCIETE DES SCIENCES HISTORIQUES ET NATURELLES DE SEMUR EN AUXOIS ET DES FOUILLES D'ALESIA. BULLETIN. see HISTORY — History Of Europe

913   FR   ISSN 0037-9379
SOCIETE FRANCAISE D'EGYPTOLOGIE. BULLETIN. 1949. 3/yr. membership. Societe Francaise d'Egyptologie, College de France, 11 Place Marcelin Berthelot, 75231 Paris Cedex 05, France. bk.rev.; illus. **Document type:** bulletin.

LA SOCIETE GUERNESIAISE. REPORT AND TRANSACTIONS. see HISTORY — History Of Europe

SOCIETE HISTORIQUE ET ARCHEOLOGIQUE DU PERIGORD. BULLETIN. see HISTORY — History Of Europe

913   FR   ISSN 0081-1181
DC2
SOCIETE NATIONALE DES ANTIQUAIRES DE FRANCE. BULLETIN. 1857. a. 250 F. Societe Nationale des Antiquaires de France., Pavillon Mollien, Palais du Louvre, Paris 75001, France. (Orders to: Diffusion de Boccard, 11 rue de Medicis, 75006 Paris, France) circ. 800. **Indexed:** Avery Ind.Archit.Per., Numis.Lit., RILA. **Document type:** bulletin.

930.1   FR   ISSN 0249-7638
GN700
SOCIETE PREHISTORIQUE FRANCAISE. BULLETIN. (Text in French; abstracts in English) 1904. q. 410 F. to individuals (foreign 460 F.); to institutions 510 F. (foreign 560 F.) (effective 1997). Societe Prehistorique Francaise, 22 rue Saint Ambroise, 75011 Paris, France. TEL 33-1-43571697. FAX 33-1-43577395. Ed. Claude Constantin. adv.; bk.rev.; bibl.; charts; illus.; index. circ. 2,000. (back issues avail.) **Indexed:** A.I.C.P., Anthropol.Lit., Art & Archaeol.Tech.Abstr., Biol.Abstr., Br.Archaeol.Abstr., Bull.Signal., GeoRef. **Document type:** bulletin, academic/scholarly publication.
   —BLDSC (2748.000000); SWETS.
   Formed by the 1978 merger of: Societe Prehistorique Francaise. Bulletin - Etudes et Travaux (ISSN 0583-8789); Societe Prehistorique Francaise. Bulletin - Comptes Rendus des Seances Mensuelles (ISSN 0373-5451); Which supersedes (in 1964): Societe Prehistorique de France. Bulletin (ISSN 0037-9514)
   Description: French research from the Palaeolithic to the Iron-Age.

SOCIETE SUISSE DES AMERICANISTES. BULLETIN/SCHWEIZERISCHE AMERIKANISTEN-GESELLSCHAFT. BULLETIN. see ANTHROPOLOGY

930.1 970.01   US
SOCIETY FOR AMERICAN ARCHAEOLOGY. ADMINISTRATIVE AND MEMBER DIRECTORY. 1994. a. $39.95 to non-members. Society for American Archaeology, 900 Second St., N.W., No. 12, Washington, DC 20002-3557. TEL 202-789-8200. FAX 202-789-0284. E-mail: publications@saa.org. Ed. Janet Walker. **Document type:** directory.
   Formerly (until 1995): Archaeologists of the Americas (ISSN 1077-2049)
   Description: Lists all SAA members and headquarters staff together with committee structure.

917   US
SOCIETY FOR AMERICAN ARCHAEOLOGY. SPECIAL PUBLICATIONS SERIES. irreg. Society for American Archaeology, 900 Second St., N.W., No. 12, Washington, DC 20002-3557. TEL 202-789-8200. FAX 202-789-0284. **Document type:** academic/scholarly publication, monographic series.

SOCIETY FOR COMMERCIAL ARCHEOLOGY. JOURNAL. see ARCHITECTURE

SOCIETY FOR COMMERCIAL ARCHEOLOGY. NEWS. see ARCHITECTURE

913   US   ISSN 0898-0004
SOCIETY FOR HISTORICAL ARCHAEOLOGY. SPECIAL PUBLICATION SERIES. 1976. irreg., latest no.7. Society for Historical Archaeology, Box 30446, Tucson, AZ 85751. TEL 520-886-8006. FAX 520-886-0812. E-mail: sha@azstarnet.com; sha_editor@cup.edu; URL: http://www.azstarnet.com/tildesha. Ed. Ronald L. Michael. R&P contact: Ronald L. Michael. illus. (back issues avail.) **Document type:** monographic series.
   Description: Each volume presents selected material culture studies from the artifact assemblages recovered from various excavated sites.

913   US   ISSN 0037-9735
CC77.H5
SOCIETY FOR HISTORICAL ARCHAEOLOGY NEWSLETTER. 1968. q. $55 to individuals; institutions $70; students $35. Society for Historical Archaeology, Box 30446, Tucson, AZ 85751. TEL 520-886-8006. FAX 520-886-0182. E-mail: sha@azstarnet.com; sha_editor@cup.edu; URL: http://www.azstarnet.com/tildesha. Ed. Norman F. Barka. tr.lit. circ. 2,500. (processed) **Document type:** newsletter.
   Description: Contains forums on archaeological conservation, urban archaeology, information on society activities, and current research.

SOCIETY FOR INDUSTRIAL ARCHEOLOGY NEWSLETTER. see TECHNOLOGY: COMPREHENSIVE WORKS

SOCIETY FOR LINCOLNSHIRE HISTORY AND ARCHAEOLOGY. ANNUAL REPORT AND STATEMENT OF ACCOUNTS. see HISTORY — History Of Europe

SOCIETY OF ANTIQUARIES OF SCOTLAND. MONOGRAPH SERIES. see HISTORY — History Of Europe

SOCIETY OF ANTIQUARIES OF SCOTLAND. PROCEEDINGS. see HISTORY — History Of Europe

SOMERSET AND DORSET NOTES AND QUERIES. see HISTORY — History Of Europe

913 500.9   UK   ISSN 0081-2056
SOMERSET ARCHAEOLOGY AND NATURAL HISTORY. 1849. a. £15 (foreign £20) (effective 1996). Somerset Archaeological & Natural History Society, Taunton Castle, Taunton, Somerset TA1 4AD, England. TEL 44-1823-272429. Ed. Tom Mayberry. bk.rev.; index, cum.index: vols.81-115, 1935-1971. circ. 1,000. **Indexed:** Br.Archaeol.Abstr., Br.Hum.Ind., Numis.Lit. **Document type:** academic/scholarly publication.
   —BLDSC (8327.823000).
   Formerly: Somersetshire Archaeological and Natural History Society. Proceedings.

914.5   IT
SOPRINTENDENZA ARCHEOLOGICA DI POMPEI. CATALOGHI. 1986. irreg., vol.5, 1993. price varies. L'Erma di Bretschneider, Via Cassiodoro 19, 00193 Rome, Italy. TEL 39-6-6874127. FAX 39-6-6874129. **Document type:** catalog.

914.5   IT
SOPRINTENDENZA ARCHEOLOGICA DI POMPEI. MONOGRAFIE. 1986. irreg., vol.10, 1995. price varies. L'Erma di Bretschneider, Via Cassiodoro 19, 00193 Rome, Italy. TEL 39-6-6874127. FAX 39-6-6874129. **Document type:** monographic series.

930.1   SA   ISSN 0038-1969
GN865.S5   CODEN: SARBAG
SOUTH AFRICAN ARCHAEOLOGICAL BULLETIN. 1945. s-a. R.110 to institutions (includes Digging Stick); Africa R.140; elsewhere R.210 ($50) (£32) (DM.76) (effective 1997). South African Archaeological Society, P.O. Box 15700, Vlaeberg 8018, South Africa. TEL 27-21-243330. FAX 27-21-246716. Ed. Judith Sealy. adv.; bk.rev.; abstr.; bibl.; charts; illus.; maps; index. circ. 1,300. **Indexed:** A.I.C.P., Abstr.Anthropol., Amer.Hist.& Life, Anthropol.Lit., Curr.Cont.Africa, GeoRef., Hist.Abstr., IBR, Ind.S.A.Per. **Document type:** academic/scholarly publication, bulletin.
   —BLDSC (8330.900000).
   Incorporates (in 1972): Goodwin Series.

SOUTH AFRICAN MUSEUM. ANNALS/SUID-AFRIKAANSE MUSEUM. ANNALE. see BIOLOGY

930.1   US
SOUTH DAKOTA ARCHAEOLOGICAL SOCIETY NEWSLETTER. 1970. q. $12 to individuals; institutions $25; students $8. Box 1257, Rapid City, SD 57709-1257. TEL 605-394-1936. FAX 605-394-1941. Ed. Michael R. Fosha. R&P contact: Michael R. Fosha. bk.rev.; film rev. (tabloid format; back issues avail.) **Indexed:** Anthropol.Lit. **Document type:** newsletter, academic/scholarly publication.
   Description: Conveys information about current research of interest to the members.

913   US   ISSN 0734-578X
F211   CODEN: SARHE4
SOUTHEASTERN ARCHAEOLOGY. 2/yr. $25 to individuals; institutions $50 (effective 1997 & 1998). Southeastern Archaeological Conference, c/o Southeastern Archaeological Survey, Box 1249, Fayetteville, AR 72702-1249. Ed. Robert C. Mainfort, Jr. R&P contact: Robert C. Mainfort. TEL 501-575-6560. adv. contact: Robert C. Mainfort. bk.rev. circ. 1,000. (back issues avail.) **Indexed:** Anthropol.Lit.
   —BLDSC (8352.354000).
   Formerly (until 1982): Bulletin of the Southeastern Archaeological Conference.
   Description: Contains articles, reports and other information pertaining to archaeological research in the southeastern region of the United States.
   Refereed Serial

ARCHAEOLOGY

930.1   SA   ISSN 1019-5785
SOUTHERN AFRICAN FIELD ARCHAEOLOGY. (Text in English) 1992. 2/yr. R.35 to individuals (outside southern Africa $25); institutions R.50 (outside southern Africa $30) (effective 1996 & 1997). Albany Museum, Somerset St., Grahamstown 6140, South Africa. TEL 27-461-22312. FAX 27-461-22398. E-mail: ambj@warthog.ru.ac.za. Eds. J.N.F. Binneman, L.E. Webley. adv.; bk.rev. **Indexed:** A.I.C.P. **Document type:** academic/scholarly publication.
—BLDSC (8352.590500).
    Description: Publishes current research projects, site reports, rack art panels, rescue excavations, contract notes and reviews.
    Refereed Serial

913   US
SOUTHERN ILLINOIS UNIVERSITY AT CARBONDALE. CENTER FOR ARCHAEOLOGICAL INVESTIGATIONS. OCCASIONAL PAPER. irreg. price varies. Southern Illinois University at Carbondale, Center for Archaeological Investigations, Carbondale, IL 62901. TEL 618-453-5031. FAX 618-453-3253. Ed. Donna Butler. R&P contact: Donna Butler. TEL 618-453-5031. adv. contact: Carolyn Taylor. circ. 500. **Indexed:** Anthropol.Lit. **Document type:** monographic series.

913   US
SOUTHERN ILLINOIS UNIVERSITY AT CARBONDALE. CENTER FOR ARCHAEOLOGICAL INVESTIGATIONS. RESEARCH PAPER. 1978. irreg. price varies. Southern Illinois University at Carbondale, Center for Archaeological Investigations, Carbondale, IL 62901. TEL 618-453-5031. FAX 618-453-3253. Ed. Donna Butler. R&P contact: Donna E. Butler. adv. contact: Carolyn Taylor. circ. 500. **Indexed:** Anthropol.Lit. **Document type:** monographic series.

913   US   ISSN 0085-6525
E78.S55
SOUTHERN INDIAN STUDIES. 1949. a. $10 to individuals; institutions $25 (includes q. Newsletter). North Carolina Archaeological Society, 109 E. Jones St., Raleigh, NC 27601-2807. TEL 919-733-7342. FAX 919-733-8653. Ed. Mark A. Mathis. bk.rev.; bibl.; illus. circ. 500. **Indexed:** Amer.Hist.& Life (1959-), Anthropol.Lit., Hist.Abstr. (1959-). **Document type:** academic/scholarly publication.
—UnCover.
    Description: Articles on the archaeology, ethnohistory and ethnography of Southern Indians and other archaeological issues.

913 570   US   ISSN 0038-4844
F778
SOUTHWESTERN LORE. 1935. q. $12.50 to individuals; institutions $25; families $15. Colorado Archaeological Society, Inc., c/o Donald C. Tucker, 4215 Balsam St., Wheatridge, CO 80033. TEL 303-431-9060. Ed. Gordon C. Tucker, Jr. bk.rev.; film rev.; bibl.; charts; illus.; cum.index: vols.1-20 (1935-1955), vols.21-30 (1955-1965), vols.31-40 (1965-1975), vols.41-50 (1975-1984), vols.51-60 (1985-1994). circ. 1,000. **Indexed:** Amer.Hist.& Life (1968-1971; 1981-1994), Anthropol.Lit., Hist.Abstr. (1968-1971; 1981-). **Document type:** academic/scholarly publication.
—UnCover.

SPIEGEL HISTORIAEL; maandblad voor geschiedenis en archeologie. see *HISTORY*

930.1   NE   ISSN 0928-9178
SPOREN IN DE TIJD. 1993. irreg. Amsterdam University Press, Prinsengracht 747-751, 1017 JX Amsterdam, Netherlands. TEL 31-20-4200050. FAX 31-20-4203214. **Document type:** monographic series.

913   PL   ISSN 0081-3834
SPRAWOZDANIA ARCHEOLOGICZNE. (Text mainly in Polish, occasionally in English; summaries in English) 1955. a. price varies. Polska Akademia Nauk, Instytut Archeologii i Etnologii (Krakow), Ul. Slawkowska 17, 31-016 Krakow, Poland. TEL 48-12-222905. (Subscr. to: Secesja, ul. Sw. Jana 12, Krakow, Poland) Ed. J. Machnik. circ. 700. **Indexed:** A.I.C.P., Br.Archaeol.Abstr., IBR. **Document type:** academic/scholarly publication.
    Description: Articles and reviews on field research in Little Poland, methodological articles.

913   AU
SPRECHENDE STEINE. 1986. a. S.40. Archaeologischer Verein Flavia Solva, Billrothgasse 15, A-8010 Graz, Austria. Ed. Gunda Pfundner. adv. circ. 500. (back issues avail.) **Document type:** academic/scholarly publication.
    Description: Archaeological information about ancient ruins in the Southern Styria region of Austria.

SRPSKA AKADEMIJA NAUKA I UMETNOSTI. ODELJENJE DRUSTVENIH NAUKA. SPOMENIK. see *SOCIAL SCIENCES: COMPREHENSIVE WORKS*

913   UK
DA670.S69
STAFFORDSHIRE ARCHAEOLOGICAL AND HISTORICAL SOCIETY. TRANSACTIONS. 1960. a. £11 to individuals; institutions £15. Staffordshire Archaeological and Historical Society, William Salt Library, Eastgate St., Stafford ST16 2LZ, England. Ed. Dr. N. Tringham. illus. circ. 300. (also avail. in microfilm from UMI; reprint service avail. from UMI) **Indexed:** Avery Ind.Archit.Per., Br.Archaeol.Abstr., Br.Hum.Ind., RILA. **Document type:** monographic series.
—BLDSC (9010.090000).
    Formerly: South Staffordshire Archaeological and Historical Society. Transactions (ISSN 0457-7817)
    Refereed Serial

913.031   YU   ISSN 0350-0241
STARINAR. (Text in Serbo-Croatian; summaries mostly in French) 1884; N.S. 1950. a. Arheoloski Institut - Institute of Archaeology, Knez Mihailova 35, 11001 Belgrade, Yugoslavia. (Subscr. to: Jugoslovenska Knjiga, Agencija za Uvoz-Izvoz, trg. Republike 5, 1100 Belgrade, Yugoslavia) Ed. Vladimir Kondic. bk.rev.; bibl.; illus. circ. 800. (back issues avail.) **Indexed:** A.I.C.P., Anthropol.Lit., Numis.Lit.
—KNAW.

913   IT   ISSN 1120-4699
STATE ARCHIVES OF ASSYRIA BULLETIN. 1987. s-a. $60. Herder Editrice e Libreria s.r.l., Piazza Montecitorio, 120, 00186 Rome, Italy. TEL 67-94628. FAX 678-47-51. (Co-publisher: Sargon) Ed. F.M. Fales. **Indexed:** Bibl.Ling., IBR. **Document type:** academic/scholarly publication.
    Description: Devoted to philological and historical studies on the documents from the Neo-Assyrian state archives.

STATNI OKRESNI ARCHIV V OLOMOUCI. ROCENKA. see *HISTORY — History Of Europe*

STEWARD ANTHROPOLOGICAL SOCIETY. JOURNAL. see *ANTHROPOLOGY*

930.1   US   ISSN 0140-654X
STONEHENGE VIEWPOINT; archaeology, astronomy, geology, and related arts and sciences. 1973. s-a. $20. 2261 Las Positas Rd., Santa Barbara, CA 93105-4116. TEL 805-687-9350. Ed. Donald L. Cyr; Pub. Joan L. Cyr. adv.; bk.rev. circ. 3,000. (back issues avail.) **Document type:** academic/scholarly publication, catalog, monographic series.
    Description: Encompasses archeology, astronomy, geology, meteorology, and related arts and sciences as applied to unsolved mysteries of the planet.

913   US
STONES AND BONES NEWSLETTER. 1959. m. $12 to individuals; institutions $17 (includes Journal of Alabama Archaeology). Alabama Archaeological Society, 13075 Moundville Archaeological Park, Moundville, AL 35474. TEL 205-371-2266. FAX 205-371-2494. Ed. McDonald Brooms. bk.rev.; charts. circ. 500. (reprint service avail. from UMI) **Document type:** newsletter.

913   IT
STUDI E MATERIALI DI ARCHEOLOGIA GRECA. 1983. irreg., no.4, 1992. price varies. (Universita de Catania, Istituto di Archeologia) L'Erma di Bretschneider, Via Cassiodoro 19, 00193 Rome, Italy. TEL 39-6-6874127. FAX 39-6-6874129. (Co-sponsor: Centro di Studi per l'Archeologia Greca) Dir. Giovanni Rizza.

913 956.91   IT   ISSN 0393-0246
STUDI EBLAITI. (Text in English, French, German, Italian) 1979. irreg. $60. (Universita di Roma "La Sapienza") Herder Editrice e Libreria s.r.l., Piazza Montecitorio 120, 00186 Rome, Italy. TEL 67-94628. FAX 678-47-51. Ed. Paolo Matthiae. circ. 1,000. (back issues avail.) **Indexed:** Anthropol.Lit., Bibl.Ling. **Document type:** academic/scholarly publication.

913 900   IT   ISSN 0585-4911
STUDI GENUENSI. (Text in Italian) 1970. a. Lit.30000 (effective 1997). Istituto Internazionale di Studi Liguri - International Institute of Ligurian Studies, Via Romana, 39, 18012 Bordighera, Italy. TEL 39-184-263601. FAX 39-184-266421. circ. 1,000. **Indexed:** M.L.A. **Document type:** academic/scholarly publication.
    Description: Contains historical studies of Genoa and Liguria (a northwestern coastal region of Italy).

930   NE
STUDIA AMSTELODAMENSIA AD EPIGRAPHICAM, IUS ANTIQUUM ET PAPYROLOGICAM PERTINENTIA. (Text in English, French, German) 1972. irreg., vol.34, 1995. price varies. J.C. Gieben, Nieuwe Herengracht 35, 1011 RM Amsterdam, Netherlands. TEL 31-20-6275170. FAX 31-20-6275170. (Dist. in N. America by: John Benjamins Publishing Co., Box 27519, Philadelphia, PA 19118-0519. TEL 215-836-1200. FAX 215-836-1204) (back issues avail.) **Document type:** monographic series.
    Description: Presents scholarly studies relating to epigraphs, ancient law, and papyrii.

913   HU   ISSN 0081-6280
STUDIA ARCHAEOLOGICA. (Text in German) 1963. irreg., vol.11, 1991. price varies. (Magyar Tudomanyos Akademia, Regeszeti Intezet) Akademiai Kiado Rt., P.O. Box 245, H-1519 Budapest, Hungary. TEL 36-1-2043976. FAX 36-1-2043973. **Indexed:** Anthropol.Lit. **Document type:** monographic series.

913   IT   ISSN 0081-6299
STUDIA ARCHAEOLOGICA. 1961. irreg. price varies. L'Erma di Bretschneider, Via Cassiodoro 19, 00193 Rome, Italy. TEL 39-6-6874127. FAX 39-6-6874129.

930.1   SP
STUDIA ARQUEOLOGICA. irreg., no.81, 1993. price varies. Universidad de Valladolid, Secretariado de Publicaciones, C. Juan Mambrilla, 14, 47003 Valladolid, Spain. TEL 983-423000. FAX 34-83-290300. TELEX 26357. **Document type:** monographic series.

930.1   NE   ISSN 0081-6396
STUDIA FRANCISCI SCHOLTEN MEMORIAE DICATA. 1952. irreg., vol.5, 1982. Nederlands Instituut voor Het Nabije Oosten - Netherlands Institute for the Near East, Witte Singel 25, P.O. Box 9515, 2300 RA Leiden, Netherlands. TEL 31-71-5272036. FAX 31-71-5272038. R&P contact: J. de Roos. adv. contact: J. de Roos. **Document type:** monographic series.

913 551   PL   ISSN 0137-530X
TN903.P7
STUDIA I MATERIALY DO DZIEJOW ZUP SOLNYCH W POLSCE. (Text in Polish; summaries in English) 1965. a. 4 Zl.($2) (effective 1996). Muzeum Zup Krakowskich - Museum of Cracovian Salt Works, Ul. Zamkowa 8, 32-020 Wieliczka, Poland. TEL 221-947. (Co-sponsor: Ministerstwo Kultury i Sztuki) Ed. Antoni Jodlowski. R&P contact: Elzbieta Benarowska-Guzik. adv. contact: Elzbieta Bendarowska-Guzik. bk.rev. circ. 400. (back issues avail.)
    Description: History of salt mines in Poland and Europe, geology of salt deposits, machines and tools used in mines. Includes ethnography, history of art and mining cartography.

STUDIA PHOENICIA. see *HISTORY — History Of The Near East*

STUDIEN ZUR GESCHICHTE NORDWEST-GRIECHENLANDS. see *CLASSICAL STUDIES*

STUDIES IN ANCIENT ORIENTAL CIVILIZATION. see *HISTORY — History Of The Near East*

ARCHAEOLOGY

913 US
STUDIES IN ARCHAEOLOGICAL SCIENCE. 1971. irreg., vol.14, 1985. Academic Press, Inc., 525 B St., Ste. 1900, San Diego, CA 92101-4495. TEL 619-231-0926. FAX 619-699-6715. (Subscr. to: Order Dept., 6277 Sea Harbor Dr., 4th Fl., Orlando, FL 32887. TEL 800-321-5068) Ed. G.W. Dimbleby. (reprint service avail. from ISI)

STUDIES IN ASIAN ART AND ARCHAEOLOGY. see *ORIENTAL STUDIES*

STUDIES IN CONSERVATION. see *ART*

930.1 BE
▼**STUDIES IN EASTERN MEDITERRANEAN ARCHAEOLOGY.** 1995. irreg. price varies. (Katholieke Universiteit Leuven, Center for Interdisciplinary Archaeological Research) N.V. Brepols, Steenweg op Tielen 68, 2300 Turnhout, Belgium. TEL 32-14-402500. FAX 32-14-428919. **Document type:** monographic series.
   Description: Reports on excavations in the eastern Mediterranean area, including archaeozoology, ancient history, architecture, archaeometry, palaeobotany and anthropology.

913 SW ISSN 0081-8232
STUDIES IN MEDITERRANEAN ARCHAEOLOGY. MONOGRAPH SERIES. (Text in English, French and German) 1962. irreg., no.123, 1996. price varies. Paul Aastroems Foerlag, William Gibsons Vaeg 11, S-433 76 Jonsered, Sweden. TEL 31-7956600. FAX 46-31-7956710. circ. 1,000. **Indexed:** Avery Ind.Archit.Per. **Document type:** monographic series.

913 SW
STUDIES IN MEDITERRANEAN ARCHAEOLOGY. POCKET-BOOK SERIES. (Text in English, French and German) 1974. irreg., no.145, 1996. Paul Aastroems Foerlag, William Gibsons vaeg 11, S-433 76 Jonsered, Sweden. TEL 46-31-7956600. FAX 46-31-7956710. circ. 1,000. **Document type:** monographic series.

913 US ISSN 0585-7023
E51
STUDIES IN PRE-COLUMBIAN ART AND ARCHAEOLOGY. 1966. irreg., no.33, 1994. price varies. Dumbarton Oaks, Publications Office, 1703 32nd St., N.W., Washington, DC 20007. TEL 202-339-6431. E-mail: DOBooks@aol.com; URL: http://members.aol.com/DOBooks/TitleList.html. Ed. Jeffrey Quilter. R&P contact: Glenn Buby. bibl.; charts; illus. circ. 1,000. (back issues avail.) **Indexed:** Anthropol.Lit. **Document type:** monographic series, academic/scholarly publication.
   Refereed Serial

913 RM ISSN 1220-4781
STUDII SI CERCETARI DE ISTORIE VECHE SI ARHEOLOGIE. (Text in Rumanian; summaries in French) 1950. 4/yr. (Academia Romana, Institutul de Arheologie Vasile Parvan) Editura Academiei Romane, Calea 13 Septembrie 13, 76117 Bucharest, Rumania. (Dist. by: Rodipet SA, Piata Presei Libere 1, sec. 1, P.O. Box 33-57, Bucharest, Rumania. TEL 401-6185103. FAX 401-2226407) Ed. Mircea Babes. bk.rev.; charts; illus.; index. **Indexed:** A.I.C.P., Anthropol.Lit., Numis.Lit.
   —BLDSC (8497.260000); KNAW.
   Formerly: Studii si Cercetari de Istorie Veche (ISSN 0039-4009)

220 IS ISSN 0081-8917
STUDIUM BIBLICUM FRANCISCANUM. COLLECTIO MAIOR. (Text in English, French, Italian) 1941. irreg., no.39, 1996. price varies. Franciscan Printing Press, P.O. Box 14064, Jerusalem 91140, Israel. TEL 972-2-6286594. FAX 972-2-6272274. circ. 1,000. (also avail. in microfiche from IDC) **Document type:** monographic series.

220 IS ISSN 0081-8925
STUDIUM BIBLICUM FRANCISCANUM. COLLECTIO MINOR. (Text in English, French, Italian) 1961. irreg., no.35, 1997. price varies. Franciscan Printing Press, P.O. Box 14064, Jerusalem 91140, Israel. TEL 972-2-6286594. FAX 972-2-6272274. circ. 1,000. **Document type:** monographic series.

220 IS ISSN 0081-8933
BS410
STUDIUM BIBLICUM FRANCISCANUM. LIBER ANNUUS. (Text in English, French, German, Italian, Latin) 1951. a., vol.45, 1995. price varies. Franciscan Printing Press, P.O. Box 14064, 91140 Jerusalem, Israel. TEL 972-2-6286594. FAX 972-2-6272274. bibl.; cum.index: 1951-1970. circ. 1,200. (also avail. in microfiche from IDC; back issues avail.) **Indexed:** Numis.Lit., RILA. **Document type:** academic/scholarly publication.

913 IS
STUDIUM BIBLICUM FRANCISCANUM. MUSEUM. (Text in English, French, Italian) 1976. irreg., no.13, 1996. price varies. Franciscan Printing Press, P.O. Box 14064, Jerusalem 91140, Israel. TEL 972-2-6286594. FAX 972-2-6272274. circ. 1,000. **Document type:** monographic series.

930.1 IT ISSN 1123-6256
▼**SUBAQUEOUS ARCHAEOLOGIST.** 1995. 3/yr. Lit.18000 (foreign Lit.25000) (effective 1997). Edipuglia s.r.l., Via Dalmazia 22-B, 70050 S. Spirito (BA), Italy. TEL 39-80-5333056. FAX 39-80-5333057.
   Description: Offers information, comments and opinions about the world of subaqueous archeology in Italy and other nations.

935 BE
▼**SUBARTU.** (Text in English) 1995. irreg. (European Centre for Upper Mesopotamian Studies) N.V. Brepols, Steenweg op Tielen 68, 2300 Turnhout, Belgium. TEL 32-14-402500. FAX 32-14-428919. bibl. **Document type:** monographic series.
   Description: Publishes studies on the archaeology, history, geography, environment, epigraphy and sociology of the Upper Mesopotamian region from prehistory to the present day.

DER SUELCHGAU. see *HISTORY — History Of Europe*

930.1 US ISSN 1079-2198
SUFFOLK COUNTY ARCHAEOLOGICAL ASSOCIATION. NEWSLETTER. 3/yr. $20 membership. Suffolk County Archaeological Association, Box 1542, Stony Brook, NY 11790-0910. TEL 516-929-8725. FAX 516-929-6967. Ed. Gaynell Stone. R&P contact: Gaynell Stone. bk.rev.; illus. **Document type:** newsletter, academic/scholarly publication.
   Description: Contains news of archaeological excavations and historic sites in Suffolk county.

914.2 942 UK ISSN 0143-4896
SUFFOLK INSTITUTE OF ARCHAEOLOGY AND HISTORY. NEWSLETTER. s-a. £12.50 (overseas £15) (effective 1996). Suffolk Institute of Archaeology and History, c/o E.A. Martin, Hon. Secy., Oak Tree Farm, Finborough Rd., Hitcham, Ipswich, Suffolk IP7 7LS, England. TEL 44-1449-741266. Ed. J. Middleton-Stewart. R&P contact: E.A. Martin. **Document type:** newsletter.

914.2 942 UK ISSN 0262-6004
SUFFOLK INSTITUTE OF ARCHAEOLOGY AND HISTORY. PROCEEDINGS. 1849. a. £12.50 (overseas £15) (effective 1996). Suffolk Institute of Archaeology and History, c/o E.A. Martin, Hon. Secy., Oak Tree Farm, Finborough Rd., Hitcham, Ipswich, Suffolk IP7 7LS, England. TEL 44-1449-741266. Ed. D. Allen. R&P contact: E.A. Martin. bk.rev. circ. 876. **Indexed:** Br.Archaeol.Abstr., Numis.Lit. **Document type:** proceedings, academic/scholarly publication.
   —BLDSC (6826.025500).
   Refereed Serial

913 IQ ISSN 0081-9271
DS67 CODEN: SUMRA9
SUMER;* journal of archaeology in Iraq. (Text in Arabic) 1945. a. ID.10000. Ministry of Culture and Information, State Organization of Antiquities and Heritage, Jamal Abdul Nasr St., Baghdad, Iraq. TEL 4158355. **Indexed:** Anthropol.Lit., GeoRef., Mid.East: Abstr.& Ind., Numis.Lit.
   —SWETS.

930.1 709 FI ISSN 0355-1822
SUOMEN MUINAISMUISTOYHDISTYKSEN AIKAKAUSKIRJA/FINSKA FORNMINNESFOERENINGENS TIDSKRIFT. (Text in English, Finnish, German and Swedish) 1874. irreg., vol.103, 1996. price varies. Suomen Muinaismuistoyhdistys - Finnish Antiquarian Society, P.O. Box 213, Nervanderinkatu 13, FIN-00101 Helsinki, Finland. Ed. Torsten Edgren. charts; illus. **Document type:** academic/scholarly publication.
   Description: Publishes contributions in archaeology, art history, and cultural history.

930.1 572 FI ISSN 0355-1806
SUOMEN MUSEO. (Text in English, Finnish and German) 1894. a. FIM 130. Suomen Muinaismuistoyhdistys - Finnish Antiquarian Society, P.O. Box 913, Nervanderinkatu 13, FIN-00101 Helsinki 10, Finland. Ed. Tuukka Talvio. illus.; cum.index: 1894-1993. **Indexed:** A.I.C.P., Anthropol.Lit., Br.Archaeol.Abstr., IBR, Numis.Lit. **Document type:** academic/scholarly publication.
   —KR SourceOne.
   Description: Publishes contributions in archaeology, anthropology, art history, and cultural history.

SUPPLEMENTUM EPIGRAPHICUM GRAECUM. see *CLASSICAL STUDIES*

913 UK ISSN 0309-7803
SURREY ARCHAEOLOGICAL COLLECTIONS. 1858. irreg. £25 (foreign £35) membership. Surrey Archaeological Society, Castle Arch, Guildford, Surrey GU1 3SX, England. TEL 44-1483-32454. FAX 44-1483-32454. Eds. G. Crocker, P. Nicolaysen. R&P contact: Glenys Crocker. bk.rev.; cum.index: vols. 1-71. (back issues avail.) **Indexed:** Br.Archaeol.Abstr., Br.Hum.Ind., Numis.Lit. **Document type:** academic/scholarly publication.
   —BLDSC (8548.340000).

913 UK ISSN 0585-9980
SURREY ARCHAEOLOGICAL SOCIETY. BULLETIN. 1965. 9/yr. membership. Surrey Archaeological Society, Castle Arch, Guildford, Surrey GU1 3SX, England. TEL 44-1483-32454. FAX 44-1483-32454. Ed. P.M. Jones. R&P contact: Glenys Crocker. adv. circ. 850. **Document type:** bulletin.
   —BLDSC (2770.580000).

913 UK ISSN 0308-342X
SURREY ARCHAEOLOGICAL SOCIETY. RESEARCH VOLUMES. 1974. irreg. membership. Surrey Archaeological Society, Castle Arch, Guildford, Surrey GU1 3SX, England. TEL 44-1483-32454. FAX 44-1483-32454. R&P contact: Glenys Crocker. **Indexed:** Br.Archaeol.Abstr. **Document type:** monographic series.
   —BLDSC (7774.150000).

913 UK ISSN 1357-7417
DA670.S97
SUSSEX PAST AND PRESENT. 1971. 3/yr. membership. Sussex Archaeological Society, Bull House, 92 High St., Lewes, Sussex BN7 1XH, England. TEL 44-1273-486260. FAX 44-1273-486990. Ed. Andy Freeman. bk.rev.; bibl. **Indexed:** Avery Ind.Archit.Per., Br.Archaeol.Abstr. **Document type:** newsletter.
   ●Also available online. Vendor(s): Information Access Co.
   Former titles (until 1994): Past and Present; (until 1993): S A S News (ISSN 0307-2568)

913 SW ISSN 0081-9921
SVENSKA INSTITUTET I ATHEN. SKRIFTER. (Latin title: Acta Instituti Atheniensis Regni Sueciae. Includes Opuscula Atheniensia) 1951. irreg., no.44, 1996. price varies. Paul Aastroems Foerlag, William Gibsons vaeg 11, S-433 76 Jonsered, Sweden. Ed. B. Alroth. bk.rev. circ. 1,000. **Document type:** academic/scholarly publication.

SVENSKA INSTITUTET I ATHEN. SKRIFTER; series prima in 4 J. see *CLASSICAL STUDIES*

913   SW   ISSN 0081-993X
DG12
SVENSKA INSTITUTET I ROM. SKRIFTER. ACTA SERIES PRIMA. (Latin title: Acta Instituti Romani Regni Sueciae. Includes Opuscula Archaeologica and Opuscula Romana) 1932. irreg., no.52, 1996. price varies. (Svenska Institutet i Rom - Swedish Institute in Rome) Paul Aastroems Foerlag, William Gibsons vaeg 11, S-433 76 Jonsered, Sweden. TEL 46-31-795-66-00. FAX 46-31-795-67-10. Ed. Brita Alroth. bk.rev. circ. 1,000. **Document type:** monographic series.

913   PL   ISSN 0082-044X
SWIATOWIT. (Text in Polish; summaries in English, French, Russian) 1899-19??; resumed 1958. irreg., vol.37, 1994. price varies. (Uniwersytet Warszawski, Instytut Archeologii) Wydawnictwa Uniwersytetu Warszawskiego, Ul. Nowy Swiat 4, 00-497 Warsaw, Poland. TEL 48-22-6253044. FAX 48-22-6253044. (Dist. by: Ars Polona, Krakowskie Przedmiescie 7, 00-068 Warsaw, Poland) Ed. Witold Hensel. R&P contact: Jolanta Okonska. circ. 500. **Indexed:** A.I.C.P., Anthropol.Lit. **Document type:** academic/scholarly publication.

913   700   FR   ISSN 0039-7946
DS94.5
SYRIA; revue d'art oriental et d'archeologie. 1920. 4/yr. (2 double nos./yr.) (Institut Francais d'Archeologie de Beyrouth) Librairie Orientaliste Paul Geuthner, 12 rue Vavin, 75006 Paris, France. TEL 33-1-46-34-71-30. FAX 33-1-43-29-75-64. TELEX 250 303 PUBLIC PARIS. Eds. E. Will, J. Caquot. bk.rev.; abstr.; illus.; index. (tabloid format; also avail. in microfiche from IDC) **Indexed:** Avery Ind.Archit.Per., Bibl.Ling., IBR, MLA Intl.Bibl., Numis.Lit. **Document type:** academic/scholarly publication.
—SWETS.

930.1   NE   ISSN 0922-3312
T M A. (Text in Dutch, occasionally in English; summaries in English) 1988. 2/yr. fl.27 (480 BEF). (Stichting ter Ondersteuning van Oudheidkundig Onderzoek) Tijdschrift voor Mediterrane Archeologie, Postbus 7030, 9701 JA Groningen, Netherlands. E-mail: t.r.hoekstra@let.rug.nl. Ed.Bd. adv.: B&W page fl.100. bk.rev.; bibl.; illus.; maps; stat.; cum. index every 5 yrs. (back issues avail.) **Document type:** academic/scholarly publication.
Description: Publishes reports, articles, reviews and commentaries on current Dutch and Belgian archaeological research in the Mediterranean region.

T R A C E. (Travaux et Recherches dans les Ameriques du Centre) see ANTHROPOLOGY

914   SP   ISSN 0213-2818
TABONA; revista de prehistoria y de arqueologia y filologia clasicas. 1972. a. $25 to individuals; institutions $30. Universidad de La Laguna, Departamento de Prehistoria, Antropologia y Paleoambiente, Secretariado de Publicaciones, San Agustin 30, 38201 La Laguna-Tenerife, Islas Canarias, Spain. TEL 922-25-81-27. adv. **Indexed:** IBR. **Document type:** academic/scholarly publication.
—CINDOC.

TALOHA. see MUSEUMS AND ART GALLERIES

TARBIZ; a quarterly for Jewish studies. see RELIGIONS AND THEOLOGY — Judaic

930.1 933   IS   ISSN 0334-4355
DS111.A1   CODEN: TEAVEY
TEL AVIV; journal of the Tel Aviv Institute of Archaeology. Variant title: Tel Aviv Journal of Archaeology. (Text in English) 1974. s-a. $34. Tel Aviv University, Institute of Archaeology, Publications Section, P.O. Box 39040, Ramat Aviv, Tel Aviv 69978, Israel. TEL 972-3-6409703. FAX 972-3-6407237. Ed. Jak Yakar. bibl.; illus. circ. 800. (back issues avail.) **Indexed:** IBR, Int.Z.Bibelwiss., Old Test.Abstr., Rel. & Theol.Abstr. **Document type:** academic/scholarly publication.
—BLDSC (8779.310000).

930.1 933   IS
TEL AVIV UNIVERSITY. INSTITUTE OF ARCHAEOLOGY. MONOGRAPH SERIES. (Text in English or Hebrew) 1973. ireg., vol.11, 1995. price varies. Tel Aviv University, Institute of Archaeology, P.O. Box 39040, Ramat Aviv, Tel Aviv 69978, Israel. TEL 972-3-6409703. FAX 972-3-6407237. (back issues avail.) **Document type:** monographic series.
Description: Publishes historical studies and reports of archaeological excavations.

930.1 933   IS
TEL AVIV UNIVERSITY. INSTITUTE OF ARCHAEOLOGY. OCCASIONAL PUBLICATIONS. (Text in English) 1993. irreg. price varies. Tel Aviv University, Institute of Archaeology, P.O. Box 39040, Ramat Aviv, Tel Aviv 69978, Israel. TEL 972-3-6409703. FAX 972-3-6407237. **Document type:** monographic series.

TENNESSEE ANTHROPOLOGICAL ASSOCIATION. MISCELLANEOUS PAPER. see ANTHROPOLOGY

TENNESSEE ANTHROPOLOGICAL ASSOCIATION. NEWSLETTER. see ANTHROPOLOGY

TENNESSEE ANTHROPOLOGIST. see ANTHROPOLOGY

TERRA AMERIGA. see ANTHROPOLOGY

TERRA SANTA. see RELIGIONS AND THEOLOGY — Roman Catholic

913 930   IT   ISSN 0452-2907
TESTIMONIA SICILIAE ANTIQUA. 1981. irreg., latest 1988. price varies. (Istituto Siciliano per la Storia Antica) Giorgio Bretschneider, Via Crescenzo 43, 00193 Rome, Italy. E-mail: bretschneider@euronet.it. **Document type:** academic/scholarly publication.

913 976.4   US   ISSN 0082-2930
F381   CODEN: BTASDX
TEXAS ARCHEOLOGICAL SOCIETY. BULLETIN. 1929. a. $25 includes newsletter. Texas Archeological Society, Center for Archeological Research, Univ. of Texas at San Antonio, San Antonio, TX 78285. TEL 512-691-4462. bk.rev. circ. 1,200. **Indexed:** A.I.C.P., Anthropol.Lit., GeoRef. **Document type:** bulletin.
—BLDSC (2776.300000); UnCover.

917   US   ISSN 0495-2944
TEXAS ARCHEOLOGICAL SOCIETY. SPECIAL PUBLICATION. 1962. irreg., no.3, 1976. $10 per no. Texas Archeological Society, Center for Archeological Research, Univ. of Texas at San Antonio, San Antonio, TX 78285. TEL 512-691-4462. **Document type:** monographic series.

913 976.4   US   ISSN 0082-2949
TEXAS ARCHEOLOGY. 1957. q. membership. Texas Archeological Society, Center for Archeological Research, Univ. of Texas at San Antonio, San Antonio, TX 78285. TEL 512-691-4462. bk.rev. circ. 1,200.

913   BE   ISSN 0775-3411
THORIKOS; preliminary reports of the excavations at Thorikos. (Supplement avail.: Thorikos-Guides) (Text in English, French) 1963. irreg., vol.9, 1990 (for years 1977-1982). 2500 BEF per vol. (Comite des Fouilles Belges en Grece - Comite voor Belgische Opgravingen in Griekenland) Editions Peeters s.p.r.l., Bondgenotenlaan 153, 3000 Leuven, Belgium. TEL 32-16-235170. FAX 32-16-228500. URL: http://www.peeters-leuven.be. adv. (back issues avail.) **Document type:** monographic series.

942   UK   ISSN 0309-9210
DA670.N89
THOROTON SOCIETY OF NOTTINGHAMSHIRE. TRANSACTIONS. 1897. a. £18 membership (effective 1996). Thoroton Society of Nottinghamshire, Nottinghamshire Archives, County House, Castle Meadow Rd., Nottingham NG2 1AG, England. Eds. A. Henstock, C. Allen. bk.rev.; cum.index: vols. 1-100. circ. 500. **Indexed:** Br.Archaeol.Abstr., Br.Hum.Ind., Numis.Lit. **Document type:** academic/scholarly publication.

THRACO-DACICA. see HISTORY — History Of Europe

930.1 948.5 SW   ISSN 1100-9586
TILLSLAGET. 1987. q. SEK 40 membership. Umeaa Arkeologifoerening, Umeaa Universitet, Institutionen foer Arkeologi, S-901 87 Umeaa, Sweden.

913   GW   ISSN 0082-450X
TIRYNS. (Text in German) 1912. irreg., vol.11, 1990. price varies. (Deutsches Archaeologisches Institut, Athens, GR) Verlag Philipp von Zabern GmbH, Philipp-von-Zabern-Platz 1-3, 55116 Mainz, Germany. TEL 06131-28747-0. FAX 06131-223710. **Document type:** monographic series.

913 700   SW   ISSN 0349-764X
TJUSTBYGDENS KULTURHISTORISKA FOERENING. AARSBOK. Cover title: Tjustbygden. 1926. a. SEK 90 membership. Tjustbygdens Kulturhistoriska Foerening, Kulbackens Museum, P.O. Box 257, S-593 01 Vaestervik, Sweden. Ed.Bd. adv. circ. 1,200.
Formerly (until 1977): Tjustbygdens Kulturhistoriska Foerening. Meddelande.

913   FR   ISSN 1161-9473
TOPOI ORIENT OCCIDENT. 1979. 1/yr. 180 F. Societe des Amis de la Bibliotheque Salomon Reinach, Maison de l'Orient Mediterraneen, 7 rue Raulin, 69007 Lyon, France. FAX 33-4-78-58-32-76. Ed. Marie-Francoise Boussac. bk.rev. **Document type:** academic/scholarly publication.
Formerly (until 1990): Societe des Amis de la Bibliotheque Salomon Reinach. Bulletin de Liaison (ISSN 0994-3269)

TOR; journal of archaeology. see HISTORY — History Of Europe

913   PL   ISSN 0860-147X
TOWARZYSTWO NAUKOWE W TORUNIU. PRACE ARCHEOLOGICZNE. (Text in Polish; summaries in German) 1938. irreg., vol.9, 1991. price varies. Towarzystwo Naukowe w Toruniu, Ul. Wysoka 16, 87-100 Torun, Poland. TEL 48-56-23941. TELEX 552388 FSBH PL. Ed. Krystyna Przewozna-Armon. circ. 750. **Document type:** monographic series.
Formerly (until 1974): Prace Prehistoryczne.

913   SP   ISSN 0211-5174
DP302.N265
TRABAJOS DE ARQUEOLOGIA NAVARRA. 1979. irreg. 2500 ptas. Gobierno de Navarra, Fondo de Publicaciones, Navas de Tolosa, 21, 31002 Pamplona, Spain. TEL 34-48-427123. **Indexed:** Anthropol.Lit.
—CINDOC.

913   SP   ISSN 0082-5638
GN835.A1   CODEN: TRPREI
TRABAJOS DE PREHISTORIA. NUEVA SERIE. 1960-1968; N.S. 1969. s-a. 5200 ptas. (foreign 7800 ptas.) (effective 1997). Centro Superior de Investigaciones Cientificas (C.S.I.C.), Centro de Estudios Historicos, Departamento de Prehistoria, Vitruvio 8, 28006 Madrid, Spain. TEL 34-1-56162833. FAX 34-1-5629634. Ed. Maria Isabel Martinez Navarrete. adv.; bk.rev.; abstr.; bibl.; charts. **Indexed:** Anthropol.Lit. **Document type:** academic/scholarly publication.
—CINDOC.
Description: Covers prehistoric research in the Iberian Peninsula, the Mediterranean, and Western Europe from the Palaeolithic period through the second Iron Age. Debates the goals and methods of archaeology in the 1990s.

913 669   UK   ISSN 0143-1250
NB1842
TRANSACTIONS OF THE MONUMENTAL BRASS SOCIETY. 1887. a. £8. Guildhall Library, Manuscripts Department, Aldermanbury, London RC2P 2EJ, England. Ed. S.G.H. Freeth. bk.rev.; cum.index. circ. 800. (back issues avail.) **Indexed:** RILA.

TRANSVAAL MUSEUM. MONOGRAPHS. see MUSEUMS AND ART GALLERIES

913   GW   ISSN 0082-643X
TRIERER GRABUNGEN UND FORSCHUNGEN. (Text in German) 1929. irreg., vol.15, 1985. price varies. (Rheinisches Landesmuseum, Trier) Verlag Philipp von Zabern GmbH, Philipp-von-Zabern-Platz 1-3, 55116 Mainz, Germany. TEL 06131-28747-0. FAX 06131-223710. index. **Indexed:** Br.Archaeol.Abstr. **Document type:** monographic series, academic/scholarly publication.

ARCHAEOLOGY

914 709 737   GW   ISSN 0041-2953
TRIERER ZEITSCHRIFT FUER GESCHICHTE UND KUNST DES TRIERER LANDES UND SEINER NACHBARGEBIETE. 1926. a. DM.88. Rheinisches Landesmuseum Trier, Weimarer Allee 1, 54290 Trier, Germany. TEL 49-651-9774-0. FAX 49-651-9774222. Ed.Bd. bk.rev. circ. 750. (back issues avail.) Indexed: Numis.Lit. **Document type:** academic/scholarly publication.

930.1   TU   ISSN 0564-5042
TURK ARKEOLOJI DERGISI/TURKISH REVIEW OF ARCHAEOLOGY. (Text in Turkish, occasionally in English, German) 1956. a. exchange basis. Ministry of Culture, General Directorate of Monuments and Museums - Kultur Bakanligi, Anitlar ve Muzeler Genel Mudurlugu, 06100 Ulus - Ankara, Turkey. TEL 90-312-3104960. FAX 90-312-3111417. Indexed: Anthropol.Lit. **Document type:** academic/scholarly publication.
   Description: Scholarly articles on archaeological projects undertaken in Turkey.

U TZ'IB. see ANTHROPOLOGY

913   UK   ISSN 0082-7355
DA990.U45   CODEN: UJAYAH
ULSTER JOURNAL OF ARCHAEOLOGY. 1938. a. £15 (effective 1998). Ulster Archaeological Society, Archaeology Dept., Queens University, Belfast BT7 1NN, N. Ireland. Ed. D. Simpson. R&P contact: F. McCormick. adv.; bk.rev.; index. circ. 550. Indexed: Br.Archaeol.Abstr., Numis.Lit. **Document type:** academic/scholarly publication.
   —BLDSC (9082.743000).

913   US
CC77.U5
UNDERWATER ARCHAEOLOGY. 1987. a. price varies. Society for Historical Archaeology, Box 30446, Tucson, AZ 85751. TEL 520-886-8006. FAX 520-886-0182. E-mail: sha@azstarnet.com; sha_editor@cup.edu; URL: http://www.azstarnet.com/tildesha. bibl.; charts; illus.; stat. circ. 2,500. (back issues avail.)
   Formerly: Society for Historical Archaeology Conference. Underwater Proceedings (ISSN 1074-3421)
   Description: Papers presented at annual conference dealing with theory, method and legal issues pertaining to underwater archaeology.

913   SP   ISSN 0067-4184
UNIVERSIDAD DE BARCELONA. INSTITUTO DE ARQUEOLOGIA Y PREHISTORIA. PUBLICACIONES EVENTUALES. 1960. irreg., no.26, 1975. 2000 ptas. (effective 1993). Universidad de Barcelona, Instituto de Arqueologia y Prehistoria, Barcelona 7, Spain. TEL 3-333-34-66. FAX 3-449-85-10.

UNIVERSIDAD DE MURCIA. ANALES DE PREHISTORIA Y ARQUEOLOGIA. see HISTORY — History Of Europe

918   PE
UNIVERSIDAD NACIONAL MAYOR DE SAN MARCOS. SEMINARIO DE HISTORIA RURAL ANDINA. SEMINARIO ARQUEOLOGIA.* 1977. irreg. Universidad Nacional Mayor de San Marcos, Seminario de Historia Rural, Av. Republica de Chile, 295, Of. 208, Apdo. 454, Lima, Peru.

918   BL
UNIVERSIDADE DE SAO PAULO. MUSEU PAULISTA. COLECAO. SERIE DE ARQUEOLOGIA. 1975. irreg. Universidade de Sao Paulo, Museu Paulista, Caixa Postal 42.503, Parque da Independencia, 04263 Sao Paulo, Brazil. Ed. Setembrino Petri. Indexed: Anthropol.Lit.
   Supersedes in part (in 1975): Museu Paulista. Colecao (ISSN 0080-6382)

913 800   IT   ISSN 0076-1818
UNIVERSITA DEGLI STUDI DI MACERATA. FACOLTA DI LETTERE E FILOSOFIA. ANNALI. 1968. a. L.60000 price varies. Universita degli Studi di Macerata, Facolta di Lettere e Filosofia, Piaggia Universita 2, 62100 Macerata, Italy. TEL 0773-4181. Ed. Giovanni Ferretti. bk.rev. circ. 500. (back issues avail.) Indexed: M.L.A.

913   GW
UNIVERSITAET BONN. SEMINAR FUER ORIENTALISCHE KUNSTGESCHICHTE. VEROEFFENTLICHUNGEN. REIHE A. NIMRUZ. 1974. irreg. price varies. Dr. Rudolf Habelt GmbH, Am Buchenhang 1, 53115 Bonn, Germany. TEL 49-228-9238322. FAX 49-228-923836. Ed. Klaus Fischer. **Document type:** monographic series, academic/scholarly publication.

930.1   GW
UNIVERSITAETSFORSCHUNGEN ZUR PRAEHISTORISCHEN ARCHAEOLOGIE. 1989. irreg., vol.42, 1997. price varies. Dr. Rudolf Habelt GmbH, Am Buchenhang 1, 53115 Bonn, Germany. TEL 49-228-9238322. FAX 49-228-923836. **Document type:** academic/scholarly publication.

UNIVERSITE CATHOLIQUE DE LOUVAIN. DEPARTEMENT D'ARCHEOLOGIE ET D'HISTOIRE DE L'ART. DOCUMENTS DE TRAVAIL. see ART

930.1 709   BE
UNIVERSITE CATHOLIQUE DE LOUVAIN. DEPARTEMENT D'ARCHEOLOGIE ET D'HISTOIRE DE L'ART. PUBLICATIONS. (Consists of 6 subseries: Aurifex, Archaeologica Transatlantica, Numismatica Lovaniensia, Braives, Arts Africains, Musicologica Neolovaniensia) (Text in English, French) 1972. irreg., no.92, 1997. price varies. Association des Diplomes Histoire Art et Archeologie, College Erasme, Place Blaise Pascal 1, 1348 Louvain-la-Neuve, Belgium. FAX 32-10-472579. E-mail: hackens@arka.ucl.ac.be. Ed. Tony Hackens. charts; illus. circ. 1,000. **Document type:** monographic series.

UNIVERSITE DE MADAGASCAR. MUSEE D'ART ET D'ARCHEOLOGIE. TRAVAUX ET DOCUMENTS. see ART

914 948   NO   ISSN 0333-130X
UNIVERSITETETS OLDSAKSAMLING. AARBOK. (Text in English, French and Norwegian) 1927. a. NOK 110 (effective 1997). Universitetet i Oslo, Oldsaksamlingen - University Museum of National Antiquities, Frederiksgate 3, 0164 Oslo 1, Norway. TEL 47-22-85-19-52. Ed. Egil Mikkelsen. R&P contact: Egil Mikkelsen. bk.rev. circ. 1,000. Indexed: Br.Archaeol.Abstr. **Document type:** academic/scholarly publication.
   Description: Contains articles on prehistoric and medieval subjects, mainly concerned with Scandinavia and Northern Europe.

913   UK
UNIVERSITY COLLEGE LONDON. INSTITUTE OF ARCHAEOLOGY. BULLETIN. 1958. a. price varies. University College London, Institute of Archaeology, 31-34 Gordon Square, London WC1H OPY, England. TEL 0171-387-7050. FAX 0171-383-2572. Ed. J.J. Wilkes. circ. 800. (also avail. in microfilm from UMI) Indexed: Anthropol.Lit., Br.Archaeol.Abstr., Geo.Abstr., IBR, Numis.Lit. **Document type:** bulletin.
   —BLDSC (2578.300000).
   Formerly: University of London. Institute of Archaeology. Bulletin (ISSN 0076-0722)

913   UK
UNIVERSITY COLLEGE LONDON. INSTITUTE OF ARCHAEOLOGY. OCCASIONAL PUBLICATION. 1977. irreg. University College London, Institute of Archaeology, 31-34 Gordon Square, London WC1H OPY, England. TEL 0171-387-7050. FAX 0171-383-2572. Indexed: Br.Archaeol.Abstr. **Document type:** monographic series.
   Formerly: University of London. Institute of Archaeology. Occasional Publication (ISSN 0141-8505)

UNIVERSITY OF ARIZONA. ANTHROPOLOGICAL PAPERS. see ANTHROPOLOGY

560   CN   ISSN 0822-2967
UNIVERSITY OF CALGARY. ARCHAEOLOGICAL ASSOCIATION. ARCHAEOLOGICAL CONFERENCE. PROCEEDINGS. 1969. a. price varies. University of Calgary, Archaeological Association, Department of Archaeology, 2920-24th Ave. N.W., Calgary, AB T2N 1N4, Canada. TEL 403-220-7120. (Subscr. to: Archaeological Association, Department of Archaeology, University of Calgary, 2500 University Dr., N.W., Calgary, AB T2N 1N4, Canada) circ. 150. Indexed: Anthropol.Lit. **Document type:** proceedings, academic/scholarly publication.
   Formerly: University of Calgary. Archaeological Association. Paleo-Environmental Workshop. Proceedings (ISSN 0068-5437)

571   US   ISSN 0068-5933
E51
UNIVERSITY OF CALIFORNIA AT BERKELEY. ARCHAEOLOGICAL RESEARCH FACILITY. CONTRIBUTIONS. 1965. irreg. price varies. University of California at Berkeley, Archaeological Research Facility, Berkeley, CA 94720. TEL 415-642-2212. circ. 400. (also avail. in microform from UMI) **Document type:** academic/scholarly publication.

913   US
UNIVERSITY OF CALIFORNIA AT LOS ANGELES. INSTITUTE OF ARCHAEOLOGY. MONOGRAPH SERIES. 1970. irreg., no.33, 1990. price varies. University of California at Los Angeles, Institute of Archaeology, 405 Hilgard Ave., Los Angeles, CA 90024-1510. TEL 213-825-7411. FAX 213-206-4723. Ed. Ernestine S. Elster. Indexed: Anthropol.Lit. **Document type:** academic/scholarly publication, monographic series.
   Formerly: University of California at Los Angeles. Institute of Archaeology. Archaeological Survey. Special Monograph Series (ISSN 0068-6204)
   Description: Publishes preliminary and final excavation reports, symposia papers and accounts of research in progress in such areas as ethnoarchaeology, archaeometry and paleodemography.

UNIVERSITY OF CALIFORNIA PUBLICATIONS. CLASSICAL STUDIES. see CLASSICAL STUDIES

UNIVERSITY OF CHICAGO ORIENTAL INSTITUTE. PUBLICATIONS. see HISTORY — History Of The Near East

913   UK   ISSN 0144-3313
UNIVERSITY OF EDINBURGH. DEPARTMENT OF ARCHAEOLOGY. OCCASIONAL PAPERS. 1978. irreg., no.18, 1995. price varies. University of Edinburgh, Department of Archaeology, Old High School, Infirmary St., Edinburgh EH1 1LT, Scotland. URL: http://www.geo.ed.ac.uk/arch/homepage.html. (Subscr. to: Oxbow Books Ltd., Park End Pl., Oxford OX1 1HN, England) (back issues avail.) **Document type:** academic/scholarly publication, monographic series.
   —BLDSC (6217.029000).

913   UK   ISSN 0266-1799
UNIVERSITY OF EDINBURGH. DEPARTMENT OF ARCHAEOLOGY. PROJECT PAPERS. 1984. irreg., no.14, 1995. price varies. Old High School, Infirmary St., Edinburgh EH1 1LT, Scotland. URL: http://www.geo.ed.ac.uk/arch/homepage.html. (Subscr. to: Oxbow Books Ltd., Park End Pl., Oxford OX1 1HN, England) (back issues avail.) **Document type:** academic/scholarly publication, monographic series.
   —BLDSC (6924.848750).

930.1   UK
UNIVERSITY OF GLASGOW. DEPARTMENT OF ARCHAEOLOGY. OCCASIONAL PAPER SERIES. irreg., no.4, 1997. £12.50. University of Glasgow, Department of Archaeology, Gregory Bldg., Glasgow G12 8QQ, Scotland. TEL 44-141-339-8855. FAX 44-141-330-3544. **Document type:** monographic series.

913   SW
UNIVERSITY OF LUND. ARCHEOLOGICAL INSTITUTE. PAPERS. YEARBOOK/MEDDELANDE FRAAN LUNDS UNIVERSITET HISTORIKA MUSEUM. (Text in English) a. A W I International AB, P.O. Box 4627, S-116 91 Stockholm, Sweden. TEL 46-8-7282500. FAX 46-8-338707. (back issues avail.) Indexed: Anthropol.Lit. **Document type:** academic/scholarly publication.

915   II   ISSN 0076-2202
UNIVERSITY OF MADRAS. ARCHAEOLOGICAL SERIES.* 1967. irreg. University of Madras, c/o Director, Publications Division, Madras 600005, Tamil Nadu, India. TEL 91-44-568778. FAX 91-44-566693.

UNIVERSITY OF MANITOBA ANTHROPOLOGY PAPERS. see ANTHROPOLOGY

UNIVERSITY OF MISSOURI MONOGRAPHS IN ANTHROPOLOGY. see ANTHROPOLOGY

ARCHAEOLOGY

913 572   US   ISSN 0162-5799
F271
UNIVERSITY OF SOUTH CAROLINA. INSTITUTE OF ARCHEOLOGY AND ANTHROPOLOGY. ANNUAL REPORT. 1976. a. free. University of South Carolina, Institute of Archeology and Anthropology, Columbia, SC 29208. TEL 803-777-8170. FAX 803-254-1338. circ. 400. **Document type:** corporate report.
    Description: Summarizes what individuals have done in their divisions for the previous year.

UNIVERZITA KOMENSKEHO. FILOZOFICKA FAKULTA. ZBORNIK: MUSAICA. see *ART*

913   PL   ISSN 0554-8195
UNIWERSYTET IM. ADAMA MICKIEWICZA. ARCHEOLOGIA. (Text in Polish; summaries in German or English) 1966. irreg., no.44, 1996. price varies. Adam Mickiewicz University Press, Nowowiejskiego 55, 61-734 Poznan, Poland. TEL 48-61-527380. FAX 48-61-527701. TELEX 413260 UAM PL. Pub. Maria Jankowska. R&P contact: Malgorzata Bis. **Document type:** academic/scholarly publication, monographic series.
    —BLDSC (9120.430000).
    Formerly (until 1975): Uniwersytet im. Adama Mickiewicza w Poznaniu. Wydzial Filozoficzno-Historyczny. Prace. Seria Archeologia (ISSN 0860-1259).
    Description: Contains current research results of the University's archaeologists, such as their Ph.D. works and monographs.

913   PL   ISSN 0083-4300
GN705
UNIWERSYTET JAGIELLONSKI. ZESZYTY NAUKOWE. PRACE ARCHEOLOGICZNE. 1960. irreg. price varies. Uniwersytet Jagiellonski, Ul. Golebia 24, 31-007 Krakow, Poland. (Dist. by: Ars Polona, Krakowskie Przedmiescie 7, 00-068 Warsaw, Poland) Ed. Janusz K. Kozlowski. circ. 700. **Indexed:** A.I.C.P.

930.1   PL   ISSN 0208-4600
CC101.P7
UNIWERSYTET WARSZAWSKI. INSTYTUT ARCHEOLOGII. STUDIA I MATERIALY ARCHEOLOGICZNE. 1981. irreg., vol.9, 1992. price varies. Wydawnictwa Uniwersytetu Warszawskiego, Ul. Nowy Swiat 4, 00-497 Warsaw, Poland. TEL 48-22-6253044. FAX 48-22-6253044. (Dist. by: Ars Polona, Krakowskie Przedmiesci 7, 00-068 Warsaw, Poland) Ed. Zofia Sztetyllo. R&P contact: Jolanta Okonska. circ. 300. **Document type:** academic/scholarly publication.
    Formerly (until no.4, 1985): Uniwersytet Warszawski. Instytut Archeologii. Studia Archeologiczne.

930.1   GW   ISSN 0940-7448
URNENFRIEDHOEFE IN NIEDERSACHSEN. 1911. irreg. Verlag Isensee, Haarenstr. 20, 26122 Oldenburg, Germany. TEL 49-441-25388. FAX 49-441-17872. **Document type:** monographic series.

913   US   ISSN 1043-1918
F51
V A S NEWSLETTER.* 1968. q. $12 membership. (Vermont Archaeological Society) Mountain Publications, 214 Jefferson Ave., Bennington, VT 05201-2325. Ed. Victor R. Rolando. bk.rev.; bibl.; charts. circ. 200. (back issues avail.) **Document type:** academic/scholarly publication, newsletter.

930.1 948.5   SW   ISSN 0347-4402
VAESTERGOETLANDS FORNMINNESFOERENINGS TIDSKRIFT. 1869. biennial. SEK 150 (effective 1990). Vaestergoetlands Fornminnesfoerening, Skaraborgs Laensmuseum, P.O. Box 253, S-532 00 Skara, Sweden.

VEREENIGING TOT BEOFENING VAN GELDERSCHE GESCHIEDENIS, OUDHEIDKUNDE EN RECHT. WERKEN. see *HISTORY — History Of Europe*

913   AU   ISSN 0042-3750
VEREIN DER FREUNDE CARNUNTUMS. MITTEILUNGEN.* 1947. 14/yr. membership. Gesellschaft der Freunde Carnuntums, Mariahilferstr. 1, 1060 Vienna, Austria. Ed. Wilhelm Herzog. circ. 700. (looseleaf format)

913 700 200   IT   ISSN 1121-9696
VETERA CHRISTIANORUM. (Text in English, French, German, Italian, Spanish) 1964. 2/yr. Lit.60000 (foreign Lit.80000) (effective 1997). (Istituto di Letteratura Cristiana Antica) Edipuglia s.r.l., Via Dalmazia 22-B, 70050 S. Spirito (BA), Italy. TEL 39-80-5333056. FAX 39-80-5333057. adv.; bk.rev. circ. 1,400. **Indexed:** Bibl.Ling., IBR, MLA Intl.Bibl., New Test.Abstr. **Document type:** academic/scholarly publication.
    —BLDSC (9222.800000); SWETS.
    Description: Covers early Christian literature, history of ancient and medieval Christianity, and archaeological documentation.

VICINO ORIENTE. see *HISTORY — History Of The Near East*

913.48   NO   ISSN 0332-608X
DL1
VIKING; tidsskrift for norroen arkeologi - journal of Norse archaeology. (Text in Norwegian; summaries in English) 1937. a. NOK 200 (effective 1997). Norsk Arkeologisk Selskap, Huk Aveny 35, N-0287 Oslo 2, Norway. TEL 47-22-43-87-92. Ed. Egil Mikkelsen. adv.; charts; illus. **Indexed:** Br.Archaeol.Abstr., NAA. **Document type:** academic/scholarly publication.
    —BLDSC (9236.374000).

930.1   PO   ISSN 0872-1653
VIPASCA; arqueologia e historia. 1992. a. Esc.1000($17) (effective 1997). Camara Municipal de Aljustrel, Unidade Arqueologica de Aljustrel, c/o Biblioteca, 7600 Aljustrel, Portugal. TEL 351-84-601480. Ed. Carlos Ramos. R&P contact: Arturo Martins. adv. contact: Arturo Martins. circ. 1,000. **Document type:** academic/scholarly publication.

913.031 666   CI   ISSN 0350-8447
DB401
VJESNIK ZA ARHEOLOGIJU I HISTORIJU DALMATINSKU. (Text in Croatian; summaries in European languages) 1878. irreg. price varies. Arheoloski Muzej (Split), Zrinsko-Frankopanska 25, P.O. Box 15, 58000 Split, Croatia. TEL 058 44-685. Ed. Emilio Marin. bk.rev. circ. 750. (back issues avail.)

VLASTIVEDNY VESTNIK MORAVSKY. see *HISTORY — History Of Europe*

913   US
VOLUMES IN HISTORICAL ARCHAEOLOGY. 1986. irreg., latest no.35. $10. University of South Carolina, South Carolina Institute of Archaeology and Anthropology, Columbia, SC 29208. TEL 803-777-8172. (Co-sponsor: Conference on Historic Site Archaeology) Ed. Stanley South. R&P contact: 803-777-8172. (back issues avail.) **Document type:** monographic series.
    Description: Covers research on historical archaeological sites in the U.S.

914 943.7   XR   ISSN 0862-2930
VYZKUMY V CECHACH. 1963. irreg., latest 1995. Ceska Akademie Ved, Archeologicky Ustav, Letenska 4, 118 01 Prague 1, Czech Republic. Ed. M. Kuna. illus. **Document type:** academic/scholarly publication.
    Supersedes: Ceskoslovenska Akademie Ved. Archeologicky Ustav. Zachranne Oddeleni. Bulletin.

930.1   US   ISSN 0738-8063
W A S NEWSLETTER. 1971. q. $12 (foreign $16) (effective Jan. 1997 & 1998). World Archaeological Society, 120 Lakewood Dr., Hollister, MO 65672. TEL 417-334-2377. Dir. Ron Miller. R&P contact: Ron Miller. adv. a page $75; adv. contact: Ron Miller. bk.rev. (processed) **Document type:** newsletter, academic/scholarly publication.
    Description: Dedicated to the study of man and his culture through the three related areas of archaeology, anthropology and art history.

913   GW   ISSN 0232-265X
WEIMARER MONOGRAPHIEN ZUR UR- UND FRUEHGESCHICHTE. 1978. irreg. price varies. Museum fuer Ur- und Fruehgeschichte Thueringens, Humboldtstr. 11, 99423 Weimar, Germany. Ed. R. Feustel.

WEN BO/JOURNAL OF MUSEUMS & ARCHAEOLOGY. see *MUSEUMS AND ART GALLERIES*

930.1   CC   ISSN 0511-4772
WENWU/CULTURAL RELICS. (Text in Chinese; table of contents in English) 1950. m. Y60 in Hong Kong & Macao; elsewhere $72 (effective 1997). Wenwu Chubanshe - Cultural Relics Publishing House, 29, Wusi Dajie, Beijing 100009, People's Republic of China. TEL 86-10-6401-0698. Ed. Yang Jin. adv.; bk.rev.; illus. circ. 15,000. **Indexed:** Amer.Hist.& Life (1955-1957), Hist.Abstr. (1955-1957), Numis.Lit. —UnCover.

915   CC   ISSN 1003-6555
WENWU CHUNQIU. (Text in Chinese) 1989. q. Y20($5) Hebei Wenwu Ju, 4 Dong Dajie, Chang'an Qu, Shijiazhuang, Hebei 050011, People's Republic of China. TEL 86-311-604-3192. Ed. Mingzhen Zheng. illus. pp./issue: 96. **Document type:** academic/scholarly publication.

931 951   CC   ISSN 1000-0194
WENWU TIANDI. (Text in Chinese) bi-m. Y13.20. Wenhua Bu, Guwenxian Yanjiushi - Ministry of Culture, China Cultural Relics Research Institute, No. 29 Wusi St., Beijing 100009, People's Republic of China. TEL 4015577. (Dist. outside China by: China International Book Trading Corp., P.O. Box 399, Beijing, P.R.C.; Dist. in US by: China Books & Periodicals, Inc., 2929 24th St., San Francisco, CA 94110) Ed. Wu Tiemei.
    —BLDSC (9295.215000).

930.10966   NR   ISSN 0331-3158
GN865.W45
WEST AFRICAN JOURNAL OF ARCHAEOLOGY. (Text in English or French) 1961. a. £N6.25. (University of Ibadan, Department of Archaeology) Ibadan University Press, University of Ibadan, Ibadan, Oyo State, Nigeria. adv.; bk.rev. **Indexed:** A.I.C.P., Anthropol.Lit., Br.Archaeol.Abstr., Curr.Cont.Africa, Documentatieblad, SSCI. **Document type:** academic/scholarly publication.
    —BLDSC (9298.685000).
    Formerly (until 1970): West African Archaeological Newsletter (ISSN 0083-8160)

WHO'S WHO IN INDIAN RELICS. see *HOBBIES*

914 943.8   PL   ISSN 0043-5082
WIADOMOSCI ARCHEOLOGICZNE/BULLETIN ARCHEOLOGIQUE POLONAIS. 1873. 2/yr. 20 Zl. (effective 1997). Panstwowe Muzeum Archeologiczne, Ul. Dluga 52, 00-241 Warsaw, Poland. TEL 48-22-8313221. FAX 48-22-8315195. TELEX 816700. (Subscr. to: Osrodek Rozpowszechniania Wydawnicts Naukowych PAN, Palac Kultury i Nauki, 00-901 Warsaw, Poland) Ed. Jan Jaskanis. adv. contact: Wojciech Brzezinski. bk.rev.; illus.; cum.index. circ. 700. **Indexed:** A.I.C.P., Anthropol.Lit., Br.Archaeol.Abstr. **Document type:** academic/scholarly publication.
    —BLDSC (9312.850000).
    Refereed Serial

WILBOUR MONOGRAPHS. see *HISTORY*

500.2 574.9   UK
WILTSHIRE ARCHAEOLOGICAL AND NATURAL HISTORY MAGAZINE. 1853. a. £18 for individual membership; institutional membership £24. Wiltshire Archaeological and Natural History Society, 41 Long St., Devizes, Wiltshire SN10 1NS, England. TEL 44-1380-727369. Ed. K. Fielden. adv.; bk.rev. circ. 1,500. **Indexed:** Br.Archaeol.Abstr., Br.Hum.Ind., Numis.Lit. **Document type:** academic/scholarly publication.
    Formed by the 1982 merger of: Wiltshire Archaeological Magazine (ISSN 0309-3476); Wiltshire Natural History Magazine (ISSN 0309-3468); Which was formerly: Wiltshire Archaeological and Natural History Magazine (ISSN 0084-0335)

913 500.2   UK
WILTSHIRE ARCHAEOLOGICAL AND NATURAL HISTORY SOCIETY. ANNUAL REPORT (YEAR). a. Wiltshire Archaeological and Natural History Society, 41 Long St., Devizes, Wiltshire SN10 1NS, England. TEL 44-1380-727369. Ed. K. Fielden. R&P contact: P.H. Robinson. **Document type:** proceedings.
    Formerly: Wiltshire Archaeological and Natural History Society. Annual Bulletin.

ARCHAEOLOGY

930.1   US   ISSN 0043-6364
E78.W8
THE WISCONSIN ARCHAEOLOGIST. 1901. q. $20 to individuals; institutions $30 (effective 1997 & 1998). Wisconsin Archaeological Society, Box 1292, Milwaukee, WI 53201. TEL 414-229-4273. Ed. David Overstreet. bk.rev.; bibl.; charts; illus.; cum.index; circ. 650 (paid). (also avail. in microfiche from BHP) **Indexed:** Abstr.Anthropol., Amer.Hist.& Life (1988-), Anthropol.Lit., Hist.Abstr. (1988-), Mich.Mag.Ind. **Document type:** academic/scholarly publication.
—UnCover.
Description: Contains original articles dealing with anthropology (ethnology, physical anthropology, archaeology) of the state of Wisconsin and adjoining regions of the U.S. and Canada. Articles of general topical or theoretical interest are also considered.
Refereed Serial

930   BN   ISSN 0352-1990
WISSENSCHAFTLICHE MITTEILUNGEN DES BOSNISCH-HERZEGOWINISCHEN LANDESMUSEUMS. ARCHAEOLOGIE. (Text in German) 1976. irreg. Zemaljski Muzej Bosne i Hercegovine, Vojvode Putnika 7, Sarajevo, Bosnia Hercegovina. Ed. Vlajko Palavestra. **Indexed:** A.I.C.P. **Document type:** academic/scholarly publication.

914.03   UK   ISSN 0084-1226
WOOLHOPE NATURALISTS' FIELD CLUB, HEREFORDSHIRE. TRANSACTIONS. 1851. a. £10 (foreign £12) (effective 1997). Woolhope Club, Hereford Library, Hereford, England. TEL 44-1568-770356. Ed. J.W. Tonkin. circ. 620. **Indexed:** Br.Archaeol.Abstr., Br.Hum.Ind., Numis.Lit. **Document type:** proceedings.

913   UK   ISSN 0143-2389
WORCESTERSHIRE ARCHAEOLOGICAL SOCIETY. TRANSACTIONS. 1923. biennial. £15. Worcestershire Archaeological Society, c/o Robin Whittaker, Ed., 14 Scobell Close, Pershore, Worcs. WR10 1QJ, England. TEL 44-1386-554886. (Subscr. addr.: c/o Wing Commander F.R. Short, 10 Sabrina Terrace, Worcester WR1 3JD, England) Pub. Alan Sutton. R&P contact: Robin Whittaker. circ. 350. (also avail. in microform from UMI) **Document type:** proceedings.
—BLDSC (9013.300000); UMI.

913   UK
WORCESTERSHIRE ARCHAEOLOGY SOCIETY. RECORDER. 1967. s-a. £2. Worcestershire Archaeological Society, c/o Robin Whittaker, Ed., 14 Scobell Close, Pershore, Worcs. WR10 1QJ, England. TEL 44-1386-554886. Pub. Alan Sutton. R&P contact: Robin Whittaker. bk.rev. circ. 400. **Indexed:** Br.Archaeol.Abstr. **Document type:** newsletter.
Former titles (until 1995): Worcestershire Archaeology and Local History Newsletter (ISSN 0143-4659); Worcestershire Archaeological Newsletter.

913   US   ISSN 1060-2887
WORLD ARCHAEOLOGICAL SOCIETY. SPECIAL PUBLICATION. 1971. irreg. price varies. World Archaeological Society, 120 Lakewood Dr., Hollister, MO 65672. TEL 417-334-2377. Ed. Ron Miller. R&P contact: Ron Miller. adv. contact: Ron Miller. bibl.; illus. **Document type:** academic/scholarly publication.
Description: Contains articles on the related fields of archaeology, anthropology, and art history that are too long for the W.A.S. Newsletter.

913   UK   ISSN 0043-8243
CC1   CODEN: WOAREN
WORLD ARCHAEOLOGY. 1969. 3/yr. £32 (U.S. and Canada $54; rest of world £32) to individuals; institutions £80 (U.S. and Canada $130; rest of world £85) (effective 1997). Routledge, 11 New Fetter Ln., London EC4P 4EE, England. TEL 44-171-583-9855. FAX 44-171-842-2298. E-mail: info.journals@routledge.com; journals.na@routledge.com; URL: http://www.routledge.com/routledge/journal/wa.html. (Subscr. to: ITPS Ltd., Cheriton House, Andover, Hants SP10 5BE, England. TEL 44-1264-342919. FAX 44-1264-342807; Subscr. in US & Canada to: 29 W. 35th St., New York, NY 10001-2299. TEL 212-244-3336. FAX 212-564-7854) Ed. Richard Bradley. adv.: page £200; trim 135 x 205. bibl.; charts; illus.; index. (also avail. in microfiche from KTO) **Indexed:** Abstr.Anthropol., Anthropol.Lit., Art & Archaeol.Tech.Abstr., Arts & Hum.Cit.Ind., ASCA, Bibl.Ling., Br.Archaeol.Abstr., Curr.Cont., Geo.Abstr., Geol.Abstr., Hum.Ind., IBR, Mid.East: Abstr.& Ind., SSCI. **Document type:** academic/scholarly publication.
—BLDSC (9352.912500); Genuine Article; KR SourceOne; SWETS; UnCover. **CCC.**
Description: Provides a broad geographic cover on archaeological topics ranging from monuments, arid environments and public health to crafts and chronology.

930.1   UK
WORLDWIDE ARCHAEOLOGY SERIES. irreg., vol.7, 1994. Ashgate Publishing Ltd. (Subsidiary of: Gower Publishing), Gower House, Croft Rd., Aldershot, Hants. GU11 3HR, England. TEL 44-1252-331551. FAX 44-1252-344405. TELEX 337210 BUREAU G. (U.S. addr.: Ashgate Publishing Company, Old Post Rd., Brookfield, Vermont 05036) **Document type:** monographic series, academic/scholarly publication.

930.1 900   GW   ISSN 1432-0320
▼**WUERZBURGER FORSCHUNGEN ZUR ALTERTUMSKUNDE.** 1996. irreg., vol.2, 1996. Ergon Verlag, Grombuehlstr. 7, 97080 Wuerzburg, Germany. TEL 49-931-280084. FAX 49-931-282872. E-mail: ergon-verlag@t-online.de. Eds. S. Boehm, U. Sinn. **Document type:** academic/scholarly publication.

913   US   ISSN 0043-9665
WYOMING ARCHAEOLOGIST. 1959. q. $15 institutional membership (Canada $19) (effective 1995). Wyoming Archaeological Society, Inc., 1617 Westridge Terr., Casper, WY 82604. TEL 307-268-2212. FAX 307-268-2224. E-mail: cbuff@acad.cc.whecn.edu. Ed. Bonnie Johnson. R&P contact: Carolyn Buff. adv. contact: Carolyn Buff. bk.rev.; illus.; maps. circ. 350. **Indexed:** Amer.Hist.& Life (1986-1991), Anthropol.Lit., Hist.Abstr. (1986-1991). **Document type:** academic/scholarly publication.
—UnCover.
Description: Provides a professional and nonprofessional look at anthropology and archaeology, focusing on Wyoming. Includes papers by professionals, graduate students and avocational archaeologists.
Refereed Serial

930.1   GW
XANTENER BERICHTE. GRABUNG, FORSCHUNG, PRAESENTATION. 1992. irreg., no.6, 1995. (Landschaftsverband Rheinland) Rheinland Verlag GmbH, Abtei Brauweiler, Postfach 2140, 50250 Pulheim, Germany. TEL 49-2234-9854265. FAX 49-2234-82503. (Dist. by: Dr. Rudolf Habelt GmbH, Am Buchenhang 1, 53115 Bonn, Germany. TEL 49-228-9238322. FAX 49-228-232017) (Co-sponsor: Archaeologischer Park Xanten) **Document type:** monographic series.

YAXKIN. see *ANTHROPOLOGY*

571 913   UK   ISSN 0084-4276
DA670.Y59
YORKSHIRE ARCHAEOLOGICAL JOURNAL. 1869. a. £20 to individuals; institutions £30. Yorkshire Archaeological Society, Claremont, 23 Clarendon Rd., Leeds LS2 9NZ, England. TEL 44-1132-457910. Ed. R.M. Butler. circ. 1,400. **Indexed:** Br.Archaeol.Abstr., Br.Hum.Ind., Numis.Lit., RILA. **Document type:** bulletin.
—BLDSC (9421.130000); KR SourceOne; UnCover.

930.1   UK
YORKSHIRE ARCHAEOLOGICAL SOCIETY. REPORT AND ACCOUNTS. a. Yorkshire Archaeological Society, Claremont, 23 Clarendon Rd., Leeds LS1 9NZ, England. TEL 44-1532-457910. **Document type:** corporate report.

930.1   UK   ISSN 1351-2676
YOUNG ARCHAEOLOGIST. 1993. q. £6 (foreign £7) (effective 1996). Council for British Archaeology, Bowes Morell House, 111 Walmgate, York YO1 2UA, England. TEL 44-1904-671417. FAX 44-1904-671384. Ed. Juliet Mather. adv. contact: Juliet Mather. bk.rev.; circ. 1,400. (back issues avail.) **Document type:** newsletter.

ZALAI GYUJTEMENY; kozlemenyek zala megye kozgyujtemenyinek kutatasaibol. see *HISTORY — History Of Europe*

913 622 669   YU   ISSN 0351-7160
ZBORNIK RADOVA MUZEJA RUDARSTVA I METALURGIJE BOR. (Text in Serbo-Croatian; summaries in English) 1980. biennial. 15000 din. Muzej Rudarstva i Metalurgije Bor - Museum of Mining and Metallurgy, Mose Pijade 19, 19210 Bor, Vojvodina, Yugoslavia. TEL 030-22-145. Ed. Ilija Jankovic. circ. 1,000.

ZEITSCHRIFT FUER AEGYPTISCHE SPRACHE UND ALTERTUMSKUNDE. see *ORIENTAL STUDIES*

913   GW   ISSN 0340-0824
D125
ZEITSCHRIFT FUER ARCHAEOLOGIE DES MITTELALTERS. 1973. a. DM.148. Rheinland Verlag GmbH, Abtei Brauweiler, Postfach 2140, 50250 Pulheim, Germany. TEL 49-2234-9854265. FAX 49-2234-82503. (Dist. by: Dr. Rudolf Habelt GmbH, Am Buchenhang 1, 53115 Bonn, Germany. TEL 49-228-9238322. FAX 49-228-232017) Ed.Bd. **Indexed:** Avery Ind.Archit.Per., Br.Archaeol.Abstr., IBR, RILA. **Document type:** academic/scholarly publication.

913   GW
ZEITSCHRIFT FUER ARCHAEOLOGIE DES MITTELALTERS. BEIHEFTE. 1981. irreg., no.9, 1995. Rheinland Verlag GmbH, Abtei Brauweiler, Postfach 2140, 50250 Pulheim, Germany. TEL 49-2234-9854265. FAX 49-2234-82503. (Dist. by: Dr. Rudolf Habelt GmbH, Am Buchenhang 1, 53115 Bonn, Germany. TEL 49-228-9238322. FAX 49-228-232017) **Document type:** monographic series.

913   GW   ISSN 0084-5299
PJ3104
ZEITSCHRIFT FUER ASSYRIOLOGIE UND VORDERASIATISCHE ARCHAEOLOGIE. vol.67, 1977. 2/yr. DM.245 (foreign DM.249) (effective 1998). Walter de Gruyter und Co., Genthiner Str. 13, 10785 Berlin, Germany. TEL 49-30-26005-0. FAX 49-30-26005251. E-mail: wdg-info@degruyter.de; URL: http://www.degruyter.de. (U.S. addr.: Walter de Gruyter, Inc., 200 Saw Mill River Rd., Hawthorne, N.Y. 10532. TEL 914-747-0110) Ed. D.O. Edzard. adv.; bk.rev. (also avail. in microfiche from BHP) **Indexed:** Bibl.Ling., IBR, M.L.A., MLA Intl.Bibl., Old Test.Abstr., Rel.Ind.One. **Document type:** academic/scholarly publication.
—SWETS. **CCC.**

913   GW   ISSN 0084-5388
PA3339
ZEITSCHRIFT FUER PAPYROLOGIE UND EPIGRAPHIK. 1967. irreg., no.119, 1997. DM.160. Dr. Rudolf Habelt GmbH, Am Buchenhang 1, 53115 Bonn, Germany. TEL 49-228-9238322. FAX 49-228-923836. **Indexed:** Bibl.Ling., IBR, Numis.Lit. **Document type:** monographic series.
—BLDSC (9475.870000); SWETS. **CCC.**

913   SZ   ISSN 0044-3476
ZEITSCHRIFT FUER SCHWEIZERISCHE ARCHAEOLOGIE UND KUNSTGESCHICHTE/REVUE SUISSE D'ART ET D'ARCHEOLOGIE. Variant title: Z A K. (Text in English, French, German, Italian) 1939. q. 75 SFr. Schweizerisches Landesmuseum - Swiss National Museum, Museumstr. 2, Postfach 6789, CH-8023 Zurich, Switzerland. TEL 41-1-2186511. FAX 41-1-2112949. Ed. Matthias Senn. bk.rev.; bibl.; charts; illus.; index. circ. 1,750. **Indexed:** Artbibl.Mod., Avery Ind.Archit.Per., Br.Archaeol.Abstr., Br.Tech.Ind., IBR, Numis.Lit., RILA, World Bibl.Soc.Sec. **Document type:** bulletin.

ZEITSCHRIFT FUER VOLKSKUNDE. see *FOLKLORE*

ARCHAEOLOGY — ABSTRACTING, BIBLIOGRAPHIES, STATISTICS

913.031   SP   ISSN 0514-7336
CC13.S66
ZEPHYRUS. (Text in English, French, Spanish) 1950. a. 6000 ptas. (effective 1995). Ediciones Universidad de Salamanca, Apdo. 325, 37080 Salamanca, Spain. TEL 34-23-294598. Dir. Maria Soledad Corchon Rodriguez. **Indexed:** Anthropol.Lit., IBR, Numis.Lit. **Document type:** academic/scholarly publication.
—BLDSC (9512.114500); CINDOC.
  Description: Contains studies on archaeology and prehistory.

ZESZYTY GLIWICKIE. see HISTORY — History Of Europe

ZESZYTY TARNOGORSKIE. see HISTORY — History Of Europe

ZGODOVINSKI CASOPIS; istoriceskij zurnal. see HISTORY — History Of Europe

931   US
ZHONGGUO WENWU BAO/CHINA'S CULTURAL RELICS NEWS. (Text in Chinese) w. $47.40. China Books & Periodicals, Inc., 2929 24th St., San Francisco, CA 94110. TEL 415-282-2994. FAX 415-282-0994. **Document type:** newspaper.

931   CC
ZHONGYUAN WENWU/RELICS OF CENTRAL CHINA. (Text in Chinese) q. $24. Henan Sheng Bowuguan - Henan Provincial Museum, No. 11, Renmin Lu, Zhengzhou, Henan 450001, People's Republic of China. TEL 555583. (Dist. in US by: China Books & Periodicals, Inc., 2929 24th St., San Francisco, CA 94110. TEL 415-282-2994) Ed. Sun Chuanxian.

913   SZ
ZUERCHER ARCHAEOLOGISCHE HEFTE. 1976. irreg., no.5, 1987. price varies. Hans Rohr Verlag, Oberdorfstr. 5, CH-8024 Zurich, Switzerland. **Document type:** monographic series.

ARCHAEOLOGY — Abstracting, Bibliographies, Statistics

913 011   US   ISSN 0743-4251
ABSTRACTS IN MARYLAND ARCHEOLOGY. 1983. a. $65. Council for Maryland Archeology, c/o James G. Gibb, 2554 Carrollton Rd., Annapolis, MD 21403. TEL 410-263-1102. Ed. James D. Sorenson. circ. 100 (paid). (back issues avail.) **Document type:** abstracting/indexing.
  Description: Abstracts of current monographs, papers, and compliance reports on Maryland archeology.

L'ANNEE PHILOLOGIQUE; bibliographie critique et analytique de l'antiquite greco-latine. see CLASSICAL STUDIES — Abstracting, Bibliographies, Statistics

ANNUAL EGYPTOLOGICAL BIBLIOGRAPHY/BIBLIOGRAPHIE EGYPTOLOGIQUE ANNUELLE/JAEHRLICHE AEGYPTOLOGISCHE BIBLIOGRAPHIE. see HISTORY — Abstracting, Bibliographies, Statistics

930.1   US   ISSN 0162-6469
ARCHAEOLOGICAL INSTITUTE OF AMERICA. ABSTRACTS OF THE GENERAL MEETING. 1975. a. $10. Archaeological Institute of America (Boston), 656 Beacon St., Boston, MA 02215. TEL 617-353-9361. FAX 617-353-6550. E-mail: AIA@BU.EDU. circ. 1,000. (back issues avail.) **Document type:** abstracting/indexing.
—BLDSC (0551.844600).
  Description: Abstracts of papers presented at their annual meeting.

ART AND ARCHAEOLOGY TECHNICAL ABSTRACTS; abstracts of the technical literature on archaeology and the fine arts. see ART — Abstracting, Bibliographies, Statistics

BIBLIOGRAPHIC GUIDE TO ANTHROPOLOGY AND ARCHAEOLOGY. see ANTHROPOLOGY — Abstracting, Bibliographies, Statistics

932   BE
BIBLIOGRAPHIE PAPYROLOGIQUE. 1941. irreg. (approx. 4/yr.). 1200 BEF. Fondation Egyptologique Reine Elisabeth, Parc du Cinquantenaire 10, 1000 Brussels, Belgium. TEL 32-2-7417364. Eds. G. Nachtergael, Al Martin. (also avail. in diskette format) **Document type:** bibliography, academic/scholarly publication.

016.9301   UK   ISSN 1367-4765
Z5132
BRITISH AND IRISH ARCHAEOLOGICAL BIBLIOGRAPHY. 1968. 2/yr. £45 to individuals; institutions £99; students £35. British Archaeological Bibliography, University College London, Rm. 101, Institute of Archaeology, 31-34 Gordon Sq., London WC1H 0PY, England. TEL 44-171-380-7532. FAX 44-171-383-2572. E-mail: tcfa266@ucl.ac.uk; tcfa316@ucl.ac.uk. Eds. Jeremy Oetgen, Isabel Holroyd. adv. contact: Isabel Holroyd. index. circ. 500. (also avail. in microform from UMI; back issues avail.) **Indexed:** A.I.C.P., Numis.Lit. **Document type:** bibliography.
● Also available on CD-ROM.
—UMI.
  Supersedes (in 1997): British Archaeological Bibliography (ISSN 0964-7104); Which supersedes (in 1992): British Archaeological Abstracts (ISSN 0007-0270).
  Description: Lists information currently being published on the archaeology of Great Britain and Ireland, with information to allow the original article to be traced and consulted.

962 932   UA
EGYPTIAN MUSEUM. LIBRARY. CATALOGUE. 1966. irreg. price varies. (Organisation des Antiquites Egyptiennes, Museums Service) Egyptian Museum, Library, Midan-el-Tahrir, Kasr el-Nil, Cairo, Egypt. TEL 20-2-5757035. Ed. Dia Abou-Ghazi. adv.; bk.rev.; index. **Document type:** academic/scholarly publication, catalog, government publication.
  Formerly: Egyptian National Museum. Library. Catalogue (ISSN 0068-5275)
  Description: Bibliography of books and articles recently acquired by the library.

F R A N C I S. 521: SOCIOLOGIE. see SOCIOLOGY — Abstracting, Bibliographies, Statistics

913 016   FR   ISSN 1157-3759
Z5118.A6
F R A N C I S. 525: PREHISTOIRE ET PROTOHISTOIRE. (Printed format ceased Jan. 1995) (Text in French, English) 1947. q. Centre National de la Recherche Scientifique, Institut de l'Information Scientifique et Technique, 2 allee du Parc de Brabois, 54514 Vandoeuvre-les-Nancy Cedex, France. TEL 83-50-46-00. FAX 83-50-46-50. adv. contact: Veronique Guinvarc'h. cum.index. **Document type:** bibliography.
● Also available online. Vendor(s): Telesystemes - Questel.
Also available on CD-ROM.
  Former titles: Bulletin Signaletique. Part 525: Prehistoire et Protohistoire (ISSN 0181-1894); (until 1979): Bulletin Signaletique. Part 525: Prehistoire.

F R A N C I S. 526: ART ET ARCHEOLOGIE; Proche-Orient, Asie, Amerique. see ART — Abstracting, Bibliographies, Statistics

INDICE HISTORICO ESPANOL. see HISTORY — Abstracting, Bibliographies, Statistics

ISTORIYA SIBIRI I DAL'NEGO VOSTOKA; tekushchii ukazatel' literatury. see HISTORY — Abstracting, Bibliographies, Statistics

948 010   DK   ISSN 0105-6492
N A A.* (Nordic Archaeological Abstracts) (Text in English) 1975. a. DKK 185 to individuals; institutions DKK 250. Nordic Archaeological Abstracts, c/o Museumstjenesten, Sjoerupvej, Lysgaard, DK-8800 Viborg, Denmark. FAX 86-623566. Eds. Else Johansen Kleppe, Jenny-Rita Naess. **Indexed:** Br.Archaeol.Abstr.
  Description: Covers prehistoric and medieval archaeology in the Nordic countries.

930   US   ISSN 0028-2812
NESTOR. (Text in English and original languages) 1957. m. (Sep.-May). $7.50 to individuals (foreign $10); institutions $12.50 (foreign $18.50) (effective 1998). Department of Classics M.L.-0226, University of Cincinnati, Cincinnati, OH 45221-0226. TEL 812-855-1421. E-mail: nestor@ucbeh.san.uc.edu; URL: http://ucaswww.mcm.uc.edu/classics/nestor/nestor.html. (Affiliate: Comite International Permanent pour les Etudes Myceniennes) Ed. Eric Cline. bk.rev.; bibl. circ. 550. (looseleaf format; also avail. in microform from UMI; diskette format; back issues avail.; reprint service avail. from UMI) **Document type:** bibliography, academic/scholarly publication.
  Description: Bibliography of material relevant to prehistoric archaeology, Homeric society, Indo-European linguistics and related fields, in the eastern Mediterranean area and southeastern Europe.

NOVAYA LITERATURA PO SOTSIAL'NYM I GUMANITARNYM NAUKAM. ISTORIYA - ARKHEOLOGIYA - ETNOGRAFIYA; bibliograficheskii ukazatel' see HISTORY — Abstracting, Bibliographies, Statistics

016.913   PL   ISSN 0137-4885
POLISH ARCHAEOLOGICAL ABSTRACTS. (Text in English) 1972. a. price varies. Polska Akademia Nauk, Instytut Historii Kultury Materialnej (Poznan), Zaklad Archeologii Wielkopolski, Ul. Zwierzyniecka 20, 60-814 Poznan, Poland. (Dist. by: Ars Polona, Krakowskie Przedmiescie 7, 00-950 Warsaw, Poland) Ed. Wojciech Dzieduszycki. abstr.; bibl. circ. 400. **Indexed:** A.I.C.P., Br.Archaeol.Abstr. **Document type:** abstracting/indexing.
—BLDSC (6543.553000).
  Description: Abstracts on all books and articles concerning Polish archaeology published in the last year in Poland.

ARCHAEOLOGY — Computer Applications

930.1   IT   ISSN 1120-6861
ARCHEOLOGIA E COLCOLATORI. a. L.48000 (effective 1997). Edizioni all'Insegna del Giglio s.a.s., Via R. Giuliani 152 r., Florence, Italy. TEL 39-55-451593. FAX 39-55-450030.

930.1 004   UK   ISSN 0305-0475
COMPUTER APPLICATIONS IN ARCHAEOLOGY. 1974. a. price varies. British Archaeological Reports, Oxford, c/o Dr. C.L.N. Ruggles, Treas., Dept. of Computing Studies, University of Leicester, Leicester LE1 7RH, England. **Indexed:** Art & Archaeol.Tech.Abstr., Br.Archaeol.Abstr. **Document type:** academic/scholarly publication.

JOURNAL OF QUANTITATIVE ANTHROPOLOGY. see ANTHROPOLOGY

SCIENCE AND ARCHAEOLOGY. see SCIENCES: COMPREHENSIVE WORKS — Computer Applications

ARCHITECTURE

see also Building and Construction; Engineering-Civil Engineering; Housing and Urban Planning; Real Estate

720   UK   ISSN 0261-6823
NA1.A1
A A FILES; annals of the Architectural Association School of Architecture. 1981. s-a. £32 (foreign £33); students £23 (foreign £24) (effective 1996). Architectural Association, 34-36 Bedford Sq., London WC1B 3ES, England. TEL 44-171-636-0974. FAX 44-171-414-0782. URL: http://www.gold.net/ellipsis/evolutionary/aa.html. Ed. Mary Wall; Pub. Mohsen Mostafavi. R&P contact: Kirsten Morphet. TEL 44-171-887-4021. bk.rev.; charts; illus.; cum.index: 1981-1991. circ. 3,500. **Indexed:** Archit.Per.Ind., Avery Ind.Archit.Per., Br.Tech.Ind., Build.Manage.Abstr., RICS. **Document type:** academic/scholarly publication.
—BLDSC (0537.071500); CISTI; Linda Hall; SWETS; UnCover.
  Formerly: A A Quarterly (ISSN 0001-0189)
  Description: Contains articles, reviews, and book reviews covering historical and contemporary architecture and related topics.

ARCHITECTURE

720 JA ISSN 0389-9160
A & U. (Architecture and Urbanism) (Text in Japanese and English; summaries in English) 1971. m. 21000 Yen($114.30) (foreign 50000 Yen). A & U Publishing Co., Ltd., 30-8 Yushima 2-chome, Bunkyo-ku, Tokyo 113, Japan. TEL 03-3816-2935. FAX 03-3816-2937. Ed. Toshio Nakamura. adv.; bk.rev.; bibl.; charts; illus.; index. circ. 25,000.
Indexed: ASCA, Avery Ind.Archit.Per., Br.Tech.Ind., Curr.Cont.
—BLDSC (1601.610000); KR SourceOne; SWETS.

720 GW
A B I. (Aktuelle Berichte und Informationen fuer Architekten und Ingenieure); Wirtschaft - Recht - Steuer. 1977. 6/yr. DM.46. Ingenieur Verlag GmbH, Rheinstr. 129c, 76275 Ettlingen, Germany. TEL 07243-39396. FAX 07243-39395. **Document type:** trade publication.

720 GW
A B I T - BUERO HEUTE. 3/yr. DM.21.80 (effective 1997). Verlagsanstalt Alexander Koch GmbH, Fasanenweg 18, 70771 Leinfelden-Echterdingen, Germany. TEL 49-711-7591-0. FAX 49-711-7591368. **Document type:** trade publication.

720 US
A C S A FACULTY DIRECTORY. a. $14.95. Association of Collegiate Schools of Architecture, Inc., 1735 New York Ave., N.W., Washington, DC 20006. TEL 202-785-2324. FAX 202-628-0448. **Document type:** directory.

720 US ISSN 0149-2446
A C S A NEWS. Key Title: News - Association of Collegiate Schools of Architecture. 1969. 9/yr. membership. Association of Collegiate Schools of Architecture, Inc., 1735 New York Ave., N.W., Washington, DC 20006. TEL 202-785-2324. FAX 202-628-0448. Ed. Thomas Gelsanliter. adv.; circ. 3,800. (controlled). (reprint service avail. from UMI)

720 DK ISSN 0908-1690
A D A. 1963. m. (10/yr.). DKK 750. (Associerede Danske Arkitekter) Visholm Media AS, Sydvestvej 49, P.O. Box 221, DK-2600 Glostrup, Denmark. Ed. Flemming Holten Nielsen. adv. contact: Knud Horn. circ. 9,000. **Document type:** trade publication.
Formerly (until 1993): D P A (ISSN 0105-6603)
Description: Features articles on subjects relevant to Danish architecture and engineering.

720 700 SA ISSN 1015-5597
A D MAGAZINE. (Art, Design, Architecture) 1986. 2/yr. R.70 (foreign R.90). ADA Magazine, P.O. Box 16093, Vlaeberg 8018, South Africa. TEL 27-21-461-9937. FAX 27-21-4619937. Ed. Jennifer Sorrell. adv.; B&W page R.5988.02, color page R.8982.03; trim 420 x 297. bk.rev. circ. 10,000. (tabloid format; back issues avail.) **Document type:** consumer publication.

720 US
A D ARCHITECTURE.* (Architectural Digest) Issued with: A D Architectural Digest, Edizione Italiana. 1987. s-a. Knapp Communications Corp., Attn.: Circulation Dept., 6300 Wilshire Blvd., Los Angeles, CA 90048. TEL 213-965-3700. FAX 213-937-5643. TELEX 901-321-2437.

A - E MARKETING JOURNAL; marketing tactics for project success. see BUSINESS AND ECONOMICS — Marketing And Purchasing

720 GW ISSN 0177-5472
A H F MITTEILUNGEN. 1981. q. (Arbeitskreis fuer Hausforschung e.V.) Jonas Verlag, Weidenhaeuserstr. 88, 35037 Marburg, Germany. TEL 49-6421-25132. **Document type:** bulletin.

720 US
A I A - D C NEWS. membership. American Institute of Architects, Washington Chapter, 1777 Church St., N.W., Washington, DC 20036. TEL 202-667-1798. FAX 202-667-4327. R&P contact: Jane Moya. circ. 1,500. **Document type:** newsletter.
Formerly: D C - A I A News.

720 US
A I A MICHIGAN MONTHLY BULLETIN. 1926. m. avail. with membership only. American Institute of Architects, Michigan Chapter, 553 E. Jefferson, Detroit, MI 48226. TEL 313-965-4100. Ed. Tim Casai. adv.; bk.rev. circ. 3,500. **Document type:** newsletter.
Formerly: M S A Monthly Bulletin (ISSN 0024-8363)

720 US ISSN 1079-3933
NA11
A I ARCHITECT. 1947. m. $48. (American Institute of Architects) American Institute of Architects Press, 1735 New York Ave., N.W., Washington, DC 20006. TEL 202-626-7465. Ed. Stephanie Stubbs. charts; illus.; circ. 56,000 (controlled). (processed) **Indexed:** Archit.Per.Ind., Avery Ind.Archit.Per.
Former titles (until 1994): Memo (Washington, 1947) (ISSN 0732-4073); A I A Memo (ISSN 0001-1487)
Description: Contains organization news.

720 GW ISSN 0173-8046
NK1700 CODEN: AITAEL
A I T. (Architektur, Innenarchitektur, Technischer Ausbau) 1890. 10/yr. DM.212 (foreign DM.260) (effective 1997). Verlagsanstalt Alexander Koch GmbH, Fasanenweg 18, 70771 Leinfelden-Echterdingen, Germany. TEL 49-711-7591-1. FAX 49-711-7591-368. Ed. Dietmar Danner. adv.; bk.rev.; charts; illus.; tr.lit.; index. circ. 16,500. **Indexed:** Avery Ind.Archit.Per., Br.Tech.Ind. **Document type:** trade publication.
—BLDSC (0785.457500); SWETS. **CCC.**
Former titles (until 1979): Architektur und Wohnwelt (ISSN 0340-3912); Architektur und Wohnform (ISSN 0003-8792)

720 690 UK ISSN 0951-5380
TH 1
A J FOCUS; products in practice. Variant title: Architects' Journal Focus. (Supplement to: Architects' Journal (ISSN 0003-8466)) 1982. m. E M A P - Construct, 151 Rosebery Ave., London EC1R 4QX, England. TEL 44-171-505-6740. FAX 44-171-505-6750. Ed. Jo White; Pub. Graham Harman. R&P contact: Graham Harman. adv. contact: Johnathon Stock. charts; illus. circ. 18,000. (back issues avail.) **Document type:** trade publication.
—BLDSC (0785.459340); CISTI; SWETS.
Formerly (until 1987): Products in Practice (ISSN 0264-1585)

A P V A NEWSLETTER. (Association for the Preservation of Virginia Antiquities) see HISTORY — History Of North And South America

720 BE
A PLUS ARCHITECTURE. Dutch edition: A Plus Architectuur. (Text in French) 1973. 6/yr. 1900 BEF (Europe 2800 BEF) (effective 1996). Centre d'Information de l'Architecture, de l'Urbanisme et du Design - Informatiecentrum voor Architectuur, Stedebouw en Design, Chaussee de Ruisbroek 83, 1190 Brussels, Belgium. TEL 32-2-3322472. FAX 32-2-3322208. Ed. Robert Courtois; Pub. Robert Courtois. adv.; circ. 13,200 (controlled). **Indexed:** Br.Tech.Ind., Mag.Ind. **Document type:** trade publication.
Formerly: A Plus.

A R I S. (Art Research in Scandinavia) see ART

720 CN ISSN 1203-1488
NA746.Q4
A R Q; revue d'architecture. (Text mainly in French, occasionally in English) 1981. bi-m. Can.$41.02 to individuals (US $60; elsewhere $70); institutions Can.$68.37 (effective 1997). Art et Architecture Quebec, 1463 rue Prefontaine, Montreal, PQ H1W 2N6, Canada. TEL 514-523-6832. E-mail: arq@sim.qc.ca. Ed. Pierre Boyer-Mercier. adv.; bk.rev. circ. 4,000. (back issues avail.) **Indexed:** Pt.de Rep. (1989-). **Document type:** trade publication.
—CISTI.
Formerly: A R Q: Architecture-Quebec (ISSN 0710-1163)

720 UK
A S C. (Architects Standard Catalogue) 1911. a. $100. Data Distribution Publications, Apex House, London Rd., Northfleet, Gravesend, Kent DA11 9JA, England. TEL 44-1322-277788. FAX 44-1322-539627. Pub. Paul Holden. R&P contact: Paul HOlden. adv. contact: Julie Skeet. circ. 19,000. **Document type:** trade publication.
Former titles: A S C Mini-File; Architects Standard Catalogues (ISSN 0066-6181)

720 UK ISSN 0956-4241
A S I JOURNAL. 1929. 5/yr. £20 (effective Mar. 1997). Architects and Surveyors Institute, St. Mary House, 15 St. Mary St., Chippenham, Wilts. SN15 3WD, England. TEL 44-1249-444505. FAX 44-1249-443602. Ed. Chris G.A. Nash. R&P contact: Chris G.A. Nash. adv.: page £475; 275 x 189; adv. contact: Linda Porter. bk.rev. circ. 6,500. **Indexed:** Archit.Per.Ind. **Document type:** trade publication.
—BLDSC (1742.170800).
Formerly (until 1988): Portico (ISSN 0032-4914)
Description: Covers architecture, surveying, engineering, environment and construction.

712 US ISSN 0192-5067
SB469
A S L A MEMBERS HANDBOOK. a. $129.95 to non-members. American Society of Landscape Architects, 4401 Connecticut Ave., N.W., Washington, DC 20008-2302. TEL 202-686-2752. adv. circ. 10,000. **Document type:** directory.

720 SW ISSN 0004-2005
A T. (Arkitekttidningen) (Supplement avail.: Arkitekttaevlingar (ISSN 0282-6747)) 1956. 12/yr. SEK 390 (foreign $590) (effective 1996). Svenska Arkitekters Riksfoerbund (SAR) - National Association of Swedish Architects, Norrlandsgatan 18, S-111 43 Stockholm, Sweden. TEL 46-8-679-27-60. FAX 46-8-611-49-30. Ed. Kerstin Persson. adv.: B&W page SEK 8700, color page SEK 15900; trim 185 x 270; adv. contact: Gerd Nystroem. bk.rev.; charts; illus.; index; circ. 5,500. **Document type:** trade publication.
Formed by the 1970 merger of: Arkitekten; Arkitekttaevlingar.
Description: Contents relates to architects' work with planning, designing and building, to research and education, housing policies, working environment and city planning.

721 US
A U A NEWS. 1986. q. $70 individual membership (foreign $80); corporate $500 (foreign $540). American Underground - Construction Association, 511 11th Ave., S., Ste. 248, Minneapolis, MN 55415. TEL 612-339-5403. FAX 612-339-3207. Ed. Susan Nelson. adv. contact: Carin Mindel. bk.rev. circ. 900. (back issues avail.) **Document type:** trade publication.

A U BIS SUPPLEMENTO TECNICO. (Arredo Urbano) see BUILDING AND CONSTRUCTION

720 SP
A V MONOGRAPHS. (Text in English, Spanish) 1985. s-m. 14500 ptas. (Europe 16500 ptas.; elsewhere 21500 ptas.) (effective 1998). Arquitectura Viva, S.L., Rosario, 31, 28005 Madrid, Spain. TEL 34-1-3669900. FAX 34-1-3640151. E-mail: aviva@compuserve.com; URL: http://www.ArquitecturaViva.com. Ed. Adela Garcia Herrera; Pub. Luis Fernandez-Galiano. R&P contact: Gina Carino. adv.: B&W page 200000, color page 225000 ptas.; trim 240 x 297. bibl.; illus. circ. 9,000. **Document type:** monographic series.
—CINDOC; SWETS.
Formerly: A y V; Monografias de Arquitectura y Vivienda (ISSN 0213-487X)
Description: Each issue covers a chosen architect, city or theme.

ARCHITECTURE

720 352.7   IC   ISSN 1022-9507
A V S. Variant title: Arkitektur Verktaekni Skipulag. (Text in Icelandic; summaries in English) 1989. q. ISK 2900($75) outside Iceland (effective through 1998). S.A.V. Ltd., Gardastraeti 17, 101 Reykjavik, Iceland. TEL 354-561-6577. FAX 354-561-6571. E-mail: skipark@centrum.is. Ed. Gestur Olafsson. R&P contact: Gestur Olafsson. adv. contact: Asdis Kristinsdottir. illus. circ. 7,000. (also avail. in microform; back issues avail.) **Document type:** academic/scholarly publication, trade publication.
    Formerly (until 1994): Arkitektur og Skipulag (ISSN 1016-7293)
    Description: Focuses on architecture, housing, urban planning and related fields.

720 694   US
A W I NEWSBRIEFS. vol.40, no.8, 1992. m. Architectural Woodwork Institute, 1952 Isaac Newton Sq., Reston, VA 20190. TEL 703-733-0600. FAX 703-733-0584. URL: http://www.awinet.org. adv. **Document type:** newsletter.
    Description: Reports association news and informs readers of events of interest, both past and forthcoming.

720 747   IT   ISSN 0001-3218
NK1700
ABITARE. (Text in English and Italian) 1961. 11/yr. L.184000 in Europe; elsewhere $115. Editrice Abitare Segesta S.p.A., Corso Monforte 15, 20122 Milan, Italy. TEL 39-2-760901. FAX 39-2-76021904. URL: http://www.think.it/abitare/Magazine.html. Ed. Italo Lupi; Pub. Renato Minetto. adv.: B&W page L.11300000, color page L.16000000; adv. contact: Alessandra Fedele. bk.rev.; abstr.; charts; illus. circ. 65,677. **Indexed:** Art Ind., Avery Ind.Archit.Per., DAAI, Search (1990-). **Document type:** consumer publication.
—BLDSC (0549.430000); KR SourceOne.
    Formerly (until 1962): Casa Novita (ISSN 1121-581X)
    Description: Presents a broad spectrum of lifestyles and living environments by reporting on houses, architecture, and places from around the world.

720   US
NA2300.C635
ABSTRACT. 1977. a. $19.95 per no. Columbia University, Graduate School of Architecture, Planning and Preservation, 400 Avery Hall, New York, NY 10027. TEL 212-854-3414. Ed. Scott Marble. **Document type:** academic/scholarly publication, monograph series.
    Supersedes (1977-1987): Precis (ISSN 0887-8781)

720   FR   ISSN 0001-3994
ACADEMIE D'ARCHITECTURE. 1840. irreg. 80 F. Academie d'Architecture, Hotel de Chaulnes, 9 place des Vosges, 75004 Paris, France. TEL 48-87-83-10. bk.rev.; illus.; stat.; index. circ. 2,000.

720   FR   ISSN 0084-5876
ACADEMIE D'ARCHITECTURE, PARIS. ANNUAIRE. irreg. free to members. Academie d'Architecture, Hotel de Chaulnes, 9 place des Vosges, 75004 Paris, France. TEL 48-87-83-10. FAX 48-87-44-42.

ACCESS AMERICA. see *HANDICAPPED — Visually Impaired*

720 370.58   US
ACCREDITED PROGRAMS IN ARCHITECTURE; and professional degrees conferred on completion of their curricula in architecture. 1940. a. free. National Architectural Accrediting Board, Inc., 1735 New York Ave., N.W., Washington, DC 20006. TEL 202-783-2007. Dir. John M. Maudlin-Jeronimo. circ. 20,000. **Document type:** catalog.
    Former titles (until 1974): Accredited Schools of Architecture; (until 1972): List of Accredited Schools of Architecture (ISSN 0077-3166)

720   UK   ISSN 0266-6200
ACROSS ARCHITECTURE. 1984. s-a. £12. Across Publications, 36 Bedford Sq., London WC1B 3ES, England. TEL 44-171-262-1557. FAX 44-171-262-1773. (Subscr. to: Across Architecture Sales, 40 Radnor Mews, London W2 2SA, England) Ed. Dimitri F. Vannas. circ. 600.
    Description: Provides a forum for discussion and debate among architectural students, and contains a lively insight into student culture at the Architectural Association.

ACTA POLYTECHNICA; prace CVUT v Praze. see *ENGINEERING*

720 690   SA   ISSN 1023-0564
ACTA STRUCTILIA; wetenskaplijke tydskrif. (Text in Afrikaans, English) 1993. irreg. Universiteit van die Oranje-Vrystaat, Posbus 339, Bloemfontein 9300, South Africa. (Co-sponsors: Departement van Argitektuur; Departement van Bourekenkunde & Konstruksiebestuur; Departement van Stads- en Streeksbeplanning) **Document type:** academic/scholarly publication.

ACTA UNIVERSITATIS WRATISLAVIENSIS. HISTORIA SZTUKI. see *ART*

ADDIS ABABA UNIVERSITY. COLLEGE OF TECHNOLOGY. LIBRARY BULLETIN. see *LIBRARY AND INFORMATION SCIENCES*

720 693   US
ADOBE JOURNAL. 1989. irreg. $17.50. Adobe Journal, Box 7725, Albuquerque, NM 87194. TEL 505-243-7801. Ed. Michael Moquin. circ. 1,500 (paid).
    Description: Covers natural building materials.

720   IS   ISSN 0334-794X
ADRICHALUT. (Text in English and Hebrew) irreg. $28. Association of Engineers and Architects in Israel, P.O. Box 3082, Tel Aviv, Israel. TEL 972-3-5240274. FAX 972-3-5235993.

720 307.1   YU   ISSN 0354-6756
AKCELERATOR; random magazin. 1994. irreg.? Zetska 2, Belgrade, Yugoslavia.

720   SZ
AKTUELLE WETTBEWERBS SCENE. (Text in French, German, Italian) 1972. 5/yr. 169 SFr. (foreign 180 SFr.). Verlag fuer Architekturinformation, Roemeralp, Asylstr. 108, CH-8032 Zurich, Switzerland. TEL 01-3886626. FAX 01-3886616. Ed. Verena Bertogg. adv. contact: adv. circ. 1,300. **Document type:** trade publication.

ALBUM, LETRAS Y ARTES. see *ART*

ALLIED ARTS NEWSLETTER. see *PUBLIC ADMINISTRATION — Municipal Government*

ALTES HAUS MODERN; Magazin fuer Modernisierung, Instandsetzung und Neubau von Haus und Wohnung. see *BUILDING AND CONSTRUCTION*

720   FR   ISSN 1165-6115
AMENAGEMENT ET MONTAGNE. 5/yr. 200 F. Edition de Meylan, 1 rue du Pre Carre, B.P. 135, 38244 Meylan Cedex, France. TEL 76-90-84-38. FAX 76-90-80-63. Ed. Denis Boutry. adv. circ. 10,000.
    Description: For building professionals in mountainous regions.

AMENAGEMENT ET NATURE. see *CONSERVATION*

AMERICAN ACADEMY IN ROME. MEMOIRS. see *ART*

AMERICAN BUILDER MAGAZINE. see *BUILDING AND CONSTRUCTION*

720   US   ISSN 1055-0674
AMERICAN BUNGALOW. q. $29.95. Brinkmann Design Offices, Inc., 123 S. Baldwin Ave., Sierra Madre, CA 91024. TEL 818-355-1651. FAX 818-355-1220. URL: http://www.ambungalow.com. Ed. George B. Murray; Pub. John Brinkmann. adv. contact: Bruce Smith. bk.rev.
—UnCover.
    Description: Aims to preserve and restore American Bungalow.

AMERICAN CONTRACTOR. see *BUILDING AND CONSTRUCTION*

720   US
AMERICAN INSTITUTE OF ARCHITECTS. FIELD REPORT. m. $20. American Institute of Architects, Colorado Chapter, 1526 15th St., Denver, CO 80202-1302. TEL 303-446-2266. Ed. Linda T. Smith. adv. circ. 1,100. **Document type:** newspaper.

720 747 690   US
AMERICAN INSTITUTE OF BUILDING DESIGN NEWSLETTER. 1989. 7/yr. members only. American Institute of Building Design, 991 Post Rd. E, Westport, CT 06880. TEL 800-366-2423. FAX 203-227-3698. Ed. Tammy J. Crosby. R&P contact: Tammy J. Crosby. adv. contact: Bobbi Currie. **Document type:** newsletter.

720   SP   ISSN 0214-4727
NA5
ANALES DE ARQUITECTURA. 1989. a. 3800 ptas. (effective 1991). Universidad de Valladolid, Secretariado de Publicaciones, Departamento de Teoria de Arquitectura y Proyectos Arquitectonicos, C. Juan Mambrilla, 14, 47003 Valladolid, Spain. TEL 983-423000. FAX 34-83-290300. TELEX 26357. **Document type:** academic/scholarly publication.
—CINDOC.

720 913 690   UK   ISSN 0951-001X
DA100
ANCIENT MONUMENTS SOCIETY TRANSACTIONS. 1924. a. £15 institutional and individual membership (effective 1997). Ancient Monuments Society, St. Ann's Vestry Hall, 2 Church Entry, London EC4V 5HB, England. TEL 44-171-236-3934. FAX 44-171-329-3677. Ed. John Bold. bk.rev.; bibl. circ. 2,000. **Indexed:** ASCA, Avery Ind.Archit.Per., Br.Archaeol.Abstr., Br.Hum.Ind., Br.Tech.Ind., Curr.Cont., Geo.Abstr.H.G. **Document type:** academic/scholarly publication.
—BLDSC (8899.200000); Genuine Article.
    Description: The history and conservation of historic buildings of all ages and types.

720   IT
ANNALI DELL'ARCHITETTURA ITALIANA CONTEMPORANEA. 1985. a. L.65000. Officina Edizioni, Via Nicola Ricciotti, 11, 00195 Rome, Italy. Eds. Marina Montuori, Giancarlo Carnevali.

712   SZ   ISSN 0003-5424
ANTHOS; vierteljahres-Zeitschrift fuer Freieausgestaltung, Gruen und Landschaftsplanung. (Text in English, French and German) 1962. q. 59 SFr. Bund Schweizer Landschaftsarchitekten, Aemtlerstr. 74, CH-8003 Zurich, Switzerland. Ed. Felix Guhl. adv.; charts; illus. circ. 5,000. **Indexed:** Avery Ind.Archit.Per., Br.Tech.Ind., Gard.Lit. (1992-), Rural Recreat.Tour.Abstr., World Agri.Econ.& Rural Sociol.Abstr. **Document type:** bulletin.
—BLDSC (1542.450000); SWETS; UnCover.

720   US   ISSN 1080-9619
APPENDX; culture - theory - praxis. 1993. a. $16.50 to individuals; institutions $25. Box 382806, Cambridge, MA 02238. URL: http://www.gsd.harvard.edu. Ed. Darell Fields. adv. contact: Milton Curry. **Document type:** academic/scholarly publication.

720   JA   ISSN 0003-7117
APPROACH. (Text in Japanese; summaries in English) 1964. q. free. Takenaka Corporation, 1-13, 4-chome, Hon-machi, Chuo-ku, Osaka 541, Japan. TEL 06-252-1201. FAX 06-271-0398. Ed. Shunichi Hirao. R&P contact: Yukio Yoshimura. bk.rev.; circ. 10,000 (controlled). pp./issue: 32. (back issues avail.) **Indexed:** Archit.Per.Ind., Ind.U.S.Gov.Per. **Document type:** academic/scholarly publication.
    Description: Covers a wide range of urban, architectural, cultural, and social subjects.

720   GW
ARBEITSKREIS FUER HAUSFORSCHUNG. BERICHTE ZUR HAUS- UND BAUFORSCHUNG. 1991. irreg., no.2, 1991. DM.56 to non-members; members DM.48. Jonas Verlag, Weidenhaeuserstr. 88, 35037 Marburg, Germany. TEL 49-6421-25132. **Document type:** monograph series.

ARCHITECTURE

720 GW ISSN 0172-2727
TH4805
ARBEITSKREIS FUER HAUSFORSCHUNG. JAHRBUCH. a. DM.56 to non-members; members DM.38. Jonas Verlag, Weidenhaeuserstr. 88, 35037 Marburg, Germany. TEL 49-6421-25132. **Document type:** bulletin.
  Former titles (until 1975): Arbeitskreis fuer Hausforschung. Bericht ueber die Tagung (ISSN 0172-2468); (until 1972): Arbeitskreis fuer Deutsche Hausforschung. Bericht ueber die Tagung (ISSN 0402-8244); Arbeitskreis fuer Deutsche Hausforschung. Niederschrift ueber die Tagung (ISSN 0172-2719)

720 IT ISSN 0394-2147
L'ARCA. (Text in English, Italian) 11/yr. L.150000($150) (effective 1996). L' Arca Edizioni S.p.A., Via Mose Bianchi 101, 20149 Milan, Italy. TEL 39-2-48014743. FAX 39-2-48014829. Ed. Cesare M. Casati. R&P contact: Titi Casati. adv.: B&W page L.5500000, color page L.9900000; adv. contact: Titi Casati. bk.rev. circ. 40,700. **Indexed:** DAAI. **Document type:** monographic series.
—BLDSC (1594.457000).
  Description: Each issue devoted to an important project theme.

720 CC
ARCH. (Text in English) 1990. irreg. Younder Hall Group, 14-F Aik San Bldg., 14 Westlands Rd., Quarry Bay, Hong Kong, People's Republic of China. TEL 852-2565-1313. FAX 852-2565-8217. Pub. Andrew Ho. adv. contact: Denise Ng. circ. 25,000.
  Description: Covers architecture, design and visual communication in Asia.

ARCH PLUS; Zeitschrift fuer Architektur, Staedtebau und Design. see BUILDING AND CONSTRUCTION

720 747 FR ISSN 0294-8567
NA2
ARCHI-CREE. bi-m. 725 F. (foreign 870 F.) (effective 1997). S.E.P., 106 bd. Malesherbes, 75017 Paris, France. TEL 33-1-42128080. FAX 33-1-46229879. Pub. Joëlle Letessier. adv.; circ. 16,227 (paid). **Indexed:** Avery Ind.Archit.Per.
—SWETS.
  Formerly: Architecture Interieure.
  Description: International architecture magazine that covers the development of architecture, draftmanship, building details and interior arrangements.

725 352.7 FR
ARCHI ECHOS. 21/yr. Editions du Gaillard, 29 rue de la Fontaine-au-Roi, 75011 Paris, France. TEL 43-38-99-77. FAX 43-38-50-13. Ed. Nathalie Catholand. circ. 7,000.

750 US ISSN 1059-9746
NA2105
ARCHIMAGE. 1981. a. free. University of Wisconsin at Milwaukee, School of Architecture and Urban Planning, Box 413, Milwaukee, WI 53201. TEL 414-229-4014. Ed.Bd. circ. 750. **Document type:** academic/scholarly publication.
  Description: Provides an intellectual forum and public record of the School of Architectural and Urban Planning.
  Refereed Serial

720 352.7 NE ISSN 0921-8041
ARCHIS. 1973. m. (Stichting Nederlands Instituut voor Architectuur en Stedebouw) Misset (Subsidiary of: Reed Elsevier plc), Postbus 4, 7000 BA Doetinchem, Netherlands. TEL 31-314-349371. FAX 31-314-363638. (Editorial add.: Stichting Nederlands Instituut voor Architectuur en Stedebouw, Jongkindstr. 5, 3015 CG Rotterdam, Netherlands. TEL 31-10-4364001) adv.: B&W page fl.3004, color fl.5749; trim 246 x 315; adv. contact: Cor van Nek. bk.rev.; illus. circ. 7,410. **Indexed:** Br.Tech.Ind., Key to Econ.Sci. **Document type:** trade publication.
—BLDSC (1597.663000); SWETS.
  Formerly (until 1986): Wonen - T A - B K (ISSN 0165-3504)
  Description: For architects, town planners, and artists.

720 NE ISSN 0044-8621
DE ARCHITECT. (Includes supplement: Architect Special) 1970. 14/yr. fl.330 (foreign fl.415) (effective 1996). Ten Hagen & Stam b.v. (Subsidiary of: Wolters Kluwer N.V.), Postbus 34, 2501 AG The Hague, Netherlands. TEL 31-70-3045700. FAX 31-70-3045812. Ed. J. Rodermond. adv.: B&W page fl.4140, color page fl.6810; trim 297 x 210; adv. contact: Herman Voois. bk.rev.; circ. 8,241 (paid). **Indexed:** Avery Ind.Archit.Per., Br.Tech.Ind., Excerp.Med. **Document type:** trade publication.
—BLDSC (1597.700000); SWETS.
  Description: For architects, interior designers, and city planners: covers architecture, building and construction.

720 352.7 AT ISSN 1037-3640
ARCHITECT (PERTH). q. Aus.$22. Royal Australian Institute of Architects, Western Australian Chapter, 22 Altona St., W. Perth, W.A. 6005, Australia. TEL 61-9-3217114. FAX 61-9-3214708. Ed. Stephen Neille. adv. circ. 2,000.
—BLDSC (1597.927000).
  Former titles (until 1986): Architect W.A. (ISSN 1037-3632); (until 1981): Architect (ISSN 0003-8393)

720 690 SA ISSN 0003-8407
ARCHITECT & BUILDER. 1951. m. R.165 in Southern Africa; elsewhere in Africa R.209; overseas R.302 (effective 1997). Laurie Wale (Pty) Ltd., P.O. Box 4591, Cape Town 8000, South Africa. TEL 27-21-4618029. FAX 27-21-4619265. Ed. Laurie Wale. adv.; bk.rev.; bibl.; charts; illus.; circ. 2,500 (paid). **Indexed:** Avery Ind.Archit.Per., Br.Tech.Ind., Ind.S.A.Per. **Document type:** trade publication.
—UnCover.
  Description: Serves the whole spectrum of the building world, including architects, contractors and engineers.

ARCHITECT, BUILDER, CONTRACTOR & DEVELOPER. see BUILDING AND CONSTRUCTION

720 AT ISSN 1034-4101
ARCHITECT DESIGNED HOUSES. 1989. s-a. Aus.$17. Architecture Media Australia, 3rd Fl., 4 Princes St., Port Melbourne, Vic. 3207, Australia. TEL 61-3-96464760. FAX 61-3-96464918. E-mail: publisher@archmedia.com.au. adv.: color page Aus.$3050; adv. contact: Carolyn Winton. circ. 31,995. **Document type:** trade publication.
  Description: Features a variety of architect designed of renovated houses with plans, photographs, lists of products used and discussion of how their designs fulfill the clients' needs.

720 352.7 AT
NA1
ARCHITECT VICTORIA. 1967. 10/yr. Aus.$75 (foreign Aus.$110). Royal Australian Institute of Architects, Victorian Chapter, 1st Fl., 41 Exhibition St., Melbourne, Vic. 8003, Australia. TEL 61-3-96548066. FAX 61-3-96503360. (Subscr. to: Anne Begg, P.O. Box 18025, Collins St. E., Melbourne, Vic. 3000, Australia. TEL 61-3-96548066) Ed. Gael Tilbrook. adv.: B&W page Aus.$1150, color page Aus.$1610; trim 220 x 186; adv. contact: Paul Andrew. bk.rev.; illus.; mkt. circ. 2,500. **Indexed:** Art Ind., Avery Ind.Archit.Per., Br.Tech.Ind. **Document type:** newsletter.
—UnCover.
  Formerly: Architect (Melbourne) (ISSN 1036-5028); Incorporates: Practice Newsletter; (in 1991): Elevations; Which was formerly (until 1985): State Electricity Commission. Newsletter.
  Description: Covers all aspects of concern to architects, including continuing education, current projects, law and finance.

720 PO
ARCHITECTI. 5/yr. Editora Triforia, Lda., Avda. Marquos de Tomar, 68, 4o Esq., 1000 Lisbon, Portugal. TEL 779-912. FAX 793-83-41. Ed. Luiz Trigueiros.

ARCHITECTS CATALOG. see BUSINESS AND ECONOMICS — Trade And Industrial Directories

666.1 US
ARCHITECTS' GUIDE TO GLASS, METAL & GLAZING. 1972. biennial. $20. U S Glass Publications, Inc., Box 569, Garrisonville, VA 22463. TEL 540-720-5584. FAX 540-720-5687. URL: http://www.woglassmag.com. Ed. Debra A. Levy. R&P contact: Meilissa Light. adv. contact: Debra Levy. bk.rev.; charts; illus.; stat.; circ. 21,000. (back issues avail.) **Document type:** trade publication.

720 US ISSN 0066-6173
ARCHITECT'S HANDBOOK OF PROFESSIONAL PRACTICE. 1917. irreg., with supplements. $200 to non-members; members $140. (American Institute of Architects) A I A Press, 1735 New York Ave., N.W., Washington, DC 20008. TEL 202-626-7575. Ed. David Haviland. R&P contact: Janet Rumbarger. TEL 202-626-7536. circ. 10,000. **Document type:** academic/scholarly publication.

720 II ISSN 0970-6852
ARCHITECTS INDIA. (Text in English) 1960. bi-m. $20. Architects Publishing Corp. of India, 51 Sujata, Ground Fl., Rani Sati Marg, Malad East, Mumbai 400 097, India. TEL 91-22-883-4442. Ed. Santosh Kumar. adv.; bk.rev.; charts; illus. circ. 5,000. **Indexed:** Archit.Per.Ind. **Document type:** trade publication.
  Formerly (until 1989): Architects Trade Journal (ISSN 0304-8594)
  Description: For architects, engineers, builders, contractors and interior designers. Includes news, technical articles and projects connected with the building industry.

720 UK ISSN 0003-8466
TH1
ARCHITECTS' JOURNAL. (Supplement avail.: A J Focus (ISSN 0951-5380)) 1895. w. £59 (U.K. students £39; all overseas £99) (includes A J Focus). E M A P - Construct, 151 Roseberry Ave., London EC1R 4QX, England. TEL 44-171-505-6740. FAX 44-171-505-6750. Ed. Paul Finch; Pub. Graham Harman. R&P contact: Graham Harman. adv. contact: Johnathon Stock. bk.rev.; bibl.; charts; illus.; index. circ. 18,000. (back issues avail.) **Indexed:** Account.& Data Proc.Abstr., Alloys Ind., Art & Archaeol.Tech.Abstr., Art Ind., Avery Ind.Archit.Per., Biodet.Abstr., Br.Ceram.Abstr., Br.Hum.Ind., Br.Tech.Ind., Build.Manage.Abstr., C.I.S. Abstr., Cadscan, Curr.Cont., Eng.Mat.Abstr., Geo.Abstr.H.G., High.Educ.Curr.Aware.Bull., HRIS, Int.Build.Serv.Abstr., Int'l.Civil Eng.Abstr., Lead Abstr., Met.Abstr., Met.Abstr.Ind., Nonfer.Met.Alert, PCC Alert, RICS, Soft.Abstr.Eng., Steels Alert, World Alum.Abstr., Zincscan. **Document type:** trade publication.
—BLDSC (1598.000000); CISTI; KR SourceOne; SWETS; UMI; UnCover. CCC.

720 GW ISSN 0044-863X
NA200
ARCHITECTURA; Zeitschrift fuer Geschichte der Baukunst. 1971. s-a. DM.105 (foreign DM.106) (effective 1996). Deutscher Kunstverlag GmbH, Nymphenburgerstr. 84, 80636 Munich, Germany. TEL 49-89-121516-0. FAX 49-89-12151616. Ed.Bd. bk.rev.; charts; illus. circ. 2,500. **Indexed:** Arts & Hum.Cit.Ind., ASCA, Avery Ind.Archit.Per., Br.Tech.Ind., Curr.Cont., IBR, Ind.Bk.Rev.Hum., RILA. **Document type:** trade publication.
—Genuine Article; KR SourceOne; SWETS.

720 HU ISSN 0066-6270
ARCHITECTURA. 1966. irreg. price varies. Magyar Tudomanyos Akademia, Prielle K. u 19-35, 1117 Budapest, Hungary. FAX 36-1-166-6466. TELEX 226-228 AKNYO H. (Co-sponsor: Magyar Epitomuveszek Szovetsege) illus. **Indexed:** Arts & Hum.Cit.Ind. **Document type:** monographic series.
  Description: Covers famous architects of the 20th Century and their works.

ARCHITECTURE

720   UK   ISSN 0003-8504
NA1
ARCHITECTURAL DESIGN. 1930. bi-m. $145 (foreign $145) (effective 1998). Academy Group Ltd., 42 Leinster Gardens, London W2 3AN, England. TEL 44-171-402-2141. FAX 44-171-723-9540. (Subscr. to: V C H Verlagsgesellschaft mbH, Postfach 101161, 69451 Weinheim, Germany. TEL 49-6201-606148. FAX 49-6201-606117; US addr.: V C H Publishers Inc., 220 E. 23rd St., New York, NY 10010-4606. TEL 212-683-8333) Ed. Maggie Toy. adv.; bk.rev.; abstr.; charts; illus.; tr.lit.; index; circ. 6,500 (paid). (back issues avail.) **Indexed:** Art Ind., Arts & Hum.Cit.Ind., Avery Ind.Archit.Per., Br.Tech.Ind., Cadscan, Curr.Cont., Lead Abstr., SSCI, World Alum.Abstr., Zincscan. **Document type:** academic/scholarly publication.
—BLDSC (1600.000000); CISTI; Genuine Article; KR SourceOne; SWETS; UncCover. **CCC.**
Description: Features current architectural thinking, criticism and achievements.

728 747   US   ISSN 0747-5179
NA7205
ARCHITECTURAL DESIGNS. 1968. bi-m. (7/yr.). $47.70; newsstand price: $4.95. Architectural Designs, Inc., 274 Riverside Ave., Westport, CT 06880-4823. TEL 203-222-1113. Ed. Carol B. Davis; Pub. Joel Davis. adv. contact: Kathleen Lappano. **Indexed:** Arts & Hum.Cit.Ind. **Document type:** consumer publication.
Formerly (until 1983): 101 Home Plans.

720   UK   ISSN 1350-7524
ARCHITECTURAL HERITAGE SOCIETY OF SCOTLAND. JOURNAL. 1972. a. £18($34) within the E.U. (effective 1996). (Architectural Heritage Society of Scotland) Edinburgh University Press, 22 George Sq., Edinburgh EH8 9LF, Scotland. TEL 44-131-650-6207. FAX 44-131-662-0053. TELEX 727442 UNIVED G. Ed. John Lowrey; Pub. Vivian C. Bone. adv. contact: Kathryn MacLean. bk.rev. circ. 1,000. **Indexed:** Archit.Per.Ind., Avery Ind.Archit.Per., RILA. **Document type:** academic/scholarly publication.
Former titles: Architectural Heritage Society of Scotland. Journal and Annual Report; Scottish Georgian Society. Annual Report and Bulletin; (until 1981): Scottish Georgian Society. Annual Report; Which incorporates: Scottish Georgian Society. Bulletin.
Description: Includes articles and essays by leading historians and researchers in Scottish architecture.

720 942   UK   ISSN 0066-622X
NA190
ARCHITECTURAL HISTORY. 1958. a. £25 (overseas £32) (includes subscr. to Newsletter) (effective 1997 & 1998). Society of Architectural Historians of Great Britain, Brandon Mead, Old Park Ln., Farnham, Surrey GU9 0AJ, England. Ed.Bd. circ. 1,150. **Indexed:** Archit.Per.Ind., Art Ind., Arts & Hum.Cit.Ind., ASCA, Avery Ind.Archit.Per., Br.Archaeol.Abstr., Br.Hum.Ind., Br.Tech.Ind., Curr.Cont., Ind.Bk.Rev.Hum., RILA. **Document type:** academic/scholarly publication.
—BLDSC (1600.200000); KR SourceOne; UnCover.

720   US   ISSN 0894-0436
TH7700
ARCHITECTURAL LIGHTING. q. $24 (Canada & Mexico $30; elsewhere $125) (effective 1996). Miller Freeman Inc. (New York) (Subsidiary of: United News & Media), One Penn Plaza, New York, NY 10119. TEL 212-714-1300. FAX 212-714-1313. (Subscr. to: Box 1061, Skokie, IL 60076-9943. TEL 800-255-2824. FAX 708-647-5972) Ed. Craig DiLouic. adv.; bk.rev.; charts; illus.; tr.lit.; index; circ. 57,000 (paid); 35,000 (controlled). (back issues avail.) **Indexed:** Search (1988-).
—SWETS; UMI; UnCover. **CCC.**
Description: Covers practical, problem-solving approaches to architectural lighting for trade professionals.

ARCHITECTURAL PSYCHOLOGY NEWSLETTER. see PSYCHOLOGY

720   US   ISSN 0003-858X
NA1   CODEN: ACURAV
ARCHITECTURAL RECORD. (Includes supplements: Record Interiors, Record Houses) 1891. 14/yr. $59 (Canada $79; elsewhere $199) (effective 1996). McGraw-Hill Companies, 1221 Ave. of the Americas, New York, NY 10020. TEL 212-512-2000. FAX 212-512-4256. URL: http://mcgraw-hill.com/corporate/news_info/locator.html. (Subscr. to: Box 516, Hightstown, NJ 08520-1450. TEL 609-426-7070) Ed.Bd.; Pub. Elaine Shusterman. adv.; bk.rev.; charts; illus.; tr.lit.; index. circ. 65,535. (also avail. in microfilm from UMI; microfiche from IDC) **Indexed:** A.S.& T.Ind., Acad.Ind., Art Ind., Arts & Hum.Cit.Ind., ASCA, Avery Ind.Archit.Per., Br.Tech.Ind., Curr.Cont., Eng.Ind., Ind.Bk.Rev.Hum., Intl.Civil Eng.Abstr., Mag.Ind., PMR, R.G.Abstr., R.G., RICS, Search (1988-), Soft.Abstr.Eng., SRI, SSCI, Tr.& Indus.Ind. **Document type:** trade publication.
●Also available online. Vendor(s): Dow Jones News Retrieval (ARCH), Knight-Ridder Information, Inc. (AR), NewsNet (BC13).
—BLDSC (1600.450000); CISTI; Genuine Article; KR SourceOne; Linda Hall; SWETS; UMI; UnCover. **CCC.**
Description: For architects and engineers on business, design, and engineering.

720 690   UK   ISSN 0003-861X
NA1
ARCHITECTURAL REVIEW. 1897. m. $85. E M A P - Architecture, 33-39 Bowling Green Ln., London EC1R 0DA, England. TEL 0171-837-1212. FAX 0171-278-4003. E-mail: lynnej@construct.emap.co.uk; URL: http://www.emap.com/construct/arhome.htm. Ed. Peter Davey. adv. contact: Neil Williams. bk.rev.; charts; illus. circ. 18,500. (also avail. in microfiche from IDC) **Indexed:** Art & Archaeol.Tech.Abstr., Art.Hosp.& Tour., Art Ind., Arts & Hum.Cit.Ind., ASCA, Avery Ind.Archit.Per., Br.Hum.Ind., Br.Tech.Ind., Cadscan, Curr.Cont., DAAI, Gard.Lit. (1992-), Ind.Bk.Rev.Hum., Lead Abstr., RICS, RILA, Search (1988-), Zincscan. **Document type:** trade publication.
●Also available online. Vendor(s): UMI.
—BLDSC (1600.475000); CISTI; Genuine Article; KR SourceOne; Linda Hall; SWETS; UMI; UnCover. **CCC.**

720   AT   ISSN 0003-8628
NA1   CODEN: ASRVA4
ARCHITECTURAL SCIENCE REVIEW. 1958. q. Aus.$35 (foreign Aus.$50) to individuals; institutions Aus.$70 (foreign Aus.$100) (effective 1996). University of Sydney, Department of Architectural Science, Sydney, N.S.W. 2006, Australia. TEL 612-3512686. FAX 612-3513031. TELEX 26169 AA. E-mail: dads@arch.su.edu.au; URL: http://www.usyd.edu/au/. Ed. H.J. Cowan. R&P contact: H.J. Cowan. adv.: page Aus.$300. bk.rev.; bibl.; charts; illus.; stat.; cum.index every 2 yrs. circ. 900. (also avail. in microform from UMI) **Indexed:** Aus.P.A.I.S., Br.Ceram.Abstr., Br.Tech.Ind., Build.Manage.Abstr., C.I.S. Abstr., Eng.Ind., IBR, Int.Build.Serv.Abstr. **Document type:** academic/scholarly publication.
—BLDSC (1600.490000); CISTI; Ei; Linda Hall; SWETS; UMI; UnCover. **CCC.**

720   US   ISSN 1068-8560
TH2235
ARCHITECTURAL SPECIFIER. 1992. 6/yr. $15 per no. Century Communications Corp., 6201 Howard St., Niles, IL 60714. TEL 847-647-1200. FAX 847-649-7055. adv.: B&W page $2880, color page $4380; trim 8 x 10 7/8. circ. 25,000 (controlled). **Document type:** trade publication.
Description: Features product news on building exterior envelope.

ARCHITECTURAL TECHNOLOGY. see BUILDING AND CONSTRUCTION

720   US   ISSN 0746-0554
NA1
ARCHITECTURE. 1913. m. $55 (Canada $64; elsewhere $85) (effective 1997). B P I Communications, Inc., 1130 Connecticut Ave., N.W., Ste. 625, Washington, DC 20036. TEL 202-828-0993. FAX 202-828-0825. URL: http://www.bpi.com/. (Subscr. to: Box 2063, Marion, OH 43302. TEL 800-347-6969) Ed. Deborah K. Dietsch; Pub. Steve Donohue. adv.: B&W page $7890; adv. contact: Marilyn Alba. bk.rev.; bibl.; charts; illus.; stat.; index. circ. 70,000. (also avail. in microform from UMI) **Indexed:** Archit.Per.Ind., Art Ind., Arts & Hum.Cit.Ind., ASCA, Avery Ind.Archit.Per., Br.Tech.Ind., Bus.Ind., Curr.Cont., Eng.Ind., Gard.Lit (1992-), Ind.Bk.Rev.Hum., R.G., Search (1988-), SSCI, Tr.& Indus.Ind.
●Also available online. Vendor(s): Information Access Co.
—BLDSC (1600.937000); CISTI; Genuine Article; KR SourceOne; Linda Hall; SWETS; UMI; UnCover. **CCC.**
Incorporates (1992-1995): Building Renovation (ISSN 1070-5988); (1920-1995): Progressive Architecture (ISSN 0033-0752); Architectural Technology; Former titles: (until 1983): A I A Journal (ISSN 0001-1479); American Institute of Architects. Journal.

720   SZ   ISSN 0379-8585
NA2542.4
ARCHITECTURE & BEHAVIOUR/ARCHITECTURE ET COMPORTEMENT. (Text in English and French) 1980. q. 70 SFr. to individuals; institutions 150 SFr. Swiss Federal Institute of Technology, Department of Architecture, C.P. 555, CH-1001 Lausanne, Switzerland. FAX 021-6176317. Ed. Kaj Noschis. adv.; bk.rev. circ. 1,000. **Indexed:** Geo.Abstr.H.G., IDA, Psychol.Abstr. (1980-). **Document type:** academic/scholarly publication.
—UnCover.

720 690   II   ISSN 0003-8652
ARCHITECTURE AND BUILDING INDUSTRY. (Text in English) 1969. m. Rs.20($7.) 87-88 New Market, Begam Bridge, Meerut, Uttar Pradesh, India. Ed. Balvir Singh. adv.; bk.rev.; bibl.; charts; illus.; index.

720   GW
ARCHITECTURE & COMPETITIONS. 1939. q. DM.98. Karl Kraemer Verlag, Schulze-Delitzsch-Str. 15, 70565 Stuttgart, Germany. TEL 49-711-78496-0. FAX 49-711-7849620. Ed. Karl Horst Kraemer. adv.; bk.rev.; charts; illus. circ. 4,000. **Indexed:** Psychol.Abstr. **Document type:** trade publication.
—BLDSC (1602.410000); SWETS.
Former titles: Architektur und Wettbewerbe (ISSN 0341-2784); Architektur Wettbewerbe (ISSN 0003-8806)
Description: Professional journal for architects and planners: theory, trends and competition results.

720   AT   ISSN 0003-8725
NA1
ARCHITECTURE AUSTRALIA. 1904. 6/yr. Aus.$45 (foreign Aus.$78). (Royal Australian Institute of Architects) Architecture Media Australia, 3rd Fl., 4 Princes St., Port Melbourne, Vic. 3207, Australia. TEL 61-3-96464760. FAX 61-3-96464918. E-mail: publisher@archmedia.com.au; URL: http://www.archmedia.com.au. Ed. P. Jackson. adv. contact: Carolyn Winton. bk.rev.; charts; illus.; index. circ. 16,733. **Indexed:** Aus.P.A.I.S., Avery Ind.Archit.Per., Br.Tech.Ind., Build.Manage.Abstr. **Document type:** trade publication.
—BLDSC (1601.870000); SWETS; UnCover.
Formerly: Architecture in Australia.
Description: Covers Australian architecture and interiors.

720   AT   ISSN 0729-8714
ARCHITECTURE BULLETIN. 1944. m. Aus.$44 (membership). Royal Australian Institute of Architects, New South Wales Chapter, 3 Manning St., Potts Point, N.S.W. 2011, Australia. TEL 02-356-2955. FAX 02-368-1164. Ed. Virginia Maxwell. adv.; bk.rev. circ. 3,000. (back issues avail.) **Document type:** trade publication.
Description: Provides information on architectural projects, issues affecting the profession, and news from the NSW Chapter of the RAIA.

ARCHITECTURE 395

720 US ISSN 0738-1131
NA730.C2
ARCHITECTURE CALIFORNIA. 1979. s-a. $34 to non-members (foreign $42); members $24; students $15 for 4 issues. American Institute of Architects, California Council, 1303 J St., Ste. 200, Sacramento, CA 95814-2916. TEL 916-448-9082. FAX 916-442-5346. Ed. Mike Martin. adv.; bk.rev. circ. 10,000. **Indexed:** Avery Ind.Archit.Per. **Document type:** trade publication.
—UnCover.
Description: Provides a forum for the exchange of ideas among architects and other disciplines on the issues currently shaping California architecture. Discusses the practice of architecture in many facets, as well as the relationship of the profession to the interests of the public.

720 FR ISSN 0003-8695
ARCHITECTURE D'AUJOURD'HUI (PARIS, 1930); recherche-formes interieures-arts-urbanisme. 1930. m. 710 F. Groupe Expansion, 25 rue Leblanc, 75842 Paris Cedex 15, France. TEL 40-60-40-60. FAX 40-60-41-27. TELEX 205 581 F. (Subscr. to: Service Abonnements B 060, 60732 Sainte Genevieve Cedex 9, France. TEL 44-89-52-30) Eds. Servan Schreiber, Francois Chaslin. adv.; bk.rev.; charts; illus.; tr.lit.; index. circ. 25,791. **Indexed:** Art Ind., ASCA, Curr.Cont., SSCI.
—BLDSC (1601.850000); KR SourceOne; SWETS; UMI. **CCC.**
Formerly: Architecture Francaise (ISSN 0003-8717)

720 FR
ARCHITECTURE ET COMMUNICATION. 4/yr. Maison de l'Architecture, 11 bd. des Recollets, 31078 Toulouse Cedex, France. TEL 61-52-29-71. FAX 61-25-01-44. Ed. Francois Linares. circ. 4,000.

720 GR ISSN 0066-6262
ARCHITECTURE IN GREECE/ARCHITECTONIKA THEMATA. (Text in Greek; summaries in English) 1967. a. $50 (effective 1997 & 1998). Architecture in Greece Press, P.O. Box 3545, 102 10 Athens, Greece. TEL 30-1-7225-930. FAX 30-1-7213-916. (Alt. addr.: 5 Kleomenous - Loukianou St., 106 75, Athens, Greece) Ed. Orestis B. Doumanis; Pub. Orestis B. Doumanis. R&P contact: Orestis B. Doumanis. adv.: B&W page $1600; color page $2000; adv. contact: Orestis B. Doumanis. bk.rev.; index. circ. 5,000. (back issues avail.) **Indexed:** Archit.Per.Ind., Avery Ind.Archit.Per., Ekist.Ind. **Document type:** trade publication.
—BLDSC (1601.960000).
Description: Covers ideas and projects influencing and shaping the human environment in Greece, along with major international trends and development. Includes architectural competitions and student activities.

720 US ISSN 1061-2963
NA2695.U6
ARCHITECTURE IN PERSPECTIVE (NO.). 1986. a. $35 to non-members; members $25. American Society of Architectural Perspectivists, c/o Alexandra Lee, 52 Broad St., Boston, MA 02109. TEL 617-951-1433. URL: http://www.asap.org. Ed. Gordon Grice. R&P contact: Alexandra Lee. **Document type:** catalog, directory.

720 US ISSN 0149-9106
NA730.M6
ARCHITECTURE MINNESOTA. 1936. bi-m. $15. American Institute of Architects, Minnesota Society, 275 Market St., Ste. 54, Minneapolis, MN 55405. TEL 612-338-6763. Ed. Linda Mack. adv.; bk.rev.; illus.; tr.lit.; cum.index. circ. 8,000. **Indexed:** Avery Ind.Archit.Per.
Formerly (until 1974): Northwest Architect (ISSN 0029-330X)

720 NZ ISSN 0113-4566
ARCHITECTURE NEW ZEALAND. 1911. 6/yr. NZ.$34.50. (N Z Institute of Architects) A G M Publishing Ltd., Private Bag 99-915, Newmarket, Auckland, New Zealand. TEL 64-9-379-5393. FAX 64-9-3089-523. Ed. Jonathan Mayo. R&P contact: Robin Beckett. adv. contact: Vanessa Mowlen. bk.rev.; charts; illus. circ. 10,000. **Indexed:** Archit.Per.Ind., RILA. **Document type:** trade publication.
—BLDSC (1601.978000); UnCover. **CCC.**
Former titles (until 1987): New Zealand Architect; New Zealand Institute of Architects Journal (ISSN 0027-7207)
Description: Aimed at professional architects. Covers practice, projects, appraisals, and architectural issues in New Zealand.

720 IS ISSN 0792-1268
NA1477
ARCHITECTURE OF ISRAEL/ADRICHALUT YISRAELIT. Variant title: A I. 1988. q. $75. Architecture of Israel, P.O. Box 302, Herziliya B, Israel. TEL 972-3-6471135. FAX 972-3-6481491. Ed. Ami Ran. adv.: page $2200; adv. contact: R. Ben Aharon. circ. 10,000. **Indexed:** Archit.Per.Ind. **Document type:** trade publication.
Description: Presents current Israeli architecture, including innovative interpretations of Western architecture and design.

720 II ISSN 0970-2369
ARCHITECTURE PLUS DESIGN. (Text in English) 1984. bi-m. Rs.430($60) Media Transasia (India) Pvt. Ltd., K-35 Green Park, New Delhi 110016, India. TEL 91-11-6868775. FAX 91-11-6867641. Ed. Svneet Paul. adv.: B&W page Rs.25000, color page $34000; trim 10 1/2 x 8 1/2; adv. contact: Vidhu Puri. bk.rev.; illus. circ. 10,000. **Document type:** trade publication.
—BLDSC (1601.075000).
Description: Contains building reviews, trends analysis, and current issue discussions for professional architects, urban designers and planners.

720 SA ISSN 0250-054X
ARCHITECTURE S.A.. (Includes supplement: Architectural Product News) (Text in English, occasionally in Afrikaans) 1915; N.S. 1978. bi-m. R.98.04 (R.124 in Africa; elsewhere R.140) (effective 1997). (Institute of South African Architects) George Warman Publications (Pty.) Ltd., P.O. Box 704, Cape Town 8000, South Africa. TEL 27-21-245320. FAX 27-21-261332. Ed. Piet de Beer. adv.; bk.rev.; bibl.; charts; illus. circ. 3,900. (also avail. in microfilm from UMI) **Indexed:** Br.Tech.Ind., Ind.S.A.Per. **Document type:** trade publication.
—BLDSC (1601.994000).
Former titles (until 1978): Plan; (until Dec. 1968): South African Architectural Record (ISSN 0038-1977)
Description: For architects and those who commission buildings in southern Africa.

374 US
ARCHITECTURE SCHOOLS: SPECIAL PROGRAMS. 1983. a. $12.95. Association of Collegiate Schools of Architecture, Inc., 1735 New York Ave., N.W., Washington, DC 20006. TEL 202-785-2324. FAX 202-628-0448. Ed. Christine Hess. circ. 500. **Document type:** directory.
Formerly: Off Campus Study Programs: U S and Abroad.

720 UK ISSN 0958-6407
ARCHITECTURE TODAY; the independent architectural magazine. 1989. 10/yr. £30 (elsewhere in the EC £35; overseas £48). Architecture Today plc., 161 Rosebery Ave., London EC1R 4QX, England. TEL 44-171-837-0143. FAX 44-171-837-0155. (Subscr. to: Reader Service Dept., 19-21 High St., Sutton, Surrey SM1 1DJ, England) Eds. Ian Latham, Mark Swenarton; Pubs. Ian Latham, Mark Swenarton. R&P contact: Ian Latham. bk.rev.; illus.; tr.lit. circ. 20,185. (back issues avail.) **Indexed:** DAAI. **Document type:** trade publication.
—BLDSC (1601.994300).
Description: Features new buildings and technical information for the practicing architect.

720 XR ISSN 0862-7010
ARCHITEKT. (Text in Czech or Slovak) 1955. fortn. 380 Kc.($37) Obec Architektu, Letenska 5, 118 45 Prague 1, Czech Republic. FAX 02-311-4926. Ed. Jiri Horsky. adv.: B&W page 52300 Kc.; 256 x 378. bk.rev. circ. 6,000.
Formerly (until 1990): Ceskoslovensky Architekt (ISSN 0009-0697)

720 GW ISSN 0003-875X
DER ARCHITEKT. 1951. m. DM.195 (foreign DM.255) (students DM.115 (foreign DM.139)) (effective 1997). (Bund Deutscher Architekten) Ernst und Sohn, Muehlenstr. 33-34, 13187 Berlin, Germany. TEL 49-30-47889200. FAX 49-30-47889284. (Subscr. to: Wiley - V C H, Postfach 101161, 69451 Weinheim, Germany. TEL 49-6201-606147. FAX 49-6201-606117; Subcsr. in the Americas to: John Wiley & Sons, Inc., 605 Third Ave., New York, NY 10158. TEL 212-850-6645. FAX 212-850-6021) Ed. Ingeborg Flagge. adv.; bk.rev.; index. circ. 8,795. **Indexed:** Br.Tech.Ind. **Document type:** trade publication.
Description: Forum for debate on a variety of architectural topics.

720 GW ISSN 0003-8768
DER ARCHITEKT UND DER BAUINGENIEUR. 1960. q. DM.11($3) (Bundesverband Freischaffender Architekten und Bauingenieure e.V.) Isar-Post, Druck- und Verlagsgesellschaft mbH, Nikolausstr. 49, Postfach 426, 84034 Landshut, Germany. Ed. A. Dahmen von Buchholz. adv.; bk.rev. circ. 2,745.

720 GW ISSN 0724-7699
ARCHITEKTENHANDBUCH SCHLESWIG-HOLSTEIN. 1977. a. DM.95. Christians & Reim Verlag GmbH, Schlossstr. 5-7, 23701 Eutin, Germany. TEL 04521-779250. FAX 04521-779260. index. (back issues avail.)

720 AU ISSN 0570-6602
ARCHITEKTUR AKTUELL; Fach-Journal. (Text in English, German) 1967. m. DM.130 (effective 1998). Springer-Verlag, Sachsenplatz 4-6, P.O. Box 89, A-1201 Vienna, Austria. TEL 43-1-3302415. FAX 43-1-3302426. E-mail: springer@springer.co.at. Ed. Liesbeth Waechter-Boehm. adv. contact: Michael Katzenberger. bk.rev. circ. 7,500. **Document type:** trade publication.

720 AU
ARCHITEKTUR UND BAU. s-a. Dynamis Werbe- und Verlagsgesellschaft mbH, Heinestr. 3, A-1020 Vienna, Austria. Ed. H. Parton. circ. 14,400.

720 690 AU ISSN 1026-8413
ARCHITEKTUR UND BAU FORUM NEWSLETTER. m. S.984. Oesterreichischer Wirtschaftsverlag, Nikolsdorfergasse 7-11, A-1051 Vienna, Austria. TEL 43-1-54664-0. FAX 43-1-54664215. E-mail: oewv@apanet.at. Ed. Guenther Greul. adv. contact: Wolfgang Duda. **Document type:** trade publication.
—BLDSC (1602.389900).

720 AU
ARCHITEKTUR UND BAU INSTALLATION. s-a. Dynamis Werbe- und Verlagsgesellschaft mbH, Heinestr. 3, A-1020 Vienna, Austria. TEL 01-2143344. FAX 01-2167929. Ed. Friedrich Hubeni. circ. 14,400.

720 AU
ARCHITEKTUR UND BAUFORUM. bi-m. Nikolsdorfergasse 7-11, A-1051 Vienna, Austria. TEL 01-555585228. FAX 01-555585347. TELEX 111669. Ed. Konrad Fischer. circ. 5,400.

720 747 SZ ISSN 1010-5778
ARCHITEKTUR UND LADENBAU; europaeische Fachzeitschrift fuer modernen Ladenbau, Schaufenster und Auslage. 1964. bi-m. 58 SFr. (foreign 83 SFr.). (Fachgruppe Ladenbau) S H Z Fachverlag AG, Alte Landstr. 43, CH-8700 Kuesnacht, Switzerland. TEL 01-9108022. FAX 01-9105155. Ed. Esther Bollmann. adv.; bk.rev. circ. 4,100. **Indexed:** Avery Ind.Archit.Per. **Document type:** trade publication.
Former titles (until 1982): Ladenbau (ISSN 0458-6123); Architektur und Ladenbau.
Description: Trade news about modern shop-design, window display and architecture.

ARCHITECTURE

720 **SZ**
ARCHITEKTUR UND TECHNIK. 1978. m. 71 SFr. B & L Verlags AG, Steinwiesenstr. 3, CH-8952 Schlieren, Switzerland. TEL 41-1-7333999. FAX 41-1-7333989. Ed. Peter Boll. adv.; bk.rev. circ. 11,500. **Document type:** trade publication.

720 **GW** **ISSN 0171-7928**
ARCHITEKTUR UND WOHNEN. (Text in German; summaries in English) 1957. bi-m. DM.88.20. Jahreszeiten Verlag GmbH, Possmoorweg 5, 22301 Hamburg, Germany. TEL 49-40-27170. FAX 49-40-27172056. TELEX 213214-JAG-D. Ed. Wolfgang Nagel; Pub. Thomas Ganske. adv. contact: Roberto Sprengel. circ. 180,000. **Document type:** consumer publication.
  Formerly (until 1971): Architektur und Kultiviertes Wohnen (ISSN 0003-8784)

720 **XR** **ISSN 0862-7002**
ARCHITECTURA. (Text in Czech or Slovak; summaries in English, French, German, Russian) 1938. a. 60 Kc.($30) Obec Architektu, Letenska 5, 118 45 Prague 1, Czech Republic. circ. 6,000. **Indexed:** Archit.Per.Ind., Avery Ind.Archit.Per., Br.Tech.Ind.
  Formerly (until 1990): Architektura C S R (ISSN 0300-5305)

720 **XO** **ISSN 0044-8680**
ARCHITEKTURA A URBANIZMUS/ARCHITECTURE AND TOWN PLANNING. (Text and summaries in Czech, English, Slovak) 1966. q. $80 (effective 1996). Slovenska Akademia Vied, Ustav Stavebnictva a Architektury, Dubravska cesta 9, 842 20 Bratislava, Slovakia. E-mail: usardula@savba.savba.sk. (Dist. by: Slovak Academic Press Ltd., P.O. Box 57, Nam. Slobody 6, 810 05 Bratislava, Slovakia. TEL 42-7-211728; Dist. in Western countries by: John Benjamins B.V., Amsteldijk 44, Amsterdam (Z.), Netherlands) Ed. M. Dulla. adv. contact: Henrieta Moravcikova. charts; illus. **Indexed:** Arts & Hum.Cit.Ind., Curr.Cont. **Document type:** academic/scholarly publication.
  Description: Publishes works on the theory of architecture, town planning and theory of creation of life environment. For architects, both in research and projects, constructors, museums and memorial personnels, university teachers students.

720 **PL** **ISSN 1232-6372**
NA6
ARCHITEKTURA - MURATOR. (Text in Polish; summaries in English) 1947. m. $100 (effective 1997). (Stowarzyszenie Architektow Polskich - SARP) Wydawnictwo Murator, Al. Wyzwolenia 6 m.43, 00-570 Warsaw, Poland. TEL 48-22-6151742. FAX 48-22-6251814. Ed. Ewa Przestaszewska-Porebska; Pub. Zygmunt Stepinski. adv.: page $2200; adv. contact: Ewa Frankowska-Bielinska. bk.rev.; abstr.; bibl.; charts; illus.; index. circ. 21,000. **Indexed:** Archit.Per.Ind., Avery Ind.Archit.Per., Br.Tech.Ind.
  Formerly (until 1994): Architektura (ISSN 0003-8814)
  Description: Includes architectural competitions, history of architecture, professional information, design, art, information about real estate.

720 **IT**
ARCHITETTI VITERBO. q. B & C s.r.l., Via Str. Teverina Km 3600, 01100 Viterbo, Italy. TEL 0761-251372. FAX 0761-352198. adv.: color page L.1300000; trim 145 x 215. circ. 5,000.

720 **IT** **ISSN 0003-8822**
ARCHITETTO. 1955. m. (10/yr.). Consiglio Nazionale di Architetti, Via S. Maria dell'Anima 10, 00186 Rome, Italy. TEL 39-6-8966009. FAX 39-6-6879520. Ed. Gianni Boeri. adv.: B&W page L.3800000, color page L.4400000. circ. 75,000. **Indexed:** Archit.Per.Ind. **Document type:** trade publication.

720 **IT**
ARCHITETTURA CRONACHE E STORIA. 1955. 11/yr. L.120000 (foreign L.180000). Via Nomentana 150, 00162 Rome, Italy. TEL 39-6-8620684. FAX 39-6-8603662. Ed. Bruno Zevi. adv.: B&W page L.4900000, color page L.6650000. bk.rev.; circ. 15,000 (paid). **Document type:** academic/scholarly publication, consumer publication.
  Refereed Serial

720 **IT**
ARCHITETTURA URBANISTICA: METODI DI PROGRAMMAZIONE E PROGETTI. 1975. irreg., no.5, 1978. price varies. Giardini Editori e Stampatori, Via Santa Bibbiana 28, 56100 Pisa, Italy. TEL 050 502531. Ed. Giacomo Donato.

720 **US** **ISSN 1066-6516**
NA1
ARCHITRONIC; the electronic journal of architecture. 1992. 3/yr. Kent State University, School of Architecture and Environmental Design, Kent, OH 44242-0001. TEL 330-672-2869. FAX 330-672-3809. E-mail: robison@saed.kent.edu; URL: http://www.saed.kent.edu/Architronic/. Ed. Elwin C. Robison. **Document type:** academic/scholarly publication.
  ●Available only online.
  —CISTI.
  Description: Explores the new ranges of architectural communication available through digital media. Serves as a platform for both presenting and reviewing research as a journal, and a forum for stimulating dialogue on emerging ideas.
  Refereed Serial

AREA (ROME, 1990); rivista internazionale di architettura e arti del progetto. see HOUSING AND URBAN PLANNING

720 **RM** **ISSN 0300-5356**
ARHITECTURA. (Text in Rumanian; summaries in English) 1906. q. $20 (effective 1995). Uniunea Arhitectilor din Romania - Union of Romanian Architects, Str. Academiei Nr. 18-20, sector 1, 70109 Bucharest, Rumania. TEL 401-6138080 ext. 183. FAX 401-3120956. Ed. Augustin Ioan. adv. contact: Mariana Celac. bk.rev.; abstr.; bibl.; illus.; stat.; index. circ. 1,000. **Indexed:** Br.Tech.Ind. **Document type:** academic/scholarly publication.

720 **CI** **ISSN 0350-3666**
ARHITEKTURA. (Text in Serbo-Croatian; summaries in English) 1949. q. $35. Savez Drustava Arhitekata Hrvatske, Trg Republike 3-I, 41000 Zagreb, Croatia. Ed. Aleksander Laslo. adv.; bk.rev.; index. circ. 2,500. **Indexed:** Br.Tech.Ind.

720 307.1 **YU** **ISSN 0354-6055**
ARHITEKTURA I URBANIZAM; casopis za prostorno planiranje, urbanizam i arhitekturu. 1960. irreg. Institut za Arhitekturu i Urbanizam Srbije, Bulevar Revolucije 73, Belgrade, Yugoslavia. Ed. Zoran Manevic.
  Formerly (until 1994): Arhitektura, Urbanizam (ISSN 0004-1238)

720 **BU** **ISSN 0324-1254**
ARKHITEKTURA. (Text in Bulgarian; summaries in English, French, German and Russian) 1954. 6/yr. $98. Suiuz na Arkhitektite v Bulgaria, Krakra 11, 1504 Sofia, Bulgaria. TEL 359-2-876513. FAX 359-2-23569. (Dist. by: Foreign Trade Co. "Hemus", 1B Raiko Daskalov Sq., 1000 Sofia, Bulgaria. TEL 359-2-871686. FAX 359-2-9803319) (Co-sponsor: Ministerstvo na Stroezhite i Arkhitekturata) Ed. Rossen Valkov. adv. circ. 4,500. **Indexed:** Archit.Per.Ind.
  —BLDSC (0010.000000).

720 690 **BW**
ARKHITEKTURA I STROITEL'STVO BELARUSI. 1970. bi-m. Izdatel'stvo Polymya, Lenina, 2, 220030 Minsk, Belarus. TEL 7-172-272719. Ed. V.M. Korneichik. circ. 2,769.
  —CISTI.
  Formerly (until 1992): Arkhitektura i Stroitel'stvo Belorussii (ISSN 0869-1975)

720 **RU** **ISSN 0235-7259**
TH4
ARKHITEKTURA I STROITEL'STVO ROSSII. 1960. m. $174 (effective 1998). Furkasovskii per., 12-5, 101000 Moscow, Russia. TEL 7-095-9249741. (Dist. by: Mezhdunarodnaya Kniga, B. Yakimanka 39, 117049 Moscow, Russia. TEL 7-095-2384967. FAX 7-095-2384634; Dist. in U.S. by: Victor Kamkin Inc., 4956 Boiling Brook Pkwy., Rockville, MD 20852. TEL 301-881-5973. FAX 301-881-1637) Ed. Aleksandr M. Sidorii. charts; illus.; index. **Indexed:** Chem.Abstr.
  —BLDSC (0011.100000).
  Formerly (until 1989): Na Stroikakh Rossii (ISSN 0027-7312)

720 **RU** **ISSN 0004-1939**
NA6
ARKHITEKTURA S.S.S.R. 1933. 6/yr. 46.80 Rub. (Gosudarstvennyi Komitet po Grazhdanskomu Stroitel'stvu i Arkhitekture) Stroiizdat, Ul. Dolgorukovskaya ul., 23a, 111442 Moscow, Russia. (Co-sponsor: Soyuz Arkitektorov) Ed. A.P. Koudriavtsev. adv.; bk.rev.; charts; illus.; index. circ. 14,250. (also avail. in microform from MIM,UMI) **Indexed:** Br.Tech.Ind.
  —Linda Hall.

720 **SW** **ISSN 0347-058X**
ARKITEKTEN. 1975. m. SEK 200 (effective 1990). Arkitektfoerbundet, P.O. Box 9097, S-102 72 Stockholm, Sweden. **Document type:** trade publication.
  Former titles (until vol.4, 1976): Tidning foer Arkitektfoerbundet; (until vol.3, 1976): Arkitekten; (until vol.1-2, 1976): Tidning foer Arkitektfoerbundet.

720 **NO** **ISSN 0004-1998**
ARKITEKTNYTT. 1951. fortn. (20/yr.). NOK 450 includes Norske Arkitektkonkurranser (in Scandinavia; elsewhere NOK 550) (effective 1996). Norske Arkitekters Landsforbund - National Association of Norwegian Architects, Josefinesgt. 34, N-0351 Oslo, Norway. TEL 47-22-60-22-90. FAX 47-22-69-59-48. (Co-sponsors: Norske Interioerarkitekters Landsforening; Norske Landskapsarkitekters Forening) Ed. Bente Sand. adv. contact: Ingrid Stenseth. bk.rev.; bibl.; illus.; index. circ. 4,700. **Document type:** trade publication.
  —CCC.

720 **SW** **ISSN 0004-2021**
NA6.S85
ARKITEKTUR; the Swedish review of architecture. (Summaries in English) 1901. 8/yr. SEK 480 (students SEK 290) (effective 1996). Arkitektur Foerlag AB, P.O. Box 1742, S-111 87 Stockholm, Sweden. TEL 46-8-679-61-05. FAX 46-8-611-52-70. Ed. Olof Hultin. adv. contact: Suzanne Murray. charts; illus.; index; circ. 6,200 (controlled). **Indexed:** Avery Ind.Archit.Per., Br.Tech.Ind. **Document type:** trade publication.
  —BLDSC (1673.600000); SWETS.
  Description: Provides varying and composite pictures of building and environment in Sweden.

720 **FI** **ISSN 0783-3660**
NA6
ARKKITEHTI/FINNISH ARCHITECTURAL REVIEW/FINSK ARKITEKTURTIDSKRIFT. 1903. 6/yr. FIM 425 in Nordic countries; elsewhere FIM 570 (effective 1998); newsstand price: FIM 60. Suomen Arkkitehtiliitto - Finnish Association of Architects, Yrjonkatu 11 A, 00120 Helsinki, Finland. TEL 358-9-584448. FAX 358-9-604479. Ed. Esa Laaksonen. adv.: B&W page FIM14000, color page FIM17500; trim 225 x 297. bk.rev.; bibl.; charts; illus. circ. 4,388. **Indexed:** Avery Ind.Archit.Per., Br.Tech.Ind. **Document type:** trade publication.
  —SWETS.
  Incorporates (1903-1951): Arkitekten (ISSN 0782-789X)

720 **FI** **ISSN 0044-8915**
ARKKITEHTIUUTISET/ARKITEKTNYTT. 1948. fortn. (16/yr.). FIM 200 in Nordic countries; elsewhere FIM 290. Suomen Arkkitehtiliitto - Finnish Association of Architects, Yrjonkatu 11 A, FIN-00120 Helsinki, Finland. TEL 358-9-584-4489. FAX 358-9-601-123. Ed. Matti Vatilo. adv.; bk.rev.; illus. circ. 3,545. **Document type:** trade publication.

720 307.1 **AG** **ISSN 0328-2384**
ARQUIS; arquitectura y urbanismo. 1993. q. Universidad de Palermo, Centro de Investigaciones en Arquitectura, C.P. 67, S.A. Florida 683, Local 18 1375 Buenos Aires, Argentina. TEL 54-1-3936303. FAX 54-1-325-7135. Ed. Daniel Silberfaden.

ARCHITECTURE

720 SP ISSN 0214-1124
ARQUITECTOS. Key Title: Boletin Informativo de la Profesion de Arquitectos. 1975. 6/yr. Consejo Superior de los Colegios de Aquitectos de Espana, Paseo de la Castellana 12, 4o, 28046 Madrid, Spain. TEL 1-435-22-00. FAX 1-575-38-39. circ. 22,400. **Indexed:** Archit.Per.Ind. **Document type:** newsletter.
—CINDOC.
 Former titles (until 1984): Consejo Superior de los Colegios de Arquitectos. Revista (ISSN 0214-1116); (until 1983): Q (ISSN 0214-1108); (until 1980): Consejo Superior de los Colegios de Arquitectos (ISSN 0210-0673)

720 SP ISSN 0004-2706
NA5
ARQUITECTURA. (Text in Spanish; summaries in English) 1918. bi-m. 12300 ptas.($106) Colegio Oficial de Arquitectos de Madrid, Barquillo 12, 28004 Madrid, Spain. TEL 521-82-00. FAX 532-54-99. Ed.Bd. adv.; bk.rev.; charts; illus. circ. 8,200. **Indexed:** Avery Ind.Archit.Per., Br.Tech.Ind.
—BLDSC (1684.720000); CINDOC; SWETS.

720 CU ISSN 1010-3821
NA5
ARQUITECTURA CUBA. (Text in Spanish; summaries in English and French) s-a. $26 in S. America; N. America $28; elsewhere $30. (Centro de Informacion de la Construccion (CIC), Departamento Editorial) Ediciones Cubanas, Obispo No. 527, Apdo. 605, Havana, Cuba. TEL 32-5556-60. bk.rev.; illus. circ. 4,500. **Indexed:** Br.Tech.Ind., IBR.

720 SP
ARQUITECTURA TECNICA. 3/yr. (Official College of Master Builders and Technical Architects) M I L M, S.L., Salamanca 31 - 3a, 46005 Valencia, Spain. TEL 6-334-07-07. Ed. D.M. Galarza.

720 SP ISSN 0214-1256
ARQUITECTURA VIVA. 1988. bi-m. 9000 ptas. (Europe 11500 ptas.; elsewhere 16500 ptas.) (effective 1998). Arquitectura Viva, S.L., Rosario, 31, 28005 Madrid, Spain. TEL 34-1-3669900. FAX 34-1-3640151. E-mail: aviva@compuser.com; URL: http://www.ArquitecturaViva.com. Ed. Adela Garcia-Herrera; Pub. Luis Fernandez Galiano. R&P contact: Gina Carino. adv.: B&W page 225000 ptas.; color page 250000 ptas.; trim 240 x 297. bk.rev.; software rev.; illus. circ. 11,000. **Document type:** trade publication.
—CINDOC; SWETS.
 Description: Covers the latest in architecture and all other inevitably related cultural and technical fields.

720 NQ
▼**ARQUITECTURA Y CONSTRUCCION.** 1996. bi-m. Imprimatur Artes Graficas, S.A., Apartado Postal 4637, Managua, Nicaragua. TEL 505-2-2660957. FAX 505-2-2668419. Dir. Sergio de Castro Lopes.

720 352.7 CU
ARQUITECTURA Y URBANISMO. q. $25 in N. America; S. America $26; Europe $28. (Ministerio de Educacion Superior) Ediciones Cubanas, Obispo No. 527, Apdo. 605, Havana, Cuba. (Alt. addr.: Apdo. 6028, CUJAE, Marianao 15, Havana, Cuba)

720 BL ISSN 0102-8979
ARQUITETURA E URBANISMO. 1984. bi-m. $93 (effective 1997). Editora Pini Ltda., Rua Anhaia, 964, Bom Retiro, 01130-900 Sao Paulo, Brazil. TEL 55-11-2248811. Ed. Mario Sergio Pini. adv. contact: Luiz Carlos F. Oliveira. **Document type:** directory.

721 690 BL ISSN 0104-1908
ARQUITETURA Y CONSTRUCAO; a revista para construir ou reformar sua casa. 1988. m. $120. Editora Abril, S.A., R. Geraldo Flausino Gomes, 61, 04573-900 Sao Paulo, SP, Brazil. TEL 011-534-5344. FAX 011-534-5638. (Subscr. to: Rua do Curtume 769, 05065-900 Sao Paulo, SP, Brazil. TEL 011-823-9100) Ed. Elda Muller. adv.; charts; illus. circ. 105,000. **Document type:** consumer publication.
 Description: Contains information on building or remodeling one's own home.

ARREDO URBANO. see BUILDING AND CONSTRUCTION

ART AND DESIGN. see ART

910 US ISSN 1060-2569
ARTISTIC TRAVELER; architecture & travel with art & photography. 1991. bi-m. $29. S & R Research, 2500 E. Fourth Plain Blvd., Ste. 104, Vancouver, WA 98661-3965. TEL 360-737-0632. E-mail: architravel@worldaccess.com. Ed. Richard Hovey; Pub. Richard Hovey. bk.rev. (back issues avail.) **Document type:** newsletter.
 Description: Aims to guide people interested in the artistic aspect of architecture to exciting visual experiences. Included is a calendar of museum exhibits and news about architectural attractions, awards and important new buildings.

ARTS ASIATIQUES. see ART

ARTS ET INDUSTRIES. see ENGINEERING

720 690 CC
ASIAN ARCHITECT & CONTRACTOR. (Text in English) 1972. m. HK.$250($65) Thomson Press Hong Kong Ltd., 202-203 Hollywood Centre, 233 Hollywood Rd., Hong Kong, People's Republic of China. TEL 852-2815-9111. FAX 852-2851-1933. Ed. Annabd Machie; Pub. J.S. Uberoi. R&P contact: Rajesh Malik. adv.: B&W page HK.$11500, color page HK.$14000; trim 209 x 279; adv. contact: Tony Snyth. circ. 16,825. **Indexed:** HongKongiana. **Document type:** trade publication.
 Formerly: Asian Architecture and Builder; Incorporates: Asia Pacific Contractor.
 Description: Covers Asian, Australian, and Pacific construction projects, plant and product news.

720.5 US ISSN 0889-3012
NA1
ASSEMBLAGE; a critical journal of architecture and design culture. 1986. 3/yr. $62 to individuals (foreign $78); institutions $125 (foreign $141); students and retired $40 (foreign $56) (effective 1997). M I T Press, 5 Cambridge Center, Cambridge, MA 02142. TEL 617-253-2889. FAX 617-577-1545. E-mail: journals-orders@mit.edu; URL: http://www-mitpress.mit.edu/journals-legacy.tcl. (Editorial addr.: 20 Hanson St. No. 4, Boston, MA 02118) Ed.Bd. R&P contact: Paul Dzus. adv. circ. 1,650. (also avail. in microform from UMI; back issues avail.; reprint service avail. from UMI) **Indexed:** Avery Ind.Archit.Per. **Document type:** academic/scholarly publication.
—BLDSC (1746.439000); SWETS; UMI; UnCover. **CCC.**
 Description: Examines the interrelationships between culture and design and between theory and material reality. Presents essays, projects and debates by scholars, theorists, and practitioners.

720 US ISSN 0848-8525
TH3401
ASSOCIATION FOR PRESERVATION TECHNOLOGY INTERNATIONAL. BULLETIN. Short title: A P T Bulletin. 1969. q. $85 (Canada $100; elsewhere $135). Association for Preservation Technology International, Box 3511, Williamsburg, VA 23187-3511. TEL 703-373-1621. FAX 888-723-4242. Ed. Diana Waite. R&P contact: Diana Waite. TEL 518-426-5935. adv. contact: Gary Maggio. bk.rev./ index. circ. 2,000. (also avail. in microfiche) **Indexed:** Amer.Hist.& Life, Art & Archaeol.Tech.Abstr., Avery Ind.Archit.Per., Hist.Abstr. **Document type:** bulletin.
—BLDSC (1581.770000); CISTI; KR SourceOne; UnCover. **CCC.**
 Formerly (until 1991): Association for Preservation Technology. Bulletin (ISSN 0044-9466)
 Description: Covers research and practical application of the principles of preservation technology to buildings, sites and objects.
 Refereed Serial

720 US ISSN 0194-410X
NA2000
ASSOCIATION OF COLLEGIATE SCHOOLS OF ARCHITECTURE. PROCEEDINGS OF THE ANNUAL MEETING. Key Title: Proceedings of the A C S A Annual Meeting. 1979. a. $30 softcover. Association of Collegiate Schools of Architecture, Inc., 1735 New York Ave., N.W., Washington, DC 20006. TEL 202-785-2324. FAX 202-628-0448. **Document type:** proceedings.

ASSOCIAZIONE PER IMOLA STORICO ARTISTICA. ATTI. see ARCHAEOLOGY

720 740 US
ATHENAEUM ANNOTATIONS. 1976. irreg. membership. Athenaeum of Philadelphia, 219 S. Sixth St., Philadelphia, PA 19106-3794. TEL 215-925-2688. circ. 1,400. **Document type:** monographic series.

AUSTRALIAN BUILDING NEWS. see BUILDING AND CONSTRUCTION

AUSTRALIAN HOME BEAUTIFUL. see INTERIOR DESIGN AND DECORATION

AWARD MAGAZINE. see BUILDING AND CONSTRUCTION

B T H - TAPETENZEITUNG. (Boden - Tapeten - Heimtextilien) see INTERIOR DESIGN AND DECORATION — Furniture And House Furnishings

720 UK ISSN 1352-2507
BARTLETT RESEARCH PAPERS. 1993. irreg. University College London, Bartlett School of Graduate Studies, Philips House, Gower St., London WC1E 6BT, England. TEL 0171-387-7050. FAX 0171-916-1887. Ed. Bev Nutt. **Document type:** academic/scholarly publication.
—BLDSC (1863.827600).

BATISSEUR EUROPEEN. see BUILDING AND CONSTRUCTION

720 SZ ISSN 0255-3104
BAUEN IN STAHL/CONSTRUIRE EN ACIER/COSTRUIRE IN ACCIAIO. (Text in French, German) 1968. q. 60 SFr. (effective 1997 & 1998). Schweizerische Zentralstelle fuer Stahlbau, Seefeldstr. 25, CH-8034 Zurich, Switzerland. TEL 41-1-2618980. FAX 41-1-2620962. Ed. Stephan Zingg. charts; illus.; cum.index. circ. 10,000. (looseleaf format; back issues avail.) **Indexed:** Alloys Ind., Eng.Mat.Abstr., Met.Abstr.Ind., Met.Abstr., Nonfer.Met.Alert, PCC Alert, Steels Alert, World Alum.Abstr. **Document type:** trade publication.
 Description: Descriptions of modern steel buildings and bridges.

720 900 572 GW
BAUERNHAEUSER AUS MITTELEUROPA; Aufmasse und Publikationen von Gerhard Eitzen. 1984. irreg. DM.25. Arbeitskreis fuer Hausforschung e.V., Nachtigallental, 55566 Sobernheim - Nahe, Germany.

720 690 AU ISSN 0005-6596
BAUFORUM; Fachzeitschrift fuer Architektur-Bautechnik-Bauwirtschaft-Industrial Design. 1967. bi-m. S.350. Architektur- und Baufachverlag Gesellschaft GmbH, Weimarer Str. 91, 1190 Vienna, Austria. Ed. Ingeborg Bugnar. adv.; bk.rev.; abstr.; charts; illus.; index. circ. 6,000. **Indexed:** Archit.Per.Ind., Avery Ind.Archit.Per., Br.Tech.Ind. **Document type:** trade publication.

720 GW
 CODEN: WZAWA9
BAUHAUS UNIVERSITAET WEIMAR. THESIS. WISSENSCHAFTLICHE ZEITSCHRIFT. (Text in English, German) 1954. 6/yr. DM.150. Bauhaus Universitaet Weimar, Coudraystr. 7, 99421 Weimar, Germany. TEL 49-3643-581150. FAX 49-3643-581156. Ed. Heidemarie Schirmer; Pub. Reiner Bensch. **Document type:** academic/scholarly publication.
—CASDDS.
 Formerly: Hochschule fuer Architektur und Bauwesen Weimar. Wissenschaftliche Zeitschrift (ISSN 0509-9773)

720 690 GW ISSN 0005-674X
NA3
BAUMEISTER; Zeitschrift fuer Architektur. (Text in German; summaries in English) 1902. m. DM.210 (students DM.150) (effective 1997). Callwey Verlag, Postfach 800409, 81604 Munich, Germany. TEL 49-89-436005-0. FAX 49-89-43600513. Ed. Wolfgang Bachmann. adv.; bk.rev.; bibl.; charts; illus.; mkt.; pat.; index circ. 17,500. **Indexed:** Art Ind., Avery Ind.Archit.Per., Br.Tech.Ind., IBR. **Document type:** trade publication.
—BLDSC (1867.600000); KR SourceOne; SWETS. **CCC.**

BAUPLAN - BAUORGA; internationale technisch-wirtschaftliche Zeitschrift. see BUILDING AND CONSTRUCTION

ARCHITECTURE

BAUTENSCHUTZ UND BAUSANIERUNG; Zeitschrift fuer Bauinstandhaltung und Denkmalpflege. see *BUILDING AND CONSTRUCTION*

720   GW   ISSN 0005-6855
TH3
BAUWELT. 1910. w. DM.374.40. Bertelsmann Fachzeitschriften GmbH, Postfach 120, 33111 Guetersloh, Germany. TEL 05241-802332. FAX 05241-73055. Ed. Peter Rumpf. adv.: B&W page DM.6640, color page DM.10830; trim 275 x 203. bk.rev.; bibl.; charts; illus.; mkt.; index. circ. 16,656. **Indexed:** Avery Ind.Archit.Per., Br.Tech.Ind., Chem.Abstr., Excerp.Med. **Document type:** trade publication.
—BLDSC (1871.000000).

720   GW   ISSN 0005-688X
DAS BAUZENTRUM. 1960. 10/yr. DM.80. Verlag das Beispiel GmbH, Spreestr. 9, 64295 Darmstadt, Germany. TEL 49-6151-33557. FAX 49-6151-313089. Ed. Otto Spies. adv.: B&W page DM.8900; trim 250 x 190. bk.rev.; circ. 40,000 (controlled). (tabloid format; reprint service avail.) **Document type:** trade publication.

720 747   US   ISSN 1046-6312
NA7205
BEAUTIFUL HOMES. 1988. a. $4.95. Archway Press, Inc., 19 W. 44th St., New York, NY 10036. TEL 212-757-5580. Ed. Richard S. Campen.
Description: Features currently popular floor plans and pictures of single family detached homes of interest to home planners and builders.

BEBYGGELSEHISTORISK TIDSKRIFT. see *HOUSING AND URBAN PLANNING*

720   NE
BERLAGE CAHIERS. (Text in English) 1992. a. price varies. (Berlage Institute Amsterdam) Uitgeverij 010, Watertorenweg 180, 3063 HA Rotterdam, Netherlands. TEL 31-10-4333509. FAX 31-10-4529825. **Document type:** monographic series.

720   SZ
THE BEST IN LEISURE AND PUBLIC ARCHITECTURE. a. $55. Rotovision S.A., Route Suisse 9, CH-1295 Mies, Switzerland. TEL 022-7553055. FAX 022-7554072. (Dist. in the U.S. by: Watson-Guptill Publications, 1515 Broadway, New York, NY 10036. TEL 800-451-1741. FAX 908-363-0338) illus.
Description: Illustrates top designs from around the world that set new standards in the architecture of leisure buildings.

720 690   US   ISSN 0743-2461
NA7205
BEST-SELLING HOME PLANS. vol.15, 1986. bi-m. $3.50 per no. Home Magazine Publishing Corp. (Subsidiary of: Hachette Filipacchi Publications (Newport Beach)), 1499 Monrovia, Newport Beach, CA 92663. TEL 714-720-5399. Ed. Inga Buell. adv. circ. 210,000.
Description: Renderings and floor plans for house designs.

BETTER HOMES AND GARDENS. see *INTERIOR DESIGN AND DECORATION*

728   US   ISSN 0731-7409
TH4816
BETTER HOMES & GARDENS REMODELING IDEAS. Key Title: Remodeling Ideas. 1945. q. (effective 1997); newsstand price: $3.99 (Canada $4.99). Meredith Corporation, Special Interest Publications, 1716 Locust St., Des Moines, IA 50336. TEL 515-284-3000. Pub. Steve Levinson. adv.: B&W page $20250; adv. contact: Peggy Leib. illus.; tr.lit.; circ. 450,000 (paid). **Document type:** consumer publication.
Formerly: Better Homes and Gardens Home Improvement Ideas.

720   YU   ISSN 0351-2592
BILTEN DOKUMENTACIJE. URBANIZAM I ARHITEKTURA/BULLETIN OF DOCUMENTATION. TOWN PLANNING AND ARCHITECTURE. 1950. bi-m. $198. Jugoslovenski Centar za Tehnicku i Naucnu Dokumentaciju - Yugoslav Center for Technical and Scientific Documentation (YCTSD), SI. Penezica-Krcuna 29-31, Box 724, 11000 Belgrade, Yugoslavia. Ed. Ljiljana Kojic-Bogdanovic.
Supersedes in part: Bilten Dokumentacije. Gradjevinarstvo i Arhitektura (ISSN 0006-260X)

721   PO   ISSN 0006-2804
BINARIO; revista de arquitectura, construcao e equipamento. (Text in Portuguese; summaries in English) 1958. m. $20. Praca de Londres 10, Lisbon 1, Portugal. Ed. Jose Luis Quintino. adv.; bk.rev.; charts; illus.; mkt.; tr.lit.; s-a. index. circ. 2,000.

720   IT
BIOARCHITETTURE. 1993. irreg. price varies. Liguori Editore s.r.l., Via Posillipo 394, 80123 Naples, Italy. TEL 39-81-7206111. FAX 39-81-7206244. Eds. Bianca Bottero, Gianni Scudo; Pub. Guido Liguori. adv. contact: Maria Liguori. **Document type:** monographic series.

712 720   NE   ISSN 0929-1806
BLAUWE KAMER PROFIEL; tijdschrift voor landschapsontwikkeling en stedebouw. 1991. bi-m. fl.115 (2300 BEF) to individuals; institutions fl.159.50 (3200 BEF). Stichting Lijn in Landschap, Herenstraat 32, 6701 DL Wageningen, Netherlands. TEL 31-317-425580. FAX 31-317-425886. E-mail: blauwekamer@gaw.nl; URL: http://www.gaw.nl/blauwekamer. Ed. Harry Haarsema. adv.: B&W page fl.1535, color page fl.3575; trim 240 x 310; adv. contact: Cathe Kwakkenbos. bk.rev.; cum.index: 1991-1995. circ. 2,000. (tabloid format; back issues avail.)
Formed by the 1993 merger of: Blauwe Kamer (ISSN 0926-1621) & Profiel (ISSN 0925-5567)
Description: Covers landscape architecture and urban planning issues, including environmental changes in urban and rural areas.

720 690   US   ISSN 0742-0552
NA705
BLUEPRINTS. 1981. q. $35 membership (effective 1998). National Building Museum, 401 F. St., N.W., Washington, DC 20001. TEL 202-272-2448. FAX 202-272-2564. Ed. Karen Eisenberg. R&P contact: Elly Mullerberg. circ. 3,000. **Indexed:** Avery Ind.Archit.Per., Br.Tech.Ind. **Document type:** newsletter, academic/scholarly publication.

BOLIGEN. see *HOUSING AND URBAN PLANNING*

BONYTT/DESIGN FOR LIVING; norsk spesialblad for arkitektur boliginnredning. see *INTERIOR DESIGN AND DECORATION*

720   US
BOSTON SOCIETY OF ARCHITECTS. CHAPTERLETTER. 1914. bi-m. $55 (foreign $75). Boston Society of Architects, 52 Broad St., Boston, MA 02109-4301. TEL 617-951-1433 ext. 221. FAX 617-951-0845. E-mail: bsarch@architects.org; URL: http://www.architects.org. Ed. Richard Fitzgerald. adv.; bk.rev. circ. 5,000. **Document type:** newsletter.

BOUW. see *BUILDING AND CONSTRUCTION*

BOUWRECHT. see *BUILDING AND CONSTRUCTION*

BRITISH ARCHAEOLOGICAL ASSOCIATION. CONFERENCE TRANSACTIONS. see *ARCHAEOLOGY*

BRITISH ARCHAEOLOGICAL ASSOCIATION. JOURNAL. see *ARCHAEOLOGY*

728   US
BUILD IT! HOME PLANS. 1990. q. newsstand price: $4.95 (Canada $5.95). Miller Freeman, Inc. (New York) (Subsidiary of: United Newspapers), One Penn Plaza, 10th Fl., New York, NY 10119. TEL 212-615-2679. FAX 212-279-3963. E-mail: wjankowski@mfi.com; URL: http://www.buildithomeplans.com. Ed. Wanda Jankowski; Pub. B. Leslie Hart. adv.; bk.rev. circ. 200,000. **Document type:** consumer publication.
Former titles: Best Home Plan Designs; Build-It Home Plan Design; Family Circle's Best Home Plan Designs.
Description: Contains drawings and photographs of plans that readers can order by mail.

BUILDCORE PRODUCT SOURCE; construction materials, equipment & furniture available in Canada. see *BUILDING AND CONSTRUCTION*

721 690   US   ISSN 0192-9070
BUILDER INSIDER. 1975. m. $15 (effective 1998). (Divibest Inc.) Michael J. Anderson, Ed. & Pub., Box 191125, Dallas, TX 75219. TEL 214-871-2913. FAX 214-871-2913. adv. contact: Michael J. Anderson. circ. 10,000. **Document type:** trade publication, newspaper.
Description: For builders, architects and remodelers.

720 690   UK   ISSN 0007-3318
NA1   CODEN: BULDBE
BUILDING; for the design and construction team. 1843. w. £98 in the UK. Builder Group plc., Builder House, 1 Millharbour, London E14 9RA, England. TEL 44-171-560-4000. FAX 44-171-560-4100. TELEX 25212 BUILD G. (Subscr. to: Building, Freepost (LE6522), Leicester LE87 4DH, England. TEL 44-1858-468811) Ed. Peter Bill; Pub. Pam Barker. adv. contact: Ben Greenish. bk.rev.; charts; illus.; mkt.; s-a. index. circ. 22,124. (also avail. in microform from UMI; reprint service avail. from UMI) **Indexed:** Abstr.Health Care Manage.Stud., Art & Archaeol.Tech.Abstr., Avery Ind.Archit.Per., Br.Hum.Ind., Br.Tech.Ind., Build.Manage.Abstr., C.I.S. Abstr., Copper Abstr., Geo.Abstr.H.G., High.Educ.Curr.Aware.Bull., INSPEC (1972-1990), Int.Build.Serv.Abstr., RICS, World Surf.Coat. **Document type:** trade publication.
—BLDSC (2359.200000); CISTI; Linda Hall; SWETS; UMI.
Formerly (until 1966): Builder (ISSN 0366-1059)
Description: Reports on all aspects of the building and construction industry.

720   SA   ISSN 0258-2228
BUILDING. 1985. bi-m. R.160 (effective 1997). Avonwold Publishing Co. (Pty) Ltd., Avonwold House, 24 Baker St., Rosebank, Johannesburg 2196, South Africa. TEL 27-11-788-1610. FAX 27-11-880-2732. (Subscr. to: P.O. Box 52068, Saxonwold 2132, South Africa) Ed. Uli Leitich. adv.; bk.rev. circ. 4,881. (back issues avail.) **Indexed:** Ind.S.A.Per. **Document type:** trade publication.
Description: Follows building concepts, structures, and materials used by the building and construction industries in South Africa.

BUILDING ACOUSTICS. see *PHYSICS — Sound*

BUILDING & CONSTRUCTION NEWS; Asia's weekly construction newspaper. see *BUILDING AND CONSTRUCTION*

720   UK   ISSN 0007-3423
BUILDING DESIGN. 1970. w. £68($178) Miller Freeman plc, Miller Freeman House, 30 Calderwood St., London SE18 6QH, England. TEL 44-181-855-7777. FAX 44-181-854-8058. Ed. Lee Mallett. adv. contact: David Jones. bk.rev.; charts; illus.; stat. circ. 29,642. (also avail. in microform from UMI; reprint service avail. from UMI) **Indexed:** Avery Ind.Archit.Per., Br.Tech.Ind., Build.Manage.Abstr., DAAI, RICS. **Document type:** trade publication.
—BLDSC (2359.710000); CISTI.

625.72 710   UK   ISSN 0969-8213
BUILDING ENGINEER. 1928. m. £8.50 (foreign £10). Incorporated Association of Architects & Surveyors, Jubilee House, Billing Brook Rd., Weston Favell, Northampton, England. Ed. Jack Scott. adv.; bk.rev.; illus. circ. 5,000. **Indexed:** Archit.Per.Ind., Br.Tech.Ind., Build.Manage.Abstr., RICS.
—BLDSC (2359.780000).
Former titles (until 1993): Architect and Surveyor (ISSN 0308-8596); (until 1977): A and S (ISSN 0308-4930); (until 1975): Architect and Surveyor (ISSN 0003-8431)

728.3   US   ISSN 0093-0938
NA7100
BUILDING IDEAS. 1937. q. (effective 1997); newsstand price: $3.99 (Canada $4.99). Meredith Corporation, Special Interest Publications, 1716 Locust St., Des Moines, IA 50336. TEL 515-284-3000. Pub. Steve Levinson. adv.: B&W page $20250; adv. contact: Peggy Leib. illus.; circ. 450,000 (paid). **Indexed:** Consum.Ind. **Document type:** consumer publication.
Formerly: Better Homes and Gardens Building Ideas.

BUILDING PRODUCTS NEWS. see *BUILDING AND CONSTRUCTION*

ARCHITECTURE

BUILDING TODAY. see *BUILDING AND CONSTRUCTION*

720 621.47 US
BUILDINGS INSIDE & OUT. 1991. s-a. free. Passive Solar Industries Council, 1511 K St., N.W., Ste. 600, Washington, DC 20005. TEL 202-628-7400. FAX 202-393-5043. adv. contact: Doug Schroeder. bk.rev. circ. 1,200. (back issues avail.) **Document type:** newsletter.
Description: Covers private and public initiatives in research and development of passive solar and climate responsive design strategies. Also includes conferences, workshops, computer tools, publications, and member news.

721 UK ISSN 0263-7960
HD7333.A3
BUILT ENVIRONMENT. 1975. q. £77.50 (effective 1997). Alexandrine Press, P.O. Box 15, 51 Commarket St., Oxford OX1 3EB, England. TEL 44-1865-724627. FAX 44-1865-792309. Eds. Peter Hall, David Banister. R&P contact: Anne Rudkin. adv.; bk.rev. circ. 645. **Indexed:** Abstr.Hyg., Avery Ind.Archit.Per., Br.Tech.Ind., Build.Manage.Abstr., Ergon.Abstr., Geo.Abstr.H.G., HRIS, IDA, Mid.East: Abstr.& Ind., RICS, Stud.Wom.Abstr.
—BLDSC (2366.039600); CISTI; Linda Hall; SWETS. **CCC.**
Formerly (until 1978): Built Environment Quarterly (ISSN 0308-1508)
Description: Covers a theme of current interest to urban, regional and environmental planners and architects.

BULLETIN MONUMENTAL. see *ARCHAEOLOGY*

BUNDESVEREINIGUNG DER LANDESENTWICKLUNGSGESELLSCHAFTEN UND HEIMSTAETTEN. MITTEILUNGEN. see *HOUSING AND URBAN PLANNING*

721 FI ISSN 0357-6574
BYGDESERIEN. (Text in Swedish) 1979. a. Aalands Folkminnesfoerbund, Aalands Museum, Obbergsvaegen 1, SF-22101 Mariehamn, Finland.

BYGG & TEKNIK. see *BUILDING AND CONSTRUCTION*

720 NO ISSN 0007-7518
NA6
BYGGEKUNST; arkitektur, form og miljoe. 1919. 8/yr. NOK 550 in Scandinavia; elsewhere NOK 630 (effective 1996). Norske Arkitekters Landsforbund - National Association of Norwegian Architects, Josefinesgt. 34, N-0351-Oslo, Norway. TEL 47-22-60-22-90. FAX 47-22-69-59-48. (Co-sponsor: Norske Landskapsarkitekter Forening, Norske Interioerarkitekters Landsforening) Ed. Bjoern Larsen. adv. contact: Ingrid Stenseth. bk.rev.; charts; illus.; index. circ. 6,000. **Indexed:** Archit.Per.Ind., Avery Ind.Archit.Per., Br.Tech.Ind. **Document type:** trade publication.
—BLDSC (2939.520000). **CCC.**

720 690 SW ISSN 0348-6885
BYGGNADSKULTUR. 1977. q. SEK 225 (effective 1996). Svenska Foereningen foer Byggnadsvaard, P.O. Box 6442, S-113 82 Stockholm, Sweden. TEL 46-8-30-37-855. FAX 46-8-30-87-99.

C O D I A. (Colegio Dominicano de Ingenieros, Arquitectos y Agrimensores) see *ENGINEERING — Civil Engineering*

720 352.7 BL
CADERNOS DE ARQUITETURA E URBANISMO. 1993. s-a. Pontificia Universidade Catolica de Minas Gerais, Av. Dom Jose Gaspar 500, 30535-610 Belo Horizonte MG, Brazil. TEL 55-31-3191220. FAX 55-31-3191225. circ. 1,000.

720 IT ISSN 1121-0745
NA1111
CALABRIA. DIPARTIMENTO ARCHITETTONICO E URBANISTICO. QUADERNI. Key Title: Rivista Semestrale del Dipartimento P.A.U. 1991. s-a. L.55000 (foreign L.100000). Rubbettino Editore, Viale dei Pini, 8, 88049 Soveria Mannelli, Italy. TEL 39-968-662034. FAX 39-968-662035. Ed. Simonetta Valtiere. abstr.; bibl.; charts; illus.; maps; stat.; index. circ. 2,000. (back issues avail.)
Description: Contains essays on the history of architecture, restoration, anthropology, economy, and human sciences.

720 US ISSN 1040-4317
CALIFORNIA ARCHITECTURE AND ARCHITECTS. 1980. irreg., no.6, 1986. price varies. Hennessey & Ingalls, Inc., 8321 Campion Dr., Los Angeles, CA 90045. TEL 310-458-9074. FAX 310-394-2928. (And: 1254 Third St. Promenade, Santa Monica, CA 90401) Ed. David Gebhard. **Document type:** monographic series.

CAMBRIDGE URBAN AND ARCHITECTURAL STUDIES. see *HOUSING AND URBAN PLANNING*

728 747 IT
CAMINO. 1978. q. L.10000 per no. Di Baio Editore s.r.l., Via Settembrini 11, 20124 Milan, Italy. TEL 02-6692254. FAX 02-6709257. Ed. Giuseppe Maria Jonghi-Lavarini. adv.: B&W page L.9500000. circ. 70,000.

720 CN ISSN 0008-2872
NA1
CANADIAN ARCHITECT. 1956. m. Can.$41($41) (foreign $82) (effective 1997). Southam Magazine Group, 1450 Don Mills Rd., Don Mills, ON M3B 2X7, Canada. TEL 416-445-6641. FAX 416-442-2214. Ed. Brownwen Ledger. adv. contact: Gord Carley. bk.rev.; charts; illus.; tr.lit.; index. circ. 10,770. **Indexed:** Art Ind., Avery Ind.Archit.Per., Br.Tech.Ind., Can.B.P.I., Can.Per.Ind.
—BLDSC (3017.180000); CISTI; KR SourceOne; SWETS; UMI; UnCover. **CCC.**
Description: Highlights innovative trends in building design, products and technology as well as innovative business techniques.

CANADIAN INTERIORS. see *INTERIOR DESIGN AND DECORATION*

728 CN
TX714
CANADIAN SELECT HOMES. 1948. 8/yr. Can.$21.35 (foreign Can.$36) (effective 1997). 25 Sheppard Ave. W., Ste. 100, North York, ON M2N 6S7, Canada. TEL 416-733-7600. FAX 416-218-3632. Ed. Barbara Dixon. adv.; bk.rev.; illus. circ. 115,000. **Indexed:** Can.B.P.I., CMI. **Document type:** consumer publication.
Former titles: Select Homes and Food (ISSN 0848-8258); Home Design and Decor (ISSN 0709-7123); Which was formed by the merger of: Select Homes (ISSN 0713-8075); Canadian Living's Food Magazine (ISSN 0831-5663); Incorporates: 1001 Decorating Ideas (ISSN 0380-6049); Cottage Country (ISSN 0709-7115); Canadian Do-It-Yourself Magazine (ISSN 0229-2491).
Description: Offers a hands-on approach to home renovation and decoration for readers with an active interest in beautifying their homes.

CASA CLAUDIA; a revista para morar melhor. see *INTERIOR DESIGN AND DECORATION*

720 IT ISSN 0008-7181
NA4
CASABELLA; rivista di urbanistica, architettura e disegno industriale. (Text in English and Italian) 1928. m. (10/yr.). L.149400. Elemond S.p.A., Via Trentacoste 7, 20134 Milan, Italy. TEL 39-2-215631. FAX 39-6-26410847. Ed. Francesco Dalco. adv.: B&W page L.9300000, color page L.12400000. bk.rev.; abstr.; charts; illus.; cum.index. circ. 38,000. **Indexed:** Art Ind., Arts & Hum.Cit.Ind., Avery Ind.Archit.Per., Br.Tech.Ind., Curr.Cont.
—BLDSC (3057.985000); KR SourceOne; SWETS.

728 747 IT
CASE AL MARE. 1980. a. L.10000. Di Baio Editore s.r.l., Via Settembrini 11, 20124 Milan, Italy. TEL 02-6692254. FAX 02-6709257. Ed. Giuseppe Maria Jonghi-Lavarini. adv.: B&W page L.9500000. circ. 48,000.

728 747 IT
CASE DI CAMPAGNA. 1979. bi-m. L.10000 per no. Di Baio Editore s.r.l., Via Settembrini 11, 20124 Milan, Italy. TEL 02-6692251. FAX 02-6709257. Ed. Giuseppe Maria Jonghi-Lavarini. adv.: B&W page L.9500000. circ. 62,000.

728 747 IT
CASE DI MONTAGNA. 1978. 3/yr. L.10000 per no. Di Baio Editore s.r.l., Via Settembrini 11, 20124 Milan, Italy. TEL 02-6692254. FAX 02-6709257. Ed. Giuseppe Maria Jonghi-Lavarini. adv.: B&W or color page L.9500000. circ. 48,000.

720 IT ISSN 0392-3355
CASTELLUM. (Text in Italian; summaries in English) 1965. s-a. L.80000. Istituto Italiano dei Castelli, Via G.A. Borgese 14, 20154 Milan, Italy. TEL 39-2-6551996. Ed. Rosalbino Fasanella; Pub. Flavio Conti. circ. 2,900. (back issues avail.) **Document type:** academic/scholarly publication.

720 VE ISSN 0506-600X
CENTRO DE INVESTIGACIONES HISTORICAS Y ESTETICAS. BOLETIN. 1964. s-a. Universidad Central de Venezuela, Facultad de Arquitectura y Urbanismo, Caracas, Venezuela. FAX 58-2-7526718. **Indexed:** Amer.Hist.& Life (1966-1974), Hist.Abstr. **Document type:** academic/scholarly publication.
Description: Presents historical research on Latin American architecture.
Refereed Serial

720 IT
CENTRO INTERNAZIONALE DI STUDI DI ARCHITETTURA "ANDREA PALLADIO" DI VICENZA. ANNALI DI ARCHITETTURA. 1959. a. L.55000. Basilica Palladiana, Domus Comestabilis, C.P. 835, 36100 Vicenza, Italy. Ed. Fernando Marias. bk.rev. **Indexed:** Avery Ind.Archit.Per., RILA.
Description: Emphasizes the study of Palladio and Renaissance architecture, with news on the activities of the center.

CERCLE HUTOIS DES SCIENCES ET BEAUX-ARTS. ANNALES. see *HISTORY — History Of Europe*

CHARETTE. see *EDUCATION*

720 UK ISSN 0141-559X
CHARLES RENNIE MACKINTOSH SOCIETY NEWSLETTER. 1973. 3/yr. £20 to individuals; libraries £30; students £10 (effective 1996). Charles Rennie Mackintosh Society, Queens Cross, 870 Garscube Rd., Glasgow G20 7EL, Scotland. TEL 44-141-946-6600. FAX 44-141-945-2321. Eds. Frank A. Walker, Patricia Douglas. bk.rev. circ. 1,500. (back issues avail.) **Indexed:** Archit.Per.Ind., DAAI. **Document type:** newsletter.
Description: Aims to foster interest in and conserve the buildings and artifacts designed by Mackintosh and his contemporaries.

728 796.5 635 XR
CHATAR & CHALUPAR; casopis pro kutily, chatare a chalupare. 1969. m. 36 Kc.($15) Ringier C.R., a.s., Domazlicka 11, 130 00 Prague 3, Czech Republic. (Subscr. to: Artia, Ve Smeckach 30, 111 27 Prague 1, Czech Republic) Ed. Josef Trnobransky. abstr.; illus.
Formerly (until 1993): Chatar (ISSN 0323-1437)

720 CC
CHINESE ARCHITECTURE/ZHONGGUO JIANZHU. (Text in English) q. Zhongguo Jianzhu Jishu Fazhan Zhongxin - China Architectural Technology Development Centre, 19 Chegongzhuang Dajie, Beijing 100044, People's Republic of China. TEL 8317744. Ed. Zhang Long.

726 704.948 UK ISSN 0262-4966
CHURCHSCAPE; annual review of the Council for the Care of Churches. 1981. a. £2.95. Council for the Care of Churches, Fielden House, Little College St., London SW1P 3SH, England. TEL 0171-222-3793. FAX 0171-222-3794. Ed. Jonathan Goodchild. adv. contact: Jonathan Goodchild. bk.rev.; bibl.; illus. circ. 1,500. **Document type:** bibliography, newsletter.
—BLDSC (3189.948000).

720 200 GW ISSN 0379-8291
CISTERCIENSER CHRONIK. 1889. s-a. DM.38. Cistercienser Abtei in Mehrerau, Postfach 420606, 50900 Cologne, Germany. TEL 0221-4201538. Ed. Hermann J. Roth. bk.rev.; bibl. **Document type:** academic/scholarly publication.

720 IT
CITTA E CAMPAGNA. m. Via Concordia 20, 00183 Rome, Italy. Dir. Mario Ciranno.

690 712 UK
CIVIC TRUST AWARDS. 1959. a. £10. Civic Trust, 17 Carlton House Terr., London SW1Y 5AW, England. TEL 0171-930-0914. FAX 0171-321-0180. Ed.Bd. (back issues avail.)

ARCHITECTURE

724.2 720.9   US   ISSN 1076-2922
NA260
▼**THE CLASSICIST.** 1995. a. $34.95 (effective 1997). (Institute for the Study of Classical Architecture) Transaction Publishers, Transaction Periodicals Consortium, Department 3092, Rutgers University, New Brunswick, NJ 08903. TEL 908-445-2280. FAX 908-445-3138. Eds. Donald M. Rattner, Richard Wilson Cameron. **Document type:** academic/scholarly publication.
   Description: Devoted to the theory and practice of architectural and artistic classicism. Contains essays on architectural theory, education, urbanism, and archeology as well as practical infomration on building technology, and a section on allied arts.
   Refereed Serial

720 700   US
CLEMSON UNIVERSITY. COLLEGE OF ARCHITECTURE. JOURNAL; a journal of educational thought. 1967. a. $6. (Clemson Architectural Foundation) Clemson University, College of Architecture, Clemson, SC 29631. TEL 803-656-3081. FAX 803-656-3896. Ed. L.G. Craig. bk.rev.; charts; illus.; stat. circ. 3,000.
   Formerly: Clemson University. College of Architecture. Semester Review (ISSN 0009-871X)

CLERK OF WORKS. see *BUILDING AND CONSTRUCTION*

720   CL   ISSN 0716-3622
COLEGIO DE ARQUITECTOS DE CHILE. REVISTA OFICIAL; ciudad y arquitectura. 1968. q. $14 (Latin America $62; Europe and US $88) (effective 1993). (Colegio de Arquitectos de Chile) Arquitable, Manuel Montt 515, Santiago, Chile. TEL 56-02-2353368. FAX 56-02-2358403. Ed. Jaime Marquez Rojas. adv. contact: Maria F. Valenzuela. circ. 3,500. **Document type:** academic/scholarly publication.

720   SP
COLEGIO OFICIAL DE DELINEANTES DE VALENCIA. BOLETIN INFORMATIVO. 4/yr. Colegio Oficial de Delineantes de Valencia - Valencia College of Draughtsmen, G.V. Marques del Turia 24; 1o 1a, 46005 Valencia, Spain. TEL 6-334-11-72. Ed. Gonzalo Divar Loyola.

720   SA
COLIMPEX ARCHITECT'S EXECUPAD. (Text in Afrikaans and English) a. Colimpex Africa (Pty) Ltd., P.O. Box 5838, Johannesburg 2000, South Africa. adv.

712   US
COLLOQUIUM ON THE HISTORY OF LANDSCAPE ARCHITECTURE. PAPERS. 1972. irreg., vol.16, 1996. price varies. Dumbarton Oaks, Research Library and Collection, 1703 32nd St., N.W., Washington, DC 20007. TEL 202-339-6431. E-mail: DOBooks@aol.com. (Subscr. to: Box 4866 Hampden Sta., Baltimore, MD 21211. TEL 410-516-6954. FAX 410-516-6998) Ed. Joachim Wolschke-Bulmahn. circ. 1,000. **Document type:** proceedings.
   Refereed Serial

720 747   US   ISSN 0195-1416
E162
COLONIAL HOMES. (Supplement avail.: Colonial Homes Classic Homes) 1975. bi-m. $14.97; newsstand price: $3.95. Hearst Corporation, Colonial Homes, 1790 Broadway, 14th Fl., New York, NY 10019. TEL 212-830-2951. FAX 212-586-3455. E-mail: colonialhomes@hearst.com; URL: http://www.hearstcorp.com. (Subscr. to: C.D.S., 1901 Bell Ave., Des Moines, IA 50315) Ed. Annette Stramesi; Pub. Brian Doyle. R&P contact: Tracy A. Keegan. adv. contact: Al Berman. circ. 601,724. (also avail. in microfiche from NBI,UMI; reprint service avail. from UMI) **Indexed:** Avery Ind.Archit.Per., Gard.Lit. (1992-), PMR. **Document type:** consumer publication.
   ●Also available online. Vendor(s): Information Access Co.
   Incorporates: American Home; **Formerly:** House Beautiful's Colonial Homes (ISSN 0164-6214)
   Description: Offers building and remodeling ideas, furniture, antiques, and collectibles.

720   CN
COLUMNS. 1978. q. free. Alberta Association of Architects, 10515 Saskatchewan Dr., Edmonton, AB T6E 4S1, Canada. TEL 403-439-1431. (Co-sponsors: Manitoba Association of Architects; Saskatchewan Association of Architects) Ed. Margaret Gates. adv. contact: Margaret Gates. circ. 190. **Document type:** newsletter.
   Formerly: Saskatchewan Association of Architects. Newsletter.

720   JA
COMMERCIAL ARCHITECTURE. 1956. 12/yr. $350. Intercontinental Marketing Corp., P.O. Box 5056, Tokyo 100-31, Japan. TEL 81-3-3661-7458. FAX 81-3-3667-9646.

700 720   US   ISSN 1058-6539
NA2340
COMPETITIONS (LOUISVILLE). 1991. q. $28. Box 20445, Louisville, KY 40250. TEL 502-451-3623. Ed. G. Stanley Collyer. R&P contact: Stanley Collyer. circ. 1,200. **Document type:** newsletter, trade publication.
   —UnCover.
   Description: For artists, planners, and architects; provides current information to the potential competition participant.

720   SP   ISSN 0214-4832
N7
COMPOSICION ARQUITECTONICA; art & architecture. (Text in English, Spanish) 1989. 3/yr. $75. (Fundacion F. Obregon Eizaguirre, Instituto de Arte y Humanidades) Comercial Atheneum S.A., Calle Rufino Gonzalez 26, 28012 Madrid, Spain. TEL 34-1-7542062. (Elsewhere: Rizzoli International Publications, 300 Park Ave. S., New York, NY 10010. TEL 212-387-3400) Ed. Javier Cenicacelaya. adv.; illus. (back issues avail.) **Indexed:** Archit.Per.Ind.
   —BLDSC (3364.948000).

CONGRES ARCHEOLOGIQUE DE FRANCE (PUBLICATION). see *ARCHAEOLOGY*

CONSTRUCTION & ENGINEERING. see *BUILDING AND CONSTRUCTION*

CONSTRUCTION HISTORY. see *BUILDING AND CONSTRUCTION*

CONSTRUCTIONAL REVIEW. see *BUILDING AND CONSTRUCTION*

720   UK
CONTEMPORARY ARCHITECTS. 1980. quinquennial. $70. St. James Press, 2-6 Boundary Row, London SE1 8HP, England. TEL 212-674-5151. Ed. Muriel Emanuel.

CONTEMPORARY ART CENTRE OF SOUTH AUSTRALIA. BROADSHEET. see *ART*

720 333.7   UK   ISSN 0958-2746
CONTEXT (LETCHWORTH). 1981. q. £36 (U.S. $93). (Association of Conservation Officers) Hau-McCartney Ltd., Heritage House, P.O. Box 21, Baldock, Herts SG7 5SH, England. TEL 44-1462-896688. FAX 44-1562-896677. Ed. Bob Kindred. adv. contact: Tony Sudweeks. bk.rev.; illus. circ. 2,000. (back issues avail.) **Document type:** bulletin.
   Description: Covers the conservation of historic buildings.

CONTRACTORS GUIDE; the guide to the roofing, insulation, siding, solar, and window industries. see *BUILDING AND CONSTRUCTION*

CORDELL'S WHO'S WHO IN BUILDING: DEVELOPERS. see *BUILDING AND CONSTRUCTION*

720   US   ISSN 0731-5384
NA1
CORNELL JOURNAL OF ARCHITECTURE. 1981. biennial. $30. Cornell University, School of Architecture, 143 E. Sibley Hall, Ithaca, NY 14853. TEL 607-255-5236. FAX 607-255-0291. Ed. Stephanie A. Goto. R&P contact: Pablo Gare. **Document type:** academic/scholarly publication.

728   US
COUNTRY STYLE HOMES, PLANS AND DESIGNS. 1991. q. $16.80. HomeStyle Publishing and Marketing Co., 213 E. 4th St., St. Paul, MN 55101. TEL 612-602-5000. FAX 612-602-5001. E-mail: feedback@homestyles.com; URL: http://www.homestyles.com. Ed. Eric Englund; Pub. Diana Jasan-Keshen. R&P contact: Diana Jasan-Keshen. adv. contact: Sheltey Junker. circ. 56,100 (paid). **Document type:** consumer publication.
   Description: Includes country estates, authentic farmhouses, ranches, Victorians, colonials and other traditionally styled designs.
   Refereed Serial

COUNTRYPOLITAN HOMES & PLANS. see *BUILDING AND CONSTRUCTION*

COURTAULD INSTITUTE ILLUSTRATION ARCHIVES. ARCHIVE 1. see *ART*

COVJEK I PROSTOR. see *ART*

720 378   US   ISSN 0277-6863
NA1
CRIT. 1976. s-a. $6. American Institute of Architecture Students, 1735 New York Ave., N.W., Washington, DC 20006. TEL 202-626-7472. FAX 202-626-7414. E-mail: aiasnatl@aol.com. Ed. Bob Dillon. adv. contact: Tom Osina. bk.rev.; film rev.; illus. circ. 10,000. (back issues avail.) **Indexed:** Avery Ind.Archit.Per. **Document type:** academic/scholarly publication.
   —BLDSC (3487.385500).
   Formerly: (no.1): Telesis (Washington) (ISSN 0364-6521)
   Description: Student journal providing a collection of art and literature reflecting current concerns, visions and opinions of architecture students in the USA.

720   IT   ISSN 0392-5803
                                                                    CODEN: CLNRDG
CRONACHE CASTELLANE. 1964. q. L.80000. Istituto Italiano dei Castelli, Via G.A. Borgese 14, 20154 Milan, Italy. TEL 39-2-3472376. circ. 2,900. (back issues avail.) **Document type:** bulletin.

720   SP   ISSN 0212-5633
NA5
EL CROQUIS; de arquitectura y diseno. (Text in English and Spanish) 1982. bi-m. (5/yr.). 20700 ptas. (Europe 26100 ptas.; N. America 29400 ptas.; elsewhere 31600 ptas.) (effective 1998). Croquis Editorial, Calle Barcelo, 15-5o, 28004 Madrid, Spain. TEL 34-1-4452149. FAX 34-1-5932192. E-mail: elcroquis@infornet.es; URL: http://www.elcroquis.es. Ed. Paloma Poveda; Pubs. Fernando Marquez Cecilia, Richard C. Levene. R&P contact: Paloma Poveda. adv. contact: Cristina Poveda. (back issues avail.) **Document type:** academic/scholarly publication.
   —CINDOC; SWETS.
   Description: Publishes information on recent works and projects in architecture, design and construction.

720.972   MX   ISSN 0185-5131
F1219.3.A6
CUADERNOS DE ARQUITECTURA MESOAMERICANA. 1984. s-a. Mex.$40 per no. (effective 1997). Universidad Nacional Autonoma de Mexico, Facultad de Arquitectura, Circuito Interior, Ciudad Universitaria, 04510 Mexico, D.F., Mexico. TEL 52-5-6220318. FAX 52-5-6160545. **Indexed:** Anthropol.Lit.
   Description: Includes articles on Mesoamerican and Prehispanic architecture. Features essays and reviews that promote building restoration.

720   SP   ISSN 1133-6129
CUADERNOS DE ARQU:TECTURA ROMANA. 1992. irreg., no.2, 1993. 1500 ptas. (effective 1997). Universidad de Murcia, Servicio de Publicaciones, Santo Cristo 1, 30080 Murcia, Spain. TEL 34-68-363014. FAX 34-68-363414. E-mail: vgm@pas.um.es; URL: http://www.um.es/-spumweb. Ed. Sebastian F. Ramallo Asensio. circ. 500. (back issues avail.) **Document type:** monographic series.
   —CINDOC.

720.902   MX   ISSN 0185-8572
CUADERNOS DE ARQUITECTURA VIRREINAL. 1985. irreg. (approx. 1/yr.). Mex.$50 per no. (effective 1997). Universidad Nacional Autonoma de Mexico, Facultad de Arquitectura, Circuito Interior, Ciudad Universitaria, 04510 Mexico, D.F., Mexico. TEL 52-5-6220318. FAX 52-5-6166545.
   Description: Includes articles on Mexican architecture based on Spanish viceroyship, XIV to XVIII centuries.

720 690   CC   ISSN 1002-8439
CUNZHEN JIANSHE/TOWN OR VILLAGE DEVELOPMENT. (Text in Chinese) bi-m. Zhongguo Jianzhu Jishu Fazhan Zhongxin - China Architectural Technology Development Centre, 19 Chegongzhuang Dajie, Beijing 100044, People's Republic of China. TEL 8992692. Ed. Ka Rucheng.

ARCHITECTURE 401

720 UK
CUSTOM HOMES BOOK OF PLANS. 1969. a. £14.95. Custom Publishing Company Ltd. (Subsidiary of: Glendower Holdings Ltd.), 45 Station Rd., Redhill, Surrey RH1 1QH, England. TEL 44-1737-767213. FAX 44-1737-771662. Ed. David Hoppit. adv.: page £2250; adv. contact: John Bailey. circ. 40,000 (controlled). **Document type:** consumer publication.
Formerly: Architectural Services Books of Plans.

720 PL
CODEN: CZTEAY
CZASOPISMO TECHNICZNE. SERIA A: ARCHITEKTURA. (Contents page in 4 languages) 1877. irreg. 20 Zl. (effective 1997). Politechnika Krakowska, Ul. Warszawska 24, 31-155 Krakow, Poland. TEL 48-12-37-42-89. FAX 48-12-335773. TELEX 322468 PK PL. E-mail: Marcinek@biblos.pk.edu.pl. bk.rev.; charts; illus.; index. circ. 12,000. **Document type:** academic/scholarly publication.
—CASDDS.
Supersedes in part: Czasopismo Techniczne (ISSN 0011-4561); Which was formerly (until 1883): Dzwignia (ISSN 1230-2791).

720 UK
D A B S COMPENDIUM. a. £60. Kemps Publishing Ltd., 11 The Swan Courtyard, Charles Edward Rd., Birmingham B26 1BU, England. TEL 44-121-765-4144. FAX 44-121-706-6210. **Document type:** trade publication.
Formerly: Kemps Borough Architects Yearbook.

720 FR
D'A - D'ARCHITECTURES. 10/yr. 7 rue de Chaillot, 75116 Paris, France. TEL 47-23-81-84. FAX 40-70-05-97. Ed. Francis Rambert. circ. 30,000.

720 GW ISSN 0942-7481
NA3
D A M ARCHITEKTUR JAHRBUCH. a. DM.58. Prestel-Verlag, Mandlstr. 26, 80802 Munich, Germany. TEL 49-89-381709-0. FAX 49-89-38170935. (Dist. in US by: TE Neues New York, 16 W. 22nd St., New York, NY 10010. TEL 212-627-9090. FAX 212-627-9511) Pub. Juergen Tesch. R&P contact: Karin Kirmaier. **Indexed:** IBR. **Document type:** trade publication.

720 690 GW ISSN 0721-1902
NA3
D B - DEUTSCHE BAUZEITUNG; Fachzeitschrift fuer Architekten und Bauingenieure. (Text in German; summaries in English) 1867. m. DM.225 (foreign DM.234; students DM.120) (effective 1997). (Bund Deutscher Baumeister, Architekten und Ingenieure e.V.) Deutsche Verlags-Anstalt GmbH, Postfach 106012, 70049 Stuttgart, Germany. TEL 49-711-2631-0. FAX 49-711-2631110. URL: http://db.bauzeitung.de. Ed. Wilfried Dechau. adv.; bk.rev.; charts; illus.; tr.lit.; index. circ. 39,102. (also avail. in microfiche from IDC) **Indexed:** Br.Tech.Ind., Excerp.Med. **Document type:** trade publication.
—BLDSC (3563.600000); SWETS. **CCC.**
Formerly: D B - Deutsche Bauzeitung - Die Bauzeitung (ISSN 0011-4766)

720 690 GW ISSN 0011-4782
D B Z. (Deutsche Bauzeitschrift); Architektur, Entwurf, Detail. 1953. m. DM.200.40. Bertelsmann Fachzeitschriften GmbH, Postfach 120, 33111 Guetersloh, Germany. TEL 05241-802332. FAX 05241-73055. Ed. Burkhard Froehlich. adv.: B&W page DM.9480, color page DM.15290; trim 297 x 225. charts; illus.; mkt.; stat.; tr.lit.; index. circ. 22,347. **Indexed:** Avery Ind.Archit.Per., Excerp.Med., INIS Atomind. **Document type:** trade publication.
—BLDSC (3563.580000); CISTI; SWETS.
Description: Covers architecture, design and detail.

720 FR ISSN 1167-0991
L R MAGAZINE. 4/yr. S.E.D.L., 28 rue Chapsal, 94340 Joinville-le-Pont, France. TEL 43-97-00-41. FAX 42-83-44-00. Ed. Francis Gilberg. circ. 3,000.

721 GW ISSN 0721-4235
NA1.A1
DAIDALOS. (Text in English and German) q. DM.170. Bertelsmann Fachzeitschriften GmbH, Postfach 120, 33111 Guetersloh, Germany. TEL 05241-802332. FAX 05241-73055. URL: http://www.fachinformation.bertelsmann.de/verlag/big/bfz/index.html. Ed. Gerrit Confurius. adv.: B&W page DM.3800, color page DM.4860; trim 297 x 245. circ. 3,475. **Indexed:** Artbibl., Avery Ind.Archit.Per., Br.Tech.Ind., RILA. **Document type:** trade publication.
—SWETS. **CCC.**
Description: Devoted to the development of architecture from classical antiquity to the present.

690 720 UK
DAILY MAIL BOOK OF HOME PLANS. 1954-1976; resumed 1978. s-a. £2.95 per no. Custom Publishing Company Ltd. (Subsidiary of: Glendower Holdings Ltd.), 45 Station Rd., Redhill, Surrey RH1 1QH, England. TEL 44-1737-771662. FAX 44-1737-771662. Ed. David Hoppit. adv.: B&W page £1600; color page £2150; adv. contact: John Bailey. illus.; circ. 7,500 (paid). (back issues avail.) **Document type:** consumer publication.
Formerly (until 1976): Daily Mail Book of Bungalow and House Plans; Formed by the merger of: Daily Mail Book of Bungalow Plans; Daily Mail Book of House Plans.

720 PR
DEARQUITECTURA. 1988. q. free. Universidad de Puerto Rico, Escuela de Arquitectura, Apdo. 21909, San Juan, PR 00931-1909. FAX 787-763-5377. Ed. Humberto Betancourt. bk.rev. **Document type:** newsletter.
Formerly: Universidad de Puerto Rico. Escuela de Arquitectura. Boletin Informativo.

720 IT
DEMETRA. 1991. s-a. L.38000 (foreign L.72000). Ordine Architetti di Enna, Via Vulturo 13, 94100 Enna, Italy. TEL 39-935-24703. (Subscr. to: Cordaro Editore, Via Calderai 80, 90133 Palermo, Italy. TEL 39-91-6176348)

723 FR ISSN 0998-5956
DEMEURE HISTORIQUE. 1966. q. 200 Fr. Association des Proprietaires de Monuments Historiques Prives, 57 quai de la Tournelle, 75005 Paris, France. Ed. Denis Picard. adv.; bk.rev.

DEMEURES ET CHATEAUX. see REAL ESTATE

725 GW ISSN 0946-4549
DENKMAL!. 1994. a. DM.16.80 (effective 1997). (Landesamt fuer Denkmalpflege Schleswig-Holstein) Westholsteinische Verlagsanstalt Boyens und Co., Am Wulf-Isebrand-Platz, 25746 Heide, Germany. TEL 49-481-6886162. FAX 49-481-6886467. **Document type:** bulletin.

DIE DENKMALPFLEGE. see ART

720 796 US
DESIGN. q. $35. National Recreation and Park Association, Park Practice Program, 2775 S. Quincy St., No. 300, Arlington, VA 22206. TEL 703-820-4940. FAX 703-671-6772. Ed. Kathleen Pleasant. illus. **Indexed:** Arts & Hum.Cit.Ind., Avery Ind.Archit.Per., Br.Rail.Bd., Cadscan, Lead Abstr., Mag.Ind., Sportsearch (1983-), Zincscan.

720 745 GR ISSN 0074-1191
NK1451
DESIGN & ART IN GREECE/THEMATA CHOROU & TECHNON. (Text in Greek; summaries in English) 1970. a. $50 (effective 1997 & 1998). Architecture in Greece Press, P.O. Box 3545, 102 10 Athens, Greece. TEL 30-1-7225-930. FAX 30-1-7213-916. Ed. Orestis B. Doumanis; Pub. Orestis B. Doumanis. R&P contact: Orestis B. Doumanis. adv.: B&W page $1600; color page $2000; adv. contact: Orestis B. Doumanis. index. circ. 5,000. (back issues avail.) **Indexed:** Avery Ind.Archit.Per., Ekist.Ind. **Document type:** trade publication.
—BLDSC (3559.905000).
Formerly: Design in Greece.
Description: Architecture and furnishings for houses, offices and shops, visual and applied arts, industrial and graphic design, and exhibitions.

DESIGN - BUILD BUSINESS. see BUILDING AND CONSTRUCTION

720 US ISSN 1054-3163
TH435
DESIGN COST & DATA; the cost estimating magazine for architects, builders and specifiers. 1958. bi-m. $64.80. L M Rector Corporation, 8602 N. 40th St., Tampa, FL 33604. TEL 813-989-9300. FAX 813-980-3982. Ed. Barb Castelli; Pub. Lee Rector. adv.: B&W page $1800, color page $2600; adv. contact: Rob Rizzi. bk.rev.; charts; illus.; index; circ. 12,500 (controlled). (also avail. in microfiche; reprint service avail. from UMI) **Indexed:** Br.Tech.Ind. **Document type:** trade publication.
—UMI. **CCC.**
Former titles: Design Cost and Data for Management of Building Design (ISSN 0739-3946); (until 1982): Design Cost and Data for Building Design Management; (until 1981): Design Cost and Data for the Construction Industry (ISSN 0192-0227); (1966-1978): Architectural Design, Cost and Data (ISSN 0003-8512)
Description: Information on cost estimating in design and construction.

720 747 690 US
DESIGN LINE. 1950. q. $48. American Institute of Building Design, 991 Post Rd. E, Westport, CT 06880. TEL 800-366-2423. FAX 203-227-3698. Ed. Tammy J. Crosby. R&P contact: Tammy J. Crosby. bk.rev. circ. 1,500. (back issues avail.) **Document type:** academic/scholarly publication.

711.05 US ISSN 1067-9359
NA9000
DESIGN METHODS; theories, research, education and practice. 1966. q. $36 (foreign $40) (effective 1997); $36 (effective 1998). Design Methods Institute, Box 3, San Luis Obispo, CA 93406. Ed. Donald P. Grant. bk.rev.; illus. circ. 1,000. **Indexed:** Archit.Per.Ind., Avery Ind.Archit.Per., DAAI. **Document type:** academic/scholarly publication.
—BLDSC (3559.993000); CISTI; SWETS; UnCover.
Former titles: Design Methods and Theories (ISSN 0147-1147); (until vol.12, 1978): D M G - D R S Journal: Design Research and Methods (ISSN 0091-0449); (until 1971): D M G Newsletter.
Description: Theories and methods of design in architecture, environmental planning, engineering, and product design.

720 FR ISSN 1143-273X
DESIGN RECHERCHES; revue scientifique trimestrielle, conception de produits - design. 1989. q. 600 F. A Jour, 11 rue du Marche St. Honore, 75001 Paris, France. TEL 42-96-67-22. FAX 40-20-07-75. Ed. Philippe Collier. **Document type:** academic/scholarly publication.

712 US
DESIGN RESEARCH NEWS. q. $24 (foreign $28). Environmental Design Research Association, Box 7146, Edmond, OK 73083-7146. TEL 405-330-4863. adv. **Document type:** bulletin.
Description: Reports on current developments in the field of environmental design research.

DESIGN SOLUTIONS. see INTERIOR DESIGN AND DECORATION

ARCHITECTURE

720 600   UK   ISSN 0142-694X
NA2750   CODEN: DSSTD5
DESIGN STUDIES. 1979. q. fl.963($553) (effective 1998). Elsevier Science Ltd., P.O. Box 800, Kidlington, Oxford OX5 1DX, England. TEL 44-1865-843000. FAX 44-1865-843010. TELEX 83111 BHPOXF G. E-mail: nlinfo-f@elsevier.nl; usinfo-f@elsevier.com; forinfo-kyf04035@niftyserve.or.jp; URL: http://www.elsevier.nl/. (Subscr. to: Elsevier Science, Regional Sales Office, P.O. Box 211, 1000 AE Amsterdam, Netherlands. TEL 31-20-4853757. FAX 31-20-4853432; Subscr. in the Americas to: Elsevier Science, Regional Sales Office, Box 945, New York, NY 10159-0945. TEL 212-633-3730. FAX 212-633-3680; Subscr. in Australasia to: Elsevier Science (Singapore) Pte Ltd, No.1 Temasek Ave., No.17-01 Millenia Tower, Singapore 039192, Singapore. TEL 65-434-3727. FAX 65-337-2230) Ed. Nigel Cross. adv.; bk.rev.; illus.; index. (also avail. in microform from UMI; back issues avail.; reprint service avail.) Indexed: A.I.Abstr., Archit.Per.Ind., Art Ind., Artbibl., Avery Ind.Archit.Per., BPIA, Br.Tech.Ind., CAD CAM Abstr., DAAI, INSPEC (1993-), Stud.Wom.Abstr., Tech.Educ.Abstr. **Document type:** academic/scholarly publication.
—BLDSC (3560.205000); AskIEEE; Ei; KR SourceOne; Linda Hall; SWETS; UMI; UnCover. **CCC.**
    ● **Description:** Promotes an understanding of the nature, effectiveness and roles of design in industry and in society by comparing applications in such areas as architecture, engineering, planning, and industrial design.
    Refereed Serial

DESIGN TIMES; beautiful interiors of the Northeast. see *INTERIOR DESIGN AND DECORATION*

DESIGN WEEK. see *ART*

DESIGN WEEK ACTION PACK. see *ART*

720 747   AT   ISSN 0810-6029
NK1490.A1
DESIGN WORLD. 1983. q. $34. Design Graphics Pty. Ltd., 6 School Rd., Ferny Creek, Vic. 3786, Australia. TEL 61-3-97551149. FAX 61-3-97551155. E-mail: email@designgraphics.com.au; URL: http://www.designgraphics.com.au. (Dist. in U.S. by: Mercury Air Freight Ltd., 2323 Randolph Ave., Avenel, NJ 07001) Ed. Colin Wood; Pub. Colin Wood. adv.; bk.rev.; circ. 25,900 (paid). Indexed: DAAI. **Document type:** consumer publication, trade publication.
—BLDSC (3560.216000); SWETS.
    ● **Description:** A vital publication for designers, design-conscious manufacturers and design management.

720 690   CN   ISSN 1181-7933
DESIGNER'S BEST HOME PLANS. 1990. a. Can.$3.50. Giroux Publishing, 102 Ellis St., Penticton, BC V2A 4L5, Canada. TEL 604-493-0942. FAX 604-493-7526. URL: cgiroux@vip.net. Ed. Michael A. Giroux. adv. contact: Dennis Thatchuk. circ. 13,500. **Document type:** consumer publication, catalog.
    ● **Description:** Features designs from Canadian home designers and the latest in housing innovations. Contains house plans for a range of styles and budgets.

DESIGNERS WEST. see *INTERIOR DESIGN AND DECORATION*

DESIGNERS WEST RESOURCE DIRECTORY. see *INTERIOR DESIGN AND DECORATION*

720 747   US
▼**DESIGNING WITH TILE & STONE.** 1995. q. Contemporary Dialysis, Inc., 6300 Variel Ave., I, Woodland Hill, CA 91367-2513. TEL 818-704-5555. FAX 818-704-6500. Pub. Jerry Fisher. adv.: page $3250; adv. contact: Steven Fisher. tr.lit. circ. 12,000. (back issues avail.) **Document type:** trade publication.
    ● **Description:** For professional architect, interior designer and specifier. Contains articles on how to select, design with, install and maintain ceramic and dimensional stone tile for residential and commercial installations both domestic and international.

DESIGNMENT. see *INTERIOR DESIGN AND DECORATION*

720   GW   ISSN 0011-9571
NA2835
DETAIL; Zeitschrift fuer Architektur & Baudetail. 1961. 8/yr. DM.162 (students DM.130) (effective 1997). Institut fuer Internationale Architektur-Dokumentation GmbH, Postfach 440261, 80751 Munich, Germany. TEL 49-89-3816200. FAX 49-89-398670. E-mail: 101553.2376@compuserve.com; URL: http://ourworld.compuserve.com/homepages/detail. adv.; bk.rev.; abstr.; charts; illus.; stat.; tr.lit.; index. Indexed: Avery Ind.Archit.Per., Br.Tech.Ind. **Document type:** trade publication.
—BLDSC (3560.720000); SWETS. **CCC.**

720   JA   ISSN 0012-4133
NA2640
DETAIL/DITERU; magazine for architects and engineers. (Text in Japanese; summaries in English) 1964. q. $16. Shokokusha Publishing Co., Ltd., 25 Sakamachi, Shinjuku-ku, Tokyo 160, Japan. TEL 81-3-3359-3231. FAX 81-3-3357-3961. Ed. Takashi Hosoda. adv.: B&W page 200000 Yen, color page 500000 Yen; adv. contact: Toshio Takahashi. illus. circ. 60,000. **Document type:** trade publication.

720   GW   ISSN 0420-1329
DEUTSCHER BAUKATALOG. a. DM.44 (DM.31 with subscr. to Detail) (effective 1997). Institut fuer Internationale Architektur-Dokumentation GmbH, Postfach 440261, 80751 Munich, Germany. TEL 49-89-3816200. FAX 49-89-398670. E-mail: 101553.2376@compuserve.com; URL: http://ourworld.compuserve.com/homepages/detail. **Document type:** trade publication.

720   GW   ISSN 0012-1215
DEUTSCHES ARCHITEKTENBLATT. 1969. m. DM.85. (Bundesarchitektenkammer) Forum-Verlag GmbH, Postfach 700262, 70572 Stuttgart, Germany. TEL 0711-7257414. FAX 0711-7257411. Ed. Reinhart Wustlich. adv. contact: Michael Schoeberl. bk.rev. circ. 91,000. Indexed: Avery Ind.Archit.Per. **Document type:** trade publication.

720   US
DIMENSION (WASHINGTON). 1994. s-a. $20 (Canada $30; elsewhere $40). Society for Environmental Graphic Design, 401 F St., N.W., Ste. 333, Washington, DC 20001. TEL 202-638-5555. FAX 202-638-0891. Ed. Scott Drummond. adv.: page $750; trim 8 1/2 x 11. circ. 1,250. **Document type:** trade publication.
    ● **Description:** Covers the design of public and commercial buildings.

DIRECTORY OF ARCHITECTS IN METROPOLITAN WASHINGTON. see *BUSINESS AND ECONOMICS — Trade And Industrial Directories*

745.2   IT
▼**DISEGNO INDUSTRIALE.** 1996. irreg. price varies. Liguori Editore s.r.l., Via Posillipo 394, 80123 Naples, Italy. TEL 39-81-7206111. FAX 39-81-7206244. **Document type:** monographic series.

DISTINGUISHED HOME PLANS & PRODUCTS - CUSTOM HOME PLANS GUIDE. see *BUILDING AND CONSTRUCTION*

720   SP   ISSN 0214-9249
DOCUMENTOS DE ARQUITECTURA. 1987. 4/yr. 8000 ptas. (Europe 12000 ptas.; America 14000 ptas.; elsewhere 17000 ptas.) (effective 1994). Colegio de Arquitectos de Almeria, Martinez Campos, 29, 04002 Almeria, Spain. TEL 34-951-231255. FAX 34-951-262265.
—CINDOC.

720   AG   ISSN 0326-8640
NA830
DOCUMENTOS DE ARQUITECTURA NACIONAL Y AMERICANA. 1973. a. $25. Instituto Argentino de Investigaciones de Historia de la Arquitectura y del Urbanismo, Casilla de Correo 120, Sucursal 48B, 1448 Buenos Aires, Argentina. FAX 54-1-8119249. Ed. Sonia Berjman. R&P contact: Ramon Gutierrez. cum.index: 1973-1980. **Document type:** academic/scholarly publication.
    Formerly: Documentos de Arquitectura Nacional. *Refereed Serial*

720 747   PL   ISSN 0209-147X
N6
DOM.* 1982. 6/yr. Wydawnictwo Arkady, Ul. Dobra 28, P.O. Box 137, 00-959 Warsaw, Poland. TEL 48-22-269441. Ed. Andrzej Jaworski. circ. 50,000.

720   US   ISSN 1041-1607
TH2170
DOME (WHEAT RIDGE). 1988. q. $40 (effective 1997). Donald R. Hoflin, Ed. & Pub., 4401 Zephyr St., Wheat Ridge, CO 80033.
—UnCover.
    ● **Description:** Deals with domes as part of the development of ultra-low-cost housing worldwide.

720   IT   ISSN 0012-5377
N4
DOMUS; architettura arredamento arte. 1928. m. (11/yr.). $175. Editoriale Domus, Via Grandi 5-7, 20089 Rozzano (MI), Italy. TEL 39-2-82472527. FAX 39-2-8255033. Ed. Mario Bellini. adv.: B&W page L.10500000, color page L.15750000. bk.rev.; illus. circ. 60,000. Indexed: Art Ind., Artbibl.Mod., Arts & Hum.Cit.Ind., Avery Ind.Archit.Per., Br.Tech.Ind., Curr.Cont., DAAI, RILA.
—BLDSC (3619.210000); KR SourceOne; SWETS.

720   IT   ISSN 1122-8938
DOMUS DOSSIER. 1993. s-a. L.18000 per no. Editoriale Domus, Via A. Grandi 5-7, 20089 Roaano (MI), Italy. TEL 39-2-26863123. FAX 39-2-8255033. Pub. Giovanna Mazzocchi Bordone. adv. contact: Giuseppe Bolandrina.

DRUSTVO KONZERVATORA SRBIJE. GLASNIK. see *CONSERVATION*

720   UK   ISSN 0307-1634
E A A REVIEW. 1957. a. £10 to non-members. Edinburgh Architectural Association, 15 Rutland Sq., Edinburgh EH1 2BE, Scotland. FAX 031-228-2188. Ed. Stuart Baxter. adv.; circ. 1,200 (controlled).
    Formerly: Edinburgh Architectural Association E A A Yearbook.
    ● **Description:** Covers new buildings and projects in the Edinburgh area. Includes a directory of architectural practices.

720   UK   ISSN 0140-5039
NA12
E A R. (Edinburgh Architecture Research) 1973. a. £10. University of Edinburgh, Department of Architecture, 20 Chambers St., Edinburgh EH1 1JZ, Scotland. FAX 0131-650-8019. TELEX 727442. E-mail: vila@caad.ed.ac.uk. circ. 250. Indexed: Avery Ind.Archit.Per., Br.Tech.Ind. **Document type:** academic/scholarly publication.
    ● **Description:** Journal of scholarly articles on architectural theory and research, with lists of current and completed postgraduate studies at the School of Architecture.
    Refereed Serial

720   SA
EDGE.* 1993. a. University of Port Elizabeth Architectural Society, Private Bag X6508, Port Elizabeth 6000, South Africa. illus. **Document type:** academic/scholarly publication.

EDILIZIA (TURIN). see *BUILDING AND CONSTRUCTION*

EDUCATIONAL FACILITY PLANNER. see *EDUCATION*

EKISTICS; problems and science of human settlements. see *HOUSING AND URBAN PLANNING*

ELEMENT UND BAU. see *BUILDING AND CONSTRUCTION*

ENERGY DESIGN UPDATE; the monthly newsletter on energy-efficient housing. see *BUILDING AND CONSTRUCTION*

ARCHITECTURE

246 460   US   ISSN 1040-6611
ENVIRONMENT AND ART LETTER; a forum on architecture and the arts for the Parish. 1988. m. $20 (effective 1997). (Archdiocese of Chicago) Liturgy Training Publications, 1800 N. Hermitage Ave., Chicago, IL 60622-1101. TEL 773-486-8970. FAX 800-933-7094. E-mail: editorial@ltp.org; orders@ltp.org. Ed. David Philippart. adv. contact: Maureen Como. bk.rev.; circ. 2,450 (paid). (back issues avail.) **Document type**: newsletter.
 Description: For architects, artists, liturgy teams, pastors, and sacristans. Provides a forum for the exchange of ideas on worship places.

ENVIRONMENT AND PLANNING B: PLANNING & DESIGN. see HOUSING AND URBAN PLANNING

ENVIRONMENTAL BUILDING NEWS; a bimonthly newsletter on environmentally sustainable design and construction. see BUILDING AND CONSTRUCTION

720 155   US
ENVIRONMENTAL DESIGN RESEARCH ASSOCIATION. ANNUAL CONFERENCE PROCEEDINGS. Short title: E D R A. Annual Conference Proceedings. (Each issue has a distinctive title) 1969. a. $50 to non-members; members $40 (effective 1995 & 1996). Environmental Design Research Association, Box 7146, Edmond, OK 73083-7146. TEL 405-330-4863. Ed.Bd. circ. 900. (back issues avail.; reprint service avail.) **Indexed**: Psychol.Abstr., Soc.Sci.Ind. **Document type**: proceedings.

720 352.7   UK   ISSN 1352-8564
▼**ENVIRONMENTS BY DESIGN**. 1996. s-a. (Kingston University, Faculty of Design) Kingston University Press, Eagle Chambers, 16-18 Eden St., Kingston-upon-Thames, Surrey KT1 1RD, England. Ed.Bd. **Document type**: academic/scholarly publication.
 —BLDSC (3791.796000).

EPITES- EPITESZETTUDOMANY/BUILDING AND ARCHITECTURAL SCIENCE. see BUILDING AND CONSTRUCTION

720   CK   ISSN 0120-6702
NA5
ESCALA; arquitectura, arte, ingenieria. 1962. bi-m. $120 (effective 1997). Calle 30, No. 17-70, Bogota, Colombia. E-mail: deserna@col-online.com. Ed. David Eduardo Serna Medina. adv.; bk.rev. circ. 16,000. **Document type**: monographic series.
 Description: Each issue covers a topic in Latin American architecture.

720   SP   ISSN 0213-3474
ESCUELA TECNICA SUPERIOR DE ARQUITECTURA DA CORUNA. BOLETIN ACADEMICO. 1985. 3/yr. 1500 ptas. Escuela Tecnica Superior de Arquitectura, Castro de Elvina, s-n, 15192 La Coruna, Spain. **Indexed**: Ind.SST.
 —CINDOC.

ESTUDOS TECNOLOGICOS. see SCIENCES: COMPREHENSIVE WORKS

ETUDES URBAINES. see HOUSING AND URBAN PLANNING

720 690   US
M DATA MONTHLY. 1982. m. $220 (foreign $250) (effective 1997). Tradeline, Inc., Box 1568, Orinda, CA 94563. TEL 510-254-1744. FAX 510-254-2744. E-mail: fpn@fmdata.com. Ed. Harriet Kroopnick. R&P contact: Harriet Kroopnick. adv. contact: Meredith Holmes. bk.rev.; cum.index: 1982-1994. circ. 7,000. (back issues avail.) **Document type**: trade publication.
 Formerly: Facilities Planning News (ISSN 1045-7089)
 Description: Reports on recently completed buildings in the areas of health care, R & D, corporate, institutional, and high-tech construction.

720   GW   ISSN 0340-2967
TH1000
F UND I-BAU; Bauen mit Systemen. 1966. q. DM.33. Element-Verlag GmbH, Zeppelinstr. 3, 71332 Waiblingen, Germany. TEL 07151-51871. FAX 07151-563343. Ed. H. Schmid. adv.; bk.rev.; abstr.; illus.; pat.; stat.; index. circ. 6,400.
 —BLDSC (3855.500000).
 Formerly: Fertigteilbau und Industrialisiertes Bauen (ISSN 0015-0231)

F X; design in business and society. see INTERIOR DESIGN AND DECORATION

720 677   US   ISSN 1045-0483
FABRICS & ARCHITECTURE. 1989. bi-m. $21 (Canada and Mexico $24; elsewhere $33). Industrial Fabrics Association International, 345 Cedar St., Ste. 800, St. Paul, MN 55101-1088. TEL 612-222-2508. FAX 612-222-8215. Ed. Jean Cook. adv. circ. 13,000. **Document type**: trade publication.
 —EMDOCS; KR SourceOne.
 Description: For architects, designers and fabric specifiers. Covers air and tension structures, awnings and canopies, banners, construction fabrics, landscaping and building codes.

FACILITIES; monthly digest for the building administration manager. see BUILDING AND CONSTRUCTION

FACILITIES DESIGN AND MANAGEMENT. see BUSINESS AND ECONOMICS — Management

720 690   US   ISSN 1049-2925
TH4311
FACILITIES PLANNING HANDBOOK. a. Tradeline, Inc., Box 1568, Orinda, CA 94563. TEL 510-254-1744. FAX 510-254-2744. E-mail: fpn@fmdata.com. Ed. Lee Ingalls. R&P contact: Lee Ingalls. adv. contact: Meredith Holmes. **Document type**: trade publication.

FACILITY MANAGEMENT JOURNAL. see BUSINESS AND ECONOMICS — Management

720   DK   ISSN 0906-2807
FAGBLADET ARTUR. Variant title: Artur. 1991. 14/yr. membership. Ansatte Arkitekters Raad, Bredgade 66, P.O. Box 1163, DK-1010 Copenhagen K, Denmark. TEL 45-33-13-12-90. adv.; B&W page DKK 6900, color page DKK 9900.

720 700   US   ISSN 0014-7001
NA4605
FAITH AND FORM. 1967. 3/yr. $24 (foreign $30) (effective 1998). Interfaith Forum on Religion, Art and Architecture (IFRAA), 25 Maple St., Auburndale, MA 02166. TEL 617-965-3018. Ed. Betty H. Meyer; Pub. Douglas Hoffman. R&P contact: Betty Meyer. adv. contact: Douglas Hoffman. bk.rev.; illus. circ. 37,500. **Indexed**: Chr.Per.Ind. **Document type**: academic/scholarly publication.
 Description: For architects, artists, clergy, temple and church administrators, liturgists, building committees, musicians and manufacturers engaged in creation and evaluation of religious art and architecture of all denominations.

720   CN   ISSN 0229-7094
FIFTH COLUMN; Canadian student journal of architecture/revue Canadienne des etudiants en architecture. (Text in English and French) 1979. s-a. Can.$18 to individuals (foreign Can.$50); libraries Can.$35 (effective 1997). School of Architecture, 815 Sherbrooke West, Montreal, PQ H3A 2K6, Canada. TEL 514-398-6700. FAX 514-398-7372. E-mail: 5column@chaussegros.architecture.mcgill.ca; URL: http://www.mcgill.caarch5column. Ed. Conor Sampson. adv.; bk.rev.; illus. circ. 250. **Indexed**: Avery Ind.Archit.Per., Br.Tech.Ind. **Document type**: academic/scholarly publication.
 Description: Promotes the study of architecture in Canada.

724   IT
FLARE; architectural lighting magazine. (Text in English, Italian) 1989. s-a. L.60000. Editrice Habitat s.r.l., Via M.M. de Taddei, 3, 20146 Milan, Italy. TEL 39-2-4814800. FAX 39-2-48193013. Ed. Piero Castiglioni. adv.; B&W page L.3300000, color page L.4400000. circ. 60,000.

720   US
▼**FLATIRON NEWS**. 1995. q. $3. Flatiron Bldg., 175 Fifth Ave., Ste. 2327, New York, NY 10010. TEL 212-627-5400. E-mail: flatiron-news@fusebox.com. Ed. Dorie Lederfajn; Pub. Michael Abramson. adv. contact: Philip Paton. bk.rev. circ. 35,000.

FLOORS. see INTERIOR DESIGN AND DECORATION

712   UK   ISSN 0963-9004
FOLLIES; the international magazine for follies, grottoes & garden buildings. 1988. q. £16.50 (U.S. $35); institutions £100 (effective 1997 & 1998). Folly Fellowship, 21 Beacon Rd., Ware, Herts. SG12 7HY, England. TEL 44-1920-487587. E-mail: follies@heritage.co.uk; URL: http://www.heritage.co.uk/heritage/follies/. Ed. Michael Cousins. adv. contact: Andrew Plumridge. circ. 1,100 (paid). **Document type**: newsletter, academic/scholarly publication.
 Description: Records and monitors architecture in the landscape, past and present, and manifestations of architectural eccentricity. Also covers architectural history. Includes news items and academic articles.

FORM; Zeitschrift fuer Gestaltung. see INTERIOR DESIGN AND DECORATION

FORM; designtidskriften. see INTERIOR DESIGN AND DECORATION

721   US   ISSN 0015-7686
FORM & FUNCTION. 1995. q. free to qualified personnel. U S G Corporation, 125 S. Franklin St., Chicago, IL 60606-4678. TEL 312-606-4181. FAX 312-606-5566. Ed. William D. Leavitt. R&P contact: William D. Leavitt. illus.; index, cum.index: 1970-1990; circ. 130,000 (controlled). (back issues avail.) **Document type**: trade publication.
 —Linda Hall; UnCover.
 Description: Carries case histories of buildings exhibiting good design and good use of U.S.G. products.

FORM & ZWECK; Fachzeitschrift fuer industrielle Formgestaltung. see BUILDING AND CONSTRUCTION

747 720   FI   ISSN 0358-8904
NK1471.F5
FORM FUNCTION FINLAND. (Text in English) 1980. q. FIM 170 (effective 1997). (Finnish Society of Crafts and Design) Design Forum Finland, Unionkatu 14, SF-00130 Helsinki 13, Finland. TEL 358-0-6220-8114. FAX 358-0-629-489. (Subscr. to: Academic Bookstore, P.O. Box 23, FIN-00371, Helsinki, Finland) Ed. Anne Stenros. R&P contact: Anne Stenros. adv.; B&W & color page FIM 9000; adv. contact: Annikki Matinmaki. bk.rev.; index. circ. 6,000. (back issues avail.) **Indexed**: DAAI. **Document type**: bulletin.
 —BLDSC (4008.307000); SWETS.
 Description: Promotes the image of the Finnish design and environmental culture abroad.

FORT; the international journal of fortification and military architecture. see MILITARY

720   NE   ISSN 0015-8372
NA6
FORUM (AMSTERDAM); driemaandelijks tijdschrift voor architectuur. Variant title: Forum voor Architectuur. 1946. 4/yr. fl.80 (foreign fl.118). Genootschap Architectura et Amicitia, Waterlooplein 211, 1011 PG Amsterdam, Netherlands. TEL 31-20-6220188. Ed. Roelof Mulder; Pub. Gerard W. Comello. adv.; illus. circ. 2,500. **Indexed**: Leg.Per, Mid.East: Abstr.& Ind.
 —SWETS.

720   US   ISSN 0734-4252
FORUM (CHICAGO, 1979). 1979. s-a. $80 membership. Society of the Architectural Historians, 1365 North Astor St., Chicago, IL 60610-2144. TEL 312-573-1365. FAX 312-573-1141. Ed. Alison K. Hoaglund. R&P contact: Elizabeth Sippel. adv. contact: Elizabeth Sippel. circ. 3,550. **Indexed**: Mag.Ind. **Document type**: bulletin.
 Description: Serves as the official bulletin for the society's Committee on Preservation.

ARCHITECTURE

720   US
NA737.W7
FRANK LLOYD WRIGHT QUARTERLY. 1990. q. $20 (with membership $40). Frank Lloyd Wright Foundation, Taliesin West, Cactus Rd. & 114th St., Scottsdale, AZ 85261-4430. TEL 602-860-2700. Ed. Dixie Legler; Pub. Suzette A. Lucas. R&P contact: Suzette Lucas. adv.; bk.rev.; illus. circ. 8,000. (back issues avail.; reprint service avail.) **Indexed:** Avery Ind.Archit.Per. **Document type:** academic/scholarly publication.
   Supersedes (1978-1982): Frank Lloyd Wright Newsletter (ISSN 0160-7375)
   Description: Contains in-depth articles about Frank Lloyd Wright, his life and work. Includes a national calendar of events.

FREUNDESKREIS BLAETTER. see *MUSEUMS AND ART GALLERIES*

720 624   CC
FUJIAN JIANZHU/FUJIAN ARCHITECTURE & CONSTRUCTION. (Text in Chinese) q. Y16 1983. Fujian Tumu Jianzhu Xuehui - Fujian Society of Civil Engineering and Architecture, 240 Beida Rd., Fuzhou, Fujian 350001, People's Republic of China. TEL 86-591-7855358. (Dist. overseas by: China Publication Trading Corporation, P.O. Box 782, Beijing, P.R. China) Ed. Zhaoyi Yuan; Pub. Zhaoyi Yuan. R&P contact: Zhaoyi Yuan. circ. 5,000.
   Refereed Serial

943   AU   ISSN 0429-8926
FUNDBERICHTE AUS OESTERREICH. 1934. a. price varies. (Bundesdenkmalamt, Abteilung fuer Bodendenkmale) Verlag Ferdinand Berger und Soehne GmbH, Wienerstr. 21-23, A-3580 Horn, Austria. TEL 43-2982-4161232. FAX 43-2982-2317235. Ed. Horst Adler. charts; illus. **Indexed:** Br.Archaeol.Abstr., Numis.Lit. **Document type:** monographic series.

G A; Internationale Zeitschrift ueber Verwendungsmoeglichkeiten von Gas im Bauwesen. (Gas und Architektur) see *HEATING, PLUMBING AND REFRIGERATION*

720   JA
G A. (Global Architecture) (Text in English, Japanese) 1977. s-a. A.D.A. Edita Tokyo Co. Ltd., 3-12-14 Sendagaya, Shibuya-ku, Tokyo 151, Japan. TEL 03-3403-1581. (US subscr. to: G A International Co., Ltd., 594 Broadway, 3rd Fl., P.O. Box 353, New York, NY 10012. TEL 212-274-9683) Ed. Yukio Futagawa. adv. contact: Tatsuo Futagawa. illus. **Indexed:** Art Ind.
   Description: For those who would like to "experience" masterpieces of modern architecture.

724   JA   ISSN 0913-1639
G A DOCUMENT. (Global Architecture) (Text in English, Japanese) 1980. irreg. A.D.A. Edita Tokyo Co. Ltd., 3-12-14 Sendagaya, Shibuya-ku, Tokyo 151, Japan. TEL 03-3403-1581. FAX 03-3497-0649. (US subscr. to: G A International Co., Ltd., 594 Broadway, 3rd Fl., P.O. Box 353, New York, NY 10012. TEL 212-274-9683) Ed. Yukio Futagawa. illus. circ. 12,000. (back issues avail.) **Indexed:** Art Ind., Avery Ind.Archit.Per., Br.Tech.Ind. **Document type:** monographic series.

720   IT
G B PROGETTI - OSSERVATORIO INTERNAZIONALE. (Gran Bazaar) (Monographic series avail.) (Text in English, Italian) 1990. m. L.120000 (foreign L.160000). Editrice Progetti, Viale Stelvio 57, 20159 Milan, Italy. TEL 2-668-021-14. FAX 2-668-021-43. Pub. Barbara Nerozzi. adv.: B&W page L.2600000, color page L.3000000; adv. contact: Dario Apollonio. circ. 22,500.
   Description: Presents a global view of the latest events concerning architecture.

GARTEN UND LANDSCHAFT; journal of landscape architecture and landscape planning. see *GARDENING AND HORTICULTURE*

GENTSE BIJDRAGEN TOT DE KUNSTGESCHIEDENIS EN OUDHEIDKUNDE. see *ART*

720 352.7   SP   ISSN 0213-4780
NA9223
GEOMETRIA. (Text in English, Spanish) 2/yr. Olmos 5, 29018 Malaga, Spain. TEL 52-29-18-38. Ed. Jose Segui. circ. 15,000.
   —CINDOC.

724 941.27   UK
GEORGIAN GROUP. SYMPOSIUM PROCEEDINGS. irreg. (approx. 1-2/yr.). price varies. Georgian Group, 6 Fitzroy Sq., London W1P 6DX, England. TEL 44-0171-387-1720. FAX 44-0171-387-1721. (back issues avail.) **Document type:** proceedings.
   Description: Publishes articles and research on Georgian architecture and craftsmanship.

724 941.27   UK
GEORGIAN GROUP. TOWN REPORTS. 1993. irreg. (approx. 1-2/yr.). £3.20 per no. Georgian Group, 6 Fitzroy Sq., London W1P 6DX, England. TEL 44-0171-387-1720. FAX 44-0171-387-1721. illus. (back issues avail.) **Document type:** monographic series.
   Description: Examines the state of towns in Britain and the effect of historical conservation policies in these areas. Contains photographic surveys.

724 941.27   UK   ISSN 0963-1070
NA966
GEORGIAN GROUP JOURNAL. 1937. a. £24 to individuals; families £38; students £15. Georgian Group, 6 Fitzroy Sq., London W1P 6DX, England. TEL 44-0171-387-1720. FAX 44-0171-387-1721. Ed. Richard Hewlings. bk.rev. circ. 3,250. (back issues avail.) **Document type:** academic/scholarly publication.
   —UnCover.
   Description: Promotes public understanding and appreciation of the classical tradition in British architecture, town planning, and decorative art, as well as the restoration and protection of this architectural and artistic heritage.

GETTY CONSERVATION INSTITUTE NEWSLETTER. see *ART*

720 666.1   GW   ISSN 0949-2720
▼**GLAS;** Architektur und Technik. 1995. bi-m. DM.75 (foreign DM.84; students DM.49.80) (effective 1997). Deutsche Verlags-Anstalt GmbH, Postfach 106012, 70049 Stuttgart, Germany. TEL 49-711-2631-0. FAX 49-711-2631110. **Document type:** trade publication.

720   GW   ISSN 0017-0852
TP845
GLASFORUM; Zeitschrift fuer Architektur, Raumgestaltung, Kunst. 1951. 6/yr. DM.84 (students DM.54) (effective 1997); newsstand price: DM.18. Verlag Karl Hofmann, Postfach 1360, 73603 Schorndorf, Germany. TEL 49-7181-402127. FAX 49-7181-402111. Ed. Dieter Schempp. adv.; bk.rev.; bibl.; illus.; index. circ. 10,500. **Indexed:** Br.Tech.Ind. **Document type:** trade publication.
   —BLDSC (4182.500000). CCC.

720   UK   ISSN 0017-0992
GLASS AGE. 1958. m. £28.50 (foreign £42). Spotlight Publications Ltd. (Subsidiary of: Morgan-Grampian plc), Ludgate House, 245 Blackfriars Rd., London SE1 9UR, England. TEL 071-620-3636. FAX 071-401-8036. Ed. Peter Butler. adv. contact: Debbie Shepherd. charts; illus.; stat. circ. 8,868. (also avail. in microform from UMI) **Indexed:** Archit.Per.Ind., Br.Tech.Ind. **Document type:** trade publication.
   —CISTI; Linda Hall; UMI.
   Description: Covers the flat glass and glazing industry, from manufacture to installation. Includes informational articles, business news, and lists of products.

GLASS MAGAZINE. see *CERAMICS, GLASS AND POTTERY*

728   US
GOOD HOUSEKEEPING HOME PLANS. 1993. a. $2.95. Hearst Corporation, Good Housekeeping, 959 Eighth Ave., New York, NY 10019. TEL 212-649-2200. FAX 212-265-3307. adv.: B&W page $10695, color page $62210; trim 8 x 10 3/4. circ. 250,000. **Document type:** consumer publication.

GOTHENBURG STUDIES IN ART AND ARCHITECTURE. see *ART*

GREAT BRITAIN. ROYAL COMMISSION ON THE HISTORICAL MONUMENTS OF ENGLAND. ANNUAL REPORT. see *ARCHAEOLOGY*

GROEN; vakblad voor de groen in stad en landschap. see *GARDENING AND HORTICULTURE*

DAS GRUNDEIGENTUM; Zeitschrift fuer die gesamte Grundstuecks-, Haus- und Wohnungswirtschaft. see *HOUSING AND URBAN PLANNING*

720   IT
GUIDE DI RICERCA STORICA E RESTAURO. 1990. irreg., no.3, 1994. price varies. Liguori Editore s.r.l., Via Posillipo 394, 80123 Naples, Italy. TEL 39-81-7206111. FAX 39-81-7206244. Ed. Giovanni Carbonara. **Document type:** monographic series.

720.7   US
NA2103
GUIDE TO ARCHITECTURE SCHOOLS. 1947. irreg. (approx. triennial). $19.95. Association of Collegiate Schools of Architecture, Inc., 1735 New York Ave., N.W., Washington, DC 20006. TEL 202-785-2324. FAX 202-628-0448. Ed. G. Martin Moeller. **Document type:** directory.
   Formerly: Guide to Architecture Schools in North America (ISSN 0092-7856)

720   US   ISSN 0740-8102
GUIDE TO GRADUATE DEGREE PROGRAMS IN ARCHITECTURAL HISTORY. 1984. biennial. $10. Society of Architectural Historians, 1365 North Astor St., Chicago, IL 60610-2144. TEL 312-573-1365. FAX 312-573-1141. **Document type:** directory, academic/scholarly publication.

344.73 620   US   ISSN 0091-8245
KF2925.3.A73
GUIDELINES FOR IMPROVING PRACTICE. ARCHITECTS AND ENGINEERS PROFESSIONAL LIABILITY. 1971. bi-m. $100. Victor O. Schinnerer & Co., Two Wisconsin Circle, Chevy Chase, MD 20815. TEL 301-961-9800. Ed. Thomas H. Porterfreld, Jr. circ. 10,500. (looseleaf format) **Document type:** trade publication.

720   US   ISSN 1089-2141
GUIDELINES LETTER; new directions and techniques in the design professions. 1972. m. $56 (Canada $70; elsewhere $76). Guidelines, Box 456, Orinda, CA 94563. TEL 510-299-1323; 800-634-7779. FAX 510-299-0181. E-mail: fsgl@aol.com. Ed. Fred Stitt. R&P contact: Martha Barrett. bk.rev.; index; circ. 3,000 (controlled). **Document type:** newsletter.
   Formerly: Guidelines Architectural Letter.
   Description: Focuses on the needs of small office practice. Includes interview excerpts, new services for architects and designers, and state-of-the-profession in the 1990's.

720 745.5   US
NK1127
THE GUILD: THE ARCHITECT'S SOURCE OF ARTISTS AND ARTISANS. 1986. a. $37.50. Guild, 931 E. Main St., Ste. 106, Madison, WI 53703. TEL 608-256-1990. FAX 608-256-1938. E-mail: guild@guild.com; URL: http://www.guild.com. Ed. Toni Fountain Sikes; Pub. Kraus Sikes. adv.; illus. circ. 10,000. **Document type:** directory.
   Supersedes in part: Guild: A Sourcebook of Artists and Artisans; Which was formerly (until 1990): Guild: A Sourcebook of American Craft Artists (ISSN 0885-3975)
   Description: Lists and displays hand-crafted work done by artists for designers and architects.

722   CC   ISSN 1000-7237
GUJIAN YUANLIN JISHU/TRADITIONAL CHINESE ARCHITECTURE AND GARDENS. (Text in Chinese) 1983. q. $20. Beijing Di'er Fangwu Xiushan Gongcheng Gongsi - Beijing No.2 House Remodeling Engineering Company, 129 Di'anmen Dongdajie, Beijing 100009, People's Republic of China. TEL 86-10-6404-1946. Ed. Xu Shuhui. circ. 10,000. **Document type:** academic/scholarly publication.

H D K MAGAZIN. (Hochschule der Kuenste Berlin) see *ART*

720   SZ   ISSN 0017-6419
HABITATION; revue bimestrielle romande. (Text in French) 1928. bi-m. 60 SFr. (foreign 80 SFr.; students 45 SFr.). Union Suisse pour l'Amelioration du Logement, Section Romande, 10 rue du Vieux-Marche, CH-1260 Nyon, Switzerland. TEL 41-22-3613616. FAX 41-22-3613617. (Co-sponsor: Federation des Architectes Suisses) Ed Francois-Joseph Z'Graggen. adv.; charts; illus.; index **Document type:** trade publication.

ARCHITECTURE

712 US
HARVARD DESIGN MAGAZINE. 1973. 3/yr. $20 (foreign $30). Harvard University, Graduate School of Design, 48 Quincy St., Cambridge, MA 02138. TEL 617-496-8728. FAX 617-496-3391. Ed. William S. Saunders. bk.rev.; charts; illus.; circ. 14,000 (paid). **Document type:** academic/scholarly publication.
Former titles: G S D News (ISSN 0746-3677); (until 1983): H G S D News.
Description: Explores major issues in architecture, landscape and urban design and planning.

DAS HAUS. see *INTERIOR DESIGN AND DECORATION*

720 NE ISSN 0017-9515
HEEMSCHUT. 1911. bi-m. fl.80 (effective 1994). (Bond Heemschut) Waanders Uitgevers, Postbus 1129, 8001 BC Zwolle, Netherlands. TEL 31-38-4658628. FAX 31-38-4655989. Ed. J. Kamerling. adv.; bk.rev.; illus. circ. 10,000. **Indexed:** Archit.Per.Ind., Avery Ind.Archit.Per.
—SWETS.

HEIMATSCHUTZ/SAUVEGARDE. see *CONSERVATION*

720 CN ISSN 1195-5899
HERITAGE CANADA. (Text in English, French) 1986. 5/yr. Can.$25. Heritage Canada, 412 MacLaren, Ottawa, ON K2P 0M8, Canada. TEL 613-237-1066. FAX 613-237-5987. E-mail: hercanat@sympatico.ca. (Subscr. to: Box 1358, Sta. N, Ottawa, ON K1P 5R4, Canada) Ed. Veronica Vaillancourt. R&P contact: Veronica Vaillancourt. adv. contact: Heather Freeman. bk.rev. circ. 3,000. (back issues avail.) **Document type:** newsletter.
Former titles: (until 1993): Impact - Heritage Canada (ISSN 0840-9676); (until 1989): Preservation Action (ISSN 0838-3073)
Description: Includes articles on heritage issues, news, activities, resources, primarily in Canada. *Refereed Serial*

720 994 AT ISSN 0157-9231
HERITAGE COUNCIL OF NEW SOUTH WALES ANNUAL REPORT. 1978. a. Heritage Council of New South Wales, G.P.O. Box 3927, Sydney, N.S.W. 2001, Australia. TEL 61-2-3912055. FAX 61-2-3912336. Ed. Murray Brown. R&P contact: Murray Brown. TEL 61-2-93912060.
Description: Informs on the activities of the Heritage Council during the year.

720 994 AT ISSN 1321-1099
HERITAGE N.S.W. 1994. q. Heritage Council of New South Wales, 1 Farrer Place, Sydney, N.S.W. 2000, Australia. TEL 61-2-93912060. FAX 61-2-93912336. E-mail: brownm@waratah.www.nsw.gov.au. Ed. Murray Brown. R&P contact: Murray Brown. TEL 61-2-93912060. circ. 5,000. (back issues avail.) **Document type:** government publication, newsletter.
Description: Provides information on activities of the Heritage Council, new publications, innovative local projects and upcoming events.

720 AT ISSN 0313-6701
HERITAGE NEWS. 1977. a. free. Australian Heritage Commission, Education and Communication Section, G.P.O. Box 1567, Canberra, A.C.T. 2601, Australia. TEL 61-6-2172111. FAX 61-6-2172095. E-mail: gchin@ahc.gov.au; URL: http://www.erin.gov.au/portfolio/ahc/ahc.html. Ed. Murray Brown. circ. 5,000. **Document type:** newsletter.
Formerly: Heritage Newsletter.

728.6 708.2 942 UK ISSN 0952-5513
HISTORIC FARM BUILDINGS GROUP. JOURNAL. 1987. a. £7.50 (includes Newsletter). Historic Farm Buildings Group, c/o Museum of English Rural Life, Box 229, Whiteknights, Reading RG6 2AG, England. TEL 01734-875123. bk.rev. **Document type:** academic/scholarly publication.
—BLDSC (4758.333000).

HISTORIC GUELPH; the royal city. see *HISTORY — History Of North And South America*

HISTORIC HAWAII MAGAZINE. see *HISTORY — History Of North And South America*

720 UK ISSN 0260-8707
HISTORIC HOUSE. 1981. q. £40 (foreign $60) (effective 1997). (Historic Houses Association) Hall - McCartney Ltd., P.O. Box 21, Heritage House, 12 Football Close, Baldock, Herts., SG7 5AH, England. TEL 44-1462-896688. FAX 44-1462-896677. Ed. Peter Sinclair; Pub. Michael McCartney. adv. contact: E.A. Goldthorpe. bk.rev. circ. 7,000. **Indexed:** Avery Ind.Archit.Per., Br.Tech.Ind. **Document type:** consumer publication.
Description: Covers a range of topics from conservation, the arts, environment and heritage to tourism and marketing for historic-home and garden owners in the U.K.

728 US ISSN 1083-379X
HISTORIC HOUSE NEWS. 1989. q. $35 includes membership. Historic House Trust of New York City, The Arsenal, Rm. 203, Central Park, New York, NY 10021. TEL 212-360-8282. FAX 212-360-8201. URL: http://www.preserve.org/hht. Ed. Valerie Kalas. R&P contact: Valerie Kalas. illus. circ. 1,500. (looseleaf format) **Document type:** newsletter.
● Also available online.
Description: Provides information relating to the 19 historic house museums located in New York City Parks. Includes articles on social history of the houses, updates on the museums and their collections, restoration projects and calendar of events at the houses.

727 977 US
HISTORIC ILLINOIS. 1978. bi-m. $10. Illinois Historic Preservation Agency, 500 E. Madison, Springfield, IL 62701-1507. TEL 217-524-6045. FAX 217-785-7937. Ed. Cynthia A. Fuener. bk.rev.; cum. index; circ. 3,800 (paid). (back issues avail) **Document type:** government publication.
Description: Reports on the efforts to promote the preservation of important buildings and other historic sites in Illinois.

HISTORIC KANSAS CITY FOUNDATION GAZETTE. see *HISTORY — History Of North And South America*

HISTORIC PALM BEACH COUNTY PRESERVATION BOARD NEWSLETTER. see *HISTORY — History Of North And South America*

725 352.7 US ISSN 1056-6309
E151
HISTORIC PRESERVATION FORUM. 1987. q. $90 membership. National Trust for Historic Preservation, 1785 Massachusetts Ave. N.W., Washington, DC 20036. TEL 202-588-6296. URL: http://www.nthp.org/. Ed. Melissa Hudgins; Pub. Melissa Hudgins. R&P contact: Melissa Hudgins. adv. contact: Melissa Hudgins. (back issues avail.)
—BLDSC (4316.083200); SWETS; UnCover.
Formerly (until 1990): Preservation Forum (ISSN 0893-9403)
Description: Serves as a forum for expressing opinions, encouraging debate, and conveying information of importance to members.

HISTORIC TRAVELER; the guide to great historic destinations. see *TRAVEL AND TOURISM*

HISTORICAL SOCIETY OF SOUTH AUSTRALIA. JOURNAL. see *HISTORY — History Of Australasia And Other Areas*

HISTORICAL SOCIETY OF SOUTH AUSTRALIA NEWSLETTER. see *HISTORY — History Of Australasia And Other Areas*

720 SZ
HOCHPARTERRE. 1988. 10/yr. 100 SFr. (foreign 130 SFr.) (effective 1997). Hochparterre AG, Ausstellungsstr. 25, CH-8005 Zurich, Switzerland. TEL 41-1-4442888. FAX 41-1-4442889. E-mail: hochparterre@access.ch; URL: http://www.hochparterre.ch. Ed. Koebi Gantenbein. adv.: B&W page 4270 SFr., color page 6920 SFr.; trim 221 x 288; adv. contact: Susanna Franzoni. bk.rev. circ. 13,000. **Document type:** trade publication.

728 US ISSN 0278-2839
TX311
HOME; creative ideas for home design. 1955. 10/yr. $21.94. Hachette Filipacchi Magazines, Inc., 1633 Broadway, New York, NY 10019. TEL 212-767-6811. FAX 212-767-5600. (Subscr. to: Box 56318, Boulder, CO 80322-6318. TEL 800-950-7370) Ed. Gale C. Steves. adv.; bk.rev. circ. 1,000,000. **Indexed:** PMR, Search (1988-). **Document type:** consumer publication.
—UMI.
Former titles: Hudson Home Magazine (ISSN 0194-1089); (until 1980): Hudson Home Guides (ISSN 0362-6520); Incorporates: Home Building and Remodeling; Home Planning and Design; Home Improvement and Repair (ISSN 0361-2813); Home Plans and Ideas; Kitchens, Baths and Family Rooms.
Description: Emphasis is on home design and architecture, including creative yet practical ideas aimed primarily at the average middle-income homeowner.

720 FR ISSN 1147-7105
HOMME ET L'ARCHITECTURE. 1969. m. 150 F. (foreign 200 F.). Conseil Regional de l'Ordre des Architectes de Paris - Ile-de-France, 140 Av. Victor Hugo, 75116 Paris, France. TEL 45-53-58-56. FAX 45-53-53-11. Ed. Jean-Philippe Pierrat. adv.; bk.rev. circ. 13,000. **Indexed:** Archit.Per.Ind., Br.Tech.Ind.
Former titles: Architectes - Architecture; Architectes (ISSN 0066-6122); (until 1969): Ordre des Architectes. Conseil Regional de Paris. Bulletin.
Description: Explores the newest architectural projects in France.

720 690 CC
HONG KONG ARCHITECTS & DESIGNERS CATALOGUE (YEAR). (Includes 2 vols.: vol. 1, Hardware & Building Supplies; vol. 2, Furniture & Soft Furnishing) (Text in English) 1976. a. HK.$550 (foreign $115.50). Far East Trade Press Ltd., Kai Tak Commercial Bldg., 2nd Fl., 317 Des Voeux Rd., Central, Hong Kong, People's Republic of China. TEL 545-3028. FAX 544-6979. (Subcr. to: Times Publishing Group, Block C, 10th Fl. Seaview Estate, 2-8 Watson Rd., North Point, Hong Kong. TEL 852-566-8381. FAX 852-508-0255; People's Republic of China) Ed. Kenneth Ho. adv.: color page HK.$6800; trim 210 x 285; adv. contact: Winnie Kwan. circ. 11,200. **Document type:** catalog.
Description: Covers commercial and domestic interiors, building supplies, home and office furnishing, landscaping, catering and hotel equipment.

HOTEL SPECIFICATION INTERNATIONAL. see *HOTELS AND RESTAURANTS*

HOUSE BEAUTIFUL. see *INTERIOR DESIGN AND DECORATION*

720 US ISSN 0073-3571
HOUSE BEAUTIFUL'S HOUSES AND PLANS. 1957. 5/yr. $2.95 per no. Hearst Corporation, 1700 Broadway, Ste. 2801, New York, NY 10019. TEL 212-903-5051. FAX 212-262-9401. Ed. Jim Kemp. circ. 200,000.

HOUSING AND PLANNING YEAR BOOK. see *HOUSING AND URBAN PLANNING*

333.7 FR ISSN 1019-679X
I C O M O S NOUVELLES/I C O M O S NEWS. q. 150 F.($32) International Council on Monuments and Sites - Counseil International des Monuments et des Sites, 75 rue du Temple, 75003 Paris, France. TEL 081-7645768. FAX 081-7646677. Ed. Roland Silve. **Document type:** newsletter.
Formerly: Icomos Information (ISSN 0394-218X)

I D. see *INTERIOR DESIGN AND DECORATION*

720 ZA ISSN 1015-0862
NA17.Z3
IN SITU. (Text in English) q. Zambia Institute of Architects, Box 76105, Ndola, Zambia. (Co-sponsor: Surveyors Institute of Zambia) **Indexed:** Archit.Per.Ind., Gas Abstr.

720 620 IT
INARCASSA. bi-m. Cassa Nazionale di Previdenza e Assistenza per gli Ingegneri e gli Architetti Liberi Professionisti, Via Salaria 229, 00199 Rome, Italy. Ed. Mauro di Martino. adv.: B&W page L.4500000. circ. 177,348.

ARCHITECTURE

720 352.7 II ISSN 0019-4409
NA1
INDIAN ARCHITECT;* a magazine for the architect, town planner and construction engineer. (Text in English) 1959. m. Rs.20($7) A 15 Pamposh Enclave, New Delhi 110 048, India. TEL 91-11-640336. Ed. D.N. Dhar. adv. contact: M. Tandon. bk.rev.; charts; illus. **Indexed:** Archit.Per.Ind., Avery Ind.Archit.Per. **Document type:** trade publication.

920 380 II
INDIAN ARCHITECTS DIRECTORY & REFERENCE BOOK. 1969. irreg. $40. Architects Publishing Corp. of India, 51 Sujata, Ground Fl., Rani Sati Marg, Malad East, Mumbai 400 097, India. TEL 91-22-8834442. Ed. A.K. Gupta. adv. circ. 5,000. **Document type:** directory.
Former titles: Indian Architects Directory (ISSN 0256-4017); All India Architects Directory (ISSN 0587-4793)
Description: Regional listing of architectural firms in India, with a separate listing of government architectural departments. Includes a special section on prize winning architects.

720 338.025 US ISSN 0737-6391
NA54.I6
INDIANA. STATE BOARD OF REGISTRATION FOR ARCHITECTS. ROSTER OF REGISTERED ARCHITECTS. 1967. biennial. State Board of Registration for Architects, 1021 State Office Bldg., Indianapolis, IN 46204. **Document type:** directory.
Formerly (until 1977): Indiana. State Board of Registration for Architects. Alphabetical Roster of Registered Architects in Good Standing and the Indiana Architectural Act (ISSN 0737-6375)

INDIANA CONSTRUCTOR. see BUILDING AND CONSTRUCTION

720 628 US ISSN 1040-5313
INDOOR AIR QUALITY UPDATE; a guide to the practical control of indoor air problems. 1988. m. $317 (foreign $377). Cutter Information Corp., 37 Broadway, Arlington, MA 02174. TEL 617-648-8700. FAX 617-648-1950. URL: http://www.cutter.com. Ed. Carlton Vogt. charts; illus. (back issues avail.) **Document type:** newsletter.
●Also available online.
—CCC.
Description: Covers current research, case studies, trends, and news in the field of indoor air quality (IAQ). Includes resource reviews, information exchange, industry events, and feature articles.

L'INDUSTRIA DELLE COSTRUZIONI. see BUILDING AND CONSTRUCTION

720 CN ISSN 1192-2168
INFO-LINK MAGAZINE. 1993. 4/yr. Can.$20. I - L Focus Inc., 3044 Bloor St. W. 270, Toronto, ON M8X 1C4, Canada. TEL 416-604-7552. FAX 416-604-2545. adv. contact: Barbara Lindenbach. circ. 47,000. (tabloid format) **Document type:** trade publication.
Description: Serves the fields of architecture, interior design, building and construction.

720 US ISSN 1047-8353
NA730.V8
INFORM (RICHMOND). (Includes directory of Virginia architecture firms) 1990. q. (plus a. directory). $16 (effective 1997). American Institute of Architects, Virginia Society, 15 S. Fifth St., Richmond, VA 23219. TEL 804-644-3041. Ed. Vernon Mays; Pub. John W. Braymer. R&P contact: Vernon Mays. adv.: B&W page $950, color page $1350; 8 1/2 x 11; adv. contact: Jonathan Dabney. bk.rev. circ. 8,000. **Indexed:** Lib.Lit. **Document type:** trade publication.
Description: Aimed at design professionals and potential clients of design services, including architecture, product design, graphic design, historic preservation, and decorative arts.

INGEGNERI ARCHITETTI COSTRUTTORI. see ENGINEERING — Civil Engineering

INGENIERIA Y ARQUITECTURA. see ENGINEERING — Civil Engineering

720 US ISSN 0020-1472
NA722
INLAND ARCHITECT. 1957. 6/yr. $50. Real Estate News Corp, 3525 W. Peterson Ave., Ste. 103, Chicago, IL 60659. TEL 312-866-9900. Pub. Steven Polydoris. adv.; bk.rev.; illus. circ. 8,000. (also avail. in microform from UMI; reprint service avail. from UMI) **Indexed:** Art Ind., Avery Ind.Archit.Per., Br.Tech.Ind., Search (1990-). —BLDSC (4514.870000); KR SourceOne; UMI; UnCover.

INSIGHTS INTO SOUTH AUSTRALIAN HISTORY. see HISTORY — History Of Australasia And Other Areas

720 069 US
INSITES. 1994. q. membership. Chicago Architecture Foundation, 224 S. Michigan Ave., Chicago, IL 60604-2501. TEL 312-922-3432. FAX 312-922-0481. URL: http://www.architecture. org. Ed. Ania Greiner. R&P contact: Ania Greiner. TEL 312-922-3432 ext.227. circ. 6,000. (tabloid format) **Document type:** newsletter.
Formerly: Chicago Architecture Foundation News.
Description: Information on Chicago architecture, educational programs, exhibitions and tours offered by the foundation.

INSTITUT FUER BAUTECHNIK. MITTEILUNGEN. see BUILDING AND CONSTRUCTION

721 YU
INSTITUT ZA ARHITEKTURU I URBANIZAM SRBIJE. ZBORNIK RADOVA. vol.7, 1975. a. Institut za Arhitekturu i Urbanizam Srbije, Bulevar Revolucije 73-II, Belgrade, Yugoslavia. Ed. N. Pejovic. charts; illus.; tr.lit.

INSTITUTION OF ENGINEERS (INDIA). ARCHITECTURAL ENGINEERING. see ENGINEERING — Civil Engineering

INSTITUTUL POLITEHNIC DIN IASI. BULETINUL. SECTIA 6: CONSTRUCTII, ARHITECTURA. see BUILDING AND CONSTRUCTION

720 GW
INTELLIGENTE ARCHITEKTUR. q. DM.84.80 (foreign DM.104) (effective 1997). Verlagsanstalt Alexander Koch GmbH, Fasanenweg 18, 70771 Leinfelden-Echterdingen, Germany. TEL 49-711-7591-0. FAX 49-711-7591368. **Document type:** trade publication.

720 US ISSN 1044-3843
NA2542.35
INTERCHANGE (POMONA). 1987. q. $10. California State Polytechnic University, College of Environmental Design, 3801 W. Temple Ave., Pomona, CA 91768. TEL 909-869-2664. FAX 909-869-4355. **Document type:** academic/scholarly publication.

INTERNATIONAL DIRECTORY OF DESIGN. see ART

720 UK ISSN 0269-0837
INTERNATIONAL DIRECTORY OF PRACTICES (YEAR). a. £45. (Royal Institute of British Architects) R I B A Publications Ltd., Finsbury Mission, 39 Moreland St., London EC1V 8BB, England. TEL 0171-2251-0791. FAX 0171-608-2375. **Document type:** directory.
Description: Covers RIBA member practices working internationally or with international offices.

INTERNATIONAL HOME PLANS; Top Designer's Collection. see HOUSING AND URBAN PLANNING

720 US ISSN 1049-6564
NA1.A1
INTERSIGHT. 1990. a. State University of New York - Buffalo, School of Architecture and Planning, Hayes Hall, Buffalo, NY 14214.

720 FR ISSN 0769-3710
INTRAMUROS. 1985. bi-m. 330 F. (foreign 430 F.). Groupe Moniteur, 17 rue d'Uzes, 75002 Paris, France. FAX 33-1-42333819. TELEX 220 528F. Ed. Chantal Clavier-Hamaide. circ. 10,000.

720 FR ISSN 0075-0018
INVENTAIRE GENERAL DES MONUMENTS ET DES RICHESSES ARTISTIQUES DE LA FRANCE. 1969. irreg. price varies. (Ministere des Affaires Culturelles) Imprimerie Nationale, B.P. 154, 59505 Douai Cedex, France. TEL 27-93-70-90. FAX 27-93-70-96. TELEX 120 389 F.

720 US ISSN 0021-0439
NA1
IOWA ARCHITECT.* 1954. q. $15 (effective 1994). (American Institute of Architects, Iowa Chapter) Mauck & Associates, 516 3d St., Ste. 200, Des Moines, IA 50309-1702. TEL 515-243-4010. FAX 515-243-6011. Ed. Paul Mankins. adv.; bk.rev.; charts; illus. circ. 5,000.
—UnCover.
Description: Covers architecture, historic renovation art, product development and design throughout the Midwest: Iowa, Missouri, Nebraska, Kansas, Minnesota, Wisconsin, Illinois, Oklahoma.
Refereed Serial

IRISH ARTS REVIEW YEARBOOK. see ART

720 IE ISSN 0021-1206
DA900.I6295
IRISH GEORGIAN SOCIETY. BULLETIN. 1958. a. $15. Irish Georgian Society, 42 Merrion Sq., Dublin 2, Ireland. TEL 01-767053. Ed. Desmond Guinness. adv.; bk.rev.; illus.; index. circ. 3,500. (also avail. in microform from UMI; reprint service avail. from UMI) **Indexed:** Archit.Per.Ind., Avery Ind.Archit.Per., Br.Tech.Ind., RILA. **Document type:** bulletin.

ISLAMIC ART AND ARCHITECTURE. see ART

720 US ISSN 1064-6906
NA7235.H3
ISLAND HOME. 1990. bi-m. $24 (foreign $54). Island Productions, Inc., 6490 S. McCarran Blvd., Ste. 30, Reno, NV 89509. TEL 702-826-2044. FAX 702-826-1971. Ed. Rob Sandler; Pub. Kathea Suzuki-Latham. R&P contact: Rob Sandler. adv. contact: Kathea Suzuki-Latham. circ. 28,450 (paid). **Document type:** consumer publication.
Formerly (until Jan. 1992): Hawaiian Island Home (ISSN 1051-3787)
Description: Architecture, design and lifestyle magazine featuring exclusive international residences on islands, art and culture, with coverage of island cuisine, fashion, travel and leisure destinations.

720 700 UK
ISSUES IN ARCHITECTURE, ART AND DESIGN. 1990. s-a. £8 to individuals; institutions £16. University of East London, Greengate House, Greengate St., London E13 OBG, England. TEL 44-181-590-7722. FAX 44-181-849-3694. E-mail: r.s.garfield@uel.ac. uk. Ed. Gillian Elinor. adv.: page £80; adv. contact: Rachel Garfield. bk.rev. (back issues avail.) **Document type:** academic/scholarly publication.

720 IT ISSN 0021-2458
ISTITUTO DI ARCHITETTURA E URBANISTICA. RASSEGNA. 1964. 3/yr. price varies. (Universita degli Studi di Roma, Facolta di Ingegneria) Edizioni Kappa s.r.l., Piazza Borghese 6, 00186 Rome, Italy. (Co-sponsor: Istituto di Architettura di Edilizie e di Tecnica Urbanistica) Ed. Federico Gorio. illus.; index, cum.index. circ. 1,500. (tabloid format)

ITEMS (PUBLIEKSEDITIE); tijdschrift voor vormgeving. see ART

ITEMS (VAKEDITIE); tijdschrift voor vormgeving. see ART

720 700 CI
IZ STAROG I NOVOG ZAGREBA. (Text in Croatian; summaries in German) 1957. quadrennial. $20. Muzej Grada Zagreba, Opaticka 20, 41000 Zagreb, Croatia. TEL 274-642. FAX 38-41-428-294. Ed. Zdenko Kuzmic. adv.; charts; illus. circ. 1,000.

720 JA ISSN 0021-4302
JAPAN ARCHITECT. International edition of: Shinkenchiku. (Text in English, Japanese) 1956. q. 21000 Yen($165) Shinkenchiku-sha Co., Ltd., 31-2, Yushima 2-chome, Bunkyo-ku, Tokyo 113, Japan. TEL 03-3811-7101. FAX 03-3812-8187. Ed. Yasuhiro Teramatsu. adv.; bk.rev.; charts; illus. circ. 18,000. (back issues avail.) **Indexed:** Art Ind., Arts & Hum.Cit.Ind., ASCA, Avery Ind.Archit.Per., Br.Tech.Ind., Curr.Cont., Search (1992-).
Description: Contains information and detailed data of selected coverage of top-level Japanese architecture, projects, city planning and new trends.

720 CC ISSN 0577-7429
JIANZHU/ARCHITECTURE. (Text in Chinese) 1954. m. Zhongguo Jianzhu Xiehui, Baiwanzhuang, Beijing 100835, People's Republic of China. TEL 8315217 Ed. Wang Mingxian.

JIANZHU JINGJI. see *BUSINESS AND ECONOMICS*

JIANZHU JISHU/ARCHITECTURAL TECHNOLOGY. see *BUILDING AND CONSTRUCTION*

JIANZHU JIXIE/CONSTRUCTION MACHINERY. see *MACHINERY*

720   CC   ISSN 0529-1399
NA1545
JIANZHU XUEBAO/ARCHITECTURAL JOURNAL. (Text in Chinese) m. Zhongguo Jianzhu Xuehui - China Architectural Society, Baiwanzhuang Jianshebu Nei, Beijing 100835, People's Republic of China. TEL 8393632. FAX 8311585. Ed. Zhang Zugang. pp./issue: 64. **Indexed:** Br.Tech.Ind.
—BLDSC (1600.310000); Linda Hall; UnCover.

720   PO   ISSN 0870-1504
JORNAL ARQUITECTOS. 1981. 10/yr. Esc.12500 to non-members. Associacao dos Arquitectos Portugueses - Portuguese Association of Architects, Rua Barata Salguiero 36, 1200 Lisbon, Portugal. TEL 3526445. FAX 543667. Ed. Michel Toussaint. adv.: B&W page Esc.155000, color page Esc.210000; 265 x 182; adv. contact: Maria de Lurdes Melo. circ. 6,200.

720   US   ISSN 0738-0895
HT166   CODEN: JAPRER
JOURNAL OF ARCHITECTURAL AND PLANNING RESEARCH. 1984-1987; resumed same year. q. $65 to individuals; institutions $114 (effective 1997). Locke Science Publishing Company, Inc., 117 West Harrison Bldg., Ste. 640-L221, Chicago, IL 60605. Ed. Andrew D. Seidel. adv.; bk.rev.; abstr.; bibl.; illus. **Indexed:** Abstr.Anthropol., Archit.Per.Ind., Arts & Hum.Cit.Ind., Br.Tech.Ind., Curr.Cont., Energy Rev., Eng.Ind., Environ.Per.Bibl. (1985-), Fam.Ind., Geo.Abstr.P.G., IDA, INSPEC (1984-), P.A.I.S., Psychol.Abstr. (1984-), Sage Urb.Stud.Abstr., Sociol.Abstr., SSCI. **Document type:** academic/scholarly publication.
—BLDSC (4947.179600); AskIEEE; CISTI; Ei; Genuine Article; KR SourceOne; SWETS; UnCover. **CCC.**
Supersedes: Journal of Architectural Research.
Description: Reports on both recent research findings and innovative practices. Provides a link between theory and practice for researchers and practicing professionals.
Refereed Serial

720   UK   ISSN 1355-6207
▼**JOURNAL OF ARCHITECTURAL CONSERVATION;** historic buildings, monuments, places and landscapes. 1995. 3/yr. £85 to institutions (outside Europe £94) (effective 1998). Donhead Publishing Ltd., 28 Southdean Gardens, Wimbledon, London SW19 6NU, England. TEL 44-181-789-0138. FAX 44-181-789-9114. (Subscr. in the U.S. to: P R G Inc., Box 1768, Rockville, MD 20849-1768. TEL 301-309-2222. FAX 301-279-7885) Ed. David Watt; Pub. Jill Pearce. adv. contact: Lindy Cornforth. bk.rev. **Document type:** academic/scholarly publication.
—BLDSC (4947.179800).
Description: Brings the results of research and innovative practice in the conservation of historic buildings, monuments, places, gardens, and landscapes to an international readership.
Refereed Serial

720   US   ISSN 1046-4883
NA1   CODEN: JAEDEW
JOURNAL OF ARCHITECTURAL EDUCATION. 1947. q. $50 to individuals (foreign $66); institutions $152 (foreign $168) (effective 1997). (Association of Collegiate Schools of Architecture, Inc.) M I T Press, 5 Cambridge Center, Cambridge, MA 02142. TEL 617-253-2889. FAX 617-577-1545. E-mail: journals-orders@mit.edu; URL: http://mitpress.mit.edu/journal-home.tcl?issn-10464883. Ed. Diane Ghirardo. R&P contact: Paul Dzus. bk.rev. (also avail. in microform from UMI; reprint service avail. from UMI) **Indexed:** Archit.Per.Ind., Art Ind., ASCA, Avery Ind.Archit.Per., Br.Tech.Ind., C.I.J.E., CAD CAM Abstr., Cont.Pg.Educ., Curr.Cont., Energy Ind., Energy Info.Abstr. **Document type:** academic/scholarly publication.
—BLDSC (4947.180000); CISTI; Genuine Article; KR SourceOne; SWETS; UMI; UnCover. **CCC.**
Former titles (until 1983): J A E (ISSN 0149-2993); (until 1974): Journal of Architectural Education (ISSN 0047-2239)
Description: Publishes articles on a wide range of topics including history, theory, practice and design.
Refereed Serial

721 624   US   ISSN 1076-0431
           CODEN: JAEIED
▼**JOURNAL OF ARCHITECTURAL ENGINEERING.** 1995. m. $131 to non-members (foreign $138), members $29 (foreign $36); CD-ROM ed. $155 to non-members (foreign $170), members $29 (foreign $51) (effective 1997). American Society of Civil Engineers, Architectural Engineering Division, 345 E. 47th St., New York, NY 10007-0335. TEL 212-705-7000. Ed. Bijan Mohraz. **Document type:** academic/scholarly publication.
●Also available on CD-ROM.
—BLDSC (4947.182000); CISTI; EMDOCS; KR SourceOne; SWETS; UnCover.
Description: Provides a multidisciplinary forum to disseminate practice-based information on the engineering and technical issues concerned with all aspects of building design.
Refereed Serial

720   UK   ISSN 1360-2365
NA1
▼**THE JOURNAL OF ARCHITECTURE.** 1996. q. £65 (foreign £110) to individuals; institutions £155 (foreign £260); print & online eds. combined £190 (foreign £315) (effective 1998). (Royal Institute of British Architects) Thomson Professional (Subsidiary of: International Thomson Publishing Group), 2-6 Boundary Row, London SE1 8HN, England. TEL 44-171-8650066. FAX 44-171-5229623. URL: http://architecture.efnspon.com. (Subscr. to: International Thomson Publishing Services Ltd., Cheriton House, North Way, Andover, Hants SP10 5BE, England. TEL 44-1264-342713. FAX 44-1264-342807; Subscr. in US & Canada to: 400 Market St., Philadelphia, PA 19106. TEL 800-552-5866) Ed.Bd. adv. contact: Gemma Heiser. bibl.; index. (back issues avail.) **Document type:** academic/scholarly publication.
●Also available online.
—BLDSC (4947.192000).
Refereed Serial

JOURNAL OF CANADIAN ART HISTORY/ANNALES D'HISTOIRE DE L'ART CANADIEN. see *ART*

JOURNAL OF DECORATIVE AND PROPAGANDA ARTS. see *ART*

JOURNAL OF URBAN DESIGN. see *HOUSING AND URBAN PLANNING*

JOURNAL OF URBAN TECHNOLOGY. see *TECHNOLOGY: COMPREHENSIVE WORKS*

720   JA   ISSN 0003-8490
KENCHIKU BUNKA/ARCHITECTURAL CULTURE. (Text in Japanese; title and summaries in English) 1947. q. $270. Shokokusha Publishing Co., Ltd., 25 Sakamachi, Shinjuku-ku, Tokyo 160, Japan. TEL 81-3-3359-3231. FAX 81-3-3357-3961. (Dist. by: Intercontinental Marketing Corp., I.P.O. Box 5056, Tokyo 100-31, Japan. TEL 81-3-3661-7458. FAX 81-3-667-9646) Ed. Hiroyoshi Tajiri. adv.: B&W page 200000 Yen, color page 500000 Yen; adv. contact: Toshio Takahashi. circ. 60,000.
—BLDSC (5089.375000).
Description: Covers the latest trends, design and technology of architecture, as well as its impact on the environment.

720   JA
KENCHIKU TECHO/ARCHITECT. 1957. m. Kinryudo Co. Ltd., 2-3, Higashi Ueno 5 chome, Taito-ku, Tokyo 110, Japan. Ed. Shigeru Kikuchi. adv. circ. 29,000.

KING SAUD UNIVERSITY. JOURNAL. ARCHITECTURE AND PLANNING. see *HOUSING AND URBAN PLANNING*

720   KO
KONCHUK MUNHWA/ARCHITECTURAL TECHNOLOGY INFORMATION. (Text in Korean) m. 273-23, 2-ga Songsu, Songdong-gu, Seoul, S. Korea. TEL 02-4684701. FAX 02-2697925.
Description: Covers architectural culture and news.

720   KO
KONGGAN/SPACE. (Text in English, Korean) 1966. m. 60000 Won (US & Canada $136). Space Group of Korea, 219 Wonseo-dong, Chongro-gu, Seoul 110-280, S. Korea. TEL 822-747-2892. FAX 822-747-2894. TELEX SPACE-K-24572. Ed. Heon-Hun Kim; Pub. Sea-Young Chang. R&P contact: Heon-Jun Kim. adv. contact: Sun-Hyung Rhee. bk.rev. circ. 5,000. **Document type:** academic/scholarly publication.
Description: Emphasizes contemporary architecture and art in evaluating Korea's past, present and future.

KULTURA. see *LITERATURE*

700 948   SZ
KUNST UND ARCHITEKTUR IN DER SUISSE/ART ET ARCHITECTURE EN SUISSE/ARTE E ARCHITETTURA IN SVIZZERA. (Text and summaries in French, German, Italian) 1950. 4/yr. 80 SFr. Gesellschaft fuer Schweizerische Kunstgeschichte - Societe d'Histoire de l'Art en Suisse, Postfach, CH-3001 Bern, Switzerland. TEL 031-3014281. FAX 031-3016991. Ed. Nott Caviezel. adv. contact: Astrid Roesli. bk.rev. circ. 10,000. (back issues avail.) **Indexed:** Archit.Per.Ind., Avery Ind.Archit.Per., RILA. **Document type:** academic/scholarly publication.
Formerly: Unsere Kunstdenkmaeler (ISSN 0566-263X)

720 700 690 352.7   GW
KUNST UND STADT. 1979. 2/yr. DM.12 per no. Kulturwerks des Berufverbandes Bildender Kuenstler Berlins GmbH, Koethenerstr. 44, 10963 Berlin, Germany. TEL 030-2611191. FAX 030-2623319. Eds. R. Krueger, E. Mueller. adv.; bk.rev. **Document type:** bulletin.
Formerly: Kunst am Bau.

KUNTATEKNIIKKA/KOMMUNTEKNIK. see *HOUSING AND URBAN PLANNING*

720   PL   ISSN 0023-5865
NA6
KWARTALNIK ARCHITEKTURY I URBANISTYKI. (Text in Polish; summaries in English) 1956. q. $52. (Polska Akademia Nauk, Komitet Architektury i Urbanistyki) Wydawnictwo Naukowe P W N, Ul. Miodowa 10, 00-251 Warsaw, Poland. TEL 48-22-312738. FAX 48-22-6954288. TELEX 813763 PWN PL. Ed. Wanda Puget. bk.rev.; charts; illus.; cum.index every 5 yrs. circ. 1,320. **Indexed:** Avery Ind.Archit.Per.

LABYRINTHOS. see *ART*

720   GW
LANDESKONSERVATOR RHEINLAND. ARBEITSHEFT DER RHEINISCHEN DENKMALPFLEGE. 1971. irreg., no.49, 1996. price varies. (Landeskonservator Rheinland) Rheinland Verlag GmbH, Abtei Brauweiler, Postfach 2140, 50250 Pulheim, Germany. TEL 49-2234-9854265. FAX 49-2234-82503. (Dist. by: Dr. Rudolf Habelt GmbH, Am Buchenhang 1, 53115 Bonn, Germany. TEL 49-228-9238322. FAX 49-228-232017) (Co-sponsor: Landschaftsverband Rheinland) **Document type:** monographic series.
Formerly: Landeskonservator Rheinland. Arbeitsheft.

THE LANDMARK (HARTFORD). see *ANTIQUES*

LANDMARKS OBSERVER. see *HISTORY — History Of North And South America*

ARCHITECTURE

712 US ISSN 0023-8023
G1
LANDSCAPE. 1951. 3/yr. $22 to individuals; institutions $42. Landscape, Box 7107, Berkeley, CA 94707. TEL 510-549-3233. FAX 510-843-7120. Ed. Rebecca McKee. bk.rev.; illus.; maps; index. circ. 4,000. (also avail. in microform from UMI) **Indexed:** Amer.Hist.& Life (1979-1994), Archit.Per.Ind., Art.Ind., Arts & Hum.Cit.Ind., Avery Ind.Archit.Per., Br.Tech.Ind., Curr.Cont., Ekist.Ind., Environ.Abstr., Environ.Per.Bibl. (1975-), Gard.Lit. (1992-), Geo.Abstr.P.G., Hist.Abstr. (1979-1994), Mid.East: Abstr.& Ind., Rural Recreat.Tour.Abstr., Sage Urb.Stud.Abstr., Sociol.Abstr., Urb.Aff.Abstr., World Agri.Econ.& Rural Sociol.Abstr. **Document type:** academic/scholarly publication.
—CIS; Genuine Article; KR SourceOne; SWETS; UMI; UnCover. **CCC.**
Description: Essays, articles, photography, and graphics on cultural geography, landscape architecture and related fields; covers city and regional planning from a social, historical, and contemporary perspective.

720 US ISSN 1071-3697
SB472.535.S66
LANDSCAPE AND NURSERY DIGEST. 1965. m. $29.95. Betrock Information Systems, Inc., 7770 Davie Rd. Ext., Hollywood, FL 33024. TEL 305-981-2821. FAX 305-981-2823. URL: http://www.betrack.com. Ed. Linda Thorne; Pub. Irv Betrock. R&P contact: Irv Betrock. adv. contact: Karen Peruzzi. circ. 16,000. **Document type:** trade publication.
Formerly: Southern Nursery Digest.
Description: Magazine for landscape architects, landscape contractors, and wholesale nurseries.

712 US ISSN 1060-9962
LANDSCAPE ARCHITECT & SPECIFIER NEWS. 1985. m. $27.95 (free to qualified personnel). Landscape Communications, Ltd., 1560 Brookhollow Drive, Ste. 222, Santa Ana, CA 92705. TEL 714-979-5276. FAX 714-979-3543. Ed. Heather Duval; Pub. George Schmok. adv. contact: Anthony Messina. **Document type:** trade publication.
Description: Publishes news of interest and use to landscape architects and others interested in the field. Contains feature articles of projects in which the design was led by a landscape architect.

720 333.7 CN ISSN 0228-6963
LANDSCAPE ARCHITECTURAL REVIEW/REVUE D'ARCHITECTURE DE PAYSAGE. (Text in English and French) 1980. 4/yr. Can.$25($25) (foreign $40). 24 Kensington Ave., Willowdale, Ont. M2M 1R6, Canada. TEL 416-223-3956. FAX 416-225-8103. Ed. Nick Van Vliet. adv.; bk.rev.; index. circ. 1,400. (back issues avail.) **Indexed:** Can.B.P.I., CMI, Gard.Lit. (1992-).
Description: A forum for the exchange, discussion and review of a broad range of ideas and topics related to the theory and practice of landscape architecture, the environmental sciences and related professions.

712 US ISSN 0023-8031
SB469
LANDSCAPE ARCHITECTURE. 1910. 12/yr. $42. American Society of Landscape Architects, 4401 Connecticut Ave., N.W., Washington, DC 20008-2302. TEL 202-686-2752. URL: http://www.asla.org/. adv.; bk.rev.; charts; illus.; tr.lit.; index. circ. 24,000. (also avail. in microfiche; back issues avail.) **Indexed:** Archit.Per.Ind., Art Ind., Arts & Hum.Cit.Ind., ASCA, Avery Ind.Archit.Per., Curr.Cont., Energy Ind., Energy Info.Abstr., Energy Rev., Environ.Per.Bibl. (1972-1993), Gard.Lit. (1992-), Geo.Abstr., Mid.East: Abstr.& Ind., Search (1991-), SSCI. **Document type:** trade publication.
—BLDSC (5153.140000); Genuine Article; KR SourceOne; Linda Hall; SWETS; UnCover.

712 US ISSN 0023-754X
SB469
LANDSCAPE ARCHITECTURE NEWS DIGEST. 1960. 8/yr. $32 to non-members. American Society of Landscape Architects, 4401 Connecticut Ave., N.W., Washington, DC 20008-2302. TEL 202-686-2752. Ed. Andy Brown. adv.; tr.lit. circ. 12,000. (looseleaf format; also avail. in microform from UMI) **Document type:** newsletter.
—UMI.
Description: Presents current news on congressional, legal, artistic, and business activities in the field of landscape architecture.

712 UK ISSN 0020-2908
SB469
LANDSCAPE DESIGN. (Supplements avail.: Landscape Design Extra, Plant User) 1934. 10/yr. £42 (U.S., Canada and Europe £50; rest of world £60; students UK £30; students Europe £40) (effective 1998). Landscape Design Trust, 13A West St., Reigate, Surrey RH2 9BL, England. TEL 44-1737-223294. FAX 44-1737-224206. Ed. Ken Fieldhouse. R&P contact: Ken Fieldhouse. adv. contact: Robert Ellis. bk.rev.; bibl.; charts; illus.; stat.; cum.index. circ. 6,500. **Indexed:** Avery Ind.Archit.Per., Br.Tech.Ind., Geo.Abstr., RICS, Rural Recreat.Tour.Abstr., World Agri.Econ.& Rural Sociol.Abstr. **Document type:** trade publication.
—BLDSC (5153.145000); SWETS; UnCover.
Formerly: Institute of Landscape Architects. Journal.

712 UK ISSN 0962-2187
LANDSCAPE DESIGN EXTRA. (Supplement to: Landscape Design) 1990. m. free with subscr. to Landscape Design. Landscape Design Trust, 13A West St., Reigate, Surrey RH2 9BL, England. TEL 44-1737-223144. FAX 44-1737-224206. Ed. Ken Fieldhouse. R&P contact: Ken Fieldhouse. adv. contact: Robert Ellis. **Document type:** bulletin.
—BLDSC (5153.145200).

LANDSCAPE HISTORY. see HISTORY

720 UK ISSN 0265-9786
LANDSCAPE ISSUES. 1984. s-a. £25. Department of Countryside and Landscape, Cheltenham and Gloucester College of Higher Education, Francis Close Hall, Swindon Rd., Cheltenham, England. TEL 44-1242-532930. FAX 44-1242-532997. E-mail: issues@chelt.ac.uk. Ed. Robert Moore. bk.rev. circ. 200. **Document type:** academic/scholarly publication.
—BLDSC (5153.146170).
Description: Publishes articles and reports on aspects of landscape architecture, countryside planning, and environmental policy.
Refereed Serial

720 712 US ISSN 0277-2426
SB469
LANDSCAPE JOURNAL; design, planning, and management of the land. 1981. s-a. $28 to individuals; institutions $69. (Council of Education in Landscape Architecture) University of Wisconsin Press, Journal Division, 114 N. Murray St., Madison, WI 53715. TEL 608-262-4952. FAX 608-262-7560. URL: http://www.wisc.edu/wisconsinpress/journals.html. Eds. Kenneth Helphand, Robert Melnick. adv.; illus. (also avail. in microform from UMI; back issues avail.; reprint service avail. from UMI) **Indexed:** Avery Ind.Archit.Per., Br.Tech.Ind., Curr.Adv.Ecol.Sci., Environ.Per.Bibl. (1985-), Gard.Lit. (1992-), Sport Fish.Abstr., Wild.Rev. **Document type:** academic/scholarly publication.
—BLDSC (5153.146300); SWETS; UMI; UnCover. **CCC.**

712 UK ISSN 0142-6397
CODEN: LAREDJ
LANDSCAPE RESEARCH. 1968. 3/yr. £42($72) to individuals; institutions £110 ($174) (effective 1997). Carfax Publishing Co., P.O. Box 25, Abingdon, Oxon OX14 3UE, England. TEL 44-1235-401000. FAX 44-1235-401550. E-mail: enquiries@carfax.co.uk. (Subscr. in N. America to: 875-81 Massachusetts Ave., Cambridge, MA 02139. FAX 617-354-6875) Ed. Paul Selman. adv.; bk.rev. circ. 650. **Indexed:** Appl.Ecol.Abstr., Archit.Per.Ind., Art.Hosp.& Tour., Biol.Abstr., Curr.Adv.Ecol.Sci., Ecol.Abstr., Energy Rev., Environ.Per.Bibl. (1981-), Forest.Abstr., Gard.Lit. (1992-), Geo.Abstr.H.G., Geo.Abstr.P.G., Rural Recreat.Tour.Abstr., World Agri.Econ.& Rural Sociol.Abstr. **Document type:** academic/scholarly publication.
—BLDSC (5153.147700); SWETS; UnCover. **CCC.**
Formerly (until 1976): Landscape Research News (ISSN 0458-7014)
Description: Deals with recent research in landscape from all disciplines.
Refereed Serial

LANDSCAPING HOMES & GARDENS. see GARDENING AND HORTICULTURE

712 GW ISSN 0323-3162
LANDSCHAFTSARCHITEKTUR; Praxismagazin fuer Landschaftsbau und Landschaftspflege. 1962. m. DM.121.20 (foreign DM.140.40) (effective 1998). Bernhard Thalacker Verlag GmbH, Postfach 8364, 38133 Braunschweig, Germany. TEL 49-531-380040. FAX 49-531-3800425. Ed. Sabine Mueller. adv.: B&W page DM.3100.80, color page DM.5170.80; trim 272 x 186; adv. contact: Bruno Steder. bk.rev. circ. 8,308. **Document type:** trade publication.
Description: Trade publication for landscape planning and design. Covers parks, other recreational areas, playgrounds, and planting. Includes reports and announcements of events and new publications.

LANDSCHAP; tijdschrift voor landschapsecologie en milieukunde. see ENVIRONMENTAL STUDIES

LEGAL HANDBOOK FOR ARCHITECTS, ENGINEERS AND CONTRACTORS. see LAW

LEICHHARDT HISTORICAL JOURNAL; Annandale, Balmain, Glebe, Leichhardt, Lilyfield, Rozelle. see HISTORY — History Of Australasia And Other Areas

720 GW
LEONARDO ONLINE; architecture with new media. 1988. bi-m. DM.96 (students DM.69) (effective 1996). W E K A Baufachverlag GmbH, Berliner Allee 28 b-c, 86153 Augsburg, Germany. TEL 49-821-5041-0. FAX 49-821-5041257. URL http://www.interest.de/weka.bau. Ed. Heike Kappel. Pub. Dieter Kleber. adv. contact: Reinhard Mueller. bk.rev. circ. 19,200. (back issues avail.) **Indexed:** A Ind., Compumath. **Document type:** trade publication.
Formerly (until 1996): Leonardo (ISSN 0935-1108)

720 747 US ISSN 0191-541X
PN2091.E4
LIGHTING DIMENSIONS. 1977. 9/yr. $40 in U.S.; Canada $49; elsewhere $62.50. Lighting Dimensions International, 32 W. 18th St., New York, NY 10011-4612. TEL 212-299-2965. FAX 212-299-2084. (Subscr. to: Lighting Dimensions, P.O. Box 425 Mt. Morris, IL 61054) Ed. Denise Tilles. adv.; bk.rev.; film rev.; play rev.; charts; illus.; tr.lit. circ. 14,000. (also avail. in microfilm from UMI; back issues avail.; reprint service avail. from UMI) **Document type:** trade publication.
—SWETS; UMI; UnCover. **CCC.**
Description: For the lighting professional. Lighting design for stage and studio, architecture and interior design.

720 IT ISSN 0024-3817
LINEASTRUTTURA.* 1966. q. L.6000. Via Ferdinando Russo 29, Naples 80123, Italy. Ed. Vera Vitolo. ad bk.rev.; bibl.; charts; illus.

723 IT ISSN 1122-0805
LINGUAGGIO DELL'ARCHITETTURA ROMANA. 1987. irreg., no.2, 1991. price varies. Casa Editrice Leo S. Olschki, Casella Postale 66, 50100 Florence, Italy. TEL 39-55-6530684. FAX 39-55-6530214. E-mail celso@olschki.it. **Document type:** monographic series

720 572 FR ISSN 0769-3397
LITHIQUES. (Text in French; summaries in English, German) 1985. q. 260 F. (foreign 360 F.). Editions Creaphis, 145 rue de Rennes, 75006 Paris, France. TEL 42-22-06-79. Eds. Pierre Gaudin, Claire Reverchon. bk.rev. (back issues avail.)

720 DK ISSN 0108-4135
NA1208
LIVING ARCHITECTURE. 1983. a. DKK 450($78) for 4 issues. Living Architecture Magazine ApS, P.O. Box 2076, Bredgade 34, DK-1260 Copenhagen, Denmark. TEL 45-33-13-76-13. FAX 45-33-32-69-89. Ed. Vibe Udsen. R&P contact: Per Nagel. adv. contact: Helle Walsted. illus. circ. 45,000. (back issues avail.) **Document type:** trade publication.
Description: Features new and traditional Scandinavian furniture, design and architecture.

ARCHITECTURE

720 747 US ISSN 1072-6063
LOG HOMES ILLUSTRATED; a complete consumer guide. 1993. bi-m. $25 (foreign $35); newsstand price: $3.99. G C R Publishing Group, Inc., 1700 Broadway, 34th Fl., New York, NY 10019. TEL 212-541-7100. FAX 212-245-1241. (Subscr. to: Box 612, Mt. Morris, IL 61054) Ed. Roland Sweet; Pub. Jason Goodman. R&P contact: Sandy Kosherick. adv. contact: Laura LaPatin. circ. 110,492. **Document type:** consumer publication.
Description: Guide to log home plans, building techniques, product reviews and decorating ideas.

720 IT ISSN 1124-9064
NA9
LOTUS INTERNATIONAL; rivista trimestrale di architettura - quarterly architectural review. (Text in English, Italian) 1963. 4/yr. L.128000 (Europe L.185500; America L.208200) (effective 1996). Elemond S.p.A., Via D. Trentacoste 7, 20134 Milan, Italy. TEL 39-2-215631. FAX 39-2-26412586. Ed. Pierluigi Nicolin. **Indexed:** Art Ind., Arts & Hum.Cit.Ind., ASCA, Avery Ind.Archit.Per., Br.Tech.Ind., Curr.Cont., SSCI.
Formerly (until 1970): Lotus (ISSN 0076-101X)

MALAYSIA SOURCE BOOK FOR ARCHITECTS AND DESIGNERS (YEAR). see *BUSINESS AND ECONOMICS — Trade And Industrial Directories*

MARMI GRANITI PIETRE; rivista specializzata del settore marmifero. see *MINES AND MINING INDUSTRY*

MARMO IN. see *BUILDING AND CONSTRUCTION*

MARMOR. see *MINES AND MINING INDUSTRY*

792 US ISSN 0025-3928
MARQUEE (SPRINGFIELD). 1968. base vol. (plus q. updates) $40 (foreign $50) (effective 1997 & 1998). Theatre Historical Society of America, York Theatre Bldg., Ste. 200, 152 N. York Rd., Elmhurst, IL 60126-2806. TEL 630-782-1800. FAX 630-782-1802. Ed. Steven Levin; Pub. Richard Sklenar. R&P contact: Richard Sklenar. adv. contact: Richard Sklenar. bk.rev.; illus.; index, cum.index: 1970-1979; circ. 1,000 (paid). (also avail. in microform from UMI; back issues avail.) **Indexed:** Avery Ind.Archit.Per. **Document type:** academic/scholarly publication.
—UMI.
Description: Features theatre buildings.

MASKAN; arkhitektura i stroitel'stvo Uzbekistana, Kazakhstana, Azerbaidzana, Kyrgyzstana, Tadzjikistana, Turkmenistana. see *BUILDING AND CONSTRUCTION*

720 IT ISSN 1121-0516
MATERIA. 1989. 4/yr. L.36000 (foreign L.45000). Quarzo s.r.l., Via Gargola 4, 42030 Viano (RE), Italy. TEL 39-536-850404. FAX 39-536-855263. Ed. Graziano Manni. adv.: B&W page L.8000000, color page L.14000000. circ. 80,000.

720 352.7 GW ISSN 0176-3539
DER MAUERANKER. 1981. q. DM.18. Interessengemeinschaft Baupflege Nordfriesland e.V., Suederstr. 30, 25821 Bredstedt, Germany. TEL 04671-2081. FAX 04671-1333. Ed. Gerd Kuehnast. adv.; bk.rev. circ. 2,500. **Document type:** bulletin.
—CCC.
Description: Provides background information and practical tips for owners and lovers of old buildings.

DAS MAUERWERK. see *BUILDING AND CONSTRUCTION*

720 700 BE
MELANGES D'HISTOIRE DE L'ARCHITECTURE. 1973. irreg. price varies. Association des Diplomes Histoire Art et Archeologie, College Erasme, Place Blaise Pascal 1, 1348 Louvain-la-Neuve, Belgium. FAX 32-10-472579. E-mail: hackens@arka.ucl.ac.be. Ed. Tony Hackens. **Document type:** monographic series.

690 669 US ISSN 0885-5781
TH1
METAL ARCHITECTURE. 1985. m. $45 (effective 1997). Modern Trade Communications, 7450 Skokie Blvd., Skokie, IL 60077. TEL 847-674-2200. FAX 847-674-3676. Ed. Bob Fittro. R&P contact: Bob Fittro. adv. contact: John Garvey. circ. 31,700. **Document type:** trade publication.

720 IT ISSN 0394-6835
METAMORFOSI; quaderni di architettura. 1985. 3/yr. L.60000 (foreign L.90000). Studio Metamorph, Viale delle Milizie 18, 00192 Rome, Italy. TEL 06-3214695. Ed. Marcello Pazzaglini. adv.; bk.rev.

720 747 US ISSN 0279-4977
N6535.N5
METROPOLIS; the magazine of architecture and design. 1981. 10/yr. $28 (foreign $45; airmail $110) (effective 1997). Bellerophon Publications, Inc., 177 E. 87th St., New York, NY 10128. TEL 212-722-5050; 800-344-3046. FAX 212-427-1938. URL: http://www.metropolismag.com; http://www.interport.net/-metropol. Ed. Susan S. Szenasy; Pub. Horace Havemeyer, III. R&P contact: Amy Firlie. adv. contact: Christy Sagalyn. bk.rev.; circ. 47,000 (paid). **Indexed:** Access (1993-), Artbibl.Mod., Avery Ind.Archit.Per., DAAI, Search (1991-). **Document type:** consumer publication.
—BLDSC (5748.937500); UnCover.
Description: Covers trends and concepts in architecture and design, with emphasis on metropolitan areas. Includes articles on neighborhoods and (or) buildings of interest, and a calendar of events.

720 FR ISSN 0223-5633
METROPOLIS. 1979. 4/yr. 27 rue du Chateau d'Eau, 75010 Paris, France. TEL 42-40-61-87. FAX 42-40-06-20. Ed. Anne Huruguen. circ. 5,000.

724 US
METROPOLITAN HISTORIC STRUCTURES ASSOCIATION. NEWS. 1976. 4/yr. $5. Metropolitan Historic Structures Association, Dyckman House Museum, 4881 Broadway, New York, NY 10034. Ed. Jane Sullivan Crowley. adv.; bk.rev. circ. 2,000.

720 690 US
MILLION DOLLAR PROJECT PLANNED LIST.* 1965. m. $150 per no. Live Leads Corp., 35 W. 76th St., 4, New York, NY 10023-1521. Ed. Thomas Szabo. circ. 100. (back issues avail.)

720 TU ISSN 1300-4212
MIMARLIK DERGISI. 1963. bi-m. $50. (T M M O B Mimarlar Odasi) Yapi Endustri Merkezi, Cumhuriyet Cad. 329, Harbiya 80230 Istanbul, Ankara, Turkey. TEL 90-212-2302919. FAX 90-212-2484814. Ed. Asli Ozbay; Pub. Semih Eryildiz. adv. contact: Mrs. Zehra Oztok Ebcim. bk.rev.; illus.; cum.index: 1963-1977, 1979-1982, 1983-1987. circ. 11,000. (back issues avail.) **Document type:** trade publication.
Description: News of current architectural issues in Turkey and the world, including planning, conservation and environmental issues.

720 US
MISSISSIPPI. STATE BOARD OF ARCHITECTURE. ANNUAL REPORT. 1935. a. 10. Board of Architecture, 239 N. Lamar St., Ste. 502, Jackson, MS 39201-1311. TEL 601-359-6020. FAX 601-359-6159.

MISSISSIPPI HISTORY NEWSLETTER. see *HISTORY — History Of North And South America*

720 690 GW
MITGLIEDERINFORMATION. bi-m. Bund Deutscher Baumeister Architekten und Ingenieure Landesverband Hessen, Am Waldacker 8, 60388 Frankfurt, Germany. TEL 06109-3103133. TELEX 4185923.

690 721 AT
MODERN BUILDING ARCHITECTURE AND ENGINEERING IN AUSTRALIA.* 1967. bi-m. J. Carroll and Co., 305 Queen St., Ste. 5, 2nd Fl., Campbelltown, N.S.W 2650, Australia. Ed. David Clifton. adv.; bk.rev. circ. 6,000.

THE MODERNIST. see *ART*

720 US ISSN 0191-4022
NA1
MODULUS. 1979. irreg. (approx a.), no.23, 1996. $25. University of Virginia, School of Architecture, Campbell Hall, Charlottesville, VA 22903. TEL 804-892-4567. E-mail: modulus@palladio.virginia.edu. (Dist. by: Princeton Architectural Press, 37 E. Seventh St., New York, NY 10003. TEL 212-995-9620. FAX 212-995-9454) Ed. Jessie Chapman. illus. **Document type:** academic/scholarly publication.

720 FR ISSN 0998-4194
MONITEUR ARCHITECTURE - A M C. 1967. 10/yr. 510 F. (foreign 610 F.). Groupe Moniteur, 17 rue d'Uzes, 75002 Paris, France. FAX 33-1-42333819. Ed. Elisabeth Allain-Dupre. bk.rev.; bibl.; illus. circ. 15,000. **Indexed:** Archit.Per.Ind., Avery Ind.Archit.Per., Br.Tech.Ind., DAAI.
—BLDSC (5908.609000); SWETS.
Former titles: A M C (ISSN 0336-1675) & Architecture Mouvement Continuite (ISSN 0336-1667)

720.92 NE
MONOGRAFIEEN VAN NEDERLANDSE ARCHITECTEN/MONOGRAPHS OF DUTCH ARCHITECTS. (Text in Dutch, English) vol.8, 1994. irreg., vol.10, 1996. Uitgeverij 010, Watertorenweg 180, 3063 HA Rotterdam, Netherlands. TEL 31-10-4333509. FAX 31-10-4529825. **Document type:** monographic series.

MONTEREY MUSEUM OF ART NEWS. see *ART*

722.6 930 NE ISSN 0169-8850
MONUMENTA GRAECA ET ROMANA. (Text in English) 1963. irreg., vol.8, 1995. price varies. E.J. Brill, P.O. Box 9000, 2300 PA Leiden, Netherlands. TEL 31-71-5353500. FAX 31-71-5317532. TELEX 39296 BRILL NL. E-mail: ejbrill@brill.nl. (In N. America: E.J. Brill, 24 Hudson St., Kinderhook, NY 12106. TEL 800-962-4406. FAX 518-758-1959) Ed. H. F. Mussche. R&P contact: Elizabeth Vennekamp. illus. (back issues avail.) **Document type:** monographic series.
Description: Scholarly monographs on topics in Greek and Roman architecture and art, particularly sculpture.
Refereed Serial

720 FR ISSN 0242-830X
N8997
MONUMENTS HISTORIQUES. 1936. bi-m. 375 F. Caisse Nationale des Monuments Historiques et des Sites, 62 rue Saint-Antoine, 75004 Paris, France. TEL 44-61-21-81. FAX 44-61-20-87. Ed. Vincent Bouvet. adv.; bk.rev.; bibl.; illus.; index. circ. 10,000. **Indexed:** Arts & Hum.Cit.Ind., ASCA, Avery Ind.Archit.Per., Br.Tech.Ind., Curr.Cont., SSCI.
—SWETS.
Former titles (until 1980): M.H. Monuments Historiques (ISSN 0153-3673); (until 1977): Monuments Historiques de la France (ISSN 0027-0768)

720 HU ISSN 0541-2439
MUEMLEKVEDELEM. 1956. q. $27. (Magyar Epitomuveszek Szovetsege, Muemleki Bizottsag) Hirlapkiado Vallalat, Blaha Lujza ter 3, 1959 Budapest 8, Hungary. TEL 1-382-399. TELEX 22-5554. (Subscr. to: Kultura, P.O.B. 149, 1389 Budapest, Hungary) (Co-sponsor: Orszagos Muemleki Felugyeloseg) Ed. Laszlo Gero. bk.rev.; abstr.; bibl.; illus.; index. circ. 1,700. **Indexed:** Art & Archaeol.Tech.Abstr., Hung.Build.Bull., Numis.Lit.

720 625 PL ISSN 0239-6866
MURATOR; domy, wnetrza , ogrody. 1983. m. $80. Wydawnictwo Murator, Ul. Al. Wyzwolenia 6 m.43, 00-570 Warsaw, Poland. TEL 48-2-6251742. FAX 48-2-6251814. Ed. Grazyna Rudolf; Pub. Zygmunt Stepinski. adv.; page $2875; adv. contact: Ewa Frankowska-Bielinska. circ. 130,000. **Indexed:** AgroLibrex.

MUSEES. see *MUSEUMS AND ART GALLERIES*

720 693 SP ISSN 1135-3384
▼**N A: NUEVA ARCHITECTURA CON ARCILLA COCIDA.** 1995. s-a. L.39000. Faenza Editrice Iberica S.L., Calle S. Vicente 62, 12001 Castellon de la Plana, Spain. TEL 34-64-216570. FAX 34-64-241010. Ed. Benjamin Caervera Canceller. adv.: color page L.2800000. circ. 14,370.

721 CC ISSN 1000-0232
NANFANG JIANZHU/SOUTH-CHINA ARCHITECTURE. (Text in Chinese) 1981. q. Y10 (effective 1994). Guangdong Sheng Tumu Jianzhu Xuehui - Guangdong Association of Architecture, No. 97, Liuhua Road, Guangzhou, Guangdong 510010, People's Republic of China. TEL 6676522. FAX 6677463. Ed. Zheng Zhenhong. adv. contact: Tian Yong. circ. 5,000. **Document type:** academic/scholarly publication.
Description: Discusses construction projects and economic theories.

ARCHITECTURE

720 US ISSN 1054-6855
E159
NATIONAL TRUST FOR HISTORIC PRESERVATION IN THE UNITED STATES. INFORMATION SERIES. 1976. irreg. $6 per no. National Trust for Historic Preservation, 1785 Massachusetts Ave., N.W., Washington, DC 20036. TEL 202-588-6286. (back issues avail.)
Formerly: National Trust for Historic Preservation. Information (ISSN 0272-6556)
Description: Provides concise information on basic and frequently used preservation techniques and issues.

NATIONAL TRUST NEWS. see HISTORY — History Of Australasia And Other Areas

712 GW ISSN 0940-6808
QH77.G3
NATURSCHUTZ UND LANDSCHAFTSPLANUNG. (Text in German; summaries in English and German) 1969. m. DM.159.60. Verlag Eugen Ulmer GmbH, Wollgrasweg 41, 70599 Stuttgart, Germany. TEL 49-711-4507-0. FAX 49-711-4507-120. (Subscr. to: Postfach 700561, 70574 Stuttgart, Germany) Ed. E. Jedicke. R&P contact: G. Friedrich. circ. 3,000. **Indexed:** Ecol.Abstr., Excerp.Med., IBR, Key Word Ind.Wildl.Res., World Agri.Econ.& Rural Sociol.Abstr. **Document type:** trade publication.
—BLDSC (6048.700000). CCC.
Former titles: Landschaft und Stadt (ISSN 0023-8058); Beitraege zur Landespflege.

725 NE
NETHERLANDS. RIJKSDIENST VOOR DE MONUMENTENZORG. JAARVERSLAG. 1974. a. Rijksdienst voor de Monumentenzorg, Postbus 1001, 3700 BA Zeist, Netherlands. TEL 31-30-6983211. FAX 31-30-6916189. Ed. M.v.d. Sluys. illus. circ. 3,000. **Document type:** government publication.

725 NE ISSN 0929-3035
NETHERLANDS. RIJKSDIENST VOOR DE MONUMENTENZORG. NIEUWSBRIEF. 1988. 6/yr. free. Rijksdienst voor de Monumentenzorg, Postbus 1001, 3700 BA Zeist, Netherlands. TEL 31-30-6983211. FAX 31-30-6916189. Ed. Olga Faber. bibl.; illus. (back issues avail.) **Document type:** government publication, newsletter.
Formerly (until 1993): R D M Z Nieuwsbrief (ISSN 0925-8183)
Description: Discusses cultural heritage, preservation and conservation issues.

NETHERLANDS INSTITUTE AT ATHENS. PUBLICATIONS. see ARCHAEOLOGY

720 UK ISSN 0262-558X
N6768
NEW ARCADIAN JOURNAL. (Each issue has distinctive title) 1981. a. £25 (foreign £30) (effective 1997). New Arcadian Press, 13 Graham Grove, Burley, Leeds LS4 2NF, England. TEL 44-113-2304608. FAX 44-1274-753236. Ed. Patrick Eyres. R&P contact: Patrick Eyres. illus. circ. 300. (back issues avail.) **Document type:** academic/scholarly publication.
Description: Explores the cultural politics of the 18th century English landscape garden and garden works by contemporary artists.
Refereed Serial

721 069 UK ISSN 0964-8011
NEW CRYSTAL PALACE MATTERS. 1980. s-a. £8 (foreign £15); newsstand price: £2.25. Crystal Palace Foundation, Crystal Palace Museum, Anerley Hill, London SE19 2BA, England. TEL 44-181-778-2173. Eds. Helen & Trevor Enefer. adv. contact: D. Pritchard. bk.rev.; charts; illus.; stat.; circ. 700 (paid). (back issues avail.) **Document type:** academic/scholarly publication.
Formerly (until 1991): Crystal Palace Matters (ISSN 0144-6401)
Description: Covers the history of Crystal Palace, social and local history, and architecture.

974.9 US
NEW JERSEY AND NATIONAL REGISTERS OF HISTORIC PLACES. 1977. biennial. $15. Department of Environmental Protection, Division of Parks and Forestry, New Jersey Historic Preservation Office, CN 404, Trenton, NJ 08625. TEL 609-292-2023. Ed. Robert W. Craig. circ. 2,000. **Document type:** government publication.
Formerly: State and National Registers of Historic Places.
Description: Lists names and addresses of properties registered as historic places and places found eligible by the State Historic Perservation Officer or determined eligible by the National Park Service.

720 US ISSN 0734-4481
NEW ORLEANS PRESERVATION IN PRINT. 1975. m. $15. Preservation Resource Center, 604 Julia St., New Orleans, LA 70130. TEL 504-581-7032. FAX 504-522-9275. Ed. Julie McCollom. adv.; bk.rev.; charts; illus. circ. 12,000. (tabloid format; back issues avail.)
Formerly: Preservation Press.

NEW STEEL CONSTRUCTION. see BUILDING AND CONSTRUCTION

720 BE
NIEUW - NEUF; architecture and design. (Supplement avail.) (Text in Dutch, French) 1965. bi-m. 2850 BEF. Socorema s.c.r.l., Rue du Merlo, 28, B-1180 Brussels, Belgium. TEL 02-376-62-28. FAX 02-376-12-80. Ed. J. Laffineur. adv.; bk.rev.; bibl.; charts; illus.; tr.lit. circ. 10,000.
Formerly: Neuf.

720 JA ISSN 1340-4210
NIHON KENCHIKU GAKKAI KEIKAKU-KEI RONBUNSHU/JOURNAL OF ARCHITECTURE, PLANNING AND ENVIRONMENTAL ENGINEERING. (Text in English, Japanese) 1936. m. 33600 Yen to non-members; members 26400 Yen (includes Nihon Kenchiku Gakkai Kozo-Kei Ronbunshu). Nihon Kenchiku Gakkai - Architectural Institute of Japan, 26-20, Shiba 5-chome, Minato-ku, Tokyo 108, Japan. TEL 81-3-3456-2051. FAX 81-3-3456-2058. bibl. **Indexed:** Abstr.J.Earthq.Eng., Concr.Abstr. **Document type:** academic/scholarly publication.
—BLDSC (4947.200600); CISTI; Linda Hall.
Supersedes (in 1994): Nihon Kenchiku Gakkai Keikaku-Kei Ronbun Hokokushu (ISSN 0910-8017); Supersedes in part (in 1985): Nihon Kenchiku Gakkai Ronbun Hokokushu (ISSN 0387-1185); Which was formerly (until 1956): Nihon Kenchiku Gakkai Ronbunshu (ISSN 0387-1177)

720 JA ISSN 1340-4202
NIHON KENCHIKU GAKKAI KOZO-KEI RONBUNSHU/JOURNAL OF STRUCTURAL AND CONSTRUCTION ENGINEERING. (Text in English, Japanese) 1936. m. 33600 Yen for non-members; members 26400 Yen (includes Nihon Kenchiku Gakkai Keikaku-Kei Ronbunshu). Nihon Kenchiku Gakkai - Architectural Institute of Japan, 26-20, Shiba 5-chome, Minato-ku, Tokyo 108, Japan. TEL 81-3-3456-2051. FAX 81-3-3456-2058. **Indexed:** C.R.I.Abstr., C.R.I.Curr.Cont.
—CISTI; Linda Hall.
Supersedes (in 1994): Nihon Kenchiku Gakkai Kozo-Kei Ronbun Hokokushu (ISSN 0910-8025); Supersedes in part (in 1985): Nihon Kenchiku Gakkai Ronbun Hokokushu (ISSN 0387-1185); Which was formerly (until 1956): Nihon Kenchiku Gakkai Ronbunshu (ISSN 0387-1177)

720 JA ISSN 0385-0870
NIKKEI ARCHITECTURE. (Text in Japanese) 1976. fortn. 20800 Yen. Nikkei Business Publications, Inc. (Subsidiary of: Nihon Keizai Shimbun, Inc.), 2-7-6, Hirakawa-cho, Chiyoda-ku, Tokyo 102, Japan. TEL 81-3-5210-8502. FAX 81-3-5210-8034. URL: http://www.nikkeibp.co.jp/. Ed. Shoji Tanabe; Pub. Shoji Tanabe. adv.; B&W page 671000 Yen, color page 973000 Yen; trim 208 x 280; adv. contact: Mitsuharu Hanagami. circ. 59,890. **Document type:** trade publication.
Description: Covers design and planning activities, as well as technological, social, economic, and legal developments relating to architecture.

720 US
▼**NO-SPACE.** 1997. q. E-mail: eknutzen@ucsd.edu; URL: http://www.geocities.com/soho/lofts/7621. Ed. Erik Knutzen. **Document type:** newsletter.
●Available only online.
Description: Theory of life in the suburbs with a focus on southern California.

720 SW ISSN 1102-5824
NORDISK ARKITEKTURFORSKNING/NORDIC JOURNAL OF ARCHITECTURAL RESEARCH. (Text in Danish, English, Norwegian, Swedish) 1987. q. SEK 290 to individuals; institutions SEK 500; students SEK 200 (effective through 1998). Nordisk Foerening foer Arkitekturforskning, Chalmers University of Technology, Dept. of Architecture, S-412 96 Goeteborg, Sweden. TEL 46-31-772-24-56. FAX 46-31-772-24-61. E-mail: redvall@arch.chalmers.se. Ed. Jerker Lundequist. adv. contact: Charistina Redvall. bk.rev. **Document type:** academic/scholarly publication.
—BLDSC (6117.947500).
Formerly (until 1992): Tidskrift foer Arkitekturforskning (ISSN 0284-2998)
Description: Acts as a forum for architectural theory, architecture criticism and debate on architecture and architectural research problems and methods in the Nordic countries.

720 NO ISSN 0332-6578
NORSKE ARKITEKTKONKURRANSER. Issued with: Arkitektnytt (ISSN 0004-1998) 1953. irreg. Norske Arkitekters Landsforbund - National Association of Norwegian Architects, Josefinesgt. 34, N-0351 Oslo, Norway. TEL 47-22-60-22-90. FAX 47-22-69-59-48. Ed. Kristin Ytreberg. illus.; index.

720 US ISSN 1045-3253
NORTH CAROLINA ARCHITECTURE. 1964. q. $30. American Institute of Architects, North Carolina Chapter, 115 W. Morgan St., Raleigh, NC 27601-1335. TEL 919-833-6656. Ed. John Roth. adv. circ. 3,500. **Indexed:** Avery Ind.Archit.Per. **Document type:** trade publication.
Former titles (until 1987): North Carolina Architect (ISSN 0029-2427); (until 1978): N C Architect (ISSN 0886-0378); (until 1977): North Carolina Architect (ISSN 0886-0386); Southern Architect.

720 US ISSN 0078-1444
N11
NORTH CAROLINA STATE UNIVERSITY. SCHOOL OF DESIGN. (STUDENT PUBLICATION MAGAZINE). 1951. irreg., vol.29, 1986. price varies. North Carolina State University, School of Design, c/o John Thomas Regan, Dean, Raleigh, NC 27695-7701. TEL 919-737-2202. adv.; bk.rev. circ. 1,000. **Indexed:** Avery Ind.Archit.Per., Br.Tech.Ind.

720 CN ISSN 0834-7816
NOVA SCOTIA ASSOCIATION OF ARCHITECTS. NEWSLETTER. m. membership. Nova Scotia Association of Architects, 1361 Barrington St., Halifax, NS B3J 1Y9, Canada. TEL 902-423-7607. FAX 902-425-7024. **Document type:** newsletter.

O P D RESTAURO. (Opificio delle Pietre Dure) see ART

720 NE ISSN 0169-6238
OASE; tijdschrift voor architectuur. 1985. q. fl.60. (Stichting Oase) Uitgeverij S U N, Postbus 1609, 6501 BP Nijmegen, Netherlands. TEL 31-24-3221700. FAX 31-24-3235493. adv. contact: Lucy Klaassen. illus. circ. 1,000. (back issues avail.) **Document type:** academic/scholarly publication.
Supersedes (1981-1985): O - Ontwerp, Onderzoek, Onderwijs (ISSN 0167-8620)

720 BL ISSN 0104-0308
NA850
OCULUM; revista de arquitectura, arte e cultura. 1985. s-a. Pontificia Universidade Catolica de Campinas, Faculdade de Arquitectura e Urbanismo, Campus 1 Rodovia D. Pedro I, km 136, 13089-500 Campina SP, Brazil. TEL 0192-52-0899. FAX 0192-55-0192. Ed. Abilio Guerra. illus. circ. 2,000.

ARCHITECTURE

720   US   ISSN 0885-5927
OCULUS. vol.58, 1996. m. $40 (effective 1996). American Institute of Architects, New York Chapter, 200 Lexington Ave., New York, NY 10016. TEL 212-683-0023. Ed. Jayne Merkel. illus. **Indexed:** Avery Ind.Archit.Per. **Document type:** newsletter.
    Description: Covers architecture in New York: what's being designed, built, published and discussed in the city, including international events and member information.

OESTERREICHISCHE INGENIEUR UND ARCHITEKTEN ZEITSCHRIFT. see *ENGINEERING*

OLD-HOUSE JOURNAL. see *BUILDING AND CONSTRUCTION*

OLD-HOUSE JOURNAL RESTORATION DIRECTORY. see *BUILDING AND CONSTRUCTION*

OLD MILL NEWS. see *HISTORY — History Of North And South America*

720   IE
▼**ONSITE IRELAND.** 1997. m. Archeire, 54 SCR Portobello, Dublin 8, Ireland. TEL 353-1-676-8996. FAX 353-1-661-3932. E-mail: pclerkin@connect.ie; URL: http://www.archeire.com/onsite/. Eds. Paul Clerkin, Beth McLendon.
● Available online only.
    Description: Covers Irish architecture: past, present and future.

OP CIT; selezione della critica d'arte contemporanea. see *ART*

OPEN HOUSE INTERNATIONAL; the journal of an association of institutes and individuals concerned with housing, design and development in the built environment. see *HOUSING AND URBAN PLANNING*

ORDINE DEGLI INGEGNERI DELLA PROVINCIA DI PALERMO. BOLLETTINO. see *BUILDING AND CONSTRUCTION*

720   HU
ORSZAGOS MUEMLEKI HIVATAL. KIADVANYOK. (Text in Hungarian; summaries in German) 1960. irreg., no.8, 1977. price varies. (Orszagos Muemlekvedelmi Bizottsag) Akademiai Kiado, Publishing House of the Hungarian Academy of Sciences, P.O. Box 245, H-1519 Budapest, Hungary. TEL 181-2134. FAX 166-6466. TELEX 22-6228 AKNYO H.
    Formerly: Orszagos Muemleki Felugyeloseg. Kiadanyok (ISSN 0073-4063)

OXONIENSIA. see *ARCHAEOLOGY*

720 747   NE
P I. (Projekt & Interieur); vakblad voor projektinrichting in Nederland en Belgie. (Text in Dutch) 1990. 6/yr. fl.103.60 (1800 BEF) (foreign fl.143). Uitgeverij Triade Benelux BV, Postbus 15341, 1001 MH Amsterdam, Netherlands. TEL 31-20-6624201. FAX 31-20-4004106. E-mail: pi@iz.nl; URL: http://www.iz.nl/PI. Ed. Olga Smalhout-Holst; Pub. Monica Kaltenschnee. R&P contact: Monica Kaltenschnee. adv.: B&W page fl.3610, color page fl.5610; trim 240 x 290; adv. contact: Peter Huiberts. bk.rev.; illus. circ. 9,965. **Document type:** trade publication.
    Description: Covers all aspects of architectural and interior design.

721   US
▶**P T I NEWSLETTER.** 1976. q. membership only. Post-Tensioning Institute, 1717 W. Northern Ave., Ste. 114, Phoenix, AZ 85021. TEL 602-870-7540. FAX 602-870-7541. Ed. Gerald J. McGuire. circ. 1,200 (controlled). (back issues avail.) **Document type:** newsletter.
    Description: Disseminates information on post-tensioned design and construction technology and developments in the post-tensioning industry. Audience is post-tensioning materials fabricators and manufacturers of prestressing materials in the US, Canada, Mexico and other countries.

720 747   CC
PACE INTERIOR ARCHITECTURE. (Editions in Chinese, English) 1988. m. Pace Publishing Ltd., Rm. 607-8, 6-F, Block B, Ming Pao Ind. Ctr., 18 Ka Yip St., Chaiwan, Hong Kong, People's Republic of China. TEL 852-2897-1688. FAX 852-2897-2888. Ed. Raka Dewan; Pub. George Lam. R&P contact: Amy Liu. adv.: color page HK.$10300; trim 213 x 285; adv. contact: Dawn Wong. circ. 44,000 (30,000 Chinese ed., 14,000 English ed.). **Document type:** trade publication.
    Description: Covers commercial interior and architectural design.

720   IT   ISSN 0031-0379
NA4
PALLADIO; * revista di storia dell'architettura e restauro. 1937; N.S. 1951-1977; resumed 1978-1980; N.S. June 1988. bi-m. De Luca Editore, Via S. Anna 16, 00186 Rome, Italy. TEL 39-6-6868678. FAX 39-6-6864430. bk.rev.; bibl.; charts; illus.; index. **Indexed:** Archit.Per.Ind., Art Ind., RILA.
—KR SourceOne; SWETS.

720   US
PAMPHLET ARCHITECTURE. 1977. irreg., no.19, 1996. $11.95 per no. Princeton Architectural Press, 37 E. Seventh St., New York, NY 10003. TEL 212-995-9620. FAX 212-995-9454. E-mail: sales@pap.designsys.com; URL: http://www.designsys.com/pap. (Dist. by: Chronicle Books, 275 Fifth St., San Francisco, CA 94103. TEL 800-722-6657) illus. (back issues avail.) **Document type:** monographic series.
    Description: Publishes the work of younger American architects.

PAMYATNIKI OTECHESTVA. see *HISTORY — History Of Europe*

720 711   IT   ISSN 0031-1731
PARAMETRO; international review of architecture and town planning. (Text in English, Italian; summaries in English, French, German, Spanish) 1971. 6/yr. Lit.162000 in Europe; Oceania Lit.242000; elsewhere Lit.202000 (effective 1997). Gruppo Editoriale Faenza Editrice S.p.A., Via Pier. de Crescenzi, 44, 48018 Faenza, Italy. TEL 39-546-663488. FAX 39-546-660440. E-mail: gefe.vendita@uno.dinamica.it; gefe.info@uno.dinamica.it. Eds. Giorgio Trebbi, Glauco Gresleri. adv.: B&W page Lit.2690000, color page Lit.3350000; adv. contact: Elvio Neri. circ. 5,000. (back issues avail.) **Indexed:** Art & Archaeol.Tech.Abstr., Avery Ind.Archit.Per., Br.Tech.Ind.
—BLDSC (6404.840000).

PARIS PROJET; amenagement urbanisme avenir. see *HOUSING AND URBAN PLANNING*

725   SZ   ISSN 1420-7095
▼**PATRIMOINE ET ARCHITECTURE.** 1996. s-a. 30 SFr. to individuals; institutions 40 SFr. (effective 1997). (Republique et Canton de Geneve, Departement des Travaux Publics et de l'Energie) Editions Medecine et Hygiene, Case Postale 456, CH-1211 Geneva 4, Switzerland. TEL 41-22-7029311. FAX 41-22-7029355. E-mail: abonnements@medecinehygiene.ch. **Document type:** academic/scholarly publication.

712 635   FR   ISSN 0395-2916
PAYSAGE ACTUALITES. 1975. 10/yr. 142 rue d'Aguesseau, 92100 Boulogne, France. TEL 46-03-15-54. FAX 46-03-97-67. Ed. Eric Burie. circ. 12,500.

720   US   ISSN 1062-8649
NA730.P4
PENNSYLVANIA ARCHITECT. q. T S G Publishing, 3090 W. Liberty Ave., Pittsburgh, PA 15216-2456. TEL 412-344-3360. FAX 412-344-3364. Ed. John A. Fatula. adv. contact: Gary Winterhalter. circ. 5,000. **Document type:** trade publication.

720   AT   ISSN 0158-7374
PERIOD BUILDING RESTORATION TRADES & SUPPLIERS DIRECTORY. 1980. a. Aus.$5.95. Mount Eagle Publications, P.O. Box 84, Heidelberg, Vic. 3084, Australia. TEL 61-3-94593911. FAX 61-3-94575249. Ed. Kennith Lloyd Jones. adv. circ. 10,000. **Document type:** directory.

724 747   UK
PERIOD HOUSE. 1989-1996. m. £20($45); newsstand price: £2.50. Essential Publishing Ltd., Topsail House, Mistley Quay, Manningtree, Essex CO11 1HD, England. TEL 44-1206-394446. (Dist. by: Comag, Tavistock Rd., W. Drayton, Middx. UB7 7QE, England. TEL 44-1895-444055. FAX 44-1895-433602; Subscr. to: P.O. Box 648, Harrow, Middx. HA1 2NW, England. TEL 44-181-863-4040) Ed. Laura Goodhart. adv.: B&W page £995, color page £1295; trim 222 x 298; adv. contact: Victoria Mottram. index; circ. 35,000 (paid). (back issues avail.) **Document type:** consumer publication.
    Former titles: Period House and Its Garden (ISSN 0966-1530); (until 1992): Old House Journal (ISSN 0961-5962)
    Description: Contains practical, technical, style and gardening features to help the period home owner get the most from their house and garden.

720 700   CI   ISSN 0553-6707
N6
PERISTIL. (Text in Croatian, English; summaries in English, German, Italian) 1954. a. Drustvo Povjesnicara Umjetnosti SR Hrvatske, Zrinski trg 11, 41000 Zagreb, Croatia. TEL 041-433-504.

THE PERMACULTURE ACTIVIST. see *AGRICULTURE*

720 690 747   UK   ISSN 0967-2176
PERSPECTIVE. 1992. bi-m. £15 (outside EC £18) (effective 1996). (Royal Society of Ulster Architects) Adleader Publications, Marlborough House, 348 Lisburn Rd., Belfast BT9 6GH. TEL 44-1232-661666. FAX 44-1232-681888. E-mail: 100654.1067@compuserve.com. Ed. Linda Brooks. R&P contact: Linda Brooks. adv. contact: Lorraine Gill. index. circ. 2,000. (back issues avail.) **Document type:** consumer publication.
    Description: Reviews recent Northern Ireland architecture. Contains news and views of importance and interest to architects and other design professionals, seeking to promote an appreciation of Northern Ireland architecture among the public.

720 690   PH   ISSN 0031-7470
TA1
PHILIPPINE ARCHITECTURE, ENGINEERING & CONSTRUCTION RECORD. (Text in English) 1953. m. P A E N C O R, Inc., 154 Araneta Ave., P.O. Box 1295, Quezon City, Philippines. TEL 2-7122239. Ed. Placido O. Urbanes Jr. adv. contact: Ambrosio Racho. charts; illus.

PICTURE HOUSE. see *MOTION PICTURES*

720 700   XV   ISSN 1318-007X
NA958
PIRANESI; 1st Middle-European architectural magazine for the culture of environment. (Text in English, German, Italian, Slovenian) 1992. s-a. DM.48. Piranesi Ltd., Bogisiceva 11, 61000 Ljubljana, Slovenia. TEL 386-61-223-039. FAX 386-61-221-226. (Dist. by: Idea Books Amsterdam, Nieuwe Herengracht 11, NL 1011 RK Amsterdam, The Netherlands) Eds. Vojteh Ravnikar, Tomaz Brate. adv.; bk.rev.; illus. circ. 2,000. **Document type:** academic/scholarly publication, monographic series.
    Description: Aims to discuss all specific features of architectural production in Middle Europe.

720 711.4   US   ISSN 1062-8657
PLACE. 1989. q. $10. American Institute of Architects, Michigan Chapter, 553 E. Jefferson St., Detroit, MI 48226. TEL 313-965-4100. Ed. Timothy Casai. adv.
    Description: Focuses on all members of the building team: the clients, architects, contractors, and developers who influence Michigan's built environment.

ARCHITECTURE

700 352.7 US ISSN 0731-0455
NA2542.35
PLACES. 1983. q. $50 (Canada $60; elsewhere $70) (effective 1997). (University of California at Berkeley, Center for Environmental Design, Pratt Institute) Design History Foundation, 110 Higgins Hall, Pratt Institute, 200 Willoughby Ave., Brooklyn, NY 11205. TEL 718-399-6090. FAX 718-399-6090. E-mail: placepratt@aol.com. (Dist. by: Eastern News, 250 W. 55th St., New York, NY 10019) Ed. Donlyn Lyndon; Pub. James F. Fulton. R&P contact: Todd W. Bressi. adv.: B&W page $1000; adv. contact: Todd W. Bressi. bk.rev.; illus. circ. 3,800. (back issues avail.; reprint service avail. from UMI) **Indexed:** Art Ind., Arts & Hum.Cit.Ind., Avery Ind.Archit.Per., Curr.Cont., DAAI, Gard.Lit. (1992-), Geo.Abstr. **Document type:** academic/scholarly publication.
—BLDSC (6506.906000); KR SourceOne; SWETS; UMI; UnCover. **CCC.**
  Description: Provides an alternative to both commercial and theoretical architecture and planning-design magazines, covering buildings, landscapes, public art, and more.

720 IE ISSN 0376-7302
PLAN. 1969. 12/yr. $50. 8-9 Sandyford Office Park, Sandyford, Dublin 18, Ireland. TEL 01-2958115. FAX 01-2959350. Ed. Emer Hughes. adv. circ. 2,778. **Indexed:** Archit.Per.Ind., Br.Tech.Ind.

720 AU
PLANEN - BAUEN - WOHNEN. bi-m. Linzerstr. 261, A-1140 Vienna, Austria. TEL 01-945288. Ed. Rudolf Tiffinger. circ. 8,000.

720 SZ
PLANEN UND BAUEN. 1968. m. 105 SFr. A N A G Annoncen und Verlags AG, Winzerstr. 112, Postfach 132, CH-8049 Zurich, Switzerland. TEL 41-1-3413080. FAX 41-1-3411811. adv. circ. 6,000. **Document type:** trade publication.

720 690 SA ISSN 0377-2780
TH119.S66
PLANNING. 1972. bi-m. R.189 (effective 1997). Avonwold Publishing Co. (Pty) Ltd., Avonwold House, 24 Baker St., Rosebank, Johannesburg 2196, South Africa. TEL 27-11-788-1610. FAX 27-11-880-2732. (Subscr. to: P.O. Box 52068, Saxonwold 2132, South Africa) Ed. C. Buchanan. circ. 3,992. (back issues avail.) **Indexed:** Br.Tech.Ind., Geo.Abstr., Ind.S.A.Per. **Document type:** trade publication.
  Description: Features architecture projects, property developments, and professional news of interest to architects in South Africa.

712 UK ISSN 0959-4361
PLANT USER. (Supplement to: Landscape Design) 1990. 2/yr. free with subscr. to Landscape Design. Landscape Design Trust, 13A West St., Reigate, Surrey RH2 9BL, England. TEL 44-1737-223144. FAX 44-1737-224206. adv. contact: Robert Ellis. **Document type:** bulletin.
—BLDSC (6523.670000).

720 IO ISSN 0126-0774
POLA. 1975. bi-m. Rps.750 per no. Yayasan Pola, Ruang 20, Departemen Arsitektur Institut Teknologi Bandung, Jalan Ganesha 10, Bandung, Indonesia. Ed. Agus Basuki. adv.; bk.rev. circ. 12,500.

720 PL ISSN 0518-3138
POLITECHNIKA GDANSKA. ZESZYTY NAUKOWE. ARCHITEKTURA. (Text in English, French, German, Polish; summaries in Russian and one West-European language) 1958. irreg. price varies. Politechnika Gdanska, Ul. G. Narutowicza 11-12, 80-952 Gdansk 6, Poland. (Dist. by: Osrodek Rozpowszechniania Wydawnictw Naukowych PAN, Palac Kultury i Nauki, 00-901 Warsaw, Poland) bibl.; charts; illus. **Document type:** academic/scholarly publication.
—Linda Hall.
  Description: Research work on town planning, ship and naval architecture and building technology.

720 PL
POLITECHNIKA KRAKOWSKA. MONOGRAFIE. SERIA: ARCHITEKTURA. (Subseries of: Politechnika Krakowska. Monografie (ISSN 0860-097X)) (Text in Polish; summaries in English, French, German, Russian) 1985. irreg. price varies. Politechnika Krakowska, Ul. Warszawska 24, 31-155 Krakow, Poland. TEL 48-12-374289. FAX 48-12-335773. TELEX 322468 PK PL. E-mail: Marcinek@biblos.pk.edu.pl. bibl.; charts; illus. circ. 200. **Document type:** academic/scholarly publication, monographic series.

720 PL ISSN 0137-1371
POLITECHNIKA KRAKOWSKA. ZESZYTY NAUKOWE. ARCHITEKTURA. (Text in Polish; summaries in English, French, German, Russian) 1956. irreg. price varies. Politechnika Krakowska, Ul. Warszawska 24, 31-155 Krakow, Poland. TEL 48-12-374289. FAX 48-12-335773. TELEX 322468 PK PL. E-mail: Marcinek@biblos.pk.edu.pl. bibl.; charts; illus. circ. 200. **Document type:** academic/scholarly publication.

720 PL ISSN 0860-0074
POLITECHNIKA SLASKA. ZESZYTY NAUKOWE. ARCHITEKTURA. 1989. irreg. Politechnika Slaska, Katowicka 7, 44-100 Gliwice, Poland. FAX 371655. TELEX 036304. (Dist. by: Ars Polona, Krakowskie Przedmiescie 7, 00-068 Warsaw, Poland) Ed. Andrzej Niezabitowski. circ. 205.

720 700 PL ISSN 0137-6233
POLITECHNIKA WROCLAWSKA. INSTYTUT ARCHITEKTURY I URBANISTYKI. PRACE NAUKOWE. KONFERENCJE. 1977. irreg., no.4, 1984. price varies. Oficyna Wydawnicza Politechniki Wroclawskiej, Wybrzeze Wyspianskiego 27, 50-370 Wroclaw, Poland. TEL 48-71-222940. FAX 48-71-223664. TELEX 712559 PWRPL. (Dist. by: Ars Polona, Krakowskie Przedmiescie 7, Warsaw, Poland) Ed. Tadeusz Izbicki. R&P contact: Halina Dudek. **Document type:** proceedings.

720 700 PL ISSN 0324-9905
POLITECHNIKA WROCLAWSKA. INSTYTUT ARCHITEKTURY I URBANISTYKI. PRACE NAUKOWE. MONOGRAFIE. (Text in Polish; summaries in English and Russian) 1969. irreg., no.15, 1992. price varies. Oficyna Wydawnicza Politechniki Wroclawskiej, Wybrzeze Wyspianskiego 27, 50-370 Wroclaw, Poland. TEL 48-71-222940. FAX 48-71-223664. TELEX 712559 PWRPL. (Dist. by: Ars Polona, Krakowskie Przedmiescie 7, Warsaw, Poland) Ed. Tadeusz Izbicki. R&P contact: Halina Dudek. adv. **Document type:** monographic series.
—Ei.

720 700 PL ISSN 0324-9891
POLITECHNIKA WROCLAWSKA. INSTYTUT ARCHITEKTURY I URBANISTYKI. PRACE NAUKOWE. STUDIA I MATERIALY. (Text in Polish; summaries in English and Russian) 1971. irreg., no.8, 1991. price varies. Oficyna Wydawnicza Politechniki Wroclawskiej, Wybrzeze Wyspianskiego 27, 50-370 Wroclaw, Poland. TEL 48-71-222940. FAX 48-71-223664. TELEX 712550 PWRPL. (Dist. by: Ars Polona, Krakowskie Przedmiescie 7, Warsaw, Poland) Ed. Tadeusz Izbicki. R&P contact: Halina Dudek. adv. **Document type:** academic/scholarly publication.

POLITECHNIKA WROCLAWSKA. INSTYTUT HISTORII ARCHITEKTURY, SZTUKI I TECHNIKI. PRACE NAUKOWE. KONFERENCJE. see *ART*

POLITECHNIKA WROCLAWSKA. INSTYTUT HISTORII ARCHITEKTURY, SZTUKI I TECHNIKI. PRACE NAUKOWE. MONOGRAFIE. see *ART*

POLITECHNIKA WROCLAWSKA. INSTYTUT HISTORII ARCHITEKTURY, SZTUKI I TECHNIKI. PRACE NAUKOWE. STUDIA I MATERIALY. see *ART*

720 IT
POLITECNICO DI TORINO. ISTITUTO DI SCIENZA DEI SISTEMI ARCHITETTONICI E TERRITORIALI DELLA FACOLTA DI ARCHITETTURA. STUDI E RECHERCHE. 3/yr. L.80000($20) Giardini Editori e Stampatori, Via Santa Bibbiana 28, 56100 Pisa, Italy. TEL 050 502531. Ed. Giacomo Donato. illus.

711 720 PL ISSN 0079-3450
POLSKA AKADEMIA NAUK. ODDZIAL W KRAKOWIE. KOMISJA URBANISTYKI I ARCHITEKTURY. TEKA. (Text in Polish; summaries in English, Russian) 1967. a. price varies. Ossolineum, Publishing House of the Polish Academy of Sciences, Pl. Solny 14a, 50-062 Wroclaw, Poland. TEL 48-71-3436961. FAX 48-71-448103. TELEX 0712771 OSS PL. Ed. Janusz Bogdanowski. **Indexed:** AgroLibrex, IBR. **Document type:** academic/scholarly publication.
—KNAW.
  Description: Presents papers on various problems of architecture: conservation, town planning, fortification and more.

727 US ISSN 1059-7239
PRACTICES. 1992. s-a. Center for the Study of Practice in Architecture, College of Design, Architecture, Art, and Planning, University of Cincinnati, Box 193713, Cincinnati, OH 45221-0016.

720 CN ISSN 0820-6848
PRAIRIE LANDSCAPE MAGAZINE. 1978. s-m. Can.$24 (foreign Can.$34) (effective 1997). (Landscape Alberta Nursery Trades Association) O T Communications, 10215 176th St., 2nd Fl., Edmonton, AB T5S 1M1, Canada. TEL 403-489-1991. FAX 403-444-2152. E-mail: lanta@planet.eon.net. Ed. Nigel Bowles; Pub. Mary-Lynn Charlton. R&P contact: Nigel Bowles. adv. contact: Mark Crncich. circ. 1,300. (back issues avail.) **Document type:** trade publication.
  Description: Provides information on the nursery trade associations of Alberta, Saskatchewan, and Manitoba.

720 US ISSN 0883-7279
NA1
PRATT JOURNAL OF ARCHITECTURE. 1985. irreg., approx. biennial. Pratt Institute, School of Architecture, Attn.: Anthony Caradonna, 200 Willoughby Ave., Brooklyn, NY 11205. TEL 718-339-4306. **Document type:** academic/scholarly publication.

PRESENZA TECNICA. see *ENGINEERING*

720 US
E151
PRESERVATION. 1949. bi-m. membership. National Trust for Historic Preservation, 1785 Massachusetts Ave., N.W., Washington, DC 20036. TEL 202-588-6000. URL: http://www.nthp.org/. Ed. Robert S. Wilson; Pub. Vin Cipolla. R&P contact: Robert S. Wilson. adv. contact: Bob A. Barron. bk.rev.; illus. circ. 225,000. (also avail. in microfilm from UMI; talking book; back issues avail.; reprint service avail.) **Indexed:** Abstr.Anthropol., Amer.Hist.& Life (1964-), Archit.Per.Ind., Art & Archaeol.Tech.Abstr., Art Ind., Arts & Hum.Cit.Ind., ASCA, Avery Ind.Archit.Per., Br.Tech.Ind., Curr.Cont., Gard.Lit. (1992-), Hist.Abstr. (1964-), Search (1988-), SSCI. **Document type:** consumer publication.
—Genuine Article; KR SourceOne; SWETS; UMI; UnCover. **CCC.**
  Formerly (until vol.48, no.4, 1996): Historic Preservation (ISSN 0018-2419); Incorporates (in 1995): Historic Preservation News (ISSN 1065-3562); Which was formerly (1961-1990): Preservation News (ISSN 0032-7735); Historic Preservation was formerly (until 1951): National Council for Historic Sites and Buildings Quarterly Report.
  Description: Focuses on preservation and restoration of structures, communities, and rural lands important to American history and culture.

720 UK ISSN 0267-4343
PRESERVATION IN ACTION. 1984. s-a. £6 (overseas £8). Architectural Heritage Fund, Clareville House, 26-27 Oxendon St., London SW1 4EC, England. TEL 44-171-925-0199. FAX 44-171-930-0295. Ed. Hilary Weir. bk.rev. circ. 2,500. **Document type:** newsletter.
  Description: Covers trusts and charitable organizations acquiring and rehabilitating buildings that merit conservation.

720.9 340 US ISSN 0882-715X
KF4310.A15
PRESERVATION LAW REPORTER. 1982. q. $95 to non-members; Forum members $55. National Trust for Historic Preservation, 1785 Massachusetts Ave. N.W., Washington, DC 20036. TEL 202-673-4000 Ed. Julia Miller. bibl.; cum.index. circ. 337. (looseleaf format; back issues avail.)

ARCHITECTURE

720.9747 US
PRESERVATION NEW YORK. 1975; N.S. 1993. q. $25 membership. Preservation League of New York State, 44 Central Ave., Albany, NY 12206. TEL 518-462-5658. FAX 518-462-5684. Ed. Jonathan Walters. R&P contact: Clark Strickland. illus. **Indexed:** Avery Ind.Archit.Per. **Document type:** newsletter.
Formerly (until 1993): Preservation League of New York State. Newsletter (ISSN 0882-7478)
Description: Reports noteworthy developments affecting historic preservation throughout New York, including articles on successful projects.

724 974.747 930.1 US ISSN 0885-7326
PRESERVATION NOTES. 1965. a. membership. Society for the Preservation of Long Island Antiquities, 93 North Country Rd., Setauket, NY 11733. TEL 516-941-9444. FAX 516-941-9184. Ed. Barbara Ferris Van Liew. adv.; bk.rev.; illus.; circ. 1,800 (controlled). (back issues avail.) **Document type:** newsletter, bulletin.
Formerly: Preservation of Long Island Antiquities; Incorporates: Society for the Preservation of Long Island Antiquities. Newsletter (ISSN 0583-9181)
Description: Reports on buildings and other sites on Long Island that have historic, cultural, or artistic importance and are endangered or have been saved. Includes a houses for sale section.

720 US
PRESERVATION PERSPECTIVE. 1981. q. $20 to individuals; institutions $35; students $10 (effective 1992). Preservation New Jersey, Inc., 149 Kearny Ave., Perth Amboy, NJ 08861-4700. TEL 908-442-1100. FAX 908-442-2442. Ed. Janice W. Stridick. R&P contact: Mary D. Krugman. adv. contact: Suzanne Rose. bk.rev.; illus.; stat.; circ. 3,000 (controlled). (looseleaf format; back issues avail.) **Document type:** newsletter.
Description: Covers architecture and historic preservation in New Jersey.

920 US ISSN 0478-1392
NA1
PRESERVATION PROGRESS (CHARLESTON). 1956. q. $25. Preservation Society of Charleston, Box 521, Charleston, SC 29402. TEL 803-722-4630. Ed. Mary Moore Jacoby. adv.; bk.rev.; illus. circ. 2,500. **Indexed:** Amer.Hist.& Life, Hist.Abstr. **Document type:** newsletter.

PRESIDENTIAL DESIGN AWARDS. see *ART*

720 UK
PRINCE OF WALES'S INSTITUTE OF ARCHITECTURE. NEWSLETTER. 2/yr. Prince of Wales's Institute of Architecture, 14 Gloucester Gate, Regent's Park, London NW1 4HG, England. TEL 44-171-916-7380. FAX 44-171-916-7381. E-mail: nicks@nwspowia.demon.co.uk; URL: http://www.cf.ac.uk/powia. **Document type:** newsletter.

720 CK ISSN 0032-9150
PROA; urbanismo, arquitectura, industrias. 1946. m. $40. Ediciones Proa, Calle 40, no. 19-52, Bogota, Colombia. Ed. Lorenzo Fonseca. adv.; bk.rev.; bibl.; charts; illus.; stat.; cum.index. circ. 15,000. **Indexed:** Archit.Per.Ind., Avery Ind.Archit.Per., Br.Tech.Ind., IBR.
—SWETS.

724 JA ISSN 0386-037X
NA673
PROCESS: ARCHITECTURE.* (Text in English, Japanese) 1977. irreg. 3000 Yen. Process Architecture Publishing Co. Ltd. - Purosesu Akitekucha, 47-2-418, Sasazuka 1-chome, Shibuya-ku, Tokyo 151, Japan. adv.; illus. **Indexed:** Art Ind., Avery Ind.Archit.Per., Br.Tech.Ind.
—BLDSC (6849.983430); KR SourceOne; SWETS; UnCover.

PRODESIGN. see *ART*

PROFESSIONAL LANDSCAPER. see *GARDENING AND HORTICULTURE*

PROFESSIONAL SERVICES MANAGEMENT JOURNAL. see *BUSINESS AND ECONOMICS — Management*

PROFESSIONS AND PROJECTS REGISTER. see *BUILDING AND CONSTRUCTION*

720 US ISSN 0190-8766
NA53
PROFILE (ATLANTA); the directory of U.S. Architectural Design Firms. 1978. a. $175 case bound; soft bound $149. Construction Market Data, Inc., 4126 Pleasantdale Rd., Ste. A8, Atlanta, GA 30340. TEL 800-949-0276. FAX 770-613-5978. E-mail: profile@cmdonl.com; URL: http://profile.cmdonl.com/aia. Ed. Dorothy A. DeGennaro; Pub. Robert G. Rogers. R&P contact: Dorothy A. Degennaro. adv.: color page $8500. circ. 18,000. **Document type:** directory.
—CISTI.
Description: Provides information on architectural design firms, listing each by city and state, and indicating key staff and their roles, staff size and type, specific project types and services.

720 XO ISSN 0322-9661
PROJEKT; revue slovenskej architektury. (Text in Czech or Slovak; summaries in English, French, German, Russian) 1959. 10/yr. $78. (Zvaz Slovenskych Architektov - Union of Slovak Architects) Obzor, Spitalska 35, 815 85 Bratislava, Slovakia. (Dist. by: Slovart, Gottwaldovo nam. 48, 805 32 Bratislava, Slovakia) Ed.Bd. circ. 5,500. **Indexed:** Avery Ind.Archit.Per.

720 690 UK ISSN 0143-8883
PROSPECT (EDINBURGH). 1979. q. £12 in E.U. nations; elsewhere £14. Royal Incorporation of Architects in Scotland, 15 Rutland Sq., Edinburgh EH1 2BE, Scotland. TEL 44-131-229-7545. FAX 44-131-228-2188. Ed. Charles McKean. adv. contact: Stan Mairs. bk.rev. circ. 5,000. (back issues avail.) **Document type:** trade publication.
Description: Reviews the recent Scottish buildings from an architectural perspective. Presents news and views concerning architects and design professionals to promote an appreciation of Scottish architecture.

720 307.1 CI ISSN 1330-0652
NA4.5 CODEN: PORREV
PROSTOR. 1993. s-a. Sveuciliste u Zagrebu, Arhitektonski Fakultet, Kaciceva 26, 10000 Zagreb, Croatia. FAX 385-41-440839. Ed. Ante Marinovic-Uzelac.
Description: Publishes results of research in all fields of architecture and urban planning.

720 SP ISSN 1133-8849
QUADERNS D'ARQUITECTURA I URBANISME. Spanish - English edition (ISSN 1133-8857) (Bilingual editions in Catalan-French or Spanish-English) 1944. q. 10000 ptas. (foreign 14000 ptas.) (effective 1996). Colegio de Arquitectos de Cataluna - Col.legi d'Arquitectes de Catalunya, Plaza Nueva, Placa Nova, 5, 08002 Barcelona, Spain. TEL 93-301-50-00. FAX 93-412-39-64. (Subscr. to: Font i Prat Associats, Subscr. Dept., Roca i Batlle 2, 08023 Barcelona, Spain) Ed. Manuel Gausa Navarro. R&P contact: Oleguer Gelpi. adv. contact: Robert Guinard. bk.rev.; illus.; index. circ. 10,000. **Indexed:** Amer.Hist.& Life (1971-1974), Archit.Per.Ind., Avery Ind.Archit.Per., Hist.Abstr. (1971-1974), Ind.SST.
—BLDSC (7167.500000); CINDOC; SWETS.
Supersedes in part (in 1985): Quaderns d'Arquitectura i Urbanisme (ISSN 0211-9595); Which was formerly (until 1980): Cuadernos de Arquitectura y Urbanismo (ISSN 0211-321X); (until 1970): Cuadernos de Arquitectura (ISSN 0011-2364)
Description: Profiles local, national, and international architectural works, accompanied by critical reflections.

720 975 US
QUAPAW QUARTER CHRONICLE. 1974. bi-m. $10 to non-members. Quapaw Quarter Association, Box 165023, Little Rock, AR 72216. Ed. C.S. Heinbockel. adv.; bk.rev.; charts; illus. circ. 15,000. (tabloid format)

720 AT ISSN 1321-8166
QUEENSLAND REVIEW. 1994. s-a. Aus.$24 to individuals; institutions and libraries Aus.$28; students Aus.$18; foreign Aus.$30. (Society of Architectural Historians) University of Queensland Press, P.O. Box 42, St. Lucia, Qld. 4067, Australia. TEL 61-7-33652452. FAX 61-7-33651988. (back issues avail.)

720 UK ISSN 0269-0829
R I B A DIRECTORY OF MEMBERS (YEAR). a. £52.50. (Royal Institute of British Architects) R I B A Publications Ltd., Finsbury Mission, 39 Moreland St., London EC1V 8BB, England. TEL 0171-251-0791. FAX 0171-608-2375. **Document type:** directory.

720 UK ISSN 0269-0810
R I B A DIRECTORY OF PRACTICES. a. £52.50. (Royal Institute of British Architects) R I B A Publications, Finsbury Mission, 39 Moreland St., London EC1V 8BB, England. TEL 44-171-251-0791. FAX 44-171-608-2375. **Document type:** directory.
Former titles: Architects; R I B A Directory of Practices.

720 UK
R I B A DRAWINGS MONOGRAPHS. irreg., no.3, 1996. (Royal Institute of British Architects) Academy Group Ltd., Academy Editions (Subsidiary of: V C H Publishing Group), 42 Leinster Gardens, London W2 3AN. (U.S. dist. by: National Book Network, Inc., 4720 Boston Way, Lanham, Maryland 20706) Ed. Jill Lever.

720 UK ISSN 0953-6973
NA12
R I B A JOURNAL. 1893. m. £66 (foreign £82). (Royal Institute of British Architects) Builder Group plc., Builder House, 1 Millharbour, London E14 9RA, England. TEL 44-171-560-4000. FAX 44-171-560-4008. URL: http://www.riba.org/riba/advice2.htm. Ed. John Welsh; Pub. Pam Barker. adv. contact: Ben Greenish. bk.rev.; charts; illus.; stat.; index. circ. 29,000. (also avail. in microform from UMI; reprint service avail. from UMI) **Indexed:** Account.& Data Proc.Abstr., Archit.Per.Ind., Art Ind., Arts & Hum.Cit.Ind., Br.Ceram.Abstr., Br.Hum.Ind., Br.Rail.Bd., Br.Tech.Ind., Build.Manage.Abstr., Curr.Cont., High.Educ.Curr.Aware.Bull., RICS, RILA, Risk Abstr. **Document type:** trade publication.
—CISTI; KR SourceOne; Linda Hall; SWETS; UMI.
Former titles (until 1987): Architect; R I B A Journal (ISSN 0035-8932)

721 UK ISSN 0265-8739
R I B A PRODUCT SELECTOR. 1982. a. £35. (Royal Institute of British Architects) R I B A Information Services, Finsbury Mission, 39 Moreland St., London EC1V 8BB, England. TEL 44-171-250-4050. FAX 44-171-490-4434. E-mail: sueq@ribac.co.uk; URL: http://www.ribac.co.uk. Ed. Sue Quirk. adv. contact: Karen Ball. circ. 20,000. **Document type:** directory.
●Also available on CD-ROM.
Description: Contains directory of products and suppliers within the UK construction industry.

RAKENNUSTAITO. see *BUILDING AND CONSTRUCTION*

RASSEGNA TECNICA DEL FRIULI VENEZIA GIULIA. see *ENGINEERING — Civil Engineering*

720 SP
RATLLES. 3/yr. Colegio Oficial de Delineantes de Barcelona - Barcelona College of Draftsmen, Mallorca 257, 2o 2a, 08008 Barcelona, Spain. TEL 3-215-06-66. FAX 3-215-92-49. Ed. Jose M. de las Heras. circ. 10,000.

720 694 US
REDWOOD NEWS. 1949. s-a. free to qualified personnel. California Redwood Association, 405 Enfrente Dr., Ste. 200, Novato, CA 94949. TEL 415-382-0662. FAX 415-382-8531. Ed. Pamela Allsebrook. R&P contact: Pamela Allsebrook. circ. 30,000. circ. 30,000 (controlled). **Document type:** trade publication.
Description: Redwood design for architects and others in the building trades.

REFURBISHMENT PROJECTS. see *BUILDING AND CONSTRUCTION*

720 UK ISSN 0306-6967
REGISTER OF ARCHITECTS. 1932. a. £40 (architects £16). Architects' Registration Council, 73 Hallam St., London W1N 6EE, England. TEL 44-171-580-5861. FAX 44-171-436-5269. circ. 31,000. **Document type:** directory.

RESIDENCES. see *INTERIOR DESIGN AND DECORATION*

RESTAURACION HOY. see *ART*

ARCHITECTURE

720.968   SA   ISSN 0037-5462
RESTORICA. (Text in Afrikaans, English) 1960. a. R.25 (effective 1995). Simon van der Stel Foundation, P.O. Box 12293, Centrahil 6006, South Africa. TEL 27-41-562849. FAX 27-41-562849. Eds. Albrecht Herholdt, Trudie Wegner. adv.; bk.rev.; illus. circ. 3,500. **Indexed:** Ind.S.A.Per. **Document type:** academic/scholarly publication.
    Supersedes: Simon van der Stel Foundation. Bulletin.
    Description: Preservation and restoration of historical buildings.
    Refereed Serial

720   SP
REVISTA BALEAR D'ARQUITECTURA. 3/yr. C. Portella 14, 07001 Palma de Mallorca, Spain. TEL 71-72-77-59. FAX 71-72-04-63. Ed. Martin Lucena.
    Description: Covers architecture, urbanism, interior design and decoration, garden and landscape architecture.

720   AG   ISSN 0327-330X
NA830
REVISTA DE ARQUITECTURA. 1904. bi-m. $60. Sociedad Central de Arquitectos, Montevideo 938, 1019 Buenos Aires, Argentina. TEL 54-1-812-3644. FAX 54-1-953-5508. Ed. Ernesto A. Grossi. adv.; illus.; circ. 8,500 (paid); 8,000 (controlled). **Indexed:** Avery Ind.Archit.Per.
    Former titles (until 1986): Sociedad Central de Arquitectos. Boletin - Architectural Society Review; (until 1955): Revista de Arquitectura.
    Description: Covers housing and urban planning, professional meetings, competitions, plans and designs.

720   SP   ISSN 0213-8948
REVISTA DE EDIFICACION. 1987. 4/yr. (Universidad de Navarra, Escuela Tecnica Superior de Arquitectura) Servicio de Publicaciones de la Universidad de Navarra, S.A., Apdo. 177, 31080 Pamplona, Spain. TEL 48-25-2700. Dir. Antonio Garcia Valcarce. **Indexed:** Ind.SST.

720   MX
REVISTA F A. irreg. (approx. 1/yr.), latest 1986. $1. Universidad Nacional Autonoma de Mexico, Facultad de Arquitectura, c/o Arq. Enrique X. de Anda, Biblioteca Lino Picaseno, Circuito Interior de Cd. Universitaria, Deleg. Coyoacan, 04510 Mexico, D.F., Mexico.

REVISTA S A I. see *ENGINEERING*

720   IT   ISSN 0080-2964
RICERCHE SULLE DIMORE RURALI IN ITALIA. 1938. irreg., no.31, 1987. price varies. (Consiglio Nazionale delle Ricerche) Casa Editrice Leo S. Olschki, Casella Postale 66, 50100 Florence, Italy. TEL 39-55-6530684. FAX 39-55-6530214. E-mail: celso@olschki.it. Eds. Lucio Gambi, Giuseppe Barbieri. circ. 1,000. **Document type:** monographic series.

720   IT
RIVISTA D'ARCHITETTURA. q. L.35000 (Europe L.70000; elsewhere L.90000). (Centro Progetto Nuovo) Editoriale d' Architettura, Via degli Alpini 5, 67051 Avezzano (Aq), Italy. TEL 0863-34163. Ed. Pino Scaglione.

RIVISTA DI STUDI LIGURI/REVUE D'ETUDES LIGURES. see *HISTORY — History Of Europe*

ROOFER MAGAZINE. see *BUILDING AND CONSTRUCTION*

ROYAL AUSTRALIAN HISTORICAL SOCIETY. TECHNICAL INFORMATION SERVICE. see *HISTORY — History Of Australasia And Other Areas*

720   UK   ISSN 0080-472X
ROYAL SOCIETY OF ULSTER ARCHITECTS. YEAR BOOK. 1928. a. free to members. Nicholson and Bass Ltd., 2 Mount Charles, Belfast BT7 1NZ, N. Ireland. Ed.Bd. adv. circ. 1,000.

720   US   ISSN 0898-4948
S A R A SCOPE. 1987. bi-m. Society of American Registered Architects, 1411 London Rd., Duluth, MN 55805. TEL 218-728-4293. FAX 218-728-5361. E-mail: SARA@protonet.com; URL: http://www.protonet.com/SARA. Ed. Raymond J. Blesener. adv.; bk.rev.; circ. 500 (controlled). (back issues avail) **Document type:** newsletter.
    Description: Covers society operations, including national, state and chapter news.

720   SI   ISSN 0217-7668
S I A YEARBOOK.* 1967. a. S.35. Singapore Institute of Architects, Publications Board, 20 Orchard Rd., 02-00 SMA House, Singapore 0923, Singapore. TEL 3388977. FAX 3368708. adv. circ. 1,700.

720   UK   ISSN 0969-4250
S P A B NEWS. 1980. q. £24. Society for the Protection of Ancient Buildings, 37 Spital Sq., London E1 6DY, England. TEL 44-171-377-1644. FAX 44-171-247-5296. (Dist. addr.: 21 Farley Hill, Luton LU1 5EE, England. TEL 44-1582-32640) Ed. Lucy Richmond. adv.; bk.rev.; circ. 5,500. (back issues avail.) **Document type:** newsletter.
—BLDSC (8361.415000).

720 974   US
S P N E A'S HISTORIC HOUSES IN NEW ENGLAND. a. free. Society for the Preservation of New England Antiquities, 141 Cambridge St., Boston, MA 02114. TEL 617-227-3956.
    Formerly: Historic Houses in New England.
    Description: Lists historic house museums in New England owned by the society and open to the public.

S.-PETERBURGSKAYA PANORAMA. see *BUILDING AND CONSTRUCTION*

S S C R JOURNAL; promotes the conservation and restoration of historic and artistic objects. (Scottish Society for Conservation and Restoration) see *ART*

690   SZ
S W B - INFORMATION. (Text in German) 1984. 4/yr. Schweizerischer Werkbund, Limmatstr. 118, CH-8031 Zurich, Switzerland. TEL 41-1-2727176. FAX 41-1-2727506. Ed.Bd. bk.rev. **Document type:** trade publication.
    Formerly: Werkbund Material.

SAN DIEGO HOME - GARDEN LIFESTYLES. see *INTERIOR DESIGN AND DECORATION*

SASKATCHEWAN. DEPARTMENT OF CULTURE AND RECREATION. ANNUAL REPORT. see *ART*

720 620   SZ   ISSN 0251-0960
TA4   CODEN: IASUD5
SCHWEIZER INGENIEUR UND ARCHITEKT/INGENIEURS ET ARCHITECTES SUISSES/INGEGNERI E ARCHITETTI SVIZZERI; Schweizerische bauzeitung - bulletin technique de la Suisse romande. 1883. w. 198 Fr. (foreign 215 Fr.). (Schweizerischer Ingenieur- und Architektenverein - Societe Suisse des Ingenieurs et des Architectes) Verlag der Akademischen Technischen Vereine, Ruedigerstr. 11, Postfach 630, CH-8021 Zurich, Switzerland. TEL 01-2015536. FAX 01-2016377. (Co-sponsors: Gesellschaft Ehemaliger Studierender der ETH Zurich, Schweizerische Vereinigung Beratender Ingenieure) Ed. H. Rudolphi. adv.; bk.rev.; bibl.; charts; illus.; index. circ. 10,222. **Indexed:** Alloys Ind., Appl.Mech.Rev., C.I.S. Abstr., Chem.Abstr., Dok.Str., Eng.Ind., Eng.Mat.Abstr., Excerp.Med., Geotech.Abstr., INSPEC, Intl.Civil Eng.Abstr., Met.Abstr.Ind., Met.Abstr., Nonfer.Met.Alert, PCC Alert, Soft.Abstr.Eng., Steels Alert, World Alum.Abstr. —CISTI; Linda Hall.
    Formerly: Schweizerische Bauzeitung (ISSN 0036-7524)

720   SZ   ISSN 0036-7370
AP32
SCHWEIZER JOURNAL. 1957. m. 215 SFr. M & T Verlag AG, Geltenwilenstr. 8a, CH-9001 St. Gallen, Switzerland. TEL 071-235555. FAX 071-236745. Ed. Dr. Hans Frey. adv.; bk.rev.; charts; illus.; index. **Indexed:** ELLIS, Excerp.Med.

SCHWEIZER KUNST/ART SUISSE/ARTE SUIZZERA. see *ART*

SEMINARIO DE ESTUDIOS DE ARTE Y ARQUEOLOGIA. BOLETIN. see *ART*

720 690   CC   ISSN 1002-8498
                                  CODEN: SJSHE4
SHIGONG JISHU/CONSTRUCTION TECHNOLOGY. (Text in Chinese) 1971. m. $36. Zhongguo Jianzhu Gongye Chubanshe, c/o Shigong Jishu Bianjibu, 19 Chegongzhuang Dajie, Xishimenwai, Beijing 100044, People's Republic of China. TEL 86-10-6839-3529. FAX 86-10-6834-8830. (Dist. overseas by: China International Book Trading Corp., P.O. Box 399, Beijing, P.R. China) Ed. Fang Yueying. adv.: page $2000; adv. contact: Ge Li. circ. 50,000. **Document type:** academic/scholarly publication.
    Description: Covers the latest developments in the field of building and construction as well as relevant policies and regulations.

721   CC   ISSN 1000-8373
SHIJIE JIANZHU DAOBAO/WORLD ARCHITECTURE HERALD. (Text in Chinese) q. Shenzhen Shiwei, Xuanchuan Shiye Fazhan Jijinhui, B-23-6, Nanyang Dasha, Shenzhen, Guangdong 518000, People's Republic of China. TEL 223401. Ed. Zhang Liangjun.

720   JA
SHINKENCHIKU/JAPAN ARCHITECT. (Text in Japanese) 1925. m. Shinkenchiku-sha,Co, Ltd. - Japan Architect Co., Ltd., 31-2, Yushima 2-chome, Bunkyo-ku, Tokyo 113, Japan. TEL 81-3-3816-2635. FAX 81-3-3816-2937. Ed. Masato Nakatani. adv.: B&W page 400000 Yen, color page 670000; trim 221 X 297; adv. contact: Masao Nakamura. circ. 87,000.

720   JA
SHOTEN KENCHIKU/COMMERCIAL ARCHITECTURE. (Text in Japanese) m. Shoten Kenchiku Sha Co., Ltd., 7-22-36 Nishi-Shinjuku, Shinjuku-ku, Tokyo 160, Japan. TEL 81-3-3363-5760. FAX 81-3-3363-5751. adv. contact: Hiroyuki Endo. circ. 60,000.
    Description: Covers architects and shop designers specializing in retail stores and restaurants.

720   CC
SICHUAN JIANZHU/SICHUAN ARCHITECTURE. (Text in Chinese) 1981. q. newsstand price: Y3. (Sichuan Tumu Jianzhu Xuehui - Sichuan Society of Civil Engineering and Architecture) Sichuan Jianzhu Zazhishe, 95, Jiefang Lu 2 Duan, Chengdu, Sichuan 610081, People's Republic of China. TEL 3332322. (Co-sponsor: Sichuan Jianzhu Gongcheng Gongsi) Ed. Tian Yingju. **Document type:** academic/scholarly publication.

720   SI   ISSN 0218-7728
NA1
SINGAPORE ARCHITECT. (Text in English) 1966. q. S.$65. Singapore Institute of Architects, Publications Board, 20 Orchard Rd., 02-00 SMA House, Singapore 0923, Singapore. TEL 65-226-2668. Ed. Robert Powell. adv.: B&W page S.$600, color page S.$1200; adv. contact: Graeme Burnett. bk.rev.; charts; illus. circ. 1,400. **Document type:** trade publication.
    Formerly (until 1994): S I A J - Singapore Institute of Architects. Journal (ISSN 0049-0520)

SINGAPORE SOURCE BOOK FOR ARCHITECTS & DESIGNERS. see *BUSINESS AND ECONOMICS — Trade And Industrial Directories*

SINTEZA; revija za likovno kulturo. see *ART*

SOCIETA DEGLI INGEGNERI E DEGLI ARCHITETTI IN TORINO. ATTI E RASSEGNA TECNICA. see *ENGINEERING — Civil Engineering*

973.9 306   US
SOCIETY FOR COMMERCIAL ARCHEOLOGY. JOURNAL. 1977. s-a. Society for Commercial Archeology, Box 2423, Atlanta, GA 30301-2423. Ed. Dwayne Jone R&P contact: Dan Hershberger. TEL 406-994-690 circ. 950 (paid). **Document type:** academic/scholarly publication.
    Supersedes in part (in 1993): Society for Commercial Archeology. News Journal (ISSN 0735-1399)
    Description: Covers roadside and commercial architecture as well as the legacy of the automobile in America.

ARCHITECTURE 415

973.9 306 US ISSN 1069-0492
E159.5
SOCIETY FOR COMMERCIAL ARCHEOLOGY. NEWS. 1977. q. $25 to individuals. Society for Commercial Archeology, Box 2423, Atlanta, GA 30301-2423. E-mail: carrot@telerama.lm.com. Ed. Greg Smith. R&P contact: Dan Hershberger. TEL 406-994-6904. bk.rev.; circ. 950 (paid). (back issues avail.) **Document type:** newsletter.
  Supersedes in part (in 1993): Society for Commercial Archeology. News Journal (ISSN 0735-1399)
  Description: Covers roadside and commercial architecture, as well as the legacy of the automobile in America.

720 352.7 CN ISSN 0228-0744
SOCIETY FOR THE STUDY OF ARCHITECTURE IN CANADA. BULLETIN/SOCIETE POUR L'ETUDE DE L'ARCHITECTURE AU CANADA. BULLETIN. (Text in English, French) 1975. q. Can.$40($45) to individuals; institutions Can.$65($70); students Can.$20($25) (effective 1997). Society for the Study of Architecture in Canada - Societe pour l'Etude de l'Architecture au Canada, Box 2302, Sta. D, Ottawa, ON K1P 5W5, Canada. Ed. Gordon W. Fulton. bk.rev.; charts; illus.; cum.index: 1980-1989; 1990-1994; circ. 500 (paid). (back issues avail.) **Document type:** academic/scholarly publication, proceedings.
  Description: Devoted to the examination of the role of the built environment in Canadian society.
  Refereed Serial

720 US ISSN 0037-9808
NA1
SOCIETY OF ARCHITECTURAL HISTORIANS. JOURNAL. 1940. q. $80 to individuals (foreign $95); institutions $150 (foreign $165); students $30 (foreign $45) (effective 1997). Society of Architectural Historians, 1365 North Astor St., Chicago, IL 60610-2144. TEL 312-573-1365. FAX 312-573-1141. URL: http://www.upenn.edu/sah/. Ed. Eve Blall. adv. contact: Elizabeth Sippel. bk.rev.; illus.; index. circ. 4,000. (also avail. in microform from UMI; reprint service avail. from UMI, ISI) **Indexed:** Amer.Bibl.Slavic & E.Eur.Stud, Amer.Hist.& Life (1963-), Art Ind., Arts & Hum.Cit.Ind., ASCA, Avery Ind.Archit.Per., Br.Archaeol.Abstr., Br.Tech.Ind., Curr.Cont., Gard.Lit. (1992-), Hist.Abstr. (1963-), Ind.Bk.Rev.Hum., Mid.East: Abstr.& Ind., RILA. **Document type:** academic/scholarly publication.
  —BLDSC (4880.770000); Genuine Article; KR SourceOne; SWETS; UMI; UnCover.

720 US ISSN 0049-1195
SOCIETY OF ARCHITECTURAL HISTORIANS. NEWSLETTER. 1957. bi-m. $80 to individuals (foreign $95); institutions $150 (foreign $165); students $30 (foreign $45) (effective 1997). Society of Architectural Historians, 1365 North Astor St, Chicago, IL 60610-2144. TEL 312-573-1365. FAX 312-573-1141. Ed. Diane Greer. adv. contact: Elizabeth Sippel. bibl.; illus. circ. 4,000. (reprint service avail. from UMI, ISI) **Indexed:** Amer.Bibl.Slavic & E.Eur.Stud. **Document type:** newsletter, bulletin.
  —BLDSC (6108.342900); CISTI.

720 942 UK
SOCIETY OF ARCHITECTURAL HISTORIANS OF GREAT BRITAIN. NEWSLETTER. 1968. s-a. £25 (overseas £32) (includes subscr. to Architectural History) (effective 1997 & 1998). Society of Architectural Historians of Great Britain, Brandon Mead, Old Park Ln., Farnham, Surrey GU9 0AJ, England. Ed.Bd. bk.rev.; bibl. circ. 1,150. **Indexed:** RILA. **Document type:** newsletter.

720.942 UK
SOCIETY OF ARCHITECTURAL HISTORIANS OF GREAT BRITAIN. OCCASIONAL PAPER. irreg. price varies. Society of Architectural Historians of Great Britain, Brandon Mead, Old Park Ln., Farnham, Surrey GU9 0AJ, England. **Document type:** monographic series.

720 651 US
SOCIETY OF DESIGN ADMINISTRATION. NATIONAL PUBLICATION. q. membership (non-members $40). Society of Design Administration, c/o Brenda L. Richards, SDA-C, JSA Inc. Architects Planners, 361 Hanover St., Portsmouth, NH 03801. TEL 603-436-2551. Ed. Molly Cowen. R&P contact: Molly Cowen. TEL 503-224-3860. adv. contact: Adele Popp.
  Formerly (until 1995): Society of Architectural Administrators. News Journal.
  Description: For administrative, secretarial, or non-technical employees of architects and architectural firms.

SOPRINTENDENZA PER I BENI CULTURALI DELLA VALLE D'AOSTA. QUADERNI. see *ART*

724 333.33 SA ISSN 1015-888X
SOUTH AFRICAN HOME OWNER. (Text in English) 1990. q. R.187.25 (effective 1997). Avonwold Publishing Co. (Pty) Ltd., Avonwold House, 24 Baker St., Rosebank, Johannesburg 2196, South Africa. TEL 27-11-788-1610. FAX 27-11-880-2732. (Subscr. to: P.O. Box 52068, Saxonwold 2132, South Africa) Ed. Christine Johnson. circ. 21,197. **Document type:** consumer publication.
  Description: Covers practical aspects of renovating, decorating and improving a house, including features on architects' plans, noteworthy projects, gardening and other subjects.

SOUTHERN GOLF - LANDSCAPE & RESORT MANAGEMENT. see *GARDENING AND HORTICULTURE*

728 US ISSN 1057-3429
NA7211
SOUTHERN LIVING HOUSE PLANS. 1987. 3/yr. newsstand price: $3.95. Southern Progress Corp., c/o H. Johnson, V.P. Circulation, 2100 Lakeshore Dr., Birmingham, AL 35209. TEL 205-877-6000. FAX 205-877-6422. Eds. Louis Joyner, Lil Petrusnek. R&P contact: Jason Burnett. adv.: B&W page $7810, color page $11000; trim 8 1/8 x 10 7/8. circ. 300,000. **Document type:** consumer publication.

721 JA
SPACIOLOGY. (Text in English) 1971. q. exchange basis. Kyoto University, Department of Architecture - Kyoto Daigaku Kogakubu Kenchikugakka, Yoshida Hon-cho, Sakyo-ku, Kyoto 606, Japan.

SPON'S ARCHITECTS' & BUILDERS' PRICE BOOK. see *BUILDING AND CONSTRUCTION*

720 CE
SRI LANKA ARCHITECT. (Text in English) 1960. q. Rs.400 (developed countries $48 or £28). Sri Lanka Institute of Architects, 120-10, Wijerama Mawatha, Colombo 7, Sri Lanka. TEL 697109. Ed. Vidura Sri Nammuni. adv.: B&W page Rs.2000, color page Rs.5000. bk.rev. circ. 1,000.
  Formerly: Sri Lanka Institute of Architects. Journal.

SRPSKA AKADEMIJA NAUKA I UMETNOSTI. ODELJENJE DRUSTVENIH NAUKA. SPOMENIK. see *SOCIAL SCIENCES: COMPREHENSIVE WORKS*

720 GW ISSN 0585-0096
STADTBAUWELT. q. DM.348.80. Bertelsmann Fachzeitschriften GmbH, Postfach 120, 33111 Guetersloh, Germany. TEL 05241-802332. FAX 05241-73055. Ed. Peter Rumpf. circ. 15,000. **Document type:** trade publication.
  —SWETS.
  Description: Trade news for architects and planners.

STAVEBNICKY CASOPIS. see *BUILDING AND CONSTRUCTION*

720 CN ISSN 0712-9092
STEEL DESIGN/CONSTRUCTION METALLIQUE. (Editions in English, French) 2/yr. free to qualified personnel. Dofasco, Inc., 1330 Burlington St. E., P.O. Box 2460, Hamilton, ON L8N 3J5, Canada. TEL 905-563-7965. Ed. W.D. Follis. R&P contact: W.D. Follis. circ. 27,573 (24,731 English ed.; 2,842 French ed.). **Document type:** newsletter, corporate report.
  Description: Describes the use of steel and steel products in contemporary architectural design.

STEUER-BRIEF FUER ARCHITEKTEN UND INGENIEURE. see *ENGINEERING*

STONE IN AMERICA. see *BUILDING AND CONSTRUCTION*

720 IT ISSN 0390-4253
STORIA ARCHITETTURA; rivista di architettura e restauro. 1982. a. (Universita di Roma, Istituto di Storia dell'Architettura) Bonsignori Editore s.r.l., Viale dei Quattro Venti, 47, 00152 Rome, Italy. TEL 06-5881496. FAX 06-5882839. **Indexed:** Avery Ind.Archit.Per., RILA. **Document type:** academic/scholarly publication.

724 US
STREAMLINE. 1987. q. $20. Art Deco Society of the Palm Beaches, 325 S.W. 29th Ave., Delray Beach, FL 33445. TEL 561-276-9925. FAX 561-276-9925. E-mail: sharon@flinet.com. Ed. Sharon Koskoff. adv. contact: Sharon Koskoff. circ. 500. **Document type:** newsletter.
  Description: Contains special events, preservation updates, stories.

STROITEL'STVO I ARKHITEKTURA. see *BUILDING AND CONSTRUCTION*

STRUCTURAL DESIGN OF TALL BUILDINGS. see *ENGINEERING — Civil Engineering*

720 IT ISSN 0081-6140
STUDI D'ARCHITETTURA ANTICA. 1966. irreg., no.5, 1974. price varies. L'Erma di Bretschneider, Via Cassiodoro, 19, 00193 Rome, Italy. TEL 39-6-6874127. FAX 39-6-6874129.

720 IT
STUDI E DOCUMENTI DI ARCHITETTURA. no.2, 1973. q. $8. Universita degli Studi di Firenze, Istituto di Composizione Architettonica, Florence, Italy. **Indexed:** Avery Ind.Archit.Per., Br.Tech.Ind.
  Supersedes: Universita degli Studi di Firenze. Istituto di Composizione Architettonica. Quaderni.

711 720 PL ISSN 0081-6566
STUDIA I MATERIALY DO TEORII I HISTORII ARCHITEKTURY I URBANISTYKI. (Text in Polish; summaries in English, Russian) 1959. irreg., no.19, 1992. price varies. (Polska Akademia Nauk) Wydawnictwo Naukowe P W N, Ul. Miodowa 10, 00-251 Warsaw, Poland. TEL 48-22-312738. FAX 48-22-6954288. (Dist. by: Ars Polona, Krakowskie Przedmiescie 7, 00-068 Warsaw, Poland)

STUDIES IN CISTERCIAN ART AND ARCHITECTURE. see *ART*

STUDIES IN THE DECORATIVE ARTS. see *ART*

720 US
STUDIO WORKS. 1994. a., vol.3, 1996. price varies. (Harvard University, Graduate School of Design) Princeton Architectural Press, 37 E. Seventh St., New York, NY 10003. TEL 212-995-9620. FAX 212-995-6454. E-mail: sales@pap.designsys.com; URL: http://www.designsys.com/pap. (Dist. by: Chronicle Books, 275 Fifth St., San Francisco, CA 94103. TEL 800-722-6657) illus. (back issues avail.) **Document type:** academic/scholarly publication.
  Description: Showcase for recent work from the design studios of the Harvard University Graduate School of Design.

721 UK ISSN 0081-9751
SURVEY OF LONDON. Title varies: Survey of London Series. 1900. irreg. (approx. biennial); vol. 43-44, 1994. price varies. (Royal Commission on Historical Monuments) Athlone Press Ltd., 1 Park Dr., London NW11 7SG, England. TEL 44-181-458-0888. FAX 44-181-201-8115. (Dist. in the U.S. by: Athelone Press, 165 First Ave., Atlantic Highlands, NJ 07718. TEL 908-872-1441) **Indexed:** Br.Archaeol.Abstr. **Document type:** monographic series.
  —CCC.
  Description: Publishes architectural studies of London buildings in various sections of the city.

ARCHITECTURE

721   UK
SURVEY OF LONDON MONOGRAPH SERIES. irreg., latest vols.17, 1991. £28. Athlone Press Ltd., 1 Park Dr., London NW11 7SG, England. TEL 44-181-458-0888. FAX 44-181-201-8115. (Subscr. to: 2B Priors Hall Farm, Widdington, Saffron Walden, Essex CB11 3SB, England; Dist in the U.S. by: Athlone Press, 165 First Ave., Atlantic Highlands, NJ 07716) illus.; index. (back issues avail.)
Document type: monographic series.
Description: Publishes architectural studies of buildings in London.

SWIMMING POOL - SPA AGE. see BUILDING AND CONSTRUCTION

720   FR
SYNDICAT NATIONAL DES ARCHITECTES D'INTERIEUR. BULLETIN. bi-m. Syndicat National des Architectes d'Interieur, 57, Bd. Richard Lenoir, 75011 Paris, France. circ. 650 (controlled).

T A B; technische Gebaeude ausruestung - Heizung, Kaelte, Elektro, Klima, Lueftung. (Technik am Bau) see HEATING, PLUMBING AND REFRIGERATION

720   IT
TE M A. (Tempo Materia Architettura); revista trimestrale di restauro. q. L.70000 (foreign L.100000) (effective 1993). (Politecnico di Milano, Facolta di Architettura) Franco Angeli, Viale Monza 106, 20127 Milan, Italy. TEL 39-2-2827651.

721   FR   ISSN 0373-0719
TH2
TECHNIQUES ET ARCHITECTURE. (Text in English, French; summaries in Spanish) 1942. bi-m. 880 F. (foreign 1010 F.). Societe Altedia Communication, 54 bis rue Dombasle, 75015 Paris, France. TEL 45-31-06-05. FAX 45-33-11-23. Ed. J.M. Hoyet. adv.; bk.rev.; index. circ. 16,800. **Indexed:** Avery Ind.Archit.Per., Br.Tech.Ind., IBR.
—BLDSC (8744.400000); SWETS; UnCover.

724   GW   ISSN 0344-9068
TECHNISCHE KULTURDENKMALE. 1966. s-a. DM.17. V.D. Linnepe Verlagsgesellschaft KG, Bahnhofstr. 28, 58119 Hagen, Germany. TEL 02331-32078. FAX 02331-32090. Eds. Friederike Kaesting, Holger Heuermann. adv.; bk.rev. circ. 3,000. (back issues avail.) **Document type:** academic/scholarly publication.

TECHNOLOGY AND CONSERVATION; of art, architecture and antiquities. see ART

TEGL. see BUILDING AND CONSTRUCTION

720   JA
TELESCOPE (TOKYO). (Text in English, Japanese) 1988. q. $45 (effective Nov. 1990). Workshop for Architecture & Urbanism, YK Aoyama Bldg., 4-7 Shibuya 2-chome, Shibuya-ku, Tokyo 150, Japan. FAX 03-3407-8753. adv.; bk.rev.; illus. circ. 3,000. (tabloid format)
Description: Highlights new architectural projects in Japan. Includes exhibitions reviews and reports.

720 700   US   ISSN 0736-1149
NA1
THRESHOLD. 1982. a. $25. (University of Illinois at Chicago, School of Architecture) Rizzoli International Publications, Inc., Threshold, 300 Park Ave. S., New York, NY 10010. TEL 212-982-2300. FAX 212-982-3866. illus.

TIMBER FRAMING. see BUILDING AND CONSTRUCTION

720 747   US   ISSN 1090-1361
TIMBER HOMES ILLUSTRATED. q. $16.97 (foreign $26.97); newsstand price: $3.99. G C R Publishing Group, Inc., 1700 Broadway, 34th Fl., New York, NY 10019. TEL 212-541-7100. FAX 212-245-1241. (Subscr. to: Box 789, Mt. Morris, IL 61054) Ed. Roland Sweet; Pub. Jason Goodman. adv. contact: Laura LaPatin. circ. 120,000 (paid). **Document type:** consumer publication.
Description: Guide to timber homes in North America. Covers traditional timber frames, log post-and-beam structures that employ elegant, majestic timbers.

TOBISHIMA GIHO, KENCHIKU/TOBISHIMA ENGINEERING REPORT, ARCHITECTURE. see ENGINEERING — Civil Engineering

720 747   US   ISSN 1059-5252
NA7205
TODAY'S FAMILY HOME PLANS. 1985. a. $3.95. Archway Press, Inc., 19 W. 44th St., New York, NY 10036. TEL 212-757-5580.
Description: Features pictures and floor plans of single family detached homes of general interest to home planners and builders.

720   US   ISSN 1050-2092
HT51
TRADITIONAL DWELLINGS AND SETTLEMENTS REVIEW. 1989. s-a. $45 to individuals; institutions $90; corporations $160 (effective 1997). International Association for the Study of Traditional Environments, Center for Environmental Design Research, 390 Wurster Hall, Department of Architecture, University of California, Berkeley, CA 94720-1839. TEL 510-642-2896. FAX 510-643-5571. E-mail: iaste@ced.berkeley.edu. Eds. Nezar AlSayyad, Jean-Paul Bourdier. R&P contact: David Moffatt. bk.rev.; circ. 350 (paid). **Document type:** academic/scholarly publication.
—BLDSC (8881.071700); UnCover.
Description: Provides a link between tradition and modernity, in any setting throughout the world.
Refereed Serial

720   IT   ISSN 0082-6006
TRATTATI DI ARCHITETTURA. 1966. irreg., latest 1995. price varies. Edizioni Il Polifilo, Via Borgonuovo 2, 20121 Milan, Italy.

TRIALOG; Zeitschrift fuer das Planen und Bauen in der Dritten Welt. see HOUSING AND URBAN PLANNING

720   IS   ISSN 0041-4549
TVAI; periodical for architecture, town planning, industrial design & the plastic arts. (Text in Hebrew; summaries in English) 1966. a. $7. Tvai, 27, Shlomo Hamelech St., Tel Aviv, Israel. TEL 03-5239152. Ed. Aba Elhanani. adv.; bk.rev.; illus. circ. 1,500.

720   FR
U I A NEWSLETTER. (Editions in English, French) 1965. bi-m. 400 F. to individuals (outside Europe 500 F.); institutions 550 F. (outside Europe 600 F.); (effective 1997). Union Internationale des Architectes - International Union of Architects, 51 rue Raynouard, 75016 Paris, France. TEL 33-1-45243688. FAX 33-1-45240278. E-mail: uia@uia-architectes.org; URL: http://www.uia-architectes.org. Ed. Catherine Hayward. bk.rev.; charts; illus. **Document type:** newsletter.
Formerly: U I A Information (ISSN 0041-6916)
Description: Contains information on worldwide architectural events and competitions.

720   SP   ISSN 0078-8732
UNIVERSIDAD DE NAVARRA. ESCUELA DE ARQUITECTURA. COLECCION DE ARQUITECTURA. 1971. irreg., no.18, 1988. price varies. Ediciones Universidad de Navarra, S.A., Apdo. 396, 31080 Pamplona, Spain. TEL 94 825 6850.
Formerly: Universidad de Navarra. Escuela de Arquitectura. Manuales: Arquitectura.

720   SP
UNIVERSIDAD DE SEVILLA. SERIE: ARQUITECTURA. irreg., latest no.11. Universidad de Sevilla, Servicio de Publicaciones, Calle Porvenir 27, 41013 Seville, Spain. TEL 34-5-4231958. FAX 34-5-4232245.
Formerly (until 1967): Universidad Hispalense. Anales. Serie: Arquitectura.

720   CK   ISSN 0120-2669
UNIVERSIDAD NACIONAL DE COLOMBIA. FACULTAD DE ARQUITECTURA. REVISTA. 1976. s-a. Col.700($2.50) (or exchange). (Universidad Nacional de Colombia, Medellin, Facultad de Arquitectura) Editorial Lealon, Biblioteca, Apdo. Aereo 1779, Medellin, Colombia. TEL 2300040. TELEX 6922 CTX MO-CO. Ed. Nora Elena Mesa Sanchez. adv.; bk.rev.; illus. circ. 1,000.

721
UNIVERSITA DEGLI STUDI DI FIRENZE. DIPARTIMENTO DI PROGETTAZIONE DELL'ARCHITETTURA. QUADERNI. 1989. a. Alinea Editrice s.r.l., Via Pierluigi da Palestrina 17-19, Rosso, 50144 Florence, Italy. TEL 39-55-333428. FAX 39-55-331013. Ed. Giuliano Maggiora.
Formerly: Universita degli Studi di Firenze. Facolta di Architettura. Quaderni di Storia dell'Architettura.

720   IT
UNIVERSITA DEGLI STUDI DI GENOVA. ISTITUTO DI PROGETTAZIONE ARCHITETTONICA. QUADERNO.* 1968. irreg. L.10500 per issue. Universita degli Studi di Genova, Istituto di Progettazione Architettonica, Via Opera Pia Cousa 11, Genoa 16145, Italy. illus.

720   IT   ISSN 0485-4152
UNIVERSITA DI ROMA. ISTITUTO DI STORIA DELL'ARCHITETTURA. QUADERNI. 1953. a. Bonsignori Editore s.r.l., Viale dei Quattro Venti, 47, 00152 Rome, Italy. TEL 06-5881496. FAX 06-5882839. (back issues avail.) **Document type:** academic/scholarly publication.

UNIVERSITY OF NEW SOUTH WALES. HANDBOOK: BUILT ENVIRONMENT. see ENVIRONMENTAL STUDIES

721 375   AT   ISSN 1036-0654
UNIVERSITY OF TECHNOLOGY, SYDNEY. FACULTY OF DESIGN ARCHITECTURE AND BUILDING HANDBOOK. 1990. a. Aus.$5 (foreign Aus.$10). University of Technology, Sydney, P.O. Box 123, City Camp, Broadway, N.S.W. 2007, Australia. TEL 61-2-330-1990. FAX 61-2-330-1551. circ. 3,000. **Document type:** catalog, academic/scholarly publication.

720   UK   ISSN 0306-0624
UNIVERSITY OF YORK. INSTITUTE OF ADVANCED ARCHITECTURAL STUDIES. RESEARCH PAPERS. 1971. irreg. price varies. University of York, Institute of Advanced Architectural Studies, The King's Manor, York YO1 2EP, England. TEL 44-1904-433988. FAX 44-1904-433949. illus. circ. 500. **Document type:** monographic series.

720   II   ISSN 0042-0824
URBAN AND RURAL PLANNING THOUGHT. (Text in English) 1958. q. Rs.40($10) School of Planning and Architecture, Indraprastha Estate, New Delhi 1, India. Ed. Prof. G.B.K. Rao. charts; illus. circ. 300. (processed) **Indexed:** Avery Ind.Archit.Per., Geo.Abstr.

URBAN DESIGN AND PRESERVATION QUARTERLY. see HOUSING AND URBAN PLANNING

720 352.7   US   ISSN 0895-8076
NA9000
URBAN DESIGN UPDATE. 1984. 6/yr. $120 (Canada $170; elsewhere $210). Institute for Urban Design, 47 Barrow St., New York, NY 10014-3736. TEL 619-455-1251. FAX 619-450-3680. (Subscr. to: 454 W. 46th St., Apt. 3CN, New York, NY 10036. TEL 212-581-5178) **Document type:** newsletter.
Description: Reports on new projects, cutting edge issues, books and other matters of interest to urban designers.

720   SW   ISSN 0281-7462
UTBLICK LANDSKAP. 1984. q. SEK 325 in Sweden; students SEK 190; other Nordic countries SEK 360; elsewhere SEK 510 (effective 1997). L A R - Landskapsarkitektarnas Riksfoerbund, Wirwachs Malmgaaard, Ansgariegatan 5, S-117 27 Stockholm, Sweden. TEL 46-8-720-66-88. FAX 46-8-668-46-70. Ed. Thorbjoern Andersson; Pub. Thorbjoern Andersson. adv.; B&W page SEK 9900, color page SEK 15500; trim 190 x 265; adv. contact: Jan Lindqvist. bk.rev. circ. 2,000.
Description: Portrays Scandinavian landscape architecture, nature conservation and town planning.

720   GW
V F A JAHRBUCH. 1985. a. DM.15. (Vereinigung Freischaffender Architekten) Sisu Steinschulte Verlag, Bismarckallee 10, 53113 Bonn, Germany. TEL 49-228-361063. FAX 49-228-351130. circ. 10,000. (back issues avail.) **Document type:** trade publication.

720   GW   ISSN 0940-3124
V F A PROFIL. 1988. m. DM.67 (foreign DM.147) (effective 1996). (Vereinigung Freischaffender Architekten) Profil Verlag GmbH, Scheideweg 160B, 26127 Oldenburg, Germany. TEL 49-441-93023-0. FAX 49-441-9302320. Ed. Hans-Peter Oswald. adv.: B&W page DM.7800, color page DM.10600; trim 185 x 260. bk.rev.; circ. 36,000 (controlled). (back issues avail.) **Document type:** trade publication
Refereed Serial

ARCHITECTURE — ABSTRACTING, BIBLIOGRAPHIES, STATISTICS

720 IT
▼VENTRE; la rinascita dell'architettura. 1995. bi-m. (Associazione d'Idee) Edizioni Libria, Via Francesco Giordani 42, 80122 Naples, Italy. TEL 39-81-7614842. Ed. Diego Lama.

VETRO SPAZIO; magazine on glass in architecture - facades, energy, renewal, interiors, new technologies. see CERAMICS, GLASS AND POTTERY

720 US ISSN 0506-8347
VIA (PHILADELPHIA). a. University of Pennsylvania, Graduate School of Fine Arts, Architecture Department, Attn. Ralph Muldrow, Philadelphia, PA 19104. TEL 215-848-7724. illus. (reprint service avail. from ISI,UMI) **Indexed**: Avery Ind.Archit.Per. **Document type**: academic/scholarly publication.

940 UK ISSN 0083-6079
VICTORIAN SOCIETY. ANNUAL. 1958. a. £20 (overseas £27). Victorian Society, 47 Linton St., London N1 7AN, England. TEL 44-181-742-3438. FAX 44-181-995-4895. Ed. Sarah Whittingham. adv. contact: Richard Seedhouse. bk.rev. circ. 3,500. **Indexed**: Archit.Per.Ind., RILA. **Document type**: academic/scholarly publication.
Description: Includes notes on the main conservation cases of the past year, plus two short articles on subjects of 19th century art and architecture.

720 FR ISSN 0049-6316
VIEILLES MAISONS FRANCAISES. 1958. 5/yr. 235 F. (Europe 315 F.; N. America 349 F.) (effective 1998). Vieilles Maisons Francaises, 93 rue de l'Universite, 75007 Paris, France. TEL 33-1-40626180. FAX 33-1-45511226. Ed. Marie-Claire Colignon; Pub. Georges De Grandmaison. adv.; bk.rev.; bibl.; charts; illus.; tr.lit. circ. 26,000. **Document type**: consumer publication.

720 IT ISSN 0042-6237
VILLEGIARDINI; casa nel verde. (Supplement avail. annually: Repertorio) 1957. 11/yr. L.173550 (foreign L.293000) (effective 1996). Elemond S.p.A., Via D. Trentacoste 7, 20134 Milan, Italy. TEL 39-2-215631. FAX 39-2-26410847. TELEX 350523 ELEPER I. Ed. Nani Prina. adv.: B&W page L.8200000, color page L.11800000; adv. contact: Nicola Minardi. charts; illus. circ. 43,000. **Indexed**: Archit.Per.Ind., Avery Ind.Archit.Per. **Document type**: consumer publication.
—SWETS.

VISION MAGAZINE. see ART

720 XV
VISION OF REALITY. (Text in English, Italian, Slovenian) 1991. irreg. DM.10. Piranesi Ltd., Bogiseva 11, 61000 Ljubljana, Slovenia. TEL 386-61-223-039. FAX 386-61-221-226. Ed. Tomaz Brate. illus.; circ. 2,000 (controlled). **Document type**: catalog.

VISWASILPI. see BUILDING AND CONSTRUCTION

728 AG ISSN 0505-7981
VIVIENDA/DWELLING; la revista de la construccion. 1960. m. $224 (effective 1997). Roberto Carmuega, Pub., Hypolito Yrigoyen 1176-80 P.B., 4396 Capital Federal, Correo Central, Buenos Aires, Argentina. TEL 54-1-3811813. FAX 54-1-3814980. E-mail: vivienda@internet.sicotel.com; URL: http://www.revistavivienda.com.ar. Ed. Daniel Carmuega. adv.: color page $1560; trim 195 x 270; adv. contact: Mario Carmuega. circ. 24,000.

720 JA
WASEDA ARCHITECTURAL NEWS. (Text in Japanese) 1977. s-a. membership. Waseda Architectural Society, Waseda Daigaku Riko-gakubu, 3-4-1- Okubo Shinjuku-ku, Tokyo 160, Japan. TEL 03-208-0640. (back issues avail.)

720 JA
WASEDA ARCHITECTURE. 1970. a. membership. Waseda Architectural Society, Waseda Daigaku Riko-gakubu, 3-4-1 Okubo Shinjuku-ku, Tokyo 160, Japan. TEL 03-208-0640. (back issues avail.)

720 SZ ISSN 0257-9332
WERK - BAUEN & WOHNEN. m. (10/yr.) 180 SFr. (foreign 190 SFr.; students 135 SFr.) (effective 1997). (Bund Schweizer Architekten - Federation des Architectes Suisses; Federation Suisse des Architectes de l'Interieur) Zollikofer AG, Fuerstenlandstr. 122, CH-9001 St. Gallen, Switzerland. TEL 41-71-2727777. FAX 41-71-2727384. adv. circ. 9,000. **Indexed**: Art Ind., Avery Ind.Archit.Per., Br.Tech.Ind., IBR, RILA. **Document type**: trade publication.
Formerly: Werk-Archithese; Which was formed by the 1977 merger of: Werk; Archithese.

720 GW ISSN 0049-7150
WERK UND ZEIT. * 1952. m. DM.36. Deutscher Werkbund e.V., Weissadlergasse 4, 6000 Frankfurt 1, Germany. Ed. Amando Kaczmarczyk. adv.; bk.rev. circ. 3,500. (back issues avail.)

720 352.7 GW
WETTBEWERBE AKTUELL. 1971. m. DM.204 (students DM.150) (effective 1997). Wettbewerbe Aktuell Verlagsgesellschaft mbH, Maximilianstr. 5, 79100 Freiburg, Germany. TEL 49-761-77455-0. FAX 49-761-7745599. URL: http://www.wettbewerbe-aktuell.de. Ed. Thomas Hoffmann-Kuhnt. adv. contact: Matthias Knecht. circ. 13,800. **Document type**: trade publication.
Formerly: Wettbewerbe (ISSN 0177-9788)
Description: Contains information on topical German architectural competitions.

720 AU
WETTBEWERBE ARCHITEKTUR JOURNAL. bi-m. Salierigasse 25, A-1180 Vienna, Austria. TEL 01-4706292. FAX 01-475314. Ed. R.J. Bahula. circ. 5,000.

720 US
WISCONSIN ARCHITECT. 1931. bi-m. $30. (A I A Wisconsin) Wisconsin Architect, Inc., 321 S. Hamilton St., Madison, WI 53703-3606. TEL 608-257-8477. Ed. Brenda Taylor; Pub. William Babcock. R&P contact: William Babcock. adv. contact: Brenda Taylor. circ. 3,700 (controlled). **Document type**: trade publication, directory.
Refereed Serial

720 747 GW
WOHN! DESIGN; internationales Magazin fuer Architektur, Wohnen und Design. 4/yr. DM.40 (effective 1997). Trend Medien Verlag GmbH, Herdweg 20, 70174 Stuttgart, Germany. TEL 49-711-18790-0. FAX 49-711-1879045. Eds. Amei Cramer, Klaus Vetterle. adv.: B&W page DM.9000, color page DM.12600; trim 199 x 278; adv. contact: Guenther Anders. circ. 90,000. **Document type**: consumer publication.

720 614.7 570 610 GW ISSN 0176-0513
WOHNUNG & GESUNDHEIT; Fachzeitschrift fuer oekologisches Bauen & Leben. (Supplement avail.) 1979. 4/yr. DM.60($45) Institut fuer Baubiologie und Oekologie, Holzham 25, 83115 Neubeuern, Germany. TEL 49-8035-2039. FAX 49-8035-8164. Ed. Anton Schneider. adv.; bk.rev.; bibl. circ. 7,500. (back issues avail.) **Document type**: trade publication.

WOOD/BOIS. see FORESTS AND FORESTRY — Lumber And Wood

WOOD DESIGN AND BUILDING. see FORESTS AND FORESTRY — Lumber And Wood

720 UK ISSN 0956-9758
NA1
WORLD ARCHITECTURE. * 1989. bi-m. £36($40) (International Academy of Architecture) Cheerman Ltd., c/o Central Books, 99 Wallis Rd., London E9 5LN, England. URL: http://www.world-architecture.co.uk/. Ed. Martin Pawley. **Indexed**: DAAI. **Document type**: trade publication.
—BLDSC (9352.912550).
Formerly: Interarchitecture (London) (ISSN 0954-8580)
Description: Profiles one contemporary architect per issue. Covers news, trends and people in the profession.

WORLD CULTURAL GUIDES. see TRAVEL AND TOURISM

720 US ISSN 1059-4396
NA737.W7
WRIGHT ANGLES. 1974. q. $35 to individuals; families $45; corporations $100. Frank Lloyd Wright Home and Studio Foundation, 951 Chicago Ave., Oak Park, IL 60302. TEL 708-848-1976. FAX 708-848-1248. Ed. Melanie Birk. bk.rev. circ. 3,200. **Document type**: newsletter.
Description: Includes a feature article on Wright's early career, architecture, decorative arts, family life or creativity; calendar of events; exhibits; education programs; news items; and other issues of interest to members.

YALE PUBLICATIONS IN THE HISTORY OF ART. see ART

720 690 * TU ISSN 1300-3437
YAPI; aylik kultur, sanat ve mimarlik dergisi. (Text in Turkish; summaries in English) 1973. m. $50 (effective 1994). Yapi Endustri Merkezi, Cumhuriyet Caddesi 329, 80230 Harbiye, Istanbul, Turkey. TEL 90-212-2474185. FAX 90-212-2471101. Ed. Ms Guner Cilgin; Pub. Dogan Hasol. adv.: B&W page £280, color page £445; adv. contact: Mrs. Zehra Oztok Ebcim. bk.rev.; illus.; index. circ. 5,000. (back issues avail.) **Document type**: trade publication.
Description: Review of culture, art and architecture.

720 US ISSN 0319-3438
YARDSTICKS FOR COSTING. Variant title: Canadian Architect's Yardsticks for Costing. 1971. a. Can.$123.05 (foreign Can.$115). R.S. Means Company Inc., 100 Construction Plaza, P.O. 800, Kingston, MA 02364. TEL 800-448-8182. Ed. Jas. A. Murray. adv. circ. 2,195.
—CISTI.
Description: Provides cost data for the Canadian construction industry.

720.6 UK ISSN 0959-3640
YORK GEORGIAN SOCIETY. ANNUAL REPORT. 1943. a. £10 membership. York Georgian Society, King's Manor, York YO1 2EW, England. Ed. Helen Kirk. R&P contact: Helen Kirk. bk.rev.; illus. circ. 600. **Indexed**: Archit.Per.Ind., RILA. **Document type**: academic/scholarly publication, corporate report.
Description: Reports on the Society's activities. Includes articles on architecture, decorative art, historic restoration work, and related subjects.

YOUR CHURCH; helping you with the business of ministry. see RELIGIONS AND THEOLOGY

604.24 GW ISSN 0932-7509
ZEICHNEN FACHZEITSCHRIFT FUER KONSTRUIEREN UND GESTALTEN. 1963. q. DM.18.50. V Z T Verlag Zeichentechnik GmbH, Neunhofer Hauptstr. 76, 90427 Nuernberg, Germany. TEL 0911-3080-460. FAX 0911-3080-400. Ed. Robert Maechtel. adv.; bk.rev.; bibl.; charts; illus.; mkt.; pat.; stat.; cum.index. circ. 7,700. **Document type**: trade publication.
Former titles: Zeichnen Fachzeitschrift fuer Alle Bereiche Technisches Zeichens; Zeichnen in Technik, Architektur, Vermessung (ISSN 0044-2046)
Description: Covers engineering design, CAD and industrial design.

720 RU ISSN 0321-5083
ZODCHESTVO. 1975. irreg. 2.96 Rub. (Soyuz Arkhitektorov Rossiiskoi Federatsii) Stroiizdat, Dolgorukovskaya ul., 23a, 111442 Moscow, Russia. TEL 7-095-2516967.
Formerly: Sovetskaya Arkhitektura.

720 IT ISSN 0394-9230
NA1.A1
ZODIAC (BILINGUAL EDITION); international architecture magazine. English edition (ISSN 0394-9249) (Text in English, Italian) 1957-1973; N.S. 1989. 2/yr. L.90000 (foreign L.100000). Editrice Abitare Segesta S.p.A., Corso Monforte 15, 20122 Milan, Italy. TEL 39-2-760901. FAX 39-2-76013109. Ed. Guido Canella. adv.: color page L.6500000; 210 x 270; adv. contact: Patrizia Cappi. bk.rev.; charts; illus.; maps; pat. circ. 10,000. **Indexed**: Art Ind. **Document type**: consumer publication.

ZONING NEWS. see HOUSING AND URBAN PLANNING

ARCHITECTURE — Abstracting, Bibliographies, Statistics

ANNUAL REGISTER OF BOOK VALUES - THE ARTS & ARCHITECTURE. see PUBLISHING AND BOOK TRADE — Abstracting, Bibliographies, Statistics

ARCHITECTURE — COMPUTER APPLICATIONS

720 US ISSN 0570-6483
Z5941
ARCHITECTURAL INDEX. 1951. a. $27. Box 1168, Boulder, CO 80306-9955. TEL 303-449-7031. FAX 303-449-3748. Ed. Ervin J. Bell; Pub. Ervin J. Bell. R&P contact: Ervin J. Bell. circ. 3,500 (paid). (back issues avail.) **Document type:** abstracting/indexing.
 Description: Index of the major US architectural journals. Articles are listed by building type, design, location and subject.

720 UK ISSN 1359-740X
Z5941
ARCHITECTURAL PUBLICATIONS INDEX. CD-ROM edition: Architectural Publications Index on Disc (UK ISSN 1357-0536) 1973. q. £180 (foreign £190); CD-ROM $700 (educational institutions $560). (British Architectural Library) R I B A Publications, Finsbury Mission, 39 Moreland St., London EC1V 8BB, England. TEL 44-171-251-0791. FAX 44-171-608-2375. Ed. C. Dembsky. adv.; illus. circ. 800. (also avail. in magnetic tape) **Document type:** abstracting/indexing.
 ●Also available online. Vendor(s): Knight-Ridder Information, Inc. (File no.179).
 Also available on CD-ROM.
 Formerly (until 1995): Architectural Periodicals Index (ISSN 0266-4380); Supersedes: R I B A Library Bulletin (ISSN 0033-6912)

ART AND ARCHITECTURE BIBLIOGRAPHIES. see *ART — Abstracting, Bibliographies, Statistics*

016.720 AT ISSN 0817-2684
AUSTRALIAN ARCHITECTURAL PERIODICALS INDEX. Abbreviated title: A A P I. 1984. a. Aus.$35 (effective 1996 & 1997). Stanton Library, Reader Services Department, P.O. Box 12, N. Sydney, N.S.W. 2059, Australia. TEL 61-2-99368400. FAX 61-2-99368440. E-mail: stanton@godzill.zeta.org.au. (also avail. in microfiche) **Document type:** abstracting/indexing.
 ●Also available online.
 Also available on CD-ROM.
 Description: Cummulative index to Australian and New Zealand architecture periodicals. Covers architecture, architects, building, interior design, conservation and restoration, and landscape architecture.

720 016.5 US ISSN 0196-0008
Z5945
AVERY INDEX TO ARCHITECTURAL PERIODICALS. 1963. a. $470 (effective 1997). (Columbia University, Avery Architectural Library) G.K. Hall & Co., MacMillan Library Reference USA, Box 159, Thorndike, ME 04986. TEL 212-654-8452; 800-223-6121. FAX 207-948-2863. URL: http://www.mir.com/thorndike. (Subscr. to: Simon & Schuster, Library Reference Order Processing, 200 Old Tappan Rd., Old Tappan, NJ 07675. TEL 800-223-2336) (also avail. in microfilm) **Document type:** abstracting/indexing.
 ●Also available online. Vendor(s): Knight-Ridder Information, Inc., Research Libraries Group Information Network.

016.7 US ISSN 0360-2699
Z5939
BIBLIOGRAPHIC GUIDE TO ART AND ARCHITECTURE. a. $410 (effective 1997). G.K. Hall & Co., MacMillan Library Reference USA, Box 159, Thorndike, ME 04986. TEL 212-654-8452; 800-223-6121. FAX 207-948-2863. URL: http://www.mir.com/thorndike. (Subscr. to: Simon & Schuster, Library Reference Order Processing, 200 Old Tappan Rd., Old Tappan, NJ 07675. TEL 800-223-2336). **Document type:** bibliography, abstracting/indexing.
 Formerly: Art and Architecture Book Guide (ISSN 0098-2822)
 Description: Lists non-journal publications on art and architecture from all historic periods and all parts of the world. Includes materials catalogued during the past year by the New York Public Library, Art and Architecture Division, with additional entries from LC MARC Tapes.

BILTEN DOKUMENTACIJE. GRADJEVINARSTVO - VISOKOGRADNJA I ZAVRSNI RADOVI U GRADJEVINARSTVU/BULLETIN OF DOCUMENTATION. CIVIL ENGINEERING - SUPERSTRUCTURES AND FINAL WORK. see *ENGINEERING — Abstracting, Bibliographies, Statistics*

BILTEN DOKUMENTACIJE. URBANIZAM I ARHITEKTURA/BULLETIN OF DOCUMENTATION. TOWN PLANNING AND ARCHITECTURE. see *ARCHITECTURE*

BIO-BIBLIOGRAPHIES IN ART AND ARCHITECTURE. see *ART — Abstracting, Bibliographies, Statistics*

721 GW ISSN 0177-8285
BULLDOK BAUSCHAEDEN. (Supplement to: Arconis (ISSN 0949-7153)) 1985. q. DM.40. (Fraunhofer Informationszentrum Raum und Bau) Fraunhofer I R B Verlag, Nobelstr. 12, 70569 Stuttgart, Germany. TEL 49-711-9702500. FAX 49-711-9702507. TELEX 7255168-IZS-D. E-mail: irb@irb.fhg.de; URL: http://www.irb.fhg.de.Ed.Bd. adv.; bk.rev. circ. 1,500. (back issues avail.) **Document type:** trade publication.

CIMAISE; arts actuels. see *ART — Abstracting, Bibliographies, Statistics*

CONTRIBUTIONS TO THE STUDY OF ART AND ARCHITECTURE. see *ART — Abstracting, Bibliographies, Statistics*

CURRENT BIBLIOGRAPHY ON SCIENCE AND TECHNOLOGY: CIVIL ENGINEERING AND ARCHITECTURE/KAGAKU GIJUTSU BUNKEN SOKUHO. DOBOKU, KENCHIKU KOGAKU HEN. see *ENGINEERING — Abstracting, Bibliographies, Statistics*

720 690 GW ISSN 0343-6403
FACHBUCHVERZEICHNIS BAUWESEN - ARCHITEKTUR (YEAR). 1900. a. DM.6. Rossipaul Kommunikation GmbH, Menzingerstr. 37, 80638 Munich, Germany. TEL 49-89-179106-0. FAX 49-89-17910622. Ed. Angela Sendlinger. circ. 30,000. **Document type:** trade publication.

721 GW ISSN 0177-3550
KURZBERICHTE AUS DER BAUFORSCHUNG. 1960. bi-m. DM.158. (Fraunhofer Informationszentrum Raum und Bau) Fraunhofer I R B Verlag, Nobelstr. 12, 70569 Stuttgart, Germany. TEL 49-711-9702500. FAX 49-711-9702507. TELEX 7255168-IZS-D. E-mail: irb@irb.fhg.de; URL: http://www.irb.fhg.de. adv.; bk.rev. circ. 1,500. (back issues avail.) **Document type:** trade publication.
 —BLDSC (5131.494000).

016.72 016.3527 US ISSN 1043-0946
NA1
SEARCH (DEVON); the magazine index for architecture, interiors, and housing magazines. 1988. a. (plus q. updates). $99 for hard copy; computerized library edition $225 (effective 1996). Search Publishing Inc., 102 Brighton Cir., Devon, PA 19333. TEL 610-889-0535. FAX 610-889-9497. E-mail: searchman@aol.com. Ed. Don Colangelo. R&P contact: Don Colangelo. circ. 1,250 (paid). (also avail. in diskette format; back issues avail.) **Document type:** abstracting/indexing.
 Description: Indexes articles and photographs.

720 316.8 SA
SOUTH AFRICA. CENTRAL STATISTICAL SERVICE. CENSUS OF ARCHITECTS AND QUANTITY SURVEYORS. (Report No. 83-01-01) every 6 years, latest 1986. R.2.31 (foreign R.2.50). Central Statistical Service - Sentrale Statistiekdiens, Private Bag X44, Pretoria 0001, South Africa. TEL 27-12-310-8911. FAX 27-12-310-8500. (Orders to: Goverment Printing Works, Private Bag X85, Pretoria 0001, South Africa) **Document type:** government publication.

ARCHITECTURE — Computer Applications

720 US ISSN 1079-9680
A C A D I A QUARTERLY. 1981. q. membership only. Association for Computer Aided Design in Architecture, c/o Skip Van Wyk, Ed., School of Architecture & Planning, Univ. of New Mexico, Albuquerque, NM 87131. TEL 505-277-2903. E-mail: vanwyk@unm.edu; URL: http://www.unm.edu/~vanwyk. (Subscr. to: Anton Harfmann, Membership Chair, Universty of Cincinnati, Box 210016, Cincinnati, OH 45221-0016) adv.: page $300; adv. contact: Skip Van Wyk. bk.rev.; circ. 280 (controlled). **Document type:** academic/scholarly publication.
 —UnCover.
 Formerly: A C A D I A Newsletter (ISSN 0896-0178)
 Description: Intended for people interested in computer applications in architecture and design.

A - E - C AUTOMATION NEWSLETTER. (Architecture, Engineering, Construction) see *ENGINEERING — Computer Applications*

720.972 MX
ARQUITECTURA MEXICANA. Short title: A M. no.2, 1987. s-a. Mex.$50 per no. (effective 1997). Universidad Nacional Autonoma de Mexico, Facultad de Arquitectura, Circuito Interior, Ciudad Universitaria, 04510 Mexico, D.F., Mexico. TEL 52-5-6220318. FAX 52-5-616-0545. Ed. Ramon Vargas Salguero.
 Formerly: Cuadernos de Arquitectura Docencia.
 Description: Covers contemporary Mexican architecture, part of the work is based on computer applications.

006.6 720 US ISSN 1057-9567
TA174
MICROSTATION MANAGER; the monthly independent publication for the MicroStation professional. 1977. m. $38.95 (foreign $59.95). MicroManagement, Inc., Box 1536, Santa Fe, NM 87501. TEL 505-982-5181. FAX 505-986-3816. E-mail: susith@aol.com. URL: http://www.copyright.com. (Subscr. to: Box 302 - Lobby A, Ann Arbor, MI 48106-0302. TEL 313-930-3799. FAX 313-930-3820) Ed. Susan Smith; Pub. Robert P. Holton. adv.: B&W page $3365, color page $4565; trim 8 1/4 x 10 7/8; adv. contact: Kyle Walkenhorst. bk.rev. circ. 21,000. **Document type:** trade publication.
 ●Also available online.
 —KR SourceOne.
 Former titles (until 1990): Design Systems Strategies (ISSN 0895-6790); A E Systems Report.
 Description: For architects and engineers who use MicroStation for CAD.

ART

see also Advertising and Public Relations; Hobbies; Museums and Art Galleries

A A T A NEWSLETTER. (American Art Therapy Association, Inc.) see *EDUCATION — Special Education And Rehabilitation*

700 US
▼**A - C JOURNAL.** 1996. s-a. Michigan Council for Arts and Cultural Affairs, 1200 Sixth St., Ste. 1180, Detroit, MI 48226. TEL 313-256-3731. FAX 313-256-3781. Ed. Jan Fedewa. circ. 12,000. **Document type:** government publication, bulletin.

A C T A NEWS. (Art Craft Teachers Association of Victoria) see *EDUCATION — Teaching Methods And Curriculum*

A D A MAGAZINE. (Art, Design, Architecture) see *ARCHITECTURE*

700 796.77 790.13 US ISSN 0899-9171
A F A S QUARTERLY. 1989. q. $16 (Canada $26; elsewhere $32). (Automotive Fine Arts Society) Bor Productions, Box 325, Lake Orion, MI 48361-0325. TEL 313-391-1378. FAX 313-391-1378. Ed. Jack Juratovic. adv. contact: Jan Taylor. bk.rev. circ. 5,000. **Document type:** consumer publication.
 Description: Informs the public about the aestheti value of automotive fine art and keeps collectors abreast of trends in value and availability.

ART   419

709   US
A G S QUARTERLY. 1977. q. $25 includes membership. Association for Gravestone Studies, c/o Lois Ahrens, Dir., 278 Main St., Ste. 207, Greenfield, MA 01301-3230. TEL 413-772-0836. FAX 413-774-5576. E-mail: ags@berkshire.net; URL: http://www.berkshire.net/ags. Ed.Bd. R&P contact: Lois Ahrens. adv. contact: Lois Ahrens. bk.rev.; bibl.; illus. circ. 1,100. **Document type:** newsletter.
  Formerly: Association for Gravestone Studies. Newsletter (ISSN 0146-5783)
  Description: Information about projects, literature and research concerning gravestones and about activities of the Association for Gravestone Studies.

700   US   ISSN 1058-9112
A GATHERING OF THE TRIBES; the multicultural arts magazine. 1991. 2/yr. $17.50; newsstand price: $10. Steve Cannon, Ed. & Pub., Box 20693, Tompkins Sq. Sta., New York, NY 10009. TEL 212-674-3778. FAX 212-674-3778. E-mail: tribes@pop.interport.net; URL: http://www.interport.net/~tribes. (Dist. by: Ubiquity Distributors, 607 DeGraw St., Brooklyn, NY 11217. TEL 718-875-5491) adv.: page $495; adv. contact: Steve Cannon. bk.rev.; dance rev, film rev, music rev, play rev, software rev, tele.rev, video rev, bibl, illus, maps, mkt, stat, tr.lit. circ. 2,000. (also avail. in video cassette; audio cassette; diskette format; back issues avail.) **Document type:** trade publication.
  ●Also available online.
  Description: Aimed at exposing intercultural and intergenerational expressions disregarding borders.

700 780   US   ISSN 8755-500X
A H A! HISPANIC ARTS NEWS. 1975. m. (9/yr.). $20 to individuals; institutions $40. Association of Hispanic Arts, 173 E. 116th St., 2nd Fl., New York, NY 10029. TEL 212-860-5445. FAX 212-427-2787. Ed. Dolores Prida. adv.; bk.rev.; charts; illus. circ. 7,000. (back issues avail.) **Document type:** newsletter.
  Formerly: Hispanic Arts (ISSN 0732-1643)
  Description: Contains opportunities for artists, calendar of events, and editorials on events affecting the arts community.

702.88   AT   ISSN 0313-5381
A I C C M BULLETIN. 1975. s-a. Aus.$75 to individuals; institutions Aus.$200; students Aus.$30. Australian Institute for the Conservation of Cultural Material, Inc., P.O. Box 1638, Canberra, A.C.T. 2601, Australia. TEL 06-243-4531. FAX 06-243-4531. E-mail: gina/drummond@awm.gov.au. adv.; bk.rev. circ. 500. (back issues avail.) **Indexed:** Art & Archaeol.Tech.Abstr. **Document type:** bulletin.
  —BLDSC (2409.316700); UnCover.
  Description: Focuses on conservation of cultural materials.
  Refereed Serial

780 700   US
A I C F NEWSLETTER. 1975. q. membership. America-Israel Cultural Foundation, 317 Madison Ave., Ste. 1605, New York, NY 10017. TEL 212-557-1600. FAX 212-557-1611. Ed. Kathleen Mellon. circ. 2,500. **Document type:** newsletter.
  Formerly: Hadashot.
  Description: Covers music, dance, film, theatre, visual arts and other creative and performing arts in Israel.

700 333.7   US   ISSN 0887-705X
A I C NEWS. 1975. bi-m. $100 membership. American Institute for Conservation of Historic and Artistic Works, 1717 K St., N.W., Ste. 301, Washington, DC 20006. TEL 202-452-9545. FAX 202-452-9328. E-mail: infoAIC@aol.com; URL: http://palimpsest.stanford.edu/aic/. Ed. Lisa Goldberg. adv.; circ. 3,000 (controlled).
  Description: Reports on conservation issues, conferences, new techniques and materials, as well as AIC activities.

A M S STUDIES IN THE EMBLEM. see *GENEALOGY AND HERALDRY*

700   UK   ISSN 0261-3425
N1
A N. (Artists Newsletter) 1980. m. £23.50 (foreign £41). A N Publications, P.O. Box 23, Sunderland, Tyne and Wear SR4 6DG, England. TEL 44-191-567-3589. FAX 44-191-564-1600. E-mail: an@anpubs.demon.co.uk. Ed. Angela Kingston; Pub. Richard Padwick. R&P contact: Hannah Firth. adv. contact: Kelly Wilson. bk.rev.; illus.; index; circ. 27,000 (paid). (back issues avail.) **Indexed:** DAAI. **Document type:** consumer publication.
  Description: Supplies information and discussion about the visual arts. Deals with issues such as contracts, studios, funding, marketing, selling, publicity, exhibiting, and salaries.
  Refereed Serial

700   US
A P A A NEWSLETTER. 1937. s-a. membership. American Physicians Art Association, 1130 N. Cabrillo, San Pedro, CA 90731. TEL 310-436-9645. FAX 310-436-7119. E-mail: cbsw70a@mail.prodigy.com. Ed. James S. Benedict. R&P contact: James S. Benedict. circ. 300. (back issues avail.) **Document type:** newsletter.
  Description: Contains news and features on the association, announcements of exhibit winners and meetings, minutes of meetings, instructions on entering art exhibits, and a catalog of entries and events.

700   SW   ISSN 0044-5711
A R I S. (Art Research in Scandinavia) (Text in English, Swedish) 1969. irreg. price varies. Lund University Press, P.O. Box 141, S-221 00 Lund, Sweden. TEL 46-46-31-20-00. FAX 46-46-30-53-38. E-mail: order@studli.se. Ed. Sven Sandstroem. illus. circ. 700. **Indexed:** IBR. **Document type:** academic/scholarly publication.

A R L I S DIRECTORY. (Art Libraries Society - UK & Ireland) see *LIBRARY AND INFORMATION SCIENCES*

A R L I S NEWSSHEET. (Art Libraries Society - UK & Ireland) see *LIBRARY AND INFORMATION SCIENCES*

700   US   ISSN 0892-3582
A S A ARTISAN. 1972. q. American Society of Artists, Inc., Box 1326, Palatine, IL 60078. TEL 312-751-2500. Ed.Bd. **Document type:** trade publication.
  Formerly (until 1982): A S A Bulletin.
  Description: Information for and about artists and craftspeople, with national calendar of events.

700   US   ISSN 0065-0129
A.W. MELLON LECTURES IN THE FINE ARTS. 1956. irreg., no.44, 1996. price varies. Princeton University Press, 41 William St., Princeton, NJ 08540. TEL 609-258-4900. FAX 609-258-6305. URL: http://pup.princeton.edu. (reprint service avail. from UMI) **Document type:** monographic series.

AARET FORTALT I BILLEDER. see *HISTORY — History Of Europe*

700 800 780   GW   ISSN 0567-4999
ABHANDLUNGEN ZUR KUNST-, MUSIK- UND LITERATURWISSENSCHAFT. no.3, 1958. irreg., vol.396, 1995. price varies. Bouvier Verlag Herbert Grundmann, Am Hof 28, 53113 Bonn, Germany. TEL 49-228-7290184. FAX 49-228-7290179. **Indexed:** M.L.A., MLA Intl.Bibl. **Document type:** monographic series.

ABRACADABRA. see *PRINTING*

700   AG
ACADEMIA NACIONAL DE BELLAS ARTES. ANUARIO.* 1973. a. $120. Academia Nacional de Bellas Artes, Sanchez de Bustamante 2663, 1425 Buenos Aires, Argentina. TEL 54-1-8022469. Ed.Bd. illus. circ. 700.

700   BE
ACADEMIAE ANALECTA. KLASSE DER SCHONE KUNSTEN. (Text in Dutch, English; summaries in English) 1938. irreg., vol.52, no.1, 1992. price varies. Koninklijke Academie voor Wetenschappen, Letteren en Schone Kunsten van Belgie, 1 Hertogsstraat, B-1000 Brussels, Belgium. FAX 32-2-5110143. (Dist. by: N.V. Brepols, Steenweg op Tielen 68, 2300 Turnhout, Belgium. TEL 32-14-402500. FAX 32-14-428919) Ed. G. Verbeke. circ. 700. (back issues avail.) **Indexed:** RILM. **Document type:** academic/scholarly publication.
  Former titles (until 1980): Koninklijke Academie voor Wetenschappen, Letteren en Schone Kunsten Van Belgie. Mededelingen. Klasse der Schone Kunsten (ISSN 0770-1349); (until 1972): Koninklijke Vlaamse Academie voor Wetenschappen, Letteren en Schone Kunsten van Belgie. Mededelingen. Klasse der Schone Kunsten (ISSN 0770-139X)

709   HU   ISSN 0001-5830
N6
ACADEMIAE SCIENTIARUM HUNGARICAE. ACTA HISTORIAE ARTIUM. (Text in English, French, German, Italian, Russian) 1953. q. $180 (effective 1997). (Magyar Tudomanyos Akademia) Akademiai Kiado Rt., P.O. Box 245, H-1519 Budapest, Hungary. TEL 36-1-2043976. FAX 36-1-2043973. Ed. Erno Marosi. adv.; bk.rev.; illus.; index. **Indexed:** Amer.Hist.& Life (1986-199?), Arts & Hum.Cit.Ind., Curr.Cont., Hist.Abstr. (1986-199?), IBR, RILA. **Document type:** academic/scholarly publication.
  —Genuine Article. **CCC**.
  Description: Presents papers on the history of art extending from the Middle Ages to contemporary art. Includes critical analyses of research publications.

700   UK
ACADEMIC FILE INTERNATIONAL NEWS & PHOTO SYNDICATION. (Former name of issuing body: Centre for Near East Asia and African Research) q. (Centre for Near East Afro-Asian Research (NEAR)) Eastern Art Publishing Group, 27 Wallorton Gardens, London SL14 8DX, England. TEL 44-81-392-1122. FAX 44-81-392-1422. E-mail: easternart@compuserve.co.uk. Eds. Sajid & Shirley Rizvi. circ. controlled.
  ●Available only online.
  Description: Online information service for the media concerning the developing world.

700   BE   ISSN 0378-7923
ACADEMIE ROYALE DES SCIENCES, DES LETTRES ET DES BEAUX-ARTS DE BELGIQUE. CLASSE DES BEAUX-ARTS. MEMOIRES. 1919. irreg. price varies. Academie Royale des Sciences, des Lettres et des Beaux-Arts de Belgique, Palais des Academies, 1 rue Ducale, 1000 Brussels, Belgium. (Dist. by: Altera Diffusion, rue Rodenbach 98, 1190 Brussels, Belgium) **Document type:** monographic series.
  —KNAW.

700 011   IT   ISSN 0394-8501
N6923.L33
ACCADEMIA LEONARDO DA VINCI: JOURNAL OF LEONARDO STUDIES AND BIBLIOGRAPHY OF VINCIANA. 1988. a. (Armand Hammer Center for Leonardo Studies, US) Giunti Gruppo Editoriale S.p.A., Via Bolognese 165, 50139 Florence, Italy. TEL 39-55-6679267. FAX 39-55-6679298. URL: http://www.giunti.it. Ed. Carlo Pedretti.

ACCADEMIA PATAVINA DI SCIENZE LETTERE ED ARTI. ATTI E MEMORIE. see *LITERATURE*

ACCADEMIA PATAVINA DI SCIENZE LETTERE ED ARTI. COLLANA ACCADEMICA. see *LITERATURE*

ACCESS (MELBOURNE). see *HANDICAPPED*

700 338   US   ISSN 1056-4101
ACCESS (SEATTLE); a guide to the visual arts in Washington State. 1972. irreg. (approx. biennial). Allied Arts of Seattle, 107 S. Main St., Ste. 201, Seattle, WA 98104. TEL 206-624-0432. circ. 5,000. **Document type:** directory.
  Description: Directory of Washington State exhibition spaces. Includes extensive addenda of arts services, organizations, education and professional training and a bibliography of additional resources.

420 ART

700　　　　　　　IT　　ISSN 1122-6218
ACOMA. 4/yr. Lit.42000 (foreign Lit.50000) (effective 1997). Giunti Gruppo Editoriale S.p.A., Via Bolonese 165, 50139 Florence, Italy. TEL 39-55-6679267. FAX 39-55-6679298. URL: http://www.giunti.it

ACTA GRAPHICA; revija za graficku tehnologiju, inzinjerstvo i dizajn - journal for graphic arts, engineering and design. see *TECHNOLOGY: COMPREHENSIVE WORKS*

709 720　　　　PL　　ISSN 0860-4746
ACTA UNIVERSITATIS WRATISLAVIENSIS. HISTORIA SZTUKI. (Text in Polish; summaries in English or German) 1988. irreg. price varies. (Uniwersytet Wroclawski) Wydawnictwo Uniwersytetu Wroclawskiego, Spolka z o.o., Pl. Uniwersytecki 9-13, 50-137 Wroclaw, Poland.
TEL 48-71-441006. FAX 48-71-402735. Eds. Zofia Ostrowska-Keblowska, Mieczyslaw Zlat. circ. 700. **Document type:** academic/scholarly publication.

ACTION (POTTS POINT). see *EDUCATION — Teaching Methods And Curriculum*

709　　　　　　　FR　　ISSN 0293-9789
ACTUALITE DES ARTS PLASTIQUES. 3/yr. 440 F. (foreign 480 F.) (effective 1997). Centre National de Documentation Pedagogique, 29 rue d'Ulm, 75230 Paris Cedex 05, France.
TEL 33-1-46349000. FAX 33-1-46345544. (Subscr. to: CNDP - Abonnement, B750, 60732 Ste. Genevieve Cedex, France. FAX 33-3-44033013) Ed. Bernard Piens.
Description: Reference collection dedicated to the development of contemporary art.

ADAM INTERNATIONAL REVIEW. see *LITERATURE*

ADORANTEN. see *ARCHAEOLOGY*

AEGYPTOLOGISCHE FORSCHUNGEN. see *HISTORY — History Of The Near East*

AERIAL. see *LITERATURE — Poetry*

AESTHETICA. PRE-PRINT. see *PHILOSOPHY*

709.2　　　　　　NE
AETA AUREA. (Text in English) 1981. irreg., vol.12, 1996. price varies. Davaco Publishers, Beukenlaan 3, 8085 RK Doornspijk, Netherlands.
TEL 31-525-661823. FAX 31-525-662153. illus. (back issues avail.) **Document type:** monographic series.
Description: Publishes monographic studies of notable Dutch painters from the 16th and 17th centuries.

700　　　　　　　EG　　ISSN 1022-5692
AFRICA 2000. q. Centro Cultural Hispano-Guineano, Apdo. 180, Malabo, Equatorial Guinea. TEL 27-20. Ed. Donato Ndongo-Bidyogo.

709.6　　　　　　US　　ISSN 0001-9933
NX587
AFRICAN ARTS. 1967. q. $42 to individuals (overseas $50); institutions $64 (overseas $72) (effective 1997). University of California at Los Angeles, James S. Coleman African Studies Center, Los Angeles, CA 90024. TEL 310-825-1218. E-mail: afriarts@ucla.edu; URL: http://www.isop.ucla.edu/jscass/afrart/afrart1.htm. Eds. Donald Cosentino, Doran Ross. adv.; bk.rev.; charts; illus.; index. circ. 5,000. (also avail. in microform from UMI; back issues avail.; reprint service avail. from UMI) **Indexed:** A.I.C.P., Acad.Ind., Anthropol.Lit., Art Ind., Art.Ind., Artbibl., Artbibl.Mod., ASCA, Avery Ind.Archit.Per., Curr.Cont.Africa, Curr.Cont., Hum.Ind., IBR, Ind.Bk.Rev.Hum., M.L.A., SSCI. **Document type:** academic/scholarly publication.
●Also available online. Vendor(s): UMI.
—BLDSC (0732.315000); KR SourceOne; UMI; UnCover.

AFRIQUE LITTERAIRE. see *LITERATURE*

AFTERIMAGES. see *LITERATURE*

700 808.8　　　　US
AFTERNOON MAGAZINE. 1995. irreg. Motley Focus Locus, 788 Columbus Ave., 7P, New York, NY 10025. E-mail: stephenw@escape.com; timber@silcom.com; URL: http://www.motley-focus.com/~timber/afternoon.html. Eds. William Timberman, Stephen Williamson.
●Available only online.
Description: International literary magazine.

700 708　　　　　CN　　ISSN 0829-4801
AGENDA. 1985. q. Can.$25. Visual Arts Ontario, 439 Wellington St. W., Toronto, ON M5V 1E7, Canada. TEL 416-591-8883. FAX 416-591-2432. Ed. Tracey Bowen. R&P contact: Hennie Wolff. adv. contact: David McClyment. circ. 3,700. **Document type:** trade publication.
Description: Includes calls for entries, job opportunities, resources, events and other news.

700 666 790.13　　　US　　ISSN 1040-8509
NC915.A35
AIRBRUSH ACTION. 1985. bi-m. $21.95 (Canada $28; elsewhere $50) (effective 1996). Airbrush Action, Inc., 1985 Swarthmore Ave., Box 2052, Lakewood, NJ 08701. TEL 908-364-2111.
FAX 908-367-5908. (Subscr. to: Box 3000, Dept. MM, Denville, NJ 07834) Ed. Clifford S. Stieglitz. adv.; bk.rev.; illus.; tr.lit. circ. 60,000. (back issues avail.) **Document type:** consumer publication, trade publication.

AISTHESIS; revista chilena de investigaciones esteticas. see *PHILOSOPHY*

AKADEMIYA NAUK AZERBAIJANA. IZVESTIYA. SERIYA YAZYKOZNANIE, LITERATURA I ISKUSSTVO. see *LINGUISTICS*

700　　　　　　　US
ALABAMA ARTS. 1971? s-a. free. State Council on the Arts, 201 Monroe St., Montgomery, AL 36130. TEL 334-242-4076. FAX 334-240-3269. Ed. Sharon Heflin. R&P contact: Sharon Heflin. illus. circ. 6,000.
Formerly: Ala-Arts (ISSN 0146-9398)

ALADIN; antiques - arts - brocante - collections - encheres. see *ANTIQUES*

792　　　　　　　US
ALASKA. STATE COUNCIL ON THE ARTS. COMMUNIQUE. Short title: A S C A Communique. 1973. m. free in Alaska; elsewhere $15. State Council on the Arts, 411 W. Fourth Ave., Ste. 1E, Anchorage, AK 99501-2343. TEL 907-279-1558.
FAX 907-279-4330. E-mail: asca@alaska.net; URL: http://www.educ.state.akus/asca/home/html. Ed. Tom Wilson. circ. 6,000. **Document type:** newsletter.
●Also available online.
Formerly: Alaska. State Council on the Arts. Bulletin; Which superseded: Arts in Alaska (ISSN 0094-3568)
Description: Provides news and opportunities fo Alaska artists.

ALBANY INSTITUTE OF HISTORY & ART. ANNUAL REPORT. see *HISTORY — History Of North And South America*

750 860 770 720　　　SP
ALBUM, LETRAS Y ARTES. bi-m. 3600 ptas. (Europe $85; elsewhere $150). Album Letras Artes, S.A., C. Juan Alvarez Mendizabal 58, 1o A, 28008 Madrid, Spain. TEL 91-559-90-27. Dir. Jesus Tablate Miquis. circ. 14,000.
Description: Covers painting, photography, architecture and literature to immerse the reader in the fundamental forms of expression and to understand art as the consequence of an age.

ALLA BOTTEGA; bimestrale di cultura ed arte. see *LITERATURE*

ALLIED ARTS NEWSLETTER. see *PUBLIC ADMINISTRATION — Municipal Government*

700 900　　　　　CN　　ISSN 1183-8086
ALPHABET CITY. 1991. a. Can.$50($50) to individuals; institutions Can.$200. Alphabet City Magazine of Toronto Inc., P.O. Box 387, Station P, Toronto, ON M5S 2S9, Canada. TEL 416-588-2827.
FAX 416-921-1754. Ed. John Knecktel; Pub. Heather Cameron. adv.: page Can.$500; adv. contact: Denis Deklerck. circ. 5,000 (paid). (tabloid format; back issues avail.) **Document type:** academic/scholarly publication.
Description: Interdisciplinary magazine of culture and politics, designed to bring academic research information to an audience of non-specialists.

700 720　　　　　IT　　ISSN 0065-6801
DG12
AMERICAN ACADEMY IN ROME. MEMOIRS. 1917. irreg. price varies. American Academy in Rome, Via Angelo Masina 5, 00153 Rome, Italy. TEL 39-6-58461. **Indexed:** Numis.Lit. **Document type:** monographic series.

701　　　　　　　US　　ISSN 1073-9300
N6505
AMERICAN ART. 1987. 3/yr. $35 to individuals; institutions $70 (foreign $80) (effective 1997). Smithsonian Institution, National Museum of American Art, 601 Indiana Ave., Ste. 200, Washington, DC 20004. TEL 202-357-1812. (Subscr. to: c/o Karen Fuchs, Membership Services, National Museum of American Art, 8th & G Streets, Washington, DC 20560) Ed. Maria Villecillo. adv.; bibl.; illus. (also avail. in microfiche; back issues avail.) **Indexed:** Acad.Ind., Amer.Hist.& Life (1987-), Art Ind., Hist.Abstr. **Document type:** academic/scholarly publication.
—BLDSC (0810.395000); KR SourceOne; UMI; UnCover.
Formerly (until 1991): Smithsonian Studies in American Art (ISSN 0890-4901)
Description: Encompasses all aspects of the nation's visual heritage from colonial to contemporary times, including new media, popular culture, and decorative arts and crafts. Primary focus is on fine arts.
Refereed Serial

700 338　　　　　US　　ISSN 0065-6968
AMERICAN ART DIRECTORY. 1898. biennial, 56th ed., 1997. $209.95. R.R. Bowker, A Division of Reed Elsevier Inc., 121 Chanlon Rd., New Providence, NJ 07974. TEL 908-464-6800. FAX 908-665-6688. TELEX 138 755. E-mail: info@bowker.com; URL: http://www.reedref.com. (Subscr. to: Order Dept., Box 31, New Providence, NJ 07974-9903. TEL 800-521-8110) index. **Document type:** directory.
Description: Identifies characteristics of art museums and libraries, enrollment and programs of art schools, major foreign institutions, and state and local systems. Indexed geographically and by institution, personnel, and subject.

709　　　　　　　US　　ISSN 0002-7359
N6505
AMERICAN ART JOURNAL. 1969. s-a. $35 (effective 1997). Kennedy Galleries, Inc., 730 Fifth Ave., New York, NY 10019. TEL 212-541-9600.
FAX 212-977-3833. Ed. Jayne A. Kuchna. bk.rev.; illus.; cum.index: vols.1-4. circ. 2,000. (also avail. in microform from UMI) **Indexed:** Amer.Hist.& Life (1970-), Art Ind., Artbibl.Mod., Artbibl., Arts & Hum.Cit.Ind., ASCA, Avery Ind.Archit.Per., Curr.Cont., Hist.Abstr. (1970-), Hum.Ind., IBR, Ind.Bk.Rev.Hum., RILA. **Document type:** academic/scholarly publication.
—BLDSC (0810.398000); KR SourceOne; UMI; UnCover.

700　　　　　　　US　　ISSN 0092-1327
N6505
AMERICAN ART REVIEW. 1973. bi-m. $21 (Canada $33; elsewhere $39). Box 480500, Kansas City, MO 64148. TEL 913-451-8801. Ed. Thomas Kellaway. adv.; bk.rev.; illus.; circ. 42,000 (paid). **Indexed:** Art Ind., Curr.Cont., Mag.Ind., RILA.
—UnCover.

| 707 | US | ISSN 0002-7375 |

N1

AMERICAN ARTIST. 1937. m. $26.95 (foreign $36.95) (effective 1997); newsstand price: $2.95. B P I Communications, Inc. (New York), 1515 Broadway, 11th Fl., New York, NY 10036. TEL 212-764-7300. FAX 212-536-5351. Ed. M. Stephen Doherty. R&P contact: Sylvia Valle. adv. contact: Irene Gruen. bk.rev.; illus.; index. circ. 145,100. (also avail. in microform (ISSN 0364-9865) from UMI; microfiche from NBI; reprint service avail.) Indexed: Acad.Ind., Art & Archaeol.Tech.Abstr., Art Ind., Art.Ind., Artbibl., Artbibl.Mod., Avery Ind.Archit.Per., Bibl.Engl.Lang.& Lit., Biog.Ind., Bk.Rev.Ind. (1965-), Child.Bk.Rev.Ind. (1965-), Mag.Ind., PMR, R.G.Abstr., R.G., Ref.Sour., TOM. **Document type:** consumer publication.
●Also available online. Vendor(s): Information Access Co.
—BLDSC (0810.410000); KR SourceOne; SWETS; UMI; UnCover. **CCC**.
 Description: Emphasizes figurative art. Includes interviews with prominent artists and articles on technical aspects of drawing and painting.

| 707 371.0025 | US | ISSN 0146-9606 |

N328

AMERICAN ARTIST DIRECTORY OF ART SCHOOLS & WORKSHOPS. 1964. a. $2.95. B P I Communications, Inc. (New York), 1515 Broadway, 11th Fl., New York, NY 10036. TEL 212-764-7300. Ed. M. Stephen Doherty. R&P contact: Sylvia Valles. adv. contact: Irene Gruen. (also avail. in microform) **Document type:** directory.
 Former titles: American Artist Art School Directory; Art School Directory.

| 741 | US | ISSN 1062-0966 |

AMERICAN CENTER FOR DESIGN JOURNAL.* a. $23. American Center for Design, 325 W. Huron St., Ste. 711, Chicago, IL 60610-3617. circ. 5,000. Indexed: DAAI. **Document type:** trade publication.
 Description: Each issue looks at a single design topic in depth. Through its broad, multidisciplinary focus, it charts a course between portfolio review periodicals and specialist scholarly journals.

| 760 974 | US | |

AMERICAN HISTORICAL PRINT COLLECTORS SOCIETY. NEWSLETTER. q. $35 includes Imprint. American Historical Print Collectors Society, Inc. (Fairfield), Box 201, Fairfield, CT 06430. TEL 810-332-3902. Ed. Donald C. O'Brien. R&P contact: Robert Braun. **Document type:** newsletter.

| 741.640 | US | ISSN 0737-6642 |

NC975

AMERICAN ILLUSTRATION.* 1959. a. $60. (Society of Illustrators) Fadner Media Enterprises, 16 W. 19th, 9th Fl., New York, NY 10011. TEL 212-647-0874. FAX 212-691-6609. (Dist. by: Watson Guptil, 1695 Oak St., Lakewood, NJ 08701. TEL 908-363-5679) Ed. Arpi Ermoyan. adv.; index. circ. 20,000. (back issues avail.) Indexed: Artbibl.
—BLDSC (4367.240000).
 Formerly: Illustrators (ISSN 0073-5477)
 Description: Features the best illustrations of the year in the following categories: advertising, book, editorial, and institutional.

| 700 | US | ISSN 0192-9968 |

AMERICAN INDIAN ART MAGAZINE. 1975. q. $20 (foreign $24). American Indian Art, Inc., 7314 E. Osborn Dr., Scottsdale, AZ 85251. TEL 602-994-5445. Ed. Roanne P. Goldfein; Pub. Mary Hamilton. R&P contact: Mary B. O'Halloran. adv. contact: Ronda Rawlins. bk.rev.; illus. circ. 29,000. (back issues avail.) Indexed: Abstr.Anthropol., Amer.Hist.& Life (1977-), Anthropol.Lit., Art Ind., Artbibl.Mod., Hist.Abstr. (1977-). **Document type:** consumer publication.
—BLDSC (0819.640000); KR SourceOne; UnCover.
 Formerly (until 1977): American Indian Art (ISSN 0362-2630)
 Description: Devoted to prehistoric, historic, and contemporary American Indian visual art.
 Refereed Serial

AMERICAN INDIAN BASKETRY AND OTHER NATIVE ARTS. see *ARTS AND HANDICRAFTS*

AMERICAN INSTITUTE FOR CONSERVATION OF HISTORIC AND ARTISTIC WORKS. ABSTRACTS OF PAPERS PRESENTED AT THE ANNUAL MEETING. see *ART — Abstracting, Bibliographies, Statistics*

| 700 333.7 | US | |

AMERICAN INSTITUTE FOR CONSERVATION OF HISTORIC AND ARTISTIC WORKS. DIRECTORY. 1973. a. $25 to individuals and non-profits; commercial $50. American Institute for Conservation of Historic and Artistic Works, 1717 K St., N.W., Ste. 301, Washington, DC 20006. TEL 202-452-9545. FAX 202-452-9328. E-mail: infoAIC@aol.com; URL: http://palimpsest.stanford.edu/aic/. adv. circ. 3,000. **Document type:** directory.
 Description: Comprehensive listing of AIC members organized by name, specialty, and geographic region; contains additional information on the AIC and the conservation field in general.

| 751.6 | US | ISSN 0197-1360 |
| | | CODEN: JAICDE |

AMERICAN INSTITUTE FOR CONSERVATION OF HISTORIC & ARTISTIC WORKS. JOURNAL. 1961. 3/yr. $73 (foreign $91). American Institute for Conservation of Historic and Artistic Works, 1717 K St., N.W., Ste. 301, Washington, DC 20006. TEL 202-452-9545. FAX 202-452-9328. E-mail: infoAIC@aol.com; URL: http://palimpsest.stanford.edu/aic/. Ed. Chandra Reedy. adv.; bk.rev.; bibl.; charts; illus.; index. circ. 3,200. (back issues avail.) Indexed: Art & Archaeol.Tech.Abstr., ASCA, Corros.Abstr.
—BLDSC (4686.640000); SWETS; UnCover.
 Formerly: American Institute for Conservation of Historic and Artistic Works. Bulletin.
 Description: Focuses on the conservation of architectural materials, archaeological objects, books and papers, paintings, photographs and sculpture.
 Refereed Serial

| 700 620 | IE | ISSN 0743-0884 |

AMERICAN INTERNATIONAL JOURNAL OF ARTS, SCIENCES, ENGINEERING AND MEDICINE. 1984. 2/yr. $100. Royal University, Ltd., 6 Lower Hatch St., Dublin 2, Ireland. FAX 353-1-6686632. Ed. C.V. Ramasastry. adv.; bk.rev. (looseleaf format) **Document type:** academic/scholarly publication.
 Description: Aimed at providing a link between research and practice for professors, consultants and researchers in various specializations.

| 741 | US | ISSN 1071-8745 |

NC1300

AMERICAN JOURNAL OF ANTHROPOMORPHICS. 1993. s-a. $40 (foreign $60) for 4 nos. (effective 1996). Med Systems Co., Box 580009, Flushing, NY 11358-0009. TEL 718-359-5741; 800-667-7943. FAX 718-359-2768. E-mail: darrell.benvenuto@f523.n278.z1.fidonet.org. Ed. Darrell Benvenuto. R&P contact: Darrell Benvenuto. adv.: B&W page $400, color page $800; adv. contact: Darrell Benvenuto. bk.rev.; illus.; circ. 8,000 (paid). (back issues avail.) **Document type:** trade publication.
●Also available online.
 Description: Reference work for freelance artists from around the world who specialize in commercial and commissioned illustration of anthropomorphics, ranging from cartoon animals to realistic illustration and representation of all sorts.

AMERICAN JOURNAL OF ART THERAPY; art in psychotherapy, education, and rehabilitation. see *EDUCATION — Special Education And Rehabilitation*

| 700 100 | US | |

AMERICAN LIVING PRESS. 1982. q. $10. Box 901, Allston, MA 02134. TEL 617-522-7782. Eds. Angela Mark, Michael Shores. illus. circ. 150. (back issues avail.)
 Formerly (until no.25, 1988): American Living.
 Description: Visual magazine depicting past, present and future.

| 700 | | ISSN 0163-8211 |

PS501

AMERICAN RAG.* 1978. q. $11. Frederick Douglass Creative Arts Center, 270 W. 96th St., New York, NY 10025. illus.

AMERICAN RESEARCH CENTER IN EGYPT. JOURNAL. see *ARCHAEOLOGY*

| 700 810 | US | |

AMERICAN REVIEW. 1977. m. $12. Allen G. Weakland, Ed. & Pub., 15 Burchfield Ave., Cranford, NJ 07016. TEL 201-276-6222. adv.; film rev.; illus. circ. 2,000. (back issues avail.; reprint service avail. from KTO) Indexed: Abstr.Engl.Stud.
 Formerly: New American Review.

| 700 338.025 | US | ISSN 0278-8128 |

NC998.5.A1

AMERICAN SHOWCASE ILLUSTRATION. 1977. a. (in 2 vols.). $75. American Showcase Inc., 915 Broadway, 14th Fl., New York, NY 10010. TEL 212-673-6600. FAX 212-673-9795. (Dist. in U.S. by: Watson-Guptill Publications, 1515 Broadway, New York, NY 10036. TEL 1-800-451-1741; Overseas & Canada: Rotovision SA, Route Suisse 9, CH-1295 Mies, Switzerland. TEL 41-22755-3055) Ed. Ann Middlebrook; Pub. Ira Shapiro. adv. contact: Rob Drasin. circ. 18,500. (back issues avail.) **Document type:** directory.
 Supersedes in part (in 1982): American Showcase (ISSN 0742-6100)
 Description: Presents trend-setting examples (4,500 images) of illustration and design for books, magazines, advertisements, posters and packaging. Lists names and addresses of over 7,000 illustrators, reps, and designers, arranged topically and by region for easy access.

AMERICAN SOCIETY OF APPRAISERS. NEWSLINE. see *BUSINESS AND ECONOMICS — Banking And Finance*

AMERICAN SOCIETY OF BOOKPLATE COLLECTORS AND DESIGNERS. YEAR BOOK. see *HOBBIES*

| 709 | US | ISSN 0890-412X |

AMERICAN UNIVERSITY STUDIES. SERIES 20. FINE ARTS. (Text in English and West European languages.) 1988. irreg. price varies. Peter Lang Publishing, Inc., 275 Seventh Ave., 28th Fl., New York, NY 10001. TEL 212-647-7700; 800-770-5264. FAX 212-647-7707. E-mail: customerservice@plang.com; URL: http://www.peterlang.com. Ed. Christopher Myers. Indexed: MLA Intl.Bibl. **Document type:** academic/scholarly publication, monographic series.
 Description: Explores a wide range of issues in the study of art.

| 704.948 | IT | ISSN 0003-1747 |

AMICO DELL'ARTE CRISTIANA. 1930. q. Lit.30000 (effective 1998). Scuola Beato Angelico, Via S. Gimignano 19, 20146 Milan, Italy. TEL 39-2-48302857. FAX 39-2-48301954. Ed. Valerio Vigorelli. adv. contact: Valerio Vigorelli. **Document type:** bulletin.

| 709 | FR | ISSN 0003-1852 |

AMIS DU CHATEAU DE PAU. BULLETIN. 1959. 2/yr. 250 F. (effective 1997). Societe des Amis du Chateau de Pau, Chateau de Pau, 64000 Pau, France. TEL 33-5-59823810. FAX 33-5-59823818. Dir. Annick Albier. adv.; bk.rev.; cum.index. circ. 1,000. (processed) **Document type:** bulletin.
 Description: Diffuses information on the cultural activities of the National Museum of the Pau Castle and its Society of Friends, provides texts of lectures, reports on trips, exhibits.

AMPERLAND; heimatkundliche Vierteljahresschrift fuer die Kreise Dachau, Freising und Fuerstenfeldbruck. see *HISTORY — History Of Europe*

| 709 | TU | ISSN 0066-1333 |

ANADOLU SANATI ARASTIRMALARI/RESEARCHES ON ANATOLIAN ART. (Text in English, Turkish; summaries in English) 1968. irreg. TL.35. Technical University of Istanbul, Department of the History of Architecture and Preservation - Istanbul Teknik Universitesi, Gumussuyu Caddesi 87, Beyoglu, Istanbul, Turkey. Ed. Dogan Kuban. circ. 1,000.

ANALES DE HISTORIA DEL ARTE. see *HISTORY*

ANDHRA PRADESH, INDIA. DEPARTMENT OF ARCHAEOLOGY AND MUSEUMS. ARCHAEOLOGICAL SERIES. see *ARCHAEOLOGY*

| 700 | NE | ISSN 0168-2997 |

ANDON. 1981. q. fl.65($50) membership. Vereniging voor Japanse Kunst - Society for Japanese Arts, Mr. Pankenstraat 12, 5571 CP Bergeijk, Netherlands. TEL 31-497-572310. FAX 31-497-573657. Ed. Henk Hernig. adv.; bk.rev.; circ. 800 (paid). **Document type:** academic/scholarly publication.
 Description: Provides a forum for the dissemination and exchange of ideas and information relating to traditional Japanese arts and crafts.

ART

810 700 US ISSN 8756-7709
ANEMONE. 1984. 4/yr. $10 to individuals; institutions $30. Anemone Press, Inc., Box 369, Chester, VT 05143. Ed. Nanette Morin. adv.; bk.rev. circ. 3,000. (back issues avail.) Indexed: Amer.Hum.Ind.

ANGELTREAD; the lyrian ruse. see LITERATURE

ANGELWATCH. see RELIGIONS AND THEOLOGY

ANIMATION JOURNAL. see MOTION PICTURES

778.53 US ISSN 1041-617X
NC1766.U5
ANIMATION MAGAZINE.* 1985. bi-m., plus supplement. $21 (Canada $30; elsewhere $39). Terry Thoren Publications, D B A Animation Magazine, 30101 Agoura Ct., Ste. 110, Agoura Hills, CA 91301-4301. TEL 818-991-2884. FAX 818-991-3773. Ed. Christine Ferriter; Pub. Rita/Street. adv.: B&W page $1800, color page $2250; trim 8 3/8 x 10 7/8; adv. contact: Linda Brown. film rev.; illus. circ. 40,000. (back issues avail.) Indexed: Art Ind. Document type: trade publication.
—BLDSC (0905.207000); KR SourceOne.
Description: Covers traditional as well as computer-generated animation. Contains columns by industry professionals and reviews coming events, news, and industry trends.

741.5 JA
ANIMEDIA. (Text in Japanese) 1981. m. 4560 Yen. Gakken Co. Ltd., 40-5, 4-chome, Kamiikedai, Ohta-ku, Tokyo 145, Japan. Ed. Keiichi Oshidari.

741.5 US ISSN 1067-0831
ANIMERICA; anime & manga monthly. 1992. m. $58 (Canada & Mexico $70; elsewhere $138). Viz Communications, Inc., Box 77010, San Francisco, CA 94107. Ed. Seiji Horibuchi; Pub. Keizo Inoue. adv.: B&W page $1300, color page $1800; trim 8 1/2 x 11; adv. contact: Lopa Mukherjee. bk.rev.; video rev.; illus.; circ. 20,000 (paid). Document type: consumer publication.
Description: News, information, interviews covering anime and manga. Includes serialized manga stories.

ANKA; revue d'art et de litterature de Turquie. see LITERATURE

700 GR ISSN 1105-0462
NX1.A1
ANNALES D'ESTHETIQUE/CHRONIKA AISTHETIKIS. (Text in English, French, German, Greek, Italian) 1962. a. Dr.2000($15) P. and E. Mixhalis Foundation, Vassilissis Sophias 79, 115 21 Athens, Greece. TEL 30-1-7218-626. Ed.Bd. bk.rev. circ. 1,000. (back issues avail.) Indexed: Phil.Ind. Document type: academic/scholarly publication.
Description: Promotes the postgraduate-level study of aesthetics.

700 FR
ANNUAIRE DE L'ART INTERNATIONAL. 1961. biennial. 350 F. Patrick Sermadiras, Ed. & Pub., 11 rue Arsene Houssaye, 75008 Paris, France. TEL 47-66-51-52. FAX 47-64-10-56. adv.; bk.rev.; illus. circ. 20,000.

700 FR ISSN 0066-3263
ANNUAIRE INTERNATIONAL DES VENTES. (Editions in French, English) 1963. a. 1200 F. Librairie Fischbacher, 33 rue de Seine, 75006 Paris, France. TEL 43-26-84-87. FAX 43-26-48-87. Ed. E. Mayer.

700 011 US ISSN 0898-7300
Z5935.3
ANNUAL BIBLIOGRAPHY OF MODERN ART. a. $250 (effective 1997). (Museum of Modern Art, Library) G.K. Hall & Co., MacMillan Library Reference USA, Box 159, Thorndike, ME 04986. TEL 212-654-8452; 800-223-6121. FAX 207-948-2863. URL: http://www.mir.com/thorndike. (Subscr. to: Simon & Schuster, Library Reference Order Processing, 200 Old Tappan Rd., Old Tappan, NJ 07675. TEL 800-223-2336) (also avail. in microform) Document type: bibliography, abstracting/indexing.
Description: Computer-derived bibliography of acquisitions catalogued in the past year by MOMA Library. Covers literature published in various languages worldwide, with emphasis on the U.S., Europe and Japan.

DER ANSCHNITT; Zeitschrift fuer Kunst und Kultur im Bergbau. see MINES AND MINING INDUSTRY

ANTHEM; the American experience in words, music and art. see LITERATURE

ANTHOLO-GEE!-ZINE. see LITERATURE

709 IT ISSN 0003-5645
ANTICHITA VIVA; rassegna d'arte. 1962. bi-m. L.130000 (foreign L.170000) (effective 1997). Casa Editrice Edam, Via Pier Capponi 24, 50132 Florence, Italy. TEL 39-55-576974. FAX 39-55-576974. Dir. Lorenzo Milone. adv.: B&W page L.2500000, color page L.2800000. bk.rev.; illus. circ. 2,000. Indexed: Artbibl.Mod., Artbibl., Avery Ind.Archit.Per., IBR, RILA.
—SWETS.

ANTIEK; tijdschrift voor liefhebbers en kenners van oude kunst en kunstnijverheid. see ANTIQUES

ANTIK & AUKTION. see ANTIQUES

ANTIKE KUNST. see ARCHAEOLOGY

ANTIKE KUNST. BEIHEFTE. see ARCHAEOLOGY

ANTIQUARIAN. see HISTORY — History Of North And South America

ANTIQUARIATO. see ANTIQUES

ANTIQUES FOLIO. see ANTIQUES

ANTIQUING DIRECTORY AND TRAVELER'S GUIDE. see ANTIQUES

700 IT ISSN 0394-0136
N1.A1
ANTOLOGIA DI BELLE ARTI. 1977. a. L.100000 (foreign L.120000). Umberto Allemandi & C. Societa Editrice, Via Mancini, 8, C.P. 1394, 10131 Turin, Italy. TEL 39-11-8199111. FAX 39-11-8193090. TELEX 224149 ALLART I. Dir. Alvar Gonzales-Palacios. R&P contact: Luigi Giannuzzi. adv. contact: Patrizia Sbodiu. Document type: academic/scholarly publication.
Description: Includes scholarly and critical articles; each issue focuses on a specific topic of art history.

ANUARIO DE INOVACOES EM COMUNICACOES E ARTES. see COMMUNICATIONS

ANZEIGER DES GERMANISCHEN NATIONALMUSEUMS UND BERICHTE AUS DEM FORSCHUNGSINSTITUT FUER REALIENKUNDE. see HISTORY — History Of Europe

700 745.1 UK ISSN 0003-6536
N1
APOLLO; the international magazine of the arts. 1925. m. £70 (U.S. & S. America $125; Canada £79; elsewhere £70) (effective 1997). Apollo Magazine Ltd., 1 Castle Ln., London SW1E 6DR, England. TEL 44-171-235-1998. FAX 44-171-235-1689. E-mail: apollomag@cityscape.co.uk (in UK); apollousa@aol.com (in US). (U.S. addr.: Box 47, North Hollywood, CA 91603-0047. TEL 818-763-7673. FAX 818-753-9492) Ed. Robin Simon; Pub. Paul Z. Josefowitz. adv.: B&W page £800 ($1320), color page £1200 ($1980); 311 x 241; adv. contact: Anthony Law. bk.rev.; illus.; index. (also avail. in microform from UMI; back issues avail.; reprint service avail. from KTO) Indexed: Art Ind., Artbibl.Mod., Arts & Hum.Cit.Ind., Avery Ind.Archit.Per., Bk.Rev.Ind. (1967-), Br.Hum.Ind., Br.Tech.Ind., Child.Bk.Rev.Ind. (1967-), Curr.Cont., DAAI, IBR, RILA. Document type: academic/scholarly publication.
—BLDSC (1568.880000); Genuine Article; KR SourceOne; SWETS; UMI.
Description: Deals with art history, antiques, and auctioneering for universities, collectors, dealers, and museums.

700 MX ISSN 0188-3992
APOYO A LA DOCENCIA. 1990. irreg. price varies. Universidad Nacional Autonoma de Mexico, Instituto de Investigaciones Esteticas, Circuito Mario de la Cueva, Zona Cultural, Ciudad Universitaria, 04510 Mexico, D.F., Mexico. TEL 52-5-6227545. FAX 52-5-6657440. E-mail: ereinoso@servidor.unam.mx.

APPLAUS; Muenchner Kulturmagazin. see THEATER

700 CN ISSN 1196-1775
APPLIED ARTS. 1986. 6/yr. Can.$37.95($47.95) (foreign $57.95) (effective 1996-1997). Applied Arts Inc., 885 Don Mills Rd., Ste. 324, Don Mills, ON M3C 1V9, Canada. TEL 416-510-0909. FAX 416-510-0913. E-mail: app-arts@interlog.com; URL: http://www.interlog.com/~app-arts. Ed. Sara Curtis; Pub. Georges Haroutiun. adv. contact: James Tenute. circ. 12,000. Document type: trade publication.
—BLDSC (1571.680100).
Formerly: Applied Arts Quarterly (ISSN 0829-9242)
Description: For designers, art directors, photographers, illustrators.

706.5 745.1 769.56 US ISSN 1051-0869
N5198
APPRAISERS STANDARD; for collectors, auctioneers, dealers, etc. 1982. 6/yr. $20 in U.S.; Canada $25; elsewhere $30. New England Appraisers Association, 5 Gill Terrace, Ludlow, VT 05149. TEL 802-228-7444. Ed. Linda L. Tucker; Pub. Linda L. Tucker. adv.; bk.rev.; circ. 1,000 (paid). (tabloid format) Document type: trade publication.
Formerly (until 1990): N E A A News (ISSN 1046-0381)
Description: Assists appraisers of all types in their profession.

ARAB LEAGUE EDUCATIONAL, SCIENTIFIC, AND CULTURAL ORGANIZATION. INFORMATION NEWSLETTER. see EDUCATION

ARCHAEOLOGIA. see ARCHAEOLOGY

ARCHAEOLOGICAL INSTITUTE OF AMERICA. ABSTRACTS OF THE GENERAL MEETING. see ARCHAEOLOGY — Abstracting, Bibliographies, Statistics

709.7 US ISSN 0003-9853
N11.A735
ARCHIVES OF AMERICAN ART JOURNAL. 1960. q. $35. Smithsonian Institution, Archives of American Art, Washington, DC 20560. TEL 202-357-2781. URL: http://www.si.edu. (Alt. addr.: 1285 Ave. of the Americas, New York, NY 10019) Ed. Robert Browny. R&P contact: D. Tell. TEL aaaem025@sivm.si.edu. bk.rev.; illus.; index. circ. 1,700. Indexed: Amer.Hist.& Life (1985-), Art Ind., Artbibl.Mod., Arts & Hum.Cit.Ind., ASCA, Avery Ind.Archit.Per., Curr.Cont., Hist.Abstr. (1985-), RILA. Document type: academic/scholarly publication.
—BLDSC (1630.950000); KR SourceOne; UnCover.
Formerly: Archives Quarterly Bulletin.

706 US ISSN 0066-6637
N7260
ARCHIVES OF ASIAN ART. 1945. a. $30. Asia Society, 725 Park Ave., New York, NY 10021-5088. TEL 212-517-8315. FAX 212-288-6400. TELEX 224953 ASIA UR. Ed. Kathryn Parker. cum.index: 1945-93. circ. 600. (back issues avail.) Indexed: Art Ind., Arts & Hum.Cit.Ind., ASCA, Avery Ind.Archit.Per., Curr.Cont.
—KR SourceOne; UnCover.
Formerly (until 1966): Chinese Art Society of America. Archives.
Description: Recent research by leading scholars on various subjects concerning Asian art.
Refereed Serial

ARCHIVES 25. see LITERATURE

ARCHIVIO PER L'ALTO ADIGE; rivista di studi alpini. see LINGUISTICS

ARCHIVIST. see HISTORY — History Of North And South America

709.4   SP   ISSN 0004-0428
N7
ARCHIVO ESPANOL DE ARTE. (Text in Spanish; abstracts in English) 1925. q. 6300 ptas. (foreign 9400 ptas.) (effective 1997). Consejo Superior de Investigaciones Cientificas (C.S.I.C.), Centro de Estudios Historicos, Centro de Estudios Historicos, Departamento de Historia del Arte "Diego Velazquez", Vitruvio 8, 28006 Madrid, Spain. TEL 34-1-5612833. FAX 34-1-5629634. Dir. Margarita M. Estella Marcos. bk.rev.; bibl.; illus.; index. (reprint service avail. from SCH) **Indexed:** Amer.Hist.& Life (1962-1972), (1989-), Art Ind., Artbibl.Mod., Arts & Hum.Cit.Ind., ASCA, Avery Ind.Archit.Per., Curr.Cont., Hist.Abstr. (1962-1972), (1989-), IBR, Ind.Bk.Rev.Hum., RILA. **Document type:** academic/scholarly publication.
—CINDOC; Genuine Article; KR SourceOne; SWETS. CCC.
Supersedes in part (in 1940): Archivo Espanol de Arte y Arqueologia (ISSN 0210-4180)
Description: Dedicated to research on the history of Spanish art, including its diffusion in America and the Philippines, and its report with other cultures.
Refereed Serial

700   SP
ARCO (YEAR). a. 3500 ptas. Feria Internacional de Arte Contemporaneo, Parque Ferial Juan Carlos I, 28067 Madrid, Spain. TEL 341-722-50-17. FAX 341-722-57-98. Dir. Rosina Gomez-Baeza. adv. circ. 4,500. **Document type:** catalog.

700 746.9   CN
AREA MAGAZINE. 1994. q. Can.$17.95($21.95) (effective Jan. 1995). Area Arts, 615 Mt. Pleasant Rd., Ste. 205, Toronto, ON M4S 3C5, Canada. TEL 416-368-9401. FAX 416-359-0755. E-mail: area.mag@canrem.com. Ed. Jason Patton; Pub. Peter Lucas. adv. contact: Jason Patton. (back issues avail.) **Document type:** consumer publication.
● Also available online.
Description: Features entertaining and insightful stories that make Toronto vibrant and unique.

700   DK   ISSN 0900-338X
ARGOS; Tidsskrift for Kunstvidenskab, visuel kommunikation og Kunstpaedagogik. 1985. irreg. DKK 78.40 (effective 1997). Odense University Press, Campusvej 55, DK-5230 Odense M, Denmark. TEL 66-157999. FAX 66-158126. E-mail: press@forlag.ou.dk. illus.

ARIEL (ENGLISH EDITION); the Israel review of arts and letters. see HUMANITIES: COMPREHENSIVE WORKS

701.1   US   ISSN 0737-0407
OA
ARISTOS. 1982. irreg. $25 (Canada $26; elsewhere $31) to individuals; libraries $35 (Canada $36; elsewhere $41) (effective 1997 & 1998). Aristos Foundation, Box 1105, Radio City Sta., New York, NY 10101. TEL 212-678-8550. E-mail: aristos@aristos.org; URL: http://www.aristos.org. Eds. Michelle Marder Kamhi, Louis Torres. R&P contact: Michelle Marder Kamhi. bk.rev.; illus. (back issues avail.) **Indexed:** Amer.Hum.Ind., Artbibl.Mod., RILA. **Document type:** academic/scholarly publication, consumer publication.
Description: Devoted to the preservation and advancement of traditional values (as opposed to modernism and post-modernism) in the arts, as well as objective standards in scholarship and criticism. Annotated table of contents.

ARIZONA ARTISTS GUILD NEWS. see MUSEUMS AND ART GALLERIES

353.9 700   US   ISSN 0098-7387
NX24.A6
ARIZONA COMMISSION ON THE ARTS. REPORT TO THE GOVERNOR (YEAR). Key Title: Report to the Governor - Arizona Commission on the Arts. a. free. Commission on the Arts, 417 W. Roosevelt St., Phoenix, AZ 85003. TEL 602-255-5882. FAX 602-256-0282. E-mail: artscomm@primenet.com; URL: http://www.state.az.us/azarts. Ed. Gary Delago. R&P contact: Mollie Lakin. TEL 602-229-8226. illus.; circ. 1,500 (controlled). **Document type:** government publication.
● Also available online.
Formerly: Arizona Commission on the Arts and Humanities. Report to the Governor.
Description: A review of the programmatic and financial community service projects supported by the commission in a given fiscal year.

700   TU   ISSN 0004-1971
ARKITEKT; yasama sanati. (Text in Turkish; summaries in English) 1931. m. DM.105($74) to Europe; North America $70 (effective 1997). Nokta Basin A.S., Buyukdere Cad. Ali Kaya Sok. 8, 80720 Levent - Istanbul, Turkey. TEL 90-212-2819916. FAX 90-212-2798512. Ed. Rifat Dedeoglu; Pub. Engin Vardar. adv. contact: Miss Nuray Berktav. bk.rev.; circ. 10,000. circ. 10,000 (paid). **Indexed:** Archit.Per.Ind.
Description: Covers architecture and the arts, decoration, interior design, antiques, archaeology.

ARLIS - N A UPDATE. see LIBRARY AND INFORMATION SCIENCES

ARMAS E TROFEUS; revista de historia, heraldica, genealogia e arte. see GENEALOGY AND HERALDRY

709.4   XO   ISSN 0044-9008
N6
ARS. (Text and summaries in English, German, Russian, Slovak) 1967. s-a. $57 in US (effective 1996). (Slovenska Akademia Vied, Ustav Dejin Umenia) Vydavatel'stvo S A P, s.r.o. - Slovak Academic Press Ltd., P.O. Box 57, Nam. Slovody 6, 810 05 Bratislava, Slovakia. TEL 42-7-211728. Ed. Jan Dekan. charts; illus. circ. 600.
—BLDSC (1697.300000).

704.948   JA   ISSN 0004-2889
N8193.A1
ARS BUDDHICA/BUKKYO GEIJUTSU. (Text in Japanese; contents page and summaries in English) 1948. bi-m. $71.75. Japan Publications Trading Co. Ltd., Box 5030, Tokyo International, Tokyo 100-31, Japan. (And: 1255 Howard St., San Francisco, CA 94103, U.S.A.) adv.; illus. circ. 1,000. (also avail. in microform)
—UnCover.

700   HU   ISSN 0133-1531
N6812
ARS HUNGARICA. (Text in Hungarian; summaries in English, French, German, Russian) 1973. 2/yr. $16 or exchange basis. Magyar Tudomanyos Akademia, Muveszettorteneti Kutato Intezete - Hungarian Academy of Sciences, Institute of Art History, Uri u. 49, 1014 Budapest, Hungary. TEL 36-1-1759011. FAX 36-1-1561849. E-mail: h4517mar@ella.hu. Ed. Maria Bernath. R&P contact: Erno Marosi. bk.rev.; circ. 500. (back issues avail.) **Indexed:** Artbibl.Mod., Avery Ind.Archit.Per., RILA. **Document type:** academic/scholarly publication.
Refereed Serial

ARS ORIENTALIS; the arts of Asia, Southeast Asia and Islam. see ORIENTAL STUDIES

700   NE
ARS PICTURAE. 1989. irreg., vol.3, 1992. price varies. Davaco Publishers, Beukenlaan 3, 8085 RK Doornspijk, Netherlands. TEL 31-525-661823. FAX 31-525-662153. (back issues avail.) **Document type:** monographic series.
Description: Publishes brief scholarly studies of the life and work of Dutch artists of the 17th century.

709   SW   ISSN 0066-7919
ARS SUETICA. (Subseries of Acta Universitatis Upsaliensis) (Text in Swedish; summaries in English or German) 1966. irreg. price varies. (Uppsala Universitet, Institute of Art History) A W I International AB, P.O. Box 4627, S-116 91 Stockholm, Sweden. TEL 46-8-7282500. FAX 46-8-338707. Ed. Rudolf Zeitler. (back issues avail.) **Document type:** monographic series.

700   RM   ISSN 1220-2789
ARS TRANSSILVANIAE. (Text in Rumanian; summaries in English, French, German) 1990. a. (Academia Romana, Institutul de Arheologie si Istoria Artei, Cluj-Napoca) Editura Academiei Romane, Calea 13 Septembrie 13, 76117 Bucharest, Rumania. (Dist. by: Rodipet SA, Piata Presei Libere 1, Sec. 1, PO Box 33-57, Bucharest, Rumania. TEL 401-6185103. FAX 401-2226407) Ed. Marius Porumb.

700   US
ARSENAL; surrealist subversion. 1970. irreg., latest 1989. $12 per no. Black Swan Press-Surrealist Editions, 1726 W. Jarvis Ave., Chicago, IL 60626. Ed. Franklin Rosemont. bk.rev.; bibl. circ. 3,000.

730   UN   ISSN 0004-5535
ART; the journal of the professional artist - le porte-parole de l'artiste professionnel. (Text in English, French; occasionally in Spanish) 1953. a. free. (International Association of Art - Association Internationale des Arts Plastiques) UNESCO Publishing, 1 rue Miollis, 75732 Paris Cedex 15, France. TEL 33-1-45684300. FAX 33-1-45685741. URL: http://www.unesco.org/publications. (Dist. in the U.S. by: Bernan Associates, 4611-F Assembly Dr., Lanham, MD 20706-4391. TEL 800-274-4888. FAX 800-865-3450) Ed. Dunbar Marshall-Malagola. circ. 2,000.

701.18   GW   ISSN 0173-2781
N3
ART. 1979. 12/yr. DM.150 (Europe DM.188.40, elsewhere DM.194.40). Gruner und Jahr AG & Co., Am Baumwall 11, 20459 Hamburg, Germany. TEL 49-40-3703-0. FAX 49-40-37035617. Ed. Axel Hecht. adv. contact: Angelika Drescher. circ. 76,213. (reprint service avail.) **Document type:** consumer publication.
—SWETS.

708.7   US   ISSN 0004-296X
N684
ART ALLIANCE BULLETIN. 1921. q. membership only. Philadelphia Art Alliance, 251 S. 18th St., Philadelphia, PA 19103. FAX 215-545-0767. Ed. Thomas W. Yanni. adv.; illus. circ. 2,500.
Description: Focuses on art exhibits in the area.

700 745.5   AT   ISSN 0313-220X
ART ALMANAC. 1978. m. Aus.$20 (foreign Aus.$30). 168 Day St., 1st fl., Sydney, N.S.W. 2010, Australia. TEL 02-267-8604. FAX 02-267-8539. Ed. Janice E. McCulloch. adv. circ. 5,500. (back issues avail.)
Description: Covers galleries and information on current exhibitions focusing on contemporary Australian art.

700   US
ART? ALTERNATIVES. 1992. a. $7.95 (foreign $17.95). Outlaw Biker Enterprises, Inc., 5 Marine View Plaza Ste. 207, Hoboken, NJ 07030. TEL 201-653-2700. Ed. Jean-Chris Miller. R&P contact: Harvey Shapiro. adv.: B&W page $1200; adv. contact: Ken Knabb. circ. 75,000. **Document type:** consumer publication.
Description: Targets the artworld subculture; features underground, low-brow and outsider art, and tattoo art.

ART & ANTIQUES. see ANTIQUES

709.94   AT   ISSN 1039-3625
N7260
ART AND ASIAPACIFIC. 1994. q. Aus.$44. Fine Arts Press Pty. Ltd., P.O. Box 480, Roseville, N.S.W. 2069, Australia. TEL 02-4171045. FAX 02-4171045. Ed. Dinah Dysart. circ. 15,000. **Document type:** consumer publication.
—UnCover.

700   US   ISSN 0197-1093
N8602
ART & AUCTION.* 1979. m. (11/yr.) $42. Auction Guild, 440 Park Ave., S. , 14 Fl, New York, NY 10016-8012. TEL 212-582-5633. FAX 212-246-3891. Ed. Amy Page; Pub. Jill Bokor. adv.; bk.rev. circ. 20,000. **Indexed:** Art & Archaeol.Tech.Abstr.
—UnCover.

709.94   AT   ISSN 0004-301X
ART AND AUSTRALIA. 1963. q. Aus.$54. Fine Arts Press Pty. Ltd., P.O. Box 480, Roseville, N.S.W. 2069, Australia. TEL 02-417-1033. FAX 02-417-1045. Ed. Dinah Dysart. adv. contact: Anna Mayo. bk.rev.; illus.; index; circ. 9,200 (paid). (tabloid format; back issues avail.) **Indexed:** Art Ind., Artbibl., Artbibl.Mod., Aus.P.A.I.S., Gdlns. **Document type:** academic/scholarly publication.
—KR SourceOne; UnCover.

ART & CRAFT; a magazine for all primary school teachers of art and craft. see ARTS AND HANDICRAFTS

700   BE
ART AND CULTURE. 1934. m. 1500 BEF($90) Palais des Beaux-Arts, 10 rue Royale, 1000 Brussels, Belgium. Ed. Claude Lorent. adv.; bk.rev.; film rev.; play rev.; illus. circ. 5,000. **Indexed:** Artbibl.
Former titles: Journal des Beaux-Arts; Beaux-Arts (ISSN 0005-7509)

424 ART

700 720 UK ISSN 0267-3991
N6480
ART AND DESIGN. 1985. bi-m. £65($135) (students £50($105)) (effective 1997). Academy Group Ltd., 42 Leinster Gardens, London W2 3AN, England. TEL 44-171-402-2141. FAX 44-171-723-9540. (Subscr. to: V C H Verlagsgesellschaft mbH, Postfach 101161, 69451 Weinheim, Germany. TEL 49-6201-606148. FAX 49-6201-606117; U.S. addr.: V C H Publishers Inc., 220 E. 23rd St., New York, NY 10010-4606. TEL 212-683-8333) Ed. Nicola Kearton. R&P contact: W. Lau. adv. contact: Nicola Kearton. circ. 5,000 (paid). (back issues avail.) **Indexed:** Art Ind., Artbibl.Mod., DAAI. **Document type:** academic/scholarly publication.
—BLDSC (1733.357430); KR SourceOne; UnCover.
Description: Provides an in-depth exploration of the underlying patterns of contemporary art.

704 II ISSN 0004-3044
ART AND LIFE. (Text mainly in English; occasionally in Bengali) 1967. a. Rs.8($1) Art Study Centre, B 20-185 Bhelupura, Varanasi 1, India. Ed. R.N. Mukerji. adv.; bk.rev.; charts; illus. circ. 100.

700 821 II ISSN 0970-1001
ART AND POETRY TODAY. (Text in English) q. Rs.80($24) Samkaleen Prakashan, 2762 Rajguru Marg, New Delhi 110 055, India. Ed. Krishan Khullar. adv.: page Rs.1000; trim 240 x 180. illus.
Formerly (until 1976): Criteria.
Description: Highlights poetry and art from all over the world.

ART & UNDERSTANDING; America's AIDS magazine. see *LITERATURE*

332.6 700 US ISSN 0161-1232
N8600
ART - ANTIQUES INVESTMENT REPORT. 1973. fortn. $125. Wall Street Reports Publishing Corp., 99 Wall St., New York, NY 10005-4393. TEL 212-747-9500.
Formed by the merger of: Art Investment Report (ISSN 0090-9211); Antiques Investment Report.
Description: Confidential bi-weekly survey designed and edited for the art connoisseur: collector, curator and dealer.

700 340 US ISSN 1362-2331
ART, ANTIQUITY, AND LAW. q. fl.355 to institutions; $182.50 to institutions in U.S. (effective 1998). Kluwer Law International (Subsidiary of: Wolters Kluwer N.V.), Postbus 85889, 2508 CN The Hague, Netherlands. TEL 31-70-3081500. FAX 31-70-3081515.

750 US ISSN 1046-4999
N8670
ART AT AUCTION IN AMERICA. 1989. a. $39.95. Frontier Publishing, Inc., 4933 W. Craig Rd., Ste. 155, Las Vegas, NV 89130. TEL 702-647-0990; 888-647-0990. FAX 702-647-0990. E-mail: frotpub@ix.netcom.com. Ed. William E. Belk; Pub. William E. Belk. adv. **Document type:** catalog.
Description: Provides comprehensive, up-to-date art guide for over 20,000 artists and 20,000 paintings sold at America's major auction houses during the previous year.

700 739.27 GW ISSN 0179-647X
ART AUREA; Schmuck Mensch Objekte. (Text in English, German) 1986. q. DM.66 (foreign DM.79). Ebner Verlag GmbH, Postfach 3060, 89020 Ulm, Germany. TEL 49-731-152028. FAX 49-731-152071. Ed. R.J. Ludwig. adv. contact: Ruth Patrick. bk.rev. circ. 16,000. **Indexed:** DAAI, IBR. **Document type:** consumer publication.

700 800 SW ISSN 1401-2979
▼**THE ART BIN.** (Text in English) 1995. bi-m. Nisus Publishing, Observatoriegatan 22, S-113 29 Stockholm, Sweden. E-mail: tallmo@nisus.se; URL: http://www.nisus.se/artbin. Ed. Karl-Erik Tallmo.
Document type: newsletter.
●Available only online.
Description: Contains cultural articles, source texts and recent artwork.

THE ART BOOK. see *PUBLISHING AND BOOK TRADE*

709 US ISSN 0004-3079
N11
ART BULLETIN. 1912. q. membership. College Art Association, 275 Seventh Ave., New York, NY 10001. TEL 212-691-1051. FAX 212-627-2381. Ed. John T. Paoletti. R&P contact: Craig Houser. adv. contact: J.C. Rafferty. bk.rev.; charts; illus.; index. circ. 9,500. (also avail. in microfilm from UMI; microfiche from IDC; reprint service avail. from KTO) **Indexed:** Acad.Ind., Art Ind., Artbibl.Mod., Artbibl., Arts & Hum.Cit.Ind., ASCA, Avery Ind.Archit.Per., Bk.Rev.Dig., Bk.Rev.Ind. (1990-), Br.Archaeol.Abstr., Br.Tech.Ind., Child.Bk.Rev.Ind. (1990-), Curr.Cont., HongKongiana, Hum.Ind., IBR, Ind.Bk.Rev.Hum., Mid.East: Abstr.& Ind., RILA. **Document type:** academic/scholarly publication.
●Also available online. Vendor(s): Information Access Co., UMI.
—BLDSC (1733.368000); KR SourceOne; SWETS; UMI; UnCover.
Description: Scholarly forum for communication; contains research articles on topics from all periods of art history.

658.91 US ISSN 0273-5652
N1
ART BUSINESS NEWS. 1974. 13/yr. $43 (effective 1996). Advanstar Communications, Inc., 7500 Old Oak Blvd., Cleveland, OH 44130. TEL 216-826-2839. FAX 216-891-2726. (Subscr. to: 1 E. First St., Duluth, MN 55082. TEL 800-346-0085) Ed. Sarah Seamark. adv.; bk.rev.; illus. circ. 33,179. (tabloid format; back issues avail.) **Document type:** trade publication.
—CCC.
Formerly (until 1980): Art Dealer and Framer (ISSN 0091-9780)
Refereed Serial

700 UK ISSN 0961-6497
ART BUSINESS TODAY. 1976. 5/yr. Fine Art Trade Guild, 16-18 Empress Pl., London SW6 1TT, England. TEL 44-171-381-6616. FAX 44-171-381-2596. Ed. Annabelle Ruston. adv. contact: Marilyn Driscoll. circ. 8,580 (controlled). **Document type:** trade publication.
—BLDSC (1733.369550).
Formerly (until 1990): Fine Art Trade Guild Journal (ISSN 0308-0854)

700 666 770 US ISSN 0893-3901
N8350
ART CALENDAR. 1986. m. $32 (Canada & Mexico $55; elsewhere $75) (effective 1997). Box 199, Upper Fairmount, MD 21867. TEL 410-651-9150. FAX 410-657-5313. E-mail: BarbDoug@dmv.com; URL: http://www.artcalendar.com. Ed. Marilyn Stevers; Pub. Barb Dougherty. R&P contact: Barb Dougherty. TEL 410-651-9151. adv. contact: Barb Dougherty. bk.rev.; circ. 20,000 (paid). **Document type:** consumer publication.
—UnCover.
Formerly: Art Calendar - D C.
Description: Lists upcoming professional opportunities in the U.S. and abroad for visual artists. Includes articles on marketing, art law, and career management.
Refereed Serial

700 US ISSN 1047-8868
ART CELLAR EXCHANGE; a service for buying and selling art. (Printed format ceased 1993.) 1989. m. Token Art Corporation, 2171 India St., Ste. H, San Diego, CA 92101. TEL 619-338-0797. FAX 619-338-0826. E-mail: ace@artcellarex.com; URL: http://www.artcellarex.com/. Ed. P.B. Van Cleve. circ. 50,000. (back issues avail.) **Document type:** newsletter.
●Available only online.
Description: For people interested in the visual art market. Provides a forum for buyers and sellers of fine art, as well as insight into the business of art.

700 US ISSN 0732-2852
NX458
ART COM: CONTEMPORARY ART COMMUNICATIONS. 1975. q. $8 per mo.; $3/hr. online. (La Mamelle, Inc.) Contemporary Arts Press, Box 3123, Rincon Annex, San Francisco, CA 94119. TEL 415-431-7524. FAX 415-431-7841. TELEX 4946074 ARTCOM. Ed. Carl E. Loeffler. adv.; bk.rev. (also avail. in microfiche; back issues avail.)
●Available only online.
Formerly (until vol.4, no.2, 1981): Mamelle Magazine: Art Contemporary.
Description: Reports on the interface between postmodern art and new communication technologies.

701 US ISSN 0195-4148
N7475
ART CRITICISM. 1979. q. $20. State University of New York at Stony Brook, Stony Brook, NY 11794. TEL 516-632-7260. Ed. Donald B. Kuspit. circ. 300. **Indexed:** Arts & Hum.Cit.Ind., ASCA, Curr.Cont. **Document type:** academic/scholarly publication.
—BLDSC (1733.374000); Genuine Article; UnCover.
Refereed Serial

706.88 US
ART DAILY. d. ArtDaily, Inc., E-mail: promotion@artdaily.com; URL: http://www.artdaily.com. illus.
●Available only online.
Description: Art news source on the net.

700 FR ISSN 0571-1509
ART DE BASSE NORMANDIE. 1956. q. 450 F. (foreign 800 F.) (effective 1997). Art de Basse-Normandie, 49 rue Canchy, 14000 Caen, C.C.P. Rouen 158 959 K, France. FAX 33-2-31502256. Ed. J. Pougheol. (back issues avail.)

700 IT
ART DIARY INTERNATIONAL. (Text in English) a. $30 (effective 1994-95). Giancarlo Politi Editore, Via Carlo Farini 68, 20159 Milan, Italy. TEL 39-2-6887341. FAX 39-2-66801290. adv.: B&W page $2600, color page $3500; trim 3 1/8 x 6 7/8. circ. 35,000. **Document type:** directory.
Description: Lists more than 30,000 addresses of artists, critics, galleries, museums, art magazines, collections and cultural institutions in 37 countries from the US to Europe and beyond.

700 IT
ART DIARY ITALIA. (Text in English, Italian) 1975. a. L.10000($28) Flash Art Books, Via Carlo Farini 68, 20159 Milan, Italy. TEL 02-6887-341. FAX 02-6680-1290. adv.: B&W page $2600, color page $3500; trim 3 1/8 x 6 7/8. circ. 35,000. **Document type:** directory.
Formerly: Art Diary.
Description: Lists more than 30,000 addresses of artists, critics, collectors, galleries, museums, alternative exhibition spaces, libraries, foundations, archives, graphic designers, art conservators, artist's agents, schools, and academies in Italy.

700 659.106 US ISSN 0735-2026
NC998.5.A1
ART DIRECTORS ANNUAL. 1921. a. $69.95. (Art Directors Club Inc.) Rotovision, S.A., 250 Park Ave. S., New York, NY 10003-1402. TEL 212-420-8798. FAX 212-460-8506. E-mail: adcny@interpost.net; URL: http://www.adcny.org. Ed. Antje Lenthe Arcia. R&P contact: Myrna Davis. TEL 212-674-0500. adv. contact: Alison Curry. circ. 15,000 (paid). **Document type:** trade publication.
Former titles: Annual of Advertising, Editorial and Television Art and Design with the Annual Copy Awards; (until 1973): Annual of Advertising, Editorial and Television Art and Design (ISSN 0066-4014).

700 SZ ISSN 1011-7822
ART DIRECTORS' INDEX TO ILLUSTRATORS. (Text in English, French, German, Spanish) 1981. a. $67.50. Rotovision S.A., Route Suisse 9, CH-1295 Mies, Switzerland. TEL 022-755-3055. FAX 022-755-4072. (Dist. in the U.S. by: Watson-Guptill Publications, 1695 Oak St., Lakewood, NJ 08701. TEL 800-451-1741. FAX 908-363-0338) illus. **Document type:** trade publication.
—BLDSC (1733.394600).
Description: Showcases the graphic designs that top illustrators from around the world select as their best work.

ART DOCUMENTATION. see *LIBRARY AND INFORMATION SCIENCES*

700   IT   ISSN 0394-0179
N4
ART E DOSSIER. 1986. m. Lit.66000 (foreign Lit.92000) (effective 1997). Giunti Gruppo Editoriale S.p.A., Via Bolognese 165, 50139 Florence, Italy. TEL 39-55-6679267. FAX 39-55-6679269. TELEX 571438. URL: http://www.giunti.it. Ed. Gioia Mori. adv.: B&W page Lit.3300000, color page Lit.5300000. circ. 55,000.

709.426   UK   ISSN 1359-8929
ART EAST. 1986. 10/yr. £15 (overseas £30) (effective 1995). B C Publications, 16C Market Pl., Diss, Norfolk IP22 3AB, England. TEL 44-1379-644200. FAX 44-1379-650480. Ed. Simon Tooth. adv.: page £600; trim 297 x 190; adv. contact: Matthew Denny. bk.rev.; film rev.; music rev.; play rev. circ. 6,000. (back issues avail.) **Document type:** consumer publication.
    Description: Covers all arts in the East Anglia area of Great Britain.

ART EDUCATION. see *EDUCATION*

ART EDUCATION. see *EDUCATION*

700   CN   ISSN 1188-4282
NX120.C2
ART ET CULTURE AU QUEBEC. 1991. biennial. Quebec dans le Monde, C.P. 8503, Sainte-Foy, PQ G1V 4N5, Canada. TEL 418-659-5540. Dir. Denis Turcotte. **Document type:** directory.
    Formerly (until 1993): Monde de la Culture au Quebec (ISSN 0847-4958)

700 387 069   FR   ISSN 0994-7957
L'ART ET LA MER. 1974. q. 100 F. Association des Peintres Officiels de la Marine, Musee de la Marine, Palais de Chaillot, 2 rue Royale, 75200 Paris Naval, France. TEL 42-60-33-30. Ed. Jean Ducros. illus. circ. 1,500.

704   FR   ISSN 0066-7951
ART ET LES GRANDES CIVILISATIONS. 1965. a. Editions Citadelles & Mazenod, 33 rue de Naples, Paris 8, France. TEL 45-22-23-66. FAX 45-22-04-27.

700 841   FR   ISSN 0518-7648
ART ET POESIE.* 1958. q. Societe des Poetes et Artistes de France, 11 rue de la Fontaine-Saint-Laurent, 58200 Cosne sur Loire, France. adv.
    —Genuine Article.

700   NE
ART EXPO YEARBOOK. a. fl.55. ArtSchool Bilthoven BV, Postbus 350, 3720 AJ Bilthoven, Netherlands. TEL 31-20-2252255. FAX 31-30-2252212.
    Description: Contains mostly figurative art by Dutch and Belgian artists.

ART HAZARDS NEWS. see *OCCUPATIONAL HEALTH AND SAFETY*

700   UK
ART HISTORIANS AND SPECIALISTS IN THE U.K.. 1991. irreg. Peter Marcan Publications, P.O. Box 3158, London SE1 4RA, England. TEL 44-171-357-0368. Ed. Peter Marcan. **Document type:** directory.
    Description: Detailed bio-bibliographical entries on some 600 individuals involved with the study of the fine and applied arts.

709   UK   ISSN 0141-6790
N7480
ART HISTORY. 1978. q. £102($182) (foreign £115) (effective 1997). (Association of Art Historians) Blackwell Publishers Ltd., 108 Cowley Rd., Oxford OX4 1JF, England. TEL 44-1865-791100. FAX 44-1865-791347. E-mail: jnlinfo@blackwellpublishers.co.uk; URL: http://www.blackwellpublishers.co.uk. Ed. Marcia Pointan. adv.; illus.; index. circ. 2,500. (also avail. in microfilm from SWZ,UMI) **Indexed:** Amer.Hist.& Life (1980-), Archit.Per.Ind., Art Ind., Artbibl.Mod., Artbibl., Arts & Hum.Cit.Ind., ASCA, Avery Ind.Archit.Per., Curr.Cont., DAAI, Hist.Abstr. (1980-), Hum.Ind., IBR, Ind.Bk.Rev.Hum., RILA. **Document type:** academic/scholarly publication. —BLDSC (1733.447000); Genuine Article; KR SourceOne; SWETS; UMI; Uncover. CCC.

709   US
ART HISTORY SERIES.* 1977. irreg. price varies. c/o D. Tiberii, 176 W. Main St., Dudley, MA 01570. Ed. Frank DiFederico. index. **Document type:** monographic series.

700   CN   ISSN 0831-2133
ART IMPRESSIONS. 1985. bi-m. Can.$22.50($27.50) (effective 1997). Branta Publishing Inc., 360 A Newkirk Rd., Richmond Hill, ON L4C 3G7, Canada. TEL 905-884-8753. FAX 905-884-1478. Ed. Michael J. Knell; Pub. C. Peter Calluori. R&P contact: Michael J. Knell. adv. contact: Michael Strachan. bk.rev. **Document type:** consumer publication.
    Description: Dedicated to the consumers and collectors of both original and limited edition reproduction art. Emphasis on figurative and impressionistic art, primarily those depicting nature or Canadian themes.

L-ART IMQADDSA; rivista biblika. see *RELIGIONS AND THEOLOGY — Roman Catholic*

709   US   ISSN 0004-3214
N1
ART IN AMERICA. 1913. m. $39.95 (foreign $69.95); newsstand price: $5. Brant Publications, Inc., 575 Broadway, 5th Fl., New York, NY 10021. TEL 212-941-2800. FAX 212-941-2819. (Subscr. to: Box 37003, Boone, IA 50037-0003. TEL 800-925-8059) Ed. Elizabeth C. Baker; Pub. Sandra Brant. R&P contact: Stephanie Rosenfeld. adv. contact: Lorrenda Newman. bk.rev.; illus. circ. 63,000. (also avail. in microform from UMI; reprint service avail. from UMI) **Indexed:** Acad.Ind., Amer.Bibl.Slavic & E.Eur.Stud., Amer.Hist.& Life (1963-1997), Art Ind., Artbibl.Mod., Arts & Hum.Cit.Ind., ASCA, Avery Ind.Archit.Per., Bk.Rev.Dig., Bk.Rev.Ind. (1975-), Chic.Per.Ind., Child.Bk.Rev.Ind. (1975-), Curr.Cont., DAAI, Film Lit.Ind. (1973-), Hist.Abstr. (1963-1997), Hum.Ind., IBR, Mag.Ind., PMR, R.G.Abstr., R.G., RILA, SSCI. **Document type:** consumer publication.
    ●Also available online. Vendor(s): Information Access Co., UMI.
    —BLDSC (1733.345000); KR SourceOne; SWETS; UMI; Uncover.
    Description: General-interest magazine covering contemporary art worldwide.

700   US
ART IN WISCONSIN.* 1984. bi-m. $15 (effective June 1993). Wisconsin Painters and Sculptors, Inc., 8872 Lime Kiln Rd., Sturgeon Bay, WI 54235-9456. Ed. Kathleen Barlament. adv. circ. 700. (looseleaf format; also avail. in diskette format)
    Formerly: Wisconsin Painters and Sculptors. Newsletter.

700   FR   ISSN 0004-3230
N1.A1
ART INTERNATIONAL. (Text in English) 1956. q. $33 to individuals; institutions $69. Archive Press, 77 rue des Archives, 75003 Paris, France. TEL 48-04-84-54. FAX 48-04-82-00. Eds. Michael Peppiatt, Jill Lloyd. adv.; bk.rev.; illus. circ. 12,000. (reprint service avail. from UMI) **Indexed:** Art Ind., Artbibl., Arts & Hum.Cit.Ind., Avery Ind.Archit.Per., Curr.Cont., Film Lit.Ind., RILA. **Document type:** academic/scholarly publication.
    —KR SourceOne; UMI; Uncover.
    Incorporating: New Lugano Review; Art Spectrum (ISSN 0304-8632)

700   US   ISSN 1046-8471
ART ISSUES. 1989. 5/yr. $25 (foreign $35). Foundation for Advanced Critical Studies, Inc., 8721 Santa Monica Blvd., Ste. 6, W. Hollywood, CA 90069. TEL 213-876-4508. FAX 213-876-5061. Ed. Gary Kornblau; Pub. Gary Kornblau. adv.; circ. 8,000 (controlled). **Document type:** academic/scholarly publication.
    —UnCover.
    Description: Critical commentary and reviews of contemporary art and popular culture.

700   US
ART JOURNAL (YEAR). 1941. q. $30 to non-members; institutions $45. College Art Association, 275 Seventh Ave., New York, NY 10001. TEL 212-691-1051. FAX 212-627-2381. Ed. Janet Kaplan. R&P contact: Craig Houser. adv. contact: J.C. Rafferty. bk.rev.; illus. circ. 11,000. (also avail. in microfilm from UMI; reprint service avail. from KTO) **Indexed:** Acad.Ind., Amer.Bibl.Slavic & E.Eur.Stud., Archit.Per.Ind., Art & Archaeol.Tech.Abstr., Art Ind., Artbibl.Mod., ASCA, Avery Ind.Archit.Per., Bk.Rev.Ind. (1965-), Br.Tech.Ind., Child.Bk.Rev.Ind. (1965-), Curr.Cont., DAAI, Hum.Ind., RILA, SSCI. **Document type:** academic/scholarly publication.
    ●Also available online. Vendor(s): Information Access Co., UMI.
    —BLDSC (1733.460000); KR SourceOne; SWETS; UMI; UnCover.
    Former titles: College Art Journal; Art Journal (ISSN 0004-3249)
    Description: Journal of ideas and opinions that focuses on critical and aesthetic issues in the visual arts of our times.

ART LAW & ACCOUNTING REPORTER. see *LAW*

ART LIBRARIES JOURNAL. see *LIBRARY AND INFORMATION SCIENCES*

ART LIBRARIES SOCIETY OF NORTH AMERICA. OCCASIONAL PAPERS. see *LIBRARY AND INFORMATION SCIENCES*

ART LIBRARIES SOCIETY OF NORTH AMERICA. TOPICAL PAPERS. see *LIBRARY AND INFORMATION SCIENCES*

700 028.1   UK
ART LINE; international art news. 1983. 8/yr. £22($50) Art Line Magazine, Phoenix House, Phoenix St., Charing Cross Rd., London WC2, England. TEL 44-171-497-3545. FAX 44-171-379-4846. Ed. Keith Patrick. bk.rev. circ. 30,000. (back issues avail.) **Indexed:** DAAI.

700   US   ISSN 0892-1202
ART LOVER'S ART AND CRAFT FAIR BULLETIN. 1977. q. $12. American Society of Artists, Inc., Box 1326, Palatine, IL 60078. TEL 312-751-2500. **Document type:** trade publication.
    Description: Listings of art and craft shows throughout the state of Illinois for visitors to shows.

ART MARKETING SOURCEBOOK. see *BUSINESS AND ECONOMICS — Trade And Industrial Directories*

702.8   US   ISSN 1066-4173
ART MATERIALS TODAY. 1993. bi-m. $39 (effective July 1994). F & W Publications, Inc., 1507 Dana Ave., Cincinnati, OH 45207. TEL 513-531-2222. FAX 513-531-1843. Ed. Cristine Antolik. adv.: color page $650; trim 8 1/2 x 11; adv. contact: Joe Wood. charts; illus.; stat.; tr.lit.; cum.index; circ. 5,000 (controlled). (back issues avail.) **Document type:** trade publication.
    Description: Gives art material retailers practical information on the best ways to run their businesses, and an overall look at the industry.

700 069   UK   ISSN 0142-6702
N1
ART MONTHLY. 1976. 10/yr. £28.50 to individuals (rest of Europe £37; N. America $55; elsewhere £49); institutions £35 (rest of Europe £45; N. America $59; elsewhere £59) (Effective Feb. 1997). Britannia Art Publications Ltd., 26 Charing Cross Rd., Ste. 17, London WC2H 0DG, England. TEL 44-171-240-0389. FAX 44-171-497-0726. Ed. Patricia Bickers. R&P contact: Letty Mooring. adv. contact: Matthew Hale. bk.rev.; cum.index: 1976-1987. circ. 4,000. (back issues avail.) **Indexed:** Art Ind., Artbibl.Mod., RILA. **Document type:** academic/scholarly publication.
    —BLDSC (1733.463200); KR SourceOne.
    Description: Contains interviews, features on new artists and trends, gallery and museum reviews from all over the world, and art market information.

426 ART

700   AT   ISSN 1033-4025
ART MONTHLY AUSTRALIA. 1987. 10/yr. Aus.$38 (foreign Aus.$80) (effective June 1997). Art Monthly Australia Pty. Ltd., c/o Canberra School of Art, G.P.O. Box 804, Canberra, A.C.T. 2601, Australia. TEL 61-6-249-3988. FAX 61-6-249-5722. E-mail: philppa.kelly@anu.edu.au; URL: http://www.anu.edu.au/ITA/AusArts/www/art.monthly/ART.MONTHLY.html. Ed. Peter Timms. R&P contact: Philippa Kelly. adv. contact: Philippa Kelly. bk.rev.; illus. circ. 4,000. (back issues avail.) **Document type:** academic/scholarly publication.
   Formerly (until 1989): Australian and International Art Monthly (ISSN 0819-5838)
   Description: News, information and discussion of current issues in the visual art world of Australia.

700   US   ISSN 0274-7073
N1
ART NEW ENGLAND; a resource for the visual arts. 1979. 6/yr. $24. Art New England, Inc., 425 Washington St., Brighton, MA 02135. TEL 617-782-3008. Eds. Stephanie Adelman, Carla Munsat. adv.; bk.rev. circ. 28,000. **Indexed:** Art Ind. **Document type:** bulletin.
   —KR SourceOne; UnCover.

700 770   NZ   ISSN 0110-1102
N7406
ART NEW ZEALAND. 1976. q. NZ.$35. Art Magazine Press Ltd., Box 10-249, Balmoral, Auckland 4, New Zealand. Ed. William Dart. adv.; bk.rev.; film rev.; play rev.; illus. circ. 4,000. **Indexed:** Artbibl.Mod., Artbibl.
   —BLDSC (1733.464500); UnCover. CCC.

700 069.5   US   ISSN 0895-4658
ART NEWS INTERNATIONAL DIRECTORY OF CORPORATE ART COLLECTIONS. 1982. biennial. $109.95. International Art Alliance, Inc., Box 1608, Largo, FL 34649. TEL 813-581-7328. FAX 813-585-6398. Ed. Shirley Reiff Howarth. adv.; circ. 3,000 (paid). (also avail. in diskette format) **Document type:** directory.
   Former titles: Art News Directory of Corporate Art Collections; Directory of Corporate Art Collections.
   Description: Indexes 1300 art collections owned by corporations around the world according to personnel, geographic location and media.

700   UK   ISSN 0960-6556
N1
THE ART NEWSPAPER (INTERNATIONAL EDITION). 1990. m. £47($69) (Can.$75) (effective 1997). Umberto Allemandi & Co. Publishing, 27-29 Vauxhall Grove, London SW815Y, England. TEL 44-171-7353331. FAX 44-171-7353332. Ed. Anna Somers Cocks. R&P contact: Anna Somers Cocks. adv. contact: Marc Owen. bk.rev.; circ. 14,000 (paid). **Indexed:** Art Ind. **Document type:** newspaper.
   —BLDSC (1733.465250); KR SourceOne.
   Incorporated (1988-1989): Journal of Art (ISSN 1044-9160)
   Description: Contains comprehensive and international coverage of the world of art: politics, economics, law, exhibitions, opinions, museums, restoration, dealers, galleries, publications and future events.

700   CK   ISSN 0121-5639
ART NEXUS; edicion internacional. (Editions in Spanish, English) 1976. q. $32 (effective 1996). Arte en Colombia Ltda., Apdo. Aereo 90193, Bogota D.E., Colombia. TEL 571-2625178. FAX 571-4136335. (U.S. addr.: 8877 Collins Ave., Ste. 809, Surfside, FL 33154. TEL 305-868-9583) Ed. Celia Sredni de Birbragher; Pub. Ivone Pini. R&P contact: Celia Sredni de Birbragher. adv. contact: Zulema Roca. bk.rev.; illus. circ. 16,000. **Indexed:** Art Ind., Artbibl., Artbibl.Mod., Hisp.Amer.Per.Ind.
   —BLDSC (1733.465270); KR SourceOne.
   Formerly (until 1991): Arte en Colombia Internacional (ISSN 0120-713X)
   Description: Covers Latin American art, architecture, films and photography.
   Refereed Serial

700   US   ISSN 1047-4994
ART OF THE WEST. 1987. bi-m. $24 (foreign $42). Duerr and Tierney Ltd., 15612 Highway 7, Ste. 235, Minnetonka, MN 55345. TEL 612-935-5850. FAX 612-935-6546. URL: http://www.aotw.com. Ed. Vicki Stavig; Pubs. Allan J. Duerr, Thomas F. Tierney. R&P contact: Thomas F. Tierney. bk.rev.; circ. 33,000 (paid). **Document type:** consumer publication.
   —UnCover.
   Description: Covers landscape and seascapes, Native American art, mountain men art, and "cowboy" art, from old wild west days to the working cowboy of today.

ART ON SCREEN; the newsletter of film & video on the visual arts. see *MOTION PICTURES*

700   US   ISSN 0278-1441
NX506
ART PAPERS; contemporary art in the U.S. 1976. bi-m. $30 (Canada & Mexico $45; elsewhere $50) (effective 1997 & 1998). Atlanta Art Papers, Inc., Box 77348, Atlanta, GA 30357. TEL 404-588-1837. FAX 404-588-1836. E-mail: cdowney@pd.org. Ed. Ruth Resnicow. R&P contact: Cathy Downey. adv.: page $480; adv. contact: Cathy Downey. bk.rev.; film rev.; play rev.; illus.; cum.index: nos. 1-15, 1991. circ. 12,000. (also avail. in microfiche from UMI) **Indexed:** Art Ind., Artbibl.Mod. **Document type:** consumer publication.
   —BLDSC (1733.465850); KR SourceOne; UMI; UnCover.
   Formed by the 1980 merger of: Contemporary Art - Southeast (ISSN 0147-6297); Atlanta Art Papers (ISSN 0271-2083); *Formerly* (until 1978): Atlanta Art Workers Coalition Newspaper.
   Description: Features current ideas about contemporary art and emerging artists in articles and interviews, original art, informed reviews, news and an extensive information section.

700   FR   ISSN 1145-3184
ART PLEIN CADRE; le magazine des professionnels de l'art et de l'encadrement. (Supplement avail.: Cadrechos) 6/yr. 400 F. 67 rue de Provence, 75009 Paris, France. TEL 42-80-27-77. FAX 40-23-08-75. Ed. Dominique Bosch. circ. 7,000. **Document type:** consumer publication, trade publication.
   Description: For professionals in the field of art and framing.

700   US
ART POLICE. Title varies with each issue: ArtPolice Comics, ArtPolice Etc. (Text in English, French, Hebrew) 1974. 3/yr. $5 to individuals; libraries $20; foreign $25. ArtPolice, Inc., 5228 43rd Ave. S., Minneapolis, MN 55417-2210. TEL 312-339-3173. Ed.Bd. circ. 1,000. (back issues avail.)
   Description: Provides venues for artists outside mainstream art publications.

700   US   ISSN 0193-6867
ART REFERENCE COLLECTION. 1980. irreg., no.5, 1984. price varies. Greenwood Press, Inc. (Subsidiary of: Greenwood Publishing Group Inc.), 88 Post Rd. W., Box 5007, Westport, CT 06881-5007. TEL 203-226-3571. FAX 203-222-1502. Ed. Pamela J. Parry.

700   US   ISSN 1050-2548
Z711.6.A76   CODEN: ARSQEP
ART REFERENCE SERVICES QUARTERLY. 1992. q. $38 to individuals (Canada $49.40; elsewhere $53.20); institutions $75 (Canada $97.50; elsewhere $105); libraries $75 (Canada $97.50; elsewhere $105) (effective 1998-1999). Haworth Press, Inc., 10 Alice St., Binghamton, NY 13904-1580. TEL 607-722-5857; 800-342-9676. FAX 607-722-6362. E-mail: getinfo@haworth.com; URL: http://www.haworth.com. Ed. Edward H. Teague; Pub. Bill Cohen. R&P contact: Ruthann Heath. adv.: B&W page $300; trim 4 3/8 x 7 1/8; adv. contact: Jackie Blakeslee. (also avail. in microform from HAW,UMI; reprint service avail. from HAW) **Indexed:** Art & Archaeol.Tech.Abstr., DAAI, INSPEC (1993-), LISA, Ref.Zh., Sage Urb.Stud.Abstr. **Document type:** academic/scholarly publication.
   —BLDSC (1733.470630); AskIEEE; Haworth; KR SourceOne; SWETS; UnCover.
   Description: Provides a forum for professionals who provide architectural and visual arts reference and information services in academic, museum, and public library settings. Includes practical and theoretical articles about a wide range of reference issues.
   Refereed Serial

700   UK
ART REVIEW;* the essential monthly guide. 1949. m. £24.50 to individuals (rest of Europe £47; elsewhere £54); institutions £35; newsstand price: £3.50. Art Review Ltd., c/o Central Books, 99 Wallis Rd., London E9 5LN, England. Ed. David Lee. adv.; bk.rev.; illus.; index. circ. 15,000. (also avail. in microfilm from UMI,BNB) **Indexed:** Art Ind., Artbibl., Artbibl.Mod., Avery Ind.Archit.Per., RILA. **Document type:** consumer publication.
   —KR SourceOne; SWETS; UMI; UnCover.
   Formerly (until Apr. 1993): Arts Review (ISSN 0004-4091)

700   US   ISSN 1068-7890
ART REVUE. 1990. q. $20. Innovative Artists Agency, 302 W. 13th St., Loveland, CO 80537. TEL 303-669-0625. FAX 303-669-0625. Ed. Jan McNutt. adv. contact: Irene Thomson. bk.rev. circ. 7,000. (back issues avail.) **Document type:** consumer publication.
   Formerly: Revue - Art in All Dimensions.

700   UK
ART SALES INDEX: OIL PAINTINGS, DRAWINGS, WATER COLOURS AND SCULPTURE. (Text in English, French; summaries in English) 1968. a. £185. Art Sales Index Ltd., 1 Thames St., Weybridge, Surrey KT13 8JG, England. TEL 44-1932-856426. FAX 44-1932-842482. Ed. Duncan Hislop; Pub. Richard Hislop. adv.; index. circ. 3,000. **Document type:** abstracting/indexing.
   ●Also available online.
   —BLDSC (1733.471510).
   Former titles: Annual Art Sales Index: Oil Paintings, Drawings, Water Colours and Sculptures; Annual Art Sales Index: Oil Paintings, Drawings and Watercolours (ISSN 0308-5910); (until 1979): Annual Art Sales Index (Year) (ISSN 0143-0688); *Formed by the merger of:* Annual Art Sales Index: Watercolours and Drawings; Annual Art Sales Index: Oil Paintings.
   Description: Contains over 120,000 sales results for over 35,000 international artists.

700   US
ART STUDENTS LEAGUE NEWS. 1948. 4/yr. free to qualified personnel. Art Students League of New York, 215 W. 57th St., New York, NY 10019. TEL 212-247-4510. Ed. Lawrence Campbell. bk.rev.; illus. circ. 7,000. **Document type:** newsletter.

700   US   ISSN 0741-496X
ART-TALK. 1981. 9/yr. $18. Box 8508, Scottsdale, AZ 85252-8508. TEL 602-948-1799. FAX 602-994-9284. Ed. Bill Macomber; Pub. Thom Romeo. adv. contact: Kathryn Young. bk.rev. circ. 40,000. **Document type:** newspaper.
   Description: Covers art news internationally and art events nationally.

ART THERAPY. see *EDUCATION — Special Education And Rehabilitation*

ART 427

700   US   ISSN 0891-9070
ART TIMES; a literary journal and resource for the arts. 1984. m. $15 (foreign $20). C S S Publications, Inc., 16 Fite Rd., Saugerties, NY 12477. TEL 914-246-6944. FAX 914-246-6944. E-mail: arttimes@mhv.net; URL: http://www.rain.org/-scultura/arttimes/arttimes. (Subscr. to: Box 730, Mt. Marion, NY 12456) Ed. Raymond J. Steiner; Pub. Cornelia Seckel. R&P contact: Cornelia Seckel. adv.: page $1045; trim 10 x 14; adv. contact: Cornelia Seckel. bk.rev.; film rev.; illus. circ. 16,000. (tabloid format; back issues avail.) **Document type:** consumer publication.
    Description: Literary essays on the various arts: visual, film, theatre, dance, and music. Includes original poetry and short fiction, arts opportunities listings and an arts calendar.

700   UK
ART WORKERS GUILD. ANNUAL REPORT. 1885. a. membership. Art Workers Guild, 6 Queen Sq., London WC1N 3AR, England. Ed. D.G. Pullen. bibl.; illus.; circ. 400 (controlled).
    Description: Covers the proceedings of the guild.

700   US   ISSN 0194-1070
ART - WORLD. 1976. a. $20. Arts Review Inc., 55 Wheatley Rd., Glen Head, NY 11545. TEL 516-626-0914. Ed. Bruce Duff Hooton. adv.; bk.rev.; illus. **Document type:** newsletter.

700   IT
ART WORLD. 1988. 3/yr. L.50000 (for 2 yrs.). Michelangelo s.r.l., Via Cimarosa 4, 20144 Milan, Italy. TEL 02-48021565. FAX 02-48009687. Ed. Marco Lupis di Santa Margherita. adv.: B&W or color page L.3600000. circ. 37,000.

700   US
ART - WORLD MUNDO - ARTE; the international Latin American news edition. (Editions in English, Spanish) 1993. m.? 580 Broadway, Ste. 304, New York, NY 10012. TEL 212-966-8661. FAX 212-344-9648. Ed. Patricia Isaza.

730 750   RM   ISSN 1220-6865
N8
ARTA. (Text and summaries in English, Rumanian) 1954. bi-m. 600 lei($39) (effective 1992). Ministerul Culturii, Piata Presei Libere 1, Sector 1, 71341 Bucharest, Rumania. TEL 401-6131380. FAX 401-31121939. (Co-sponsor: Soros Foundation for an Open Society) Ed. Calin Dan. adv.; bk.rev. circ. 2,500. **Indexed:** Artbibl.Mod., RILA.
    Formerly: Arta Plastica Review.
    Description: Covers modern and contemporary visual arts in Rumania and abroad; painting, sculpture, graphics, decorative arts, design, video, installations, performances, film, theater, photography.

700   AT
▼**ARTBEAT.** 1995. q. Department of Communications and the Arts, G.P.O. Box 2154, Canberra, A.C.T. 2601, Australia. TEL 61-6-2791253. E-mail: artbeat@dca.gov.au; URL: http://www.dca.gov.au/artbeat.html. Ed. Cinden Lester. **Document type:** newsletter.
●Available only online.
    Description: Cultural newsletter focusing primarily on federal cultural policy, projects and activities.

745.2   IT
ARTE. 1970. 11/yr. L.78000 (foreign L.140000) (effective 1997). Editoriale Giorgio Mondadori S.p.A., Via A. Ponti, 10, 20143 Milan, Italy. TEL 02-891661. FAX 02-89125888. Ed. Mario Pancera. adv.; bk.rev.; charts; illus. circ. 40,000. **Indexed:** Artbibl., Artbibl.Mod., RILA.
    Formerly: BolaffiArte (ISSN 0045-236X)

709   SA   ISSN 0004-3389
DE ARTE. (Text in Afrikaans, English) 1967. a. R.18.50 (overseas $5.95(£4.40)) (effective 1997). (University of South Africa, Department of Art History and Fine Arts) Unisa Press, Periodicals, P.O. Box 392, Pretoria 0001, South Africa. TEL 27-12-4293111. FAX 27-12-4293221. TELEX 350068. E-mail: unisa-press@unisa.ac.za. Ed. B. van Haute. adv.; bk.rev.; play rev.; bibl.; illus.; circ. 2,000 (paid). (back issues avail.) **Indexed:** IBR, Ind.S.A.Per. **Document type:** academic/scholarly publication.
    Description: Articles cover a wide range within art and architectural history as well as applied arts.
    Refereed Serial

704.948   IT   ISSN 0004-3400
N7810
ARTE CRISTIANA; rivista internazionale di storia dell'arte e di arti liturgiche. 1913; N.S. 1983. bi-m. Lit.100000 (foreign Lit.150000) (effective 1998). Scuola Beato Angelico, Viale S. Gimignano 19, 20146 Milan, Italy. TEL 39-2-48302857. FAX 39-2-48301954. Ed. Valerio Vigorelli. adv. contact: Valerio Vigorelli. bk.rev.; bibl.; charts; index, cum.index. **Indexed:** Artbibl.Mod., Avery Ind.Archit.Per., RILA. **Document type:** academic/scholarly publication.

709 913   IT   ISSN 0391-9110
ARTE E ARCHEOLOGIA; studi e documenti. 1972. irreg., no.24, 1985. price varies. Casa Editrice Leo S. Olschki, Casella Postale 66, 50100 Florence, Italy. TEL 39-55-6530684. FAX 39-55-6530214. E-mail: celso@olschki.it. **Document type:** monographic series.

700   IT
ARTE & CORNICE. (Text in Italian; summaries in English) 1984. q. L.30000 (foreign L.40000). Rima Editrice s.r.l., Viale Sarca 235-3, 20126 Milan, Italy. TEL 02-66103539. FAX 02-66103558. circ. 9,800.
    Formerly: Aste e Cornici (ISSN 0393-439X)
    Description: Covers all aspects of frames.

700   BL   ISSN 0103-8508
ARTE E CULTURA DA AMERICA LATINA. 1990. s-a. 30 BTN($20) Sociedade Cientifica de Estudos da Arte, Rua Domingos Cordeiro 76, 05688 Sao Paulo SP, Brazil.

700   CK   ISSN 0121-506X
NX535.A1
ARTE FACTO. 1992. s-a. Universidad Nacional de Colombia, Facultad de Artes, Apdo. Aereo 50211, Santafe de Bogota, Colombia. circ. 1,000.

700   SP   ISSN 0212-7342
ARTE GALICIA; revista de informacion de las artes plasticas gallegas. 1979. q. 1500 ptas. Sociedad Artistica Ferrolana, Apdo. 339, 15480 Ferrol, Spain. TEL 39-81-353474. adv.: B&W page 20000 ptas.; adv. contact: Gonzalo Palmeiro. circ. 3,000.

760   SP
ARTE GRAFICO EN MADRID. biennial. Fundacion C E I M, Diego de Leon 50, 28006 Madrid, Spain.

700   SP   ISSN 1131-5598
ARTE, INDIVIDUO Y SOCIEDAD. 1988. a. 2000 ptas.($22) (effective 1997). Universidad Complutense, Departamento de Didactica de Expresion Plastica, Servicio de Publicaciones, Calle Isaac Peral s-n, Ciudad Universitaria, 28040 Madrid, Spain. TEL 34-1-3946934. FAX 34-1-3946954. (back issues avail.)
—CINDOC.
    Description: Focuses on artistic education analyzing aesthetic, behaviour and social environment on individuals.

709   IT   ISSN 0004-3443
N4
ARTE LOMBARDA; rivista di storia dell'arte. (Text in English, French, German, Italian) 1955. 3/yr. Lit.330000 (foreign Lit.395000) (effective 1998). Istituto per la Storia dell'Arte Lombarda, Palazzo Reale, Piazza Duomo 14, 20122 Milan, Italy. TEL 39-2-878475. FAX 39-2-86463412. Ed. Maria Luisa Gatti Perer. bk.rev.; bibl.; illus.; index, cum.index. circ. 1,000. (back issues avail.) **Indexed:** Artbibl.Mod., Avery Ind.Archit.Per., IBR, RILA. —SWETS.

700   IT   ISSN 0393-7267
N5950
ARTE MEDIEVALE. 1987. s-a. price varies. Istituto della Enciclopedia Italiana, Piazza della Enciclopedia Italiana 4, 00186 Rome, Italy. TEL 39-6-68984. FAX 39-6-68982175. Ed. Angiola Maria Romanini. **Document type:** academic/scholarly publication.
    Description: International review of medieval art, with contributions in original language.

700   IT   ISSN 0390-1319
ARTE NAIVE. s-a. L.15000 (foreign L.20000) (effective 1995). Artigianato Grafico Editoriale s.n.c., Via Casorati, 29, 42100 Reggio Emilia, Italy. FAX 39-522-921169.

701.18   IT
ARTE NUOVA. 1971. m. L.1500. Corso Matteotti 11, 60035 Jesi, Italy. Ed. Armando Ginesi. adv.; bk.rev.; charts; illus.
    Formerly: Arte Nuova Oggi (ISSN 0044-9067)

700   IT
ARTE STAMPA. 1950. 3/yr. L.30000. Editrice Liguria, Via de Mari 4, 17100 Savona, Italy. TEL 019-829917. FAX 019-387798.
    Formerly: Arte Stampa Liguria

700   BL   ISSN 0102-6550
NX533.A1   CODEN: ARTEES
ARTE U N E S P. (Text in Portuguese; summaries in English, Portuguese) 1985. A. $30 or exchange basis. Universidade Estadual Paulista, Av. Vicente Ferreira 1278, Caixa Postal 71, 17515-901 Marilia SP, Brazil. TEL 55-144-222504. FAX 55-144-222504. E-mail: uespr@brfapesp.bitnet. **Document type:** academic/scholarly publication.
    Description: Covers Brazilian art, including its history, origin and style.

709   IT   ISSN 0392-5234
N6921
ARTE VENETA; rivista di storia dell'arte. 1947. a. L.140000. Gruppo Editoriale Electa Periodici s.r.l., Via Trantacoste, 7, Milan, Italy. Ed. Rodolfo Pallucchini. adv. circ. 2,500. (reprint service avail. from SWZ) **Indexed:** Art & Archaeol.Tech.Abstr., Artbibl.Mod., Avery Ind.Archit.Per., RILA.

700 913   BO   ISSN 0587-5447
N7
ARTE Y ARQUEOLOGIA. 1969-1983 (vol.9); resumed 1986. biennial. $10. (Universidad Mayor de San Andres, Instituto de Estudios Bolivianos) Museo Nacional de Arte, Casilla Postal 609, La Paz, Bolivia. Ed. Teresa Gisbert. adv. circ. 500. **Indexed:** Amer.Hist.& Life, Hist.Abstr.

709.04   BE   ISSN 0771-761X
N6758
ARTEFACTUM. (Text in Dutch, English, French, German) 1983. 5/yr. $40. Artefactum S.A., Amerikalei 125, B-2000 Antwerp, Belgium. TEL 32-3-2382089. FAX 32-3-2374079. Ed. Erno Vroonen; Pub. Lieve De Deyne. adv.; bk.rev. circ. 10,000. (back issues avail.) **Indexed:** Art Ind.
—KR SourceOne.
    Description: Covers contemporary art in Europe.

ARTEMIS - ARTISTS AND WRITERS; artists and writers from the Blue Ridge Mountains. see *LITERATURE — Poetry*

700   BL   ISSN 0004-3486
ARTES.* 1965. m. Cr.$18.($16) Rua Nestor Pestana 30.21 Conj. 216, Sao Paulo 3 S.P., Brazil. bk.rev.; film rev.; play rev. circ. 15,000.

700   SP
LAS ARTES; catalogo de pintores, escultores y ceramistas en Mallorca. a. Basilio Baltasar Ediciones, C. Serinya 9, 2o 2a, 07003 Palma de Mallorca, Spain. TEL 72-79-39. FAX 72-72-34.

709.72   MX   ISSN 0300-4953
N7
ARTES DE MEXICO. (Text in English, Spanish) 1957; N.S. 1988. q. Mex.$600 (foreign $150) per 6 nos. (effective 1997 & 1998). Artes de Mexico y del Mundo S.A., Plaza Rio de Janeiro 52, Col. Roma, 06700 Mexico, D.F., Mexico. TEL 52-5-2083205. FAX 52-5-5255925. E-mail: artesmex@internet.com.mx. Eds. Alberto Ruy Sanchez, Margarita de Ovalle; Pub. Alberto Ruy Sanchez. R&P contact: Teresa Vergara. adv. contact: Margarita de Orellana. bk.rev.; illus.; circ. 20,000 (paid). **Indexed:** Art Ind., Hisp.Amer.Per.Ind. (1970-). **Document type:** academic/scholarly publication.
—KR SourceOne.
    Description: Covers prehistoric art to modern film, colonial paintings to ritual art, Chiapan textiles to viceroyal palaces, architecture to silver works.
    Refereed Serial

ARTES INTERNATIONAL; an international reader of literature, art and music. see *LITERARY AND POLITICAL REVIEWS*

ULRICH'S INTERNATIONAL PERIODICALS DIRECTORY 1998

A

700   EC   ISSN 0257-1625
ARTESANIAS DE AMERICA. 1979. 3/yr. $12 (effective 1997). Centro Interamericano de Artesanias y Artes Populares, Hermano Miguel 3-23 (Escalinata), Apdo. 01.01.1943, Cuenca, Ecuador. TEL 593-7-829451. FAX 593-7-831450. Ed. Joaquin Moreno. adv. contact: Manual Jadan. bk.rev. circ. 2,000. **Indexed:** IBR. **Document type:** academic/scholarly publication.
     Formerly (until 1982): Centro Interamericano de Artesanias y Artes Populares. Boletin de Informacion.

709   CN   ISSN 1192-7712
N1
ARTFOCUS. 1983. q. Can.$18 (foreign Can.$25). Fleisher Fine Arts Inc., 15 McMurrich St., Ste. 706, Toronto, ON M5R 3M6, Canada. TEL 416-925-5564. FAX 416-925-2972. E-mail: info@artfocus.com; URL: http://www.artfocus.com. (Subscr. to: Box 1063, Sta. F, Toronto, ON M4Y 2T7, Canada) Ed. Pat Fleisher. adv.: B&W page Can.$1400, color page Can.$2000; trim 8 1/2 x 11. bk.rev. circ. 10,000. (back issues avail.) **Document type:** consumer publication.
     Supersedes (in 1992): Artpost Magazine (ISSN 0829-0784)
     Description: Contemporary and historical art exhibited in Canada and abroad.

700   US   ISSN 0004-3532
N1
ARTFORUM. 1962. m. (10/yr.). $52 to individuals (foreign $80); institutions $66 (foreign $99). Artforum International Magazine, Inc., 65 Bleecker St., New York, NY 10012. TEL 212-475-4000. FAX 212-529-1257. (Subscr. to: Box 3000, Denville, NJ 07834) Ed. Jack Bankowsky; Pub. Anthony Korner. R&P contact: Elizabeth Franzen. adv.; bk.rev.; film rev.; play rev.; abstr.; bibl.; charts; illus. circ. 27,000. (also avail. in microform from UMI; microfiche; back issues avail.) **Indexed:** Acad.Ind., Amer.Bibl.Slavic & E.Eur.Stud., Art Ind., Artbibl., Artbibl.Mod., Arts & Hum.Cit.Ind., ASCA, Avery Ind.Archit.Per., Curr.Cont., DAAI, Film Lit.Ind. (1973-), Hum.Ind., Ind.Bk.Rev.Hum., RILA, RILM. **Document type:** trade publication.
     ●Also available online. Vendor(s): Information Access Co.
     —BLDSC (1733.743000); KR SourceOne; UnCover.
     Description: Offers coverage of the contemporary art world, with sections on architecture, music, advertising and reviews of contemporary exhibitions worldwide.

741.6 096   US   ISSN 1076-8912
ARTHUR RACKHAM SOCIETY NEWSLETTER. 1984. irreg., approx. q., no.20, 1995. $20 (£15($22.50) outside US) (effective 1996 & 1997). Arthur Rackham Society, 1240 Devil's Gulch Rd., Estes Park, CO 80517. TEL 970-586-4092. FAX 970-586-4092. (In U.K.: c/o Richard Riall, Garden Cottage, 7 Gardeners Hill Rd., Boundstone, Near Farnham, Surrey GU10 4RL, England) Ed. Dorothy S. Gibbs. R&P contact: Dorothy S. Gibbs. bk.rev.; bibl.; illus. circ. 150. **Document type:** newsletter.
     Description: Covers the life and works of English illustrator Arthur Rackham, and activities of the society.

709.5   SZ   ISSN 0004-3648
N8
ARTIBUS ASIAE; quarterly of Asian art and archaeology for scholars and connoisseurs. (Text in English, French, German) 1925. q. 124.50 SFr.($92.50) (effective 1997). Museum Rietberg Zurich, Gablerstr. 15, CH-8002 Zurich, Switzerland. TEL 41-1-2024528. FAX 41-1-2025201. Ed. Thomas Lawton; Pubs. Elizabeth Hefti, Eberhard Fischer. bk.rev.; bibl.; charts; illus.; index. (reprint service avail. from SCH) **Indexed:** Art Ind., Artbibl., Artbibl.Mod., Arts & Hum.Cit.Ind., ASCA, Avery Ind.Archit.Per., Curr.Cont., IBR, Ind.Bk.Rev.Hum. **Document type:** academic/scholarly publication.
     —BLDSC (1734.080000); KR SourceOne; SWETS; UnCover.

709.5   SZ
ARTIBUS ASIAE SUPPLEMENTA. 1937. a. price varies. Museum Rietberg Zurich, Gablerstr. 15, CH-8002 Zurich, Switzerland. TEL 41-1-2024564. FAX 41-1-2025201. Ed. Thomas Lawton; Pubs. Elizabeth Hefti, Eberhard Fischer. bibl.; illus. **Document type:** academic/scholarly publication.
     Description: Series of full-length books dealing with similar topics to "Artibus Asiae".

700   AU   ISSN 0391-9064
NX1.A1
ARTIBUS ET HISTORIAE; international journal for visual arts. (Text in English, French, German or Italian; summaries in English) 1980. s-a. S.1590($156) (International Institute for Art History Research) Irsa Verlag Gmbh, Ruedengasse 6, A-1030 Vienna, Austria. TEL 43-1-7130136. FAX 43-1-7130130. Ed. Jozef Grabski. **Indexed:** Amer.Hist.& Life (1989-1995), Art Ind., Artbibl.Mod., Avery Ind.Archit.Per., Hist.Abstr. (1989-1995), IBR, RILA, RILM. **Document type:** academic/scholarly publication.
     —BLDSC (1734.085000); KR SourceOne; SWETS; UnCover.
     Description: Covers a broad range of subjects, including photography and film, as well as traditional topics of scholarly art research.

700   CN   ISSN 0847-3277
ARTICHOKE; writings about the visual arts. 1989. 3/yr. Can.$20($30) (effective 1997). Artichoke Publishing, 102-1625-15 Ave. S.E., Calgary, AB T3C 0Y3, Canada. TEL 604-683-1941. FAX 604-683-1941. (Subscr. to: 901 Jervis St., Ste 208, Vancouver, BC V6E 2B6, Canada) Ed. Paula Gustafson. adv.; bk.rev.; circ. 1,000 (paid). (back issues avail.) **Document type:** consumer publication.
     Description: Western Canada's only visual arts magazine.

700   US
ARTIFACTS (COLUMBIA). 1976. 4/yr. Arts Commission, 1800 Gervais St., Columbia, SC 29201. TEL 803-734-8696. FAX 803-734-8526. Ed. Jayne Darke. bk.rev.; bibl.; stat. circ. 17,000. **Document type:** government publication, newspaper.

700   SZ   ISSN 0004-3842
N3
ARTIS. 1948. m. 78 SFr. (foreign 84 SFr.). Hallwag AG, Nordring 4, CH-3001 Bern, Switzerland. TEL 41-31-3323131. FAX 41-31-3314133. TELEX 912661-HAWA-CH. Ed. Peter Vetsch. adv. contact: Hans Bueschi. bk.rev.; bibl.; illus.; mkt.; index. circ. 11,000. (back issues avail.) **Indexed:** IBR. **Document type:** bulletin.
     Formerly: Speculum Artis.

700   UK   ISSN 0004-3877
N1
THE ARTIST. 1931. m. $50. The Artists' Publishing Co. Ltd., 63-65 High St., Tenterden, Kent TN30 6BD, England. TEL 44-1580-763673. FAX 44-1580-765411. Ed. Sally Bulgin; Pub. Irene Briers. R&P contact: Sally Bulgin. adv. contact: Tim Fleming. illus. circ. 17,000. **Indexed:** Avery Ind.Archit.Per. **Document type:** bulletin.
     —BLDSC (1735.280000); KR SourceOne; SWETS; UMI; UnCover.
     Incorporates: Art and Artists (ISSN 0004-3001)

700   CC
ARTIST/MEI SHU CHIA. (Text in Chinese; table of contents in English) bi-m. HK.$108. Artist Publishing Co., 2F, Hong Kong Diamond Exchange Bldg., 8-10 Duddell St., Central, Hong Kong, People's Republic of China. TEL 570-6249. adv.; illus.

700   IT   ISSN 1120-2459
ARTISTA. 1989. a. Casa Editrice le Lettere, Costa S. Giorgio 28, 50125 Florence, Italy.

769.56 383   US   ISSN 1181-9456
ARTISTAMP NEWS. 1971. s-a. Can.$12 for 3 issues (effective 1997). P.O. Box 3655, Vancouver, BC V6B 3Y8, Canada. TEL 604-885-7156. FAX 604-885-7183. Ed. Ed Varney. bk.rev.; illus.; circ. 100 (paid). (looseleaf format; back issues avail.) **Document type:** newsletter.
     Formerly (until 1991): Banana Rag.
     Description: Focuses on the emerging field of stamps by artists, with information and news of shows and projects, profiles of artists and reproductions of their works.

791.060489   DK
ARTISTERNE. 1982. a. free to institutions. Dansk Artist Forbund, Vendersgade 24, DK-1363 Copenhagen K, Denmark. TEL 45-33-32-66-77. FAX 45-33-33-73-30. Ed. Nick Olander. illus. circ. 13,000.
     Formerly (until 1985): Show-Guide (ISSN 0109-8411)

ARTISTIC TRAVELER; architecture & travel with art & photography. see ARCHITECTURE

700   US   ISSN 1075-0894
N8600
ARTIST'S AND GRAPHIC DESIGNER'S MARKET; where and how to sell your illustrations, fine art, graphic design and cartoons. 1979. a. $24.99. F & W Publications, Inc., 1507 Dana Ave., Cincinnati, OH 45207. TEL 513-531-2222. FAX 513-531-4082. Ed. Mary Cox. illus.
     Formerly: Artist's Market (ISSN 0161-0546); Which supersedes in part: Art and Crafts Market (ISSN 0147-2461); Former titles: Artist's and Photographer's Market (ISSN 0146-8294); Artist's Market (ISSN 0361-607X); (until 1973): Cartoonists' Market.
     Description: Lists 2500 places to sell art for ads, albums, cartoons, graphic designs, greeting cards, illustrations, galleries and posters-prints.

760   UK   ISSN 0269-4697
THE ARTIST'S AND ILLUSTRATOR'S MAGAZINE. 1986. m. £23.10 (foreign £32) (effective 1997). Quarto Magazines plc, The Fitzpatrick Bldg., 188-194 York Way, London N7 9QR. TEL 49-171-700-8500. FAX 49-171-700-4985. (Subscr. to: Tower House, Sovereign Park, Market Harborough, Leicestershire LE16 9EF, England. TEL 44-1858-435307) Ed. Laura Gascgoine; Pub. Marion Hasson. R&P contact: Marion Hasson. adv.: B&W page £949, color page £1552; trim 297 x 210; adv. contact: Paul Harris. bk.rev.; cum.index. (back issues avail.) **Document type:** consumer publication.
     Description: Focuses on painting and drawing techniques and includes interviews with artists, product reviews and practical demonstrations.

700   UK   ISSN 1355-0187
ARTIST'S BOOK YEARBOOK. a. £10 (Europe £13; U.S. £14; elsewhere £15) (effective 1997). Magpie Press, 1 Hermitage Cottage, Clamp Hill, Stanmore, Mddx. HA7 3JW, England. FAX 44-181-954-0670. Ed. Tanya Peixoto. R&P contact: Tanya Peixoto. adv. contact: Gary Donaldson. circ. 1,000 (paid). **Document type:** directory.
     Refereed Serial

748.5   CN
ARTISTS IN STAINED GLASS. JOURNAL. 1978. q. Can.$40 (US Can.$50, elsewhere Can.$65) (effective 1997). Artists in Stained Glass, 35 McCaul St., Toronto, ON M5T 1V7, Canada. TEL 519-334-3119. FAX 416-977-3552. Ed. Virginia Smith. adv. contact: Virginia Smith. circ. 300. (back issues avail.) **Document type:** bulletin.
     Formerly (until 1996): Artists in Stained Glass. Bulletin (ISSN 0841-8039)
     Description: Promotes stained glass as an art form.

750   US   ISSN 0741-3351
N7430
ARTIST'S MAGAZINE. 1984. m. $27. F & W Publications, Inc., 1507 Dana Ave., Cincinnati, OH 45207. TEL 513-531-2222. FAX 513-531-4082. (Subscr. to: Box 2120, Harlan, IA 51593) Ed. Sandra Carpenter. adv.; bk.rev.; illus. circ. 230,104. **Indexed:** Ind.How To Do It (1989-).
     —UMI; UnCover.
     Description: How-to publication for beginning, intermediate and advanced artists.

700   GW   ISSN 1015-9797
▼**ARTIUM.** (Text in English, German) 1995. 3/yr. DM.50 (effective 1997). Art Center GmbH, Koehlerweg 16, 61440 Oberursel, Germany. TEL 49-6171-52508. FAX 49-6171-56812. Ed. Maria Burghagen. adv. **Document type:** academic/scholarly publication.
     Description: Covers art of the 19th and 20th centuries.

700   US
ARTLETTER. 1980. bi-m. $35. Virginia Beach Center for the Arts, 2200 Park Ave., Virginia Beach, VA 23451. TEL 804-425-0000. Dir. Helen Snow. circ. 2,500. (back issues avail.) **Document type:** newsletter.

700 370   AT   ISSN 0727-1239
ARTLINK. 1981. q. Aus.$40 to individuals; institutions Aus.$70; schools Aus.$45 (effective 1997). Art Link Australia, 363 Esplanade, Henley Beach, S.A. 5022, Australia. TEL 61-8-356-8511. FAX 61-8-235-1280. E-mail: artlink@webmedia.com.au. Ed. Stephanie Britton. R&P contact: Stephanie Britton. adv. contact: Stephanie Britton. bk.rev.; illus. circ. 3,000. (back issues avail.) **Document type:** consumer publication.
—CCC.
Description: Covers contemporary art in Australia, all media including electronic, with comment on new work, industry issues, information and publications.

700   US
▼**ARTNET MAGAZINE**. 1996. d. free. ArtNet, 145 E. 57th St., 9th Fl., New York, NY 10022. TEL 212-497-9700. FAX 212-497-9707. E-mail: artnet@artnet.com; URL: http://www.artnet.com/magazine.html. Ed. Walter Robinson; Pub. Hans Neuendorf. R&P contact: William Brewster Fine. adv. contact: William Brewster Fine. bk.rev.; illus. **Document type:** trade publication.
●Available only online.
Description: Includes fine art news, reviews, features, images, auction reports, letters from London, Paris and Tokyo.

707.4 701.18   US   ISSN 0004-3273
N1
ARTNEWS. 1902. 11/yr. $39.95. Artnews Associates, 48 W. 38th St., New York, NY 10018. TEL 212-398-1690. FAX 212-819-0394. (Subscr. to: Artnews Subscription Service, Box 56590, Boulder, CO 80322. TEL 800-284-4625) Ed. Milton Esterow; Pub. Milton Esterow. R&P contact: Grace Scalera. adv. contact: Arnold Obler. bk.rev.; illus. circ. 75,000. (also avail. in microform from UMI,MIM; back issues avail.; reprint service avail. from UMI) **Indexed:** Art & Archaeol.Tech.Abstr., Art Ind., Artbibl.Mod., ASCA, Biodet.Abstr., Bk.Rev.Ind. (1986-), Child.Bk.Rev.Ind. (1986-), Curr.Cont., DAAI, Ind.Bk.Rev.Hum., Mag.Ind., Mid.East: Abstr.& Ind., PMR, R.G., RILA. **Document type:** consumer publication, newsletter.
—BLDSC (1733.465000); KR SourceOne; SWETS; UMI; UnCover.
Description: General interest art magazine, containing profiles of artists, surveys of gallery exhibits, and international art news.

700   US   ISSN 0145-7241
N1
ARTNEWSLETTER; the international bi-weekly business report on the art market. 1975. bi-w. $249 (foreign $277). Artnews Associates, 48 W. 38th St., New York, NY 10018. TEL 212-398-1690. Ed. Barbara Pollack; Pub. Milton Esterow. R&P contact: Grace Scalera. **Document type:** newsletter.

800   US   ISSN 1085-3391
▼**ARTNOIR SHOWCASE**. 1995. m. free. 1323 S.E. 17th St., Ste. 138, Fort Lauderdale, FL 33316. TEL 954-523-9673. FAX 954-523-9673. E-mail: artnoir@artnoir.com; URL: http://www.artnoir.com. Ed. Coni Porter Uzelac. R&P contact: Coni Porter Uzelac. adv. contact: Coni Porter Uzelac. **Document type:** academic/scholarly publication.
●Available only online.
Description: For artists, art historians, educators, collectors, museums, and galleries, especially those interested in the art of the diaspora including African American, Afro-Caribbean, Brazilian, Polynesian and Micronesian.

700   US
ARTPLUS.* 1990. q. $5 per no. (Boca Museum) G S & J Publishing, Inc., 5212 N.W. 54th Ave., Pompano Beach, FL 33073-3755. TEL 305-977-5901. Ed. Carol Hobbs. circ. 5,000.
Description: Covers artists, collectors, dealers, fashion, travel and dining.

705 706   AT   ISSN 0066-8095
ARTS. 1958. a. Aus.$10 to individuals; institutions Aus.$12 (effective 1997). University of Sydney, Arts Association, Sydney, N.S.W., Australia. TEL 61-2-93512656. FAX 61-2-93512434. TELEX AA 26169 UNISYD. Ed. Geoffrey Little. R&P contact: Geoffrey Little. bk.rev. circ. 500. **Document type:** academic/scholarly publication.
Description: Inaugural lectures, special lectures, occasional papers to graduates and faculty of arts, and research papers in arts.

700   US
ARTS (MINNEAPOLIS). 1983. m. membership. Minneapolis Institute of Arts, 2400 Third Ave. S., Minneapolis, MN 55404. TEL 612-870-3046. FAX 612-870-3004. Pub. Scott Sayre. R&P contact: Ann Dankowski. adv. circ. 20,000. (reprint service avail.) **Document type:** newsletter.

700   BE
ARTS AFRICAINS. irreg. price varies. Association des Diplomes Histoire Art et Archeologie, College Erasme, Place Blaise Pascal 1, 1348 Louvain-la-Neuve, Belgium. FAX 32-10-472579. E-mail: hackens@arka.ucl.ac.be. Ed. Tony Hackens. **Document type:** monographic series.
Description: Scholarly monographs on topics in African art.

ARTS ALIVE!; a magazine promoting the Arts. see THEATER

700   JO
ARTS AMATEURS/HUWAT AL-FUNOUN.* (Text in Arabic; supplements in English, German) 1968. m. Club of Arts Amateurs, P.O. Box 6370, Amman, Jordan. Ed. Nayef Kamal Naanah. adv.; bk.rev. circ. 10,000.

700 352   US   ISSN 1047-3297
ARTS AND CULTURE FUNDING REPORT. 1989. m. $138. Education Funding Research Council, 4301 Fairfax Dr. No. 875, Arlington, VA 22203-1627. TEL 703-528-1000. FAX 703-528-6060. Ed. Carol Dana; Pub. James J. Marshall. R&P contact: Donald Hoffman. **Document type:** newsletter.
—CCC.
Description: Reports on federal, state and private financial aid to arts and cultural projects.

ARTS & LEISURE TIMES. see LEISURE AND RECREATION

ARTS AND MEDIA SERIES. see COMMUNICATIONS

701.18 745.1   BE
ARTS, ANTIQUES ET AUCTIONS. (Text in Dutch, English, French) 1971. m. (10/yr.). 3000 BEF. Arts Antiques Auctions S.A., Boite 22, 79 Bd. Ed. Machtens, 1080 Brussels, Belgium. TEL 32-2-4108686. FAX 32-2-4108289. Ed. J.P. Corne. adv.: B&W page 39500 BEF, color page 58000 BEF; trim 295 x 215; adv. contact: J. Van Hecke-Corne. bk.rev. circ. 10,000.
Description: Publishes information on public sales, antiques fairs and markets, and art expositions in Belgium and abroad.

709.5   FR   ISSN 0004-3958
N2
ARTS ASIATIQUES. (Text in French; occasionally in English) 1954. irreg., vol.52, 1997. 225 F. (Ecole Francaise d'Extreme Orient, Jean Maisonneuve Librarie d'Amerique et d'Orient) Editions d' Amerique et d'Orient, 11 rue Saint Sulpice, 75006 Paris, France. TEL 33-1-43268635. FAX 33-1-43545954. Eds. Jean Filliozat, Jeannine Auboyer. adv.; bk.rev.; charts; illus. circ. 1,500. (reprint service avail. from KTO) **Indexed:** Art Ind., Avery Ind.Archit.Per., IBR.
—KR SourceOne; SWETS.

700   CN   ISSN 0704-7916
NX513.A3
ARTS ATLANTIC; Atlantic Canada's journal of the arts. 1977. 3/yr. Can.$19.95 for 4 nos. (foreign Can.$29.95) (effective 1997). ARTSatlantic Inc., 145 Richmond St., Charlottetown, PQ C1A 1J1, Canada. TEL 902-628-6138. FAX 902-566-4648. Ed. Joseph Sherman. R&P contact: Joseph Sherman. adv.: page Can.$800; trim 8 3/8 x 10 7/8; adv. contact: Ellen MacPhail. bk.rev.; film rev.; play rev.; bibl.; illus. circ. 3,000. (also avail. in microfilm from MML; back issues avail.; reprint service avail. from MMI) **Indexed:** Art Bibl., Can.B.P.I., Can.Per.Ind., CMI. **Document type:** trade publication.
—BLDSC (1736.110000).
Description: Features the region's fine arts, cinema and video, crafts, performance, and related creativity.

700   CN   ISSN 0843-2260
ARTS BEAT. 1973. bi-m. Can.$25 (foreign Can.$35) (effective 1997). Hamilton & Region Arts Council, 2 King St. W., Hamilton, ON L8P 1A1, Canada. TEL 905-529-9485. FAX 905-529-0238. E-mail: harac@netaccess.on.ca; URL: http://www.netaccess.on.ca/~harac. Ed. Ivan Jurakic. R&P contact: Ivan Jurakic. adv. contact: Ivan Jurakic. bk.rev.; circ. 3,000 (paid). (tabloid format; back issues avail.) **Document type:** newsletter.
Former titles (until 1987): Art-i-fact (ISSN 0843-2252); (until 1981): Art-i-fact Bulletin (ISSN 0382-8638); (until 1975): Art-i-fact (ISSN 0315-7202)
Description: Dedicated to promoting an understanding and appreciation of the arts in all disciplines within the greater Hamilton area, including: craft, dance, literature, music theater and visual arts.
Refereed Serial

700   AT
ARTS COUNCIL OF AUSTRALIA. ANNUAL REPORT. 1948. a. Arts Council of Australia, Ste. 605, 6th Fl., Phoenix House, c/o Pier 5, Hickson Rd., Millers Point, N.S.W. 2000, Australia. Ed. Jennifer Bott. circ. 1,500.

700   UK
ARTS COUNCIL OF ENGLAND. ANNUAL REPORT AND ACCOUNTS. (Former name of issuing body: Arts Council of Great Britain) 1945. a. free. Arts Council of England, 14 Great Peter St., London SW1P 3NQ, England. TEL 44-171-333-0100. FAX 44-171-973-6590. TELEX 9312102069 AC G. Pub. Caroline Leech. **Document type:** corporate report, government publication.
Formerly: Arts Council of Great Britain. Annual Report and Accounts (ISSN 0066-8133)
Description: Provides an overview of the council's work and records of grants and guarantees offered in the support of the arts.

700   FR   ISSN 0337-1603
NX588.75
ARTS D'AFRIQUE NOIRE. 1971. q. 295 F.($66) (effective 1997). P.O. Box 24, 95400 Arnouville, France. Ed. Raoul Lehuard; Pub. Raoul Lehuard. R&P contact: Raoul Lehuard. illus.; index. **Indexed:** Anthropol.Lit., Art Ind. **Document type:** academic/scholarly publication, monographic series.
—KR SourceOne.

745.5 707   US   ISSN 1063-2913
NK1160
ARTS EDUCATION POLICY REVIEW. 1899. bi-m. $36 to individuals; institutions $63. (Helen Dwight Reid Educational Foundation) Heldref Publications, 1319 Eighteenth St., N.W., Washington, DC 20036-1802. TEL 202-296-6267. FAX 202-296-5149. (Co-sponsor: Music Educators National Conference) Ed. Sheila Barrows. adv. contact: Raymond Rallo. bk.rev.; illus. circ. 1,400. (also avail. in microform from UMI; reprint service avail.) **Indexed:** Art Ind., Bk.Rev.Ind. (1975-1977), C.I.J.E., Educ.Ind., Graph.Arts Abstr., Mag.Ind., Per.Islam. (1994-), R.G., R.G.Abstr. **Document type:** academic/scholarly publication.
●Also available online. Vendor(s): Information Access Co., UMI.
Also available on CD-ROM. Producer(s): UMI.
—BLDSC (1736.238000); KR SourceOne; SWETS; UMI; UnCover. CCC.
Former titles: Design for Arts in Education (ISSN 0732-0973); Design (ISSN 0011-9253)
Refereed Serial

ARTS ET METIERS. see ENGINEERING — Mechanical Engineering

709   FR
ARTS ET SOCIETE. 1976. a. price varies. (Universite de Rennes II (Universite de Haute Bretagne), Centre de Recherches sur les Arts Anciens et Modernes de l'Ouest de la France) Presses Universitaires de Rennes, Campus Rennes 2 - La Harpe, 2 rue du Doyen D. Leroy, 35044 Rennes Cedex, France. TEL 33-2-99546638. FAX 33-2-99330795. Ed. X. Barral i. Altet. bk.rev. **Indexed:** RILA.
Formerly: Arts de l'Ouest (ISSN 0220-2220)
Description: Collection which covers painting, architecture, applied arts and archaeology.

THE ARTS IN PSYCHOTHERAPY; an international journal. see PSYCHOLOGY

430 ART

700   NX1   US   ISSN 0897-859X
ARTS INDIANA MAGAZINE. (Annual literary supplement avail.: Hopewell Review) 1979. bi-m. $18 (foreign $48). Arts Indiana, Inc., 47 S. Pennsylvania, Ste. 701, Indianapolis, IN 46204. TEL 317-632-7894. FAX 317-632-7966. Ed. Lou Harry. R&P contact: Orval Schierholz. adv. contact: Kay Ivcevich. bk.rev. circ. 25,000. **Indexed:** Amer.Hum.Ind. **Document type:** consumer publication.
    Formerly (until 1987): Arts Insight (ISSN 0738-9787)
    Description: Devoted to statewide coverage of the visual, literary, and performing arts in Indiana.

ARTS INTERNATIONAL. see *LITERATURE*

700   US
ARTS LINK; news for arts leaders. m. membership. Americans for the Arts, 927 15 St., N.W., Washington, DC 20005. TEL 202-371-2830. FAX 202-371-0424. Ed. Jenifer Neiman. adv. circ. 5,000. **Document type:** newsletter.
    Former titles: A C A Update (ISSN 1054-3570); (until 1979): Update (New York); A C A Word from Washington (ISSN 0300-7065)
    Description: Provides, in summary form, current legislative reports and arts news for arts leaders.

700   US   ISSN 0004-4059
N1
ARTS MAGAZINE (NEW YORK).* 1926. 10/yr. $34.95. Arts Communications Group, 150 Greenway Ter., Apt. 44W, Forest Hills, NY 11375-5212. TEL 212-431-4410. FAX 212-431-4682. Ed. Barry Schwabsky. adv.; bk.rev.; illus. circ. 22,000. (also avail. in microform from UMI) **Indexed:** Acad.Ind., Art Ind., Artbibl.Mod., Arts & Hum.Cit.Ind., Avery Ind.Archit.Per., Curr.Cont., DAAI, Hum.Ind., R.G., RILA.
    —KR SourceOne; UMI; UnCover.
    Description: Covers 20th century art, architecture and design. Contains profiles of artists, and reviews of gallery exhibits.

700 792.800   UK
ARTS NEWS. 1986. q. £4 to non-members (members £2.50) per no. National Campaign for the Arts, Francis House, Francis St., London SW1P 1DE, England. TEL 44-171-828-4448. FAX 44-171-931-9959. E-mail: nca@ecna.org; URL: http://www.ecna.org/nca. **Document type:** bulletin.
    Formerly (until 1996): N C A News (ISSN 0957-9044)

700 960   US   ISSN 1044-8640
ARTS OF AFRICA. 1987. a. $40 (effective 1998). African Studies Association, Credit Union Bldg., Emory University, Atlanta, GA 30322. E-mail: ckoch@emory.edu. R&P contact: Christopher Koch. **Document type:** academic/scholarly publication.

709.5   CC   ISSN 0004-4083
NX572
ARTS OF ASIA. 1971. 6/yr. HK.$500($65) Arts of Asia Publications Ltd., 1309 Kowloon Centre, 29-39 Ashley Rd., Kowloon, Hong Kong, People's Republic of China. TEL 852-2376-1002. FAX 852-2376-3713. URL: http://www.hk.linkage.net/~artsasia. Ed. Mrs. Tuyet Nguyet. adv. contact: Robin Markbreiter. bk.rev.; illus.; index every 3 yrs. circ. 18,000. (back issues avail.) **Indexed:** Art & Archaeol.Tech.Abstr., Art Ind., Artbibl.Mod., Artbibl., Arts & Hum.Cit.Ind., ASCA, Avery Ind.Archit.Per., Curr.Cont. **Document type:** academic/scholarly publication.
    —BLDSC (1736.090000); Genuine Article; KR SourceOne; SWETS; UnCover.

700   II
ARTS OF HIMACHAL. 1975. irreg. price varies. State Museum, Simla, Department of Languages and Cultural Affairs, Simla, Himachal Pradesh, India. Ed. Vishwa Chander Ohri. circ. 1,000. **Document type:** monographic series.

700   US   ISSN 0740-9214
N1
ARTS QUARTERLY. 1978. q. $10 (foreign $15). New Orleans Museum of Art, Box 19123, New Orleans, LA 70179. TEL 504-488-2631. FAX 504-484-6662. Ed. Wanda O'Shello. R&P contact: Wanda O'Shello. adv. contact: Karron Lane. bk.rev.; illus. circ. 20,000. (tabloid format; back issues avail.) **Indexed:** RILA. **Document type:** newsletter.

700   JM
ARTS REVIEW. 1976. 3/yr. J.$0.50. University of the West Indies, Creative Arts Centre, P.O. Box 97, Mona, Kingston 7, Jamaica, W.I.

700   NE   ISSN 0926-7069
ARTSCHOOL MAGAZINE. 1986. 6/yr. fl.60 (foreign fl.120). ArtSchool Bilthoven BV, Postbus 350, 3720 AJ Bilthoven, Netherlands. TEL 31-30-2252255. FAX 31-30-2252212. Ed. Anton Kriegsman. adv.: B&W page fl.2100, color page fl.3575; trim 199 x 277; adv. contact: N. Kriegsman. bk.rev.; index. circ. 16,000. (back issues avail.) **Document type:** consumer publication.
    Formerly (until 1992): Tekenen en Schilderen.

ARTSFOCUS. see *MUSEUMS AND ART GALLERIES*

708   IT
ARTSHOW; guida alle mostre d'arte. 1986. 8/yr. L.25000 (foreign L.33000). Artshow Edizioni s.r.l., Viale Monza 48, 20127 Milan, Italy. TEL 39-2-26826502. FAX 39-2-26826498. Ed. Giulio Ciavoliello. adv.: B&W page L.1600000; adv. contact: Pia Quarzo Cerina. circ. 40,000. **Document type:** consumer publication.

700   AT   ISSN 1033-7318
ARTSLINE. 1989. q. free. Western Australia Department for the Arts, Alexander Library Bldg., Perth Cultural Centre, P.O. Box 8349, Perth, W.A. 6849, Australia. TEL 61-9-4271222. FAX 61-9-4271233. Ed. Mary Wright. bibl.; charts; illus. **Document type:** government publication, newsletter.
    —BLDSC (1736.862850).
    Description: Highlights role and functions of the department.

700   US   ISSN 1064-6620
ARTSOURCE QUARTERLY; a guide to marketing art. 1991. q. $19. ArtNetwork Press, 18757 Wildflower Dr., Box 1268, Penn Valley, CA 95946. TEL 916-432-7630. FAX 916-432-7633. Ed. Constance Smith. adv. contact: Sarah Meyers. (back issues avail.) **Document type:** newsletter.
    Description: Focuses on the latest marketing information for fine artists, including interviews with artworld professionals, and strategies to make more sales.

700   US   ISSN 1065-1543
N6512
ARTSPEAK; an international gallery review. 1978. m. $30 (Canada $35; elsewhere $40). 420 Fifth Ave., 26th Fl., New York, NY 10018. TEL 212-924-6531. E-mail: artliaison@artliaison.dorsai.org. Pub. Lillian Firestone. adv.; bk.rev. circ. 45,000. (tabloid format; back issues avail.) **Document type:** consumer publication.
    ●Also available online.
    Description: Provides art, art reviews and services to the art community.

700   AT   ISSN 0311-0095
ARTVIEWS. 1972? irreg. Aus.$0.40 per no. Artists' Guild of Australia, 156 Banksia St., Pagewood, N.S.W. 2035, Australia.

709.7   US   ISSN 0004-4121
N1
ARTWEEK; West Coast art news criticism. 1970. m. $30 to individuals; institutions $34. Spaulding - Devlin, Inc., 2149 Paragon Dr., Ste. 100, San Jose, CA 95131. TEL 408-279-2293. FAX 408-279-2432. Ed. Meredith Tromble; Pub. Kitty Spaulding. R&P contact: Kitty Spaulding. TEL 408-441-7065. adv. contact: Kitty Spaulding. bk.rev.; illus.; cum.index: vols.1-7, 1977. circ. 14,500. (also avail. in microform from UMI,MIM) **Indexed:** Art Ind., Artbibl., Chic.Per.Ind., Mag.Ind., R.G., RILA. **Document type:** trade publication.
    —BLDSC (1736.865000); KR SourceOne; UMI.
    Description: Includes commentary and reviews, interviews, and regular features.

ARTWORK; the North's independent free arts newspaper. see *ARTS AND HANDICRAFTS*

700   AT   ISSN 1323-5885
ARTWORKER. 1986. q. Aus.$35 individual membership; institutional Aus.$60 (effective Feb. 1997). Queensland Artworkers Alliance Inc., 497 Adelaide St., Brisbane, Qld., 4000, Australia. TEL 61-7-38322230. FAX 61-7-38322231. E-mail: qaa@thehub.com.au. Ed. Lindy Johnson. R&P contact: Lindy Johnson. adv.: B&W page Aus.$300; trim 210 x 297; adv. contact: Lindy Johnson. circ. 1,000 (controlled). **Document type:** newsletter.
    Formerly: Queensland Artworkers Alliance Newsletter.
    Description: Provides membership information, issue-based articles, and specialist industry columns.

700 374   AT
ARTWORKS. 1978. 2/yr. Aus.$5. Waverley-Woollahra Arts Centre Co-op Ltd., 138 Bondi Rd., Bondi, N.S.W. 2026, Australia. Eds. Brigid Phecan, Susan Parker. adv. circ. 6,000. (back issues avail.) **Document type:** academic/scholarly publication.

700   US   ISSN 1062-8312
N6750
ARTWORLD EUROPE. 1990. bi-m. $59. Humanities Exchange, Inc., Box 1608, Largo, FL 34649. TEL 813-581-7328. FAX 813-585-6398. Ed. S.R. Howarth. bk.rev. circ. 1,000. (back issues avail.) **Document type:** newsletter.
    Description: Covers European art world including exhibitions, museum renovations, art fairs, galleries, restorations, and interviews with art professionals.

700   US   ISSN 1057-5413
ARTWORLD HOTLINE. 1991. m. $26. ArtNetwork Press, 18757 Wildflower Dr., Box 1268, Penn Valley, CA 95946. TEL 916-432-7630. FAX 916-432-7633. **Document type:** newsletter.
    Description: Provides current information and opportunities in the areas of percentages for arts commissions, gallery calls, fellowships; lists representatives looking for artists, residencies, grants and more.

700   JA
ASAHI GRAPH BESSATU BIJUTU. (Text in Japanese) 1977. 9/yr. Asahi Shimbun Publishing Co., 3-2, Tsukiji 5-chome, Chuo-ku, Tokyo 104-11, Japan. (Subscr. to: Oversea Courier Service Co., Ltd., 9, Shibaura 2-chome, Minato-ku, Tokyo 108, Japan) Ed. Yoshio Nagata.
    Formerly: Asahi Graph Bessatsu.

ASIA INSTITUTE. BULLETIN. see *ORIENTAL STUDIES*

ASIAN ART AND CULTURE. see *ORIENTAL STUDIES*

700 069   NE   ISSN 0925-6741
ASPECTEN VAN DE VERZAMELING BEELDHOUWKUNST EN KUNSTNIJVERHEID. (Text in Dutch, English) 1990. irreg., vol.6, 1995. price varies. (Rijksmuseum Amsterdam) Waanders Uitgevers, Postbus 1129, 8001 BC Zwolle, Netherlands. TEL 31-38-4658628. FAX 31-38-4655989. illus. **Document type:** monographic series.

ASSOCIATION INTERNATIONALE D'ETUDES DU SUD-EST EUROPEEN. BULLETIN. see *HISTORY — History Of Europe*

700   UK   ISSN 0307-9163
ASSOCIATION OF ART HISTORIANS. BULLETIN. 1975. 3/yr. £18 to non-members; in Europe £22; in the US £26. Association of Art Historians, Dog and Partridge House, Byley, Ches. CW10 9NJ, England. TEL 44-1606-835517. FAX 44-1606-834799. Ed. Jannet King. R&P contact: Jannet King. adv. contact: Jannnet King. circ. 1,500. **Document type:** bulletin, newsletter.

741.6   UK   ISSN 0958-3726
ASSOCIATION OF ILLUSTRATORS. JOURNAL. 1990. bi-m. membership. Association of Illustrators, 1 Colville Place, London W1P 1HN, England. TEL 071-636-4100. **Indexed:** DAAI.

700   PE
ASTERISCO; revista de actualidad y cultura. (Special editions avail.) irreg., latest no.5, 1992. Ediciones Fragor, Jiron Jose de Sucre 1083, Huaras, Peru. TEL 72-1177. Dir. Francisco Gonzales. illus.

THE ASTROPHYSICIST'S TANGO PARTNER SPEAKS. see *LITERATURE — Poetry*

ART

700   GW   ISSN 0176-8530
ATELIER; die Zeitschrift fuer Kuenstler. 1982. bi-m. DM.42($30) (foreign DM.48). Atelier Verlag KG, Industriestr. 170, 50999 Cologne, Germany. TEL 49-221-410177. FAX 49-221-410177. Ed. Bence Fritzsche. adv.; bk.rev. circ. 7,600. **Document type**: consumer publication.
   Description: Information for visual artists. Includes a calendar of art competitions.

ATENEO VENETO; rivista di scienze, lettere ed arti. see *SCIENCES: COMPREHENSIVE WORKS*

700 850   IT   ISSN 1122-6250
ATHANOR. (Text in English, French, Italian) 1990. a. Lit.35000 (foreign Lit.45000) (effective 1998). (Universita di Bari) Angelo Longo Editore, Via Paolo Costa 33, 48100 Ravenna, Italy. TEL 39-544-217026. FAX 39-544-217554. E-mail: longo-ra@linknet.it. Ed. Augusto Ponzio. circ. 2,000. Indexed: MLA Intl.Bibl. **Document type**: academic/scholarly publication.
   Description: Studies on philosophy, language, literature, and art.

ATHENAEUM ANNOTATIONS. see *ARCHITECTURE*

700   IT
ATLANTI DI RESTAURO. irreg. Stefano Patacconi Editore, Corso d'Augusto 115, Rimini, Italy. TEL 39-541-27756. FAX 39-541-54208. Eds. Alfredo Bellandi, Franco Faranda. **Document type**: monographic series.

700   UK   ISSN 0267-484X
ATLAS. 1985. irreg. 16 Talfourd Rd., London SE15 5NY, England. URL: http://www.ruskin-sch.ox.ac.uk/cooker. Ed. Jake Tilson. adv. circ. 2,500. (back issues avail.)

706.5   IT
AUCTION BOOK/LIBRO DELLE ASTE; worldwide contemporary art results - risultati delle aste d'arte contemporanea nel mondo. a. $15 (effective 1994-95). Giancarlo Politi Editore, Via Carlo Farini 68, 20159 Milan, Italy. TEL 39-2-6887341. FAX 39-2-66801290. Ed. Gilda Williams. adv.: B&W page $2600, color page $3500; trim 3 1/8 x 6 7/8. circ. 20,000. **Document type**: directory.
   Description: Presents a collection of selling prices from the principal international auction houses.

700 330   UK   ISSN 0144-3690
N6505
AUCTION PRICES OF AMERICAN ARTISTS. biennial. $40. Art Sales Index Ltd., 1 Thames St., Weybridge, Surrey KT13 8JG, England. TEL 44-1932-556426. FAX 44-1932-842482. Ed. Duncan Hislop. **Document type**: catalog.
   Description: Sales results from over 5,000 American artists.

700 860   DR
AUDITORIUM; revista cultural informativa. bi-m. newsstand price: RD.$30. Direccion General de Bellas Artes, c/o Palacio de Bellas Artes, Av. Maximo Gomez 2, Santo Domingo, Dominican Republic. TEL 809-682-1325. FAX 809-682-8622.

700   IT
AURORA. bi-m. Via S. Giovanni in Laterno 276, 00184 Rome, Italy. Ed. Vincenzo Lo Faro. Indexed: RILM.

AURORA; Jahrbuch der Eichendorff-Gesellschaft. see *LITERATURE*

AURORA-BUCHREIHE. see *LITERATURE*

700   GW   ISSN 0067-0642
AUS FORSCHUNG UND KUNST. 1968. irreg., no.29, 1995. price varies. (Geschichtsverein fuer Kaernten, AU) Dr. Rudolf Habelt GmbH, Am Buchenhang 1, 53115 Bonn, Germany. TEL 49-228-9238322. FAX 49-228-923836. Ed. Gotbert Moro. Indexed: IBR. **Document type**: monographic series.

AUSGABE; ein Literatur- und Kunstmagazin. see *LITERATURE*

AUSTRALIAN ABORIGINAL STUDIES. see *ANTHROPOLOGY*

AUSTRALIAN ANTIQUE COLLECTOR. see *ANTIQUES*

706.5   AT   ISSN 0819-923X
AUSTRALIAN ART AUCTION RECORDS. 1975. biennial. Aus.$75 (CD-ROM Aus.$400). Australian Art Sales, P.O. Box 50, Sutherland, N.S.W. 2232, Australia. TEL 61-2-92677363. Ed. Edward D. Craig. R&P contact: Edward D. Craig. circ. 1,500 (paid). **Document type**: consumer publication, directory.
• Also available on CD-ROM.
   Description: Records of auction prices for works of art. Includes biographical details of artists.

700 370   AT   ISSN 1032-1942
AUSTRALIAN ART EDUCATION. 1976. 3/yr. Aus.$40. Australian Institute of Art Education, c/o Lee Emery, Ed., University of Melbourne, Faculty of Education, Parkville, Vic. 3052, Australia. TEL 61-3-344-8386. FAX 61-3-349-4290. (Subscr. to: Ms. Cindy Hales, Deception Bay State High School, Deception Bay, Qld. 4508, Australia) bk.rev.; abstr.; bibl.; charts; illus. circ. 500. Indexed: C.I.J.E. **Document type**: academic/scholarly publication.
—UnCover.
   Formerly (until 1988): Institute of Art Education. Journal (ISSN 0729-5995)
   Description: Devoted to the scholarly examination of issues in art education both in Australia and overseas.
   Refereed Serial

750   AT   ISSN 0813-8095
AUSTRALIAN ARTIST. 1984. m. Aus.$49.50($85) Elladrent Pty. Ltd., P.O. Box 978, Chatswood, N.S.W. 2057, Australia. TEL 61-2-94916333. FAX 61-2-94115175. Ed. Vincent Miller. R&P contact: Terri Dodd. adv.: color page Aus.$1600; adv. contact: Vincent Miller. circ. 20,000 (paid). (back issues avail.) **Document type**: consumer publication.
—UnCover.
   Description: Devoted to developing artistic and creative talents of Australian painters.

AUSTRALIAN CREATIVE. see *ADVERTISING AND PUBLIC RELATIONS*

700   AT   ISSN 0314-6464
N7400
AUSTRALIAN JOURNAL OF ART. 1978. a. Aus.$15. Art Association of Australia, c/o Dept. of Art History, City Art Institute, P.O. Box 259, Paddington, N.S.W. 2021, Australia. TEL 02-339-9555. FAX 02-3399506. Eds. Margaret Plant, John Gregory. adv.; bk.rev. circ. 800. (back issues avail.)
—BLDSC (1803.520000); UnCover.

700 600   AT
AUSTRALIAN NETWORK FOR ART AND TECHNOLOGY NEWSLETTER. 1988. q. $20 to individuals; institutions $40. Australian Network for Art and Technology, P.O. Box 8029, Hindley St., Adelaide, S.A. 5000, Australia. TEL 61-8-82319037. FAX 61-8-82117323. E-mail: anat@camtech.net.au; URL: http://www.va.com/anat/. Ed. Amanda McDonald Crowley. **Document type**: newsletter.
• Also available online.

AUTHORS & ARTISTS FOR YOUNG ADULTS. see *CHILDREN AND YOUTH — For*

AVANT GARDE CRITICAL STUDIES. see *LITERATURE*

AXIS; world design journal. see *INTERIOR DESIGN AND DECORATION*

AZTLAN; a journal of Chicano studies. see *ETHNIC INTERESTS*

AZURE MAGAZINE. see *INTERIOR DESIGN AND DECORATION*

B C A NEWS. (Business Committee for the Arts, Inc.) see *BUSINESS AND ECONOMICS*

B C A T A JOURNAL FOR ART TEACHERS. (B.C. Art Teachers' Association) see *EDUCATION — Teaching Methods And Curriculum*

B L A C. (Black Literature and Arts Congress) see *ETHNIC INTERESTS*

BABY SPLIT BOWLING NEWS. see *LITERATURE*

700 910   SP   ISSN 0212-5099
BAETICA;* estudios de arte, geografia e historia. 1978. a. Universidad de Malaga, Facultad de Geografia e Historia, Apdo. Correos 3149, 29080 Malaga, Spain.
—CINDOC.

BAKUNIN. see *LITERATURE*

860 700 100   SP   ISSN 0214-9982
BALSA DE LA MEDUSA. 1987. q. 2500 ptas. (Europe 3500 ptas.; America 4000 ptas.). Visor Distribuciones S.A., Tomas Breton, 55, 28045 Madrid, Spain. TEL 341-468-11-02. FAX 341-468-10-98. Ed. Carlos Thiebaut. bk.rev. circ. 3,500.
—CINDOC.
   Description: Focuses on cultural and social criticism in the fields of communication, art criticism, philosophy and literature.

BAMPTON LECTURES IN AMERICA. see *RELIGIONS AND THEOLOGY*

BANGLADESH LALIT KALA. see *MUSEUMS AND ART GALLERIES*

769   CC   ISSN 1000-4378
BANHUA YISHU/ART OF PRINTS. (Text in Chinese) q. Shanghai Renmin Meishu Chubanshe - Shanghai People's Art Publishers, No.33, Alley 672, Changle Road, Shanghai 200040, People's Republic of China. TEL 4374528. Ed. Lu Zongduo.

BARBACANE; revue des pierres et des hommes. see *LITERATURE*

BARBADOS MUSEUM AND HISTORICAL SOCIETY. JOURNAL. see *HISTORY — History Of North And South America*

700   IO   ISSN 0005-6138
AP95.I5
BASIS; majalah bulanan kebudayaan umum/monthly for culture in general. 1951. m. $20. Yayasan Badan Penerbit Basis, Abu Bakar Ali 14, Yogyakarta, Indonesia. TEL 88283. Ed. Dick Hartoko. adv.; bk.rev.; illus.; index. circ. 3,000. Indexed: Bibl.Ling.

705   SP   ISSN 0210-0274
BATIK; panorama general de las artes - arte, diseno, arquitectura. 1973. bi-m. 4000 ptas.($70) Publiart S.A., Rambla prat. 6 pral. 1a, 08012 Barcelona, Spain. TEL 3-217-45-20. Ed. Manuel Rufi-Gibert. adv.; bk.rev. circ. 5,000.

700   GW   ISSN 0341-9150
N6873
BAYERISCHE DENKMALPFLEGE. JAHRBUCH. 1947. a. DM.60. (Bayerisches Landesamt fuer Denkmalpflege) Deutscher Kunstverlag GmbH, Nymphenburgerstr. 84, 80636 Munich, Germany. TEL 49-89-121516-0. FAX 49-89-12151616. Indexed: IBR. **Document type**: bulletin.

700   GW
BAYERISCHE STAATSGEMAELDESAMMLUNGEN. JAHRESBERICHT. 1972. a. membership. Bayerische Staatsgemaeldesammlungen, Barer Str. 29, 80799 Munich, Germany. TEL 49-89-238050. Ed.Bd. circ. 1,500. **Document type**: corporate report.

BEATTHIEF. see *MUSIC*

709   FR   ISSN 0757-2271
N1
BEAUX ARTS MAGAZINE; actualite des arts. 11/yr. 345 F. (effective 1995). Editions Nuit et Jour, 9 rue Christiani, 75018 Paris, France. TEL 49-25-17-17. Ed. Jean-Noel Beyler. Indexed: Art Ind., IBR.
—KR SourceOne; SWETS; UnCover.

740 810   US
BEBOP DRAWING CLUB BOOK. 1974. irreg. Artman's Press, 1442A Walnut St., Berkeley, CA 94709. Ed. Glenn Myles. illus.

700   SW   ISSN 1103-4920
BECKERELL. 1991. q. SEK 99. Beckerell, P.O. Box 17127, S-200 10 Malmoe, Sweden. TEL 46-40-30-72-77. FAX 46-40-30-15-07.
   Description: Each issue features interviews with a number of real and unreal artists. The subject matter is a mixture from light to serious, cartoons to discussions of art theory.

ART

700 GW ISSN 0067-5121
BEITRAEGE ZUR KUNST DES CHRISTLICHEN OSTENS. 1964. irreg. price varies. Verlag Aurel Bongers, Postfach 100264, 45602 Recklinghausen, Germany. illus. **Document type:** monographic series.

700 SP
BELART BELLAS ARTES. 1993. m. 4000 ptas.($80) Ediciones Jardin S.L., C. Ferraz, 11 1o, 28008 Madrid, Spain. TEL 34-1-5470529. FAX 34-1-5415055. Ed. Mariano Alonso. adv. contact: Gema Alonso. circ. 150,000. (back issues avail.) **Document type:** consumer publication.
Description: Reports on art, including information on exhibitions of national and international art.

741.5 NR
BENBELLA AND LULU. 1989. fortn. £N12. Daily Times of Nigeria Ltd., Publications Division, New Isheri Rd., P.M.B. 21340, Agidingbi, Ikeja, Lagos State, Nigeria. TEL 234-64-900850-9. FAX 234-64-21333. circ. 10,000. **Document type:** consumer publication.

745.5 694 GW ISSN 0343-1711
BERGISCHE HANDWERK. 1947. m. (Kreishandwerkerschaft Remscheid) J.F. Ziegler KG Druckerei und Verlag, Konrad-Adenauer-Str. 2-4, 42853 Remscheid, Germany. TEL 02191-909-0. FAX 02191-909266. Ed. J.F. Ziegler. adv.; bk.rev. circ. 3,000. (back issues avail.) **Document type:** newsletter.

BERGOMUM; studi di letteratura, storia ed arte. see HISTORY — History Of Europe

700 SZ ISSN 1010-559X
BERNER KUNSTMITTEILUNGEN. (Text in German) 1955. 5/yr. Kunstmuseum Bern, Hodlerstr. 12, CH-3011 Bern, Switzerland. TEL 41-31-3110944. FAX 41-31-3117263. (Co-sponsors: Bernische Kunstgesellschaft; Verein der Freunde des Berner Kunstmuseums) Ed. Therese Bhattacharya-Stettler. adv.; illus.; cum.index. circ. 4,500. (back issues avail.) **Indexed:** Artbibl.Mod., RILA. **Document type:** bulletin.
Formerly (until 1970): Kunstmuseum Bern. Mitteilungen (ISSN 0405-5888)

BEST EDITORIAL CARTOONS OF THE YEAR. see LITERARY AND POLITICAL REVIEWS

BEST IN COVERS AND POSTERS. see PUBLISHING AND BOOK TRADE

THE BEST IN MODERN JEWELERY DESIGN. see JEWELRY, CLOCKS AND WATCHES

BIBLIOTECA NAPOLETANA DI STORIA E ARTE. see HISTORY — History Of Europe

700 PL ISSN 0067-7698
BIBLIOTEKA KRAKOWSKA. 1897. irregl., vol.122, 1981. price varies. Towarzystwo Milosnikow Historii i Zabytkow Krakowa, Ul. Sw. Jana 12, 31-018 Krakow, Poland. TEL 48-12-212783. (Dist. by: Ars Polona-Ruch, Krakowskie Przedmiescie 7, Warsaw, Poland) Ed. Janina Bieniarzowna.

709 IT ISSN 0940-7855
BIBLIOTHECA HERTZIANA. ROEMISCHES JAHRBUCH. (Text in English, German, Italian) 1937. irreg., no.31, 1996. price varies. Bibliotheca Hertziana, Via Gregoriana 28, 00187 Rome, Italy. TEL 39-6-69993258. FAX 39-6-69993333. E-mail: kliemann@biblhertz.it. illus. circ. 300. (back issues avail.) **Indexed:** Art Ind., IBR. **Document type:** academic/scholarly publication.
—BLDSC (8020.822000); KR SourceOne.
Formerly: Roemisches Jahrbuch fuer Kunstgeschichte (ISSN 0342-2046)
Description: Art history focusing on Rome and Italy.
Refereed Serial

BIBLIOTHEQUE DU C N A M. see ENGINEERING — Mechanical Engineering

700 JA ISSN 0287-2218
NX8.J3
BIJUTSU TECHO. (Text in Japanese; summaries in English) 1948. m. 18000 Yen. Bijutsu Shuppan-sha, Inaoka Bldg., 2-36 Kanda, Jinbo-cho, Chiyoda-ku, Tokyo 101, Japan. TEL 03-3234-2151. FAX 03-3234-9451. adv.; bk.rev.; film rev.; play rev. (back issues avail.)
Description: Covers contemporary art.

740 SW ISSN 0349-2117
BILD I SKOLAN. 1929. 4/yr. SEK 150 (effective 1996). Laerarfoerbundet, c/o Arne Kochum, Otto Bondes Vaeg 117, S-184 62 Aakersberga. TEL 46-8-540-620-51. FAX 46-8-540-866-41. Ed. Arne Kochum. adv.: B&W page SEK 4000, color page SEK 5000; trim 184 x 272; adv. contact: Annelie Bjoernsdotter-Lundqvist. circ. 2,900. cols./p.: 4; pp./issue: 44.

741.5 SW ISSN 0347-7096
BILD OCH BUBBLA/PICTURE AND CAPTION. 1968. 6/yr. SEK 190 (effective 1996). Seriefraemjandet, P.O. Box 8135, S-104 20 Stockholm, Sweden. TEL 46-8-653-26-73. Ed. Daniel Atterbom. **Indexed:** Child.Lit.Abstr. **Document type:** trade publication.
Formerly (until 1977): Thud (ISSN 0346-3133)

750 331.8 SW ISSN 0348-0615
BILDKONSTNAEREN. 1976. q. SEK 125. Svenska Konstnaersfoerbundet (SK), P.O. Box 4047, S-400 40 Goeteborg, Sweden. TEL 46-31-42-47-31.

700 NO ISSN 0332-723X
BILLEDKUNSTNEREN. 1975. 10/yr. NOK 250. Norske Billedkunstneres Fagorganisasjon, Kongensgt. 3, N-0153 Oslo 1, Norway. **Document type:** trade publication.

709 PL ISSN 0006-3967
BIULETYN HISTORII SZTUKI. (Text in Polish; summaries in English) 1932. q. $20. Polska Akademia Nauk, Instytut Sztuki - Polish Academy of Science, Institute of Art, Ul. Dluga 28, 00-950 Warsaw, Poland. TEL 48-22-313271. FAX 48-22-313149. (Dist. by: AMOS, ul. Zuga 12, 01-806 Warsaw, Poland. TEL 48-22-346521) Ed. Piotr Paszkiewicz. bk.rev.; bibl.; charts; illus.; index. circ. 1,000. **Indexed:** Amer.Hist.& Life (1984-1985), (1987-1988), (1992-), Artbibl.Mod., Artbibl., Avery Ind.Archit.Per., Hist.Abstr. (1984-1985), (1987-1988), (1992-), IBR, RILA.
Description: Covers history of Polish and world art.

BIZA NEIRA (BISE NOIRE); sur l'Auvergne et la civilisation Auvergnate. see HISTORY — History Of Europe

BLACK BEAR REVIEW. see LITERATURE — Poetry

BLACK CROSS MAGAZINE; journal of heavy poetry & art. see LITERATURE

BLACKFLASH. see PHOTOGRAPHY

BLADES; a tiny handmade magazine. see LITERATURE — Poetry

BLAETTER DER FREIEN VOLKSBUEHNE BERLIN. see THEATER

BLAETTER FUER HEIMATKUNDE. see HISTORY

BODENSEE HEFTE; Zeitschrift der Euro-Region Bodensee. see GEOGRAPHY

700 350 NE ISSN 0925-0239
BOEKMANCAHIER; kwartaalschrift voor kunst, onderzoek en beleid. (Text mainly in Dutch, occaisonally in English) 1988. q. fl.70 to individuals (foreign fl.85); institutions fl.90 (foreign fl.105) (effective 1998). Boekmanstichting, Herengracht 415, 1017 BP Amsterdam, Netherlands. TEL 31-20-6243736. FAX 31-20-6385239. E-mail: e.boekman@inter.nl.net. Ed. I. van Hamersveld. adv.: B&W page fl.575; adv. contact: S. Hoogervorst. bk.rev.; abstr.; bibl.; illus.; index. (back issues avail.) **Document type:** academic/scholarly publication. —SWETS.
Description: Publishes articles on art and culture, research and management, including national and international policy issues.

BOKVAENNEN. see PUBLISHING AND BOOK TRADE

700 PR ISSN 0006-6206
BOLETIN DE ARTE. 1966. q. free. Asociacion Puertorriquena de la Unesco, Box 1361, San Juan, PR 00902. Ed. Antonio J. Molina. bk.rev.; bibl. circ. 3,000.

BOLLETTINO LIGUSTICO PER LA STORIA E LA CULTURA REGIONALE. see HISTORY — History Of Europe

730 808 US ISSN 0743-3204
NX458
BOMB; artists, writers, actors, directors. 1981. q. $18 (effective 1997). New Art Publications, Inc., 594 Broadway, No. 905, New York, NY 10012-3233. TEL 212-431-3943. FAX 212-431-5880. E-mail: bomb@nyo.com; URL: http://www.bombsite.com. (Subscr. to: Box 2003, Canal St. Sta., New York, NY 10013) Ed. Betsy Sussler. R&P contact: Jay Berman. adv. contact: Maryann Monforton. illus. circ. 60,000. (back issues avail.) **Indexed:** Amer.Hum.Ind., Artbibl.Mod. **Document type:** consumer publication.
Description: Original fiction, poetry, essays, interviews and dialogues between artists, fiction writers, musicians, playwrights, directors, actors, photographers, and musicians.

701 II
BOMBAY ART SOCIETY'S ART JOURNAL. 1971. q. Rs.4. Bombay Art Society, Jehangir Art Gallery, 16-B Mahatma Gandhi Rd., Bombay 400 001, India. Ed. Gopal S. Adivrekar. adv.; illus.

700 792 CN ISSN 0831-2559
BORDER CROSSINGS. 1982. q. $23 (foreign $23) (effective 1997). Arts Manitoba Publications Inc., 500 - 70 Arthur St., Winnipeg, MB R3B 1G7, Canada. TEL 204-942-5778. FAX 204-949-0793. Ed. Meeka Walsh. R&P contact: Meeka Walsh. adv.; bk.rev.; index; circ. 3,300 (paid). **Indexed:** Can.B.P.I., Can.Lit.Ind. **Document type:** trade publication.
●Also available online.
Formerly: Arts Manitoba.
Description: Publication featuring articles, artists' profiles and interviews covering the full range of the contemporary arts (visual, performing and literary) in Canada. Also feature articles on American and international art.

700 301.16 CN ISSN 0826-967X
BORDER - LINES. 1984. q. Can.$20($20) to individuals (foreign Can.$25); institutions Can.$35 (foreign Can.$40); low-income persons Can.$16 (foreign Can.$21) (effective 1997 & 1998). 400 Dovercourt Rd., Toronto, ON M6J 3E7, Canada. TEL 416-534-3224. FAX 416-534-2301. E-mail: borderln@idirect.com; URL: http://www.interlog.com/kavik/border.htm. Ed. Julie Jenkinson. adv.: page Can.$500; adv. contact: Karen Cowitz. bk.rev.; circ. 2,000 (paid); 1,000. (also avail. in microfilm; back issues avail.) **Indexed:** Alt.Press Ind., Amer.Hist.& Life, Can.B.P.I., Hist.Abstr.
Description: An interdisciplinary magazine committed to exploring all aspects of culture - including popular culture, fine arts, visual arts, gender, literature, multi-culturalism, mass communications and political culture.

BRABANT CULTUREEL. see HUMANITIES: COMPREHENSIVE WORKS

BRAUNSCHWEIGISCHE HEIMAT; Zeitschrift fuer Natur- u. Heimatpflege, Landes- u. Volkskunde, Geschichte, Kunst u. Kultur Ostfalens. see HISTORY — History Of Europe

700 BL ISSN 0103-9636
NX533.A1
BRAZILIAN ART RESEARCH YEARBOOK. 1992. a. Universidade de Sao Paulo, School of Communication and Arts, Av. Prof. Lucio Martins Rodrigues, 443, Butanta, SP, Brazil. Ed. Jose Marques de Melo; Pub. Mirian Rejowski de Carvalho.

BRITISH ARCHAEOLOGICAL ASSOCIATION. CONFERENCE TRANSACTIONS. see ARCHAEOLOGY

BRITISH ARCHAEOLOGICAL ASSOCIATION. JOURNAL. see ARCHAEOLOGY

BRITISH SCHOOL AT ATHENS. ANNUAL. see ARCHAEOLOGY

THE BROKEN FIDDLE. see LITERARY AND POLITICAL REVIEWS

BROOKGREEN JOURNAL. see GARDENING AND HORTICULTURE

700 US
BROOKLYN JOURNAL OF ARTS & URBAN AFFAIRS. m. Brooklyn Journal Publications, Inc., 129 Montague St., Brooklyn, NY 11201. TEL 718-624-6033. FAX 718-875-5302.

741.61   US
BROWN LINES. 6/yr. Ken Brown Studio of Calligraphic Art, Box 637, Hugo, OK 74743. TEL 405-326-7544. FAX 405-326-6366. Ed. Ken Brown. circ. 5,000.

700   GW   ISSN 0720-0056
BRUCKMANNS PANTHEON; internationale Jahres Zeitschrift fuer Kunst. (Text and summaries in English, French, German) 1928. a. DM.98. F. Bruckmann Muenchen Verlag und Druck GmbH, Nymphenburgerstr. 86, 80636 Munich, Germany. TEL 49-89-125701. FAX 49-89-1257269. Ed. Erhardt D. Stiebner. adv.; bk.rev.; abstr.; bibl.; illus.; index. circ. 2,000. (reprint service avail. from KTO) **Indexed:** Art Ind., Artbibl., Artbibl.Mod., Arts & Hum.Cit.Ind., Avery Ind.Archit.Per., Curr.Cont., IBR, Ind.Bk.Rev.Hum., RILA. **Document type:** consumer publication.
—Genuine Article; KR SourceOne. **CCC.**
Formerly: Pantheon (ISSN 0031-0999)

DIE BRUECKE; Kaerntner Kulturzeitschrift. see LITERARY AND POLITICAL REVIEWS

708   GW   ISSN 0572-7146
BRUECKE-ARCHIV. 1967. irreg., no.9, 1977. price varies. Bruecke-Museum, Bussardsteig 9, 14195 Berlin, Germany. Ed. Magdalena Moeller. illus. **Indexed:** RILA.

700   US
BRUSHSTROKES. s-a. membership. Children's Art Exchange, Box 503, Middlebury, VT 05753. TEL 802-388-3023. **Indexed:** World Surf.Coat.
Formerly: Children's Art Exchange Newsletter.

700   US
BRUTARIAN. 1991. q. $12 (foreign $20); newsstand price: $4. Box 25222, Arlington, VA 22202-9998. TEL 703-360-2514. Ed. Dominick J. Salemi. adv.: page $300. bk.rev. circ. 3,000. (back issues avail.)

700 913   HU   ISSN 0133-5545
BULLETIN DU MUSEE HONGROIS DES BEAUX-ARTS. (Text in French, Hungarian) 1947. s-a. only on exchange basis. Szepmuveszeti Muzeum - Musee des Beaux-Arts, Dozsa Gyorgy ut 41, 1146 Budapest XIV, Hungary. TEL 36-1-3439759. FAX 36-1-3438298. Ed. Zsuzsa Gonda. R&P contact: Anna Marangi. circ. 700. **Indexed:** Art & Archaeol.Tech.Abstr., Artbibl.Mod., RILA. **Document type:** bulletin.

BULLETIN MONUMENTAL. see ARCHAEOLOGY

709   NZ   ISSN 0110-4888
BULLETIN OF NEW ZEALAND ART HISTORY. 1972. a. price varies. University of Otago, Hocken Library, P.O. Box 56, Dunedin, New Zealand. FAX 64-3-4795078. TELEX 03-4791-100. E-mail: hocken@library.otago.ac.nz. Ed.Bd. R&P contact: S.R. Strachan. bk.rev. circ. 200. **Indexed:** Artbibl.Mod. **Document type:** bulletin.
—UnCover.
Description: Chronicles the history of art in New Zealand, as well as production and activities of artists and museums in other countries which influence New Zealand art.

BULLETTINO STORICO EMPOLESE. see HISTORY — History Of Europe

BUNKAZAI HOZON SYUHUKU GAKKAISI. see ANTIQUES

BURGEN UND SCHLOESSER. see HISTORY — History Of Europe

BURGENBOTE; Oesterreichs Bindenschild. see CONSERVATION

745.1   UK   ISSN 0007-6287
N1
BURLINGTON MAGAZINE. 1903. m. $393 (effective 1997). Burlington Magazine Publications Ltd., 14-16 Duke's Rd., London WC1H 9AD, England. TEL 44-171-388-1228. FAX 44-171-388-1230. E-mail: burlington@compuserve.com. Ed. Caroline Elam. R&P contact: Caroline ELam. adv. contact: Mike Ross. bk.rev.; illus.; index, cum.index every 10 yrs.: 1963-1972, 1973-1982. (also avail. in microfilm; microfiche from IDC; reprint service avail. from KTO) **Indexed:** Art & Archaeol.Tech.Abstr., Art Ind., Artbibl.Mod., Artbibl., Arts & Hum.Cit.Ind., ASCA, Avery Ind.Archit.Per., Bibl.Engl.Lang.& Lit., Bk.Rev.Ind. (1968-), Br.Hum.Ind., Br.Tech.Ind., Child.Bk.Rev.Ind. (1968-), Curr.Cont., DAAI, IBR, Ind.Bk.Rev.Hum., RILA, SSCI. **Document type:** academic/scholarly publication.
—BLDSC (2931.650000); KR SourceOne; SWETS; UMI; UnCover.
Description: Fine art magazine, international in scope, covering all periods from antiquity to the present day.
Refereed Serial

BUSINESS & TEACHER DIRECTORY (YEAR). see ARTS AND HANDICRAFTS

760   UK   ISSN 0963-6153
BUSINESS RATIO REPORT: DESIGN CONSULTANTS; an industry sector analysis. 1988. a. I C C Business Publications (Subsidiary of: I C C Information Group), Field House, 72 Oldfield Rd., Hampton, Mddx. TW18 1BR, England. TEL 44-181-783-0922. FAX 44-181-783-1940. charts; stat. **Document type:** trade publication.
Formerly (until 1989): Business Ratio Report. Design Consultancies (ISSN 0953-8143)

700   PL   ISSN 0067-947X
BYDGOSKIE TOWARZYSTWO NAUKOWE. WYDZIAL NAUK HUMANISTYCZNYCH. PRACE. SERIA D (SZTUKA). irreg., no.3, 1965. price varies. Bydgoskie Towarzystwo Naukowe, Jezuicka 4, Bydgoszcz, Poland. (Dist. by: Ars Polona-Ruch, Krakowskie Przedmiescie 7, Warsaw, Poland)

BYZANTION; revue internationale des etudes byzantines. see ORIENTAL STUDIES

700   US
C A A NEWSLETTER (NEW YORK). 6/yr. membership. College Art Association, 275 Seventh Ave., New York, NY 10001. TEL 212-691-1051. FAX 212-627-2381. Ed. Jessica Tagliaferro. R&P contact: Jessica Tagliaferro. adv. contact: J.C. Rafferty. bibl. circ. 13,000. **Document type:** newsletter.

700 793.3 780 792   US
C A NEWS. 1985. q. $15 to individuals; institutions $50. Christians in the Arts Networking, Inc., 9 Court St., 2nd Fl., Box 242, Arlington, MA 02174-0003. TEL 617-646-1541. FAX 617-646-7725. Ed. Brian Emmet. bk.rev. circ. 750. (back issues avail.) **Document type:** newsletter.
Description: Highlights conferences and other events around the world. Looks at other organizations and what they are doing.

700 069   CN   ISSN 0829-2906
C MAGAZINE; international contemporary art. 1970. q. Can.$25.68 to individuals (foreign $28); institutions Can.$36.38 (foreign $38). C Arts Publishing and Production, Inc., P.O. Box 5, Stn. B, Toronto, ON M5T 2T2, Canada. TEL 416-539-9495. FAX 416-539-9903. E-mail: cmag@istar.ca. Ed. Joyce Mason. R&P contact: Joyce Mason. adv. contact: Deirdre Millin. bk.rev. circ. 5,000. (also avail. in microfiche; back issues avail.) **Indexed:** Can.B.P.I., CMI. **Document type:** consumer publication.
Formerly (until 1984): Impressions.
Description: Provides a forum for the presentation of contemporary art and the discussion of issues surrounding art in our culture.

700 301.412   US
C W A O NEWS. 1982. m. $10 to individuals; organizations $25. Coalition of Women's Art Organizations, 123 E. Beutel Rd., Port Washington, WI 53074-1103. TEL 414-284-4458. FAX 414-284-8875. E-mail: dprovis@omnifest.uwm.edu. Ed. Dorothy Provis. circ. 175 (paid). **Document type:** newsletter.
Description: Provides current information on pending legislation (federal and state) concerning arts and network with arts advocacy groups.

709 069   NE
CAHIER VINCENT. no.3, 1991. irreg., no.6, 1995. (Rijksmuseum Vincent van Gogh) Waanders Uitgevers, Postbus 1129, 8001 BC Zwolle, Netherlands. TEL 31-38-4658628. FAX 31-38-4655989. **Document type:** monographic series.

CAHIERS ALSACIENS D'ARCHEOLOGIE D'ART ET D'HISTOIRE. see ARCHAEOLOGY

CAHIERS BOURBONNAIS; arts, lettres, regionalisme. see LITERATURE

CAHIERS DE CIVILISATION MEDIEVALE. see HISTORY

CAHIERS DE CIVILISATION MEDIEVALE. SUPPLEMENT. see HISTORY

CAHIERS DE L'IROISE. see HISTORY — History Of Europe

THE CAIRN. see MUSEUMS AND ART GALLERIES

CALABRIA LIBRI; panorama bibliografico e di vita culturale. see BIBLIOGRAPHIES

700   IT   ISSN 0008-056X
CALABRIA NOBILISSIMA. (Text in French, Italian, Latin) 1947. s-a. L.10000($8) Giornalista Mario Borretti, Via G. de Rada 10, Cosenza 87100, Italy. Ed. Raffaele Borretti. adv.; bk.rev.; bibl.; illus. circ. 1,000.

CALCUTTAN. see POLITICAL SCIENCE

700   US
CALIFORNIA ART REVIEW.* 1989. irreg. $49.95 paperback; hardbound $59.95. American References Publishing Corp., 2210 N. Burling St., Chicago, IL 60614-3712. Ed. Les Krantz. illus.
Description: Lists museums, galleries, art associations, and museum personnel alphabetically by city. Includes addresses, telephone numbers, admissions information, history, and information about types of displays. Lists artists, including medium, address, gallery affiliations, birthdate, awards, education, and short profiles of work. Also lists media who report on the art scene, with names, addresses, and telephone numbers.

709   US   ISSN 0068-5909
CALIFORNIA STUDIES IN THE HISTORY OF ART. (Supplementary Discovery Series avail.) 1962. irreg. no.35, 1996. price varies. University of California Press, 2120 Berkeley Way, Berkeley, CA 94720. TEL 510-642-4247. FAX 510-643-7127. (Orders to: California-Princeton Fulfillment Services, 1455 Lower Ferry Rd., Ewing, NJ 08618. TEL 800-777-4726. FAX 800-999-1958) (back issues avail.) **Document type:** monographic series.
Description: Publishes research on the history of all forms of Western art.
Refereed Serial

700   US   ISSN 0147-1627
PS508.W7
CALYX; a journal of art & literature by women. 1976. 2/yr. $19.50 to individuals for 3 nos. Calyx, Inc., Box B, Corvallis, OR 97339. TEL 541-753-9384. FAX 541-753-0515. Ed. Magarita Donnelly. R&P contact: Margarita Donnelly. adv.: B&W page $550; adv. contact: Teri Mae Rutledge. bk.rev.; illus. circ. 4,500. (back issues avail.) **Indexed:** Amer.Hum.Ind., Fem.Per., Hum.Ind., Mid.East: Abstr.& Ind., Stud.Wom.Abstr. **Document type:** trade publication.
—UnCover.
Description: Publishes literature and art by women with interest in work by women; includes strong emphasis on work by women of color.
Refereed Serial

CAMERAWORK; a journal of photographic arts. see PHOTOGRAPHY

CAMPUS REVIEW. see LITERARY AND POLITICAL REVIEWS

700 780 792   CN   ISSN 0576-4300
CANADA COUNCIL ANNUAL REPORT AND SUPPLEMENT/RAPPORT ANNUEL DU CONSEIL DES ARTS DU CANADA ET SON SUPPLEMENT. (Text in English, French) 1958. a. free. Canada Council for the Arts, Box 1047, 350 Albert St., Ottawa, ON K1P 5V8, Canada. TEL 613-566-4365; 800-263-5588. FAX 613-566-4407. charts; stat. circ. 5,000. **Document type:** corporate report.

CANADA'S CULTURE, HERITAGE AND IDENTITY: A STATISTICAL PERSPECTIVE/LE CANADA, SA CULTURE, SON PATRIMOINE ET SON IDENTITE: PERSPECTIVE STATISTIQUE. see *PUBLIC ADMINISTRATION — Abstracting, Bibliographies, Statistics*

700   CN   ISSN 0825-3854
CANADIAN ART. 1984. q. Can.$25.68 (US Can.$32; elsewhere Can.$40) (effective 1997). Canadian Art Foundation, 70 The Esplanade, 2nd Fl., Toronto, ON M5E 1R2, Canada. TEL 416-368-8854. FAX 416-368-6135. Ed. Richard Rhodes; Pub. Wendy Ingram. R&P contact: Wendy Ingram. adv. contact: Wendy Ingram. bk.rev.; circ. 18,000 (paid); 4,000. (also avail. in microform from MML; back issues avail.) Indexed: Art Ind., Artbibl.Mod., Can.B.P.I. Document type: consumer publication.
—KR SourceOne.

706.5   CN   ISSN 0229-8961
N6540
CANADIAN ART SALES INDEX. 1980. a. Can.$45. Westbridge Publications Ltd., 2339 Granville St., Vancouver, BC V6H 3G4, Canada. TEL 604-736-1014. FAX 604-734-4944. Ed. Anthony R. Westbridge. adv. circ. 2,000. (back issues avail.) Document type: directory.

700 069   CN   ISSN 0383-5405
CANADIAN ARTISTS SERIES. French edition: Collection: Artistes Canadiens (ISSN 0384-3521) 1973. irreg., no.10, 1985. Can.$8.95. National Gallery of Canada, Publications Division, c/o Irene Lillico, 380 Sussex Dr., Ottawa, ON K1N 9N4, Canada. TEL 613-990-0537. FAX 613-990-7460. illus. circ. 5,000. Document type: catalog.
Description: Examines life and work of significant Canadian artists and their contributions to art in Canada.

CANADIAN JOURNAL OF NETHERLANDIC STUDIES/REVUE CANADIENNE D'ETUDES NEERLANDAISES. see *LITERATURE*

CANADIAN REVIEW OF ART EDUCATION RESEARCH AND ISSUES/REVUE CANADIENNE D'EDUCATION ARTISTIQUE RECHERCHE ET QUESTIONS D'ACTUALITE ARTISTIQUE. see *EDUCATION*

CANADIAN SOCIETY FOR EDUCATION THROUGH ART. JOURNAL. see *EDUCATION*

CANADIAN SOCIETY FOR EDUCATION THROUGH ART. VIEWPOINTS. see *EDUCATION*

CANTRILLS FILMNOTES. see *MOTION PICTURES*

CANVAS (MADISON). see *LITERATURE*

CAPILANO REVIEW. see *LITERATURE*

CARDOZO ARTS & ENTERTAINMENT LAW JOURNAL. see *LAW*

CARIBBEAN STUDIES/ESTUDIOS DEL CARIBE/ESTUDES DES CARAIBES. see *SOCIAL SCIENCES: COMPREHENSIVE WORKS*

700   US   ISSN 0741-0085
CB235
CARIBE MAGAZINE; visual arts in the Caribbean. 1977. irreg. $3 per no. Caribbean Cultural Center, 408 W. 58th St., New York, NY 10019. TEL 212-307-7420. Ed. Marta Vega. bk.rev.; charts; illus. circ. 2,500. Indexed: A.I.C.P.
Formerly: Pre-Columbian Research Resources Review.
Description: Explores the African Diaspora and the cultures of all its descendants residing in the Americas, the Caribbean, and around the world.

800 500 700   US   ISSN 0008-6681
AS36
CARNEGIE MAGAZINE; dedicated to art, science, literature and music. 1927. bi-m. $12. Carnegie Museums of Pittsburgh, 4400 Forbes Ave., Pittsburgh, PA 15213. TEL 412-622-3315. FAX 412-622-1907. E-mail: carnegiemag@clpgh.org; URL: http://www.clpgh.cmag/. Ed. R. Jay Gangewere. R&P contact: R. Jay Gangewere. adv.: B&W page $1600, color page $2800; trim 8 1/4 x 10 7/8. bk.rev.; illus.; index. circ. 30,000. (also avail. in microform from UMI; reprint service avail. from UMI) Indexed: Artbibl.Mod., Avery Ind.Archit.Per., RILA. Document type: consumer publication.
—UMI; UnCover.
Incorporates: Carnegie. Annual Report.
Description: Articles and photography on the arts, natural history, science, literature, and music, with regular editorial and news columns.

700   CN   ISSN 1191-8594
CARNET;* a trade magazine for visual artists - une revue pour les artistes visuels. (Text in English, French) 1975. s-a. Can.$25 membership. Canadian Artists Representation - Front des Artistes Canadiens, 189 Laurier Ave. E., Ottawa, ON K1N 6P1, Canada. TEL 416-360-0780. FAX 416-360-0781. Ed. Sandra Lewis. adv. contact: Sandra Lewis. circ. 2,500. (back issues avail.) Document type: bulletin.
Incorporates: Studio File (ISSN 1185-3476); Which was formerly: Arterra (ISSN 0828-3699); C A R F A C Manitoba News Bulletin (ISSN 0225-4816); (until 1978): Touch - Touche (ISSN 0708-9953); Former titles: Art Action (ISSN 0842-1846); C A R F A C News (ISSN 0705-2634); C A R News (ISSN 0705-2634).
Description: Articles on cultural policy, professional development, programs for artists, special projects, members' shows and opportunities.

CARRIZOS. see *LITERATURE*

700   IT   ISSN 0392-3347
CARROBBIO. 1975. a. L.81000 (effective 1997). Patron Editore, Via Badini 12, 40050 Quarto Inferiore (BO), Italy. TEL 39-51-767003. FAX 39-51-768252.

700   US   ISSN 0740-0780
CARROUSEL ART. 1978. 4/yr. $25. Cameo Productions, Box 992, Garden Grove, CA 92642. TEL 714-530-2991. Ed. Sondra L. Evans. adv.; bk.rev.; illus. circ. 1,200. (back issues avail.)
Description: Photographic and historical documentation of antique merry-go-rounds and the artists who created them.

704.948 701.18   DR
CARTA DE ARAWAK. 1985. m. Av. Pasteur 104, Santo Domingo, Dominican Republic. Dir. Efraim Castillo.

CARTE SEGRETE; rivista-libro di letteratura ed arte. see *LITERATURE*

741.5 658.8   US
▼**CARTOON OPPORTUNITIES.** 1995. m. $60. Box 248, Chalfont, PA 18914. TEL 215-822-9158. FAX 215-723-9788. Ed. Bradley Keough; Pub. Bill Keough. R&P contact: Bradley Keough. adv. contact: Bill Keough. bk.rev. Document type: bulletin.
Description: Publishes listings of markets that buy cartoons as well as tips on how to draw and market cartoons.

CARTOON TIMES. see *MUSEUMS AND ART GALLERIES*

700 808.87   US
CARTOON TIPS. 1936. m. $50. Hartman Publishing Co., Box 30367, Lincoln, NE 68503. TEL 308-453-3191. Ed. George Hartman. adv. contact: George Hartman. circ. 300. (tabloid format; back issues avail.) Document type: newsletter, trade publication.
Formerly: Cartoon World.
Description: Articles on cartooning, gagwriting, and listings of new cartoon magazines and T.J. markets.

CARTOONIST AND COMIC ARTIST MAGAZINE. see *LITERARY AND POLITICAL REVIEWS*

741.5   US   ISSN 0008-7068
NC1300
CARTOONIST PROFILES. 1969. q. $25 to institutions. Box 325, Fairfield, CT 06430. Ed. Jud Hurd. adv.; charts; illus. (also avail. in microform from UMI)
—UMI; UnCover.

709 913   FR   ISSN 0076-230X
DP1
CASA DE VELASQUEZ, MADRID. MELANGES/CASA DE VELASQUEZ, MADRID. MISCELLANIES. (Text in French, Spanish) 1965. a. price varies. De Boccard Edition, 11 rue de Medicis, 75006 Paris, France. Indexed: Amer.Hist.& Life (1969-1973), Hist.Abstr. (1969-1973).
—BLDSC (5536.811000); CINDOC.

CATALOGO DANTE. see *LITERATURE*

708   MX   ISSN 0187-9766
CATALOGO DE LAS EXPOSICIONES DE ARTE. (Supplement to: Universidad Nacional Autonoma de Mexico. Instituto de Investigaciones Esteticas. Anales (ISSN 0185-1276)) 1937. a. Universidad Nacional Autonoma de Mexico, Instituto de Investigaciones Esteticas, Circuito Mario de la Cueva, Zona Cultural, Ciudad Universitaria, 04510 Mexico, D.F., Mexico. TEL 52-5-6227545. FAX 52-5-6657440. E-mail: ereinoso@servidor.unam.mx. Ed.Bd.

750   IT   ISSN 0394-0519
N6917
CATALOGO DELL'ARTE ITALIANA DELL'OTTOCENTO. 1964. a. L.140000. Editoriale Giorgio Mondadori S.p.A., Via A. Ponti 10, 20143 Milan, Italy. TEL 02-891661. FAX 02-89125888. Ed. P. Bozzia. adv.; illus.
Former titles (until 1983): Catalogo della Pittura Italiana dell'Ottocento (ISSN 0394-0500); Catalogo Bolaffi della Pittura Italiana dell'Ottocento (ISSN 0394-0497)

700   IT
CATALOGO DELL'ARTE MODERNA ITALIANA. 1962. a. L.150000. Editoriale Giorgio Mondadori S.p.A., Via A. Ponti, 10, 20143 Milan, Italy. TEL 02-891661. FAX 02-89125888. Ed. P. Bozzia. adv.; illus.
Former titles: Catalogo Nazionale Bolaffi d'Arte Moderna; (until 1970): Catalogo Bolaffi d'Arte Moderna (ISSN 0576-8861); (until 1963): Collezionista d'Arte Moderna.

760   IT
CATALOGO DELLA GRAFICA ITALIANA. 1970. a. L.120000. Editoriale Giorgio Mondadori S.p.A., Via A. Ponti, 10, 20143 Milan, Italy. TEL 02-891661. FAX 02-89125888. Ed. P. Bozzia. adv.; illus.
Former titles: Catalogo Nazionale Bolaffi della Grafica; Catalogo Bolaffi della Grafica Italiana.

700   SP
CATALOGO NACIONAL DE ARTE CONTEMPORANEO. a. Iberico 2000, S.A., Joaquin Montes Jovellar 4, 1o Dcha., Madrid, Spain. TEL 91-261-82-68.

700 746   SZ   ISSN 1420-6021
CATALOGUE BIENNALE INTERNATIONALE DE LAUSANNE. (Text in English, French) 1962. biennial. 30 SFr. International Centre of Ancient and Modern Tapestry - Centre International de la Tapisserie Ancienne et Moderne, 4 Av. Villamont, CH-1005 Lausanne, Switzerland. TEL 41-21-3230757. FAX 41-21-3230721. adv. circ. 7,000. Document type: monographic series.
Formerly: Biennale Internationale de la Tapisserie (ISSN 0067-849X)

700 808.81   US   ISSN 0739-8506
CATALYST (SEATTLE). 1980. s-a. $8 (foreign $11). Laocoon Books, Box 20518, Seattle, WA 98102. TEL 206-323-7268. Ed. M. Kettner. circ. 2,000. (back issues avail.)
Description: Literary erotica in irregular collections, with emphasis on modern poetry and illustrated art.

THE CELATOR; journal of ancient and medieval art and artifacts. see *NUMISMATICS*

700   AT
CELEBRITY, PEOPLE, EVENTS NEWS. 1990. w. Aus.$1200. H W W Pty. Ltd. (Horan Wall & Walker), 15-19 Prospect St., Surry Hills, N.S.W. 2010, Australia. TEL 61-2-93609360. FAX 61-2-93805533. URL: http://www.hww.com.au. Document type: bulletin.
Formerly: Media Futures (ISSN 1037-3381); Supersedes: MediaFax (ISSN 1035-0802)

700   US
CENTER OF ATTENTION. 1977. m. $25. ArtsCenter, 300-G E. Main St., Carrboro, NC 27510. TEL 919-929-2787. Ed. Bett Wilson. illus. circ. 3,000.
Formerly: Artscope.

705   US
CENTRAL HALL ARTISTS NEWSLETTER.* 1974. q. $1. Central Hall Artists Inc., c/o L. Cohen, 84 Allenwood Rd., Great Neck, NY 11023. Ed.Bd. adv.; illus. circ. 1,000.

700   780   CM
CENTRE CULTUREL FRANCAIS DE YAOUNDE. PROGRAMME SAISON. (Text in French) a. Centre Culturel Francais de Yaounde, B.P. 513, Yaounde, Cameroon.

CENTRE D'HISTOIRE ET D'ART DE LA THUDINIE. PUBLICATIONS. see *HISTORY — History Of Europe*

CENTRE INTERNATIONAL D'ETUDE DES TEXTILES ANCIENS. BULLETIN. see *TEXTILE INDUSTRIES AND FABRICS*

CENTRO CAMUNO DI STUDI PREISTORICI. ARCHIVI. see *ARCHAEOLOGY*

CENTRO CAMUNO DI STUDI PREISTORICI. BOLLETTINO. see *ARCHAEOLOGY*

CENTRO CAMUNO DI STUDI PREISTORICI. STUDI CAMUNI. see *ARCHAEOLOGY*

709 913   IT
CENTRO CAMUNO DI STUDI PREISTORICI. SYMPOSIA. (Text in various languages) irreg., vol.3, 1983. L.200000. Centro Camuno di Studi Preistorici, Edizioni del Centro, Capo di Ponte, 25044 Brescia, Italy. TEL 39-364-42091. FAX 39-364-42572. E-mail: ccsp@globalnet.it; URL: http://ccsp.lo.it

700 900 011   IT
CENTRO DI CULTURA E STORIA AMALFITANA. RASSEGNA. 1981; N.S. 1991. s-m. L.30000($20) Centro di Cultura e Storia Amalfitana, Via Annunziatella 44, 84011 Amalfi, Italy. TEL 089-871170. FAX 089-873143. (Co-sponsor: Ministero Beni Culturali e Ambientali - Rome) Ed. Andrea Cerenza. bk.rev.; bibl. circ. 1,000. **Document type:** monographic series.
Description: Contains articles and research on the history and civilization of the Amalfi region.

CHANGJIANG WENYI/YANGTZE LITERATURE AND ART. see *LITERATURE*

CHANOYU QUARTERLY; tea and the arts of Japan. see *ORIENTAL STUDIES*

700   DK   ISSN 0109-3479
CHARLOTTENBORG FORAARSUDSTILLINGEN. 1984. a. Nyhavn 2, DK-1051 Copenhagen K, Denmark.

700 363.49   US   ISSN 1083-8872
CHEROTIC REVOLUTIONARY. 1991. irreg., latest no.6, 1996. $5 per no. Inter - Relations, Inc., Box 11445, Berkeley, CA 94712. TEL 510-526-7858. FAX 519-524-2053. E-mail: fmoore@lanminds.com; URL: http://users.lanminds.com/~fmoore. Eds. Frank Moore, Linda Mac. R&P contact: Linda Mac. adv. contact: Linda Mac. bk.rev.; film rev.; play rev.; video rev, music rev. circ. 500. (back issues avail.) **Document type:** newsletter.
Description: Zine about the edge for and by people on the edge... if not over the edge.

NE   ISSN 1380-7811
▼**CHIASMA.** 1995. irreg., vol.3, 1996. Editions Rodopi B.V., Keizersgracht 302-304, 1016 EX Amsterdam, Netherlands. TEL 31-20-6227507. FAX 31-20-6380948. E-mail: F.van.der.Zee.@Rodopi.nl. (In N. America: 2015 S. Park Pl., Atlanta, GA 30339. TEL 800-225-3998. FAX 770-933-9644) (back issues avail.) **Document type:** monographic series.

700   US
CHICAGO ART REVIEW.* irreg., 4th ed., 1989. $29.95 paperback; hardbound $39.95. American References Publishing Corp., 2210 N. Burling St., Chicago, IL 60614-3712. Ed. Les Krantz. illus.
Description: Lists museums, galleries, art associations, and museum personnel alphabetically by city, including addresses, telephone numbers, admission information, history, and information about types of displays. Lists artists, including medium, address, gallery affiliations, birthdate, awards, education, and short profiles.

700 658   US
CHICAGO ARTISTS' NEWS. 1975. m. $35 to individuals; organizations $45. Chicago Artists' Coalition, 11 E. Hubbard St., 7th Fl., Chicago, IL 60611. TEL 312-670-2060. FAX 312-670-2521. URL: http://www.caconline.or/home.html. Ed. Jeff Abell. R&P contact: Jeff Abell. adv. contact: Jeff Abell. bk.rev.; circ. 3,000 (paid). **Document type:** newsletter.
●Also available online.
Formerly (until Jan. 1990): C A C News (ISSN 0890-5908)
Description: Feature articles, list of gallery openings, jobs, space, opportunities including grants information, exhibitions, lectures, workshops, and other information of concern to artists.
Refereed Serial

709   US   ISSN 1045-1382
N6487.C52
CHICAGO INTERNATIONAL NEW ART FORMS EXPOSITION.* 1986. a. Lakeside Group Inc., General Delivery, Lakeside, MI 49116-9999.

CHILDREN'S WRITER'S AND ILLUSTRATOR'S MARKET. see *PUBLISHING AND BOOK TRADE*

CHINA INSTITUTE IN AMERICA. BULLETIN.. see *ORIENTAL STUDIES*

750   US   ISSN 0889-8189
CHINA PAINTER. 1967. bi-m. $30 (foreign $35) (effective 1997). World Organization of China Painters, 2641 N.W. 10, Oklahoma City, OK 73107. TEL 405-521-1234. FAX 405-521-1265. URL: http://www.theshop.wet@wocporg. Ed. Pat Dickerson. adv. circ. 8,000. (back issues avail.)
Description: Covers all aspects of the fine art of porcelain china painting.

700   KN
CHOSON YESUL/KOREAN ARTS. (Text in Korean) m. Central Committee of the General Federation of Literature and Arts of Korea, Pyongyang, N. Korea.

DIE CHRISTENGEMEINSCHAFT; Monatsschrift zur religioesen Erneuerung. see *RELIGIONS AND THEOLOGY*

CHRISTIAAN DE WET ANNALE. see *HISTORY — History Of Africa*

704.948 200   US   ISSN 1080-7608
CHRISTIANITY AND THE ARTS. 1994. q. $21 (Canada $25; elsewhere $30) (effective 1997). Christianity and the Arts, Box 118088, Chicago, IL 60611. TEL 312-642-8606. FAX 312-266-7719. E-mail: chrnarts@aol.com; URL: http://members.aol.com/chrarts/chrnarts.html. Ed. Marci Whitney-Scheneck; Pub. Marci Whitney-Scheneck. adv.: page $400; trim 8 1/2 x 11; adv. contact: Marci Whitney-Scheneck. bk.rev.; music rev.; video rev. circ. 5,000. **Document type:** consumer publication.
Description: Explores Christian expression (art, dance, music, literature, films, and drama) for Protestants, Catholics, and Orthodox.

700   UK   ISSN 0266-1217
N8610
CHRISTIE'S INTERNATIONAL MAGAZINE. 1984. 10/yr. £44($65) Christie's, 8 King St., St. James's, London SW1Y 6QT, England. TEL 0171-839-9060. FAX 0171-839-1611. URL: http://www.christies.com. Ed. Meredith Etherington-Smith. adv.: B&W page £2600, color page £4000; trim 232 x 297. circ. 50,000.

CHRONICA. see *HISTORY — History Of Europe*

CHURCHSCAPE; annual review of the Council for the Care of Churches. see *ARCHITECTURE*

CIBA COLLECTION OF MEDICAL ILLUSTRATIONS. see *MEDICAL SCIENCES*

CINMAY SMRTI PATHAGARA. see *LITERATURE*

700   IT
CITTA DI RIGA; periodica quadrimestrale d'arte. no.2, 1977. 3/yr. Nuova Foglio S.p.A., Piane di Chienti 12, 62010 Pollenza (Macerata), Italy. Ed. Elisabetta Rasy.

CITTA DI VITA; bimestrale di religione arte e scienza. see *RELIGIONS AND THEOLOGY*

700   IT
LA CIVETTA. no.2, 1974. irreg., no.6, 1977. price varies. Giardini Editori e Stampatori, Via Santa Bibbiana 28, 56100 Pisa, Italy. TEL 050 502531. Ed. Nicola Micieli.

700 945   IT   ISSN 0069-4355
CIVILTA VENEZIANA. FONTI E TESTI. SERIE PRIMA: FONTI E TESTI PER LA STORIA DELL'ARTE VENETA. 1959. irreg., no.8, 1972. price varies. (Fondazione Giorgio Cini) Casa Editrice Leo S. Olschki, Casella Postale 66, 50100 Florence, Italy. TEL 39-55-6530684. FAX 39-55-6530214. E-mail: celso@olschki.it. circ. 1,000. **Document type:** monographic series.

THE CLASSICIST. see *ARCHITECTURE*

940   NE
CLAVIS KLEINE KUNSTHISTORISCHE MONOGRAFIEEN. 1984. a. price varies. Clavis Stichting Publicaties Middeleeuwse Kunst, Postbus 1521, 3500 BM Utrecht, Netherlands. **Document type:** monographic series.

940   NE
CLAVIS KUNSTHISTORISCHE MONOGRAFIEEN. 1984. a. price varies. Clavis Stichting Publicaties Middeleeuwse Kunst, Postbus 1521, 3500 BM Utrecht, Netherlands. **Document type:** monographic series.

CLEMSON UNIVERSITY. COLLEGE OF ARCHITECTURE. JOURNAL; a journal of educational thought. see *ARCHITECTURE*

CLOCKWATCH REVIEW; a journal of the arts. see *LITERATURE*

COLECCION ETHOS. see *MUSIC*

790.132   CN   ISSN 1196-4812
COLLECTIBLES CANADA. 1982. 6/yr. Can.$16.95 (foreign Can.$27.99) (effective 1997). Trajan Publishing Corp., 202-103 Lakeshore Rd., St. Catharines, ON L2N 2T6, Canada. TEL 905-646-7744. FAX 905-646-0995. Ed. Bret Evans. adv. contact: Clark Cooper. bk.rev.; circ. 7,500 (paid). (back issues avail.) **Document type:** consumer publication.
Supersedes in part (in 1993): Insight on Collectables (ISSN 0836-5873); Which was formerly (until 1987): Insight (ISSN 0833-4447); (until 1986): Insight on Collectables (ISSN 0714-8992).
Description: Features limited edition art and Royal Doulton. Coverage includes artist features, new products, trade and show news.

COLLECTIONS (COLUMBIA). see *MUSEUMS AND ART GALLERIES*

COLLECTOR. see *ADVERTISING AND PUBLIC RELATIONS*

COLLECTOR EDITIONS. see *HOBBIES*

700 340   US   ISSN 0888-4226
K1
COLUMBIA - V L A JOURNAL OF LAW & THE ARTS. 1974. q. $35 (foreign $43) (effective 1996). Columbia University School of Law, 435 W. 116th St., Box D28, New York, NY 10027. TEL 212-663-8719. Ed.Bd. adv.; bk.rev.; index. circ. 750. (also avail. in microfiche from WSH; microfilm from WSH; back issues avail.; reprint service avail. from WSH) **Indexed:** C.L.I., L.R.I., Leg.Per. **Document type:** academic/scholarly publication.
—BLDSC (3323.920000); KR SourceOne; UnCover.
Formerly: Art and the Law (ISSN 0743-5266)

COMIC ART STUDIES. see *LIBRARY AND INFORMATION SCIENCES*

741.5 070.5   US   ISSN 0194-7869
COMICS JOURNAL; the magazine of comics news & criticism. 1976. m. $35 (foreign $40). Fantagraphics Books, Inc., 7563 Lake City Way, Seattle, WA 98115. TEL 206-524-1967. FAX 206-524-2104. E-mail: fgraphic@halcyon.com; URL: http://www.halcyon.com/fgraphic/home.html. Ed. Tom Spurgeon. R&P contact: Gary Groth. adv.: page $200; trim 8 3/8 x 10 7/8; adv. contact: Rhea Patton. bk.rev.; film rev.; illus. circ. 12,000. (back issues avail.) Document type: trade publication. —UnCover.

COMICS RETAILER. see BUSINESS AND ECONOMICS — Small Business

700   US   ISSN 0887-8943
COMICS VALUES MONTHLY. 1986. m. newsstand price: $3.95. Sunrise Publications, 15 Danbury Rd., Ridgefield, CT 06877. TEL 203-438-9652. FAX 203-438-6744.

COMITATUS; a journal of Medieval and Renaissance studies. see LITERATURE

700   IT
▼**COMMENTARI D'ARTE**; rivista di critica e storia dell'arte. 1995. a.? L.120000 (foreign $100). De Luca Editore, Via di S. Anna 16, 00186 Rome, Italy. TEL 39-6-6868678. FAX 39-6-6864430. Ed. Stefania Petrillo. adv.

COMPETITIONS (LOUISVILLE). see ARCHITECTURE

700   AT   ISSN 1322-3267
COMPETITIONS AND FINANCIAL OPPORTUNITIES FOR ARTISTS. a. Aus.$35 individual membership; institutional Aus.$60. Queensland Artworkers Alliance Inc., 497 Adelaide St., Brisbane, Qld. 4000, Australia. TEL 48-7-38322230. FAX 61-7-38322231. E-mail: qaa@thehub.com.au. Ed. Lindy Johnson. R&P contact: Lindy Johnson. adv.: B&W page Aus.$300; trim 210 x 297. circ. controlled. Document type: directory.
    Formerly: Creative Culture.
    Description: Listings of art competitions, prizes, awards, scholarships, grants, fellowships, foundations and professional opportunities for visual artists.

700 810   US   ISSN 1048-8790
NX504
CONCEPTIONS SOUTHWEST; publicacion de literatura y arte de la Universidad de Nuevo Mexico. (Text in English, Spanish) 1977. s-a. $5. University of New Mexico, Student Publications Board, Box 20, Albuquerque, NM 87131. TEL 505-277-7525. circ. 700. (back issues avail.)
    Description: Fine arts magazine publishing work of the University of New Mexico staff, faculty and alumni.

CONFERENCE ON EDITORIAL PROBLEMS: UNIVERSITY OF TORONTO. see LITERATURE

CONNAISSANCE DE L'EURE. see HISTORY

700   FR   ISSN 0293-9274
CONNAISSANCE DES ARTS. 1952. m. 520 F. Societe Francaise de Promotion Artistique, 25 rue de Ponthieu, 75008 Paris, France. TEL 43-59-62-00. FAX 42-56-43-35. Ed. Philip Jodidio. adv. contact: Carl Bocksch-Juul. bk.rev.; bibl.; illus.; mkt. circ. 47,053. Indexed: Art & Archaeol.Tech.Abstr., Art Ind., Artbibl.Mod., Arts & Hum.Cit.Ind., ASCA, Avery Ind.Archit.Per., Br.Tech.Ind., Curr.Cont., DAAI, Geo.Abstr., RILA.
—BLDSC (3417.568000); SWETS.
    Former titles: Connaissance des Arts-Plaisir; Plaisir de France (ISSN 0032-048X); Connaissance des Arts (ISSN 0010-5988)

CONNECTICUT HISTORICAL SOCIETY. BULLETIN. see HISTORY. — History Of North And South America

CONSEQUENCES. see LITERATURE

CONSTRUCTIVE CRITICISM; a journal of construct psychology and the arts. see PSYCHOLOGY

700   AT   ISSN 0819-677X
CONTEMPORARY ART CENTRE OF SOUTH AUSTRALIA. BROADSHEET. 1954. q. Aus.$15. Contemporary Art Centre of South Australia, 14 Porter St., Parkside, S.A. 5063, Australia. E-mail: cacsa@camtech.net.au. Ed. Bala Starr. R&P contact: Joanne Harris. adv. contact: Joanne Harris. bk.rev. circ. 7,000. (back issues avail.) Document type: newspaper.
    Formerly: Contemporary Art Society of Australia. Broadsheet.
    Description: Covers contemporary art, popular culture, film and architecture.

760 002.075   US   ISSN 1066-9434
NE508
CONTEMPORARY IMPRESSIONS.* 1993. s-a. $50 to institutions (Canada $53; elsewhere $58) (effective 1996). American Print Alliance, 302 Larkspur Turn, Peachtree City, GA 30269-2210. TEL 202-544-2439. Ed. Carol Pulin. R&P contact: Carol Pulin. adv. contact: Carol Pulin. bk.rev.; illus. circ. 2,000. (back issues avail.) Indexed: Artbibl.Mod.
    Description: Contains critical writing on prints, paperworks and artists' books for artists, collectors and the educated public; includes an original print each year.

760 686.2   US   ISSN 1046-9087
CONTEMPORARY PRINT PORTFOLIO; a guide to prices, new editions & sources. 1990. a. $85 (foreign $100). Bon a Tirer Publishing, Box 3480, Shawnee Mission, KS 66203. TEL 913-631-4991. Ed. Joseph E. Zanatta.

700 384.55   UK
CONTEMPORARY VISUAL ARTS. vol.3, 1995. q. £16 to individuals (U.S. $32); institutions £20 (U.S. $42). Gordon & Breach Magazines Unlimited, 197 Knightsbridge, 8th Fl. N., London SW7 1RB, England. TEL 44-171-823-8373. FAX 44-171-823-7969. E-mail: cva@gbhap.com; URL: http://www.gbhap.com/cont.visarts. (Subscr. to: Brookland Mailing Service, Unit 5, Parkway Trading Estate, St. Werburghs Rd., Bristol BS2 9BR, England. TEL 44-117-9555215. FAX 44-117-9541485; U.S. subscr. to: G & B Magazines Inc., Box 32160, Newark, NJ 07102) Ed. Keith Patrick; Pub. Lynne Green. R&P contact: Dawn Fulcher. adv. contact: Michael Boag. bk.rev.; illus. Document type: consumer publication.
    Formerly (until Apr. 1997, no.14): Contemporary Art (ISSN 0968-6711)
    Description: Provides an overview of art today, covering video, film, photography, performance and installation as well as painting and sculpture. Focuses on British art but also looks at significant international developments.

CONTENUTI; trimestrale di lettere e arti. see LITERATURE

CONTEXT SOUTH. see LITERATURE — Poetry

150   UK   ISSN 0069-973X
CONTROL MAGAZINE. 1965. a. £8. 5 London Mews, London W.2. England. Ed. S. Willats. circ. 750. Indexed: Artbibl.

700 800   US
CORADDI. 1897. bi-m. $4. (University of North Carolina at Greensboro, University Media Board) Coraddi Publications, Elliott Center, Rm 205, Greensboro, NC 27412. TEL 919-379-5572. Ed. Elizabeth House. adv.; bk.rev.; illus. circ. 4,000.

700   IE   ISSN 0332-2580
CORK REVIEW. 1979-1981 (vol.2, no.3); resumed. a. I£4.95. Triskell Arts Centre, Tobin St., Cork, Ireland. TEL 021-272022. FAX 021-275945. Ed. Liz McAvoy. adv. contact: Dermot O'Gara. bk.rev.; illus. circ. 2,000. Document type: consumer publication.

700   DK   ISSN 0107-9794
N7018.5.C6
CORNER. 1986. a. DKK 30. Tofte Baeksvej 2, DK-2800 Lyngby, Denmark. Ed. Uffe Thorlacius.

CORNFIELD REVIEW; an annual of the creative arts. see LITERATURE

730   IT   ISSN 0528-5658
CORPUS DELLA SCULTURA ALTOMEDIEVALE. 1959. irreg., no.13, 1991. price varies. Centro Italiano di Studi sull'Alto Medioevo, Palazzo Ancaiani, 06049 Spoleto, Italy. TEL 39-743-220418. FAX 39-743-223507. Document type: monographic series.

091   BE
CORPUS OF THE ILLUMINATED MANUSCRIPTS OF THE LOW COUNTRIES. (Text in English) 1985. irreg., vol.9, 1996. price varies. (Katholieke Universiteit Leuven) Editions Peeters s.p.r.l., Bondgenotenlaan 153, 3000 Leuven, Belgium. TEL 32-16-235170. FAX 32-16-228500. URL: http://www.peeters-leuven.be. (back issues avail.) Document type: monographic series.

700   FR
CORPUS VITREARUM. biennial. price varies. C N R S Editions, 20-22 rue St. Amand, 75015 Paris, France. TEL 45-33-16-00. FAX 45-33-92-13. TELEX 200 356 F. adv.; bk.rev.; index; circ. 1,500 (controlled).

700 943   GW   ISSN 0232-1459
CORPUS VITREARUM MEDII AEVI. 1976. irreg., no.16, 1993. Akademie Verlag GmbH, Muehlenstr. 33-34, 13187 Berlin, Germany. TEL 49-30-47889348. FAX 49-30-47889357. E-mail: info@akademie-verlag.de. Document type: monographic series.

700   SP   ISSN 0213-7690
CORREO DEL ARTE; revista mensual de las artes plasticas. 1980. m. (10/yr.) $70 (effective 1997). Movipress 2000 S.l., Garcia de Paredes 61, 28010 Madrid, Spain. TEL 34-1-3991439. FAX 34-1-3995049. Ed. Antonio Morales. adv. circ. 5,000.
    Description: Covers painting, sculpture, photography, design and architecture.

CORRIERE DEL MEZZOGIORNO; il tridente. see POLITICAL SCIENCE

700 913   IT
CORSI INTERNAZIONALI DI CULTURA SULL'ARTE RAVENNATE E BIZANTINA. ATTI. (Text in English, French, German, Italian) 1953. irreg., no.42, 1996. Lit.180000 (effective 1997). Angelo Longo Editore, Via Paolo Costa 33, 48100 Ravenna, Italy. TEL 39-0544-217026. FAX 39-544-217554. E-mail: longo-ra@linknet.it. (Co-sponsor: Universita di Bologna) Ed. Alfio Longo. circ. 1,500. Document type: academic/scholarly publication.
    Description: Studies on Byzantine culture, art and history.

700   FR   ISSN 0152-3791
LA COTE DES ARTS; actualite artistique et culturelle. 1977. m. 450 F. (foreign 600 F.). Cote des Arts, 31 rue Dieude, BP 40, 13251 Marseille Cedex 20, France. TEL 91-33-91-62. FAX 91-33-36-64. Ed. Luc Elysee Serraf. adv.; bk.rev. circ. 12,000.
—CCC.

709   UK   ISSN 0307-8051
COURTAULD INSTITUTE ILLUSTRATION ARCHIVES. ARCHIVE 1. irreg. $30 per no. (Courtauld Institute, University of London) Harvey Miller Publishers, 197 Kightsbridge, 8th fl., London SW7 1RB, England. TEL 44-171-584-7676. FAX 44-171-823-7969. E-mail: sarah.kane@gbhap.com. Ed. Elly Miller. Document type: academic/scholarly publication.
    Description: Pictorial study archive of cathedrals and monastic buildings in the British Isles.

709   UK   ISSN 0307-806X
COURTAULD INSTITUTE ILLUSTRATION ARCHIVES. ARCHIVE 2. irreg. $30 per no. (Courtauld Institute, University of London) Harvey Miller Publishers, 197 Knightsbridge, 8th fl., London SW7 1RB, England. TEL 44-171-584-7676. FAX 44-171-823-7969. E-mail: sarah.kane@gbhap.com. Ed. Elly Miller. Document type: academic/scholarly publication.
    Formerly: 15th and 16th Century Sculpture in Italy.
    Description: Pictorial study archive of 15th and 16th century sculpture in Italy.

720 709   UK   ISSN 0307-8078
COURTAULD INSTITUTE ILLUSTRATION ARCHIVES. ARCHIVE 3. irreg. $30 per no. (Courtauld Institute, University of London) Harvey Miller Publishers, 197 Knightsbridge 8th fl., London SW7 1RB, England. TEL 44-171-584-7676. FAX 44-171-823-7969. E-mail: sarah.kane@gbhap.com. Ed. Elly Miller. Document type: academic/scholarly publication.
    Description: Pictorial study archive of medieval architecture and sculpture in Europe.

709 UK ISSN 0307-8086
**COURTAULD INSTITUTE ILLUSTRATION ARCHIVES.
ARCHIVE 4.** irreg. $30 per no. (Courtauld Institute, University of London) Harvey Miller Publishers, 197 Knightsbridge 8th fl., London SW19 5BD, England. TEL 44-171-584-7676. FAX 44-171-823-7969. E-mail: sarah.kane@gbhap.com. Ed. Elly Miller. **Document type:** academic/scholarly publication.
Description: Pictorial study archive of early 18th and 19th century in the U.K.

700 CI ISSN 0011-0728
COVJEK I PROSTOR. (Text in Serbo-Croatian; summaries in English) 1953. m. $35. Savez Drustava Arhitekata Hrvatske, Trg Republike 3-I, 41000 Zagreb, Croatia. Ed. Tomislav Premerl. adv.; bk.rev. circ. 3,000. **Indexed:** Br.Tech.Ind.

COWBOY ARTISTS OF AMERICA NEWSLETTER. see *MUSEUMS AND ART GALLERIES*

CRAFT ARTS INTERNATIONAL MAGAZINE. see *ARTS AND HANDICRAFTS*

760 659 US
CRAP HOUND. 1994. irreg., latest no.4. $5 per issue. Box 40373, Portland, OR 97240-0373. Ed. Sean Tejaratchi. illus.
Description: Adult zine that includes graphics from advertising of the 1930s to 1950s positioned so as to give them new meaning.

760 JA
CREATION; international graphic design, art & illustration. 1989. q. 3200 Yen. Recruit Co., Ltd., 8-4-17 Ginza, Chuo-ku, Tokyo 104, Japan. TEL 81-3-3575-7074. FAX 81-3-3575-7077. Ed. Yusaku Kamekura. circ. 10,000. (back issues avail.) **Document type:** consumer publication.
Description: Features highly acclaimed graphic designers, illustrators and artists from all over the world.

700 FR ISSN 0293-0196
CREATIONS. (Supplement avail.) 1959. 6/yr. 181 F. Ecole Moderne Francaise - Pedagogie Freinet, B.P. 109, 06322 Cannes - La Bocca Cedex, France. illus.
Formerly: Art Enfantin (ISSN 0004-3133)
Description: Contains children's art work.

THE CREATIVE HANDBOOK. see *ARTS AND HANDICRAFTS*

700 770 338.025 US ISSN 1081-1702
TR690.4
CREATIVE OPTIONS FOR BUSINESS AND ANNUAL REPORTS; photography, illustration & graphic design. 1981. a. $37.50. American Showcase Inc., 915 Broadway, 14th Fl., New York, NY 10010. TEL 212-673-6600. FAX 212-673-9795. (Dist. in U.S. by: Watson-Guptill Publications, 1515 Broadway, New York, NY 10036. TEL 1-800-451-1741; Overseas & Canada: Rotovision SA, Route Suisse 9, CH-1295 Mies, Switzerland. TEL 41-22755-3055) Ed. Ann Middlebrook; Pub. Ira Shapiro. adv. contact: Rob Drasin. **Document type:** directory.
Formerly: Corporate Showcase (ISSN 0742-9975)
Description: Photographers, illustrators and graphic designers serving the corporate market display their best work through over 650 4-color images. Also featured are comprehensive listings of 16,000 photographers, reps, stock photo agencies, film-photo support services, illustrators and graphic designers whose names and addresses are arranged topically and by region for easy access.

CREATIVE SOURCE AUSTRALIA; the wizards of Oz. see *ARTS AND HANDICRAFTS*

CREATIVE WOMAN. see *WOMEN'S INTERESTS*

CREATIVITY. see *ADVERTISING AND PUBLIC RELATIONS*

CRESCENDO (INTERLOCHEN). see *EDUCATION*

701.18 IT ISSN 0011-1511
N4
CRITICA D'ARTE.* 1935; N.S. 1954-1989 (Apr.); resumed 1990. q. L.36000($35) Casa Editrece Ponte alle Grazie, Via del Giglio 15, 50123 Florence, Italy. TEL 055-23458911. Ed. Carlo Ludovico Ragghianti. adv.; bk.rev.; abstr.; bibl.; illus.; index. circ. 11,000. **Indexed:** Artbibl.Mod.; Arts & Hum.Cit.Ind., Avery Ind.Archit.Per., Curr.Cont., RILA.

CRONACHE DI ARCHEOLOGIA. see *ARCHAEOLOGY*

CROSSCURRENTS. see *MUSIC*

CROSSCURRENTS; a quarterly. see *LITERATURE*

700 AG ISSN 0070-1688
CUADERNOS DE HISTORIA DEL ARTE. 1961-1967?; resumed 1988. irreg., no.14, 1992. $10 per no. (Instituto de Historia del Arte) Universidad Nacional de Cuyo, Facultad de Filosofia y Letras, Centro Universitario, Parque General San Martin, 5500 Mendoza, Argentina. TEL 54-61-230915. FAX 54-61-380457. Ed.Bd. bk.rev. **Document type:** academic/scholarly publication.
● Also available on CD-ROM.
Description: Covers general art and Argentine art, particularly from Mendoza.

709 MX ISSN 0185-1691
CUADERNOS DE HISTORIA DEL ARTE. 1973. irreg., latest 1990. price varies. Universidad Nacional Autonoma de Mexico, Instituto de Investigaciones Esteticas, Circuito Mario de la Cueva, Zona Cultural, Ciudad Universitaria, 04510 Mexico, D.F., Mexico. TEL 52-5-6227545. FAX 52-5-6227440. E-mail: ereinoso@servidor.unam.mx.

CUBA INTERNACIONAL. see *POLITICAL SCIENCE*

700 US ISSN 0882-4371
AC5
CULTURAL CRITIQUE; an international journal of cultural studies. 1985. 3/yr. $40 to individuals; institutions $78 (effective 1998). (Society for Cultural Critique) Oxford University Press, Journals, 2001 Evans Rd., Cary, NC 27513. TEL 919-677-0977; 800-852-7323. FAX 919-677-1714. E-mail: jnlorders@oup-usa.org; URL: http://www.oup-usa.org/. (Subscr. in N. America to: Oxford University Press, Journals, Great Clarendon St., Oxford OX2 6DP, England. TEL 44-1865-267907. FAX 44-1865-267485) Ed. Abdul R. Jan Mohamed. circ. 700. (also avail. in microfiche from UMI) **Indexed:** Amer.Hist.& Life (1989-), Arts & Hum.Cit.Ind., ASCA, Curr.Cont., Hist.Abstr. (1989-), IBR, Int.Polit.Sci.Abstr., Left Ind. (1985-), MLA Intl.Bibl., Per.Islam. (1994-1995), Sociol.Abstr., SSCI. **Document type:** academic/scholarly publication.
—BLDSC (3491.661600); Genuine Article; SWETS; UMI; UnCover. CCC.
Description: Investigates the broad terrain of cultural interpretation currently defined by the conjunction of literary, philosophical, anthropological, and sociological studies of Marxist, feminist, psychoanalytic, and post-structural methods.

700 UK ISSN 0954-8963
NX543
CULTURAL TRENDS. q. £84($129) to individuals; institutions £84 ($129) (effective 1997). (Policy Studies Institute) Carfax Publishing Co., P.O. Box 25, Abingdon, Oxon. OX14 3UE, England. TEL 44-1235-401000. FAX 44-1235-401550. E-mail: enquiries@carfax.co.uk. (Subscr. in N. America to: Carfax Publishing Co., 875-81 Massachusetts Ave., Cambridge, MA 02139) **Document type:** academic/scholarly publication.
—BLDSC (3491.668463). CCC.
Description: Presents independent research on essential statistics about the arts and cultural industries in the U.K.
Refereed Serial

700 780 UK
CULTURAL TRENDS IN SCOTLAND. a. Policy Studies Institute, 100 Park Village E., London NW1 3SR, England. TEL 44-171-468-0468. FAX 44-171-388-0914. (Dist. by: BEBC Distribution Ltd., P.O. Box 1496, Poole BH12 3YD, England; Subscr. to: Carfax Publishing Co. Ltd., P.O. Box 25, Abingdon, Oxford OX14 3UE, England) (Co-sponsor: Scottish Arts Council) **Document type:** directory.

700 NE
CULTURELE MARKETING NIEUWSBRIEF. 1992. m. fl.125. Bureau Menno Heling Culturele Marketing, Prinsengracht 1087, 1017 JH Amsterdam, Netherlands. TEL 31-20-6235001. FAX 31-20-6382196. Ed. Lex Hermans. bk.rev.; charts; stat.; circ. 500 (paid). (back issues avail.) **Document type:** newsletter.
Description: Deals with marketing the arts and culture. For professionals in museums and stage arts institutions.

700 IT ISSN 0011-6726
D'ARS; periodico d'arte contemporanea. 1960. q. L.90000 (Europe L.105000; America, Africa, Asia $100) (effective 1997). Via Giardino A. Calderini 3, 20123 Milan, Italy. TEL 39-2-860290. FAX 39-2-865997. Ed. M.C. Spasciani. adv.; bk.rev. circ. 5,000.

700 SP ISSN 0211-0768
D'ART. (Text in Catalan, Spanish) 1972. a. 1500 ptas.($12.50) (foreign 2000 ptas.). Universidad de Barcelona, Departament d'Historia de l'Art, Facultat de Geografia i Historia, Baldiri Reixach s.n., 08028 Barcelona, Spain. TEL 440-92-00. Ed. Dr. Pere Salabert. bk.rev. circ. 1,000. (back issues avail.)
—CINDOC.
Description: Includes a list and short abstract of the theses (first degree and doctoral dissertations) that have been read at the History of Art Department of the University of Barcelona.

D B C C PHOTOGRAPHIC SOCIETY. NEWSLETTER. (Dayton Beach Community College) see *PHOTOGRAPHY*

DADA - SURREALISM. see *LITERATURE*

DANDELION. see *LITERATURE — Poetry*

DANDELION ARTS MAGAZINE. see *LITERATURE — Poetry*

700 CC
DANGDAI MEISUJIA/MODERN ARTIST. (Text in Chinese) q. Sichuan Art Academy, Huangjiaoya, Chongqing, Sichuan 630050, People's Republic of China. TEL 25423-25.

DANGDAI WENYI TANSUO/CONTEMPORARY LITERATURE AND ART STUDY. see *LITERATURE*

DANSK MOENSTERTIDENDE. see *PATENTS, TRADEMARKS AND COPYRIGHTS*

700 II ISSN 0045-9658
DARSHAK; a Bengali fortnightly on art news & views. (Text in Bengali) 1960. fortn. Rs.10($2) Nabya Bangla Natya Parishad, 9-3 Tamar Lane, Calcutta 700009, India. Eds. Deb Kumar Basu, Rabi Mitra. adv.; bk.rev.; illus. circ. 2,000.

700 800 CC
DAZHONG WENYI. (Text in Chinese) m. newsstand price: Y2.88. Hebei Sheng Qunzhong Yishu-guan, 10 Hongguang Jie, Xinhua Xilu, Shijiazhuang, Hebei 050081, People's Republic of China. TEL 86-311-3034491. Ed. Tian Zhongxin. adv. circ. 20,000.

700 US
DEAF ARTISTS OF AMERICA NEWSLETTER. 1986. 4/yr. $10 (foreign $15). Deaf Artists of America, Inc., 302 Goodman St., N., Ste. 205, Rochester, NY 14607-1149. TEL 716-244-3460 TTY. FAX 716-244-3690. Ed. Tom Willard. adv.; bk.rev. circ. 1,000. (back issues avail.) **Document type:** newsletter.
Former titles (until 1993): Uncharted; Deaf Artists of America News (ISSN 0887-638X)
Description: News and feature articles for and about America's deaf and hard-of-hearing visual artists, performers, writers, arts educators and arts administrators.

DECISION; Zeitschrift fuer deutsche und franzoesische Literatur. see *LITERATURE*

745 US ISSN 0884-4011
DECORATIVE ARTS SOCIETY NEWSLETTER. 1975. 3/yr. $20 to individuals; institutions $25. Decorative Arts Society, c/o Cooper-Hewitt National Design Museum, 2 E. 91st St., New York, NY 10128. Ed. Elizabeth J. Kannan. **Indexed:** DAAI. **Document type:** newsletter.
Formerly (until 1978): Decorative Arts Newsletter (ISSN 0740-5634)
Description: Provides a forum for those interested in European and American decorative arts of all periods.

DECORATIVE ARTS SOCIETY, 1850 TO THE PRESENT. JOURNAL. see *ARTS AND HANDICRAFTS*

700　　　　　　GW　　ISSN 0342-1732
DEIKE-PRESS; international clip art service. 1923. 6/yr. Verlag Horst Deike KG, Postfach 100452, 78404 Konstanz, Germany. TEL 07531-8155-0. FAX 07531-815581. Ed. Wolfgang Deike. circ. 1,500. **Document type:** consumer publication.

700　　　　　　RU
DEKORATIVNOE ISKUSSTVO - DIALOG ISTORII I KULTURY. (Text in Russian; summaries in English) 1957. s-a. price varies. Izdatel'stvo D I - D I K, Ul. Tverskaya, 9, 103009 Moscow, Russia. TEL 7-95-2291910. FAX 7-95-2292760. (Dist. by: Mezhdunarodnaya Kniga, B. Yakimanka 39, 117049 Moscow, Russia; Dist. in U.S. by: Victor Kamkin Inc., 4956 Boiling Brook Pkwy, Rockville, MD 20852. TEL 301-881-5973) Ed. Aider Kurkchi. adv.; illus.; index. circ. 3,000. **Document type:** academic/scholarly publication.
　Formed by the 1994 merger of: Dialog Istorii i Kultury & Dekorativnoe Iskusstvo (ISSN 0869-4494); Which was formerly (until 1991): Dekorativnoe Iskusstvo S S S R (ISSN 0130-3031)
　Description: Deals with the history and theory of fine arts, includes articles on painting and sculpture.

700 574　　　　GW　　ISSN 0724-2689
NX456
DELFIN; eine deutsche Zeitschrift fuer Konstruktion, Analyse und Kritik. 1983. s-a. DM.27($15) Poiesis Verlag, Postfach 2104, Marderstr. 17, 33378 Rheda-Wiedenbrueck, Germany. Eds. Gebhard Rusch, Siegfried J. Schmidt. adv.; bk.rev.; bibl.; circ. 900. (back issues avail.)
　Description: Covers essays in philosophy, science, politics, literature, art and architecture, which broaden our thoughts and views.

686.3 095　　　GW　　ISSN 0341-2474
DENKMAELER DER BUCHKUNST. 1976. irreg., vol.12, 1996. price varies. Anton Hiersemann Verlag, Rosenbergstr. 113, 70193 Stuttgart, Germany. TEL 49-711-638265. FAX 49-711-6369010. (Subscr. to: Postfach 140155, 70071 Stuttgart, Germany) **Document type:** monographic series.

709　　　　　　GW　　ISSN 0947-031X
N3
DIE DENKMALPFLEGE. 1934. s-a. DM.53 (foreign DM.54) (effective 1996). (Vereinigung der Landesdenkmalpfleger in der Bundesrepublik Deutschland) Deutscher Kunstverlag GmbH, Nymphenburgerstr. 84, 80636 Munich, Germany. TEL 49-89-121516-0. FAX 49-89-12151616. Ed. J. Habich. adv.; bk.rev.; bibl.; index. circ. 1,800. **Indexed:** Archit.Per.Ind., Art & Archaeol.Tech.Abstr., Artbibl.Mod., Arts & Hum.Cit.Ind., Arts & Hum.Cit.Ind., ASCA, Avery Ind.Archit.Per., Curr.Cont., RILA. **Document type:** bulletin.
　—Genuine Article.
　Formerly (until 1993): Deutsche Kunst und Denkmalpflege (ISSN 0012-0375)

751.6　　　　　GW　　ISSN 0340-2495
DENKMALPFLEGE IN BADEN-WUERTTEMBERG. 1972. q. free. Landesdenkmalamt Baden-Wuerttemberg, Moerikestr. 12, 70178 Stuttgart, Germany. bk.rev.; illus. circ. 20,000. **Indexed:** Art & Archaeol.Tech.Abstr., IBR. **Document type:** bulletin.

751.6　　　　　GW
DENKMALPFLEGE IN SACHSEN-ANHALT. 1993. s-a. DM.22. (Landesamt fuer Denkmalpflege) Verlag fuer Bauwesen GmbH, Am Friedrichshain 22, 10407 Berlin, Germany. TEL 49-30-42151-0. FAX 49-30-42151468. circ. 1,000. **Document type:** bulletin.

354.489 700　　　DK　　ISSN 0107-2951
DENMARK. STATENS KUNSTFOND. BERETNING. 1959. a. free. Statens Kunstfond - Danish Arts Foundation, Sankt Annae Plads 10B, DK-1250 Copenhagen K, Denmark. TEL 45-33-11-36-01. FAX 45-33-11-35-06. Ed. Vibeke Jakobsen. circ. 1,800. **Document type:** bulletin.

DESIGN & ART IN GREECE/THEMATA CHOROU & TECHNON. see ARCHITECTURE

745 709　　　　US　　ISSN 0747-9360
DESIGN ISSUES; a journal of history, theory and criticism. 1984. 3/yr. $38 to individuals (foreign $54); institutions $88 (foreign $104); students and retired $22 (foreign $38) (effective 1997). M I T Press, 5 Cambridge Center, Cambridge, MA 02142. TEL 617-235-2889. FAX 617-577-1545. E-mail: journals-orders@mit.edu; URL: http://www-mitpress.mit.edu. (Editorial addr.: 110 Margaret Morrison, Carnegie Mellon University, Pittsburgh, PA 15213) Ed.Bd. R&P contact: Paul Dzus. adv.; bk.rev. circ. 1,400. (also avail. in microfilm from UMI; reprint service avail. from UMI) **Indexed:** Art Ind., Artbibl.Mod., ASCA, Curr.Cont., DAAI. **Document type:** academic/scholarly publication.
　—BLDSC (3559.976000); Genuine Article; KR SourceOne; SWETS; UMI; UnCover. **CCC.**
　Description: Presents a scholarly forum for the history, theory, and criticism of design. Provokes inquiry into the cultural and intellectual role of non-architectural fields, from graphic design to industrial design.
　Refereed Serial

741　　　　　　US　　ISSN 1054-7746
NK1170
DESIGN STATEMENTS.* 1985. 3/yr. $25. American Center for Design, 325 W. Huron St., Ste. 711, Chicago, IL 60610-3617. TEL 312-787-2018. FAX 312-649-9518. adv. contact: Mary Davis. bk.rev. circ. 3,000. **Indexed:** DAAI. **Document type:** trade publication.
　Description: For product and communication design professionals, educators and students.

700　　　　　　UK　　ISSN 0950-3676
DESIGN WEEK. (Supplement avail.) 1986. w. £105 (includes q. supplement, Design Week Action Pack). Centaur Publishing, St. Giles House, 50 Poland St., London W1V 4AX, England. TEL 44-171-439-4222. FAX 44-171-734-1770. Ed. Lynda Relph-Knight; Pub. Roger Beckett. adv. contact: Jessica MacDermott. bk.rev. circ. 10,406. (also avail. in microform from UMI) **Indexed:** DAAI. **Document type:** trade publication.
　—BLDSC (3560.215000); UMI.
　Description: Dedicated to design, news, and features about the industry worldwide.

700　　　　　　UK
DESIGN WEEK ACTION PACK. q. free with subscr. to Design Week (ISSN 0950-3676). Centaur Publishing, 50 Poland St., London W1V 4AX, England. TEL 44-171-439-4222. FAX 44-171-734-1770. Ed. Lynda Relph Knight; Pub. Roger Beckett. adv. contact: Jessica MacDermott. circ. 8,500. (back issues avail.) **Document type:** trade publication.
　Description: Aimed at designers, graphic artists, and home-design consultants.

702.8　　　　　GW　　ISSN 0930-2417
DESIGNERS DIGEST; magazin fuer Gestaltung und Technik. 1987. bi-m. DM.64; newsstand price: DM.16. Verlag Design und Technik GmbH, A.-Paul-Weber-Str. 5, 21493 Schretstaken, Germany. TEL 089-7917045. FAX 089-791-8883. circ. 35,000. (back issues avail.)
　Incorporates: Grafik Design und Technik.

700　　　　　　US
DESTROY ALL COMIC BOOKS.* 6/yr. $9. 52 Davie Cir., No. A, Chapel Hill, NC 27514-5901. Ed. Jeff Levine. **Document type:** newsletter.
　Description: Information on the alternative comics scene.

700　　　　　　US
DETROIT FOCUS QUARTERLY; a visual arts publication. 1982. q. $15. Detroit Focus Gallery, Box 32823, Detroit, MI 48232-0823. TEL 313-965-3245. Ed. Vince Carducci. adv. contact: Christine Welch. bk.rev. circ. 3,000. **Document type:** newsletter.

700　　　　　　US　　ISSN 0011-9636
N560
DETROIT INSTITUTE OF ARTS. BULLETIN. 1919. 2/yr. $16 (foreign $20). Detroit Institute of Arts, 5200 Woodward Ave., Detroit, MI 48202. TEL 313-833-1368. FAX 313-833-9169. E-mail: jruskin@cms.cc.wayne.edu. Ed. Maya Hoptman. R&P contact: Maya Hoptman. illus. circ. 5,000. (also avail. in microfiche; reprint service avail. from UMI) **Indexed:** Art Ind., Artbibl.Mod., RILA. **Document type:** academic/scholarly publication.
　—KR SourceOne; UMI; UnCover.
　Description: Devoted to the study of objects in the Museum's permanent collection.

700　　　　　　GW　　ISSN 0012-0693
DIE DEUTSCHE SCHRIFT; Zeitschrift zur Foerderung von Gotisch, Schwabacher und Fraktur. 1924. 4/yr. DM.44. Bund fuer Deutsche Schrift und Sprache, Postfach 1110, 2907 Uhlhorn, Germany. Ed. Wolfgang Hendlmeier. adv.; bk.rev.; illus. circ. 2,000. **Document type:** academic/scholarly publication.

700　　　　　　GW　　ISSN 0044-2135
N3
DEUTSCHER VEREIN FUER KUNSTWISSENSCHAFT. ZEITSCHRIFT. 1934. a. price varies. (Deutscher Verein fuer Kunstwissenschaft e.V.) Deutscher Verlag fuer Kunstwissenschaft GmbH, Charlottenstr. 13, 10969 Berlin, Germany. TEL 49-30-25913864. FAX 49-30-25913537. illus. circ. 1,600. (back issues avail.; reprint service avail.) **Indexed:** Art Ind., IBR, RILA. **Document type:** academic/scholarly publication.
　—BLDSC (9442.195000); Genuine Article; KR SourceOne; SWETS. **CCC.**
　Formerly: Zeitschrift fuer Kunstwissenschaft.

700 800　　　　UK　　ISSN 0309-7994
DEVONSHIRE ASSOCIATION FOR THE ADVANCEMENT OF SCIENCE, LITERATURE AND ART. REPORT AND TRANSACTIONS. 1862. a. £12 worldwide (effective 1997). Devonshire Association, 7 Cathedral Close, Exeter, Devon EX1 1EZ, England. TEL 44-1392-52461. FAX 44-1392-52461. Ed. T.A. Greeves. bk.rev.; circ. 1,200 (paid). **Indexed:** Numis.Lit., RILA. **Document type:** proceedings.
　—BLDSC (7638.200000).
　Description: Publishes original papers about the county of Devon.
　Refereed Serial

DIABLO ARTS MAGAZINE. see THEATER

701.18　　　　　US　　ISSN 0279-568X
DIALOGUE (COLUMBUS); arts in the Midwest. 1978. bi-m. $16 to individuals (Canada & Mexico $41; elsewhere $46); institutions $20 (Canada & Mexico $45; elsewhere $50) (effective 1997 & 1998). Dialogue Inc., Box 2572, Columbus, OH 43216-2572. TEL 614-621-3704. FAX 614-621-2448. E-mail: dialogarts@aol.com. Ed. Lorrie Dirkse. R&P contact: Lorrie Dirkse. adv.: page $600; 9 1/2 x 12 1/2; adv. contact: Diane Emrick. bk.rev. circ. 10,000. (also avail. in microfiche; back issues avail.)
　Description: Covers arts in Ohio, Illinois, and Indiana, and offers regional arts criticism, news, exhibition previews, and artist opportunities.

920 830　　　　GW　　ISSN 0070-4695
DICHTER UND ZEICHNER. 1963. irreg. price varies. Graphikum Verlag, Wilhelm-Baum-Weg 31, 37077 Goettingen, Germany. Ed. Anna-Helene Kurz. circ. 1,500. **Document type:** monographic series.

700 920　　　　US
DICTIONARY OF CONTEMPORARY AMERICAN ARTISTS. 1971. irreg., latest 1994. $85. St. Martin's Press, Scholarly and Reference Division, 175 5th Ave., New York, NY 10010. TEL 212-982-3900. FAX 212-777-6359. Ed. Paul Cummings. **Document type:** academic/scholarly publication.
　Description: Profiles painters, sculptors and printmakers chosen on the basis of representation in museums, public and international exhibitions, influence as teachers, recognition received from fellow artists, dealers, critics and others with a professional interest in fine arts.

700　　　　　　FR　　ISSN 0070-4776
DICTIONNAIRE DES VALEURS DES MEUBLES ET OBJETS D'ART. 1965. irreg. Librairie Fischbacher, 33 rue de Seine, 75006 Paris, France. TEL 43-26-84-87. FAX 43-26-48-87. Ed. E. Mayer.

DIETSCHE WARANDE EN BELFORT; tijdschrift voor letterkunde en geestesleven. see LITERARY AND POLITICAL REVIEWS

760 770 US
DIRECT STOCK. 1992. a. $24.95. Watson - Guptill Publications, 1515 Broadway, New York, NY 10036. TEL 212-764-7300. (Orders to: 1695 Oak St., Lakewood, NJ 08701. TEL 800-451-1741. FAX 908-363-0338). illus. **Document type:** catalog, trade publication.
  Description: Catalogs stock photographs available to graphic designers for purchase.

DIRECTORY OF CARTOONISTS - GAGWRITERS - SHORT HUMOR MARKETS. see BUSINESS AND ECONOMICS — Trade And Industrial Directories

700 CN ISSN 0832-865X
DIRECTORY OF THE ARTS. (Text in English, French) s-a. Can.$30 to non-members; members Can.$25. Canadian Conference of the Arts, 189 Laurier Ave. E., Ottawa, ON K1N 6P1, Canada. TEL 613-238-3561. FAX 613-238-4849. E-mail: cca@mail.culturenet.ca. Ed. Sharon Griffiths. **Document type:** directory.
  Incorporates: Who's Who: A Guide to Federal and Provincial Departments and Agencies, Their Funding Programs and the People Who Head Them (ISSN 0384-2355); Who Does What: A Guide to National Associations, Service Organizations and Unions Operating in the Arts (ISSN 0700-2661)
  Description: Offers a comlete guide to federal and provincial government agencies related to arts and culture, and national and provincial arts service organizations.

700 808.81 US
DISCRETE EPHEMERA. 1990. triennial. $25. Atomic Art, Scud Towers, 2418 Western Ave., Seattle, WA 98121. TEL 206-728-9245. adv.; illus. circ. 500.

700 IT
DISEGNO E PITTURA. Italian translation of: Artist's and Illustrator's Magazine (UK ISSN 0269-4697) 1986. m. L.72000 (foreign L.144000). Golf News, s.r.l., Via Scarlatti 30, 20124 Milan, Italy. TEL 39-2-6692299. FAX 39-2-6692306. (Dist. by: Parrini Distribuzione Piazza Indipendenza, 11B Rome, Italy) Ed. Sandro Bellenghi; Pub. Pat Nesi. adv. contact: Giampaola Corsini. bk.rev. circ. 26,000.
  Formerly: Disegnare e Dipingere.
  Description: Articles describing techniques of drawing, designing, and painting. Features selected artists and their work methods.

DOCUMENTATION AND REGISTRATION OF ROCK ART IN TANUM. see ARCHAEOLOGY

DOCUMENTI E RICERCHE D'ARTE ALESSANDRINA. see ARCHAEOLOGY

700 770 NE ISSN 1068-6894
DOCUMENTING THE IMAGE SERIES. 1994. irreg, latest vol.4. £29. Gordon and Breach - Harwood Academic, Amsteldisk 166, 1st Fl., 1079 LH Amsterdam, Netherlands. (Subscr. to: International Publishers Distributor, Box 32160, Newark, NJ 07102. TEL 800-545-8398. FAX 215-750-6343) **Document type:** monographic series.

700 800 US ISSN 1071-8613
NX504
DOCUMENTS (NEW YORK).* 1992. 2/yr. $20 to individuals (foreign $45); institutions $50 (foreign $75). Documents Magazine Inc., 60 W. 13th St., Apt. 7B, New York, NY 10011-7917. TEL 212-614-0935. FAX 212-254-3154. (Dist. by: Bernhard DeBoer Inc., 113 E. Centre St., Nutley, NJ 07110. TEL 201-667-9300) Ed. Jim Marcovitz. adv. contact: Madeleine Leskin. bk.rev.; film rev.; illus. circ. 3,000. (back issues avail.)
  Description: Provides a forum for the emerging voices in the fields of art, independent film, video, architecture and cultural criticism.

705 DR
DOMINICAN REPUBLIC. DIRECCION GENERAL DE BELLAS ARTES. CATALOGO DE LA BIENAL DE ARTES PLASTICAS. irreg. Direccion General de Bellas Artes, Santo Domingo, Dominican Republic. illus.

700 CC
DONGHUA DAWANG. (Text in Chinese) bi-m. Shanghai Renmin Meishu Chubanshe - Shanghai People's Art Publishers, No.33, Alley 672, Changle Road, Shanghai 200040, People's Republic of China. TEL 4374528. Ed. Huang Qianggen.

DOODGEWOON; tijdschrift over de dood. see PHILOSOPHY

700 FR ISSN 1161-3122
DOSSIER DE L'ART. 10/yr. 380 F. (foreign 430 F.) (effective 1997). Editions Faton S.A., 25 rue Berbisey, 21000 Dijon, France. TEL 33-3-80404104. (Subscr. to: 1 rue des Artidans, B.P. 90, 21803 Quetigny Cedex, France. TEL 33-3-80489848. FAX 33-3-80489846)

700 FR ISSN 0756-5860
LES DOSSIERS DE L'ART PUBLIC. (Text in English, French) 1983. irreg., latest no.6, 1991. 120 F. Association pour la Promotion de l'Art Public (A.P.A.P.), 71 rue d'Hautpoul, 75019 Paris, France. TEL 1-42-41-13-61. FAX 1-42-41-77-18. Ed. Herve Bechy. bk.rev. circ. 2,000.

DOUBLETAKE. see LITERARY AND POLITICAL REVIEWS

DRAGON. see LITERATURE

740 US ISSN 0191-6963
NC1
DRAWING; the international review. 1979. bi-m. $50 includes membership. Drawing Society, Inc., 15 Penn Plaza, Box 66, 415 Seventh Ave., New York, NY 10001-2007. TEL 212-563-4822. FAX 212-563-4829. Ed. Michael Flack. adv.; bk.rev. circ. 1,100. **Indexed:** Art & Archaeol.Tech.Abstr., Art Ind., Artbibl., Artbibl.Mod., Avery Ind.Archit.Per., RILA RILM. **Document type:** academic/scholarly publication.
  —BLDSC (3623.303000); KR SourceOne; UnCover.

DRUNKEN BOAT. see LITERARY AND POLITICAL REVIEWS

DRUSTVO KONZERVATORA SRBIJE. GLASNIK. see CONSERVATION

700 800 BE ISSN 0012-6799
DRYADE; revue artistique et litteraire. 1955. q. 250 Fr. Georges Bouillon, Ed. & Pub., 40 rue de Vieux-Virton, B-6762 Virton, Belgium. adv.; bk.rev.; illus.; play rev. circ. 1,100.

700 SZ ISSN 0012-6837
AP32
DU; die Zeitschrift der Kultur. (Text in German; summaries in English) 1941. m. 150 SFr. (effective 1997); newsstand price: 20 SFr. T A Media AG, Werdstr. 21, CH-8021 Zurich, Switzerland. TEL 41-1-2484111. FAX 41-1-2485314. URL: http://www.dumag.ch. Ed. Dieter Bachmann. adv. contact: Yvonne Philipp. bk.rev.; illus.; rec.rev.; index. circ. 28,027. **Indexed:** Archit.Per.Ind., Art Ind., Artbibl.Mod., Artbibl., Avery Ind.Archit.Per. **Document type:** consumer publication.
  —BLDSC (3630.530000); KR SourceOne; SWETS.
  Formerly: Du-Atlantis.

DUITSE KRONIEK. see POLITICAL SCIENCE — International Relations

DUMBARTON OAKS CONFERENCE PROCEEDINGS. see ARCHAEOLOGY

DUNHUANG YANJIU/DUNHUANG STUDIES. see ARCHAEOLOGY

700 CC ISSN 1000-6028
DUO YUN. (Text in Chinese) s-a. Shanghai Shu Hua Chubanshe - Shanghai Calligraphy and Painting Publishers, 81 Qinzhou S. Rd., Shanghai 200233, People's Republic of China. TEL 86-21-6451-9008. Ed. Lu Fusheng.

707 CN
E V A: THE ELECTRONIC VISUAL ARTS JOURNAL. 1993. 2/yr. University of Western Ontario, 1341 Birmingham St., Halifax N.S., B3J 2J3, Canada. E-mail: eva@bosshog.arts.uwo.ca; URL: http://www.uwo.ca/visarts/eva.html. Eds. Arthur R. Meads, Sam Gerszon.
●Available only online.
  Description: Dedicated to the exploration of the visual arts.

ART 439

EARLY DRAMA, ART, AND MUSIC REVIEW. see THEATER

EARTHSONG. see MUSEUMS AND ART GALLERIES

700 956 UK ISSN 0269-8404
N7260
EASTERN ART REPORT. (Former name of issuing body: Centre for Near East Asia and African Research) 1989. bi-m. £25 to individuals in U.K. (rest of Europe £35, U.S. $75, elsewhere £45); institutions (U.K. £40, rest of Europe £60, U.S. $130, elsewhere £80) (effective 1996). (Centre for Near East Afro-Asia Research (NEAR)) Eastern Art Publishing Group, P.O. Box 13666, London SW14 8WF, England. TEL 44-181-392-1122. FAX 44-181-392-1422. E-mail: easternart@compuserve.com. Eds. Sajid & Shirley Rizvi. adv. circ. 9,000. (back issues avail.) **Indexed:** Per.Islam. (1990-). **Document type:** academic/scholarly publication, monographic series.
  Description: Combines scholarly articles on the visual arts of Africa, the Far East, South and Southeast Asia (including China and Japan) with exclusive interviews, previews of exhibitions, art events, books and exhibition catalogs.
  Refereed Serial

740 UK ISSN 1358-6688
▼**THE EDGE.** 1995. bi-m. £18($36); newsstand price: £2.75. Calligraphy and Lettering Arts Society, 54 Boileau Rd., London SW13 9BL, England. TEL 44-181-741-7886. FAX 44-181-741-7886. E-mail: 101344.3245@compuserve.com. Ed. Sue Cavendish. adv.; bk.rev.; illus.; index; circ. 1,500 (paid). (back issues avail.) **Document type:** newsletter.
  Description: Discusses various aspects of caligraphy, present and historic. Updates readers on forthcoming events of interest.

700 NE
EDITIE COLLECTION D'ART. 8/yr. Collection d'Art Galerie, Keizersgracht 516, 1017 EJ Amsterdam, Netherlands. bk.rev. circ. 1,500.

EDITOR'S CHOICE; fiction, poetry and art from the U.S. small press. see LITERATURE

EIGHTEENTH CENTURY: A CURRENT BIBLIOGRAPHY. see BIBLIOGRAPHIES

EIGHTEENTH CENTURY LIFE. see HISTORY — History of Europe

EIGHTEENTH-CENTURY STUDIES. see HISTORY

EMBLEMATICA; an interdisciplinary journal for emblem studies. see HISTORY — History Of Europe

808 US ISSN 1045-3717
NC997.A1
EMIGRE. 1982. q. $28 (Canada $35, elsewhere $58). Emigre Graphics, 4475 D St., Sacramento, CA 95819. TEL 916-451-4344. FAX 916-451-4351. Ed. Rudy Vander Lans. R&P contact: Rudy Vander Lans. adv.; bk.rev. circ. 7,000. (back issues avail.) **Indexed:** DAAI, MLA Intl.Bibl. **Document type:** trade publication.
  Description: Features both established and emerging graphic design talents from around the world. Focuses on a specific design topic and showcases works, often experimental in nature.

EMPA. see MUSEUMS AND ART GALLERIES

701 US ISSN 0276-2374
NX1 CODEN: ESAREN
EMPIRICAL STUDY OF THE ARTS. 1982. 2/yr. $88 (effective 1997). Baywood Publishing Co., Inc., 26 Austin Ave., Box 337, Amityville, NY 11701. TEL 516-691-1270. FAX 516-691-1770. E-mail: baywood@baywood.com; URL: http://baywood.com. Ed. Colin Martindale. R&P contact: Julie Krempa. adv. contact: Michelle Satchell. bk.rev. (back issues avail.) **Indexed:** Psychol.Abstr. (1983-). **Document type:** academic/scholarly publication.
  —BLDSC (3737.024200). **CCC.**
  Description: Covers the fields of anthropology, applied aesthetics, psychology, semiotics and discourse analysis, sociology, and computational stylistics.

EMPLOYMENT OPPORTUNITIES (ENGLEWOOD). see OCCUPATIONS AND CAREERS

ENCYCLIA. see SCIENCES: COMPREHENSIVE WORKS

700   FR   ISSN 0248-6156
L'ENNEMI. 1980. a. 100 F. Christian Bourgois Editeur, 116 rue du Bac, 75007 Paris Cedex 13, France. TEL 1-45-44-09-13. FAX 1-45-44-87-86. Ed. Gerard-Georges Lemaire. illus. circ. 2,000. **Document type:** monographic series.
     Incorporates: Alea (ISSN 0249-3446)

700 808.8   US   ISSN 1090-0020
ENTERZONE. 1994. q. 1017 Bayview Ave., Oakland, CA 94610-4032. E-mail: info@ezone.org; URL: http://ezone.org/ez. Ed. Christian Crumlish. ●Available only online.
     Description: Covers arts, literature, and media.

ENVIRONMENT AND ART LETTER; a forum on architecture and the arts for the Parish. see ARCHITECTURE

700 150.19   AG
EOS; revista Argentina de arte y psicoanalisis. 1991. a.? Fundacion Banco Credito Argentino, 11 de Septiembre 1990, 1428 Buenos Aires, Argentina. TEL 783-3819. Ed.Bd.

700   US   ISSN 1044-0224
N7668.H6
EQUINE IMAGES. 1986. bi-m. $29.95 (foreign $41.95) (Canada $39.95). Heartland Communications Group, Inc., 1003 Central Ave., Fort Dodge, IA 50501. TEL 515-955-1600. FAX 800-247-2000. URL: http://www.equineimages.com.
     Description: Equine artwork, antiques and collectibles reflecting the horse loving equestrian lifestyle.

700 200   US   ISSN 1049-4782
ERRANT NEWS. 1989. irreg. $1 per no. Sally Goodspeed, Ed. & Pub., 2318 N. Charles St., Baltimore, MD 21218. bk.rev. (back issues avail.)
     Description: Looks at mythology and the Bible through the iconography of ancient art.

740   CC   ISSN 1003-0468
ERTONG MANHUA/CHILDREN'S CARTOON. (Text in Chinese) 1980. m. Renmin Meishu Chubanshe - People's Fine Arts Publishers, 32 Beizongbu Hutong, Beijing 100735, People's Republic of China. TEL 552296. Ed. Ding Wu. **Document type:** consumer publication.

700   VE
ESCRITOS. 1986. s-a. $30 (effective 1997). Universidad Central de Venezuela, Facultad de Humanidades y Educacion, Escuela de Artes, P.O. Box 47.687, 1041-A Caracas, Vezenuela. TEL 58-2-694926. FAX 58-2-6052862. (Subscr. to: P.O. Box 52055, 1050 Caracas, Venezuela) Ed. Catalina Gaspar. adv.: page $200. bk.rev.
     Description: Covers art, theatre, music, dance and literature.
     Refereed Serial

700 500   US   ISSN 0361-5634
AS36
ESSAYS IN ARTS AND SCIENCES. 1971. a. $10 (foreign $15) (effective 1997). University of New Haven, School of Arts and Sciences, West Haven, CT 06516. TEL 203-932-7371. FAX 203-932-1469. Ed. David E.E. Sloane. R&P contact: David E.E. Sloane. adv.; bk.rev.; circ. 300 (paid). **Indexed:** Abstr.Engl.Stud., M.L.A., Mid.East: Abstr.& Ind., MLA Intl.Bibl. **Document type:** academic/scholarly publication.
    —BLDSC (3811.675500); UnCover.
     Description: Features scholarly articles in the arts and sciences.
     Refereed Serial

800   FR   ISSN 0998-8041
L'ESTAMPILLE - L'OBJET D'ART; art antiquites et artisanat. 1969. m. (11/yr.) 420 F. (foreign 475 F.) (effective 1997). Editions Faton S.A., 25 rue Berbisey, 21000 Dijon, France. TEL 33-3-80404104. (Subscr. to: 1 rue des Artisans, B.P. 90, 21803 Quetigny Cedex, France. TEL 33-3-80489845. FAX 33-3-80489846) Ed. Louis Faton. adv.; bk.rev. circ. 50,000.
     Formed by the merger of: Estampille (ISSN 0184-7724) & Objet d'Art (ISSN 0988-8519)

701.17 111.85
801.93   XR   ISSN 0014-1291
BH6
ESTETIKA/AESTHETICS. (Text in Czech, English, German, Slovak; summaries in English, German) 1964. q. DM.92. Czech Academy of Sciences, Institute of the History of Art, Husova 4, 110 00 Prague, Czech Republic. TEL 420-2-2319352. FAX 420-2-24229436. (Dist. by: Kubon and Sagner, P.O. Box 340108, D-3000 Munich 34, Germany) Ed. Helena Lorenzova. bk.rev.; charts; illus.; tr.lit.; index. circ. 1,400. **Document type:** academic/scholarly publication.
    —CCC.
     Description: Contains studies and articles on general aesthetics and the theory and history of art.

709   MX   ISSN 0071-1659
ESTUDIOS DE ARTE Y ESTETICA. 1958. irreg., latest 1988. price varies. Universidad Nacional Autonoma de Mexico, Instituto de Investigaciones Esteticas, Circuito Mario de la Cueva, Zona Cultural, Ciudad Universitaria, 04510 Mexico, D.F., Mexico. TEL 52-5-6227545. FAX 52-5-6657440. E-mail: ereinoso@servidor.unam.mx.

709   MX   ISSN 0071-1748
ESTUDIOS Y FUENTES DEL ARTE EN MEXICO. 1955. irreg., latest 1989. price varies. Universidad Nacional Autonoma de Mexico, Instituto de Investigaciones Esteticas, Circuito Mario de la Cueva, Zona Cultural, Ciudad Universitaria, 04510 Mexico, D.F., Mexico. TEL 52-5-6227545. FAX 52-5-6657440. E-mail: ereinoso@servidor.unam.mx.

700 800   PO   ISSN 0870-8584
ESTUDOS ITALIANOS EM PORTUGAL. (Text in Italian, Portuguese) 1939. irreg., no. 32, 1969. Esc.150($5.50) (Istituto Italiano di Cultura in Portogallo) Papelaria Fernandes, Largo do Rato 13, Lisbon 2, Portugal. bk.rev.; bibl.; illus.; stat.; tr.lit.; cum.index. circ. 500. (tabloid format; also avail. in cards) **Indexed:** Amer.Hist.& Life (1982-), Hist.Abstr. (1982-).

700   CN   ISSN 0835-7641
ETC. MONTREAL. 1987. q. Can.$28 to individuals (foreign Can.$39); institutions Can.$48 (foreign Can.$39) (effective 1997). Revue d'Art Contemporain Etc Inc., 1435 De Bleury, Ste. 806, Montreal, PQ H3A 2H7, Canada. TEL 514-848-1125. FAX 514-848-0071. Ed. Isabelle Lelarge. adv.; bk.rev. circ. 2,500.
     Description: Deals with contemporary art and art criticism.

ETHNOARTS INDEX. see ART — Abstracting, Bibliographies, Statistics

709   BE   ISSN 0071-1969
ETUDES D'HISTOIRE DE L'ART. 1964. irreg., vol.7, 1993. price varies. (Institut Historique Belge de Rome - Belgische Historisch Instituut te Rome) N.V. Brepols, Steenweg op Tielen 68, 2300 Turnhout, Belgium. TEL 32-14-402500. FAX 32-14-428919. circ. controlled. (back issues avail.) **Document type:** monographic series.
     Description: Studies on art history, with emphasis on the relations between Belgian artists and Italy.

EUROPEAN AND AMERICAN PAINTING, SCULPTURE AND DECORATIVE ARTS, VOLUME 1: 1300-1800. see MUSEUMS AND ART GALLERIES

EUROPEAN CREATIVE HANDBOOK. see ARTS AND HANDICRAFTS

741.5   UK   ISSN 0378-9012
EUROPEAN ILLUSTRATION. (Text in English, French, German) 1975. a. £38. 80 Charlotte St., London W1A 1AQ, England. Ed. Edward Booth-Clibborn. illus. circ. 10,000.

EUROPEAN MEDIA ART FESTIVAL. see MOTION PICTURES

EUROPEAN PHOTOGRAPHY. see PHOTOGRAPHY

EUROPEAN STUDIES JOURNAL. see HISTORY — History Of Europe

EVALUATOR. see ANTIQUES

700 800   IT
EVENTI E INTERVENTI. irreg., latest no.8. price varies. Angelo Longo Editore, Via Paolo Costa 33, 48100 Ravenna, Italy. TEL 39-544-217026. FAX 39-544-217554. E-mail: longo-ra@linknet.it. Ed. Alfio Longo. circ. 1,500. **Document type:** academic/scholarly publication.

EXETER STUDIES IN AMERICAN & COMMONWEALTH ARTS. see LITERATURE

760   GW   ISSN 0172-2859
EXLIBRISKUNST UND GRAPHIK. JAHRBUCH. 1891. a. DM.120 to members; non-members DM.150 (effective 1996). Deutsche Exlibris-Gesellschaft e.V., Am Loewentor 46, 56075 Koblenz, Germany. TEL 49-261-57885. FAX 49-261-57885. Ed. Birgit Goebel. adv. **Document type:** bulletin.
     Formerly: Exlibriskunst und Graphik (ISSN 0075-2630)
     Refereed Serial

EXPLORING (SAN FRANCISCO). see SCIENCES: COMPREHENSIVE WORKS

700   US   ISSN 1063-1321
EXPOSE.* 1994. bi-m. $9.85 (foreign $29). 775 Pleasant St., Boulder, CO 80302-6925. TEL 303-939-9688; 800-638-3826. Dir. Brian Roberts. adv. contact: Linda Hull. (back issues avail.)

EXPRESSION; revue culturelle feminine internationale. see WOMEN'S INTERESTS

709.04   AT   ISSN 0818-8734
EYELINE. 1987. 3/yr. Aus.$20 to individuals; institutions Aus.$33 (effective 1997). Eyeline Publishing Ltd., c/o Academy of the Arts - Visual Arts, Park Rd., Kelvin Grove, Qld. 4059, Australia. TEL 61-7-38645521. FAX 61-7-38643974. Ed. Sarah Follent. R&P contact: Sarah Follent. TEL 61-7-38645520. adv.: B&W page Aus.$400, color page Aus.$1400; trim 248 x 288; adv. contact: Debra Beattie. bk.rev.; film rev.; circ. 2,000 (controlled). (back issues avail.)
     Description: Covers contemporary visual art, craft, design, visual culture. Includes artist monographs, specialist columns, and researched articles.

700 800 808.81   US   ISSN 0899-630X
F A R C E. 1988. irreg. $12 for 4 nos. (The Paper Plant) Fine Arts Research and Communications Enterprises, Box 543, Raleigh, NC 27602. TEL 919-834-9203. Ed. John Dancy-Jones. adv.; bk.rev.; index. circ. 1,000. (back issues avail.)
     Description: Forum for non-established artists and writers, local and non-local.

700 378   US   ISSN 1090-3372
F A T E IN REVIEW. 1975. a. $10 per no. Foundations in Art Theory and Education, Art Department FAA 216, Eastern Illinois Univ., Charleston, IL 61920. TEL 808-956-5250. FAX 808-956-9043. URL: http://www.louisville.edu/groups/finearts-www/FATE.html. Ed. Laura Ruby. R&P contact: Laura Ruby. bk.rev. circ. 700. **Document type:** academic/scholarly publication.
     Description: Contains articles on college level core courses in studio, art history and critical studies in visual art and design.
     Refereed Serial

700 055.1   IT   ISSN 0394-0462
N4
F M R (ENGLISH EDITION). French edition (ISSN 0394-0454) Italian edition (ISSN 0393-0033) (Editions in English, French, Italian, Spanish) 1982. bi-m. L.160000($90) in Europe; N. America $114; elsewhere $126. Franco Maria Ricci S.p.A., Via Montecuccoli, 32, 20147 Milan, Italy. TEL 39-2-48301-246. FAX 39-2-48301-473. (Subscr. to: Speedimpex-FMR, 35-02 48th Ave., Long Island City, NY 11101. TEL 718-392-0034. FAX 718-361-0815) Ed. Laura Casalis; Pub. Franco Maria Ricci. R&P contact: Massimo Navoni. adv. circ. 43,000. **Indexed:** Art Ind., Artbibl.Mod., DAAI. **Document type:** consumer publication.

FABERS HEFTE. see MUSIC

700   US
FACE; the face of the congress. 1992. q. $10 (effective Jan. 1993). Fa Ga Ga Ga, Box 1382, Youngstown, OH 44501. TEL 216-744-4116. Eds. Mark Corroto and Melinda Otto Corroto. bk.rev. circ. 175.

FAENZA; rivista di studi di storia e di tecnica dell'arte ceramica. see CERAMICS, GLASS AND POTTERY

FANTASIA. see LITERATURE — Science Fiction, Fantasy, Horror

700 800   US   ISSN 1075-5713
FARM. 1987. irreg., no.7, 1995. $13 (effective 1995). (Instituting Contemporary Idea) Feature, 76 Greene St., New York, NY 10012. TEL 212-941-7077. FAX 212-431-7187. circ. 750. **Document type:** academic/scholarly publication. **Description:** Focuses on contemporary art and fiction.

701.18   IT   ISSN 1121-0052
IL FAUNO; mensile indipendente di cultura. 1954. m. L.20000. Fauno Editore, Borgo Tegolaio 5, 50125 Florence, Italy. Ed. Giovanni Arcidiacono. circ. 3,000.

700 913   IT   ISSN 0391-7517
FELIX RAVENNA; RIVISTA DI ANTICHITA RAVENNATI, CRISTIANE E BIZANTINE. 1977. a., latest no.139-140, 1990. L.50000 (foreign L.55000). (Universita degli Studi di Bologna, Istituto di Antichita Ravennati e Bizantine) Edizioni del Girasole, s.r.l., Via P. Costa 10, 48100 Ravenna, Italy. TEL 39-544-212830. FAX 39-544-38432. E-mail: info@europart.it; URL: http://www.europart.it/girasole. (Co-sponsor: Fondazione Cassa di Risparmio, Ravenna) Ed. Raffaella Farioli Campanati. R&P contact: Ivan Simonini. bk.rev. circ. 500. **Indexed:** Avery Ind.Archit.Per., RILA. **Document type:** monographic series, academic/scholarly publication. **Description:** Covers ancient art and archaeology, and old Christian and Byzantine art from all over the world.

DAS FENSTER; Tiroler Kulturzeitschrift. see LITERATURE

700   FR   ISSN 0557-5737
FER DE LANCE; * rythmes et couleurs. 1955. q. 180 F.($48) Editions de la Diaspora Francaise, 5 rue La Bruyeere, 75009 Paris, France. Ed. Marie Noelle Collen. adv.; bk.rev. circ. 31,000.

745   US   ISSN 0164-324X
TT697
FIBERARTS. 1974. 5/yr. $22 (foreign $27). 50 College St., Asheville, NC 28801. TEL 704-253-0467. FAX 704-253-7952. E-mail: larkmail@larkbooks.com; URL: http://www.larkbooks.com. Ed. Ann Batchelder; Pub. Rob Pulleyn. R&P contact: Nancy Orban. adv. contact: Jacqueline Corbett. bk.rev.; illus. circ. 25,000. **Indexed:** Art & Archaeol.Tech.Abstr., Art Ind., DAAI, Ind.How To Do It (1990-), Text.Tech.Dig. **Document type:** trade publication.
—BLDSC (3914.690000); KR SourceOne; UnCover. **Formerly** (until 1975): Fibercraft Newsletter. **Description:** For enthusiasts of contemporary weaving, handmade clothing, crochet, needlework, quilting, dyeing, tapestry, and basketry. Covers profiles and interviews with individual artists, including photo portfolios of their work, techniques, and life-styles.

709   SW   ISSN 0071-481X
N25
FIGURA. NOVA SERIES; Uppsala studies in the history of art. (Subseries of: Acta Universitatis Upsaliensis) (Text in English or German) 1951-1959 (nos.1-12); N.S. 1959. irreg. price varies. (Uppsala Universitet, Institute of Art History) A W I International AB, Box 4627, S-116 91 Stockholm, Sweden. TEL 46-8-7282500. FAX 46-8-338707. Ed. Rudolf Zeitler. (back issues avail.) **Document type:** monographic series.
—KNAW.

FIKRUN WA FANN. see LITERARY AND POLITICAL REVIEWS

FILM AUSTRALIA EDUCATION CATALOGUE. see MOTION PICTURES

FILOZOFSKI FAKULTET - ZADAR. RAZDIO POVIJESNIH ZNANOSTI. RADOVI. see ARCHAEOLOGY

700   UK
FINE ART TRADE GUILD. DIRECTORY. 1910. a. Fine Art Trade Guild, 16-18 Empress Pl., London SW6 1TT, England. TEL 0171-381-6616. FAX 0171-381-2596. Ed. Vanessa Giles. adv. contact: Marilyn Driscoll. circ. 1,800 (controlled). **Document type:** trade publication. **Formerly** (until 1996): Picture and Prints Directory.

FIREWEED; a feminist quarterly of writing, politics, art & culture. see WOMEN'S INTERESTS

700   IT
FLASH ART CHINESE. (Text in Chinese) q. $25 (effective 1994-95). Giancarlo Politi Editore, Via Carlo Farini 68, 20159 Milan, Italy. TEL 39-2-6887341. FAX 39-2-66801290.

700   IT   ISSN 0394-1493
N1.A1
FLASH ART INTERNATIONAL. Italian edition: Flash Art Italia. (Text in English) 1980. 6/yr. $50 for 8 nos. (effective 1994-95). Giancarlo Politi Editore, Via Carlo Farini 68, 20159 Milan, Italy. TEL 39-2-6887341. FAX 39-2-66801290. (US subscr. to: c/o European Publishers, 799 Broadway, Rm. 226, New York, NY 10003) Eds. Giancarlo Politi, Helena Kontova. adv.: B&W page $3200, color page $4300; trim 7 1/16 x 9 5/8. bk.rev.; charts; illus. circ. 50,000. **Indexed:** Art Ind., DAAI.
—BLDSC (3950.021000); KR SourceOne; SWETS; UnCover. **Description:** Contains news of the contemporary art world.

700   IT
N1.A1
FLASH ART ITALIA. English edition: Flash Art International. 1967. 8/yr. $50 (effective 1994-95). Giancarlo Politi Editore, Via Carlo Farini 68, 20159 Milan, Italy. TEL 39-2-6887341. FAX 39-2-66801290. (U.S. subscr.: c/o European Publishers, 799 Broadway Rm. 226, New York, NY 10003) Eds. Giancarlo Politi, Helena Kontova. bk.rev.; charts; illus. circ. 40,000. **Indexed:** Artbibl., RILA. **Formed by the merger of** (1973-1979): Heute Kunst (ISSN 0391-6472); Flash Art (Edizione Italiana) (ISSN 0015-3524); Which was formerly (until 1967): Flash (ISSN 0394-1485) **Description:** Presents the full spectrum of international contemporary art, with a special focus on Italy. Includes design, fashion, literature and philosophy.

FLORIDA FOLKLIFE RESOURCE DIRECTORY. see FOLKLORE

700 790.1   CN
FOCUS ON FESTIVALS. 1980. 3/yr. Can.$20 membership (effective 1997). Associated Manitoba Arts Festivals, Inc., 424 - 100 Arthur St., Winnipeg, MB R3B 1H3, Canada. TEL 204-945-4578. FAX 204-948-2073. Ed. Karen Oliver; Pub. Karen Oliver. adv. contact: Karen Oliver. circ. 500. (back issues avail.) **Document type:** newsletter. **Description:** News about Manitoba's 38 local community arts festivals, the Manitoba Community Arts Development, and provincial festival events.

FOGLIO; Seiten der Sinne. see LITERARY AND POLITICAL REVIEWS

709   PL   ISSN 0071-6723
N6
FOLIA HISTORIAE ARTIUM. (Text in Polish; summaries in French) 1964. a. price varies. Polska Akademia Nauk, Oddzial w Krakowie, Komisja Teorii i Historii Sztuki, Ul. Slawkowska 17, 31-016 Krakow, Poland. TEL 48-12-224853. FAX 48-12-222791. Ed. L. Kalinowski. **Indexed:** Amer.Hist.& Life (1990-), Artbibl.Mod., Artbibl., Avery Ind.Archit.Per., Hist.Abstr. (1990-), IBR, RILA. **Document type:** academic/scholarly publication.
—KNAW. **Description:** Papers concerning European and occasionally Eastern art from early Christianity to modern times.

ART 441

745 069   US   ISSN 1067-3067
NK805
FOLK ART. 1971. q. membership. Museum of American Folk Art, 61 W. 62nd St., New York, NY 10023. TEL 212-977-7170. FAX 212-977-8134. Ed. Rosemary Gabriel. adv.; bk.rev.; illus. circ. 10,000. **Indexed:** Art Ind., Artbibl.Mod., Artbibl., RILA. **Document type:** bulletin.
—BLDSC (3974.571210); KR SourceOne; UnCover. **Formerly** (until 1992): Clarion.

700 709   US   ISSN 0738-8357
FOLK ART FINDER. 1980. q. $14 (Canada $18; elsewhere $24). (Folk Art Finder) Gallery Press, One River Rd., Essex, CT 06426. TEL 860-767-0313. Ed. Florence Laffal. adv.; bk.rev.; illus.; index. (back issues avail.) **Document type:** newsletter. **Description:** Features articles on folk artists, reader exchange, topical news, exhibition calendar, commentary, new finds and new directions in folk and outsider art.

745   US   ISSN 1043-5026
FOLK ART MESSENGER. 1987. q. $25 (foreign $35). Folk Art Society of America, Box 17041, Richmond, VA 23226. TEL 804-285-4532. FAX 804-285-4532. E-mail: fasa@folkart.org; URL: http://www.folkart.org. Ed. Ann Oppenhimer; Pub. Ann Oppenheimer. R&P contact: Ann Oppenhimer. bk.rev.; illus.; cum.index: 1987-1994; circ. 1,000 (paid). (back issues avail.) **Document type:** academic/scholarly publication, newsletter. **Description:** Promotes the discovery, study and documentation of folk and self-taught art, folk artists and folk art environments, with an emphasis on the contemporary. *Refereed Serial*

709 900   IT
FONTI E STUDI PER LA STORIA DI BOLOGNA E DELLE PROVINCE EMILIANE E ROMAGNOLE. 1969. irreg., vol.7, 1981. price varies. Alfa Edizioni, Via Santo Stefano 13, I-40125 Bologna, Italy. circ. 4,000.

700   US   ISSN 0890-2992
FOR YOUR INFORMATION (NEW YORK); practical information for those who create and work in the arts. Short title: F Y I. 1985. q. $15 contribution; libraries $50 (effective 1994). New York Foundation for the Arts, 155 Ave. of the Americas, New York, NY 10013. TEL 212-366-6900. FAX 212-366-1778. URL: http://www.artswire.org/artswire/www/nyfa.html. Ed. Joseph Hannan. R&P contact: Joseph Hannan. adv. contact: Shu-Mei Chan. bk.rev. circ. 28,000. (back issues avail.) **Document type:** newsletter. **Description:** Condensed information on issues, events, and opportunities for artists and arts workers. Includes funding deadlines and information on residencies. *Refereed Serial*

FORM FUNCTION FINLAND. see ARCHITECTURE

760 655   GW   ISSN 0015-7759
FORMAT;* Zeitschrift fuer verbale und visuelle Kommunikation. 1964. bi-m. DM.92. Verlag Dieter Gitzel, Friedhofstr. 29, Postfach 27, 6729 Rheinzabern, Germany. Ed. D. Gitzel. adv.; bk.rev.; charts; illus.; tr.lit. circ. 4,000.

709 913   GW   ISSN 0532-2189
N3
FORSCHUNGEN ZUR KUNSTGESCHICHTE UND CHRISTLICHEN ARCHAEOLOGIE. irreg., vol.18, 1997. price varies. Franz Steiner Verlag Wiesbaden GmbH, Birkenwaldstr. 44, 70191 Stuttgart, Germany. TEL 49-711-2582-0. FAX 49-711-2582390. (Subscr. to: Postfach 101061, 70009 Stuttgart, Germany) Eds. Richard Hamann-MacLean, Otto Feld. R&P contact: Sabine Koerner. **Indexed:** Avery Ind.Archit.Per. **Document type:** monographic series.

FOTOGRAF. see PHOTOGRAPHY

700   SA
FOUNDATION FOR THE CREATIVE ARTS. ANNUAL REPORT/STIGTING VIR DIE SKEPPENDE KUNSTE. JAARVERSLAG. 1994. a. Foundation for the Creative Arts, P.O. Box 91122, Auckland Park 2006, South Africa. illus. **Document type:** corporate report.

FRANK; an international journal of contemporary writing and art. see LITERARY AND POLITICAL REVIEWS

FRANKLIN MINT ALMANAC. see NUMISMATICS

ART

760 US
FREELANCER'S NEWS. 1989. 8/yr. $25. Creative Independent Communications, Inc., Box 437, Murray Hill Sta., New York, NY 10156-0437. TEL 212-686-3514. Ed. Barbara Gordon.
Description: Discusses marketing and selling, trade practices, case histories in the freelance graphic arts field.

700 US ISSN 0071-9382
FREER GALLERY OF ART, WASHINGTON, D.C. OCCASIONAL PAPERS. 1947. irreg. vol.4, 1971. Freer Gallery of Art, Smithsonian Institution, Jefferson Dr., S.W. at 12th St., Washington, DC 20560. TEL 202-357-1432.

700 US
FRIENDS OF FRENCH ART; art de vivre into art conservation. 1979. a. $40 donation. Villa Narcissa, 100 Vanderlip Dr., Rancho Palos Verdes, CA 90275. TEL 310-377-4444. FAX 310-377-4584. Ed. Elin Vanderlip. circ. 10,000.
Description: Covers annual trip to France to raise money for art conservation and restoration, and exchange of art conservation students to museums.

700 UK ISSN 0962-0672
FRIEZE; contemporary art and culture. 1991. bi-m. £25.50 to individuals (foreign £29($44)); institutions £30 (foreign £33($50)) (effective 1997); newsstand price: £3.95 ($6). Durian Publications, 21 Denmark St., London WC2H 8NA, England. TEL 44-171-379-1533. FAX 44-171-379-1521. E-mail: editors@frieze.demon.co.uk. Ed. Matthew Slotover. R&P contact: Matthew Slotover. adv.: page $2,400; trim 300 x 230; adv. contact: Michael Benevento. (back issues avail.) **Document type:** consumer publication.
—BLDSC (4039.170000).
Description: Covers international contemporary art and the culture it reflects.

FRITID & KULTUR I SVERIGE. see *LEISURE AND RECREATION*

FUCK. see *LITERARY AND POLITICAL REVIEWS*

FUEHRER ZU ARCHAEOLOGISCHEN DENKMAELERN IN DEUTSCHLAND. see *ARCHAEOLOGY*

FUNDE UND AUSGRABUNGEN IM BEZIRK TRIER. see *ARCHAEOLOGY*

FUOCO; rassegna di cultura e d'arte. see *LITERARY AND POLITICAL REVIEWS*

FYNSKE MINDER. see *HISTORY — History Of Europe*

G L B. (Gymnasiets Laerere i Billedkunst) see *EDUCATION*

741.5 808.87 US
GAG RECAP. 1954. m. $50 (foreign $60). Gag Recap Publishers, 12 Hedden Pl., New Providence, NJ 07974-1724. TEL 908-464-1158. Ed. Al Gottlieb. (back issues avail.) **Document type:** newsletter, trade publication.
Description: Market information for cartoonists and gagwriters.

759.2 UK ISSN 1351-2021
GAINSBOROUGH'S HOUSE REVIEW. 1989. a. £5.95($10) to individuals; libraries £8.95($15) (effective 1997). Gainsborough's House Society, 46 Gainsborough St., Sudbury, Suffolk CO10 6EU, England. TEL 44-1787-372958. FAX 44-1787-376991. Ed. Hugh Belsey. R&P contact: Hugh Belsey. adv. contact: Jennifer Prowse. illus. circ. 700. (back issues avail.) **Document type:** academic/scholarly publication.
Formerly (until 1992): Gainsborough's House Society Annual Report (ISSN 0960-8176)
Description: Includes articles on aspects of the life and work of Thomas Gainsborough and related subjects.

700 001.3 NE
GALATEA. 1996. q. Vrije Universiteit Amsterdam, Word & Image Studies, E-mail: galatea@let.vu.nl; URL: http://www.let.vu.nl/e-zine/galatea.
●Available only online.
Description: Interdisciplinary contributions on culture, literature and the arts.

700 CN ISSN 0838-1658
GALLERIE: WOMEN ARTISTS MONOGRAPHS. 1988. irreg. Gallerie Publications, 2901 Panorama Dr., North Vancouver, BC V7G 2A4, Canada. TEL 604-929-8706. Ed. Caffyn Kelley. adv.; bk.rev. circ. 2,500. **Indexed:** Can.Wom.Per.Ind. **Document type:** monographic series.
Formerly (until Sep. 1990): Gallerie: Women's Art.
Description: Women artists from across North America discuss their art and concerns in a series of books.

THE GARRETT COUNTY JOURNAL. see *LITERATURE*

EL GATO TUERTO/ONE-EYED CAT; gaceta de arte, literatura, etcetera, etcetera. see *LITERATURE*

701.18 FR ISSN 1169-2294
GAZETTE DE L'HOTEL DROUOT; l'hebdomadaire des ventes publiques. 1891. w. 550 F. (foreign 780 F.). 10 rue du Faubourg Montmartre, 75009 Paris, France. TEL 47-70-93-00. FAX 47-70-93-94. Ed. Jacques Boussac. adv. circ. 78,000.
Formerly (until 1891): Hotel Drouot (ISSN 1169-2286)
Description: Includes news of art, antiques, auctions.

700 FR ISSN 0016-5530
N2
GAZETTE DES BEAUX ARTS. (Text in English, French) 1859. 10/yr. 1400 F. (effective 1996). B.P. 87, 05003 Gap Cedex, France. TEL 45-61-61-70. FAX 45-61-61-71. TELEX 644 646. Ed. Francois Souchal. bk.rev.; illus.; index. circ. 1,650. (also avail. in microfilm from PMC; reprint service avail. from KTO) **Indexed:** Art Ind., Artbibl.Mod., Arts & Hum.Cit.Ind., Avery Ind.Archit.Per., Curr.Cont., IBR, RILA. **Document type:** academic/scholarly publication.
—BLDSC (4093.250000); KR SourceOne; SWETS; UnCover.
Description: Scholarly journal with research articles on topics through the early 20th century.

701.18 JA ISSN 0435-1657
GEIJUTSU SHINCHO. 1950. m. Shincho-Sha, 71 Yaraicho, Shinjuku-ku, Tokyo 162, Japan. TEL 03-3266-5381. FAX 03-3266-5387. TELEX 27433. Ed. Midori Yamakawa. adv. circ. 150,000.
Description: Covers fine arts, music, architecture, drama and design.

GENAVA; revue d'archeologie et d'histoire de l'art. see *ARCHAEOLOGY*

GENERATOR. see *LITERATURE — Poetry*

700 720 BE ISSN 0772-7151
N9
GENTSE BIJDRAGEN TOT DE KUNSTGESCHIEDENIS EN OUDHEIDKUNDE. (Text and summaries in Dutch, English, French, German) 1934. irreg., vol.30, 1992. 1500 BEF. (Rijksuniversiteit te Gent, Sectie Kunstgeschiedenis en Oudheidkunde) Editions Peeters s.p.r.l., Bondgenotenlaan 153, 3000 Leuven, Belgium. TEL 32-16-235170. FAX 32-16-228500. URL: http://www.peeters-leuven.be. Ed. J. Vander Auwera. illus. circ. 120. (back issues avail.) **Document type:** academic/scholarly publication.

700 US ISSN 0147-1902
N514.A8
GEORGIA MUSEUM OF ART. BULLETIN. (Text mainly in English) 1974. a. $10. Georgia Museum of Art, University of Georgia, Athens, GA 30602. TEL 706-542-4662. E-mail: jdeprima@uga.cc.uga.edu. Ed. William Eiland. R&P contact: Annelies Mondi. circ. 1,000. (back issues avail.) **Indexed:** Artbibl.Mod., RILA. **Document type:** bulletin.
Description: Contains an annual report and scholarly articles dealing with works from the museum's collections.

709 940 US ISSN 0016-920X
N6280
GESTA. 1963. s-a. $35 to individuals (foreign $40); institutions $50; students $15 (effective 1998). International Center of Medieval Art, The Cloisters, Fort Tryon Park, New York, NY 10040. TEL 212-928-1146. FAX 212-928-1146. E-mail: 73430.2037@compuserve.com; URL: http://www.medievalart.org. Ed. Dale Kinney. R&P contact: Nancy Wu. adv. contact: Dale Kinney. bibl.; charts; illus.; cum.index. circ. 975. **Indexed:** Art Ind., Arts & Hum.Cit.Ind., ASCA, Avery Ind.Archit.Per., Br.Archaeol.Abstr., Curr.Cont., IBR, RILA. **Document type:** academic/scholarly publication.
—BLDSC (4163.300000); Genuine Article; KR SourceOne; SWETS; UnCover.

751.6 US ISSN 0898-4808
N8554
GETTY CONSERVATION INSTITUTE NEWSLETTER. 1986. 3/yr. free. Getty Conservation Institute, 1200 Getty Center Dr., Ste. 700, Los Angeles, CA 90049-1657. TEL 310-440-7325. FAX 310-440-7702. Ed. Jeffrey Levin. illus.; tr.lit. circ. 8,000. (back issues avail.) **Document type:** newsletter.
Description: Covers the institute's activities in the conservation of objects and collections, sites and monuments, and historic structures and cities. Includes scientific research, conservation education, information documentation and public awareness programs.

700 GW ISSN 0342-104X
GIESSENER BEITRAEGE ZUR KUNSTGESCHICHTE. 1970. irreg., vol.9, 1994. DM.45. Wilhelm Schmitz Verlag, Staufenbergerweg 22, 35457 Lollar, Germany. TEL 49-6406-2324. **Document type:** monographic series.

790.132 CN
GIFT AND COLLECTIBLES RETAILER. 1982. 6/yr. Can.$14.95 (effective 1997). Trajan Publishing Corp., 103 Lakeshore Rd., Ste. 202, St. Catharines, ON L2N 2T6, Canada. TEL 905-646-7744. FAX 905-646-0995. Ed. Bret Evans; Pub. Paul Fiocca. adv.: B&W page Can.$1095; trim 8 1/8 x 10 3/4; adv. contact: Cyndi Hood. **Document type:** trade publication.
Formerly: Canadian Collectibles Retailer (ISSN 1196-4820); Supersedes in part (in 1993): Insight on Collectables (ISSN 0836-5873); Which was formerly (until 1987): Insight (ISSN 0833-4447); (until 1986): Insight on Collectables (ISSN 0714-8992).

700 IQ
GILAGAMESH; journal of modern Iraqi arts. (Text in English) 1986. q. ID.5($20) Dar Al-Ma'mum for Translation & Publishing, P.O. Box 8018, Baghdad, Iraq. TEL 9641-5383171. TELEX 212984 MAMUN IK. Ed. Naji al-Hadithi. adv.; bk.rev. circ. 15,000.

THE GILCREASE JOURNAL. see *HISTORY — History Of North And South America*

700 IT ISSN 0394-0543
N6911
IL GIORNALE DELL'ARTE; mensile di informazione, cultura, economia. 1983. m. L.90000 (foreign L.100000). Umberto Allemandi & C. Societa Editrice, Via Mancini, 8, C.P. 1394, 10131 Turin, Italy. TEL 39-11-8199111. FAX 39-11-8193090. Ed. Gianna Marini. R&P contact: Luigi Giannuzzi. adv. contact: Patrizia Sbodiu. bk.rev.; illus. circ. 23,500. **Document type:** consumer publication.
Description: Provides comprehensive coverage of the art world, including news of exhibitions, books, restoration, archaeology, galleries, the marketplace, and auction results.

GIUSTIZIA NUOVA. see *LAW*

700 666.1 US ISSN 0278-9426
NK5112
GLASS ART SOCIETY JOURNAL. 1981. a. $40 to individuals in N. America; elsewhere $50 (effective 1997). Glass Art Society, 1305 Fourth Ave., Ste. 711, Seattle, WA 98101-2401. TEL 206-382-1305. FAX 206-382-2630. Ed. Tina Oldknow. adv. contact: Meredith Chernick. charts; illus.; tr.lit. circ. 1,500. (back issues avail.) **Indexed:** DAAI. **Document type:** academic/scholarly publication.

GLASS CHERRY; a poetry magazine. see *LITERATURE — Poetry*

GLENDORA REVIEW; african quarterly on the arts. see *LITERATURE*

700 US ISSN 1082-8338
GLOBAL MAIL; * the hole to the underground. 1992. 3/yr. $9 (foreign $12) (effective through 1996); newsstand price: $3. Soapbox June, Box 410837, San Francisco, CA 94141-0837. E-mail: soapbox@well.sf.ca.us. Ed. Ashley Parker Owens. circ. 5,000. (also avail. in diskette format; back issues avail.) **Document type:** consumer publication, directory.
●Also available online.
Description: Provides more than 700 listings of cultural projects from over 40 nations for artists, activists, writers, and publishers.

700 AT ISSN 1324-8030
▼**GLOBE E JOURNAL OF CONTEMPORARY ART.** 1995. 3/yr. Monash University, Visual Arts Department, Wellington Rd., Clayton, Vic. 3168, Australia. TEL 61-3-99054222. FAX 61-3-99054209. E-mail: globe@arts.monash.edu.au; URL: http://www.arts.monash.edu.au/visarts/globe/ghome.html. (Co-sponsor: Vicarts, Gordon Darling Foundation, Australian Council) Ed. Robert Schubert. **Document type:** academic/scholarly publication.
●Available only online.
Description: Covers contemporary visual culture from an Australian perspective.

GLOSSOLALIA. see *LITERATURE*

GNOME BAKER. see *LITERATURE*

651.6 SW ISSN 0284-6578
GOETEBORG STUDIES IN CONSERVATION. (Subseries of Acta Universitatis Gothoburgensis) 1988. irreg., no.3, 1996. price varies; also exchange basis. Acta Universitatis Gothoburgensis, P.O. Box 5096, S-402 22 Goeteborg, Sweden. TEL 46-31-7731733. FAX 46-31-163797. Ed. Jan Rosvall. **Document type:** monographic series.
—BLDSC (4201.960000).

700 US ISSN 0160-6298
NE85
GORDON'S PRINT PRICE ANNUAL (YEAR).* 1978. a. (plus 1 update). $225 (with update $299) (cum. CD-ROM $595) (effective 1996). Gordon's Art Reference, Inc., 306 W. Coronado Rd., Phoenix, AZ 85003-1147. TEL 941-434-6842. FAX 941-434-6969.
●Also available on CD-ROM.
Description: Lists over 35,000 prints sold during the past year in the world's major auctions and galleries.

709 720 SW ISSN 0348-4114
GOTHENBURG STUDIES IN ART AND ARCHITECTURE. (Subseries of Acta Universitatis Gothoburgensis) 1978. irreg., no.3, 1985. price varies; also exchange basis. Acta Universitatis Gothoburgensis, P.O. Box 5096, S-402 22 Goeteborg, Sweden. TEL 46-31-7731733. FAX 46-31-163797. Ed. Maj-Brit Wadell. **Document type:** monographic series.

700 SP ISSN 0017-2715
N7
GOYA; revista de arte. 1954. bi-m. $70 (effective Jan. 1996). Fundacion Lazaro Galdiano, Serrano 122, Madrid, Spain. TEL 34-1-5635535. FAX 34-1-5617793. Dir. Araceli Pereda Alonso. adv.; bk.rev.; illus. circ. 2,000. **Indexed:** Amer.Hist.& Life, Art Ind., Artbibl., Artbibl.Mod., Arts & Hum.Cit.Ind., ASCA, Avery Ind.Archit.Per., Curr.Cont., Hist.Abstr., IBR, RILA, SSCI. **Document type:** academic/scholarly publication.
—BLDSC (4206.100000); CINDOC; Genuine Article; KR SourceOne; SWETS.

GRAMMATEION; the St. Michael's Journal of the Arts. see *LITERARY AND POLITICAL REVIEWS*

GRAND STREET. see *LITERATURE*

760 US
GRAPHIC ARTISTS GUILD. DIRECTORY OF ILLUSTRATIONS. a. (Graphic Artists Guild) Serbin Communications, Inc., 511 Olive St., Santa Barbara, CA 93101. TEL 805-963-0439. (Alt. addr.: Graphic Artists Guild, 11 W. 20th St., 8th Fl., New York, NY 10011-3704. TEL 212-463-7730. FAX 212-463-8779) **Document type:** trade publication.

700 CN
GRAPHIC EXCHANGE. 1991. 6/yr. Can.$29. Brill Communications, 348 Danforth Ave., Box 65090, Toronto, Ont. M4K 3Z2, Canada. TEL 416-961-1325. FAX 416-961-0941. E-mail: gxo@tube.com. Ed. Dan Brill; Pub. Dan Brill. adv.: color page Can.$3600; trim 8 1/4 x 10 3/4. circ. 11,143.

700 US
GRAPHIC WORK OF BIRGER SANDZEN. 1952. irreg., 3rd ed., 1983. $4. Birger Sandzen Memorial Foundation, Box 348, Lindsborg, KS 67456-0348. TEL 913-227-2220. FAX 913-227-4170. Ed. Charles P. Greenough, 3rd. adv. contact: Larry Griffis. bk.rev.; circ. 2,000 (paid). **Document type:** catalog.
Description: A catalog of the prints produced by Birger Sandzen by year, title, size, and number of editions.

760 UK ISSN 1350-0937
NC997.A1
GRAPHICS INTERNATIONAL; the magazine for the creative graphic design business. Variant title: Graphics. 1988. 10/yr. £32.50($52.50) (effective 1997); newsstand price: £2.50. Creative Magazines Ltd., 35 Britannia Row, London N1 8QH, England. TEL 44-171-226-1739. FAX 44-171-226-1540. E-mail: 71333.3134@compuserve.com. Ed. Penelope Foulkes; Pub. Robert T. Prior. adv.: page £945; trim 380 x 275; adv. contact: Lawrence McAlister. bk.rev.; software rev.; illus. circ. 8,000. (back issues avail.) **Indexed:** Br.Ceram.Abstr., DAAI. **Document type:** trade publication.
Formerly (until Aug. 1992): Hot Graphics (ISSN 0962-7308)
Description: Presents innovative corporate identity, packaging, graphic design, illustration, and computer graphics work from the international circuit.

760 UK ISSN 0142-8853
GRAPHICS WORLD. 1977. bi-m. £28.50 (Europe 47.25; elsewhere £52.50). Datateam Publishing Ltd., Attn: Rob Foreman, Fairmeadow, Maidstone, Kent ME14 IN9, England. TEL 01622-687031. FAX 01622-757646. Ed. Charles Walker; Pub. Nick Carpenter. adv. contact: Barry Morgan. circ. 7,000. **Indexed:** Abstr.Bull.Inst.Pap.Chem., Artbibl.Mod., BMT, DAAI, Fluidex, Graph.Arts Lit.Abstr., Print.Abstr., WPM. **Document type:** trade publication.
—SWETS.

760 659.1 SZ ISSN 0017-3452
N8 CODEN: GRPHAB
GRAPHIS; international journal of visual communication. (Text in English, French and German) 1944. bi-m. 156 SFr.($108) B. Martin Pedersen Graphis Press Corp, Dufourstr. 107, CH-8008 Zurich, Switzerland. TEL 212-532-9387. FAX 212-213-3229. (U.S. address: Graphis US Inc., 141 Lexington Ave., New York, NY 10016) Ed. B. Martin Pedersen. adv.; bk.rev.; illus.; stat.; index. cum.index: 1944-1953. circ. 20,000. **Indexed:** Art Ind., Artbibl.Mod., Arts & Hum.Cit.Ind., ASCA, Child.Lit.Abstr., Curr.Cont., DAAI, Film Lit.Ind. (1973-).
—BLDSC (4212.527000); CASDDS; KR SourceOne; SWETS; UnCover.
Description: Information about design, graphics and illustration.

700 SZ
GRAPHIS ANNUAL REPORTS. 1991. a. $75. B. Martin Pedersen Graphis Press Corp., Dufourstr. 107, CH-8008 Zurich, Switzerland. (Dist. in the U.S. by: Watson-Guptill Publications, 1695 Oak St., Lakewood, NJ 08701. TEL 800-451-1741. FAX 908-363-0338) Ed. B. Martin Pedersen. illus. **Document type:** trade publication.
Description: Reviews how successful corporate publications were designed.

700 SZ
GRAPHIS CORPORATE IDENTITY. 1993. a. $75. B. Martin Pedersen Graphis Press Corp., Dufourstr. 107, CH-8008 Zurich, Switzerland. (Dist. in the U.S. by: Watson-Guptill Publications, 1695 Oak St., Lakewood, NJ 08701. TEL 800-451-1741. FAX 908-363-0338) Ed. B. Martin Pedersen. illus. **Document type:** trade publication.
Description: Takes an in-depth look at the corporate-identity programs of 50 design firms from around the world.

659.1 760 SZ ISSN 1012-9340
GRAPHIS DESIGN; international annual of design and illustration. (Text in English, French, German) 1952. a. $69. B. Martin Pedersen Graphis Press Corp., Dufourstr. 107, CH-8008 Zurich, Switzerland. (Dist. in the U.S. by: Watson-Guptill Publications, 1695 Oak St., Lakewood, NJ 08701. TEL 800-451-1741. FAX 908-363-0338) Ed. B. Martin Pedersen. index. circ. 16,000. **Document type:** trade publication.
—BLDSC (4212.528250).
Formerly: Graphis Annual (ISSN 0072-5528)
Description: Presents more than 800 examples of excellence in illustrative and photographic visual communication from around the world.

700 686.2 SZ
GRAPHIS LETTERHEAD. 1993. a. $69. B. Martin Pedersen Graphis Press Corp., Dufourstr. 107, CH-8008 Zurich, Switzerland. (Dist. in the U.S. by: Watson-Guptill Publications, 1695 Oak St., Lakewood, NJ 08701. TEL 800-451-1741. FAX 908-363-0338) Ed. B. Martin Pedersen. illus.; index. **Document type:** trade publication.
Description: Reproduces the best stationery designs created during the previous two years from around the world. Presents ideas to guide graphic design professionals in this area of corporate identity.

700 686.2 SZ
GRAPHIS LOGO. 1993. a. $60. B. Martin Pedersen Graphis Press Corp., Dufourstr. 107, CH-8008 Zurich, Switzerland. (Dist. in the U.S. by: Watson-Guptill Publications, 1695 Oak St., Lakewood, NJ 08701. TEL 800-451-1741. FAX 908-363-0338) Ed. B. Martin Pedersen. illus.; index. **Document type:** trade publication.
Description: Features more than 300 innovative, top-quality corporate logos and brand trademarks from around the world. Presents ideas for running a successful corporate identity program.

769.5 SZ ISSN 1021-2892
GRAPHIS POSTERS; international annual of poster art. (Text in English, French and German) 1973. a. 123 Fr.($69) B. Martin Pedersen Graphis Press Corp, Dufourstr. 107, CH-8008 Zurich, Switzerland. (Dist. in the U.S. by: Watson-Guptill Publications, 1695 Oak St., Lakewood, NJ 08701. TEL 800-451-1741. FAX 908-363-0338) Ed. B. Martin Pedersen. illus. circ. 8,500. **Document type:** trade publication.
—BLDSC (4212.529500).

760 746.92 SZ
GRAPHIS T - SHIRT DESIGN. 1994. a. $75. B. Martin Pedersen Graphis Press Corp., Dufourstr. 107, CH-8008 Zurich, Switzerland. (Dist. in the U.S. by: Watson-Guptill Publications, 1695 Oak St., Lakewood, NJ 08701. TEL 800-451-1741. FAX 908-363-0338) Ed. B. Martin Pedersen. illus. **Document type:** trade publication.
Description: Presents innovative T-shirt designs in creative fashion photographs.

700 GW ISSN 0342-3158
GRAPHISCHE KUNST; Zeitschrift fuer Graphikfreunde. (Each no. issued in 4 sections) 1973. s-a. DM,50. Edition Curt Visel, Weberstr. 36, 87700 Memmingen, Germany. TEL 49-8331-2853. FAX 49-8331-490364. Ed. Curt Visel. bk.rev.; illus. circ. 1,000. (also avail. in microfilm from BHP) **Indexed:** Artbibl.Mod., IBR. **Document type:** consumer publication.
—SWETS.
Description: Covers graphics and book illustration of this century.

700 SP ISSN 0210-1254
GUADALIMAR; revista de las artes. 1975. bi-m. 5400 ptas. (Europe 7000 ptas.; elsewhere 15000 ptas.) Miguel Fernandez-Braso, Ed. & Pub., Villanueva 22, 28001 Madrid, Spain. TEL 91-275-04-27.
—CINDOC.
Description: Covers artistic creation in the plastic arts.

700 CC ISSN 1003-3343
GUANG YU YING/LIGHT AND SHADOW. (Text in Chinese) 1981. q. Jiangsu Renmin Chubanshe, Qikan Bu - Jiangsu People's Publishing House, 165 Zhongyang Lu, Nanjing, Jiangsu 210009, People's Republic of China. TEL 634748. Ed. Xiao Zhuang.

444 ART

700 IT
GUIDA ALLE ACCADEMIE DI BELLE ARTI IN ITALIA. 1992? biennial. Giancarlo Politi Editore, Via Carlo Farini 68, 20159 Milan, Italy. TEL 39-2-6887341. FAX 39-2-68801290.

700 FR ISSN 0533-5167
GUIDE EMER. (Text in Dutch, English, French, German, Italian, Spanish) 1947. biennial. 330 F. Editions Emer, 47 rue des Tournelles, 75003 Paris, France. TEL 42-47-17-15. FAX 42-74-07-99. Ed. Virginie Mantoine; Pub. Louis Giscard d'Estaing. adv.; circ. 10,000 (paid). **Document type:** directory.
  Formerly: Guide Europeen de l'Amateur d'Art, de l'Antiquaire et du Bibliophile (ISSN 0066-3069)

700 FR
GUIDE INTERNATIONAL DES EXPERTS & SPECIALISTES; guide juridique de l'art - liste des catalogues raisonnes. a. Editions des Catalogues Raisonnes, 18 rue Godefroy Cavaignac, 75011 Paris, France. TEL 1-43-56-29-50. FAX 1-43-56-29-27. Ed. Armand Israel.

700 350.6 US
GUIDE TO ARTS ADMINISTRATION TRAINING RESEARCH (YEARS). 1975. biennial. price varies. Americans for the Arts, 927 15 St., N.W., Washington, DC 20005. TEL 202-371-2830. FAX 202-371-0424. Ed. E. Arthur Prieve. circ. 1,500. **Document type:** consumer publication.
  Formerly: Survey of Arts Administration Training.

GUIDE TO LITERARY AGENTS. see *PUBLISHING AND BOOK TRADE*

700 NX398 US ISSN 0360-3407
GUIDE TO NATIONAL ENDOWMENT FOR THE ARTS. Cover title: National Endowment for the Arts. A New Look. 1972. a. free. U.S. National Endowment for the Arts, Public Information Office, 1100 Pennsylvania Ave., N.W., Washington, DC 20506. TEL 202-682-5400. URL: http://www.arts.endow. gov. circ. 20,000. **Document type:** government publication.
  Formerly: National Endowment for the Arts. Guide to Programs (ISSN 0547-6658)

760 US
GUILD NEWS. q. $15 (effective 1995). Graphic Artists Guild, 11 W. 20th St., 8th Fl., New York, NY 10011-3704. TEL 212-463-7730. FAX 212-463-8779. E-mail: paulatgag@aol.com; URL: http://www.gag.org/. Ed. Paul Basista. adv. contact: Carla Strickland. bk.rev.; circ. 5,000 (controlled). (tabloid format) **Document type:** newspaper.
  Description: Covers legal and industry issues in visual communications.
  Refereed Serial

THE GUILD: THE ARCHITECT'S SOURCE OF ARTISTS AND ARTISANS. see *ARCHITECTURE*

THE GUILD: THE DESIGNER'S REFERENCE BOOK OF ARTISTS. see *INTERIOR DESIGN AND DECORATION*

790 US
GUILDNOTES. q. $60. National Guild of Community Schools of the Arts, Box 8018, Englewood, NJ 07631-8018. TEL 201-871-3337. Ed. Lolita Mayadas. **Document type:** newsletter.
  Description: Information about issues, programs and funding related to community arts schools.

GUNMA UNIVERSITY, FACULTY OF EDUCATION. ANNUAL REPORT: ART, TECHNOLOGY, HEALTH & PHYSICAL EDUCATION, AND SCIENCE OF HUMAN LIVING SERIES. see *EDUCATION — Higher Education*

700 CC ISSN 1005-6912
GUOHUA JIA. (Text in Chinese) q. $28.30. Tianjin Renmin Meishu Chubanshe - Tianjin People's Fine Art Publishing House, 150 Machang Dao, Heping Qu, Tianjin 300050, People's Republic of China. TEL 86-2-328-0984. FAX 86-2-3313358. (Dist. overseas by: China International Book Trading Corp., P.O. Box 399, Beijing 100044, P.R. China) Ed. Du Ziling.
  Formerly: Yingchun Hua.
  Description: Covers traditional Chinese painting.

700 792 780 720 GW ISSN 0947-3882
H D K MAGAZIN. 1975. s-a. free. Hochschule der Kuenste Berlin, Presse- und Informationsstelle, Ernst-Reuter-Platz 10, 10587 Berlin, Germany. TEL 49-30-31852450. FAX 49-30-3185-2635. URL: http://www.hdk-berlin.de. Ed. Verena Tafel. bk.rev. circ. 4,800. (back issues avail.) **Document type:** academic/scholarly publication.
  Formerly: H D K Info.

745.5 GW
H K H PERSPEKTIVEN. (Holz und Kunststoffverarbeitende Handwerk) 1973. m. Fachverband Holz und Kunststoff Nordrhein-Westfalen, Kreuzstr. 108-110, 44137 Dortmund, Germany. TEL 0231-9120100. FAX 0231-91201010. Ed. Ralf Bickert. adv.
  Formerly: Info Holz und Kunststoff.

741.6 GW
H S AKTUELL. 1985. bi-m. Heinrich Schmid GmbH und Co., Lederstr. 33, 72764 Reutlingen, Germany. TEL 07121-326111. FAX 07121-326165. bk.rev.; illus. circ. 4,000. (back issues avail.) **Document type:** consumer publication.

741.5 US
H U P. 1985. biennial. $6. Last Gasp of San Francisco, 777 Florida St., San Francisco, CA 94110. TEL 415-824-6636. FAX 415-824-1836. Ed. R. Crumb. circ. 25,000. (back issues avail.)
  Description: Contains cartoon art for adults.

745.5 DK ISSN 0903-0425
HAAND OG VAERK. * 1967. 7/yr. Haandvaerkerforeningen i Kjoebenhavn, Bredgade 41, DK-1260 Copenhagen K, Denmark. adv. circ. 3,700.

745 DK ISSN 0109-4564
HAANDVAERKSHISTORISK TIDSSKRIFT. 1983. q. membership. Haadverkshistorisk Selskab, c/o Birgit C. Villumsen, Illerupvej 2, Foerlev, 8660 Skanderborg, Denmark. illus.

709.4 GW ISSN 0072-9205
HABELTS DISSERTATIONSDRUCKE. REIHE KUNSTGESCHICHTE. 1953. irreg., no.8, 1985. price varies. Dr. Rudolf Habelt GmbH, Am Buchenhang 1, 53115 Bonn, Germany. TEL 49-228-9238322. FAX 49-228-923836. **Document type:** monographic series.

700 DK ISSN 0085-1361
HAFNIA: COPENHAGEN PAPERS IN THE HISTORY OF ART. (Text in English, French, German) 1970. irreg. DKK 175. Koebenhavns Universitet, Institute of Art History, Njalsgade 80, 2300 Copenhagen S, Denmark. (Dist. by: Rosenkilde og Bagger Forlag, 3 Kron-Prinsens-Gade, Copenhagen K, Denmark) Eds. Oystein Hjort, Marianne Marcussen. circ. 600. **Indexed:** Artbibl.Mod., Avery Ind.Archit.Per., NAA, RILA.

700 069 US ISSN 1065-819X N526
HARVARD UNIVERSITY ART MUSEUMS REVIEW. 1992. s-a. free. Harvard University Art Museums, 32 Quincy St., Cambridge, MA 02138. TEL 617-495-4336. FAX 617-495-9936. Ed. Evelyn Rosenthal. circ. 5,000. (tabloid format; back issues avail.) **Document type:** academic/scholarly publication.
  Formerly: Harvard University Art Musuems. News.
  Description: Provides information on research, collections, and activities.

HARVESTER. see *LITERATURE*

HAWAII ANTIQUES, ART, & COLLECTIBLES QUARTERLY. see *ANTIQUES*

700 UK ISSN 1353-9760
HEADPRESS. 1991. q. £14($40) (rest of Europe £20). Headpress, 40 Rossall Ave., Radcliffe, Manchester M26 IJD, England. TEL 44-161-796-1935. FAX 44-161-796-1935. Ed. David Kerekes. adv.; bk.rev.; film rev.; illus. circ. 3,000. **Document type:** consumer publication.
  Description: Covers bizarre culture, deviant conceptions and cinematic extremes, including artist interviews.

HEDGEHOG. see *LITERATURE — Poetry*

HENRY'S AUKTIONEN. see *ANTIQUES*

700 669 GW ISSN 0942-7511
HEPHAISTOS; internationale Zeitschrift fuer Metallgestalter. 1992. 6/yr. DM.150 (students DM.120). Verlag Hephaistos, Sudetenstr. 74, 82538 Geretsried, Germany. TEL 08171-32501. FAX 08171-80646. Ed. Peter Elgass. adv.: B&W page DM.900; adv. contact: Peter Elgass. circ. 2,000. **Document type:** trade publication.

709 US ISSN 0899-9856
HERMENEUTICS OF ART. irreg. Peter Lang Publishing, Inc., 275 Seventh Ave., 28th Fl., New York, NY 10001. TEL 212-647-7700; 800-770-5264. FAX 212-647-7707. URL: http://www.peterlang.com. Ed. Moshe Barasch. **Document type:** academic/scholarly publication, monographic series. —BLDSC (4300.075200).
  Description: Presents original research in the history and theoretical foundations of the visual arts.

700 800 GW ISSN 0946-9923
HERZOG AUGUST BIBLIOTHEK. AUSSTELLUNGSKATALOGE. irreg., vol.74, 1996. price varies. Harrassowitz Verlag, 65174 Wiesbaden, Germany. TEL 49-611-530-0. FAX 49-611-530570. E-mail: verlag@harrassowitz.de; URL: http://www.harrassowitz.de. R&P contact: Albrecht Weddigen. adv. contact: Albrecht Weddigen. **Document type:** monographic series.

700 SW ISSN 1103-1832
HETEROGENESIS. (Text in Spanish, Swedish) 1992. q. SEK 150 (effective 1997). Konstfoereningen Mulato Gil, Box 4028, S-227 21 Lund, Sweden. TEL 46--46-15-93-07. FAX 46-46-14-65-82. E-mail: lunds.tidskriftverkstad@mailbox.swipnet.se.

700 US
HIBELETTER; current events of the Edna Hibel Society. 1978. q. free to members. Edna Hibel Society, Box 9721, Coral Springs, FL 33075. TEL 305-731-6699. Ed. Ralph Burg. illus. circ. 4,500. **Document type:** newsletter.
  Formerly: Edna Hibel Society Newsletter.
  Description: Features a variety of subjects relating to Edna Hibel.

HIGHLANDER. see *GEOGRAPHY*

HIRMAGAZIN - MAGYAR IPARSZOVETSEG. see *LABOR UNIONS*

700 NX7 US ISSN 0738-5625
HISPANIC AMERICAN ARTS; * all you want or must know, about everything, in all the fields of Hispanic American arts. (Text in Spanish, English) 1974. 3/yr. $42. E. Darino, Ed. & Pub., 222 Park Ave. S., Apt. 2A, New York, NY 10003. bk.rev.; film rev.; play rev.; bibl.; illus.; index.

700 N7480 FR ISSN 0992-2059
HISTOIRE DE L'ART; revue de recherche et d'information. 1988. 3/yr. 280 F. (foreign 330 F.) (effective 1996). (Association des Professeurs d'Archeologie et d'Histoire de l'Art des Universites) A.P.A.H.A.U., Centre d'Histoire, 3 rue Michelet, 75006 Paris, France. TEL 33-1-40469390. FAX 33-1-40070179. Ed. Francoise Levaillant. adv. **Document type:** academic/scholarly publication.

HOCHSCHULE FUER MUSIK UND DARSTELLENDE KUNST MOZARTEUM IN SALZBURG. JAHRESBERICHT. see *EDUCATION*

741.5 US ISSN 1074-7354
HOGAN'S ALLEY; the magazine of the cartoon arts. 1994. s-a. $18.95 (foreign $27.95) for 4 issues; newsstand price: $5.95. Bull Moose Publishing Corp., Box 47684, Atlanta, GA 30368. TEL 770-458-2624. FAX 770-458-3657. E-mail: 71061.43@compuserve.com. Eds. Tom Heintjes, Rick Marschall. adv.: B&W page $250; trim 8 1/4 x 10 3/4; adv. contact: Rick Marshall. bk.rev. illus.; circ. 5,000 (paid). (back issues avail.) **Document type:** consumer publication.
  ●Also available online. Vendor(s): CompuServe, Inc. (FUNFOR).
  Description: Focuses on cartooning with special emphasis on newspaper strips.

700 UK
▼HOLLIS ARTS FUNDING HANDBOOK. 1996. a. £55 (fund-seeking organizations £35). Hollis Directories Ltd., Harlequin House, 7 High St., Teddington, Mddx. TW11 8EL, England. TEL 44-181-9777711. FAX 44-181-9771133. Document type: directory.
Description: Guide to arts funding in UK.

700 US ISSN 0360-4756
N576.H6
HONOLULU ACADEMY OF ARTS. JOURNAL. 1974. irreg., vol.4, 1986. Honolulu Academy of Arts, 900 S. Beretania St., Honolulu, HI 96814. Document type: monographic series.

700 780 US
HOOK; art, ideas & evolution. d. Market Vision Studios, Trent Bldg., 50 S. Buckhout St., Irvington, NY 10533. E-mail: webmaster@thehook.com; URL: http://www.thehook.com. music rev.
●Available only online.
Description: On-line arts and entertainment e-zine featuring art, music, interactive shockwave games, QTVR demos, audio and video clips, and more.

700 US ISSN 1069-6636
NX1
HOPEWELL REVIEW; new work by Indiana's best writers. (Supplement to: Arts Indiana (ISSN 0897-859X)) 1989. a. $6.95. Arts Indiana, Inc., 47 S. Pennsylvania St., Ste. 701, Indianapolis, IN 46204-3622. TEL 317-632-7894. FAX 317-632-7966. Ed. Joseph F. Trimmer. R&P contact: Elizabeth Wiener. adv. contact: Kay Ivcevich. Document type: consumer publication.

HRVATSKA REVIJA. see LITERARY AND POLITICAL REVIEWS

700 CC ISSN 1000-4815
HUALANG/GALLERY. (Text in Chinese) q. Guangdong Lingnan Meishu Chubanshe, No. 11, Shuiyin Lu, Huanshi Donglu, Guangzhou, Guangdong 510075, People's Republic of China. TEL 768688. Ed. Lin Kangsheng.

HUDEBNI VYCHOVA. see EDUCATION

HUESO HUMERO. see LITERATURE

HUMBOLDT (PORTUGUESE EDITION); revista para o mondo Luso-Brasileiro. see LITERARY AND POLITICAL REVIEWS

HUNT INSTITUTE FOR BOTANICAL DOCUMENTATION. BULLETIN. see BIOLOGY — Botany

HUNTINGTON LIBRARY QUARTERLY; studies in English and American literature, history, and art. see LITERATURE

HVEDEKORN. see LITERATURE

700 500 MX ISSN 0536-2571
I C A C H;* organo de divulgacion cultural. no.7, 1973. s-a. Instituto de Ciencias y Artes de Chiapas, 2a y 3a Oriente, Tuxtla, Gutierrez, Chiapas, Mexico.

700 792 UK
◀I C A MONTHLY BULLETIN. 1977. m. £25 membership. Institute of Contemporary Arts, The Mall, London SW1, England. TEL 44-171-930-0493. FAX 44-171-873-0051. E-mail: info@ica.org.uk; URL: http://www.illumin.co.uk/ica/. illus. circ. 31,000. Document type: bulletin.
Formerly (until Oct. 1977): I C A Quarterly.
Description: Gallery, theater, cinema and talks, events and news of the Institute of Contemporary Arts.

700 913 US
C S NEWSLETTER. 1982. biennial. membership. International Catacomb Society, 61 Beacon St., Boston, MA 02108. TEL 617-742-1285. circ. 1,000. (back issues avail.) Document type: newsletter.

343 700 US ISSN 8756-7172
N8554
I F A R REPORTS; and the art loss register. 1977. 10/yr. $65 (foreign $85) (effective 1997). International Foundation for Art Research, Inc., 500 Fifth Ave., Ste 1234, New York, NY 10110. TEL 212-391-6234. FAX 212-391-8794. Ed. Constance Lowenthal. R&P contact: Constance Lowenthal. cum.index. circ. 1,200. Document type: newsletter.
Formed by the merger of: Art Research News & Stolen Art Alert (ISSN 0197-0208); Supersedes (1979-1984): Art Theft Archive Newsletter.
Description: Articles on art theft, authentication and fraud as well as the stolen art alert, a catalogue of art theft reports and recovery listing.

I F O STUDIEN ZU KULTUR UND WIRTSCHAFT. see BUSINESS AND ECONOMICS

700 020 US ISSN 0741-2940
NE3000
I S C A QUARTERLY. 1982. q. $90 (foreign $110). International Society of Copier Artists, 759 President St., Brooklyn, NY 11215. TEL 718-638-3264. Ed. Louise Neaderland; Pub. Louise Neaderland. R&P contact: Louise Neaderland. circ. 125 (paid). (back issues avail.)
Description: Promotes xerography as a creative tool and art form for prints and artists' books.

769.562 NE
I U O M A MAGAZINE. (Text in English) 1991. a. membership. International Union of Mail Artists, P.O. Box 10388, 5000 JJ Tilburg, Netherlands. Ed. Ruud Janssen. illus.; index. circ. 10,000.
Description: Discusses international projects and activities of the union and its members, with addresses, calls for submissions and notices of projects.

IBDA/INNOVATION. see LITERATURE

ICARUS. see LITERATURE

760 659.1 UK
ICOGRADA MESSAGE BOARD. 1963. q. £30 to qualified personnel (free to member associates). International Council of Graphic Design Associations, P.O. Box 398, London W11 4UG, England.
TEL 44-171-603-8494. FAX 44-171-371-6040. E-mail: 106065.2235@compuserve.com. Dir. Mary V. Mullin. R&P contact: Mary V. Mullin. bk.rev. circ. 2,200. (back issues avail.) Document type: newsletter.
Description: Contains articles on professional design, new designs, an international design calendar, information relating to intellectual property, reproduction rights, and copyright issues, educational matters, and news of members.

ICONOGRAPHIA FRANCISCANA. see RELIGIONS AND THEOLOGY — Roman Catholic

704.948 SW ISSN 0106-1348
N7957
ICONOGRAPHISKE POST; nordisk tidskrift foer bildtolkning - Nordic iconographic review. Variant title: I C O Den Iconographiske Post. (Text in Danish, Norwegian, Swedish; summaries and captions in English) 1970. q. SEK 150 within the Nordic countries; elsewhere SEK 180.
Riksantikvarieaembetet - Central Board of National Antiquities, P.O. Box 5405, S-114 84 Stockholm, Sweden. TEL 46-8-783-90-62.
FAX 46-8-783-90-88. Ed. Ingalill Pegelow. bk.rev.; bibl.; illus.; cum.index: 1970-1974, 1975-1984. circ. 1,500. Indexed: NAA, RILM.
—SWETS.

704.948 NE
ICONOGRAPHY OF RELIGIONS. (Consists of 24 Sections and Supplements) 1973. irreg., latest 1996. price varies. (Rijksuniversiteit te Groningen, Institute of Religious Iconography) E.J. Brill, P.O. Box 9000, 2300 PA Leiden, Netherlands.
TEL 31-71-5353500. FAX 31-71-5317532. TELEX 39296 BRILL NL. E-mail: ejbrill@brill.nl. (In N. America: E.J. Brill, 24 Hudson St., Kinderhook, NY 12106. TEL 800-962-4406. FAX 518-758-1959) Ed.Bd. R&P contact: Elizabeth Vennekamp. illus. Document type: monographic series.
Description: Scholarly studies discussing religious iconography in traditions from all parts of the world.
Refereed Serial

704.948 299.92 NE
ICONOGRAPHY OF RELIGIONS. SECTION 2, NEW ZEALAND. 1986. irreg. price varies. (Rijksuniversiteit te Groningen, Institute of Religious Iconography) E.J. Brill, P.O. Box 9000, 2300 PA Leiden, Netherlands. TEL 31-71-5353500. FAX 31-71-5317532. TELEX 29296 BRILL NL. E-mail: ejbrill@brill.nl. (In N. America: E.J. Brill, 24 Hudson St., Kinderhook, NY 12106. TEL 800-962-4406. FAX 518-758-1959) R&P contact: Elizabeth Vennekamp. illus. Document type: monographic series.
Description: Scholarly monographs on topics in religious iconography.
Refereed Serial

704.948 299.92 NE ISSN 0169-8087
ICONOGRAPHY OF RELIGIONS. SECTION 5, AUSTRALIA. 1974. irreg. price varies. (Rijksuniversiteit te Groningen, Institute of Religious Iconography) E.J. Brill, P.O. Box 9000, 2300 PA Leiden, Netherlands. TEL 31-71-5353500. FAX 31-71-5317532. TELEX 39296 BRILL NL. E-mail: ejbrill@brill.nl. (In N. America: E.J. Brill, 24 Hudson St., Kinderhook, NY 12106. TEL 800-962-4406. FAX 518-758-1959) R&P contact: Elizabeth Vennekamp. illus. Document type: monographic series.
Description: Scholarly monographs on the iconography of Australian aboriginal religions.
Refereed Serial

704.948 299.6 NE ISSN 0169-8230
ICONOGRAPHY OF RELIGIONS. SECTION 7, AFRICA. 1974. irreg., latest 1985. price varies. (Rijksuniversiteit te Groningen, Institute of Religious Iconography) E.J. Brill, P.O. Box 9000, 2300 PA Leiden, Netherlands. TEL 31-71-5353500. FAX 31-71-5317532. TELEX 39296 BRILL NL. E-mail: ejbrill@brill.nl. (In N. America: E.J. Brill, 24 Hudson St., Kinderhook, NY 12106. TEL 800-962-4406. FAX 518-758-1959) R&P contact: Elizabeth Vennekamp. illus. Document type: monographic series.
Description: Scholarly monographs on the iconography of African religions.
Refereed Serial

704.948 299.797 NE ISSN 0169-9628
ICONOGRAPHY OF RELIGIONS. SECTION 8, ARCTIC PEOPLES. 1985. irreg., no.2, 1985. price varies. (Rijksuniversiteit te Groningen, Institute of Religious Iconography) E.J. Brill, P.O. Box 9000, 2300 PA Leiden, Netherlands. TEL 31-71-5353500. FAX 31-71-5317532. TELEX 39296 BRILL NL. E-mail: ejbrill@brill.nl. (In N. America: E.J. Brill, 24 Hudson St., Kinderhook, NY 12106. TEL 800-962-4406. FAX 518-758-1959) R&P contact: Elizabeth Vennekamp. illus. Document type: monographic series.
Description: Scholarly monographs on the iconography of Eskimo and Arctic religions.
Refereed Serial

704.948 299.8 NE ISSN 0921-0334
ICONOGRAPHY OF RELIGIONS. SECTION 9, SOUTH AMERICA. 1987. irreg., vol.2, 1990. price varies. (Rijksuniversiteit te Groningen, Institute of Religious Iconography) E.J. Brill, P.O. Box 9000, 2300 PA Leiden, Netherlands. TEL 31-71-5353500. FAX 31-71-5317532. TELEX 39296 BRILL NL. E-mail: ejbrill@brill.nl. (In N. America: E.J. Brill, 24 Hudson St., Kinderhook, NY 12106. TEL 800-962-4406. FAX 518-758-1959) R&P contact: Elizabeth Vennekamp. illus. Document type: monographic series.
—CCC.
Description: Scholarly monographs on the iconography of South American Indian religions.

704.948 299.7 NE ISSN 0169-8184
ICONOGRAPHY OF RELIGIONS. SECTION 10, NORTH AMERICA. 1973. irreg., latest 1987. price varies. (Rijksuniversiteit te Groningen, Institute of Religious Iconography) E.J. Brill, P.O. Box 9000, 2300 PA Leiden, Netherlands. TEL 31-71-5353500. FAX 31-71-5317532. TELEX 39296 BRILL NL. E-mail: ejbrill@brill.nl. (In N. America: E.J. Brill, 24 Hudson St., Kinderhook, NY 12106. TEL 800-962-4406. FAX 518-758-1959) R&P contact: Elizabeth Vennekamp. illus. Document type: monographic series.
Description: Scholarly monographs on the iconography of indigenous North American religions.
Refereed Serial

704.948 299.7   NE   ISSN 0169-9970
ICONOGRAPHY OF RELIGIONS. SECTION 11, ANCIENT AMERICA. irreg., vol.4, 1981. price varies. (Rijksuniversiteit te Groningen, Institute of Religious Iconography) E.J. Brill, P.O. Box 9000, 2300 PA Leiden, Netherlands. TEL 31-71-5353500. FAX 31-71-5317532. TELEX 39296 BRILL NL. E-mail: ejbrill@brill.nl. (In N. America: E.J. Brill, 24 Hudson St., Kinderhook, NY 12106. TEL 800-962-4406. FAX 518-758-1959) R&P contact: ELizabeth Vennekamp. illus. **Document type:** monographic series.
  Description: Scholarly monographs on the iconography of pre-Columbian American religions.
  Refereed Serial

704.948 299.5   NE   ISSN 0169-9725
ICONOGRAPHY OF RELIGIONS. SECTION 12, EAST AND CENTRAL ASIA. irreg., latest 1988. price varies. (Rijksuniversiteit te Groningen, Institute of Religious Iconography) E.J. Brill, P.O. Box 9000, 2300 PA Leiden, Netherlands. TEL 31-71-5353500. FAX 31-71-5317532. TELEX 39296 BRILL NL. E-mail: ejbrill@brill.nl. (In N. America: E.J. Brill, 24 Hudson St., Kinderhook, NY 12106. TEL 800-962-4406. FAX 518-758-1959) R&P contact: Elizabeth Vennekamp. illus. **Document type:** monographic series.
  Description: Scholarly monographs on the iconography of East and Central Asian religions, including Chinese and Korean Buddhism, Confucianism, and other religious traditions.
  Refereed Serial

704.948 294   NE   ISSN 0169-8133
ICONOGRAPHY OF RELIGIONS. SECTION 13, INDIAN RELIGIONS. 1973. irreg., vol.18, 1996. price varies. (Rijksuniversiteit te Groningen, Institute of Religious Iconography) E.J. Brill, P.O. Box 9000, 2300 PA Leiden, Netherlands. TEL 31-71-5353500. FAX 31-71-5317532. TELEX 39296 BRILL NL. E-mail: ejbrill@brill.nl. (In N. America: E.J. Brill, 24 Hudson St., Kinderhook, NY 12106. TEL 800-962-4406. FAX 518-758-1959) R&P contact: Elizabeth Vennekamp. illus. **Document type:** monographic series.
  Description: Scholarly monographs on the iconography of Indian religions, including Buddhism, Jainism, Sikhism, in India and neighboring geographical regions.
  Refereed Serial

704.948 299.15   NE   ISSN 0169-9873
ICONOGRAPHY OF RELIGIONS. SECTION 14, IRAN. 1980. irreg., latest 1986. price varies. (Rijksuniversiteit te Groningen, Institute of Religious Iconography) E.J. Brill, P.O. Box 9000, 2300 PA Leiden, Netherlands. TEL 31-71-5353500. FAX 31-71-5317532. TELEX 39296 BRILL NL. E-mail: ejbrill@brill.nl. (In N. America: E.J. Brill, 24 Hudson St., Kinderhook, NY 12106. TEL 800-962-4406. FAX 518-758-1959) R&P contact: Elizabeth Vennekamp. illus. **Document type:** monographic series.
  Description: Scholarly monographs on the iconography of Iranian religions, including Zoroastrianism and Parsism.
  Refereed Serial

704.948 299.35   NE   ISSN 0169-8036
ICONOGRAPHY OF RELIGIONS. SECTION 15, MESOPOTAMIA AND THE NEAR EAST. 1976. irreg., latest 1990. price varies. (Rijksuniversiteit te Groningen, Institute of Religious Iconography) E.J. Brill, P.O. Box 9000, 2300 PA Leiden, Netherlands. TEL 31-71-5353500. FAX 31-71-5317532. TELEX 39296 BRILL NL. E-mail: ejbrill@brill.nl. (In N. America: E.J. Brill, 24 Hudson St., Kinderhook, NY 12106. TEL 800-962-4406. FAX 518-758-1959) R&P contact: Elizabeth Vennekamp. illus. **Document type:** monographic series.
  Description: Scholarly monographs on the religious iconography of the ancient Near East.
  Refereed Serial

704.948 299.32   NE   ISSN 0169-8338
ICONOGRAPHY OF RELIGIONS. SECTION 16, EGYPT. 1982. irreg., vol. 10, 1988. price varies. (Rijksuniversiteit te Groningen, Institute of Religious Iconography) E.J. Brill, P.O. Box 9000, 2300 PA Leiden, Netherlands. TEL 31-71-5353500. FAX 31-71-5317532. TELEX 39296 BRILL NL. E-mail: ejbrill@brill.nl. (In N. America: E.J. Brill, 24 Hudson St., Kinderhook, NY 12106. TEL 800-962-4406. FAX 518-758-1959) R&P contact: Elizabeth Vennekamp. illus. **Document type:** monographic series.
  Description: Scholarly monographs on the religious iconography of ancient Egypt.
  Refereed Serial

704.948 292   NE   ISSN 0169-9822
ICONOGRAPHY OF RELIGIONS. SECTION 17, GREECE AND ROME. 1976. irreg., latest 1988. price varies. (Rijksuniversiteit te Groningen, Institute of Religious Iconography) E.J. Brill, P.O. Box 9000, 2300 PA Leiden, Netherlands. TEL 31-71-5353500. FAX 31-71-5317532. TELEX 39296 BRILL NL. E-mail: ejbrill@brill.nl. (In N. America: E.J. Brill, 24 Hudson St., Kinderhook, NY 12106. TEL 800-962-4406. FAX 518-758-1959) R&P contact: Elizabeth Vennekamp. illus. **Document type:** monographic series.
  Description: Scholarly monographs on the religious iconography of ancient Greece and Rome.
  Refereed Serial

704.948 299.32   NE   ISSN 0169-9679
ICONOGRAPHY OF RELIGIONS. SECTION 19, ANCIENT EUROPE. 1985. irreg. price varies. (Rijksuniversiteit te Groningen, Institute of Religious Iconography) E.J. Brill, P.O. Box 9000, 2300 PA Leiden, Netherlands. TEL 31-71-5353500. FAX 31-71-5317532. TELEX 39296 BRILL NL. E-mail: ejbrill@brill.nl. (In N. America: E.J. Brill, 24 Hudson St., Kinderhook, NY 12106. TEL 800-962-4406. FAX 518-758-1959) R&P contact: Elizabeth Vennekamp. illus. **Document type:** monographic series.
  Description: Scholarly monographs on the iconography of ancient European religions.
  Refereed Serial

704.948 299.932   NE   ISSN 0169-8435
ICONOGRAPHY OF RELIGIONS. SECTION 20, MANICHAEISM. 1982. irreg. price varies. (Rijksuniversiteit te Groningen, Institute of Religious Iconography) E.J. Brill, P.O. Box 9000, 2300 PA Leiden, Netherlands. TEL 31-71-5353500. FAX 31-71-5317532. TELEX 39296 BRILL NL. E-mail: ejbrill@brill.nl. (In N. America: E.J. Brill, 24 Hudson St., Kinderhook, NY 12106. TEL 800-962-4406. FAX 518-758-1959) R&P contact: Elizabeth Vennekamp. illus. **Document type:** monographic series.
  Description: Scholarly monographs on the religious iconography of Manichaeism.
  Refereed Serial

704.948 299.932   NE   ISSN 0169-9776
ICONOGRAPHY OF RELIGIONS. SECTION 21, MANDAEISM. 1978. irreg. price varies. (Rijksuniversiteit te Groningen, Institute of Religious Iconography) E.J. Brill, P.O. Box 9000, 2300 PA Leiden, Netherlands. TEL 31-71-5353500. FAX 31-71-5317532. TELEX 39296 BRILL NL. E-mail: ejbrill@brill.nl. (In N. America: E.J. Brill, 24 Hudson St., Kinderhook, NY 12106. TEL 800-962-4406. FAX 518-758-1959) R&P contact: Elizabeth Vennekamp. illus. **Document type:** monographic series.
  Description: Scholarly monographs on the religious iconography of Mandaeism.
  Refereed Serial

704.948 297   NE   ISSN 0169-8389
ICONOGRAPHY OF RELIGIONS. SECTION 22, ISLAM. 1970. irreg., latest 1985. price varies. (Rijksuniversiteit te Groningen, Institute of Religious Iconography) E.J. Brill, P.O. Box 9000, 2300 PA Leiden, Netherlands. TEL 31-71-5353500. FAX 31-71-5317532. TELEX 39296 BRILL NL. E-mail: ejbrill@brill.nl. (In N. America: E.J. Brill, 24 Hudson St., Kinderhook, NY 12106. TEL 800-962-4406. FAX 518-758-1959) R&P contact: Elizabeth Vennekamp. illus. **Document type:** monographic series.
  Description: Scholarly monographs on the religious iconography of Islam.
  Refereed Serial

704.498 296   NE   ISSN 0169-8281
ICONOGRAPHY OF RELIGIONS. SECTION 23, JUDAISM. 1975. irreg., vol.5, 1987. price varies. (Rijksuniversiteit te Groningen, Institute of Religious Iconography) E.J. Brill, P.O. Box 9000, 2300 PA Leiden, Netherlands. TEL 31-71-5353500. FAX 31-71-5317532. TELEX 39296 BRILL NL. E-mail: ejbrill@brill.nl. (In N. America: E.J. Brill, 24 Hudson St., Kinderhook, NY 12106. TEL 800-962-4406. FAX 518-758-1959) Ed.Bd. R&P contact: Elizabeth Vennekamp. illus. **Document type:** monographic series.
  Description: Scholarly monographs on topics in the iconography of Judaism.
  Refereed Serial

704.948 246   NE   ISSN 0169-992X
ICONOGRAPHY OF RELIGIONS. SECTION 24, CHRISTIANITY. irreg., latest 1981. price varies. (Rijksuniversiteit te Groningen, Institute of Religious Iconography) E.J. Brill, P.O. Box 9000, 2300 PA Leiden, Netherlands. TEL 31-71-5353500. FAX 31-71-5317532. TELEX 39296 BRILL NL. E-mail: ejbrill@brill.nl. (In N. America: E.J. Brill, 24 Hudson St., Kinderhook, NY 12106. TEL 800-962-4406. FAX 518-758-1959) R&P contact: Elizabeth Vennekamp. illus. **Document type:** monographic series.
  Description: Scholarly monographs on topics in Christian iconography.
  Refereed Serial

704.948   NE
ICONOGRAPHY OF RELIGIONS. SUPPLEMENTS. 1980. irreg. price varies. (Rijksuniversiteit te Groningen, Institute of Religious Iconography) E.J. Brill, P.O. Box 9000, 2300 PA Leiden, Netherlands. TEL 31-71-5353500. FAX 31-71-5317532. TELEX 39296 BRILL NL. E-mail: ejbrill@brill.nl. (In N. America: E.J. Brill, 24 Hudson St., Kinderhook, NY 12106. TEL 800-962-4406. FAX 518-758-1959) R&P contact: Elizabeth Vennekamp. illus. **Document type:** monographic series.
  Refereed Serial

709.37   NE
ICONOLOGICAL STUDIES IN ROMAN ART. (Text in English) 1994. irreg., vol.3, 1994. fl.85 per vol. J.C. Gieben, Nieuwe Herengracht 35, 1011 RM Amsterdam, Netherlands. TEL 31-20-6275170. FAX 31-20-6275170. (Dist. in N. America by: John Benjamins Publishing Co., Box 27519, Philadelphia, PA 19118-0519. TEL 215-836-1200. FAX 215-836-1204) Ed. F.J.G.M. Miller. illus. (back issues avail.) **Document type:** academic/scholarly publication.

700   IT
ICONOSTASI; stagioni e territori dell'arte. 1992. q.? L.25000 per no. Edizioni Quattroventi, Via Dini 16, Casella Postale 156, 61029 Urbino, Italy. TEL 0722-2588. FAX 0722-320998. Ed. Mariano Apa.

700   GW
IKONENKALENDER. a. DM.36. Verlag Aurel Bongers, Postfach 100264, 45602 Recklinghausen, Germany. illus. **Document type:** bulletin.

700   PL   ISSN 0860-5769
IKONOTHEKA. (Text in Polish; summaries in German, French) 1990. irreg., vol.6, 1993. price varies. Uniwersytet Warszawski, Instytut Historii Sztuki, Ul. Krakowskie Przemiescie 26-28, 00-927 Warsaw, Poland. Ed. Maria Poprzecka. circ. 500.

700   US   ISSN 0445-3387
AM101
ILLINOIS. STATE MUSEUM. HANDBOOK OF COLLECTIONS. 1963. irreg., no.6, 1988. Illinois State Museum, Springfield, IL 62706. TEL 217-782-7386. FAX 217-782-1254. E-mail: editor@museumstate.il.us; URL: http://www.museum.state.il.us. Ed. Kimberly K. Britton. R&P contact: Ed Munyer. **Document type:** monographic series.

760   JA
ILLUSTRATION IN JAPAN. (Text in Japanese and English) 1972. a. (Daiichi Shuppan Center) Kodansha Ltd., 12-21, Otowa, 2-chome, Bunkyo-ku Tokyo 112, Japan.

700　　　　　　GW　　ISSN 0019-2457
NC960
ILLUSTRATION 63; Zeitschrift fuer die Buchillustration. 1963. 3/yr. DM.178. Edition Curt Visel, Weberstr. 36, 87700 Memmingen, Germany. TEL 49-8331-2853. FAX 49-8331-490364. Ed. Curt Visel. bk.rev.; illus. circ. 700. **Indexed:** Artbibl.Mod., IBR. **Document type:** consumer publication.
  Description: Covers the art of graphic prints within this century.

741.6　　　　　US　　ISSN 0019-2465
NC997.A1
ILLUSTRATOR. 1916. a. $8 for 4 yrs. Art Instruction Schools, 3309 Broadway St., N.E., Minneapolis, MN 55413-1754. TEL 612-362-5060; 800-788-9532. FAX 612-362-5260. Ed. Steve Unverzagt; Pub. Steve Unverzagt. adv.; bk.rev.; illus. circ. 30,000. (tabloid format) **Document type:** academic/scholarly publication.

700 946　　　　SP　　ISSN 0213-392X
N7101
IMAFRONTE. 1955. irreg., no.11, 1995. 2000 ptas. (effective 1997). Universidad de Murcia, Departamento de Historia del Arte, Servicio de Publicaciones, Santo Cristo 1, 30080 Murcia, Spain. TEL 34-68-363014. FAX 34-68-363414. E-mail: vgm@pas.um.es; URL: http://www.um.es/~spumweb. Ed. Jesus Rivas Carmona. circ. 500. (back issues avail.) **Document type:** academic/scholarly publication.
  —CINDOC.
  Supersedes in part (in 1985): Universidad de Murcia. Anales. Filosofia y Letras (ISSN 0463-9863)
  Description: Covers the history of Murcian and Baroque art.

IMAGE (KENNETT SQUARE); a journal of the arts & religion. see RELIGIONS AND THEOLOGY

700　　　　　　SA　　ISSN 1021-1497
IMAGE & TEXT. 1992. a. R.20 (effective 1997). University of Pretoria, Faculty of Arts: Visual Art & Art History, Pretoria 0002, South Africa. TEL 27-12-4202286. FAX 27-12-4203686. TELEX 3-22723 SA. E-mail: sauthoff@libarts.up.ac.za. Ed. Marian D. Sauthoff. bk.rev. circ. 2,000. **Document type:** academic/scholarly publication.
  Description: Communicates ideas, opinions, experiences and research finding relating to design, with a focus on the South African context.
  Refereed Serial

IMPERIAL RUSSIAN JOURNAL. see HISTORY — History Of Europe

700 808.81　　　US　　ISSN 1044-7490
IMPETUS. 1984. irreg. $20 (foreign $30). Impetus Implosion Press, 4975 Comanche Trail, Stow, OH 44224. TEL 216-688-5210. FAX 216-688-5120. E-mail: IMPETUS@aol.com. Ed. Cheryl A Townsend. adv.; bk.rev. circ. 1,000. (back issues avail.)
  Description: Social protest expressed through the means of poetry, artwork, editorials and articles.

IMPREMPRES; tecnicas equipos para las artes graficas e industrias de la transformacion del papel y carton. see PAPER AND PULP

700 950　　　　　US
IMPRESSIONS (NEW YORK). 1976. s-a. membership. Ukiyo-e Society of America, Inc., Box 665, F.D.R. Sta., New York, NY 10150. Ed. Henry D. Smith. R&P contact: Henry D. Smith. circ. 400. (back issues avail.) **Document type:** academic/scholarly publication.
  Description: Devoted to the study and art of Japanese woodblock prints.

760　　　　　　SZ
IMPRESSUM 2 - CARTOONISTEN, ILLUSTRATOREN, ARCHIVE. (Text in French, German) irreg. 110 SFr. Medienpublikationen Hildegard Schulthess-Eberle, Aescherweg 20, CH-5725 Leutwil, Switzerland. TEL 41-62-7676070. FAX 41-62-7676077. **Document type:** directory.
  Description: Directory of illustrators and other graphic arts information in Switzerland.

700 800　　　　SA　　ISSN 1021-8629
IMPRINT; a magazine of the arts. 1993. 3/yr. R.22.80. P.O. Box 5091, Rivonia 2128, South Africa. illus.

760 974　　　　US　　ISSN 0277-7061
NE505
IMPRINT (FAIRFIELD). 1976. s-a. $35 (foreign $45) includes Newsletter. American Historical Print Collectors Society, Inc., Box 201, Fairfield, CT 06430. TEL 810-332-3902. Ed. Sue Raincy. R&P contact: Sue Rainey. TEL 804-293-4979. bk.rev.; illus. circ. 600. (back issues avail.) **Indexed:** Amer.Hist.& Life (1984-), Hist.Abstr., RILA. **Document type:** academic/scholarly publication.
  —UnCover.
  Description: Scholarly articles concerning history, meanings, and techniques of prints made in America or about American subjects before 1900.

IN; German - American cultural review. see LITERARY AND POLITICAL REVIEWS

700　　　　　　US
IN BRIEF (SAN FRANCISCO, 1974). 1974. q. $12 membership. Artists in Print, Inc., 665 Third St., Ste. 530, San Francisco, CA 94107. TEL 415-243-8244. FAX 415-495-3155. Ed. R. Biggs. adv.; bk.rev.; illus.; stat.; tr.lit. circ. 3,000. **Indexed:** Child.Lit.Abstr., New Per.Ind. **Document type:** newsletter.
  Formerly: Graphiti.

IN FOCUS (LOS ANGELES). see MOTION PICTURES

391　　　　　　US
▼**IN THE FLESH.** 1995. q. newsstand price: $6.95. Outlaw Biker Enterprises, Inc., 5 Marine View Plaza, Ste.207, Hoboken, NJ 07030. TEL 201-653-2700. FAX 201-653-7892. Ed. Jean-Chris Miller; Pub. Casey Exton. **Document type:** consumer publication.
  Description: Covers piercings, tatoos, and other art that modifies the human body.

700 001.3　　　　IT
L'INCONTRO DELLE GENTI; rivista di scienze lettere ed arte. (Text in English and Italian; summaries in English, French and German) 1967. bi-m. L.30000($25) E.R.A. Incontro s.r.l., Via XX Settembre 44, 00187 Roma, Italy. TEL 06-486866. FAX 06-48286599. Ed. Enrico Sciubba. adv.; bk.rev. circ. 5,000. (back issues avail.)

306.4　　　　　SW　　ISSN 1103-0674
INDEX; contemporary art and culture. (Text in English and Swedish) 1978. 4/yr. SEK 250 to individuals in Scandinavia and Baltics (elsewhere SEK 300); institutions SEK 300 (elsewhere SEK 350); students SEK 200 (effective 1998). Stiftelsen foer Visuella Studier, P.O. Box 15152, S-104 65 Stockholm, Sweden. TEL 46-8-641-62-26. FAX 46-8-641-96-08. E-mail: magazine.index@mbox200.swipnet.se. Ed. Sara Arrhenius. adv.: B&W page SEK 5000, color page SEK 9000; trim 215 x 260; adv. contact: Mattias Givell. **Document type:** consumer publication.
  Former titles (until 1992): Bildtidningen (ISSN 1100-5203); (until 1989): Bild (ISSN 0283-6041); (until 1985): Fotograficentrums Bildtidning (ISSN 0348-3959)
  Description: Focuses on contemporary Scandinavian and international art, media, and culture.

700　　　　　　US
▼**INDEX.** 1996. bi-m. $25 (foreign $50). 526 W. 26th St., Ste. 920, New York, NY 10001. TEL 212-243-1428. FAX 212-243-1603. E-mail: phcell@pipeline.com. Ed. Bob Nickas; Pub. Peter Halley. adv. contact: Ariana Speyer. film rev.; music rev. circ. 6,000. (tabloid format) **Document type:** consumer publication.
  Description: Covers the art, music and film scene. Publishes extensive interviews with performers, artists and film-makers, reviews of cultural events, fabulations and critical essays.

700　　　　　　II　　ISSN 0970-8413
INDIAN AND WORLD ARTS & CRAFTS. (Text in English) 1982. m. $25. RHYTHM - Pandanallur International School of Bharatanatyam, 197 Kohat Enclave, Pitampura, Delhi 110034, India. TEL 91-11-719-3716. Ed. M.R. Dinesh. R&P contact: M.R. Dinesh. adv. **Document type:** consumer publication.
  Description: Tabloid news and feature magazine on arts, theatre, crafts and culture.

INDIAN ARTIST; the magazine of contemporary native American art, music, literature, photography, film, theater and dance. see ETHNIC INTERESTS

INFOFAX: FOTOGRAFIE. see PHOTOGRAPHY

INSIGHT MAGAZINE; entertainment aimed at you. see MUSIC

INSITES. see ARCHITECTURE

INSTITUT ARCHEOLOGIQUE DU LUXEMBOURG. BULLETINS; archeologie-art-histoire-folklore. see ARCHAEOLOGY

700　　　　　　BE　　ISSN 0085-1892
N13
INSTITUT ROYAL DU PATRIMOINE ARTISTIQUE. BULLETIN/KONINKLIJK INSTITUUT VOOR HET KUNSTPATRIMONIUM. BULLETIN. (Text and summaries in Dutch, French) 1958. a., latest vol.25, 1993 (for the year 1995). price varies. Institut Royal du Patrimoine Artistique, 1 Parc du Cinquantenaire, 1000 Brussels, Belgium. TEL 32-2-7396711. FAX 32-2-7320105. Ed. Jacques Debergh. R&P contact: Mrs. L. Masschelein-Kleiner. circ. 1,100. (back issues avail.) **Indexed:** Art & Archaeol.Tech.Abstr., RILA. **Document type:** bulletin.
  —Linda Hall; SWETS.
  Description: Covers topics relating to Belgian art and conservation.
  Refereed Serial

700　　　　　　US
INSTITUTE ITEMS. m. $50. Art and Creative Materials Institute, 100 Boylestion St., Ste. 1050, Boston, MA 02116-4610. TEL 617-426-6400. FAX 617-426-6639. Ed. Debbie Gustafson. tr.lit. circ. 350. (back issues avail.) **Document type:** newsletter.
  Description: Keeps members updated on issues of interest, including legislation and regulations, association services, etc.

INSTITUTO BRASIL - ESTADOS UNIDOS. BOLETIM. see EDUCATION

INSTITUTO CARO Y CUERVO. NOTICIAS CULTURALES. see LITERATURE

INTANGIBLE. see LITERATURE

INTERACTA. see EDUCATION — Teaching Methods And Curriculum

INTERFERENCES, ARTS, LETTRES. see LITERATURE

796.56 383　　　CN
INTERNATIONAL ART POST. 1988. irreg., latest vol.7, no.2. Can.$25. Banana Productions, P.O. Box 807, Sechelt, BC V0N 3A0, Canada. TEL 604-885-7156. FAX 604-885-7183. Ed. Anna Banana. circ. 500 (paid).
  Description: Presents full-color gummed stamps by artists, cooperatively published.

700　　　　　　UK　　ISSN 1355-6169
INTERNATIONAL ARTS MANAGER. 1987. 10/yr. £40 (foreign £45). Arts Publishing International, 4 Assam St., London E1 7QS, England. TEL 44-171-247-0066. FAX 44-171-247-6868. E-mail: post@api.co.uk. Ed. Marika Thorogood; Pub. Martin Huber. adv.: B&W page £830; color page £2950; adv. contact: Bill Richards. circ. 4,500. **Document type:** trade publication.
  Description: Contains news and feature articles on performing arts managers, venues, and companies from all parts of the world.

700　　　　　　US
INTERNATIONAL ASSOCIATION FOR THE FANTASTIC IN THE ARTS NEWSLETTER. 1987. q. membership. International Association for the Fantastic in the Arts, College of Humanities, Florida Atlantic University, 500 N.W. 20th St., B-9 HU-50, Boca Raton, FL 33431. TEL 407-367-3838. Ed. Robert Collins. film rev.; bibl. circ. 400. (back issues avail.) **Document type:** newsletter.

700　　　　　　FR
INTERNATIONAL ASSOCIATION OF PERFORMING ARTS LIBRARIES AND MUSEUMS. CONGRESS PROCEEDINGS. (Publisher of Proceedings varies) 1957. biennial. International Association of Performing Arts Libraries and Museums, 1 rue de Sully, 75004 Paris, France. **Document type:** proceedings.
  Formerly: International Society for Performing Arts Libraries and Museums. Congress Proceedings (ISSN 0074-7882)

448 ART

700   US   ISSN 0074-1922
INTERNATIONAL AUCTION RECORDS.* 1967. a. $179. Editions Publisol, 151 Tremont St., Apt. 7E, Boston, MA 02111-1106. TEL 617-536-3726. Ed. E. Mayer. adv. contact: Gregory Morson. illus. circ. 5,000.
  Description: Information on today's worldwide market values for authenticated works of art.

709   US
INTERNATIONAL CENTER OF MEDIEVAL ART. NEWSLETTER. 3/yr. membership. International Center of Medieval Art, The Cloisters, Fort Tryon Park, New York, NY 10040. TEL 212-928-1146. FAX 212-928-1146. E-mail: 73430.2037@compuserve.com; URL: http://www.medievalart.org. Ed. Judith Oliver. **Document type:** newsletter.

INTERNATIONAL CHINESE SNUFF BOTTLE SOCIETY. JOURNAL. see *ANTIQUES*

709   FR   ISSN 0074-4190
INTERNATIONAL CONGRESS ON THE HISTORY OF ART. PROCEEDINGS. 1873. quinquennial, 1968, 22nd, Budapest. 75 F. Orient - Express, c/o Institut d'Art et d'Archeologie, 3 rue Michelet, 75006 Paris, France. FAX 44-07-01-79. Ed. Eric Jean. **Document type:** newsletter.

700   JA
INTERNATIONAL DESIGN YEARBOOK. a. 13800 Yen. Bijutsu Shuppan-sha, Inaoka Bldg., 2-36 Kanda, Jinbo-cho, Chiyoda-ku, Tokyo 101, Japan. TEL 03-3234-2151. FAX 03-3234-9451.

700   GW   ISSN 0074-4565
INTERNATIONAL DIRECTORY OF ARTS. (In 3 vols.) (Text in English, French, German, Italian, Spanish) 1949. biennial, 1996, 23rd ed., DM.448. K.G. Saur Verlag KG, A member of the Reed Elsevier plc group, Ortlerstr. 8, 81373 Munich, Germany. TEL 49-89-769021321. FAX 49-89-76902150. E-mail: 100730.1341@compuserve.com; URL: http://www.reedref.com. (Subscr. to: Postfach 701620, 81316 Munich, Germany; N. America subscr. to: K.G. Saur, A Reed Reference Publishing Company, 121 Chanlon Rd., Box 31, New Providence, NJ 07974-9903, USA. TEL 908-464-6800) Ed. Michael Zils. adv.; index. circ. 10,000. **Document type:** directory.
  Description: Comprehensive guide to art sources and markets in 137 countries. Contains over 150,000 names and addresses of art restorers, publishers, libraries, art dealers and galleries, museums, associations.

700   US
INTERNATIONAL DIRECTORY OF CHRISTIAN ARTS ORGANIZATIONS. 1991. irreg. $35. Christians in the Arts Networking Inc., 9 Washington Ave., Box 242, Arlington, MA 02174-0003. TEL 617-646-1541. FAX 617-696-7725. adv.; B&W page $375. **Document type:** directory.
  Description: Lists Christian arts organizations, including contact information, activities and publications.

741.4   US   ISSN 1068-7688
INTERNATIONAL DIRECTORY OF DESIGN. 1992. a. (CD-ROM s-a.) $75 paperbound (hardbound $105; CD-ROM $140) (effective 1997). Penrose Press, Box 470925, San Francisco, CA 94147. TEL 415-567-4157. FAX 415-567-4165. URL: http://www.penrose-press.com/idd/. Ed. Ray Lauzzana; Pub. Ray Lauzzana. R&P contact: Denise Penrose. **Document type:** directory.
  ●Also available online.
  ●Also available on CD-ROM.
  Description: Guide to more than 3000 design education programs around the world.

INTERNATIONAL FEDERATION OF LIBRARY ASSOCIATIONS AND INSTITUTIONS. SECTION OF ART LIBRARIES. NEWSLETTER. see *LIBRARY AND INFORMATION SCIENCES*

760   DK   ISSN 0020-6830
INTERNATIONAL GRAFIK; original graphics review. (No issues in 1975) (Text in Danish, English, French and German) 1969. s-a. DKK 60. Box 109, 9900 Frederikshavn, Denmark. Eds. Helmer Fogedgaard, Klaus Roedel. adv.; illus.; index.

INTERNATIONAL JOURNAL OF ARTS MEDICINE. see *MEDICAL SCIENCES*

700   GW   ISSN 0940-7391
CC135
INTERNATIONAL JOURNAL OF CULTURAL PROPERTY. (Text in English) 1992. s-a. DM.253 (foreign DM.257) (effective 1998). (International Cultural Property Society) Walter de Gruyter und Co., Genthiner Str. 13, 10785 Berlin, Germany. TEL 49-30-26005-0. FAX 49-30-2600525. E-mail: wdg-info@degruyter.de; URL: http://www.degruyter.de. (U.S. addr.: Walter de Gruyter, Inc., 200 Saw Mill River Rd., Hawthorne, NY 10532. TEL 914-747-0110) Ed. Norman Palmer. **Indexed:** Anthropol.Lit. **Document type:** academic/scholarly publication.
  —BLDSC (4542.181000); SWETS; UnCover. **CCC.**

INTERNATIONAL QUARTERLY (TALLAHASSEE); literature and art in all genres in original English and in translation from any language and for and from all countries for discerning general readers. see *LITERATURE*

700   US   ISSN 1045-0920
NX164.N4
INTERNATIONAL REVIEW OF AFRICAN AMERICAN ART; an international publication. 1976. q. $36. University Museum, Hampton University, Hampton, VA 23668-0101. TEL 804-727-5142. FAX 804-727-5084. Ed. Juliette Bowles; Pub. Jeanne Zeidler. R&P contact: Juliette Bowles. adv. contact: Karen Costa. bk.rev.; illus. circ. 5,000. **Indexed:** Amer.Hum.Ind., Art Ind., Arts & Hum.Cit.Ind., ASCA, Curr.Cont. **Document type:** academic/scholarly publication.
  —KR SourceOne; UnCover.
  Formerly: Black Art (ISSN 0145-8116)
  Description: Covers art and culture of black people in the Americas.

702   US   ISSN 1065-643X
INTERNATIONAL TATTOO ART. 1992. m. newsstand price: $4.99. Mavety Media Group Ltd., 462 Broadway, New York, NY 10013. TEL 212-966-8400. FAX 212-960-9366. adv. **Document type:** consumer publication.

INTERPLAY; proceedings of symposia in comparative literature and the arts. see *LITERATURE*

INTERSPECIES NEWSLETTER. see *COMMUNICATIONS*

700 900 100   IT
INTERVENTI CLASSENSI. irreg., latest no.16. price varies. Angelo Longo Editore, Via Paolo Costa 33, 48100 Ravenna, Italy. TEL 39-544-217026. FAX 39-544-217554. E-mail: longo-ra@linknet.it. Ed. Alfio Longo. circ. 3,500. **Document type:** academic/scholarly publication.
  Description: Studies on art, history, collection of classic libraries

700   CN   ISSN 0831-6708
INUIT ART QUARTERLY. 1986. q. Can.$26.75 (U.S. $25; elsewhere Can.$39) (effective 1997 & 1998). Inuit Art Foundation, 2081 Merivale Rd., Nepean, ON K2G 1G9, Canada. TEL 613-224-8189. FAX 613-224-2907. E-mail: inuitart@intranet.ca; URL: http://www.inuitart.org. Ed. Marybelle Mitchell. R&P contact: Matthew Fox. adv. contact: Sheila Sturk-Green. bk.rev.; circ. 1,923 (paid); 1,862 (controlled). **Indexed:** Art Ind. **Document type:** academic/scholarly publication.
  —KR SourceOne. **CCC.**
  Description: Features, profiles and news about Inuit art and artists as well as reviews of exhibitions.

INVENTAIRE GENERAL DES MONUMENTS ET DES RICHESSES ARTISTIQUES DE LA FRANCE. see *ARCHITECTURE*

INVESTING IN ART. see *BUSINESS AND ECONOMICS — Investments*

700 500   US   ISSN 0021-0331
PS536.2
IO. 1964. a. $40 (foreign $50). (Society for the Study of Native Arts and Sciences) North Atlantic Books, Box 12327, Berkeley, CA 94712. TEL 510-559-8277. FAX 510-559-8279. Ed. Richard Grossinger; Pub. Richard Glassinger. R&P contact: Lindy Hough. illus. circ. 3,000. (tabloid format; back issues avail.)

700 720 069 708   IE   ISSN 0791-3540
N6782
IRISH ARTS REVIEW YEARBOOK. 1984. a. I£30 in Ireland & U.K. (Europe I£32; elsewhere I£35) for hardcover ed.; softcover ed. I£20 in Ireland & U.K. (Europe I£22; elsewhere I£25) (effective 1997 & 1998). State Apartments, Dublin Castle, Dublin 2, Ireland. TEL 353-1-679-3503. FAX 353-1-679-3503. (Subscr. to: P.O. Box 3500, Dublin 4, Ireland) Ed. Homan Potterton. adv. contact: Vera Finnegan. bk.rev./; illus.; circ. 3,000 (paid). (back issues avail.) **Indexed:** Artbibl.Mod., DAAI, RILA. **Document type:** academic/scholarly publication.
  —BLDSC (4568.875000).
  Formerly: Irish Arts Review (ISSN 0790-178X)
  Description: Discusses Irish visual and decorative arts from pre-history to the present.
  Refereed Serial

ISLAM AND THE MODERN AGE. see *RELIGIONS AND THEOLOGY — Islamic*

709 956   US   ISSN 0742-1125
ISLAMIC ART AND ARCHITECTURE. 1981. irreg. price varies. Mazda Publishers, Box 2603, Costa Mesa, CA 92626. TEL 714-751-5252. Ed. A. Daneshvari. **Indexed:** Avery Ind.Archit.Per.

ISLANDS; a New Zealand quarterly of arts and letters. see *LITERATURE*

ISSUES IN ARCHITECTURE, ART AND DESIGN. see *ARCHITECTURE*

ISTITUTO NAZIONALE DI ARCHEOLOGIA E STORIA DELL'ARTE. RIVISTA. see *ARCHAEOLOGY*

709 940   IT   ISSN 0393-0904
ISTITUTO SICILIANO DI STUDI BIZANTINI E NEOELLENICI. MONUMENTI. 1962. irreg., no.5, 1997. Istituto Siciliano di Studi Bizantini e Neoellenici, Via Noto, 34, 90141 Palermo, Italy. TEL 39-91-6259541. FAX 39-91-6259541. **Document type:** monographic series.

ISTRA; kultura, knjizevnost drustvena pitjana. see *LITERATURE*

700   IT   ISSN 0394-4573
N4
ITALY. MINISTERO PER I BENI CULTURALI E AMBIENTALI. BOLLETTINO D'ARTE. Short title: Bollettino d'Arte. (Irreg. supplement avail. (ISSN 0394-4611)) 1907. bi-m. L.260000 (foreign L.300000) (effective 1993). Ministero per i Beni Culturali e Ambientali, Ufficio Centrale per i Beni Ambientali, Architettonici, Archeologici, Artistici e Storici, Via di San Michele, 22, 00153 Rome, Italy. TEL 5843-2420. FAX 5843-2352. Ed. Francesco Sisinni. bk.rev.; bibl.; illus. **Indexed:** Art Ind., Artbibl.Mod., Avery Ind.Archit.Per., Numis.Lit., RILA, RILM.
  —KR SourceOne; SWETS.
  Formerly (until 1975): Italy. Ministero della Pubblica Istruzione. Bollettino d'Arte (ISSN 0391-9854)

745 620   NE   ISSN 0167-9082
ITEMS (PUBLIEKSEDITIE); tijdschrift voor vormgeving. (Text in Dutch, summaries in English) 1982. 8/yr. fl.105 (foreign fl.140); newsstand price: fl.14.50. Uitgeverij B I S, Postbus 15751, 1001 NG Amsterdam, Netherlands. TEL 31-20-6205171. FAX 31-20-6279251. E-mail: BISPUB@XS4ALL.NL. Ed. Renny Ramakers. adv. contact: Volkert Vos. bk.rev.; illus.; circ. 10,000 (paid). (tabloid format) **Document type:** trade publication.
  Incorporates (1985-1993): Industrieel Ontwerpen (ISSN 0920-0118)
  Description: Covers news in the fields of design, visual communication and architecture.

745 620   NE   ISSN 1381-4249
ITEMS (VAKEDITIE); tijdschrift voor vormgeving. 1993. 8/yr. fl.165 (foreign fl.210); newsstand price: fl.23.50. Uitgeverij B I S, Postbus 15751, 1001 NG Amsterdam, Netherlands. TEL 31-20-6205171. FAX 31-20-6279251. E-mail: BISPUB@XS4ALL.NL. Ed. Renny Ramakers. adv. contact: Volkert Vos. illus. (tabloid format) **Document type:** trade publication.
  —BLDSC (4588.584000).
  Description: News and information in the fields of design, visual communication and architecture for design professionals.

| 700 | | IT | ISSN 0390-2498 |

ITERARTE. 1974. bi-m. L.6000. Circolo Artistico di Bologna, Via Clavature 8, Bologna, Italy. Ed. Giovanni M. Accame. adv.; illus.

IZ STAROG I NOVOG ZAGREBA. see *ARCHITECTURE*

THE J. PAUL GETTY MUSEUM JOURNAL. see *MUSEUMS AND ART GALLERIES*

| 700 | | BE | ISSN 0066-3174 |

JAARBOEK DER SCHONE KUNSTEN/ALGEMEEN JAARBOEK DER SCHONE KUNSTEN. (Text in Dutch, French) 1928. a. 450 Fr.($15) Editions ARTO, 85 Avenue Winston Churchill, 1180 Brussels, Belgium. adv.; bk.rev. circ. 4,000.
Formerly: Dessinateurs, Peintres et Sculpteurs de Belgique (ISSN 0070-3869)

| 700 616.89 | | JA | ISSN 0916-6688 |
| RC489.A7 | | | |

JAPANESE BULLETIN OF ARTS THERAPY. (Text in Japanese and other languages) 1969. a. 7000 Yen. Societe Japonaise de Psychopathologie de l'Expression, c/o Neuropsychiatric Research Institute, 91 Bentencho, Shinjuku-ku, Tokyo 162, Japan. TEL 81-3-3260-9171. FAX 81-3-3260-9191. Ed. Dr. Yoshihito Tokuda. adv.; bk.rev.; bibl.; charts; illus.; stat.; circ. 4,500 (controlled). (back issues avail.) **Document type:** academic/scholarly publication.

JAPANESE SWORD SOCIETY OF THE U S BULLETIN. see *ANTIQUES*

JASZKUNSAG; social and artistic journal. see *LITERATURE*

| 700 890 491.93 | | CN | ISSN 0448-9179 |
| 780 | | | |

JAUNA GAITA. (Text in Latvian; summaries in English) 1955. bi-m. Can.$30($30) (effective 1995). 23 Markland Drive, Etobicoke, ON M9C 1M8, Canada. TEL 416-621-0898. (Subscr. to: Ms. I. Bulmanis, 23 Markland Dr., Etobicoke, ON M9C 1M8, Canada) Ed. L. Zandbergs. bk.rev.; cum.index. circ. 1,200. (back issues avail.) **Indexed:** M.L.A., MLA Intl.Bibl.

JEOPARDY. see *LITERATURE*

| 700 | | IS | ISSN 0792-0660 |
| N7415 | | | |

JEWISH ART. (Text in English, French) 1974. a. price varies. (Hebrew University of Jerusalem, Center for Jewish Art) Magnes Press, Hebrew University, Jerusalem, P.O. Box 7695, Jerusalem, Israel. TEL 972-2-5660341. FAX 972-5633370. Ed. Bezalel Narkiss. bk.rev.; bibl.; illus. circ. 2,000. (also avail. in microform from UMI; back issues avail.; reprint service avail. from UMI) **Indexed:** Art Ind., Artbibl.Mod., Arts & Hum.Cit.Ind., ASCA, Avery Ind.Archit.Per., Curr.Cont., Ind.Jew.Per., RILA. **Document type:** academic/scholarly publication.
—BLDSC (4668.351250); KR SourceOne.
Formerly: Journal of Jewish Art (ISSN 0160-208X)

| 750 | | CC | |

JIANGSU HUAKAN/JIANGSU PICTORIAL. (Text in Chinese) m. $67.50. Jiangsu Meishu Chubanshe, 165 Zhongyang Lu, Nanjing, Jiangsu 210009, People's Republic of China. TEL 306301. (Dist. in US by: China Books & Periodicals, Inc., 2929 24th St., San Francisco, CA 94110. TEL 415-282-2994) Ed. Liu Dianzhang.

| 700 | | NE | ISSN 0168-9193 |

JONG HOLLAND; tijdschrift vor kunst en voormgeving na 1850. (Text in Dutch; summaries in English) 1985. q. fl.63 (foreign fl.95) (effective 1997); newsstand price: fl.18.50. Stichting Jong Holland, Postbus 90418, 2509 LK The Hague, Netherlands. TEL 31-70-3852415. FAX 31-70-3852415. Ed. Patricia van Ulzen. R&P contact: Patricia van Ulzen. adv.; bk.rev. circ. 1,850. **Document type:** consumer publication, academic/scholarly publication.
—SWETS.
Description: Publishes studies of art and design after 1850, including critical appraisals of individual artists and thematic studies.
Refereed Serial

| 701.1 | | US | ISSN 0021-8529 |
| N1 | | | |

JOURNAL OF AESTHETICS AND ART CRITICISM. 1941. q. $36 to nonmember individuals; institutions $67. (American Society for Aesthetics) University of Wisconsin Press, Journal Division, 114 N. Murray St., Madison, WI 53715. TEL 608-262-5839. FAX 608-262-7560. Ed. Philip Alperson. adv.: page $235; 5 1/2 x 8. bk.rev.; bibl.; index. circ. 2,700. (also avail. in microform from MIM,UMI; reprint service avail. from UMI) **Indexed:** Abstr.Engl.Stud., Acad.Ind., Amer.Bibl.Slavic & E.Eur.Stud., Art Ind., Arts & Hum.Cit.Ind., ASCA, Avery Ind.Archit.Per., Bk.Rev.Dig., Bk.Rev.Ind. (1965-), Can.Rev.Comp.Lit., Child.Bk.Rev.Ind. (1965-), Curr.Cont., Film Lit.Ind. (1973-), Hum.Ind., IBR, Ind.Bk.Rev.Hum., M.L.A., MLA Intl.Bibl., Music Ind., Phil.Ind., Psychol.Abstr., RILA, RILM, SSCI. **Document type:** academic/scholarly publication.
—BLDSC (4919.985000); KR SourceOne; SWETS; UMI; UnCover.
Description: Takes an interdisciplinary approach to exploring aesthetics, as related to visual arts, literature, music, and theater.

JOURNAL OF ART AND DESIGN EDUCATION. see *EDUCATION — Teaching Methods And Curriculum*

JOURNAL OF ART & ENTERTAINMENT LAW. see *LAW*

| 709 | | JA | ISSN 0021-907X |

JOURNAL OF ART HISTORY/BIJUTSU SHI. (Text in Japanese; title in English) 1950. q. $22.25. Japan Art History Society - Bijutsu-shi Gakkai, c/o Tokyo National Research Institute of Cultural Properties, Ueno Park, Tokyo, Japan. Ed. Kaho Yonezawa. illus.; index. circ. 800.
—UnCover.

| 707 | | JA | ISSN 0021-9088 |

JOURNAL OF ART STUDIES/BIJUTSU KENKYU. (Text in Japanese; title and summaries in English) 1932. bi-m. 2266 Yen per copy. Japan Publications Trading Co. Ltd., Box 5030, Tokyo International, Tokyo 100-31, Japan. (Or: 1255 Howard St., San Francisco, CA 94103) illus.; index. circ. 600.

| 700 720 | | CN | ISSN 0315-4297 |
| N6540 | | | |

JOURNAL OF CANADIAN ART HISTORY/ANNALES D'HISTOIRE DE L'ART CANADIEN. (Text in English, French) 1974. s-a. Can.$25($30) (foreign $30) (effective 1997). Concordia University, 1455 boul. de Maisonneuve Ouest, S-VA 432, Montreal, PQ H3G 1M8, Canada. TEL 514-848-4699. FAX 514-848-8627. E-mail: spaik@gemini.concordia.ca. Ed. Sandra Paikowsky; Pub. Sandra Paikowsky. R&P contact: Brenda Dionne Hutchinson. adv. contact: Brenda Dionne Hutchinson. bk.rev.; bibl.; charts; illus.; index. circ. 700. (also avail. in microfilm from MML; back issues avail.) **Indexed:** Amer.Hist.& Life (1994-), Art Ind., Artbibl.Mod., Arts & Hum.Cit.Ind., Avery Ind.Archit.Per., Br.Tech.Ind., Can.B.P.I., Can.Per.Ind., Curr.Cont., Hist.Abstr. (1994-), Pt.de Rep. (1983-), RILA. **Document type:** academic/scholarly publication.
—Genuine Article; KR SourceOne; UnCover.
Description: Devoted to the publications of scholarly articles on the history of Canadian art, architecture and the decorative arts.
Refereed Serial

| 700 | | US | ISSN 0897-2400 |
| N6480 | | | |

JOURNAL OF CONTEMPORARY ART. 1988. s-a. $14. Box 1472, New York, NY 10023-1472. TEL 212-925-7576. FAX 212-799-1458. E-mail: jca@thing.net; URL: htp://www.thing.net/jca. Ed. Klaus Ottmann. adv.; illus.; cum.index: vols.1-4. circ. 3,000. **Indexed:** Art Ind.
—KR SourceOne; UnCover.
Description: Devoted exclusively to art projects and interviews with contemporary artists.

JOURNAL OF CULTURAL ECONOMICS. see *BUSINESS AND ECONOMICS — Economic Systems And Theories, Economic History*

| 700 720 069 | | US | ISSN 0888-7314 |
| NK1 | | | |

JOURNAL OF DECORATIVE AND PROPAGANDA ARTS. (Supplements avail.) 1986-1990 (no.17); resumed no.18, 1992. a. $19 to individuals (foreign $24); institutions $25 (foreign $30) (effective 1996). Wolfson Foundation of Decorative and Propaganda Arts, Inc., 2399 N.E. Second Ave., Miami, FL 33137. TEL 305-573-9170. FAX 305-573-0409. Ed. Cathy Leff. R&P contact: Cathy Leff. adv.: B&W page $250; color page $400. circ. 5,000. (back issues avail.) **Indexed:** DAAI, Per.Islam. (1994-), RILA. **Document type:** academic/scholarly publication.
—BLDSC (4967.900000); UnCover.
Description: Contains scholarly articles of international scope on decorative and propaganda arts, including architecture and design, from 1875 to 1945.

JOURNAL OF DESIGN & TECHNOLOGY EDUCATION. see *EDUCATION — Teaching Methods And Curriculum*

| 700 747 | | UK | ISSN 0952-4649 |
| NK1175 | | | |

JOURNAL OF DESIGN HISTORY. 1988. q. £80 (foreign $115) (effective 1998). (Design History Society) Oxford University Press, Academic Division, Great Clarendon St., Oxford OX2 6DP, England. TEL 44-1865-267907. FAX 44-1865-267485. TELEX 8373300-OXPRES-G. E-mail: jnl.info@oup.co.uk; URL: http://www.oup.co.uk/journals. (U.S. subscr. to: Oxford University Press Inc., 2001 Evans Rd., Cary, NC 27513. TEL 800-852-7323. FAX 919-677-1714) Ed.Bd.; Pub. Philip Joseph. R&P contact: Joolz Longley. adv. contact: Jane Parker. bk.rev.; illus. circ. 925. **Indexed:** Amer.Hist.& Life (1988-), Art Ind., DAAI, Hist.Abstr. (1988-). **Document type:** academic/scholarly publication.
—BLDSC (4968.815000); KR SourceOne; SWETS; UMI; UnCover. **CCC**.
Description: Provides a forum for dialog and debate, for publishing new research, and for addressing current issues of interest on a wide and interdisciplinary basis.

JOURNAL OF EARLY SOUTHERN DECORATIVE ARTS. see *ANTIQUES*

JOURNAL OF EUROPEAN STUDIES. see *HISTORY — History Of Europe*

JOURNAL OF MEDIEVAL AND EARLY MODERN STUDIES. see *HUMANITIES: COMPREHENSIVE WORKS*

JOURNAL OF MULTICULTURAL AND CROSS-CULTURAL RESEARCH IN ART EDUCATION. see *EDUCATION*

JOURNAL OF PRE-RAPHAELITE STUDIES. see *LITERATURE*

| 510 | | US | |

JOURNAL OF REGIONAL CRITICISM. 1979. irreg. price varies. (Institute of Martial Arts, Inc.) Arjuna Library Press, 1025 Garner St., D, Space 18, Colorado Springs, CO 80905-1774. TEL 719-475-2787. Ed. Joseph A. Uphoff, Jr. (looseleaf format) **Document type:** proceedings, academic/scholarly publication.
Description: Manuscript copy on proceedings in surrealist theory, metamathematics, experiments in poetics of representational and dynamic forms, abstract and symbolic arts, metalogic of criticism, and analytical Labanotation (differential algebra) in dance and martial arts.

| 700 300 | | US | ISSN 1057-0292 |

JOURNAL OF SOCIAL THEORY IN ART EDUCATION. 1981. a. $15. (Caucus of Social Theory and Art Education) National Art Education Association, 1916 Association Dr., Reston, VA 20191-1590. TEL 703-860-8000. (Subscr. to: Connie Landis, CSTAE Treas., 3026 Stinson Ave., Billings, MT 59102) Ed. Janice Davenport. R&P contact: Cam Luccarelli. adv. contact: Janice Davenport. circ. 150. **Indexed:** C.I.J.E. **Document type:** academic/scholarly publication.
Description: Promotes the use of theoretical concepts from the social sciences to study visual culture and the teaching of art.

| 700 | | GW | ISSN 0933-307X |

JUNGE KUNST. 1987. 4/yr. DM.39 (Europe DM.47). Verlagsgesellschaft Ritterbach mbH, Postfach 1820, 50208 Frechen, Germany. TEL 49-2234-1866-0. FAX 49-2234-186690. Ed. Barbara Rotzoll-Golly. R&P contact: Johannes Taube. adv. contact: Franziska Burgwinkel. **Document type:** consumer publication.

700 US ISSN 1077-8411
JUXTAPOZ. 1994. q. $14.50 (Canada $18.50; elsewhere $25) (effective 1997); newsstand price: $3.95. High Speed Productions, Inc., 1303 Underwood Ave., San Francisco, CA 94124-3308. TEL 415-822-3083. FAX 415-822-8359. URL: http://www.juxtapoz.com. (Dist. by: Kable News Co. Inc., 641 Lexington Ave., New York, NY 10022. TEL 212-768-1000. FAX 212-768-1063; Alt. addr.: Box 884570, San Francisco, CA 94188-4570) Ed. Kevin Thatcher; Pub. Edward Riggins. adv.: B&W page $2000; trim 8 1/2 x 10 7/8; adv. contact: Steve Timble. video rev.; circ. 35,000 (paid). (back issues avail.)
 Description: Offers a gallery of underground artists. Includes full color layouts featuring painters, sculptors, cartoonists, and photographers along with portfolios, sketches, interviews and reviews.

700 FI ISSN 0075-4633
JYVASKYLA STUDIES IN THE ARTS. 1967. irreg. price varies; available on exchange. Jyvaskylan Yliopisto - University of Jyvaskyla, Publications Center, PL 35, 40100 Jyvaskyla 10, Finland. TEL 941-601-211. FAX 603-371. TELEX 28219 JYK SF. Eds. Erkki Pekkila, Kalevi Poykko. circ. 450.

914 700 BE ISSN 0022-7277
NX5
K & C. (Kunst en Cultuur) 1968. m. 1500 BEF. Palais des Beaux Arts, Koningsstraat 10, 1000 Brussels, Belgium. Ed. Frans Boenders. adv.; bk.rev.; film rev.; play rev.; bibl.; illus. circ. 500.

K W M NEWSLETTER. (Kendall Whaling Museum) see *MUSEUMS AND ART GALLERIES*

KALAVA HA SAHITYAYA. see *LITERATURE*

KALDRON. see *LITERATURE — Poetry*

THE KALEIDOSCOPE (AKRON); international magazine of literature, fine arts and disability. see *HANDICAPPED*

700 AT ISSN 0047-312X
KALORI. 1959. q. Aus.$10. Royal South Australian Society of Arts, 122 Kintore Ave., North Terr., Adelaide, S.A. 5000, Australia. TEL 61-8-223-4704. Ed. P.W. Griscti. adv.; bk.rev. circ. 800. **Document type:** academic/scholarly publication.

KANINA; revista de artes y letras. see *LITERATURE*

700 PL ISSN 0075-5257
KATALOG ZABYTKOW SZTUKI W POLSCE. 1953. irreg. price varies. (Polska Akademia Nauk, Instytut Sztuki) Wydawnictwa Artystyczne i Filmowe, Pulawska 61, 02-595 Warsaw, Poland. TEL 048-22-45-53-01. FAX 48-22-455584. (Dist. by: Ars Polona-Ruch, Krakowskie Przedmiescie 7, Warsaw, Poland) Ed. Jerzy Zygmunt Lozinski. circ. 3,250. **Document type:** catalog.
 Description: Each volume covers a part of Poland's territory and contains inventory descriptions of architecture, sculpture, painting and objects of applied art.

KAYHAN KARIKATUR. see *LITERARY AND POLITICAL REVIEWS*

741.092 US ISSN 0163-1861
N6537.K44
KENT COLLECTOR. 1974. 3/yr. $15. State University of New York at Plattsburgh, Rockwell Kent Gallery, SUNY-Plattsburgh, Plattsburgh, NY 12901. TEL 518-564-2813. Ed. Marguerite Eisinger. R&P contact: Marguerite Eisinger. adv. contact: Marguerite Eisinger. bk.rev. circ. 225. **Document type:** academic/scholarly publication, newsletter.
 Description: Devoted to the life and work of Rockwell Kent and the American art of the first half of the twentieth century.

KENYA NATIONAL ACADEMY OF SCIENCE. ANNUAL REPORT. see *SCIENCES: COMPREHENSIVE WORKS*

KERAMISCHE ZEITSCHRIFT. see *CERAMICS, GLASS AND POTTERY*

700 RU ISSN 0131-7555
KHUDOZHNIK. 1958. q. $96 (effective 1998). (Soyuz Khudozhnikov Rossiiskoi Federatsii) Izdatel'stvo Khudozhnik, Ul. Chernyakhovskogo, 4a, 125319 Moscow, Russia. TEL 095-1512502. (Dist. in U.S. by: Victor Kamkin Inc., 4956 Boiling Brook Pkwy., Rockville, MD 20852. TEL 301-881-5973. FAX 301-881-5973) illus.; index. **Indexed:** Numis.Lit. —BLDSC (0396.370000).

700 800 SU ISSN 1018-3612
KING SAUD UNIVERSITY. JOURNAL. ARTS. Key Title: Majallat Jami'at al-Malik Sa'ud, al-Adab. (Other sections avail.: Administrative Sciences, Agricultural Sciences, Architecture and Planning, Computer and Information Sciences, Educational Sciences and Islamic Studies, Engineering Sciences, Science) (Text in Arabic, English) 1989. s-a. $10. King Saud University, University Libraries, P.O. Box 22480, Riyadh 11495, Saudi Arabia. TEL 966-1-4676148. FAX 966-1-4676162. TELEX 401019 KSU SJ. Ed. Khalid A. Al-Hamoudi. R&P contact: Saad A. Al-Dobaian. charts; illus. circ. 3,000. **Document type:** academic/scholarly publication.
 Refereed Serial

700 SP ISSN 0214-7955
N7109.P25
KOBIE, REVISTA DE BELLAS ARTES Y CIENCIAS: SERIE BELLAS ARTES. Key Title: Kobie. Arte Ederrak. (Text in English, German, Spanish; summaries in Basque, English, French, German) 1969. a. 2500 ptas. Diputacion Foral de Bizkaia, Departamento de Cultura, P.O. Box 97, Bilbao, Spain. TEL 34-4-4157217. FAX 34-4-4162981. (back issues avail.)
—CINDOC.
 Supersedes in part (in 1984): Kobie (ISSN 0211-1942)

KODIKAS - CODE - ARS SEMEIOTICA; an international journal of semiotics. see *COMMUNICATIONS*

KODIKAS - CODE SUPPLEMENT. see *COMMUNICATIONS*

700 JA ISSN 0023-2785
N8
KOKKA/ESSENCES OF JAPAN. (Text in Japanese) 1889. m. $405. Asahi Shimbun Publishing Co., 3-2, Tsukiji 5-chome, Chuo-ku, Tokyo 104-11, Japan. (Order to: Japan Publications Trading Co., Ltd., Box 5030, Tokyo International, Tokyo, Japan) Ed. Yuzo Yamane. circ. 2,000. (also avail. in microform from CHL)

709 GW ISSN 0075-6563
KOLLOQUIUM UEBER SPAETANTIKE UND FRUEHMITTELALTERLICHE SKULPTUR. (Text in German) 1968. irreg. price varies. Verlag Philipp von Zabern GmbH, Philipp-von-Zabern-Platz 1-3, 55116 Mainz, Germany. TEL 06131-28747-0. FAX 06131-223710. Ed. Vladimir Milojcic. **Document type:** monographic series.

KONGGAN/SPACE. see *ARCHITECTURE*

700 BE ISSN 0770-0849
KONINKLIJKE ACADEMIE VOOR WETENSCHAPPEN, LETTEREN EN SCHONE KUNSTEN VAN BELGIE. VERHANDELINGEN. KLASSE DER SCHONE KUNSTEN. (Text in Dutch, English, French, German) 1943. irreg., no.55, 1991. price varies. Koninklijke Academie voor Wetenschappen, Letteren en Schone Kunsten van Belgie, 1 Hertogsstraat, B-1000 Brussels, Belgium. (Dist. by: N.V. Brepols, Steenweg op Tielen 68, 2300 Turnhout, Belgium. TEL 32-14-402500. FAX 32-14-428919) (back issues avail.) **Document type:** monographic series.
—KNAW.
 Formerly (until 1972): Koninklijke Vlaamse Academie voor Wetenschappen, Letteren en Schone Kunsten van Belgie. Verhandelingen. Klasse der Schone Kunsten (ISSN 0770-089X)

709 NO ISSN 0023-3609
N8
KONSTHISTORISK TIDSKRIFT. (Text in English, French, German and Scandinavian languages; summaries in English.) 1932. q. NOK 545 in Nordic countries; elsewhere $97 (effective 1997). (Konsthistoriska Saellskapet) Scandinavian University Press, P.O. Box 2959 Toeyen, N-0608 Oslo, Norway. TEL 47-22-57-54-00. FAX 47-22-57-53-53. E-mail: mail@scup.no; URL: http://www.scup.no. (U.S. addr.: 875 Massachusetts Ave., Ste. 84, Cambridge, MA 02139. TEL 617-497-6515. FAX 617-354-6875) Ed. Hans Henrik Brummer. adv.; bk.rev.; bibl.; illus. circ. 500. **Indexed:** Art Ind., Artbibl., Artbibl.Mod., Arts & Hum.Cit.Ind., ASCA, Avery Ind.Archit.Per., Curr.Cont., Ind.Bk.Rev.Hum., RILA. **Document type:** academic/scholarly publication.
—Genuine Article; KR SourceOne; SWETS. **CCC.**

750 SW ISSN 0283-2887
KONSTNAEREN. 1940. bi-m. SEK 220; newsstand price: SEK 45. Konstnaernas Riksorganisation (KRO), Enkehuset, Nortullsg. 45, S-113 45 Stockholm, Sweden. Ed. Birgitta Gustafsson. adv.: B&W page SEK 8200, color page SEK 11100; trim 190 x 230; adv. contact: Mats Broden. circ. 4,300. cols./p.: 4; pp./issue: 32.
 Former titles (until 1985): K R O - Konstnaeren; (until 1979): Konstnaeren; (until no.4, 1976): Medlemsblad - K R O.

720 SW ISSN 0347-4453
KONSTPERSPEKTIV; Nordens stoersta konsttidskrift. 1975. q. SEK 250 (members, art students and artists SEK 200) (effective 1995). Sveriges Konstfoereningars Riksfoerbund, P.O. Box 60065, S-216 10 Malmoe, Sweden. TEL 46-40-16-41-10. FAX 46-46-16-26-07. Ed. Uno Kampmark. adv. contact: Monica Larsson. (also avail. in audio cassette)

720 SW ISSN 1101-8623
KONSTTIDNINGEN. 1990. q. SEK 170 (effective 1996). Vindel AB, c/o Lars Kolberg, Ehrensvaerdsgatan 3, S-112 35 Stockholm, Sweden. TEL 46-8-651-70-17. FAX 46-8-651-70-17. (Subscr. to: Foerlagsdata RK AB, Box 982, S-721 23 Vaesteraas, Sweden. TEL 46-21-554-21)

700 745.1 SW ISSN 1103-663X
KONSTVAERLDEN; auktioner, design antikviteter, debatt. 1992. bi-m. SEK 270 (foreign SEK 390) (effective 1997). LotsatorGruppen AB, Box 5111, S-102 43 Stockholm, Sweden. TEL 46-8-661-62-11. FAX 46-8-661-62-11. (Subscr. to: Pressdata, Box 3263, S-103 65 Stockholm, Sweden. TEL 46-8-98-88-80) Ed. Goeran Hellstroem. circ. 18,000.

700 PL ISSN 1230-6142
NK7
KONTEKSTY; polska sztuka ludowa. (Text in Polish; summaries in English) 1947. q. $20. Polska Akademia Nauk, Instytut Sztuki, Ul. Dluga 28, 00-950 Warsaw, Poland. TEL 48-22-313271. FAX 48-22-313149. (Dist. by: AMOS, ul. Zuga 12 01-806 Warsaw, Poland. TEL 48-22-346521) Eds. Aleksander Jackowski, Zbigniew Benedyktowicz. bk.rev.; illus.; index. circ. 1,000. (reprint service avail.) **Indexed:** Artbibl.Mod., IBR, M.L.A., MLA Intl.Bibl. **Document type:** academic/scholarly publication.
 Formerly (until 1990): Polska Sztuka Ludowa (ISSN 0032-3721)
 Description: Covers Polish folk art.

701 AU ISSN 0023-3757
KONTUR;* Zeitschrift fuer Kunsttheorie. no.47, 1973. 10/yr. S.80($4) H. Kuchling, Linzerstr. 392, A-1014 Vienna, Austria.

KOREANA; a quarterly on Korean culture. see *ORIENTAL STUDIES*

709 GW ISSN 0340-7403
KRITISCHE BERICHTE; Zeitschrift fuer Kunst- und Kulturgeschichte. 1973. q. DM.58 (foreign DM.63). (Ulmer Verein, Verband fuer Kunst- und Kulturwissenschaften) Jonas Verlag, Weidenhaeuserstr. 88, 35037 Marburg, Germany. TEL 49-6421-25132. Ed.Bd. adv.; bk.rev. circ. 1,500. **Indexed:** Artbibl.Mod. **Document type:** academic/scholarly publication.

709 NE ISSN 0166-0381
KRONIEK VAN HET REMBRANDTHUIS. (Text in Dutch; summaries in English) 1946. 2/yr. fl.35 (effective 1996). Vereniging van Vrienden van Museum Het Rembrandthuis, Jodenbreestraat 4-6, 1011 NK Amsterdam, Netherlands. TEL 31-20-6384668. FAX 31-20-6232246. Ed. M.E.A. Enklaar. adv.; illus. (X) **Document type:** academic/scholarly publication.
 Formerly (until 1969): Vriendenkring van Het Rembrandthuis. Kroniek (ISSN 0042-9171)
 Description: Covers Rembrandt and his surroundings, including his redecessors, pupils and followers, 17th century art, etching techniques, and history.

KUENSTLER JAHRBUCH. see BUSINESS AND ECONOMICS — Trade And Industrial Directories

700 GW ISSN 0934-1730
KUENSTLER - KRITISCHES LEXIKON DER GEGENWARTSKUNST. 1988. q. DM.214. W B Verlag, Nymphenburgstr. 84, 80636 Munich, Germany. Ed. Detlef Bluemler. **Document type:** academic/scholarly publication.

700 331.8 GW ISSN 0946-3100
DIE KUENSTLERGILDE; bildende Kunst, Literatur, Musik, Photographie, Publizistik, Theater. 1954. q. DM.60 (effective 1997). Kuenstlergilde e.V., Hafenmarkt 2, 73728 Esslingen, Germany. TEL 49-711-3969010. FAX 49-711-39690123. Ed. Samuel Beer. adv.: B&W page DM.900; trim 258 x 180. bk.rev. circ. 1,800. **Document type:** newsletter.

700 830 GW
KULTUR NEWS. 1991. m. DM.12. Kulturring in Berlin e.V., Friedrichstr. 120, 10117 Berlin, Germany. TEL 49-30-2826343. FAX 49-30-2826343. Ed. Ulrich Becker. R&P contact: Ulrich Becker. adv.: page DM.180; adv. contact: Ulrich Becker. bk.rev.; bibl.; film rev.; illus.; music rev.; play rev.; circ. 1,500. (back issues avail.) **Document type:** newsletter.
 Formerly: Kulturbund Informationen.

KULTUR UND TECHNIK. see MUSEUMS AND ART GALLERIES

KULTURA. see LITERATURE

700 AU ISSN 0023-5121
KULTURBERICHTE AUS NIEDEROESTERREICH. Variant title: N O Kulturberichte. (Supplement to: Amtliche Nachrichten) 1950. m. S.36. Amt der Niederoesterreichische Landesregierung, Presseabteilung, Herrengasse 11, A-1014 Vienna, Austria. Eds. Gottfried Kapf, Heinz-Werner Eckhardt. charts; illus.

700 GW ISSN 0724-343X
DD260.3
KULTURCHRONIK; Nachrichten und Berichte aus Deutschland. English edition (ISSN 0934-1706) (Text in English, French, German, Russian and Spanish) 1983. bi-m. free. Inter Nationes e.V., Kennedyallee 91-103, 53175 Bonn, Germany. TEL 49-228-880-0. FAX 49-228-880457. TELEX 17228308. Ed. Dieter Benecke. bk.rev.; bibl.; illus. circ. 45,000. **Document type:** consumer publication.
 Description: Devoted to news and views concerning art, literature, theatre, education and science, architecture, photography, film, television and music in Germany. Includes list of events and exhibitions.

700 II ISSN 0023-5342
KUMAR. (Text in Gujarati) 1924. m. Rs.24($6) Kumar Karyalaya Ltd., 1454 Raipur, Ahmedabad 1, India. Ed. B. Rawat. adv.; bk.rev.; illus. circ. 5,500.

709 913 SW ISSN 0083-6737
KUNGLIGA VITTERHETS HISTORIE OCH ANTIKVITETS AKADEMIEN. ANTIKVARISKT ARKIV. (Text in English, German and Swedish) 1954. irreg., no.78, 1995. price varies. Kungliga Vitterhets, Historie- och Antikvitets Akademien - Royal Academy of Letters, History and Antiquities, P.O. Box 5622, S-114 86 Stockholm, Sweden. Dist. by: Almqvist & Wiksell International, P.O. Box 4627, S-116 91 Stockholm, Sweden. TEL 46-8-7282500. FAX 46-8-338707) index.
 —KNAW.

700 SZ ISSN 1013-6940
DAS KUNST-BULLETIN. 1968. m. 44 SFr. (Europe 55 SFr.) (effective 1996). Schweizerischer Kunstverein, Postfach, CH-8026 Zurich, Switzerland. TEL 41-1-2416300. FAX 41-1-2416373. (Subscr. to: Zuerichsee Zeitschriften Verlag, Seestr. 86, CH-8712 Staefa, Switzerland. TEL 41-1-9285521) Ed. Claudia Jolles. adv. contact: Kurt Eberle. bk.rev. circ. 19,000. **Document type:** bulletin.

KUNST EN WETENSCHAP. see SCIENCES: COMPREHENSIVE WORKS

KUNST IN KOELN. see MUSEUMS AND ART GALLERIES

705 AU ISSN 0075-7241
KUNST-KATALOG: AUKTIONEN. 1947. irreg. price varies. Dorotheum, Dorotheergasse 17, A-1011 Vienna, Austria. TEL 43-1-51560-0. FAX 43-1-51560443. E-mail: marketing.dorotheum@telecom.at; URL: http://www.dorotheum.com. Ed. Dieter Rauch. adv. contact: Reinier Heere. bk.rev. circ. 2,000. **Document type:** catalog.

700 NO ISSN 0023-5415
N8
KUNST OG KULTUR; Norwegian journal for pictorial art, architecture and handicrafts. (Text in Norwegian; summaries in English) 1911. q. NOK 525 in Nordic countries; elsewhere $115 (effective 1997). (National Gallery of Art) Scandinavian University Press, P.O. Box 2959 Toeyen, N-0608 Oslo, Norway. TEL 47-22-57-54-00. FAX 47-22-57-53-53. E-mail: mail@scup.no; URL: http://www.scup.no. (US addr.: 875 Massachusetts Ave., Ste. 84, Cambridge, MA 02139. TEL 617-497-6515. FAX 617-354-6875) Eds. Knut Berg Nils Messel. adv.; bk.rev.; illus.; index. circ. 1,000. Indexed: Artbibl, IBR. **Document type:** academic/scholarly publication.
 Description: Devoted to pictorial art, architecture and handicraft.

700 DK ISSN 0454-6520
KUNST OG MUSEUM. 1966. a. DKK 60. (Foreningen af Danske Kunstmuseer) Museumstjenesten, Sjoerupvej 1, Lysgaard, 8800 Viborg, Denmark. illus.

704.948 AU ISSN 0023-5431
KUNST UND KIRCHE; Oekumenische Zeitschrift fuer Architektur und Kunst. 1923. q. S.378. Landesverlag, Landstr. 41, A-4020 Linz, Austria. Ed.Bd. adv.; bk.rev.; illus.; index. **Indexed:** Artbibl.Mod., Artbibl., Avery Ind.Archit.Per., CERDIC. —BLDSC (5129.800000).

700 800 GW ISSN 0946-5243
KUNST UND KULTUR. 9/yr. DM.50. Industriegewerkschaft Medien, Postfach 102451, 70020 Stuttgart, Germany. TEL 49-711-20180. FAX 49-711-2018262. circ. 20,000. **Document type:** consumer publication.

KUNST UND STADT. see ARCHITECTURE

720 730 SZ ISSN 0023-5458
KUNST UND STEIN. 1956. bi-m. 75 SFr. to members; non-members 81 SFr.; foreign 90 SFr. (Verband Schweizer Bildhauer- und Steinmetzmeister) Verlag Kunst und Stein, Postfach 6922, Schwarztorstr. 26, CH-3001 Bern, Switzerland. TEL 41-31-3822322. FAX 41-31-3822670. Ed. Thomas Gfeller. adv.; bk.rev. circ. 1,800. **Document type:** consumer publication.

707 370 GW ISSN 0170-6225
KUNST UND UNTERRICHT; Zeitschrift fuer Kunstpaedagogik. 1968. 10/yr. DM.143.60 (foreign DM.153.60). Erhard Friedrich Verlag GmbH, Im Brande 17, 30926 Seelze, Germany. TEL 49-511-40004-0. FAX 49-511-40004170. (Subscr. to: Postfach 100150, 30917 Seelze, Germany) Ed.Bd. adv.; bibl.; charts; illus.; index. circ. 15,000. **Indexed:** IBR. **Document type:** academic/scholarly publication.

705 DK ISSN 0107-6957
KUNSTAVISEN. 1981. m. DKK 320. Kunst-Avisen, Greve Strandvej 31, DK-2670 Greve, Denmark. TEL 45-42-60-11-00. FAX 45-42-60-45-10. Ed. Kurt Faurholm. adv.; illus. circ. 6,000. **Document type:** newspaper.

700 NE ISSN 0165-1129
KUNSTBEELD. 1976. 11/yr. fl.155. Bohn Stafleu van Loghum B.V. (Subsidiary of: Wolters Kluwer N.V.), Postbus 246, 3990 GA Houten, Netherlands. TEL 31-3403-95711. FAX 31-3403-50903. (Editorial addr.: J. Verhulststraat 101, 1071 MX Amsterdam, Netherlands. TEL 31-20-6734222) Ed. F. Duister. adv.; circ. 9,500 (paid). **Document type:** consumer publication.
 —SWETS.

700 GW ISSN 0023-5504
DER KUNSTHANDEL; Zeitschrift fuer Bild und Rahmen. 1908. m. DM.240 (foreign DM.252) (effective 1997). Huethig GmbH, Postfach 102869, 69018 Heidelberg, Germany. TEL 49-6221-489293. FAX 49-6221-489481. E-mail: cohenm@huethig.de. Eds. Horst Weidmann, Astrid Kehsler. adv.: B&W page DM.1800; trim 210 x 297; adv. contact: Micheline Cohen. bk.rev.; charts; illus. circ. 4,000. **Document type:** trade publication.

709 AU ISSN 0075-2312
KUNSTHISTORISCHE SAMMLUNGEN IN WIEN. JAHRBUCH. 1926. a. price varies. (Kunsthistorisches Museum in Wien) Verlag Anton Schroll und Co., Spengergasse 39, A-1051 Vienna, Austria. FAX 43-1-544564166. Ed. Georg Kugler. R&P contact: Georg Kugler. **Indexed:** Art Ind., Artbibl.Mod., IBR, Numis.Lit., RILA. **Document type:** academic/scholarly publication.
 —KR SourceOne.

700 900 IT
KUNSTHISTORISCHES INSTITUT IN FLORENZ. MITTEILUNGEN. (Text in English, German, Italian) 1908. 3/yr. DM.170. Kunsthistorisches Institut in Florenz, Via G. Giusti 44, 50121 Florence, Italy. TEL 39-55-2491147. FAX 39-55-2491155. Eds. Max Seidel, Wolfger A. Bulst. bibl.; illus.; index; circ. 900 (controlled). (reprint service avail. from SWZ) **Indexed:** Art Ind., Curr.Cont., RILA. **Document type:** academic/scholarly publication.

705 AU ISSN 0454-6601
N6836.L5
KUNSTJAHRBUCH DER STADT LINZ. 1961. a. S.250. Stadtmuseum Linz, Bethlehemstr. 7, A-4020 Linz, Austria. Ed. W. Katzinger. bk.rev. circ. 450. **Indexed:** Artbibl.Mod., RILA. **Document type:** academic/scholarly publication.
 Formerly: Linzer Jahrbuch fuer Kunstgeschichte (ISSN 0075-9732)

700 SZ ISSN 0023-5512
KUNSTNACHRICHTEN. 1963. bi-m. 19.80 Fr. Edition Kunstkreis im Ex Libris Verlag, Postfach, 8010 Zurich, Switzerland. Ed. P.F. Althaus. bk.rev.; illus. circ. 10,000. (tabloid format)

706.5 GW ISSN 0174-352X
KUNSTPREIS-JAHRBUCH. (In three volumes) a. DM.248 (foreign DM.256). Weltkunst Verlag GmbH, Nymphenburgerstr. 84, 80636 Munich, Germany. TEL 49-89-126990-0. FAX 49-89-12699011. Ed. Eleonore Pichelkastner. adv.; illus. circ. 9,000. **Document type:** catalog.
 Formerly: Art-Price Annual.
 Description: Verified art auction results from international auction houses.

700 NE ISSN 0166-7297
KUNSTSCHRIFT. 1957. 6/yr. fl.94.50 includes Tentoonstellingsboekje. (Openbaar Kunstbezit) S D U Uitgeverij Koninginnegracht, Postbus 30446, 2500 GK The Hague, Netherlands. TEL 31-70-3429700. FAX 31-70-3634903. Ed. M. Haveman. adv. circ. 19,500. **Document type:** consumer publication.
 —SWETS.
 Formerly (until 1980): Openbaar Kunstbezit (ISSN 0166-7394)

700 371.33 GW
KUNSTSTUNDE; Unterrichtsbeispiele zur aesthetischen Erziehung. 1980. 2/yr. DM.24 (effective 1998). A L S Verlag GmbH, Voltastr. 3, 63128 Dietzenbach, Germany. TEL 49-6074-82160. FAX 49-6074-27322. Ed. Ingrid Kreide. illus.; cum.index: 1980-1996. circ. 8,000. (looseleaf format; back issues avail.) **Document type:** academic/scholarly publication.

701 GW ISSN 0723-6638
KURT-SCHWITTERS-ALMANACH. 1982. a. DM.24.80 per no. Postscriptum-Verlag GmbH, Annenstr. 8, 30171 Hannover, Germany. TEL 0511-713686. Ed. Michael Erlhoff. circ. 1,500.

KYOWA HAKKO KOGYO. ANNUAL REPORT. see ADVERTISING AND PUBLIC RELATIONS

700 720 900 800   IT   ISSN 0393-0807
N6916
LABYRINTHOS. (Text in English, French, German, Italian) 1982. s-a. L.50000. Casa Editrice Vallecchi, Viale Milton 7, 50129 Florence, Italy. Ed. Gian Lorenzo Mellini. adv.; bk.rev. circ. 2,000. (back issues avail.) **Indexed:** Avery Ind.Archit.Per., RILA.

709   II   ISSN 0458-6506
LALIT KALA. 1955. irreg., no.27, 1993. Rs.250. National Academy of Art - Lalit Kala Akademi, Rabindra Bhavan, New Delhi 110001, India. —UnCover.
Description: Covers ancient Indian art and archaeology.

709   II   ISSN 0023-7396
N1
LALIT KALA CONTEMPORARY. (Text in English) 1962. s-a. Rs.60. National Academy of Art - Lalit Kala Akademi, Rabindra Bhavan, New Delhi 110001, India. Ed. S.A. Krishnan. adv.; bk.rev.
Description: Devoted to contemporary Indian art.

LANTERN; cultural journal. see EDUCATION

700   SP   ISSN 0212-1700
LAPIZ; revista internacional de arte. 1982. m. (10/yr.). 9000 ptas. (Europe 11500 ptas.; America 17600 ptas.) (effective 1995). Publicaciones de Estetica y Pensamiento, S.L., Gravina 10, 1o, 28004 Madrid, Spain. TEL 91-522-29-72. FAX 91-522-47-07. Ed. Jose Alberto Lopez. adv.: page 290000 ptas.; trim 242 x 287; adv. contact: Isabel de Busto. circ. 18,000.
—CINDOC; SWETS.
Description: Informs on developments in the plastic arts, both in Spain and abroad.

700   US   ISSN 0362-7047
N6995.L3
LATVJU MAKSLA. (Text in Latvian) 1975. irreg. $12 per no. American Latvian Association in the United States, Inc., Latvian Institute, 400 Hurley Ave., Box 4578, Rockville, MD 20849-4578. TEL 301-340-1914. FAX 301-762-5438. Ed. Arnold Sildegs. R&P contact: Arnold Sildegs. TEL 616-344-5373. adv. contact: Arnold Sildegs. bk.rev.; illus.; circ. 1,500 (paid). **Document type:** monographic series.

LAZIO IERI E OGGI; rivista mensile di cultura, arte, turismo. see TRAVEL AND TOURISM

741   GW
LEHRHILFEN BILDENDE KUNST. KUENSTLER UND WERK. 1970. s-a. DM.40. Kallmeyer'sche Verlagsbuchhandlung GmbH, Im Brande 19, 30926 Seelze, Germany. TEL 49-511-40004175. FAX 49-511-40004176. Ed. Johannes Eucker. (looseleaf format; reprint service avail.) **Document type:** academic/scholarly publication.
Former titles (until 1994): Lernhilfen fuer Bildende Kunst (ISSN 0935-8811); Lehrbogen fuer Kunsterziehung (ISSN 0932-7959); Zeichenwerk (ISSN 0084-523X)

LEIDSE UNIVERSITEITSBIBLIOTHEEK. KUNSTPUBLIKATIES. see LIBRARY AND INFORMATION SCIENCES

750   UK   ISSN 0024-0710
LEISURE PAINTER. 1967. m. $50. Artists' Publishing Co. Ltd., Caxton House, 63-65 High St., Tenterden, Kent TN30 6BD, England. TEL 44-1580-763315. FAX 44-1580-765411. Ed. Irene Briers. adv. contact: Tim Fleming. bk.rev.; illus. circ. 23,000. **Document type:** consumer publication.
Description: Provides painting instruction and guidance.

LEODIUM. see HISTORY — History Of Europe

705   US   ISSN 0024-094X
N6490   CODEN: LEONDP
LEONARDO: ART SCIENCE AND TECHNOLOGY; oriented towards readers interested in the application of contemporary science and technology to music and the arts. 1966. 5/yr. $58 to individuals (foreign $80); institutions $330 (foreign $352); students $48 (foreign $70) includes Leonardo Musical Journal (effective 1997). (International Society for the Arts, Sciences and Technology) M I T Press, 5 Cambridge Center, Cambridge, MA 02142. TEL 617-253-2889. FAX 617-577-1545. E-mail: journals-orders@mit.edu; URL: http://www-mitpress.mit.edu. Ed. Roger L. Malina. R&P contact: Paul Dzus. adv.; bk.rev.; illus. circ. 2,500. (also avail. in microfilm from UMI; back issues avail.) **Indexed:** Abstr.Hum.Comp.Inter., Art & Archaeol.Tech.Abstr., Arts & Hum.Cit.Ind., Curr.Cont., INSPEC (1993-). **Document type:** academic/scholarly publication.
—BLDSC (5182.600000); AskIEEE; Genuine Article; KR SourceOne; SWETS; UMI; UnCover. **CCC.**
Description: Devoted to the interrelationships between art, science and technology. Contains articles about technical aspects of art, on general developments and new materials, and on techniques of use to artists.
Refereed Serial

709.94   UK
LEONARDO DA VINCI SOCIETY NEWSLETTER. 1982. 2/yr. £5 membership. Leonardo da Vinci Society, c/o Francis Ames-Lewis, Ed., Dept. of History of Art, Birkbeck College, 43 Gordon Sq., London WC1H 0PD, England. TEL 44-171-631-6108. FAX 44-171-631-6107. E-mail: f.ames-lewis@hart.bbk.ac.uk. R&P contact: Francis Ames-Lewis. bibl. circ. 150. (back issues avail.) **Document type:** newsletter.
Supersedes in part (in 1989): Newsletter for Leonardisti (ISSN 0741-9597)
Description: Includes a current select bibliography, news of events, exhibitions, conferences and lectures on Leonardo da Vinci.

LEONARDO MUSIC JOURNAL. see MUSIC

700   RU   ISSN 0024-1199
LETOPIS' PECHATNYKH PROIZVEDENII IZOBRAZITEL'NOGO ISKUSSTVA. 1934. q. $4.80. (Komitet po Pechati Soveta Ministrov) Izdatel'stvo Kniga, 50, Gorky St., 125047 Moscow, Russia. bibl.; index. circ. 945.

700 800   DR
LETRA GRANDE, ARTE Y LITERATURA. 1980. m. $65. Leonardo da Vinci 13, Mirador del Sur, Santo Domingo, Dominican Republic. TEL 809-531-2225. FAX 809-541-2855. Dir. Juan Ramon Quinones M. adv. contact: Berenice Canaham.

LETRAS DEL ECUADOR. see LITERATURE

LETRAS E ARTES. see LITERATURE

700   US
LETTER ARTS' BOOK CLUB NEWSLETTER. 1980. q. $7.50 (effective 1997). Letter Arts' Book Club, Inc., 1833 Spring Garden St., Greensboro, NC 27403. TEL 910-272-7604. FAX 910-272-9015. E-mail: JNEALBOOKS@AOL.com. Ed. John Neal. bk.rev. circ. 5,000. **Document type:** newsletter.
Description: How-to articles for calligraphers, marblers, book-binders, illuminators.

741.61   US   ISSN 1076-7339
Z43.A1
LETTER ARTS REVIEW. 1982. q. $42 (Canada and Mexico $45; elsewhere $62). Letters Arts Review, vnc., 1624 24th Ave., S.W., Norman, OK 73072-5709. TEL 405-364-8794. FAX 405-364-8914. E-mail: letterarts@netplus.net; URL: http://www.letterarts.com. Ed. Karyn L. Gilman. Pub. Karyn L. Gilman. R&P contact: Karyn L. Gilman. adv. contact: Karyn L. Gilman. bk.rev.; index, cum.index etc. 5,000. (back issues avail.) **Indexed:** Art Ind., DAAI.
—BLDSC (5185.126770); KR SourceOne; UnCover.
Former titles (until vol.11, no.2, 1994): Calligraphy Review (ISSN 0895-7819); (until 1987) Calligraphy Idea Exchange (ISSN 0737-318X)
Description: Dedicated to the art and craft of hand lettering. Provides in-depth articles and quality reproductions about artists, calligraphic works past, present and future, typography, artists' books, practical commercial applications, and unbiased book and exhibition reviews.

LETTER BOMB. see COMMUNICATIONS — Postal Affairs

745   US
LETTERHEADS; the international annual of letterhead design. 1977. a. $19.95 (effective 1996). Art Direction Book Co., Inc., 456 Glenbrook Rd., Glenbrook, CT 06906-1800. TEL 203-353-1441. FAX 203-353-1371. Ed. Don Barron. adv.; circ. 6,200 (paid). **Document type:** trade publication.

LETTRES EOLIENNES/EOLIKA GRAMMATA; revue bimensuelle d'art de Lesbos. see LITERATURE

700   US
▼**LEXXICON.COM.** 1996. bi-m. Box 387, Newnan, GA 30364. E-mail: linda@lexxicon.com; URL: http://www.lexxicon.com. Ed. Linda Devault Anderson.
●Available only online.
Description: Covers art in all its forms.

792 780 700   CN   ISSN 0227-227X
LIAISON; la revue des arts en Ontario francais. 1978. 5/yr. Can.$26 (effective 1996). Editions L' Interligne, 282 Dupuis, Ste. 202, Vanier, ON K1L 7H9, Canada. TEL 613-748-0850. FAX 613-748-0852. Ed. Paul-F. Sylvestre. R&P contact: Paul-Francois Sylvestre. adv. contact: Rachel Carriere. bk.rev.; illus. circ. 1,400. **Indexed:** Rehabil.Lit. **Document type:** consumer publication.
Description: Artistic and cultural activities by Franco-Ontariens; includes creative writing, profiles of artists, current events.

700   CC
LIANHUAN HUABAO/PICTURE STORIES. (Text in Chinese) m. $90. Renmin Meishu Chubanshe - People's Fine Arts Publishers, 32 Beizongbu Hutong, Beijing 100735, People's Republic of China. TEL 5122587. (Dist. in US by: China Books & Periodicals, Inc. 2929 24th St., San Francisco, CA 94110. TEL 415-282-2994) Ed. Meng Qingjiang. illus.

740 800   CC
LIANHUANHUA YISHU/ART OF PICTORIAL STORIES. (Text in Chinese) q. Zhongguo Lianhuanhua Chubanshe, 7 Banqiao Nanxiang, Beixinqiao, Beijing 100007, People's Republic of China. TEL 4014830. Ed. Jiang Weipu.

700   US
LIBRARY OF GREAT PAINTERS. irreg. $49.50. Harry N. Abrams, Inc., 100 Fifth Ave., New York, NY 10011. TEL 212-206-7715. FAX 212-654-8437. TELEX 175975. **Document type:** monographic series.

LICHTUNGEN; Zeitschrift fuer Literatur, Kunst und Zeitkritik. see LITERATURE

700   NE   ISSN 0925-8191
LIER EN BOOG; series of philosophy of art & art theory. (Text in English) 1975. 2/yr. fl.45. Postbus 1718, 1000 BS Amsterdam, Netherlands. FAX 31-20-6221787. E-mail: lierboog@dds.nl. Eds. Annette Balhema, Henu Slager. adv. contact: Henu Slager. bk.rev. circ. 1,000. **Document type:** academic/scholarly publication.
Refereed Serial

700   US   ISSN 0161-4223
LIGHTWORKS; illuminating thresholds of new art. 1975. irreg., no.22, 1997. $20 to individuals; institutions $25 (for 4 nos.) (effective 1997). Lightworks Magazine, Inc., Box 1202, Birmingham, MI 48012-1202. TEL 248-626-8026. FAX 248-737-0046. Ed. Andrea D. Martin; Pub. Charlton Burch. bk.rev.; film rev.; illus. circ. 2,000. (back issues avail.)
—BLDSC (5215.530000); UnCover.
Description: Presents approaches to new and experimental art including intermedia artforms, photography, xerography, artist's books, mail art and fringe research. The accent is on far-reaching exploration within the creative arts.
Refereed Serial

700 AT ISSN 1327-5445
LIKE, ART MAGAZINE. 1988. q. Aus.$20 to individuals (foreign Aus.$45); institutions Aus.$30 (foreign Aus.$55); newsstand price: Aus.$6. Royal Melbourne Institute of Technology, Faculty of Art & Design, G.P.O. Box 2476V, Melbourne, Vic. 3001, Australia. TEL 61-3-96601779. FAX 61-3-96601779. E-mail: like@rmit.edu.au. Ed. Robyn McKenzie. adv.: page Aus.$600; trim 340 x 240; adv. contact: Sarah Ritson. bk.rev.; film rev.; illus.; index. circ. 1,000.
Formerly: Agenda: Australian Contemporary Art (ISSN 1033-1115)
Description: Discusses contemporary visual art and culture.

701.18 IT ISSN 0391-6553
LINEA ESTETICA. 1963. bi-m. L.13500. Sindacato Nazionale Estetisi Diplomati, Via Gustavo Modena 16, 20129 Milano, Italy. Ed. Vincenzo Coratelli. adv.; bk.rev. circ. 10,000.

LINEASTRUTTURA. see ARCHITECTURE

700 IT
LINEAVERDE; periodico di arte attualita e cultura. 1973. bi-m. free. Rossieditore, Casella Postale 1008, Via L. Giordano 56, 80127 Vomero (Naples), Italy. TEL 39-81-5569132. FAX 39-81-5569132. Ed. Paolo Rossi. adv. contact: Paolo Rossi. bk.rev. circ. 3,000. (also avail. in microform) Document type: academic/scholarly publication, newsletter.

700 SP ISSN 0211-2574
LINO: REVISTA DE ARTE. 1980. a. price varies. Universidad de Oviedo, Servicio de Publicaciones, C. Arguelles 19, 33003 Oviedo, Spain. TEL 34-85-210160. FAX 34-85-218352. Ed. Carlos Cid Priego.
—CINDOC.

LITERATURA I MASTATSTVA. see LITERATURE

LITERATURE AND THE VISUAL ARTS: NEW FOUNDATIONS. see LITERATURE

LITERATURNAYA ROSSIYA. see LITERARY AND POLITICAL REVIEWS

LITHOPHANE COLLECTOR'S CLUB BULLETIN. see MUSEUMS AND ART GALLERIES

700 800 US ISSN 0271-7735
PS571.K2
LITTLE BALKANS REVIEW; Southeast Kansas literary and graphics quarterly. 1980. q. $10. Little Balkans Press, Inc., 601 Grandview Heights Terrace, Pittsburg, KS 66762. Ed. Gene DeGruson. adv.; bk.rev.; illus.; index. circ. 1,500. (back issues avail.) Indexed: Ind.Amer.Per.Verse, Vert.File Ind.

700 500.9 US ISSN 0024-5283
QH1 CODEN: LIMUAR
THE LIVING MUSEUM. (Braille and Inkprint Editions) 1939. q. free. Illinois State Museum, Springfield, IL 62706. TEL 217-782-7386. FAX 217-782-1254. E-mail: editor@museum.state.il.us; URL: http://www.museum.state.il.us. Ed. Kimberly K. Britton. R&P contact: Ed Munyer. illus.; index, cum.index: 1939-1955. circ. 19,000. Indexed: Biol.Abstr., Biol.Dig., Sport Fish.Abstr., Wild.Rev. Document type: academic/scholarly publication.
—Linda Hall; UnCover.
Description: Describes Illinois' natural history, art, and anthropology.

700 FR
LIVRE DU CONGRES L'A F T P V. (Text in French) biennial. 800 F. (Etudes et Realisation de la Couleur) E R E C, 68, rue Jean Jaures, 92800 Puteaux, France. TEL 47730123. Ed. Annik Chauvel. circ. 800.
Description: Gathers the full text of the lectures pronounced during the AFTPV Congress.

LOST GENERATION JOURNAL. see LITERATURE

700 DK ISSN 0024-6891
NX28.S8
LOUISIANA-REVY. 1960. 3/yr. DKK 225. Louisiana Museum of Modern Art, Gl. Strandvej 13, 3050 Humlebaek, Denmark. FAX 45-42-193505. Ed. Kjeld Kjeldsen. adv.; illus.; index, cum.index: vols.1-35. circ. 40,000. Indexed: Artbibl., Artbibl.Mod. Document type: catalog.

THE LOW COUNTRIES; arts and society in Flanders and The Netherlands: a yearbook. see HUMANITIES: COMPREHENSIVE WORKS

LUMINA. see LITERATURE

700 SW ISSN 1100-2859
LUND STUDIES IN ART HISTORY. (Text in English, French, Swedish) 1988. irreg. price varies. Lund University Press, P.O. Box 141, S-221 00 Lund, Sweden. TEL 46-46-31-20-00.
FAX 46-46-30-53-30. E-mail: order@studli.se. Eds. S-Aa Nilsson, Sven Sandstroem. Document type: academic/scholarly publication.

LYLE OFFICIAL REVIEW ANTIQUES PRICE GUIDE. see ANTIQUES

700 BL ISSN 0104-320X
M A C REVISTA.* (Text in Portuguese; summaries in English, Spanish) 1992. a. $6. Universidade de Sao Paulo, Museu de Arte Contemporanea, Rua da Reitoria, 160, 05508-900 Sao Paulo SP, Brazil. TEL 55-11-818-3538. FAX 55-11-2120218. Eds. Lisbeth Rebollo Goncalves, Vera Filinto. circ. 2,000. Document type: academic/scholarly publication.

731.76 US ISSN 0192-2491
M B NEWS. 1944. m. $45 in U.S.; Canada $70; Europe, SA, Australia, New Zealand $85; elsewhere $97 (effective 1997). Monument Builders of North America, 3158 S. River Rd., Ste. 224, Des Plaines, IL 60018. TEL 847-803-8800; 800-233-4472. FAX 847-803-8233. Ed. Donna D. Jones. adv. contact: Donna D. Jones. bk.rev. circ. 1,400. Document type: trade publication.
Formerly: Monument Builder News.
Description: For monument retailers, wholesalers and quarriers. Includes news of the trade, meetings, features and memorial designs.

700 US
M C A C A BULLETIN. bi-m. Michigan Council for Arts and Cultural Affairs, 1200 Sixth St., Ste. 1180, Detroit, MI 48226. TEL 313-256-3731. FAX 313-256-3781. circ. 12,000. Document type: government publication, bulletin.
Formerly: M C A News.

MACEDONIAN REVIEW; history, culture, literature, arts. see LITERATURE

700 FR ISSN 0397-5770
MACULA. 1976. q. 175 F. 6 rue Coetlogon, 75006 Paris, France. Ed. Bd. illus. Indexed: Arts & Hum.Cit.Ind., Curr.Cont., RILA.

790.2 700.74 NE ISSN 0167-9813
MAGAZIJN; uitgaan in Rotterdam. 1970. 10/yr. fl.32.50($30) (single issue free locally). V V V Rotterdam, Cool Singel 67, 3012 AC Rotterdam, Netherlands. TEL 31-10-4023228. FAX 31-10-4130589. Ed. Peter Snel. R&P contact: Peter Snel. adv.; illus. circ. 50,000. cols./p.: 6; pp./issue: 32. (tabloid format) Document type: newspaper.
Description: Covers what's going on in theaters, concert halls, galleries, museums.

700 PL ISSN 1231-6709
MAGAZYN SZTUKI. 1993. q. 40 Zl. (in US $40). Ryszard Ziarkiewicz, Ed. & Pub., Ul. Zakopianska 32b-4, 80-142 Gdansk, Poland. TEL 48-58-321001. FAX 48-58-321001. adv. contact: Beata Maciejewska. circ. 1,000. (back issues avail.)
Description: Presents contemporary art - Polish and international as well.

700 US ISSN 0196-8432
MAGIC CHANGES;* the biannual for independent artists. 1979. s-a. $5. (Order of the Celestial Otter) Celestial Otter Press, c/o John Sennett, Ed., 601 Fairbanks Ct., No. V2, Schaumberg, IL 60194-5128. TEL 708-416-3111. adv. contact: Kaela Sennett. bk.rev. circ. 500. (back issues avail.)

MAGICAL BLEND; a transformative journey. see NEW AGE PUBLICATIONS

MAGIRA. see LITERATURE — Science Fiction, Fantasy, Horror

745 HU ISSN 1217-9833
MAGYAR NEPMUVESZET. (Text in Hungarian; summaries in English, German) 1951-1955; resumed 1994. a. 550 Ft. or exchange basis. Neprajzi Muzeum - Ethnographical Museum, Kosuth Lajos ter 12, 1055 Budapest, Hungary. TEL 36-1-326340. FAX 36-2-692419. Ed. Attila Selmeczi-Kovacs. Document type: monographic series.

709 943 HU ISSN 0076-2490
MAGYARORSZAG MUEMLEKI TOPOGRAFIAJA. (Text in Hungarian; summaries in English, German, Russian) 1956. irreg., vol.11, 1987. price varies. (Magyar Tudomanyos Akademia) Akademiai Kiado Rt., P.O. Box 245, H-1519 Budapest, Hungary. TEL 36-1-2043976. FAX 36-1-2043973.

790 910.03 US ISSN 0149-0729
MAHOGANY. 1977. w. free. Ike DuBose, 1520 Royster, Ft. Worth, TX 76134. adv. circ. 150,000.

700 793.3 UK ISSN 0959-0013
MAILOUT; arts work with people. 1988. bi-m. £21 (Europe £25.75; U.S. £30.20; Australia £31.50) (effective 1997); newsstand price: £3.50. Mailout Trust, Kirklees Media Centre, 7 Northumberland St., Huddersfield HD1 1RL, England. TEL 44-1484-469009. FAX 44-1484-469009. E-mail: mailout@architechs.uk. (Distr. addr.: Corby Community Arts, Canada Sq., Corby, Northants NN18 9JF, England. FAX 44-1536-460777) Ed. Victoria Minton. R&P contact: Victoria Minton. adv.: page £300; adv. contact: Victoria Minton. bk.rev.; film rev.; music rev.; illus.; cum.index; circ. 7,500. (back issues avail.) Document type: bulletin.
Description: Covers all forms of participatory arts work.
Refereed Serial

MAIN DE SINGE. see LITERARY AND POLITICAL REVIEWS

MAINFRAENKISCHES JAHRBUCH FUER GESCHICHTE UND KUNST. see HISTORY — History Of Europe

943 913 709 GW ISSN 0076-2792
DD901.M2
MAINZER ZEITSCHRIFT; Mittelrheinisches Jahrbuch fuer Archaeologie, Geschichte und Kunst. 1906. a. DM.96 (effective 1995). Mainzer Altertumsverein e.V., Rheinallee 3b, 55116 Mainz, Germany. Ed. Friedrich Schuetz. circ. 770. Indexed: Br.Archaeol.Abstr., IBR, RILA. Document type: academic/scholarly publication.
—BLDSC (5352.670000).

700 605.4 UK ISSN 1365-8190
MAKE; the magazine of womens art. 1983. bi-m. £18 (Europe £23; rest of world £28) to individuals; institutions £33(Europe £43; rest of world £43) (effective 1997); newsstand price: £2.75. (Arts Council of England) Women's Art Library, Fulham Palace, Bishops Ave., London SW6 6EA, England. TEL 44-171-384-1110. FAX 44-171-384-1110. (Distr. by: Central Books, 99 Wallis Rd., London E9 5LN, England. TEL 44-181-986-4854. FAX 44-181-533-5821) Ed. Heidi Reitmaier. adv.: B&W page £415; 316 x 236; adv. contact: Helena Swatton. bk.rev.; video rev. circ. 19,000. (back issues avail.) Indexed: Art Ind., Fem.Per. Document type: academic/scholarly publication.
—BLDSC (5353.694910).
Formerly (until 1996): Women's Art Magazine (ISSN 0961-1460)
Description: Publishes critical debates, themes between art history and feminism, exhibition reviews, and interviews. Also contains a full listing for art historians, librarians, academics, artists, students, and others interested in issues relating to women's art.

700 808.81 US ISSN 0888-0972
MALLIFE. 1981. s-a. $10. Bomb Shelter Props, Box 17686, Phoenix, AZ 85011. TEL 602-253-4430. Ed. Mike Miskowski. adv.; bk.rev.; film rev. circ. 300. (back issues avail.)
Description: Writing and art dealing with greed inherent in capitalist economies.

ART

700 895.1   CC
MANG YUAN. (Text in Chinese) bi-m. Y3 per no. Henan Sheng Wenlian, No. 34, Jing 7 Lu, Zhengzhou, Henan 450003, People's Republic of China. TEL 334646. (Dist. overseas by: China Publications Foreign Trade Corp., P.O. Box 782, Beijing, P.R.C.) Ed. Qian Jiyang. illus.
Description: Literary magazine.

700   US
MANHATTAN ARTS INTERNATIONAL. 1983. 4/yr. $12 (foreign $30) (effective 1997). 200 E. 72nd St., Ste. 26L, New York, NY 10021. TEL 212-472-1660. FAX 212-794-0324. Ed. Renee Phillips. adv.; bk.rev.; circ. 10,000 (paid); 40,000. (back issues avail.) **Document type:** consumer publication.
Formerly: Manhattan Arts.
Description: Promotes new artists on the horizon. Covers art trends and collecting, and includes interviews with world art leaders and reviews of exhibitions.

MANILA REVIEW; Philippines journal of literature and the arts. see *LITERATURE*

700   GW   ISSN 0178-3556
MANIPULATOR. (Text in English, German, Italian; summaries in English) 1982. q. DM.72 (foreign DM.90). Moser und Colby GmbH, Duisburgerstr. 44, 40477 Duesseldorf, Germany. TEL 0211-4982068. FAX 0211-4983424. Ed. Wilhelm Moser. adv. circ. 24,000. (back issues avail.)

MANUSKRIPTE; Zeitschrift fuer Literatur, Kunst, Kritik. see *LITERATURE*

070.5   UK
MARCAN HANDBOOK OF ARTS ORGANISATIONS. 1983. triennial. £20. Peter Marcan Publications, P.O. Box 3158, London SE1 4RA, England. TEL 44-171-357-0368. circ. 750. **Document type:** directory.
Formerly: Arts Address Book.
Description: Covers national and international organizations in all areas of the arts, pure and applied, with details of activities and publications.

700   II   ISSN 0025-2913
N1
MARG. Variant title: Marg Art Magazine. (Text in English) 1946. q. $45. (National Centre for the Performing Arts) Marg Publications, Army-Navy Bldg., 3rd Fl., 148 Mahatma Gandhi Rd., Fort, Mumbai 400 001, India. TEL 91-22-2842520. FAX 91-22-2049522. TELEX 01182618. Ed. Pratapaditya Pal. adv.; bk.rev.; illus. circ. 3,000. (back issues avail.) **Indexed:** Art & Archaeol.Tech.Abstr., Art Ind., Artbibl.Mod., Br.Tech.Ind., Geo.Abstr., IBR. **Document type:** academic/scholarly publication.
—KR SourceOne; UnCover.

709   US   ISSN 0277-8726
E159.5
MARKERS. 1979. a. $37 to non-members; members $32. Association for Gravestone Studies, c/o Lois Ahrens, Dir., 278 Main St., Ste. 278, Greenfield, MA 01301-3230. TEL 413-772-0836. E-mail: ags@berkshire.net; URL: http://www.berkshire.net/ags. Ed. Richard E. Meyer. R&P contact: Lois Ahrens. **Indexed:** Amer.Hist.& Life (1979-), Hist.Abstr. (1979-), MLA Intl.Bibl. **Document type:** academic/scholarly publication.
Description: Scholarly articles relating to many aspects of funerary art, preservation, and history in different parts of the United States.

701 709   XR
MASARYKOVA UNIVERZITA. FILOZOFICKA FAKULTA. SBORNIK PRACI. F: RADA UMENOVEDNA. (Text in Czech; summaries in various languages) 1957. irreg. (approx. a.). price varies. Masarykova Univerzita, Filozoficka Fakulta, A. Novaka 1, 660 88 Brno, Czech Republic. TEL 420-5-41121102. FAX 420-5-41121406. E-mail: exchange@phil.muni.cz. R&P contact: Ivan Seidl. TEL 420-5-41121337. bk.rev. **Document type:** academic/scholarly publication.
Formerly: Univerzita J.E. Purkyne. Filozoficka Fakulta. Sbornik Praci. F: Rada Umenovedna (ISSN 0231-5025)
Description: Articles about the theory and history of the arts.

MASK LORE. see *PHILATELY*

741   US   ISSN 0025-5025
NC1
MASTER DRAWINGS; devoted exclusively to the study and illustration of drawings. 1963. q. $60 (foreign $65) (effective 1997). Master Drawings Association, Inc., 29 E. 36th St., New York, NY 10016. TEL 212-685-0008. FAX 212-685-4740. Ed. Anne-Marie Logan. adv.; bk.rev.; illus.; index, cum.index: 1963-1983. circ. 1,250. (back issues avail.; reprint service avail.) **Indexed:** Art.Ind., Art Ind., Arts & Hum.Cit.Ind., ASCA, Avery Ind.Archit.Per., Br.Tech.Ind., Curr.Cont., IBR, Ind.Bk.Rev.Hum., RILA. **Document type:** academic/scholarly publication.
—KR SourceOne; SWETS; UnCover.

708 069   CN   ISSN 0383-5391
MASTERPIECES IN THE NATIONAL GALLERY OF CANADA/CHEFS-D'OEUVRE DE LA GALERIE NATIONALE DU CANADA. (Text in English, French) 1971. irreg., no.12, 1978. Can.$1.95. National Gallery of Canada, Publications Division, c/o Irene Lillico, 380 Sussex Dr., Ottawa, ON K1N 9N4, Canada. TEL 613-990-0537. FAX 613-990-7460. (Dist. by: University of Chicago Press, 5801 Ellis Ave., Chicago, IL 60637-1496) Eds. Charles Hill, Michael Pantazzi. illus. circ. 5,000. **Document type:** monographic series.
Description: Details study, history and criticism of individual paintings in the National Gallery's collection.

MATERIALI E STRUTTURE; problemi di conservazione. see *CONSERVATION*

MATRIART; a Canadian feminist art journal. see *WOMEN'S STUDIES*

718   FR   ISSN 0025-6072
MAUSOLEE; arts et techniques des roches de qualite. 1933. m. 805 F. (effective 1997). Societe Le Mausolee, B.P. 8, 69702 Givors Cedex, France. TEL 33-4-72248933. FAX 33-4-72246193. Ed. Claude Gargi. adv. contact: Jacqueline Martin. charts; illus. circ. 4,500. **Indexed:** GeoRef.
—BLDSC (5413.279600).

700   IE   ISSN 0332-4869
MAYNOOTH REVIEW. 1975. s-a. £6. St. Patrick's College, Maynooth, Co. Kildare, Ireland. Ed. Dr. Martin Pulbrook. circ. 300. (back issues avail.) **Indexed:** M.L.A., MLA Intl.Bibl.

500 808   US   ISSN 0272-5657
ME. Variant title: Dirigo Me. (Text in English, French, Italian) 1980. irreg., approx. q. $20. (International Mail Art Network) Pittore Euforico, Box 182, Bowdoinham, ME 04008-0182. TEL 207-666-8453. Ed. Carlo Pittore. adv.; bk.rev.; illus. circ. 1,000. (tabloid format; back issues avail.) **Document type:** newsletter.
Formerly: Me, Too.

THE MEDAL. see *NUMISMATICS*

MEDIA AND ARTS LAW REVIEW. see *LAW*

MEDIAEVALIA. see *HISTORY — History Of Europe*

709   IT
MEDIAEVALIA. 1983. irreg., vol.3, 1990. price varies. (Universita di Roma "La Sapienza") L'Erma di Bretschneider, Via Cassiodoro 19, 00193 Rome, Italy. TEL 39-6-6874127. FAX 39-6-6874129. Dir. Angiola Maria Romanini.
Description: Covers the history of medieval art.

MEDIAEVALIA GRONINGANA. see *HISTORY — History Of Europe*

384.55 700   NE   ISSN 0920-7864
MEDIAMATIC. 1986. 4/yr. fl.75. Stichting Mediamatic, Postbus 17090, 1001 JL Amsterdam, Netherlands. TEL 31-20-6384534. FAX 31-20-6237760. Ed.Bd. adv.; bk.rev.
—SWETS.

MEDIEVAL ACADEMY BOOKS. see *HISTORY — History Of Europe*

MEDIEVALIA ET HUMANISTICA; studies in medieval and renaissance culture. see *HISTORY — History Of Europe*

700 750   CC   ISSN 1003-1774
MEISHU/ART. (Text in Chinese; table of contents in English) 1954. m. Y32.60($90) Wenlian Dalou, 13th Floor, 10 Nongzhanguan Nanli, Beijing 100026, People's Republic of China. TEL 5003278. (Dist. outside China by: China International Book Trading Corp., P.O. Box 399, Beijing, P.R.C.; Dist. in US by: China Books & Periodicals, Inc., 2929 24th St., San Francisco, CA 94110. TEL 415-282-2994) Ed. Shao Dazhen. bk.rev.; illus.
Description: Covers art history, painting. Includes interviews with artists and articles on the art world.

700   CC
MEISHU DAGUAN. (Text in Chinese) m. Liaoning Meishu Chubanshe, 29 Minzu Beijie, Heping-qu, Shenyang, Liaoning 110001, People's Republic of China. TEL 433151. Ed. Zhang Xiushi.

700   CC
MEISHU GENGYUN. (Text in Chinese) q. Shanxi Meishu Yuan - Shanxi Fine Art Institute, 46 Yingze Dajie, Taiyuan, Shanxi 030001, People's Republic of China. TEL 441545. Ed. Zhao Jing.

700   CC
MEISHU JIE/AIR CIRCLE. (Text in Chinese) bi-m. Guangxi Wenlian, 28 Jianzheng Lu, Nanning, Guangxi 530023, People's Republic of China. TEL 27225. Ed. Guo Ling.

709   CC   ISSN 1002-9680
MEISHU SHILUN/HISTORY OF ARTS. (Text in Chinese) 1981. q. $23.70. (Zhongguo Yishu Yanjiuyuan, Meishu Yanjiusuo - Chinese Academy of Arts, Institute of Fine Art) Meishu Shilun Bianjibu, 17 Qianhai Xijie, Beijing 100009, People's Republic of China. TEL 651128. (Dist. in US by: China Books & Periodicals, Inc., 2929 24th St., San Francisco, CA 94110. TEL 415-282-2994) Ed. Shui Tianzhong.

701   CC   ISSN 0461-6855
MEISHU YANJIU/ART RESEARCH. (Text in Chinese; table of contents in English) 1957. q. Y14($33) Zhongyang Meishu Xueyuan - Central Academy of Arts, 5 Xiaowei Hutong, Dongcheng Qu, Beijing 100730, People's Republic of China. (Dist. outside China by: China International Book Trading Corp., P.O. Box 399, Beijing, P.R.C.; Dist. in US by: China Books & Periodicals, Inc., 2929 24th St., San Francisco, CA 94110. TEL 415-282-2994) Eds. Tong Jinghan, Du Zhesen. illus.
Description: Covers art, art education, and art criticism worldwide.

070.5 700   CC   ISSN 1003-045X
MEISHU ZHI YOU/FRIEND OF FINE ARTS. (Text in Chinese) 1982. bi-m. Y5.88. Renmin Meishu Chubanshe, 32 Beizongbu Hutong, Beijing 100735, People's Republic of China. TEL 5122583. Eds. Shen Peng, Wu Baolun. circ. 50,000.

750   CC   ISSN 1003-5605
MEIYUAN/CENTRE OF FINE ARTS BIMONTHLY. Variant title: Lu Xun Meishu Xueyuan Xuebao. (Text in Chinese; table of contents in English) 1980. bi-m. Y88.80. Lu Xun Meishu Xueyuan, 19 Sanhao Jie, Heping Qu, Shenyang, Liaoning 110003, People's Republic of China. TEL 3920125. FAX 390334. (Dist. outside China by: China Publications Foreign Trade Corp., P.O. Box 782, Beijing, P.R. China. TEL 3832058) Ed. Song Huimin. adv. contact: Li Fengying. bk.rev.; illus.; circ. 11,000 (paid). **Document type:** academic/scholarly publication.
Description: Covers traditional Chinese painting. Refereed Serial

MELANGES D'HISTOIRE DE L'ARCHITECTURE. see *ARCHITECTURE*

MEMOIRES DE LA DELEGATION ARCHEOLOGIQUE FRANCAISE EN IRAN. see *ARCHAEOLOGY*

MERVYN PEAKE REVIEW. see *LITERATURE — Science Fiction, Fantasy, Horror*

MESH; film - video - multimedia - art. see *MOTION PICTURES*

| 700 | FR | ISSN 0152-2418
METIERS D'ART. 1977. q. 200 F. (foreign 270 F.). Societe d'Encouragement aux Metiers d'Art, 20 rue de la Boetie, 75008 Paris, France. TEL 49-24-01-03. FAX 49-24-98-54.
   Description: Forum by which artists can present their artistic works. Informs readers about the profession and opportunities available in the art world.

| 700 | NE | ISSN 0168-9053
METROPOLIS M; tijdschrift over hedendaagse kunst. 1979. bi-m. fl.80($65) Stichting Metropolis M, Postbus 19263, 3501 DG Utrecht, Netherlands. TEL 31-30-324125. FAX 31-30-369161. (Subscr. addr.: Metropolis M c/o Brouwer Offset, Postbus 9151, 3506 GD Utrecht, Netherlands. TEL 31-30-457390. FAX 31-30-435024) adv.: B&W page fl.1070, color page fl.1256; adv. contact: Peter Nijenhuis. index. (back issues avail.)
   —SWETS.
   Description: Covers contemporary art.

MICHIGAN ACADEMICIAN. see *SCIENCES: COMPREHENSIVE WORKS*

| 700 | US |
MICHIGAN ART FAIRS. a. Michigan Council for Arts and Cultural Affairs, 1200 Sixth St., Ste. 1180, Detroit, MI 48226. TEL 313-256-3731. FAX 313-256-3781. circ. 20,000. **Document type:** government publication, catalog.

| 340 700 | US |
MICHIGAN COUNCIL FOR THE ARTS. LEGISLATIVE REPORT. 1969. a. free. Michigan Council for the Arts, 1200 Sixth St., Detroit, MI 48226. TEL 313-256-3731. FAX 313-256-3781. Ed. Martha Gibiser Shea. circ. 500.

| 709 | US |
MICHIGAN STATE UNIVERSITY. MUSEUM PUBLICATIONS. FOLK ART SERIES. irreg. price varies. Michigan State University, Museum, East Lansing, MI 48824. TEL 517-355-2370. **Document type:** monographic series.

MIDATLANTIC ANTIQUES MAGAZINE; monthly guide to antiques, auctions, art & collectibles. see *ANTIQUES*

MIDCOASTER. see *LITERATURE*

| 700 745.5 | US |
MIDWEST ART FARE. 1970. m. $9. Manfred Kiess, Ed. & Pub., 1056 56th St., Des Moines, IA 50311. TEL 515-274-0675. circ. 300. (looseleaf format)

| 700 069 | US |
MIDWEST MUSEUM BULLETIN. 1979. bi-m. free to members. Midwest Museum of American Art, 429 S. Main St., Box 1812, Elkhart, IN 46515. TEL 219-293-6660. Ed. Brian D. Byrn. circ. 550. **Document type:** bulletin.
   Description: Reviews of exhibitions, schedule of events, film showing, lectures and classes for members and interested public.

| 700 | UK | ISSN 1352-3996
MILLER'S PICTURE PRICE GUIDE. 1993. a. Reed International, Michelin House, 81 Fulham Rd., London SW3 6RB, England. **Document type:** catalog.

| 700 | IT |
MINIATURA E ARTI MINORI IN CAMPANIA. no.10, 1975. irreg., no.13, 1978. price varies. (Banca Sannitica) Societa Editrice Napoletana s.r.l., Corso Umberto I 34, 80138 Naples, Italy. Ed. Mario Rotili.

MINIATURE COLLECTOR; the magazine for the artist, hobbyist and collector. see *HOBBIES*

| 700 | US | ISSN 0076-9096
MINNEAPOLIS INSTITUTE OF ARTS. ANNUAL REPORT. 1961. a. Minneapolis Institute of Arts, 2400 Third Ave. S., Minneapolis, MN 55404. TEL 612-870-3046. FAX 612-870-3004. Ed. Lizanne Hart. circ. 15,000. **Document type:** corporate report.

| 708 700 | US | ISSN 0076-910X
MINNEAPOLIS INSTITUTE OF ARTS. BULLETIN. 1955. irreg. $10. Minneapolis Institute of Arts, 2400 Third Ave. S., Minneapolis, MN 55404. TEL 612-870-3029. FAX 612-870-3004. circ. 1,000. **Indexed:** Art Ind., Artbibl.Mod., RILA. **Document type:** bulletin.
   —KR SourceOne; UMI.

| 700 | US | ISSN 1060-3107
MINNESOTA ARTS DIRECTORY. 1977. a. (plus update). $11.95 (foreign $13.95) (effective 1997). New North Publishing, Box 580320, Minneapolis, MN 55458-0320. TEL 612-871-0813. Ed. James W. Schiller; Pub. James W. Schiller. adv. contact: James W. Schiller. circ. 7,500. **Document type:** directory.
   Formerly (until 1989): Minnesota Arts Fairs.
   Description: Lists arts and crafts fairs and festivals in Minnesota, Wisconsin, Iowa and the Dakotas, as well as more than 400 artists, artisans, suppliers, arts organizations and services in the region.

MINT MUSEUM MEMBERNEWS. see *MUSEUMS AND ART GALLERIES*

| 700 | CC | ISSN 1003-2568
MINZU YISHU/MINORITY ART. (Text in Chinese) 1985. q. newsstand price: Y2. Guangxi Yishu Yanjiusuo - Guangxi Art Institute, 13 Minzhu Lu, Nanning, Guangxi 530023, People's Republic of China. TEL 0771-5860143. (Dist. overseas by: China Foreign Trade Publishing Company, P.O. Box 782, Beijing, P.R. China) Eds. Zhou Minzhen, Pan Jian. bk.rev.; circ. 2,000 (paid). **Document type:** academic/scholarly publication.
   Description: Covers Chinese minority art, including music, theatre, folk art and dances.

| 700 808.81 | US |
MIRAGE; the magazine of the arts. a. Cochise College, Douglas, AZ 85607. TEL 520-364-7943. Eds. Norman Bates, Mark Litwicki. illus. circ. 2,000.
   Description: Showcases talent from all parts of Cochise county in Southern Arizona.

| 791.43 | US |
▼**MIRROR MAGAZINE.** 1996. q. Box 182, Bolinas, CA 94118. E-mail: joelb@mirrormagazine.com; URL: http://www.mirrormagazine.com. Ed. Joel Braverman. film rev.
●Available only online.
   Description: Covers new art, original writing, music, fiction, poetry, restaurant, bar and movies.

| 700 N8.H4 | IS | ISSN 0334-9810
MISHKAFAYIM. 1987. q. IS.51. Israel Museum, Youth Department, P.O. Box 71117, Jerusalem 91710, Israel. TEL 972-2-708823. FAX 972-2-631833. (Subscr. to: 5 Mikunis St., Tel Aviv 67772, Israel) Ed. Tamir Rauner. adv. circ. 16,000.
   Description: Art for the general public.

MISSISSIPPI HISTORY NEWSLETTER. see *HISTORY — History Of North And South America*

| 700 069 NK1073.6.A1 | KO | ISSN 0540-4568
MISUL CHARYO/NATIONAL MUSEUM JOURNAL OF ARTS. Key Title: Misur Jaryo. (Text in Korean; summaries in Korean or English) 1960. s-a. National Museum of Korea, Department of Fine Arts - Gujrib Juhhah Bagmurgwan, 1 Sejong-no, Chongno-gu, Seoul 110 050, S. Korea. TEL 02-720-4723. illus.

| 220.93 930.1 | AU | ISSN 1025-6555
▼**MITTEILUNGEN ZUR CHRISTLICHEN ARCHAEOLOGIE.** 1995. a. Verlag der Oesterreichischen Akademie der Wissenschaften, Postfach 471, A-1011 Vienna, Austria. TEL 43-1-51581401. FAX 43-1-51581400. E-mail: verlag@oeaw.ac.at; URL: http://www.oeaw.ac.at/einheiten/verlag. Eds. Renate Pillinger, Erich Renhart. **Document type:** academic/scholarly publication.

| 700 | CN |
MIX; the magazine of artist-run culture. (Text in English, French) 1976. 4/yr. Can.$20 to individuals (foreign Can.$25); institutions Can.$30 (foreign Can.$35) (effective 1996-1997). Parallelogramme Artist-Run Culture and Publishing Inc., 401 Richmond St. W., Ste. 446, Toronto, ON M5V 3A8, Canada. TEL 416-506-1012. FAX 416-340-8458. E-mail: mixadmin@web.net; URL: www.web.net/mix/. Ed. Margaret Christakos. R&P contact: Margaret Christakos. adv. contact: Lorne Fromer. bk.rev. circ. 5,000. (also avail. in microfilm) **Indexed:** Artbibl.Mod., Can.B.P.I. **Document type:** consumer publication.
   Formerly (until 1995): Parallelogramme (ISSN 0703-8712)
   Description: Covers contemporary art including performance, video, film, photography, installation, painting, sculpture and mixed media.

| 700 370 | US |
MIXED MEDIA. q. free. Maine Art Education Association, Box 10463, Portland, ME 04104. Ed. Diane Noble. adv. circ. 700.

| 700 | JA |
MIZUE. (Text in Japanese) 1905. q. 2800 Yen. Bijutsu Shuppan-Sha Ltd., Inaoka Bldg., 2-36, Kanda, Jimbo-cho, Chiyoda-ku, Tokyo 101, Japan. TEL 03-3234-2151. FAX 03-3234-9451. Ed. Tatsumi Shinoda. circ. 30,000. **Indexed:** Sugar Ind.Abstr.

| 700 920 N40 | US | ISSN 1052-1712
MODERN ARTS CRITICISM. 1990. a. $67. Gale Research, 835 Penobscot Bldg., 645 Griswold St., Detroit, MI 48226-4094. TEL 313-961-2242; 800-877-4253. FAX 800-414-5043. E-mail: daniel_snyder@gale.com. Ed. Joann Prosyniuk.
   Description: Provides excerpted critical assessments of approximately 25 visual artists from the beginning of modern era to the present.

| 709 720 | US |
THE MODERNIST.* 1981. q. $20. Art Deco Society of New York, c/o William Weber, 55 Lincoln Ave., Bergenfield, NJ 07621-2517. Ed. Glenn Loney. adv.: bk.rev. circ. 1,000. (back issues avail.)
   Formerly: Art Deco News (ISSN 0743-3522)
   Description: Surveys modern movements in the arts, architecture, design, and performance past, present, and future, through features, photo-essays, critiques, news and notes.

MODO; mensile di informazione sul design. see *TECHNOLOGY: COMPREHENSIVE WORKS*

| 700 850 | IT |
▼**MONDO ARTE.** 1995. bi-m. newsstand price: L.8000. Sistemi Comunicativi Multimediali s.r.l., Via P.G.A. Filippini 130, 00144 Rome, Italy. TEL 39-6-5295888. FAX 39-6-5293621. Ed. Francesca Zema. adv. **Document type:** consumer publication.

| 700 | US | ISSN 0544-845X
MONOGRAPHS ON AMERICAN ART. 1968. irreg., no.4, 1975. price varies. Sheldon Memorial Art Gallery, 12th & R. Sts., University of Nebraska, Lincoln, NE 68588. TEL 402-472-2461. illus. **Document type:** monographic series.

| 700 | US | ISSN 1053-976X
MONOGRAPHS ON THE FINE ARTS. irreg. price varies. (College Art Association of America) University of Washington Press, Box 50096, Seattle, WA 98145. TEL 206-543-8870. FAX 206-543-3932. Ed.Bd. **Document type:** monographic series.
   —BLDSC (5915.436300).
   Formerly: Monographs on Archaeology and Fine Arts (ISSN 0077-0981)

| 708.1 745.5 | US |
MONTEREY MUSEUM OF ART NEWS. 1986. bi-m. $35 (families $50) (effective 1997). Monterey Museum of Art, 559 Pacific St., Monterey, CA 93940. TEL 408-372-5477. FAX 408-372-5680. Ed. Richard Gadd. adv. contact: Pat Seiling. circ. 3,000. **Document type:** newsletter.
   Formerly: Monterey Peninsula Museum of Art News.
   Description: Exhibitions at and acquisitions by the museum; activity and program information.

| 700 | JA | ISSN 0910-4364
MONTHLY ART/GEKKAN BIJUTSU. (Text in Japanese) 1975. m. 21600 Yen. Jitsugyo no Nihon Sha, Ltd., 3-9 Ginza, 1-chome, Chuo-ku, Tokyo 104, Japan. TEL 81-3-3563-5636. FAX 81-3-3562-3200. E-mail: lebo2234@niftyserve.or.jp. Ed. Minoru Nakano.

MONUMENTA ARTIS ROMANAE. see *ARCHAEOLOGY*

| 730 | IT | ISSN 0545-008X
MONUMENTI ETRUSCHI. 1968. irreg., no.7, 1992. price varies. Casa Editrice Leo S. Olschki, Casella Postale 66, 50100 Florence, Italy. TEL 39-55-6530684. FAX 39-55-6530214. URL: celso@olschki.it. **Document type:** monographic series.

MOONDANCE; celebrating creative women. see *WOMEN'S INTERESTS*

MOSAIC (ST. PETERSBURG). see *MUSEUMS AND ART GALLERIES*

456   ART

700　　　　　　IT　ISSN 0394-4271
N4
MOSTRE E MUSEI. 1975. irreg., no.8, 1983. price varies. Societa Editrice Napoletana s.r.l., Corso Umberto I 34, 80138 Naples, Italy. Ed. Raffaello Causa.

700 800 780　　US　ISSN 8756-890X
MOVEMENTS IN THE ARTS. 1985. irreg. price varies. Greenwood Press, Inc. (Subsidiary of: Greenwood Publishing Group Inc.), 88 Post Rd. W., Box 5007, Westport, CT 06881-5007. TEL 203-226-3571. FAX 203-222-1502.

MUDFISH; art and poetry. see LITERATURE — Poetry

709　　　　　　GW　ISSN 0077-1899
N9
MUENCHENER JAHRBUCH DER BILDENDEN KUNST. 1950. a. DM.154. Staatliche Kunstsammlungen Bayerns, Prinzregentenstr. 3, 80538 Munich, Germany. TEL 49-89-211241. FAX 49-89-21124201. Eds. Konrad Renger, Lorenz Seelig. R&P contact: Lorenz Seelig. **Indexed:** Art Ind., Artbibl.Mod., IBR, RILA. **Document type:** academic/scholarly publication.
—BLDSC (5983.735000); KR SourceOne; SWETS.
Description: Art historical journal with emphasis on archeology, architecture, painting and sculpture.
Refereed Serial

MUENCHENER KULTURFUEHRER MIT THEATERPLAN. see GENERAL INTEREST PERIODICALS — Germany

704.9　　　　　GW　ISSN 0027-299X
N3
DAS MUENSTER; Zeitschrift fuer Christliche Kunst und Kunstwissenschaft. (Text in German; summaries in English and French) 1947. q. DM.58. Verlag Schnell und Steiner GmbH, Leibnizstr. 13, 93009 Regensburg, Germany. TEL 49-941-78785-0. FAX 49-941-7878516. adv. contact: Dagmar Hackner. bk.rev.; bibl.; illus.; index. circ. 2,500. **Indexed:** Artbibl.Mod., Br.Tech.Ind., CERDIC, IBR, RILA. **Document type:** bulletin.
—BLDSC (5985.550000).

704.948 297.38　NE　ISSN 0732-2992
N6260
MUQARNAS; an annual on Islamic art and architecture. (Supplement avail. (ISSN 0921-0326)) 1983. a., vol.13, 1996. fl.85($55) (effective 1996). E.J. Brill, P.O. Box 9000, 2300 PA Leiden, Netherlands. TEL 31-71-5353500. FAX 31-71-5317532. TELEX 39296 BRILL NL. E-mail: ejbrill@brill.nl. (In N. America: E.J. Brill, 24 Hudson St., Kinderhook, NY 12106. TEL 800-962-4406. FAX 518-758-1959) Ed. Gulru Necipoglu. R&P contact: Elizabeth Vennekamp. illus.; cum.index: vols.1-10 in vol.10. (back issues avail.) **Indexed:** Archit.Per.Ind. **Document type:** academic/scholarly publication.
—BLDSC (5985.860000). CCC.
Description: Scholarly contributions on historical, cultural and technical aspects of Islamic art, ceramics and architecture, from all regions of the Islamic world, in the medieval and modern periods. Serves as a forum for discussion among scholars and students in the Western and Islamic world.
Refereed Serial

704.948 297.38　NE　ISSN 0921-0326
MUQARNAS, SUPPLEMENTS. Key Title: Studies in Islamic Art and Architecture. Supplements to Muqarnas. (Supplement to: Muqarnas (ISSN 0732-2992)) 1987. irreg., no.6, 1992. price varies. E.J. Brill, P.O. Box 9000, 2300 PA Leiden, Netherlands. TEL 31-71-5353500. FAX 31-71-5317532. TELEX 39296 BRILL NL. E-mail: ejbrill@brill.nl. (In N. America: E.J. Brill, 24 Hudson St., Kinderhook, NY 12106. TEL 800-962-4406. FAX 518-758-1959) R&P contact: Elizabeth Vennekamp. illus. (back issues avail.) **Document type:** monographic series.
—BLDSC (8490.785400).
Description: Scholarly historical examinations of topics and issues in Islamic art, architecture and culture.
Refereed Serial

700　　　　　　JA　ISSN 0288-6030
MUSASHINO ART UNIVERSITY. BULLETIN. (Text in Japanese; summaries in English) 1963. irreg., no.25, 1994. free. Musashino Art University, 1-736 Ogawa-machi, Kodaira-shi, Tokyo 187, Japan. illus. **Document type:** bulletin.
—BLDSC (2623.550000).

913 708　　　　US　ISSN 0077-2194
N584.M5
MUSE (COLUMBIA). 1967. a. $12. University of Missouri at Columbia, Museum of Art and Archaeology, One Pickard Hall, Columbia, MO 65211. TEL 573-882-3591. FAX 573-884-4039. Dir. Marlene Perchinske. circ. 2,500. **Indexed:** Numis.Lit., RILA. **Document type:** academic/scholarly publication.

MUSEA NOSTRA. see MUSEUMS AND ART GALLERIES

709.4　　　　　FR　ISSN 1141-4782
MUSEE INGRES. BULLETIN. (Special nos. avail.) 1956. a. 120 F. Societe des Amis du Musee d'Ingres, 7 rue Emile Pouvillon, 82000 Montauban, France. Ed. Evelyne Dayrens. bk.rev.; illus. circ. 800. **Indexed:** RILA. **Document type:** bulletin.
Description: Discusses new acquisitions by the Musee d'Ingres and covers special exhibits. Reviews the year's news of the museum.

MUSEES. see MUSEUMS AND ART GALLERIES

700 913　　　　CL　ISSN 0716-1530
F2230.1.A7
MUSEO CHILENO DE ARTE PRECOLOMBINO. BOLETIN. 1986. irreg. $9 (foreign $15). Museo Chileno de Arte Precolombino, Bandera 361, Casilla 3687, Santiago, Chile. TEL 695-3851. FAX 697-2779. Ed. Jose Berenguer R. circ. 500. (back issues avail.) **Indexed:** Anthropol.Lit. **Document type:** bulletin, academic/scholarly publication.
Description: Contains essays, research reports, and commentary on aboriginal art of the Americas, namely pre-European art.

MUSEU DE ARQUEOLOGIA E ETNOLOGIA. REVISTA. see ARCHAEOLOGY

700 069　　　　SP　ISSN 1133-6455
MUSEU NACIONAL D'ART DE CATALUYNA. BUTLLETI. (Text in Catalan, English, French, German, or Spanish; summaries in Catalan, English, and Spanish) 1993. a. 7500 ptas. (effective 1997). Museu Nacional d'Art de Catalunya, Palau Nacional, Parc de Montjuic, 08038 Barcelona, Spain. TEL 34-3-4237199. FAX 34-3-3255773. Ed. Eduard Carbonell Esteller; Pub. Maria Montserrat Guma. bk.rev. circ. 1,500. **Document type:** bulletin, bibliography.
Description: Includes papers on art history and museology, museum news and research works on the collection, exhibition reviews and studies of art from other collections.

MUSEUM FUER VOELKERKUNDE, BERLIN. VEROEFFENTLICHUNGEN. NEUE FOLGE. ABTEILUNG: AMERIKANISCHE NATURVOELKER. see ANTHROPOLOGY

MUSEUM NOTES (SPOKANE). see MUSEUMS AND ART GALLERIES

MUSEUM OF FAR EASTERN ANTIQUITIES. BULLETIN. see MUSEUMS AND ART GALLERIES

MUSEUM YEAR. see MUSEUMS AND ART GALLERIES

MUSIC OF THE SPHERES; a quarterly magazine of art and music for the New Age. see NEW AGE PUBLICATIONS

MUSICA, CINEMA, IMMAGINE, TEATRO. see MUSIC

MUSICWORKS; journal of sound explorations. see MUSIC

709　　　　　　HU　ISSN 0027-5247
MUVESZETTORTENETI ERTESITO/BULLETIN FOR HISTORY OF ARTS. (Text in Hungarian; summaries occasionally in English, French or German) 1952. q. $48 (effective 1998). (Magyar Tudomanyos Akademia) Akademiai Kiado Rt., P.O. Box 245, H-1519 Budapest, Hungary. TEL 36-1-2043976. FAX 36-1-2043973. Ed. Miklos Mojzer. adv.; bk.rev.; charts; illus.; index. **Indexed:** Amer.Hist.& Life (1993-), Artbibl.Mod., Hist.Abstr. (1993-), Numis.Lit., RILA.

700　　　　　　IR　ISSN 1010-6618
MUZAH'HA. 1962. m. Sazman-i Miras-i Farhangi Kishvar, Idarah-i Kull-i Muzah'ha-yi, 60 Khayaban-e-Laristan, Ustad Mutahhari Ave., Tehran, Iran.
Supersedes (1962-1977): Hunar va Mardum - Art and People (ISSN 1010-6464)

700　　　　　　PL　ISSN 0068-4678
MUZEUM GORNOSLASKIE W BYTOMIU. ROCZNIK. SERIA SZTUKA. (Text in Polish; summaries in German and English) 1964. irreg. $15 price varies. Muzeum Gornoslaskie, Pl. Sobieskiego 2, 41-902 Bytom, Poland. TEL 48-32-81-34-01.

MUZEUM NARODOWE W KRAKOWIE. KATALOGI ZBIOROW/NATIONAL MUSEUM IN CRACOW. CATALOGUES OF THE COLLECTIONS. see MUSEUMS AND ART GALLERIES

700 370　　　　US　ISSN 0160-6395
N105
N A E A NEWS. 1958. bi-m. $50 membership. National Art Education Association, 1916 Association Dr., Reston, VA 20191-1590. TEL 703-860-8000. Ed. Janice Davenport. R&P contact: Cam Luccarelli. adv. contact: Janice Davenport. bk.rev. circ. 16,000. **Document type:** newsletter.
—BLDSC (6011.377000).
Description: List of current association events and news affecting visual art education.

702.8　　　　　US
N A M T A NEWS & VIEWS. 1960. m. membership. National Art Materials Trade Association, 178 Lakeview Ave., Clifton, NJ 07011. TEL 201-546-6400. FAX 201-546-0393. Ed. John R. Luciano. bk.rev. circ. 1,500. **Document type:** trade publication, newsletter.

700 780　　　　US　ISSN 0894-8585
N D. 1982. 2/yr. $9. N D, Box 4144, Austin, TX 78765. TEL 512-440-7609. FAX 512-416-8007. E-mail: plunkett@ND.org. Ed. Daniel Plunkett. adv.; bk.rev.; music rev.; circ. 3,000 (paid). **Document type:** consumer publication.
Description: Devoted to documenting experimental works and artists. Serves as a forum for exchange and contact within the international community of artists, networkers and musicians.

700　　　　　　GW　ISSN 0935-2341
N I K E. (Text in English, German) 1983. 10/yr. DM.410 (foreign DM.460). Verlag Gerhard Goetze, Leopoldstr. 62, 80802 Munich, Germany. TEL 089-340013. FAX 089-340069. Ed. Gerhard Goetze. adv.; bk.rev. circ. 10,000. **Indexed:** RILA. **Document type:** consumer publication.
Formerly (until 1985): Neue Kunst in Europa (ISSN 0175-0038)

N O I INTERNATIONAL; Mensch, Gesellschaft, Kultur, Umwelt. see LITERATURE

750　　　　　　UK
N P G TRIENNIAL REPORT. triennial. National Portrait Gallery, St. Martin's Pl., London WC2H 0HE, England. TEL 44-171-306-0055. **Document type:** monographic series.

709.4　　　　　IT　ISSN 0027-7835
NK155.Z9
NAPOLI NOBILISSIMA; rivista di arti figurative, archeologia ed urbanistica. vol.5,1966. m. Societa l'Arte Tipografica, Via S. Biagio dei Librai 39, 80100 Naples, Italy. Ed. Roberto Pane. illus. **Indexed:** RILA.

THE NATION. see LITERARY AND POLITICAL REVIEWS

700　　　　　　US　ISSN 0191-0825
THE NATIONAL ACADEMY. ANNUAL EXHIBITION CATALOGUE. 1826. a. $10. The National Academy, 1083 Fifth Ave., New York, NY 10128. TEL 212-369-4880. FAX 212-360-6795. Ed. Virginia Levie. R&P contact: Virginia Levie. adv. contact: Molly McCray. (back issues avail.) **Document type:** academic/scholarly publication, catalog.

700　　　　　　US　ISSN 0190-8049
N6505
NATIONAL ARTS GUIDE.* 1979. bi-m. $50. National Arts Guide, Inc., 209 Lake Shore Dr., Chicago, IL 60611. TEL 312-642-9001.

NATIONAL ASSOCIATION OF SCHOOLS OF ART AND DESIGN. DIRECTORY. see EDUCATION — Guides To Schools And Colleges

707.4　　　　　US
NATIONAL ASSOCIATION OF WOMEN ARTISTS. ANNUAL EXHIBITION CATALOG. 1889. a. $9. National Association of Women Artists, 41 Union Sq., W., Rm 906, New York, NY 10003. TEL 212-675-1616. FAX 212-675-1616. E-mail: nawomena@msn.com adv.; circ. 1,000 (controlled). **Document type:** catalog

NATIONAL DIRECTORY OF ART & ANTIQUES BUYERS & SPECIALISTS. see *ANTIQUES*

700 374 US ISSN 1043-092X
NX396.6
NATIONAL DIRECTORY OF ART INTERNSHIPS. 1983. biennial, 6th ed. 1995-1997. $50 (effective 1996). National Network for Artist Placement, 935 W. Avenue 37, Los Angeles, CA 90065. TEL 213-222-4035. Ed. Warren Christensen. **Document type:** directory.

700 US
NATIONAL DIRECTORY OF ARTS AND EDUCATION SUPPORT BY BUSINESS CORPORATIONS. (Subseries of: Arts Patronage Series) 1979. biennial or triennial, latest 1989-90. $60. Washington International Arts Letter, 326 N. Johnson St., Des Moines, IA 52245-2634. TEL 319-358-6777. Ed. Nancy A. Fandel. **Document type:** directory.
Formerly: National Directory of Arts Support by Business Corporations; Supersedes in part: Arts Support by Private Foundations and Business Corporations.

700 US ISSN 0270-5966
NX398
NATIONAL DIRECTORY OF GRANTS AND AID TO INDIVIDUALS IN THE ARTS, INTERNATIONAL. 1970. triennial or quadrennial, latest 8th ed., 1993. $30. Washington International Arts Letter, 326 N. Johnson St., Des Moines, IA 52245-2834. TEL 319-358-6777. Ed. Nancy A. Fandel. (reprint service avail. from UMI) **Document type:** directory.
Formerly: Grants and Aid to Individuals in the Arts.

700 792.8 US ISSN 0882-245X
NX398
NATIONAL FOUNDATION FOR ADVANCEMENT IN THE ARTS. ANNUAL REPORT. 1981. a. free. National Foundation for Advancement in the Arts, 800 Brickell Ave. No. 5, Miami, FL 33131-2944. TEL 305-377-1140. FAX 305-377-1149. Ed. Suzette L. Prude. R&P contact: Suzette L. Prude. circ. 1,000 (controlled). **Document type:** corporate report.

708.1 069 UK ISSN 0140-7430
ND1630
NATIONAL GALLERY, LONDON. TECHNICAL BULLETIN. 1977-1989; N.S. 1993. a. £19.50. National Gallery Publications Ltd., 5-6 Pall Mall East, London SW1Y 5BA, England. TEL 44-171-839-8544. FAX 44-171-930-0108. Ed. Ashok Roy; Pub. Patricia Williams. R&P contact: Jan Green. illus. circ. 2,000. (back issues avail.) **Indexed:** Art & Archaeol.Tech.Abstr., RILA. **Document type:** academic/scholarly publication.
—BLDSC (6023.980000).
Description: Technical studies of easel paintings and articles in museology.

700 US ISSN 0091-7222
N856
NATIONAL GALLERY OF ART. ANNUAL REPORT. 1970. a. price varies. National Gallery of Art, Washington, DC 20565. TEL 202-842-6200. illus. circ. 5,500. **Document type:** corporate report.
—KR SourceOne.

NATIONAL GALLERY OF CANADA CATALOGUE. CANADIAN ART. see *MUSEUMS AND ART GALLERIES*

700 JA ISSN 0914-7489
N8.J28
NATIONAL MUSEUM OF MODERN ART, TOKYO. BULLETIN. (Text in Japanese, summaries in English) 1987. biennial. National Museum of Modern Art, Tokyo, 3 Kitanomaru Koen, Chiyoda-ku, Tokyo 102, Japan. TEL 81-3-3214-2561. FAX 81-3-3213-1340. circ. 1,000. **Document type:** academic/scholarly publication, bulletin.
Description: Publishes research articles on modern and contemporary arts including crafts and films.

NATIONAL PALACE MUSEUM. MONTHLY OF CHINESE ART. see *MUSEUMS AND ART GALLERIES*

750 UK
NATIONAL PORTRAIT GALLERY. REPORT. a. National Portrait Gallery, St. Martin's Pl., London WC2H 0HE, England. TEL 44-171-306-0055. **Document type:** corporate report.

709 NE ISSN 0169-6726
N5
NEDERLANDS KUNSTHISTORISCH JAARBOEK. (Text in Dutch; summaries in English) 1950. a. fl.183.95. Waanders Uitgevers, Postbus 1129, 8001 BC Zwolle, Netherlands. TEL 31-38-4658628. FAX 31-38-4655989. Ed.Bd. circ. 550. (back issues avail.) **Indexed:** Art Ind., Artbibl.Mod., IBR, RILA.
—KR SourceOne; SWETS.

700 800 LU
NEEUROPA. 1971. bi-a. $50. Europeditor, P.O. Box 212, Luxembourg, Luxembourg. Eds. Georges Astalos, Pino Mariano. adv.; bk.rev. circ. 10,000.

700 US
NETSHAKER. 1992. s-a. $12. Netshaker Press, Box 370, Etna, NH 03750-0370. TEL 603-448-4797. Ed. Chuck Welch.
Description: Covers outsider art, mail art, e-mail art and zines.

700 GW ISSN 0941-6501
N3
NEUE BILDENDE KUNST. 1953. bi-m. DM.84 (Switzerland 84 SFr.; Austria S.672; elsewhere $66) (effective 1997). (Verband Bildender Kuenstler) Neue Bildende Kunst Redaktion GmbH, Christburgerstr. 11, 10405 Berlin, Germany. TEL 49-30-4413177. FAX 49-30-4413176. E-mail: nbk.bln@t-online.de; URL: http://www.hso.ch/nbk. Ed. Matthias Fluegge. adv.: B&W page DM.1890, color page DM.3090; trim 280 x 213; adv. contact: Ursula Wolf. bk.rev.; charts; illus. circ. 10,000. **Indexed:** Art & Archaeol.Tech.Abstr., Artbibl.Mod., Artbibl., IBR, RILA. **Document type:** consumer publication.
Formerly (until 1990): Bildende Kunst (ISSN 0006-2391)
Description: Provides reports, criticism, essays, interviews, news and reviews of contemporary art as well as an international exhibition calendar.

NEW ARCADIAN JOURNAL. see *ARCHITECTURE*

700 US ISSN 0886-8115
N6512
NEW ART EXAMINER; independent voice of the visual arts. 1973. 10/yr. $35 (Canada $53; elsewhere $68). Chicago New Art Association, 314 W. Institute Pl., Chicago, IL 60610-3007. TEL 312-649-9900. FAX 312-649-9935. E-mail: examiner@cnaa.tezcat. com. Ed. Kathryn Hixson; Pub. Grant Samuelson. R&P contact: Grant Samuelson. adv. contact: Mari Eastman. bk.rev.; illus.; circ. 20,000 (paid). (back issues avail.) **Indexed:** Art Ind., Art.Ind., Artbibl.Mod., Artbibl., Avery Ind.Archit.Per., RILA. **Document type:** trade publication.
—BLDSC (6082.090000); KR SourceOne.
Description: Commentary on and analysis of the exhibition and making of the visual arts.

NEW COLLAGE MAGAZINE. see *LITERATURE*

700 792 NR ISSN 0331-7080
NEW CULTURE; a review of contemporary African arts. (Text in English) 1978. 10/yr. £N15($40) African Designs Development Centre Ltd., New Culture Studios, N6A Adeola Crescent, Oremji, P.M.B. 5162, Ibadan, Oyo State, Nigeria. Ed. D. Nwoko. bk.rev. (back issues avail.)

NEW DEPARTURES; international review of literature & the lively arts. see *LITERATURE*

701.18 UK
NEW ENGLISH ART CLUB. a. Federation of British Artists, 17 Carlton House Terrace, London SW1Y 5BD, England. TEL 0171-930-6844. FAX 0171-839-7830. **Document type:** catalog.

700 US
NEW HAMPSHIRE ARTS. vol.4, 1987. q. free. State Council on the Arts, 40 N. Main St., Concord, NH 03301. TEL 603-271-2789. FAX 603-271-3584. E-mail: sylvester@lilac.nhsl.lib.nh.us. Ed. Audrey V. Sylvester. R&P contact: Audrey V. Sylvester. bk.rev. circ. 5,000. (tabloid format; back issues avail.) **Document type:** newsletter.
Formerly: Artsheaf.
Description: Provides information of interest to artists and art organizations in New Hampshire.

NEW MUSE OF CONTEMPT. see *LITERATURE*

700 US ISSN 0737-5387
NX504
NEW OBSERVATIONS. 1982. q. $22 (foreign $38). New Observations Ltd., 611 Broadway, No. 701, New York, NY 10012. TEL 212-677-8561. E-mail: newobs@inch.com; URL: http://plexus.org/newobs. Ed. Diane R. Karp. R&P contact: Erika Knerr. circ. 1,500 (paid). (back issues avail.)
—UnCover.
Description: Centers on contemporary visual art from the artist's perspective.
Refereed Serial

THE NEW RENAISSANCE; an international magazine of ideas and opinions, emphasizing literature & the arts. see *LITERATURE*

700 900 400 SW
NEW SOCIETY OF LETTERS AT LUND. PUBLICATIONS. (Text in English, German or Swedish; summaries in English or German) 1921. irreg. Lund University Press, P.O. Box 141, S-221 00 Stockholm, Lund, Sweden. TEL 46-46-31-20-00. FAX 46-46-30-53-38. E-mail: order@studli.se; URL: http://www.studli.se/. Ed. Bo Westerhult. **Document type:** monographic series.

700 US
NEW YORK ART REVIEW.* irreg., 3rd ed., 1988. $49.95 paperback; hardbound $59.95. American References Publishing Corp., 2210 N. Burling St., Chicago, IL 60614-3712. Ed. Les Krantz. illus.
Description: Lists museums, galleries, art associations, and museum personnel alphabetically by city, including addresses, telephone numbers, admission information, history, and information on types of displays. Lists artists, including medium, address, gallery affiliations, birthdate, awards, education, and short profiles.

700 800 361.8 US
NEWORLD;* the multicultural magazine of the arts. 1974. bi-m. $7.50. Inner-City Cultural Center, Box 272, Los Angeles, CA 90078-0272. TEL 213-387-1161. (Subscr. to: 6331 Hollywood Blvd., Ste. 624, Los Angeles, CA 90028) Ed. Fred Beauford. adv.; bk.rev.; film rev.; play rev. circ. 10,000. (back issues avail.)
Formerly: New World Quarterly of the Inner-City Cultural Center.

016 700 US ISSN 0737-4003
NEWSBANK REVIEW OF THE ARTS: FINE ARTS AND ARCHITECTURE. 1972. m. (q. and a. cums.). price varies. NewsBank, Inc., 58 Pine St., New Canaan, CT 06840-5426. TEL 203-966-1100. FAX 203-966-6254. Ed. Jim Branch. cum.index (paper or CD-ROM). (also avail. in microfiche)
Supersedes in part: NewsBank Review of the Arts.

700 930.1 950 US ISSN 8755-4593
NEWSLETTER EAST ASIAN ART & ARCHAEOLOGY. Short title: Newsletter E A A A. 1977. 3/yr. $12 (foreign $15) (effective 1997). University of Michigan, History of Art Department, Tappan Hall, Rm. 50, University of Michigan, Ann Arbor, MI 48109-1357. TEL 313-936-2539. FAX 313-647-4121. E-mail: wholden@umich.edu; URL: http://www.umich.edu/~hartspc.NEAAA. Ed. Wendy Holden. adv. contact: Wendy Holden. bk.rev. circ. 450. (back issues avail.) **Document type:** newsletter.
Description: Informs readers about Asian art activities regarding worldwide exhibitions, symposia, lectures, and book dealers.

700 US ISSN 0085-4174
NEWSLETTER ON CONTEMPORARY JAPANESE PRINTS. 1971. irreg. free. Helen & Felix Juda Collection, 644 S. June St., Los Angeles, CA 90005. Ed. Irene Drori. illus. **Document type:** newsletter.

700 IT ISSN 0394-6428
NEXT. (Text in English, French, Italian) 1985. q. $40 (effective 1995-96). Joyce & Co. - Associazione Culturale, Via Natale del Grande 51, 00153 Rome, Italy. TEL 39-6-5899285. Eds. Anna Di Biagio, Emma Ercoli. adv.: B&W page L.1200000, color page L.1500000. **Document type:** consumer publication.

709 GW ISSN 0078-0537
N3
NIEDERDEUTSCHE BEITRAEGE ZUR KUNSTGESCHICHTE.
1961. a. DM.65. (Niedersaechsisches
Landesmuseum, Hannover) Deutscher Kunstverlag
GmbH, Nymphenburgerstr. 84, 80636 Munich,
Germany. TEL 49-89-121516-0.
FAX 49-89-12151616. Ed. Heide Grape-Albers.
circ. 800. **Indexed:** Artbibl.Mod., Avery Ind.Archit.Per.,
IBR, NAA, RILA. **Document type:** academic/scholarly
publication.

740 CC
NIENHUA YISHU/ART OF NEW YEAR PICTURE. (Text in
Chinese) s-a. Tianjin Renmin Meishu Chubanshe -
Tianjin People's Fine Art Publishers, 150 Machang
Dao, Heping Qu, Tianjin 300050, People's Republic
of China. TEL 313820. Ed. Qing Baiyin.

700 JA ISSN 0914-7829
NIKKEI ART. (Text in Japanese) 1988. m. 17500 Yen.
Nikkei Business Publications, Inc. (Subsidiary of:
Nihon Keizai Shimbun, Inc.), 2-7-6, Hirakawa-cho,
Chiyoda-ku, Tokyo 102, Japan.
TEL 81-3-5210-8322. FAX 81-3-5210-8119. URL:
http://www.nikkeibp.co.jp/. Ed. Takehiko Katsuo;
Pub. Katsutoshi Kimura. adv.: B&W page
340000 Yen; color page 455000 Yen; trim
180 x 280; adv. contact: Tatsuya Saito. mkt.; illus.
circ. 12,406. **Document type:** trade publication.
Description: Contains specialized information on
the art market for collectors and investors, including
current market values of paintings, sculptures,
prints, ceramics, and antiques.

700 FR ISSN 1155-1240
NINETY; des annees 90 - art in the 90's. bi-m. 540 F.
(Europe 590 F.; elsewhere 690 F.). Eighty
Magazine, 33 rue de la Breche aux Loups, 75012
Paris, France. TEL 43-40-80-82. Ed. Catherine
Flohic.
Formerly: Eighty (ISSN 0294-1880)

700 GW
NO NEWS. 1986. q. DM.85. No-Institute, Niederfeldstr.
35, 34128 Kassel, Germany. TEL 49-561-884694.
FAX 49-561-884694. Ed. Juergen Olbrich. (back
issues avail.) **Document type:** bulletin.
Formerly: Tiegel und Tumult.

709 SP ISSN 0213-2214
N7101
NORBA: ARTE. 1980. irreg., no.10, 1990. Universidad
de Extremadura, Departamento de Historia del Arte,
Servicio de Publicaciones, Calle Pizarro, 8, 10071
Caceres, Spain. TEL 927-247650. Ed. Maria del
Mar Lonzano Bartolozzi. illus.
—CINDOC.
Supersedes in part (in 1983): Norba (ISSN
0211-0636)
Description: Covers art history, with preference to
aspects of Spanish art: theory, analysis,
documentation, commentaries.

**NORDISK TIDSKRIFT FOR VETENSKAP, KONST OCH
INDUSTRI.** see *LITERARY AND POLITICAL REVIEWS*

700 NO ISSN 0803-6160
N7068
NORSK KUNSTAARBOK/YEARBOOK OF NORWEGIAN ART.
Variant title: Kunstaarbok. (Text in English,
Norwegian) 1992. a. NOK 325 in Nordic countries;
elsewhere $65 (effective 1997). (K I K -
Kunstnernes Informasjonskontor) Scandinavian
University Press, P.O. Box 2959 Toeyen, N-0608
Oslo, Norway. TEL 47-22-57-54-00.
FAX 47-22-57-53-53. E-mail: mail@scup.no; URL:
http://www.scup.no. (US addr.: 875 Massachusetts
Ave., Ste. 84, Cambridge, MA 02139. TEL
617-497-6515. FAX 617-354-6875) **Document
type:** academic/scholarly publication.
Description: Contains an overview of contemporary
Norwegian art; visual arts, applied art, photography.
Reviews important exhibitions in Norway.

384 NO ISSN 0804-8452
P92.N8
NORSK MEDIETIDSSKRIFT. 1994. s-a. NOK 160 to
individuals; institutions NOK 300; students NOK
130 (effective 1997). Novus Forlag, P.O. Box 748
Sentrum, N-0106 Oslo, Norway.
TEL 47-2271-7450. FAX 47-2271-8107. E-mail:
novus@novus.no; URL: http://www.sn.no/novus. Ed.
Kathrine Skretting.

700 US ISSN 0749-6400
NORTH LIGHT. 13/yr. F & W Publications, Inc., 1507
Dana Ave., Cincinnati, OH 45207.
TEL 513-531-2222. FAX 513-531-4082. Ed. Libby
Fellerhoff. circ. 64,000.

700 808 US ISSN 0739-2974
NX456
NORTHERN LIGHTS STUDIES IN CREATIVITY. 1984.
irreg., no.3, 1991. University of Maine, Presque Isle,
181 Main St., Presque Isle, ME 04769.
TEL 207-762-0311. Ed. Stanley Scott. adv.; bk.rev.
circ. 500. (back issues avail.)

NORTHWEST REVIEW. see *LITERATURE*

700 IT ISSN 0029-3814
NOSTRO TEMPO; settimanale cattolico. 1946. bi-m.
L.32000. Centro Giornali Cattolici, Corso Matteotti
11, 10121 Turin, Italy. Ed. Domenico Agasso. adv.;
bk.rev.; film rev.; illus.; index.

700 IT ISSN 0029-4322
NOTIZIARIO D'ARTE. (Text in Italian; summaries in
English, French and German) 1949. bi-m.
L.2000($7) Ennio Francia Ed. & Pub., Via del
Babuino 197, Rome, Italy. adv.; bk.rev.; bibl.; illus.
circ. 2,000.

700 708.5 IT ISSN 0391-3716
NOTIZIARIO VINCIANO. 1977. q. Centro Ricerche
Leonardiane, Contrada del Carmine, 37, 25122
Brescia, Italy. TEL 030-55322. Eds. Giovanni De
Toni, Antonio De Toni. bibl.; illus. circ. 200. (back
issues avail.)

709 IT ISSN 0391-4364
N380
NOTIZIE DA PALAZZO ALBANI. 1972. 2/yr. L.50000
(foreign L.50000). (Universita degli Studi di Urbino,
Istituto di Storia dell'Arte Medievale e Moderna)
Argalia Editore, Via del Balestriere 2, Urbino, Italy.
bk.rev.; illus. **Indexed:** RILA.

NOUVELLE REVUE NEUCHATELOISE. see *HISTORY —
History Of Europe*

760 FR ISSN 0029-4888
NE1
NOUVELLES DE L'ESTAMPE. 1963. 5/yr. 370 F. (EU
470 F.) (foreign 490 F.) (effective 1997-1998).
Comite National de la Gravure Francaise, 58 rue de
Richelieu, 75002 Paris, France.
TEL 33-1-47038388. FAX 33-1-47038307. Ed.
Laure Beaumont-Maillet. R&P contact: Gerard Sourd.
adv.: B&W page 5000 F., color page 12000 F.; adv.
contact: Gerard Sourd. bk.rev. circ. 1,200.
(processed) **Indexed:** Artbibl.Mod., Artbibl., IBR, RILA.
Document type: academic/scholarly publication,
bibliography.
—BLDSC (6176.773000); SWETS.

700 CK ISSN 0029-4969
NOVA; * revista de arte y literatura. 1964. bi-m.
Col.$3.50. Apartado Aereo 15858, Bogota,
Colombia. Ed. David Consuegra U. adv.; charts; illus.

NOVUM. see *ADVERTISING AND PUBLIC RELATIONS*

NUEVA LUZ. see *PHOTOGRAPHY*

LA NUEZ; revista internacional de arte y literatura. see
LITERATURE — Poetry

700 800 301 200 IT
BR738.6
NUOVA EUROPA; rivista internazionale di cultura. 1960.
bi-m. L.50000 (foreign L.70000) (effective 1997).
(Centro Studi Russia Cristiana) R.C. Edizioni s.r.l., Via
Ponzio, 44, 20133 Milan, Italy.
TEL 39-2-2663432. FAX 39-2-2365011. E-mail: r.
c.edizioni@enter.it. Ed. Romano Scalfi. adv. contact:
Stefania Rafaelli. bk.rev.; index. circ. 6,500. **Indexed:**
CERDIC. **Document type:** academic/scholarly
publication, trade publication.
Former titles: Altra Europa (ISSN 1120-0685);
(until 1985): Centro Studi Russia Cristiana. Rivista
(ISSN 0391-2795); (until 1976): Russia Cristiana
(ISSN 0485-7348); (until 1965): Russia Cristiana
Ieri e Oggi (ISSN 1120-0693).

NUOVA RASSEGNA; periodico di attualita, lettere, arti,
cinema, teatro. see *LITERARY AND POLITICAL
REVIEWS*

NY CARLSBERG GLYPTOTEK. MEDDELELSER. see
ARCHAEOLOGY

751.6 IT ISSN 1120-2513
O P D RESTAURO. (Opificio delle Pietre Dure) 1986;
N.S. 1989. a. L.90000 (foreign L.110000).
(Ministero per i Beni Culturali e Ambientali) Centro
Di della Edifimi s.r.l., Lungarno Serristori, 35, 50125
Florence, Italy. TEL 55-2342668.
FAX 55-2342667. (Subscr. to: Centro Di, Via
de'Renai 20r, 50125 Florence, Italy) Ed. Giorgio
Bonsanti. adv.; bk.rev. **Document type:**
academic/scholarly publication.
Description: Covers art restoration technique and
history and the activities of the Opificio.

700 800 AU ISSN 0253-7435
OBEROESTERREICH; Kulturzeitschrift. q. S.396.
Landesverlag, Landstr. 41, A-4020 Linz, Austria. Ed.
Otto Wutzel. illus.

700 CC
THE OBSERVATION POST/CH'UN CH'IU. (Text in
Chinese) m. 60 Leighton Rd., 6th Fl., Hong Kong,
People's Republic of China. TEL 5-765123.

740 XV
OBVESTILA. (Text in Slovenian; summaries in English)
1975. irreg. (4-5/yr.). free. Drustvo Exlibris
Sloveniae, Trubarjeva 14, 61000 Ljubljana,
Slovenia. TEL 061 312-332. (looseleaf format)

700 PL ISSN 0029-8247
DK409
OCHRONA ZABYTKOW. (Text in Polish; summaries in
English) 1948. q. $17. Ministerstwo Kultury i
Sztuki, Generalny Konserwator Zabytkow, Osrodek
Dokumentacji Zabytkow, c/o Redakcja, Ul.
Mazowiecka 11, 00-052 Warsaw, Poland.
TEL 48-22-270038. (Dist. by: Ars Polona-Ruch,
Krakowskie Przedmiescie 7, Warsaw, Poland)
bk.rev.; abstr.; bibl.; charts; illus.; index. circ. 1,450.
(also avail. in microfilm) **Indexed:** Art &
Archaeol.Tech.Abstr., Avery Ind.Archit.Per. **Document
type:** bulletin.
—BLDSC (6235.122000).
Description: Covers restoration techniques,
procedures, and projects.

700 800 US ISSN 0162-2870
NX1
OCTOBER. 1976. q. $35 to individuals (foreign $51);
institutions $98 (foreign $114); students and
retired $25 (foreign $41) (effective 1997). M I T
Press, 55 Hayward St., Cambridge, MA 02142.
TEL 617-253-2889. FAX 617-577-1545. E-mail:
journals-orders@mit.edu; URL: http://www-mitpress.
mit.edu. (Editorial addr.: 225 Lafayette St., No.
1012, New York, NY 10012) Ed.Bd. R&P contact:
Paul Dzus. illus. circ. 4,000. (also avail. in microform
from UMI; reprint service avail. from UMI) **Indexed:**
Alt.Press Ind., Artbibl.Mod., Arts & Hum.Cit.Ind.,
Curr.Cont., Film Lit.Ind. (1986-), MLA Intl.Bibl., RILA.
—BLDSC (6235.151490); Genuine Article; KR
SourceOne; SWETS; UMI; UnCover. **CCC.**
Description: Presents current texts by and about
leading contemporary artists, scholars and critics.
Topics include film, painting, music, photography
and more.

700 949.2 NE ISSN 0923-0033
OCULI. 1987. irreg., vol.6, 1996. price varies. John
Benjamins Publishing Co., Amsteldijk 44, P.O. Box
75577, 1070 AN Amsterdam, Netherlands.
TEL 31-20-6738156. FAX 31-20-6739956. (In N.
America: Box 27519, Philadelphia, PA
19118-0519. TEL 215-836-1200. FAX
215-836-1204) (Co-publisher: Forsten) Eds. Rob
Ruurs, Bert W. Meijer. **Document type:** monographic
series.
—BLDSC (6235.156000).
Description: Historical research in the arts of the
Low Countries, from the 14th and 15th centuries to
the present. Includes monographs, catalogues, and
critical studies.

709 DK ISSN 0078-3285
ODENSE UNIVERSITY STUDIES IN ART HISTORY. (Text in
German and Italian) 1970. irreg., latest 1986. price
varies. Odense University Press, Campusvej 55,
DK-5230 Odense M, Denmark. TEL 66-157999.
FAX 66-158126. E-mail: press@forlag.ou.dk. (back
issues avail.)

ODRA; miesiecznik spoleczno-kulturalny. see
LITERATURE

700 FR ISSN 0029-862X
L'OEIL; revue internationale d'art. 1955. 10/yr. 136 SFr. Editions Gallimard, 5 rue Sebastien-Bottin, 75007 Paris, France. TEL 33-1-46598900. Ed. Guy Boyer. adv.; bk.rev.; illus. circ. 30,000. **Indexed:** Art Ind., Artbibl.Mod., Artbibl., ASCA, Avery Ind.Archit.Per., Chic.Per.Ind., Curr.Cont., IBR, Pt.de Rep. (1979-), RILA.
—BLDSC (6235.263900); KR SourceOne; SWETS.

700 900 AU ISSN 0029-9626
N3
OESTERREICHISCHE ZEITSCHRIFT FUER KUNST UND DENKMALPFLEGE. 1856. 5/yr. S.350. (Oesterreichisches Bundesdenkmalamt) Verlag Anton Schroll und Co., Spengergasse 39, A-1051 Vienna, Austria. FAX 43-1-544564166. Ed. Ernst Bacher. R&P contact: Eckart Vancsa. adv.; bk.rev.; charts; illus. circ. 150. **Indexed:** Amer.Hist.& Life, Artbibl.Mod., Avery Ind.Archit.Per., Hist.Abstr., IBR, RILA. **Document type:** academic/scholarly publication.
—SWETS.

OESTERREICHISCHES MUSEUM FUER VOLKSKUNDE. VEROEFFENTLICHUNGEN. see *FOLKLORE*

709 US ISSN 0731-3284
NX24.03
OHIO ARTS COUNCIL. BIENNIAL REPORT. 1965. biennial. membership only. Ohio Arts Council, 727 E. Main St., Columbus, OH 43205. TEL 614-466-2613. Ed.Bd. stat. circ. 500. **Document type:** corporate report.
Formerly: Ohio Arts Council. Annual Report.

OKTOBAR; list za knjizevnost, umetnost i kulturu. see *LITERATURE*

700 DK ISSN 0108-3511
OMKRING ET KUNSTVAERK. 1980. irreg. DKK 2 per no. Randers Kunstmuseum, Stemannsgade 2, 8900 Randers, Denmark. Ed. Nina Hobolth. illus.

700 GW
ON - OPEN NET MAG. (Text in English) 1991. s-a. DM.5. Edition Kunst - Bahnhausen, Postfach 2631, 32383 Minden, Germany. Ed. Jo Klaffki. circ. 400. **Document type:** bulletin.

769 US
NE1
ON PAPER; the journal of prints, drawings, and photography. 1970. bi-m. $60 (effective 1997). Fanning Publishing Co., Inc., 39 E. 78th St., New York, NY 10021. TEL 212-988-5959. FAX 212-988-6107. Ed. Faye Hirsch; Pub. Gabriella Fanning. R&P contact: Jacqueline Brody. adv.; bk.rev.; illus. circ. 5,000. (looseleaf format) **Indexed:** Art Ind., Artbibl., Artbibl.Mod., Avery Ind.Archit.Per., RILA.
—KR SourceOne; UnCover.
Formerly (until 1996): Print Collector's Newsletter (ISSN 0032-8537)

700 CN ISSN 0701-5429
ONTARIO ARTS COUNCIL. ANNUAL REPORT/CONSEIL DES ARTS DE L'ONTARIO. RAPPORT ANNUEL. (Text in English, French) 1963. a. free. Ontario Arts Council - Conseil des Arts de l'Ontario, Ste. 500, 151 Bloor St. W., Toronto, ON M5S 1T6, Canada. TEL 416-961-1660; 800-387-0058. FAX 416-961-7796. circ. 3,500.

700 IT ISSN 0030-3305
OP CIT; selezione della critica d'arte contemporanea. 1964. 3/yr. L.16000 (foreign L.24000). Edizioni il Centro, Via Vincenzo Padula, 2, 80123 Naples, Italy. Ed. Renato De Fusco. adv.; bk.rev.; bibl. circ. 1,000. **Indexed:** Artbibl.Mod., Artbibl., Hisp.Amer.Per.Ind. (1986-), MLA Intl.Bibl. **Document type:** academic/scholarly publication.
—BLDSC (6265.550000).

700 IT
OPEN; bimestrale di cultura ed arte. 1993. bi-m. L.15000. Edizioni Il Grappolo, Casella Postale Aperta, 84080 Piazza del Galdo (SA), Italy. TEL 39-89-894457. Ed. Antonio Corbisiero. adv.: B&W page L.100000; 150 x 210. bk.rev. circ. 10,000.

708.9493 BE
OPENBAAR KUNSTBEZIT IN VLAANDEREN. (Text in Dutch) 1963. q. 1100 BEF. Openbaar Kunstbezit in Vlaanderen v.z.w., Grote Markt 46, 9100 Sint-Niklaas, Belgium. TEL 32-3-7601640. FAX 32-3-7601641. Ed. Rudy Vercruysse; Pub. Rudy Vercruysse. R&P contact: Rudy Vercruysse. adv.: B&W page 72000 BEF; adv. contact: Jan Bergmans. bk.rev.; index. (back issues avail.) **Document type:** consumer publication.
Description: Presents art in Belgian museums and public collections.

ORIENS. see *ORIENTAL STUDIES*

ORIENTAL ART; devoted to the study of all forms of Oriental art. see *ORIENTAL STUDIES*

700 US ISSN 0078-6551
ORIENTAL STUDIES. no.8, 1970. irreg. price varies. Freer Gallery of Art, Smithsonian Institution, Jefferson Dr., S.W. at 12th St., Washington, DC 20560. TEL 202-357-1432.

950 CC ISSN 0030-5448
DS501
ORIENTATIONS. (Text in English) 1970. 11/yr. $100 (effective 1996). Orientations Magazine Ltd., 14th Fl., 200 Lockhart Rd., Hong Kong, People's Republic of China. TEL 852-2511-1368. FAX 852-2507-4620. E-mail: info@orientations.com.hk; URL: http://www.orientations.com.hk/. Ed. Elizabeth Knight. R&P contact: Elizabeth Knight. adv.; bk.rev.; illus.; index. circ. 10,812. (back issues avail.) **Indexed:** Art & Archaeol.Tech.Abstr., Artbibl.Mod., So.Pac.Per.Ind. **Document type:** consumer publication.
—BLDSC (6291.220100); SWETS; UnCover.
Description: For collectors and connoisseurs of Asian art. Presents the ancient arts of painting, calligraphy, bronzes, and ceramics, as well as the decorative arts and crafts. Includes coverage of contemporary artists.

700 US ISSN 0030-5529
THE ORIGINAL ART REPORT; committed to the preservation, comprehension, and progress of artists, art, and the broader society. Abbreviated title: T O A R. 1967. irreg. (12 nos./vol.) $31 per vol. 3024 Sunnyside Dr., Rockford, IL 61114-6025. Ed. Frank Salantrie; Pub. June Salantrie. bk.rev. (back issues avail.) **Document type:** newsletter.
Description: Probes the way art works in the real world. Contains objective and subjective opinions and inquiries based on generally available knowledge, usually with a twist.

700 333.7 US
▼**THE ORLO EXPRESS.** 1995. s-a. $10. Orlo, Box 10342, Portland, OR 97210. TEL 503-242-2330. FAX 503-243-2645. E-mail: orlo@teleport.com; URL: http://www.teleport.com/~orlo/. illus. (tabloid format) **Document type:** newsletter.
Description: Publishes news and information on the organization's grassroots environmental activities, including performances.

ORNAMENT; a quarterly of jewelry and personal adornment. see *JEWELRY, CLOCKS AND WATCHES*

730 PL ISSN 1230-6703
ORONSKO; kwartalnik rzezby. (Text in Polish; summaries in English) 1990. q. 10 Zl. (effective 1997). Centrum Rzezby Polskiej, Ul. Topolowa 1, 26-681 Oronsko, Poland. TEL 48-48-3621916. FAX 48-48-3621916. Ed. Tomasz Palacz. adv.; bk.rev. circ. 500. **Document type:** newsletter.
Description: Devoted to contemporary sculpture.

700 800 BN
OSNOVAC. (Text in Serbo-Croatian) 1977. q. Udruzena Osnovna Skola, M. Tita 8, Derventa, Bosnia Hercegovina. TEL 074-833-934.

ART 459

709 NE ISSN 0030-672X
DJ1
OUD-HOLLAND; driemaandelijks tijdschrift voor Nederlandse kunstgeschiedenis. (Text in Dutch; summaries in English) 1885. q. fl.120 (foreign fl.140). (Stichting tot Exploitatie van het Rijksbureau voor Kunsthistorische Documentatie) Uitgeverij Nauta, Postbus 1, 7200 AA Zutphen, Netherlands. TEL 31-5750-13614. Ed.Bd. bk.rev.; illus.; index. circ. 750. (reprint service avail. from KTO) **Indexed:** Art Ind., Artbibl.Mod., Artbibl., Arts & Hum.Cit.Ind., ASCA, Avery Ind.Archit.Per., Curr.Cont., IBR, RILA. **Document type:** academic/scholarly publication.
—KR SourceOne; SWETS.

OUROBOROS. see *LITERATURE*

700 709 UK ISSN 0142-6540
N1
OXFORD ART JOURNAL. 1978. s-a. £53 (foreign $94) (effective 1998). Oxford University Press, Academic Division, Great Clarendon St., Oxford OX2 6DP, England. TEL 44-1865-267907. FAX 44-1865-267485. TELEX 837330-OXPRES-G. E-mail: jnl.info@oup.co.uk; URL: http://www.oup.co.uk/journals. (U.S. subscr. to: Oxford University Press Inc., 2001 Evans Rd., Cary, NC 27513. TEL 800-852-7323. FAX 919-677-1714) Ed.Bd.; Pub. Philip Joseph. R&P contact: Joolz Longley. adv. contact: Jane Parker. bk.rev.; illus.; cum.index. circ. 900. (also avail. in microform; back issues avail.) **Indexed:** Amer.Hist.& Life (1987-), Art Ind., Artbibl.Mod., Arts & Hum.Cit.Ind., ASCA, Avery Ind.Archit.Per., Curr.Cont., DAAI, Hist.Abstr. (1987-), RILA. **Document type:** academic/scholarly publication.
—BLDSC (6320.597000); Genuine Article; KR SourceOne; SWETS; UMI; UnCover. **CCC**.
Description: Addresses historical and philosophical issues concerning visual culture while seeking to provide an alternative to mainstream art history journals.

790 800 US ISSN 1067-2222
NX504
P - FORM; a journal of interdisciplinary and performance art. 1986. q. $13 to individuals (Canada and Mexico $20; elsewhere $30); institutions $20 (Canada de Mexco $30; elsewhere $40) (effective 1997). Randolph Street Gallery, 756 N. Milwaukee Ave., Chicago, IL 60622. TEL 312-666-7737. FAX 312-666-8986. E-mail: randolph@merle.acns.nwu.edu; kthompson@u.washington.edu; URL: http://fileroom.aaup.uic.edu/RSG/pformhomepage.html. Ed. Ken Thompson. adv.: B&W page $220, trim 10 x 7 1/2; adv. contact: Ken Thompson. bk.rev.; play rev.; illus. circ. 1,500. (back issues avail.) **Document type:** academic/scholarly publication.
Description: Covers the experimental time-based arts, including performance, video, audio or sound art, theater, dance and film.
Refereed Serial

700 FR
P L G. (Plein la Gueule) 1978. 4/yr. 180 F. (foreign 200 F.). Association pour la Promotion des Jeunes Auteurs de la Bande Dessinee, 3 rue de la Vanne, 92120 Montrouge, France. TEL 33-1-46556604. FAX 33-1-46556604. Ed. Philippe Morin; Pub. Pierre-Marie Jamet. R&P contact: Frederic Debomy. adv. contact: Dominique Poncet. bk.rev. circ. 1,500. **Document type:** monographic series.
Formerly: P L G P U R (ISSN 0223-0844)
Description: Contains interviews with comic book authors.

740 US ISSN 1018-4252
N7410
PACIFIC ARTS. 1975. a., nos.9-10, 1994. $40 membership (artists $30). Pacific Arts Association, c/o Metropolitan Museum of Art, Dept. AAOA, 1000 Fifth Ave., New York, NY 10028. Ed. Philip J.C. Dark. bk.rev.; film rev.; bibl. circ. 300. **Indexed:** A.I.C.P., Anthropol.Lit., So.Pac.Per.Ind.
—BLDSC (6328.768000).
Formerly (until no.29, 1989): Pacific Arts Newsletter (ISSN 0111-5774)
Description: Articles, commentary and reviews about research museums, exhibitions, and publications on Pacific arts and material culture.

460 ART

700 US
N7410
PACIFIC ARTS NEWSLETTER. 1993. q. Pacific Arts Association, c/o Metropolitan Museum of Art, Dept. AAOA, 1000 Fifth Ave., New York, NY 10028. FAX 808-521-6591. Eds. Mike Gunn, Virginia Lee Webb. **Document type:** newsletter.
  Description: Publishes news, bibliographical notes, association events and matters.

700 US
PAINT RAG. 1926. m. $25 membership only. Association of Hawaii Artists, Box 10202, Honolulu, HI 96816. TEL 808-396-7494. Ed. Leslie Tomomatsu. adv. circ. 500. **Document type:** newsletter.
  Description: To promote and stimulate growth and ability among members of the art community, and to contribute to the cultural life of the state of Hawaii.

PALAESTRA. see *LITERATURE*

700 BE
PALAIS DES BEAUX-ARTS. m. 400 BEF. Palais des Beaux-Arts - Charleroi, Place du Manege, 6000 Charleroi, Belgium. TEL 32-71-314420. FAX 32-71-334207. adv. (tabloid format; back issues avail.)
  Formerly (until 1992): Vie et Culture.

700 SW ISSN 0031-0352
N8
PALETTEN. 1940. q. SEK 250 (students, artists, members of art organizations SEK 200) (effective 1996). Stiftelsen Paletten, Karl Gustavsgatan 10 C, S-411 25 Goeteborg, Sweden. TEL 46-31-711-87-39. FAX 46-31-711-77-85. E-mail: paletten@netg.se. adv. contact: Gunnilla Hylten-Cavallius. bk.rev.; illus. circ. 5,500. **Indexed:** Artbibl.Mod., Artbibl. **Document type:** bulletin.

700 913 RU
PAMYATNIKI KUL'TURY. NOVYE OTKRYTIYA/MONUMENTS OF CULTURE. NEW DISCOVERIES. (Text in Russian; summaries in English) 1974. irreg. price varies. (Rossiiskaya Akademiya Nauk, Nauchnyi Sovet po Istorii Mirovoi Kul'tury) Izdatel'stvo Nauka, S.-Peterburgskoe Otdelenie, Mendeleevskaya liniya, 1, 199034 St. Petersburg B-34, Russia. (Dist. by: Mezhdunarodnaya Kniga, B. Yakimanka 39, 117049 Moscow, Russia) Ed.Bd. illus.

PAN; c'est myotique! see *LINGUISTICS*

PANDULIPI. see *LITERARY AND POLITICAL REVIEWS*

700 CN ISSN 0318-7020
NX456
PARACHUTE (MONTREAL); contemporary art magazine. (Text in English, French) 1975. q. Can.$34 to individuals (foreign Can.$44); institutions Can.$50 (foreign Can.$60). Editions Parachute, 4060 bd. St. Laurent, Ste. 501, Montreal, PQ H2W 1Y9, Canada. TEL 514-842-9805. FAX 514-287-7146. E-mail: parachut@citenet.net. Ed. Chantal Pontbriand. R&P contact: Colette Tougas. adv. contact: Colett Tougas. bk.rev. circ. 5,000. (back issues avail.) **Indexed:** Artbibl.Mod., Can.Per.Ind., Pt.de Rep. (1983-), RADAR, RILA. **Document type:** academic/scholarly publication.
  —BLDSC (6404.710000); UnCover.
  Description: Presents contemporary Canadian and international art and criticism. Includes articles, interviews, exhibition reviews, and a debate section.

PARAGONE; rivista mensile di arte figurativa e letteratura. see *LITERATURE*

PARALLAX. see *LITERATURE*

700 SZ ISSN 0256-0917
PARKETT. (Text in English, German) 1984. 3/yr. 98 SFr. (Europe 115 SFr.; U.S. and Canada $75) (effective 1997). Parkett Verlag AG, Quellenstr. 27, CH-8005 Zurich, Switzerland. TEL 41-1-2718140. FAX 41-1-2724301. (Subscr. in US to: Parkett Publishers, 636 Broadway, 12th Fl., New York, NY 10012. TEL 212-673-2660. FAX 212-673-2887) Ed. Bice Curiger; Pub. Dieter von Graffenried. adv.; bk.rev.; illus.; cum.index: nos.1-25. circ. 10,000. **Indexed:** Art Ind., Artbibl. **Document type:** consumer publication.
  —BLDSC (6406.771000); KR SourceOne; SWETS.
  Description: Documents European and American contemporary art. Each issue covers several important artists and is produced in close collaboration with those artists.

700 860 SP ISSN 1130-0388
EL PASEANTE. 1985. q. europe 4500 ptas.; elsewhere 8000 ptas. Ediciones Siruela, S.A., Pl. de Manuel Becera 15, El Pabellon, 28028 Madrid, Spain. TEL 91-355-57-20. FAX 91-355-22-01. Dir. Jacobo Fitz-James Stewart. adv. contact: Mamen Fernandez Damborenea. circ. 15,000.
  Description: Reviews the main cultural features of our times, from literary creation to the plastic arts.

PASSAGEN; Zeitschrift fuer Literatur und Kunst. see *LITERATURE*

PEN WORLD. see *HOBBIES*

PENFINDER. see *HOBBIES*

PEQUOD. see *LITERATURE*

700 CN
PERFORMANCE (ROYAL THOMSON - MASSEY HALL EDITION). 1982. bi-m. St. Clair Group, 30 St. Clair Ave. W., Ste. 805, Toronto, ON M4V 3A1, Canada. TEL 416-926-7595. FAX 416-926-0407. Ed. Laurie Payne. adv. **Document type:** consumer publication.
  Formerly: Bravo (ISSN 0714-6981)

PERISTIL. see *ARCHITECTURE*

PESARO CITTA E CONTA. see *HISTORY — History Of Europe*

700 CI ISSN 0031-6296
PETNAEST DANA/FIFTEEN DAYS; casopis za kulturu i umjetnost. (Text in Croatian) 1973. bi-m. $20. Radnicko Sveuciliste "Mosa Pijade", Proletarskih Brigada 68, 41000 Zagreb, Croatia. Ed. Slavko Kovac. bk.rev.; illus.; cum.index. circ. 2,000.
  Formerly: Petnaest - Fifteen Dana.

PHAROS. see *ARCHAEOLOGY*

PHILANTHROPIC DIGEST. see *SOCIAL SERVICES AND WELFARE*

709 US ISSN 0193-8061
N5300
PHOEBUS (TEMPE); a journal of art history. 1978. a. $12. Arizona State University, School of Art, Tempe, AZ 85281. TEL 602-965-6439. Ed. Anthony Lacy Gully. bk.rev.; illus. circ. 1,200. **Indexed:** RILA.

PHOTOGRAPH COLLECTOR; for collectors, curators and dealers. see *PHOTOGRAPHY*

PHOTOGRAPHIC ART MARKET: AUCTION PRICES (YEAR). see *PHOTOGRAPHY*

700 001.644 JA
PICABIA. 1989. 6/yr. 13680 Yen. Rikuyo-sha Publishing Inc., Shizuoka Bank Bldg., 2-19-12 Shinjuku, Shinjuku-ku, Tokyo 160, Japan. TEL 03-3354-4020. FAX 03-3352-3106. Ed. Takashi Hirabayashi.
  Description: For those concerned with graphic design.

709 BE
▼**PICTURA NOVA;** studies in 16th and 17th century Flemish painting and drawing. (Text in English, German) 1996. irreg., vol.3, 1997. price varies. N.V. Brepols, Steenweg op Tielen 68, 2300 Turnhout, Belgium. TEL 32-14-402500. FAX 32-14-428919. Eds. Hans Vlieghe, Katlijne van der Stighelen. bibl.; illus. (back issues avail.) **Document type:** monographic series.
  Description: Publishes monographic studies of specific artists and studies on various themes and topics in Flemish painting and drawing of the 16th and 17th centuries.
  Refereed Serial

PICTURES QUARTERLY. see *PHOTOGRAPHY*

700 BL ISSN 0104-3358
PIRACEMA; arte e cultura. 1993. Instituto Brasileiro de Arte e Cultura, Palacio Gustavo Capanema, Rua da Imprensa 16, 7o andar, 20030-120 Rio de Janeiro RJ, Brazil. TEL 55-21-2976116. FAX 55-21-2624895. Ed. Ivan Junqueira.

PIRANESI; 1st Middle-European architectural magazine for the culture of environment. see *ARCHITECTURE*

PITANJA; mjesecnik: drustvo, znanost, kultura. see *LITERATURE*

700 GW ISSN 0945-9936
PLAKAT JOURNAL. (Text in English, German) 1994. q. DM.65 (Europe DM.75; elsewhere $65) (effective 1997). PlakatKonzepte Grohnert und Weigelt, Oskar-Winter-Str. 3, 30161 Hannover, Germany. TEL 49-511-628376. FAX 49-511-628377. **Document type:** consumer publication.

PLANET; the Welsh internationalist. see *LITERATURE*

PLASTYKA I WYCHOWANIE W SZKOLE. see *EDUCATION*

700 GW ISSN 0938-6602
DAS PLATEAU. 1990. bi-m. DM.120. Radius-Verlag GmbH, Olgastr. 114, 70180 Stuttgart, Germany. TEL 49-711-6076666. FAX 49-711-6075555. Ed. Wolfgang Erk. circ. 1,500. **Document type:** bulletin.
  Description: Contains essays on general cultural interests.

PLEINE MARGE; cahiers de litterature, d'arts plastiques et de critique. see *LITERATURE*

PLUG; cultureel informatieblad voor houders van een Cultureel Jongeren Pasport in Noord-Holland. see *THEATER*

700 IT ISSN 0079-242X
POCKET LIBRARY OF STUDIES IN ART. 1948. irreg., vol.30, 1996. price varies. Casa Editrice Leo S. Olschki, Casella Postale 66, 50100 Florence, Italy. TEL 39-55-6530684. FAX 39-55-6530214. E-mail: celso@olschki.it. circ. 1,200. **Document type:** monographic series.

POETS, PAINTERS, COMPOSERS. see *LITERATURE*

POLICORDO; revista quadrimestrale di cultura, letteratura, arte. see *HUMANITIES: COMPREHENSIVE WORKS*

700 IT ISSN 0391-8653
POLIEDRO;* rassegna mensile d'arte. (Text in French and Italian; summaries in Italian) 1964. m. L.10000. Michele Calabrese, Ed. & Pub., Via Calpurnio Pisone 111, 00175 Rome, Italy. adv.; bk.rev.; illus. circ. 51 (controlled).

700 MX ISSN 1405-0560
POLIESTER; pintura y no pintura. (Text in English, Spanish) 1992. q. Mex.$120($40) (Europe & Latin America $50) (effective 1997 & 1998). Michoacan 139, Col. Condesa, 06140 Mexico DF, Mexico. TEL 52-5-2565681. FAX 525-2114039. E-mail: poliester@intranet.com.mx. Ed. Kurt Hollander. adv. contact: Gabriela Salinas.
  Description: Covers contemporary art of the Americas. Includes interviews with curators and reviews of exhibitions.

POLITECHNIKA WROCLAWSKA. INSTYTUT ARCHITEKTURY I URBANISTYKI. PRACE NAUKOWE. KONFERENCJE. see *ARCHITECTURE*

POLITECHNIKA WROCLAWSKA. INSTYTUT ARCHITEKTURY I URBANISTYKI. PRACE NAUKOWE. MONOGRAFIE. see *ARCHITECTURE*

POLITECHNIKA WROCLAWSKA. INSTYTUT ARCHITEKTURY I URBANISTYKI. PRACE NAUKOWE. STUDIA I MATERIALY. see *ARCHITECTURE*

709 720   PL   ISSN 0860-1194
POLITECHNIKA WROCLAWSKA. INSTYTUT HISTORII ARCHITEKTURY, SZTUKI I TECHNIKI. PRACE NAUKOWE. KONFERENCJE. 1985. irreg. price varies. Oficyna Wydawnicza Politechniki Wroclawskiej, Wybrzeze Wyspianskiego 27, 50-370 Wroclaw, Poland. TEL 48-71-222940. FAX 48-71-223664. TELEX 71-2559 PWRPL. (Dist. by: Ars Polona, Krakowskie Przedmiescie 7, Warsaw, Poland) R&P contact: Halina Dudek. adv. **Document type:** proceedings.

709 720   PL   ISSN 0324-9662
POLITECHNIKA WROCLAWSKA. INSTYTUT HISTORII ARCHITEKTURY, SZTUKI I TECHNIKI. PRACE NAUKOWE. MONOGRAFIE. (Text in Polish; summaries in English and Russian) 1971. irreg., no.18, 1994. price varies. Oficyna Wydawnicza Politechniki Wroclawskiej, Wybrzeze Wyspianskiego 27, 50-370 Wroclaw, Poland. TEL 48-71-222940. FAX 48-71-223664. TELEX 71-22-54 PWRPL. (Dist. by: Ars Polona, Krakowskie Przedmiescie 7, Warsaw, Poland) Ed. Maria Lyko. R&P contact: Halina Dudek. adv. circ. 530. **Document type:** monographic series.

709 720   PL   ISSN 0324-9654
POLITECHNIKA WROCLAWSKA. INSTYTUT HISTORII ARCHITEKTURY, SZTUKI I TECHNIKI. PRACE NAUKOWE. STUDIA I MATERIALY. (Text in Polish; summaries in English and Russian) 1972. irreg., no.11, 1989. price varies. Oficyna Wydawnicza Politechniki Wroclawskiej, Wybrzeze Wyspianskiego 27, 50-370 Wroclaw, Poland. TEL 48-71-222940. FAX 48-71-223664. TELEX 712559 PWRPL. (Dist. by: Ars Polona, Krakowskie Przedmiescie 7, Warsaw, Poland) R&P contact: Halina Dudek. adv. circ. 390. **Document type:** academic/scholarly publication.

700   AU   ISSN 0259-0824
POLYAISTHESIS; Beitraege zur Integration der Kuenste und der Wissenschaften und zu ihrer Umsetzung in die Paedagogische Praxis. 1986. a. price varies. (Internationale Gesellschaft fuer Polyaesthetische Erziehung) Oesterreichischer Kunst- und Kulturverlag, Postfach 17, A-1016 Vienna, Austria. **Indexed:** IBR. **Document type:** academic/scholarly publication.
—SWETS.

POLYMERS PAINT COLOR YEAR BOOK. see *PAINTS AND PROTECTIVE COATINGS*

700 943   GW   ISSN 0032-4167
POMMERN; Kunst - Geschichte - Volkstum. 1963. q. DM.37 (effective 1997). Pommersche Zentralverband e.V., Schloss Rantzabau, Daenischestr. 44, 24103 Kiel, Germany. Ed. Helga Wetzel. adv.; bk.rev.; abstr.; bibl.; charts; illus. circ. 1,500. **Document type:** bulletin.
—BLDSC (6549.505000).
Formerly: Unser Pommern.

800 700   US
POSTCARD ART - POSTCARD FICTION. 1974. irreg. (1-2/yr.) $5. Martha Rosler, Ed. & Pub., 143 McGuinness Blvd., Brooklyn, NY 11222. TEL 718-383-2277. circ. 600.

709   PL   ISSN 0079-466X
POZNANSKIE TOWARZYSTWO PRZYJACIOL NAUK. KOMISJA HISTORII SZTUKI. PRACE. (Text in Polish; summaries in French) 1923. irreg., vol.20, 1994. price varies. Poznanskie Towarzystwo Przyjaciol Nauk, Komisja Historii Sztuki, Ul. Mielzynskiego 27-29, 61-725 Poznan, Poland. (Dist. by: Ars Polona, Krakowskie Przedmiescie 7, 00-068 Warsaw, Poland) charts; illus. **Document type:** monographic series.

060 709   PL   ISSN 0138-0516
PRACE POPULARNONAUKOWE. ZABYTKI POLSKI POLNOCNEJ. (Subseries of: Prace Popularnonaukowe (ISSN 0079-4805)) 1975. irreg., no.9, 1991. price varies. Towarzystwo Naukowe w Toruniu, Ul. Wysoka 16, 87-100 Torun, Poland. TEL 48-56-23941. TELEX 552388 FSBH PL. Ed. Cecylia Iwaniszewska. circ. 7,000. **Document type:** monographic series.

PRAIRIE DOG. see *LITERATURE*

PRATIBHA INDIA; journal of Indian art, culture and literature. see *LITERATURE*

PRATO - STORIA ED ARTE. see *HISTORY — History Of Europe*

700 800   IT   ISSN 1124-5093
PRAZ!. (Text in Italian and language of author) 1994. 3/yr. L.40000 (foreign L.80000) (effective 1997). Semar Editore, Via di Torre Argentina 47, 00186 Rome, Italy. TEL 39-6-6876523. FAX 39-6-68308601. Ed. Mattia Carratello. adv.: page $1200. bk.rev.; abstr.; bibl.; illus.; index, cum.index; circ. 5,000 (paid). (also avail. in diskette format; back issues avail.) **Document type:** monographic series.
Description: Covers literature, criticism, art, poetry and music fields.

PRESENT; international trade magazine for giftware and christmas items. see *ARTS AND HANDICRAFTS*

700   CN
PRESENTERS HANDBOOK/GUIDE DU DIFFUSEUR. (Editions in English, French) 1975. irreg., latest Spring, 1992. Can.$20 (US Can.$25; elsewhere $30). Canada Council for the Arts, Box 1047, 350 Albert St., Ottawa, ON K1P 5V8, Canada. TEL 613-566-4414. FAX 613-566-4404. URL: http://www.canadacouncil.ca. **Document type:** academic/scholarly publication.
Former titles: Sponsors' Handbook for the 80's - Guide du Commanditaire; Sponsors' Handbook for Touring Attractions.

700   US   ISSN 1049-541X
PRESIDENTIAL DESIGN AWARDS. 1984. quadrennial. free. National Endowment for the Arts, Publication Office, 1100 Pennsylvania Ave., N.W., Washington, DC 20506. TEL 202-682-5437. FAX 202-682-5669. **Document type:** government publication.

PREVUE. see *MOTION PICTURES*

PRIMEVAL SCULPTURE. see *ANTHROPOLOGY*

PRIMI PIANI; mensile d'arte, costume, cultura, scienza, spettacolo e turismo. see *MUSIC*

PRINCETON ESSAYS ON THE ARTS. see *HUMANITIES: COMPREHENSIVE WORKS*

700 913   US   ISSN 0079-5208
PRINCETON MONOGRAPHS IN ART AND ARCHAEOLOGY. 1932. irreg., no.46, 1988. price varies. Princeton University Press, 41 William St., Princeton, NJ 08540. TEL 609-258-4900. FAX 609-258-6305. URL: http://pup.princeton.edu. (reprint service avail. from UMI) **Document type:** monographic series.
—BLDSC (6612.939000).

741.6   UK   ISSN 0265-8305
NE1
PRINT QUARTERLY. 1984. q. £40 (Europe £48; U.S. and Canada $70) (effective 1997). Print Quarterly Publications, 80 Carlton Hill, London NW8 0ER, England. TEL 44-171-625-6332. FAX 44-171-624-0960. Ed. David Landau. R&P contact: David Landau. adv. contact: Carolyn Gill. bk.rev. circ. 1,300. **Indexed:** Amer.Hist.& Life (1984-), Art Ind., Artbibl.Mod., Arts & Hum.Cit.Ind., ASCA, Avery Ind.Archit.Per., Curr.Cont., Hist.Abstr. (1984-), RILA. **Document type:** academic/scholarly publication.
—BLDSC (6613.218000); Genuine Article; KR SourceOne; SWETS; UnCover.
Description: Devoted to the history of prints and printmaking from the fifteenth century to the present.

760   UK   ISSN 0960-9253
NE1
PRINTMAKING TODAY. 1990. q. £16 to individuals. N. America $32.50; elsewhere £22.50); institutions £18.50 (N. America $39.50). Farrand Press, 50 Ferry St., Isle of Dogs, London E14 3DT, England. TEL 44-171-515-7322. FAX 44-171-537-3559. Ed. Rosemary Simmons. adv. contact: Geoff Munday. bk.rev.; circ. 1,750 (paid). **Document type:** academic/scholarly publication.
—BLDSC (6615.285000).
Description: Reports on contemporary international printmaking.

700   US   ISSN 0734-2721
NE491
PRINTWORLD DIRECTORY OF CONTEMPORARY PRINTS AND PRICES. 1982. a. $259.95. Printworld, 881 Jefferson Way, West Chester, PA 19380. TEL 800-788-9101. FAX 215-431-6653. Pub. Selma Smith. **Document type:** directory.
Description: Lists prints and their artists and provides current addresses of galleries and publishers.

PRISMA (KASSEL). see *SCIENCES: COMPREHENSIVE WORKS*

700   BU   ISSN 0032-9371
PROBLEMI NA IZKUSTVOTO/PROBLEMS OF ART. (Summaries in English, French, German and Russian) 1968. q. 1.80 lv. per no. (Bulgarska Akademiia na Naukite, Institut za Izkustvoznanie) Publishing House of the Bulgarian Academy of Sciences, Acad. G. Bonchev St., Bldg. 6, 1113 Sofia, Bulgaria. (Dist. by: Hemus, 6, Rouski Blvd., 1000 Sofia, Bulgaria) Ed. A. Stoikov. bk.rev.; film rev.; play rev.; illus. circ. 1,360. (reprint service avail. from IRC) **Indexed:** Artbibl., Artbibl.Mod., RILA.
—BLDSC (0133.109000).

747 720   NZ   ISSN 1171-8897
PRODESIGN. 1992. 6/yr. NZ.$36.95. A G M Publishing Ltd., Private Bag 99-915, Newmarket, Auckland, New Zealand. TEL 64-9-379-5393. FAX 64-9-308-9523. Eds. Robin Beckett, Kristy Robertson; Pub. Robin Beckett. R&P contact: Robin Beckett. adv. contact: Stephaniie Watson. charts; illus.; tr.lit. circ. 8,500. **Document type:** trade publication.
Description: For the professional design community as well as their clients. Provides information, comment and debate on design and design matters including new products and projects, key issues, events and awards, overseas trends, people and practice profiles, professional development and education.

700   IT
▼**PROGETTO RESTAURO.** 1995. 3/yr. L.20000 (foreign L.30000). Poligrafo Casa Editrice, Via Turazza 19, 35128 Padua, Italy. TEL 39-49-776986. FAX 39-49-772523. Ed. Giulio Bresciani Alvarez.

700   UY
PROGRAMA; por un programa de trabajo de la cultura. bi-m. Urg.$360($10) Editorial Imago s.r.l., Treinta y Tres 1324, Montevideo, Uruguay. Ed. Luis Carrizo.

720   PL   ISSN 0033-0957
N6
PROJEKT; sztuka wizualna i projektowanie. (Text in English, Polish) 1956. bi-m. $48. Visual Art Foundation "Project", Ul. Nowy Swiat 7-6, 00-793 Warsaw, Poland. TEL 312-2823107. FAX 312-2823108. (Dist. by: Ars Polona, Krakowskie Przedmiescie 7, Warsaw, Poland; Subscr. in U.S. to: Andy Grafik Co. Publishing House, 4901 W. Roscoe St., Chicago, IL 60641) Eds. Tadeusz Kielan, Krzysztof Stanislawski. adv.; bk.rev.; illus.; index. circ. 12,000. **Indexed:** Artbibl.Mod.
Description: Visual art and design from Poland and other countries. Includes contemporary poster, painting, drawing, sculpture, graphic, photography and experimental art.

709   IT   ISSN 0394-0802
N4
PROSPETTIVA; rivista di storia dell'arte antica e moderna. 1975. q. L.140000 (foreign L.180000) (effective 1994). (Universita degli Studi di Siena, Facolta di Lettere) Centro Di della Edifimi s.r.l., Lungarno Serristori 35, 50125 Florence, Italy. TEL 55-2342668. FAX 55-2342667. (Subscr. to: Centro Di, Via de'Renai 20r, 50125 Florence, Italy) Ed. Luciano Bellosi. adv.; bk.rev.; illus. circ. 600. **Indexed:** ASCA, Avery Ind.Archit.Per., Curr.Cont., RILA. **Document type:** academic/scholarly publication.
—SWETS.
Description: Covers methodological problems, essays, contributions, and exhibitions. Includes art history from antiquity up to modern times.

PROTOKOLLE; Wiener Halbjahresschrift fuer Literatur, Bildende Kunst und Musik. see *LITERATURE*

462 ART

741.5 US ISSN 1087-9013
▼PROTOONER. (Text in English, French, German) 1995. m. $50 (Canada $55) (effective Mar. 1995). Protooner, Box 2270, Daly City, CA 94017-2270. TEL 415-755-4827. FAX 415-755-3005. Ed. Joyce Miller; Pub. Ladd A. Miller. adv. contact: Joyce Miller. bibl.; illus.; circ. 525 (paid). (back issues avail.) **Document type:** trade publication.
Description: For cartoonists producing a variety of nationally known cartoons accompanied by short comments on their history and origin. Also includes a list of publications advertising for cartoons to be submitted.
Refereed Serial

700 800 US ISSN 1053-5012
PROVINCETOWN ARTS. 1985. a. $10 (effective 1998). Christopher Busa, Ed. & Pub., 650 Commercial St., Box 35, Provincetown, MA 02657. TEL 508-487-3167. FAX 508-487-8634. R&P contact: Christopher Busa. adv.: B&W page $990, color page $1300; trim 9 x 12; adv. contact: Michelle Weinberg. bk.rev.; illus. circ. 8,000. **Document type:** trade publication.
Description: Covers artists and writers in and around Provincetown, with interviews, essays, discussions of current gallery offerings, fiction, poetry and a calendar of exhibitions.

PROZA; literary and art magazine. see *LITERATURE*

701.18 US ISSN 1062-5089
N8908.A1
PUBLIC ART ISSUES. 1983. 4/yr. free. Public Art Fund Inc., 1 E. 53rd St., 11th Fl., New York, NY 10022. TEL 212-980-4575. FAX 212-980-3610. circ. 2,000. **Document type:** newsletter.
Former titles: In Process (ISSN 1060-6734); (until 1991): Public Art Fund Newsletter.
Description: Covers issues related to the field of public art.

700 US ISSN 1040-211X
N8700
PUBLIC ART REVIEW. 1989. s-a. $17 (foreign $28) (effective 1997). Forecast Public Artworks, 2324 University Ave. W., Ste. 102, St. Paul, MN 55114-1802. TEL 612-641-1128. FAX 612-641-0028. E-mail: forecast@mtn.org. Ed. Jack Becker. R&P contact: Jack Becker. bk.rev.; circ. 5,000 (paid). **Indexed:** Art Ind. **Document type:** academic/scholarly publication.
—BLDSC (6962.791300); KR SourceOne; UnCover.
Description: Critical dialogue, reviews, profiles and listings on public art.

700 US
PUBLIC ILLUMINATION MAGAZINE. 1979. irreg. $3 for 2 nos. 30-73 47th St., Long Island City, NY 11103. TEL 718-721-0946. Ed. Zagreus Bowery; Pub. Zagreus Bowery. R&P contact: Ron Kolm. circ. 1,000.
Description: Contains dada art submitted and published pseudonymously.

700 070.5 US ISSN 0885-6370
NC975
PUBLICATION DESIGN ANNUAL.* a. (Society of Publication Designers) Rockport Publishers, 33 Commercial St., Gloucester, MA 01930-5040. TEL 508-546-9590. FAX 212-979-2207. (Dist. by: Watson-Guptill Publications, Inc., 1515 Broadway, New York, NY 10036)

PUNCTURE; a magazine of music and the arts. see *MUSIC*

PUNGOLO VERDE; arti-scienza e lettere. see *LITERARY AND POLITICAL REVIEWS*

700 IT
QUADERNI DI STORIA DELL'ARTE. 1966. irreg., no.15, 1988. price varies. Universita degli Studi di Parma, Istituto di Storia dell'Arte, P.le della Pace 7A, 43100 Parma, Italy. TEL 0521-283089. FAX 0521-207125.

700 UK ISSN 0958-0433
R S A JOURNAL. 1852. 10/yr. £60 within E.U.; elsewhere £70 (effective 1997). Royal Society for the Encouragement of Arts, Manufactures and Commerce, 8 John Adam St., London WC2N 6EZ, England. TEL 44-171-930-5115. FAX 44-171-839-7831. E-mail: editor@rsa-journal.demon.co.uk; URL: http://www.cs.mdx.ac.uk/rsa/. Ed. Imogen McEvedy. adv.; bk.rev.; charts; illus.; index. circ. 21,000. (also avail. in microfilm from UMI,PMC; reprint service avail. from UMI) **Indexed:** Account.& Data Proc.Abstr., Archit.Per.Ind., Artbibl.Mod., Br.Archaeol.Abstr., Br.Ceram.Abstr., Br.Hum.Ind., Br.Tech.Ind., Build.Manage.Abstr., Chem.Abstr., DAAI, Ecol.Abstr., Field Crop Abstr., Geo.Abstr.P.G., Herb.Abstr., IBR, IDA, Ind.Bk.Rev.Hum., Met.Abstr., Mgmt.& Market.Abstr., MLA Intl.Bibl., RICS, RILA, Rural Recreat.Tour.Abstr., So.Pac.Per.Ind., W.R.C.Inf., World Agri.Econ.& Rural Sociol.Abstr. **Document type:** bulletin.
—BLDSC (8036.704200); CISTI; Linda Hall; SWETS; UMI; UnCover.
Formerly: Royal Society of Arts. Journal (ISSN 0035-9114)

R S V P: THE DIRECTORY OF ILLUSTRATION AND DESIGN. see *BUSINESS AND ECONOMICS — Trade And Industrial Directories*

RABENFLUG; Literatur - Kunst - Geschichte. see *LITERATURE*

700 800 851 IT
RADAR - SEI; rivista mensile di attualita-arte-cultura. 1973. m. L.35000. Organizzazione "X" di Armando Rositani, Corso Cavour, 113, 70121 Bari, Italy. TEL 39-80-5214363. FAX 39-80-5214363. Ed. Armando Rositani. adv. contact: Mariuccia Verrone. bk.rev. circ. 6,000. (back issues avail.)

706 US ISSN 0886-7771
NX510.C2
RADIUS (SAN FRANCISCO);* resources for local arts. 1985. bi-m. $30. California Assembly of Local Arts Agencies, 870 Market St., Ste. 714, San Francisco, CA 94102. TEL 415-979-2345. FAX 415-394-5000. Ed. Ken Larsen. adv.; bk.rev. circ. 2,000. (back issues avail.) **Document type:** trade publication.
Description: Presents information for funding and services as well as programs for local arts groups.

700 CV ISSN 0258-5324
RAIZES. 1977. q. C.P. 98, Praia, Sao Tiago, Cape Verde Islands. TEL 319. Ed. Arnaldo Franca. circ. 1,500.

750 800 780 CN ISSN 0834-3551
NX1
RAMPIKE MAGAZINE. (Text in English and French) 1979. s-a. Can.$14($14) (foreign $16) (effective 1997). (Ontario Arts Council) Rampike, 81 Thorneloe Cres., Sault-St. Marie, ON P6A 4J4, Canada. TEL 705-949-6498. URL: http://www.auc.on.ca. Ed. Karl E. Jirgens. adv.; cum.index: 1979-1984. circ. 2,000. (back issues avail.) **Indexed:** Artbibl.Mod.
Description: Thematic art and writing journal featuring select international talent.

709
RASSEGNA D'ARTE.* L.2000. G. Alparone, Ed. & Pub., Viale Cavalleggeri Aosta, 77, 80124 Naples, Italy. illus.

700 IT ISSN 0033-9857
RASSEGNA SOVIETICA; rivista bimestrale di cultura. 1949. bi-m. L.20000. Associazione Italiana per i Rapporti Culturali con l'Unione Sovietica, Piazza di Campitelli 2, 00186 Rome, Italy. Ed. Umberto Cerroni. bk.rev. circ. 2,000.

700 UK ISSN 0955-1182
RAW VISION; international journal of intuitive and visionary art. 1989. 4/yr. £20 to individuals in U.K. (Europe £26; U.S. $38; Canada $47; Australia, Japan, Africa £30); institutions in U.K. £30 (Europe £36; U.S. $55; Canada $66; Australia, Japan, Africa £40) (effective 1997). Raw Vision Ltd., 42 Llanvanor Rd., London NW2 2AP, England. TEL 44-1923-856644. FAX 44-1923-859897. (US subscr. to: Raw Vision, 163 Amsterdam Ave., 203, New York, NY 10023-5001. TEL 212-714-8381) Ed. John Maizels. R&P contact: John Maizels. **Document type:** academic/scholarly publication.
—UnCover.

RAZVITOK. see *LITERATURE*

730 929.82 US ISSN 1069-1855
RECOGNITION REVIEW. 1979. m. $42. Awards and Recognition Association (A R A), 35 E. Wacker Dr., Ste. 500, Chicago, IL 60601. TEL 800-344-2148. FAX 312-236-1140. Ed. Tim Noworyta; Pub. Ralph Bloch. adv.; tr.lit. circ. 8,500. (tabloid format)
Former titles (until 1993): T D M A Today; Trophy Dealer; T D M A Newsletter (ISSN 1063-8261)

720 IT
RECUPERO E CONSERVAZIONE. 1994. bi-m. L.60000 (foreign L.90000). Eredi de Lettera Editore, Via Bazzini 17, 20131 Milan, Italy. TEL 39-2-2666345. FAX 39-2-2664781. Ed. Fiorino Ivan De Lettera. adv.

RED BASS. see *LITERARY AND POLITICAL REVIEWS*

700 US ISSN 1054-3465
REFLEX MAGAZINE;* the northwest's forum on the visual arts. 1987. m. (except Jan. & Jul.). $18 to individuals; institutions and foreign $35. Xelfer, 1011 W. Armour St., Seattle, WA 98119-2234. TEL 206-682-7688. FAX 206-682-6912. Ed. John Boylan. adv.: B&W page $700; adv. contact: Jim Demetre. bk.rev.; illus.; circ. 1,000 (paid); 7,000 (controlled). (back issues avail.) **Document type:** newspaper.
Description: Contains news, criticism, and analysis on Northwest art and art issues, with interviews, features and a comprehensive regional calendar of exhibitions.

RENAISSANCE QUARTERLY. see *LITERATURE*

700 FR ISSN 0761-4241
REPERES (PARIS, 1947); cahiers d'art contemporain. 1947. irreg., no.87, 1996. price varies. Galerie Lelong, 13 rue de Teheran, 75008 Paris, France. TEL 33-1-45-63-13-19. FAX 33-1-42-89-34-33. Ed. Daniel Lelong. illus. **Indexed:** Artbibl.Mod.
Formerly (until 1982): Derriere le Miroir (ISSN 0011-9113)

700 800 SP ISSN 0080-1763
RESENA DE LITERATURA, ARTE Y ESPECTACULOS. 1964. 10/yr. 5500 ptas.($54) (Europe $76; Latin America $85; US $89; Asia $112) (effective 1995). Centro Loyola de Estudios y Comunicacion Social, Pablo Aranda 3, 28006 Madrid, Spain. TEL 341-562-49-30. FAX 341-563-40-73. Ed. Luis Urbez. R&P contact: Luis Urbez. adv.; cum.index: 1964-1973. circ. 3,000. **Document type:** academic/scholarly publication.
—CINDOC.
Description: Critiques plastic arts, cinema, television, theater, music, fiction and poetry.

700 720 CK ISSN 0121-5264
RESTAURACION HOY. 1986. s-a. $40 for 2 yrs. (Instituto Colombiano de Cultura) Centro Nacional de Restauracion, Calle 9, no. 8-31, Bogota, Colombia. TEL 2848595. FAX 2828759. Ed. Beatriz Restrepo. bk.rev. circ. 1,000. **Document type:** academic/scholarly publication.

751.6 GW ISSN 0933-4017
RESTAURO; Zeitschrift fuer Kunsttechniken, Restaurierung und Museumsfragen. q. DM.161 (students DM.129.50) (effective 1997). Callwey Verlag, Postfach 800409, 81604 Munich, Germany. TEL 49-89-436005-0. FAX 49-89-43600513. Ed.Bd. adv.; bk.rev.; illus. circ. 5,500. (back issues avail.) **Indexed:** Art & Archaeol.Tech.Abstr., RILA. **Document type:** trade publication.
—SWETS. **CCC.**
Formerly: Maltechnik-Restauro (ISSN 0025-1445)

REVISTA CAMPINENSE DE CULTURA. see *LITERATURE*

REVISTA CANADIENSE DE ESTUDIOS HISPANICOS. see *LITERATURE*

REVISTA COMUNICACOES E ARTES. see *COMMUNICATIONS*

REVISTA CULTULUI MOZAIC/REVIEW OF THE MOSAIC CREED. see *RELIGIONS AND THEOLOGY — Judaic*

ART

700   AG   ISSN 0327-3687
REVISTA DE ESTETICA/AESTHETICS MAGAZINE. (Text in English and Spanish) 1983. biennial. no.9, 1994. $15. Centro de Arte y Comunicacion, Escuela de Altos Estudios - Center of Art and Communication, Elpidio Gonzalez 4070, 1407 Buenos Aires, Argentina. TEL 54-1-5674594. FAX 54-1-5663867. TELEX 18660 DELPHI AR. Ed. Jorge Glusberg. circ. 3,000. (also avail. in microform)

REVISTA DO PATRIMONIO. see HISTORY — History Of North And South America

700   BE   ISSN 0035-077X
N2
REVUE BELGE D'ARCHEOLOGIE ET D'HISTOIRE DE L'ART/BELGISCH TIJDSCHRIFT VOOR OUDHEIDKUNDE EN KUNSTGESHIEDENIS. 1931. a. 1200 BEF. Academie Royale d'Archeologie de Belgique - Koninklijke Academie voor Oudheidkunde van Belgie, Av. A. Huysmans 87, Bte. 6, 1050 Brussels, Belgium. Dir. J. Dosogne-Lafontaine. bk.rev.; bibl.; illus.; cum.index: vols.1-59, 1931-1990. circ. 400. (reprint service avail. from KTO) **Indexed:** Art & Archaeol.Tech.Abstr., Art Ind., Artbibl.Mod., Avery Ind.Archit.Per., IBR, RILA. **Document type:** academic/scholarly publication, bulletin.
—KR SourceOne.
Description: Publishes topics relating to archaeology and art history, with particular emphasis on Belgium and Belgian art.

REVUE D'ESTHETIQUE. see PHILOSOPHY

LA REVUE DE BELLES-LETTRES. see LITERARY AND POLITICAL REVIEWS

700   FR   ISSN 0035-1326
REVUE DE L'ART. (Text in French; summaries in English and German) 1968. q. 430 F. to individuals (foreign 520); agencies 387 F. (foreign 468 F.) (effective 1998). (Comite Francais d'Histoire de l'Art) Presses Universitaires de France, Departement des Revues, 14 av. du Bois-de-l'Epine, 91003 Evry Cedex, France. TEL 33-1-60778205. FAX 33-1-60792045. TELEX PUF 600 474 F. Ed. Andre Chastel. bk.rev.; abstr.; charts; illus. **Indexed:** Art & Archaeol.Tech.Abstr., Art Ind., Artbibl.Mod., Arts & Hum.Cit.Ind., ASCA, Avery Ind.Archit.Per., Curr.Cont., IBR, RILA.
—BLDSC (7891.180000); KR SourceOne; SWETS.
Description: Presents for reflection and criticism those activities, proceedings and interpretations roused or being roused by art and its history as well as works and their creators throughout time and civilization.

700 930.1 780.01   BE   ISSN 0080-2530
CC3
REVUE DES ARCHEOLOGUES ET HISTORIENS D'ART DE LOUVAIN. 1968. a. 2000 BEF. Association des Diplomes Histoire Art et Archeologie, College Erasme, Place Blaise Pascal 1, 1348 Louvain-la-Neuve, Belgium. TEL 32-10-474880. FAX 32-10-472519. E-mail: hackens@arka.ucl.ac.be. Eds. Tony Hackens, Ghislaine Moucharte. bk.rev. circ. 1,000. **Indexed:** Art & Archaeol.Tech.Abstr., Avery Ind.Archit.Per., Numis.Lit., RILA. **Document type:** academic/scholarly publication.

700 960   FR   ISSN 1157-4127
NX588.75
REVUE NOIRE; art contemporain africain - African contemporary art. (Text in English, French) 1991. q. 400 F. (Europe & Africa 460 F.; elsewhere 540 F.) (effective 1997). 8 rue Cels, 75014 Paris, France. TEL 33-1-43209200. FAX 33-1-43229260. E-mail: renoir@club-internet.fr; URL: http://rio.net/revuenoire. Ed. N'Gone Fall; Pub. Jean Loup Pivin. R&P contact: Pascal Martin Saint Leon. adv.; bk.rev.; illus. (back issues avail.) **Indexed:** Curr.Cont.Africa.

709   RM   ISSN 0556-8080
REVUE ROUMAINE D'HISTOIRE DE L'ART. SERIE BEAUX-ARTS. 1963. a. 50 lei($45) (Academia Romana, Institutul de Istoria Artei George Oprescu) Editura Academiei Romane, Calea 13 Septembrie 13, 76117 Bucharest, Rumania. (Dist. by: Rodipet SA, Piata Presei Libere 1, Sec.1, P.O. Box 33-57, Bucharest, Rumania. TEL 401-6185103. FAX 401-2226407) Ed. Remus Niculescu. **Indexed:** Avery Ind.Archit.Per., Numis.Lit., RILA.
—KNAW.
Formerly: Revue Roumaine de l'Histoire de l'Art. Serie Arts Plastiques (ISSN 0080-262X)

709   RM   ISSN 0080-2638
REVUE ROUMAINE D'HISTOIRE DE L'ART. SERIE THEATRE, MUSIQUE, CINEMATOGRAPHIE. 1963. a. (Academia Romana, Institutul de Istoria Artei George Oprescu) Editura Academiei Romane, Calea 13 Septembrie 13, 76117 Bucharest, Rumania. (Dist. by: Rodipet SA, Piata Presei Libere 1, Sec. 1, Box 33-57, Bucharest, Rumania. TEL 401-6185103. FAX 401-2226407) Ed. Ion Zamfirescu. **Indexed:** Artbibl.Mod.
—KNAW.

750
RICERCHE SUL '600 NAPOLETANO. a. L.120000. Via G. Revere 1, 20123 Milan, Italy. TEL 4694042. (U.S. addr.: Alfredo De Palchi, Union Square Art Books, 33 Union Sq., New York, NY 10003) Ed. Giuseppe DeVito. circ. 1,000.

709.4   NE   ISSN 0165-9510
RIJKSMUSEUM. BULLETIN. Key Title: Bulletin van het Rijksmuseum. (Text in Dutch; summaries in English) 1953. q. fl.42.25. S D U Uitgeverij, Chr. Plantijnstraat 2, 2515 TZ The Hague, Netherlands. TEL 31-70-3789911. FAX 31-70-3475778. (Prepared by: Rijksmuseum, Amsterdam) bk.rev.; illus.; index. circ. 2,500. **Indexed:** Art Ind., Avery Ind.Archit.Per., RILA. **Document type:** bulletin.
—KR SourceOne; SWETS.
Former titles: Netherlands. Rijksmuseum Amsterdam. Bulletin (ISSN 0569-9665); Netherlands. Rijksmuseum. Bulletin (ISSN 0028-3002)

RIJKSMUSEUMKUNSTKRANT. see MUSEUMS AND ART GALLERIES

700   IS
RIMONIM. 1983. irreg., vol.4, 1994. $13. Society for Jewish Art, P.O. Box 4262, Jerusalem, Israel. TEL 02-634797. Ed. Bezalel Narkiss. circ. 1,000. **Document type:** bulletin.
Description: Studies forms and styles of Jewish art through the ages.

700   BL
RIO ARTES. 1991. m. Cr.$20000. Rua Rumania 14, 22240 Laranjeiras, RJ, Brazil. TEL 285-5344. Ed. Wilson Coutinho. (tabloid format)
Formerly (until 1992): Rio Artes e Literatura.

RIVER STYX. see LITERARY AND POLITICAL REVIEWS

700   IT   ISSN 1122-0732
RIVISTA D'ARTE; studi documentari per la storia delle arti in Toscana. 1903; N.S. 1984. a. L.105000 (foreign L.128000)($86) (effective 1997). (Fondazione Horne) Casa Editrice Leo S. Olschki, Casella Postale 66, 50100 Florence, Italy. TEL 39-55-6530684. FAX 39-55-6530214. E-mail: celso@olschki.it. Ed. Umberto Baldini. adv. circ. 1,000. **Indexed:** Amer.Hist.& Life (1986-1988), (1990-1992), Artbibl.Mod., Hist.Abstr. (1990-1992), IBR, RILA. **Document type:** academic/scholarly publication.

RIVISTA DALMATICA. see HISTORY — History Of Europe

700   IT
RIVISTA DI ARTE E CRITICA. 1993. q. L.30000. Associazione Art e Critica, Via San Calepodio 28, 00152 Rome, Italy. TEL 39-6-5803377. Ed. Daniela Bigi; Pub. Roberto Lambarelli.

701   IT   ISSN 0393-9858
RIVISTA DI PSICOLOGIA DELL'ARTE. 1979. a. Lit.30000 (foreign $30) (effective 1997). Jartrakor, Via dei Pianellari 20, 00186 Rome, Italy. TEL 39-6-68307590. FAX 39-6-6867824. E-mail: sergio.lombardo@iol.it. Ed. Sergio Lombardo. R&P contact: Sergio Lombardo. adv.; bk.rev. circ. 3,000. (back issues avail.) **Indexed:** Psychol.Abstr. **Document type:** academic/scholarly publication.
Description: Publishes experimental and theoretical studies in the field of psychology of art and empirical aesthetics.

700 930.1   IT
RIVISTA INGALINA E INTEMELIA. 1946. a. Lit.80000($50) (effective 1997). Istituto Internazionale di Studi Liguri - International Institute of Ligurian Studies, Via Romana 39, 18012 Bordighera (IM), Italy. TEL 39-184-263601. FAX 39-184-266421. index. circ. 2,000. (back issues avail.) **Document type:** academic/scholarly publication.
Description: Covers art, handicrafts, archaeology, history and architecture of west of Liguria.

ROCK ART RESEARCH. see ANTHROPOLOGY

700   US
ROCKHURST REVIEW; a fine arts journal. 1988. a. Rockhurst College Press, Van Ackeran 215, 1100 Rockhurst Rd., Kansas City, MO 64110. Ed. Patricia Cleary Miller.
Description: Presents poetry, prose, photography and drawings.

709   PL   ISSN 0080-3472
N9.6
ROCZNIK HISTORII SZTUKI. (Text in Polish; summaries in English, French and German) 1956. a. price varies. (Polska Akademia Nauk, Instytut Sztuki) Ossolineum, Publishing House of the Polish Academy of Sciences, Pl. Solny 14a, 500626 Wroclaw, Poland. TEL 48-71-3436961. FAX 48-71-448103. TELEX 0712771 OSS PL. Ed. Andrzej Ryszkiewicz. circ. 500. **Indexed:** Artbibl.Mod., Avery Ind.Archit.Per., RILA. **Document type:** academic/scholarly publication.
Description: Devoted to the past and contemporary history of art in Poland and Europe.

700 780 792   CN
RODMAN HALL BULLETIN. 1970. m. free. Rodman Hall Arts Centre, 109 St. Paul Crescent, St. Catharins, Ont. L2S 1M3, Canada. TEL 416-684-2925. FAX 416-682-2950. circ. 1,500. (back issues avail.) **Document type:** bulletin.

ROEMISCHE BRONZEN AUS DEUTSCHLAND. see ARCHAEOLOGY

741.5 800   NR
ROMANCE OF LIFE. 1989. irreg. £N3. Daily Times of Nigeria Ltd., Publications Division, New Isheri Rd., P.M.B. 21340, Agidingbi, Ikeja, Lagos State, Nigeria. TEL 234-64-900850-9. FAX 234-64-21333. Ed. David Ajoboye. **Document type:** consumer publication.

ROMANIA LITERARA. see LITERATURE

729.5 733   DK   ISSN 0107-2366
NK1285
ROMANSKE STENARBEJDER. 1981. irreg. price varies. Forlaget Hikuin, Moesgaard, DK-8270 Hoejbjerg, Denmark. TEL 45-86-667666. FAX 45-86-667611. Ed. Jens Vellev. illus.
Description: Publishes articles on art in Danish Romanesque churches.

850   IT
ROMANTICISMO E DINTORNI. 1984. irreg., no.5, 1994. price varies. Liguori Editore s.r.l., Via Posillipo 394, 80123 Naples, Italy. TEL 39-81-7206111. FAX 39-81-7206244. Ed.Bd.; Pub. Guido Liguori. adv. contact: Maria Liguori. **Document type:** monographic series.

570 700   CN   ISSN 0035-8495
AM101
ROTUNDA. 1968. 3/yr. $12.84 to non-members (foreign $18) (effective 1997). Royal Ontario Museum, Publications, 100 Queen's Park, Toronto, ON M5S 2C6, Canada. TEL 416-586-5590. FAX 416-586-5887. E-mail: sandras@rom.on.ca. Ed. Sandra Shaul. R&P contact: Sandra Shaul. adv.; bk.rev.; charts; illus.; stat.; index. circ. 25,000. **Indexed:** Amer.Hist.& Life (1987-1989), Can.B.P.I., Can.Per.Ind., CMI, Hist.Abstr. (1987-1989). **Document type:** consumer publication.
Description: Reports the latest information on the endeavours of humankind and the ways of nature, both past and present.

750   UK
ROYAL INSTITUTE OF OIL PAINTERS. EXHIBITION CATALOGUE. a. £2. Federation of British Artists, 17 Carlton House Terrace, London SW1Y 5BD, England. TEL 0171-930-6844. FAX 0171-839-7830. **Document type:** catalog.

ART

706   UK
ROYAL SOCIETY OF BRITISH ARTISTS. PUBLICATION. 1890. a. £2. Federation of British Artists, 17 Carlton House Terrace, London SW1Y 5BD, England. TEL 0171-930-6844. FAX 0171-839-7830. circ. 5,000. **Document type:** trade publication.

706   UK
ROYAL SOCIETY OF MARINE ARTISTS. EXHIBITION CATALOGUE. 1946. a. £2. Federation of British Artists, 17 Carlton House Terrace, London SW1Y 5BD, England. TEL 0171-930-6844. FAX 0171-839-7830. **Document type:** catalog.

700   UK
ROYAL SOCIETY OF MINIATURE PAINTERS, SCULPTORS AND GRAVERS. PUBLICATION. 1895. a. £3. Royal Society of Miniature Painters, Sculptors and Gravers, Westminster Gallery, Westminster Central Hall, Storey's Gate, London SW1H 9NH, England. TEL 44-1747-860311. Ed. Suzanne Lucas. R&P contact: Suzanne Lucas. **Document type:** catalog.

757   UK
ROYAL SOCIETY OF PORTRAIT PAINTERS. PUBLICATION. 1981. a. £4. Federation of British Artists, 17 Carlton House Terrace, London SW1Y 5BD, England. TEL 0171-930-6844. FAX 0171-839-7830. **Document type:** trade publication.

746.92 770   US
▼**RUSE MAGAZINE.** 1996. q. 40 Lucky Dr., Greenbrae, CA 94904. E-mail: fiend@miso.co.kr; URL: http://www.ruse.com. Ed. Shawn C. Kim.
● Available only online.
Description: Covers fashion, arts, culture, photography, design, video and film and more.

700   US
RUSS COCHRAN NEWSLETTER. 1973. s-a. $1. Russ Cochran Publisher, Ltd., Box 469, W. Plains, MO 65775-0469. TEL 417-256-2224. FAX 417-256-5555. Ed. Russ Cochran. circ. 8,000. **Document type:** newsletter.
Description: Updates on the progress of reprinting the complete EC comic book line. Introduces new products in the comic line.

RUSTIC RUB. see LITERATURE — Poetry

S A C NEWSMONTHLY; national news and listings of art & craft shows. (Southern Art and Crafts) see ARTS AND HANDICRAFTS

S P N E A NEWS. (Society for the Preservation of New England Antiquities) see HISTORY

751.6   UK   ISSN 0959-2369
S S C R JOURNAL; promotes the conservation and restoration of historic and artistic objects. 1980. q. £35 to individuals (overseas £38); institutions £70 (overseas £75); students £20 (overseas £23) (effective 1997 & 1998). Scottish Society for Conservation and Restoration, The Glasite Meeting House, 33 Barony St., Edinburgh EH3 6NX, Scotland. TEL 44-131-556-8417. FAX 44-131-557-5977. E-mail: admin@sscr.demon.co.uk. Ed. Jane Hutchison. R&P contact: Jane Hutchison. adv. contact: Wendi Davidson. bk.rev. circ. 400. **Indexed:** Art & Archaeol.Tech.Abstr. **Document type:** academic/scholarly publication.
Former titles (until 1990): Scottish Society for Conservation and Restoration. Bulletin (ISSN 0264-9039); (until 1983): Scottish Society for Conservation and Restoration. Newsletter (ISSN 0261-703X); (until 1980): Scottish Society for the Conservation and Restoration of Historic and Artistic Works. Newsletter (ISSN 0260-5597); (until 1979): S S C R Newsletter.
Refereed Serial

SABAZIA. see HISTORY

700   US   ISSN 0741-9163
SACRED ART JOURNAL;* Orthodox liturgical arts. 1979. q. $25 (foreign $37). (St. John of Damascus Association of Orthodox Iconographers, Iconologists, and Architects) Antakya Press, Box 1128, Torrance, CA 90505-6359. TEL 412-238-3677. FAX 412-238-2102. Eds. Rev. George Geha, Paul D. Garrett. adv.; bk.rev.; cum.index: 1979-1987. circ. 1,000. (back issues avail.)
Description: Presents the liturgical arts of the Eastern Churches with emphasis on the painting of the Panel icons.

709   IT   ISSN 0392-713X
N4
SAGGI E MEMORIE DI STORIA DELL'ARTE. 1957. irreg., no.19, 1995. price varies. (Fondazione Giorgio Cini, Centro di Cultura e Civilta) Casa Editrice Leo S. Olschki, Casella Postale 66, 50100 Florence, Italy. TEL 39-55-6530684. FAX 39-55-6530214. E-mail: celso@olschki.it. circ. 500. **Indexed:** Artbibl.Mod., RILA. **Document type:** monographic series.

700   US   ISSN 0749-6435
SALOME; a journal of the performing arts. 1975. q. $12. Ommation Press, 5548 N. Sawyer Ave., Chicago, IL 60625. Ed. Effie Mihopoulos. adv.; bk.rev.; film rev. circ. 1,000. **Indexed:** A.I.P.P.
—BLDSC (8071.170000).
Description: Interviews, reviews, photo documentation and artwork concerning the performing arts.

700   US
SALON (FORT COLLINS); journal of aesthetics. 1988. q. $20 (foreign $30). Pat Hartman, Ed. & Pub., 305 W. Magnolia, No. 386, Ft. Collins, CO 80521. TEL 970-224-3116. R&P contact: Pat Hartman. adv. contact: Pat Hartman. bk.rev. **Document type:** newsletter.
Description: Arts journal with a libertarian slant.

SALT E-ZINE. see MUSIC

SAMNIUM. see HISTORY — History Of Europe

700   US   ISSN 0581-4766
HV97.S25
SAMUEL H. KRESS FOUNDATION. ANNUAL REPORT. 1963. a. Samuel H. Kress Foundation, 174 E. 80th St., New York, NY 10021. TEL 212-861-4993. FAX 212-628-3146. circ. 2,500. **Document type:** corporate report.
Description: Describes the foundation's grant programs in art history, conservation and preservation.

700   PE   ISSN 0254-8151
SAN MARCOS. 1947. q. Universidad Nacional Mayor de San Marcos, Ave. Republica de Chile 295, Of. 506, Lima, Peru. Ed. Juan de Dios Guevara. bk.rev.; bibl.

700 810   US
SANDBOX MAGAZINE. 2/yr. $8 (Canada & Mexico $11; elsewhere $17); newsstand price: $5. Sandbox Open Arts Inc., Box 150098, Brooklyn, NY 11215-0098. E-mail: sandbox@echonyc.com; URL: http://www.echonyc.com/~sandbox. Ed. Sylvie Myerson; Pubs. Vidyut Jain, Sylvie Myerson. **Document type:** consumer publication.
Description: Fosters collaboration between visual artists, performance artists, writers and musicians.

700 810   US
SANDBOX WEB-ZINE. 2/yr. Sandbox Open Arts Inc., Box 150098, Brooklyn, NY 11215-0098. E-mail: sandbox@echonyc.com; URL: http://www.echonyc.com/~sandbox. Ed. Sylvie Myerson. **Document type:** consumer publication.
● Available only online.
Description: Presents articles, reviews and interactive art exploiting the creative potential of the World Wide Web.

SANTO; rivista francescana di storia dottrina arte. see HISTORY — History Of Europe

700   CN
SASKATCHEWAN. DEPARTMENT OF CULTURE AND RECREATION. ANNUAL REPORT.* 1972. a. free. Saskatchewan Government Printing Co., 2005 Eighth Ave., Regina, SK S4R 7B2, Canada. TEL 306-787-5759. Ed. Rick Folk. illus. circ. 800. **Document type:** government publication.
Formerly: Saskatchewan. Department of Culture and Youth. Annual Report (ISSN 0317-4344)

354   CN   ISSN 0701-6433
NX28.C32
SASKATCHEWAN CENTRE OF THE ARTS. ANNUAL REPORT. a. Saskatchewan Centre of the Arts, 200 Lakeshore Dr., Regina, SK S4P 3V7, Canada. TEL 306-584-5050. adv. contact: Louise Yates. **Document type:** corporate report.

709.9   JM   ISSN 0036-5068
F1601
SAVACOU; a journal of the Caribbean artists movement. 1970. irreg. (1-2/yr.). $15. (Caribbean Artists Movement) Savacou Publications, Box 170, Mona, Kingston 7, Jamaica, W.I. Ed. Edward Kamau Brathwaite. adv.; bk.rev.; bibl. circ. 2,000. **Indexed:** M.L.A., MLA Intl.Bibl.

391   US   ISSN 1072-8384
SAVAGE. 1994. 6/yr. $24.95 (effective 1996); newsstand price: $4.99. Paisano Publications, Inc., Box 1050, Agoura Hills, CA 91376-1050. TEL 818-889-8740. FAX 818-889-4726. Ed. Keith Ball; Pub. Joseph Teresi. R&P contact: Brian Wood. adv. contact: Lizette Hottinger. illus. **Document type:** consumer publication.

709   DK   ISSN 0906-3447
NK1160
SCANDINAVIAN JOURNAL OF DESIGN HISTORY. (Text in English) 1991. irreg. DKK 188 (effective 1998). (Danish Museum of Decorative Art) Rhodos, International Science and Art Publishers, Strandgade 36, 1401 Copenhagen, Denmark. TEL 45-31-54-30-20. FAX 45-32-95-47-42. Ed. Mirjam Gelfer-Joergensen. R&P contact: Niels Blaedel. bk.rev. **Indexed:** Amer.Hist.& Life (1991-), DAAI, Hist.Abstr. (1991-). **Document type:** academic/scholarly publication.
—BLDSC (8087.505530).

700 780   SZ   ISSN 1016-9415
SCENES MAGAZINE; mensuel suisse d'information culturelle. 1986. m. 100 SFr. (effective 1996). Case Postale 129, CH-1211 Geneva 4, Switzerland. TEL 41-22-3469643. Ed. F. Frederich. adv.; bk.rev. circ. 5,000. **Document type:** consumer publication.

943   IT   ISSN 0036-6145
SCHLERN; Zeitschrift fuer Suedtiroler Landeskunde. (Text in German) 1920. m. L.107200 (effective 1995). Verlagsanstalt Athesia, Lauben, 41, Postfach 417, 39100 Bozen, Sudtirol, Italy. TEL 39-471-925111. FAX 39-471-925569. Ed. Dr. Hans Griessmair. adv. contact: Ilse Egger. bk.rev.; illus.; index, cum.index. circ. 1,600. (back issues avail.) **Indexed:** IBR. **Document type:** consumer publication.

700 371.3   US   ISSN 1060-832X
N1
SCHOLASTIC ART. 1970. 6/yr. $7.45 to students. Scholastic Inc., 555 Broadway, New York, NY 10012-3999. TEL 212-343-6100. Ed. Margaret Howlett. bibl.; illus.; index, circ. 205,000. (also avail. in microfilm from UMI; reprint service avail. from UMI) **Indexed:** Ind.Child.Mag. **Document type:** trade publication.
—KR SourceOne; UMI.
Formerly: Art and Man (ISSN 0004-3052); Incorporates: Artist Junior (ISSN 0004-3893)
Description: Geared toward ages 11-18.

700   GW   ISSN 0080-7176
Z5961.G4
SCHRIFFTUM ZUR DEUTSCHEN KUNST. 1934; N.S. 1962. irreg., vol.59, 1997. price varies. (Deutscher Verein fuer Kunstwissenschaft e.V.) Deutscher Verlag fuer Kunstwissenschaft GmbH, Charlottenstr. 13, 10969 Berlin, Germany. TEL 49-30-25913864. FAX 49-30-25913537. **Document type:** bibliography.

700 720   SZ   ISSN 1016-2879
SCHWEIZER KUNST/ART SUISSE/ARTE SUIZZERA.* (Text in French, German and Italian) 1972. m. 16 SFr. Gesellschaft Schweizerischer Maler, Bildhauer und Architekten, Postfach, CH-4007 Basel, Switzerland. Ed.Bd. adv.; bk.rev.; bibl.; illus.

751.6   FR   ISSN 0988-3789
SCIENCE ET TECHNOLOGIE DE LA CONSERVATION ET DE LA RESTORATION DES OEUVRES D'ART ET DU PATRIMOINE. 1988. s-a. 160 F. (Etudes et Realisations de la Couleur) E R E C, 68, rue Jean Jaures, 92800 Puteaux, France. TEL 47-73-01-23. FAX 49-00-05-91. Ed. Annik Chauvel. circ. 5,000.

700   NE   ISSN 0080-8350
SCRIPTA ARTIS MONOGRAPHIA. (Text in English, French and German) 1968. irreg. price varies (approx. $25 per no.). A P A, Postbus 122, 3600 AC Maarssen, Netherlands. TEL 31-30-436166. FAX 31-30-420250. **Document type:** monographic series.

730 US ISSN 0889-728X
NB1
SCULPTURE. 1982. 10/yr. $45 in N. America; elsewhere $75. International Sculpture Center, 1050 17th St., N.W., Ste. 250, Washington, DC 20036. TEL 202-785-1144. FAX 202-785-0810. adv. contact: Arlene Epstein. bk.rev. circ. 22,000. **Indexed:** Art Ind. **Document type:** consumer publication.
—BLDSC (8213.295000); KR SourceOne; UnCover.
  Former titles (until Jan. 1987): International Sculpture (ISSN 0887-5472); (until Apr. 1985): Sculptors International (ISSN 0730-675X); (until 1981): International Sculpture Center Bulletin (ISSN 0277-240X); National Sculpture Center Bulletin (ISSN 0891-1983)
  Description: Devoted to issues and ideas in contemporary sculpture. Features criticisms, legal issues and aesthetics, events, commissions and exhibition reviews.

730 US ISSN 0747-5284
NB1
SCULPTURE REVIEW. 1951. q. $19 (foreign $25) (effective 1997). National Sculpture Society, 1177 Ave. of the Americas, New York, NY 10036. TEL 212-764-5645. FAX 212-764-5651. Ed. David Finn; Pub. Stanley Bleifeld. R&P contact: Amy Kelly. adv.: B&W page $1210; adv. contact: Amy Kelly. bk.rev.; illus.; cum.index. circ. 6,500. (also avail. in microform from UMI; back issues avail.; reprint service avail. from UMI) **Indexed:** Art Ind., ASCA, Avery Ind.Archit.Per., Bk.Rev.Ind. (1980-), Child.Bk.Rev.Ind. (1980-), Curr.Cont., Numis.Lit. **Document type:** consumer publication.
●Also available on CD-ROM.
—BLDSC (8213.297000); Genuine Article; KR SourceOne; SWETS; UMI; UnCover.
  Former titles: Sculpture (ISSN 0272-6807); (until 1971): National Sculpture Review (ISSN 0028-0127)
  Description: Primary mission is to educate and inform the public of contemporary figurative sculpture. Publishes educational articles, candid interviews, and historical essays in every issue, highlighted by photography. Annual collectors' issue and special features on conservation, reliefs, and the history of sculpture tools.

700 US
SEATTLE ARTS. 1972. bi-m. free in the U.S. (foreign $20). City of Seattle Arts Commission, 312 First Ave., N., Seattle, WA 98109-4501. TEL 206-684-7306. FAX 206-684-7172. URL: http://www.pan.ci.seattle.wa.us. Ed. Daria DeCooman. adv.; illus, stat. circ. 12,000. (tabloid format) **Document type:** newsletter, government publication.
  Formerly: Seattle and King County Arts Commission. Newsletter.
  Description: Provides news about the commission's activities and achievements, along with job and volunteer positions available in the arts.

SECOND SHIFT. see WOMEN'S INTERESTS

700 SP ISSN 0487-3491
SEMINARIO DE ARTE ARAGONES. 1945. a. 3000 ptas. per no. (effective 1997). Institucion Fernando el Catolico, Plaza de Espana 2, 50071 Zaragoza, Spain. TEL 34-976-288878. FAX 34-976-288869. E-mail: ifc@mail.sendanet.es. Ed. Gonzalo Borras Gualis. R&P contact: Felix Sanchez. adv. contact: Maria-Luz Cortes. circ. 750. **Document type:** academic/scholarly publication.
—CINDOC.
  Refereed Serial

700 720 SP ISSN 0210-9573
SEMINARIO DE ESTUDIOS DE ARTE Y ARQUEOLOGIA. BOLETIN. 1939. a. 4000 ptas. (foreign 6000 ptas.). Universidad de Valladolid, Secretariado de Publicaciones, C. Juan Mambrilla, 14, 47003 Valladolid, Spain. FAX 34-83-290300. TELEX 26357. **Indexed:** Numis.Lit. **Document type:** bulletin, academic/scholarly publication.
—CINDOC.

741.5 DK ISSN 0109-3797
SERIE KUREREN; Fokus pa Tegneseriemediet. 1984. bi-m. Viking, Gabelsparken 81, 6740 Bramming, Denmark. illus.

700 IT
SETTORE CULTURA E SPETTACOLO. RASSEGNA DI STUDI E DI NOTIZIE. 1973. a. L.25000 or exchange basis. Settore Cultura e Spettacolo, Civiche Raccolte d'Arte Applicata ed Incisioni, Castello Sforzesco, 20121 Milan, Italy. FAX 39-2-8693071. Ed. Claudio Salsi. R&P contact: Roberto Alberti. illus. circ. 750. **Document type:** academic/scholarly publication.
  Description: Articles deal with objects and collections of the organization, essays on related subjects and on new acquisitions.
  Refereed Serial

SHANGHAI YISHUJIA/SHANGHAI ARTIST. see THEATER

SHAONIAN WENYI/JUVENILE LITERATURE. see CHILDREN AND YOUTH — For

700 CC ISSN 1000-8683
SHIJIE MEISHU/WORLD ART. (Text in Chinese) 1979. q. Y3.20($33) (Zhongyang Meishu Xueyuan - Central Academy of Fine Arts) Renmin Meishu Chubanshe, 32 Beizongbu Hutong, Beijing 100735, People's Republic of China. (Dist. outside China by: China International Book Trading Corp., P.O. Box 399, Beijing, P.R.C.; Dist. in US by: China Books & Periodicals, Inc., 2929 24th St., San Francisco, CA 94110. TEL 415-282-2994)
  Description: Introduces to Chinese readers foreign art streams and schools, foreign artists and their works, art history and theories, as well as art techniques and materials.

700 CC ISSN 1000-4483
SHIYONG MEISHU/APPLIED FINE ART. (Text in Chinese) q. Shanghai Renmin Meishu Chubanshe - Shanghai People's Art Publishers, No.33, Alley 672, Changle Road, Shanghai 200040, People's Republic of China. TEL 4374528. Ed. Zhou Feng.

SHORT STUDIES IN SPANISH. see LINGUISTICS

741.61 CC ISSN 1000-6214
SHU YU HUA/CALLIGRAPHY AND PAINTING. (Text in Chinese) bi-m. Shanghai Shu Hua Chubanshe - Shanghai Calligraphy and Painting Publishers, 81 Qinzhou S. Rd., Shanghai 200233, People's Republic of China. TEL 86-21-6451-9008.

741.61 CC ISSN 1000-6036
SHUFA/CALLIGRAPHY. (Text in Chinese) 1978. bi-m. $75.60. Shanghai Shu Hua Chubanshe - Shanghai Calligraphy and Painting Publishers, 81 Qinzhou S. Rd., Shanghai 200233, People's Republic of China. TEL 86-21-6451-9008. (Dist. outside China by: China International Book Trading Corp., P.O. Box 2820, Beijing, P.R.C.; Dist. in US by: China Books & Periodicals, Inc., 2929 24th St., San Francisco, CA 94110. TEL 415-282-2994) Ed. Lu Fusheng. illus.
  Description: Covers Chinese calligraphy, both ancient and modern, traditional and avant-garde. Includes numerous samples of calligraphy.

741.61 US
SHUFA BAO/CALLIGRAPHIC ART WEELY. (Text in Chinese) 1984. w. Y35.10 (foreign $32.12) (effective 1998). (Hubei Shufajia Xiehui) Shufa Baoshe, No. 4, Shuiguo Hu Heng Lu, Wuhan, Hubei 430071, People's Republic of China. TEL 86-27-781-7557. FAX 86-27-783-4954. (Dist. overseas by: China International Book Trading Corp., P.O. Box 399, Beijing 100044, P.R. China) adv.; circ. 150,000 (paid). **Document type:** newspaper.
  Description: Covers calligraphy and seal cutting art as well as trends and activities home and abroad.

741.61 CC ISSN 1004-213X
SHUFA SHANGPING/CALLIGRAPHY APPRECIATION AND REVIEW. (Text in Chinese) 1988. q. Y80. Zhongguo Shufajia Xiehui, Heilongjiang Fenhui - China Calligraphers' Association, Heilongjiang Chapter, Fu 16, Yaojing Jie, Nangang-qu, Harbin, Heilongjiang 150006, People's Republic of China. TEL 330933. Ed. Li Kemin. circ. 20,000. **Document type:** academic/scholarly publication.

741.61 CC ISSN 1000-6044
NK3634.A2
SHUFA YANJIU/STUDIES IN CALLIGRAPHY. (Text in Chinese) 1979. q. $36. Shanghai Shu Hua Chubanshe - Shanghai Calligraphy and Painting Publishers, 81 Qinzhou S. Rd., Shanghai 200233, People's Republic of China. TEL 86-21-6451-9008. (Dist. in US by: China Books & Periodicals, Inc., 2929 24th St., San Francisco, CA 94110. TEL 415-282-2994)
—UnCover.

792 CC
SICHUAN XIJU/SICHUAN THEATRE. (Text in Chinese) bi-m. Chuanju Yishu Yanjiushi - Sichuan Drama Research Office, 21, Dongchengen Nanjie, Chengdu, Sichuan 610015. TEL 665915. Ed. Wang Ding'ou.

709 TH ISSN 0037-5314
SILPAKON.* (Text in Thai; table of contents in English) 1957. bi-m. B.40($3.) Government House Press, Fine Arts Department, Thanon Na Phra That, Bangkok, Thailand. Ed. Nai Prapat Treenarong. charts; illus.; index. circ. 1,000.

709 NE ISSN 0037-5411
N5
SIMIOLUS; Netherlands quarterly for the history of art. (Text in English) 1966. q. fl.95 to individuals; institutions fl.160; European students fl.50 (effective 1997). Foundation for Dutch Art - Historical Publications, Kromme Nieuwegracht 29, 3512 HD Utrecht, Netherlands. TEL 31-30-392278. FAX 32-30-392167. Ed. Peter Hecht. adv.; bk.rev.; bibl.; illus. circ. 950. (back issues avail.; reprint service avail. from SWZ) **Indexed:** Art Ind., Artbibl., Artbibl.Mod., Arts & Hum.Cit.Ind., ASCA, Curr.Cont., IBR, Ind.Bk.Rev.Hum., RILA. **Document type:** academic/scholarly publication.
—BLDSC (8284.200000); KR SourceOne; SWETS; UnCover.

700 720 XV ISSN 0049-0601
N6
SINTEZA; revija za likovno kulturo. (Text in Slovenian; summaries in English and Serbo-Croatian) 1964. q. $40. Revija Sinteza, Erjavceva Cesta 15-1, 61000 Ljubljana, Slovenia. TEL 061 221-596. Ed. Stane Bernik. adv.; bk.rev.; index. circ. 1,700. **Indexed:** Artbibl.Mod., Br.Tech.Ind.

700 US
SKETCH BOARD BULLETIN. a. $10. Kappa Pi International Honorary Art Fraternity, 9321 Paul Adrian Dr., Crestwood, MO 63126. Ed. Arthur B. Kennon. **Document type:** academic/scholarly publication, directory, newsletter.

700 US
SKETCH BOOK. 1937. a. $10. Kappa Pi International Honorary Art Fraternity, 9321 Paul Adrian Dr., Crestwood, MO 63126. Ed. Arthur B. Kennon. circ. 2,000 (controlled). **Document type:** academic/scholarly publication, directory, newsletter.

391 US ISSN 1061-3013
SKIN ART. 1992. 9/yr. $32.95 (foreign $42.95). Outlaw Biker Enterprises, Inc., 5 Marine View Plaza, Ste. 207, Hoboken, NJ 07030. TEL 201-653-2700. Ed. Casey Exton. adv. contact: Ken Knabb. illus. **Document type:** consumer publication.

391 US
SKIN ART MAGAZINE. 1993. 9/yr. Outlaw Biker Enterprises, Inc., 5 Marine View Plaza, Ste. 207, Hoboken, NJ 07004. TEL 201-653-2700. adv. contact: Ken Knabb. illus. **Document type:** consumer publication.
  Formerly: Skin Art Presents (ISSN 1067-2060)

741 960 SA
SKOTAVILLE GRAPHIC SERIES. irreg., latest no.2. Skotaville Publishers, P.O. Box 32483, Braamfontein 2017, South Africa. (Dist. outside Africa by: African Books Collective Ltd., The Jam Factory, 27 Park End St., Oxford OX1 1HU, England. TEL 0865-726686. FAX 0865-796298) **Document type:** monographic series.

730 DK ISSN 0107-4911
NB198
SKULPTUR VEKSOELUND. 1978. a. DKK 25. Veksoelund, c/o Poul Hansen, Kirkestraede 6, 3670 Veksoe, Denmark. illus.

466 ART

708 CN ISSN 0821-2287
SLATE. 1979. 8/yr. Can.$22 (foreign Can.$30) (effective 1997). Slate, 155 King St. E., Kingston, ON K7L 2Z9, Canada. TEL 613-542-3717. FAX 613-542-1447. E-mail: admin@slateartguide.com; URL: http://www.slateartguide.com. Ed. Allan Lochhead. adv.; maps; circ. 150 (paid); 12,100 (controlled).
  Formerly (until 1982): Slate Gallery Guide (ISSN 0821-2279); (until 1981): Slate (ISSN 0821-2260)
  Description: Lists gallery exhibitions, studio shows, opening receptions and events.

SLIPSTREAM (NIAGARA FALLS). see LITERATURE — Poetry

SLOVENSKE POHLADY NA LITERATURU A UMENIE. see LITERATURE

700 GW
SMILE; international culture mag. (Text in English, German) 1984. s-a. DM.10. Edition Kunst - Bahnhausen, Postfach 2631, 32383 Minden, Germany. Ed. Jo Klaffki. **Document type:** bulletin.

SOCIETA PER GLI STUDI STORICI, ARCHEOLOGICI ED ARTISTICI DELLA PROVINCIA DI CUNEO. BOLLETTINO. see ARCHAEOLOGY

SOCIETA PIEMONTESE DI ARCHEOLOGIA E BELLE ARTI. BOLLETTINO. see ARCHAEOLOGY

709 943 BE
SOCIETE D'ART ET D'HISTOIRE DU DIOCESE DE LIEGE. BULLETIN. 1881. 600 Fr. Societe d'Art et d'Histoire du Diocese de Liege, Rue Bonne Fortune 6, 4000 Liege, Belgium. cum.index: vols.16-55. circ. 3,500. **Document type:** bulletin.

SOCIETE DES ANTIQUAIRES DE L'OUEST. BULLETIN. see HISTORY — History Of Europe

SOCIETE DES SCIENCES, LETTRES ET ARTS DE BAYONNE. BULLETIN. see LITERATURE

SOCIETY FOR ARMENIAN STUDIES. JOURNAL. see ETHNIC INTERESTS

741 370 UK ISSN 0037-9743
Z43.A1
SOCIETY FOR ITALIC HANDWRITING. JOURNAL. 1962. a. £12($20) Society for Italic Handwriting, 205 Dyas Ave., Great Barr, Birmingham B42 1HN, England. TEL 44-121-358-0032. URL: http://www.argonet.co.uk/users/quilljar/sih.html. Ed. John Fricker. adv.; bk.rev.; charts; illus. circ. 1,200. **Indexed:** RILA. **Document type:** newsletter.
  Description: Promotion of the use of italic handwriting for everyday use in educational and other areas.

741 370 UK ISSN 1358-3921
SOCIETY FOR ITALIC HANDWRITING. NEWSLETTER. q. Society for Italic Handwriting, 205 Dyas Ave., Great Barr, Birmingham B42 1HN, England. TEL 44-121-358-0032. URL: http://www.argonet.co.uk/users/quilljar/sih.html. Ed. Nicholas Caulkin. charts; illus. **Document type:** newsletter.
  Formerly: Society for Italic Handwriting. Bulletin (ISSN 0264-3898)
  Description: Information on the use of italic handwriting and news about the Society.

SOCIETY FOR RENAISSANCE STUDIES. BULLETIN. see LITERATURE

750 US
SOCIETY OF ANIMAL ARTISTS NEWSLETTER.* 1960. 4/yr. membership. Society of Animal Artists, Box 167, Bronx, NY 10464-0167. Ed. Patricia Bott. adv.; bk.rev.; illus.; stat. circ. 200. **Document type:** newsletter.

SOCIETY OF PHOTOGRAPHER AND ARTIST REPRESENTATIVES. NEWSLETTER. see PHOTOGRAPHY

706 UK
SOCIETY OF WILDLIFE ARTISTS. PUBLICATION. a. £1. Federation of British Artists, 17 Carlton House Terrace, London SW1Y 5BD, England. TEL 0171-930-6844. FAX 0171-839-7830. **Document type:** catalog.
  Description: Catalog for annual exhibition in July or August.

708 FR
SON!.* no.3, 1984. bi-m. 63 av. de Champs-Elysees, 75008 Paris, France. Ed. Frank Tenot.

709 726 IT
SOPRINTENDENZA PER I BENI CULTURALI DELLA VALLE D'AOSTA. QUADERNI. 1981. irreg., no.7, 1992. price varies. L'Erma di Bretschneider, Via Cassiodoro 19, 00193 Rome, Italy. TEL 39-6-6874127. FAX 39-6-6874129. **Document type:** monographic series.

700 745.1 US ISSN 1056-7143
N8604.S66
SOTHEBY'S NEWSLETTER. 1973. 7/yr. $25 in U.S. & Canada; elsewhere $35. Sotheby's Inc., 1334 York Ave., New York, NY 10021. TEL 212-606-7000. Ed. Lynn Stowell Pearson. circ. 55,000. **Document type:** newsletter.

709 US ISSN 0737-4453
SOURCE: NOTES IN THE HISTORY OF ART. 1981. q. $25 (Canada & Mexico $28; elsewhere $30) (effective 1996-97). Ars Brevis Foundation, Inc., 1 E. 87th St., Ste. 8A, New York, NY 10128. TEL 212-369-1667. FAX 212-360-6494. Ed. Laurie Adams; Pub. Susan Weber. R&P contact: Susan Weber. circ. 1,000 (paid). **Indexed:** Arts & Hum.Cit.Ind., ASCA, Avery Ind.Archit.Per., Curr.Cont., RILA. **Document type:** academic/scholarly publication.
  —BLDSC (8330.575100); Genuine Article; UnCover.
  Description: Scholarly journal devoted to short notes, articles and reviews in art history and archaeology.
  Refereed Serial

700 US ISSN 1043-5158
N1
SOUTHEASTERN COLLEGE ART CONFERENCE REVIEW. Abbreviated short title: S E C A C Review. 1967. a. $30 (foreign $35) (effective 1996). Southeastern College Art Conference Review, Box 508, Chapel Hill, NC 27516-0508. TEL 910-929-0547. Ed. Floyd W. Martin. bk.rev.; illus. circ. 500. **Indexed:** Avery Ind.Archit.Per., RILA. **Document type:** academic/scholarly publication.
  —BLDSC (8352.357000).
  Formerly (until 1976): S E C A C Review and Newsletter (ISSN 0584-4118)

700 800 US ISSN 0886-067X
SOUTHEASTERN FRONT. 1993. irreg.? free. Southeastern Front, 565 17th St., N.W., Cleveland, TN 37311. TEL 615-479-3244. Ed. Robin Merritt. adv.; bk.rev. circ. 1,500.
  Description: Publishes new art, fiction and poetry.

705 US ISSN 0192-4214
N6525
SOUTHWEST ART. 1971. m. $32. Cowles Enthusiast Media, Collectibles Group (Houston), Box 460535, Houston, TX 77256-0535. TEL 713-850-0500. FAX 713-850-1314. Ed. Susan Hallsten McGarry; Pub. Joel Kessler. adv.; bk.rev. circ. 70,698. **Indexed:** Access (1975-), Art Ind., Artbibl.Mod., Artbibl., Chic.Per.Ind. **Document type:** consumer publication.
  —BLDSC (8356.280000); KR SourceOne; UnCover.
  Former titles: Southwest Art Magazine (ISSN 0091-8830); Southwest Art Gallery; Incorporates (1985-1987): Western Art Digest (ISSN 0883-8992); Which was formed by the merger of (1977-1985): Art West; Artist of the Rockies and the Golden West (ISSN 0364-3379); Which were formerly: Artists of the Rockies.
  Description: Focuses on representational arts west of the Mississippi River. Includes interviews with painters, sculptors, museum professionals, collectors and dealers.

SPANNER (LONDON, 1974). see LITERARY AND POLITICAL REVIEWS

740 US
SPANNER N Y C. 1978. s-a. $4 per no. Aloes Books U S A, Box 5, Canal St. Sta., New York, NY 10013. Eds. Dick Miller, Terry Slotkin. illus. circ. 1,000.

700 001.3 BE
SPECTRAAL. (Text in Dutch) 1978. q. 350 BEF. Rijsenbergstraat 390, 9000 Gent, Belgium. TEL 32-9-2227022. Ed. Lisette De Backer. adv.: page 4500 BEF; adv. contact: Lisette De Backer. bk.rev. (back issues avail.) **Document type:** newsletter.

800 US ISSN 0038-7061
LH1.C224
SPECTRUM (AMHERST). 1967. a. $5. University of Massachusetts, Spectrum, R.S.O. No. 125, Student Union, Amherst, MA 01003. TEL 413-545-2240. Ed. Heather A. Bell. bk.rev.; illus. circ. 11,000.
  Description: Publishes student works in arts and literature.

SPECULUM; a journal of Medieval studies. see HISTORY — History Of Europe

708.1 US ISSN 0733-866X
N582.L25
SPENCER MUSEUM OF ART. REGISTER. 1951. a. $12 (foreign $15). University of Kansas, Spencer Museum of Art, Lawrence, KS 66045. TEL 913-864-4710. FAX 913-864-3112. URL: htt://www.falconcc.ukans.edu/~sma. Ed. Sally Hayden. illus. circ. 900. **Indexed:** Artbibl.Mod., RILA. **Document type:** academic/scholarly publication.
  —UnCover.
  Formerly: University of Kansas. Museum of Art. Register (ISSN 0041-9672)
  Description: Scholarly articles on works of art in the collection along with the museum annual report.

700 800 FR ISSN 0755-964X
SPHINX WOMEN'S INTERNATIONAL LITERARY ART REVIEW. 1984. a. 135 Fr. Sphinx International, 175 Ave. Ledru-Rollin, 75011 Paris, France. Ed. Carol Pratl. adv.; bk.rev.; illus. circ. 3,000. (back issues avail.)

354 CN
SPOTLIGHT. Cover title: Saskatchewan Centre Spotlight. 5/yr. Saskatchewan Centre of the Arts, 200 Lakeshore Dr., Regina, SK S4P 3V7, Canada. TEL 306-565-4500. FAX 306-565-3274. adv.: page Can.$720; trim 8 1/2 x 5 1/2; adv. contact: Louise Yates.
  Description: Contains a regular calendar of upcoming performances, local arts information, program performance details, a restaurant guide as well as other related articles.

SPRINGER HEFTE FUER GEGENWARTSKUNST. see HISTORY

700 780 YU ISSN 0081-4008
SRPSKA AKADEMIJA NAUKA I UMETNOSTI. ODELJENJE LIKOVNE I MUZICKE UMETNOSTI. POSEBNA IZDANJA. (Text in Serbo-Croatian; summaries in English, French, German or Russian) 1954. irreg. price varies. Srpska Akademija Nauka i Umetnosti, Knez Mihailova 35, 11001 Belgrade, Serbia, Yugoslavia. (Dist. by: Prosveta, Terazije 16, Belgrade, Serbia, Yugoslavia) circ. 1,000.

700 GW ISSN 0585-0118
STAEDEL JAHRBUCH. 1967. biennial. DM.154. (Staedelsches Museum-Verein und Stadt Frankfurt am Main) Prestel-Verlag, Mandlstr. 26, 80802 Munich, Germany. TEL 49-89-381709-0. FAX 49-89-38170935. Ed. Michael Maegraith; Pub. Juergen Tesch. R&P contact: Karin Kiermaier. **Indexed:** Artbibl.Mod., IBR, RILA. **Document type:** monographic series.
  —BLDSC (8425.890000).
  Description: Art historical journal with emphasis on archeology, architecture, painting and sculpture.

STATE ARTS AGENCY DIRECTORY. see BUSINESS AND ECONOMICS — Trade And Industrial Directories

709 DK
N1915
STATENS MUSEUM FOR KUNST. JOURNAL. (Text in English) 1917. a. DKK 248. Statens Museum for Kunst, Soelvgade 48-50, DK-1307 Copenhagen K, Denmark. FAX 45-33-14-23-26. Ed. Kasper Monrad. illus. **Indexed:** Artbibl.Mod., RILA. **Document type:** academic/scholarly publication.
  —BLDSC (5130.750000).
  Formerly (until 1993): Kunstmuseets Aarsskrift (ISSN 0107-8933)

STERZ; Zeitschrift fuer Literatur, Kunst und Kulturpolitik. see LITERATURE

ART   467

745.5   SW
STOCKHOLMS-FOERETAGAREN. 1970. q. SEK 25. Stockholms Stads Hantverksfoerening - Stockholm Craft and Small Industry Association, Goetgatan 61, 11621 Stockholm, Sweden. TEL 4-608-644-0090. FAX 4-608-643-7134. Ed. Haakan Wallensten. adv.; bk.rev. circ. 4,110. **Document type:** newsletter.

700 745.4 780 792   KR
STOHOLOSNYK/STOGOLOSNIK; aktualna svitova kultura. (Text in Ukrainian) 1994. q. $40 (effective 1996). Ukrainoznavstvo, Pubachov St., 12-2, 252 050 Kiev, Ukraine. FAX 38-44-2206474. Ed. Olga Korniyakova. circ. 5,000.

709   IT   ISSN 0587-1131
STORIA DELL'ARTE. 1969. 3/yr. L.120000 (foreign L.140000) (effective 1996). Nuova Italia Editrice S.p.a., Via Ernesto Codignola, 50018 Scandicci (FI), Italy. Ed.Bd. **Indexed:** Art Ind., Artbibl.Mod., Artbibl., Arts & Hum.Cit.Ind., ASCA, Avery Ind.Archit.Per., Curr.Cont., RILA.

709   IT
STORIA DELL'ARTE E DELLA CRITICA D'ARTE. 1990. irreg., no.7, 1996. price varies. Liguori Editore s.r.l., Via Posillipo 394, 80123 Naples, Italy. TEL 39-81-7206111. FAX 39-81-7206244. Ed. Alfredo De Paz; Pub. Guido Liguori. adv. contact: Maria Liguori. **Document type:** monographic series.

700   IT   ISSN 0081-5845
STORIA DELLA MINIATURA. STUDI E DOCUMENTI. 1962. irreg., no.7, 1992. price varies. Casa Editrice Leo S. Olschki, Casella Postale 66, 50100 Florence, Italy. TEL 39-55-6530684. FAX 39-55-6530214. E-mail: celso@olschki.it. circ. 1,000. **Document type:** monographic series.

LO STRANIERO/STRANGER/ETRANGER/FREMDE/ EXTRANJERO. see *LITERARY AND POLITICAL REVIEWS*

STREAMLINE. see *ARCHITECTURE*

700 371.42   US
STREET ARTISTS' NEWSLETTER. 1979. a. $25 membership (effective 1995). (Street Artist's Guild) Folk Arts Network, Inc., Box 380867, Cambridge, MA 02238. TEL 617-522-3407. (Subscr. to: Box 380570, Cambridge, MA 02238) Ed. Stephen Baird. adv.; bk.rev. circ. 1,000. (looseleaf format; back issues avail.) **Document type:** newsletter.
  Description: Covers locations, legal issues, profiles and reviews. Includes festival and event listings.

709 707   CN   ISSN 0081-6027
STRUCTURIST. 1960. biennial. Can.$28 to individuals; institutions Can.$52. Eli Bornstein, Ed. & Pub., Box 378, RPO University, University of Saskatchewan, Saskatoon, SK S7N 4J8, Canada. TEL 306-966-4198. FAX 306-966-8670. bk.rev.; cum.index: nos.1-30. circ. 1,200. (also avail. in microform from UMI; back issues avail.; reprint service avail. from UMI) **Indexed:** Art Ind., Artbibl.Mod., Avery Ind.Archit.Per. **Document type:** academic/scholarly publication.
●Also available online.
Also available on CD-ROM. Producer(s): H.W. Wilson.
—BLDSC (8479.320000); KR SourceOne; UMI; UnCover.

STUDI BITONTINI. see *HISTORY — History Of Europe*

709   IT
STUDI DI STORIA DELL'ARTE. (Text in English, French, German, Italian) 1990. a. L.100000. Ediart, Via XXV Aprile 11A, 06059 Todi (Perugia), Italy. TEL 075-8942411. Ed. Filippo Todini. bk.rev.; index. circ. 1,000. (back issues avail.)

709   IT
STUDI DI STORIA DELLE ARTI. 1977. a. L.20000($15) (effective 1993). Istituto di Storia dell'Arte, Universita di Genova, Via Balbi 4, 16126 Genoa, Italy. TEL 010-2099749. Ed. Gildo Fossati. circ. 1,000. (back issues avail.) **Indexed:** RILA. **Document type:** academic/scholarly publication.

709 701.18   IT
STUDI E TESTI DI STORIA E CRITICA DELL'ARTE. 1975. irreg., no.12, 1984. price varies. Societa Editrice Napoletana s.r.l., Corso Umberto I 34, 80138 Naples, Italy.

709   PL
STUDIA NAD SZTUKA RENESANSU I BAROKU/STUDIES IN ART OF RENAISSANCE AND BAROQUE. Katolicki Uniwersytet Lubelski, Towarzystwo Naukowe, Ul. Gliniana 21, 20-616 Lublin, Poland. TEL 55-01-93. Ed. Antoni Maslinski.

701   PL   ISSN 0081-7104
STUDIA Z HISTORII SZTUKI. (Text in Polish; summaries in English, French and German) 1953. irreg., vol.49, 1995. price varies. Polska Akademia Nauk, Instytut Sztuki, Ul. Dluga 26-28, 00-950 Warsaw, Poland. TEL 48-22-313271. FAX 48-22-313149. **Document type:** monographic series.

709   GW   ISSN 0081-7228
STUDIEN ZUR DEUTSCHEN KUNSTGESCHICHTE. 1894. irreg., no.360, 1997. price varies. Verlag Valentin Koerner GmbH, Postfach 100164, 76482 Baden-Baden, Germany. TEL 49-7221-22423. FAX 49-7221-38697. circ. 1,000. (reprint service avail. from KTO) **Document type:** monographic series. **Description:** Concerning the history of German art.

700   GW   ISSN 0175-9558
STUDIEN ZUR KUNSTGESCHICHTE. irreg., vol.89, 1994. price varies. Georg Olms Verlag, Hagentorwall 7, 31134 Hildesheim, Germany. TEL 49-5121-1501-0. FAX 49-5121-150150. (US subscr. to: 350 Fifth Ave., Ste. 3304, New York, NY 10118-0069. TEL 800-920-9334) **Document type:** monographic series.

709 950   GW   ISSN 0170-3684
STUDIEN ZUR OSTASIATISCHEN SCHRIFTKUNST. 1970. irreg., vol. 4, 1985. price varies. Franz Steiner Verlag Wiesbaden GmbH, Birkenwaldstr. 44, 70191 Stuttgart, Germany. TEL 49-711-2582-0. FAX 49-711-2582390. (Subscr. to: Postfach 101061, 70009 Stuttgart, Germany) Ed. Dietrich Seckel. R&P contact: Sabine Koerner. **Document type:** monographic series.

091 745.6   NE
STUDIES AND FACSIMILES OF NETHERLANDISH ILLUMINATED MANUSCRIPTS. (Text in English) 1986. irreg., vol.3, 1991. price varies. Davaco Publishers, Beukenlaan 3, 8085 RK Doornspijk, Netherlands. TEL 31-525-661823. FAX 31-525-662153. **Document type:** monographic series.

STUDIES IN AESTHETICS. see *PHILOSOPHY*

700 200   US
STUDIES IN ART AND RELIGIOUS INTERPRETATION. 1982. irreg., latest no.19. $49.95 per no. Edwin Mellen Press, 415 Ridge St., Box 450, Lewiston, NY 14092. TEL 716-754-2788. FAX 754-4056. **Document type:** monographic series.

STUDIES IN ART EDUCATION; a journal of issues and research in art education. see *EDUCATION*

STUDIES IN ASIAN ART AND ARCHAEOLOGY. see *ORIENTAL STUDIES*

700   US
STUDIES IN BRITISH ART. irreg., latest 1992. price varies. (Paul Mellon Centre for Studies in British Art) Yale University Press, Box 209040, New Haven, CT 06520. TEL 203-432-0940. **Document type:** monographic series.

700 720   US
STUDIES IN CISTERCIAN ART AND ARCHITECTURE. 1982. irreg., vol.4, 1993. price varies. Cistercian Publications, Kalamazoo, MI 48008. E-mail: trappist@ultranet.com; URL: http://www.ultranet.com/~trappist/. Ed. Meredith Parsons Lillich. R&P contact: E. Royanne Elder. circ. 1,000. **Document type:** academic/scholarly publication, monographic series.

751.6 913   UK   ISSN 0039-3630
N8560   CODEN: SCONAH
STUDIES IN CONSERVATION. (Text in English; summaries in French, German, Spanish) 1952. q. £35 (effective 1997). International Institute for Conservation of Historic and Artistic Works, 6 Buckingham St., London WC2N 6BA, England. TEL 44-171-839-5975. FAX 44-171-976-1564. E-mail: iicon@compuserve.com. Ed.Bd. adv.; bk.rev.; illus.; index. circ. 5,000. (back issues avail.) **Indexed:** AESIS, Anthropol.Lit., Art & Archaeol.Tech.Abstr., Art Ind., Arts & Hum.Cit.Ind., ASCA, Avery Ind.Archit.Per., Br.Archaeol.Abstr., Chem.Abstr., Curr.Cont., Forest Prod.Abstr., Numis.Lit., World Surf.Coat. **Document type:** academic/scholarly publication.
—BLDSC (8490.290000); CASDDS; Genuine Article; KR SourceOne; Linda Hall; SWETS; UnCover.
  Description: Contains original work and reviews on advances in conservation and restoration, covering both practical and scientific aspects, together with technical research on materials and methods of fabrication.
Refereed Serial

769.9492   NE
▼**STUDIES IN DUTCH GRAPHIC ART.** (Text in English) 1996. irreg. (Museum Het Rembrandthuis) Waanders Uitgevers, Postbus 1129, 8001 BC Zwolle, Netherlands. (Co-sponsor: Rembrandt Information Center) illus. **Document type:** academic/scholarly publication.

704   US   ISSN 0148-1029
NX1
STUDIES IN ICONOGRAPHY. vol.9, 1983. a. $12 to individuals; institutions $25. Arizona State University, School of Art, Tempe, AZ 85287. TEL 602-965-6439. Ed. Anthony Lacy Gully. **Indexed:** Artbibl.Mod., Avery Ind.Archit.Per., M.L.A., MLA Intl.Bibl., RILA.
—BLDSC (8490.714000).

700   US   ISSN 1058-997X
N6512
STUDIES IN MODERN ART. 1991. a. $25. Museum of Modern Art, 11 W. 53rd St., New York, NY 10019-5498. TEL 212-708-9730. FAX 212-708-9779. TELEX 62370 MODART. Ed. John Elderfield. **Indexed:** Art Ind.
—KR SourceOne.
  Description: Devoted to modern and contemporary art. Concentrates on the museum's collection and programs as well as topics broadly related to the museums holdings. Each issue focuses on a single topic, such as an historical period, a movement, technique or individual work.

STUDIES IN PRE-COLUMBIAN ART AND ARCHAEOLOGY. see *ARCHAEOLOGY*

740 745.1 720   US   ISSN 1069-8825
NK1
STUDIES IN THE DECORATIVE ARTS. 1993. s-a. $30 (Canada & Mexico $35; elsewhere $37) (effective 1997). Bard Graduate Center for Studies in the Decorative Arts, 18 W. 86th St., New York, NY 10024. TEL 212-501-3058. FAX 212-501-3089. E-mail: sherrill@bgc.bard.edu; URL: http://www.bard.edu/bgc. Ed. Sarah B. Sherrill. R&P contact: Sarah B. Sherrill. bk.rev.; circ. 420 (paid). (back issues avail.) **Indexed:** Amer.Hist.& Life (1993-), Artbibl.Mod., Hist.Abstr. (1993-), RILA. **Document type:** academic/scholarly publication.
—BLDSC (8490.330500).
  Description: Publishes new research and interpretation in the history of the decorative arts. Studies all periods and cultures.
Refereed Serial

708   US   ISSN 0091-7338
N386.U5
STUDIES IN THE HISTORY OF ART. 1971. irreg. price varies. National Gallery of Art, Washington, DC 20565. TEL 301-322-5900. (Subscr. to: 2000B South Club Dr., Landover, MD 20785; Dist. by: University Press of New England, Box 979, Hanover, NH 03755) charts; illus. circ. 6,000. **Indexed:** Art Ind., Artbibl.Mod., Arts & Hum.Cit.Ind., ASCA, Avery Ind.Archit.Per., Curr.Cont., RILA.
—BLDSC (8490.653000); KR SourceOne; UnCover.
  Formerly: Report and Studies in the History of Art (ISSN 0080-1240)

709 730 N8	RM ISSN 0039-3983	

STUDII SI CERCETARI DE ISTORIA ARTEI. SERIA ARTA PLASTICA. (Text in Rumanian; summaries in English, French, German, Russian) 1954. a. (Academia Romana, Institutul de Istoria Artei George Oprescu) Editura Academiei Romane, Calea 13 Septembrie 13, 76117 Bucharest, Rumania. (Dist. by: Rodipet SA, Piata Presei Libere 1, Sec. 1, P.O. Box 33-57, Bucharest, Rumania. TEL 401-6185103. FAX 401-2226407) Ed. Remus Niculescu. bk.rev.; illus.; index. Indexed: Numis.Lit., RILA.

700   IS   ISSN 0792-4038
STUDIO. 1989. m. IS.220($72) Havatzeleth Cultural and Educational Institutes of Hashomer Hatzair, P.O. Box 23570, Tel Aviv 61231, Israel. TEL 972-3-2512207. FAX 972-3-2512202. E-mail: studio@netvision.net.il. Ed. Sarah Breitberg-Semel. adv. contact: Yossi Peled. bk.rev.; film rev.; illus. circ. 4,000. (back issues avail.) **Document type:** academic/scholarly publication, consumer publication.
Refereed Serial

700   US
STUDIO OZ. q. free. InterCity Oz, E-mail: kyoung@interoz.com; URL: http://interoz.com/studiooz. **Document type:** bulletin.
●Available only online.
Description: Features highly acclaimed artists mostly from the southwestern United States.

SUEDOSTDEUTSCHES KULTURWERK. VEROEFFENTLICHUNGEN. REIHE A: KULTUR UND DICHTUNG. see *HISTORY — History Of Europe*

700 658.8   US
SUNSHINE ARTIST; America's premier show & festival guide for artists and craftspeople. 1972. m. $29.95. Palm House Publishing, Inc., 2600 Temple Dr, Winter Park, FL 32789-1371. TEL 407-539-1399. FAX 407-539-1499. Ed. Amy Detwiler; Pub. David F. Cook. adv.: color page $1195; adv. contact: Christi Ashly. circ. 15,000 (paid). (back issues avail.) **Document type:** trade publication.
Formerly: Sunshine Artists U S A (ISSN 0199-9370)

SUOMEN MUINAISMUISTOYHDISTYKSEN AIKAKAUSKIRJA/FINSKA FORNMINNESFOERENINGENS TIDSKRIFT. see *ARCHAEOLOGY*

SUOMEN MUSEO. see *ARCHAEOLOGY*

745   US   ISSN 0197-4483
SURFACE DESIGN JOURNAL. 1973. q. $45 (foreign $51). Surface Design Association, P.O. Box 20799, Oakland, CA 94620. TEL 707-829-3110. FAX 707-829-3285. Ed. Patricia Malarcher. R&P contact: Patricia Malarcher. adv. contact: Joy Stocksdale. bk.rev.; illus. circ. 4,000. (back issues avail.) **Document type:** trade publication.
—BLDSC (8547.820000); KR SourceOne; UnCover.
Description: Contains articles on artists, design, inspiration, technique, and education.

700   GW   ISSN 0172-3456
SYMBOL; Kunst im Rheinland. 1971. q. DM.3. Ubierring 6-8, 50678 Cologne, Germany. TEL 0221-314499. FAX 0221-314499. Ed. Wolfgang Wangler. adv.; bk.rev. (back issues avail.)

700   NE   ISSN 0923-9073
SYMBOLA ET EMBLEMATA. 1989. irreg., vol.7, 1995. price varies. E.J. Brill, P.O. Box 9000, 2300 PA Leiden, Netherlands. TEL 31-71-5353500. FAX 31-71-5317532. TELEX 39296 BRILL NL. E-mail: ejbrill@brill.nl. (In N. America: E.J. Brill, 24 Hudson St., Kinderhook, NY 12106. TEL 800-962-4406. FAX 518-758-1959) R&P contact: Elizabeth Vennekamp. illus. (back issues avail.) **Document type:** monographic series.
—BLDSC (8581.690000).
Description: Scholarly monographs and papers on the history of emblems in Europe.
Refereed Serial

SYMMETRY: CULTURE AND SCIENCE. see *SCIENCES: COMPREHENSIVE WORKS*

SYRIA; revue d'art oriental et d'archeologie. see *ARCHAEOLOGY*

700   PL   ISSN 0324-8232
N6
SZTUKA. (Text in Polish; summaries in English, French) 1974. m. 24 ZI.($48) Studio Wydawnicze "Sztuka", Ul. Miodowa 12 m. 57, 00-261 Warsaw, Poland. Ed. Andrzej Skoczylas. bk.rev.; bibl.; illus. Indexed: Artbibl.Mod., Artbibl.
Formerly: Przeglad Artystyczny (ISSN 0033-2011)
Description: Color and black and white pictures, critical and theoretical texts on contemporary art in Poland and in the world; reviews, interviews, and chronicles.

700   NE
T A M BULLETIN. (Text in English) 1984. bi-m. free. Travelling Art Mail, c/o T A M, Postbus 10388, 5000 JJ Tilburg, Netherlands. TEL 31-13-5366103. E-mail: TAM@dds.nl. Ed. Ruud Janssen. bk.rev.; illus.; stat.; circ. controlled. **Document type:** bulletin.
●Also available online.
Description: Features mail-art news, projects and publications through a computer bulletin board service.

740   SP   ISSN 0210-3761
T G; revista de las artes decorativas. 1968. bi-m. 2.700 ptas.($42) in Europe; U.S. $55. (Tapicerias Gancedo) Ediciones Sohail, Velazquez 21, 28001 Madrid, Spain. TEL 1-275-38-28. Ed. Jose Gancedo Baga. adv.; bk.rev.; illus.; circ. 10,000 (controlled).

700   NE   ISSN 0166-4492
TABLEAU. (Text in Dutch, English) 1978. bi-m. fl.90 (Belgium 1950 BEF; elsewhere fl.140). Tableau Fine Arts Magazine B.V., Grote Haven 1, 2851 BM Haastrecht, Netherlands. TEL 31-182-501066. FAX 31-182-501992. (Subscr. to: Betapress Abonnementen Services, Postbus 97, 5126 ZH Gilze, Netherlands. TEL 31-161-457901. FAX 31-161-452913) Eds. Anja renkel, Anneliese Hamming; Pub. Jaap Verhage. adv.: color page fl.3500; adv. contact: Mrs. Janny Verhage-Bisdom. illus.; circ. 23,000 (paid). (back issues avail.) **Document type:** consumer publication.
—SWETS.
Description: Covers the international art world, including museum and gallery exhibitions, auctions, art and antiques fairs, and profiles of artists.

TABLEAU (WINNIPEG); involving people in the visual arts. see *MUSEUMS AND ART GALLERIES*

700   FI   ISSN 0039-8977
N8
TAIDE. (Text in Finnish; summaries in English) 1960. bi-m. FIM 400. Art Publishing TAIDE, Kasarmikatu 23A, 00130 Helsinki, Finland. TEL 358-0-626467. FAX 358-0-626482. Ed. Jyrki Siukonen. adv.; bk.rev.; illus. circ. 6,500. Indexed: Artbibl.Mod. **Document type:** academic/scholarly publication.
—BLDSC (8598.502700).

TALOHA. see *MUSEUMS AND ART GALLERIES*

TAMIL KALAI; research journal on Tamilology. see *HISTORY — History Of Asia*

700   TS
AL-TASHKIL. 1987. irreg. free. Emirates Society for Fine Arts, Cultural Group, P.O. Box 2355, Sharjah, United Arab Emirates. TEL 375262. Ed. Muhammas Yussif Ali. circ. 500.
Description: Covers fine arts activities in the U.A.E., including exhibition listings and cinema.

391   US   ISSN 1041-3146
GT2345
TATTOO; magazine of skin art. m. $34.95 (foreign $46.95) (effective 1996). Paisano Publications, Inc., Box 1050, Agoura Hills, CA 91376-1050. TEL 818-889-8740. FAX 818-889-4726. Ed. Keith Ball; Pub. Joseph Teresi. R&P contact: Brian Wood. adv. contact: Lizette Hottinger. circ. 131,664 (paid). **Document type:** consumer publication.

391   US   ISSN 1079-9443
TATTOO FLASH. bi-m. $24.90 (effective 1996); newsstand price: $4.99. Paisano Publications, Inc., Box 1050, Agoura Hills, CA 91376-1050. TEL 818-889-8740. FAX 818-889-4726. Ed. Keith Ball; Pub. Joseph Teresi. R&P contact: Brian Wood. adv. contact: Lizette Hottinger. **Document type:** consumer publication.
Formerly: Flash (Agoura Hills) (ISSN 1070-1184)

700   US   ISSN 1047-1499
TATTOO REVIEW. 9/yr. $32.95. Outlaw Biker Enterprises, Inc., 5 Marine View Plaza, Ste. 207, Hoboken, NJ 07030. TEL 201-653-2700. Ed. Jean-Chris Miller; Pub. Casey Exton. adv. contact: Ken Knabb. circ. 170,000. (back issues avail.) **Document type:** consumer publication.

702   US
TATTOO REVIEW SPECIALS. q. newsstand price: $5.95. Outlaw Biker Enterprises, Inc., 5 Marine View Plaza, Ste. 207, Hoboken, NJ 07030. TEL 201-653-2700. Ed. Jean-Chris Miller; Pub. Casey Exton. adv. contact: Ken Knabb. **Document type:** consumer publication.

391.65   CN
▼**TATTOOS.COM EZINE.** 1995. d. 2234 Kingston Rd., Toronto, ON M1N 1Y9, Canada. E-mail: tats@inforamp.net; URL: http://tattoos.com. Ed. Damian McGrath.
●Available only online.
Description: Covers tattoos and body modification.

702   US   ISSN 1070-7247
TATTOOS FOR MEN. 1993. bi-m. newsstand price: $5.95. Outlaw Biker Enterprises, Inc., 5 Marine View Plaza, Ste. 207, Hoboken, NJ 07030. TEL 201-653-2700. FAX 201-653-7892. Ed. Jean-Chris Miller; Pub. Casey Exton. adv. contact: Ken Knabb. **Document type:** consumer publication.

702   US
TATTOOS FOR WOMEN. bi-m. newsstand price: $5.95. Outlaw Biker Enterprises, Inc., 5 Marine View Plaza, Ste. 207, Hoboken, NJ 07030. TEL 201-653-2700. FAX 201-653-7892. Ed. Jean-Chris Miller; Pub. Casey Exton. adv. contact: Ken Knabb. **Document type:** consumer publication.

700   US
TATTOOTIME.* 1982. irreg. Hardy Marks Publications, 766 Francisco St., San Francisco, CA 94133-1615. FAX 808-737-7033. Ed. D.E. Hardy. circ. 10,000.

751.6 720   US   ISSN 0146-1214
N8554   CODEN: TECODM
TECHNOLOGY AND CONSERVATION; of art, architecture and antiquities. 1976. q. $28 (foreign $60) (effective 1997). Technology Organization Inc., 76 Highland Ave., Somerville, MA 02143. TEL 617-623-4488. Ed. Susan E. Schur; Pub. Susan E. Schur. adv. contact: Susan E. Schur. bk.rev.; illus.; tr.lit. circ. 15,500. Indexed: Abstr.Anthropol., Art & Archaeol.Tech.Abstr., Art Ind., Avery Ind.Archit.Per., Br.Archaeol.Abstr., Br.Tech.Ind., Chem.Abstr., Graph.Arts Lit.Abstr., RILA. **Document type:** trade publication.
—BLDSC (8758.570000); CISTI; KR SourceOne; SWETS; UnCover.
Description: Covers the analysis, preservation, restoration, security, environmental protection, and documentation of art (paintings, sculptures, textiles, ceramics, antiquities etc.), photography, manuscripts, books, and architecture (buildings, monuments, historic sites).

740   SW   ISSN 0347-7673
TECKNAREN. 1977. 6/yr. SEK 220 to non-members (effective 1996). Foereningen Svenska Tecknare, Goetgatan 48, S-118 26 Stockholm, Sweden. TEL 46-8-642-75-80. FAX 46-8-641-75-14. Ed. Lena Andersson. R&P contact: Lena Andersson. adv.; bk.rev. circ. 1,208. **Document type:** trade publication.
Description: Forum for debate, feature stories, and news relevant to professional illustrators and graphic designers.

620 645   RU   ISSN 0040-2230
TS149   CODEN: TKESBG
TEKHNICHESKAYA ESTETIKA. (Text in Russian; summaries in English, French, German) 1964. m. 37.50 Rub. Izdatel'stvo Kniga, 50, Gorky St., 125047 Moscow, Russia. illus.; index. Indexed: Chem.Abstr.

700   IT
TEMA CELESTE; arte contemporanea. 1983. 5/yr. L.50000($40) Prisma s.r.l., Via Agusta 17, 96100 Syracuse, Italy. TEL 931-491-597. FAX 931-491-491. (Edit. addr.: Via Sambuco 15, 20122 Milan, Italy. TEL 39-2-89400950. FAX 39-2-89402331) Ed. Demetrio Paparoni. adv.

ART 469

700　　　　　　SZ　ISSN 1016-0809
TEMPORALE; rivista d'arte e di cultura. 1983. q. 36 SFr. Edizioni Dabbeni - Lugano, Casella Postale 2461, 6900 Lugano, Switzerland. TEL 091-23-29-80. FAX 091-23-12-11. Ed. Stefano Dabbeni.

700　　　　　　US
TENNESSEE ARTS REPORT. 1974. q. free. Tennessee Arts Commission, 401 Charlotte Ave., Nashville, TN 37243-0780. TEL 615-741-1701. FAX 615-741-8559. URL: http://www.arts.state.tn.us. Ed. Stephanie Tallman. bk.rev.; film rev.; play rev. circ. 4,000. (tabloid format; back issues avail.; reprint service avail. from UMI) **Document type**: government publication, newsletter.

TERRA PLANA. see TRAVEL AND TOURISM

700　　　　　　IT　ISSN 1123-4695
TERRE DEL FUOCO. 1993. s-a. L.25000 (foreign L.43000) (effective 1996). Cooperativa Libraria Universitaria Editrice Bologna, Via Marsala 24, 40126 Bologna BO, Italy. TEL 39-51-220736. FAX 39-51-237758.

709.04　　　　　　NO　ISSN 0802-7323
N3128
TERSKEL/THRESHOLD. 1990. s-a. NOK 50 per no. Museet for Samtidskunst, Bankplassen 4, P.O. Box 8191, Dep 0034, Oslo, Norway. TEL 47-22-33-58-20. FAX 47-22-33-57-90. Ed. Per Bj. Boym. **Document type**: academic/scholarly publication, catalog.

753　　　　　　IT　ISSN 0390-0355
TERZO OCCHIO; rivista trimestrale d'arte contemporanea. 1975. q. L.50000. Edizioni Bora S.N.C., Via Jacopo di Paolo, 42, 40128 Bologna, Italy. TEL 39-51-356133. FAX 39-51-374394. Ed. Patrizia Bonfiglioli. adv.; bk.rev.; illus. circ. 10,000.

700　　　　　　GW　ISSN 0940-9459
TEXTE ZUR KUNST. 1991. q. DM.100 (students DM.90; overseas DM.130(students DM.120)) (effective 1997). Texte zur Kunst Verlag GmbH und Co. KG, Gereonshof 30, 50670 Cologne, Germany. TEL 49-221-1390445. FAX 49-221-138229. Eds. Stefan Germer, Isabelle Graw. adv. contact: Juergen Bahr. **Document type**: academic/scholarly publication.

TEXTILE MUSEUM JOURNAL. see TEXTILE INDUSTRIES AND FABRICS

700　　　　　　TS
THAQAFA WA FANN/CULTURE AND ART. (Text in Arabic) 1989. d. Cultural Foundation, Culture and Arts Department, P.O. Box 2380, Abu Dhabi, United Arab Emirates. TEL 215300. FAX 336059. TELEX 2214 CULCEN EM. circ. 500 (controlled).
Description: Covers the activities of the foundation: exhibitions, film series, lectures, meeting, publications.

THEORIE UND GESCHICHTE DER LITERATUR UND DER SCHOENEN KUENSTE. see LITERATURE

700　　　　　　CN
THERE AND BACK: TOUR ORGANIZERS HANDBOOK/ALLER RETOUR: GUIDE DU DIRECTEUR DE TOURNEES. (Text in English, French) 1977. irreg., latest Spring 1992. Can.$18 (US Can.$25; elsewhere Can.$30). Canada Council for the Arts, Box 1047, 350 Albert St., Ottawa, ON K1P 5V8, Canada. TEL 613-566-4414. FAX 613-566-4404. URL: http://www.canadacouncil.ca. **Document type**: academic/scholarly publication.
Formerly: Tour Organizers Handbook.

700　　　　　　UK　ISSN 0952-8822
NX596.3.A1
THIRD TEXT; third world perspectives on contemporary art & culture. 1987. q. £26 to individuals (U.S. $55; elsewhere £40); institutions £52 (U.S. $120; elsewhere £70) (effective 1997). Kala Press, P.O. Box 3509, London NW6 3PJ, England. TEL 44-171-372-0826. (Subscr. to: Carfax Publishing Co., P.O. Box 25, Abingdon, Oxfon. OX14 3UE, England. TEL 44-1235-555335. FAX 44-1235-401550; U.S. subscr. to: Carfax Publishing Co., Box 2025, Dunnellon, FL 34430-2025) Ed. Rasheed Araeen. adv. contact: Pamela Courtney. bk.rev. circ. 2,500. **Indexed**: Art Ind., Left Ind., Per.Islam. (1990-). **Document type**: academic/scholarly publication.
—BLDSC (8820.143200); KR SourceOne; UnCover. CCC.
Description: Scholarly journal focusing on the fields of art criticism, art history and cultural studies. Refereed Serial

THORVALDSENS MUSEUM. MEDDELELSER. see MUSEUMS AND ART GALLERIES

THRESHOLD. see ARCHITECTURE

TIDSKRIFTEN 90TAL OM LITTERATUR OCH KONST. see LITERATURE

TIROLER HEIMATBLAETTER. see HISTORY — History Of Europe

TJABE RAWIT; verhaltenkrant met een indische achtergrond. see LITERARY AND POLITICAL REVIEWS

TJUSTBYGDENS KULTURHISTORISKA FOERENING. AARSBOK. see ARCHAEOLOGY

738　　　　　　US　ISSN 0199-4514
TOLE WORLD; decorative painting projects & ideas. 1977. bi-m. $24. E G W Publishing Co., 1041 Shary Circle, Concord, CA 94518. TEL 510-671-9852. FAX 510-671-0692. Ed. Judy Swager. adv.; circ. 90,000 (paid). (back issues avail.) **Indexed**: Ind.How To Do It (1990-). **Document type**: consumer publication.

702.8　　　　　　DK　ISSN 0900-3347
TOOLS; tools design journal. 1985. bi-m. DKK 400. Designlab A-S, Antoinettevej 5, DK-2500 Valby, Denmark. Ed. Per Mollerup. adv.; bk.rev. circ. 8,000.

700 800 301　　　　　　IT　ISSN 0392-498X
IL TORCHIO ARTISTICO E LETTERARIO; organo ufficiale di stampa dell'Accademia Culturale d'Europa. 1978. m. L.20000. Accademia Culturale d'Europa, Viale IV Novembre 1, 01030 Bassano Romano (VT), Italy. TEL 0761 634115. Ed. Rino Pompei. bk.rev. (back issues avail.)

700　　　　　　PL　ISSN 0082-5514
TOWARZYSTWO NAUKOWE W TORUNIU. KOMISJA HISTORII SZTUKI. TEKA. (Subseries of Towarzystwo Naukowe w Toruniu. Wydzial Filologiczno-Filozoficzny. Prace) (Text in Polish; summaries in French) 1959. irreg., vol.8, 1992. price varies. Towarzystwo Naukowe w Toruniu, Ul. Wysoka 16, 87-100 Torun, Poland. TEL 48-56-23941. TELEX 552388 FSBH PL. Ed. Marian Szarmach. circ. 600. **Document type**: monographic series.

700 808.87　　　　　　US
TRADE JOURNAL RECAP. 1973. m. $20. Gag Recap Publishers, 12 Hedden Pl., New Providence, NJ 07974-1724. TEL 908-464-1158. Ed. Al Gottlieb. (back issues avail.) **Document type**: trade publication, newsletter.
Description: Describes cartoons printed in trade journals and house organs during the previous months. Includes frequency of publication, issue date, cartoon editor, address, price paid, and cartoonist's name.

700 800　　　　　　US
▼**TRANS**; art.cultures.media. (Text in English, Spanish) 1995. 3/yr. $40. Passim Inc., 109 W. 17th St., New York, NY 10011. TEL 212-929-0226. FAX 212-924-6779. E-mail: trans@echonyc.com; URL: http://www.echonyc.com/-trans. Ed. Sandra Antelo-Suarez. illus. **Document type**: academic/scholarly publication.
●Also available online.

700　　　　　　AG
TRASTIENDA; revista del mercado de arte y antiguedades. m.? $40. Tte. Gral. Peron 1454, 1o '6', 1037 Buenos Aires, Argentina. Ed. Julia Raggi; Pub. Mario Gilardoni.

TRAVAUX D'HUMANISME ET RENAISSANCE. see HISTORY — History Of Europe

TRIBUS; Jahrbuch des Linden-Museums Stuttgart. see ANTHROPOLOGY

TRICYCLE; the Buddhist review. see RELIGIONS AND THEOLOGY — Buddhist

TRIERER ZEITSCHRIFT FUER GESCHICHTE UND KUNST DES TRIERER LANDES UND SEINER NACHBARGEBIETE. see ARCHAEOLOGY

TRIVIUM. see LITERATURE

750 730　　　　　　FR
TROUVAILLES. m. 80 F. Joel Garcia, 1-3 rue du Depart, 75014 Paris, France. Eds. Anne Vaujour, Rene Margeridon. adv.; illus.
Description: Antiques in painting, sculpture, decorations.

745.1 070.5　　　　　　US
THE TRUMPET (NEW YORK). 1986. q. free. Swann Galleries, Inc., 104 E. 25th St., New York, NY 10010-2977. TEL 212-254-4710. FAX 212-979-1017. Ed. Caroline Birenbaum. illus. circ. 38,000. **Document type**: newsletter.
Description: Provides news of forthcoming sales of rare books, photographs, autographs and art at auctions, as well as brief notes on recently held sales, and the prices brought in by notable pieces.

700　　　　　　GW
TUDUV-STUDIE. REIHE KUNSTGESCHICHTE. 1979. irreg. price varies. Tuduv Verlagsgesellschaft mbH, Gabelsbergerstr. 15, 80333 Munich, Germany.

700 780 792　　　　　　UK　ISSN 0260-8383
TUITION, ENTERTAINMENT, NEWS, VIEWS. 1976? 2/yr. £0.20. Oxford Area Arts Council, Old Fire Station Arts Centre, Oxford, England. illus.
Formerly: Oxford Area Arts Council. Newsletter.

700 915.6　　　　　　TU
TURKISH TREASURES; culture-art-tourism magazine. (Text in English) 1978. q. TL.100($4) Ilbas A.S., Alaykosku Cad. 9 Cagaloglu, Istanbul, Turkey. Ed. Nevzat Ilhan.

700　　　　　　US
TURNBERRY.* q. G S & J Publishing, Inc., 5212 N.W. 54th Ave., Pompano Beach, FL 33073-3755. TEL 305-977-5901. circ. 5,000 (controlled).

709　　　　　　RU　ISSN 0131-6877
TVORCHESTVO. 1957. q. $58 (effective 1998). (Soyuz Khudozhnikov Rossiiskoi Federatsii) Izdatel'stvo Khudozhnik, Ul. Chernyakhovskogo, 4a, 125319 Moscow, Russia. TEL 095-151-2502. (Dist. in U.S. by: Victor Kamkin Inc., 4956 Boiling Brook Pkwy., Rockville, MD 20852. TEL 901-881-5973. FAX 301-881-1637) Ed. Alexander Rozhin. bk.rev.; illus.; index. circ. 14,000. **Indexed**: Artbibl., Artbibl.Mod., Numis.Lit.

XXIST CENTURY; a new quarterly of art, politics, literature and ideas. see LITERATURE

790　　　　　　US
U N I M A - U S A MEMBERSHIP GUIDE AND DIRECTORY. 1966. a. membership. Union Internationale de la Marionette, 1404 Spring St., N.W., Atlanta, GA 30309-2820. TEL 404-873-3089. FAX 404-873-9907. Eds. Mark Smythe, Angela Benefield. **Document type**: directory.
Description: Lists North American puppeteers for persons who use their art to promote international and intercultural peace and understanding.

470 ART

700 US ISSN 0899-1782
N6505
U S ART. 1982. 12/yr. $32.95 (effective 1997). MSP Communications, 220 S. 6th St., Ste. 500, Minneapolis, MN 55402. TEL 612-339-7571. FAX 612-339-5806. Ed. Frank Sisser. adv.; bk.rev. circ. 55,000. **Document type:** consumer publication.
Formerly: Midwest Art (ISSN 0744-6217)
Description: For collectors and enthusiasts of limited-edition realist print art in America, including wildlife, landscape, Americana, Western, still-life and florals.

ULM UND OBERSCHWABEN; Zeitschrift fuer Geschichte und Kunst. see HISTORY — History Of Europe

700 US ISSN 0160-0699
UMBRELLA. 1978. s-a. $18 to individuals (foreign $20); institutions $25 (foreign $30) (effective 1997). Umbrella Associates, Box 3640, Santa Monica, CA 90408. TEL 310-399-1146. FAX 310-399-5070. E-mail: umbrella@ix.netcom.com; URL: http://colophon.com/journal. Ed. Judith A. Hoffberg; Pub. Judith A. Hoffberg. adv.; bk.rev.; illus.; circ. 500 (paid). (back issues avail.) **Document type:** newsletter.
Description: Covers news and publications made by artists, including photography and mail art.

709 XR ISSN 0049-5123
N6
UMENI/ARTS. (Text and summaries in Czech, English, German) 1952. q. DM.291. Ceska Akademie Ved, Ustav Dejin Umeni, Husova 4, 110 00 Prague 1, Czech Republic. TEL 231-29-51. (Dist. in Western countries by: Kubon & Sagner, P.O. Box 34 01 08, 8000 Munich 34, Germany) Ed. Rostislav Svacha. illus. circ. 14,000. (also avail. in microfiche from NRP) **Indexed:** Artbibl.Mod., Artbibl, Avery Ind.Archit.Per., IBR, RILA.
Description: Specialized studies and essays dealing with the history of the arts in general; studies on Bohemian and Central European painting, sculpture, architecture and applied arts.

700 YU ISSN 0041-6320
UMETNOST; casopis za likovne umetnosti i kritiku. (Text in Serbo-Croatian; summaries in English and French) vol.2, 1966. bi-m. 160 din.($9.20) Turisticka Stampa, Knez Mihailova 21, Belgrade, Yugoslavia. Ed. Zivojin Turinski.

700 MP
UNDESNIY SOYOLYN DZAM/ROAD OF NATIONAL CULTURE. (Text in Mongolian) bi-m. Culture and Art Development Committee, Ulan Bator, Mongolia.

UNIR: ECHO DE SAINT LOUIS. see LITERATURE

UNIROD. see LITERATURE

702.8 363.6 UK
UNITED KINGDOM INSTITUTE FOR CONSERVATION OF HISTORIC AND ARTISTIC WORKS OF ART. OCCASIONAL PAPERS.* irreg., no.11, 1992. United Kingdom Institute for Conservation of Historic and Artistic Works of Art, 6 Whitehorse Mews, London SE1 7QD, England. Ed. Christine Daintith. **Document type:** monographic series.

700 US ISSN 0083-2103
NX22
U.S. NATIONAL ENDOWMENT FOR THE ARTS. ANNUAL REPORT. 1967. a. free. U.S. National Endowment for the Arts, Public Information Office, 1100 Pennsylvania Ave., N.W., Washington, DC 20506. TEL 202-682-5400. circ. 4,000 (controlled). **Document type:** government publication, corporate report.
Description: Lists grants awarded to artists and arts organizations; contains names, funded amount, and a brief description of the grant.

700 378 US
▼**U.S. NATIONAL ENDOWMENT FOR THE ARTS. GRANTS TO ORGANIZATIONS.** 1997. a. U.S. National Endowment for the Arts, Public Information Office, 1100 Pennsylvania Ave., N.W., Washington, DC 20506. TEL 202-682-5400. URL: http://www.arts.endow.gov.
Description: Covers the new general guideline for grants to be given in four categories: Heritage & Preservation, Creation & Presentation, Education & Access, and Planning & Stabilization. Since guidelines are no longer divided according to disciplines (visual arts, dance, music, theater etc.), this publication covers eligibility and application information for all organizations involved in these areas.

700 SP ISSN 0210-962X
NX7 CODEN: CAUGFB
UNIVERSIDAD DE GRANADA. CUADERNOS DE ARTE. 1974. a., no.26, 1995. Universidad de Granada, Departamento de Historia del Arte, Servicio de Publicaciones, Antiguo Colegio Maximo, Campus de Cartuja, 18071 Granada, Spain. TEL 34-58-243930. FAX 34-58-242827. Ed. Antonio Moreno Garrido. illus. **Document type:** academic/scholarly publication.
—CINDOC.

700 800 GT
UNIVERSIDAD DE SAN CARLOS. REVISTA; artes - literatura - ciencias humanas. m. Universidad de San Carlos de Guatemala, Ciudad Universitaria, zona 12, Edificio de Rectoria, Of. 307, Guatemala, Guatemala. Ed. Julio Penados del Barrio. bibl.; illus. circ. 2,000.

700 SP
UNIVERSIDAD DE SEVILLA. SERIE: BELLAS ARTES. irreg. Universidad de Sevilla, Servicio de Publicaciones, Calle Porvenir 27, 41013 Seville, Spain. TEL 34-5-4231958. FAX 34-5-4232245. illus.

700 300 BO ISSN 0041-8609
UNIVERSIDAD MAYOR DE SAN ANDRES. GACETA UNIVERSITARIA.* m. Universidad Mayor de San Andres, Departamento de Relaciones Publicas, Casilla 4787, La Paz, Bolivia. Ed. Abel Elias Sainz. charts; illus.

700 MX ISSN 0188-9583
UNIVERSIDAD NACIONAL AUTONOMA DE MEXICO. ESCUELA NACIONAL DE ARTES PLASTICAS. REVISTA. s-a. Mex.$30($8) (effective 1997). Ave. Constitucion 600, Barrio de la Concha, Xochimilco, 16210 Mexico, D.F., Mexico. TEL 52-5-6762621. FAX 52-5-6530281. Ed. Fernando Alba Aldave.
Description: Publishes original articles and case reports on sculpture, painting and art related issues.

700 MX ISSN 0185-1276
N16
UNIVERSIDAD NACIONAL AUTONOMA DE MEXICO. INSTITUTO DE INVESTIGACIONES ESTETICAS. ANALES. (Supplement avail.: Catalogo de las Exposiciones de Arte (ISSN 0187-9766)) 1937. s-a. Mex.$150($60) (effective 1997). Universidad Nacional Autonoma de Mexico, Instituto de Investigaciones Esteticas, Circuito Mario de la Cueva, Zona Cultural, Ciudad Universitaria, 04510 Mexico, D.F., Mexico. TEL 52-5-6227545. FAX 52-5-6657440. E-mail: ereynoso@servidor.unam.mx. Ed.Bd. circ. 1,500. (bibl) **Indexed:** Hisp.Amer.Per.Ind. (1970-), IBR. **Document type:** academic/scholarly publication.
Description: Publishes articles, notes and news on Mexican and Latin American art.

700 MX ISSN 0185-1799
UNIVERSIDAD NACIONAL AUTONOMA DE MEXICO. INSTITUTO DE INVESTIGACIONES ESTETICAS. MONOGRAFIAS DE ARTE. 1977. irreg., latest, 1990. price varies. Universidad Nacional Autonoma de Mexico, Instituto de Investigaciones Esteticas, Circuito Mario de la Cueva, Zona Cultural, Ciudad Universitaria, 04510 Mexico, D.F., Mexico. TEL 52-5-6227545. FAX 52-5-6657440. E-mail: ereinoso@servidor.unam.mx. **Document type:** monographic series.

701.18 IT
UNIVERSITA DEGLI STUDI DI PARMA. ISTITUTO DI STORIA DELL'ARTE. CATALOGHI. (Each issue devoted to an individual artist) 1968. irreg., no.26, 1975. price varies. Universita degli Studi di Parma, Istituto di Storia dell'Arte, Piazzale della Pace 7A, 43100 Parma, Italy. TEL 0521-283089. FAX 0521-207125. bk.rev.; bibl.; illus. circ. 1,000.

707 IT ISSN 0557-3122
UNIVERSITA DEGLI STUDI DI ROMA. SEMINARIO DI ARCHEOLOGIA E STORIA DELL'ARTE GRECA E ROMANA. STUDI MISCELLANEI. 1961. irreg., vol.30, 1996. price varies. L'Erma di Bretschneider, Via Cassiodoro, 19, 00193 Rome, Italy. TEL 39-6-6874127. FAX 39-6-6874129.

709 GW
UNIVERSITAET BONN. SEMINAR FUER ORIENTALISCHE KUNSTGESCHICHTE. VEROEFFENTLICHUNGEN. REIHE B. ANTIQUITATES ORIENTALES. 1977. irreg. price varies. Dr. Rudolf Habelt GmbH, Am Buchenhang 1, 53115 Bonn, Germany. TEL 49-228-9238322. FAX 49-228-923836. **Document type:** monographic series.

700 AU
UNIVERSITAET INNSBRUCK. KUNSTGESCHICHTLICHE STUDIEN. (Subseries of: Universitaet Innsbruck. Veroeffentlichungen) 1972. irreg. price varies. Oesterreichische Kommissionsbuchhandlung, Maximilianstr. 17, A-6020 Innsbruck, Austria. Ed. Otto Lutterotti.

709 950 GW ISSN 0170-3692
UNIVERSITAET ZU KOELN. KUNSTHISTORISCHES INSTITUT. ABTEILUNG ASIEN. PUBLIKATIONEN. irreg., vol.6, 1990. price varies. Franz Steiner Verlag Wiesbaden GmbH, Birkenwaldstr. 44, 70191 Stuttgart, Germany. TEL 49-711-2582-0. FAX 49-711-2582390. (Subscr. to: Postfach 101061, 70009 Stuttgart, Germany) Ed.Bd. R&P contact: Sabine Koerner. **Document type:** monographic series.
Description: Asian art history.

UNIVERSITAS (GERMAN EDITION); Zeitschrift fuer interdisziplinaere Wissenschaft. see SCIENCES: COMPREHENSIVE WORKS

709 BE
UNIVERSITE CATHOLIQUE DE LOUVAIN. DEPARTEMENT D'ARCHEOLOGIE ET D'HISTOIRE DE L'ART. DOCUMENTS DE TRAVAIL. 1970. irreg., no.29, 1997. price varies. Association des Diplomes Histoire Art et Archeologie, College Erasme, Place Blaise Pascal 1, 1348 Louvain-la-Neuve, Belgium. FAX 32-10-472579. E-mail: hackens@arka.ucl.ac.be. Ed. Tony Hackens. **Document type:** monographic series.

709 913 MG
UNIVERSITE DE MADAGASCAR. MUSEE D'ART ET D'ARCHEOLOGIE. TRAVAUX ET DOCUMENTS. 1970. irreg., no.26, 1987. FMG.3000. Universite de Madagascar, Musee d'Art et d'Archeologie, B.P. 564 Isoraka, Antananarivo, Madagascar.
Description: Ancient and contemporary geography, art, history and ethnology of Madagascar.

UNIVERSITE DE POITIERS. CENTRE D'ETUDES SUPERIEURES DE CIVILISATION MEDIEVALE. PUBLICATIONS. see HISTORY

700 CN ISSN 0315-940X
UNIVERSITIES ART ASSOCIATION OF CANADA. JOURNAL/ASSOCIATION D'ART DES UNIVERSITES DU CANADA. JOURNAL. (Text in English and French) 1972. 4/yr. Can.$10. Universities Art Association of Canada, c/o Department of Fine Arts, University of Waterloo, Waterloo, ON N2L 3G1, Canada. TEL 519-888-4567. FAX 519-746-4982. E-mail: jmcoutu@artsech.watstar.uwaterloo.ca. Ed. Joan Coutu. adv.; bk.rev. circ. 350. **Document type:** newsletter.

UNIVERSITY OF CALIFORNIA AT LOS ANGELES. FOWLER MUSEUM OF CULTURAL HISTORY. MONOGRAPH SERIES. see MUSEUMS AND ART GALLERIES

UNIVERSITY OF CALIFORNIA AT LOS ANGELES. FOWLER MUSEUM OF CULTURAL HISTORY. OCCASIONAL PAPERS. see MUSEUMS AND ART GALLERIES

700 378 US
UNIVERSITY OF ILLINOIS AT URBANA-CHAMPAIGN. SCHOOL OF ART AND DESIGN. NEWSLETTER. 1951. a. free. University of Illinois at Urbana-Champaign, Continuing Education and Public Service-Visual Arts, 123 Fine and Applied Arts Bldg., Champaign, IL 61820. TEL 217-333-2439. FAX 217-244-7388. Ed. Carol Fisher. circ. 6,000 (controlled). (tabloid format)
Formerly (until 1976): University of Illinois at Urbana-Champaign. Department of Art. Newsletter (ISSN 0073-5256)
Description: Contains information on the school for faculty and students.

UNIVERSITY OF KENTUCKY ART MUSEUM NEWSLETTER. see *MUSEUMS AND ART GALLERIES*

700 AT ISSN 1322-9575
UNIVERSITY OF NEW SOUTH WALES. HANDBOOK: ART AND SOCIAL SCIENCES. 1976. a. Aus.$6. University of New South Wales, Sydney, N.S.W. 2052, Australia. TEL 61-2-385-2840. FAX 61-2-662-2163.
Former titles (until 1993): University of New South Wales. Faculty Handbooks: Art and Social Sciences (ISSN 1037-9843); (until 1992): University of New South Wales. Faculty Handbooks: Arts (ISSN 0811-7608)

700 913 780 XO ISSN 0083-4130
UNIVERZITA KOMENSKEHO. FILOZOFICKA FAKULTA. ZBORNIK: MUSAICA. (Text in Czech or Slovak; summaries in English and German) 1961. irreg. exchange basis. Univerzita Komenskeho, Filozoficka Fakulta, c/o Ustredna Kniznica Filozofickej Fakulty, Gondova 2, 818 01 Bratislava, Slovakia. circ. 700. **Document type:** academic/scholarly publication.
Description: Discusses philosophic aspects of the study and teaching of art.

700 PL ISSN 0556-1019
UNIWERSYTET IM. ADAMA MICKIEWICZA. HISTORIA SZTUKI. (Text in Polish; summaries in German or English) 1959. irreg., no.25, 1996. price varies. Adam Mickiewicz University Press, Nowowiejskiego 55, 61-734 Poznan, Poland. TEL 48-61-527380. FAX 48-61-527701. TELEX 413260 UAMPL. Pub. Maria Jankowska. R&P contact: Malgorzata Bis. **Document type:** academic/scholarly publication, monographic series.
—BLDSC (9120.470300).
Former titles (until 1969): Uniwersytet im. Adama Mickiewicza w Poznaniu. Wydzial Filozoficzno-Historyczny. Prace. Seria Historia Sztuki (ISSN 0860-1399); Uniwersytet im. Adama Mickiewicza w Poznaniu. Zeszyty Naukowe. Historia Sztuki (ISSN 0083-4270)
Description: Contains current research results of the university's scholars of history of art, their Ph.D. works and monographs. Each volume contains the work of one author.

709 PL ISSN 0083-4424
UNIWERSYTET JAGIELLONSKI. ZESZYTY NAUKOWE. PRACE Z HISTORII SZTUKI. (Text in Polish; summaries in French and Russian) 1962. irreg., no.157 1983. price varies. Uniwersytet Jagiellonski, Ul. Golegia 24, 31-007 Krakow, Poland. (Dist. by: Ars Polona, Krakowskie Przedmiescie 7, 00-068 Warsaw, Poland)

UPSTATE MAGAZINE. see *GENERAL INTEREST PERIODICALS — United States*

700 780 US
URBAN DESIRES. 1994. bi-m. 54 W. 21st St., Ste. 903, New York, NY 10010. E-mail: gaby@desires.com; URL: http://www.desires.com. Ed. Gabrielle Shannon.
●Available only online.
Description: Contains works by artists and musicians.

URBANUS MAGAZINE. see *LITERATURE*

UTTERANTS…. see *LITERATURE*

700 SW ISSN 0283-751X
VALOER; konstvetenskapliga studier. 1986. irreg. (4-5/yr.). SEK 150 (effective 1997). Foereningen Valoer, Konstvetenskapliga Institutionen, Slottet, Soedra tornet, inngaang HO, S-752 37 Uppsala, Sweden. TEL 46-18-18-28-88. FAX 46-18-18-28-92. E-mail: Britt-Inger.Johansson@konstvet.uu.se. Ed. Britt-Inger Johansson. R&P contact: Eva-Lena Karlsson. bk.rev.; circ. 500 (paid); 50 (controlled). **Document type:** academic/scholarly publication.
Description: Features articles on architecture and fine and decorative arts. Publishes results of art historical research in progress and gives accounts of conferences.
Refereed Serial

700 IT
VENEZIE FRANCESCANE; rivista di storia, arte e cultura. N.S. 1984-1989; resumed. irreg. L.25000 (foreign L.50000). Istituto Storico Francescano Venete, Via S. Francesco 118, 35121 Padua, Italy. TEL 39-49-656092. Ed. Antonio Rigon. (back issues avail.) **Document type:** monographic series.

700 BE ISSN 0042-3440
VENT - ART.* 1967. q. 40 F. c/o Jean Schwartz, 36 rue de la Laiterie, Brussels 7, Belgium. Ed. Joan Marti. adv.; illus.

VENUE MAGAZINE. see *THEATER*

VEREIN FUER VOLKSKUNDE IN WIEN. SONDERSCHRIFTEN.. see *FOLKLORE*

700 GW
VERNISSAGE. irreg. (12-15/yr.). Vereinigte Verlagsanstalten GmbH, Hoeherweg 278, 40231 Duesseldorf, Germany. TEL 49-211-7357-0. FAX 49-211-7357223. circ. 27,000. **Document type:** bulletin.

VERSCHILIG; jong kultuurtijdschrift. see *LITERARY AND POLITICAL REVIEWS*

745 US
VESTERHEIM ROSEMALING LETTER. 1968. q. $35 includes membership (Canada and Mexico $39; elsewhere $40) (effective 1997). Vesterheim Norwegian-American Museum, Box 379, 502 Water St., Decorah, IA 52101. TEL 319-382-9681. FAX 319-382-8828. Ed. Sara Tollefson. illus.; maps. circ. 1,600. (looseleaf format; back issues avail.) **Document type:** newsletter.
Description: Covers rosemaling, decorative Norwegian folk paintings.

700 800 IT ISSN 0393-6147
IL VESUVIO; fiaccola ercolanese. Variant title: Vesuv. 1964. d. $50. Via Liberta, 80040 San Sebastiano (NA), Italy. FAX 39-81-7715870. Ed. Vincenzo Ascione. adv.; bk.rev.; illus.

VETERA CHRISTIANORUM. see *ARCHAEOLOGY*

700 800 780 792.8 US ISSN 1077-6788
VICE; art and entertainment magazine. 1994. m. $36 (foreign $46); newsstand price: $2. Vice Publishing, Inc., Box 20281, New York, NY 10011-0003. TEL 212-727-2787. FAX 212-727-3190. E-mail: vice@nycnet.com. Ed. William A. Zeoli; Pub. William A. Zeoli. adv.: page $989; trim 7 3/4 x 10; adv. contact: William A. Zeoli. bk.rev.; dance rev.; film rev.; music rev.; play rev.; tele.rev.; video rev.; bibl.; illus.; tr.ut. circ. 25,000. (back issues avail.)
●Also available online.
Description: Art and entertainment magazine for gay men, thirty and over. Aims to present the arts in all their many forms while providing enlightening and lively entertainment.

VICE VERSA MAGAZINE. see *LITERATURE*

VIDEO GUIDE. see *COMMUNICATIONS — Video*

700 CN ISSN 0042-5435
NX2
VIE DES ARTS. (Text in French) 1956. q. Can.$24 (foreign Can.$39). Societe la Vie des Arts, 200 St-Jacques St., Ste. 600, Montreal, PQ H2Y 1M1, Canada. TEL 514-282-0205. FAX 514-282-0235. URL: http://www.sciencetech.com./vie.html. Ed. Bernard Levy. adv.; bk.rev.; illus.; cum.index: 1956-66, 1966-76, 1976-86, 1986-91. circ. 7,500. (also avail. in microfilm from BNQ) **Indexed:** Artbibl., Artbibl.Mod., Can.B.P.I., Can.Per.Ind., Pt.de Rep. (1979-), RADAR. **Document type:** consumer publication.
Description: Features articles on artists, the art market, and trends in contemporary art and architecture in Canada and around the world.

VIEWFINDER JOURNAL OF FOCAL POINT GALLERY. see *PHOTOGRAPHY*

VISAGES DU VINGTIEME SIECLE; revue de "La Legion Violette". see *HUMANITIES: COMPREHENSIVE WORKS*

700 720 PH ISSN 0042-692X
VISION MAGAZINE. (Text in English, Filipino) 1964. s-a. $22. University of Santo Tomas, College of Architecture and Fine Arts, Espana St., Sampaloc, Manila, Philippines. TEL 7314343. Ed. Pebbles B. Tan-Gatue. bk.rev.; charts; illus. circ. 3,000.
Description: Serves as a gallery of the students' best works. Features articles related to architecture and fine arts.

700 US ISSN 0892-6905
VISIONS: AN ART QUARTERLY.* 1986. q. $16. L A Artcore, 420 E. Third St., Ste. 110, Los Angeles, CA 90013-1644. TEL 213-628-6164. FAX 213-620-1277. Ed. Peter Frank. adv.; bk.rev.; circ. 12,000 (controlled).

741.67 301.16 SP ISSN 1133-0422
VISUAL. 11/yr. Ferraz 11, 1o Dcha., 28008 Madrid, Spain. TEL 1-541-34-00. FAX 1-248-11-23. Ed. Alvaro Sobrino. circ. 7,500.
—SWETS.

709.716 CN ISSN 0704-0512
VISUAL ARTS NEWS. 1978. q. Can.$12.50($16) (foreign Can.$18) (effective 1996-1997). Visual Arts Nova Scotia, 1809 Barrington St., Ste. 901, Halifax, NS B3J 3K8, Canada. TEL 902-423-4694. FAX 902-422-0881. E-mail: vans@fox.nstn.ca. Ed. Gil McElroy. adv. contact: Kim Goodson. circ. 650. (back issues avail.) **Document type:** newsletter.
Description: Offers features, interviews and reviews with a focus on living Nova Scotian artists. Promotes a knowledge of the artists and their work.

VISUAL ARTS RESEARCH; educational, historical, philosophical and psychological perspectives. see *EDUCATION — Teaching Methods And Curriculum*

700 NE ISSN 0197-3762
N3998 CODEN: VRVRDZ
VISUAL RESOURCES; an international journal of documentation. (Text in English and Western European languages) 1980. 4/yr. $108 (effective 1998). Gordon and Breach - Harwood Academic, Amsteldisk 166, 1st Fl., 1079 LH Amsterdam, Netherlands. (Subscr. to: International Publishers Distributor, Box 32160, Newark, NJ 07102. TEL 800-545-8398. FAX 215-750-6343) Eds. Christine L. Sundt, Helene E. Roberts. adv.; bk.rev.; illus.; index. (also avail. in microfilm; microfiche; back issues avail.) **Indexed:** Art Ind., Artbibl.Mod., INSPEC, RILA.
—BLDSC (9241.320000); KR SourceOne; UnCover. CCC.
Refereed Serial

700 020   US   ISSN 1046-9001
N72.P5
VISUAL RESOURCES ASSOCIATION BULLETIN. Variant title: V R A Bulletin. 1974. q. $55 membership (foreign individuals $70; institutions $75). Visual Resources Association, Tappan Hall, Rm. 20, History of Art Department, University of Michigan, Ann Arbor, MI 48109. TEL 313-763-6114. FAX 313-747-4123. E-mail: VRAL@UAFSYB. (Subscr. to: Lynda White, Assistant Fine Arts Librarian, Fiske Kimball Fine Arts Library, Bayly Dr., University of Virginia, Charlottesville, VA 22903) Ed. Joy Blouin. R&P contact: Joy Blouin. index. circ. 769. (back issues avail.) **Document type:** bulletin.
—BLDSC (9258.707025); UnCover.
Formerly (until 1989): International Bulletin for Photographic Documentation of the Visual Arts.
Description: Contains association news, updates readers on conferences and workshops, and provides information on various aspects of managing visual resources collections.

VISUALLY SPEAKING. see EDUCATION — Teaching Methods And Curriculum

VISWA RACHANA/WORLD WRITING; illustrated fortnightly. see LITERATURE

700   AU
VIVE LE DISCOURS DES PICTURES. 1984. irreg. no.5, 1989. DM.10. Linzergasse 8, A-5020 Salzburg, Austria. TEL 43-662-884441. Ed. Astrit Schmidt-Burkhardt. circ. 500 (paid). (back issues avail.) **Document type:** bulletin.

700   BE   ISSN 0042-7683
VLAANDEREN; tijdschrift voor kunst en cultuur. (Text mainly in Dutch; occasionally in English, French and German) 1951. bi-m. $35. Christelijk Vlaams Kunstenaarsverbond vzw, c/o Dirk Rommens, Sec., Sint-Pietersstraat 39, 8520 Kuurne, Belgium. TEL 32-56-357866. FAX 32-56-357866. E-mail: dirk.rommens@ping.be; URL: http://www.ping.be/vlaanderen. Ed. Jean-Luc Meulemeester. adv. contact: Adiel Van Daele. bk.rev.; charts; illus.; tr.lit.; index. circ. 4,000.
Formerly: West-Vlaanderen.
Description: Publishes thematic articles about art, culture, and cultural events.

740 747 688   UK
THE VOLUME FRAMER. 1986. m. free to qualified personnel. Vic Faulkner Associates, 45 Longfield Dr., Amersham., Bucks. HP6 5H6, England. TEL 44-1494-791451. FAX 44-1494-778224. E-mail: Vic_Faulkner@compuserve.com. Ed. Vic Faulkner; Pub. Vic Faulkner. adv.: page $1200; adv. contact: Vic Faulkner. bk.rev.; circ. 5,000 (controlled). (avail. only by fax; back issues avail.) **Document type:** trade publication.
Former titles: Framing and Art (ISSN 0957-929X); (until 1989): Framing, Fine Art and Wall Decor (ISSN 0952-3197); (until 1987): Framing and Wall Decor.
Description: Informs industry leaders in the volume picture framing industry on key issues and current affairs.

700   NE   ISSN 0169-6858
VORM EN INDUSTRIE IN NEDERLAND. 1984. irreg. Uitgeverij 010, Watertorenweg 180, 3063 HA Rotterdam, Netherlands. TEL 31-10-4333509. FAX 31-10-4529825.

700   US   ISSN 1051-9556
VUE.* 1985. q. $20. Vue Publishing Company, Inc., 3131 N.E. Seventh Ave., Apt. A, Miami, FL 33137-4253. TEL 908-388-8883. FAX 305-531-3301. Ed. Bob Hesson; Pub. John Caliste. adv.: B&W page $1500, color page $2000; trim 8 1/2 x 11. circ. 40,000.
Description: Covers the visual, performing, literary and design arts. Includes controversial topics and reviews and previews of events.

VYTVARNA VYCHOVA; casopis pro vytvarnou a obecne estetickouvychovu skoli a mimoskIni. see EDUCATION

700   XO   ISSN 0042-9392
VYTVARNICTVO, FOTOGRAFIA, FILM; mesacnik pre zaujmovu umelecku cinnost. (Text in Czech or Slovak; summaries in English, German, Russian) 1963. m. $58. (Osvetovy Ustav - Cultural Institute) Obzor, Spitalska ul. 35, 815 85 Bratislava, Slovakia. (Dist. by: Slovart, Gottwaldovo nam. 48, 805 32 Bratislava, Slovakia) Ed. Jaroslav Ciljak. illus.; index.

700   XO   ISSN 0139-7214
VYTVARNY ZIVOT. (Text in Czech or Slovak; summaries in English, German, Russian) 10/yr. $102. Slovenska Vytvarna Unia, Dostojeskeho rad 2, 811 09 Bratislava, Slovakia. **Indexed:** Artbibl.Mod.

700   US   ISSN 1052-0066
N8554
W A A C NEWSLETTER. 1979. 3/yr. $30 in the U.S. and Canada; elsewhere $35. Western Association for Art Conservation, 5905 Wilshire Blvd., Los Angeles, CA 90036. TEL 602-433-0461. Ed. Carolyn Tallent. bk.rev.; film rev.; bibl.; illus.; tr.lit.; cum.index: 1978-1988. circ. 400. **Document type:** newsletter.
●Also available online.
Description: Serves professionals in conservation and restoration of artistic and cultural works with news, ideas, and information.

800 792 780   MW
W A S I. (Text in English; occasionally in Chiyao) 1992. 3/yr. (Writers and Artists Services International) P.O. Box 317, Zomba, Malawi. Ed. Steve Chimombo. bk.rev.
Description: Covers art, literature, music and drama. Aims to include Chiyao language and literature, putting it on the national scene.

709   GW
WALLRAF-RICHARTZ-JAHRBUCH; WESTDEUTSCHES JAHRBUCH FUER KUNSTGESCHICHTE. NEUE FOLGE. 1924. a. DM.148. (Freunde des Wallraf-Richartz-Museums) DuMont Buchverlag, Mittelstr. 12-14, 50672 Cologne, Germany. TEL 49-221-2053246. FAX 49-221-2053294. circ. 800. **Indexed:** Artbibl.Mod., Avery Ind.Archit.Per., IBR, RILA. **Document type:** academic/scholarly publication.
—BLDSC (9261.630000); KR SourceOne.
Formerly (until 1979): Wallraf-Richartz-Jahrbuch; Westdeutsches Jahrbuch fuer Kunstgeschichte (ISSN 0083-7105)

709   US   ISSN 0083-7148
WALTER W.S. COOK ALUMNI LECTURE. 1960. irreg. $5. (New York University, Institute of Fine Arts) J. J. Augustin, Inc., Box 311, Locust Valley, NY 11560. TEL 516-676-1510. index.

708.1   US   ISSN 0043-0188
N5220
WALTERS ART GALLERY. BULLETIN. 1948. m. (10/yr.). $12 (foreign $15). Walters Art Gallery, 600 N. Charles St., Baltimore, MD 21201-5185. TEL 410-547-9000. FAX 410-783-7969. Ed. Nini Sarmiento. illus. circ. 1,000. **Indexed:** Artbibl.Mod., RILA. **Document type:** bulletin.
Description: Reviews exhibitions and events at the Walters Art Gallery.

705 709   US   ISSN 0083-7156
N5220
WALTERS ART GALLERY. JOURNAL. 1938. a. (occasionally biennial). $42 (foreign $43). Walters Art Gallery, 600 N. Charles St., Baltimore, MD 21201-5185. TEL 410-547-9000. FAX 410-783-7969. Ed. William R. Johnston. illus. circ. 1,000. **Indexed:** Art & Archaeol.Tech.Abstr., Art Ind., Artbibl.Mod., RILA. **Document type:** academic/scholarly publication.
—KR SourceOne.
Description: Covers art history, particularly that of pieces in the Walters collection.

700   US   ISSN 0043-0609
NX1
WASHINGTON INTERNATIONAL ARTS LETTER. Short title: Arts Letter. 1962. q. $124. (Allied Business Consultants, Inc.) Washington International Arts Letter, 326 N. Johnsonn St., Des Moines, IA 52245. TEL 319-358-6777. Ed. Nancy A. Fandel. bk.rev.; charts; illus. circ. 13,220. (also avail. in microform from UMI)
—UMI.

700   US   ISSN 0163-903X
WASHINGTON REVIEW. 1975. bi-m. $12 (effective 1998). Friends of the Washington Review of the Arts, Inc., Box 50132, Washington, DC 20091-0132. TEL 202-638-0515. Ed. Clarissa Wittenberg. R&P contact: Mary Swirt. adv. contact: Mary Swirt. bk.rev.; film rev.; play rev.; illus. circ. 1,500. (tabloid format; also avail. in microform; back issues avail.) **Indexed:** A.I.P.P., Amer.Hum.Ind.
Former titles: Washington Review: a Quarterly Review of the Arts; Washington Review of the Arts.
Description: Contains fiction, short stories, poetry, essays and art.

750   US   ISSN 1053-3915
ND1700
WATERCOLOR. q. $21 (Canada $46) (effective 1997); newsstand price: $5.95. B P I Communications, Inc. (New York), 1515 Broadway, New York, NY 10036. TEL 212-536-5164. FAX 212-536-5294.
Description: Showcase of specially commissioned artists and step-by-step demonstrations totally devoted to watercolor.

750   US   ISSN 1079-5936
WATERCOLOR MAGIC. 1993. q. $14.99; newsstand price: $3.99. F & W Publications, Inc., 1507 Dana Ave., Cincinnati, OH 45236. TEL 513-531-2222. FAX 513-531-1843. (Subscr. to: Box 5439, Harlan, IA 51593. TEL 800-811-9834) Ed. Sandra Carpenter; Pub. Jeffry Lapin. adv. (back issues avail.) **Document type:** consumer publication.

750   CN
WATERCOLOUR NEWS.* (Text in English, French) 3/yr. Can.$30 membership. Canadian Society of Painters in Water Colour - Societe Canadienne de Peintres en Aquarelle, 439 Wellington St. W., Toronto, ON M5V 1E7, Canada. TEL 416-638-1983. FAX 416-630-8349. Ed. Janet Baker. adv. circ. 400. (back issues avail.) **Document type:** newsletter.
Description: For professional watercolour artists and those interested in the form.

DIE WEBEREIZEITUNG. see GENERAL INTEREST PERIODICALS — Germany

WEIMAR AND NOW: GERMAN CULTURAL CRITICISM. see LITERATURE

WELTKUNST; the world art review. see ANTIQUES

WENYI BAO/LITERATURE & ART GAZETTE. see LITERATURE

700   CC   ISSN 0510-0380
WENYI XUEXI/ART STUDIES. (Text in Chinese) 1954. m. Zhongguo Wenlian Chuban Gongsi, 10 Nongzhuguan Nanli, Beijing 100026, People's Republic of China. TEL 5005588.

WENYI YANJIU/LITERATURE AND ART STUDIES. see LITERATURE

WEST COAST PEDDLER; oldest journal of antiques, art & collectibles in the Pacific states. see ANTIQUES

700   US   ISSN 0043-3357
N6530.C2
WESTART; West Coast's art news scene. 1962. s-m. $16. WestArt Publications, Box 6868, Auburn, CA 95604. Ed. Martha Garcia; Pub. Bud Pisarek. adv.: page $420; adv. contact: Martha Garcia. bk.rev.; illus.; circ. 4,000 (paid). (tabloid format; also avail. in microform from UMI; reprint service avail. from UMI) **Indexed:** Cal.Per.Ind. (1978-). **Document type:** newspaper, trade publication.
—UMI.

700   CN   ISSN 1191-3371
WESTBRIDGE ART MARKET REPORT; the newsletter for fine art collectors and investors. 1974. bi-m. Can.$54($54) (foreign $86). Westbridge Publications, 2339 Granville St., Vancouver, BC V6H 3G4, Canada. TEL 604-736-1014. FAX 604-734-4944. Ed. Anthony R. Westbridge. adv.; bk.rev. circ. 500. (back issues avail.) **Document type:** newsletter.
Former titles (until 1992): Fine Art and Auction Review (ISSN 0833-0891); Antiques and Art (ISSN 0703-5748); Antiques Gazette.

700 800 280 770   US   ISSN 0508-6191
WESTWIND (LOS ANGELES); U C L A's journal of the arts. 1957. a. $15 (foreign $20). University of California at Los Angeles, A-265 Murphy Hall, 405 Hilgard Ave., Los Angeles, CA 90095. TEL 310-206-1225. E-mail: westwind@hup.ucla.edu. R&P contact: Paul Hellyer. adv.: page $140; 9 x 6; adv. contact: Paul Hellyer. circ. 1,100. **Document type:** academic/scholarly publication.
Refereed Serial

700   UK   ISSN 0269-9214
WESTWORDS. 1987. 2/yr. £5. 15 Trelawney Rd., Peverell, Plymouth, Devonshire PL3 4JS, England. TEL 0752-262877. Ed. David Woolley. adv.; bk.rev. circ. 450. (back issues avail.)

WHAT DID I EAT LAST NIGHT?. see *LITERATURE*

700
WHAT'S UP AT CHEEKWOOD. 1961. bi-m. membership. Tennessee Botanical Gardens & Museum of Art, 1200 Forrest Park Dr., Nashville, TN 37205. TEL 615-353-2163. FAX 615-353-2168. Ed. Martha Farabee. adv. contact: Sherry Brown. circ. 7,400. **Document type:** newsletter.
Former titles: Cheekwood - Tennessee Botanical Gardens and Museum of Art; Cheekwood - Tennessee Botanical Gardens and Fine Arts Center (Calendar); Cheekwood Mirror.
Description: Informs members of happenings and exhibits at Cheekwood.
Refereed Serial

WHETSTONE (BARRINGTON). see *LITERATURE*

500   US   ISSN 0190-9835
N1
WHITE WALLS; a journal of language and art. 1978. 3/yr. $15 to individuals (overseas $30); institutions $18 (overseas $35) (effective 1994). White Walls, Inc., Box 8204, Chicago, IL 60680. TEL 312-528-1526. Ed. Mary Patten. adv.: B&W page $180. circ. 1,400. (back issues avail.) **Indexed:** Artbibl.Mod. **Document type:** monographic series.
Description: Run by artists, supports and publishes artwork that explores relationships between language, visual arts, and contemporary culture.

WHOLE ARTS DIRECTORY. see *BUSINESS AND ECONOMICS — Trade And Industrial Directories*

WHO'S WHO IN ART. see *BIOGRAPHY*

706.5   US
WHO'S WHO IN ART MATERIALS. a. $110 to non-members. National Art Materials Trade Association, 178 Lakeview Ave., Clifton, NJ 07011. TEL 201-546-6400. FAX 201-546-0393. Ed. John R. Luciano. circ. 2,000. **Document type:** trade publication, directory.
Description: Geared to manufacturers and representatives, retailers, wholesalers, importers and publishers of art materials.

700   AU   ISSN 0083-9981
N9
WIENER JAHRBUCH FUER KUNSTGESCHICHTE. (Text in English and German) 1921. a. (Bundesdenkmalamt Wien) Boehlau Verlag GmbH & Co.KG., Sachsenplatz 4-6, A-1201 Vienna, Austria. TEL 43-1-3302427-0. FAX 43-1-3302432. TELEX 114-506-SPRIW-A. (Co-sponsor: Universitaet Wien. Kunsthistorisches Institut) Eds. E. Frodl-Kraft, G. Schmidt. bk.rev.; illus. circ. 500. **Indexed:** Artbibl.Mod., IBR, RILA. **Document type:** academic/scholarly publication.

700   AU
WIENZEILE; internationales kunstmagazin. q. V I Z A Literaturfoerderungsverein, Hahngasse 15, A-1090 Vienna, Austria. TEL 01-315222. Ed.Bd. circ. 3,000. **Document type:** consumer publication.

WILBOUR MONOGRAPHS. see *HISTORY*

700   US   ISSN 1084-7855
N7660
WILDLIFE ART. 1982. bi-m. $32.95. Pothole Publications, Inc., Box 16246, St. Louis Park, MN 55416-0246. TEL 612-927-9056; 800-221-6547. FAX 612-927-9056. Ed. Robert J. Koenke; Pub. Robert J. Koenke. adv. contact: Pat Jewett. bk.rev.; circ. 55,000 (paid). **Document type:** consumer publication.
—UnCover.
Formerly: Wildlife Art News (ISSN 0746-9640)
Description: For wildlife art collectors. Contains interviews with artists, a calendar of events and business news.

700 975   US
WILLIAMSBURG DECORATIVE ARTS SERIES. 1974. irreg., latest 1997. price varies. Colonial Williamsburg Foundation, Box 1776, Williamsburg, VA 23187-1776. TEL 757-220-7342.

WINDHAM PHOENIX. see *LITERATURE*

WINDSCRIPT. see *LITERATURE*

WISCONSIN ACADEMY OF SCIENCES, ARTS AND LETTERS. TRANSACTIONS. see *SCIENCES: COMPREHENSIVE WORKS*

WISCONSIN ACADEMY REVIEW. see *LITERARY AND POLITICAL REVIEWS*

WITTENBERG REVIEW OF LITERATURE AND ART. see *LITERATURE*

741.5   US   ISSN 0892-9807
NC1300
WITTYWORLD; international cartoon bulletin. (Includes a magazine and 11 bulletins.) 1987. 11/yr. $56 (foreign $64) (effective 1997). WittyWorld Publications, 214 School St., North Wales, PA 19454. TEL 215-699-2626. FAX 215-699-0627. (Box 1458, North Wales, PA 19454) Ed. Joseph George Szabo; Pub. Joseph George Szabo. adv. contact: Flora Toth. bk.rev.; video rev.; illus. circ. 5,000. **Document type:** trade publication, bulletin.
Description: Covers all aspects of cartooning art: political, comic strip, animation, and caricature. Includes interviews with leading cartoonists, dates and reports on competitions, and examples of cartoons.

WOMAN OF POWER; a magazine of feminism, spirituality, and politics. see *WOMEN'S STUDIES*

700   US   ISSN 0270-7993
N72.F45
WOMAN'S ART JOURNAL. 1980. s-a. $16 to individuals; institutions $25 (effective 1997). Woman's Art, Inc., 1711 Harris Rd., Laverock, PA 19038-7208. TEL 215-233-0639. FAX 215-233-0639. Ed. Elsa Honig Fine; Pub. Elsa Honig Fine. adv.; bk.rev. circ. 4,000. (also avail. in microform from UMI; back issues avail.) **Indexed:** Art Ind., Artbibl.Mod., Arts & Hum.Cit.Ind., ASCA, Curr.Cont., Fem.Per., RILA. **Document type:** academic/scholarly publication.
—BLDSC (9343.171900); Genuine Article; KR SourceOne; UMI; UnCover.
Description: Covers women in all areas of the visual arts. Each issue features articles ranging in subject from antiquity to the present, along with about 20 book and catalogue reviews.
Refereed Serial

704.042   US
N6512
WOMEN ARTISTS NEWS BOOK REVIEW. 1975. a. $6 to individuals; institutions $7 (effective 1997). (Midmarch Associates) Midmarch Arts Press, 300 Riverside Drive, New York, NY 10025. TEL 212-666-6990. Ed. Sylvia Moore. adv.; bk.rev.; illus.; index. circ. 5,000. (back issues avail.) **Indexed:** Alt.Press Ind., Art Ind., Artbibl., Artbibl.Mod., Fem.Per., RILA. **Document type:** trade publication.
—KR SourceOne; UnCover.
Former titles: Women Artists News (ISSN 0149-7081); N A W A News; Women Artist Newsletter (ISSN 0361-9117)
Description: Includes essays on art, women artists, women's issues and literature.

700   US   ISSN 1058-7217
N858.N36
WOMEN IN THE ARTS. 1983. q. membership. National Museum of Women in the Arts, 1250 New York Ave. N.W., Washington, DC 20005-3920. TEL 202-783-5000. FAX 202-393-3234. URL: http://www.nmwa.org. Ed. Laureen Schipsi. R&P contact: Randi Greenberg. adv. contact: Mary-Frances Wain. circ. 60,000 (controlled). **Document type:** academic/scholarly publication.
Formerly (until 1991): National Museum of Women in the Arts News (ISSN 0891-1827)
Description: Provides information on museum activities related to promoting knowledge about women in the arts, notices of exhibitions across the country of works by women artsts, and articles on women's contributions to the arts.

700 301.412   US
WOMEN IN THE ARTS NEWSLETTER. 1971. bi-m. $9 to individuals; institutions $15 (foreign $19). Women in the Arts Foundation, Inc., 1175 York Ave., No. 2G, c/o R. Crown, New York, NY 10021. TEL 212-751-1915. FAX 212-751-1915. Ed. Erin Butler. adv.; bk.rev. circ. 300. **Document type:** newsletter.
Formerly: Women in the Arts Bulletin - Newsletter.

700 301.412   US
WOMEN'S CAUCUS FOR ART. HONOR AWARDS CATALOGUE. 1980. a. $8 to non-members. Women's Caucus for Art, Moore College of Art, 20th & The Parkway, Philadelphia, PA 19103. TEL 215-854-0922. bibl. circ. 4,000. (back issues avail.) **Document type:** catalog.
Description: Honors five women for their life work in the visual arts. Includes essays and a chronology.

700 301.412   US   ISSN 1052-4959
NX180.F4
WOMEN'S CAUCUS FOR ART. NATIONAL UPDATE. 1978. q. membership. Women's Caucus for Art, Moore College of Art, 20th & The Parkway, Philadelphia, PA 19103. TEL 215-854-0922. circ. 4,000. (tabloid format)
Description: Contains information of interest to women in all visual arts professions. Includes short articles and new material, as well as job listings and exhibition opportunities.

709.94   SZ   ISSN 1321-0505
WORLD ART. 1994. q. 84 SFr.; newsstand price: 16 SFr. G & B Arts International Ltd., St. Johanns Vorstadt 19, Postfach, CH-4004 Basel, Switzerland. TEL 41-61-2610138. FAX 41-61-2610173. Eds. Ray Edgar, Sarah Bayliss; Pub. Ashley Crawford. adv. contact: Anna Mayo. bk.rev.; illus. circ. 20,000. **Document type:** consumer publication.
Description: Presents issues and developments in contemporary arts and visual culture. Includes international artist profiles and interviews.

700 790   NE   ISSN 0084-1498
WORLD COLLECTORS ANNUARY. (Text in English) 1950. a., latest vol.44 (for years 1993-1995). $195. World Collectors Publishers, P.O. Box 23, 6500 AA Nijmegen, Netherlands. FAX 31-243-237747. Ed. M.J. van Laake. adv.; cum.index (1946-1982). circ. 1,000.
Description: Alphabetical listing of each object (painting, drawing, pastel, gouache, and watercolor) sold at auction, with price realized (and conversion into U.S. dollars), factual and scholarly description, and provenance index.

WORLD CULTURAL GUIDES. see *TRAVEL AND TOURISM*

700 745.1   US
WORLD FINE ART. 1982. bi-m. $75 (effective 1996 & 1997). Art Baron Management Corp., Box 5365, Scottsdale, AZ 85261. TEL 602-957-3215. Ed. Steve Shipp; Pub. Jeff Coffin. R&P contact: Steve Shipp. bk.rev. **Document type:** newsletter.

700   IS
WORLD OF ART. (Text in Hebrew) 1977. s-a. IS.60($30) World of Art Inc., 190 Ben-Yehuda St., Tel Aviv 63471, Israel. TEL 3-5237115. FAX 3-5272570. Ed. Joseph A. Melamed. adv.; bk.rev. circ. 4,000. (back issues avail.) **Indexed:** Ind.Heb.Per.

THE WORLD OF TRIBAL ARTS. see *MUSEUMS AND ART GALLERIES*

474 ART

700　　　　　　PL　ISSN 0084-2982
WROCLAWSKIE TOWARZYSTWO NAUKOWE. KOMISJA HISTORII SZTUKI. ROZPRAWY. (Text in Polish; summaries in English and French) 1960. irreg., vol.12, 1991. price varies. Wroclawskie Towarzystwo Naukowe, Komisja Historii Sztuki, Ul. Parkowa 13, 50-016 Wroclaw, Poland. TEL 48-71-484061. circ. 1,000. **Document type:** monographic series.
   Description: Monographs and studies in Polish painting, sculpture, artistics industry and handicraft on comparative background.

WYDZIAL FILOLOGICZNO-FILOZOFICZNY. PRACE. see *PHILOSOPHY*

730　　　　　　PL　ISSN 0860-9071
WYZSZA SZKOLA PEDAGOGICZNA IM. KOMISJI EDUKACJI NARODOWEJ W KRAKOWIE. ROCZNIK NAUKOWO-DYDAKTYCZNY. PRACE Z WYCHOWANIA PLASTYCZNEGO. 1988. irreg. price varies. Wydawnictwo Naukowe W S P, Ul. Karmelicka 41, 31-128 Krakow, Poland. TEL 33-78-20. (Co-sponsor: Ministerstwo Edukacji Nrodowej)

XALMAN. see *LITERATURE*

XERO; quaderni di Heliopolis, see *LITERATURE — Poetry*

700　　　　　　CC
XIN MEISHU/NEW FINE ART. (Text in Chinese) q. Zhejiang Meishu Xueyuan - Zhejiang Academy of Fine Art, Hangzhou, Zhejiang 310002, People's Republic of China. TEL 774348. Ed. Xiao Feng.

700　　　　　　CC
XIZANG YISHU YANJIU/TIBETAN ART STUDIES. (Editions in Chinese, Tibetan) Chinese ed. q.; Tibetan ed. s-a. Y20 (foreign $24) for Chinese ed.; Tibetan ed. Y10 (foreign $12). Xizang Zizhiqu Minzu Yishu Yanjiusuo, Wenhuating Yuan Nei, 2 Duodi Lu, Lhasa, Xizang (Tibet) 850000, People's Republic of China. TEL 6326538. (Dist. overseas by: Jiangsu Publications Import & Export Corp., 56 Gao Yun Ling, Nanjing, Jiangsu, P.R.C.) Eds. Liu Zhiqun, Da Wa Sang Bu.
   Description: Covers Tibetan culture, including music and dance, literature, painting and artists.

700 792　　　　　AT　ISSN 0817-4628
XPRESS.* 1986. bi-m. Aus.$48. A & E Xpress, P.O. Box 1195, Potts Point, N.S.W. 2011, Australia. TEL 02 358 4077. (Subscr. to: P.O. Box 1195, Potts Point, N.S.W. 2011, Australia) Ed. Alexandra Morphett. adv.; bk.rev. (back issues avail.)
   Description: Discusses popular culture topics including art, fashion design and theatre.

700　　　　　　US　ISSN 0084-3415
YALE PUBLICATIONS IN THE HISTORY OF ART. 1939. irreg., latest 1992. price varies. Yale University Press, Box 209040, New Haven, CT 06520. TEL 203-432-0940.

YAPI; aylik kultur, sanat ve mimarlik dergisi. see *ARCHITECTURE*

700 801　　　　　US　ISSN 1074-5629
YEFIEF; a narrative of culture at the end of the century. 1994. a. $9 (foreign $12) (effective 1998). Images for Media, Box 8505, Santa Fe, NM 87504. TEL 505-753-3648. FAX 505-753-7049. E-mail: arr@imagesformedia.com; URL: http://www.imagesformedia.com. Ed. Ann Racuya-Robbins; Pub. Ann Racuya-Robbins. R&P contact: Ann Racuya-Robbins. adv. contact: Ann Racuya-Robbins. bk.rev. circ. 2,000. (back issues avail.) **Document type:** trade publication.
   Description: Containing fine art, literature and new forms. Constructed to create a narrative of culture at the end of the century, a narrative that draws on the diversity of contemporary life to ask, When we speak what language do we make?

YINGJU YISHU/ART OF FILM AND DRAMA. see *MOTION PICTURES*

700　　　　　　CC　ISSN 1003-9104
YISHU BAIJIA/HUNDRED SCHOOLS IN ART. (Text in Chinese) 1985. q. $50. Jiangsu Sheng Wenhua Yishu Yanjiusuo - Jiangsu Provincial Institute of Culture and Art, 1 Qingdao Lu, Nanjing, Jiangsu 210008, People's Republic of China. TEL 86-25-6632175. Ed. Weidong Su. R&P contact: Weidong Su. adv.: page $600; adv. contact: Shangxian Zheng. bk.rev. circ. 3,000. **Document type:** academic/scholarly publication.
   Refereed Serial

700　　　　　　CC
YISHU SHIJIE/ART WORLD. (Text in Chinese) bi-m. Y8.40($24.30) Shanghai Wenyi Chubanshe, 74 Shaoxing Lu, Shanghai 200020, People's Republic of China. TEL 372608. (Dist. outside China by: China International Book Trading Corp., P.O. Box 399, Beijing, P.R.C.; Dist. in US by: China Books & Periodicals, Inc., 2929 24th St., San Francisco, CA 94110. TEL 415-282-2994) Eds. Nie Wenhui, Tang Zongliang. adv.; illus.

700　　　　　　CC
YISHU YU SHIDAI. (Text in Chinese) bi-m. Hubei Sheng Wenlian, 1 Dongting 2 Lu, Donghu, Wuchang, Wuhan, Hubei 430071, People's Republic of China. TEL 356377. Ed. Chen Dongcheng.

700　　　　　　CC
YISHUJIA/ARTIST. (Text in Chinese) bi-m. Y1.50 per no. (Tianjin Wenxue Yishujie Lianhehui - Tianjin Federation of the Literary and Art Circle) Yishujia Zazhishe, 237 Xinhua Lu, Heping Qu, Tianjin 300040, People's Republic of China. Ed. Feng Jicai. illus.
   Description: Presents profiles, interviews, and biographical articles about Chinese and foreign artists in all media. Also contains articles and discussion on issues pertaining to art and society.

700　　　　　　CH　ISSN 1016-4170
YISHUJIA/ARTIST. (Text in Chinese) 1975. m. NT.$2300($87) (effective Jan. 1995). Artist Magazine, 6F, 147 Chungking S. Rd. Sec. 1, Taipei, Taiwan, Republic of China. TEL 02-371-9692. FAX 02-331-7096. Ed. Flora Yang; Pub. Ho Cheng Kuang. adv.: color page $550; adv. contact: Grace Huang. bk.rev.; illus. circ. 22,000.

700　　　　　　UK　ISSN 0951-9084
YORKSHIRE ARTSCENE. 1976. 10/yr. £12. (Yorkshire and Humberside Arts) White Knight Music Ltd., Dean Clough Industrial Park, Halifax, W. Yorks HX3 5AX, England. TEL 44-1422-322527. FAX 44-1422-322518. Ed. Vic Allen. adv.: B&W page £385, color page £655; adv. contact: David Nesbitt. bk.rev.; abstr.; bibl.; film rev.; illus.; music rev.; play rev. circ. 25,000. (back issues avail.) **Document type:** consumer publication.
   Formerly (until 1986): Arts Yorkshire (ISSN 0264-7699)

YUNYI KHUDOZHNIK. see *CHILDREN AND YOUTH — For*

730　　　　　　CC　ISSN 1001-3296
ZAOXING YISHU YANJIU. (Subseries of: Fuyin Baokan Ziliao) (Text in Chinese) 1978. q. $30.02. Zhongguo Renmin Daxue, Shubao Ziliao Zhongxin - China People's University, Book & Newspaper Information Center, 3 Zhang Zizhong Rd., P.O. Box 1122, Beijing 100007, People's Republic of China. TEL 86-10-4015080. (Dist. in US by: China Publications Service, Box 49614, Chicago, IL 60649. TEL 312-288-3291. FAX 312-288-8570) pp./issue: 120.
   Description: Covers paintings, calligraphy, sculpture, handcrafts, photography and other art forms.

709　　　　　　YU　ISSN 0514-616X
ZBORNIK ZASTITE SPOMENIKA KULTURE/RECUEIL DES TRAVAUX SUR LA PROTECTION DES MONUMENTS HISTORIQUES. 1950. a. Republicki Zavod za Zastitu Spomenika Kulture, Kalegdan 14, Belgrade, Yugoslavia. Ed. Jovan Sekulic.

700　　　　　　SZ
ZEICHNEN UND GESTALT. (Supplement to: Schweizerische Lehrerzeitung) 1912. 3/yr. 6 SFr. Gesellschaft Schweizerischer Zeichenlehrer, Im Geeren 7, CH-8112 Otelfingen, Switzerland. TEL 01-8441209. Ed. M. Poertner-Hayoz. circ. 1,000. **Document type:** bulletin.

ZEITSCHRIFT FUER AESTHETIK UND ALLGEMEINE KUNSTWISSENSCHAFT. see *PHILOSOPHY*

709　　　　　　GW　ISSN 0044-2992
N3
ZEITSCHRIFT FUER KUNSTGESCHICHTE. (Text in English, French, German and Italian) 1932. 4/yr. DM.190.20 (foreign DM.192) (effective 1996). Deutscher Kunstverlag GmbH, Nymphenburgerstr. 84, 80636 Munich, Germany. TEL 49-89-121516-0. FAX 49-89-12151616. Ed.Bd. bk.rev.; charts; illus.; index. circ. 900. (reprint service avail. from KTO) **Indexed:** Amer.Hist.& Life (1987-), Art Ind., Artbibl.Mod.; Arts & Hum.Cit.Ind., ASCA, Avery Ind.Archit.Per., Curr.Cont., Hist.Abstr. (1987-), IBR, Ind.Bk.Rev.Hum., New Test.Abstr., RILA. **Document type:** academic/scholarly publication.
   —Genuine Article; KR SourceOne; SWETS. **CCC**.

700　　　　　　GW　ISSN 0931-7198
N8554
ZEITSCHRIFT FUER KUNSTTECHNOLOGIE UND KONSERVIERUNG. 1987. s-a. DM.90. (Deutscher Restauratorenverbandes e.V.) Wernersche Verlagsgesellschaft mbH, Liebfrauenring 17-19, 67547 Worms, Germany. TEL 06241-43574. FAX 06241-45564. Ed. Juergen Hirschauer. adv. contact: Juergen Hirschauer. **Document type:** bulletin.
   —BLDSC (9468.430000).

704.918　　　　　GW　ISSN 0930-6897
NX655
ZEITSCHRIFT FUER OSTKIRCHLICHE KUNST HERMENEIA; Beitraege zu Kultur und Kunst, Ikonen und Theologie des christlichen Ostens. 1985. q. DM.70. Typos Verlag, Gruener Weg 40a, 44791 Bochum, Germany. TEL 49-234-501932. FAX 49-234-503576. E-mail: 101763.2306@compuserve.com. Ed. Nikolaus Thon. R&P contact: Nikolaus Thon. adv. contact: Kerstin Keller. bk.rev. circ. 1,000. (back issues avail.) **Document type:** academic/scholarly publication.
   Description: Presents information on all aspects of Orthodox and Eastern Orthodox sacred art, hagiography, liturgy and liturgical music.

ZEITSCHRIFT FUER SCHWEIZERISCHE ARCHAEOLOGIE UND KUNSTGESCHICHTE/REVUE SUISSE D'ART ET D'ARCHEOLOGIE. see *ARCHAEOLOGY*

760　　　　　　CC　ISSN 1005-0787
ZHONGGUO BANHUA. (Text in Chinese) q. Renmin Meishu Chubanshe - People's Fine Arts Publishers, 32 Beizongbu Hutong, Beijing 100735, People's Republic of China. TEL 5122583. Ed. Liu Yushan.
   Formerly: Banhua Shijie.

750　　　　　　CC
ZHONGGUO HUA/CHINESE PAINTING. (Text in Chinese) 1957. q. (Zhongguo Beijing Huayuan) Zhongguo Hua Bianjibu, 13 Yu'er Hutong, Di'anmen, Beijing 100009, People's Republic of China. TEL 86-10-4040179. FAX 86-10-4035322. (Dist. in US by: China Books & Periodicals, Inc., 2929 24th St., San Francisco, CA 94110. TEL 415-282-2994. FAX 415-282-0994) Ed. Wen Guanwang. **Document type:** academic/scholarly publication.
   Description: Focuses on traditional Chinese painting and artists.

740　　　　　　CC
ZHONGGUO LIANHUANHUA/CHINESE PICTURE STORIES. (Text in Chinese) m. Zhongguo Lianhuanhua Chubanshe, 7 Banqiao Nanxiang, Beixinqiao, Beijing 100007, People's Republic of China. TEL 4014830. Ed. Jiang Weipu.

741.5　　　　　CC　ISSN 1005-6955
ZHONGGUO MANHUA/CHINA CARTOONS. (Text in Chinese) bi-m. $16.20. Tianjin Renmin Meishu Chubanshe - Tianjin People's Fine Art Publishing House, 150 Machang Dao, Heping Qu, Tianjin 300050, People's Republic of China. TEL 86-2-3313358. (Dist. overseas by: China International Book Trading Corp., P.O. Box 399, Beijing 100044, P.R. China) Ed. Liu Jingping.

741.61　　　　　US
ZHONGGUO SHUFA/CHINESE CALLIGRAPHY. (Text in Chinese) bi-m. $30.50. Zhongguo Zhufajia Xiehui, 2 Shatan Beijie, Beijing 100009, People's Republic of China. (Dist. overseas by: China International Book Trading Corp., P.O. Box 399, Beijing 100044, P.R. China; Dist. in US by: China Books & Periodicals, Inc., 2929 24th St., San Francisco, CA 94110. TEL 415-282-2994. FAX 415-282-0994) illus.

750		CC	

ZHONGGUO SHUHUA/CHINESE CALLIGRAPHY AND PAINTING. (Text in Chinese; table of contents in English) m. Y96. Renmin Meishu Chubanshe, 32 Beizongbu Hutong, Beijing 100735, People's Republic of China. TEL 5122583. Ed. Shen Peng. illus. (tabloid format)
Description: Covers Chinese painting.

700		CC	ISSN 1003-0433

ZHONGGUO YISHU/CHINESE ART. (Text in Chinese) q. Renmin Meishu Chubanshe, 32 Beizongbu Hutong, Beijing 100735, People's Republic of China. TEL 5122375. Ed. Chen Yunhe.

750		CC	ISSN 1005-6920

ZHONGGUO YOUHUA/CHINA OIL PAINTING. (Text in Chinese) q. $26.60. Tianjin Renmin Meishu Chubanshe - Tianjin People's Fine Art Publishing House, 150 Machang Dao, Heping Qu, Tianjin 300050, People's Republic of China. TEL 86-2-3313358. FAX 86-2-3313358. (Dist. overseas by: China International Book Trading Corp., P.O. Box 399, Beijing 100044, P.R. China) Ed. Du Ziling.

740		US	ISSN 0412-3662

ZHUANGSHI/DECORATION. (Text in Chinese) q. (Zhongyang Gongyi Meishu Xueyuan) China Books & Periodicals, Inc., Beijing, People's Republic of China. (Dist. overseas by: China International Book Trading Corp., P.O. Box 399, Beijing 399, P.R. China; China Books & Periodicals, Inc., 2929 24th St., San Francisco, CA 94110. TEL 415-282-2994. FAX 415-282-0994) illus. pp./issue; 56.
Description: Covers decorative art and design as well as advertising designs

ZIPZAP. see *LITERATURE*

700		FR	ISSN 0044-4952
N2			

ZODIAQUE. 1951. q. 430 F. (foreign 481 F.). Editions Zodiaque, Abbaye de la Pierre Qui Vire, F-89630 St. Leger Vauban, France. TEL 86-32-21-23. FAX 86-32-22-33. Ed. Nicolas Maire. bk.rev.; index. circ. 10,000. (back issues avail.) Indexed: Artbibl.Mod.

760		JA	ISSN 0387-5512
QA90			

ZUGAKU KENKYU/JOURNAL OF GRAPHIC SCIENCE OF JAPAN. (Text in Japanese; summaries in English) 1967. s-a. Nihon Zugakkai - Japan Society for Graphic Science, c/o Tokyo Daigaku Kyoyogakubu, 8-1, Komaba 3-chome, Meguro-ku, Tokyo 153, Japan. abstr. Indexed: Jap.Per.Ind.

740		NE	

ZWART EN WIT. 3/yr. fl.60. Ravenberg Pers, Paasberg 26, 6862 CC Oosterbeek, Netherlands. circ. 500.

ZYZZYVA. see *LITERATURE*

790 900		FR	ISSN 0181-687X

4 TAXIS. (Text in English, French, Spanish) 1978. q. 490 F. (foreign 680 F.). Michel Aphesbero, Ed. & Pub., 3 rue Canihac, 33000 Bordeaux, France. TEL 56-92-74-60. adv.; illus. circ. 1,000.

700		US	

▼**15 CREDIBILITY STREET.** 1995. q. Wright Hall, Smith College, Northampton, MA 01063. E-mail: tshortel@sophia.smith.edu; URL: http://www.smith.edu/15cst. Ed. Timothy Shortell.
●Available online only.
Description: Publishes innovative, modern art and theory, including graphic art, music, poetry, short fiction, essays and manifestoes.

759.05		NE	

19TH CENTURY MASTERS. (Text in Dutch, English) 1993. irreg., vol.2, 1993. fl.27.85 per no. (Van Gogh Museum) Waanders Uitgevers, Postbus 1129, 8001 BC Zwolle, Netherlands. TEL 31-38-4658628. FAX 31-38-4655989. illus.
Document type: monographic series.

760		US	

100 SHOW.* 1979. a. $30. American Center for Design, 325 W. Huron St., Ste. 711, Chicago, IL 60610-3617. TEL 312-787-2018. FAX 312-649-9518. (Dist. in the U.S. by: Watson-Guptill Publications, 1695 Oak St., Lakewood, NJ 08701. TEL 800-451-1741. FAX 908-363-0338) Document type: trade publication.
Description: Reproduces the 100 graphic designs, from all areas of specialty, that won rigorous industry competitions.

360 DEGREES: ART & LITERARY REVIEW. see *LITERATURE*

2029 MAGAZIN. see *PHOTOGRAPHY*

ART — Abstracting, Bibliographies, Statistics

016.7516		US	
AM141			

AMERICAN INSTITUTE FOR CONSERVATION OF HISTORIC AND ARTISTIC WORKS. ABSTRACTS OF PAPERS PRESENTED AT THE ANNUAL MEETING. Key Title: Abstracts of Papers Presented at the Annual Meeting- American Institute for Conservation of Historic and Artistic Works. a. $10 (price varies). American Institute for Conservation of Historic and Artistic Works, 1717 K St., N.W., Ste. 301, Washington, DC 20006. TEL 202-452-9545. FAX 202-452-9328. E-mail: infoAIC@aol.com; URL: http://palimpsest.stanford.edu/aic/. circ. 1,200. Indexed: Art & Archaeol.Tech.Abstr. **Document type:** abstracting/indexing.
Formerly: American Institute for Conservation of Historic and Artistic Works. Preprints of Papers Presented at the Annual Meeting (ISSN 0272-3727)

ANNUAL REGISTER OF BOOK VALUES - THE ARTS & ARCHITECTURE. see *PUBLISHING AND BOOK TRADE — Abstracting, Bibliographies, Statistics*

700 571 016		US	ISSN 0004-2994
AM1			CODEN: AATABU

ART AND ARCHAEOLOGY TECHNICAL ABSTRACTS; abstracts of the technical literature on archaeology and the fine arts. (Text in English; titles in English and original languages) 1955. s-a. $75 to individuals; institutions $125 (effective 1997). Getty Conservation Institute, 1200 Getty Center Dr., Ste. 700, Los Angeles, CA 90049-1657. TEL 310-440-7325. FAX 310-440-7702. (Co-sponsor: International Institute for Conservation of Historic and Artistic Works (London)) index. circ. 1,200. Indexed: AESIS, Chem.Abstr., Forest Prod.Abstr., RILA, Text.Tech.Dig., World Surf.Coat., World Surf.Coat. **Document type:** abstracting/indexing.
—BLDSC (1733.350000).
Formerly: I I C Abstracts.

016 700 720		US	

ART AND ARCHITECTURE BIBLIOGRAPHIES. 1973. irreg., no.5, 1978. price varies. Hennessey & Ingalls, Inc., 8321 Campion Dr., Los Angeles, CA 90045. TEL 310-458-9074. FAX 310-394-2928. (And: 1254 Third St. Promenade, Santa Monica, CA 90401) **Document type:** bibliography.

700 016		US	ISSN 0004-3222
Z5937			

ART INDEX. CD-ROM edition (US ISSN 1076-7290) 1929. q. (with a. cumulations); m. on CD-ROM. service basis for print version; $1495 for CD-ROM. H.W. Wilson Co., 950 University Ave., Bronx, NY 10452. TEL 718-588-8400; 800-367-6770. FAX 718-590-1617. TELEX 4990003HWILSON. Ed. Alison Dickey. (also avail. in magnetic tape)
Document type: abstracting/indexing.
●Also available online. Vendor(s): Knight-Ridder Information, Inc., OCLC, Ovid Technologies, Inc., Wilsonline (File ART).
Also available on CD-ROM. Producer(s): SilverPlatter Information, Inc., H.W. Wilson (WILSONDISC).
—BLDSC (1733.450000); UnCover.
Description: Author and subject index to domestic and foreign art periodicals and museum bulletins covering archaeology, architecture, art history, city planning, crafts, graphic arts, industrial design, and interior design.

700 016		UK	ISSN 0307-9961
Z5937			

ARTBIBLIOGRAPHIES CURRENT TITLES. 1972. bi-m. price varies. A B C - Clio Ltd., 35A Great Clarendon St., Oxford OX2 6AT, England. TEL 44-1865-311350. FAX 44-1865-311358. (All subscr. to: A B C - Clio, 130 Cremona, Box 1911, Santa Barbara, CA 93116-1911. TEL 805-968-1911. FAX 805-685-9685) Ed. Tony Sloggett. **Document type:** abstracting/indexing, bibliography.
Description: Provides tables of contents to key art journals.

700 016		UK	ISSN 0300-466X
Z5935			

ARTBIBLIOGRAPHIES MODERN. 1969. s-a. price varies. A B C - Clio Ltd., 35A Great Clarendon St., Oxford OX2 6AT, England. TEL 44-1865-311350. FAX 44-1865-311358. (All subscr. to: A B C - Clio, 130 Cremona, Box 1911, Santa Barbara, CA 93116-1911. TEL 805-968-1911. FAX 805-685-9685) Ed. Tony Sloggett. **Document type:** abstracting/indexing, bibliography.
●Also available online. Vendor(s): Knight-Ridder Information, Inc. (File no.56).
Also available on CD-ROM.
Supersedes: L O M A Literature on Modern Art (ISSN 0090-7235)
Description: Indexes and abstracts current literature on 20th century art and design.

001.3 016		US	ISSN 0162-8445
Al3			

ARTS & HUMANITIES CITATION INDEX. Short title: A & H C I. (Includes: Source Index, Citation Index, Corporate Index, and Permuterm Subject Index) 1976. 3/yr. including annual cum. $6490. Institute for Scientific Information, 3501 Market St., Philadelphia, PA 19104. TEL 215-386-0100. FAX 215-386-2911. (UK addr.: Brunel Science Park, Brunel University, Uxbridge UB8 3PQ, England) cum.index: 1975-79, 1980-89. (also avail. in magnetic tape) **Document type:** academic/scholarly publication, bibliography.
●Also available online. Vendor(s): Knight-Ridder Information, Inc. (File no.439), Ovid Technologies, Inc. (AHCI).
Also available on CD-ROM. Producer(s): Institute for Scientific Information (A&HCI/CDE).
—BLDSC (1735.800000).
Description: Multidisciplinary indexing of all fields of arts and humanities, including dance, film, radio and television, language, music and literature.

700 016		FR	ISSN 1150-1588
Z5937			

B H A. (Bibliography of the History of Art) (Text in English, French) 1990. q. 2285 F.($425) Centre National de la Recherche Scientifique, Institut de l'Information Scientifique et Technique, 2 allee du Parc de Brabois, 54514 Vandoeuvre-Les-Nancy Cedex, France. TEL 83-50-46-00. FAX 83-50-46-50. (Co-publisher: J. Paul Getty Trust, Art History Information Program) (Co-sponsors: College Art Association of America; Art Libraries Association of North America; International Committee for the History of Art) Eds. Michael Rinehart, Maryse Bideault. adv. contact: Veronique Guinvarc'h. bk.rev.; abstr.; index. circ. 1,000. (back issues avail.)
●Also available online. Vendor(s): Knight-Ridder Information, Inc. (File no.191, Art Literature International), Telesystemes - Questel.
Formed by the merger of (1910-1990): Bulletin Signaletique. Part 530: R A A (Repertoire d'Art et d'Archeologie. Nouvelle Serie) (ISSN 0080-0953); (1971-1990): R I L A (Repertoire International de la Litterature de l'Art) (ISSN 0145-5982)
Description: Covers the current literature of Western art from late antiquity to the present, including the entire artistic production of the European and New World successors to the Greco-Roman world and those peoples and cultures that are studied in relation to them.

097 016		DK	

BIBLIOGRAFI OVER EUROPAEISKE KUNSTNERES EX LIBRIS/EUROPAEISCHE EX LIBRIS/EUROPEAN BOOK PLATES/EX LIBRIS D'EUROPE. (Text in Danish, English, French, German) 1967. a. (latest 1978, combines 1976-77). DKK 120. Klaus Roedel, Ed. & Pub., P.O. Box 109, DK-9900 Frederikshavn, Denmark. circ. 300. **Document type:** bibliography.

ART — COMPUTER APPLICATIONS

700 016   GW
BIBLIOGRAPHIE DER ANTIQUARIATS-, AUKTIONS- UND KUNSTKATALOGE. 1975. irreg. $75. Lausner Weg 36b, 04207 Leipzig, Germany. FAX 49-341-4213818. Ed. Gerhard Loh; Pub. Gerhard Loh. **Document type:** bibliography.

700 720   US   ISSN 1055-6826
BIO-BIBLIOGRAPHIES IN ART AND ARCHITECTURE. 1991. irreg. price varies. Greenwood Press, Inc. (Subsidiary of: Greenwood Publishing Group Inc.), 88 Post Rd. W., Box 5007, Westport, CT 06881-5007. TEL 203-226-3571. FAX 203-222-1502. **Document type:** bibliography, monographic series.

CANADIAN ART SALES INDEX. see *ART*

700 720   FR   ISSN 0009-6830
CIMAISE; arts actuels. (Text in English, French) 1953. bi-m. 350 F. to individuals (foreign 450 F.); agencies 280 F. (foreign 360 F.) (effective 1998). Cimaise S.A.R.L., 95 rue Vieille du Temple, 75003 Paris, France. TEL 33-1-42744092. FAX 33-1-42744092. Ed. Martine Arnault-Tran; Pub. Rene Barzilay. R&P contact: B. Solleau. adv. contact: Rene Barzilay. bk.rev.; bibl.; illus. circ. 15,000. (reprint service avail. from ISI) **Indexed:** Art Ind., Artbibl.Mod., Artbibl., ASCA, Curr.Cont. **Document type:** abstracting/indexing.
—BLDSC (3198.250000); Genuine Article; KR SourceOne; SWETS; UnCover.
Description: Focuses on contemporary art and exhibits.

700 720   US
CONTRIBUTIONS TO THE STUDY OF ART AND ARCHITECTURE. 1992. irreg. price varies. Praeger Publishers (Subsidiary of: Greenwood Publishing Group Inc.), 88 Post Rd. W., Box 5007, Westport, CT 06881-5007. TEL 203-226-3571. FAX 203-222-1502. **Document type:** monographic series.

700   UK   ISSN 0953-0681
NK1160
DESIGN AND APPLIED ARTS INDEX. Short title: D A A I. 1987. s-a. price varies. Design Documentation, Old Manor Lodge, Bodiam, Robertsbridge, E. Sussex TN32 5UJ, England. TEL 0580-830877. FAX 0435-863184. Ed. C.J. Mees. adv.; bk.rev. **Document type:** abstracting/indexing.
●Also available on CD-ROM.
—BLDSC (3559.886400).
Description: Annotated index to 300 current international architecture, design and crafts journals.

011 700   US   ISSN 0893-0120
N5310.7
ETHNOARTS INDEX. 1983. q. $60 (foreign $65). Data Arts, Box 30789, Seattle, WA 98103. TEL 206-783-9580. Ed. Eugene C. Burt. bk.rev.; bibl. circ. 100. (back issues avail.) **Indexed:** Anthropol.Lit. **Document type:** abstracting/indexing.
Formerly: Tribal Arts Review (ISSN 0748-0024)
Description: Abstracting and indexing publications on the art of the indigenous peoples of Africa, Oceania, and the Americas.

EX-LIBRIS FRANCAIS. see *PUBLISHING AND BOOK TRADE — Abstracting, Bibliographies, Statistics*

700 913 016   FR   ISSN 1157-3767
Z5132
F R A N C I S. 526: ART ET ARCHEOLOGIE; Proche-Orient, Asie, Amerique. (Printed format ceased Jan. 1995) 1947- q. Centre National de la Recherche Scientifique, Institut de l'Information Scientifique et Technique, 2 allee du Parc de Brabois, 54514 Vandoeuvre-les-Nancy Cedex, France. TEL 83-50-46-00. FAX 83-50-46-50. adv. contact: Veronique Guinvarc'h. cum.index. **Indexed:** Br.Archaeol.Abstr. **Document type:** bibliography.
●Also available online. Vendor(s): Telesystemes - Questel.
Also available on CD-ROM.
Formerly: Bulletin Signaletique. Part 526: Art et Archeologie (ISSN 0007-5612)

700 011   US
FINE ARTS PERIODICALS;* an international directory of the visual arts. irreg. $89. Peri Press, 20 Shad Way, Voorheesville, NY 12186-4940. TEL 518-765-3163; 800-677-4992. FAX 518-765-3158. Ed. Doris Robinson. index. **Document type:** directory.
Description: Covers more than 2700 current fine arts publications, classified by subject, indicating the scope, purpose and focus of each title. Indexed by title, publisher, subject, country and ISSN.

700 686.2   SZ
GRAPHIC DESIGNERS' INDEX. 1986? a. $67.50. Rotovision S.A., Route Suisse 9, CH-1295 Mies, Switzerland. TEL 022-7553055. FAX 022-7554072. (Dist. in the U.S. by: Watson-Guptill Publications, 1695 Oak St., Lakewood, NJ 08701. TEL 800-451-1741. FAX 908-363-0338). illus. **Document type:** trade publication, abstracting/indexing.
Description: Presents the latest trends in art direction; computer graphics; and corporate, display, environmental, packaging, industrial, interior, and textile design. Lists major photographers and illustrators.

700 800   GR   ISSN 0256-3606
GREECE. NATIONAL STATISTICAL SERVICE. CULTURAL STATISTICS. (Text in Greek) 1973. a. $6. National Statistical Service of Greece, Statistical Information and Publications Division - Ethniki Statistiki Yperesia tes Ellados, 14-16 Lykourgou, 101 66 Athens, Greece. TEL 30-1-3289-397. FAX 30-1-3241-102. TELEX 216734 ESYE GR. (back issues avail.) **Document type:** government publication.

011 700   US   ISSN 0893-0139
N8580
INDEX TO REPRODUCTIONS IN ART PERIODICALS. 1987. q. $50 (foreign $60). Data Arts, Box 30789, Seattle, WA 98103. TEL 206-783-9580. Ed. Eugene C. Burt. **Document type:** abstracting/indexing.
Description: Provides cover-to-cover indexing of art reproduced in five art periodicals (Art in America, American Craft, Arts of Asia, African Arts, American Indian Art). Indexes by artist, title, media, and subject.

016.7   SP   ISSN 0214-7548
INDICE ESPANOL DE HUMANIDADES. SERIES A: ART. 1978. a. 9000 ptas. or exchange basis (effective 1997). Centro de Informacion y Documentacion Cientifica (Cindoc), Joaquin Costa 22, 28002 Madrid, Spain. TEL 34-3-5635482. FAX 34-1-5642644. E-mail: sdi@cindoc.csic.es. Ed. Teresa Abejon. circ. 250. **Document type:** abstracting/indexing.
●Also available online.
Also available on CD-ROM.
Supersedes in part (in 1989): Indice Espanol de Humanidades (ISSN 0210-8488)

700   CN   ISSN 0825-8708
NX513.A3
INTER. (Text in French) 1978. 3/yr. Can.$30 to individuals (foreign Can.$50); institutions $60 (foreign Can.$75) (effective 1997). Les Editions Intervention, 374-227, Haute-Ville, PQ G1R 4P8, Canada. TEL 418-529-9680. FAX 418-529-6933. E-mail: edinter@total.net. Ed.Bd. R&P contact: Richard Martel. adv.: B&W page Can.$625; trim 210 x 310. circ. 1,200. **Document type:** abstracting/indexing.
Formerly (until 1984): Intervention (ISSN 0705-1972)

KUNGLIGA VITTERHETS HISTORIE OCH ANTIKVITETS AKADEMIEN. AARSBOK. see *HISTORY — History Of Europe*

948.5 745.1   SW   ISSN 0083-6761
KUNGLIGA VITTERHETS HISTORIE OCH ANTIKVITETS AKADEMIEN. HANDLINGAR. ANTIKVARISKA SERIEN/ROYAL ACADEMY OF LETTERS, HISTORY AND ANTIQUITIES. PROCEEDINGS. ANTIQUARIAN SERIES. (Text in English, French, German and Swedish) 1954. irreg., no.40, 1996. price varies. Kungliga Vitterhets, Historie- och Antikvitets Akademien, P.O. Box 4627, S-11691 Stockholm, Sweden. (Dist. by: Almqvist & Wiksell International, P.O. Box 4627, S-116 91 Stockholm, Sweden. TEL 46-8-7282500. FAX 46-8-338707)

KUNGLIGA VITTERHETS HISTORIE OCH ANTIKVITETS AKADEMIEN. KONFERENSER. see *MEETINGS AND CONGRESSES*

700 330   US   ISSN 0747-6566
N8602
LEONARD'S ANNUAL PRICE INDEX OF ART AUCTIONS. 1981. a. $219. Auction Index, Inc., 30 Valentine Park, Newton, MA 02165. TEL 617-964-2867. FAX 617-969-9912. **Document type:** abstracting/indexing.
Formerly (until 1982): Leonard's Annual Index of Art Auctions (ISSN 0733-5342)
Description: Listings of sales from nineteen major American auction galleries.

OESTERREICHISCHE VOLKSKUNDLICHE BIBLIOGRAPHIE. see *FOLKLORE — Abstracting, Bibliographies, Statistics*

SANTO; rivista francescana di storia dottrina arte. see *HISTORY — History Of Europe*

740   XO
SLOVENSKA NARODNA BIBLIOGRAFIA SERIA G: GRAFIKA. (Text in Czech, English, French, German, Russian, Slovak; summaries in English, French, German, Slovak) 1975. a. Matica Slovenska, Slovenska Narodna Kniznica, Ul. L. Novomeskeho 32, 036 52 Martin, Slovakia. TEL 0842-313-71. FAX 0842-324-54. TELEX 075 331. Ed. Anna Kucianova. (back issues avail.) **Document type:** bibliography.
Formerly (until 1985): Katalog Slovenskych Plagatov.

TURKEY. DEVLET ISTATISTIK ENSTITUSU. KULTUR ISTATISTIKLERI/TURKEY. STATE INSTITUTE OF STATISTICS. CULTURAL STATISTICS. see *STATISTICS*

016.7   US
WILSON ABSTRACTS. Variant title: Wilson Art Abstracts. (Not avail. in print format) 1994. m., 9/yr., and q. versions avail. $2495 for m.; 9/yr. $1875; q. $1245. H.W. Wilson Co., 950 University Ave., Bronx, NY 10452. TEL 718-588-8400; 800-367-6770. FAX 718-590-1617. TELEX 4990003HWILSON. **Document type:** abstracting/indexing.
●Also available online. Vendor(s): Knight-Ridder Information, Inc., OCLC, Ovid Technologies, Inc., Wilsonline (File ART).
Also available on CD-ROM. Producer(s): SilverPlatter Information, Inc., H.W. Wilson (WILSONDISC).

ART — Computer Applications

A S I F A NEWS. (Association Internationale du Film d'Animation) see *MOTION PICTURES*

BEFORE & AFTER; how to design cool stuff. see *COMPUTERS — Computer Graphics*

700 384.3   SZ
▼**BURTZ BIRTUAL ATELIER.** 1995. m. Keltenstr. 23, CH-8044 Zurich, Switzerland. E-mail: burtz@burtz.ch; URL: http://www.burtz.ch. Ed. Marcy Burt Butz.
●Available only online.
Description: Provides a creative forum for ideas, pre-press publications, projects and progressive programming. Exhibitions of unusual digital painting and extensive commentary on the potential and problems inherent in Internet art.

006.6   US   ISSN 1063-312X
N7433.8
COMPUTER ARTIST. 1992. bi-m. $29.70 (Canada $34.95; elsewhere $54.95) (effective 1997). PennWell Publishing Co. (Nashua), 10 Tara Blvd., 5th Fl., Nashua, NH 03062-2801. TEL 603-891-9168. FAX 603-891-0539. (Subscr. to: Box 1260, Tulsa, OK 74101. TEL 918-835-3161. FAX 918-832-9295) Ed. Tom McMillan. adv. circ. 20,000. **Document type:** trade publication.
—KR SourceOne.
Description: Covers art and drawing packages, animation programs, page makeup software, color printers, monitors, input devices, scanners, equipment reviews and interviews.

ARTS AND HANDICRAFTS

700   NE   ISSN 1048-6798
N380   CODEN: CHIAEF
COMPUTERS AND THE HISTORY OF ART. 1990. 2/yr. $65 (effective 1998). Gordon and Breach - Harwood Academic, Amsteldisk 166, 1st Fl., 1079 LH Amsterdam, Netherlands. (Subscr. to: International Publishers Distributor, Box 32160, Newark, NJ 07102. TEL 800-545-8398. FAX 215-750-6343) Ed. William Vaughan. (also avail. in microform) **Indexed:** Art Ind.
—BLDSC (3394.708000); KR SourceOne; SWETS. CCC.
Refereed Serial

CREATIVE TECHNOLOGY. see *COMPUTERS — Computer Graphics*

D T & G JOURNAL OF DESIGN, TYPOGRAPHY & GRAPHICS. see *COMPUTERS — Computer Networks*

006.6   UK   ISSN 1361-5556
▼**INTERNATIONAL JOURNAL OF VISUAL COMPUTING.** 1997. q. £30 to individuals; institutions £60 (effective 1997). Intellect, Earl Richards Rd. N., Exeter, Devon EX2 6AS, England. TEL 44-1392-475110. FAX 44-1392-475110. E-mail: intellect@dial.pipex.uk; URL: http://www.intellect-net.com/. Ed. Stuart Mealing. **Document type:** academic/scholarly publication.
Description: Covers the meeting ground between art, design and science where computers are used to visual ends.
Refereed Serial

700 800   US   ISSN 0927-3034
P98   CODEN: LADEEI
LANGUAGES OF DESIGN; formalisms for word, images and sound. 1992. q. $81 to individuals; institutions $165 (effective 1997). Penrose Press, Box 470925, San Francisco, CA 94147. E-mail: lauzzana@netcom.com; URL: http://www.penrose-press.com. Ed. Ray Lauzzana; Pub. Ray Lauzzana. R&P contact: Denise Penrose. adv. contact: Denise Penrose. bk.rev. circ. 500. (also avail. in microform from UMI; back issues avail.) **Indexed:** INSPEC (1993-). **Document type:** academic/scholarly publication.
—BLDSC (5155.713500); AskIEEE; Ei; KR SourceOne; SWETS.
Description: Interdisciplinary journal devoted to research in formal languages and their use for the generation and analysis of words, images and sound in both literary works and "nonliterary texts," music and visual art, as well as applications of computational methods in visual, audio and textual analyses.
Refereed Serial

705   US   ISSN 1071-4391
NX21.2.I59
▼**LEONARDO ELECTRONIC ALMANAC.** 1993. m. $15 to Leonardo-ISAST members; others $30. (International Society for the Arts, Sciences, and Technology (ISAST)) M I T Press, 5 Cambridge Center, Cambridge, MA 02142. TEL 617-253-2889. FAX 617-577-1545. E-mail: journals-orders@mit.edu; URL: http://www-mitpress.mit.edu/jrnls-catalog/leonardo-almanac.html. Ed. Craig Harris.
•Available only online.
Description: Serves as an interdisciplinary forum for people interested in the use of new media in contemporary artistic expression, especially involving 20th century science and technology.

MEDIAMATIC. see *ART*

700 338.025   US   ISSN 1063-6471
P93.5
NEW MEDIA SHOWCASE; the digital sourcebook. 1990. a. $35. American Showcase Inc., 915 Broadway, 14th Fl., New York, NY 10010. TEL 212-673-9795. FAX 212-673-9795. (Dist. by: Watson-Guptill Publications, 1515 Broadway, New York, NY 10036. TEL 1-800-451-1741; Overseas & Canada dist. by: Rotovision SA, Route Suisse 9, CH-1295 Mies, Switzerland. TEL 41-222755-4072) Ed. Ann Middlebrook; Pub. Ira Shapiro. adv. contact: Rob Drasin. **Document type:** directory.
Description: Devoted to the artists, producers and designers working with the digital technology. Topics covered include electronic imaging, interactive multimedia, production facilities, and professional resources. Also contains more than 6,000 names, addresses and phone numbers of professionals working in the categories listed above, sorted topically and by alphabetical index for easy access.

651.8 700   UK   ISSN 0030-9362
PAGE. 1969. 4/yr. £4. Computer Arts Society, 50-51 Russell Square, London WC1B 4JX, England. Ed. John Lansdown. adv.; bk.rev.; bibl.; illus. circ. 1,000. (looseleaf format) **Indexed:** Comput.Cont., INSPEC.
—AskIEEE; KR SourceOne.

PHOTOSHOP TIPS & TRICKS. see *COMPUTERS — Computer Networks*

700   CN
PIXEL - THE COMPUTER ANIMATION DIRECTORY. $89. Pixel - The Computer Animation News People, 109 Venderhoof St., Ste. 2, Totonto, ON M4G 2H7, Canada. TEL 416-424-4657. FAX 416-424-1812. E-mail: pixel@inforamp.net. Ed. Robi Roncarelli; Pub. Robi Roncarelli. (also avail. in diskette format; printed format avail. on request) **Document type:** directory.
•Also available online.
Former titles: Directory of Computer Animation Producers (ISSN 1202-5941) & International Directory of Computer Animation Producers (ISSN 0840-5905)

700   CN   ISSN 0835-8095
PIXEL - THE COMPUTER ANIMATION NEWSLETTER. (Print edition ceased) 1984. m. $345. Pixel - The Computer Animation News People, 109 Vanderhoof Ave., Ste. 2, Toronto, ON M4G 2H7, Canada. TEL 415-424-4657. FAX 416-424-1812. E-mail: pixel@inforamp.net. Ed. Robi Roncarelli. **Document type:** newsletter.
•Also available online.
Also available on CD-ROM.
Description: Includes information on trends, market developments, and the general industry.

700   CN   ISSN 1202-1156
RONCARELLI REPORT ON THE COMPUTER ANIMATION INDUSTRY. 1984. a. $1295. Pixel - The Computer Animation News People, 109 Venderhoof Ave., Ste. 2, Toronto, ON M4G 2H7, Canada. TEL 415-424-4657. FAX 415-424-1812. E-mail: pixel@inforamp.net. Ed. Robi Roncarelli; Pub. Robi Roncarelli. (back issues avail.)
Formerly: (until 1992): Roncarelli Report (ISSN 0838-2271)
Description: Report and analysis of the current state of the global computer animation industry with comments and forecasts.

SILICON GRAPHICS WORLD. see *COMPUTERS — Computer Graphics*

700 001.644 780   US   ISSN 0748-2043
SMALL COMPUTERS IN THE ARTS NEWS.* Abbreviated title: S C A N. 1982. 3/yr. $15. Small Computers in the Arts Network, Inc., 209 Upland Rd., Merton Sta., PA 19066-1821. Ed. Dick Moberg. adv.; bk.rev. circ. 350.
—BLDSC (6842.347000).
Description: Contains articles about music and graphics education, music synthesis and composition, and each issue features an artist and his or her work.

700   IT
STANZA ROSSA; rivista d'arte dell'era virtuale. 1992. bi-m. L.24000 (foreign L.60000). Edizioni dell'Ortica s.n.c., Piazza di Porta Mascarelia, 7, 40126 Bologna, Italy. TEL 39-51-347328. Ed. Stefano Righetti. adv.: page L.1000000; adv. contact: Alessandro Finelli. circ. 1,500. (also avail. in diskette format; back issues avail.) **Document type:** academic/scholarly publication.
Description: Specializes in computer art, communication, art and technology, multimedia, virtual reality, mass media and video.

621.3 001.6   US   ISSN 1042-2994
NX260
SYMPOSIUM ON SMALL COMPUTERS IN THE ARTS. PROCEEDINGS.* 1981. a. Small Computers in the Arts Network, Inc., 209 Upland Rd., Merton Sta., PA 19066-1821. **Document type:** proceedings.

700   US
TECH TIPS. 1989. q. $100. Apollo Graphics Ltd., 1085 Industrial Blvd., Southampton, PA 18966. TEL 215-953-0500. FAX 215-953-1144. Ed. Roy J. Innella. tr.lit. circ. 3,000. (back issues avail.) **Document type:** newsletter.
Description: To enlighten art directors, advertising managers and those in advertising of the complexities and possible pitfalls of producing a project.

TECHNOLOGY WATCH; for the graphic arts and information industries. see *COMPUTERS — Computer Graphics*

ARTIFICIAL INTELLIGENCE

see *Computers–Artificial Intelligence*

ARTS AND HANDICRAFTS

A F D A FORUM. (American Fish Decoy Association) see *HOBBIES*

745.5   US   ISSN 0278-9507
NK4005
AMERICAN CERAMICS.* 1982. q. $24. 9 E. 45th St., 6th Fl., New York, NY 10017-2403. TEL 212-944-2180. Ed. Michael McTwigan. adv.; bk.rev.; illus. circ. 6,000. **Indexed:** Alloys Ind., Art Ind., Artbibl.Mod., DAAI, Eng.Mat.Abstr., Met.Abstr.Ind., Met.Abstr., Nonfer.Met.Alert; PCC Alert, Steels Alert, World Alum.Abstr.
—BLDSC (0812.070000); KR SourceOne; UnCover.

745.5   US   ISSN 0194-8008
NK1
AMERICAN CRAFT. 1941. bi-m. $40 (foreign $55) (effective 1996). American Craft Council, 72 Spring St., New York, NY 10012. TEL 212-274-0630. FAX 212-274-0650. Ed. Lois Moran; Pub. Lois Moran. adv. contact: Don Zanone. bk.rev.; illus. circ. 40,000. (also avail. in microform from UMI,MIM; reprint service avail. from UMI) **Indexed:** Art Ind., Artbibl.Mod., Avery Ind.Archit.Per., Bk.Rev.Ind. (1965-), Child.Bk.Rev.Ind. (1965-), DAAI, Ind.Bk.Rev.Hum., Mag.Ind., Media Rev.Dig., PMR, R.G.Abstr., R.G. **Document type:** consumer publication.
•Also available online. Vendor(s): UMI.
Also available on CD-ROM. Producer(s): UMI.
—BLDSC (0812.660000); KR SourceOne; SWETS; UMI; UnCover.
Former titles: Craft Horizons with Craft World (ISSN 0164-9191); (until 1979, vol.39, no.3): Craft Horizons (ISSN 0011-0744); *Incorporates:* Craft World.
Description: Covers a variety of crafts, including fiber, clay, metal, wood, and glass. Includes artist profiles, exhibition reviews, lists of museum and gallery exhibits, and discussions of historical as well as contemporary crafts.

746.41 745.5   US
AMERICAN INDIAN BASKETRY AND OTHER NATIVE ARTS. 1979. 4/yr. $30. (Institute for the Study of Traditional American Indian Arts) John M. Gogol, Ed. & Pub., Box 66124, Portland, OR 97266. TEL 503-233-8131. adv.; bk.rev.; bibl.; illus. circ. 5,000. (back issues avail.) **Indexed:** A.I.C.P., Anthropol.Lit.
Formerly: American Indian Basketry.

AMERICAN JOURNAL OF ART THERAPY; art in psychotherapy, education, and rehabilitation. see *EDUCATION — Special Education And Rehabilitation*

745.5   US   ISSN 1078-8425
▼**AMERICAN STYLE.** 1995. q. $28. Box 96063, Washington, DC 20078-7115. TEL 800-555-3721. Ed. W. Rosen.

AMPERSAND. see *PUBLISHING AND BOOK TRADE*

745.5   CN   ISSN 1189-4555
ANNUAL CRAFT SHOWS IN ONTARIO. 1975. a. Can.$14 to non-members; members Can.$10 (effective 1997). Ontario Crafts Council, Chalmers Bldg., 35 McCaul St., Toronto, On M5T 1V7, Canada. TEL 416-977-3551. FAX 416-977-3552. Ed. Jane Moore. circ. 2,000. **Document type:** directory.
Description: Designed for craftspeople looking for shows as a market for their work.

745.5   US   ISSN 0889-177X
ANVIL'S RING. 1973. q. $35 to individuals; libraries $25; foreign $50. Artists-Blacksmith Association of North America, Box 206, Washington, MO 63090. TEL 314-390-2133. FAX 314-390-2133. Ed. Jim MacCarty. adv.; bk.rev.; charts; illus.; tr.lit.; circ. 3,500 (paid). (back issues avail.) **Document type:** trade publication.
Description: Blacksmithing, metal arts, tools technique, design and events.

ARTS AND HANDICRAFTS

A

ARIADNE. see *INTERIOR DESIGN AND DECORATION*

ART ALMANAC. see *ART*

745.5 707   UK   ISSN 0262-7035
ART & CRAFT; a magazine for all primary school teachers of art and craft. 1936. m. £25.20. Scholastic Ltd., Westfield Rd., Southam, Leamington Spa, Warks CV33 0JH, England. TEL 44-1926-813910. FAX 44-1926-817727. Ed. Sian Morgan. adv. contact: Chris Pratt. bk.rev.; illus. circ. 15,773. (also avail. in microform from UMI) **Document type:** academic/scholarly publication. —SWETS; UMI.
   Formerly: Art and Craft in Education (ISSN 0004-3028)

ART & DESIGN COURSES. see *EDUCATION — Teaching Methods And Curriculum*

ART REVUE. see *ART*

ART TIMES; a literary journal and resource for the arts. see *ART*

745.5   IT   ISSN 0391-707X
ARTIGIANATO OGGI. 1977. m. L.10000. Confederazione Nazionale Artigianato, Via Santa Prassede 24, Rome, Italy. TEL 6-47-57-441. Ed. Sergio Cecchini. adv.; bk.rev. circ. 200,000.

ARTISTS IN STAINED GLASS. JOURNAL. see *ART*

ARTS BEAT. see *ART*

ARTS EDUCATION POLICY REVIEW. see *ART*

745.5   US   ISSN 1071-6289
ARTS 'N CRAFTS SHOWGUIDE; a market guide to arts, crafts fairs and other events. 1985. 6/yr. $21.95. A C N Publications, Box 25, Jefferson City, MO 65102. TEL 314-636-0491. FAX 314-636-2112. E-mail: acnpubs@email.plnet.net. (Street addr.: 208E E. High St., Jefferson City, MO 65101) Ed. Dan Engle. adv. contact: Dan Engle. bk.rev. circ. 10,000. **Document type:** consumer publication, trade publication.
   Former titles (until vol.6, no.5, 1991): A C N Showtime; A C N Art and Craft News.
   Description: Lists national art and craft events, fairs, and festivals. Contains information, opportunities, resources and a nationwide show list.

745.5   UK
ARTWORK; the North's independent free arts newspaper. 1983. bi-m. £7 (single copies SAE). Famedram Publishers Ltd., P.O. Box 3, Ellon, Aberdeenshire AB41 9EA, Scotland. TEL 44-1651-842429. FAX 44-1651-842180. E-mail: ramedram@artwork.co.uk; URL: http://www.artwork.co.uk/diary. Ed. Bill Williams; Pub. Bill Williams. R&P contact: Eleanor Stewart. adv. contact: Gil Livingston. bk.rev. circ. 20,000. (tabloid format; also avail. in diskette format; back issues avail.) **Document type:** newspaper.
   Description: Informs readers about arts and handicrafts shows and events.

745.5   AT   ISSN 1322-8099
THE AUSTRALIAN WOMEN'S WEEKLY HANDMADE; craft, decorating, fashion. 1984. bi-m. Aus.$36.70 (foreign Aus.$55.50). Australian Consolidated Press Pty. Ltd., G.P.O. Box 4088, Sydney, N.S.W. 1028, Australia. TEL 61-2-92828000. FAX 61-2-92643614. (Subscr. to: G.P.O. Box 5252, Sydney, N.S.W. 2001, Australia. TEL 61-2-92600012) Ed. Mary Coleman. R&P contact: Caroline Halliday. adv. contact: Robyn Blunt. bk.rev. circ. 70,000. (back issues avail.) **Document type:** consumer publication.
   Description: Craft magazine filled with fashion (including free, full-sized patterns), needlework, home decorating, and creative craft projects, for crafts people of all levels.

AZURE MAGAZINE. see *INTERIOR DESIGN AND DECORATION*

745.5   US   ISSN 1049-9970
BALLOONS AND PARTIES TODAY.* 1986. bi-m. $29.95. Festivities Publications, Inc., 815 Haines St., Jacksonville, FL 32206-6050. TEL 904-634-1902. FAX 904-633-8764. Ed. April Anderson; Pubs. Debra and David Paulk. adv. contact: Greg Smith. tr.lit. circ. 7,000. (back issues avail.) **Document type:** trade publication.
   Formerly: Balloons Today.
   Description: Presents full color designs and decorations using balloons. Geared towards retailers selling balloons and party supplies and trade managers for industry.

745.592   US
BASKET BITS. 1989. q. $14. Jim Rutherford, Ed. & Pub., Box 8, Loudonville, OH 44842. TEL 419-994-3256. adv. circ. 1,800.
   Description: Provides step-by-step instructions for basket weaving. Includes interviews with basket makers and basketry suppliers, and a calendar of events.

745.5   JA
BENIBANA. 1974. irreg. free. Tsutomu Yamaguchi, Ed. & Pub., 32 Koyama-Minami, Kamifusa-cho, Kita-ku, Kyoto 603, Japan. TEL 81-75-451-3568. Ed. Tsutomu Yamaguchi. R&P contact: Tsutomu Yamaguchi. index. circ. 300. **Document type:** monographic series.
   Description: Focuses on the techniques and history of paper-making, dyeing and textiles in China and Japan.

745.5   US   ISSN 0731-5376
TT1
BETTER HOMES AND GARDENS COUNTRY CRAFTS. Key Title: Country Crafts. 1981. a. (effective 1996-1997); newsstand price: $4.99 (Canada $5.99). Meredith Corporation, Special Interest Publications, 1716 Locust St., Des Moines, IA 50336. TEL 515-284-3000. Ed. Marjoan Schaefer; Pub. Steve Levinson. adv.: B&W page $14550, color page $19300; adv. contact: Peggy Leib. circ. 400,000 (paid). **Document type:** consumer publication.

745.5   US   ISSN 1085-1526
BETTER HOMES AND GARDENS CROSS-STITCH CHRISTMAS. Key Title: Cross-Stitch Christmas. 1990. a. (effective 1996-1997); newsstand price: $4.99 (Canada $5.99). Meredith Corporation, Special Interest Publications, 1716 Locust St., Des Moines, IA 50309. TEL 515-284-3000. Ed. Marjoan Scharfer; Pub. Steve Levinson. adv.: B&W page $14550, color page $19300; trim 8 x 10 1/2; adv. contact: Peggy Leib. circ. 600,000 (paid). **Document type:** consumer publication.
   Description: Devoted to cross-stitch projects for Christmas. Includes instructions, charts and photographs for each project.

698.3 745.5   US   ISSN 1056-716X
BETTER HOMES AND GARDENS DECORATIVE WOODCRAFTS. 1991. bi-m. $29.97 (effective 1997). Meredith Corporation, Crafts Group, 1912 Grand Ave., Des Moines, IA 50309-3379. TEL 515-284-3236. Ed. Beverly Rivers; Pub. Bill Reed. adv. contact: Maureen Ruth. circ. 300,000. **Document type:** consumer publication.

BETTER HOMES AND GARDENS FLORAL & NATURE CRAFTS. see *GARDENING AND HORTICULTURE*

745.5   US   ISSN 0278-7490
TT1
BETTER HOMES AND GARDENS HOLIDAY CRAFTS. Key Title: Holiday Crafts. 1974. s-a. (effective 1996-1997); newsstand price: $4.99 (Canada $5.99). Meredith Corporation, Special Interest Publications, 1716 Locust St., Des Moines, IA 50336. TEL 515-284-3000. Ed. Linda Stueve; Pub. Steve Levinson. adv.: B&W page $14550, color page $19300; adv. contact: Peggy Leib. circ. 400,000 (paid). **Document type:** consumer publication.

745.5   US
BETTER HOMES AND GARDENS SANTA CLAUS. Variant title: Santa Claus. 1991. a. (effective 1996-1997); newsstand price: $4.99 (Canada $5.99). Meredith Corporation, Special Interest Publications, 1716 Locust St., Des Moines, IA 50309. TEL 515-284-3000. FAX 515-284-2700. Ed. Marjoan Schaefer; Pub. Steve Levinson. adv.: B&W page $14550; color page $19300; trim 8 x 10 1/2; adv. contact: Peggy Leib. circ. 350,000 (paid). **Document type:** consumer publication.
   Description: Contains 40 to 50 crafts projects featuring Santa Claus.

745.5   US
BETTER HOMES AND GARDENS VICTORIAN TREASURES. Variant title: Victorian Treasures. a. (effective 1996-1997); newsstand price: $4.99 (Canada $5.99). Meredith Corporation, Special Interest Publications, 1716 Locust St., Des Moines, IA 50336. TEL 515-284-3000. Ed. Linda Stueve; Pub. Steve Levinson. adv.: B&W page $14550, color page $19300; adv. contact: Peggy Leib. circ. 400,000 (paid). **Document type:** consumer publication.
   Formerly (until Jan. 1996): Better Homes and Gardens Victorian Hearts and Flowers.

BRIDAL CRAFTS. see *MATRIMONY*

745.5 747 700   US
BUSINESS & TEACHER DIRECTORY (YEAR).* 1991. a. $10 (effective Oct. 1995). Society of Decorative Painters, 303 N. McLean Blvd., Wichita, KS 67203-5916. TEL 316-283-9665. FAX 316-283-5048. Ed. Julie Vosberg. adv. contact: Cheryl Capps. circ. 4,000 (controlled). **Document type:** directory, trade publication.
   Description: Lists artists, teachers, retailers, wholesalers, manufacturers, importers, exporters, and publishers in the decorative painting industry.

745.5   US
BUTTERFLY NET. 1977. 6/yr. $20 membership. Fenton Art Glass Collectors of America, Inc., Box 384, Williamstown, WV 26187-0384. TEL 304-375-6196. Ed. Ferill J. Rice. R&P contact: Art Gilbert. adv. contact: Debbie Nielsen. circ. 3,600. **Document type:** academic/scholarly publication, newsletter.
   Description: Includes informative articles on Fenton glass and advertising listings from members showing items wanted or for sale.

CANADA QUILTS MAGAZINE. see *NEEDLEWORK*

CANADIAN BOOKBINDERS & BOOK ARTISTS GUILD NEWSLETTER. see *PUBLISHING AND BOOK TRADE*

745.531   CN   ISSN 0045-5121
CANADIAN LEATHERCRAFT. 1951. q. Can.$25 membership. Canadian Society of Creative Leathercraft, c/o Lois MacPherson, 1506 - 205 Queen Mary Dr., Oakville, ON L6K 3K8, Canada. Eds. Betsy Rennie, Lois MacPherson. adv.; bk.rev.; circ. 90 (controlled). **Document type:** newsletter.

745.5   US
CANDLE INFO MAPPING NEWSLETTER. 1985. biannual. $7. Update Publicare Co., Prosperity & Profits Unlimited Distribution Services, Box 416, Denver, CO 80201. TEL 303-575-5676. Ed. A.C. Doyle. circ. 600. **Document type:** newsletter.
   Formerly: Candle Makers Instruction Etc. Update.

745.5   US   ISSN 0009-0190
CERAMIC ARTS & CRAFTS. (Editions in English and Spanish) 1955. m. $23.50 (foreign $30.90) (effective 1997). Scott Publications, 30595 Eight Mile Rd., Livonia, MI 48152-1798. TEL 248-477-6650. FAX 248-477-6795. Ed. Bill Thompson; Pub. Robert Keessen. adv. contact: Jim Mac. illus.; tr.lit. circ. 38,000. (also avail. in microfilm from UMI) **Indexed:** Ind.How To Do It (1990-). **Document type:** consumer publication.

698.3   US   ISSN 0577-9294
TT199.7
CHIP CHATS. 1953. bi-m. $11 (foreign $14). (National Wood Carvers Association) Edward F. Gallenstein, Ed. & Pub., 7424 Miami Ave., Cincinnati, OH 45243. TEL 513-561-0627. R&P contact: Edward F. Gallenstein. bk.rev.; circ. 55,000 (paid). (back issues avail.) **Indexed:** Ind.How To Do It (1990-). **Document type:** trade publication.

ARTS AND HANDICRAFTS

CHRISTMAS: YEAR ROUND NEEDLEWORK & CRAFT IDEAS. see *NEEDLEWORK*

745.5 US
CLIP ART SERIES. irreg., approx. 4/yr. $6.99 per no. F & W Publications, Inc., North Light Books, 1507 Dana Ave., Cincinnati, OH 45207. TEL 800-289-0963. FAX 513-531-4082. Ed. David Lewis. R&P contact: Jenny Walsh.

COLLECTIONS (COLUMBIA). see *MUSEUMS AND ART GALLERIES*

745.5 US ISSN 0897-7216
TT25.W55
COLONIAL WILLIAMSBURG HISTORIC TRADES. 1988. irreg. price varies. Colonial Williamsburg Foundation, Box 1776, Williamsburg, VA 23187-1776. TEL 757-220-7342.
 Description: Presents articles on crafts practiced in Colonial America.

745.5 US
CONTEMPORARY FOLK ART. 1993. q. $3.95 per no. Long Publications, Inc., 8393 E. Holly Rd., Holly, MI 48442. TEL 313-634-9675. FAX 313-634-0301.

745.5 US ISSN 1047-4625
TT23
COUNTRY FOLK ART MAGAZINE. 1988. bi-m. $22.95 (effective 1997). Long Publications, Inc., 8393 E. Holly Rd., Holly, MI 48442. TEL 248-634-9675. FAX 248-634-0301. Ed. Rhonda Blakely. circ. 360,000. **Document type:** consumer publication.

745.5 US
COUNTRY HOME FOLK CRAFTS. 1994. bi-m. $24.97; newsstand price: $4.95. Meredith Corporation, Special Interest Publications, 1716 Locust St., Des Moines, IA 50336. TEL 515-284-3000. Ed. Molly Culbertson; Pub. Joe Lagani. adv.: B&W page $4875. **Document type:** consumer publication.

745.5 US ISSN 1047-3955
COUNTRY SAMPLER. 1984. bi-m. $23.97 (Canada $33.97; elsewhere $53.97); newsstand price: $4.99. Sampler Publications, Inc., 707 Kautz Rd., St. Charles, IL 60174. TEL 630-377-8000. FAX 630-377-8194. URL: http://www.sampler.com. (Subscr. to: Box 420235, Palm Coast, FL 32142-0235) adv. circ. 550,000. **Document type:** consumer publication.
 Description: Contains information about country home accessories and crafts.

COUNTRY SAMPLER'S DECORATING IDEAS. see *INTERIOR DESIGN AND DECORATION*

745.5 AT ISSN 0813-6734
CRAFT A.C.T.. (Australian Capital Territory) 1974. m. Aus.$20. Crafts Council of the ACT Inc., P.O. Box 720, Dickson, A.C.T. 2602, Australia. TEL 64-6-2412373. FAX 64-6-2416743. circ. 350. (back issues avail.)

745.5 746 US
CRAFT AND NEEDLEWORK AGE. 1946. m. $20. Hobby Publications, Inc., 225 Gordons Corner Plaza, Box 420, Manalapan, NJ 07726. TEL 908-446-4900. FAX 908-446-5488. Ed. Karen Ancona; Pub. David Gherman. adv. contact: Tammy Keck. bk.rev.; illus.; mkt.; stat.; tr.mk. circ. 33,000. **Document type:** trade publication.
 Former titles: Craft and Needlework Age - World of Miniatures (ISSN 0744-2319); Craft, Model and Hobby Industry (ISSN 0011-0752)

745.5 700 AT ISSN 0814-6586
CRAFT ARTS INTERNATIONAL MAGAZINE. 1984. q. Aus.$40($72) Craft-Art Pty. Ltd., P.O. Box 363, Neutral Bay Junction, N.S.W. 2089, Australia. TEL 61-2-908-4797. FAX 61-2-953-1576. Ed. Ken Lockwood. adv. contact: Jenie Thomas. (back issues avail.) Indexed: DAAI. **Document type:** academic/scholarly publication, consumer publication.
 —BLDSC (3486.577500).
 Formerly: Craft Arts Magazine.
 Description: Specialises in the presentation and documentation of creative works, with emphasis on the visual and applied arts. Examines concepts that challenge conventional aesthetic experience.

745.5 US ISSN 1193-3208
CRAFT CONNECTION. 1974. q. $35 (effective 1997). Minnesota Crafts Council, Hennepin Center for the Arts, 528 Hennepin Ave., Rm. 216, Minneapolis, MN 55403. TEL 612-333-7789. FAX 612-332-8131. E-mail: mncraft@mth.org; URL: http://www.mth.org/mncrafts. R&P contact: David Glenn. bk.rev. circ. 4,000. (tabloid format) **Document type:** newspaper.
 Description: Contains interviews with artists, reviews of exhibits, grant information for artists, calendar listings of festivals, exhibitions and workshops, and general news of interest to professionals in the arts and crafts industry.

745.5 292 US ISSN 1074-7966
CRAFT - CRAFTS. 1994. q. $15 (foreign $20) (effective Feb. 1997). Box 441, Ponderay, ID 83852. TEL 208-263-6885 ext. 4535. Ed. InaRae Ussack; Pub. InaRae Ussack. R&P contact: InaRae Ussack. adv. contact: Inarae Ussack. bk.rev. circ. 500. **Document type:** consumer publication.
 Description: Discusses needlework, jewelry making, and other crafts for Pagans, Wiccans, and followers of other Earth religions. Publishes poetry and recipes.

745.5 338 US ISSN 1046-9699
CRAFT MARKETING NEWS. 1984. bi-m. $17.95 (foreign $50) (effective 1997). Front Room Publishers, Box 1541, Clifton, NJ 07015-1541. TEL 201-773-4215. FAX 201-815-1235. E-mail: rjp@intac.com; URL: http://www.intac.com/~rjp. Ed. Adele Patti. adv. contact: Bob Patti. bk.rev. circ. 2,500. (paid). (looseleaf format; back issues avail.) **Document type:** newsletter, trade publication.
 Formerly: Front Room News.
 Description: Contains information on crafts marketing: wholesale sales to shops and galleries.

745.5 US ISSN 1053-2013
CRAFT RELATED NEWSLETTERS, PERIODICALS & PUBLICATIONS; an updating reference. 1990. biennial. $11.95. Continnuus, c/o Prosperity & Profits Unlimited Distribution Services, Box 416, Denver, CO 80201-0416. TEL 303-575-5676. Ed. A.C. Doyle. R&P contact: A. Doyle. circ. 2,000.
 Description: Lists references for crafts, crafts patterns, products, and fairs.

745.5 US ISSN 1059-8766
CRAFT SUPPLY MAGAZINE; the industry source for the gift producer. 1989. bi-m. $40. Hobby Publications, Inc., 225 Gordon's Corner Plaza, Box 420, Manalapan, NJ 07726. TEL 908-446-4900. FAX 908-446-5488. Ed. Maria Nerius. adv.; bk.rev. circ. 8,500. **Document type:** trade publication.
 Formed by the Oct. 1991 merger of: Craft Supply Report & Craft Supply Directory.
 Description: Geared toward the professional maker of hand crafted gifts. Addresses market concerns such as the availability of supplies, development of markets, show schedules, and trends in home decor.

745.5 700 AT ISSN 0158-7048
CRAFT VICTORIA. (Supplement avail.) 1970. 3/yr. membership. Crafts Council of Victoria, 114 Gertrude St., Fitzroy, Vic. 3065, Australia. TEL 61-3-94173111. FAX 61-3-94197295. Ed. Robert Buckingham; Ed. Suzie Attiwill. R&P contact: Robert Buckingham. adv. contact: Caterina Nuccitelli. bk.rev. circ. 1,600. **Document type:** newsletter.
 Description: Features articles, exhibition reviews, critical writing and debate. Supplement focuses on business opportunities, promotion, marketing and profession development.

745.5 SA ISSN 1023-5248
CRAFTART; a quarterly publication promoting South African crafts. 1994. q. R.19.50($10) per issue. CraftArt Publishers, P.O. Box 650737, Benmore 2010, South Africa. illus.

790 US
CRAFTING TRADITIONS. 1983. bi-m $16.98 (Canada $24.59; elsewhere $25.98); newsstand price: $2.99. Reiman Publications, LP, 5400 S. 60th St., Greendale, WI 53129. TEL 414-423-0100. FAX 414-423-1143. (Subscr. to: Box 996, Greendale, WI 53129) Ed. Kathleen Zimmer. illus.; circ. 500,000 (paid). **Document type:** consumer publication.
 —UMI.
 Formerly (until 1995): Country Handcrafts (ISSN 0745-3116)
 Description: Craft ideas and projects for memorable holidays and family occasions.

745 US ISSN 0897-6341
CRAFTRENDS. 1982. m. $26. P J S Publications, Inc., 2 News Plaza, Box 1790, Peoria, IL 61656-3435. TEL 309-682-6626. FAX 309-682-7394. Ed. Bill Gardner. adv.; bk.rev.; circ. 31,472 (controlled). **Document type:** trade publication.

745 UK ISSN 0306-610X
TT1
CRAFTS; the decorative & applied arts magazine. 1973. 6/yr. £25 to individuals in the U.K. and Ireland (overseas £35); institutions in the U.K. and Ireland £35 (overseas £45); newsstand price: £4.50. Crafts Council, 44a Pentonville Rd., London N1 9BY, England. TEL 44-171-278-7700. FAX 44-171-837-6891. E-mail: crafts@craftscouncil.org.uk; URL: http://www.craftscouncil.org.uk. Ed. Geraldine Rudge; Pub. Andrew Ryan. R&P contact: Andrew Ryan. TEL 44-171-806-2540. adv. contact: Georgina Harman. bk.rev.; illus.; index. circ. 14,000. (also avail. in microform from UMI; reprint service avail. from UMI) Indexed: Art Ind., DAAI. **Document type:** trade publication.
 —BLDSC (3486.750000); KR SourceOne; SWETS; UMI; UnCover. **CCC.**
 Description: Britain's decorative arts publication featuring work by craftsmen and women worldwide; includes shopping guide and calendar of craft events.

745.5 US ISSN 0148-9127
TT1
CRAFTS. 1978. m. $21.98. K-III Communications Corp., 745 Fifth Ave., New York, NY 10151. TEL 212-745-0100. Ed. Judith Brassart. adv.; bk.rev.; illus. circ. 406,042. Indexed: Consum.Ind., Ind.How To Do It (1991-). **Document type:** consumer publication.
 Description: Covers general handicrafts, including needlecrafts, tile painting, doll making, kids' crafts, and gift giving crafts.

745.5 UK
CRAFTS BEAUTIFUL. 1993. m. £24.50 (Europe £37.20, U.S. £39.50, elsewhere £55.70); newsstand price: £2.40. Maze Media Ltd., Castle House, 97 High St., Colchester, Essex CO1 1TH, England. TEL 44-1255-676815. FAX 44-01206-769512. E-mail: mail@maze.u-net.com. (Dist. by: UMD, 16-28 Tabernacle St., London EC2A 4BN, England. TEL 0171-638-4666. FAX 0171-638-4665) Ed. Helen Stuttle; Pub. Matthew Tudor. adv.: B&W page £425, color page £670; trim 297 x 210; adv. contact: Martin Lack. bk.rev.; circ. 30,000 (paid). (back issues avail.) **Document type:** consumer publication.
 Description: Contains regular features on stencils, rubber stamping, decoupage, stitching, home decorations, knitting, quilling, ceramics, quilting, painting, doughcraft and plastecrafts. Includes giveaways, competitions, draws, and free patterns each month.

745.5 IE
CRAFTS COUNCIL. NEWSLETTER. 1992. q. £8 (Europe I£10; rest of world I£12). Crafts Council, Castle Yard, Kilkenny, Ireland. TEL 353-56-618048. FAX 353-56-63754. Ed. Nuala McGrath. R&P contact: Nuala McGrath. circ. 1,500. (looseleaf format; back issues avail.) **Document type:** newsletter.

745.5 US ISSN 0273-7957
CRAFTS FAIR GUIDE. 1974. q. $42.50. Box 688, Corte Madera, CA 94976. TEL 415-924-3259; 800-871-2341. FAX 415-924-3259. Eds. Lee & Dianne Spiegel. adv.; bk.rev. circ. 4,500.
 Description: Reviews, rates, and evaluates arts and crafts fairs in the Western states.

745.5 US ISSN 0146-6607
TT855
CRAFTS 'N THINGS. 1975. 10/yr. $18.97. Clapper Communications Companies, 2400 E. Devon Ave., Ste. 375, Des Plaines, IL 60018-4618. TEL 847-635-5800. FAX 847-635-6311. URL: http://www.craftnet.org/crafts-n-things. Ed. Julie Stephani. adv. contact: Stuart Hochwert. bk.rev.; illus.; index. circ. 310,000. (back issues avail.) Indexed: Bk.Rev.Ind. (1978-1985), Ind.How To Do It (1978-1985), Mag.Ind., MELSA. **Document type:** consumer publication.
 ●Also available online.
 —UMI; UnCover.
 Incorporates (1967-1986): Creative Crafts and Miniatures; Which was formed by the merger of: Creative Craft (ISSN 0011-0884); Miniature Magazine (ISSN 0162-5632)

ARTS AND HANDICRAFTS

745.5   US   ISSN 0899-9724
CRAFTS NEWS. 1986. q. $35. Crafts Center, 1001 Connecticut Ave., Ste. 525, Washington, DC 20036. TEL 202-728-9603. FAX 202-296-2452. Ed. Nina Smith. adv. contact: Evelyn Mendoza. circ. 6,000. (back issues avail.) **Document type:** newsletter.
   Description: International crafts effort, artisan profiles, sources of technical assistance, equipment, materials, trends, trade issues, and microcredit information.

745.5   US   ISSN 0160-7650
THE CRAFTS REPORT. 1974. m. $29 (effective 1995); newsstand price: $4.50. Crafts Report Publishing Co., Inc., Box 1992, Wilmington, DE 19899-1992. TEL 302-656-2209; 800-777-7098. FAX 302-656-4894. Ed. Marilyn Stevens. adv. contact: Mary Ann Parker. bk.rev./ illus. circ. 23,000. (tabloid format; also avail. in microform from UMI; reprint service avail. from UMI) **Indexed:** DAAI. **Document type:** newspaper.
   —UMI; UnCover.
   Incorporates: Working Craftsman (ISSN 0149-0206)
   Description: Business newsmonthly for professional craftspersons, gallery and shop owners. Covers sales and marketing, management, finance and crafts industry trends. Lists fairs and shows throughout the US, and reports on issues such as taxes, health, law, copyright, and computers.

745.5   UK   ISSN 0953-9190
THE CRAFTSMAN MAGAZINE. 1983. bi-m. £13 (foreign £25) (effective 1996). P S B Design and Print Consultants Ltd., P.O. Box 5, Lowthorpe, Driffield, E. Yorks YO25 8JD, England. TEL 44-1377-255213. FAX 44-1377-255730. Ed. Angie Boyer. R&P contact: Paul Boyer. adv. contact: Andrea Garnett. bk.rev. circ. 15,000. (back issues avail.) **Document type:** consumer publication.

745.5   UK   ISSN 0968-4506
CRAFTWORKER'S YEAR BOOK. 1981. a. £14.25 (U.S. $30) (effective 1997). The Write Angle Press, 44 Kingsway, Stoke-on-Trent ST4 1JH, England. TEL 44-1782-749919. FAX 44-1782-747061. Ed. Charles Wallin. R&P contact: Philip Stanbridge. adv. contact: Philip Stanbridge. circ. 3,000 (paid). **Document type:** directory.
   Formerly: Craftman's Directory (Year) Part 1 (ISSN 0261-2135)
   Description: Contains business advice and comprehensive data for British professional craftworkers.

745.5   US
CRAFTWORKS. 1985. 10/yr. $35. All American Crafts, Inc., 243 Newton-Sparta Rd., Newton, NJ 07860-2748. TEL 201-383-8080. Ed. Jane Guthrie. adv. contact: Lee Jaworski. bk.rev.; illus. circ. 325,000. **Document type:** consumer publication.
   Formerly: Craftworks for the Home (ISSN 0891-0588)
   Description: For craft enthusiasts, featuring original craft projects, designs, instructions, and diagrams for all skill levels.

700   UK
THE CREATIVE HANDBOOK. 1973. a. £112. Reed Information Services, Division of Reed Telepublishing Ltd. (Subsidiary of: Reed Elsevier group), Windsor Court, E. Grinstead House, E. Grinstead, W. Sussex RH19 1XA, England. TEL 01342-335832. FAX 01342-335948. TELEX 95127-INFSER-G. E-mail: http://www.reedinfo.co.uk. Ed. Claire Crossfield; Pub. Richard Woolley. adv.: B&W page £2850, color page £4750; trim 270 x 130; adv. contact: Jerry Odlin. circ. 11,000. **Document type:** directory.
   Description: Lists photographers, illustrators, design consultants and other creative services.

745.5   US   ISSN 1062-8207
CREATIVE OUTLETS. 1984. q. $5 per issue. Country Press, Box 5024, Durango, CO 81301. Ed. J.L. Walker. adv.; bk.rev. **Document type:** newsletter.
   Description: Dedicated to home based business with an emphasis on the arts and crafts industry. Features listings of shops and shows buying or consigning handicrafts.

700 770   AT   ISSN 0726-3589
CREATIVE SOURCE AUSTRALIA; the wizards of Oz. 1980. every 18 mos. $70. Armadillo Publishers Pty. Ltd., 11 Dingley Dell Rd., Warrandyte North, Melbourne, Vic. 3113, Australia. TEL 61-3-98444558. FAX 61-3-94895576. Ed. Elaine Howell; Pub. Elaine Howell. R&P contact: Elaine Howell. adv. contact: Elaine Howell. illus. circ. 4,000. (back issues avail.) **Document type:** directory.
   Description: Comprehensive source of what's happening in Australia's creative circles today.

745.5 790.132   UK   ISSN 0262-7140
CRESTED CIRCLE; a bi-monthly magazine for collectors of the products of the crested china manufacturers. 1980. bi-m. £4. c/o F. Owen, 26 Urswick Rd., Dagenham, Essex RM9 6EA, England. adv.; bk.rev. circ. 400.

CROCHET HOME. see NEEDLEWORK

CROSS QUICK - CROSS STITCH. see NEEDLEWORK

CROSS STITCH. see NEEDLEWORK

CROSS STITCH & COUNTRY CRAFTS. see NEEDLEWORK

CROSS-STITCH COLLECTION. see NEEDLEWORK

CROSS STITCH! MAGAZINE. see NEEDLEWORK

745.5   US   ISSN 1054-1551
CROSS STITCH SAMPLER. 1991. 6/yr. $19.98. N K S Publishing, 707 Kautz Rd., St. Charles, IL 60174. TEL 708-377-8000. FAX 708-377-8194. Ed. Deborah A. Novak. adv. contact: Deborah A. Novak. circ. 98,000 (paid). **Indexed:** Ind.How To Do It (1991-). **Document type:** consumer publication.
   Description: Features designer cross stitch and counted threadprojects with instructions and recommendations.

CROSS-STITCHER. see NEEDLEWORK

CROSS-STITCHER. see NEEDLEWORK

745.5   US   ISSN 0893-1097
DECORATIVE ARTIST'S WORKBOOK. 1987. bi-m. $19. F & W Publications, Inc., 1507 Dana Ave., Cincinnati, OH 45207. TEL 513-531-2222. FAX 513-531-4082. Ed. Sandra Carpenter. circ. 85,000. (also avail. in microform from UMI) **Indexed:** Ind.How To Do It (1990-).
   —UMI.

745.0941   UK   ISSN 0260-9568
DECORATIVE ARTS SOCIETY, 1850 TO THE PRESENT. JOURNAL. 1976. a. £10 to individuals; institutions £20 (effective Apr. 1996). Decorative Arts Society, 1850 to the Present, c/o Helen Grogan, Hon. Secy., P.O. Box 844, Lewes, E. Sussex BN7 3NG, England. TEL 44-1798-831734. (Subscr. to: 47 Coombe Crescent, Bury, Pulborough, W. Sussex RH20 1PE, England. TEL 44-178-831731) adv.: page £120. bk.rev./ bibl.; illus.; cum.index. circ. 500. **Document type:** academic/scholarly publication.
   —BLDSC (4732.675000).
   Formerly (until 1978): Decorative Arts Society 1890 - 1940. Bulletin.

745.592   US   ISSN 0746-9624
DOLL CRAFTER. 1983. m. $38.80 (foreign $48.80) (effective 1997). Scott Publications, 30595 Eight Mile Rd., Livonia, MI 48152-1798. TEL 248-477-6650. FAX 248-477-6795. Ed. Barbara Campbell. adv. circ. 9,700,000. **Indexed:** Ind.How To Do It (1990-). **Document type:** consumer publication.
   Description: For the doll creator and collector.

DOLLMAKING. see HOBBIES

745.5   GW   ISSN 0720-0528
DRECHSELN. 1878. q. DM.46.75. Kettler Verlag, Robert-Bosch-Str. 14, 59199 Boenen, Germany. TEL 02383-5118. FAX 02383-3052. Eds. Gisela Aurich, Martin Nolte. adv.; bk.rev. circ. 975.
   Former titles (until 1991): Holz und Elfenbein; Deutsche Drechsler Zeitung.
   Description: Covers all aspects of the art and craft of lathe-turning.

745.5 800   UK
DUE SOUTH; the biggest guide to what's on in the South. 1984. m. £8.50. Lastcode Ltd., 106 St. Mary's Rd., Southampton, Hampshire SO2 0AN, England. TEL 0703-332233. Ed. Sally O'Shaughnessy. circ. 16,000. (back issues avail.)

E M: EBONY MAN. see ETHNIC INTERESTS

EARLY AMERICAN HOMES; magazine of authentic colonial design, decorating, fine crafts and reproductions. see INTERIOR DESIGN AND DECORATION — Furniture And House Furnishings

EESTI NAINE; a magazine for women. see WOMEN'S INTERESTS

745.5   FR   ISSN 1256-7531
ENCADREMENT DECORATION. le magazine professionel du cadre et du decor interieur. 1990. q. 200 (foreign 270 F.). Revue de l'Encadrement, 132 bis av. Foch, 94100 St.-Maur-des-Fosses, France. TEL 48-85-12-30. FAX 48-85-38-94. Ed. Claude Lombard. adv.: B&W page 9000 F., color page 13500 F.; 210 x 297; adv. contact: Claude Lombard. bk.rev.; circ. 5,000 (paid). cols./p.: 3; pp./issue: 48. (back issues avail.) **Document type:** trade publication.
   Formerly (until 1994): Revue de l'Encadrement et de la Dorure.
   Description: Covers the training for many types of handicrafts, along with conservation issues and decorative techniques.

700   UK   ISSN 1356-7772
EUROPEAN CREATIVE HANDBOOK. 1993. a. £90. Reed Information Services, Division of Reed Telepublishing Ltd. (Subsidiary of: Reed Elsevier group), Windsor Court, E. Grinstead House, E. Grinstead, W. Sussex RH19 1XA, England. TEL 01342-326972. FAX 01342-335612. E-mail: http://www.reedinfo.co.uk. Ed. Claire Crossfield; Pub. Richard Woolley. adv.: B&W page £1525, color page £2500; trim 270 x 130; adv. contact: Jerry Odlin. circ. 5,000. **Document type:** directory.

745.5 738   UK   ISSN 0264-5041
EUROPEAN TABLEWARE BUYERS GUIDE. 1971. a. £46 (overseas £56) (effective 1997). Argus Business Media Ltd. (Subsidiary of: D M G Exhibitions Group Ltd.), Queensway House, 2 Queensway, Redhill, Surrey RH1 1QS, England. TEL 44-1737-768611. FAX 44-1737-761989. Ed. Stephen Wadey; Pub. Anthony J.E. Pike. adv. contact: Robin Beaman. **Document type:** trade publication.
   Former titles: Tableware Reference Book; Tableware and Pottery Gazette Reference Book (ISSN 0082-1438)

292 398   UK
EVERLASTING CIRCLE. irreg. free. Acca and Adda, B C M Akademia, London WC1N 3XX, England. Ed. S. Bate. **Document type:** newsletter.
   Description: Reviews and reports Ebat (Pagan bard) music and folklore and folk events.

792   US   ISSN 1067-1846
FAIRS AND FESTIVALS (YEAR). 1977. a. $18.50. Arts Extension Service, Division of Continuing Education, University of Massachusetts, Amherst, MA 01003. TEL 413-545-2360. FAX 413-545-3351. E-mail: aes@admin.umass.edu. Ed. Clare Wood. R&P contact: Clare Wood. adv. contact: Clare D. Wood. bibl.; index. circ. 2,500. **Document type:** directory.
   Former titles: Fairs and Festivals (Year): Northeast and Southeast (ISSN 1059-5929); (until 1991): Fairs and Festivals in the Northeast (ISSN 1051-9505); Incorporates (in 1991): Fairs and Festivals in the Southeast (ISSN 1051-9513)
   Description: Calendar listing of regional festivals for craftspeople, vendors, performers, media, and the arts-loving public.

FINE TOOL JOURNAL. see ANTIQUES

745.5 677.11   US   ISSN 1078-0335
FLAX CRAFT. 1993. q. $7.50 (Can.$10) (effective 1996). Virginia Handy, Ed. & Pub., 3503 Edwards Rd., Sodus, MI 49126-9707. TEL 616-944-5719. FAX 616-944-5719. (Alt. addr.: 4286 Watson Rd., Eau Claire, MI 49111) Ed. Virginia Handy. adv.; bibl.; circ. 75 (paid); 50 (controlled). (back issues avail.) **Document type:** newsletter.
   Description: Covers the growing and processing of the plant for linen and the use of the fiber for spinning, weaving, and related crafts.

ARTS AND HANDICRAFTS

745.92   UK   ISSN 0046-421X
THE FLOWER ARRANGER. 1961. q. £8.50 (foreign £10) (effective 1996). National Association of Flower Arrangement Societies, 21 Denbigh St., London SW1V 2HF, England.
TEL 44-171-828-5145. (Subscr. to: Taylor Bloxham Ltd., Nugent St., Leicester LE3 5HH, England) Ed. Jill Grayston. R&P contact: Jill Grayston. adv.; bk.rev.; illus.; index. circ. 55,000. **Document type:** consumer publication.

FORM; designtidskriften. see *INTERIOR DESIGN AND DECORATION*

372.5 700   NO   ISSN 0805-9144
                              CODEN: IEKRDI
FORM; et fagpedagogisk tidsskrift. 1967. bi-m. NOK 200 (effective 1997). Landslaget Forming i Skolen, Kongensgate 4, N-153 Oslo, Norway. TEL 47-22-42-29-71. FAX 47-22-41-93-83. Tone Vestoel. adv. contact: Berit Landet Holoyen. bk.rev. circ. 2,100. (back issues avail.) **Document type:** academic/scholarly publication.
—CASDDS. **CCC.**
    Former titles (until 1995): Forming i Skolen (ISSN 0333-2217); (until 1981): Ide og Form (ISSN 0046-8525)

FUSIONS. see *CERAMICS, GLASS AND POTTERY*

658.8   US   ISSN 1050-0316
GIFT BASKET REVIEW. * 1990. m. $29.95. Festivities Publications, Inc., 815 Haines St., Jacksonville, FL 32206-6050. TEL 904-634-1902. FAX 904-633-8764. Ed. Sin-Ting Mary Liu; Pub. Debra & David Paulk. adv. contact: Ann Saporito. circ. 15,000. **Document type:** trade publication.
    Description: Features full color design ideas for gift baskets. For retailers and distributors in the gift industries.

745.5 666   US   ISSN 1041-6684
TT298
GLASS PATTERNS QUARTERLY. 1985. q. $24 (foreign $29). Glass Patterns Quarterly, Inc., 8300 Hidden Valley Rd., Box 69, Westport, KY 40077. TEL 502-222-5631. FAX 502-222-4527. E-mail: gpq@aol.com. Ed. Maureen James; Pub. Steven V. James. R&P contact: Maureen James. adv. contact: Sarah Martin. bk.rev.; index. circ. 40,600. **Document type:** consumer publication.
    Description: Contains step-by-step instructions, how-to-to photos, and patterns for creating more than a dozen projects each issue.

748   US   ISSN 0017-1077
GLASS WORKSHOP. * 1969. q. $8. Stained Glass Club, 8 Frasco Ln., Norwood, NJ 07648-2407. Ed. Dr. S. Isenberg. adv.; bk.rev.; illus. circ. 2,000.

745.5   DK   ISSN 0105-9416
HAANDVAERKET AND MASKINEN. 1976. 6/yr. Postboks 92, DK-2900 Hellerup, Denmark.

745.5   UK   ISSN 0142-0798
NK2808
HALI; the international magazine of antique carpet and textile art. 1978. bi-m. £62($118) (Germany DM.190; rest of Europe £68; elsewhere £84). Hali Publications Ltd., Kingsgate House, Kingsgate Pl., London NW6 4TA, England. TEL 44-171-3289341. FAX 44-171-3725924. (Addr. in N. America: c/o I.M.P. Building C1D, 145 Ave. and Hook Creek Blvd., Valley Steam, NY 11581, USA) Ed. Daniel Shaffer; Pub. Sebastian Ghandchi. R&P contact: Sebastian Ghandchi. adv. contact: conrad Shouldice. bk.rev.; bibl.; illus.; stat.; tr.lit.; index; circ. 7,500 (paid). (back issues avail.) **Indexed:** Art & Archaeol.Tech.Abstr., Art Ind., Artbibl.Mod., Per.Islam. (1991-). **Document type:** academic/scholarly publication.
—BLDSC (4240.375000); KR SourceOne; UnCover.
    Description: Covers all aspects of fine antique carpets and textiles, providing scholarly research, reviews of public and private exhibitions, and marketplace news.

HAND PAPERMAKING. see *PAPER AND PULP*

745.5   US   ISSN 1072-0529
HANDCRAFT ILLUSTRATED. 1993. bi-m. $24.95 (Canada $27.95; elsewhere $39.95). Natural Health L.P., 17 Station St., Box 1200, Brookline, MA 02147. TEL 617-232-1000. FAX 617-325-1572. (Subscr. to: Box 7448, Red Oak, IA 51591-0448) Ed. Carol Endler Sterbenz. **Document type:** consumer publication.
    Description: Presents detailed instructions and advice on craft ideas, including flower arrangement, framing, gilding, antiquing, wreath making and similar projects.

745.5 790   US   ISSN 0897-5345
HANDS ON GUIDE. 1988. m. $28. 255 Cranston Crest, Escondido, CA 92025-7037. TEL 619-747-8206. Ed. Christel Luther. R&P contact: Christel Luther. adv. circ. 2,000. (tabloid format) **Document type:** directory, trade publication.
    Description: A Western states events guide for vendors, exhibitors and shoppers.

745.5   US   ISSN 0198-8212
TT848
HANDWOVEN. 1979. 5/yr. $22 (foreign $28). Interweave Press, Inc., 201 E. Fourth St., Loveland, CO 80537. TEL 970-669-7672. FAX 970-667-8317. Ed. Jean Scorgie; Pub. Linda C. Ligon. R&P contact: Karen Evanson. adv. contact: Sharon Altergott. bk.rev.; illus. circ. 36,000. **Indexed:** Ind.How To Do It (1979-). **Document type:** consumer publication.
—UnCover.
    Incorporates (in 1981): Interweave (ISSN 0198-8220)
    Description: Provides woven projects, step-by-step instructions, in-depth articles, reviews, columns, tips and product information. Features cover special techniques, history, people and weaving lore. Projects include fashions, fabrics and accessories for the home.

745.5   SW   ISSN 0345-4649
HEMSLOEJDEN. 1933. 6/yr. SEK 245 in Sweden; Nordic and Baltic countries SEK 268; elsewhere SEK 345 (effective 1998); newsstand price: SEK 45. Svenska Hemslojdsfoereningarnas Riksfoerbund - S H R, Kungsgatan 51, S-903 26 Umeaa, Sweden. TEL 46-90-14-59-25. FAX 46-90-14-59-23. E-mail: hemslojden@tidskriften.shrslojd.se. Ed. Katarina Aagren. R&P contact: Katarina Aagren. adv. contact: Ulla Segerstedt. bk.rev. circ. 20,000.

745.5   GW
HOBEL UND SPAN; Holz- und Kunststoffverarbeitendes Handwerk Rheinland-Pfalz. 1951. m. Landesfachverband Holz und Kunststoff Rheinland-Pfalz, Postfach 946, 56009 Koblenz, Germany. TEL 0261-34445.

HOOKED ON CROCHET!. see *NEEDLEWORK*

745.5   US
HORIZONS (ELMWOOD PARK). 1982. 4/yr. membership only. Hobby Industry Assn., 319 E. 54th St., Box 348, Elmwood Park, NJ 07407. TEL 201-794-1133. FAX 201-797-0657. Ed. Hope Crawley. circ. 4,000. (tabloid format; back issues avail.) **Document type:** newsletter.
    Description: Provides information regarding the Association and industry events.

746 746   DK   ISSN 0108-481X
HUSFLID. Variant title: Dansk Husflid. 1881. bi-m. DKK 170 membership (retired DKK 102; families DKK 255; youth DKK 85) (effective 1996). Dansk Husflidsselskab, Tyrebakken 11, DK-5300 Kerteminde, Denmark. TEL 45-65-32-20-96. FAX 45-65-32-56-11. Ed. Ib Solvang. adv.: B&W page DKK 3100, color page DKK 4740; trim 191 x 261; adv. contact: Inge Bay. circ. 7,000.
    Formerly (until 1972): Dansk Husflidstidende.

INDIAN ARTS & CRAFTS ASSOCIATION NEWSLETTER. see *ETHNIC INTERESTS*

745.5 700   US
INFORM (SYRACUSE). 1981. q. $30 membership. Empire State Crafts Alliance, Inc., 320 Montgomery St., Syracuse, NY 13202-2010. TEL 315-472-4245. Ed. Megan White. R&P contact: Megan White. adv.; bk.rev. circ. 1,100. **Indexed:** Paper & Bd.Abstr. **Document type:** newsletter.
    Formerly: Information (Poughkeepsie).

INK & GALL; the marbling journal. see *PUBLISHING AND BOOK TRADE*

INSTRUMENTENBAU REPORT; aktuelle Informationen fuer Musikfreunde und Instrumentenbauer. see *MUSIC*

745.5   US
INTERNATIONAL DIRECTORY OF RESOURCES FOR ARTISANS. irreg., latest 1994. $50. Crafts Center, 1001 Connecticut Ave., Ste. 525, Washington, DC 20036. TEL 202-729-9603. FAX 202-296-2452. Ed. Caroline Ramsay. adv. contact: Nina Smith. **Document type:** directory.
    Description: Lists more than 6000 organizations that offer assistance in finding new craft products, markets, and sources of funding and technical assistance, materials, tools and publications.

INUIT ART QUARTERLY. see *ART*

ITALIC HANDWRITING NEWSLETTER; a newsletter for people who care about legibility. see *EDUCATION — Teaching Methods And Curriculum*

745.5   US   ISSN 0075-4250
                              CODEN: JGLSAE
JOURNAL OF GLASS STUDIES. 1959. a. $42.50 (foreign $43.50). Corning Museum of Glass, One Museum Way, Corning, NY 14830-2253. TEL 607-937-5371. FAX 607-937-3352. Ed. David B. Whitehouse. cum.index: vols.1-15. circ. 1,500. (also avail. in microform from UMI; reprint service avail. from UMI) **Indexed:** A.I.C.P., Art & Archaeol.Tech.Abstr., Art Ind., Artbibl.Mod., Arts & Hum.Cit.Ind., ASCA, Br.Archaeol.Abstr., Bull.Signal., Chem.Abstr., Curr.Cont., Numis.Lit, RILA. **Document type:** academic/scholarly publication.
—CASDDS; KR SourceOne; UMI; UnCover. **CCC.**
    Description: Articles on the artistic, historical, and archeological aspects of glass from classical antiquity through the 19th century.

KEEPSAKE CALENDAR; (year) cross-stitch collection. see *NEEDLEWORK*

745.5   SZ   ISSN 0023-0553
NK3700
KERAMIK-FREUNDE DER SCHWEIZ. MITTEILUNGSBLATT/AMIS SUISSES DE LA CERAMIQUE. BULLETIN. (Text in English, French, German and Italian) 1946. irreg. membership. Plattenstr. 86, CH-8032 Zurich, Switzerland. TEL 41-1-2612155. Ed. Rudolf Schnyder. R&P contact: Rudolf Schnyder. bk.rev.; abstr.; charts; illus.; mkt. **Indexed:** Artbibl.Mod., RILA. **Document type:** bulletin.

745.5   GW   ISSN 0172-6102
KERAMIKMAGAZIN. 6/yr. DM.64 (Europe DM.69; overseas DM.82). Verlagsgesellschaft Ritterbach mbH, Postfach 1820, 50208 Frechen, Germany. TEL 49-2234-1866-0. FAX 49-2234-186690. Ed. Gabi Dewald. **Document type:** consumer publication.
    Incorporates (in 1991): Keramik Creativ (ISSN 0720-9126)

745.5   AU
KERAMISCHE RUNDSCHAU KLIMA UND RAUM. Short title: K und R. 12/yr. S.1050 (effective 1997). Verlag Lorenz, Ebendorferstr. 10, A-1010 Vienna, Austria. TEL 43-1-4056695. FAX 43-1-4068693. adv.: B&W page S.17200, color page S.31900. circ. 2,200. **Indexed:** Br.Ceram.Abstr. **Document type:** trade publication.

745.5   NO   ISSN 0333-1059
KUNSTHAANDVERK. 1980. q. NOK 215 to individuals; institutions NOK 265 (effective 1997). Norske Kunsthandverkeres Formidlingssentral, Kongensgt. 3, N-153 Oslo, Norway. TEL 47-2-33-59-90. FAX 47-2-42-39-37. Ed. Ellen J. Lerberg. adv.: B&W page NOK 4000. bk.rev. circ. 3,000. **Indexed:** DAAI.

745.5   GW   ISSN 0941-9179
NK925
KUNSTHANDWERK UND DESIGN. 1965. bi-m. DM.84 (Europe DM.105; overseas DM.115). Verlagsgesellschaft Ritterbach mbH, Postfach 1820, 50208 Frechen, Germany. TEL 49-2234-1866-0. FAX 49-2234-186690. Ed. Uta Klotz. adv.; bk.rev. circ. 7,600. **Document type:** consumer publication.
—BLDSC (5130.688800).
    Formerly: Kunst und Handwerk (ISSN 0454-6539)

LADY'S CIRCLE PATCHWORK QUILTS. see *NEEDLEWORK*

ARTS AND HANDICRAFTS

745.5 685 US
LEATHER CRAFTERS & SADDLERS JOURNAL. 1956. bi-m. $24 in the U.S.; Canada $28; elsewhere $34. Leather Crafters and Saddlers Journal Inc., 331 Annette Ct., Rhinelander, WI 54501-2902. TEL 715-362-5393. FAX 715-362-5391. Ed. William R. Reis. adv.; bk.rev.; charts; illus.; tr.lit.; index; circ. 7,500 (paid). (also avail. in microform from UMI; reprint service avail.) Indexed: Ind.How To Do It (1990-). **Document type:** consumer publication.
—UMi.
Former titles: Leather Crafters Journal (ISSN 1056-4225); (until no.2, 1991): Leather Craftsman (ISSN 1047-9805); Make it with Leather (ISSN 0738-4718); Craftsman (ISSN 0011-0779)

745.5 IT ISSN 0393-8190
NX4
M C M : LA STORIA DELLE COSE; rivista delle arti minori. (Text in Italian; summaries in English and Italian) 1985. q. L.50000 (foreign L.90000) (effective 1997). Maria Cristina de Montemayor Editore, Viale Alessandro Volta, 173, 50131 Florence, Italy. TEL 39-55-224227. Ed. Maria Cristina de Montemayor. adv.; B&W page L.2000000, color page L.3000000; 200 x 260; adv. contact: Marino Giani. bk.rev. circ. 10,000. (back issues avail.) **Document type:** newspaper.
Description: Includes news on a wide variety of topics: the history of painting, the art of hand blown glass, tapestries, making and working with metals and fabrics, clay, pottery, fiber, gold, silver, wood and mosaic.

745.5 US ISSN 1045-2702
MATTER.* 1989. m. $18 (free to qualified personnel). G L M Publications (Subsidiary of: George Little Management, Inc.), 10 Bank St., Ste. 1200, White Plains, NY 10606-1952. (Subscr. to: Box 482, Winchester, MA 08190) Ed. Karen Gaspin. circ. controlled.
Description: Covers the crafts industry.

745.5 AT
MELBOURNE SHEEP AND WOOL. 1878. a. Aus.$45. Australian Sheep Breeders Association Inc., Royal Melbourne Showgrounds, Epsom Rd., Ascot Vale, Vic. 3032, Australia. TEL 61-3-92817518. FAX 61-3-3762973. Ed. Peter Fraser. circ. 700. (back issues avail.) **Document type:** catalog.
Formerly: Weekly Times Melbourne Sheep and Woolcraft Show.

745.5 669 US ISSN 0270-1146
NK6400
METALSMITH. 1979. q. $26 to non-members (Canada $34; elsewhere $68). Society of North American Goldsmiths, 5009 Londonderry Dr., Tampa, FL 33647. TEL 813-977-5326. FAX 813-977-8462. Ed. Frank Lewis. adv.; B&W page $710, color page $1288; trim 8 3/8 x 10 7/8; adv. contact: Bob Mitchell. bk.rev.; charts; illus.; index. circ. 13,300. (back issues avail.) Indexed: Art Ind., DAAI. **Document type:** trade publication.
—BLDSC (5699.610000); KR SourceOne; UnCover.
Former titles: Golddust & Goldsmith's Journal (ISSN 0197-0127)
Description: Devoted solely to the metal arts.

MINNESOTA ARTS DIRECTORY. see ART

MONTEREY MUSEUM OF ART NEWS. see ART

745.5 US ISSN 0739-1544
NK4005
N C E C A JOURNAL.* 1980. a. $35 (foreign $45; students $25) includes membership. (National Council on Education for the Ceramic Arts) Key Connection, 1809 W. Main St. 185, Carbondale, IL 62901-2123. (Membership addr.: c/o Regina Brown, Exec.Sec., Box 1677, Bandon, OR 94711) Ed. Linda Mosley. charts; illus. circ. 3,000.
Description: Record of the annual conference proceedings.

745.5 US
N C E C A NEWS.* 1977. q. membership. (National Council on Education for the Ceramic Arts) Key Connection, 1809 W. Main St. 185, Carbondale, IL 62901-2123. (Membership addr.: c/o Regina Brown, Exec.Sec., Box 1677, Bandon, OR 97411) circ. 3,000. **Document type:** newsletter.
Formerly (until 1986): N C E C A Newsletter (ISSN 0739-1552)
Description: Includes pertinent information about the annual conference, other NCECA activities, and news from the membership.

745 RU ISSN 0235-5051
NARODNOE TVORCHESTVO. (Text in Russian) 1937. bi-m. $58 (effective 1998). Tsentr Russkogo Fol'klora - Centre of Russian Folklore, Kropotkinskii per., 10, 119034 Moscow, Russia. TEL 7-095-2468417. FAX 7-095-2463389. (Dist. by: Mezhdunarodnaya Kniga, B. Yakimanka 39, 117049 Moscow, Russia. TEL 7-095-2384967. FAX 7-095-2384634) (Co-sponsor: Ministerstvo Kul'tury Rossiiskoi Federatsii) Ed. Anatoli Kargin. adv.: page $300; adv. contact: Anatoli Kargin. circ. 10,000.

745.5 SA ISSN 1015-2369
NATIONAL CERAMICS QUARTERLY. (Text in English) 1974. q. $20. (Association of Potters of Southern Africa) Guassardo - National Ceramics, P.O. Box 568, Anerley 4230, Natal, South Africa. TEL 27-39-6813216. FAX 27-39-6813216. Ed. Michael Guassardo. adv.; bk.rev.; circ. 2,000 (paid).
Supersedes (in 1984): Sgraffiti.
Description: Brings the reader up-to-date on news from around the world, new technical developments, an in-depth look at ceramics in the home, the people who make them, as well as the firms that supply the necessary materials.

NEEDLEWORK. see NEEDLEWORK

700 GW ISSN 0723-2454
NK5100
NEUES GLAS/NEW GLASS; magazine on contemporary glass art. (Text in English, German) 1980. q. DM.66 (Europe DM.70; overseas DM.76). Verlagsgesellschaft Ritterbach mbH, Postfach 1820, 50208 Frechen, Germany. TEL 49-2234-1866-0. FAX 49-2234-186690. Ed. Uta Klotz. circ. 9,000. (back issues avail.) Indexed: Art Ind., Artbibl.Mod., DAAI. **Document type:** consumer publication.
—BLDSC (6077.985500); KR SourceOne.

745.5 US ISSN 0275-469X
NK5110
NEW GLASS REVIEW. 1976. a. $8.50 (foreign $10.75). Corning Museum of Glass, One Museum Way, Corning, NY 14830-2253. TEL 607-937-5371. FAX 607-937-3352. Ed. David B. Whitehouse. (reprint service avail. from UMI) Indexed: Artbibl.Mod., DAAI. **Document type:** academic/scholarly publication.
—BLDSC (6084.217500).
Formerly (until 1979): Contemporary Glass; **Supersedes** (in 1978): Contemporary Glass Microfiche Program.
Description: Compendium of contemporary glass made in previous calendar year.

NEW IDEA. see HOME ECONOMICS

745.5 NZ ISSN 1173-5279
NEW ZEALAND POTTER. 1958. 3/yr. NZ.$33 (foreign NZ.$45). New Zealand Potter Publications Ltd., P.O. Box 881, Auckland, New Zealand. TEL 64-9-3798665. FAX 64-9-3093247. Ed. Howard Willims. R&P contact: Cecilia Parkinson. adv.; B&W page NZ.$485, color page NZ.$759; adv. contact: Cecilia Parkinson. bk.rev.; charts; illus.; tr.lit.; cum.index. circ. 6,000. (back issues avail.) Indexed: Pinpointer. **Document type:** abstracting/indexing, consumer publication.
—UnCover. CCC.
Former titles: Potter (ISSN 0113-583X); (until 1975): New Zealand Potter (ISSN 0028-8608)

NORTHEAST - JOURNAL OF ANTIQUES & ART; antiques - art - historic homes - country life - preservation & restoration. see ANTIQUES

745.582 US ISSN 1074-8067
NOTES FROM A BEADERWORKER'S JOURNAL. 1989. q. $20. Center for the Study of Beadwork, Box 13719, Portland, OR 97213. TEL 503-248-1848. FAX 503-248-1011. Ed. Alice Scherer. adv.: page $125. bk.rev. circ. 650. **Document type:** newsletter.
Description: Devoted to keeping readers up-to-date on the activities of the center and on information from the field worldwide.

745.5 338 CN ISSN 1193-011X
NOVA SCOTIA CRAFT NEWS. 1973. q. Can.$53.50 (effective 1997). Nova Scotia Designer Crafts Council, Ste. 901, 1809 Barrington St., Halifax, NS B3J 3K8, Canada. TEL 902-423-3837. FAX 902-422-0881. E-mail: nsdcc@isisnet.com; URL: http://www.isisnet.com/nsdcc. R&P contact: Susan Hanranan. adv.: B&W page Can.$219.35; adv. contact: Pat Chambers. circ. 500. (also avail. in diskette format; back issues avail.) **Document type:** newsletter.
Former titles (until 1992): Nova Scotia Designer Crafts Council. Newsletter (ISSN 0834-3829); (until 1986): N S D C C Newsletter (ISSN 0834-3136); (until 1985): N S D C Newsletter (ISSN 0709-0374)

745.5 AT ISSN 1038-1856
OBJECT. 1964. q. Aus.$28 to individuals; institutions Aus.$44. Centre for Contemporary Craft, Level 3, 88 George St., The Rocks, Sydney, N.S.W. 2000, Australia. TEL 61-2-92479126. FAX 61-2-92472641. E-mail: cfcc@cfcc.com.au. Ed. Ian Were. adv. contact: Angela Robertson. bk.rev. circ. 6,000. **Document type:** academic/scholarly publication.
Formerly (until 1995): Crafts New South Wales (ISSN 0726-6758)
Description: Presents critical and theoretical writing on crafts-based art and design issues.
Refereed Serial

745.5 SP ISSN 1135-1152
OFICIO Y ARTE; noticias de artesania. 1992. bi-m. 2100 ptas. in Europe 2600 ptas.; elsewhere 3800 ptas. (effective 1997). Organizacion de los Artesanos de Espana, Camino de la Iglesia 38, 15009 A Coruna, Spain. TEL 34-81-288104. FAX 34-81-133569. Dir. Manual Gonzalez Arias. adv.: page 57200 ptas.; trim 257 x 181; adv. contact: Manuel Gonzalez Arias. circ. 5,000. **Document type:** bulletin.
Description: Provides information on exhibitions, galleries, shops, fairs, museums, technical articles and more.

745.5 CN ISSN 0229-1320
ONTARIO CRAFT. 1981. 4/yr. Can.$19($21.48) (effective 1998). Ontario Crafts Council, Chalmers Bldg., 35 McCaul St., Toronto, ON M5T 1V5, Canada. TEL 416-977-3551. FAX 416-977-3552. Ed. Anne McPherson. adv.: B&W page Can.$930; trim 8 1/8 x 11; adv. contact: Susan Browne. illus. circ. 4,000. (reprint service avail. from MML) Indexed: Can.B.P.I., CMI, DAAI. **Document type:** consumer publication.
Incorporates (1975-1996): Craftnews (ISSN 0319-7832); **Supersedes:** Craftsman (ISSN 0319-7840)

745.5 US ISSN 0030-901X
PACK-O-FUN. 1951. 6/yr. $14.97. Clapper Communications Companies, 2400 E. Devon Ave., Ste. 375, Des Plaines, IL 60018-4618. TEL 847-635-5800. FAX 847-635-6311. URL: http://www.craftnet.org/pack-o-fun. Ed. Bill Stephani. adv. contact: Stuart Hochwert. circ. 102,000. (back issues avail.) **Document type:** consumer publication.
●Also available online.
—UMi.

745.5 US ISSN 1079-6819
PAINTING. 1985. 6/yr. $21.95 (includes Source Guide). Clapper Communications Companies, 2400 E. Devon Ave., Ste. 375, Des Plaines, IL 60018-4618. TEL 847-635-5800; 800-272-3871. FAX 847-635-6311. URL: http://www.craftnet.org/painting. Ed. Beth Browning. adv. contact: Stuart Hochwert. bk.rev.; circ. 100,000 (paid). (back issues avail.) **Document type:** consumer publication.
●Also available online.
—Ei.
Former titles (until 1995): Decorative Arts Painting (ISSN 1067-0068); (until 1993): Decorative Arts Digest (ISSN 0888-076X)
Description: Directed toward those interested in learning, or increasing skills, in tole and decorative painting.

ARTS AND HANDICRAFTS 483

745.5   US
PAINTWORKS. 1991. 9/yr. $44.55. All American Crafts, Inc., 243 Newton-Sparta Rd., Newton, NJ 07860. TEL 201-383-8080. FAX 201-383-8133. adv.: B&W page $900, color page $1500; trim 7 7/8 x 10 1/2; adv. contact: Robert Becker. circ. 170,000. **Document type:** consumer publication.
    Description: Features craft and decorative painting for painters and hobbyists.

745.5   MX
PEQUENA DIANA. 1984. m. Lucio Blanco 435, Col. Juan Tlihuaca, 02400 Mexico D.F., Mexico. TEL 5-352-6056. Ed. Javier Ortiz Camorlinga. circ. 200,000.

PERISTIL. see *ARCHITECTURE*

745.5   US   ISSN 1052-9977
PICTURE FRAMING MAGAZINE. m. $20. Hobby Publications, Inc., 225 Gordons Corner Plaza, Box 420, Manalapan, NJ 07726. TEL 908-446-4900. FAX 908-446-5488. Ed. Laura Caiaccia. circ. 27,632.
    Description: For independent retailers, gallery owners, chain store buyers, wholesalers, manufacturers and designers of frames and related framing supplies. Editorial emphasis is on education and technique in custom framing.

PIECEWORK; all this by hand. see *NEEDLEWORK*

PLASTIC CANVAS! MAGAZINE. see *NEEDLEWORK*

PLASTIC CANVAS WORLD. see *NEEDLEWORK*

745.5   UK   ISSN 0144-2937
POPULAR CRAFTS. 1974. m. £22.80 (Europe £33.30; U.S. $49) (effective 1996). Nexus Special Interests Ltd., Nexus House, Boundary Way, Hemel Hempstead, Herts HP2 7ST, England. TEL 44-1442-66551. FAX 44-1442-66998. (Subscr. to: Nexus Subscription Services, Queensway House, 2 Queensway, Redhill, RH1 1QS, Surrey, England. TEL 44-1737-768611; Subscr. in US to: Wise Owl Worldwide Publications, 4314 W. 238th St., Torrance, CA 90505-4509. TEL 310-375-6258. FAX 310-375-0548) Ed. Brenda Ross. adv.; bk.rev.; index. **Document type:** consumer publication.
—BLDSC (6550.325000).
    Incorporates: Gem Craft (ISSN 0140-5977)
    Description: Offers advice and projects for arts and crafts enthusiasts.

745.5   UK
POPULAR CRAFTS PROJECTS. (Supplements avail.: Popular Crafts Projects: Projects for the Home (ISSN 0968-6002); Popular Crafts Projects: Projects for Christmas (ISSN 0966-6125)) bi-m. Nexus Special Interests Ltd., Nexus House, Boundary Way, Hemel Hempstead, Herts. HP2 7ST, England. TEL 44-1442-66551. FAX 44-1442-66998. (Subscr. to: Argus Subscription Services, Queensway House, 2 Queensway, Redhill, Surrey, England. TEL 44-1737-768611) **Document type:** consumer publication.
    Description: Offers a wide variety of arts and crafts projects for all times of the year.

745.5   UK   ISSN 0969-6946
POPULAR PATCHWORK. 1993. 7/yr. £18.20 (Europe £22.80; U.S. $40.50) (effective 1996). Nexus Special Interests Ltd., Nexus House, Boundary Way, Hemel Hempstead, Herts HP2 7ST, England. TEL 44-1442-66551. FAX 44-1442-66998. (Subscr. to: Nexus Subscription Services, Queensway House, 2 Queensway, Redhill, Surrey, England. TEL 44-1737-768611; Subscr. in US to: Wise Owl Worldwide Publications, 4314 W. 238th St., Torrance, CA 90505-4509. TEL 310-375-6258. FAX 310-375-0548) **Document type:** consumer publication.
    Description: Offers clear instruction for patchwork quilt projects for beginners and experts alike.

738.15   NO   ISSN 0333-4872
PORSELENSMALING. (Editions in English, German) 1980. 6/yr. NOK 235 in Scandinavia; elsewhere NOK 295 (effective 1997). (Union of Educational Officers of China Decorating) Tema Forlag, N-2260 Kirkenaer, Norway. TEL 47-62-9415-66. FAX 47-62-94-11-70. Ed. Helene Loevenskiold. adv.: B&W page NOK 5020, color page NOK 9610; trim 264 x 185; adv. contact: Bjoern Thore Skulstad. circ. 13,440.
    Description: Publishes articles on methods and techniques of painting porcelain.

745.5   US
POTPOURRI SIMPLE & EASY UPDATE. 1992. a. $5. Prosperity & Profits Unlimited Distribution Services, Box 416, Denver, CO 80201-0416. TEL 303-575-5576. Ed. A. Doyle. circ. 3,200 (paid). (looseleaf format) **Document type:** newsletter.
    Description: Offers potpourri recipes.

745.5   AT   ISSN 0048-4954
POTTERY IN AUSTRALIA. 1962. q. Aus.$52 (foreign Aus.$64) (effective 1996). Potters' Society of Australia, P.O. Box 937, Crows Nest, N.S.W. 2065, Australia. TEL 61-2-99013353. FAX 61-2-4361681. Ed. Christina Fitzgerald. adv. contact: Sandi Cullen. cum.index: 1962-1995. circ. 5,000. Indexed: DAAI, Gdlns, Pinpointer. **Document type:** consumer publication, trade publication.
—BLDSC (6566.100000); UnCover.

745.5   GW   ISSN 0032-7697
PRESENT; international trade magazine for giftware and christmas items. (Text in German, captions in English) 1925. m. DM.117 (foreign DM.123) (effective 1997). (Verband der Korbwaren-, Korbmoebel- und Kinderwagenindustrie e.V.) Meisenbach GmbH, Hainstr. 18, 96047 Bamberg, Germany. TEL 49-951-861135. FAX 49-951-861158. (Subscr. to: Postfach 2069, 96011 Bamberg, Germany) Ed. Christine Dicker. adv.: B&W page DM.3415, color page DM.5596; trim 260 x 184; adv. contact: Rita Engl. mkt. circ. 6,540. **Document type:** trade publication.

745.5   IT
QUADERNI DELL'EMILCERAMICA. no.14. 2/yr. Lit.8000 per no. (effective 1997). Gruppo Editoriale Faenza Editrice S.p.A., Via Pier. de Crescenzi, 44, 48018 Faenza RA, Italy. TEL 39-546-663488. FAX 39-546-660440. E-mail: gefe.vendita@uno.dinamica.it; gefe.info@uno.dinamica.it. Ed. Francesco Liverani.

QUEENSLAND BOOKBINDERS' GUILD. NEWSLETTER. see *PUBLISHING AND BOOK TRADE*

QUICK & EASY PLASTIC CANVAS. see *NEEDLEWORK*

745.5   US   ISSN 0899-0581
QUILTMAKERS TIME. 1972. irreg., no.3, 1986. $3.95. Sally Goodspeed, Ed. & Pub., 238 N. Charles St., Baltimore, MD 21218. bk.rev.; illus.
    Description: Publishes articles and essays on the historical origin and evolution of the decorative arts, with instructional drawings and patterns. Includes an ongoing biographical study of the Lincoln family.

745.5 738.1   UK   ISSN 0953-0436
REAL POTTERY; a review of craft pottery. 1954. irreg., approx. a. £10. Northfields Studio, Northfields, Tring, Herts. HP23 5QW, England. TEL 01442-85229. Ed. M. Fieldhouse. adv.; bk.rev.; illus.; index. circ. 2,500. (also avail. in microfilm from UMI; reprint service avail. from UMI) Indexed: Br.Ceram.Abstr.
—UMI.
    Former titles: Pottery Quarterly (ISSN 0032-5678); Real Pottery.

RECIPE GREETINGS UPDATE. see *HOME ECONOMICS*

745.5   US   ISSN 1073-2527
RODALE'S QUICK & EASY CRAFT COLLECTION. 1992. q. $3.50 per no. Rodale Press, Inc., 33 E. Minor St., Emmaus, PA 18049. TEL 610-967-5171. FAX 610-967-7725. **Document type:** consumer publication.
    Description: Ideas and projects for crafts enthusiasts.

745.5   II   ISSN 0035-8215
N8
ROOPA-LEKHA; an illustrated journal of Indian arts and crafts. 1929. s-a. $20. All-India Fine Arts and Crafts Society, Rafi Marg, New Delhi 1, India. Ed. S.S. Bhagat Secy. adv.; bk.rev.; illus. circ. 1,000.

730   US   ISSN 0746-7672
RUBBERSTAMPMADNESS. 1980. bi-m. $24 (foreign $30) (effective 1996). Rubberstampmadness, Inc., 408 S.W. Monroe, Ste. 210, Corvallis, OR 97330. TEL 541-752-0075. FAX 541-752-5475. E-mail: rsmadness@proaxis.com. Ed. Roberta Sperling; Pub. Michael Malan. R&P contact: Roberta Sperling. adv. contact: Susan Shumway. bk.rev.; circ. 21,000 (paid). **Document type:** consumer publication.
    Description: Devoted to the creative use of artistic rubber stamps. Includes stories on artists using stamps and provides hints on ways to use rubber stamps.
    Refereed Serial

790.13 700 745.5   US
S A C NEWSMONTHLY. (Southern Art and Crafts); national news and listings of art & craft shows. 1986. m. $24 (effective 1996-1997); newsstand price: $3. S A C, Inc., Box 159, Bogalusa, LA 70429-0159. TEL 504-732-2322; 800-825-3722. FAX 504-732-3744. (Alt addr.: 414 Ave. B, Bogalusa, LA 70427) Ed. Wayne Smith; Pub. Wayne Smith. R&P contact: Wayne Smith. adv. contact: Sue Martin. bk.rev. circ. 500. cols./p.: 4; pp./issue: 64. (tabloid format; back issues avail.) **Document type:** newsletter.
    •Also available online.
    Incorporates: Art and Crafts Catalyst; Former titles: National Arts and Crafts Network; National Calendar of Open Competitive Exhibitions; Lisa's Report; Craft Show Bulletin.
    Description: Lists art and crafts shows and festivals nationwide.

700   AT   ISSN 0819-2936
S.A. CRAFTS. (South Australia) 1985. q. $65. Crafts Council of South Australia Inc., P.O. Box 8067, Station Arcade, S.A. 5000, Australia. TEL 61-8-84101822. FAX 61-8-82310434. Ed. Gail Fairlamb. R&P contact: Gail Fairlamb. adv. contact: Bernadette Irwin. bk.rev. circ. 500. (back issues avail.)
    Formerly (until June 1986): S.A. Crafts News (ISSN 0814-9933)
    Description: Focuses on CCSA projects, national and state crafts news. Provides current information on funding opportunities, workshops, exhibitions, and festivals.

700 746   US
S A G A NEWS. Variant title: SagaNews. 1979. q. $28 membership (foreign $32) (effective 1997). Smocking Arts Guild of America, 1926 Waukegan Rd., Glenview, IL 60025-1770. TEL 847-657-6804. FAX 847-699-6369. Ed. Laura Sencabaugh. R&P contact: Patricia Sistler. bk.rev. circ. 4,000 (paid). **Document type:** newsletter.
    Formerly (until Jan. 1988): Smocking Arts.

745.5 669   US
S N A G NEWSLETTER. bi-m. $55 membership (Canada $65; elsewhere $68); student $40 (Canada $50; elsewhere $53) (effective 1997). Society of North American Goldsmiths, 5009 Londonderry Dr., Tampa, FL 33647. TEL 813-977-5326. FAX 813-977-8462. **Document type:** newsletter.
    Description: Features information on exhibitions, workshops, conferences, and job opportunities throughout North America.

745.5   US   ISSN 0748-8378
S P A C E S; notes on America's folk art environments. 1982. irreg. $15 to individuals; institutions $25. Saving and Preserving Art and Cultural Environments, 1804 N. Van Ness, Los Angeles, CA 90028. TEL 213-463-1629. bk.rev.; film rev.; bibl.; illus. circ. 1,000. (back issues avail.) **Document type:** newspaper.

745.5   US
SCENTERPIECE UPDATE. 1990. a. $5. Continnuus, c/o Prosperity & Profits Unlimited Distribution Services, Box 416, Denver, CO 80201-0416. TEL 303-575-5676. Ed. A. Doyle. R&P contact: A. Doyle. (looseleaf format) **Document type:** newsletter.
    Description: Contains potpourri recipes and explains the origins of various fragrances.

ARTS AND HANDICRAFTS

DIE SCHAULADE; international trade magazine for table top, household goods, giftware and living accessories. see CERAMICS, GLASS AND POTTERY.

SCHOOL ARTS; the art education magazine for teachers. see EDUCATION — Teaching Methods And Curriculum

745.5   UK   ISSN 0144-1302
SCOTTISH POTTERY HISTORICAL REVIEW. 1980. a. Scottish Pottery Society, c/o Mr. Graeme Cruickshank, 21 Warrender Park Terrace, Edinburgh, Scotland. adv.; bk.rev. circ. 300.

745.5   US   ISSN 1072-4478
NX1
SEVEN ARTS. 1988. m. $15. Penn Communications Group, Inc., 260 S. Broad St., Philadelphia, PA 19102. TEL 215-735-6900. FAX 215-735-7247. E-mail: editorial@sevenarts.voicenet.com; URL: http://sevenarts.voicenet.com. Ed. Virginia Moles; Pub. Lawrence Wexler. R&P contact: Virginia Moles. adv. contact: Thomas Curry. illus. **Document type:** consumer publication.
  Formerly (until Oct. 1993): Applause.
  Description: Covers regional and local arts and entertainment, and serves as program guide for WHYY TV12 and radio station 91 FM.

SHUTTLE CRAFT GUILD. MONOGRAPHS. see NEEDLEWORK

SIMPLY CROSS STITCH. see NEEDLEWORK

372.55   DK   ISSN 0106-9608
SLOEJD. 1978. 6/yr. DKK 340 (effective 1997). Danmarks Sloejdlaererforening, Finlandsvej 1, DK-4270 Hoeng, Denmark. TEL 45-58-85-08-95. Ed. Emil Baad. adv.; bk.rev. circ. 2,596. (back issues avail.)

745 746   SW   ISSN 0346-0509
SLOEJDFORUM. 1973. 6/yr. SEK 280 (effective 1997); newsstand price: SEK 50. Laerarfoerbundet, P.O. Box 3263, S-103 65 Stockholm, Sweden. TEL 46-587-600-15. FAX 46-8-58036457. E-mail: hasse.hedstrom@mailbox.swipnet.se. Ed. Hasse Hedstroem. adv.; B&W page SEK 5600, color page SEK 8400; trim 182 x 266; adv. contact: Lisen Skeppstedt. cols./p.: 2; pp./issue: 50.
  Formed by the 1973 merger of: Svensk Sloejdtidning (ISSN 0039-6710); Sloejdlaeraren.

745.5922   US
SOFT DOLLS & ANIMALS. q. $163.95 (foreign $$20.95) (effective 1997). Scott Publications, 30595 Eight Mile Rd., Livonia, MI 48152-1798. TEL 810-477-6650; 800-458-8237. FAX 810-477-6795.
  Description: Contains full details on how professionals create cloth dolls and animals. Provides ideas and possible projects.

745.5   UK
SOURCES. 1994. a. £25 to non-members. Fine Arts Trade Guild, 16-18 Empress Pl., London SW6 1TT, England. TEL 44-171-381-6616. FAX 44-171-381-2596. Ed. Vanessa Giles. circ. 2,000 (controlled). **Document type:** bulletin.

745.5   US   ISSN 0198-8239
TT847
SPIN-OFF; the magazine for handspinners. 1977. q. $21 (foreign $26). Interweave Press, Inc., 201 E. Fourth St., Loveland, CO 80537. TEL 970-669-7672. FAX 970-667-8317. Ed. Linda C. Ligon; Pub. Linda C. Ligon. R&P contact: Karen Evanson. adv. contact: Sharon Altergott. circ. 18,000. **Indexed:** Ind.How To Do It (1978-). **Document type:** consumer publication.
  —UnCover.
  Description: Offers new ideas, approaches and special projects to the hand spinner.

745.5   US   ISSN 1067-8867
NK5300
STAINED GLASS; devoted to the craft of stained and decorative art glass. 1906. q. $30 to individuals (foreign $46); libraries and educational institutions $22.50 (foreign $34.50) (effective 1998); newsstand price: $8.50. Stained Glass Association of America, 6 S.W. Second St., Ste. 7, Lees Summit, MO 64063-2352. TEL 816-524-9313; 800-438-9581. FAX 816-524-9405. E-mail: sgmagaz@kcnet.com; URL: http://www.art.glassworld.com/mag/sglass/sglass.html. Ed. Richard Gross. R&P contact: Katei Gross. adv. contact: Katei Gross. bk.rev.; bibl.; illus.; index, cum.index. circ. 1906-1987. circ. 6,000. (also avail. in microfilm; microfiche) **Indexed:** Art Ind., Artbibl.Mod., ASCA, Avery Ind.Archit.Per., DAAI. **Document type:** trade publication.
  —BLDSC (8430.013000); KR SourceOne; UnCover.
  Former titles (until 1990): Stained Glass Quarterly (ISSN 0895-7002); (until 1986): Stained Glass (ISSN 0038-9161)
  Description: Preserves the techniques of the past and illustrates the trends of the future in stained glass crafts. For hobbyists, professional artists, interior decorators, architects, and restoration specialists.

745.5   RU   ISSN 0131-9582
CODEN: STKRAQ
STEKLO I KERAMIKA. 1944. m. $173 (effective 1998). Ministerstvo Promyshlennosti Stroitel'nykh Materialov, Moscow, Russia. Ed. N.N. Rokhlin. bk.rev.; abstr.; charts; illus.; stat.; index. circ. 7,160. **Indexed:** Alloys Ind., Br.Ceram.Abstr., Ceram.Abstr., Chem.Abstr., Eng.Mat.Abstr., INSPEC, ISMEC, Met.Abstr., Met.Abstr.Ind., Nonfer.Met.Alert, PCC Alert, Steels Alert, World Alum.Abstr.
  —BLDSC (0169.000000); AskIEEE; CASDDS; CISTI; KR SourceOne. **CCC.**

STOHOLOSNYK/STOGOLOSNIK; aktualna svitova kultura. see ART

745.5   US   ISSN 0091-6641
NK3700
STUDIO POTTER. 1972. s-a. $25 (foreign $28) (effective 1996). Studio Potter, Box 70, Goffstown, NH 03045. TEL 603-774-3582. FAX 603-774-6313. Ed. Gerry Williams. bk.rev.; cum.index in vol.5. circ. 6,000. (back issues avail.) **Indexed:** Art Ind., DAAI. **Document type:** academic/scholarly publication.
  —BLDSC (8500.628600); KR SourceOne; UnCover.
  Description: Devoted to the interests of working potters and ceramic artists, covering technology, aesthetics, history, and biography. Each issue explores a single theme.

STYLE 1900; the quarterly journal of the arts and crafts movement. see ANTIQUES

SYMPOSIUM ON THE ART OF SCIENTIFIC GLASSBLOWING PROCEEDINGS. see CERAMICS, GLASS AND POTTERY

745.5   FI   ISSN 1235-6875
TAITO. 1907. 6/yr. FIM 280 in EU countries; other European countries FIM 310; elsewhere FIM 325. Kasi- ja Taideteollisuusliitto - Finnish Crafts and Arts Organization, P.O. Box 186, Kalevankatu 61, FIN-00181 Helsinki, Finland. TEL 358-9-694-0012. FAX 358-9-694-0067. E-mail: sirpa.stark@edita.fi; URL: http://www.edita.fi/taito. Ed. Marketta Luutonen. adv. contact: Sirpa Stark. circ. 10 500 (controlled).
  Incorporates (1935-1990): Kotiteollisuus - Vaar Hoemsleojd (ISSN 0355-7421)
  Description: Contains articles on Finnish handicrafts, events, interviews, and gives instruction on patterns and models for weaving, knitting, woodwork and other related handicrafts.

TEXTILE FIBRE FORUM; the fibre magazine of the Australian region. see TEXTILE INDUSTRIES AND FABRICS

TEXTILE FORUM. see TEXTILE INDUSTRIES AND FABRICS

TEXTILE MUSEUM JOURNAL. see TEXTILE INDUSTRIES AND FABRICS

TIMBERTIMES; logging & lumbering - history & modeling. see HOBBIES

745.92   JA
TOKYO NO IKEBANA. (Text in Japanese) a. Tokyo-to Kado Kyokai, c/o Shinkosha Bldg., 2-1-8 Koraku, Bunkyo-ku, Tokyo, Japan. illus.
  Description: Concerns flower arrangement.

745.5   UK   ISSN 0951-6751
TORQUAY POTTERY COLLECTORS SOCIETY. MAGAZINE. 1976. a. £12. Torquay Pottery Collectors Society, c/o Virginia Brisco, Ed., 218 Sandridge Rd., St. Albans, Herts., England. adv.; bk.rev.; illus. circ. 1,100. **Document type:** newsletter.
  Formerly: Torquay Pottery Collectors Society. Newsletter (ISSN 0143-5590)
  Description: History of the potteries that operated in South Devon, England from 1870 to 1970.

745 398   PL   ISSN 0860-4126
TWORCZOSC LUDOWA. 1986. q. $10. Stowarzyszenie Tworcow Ludowych, Zarzad Glowny, Ul. Grodzka 14, 20-112 Lublin, Poland. TEL 48-81-24974. bk.rev.; bibl.; illus.
  Description: Covers folk art and folk culture.

VAEVMAGASINET; Scandinavian weaving magazine. see NEEDLEWORK

VESTERHEIM ROSEMALING LETTER. see ART

745.5   RM
VIATA C M. 1953. m. Calea Plevnei 46, Bucharest, Rumania. Ed. Marin Petre. circ. 65,000.
  Formerly (until 1991): Viata Cooperatiei Mestesugaresti.

VISUAL ARTS NEWS. see ART

745.5   NE   ISSN 0927-748X
VORMEN UIT VUUR. 1953. q. fl.70 to individuals; institutions fl. 100. Nederlandse Vereniging van Vrienden van Ceramiek en Glas - Dutch Society of Friends of Ceramics and Glass, c/o M. Broekema, Sec., Da Costalaan 10, 1215 BZ Hilversum, Netherlands. TEL 31-35-231704. (Editorial addr.: Mrs. K. Gaillard, Osterdreef 71, 2153 AX Nieuw Vennep, Netherlands) adv.; bk.rev.; cum.index. circ. 700. (back issues avail.) **Document type:** academic/scholarly publication, bulletin.
  Former titles (until 1992): Nederlandse Vereniging van Vrienden van de Ceramiek. Mededelingen (ISSN 0920-1009); (until 1979): Vrienden van de Nederlandse Ceramiek. Mededelingenblad (ISSN 0165-814X); Vereniging van Vrienden van de Nederlandse Ceramiek. Mededelingenblad (ISSN 0042-3858)
  Description: Covers all types of glass and ceramics, from all periods.

WHO'S WHO IN ART MATERIALS. see ART

WOODCARVING. see BUILDING AND CONSTRUCTION — Carpentry And Woodwork

745.5   US   ISSN 1069-6105
YIPPY YI YEA MAGAZINE; western style, coast to coast. 1992. s-a. $9 (effective 1997); newsstand price: 4.95. Long Publications, Inc., 8393 E. Holly Rd., Holly, MI 48442. TEL 248-634-9675. FAX 248-634-0301. Ed. Cheryl Anderson. adv.: B&W page $895, color page $1095; trim 8 1/8 x 10 1/8; adv. contact: Mary Ellen Krause. circ. 80,000. **Document type:** consumer publication.

747   CC
YISHU - SHENGHUO/ART - LIFE. (Text in Chinese) q. Y350001. Fujian Sheng Gongyi Meishu Xuexiao, 22 Hexi Lu, Fuzhou, Fujian 350001, People's Republic of China. TEL 534506. (Dist. overseas by: Jiangsu Publications Import & Export Corp., 56 Gao Yun Ling, Nanjing, Jiangsu, P.R.C.) Ed. Zheng Likuo.
  Description: Covers researches in arts and crafts, interior design and design of daily utensils.

745 398   RU   ISSN 0204-3432
ZHIVAYA STARINA. (Text in Russian) 1890. q. $68 (effective 1998). Tsentr Russkogo Fol'klora - Centre of Russian Folklore, Kropotkinskii per., 10, 119034 Moscow, Russia. TEL 7-095-2468417. FAX 7-095-2463389. (Dist. by: Mezhdunarodnaya Kniga, B. Yakimanka 39, 117049 Moscow, Russia. TEL 7-095-2384967. FAX 7-095-2384634) (Co-sponsor: Ministerstvo Kul'tury Rossiiskoi Federatsii) Ed. N.I. Tolstoi. adv.: page $600; adv. contact: Anatoli Kargin. bk.rev.; index. circ. 3,000.
  Description: Covers traditional Slavik culture and folk arts.

ARTS AND HANDICRAFTS —
Abstracting, Bibliographies, Statistics

745.5 EC
CENTRO INTERAMERICANO DE ARTESANIAS Y ARTES POPULARES. CENTRO DE DOCUMENTACION. BOLETIN. 1991. 3/yr. exchange basis. Centro Interamericano de Artesanias y Artes Populares, Hermano Miguel 3-23 (Escalinata), Apdo. 01.01.1943, Cuenca, Ecuador. TEL 593-7-829451. FAX 593-7-831450. Ed. Joaquin Moreno. adv. contact: Manual Jadan. circ. 1,000. **Document type:** bulletin.

CLOTHING AND TEXTILE ARTS INDEX. see *CLOTHING TRADE — Abstracting, Bibliographies, Statistics*

HANDICRAFT - HOBBY INDEX; a current periodical index to doing, making, and building. see *HOW-TO AND DO-IT-YOURSELF — Abstracting, Bibliographies, Statistics*

745.5 011 AT ISSN 1034-8174
INDEX TO CRAFT JOURNALS. 1979. irreg., latest 1989-90. Aus.$118 (foreign Aus.$125). Craft of Australia, Level 5, 414-418 Elizabeth St., Surry Hill, N.S.W. 2010, Australia. TEL 61-2-211-1445. FAX 61-2-211-1443. Ed. Beth Hatton. circ. 140. (back issues avail.) **Document type:** abstracting/indexing.
Description: Access to information in 74 craft periodicals classified by authors, craftsperson's name, subject heading, studio-workshop name.

745.5097 CN ISSN 1192-4373
TERRES EN VUES/ASSI NUKUAN. (Text in French and several native languages) q. Can.$20; newsstand price: Can.$6. Terres en Vues - Societe pour la Diffusion de la Culture Autochtone, 770 rue Rachel E., Montreal, PQ H2S 2H5, Canada. TEL 514-521-2714. FAX 514-521-9480. Ed. Andre Dudemaine; Pub. Danie Corvec. adv.: page Can.$1000; adv. contact: Andre Dudemaine. bk.rev.; film rev.; music rev.; play rev.; video rev. circ. 3,000. (back issues avail.)
Description: American Native people's cultural magazine with a focus on arts, handicraft, lifestyle and festivals.

ASTROLOGY

see also New Age Publications

133.5 US ISSN 1049-6181
A F A N NEWSLETTER.* 1988. q. membership. (Association for Astrological Networking) Matrix Software, 315 Marion Ave., Big Rapids, MI 49307. TEL 616-796-2483. Ed. Gloria Star. **Document type:** newsletter.

133.5 IT
ALTRA; rivista trimestrale di astrologia, psicologia, spiritualita. 1992. q. L.10000 per no. Jupiter Edizioni, C.P. 25, 56026 S. Bernedetto (Pisa), Italy. Ed. Gabriella Verdone.

133.5 US ISSN 0002-7529
AMERICAN ASTROLOGY. 1933. m. $18.98. (American Astrology Inc.) Starlog Group, Inc., 475 Park Ave. S., 8th Fl., New York, NY 10016. Eds. Ken Irving, Lee Chapman. adv.; bk.rev. circ. 185,000. (also avail. in microform from UMI) **Document type:** consumer publication.

133.5 US ISSN 0516-9550
AMERICAN ASTROLOGY DIGEST. 1956. a. $2. (American Astrology, Inc.) Starlog Group, Inc., 475 Park Ave. S., 8th Fl., New York, NY 10016. TEL 212-689-2830. FAX 212-889-7933. Eds. Lee Chapman, Ken Irving. adv.; charts; illus.; tr.lit. **Document type:** consumer publication.

133.5 US ISSN 1053-0584
BF1651
ASPECTS (ENCINO); astrological magazine. 1975. q. $25. Aquarius Workshops, Inc., Box 260556, Encino, CA 91426. TEL 818-782-5573. Ed. Karen McCauley. adv.; bk.rev.; charts. circ. 1,500. (back issues avail.) **Document type:** trade publication.

133.5 IT ISSN 0392-226X
ASTRA. 1977. m. L.48000. Rizzoli Editore-Corriere della Sera, Via A. Rizzoli 2, 20132 Milan, Italy. TEL 02-2588. Ed. Rudy Stauder. adv.: B&W page L.12900000; adv. contact: Flavio Biondi. circ. 159,172.

133.5 IT
ASTRELLA. m. L.3500 per no. Edizioni Internazionale Cioe s.r.l., Via Giovanni Fabroni 24, 00191 Rome, Italy. TEL 06-3287250. FAX 06-3274576. Ed. Fabio Piscopo. adv.: B&W or color page L.6500000. **Document type:** consumer publication.

133.5 FR
ASTRES. 1948. m. 169 F. G. Gourdon, Ed. & Pub., 10 rue de Crussol, 75544 Paris Cedex 11, France. TEL 16-1-48-05-4110. FAX 16-1-49-23-5360. adv.; illus. circ. 110,000.

133.5 US
ASTRO ANALYTICS NEWSLETTER. 1978. 4/yr. Box 16927, Encino, CA 91416-6927. TEL 818-997-8684. Ed. Craig Greeno. bk.rev. circ. 4,000. **Document type:** newsletter.
Formerly: Astro Analytics.
Description: Features articles, comments, astrological product reviews, and other related items.

133.5 US ISSN 1074-6196
ASTRO DIGEST. 1994. bi-m. $1.99. J M T Publications, 350 Theodore Fremd Ave., Rye, NY 10580. TEL 914-967-1565. FAX 914-967-1565. circ. 100,000. **Document type:** consumer publication.

THE ASTRO-INVESTOR; a newsletter for investors. see *BUSINESS AND ECONOMICS — Investments*

133.5 YU
ASTRO ONA. 1990. bi-m. Revijalna Stampa, Trg Nikole Pasica 7, Belgrade, Yugoslavia. Ed. Rade Atic.

133.5 US ISSN 1066-2405
ASTRO SIGNS. (Includes 12 m. issues for each sign) 1986. m. $12. T-Square Publications, 350 Theodore Fremd Ave., Rye, NY 10580. TEL 914-967-1565. FAX 914-967-1682. Ed. Rochelle Gordon. adv. circ. 1,500,00.

133.5 YU
▼**ASTRO SVET.** 1995. m. Drustvo Astrologa Jugoslavije, Filipa Visnjica 1-a, Novi Sad, Yugoslavia. Ed. Zlatko Zatkovic.

133.5 IT ISSN 1121-5461
ASTRODONNA. 1990. m. L.6000 per no. Dellaschiava S.p.A., Viale Stelvio 57, 20159 Milan, Italy. TEL 39-2-6988. FAX 39-2-6988337. Ed. Patrizia Pontremoli. adv.: color page L.15000000. **Document type:** consumer publication.
Formerly (until 1991): Astrocosmo (ISSN 1120-7922)

133.5 US
ASTROFLASH. 1979. q. $6 (free to customers). (Astro Communications Services) A C S Publications, Box 34487, San Diego, CA 92163-4487. TEL 619-492-9919. URL: http://www.astro.com. Ed. Maritha Pottenger; Pub. Maria Kay Simms. R&P contact: Maritha Pottenger. adv. contact: Nadine MacLane. bk.rev.; illus. circ. 20,000. **Document type:** consumer publication, newsletter.
Description: Contains astrological articles on beginning and intermediate topics.

133.5 SZ ISSN 0257-9235
ASTROLOG; Fachzeitschrift fuer astrologische Psychologie. 1981. 6/yr. 10 SFr. Astrologisch-Psychologisches Institut, Obertilistr. 4, Postfach 614, CH-8134 Adliswil, Switzerland. TEL 41-1-7103776. FAX 41-1-7103786. **Document type:** newsletter.

133.5 II ISSN 0004-6140
BF1651
ASTROLOGICAL MAGAZINE. (Text in English) 1895. m. Rs.1575($45) Raman Publications "Sri Rajeswari", 115-1, New Extension, Seshadripuram, Bangalore 560 020, India. TEL 91-80-3348646. FAX 91-80-3345626. Ed. B.V. Raman. R&P contact: Gayatri Devi Vasudev. adv.; bk.rev.; index. circ. 25,000. (tabloid format) **Document type:** newspaper.

133.5 US ISSN 0044-9784
BF1651
ASTROLOGICAL REVIEW.* 4/yr. $20. Astrologers' Guild of America, 5 Fair Meadow Dr., Brewster, NY 10509. Ed. Susanne Neuschulz.

133.5 SZ
ASTROLOGIE HEUTE. 1986. bi-m. 65 SFr. (effective 1997). Astrodata AG, Chilenholzstr. 8, CH-8907 Wettswil, Switzerland. TEL 41-1-4921515. FAX 41-1-4935135. E-mail: astrologieheute@compuserve.com. Ed. Claude Weiss; Pub. Armando Bertozzi. adv.; bk.rev.; circ. 11,000 (paid). (back issues avail.) **Document type:** consumer publication. *Refereed Serial*

133.5 US
ASTROLOGY AND PSYCHIC NEWS. vol.66, no.18, 1989. q. membership. California Astrology Association, Department V, Box 810, N. Hollywood, CA 91603. (back issues avail.)

133.5 US
ASTROLOGY ANNUAL. a. Hachette Filipacchi Magazines, Inc., 1633 Broadway, 45th Fl., New York, NY 10009. TEL 212-767-6000. **Document type:** consumer publication.

133.5 US
ASTROLOGY DIRECTORY. a. $6.50. Ghost Research Society, Box 205, Oak Lawn, IL 60454-0205. TEL 708-425-5163. **Document type:** directory.
Description: Contains names of individuals, groups, organizations, and publications on the subject.

133.5 US ISSN 0004-6191
ASTROLOGY GUIDE.* 1937. bi-m. $7.50. Sterling - Macfadden Partnership, 35 Wilbur St., Lynbrook, NY 11563. TEL 516-593-1220. adv.; bk.rev.; charts; illus. **Document type:** consumer publication.

133.5 UK
ASTROLOGY QUARTERLY. 1926. q. £18 for UK and Europe; U.S., Canada, India, S. Africa, S. America £21; Far East, Australia, N. Zealand, S.E. Asia, Japan £23 (effective March 1997). Astrological Lodge of London, 50 Gloucester Pl., London W1H 4EA, England. Ed. Gerasime Patilas. adv. contact: Patricia Green. bk.rev.; charts; index. circ. 700. **Document type:** academic/scholarly publication.
Formerly: Astrology (ISSN 0004-6183)

133.5 US ISSN 0195-0851
BF1651
ASTROLOGY: YOUR DAILY HOROSCOPE. m. $10.95. Hachette Filipacchi Magazines, Inc., 1633 Broadway, 45th Fl., New York, NY 10009. TEL 212-767-6000. illus. **Document type:** consumer publication.
—UMI.

133.5 US
ASTROTALK BULLETIN. 1983. q. $9.95 (foreign $17.95) for 6 nos. Matrix Software, 315 Marion Ave., Big Rapids, MI 49307. TEL 616-796-2483. FAX 616-796-3060. Ed. Michael Erlewine. bk.rev.; illus.; stat. circ. 1,000. **Document type:** bulletin.
Formerly: Astro Talk (ISSN 0740-6738)
Description: Bulletin for the Matrix user's group with information on the developments in the Matrix software field. Includes astrological and time cycles, and stock market correspondence to cyclical data.

133.5 GW
ASTROWOCHE. w. (Thu.) DM.135.20 (foreign DM.213.20) (effective 1997); newsstand price: DM.2.60. Astro Zeitschriftenverlags GmbH, Medienstr. 5, 94036 Passau, Germany. TEL 49-851-802201. FAX 49-851-802837. (Subscr. to: P M S GmbH, Postfach 290180, 47261 Duisburg, Germany. TEL 49-203-76908-0. FAX 49-203-7690830) Ed. Tonio Montel. adv. contact: Walter Krey. circ. 60,585. **Document type:** consumer publication.

133.5 FR ISSN 0007-9596
CAHIERS ASTROLOGIQUES; revue d'astrologie traditionnelle. 1938. 6/yr. 120 F. Editions des Cahiers Astrologiques, 7 rue Condorcet, 75009 Paris, France. Ed. Paul Rogel. adv.; bk.rev.; abstr.; bibl.; charts; illus.; stat.; index. circ. 1,200.

CHURCH OF LIGHT QUARTERLY. see *NEW AGE PUBLICATIONS*

ASTROLOGY

133.5 US ISSN 1066-4920
BF1621
CONSIDERATIONS. 1983. q. $30 (foreign $35). Box 491, Mount Kisco, NY 10549. Ed. Kenneth Gillman. bk.rev.; illus.; circ. 1,500 (paid). **Document type:** academic/scholarly publication.

133.5 UK ISSN 0260-8790
BF1651
CORRELATION; journal of research into astrology. 1981. s-a. £11 to EU residents and NCGR members; elsewhere £12 (effective May 1997). Astrological Association of Great Britain, 396 Caledonian Rd., London N1 1DN, England. TEL 44-171-700-3746. FAX 44-171-700-6479. E-mail: astrological.association@zetnet.co.uk; URL: http://www.astrologer.com/aanet/. Ed. Rudolf Smit. adv.; bk.rev.; abstr.; charts; index. circ. 400. (back issues avail.) **Document type:** academic/scholarly publication.
Description: Provides articles on research and on methodological and philosophical areas related to astrology.
Refereed Serial

133.5 US ISSN 0018-5116
DELL HOROSCOPE. Key Title: Horoscope. 1935. 12/yr. $23.88. Dell Magazines (Subsidiary of: Crosstown Publications), 1270 Ave. of the Americas, New York, NY 10020. TEL 212-698-1313. FAX 212-698-1198. (Subscr. to: Box 53352, Boulder, CO 80322-3352) Ed. Ronnie Grishman; Pub. Peter Kanter. R&P contact: Cynthia Manson. adv. contact: Francine Moore. bk.rev.; charts; illus. circ. 150,000. (also avail. in microform from UMI; reprint service avail. from UMI) **Document type:** consumer publication.

133.5 US
DELL HOROSCOPE PURSE BOOKS. a. Dell Magazines, 1270 Ave. of the Americas, New York, NY 10020. TEL 212-698-1313. FAX 212-698-1198. Ed. Ronnie Grishman; Pub. Peter Kanter. R&P contact: Cynthia Manson. adv. contact: Francine Moore. **Document type:** consumer publication.

133.5 IT
ESOTERICA.* 1989. m. L.35000. Editoriale Domani Coop.r.l., Viale Mazzini 145, 00195 Rome, Italy. TEL 06-3207101. Ed. Salvatore Puzzo. adv.: B&W page L.3000000. circ. 38,000.

133.5 332.6 US ISSN 1055-8527
FINANCIAL CYCLES; wealth creation & investment success through person-centered financial astrology. 1988. m. $55 (foreign $79). Bost Communications - Support of Nature, Box 1657, Sarasota, FL 34230-1657. TEL 941-953-3545. FAX 941-953-3732. E-mail: timbost@pipeline.com. Ed. Timothy Lee Bost; Pub. Timothy Lee Bost. R&P contact: Timothy Lee Bost. adv. contact: Timothy Lee Bost. bk.rev.; charts; illus. circ. 125. (back issues avail.; reprint service avail.) **Document type:** newsletter.
Description: Explores the use of technical analysis and financial astrology in promoting the esoteric understanding of economic trends, geocosmic cycles, geopolitical events, and market movements.

133.5 UK ISSN 0071-8084
FOULSHAM'S ORIGINAL OLD MOORE'S ALMANACK. 1697. a. 65p. W. Foulsham & Co. Ltd., Yeovil Rd., Slough SL1 4JH, England. TEL 0753-26769. TELEX 849041 SHARET G.
Description: Contains astrological predictions for a twelve month period.

133.5 US
GEOCOSMIC. 1978. 2/yr. $35 membership. National Council for Geocosmic Research, Inc., P.O. Box 1220, Dunkirk, MD 20754-1220. TEL 301-812-2593. E-mail: ncgr@allware.com; URL: http://www.geocosmic.org. Ed. Frances McEvoy; Pub. Mary Downing. R&P contact: Mary Downing. adv. contact: Arlene Nimark. bk.rev.; bibl.; charts; illus.; stat. circ. 3,000. (back issues avail.) **Document type:** academic/scholarly publication.
Formerly: Geocosmic News.

133.5 FR
GUIDE ASTROLOGIQUE. (Supplement to: Astre) 1970. a. 26 F. G. Gourdon, Ed. & Pub., 10 rue de Crussol, 75544 Paris Cedex II, France. TEL 48-05-41-10. FAX 49-23-53-60. adv.; illus. circ. 120,000.

133.5 CE
GUPTA GAVESANA. (Text in Sinhalese) 1978. m. Rs.2.50. Sithumina, 105 2-2 Jayantha Weerasekera Mawatha, Colombo 10, Sri Lanka. Ed. B.M.C. Mohotti. adv.; bk.rev. circ. 10,000.

133.5 FR ISSN 0982-3689
HOROSCOPE. m. 165 F. (foreign 215 F.). Editions Nuit et Jour, 9 rue Christiani, 75018 Paris, France. TEL 49-25-17-17. adv. circ. 160,000.

133.5 CN ISSN 0018-5124
HOROSCOPE QUOTIDIEN ECLAIR. (Text in French) 1956. m. Can.$32.99 (effective 1997). SuperMagazine Inc., 9125 Pascal-Gagnon, Bur. 212, St-Leonard, PQ H1P 1Z4, Canada. TEL 514-955-0305. FAX 514-321-9550. Ed. Gilbert Grou. R&P contact: Celine Forest. adv. contact: Claude David. circ. 35,000. **Document type:** consumer publication.

133.5 BL ISSN 0104-1576
HOROSCOPO; a revista dos astros. 1972. m. Editora Azul, S.A., Av. Naçoes Unidas, 5777, 05479-900 Sao Paulo, SP, Brazil. TEL 55-11-8673000. FAX 55-11-8673311. TELEX 55-11-83178-EDAZ. E-mail: benjamin.goncalvez@email.abril.com.br. Ed. Lana Nowikow. R&P contact: Benjamin Goncalvez. TEL 55-11-8673311. adv.: Color page $55000; 134 x 190; adv. contact: Enio Vergeiro. illus.; circ. 118,027 (paid). **Document type:** consumer publication.
Former titles (until 1990): Horoscopo Caricia; (until 1986): Horoscopo Capricho.
Description: Covers the zodiac and astrology. Includes feature articles on each zodiac sign and daily horoscopes.

133.5 615.89 IT
INCANTESIMO. 1992. m. Editrice Marduk, Via Samminiatese 64, 56027 San Miniato (Pisa), Italy. TEL 39-571-43421. Ed. Massimo Benedetti. adv. contact: Lino Ieva.

J. GRUBER'S HAGERS-TOWN TOWN AND COUNTRY ALMANACK. see *ENCYCLOPEDIAS AND GENERAL ALMANACS*

133.5 II
JANMABHOOMI KHAGOL SIDDHA SUKSHMA NIRAYANA BHARATIYA PANCHANG (GUJARATI EDITION). (Editions in Gujarati, Hindi) 1943. a. Rs.20 (foreign Rs.120). Saurashtra Trust, Janmabhoomi Bhavan, Janmabhoomi Marg, Fort, Bombay 400 001, India. TEL 022-2870831. FAX 022-2874097. TELEX 11-86859-BHOO-IN. Ed. Jyoti Bhatt. adv.; bk.rev. circ. 50,000. (also avail. in microfilm; back issues avail.)
Description: Annual almanac of astrology-palmistry.

133.5 II
JANMABHOOMI KHAGOL SIDDHA SUKSHMA NIRAYANA BHARATIYA PANCHANG (HINDI EDITION). (Editions in Gujarati, Hindi) 1991. a. Rs.12 (foreign Rs.60). Saurashtra Trust, Janmabhoomi Bhavan, Janmabhoomi Marg, Fort, Bombay 400 001, India. TEL 2870831. TELEX 11-86859-BHOO-IN. Ed. Jyoti Bhatt. adv.; bk.rev. circ. 7,500. (also avail. in microfilm)
Description: Annual almanac of astrology-palmistry.

133.5 II
JANMABHOOMI PANCHANG. (Text in Gujarati) 1945. a. Rps.80. Saurashtra Trust, Janmabhoomi Bhavan, Janmabhoomi Marg, Fort, Bombay 400 001, India. TEL 2870831. TELEX 11-86859 BHOO IN. Ed. Jyoti Bhatt. adv. circ. 47,000.
Description: Annual almanac with special interest articles on astrology.

133.5 NE ISSN 0022-7463
DE KAARSVLAM. German edition: Flamme. 1947. m. fl.44. Mellie Uyldert, Ed.& Pub., Lomanlaan 7, Bussum, Netherlands. bk.rev.; film rev.; play rev. circ. 4,000.

133.5 640 II
KALNIRNAY. (Text in English, Hindi, Marathi, Kanada, Gujarati) 1973. a. Rs.10($4) Sumangal Publishing Co., 172 M.M.G.S. Marg, Box 5547, Dadar, Bombay 400 014, India. TEL 91-022-4130885. FAX 91-022-4146939. Ed. Jayant Salgaonkar. adv.

133.5 US ISSN 0047-3650
KOSMOS. 1968. q. $30. International Society for Astrological Research, Inc., Box 38613, Los Angeles, CA 90038-0613. TEL 805-525-0461. FAX 805-525-0461. E-mail: raymondmerriman@msn.com; URL: http://stars.org/isar/. Ed. Kim Rogers-Gallagher. R&P contact: Marguerite Dar Boggia. adv. contact: Kim Rogers-Gallagher. bk.rev.; charts; illus.; circ. 1,000 (controlled). **Document type:** academic/scholarly publication.
Description: Contains timed birthdates of known personalities and persons listed by categories.
Refereed Serial

133.5 US
LAKEWOODS ASTROLOGICAL GUIDES.* 1979. a. Lakewood Books, c/o Stephens, Step 857, 3630 Orchard St., Orchard, NY 11957-1284. TEL 516-749-1122. Ed. Don Wigal. circ. 10,000.

133.5 IT
LINGUAGGIO ASTRALE. 1971. q. L.80000. Centro Italiano di Astrologia (CIDA), Via Giacinto Collegno 12 bis, 10143 Turin, Italy. TEL 39-11-4376192. Ed. Grazia Mirti. R&P contact: Grazia Mitri. adv. circ. 2,000. (back issues avail.) **Document type:** academic/scholarly publication.

133.5 II
MATHAJOTHIDAM; astrological Tamil monthly. (Text in Tamil) 1949. m. 3 Arasamaram, Vellore, N.A.A. Dist., Pin 632 004, India. Ed. A.K. Thulasiraman; Pub. A.K. Thulasiraman. circ. 8,000.

133.5 US
MIDNIGHT HOROSCOPE.* 1980. 4/yr. $9.97 for 8 issues. Globe Communications Corp. (New York), 3 E. 54th St., 15th Fl., New York, NY 10022-3108. TEL 800-472-7744. Ed. Carlson Wade. adv.; bk.rev.; illus. circ. 50,000.

133.5 US
MINI EXAMINER. 1979. bi-w. $17. Box 3893, Chatsworth, CA 91313. TEL 818-347-6949. Ed. Irene Hamlen Stephenson. (looseleaf format; back issues avail.) **Document type:** newsletter.
Description: Applies biorhythm character and compatibility analysis to relationships to determine whether they will work.

133.5 US ISSN 1079-1345
THE MOUNTAIN ASTROLOGER. 1988. 10/yr. $35 in U.S.; Canada $50 (effective 1996). Box 970, Cedar Ridge, CA 95924-0970. TEL 916-477-8839. E-mail: TMAMary@aol.com; URL: http://www.mountainastrologer.com/. Ed. Kate Sholly; Pub. Tem Tarriktar. adv.; bk.rev.; charts; illus.; stat. circ. 15,000. (back issues avail.) **Document type:** bulletin.

133.5 US ISSN 0892-5429
MUTABLE DILEMMA. 1977. q. $20 (foreign $30) (effective 1997). Los Angeles Community Church of Religious Science, 838 Fifth Ave., Los Angeles, CA 90005. TEL 213-487-1000. FAX 213-487-7853. E-mail: 71267.2075@compuserve.com. Ed. Mark Pottenger. R&P contact: Mark Pottenger. bk.rev. circ. 250. (back issues avail.) **Document type:** academic/scholarly publication.

133.5 US ISSN 0296-5569
N C G R JOURNAL. 1984. 2/yr. $35 membership. National Council for Geocosmic Research, Inc., P.O. Box 1220, Dunkirk, MD 20754-1220. TEL 301-812-2593. E-mail: ncgr@allware.com; URL: http://www.ncgr.org/www/Publi.htm. Ed. Loraine Welsh; Pub. Mary Downing. R&P contact: Mary Downing. adv. contact: Arlene Nimark. bk.rev. circ. 3,000. (back issues avail.) **Document type:** academic/scholarly publication.
Description: Education and research regarding the correspondence between events in the cosmos and events on earth.

133.5 US
NATIONAL COUNCIL FOR GEOCOSMIC RESEARCH. MEMBERLETTER. 1984. m. membership. National Council for Geocosmic Research, Inc., P.O. Box 1220, Dunkirk, MD 20754-1220. TEL 301-812-2593. E-mail: ncgr@allware.com; URL: http://www.geocosmic.org. Ed. Martha Ramsey; Pub. Mary Downing. R&P contact: Mary Downing. adv. contact: Arlene Nimark. bk.rev. circ. 3,000. **Document type:** newsletter.

ORACLE. see *PARAPSYCHOLOGY AND OCCULTISM*

133.5 　　　IT
OROSCOPO DELLA SETTIMANA. 1990. w. L.54000 (foreign L.88000). Casa Editrice Universo S.p.A., Via 9a Strada Torre 3, 20090 Milan San Felice, Italy. TEL 02-7533741. FAX 02-7533880. Eds. Nicola De Feo, Sergio Del Duca. adv.: B&W page L.2500000, color page L.3000000. circ. 70,000. **Document type:** consumer publication.

133.5   338.025   US
POWER AGENT. (Part of: The Industry's Edge Series) 1993. 4/yr. $25. Canoco Publishing, 11611 Chenault St., Ste. 118, Los Angeles, CA 90049. TEL 310-471-2287. FAX 310-471-1944. E-mail: industryedge@earthlink.net; URL: http://www.hollywoodnetwork.com/astrohollywood. adv.: B&W page $600; adv. contact: Taaffe O'Connell. circ. 20,000. **Document type:** directory.
Formerly: Taaffe O'Connell's Astro Agents (ISSN 1065-7584)
Description: Comprehensive listing of Hollywood's agents with their astrological signs, addresses and phone numbers, sign descriptions and agency breakdowns.

133.5 　　　II
POYYAMOZHI; astrological Tamil monthly. (Text in Tamil) 1972. m. Rs.36. P. Adimoolam, Ed.& Pub., 64 Gaudiamath Rd., Madras 600 014, India. FAX 868780. adv.; bk.rev.; charts; illus. circ. 2,500.

133.5 　　　UK 　　ISSN 0079-4953
PREDICTION ANNUAL. a. £3.95. Link House Magazines Ltd., Link House, Dingwall Ave., Croydon, Surrey CR9 2TA, England. TEL 44-181-686-2599. FAX 44-181-781-1159. Ed. Jo Logan. adv.; bk.rev. **Document type:** consumer publication.
Description: Presents astrological forecasts for each sign of the Zodiac; includes Tarot card projections.

133.5 　　　FR 　　ISSN 1247-9772
QUEL AVENIR MAGAZINE. 1986. m. 190 F. G. Gourdon, Ed.& Pub., 10 rue de Crussol, 75554 Paris Cedex 11, France. TEL 16-1-48-05-4110. FAX 16-1-49-23-5360. adv.; illus. circ. 105,000.
Formerly (until 1993): Quel Avenir Madame (ISSN 0764-8812)

133.5 　　　UK
RAPHAEL'S ASTROLOGICAL ALMANAC. 1819. a. £2.50. W. Foulsham & Co. Ltd., Yeovil Rd., Slough SL1 4JH, England. TEL 0753-26769. TELEX 849041 SHARET G.
Description: Provides reference material for the astrologer as well as predictions for the year ahead.

133.5 　　　IT
SESTILE. 1992. m. (11/yr.). L.40000 (effective 1995). Centro Italiano di Astrologia (CIDA), Via Giacinto Collegno 12 bis, 10143 Turin, Italy. TEL 39-11-4376192. Ed. Grazia Mirti. **Document type:** trade publication.
Description: Covers professional astrology.

133.5 　　　US
SIDEREALIST. 4/yr. $14.50. Sidereal Registry & Exchange, 11 Valley St., Endwell, NY 13760. Ed. Norman Bones.

STAR BEACON. see *NEW AGE PUBLICATIONS*

133.5 　　　US
STARSCROLL. m. newsstand price: $0.89. Twelve Signs, Inc., 3369 S. Robertson Blvd., Los Angeles, CA 90034. TEL 310-553-8000. FAX 310-836-0110. Pub. Richard W. Houseman. **Document type:** consumer publication.

133.5 　　　US
STARSIGNS. m. newsstand price: $0.99. Twelve Signs, Inc., 3369 S. Robertson Blvd., Los Angeles, CA 90034. TEL 310-553-8000. FAX 310-836-0110. Pub. Richard W. Housman. **Document type:** consumer publication.

133.5 　　　US
STELLIUM QUARTERLY; an astrological journal. 1975. q. $6.50. Stellium Inc., 257 Vista Rio Circle, El Paso, TX 79912-2125. Ed. Katherine Boehrer. adv.; bk.rev.; charts; illus. (back issues avail.)

133.5 　　　CE
SUBASETHA. (Text in Sinhala) 1967. w. Lake House, D.R. Wijewardene Mawatha, P.O. Box 248, Colombo 10, Sri Lanka. TEL 1-21181. Ed. K. Chandra Sri Kularatne. circ. 80,000.

133.5 　　　NE 　　ISSN 0925-2878
SYMBOLON; tijdschrift voor astrologie en haar raakvlakken. 1990. 4/yr. fl.43.50. Amsterdamseweg 479, 1181 BR Amstelveen, Netherlands. TEL 31-20-6436979. FAX 31-20-6417310. Ed. A.J. Hamaker. adv.: B&W page fl.450. bk.rev. circ. 1,200.
Description: Covers serious astrological subjects for professional astrologers.

TAAFFE O'CONNELL'S ASTRO CASTER; a comprehensive listing of over 700 Hollywood casting agents, their astrological signs, address & phone numbers, sign descriptions, show assignments and studio breakdowns. see *BUSINESS AND ECONOMICS — Trade And Industrial Directories*

133.5 　　　US 　　ISSN 1067-1439
BF1651
TODAY'S ASTROLOGER. 1938. m. $35. American Federation of Astrologers, Inc., 6535 S. Rural Rd., Box 22040, Tempe, AZ 85285. TEL 602-838-1751. FAX 602-838-8293. E-mail: afa@msn.com. Ed. Kris Brandt Riske. R&P contact: Kris Brandt Riske. bk.rev.; charts; index; circ. 2,700 (controlled). (back issues avail.) **Document type:** academic/scholarly publication.
Formerly: American Federation of Astrologers Bulletin (ISSN 0735-4797)
Description: Contains astrological articles, data information, news releases and a calendar of activities of members and affiliates.

133.5 　　　DK 　　ISSN 0108-2450
TRIGON; magazine for professional astrology. 1981. 3/yr. DKK 65. Forlaget Stjernerne, Irene Christensen Instituttet, Nr. Farimagsgade 63-1, 1364 Copenhagen K, Denmark. FAX 33141303. Ed. Christian Borup. adv.; bk.rev.; illus. circ. 1,000.

133.5 　　　IT
TUTTOSTELLE.* 1986. m. L.24000 (foreign L.33000). Editoriale Albero S.r.l., Via Branda Castiglioni 2a, 20156 Milan, Italy. TEL 2046510. Ed. G. Carlo Botteri.

133.5   613.26   US
VEGETARIAN ASTROLOGER. irreg. 4216 Tod Ave., East Chicago, IN 46312. TEL 219-397-9297. Ed. Ted PanDeva.

133.5 　　　FR
VOTRE SIGNE ASTRAL ET VOUS. 1949. a. 28 F. G. Gourdon, Ed.& Pub., 10 rue de Crussol, 75554 Paris Cedex 11, France. TEL 16-1-48-05-4110. FAX 16-1-49-23-5360. adv.; illus. circ. 55,000.
Formerly: Astral (ISSN 1250-5005)

133.5 　　　US 　　ISSN 0747-8968
WELCOME TO PLANET EARTH; journal of new astrology in the contemporary world. 1979. m. $25. Great Bear Press, Box 5164, Eugene, OR 97405. Ed. Mark Lerner. bk.rev. circ. 2,100.
Former titles: Pass the Word; Great Bear.
Description: Includes information on workshops, services, other periodicals. New age topics are covered as well.

133.5 　　　US
WHITE SUN. 1977. 4/yr. $18. D.O.M.E. Inner Guide Meditation Center, Box 46146, Los Angeles, CA 90046-2015. TEL 213-851-9333. Ed. Ed Steinbrecher. R&P contact: Stephen Conners. bk.rev.; illus. circ. 10,000. **Document type:** newsletter.
Former titles: Aquarian Changes; Domesday Book.

133.5 　　　US 　　ISSN 0044-1082
BF1651
YOUR PERSONAL ASTROLOGY MAGAZINE.* 1939. q. $5. Sterling - Macfadden Partnership, 35 Wilbur St., Lynbrook, NY 11563. TEL 516-593-1220. Ed. Marsha Kaplan. adv.; bk.rev.; charts. **Document type:** consumer publication.

ASTRONOMY

520 　　　US 　　ISSN 1046-5200
A A S JOB REGISTER. 1980. m. membership only. American Astronomical Society, c/o Dawn Marie Craig, 2000 Florida Ave., N.W., Ste. 400, Washington, DC 20009. TEL 202-328-2010. FAX 202-234-2560. Ed. Judy Johnson. adv. circ. 2,000. (looseleaf format; back issues avail.)
Description: Covers current job openings in astronomy for Ph.D. astronomers.

520 　　　US 　　ISSN 8750-9350
A A S NEWSLETTER. 197? 5/yr. membership. American Astronomical Society, c/o Lynn Scholz, 2000 Florida Ave., N.W., Ste. 400, Washington, DC 20009. TEL 202-328-2010. FAX 202-234-2560. URL: http://www.aas.org. Ed. Robert W. Milkey. R&P contact: Robert W. Milkey. circ. 6,000. **Document type:** newsletter.

520 　　　US
A A V S O ALERT NOTICES. 1974. irreg. $10 to individuals (foreign $15); institutions $15 (foreign $20). American Association of Variable Star Observers, 25 Birch St., Cambridge, MA 02138-1205. TEL 617-354-0484. FAX 617-354-0665. Ed. Janet A. Mattei. circ. 600.
Description: Alerts those interested to the discovery of novae, unusual activities of variable stars, and special requests from astronomers for simultaneous AAVSO observations.

523.8 　　　US
A A V S O BULLETIN: PREDICTED DATES OF MAXIMA AND MINIMA OF LONG PERIOD VARIABLE STARS. 1937. a. $25 to individuals (foreign $30); institutions $40 (foreign $45). American Association of Variable Star Observers, 25 Birch St., Cambridge, MA 02138. TEL 617-354-0484. Ed. Janet A. Mattei. circ. 1,500. (looseleaf format; back issues avail.) Indexed: Astron. & Astrophys.Abstr, INSPEC (1981-). **Document type:** bulletin.
—CISTI; Linda Hall.
Formerly: A A V S O Bulletin (ISSN 0516-9518)
Description: Annual predicted dates of maxima and minima of 600 long period variable stars.
Refereed Serial

520 　　　US 　　ISSN 0197-2979
　　　　　　　　　　CODEN: AACID5
A A V S O CIRCULAR. 1970. 12/yr. $25 to individuals (foreign $30); institutions $40 (foreign $45). American Association of Variable Star Observers, 25 Birch St., Cambridge, MA 02138. TEL 617-354-0484. Ed. John Bortle. Indexed: INSPEC (1981-).
—AskIEEE; CISTI; KR SourceOne.
Description: Monthly preliminary observations of some eruptive and other interesting variable stars. Director's request for more data on selected variable stars.

520 　　　US
A A V S O EPHEMERIDES FOR R R LYRAE STARS AND ECLIPSING BINARIES. 1981. a. $10 to individuals (foreign $15); institutions $35 (foreign $40). American Association of Variable Star Observers, 25 Birch St., Cambridge, MA 02138. TEL 617-354-0484.

522 　　　US
A A V S O PHOTOELECTRIC PHOTOMETRY NEWSLETTER. 1979. irreg. (3-4/yr.). $10 to individuals (foreign $15); institutions $15 (foreign $20). American Association of Variable Star Observers, 25 Birch St., Cambridge, MA 02138. TEL 617-354-0484. FAX 617-354-0665. circ. 200. (looseleaf format; back issues avail.) **Document type:** newsletter.
Description: Contains brief reports on small-amplitude variables, requests for PEP observations, and photoelectric hardware and software.

523.8 　　　US
A A V S O REPORTS AND MONOGRAPHS. irreg. $10 (foreign $15). American Association of Variable Star Observers, 25 Birch St., Cambridge, MA 02138. TEL 617-354-0484. Ed. Janet A. Mattei. circ. 1,000. (back issues avail.) Indexed: Astron.& Astrophys.Abstr., INSPEC. **Document type:** monographic series.
—AskIEEE; KR SourceOne.
Formerly: A A V S O Report (ISSN 0097-5265); Supersedes (1949-1966): American Association of Variable Star Observers. Quarterly Report.
Description: Reports: Computer-generated light curves of variables in the AAVSO observing program, usually covering an interval of 1000 days. Monographs: Computer-generated, long-term (20 years plus) light curves of variable stars, one star per monograph.
Refereed Serial

ASTRONOMY

520   FR
A G B NEWSLETTER. (Asymptotic Giant Branch) 1994. m. University of Grenoble, E-mail: agbnews@gag.observ-gr.fr; URL: http://gag.observ-gr.fr/liens/agbnews.html. Eds. Thierry Forveille, Claudine Kahane. **Document type:** newsletter.
●Available only online.
Description: Covers stellar evolution on the asymptotic giant branch and beyond.

520   US
A S P CATALOG. 1976. s-a. free. Astronomical Society of the Pacific, 390 Ashton Ave., San Francisco, CA 94112. TEL 415-337-1100. FAX 415-337-5205. circ. 300,000. **Document type:** catalog.
Formerly: A S P Selectory.
Description: Annotated listings of educational materials in astronomy.

520   US   ISSN 0733-6314
ABRAMS PLANETARIUM SKY CALENDAR; an aid to enjoying the changing sky. 1969. q. $7.50. Michigan State University, Talbert & Leota Abrams Planetarium, East Lansing, MI 48824. TEL 517-355-4676. E-mail: griffi24@pilot.msu.edu; URL: http://www.pa.msu.edu/skycal2.html. Ed. Robert C. Victor. circ. 15,000. (looseleaf format; back issues avail.)
Description: Provides a night-by-night description of noteworthy sky events and includes a simplified star chart of the month's evening sky. On the calendar, text and drawings guide to bright planets at dusk and dawn, to the bright zodiac stars as the moon passes them, and to sights that can be enjoyed with binoculars.

ACADEMIE SERBE DES SCIENCES ET DES ARTS. CLASSE DES SCIENCES MATHEMATIQUES ET NATURELLES. BULLETIN. SCIENCES MATHEMATIQUES. see *MATHEMATICS*

520   PL   ISSN 0001-5237
                  CODEN: AASWAM
ACTA ASTRONOMICA; an international quarterly journal. (Text in English) 1925. q. $130 (effective 1998). Copernicus Foundation for Polish Astronomy, Al. Ujazdowskie 4, 00-478 Warsaw, Poland. TEL 48-22-6295346. FAX 48-2-26294967. E-mail: acta@sirius.astrouw.edu.pl. (Dist. by: Mezhdunarodnaya Kniga, B. Yakimanka 39, 117049 Moscow, Russia. TEL 7-095-2384967. FAX 7-095-2384634) Eds. Marcin Kubiak, Andrzej Udalski. adv.; bk.rev.; circ. 250 (paid). **Indexed:** ASCA, Chem.Abstr., Curr.Cont., Ind.Sci.Rev., INIS Atomind., INSPEC (1969-), Int.Aerosp.Abstr., Meteor.& Geoastrophys.Abstr. **Document type:** academic/scholarly publication.
—BLDSC (0596.800000); AskIEEE; CASDDS; CISTI; Genuine Article; KR SourceOne; Linda Hall; SWETS; UnCover.
Description: Publishes original, scientific papers from the domain of astrophysics and astronomy.
Refereed Serial

523.01   SI   ISSN 0218-0251
ADVANCED SERIES IN ASTROPHYSICS AND COSMOLOGY. (Text in English) 1984. irreg., vol. 9, 1993. price varies. World Scientific Publishing Co. Pte. Ltd., Farrer Rd., P.O. Box 128, Singapore 9128, Singapore. TEL 65-3825663. FAX 65-3825919. TELEX RS 28561 WSPC. E-mail: wspcsl@singnet.com.sg.; sales@wspc2.demon.co.uk; wspc@wspc.com; URL: http://www.signet.com.sg/~wspclib/. (UK addr.: 57 Shelton St., Covent Garden, London WC2H 9HE, England. TEL 44-171-836-0888. FAX 44-171-836-2020; US addr.: 1060 Main St., River Edge, NJ 07661. TEL 800-227-7562. FAX 201-487-9656) **Document type:** monographic series.
—BLDSC (0696.927200).

500.5   GW   ISSN 1430-9602
▼**ADVANCES IN SPATIAL SCIENCE.** 1995. irreg. Springer-Verlag, Heidelberger Platz 3, 14197 Berlin, Germany. TEL 49-30-82787-0. FAX 49-30-82787448. E-mail: subscriptions@springer.de; URL: http://www.springer.de. (Subscr. in N. America to: Springer-Verlag New York, Inc., 333 Meadowlands Pkwy., Secaucus, NJ 07094. TEL 212-460-1500. FAX 212-473-6272) Ed.Bd.
Document type: monographic series.
Description: Publishes relevant research in this area of economics.

520   SP
AGRUPACION ASTRONOMICA DE SABADELL. CIRCULAR INFORMATIVA. no.267, 1981. 1/yr. 9700 ptas. membership. Agrupacion Astronomica de Sabadell, Casilla 50, 08200 Sabadell, Spain. TEL 7255373.
Formerly: Agrupacion Astronomica de Sabadell. Circular Mensual.

THE AIR ALMANAC. see *AERONAUTICS AND SPACE FLIGHT*

AKADEMIYA NAUK TAJIKISTANA. DOKLADY. see *MATHEMATICS*

520   DK   ISSN 0905-8958
AKTUEL ASTRONOMI. 1977. q. DKK 215($26) (Tycho Brahe Planetarium) I S Astronomisk Forlag, Gl. Kongevej 10, DK-1610 Copenhagen V, Denmark. FAX 45-33-14-28-88. E-mail: tycho@inet.uni-c.dk; URL: http://www.astro.ku.dk/tycho.html. Ed. Henry Noergaard. R&P contact: Henry Noergaard. adv.; bk.rev.; illus. circ. 12,000. **Document type:** academic/scholarly publication.
Former titles (until 1991): Astronomi og Rumfart (ISSN 0107-2862); (until 1980): Dansk Amatoer Astronomi (ISSN 0105-9815)

520   PH   ISSN 0569-0838
ALMANAC FOR GEODETIC ENGINEERS. (Text in English) a. P.40. Philippine Atmospheric, Geophysical and Astronomical Services Administration, 1424 Quezon Ave., Quezon City 1101, Philippines. TELEX 42021-PAGASA-PM. Dir. Roman L. Kintanar. circ. 1,500. **Document type:** government publication.
Description: Data of the sun and selected stars for surveying purposes.

528.6   SP   ISSN 0210-735X
ALMANAQUE NAUTICO. 1792. a. 1976 ptas. (effective 1996). Real Instituto y Observatorio de la Armada, Cecilio Pujazon s-n, 11110 San Fernando (Cadiz), Spain. illus.; circ. 3,000 (paid). **Indexed:** Ind.SST. **Document type:** government publication.
Formerly: Almanaque Nautico para Uso de los Navegantes (ISSN 0210-7341)
Description: Provides data required for astronomical navigation at sea.

520 036   SP   ISSN 0210-8046
ALMANAQUE NAUTICO REDUCIDO PARA USO CON MAQUINAS DE CALCULAR. 1979. a. 884 ptas. (effective 1996). Real Instituto y Observatorio de la Armada, Cecilio Pugazon, s-n, 11100 San Fernando, Cadiz, Spain. circ. 350 (paid). **Indexed:** Ind.SST. **Document type:** government publication.
Description: Provides the data and formulae required for astronomical navigation at sea using programmable calculators.

520   US   ISSN 0271-9053
QB835   CODEN: JAAODA
AMERICAN ASSOCIATION OF VARIABLE STAR OBSERVERS. JOURNAL. 1972. 2/yr. $25 to individuals (foreign $30); institutions $40 (foreign $45). American Association of Variable Star Observers, 25 Birch St., Cambridge, MA 02138. TEL 617-354-0484. E-mail: aavso@aavso.org; URL: http://www.aavso.org/journal.html. Ed. Charles A. Whitney. bk.rev.; index. circ. 1,500. (back issues avail.) **Indexed:** Astron.& Astrophys.Abstr., INSPEC (1980-). **Document type:** academic/scholarly publication.
—AskIEEE; CISTI; KR SourceOne; Linda Hall.
Description: Scientific papers on variable star research, AAVSO activities, and letters to editor.
Refereed Serial

520   US   ISSN 0271-8480
AMERICAN ASSOCIATION OF VARIABLE STAR OBSERVERS. SOLAR BULLETIN. 1945. 12/yr. $25 to individuals (foreign $30); institutions $40 (foreign $45). American Association of Variable Star Observers, 25 Birch St., Cambridge, MA 02138. TEL 617-354-0484. FAX 617-354-0665. Ed. Peter O. Taylor. circ. 300. (looseleaf format) **Indexed:** INSPEC. **Document type:** bulletin.
Description: Daily American and international sunspot numbers; sudden ionospheric disturbance data.

520   US   ISSN 0002-7537
                  CODEN: AASBAR
AMERICAN ASTRONOMICAL SOCIETY. BULLETIN. 1969. q. $53 (foreign $63) (effective 1998). American Institute of Physics, One Physics Ellipse, College Park, MD 20740-3843. TEL 301-209-3000. E-mail: ssavoy@aas.org; URL: http://www.aas.org/publications/baas/baas.html. (Subscr. to: AIP Member and Subscriber Service, 500 Sunnyside Blvd., Woodbury, NY 11797-2999. TEL 516-576-2411. FAX 516-576-2374) Ed. P.B. Boyce. abstr. (also avail. in microfilm from AIP) **Indexed:** INIS Atomind., INSPEC (1969-1991). **Document type:** bulletin.
—BLDSC (2386.200000); CISTI; KR SourceOne; Linda Hall; SWETS; UnCover.

AMERICAN SOCIETY FOR PHOTOGRAMMETRY AND REMOTE SENSING. FALL CONVENTION. TECHNICAL PAPERS. see *GEOGRAPHY*

ANG TAGAMASID. see *METEOROLOGY*

520 523.01   US   ISSN 0066-4146
QB1   CODEN: ARAAAJ
ANNUAL REVIEW OF ASTRONOMY AND ASTROPHYSICS. 1963. a. $70 to individuals (foreign $75); institutions $140 (foreign $150) (effective 1998). Annual Reviews Inc., 4139 El Camino Way, Box 10139, Palo Alto, CA 94303-0139. TEL 650-493-4400; 800-523-8635. FAX 650-424-0910. E-mail: service@annurev.org; URL: http://www.annurev.org. Ed. Geoffrey Burbidge; Pub. John S. McNeil. R&P contact: Jeanne Kunz. bibl.; index, cum.index. (also avail. in microfilm from UMI; back issues avail.; reprint service avail.) **Indexed:** ASCA, Chem.Abstr., Curr.Cont., Ind.Sci.Rev., INSPEC, Int.Aerosp.Abstr., M.M.R.I., Nucl.Sci.Abstr., Phys.Ber. **Document type:** academic/scholarly publication.
—CASDDS; CISTI; Genuine Article; Linda Hall; SWETS; UMI; UnCover. **CCC.**
Description: Original critical reviews of the significant primary literature and current developments in astronomy and astrophysics.

ANNUAL REVIEW OF EARTH AND PLANETARY SCIENCES. see *EARTH SCIENCES*

520 551   US   ISSN 0270-7179
ANTARCTIC METEORITE NEWSLETTER. 1978. 2/yr. free. Antarctic Meteorite Program, Code SN2, NASA, Johnson Space Center, Houston, TX 77058. TEL 713-483-5135. FAX 713-483-5347. E-mail: mlindstrom@snmail.jsc.nasa.gov; URL: http://www.corator.jcs.nasa.gov/curator/curator.htm. Ed. Marilyn M. Lindstrom. circ. 600. **Document type:** newsletter, government publication, catalog.
Description: Lists classifications and descriptions of meteorites returned as part of the US Antarctic Meteorite Program.

ARCHAEOASTRONOMY. see *ARCHAEOLOGY*

520   UK   ISSN 0142-7253
GN799.A8   CODEN: ARHADN
ARCHAEOASTRONOMY. (Supplement to: Journal for the History of Astronomy) 1979. a. £19($38) (effective 1998). Science History Publications Ltd., 16 Rutherford Rd., Cambridge CB2 2HH, England. TEL 44-1223-565532. FAX 44-1223-565532. Ed. C.L.N. Ruggles; Pub. Bernard Hoskin. R&P contact: Bernard Hoskin. adv. contact: Bernard Hoskin. bk.rev.; illus.; index. circ. 600. (back issues avail.) **Indexed:** Abstr.Anthropol., Anthropol.Lit., Br.Archaeol.Abstr., INSPEC (1979-1993). **Document type:** academic/scholarly publication.
—BLDSC (1594.520000); AskIEEE; CISTI; KR SourceOne; Linda Hall; UnCover. **CCC.**
Description: Devoted to pre-written astronomy.
Refereed Serial

ARCHAEOASTRONOMY & ETHNOASTRONOMY NEWS. see *ARCHAEOLOGY*

520   GW   ISSN 0570-6262
ARCHENHOLD-STERNWARTE. VORTRAEGE UND SCHRIFTEN. 1959. irreg., vol.7, no.70, 1989. price varies. Archenhold-Sternwarte, Alt-Treptow 1, 12435 Berlin, Germany. TEL 49-30-2727493. FAX 49-30-2318083. Ed. D.B. Herrmann. adv.; bk.rev. circ. 1,500. **Document type:** monographic series.
—Linda Hall.
Description: Documents the history of astronomy.

ASTRONOMY

520   PE   ISSN 0044-9318
ASOCIACION PERUANA DE ASTRONOMIA. BOLETIN.* 1947. q. Juan Fanning, Ed.& Pub., 354 Miraflores, Lima 18, Peru. Ed. Gustavo A. Estremadoyro. bk.rev. (processed) **Indexed:** A.I.C.P.

523   US   ISSN 0039-2502
QB1   CODEN: STASAD
ASSOCIATION OF LUNAR AND PLANETARY OBSERVERS. JOURNAL. Variant title: Strolling Astronomer. 1947. q. $16 in US, Canada and Mexico; elsewhere $20. Association of Lunar and Planetary Observers, Box 16131, San Francisco, CA 94116. TEL 415-566-5786. FAX 415-731-8242. E-mail: 73737.1102@compuserve.com; URL: http://www.LPL.Arizona.edu/~rhill/alpo/member.html. Ed. John E. Westfall. adv.; bk.rev.; charts; illus.; stat.; circ. 600 (paid). **Indexed:** Astron.& Astrophys.Abstr., INSPEC (1982-). **Document type:** academic/scholarly publication.
—AskIEEE; KR SourceOne; Linda Hall; UnCover.

522.1   FR   ISSN 0249-7522
ASSOCIATION POUR LE DEVELOPPEMENT INTERNATIONAL DE L'OBSERVATOIRE DE NICE. BULLETIN. (Text in English, French) 1964. a. 50 F. Association pour le Developpement International de l'Observatoire de Nice, B.P. 139, F-06003 Nice, France. charts; illus. circ. 400. **Document type:** bulletin.
—CISTI.
Formerly (until 1974): Association pour le Developpement International de l'Observatoire de Nice. Bulletin d'Information (ISSN 0004-5861)

520   SW   ISSN 0280-7173
ASTRO. 1982. q. SEK 170 membership (effective 1995). Svensk Amatoerastronomisk Foerening (SAAF), c/o Jan Persson, Eklanda Skale 11, S-431 49 Moelndal, Sweden. TEL 46-31-27-78-20. E-mail: jan.persson@space.se. Ed. Jan Persson. adv.; bk.rev. **Document type:** bulletin.

522.63   US   ISSN 0094-1417
QB121
ASTROGRAPH.* 1973. bi-m. $10 (foreign $15). Box 369, Dumfries, VA 22026-0369. TEL 703-892-6846. Ed. Robert C. Price. adv.: color page $625. bk.rev. circ. 1,200.
Description: Covers astrophotography: astronomical photography of the Moon, planets, galaxies, nebulae and stars.

520   FR   ISSN 0398-074X
ASTROLAB. (Text mainly in French; summaries in English, Italian, Spanish) 1976. a. 240 F. (effective 1997). Philippe Bury, Ed.& Pub., 185 rue de Solignac, 87000 Limoges, France. E-mail: philippe.bury@0555312059.minicom.atlas.fr. adv.; bk.rev.
Description: Practical and theoretical ideas on astronomy and space. Includes new books and materials available.

520   FR   ISSN 0764-2997
ASTROLETTRE. 1984. irreg. (approx. 5/yr.). 80 F. (effective 1997). Philippe Bury, Ed. & Pub., 185 rue de Solignac, 87000 Limoges, France. E-mail: philippe.bury@0555312059.minicom.atlas.fr. adv.; bk.rev.

520   UK   ISSN 0950-138X
THE ASTRONOMER. 1964. m. £21 (Europe £25; elsewhere £28) (effective 1997-1998). 16 Westminster Close, Basingstoke, Hants. RG22 4PP, England. TEL 44-1256-471074. FAX 44-1256-471074. E-mail: guy@tahq.demon.co.uk; URL: http://www.demon.co.uk/astronomer/. (Subscr. to: Peter Meadows, 250 Linnet Dr., Chelmsford CM2 8AJ, England) Ed. Guy Hurst; Pub. Guy Hurst. adv. contact: Peter Meadows. bk.rev.; charts; illus.; stat.; circ. 300. circ. 300 (paid). (back issues avail.) **Indexed:** INSPEC (1985-). **Document type:** academic/scholarly publication.
●Also available online.
—BLDSC (1749.760000); AskIEEE; KR SourceOne.
Refereed Serial

520   NO   ISSN 0802-7587
ASTRONOMI. 1971. q. NOK 250. Norsk Astronomisk Selskap, P.O. Box 250, 1029 Blindern, N-0315 Oslo 3, Norway. Ed. Arild Mikalsen. adv.; bk.rev. circ. 1,100.
Former titles (until 1989): Amatoerastronomen (ISSN 0802-7609); (until 1972): Amatoerkontakt (ISSN 0802-7595)

522   629.4   SW   ISSN 1104-1242
ASTRONOMI- OCH RYMDFART. 1977. q. SEK 200. Astronomi- och Rymdfartsfremjandet - Swedish Astronomy and Space Association, P.O. Box 7220, S-402 34 Goeteborg, Sweden. TEL 46. Ed. Thommy Eriksson. adv.; bk.rev. circ. 1,200. **Document type:** bulletin.
Formerly (until 1993): Aurora (ISSN 1101-1718)

520   IT
L'ASTRONOMIA (MILAN). 1979. m. Lit.8000 per no. (effective 1997). Media Presse Edizioni, Via Nino Bixio 30, 20129 Milan, Italy. TEL 39-2-2043941. FAX 39-2-2046507. Ed. Corrado Lamberti; Pub. Cesare Vacchelli. R&P contact: Corrado Lamberti. adv.: B&W page L.3100000; adv. contact: Luigi Vacchelli. bk.rev. circ. 70,000.

523   US   ISSN 0737-6421
QB8.U6   CODEN: ASALET
THE ASTRONOMICAL ALMANAC. 1855. a. $29 (effective 1995). U.S. Naval Observatory, Department of the Navy, Washington, DC 20392. (Subscr. also to: Superintendent of Documents, U.S. Government Printing Office, Box 371954, Pittsburgh, PA 15250-7954. TEL 202-512-1800. FAX 202-512-2250; Subscr. in the U.K. to: H.M.S.O. Publications Centre, P.O. Box 276, London SW8 5DT, England. TEL 0171-873-9090. FAX 0171-873-8200) (Co-sponsor: H.M. Nautical Almanac Office (UK)) (back issues avail.) **Indexed:** INSPEC. **Document type:** government publication.
—BLDSC (1749.780000); CISTI.
Supersedes: Astronomical Ephemeris (ISSN 0066-9962); American Ephemeris and Nautical Almanac (ISSN 0065-8189); Nautical Almanac and Astronomical Ephemeris.
Description: Contains precise ephemerides of the sun, moon, and planets and satellites, as well as data for eclipses and other astronomical phenomena.

520   NE   ISSN 1055-6796
QB1   CODEN: AATREG
ASTRONOMICAL AND ASTROPHYSICAL TRANSACTIONS. 1991. 12/yr. (in 3 vols., 4 nos./vol.). $144 (effective 1998). (Eurasian Astronomical Society, UR) Gordon and Breach - Harwood Academic, Amsteldisk 166, 1st Fl., 1079 LH Amsterdam, Netherlands. (Subscr. to: International Publishers Distributor, Box 32160, Newark, NJ 07102. TEL 800-545-8398. FAX 215-750-6343) Ed N.G. Bochkarev. (also avail. in microform) **Indexed:** INSPEC (1992-). **Document type:** academic/scholarly publication.
—BLDSC (1749.790000); AskIEEE; CASDDS; CISTI; KR SourceOne. **CCC**.
Description: Covers all modern and classical fields of astronomy and astrophysics. Includes astronomical instrumentation and related fundamental sciences.
Refereed Serial

520   II   ISSN 0066-9970
ASTRONOMICAL EPHEMERIS OF GEOCENTRIC PLACES OF PLANETS. (Text in English; summaries in Hindi) 1942. a. Rs.13. Shree Jiwaji Observatory, Ujain, Madhya Pradesh, India. Ed. Jyotishstracharya K. K. Joshi. circ. 500. **Document type:** government publication.

520   US   ISSN 0004-6256
QB1   CODEN: ANJOAA
ASTRONOMICAL JOURNAL. 1849. m. $340 (foreign $445) (effective 1998). (American Astronomical Society) American Institute of Physics, One Physics Ellipse, College Park, MD 20740-3843. TEL 301-209-3000. E-mail: astroj@astroj.washington.edu; URL: http://www.astro.washington.edu/astroj/index.html. (Subscr. to: University of Chicago Press, 5801 S. Ellis Ave., Chicago, IL 60637) Ed. P.W. Hodge. abstr.; bibl.; charts; index, cum.index: vols.1-50, 1849-1944; vols.51-80, 1944-1975. (also avail. in microform from AIP; back issues avail.) **Indexed:** Appl.Mech.Rev., ASCA, C.P.I., Chem.Abstr., Comput.Rev., Curr.Cont., Gen.Phys.Adv.Abstr., Ind.Sci.Rev., INIS Atomind., INSPEC (1977-), Math.R., Meteor.& Geoastrophys.Abstr., Phys.Ber., Sci.Cit.Ind. **Document type:** academic/scholarly publication.
—BLDSC (1752.000000); AskIEEE; CASDDS; CISTI; Genuine Article; KR SourceOne; Linda Hall; SWETS; UnCover. **CCC**.
Refereed Serial

520   XO   ISSN 0862-920X
ASTRONOMICAL OBSERVATORY ON SKALNATE PLESO. CONTRIBUTIONS. (Text in English; summaries in Russian and Slovak) vol.8, 1977. irreg. price varies. (Slovenska Akademia Vied, Astronomicky Ustav) Veda, Publishing House of the Slovak Academy of Sciences, Bradacova 7, 852 86 Bratislava, Slovakia. (Dist. by: Slovart, Nam. Slobody 6, 817 64 Bratislava, Slovakia)
—CISTI.
Formerly (until 1990): Astronomicke Observatorie na Skalnatom Plese. Prace (ISSN 0583-466X)

523   US   ISSN 0083-2421
QB9
ASTRONOMICAL PHENOMENA. 1951. a. $4.25 for 1995 edition; 1996 edition $5. U.S. Naval Observatory, Department of the Navy, Washington, DC 20392. TEL 202-783-3238. (Dist. by Bernan, 4611-F Assembly Dr., Lanham, MD 20706. TEL 800-274-4447. FAX 301-459-0056; Subscr. in the U.K. to: H.M.S.O. Publications Centre, P.O. Box 276, London SW8 5DT, England. TEL 0171-873-9090. FAX 0171-873-8200) (Co-sponsor: H.M. Nautical Almanac Office (UK)) (back issues avail.) **Document type:** government publication.
—CISTI.
Description: Preprints data from the Astronomical Almanac, including the calendar, anniversaries and festivals, chronological eras and cycles, equinoxes and solstices, phase of the moon, visibility and configurations of the planets, elipses, equation of time and declination of the sun, rising and setting of the sun and moon, and the position of the Polaris.

520   AT   ISSN 1323-3580
QB1.A37   CODEN: PASAFO
ASTRONOMICAL SOCIETY OF AUSTRALIA. PUBLICATIONS. 1966. 3/yr. Aus.$160 (effective 1997). C.S.I.R.O. Publishing, 150 Oxford St., Collingwood, Vic. 3066, Australia. TEL 61-3-96627500. FAX 61-3-96627611. E-mail: michelle@physics.usyd.edu.au; URL: http://www.publish.csiro.au/journals/pasa/index.html. (Subscr. to: CSIRO Publications Sales, P.O. Box 89, East Melbourne, Vic. 3002, Australia. TEL 61-3-4187217. FAX 61-3-4190459) Ed. M.C. Storey. adv.; bk.rev.; abstr.; bibl.; charts; stat. circ. 600. (back issues avail.; reprint service avail. from ISI) **Indexed:** ASCA, Astron.& Astrophys.Abstr., Chem.Abstr., Curr.Cont., Ind.Sci.Rev., INSPEC (1968-), Sci.Cit.Ind. **Document type:** academic/scholarly publication.
●Also available online.
—BLDSC (7027.800000); AskIEEE; CASDDS; CISTI; Genuine Article; KR SourceOne; Linda Hall; UnCover.
Formerly: Astronomical Society of Australia. Proceedings (ISSN 0066-9997).
Description: Publishes articles on original astronomical research, including instrumentation and software development.
Refereed Serial

520   II   ISSN 0304-9523
QB1   CODEN: BANID3
ASTRONOMICAL SOCIETY OF INDIA. BULLETIN. (Text in English) 1973. q. Rs.100($5) to individuals (foreign $30); institutions Rs.150 (foreign $70) (effective 1997 & 1998); newsstand price: Rs.50. Astronomical Society of India, Indian Institute of Astrophysics, Koramangala, Bangalore 560 034, India. TEL 91-80-5530672. FAX 91-80-5534043. TELEX 0845-2763-IIAB-IN. E-mail: vinod@iiap.ernet.in. Ed. Vinod Krishan. adv.; bk.rev. circ. 900. (reprint service avail.) **Indexed:** Astron.& Astrophys.Abstr., Chem.Abstr., Indian Sci.Ind., INSPEC (1977-). **Document type:** bulletin.
—AskIEEE; CASDDS; CISTI; KR SourceOne; Linda Hall; UnCover.
Refereed Serial

ASTRONOMY

520   JA   ISSN 0004-6264
QB1   CODEN: PASJAC
ASTRONOMICAL SOCIETY OF JAPAN. PUBLICATIONS/NIHON TENMON GAKKAI OBUN KENKYU HOKOKU. (Text and summaries in English) 1949. bi-m. 22,000 Yen. Nihon Tenmon Gakkai - Astronomical Society of Japan, c/o National Astronomical Observatory, 21-1, Osawa 2-chome, Mitaka-shi, Tokyo 181, Japan. (Dist. by: Maruzen Co., Ltd., Daisan Maruzen Biru, 16-1, Nihonbashi 2-chome, Chuo-ku, Tokyo 103, Japan) Ed. N. Arimoto. adv. (reprint service avail. from ISI) **Indexed:** ASCA, Chem.Abstr., Curr.Cont., Ind.Sci.Rev., INSPEC (1968-), Jap.Per.Ind., JTA, Phys.Ber., Sci.Cit.Ind. —BLDSC (7029.000000); AskIEEE; CASDDS; CISTI; Genuine Article; KR SourceOne; Linda Hall; SWETS; UnCover.

520   US
ASTRONOMICAL SOCIETY OF NEW YORK. NEWSLETTER. 1976. s-a. $12. L. Davis Press, Inc., 1125 Oxford Pl., Schenectady, NY 12308. TEL 518-374-5636. Ed. A.G. Davis Philip. circ. 100. **Indexed:** Astron.& Astrophys.Abstr. **Document type:** newsletter.

520   AT   ISSN 0044-9806
ASTRONOMICAL SOCIETY OF SOUTH AUSTRALIA. BULLETIN. 1892. m. Aus.$35. Astronomical Society of South Australia, G.P.O. Box 199, Adelaide, S.A. 5001, Australia. TEL 61-8-83381231. FAX 61-8-83794145. E-mail: assa@gist.net.au; URL: http://www.gist.net.au/assa/. Ed. Dean Davidson. R&P contact: Dean Davidson. bk.rev. circ. 450. **Document type:** newsletter.

520   SA   ISSN 0024-8266
                              CODEN: MASAAK
ASTRONOMICAL SOCIETY OF SOUTHERN AFRICA. MONTHLY NOTES. Short title: M N A S S A. 1940. bi-m. $30 (effective 1998). Astronomical Society of Southern Africa, P.O. Box 9, Observatory 7935, South Africa. TEL 27-21-5315250. FAX 27-21-473639. TELEX 520 309. Ed. Auke Slotegraaf. R&P contact: Cliff Turk. adv. contact: Cliff Turk. bk.rev.; bibl.; charts; illus. circ. 650. **Indexed:** Astron.& Astrophys.Abstr., INSPEC (1968-). **Document type:** academic/scholarly publication. —AskIEEE; CISTI; KR SourceOne; UnCover.
      Refereed Serial

520   US   ISSN 0004-6280
QB1   CODEN: PASPAU
ASTRONOMICAL SOCIETY OF THE PACIFIC. PUBLICATIONS. 1889. m. $80 to non-research libraries, other institutions $190, membership for individuals (includes Mercury magazine). Astronomical Society of the Pacific, 390 Ashton Ave., San Francisco, CA 94112. TEL 415-337-1100. FAX 415-337-5205. E-mail: pasp@stsci.edu; URL: http://www.stsci.edu/pasp/. Ed. Howard Bond. illus.; cum.index: vols.1-94. circ. 3,000. (also avail. in microfiche; reprint service avail. from UMI) **Indexed:** ASCA, Astron.& Astrophys.Abstr., Chem.Abstr., Ind.Sci.Rev., INSPEC (1968-), Math.R., Phys.Ber. **Document type:** bulletin. —BLDSC (7030.000000); AskIEEE; CASDDS; CISTI; Ei; KR SourceOne; Linda Hall; SWETS; UMI; UnCover. **Description:** Research reports, PhD abstracts and review articles in astronomy and astrophysics.

520   AT   ISSN 0067-0006
QB4.9.A8
ASTRONOMICAL SOCIETY OF VICTORIA. ASTRONOMICAL YEARBOOK. 1964. a. Aus.$15. Astronomical Society of Victoria, G.P.O. Box 1059J, Melbourne, Vic. 3001, Australia. URL: http://www.gsat.net.au/astrovic. Ed. Steven Pattie. R&P contact: Steven Pattie. index. circ. 850. **Document type:** academic/scholarly publication.
    Description: Contains data for local observations and other general astronomical information, as well as informative summaries of various celestial objects.

520   BU   ISSN 0068-3639
ASTRONOMICHESKI KALENDAR NA OBSERVATORIIATA V SOFIA. 1954. a. 1.26 lv. (Bulgarska Akademiia na Naukite, Sektsiia po Astronomiia) Publishing House of the Bulgarian Academy of Sciences, Acad. G. Bonchev St., Bldg. 6, 1113 Sofia, Bulgaria. (Dist. by: Hemus, 6, Rouski Blvd., 1000 Sofia, Bulgaria) Ed. L. Levicharska. circ. 2,640. (reprint service avail. from IRC)

520   RU   ISSN 0320-930X
QB1   CODEN: ASVEA7
ASTRONOMICHESKII VESTNIK. English translation: Solar System Research (US ISSN 0038-0946) (Text in Russian; summaries in English) 1967. q. 11.40 Rub. Izdatel'stvo Nauka, 90 Profsoyuznaya ul., 117864 Moscow, Russia. TEL 234-05-84. Ed. Michael Ya. Marov. circ. 2,300. (back issues avail.) **Indexed:** Chem.Abstr., INIS Atomind., INSPEC (1969-).
—AskIEEE; CASDDS; CISTI; KNAW; KR SourceOne; Linda Hall. **CCC.**

520   RU   ISSN 0004-6299
                              CODEN: ASZHA2
ASTRONOMICHESKII ZHURNAL. English translation: Astronomy Reports (US ISSN 1063-7729) 1924. bi-m. $240 (effective 1998). (Rossiiskaya Akademiya Nauk, Astrosovet) Izdatel'stvo Nauka, 90 Profsoyuznaya ul., 117864 Moscow, Russia. (Dist. by: Mezhdunarodnaya Kniga, ul. B. Yakimanka 39, 117049 Moscow, Russia) Ed. E.R. Mustel. bk.rev.; index. (tabloid format) **Indexed:** ASCA, Chem.Abstr., Curr.Cont., Ind.Sci.Rev., INIS Atomind., INSPEC (1968-), Math.R., Meteor.& Geoastrophys.Abstr., Phys.Ber., Sci.Cit.Ind., Zent.Math.
—BLDSC (0013.000000); AskIEEE; CASDDS; CISTI; Genuine Article; KR SourceOne; Linda Hall. **CCC.**

520   FR   ISSN 0004-6302
QB1
ASTRONOMIE. 1882. m. (10/yr.). 510 F. (effective 1997). Societe Astronomique de France, 3 rue Beethoven, 75016 Paris, France. TEL 01-42-24-13-74. FAX 01-42-30-75-47. Ed. M. Gros. R&P contact: Elisabeth Sable. adv.; bk.rev.; bibl.; charts; illus.; index. circ. 2,600. **Indexed:** Astron.& Astrophys.Abstr., Bull.Signal., INSPEC (1984-), Ref.Zh. **Document type:** bulletin.
—AskIEEE; KR SourceOne; Linda Hall. **CCC.**

520   FR   ISSN 0989-6236
ASTRONOMIE ET SCIENCES HUMAINES. 1988. s-a. 100 F. Observatoire Astronomique de Strasbourg, 11 rue de l'Universite, 67000 Strasbourg, France. FAX 88-25-01-60. TELEX 890506 STAROB S. E-mail: gerard@simbad.u-strasbg.fr. Ed. Gerard Jasniewicz. circ. 450. **Document type:** proceedings.
—CISTI.

520   CN   ISSN 1183-5362
ASTRONOMIE QUEBEC. 1972. bi-m. Can.$32. Editions Astronomique Inc., 4545 Ave. Pierre de Coubertin, Montreal, PQ H1V 3R2, Canada. TEL 514-252-3038. FAX 514-251-8038. Ed. Jean-Pierre Urbain. adv.: B&W page Can.$625. illus. circ. 2,500. **Indexed:** Pt.de Rep. (1991-).
    Formerly: Quebec Astronomique (ISSN 0318-0492)
    Description: Disseminates astronomical and astronautical information including observation reports, member news, general information, and more.

520   GW   ISSN 0948-4388
ASTRONOMIE UND RAUMFAHRT. (Text in German; summaries in English, Russian) 1964. bi-m. DM.12. Erhard Friedrich Verlag GmbH, Im Brande 15, 30926 Seelze, Germany. TEL 49-511-40004-0. FAX 49-511-40004170. (Subscr. to: Postfach 100150, 30917 Seelze, Germany) bk.rev.; bibl.; charts; illus.; stat.; index. circ. 3,500.
—CISTI.
    Formerly: Astronomie in der Schule (ISSN 0004-6310)

520   GW   ISSN 0067-0014
ASTRONOMISCHE GRUNDLAGEN FUER DEN KALENDER. 1949. a. DM.109 (including diskette DM.289,75) (effective 1997 & 1998). (Astronomisches Rechen-Institut) Verlag G. Braun GmbH, Karl-Friedrich-Str. 14-18, 76133 Karlsruhe, Germany. TEL 49-721-165-0. FAX 49-721-165855. TELEX 7826904-VGB-D. Ed. T. Lederle. circ. 1,000. **Document type:** bulletin.

520   GW   ISSN 0004-6337
QB1   CODEN: ASNAAN
ASTRONOMISCHE NACHRICHTEN; a journal on all fields of astronomy. (Text and summaries in English, German) 1821. bi-m. DM.195 (foreign DM.207) to individuals; institutions DM.645 (foreign DM.675) (effective 1997). (Astrophysikalisches Institut Potsdam) Akademie Verlag GmbH, Muehlenstr. 33-34, 13187 Berlin, Germany. TEL 49-30-47889348. FAX 49-30-47889357. E-mail: info@akademie-verlag.de. (Subscr. in the Americas to: John Wiley & Sons, Inc., 605 Third Ave., New York, NY 10158. TEL 212-850-6645. FAX 212-850-6021) Ed.Bd. charts; illus.; index. circ. 350. **Indexed:** ASCA, Chem.Abstr., Curr.Cont., Ind.Sci.Rev., INIS Atomind., INSPEC (1976-), Math.R., Phys.Ber., Sci.Cit.Ind., SSCI, Zent.Math. **Document type:** academic/scholarly publication.
—AskIEEE; CASDDS; CISTI; Genuine Article; KR SourceOne; Linda Hall; UnCover. **CCC.**

520   SW   ISSN 0004-6345
                              CODEN: ANTKBF
ASTRONOMISK TIDSSKRIFT. (Supplement avail.) 1916. 4/yr. SEK 200 membership (effective 1997). Astronomiska Observatoriet, Box 515, S-751 20 Uppsala, Sweden. TEL 46-18-30-28-65. FAX 46-18-52-75-83. E-mail: gunnar.welin@astro.uu.se. (Co-sponsors: Norsk Astronomisk Selskap, Oslo; Dansk Astronomisk Selskab, Copenhagen) Ed. Gunnar Welin. adv.; bk.rev.; charts; illus.; index; circ. 2,500. circ. 2,800 (paid). **Indexed:** INIS Atomind., INSPEC (1974-1988). **Document type:** academic/scholarly publication.
—CISTI; Linda Hall.
    Formerly (until 1968): Nordisk Astronomisk Tidsskrift (ISSN 0909-4865)
    Description: Contains news on astronomy, articles on the history of astronomy, society activities and other things of interest to amateur astronomers.

520   US   ISSN 0091-6358
QB1   CODEN: ASTRD5
ASTRONOMY. 1973. m. $34.95 (effective 1996). Kalmbach Publishing Co., 210272 Crossroads Cir., Waukesha, WI 53187. TEL 414-796-8776. FAX 414-796-1142. URL: http://www.kalmbach.com/astro/astronomy.html. Ed. Robert Burnham. adv.; bk.rev.; charts; illus.; index. circ. 170,000. (back issues avail.; reprint service avail. from UMI) **Indexed:** Acad.Ind., Bk.Rev.Ind. (1989-), Child.Bk.Rev.Ind. (1989-), Gen.Sci.Ind., GeoRef., Ind.How To Do It (1980-), INSPEC (1976-), Mag.Ind., PMR, R.G.Abstr., R.G. **Document type:** consumer publication.
● Also available online. Vendor(s): Information Access Co., UMI.
—BLDSC (1762.960000); AskIEEE; CISTI; Ei; KR SourceOne; Linda Hall; SWETS; UMI; UnCover.
    Description: Explores the planets, stars, and galaxies, and probes other facets of space. Includes monthly star charts with tips about star-gazing.

520 523.01   GW   ISSN 0004-6361
QB1   CODEN: AAEJAF
ASTRONOMY AND ASTROPHYSICS; a European journal. Online edition (GW ISSN 1432-0746) (Text in English, French or German; summaries in English) 1969. 36/yr. DM.4670.40 (foreign DM.4852.20) (effective 1998). (European Southern Observatory) Springer-Verlag, Heidelberger Platz 3, 14197 Berlin, Germany. TEL 49-30-82787-0. FAX 49-30-82787448. E-mail: subscriptions@springer.de; URL: http://link.springer.de. (Subscr. in N. America to: Springer-Verlag New York, Inc., 333 Meadowlands Pkwy., Secaucus, NJ 07094. TEL 212-460-1500. FAX 212-473-6272) Eds. J. Lequeux, H. Habins. adv.; bibl.; charts; illus.; index, cum.index. (also avail. in microform from UMI; reprint service avail. from ISI) **Indexed:** Appl.Mech.Rev., ASCA, Chem.Abstr., Compumath, Curr.Cont., Ind.Sci.Rev., INIS Atomind., INSPEC (1970-), Math.R., Meteor.& Geoastrophys.Abstr., Sci.Cit.Ind. **Document type:** academic/scholarly publication.
● Also available online.
—BLDSC (1762.970000); AskIEEE; CASDDS; CISTI; Ei; Genuine Article; KR SourceOne; Linda Hall; SWETS; UMI; UnCover. **CCC.**
    Supersedes: Zeitschrift fuer Astrophysik.
    Description: Presents papers on all aspects of astronomy and astrophysics - theoretical, observational, and instrumental - regardless of the techniques used - optical, radio, particles, space vehicles, and numerical analysis.

ASTRONOMY

520   GW   ISSN 0935-4956
QB1   CODEN: AASREB
THE ASTRONOMY AND ASTROPHYSICS REVIEW. Online edition (GW ISSN 1432-0754) (Text in English) 1989. q. DM.416 (foreign DM.420.60) (effective 1998). Springer-Verlag, Heidelberger Platz 3, 14197 Berlin, Germany. TEL 49-30-82787-0. FAX 49-30-82787448. E-mail: subscriptions@springer.de; URL: http://link.springer.de; http://www.springer-ny.com/physics/journals.htm. (Subscr. in N. America to: Springer-Verlag New York, Inc., 333 Meadowlands Pkwy., Secaucus, NJ 07094. TEL 212-460-1500. FAX 212-473-6272) Ed. L. Woltjer. (back issues avail.) **Indexed:** ASCA, Curr.Cont., INSPEC (1989-). **Document type:** academic/scholarly publication.
●Also available online.
—BLDSC (1762.971700); AskIEEE; CISTI; Ei; Genuine Article; KR SourceOne; Linda Hall; SWETS; UMI; UnCover. **CCC**.

520   FR   ISSN 0365-0138
QB1   CODEN: AAESB9
ASTRONOMY AND ASTROPHYSICS SUPPLEMENT SERIES; a European journal. (Text in English) 15/yr. 1060 F. to individuals; institutions 5150 F. (effective 1997). Editions de Physique, 7 av.du Hoggar, B.P. 112, Z.I. de Courtaboeuf, 91944 Les Ulis cedex A, France. TEL 33-1-69-07-36-88. FAX 33-1-69-28-84-91. TELEX 602 321 F. E-mail: customers@ed-phys.fr; URL: http:www.ed-phys.fr. index. (back issues avail.) **Indexed:** ASCA, Chem.Abstr., Compumath, Curr.Cont., Ind.Sci.Rev., INIS Atomind., INSPEC (1980-), Phys.Ber. **Document type:** academic/scholarly publication.
●Also available online.
—BLDSC (1762.972000); AskIEEE; CASDDS; CISTI; Genuine Article; KR SourceOne; Linda Hall; SWETS; UnCover. **CCC**.
Description: Observation data and original articles on astronomy and astrophysics.

520   UK   ISSN 1366-8781
QB1   CODEN: QJRAAK
ASTRONOMY & GEOPHYSICS; journal of the Royal Astronomical Society. 1960. q. £40 to individuals in the EU (N. America $70; elsewhere £45); institutions in the EU £92 (N. America $161; elsewhere £102) (effective 1997). (Royal Astronomical Society) I O P Publishing Ltd., Dirac House, Temple Back, Bristol BS1 6BE, England. TEL 44-117-929-7481. FAX 44-117-929-4318. E-mail: custserv@ioppublishing.co.uk; URL: http://www.iop.org/mags/ag. (Editorial addr.: Department of Earth Sciences, University of Leeds, Leeds LS2 9JT, England. TEL 44-113-233-5251. FAX 44-113-233-5259) Ed. Sue Bowler; Pub. Chris Manning. R&P contact: Mark Ware. adv. contact: Martine Cariou-Keen. bibl.; index. circ. 3,135. (also avail. in microform from UMI; back issues avail.; reprint service avail. from ISI) **Indexed:** ASCA, Curr.Cont., Deep Sea Res.& Oceanogr.Abstr., GeoRef., Ind.Sci.Rev., INSPEC, Math.R., Phys.Ber., Sci.Cit.Ind. **Document type:** academic/scholarly publication.
●Also available online.
—BLDSC (1762.975000); AskIEEE; CASDDS; CISTI; Genuine Article; KR SourceOne; Linda Hall; SWETS; UMI; UnCover.
Formerly (until 1997): Royal Astronomical Society. Quarterly Journal (ISSN 0035-8738)
Description: Publishes scientific articles on major developing themes in astronomy and geophysics in a succinct, readable, and accessible format.
Refereed Serial

520   IE   ISSN 0791-8062
ASTRONOMY & SPACE. 1990. bi-m. I£10. Astronomy Ireland, P.O. Box 2888, Dublin 1, Ireland. TEL 353-1-4598883. FAX 353-1-4599933. E-mail: ai@iol.ie; URL: http://www.iol.ie/-al/. Ed. David Moore. R&P contact: David Moore. adv. contact: Jan Trzcinski. bk.rev. **Document type:** bulletin.
Description: Covers Irish and international astronomy and space news.

520   RU   ISSN 1063-7737
QB1   CODEN: ALETEO
ASTRONOMY LETTERS. English translation of: Pis'ma v Astronomicheskii Zhurnal (RU ISSN 0320-0108) 1975. bi-m. $980 to institutions (effective 1997). (Rossiiskaya Akademiya Nauk) Maik Nauka - Interperiodica, Mezhdunarodnyi Otdel, Ul. Profsoyuznaya, 90, 117864 Moscow, Russia. (Subscr. to: American Institute of Physics, Member and Subscriber Services, 500 Sunnyside Blvd., Woodbury, NY 11797-2999, U.S.A.. TEL 516-576-2270. FAX 516-349-9704) Ed. P. Schippuick. bibl.; charts; illus.; index. (also avail. in microform from AIP; back issues avail.) **Indexed:** ASCA, C.P.I., Curr.Cont., Gen.Phys.Adv.Abstr., Ind.Sci.Rev., INSPEC (1975-), Int.Aerosp.Abstr., Phys.Ber., Sci.Cit.Ind., SSCI. **Document type:** academic/scholarly publication.
—BLDSC (0404.773000); AskIEEE; CISTI; Genuine Article; KR SourceOne; SWETS; UnCover. **CCC**.
Formerly: Soviet Astronomy Letters (ISSN 0360-0327)

520   UK   ISSN 0951-9726
                                 CODEN: ASNOEZ
ASTRONOMY NOW. 1987. m. £25 (E.C. nations £29; elsewhere £36($55)) (effective 1998). 124C Landor Rd., London SW9 9JB, England. Ed. Pam Spence; Pub. Chris Courtiour. adv. contact: Lucien Taylor. bk.rev.; index. circ. 25,000. (back issues avail.) **Indexed:** INSPEC (1988-). **Document type:** academic/scholarly publication.
—BLDSC (1762.979200); AskIEEE; CISTI; Ei; KR SourceOne; Linda Hall; SWETS.
Description: Covers information for amateur astronomers as well as people with a general interest in astronomy.

520   RU   ISSN 1063-7729
QB1   CODEN: ATROES
ASTRONOMY REPORTS. English translation of: Astronomicheskii Zhurnal (RU ISSN 0004-6299) 1957. bi-m. $1490 (foreign $1515) (effective 1997). (Rossiiskaya Akademiya Nauk) Maik Nauka - Interperiodica, Mezhdunarodnyi Otdel, Ul. Profsoyuznaya, 90, 117864 Moscow, Russia. TEL 301-209-3000. (Subscr. to: American Institute of Physics, Member and Subscriber Services, 500 Sunnyside Blvd., Woodbury, NY 11797-2999, U.S.A.. TEL 516-576-2411. FAX 516-576-2374) Ed. M. Damashek. bk.rev.; bibl.; charts; illus.; index. (also avail. in microform from AIP; back issues avail.) **Indexed:** C.P.I., Gen.Phys.Adv.Abstr., INSPEC (1993-), Int.Aerosp.Abstr., Math.R., Meteor.& Geoastrophys.Abstr., Phys.Ber. **Document type:** academic/scholarly publication.
—BLDSC (0404.775000); AskIEEE; CISTI; KR SourceOne; Linda Hall; SWETS; UnCover. **CCC**.
Former titles: Soviet Astronomy; Soviet Astronomy A.J. (ISSN 0038-5301)

520   US
ASTRONOMY THROUGH PRACTICAL INVESTIGATION. 1973. base vol. (plus a. update). $1 per no. L.S.W. Publications, Inc., Box 82, Mattituck, NY 11952. Ed.Bd. circ. 1,000.

523.013   NE   ISSN 0927-6505
                                 CODEN: APHYEE
ASTROPARTICLE PHYSICS. (Text in English) 1992. 8/yr. fl.879($505) to institutions; with New Astronomy fl.2445 ($1411) (effective 1998). North-Holland (Subsidiary of: Elsevier Science B.V.), P.O. Box 211, 1000 AE Amsterdam, Netherlands. TEL 31-20-4853911. FAX 31-20-4853598. TELEX 18582 ESPA NL. (Subscr. in the Americas to: Elsevier Science, Regional Sales Office, Box 945, New York, NY 10159-0945. TEL 212-633-3730. FAX 212-633-3680; Subscr. in Australasia and the Far East to: Elsevier Science (Singapore) Pte Ltd, No.1 Temasek Ave., No.17-01 Millenia Tower, Singapore 039192, Singapore. TEL 65-434-3727. FAX 65-337-2230; Subscr. in Japan to: Elsevier Science Japan, 9-15 Higashi-Azabu 1-chome, Minato-ku Tokyo 106, Japan. TEL 81-3-5561-5033. FAX 81-3-5561-5047) Ed.Bd. illus. (also avail. in microform from UMI; back issues avail.) **Indexed:** ASCA, Curr.Cont., INSPEC (1992-). **Document type:** academic/scholarly publication.
—AskIEEE; CISTI; Genuine Article; KR SourceOne; SWETS.
Description: Publishes experimental and theoretical research papers focusing on new developments in high energy cosmic ray physics and astrophysics, particle cosmology and astrophysics, neutrino and gamma-ray astronomy, and relevant advances in instrumentation and detectors.
Refereed Serial

523.01   US   ISSN 0004-637X
QB1   CODEN: ASJOAB
THE ASTROPHYSICAL JOURNAL; an international review of astronomy and astronomical physics. (Supplement Series avail.; s-a. video supplement avail.) 1895. 3/m. $1050 (Canada $1123; elsewhere $1050) to non-member individuals & institutions; Libraries in many developing nations $345 (effective 1998). (American Astronomical Society) University of Chicago Press, Journals Division, Box 37005, Chicago, IL 60637. TEL 773-753-3347. FAX 773-753-0811. TELEX 25-4603. E-mail: apj@journals.uchicago.edu; URL: http://supernova.aas.org/apj/apj.html; http://journals.uchicago.edu/ApJ/journal. Eds. Helmut Abt, A. Dalgarno. bk.rev.; bibl.; charts; illus.; biennial index, cum.index. circ. 3,000. (also avail. in microform from PMC,UMI; reprint service avail. from ISI,UMI) **Indexed:** ASCA, Chem.Abstr., Chem.Cit.Ind., Chem.Titles, Curr.Cont., Ind.Sci.Rev., INIS Atomind., INSPEC (1968-), Math.R., Phys.Ber., Sci.Cit.Ind. **Document type:** academic/scholarly publication.
—BLDSC (1764.000000); AskIEEE; CASDDS; CISTI; Ei; Genuine Article; KR SourceOne; Linda Hall; SWETS; UMI; UnCover. **CCC**.
Refereed Serial

523.01   US   ISSN 0067-0049
QB1   CODEN: APJSA2
ASTROPHYSICAL JOURNAL. SUPPLEMENT SERIES. (Supplement to: Astrophysical Journal) 1953. m. $200 to non-member individuals & institutions worldwide (Canada $214; developing nations $70) (effective 1998). (American Astronomical Society) University of Chicago Press, Journals Division, 37005, Chicago, IL 60637. TEL 773-753-3347. FAX 773-753-0811. TELEX 25-4603. E-mail: subscriptions@journals.uchicago.edu; URL: http://www.journals.uchicago.edu/. Ed. Helmut Abt. cum.index. circ. 1,000. (also avail. in microfiche; reprint service avail. from UMI,ISI) **Indexed:** ASCA, Chem.Abstr., Chem.Cit.Ind., Curr.Cont., Ind.Sci.Rev., INSPEC (1968-), Phys.Ber., Sci.Cit.Ind. **Document type:** academic/scholarly publication.
—BLDSC (1765.000000); AskIEEE; CASDDS; CISTI; Genuine Article; KR SourceOne; SWETS; UnCover. **CCC**.
Refereed Serial

ASTRONOMY

523.01 NE ISSN 0888-6512
QB460 CODEN: ALECE7
ASTROPHYSICAL LETTERS AND COMMUNICATIONS.
1967. 6/yr. $276 (effective 1998). Gordon and Breach - Harwood Academic, Amsteldisk 166, 1st Fl., 1079 LH Amsterdam, Netherlands. URL: http://www.gbhap-co.com/journals/105/index.htm. (Subscr. to: International Publishers Distributor, Box 32160, Newark, NJ 07102. TEL 800-545-8398. FAX 215-750-6343) Ed. Giorgio G.C. Palumbo. adv.; bk.rev.; index. (also avail. in microform) **Indexed:** ASCA, Astron.& Astrophys.Abstr., Chem.Abstr., Curr.Cont., Ind.Sci.Rev., INIS Atomind., INSPEC (1968-), Phys.Ber., Sci.Cit.Ind. **Document type:** academic/scholarly publication.
—BLDSC (1765.021000); AskIEEE; CASDDS; CISTI; KR SourceOne; Linda Hall; SWETS; UnCover. **CCC.**
   Formerly: Astrophysical Letters (ISSN 0004-6388)
   Refereed Serial

523.01 US ISSN 0571-7256
QB461 CODEN: ATPYAA
ASTROPHYSICS. English translation of: Astrofizika (AI ISSN 0571-7132) 1965. q. $1125 (foreign $1315) (effective 1998). (Armenian Academy of Sciences, AI) Plenum Publishing Corp., Consultants Bureau, 233 Spring St., New York, NY 10013-1578. TEL 212-620-8468. FAX 212-463-0742. TELEX 23-421139. Ed. L.V. Mirzoyan. bk.rev.; charts; illus.; index. (also avail. in microform from UMI; back issues avail.) **Indexed:** Appl.Mech.Rev., Energy Res.Abstr., INIS Atomind., INSPEC (1968-), Math.R. **Document type:** academic/scholarly publication.
—BLDSC (0404.780000); AskIEEE; KR SourceOne; SWETS; UMI. **CCC.**
   Refereed Serial

520 NE ISSN 1071-703X
QB460 CODEN: SSRVDZ
ASTROPHYSICS AND SPACE PHYSICS REVIEWS. vol.3, 1984. 4/yr. $197 (effective 1998). Gordon and Breach - Harwood Academic, Amsteldisk 166, 1st Fl., 1079 LH Amsterdam, Netherlands. (Subscr. to: International Publishers Distributor, Box 32160, Newark, NJ 07102. TEL 800-545-8398. FAX 215-750-6343) Ed. R.A. Syunyaev. index. (also avail. in microform; back issues avail.) **Indexed:** INSPEC. **Document type:** academic/scholarly publication.
—CASDDS; CISTI; UnCover. **CCC.**
   Formerly: Soviet Scientific Reviews. Section E. Astrophysics and Space Physics Reviews (ISSN 0143-0432)
   Refereed Serial

523.01 NE ISSN 0004-640X
QB460 CODEN: APSSBE
ASTROPHYSICS AND SPACE SCIENCE; an international journal of cosmic physics. (Supplement avail.: Experimental Astronomy (ISSN 0922-6435)) (Text in English) 1968. 24/yr. fl.5988 to institutions; $3072 to institutions in U.S. (effective 1998). Kluwer Academic Publishers, Postbus 17, 3300 AA Dordrecht, Netherlands. TEL 31-78-6392392. FAX 31-78-6392254. TELEX 29245 KAPG NL. E-mail: services@wkap.nl; URL: http://www.wkap.nl/kapis/CGI-BIN/WORLD/journalhome.htm?004-640X. (Dist by: Kluwer Academic Publishers Group, Box 322, 3300 AH Dordrecht, Netherlands. TEL 31-78-6392392. FAX 31-78-6546474; N. America dist. addr.: Box 358, Accord Sta., Hingham, MA 02018-0358. TEL 617-871-6600. FAX 617-871-6528) Eds. John Dyson, Juergen Rahe. adv.; bk.rev.; illus.; index. (also avail. in microform from UMI) **Indexed:** ASCA, Astron.& Astrophys.Abstr., Chem.Abstr., Curr.Cont., Geophys.Abstr., Ind.Sci.Rev., INIS Atomind., INSPEC (1968-), Math.R., Meteor.& Geoastrophys.Abstr., Phys.Ber., Sci.Cit.Ind., Zent.Math. **Document type:** academic/scholarly publication.
—BLDSC (1765.048000); AskIEEE; CASDDS; CISTI; Ei; Genuine Article; KR SourceOne; Linda Hall; SWETS; UMI; UnCover. **CCC.**
   Incorporates (1970-1972): Cosmic Electrodynamics; (1975-1981): Space Science Instrumentation (ISSN 0377-7936)
   Description: Publishes original contributions in the entire domain of astrophysics and related fields, including observational and theoretical papers, as well as discussions of techniques and instrumentation.
   Refereed Serial

520 523.01 NE ISSN 0067-0057
CODEN: ASSLAD
ASTROPHYSICS AND SPACE SCIENCE LIBRARY; a series of books on the developments of space science and of general astronomy and astrophysics published in connection with the journal Space Science Reviews. 1965. irreg., vol.205, 1995. price varies. Kluwer Academic Publishers, Postbus 17, 3300 AA Dordrecht, Netherlands. TEL 31-78-6392392. FAX 31-78-6392254. TELEX 29245 KAPG NL. E-mail: services@wkap.nl; URL: http://www.wkap.nl. (Dist. by: Kluwer Academic Publishers Group, P.O. Box 322, 3300 AH Dordrecht, Netherlands. TEL 31-78-6392392. FAX 31-78-6546474; N. America dist. addr.: Box 358, Accord Sta., Hingham, MA 02018-0358. TEL 617-871-6600. FAX 617-871-6528) Ed. C. de Jager. (back issues avail.) **Indexed:** Appl.Mech.Rev., Chem.Abstr., GeoRef., INSPEC, Math.R., Phys.Ber. **Document type:** monographic series.
—BLDSC (1765.050000); AskIEEE; CASDDS; CISTI; Ei; KR SourceOne.
   Refereed Serial

520 SP ISSN 0210-4105
ASTRUM. 1960. bi-m. 9700 ptas. membership. Agrupacion Astronomica de Sabadell, Casilla 50, 08200 Sabadell, Spain. TEL 7255373. adv.; abstr.; bibl.; illus.; stat. circ. 2,000.
—BLDSC (1765.200000).

551.56 NO ISSN 0373-4854
AURORAL OBSERVATORY. MAGNETIC OBSERVATIONS. (Text in English) 1932. a. free. University of Tromsoe, Auroral Observatory, 9001 Tromsoe, Norway. FAX 47-83-89-85-2.
—BLDSC (5337.650000). **CCC.**
   Formerly (until 1971): Norske Institutt for Kosmisk Fysikk. Magnetic Observations.

AUSTRALIAN JOURNAL OF PHYSICS. see *PHYSICS*

520 II
BHAGYAVATI PANCHANGA. (Text in Manipuri; summaries in major Indian languages) 1930. a. Rs.5. Bhagyavati Library, Sagolband Rd., Meino Lane, Manipur State, Imphal 795001, India. Ed. Shri Utsam Jatra Singh. adv. circ. 5,000.

BOLETIM I G - U S P. PUBLICACAO ESPECIAL. see *EARTH SCIENCES*

BOLETIM I G - U S P. SERIE CIENTIFICA. see *EARTH SCIENCES*

BOLETIM I G - U S P. SERIE DIDATICA. see *EARTH SCIENCES*

520 SP ISSN 1132-2306
BOLETIN DE ASTRONOMIA. 1977. q. exchange basis. Sociedad de Ciencias Aranzadi, Seccion Astronomia, Plaza de I. Zuloaga (Museo), 20003 Donostia-San Sebastian, Spain. TEL 943-42-29-45. FAX 943-42-13-16. **Document type:** bulletin.
   Former titles (until 1987): Sociedad de Ciencias Aranzadi. Seccion de Astronomia. Circular; (until 1979): Asociacion Guipuzcoana de Astronomia. Circular (ISSN 1132-2314)

520 UK ISSN 0068-130X
CODEN: BAAHAY
BRITISH ASTRONOMICAL ASSOCIATION. HANDBOOK. 1922. a. £8.75 (effective 1995-1996). British Astronomical Association, Burlington House, Piccadilly, London W1V 9AG, England. TEL 44-171-734-4145. Ed. N.J. Goodman. adv. circ. 4,000. **Indexed:** INSPEC. **Document type:** academic/scholarly publication.
—BLDSC (4244.000000); CISTI; Linda Hall.
   Formerly: British Astronomical Association. Observer's Handbook.
   Description: Provides astronomical data.
   Refereed Serial

520 UK ISSN 0007-0297
QB1 CODEN: JBAAA6
BRITISH ASTRONOMICAL ASSOCIATION. JOURNAL. 1890. bi-m. £33.75 (effective 1995-1996). British Astronomical Association, Burlington House, Picadilly, London W1V 9AG, England. TEL 44-171-734-4145. E-mail: 100257.735@compuserve.com; URL: http://www.star.ncl.ac.uk/~hwm/. Ed. H. McGee. adv.; bk.rev.; index. circ. 3,500. **Indexed:** INSPEC (1968-). **Document type:** academic/scholarly publication.
—BLDSC (4713.000000); AskIEEE; CISTI; KR SourceOne; Linda Hall; UnCover.

520 UK ISSN 0004-6248
QB1 CODEN: CABCAZ
BULLETIN OF THE ASTRONOMICAL INSTITUTES OF CZECHOSLOVAKIA. (Text mainly in English; occasionally in French, German, or Russian; summaries in English, French, German, Russian) 1947. bi-m. $156. (Czech Academy of Sciences, Astronomical Institute, CS) W.B. Saunders Co. Ltd. (Subsidiary of: Harcourt Brace & Company Ltd.), 24-28 Oval Rd., London NW1 7DX, England. TEL 44-171-267-4466. FAX 44-171-482-2293. URL: http://www.hbuk.co.uk/wbs/. (Subscr. to: Harcourt Brace & Company Ltd., Foots Cray High St., Sidcup, Kent DA14 5HP, England. TEL 44-181-300-3322; Alt. addr.: Budecska 6, 120 23 Prague, Czech Republic) Ed. S. Kriz. adv.; bk.rev.; charts; illus.; stat.; index. circ. 1,000. **Indexed:** Chem.Abstr., Curr.Cont., Ind.Sci.Rev., INIS Atomind., INSPEC (1971-), Ref.Zh., Sci.Cit.Ind. **Document type:** academic/scholarly publication.
—AskIEEE; CASDDS; CISTI; KR SourceOne; Linda Hall; UnCover. **CCC.**
   Description: Devoted to astronomy and astrophysics. Presents original scientific papers by Czech astronomers and, occasionally, foreign authors.

520 SP ISSN 1132-7502
CARLSBERG MERIDIAN CATALOGUE LA PALMA. 1985. a. Real Instituto y Observatorio de la Armada, Cecilio Pujazon, s-n, 11110 San Fernando (Cadiz), Spain. circ. 500 (paid). **Document type:** government publication.

523.75 FR ISSN 0373-7713
CARTES SYNOPTIQUES DE LA CHROMOSPHERE SOLAIRE ET CATALOGUES DES FILAMENTS ET DES CENTRES D'ACTIVITE. 1919. biennial. free. Observatoire de Paris, Section d'Astrophysique de Meudon, 5 place Jules Janssen, 92195 Meudon Principal Cedex, France. TEL 33-1-45077800. FAX 33-1-45077959. TELEX 634 103 OBSASTR. Ed. Z. Mouradian. circ. 300. **Indexed:** Astron.& Astrophys.Abstr. **Document type:** academic/scholarly publication.
   Formerly: Cartes Synoptiques de la Chromosphere Solaire (ISSN 0085-4778)

520 CN ISSN 0715-4747
CASSIOPEIA. (Text in English, French) 1973. q. free. Canadian Astronomical Society - Societe Canadienne d'Astronomie, c/o Dept. of Mathematics, Physics & Engineering, Mount Royal College, 4825 Richard Rd., S.W., Calgary, AB T3E 6K6, Canada. TEL 403-240-6029. FAX 430-240-6664. Ed. Jack Penfold. R&P contact: Jack Penfold. bk.rev.; index; circ. 400 (controlled). **Document type:** newsletter.
—CISTI.

520 NE ISSN 0923-2958
QB351 CODEN: CLMCAV
CELESTIAL MECHANICS AND DYNAMICAL ASTRONOMY; an international journal of space dynamics. (Text in English) 1969. m. fl.2100 to institutions; $1077 to institutions in U.S. (effective 1998). Kluwer Academic Publishers, Postbus 17, 3300 AA Dordrecht, Netherlands. TEL 31-78-6392392. FAX 31-78-6392254. TELEX 29245 KAPG NL. E-mail: services@wkap.nl; URL: http://www.wkap.nl/kapis/CGI-BIN/WORLD/journalhome.htm?0923-2958. (Dist. by: Kluwer Academic Publishers Group, P.O. Box 322, 3300 AH Dordrecht, Netherlands. TEL 31-78-6392392. FAX 31-78-6546474; N. America dist. addr.: Box 358, Accord Sta., Hingham, MA 02018-0358. TEL 617-871-6600. FAX 617-871-6528) Ed. J. Henrard. adv.; bk.rev.; illus. (also avail. in microform from UMI; reprint service avail. from SWZ) **Indexed:** Appl.Mech.Rev., Astron.& Astrophys.Abstr., Curr.Cont., Ind.Sci.Rev., INSPEC (1969-), Int.Aerosp.Abstr., Math.R., Nucl.Sci.Abstr., Phys.Ber., Sci.Cit.Ind., Zent.Math. **Document type:** academic/scholarly publication.
—AskIEEE; CISTI; Genuine Article; KR SourceOne; Linda Hall; SWETS; UMI; UnCover. **CCC.**
   Formerly: Celestial Mechanics (ISSN 0008-8714)
   Refereed Serial

ASTRONOMY

520 — RM
CENTRE DE L'ASTRONOMIE ET DES SCIENCES SPATIALES. OBSERVATIONS SOLAIRES. (Text in French) 1956. a. (Institutul Astronomic Din Bucuresti) Editura Academiei Romane, Calea 13 Septembrie 13, 76117 Bucharest, Rumania. (Dist. by: Rodipet SA, Piata Presei Libere 1, Sec. 1, P.O. Box 33-57, Bucharest, Rumania. TEL 401-6185103. FAX 401-2226407) Ed. Georgeta Maris. bk.rev. circ. 500. **Indexed:** Astron.& Astrophys.Abstr., Bull.Signal., Ref.Zh.
  Formerly: Institutul Astronomic din Bucuresti. Observations Solaires (ISSN 0068-3094)

522 — RM — ISSN 0256-5277
CENTRUL DE ASTRONOMIE SI STIINTE SPATIALE. ANUARUL ASTRONOMIC. 1940. a. (Institutul Astronomic din Bucuresti) Editura Academiei Romane, Calea 13 Septembrie 13, 76117 Bucharest, Rumania. (Dist. by: Rodipet SA, Piata Presei Libere 1, P.O. Box 33-57, Bucharest, Rumania. TEL 401-6185103. FAX 401-2226407) circ. 1,600. **Indexed:** Astron.& Astrophys.Abstr., Bull.Signal., Ref.Zh.
  Formerly: Institutul Astronomic din Bucuresti. Anuarul (ISSN 0068-3086)

520 — UK — ISSN 0275-1062
QB1 — CODEN: CASGEY
CHINESE ASTRONOMY AND ASTROPHYSICS. (Selected English translation of: Tianwen Xuebao (ISSN 0001-5245), Tianti Wuli Xuebao (ISSN 0253-2379), and Kongjian Kexue Xuebao (ISSN 0154-6124), all published in the People's Republic of China.) 1977. q. fl.1819($1045) (effective 1998). Elsevier Science Ltd., Pergamon, P.O. Box 800, Kidlington, Oxford OX5 1DX, England. TEL 44-1865-843000. FAX 44-1865-843010. E-mail: nlinfo-f@elsevier.nl; usinfo-f@elsevier.com; forinfo-kyf04035@niftyserve.or.jp; URL: http://www.elsevier.nl/. (Subscr. to: Elsevier Science, Regional Sales Office, P.O. Box 211, 1000 AE Amsterdam, Netherlands. TEL 31-20-4853773. FAX 31-20-4853432; Subscr. in the Americas to: Elsevier Science, Regional Sales Office, Box 945, New York, NY 10159-0945. TEL 212-633-3730. FAX 212-633-3680; Subscr. in Australasia and the Far East to: Elsevier Science (Singapore) Pte Ltd, No.1 Temasek Ave., No.17-01 Millenia Tower, Singapore 039192, Singapore. TEL 65-434-3727. FAX 65-337-2230) Ed. Wang Shouguan. adv. (also avail. in microfilm from UMI) **Indexed:** Curr.Cont., INSPEC (1985-), Int.Aerosp.Abstr., Math.R., Phys.Ber. **Document type:** academic/scholarly publication.
  —BLDSC (3180.272500); AskIEEE; CISTI; KR SourceOne; UMI; UnCover. **CCC.**
  Formerly: Chinese Astronomy (ISSN 0146-6364)
  Description: Presents the results of current Chinese research in all disciplines of astronomy and astrophysics.
  Refereed Serial

520 — FR — ISSN 0373-9139
CIEL ET ESPACE. 1947. m. 310 F. (foreign 493 F.). Association Francaise d'Astronomie, Observatoire du Parc Montsouris, 17 rue Emile-Deutsch de la Meurthe, 75014 Paris, France. TEL 45-89-81-44. FAX 45-65-08-95. Ed. Alain Cirou. adv. contact: Didier Renondin. bk.rev. circ. 70,000. **Indexed:** INSPEC (1982-1990). **Document type:** newspaper.
  —BLDSC (3192.990000).

520 551 — BE — ISSN 0009-6709
QB1 — CODEN: CIELAV
CIEL ET TERRE. 1880. bi-m. 1500 BEF to individuals (Within European Union 1950 BEF, elsewhere 2100 BEF); institutions 1350 BEF (within EU 1750 BEF; elsewhere 1900 BEF) (effective 1998). Societe Royale Belge d'Astronomie, de Meteorologie et de Physique du Globe, 3 av. Circulaire, 1180 Brussels, Belgium. TEL 32-2-3730253. FAX 32-2-374-9822. TELEX 21565 OBSBEL. Dir. R. Dejaiffe. adv.; bk.rev.; illus.; index. circ. 1,200. **Indexed:** Astron.& Astrophys.Abstr., Chem.Abstr., GeoRef., INSPEC (1970-), Meteor.& Geoastrophys.Abstr. **Document type:** academic/scholarly publication.
  —BLDSC (3193.000000); AskIEEE; CISTI; KR SourceOne; Linda Hall.
  Refereed Serial

520 — IT
▼**IL CIELO**; l'astronomia; gli uomini, gli strumenti, le tecniche. 1996. 11/yr. L.68000; newsstand price: L.10000. Biroma Editore, Via San Pio X, 108, 35015 Galliera Veneta, Padova, Italy. TEL 39-49-9422177. E-mail: mc2212@mclink.it; URL: http://www.mclink.it/com/biroma/ilcielo. Ed. Dr. Gastone Favero.

520 — CK — ISSN 0120-2758
COLOMBIA. OBSERVATORIO ASTRONOMICO NACIONAL. ANUARIO. a. $1.50 or exchange basis. Universidad Nacional de Colombia, Observatorio Astronomico Nacional, Apdo. Aereo 2584, Bogota, Colombia.

522.1 — CK — ISSN 0067-9518
COLOMBIA. OBSERVATORIO ASTRONOMICO NACIONAL. PUBLICACIONES. (Text in Spanish or English; summaries in Spanish and English) 1967. irreg., no.6, 1980. Universidad Nacional de Colombia, Observatorio Astronomico Nacional, Apdo. Aereo 2584, Bogota, Colombia. circ. 500.
  —CISTI.

520 551.6 — CE
COLOMBO OBSERVATORY. REPORT. (Text in English) a. Colombo Observatory, Bauddhaloka Mawatha, Colombo 7, Sri Lanka. charts; illus.; stat.

523.01 — NE — ISSN 0146-2970
QB461 — CODEN: COASD9
COMMENTS ON ASTROPHYSICS. 1969. 6/yr. (in 1 vol., 6 nos./vol.) $230 (effective 1998). Gordon and Breach - Harwood Academic, Amsteldisk 166, 1st Fl., 1079 LH Amsterdam, Netherlands. (Subscr. to: International Publishers Distributor, Box 32160, Newark, NJ 07102. TEL 800-545-8398. FAX 215-750-6343) Ed.Bd. adv.; charts; illus. (also avail. in microform) **Indexed:** Chem.Abstr., Curr.Cont., GeoRef., INIS Atomind., INSPEC (1976-), Phys.Ber. **Document type:** academic/scholarly publication.
  —BLDSC (3336.023000); AskIEEE; CASDDS; CISTI; KR SourceOne; Linda Hall; SWETS; UnCover. **CCC.**
  Incorporates: Earth and Extraterrestrial Sciences (ISSN 0070-7902); **Formerly:** Comments on Astrophysics and Space Physics (ISSN 0010-2679)
  Refereed Serial

520 — US — ISSN 0889-9630
COMPARATIVE EPHEMERIS (YEAR). 1979. a. $12. Astronomical Data Service, 3922 Leisure Lane, Colorado Springs, CO 80917. TEL 719-597-4068. (Subscr. to: Box 26180, Colorado Springs, CO 80936)
  Description: Provides the daily celestial positions of the sun, moon, Mercury, Venus, Mars, Jupiter and Saturn arranged side-by-side, on two facing pages per month, for easy comparison of positions and sight recognition of phenomena.

520.09 — NE
CORPUS DES ASTRONOMES BYZANTINS. (Text in English, French) 1983. irreg., vol.6, 1993. price varies. J.C. Gieben, Nieuwe Herengracht 35, 1011 RM Amsterdam, Netherlands. TEL 31-20-6275170. FAX 31-20-6275170. (Dist. in N. America by: John Benjamins Publishing Co., Box 27519, Philadelphia, PA 19118-0519. TEL 215-836-1200. FAX 215-836-1204) (Co-publisher: A.M. Hakkert, Calle Alfambra, 26, 35010 Las Palmas de Gran Canaria, Spain) Ed. Anne Tihon. (back issues avail.) **Document type:** monographic series.
  Description: Publishes scholarly studies of Byzantine astronomers and their work, and critical editions of important texts.

CURRENT PAPERS IN PHYSICS; containing about 78,000 titles of research articles from the world's physics journals. see *PHYSICS — Abstracting, Bibliographies, Statistics*

520 — NE — ISSN 0732-4421
QB1
CURRENT TOPICS IN CHINESE SCIENCE. SECTION E: ASTRONOMY. 1982. irreg., vol.3, 1985. Gordon and Breach - Harwood Academic, Amsteldisk 166, 1st Fl., 1079 LH Amsterdam, Netherlands. (Subscr. to: International Publishers Distributor, Box 32160, Newark, NJ 07102. TEL 800-545-8398. FAX 215-750-6343) (also avail. in microform) **Document type:** monographic series.
  —CISTI. **CCC.**
  Refereed Serial

520 — JA
DAIKIKYU SHINPOJUMU. (Text in Japanese) a. Institute of Space and Astronautical Science - Uchu Kagaku Kenkyujo, 1-1, Yoshinodai 3-chome, Sagamihara-shi, Kanagawa-ken 229, Japan.
  Description: Contains papers on observation balloons.

520 — UK — ISSN 0260-7794
DARLINGTON ASTRONOMICAL SOCIETY. NEWSLETTER. 1980. irreg. membership. Darlington Astronomical Society, c/o Paul Tate, Ed., 59 Eden Cres., Darlington Co., Durham DL1 5TN, England. adv.; bk.rev.; illus. **Document type:** newsletter.

DIRECTORY OF PHYSICS & ASTRONOMY STAFF (YEAR). see *EDUCATION — Higher Education*

523.01 — CN — ISSN 0078-6950
QB4
DOMINION ASTROPHYSICAL OBSERVATORY, VICTORIA. PUBLICATIONS. 1918. irreg. exchange basis. (National Research Council of Canada) Dominion Astrophysical Observatory, Herzberg Institute of Astrophysics, Victoria, B.C., Canada. TEL 250-363-0001. **Indexed:** INSPEC (1968-).
  —BLDSC (7057.000000); AskIEEE; CISTI; KR SourceOne. **CCC.**

520 — IE — ISSN 0070-7643
DUNSINK OBSERVATORY. PUBLICATIONS; communications of the Dublin Institute for Advanced Studies, Series C. 1960. irreg., vol.1, no.7. price varies. Dublin Institute for Advanced Studies, 10 Burlington Rd., Dublin 4, Ireland. TEL 353-1-680748. FAX 353-1-680561. **Document type:** monographic series.
  —CISTI.

523.01 — GW
▼**E S O ASTROPHYSICS SYMPOSIA.** (European Southern Observatory) (Text in English) 1995. irreg. DM.48. Springer-Verlag, Heidelberger Platz 3, 14197 Berlin, Germany. TEL 49-30-82787-0. FAX 49-30-82787448. (Subscr. in N. America to: Springer-Verlag New York, Inc., 333 Meadowlands Pkwy., Secaucus, NJ 07094. TEL 212-460-1500. FAX 212-473-6272) Ed. P. Crane. **Document type:** monographic series.

522.1 — GW — ISSN 0108-9358
E S O FOELGEFORSKNING; bevillinger til stoette af astronomiske forskningsprojekter ved det europaeske Sydobservatorium. 1981. a. free. European Southern Observatory, Karl-Schwarzschild-Str. 2, 85748 Garching, Germany. TEL 49-89-3202362. Ed. M-H. Ulrich Demoulin. R&P contact: R.M. West. illus. **Document type:** bulletin.

520 — US — ISSN 1040-3124
QC801 — CODEN: EARSEJ
EARTH IN SPACE. 9/yr. (Sep.-May). $12 (foreign $16) (effective 1995-1996). American Geophysical Union, 2000 Florida Ave., N.W., Washington, DC 20009. TEL 202-462-6900; 800-966-2481. FAX 202-328-0566. TELEX 710-822-9300. E-mail: cust__ser@kosmos.agu.org; URL: http://www.agu.org. (Addr. in Europe: A G U European Office, Postfach 49, 37189 Katlenburg-Lindau, Germany. TEL 49-5556-1440. FAX 49-5556-4709)
  —UnCover.
  Description: Designed to stimulate educators and top high school students by providing a window on current earth and space science.

ASTRONOMY

523.3 NE ISSN 0167-9295
QB581 CODEN: EMPLD3
EARTH, MOON AND PLANETS; an international journal of comparative planetology. (Text in English) 1969. m. fl.2280 to institutions; $1170 to institutions in U.S. (effective 1998). Kluwer Academic Publishers, Postbus 17, 3300 AA Dordrecht, Netherlands. TEL 31-78-6392392. FAX 31-78-6392254. TELEX 29245 KAPG NL. E-mail: services@wkap.nl; URL: http://www.wkap.nl/kapis/CGI-BIN/WORLD/journalhome.htm?0167-9295. (Dist. by: Kluwer Academic Publishers Group, P.O. Box 322, 3300 AH Dordrecht, Netherlands. TEL 31-78-6392392. FAX 31-78-6546474; N. America dist. addr.: Box 358, Accord Sta., Hingham, MA 02018-0358. TEL 617-871-6600. FAX 617-871-6528) Ed. Z. Kopal. adv.; bk.rev.; bibl.; illus.; index. (also avail. in microform from UMI; reprint service avail. from SWZ) **Indexed**: ASCA, Astron.& Astrophys.Abstr., Chem.Abstr., Curr.Adv.Ecol.Sci., Curr.Cont., Deep Sea Res.& Oceanogr.Abstr., Ecol.Abstr., Geo.Abstr.H.G., Geo.Abstr.P.G., Geol.Abstr., Geophys.Abstr., GeoRef., Ind.Sci.Rev., INIS Atomind., INSPEC (1969-), Int.Aerosp.Abstr., Phys.Ber., Sci.Cit.Ind., Zent.Math. **Document type**: academic/scholarly publication.
—BLDSC (3643.195000); AskIEEE; CASDDS; CISTI; Genuine Article; KR SourceOne; Linda Hall; SWETS; UMI; UnCover. **CCC**.
Former titles: Moon and the Planets (ISSN 0165-0807); Moon (ISSN 0027-0903)
Refereed Serial

EARTH SPACE REVIEW. see *EARTH SCIENCES*

528.6 SP ISSN 0080-5971
EFERMERIDES ASTRONOMICAS. 1971. a. 1976 ptas. (effective 1996). Real Instituto y Observatorio de la Armada, Cecilio Pugazon, s-n, 11100 San Fernando (Cadiz), Spain. circ. 700 (paid). **Indexed**: Ind.SST. **Document type**: government publication.
Description: Provides the high accuracy data require for astronomical observations.

520 FR ISSN 0769-1041
QB404
EPHEMERIDES OF THE FAINT SATELLITES OF JUPITER AND SATURN. (Text in English, French) 1985. a. 55 F. Bureau des Longitudes, 77 av. Denfert-Rochereau, 75014 Paris, France. Ed. J.E. Arlot.

520 FR
EPHEMERIDES OF THE SATELLITES OF MARS, JUPITER, SATURN AND URANUS. 1986. a. 200 F. Bureau des Longitudes, 77 av. Denfert-Rochereau, 75014 Paris, France. (Subscr. to: Editions de Physique, Z.I. de Courtaboeuf, B.P. 112, 91940 les Ulis Cedex, France) Ed. J.E. Arlot.

520 AT ISSN 0312-1305
EPHEMERIS.* a. Aus.$8. Astronomical Society of New South Wales Incorporated, c/o Astronomical Society of S.A., G.P.O. Box 199, Adelaide, S.A. 5001, Australia. Ed. Peter Northfield. circ. 1,000.
Formerly (until 1973): Yearbook of Astronomy. Ephemeris (ISSN 0312-1291)
Description: Data book on predicted astronomical phenomena occurring during the year. Contains physical details of the solar system.

EPIMENIDES/EPIMENIS. see *TRANSPORTATION — Ships And Shipping*

520 GW ISSN 0531-4496
QB82.G42
EUROPEAN SOUTHERN OBSERVATORY. ANNUAL REPORT. (Text in English, French and German) 1964. a. free. European Southern Observatory, Karl-Schwarzschild-Str. 2, 85748 Garching, Germany. TEL 49-89-3202362. circ. 1,600.
—BLDSC (1245.600000); CISTI.

520 681.2 NE ISSN 0922-6435
QB84.5 CODEN: EXASER
EXPERIMENTAL ASTRONOMY; an international journal on astronomical instrumentation and data analysis. (Supplement to: Astrophysics and Space Science (ISSN 0004-640X)) (Text in English) 1989. q. fl.520 to institutions; $267 to institutions in U.S. (effective 1998). Kluwer Academic Publishers, Postbus 17, 3300 AA Dordrecht, Netherlands. TEL 31-78-6392392. FAX 31-78-6392254. TELEX 29245 KAPG NL. E-mail: services@wkap.nl; URL: http://www.wkap.nl/kapis/GCI-BIN/WORLD/journalhome.htm?0922-6435. (Dist. by: Kluwer Academic Publishers Group, P.O. Box 322, 3300 AH Dordrecht, Netherlands. TEL 31-78-6392392. FAX 31-78-6546474; N. America dist. addr.: Box 358, Accord Sta., Hingham, MA 02018-0358. TEL 617-871-6600. FAX 617-871-6528) Ed.Bd. (also avail. in microform from UMI; back issues avail.) **Indexed**: INSPEC (1989-). **Document type**: academic/scholarly publication.
—BLDSC (3838.744000); AskIEEE; CISTI; KR SourceOne; Linda Hall; SWETS; UMI; UnCover. **CCC**.
Description: Publishes short and long research articles, research letters and reviews on advances in astronomical detection techniques, in instruments and in techniques of data analysis and image-processing.
Refereed Serial

520 US ISSN 0146-7662
EYEPIECE. 1954. m. $40 (includes subscr. to Sky and Telescope). Amateur Astronomers Association, 1010 Park Ave., New York, NY 10028. TEL 212-535-2922. E-mail: RN.5305@ROSE.COM. Ed. Jack Dittrick. circ. 700. (back issues avail.) **Document type**: newsletter.
Incorporates: Urban Observers.
Description: News on astronomy and related topics for astronomers in New York metropolitan area.

520 UK
F A S HANDBOOK. 1977. a. £2.80. Federation of Astronomical Societies, 17 Havelock St., Thornton, Bradford, W. Yorkshire BD13 3HA, England. Ed. Brian Jones. adv. circ. 300.
Description: Provides data on suppliers, places to visit, speakers, information sources, astronomical organizations, mainly within the UK.

520 SP ISSN 0210-8127
FENOMENOS ASTRONOMICOS. 1980. biennial. 354 ptas. (effective 1996). Real Instituto y Observatorio de la Armada, Cecilio Pujazon s-n, 11110 San Fernando (Cadiz), Spain. circ. 250 (paid). **Indexed**: Ind.SST. **Document type**: government publication.
Description: Provides information on the principal phenomena of the Sun and the Moon.

FOUNDATIONS OF PHYSICS; an international journal devoted to the conceptual and fundamental theories of modern physics, biophysics, and cosmology. see *PHYSICS*

523.01 NE ISSN 0094-5846
QC801 CODEN: FNCPAX
FUNDAMENTALS OF COSMIC PHYSICS. 12/yr. (in 3 vols., 4 nos./vol.). $407 (effective 1998). Gordon and Breach - Harwood Academic, Amsteldisk 166, 1st Fl., 1079 LH Amsterdam, Netherlands. URL: http://www.gbhap-us.com/journals/133/index.htm. (Subscr to: International Publishers Distributor, Box 32160, Newark, NJ 07102. TEL 800-545-8398. FAX 215-750-6343) Eds. V. Canuto, Bruce Elmegreen. adv.; index. (also avail. in microform) **Indexed**: Chem.Abstr., INSPEC, Int.Aerosp.Abstr., Phys.Ber. **Document type**: academic/scholarly publication.
—BLDSC (4056.092000); AskIEEE; CASDDS; CISTI; KR SourceOne; Linda Hall; SWETS; UnCover. **CCC**.
Refereed Serial

520 530 GW
GAUSS - GESELLSCHAFT. MITTEILUNGEN. 1964. a. DM.50($30) to non-members (effective 1997). Gauss-Gesellschaft e.V., Herzberger Landstr. 180, 37075 Goettingen, Germany. Ed. H.H. Voigt. adv.; bk.rev. (back issues avail.) **Document type**: bulletin.

520 JA ISSN 0288-4216
GEKKAN TENMON. (Text in Japanese) 1934. m. 6600 Yen($99) Chijin Shokan Co., Ltd., 15 Naka-machi, Shinjuku-ku, Tokyo 162, Japan. TEL 03-3235-4422. FAX 03-3235-8984. Ed. Akira Tsuda. adv.; bk.rev.
—CISTI.

551 523.01 NE ISSN 0165-1307
QB84.5 CODEN: GAMOD3
GEOPHYSICS AND ASTROPHYSICS MONOGRAPHS; a series of graduate-level textbooks and monographs on plasma astrophysics and geophysics, including magnetospheric, solar, and stellar physics. (Text in English) 1972. irreg. price varies. Kluwer Academic Publishers, Postbus 17, 3300 AA Dordrecht, Netherlands. TEL 31-78-6392392. FAX 31-78-6392254. TELEX 29245 KAPG NL. E-mail: services@wkap.nl; URL: http://www.wkap.nl. (Dist. by: Kluwer Academic Publishers Group, P.O. Box 322, 3300 AH Dordrecht, Netherlands. TEL 31-78-6392392. FAX 31-78-6546474; N. America dist. addr.: Box 358, Accord Sta., Hingham, MA 02018-0358. TEL 617-871-6600) Ed. B.M. McCormac. **Document type**: monographic series.
—CISTI.
Refereed Serial

520 IT ISSN 0390-1106
QB33.I8
GIORNALE DI ASTRONOMIA. 1975. q. L.9000. Societa Astronomica Italiana, Via Brera 28, 20121 Milan, Italy. Ed. Mario Rigutti. bk.rev.
—CISTI.

GRADUATE PROGRAMS: PHYSICS, ASTRONOMY, AND RELATED FIELDS (YEAR). see *EDUCATION — Higher Education*

520 530 US
THE GRADUATE SERIES IN ASTRONOMY. 1992? irreg. price varies. (Institute of Physics, UK) I O P Publishing, c/o A I D C, 2 Wintersport Ln., Box 20, Williston, VT 05495-0020. TEL 800-632-0880. FAX 802-862-0095. (Orders outside the U.S. to: I O P Publishing Ltd., Techno House, Redcliffe Way, Bristol, Avon BS1 6NX, England. TEL 44-117-929-7581. FAX 44-117-929-4318) Eds. R.J. Taylor, R.E. White. **Document type**: monographic series.
Description: Covers all aspects of theoretical and experimental astronomy and astrophysics for graduate students.

520 GR ISSN 0072-7385
GREEK NATIONAL COMMITTEE FOR ASTRONOMY. ANNUAL REPORTS OF THE ASTRONOMICAL INSTITUTES OF GREECE. (Text in English) 1960. a. exchange basis. Greek National Committee for Astronomy, 14 Anagnostopolou St., GR 106 73 Athens, Greece.

520 US ISSN 0195-3982
QB1
GRIFFITH OBSERVER. 1937. m. $18 (Canada $25; Mexico $26; elsewhere $30) (effective 1998). Griffith Observatory, 2800 E. Observatory Rd., Los Angeles, CA 90027. TEL 213-664-1181. FAX 213-663-4323. E-mail: info@GriffithObs.org; URL: http://www.griffithobs.org/Observer.html. Ed. E.C. Krupp. R&P contact: E.C. Krupp. TEL 213-662-6885. bk.rev.; index; circ. 3,500 (paid). **Document type**: consumer publication.
—CISTI; UnCover.
Description: Charts, photographs, and illustrative articles on astronomy and related sciences, with monthly sky calendar and illustration of celestial events.

523.3 GW
GRUPPE BERLINER MONDBEOBACHTER. PROTOKOLL DER SITZUNG. 1954. m. Wilhelm-Forster-Sternwarte e.V., Munsterdamm 90, 12169 Berlin, Germany. TEL 49-30-790093-0. FAX 49-30-790093-12. Ed. Adolf Voigt. adv. contact: Jochen Rose. bk.rev. circ. 650. **Document type**: academic/scholarly publication.

520 BE ISSN 0772-6422
HEELAL. (Text in Dutch) 1956. m. 800 BEF (foreign 1000 BEF) (effective 1996 & 1997). Vereniging voor Sterrenkunde v.z.w., Brieversweg 147, 8310 Brugge, Belgium. TEL 32-50-358872. FAX 32-50-355007. E-mail: heelal@club.innet.be. Ed. Claude Doom. adv.; B&W page 8000 BEF; adv. contact: Frank Tamsin. bk.rev.; illus.; index; circ. 1,900 (paid). (back issues avail.) **Document type**: consumer publication, newsletter.
Description: Covers topics of interest to amateur astronomers.
Refereed Serial

520   JA   ISSN 0389-7605
HOKKYOKUSEI HOIKAKUHYO/POLARIS ALMANAC FOR AZIMUTH DETERMINATION. (Text in Japanese) a. 650 Yen. Kaijo Hoan Kyokai, Suirobu - Maritime Safety Agency Association, 3-1, Tsukiji 5-chome, Chuo-ku, Tokyo 104, Japan. charts; stat. **Document type:** government publication.

520   JA
HOSHI. (Text in Japanese) irreg. Kawasaki Tenmon Dokokai - Kawasaki Astronomical Circle, c/o Mr. Mikio Kawamura, 5-224, Hosoyama, Asao-ku, Kawasaki-shi, Kanagawa-ken 215, Japan.
 Description: Contains news of the organization and relevant subjects.

520   JA   ISSN 0389-2131
HOSHI NO TECHO. (Text in Japanese) 1978. q. 3200 Yen. Kawade Shobo Shinsha, 32-2, Sendagaya 2-chome, Shibuya-ku, Tokyo 151, Japan.

523.51   JA   ISSN 0389-0341
HOSHI NO TOMO/FRIEND OF STARS. (Text in Japanese) 1950? a. 3600 Yen membership. Nippon Ryusei Kenkyukai - Nippon Meteor Society, Yabu Tenmondai, 878 Maruyama-cho, Omihachiman-shi, Shiga-ken 523, Japan. TEL 0748-32-4539. FAX 0748-33-4892. Ed. Yasuo Yabu.

520 551.22   CI   ISSN 0351-2657
HVAR OBSERVATORY BULLETIN. (Text in English; summaries in Croatian, English) 1977. a. free. Hvar Observatory, Faculty of Geodesy, Kaciceva 26, 41000 Zagreb, Croatia. FAX 38-41-445-410. TELEX 22203 IFS YU. Ed. Vladis Vujnovic. circ. 400. (back issues avail.) **Indexed:** Astron.& Astrophys.Abstr., Int.Aerosp.Abstr., Ref.Zh.
 —AskIEEE; CISTI; KR SourceOne.
 Description: Highlights solar and stellar physics.

520 551.5   JA   ISSN 0919-8296
QC484.8
I C R R ANNUAL REPORT. (Text in English) a. University of Tokyo, Institute for Cosmic Ray Research - Tokyo Daigaku Uchusen Kenkyujo, 2-1, Midori-machi 3-chome, Tanashi-shi, Tokyo 188, Japan. **Document type:** academic/scholarly publication.
 Description: Contains research activities of the institute.

532.019   JA
I C R R HOKOKU. English edition: I C R R Report. (Text in Japanese) 1976. 10/yr. University of Tokyo, Institute for Cosmic Ray Research - Tokyo Daigaku Uchusen Kenkyujo, 2-1, Midori-machi 3-chome, Tanashi-shi, Tokyo 188, Japan.

520   JA
I C R R NEWS. (Text in Japanese) 4/yr. University of Tokyo, Institute for Cosmic Ray Research - Tokyo Daigaku Uchusen Kenkyujo, 2-1, Midori-machi 3-chome, Tanashi-shi, Tokyo 188, Japan.
 Description: Covers ICRR news and activities.

532.019   JA   ISSN 1340-3745
                       CODEN: ICRPEY
I C R R REPORT. Japanese edition: I C R R Hokoku. (Text in English) 1976. approx. 30/yr. University of Tokyo, Institute for Cosmic Ray Research - Tokyo Daigaku Uchusen Kenkyujo, 2-1, Midori-machi 3-chome, Tanashi-shi, Tokyo 188, Japan. **Indexed:** Chem.Abstr.
 —CASDDS.

520   JA
I S A S LUNAR AND PLANETARY SYMPOSIUM. PROCEEDINGS. (Text and summaries in English) a. Institute of Space and Astronautical Science - Uchu Kagaku Kenkyujo, 1-1, Yoshinodai 3-chome, Sagamihara-shi, Kanagawa-ken 229, Japan.

520   JA   ISSN 0285-2861
I S A S NYUSU. (Text in Japanese) 1981. m. Institute of Space and Astronautical Science - Uchu Kagaku Kenkyujo, 1-1, Yoshinodai 3-chome, Sagamihara-shi, Kanagawa-ken 229, Japan.
 Description: News of the institute.

520   JA
I S A S RESEARCH NOTE. (Text and summaries in English and Japanese) 1981. irreg. Institute of Space and Astronautical Science - Uchu Kagaku Kenkyujo, 1-1, Yoshinodai 3-chome, Sagamihara-shi, Kanagawa-ken 229, Japan.

523.2   US   ISSN 0019-1035
QB1   CODEN: ICRSA5
ICARUS (SAN DIEGO); international journal of solar system studies. 1962. m. $1572 (foreign $1761) (effective 1997). (American Astronomical Society, Division for Planetary Sciences) Academic Press, Inc., Journal Division, 525 B St., Ste. 1900, San Diego, CA 92101-4495. TEL 619-230-1840. FAX 619-699-6800. E-mail: apsubs@acad.com; URL: http://www.apnet.com/www/journal/is.htm; http://www.idealibrary.com/. (Subscr. to: Box 861213, Orlando, FL 32886-1213. TEL 407-347-4040. FAX 407-363-9661) Ed. Joseph A. Burns. adv.; bibl.; charts; index. (back issues avail.) **Indexed:** Chem.Abstr., Chem.Cit.Ind., Deep Sea Res.& Oceanogr.Abstr., Ind.Sci.Rev., INIS Atomind., INSPEC (1968-), Meteor.& Geoastrophys.Abstr., Phys.Ber., Sci.Cit.Ind. **Document type:** academic/scholarly publication.
 ●Also available online.
 —BLDSC (4360.250000); AskIEEE; CASDDS; CISTI; Ei; Genuine Article; KR SourceOne; Linda Hall; SWETS; UnCover. **CCC.**
 Description: Publishes original contributions in the field of planetary science. Reports the results of new research-observational, experimental, or theoretical - concerning the astronomy, geology, meteorology, physics, chemistry, biology, and other scientific aspects of the solar or extrasolar systems.
 Refereed Serial

IKOMAYAMA UCHU KAGAKUKAN NYUSU. see *MUSEUMS AND ART GALLERIES*

528   II
INDIAN ASTRONOMICAL EPHEMERIS. 1958. a. Rs.100. Meteorological Department, Lodi Rd., New Delhi 110003, India. (Dist. by: Controller of Publications, Government of India, Civil Lines, Delhi 110 054, India) index. circ. 375.
 Formerly: Indian Ephemeris and Nautical Almanac (ISSN 0537-1546)

523.01   II   ISSN 0367-8393
QC801   CODEN: IJRSAK
INDIAN JOURNAL OF RADIO & SPACE PHYSICS. (Text in English) 1972. bi-m. Rs.250($120) Council of Scientific and Industrial Research, Publications & Information Directorate, Hillside Rd., New Delhi 110012, India. TEL 91-11-5786301. FAX 91-11-5787062. TELEX 031-77271 PID IN. E-mail: pid@sirnetd.ernet.in. (Co-sponsor: Indian National Science Academy) Ed. R.P. Goal. illus. **Indexed:** Chem.Abstr., Curr.Cont., Ind.Sci.Rev., INIS Atomind., INSPEC, Sci.Cit.Ind. **Document type:** academic/scholarly publication.
 —BLDSC (4420.900000); AskIEEE; CASDDS; CISTI; Ei; Genuine Article; KR SourceOne; Linda Hall; UnCover.

520   HU   ISSN 0374-0676
INFORMATION BULLETIN ON VARIABLE STARS. (Text in English and French) 1961. irreg., approx. 200/yr. 1600 BEF($65) Hungarian Academy of Sciences, Konkoly Observatory, International Astronomical Union, Box 67, 1525 Budapest, Hungary. TELEX 61-227460 KONOB H. Eds. K. Olah, L. Szabados. circ. 500. (back issues avail.) **Indexed:** INSPEC. **Document type:** bulletin.
 —BLDSC (4485.560000); AskIEEE; CISTI; KR SourceOne.
 Refereed Serial

INSTITUT ROYAL METEOROLOGIQUE DE BELGIQUE. BULLETIN MENSUEL: OBSERVATIONS IONOSPHERIQUES ET DU RAYONNEMENT COSMIQUE/KONINKLIJK METEOROLOGISCH INSTITUUT VAN BELGIE. MAANDBULLETIN: WAARNEMINGEN VAN DE IONOSFEER EN DE KOSMISCHE STRALING. see *METEOROLOGY*

INSTITUT ROYAL METEOROLOGIQUE DE BELGIQUE. BULLETIN QUOTIDIEN DU TEMPS/KONINKLIJK METEOROLOGISCH INSTITUUT VAN BELGIE. DAGELIJKS WEERBULLETIN. see *METEOROLOGY*

520   RU   ISSN 0002-3302
                       CODEN: BTASAU
INSTITUT TEORETICHESKOI ASTRONOMII. BYULLETEN'. (Text in Russian; summaries in English) 1924. s-a. (Akademiya Nauk S.S.S.R., Institut Teoreticheskoi Astronomii, Leningradskoe Otdelenie) Izdatel'stvo Nauka, 90 Profsoyuznaya ul., 117864 Moscow, Russia. Ed. S.S. Lavrov. circ. 1,000. **Indexed:** Astron.& Astrophys.Abstr., INSPEC (1971-1982), Ref.Zh.

ASTRONOMY   495

520   JA   ISSN 0285-6808
                       CODEN: IASRDU
INSTITUTE OF SPACE AND AERONAUTICAL SCIENCE. REPORT. (Text in English) 1921. irreg. Institute of Space and Aeronautical Science - Uchu Kagaku Kenkyujo, 1-1, Yoshinodai 3-chome, Sagamihara-shi, Kanagawa-ken 229, Japan. index. **Indexed:** INSPEC. **Document type:** academic/scholarly publication.
 —BLDSC (7522.724000); CASDDS; CISTI; Linda Hall.
 Former titles (until 1981): University of Tokyo. Institute of Space and Aeronautical Science. Report (ISSN 0372-1418); (until 1965): University of Tokyo. Aeronautical Research Institute. Report (ISSN 0376-1061)

520   JA   ISSN 0288-433X
INSTITUTE OF SPACE AND ASTRONAUTICAL SCIENCE. REPORT. SPECIAL PUBLICATION. (Text and summaries in English) 1983. a. Institute of Space and Astronautical Science - Uchu Kagaku Kenkyujo, 1-1, Yoshinodai 3-chome, Sagamihara-shi, Kanagawa-ken 229, Japan.
 —BLDSC (7522.724500).

520 910.02   SP   ISSN 0213-6198
INSTITUTO DE ASTRONOMIA Y GEODESIA. PUBLICACION. 1949. irreg., no.188, 1996. free. Instituto de Astronomia y Geodesia, c/o Fac. de Matematicas, Univ. Complutense de Madrid, 28040 Madrid, Spain. TEL 34-1-3944615. FAX 34-1-3944607. E-mail: flora@iagmat1.mat.ucm.es. **Indexed:** Ind.SST.
 —CISTI.
 Formerly (until 1985): Seminario de Astronomia y Geodesia. Publicacion (ISSN 0211-8289)

520   US   ISSN 0081-0304
                       CODEN: IANUAB
INTERNATIONAL ASTRONOMICAL UNION. CENTRAL BUREAU FOR ASTRONOMICAL TELEGRAMS. CIRCULAR. 1922. irreg., no.6556, 1997. price varies. Smithsonian Institution Astrophysical Observatory, 60 Garden St., Cambridge, MA 02138. TEL 617-495-7280. FAX 617-495-7231. TELEX 710-320-6842 ASTROGRAM CAM. E-mail: iausubs@cfa.harvard.edu. (Co-sponsor: International Astronomical Union) Ed. B.G. Marsden. R&P contact: B.G. Marsden. TEL 617-495-7244. circ. 600.
 ●Also available online.
 —AskIEEE; CISTI; KR SourceOne.
 Formerly (until 1964): Union Astronomique Internationale. Bureau Central de Telegrammes Astronomiques. Circulaire.

520   NE
INTERNATIONAL ASTRONOMICAL UNION. GENERAL ASSEMBLY. HIGHLIGHTS. triennial, 7th, 1985. price varies. Kluwer Academic Publishers, Postbus 17, 3300 AA Dordrecht, Netherlands. TEL 31-78-6392392. FAX 31-78-6392254. TELEX 29245 KAPG NL. E-mail: services@wkap.nl; URL: http://www.wkap.nl. (Dist. by: Kluwer Academic Publishers Group, P.O. Box 322, 3300 AH Dordrecht, Netherlands. TEL 31-78-6392392. FAX 31-78-6546474; N. America dist. addr.: Box 358, Accord Sta., Hingham, MA 02018-0358. TEL 617-871-6600) **Document type:** proceedings.
 Formerly: International Astronomical Union. General Assembly. Proceedings.
 Refereed Serial

520   US   ISSN 0736-6884
                       CODEN: MPCIB2
INTERNATIONAL ASTRONOMICAL UNION. MINOR PLANET CENTER. MINOR PLANET CIRCULARS - MINOR PLANETS AND COMETS. 1947. irreg. (approx. m.), no.28908, 1997. (International Astronomical Union, Commission 20) Smithsonian Institution Astrophysical Observatory, 60 Garden St., Cambridge, MA 02138. TEL 617-495-7280. FAX 617-495-7231. TELEX 710-320-6842 ASTROGRAM CAM. E-mail: iausubs@cfa.harvard.edu; URL: http://cfa-www.harvard.edu/cfa/ps/services/MPC.html. Ed. Brian G. Marsden. R&P contact: Brian G. Marsden. TEL 617-495-7244. circ. 250. **Indexed:** INSPEC.
 ●Also available online.
 —AskIEEE; KR SourceOne.
 Former titles (until 1978): Cincinnati Observatory. Minor Planet Circulars; Smithsonian Institution. Astrophysical Observatory. Minor Planet Circulars - Minor Planets and Comets.

ASTRONOMY

520   NE   ISSN 0074-1809
CODEN: IASYAE
INTERNATIONAL ASTRONOMICAL UNION. PROCEEDINGS OF SYMPOSIA. 1955. irreg., 158th, 1993, Sydney. price varies. Kluwer Academic Publishers, Postbus 17, 3300 AA Dordrecht, Netherlands. TEL 31-78-6392392. FAX 31-78-6392254. TELEX 29245 KAPG NL. E-mail: services@wkap.nl; URL: http://www.wkap.nl. (Dist. by: Kluwer Academic Publishers Group, P.O. Box 322, 3300 AH Dordrecht, Netherlands. TEL 31-78-6392392. FAX 31-78-6546474; N. America dist. addr.: Box 358, Accord Sta., Hingham, MA 02018-0358. TEL 617-871-6600. FAX 617-871-6528) **Indexed:** Chem.Abstr., INSPEC. **Document type:** proceedings.
—BLDSC (8584.000000); AskIEEE; CASDDS; CISTI; Genuine Article; KR SourceOne.
Refereed Serial

520   NE   ISSN 0080-1372
INTERNATIONAL ASTRONOMICAL UNION. TRANSACTIONS. (Issued in two parts: Part A: Reports, Part B: Proceedings) 1922. triennial, vol.22A, 1994. price varies. Kluwer Academic Publishers, Postbus 17, 3300 AA Dordrecht, Netherlands. TEL 31-78-6392392. FAX 31-78-6392254. TELEX 29245 KAPG NL. E-mail: services@wkap.nl; URL: http://www.wkap.nl. (Dist. by: Kluwer Academic Publishers Group, P.O. Box 322, 3300 AH Dordrecht, Netherlands. TEL 31-78-6392392. FAX 31-78-6546474; N. America dist. addr.: Box 358, Accord Sta., Hingham, MA 02018-0358. TEL 617-871-6600. FAX 617-871-6528) **Indexed:** INSPEC. **Document type:** proceedings.
Formerly: International Astronomical Union. Transactions and Highlights; *Incorporating:* Reports on Astronomy.
Refereed Serial

520   US   ISSN 0736-6922
CODEN: ICOQDL
INTERNATIONAL COMET QUARTERLY. 1979. q (plus a handbook). $31 (foreign $46). International Comet Quarterly, Smithsonian Astrophysical Observatory, M.S.18, 60 Garden St., Cambridge, MA 02138. TEL 617-495-7440. E-mail: icq@cfa.harvard.edu; URL: http://cfa-www.harvard.edu/cfa/ps/icq.html. Ed. Daniel W.E. Green. R&P contact: Daniel W.E. Green. adv.; bk.rev.; charts; illus.; index. circ. 500. (back issues avail.) **Indexed:** Astron.& Astrophys.Abstr., INSPEC. **Document type:** academic/scholarly publication.
—AskIEEE; KR SourceOne; Linda Hall; UnCover.
Description: Includes photometric observations of comets, general reviews of recent studies and observations, and reviews and research articles by cometary astronomers on various aspects of cometary research.
Refereed Serial

525.3 551   FR
INTERNATIONAL EARTH ROTATION SERVICE. ANNUAL REPORT. (Text in English) 1964. a. avail. on exchange or request. International Earth Rotation Service (IERS), c/o Dr. M. Feissel, Paris Observatory, 61 av. de l'Observatoire, 75014 Paris, France. TEL 40-51-22-26. FAX 40-51-22-91. TELEX 270-776 OBS. **Document type:** academic/scholarly publication.
Former titles: International Polar Motion Service. Annual Report; Bureau International de l'Heure. Rapport Annuel (ISSN 0074-7432)

525.3   FR
INTERNATIONAL EARTH ROTATION SERVICE. MONTHLY BULLETIN. (Text in English) 1962. m. avail. on exchange or request. International Earth Rotation Service (IERS), c/o Dr. M. Feissel, 61 av. de l'Observatoire, 75014 Paris, France. TEL 40-51-22-26. FAX 40-51-22-91. TELEX 270-776 OBS. **Document type:** bulletin.
Former titles: Bureau International de l'Heure. Circulaire D; International Polar Motion Service. Monthly Notes (ISSN 0020-8337)

520   FR
INTERNATIONAL EARTH ROTATION SERVICE. SPECIAL BULLETIN C. irreg. International Earth Rotation Service (IERS), 61 av. de l'Observatoire, 75014 Paris, France. TEL 40-51-22-26. FAX 40-51-22-91. TELEX 270-776 OBS. **Document type:** bulletin.

520   FR
INTERNATIONAL EARTH ROTATION SERVICE. SPECIAL BULLETIN D. irreg. International Earth Rotation Service (IERS), 61 av. de l'Observatoire, 75014 Paris, France. TEL 40-51-22-26. FAX 40-51-22-91. TELEX 270-776 OBS. **Document type:** bulletin.

520   FR   ISSN 1019-4568
INTERNATIONAL EARTH ROTATION SERVICE. TECHNICAL NOTES. 1989. irreg. International Earth Rotation Service (IERS), c/o Dr. M. Feissel, 61 av. de l'Observatoire, 75014 Paris, France. TEL 40-51-22-26. FAX 40-51-22-91. TELEX 270-776 OBS. **Document type:** monographic series.
—CISTI.

520   US
INTERNATIONAL EARTH ROTATION SERVICE. WEEKLY BULLETIN A. w. (International Earth Rotation Service (IERS), FR) U.S. Naval Observatory, c/o Dr. D.D. McCarthy, Department of the Navy, Washington, DC 20392-5100. TEL 202-762-1837. **Document type:** bulletin, government publication.

520   UK   ISSN 0021-1052
QB1   CODEN: IRAJAW
THE IRISH ASTRONOMICAL JOURNAL. 1950. s-a. £22($35) to individuals in Europe (U.S. & Canada £28.50($45); elsewhere £30($47.50)); institutions in Europe £28($44) (U.S. & Canada £34.50($54.50); elsewhere £36.50(57.50)) (effective 1998). Armagh Observatory, College Hill, Armagh BT61 9DG, N. Ireland. TEL 44-1861-522928. FAX 44-1861-527174. E-mail: iaj@star.arm.ac.uk; URL: http://www.star.arm.ac.uk/iaj/home.html. Ed. A.D. Andrews. R&P contact: A.D. Andrews. adv. contact: A.G. Gunn. bk.rev. circ. 600. (back issues avail.) **Indexed:** Astron.& Astrophys.Abstr., INSPEC, Int.Aerosp.Abstr. **Document type:** academic/scholarly publication.
—BLDSC (4569.000000); AskIEEE; CISTI; KR SourceOne; Linda Hall; UnCover.
Description: Contains astronomical research papers and review papers by specialists, as well as articles and news for the general scientific community.
Refereed Serial

520 530   TU   ISSN 1015-5295
Q69   CODEN: IUFDEU
ISTANBUL UNIVERSITESI FEN FAKULTESI ASTRONOMI VE FIZIK DERGISI/ISTANBUL UNIVERSITY FACULTY OF SCIENCE JOURNAL OF ASTRONOMY AND PHYSICS. (Text in English, summaries in Turkish) 1923. a. exchange basis. Istanbul Universitesi Fen Fakultesi, Dergi Editor Kurulu, 34459 Vezneciler - Istanbul, Turkey. TEL 90-212-5118480. FAX 90-212-5190834. E-mail: IK001@TRIUVM 11. Ed. Hulya Senkon. circ. 200. **Document type:** academic/scholarly publication.
—BLDSC (4947.545000); CASDDS; KNAW; Linda Hall.
Former titles (until vol.54, 1989): Istanbul University. Faculty of Science. Review. Serie C (ISSN 0253-2638); (until 1980): Istanbul Universitesi Fen Fakultesi Mecmuasi, Serie C - Astronomie, Physique, Chimie (ISSN 0444-7298); *Which supersedes in part* (in 1954): Istanbul Universitesi Fen Fakultesi Mecmuasi, Seri A - Matematik, Fizik, Kimya (ISSN 0367-7745); *Which supersedes in part* (in 1940): Istanbul Universitesi Fen Fakultesi Mecmuasi (ISSN 0368-0630)
Description: Publishes articles on topics in astronomy and physics.

520   RU   ISSN 0202-0742
QB3   CODEN: INTAC6
ITOGI NAUKI I TEKHNIKI: ASTRONOMIYA. 1965. irreg., latest vol.36, 1989. 5.40 Rub. Vsesoyuznyi Institut Nauchno-Tekhnicheskoi Informatsii (VINITI), Baltiiskaya ul. 14, Moscow A-219, Russia. **Indexed:** Zent.Math.
—CASDDS; CISTI; Linda Hall. **CCC.**

520   RU   ISSN 0202-0734
TL787   CODEN: IIKPA3
ITOGI NAUKI I TEKHNIKI: ISSLEDOVANIE KOSMICHESKOGO PROSTRANSTVA. 1971. irreg., latest vol.30, 1989. 6.60 Rub. Vsesoyuznyi Institut Nauchno-Tekhnicheskoi Informatsii (VINITI), Baltiiskaya ul. 14, Moscow A-219, Russia. (Subscr. to: Mezhdunarodnaya Kniga, Dimitrova ul. 39, 113095 Moscow, Russia) **Indexed:** Chem.Abstr., INSPEC.
—AskIEEE; CASDDS; CISTI; KR SourceOne; Linda Hall. **CCC.**

520   UK
J C M T NEWSLETTER. q. Royal Observatory Edinburgh, Blackford Hill, Edinburgh EH9 3HJ, Scotland. TEL 031-668-8100. FAX 031-662-1668. E-mail: user@star.roe.ac.uk. **Document type:** newsletter.

520   US
J G R: JOURNAL OF GEOPHYSICAL RESEARCH: PLANETS. m. $480 (foreign $498); with fiche $516 (foreign $534) (effective 1996). American Geophysical Union, 2000 Florida Ave., N.W., Washington, DC 20009. TEL 202-462-6900; 800-966-2481. FAX 202-328-0566. TELEX 710-822-9300. E-mail: cust_ser@kosmos.agu.org; URL: http://www.agu.org. (Addr. in Europe: A G U European Office, Postfach 49, 37189 Katlenburg-Lindau, Germany. TEL 49-5556-1440. FAX 49-5556-4709) (also avail. in microform from AGU) **Indexed:** Chem.Cit.Ind., Curr.Cont. **Document type:** academic/scholarly publication.
Supersedes in part (in 1991): J G R: Journal of Geophysical Research: Solid Earth and Planets.
Description: Covers the geology, geophysics, and geochemistry of planets (except Earth), satellites, and small bodies (including dust, meteorites, and rings).

520   UK   ISSN 0021-8286
QB15   CODEN: JHSAA2
JOURNAL FOR THE HISTORY OF ASTRONOMY. 1970. 4/yr. £65($130) (effective 1998). Science History Publications Ltd., 16 Rutherford Rd., Cambridge CB2 2HH, England. TEL 44-1223-565532. FAX 44-1223-565532. Ed. M.A. Hoskin; Pub. Bernard Hoskin. R&P contact: Bernard Hoskin. adv. contact: Bernard Hoskin. bk.rev.; bibl.; charts; illus.; index. circ. 650. (back issues avail.) **Indexed:** Abstr.Anthropol., Amer.Hist.& Life (1974-), Br.Archaeol.Abstr., Hist.Abstr. (1974-), INSPEC, Math.R., Mid.East: Abstr.& Ind. **Document type:** academic/scholarly publication.
—BLDSC (5000.580000); AskIEEE; CISTI; KR SourceOne; Linda Hall; SWETS; UnCover. **CCC.**
Description: History of astronomy, astrophysics, cosmology and related sciences.
Refereed Serial

523.01   II   ISSN 0250-6335
QB460   CODEN: JASRD7
JOURNAL OF ASTROPHYSICS AND ASTRONOMY. (Text in English) 1980. 4/yr. Rs.150($100) (effective 1997). Indian Academy of Sciences, C.V. Raman Avenue, P.B. No. 8005, Bangalore 560 080, India. TEL 91-80-3342546. FAX 91-80-3346094. TELEX 0845-2178-ACAD-IN. E-mail: jaa@ias.ernet.in. Ed. G. Srinivasan. illus. circ. 800. (back issues avail.) **Indexed:** ASCA, Chem.Abstr., Curr.Cont., Ind.Sci.Rev., INIS Atomind., INSPEC, Int.Aerosp.Abstr., Phys.Ber., Sci.Cit.Ind. **Document type:** academic/scholarly publication.
—BLDSC (4947.550000); AskIEEE; CASDDS; CISTI; Genuine Article; KR SourceOne; Linda Hall; SWETS; UnCover.

JOURNAL OF ATMOSPHERIC AND SOLAR - TERRESTRIAL PHYSICS. see *EARTH SCIENCES — Geophysics*

JOURNAL OF MATHEMATICAL SCIENCES. see *MATHEMATICS*

520   IQ   ISSN 1012-3431
CODEN: JSAREA
JOURNAL OF SPACE ASTRONOMY RESEARCH. (Text in Arabic, English) 1984. s-a. ID.5($15) to individuals; institutions $50. Scientific Research Council, Space and Astronomy Research Center, Jadiriyah P.O. Box 2441, Baghdad, Iraq. TELEX 213976 SR IK. circ. 500. **Indexed:** INSPEC, Int.Aerosp.Abstr. **Document type:** academic/scholarly publication.

KAIJO HOANCHO. SUIROBU KANSOKU HOKOKU. TENMON SOKUCHI HEN/DATA REPORT OF HYDROGRAPHIC OBSERVATIONS. SERIES OF ASTRONOMY AND GEODESY. see *EARTH SCIENCES — Geophysics*

ASTRONOMY

520 530   US   ISSN 0884-5913
QB460   CODEN: KPCBEU
KINEMATICS AND PHYSICS OF CELESTIAL BODIES. English translation of: Kinematika i Fizika Nebesnykh Tel (KR ISSN 0233-7665) 1985. bi-m. $965 (effective 1998). (Ukrainian Academy of Sciences, Division of Physics and Astronomy, KR) Allerton Press, Inc., 150 Fifth Ave., New York, NY 10011. TEL 212-924-3950. FAX 212-463-9684. Ed. Ya.S. Yatskiv. **Indexed:** INSPEC (1987-). **Document type:** academic/scholarly publication.
—BLDSC (0415.405000); AskIEEE; CISTI; KR SourceOne; UnCover. **CCC.**
     Description: Covers solar physics, astronomic catalogs and databases, positional and theoretical astronomy, stars and interstellar space, planetary physics, earth rotation and geodynamics, galactic structure and dynamics.

522.1   JA   ISSN 0915-8863
KOKURITSU TENMONDAI NYUSU. (Text in Japanese) 1988. bi-m. National Astronomical Observatory - Kokuritsu Tenmondai, 21-1, Osawa 2-chome, Mitaka-shi, Tokyo 181, Japan.
FAX 81-422-34-3690.
     Description: News of the observatory.

520   KO   ISSN 0253-3065
QB1   CODEN: CHACDE
KOREAN ASTRONOMICAL SOCIETY. JOURNAL. (Text in English) 1968. s-a. 10000 Won($20) (free to members). Seoul National University, San 56-1, Sinlim-dong, Kwanak-ku, Seoul 151-742, S. Korea. TEL 02-884-9055. FAX 02-887-1435. Ed. Minn Y.K. circ. 500. **Indexed:** INIS Atomind., INSPEC (1987-). **Document type:** academic/scholarly publication.
—BLDSC (4811.900000); AskIEEE; CISTI; KR SourceOne.
     Description: Covers the entire domain of astronomy, astrophysics and related fields.

520   KR   ISSN 0235-1552
KOSMICHESKAYA NAUKA I TEKHNIKA; respublikanskii mezhvedomstvennyi sbornik nauchnykh trudov. (Text in Russian) 1973. a. (Akademiya Nauk Ukrainy, Komissiya Kosmicheskikh Issledovanii, Institut Metallofiziki) Vidavnitstvo Naukova Dumka, Vul. Tereshchenkivska 3, 252601 Kiev, Ukraine. TEL 044-224-4068. FAX 044-224-7060. (Dist. by: Mezhdunarodnaya Kniga, B. Yakimanka 39, 117049 Moscow, Russia) Ed. B.G. Bar'yakhtar.
—CISTI; Linda Hall. **CCC.**
     Formerly (until 1986): Kosmicheskie Issledovaniya na Ukraine (ISSN 0321-4508)

520   XO   ISSN 0323-049X
KOZMOS. 1970. bi-m. $26. Slovenska Ustredna Hvezdaren, 947 01 Hurbanovo, Slovakia.

523   RU   ISSN 0367-8466
QB1   CODEN: IKAOAW
KRYMSKAYA ASTROFIZICHESKAYA OBSERVATORIYA. IZVESTIYA. English translation: Russian Academy of Sciences. Crimean Astrophysical Observatory. Bulletin (US ISSN 0190-2717) (in Russian; summaries in English and Russian) 1946. s-a. exchange basis. (Rossiiskaya Akademiya Nauk, Krymskaya Astrofizicheskaya Observatoriya) Izdatel'stvo Nauka, 90 Profsoyuznaya ul., 117864 Moscow, Russia. TEL 234-05-84. (Dist. by: Mezhdunarodnaya Kniga, ul. Dimitrova D.39, 113095 Moscow, Russia) Ed. A.B. Severnii. **Indexed:** Chem.Abstr., INIS Atomind., INSPEC, Int.Aerosp.Abstr.
—AskIEEE; CASDDS; CISTI; KNAW; KR SourceOne.

520   JA   ISSN 0388-0230
KYOTO UNIVERSITY. DEPARTMENT OF ASTRONOMY. CONTRIBUTIONS. (Text and summaries in English) 1960. irreg. Kyoto University, Faculty of Science, Department of Astronomy - Kyoto Daigaku Rigakubu Uchu Butsurigakka, Oiwake-cho, Kita-Shirakawa, Sakyo-ku, Kyoto-shi, Kyoto-fu 606, Japan.
TEL 81-75-753-3900. FAX 81-75-753-3897.
E-mail: ikemura@kusastro.kyoto-u.ac.jp. **Document type:** academic/scholarly publication.

522.1   JA   ISSN 0388-2349
KYOTO UNIVERSITY. KWASAN AND HIDA OBSERVATORIES. CONTRIBUTIONS. (Text and summaries in English) 1948. irreg. Kyoto University, Faculty of Science, Kwasan Observatory - Kyoto Daigaku Rigakubu Fuzoku Kazan Tenmondai, Omine-cho, Kita-Kazan, Yamashina-ku, Kyoto-shi, Kyoto-fu 607, Japan. Ed. Mitsugu Makita. **Document type:** academic/scholarly publication.
—CISTI; Linda Hall.

523.4   US   ISSN 0730-966X
   CODEN: LPIRDG
L P I TECHNICAL REPORT. 1981. irreg. (5-10/yr.). Lunar and Planetary Institute, 3600 Bay Area Blvd., Houston, TX 77058-1113. TEL 713-486-2172. FAX 713-486-2186. circ. 300. **Indexed:** INSPEC. **Document type:** academic/scholarly publication.
● Also available online.
—CISTI.

520   US   ISSN 0075-7896
LANDOLT-BOERNSTEIN, ZAHLENWERTE UND FUNKTIONEN AUS NATURWISSENSCHAFTEN UND TECHNIK. NEUE SERIE. GROUP 6: ASTRONOMY. 1965. irreg. price varies. Springer-Verlag, 175 Fifth Ave., New York, NY 10010. TEL 212-460-1500. FAX 212-473-6272. (Also: Berlin, Heidelberg, Tokyo and Vienna) (reprint service avail. from ISI) **Document type:** academic/scholarly publication.

520   US   ISSN 0075-9325
LICK OBSERVATORY. PUBLICATIONS. (At head of title: University of California) 1892. irreg., vol.23, 1981. price varies. Lick Observatory, Library, University of California, Santa Cruz, CA 95064.
TEL 408-429-2201. Ed.Bd. **Indexed:** Astron.& Astrophys.Abstr. **Document type:** bulletin.
—CISTI.

520   US   ISSN 0889-9622
QB601
LOCAL PLANET VISIBILITY REPORT (YEAR). 1978. a. $15. Astronomical Data Service, 3922 Leisure Ln., Colorado Springs, CO 80917. TEL 719-597-4068. (Subscr. to: Box 26180, Colorado Springs, CO 80936)
     Description: Contains local visibility information for each of five planets, Mercury, Venus, Mars, Jupiter, and Saturn, computed for your latitude, longitude, and time zone.

523.4   US   ISSN 0891-4664
   CODEN: LPIBE3
LUNAR AND PLANETARY INFORMATION BULLETIN. 1970. q. free. Lunar and Planetary Institute, 3600 Bay Area Blvd., Houston, TX 77058-1113.
TEL 713-486-2172. FAX 713-486-2186. E-mail: thompson@lpi.jsc.nasa.gov; URL: http://cass.jsc.nasa.gov/pub/publications/publications.html. Ed. Pamela B. Thompson. bk.rev. circ. 5,500. **Indexed:** INSPEC (1985-). **Document type:** bulletin.
● Also available online.
—BLDSC (5304.785000); AskIEEE; KR SourceOne; Linda Hall.

MAJALLAH-I FIZIK/IRANIAN JOURNAL OF PHYSICS. see PHYSICS

MANITOBA MUSEUM OF MAN AND NATURE. HAPPENINGS. see MUSEUMS AND ART GALLERIES

520   US   ISSN 0047-6773
QB1   CODEN: MRCYAT
MERCURY (SAN FRANCISCO). 1972. bi-m. $35 to individuals and non-research libraries (foreign $44); institutions $190 (includes Publications of the A S P). Astronomical Society of the Pacific, 390 Ashton Ave., San Francisco, CA 94112.
TEL 415-337-1100. FAX 415-337-5205. URL: http://www.aspky.org/subpages/mercury.html. Ed. George Musser. adv.; bk.rev.; charts; illus.; index; cum.index. circ. 7,000. (back issues avail.; reprint service avail. from UMI) **Indexed:** Astron.& Astrophys.Abstr., C.I.J.E., Gen.Sci.Ind., INSPEC. **Document type:** consumer publication.
—BLDSC (5679.850000); AskIEEE; CISTI; KR SourceOne; Linda Hall; SWETS; UMI; UnCover.
     Description: Nontechnical magazine about astronomy for the general reader or amateur astronomer.

520   GW   ISSN 0722-6691
QB1   CODEN: MESSE4
THE MESSENGER/MENSAJERO. (Text in English; abstracts occasionally in Spanish) 1974. q. free. European Southern Observatory, Karl-Schwarzschild-Str. 2, 85748 Garching, Germany. TEL 49-89-3202362. E-mail: ips@eso.org; URL: http://www.hq.eso.org/messenger.html. Ed. M.H. Ulrich. **Indexed:** INSPEC (1988-). **Document type:** bulletin.
—BLDSC (5682.690000); AskIEEE; KR SourceOne. **CCC.**
     Description: Covers research and findings of astronomical and astrophysical observatories in Europe and of the European Southern Observatory in La Silla, Chile. Includes reports and list of events.

523.5   US   ISSN 0146-9959
METEOR NEWS. 1970. irreg. (3-4/yr.). $6 (foreign $9; air mail $12). Callahan Astronomical Society, 3859 Woodland Heights, Callahan, FL 32011.
TEL 904-879-2646. Ed. Karl Simmons; Pub. Wanda Simmons. adv.; bk.rev.; charts; cum.index every 5 yrs.; circ. 350 (paid). (processed) **Document type:** newsletter.
     Description: Reports on meteor observations and meteorite falls worldwide.

523.4 550   US   ISSN 1086-9379
QB741   CODEN: MPSCFY
METEORITICS AND PLANETARY SCIENCE. 1953. bi-m (plus a suppl.). $330 to institutions in U.S., Canada and Mexico; elsewhere $345 (effective 1998). Meteoritical Society, c/o Hazel Sears, Business Editor, Department of Chemistry and Biochemistry, University of Arkansas, Fayetteville, AR 72701.
TEL 501-575-7625. FAX 501-575-7778. E-mail: meteor@comp.uark.edu; URL: http://www.uark.edu/meteor; http://www.meteorite.ch/metsoc2.htm. Ed. Derek W. Sears. adv. contact: Hazel Sears. bk.rev.; charts; illus.; stat.; index; circ. 1,200 (paid). (also avail. in microform from UMI; back issues avail.) **Indexed:** ASCA, Chem.Abstr., Curr.Cont., Deep Sea Res.& Oceanogr.Abstr., Geol.Abstr., GeoRef., Ind.Sci.Rev., INSPEC, Int.Aerosp.Abstr., Mineral.Abstr., Sci.Cit.Ind. **Document type:** academic/scholarly publication.
—BLDSC (5703.350000); AskIEEE; CASDDS; CISTI; Genuine Article; KR SourceOne; Linda Hall; UMI; UnCover. **CCC.**
     Formerly (until 1996): Meteoritics (ISSN 0026-1114)
     Description: Publishes primary research articles and invited reviews in such areas as asteroids, comets, craters, interplanetary dust, interstellar medium, lunar samples, meteors, meteorites, natural satellites, planets, tektites and the origin and history of the Solar System.
Refereed Serial

520   GW   ISSN 0944-1999
MITTEILUNGEN ZUR ASTRONOMIEGESCHICHTE. Online edition: Electronic Newsletter for the History of Astronomy. 1992. s-a. DM.5. Astronomische Gesellschaft, Arbeitskreis Astronomiegeschichte, Otterkiez 14, 14478 Potsdam, Germany.
TEL 49-331-863199. E-mail: wdi@potsdam.ifag.de; URL: http://www.astro.uni-bonn.de/~pbrosche/aa/aa-ejourn.html. Ed. Wolfgang R. Dick. **Document type:** newsletter.
● Also available online.
     Description: Contains news from all fields of the history of astronomy.

520 551   JA   ISSN 0916-6343
QB330
MIZUSAWA ASTROGEODYNAMICS OBSERVATORY. ANNUAL REPORT. (Text in English) 1988. a. National Astronomical Observatory, Division of Earth Rotation, Mizusawa Astrogeodynamics Observatory - Kokuritsu Tenmondai Chikyu Kaiten Kenkyukei Mizusawa Kansoku Senta, 2-12, Hoshigaoka-machi, Mizusawa-shi, Iwate-ken 023, Japan.
TEL 81-197-22-7111. FAX 81-197-22-7120. E-mail: manabe@miz.nao.ac.jp. Ed. Seiji Manabe. circ. 200. **Document type:** bulletin.
     Description: Annual summary of the time service and geophysical observations performed in the Mizusawa Astronomical Observatory.

ASTRONOMY

520   UK   ISSN 0141-1128
MONOGRAPHS ON ASTRONOMICAL SUBJECTS. 1975. irreg., no.9, 1983. price varies. Oxford University Press, Walton St., Oxford OX2 6DP, England. TEL 44-1865-56767. FAX 44-1865-56646. (Subscr. in US to: Oxford University Press Inc., 2001 Evans Rd., Cary, NC 27513. TEL 919-677-0977. FAX 919-677-1714) Ed. A.J. Meadows. **Document type:** monographic series.
—CISTI.
Refereed Serial

MOSKOVSKII UNIVERSITET. VESTNIK. SERIYA 3: FIZIKA, ASTRONOMIYA. see *PHYSICS*

MOZAMBIQUE. INSTITUTO NACIONAL DE METEOROLOGIA. INFORMACOES DE CARACTER ASTRONOMICO. see *EARTH SCIENCES — Geophysics*

520   US   ISSN 0894-5985
N R A O NEWSLETTER. 1981. q. free to qualified personnel. National Radio Astronomy Observatory, 520 Edgemont Rd., Charlottesville, VA 22903. TEL 804-296-0211. FAX 804-296-0278. circ. 700. **Document type:** newsletter.
Description: Covers news, policies and instrumentation of interest to NRAO employees, telescope users, and others in the astronomical community.

522.1   JA
N R O GIJUTSU HOKOKU/N R O TECHNICAL REPORT. (Text in English, Japanese; summaries in English) 1981. irreg. National Astronomical Observatory, Nobeyama Radio Observatory - Kokuritsu Tenmondai Nobeyama Uchu Denpa Kansokujo, Nobeyama, Minami-Makimura, Minami-Saku-gun, Nagano-ken 384-13, Japan. **Document type:** academic/scholarly publication.

522.1   JA   ISSN 0911-5501
N R O REPORT. (Text and summaries in English) 1982. irreg. National Astronomical Observatory, Nobeyama Radio Observatory - Kokuritsu Tenmondai Nobeyama Uchu Denpa Kansokujo, Nobeyama, Minami-Makimura, Minami-Saku-gun, Nagano-ken 384-13, Japan.
Description: Contains original research papers.

522.1   JA
N R O YUZAZU MITINGU. (Text in Japanese) 1983. a. National Astronomical Observatory, Nobeyama Radio Observatory - Kokuritsu Tenmondai Nobeyama Uchu Denpa Kansokujo, Nobeyama, Minami-Makimura, Minami-Saku-gun, Nagano-ken 384-13, Japan. **Document type:** proceedings.
Description: Contains proceedings from the observatory's users' meeting.

520   US
N T I S ALERTS: ASTRONOMY & ASTROPHYSICS. w. $140 (outside N. America $195). U.S. National Technical Information Service, 5285 Port Royal Rd., Springfield, VA 22161. TEL 703-487-4650. FAX 703-321-8547. TELEX 64617. bibl. (also avail. in microform from NTI) **Document type:** abstracting/indexing, government publication.

520 551   JA   ISSN 0915-3780
NATIONAL ASTRONOMICAL OBSERVATORY. MIZUSAWA ASTROGEODYNAMICS OBSERVATORY. MIZUSAWA KANSOKU CENTER. TECHNICAL REPORT. (Text and summaries in Japanese) 1988. a. National Astronomical Observatory, Mizusawa Astrogeodynamics Observatory, Mizusawa Kansoku Center - Kokuritsu Tenmondai, 2-12 Hoshigaoka, Mizusawa, Iwate-ken 023, Japan. TEL 0197-22-7111. FAX 0197-22-7120. TELEX 837628-ILSMIZ-J. Ed. T. Tsubokawa. **Document type:** academic/scholarly publication.

522.1   JA   ISSN 0915-3640
QB4.K68   CODEN: PNAJEH
NATIONAL ASTRONOMICAL OBSERVATORY. PUBLICATIONS/KOKURITSU TENMONDAI OBUN HOKOKU. (Text in English) 1922. 2/yr. exchange basis. National Astronomical Observatory - Kokuritsu Tenmondai, 21-1, Osawa 2-chome, Mitaka-shi, Tokyo 181, Japan. FAX 81-422-34-3690. **Indexed:** Chem.Abstr., INSPEC, Int.Aerosp.Abstr.
—BLDSC (7096.853000); AskIEEE; CASDDS; CISTI; KR SourceOne.
Former titles (until 1989): National Astronomical Observatory. Annals; Tokyo Astronomical Observatory. Annals (ISSN 0082-4704); Supersedes (in 1937): Observatoire Astronomique de Tokyo. Annales.

520   JA   ISSN 0915-6321
QB1   CODEN: KTENE2
NATIONAL ASTRONOMICAL OBSERVATORY. REPORT. (Text in Japanese) 1932. 2/yr. available on exchange basis only. National Astronomical Observatory - Kokuritsu Tenmondai, 21-1, Osawa 2-chome, Mitaka-shi, Tokyo 181, Japan. FAX 81-422-34-3690. **Indexed:** INSPEC.
—BLDSC (7560.025000); AskIEEE; KR SourceOne.
Formerly (until 1989): Tokyo Astronomical Observatory. Report (ISSN 0374-4639)

520   JA   ISSN 0915-0021
NATIONAL ASTRONOMICAL OBSERVATORY. REPRINT. (Text in English) 1938. irreg., latest 1997. exchange basis. National Astronomical Observatory - Kokuritsu Tenmondai, 21-1, Osawa 2-chome, Mitaka-shi, Tokyo 181, Japan. FAX 81-422-34-3690. **Indexed:** Int.Aerosp.Abstr.
—CISTI.
Formerly (until 1988): Tokyo Astronomical Observatory. Reprints (ISSN 0082-4712)

THE NAUTICAL ALMANAC. see *TRANSPORTATION — Ships And Shipping*

528.3   GW   ISSN 0077-6211
NAUTISCHES JAHRBUCH, ODER EPHEMERIDEN UND TAFELN. a. DM.43.70. Bundesamt fuer Seeschiffahrt und Hydrographie, Bernhard-Nocht-Str. 78, 20359 Hamburg, Germany. TEL 49-40-3190-0. FAX 49-40-3190-5000. TELEX 211138-BSHHH-D. circ. 5,200. **Document type:** academic/scholarly publication.

520   NE   ISSN 1384-1092
▼**NEW ASTRONOMY.** Online edition (NE ISSN 1384-1076) (Text in English) 1996. 8/yr. fl.800($460) (effective 1998). Elsevier Science B.V., P.O. Box 211, 1000 AE Amsterdam, Netherlands. TEL 31-20-4853911. FAX 31-20-4853705. E-mail: nlinfo-f@elsevier.nl; usinfo-f@elsevier.com; forinfo-kyf04035@niftyserve.or.jp; URL: http://www.elsevier.nl:80/inca/publications/5/2/5/6/5/4/525654.html. (Subscr. in the Americas to: Elsevier Science, Regional Sales Office, Box 945, New York, NY 10159-0945. TEL 212-633-3730. FAX 212-633-3680; Subscr. in Australasia and the Far East to: Elsevier Science (Singapore) Pte Ltd, No.1 Temasek Ave., No.17-01 Millenia Tower, Singapore 039192, Singapore. TEL 65-434-3727. FAX 65-337-2230; Subscr. in Japan to: Elsevier Science Japan, 9-15 Higashi-Azabu 1-chome, Minato-ku, Tokyo 106, Japan. TEL 81-3-5561-5033. FAX 81-3-5561-5047) Ed. Michiel Kolman. (back issues avail.) **Document type:** academic/scholarly publication.
●Also available online.
Description: Publishes original research in astronomy and astrophysics; the online edition includes links to major scientific data centers.
Refereed Serial

522.1   JA   ISSN 0911-5870
NOBEYAMA NEWSLETTER. (Text in English) 1985. s-a. National Astronomical Observatory, Nobeyama Radio Observatory - Kokuritsu Tenmondai Nobeyama Uchu Denpa Kansokujo, Nobeyama, Minami-Makimura, Minami-Saku-gun, Nagano-ken 384-13, Japan. **Document type:** newsletter.
—CISTI.

522.1   JA   ISSN 0911-5242
NOBEYAMA UCHU DENPA KANSOKUJO NYUSU. (Text in Japanese) 1982. irreg. National Astronomical Observatory, Nobeyama Radio Observatory - Kokuritsu Tenmondai Nobeyama Uchu Denpa Kansokujo, Nobeyama, Minami-Makimura, Minami-Saku-gun, Nagano-ken 384-13, Japan.
Description: News of the observatory.

NOTIZIARIO U F O; Italy's international U F O news. see *AERONAUTICS AND SPACE FLIGHT*

520   GW   ISSN 0078-2246
NOVA KEPLERIANA. NEUE FOLGE. (Subseries of: Bayerische Akademie der Wissenschaften. Mathematisch-Naturwissenschaftliche Klasse. Abhandlungen. Neue Folge) (Text in German; summaries partly in English) 1969. irreg., no.7, 1980. price varies. (Kepler-Kommission) C.H. Beck'sche Verlagsbuchhandlung, Wilhelmstr. 9, 80801 Munich, Germany. TEL 089-38189-338. FAX 089-38189-398. **Document type:** monographic series.

NOVOSTI KOSMONAVTIKI. see *AERONAUTICS AND SPACE FLIGHT*

520   IT
NUOVO ORIONE. 1977. m. L.67000. Sirio s.r.l., Via Bronzino 3, 20133 Milan, Italy. TEL 02-2046510. FAX 02-2049593. Ed. Paola Dameno. adv.: B&W page L.1500000, color page L.2500000. circ. 30,000. **Document type:** consumer publication.

520   FR   ISSN 0769-0878
OBSERVATIONS ET TRAVAUX. q. 135 F. (effective 1997). Societe Astronomique de France, 3 rue Beethoven, 75016 Paris, France. TEL 01-42-24-13-74. FAX 01-42-30-75-47. Ed. B. Rousseau. R&P contact: Elisabeth Sable. **Document type:** bulletin.
—CISTI.

520   AE   ISSN 0065-6232
OBSERVATOIRE ASTRONOMIQUE D'ALGER. ANNALES. Variant title: Universite d'Alger. Observatoire Astronomique. Annales. irreg., no.5, 1979. Universite d'Alger, Observatoire Astronomique, Bouzareah, Algeria.

520   SZ
OBSERVATOIRE DE GENEVE. PRE-PUBLICATIONS. SERIE C. (Text in English and French) 1986. irreg. (approx. 4/yr.). free or avail. on exchange. Observatoire de Geneve, CH-1290 Sauverny, Switzerland.

520   SZ   ISSN 0085-0942
OBSERVATOIRE DE GENEVE. PUBLICATIONS. SERIE A. (Text in English, French) 1928. irreg. (approx. a). 15 Fr. Observatoire de Geneve, CH-1290 Sauverny, Switzerland. **Indexed:** Astron.& Astrophys.Abstr., Bull.Signal.
Description: Astronomical and astrophysical research.

520   SZ   ISSN 0435-2939
OBSERVATOIRE DE GENEVE. PUBLICATIONS. SERIE B. (Text in English and French) 1967. irreg. price varies. Observatoire de Geneve, CH-1290 Sauverny, Switzerland. **Indexed:** Astron.& Astrophys.Abstr., Bull.Signal.
Description: Astronomical and astrophysical research.

523.8   FR   ISSN 1169-8837
QB1   CODEN: BICSDY
OBSERVATOIRE DE STRASBOURG. CENTRE DE DONNEES ASTRONOMIQUES DE STRASBOURG. INFORMATION BULLETIN. (Text in English, French) 1971. 2/yr. free to qualified personnel. Observatoire de Strasbourg, 11 rue de l'Universite, 67000 Strasbourg, France. TEL 33-3-88150720. FAX 33-3-88150760. E-mail question@simbad.u-strasbg.fr; URL: http://cdsweb.u-strasbg.fr/cds.html. Ed. Francoise Genova. abstr.; bibl. circ. 550. (back issues avail.) **Indexed:** INSPEC. **Document type:** bulletin, newsletter.
●Also available online.
—BLDSC (2862.273320); AskIEEE; CISTI; KR SourceOne.
Formerly: Observatoire de Strasbourg. Centre de Donnees Stellaires. Information Bulletin (ISSN 0242-6536)
Description: Provides information about astronomical catalogues and data sets and news about the activities of the center.
Refereed Serial

ASTRONOMY

522.1   SP   ISSN 0373-5125
OBSERVATORIO ASTRONOMICO DE MADRID. ANUARIO. 1860; N.S. 1907. a. 800 ptas. Observatorio Astronomico Nacional, Alfonso XII No. 3, 28014 Madrid, Spain. (Co-sponsor: Instituto Geografico Nacional) **Indexed:** Ind.SST, Ind.SST.
    Formerly (1860-1926): Observatorio de Madrid. Anuario (ISSN 0210-7619); Incorporates (1862-1905): Observatorio de Madrid. Observaciones Meteorologicas (ISSN 0214-1671)

520   AG   ISSN 0302-2277
QB1
OBSERVATORIO ASTRONOMICO MUNICIPAL DE ROSARIO. BOLETIN. (Text in Spanish; summaries in English) irreg. Observatorio Astronomico Municipal de Rosario, Parque Urquiza, Rosario, Argentina. illus.
—CISTI.

520 551   SP   ISSN 0212-9760
OBSERVATORIO DE EBRO. PUBLICACIONES. MEMORIA. 1906. irreg. free. Observatorio Fisica Cosmica del Ebro, 43520 Roquetas (Tarragona), Spain. TEL 34-77-500511. FAX 34-77-504660. Ed. L.F. Alberca. **Indexed:** Ind.SST. **Document type:** monographic series.

522.1   BL
OBSERVATORIO NACIONAL RIO DE JANEIRO. EFEMERIDES ASTRONOMICAS. 1885. a. Cr.$20. Observatorio Nacional, Coordenacao de Informacao e Documentacao, Rua General Jose Cristino, 77, 20921 Sao Cristovao, Brazil.
    Formerly (until 1977): Observatorio Nacional Rio de Janeiro. Anuario.

520 551   BL
OBSERVATORIO NACIONAL RIO DE JANEIRO. PUBLICACOES. (Text in English, French, Portuguese) 1977; N.S. 1980. irreg. free. Observatorio Nacional, Coordenacao de Informacao e Documentacao, Rua General Jose Cristino, 77, 20921 Sao Cristovao, Brazil.

520   UK   ISSN 0029-7704
QB1   CODEN: OBSEAR
OBSERVATORY. 1877. bi-m. £10($20) to individuals; institutions £24($48) (effective 1997). c/o Dr. D.J. Stickland, Ed., Space and Astrophysics Div., Rutherford Appleton Laboratory, Chilton, Didcot, Oxon OX11 0QX, England. FAX 44-1235-445848. R&P contact: D.J. Strickland. adv.; bk.rev.; illus.; index, cum.index. circ. 3,300. **Indexed:** ASCA, Astron.& Astrophys.Abstr., Chem.Abstr., Curr.Cont., Ind.Sci.Rev., INSPEC, Math.R., Meteor.& Geoastrophys.Abstr., Sci.Cit.Ind. **Document type:** academic/scholarly publication.
    —BLDSC (6206.000000); AskIEEE; CASDDS; CISTI; Genuine Article; KR SourceOne; Linda Hall; SWETS; UnCover.
    Refereed Serial

520   PL   ISSN 0075-7047
OBSERWATORIUM KRAKOWSKIE. ROCZNIK ASTRONOMICZNY. DODATEK MIEDZYNARODOWY/SUPPLEMENTO AD ANNUARIO CRACOVIENSE. Key Title: Rocznik Astronomiczny Obserwatorium Krakowskiego. Dodatek Miedzynarodowy. Cover title: S A C - Rocznik Astronomiczny Obserwatorium Krakowskiego. (Text in English) 1922. a. $13 per issue. Uniwersytet Jagiellonski, Oberwatorium Krakowskie - Jagiellonian University, Astronomical Observatory, Ul. Orla 171, 30-244 Krakow, Poland. TEL 48-12-251294. FAX 48-12-251318. E-mail: sac@oa.uj.edu.pl; URL: http://www.oa.uj.eud.pl/ktt.rcznk.html. Ed. Maria Kurpinska-Winiarska. R&P contact: Maria Kurpinska-Winiarska. circ. 400. **Document type:** academic/scholarly publication.
    ●Also available online.

520   US   ISSN 0737-6766
OCCULTATION NEWSLETTER. 1974. q. $20 (foreign $25). International Occultation Timing Association, 2760 S.W. Jewell Ave., Topeka, KS 66611-1614. TEL 913-232-3693. Ed. Rex L. Easton. charts; stat.; circ. 350 (paid). (looseleaf format; back issues avail.) **Document type:** newsletter.
    Description: Reports, predictions, methods of observing lunar occultations, asteroidal occultations, lunar and solar eclipses.

ODYSSEY (PETERBOROUGH); the young people's magazine of astronomy and outer space. see CHILDREN AND YOUTH — For

520   SZ   ISSN 0030-557X
ORION. (Text in French and German) 1943. 6/yr. 60 SFr. (foreign 65 SFr.) (effective 1997). Societe Astronomique de Suisse - Schweizerische Astronomische Gesellschaft, c/o Sue Kernen, Gristenbuehl 13, CH-9315 Neukirch, Switzerland. TEL 41-71-4771743. Ed. N. Cramer. adv.; bk.rev.; charts; illus.; index. circ. 2,800. (also avail. in microfiche) **Indexed:** R.G.Abstr. **Document type:** newsletter.
—CISTI.

520   AT   ISSN 0079-1067
PERTH OBSERVATORY. COMMUNICATIONS. 1964. irreg., no.5, 1986. exchange basis. (Perth Observatory) Western Australia Government Printer, Bickley, W.A. 6076, Australia. TEL 09-293-8255. FAX 09-293-8138. circ. 200. **Indexed:** Astron.& Astrophys.Abstr.
    Description: Documents position of comets and minor planets.

520   US   ISSN 1093-118X
PHOTOGRAPHER'S ALMANAC OF THE SUN & MOON (YEAR). 1988. a. $20. Astronomical Data Service, 3922 Leisure Ln., Colorado Springs, CO 80917. TEL 719-597-4068. (Subscr. to: Box 26180, Colorado Springs, CO 80936)
    Description: Computed for the purchaser's latitude, longitude, and time zone, and contains everything about the daily astronomical circumstances of sunlight and moonlight that a landscape photographer might need to know.

PHYSICS ABSTRACTS. see PHYSICS — Abstracting, Bibliographies, Statistics

PHYSICS AND CHEMISTRY IN SPACE. see CHEMISTRY

520   RU   ISSN 0320-0108
QB1   CODEN: PAZHDA
PIS'MA V ASTRONOMICHESKII ZHURNAL. English translation: Astronomy Letters (US ISSN 1063-7737) (Text in Russian; summaries in English) 1975. m. $245 (effective 1998). (Rossiiskaya Akademiya Nauk, Astrosovet) Izdatel'stvo Nauka, 90 Profsoyuznaya ul., 117864 Moscow, Russia. TEL 234-05-84. (Dist. by: Mezhdunarodnaya Kniga, ul. Dimitrova D.39, 113095 Moscow, Russia) Ed. B.Ju. Levin. **Indexed:** Chem.Abstr., INSPEC, Phys.Ber., Sci.Cit.Ind. **Document type:** academic/scholarly publication.
    —BLDSC (0129.487700); AskIEEE; CASDDS; CISTI; KNAW; KR SourceOne; Linda Hall. CCC.

520   US   ISSN 0090-3213
QB1
PLANETARIAN. 1972. q. $40. International Planetarium Society, Griffith Observatory, 2800 E. Observatory Rd., Los Angeles, CA 90027. FAX 818-708-7314. E-mail: jmosley@griffithObs.ogr; URL: http://www.griffithobs.org/IPSPlanetarian.html. Ed. John E. Mosley. R&P contact: John Mosley. adv.; bk.rev.; illus.; index. circ. 750. (also avail. in microform from UMI; reprint service avail. from UMI) **Document type:** academic/scholarly publication.
    —CISTI; Linda Hall; UMI; UnCover.

520 550   UK   ISSN 0032-0633
QC801   CODEN: PLSSAE
PLANETARY AND SPACE SCIENCE. 1959. m. fl.3647($2096) (effective 1998). (European Geophysical Society, Planetary and Solar Systems Sciences Section) Elsevier Science Ltd., Pergamon, P.O. Box 800, Kidlington, Oxford OX5 1DX, England. TEL 44-1865-843000. FAX 44-1865-843010. E-mail: nlinfo-f@elsevier.nl; usinfo-f@elsevier.com; forinfo-kyf04035@niftyserve.or.jp; URL: http://www.elsevier.nl/; http://www.copernicus.org/EGGS/egsga/638.htm. (Subscr. to: Elsevier Science, Regional Sales Office, P.O. Box 211, 1000 AE Amsterdam, Netherlands. TEL 31-20-4853757. FAX 31-20-4853432; Subscr. in the Americas to: Elsevier Science, Regional Sales Office, Box 945, New York, NY 10159-0945. TEL 212-633-3730. FAX 212-633-3680; Subscr. in Australasia and the Far East to: Elsevier Science (Singapore) Pte Ltd, No.1 Temasek Ave., No.17-01 Millenia Tower, Singapore 039192, Singapore. TEL 65-434-3727. FAX 65-337-2230) Ed. Marcello Coradini. adv.; bk.rev. circ. 1,250. (also avail. in microfilm from UMI; back issues avail.) **Indexed:** Appl.Mech.Rev., ASCA, Chem.Abstr., Chem.Cit.Ind., Curr.Cont., Environ.Per.Bibl., Excerp.Med., GeoRef., Ind.Sci.Rev., INSPEC, Int.Aerosp.Abstr., Meteor.& Geoastrophys.Abstr., Phys.Ber., Sci.Cit.Ind., SSCI. **Document type:** academic/scholarly publication.
    —BLDSC (6508.320000); AskIEEE; CASDDS; Ei; Genuine Article; KR SourceOne; Linda Hall; SWETS; UMI; UnCover. **CCC.**
    Description: Publishes papers in cosmology and origins; small bodies, dust and rings; terrestrial planets and satellites; outer planets; planetary atmospheres, magnetospheres and ionospheres; exobiology; celestial mechanics; and the history of planetary and space research.
    Refereed Serial

522   US   ISSN 0736-3680
QB600
PLANETARY REPORT. 1980. bi-m. $25 (Canada $35; elsewhere $45). Planetary Society, 65 N. Catalina Ave., Pasadena, CA 91106-2301. TEL 818-793-5100. FAX 818-793-5568. TELEX 757511. E-mail: tps@mars.planetary.org; URL: http://planetary.org/tps/. Ed. Charlene M. Anderson. R&P contact: Charlene M. Anderson. bk.rev.; charts; illus.; circ. 100,000 (paid). (back issues avail.)
    ●Also available online.
    —BLDSC (6508.350000); UnCover.
    Description: Focuses on planetary exploration and the search for extraterrestrial intelligence.

POLISH ACADEMY OF SCIENCES. BULLETIN. MATHEMATICS. see MATHEMATICS

520   UK   ISSN 0261-0892
POPULAR ASTRONOMY. 1953. q. £12. Society for Popular Astronomy, 36 Fairway, Keyworth, Nottingham NG12 5DU, England. Ed. Tom Hosking. adv. contact: Stewart McLaughlin. bk.rev.; illus.; circ. controlled. **Document type:** bulletin.
    Formerly: Hermes.

520   PL   ISSN 0032-5414
QB1   CODEN: PYAIAJ
POSTEPY ASTRONOMII. 1953. q. Zl.($46) (effective 1998). Polskie Towarzystwo Astronomiczne - Polish Astronomical Society, Ul. Bartycka 18, 00-716 Warsaw, Poland. TEL 48-22-410041. FAX 48-22-410046. E-mail: aw@astri.uni.torun.pl. (Dist. by: Ars Polona, Krakowskie Przedmiescie 7, 00-068 Warsaw, Poland; Dist. also by: Mezhdunarodnaya Kniga, B. Yakimanka 39, 117049 Moscow, Russia. TEL 7-095-2384967. FAX 7-095-2384634) Ed. A. Woszczyk. R&P contact: A. Woszczyk. adv.; bk.rev.; charts; illus.; index. circ. 1,000. **Indexed:** Chem.Abstr., INSPEC. **Document type:** academic/scholarly publication.
    —CASDDS; CISTI; KR SourceOne; Linda Hall.
    Description: Contains review articles, news, people in astronomy, astronomical centers in Poland, occasionally interviews.
    Refereed Serial

520   FR   ISSN 0154-4101
PULSAR. 1910. bi-m. 180 F. Societe d'Astronomie Populaire, 1 Av. Camille Flammarion, 31500 Toulouse, France. Ed. Christian Sanchez. adv.; bk.rev.; bibl.; charts; illus.; index, cum.index. circ. 1,500.
—CISTI.
    Formerly: Societe d'Astronomie Populaire de Toulouse. Bulletin Mensuel (ISSN 0037-900X)

ASTRONOMY

520 US
▼**QUE TAL? IN THE CURRENT SKIES.** 1996. m. free. Kansas City Missouri School District Planetarium, E-mail: starwalk@gvi.net; URL: http://oz.sunflower.org/~starwalk/current__sky.html. Ed. Bob Riddle. illus.; maps. (back issues avail.) **Document type:** newsletter.
●Available only online.
Description: Information on astronomy and related subjects.

QUEST (GRAND RAPIDS); the history of spaceflight magazine. see *AERONAUTICS AND SPACE FLIGHT*

520 SP
REAL INSTITUTO Y OBSERVATORIO DE LA ARMADA. BOLETIN ASTRONOMICO. 1966. a? Real Instituto y Observatorio de la Armada, San Fernando (Cadiz), Spain. circ. 100. (back issues avail.) **Indexed:** Ind.SST.
Formerly: Instituto y Observatorio de Marina. Boletin Astronomico (ISSN 0210-6493)

520 SP ISSN 1131-5040
REAL OBSERVATORIO DE LA ARMADA. BOLETIN. 1986. irreg. (2-5/yr.). Real Instituto y Observatorio de la Armada, Cecilio Pugazon, s-n, 11100 San Fernando (Cadiz), Spain. circ. 100. **Indexed:** Ind.SST. **Document type:** government publication.
—CISTI.
Supersedes (1966-1984): Real Observatorio de la Armada. Boletin Astronomico; **Incorporates** (1952-1967): Instituto y Observatorio de Marina de San Fernando. Seccion de Astronomia. Serie A: Movimientos Propios Estelares (ISSN 0558-3985); (1953-1981): Instituto y Observatorio de Marina de San Fernando. Seccion de Astronomia. Serie B: Pequenos Planetas (ISSN 0558-3993); (1957-1983): Instituto y Observatorio de Marina de San Fernando. Seccion de Astronomia. Serie C: Rotacion de la Tierra (ISN 0210-6485); Which was formerly (until 1969): Serie C: Servicio de Hora (ISSN 0210-6485); And (1964-1981): Instituto y Observatorio de Marina de San Fernando. Seccion de Astronomia. Serie D: Ocultaciones de Estrella por la Luna (ISSN 0210-8119).
Description: Helps use and understand concepts in other technical publications of the ROA. Presents scientific work done at the ROA.

520 US ISSN 0034-2963
REFLECTOR NEWSLETTER. 1956. q. $4 to non-members. Astronomical League, 5027 W. Stanford, Dallas, TX 75209-3319. TEL 214-357-2744. Ed. Ed Flaspoehler. R&P contact: Edward Flaspoehler. adv. contact: Edward Fraspoehler. bk.rev.; charts; illus.; stat. circ. 14,000. **Document type:** newsletter.
●Also available online. Vendor(s): CompuServe, Inc.
Description: Covers amateur astronomy news.

REVIEWS OF GEOPHYSICS. see *EARTH SCIENCES — Geophysics*

520 AG ISSN 0044-9253
REVISTA ASTRONOMICA. 1929. q. $20. Asociacion Argentina Amigos de la Astronomia, Correo Central, Casilla 369, 1000 Buenos Aires, Argentina. TEL 54-1-8633366. E-mail: revast@aaaa.org.ar. Ed. Cristian Rusquellas. R&P contact: Cristian Rusquellas. adv. contact: Jose Aiani. bk.rev. circ. 1,000. (back issues avail.) **Document type:** academic/scholarly publication.
Description: Covers amateur astronomy, observation guides, telescopes and the ephemerides.

520 MX ISSN 0185-1101
QB1 CODEN: RMAAD4
REVISTA MEXICANA DE ASTRONOMIA Y ASTROFISICA. (Text in English; summaries in English and Spanish) 1974. s-a. $40 (effective 1998) (free to qualified personnel). Universidad Nacional Autonoma de Mexico, Instituto de Astronomia, Apdo. Postal 70-264, 04510 Mexico DF, Mexico. TEL 52-5-6223900. FAX 52-5-616-0653. E-mail: rmaa@astroscu.unam.mx. Ed.Bd. R&P contact: Silvia Torres-Peimbert. cum.index: 1974-1994. circ. 850. **Indexed:** ASCA, Astron.& Astrophys.Abstr., Chem.Abstr., Curr.Cont., INSPEC (1974-), Math.R., Phys.Ber., Sci.Cit.Ind. **Document type:** academic/scholarly publication.
—AskIEEE; CASDDS; CISTI; Genuine Article; KR SourceOne; Linda Hall; UnCover.
Description: Includes original research papers.
Refereed Serial

520 523.01 MX ISSN 1405-2059
CODEN: RMAAF6
▼**REVISTA MEXICANA DE ASTRONOMIA Y ASTROFISICA SERIE DE CONFERENCIAS.** 1995. irreg. vol.5, 1996. $40 (free to qualified personnel). Universidad Nacional Autonoma de Mexico, Instituto de Astronomia, Apdo. Postal 70-264, 04510 Mexico DF, Mexico. TEL 52-5-6223900. FAX 52-5-616-0653. E-mail: rmaa@astroscu.unam.mx. Ed. Silvia Torres-Peimbert. **Document type:** proceedings.
—AskIEEE; CASDDS; CISTI; KR SourceOne.

520 XR ISSN 0035-5550
RISE HVEZD.* (Text in Czech or Slovak) 1920. m. $21.70. Informacni a Poradenske Stredisko pro Misti Kulturu, Ul. Blanicka 4, 120 21 Prague 2, Czech Republic. Ed. Eduard Skoda. bk.rev.; film rev.; bibl.; charts; index. circ. 5,000. **Document type:** consumer publication.
Description: Astronomical journal for amateurs.

520 RM ISSN 1220-5168
ROMANIAN ASTRONOMICAL JOURNAL. (Text in English, French; summaries in English) 1991. s-a. (Academia Romana, Observatul Astronomic) Editura Academiei Romane, Calea 13 Septembrie 13, 76117 Bucharest, Romania. TEL 6507680. (Dist. by: Rodipet SA, Piata Presei Libere 1, Sec. 1, PO Box 33-57, Bucharest, Rumania. TEL 401-6185103. FAX 401-2224126) Ed. Arpad Pal.
—BLDSC (8019.586000); CISTI; Linda Hall.
Supersedes (1956-1974): Studii si Cercetari de Astronomie (ISSN 0039-3894); Which was formerly (until 1963): Studii si Cercetari de Astronomie si Seismologie (ISSN 1220-062X)

520 551.5 UK ISSN 0035-8711
QB1 CODEN: MNRAA4
ROYAL ASTRONOMICAL SOCIETY. MONTHLY NOTICES. 1827. 36/yr. £1750($3104) (foreign £1870) (effective 1998). Blackwell Science Ltd., Osney Mead, Oxford OX2 0EL, England. TEL 44-1865-206206. FAX 44-1865-721205. E-mail: journals.cs@blacksci.co.uk; URL: http://www.black.co.uk. Ed. Prof. A.C. Fabian; Pub. Allen Stevens. R&P contact: Sarah Pollard. adv. contact: Martine Cariou-Keen. illus.; index, cum.index: vols.1-91, 1827-1931 (in 4 vols.). circ. 1,115. (also avail. in microform from UMI; back issues avail.; reprint service avail. from ISI) **Indexed:** ASCA, Chem.Abstr., Chem.Cit.Ind., Curr.Cont, GeoRef., Ind.Sci.Rev., INSPEC, Int.Aerosp.Abstr., Math.R., Phys.Ber., Sci.Cit.Ind. **Document type:** academic/scholarly publication.
—BLDSC (5943.000000); AskIEEE; CASDDS; CISTI; Ei; Genuine Article; KR SourceOne; Linda Hall; SWETS; UMI; UnCover. CCC.
Refereed Serial

520 CN ISSN 0035-872X
QB1 CODEN: JRASA2
ROYAL ASTRONOMICAL SOCIETY OF CANADA. JOURNAL. 1907. bi-m. Can.$80($80) to institutions (effective 1998). Royal Astronomical Society of Canada - Societe Royale d'Astronomie du Canada, 136 Dupont St., Toronto, ON M5R 1V2, Canada. TEL 416-924-7973. FAX 416-924-2911. E-mail: rasc@istar.ca; URL: http://apwww.stmarys.ca/rasc/nat/journal/journal.html. (Subscr. to: University of Toronto Press, Journals Department, 5201 Dufferin St., North York, ON M3H 5T8, Canada. TEL 416-667-7810. FAX 416-667-7881) Ed. David G. Turner. bk.rev.; bibl.; illus.; index, cum.index: vols.1-25, 26-60. circ. 2,950. (also avail. in microform from UMI) **Indexed:** ASCA, Astron.& Astrophys.Abstr., Chem.Abstr., Curr.Cont., INIS Atomind., INSPEC, Int.Aerosp.Abstr. **Document type:** academic/scholarly publication.
—BLDSC (4854.000000); AskIEEE; CASDDS; CISTI; KR SourceOne; Linda Hall; SWETS; UnCover.
Incorporates (1978-1997): Royal Astronomical Society of Canada. Bulletin (ISSN 1187-1571); Which was formerly (until 1991): Royal Astronomical Society of Canada. Newsletter (ISSN 0846-8877); (until 1989): Royal Astronomical Society of Canada. National Newsletter (ISSN 0846-8494).
Description: Contains articles on Canadian astronomers and current activities of the RASC, research and review papers by professional and amateur astronomers, and articles of a historical, biographical, or educational nature of general interest to the astronomical community.

522 CN ISSN 0080-4193
QB9
ROYAL ASTRONOMICAL SOCIETY OF CANADA. OBSERVER'S HANDBOOK. 1908. a. Can.$18.14($16.95) Royal Astronomical Society of Canada, 136 Dupont St., Toronto, ON M5R 1V2, Canada. TEL 416-924-7973. FAX 416-924-7973. E-mail: rasc@istar.ca; URL: http://www.rasc.ca/info.html. Ed. Dr. Roy L. Bishop. index. circ. 16,000. (also avail. in microform from UMI)
—BLDSC (6208.000000); CISTI; Linda Hall.

ROYAL IRISH ACADEMY. PROCEEDINGS. SECTION A: MATHEMATICAL AND PHYSICAL SCIENCES. see *MATHEMATICS*

520 US ISSN 0190-2717
QB1 CODEN: BCAOD4
RUSSIAN ACADEMY OF SCIENCES. CRIMEAN ASTROPHYSICAL OBSERVATORY. BULLETIN. Key Title: Bulletin of the Crimean Astrophysical Observatory. English traslation of: Russian Academy of Sciences. Krymskaya Astrofizicheskaya Observatoriya. Izvestiya. 1977. irreg., latest vol.92. $250 (effective 1998). (Russian Academy of Sciences, Crimean Astrophysical Observatory, RU) Allerton Press, Inc., 150 Fifth Ave., New York, NY 10011. TEL 212-924-3950. FAX 212-463-9684. Ed. N.V. Steshenko. **Indexed:** INSPEC (1979-), Phys.Ber. **Document type:** academic/scholarly publication.
—BLDSC (0409.150000); AskIEEE; CISTI; KR SourceOne. CCC.
Formerly: Academy of Sciences of the U S S R. Crimean Astrophysical Observatory. Bulletin.
Description: Emphasis on solar astrophysics, stellar spectroscopy, extra galactic radio sources, astrophysical equipment.

520 SA ISSN 1017-7787
S A A O NEWSLETTER. (Text in English) 1983. s-a. free. South Africa Astronomical Observatory, P.O. Box 9, Observatory 7935, South Africa. TEL 27-21-470025. FAX 27-21-473639. TELEX 5-20309 SA. E-mail: ethleen@saao.ac.za; URL: http://www.saao.ac.za. Ed. Ethleen Lastovica. circ. 700. (back issues avail.) **Document type:** newsletter.
●Also available online.

520 JA
S P A R C JIMUKYOKUHO/S P A R C NEWS. (Text in Japanese) 1967. irreg. Space Research Co-Operative Association - Uchu Kukan Kenkyusha Kyogikai, Nagoya Daigaku Rigakubu Butsurigaku Kyoshitsu, Furo-cho, Chikusa-ku, Nagoya-shi, Aichi-ken 464, Japan.
Description: Contains news of the association.

SANKT-PETERBURGSKII UNIVERSITET. VESTNIK. SERIYA: MATEMATIKA, MEKHANIKA I ASTRONOMIYA. see *MATHEMATICS*

520 FR ISSN 0769-1025
SATELLITES DE SATURNE I TO VIII. (Text in French) 1985. a. 55 F. Bureau des Longitudes, 77 av. Denfert-Rochereau, 75014 Paris, France. (Subscr. to: A F A, 17 rue Deutch de la Meurthe, F-75014 Paris, France) Ed. J.E. Arlot.

520 FR ISSN 0769-1033
SATELLITES GALILEENS DE JUPITER; phenomenes et configurations. (Text in English, French) 1979. a. 55 F. Bureau des Longitudes, 77 av. Denfert-Rochereau, 75014 Paris, France. (Subscr. to: 17 rue Deutsche-de-la-Meurthe, 75014 Paris, France) Ed. J.E. Arlot.

SCIENCE IN CHINA. SERIES A: MATHEMATICS, PHYSICS, ASTRONOMY. see *MATHEMATICS*

520 US
SELENOLOGY. 1982. q. $12. American Lunar Society, Box 209, E. Pittsburgh, PA 15112. TEL 412-829-8901. Ed. Francis G. Graham. bk.rev. circ. 200. (also avail. in microform) **Document type:** academic/scholarly publication.
Description: Devoted to the science of the Earth's moon.

520 JA ISSN 0386-0817
SENDAI ASTRONOMIAJ REPORTOJ. (Text and summaries in English) 1930. irreg. free. Tohoku Daigaku, Rigakubu - Tohoku University, Faculty of Science, Aoba, Aramaki, Sendai-shi, Miyagi-ken 980 Japan. Ed. Mine Takeuti. **Indexed:** INIS Atomind. **Document type:** academic/scholarly publication.
—BLDSC (8241.070000).

ASTRONOMY 501

520　　　　　　US　　ISSN 0037-6604
QB1　　　　　　　　CODEN: SKTEA3
SKY & TELESCOPE; the essential magazine of astronomy. 1941. m. $33 (Canada $43; elsewhere $50). Sky Publishing Corp., 49 Bay State Rd., Cambridge, MA 02138. TEL 617-864-7360. FAX 617-864-6117. E-mail: postmaster@skypub.com; skytel@skypub.com; URL: http://www.skypub.com/s__t/s__t.shtlm. (Subscr. to: Box 9111, Belmont, MA 02178) Ed. Leif J. Robinson. adv. contact: Kim Bennett. bk.rev.; film rev.; charts; illus.; s-a. index; circ. 106,000 (paid). (also avail. in microform from UMI; reprint service avail.) **Indexed:** Acad.Ind., ASCA, Astron.& Astrophys.Abstr., Biog.Ind., Bk.Rev.Ind. (1965-), Child.Bk.Rev.Ind. (1965-), Curr.Cont., Gen.Sci.Ind., GeoRef., Ind.How To Do It (1978-), INSPEC, Int.Aerosp.Abstr., Mag.Ind., PMR, R.G.Abstr., R.G. **Document type:** academic/scholarly publication.
●Also available online. Vendor(s): Information Access Co., UMI.
—BLDSC (8309.000000); AskIEEE; CISTI; KR SourceOne; Linda Hall; SWETS; UMI; UnCover. **CCC**.
Former titles: Telescope: Drama of the Skies; Sky (ISSN 0361-8242)
Description: Discusses astronomy and space science. Contains items by leading professionals, activities of amateur astronomers and current celestial events.

520　　　　　　US
▼**SKY WATCH**. 1996. a. $3.95. Sky Publishing Corporation, 49 Bat St., Cambridge, MA 02138. TEL 617-864-7360; 800-253-0245. FAX 617-864-6117. E-mail: orders@skypup.com; URL: http://www.skypub.com/. (Subscr. to: Box 9111, Belmont, MA 02178) illus. circ. 75,000.
Description: Features coverage of celestial and space highlights throughout the year and answers the most common questions asked by newcomers to astronomy.

520　　　　　　JA　　ISSN 0911-7652
SKY WATCHER. (Text in Japanese) 1983. m. 620 Yen. (Rippu Shobo Inc.) Rippu Shobo Inc., 5-8, Kamimeguro 5-chome, Meguro-ku, Tokyo 153, Japan. TEL 03-5721-0561. Ed. Masaya Kawaguchi. adv.; bk.rev. **Document type:** consumer publication.

520　　　　　　US　　ISSN 0889-9614
SKYWATCHERS ALMANAC (YEAR). 1976. a. $20. Astronomical Data Service, 3922 Leisure Lane, Colorado Springs, CO 80917-3502. TEL 719-597-4068. (Subscr. to: Box 26180, Colorado Springs, CO 80936) Ed. Roger L. Mansfield. (back issues avail.)
Description: Provides information about the sun, moon, planets, stars, and constellations in an easy-to-use, quick-reference format. Computed for purchaser's latitude and longitude.

520　　　　　　IT　　ISSN 0037-8720
　　　　　　　　　　　CODEN: MSATAB
SOCIETA ASTRONOMICA ITALIANA. MEMORIE. (Text in English, French and Italian) 1920. q. L.30000. Societa Astronomica Italiana, Via Brera 28, 20121 Milan, Italy. Dir. L. Gratton. bk.rev.; charts; illus.; index. circ. 400. **Indexed:** Bull.Signal., Chem.Abstr, INSPEC, Int.Aerosp.Abstr., Math.R.
—BLDSC (5675.055000); AskIEEE; CASDDS; CISTI; KR SourceOne; UnCover.

SOCIETA ITALIANA DI FISICA. NUOVO CIMENTO B; general physics, relativity, astronomy and mathematical physics and methods. see *PHYSICS*

520　　　　　　FR　　ISSN 0081-0738
SOCIETE ASTRONOMIQUE DE BORDEAUX. BULLETIN.* 1961. a. price varies. Societe Astronomique de Bordeaux, Hotel des Societes Savantes, 71 rue du Loup, Bordeaux, France.

523.01 551　　　US
QB524
SOLAR-GEOPHYSICAL DATA. PART 1 - PROMPT REPORTS. 1957. m. (plus a. descriptive text issue) $60 (foreign $66). U.S. National Geophysical Data Center, National Oceanic and Atmospheric Administration, 325 Broadway, Boulder, CO 80303-3328. TEL 303-497-6836. FAX 303-497-6513. E-mail: info@mail.ngdc.noaa.gov. (also avail. in microfiche from NTI) **Document type:** government publication.
●Also available on CD-ROM.
Description: Presents historical data on the sun's activity and effects on the Earth.

523.01 551　　　US
QB524
SOLAR-GEOPHYSICAL DATA: PART 2 - COMPREHENSIVE REPORTS. 1955. m. $60 (foreign $66). U.S. National Geophysical Data Center, National Oceanic and Atmospheric Administration, 325 Broadway, Boulder, CO 80303-3328. TEL 303-497-6836. FAX 303-497-6513. E-mail: info@mail.ngdc.noaa.gov. Eds. Helen E. Coffey, John A. McKinnon. circ. 800. (also avail. in microfiche from NTI) **Document type:** government publication.
●Also available on CD-ROM.
Description: Presents historical data on the sun's activity and effects on the Earth.

523.01　　　　　NE　　ISSN 0038-0938
QB521　　　　　　　　CODEN: SLPHAX
SOLAR PHYSICS; a journal for solar and solar-stellar research and the study of solar terrestrial physics. 1967. 14/yr. fl.4340 to institutions; $2226 to institutions in U.S. (effective 1998). Kluwer Academic Publishers, Postbus 17, 3300 AA Dordrecht, Netherlands. TEL 31-78-6392392. FAX 31-78-6392254. TELEX 29245 KAPG NL. E-mail: services@wkap.nl; URL: http://www.wkap.nl/kapis/CGI-BIN/WORLD/journalshome.htm?0038-0938. (Dist. by: Kluwer Academic Publishers Group, P.O. Box 322, 3300 AH Dordrecht, Netherlands. TEL 31-78-6392392. FAX 31-78-6546474; N. America dist. addr.: Box 358, Accord Sta., Hingham, MA 02018-0358. TEL 617-871-6600. FAX 617-871-6528) Eds. C. De Jager, Z. Svestka. adv.; bk.rev.; illus.; index, cum.index vols. 1-100. (also avail. in microform from UMI; reprint service avail. from SWZ) **Indexed:** ASCA, Astron.& Astrophys.Abstr., Bull.Signal., Chem.Abstr., Curr.Cont., Eng.Ind., IBR, IBZ, Ind.Sci.Rev., INIS Atomind., INSPEC, Int.Aerosp.Abstr., Meteor.& Geoastrophys.Abstr., Phys.Ber., Ref.Zh., Sci.Cit.Ind. **Document type:** academic/scholarly publication.
—BLDSC (8327.205000); AskIEEE; CASDDS; CISTI; Genuine Article; KR SourceOne; Linda Hall; SWETS; UMI; UnCover. **CCC**.
Description: Publishes the results of fundamental research on the Sun.
Refereed Serial

621.47 523.01　　RU　　ISSN 0038-0946
QB501　　　　　　　　CODEN: SSYRAL
SOLAR SYSTEM RESEARCH. English translation of: Astronomicheskii Vestnik (RU ISSN 0320-930X) 1967. bi-m. $1245 in US; elsewhere $1445 (effective 1998). (Russian Academy of Sciences, Institute of Applied Mathematics) Maik Nauka - Interperiodica, Mezhdunarodnyi Otdel, Ul. Profsoyuznaya, 90, 117864 Moscow, Russia. TEL 7-095-3360066. FAX 7-095-3360066. E-mail: info@plenum.com; URL: http://ns1.info.com:6800/cgi/getarec?ple2000246. (Dist. by: Plenum Publishing Corp., 233 Spring St., New York, NY 10013-1578, U.S.A.. TEL 212-620-8468. FAX 212-463-0742) Ed. Michail Ya. Marov. (also avail. in microfilm from UMI; back issues avail.) **Indexed:** Eng.Ind., INSPEC (1972-), Sci.Res.Abstr. **Document type:** academic/scholarly publication.
—BLDSC (0420.825000); AskIEEE; CISTI; KR SourceOne; SWETS; UMI; UnCover. **CCC**.
Refereed Serial

520　　　　　　UK　　ISSN 0144-4492
SOLAR SYSTEM TODAY. 1979. q. £3. Bretmain, 996 Hamilton Rd., Felixstowe, England.

520　　　　　　GW　　ISSN 0721-0094
SONNE; Mitteilungsblatt der Amateursonnenbeobachter. (Text in German; abstracts in English) 1977. q. DM.30($22) (effective 1997). Vereinigung der Sternfreunde e.V., Fachgruppe Sonne, c/o Wilhelm-Foerster-Sternwarte e.V., Munsterdamm 90, 12169 Berlin, Germany. URL: http://neptun.uni-sw.gwdg.de/sonne.html. Ed. Peter Voelker. adv. contact: Robert Hilz. bk.rev.; abstr.; bibl.; charts; illus.; stat.; index. circ. 350. (back issues avail.) **Indexed:** Astron.& Astrophys.Abstr. **Document type:** bulletin.
Description: Observations of the sun.

522.19687　　　　SA　　ISSN 0250-0671
SOUTH AFRICAN ASTRONOMICAL OBSERVATORY. ANNUAL REPORT. Key Title: Report for the Year Ending - South African Astronomical Observatory. (Text in English) 1977. a. South African Astronomical Observatory, Foundation for Research and Development, P.O. Box 9, Observatory 7935, South Africa. TEL 27-21-470025. FAX 27-21-473639. TELEX 5-20309 SA. E-mail: ethleen@saao.ac.za. Ed. R.S. Stobie. R&P contact: R.S. Stobie. **Document type:** corporate report.
—BLDSC (7608.820000).

520　　　　　　NZ　　ISSN 0049-1640
QB1
SOUTHERN STARS. 1934. q. NZ.$50 to non-members. Royal Astronomical Society of New Zealand (Inc.), P.O. Box 3181, Wellington, New Zealand. TEL 64-4-5276398. FAX 64-4-5276374. E-mail: edwin.budding@cit.ac.nz. Ed Edwin Budding. adv.: page N.Z.$50. bk.rev.; software rev.; cum.index every 2 yrs.; circ. 450 (paid). **Indexed:** Astron.& Astrophys.Abstr. **Document type:** academic/scholarly publication.
—BLDSC (8356.000000); CISTI; Linda Hall; UnCover. **CCC**.
Description: Covers astronomical research and reports especially as caried out in New Zealand.
Refereed Serial

520　　　　　　JA
SPACE RESEARCH IN JAPAN. (Text in English) 2/yr. (Nihon Gakujutsu Kaigi, Uchu Kukan Kenkyu Renraku linkai - Science Council of Japan, Japan National Committee for Space Research) Institute of Space and Astronautical Science, Uchu Kagaku Kenkyujo, 1-1, Yoshinodai 3-chome, Sagamihara-shi, Kanagawa-ken 229, Japan. abstr.

520 629.4　　　　NE　　ISSN 0038-6308
QB1　　　　　　　　CODEN: SPSRA4
SPACE SCIENCE REVIEWS. (Text in English) 1962. 16/yr. fl.2544 to institutions; $1306 to institutions in U.S. (effective 1998). Kluwer Academic Publishers, Postbus 17, 3300 AA Dordrecht, Netherlands. TEL 31-78-6392392. FAX 31-78-6392254. TELEX 29245 KAPG NL. E-mail: services@wkap.nl; URL: http://www.wkap.nl/kapis/CGI-BIN/WORLD/journalhome.html?0038-6308. (Dist. by: Kluwer Academic Publishers Group, P.O. Box 322, 3300 AH Dordrecht, Netherlands. TEL 31-78-6392392. FAX 31-78-6546474; N. America dist. addr.: Box 358, Accord Sta., Hingham, MA 02018-0358. TEL 617-871-6600. FAX 617-871-6528) Ed. C. de Jager. adv.; bk.rev.; illus. (also avail. in microform from UMI,PMC; reprint service avail. from SWZ) **Indexed:** ASCA, Astron.& Astrophys.Abstr., Bull.Signal., Chem.Abstr., Curr.Cont., IBR, IBZ, Ind.Sci.Rev., INIS Atomind., INSPEC, Int.Aerosp.Abstr., Meteor.& Geoastrophys.Abstr., Phys.Ber., Ref.Zh., Sci.Cit.Ind. **Document type:** academic/scholarly publication.
—AskIEEE; CISTI; Genuine Article; KR SourceOne; Linda Hall; SWETS; UMI; UnCover. **CCC**.
Description: Publishes review papers on scientific research carried out by means of rockets, rocket-propelled vehicles, stratospheric balloons, and at observatories on the Earth.
Refereed Serial

520　　　　　　UK　　ISSN 1353-7784
SPECTRUM. 1979. q. free. Royal Greenwich Observatory, Madingley Rd., Cambridge CB3 0EZ, England. E-mail: spectrum@ast.cam.ac.uk. Ed. Mark Casali. circ. 2,000. (back issues avail.) **Document type:** newsletter.
—CISTI.
Formed by the 1994 merger of: Gemini & U K I R T Newsletter; Which was formerly (until 1993): J C M T - U K I R T Newsletter (ISSN 0963-2700); Which was formed by the 1990 merger of: U K I R T Newsletter (ISSN 0143-0599); Protostar (ISSN 0267-1247)

520　　　　　　US　　ISSN 0893-4614
STAR TECH; the real cosmic connection. 1987. m. $16.50 (foreign $25). Richard Nolle, Ed. & Pub., Box 26599, Tempe, AZ 85285-6599. TEL 602-838-3245. (back issues avail.)
Description: For people who are interested in contemporary ideas, techniques, and tools for understanding the connections between human experience and the cosmic environment.

ASTRONOMY

520 US ISSN 0889-3098
STARDATE. 1972. bi-m. $18. University of Texas, Austin, McDonald Observatory, Austin, TX 78712. TEL 512-471-5285. FAX 512-471-5060. TELEX 9108741351. URL: http://www.as.utexas.edu/mcdonald/mcdonald.html. Ed. Doug Addison; Pub. Sandra Barnes. bk.rev.; circ. 10,500 (paid). **Document type:** consumer publication.
Formerly: McDonald Observatory News.

520 GW ISSN 0039-1263
QB1 CODEN: STUWAN
STERNE UND WELTRAUM; Zeitschrift fuer Astronomie. 1962. m. DM.125 (foreign DM.140) (effective 1997). (Max-Planck-Institut fuer Astronomie) Verlag Sterne und Weltraum Dr. Vehrenberg GmbH, Portiastr. 10, 81545 Munich, Germany. TEL 49-89-646947. FAX 49-89-6423409. Ed.Bd. adv.; bk.rev.; abstr.; charts; illus.; index. circ. 16,000. (back issues avail.) **Document type:** bulletin.
—AskIEEE; CASDDS; CISTI; KR SourceOne; Linda Hall; SWETS. **CCC.**
Incorporates (1921-1997): Sterne (ISSN 0039-1255)

520 AU ISSN 0039-1271
DER STERNENBOTE; Oesterreichische Astronomische Monatsschrift. 1958. m. S.195 (effective 1997). Astronomisches Buero, Hasenwartgasse 32, A-1238 Vienna, Austria. TEL 43-1-8893541. FAX 43-1-8893541. E-mail: astbuero@astronomisches-buero-wien.or.at; URL: http://members.ping.at/astbuero. Ed. Hermann Mucke. R&P contact: Hermann Mucke. adv.; bk.rev.; bibl. circ. 2,000. (processed) **Document type:** bulletin.

STONEHENGE VIEWPOINT; archaeology, astronomy, geology, and related arts and sciences. see *ARCHAEOLOGY*

520.09 NE ISSN 0925-6806
STUDIA COPERNICANA - BRILL SERIES. 1991. irreg. price varies. E.J. Brill, P.O. Box 9000, 2300 PA Leiden, Netherlands. TEL 31-71-5353500. FAX 31-71-5317532. TELEX 39296 BRILL NL. E-mail: ejbrill@brill.nl. (In N. America: E.J. Brill, 24 Hudson St., Kinderhook, NY 12106. TEL 800-962-4406. FAX 518-758-1959) Ed. Pawel Czartoryski. R&P contact: Elizabeth Vennekamp. **Document type:** monographic series.
Refereed Serial

520 PL ISSN 0082-5573
STUDIA SOCIETATIS SCIENTIARUM TORUNENSIS. SECTIO F. ASTRONOMIA. (Text in English; summaries in Polish) 1956. irreg., vol.6, no.4, 1987. price varies. Towarzystwo Naukowe w Toruniu, Ul. Wysoka 16, 87-100 Torun, Poland. TEL 48-56-23941. TELEX 552388 FSBH PL. Ed. Cecylia Iwaniszewska. charts; illus.; index. circ. 650. **Document type:** monographic series.

520 JA ISSN 0288-1977
TENMON GAIDO/GUIDE TO ASTRONOMY. (Text in Japanese) 1965. m. 14460 Yen. Seibundo Shinkosha Publishing Co. Ltd., 1-13-7 Yayoi-cho, Nakano-ku, Tokyo 164, Japan. Ed. Yukihiro Takatsuki. circ. 200,000.

520 JA ISSN 0374-2466
CODEN: TGEPAC
TENMON GEPPO/ASTRONOMICAL HERALD. (Text in Japanese) 1908. m. 8400 Yen. Nihon Tenmon Gakkai - Astronomical Society of Japan, c/o National Astronomical Observatory, 21-1, Osawa 2-chome, Mitaka-shi, Tokyo 181, Japan. Ed. Y. Suematsu. adv.; bk.rev.; index. circ. 3,000. **Indexed:** Chem.Abstr., INIS Atomind., INSPEC (1970-1991), Jap.Per.Ind.
—AskIEEE; CASDDS; CISTI; KR SourceOne.

523.51 JA ISSN 0388-5852
TENMON KAIHO/ASTRONOMICAL CIRCULAR. (Text in Japanese) 1950. q. Nippon Ryusei Kenkyukai - Nippon Meteor Society, Yabu Tenmondai, 878 Maruyama-cho, Omihachiman-shi, Shiga-ken 523, Japan. TEL 0748-32-4539. FAX 0748-33-4892. Ed. Yasuo Yabu. **Document type:** academic/scholarly publication.
Formerly: Tenmon Sokuho.

523.01 CC ISSN 0253-2379
QB461 CODEN: TWXUDX
TIANTI WULI XUEBAO/ACTA ASTROPHYSICA SINICA. (Partial English translation: Chinese Astronomy and Astrophysics (ISSN 0275-1062) (Text in Chinese; summaries in English) 1980. q. $62.40. Science Press, Marketing and Sales Department, 16 Donghuangchenggen North St., Beijing 100717, People's Republic of China. TEL 4010642. FAX 4019810. adv. circ. 6,000. **Indexed:** Chem.Abstr., INSPEC (1984-), Math.R. **Document type:** academic/scholarly publication.
—AskIEEE; CASDDS; CISTI; KR SourceOne; Linda Hall.
Description: Contains articles on theoretical and observational astrophysics, astronomical methods and techniques, and research notes.
Refereed Serial

520 CC
TIANWEN AIHAOZHE/AMATEUR ASTRONOMER. (Text in Chinese) m. $0.40 per no. Guoji Shudian, Qikan Bu - China International Book Trading Corp., Chegongzhuang Xilu 21, P.O. Box 399, Beijing 100044, People's Republic of China.

520 CC ISSN 0001-5245
QB1 CODEN: TIWHAO
TIANWEN XUEBAO/ACTA ASTRONOMICA SINICA. Partial English translation: Chinese Astronomy and Astrophysics (CC ISSN 0275-1062) (Text in Chinese; summaries in English) 1953. q. $63.20. Science Press, Marketing and Sales Department, 16 Donghuangchenggen North St., Beijing 100717, People's Republic of China. TEL 4010642. FAX 4019810. adv. circ. 7,000. **Indexed:** INSPEC (1979-), Zent.Math. **Document type:** academic/scholarly publication.
—BLDSC (0598.500000); AskIEEE; CISTI; KR SourceOne; Linda Hall.
Description: Includes papers on theoretical astronomy, analysis of astronomical observations, application of the results of astronomical study, development of astronomical instruments, and the history of astronomy.
Refereed Serial

520 CC ISSN 1000-8349
TIANWENXUE JINZHAN/PROGRESS IN ASTRONOMY. (Text in Chinese; summaries in English) 1983. q. $45.60. (Chinese Academy of Sciences, Shanghai Astronomical Observatory) Science Press, Marketing and Sales Department, 16 Donghuangchenggen North St., Beijing 100717, People's Republic of China. TEL 4010642. FAX 4019810. adv. circ. 5,000. **Document type:** academic/scholarly publication.
—BLDSC (6865.928000).
Refereed Serial

TOHOKU UNIVERSITY. SCIENCE REPORTS. SERIES 8: PHYSICS AND ASTRONOMY. see *PHYSICS*

UCHU SEIBUTSU KAGAKU/BIOLOGICAL SCIENCE IN SPACE. see *BIOLOGY*

520 AT ISSN 0049-5506
UNIVERSE.* 1955. m. Aus.$24. Astronomical Society of New South Wales Incorporated, c/o Astronomical Society of S.A., G.P.O. Box 199, Australia. Ed. Peter Northfield. bk.rev. circ. 300.
Description: Provides information for members on astronomy and related topics.

521 372 US ISSN 0890-6866
UNIVERSE IN A CLASSROOM; a newsletter on astronomy for teachers. 1984. 3/yr. free to qualified personnel. Astronomical Society of the Pacific, 390 Ashton Ave., San Francisco, CA 94112. TEL 415-337-1100. FAX 415-337-5205. Ed. George Musser. illus. circ. 15,000. **Document type:** newsletter.
Description: For teachers of astronomy for grades 3-12, with information, activities and resource lists.

520 CL ISSN 0069-3553
UNIVERSIDAD DE CHILE. DEPARTAMENTO DE ASTRONOMIA. PUBLICACIONES. (Text and summaries in Spanish and English) 1967. irreg. free or exchange basis. (Universidad de Chile, Departamento de Astronomia) Editorial Universitaria, Avda. Santa Maria 1990, Casilla 3444 Correo Central, Santiago, Chile. Ed. Hugo Moreno. circ. 700. **Indexed:** Astron.& Astrophys.Abstr., Bull.Signal.
—CISTI.

520 MX ISSN 0185-2752
UNIVERSIDAD DE GUADALAJARA. INSTITUTO DE ASTRONOMIA Y METEOROLOGIA. BOLETIN INFORMATIVO MENSUAL. 1965. m. Mex.$180 (foreign $36) (effective 1997). Universidad de Guadalajara, Instituto de Astronomia y Meteorologia, Av. Vallarta Num. 2602, 44110 Guadalajara, Jal., Mexico. TEL 52-3-6164937. FAX 52-3-6159829. E-mail: dalba@udgserv.cencar.udg.mx. Ed.Bd. charts. circ. 150. (processed) **Document type:** bulletin.
Formerly: Universidad de Guadalajara. Instituto de Astronomia y Meteorologia. Informacion (ISSN 0041-8404)
Description: Covers astronomy news, astronomical phenomena, climatology, regional meteorological information, popularization articles on astronomy and meteorology.

520 BL ISSN 0100-5545
QB82.B672
UNIVERSIDADE DE SAO PAULO. INSTITUTO ASTRONOMICO E GEOFISICO. ANUARIO ASTRONOMICO. 1930-38; N.S. 1953; N.S. 1974. a. Cr.$130($6) Universidade de Sao Paulo, Instituto Astronomico e Geofisico, Biblioteca, Caixa Postal 30627, 01051 Sao Paulo, SP, Brazil. Ed. Paulo Benevides Soares. circ. 2,000. **Indexed:** Astron.& Astrophys.Abstr., Bull.Signal., Ref.Zh.
—CISTI; Linda Hall.
Formerly: Sao Paulo, Brazil (State). Observatorio. Anuario Astronomico (ISSN 0080-6412)

520 BE
UNIVERSITEIT TE GENT. STERRENKUNDIG OBSERVATORIUM. MEDEDELINGEN. (Text and summaries in Dutch, English) 1939. irreg. free. Universiteit te Gent, Sterrenkundig Observatorium, Krijgslaan 281, B-9000 Ghent, Belgium. TEL 32-9-2644798. FAX 32-9-2644989. **Document type:** academic/scholarly publication.
Formerly: Rijksuniversiteit te Gent. Sterrenkundig Observatorium. Mededelingen: Astronomie (ISSN 0072-4432)

520 YU ISSN 0350-3283
UNIVERSITY OF BELGRADE. FACULTY OF SCIENCES. DEPARTMENT OF ASTRONOMY. PUBLICATIONS. (Text and summaries in English, Russian) 1969. a. free. Univerzitet u Beogradu, Prirodno-Matematicki Fakultet, Katedra za Astronomiju, Studentski trg 16, 11000 Belgrade, Yugoslavia. Ed. Branislav Sevarlic. bibl.; charts; illus. circ. 500.
—CISTI.

UNIVERSITY OF BRITISH COLUMBIA. PHYSICS SOCIETY. JOURNAL. see *PHYSICS*

523.01 UK
UNIVERSITY OF LEICESTER. X-RAY ASTRONOMY GROUP. SPECIAL REPORT. irreg. £20. University of Leicester, X-Ray Astronomy Group, Leicester LE1 7RH, England. **Document type:** academic/scholarly publication, monographic series.

523.51 US ISSN 0085-3968
UNIVERSITY OF NEW MEXICO. INSTITUTE OF METEORITICS. SPECIAL PUBLICATION. 1970. irreg. (2-4/yr.). $10 per issue (or exchange basis). University of New Mexico, Institute of Meteoritics, Albuquerque, NM 87131. TEL 505-277-2747. FAX 505-277-3577. Ed. James J. Papike. circ. 1,000. (back issues avail.) **Indexed:** GeoRef.
Refereed Serial

520 JA ISSN 0563-8038
UNIVERSITY OF TOKYO. DEPARTMENT OF ASTRONOMY. CONTRIBUTIONS. (Text and summaries in English) 1959. irreg. University of Tokyo, Faculty of Science, Department of Astronomy - Tokyo Daigaku Rigakubu Tenmongaku Kyoshitsu, c/o Faculty of Science - Library, 3-1, Hongo 7-chome, Bunkyo-ku, Tokyo 113, Japan. **Document type:** academic/scholarly publication.

520 MX ISSN 0374-0501
UNIVERSO. vol.27, 1973. q. Mex.$32($12) Sociedad Astronomica de Mexico, Jardin Felipe Xicotencatl, Mexico 13, D.F., Mexico. Ed. Antonio R. Viaud. charts; illus.

ASTRONOMY — COMPUTER APPLICATIONS   503

520   PL   ISSN 0554-8233
UNIWERSYTET IM. ADAMA MICKIEWICZA. ASTRONOMIA. (Text in English or Polish; summaries in English) 1964. irreg., no.4, 1992. price varies. Adam Mickiewicz University Press, Nowowiejskiego 55, 61-734 Poznan, Poland. TEL 48-61-527380. FAX 48-61-527701. TELEX 413260 UAMPL. Pub. Maria Jankowska. R&P contact: Malgorzata Bis. **Document type:** academic/scholarly publication, monographic series.
 Formerly (until 1976): Uniwersytet im. Adama Mickiewicza w Poznaniu. Wydzial Matematyki, Fizyki i Chemii. Prace. Seria Astronomia (ISSN 0208-6492)
 Description: Contains current research results of the university's astronomers, their Ph.D. works, monographs and scientific works.

520   PL   ISSN 0042-0794
QB1
URANIA. (Text in Polish; contents page in English and Russian) 1922. m. 588 Zl.($13.20) Polskie Towarzystwo Milosnikow Astronomii - Polish Association of Friends of Astronomy, Ul. Solskiego 30 m. 8, 31-027 Krakow, Poland. TEL 386-25. (Dist. by: Ars Polona - Ruch, Krakowskie Przedmiescie 7, Warsaw, Poland) Ed. K. Ziolkowski. adv.; bk.rev.; charts; illus.; index. circ. 3,500. **Indexed:** Astron.& Astrophys.Abstr., GeoRef.
 —CISTI.
 Description: Popular scientific magazine dealing with different aspects of astronomic research and space conquest.

522.1   VC
VATICAN OBSERVATORY ANNUAL REPORT. (Text in English) 1970. a. free. Specola Vaticana - Vatican Observatory, 00120 Vatican City (Rome), State of the Vatican City. TEL 39-6-69885266. FAX 39-6-69884671. (U.S. addr.: Vatican Observatory Research Group, Steward Observatory, University of Arizona, Tucson, AZ 85721) Ed. George V. Coyne. circ. 500. (back issues avail.) **Indexed:** Astron. & Astrophys.Abstr. **Document type:** academic/scholarly publication.
 —CISTI.
 Supersedes in part (in 1994): Vatican Observatory Publications (ISSN 0083-5293)

520   GW   ISSN 0340-9821
VEROEFFENTLICHUNGEN DER ASTRONOMISCHEN INSTITUT DER UNIVERSITAET BONN. (Text in German; summaries in English) 1930. irreg. price varies. (Astronomische Institut der Universitaet Bonn-Sternwarte) Ferd. Duemmlers Verlag, Kaiserstr. 31-37, 53113 Bonn, Germany. (Subscr. to: Postfach 1480, 53004 Bonn, Germany)

520   US
VIA STELLARIS. 1958. m. $10. Von Braun Astronomical Society, Inc., Box 1142, Huntsville, AL 35807. TEL 205-539-0316. Ed. Crystal Kitchens. bk.rev. circ. 200. (looseleaf format) **Document type:** newsletter.
 Description: Information on astronomy and astrophotography. Includes calendar of local events and meetings.

520   UK   ISSN 0083-6656
QB1   CODEN: VASTA6
VISTAS IN ASTRONOMY; an international review journal. 1958. q. fl.1045($601) to institutions (effective 1998). Elsevier Science Ltd., Pergamon, P.O. Box 800, Kidlington, Oxford OX5 1DX, England. TEL 44-1865-843000. FAX 44-1865-843010. E-mail: nlinfo-f@elsevier.nl; usinfo-f@elsevier.com; forinfo-kyf04035@niftyserve.or.jp; URL: http://www.elsevier.nl:80/inca/publications/store/4/2/6/426.pub.shtml. (Subscr. to: Elsevier Science, Regional Sales Office, P.O. Box 211, 1000 AE Amsterdam, Netherlands. TEL 31-20-4853757. FAX 31-20-4853432; Subscr. in the Americas to: Elsevier Science, Regional Sales Office, Box 945, New York, NY 10159-0945. TEL 212-633-3730. FAX 212-633-3680; Subscr. in Australasia and the Far East to: Elsevier Science (Singapore) Pte Ltd, No.1 Temasek Ave., No.17-01 Millenia Tower, Singapore 039192, Singapore. TEL 65-434-3727. FAX 65-337-2230) Ed.Bd. index. (also avail. in microfilm from UMI) **Indexed:** Chem.Abstr., GeoRef., INSPEC, Int.Aerosp.Abstr., Math.R., Phys.Ber. **Document type:** academic/scholarly publication.
 —BLDSC (9241.180000); AskIEEE; CASDDS; CISTI; KR SourceOne; Linda Hall; UMI; UnCover. **CCC.**
 Incorporates (1977-1991): Astronomy Quarterly (ISSN 0364-9229)
 Refereed Serial

520   RU
VSELENNAYA I MY; al'manakh. (Text in Russian; summaries in English) 1993. irreg. Astronomicheskie Obshchestvo - Astronomical Society, University prosp. 13, 119899 Moscow, Russia. TEL 7-095-9391626. FAX 7-095-9328841. E-mail: konon@sai.msu.su. Ed. E.V. Kononovich. (back issues avail.)
 Description: Covers astronomy for general audience, teachers, and students.

520   IE   ISSN 0043-1680
WEBB SOCIETY QUARTERLY JOURNAL. 1969. q. £12($22) (effective 1996). Webb Society, c/o M.B. Swan, Ed., Carroweragh, Kilshanny, Kilfenora, Co. Clare, Ireland. TEL 353-65-71946. FAX 44-1705-862466. E-mail: 100014.3650@compuserve.com; URL: http://www.webbsociety.org. adv.; bk.rev.; charts; cum.index. circ. 450. (processed) **Document type:** academic/scholarly publication.
 Description: Intended as educational, for advanced amateur astronomers, membership world-wide.

ZEITSCHRIFT FUER NATURFORSCHUNG. SECTION A: A JOURNAL OF PHYSICAL SCIENCES. see PHYSICS

520   RU   ISSN 0044-3948
QB1   CODEN: ZEVSAM
ZEMLYA I VSELENNAYA. 1965. bi-m. $87 (effective 1998). (Rossiiskaya Akademiya Nauk) Izdatel'stvo Nauka, 90 Profsoyuznaya ul., 117864 Moscow, Russia. TEL 234-05-84. (Dist. by: Mezhdunarodnaya Kniga, ul. Dimitrova D.39, 113095 Moscow, Russia) Ed. D.Ja. Martinov. index. circ. 20,000. **Indexed:** Biol.Abstr., Chem.Abstr., Int.Aerosp.Abstr.
 —BLDSC (0072.080000); CISTI; KNAW; Linda Hall.

520   NE   ISSN 0165-0211
ZENIT. 1974. m. fl.95 (effective 1996). Stichting "De Koepel", Zonnenburg 2, 3512 NL Utrecht, Netherlands. TEL 31-30-2311360. FAX 31-30-2342852. Ed. E. Mathlener. adv.; bk.rev.; charts; illus.; index; circ. 7,500 (paid). **Indexed:** Astron.& Astrophys.Abstr., Excerp.Med. **Document type:** consumer publication.
 —CISTI; Linda Hall; SWETS.
 Supersedes: Hemel en Dampkring (ISSN 0018-0289); Macro (Utrecht).

ASTRONOMY — Abstracting, Bibliographies, Statistics

520 523.01 016   US   ISSN 0067-0022
Z5153
ASTRONOMY AND ASTROPHYSICS ABSTRACTS. (Published for Astronomisches Recheninstitut) 1969. irreg., vol.61, 1995. price varies. Springer-Verlag, 175 Fifth Ave., New York, NY 10010. TEL 212-460-1500. FAX 212-473-6272. (Also: Berlin, Heidelberg, Tokyo and Vienna) (reprint service avail. from ISI) **Indexed:** Phys.Ber. **Document type:** abstracting/indexing.
 —BLDSC (1762.971000); CISTI; Linda Hall. **CCC.**
 Supersedes: Astronomischer Jaresbericht.

523.019   JA
COSMIC RAY INTENSITY. (Text in English) 1959. irreg., no.37, 1996. Science Council of Japan, International Committee on Solar-Terrestrial Physics - Nihon Gakujutsu Kaigi, Kokusai Chikyu Kansoku Tokubetsu linkai, 22-34, Roppongi 7-chome, Minato-ku, Tokyo 106, Japan. stat.

METEOROLOGICAL AND GEOASTROPHYSICAL ABSTRACTS. see METEOROLOGY — Abstracting, Bibliographies, Statistics

520   JA
NIHON TENMON KENKYUKAI KANSOKU GEPPO/JAPAN ASTRONOMICAL STUDY ASSOCIATION. MONTHLY BULLETIN. (Text in Japanese) 1964. m. Nihon Tenmon Kenkyukai - Japan Astronomical Study Association, c/o Kokuritsu Kagaku Hakubutsukan, Rikagaku Kenkyubu, 7, Ueno Koen, Taito-ku, Tokyo 110, Japan. stat. **Document type:** bulletin.

P A S C A L E 48: ENVIRONNEMENT COSMIQUE TERRESTRE, ASTRONOMIE ET GEOLOGIE EXTRATERRESTRE. see EARTH SCIENCES — Abstracting, Bibliographies, Statistics

520   PH   ISSN 0115-1207
PHILIPPINE ASTRONOMICAL HANDBOOK. (Text in English) 1950. a. P.40($1.50) Philippine Atmospheric, Geophysical and Astronomical Services Administration, 1424 Quezon Ave., Quezon City 1101, Philippines. TELEX 42021-PAGASA-PM. Dir. Roman L. Kintanar. circ. 300. **Document type:** government publication.
 Description: Annual publication containing data on the sun, moon, planets and eclipses.

523.7   JA   ISSN 0048-6167
QUARTERLY BULLETIN ON SOLAR ACTIVITY. (Text in English, French) 1928. q. $30. (International Astronomical Union) National Astronomical Observatory, Kokuritsu Tenmondai, 21-1, Osawa 2-chome, Mitaka-shi, Tokyo 181, Japan. FAX 81-422-34-3700. bk.rev.; charts; stat. circ. 400. **Document type:** bulletin.

520 016   RU   ISSN 0486-2236
REFERATIVNYI ZHURNAL. ASTRONOMIYA. 1953. m. $674 (effective 1998). Vsesoyuznyi Institut Nauchno-Tekhnicheskoi Informatsii (VINITI), Baltiiskaya ul., 14, Moscow A-219, Russia. (Subscr. to: Mezhdunarodnaya Kniga, Dimitrova ul. 39, 113095 Moscow, Russia) **Document type:** abstracting/indexing.
 —CISTI; Linda Hall.

629.13 016   RU   ISSN 0034-2408
REFERATIVNYI ZHURNAL. ISSLEDOVANIE KOSMICHESKOGO PROSTRANSTVA. 1964. m. $341 (effective 1998). Vsesoyuznyi Institut Nauchno-Tekhnicheskoi Informatsii (VINITI), Baltiiskaya ul., 14, Moscow A-219, Russia. (Dist. by: Mezhdunarodnaya Kniga, B. Yakimanka 39, 117049 Moscow, Russia) **Document type:** abstracting/indexing.

523.53   JA   ISSN 0385-0994
RYUSEIJIN KAIHO/CIRCULAR OF METEORIC DUST. (Text in Japanese) 1964. bi-m. Morikubo Shigeru, Ed. & Pub., 1058, Oigawa, Atsugi-shi, Kanagawa-ken 243-02, Japan. stat.

523.58 551.527   JA
SOLAR TERRESTRIAL ACTIVITY CHART. (Text in English) a. Nihon Gakujutsu Kaigi, Joho Kokusaika - Science Council of Japan, Science Information and International Affairs Division, 22-34, Roppongi 7-chome, Minato-ku, Tokyo 106, Japan. charts; stat.

522   PH   ISSN 0115-3307
QB216
TABLE OF SUNRISE, SUNSET, TWILIGHT, MOONRISE AND MOONSET. (Text in English) a. P.40($1.50) Philippine Atmospheric, Geophysical and Astronomical Services Administration, 1424 Quezon Ave., Quezon City 1101, Philippines. TELEX 42021-PAGASA-PM. Dir. Roman L. Kintanar. circ. 450. **Document type:** government publication.
 Description: Sunrise and moonrise data for the Philippines.

520   JA
TAIYOKEI KAGAKU SHINPOJUMU. (Text in Japanese) a. Institute of Space and Astronautical Science - Uchu Kagaku Kenkyujo, 1-1, Yoshinodai 3-chome, Sagamihara-shi, Kanagawa-ken 229, Japan. abstr.
 Description: Contains abstracts from the Institute's symposium on solar system sciences.

ASTRONOMY — Computer Applications

522   US   ISSN 1074-875X
QB127.4
C C D ASTRONOMY; the magazine of electronic imaging. 1994. q. $22 (foreign $33); newsstand price: $5.95. Sky Publishing Corp., 49 Bay State Rd., Cambridge, MA 02138-1200. TEL 617-864-7360. FAX 617-576-0336. E-mail: ccda@skypub.com. URL: http://www.skypub.com. (Subscr. to: Box 9111, Belmont, MA 02178) Ed. Laurence A. Marschall; Pub. Richard Tresch Fienberg. adv. contact: Kim Bennett. bk.rev.; circ. 9,380 (paid). (also avail. in microform from UMI; back issues avail.; reprint service avail.) **Indexed:** Ind.How To Do It. **Document type:** consumer publication.
 —SWETS; UMI.
 Description: Covers all facets of electronic imaging and its applications in astronomy, highlighting the recreational, scientific, and aesthetic aspects of the C.C.D. revolution.

AUTOMATION

see Computers–Automation

AUTOMOBILES

see Transportation–Automobiles

BAKERS AND CONFECTIONERS

see Food and Food Industries–Bakers and Confectioners

BALL GAMES

see Sports and Games–Ball Games

BANKING AND FINANCE

see Business and Economics–Banking and Finance

BEAUTY CULTURE

see also Beauty Culture–Perfumes and Cosmetics

646.7   US
A A C S NEWS REPORT. m. American Association of Cosmetology Schools, c/o Ronald E. Smith, 901 N. Washington St., Ste. 206, Alexandria, VA 22314-1535. TEL 703-683-1700. FAX 703-683-2376. adv. **Document type:** newsletter.
Former titles: A A C S News; N A A C S News.

646.7   SA
AESTHETICS; professional hair, beauty, nails. 1994. m. R.114. Toxic Ratman Publishing Corp., P.O. Box 1707, Fourways 2055, South Africa. adv.; illus. **Document type:** trade publication.

AGRO FOOD INDUSTRY HI-TECH. see *AGRICULTURE*

646.7   IT   ISSN 1121-9580
ALLURE CLUB. 1993. bi-m. L.130000 (effective 1997). Target s.r.l., Via Bondi 23-2, 40138 Bologna, Italy. TEL 39-51-342426. FAX 39-51-34554. Ed. Rosetta Sannelli; Pub. Luciano Parisini. R&P contact: Diana Baravelli. **Document type:** consumer publication, trade publication.
Description: For operators in the accessory business: firm managers, beauty consultants, retailers and business agents.

646.7   MX
ALTO PEINADO. 1969. m. Mex.$120($70) Editorial Famari, Norte 72-A, no. 6120, Col. Gertrudiz Sanchez, C.P. 07830 Mexico, D.F., Mexico. TEL 760-9391. FAX 751-5918. Ed. Francisco Martinez Rios. adv.; film rev.; illus. **Document type:** consumer publication.

646.724   US   ISSN 0741-5737
TT950
AMERICAN SALON. (Supplement avail.: American Salon Distributor - Manufacturer News Edition) 1877. m. $24 (Canada $34; elsewhere $39) (effective 1996). (National Hairdressers and Cosmetologists Association) Advanstar Communications, Inc., 7500 Old Oak Blvd., Cleveland, OH 44130. TEL 216-826-2839. FAX 216-891-2726. (Subscr. to: 131 W. First St., Duluth, MN 55082. TEL 218-723-9477) Ed. Mathy McFarland. adv.; bk.rev.; illus.; tr.lit. circ. 130,032. (also avail. in microfilm from UMI; back issues avail.) **Document type:** trade publication.
—UMI. **CCC.**
Formerly: American Hairdresser - Salon Owner (ISSN 0095-1404); Which incorporated: Salon Owner (ISSN 0036-3553); Which was formerly: American Hairdresser.
Description: Focuses on management and technical information emphasizing the full service salon concept.

646.7   US
AMERICAN STYLIST. 1993. bi-m. $9.99; newsstand price: $1.99. Advanstar Communications, Inc., 7500 Old Oak Blvd., Cleveland, OH 44130. TEL 216-243-8100. FAX 216-891-2651. (Subscr. to: Box 6057, Duluth, MN 55806-9781. TEL 800-346-0085 ext. 477. FAX 218-723-9433; Editorial addr.: 270 Madison Ave., New York, NY 10016) Ed. Kathy McFarland; Pub. Marianne Dougherty. tr.lit. (back issues avail.) **Document type:** trade publication.
Description: Offers technical and business education, information on new products, educational opportunities and news about the industry.

646.724   AT
AUSTRALIAN PROFESSIONAL HAIRDRESSER. q. Aus.$35. T M P C (The Magazine Publishing Company), 34 Station St., P.O. Box 406, Nundah, Qld. 4012, Australia. TEL 61-7-32665000. FAX 61-7-32665577. E-mail: tmpc@powerup.com.au; URL: http://www.ausmall.com.au/magazine. Ed. Lesley Goodwin. adv.: B&W page Aus.$1581, color Aus.$2415; trim 275 x 210; adv. contact: Alan Kirk. circ. 2,000. **Document type:** trade publication.
Formerly: Queensland Professional Hairdresser.

646.7   GW
AYK AKTIV. q. (Ayk Beauty Sun-Sonnenstudios) Vereinigte Verlagsanstalten GmbH, Hoehrweg 278, 40231 Duesseldorf, Germany. TEL 49-211-7357-0. FAX 49-211-7357223. circ. 100,000. **Document type:** newsletter.

646.7 658.8   UK
BABY CARE PRODUCTS: THE INTERNATIONAL MARKET. (Subseries of: Market Direction reports) a. £2500($3000) (effective 1997). Euromonitor, 60-61 Britton St., London EC1M 5NA, England. TEL 44-171-251-8024. FAX 44-171-608-3149. E-mail: info@euromonitor.com; URL: http://www.euromonitor.com. (Addr. in N. America: Euromonitor International, 122 S. Michigan Ave., Ste. 1200, Chicago, IL 60603. TEL 800-577-3876. FAX 312-922-1157) (looseleaf format) **Document type:** trade publication.
•Also available online. Vendor(s): Data-Star, Knight-Ridder Information, Inc.
Description: Analyzes the markets for baby-care toiletries for France, Germany, Italy, Spain, the U.K., the U.S., Japan & Canada.

646.7 658.8   UK
BATH AND SHOWER PRODUCTS: THE INTERNATIONAL MARKET. (Subseries of: Market Direction reports) a. £2250($4500) (effective 1997). Euromonitor, 60-61 Britton St., London EC1M 5NA, England. TEL 44-171-251-8024. FAX 44-171-608-3149. E-mail: info@euromonitor.com; URL: http://www.euromonitor.com. (Addr. in N. America: Euromonitor International, 122 S. Michigan Ave., Ste. 1200, Chicago, IL 60603. TEL 800-577-3876. FAX 312-922-1157) (looseleaf format) **Document type:** trade publication.
•Also available online. Vendor(s): Data-Star, Knight-Ridder Information, Inc.
Description: Analyzes the bath and shower products market segment for France, Germany, Italy, Spain, the U.K., the U.S., and Japan.

646.7   SZ
BEAUTE INFORMATION. (Text in French, German, Italian) q. Rue Viguet 6, Case Postale 177, CH-1211 Geneva 26, Switzerland. TEL 022-432948. FAX 022-435644. Ed. Monique Raffier. circ. 127,200.

646.7 668.5   FR   ISSN 0408-7496
BEAUTERAMA. 1960. bi-m. 380 F. (foreign 650 F.). 116 quai Louis Bleriot, 75016 Paris, France. TEL 45202136. Ed. Chantal Le Creurer. adv.: B&W page 15200 F., color page 18100 F.; trim 225 x 320. circ. 5,000. **Document type:** catalog, directory.

646.7 053.1   AU
BEAUTY. 1982. m. S.380 (foreign S.600). H.J. Pichler Verlagsgesellschaft, Muthgasse 109, Postfach 16, A-1195 Vienna, Austria. TEL 43-1-31851510. FAX 43-1-375736. Ed. Hans Pichler. adv.: B&W page S.57000; trim 213 x 285; adv. contact: Hans Pichler. bk.rev.; circ. 80,000. (back issues avail.) **Document type:** consumer publication.
Formerly (until 1992): Neue Beauty.

646.7   GW
BEAUTY CARE SUPPLY GUIDE. (Text in English) 1989. a. $50 (effective 1997). Made in Europe Marketing Organisation GmbH, Hahnstr. 70, 60528 Frankfurt a.M., Germany. TEL 49-69-6680380. FAX 49-69-66803838. E-mail: 100734.3642@compuserve.com; URL: http://www.miesys.com. Ed. Martin Romer; Pub. Martin Romer. R&P contact: Martin Romer. adv. contact: Franziska Bastanier. circ. 15,000. (back issues avail.) **Document type:** catalog, directory.
•Also available on CD-ROM.
Description: International purchasing handbook for importers, distributors, agents and traders in over 180 countries.

646.72   US   ISSN 1052-4169
BEAUTY EDUCATION. 1948. m. Milady Publishing Company (Subsidiary of: Delmar Publishers Inc.), 3 Columbia Cir., Box 125-19, Albany, NY 12212-2519. TEL 518-464-3569; 800-998-7498. FAX 518-464-0358. (Subscr. to: Beauty Education, Box 640, Holmes, PA 19043) Ed. Susan Pena; Pub. Barbara Leto. adv.; bk.rev.; illus. circ. 4,000. **Document type:** trade publication.
Formerly: National Beauty School Journal (ISSN 0027-8769)
Description: Contains articles, news, and departments on cosmetology education and beauty culture for cosmetology educators.

646.7   GW   ISSN 0944-0364
BEAUTY FORUM. 1985. m. DM.99 (foreign DM.111) (effective 1997). Verlag G. Braun GmbH, Karl-Friedrich-Str. 14-18, 76133 Karlsruhe, Germany. TEL 49-721-165-0. FAX 49-721-165148. Ed. Ulrike Hemer-Seitz. adv. contact: Diana Konrad. **Document type:** consumer publication.

646.7 658   US   ISSN 1078-1781
BEAUTY INC.. 1994. bi-m. free. Beauty & Barber Supply Institute, Inc., 11811 N. Tatum Blvd., Ste. 1085, Phoeniz, AZ 85028-1625. TEL 602-404-1800. FAX 602-404-8900. E-mail: denise@bbsi.org; URL: http://www.bbsi.org. Ed. Denise M. Rucci; Pub. Frederic P. Polk. R&P contact: Denise M. Rucci. adv. contact: Diane Haggard. circ. 5,000. (controlled). **Document type:** trade publication.
Description: Covers beauty and barber supplies distribution trends, regulations, technology, and trade show news.
Refereed Serial

646   IT   ISSN 0392-2669
BEAUTY-LINE. 1974. 11/yr. L.70000 (foreign L.120000). SEPEM s.r.l., Via Grado 9, 20125 Milan, Italy. TEL 39-2-26825530. FAX 39-2-26823952. Ed. Franco Mattei. adv. circ. 35,000.
Description: Covers hairdressing, aesthetics and perfumery.

646.72   SP
BELLEZA Y MODA. 1966. m. 3300 ptas. (foreign 15515 ptas.); newsstand price: 375 ptas. R B A Revistas, S.A., Perez Galdos 36, 08012 Barcelona, Spain. TEL 34-3-4157374. FAX 34-3-2177378. (Dist. by: Midesa, Ctra. Irun, 13350, 28034 Madrid, Spain. TEL 34-1-6621000. FAX 34-1-6621462; Alt. addr. Avda. Principe de Asturias, 66-4o 3o 08012 Barcelona, Spain. TEL 34-3-4152322. FAX 34-3-2380730) Ed. Silvia Arenas. adv.: page 760000 ptas.; trim 230 X 297; adv. contact: Adriana Hernandez. charts; illus.; pat.; tr.lit.; tr.mk.; circ. 26,481 (paid). (back issues avail.) **Document type:** consumer publication.
Former titles: Belleza y Moda - Votre Beaute & Belleza y Moda (ISSN 0005-8629)

BIBA. see *CLOTHING TRADE — Fashions*

646.7 910.03   US   ISSN 1058-0956
BLAC-TRESS. bi-m. $17.77. Harris Publications, Inc., 1115 Broadway, 8th Fl., New York, NY 10010. TEL 212-807-7100. FAX 212-627-4678. **Document type:** consumer publication.

646.724   UK   ISSN 0263-3213
BLACK BEAUTY & HAIR. 1982. q. £11($20) Hawker Consumer Publishing Ltd., 13 Park House, 140 Battersea Park Rd., London SW11 4NB, England. TEL 0171-720-2108. FAX 0171-498-0266. Ed. Irene Shelley; Pub. Pat Petker. adv. contact: Pat Petker. circ. 21,101 (paid). (back issues avail.) **Document type:** consumer publication.

BEAUTY CULTURE

646.724 910.03 US
BLACK BEAUTY HANDBOOK. 1987. 2/yr. $0.99 per no. Beauty Handbook Corporation, 74 Holly Hill Ln., 3rd Fl., Greenwich, CT 06830-6098. TEL 203-869-5553. Ed. Andrea Sercu. circ. 500,000.

646.7 SA
BLACK SALON. 1994. m. R.60. Toxic Ratman Publishing Corp., P.O. Box 1707, Fourways 2055, South Africa. adv.; illus. **Document type:** trade publication.

BOA FORMA. see *PHYSICAL FITNESS AND HYGIENE*

646.7 613.7 II
BODY & BEAUTY CARE. (Text in English) 1982. fortn. Publicity Society of India Ltd., Free Press House, 215 Nariman Point, Bombay 400 021, India. TEL 2853335. Ed. M.S. Kamath; Pub. R. Mani. adv.: B&W page Rs.9000, color page Rs.18000; trim 163 x 240.

BRITAIN'S TOP TOILETRY AND DETERGENT COMPANIES. see *BUSINESS AND ECONOMICS — Trade And Industrial Directories*

BURDA INTERNATIONAL. see *CLOTHING TRADE*

646.7 SZ
BURDA MODEN (ARABIC EDITION). 1985. m. DM.105.60. I P M International Press & Marketing S.A., 2 Cours de Rive, CH-1204 Geneva, Switzerland. TEL 022-3105357. FAX 022-3105327. TELEX 423052-CH. (Subscr. to: Verlag Aenne Burda GmbH, Am Kestendamm 2, 77652 Offenburg, Germany) Ed. A. Hazan. circ. 94,092. **Document type:** consumer publication.

343.794 US
CALIFORNIA. STATE BOARD OF BARBERING AND COSMETOLOGY. RULES AND REGULATIONS. 1929. irreg. free. State Board of Barbering and Cosmetology, 400 R St. No. 4080, Sacramento, CA 95814-6213. TEL 916-445-7061. **Document type:** government publication.
Formerly: California. State Board of Cosmetology. Rules and Regulations (ISSN 0094-4327)
Description: Alerts readers to updates and revisions in the California state rules and regulations affecting the barber and cosmetology sectors.

646.724 US
CALIFORNIA STYLIST & SALON. m. $15 (foreign $30) (effective 1997). Holland Graphics, 1750 S.W. Skyline Blvd., Ste. 24, Portland, OR 97221-2533. TEL 503-297-7010. FAX 503-297-7022. E-mail: hollandgfx@aol.com. Ed. Linda Holland. adv. contact: Joel Holland. circ. 41,000. (tabloid format; back issues avail.)
Description: Official publication for the cosmetology unit of the California Dept. of Consumer Affairs.

646.7 US ISSN 1041-0430
CAMEO; exaltation of woman. 1988. bi-m. $6 per no. Pygmalion Publications, 7 Morningwood Dr., Laguna Niguel, CA 92677. TEL 714-661-1674. Ed. Daniel Nicolas. adv. circ. 100,000.
Description: Covers hair styles, manicures, skin care, makeup and fashion.

CHIMICA OGGI/CHEMISTRY TODAY. see *CHEMISTRY*

CLIN D'OEIL. see *CLOTHING TRADE — Fashions*

646.742 GW
CLIPS. 1984. m. DM.140 (effective 1997). Clips Verlags GmbH, Wilhelm-Backhaus-Str. 2, 50931 Cologne, Germany. TEL 49-221-944067-0. FAX 49-221-94406710. Ed. Heidrun Barbie. adv.: B&W page DM.3589, color page DM.6281; trim 230 x 297; adv. contact: Gaby Contoli. bk.rev.; charts; illus.; tr.lit.; index. circ. 28,619. **Document type:** trade publication.
Incorporates (1947-1993): Frisur und Kosmetik (ISSN 0323-410X); Which was formerly: Frisur (ISSN 0016-1489)
Description: Trade publication for hairdressers and beauty salons. Covers new fashion hairstyles, hair care, beauty care, reports of events, tips, and new cosmetic products.

646.724 NE ISSN 0165-3679
COIFFURE; vaktijdschrift voor de kapper/ondernemer. 1972. m. fl.174.50. Samsom Bedrijfsinformatie B.V. (Subsidiary of: Wolters Kluwer N.V.), Postbus 4, 2400 MA Alphen aan den Rijn, Netherlands. TEL 31-172-466775. FAX 31-172-440681. Ed. N. Bruinenga; Pub. E. Stolwerk. adv.; bk.rev.; index; circ. 4,430 (controlled). **Document type:** trade publication.

646.7 GR
COIFFURE AND NAIL DESIGN. q.? free to qualified personnel. I.C.O. International, 3A Barbanou, P.O. Box 190 25, 117 10 Athens, Greece. TEL 30-1-9010-016. FAX 30-1-9016-663. adv.: B&W page DM.1800; color page DM.2000. **Document type:** trade publication.

646.724 FR ISSN 0751-5960
COIFFURE DE PARIS. 1909. 11/yr. $75. Coiffure de Paris SA., 38 rue Jean Mermoz, 75008 Paris, France. TEL 43-12-87-03. FAX 43-12-87-57. Ed. M. Vincent. adv.; illus. circ. 35,000.
Formerly (until 1969): Hebdo Coiffure (ISSN 0010-034X)
Description: Discusses hairdressing techniques.

382 FR ISSN 1161-899X
COIFFURE ET STYLES. 1946. m. 285 F. (Federation Nationale de la Coiffure) S.E.I.D., 1-3 Place de la Bourse, 75002 Paris, France. TEL 42 61 53 24. Dir. Marc Betbeder. adv. circ. 37,300.
Formerly (until 1991): Coiffeur de France (ISSN 0750-3563)
Description: Information about laws concerning hairdressers, hair fashion and beauty profession news.

646.7 NE ISSN 0927-7927
COIFFURE GALLERY. 1979. 4/yr. fl.152.50. Samsom Bedrijfsinformatie B.V. (Subsidiary of: Wolters Kluwer N.V.), Postbus 4, 2400 MA Alphen aan den Rijn, Netherlands. TEL 31-172-466775. FAX 31-172-440681. Ed. N. Bruinenga. adv.; illus. circ. 2,200. **Document type:** trade publication.
Formerly: Photo Gallery.

646.7 SP ISSN 0214-5790
COIFFURE PROFESSIONNELLE. 1983. 11/yr. Prensa Hispanoamericana, S.A., Gascuena 21, 28022 Madrid, Spain. TEL 1-747-80-00. FAX 1-747-90-56. Ed. Angeles M. Martinez. circ. 17,000.

646.7 US
COLOR NEWS. 1986. q. $20. Pantone, Inc., 590 Commerce Blvd., Carlstadt, NJ 07072. TEL 201-935-5500. FAX 201-896-0242. Ed. Leatrice Eiseman. stat. circ. 100,000. (back issues avail.) **Document type:** newsletter.
Description: Examines all aspects of color in everyday life, both professional and personal.

668.5 US ISSN 0589-8447
COSMETIC WORLD. 1967. w. $175 (foreign $250) (effective 1997). Ledes Group, Inc., 530 Fifth Ave., Ste. 430, New York, NY 10036-5101. TEL 212-840-8800. FAX 212-840-7246. Ed. John G. Ledes. adv.: B&W page $2350; trim 7 x 10. bk.rev. circ. 5,048. (back issues avail.) **Document type:** newsletter, trade publication.
Description: Covers marketing, sales, retailing and technical management of the cosmetic, fragrance and toiletry industry.

646.7 US
COSMETICS: LATIN AMERICAN INDUSTRIAL REPORT. (Avail. for each of 22 Latin American countries) 1985. a. $435 per country report. Aquino Productions, Box 125, Rochester, VT 05767.

646.7 UK
CUTTING EDGE. 11/yr. 32 Vauxhall Bridge Rd., London SW1V 2SS, England. TEL 071-973-6636. FAX 071-233-5081. Ed. Damian Hockney. circ. 25,000.

646.7 658.8 UK
DEODORANTS: THE INTERNATIONAL MARKET. (Subseries of: Market Direction reports) a. £2250($4500) (effective 1997). Euromonitor, 60-61 Britton St., London EC1M 5NA, England. TEL 44-171-251-8024. FAX 44-171-608-3149. E-mail: info@euromonitor.com; URL: http://www.euromonitor.com. (Addr. in N. America: Euromonitor International, 122 S. Michigan Ave., Ste. 1200, Chicago, IL 60603. TEL 800-577-3876. FAX 312-922-1157) (looseleaf format) **Document type:** trade publication.
●Also available online. Vendor(s): Data-Star, Knight-Ridder Information, Inc.
Description: Analyzes the deodorants market segment for France, Germany, Italy, Spain, the U.K., the U.S., and Japan.

646.7 US
DERMASCOPE; the encyclopedia of aesthetics. 1973. bi-m. $35 (Canada $55; elsewhere $75). Aestheticians International Association, Dermascope Magazine, 3939 E. Hwy. 80, Ste. 408, Mesquite, TX 75150. TEL 972-682-9510; 800-961-3777. FAX 972-686-5901. URL: http://www.dermascope.com. Ed. Saundra Wallens. adv. contact: Glenn Dietel. bk.rev. circ. 15,000. (back issues avail.) **Document type:** trade publication.
Description: Covers a wide variety of subjects related to skin care, make up and body spa therapy with related subjects which affect the beauty and aging of the skin.

DETOUR. see *WOMEN'S INTERESTS*

646.7 US ISSN 1073-290X
DR. HAIR COSMETOLOGY NEWS JOURNAL. 1994. bi-m. $12. (Dr. Hair Product Company) Michael's Hair Design Studio, 12777 Jones Rd., Ste. 425, Houston, TX 77070. TEL 713-897-9171. FAX 713-370-8887. E-mail: 74104.2317@compuserve.com. Ed. R. Michael Tucker. adv.: page $380. charts; illus. circ. 1,500. **Document type:** consumer publication.
Description: Acts as a forum for professional and student cosmetologists.

EBONY. see *ETHNIC INTERESTS*

646.724 FR ISSN 1153-950X
ECLAIREUR DES COIFFEURS. 1904. 44/yr. 250 F. (foreign 380 F.) 60-62 rue du Faubourg St. Martin, 75010 Paris, France. Ed. P. Salomon. adv. circ. 36,000.

ELECTROLYSIS WORLD. see *MEDICAL SCIENCES — Dermatology And Venereology*

ELEGANTISSIMA. see *CLOTHING TRADE — Fashions*

ELLE; Hong Kong. see *WOMEN'S INTERESTS*

646.7 IT
ESTETICA BEAUTY; rivista professionale di bellezza. bi-m. Edizioni E.S.A.V. s.r.l., Via Cavour 50, 10123 Turin, Italy. TEL 011-8398657. FAX 011-812-5661. TELEX 224067 ESATO I. Ed. A. Valle. adv.: color page L.4300000; trim 187 x 257. circ. 14,466.

646 IT
ESTETICA MODACAPELLI/ESTETICA HAIRFASHION. (Editions in English, German, Italian, Portuguese, Spanish) 1946. bi-m. L.117000($97) (effective Jan. 1992). Edizioni E.S.A.V. S.r.l., Via Cavour 50, 10123 Turin, Italy. TEL 011-8398657. FAX 011-8125661. TELEX 224067 ESATO I. Ed. Roberto Pissimiglia. adv.: B&W page L.4200000, color page L.5800000; trim 187 x 257. circ. 95,000. Indexed: Artbibl.Mod.
Description: Presents hairstyles from all over the world. Contains news, tips, reports, and techniques.

646.72 NE ISSN 0014-1321
ESTHETICIENNE. 1965. m. fl.127.20. Koggeschip Vakbladen B.V., Postbus 1198, 1000 BD Amsterdam, Netherlands. TEL 31-20-6916666. FAX 31-20-6960396. Ed. Marco D.M. Jouret; Pub. E.A. van Trigt. adv. contact: Ronald Vedder. illus. circ. 7,500. **Document type:** trade publication.

646.7 FR ISSN 0220-1941
ESTHETIQUE. 1969. 11/yr. 8 rue Fort-Notre-Dame, 13007 Marseille, France. TEL 91-33-45-20. FAX 91-54-48-06. Ed. J.M. Mondoloni. circ. 6,500.
Formerly (until 1976): Revue Francaise de l'Esthetique (ISSN 0220-195X)

BEAUTY CULTURE

646.7   SP
ESTILISMO.* 11/yr. Ediciones Tecno-Imagen S.A., Avda. Valdelaparra 27, local 10, 28100 Madrid, Spain. TEL 1-302-80-81. FAX 1-766-20-43. Ed. Arturo Munoz. circ. 15,000.

EVA. see CLOTHING TRADE — Fashions

FASHIONSTANCE. see CLOTHING TRADE — Fashions

FORMA IN MODO NATURALE. see PHYSICAL FITNESS AND HYGIENE

646.742   GW   ISSN 0724-1291
FRISEURWELT AKTUELL. 1949. m. DM.132 (foreign DM.155) (effective 1997). Terra Verlag GmbH, Postfach 102144, 78421 Konstanz, Germany. TEL 49-7531-812244. FAX 49-7531-812299. Ed.Bd. adv.; bk.rev.; charts; illus.; stat.; tr.lit. circ. 30,000. **Document type:** trade publication. —CCC.
   Formerly (until 1983): Friseurwelt (ISSN 0016-1470)

646.724   DK
FRISOERFAGET. 1959. 11/yr. DKK 440($13) (ReproHuset) OR2 Grafisk Hus A-S, Smallegade 10, 1 tv., DK-2000 Frederiksberg, Denmark. TEL 45-97-22-48-85. FAX 45-97-22-01-80. E-mail: reprohus@postl.tele.dk. Ed. Benny Rosborg. R&P contact: Karen Linger. adv.: B&W page DKK 6050, color page DKK 14000; trim 190 x 277; adv. contact: Helle Jensen. circ. 6,200. **Document type:** trade publication.
   Formerly: Frisoerfagene (ISSN 0901-2737)

GLAMOUR. see CLOTHING TRADE — Fashions

646.7   MP
GOO MARAL/BEAUTIFUL DOE. (Text in Mongolian) 1990. bi-m. Association of Women, Ulan Bator, Mongolia. TEL 21035. circ. 50,000.

646.7   US
GREEN BOOK (CLEVELAND); the annual manufacturer's & distributor's marketing & reference guide for the professional salon industry. a. $70 (effective 1996). Advanstar Communications, Inc., 7500 Old Oak Blvd., Cleveland, OH 44130. TEL 216-826-2839. FAX 216-891-2726. (Subscr. to: 131 W. First St., Duluth, MN 55802. TEL 800-346-0085) Ed. Susan Sommers. circ. 1,036. **Document type:** directory, trade publication.
   Description: Marketing and buying guide providing listings of distributors, manufacturers, products and services, key executives and demographics.

646   IT
LA GRIFFE; moda & immagine. (Text in English, French, German, Italian and Spanish) 1960. bi-m. L.160000 (foreign $200). Fregoli Editore s.r.l., Via Lanino 5, 20144 Milan, Italy. TEL 02-48952284. FAX 02-48952716. adv. circ. 18,000.
   Former titles (until 1988): Zeffiro Italia; Zeffiro.

646.724   UK   ISSN 0143-7968
HAIR. 1977. bi-m. £12.60 (foreign £16.20) (effective 1996). I P C Magazines, Southbank Publishing Group (Subsidiary of: Reed Elsevier group), King's Reach Tower, Stamford St., London SE1 9LS, England. TEL 44-171-261-5000. FAX 44-1444-445599. TELEX 892084 REEDBP G. (Dist. by: Quadrant Subscription Services, Oakfield House, Perrymount Rd., Haywards Heath, W. Sussex RH16 3DH, England. TEL 44-1444-445555) Ed. Annette Dennis. adv. contact: Christina Michell. circ. 174,443. **Document type:** consumer publication.

646.7   JA
HAIR & BEAUTY. (Text in Japanese) 4/yr. Kodansha Ltd., 12-21 Otowa 2-chome, Bunkyo-ku, Tokyo 112, Japan. TEL 03-5395-3445. FAX 03-3945-4821. TELEX J34509 KODANSHA. Ed. Takashi Sasagawa. circ. 150,000. **Document type:** consumer publication.
   Description: Beauty magazine for 15-28 years old.

646.7 658.8   UK
HAIR CARE PRODUCTS: THE INTERNATIONAL MARKET. (Subseries of: Market Direction reports) a. £2500($5000) (effective 1997). Euromonitor, 60-61 Britton St., London EC1M 5NA, England. TEL 44-171-251-8024. FAX 44-171-608-3149. E-mail: info@euromonitor.com. (Addr. in N. America: Euromonitor International, 122 S. Michigan Ave., Ste. 1200, Chicago, IL 60603. TEL 800-577-3876. FAX 312-922-1157) (looseleaf format) **Document type:** trade publication.
   ●Also available online. Vendor(s): Data-Star, Knight-Ridder Information, Inc.
   Description: Analyzes the markets for hair-care products in France, Germany, Italy, Spain, the U.K., the U.S., Japan, and Canada.

646.7   US   ISSN 0887-803X
HAIR INTERNATIONAL NEWS. bi-m. $25. (Associated Master Barbers and Beauticians of America) Hair International, Box 273, Palmyra, PA 17078-0273. Ed. Franz Singer. adv. contact: Linda Yiengst. circ. 700. (back issues avail.)

646.7 910.03   US
HAIR TODAY. bi-m. Alfond Publications, 315 E. 65th St., Ste. 3H, New York, NY 10021-6848. TEL 212-744-8981. FAX 212-744-8478. Ed. Anne Alfond. adv.; bk.rev. circ. 150,000. **Document type:** consumer publication.
   Former titles: Unique Hair Today; (until 1993): Black Hair Today - Beauty and Lifestyles.

646.724   UK   ISSN 0143-6910
HAIRDRESSERS' JOURNAL INTERNATIONAL. 1882. w. £65. Reed Business Information (Subsidiary of: Reed Elsevier group), Quadrant House, The Quadrant, Sutton, Surrey SM2 5AS, England. TEL 44-181-652-3500. Ed. Sonia Young. adv.; bk.rev.; illus.; tr.mk. circ. 15,500. **Document type:** trade publication.
   Formerly: Hairdressers' Journal (ISSN 0017-6761)

646.724   UK   ISSN 0954-2787
HAIRFLAIR. 1982. m. £21 (foreign £35); newsstand price: £1.80. Hair and Beauty Ltd., 27 Maddox St., 4th Fl., London W1R 9LE, England. TEL 44-171-493-3533. FAX 44-171-499-6686. Ed. Joani Walsh; Pub. James Kimber. adv.: B&W page £1000, color page £1725; trim 209 x 295; adv. contact: Darren Newton. circ. 56,000 (paid). **Document type:** consumer publication.

646.724 746.92   AT   ISSN 1320-9469
HAIRTELL. 1959. m. Aus.$40 (foreign Aus.$55) to non-members. Professional Hairdressers' Association, Level 10, 60 Pitt St., Sydney, N.S.W. 2000, Australia. TEL 61-2-92475500. FAX 61-2-92475553. Ed. Linden Swan. adv.; cum.index. circ. 1,600. **Document type:** newsletter, trade publication.
   Formerly (until vol.30, no.4, 1989): Hair Fashions Magazine.
   Description: Provides industrial news of the hairdressing and industry.

646.724   IC
HAR OG FEGURD/HAIR AND BEAUTY MAGAZINE; timarit harsnyrtiidnadarins og Felags Islenskra Snyrtifraedinga. 1980. 3/yr. ISK 1400($27) (effective 1996). Timaritid Har og Fegurd, Skulagata 54, IS-105 Reykjavik, Iceland. TEL 354-562-8141. FAX 354-562-8141. E-mail: pmelsted@vortex.is; URL: http://www.vortex.is/fashion. Ed. Petur Melsted.
   Description: Publishes articles and other information on fashion in hair styling, clothes design, cosmetics and make-up, as well as on environmental protection.

646.7   IE
HEALTH & BEAUTY. 1985. 6/yr. I£20 in Ireland & U.K.; elsewhere I£30 (effective 1997). H B Publications, 10 Woodford, Brewery Rd., Blackrock, Co. Dublin, Ireland. TEL 2945095. Ed. Max Stephenson. adv.: B&W page I£450, color page I£800; adv. contact: David Briggs. bk.rev. circ. 11,000. **Document type:** consumer publication.
   Description: Covers health, beauty, fitness, slimming, diet, nutrition, and more.

646.7   UK
HEALTH & BEAUTY SALON; for health and beauty therapists. 1980. m. £31. Reed Business Information (Subsidiary of: Reed Elsevier group), Quadrant House, The Quadrant, Sutton, Surrey SM2 5AS, England. TEL 44-181-652-3500. FAX 44-181-652-3958. Ed. Jayne Fisher. adv. contact: Steve James. illus. circ. 9,100. **Document type:** trade publication.
   Formerly: Beauty Salon (ISSN 0261-4146)

646.7   AT
HIGHLIGHTS. 1992. s-a. Aus.$60. Highlights Publications, 40 George St., Liechhardt, N.S.W. 2040, Australia. TEL 61-2-5643617. FAX 61-2-5645418. Ed. Mark Stapleton; Pub. Mark Stapleton. adv.: page Aus.$3000; trim 240 x 330; adv. contact: Mark Stapleton. circ. 10,000. (back issues avail.) **Document type:** trade publication.

646.724 338   US   ISSN 0277-0334
HOW TO DOUBLE YOUR INCOME; monthly report for hairstylists. 1981. m. $49.50. 7112 N. 15th Pl., Phoenix, AZ 85020-5416. TEL 800-486-3033. FAX 602-395-9624. Ed. E. Kenneth Lange. adv.; bk.rev. circ. 1,560.
   Description: Provides technical, promotional and motivational materials for the professional hairstylist and-or salon owner.

646.724   US   ISSN 1056-4632
HYPE HAIR; for Black teens. 1992. bi-m. $18 (foreign $23). Word Up! Publications, Inc., 210 Rte. 4 E., Ste. 401, Paramus, NJ 07652. TEL 201-843-4004. FAX 201-843-8636. circ. 75,000. **Document type:** consumer publication.
   Description: Covers beauty haircare for African American women.

I F M T MAGAZINE. (International Fashion Model & Talent) see CLOTHING TRADE — Fashions

646.7   UK
INSTITUTE OF ELECTROLYSIS. LIST OF QUALIFIED OPERATORS. SYLLABUS PROSPECTUS. 1962. a. membership. Institute of Electrolysis, 251 Seymour Grove, Manchester M16 ODS, England. circ. (controlled). **Document type:** newsletter.

INTERNATIONAL DIRECTORY OF PAGEANTS. see WOMEN'S INTERESTS

646   CN   ISSN 1189-4695
JUST YOU NOW. 1982. 4/yr. Can.$14.95 for 8 issues. Family Communications, Inc., 37 Hanna Ave., Toronto, ON M6K 1X1, Canada. Ed. Bettie Bradley. circ. 226,000. (back issues avail.) **Indexed:** Can.B.P.I. **Document type:** consumer publication.
   Former titles: You - Verve (ISSN 0841-6648); Formed by the merger of: You (ISSN 0828-1238); Verve (ISSN 0829-7762); Which was formerly: All about You.

646.724   FI   ISSN 0022-7714
KAHERTAJA. 1917. 6/yr. FIM 660. Suomen Kahertajaliitto - Finnish Hairdressers Association, Makelankatu 54 A, FIN-00510 Helsinki, Finland. TEL 358-0-735008. FAX 358-0-715276. Ed. Juhani Lehtonen. R&P contact: Juhani Lehtonen. adv. contact: Jari Makelainen. bk.rev.; illus. circ. 2,200. **Document type:** trade publication.
   Description: Geared towards the hairdressing trade. Presents latest news in the industry plus a calendar of events.

646.724   GW   ISSN 0022-8176
KAMM UND SCHERE; Zeitschrift fuer den jungen Friseur 1959. 6/yr. DM.39.60 (foreign DM.47) (effective 1997). Terra Verlag GmbH, Postfach 102144, 78421 Konstanz, Germany. TEL 49-7531-8122-0. FAX 49-7531-812299. Eds. Susanne Reiss, Renate Probst. adv.; bk.rev. circ. 29,800. **Document type:** trade publication. —CCC.

646.7   BE   ISSN 0775-8952
KAPPER EN KAPSELS; maandblad van het kappersvak. French edition: Coiffeur et Coiffures (ISSN 0775-8944) 1949. 9/yr. A.P.I.C., Dieweg 294, Brussels 1180, Belgium. TEL 32-2-3754444. FAX 32-2-3755257. adv.: B&W page 32100 BEF; color page 64200 BEF; trim 210 x 297. circ. 10,900. (6,000 Dutch ed.; 4,900 French ed.). **Document type:** trade publication.
   Supersedes (in 1988): Kapper (ISSN 0775-8936); Coiffeur (ISSN 0775-8928)
   Description: For the hairdressing trade.

BEAUTY CULTURE

646.72 **FI** **ISSN 0047-3308**
KAUNEUS JA TERVEYS. 1956. m. FIM 495. A-Lehdet Oy, Hitsaajankatu 7, FIN-00081 A-Lehdet, Finland. FAX 358-0-786-858. Ed. Irmeli Castren. circ. 60,505. **Document type:** consumer publication.
  Description: Offers expert advice on beauty care, human relations, mental health and physical exercise.

646.7 **UK**
KEY NOTE MARKET REPORT: BATHS & SANITARYWARE. Variant title: Baths & Sanitaryware. irreg., no.7, 1993. £205. Key Note Ltd., Field House, 72 Oldfield Rd., Hampton, Middlesex TW12 2HQ, England. TEL 44-181-783-0755. FAX 44-181-783-0049. **Document type:** trade publication.
  ●Also available online.
  Also available on CD-ROM.
  Formerly: Key Note Report: Baths and Sanitaryware (ISSN 0957-7300)

646.7 **UK**
KEY NOTE MARKET REPORT: TOILETRIES. Variant title: Toiletries. irreg., no.10, 1994. £285. Key Note Ltd., Field House, 72 Oldfield Rd., Hampton, Middlesex TW12 2HQ, England. TEL 44-181-783-0755. FAX 44-181-783-0049. **Document type:** trade publication.
  ●Also available online.
  Also available on CD-ROM.
  Formerly: Key Note Report: Toiletries.

KIELS FEINE ADRESSEN. see *GENERAL INTEREST PERIODICALS — Germany*

KOELN - BONNS FEINE ADRESSEN. see *GENERAL INTEREST PERIODICALS — Germany*

KOSMETIK INTERNATIONAL. see *BEAUTY CULTURE — Perfumes And Cosmetics*

646.7 **TH**
THE LADY. (Text in Thai) m. 77 Rama V Rd., Bangkok, Thailand. Ed. Princess Ngarmchitr Prem Purachatra.

646.724 **GW** **ISSN 0723-7928**
LEHRER IM BERUFSFELD KOERPERPFLEGE. 1959. 6/yr. DM.57 (foreign DM.62.40) (effective 1997). Terra Verlag GmbH, Postfach 102144, 78421 Konstanz, Germany. TEL 49-7531-8122-0. FAX 49-7531-812299. Ed. Klaus Oligmueller. adv.; bk.rev.; illus.; index. circ. 1,000. (tabloid format) **Document type:** trade publication.
  Former titles: Lehrer in Friseurklassen (ISSN 0024-0605); Mitteilungsblatt der Lehrer im Deutschen Friseurhandwerk.

LOOKING FIT. see *PHYSICAL FITNESS AND HYGIENE*

LUMIERE. see *CLOTHING TRADE — Fashions*

646.7 658.8 **UK**
MAKE-UP AND COLOUR COSMETICS: THE INTERNATIONAL MARKET. (Subseries of: Market Direction reports) a. £2500($5000) (effective 1997). Euromonitor, 60-61 Britton St., London EC1M 5NA, England. TEL 44-171-251-8024. FAX 44-171-608-3149. E-mail: info@euromonitor.com; URL: http://www.euromonitor.com. (Addr. in N. America: Euromonitor International, 122 S. Michigan Ave., Ste. 1200, Chicago, IL 60603. TEL 800-577-3876. FAX 312-922-1157) (looseleaf format) **Document type:** trade publication.
  ●Also available online. Vendor(s): Data-Star, Knight-Ridder Information, Inc.
  Description: Analyzes the make-up and color cosmetics market segments for France, Germany, Italy, Spain, the U.K., the U.S., Japan, and Canada.

646.7 613.7 **UK**
MARIE CLAIRE HEALTH & BEAUTY. 1994? m. I P C Magazines (Subsidiary of: Reed Elsevier group), King's Reach Tower, Stamford St., London SE1 9LS, England. TEL 071-261-6575. TELEX 892084 REEDBP G. (Dist. by: Quadrant Subscription Services, Oakfield House, Perrymount Rd., Haywards Heath, W. Sussex RH16 3DH, England. TEL 0444-440421) **Document type:** consumer publication.

606.7 658.8 **UK**
MEN'S TOILETRIES: THE INTERNATIONAL MARKET. (Subseries of: Market Direction reports) a. £2250($4500) (effective 1997). Euromonitor, 60-61 Britton St., London EC1M 5NA, England. TEL 44-171-251-8024. FAX 44-171-608-3149. E-mail: info@euromonitor.com; URL: http://www.euromonitor.com. (Addr. in N. America: Euromonitor International, 122 S. Michigan Ave., Ste. 1200, Chicago, IL 60603. TEL 800-577-3876. FAX 312-922-1157) (looseleaf format) **Document type:** trade publication.
  ●Also available online. Vendor(s): Data-Star, Knight-Ridder Information, Inc.
  Description: Analyzes the market for men's toiletries for France, Germany, Italy, Spain, the U.K., the U.S., and Japan.

MODA TOP. see *CLOTHING TRADE — Fashions*

646.72 **US** **ISSN 0148-4001**
RL76.A1
MODERN SALON MAGAZINE. 1924. m. $20 (Canada $29.50; elsewhere $36) (effective 1995). Vance Publishing Corporation (Lincolnshire), Box 1414, Lincolnshire, IL 60069-1414. TEL 708-634-2600; 800-621-2845. FAX 708-634-4379. Ed. Mary Atherton. adv.; bk.rev.; illus.; tr.lit.; index. circ. 133,000. (also avail. in microform from UMI) —UMI. **CCC.**
  Incorporates: Visions (Lincolnshire); **Formerly** (until 1977): Modern Beauty Shop (ISSN 0026-7511)
  Description: Features hair styles and business trends.

646.7 **MP**
MONGOLJIN GOO/MONGOLIAN BEAUTY. (Supplyment to: Goo Maral) (Text in Mongolian) bi-m. P.O. Box 2106-44, 44-303, Ulan Bator, Mongolia. TEL 21035. Ed. B. Enhtuyaa.

MUENCHENS FEINE ADRESSEN. see *GENERAL INTEREST PERIODICALS — Germany*

646.7 **US** **ISSN 1064-5926**
N A C C A S REVIEW. 1981. q. $45. National Accrediting Commission of Cosmetology Arts & Sciences, 901 N. Stuart St., Ste. 900, Arlington, VA 22203-1816. TEL 703-527-7600. FAX 703-527-8811. Ed. Clifford A. Culbreath. R&P contact: Clifford A. Culbreath. adv. circ. 2,000. (back issues avail.) **Document type:** trade publication.
  Description: Covers issues relating to the development and implementation of standards in post-secondary education in cosmetology.

646.7 **US**
N I C BULLETIN. 1954. bi-m. membership. National - Interstate Council of State Boards of Cosmetology, Box 11390, Columbia, SC 29211. E-mail: brookstg@global2000.net. (Subscr. to: T. Gerald Brooks, Ed., 8 Hills Rd., Ballston Lake, NY 12019-9231. TEL 518-899-5798. FAX 518-899-5702) Ed. Gerald Brooks. circ. 600. **Document type:** bulletin.
  Formerly: National Interstate Council of State Boards of Cosmetology. Bulletin.
  Description: Covers topics relating to cosmetology licensing, testing, regulation and enforcement.

624.7 **US** **ISSN 0896-193X**
NAILS. 1983. m. (plus Factbook in July). $38 (Canada $57; elsewhere $87). Bobit Publishing Company, 2512 Artesia Blvd., Redondo Beach, CA 90278-3210. TEL 310-376-8788. FAX 310-376-9043. E-mail: chris@bobit.com. Ed. Cyndy Drummey. adv. circ. 50,000.
  Description: Provides business advice for professional manicurists, nail salon owners, and beauty supply distributors. Includes information on new products and application techniques.

NATIONAL ALOPECIA AREATA FOUNDATION NEWSLETTER. see *MEDICAL SCIENCES — Dermatology And Venereology*

646.7 **US**
NATIONAL BEAUTY NEWS.* m. National Beauty News, Inc., 10405 E. 55th Pl., Apt. B, Tulsa, OK 74146-6502. TEL 918-583-5708. FAX 918-582-0099. Ed. John Alexander. circ. 27,500.

646.7 **UK**
NATIONAL HAIRDRESSER. 1974. q. membership. National Hairdressers Federation, 11 Goldington Rd., Bedford, England. TEL 44-1234-360332. FAX 44-1234-269337. Ed. R.J. Seymour. R&P contact: John Patterson. adv.; bk.rev. circ. 11,500. **Document type:** newsletter.

646.7 **US**
NEW ENGLAND BEAUTY JOURNAL. m. $18. Bay Colony Publications, 105 Orchard St., Lynn, MA 01905. TEL 617-592-9157. (tabloid format)
  Description: For the hair salon trade.

646.724 **US**
NORTHWEST STYLIST & SALON. 1983. m. $15 (foreign $30) (effective 1997). Holland Graphics, 1750 S.W. Skyline Blvd., Ste. 24, Portland, OR 97221-2533. TEL 503-297-7010. FAX 503-297-7022. E-mail: hollandgfx@aol.com. Ed. Linda Holland. R&P contact: Linda Holland. adv. contact: Joel Holland. bk.rev. circ. 22,000. (tabloid format; back issues avail.) **Document type:** trade publication.
  Description: For salon and beauty school owners, practitioners, and students in Oregon, Idaho, and Washington.

646.72 **FR** **ISSN 0029-490X**
NOUVELLES ESTHETIQUES. (Editions in English, French, Greek, Italian, Spanish) 1952. 11/yr. 250 F. Societe d'Edition Les Nouvelles Esthetiques, 7 av. Stephane Mallarme, 75017 Paris, France. TEL 43-80-06-47. FAX 43-80-83-63. Ed. M. Pierantoni. adv.; bk.rev.; illus. circ. 35,000 (15,000 French ed., 8,000 English ed., 6,000 Spanish ed., 6,000 Italian ed.). (tabloid format)

646.7 **IT**
NOUVELLES ESTHETIQUES (ITALIAN EDITION). 9/yr. L.100000 (Europe L.160000; elsewhere L.175000) (effective 1995). A L A Editrice s.r.l., Via Macedonio Melloni 36, 20129 Milan, Italy. TEL 39-2-747656. FAX 39-2-70100018. Ed. Nennella Santelli. **Document type:** trade publication.

646.724 **AU** **ISSN 0029-9065**
DER OESTERREICHISCHE FRISEUR; offizielles Fachorgan der Friseure Oesterreichs. 1948. m. S.490 (Europe S.570; overseas S.600). Landesinnung Wien der Friseure, Mollardgasse 1, A-1060 Vienna, Austria. TEL 0222-5870420. FAX 0222-587042018. adv. circ. 4,800. **Document type:** trade publication.
  Description: Trade publication for hairdressers and owners of beauty salons. Covers new hair fashions, product information, sales promotion, and association news. Includes reports and announcements of events and exhibitions, classified ads, list of courses.

606.7 658.8 **UK**
ORAL HYGIENE PRODUCTS: THE INTERNATIONAL MARKET. (Subseries of: Market Direction reports) a. £2500($5000) (effective 1997). Euromonitor, 60-61 Britton St., London EC1M 5NA, England. TEL 44-171-251-8024. FAX 44-171-608-3149. E-mail: info@euromonitor.com; URL: http://www.euromonitor.com. (Addr. in N. America: Euromonitor International, 122 S. Michigan Ave., Ste. 1200, Chicago, IL 60603. TEL 800-577-3876. FAX 312-922-1157) (looseleaf format) **Document type:** trade publication.
  ●Also available online. Vendor(s): Data-Star, Knight-Ridder Information, Inc.
  Description: Analyzes the oral-hygiene products market segment for France, Germany, Italy, Spain, the U.K., the U.S., Japan, and Canada.

PAGEANTRY; the magazine for the pageant, talent, and fashion industry. see *CLOTHING TRADE — Fashions*

646.7 **GW**
PASSION LADY. (Text in English) q. DM.59.50. Trend Design GmbH, Bruederstr. 16, 32052 Herford, Germany. TEL 05221-54900. FAX 05221-56890. **Document type:** trade publication.

646.7 **GW**
PASSION MEN; international hair magazine. (Text in English) q. DM.49.50. Trend Design GmbH, Bruederstr. 16, 32052 Herford, Germany. TEL 05221-54900. FAX 05221-56890. **Document type:** trade publication.

BEAUTY CULTURE

646.724   SP   ISSN 1134-5608
PELUQUERIAS DE GRAN SELECCION; revista tecnica del peinado. Issued with: Revista Tecnica de Peluqueria y Belleza. (Text in English, French, Italian, Spanish) 1969. m. $79 (effective Jan. 1997). Alcolea, 43, 08014 Barcelona, Spain. TEL 34-3-3394907. FAX 34-3-4111994. E-mail: info@hair-styles.com; URL: http://www.hair-styles.com/. Ed. Juan Prat; Pub. Luis Llongueras Batlle. adv. contact: Pauli Sole. film rev.; play rev.; illus. circ. 25,000. **Document type:** trade publication.
  Description: Contains hairstyles and how to do them.

646.7 658.8   UK
PERFUMES AND FRAGRANCES: THE INTERNATIONAL MARKET. (Subseries of: Market Direction reports) a. £2500($5000) (effective 1997). Euromonitor, 60-61 Britton St., London EC1M 5NA, England. TEL 44-171-251-8024. FAX 44-171-608-3149. E-mail: info@euromonitor.com; URL: http://www.euromonitor.com. (Addr. in N. America: Euromonitor International, 122 S. Michigan Ave., Ste. 1200, Chicago, IL 60603. TEL 800-577-3876. FAX 312-922-1157) (looseleaf format) **Document type:** trade publication.
  ●Also available online. Vendor(s): Data-Star, Knight-Ridder Information, Inc.
  Description: Analyzes the market segment for perfumes and fragrances for France, Germany, Italy, Spain, the U.K., the U.S., Canada, and Japan.

POINT OF VIEW. see *CLOTHING TRADE — Fashions*

PUI BELLA. see *WOMEN'S INTERESTS*

646.72   SA   ISSN 0036-0759
S.A. HAIRDRESSING AND BEAUTY CULTURE. Title varies: South African Hairdressing and Beauty Culture. (Text in English) 1946. m. R.62.70 (R.72 in Africa; elsewhere R.92) (effective 1996). (S A Hairdressers & Cosmetologists Association) Trade Foucs Publications, P.O. Box 11800, Selcourt 1567, South Africa. Ed. Tessa O'Hara. adv.; bk.rev.; charts; illus. circ. 2,200. **Document type:** trade publication.
  Description: Journal for the hairdressing and cosmetology industry.

646.7   IT
SALON. 10/yr. Via R. Gessi 28, 20146 Milan, Italy. TEL 2-42-39-443. FAX 2-41-23-405. Ed. Giuseppe Tirabasso. circ. 13,000.

646.7   PL   ISSN 1230-9656
SALON I ELEGANCJA. 1993. m. free distr. to beauty parlors. Warsaw Voice S.A., Ksiecia Janusza 64, 01-452 Warsaw, Poland. TEL 48-22-366377. FAX 48-22-371995. adv.: page 5500 Zl.; 180 x 261; adv. contact: Barbara Milczarek. illus. **Document type:** trade publication.
  Description: Covers cosmetics, skin care and biological restoration.

646.7   CN   ISSN 1197-1495
SALON MAGAZINE.* 1992. 6/yr. Can.$20 (US Can.$30, elsewhere Can.$40). Salon Communications Inc., 411 Richmond St. E., Ste. 300, Toronto, ON M5A 3S5, Canada. TEL 416-869-3131. FAX 416-869-3008. E-mail: salon@informap.net. Ed. Alison Wood; Pub. Greg Robins. adv.: B&W page Can.$2630, color page Can.$3200; trim 8 1/8 x 10 7/8. circ. 27,000.

646.7   US   ISSN 1071-5606
SALON NEWS. 1993. m. $24 (foreign $60) (effective 1995). Fairchild Publications (Subsidiary of: Capital Cities - A B C, Inc.), 7 W. 34th St., New York, NY 10001. TEL 212-630-4000.

646.7   US
SALON REPORT.* q. Salon Development Corporation, 1381 Summit Ave., St. Paul, MN 55105-2219. TEL 612-690-1613. Ed. Bill Perron. **Document type:** newsletter.

646.7   US
SALON TECHNOLOGIES; information for the beauty professional. 1991. bi-m. $16. Marie Provenzano, Inc., Box 841224, Pembroke Pines, FL 33024. TEL 305-437-4580. Ed. Marie Provenzano. adv.: B&W page $1841, color page $2577; trim 10 1/2 x 13 1/2. circ. 20,000. **Document type:** trade publication, newspaper.
  Description: Provides information for beauty salon owners and employees in the Southeastern U.S.

646.7   US   ISSN 0743-6394
SALON TODAY. bi.m. $42 (foreign $60) (effective 1995). Vance Publishing Corporation (Lincolnshire), Box 1414, Lincolnshire, IL 60069-1414. TEL 708-634-2600; 800-621-2845. FAX 708-634-4379. Ed. Alfonso Pena-Ramos. circ. 40,000. **Document type:** trade publication.

646.727   DK   ISSN 0109-596X
SAMMENSLUTNINGEN AF DANSKE FODPLEJERE - FAGTIDSSKRIFT. 1976. q. Sammenslutningen af Danske Fodplejere, c/o Hartvig Pedersen, Tegelvaerksvej 20, Brundby, DK-8791 Tranebjerg, Denmark.
  Former titles (until 1983): Fodplejeren (ISSN 0107-3362); (until 1978): Fodspecialisten (ISSN 0107-4148)

646.7   NE   ISSN 0168-9630
DE SCHOONHEIDSPECIALIST. (Text in Dutch) 1966. m. fl.125 (foreign fl.175). (Algemene Nederlandse Branche Organisatie Schoonheidsverzorging - Dutch Association of Beauty Therapists) Uitgeverij Lakerveld B.V., Mangaanstraat 86, Postbus 43250, 2504 AG The Hague, Netherlands. TEL 31-70-3218218. FAX 31-70-3298744. E-mail: publish@lakerveld.nl; URL: http://www.lakerveld.nl. Ed. Esseline Braakhekke; Pub. Ad van Gaalen. R&P contact: Ad van Gaalen. adv. contact: Hans de Jong. illus. circ. 9,000. (back issues avail.) **Document type:** trade publication.
  Description: Business magazine for beauty therapists.

646.7 658.8   UK
SKIN CARE: THE INTERNATIONAL MARKET. (Subseries of: Market Direction reports) a. latest 1997. £2500($5000) (effective 1997). Euromonitor, 60-61 Britton St., London EC1M 5NA, England. TEL 44-171-251-8024. FAX 44-171-608-3149. E-mail: info@euromonitor.com; URL: http://www.euromonitor.com. (Addr. in N. America: Euromonitor International, 122 S. Michigan Ave., Ste. 1200, Chicago, IL 60603. TEL 800-577-3876. FAX 312-922-1157) (looseleaf format) **Document type:** trade publication.
  ●Also available online. Vendor(s): Data-Star, Knight-Ridder Information, Inc.
  Description: Analyzes the skin-care products market for France, Germany, Italy, Spain, the U.K., the U.S., Japan, and Canada.

646.724   US   ISSN 1042-5276
SOPHISTICATE'S BLACK HAIR;* styles and care guide. bi-m. $3.50. Associated Publications, 875-N. Michigan Ave., Ste. 3434, Chicago, IL 60611-1901. TEL 312-266-8680.

646.724   US   ISSN 1041-7125 TT950
SOPHISTICATE'S HAIRSTYLE GUIDE.* bi-m. $17.65. Associated Publications, 875 N. Michigan Ave., Ste. 3434, Chicago, IL 60610. TEL 312-266-8680.

646.724   DK   ISSN 0038-7266
SPEJLET. 1912. m. DKK 175 (effective 1997). Dansk Frisoerforbund - Union of Danish Hairdressers and Beauticians, Lersoe Parkalle 21, DK-2100 Copenhagen OE, Denmark. FAX 35-82-14-62. Ed. Poul Monggaard. adv.; bk.rev. circ. 5,000.

646.7   US
STAR HAIRDO. bi-m. newsstand price: $2.95. G C R Publishing Group, Inc., 1700 Broadway, 34th Fl., New York, NY 10019. TEL 212-541-7100. FAX 212-245-1241. Pub. Jason Goodman.

646.724   IT
STUDIO. 1981. m. L.59000 (Europe L.90000). Studio s.r.l., Corso Casale 410 20, 10132 Turin, Italy. TEL 39-11-8981502. FAX 39-11-8987073. TELEX 216258 STUDIO I. Ed. Fernando Trono. adv.: B&W page L.3500000, color page L.4800000. circ. 24,000.

646.724   IT
STUDIO U S A; hair fashion. (Text in English) bi-m. (7/yr.). Studio s.r.l., Corso Casale 410, Turin, Italy. TEL 11-898-1502. FAX 11-898-7073. adv.: B&W page $4000, color page $6000; trim 9 1/8 x 11 3/8.
  Description: Covers new hairstyles and makeup from America and Europe. Includes personality profiles and interviews.

646.7   GW
STYLE. q. DM.36 (foreign DM.40). Feldstr. 75, 40479 Duesseldorf, Germany. TEL 0211-4912448. FAX 0211-4982844. Ed. Brigitte Schiller-Domke. adv. contact: Karin Schulz. circ. 93,922. **Document type:** consumer publication.

646.7 658.8   UK
SUN CARE: THE INTERNATIONAL MARKET. (Subseries of: Market Direction reports) a. £1595($3190) (effective 1997). Euromonitor, 60-61 Britton St., London EC1M 5NA, England. TEL 44-171-251-8024. FAX 44-171-608-3149. E-mail: info@euromonitor.com; URL: http://www.euromonitor.com. (Addr. in N. America: Euromonitor International, 122 S. Michigan Ave., Ste. 1200, Chicago, IL 60603. TEL 800-577-3876. FAX 312-922-1157) (looseleaf format) **Document type:** trade publication.
  ●Also available online. Vendor(s): Data-Star, Knight-Ridder Information, Inc.
  Description: Analyzes the market for sunscreen products for France, Germany, Italy, Spain, the U.K., the U.S., and Japan.

646.7   SW   ISSN 0346-0657
SVENSKA FRISOERTIDNINGEN. 1902. m. SEK 400. Sveriges Frisoerfoeretagare, Frisoerernas Hus, Per Ekstroems Vaeg 3, S-161 55 Bromma, Sweden. FAX 8-879562. Ed. Christer Wistroem. adv. circ. 9,000.

646.7   SZ
SWISS HAIR PROFESSIONAL. (Text in French, German, Italian) m. 168 SFr. (foreign 210 SFr.) (effective 1997). Schweizerischer Coiffeurmeister Verband - Swiss Association of Master Hairdressers, Moserstr. 52, CH-3014 Bern, Switzerland. TEL 41-31-3327942. FAX 41-31-3314500. Ed. Rolf Fauser. adv. contact: Monika Moser. circ. 10,000. **Document type:** trade publication.
  Formerly: Swiss Hair Intern.
  Description: Magazine for hairdressers, covering information about new hairstyles and association activities.

646.7   SZ
SWISS HAIR SHOP. (Editions in French, German and Italian) 1991. 24/yr. 168 SFr. (foreign 210 SFr.) (effective 1997). Schweizerischer Coiffeurmeister Verband - Swiss Association of Master Hairdressers, Moserstr. 52, CH-3014 Bern, Switzerland. TEL 41-31-3327942. FAX 41-31-3314500. Ed. Rolf Fauser. adv. circ. 10,000. **Document type:** bulletin.
  Description: Presents information on the activities of SAMH for fellow hairdressers.

646.7   SP
TOCADO. 1956. 11/yr. 7000 ptas. (effective 1995) 7700 ptas. (effective 1996). Ediciones Tocado, Rep. Argentina 270 ent. 3o, 08023 Barcelona, Spain. TEL 34-3-4173950. FAX 34-3-4174324. Ed. Jaime Juez Cosin; Pub. Antonio Castro Morera. adv.: B&W page 95000 ptas., color page 130000 ptas.; 220 x 300; adv. contact: Agustin Angosta. circ. 15,000. **Document type:** trade publication.

646.724   GW   ISSN 0178-9805
TOP HAIR. (Editions in Dutch and German) 1883. s-m. DM.188.40 (combined subscr. with Madame DM.280.80). Magazinpresse Verlag GmbH, Elisenstr. 3, 80335 Munich, Germany. TEL 089-55135-0. FAX 089-55135-299. (Subscr. in US to: GLP International, 153 S. Dean St., Englewood, NJ 07631. TEL 201-871-1010. FAX 201-871-0870) Ed. Rolf Wilms. adv.: B&W page DM.4719, color page DM.8484; adv. contact: Maritta Obytz-Nehry. circ. 42,000. **Document type:** consumer publication.
  Formed by the 1985 merger of: Friseurhandwerk Friseurspiegel (ISSN 0016-1454); Deutsche Friseur-Zeitung (ISSN 0724-9799); Which was formerly (1956-1980): Deutsche Friseur-Zeitung. Hauptausgabe (ISSN 0011-491X)

646.7   GW
TOP TAN. 6/yr. DM.60 (foreign DM.73.80) (effective 1997). Terra Verlag GmbH, Postfach 102144, 78421 Konstanz, Germany. TEL 49-7531-8122-0. FAX 49-7531-812299. Ed. Christel Mampell. **Document type:** trade publication.

BEAUTY CULTURE — PERFUMES AND COSMETICS 509

646.724 US ISSN 1076-8092
TRY IT YOURSELF HAIR; for Black teens. 1992. bi-m. $18 (foreign $23). Word Up! Publications, Inc., 210 Rte. 4E., Ste. 401, Paramus, NJ 07652. TEL 201-843-4004. FAX 201-843-8636. circ. 75,000. **Document type:** consumer publication.
  Description: Haircare for African American women.

TWOJ STYL. see CLOTHING TRADE — Fashions

646.7 SP
ULTIMO GRITO.* 4/yr. Blasco de Garay 18, 28015 Madrid, Spain. TEL 1-593-17-16.

646.724 305.4 US ISSN 1069-4889
UNIQUE HAIR & BEAUTY.* 1993. bi-m. newsstand price: $3.50. Larry Flynt Publications, Inc., 8484 Wilshire Blvd., Ste. 900, Beverly Hills, CA 90211-3227. TEL 310-858-7100. FAX 310-275-3857. adv. **Document type:** consumer publication.

646.7 CN
VISAGE. (Text in English, French) 1989. bi-m. $19 (foreign $28). Literati Publishing Corp., 50 Charles St. E., Ste. 966, Toronto, ON M4Y 2N9, Canada. TEL 416-963-9709. FAX 416-963-5119. Ed. Linda Wright. adv. circ. 31,491.

VIVERSANI E BELLI; settimanale di salute e belezza. see PHYSICAL FITNESS AND HYGIENE

VOGUE AUSTRALIA. see CLOTHING TRADE — Fashions

VOGUE ITALIA. see CLOTHING TRADE — Fashions

646.72 FR ISSN 0042-8965
RA778.A1
VOTRE BEAUTE. 1933. 10/yr. $45. Votre Beaute S.A., 38 rue Jean-Mermoz, 75008 Paris, France. TEL 43-12-87-00. FAX 43-12-87-59. adv.; bk.rev. circ. 100,000.

646.7 JA
WOMEN'S GRAPHIC BEAUTY/FUJINGAHO BEAUTY. (Text in Japanese) 1951. m. 14400 Yen. Fujin Gaho Sha, 9-1, 2-chome, Nishi-Shimbashi, Minato-ku, Tokyo, Japan. Ed. Jun Hosokawa.

646.7 CC
YOUNG GIRL MAGAZINE. (Text in Chinese) 1987. bi-w. B2, 14-F, Fuk Keung Ind. bldg., 66-68 Tong Mei Rd., Taikoktsui Kowloon, Hong Kong, People's Republic of China. TEL 3910668. FAX 7893868. Ed. Vincent Leung. circ. 65,000.

646.724 UK ISSN 0955-0372
YOUR HAIR. 1978. m. £16. Health Digest Publications, 10 Woodberry Way, London E4, England. Ed. Pat Herbert.
  Incorporates: Hair Fashion and Style.

646.7 613.7 US
ZDROWIE, URODA I ZYCIE. (Text in Polish) 1988. m. $25. Back to Nature, Inc., 5627 N. Milwaukee, Chicago, IL 60646. TEL 312-585-0402. Ed. Barbara Radlinski; Pub. Marcin Hencz. R&P contact: Marcin Hencz. adv.: page $325; adv. contact: Barbara Radlinski. circ. 15,000. (back issues avail.) **Document type:** consumer publication.
  Description: Provides health, fitness and beauty tips.

646.7 IT
ZEFFIRO CAPELLI & COMPANY. 6/yr. L.67500 (Europe L.90000) (effective 1994). Via Cavour 46, 10123 Turin, Italy. TEL 11-83-66-63. FAX 11-83-79-67. Ed. Paola Gallotti. circ. 24,500.

ZEST; the health and beauty magazine. see WOMEN'S INTERESTS

BEAUTY CULTURE — Abstracting, Bibliographies, Statistics

668.5 US ISSN 0275-7044
CODEN: CACCD9
C A SELECTS. COSMETIC CHEMICALS. s-w. $240 to non-members; members $70 (effective 1998). Chemical Abstracts Service (Subsidiary of: American Chemical Society), 2540 Olentangy River Rd., Box 3012, Columbus, OH 43210-0012. TEL 714-447-3600. FAX 714-447-3713. TELEX 6842086. **Document type:** abstracting/indexing.
  Description: Covers the synthesis or manufacture of chemical substances of use in cosmetics; formulation of cosmetic preparations.

C A SELECTS PLUS. FLAVORS & FRAGRANCES. see CHEMISTRY — Abstracting, Bibliographies, Statistics

646.7 316.8 SA
SOUTH AFRICA. CENTRAL STATISTICAL SERVICE. CENSUS OF SOCIAL, RECREATIONAL AND PERSONAL SERVICES - HAIRDRESSING AND BEAUTY SERVICES. (Report No. 95-01-01) irreg., latest 1988. R.4.40 (foreign R.4.80). Central Statistical Service - Sentrale Statistiekdiens, Private Bag X44, Pretoria 0001, South Africa. TEL 27-12-310-8911. FAX 27-12-310-8500. (Orders to: Government Printing Works, Private Bag X85, Pretoria 0001, South Africa) **Document type:** government publication.

BEAUTY CULTURE — Perfumes And Cosmetics

338.4 646.7 643 US ISSN 1086-122X
ACUPOLL REPORTS - HEALTH & BEAUTY AIDS, HOUSEHOLD PRODUCTS. 1991. m. $1995 (effective 1997). Marketing Intelligence Service Ltd., 6473D Rte. 64, Naples, NY 14512-9726. TEL 716-374-6326. FAX 716-374-5217. E-mail: mktgintelsvc@cis.compuserve.com; URL: http://ourworld.compuserve.com/homepages/mktg/Ntelsvc. Ed. Kim Cruise. **Document type:** newsletter.
  Description: Offers accurate and reliable quantitative data on the consumer appeal of the most significant and innovative health and beauty aid products entering test market or national distribution.

668.5 AU
AESTHETIK. bi-m. Ziegelofengasse 31, A-1050 Vienna, Austria. TEL 01-551345. Ed. Gerhard Schuppich. circ. 1,200.

688.5 IT ISSN 1120-5415
ALLURE. (In 2 editions: trade and consumer) 1985. 10/yr. L.130000. Target s.r.l., Via Bondi 23, 2, 40138 Bologna, Italy. TEL 39-51-342426. FAX 39-51-345554. Ed. Rosetta Sannelli; Pub. Luciano Parisini. R&P contact: Diana Baravelli. adv.: B&W page L.8230000, color page L.9100000; 220 x 297; adv. contact: Alessandro Parisini. circ. 35,000 (controlled). **Document type:** consumer publication, trade publication.
  Description: For operators in the perfume business: firm managers, beauty consultants, retailers and business agents.
  Refereed Serial

668.5 612.86 US
AROMA-CHOLOGY REVIEW. 1987. q. $40. Olfactory Research Fund Ltd., 145 E. 32nd St., New York, NY 10016. TEL 212-725-2755. FAX 212-779-9058. Ed. Annette Green.
  Formerly (until 1992): Focus on Fragrance.
  Description: Reports on the latest research in olfaction.

668.55 UK
AVON CONTACT. 1966. m. free. Avon Cosmetics Ltd., Nunn Mills Rd., Northampton, England. TEL 44-1604-232425. FAX 44-1604-618628. Ed. Judith Wojtowicz. R&P contact: Judith Wojtowicz. bk.rev. circ. 3,000. **Document type:** newspaper.

BEAUTERAMA. see BEAUTY CULTURE

668.55 GW ISSN 0932-7398
BEAUTY; Cosmetic Fachjournal. 1987. q. DM.28 (foreign DM.32). Beauty Verlag GmbH, Ringstr. 52, 83355 Grabenstaett, Germany. TEL 08661-239. FAX 08661-1450. Eds. Peter Woelk, Helgard Keese. circ. 30,000. (back issues avail.)

668.54 668.55 US ISSN 0887-414X
BEAUTY AGE.* 1985. bi-m. $25. 347 Varick St., Apt. 417A, Jersey City, NJ 07302-3459. TEL 212-580-2756. Ed. Paul M. Cohen. adv. circ. 27,719. (back issues avail.)
  Description: Describes cosmetic, fragrance and cosmetic accessory products.

668.5 UK ISSN 0960-3751
BEAUTY COUNTER. 1962. m. £58 (overseas £68) (includes Community Pharmacy). Miller Freeman plc, Sovereign Way, Tonbridge, Kent TN9 1RW, England. TEL 44-1732-364422. FAX 44-1732-361534. Ed. Jo Webb. adv. contact: Kate Haysom. circ. 13,813 (controlled). **Document type:** trade publication.
  ●Also available online. Vendor(s): Information Access Co.
  Former titles: Beauty Counter and Perfumery and Toiletries Buyer (ISSN 0263-6085); Beauty Counter and Toiletries Buyer.
  Description: Contains information for managers of retail pharmacies, department stores, and grocery buying departments.

668.5 US ISSN 0005-7487
BEAUTY FASHION. 1916. 12/yr. $25 (Canada & Mexico $50; elsewhere $175). Beauty Fashion, Inc., 530 5th Ave., 4th Fl., New York, NY 10036-5101. TEL 212-840-8800. FAX 212-840-7246. Ed. John G. Ledes; Pub. George Ledes. R&P contact: John G. Ledes. adv. contact: George Ledes. bk.rev. circ. 18,396. **Document type:** trade publication.
  Description: Covers perfumes, cosmetics, skincare and toiletries.

668.5 UK
BEAUTY MAGAZINE. m. (11/yr.). £49 (foreign £89). Cosmetics Communications Ltd., 335 Linen Hall, 162-168 Regent St., London W1R 5TB, England. TEL 44-171-434-1530. FAX 44-171-437-0915. Ed. Tonya Meli. adv. contact: Vivien Brockwell. circ. 13,200 (controlled). **Document type:** trade publication.
  Description: Provides trade information for beauty sales personnel.

BLACK BEAUTY & HAIR. see BEAUTY CULTURE

338.5 UK ISSN 1357-6801
BUSINESS RATIO PLUS: THE TOILETRIES AND COSMETICS INDUSTRY. 1978. a. £195. I C C Business Publications (Subsidiary of: I C C Information Group), Field House, 72 Oldfield Rd., Hampton, Mddx. TW12 2HQ, England. TEL 44-181-783-0922. FAX 44-181-783-1940. **Document type:** trade publication.
  Formerly (until 1994): Business Ratio Report: Toiletries and Cosmetics Industry (ISSN 0261-9636).

668.55 UK
C I DIRECTORY. (Cosmetics International) a. £85 (includes Cosmetics International). Cosmetics Communications Ltd., 335 Linen Hall, 162-168 Regent St., London W1R 5TB, England. TEL 44-171-434-1530. FAX 44-171-437-0915. **Document type:** directory, trade publication.

338.4 646.7 615 US ISSN 1086-119X
CATEGORY REPORT - HEALTH & BEAUTY AIDS. m. $1000 (effective 1997). Marketing Intelligence Service Ltd., 6473D Route 64, Naples, NY 14512-9726. TEL 716-374-6326. FAX 716-374-5217. E-mail: mktgintelsvc@cis.compuserve.com; URL: http://ourworld.compuserve.com/homepages/mktgintelsvc.com. Ed. Kim Cruise. **Document type:** newsletter.
  Description: Contains detailed product and packaging description and analysis of new foreign and domestic consumer packaged goods.

338.4 643 636.088 US ISSN 1086-1203
CATEGORY REPORT - HOUSEHOLD, PET & MISCELLANEOUS PRODUCTS. m. $1000 (effective 1997). Marketing Intelligence Service Ltd., 6473D Route 64, Naples, NY 14512-9726. TEL 716-374-6326. FAX 716-374-5217. E-mail: mktgintelsvc@cis.compuserve.com; URL: http://ourworld.compuserve.com/homepages/mktgintelsvc. Ed. Kim Cruise. (back issues avail.) **Document type:** newsletter.
  Description: Contains detailed product and packaging description and analysis of new foreign and domestic consumer packaged goods.

CHEMEXCIL EXPORT BULLETIN. see BUSINESS AND ECONOMICS — International Commerce

BEAUTY CULTURE — PERFUMES AND COSMETICS

668.5 GR
CHRYSES SELIDES ESTHITIKIS/AESTHETIC GOLDEN PAGES. 1985. bi-m. Dr.1500($20) I C O International, 3A Barbanou St., P.O. Box 190.25, 117 10 Athens, Greece. TEL 30-1-9017-806. FAX 30-1-9016-663. Ed. Stella Tsirimocou; Pub. Dimitrios E. Tsirimocos. adv.: B&W page DM.2200, color page DM.2400; 230 x 305. bk.rev. circ. 10,000. (back issues avail.) Document type: directory.
   Description: Lists beauticians and cosmetologists in Greece and Cyprus.

668.55 IT
COSMESI. 1969. 2/yr. Schwegler Editore s.n.c., Via Senato 18, 20121 Milan, Italy. TEL 2-79-50-75. FAX 2-76-00-68-92. Ed. Carla Catani. adv. circ. 12,000.

668.55 US ISSN 0275-4681
COSMETIC INSIDER'S REPORT; a twice-monthly newsletter for the cosmetic industry executive. 1981. s-m. $145 (effective 1996). Advanstar Communications, Inc., 7500 Old Oak Blvd., Cleveland, OH 44130. TEL 216-826-2839. FAX 216-891-2726. (Subscr. to: 131 W. First St., Duluth, MN 55802. TEL 218-723-9838) Ed. Don Davis. circ. 350. **Document type:** trade publication.
●Also available online. Vendor(s): Data-Star, Information Access Co., Knight-Ridder Information, Inc.
—CCC.
   Description: Interprets as well as reports developments relating to new products, key personnel changes, regulation, and mergers and acquisitions in the marketing field.

668.55 658 GW ISSN 0947-0603
COSMETIC MANAGEMENT INTERNATIONAL. bi-m. DM.72. Kosmetik International Verlag GmbH, Schulstr. 12, 76532 Baden-Baden, Germany. TEL 49-7221-5079-0. FAX 49-7221-507950. Ed. Heinrich Grossman. adv.: B&W page DM.2355, color DM.4155; trim 160 x 257; adv. contact: Birgit Hartmann. circ. 5,700. **Document type:** trade publication.

668.5 IT
COSMETIC NEWS. 1978. 6/yr. L.60000 (foreign L.100000) (effective 1996). Sepem s.r.l., Via Grado 9, 20125 Milan, Italy. TEL 39-2-26825553. FAX 39-2-26823952. Ed. Franco Mattei. R&P contact: Franco Mattei. adv.: B&W page L.850000, color page L.1200000. bk.rev.; circ. 3,000 (controlled).

668.55 UK
COSMETIC PRODUCTS REPORT. m. £175($395) (rest of Europe £199; elsewhere £235). Cosmetics Communications Ltd., 335 Linen Hall, 162-168 Regent St., London W1R 5TB, England. TEL 44-171-434-1530. FAX 44-171-437-0915. **Document type:** trade publication.
   Formerly: C I New Products Report.
   Description: Covers all product launches of cosmetics worldwide.

COSMETIC SCIENCE AND TECHNOLOGY SERIES. see MEDICAL SCIENCES

668.5 UK ISSN 0305-0319
TP983 CODEN: CSWNAR
COSMETIC WORLD NEWS; the international news magazine of the perfumery, cosmetics and toiletries industry. 1950. 6/yr. $192. World News Publications, 130 Wigmore St., London W1H OAT, England. FAX 44-171-487-5436. Ed. M.A. Murray-Pearce. adv.; bk.rev.; abstr. circ. 6,000. (also avail. in microform from UMI; reprint service avail. from UMI) Indexed: Chem.Abstr., Key to Econ.Sci., PROMT. **Document type:** trade publication.
●Also available online. Vendor(s): Information Access Co.
—BLDSC (3477.177000); UMI.
   Formerly (until 1974): International Perfumer (ISSN 0020-8248)

668.5 SP ISSN 0212-3991
COSMETICA Y AROMATICA. 1983. 6/yr. Travesera de Gracia 15, 08021 Barcelona, Spain. TEL 3-204-79-33. FAX 3-209-69-18.

668.5 US ISSN 0361-4387
TP983 CODEN: CTOIDG
COSMETICS AND TOILETRIES; the international journal of cosmetic technology. 1906. m. $79 (Canada $109; elsewhere $156) (effective 1996 & 1997). Allured Publishing, 362 S. Schmale Rd., Carol Stream, IL 60188-2787. TEL 708-653-2155. FAX 708-653-2192. Ed. Cynthia Urbano. adv.; bk.rev.; abstr.; bibl.; charts; illus.; mkt.; tr.lit.; index. circ. 3,000. (also avail. in microform from UMI; reprint service avail. from UMI) Indexed: A.S.& T.Ind., Chem.Abstr., I.P.A., PROMT. **Document type:** trade publication.
●Also available online. Vendor(s): Information Access Co.
—BLDSC (3477.184500); CASDDS; CISTI; Ei; KR SourceOne; Linda Hall; SWETS; UnCover. CCC.
   Former titles (until 1975): Cosmetics and Perfumery (ISSN 0090-6581); American Perfumer and Cosmetics (ISSN 0003-0392); (1960-1962): American Perfumer (ISSN 0096-0896); American Perfumer and Aromatics (ISSN 0517-4252); American Perfumer and Essential Oil Review (1940) (ISSN 0161-9977); (1936-1939): American Perfumer, Cosmetics, Toilet Preparations; American Perfumer (1936) (ISSN 0096-087X); American Perfumer and Essential Oil Review (1906) (ISSN 0096-0888); American Perfumer (1906) (ISSN 0162-8593).
   Description: Covers ingredient application, formulation ideas and research.

668.55 UK ISSN 0963-6137
CODEN: COSIDZ
COSMETICS INTERNATIONAL; the news bulletin of the cosmetics industry. 1975. s-m. £235 (rest of Europe £285; N. America $495; elsewhere £298) (includes C I Directory). Cosmetics Communications Ltd., 335 Linen Hall, 162-168 Regent St., London W1R 5TB, England. TEL 44-171-434-1530. FAX 44-171-437-0915. Ed. Charlotte Coleman. adv.: B&W page £775, color page £975. **Document type:** newsletter.
●Also available online. Vendor(s): Information Access Co., Lexis-Nexis.
—BLDSC (3477.187000); SWETS.
   Description: Covers market trends, mergers, acquisitions, financial reports and company profiles.

668.5 FR ISSN 0980-0875
COSMETIQUE NEWS. 1986. 22/yr. Publications Professionnelles Europeennes, 175-177 rue d'Aguesseau, 92100 Boulogne, France. TEL 433-1-41-86-71-64. FAX 33-1-41-86-71-60. Ed. Sabine Chabbert. circ. 11,000.

D C A T DIGEST. (Drug, Chemical and Allied Trades Association) see PHARMACY AND PHARMACOLOGY

D W: DROGISTEN WEEKBLAD; onafhankelijk vakblad voor drogisterij, parfumerie, reformzaak. see PHARMACY AND PHARMACOLOGY

DIARY. see CLOTHING TRADE — Fashions

668.5 GW ISSN 0012-5881
CODEN: DRFSDW
DRAGOCO REPORT; for our friends in the perfume, cosmetics, and toilet goods industries. (Editions in English, French, German, Spanish) 1956. 6/yr. free. Dragoco Gerberding & Co. AG, Dragocostr., 37601 Holzminden, Germany. TEL 49-5531-97-0. FAX 49-5531-971391. (US addr.: Dragoco, Inc., Gordon Dr., Totowa, NJ 07512. TEL 201-256-3850) Eds. Katja Seibicke, Marlies Knirsch. bibl.; charts; illus.; stat. circ. 16,000. Indexed: Chem.Abstr., I.P.A. **Document type:** trade publication.
●Also available online.
—CCC.

615 668.5 US ISSN 0732-0760
TP200
DRUG AND COSMETIC CATALOG. 1931. a. $20 (effective 1996). Advanstar Communications, Inc., 7500 Old Oak Blvd., Cleveland, OH 44130. TEL 216-826-2839. FAX 216-891-2726. (Subscr. to: 131 W. First St., Duluth, MN 55802. TEL 800-346-0085) Ed. Donald A. Davis. circ. 14,145. **Document type:** catalog, trade publication.
   Description: Annual directory of the drug and cosmetic industry.

615.1 668.5 US ISSN 0012-6527
RS1 CODEN: DCINAQ
DRUG AND COSMETIC INDUSTRY. Abbreviated title: D C I. 1914. m. $39 (in Canada $59; elsewhere $99) (effective 1996). Advanstar Communications, Inc., 7500 Old Oak Blvd., Cleveland, OH 44130. TEL 216-826-2839. FAX 216-891-2726. (Subscr. to: 131 W. First St., Duluth, MN 55802. TEL 800-346-0085) Ed. Karen Hoppe. adv.; bk.rev.; abstr.; illus.; mkt.; pat.; tr.mk.; index. circ. 14,145. (also avail. in microform from PMC,UMI) Indexed: B.P.I., Biol.Abstr., Biotech.Abstr., Bus.Ind., Cadscan, Chem.Abstr., Curr.Cont., Curr.Pack.Abstr., Hlth.Ind., I.P.A., Int.Packag.Abstr., Lead Abstr., PROMT, Tr.& Indus.Ind., Zincscan. **Document type:** trade publication.
●Also available online. Vendor(s): Information Access Co., Knight-Ridder Information, Inc., UMI.
—BLDSC (3628.000000); CASDDS; CISTI; KR SourceOne; Linda Hall; SWETS; UMI; UnCover. CCC.
   Description: Formulation, raw material procurement, production and packaging for marketers and manufacturers of cosmetics, personal products and OTC pharmaceuticals.

668.5 UK ISSN 1364-9922
ESPRIT. 1988. m. £92 in U.K. and Europe; elsewhere £118 (effective 1997). Sandron Publishing, Bouverie House, 43A Effra Rd., Wimbledon, London SW19 8PS, England. TEL 44-181-543-9799. FAX 44-181-540-6519. Ed. Lorraine Wilson-Morris; Pub. Andrea Jones. R&P contact: Andrea Jones. adv.: B&W page £1580, color page £1995; adv. contact: Jonathan Charles. circ. 9,000. Indexed: Arts & Hum.Cit.Ind. **Document type:** trade publication.
   Description: Information source for the perfumery, cosmetics, skincare and premium toiletries industry.

668.5 SP ISSN 1130-0590
ESTETICA ESPANOLA. 1986. bi-m. 4700 ptas. (Europe 7000 ptas.) (effective 1994). National Federation of Beauticians, San Bernardo 8, 3o, 28015 Madrid, Spain. TEL 1-521-24-34. FAX 1-521-37-65. Ed. G. Garcia Vaquero. adv.; bk.rev. circ. 7,000.

668.5 SP ISSN 0214-5774
ESTETICA PROFESIONAL. 1977. 11/yr. Prensa Hispanoamericana, S.A., Gascuena 21, 28022 Madrid, Spain. TEL 1-747-80-00. FAX 1-747-90-56. Ed. Maria Mugico. circ. 20,000.

668.5 FR ISSN 1146-5794
ESTHETICA PROFESSIONNEL. 1985. 10/yr. 58 rue Saint Georges, 75009 Paris, France. TEL 42-85-51-00. FAX 42-85-41-45. TELEX 281 078 F. Ed. Joelle Ilous. circ. 10,000.
   Formerly (until 1990): Esthetica (ISSN 0769-6507)

668.5 UK ISSN 0957-1515
EUROPEAN COSMETIC MARKETS. 1983. m. £650 (foreign £695) (effective 1997). Wilmington Publishing, Wilmington House, Church Rd., Dartford, Kent UA2 7EF, England. TEL 44-1322-277788. FAX 44-1322-276476. Ed. Charlotte Sharpe. adv.; circ. 5,000 (paid). **Document type:** trade publication.
●Also available online. Vendor(s): Information Access Co.
—BLDSC (3829.688620); SWETS.
   Description: Publishes market reports, along with news and product launches in the cosmetics industry.

380 688.55 658.8 UK ISSN 0952-9578
EUROPEAN COSMETICS AND TOILETRIES MARKETING DIRECTORY. 2nd edition, 1993. irreg. £160($335) Euromonitor, 60-61 Britton St., London EC1M 5NA, England. TEL 44-171-251-8024. FAX 44-171-608-3149. E-mail: info@euromonitor.com; URL: http://www.euromonitor.com. (Addr. in N America: Euromonitor International, 122 S. Michigan Ave., Ste. 1200, Chicago, IL 60603. TEL 800-577-3876. FAX 312-922-1157) **Document type:** directory.
   Description: Covers the cosmetics industry and market in Europe and provides the names and addresses of major manufacturers.

BEAUTY CULTURE — PERFUMES AND COSMETICS

688.55 658.8   UK
EUROPEAN COSMETICS AND TOILETRIES REPORT (YEAR). irreg., latest 1993. £450($900) (effective 1997). Euromonitor, 60-61 Britton St., London EC1M 5NA, England. TEL 44-171-251-8024. FAX 44-171-608-3149. E-mail: info@euromonitor.com; URL: http://www.euromonitor.com. (Addr. in N. America: Euromonitor International, 122 S. Michigan Ave., Ste. 1200, Chicago, IL 60603. TEL 800-577-3876. FAX 312-922-1157) charts; stat. **Document type**: trade publication.
   Description: Examines trends and developments in the cosmetics and toiletries industry and addresses current issues, such as packaging and environmental awareness.

668.5   IT
EXPORT MAGAZINE - BEAUTY DISTRIBUTOR. (Text in English, Italian) 10/yr. Via R. Gessi 28, 20146 Milan, Italy. TEL 2-42-39-443. FAX 2-412-34-05. Ed. Giuseppe Tirabasso. circ. 15,000.

668.5   US   ISSN 1070-1281
KF3896.A15
F M A REGULATORY AND LEGISLATIVE UPDATE. 1990. q. Fragrance Materials Association of the United States, 1620 I St., N.W., Ste. 950, Washington, DC 20006. TEL 202-293-5800. FAX 202-463-8998. Ed. Glenn Roberts. circ. 300. (looseleaf format; back issues avail.) **Document type**: newsletter.
   Former titles (until 1991): F M A Update, Regulatory and Legislative News (ISSN 1070-1273); (until 1990): F M A Regulatory Update (ISSN 1070-1265)

668.55 658   GW
FAIR CATALOGUE K I LIVE. (Kosmetik International) a. Kosmetik International Verlag GmbH, Schulstr. 12, 76532 Baden-Baden, Germany. TEL 49-7221-5079-0. FAX 49-7221-507950. Ed. Heinrich Grossmann. adv.: B&W page DM.2116, color page DM.3856; trim 200 x 280; adv. contact: Birgit Hartmann. circ. 20,000. **Document type**: trade publication.
   Former titles: Program K I Live; Treffpunkt Kosmetik International.

FARMACIA DISTRIBUICAO. see PHARMACY AND PHARMACOLOGY

FINANCIAL SURVEY. THE TOILETRIES AND COSMETICS INDUSTRY; company data for success. see BUSINESS AND ECONOMICS — Trade And Industrial Directories

FLAVOUR & FRAGRANCE JOURNAL. see CHEMISTRY — Organic Chemistry

FOOD AND DRUG LAW JOURNAL. see LAW

FOOD, DRUG, COSMETIC, AND MEDICAL DEVICE LAW DIGEST. see LAW

FOR FORMULATION CHEMISTS ONLY. see CHEMISTRY — Analytical Chemistry

668.5   US
FRAGRANCE FORUM. q. $100 to non-members (foreign $130); members $75 (foreign $105). Fragrance Foundation, 145 E. 32nd St., New York, NY 10016. TEL 212-725-2755. FAX 212-779-9058. Ed. Annette Green. bk.rev.; charts; illus. (back issues avail.) **Document type**: newsletter.
   Description: Provides information on the marketing of fragrance in the 90s. Addresses changing trends, technologies, sociological developments and future markets.

668.5   SZ
FUER SIE MADAME. (Text in French, German) 10/yr. Merkurstr. 34, CH-8032 Zurich, Switzerland. TEL 01-2524522. FAX 01-2611986. Ed. Rene Boser. circ. 100,000.

668.55   US
GRAYSON REPORT. 1972. bi-m. $45 (effective 1988). Grayson Associates, Inc., 108 Loma Media Rd., Santa Barbara, CA 93103. TEL 805-564-1313. FAX 805-564-8800. Ed. Suzanne Grayson. **Document type**: trade publication.
   Description: Covers marketing analysis for the cosmetics and toiletries industry.

GUIDE INTERNATIONAL DE LA PARFUMERIE/GENERAL DIRECTORY OF THE PERFUME AND COSMETIC INDUSTRY. see BUSINESS AND ECONOMICS — Trade And Industrial Directories

HOUSEHOLD & PERSONAL PRODUCTS INDUSTRY; the magazine for the detergent, soap, cosmetic and toiletry, wax, polish and aerosol industries. see BUSINESS AND ECONOMICS — Marketing And Purchasing

668.54   IT
IMAGINE. 1975. 10/yr. (Federazione Nazionale Profumieri Italiani) Edizioni Pi-Erre, Corso Venezia 49, 20121 Milan, Italy. TEL 2-77-50-203. Ed. Luciano Parisini. adv.; illus. circ. 12,000.

668.54   II   ISSN 0019-607X
CODEN: IPERAS
INDIAN PERFUMER. (Text in English) 1957. q. Rs.350($75) (effective 1992). Essential Oil Association of India, Dua Complex, 24 Veer Savarkar Block, Sakarpur, Vikas Marge, Delhi 110 092, India. FAX 11-2204284. TELEX 31-62434 SIVA IN. Ed. S.N. Sobti. adv.; bk.rev.; abstr.; charts; illus.; pat.; stat. circ. 500. **Indexed**: Biol.Abstr., Chem.Abstr., Curr.Cont., Rice Abstr.
—BLDSC (4425.500000); CASDDS.

668.5   UK   ISSN 1363-0407
INSIDE COSMETICS. 10/yr. £58 (E.U. £71; rest of world $126) (effective 1997). Miller Freeman Technical Ltd. (Subsidiary of: Miller Freeman plc), Miller Freeman House, 30 Calderwood St., London SE18 6QH, England. TEL 44-181-855-7777. FAX 44-181-316-3017. E-mail: edit@ic.mfplc.co.uk. (Subscr. to: Royal Sovereign House, 40 Beresford St., Woolrich, London SE1 6BQ, England. TEL 44-181-855-7777) Ed. Gerry Duggin. adv. contact: Jim Howard. circ. 3,500. **Indexed**: I.P.A. **Document type**: trade publication.
—BLDSC (4518.151829).
   Formerly: C T M S (ISSN 0952-519X)

668.5   UK   ISSN 0142-5463
TP983   CODEN: IJCMDW
INTERNATIONAL JOURNAL OF COSMETIC SCIENCE. bi-m. £345 (foreign $575) (effective 1998). (Society of Cosmetic Chemists) Thomson Science (Subsidiary of: International Thomson Publishing Group), 2-6 Boundary Row, London SE1 8HN, England. TEL 44-171-8650066. FAX 44-171-5229623. TELEX 290164 CHAPMA G. E-mail: journal@rapidcom.co.uk; URL: http://www.thomsonscience.com. (Dist. by: International Thomson Publishing Services Ltd., Cheriton House, North Way, Andover, Hants. SP10 5BE, England. TEL 44-1264-342713. FAX 44-1264-342807; Subscr. in US & Canada to: 400 Market St., Philadelphia, PA 19106. TEL 800-552-5866) Ed. J.M. Blakeway. adv. circ. 2,750. (back issues avail.; reprint service avail. from ISI) **Indexed**: ASCA, Biol.Abstr., Biotech.Abstr., C.I.S. Abstr., Chem.Abstr., Curr.Adv.Ecol.Sci., Curr.Cont., Excerp.Med., I.P.A., Ind.Med., Ind.Sci.Rev., Sci.Cit.Ind. **Document type**: academic/scholarly publication.
●Also available online.
—BLDSC (4542.178400); ADONIS; CASDDS; CISTI; Ei; SWETS; UMI. **CCC**.
   Description: Provides a current presentation of pure and applied scientific research in cosmetics, toiletries, perfumery, and allied fields.
   Refereed Serial

INTERNATIONAL PHARMACEUTICAL REGULATORY MONITOR; a legal, medical & scientific information series for the pharmaceutical and biotech industry. see PHARMACY AND PHARMACOLOGY

INTERNATIONAL PRODUCT ALERT. see BUSINESS AND ECONOMICS — Marketing And Purchasing

668.55   JA   ISSN 0287-1238
CODEN: NKKAEV
JAPANESE COSMETIC SCIENCE SOCIETY. JOURNAL. 1976. q. 12000 Yen (effective till 1996). Japanese Cosmetic Science Society, 3-3165 Higashi-Tamagaw Gakuen, Machida-shi, Tokyo 194, Japan. FAX 81-427-23-3585. (Dist. by: Business Center for Academic Societies Japan, 5-16-9 Honkomagome, Bunkyo-ku, Tokyo 113, Japan. TEL 03-5814-5811) adv.; bk.rev. **Document type**: academic/scholarly publication.
—BLDSC (4809.253000); CASDDS.

668.54   US   ISSN 1041-2905
TP958   CODEN: JEOREG
JOURNAL OF ESSENTIAL OIL RESEARCH. 1989. bi-m. $230 in US & Canada; elsewhere $260 (effective 1996 & 1997). Allured Publishing, 362 S. Schmale Rd., Carol Stream, IL 60188-2787. TEL 708-653-2155. FAX 708-653-2192. **Indexed**: Food Sci.& Tech.Abstr., I.P.A. **Document type**: academic/scholarly publication.
—BLDSC (4979.550000); CASDDS; CISTI; Ei; Linda Hall; SWETS; UnCover. **CCC**.
   Description: Contains original research papers on all aspects of production, processing and analysis of essential oils and related natural products relative to their use in flavor and fragrances.

668.5   UK
KEY NOTE MARKET REPORT: COSMETICS & FRAGRANCES. Variant title: Cosmetics & Fragrances. irreg., no.11, 1995. £285. Key Note Ltd., Field House, 72 Oldfield Rd., Hampton, Middlesex TW12 2HQ, England. TEL 44-181-783-0755. FAX 44-181-783-0049. **Document type**: trade publication.
●Also available online.
Also available on CD-ROM.
   Formerly (until 1995): Key Note Report: Cosmetics and Fragrances.

668.5   UK
KEY NOTE MARKET REVIEW: U K TOILETRIES & COSMETICS MARKET. Variant title: U K Toiletries & Cosmetics Market. 1992. irreg. £375. Key Note Ltd., Field House, 72 Oldfield Rd., Hampton, Middlesex TW12 2HQ, England. TEL 44-181-783-0755. FAX 44-181-783-1940. **Document type**: trade publication.
●Also available online.
Also available on CD-ROM.

668.5   NE   ISSN 0165-2192
KOSMETIEK; vakblad voor de cosmeticabranche. (Supplement avail.: Kosmetiek Apropos (ISSN 1381-8864)) 1972. m. fl.86.75. Samsom BedrijfsInformatie B.V. (Subsidiary of: Wolters Kluwer N.V.), Postbus 4, 2400 MA Alphen aan den Rijn, Netherlands. TEL 31-172-446954. FAX 31-172-422804. Ed. P. Weijers. R&P contact: E. Stolwerk. adv. contact: N. van der Does. circ. 4,000. **Indexed**: Key to Econ.Sci. **Document type**: trade publication.

668.5   NE   ISSN 1381-8864
KOSMETIEK APROPOS. (Supplement to: Kosmetiek (ISSN 0165-2192)) 1987. 6/yr. Samsom BedrijfsInformatie B.V. (Subsidiary of: Wolters Kluwer N.V.), P.O. Box 4, 2400 MA Alphen aan den Rijn, Netherlands. TEL 31-172-446954. FAX 31-172-422804. Ed. P. Weijers. R&P contact: E. Stolwerk. adv. contact: N. van der Does. illus. circ. 10,000. **Document type**: trade publication.

668.5   GW   ISSN 0342-2976
KOSMETIK INTERNATIONAL. 1951. m. DM.91.80. Kosmetik International Verlag GmbH, Schulstr. 12, 76532 Baden-Baden, Germany. TEL 49-7221-5079-0. FAX 49-7221-507950. Ed. Heinrich Grossmann. adv.: B&W page DM.4630; trim 200 x 280; adv. contact: Birgit Hartmann. bk.rev.; illus. circ. 22,500. **Document type**: trade publication.
   Formerly: Kosmetikerinnen-Fachzeitung - Parfuemerie Journal (ISSN 0023-4176)

668.55   GW
KOSMETIK REPORT; aktuelle Informationen. 1971. 3/mo. DM.1212.60 (effective 1996). Orbis Werbung, Neuhauserstr. 21, 78464 Konstanz, Germany. TEL 49-7531-882247. FAX 49-7531-812299. Ed. Sabine Bursy. adv. circ. 750. **Document type**: trade publication.

668.55   GW
KOSMETIKJAHRBUCH. a. DM.89. Verlag fuer Chemische Industrie H. Ziolkowsky GmbH, Beethovenstr. 16, 86150 Augsburg, Germany. TEL 49-821-519345. FAX 49-821-517953. Ed. Bernd Ziolkowsky. **Document type**: trade publication.

BEAUTY CULTURE — PERFUMES AND COSMETICS

668.5 US ISSN 0740-3852
LOOKOUT - NONFOODS. 1978. s-m. $600 (effective 1997). Marketing Intelligence Service Ltd., 6473D Route 64, Naples, NY 14512-9726. TEL 716-374-6326. FAX 716-374-5217. E-mail: mktgintelsvc@cis.compuserve.com; URL: http://ourworld.compuserve.com/homepages/mktgintelsvc. Ed. Philip Schreur. **Document type:** newsletter.
●Also available online.
—CCC.
Supersedes in part: Lookout (Naples).
Description: Reviews the most innovative and influential new product entries, complete with analyses and illustrations.

668.54 668.55 SP
N C P DOCUMENTA. (Noticias de Cosmetica y de Perfumeria) 1977. m. 600 ptas.($8) (or membership). (Sociedad Espanola de Quimicos Cosmeticos) Romargraf S.A., Juventud 55, Hospitalet del Llobregat, Barcelona, Spain. Ed.Bd. charts.

688.55 US ISSN 1049-4553
NAILPRO. 1990. m. $31. Creative Age Publications, Inc., 7628 Densmore Ave., Van Nuys, CA 91406-2042. TEL 818-782-7328. FAX 818-782-7450. Ed. Linda W. Lewis; Pub. Deborah Carver. R&P contact: Andrea Sercu. adv.: B&W page $3661, color page $4822; trim 8 x 10 3/4; adv. contact: Lester G. Alvarado. circ. 48,118 (controlled). **Document type:** trade publication.
Formerly: N - The Magazine for Nail Professionals.
Description: Covers the technical, business and management aspects of the nail-care industry, with emphasis on how to effectively build a nail salon business.

NIEUWE DROGIST. see PHARMACY AND PHARMACOLOGY

668.5 SP ISSN 0213-1579
NOTICIAS DE COSMETICA Y DE PERFUMERIA. Short title: N C P. (Includes supplements) 1971. m. free. (Sociedad Espanola de Quimicos Cosmeticos) Romargraf S.A., Juventud 55-57, Hospitalet del Llobregat, Barcelona, Spain. Ed. Miguel Margalef. adv.; bk.rev.; abstr.; pat.; stat.; illus.; index. circ. 3,000. (back issues avail.)

668.5 SP ISSN 0210-4245
NUEVA ESTETICA. 1964. m. (10/yr.). $135. Ediciones Tecnicas Especializadas, Travesera de Gracia 15, 4, 08021 Barcelona, Spain. TEL 3-2097933. FAX 3-2096918. Ed. Alejandra Puig. adv.; bk.rev.; abstr.; illus.; index. circ. 15,000. (back issues avail.)

668.5 IT
NUOVE ARMONIE; listino ufficiale dei prezzi dei prodotti della profumeria in Italia. 1959. q. L.8000. Associazione Profumieri Milano, Corso Venezia 47, 20122 Milan, Italy. Ed. Mario Verducci. adv. circ. 7,000.

OESTERREICHISCHE DROGEN ZEITUNG. see PHARMACY AND PHARMACOLOGY

668.5 AU
OESTERREICHISCHE KOSMETIKER - FUSSPFLEGER - MASSEUR. m. Kaigasse 31, A-5020 Salzburg, Austria. TEL 0662-843457. Ed. Marga Schicho. **Document type:** trade publication.

668.5 PO
OLEOS E SABOES. 6/yr. Rua Rosa Araujo 49 B, Lisbon, Portugal.

668.54 GW ISSN 0723-1989
PARFUEMERIE AKTUELL. 1982. 7/yr. DM.70 (foreign DM.87) (effective 1997). Terra Verlag GmbH, Postfach 102144, 78421 Konstanz, Germany. TEL 49-7531-8122-0. FAX 49-7531-812299. Eds. Heidi Stolz, Susanne Reiss. circ. 17,000. **Document type:** consumer publication.
—CCC.

668.5 GW ISSN 0031-1952
TP983 CODEN: PAKOAL
PARFUEMERIE UND KOSMETIK. 1919. 11/yr. DM.322.30 (foreign DM.335.50) (effective 1997). Huethig GmbH, Postfach 102869, 69018 Heidelberg, Germany. TEL 49-6221-489307. FAX 49-6221-489481. Ed. Monika Herzberger. adv.: B&W page DM.3000; trim 210 x 297; adv. contact: Karl Dietzow. bk.rev.; abstr.; bibl.; charts; index. circ. 3,322. **Indexed:** Biotech.Abstr., Chem.Abstr., I.P.A., Key to Econ.Sci. **Document type:** trade publication.
—BLDSC (6406.575000); CASDDS; Ei; SWETS. CCC.
Description: Discusses recent technical and scientific advances affecting the perfume and cosmetics industries.

668.5 FR ISSN 0751-5537
PARFUMS-BEAUTE. 1931. a. 570 F. Editions Louis Johanet, 68 rue Boursault, 75017 Paris, France.

668.5 FR
TP983 CODEN: PCARDV
PARFUMS, COSMETIQUES, ACTUALITES; partenaire des industries cosmetiques et aromatiques. bi-m. 815 F. (foreign 1090 F.). Societe d'Expansion Technique et Economique S.A., 4 rue de Seze, 75009 Paris, France. TEL 33-1-44945060. FAX 33-1-44945075. TELEX EDISETE 650896F. Ed. Francoise Basset. adv.; charts; illus.; tr.lit. **Indexed:** Chem.Abstr., Key to Econ.Sci., PROMT. **Document type:** trade publication.
—BLDSC (1684.353000); CASDDS; CISTI; Ei; Linda Hall. CCC.
Former titles (until Sep. 1995): Parfums, Cosmetiques, Aromes (ISSN 0337-3029); (until 1975): Parfums, Cosmetiques, Savons de France (ISSN 0031-1960); Which was formed by the merger of (1958-1970): Parfumerie, Cosmetique, Savons (ISSN 0369-9099); (1957-1970): France et Ses Parfums (ISSN 0532-9094)

646 US ISSN 0272-2666
TP983 CODEN: PEFLDI
PERFUMER & FLAVORIST. 1974. bi-m. $110 in U.S. & Canada; elsewhere $150 (effective 1996 & 1997). Allured Publishing, 362 S. Schmale Rd., Carol Stream, IL 60188-2787. TEL 708-653-2155. FAX 708-653-2192. Ed. Stanley E. Allured. adv. contact: Stanley E. Allured. bk.rev. circ. 2,600. (also avail. in microform from UMI; reprint service avail. from UMI) **Indexed:** Chem.Abstr., Food Sci.& Tech.Abstr., Forest.Abstr., Forest Prod.Abstr., Hort.Abstr., I.P.A. **Document type:** trade publication.
●Also available online.
—BLDSC (6423.950000); CASDDS; CISTI; Linda Hall; SWETS; UMI. CCC.
Formerly (until 1979): Perfumer and Flavorist International (ISSN 0361-8587)
Description: International business magazine for the flavor and fragrance industry. Covers the creative, scientific and commercial aspects of this business.

668.54 SP
PERFUMERIA AL DIA. 6/yr. Via Agusta 59, 8o Of. 812, 08006 Barcelona, Spain. TEL 3-2378865. FAX 3-415-86-88. Ed. Salvador Beltran Nunez. circ. 20,000.

668.5 MX ISSN 0185-6588
PERFUMERIA MODERNA/MODERN PERFUMING. 1969. m. $50. Bravo Grupo Editorial, S.A., Jose Maria Bustillos 49, Col. Algarin, 06880 Mexico, D.F., Mexico. TEL 5-530-6062. FAX 5-538-8679. Ed. Lazaro Bravo Bernabe. adv. circ. 5,000.
Description: Suppliers' guide to perfumes, cosmetics, aerosols, detergents, insecticides, pharmaceuticals, and chemical products.

668.5 GR
PERFUMERY. q? free to qualified personnel. I C O International, 3A Barbanou, P.O. Box 190 25, 117 10 Athens, Greece. TEL 30-1-9017-806. FAX 30-1-9016-663. adv.: B&W page DM.1800; color page DM.2000. circ. 10,000 (controlled). **Document type:** trade publication.

668.55 615 SA ISSN 1015-4760
CODEN: PCRVDQ
PHARMACEUTICAL & COSMETIC REVIEW; devoted to the manufacture & marketing of medicines, toiletries, soaps, detergents in South Africa. 1974. bi-m. R.201.49 outside South Africa (effective 1997). National Publishing (Pty) Ltd., P.O. Box 2271, Clareinch 7740, South Africa. TEL 27-21-611140. FAX 27-21-611389. (Co-sponsors: Aerosol Manufacturers' Association; Society of Cosmetic Chemists; South African Association of Industrial Flavor and Fragrance Manufacturers) Ed. Lindy Hughson. adv.; illus. circ. 1,831. **Indexed:** I.P.A., Ind.S.A.Per. **Document type:** trade publication.
—BLDSC (6442.750000).
Formerly: South African Pharmaceutical and Cosmetic Review (ISSN 0257-2028)
Description: Reports on new equipment, ingredients, processes, packaging materials, legislative and marketing trends and overseas developments for manufacturers, packers and distributors of pharmaceutical, cosmetic and related products.

668.5 SP
PINKER ESTETICA. 12/yr. Ediciones Tecnicas Doria, Avda. Puerta del Angel 7, 08002 Barcelona, Spain. TEL 34-3-3187489. FAX 34-3-3011105. Ed. Maria Jesus Jimenez. **Document type:** consumer publication, trade publication.

PRODUCT ALERT. see FOOD AND FOOD INDUSTRIES

646.72 GW ISSN 0944-4025
CODEN: ANKODI
PROFI KOSMETIK; internationale Fachzeitschrift fuer Kosmetik in Theorie und Praxis. 1956. m. DM.72 (foreign DM.91) (effective 1997). Terra Verlag GmbH, Postfach 102144, 78421 Konstanz, Germany. TEL 49-7531-8122-0. FAX 49-7531-812299. Eds. Heidi Stolz, Gudrun Enders. adv.; bk.rev.; illus.; stat. circ. 15,300. **Document type:** trade publication.
—CASDDS. CCC.
Former titles: Kosmetik Journal (ISSN 0342-2968); Angewandte Kosmetik (ISSN 0003-3138)

668.5 SP
REGIA, BELLEZA Y PERFUMES. 6/yr. Hermano Julio 26, Barcelona, Spain. TEL 3-380-10-35. Ed. R. Planas Buera.

668.5 664.5 IT ISSN 0035-6948
RIVISTA ITALIANA ESSENZE, PROFUMI, PIANTE OFFICIANALI, AROMI, SAPONI, AEROSOL, COSMETICI. Short title: Rivista Italiana Eppos. (Supplement avail.: Symposium on Essential Oils. Proceedings) 1919-1981; resumed 1990. 3/yr. L.150000. Istituto Tetrahedron, Via Capitani di Mozzo, 12, 24030 Mozzo (BG), Italy. TEL 39-35-468511. FAX 39-35-463803. Ed. Enrico Colombo. adv. contact: Silvia Sarlo. bk.rev.; abstr.; charts; illus.; mkt.; index. circ. 5,000. **Indexed:** Biol.Abstr., Chem.Abstr., Food Sci.& Tech.Abstr., I.P.A. **Document type:** academic/scholarly publication.
—CISTI.
Description: Publishes original papers and reviews on; aroma, medicinal plants, sensory analysis, essences, ingredients and additives, perfumes, instrumental analysis, hygiene, microbiology and chemometrics.
Refereed Serial

668.5 GW ISSN 0942-7694
TP1 CODEN: SOFJEE
S OE F W JOURNAL. 1874. 15/yr. DM.384 (effective 1997). (Specialists in Soaps, Perfumes, Detergents (SEPAWA)) Verlag fuer Chemische Industrie H. Ziolkowsky GmbH, Beethovenstr. 16, 86150 Augsburg, Germany. TEL 49-821-519345. FAX 49-821-517953. (Co-sponsor: Vereinigung der Seifen-, Parfuem-, und Waschmittelfachleute e.V.) Ed. Bernd Ziolkowsky. adv.; bk.rev.; bibl.; charts; illus.; mkt.; pat.; tr.mk.; index. circ. 3,000. **Indexed:** Biol.Abstr., Biotech.Abstr., Chem.Abstr., Excerpt.Med., Food Sci.& Tech.Abstr., Forest Prod.Abstr., I.P.A., Int.Packag.Abstr., Key to Econ.Sci., Nutr.Abstr., PROMT. **Document type:** trade publication.
—BLDSC (8321.483000); CASDDS; CISTI; Linda Hall; SWETS. CCC.
Formerly (until 1991): Seifen, Oele, Fette, Wachse (ISSN 0173-5500)

668.55   JA
SHISEIDO ANNUAL REPORT. a. Shiseido Co. Ltd., 7-5-5 Ginza, Chuo-ku, Tokyo 104-10, Japan. TEL (03) 572-5111. FAX 03-572-6973. **Document type:** corporate report.
   Description: Offers a review of the year's highlights, economic status of the company, market trends, and future plans.

668.55   JA
SHISEIDO SEMI-ANNUAL REPORT. s-a. Shiseido Co. Ltd., 7-5-5, Ginza, Chuo-Ku, Tokyo 104, Japan. TEL 03(572)5111. FAX 03-572-6973. TELEX J24548. **Document type:** corporate report.

668.5   US
SHOPTALK (CHICAGO); journal of cosmetology for today's professional. 1981. 8/yr. $42 (renewal $32); Canada $52; elsewhere $107. Shoptalk Publications, Inc., 228 S. Wabash Ave., 10th Fl., Chicago, IL 60604-2318. TEL 312-939-8600; 888-266-6329. FAX 312-939-6181. E-mail: 101660,2577@compuserve.com. Ed. Ann McMikel. R&P contact: A.J. Thompson. adv.: color page $5763; adv. contact: Tina Bell. bk.rev.; charts; illus.; stat.; tr.lit.; index, cum.index: 1981-84; circ. 35,000 (paid). (back issues avail.) **Document type:** trade publication.
   Description: Covers skin care, nails, hairstyle, braiding and more.

SKIN INC; business and science for skin care professionals. see *MEDICAL SCIENCES — Dermatology And Venereology*

668.5   US   ISSN 0091-1372
TP1   CODEN: SCCSC8
SOAP, COSMETICS, CHEMICAL SPECIALTIES. 1925. m. $60. P T N Publishing Corp., 445 Broadhollow Rd., Melville, NY 11747-3601. Ed. Anita Shaw; Pub. Ken Carroll. adv.; bk.rev.; bibl.; illus.; mkt.; pat.; tr.lit.; tr.mk. circ. 17,050. (also avail. in microform from UMI,PMC; reprint service avail. from UMI) **Indexed:** A.S.& T.Ind., Art & Archaeol.Tech.Abstr., ASCA, Biol.Abstr., Bus.Ind., Chem.Abstr., Curr.Cont., Curr.Pack.Abstr., Excerp.Med., Hlth.Ind., I.P.A., PROMT, Risk Abstr., Text.Tech.Dig., Tr.& Indus.Ind. **Document type:** trade publication.
●Also available online. Vendor(s): Information Access Co., Lexis-Nexis.
—BLDSC (8315.150000); CASDDS; CISTI; Ei; Linda Hall; SWETS; UMI; UnCover.
   Formerly: Soap and Chemical Specialties (ISSN 0037-7481)
   Description: Edited for manufacturers of detergents, soaps, cosmetics, aerosols, waxes, polishers, insecticides, disinfectants, and other chemical specialty products.

668.5   UK   ISSN 0037-749X
                                      CODEN: SSPCD2
SOAP, PERFUMERY & COSMETICS. 1928. m. £60($195) (foreign £125). Wilmington Business Publishing, Apex House, London Rd., Northfleet, Kent DA11 9JA, England. TEL 44-1322-277788. FAX 44-1474-569418. E-mail: wbp@wilmington.co.uk. Ed. Liz Jones. adv.; bk.rev.; abstr.; bibl.; charts; illus.; mkt.; pat.; tr.mk.; index. circ. 3,400. **Indexed:** Br.Tech.Ind., Chem.Abstr., Curr.Pack.Abstr., I.P.A., Int.Packag.Abstr., Key to Econ.Sci., PROMT. **Document type:** directory, trade publication.
●Also available online. Vendor(s): Information Access Co.
—BLDSC (8316.000000); CISTI; Linda Hall; SWETS; UnCover.
   Incorporating: Soap Trade Review.

668.5   II   ISSN 0379-5608
                                      CODEN: SDTRDU
SOAPS, DETERGENTS & TOILETRIES REVIEW. (Text in English) 1965. m. $50. Wadera Publications, General Assurance Bldg., 1st Fl., 232 Dr. D.N. Rd., Bombay 400 001, India. Ed. Roshanlal Wadhera. circ. 4,000. **Indexed:** Chem.Abstr.
—BLDSC (8317.600000); CASDDS.

SOCIEDAD ARGENTINA PARA LA INVESTIGACION DE PRODUCTOS AROMATICOS. ANALES. see *BIOLOGY — Botany*

668.5   US   ISSN 0037-9832
TP983.A1   CODEN: JSCCA5
SOCIETY OF COSMETIC CHEMISTS. JOURNAL. 1947. bi-m. $200. Society of Cosmetic Chemists, 120 Wall St., New York, NY 10005-4088. TEL 212-668-1500. FAX 212-668-1504. URL: http://www.scconline.org. Ed. Randall Wickitt. adv.: page $450; trim 6 3/4 x 9 3/4; adv. contact: William DeVita. bk.rev. circ. 4,200. (also avail. in microform from PMC) **Indexed:** ASCA, Chem.Cit.Ind., Curr.Cont., I.P.A. **Document type:** academic/scholarly publication.
—BLDSC (4884.000000); CASDDS; CISTI; Ei; Genuine Article; SWETS; UnCover. CCC.

SVENSK FAERGHANDEL; tapet - parfym. see *PAINTS AND PROTECTIVE COATINGS*

T W DERMATOLOGIE; Fachzeitschrift fuer kosmetische Dermatologie. see *MEDICAL SCIENCES — Dermatology And Venereology*

668.5   SP   ISSN 0213-0858
TIENDAS DE DROGUERIA & PERFUMERIA; revista professional del sector de la drogueria y perfumeria. Variant title: Drogueria e Perfumeria. 1985. m. 12900 ptas. (foreign 23000 ptas.) (effective 1997). Tecnipublicaciones S.A., C. Albacete 5, 28027 Madrid, Spain. TEL 34-1-3261440. FAX 34-1-3262407. adv. circ. 15,000. **Document type:** trade publication.

668.5   US   ISSN 0279-1110
TOILETRIES, FRAGRANCES AND SKIN CARE: THE ROSE SHEET. 1980. w. $580 (foreign $705) (effective Jan. 1996). F-D-C Reports, Inc., 5550 Friendship Blvd., Ste. 1, Chevy Chase, MD 20815. TEL 800-332-2181. FAX 301-664-7238. Ed. Holly Mead. R&P contact: Meghanne Malone. (looseleaf format; back issues avail.; reprint service avail.) **Document type:** trade publication, newsletter.
●Also available online. Vendor(s): Data-Star (FDCR), Knight-Ridder Information, Inc. (File no.187), Lexis-Nexis, Ovid Technologies, Inc. (FDCR).
—CCC.
   Description: Provides executives in the toiletries, fragrances, skin care and related industries with specialized regulatory, legislative, scientific, financial and legal news.

668.3   IT
UP - BEAUTY & BIJOUX. 6/yr. Radicchi Editore s.r.l., Via S.G.B. de la Salle 4, 20132 Milan, Italy. TEL 2-26-30-03-30. Ed. Rossella Radicchi.

668.5   SP
VENTAS DE PERFUMERIA Y COSMETICA. (Supplements avail.: Quien es Quien, Diccionario de la Cosmetica de Tratamiento, Diccionario de Fragrancias) 1980. 12/yr. 9200 ptas. (foreign 19800 ptas.). Ediciones 4 Mas 4, C. Del Pisuerga, 19-21, 08028 Barcelona, Spain. TEL 34-3-4482978. FAX 34-3-3341253. Ed. Carles Solsona; Pub. Antonio Bergillos. adv.: color page 225000 ptas.; adv. contact: Francisco Borroso. circ. 8,000. **Document type:** trade publication.
   Description: Covers retail trade in perfumes and cosmetics.

668.5 667   GW   ISSN 0171-4341
WER UND WAS IN DER DEUTSCHEN KOERPERPFLEGE-, WASCH- UND REINIGUNGSMITTEL-INDUSTRIE. biennial. DM.198 (effective 1997). B. Behr's Verlag GmbH, Averhoffstr. 10, 22085 Hamburg, Germany. TEL 49-40-2270080. FAX 49-40-2201091. E-mail: behrs@behrs.de; URL: http://www.behrs.de. **Document type:** directory.

665.5   US   ISSN 1073-3086
WOMAN'S DAY BEAUTY. vol.5, no.1, 1995. q. (Mary Kay Cosmetics) Hachette Filipacchi Magazines, Inc., 1633 Broadway, New York, NY 10019. TEL 212-767-6000. FAX 212-767-5619. Ed. Nancy Kalish; Pub. Beth-Ann Burgon. **Document type:** consumer publication.

668.5   CC   ISSN 1004-5163
ZHONGGUO HUAZHUANGPIN/CHINA COSMETICS REVIEW. (Text in Chinese) bi-m. (Guonei Maoyi Bu, Zhongguo Baihuo Fangzhipin Gongsi) Zhongguo Huazhuangpin Bianjibu, Guonei Moyi Bu Nei, 45 Fuxingmennei Dajie, Beijing 100801, People's Republic of China. TEL 86-10-6018261. FAX 81-10-6018261. (Dist. overseas by: China International Book Trading Corp., P.O. Box 399, Beijing 100044, P.R. China) Ed. Jin Guoliang. pp./issue: 48. **Document type:** consumer publication.

BEVERAGES

see also Food and Food Industries; Packaging

338.47   US
A B A NEWSLETTER. 1983. m. $38 membership. American Bartenders' Association, Box D, Plant City, FL 33564. TEL 800-935-3232. FAX 813-752-2768. Ed. Linda Harrell. bk.rev. **Document type:** newsletter.

A PROPOS CULINA; Beitraege zur Kulturgeschichte des Essens und Trinkens. see *SOCIAL SCIENCES: COMPREHENSIVE WORKS*

663.3   US   ISSN 0149-7308
A S B C NEWSLETTER. q. $125 to non-members (foreign $131); individual members $85; corporate members $185; student members $25. American Society of Brewing Chemists, 3340 Pilot Knob Rd., St. Paul, MN 55121-2097. TEL 612-454-7250. FAX 612-454-0766. URL: http://www.scisoc.org/asbc. Ed. Jenette Wheeler. R&P contact: Jenette Wheeler. adv. contact: Amy Hope. **Document type:** newsletter.

ACUPOLL REPORTS - FOODS & BEVERAGES. see *FOOD AND FOOD INDUSTRIES*

663   NE   ISSN 0929-6247
AD FUNDUM. (Text in Dutch) 1993. m. fl.105 (foreign fl.145) (free to qualified personnel). Uitgeverij Lakerveld B.V., Mangaanstraat 86, Postbus 43250, 2504 AG The Hague, Netherlands. TEL 31-70-3218218. FAX 31-70-3298744. E-mail: publish@lakerveld.nl; URL: http://www.lakerveld.nl. Ed. Willem Verstraaten; Pub. Ad van Gaalen. R&P contact: Ad van Gaalen. adv. contact: Hans de Jong. illus.; circ. 1,000 (paid), 3,000 (controlled). (back issues avail.) **Document type:** trade publication.
   Description: Business magazine for the beverage trade.

663 616.861   US   ISSN 1067-3105
ALCOHOL ISSUES INSIGHTS. 1983. m. $240. Beer Marketer's Insights, Inc., Box 264, West Nyack, NY 10994. TEL 914-524-2337. Ed. Eric Shepard. (back issues avail.) **Document type:** newsletter.
   Description: Covers alcohol policy issues, including excise tax, drunk driving laws, advertising and availability restrictions, and alcohol and health.

663   US   ISSN 0889-3519
ALCOHOLIC BEVERAGE EXECUTIVES' NEWSLETTER. 1940. w. $275 (foreign $300). Alcoholic Beverage Executives' Newsletter, Inc., Box 3188, Omaha, NE 68103-0188. TEL 402-397-5514. FAX 402-397-3843. Ed. Patricia Kennedy; Pub. Patricia Kennedy. R&P contact: Patricia Kennedy. adv. (looseleaf format; back issues avail.) **Document type:** newsletter.

663.4   US
ALE STREET NEWS. vol.2, 1993. bi-m. $16.95 (effective 1997). Tuscarora Inc., Box 1125, Maywood, NJ 07607. TEL 201-368-9100; 800-351-2537. FAX 201-368-9101. E-mail: info@alestreetnews.com; URL: http://www.alestreetnews.com. Ed. Tony Forder; Pubs. Tony Forder, Jack Babin. adv. contact: Jack Babin. circ. 100,000 (controlled). **Document type:** newspaper, trade publication.

663.4   US
ALEPHENALIA BEER NEWS. 1980. a. free. Merchant du Vin Corp., 140 Lakeside Ave., No. 300, Seattle, WA 98122-6538. TEL 206-322-5022. FAX 206-322-5185. E-mail: info@mdv-beer.com. Ed. Charles S. Finkel. R&P contact: Rose Ann Finkel. bk.rev. circ. 33,000. (tabloid format) **Document type:** newsletter, consumer publication.

663.1   GW   ISSN 0002-5496
ALKOHOL-INDUSTRIE; deutsche Spirituosen-Zeitung und Brennerei-Zeitung. (Supplements: Junge Destillateur und Brenner Spirituosen Verkauf) 1887. s-m. DM.200 (foreign DM.220). Team Verlag GmbH und Fachzeitschriften KG, Auwanne 19, 63791 Karlstein, Germany. Ed. Horst P. Czerner. adv.; bk.rev.; charts; illus.; mkt.; pat.; index. circ. 3,000. **Indexed:** Biol.Abstr., Chem.Abstr., Food Sci.& Tech.Abstr. **Document type:** trade publication.
—BLDSC (0788.540000); CISTI.

BEVERAGES

ALT OM MAD. see *FOOD AND FOOD INDUSTRIES*

663.2 634.8 FR ISSN 0769-8372
AMATEUR DE BORDEAUX. 1981. 5/yr. Societe d'Editions Specialisees, 22 rue des Reculettes, 75013 Paris, France. TEL 43-31-44-99. FAX 43-31-41-15. **Document type:** consumer publication.
Description: Cultivates the art of the good life in the heart of the Bordeaux wine country.

663.3 US ISSN 1055-470X
HD9397.U5
AMERICAN BREWER; the business of beer, a micro-brewer - pub brewing magazine. 1983. 5/yr. $24 (foreign $40). American Brewer Inc., Box 510, Hayward, CA 94543-0510. TEL 510-538-9500. FAX 510-538-7644. E-mail: bill@ambrew.com; URL: http://www.ambrew.com. Ed. Jim Dorsch; Pub. Bill Owens. R&P contact: Bill Owens. adv. contact: Jim Dorsch. bk.rev.; circ. 18,000 (paid). **Document type:** consumer publication, trade publication.
—CCC.
Formed by the 1987 merger of (1986-1987): Amateur Brewer (ISSN 0887-7416); Home Fermenter's Digest (ISSN 0742-4590)
Description: Covers styles and varieties of beers as well as personalities who have shaped the industry.

AMERICAN BREWERIANA JOURNAL. see *HOBBIES*

AMERICAN INSTITUTE OF WINE & FOOD. NEW YORK AREA CHAPTER. NEWS. see *FOOD AND FOOD INDUSTRIES*

663.2 634.8 US ISSN 0002-9254
CODEN: AJEVAC
AMERICAN JOURNAL OF ENOLOGY AND VITICULTURE. 1954. q. $155 (foreign $175) (effective 1997). American Society for Enology and Viticulture, Box 1855, Davis, CA 95617. TEL 916-753-3142. FAX 916-753-3318. Ed. JoAnne Rantz. adv.; abstr.; bibl.; charts; index. circ. 3,300. (also avail. in microfilm from UMI; reprint service avail. from UMI) **Indexed:** Agri.Eng.Abstr., ASCA, Biodet.Abstr., Biol.Abstr., Biotech.Abstr., Chem.Abstr., Crop Physiol.Abstr., Curr.Adv.Ecol.Sci., Curr.Cont., Curr.Pack.Abstr., Excerp.Med., Food Sci.& Tech.Abstr., Helminthol.Abstr., Hort.Abstr., Ind.Sci.Rev., Irr.& Drain.Abstr., Nutr.Abstr., Plant Breed.Abstr., Plant Grow.Reg.Abstr., Sci.Cit.Ind., Soils & Fert., VITIS. **Document type:** academic/scholarly publication.
—BLDSC (0824.525000); CASDDS; CISTI; EMDOCS; Genuine Article; Linda Hall; SWETS; UMI; UnCover.
Description: Examines grape growing and wine making research.
Refereed Serial

663.3 US ISSN 0361-0470
CODEN: JSBCD3
AMERICAN SOCIETY OF BREWING CHEMISTS. JOURNAL. 1942. q. $115 to non-members (foreign $124); individual members $85; corporate members $185; student members $25. American Society of Brewing Chemists, 3340 Pilot Knob Rd., St. Paul, MN 55121-2097. TEL 612-454-7250. FAX 612-454-0766. URL: http://www.scisoc.org/asbc. Ed. P.L. Freeman; Pub. Steven C. Nelson. R&P contact: Ina Pfefer. adv. contact: Amy Hope. charts; index, cum.index: 1940-1945, 1955-1964. circ. 850. (back issues avail.) **Indexed:** Alloys Ind., ASCA, Chem.Abstr., Curr.Cont., Curr.Pack.Abstr., Eng.Mat.Abstr., Food Sci.& Tech.Abstr., Ind.Sci.Rev., Met.Abstr., Met.Abstr.Ind., Nonfer.Met.Alert, PCC Alert, Steels Alert, World Alum.Abstr. **Document type:** proceedings.
—BLDSC (4692.545000); CASDDS; CISTI; Genuine Article; Linda Hall; SWETS; UnCover. **CCC.**
Formerly (until vol.34, 1976): American Society of Brewing Chemists. Proceedings (ISSN 0096-0845)
Refereed Serial

663.2 664 US ISSN 0892-7642
AMERICAN WINE & FOOD. 1987. m. membership. American Institute of Wine and Food, 1550 Bryant St., San Francisco, CA 94103. TEL 415-255-3000.

663.2 641.5 US
AMERICAN WINE ON THE WEB. 1988. 12/yr. Box 5068, Lake Gregory, CA 92325. TEL 909-338-9776. FAX 909-338-4956. URL: http://www.2way.com/food/wine. Ed. Richard Jones; Pub. Gerry Troy. R&P contact: Gerry Troy. adv. contact: Gerry Troy. **Document type:** newsletter.
●Available only online.
Former titles (until 1995): Southwest Internacional Wine and Food Review; Southwest International Wine.
Description: Covers the wine industry in the Americas. Focuses on new wine releases, winery profiles, wine art, and wine events.

663.2 US ISSN 0149-6778
AMERICAN WINE SOCIETY BULLETIN. 1973. irreg. $3. American Wine Society, 3006 Latta Rd., Rochester, NY 14612. TEL 716-225-7613. Pub. Angel Nardone. R&P contact: Angel Nardone. circ. 3,000. (back issues avail.) **Document type:** bulletin.

663 US ISSN 0364-698X
TP544.A46
AMERICAN WINE SOCIETY JOURNAL. vol.6, 1974. q. $36 includes manual & bulletin. American Wine Society, 3006 Latta Rd., Rochester, NY 14612. TEL 716-225-7613. Ed. Jane Moulton; Pub. Angel Nardone. R&P contact: Angel Nardone. **Indexed:** Bibl.Agri.
Description: Contains articles on all aspects of wine appreciation, grape growing, winemaking, travel, health, and food.

663.2 US ISSN 0149-676X
AMERICAN WINE SOCIETY MANUAL. irreg. price varies. American Wine Society, 3006 Latta Rd., Rochester, NY 14612. TEL 716-225-7613. R&P contact: Angel Nardone. (back issues avail.)

663.2 US
AMERICAN WINE SOCIETY NEWS. vol.4, 1990. q. membership. American Wine Society, 3006 Latta Rd., Rochester, NY 14612. TEL 716-225-7613. Ed. Robert Miller; Pub. Angel Nardone. R&P contact: Angel Nardone. adv. contact: Angel Nardone.
Description: Contains news of the society; profiles the society's members; and lists calendar of events.

663.2 IT
ANNUARIO DEI VINI ITALIANI. a. Luca Maroni Editore, Via Rodolfo Benini 24, 00191 Rome, Italy. TEL 39-6-8271061. FAX 39-6-8271061. Ed. Fabio Rizzari. **Document type:** directory.
Description: Reports on the products of 181 wineries, listed by region.

663.3 YU
APA. 1975. m. Apatinska Privara, Trg Oslobodenja 5, Apatin, Yugoslavia. Ed. Dusanka Kupresanin.

APERITIF; tidningen foer an baettre restaurang- och. see *HOTELS AND RESTAURANTS*

663 US
APPELLATION; wine country living. 1993. bi-m. $18. Appellation Magazine Co., Box 516, Napa, CA 94559. TEL 707-963-3393. FAX 707-963-2250. Ed. Mary Chesterfield; Pub. Jack C. Morgan. R&P contact: Dick Dee. adv.: B&W page $4500, color page $6000. circ. 125,000. **Document type:** consumer publication.
Formerly (until 1977): Napa Valley Appellation (ISSN 1072-5717)

663.1 US ISSN 0164-6281
ARIZONA BEVERAGE ANALYST. 1936. m. $15. Bell Publications, Beverage Analyst Group, 2403 Champa St., Denver, CO 80205. TEL 303-296-1600. FAX 303-295-2159. Ed. Sherry Smith. R&P contact: Larry Bell. adv. contact: Sherry Smith. bk.rev.; illus. circ. 2,500. **Document type:** trade publication.
Formerly (until 1977): Arizona Beverage Journal (ISSN 0004-1432)
Description: Examines the liquor industry.

ART CULINAIRE; the international magazine in good taste. see *FOOD AND FOOD INDUSTRIES*

THE ART OF EATING. see *FOOD AND FOOD INDUSTRIES*

663 UK ISSN 1354-7240
ASIA - PACIFIC DRINKS BUYER. (Text in English; summaries in Chinese, Japanese, Korean, Thai) 1994. bi-m. $80 (outside Europe $110). Crier Publications Ltd., Arctic House, Rye Ln., Dunton Green, Sevenoaks, Kent TH14 5HB, England. TEL 44-1732-451515. FAX 44-1732-451383. E-mail: antk@crier.demon.co.uk. Ed. Heather Buckle; Pub. John Whitbread. adv. contact: Philip McLean. circ. 10,200. (back issues avail.) **Document type:** trade publication.
Description: Discusses matters of interest to major purchasing companies of drinks in all Asian and Pacific nations.

663.3 SP
ASOCIACION ESPANOLA DE TECNICOS DE CERVEZA Y MALTA. ANUARIO. a. Asociacion Espanola de Tecnicos de Cerveza y Malta, Ramirez de Prado 8, 1o F, 28045 Madrid, Spain. TEL 34-1-5277255. FAX 34-1-5285507. adv.: B&W page 54000 ptas.

663 GT ISSN 0066-8567
ASOCIACION NACIONAL DEL CAFE. DEPARTAMENTO DE ASUNTOS AGRICOLAS. INFORME ANUAL. 1962. a. free. Asociacion Nacional del Cafe, Departamento de Asuntos Agricolas, Edificio Etisa, Plazuela Espana, Zona 9, Guatemala, Guatemala.
Formerly: Asociacion Nacional del Cafe. Departamento de Asuntos Agricolas. Annual Memory.

ASSAM DIRECTORY & TEA AREAS HANDBOOK. see *BUSINESS AND ECONOMICS — Trade And Industrial Directories*

338.47 US
ASSOCIATION OF WINE SUPPLIERS. BANKRUPTCY UPDATE. irreg. Association of Wine Suppliers, 21 Tamal Vistal Blvd., No. 196, Corte Madera, CA 94925. TEL 415-924-2640.

663 US ISSN 0044-9881
ATLANTIC CONTROL STATES BEVERAGE JOURNAL. (North Carolina, Virginia and West Virginia Editions) 1967. m. $12. Club & Tavern, Inc., 3 12th St., Wheeling, WV 26003. TEL 304-232-7620. FAX 304-233-1236. Ed. Arnold Lazarus. adv.; bk.rev. circ. 6,379. **Document type:** trade publication.
Description: News publication for West Virginia, Virginia and North Carolina liquor licenses and restaurants.

ATTERBURY LETTER - WINE, DINING & TRAVEL. see *TRAVEL AND TOURISM*

663.2 AT ISSN 1033-7954
HD9388.A8
AUSTRALIAN AND NEW ZEALAND WINE INDUSTRY DIRECTORY. 1983. a. Aus.$65 (foreign Aus.$75). Winetitles, P.O. Box 1140, Marleston, S.A. 5033, Australia. TEL 61-8-82346055. FAX 61-8-82346050. E-mail: editor@winetitles.com.au; URL: http://www.winetitles.com.au. Ed. Michael Major; Pub. Paul Clancy. adv.: B&W page Aus.$1400, color page Aus.$1750; adv. contact: Paul Clancy. maps, stat. circ. 2,500. **Document type:** directory, trade publication.
Formerly (until 1987): Australian Wine Industry Directory (ISSN 0811-1324)
Description: Directory of all wineries in Australia and New Zealand, personnel, suppliers, consultants, distributors.

663.2 630 AT ISSN 0819-2421
AUSTRALIAN AND NEW ZEALAND WINE INDUSTRY JOURNAL. 1986. q. Aus.$60 (foreign Aus.$90). Winetitles, P.O. Box 1140, Marleston, S.A. 5033, Australia. TEL 61-8-82346055. FAX 61-8-82346050. E-mail: editor@winetitles.com.au; URL: http://www.winetitles.com.au. Ed. Michael Major; Pub. Paul Clancy. adv.: B&W page Aus.$1185, color page Aus.$1550; adv. contact: Paul Clancy. index. circ. 2,500. (back issues avail.) **Indexed:** Food Sci.& Tech.Abstr. **Document type:** trade publication.
—BLDSC (1797.360000); UnCover.
Formerly: Australian Wine Industry Journal (ISSN 0817-427X)
Description: Technical and scientific journal of winemaking and grapegrowing. Contains papers, industry news, market reports, new products.
Refereed Serial

AUSTRALIAN HOTELIER. see *HOTELS AND RESTAURANTS*

BEVERAGES

663.2   AT   ISSN 0816-0805
AUSTRALIAN WINE RESEARCH INSTITUTE TECHNICAL REVIEW. 1981. bi-m. Aus.$45 (students Aus.$22.50) (effective July 1992). Australian Wine Research Institute, P.O. Box 197, Glen Osmond, S.A. 5064, Australia. TEL 61-8-83036600. FAX 61-8-83036601. Ed. Creina Stockley. R&P contact: Creina Stockley. bk.rev.; abstr.; circ. 925 (controlled). (back issues avail.) Document type: academic/scholarly publication.
    Description: Technical abstracts for winemakers, research articles, and industry news.
    Refereed Serial

AUSTRIA. HOEHERE BUNDESLEHRANSTALT UND BUNDESAMT FUER WEIN- UND OBSTBAU. MITTEILUNGEN KLOSTERNEUBURG; Rebe und Wein, Obstbau und Fruechteverwertung. see AGRICULTURE — Crop Production And Soil

663.2   CN   ISSN 1188-1348
B C WINE TRAILS. Key Title: British Columbia Wine Trails. 1991. q. Can.$10($12) (effective Jan. 1995). Wine Trails Publishing, P.O. Box 1077, Summerland, BC V0H 1Z0, Canada. TEL 604-494-7733. FAX 604-494-7737. Ed. Dave Gamble; Pub. Dave Gamble. adv.: B&W page Can.$1375; trim 11 1/2 X 15 1/2; adv. contact: Dave Gamble. bk.rev. circ. 15,000. (tabloid format; back issues avail.) Document type: consumer publication, trade publication.
    Description: Guides readers into the vineyards, cellars and tasting roads of British Columbia wineries.

663.2   IT
BACCHUS. Italian edition: Civilta del Bere. (Text in German) 1978. s-a. DM.20. Editoriale Lariana s.r.l., Via Ciro Menotti 11-D, 20129 Milan, Italy. TEL 39-2-76110303. FAX 39-2-713847. Ed. Pino Khail. adv.: B&W page L.7256000, color page L.10884000; adv. contact: Antonella Khail. circ. 46,000. Document type: trade publication.
    Description: Explores Italian wines and food.

663   GW   ISSN 0172-0937
BADISCHE WINZER. m. (Badischer Weinbauverband e.V.) Badischer Landwirtschafts Verlag GmbH, Friedrichstr. 43, 79098 Freiburg im Breisgau, Germany. Ed. Manfred Zimper. adv. circ. 23,000. Document type: trade publication.

663.3   US
BARLEYCORN; celebrating & exploring the brewing arts. 1990. 8/yr. $20 (Canada $30; elsewhere $50). George Rivers, Ed. & Pub., Box 549, Frederick, MD 21705. TEL 301-831-3759. FAX 301-831-6376. R&P contact: Geroge Rivers. adv. contact: Mike Horkan. illus. circ. 50,000. Document type: consumer publication.

663.2   CN   ISSN 0228-5452
LA BARRIQUE. 1971. 7/yr. Can.$23. Kylix Media Inc., 5165 Sherbrooke St. W., Ste. 414, Montreal, PQ H4A 1T6, Canada. TEL 514-481-5892. FAX 514-481-9699. E-mail: ryann@odyssee.net. Ed. Nicole Barrette-Ryan. adv. circ. 11,045. (back issues avail.) Document type: consumer publication.
    Description: Wine and spirits information for consumers and restaurateurs in the Quebec province.

663   US   ISSN 0199-8404
BARTENDER; the authority on bartending and on-premise. 1979. 4/yr. $25 (foreign $35). Foley Publishing Corp., Box 158, Liberty Corner, NJ 07938. TEL 908-766-6006. FAX 908-766-6607. E-mail: barmag@aol.com; URL: http://www.bartender.com. Ed. Jaclyn Wilson Foley; Pub. Raymond Foley. adv. contact: Raymond Foley. bk.rev.; circ. 13,575 (paid); 130,703 (controlled). (back issues avail.) Document type: trade publication.
    Description: For the full service on-premise industry.

BARTENDER INTERNATIONAL. see OCCUPATIONS AND CAREERS

BARTENDEREN. see OCCUPATIONS AND CAREERS

663.2   US
    SB387
THE BAXEVANIS AMERICAN WINE REVIEW. 1974. bi-m. $25 (effective 1994-1995). John J. Baxevanis, Ed. & Pub., 1947 Hillside Dr., Stroudsburg, PA 18360. TEL 717-424-6076. adv.; bk.rev.; index, cum.index: 1974-1984; circ. 2,500 (paid). Document type: newsletter.
    Formerly (until 1994): Vinifera Wine Growers Journal (ISSN 0095-3563)
    Description: Informs, educates, and fosters discourse on the wines and geography of the world's major and minor wine-producing regions.

BAY FOOD. see FOOD AND FOOD INDUSTRIES

663   US   ISSN 0005-7533
                CODEN: BBDSDO
BEBIDAS. (Text in Spanish) 1942. bi-m. $18. Global Beverage Publishers Inc., Box 16116, Cleveland, OH 44116. TEL 216-331-9100. FAX 216-331-9020. Ed. William R. Dolan. adv.: B&W page $2750; trim 8 1/4 x 11 1/4; adv. contact: William R. Dolan. bk.rev. circ. 9,500. Document type: trade publication.
    Description: Written for producers and distributors of soft drinks, beer, bottled water and juice in 22 countries of Latin America plus Spain and Portugal.

663   MX   ISSN 0188-8080
BEBIDAS MEXICANAS. bi-m. $25 (foreign $55) (effective 1996 & 1997). Alfa Editores Tecnicos S.A., Libertad No. 107-402, 03660 Mexico DF, Mexico. TEL 525-579-3333. FAX 525-532-9504. Ed. Alejandro Garduno-Torres. R&P contact: Alfredo Remes. adv.: B&W page $504, color page $756. circ. 5,000 (controlled). Document type: trade publication.
    Description: Presents technological, legal, business and marketing aspects of the beverage sector.
    Refereed Serial

663.4   US   ISSN 1067-4160
BEER; the magazine. 1993. 5/yr. $18 (effective 1997). Box 717, Hayward, CA 94543-0717. TEL 510-538-7644; 800-646-2701. FAX 510-538-7644. E-mail: btm@AmBrew.com; URL: http://www.ambrew.com/. Ed. Jim Dorsch; Pub. Bill Owens. R&P contact: Melora Janisch. bk.rev. circ. 50,000. (tabloid format) Document type: consumer publication.
    Description: For people who love beer; contains news from lambics to lagers.

663.4 642.5   US
BEER & TAVERN CHRONICLE. 1994. m. $30 (Canada $36; rest of world $50). Beer & Tavern Chronicle, Inc., 244 Madison Ave., Ste. 164, New York, NY 10016. TEL 212-685-8334; 800-343-4677. E-mail: gsmithbeer@aol.com. Ed. Gregg Smith; Pub. Liz Branch. R&P contact: Gregg Smith. adv. contact: Liz Branch. circ. 120,000. Document type: newspaper.

BEER CANS & BREWERY COLLECTIBLES. see HOBBIES

663.4   US
▼**BEER CONNOISSEUR**. 1997. q. $17.50. 2102 S. Arlington Heights Rd., Arlington Heights, IL 60005. Document type: consumer publication.

662.3 658.8   US
BEER HANDBOOK. a. $350 (for Aug. 1997 ed.). Adams Trade Press, 2101 S. Arlington, Ste. 150, Arlington Heights, IL 60005. TEL 800-396-3939. charts; stat. Document type: trade publication.
    Description: Reports trends, statistics, and analyses for the beer industry.

663.4   US
BEER INDUSTRY UPDATE. 1982. a. $750. Beer Marketer's Insights, Inc., Box 264, West Nyack, NY 10994. TEL 914-624-2337. Ed. Jerry Steinman. charts. (back issues avail.) Document type: trade publication.
    Description: Statistical overview of US beer industry, with written analysis. Provides data for total beer shipments by state, brewer and region.

663.3   US   ISSN 0300-7480
BEER MARKETER'S INSIGHTS. 1970. 23/yr. $385. Beer Marketer's Insights, Inc., Box 264, West Nyack, NY 10994. TEL 914-624-2337. Ed. Jerry Steinman. bk.rev.; stat. (processed; back issues avail.) Document type: newsletter.
    Description: Analyzes shipments, sales in beer industry (domestic and import), plus social, political, legal trends which affect sales.

663.4 310   US   ISSN 0164-4831
BEER STATISTICS NEWS. 1974. 24/yr. $315. Beer Marketer's Insights, Inc., Box 264, West Nyack, NY 10994. TEL 914-624-2337. Ed. Eric Shepard. charts. Document type: bulletin.
    Description: Reports shipments by major brewers in 39 states. Includes state, region, summary reports with graphs, maps, written analysis.

663.4 658.8   UK
BEER: THE INTERNATIONAL MARKET. (Subseries of: Market Direction reports) a. £2500($5000) (effective 1996). Euromonitor, 60-61 Britton St., London EC1M 5NA, England. TEL 44-171-251-8024. FAX 44-171-908-3149. E-mail: info@euromonitor.com; URL: http://www.euromonitor.com. (Addr. in N. America: Euromonitor International, 122 S. Michigan Ave., Ste. 1200, Chicago, IL 60603. TEL 800-577-3876. FAX 312-922-1157) (looseleaf format) Document type: trade publication.
    ●Also available online. Vendor(s): Data-Star, Knight-Ridder Information, Inc.
    Description: Analyzes the beer markets in France, Germany, Italy, Spain, the U.K., the U.S., Japan, and Canada.

BEST 'N' MOST IN D F S. see BUSINESS AND ECONOMICS — International Commerce

658.8   US
BEVERAGE ALCOHOL BUSINESS SCENE.* 1963. m. (8/yr.) $30. Diamond Publications, Box 398, Hopkins, MN 55343-0398. TEL 612-449-9446. FAX 612-449-9447. Ed. Gary L. Diamond. adv. circ. 26,000. Document type: trade publication.
    Former titles: Spirits, Wine and Beer Marketing in Iowa (ISSN 0747-3214); Iowa Beverage Journal (ISSN 0191-4650)
    Description: For beverage alcohol licensees buying at least $1,000,000 of liquor, wine and or beer at wholesale prices.

338.47   US   ISSN 0736-220X
BEVERAGE ALCOHOL MARKET REPORT. 1982. 26/yr. $195 (foreign $215) (effective January 1996). Peregrine Communications, 160 E. 48th St., New York, NY 10017. TEL 212-371-5237. Ed. Perry Luntz; Pub. Perry Luntz. R&P contact: Perry Luntz. adv.; bk.rev.; charts; stat. circ. 3,000. Document type: newsletter.
    Description: For executives in the international beer, wine and spirits industries, including producers, wholesalers and retailers.

663 658   US
    HD9350.1
BEVERAGE & FOOD DYNAMICS. 1934. 9/yr. $35 (Canada and Mexico $50; elsewhere $75) (free to qualified personnel) (effective 1997). Hunter Publishing Limited Partnership, 2101 S. Arlington Heights Rd., Ste. 150, Arlington Heights, IL 60005. TEL 847-427-9512. FAX 847-427-2097. Ed. Richard Brandes; Pub. Seymour Leikind. adv. contact: John Pennacchio. charts; illus.; stat.; circ. 75,000 (controlled). Document type: trade publication.
    Former titles (until June 1994): Jobson's Beverage Dynamics (ISSN 1046-1973); (until 1989): Liquor Store (ISSN 1058-5273); (until 1984): Liquor Store Magazine (ISSN 0024-4236)
    Description: Covers the retail trade in specialty food items, sundries, gourmet and deli products, and the beverage trade, including alcohol.

663 664   II   ISSN 0970-6194
BEVERAGE AND FOOD WORLD. (Text in English) vol.3, 1974. bi-m. Rs.180($30) Amalgamated Press, Narang House, 41 Ambalal Doshi Marg, Fort, Mumbai 400 001, India. TEL 91-22-2650268. FAX 91-22-2641275. Ed. Norman da Silva. adv.: B&W page Rs.5000($300), color page Rs.7500($375); trim 240 x 186. circ. 5,000. Document type: trade publication.
    Incorporates: Brewer - Distiller and Bottler.
    Description: Provides information on processed foods and beverage products, equipment, and ingredients.

516 BEVERAGES

663 US
BEVERAGE BEACON - LEDGER. 1970. m. $12 (effective 1997). 6601 S. Hoover St., Los Angeles, CA 90044-3695. TEL 213-778-7522. FAX 213-778-2725. Ed. Samuel King; Pub. Samuel King. R&P contact: Samuel King. adv. contact: Mike Johnson. bk.rev. circ. 10,000. (tabloid format; back issues avail.) **Document type:** trade publication.
Incorporates: Beverage Ledger.

663.1 US ISSN 0006-0356
BEVERAGE BULLETIN. 1936. m. $24; newsstand price: $3. California Beverage Publications, Inc., 6310 San Vicente Blvd., Ste. 530, Los Angeles, CA 90048-5426. TEL 213-930-4831. FAX 213-930-4835. Ed. Michael Lynn; Pub. Dan Bolton. R&P contact: Dan Bolton. adv.: page $3529; 10 x 14; adv. contact: Mike Chu. illus. circ. 16,000. (tabloid format) **Document type:** newspaper, trade publication.

663 US
BEVERAGE COMMUNICATOR. 1972. q. $18 (foreign $20). Beverage Communicator, Inc., 5 Barker Ave., Ste. 501, White Plains, NY 10601. TEL 914-761-7700. FAX 914-997-2617. circ. 6,250.

663.6 US ISSN 0148-6187
HD9348.U5 CODEN: BEVIAY
BEVERAGE INDUSTRY. (Supplement avail.: Beverage Industry Annual Manual (ISSN 8755-0717)) 1946. m. $55 (foreign $110) (free to qualified personnel) (effective 1996). Stagnito Publishing Company, 1935 Shermer Rd., Ste. 100, Northbrook, IL 60062. TEL 847-205-5660. FAX 847-205-5680. Ed. Joan Hollaran; Pub. Tom Bachmann. R&P contact: Joan Hollaran. adv. contact: Anngail Norris. illus. circ. 28,987. (also avail. in microform from UMI) **Indexed:** B.P.I., Bus.Ind., Chic.Per.Ind., Curr.Pack.Abstr., Hospit.Ind., Int.Packag.Abstr., PROMT, SRI, Tr.& Indus.Ind. **Document type:** trade publication.
●Also available online. Vendor(s): Information Access Co.
—BLDSC (1947.255000); KR SourceOne; UMI; UnCover.
Former titles (until 1973): Soft Drink Industry (ISSN 0038-0547); (until 1966): Bottling Industry.
Description: Edited for executives in beverage markets, with emphasis on marketing, technology, and distribution activities.

663 US ISSN 8755-0717
HD9348.U5
BEVERAGE INDUSTRY ANNUAL MANUAL. (Supplement to: Beverage Industry (ISSN 0148-6187)) 1967. a. $55 (effective 1995). Stagnito Publishing Company, 1935 Shermer Rd., Ste. 100, Northbrook, IL 60062. TEL 847-205-5600. FAX 847-205-5680. Ed. Joan Hollaran; Pub. Tom Bachmann. adv. contact: Anngail Norris. stat. circ. 27,000. **Indexed:** SRI. **Document type:** trade publication.
Description: Contains statistical material for beverage industry executives and department managers.

663.1 US ISSN 1054-0423
BEVERAGE INDUSTRY NEWS. 1935. m. $49. B I N Publications, 703 Market St., Ste.251, San Francisco, CA 94103. TEL 415-495-8984. FAX 415-546-6213. Ed. David L. Page; Pub. David L. Page. R&P contact: David L. Page. adv. contact: David L. Page. bk.rev.; abstr.; bibl.; charts; illus.; stat.; index. circ. 10,000. **Document type:** trade publication.
Incorporates (1970-1994): Beverage Industry News Merchandiser (ISSN 0271-9894); Formerly (until 1988): Beverage Industry News of California (ISSN 0274-9041)
Description: Covers all news relevant to the alcoholic beverage industry.

663 US ISSN 1057-5030
HD9348.U5
THE (YEAR) BEVERAGE MARKETING DIRECTORY. 1978. a., 15th ed., 1993. $745 softcover; hardcover $765. Beverage Marketing Corporation, 2670 Commercial Ave., Mingo Junction, OH 43938. TEL 614-598-4133. FAX 614-598-3977. Ed. Terry Welling. adv. circ. 2,300. (also avail. in diskette format) **Document type:** directory, trade publication.
Former titles (until 1991): National Beverage Marketing Directory (ISSN 0197-3061); (until 1980): National Beverage Marketing Directory of Telephone Numbers and Addresses (ISSN 0160-9580)
Description: Guide to the beverage industry in the United States and Canada. Comprehensive company-by-company listing of more than 12,000 producers, bottlers, importers, wholesalers and distributors in every beverage category.

663 US ISSN 0006-0372
BEVERAGE MEDIA. 1936. m. $78. (Beverage Network) Beverage Media, Ltd., 161 Ave. of the Americas, New York, NY 10013. TEL 212-734-0322. FAX 212-620-0473. Ed. William G. Slone. adv.; bk.rev.; illus.; mkt.; stat.; tr.lit. circ. 7,800. **Document type:** trade publication.

663.6 US ISSN 0098-2318
TP659.A1 CODEN: BEWODQ
BEVERAGE WORLD (ENGLISH EDITION); magazine of the beverage industry. 1882. m. $45 (foreign $55). Strategic Business Communications, 226 W. 26th St., New York, NY 10011. TEL 212-822-5930. FAX 212-822-5931. Ed. Havis Dawson. adv.; charts; illus.; mkt.; pat.; tr.lit.; tr.mk.; index. circ. 33,000. (also avail. in microfilm from UMI; reprint service avail. from UMI) **Indexed:** B.P.I., BPIA, Bus.Ind., Curr.Pack.Abstr., Excerp.Med., Hospit.Ind., Int.Packag.Abstr., P.A.I.S., PROMT, Tr.& Indus.Ind. **Document type:** trade publication.
●Also available online. Vendor(s): Information Access Co., Knight-Ridder Information, Inc., Lexis-Nexis, UMI.
—BLDSC (1947.265000); KR SourceOne; Linda Hall; SWETS; UMI; UnCover.
Former titles: Soft Drinks (ISSN 0038-0571); National Bottler's Gazette.

663 US ISSN 1076-8149
BEVERAGE WORLD EN ESPANOL. (Text in Spanish) 1946-1989; resumed 1994. bi-m. Strategic Business Communications, 226 W. 26th St., New York, NY 10011. TEL 212-822-5930. FAX 212-822-5931. circ. 10,600. **Document type:** trade publication.

663 US ISSN 1076-5271
TP500
BEVERAGE WORLD INTERNATIONAL. 1983. bi-m. Strategic Business Communications, 226 W. 26th St., New York, NY 10011. TEL 212-822-5930. FAX 212-822-5931. Ed. Michael Edison. adv. circ. 20,153. **Document type:** trade publication.

338.47 US
BEVERAGE WORLD'S DATABANK. 1984. a. $49. Strategic Business Communications, 226 W. 26th St., New York, NY 10011. TEL 212-822-5930. FAX 212-822-5931. Ed. Sandy Beckerman. adv. circ. 28,013. **Document type:** trade publication.
Former titles: Beverage World's Daily Desk Reference Living Directory; Beverage World's Living Directory.

663 US
BEVERAGES: LATIN AMERICAN INDUSTRIAL REPORT. (Avail. for each of 22 Latin American countries) 1985. a. $435 per country report. Aquino Productions, Box 125, Rochester, VT 05767. Ed. Andres C. Aquino.

663 GW ISSN 0937-1958
BIER & GETRAENKE. 1990. m. DM.140 (foreign DM.183) (effective 1997). Verlag Hans Carl GmbH, Andernacherstr. 33a, 90411 Nuernberg, Germany. TEL 49-911-95285-0. FAX 49-911-9528548. Ed. Guenter Schmiedel. adv.: B&W page DM.4660, color page DM.7000; trim 185 x 275; adv. contact: Corinna Thoenissen. circ. 9,600. **Document type:** trade publication.
Description: Provides information for the beer and beverage specialist wholesale trade.

641 GW ISSN 0341-4914
DER BIERGROSSHANDEL. 1949. s-m. DM.23.20 per mo. (foreign DM.25.10) (effective 1997). Matthaes Verlag GmbH, Postfach 103144, 70027 Stuttgart, Germany. TEL 49-711-2133-0. circ. 10,600. **Indexed:** Food Sci.& Tech.Abstr., Key to Econ.Sci. **Document type:** newspaper.

663 CN
BILLY'S BEST BOTTLES. 1973. bi-m. Can.$40 (foreign Can.$50) (effective 1997). Best Bottles Inc., Box 21011, Stratford, ON N5A 7V4, Canada. TEL 519-273-5517. FAX 519-273-5517. Ed. William Munnelly; Pub. William Munnelly. bk.rev. circ. 5,000. (back issues avail.) **Document type:** newsletter.
Former titles: Best Bottles Wineletter (ISSN 1196-9539); (until 1987): Best Bottles (ISSN 0827-7478); (until 1984): William Munnelly's Private Guide to the Best Bottles (ISSN 0827-746X)
Description: Review of all wines sold in Canada as well as restaurant and travel tips.

BINSTED'S BOTTLING DIRECTORY (YEAR). see *BUSINESS AND ECONOMICS* — *Trade And Industrial Directories*

663.3 FR ISSN 1266-2925
CODEN: BOSSBI
BIOS; boissons conditionnement. Key Title: Boissons Bios Conditionnement. (Text in French; summaries in English, French, German) 1970. 7/yr. 490 F. (foreign 650 F.) (effective 1997). P C I Presse et Communication de l'Institut, 24 rue de Dunkerque, 75010 Paris, France. TEL 33-1-45267865. FAX 33-1-42806436. Ed. Frederic Reux; Pub. Robert Brissart. adv.: B&W page 6200 F., color page 13000 F.; 175 x 260; adv. contact: Catherine Leclercq-Bourdon. bk.rev.; abstr.; bibl.; stat.; tr.lit.; index. circ. 3,000. **Indexed:** Biol.Abstr., Biol.Dig., Chem.Abstr., Curr.Biotech.Abstr., Dairy Sci.Abstr., Food Sci.& Tech.Abstr., Packag.Sci.Tech. **Document type:** trade publication.
—BLDSC (2121.200000); CASDDS; CISTI.
Former titles (until 1995): Bios Boissons (ISSN 1252-1248); (until 1993): Bios (ISSN 0366-2284); (until 1972): Cahiers de Bio (ISSN 0150-648X); Bios Brasserie Malterie Biotechnique (ISSN 1274-0225).
Description: Deals with the evolutions and the technological innovations in the following sectors: raw materials and ingredients; manufacturing processes; packaging and bottling; packing; handling and logistics; control, measurement, analysis and hygiene.

663.4 IT ISSN 0006-3770
BIRRA E MALTO. 1954. 3/yr. free to qualified personnel. Associazione Italiana Tecnici Birra e Malto - Italian Brewmasters Association, Via Trento 79, 32034 Pedavena (BL), Italy. Ed. Tullio Zangrando. adv.; bk.rev. circ. 950. **Indexed:** Food Sci.& Tech.Abstr. **Document type:** academic/scholarly publication.
—BLDSC (2094.080000).
Description: Publishes articles on the art and science of brewing and technological progress.

663 FR ISSN 0760-1999
BOISSONS DE FRANCE - JEAN PRIMUS. 1936. m. 136 F. Federation Nationale des Boissons, 49 rue de la Glaciere, 75013 Paris, France. TEL 45-87-21-41. FAX 45-87-11-69. TELEX 260 076 F. Ed. Claude Boissin. adv.; bk.rev.; bibl.; charts; illus.; stat.; index. circ. 7,000.
Formerly: Boissons de France "Saines et Legeres" (ISSN 0006-5803)

BON VIVANT. see *TRAVEL AND TOURISM*

663.19 US
BOTTLED WATER REPORTER. 6/yr. $50 (foreign $100). International Bottled Water Association, 113 N. Henry St., Alexandria, VA 22314-2973. TEL 703-683-5213. FAX 703-683-4074. Ed. Lisa M. Prats. adv. contact: Ann F. Carberry. bk.rev. circ. 3,000. **Document type:** trade publication.

663 FR ISSN 0298-7449
LE BOUILLEUR DE FRANCE.* q. Editions Generales et Corporatives, s.a.r.l., 156 rue du Faubourg Poisssoniere, 75010 Paris, France. TEL 33-5-45221019. adv. circ. 30,000.

BEVERAGES

663.2 SP ISSN 0211-1071
BOUQUET. 1980. 12/yr. Ediciones Sociales S.L., Rosellon 186-4o, 08036 Barcelona, Spain. TEL 3-323-14-91. FAX 3-454-86-65. Ed. Julio Cayuela Torno. **Document type:** consumer publication.

663.1 GW ISSN 0006-9159
CODEN: BWWSAP
DIE BRANNTWEINWIRTSCHAFT; Zeitschrift fuer Spirituosindustrie. 1857. s-m. DM.256.80 (foreign DM.305) (effective 1997). Versuchs- und Lehranstalt fuer Spiritusfabrikation und Fermentationstechnologie, Seestr. 13, 13353 Berlin, Germany. TEL 49-30-4509-0. FAX 49-30-4536067. TELEX 184403-VLSF-D. Ed. Klaus-Dieter Schuenemann. adv.; bk.rev.; charts; illus.; pat.; tr.lit.; index. circ. 3,000. **Indexed:** Biol.Abstr., C.I.S. Abstr., Chem.Abstr., Food Sci.& Tech.Abstr., VITIS. **Document type:** trade publication.
—BLDSC (2271.000000); CASDDS.

663.3 GW ISSN 0179-2466
CODEN: MONBAS
BRAUEREI-FORUM; Fachzeitung fuer Brauereien, Maelzereien und Getraenkeindustrie. 1903. fortn. DM.225 (effective 1997). Versuchs- und Lehranstalt fuer Brauerei in Berlin, Seestr. 13, 13353 Berlin, Germany. FAX 49-30-4536069. adv.; bk.rev. circ. 5,200. **Indexed:** Anal.Abstr., Biol.Abstr., Chem.Abstr., Dairy Sci.Abstr., Field Crop Abstr., Food Sci.& Tech.Abstr., Herb.Abstr., Packag.Sci.Tech. **Document type:** trade publication.
—BLDSC (2275.901000); CASDDS; CISTI; Linda Hall.
Incorporates (in 1986): Tageszeitung fuer Brauerei (ISSN 0039-8942); Which was formerly: Forum der Brauerei; Monatsschrift fuer Brauerei (ISSN 0369-1233)

663.3 GW ISSN 0172-0589
BRAUEREI JOURNAL. 1882. 21/yr. DM.69. (Bundesverband Deutscher Mittelstandsbrauereien e.V.) Dreistern Verlag GmbH, Andreas-Hofer-Str. 1, 81547 Munich, Germany. TEL 089-6970372. FAX 089-6970141. Ed. Dr. Guenter Thoss. adv.; charts; illus. **Indexed:** C.I.S. Abstr. **Document type:** trade publication.
Incorporating: Brauereibesitzer und Braumeister (ISSN 0006-9280)

663.3 SZ ISSN 1018-2535
CODEN: BRGRED
BRAUEREI UND GETRAENKE-RUNDSCHAU/REVUE DE LA BRASSERIE ET DES BOISSONS/RIVISTA DELLE BIRRERIE E DELLE BEVANDE. 1890. m. 158 SFr. Brauerei und Getranke-Rundschau, Bahnhofplatz 9, Postfach 6325, CH-8023 Zurich, Switzerland. TEL 41-1-2212184. FAX 41-1-2116206. (Co-sponsors: Verband Schweizerischer Brauereien; Schweizerische Braumeistervereinigung) Ed. H. Pfenninger. R&P contact: Uta Luettgen. adv. contact: Uta Luettgen. bk.rev.; abstr.; bibl.; charts; illus.; pat.; stat.; tr.mk.; index, cum.index. **Indexed:** Biol.Abstr., Chem.Abstr., Food Sci.& Tech.Abstr. **Document type:** trade publication.
—BLDSC (2275.904500); CASDDS.
Supersedes: Schweizer Brauerei-Rundschau (ISSN 0036-7311)

663.3 GW ISSN 0068-0710
BRAUEREIEN UND MAELZEREIEN IN EUROPA. 1910. a. DM.425 (effective 1997). Verlag Hoppenstedt GmbH, Havelstr. 9, 64295 Darmstadt, Germany. TEL 49-6151-380-0. FAX 49-6151-380-360. adv. circ. 2,000. **Document type:** directory.

663.4 GW ISSN 0341-7115
CODEN: BRINDA
BRAUINDUSTRIE. 1915. m. DM.93. Verlag W. Sachon, Schloss Mindelburg, 87714 Mindelheim, Germany. TEL 49-8261-999-0. FAX 49-8261-999-132. TELEX 539624. E-mail: sachon@t-online.de; URL: http://www.sachon.de. Ed. Joerg Bueckle. adv. contact: Ingeborg Rodriguez. bk.rev.; index. circ. 7,437. **Indexed:** Chem.Abstr., Packag.Sci.Tech. **Document type:** trade publication.
—BLDSC (2275.930000); CASDDS; CISTI.
Formerly: Brauer und Maelzer (ISSN 0045-2718)

663.3 GW ISSN 0724-696X
CODEN: BRUWAQ
BRAUWELT; Zeitschrift fuer das gesamte Brauwesen und die Getraenkewirtschaft. (English supplement avail.) (Text in German; summaries in English and French) 1861. 3/m. DM.226 (foreign DM.297) (effective 1997). Verlag Hans Carl GmbH, Andernacherstr. 33a, 90411 Nuernberg, Germany. TEL 49-911-95285-0. FAX 49-911-9528548. Ed. Karl-Ullrich Heyse. adv.: B&W page DM.4335, color page DM.6780; trim 185 x 275; adv. contact: Corinna Thoenissen. bk.rev.; abstr.; charts; illus.; pat.; tr.lit.; index. circ. 7,936. **Indexed:** C.I.S. Abstr., Chem.Abstr., Excerp.Med., Food Sci.& Tech.Abstr., Int.Packag.Abstr., Nutr.Abstr. **Document type:** trade publication.
—BLDSC (2277.049000); CISTI; Linda Hall. **CCC**.
Incorporates (in 1993): Getraenketechnik.

663.3 GW
BRAUWELT - BREVIER (YEAR). a. Verlag Hans Carl GmbH, Andernacherstr. 33a, 90411 Nuernberg, Germany. TEL 49-911-95285-0. FAX 49-911-9528548. Ed. K.-U. Heyse. **Document type:** trade publication.

663.3 GW ISSN 0934-9340
HD9397.A1 CODEN: BRINEB
BRAUWELT INTERNATIONAL. (Text in English) 1983. 5/yr. DM.133 (effective 1996). Verlag Hans Carl GmbH, Andernacherstr. 33a, 90411 Nuernberg, Germany. TEL 49-911-95285-0. FAX 49-911-9528548. Ed. Karl-Ullrich Heyse. adv.: B&W page DM.4305, color page DM.6750; trim 185 x 275; adv. contact: Korinna Thoenissen. index. circ. 11,418. (back issues avail.) **Indexed:** Food Sci.& Tech.Abstr. **Document type:** trade publication.
—BLDSC (2277.110000).

663.3 NE
BREW-INFO; monthly industry review. (Supplement avail.) 1952. m. fl.400. (Brewing Research Foundation International, UK) European Brewery Convention, P.O. Box 510, 2380 BB Zoeterwoude, Netherlands. TEL 31-71-456047. FAX 31-71-410013. TELEX 39390 HENB NL. bk.rev.; circ. 400 (controlled). **Indexed:** Agri.Eng.Abstr.
● Also available online.
Former titles: Brewing Research Foundation. Current Awareness Monthly; Brewing Research Foundation. Bulletin of Current Literature; Brewing Industry Research Foundation. Bulletin of Current Literature (ISSN 0300-4619)

663 US ISSN 1079-414X
BREW: TRAVELING AMERICA'S BREWPUBS AND MICROBREWERIES. 1994. 6/yr. $24.79 (Canada $39.79; foreign $44.79) (effective 1997); newsstand price: $5.50. 1120 Mulberry, Des Moines, IA 50309. TEL 515-243-9429. FAX 515-243-4517. E-mail: brewmag@netins.net; URL: http://www.brewmag.com. Ed. Beverly Walsmith; Pub. Don Walsmith. adv.; bk.rev. (back issues avail.) **Document type:** consumer publication.
● Also available online.
Description: Covers microbreweries, brewpubs, and appreciation of traditional style beers and ales.

663.4 US ISSN 1081-826X
TP570
BREW YOUR OWN; the how-to homebrew beer magazine. m. $44.95 (Canada & Mexico $60.95; elsewhere $80.95). 216 F St., Ste. 160, Davis, CA 95616. TEL 916-758-4596. FAX 916-758-7477. Ed. Craig Bystrinski; Pub. Carl Landau. adv. contact: Corey Gerhard. **Document type:** consumer publication.
Description: Provides practical hands-on tips and techniques to brew great tasting beer for hobbyists who make their own beer.

663.3 UK ISSN 0006-9736
TP500 CODEN: BREWDH
BREWER. 1910. m. £49 (foreign £66). Brewers Guild Publications Ltd., 8 Ely Pl., Holborn, London EC1N 6SD, England. TEL 44-171-405-4565. FAX 44-171-831-4995. Ed. A. Duckworth. adv.; bk.rev.; charts; illus.; stat.; index. circ. 2,500. **Indexed:** Biol.Abstr., Curr.Pack.Abstr., Food Sci.& Tech.Abstr., Packag.Sci.Tech. **Document type:** trade publication.
—BLDSC (2279.830000); CASDDS; CISTI.
Formerly: Brewers' Guild Journal.

663 US
BREWERS ALMANAC. 1946. a. $170 (effective Sep. 1996). Beer Institute, 122 C St., N.W., Ste. 750, Washington, DC 20001-2109. TEL 202-737-2337. FAX 202-737-7004. URL: http://www.beerinst.org. Ed. Matthew A. Hein. charts; stat. circ. 1,400. **Document type:** trade publication.
Description: Documents historical and current information on the American brewing industry.

663.3 US ISSN 0006-971X
TP500 CODEN: BRDGAT
BREWERS DIGEST. (Annual Buyers' Guide and Directory avail.) 1926. m. $25. Siebel Publishing Co., Inc., 4049 W. Peterson Ave., Chicago, IL 60646. TEL 312-463-3401. Ed. Clarence Allie; Pub. Leonard Kay. R&P contact: Leonard Kay. TEL 773-463-7484. adv. contact: Leonard Kay. bk.rev.; abstr.; bibl.; illus.; stat.; tr.lit.; index. circ. 2,791. **Indexed:** Biol.Abstr., Chem.Abstr., Curr.Cont., Curr.Pack.Abstr., Food Sci.& Tech.Abstr., Int.Packag.Abstr., Nutr.Abstr. **Document type:** trade publication.
—BLDSC (2280.000000); CASDDS; CISTI; Linda Hall.

663.3 US
BREWERS DIGEST ANNUAL BUYERS GUIDE AND BREWERY DIRECTORY. Variant title: Brewers Digest Brewery Directory. 1926. a. $50. Siebel Publishing Co., Inc., 4049 W. Peterson Ave., Chicago, IL 60646. TEL 312-463-3401. Ed. Dori Whitney; Pub. Leonard Kay. adv. circ. 3,104. **Document type:** trade publication, directory.

663.3 UK ISSN 0006-9728
TP500
BREWERS' GUARDIAN. 1871. m. £45 (rest of Europe £72; elsewhere £85) (effective 1996). Hampton Publishing Ltd., 97 Station Rd., Hampton, Mddx. TW12 2BD, England. TEL 0181-941-7750. FAX 0181-941-7721. Ed. Graham Large. adv. contact: Heidi Urban. charts; illus.; mkt.stat.; tr.lit.; index. circ. 2,800. (also avail. in microform from UMI; reprint service avail. from UMI) **Indexed:** Biol.Abstr., Chem.Abstr., Curr.Pack.Abstr., Food Sci.& Tech.Abstr., Int.Packag.Abstr., Packag.Sci.Tech. **Document type:** trade publication.
—BLDSC (2281.000000); CISTI; UMI.

663.3 UK ISSN 0309-7625
BREWERS GUILD DIRECTORY. 1923. a. £45 to non-members. Brewers' Guild Publications Ltd., 8 Ely Pl., London EC1N 6SD, England. TEL 44-171-405-4565. FAX 44-171-831-4995. Ed. J.A. Barker. adv. contact: Julie Barker. circ. 2,000. **Document type:** directory.

663.3 UK
BREWERY MANUAL & WHO'S WHO IN BRITISH BREWING & SCOTCH WHISKEY DISTILLING. 1915. a. £62. Hampton Publishing Ltd., 97 Station Rd., Hampton, Mddx. TW12 2AZ, England. TEL 0181-941-7750. FAX 0181-941-7721. Ed. Graham Large. adv. contact: Heidi Urban. **Document type:** directory.
Description: Gives names, addresses, financial details and personnel of all British breweries and Scotch whisky distillers maltsters and hop merchants. Lists all brands, wholesalers, organizations, conferences and conventions. Contains material of interest to beer importers, pub operators, cider makers, and manufacturers of soft drinks.

663 GW
BREWING AND BEVERAGE INDUSTRY INTERNATIONAL. (Text in English) 1989. 4/yr. DM.10. Verlag W. Sachon, Schloss Mindelburg, 87714 Mindelheim, Germany. TEL 49-8261-999-0. FAX 49-8261-999-132. E-mail: sachon@t-online.de; URL: http://www.sachon.de. Eds. Joerg Bueckle, Wolfgang Burkart. adv. contact: Ingeborg Rodriguez. circ. 9,429. (back issues avail.) **Document type:** trade publication.

BEVERAGES

663.1 — UK — ISSN 0308-1265
CODEN: BDINDE
BREWING & DISTILLING INTERNATIONAL. 1865. m. £48 (foreign £80) (effective 1997). Brewery Traders Publications Ltd., Southbound House, 163 Burton Rd., Burton-upon-Trent, Staffs. DE14 3DP, England. TEL 44-1283-566784. FAX 44-1283-510674. Ed. B.J. Stephens; Pub. Wilf Hipkins. R&P contact: B.J. Stevens. adv. contact: Kath Adkin. bk.rev.; charts; illus.; mkt.; tr.lit. circ. 3,752. **Indexed:** Chem.Abstr., Food Sci.& Tech.Abstr., Int.Packag.Abstr., Nutr.Abstr., Packag.Sci.Tech. **Document type:** trade publication.
—BLDSC (2282.700000); CISTI.
Formerly (until 1974): International Brewing and Distilling (ISSN 0020-6210)
Description: Covers news, views new products and plant applications. Includes regular technical features on all aspects of the brewing and distilling processes.

663.3 — CN — ISSN 0068-094X
BREWING AND MALTING BARLEY RESEARCH INSTITUTE. ANNUAL REPORT. 1952. a. free to qualified persons. Brewing and Malting Barley Research Institute, 206-167 Lombard Ave., Winnipeg, MB R3B 0T6, Canada. TEL 204-942-1407. Ed. N.T. Kendall. circ. 700 controlled. **Indexed:** Food Sci.& Tech.Abstr. **Document type:** corporate report.

663 — US — ISSN 1072-5806
BREWING TECHNIQUES; the art and science of small-scale brewing. 1993. bi-m. $33 (Canada $40; elsewhere $48) (effective 1996). New Wine Press, Inc., 1127 Lincoln St., Eugene, OR 97401. TEL 541-687-2993; 800-427-2993. FAX 541-687-8534. E-mail: bteditor@aol.com; URL: http://brewtechniques.com/brewingtechniques. (Subscr. to: Box 3222, Eugene, OR 97403) Ed. Stephen A. Mallery; Pub. Stephen A. Mallery. adv. contact: Stephen A. Mallery. bk.rev.; circ. 12,000 (paid). **Document type:** consumer publication.
Refereed Serial

663.2 658.8 — UK
BRITAIN'S DRINKS INDUSTRY. 1985. irreg., latest 1991. £50. Jordan & Sons Ltd., 21 St. Thomas St., Bristol BS1 6JS, England. TEL 44-117-923-0600. FAX 44-117-923-0063. **Document type:** directory.
Formerly: Britain's Wine Industry.
Description: An overview of the drinks industry, including financial analysis, market share trends, comparison tables, financial profiles of top companies and sales and marketing information.

663 — BE
HET BROUWERSBLAD. French edition: Journal du Brasseur. (Text in Flemish) 1893. 4/yr. 1200 BEF (foreign 2000 BEF). Confederation des Brasseries de Belgique - Belgian Brewers' Association, Maison des Brasseurs, Grand'Place 10, 1000 Brussels, Belgium. TEL 32-2-511-49-59.
FAX 32-2-511-32-87. Ed. Michel Brichet. adv.; bk.rev. circ. 4,000. **Document type:** trade publication.
Former titles: Kleine Brouwersblad; Renseignements Techniques.

663.2 634.8 — FR — ISSN 0029-7127
CODEN: BLOVAJ
BULLETIN DE L'O I V; revue internationale. (Text in English, French) 1928. bi-m. 690 F. (foreign 840 F.) (effective 1997). Office International de la Vigne et du Vin, 18 rue d'Aguesseau, 75008 Paris, France. TEL 33-1-44948080.
FAX 33-1-42669063. E-mail: OIV101675.2013@compuserve.com. Ed. M.J. Deshayes. bk.rev.; abstr.; bibl.; charts; index. circ. 1,000. **Indexed:** Biol.Abstr., Chem.Abstr., Food Sci.& Tech.Abstr., Helminthol.Abstr., Hort.Abstr., Plant Grow.Reg.Abstr., VITIS. **Document type:** bulletin.
—BLDSC (2668.300000); CASDDS; SWETS.

663.3 658.8 — UK — ISSN 1354-8743
BUSINESS RATIO PLUS: BREWERS. 1974. a. I C C Business Publications Ltd., Field House, 72 Oldfield Rd., Hampton, Mddx. TW12 2HQ, England. TEL 44-181-783-0922. FAX 44-181-783-1940. charts; stat. **Document type:** trade publication.
Formerly (until 1993): Business Ratio Report: Brewers (ISSN 0261-748X)

663.2 — UK — ISSN 1354-8727
BUSINESS RATIO PLUS: WINE & SPIRIT MERCHANTS. 1973. a. £195. I C C Business Publications (Subsidiary of: I C C Information Group), Field House, 72 Oldfield Rd., Hampton, Mddx. TW12 2HQ. TEL 44-181-783-0922. FAX 44-181-783-1940. **Document type:** trade publication.
Formerly (until 1995): Business Ratio Report: Wine and Spirit Merchants (ISSN 0261-9695)

338.7 663.1 658.8 — UK — ISSN 0261-7803
BUSINESS RATIO REPORT: DISTILLERS; an industry sector analysis. 1973. a. I C C Business Ratios Ltd., Freepost, Field House, Hampton, Mddx. TW12 1BR, England. TEL 081-783-0977. FAX 081-783-1940. charts; stat. **Document type:** trade publication.

663.2 — US — ISSN 0883-4423
TP557
CALIFORNIA WINE WINNERS; the best from the competitions. 1983. a. $8.95 (effective 1996 to 1998). Varietal Fair, 4022 Harrison Grade Rd., Sebastopol, CA 95472. TEL 707-874-3105. FAX 707-874-1323. Eds. T. Ahlstrom, J.T. Devine. R&P contact: T. Ahlstrom. adv. contact: J.T. Devine. circ. 11,000 (paid). (back issues avail.) **Document type:** consumer publication, trade publication.
Description: Covers the major Western wine judgings and reports on specific awards given during each contest.

663 — UK — ISSN 0956-8018
CAN MAKERS REPORT. 1981. biennial. free. Can Makers Information Service, 1 Chelsea Manor Gardens, London SW3 5PN, England. TEL 44-171-351-2400. FAX 44-171-352-6246. circ. 3,000 (controlled). **Document type:** trade publication.
—BLDSC (3016.406400).

338.4 641.2 — US — ISSN 1086-1173
CATEGORY REPORT - BEVERAGES. m. $1000 (effective 1997). Marketing Intelligence Service Ltd., 6473D Route 64, Naples, NY 14512-9726.
TEL 716-374-6326. FAX 716-374-5217. E-mail: mktgINTELsvc@cis.compuserve.com; URL: http://ourworld.compuserve.com/homepages/mktgintelsvc. Ed. Kim Cruise. **Document type:** newsletter.
Description: Contains detailed product and packaging description and analysis of new foreign and domestic consumer packaged goods.

663.3 — US — ISSN 1086-2587
CELEBRATOR BEER NEWS. 1988. bi-m. $16.95 (Canada $19; elsewhere $28) (effective 1997). Celebrator Publications, Box 375, Hayward, CA 94543. TEL 510-670-0121. FAX 510-670-0639. E-mail: tdalldorf@celebrator.com; URL: http://www.celebrator.com/celebrator/. Ed. Tom Dalldorf; Pub. Tom Dalldorf. R&P contact: Georgia Weathers. adv. contact: Georgia Weathers. bk.rev. circ. 50,000. (back issues avail.) **Document type:** newspaper, consumer publication.

663 674.94 — US
CELLAR NOTES.* 1981. bi-m. $15. Cellar Notes Inc., 5 Muirfield Ln., St. Louis, MO 63141-7355.
TEL 314-576-4143. Ed. Eileen M. Carr. bk.rev. circ. 400. (back issues avail.)

663.3 — BE
CODEN: CERBE8
CEREVISIA; Belgian journal of Brewing and Biotechnology. (Text in Dutch, English, French, German) 1939. q. 2500 BEF (foreign 3000 BEF) (effective 1996 & 1997). Groene Dreef 11, 9830 Sint-Martens-Latem, Belgium. TEL 32-9-2825695. FAX 32-9-2216370. Eds. J. Lenges, E. Van Schoonenbeerghe; Pub. Jacques Vander Stricht. adv.: B&W page 12500 BEF, color page 22500 BEF; trim 297 x 210; adv. contact: Jacques Vander Stricht. bk.rev.; abstr.; charts; illus.; tr.lit.; index. circ. 2,000. (also avail. in microform; reprint service avail. from UMI) **Indexed:** Biol.Abstr., Chem.Abstr., Curr.Adv.Ecol.Sci., Curr.Biotech.Abstr., Curr.Cont., Dairy Sci.Abstr., Food Sci.& Tech.Abstr., Nutr.Abstr., Packag.Sci.Tech. **Document type:** bulletin, abstracting/indexing, proceedings, academic/scholarly publication.
—BLDSC (3120.050000); CASDDS; CISTI; Linda Hall; SWETS.
Formerly (until 1995): Cerevisia and Biotechnology (ISSN 0778-2640); Formed by the 1991 merger of: Belgian Journal of Food Chemistry and Biotechnology (ISSN 0773-6177); Which was formerly (1946-1985): Revue des Fermentations et des Industries Alimentaires (ISSN 0035-2071); And: Cerevisia (ISSN 0770-1713); Which was formed by the 1976 merger of: Fermentatio (ISSN 0015-0053); And: B I F (ISSN 0773-4964); Which was formerly: Association des Anciens Etudiants en Brasserie de Bruxelles. Bulletin.
Description: Covers developments in the brewing sciences and other sectors of fermentation and non-alcoholic beverage technology.

663.3 — SP — ISSN 0300-4481
CODEN: CEMADD
CERVEZA Y MALTA. 1964. q. 1000 ptas.($110) (effective 1997). Asociacion Espanola de Tecnicos de Cerveza y Malta, Ramirez de Prado, 8-1o F, 28045 Madrid, Spain. TEL 34-1-5277255. FAX 34-1-5285507. Ed. Salvador Martin Aparicio. adv.: B&W page 54000 ptas. bk.rev.; abstr.; bibl.; charts; illus.; pat.; stat.; cum.index; circ. 1,500 (controlled). **Indexed:** Chem.Abstr., Ind.SST. **Document type:** trade publication.
—BLDSC (3120.245600); CASDDS. CCC.
Description: Contains scientific, technical and professional articles about the beer and malt industry.

663 — UK
▼**CHINESE DRINKS BUYER.** (Text in Chinese) 1996. q. free. Crier Publications Ltd., Artic House, Rye Ln., Dunton Green, Sevenoaks, Kent TH14 5HB, England. TEL 44-1732-451515. FAX 44-1732-451383. Ed. Heather Buckle; Pub. John Whitbread. adv. contact: Philip McLean. circ. 11,000. **Document type:** trade publication.
Description: Discusses matters of interest to major purchasing companies of drinks in China.

641 — IT
CIVILTA DEL BERE; mensile di informazione, documentazione e difesa della qualita. German edition: Bacchus. 1974. m. (11/yr.). L.130000 in U.S. Editoriale Lariana s.r.l., Via Ciro Menotti 11-D, 20129 Milan, Italy. TEL 39-2-76110303. FAX 39-2-713847. Ed. Bruno Donati. adv.: B&W page L.7256000, color page L.10884000; adv. contact: Antonella Khail. illus. circ. 49,000. **Document type:** trade publication.
Description: Covers winemaking, wines, alcoholic beverages and food.

663 — US
CLOCKDIAL. 1938. q. Dr Pepper - Cadbury North America, Box 655086, Dallas, TX 75265-5086. TEL 214-360-7000. FAX 214-360-7981. Ed. Jill Haerle. R&P contact: Jill Haerle. circ. 16,000. **Document type:** trade publication.
Description: For the employees and management of Dr Pepper bottling plants worldwide.

663 — GW
COCA-COLA JOURNAL. 1934. bi-m. free. Coca-Cola GmbH, Max-Keith-Str. 66, 45136 Essen, Germany. TEL 49-201-8211490. FAX 49-201-8211110. Ed. Ursula Kindenberg. circ. 16,000. (back issues avail.) **Document type:** corporate report.

BEVERAGES

663   SZ
COCKTAIL BAR. (Text in French, German, Italian) q. Gastronomie & Tourisme SA, Case Postale 231, CH-6963 Lugano-Pregassona, Switzerland. TEL 41-91-9413828. FAX 41-91-9413825. Ed. Alberto Dell'Acqua. **Document type:** trade publication.

663.1   AT
▼**COCTAIL OF THE WEEK NEWSLETTER.** 1996. w. Box 2577, Taren Point Business Ctr., N.S.W. 2229, Australia. E-mail: berghous@ozemail.com.au; URL: http://www.ozemail.com.au/~berghous/drink.html. Ed. David Berghouse. **Document type:** newsletter.
●Available only online.
Description: Introduces a new cocktail each week, plus "Know Your Cocktails" and everything for the home bar.

663.93   US
▼**COFFEE JOURNAL.** * 1995. q. $12.97; newsstand price: $3.95. Tiger Oak Publications, Inc., 123 N. 3rd St., Ste. 508, Minneapolis, MN 55401-1664. TEL 612-338-4125. FAX 612-338-0532. Ed. Susan Bonne; Pub. R. Craig Bednar. adv. contact: 125,000. **Document type:** consumer publication.
Description: Devoted to gourmet coffees: includes bean and product suggestions, interviews, fiction, and unique recipes.

663   US   ISSN 0010-1516
COLORADO BEVERAGE ANALYST. 1936. m. $16. Bell Publications, Beverage Analyst Group, 2403 Champa St., Denver, CO 80205. TEL 303-296-1600. FAX 303-295-2159. Ed. Sherry Smith. R&P contact: Larry Bell. adv.; illus.; stat.; tr.lit. circ. 2,200. **Document type:** trade publication.

COMPENSATION IN FOOD & BEVERAGE PROCESSING. see *BUSINESS AND ECONOMICS — Labor And Industrial Relations*

663   US   ISSN 0191-8818
CONNECTICUT BEVERAGE JOURNAL. 1945. m. $25. Beverage Publications, Inc., 2508 Whitney Ave., Ste. C, Box 5157, Hamden, CT 06518. FAX 203-288-2693. Ed. Gerald P. Slone. adv. contact: Noreen Hartmann. circ. 5,636. **Document type:** trade publication.

663.2 686.2   US   ISSN 0161-6668
CONNOISSEURS GUIDE TO CALIFORNIA WINE. 1974. m. $45 (foreign $70). Box V, Alameda, CA 94501. TEL 510-865-3150. Eds. Charles Olken, Earl Singer. index. circ. 11,000. (looseleaf format; back issues avail.) **Document type:** newsletter.

663.2   IT
CORRIERE VINICOLO; commercio vinicolo. (Supplements avail.) 1928. w. L.280000 including a. supplement Enotria e Codico della Vite e del Vinon (effective 1997). Unione Italiana Vini, Via S. Vittore al Teatro 3, Milan, Italy. TEL 39-2-801595. FAX 39-2-866226. TELEX 39-2-313681. Ed. Marco Mancini. adv.; bk.rev.
Description: Discusses viticulture.

663   FR   ISSN 1257-2187
LA COTE DES VINS. s-m. 989 F. (foreign 1300 F.) (effective 1997). Jour-Azur S.A., 17 rue d'Uzes, 75108 Paris Cedex 02, France. TEL 33-1-40133500. FAX 33-1-40419363. **Document type:** newsletter.

663.2   UK   ISSN 0954-4240
DECANTER; the world's best wine magazine. 1975. m. £35.40 (rest of Europe £46; elsewhere £72) (effective 1996). Decanter Magazine Ltd. (Subsidiary of: Link House Magazines), Priory House, 8 Battersea Park Rd., London SW8 4BG, England. TEL 0171-627-8181. FAX 0171-738-8688. TELEX 964240 CWEASY G. (Subscr. to: 120-126 Lavender Ave., Mitcham, Surrey CR4 3HP, England. TEL 0181-646-6672. FAX 0181-648-4873; N. American subscr. to: Fulco, Box 3000, Denville, NJ 07834. TEL 800-875-2997) Ed. Jonathan Goodall; Pub. Sarah Kemp. adv.; B&W page £895, color page £1915; trim 297 x 210; adv. contact: Stephen Hobley. bk.rev.; illus.; tr.lit.; circ. 35,000 (paid). Indexed: Art.Hosp.& Tour. **Document type:** consumer publication.
Former titles (until 1985): Decanter Magazine (ISSN 0141-6014); (until 1975): Wine-Butler (ISSN 0043-5783)
Description: Discusses wine and wine making.

663   US
DELAWARE BEVERAGE MONTHLY. 1984. m. $38 (effective 1997). Melton Communications Inc., 1518 N. Van Buren St., Wilmington, DE 19806. TEL 302-655-2800. FAX 302-655-2805. Ed. Dale W. Melton; Pub. Dale W. Melton. adv. contact: Fran Baldt. circ. 1,800 (controlled). **Document type:** trade publication.
Description: For alcoholic beverage licensees in the state of Delaware.

DESKTOP PRODUCTS GUIDE. see *BUSINESS AND ECONOMICS — Trade And Industrial Directories*

663   GW   ISSN 0724-4266
DEUTSCHE GETRAENKE WIRTSCHAFT; Fachzeitschrift und Mitteilungsblatt fuer die Getraenkewirtschaft. 1928. m. DM.78 (foreign DM.88) (effective 1997). (Raabe-Gesellschaft) D G W Verlag Monika Busch und Timur Dosdogru GbR, Selbeckerstr. 103, 58091 Hagen, Germany. TEL 49-2331-71084. FAX 49-2331-72853. Eds. Monika Busch, Timur Dosdogru. adv.: B&W page DM.5557.60, color page DM.9395.70; trim 210 x 280. circ. 22,000. Indexed: Food Sci.& Tech.Abstr. **Document type:** trade publication.
Formerly (until 1983): Deutsche Getraenke-Industrie (ISSN 0012-0227)
Description: Covers beer, wine, champagne, spirits, trade fairs, management and news.

663   GW   ISSN 0944-3177
DER DEUTSCHE WEINBAU (NEUSTADT). 1993. 24/yr. DM.132 (foreign DM.184.80) (effective 1997). Meininger Verlag GmbH, Maximilianstr. 7-17, 67433 Neustadt, Germany. TEL 49-6321-8908-0. FAX 49-6321-890873. Ed. Rudolf Nickenig. circ. 9,624. Indexed: Food Sci.& Tech.Abstr. **Document type:** trade publication.
—BLDSC (3575.570000); SWETS.

663.4   GW   ISSN 0172-3774
DEUTSCHER BRAUMEISTER- UND MALZMEISTER-BUND. MITTEILUNGSBLATT. 4/yr. (plus a. issue) DM.128 (annual issue DM.55) (effective 1997). Verlag Hans Carl GmbH, Andernacherstr. 33a, 90411 Nuernberg, Germany. TEL 49-911-95285-0. FAX 49-911-9528548. Eds. Karlheinz Limpert, Karl-Ullrich Heyse. adv.: B&W page DM.2310, color page DM.4200; trim 185 x 275; adv. contact: Korinna Thoenissen. circ. 3,525. **Document type:** newsletter.

DIRECTORIO DE LA INDUSTRIA MEXICANA DE BEBIDAS. see *BUSINESS AND ECONOMICS — Trade And Industrial Directories*

663   GW   ISSN 0344-6816
DER DOEMENSIANER. 1960. q. DM.48. Verlag W. Sachon, Schloss Mindelburg, 87714 Mindelheim, Germany. TEL 49-8261-999-0. FAX 49-8261-999-132. E-mail: sachon@t-online.de; URL: http://www.sachon.de. Ed. G. Zentgraf. adv. contact: Ingeborg Rodriguez. circ. 3,311. **Document type:** trade publication.

DRAM SHOP AND ALCOHOL REPORTER. see *LAW*

663 658.8   NE   ISSN 0165-2745
DRANKENDETAIL. 1902. 10/yr. fl.105 (Europe fl.149; elsewhere fl.169). Theo Jaegers B.V., Postbus 37, 3990 DA Houten, Netherlands. TEL 31-30-6371780. FAX 31-30-6351034. Ed. Theo Jaegers. R&P contact: Theo Jaegers. adv.: B&W page fl.1690,color page fl.2710; bleed 218 x 291. bk.rev.; illus. circ. 2,500. **Document type:** trade publication.
Formerly (until 1978): Gastrovin.
Description: For specialized retailers of wine, spirits, beer and non-alcoholic beverages, their suppliers, and allied trades.

663   UK   ISSN 0951-7723
THE DRINK FORECAST. q. £695 (effective 1998). N T C Publications Ltd., P.O. Box 69, Henley-on-Thames, Oxon RG9 1GB, England. TEL 44-1491-411000. FAX 44-1491-571188. **Document type:** trade publication.
Description: Provides a monitor of trends in all the main alcoholic and soft drink sectors.

663   GW   ISSN 1433-1594
▼**DRINK TECHNOLOGY AND MARKETING.** (Text in English) 1997. q. DM.90 (foreign $56) (effective 1998). Dr. Harnisch Verlagsgesellschaft mbH, Blumenstr. 15, 90402 Nuernberg, Germany. TEL 49-911-2018-0. FAX 49-911-2018100. E-mail: uepost@aol.com. **Document type:** trade publication.

663   GW
DRINKS. 1985. bi-m. DM.55. (Deutsche Barkeeper Union e.V.) Dieter Knauer Verlags GmbH, Rostocker Str. 3, 63073 Offenbach-Main, Germany. TEL 069-89-16-09. circ. 5,300.

663.1   UK   ISSN 0012-625X   HD9390.A1
DRINKS INTERNATIONAL. 1967. 10/yr. £45 (foreign £75). Reed Business Publishing Ltd., Reed Publishing Services Ltd., 7-11, St. John's Hill, London SW11 1TE, England. TEL 44-181-228 3344. FAX 44-181-350-1586. Ed. Pamela Massingham. adv. circ. controlled. **Document type:** trade publication.
Description: Covers all aspects of the beverage trade worldwide.

641   NE   ISSN 0921-8386
DRINKS - SLIJTERSVAKBLAD; trade magazine for wines, spirits, beer and other beverages. 1952. m. fl.105 (effective 1993). (Vereniging Nederlands Slijters-wijnhandelaren) Vaktechnische Uitgeverij Sri, Hemonystraat 11, 1074 BK Amsterdam Z, Netherlands. FAX 31-20-6442733. Ed. Herbert Noord. adv.; bk.rev.; illus. circ. 3,000. Indexed: Key to Econ.Sci. **Document type:** trade publication.
Formerly (until 1986): Slijtersvakblad (ISSN 0165-8700)

663.2   GW   ISSN 0172-391X
E W R; Schriftenreihe zum europaeischen Weinrecht. 1979. irreg. (Institut fuer Weinrecht der Gesellschaft fuer Rechtspolitik, Trier) Deutscher Fachverlag GmbH, Mainzer Landstr. 251, 60326 Frankfurt a.M., Germany. TEL 49-69-75951173. FAX 49-69-75951170. Indexed: ELLIS. **Document type:** monographic series.

663.2   IT   ISSN 0390-2048
ENOHOBBY. 1974. m. Via San Tarcisio 5, 00178 Rome, Italy. Ed. Franco Tomassoli.

ENOTECA WINE AND FOOD MAGAZINE; for the connoisseur in you. see *HOTELS AND RESTAURANTS*

663.2   IT   ISSN 0392-176X
ENOTECNICO. 1890. 10/yr. L.55000($24) Associazione Enotecnici Italiani, Viale Murillo 17, 20149 Milan, Italy. TEL 2-40072460. FAX 2-48704951. Ed. Giuseppe Martelli. adv.; bk.rev.; charts; illus.; stat. circ. 6,500. Indexed: Food Sci.& Tech.Abstr.
—BLDSC (3775.695000).

641   IT
ENOTRIA; annuario della vite e del vino. (Supplement to: Corriere Vinicolo) 1920. a. Unione Italiana Vini, Via San Vittore al Teatro 3, 20123 Milan, Italy. TEL 2-801595. FAX 2-866226. TELEX 313681. Ed. Marco Mancini. adv.: B&W page L.2200000, color page L.3000000. circ. 30,000.

EPICUREAN. see *FOOD AND FOOD INDUSTRIES*

641.3   GW   ISSN 0342-2232
DAS ERFRISCHUNGSGETRAENK - MINERALWASSER-ZEITUNG. 1948. m. DM.21.90 per mo. (foreign DM.23.50) (effective 1997). (Bundesverband der Deutschen Erfrischungsgetraenke-Industrie e.V.) Matthaes Verlag GmbH, Postfach 103144, 70027 Stuttgart, Germany. TEL 49-711-2133-0. FAX 49-711-2133290. Ed. Roswitha Volkhardt; Pub. Amalie Marga Matthaes. adv.: B&W page DM.3400, color page DM.5620; trim 187 x 262; adv. contact: Rudolf Goeth. circ. 3,293. Indexed: Food Sci.& Tech.Abstr. **Document type:** newspaper.
Formerly (until 1968): Mineralwasser-Zeitung (ISSN 0343-110X)

ESSEN UND TRINKEN. see *FOOD AND FOOD INDUSTRIES*

BEVERAGES

663 SP
ETIQUETA DE EDICIONES MARCO REAL. 1993. bi-m. Ediciones Marco Real, S.A., Valentin Beato, 11, 28037 Madrid, Spain. TEL 327-00-44. FAX 204-12-08. TELEX 42677 EMR. **Document type:** consumer publication.
Description: Covers gastronomy, wines, beer and spirits.

663.3 UK ISSN 0071-2531
EUROPEAN BREWERY CONVENTION. PROCEEDINGS OF THE INTERNATIONAL CONGRESS. (Text in English, French, German) 1950. biennial, 24th, 1993, Oslo. £75. I R L Press Ltd. (Subsidiary of: Oxford University Press), Walton St., Oxford OX2 6 DP, England. TEL 44-1865-56767. FAX 44-1865-56646. TELEX 837330 OXPRESS GB. (In U.S.: Box Q, Maclean, VA 22101-0850) circ. 1,500. (back issues avail.) **Indexed:** Chem.Abstr., Food Sci.& Tech.Abstr. **Document type:** proceedings.
—BLDSC (6843.301000).
Refereed Serial

663 UK ISSN 1351-4911
EUROPEAN DRINKS BUYER. (Text in English; summaries in French, German, Italian, Spanish) 1991. bi-m. £50 (outside Europe £70). Crier Publications Ltd., Arctic House, Rye Ln., Dunton Green, Sevenoaks, Kent TN14 5HB, England. TEL 01732-451515. FAX 01732-451383. E-mail: antk@crier.demon.co.uk. Ed. Heather Buckle; Pub. John Whitbread. adv. contact: Philip McLean. circ. 10,942. (back issues avail.) **Document type:** trade publication.
Description: Discusses matters of interest to major companies purchasing drinks in all European nations.

663 658.8 UK
EUROPEAN DRINKS MARKETING DIRECTORY. 3rd edition, 1993. irreg., 4th ed., 1996. £215($430) (effective 1996). Euromonitor, 60-61 Britton Rd., London EC1M 5NA, England. TEL 44-171-251-8024. FAX 44-171-608-3149. E-mail: info@euromonitor.com; URL: http://www.euromonitor.com. (Addr. in N. America: Euromonitor International, 133 S. Michigan Ave., Ste. 1200, Chicago, IL 60603. TEL 800-577-3876. FAX 312-922-1157) stat. **Document type:** directory.
Description: Compiles company details and financial data on European retailers, wholesalers, and manufacturers of beverages.

EUROPEAN FOOD AND DRINK REVIEW; quarterly review of food and drink technology. *see FOOD AND FOOD INDUSTRIES*

663 CK ISSN 0084-7941
FEDERACION NACIONAL DE CAFETEROS DE COLOMBIA. BOLETIN DE INFORMACION ESTADISTICA SOBRE CAFE. a. Federacion Nacional de Cafeteros de Colombia, Departamento de Informacion Cafetera, Calle 73 No. 8-13, piso 10 B, Bogota D.E., Colombia.

663.63 FR ISSN 0074-5952
FEDERATION INTERNATIONALE DES PRODUCTEURS DE JUS DE FRUITS. COMPTE-RENDU DU CONGRES/INTERNATIONAL FEDERATION OF FRUIT JUICE PRODUCERS. PROCEEDINGS OF CONGRESS. 1948. irreg., 12th, Interlaken. 380 F. (effective 1997). Federation Internationale des Producteurs de Jus de Fruits - International Federation of Fruit Juice Producers, 10 rue de Liege, 75009 Paris, France. TEL 33-1-48743116. FAX 33-1-53219588. **Document type:** proceedings.

663.3 UK ISSN 0957-7041
TP500 CODEN: FEREEG
FERMENT. 1988. bi-m. £115. Institute of Brewing, 33 Clarges St., London W1Y 8EE, England. TEL 44-171-499-8144. FAX 44-171-499-1156. Ed. T.R. Wainwright. adv. contact: F. Bolton. circ. 4,200. (back issues avail.) **Indexed:** Biol.Abstr. (1990-), Chem.Abstr., Food Sci.& Tech.Abstr. **Document type:** academic/scholarly publication.
—BLDSC (3906.955000); CISTI.
Description: For personnel in brewing and related industries; all aspects of practical brewing science, technology, and training.

663.3 FR ISSN 0758-0088
LA FEUILLE DE HOUBLON. 1990. m. 300 F. (foreign 500 F.) (effective 1998). P H C Editions, 64 rue de la Rochefoucauld, 75009 Paris, France. TEL 33-1-40160388. FAX 33-1-40160460. Ed. Philippe Carpentier; Pub. Jean-Philippe de Contances. adv.: B&W page 17000 F., color page 22000 F.; trim 300 x 420; adv. contact: Nathalie Leveille. circ. 20,000. (tabloid format; back issues avail.) **Document type:** bulletin.
Description: Contains trade articles about beer and other beverages for brewers, wholesalers, and pub owners.

663.2 US ISSN 1045-0971
FINE WINE FOLIO; an appreciation of vineyards and vintages. 1988. m. $46.50 (foreign $57) (effective 1997-98). Holland & Edwards Publishing Inc., 250 Mercer St., A203, New York, NY 10012. TEL 212-673-5773. FAX 212-995-8956. Ed. Edward Holland; Pub. Edward Holland. R&P contact: Edward Holland. adv. contact: Edward Holland. circ. 75,000 (paid). (back issues avail.) **Document type:** consumer publication.
Description: Each issue is a profile of one of the world's wine-production areas; including leading producers and their labels, information on recent vintages.

658.8 GW ISSN 0947-4560
FIZZ; fuer die Szenengastronomie. m. DM.99.60 (foreign DM.126) (effective 1997). Meininger Verlag GmbH, Maximilianstr. 7-17, 67433 Neustadt, Germany. TEL 49-6321-8908-0. FAX 49-6321-8908-73. Ed. Annette Koenig. circ. 9,265. **Document type:** trade publication.
Former titles: Getraenke Gastronomie (ISSN 0937-3926); Getraenke.

663.63 GW ISSN 0015-4539
CODEN: FLOBA3
FLUESSIGES OBST. 1930. m. DM.241.50 (Europe DM.261; overseas DM.284) (effective 1996). (Verband der Deutschen Fruchtsaft-Industrie e.V.) Verlag Fluessiges Obst GmbH, Diezer Str. 5, 56370 Schoenborn, Germany. TEL 49-6486-8016. FAX 49-6486-6220. Ed. Evi Friedel; Pub. Philipp Possmann. R&P contact: Evi Friedel. adv.: B&W page DM.3457, color page DM.5017; trim 250 x 175; adv. contact: Sybille Schaefer. bk.rev.; index. circ. 1,850. **Indexed:** Chem.Abstr., Food Sci.& Tech.Abstr., INIS Atomind., VITIS. **Document type:** trade publication.
—BLDSC (3962.280000); CASDDS; Linda Hall. CCC.

FOCUS ON FOOD & BEVERAGE. *see FOOD AND FOOD INDUSTRIES*

FOOD & BEVERAGE MARKETING; the national publication for food, beverage, beer, wine, liquor & tobacco marketing executives. *see FOOD AND FOOD INDUSTRIES*

FOOD AND BEVERAGE MARKETPLACE. *see BUSINESS AND ECONOMICS — Trade And Industrial Directories*

FOOD & BEVERAGE NEWS. *see LAW*

663 664 CN ISSN 1188-5335
FOOD & DRINK/BON VERRE, BONNE TABLE. 1988. q. free. Liquor Control Board of Ontario, 55 Lake Shore Blvd., E., Toronto, ON M5E 1A4, Canada. TEL 416-864-6630. FAX 416-365-5935. Ed. Michelle Oosterman; Pub. Debbie Costa. circ. 300,000. **Document type:** consumer publication.

FOOD AND DRINK TRADE HANDBOOK. *see FOOD AND FOOD INDUSTRIES*

FOOD & DRINK WEEKLY. *see FOOD AND FOOD INDUSTRIES*

FOOD AND LIQUOR RETAILER. *see FOOD AND FOOD INDUSTRIES — Grocery Trade*

FOOD & WINE. *see FOOD AND FOOD INDUSTRIES*

663 664 UK
FOOD FROM GREECE;* annual review for the Greek production of food and wines. (Text in English, French, German) 1986. a. K. Korovilas & Co., c/o Robert G. Horsfield, Daisy Bank, Chinley via Stockport, England. Ed. Guido Cioffi. adv.; bk.rev. circ. 4,000. (back issues avail.)

FOOD MANAGEMENT. *see FOOD AND FOOD INDUSTRIES*

663.2 US ISSN 0364-9474
TP544
FRIENDS OF WINE.* 1964. bi-m. $18. Les Amis du Vin, O A Picone, 5015 Glenoak Dr., Louisville, OH 44641-8831. TEL 301-588-0980. Ed. Ronald J. Fonte. adv.; bk.rev. circ. 80,000. (also avail. in microfiche from UMI; reprint service avail. from UMI) **Indexed:** Consum.Ind.
—UMI.

663.6 658.8 UK
FRUIT JUICES: THE INTERNATIONAL MARKET. (Subseries of: Market Direction reports) a. £2500($5000) (effective 1997). Euromonitor, 60-61 Britton St., London EC1N 5NA, England. TEL 44-171-251-8024. FAX 44-171-608-3149. E-mail: info@euromonitor.com; URL: http://www.euromonitor.com. (N. American addr.: Euromonitor International, 122 S. Michigan Ave., Ste. 1200, Chicago, IL 60603. TEL 800-577-3876. FAX 312-922-1157) (looseleaf format) **Document type:** trade publication.
●Also available online. Vendor(s): Data-Star, Knight-Ridder Information, Inc.
Description: Analyzes the fruit-juice markets in France, Germany, Italy, Spain, the U.K., the U.S., Japan, and Canada.

663.63 GW ISSN 0939-4435
CODEN: FRPREY
FRUIT PROCESSING. (Text in English) 1991. m. DM.172 (Europe DM.185) (effective 1996). Verlag Fluessiges Obst GmbH, Diezer Str. 5, 56370 Schoenborn, Germany. TEL 49-6486-8016. FAX 49-6486-6220. Ed. Evi Friedel; Pub. Philipp Possmann. R&P contact: Evi Friedel. adv.: B&W page DM.3885, color page DM.5430; trim 175 x 250; adv. contact: Sybille Schaefer. bk.rev.; abstr.; bibl.; charts; illus.; tr.lit.; circ. 3,758. (back issues avail.) **Indexed:** Food Sci.& Tech.Abstr. **Document type:** trade publication.
—BLDSC (4042.870000); CASDDS. **CCC.**

663 UK
GASTRONOMIQUE. q. National Press Publishers, Peel House, 5 Balfour St., Weybridge, Surrey KT13 8HE, England. TEL 44-1932-859155. FAX 44-1932-859661. Ed. Chris Locke. circ. 10,000. **Document type:** consumer publication.

663 GW
GAULT MILLAU WEINGUIDE DEUTSCHLAND. a. DM.48. Wilhelm Heyne Verlag, Tuerkenstr. 5-7, 80333 Munich, Germany. TEL 49-89-28635301. FAX 49-89-28635304. Ed. Johannes Heyne. (back issues avail.) **Document type:** consumer publication, directory.

663 US ISSN 1074-0759
GEORGE WELLS' WASHINGTON BEVERAGE INSIGHT. 1974. w. $375 (foreign $425) (effective 1995). George Wells & Associates, 2942 S. Columbus St., Ste. A-2, Arlington, VA 22206. TEL 703-671-8140. Ed. George Wells; Pub. George Wells. R&P contact: George Wells. tr.lit.; index. (looseleaf format) **Document type:** newsletter.
●Also available online. Vendor(s): Information Access Co., NewsNet.
Formerly: Washington Beverage Insight (ISSN 0890-8060)
Description: Covers national legislation, regulation and litigation affecting the soft drink and alcoholic beverage industries.

663 GW ISSN 0072-422X
HD9397.G2
GESELLSCHAFT FUER DIE GESCHICHTE UND BIBLIOGRAPHIE DES BRAUWESENS. JAHRBUCH. 1928. a. DM.73.50. Gesellschaft fuer die Geschichte und Bibliographie des Brauwesens e.V., Seestr. 13, 1000 Berlin 65, Germany. TEL 030-4509264. FAX 030-4536069. Ed. Hans G. Schultze-Berndt. bk.rev. circ. 800. **Document type:** bibliography.

663 AU
GETRAENKE. 1949. 11/yr. S.363 (foreign S.600). Verband der Getraenkehersteller Oesterreichs, Zaunergasse 1-3, A-1030 Vienna, Austria. TEL 43-1-7131505. FAX 43-1-7133946. E-mail: bier-fruchtsaft-limonade@getraenkeverband-austria.telecom.at. Ed. Leopold Wurstbauer. adv.: B&W page S.5820, color page S.13320; adv. contact: Andreas Lichal. circ. 1,200. **Document type:** trade publication.

BEVERAGES

663 GW ISSN 1431-4428
▼**GETRAENKE! TECHNOLOGIE UND MARKETING.** 1997. 5/yr. DM.90 (foreign DM.102) (effective 1998). Dr. Harnisch Verlagsgesellschaft mbH, Blumenstr. 15, 90402 Nuernberg, Germany. TEL 49-911-2018-0. FAX 49-911-2018100. E-mail: uepost@aol.com. **Document type:** trade publication.

663 GW ISSN 0947-5141
GETRAENKE ZEITUNG. 1968. 24/yr. DM.154.80 (foreign DM.207.60) (effective 1997). Meininger Verlag GmbH, Maximilianstr. 7-17, 67433 Neustadt, Germany. TEL 49-6321-8908-0. FAX 49-6321-890873. Ed. Reiner Mihr. adv. circ. 13,050. **Document type:** trade publication.
—CCC.
 Former titles (until 1994): Getraenke Handel (ISSN 0937-390X); Getraenke Revue (ISSN 0343-3919)

663 GW ISSN 0724-6153
GETRAENKEFACHGROSSHANDEL. 1982. 11/yr. DM.67. Verlag W. Sachon, Schloss Mindelburg, 87714 Mindelheim, Germany. TEL 49-8261-999-0. FAX 49-8261-999-132. E-mail: sachon@t-online.de; URL: http://www.sachon.de. Ed. Friederike Ott. adv. contact: Ingeborg Rodriguez. circ. 16,183. **Document type:** trade publication.

663 GW ISSN 0016-9331
GETRAENKEHANDEL. 1966. q. DM.48. Zeitungs- und Zeitschriftenverlag Heinrichs, Brueggekamp 1, 30890 Barsinghausen, Germany. TEL 49-5105-2289. Ed. G. Heinrichs; Pub. G. Heinrichs. adv.; bk.rev.; illus.; mkt.; tr.lit. circ. 3,900. (processed) **Document type:** trade publication.

663 GW ISSN 0016-9323
GETRAENKEINDUSTRIE. 1946. m. DM.74. Verlag W. Sachon, Schloss Mindelburg, 87714 Mindelheim, Germany. TEL 49-8261-999-0. FAX 49-8261-999-132. E-mail: sachon@t-online.de; URL: http://www.sachon.de. Ed. Wolfgang Burkart. adv. contact: Ingeborg Rodriguez. abstr.; illus. circ. 10,225. **Document type:** trade publication.
—BLDSC (4165.150000).

663 GW ISSN 0721-8389
GETRAENKEMARKT; Zeitschrift fuer Marketing und Technik im Getraenkehandel. 1981. m. DM.114 (foreign DM.136) (effective 1997). Verlag Hans Carl GmbH, Andernacherstr. 33a, 90411 Nuernberg, Germany. TEL 49-911-95285-0. FAX 49-911-9528548. Ed. Guenter Schmiedel. adv.: B&W page DM.6920, color page DM.9560; trim 191 x 268; adv. contact: Korinna Thoenissen. bk.rev. circ. 17,380. (back issues avail.) **Document type:** trade publication.
—CCC.

663 GW ISSN 0943-4704
GETRAENKEREPORT; fuer Handel und Gastronomie. 1991. 6/yr. DM.50. L F G Verlag, Augustenstr. 33, 80333 Munich, Germany. TEL 49-89-542629-0. FAX 49-89-54262928. Ed. Frank J. Gindler. circ. 27,000. **Document type:** trade publication.

663.1 IT ISSN 0017-0119
GIORNALE DEI DISTILLATORI (NUOVO); alcoli - acquaviti - liquori. 1962. m. L.90000 (foreign L.170000). Guido Scialpi Editore, Via Ugo de Carolis 7, 00136 Rome, Italy. TEL 39-6-33679865. FAX 39-6-33679865. Ed. Guido Scialpi. adv.: page L.1200000. bk.rev.; stat. circ. 3,000. **Document type:** newspaper.
 Description: Covers economic, technical and legislative information in the distillation and liqueur industry.

663 US
GOLDEN STATE BEVERAGE TIMES.* 1991. m. Diamond Publications, Box 398, Hopkins, MN 55343-0398. TEL 612-449-9446. FAX 612-449-9447. adv.: B&W page $1725, color page $2475; trim 8 1/2 x 11. circ. 13,500.
 Description: Covers problems, trends and purchasing information for the alcoholic beverage industry.

663.4 UK ISSN 0265-0681
GOOD BEER GUIDE. 1974. a. £10.99. (Campaign for Real Ale Ltd.) C A M R A Books, 230 Hatfield Rd., St. Albans, Herts. AL1 4LW, England. TEL 44-1727-867201. FAX 44-1727-867670. E-mail: camra@camra.org.uk; URL: http://www.camra.org.uk. Ed. Jeff Evans. bk.rev. circ. 60,000. (back issues avail.) **Document type:** consumer publication.

GOURMET FARE MAGAZINE. see *FOOD AND FOOD INDUSTRIES*

641.2 US
GRAPE 'ZINE; eccentric but essential. 1993. m. $35 to individuals; institutions $60. Grape'Zine, Suffolk St., Sag Harbor, NY 11963. TEL 516-725-3387. FAX 516-725-3387. E-mail: 74003.3001@compuserve.com. Ed. Michael Todd; Pub. Michael Todd. R&P contact: Michael Todd. adv. circ. 40,000. **Document type:** trade publication, consumer publication.
 Description: Covers wine of the world and local foods.

663 US ISSN 1071-3573
TP577
GRASS ROOTS INTERNATIONAL BEER RESOURCE DIRECTORY. 1993. a. $20. Grass Roots Productions, 444 W. 54th St., New York, NY 10019. TEL 212-957-8386. Ed. Heather Wood. **Document type:** directory.
 Description: Covers everything of interest to the beer-lover.

663.4 US
GREAT LAKES BREWING NEWS. 1996. bi-m. $15 (Canada $20; elsewhere $50). Bill Metzger, Ed. & Pub., 214 Muegel Rd., East Amherst, NY 14051. TEL 716-689-5841. FAX 716-689-5789. E-mail: glbrewing@aol.com. R&P contact: Bill Metzger. adv. contact: Bill Metzger. circ. 40,000. **Document type:** consumer publication.
 Description: Covers news of interest to and about microbreweries across the US. Discusses the history of brewing.

663.3 GD
GRENADA BREWERIES ANNUAL REPORT. a. Grenada Breweries, Grand Anse, St. George's, Grenada, W.I. **Document type:** corporate report.

663 UK
GRIST INTERNATIONAL. 6/yr. 2 Balfour Rd., Highbury, London N5 2HB, England. TEL 071-359-8323. FAX 071-354-3962. Ed. Elisabeth Baker. circ. 2,500. **Document type:** trade publication.

663.2 IT
GUIDA AI VINI DEL MONDO. (Text in Italian, Spanish) 1992. biennial. Lit.59000 to non-members; members Lit.50000 (effective 1997). Arcigola Slow Food Editore, Via della Mendicita Istruita 45, 12042 Bra (CN), Italy. TEL 39-172-412519. FAX 39-172-411218. E-mail: slowinfo@slow-food.com; URL: http://www.slow-food.com. Ed. Carlo Petrini. adv. circ. 20,000.
 Description: Lists wineries and wines by country, from all over the world.

GUIDE TO THE WINELANDS OF THE CAPE. see *TRAVEL AND TOURISM*

663.3 UK
GUINNESS GLOBE. 1984. m. free. Guinness Brewing Worldwide, Park Royal Brewery, London NW10 7RR, England. TEL 44-181-965-1882. TELEX 23882. Ed. Claire Grundy. R&P contact: Claire Grundy. circ. 8,500. **Document type:** newspaper.
 Description: Presents news and information of interest to employees and pensioners of Guiness Brewing and associated companies worldwide.

663.2 UK
HARPERS WINE AND SPIRIT DIRECTORY. 1914. a. £70. Harper Trade Journals Ltd., Harling House, 47-51 Great Suffolk St., London SE1 OBS, England. TEL 4-171-261-1604. FAX 44-171-633-0281. Ed. Patrick Straker; Pub. Anthony Hawser. R&P contact: Anthony Hawser. adv. contact: John Burnyeat. circ. 3,500. (back issues avail.) **Document type:** trade publication, directory.
—BLDSC (4264.949500).
 Former titles: Harpers Wine and Spirit Annual (ISSN 0952-0856); Harpers Directory of the Wine and Spirit Trade; Harpers Directory and Manual of the Wine and Spirit Trade (ISSN 0073-0408)
 Description: Lists distilleries, wineries, shippers, wholesalers, trade agencies and associations connected to the wine and spirit industry worldwide,

663.1 UK
HARPERS WINE AND SPIRIT WEEKLY. 1878. w. £95 includes Directory. Harper Trade Journals Ltd., Harling House, 47-51 Great Suffolk St., London SE1 OBS, England. TEL 44-171-261-1604. FAX 44-171-633-0281. Ed. Patrick Straker; Pub. Anthony Hawser. R&P contact: Anthony Hawser. adv. contact: John Burnyeat. bk.rev.; mkt.; stat.; tr.mk. **Document type:** trade publication.
 Formerly (until Sep. 1996): Harpers Wine and Spirit Gazette (ISSN 0017-7903)

HARVEST (LAKEVILLE-MIDDLEBORO). see *AGRICULTURE*

663 US ISSN 0017-8543
HAWAII BEVERAGE GUIDE. 1949. m. $32. (Associated Beverage Publications) Service Publications, Inc. (Honolulu), Box 853, Honolulu, HI 96808. TEL 808-591-0049. FAX 808-591-0038. Ed. Campbell Mansfield. adv.; stat. circ. 1,950. **Document type:** trade publication.
 Description: Focuses on beverage products. Covers all aspects of the industry.

663.9 658.8 UK
HOT DRINKS: THE INTERNATIONAL MARKET. (Subseries of: Market Direction reports) 1986. a. £2500($5000) (effective 1997). Euromonitor, 60-61 Britton St., London EC1M 5QU, England. TEL 44-171-251-8024. FAX 44-171-608-3149. E-mail: info@euromonitor.com; URL: http://www.euromonitor.com. (Addr. in N. America: Euromonitor International, 122 S. Michigan Ave., Ste. 1200, Chicago, IL 60603. TEL 800-577-3876. FAX 312-922-1157) (looseleaf format) **Document type:** trade publication.
 Formerly: Hot Beverages: The International Market.
 Description: Analyzes the market for hot beverages in France, Germany, Italy, Spain, the U.K., the U.S., and Japan.

663.19 US ISSN 1058-3289
I B W A NEWS. 1980. bi-m. International Bottled Water Association, 113 N. Henry St., Alexandria, VA 22314. TEL 703-683-5213. FAX 703-683-4074. Ed. Ann F. Carberry. circ. 2,500 (controlled). **Document type:** newsletter.
 Description: Covers the events and activities of the IBWA and the bottled water industry throughout the world.

663.19 US
I B W A TECHNICAL BULLETIN. 1980. q. International Bottled Water Association, 113 N. Henry St., Alexandria, VA 22314. TEL 703-683-5213. FAX 703-683-4074. Ed. Tyrone P. Wilson. circ. 2,500 (controlled). **Document type:** newsletter.
 Description: Covers technical subjects pertaining to the bottled water industry worldwide.

663 US ISSN 0019-1892
ILLINOIS BEVERAGE JOURNAL. 1944. m. $30. Illinois Beverage Media, Inc., 2260 Bracken Lane, Northfield, IL 60093-2903. TEL 708-441-7776. Ed. Jim O'Brien. adv. circ. 6,000. **Document type:** trade publication.
 Description: Trade magazine for the beverage alcohol industry in Illinois.

IMBOTTIGLIAMENTO. see *PACKAGING*

522 BEVERAGES

663 338.47 US
IMPACT (NEW YORK); U S news and research for the wine, spirits and beer industries. Variant title: Impact Newsletter. 1970. s-m. $375 (Canada $395; overseas $415). M. Shanken Communications, Inc., 387 Park Ave. S., New York, NY 10016. TEL 212-684-4224. FAX 212-684-5424. TELEX 422687 MSHANK UI. (Subscr. to: Box 10862, Riverton, NJ 08077. FAX 212-481-0722) Ed. Marvin R. Shanken. adv.; bk.rev.; index. (back issues avail.) **Document type:** trade publication.
 Former titles: Impact: Wine and Spirits Newsletter (ISSN 0363-9444); Impact Alcoholic Beverage Newsletter.
 Description: Focuses on news related to the United States alcoholic beverage industry.

663 338.47 US ISSN 0268-8212
IMPACT INTERNATIONAL; global news and research for the international drinks executive. 1986. s-m. $425. M. Shanken Communications, Inc., 387 Park Ave. S., New York, NY 10016. TEL 212-684-4224. FAX 212-684-5424. TELEX 422687 MSHANK UI. (Subscr. to: Box 10862, Riverton, NJ 08077. FAX 212-481-0722) adv.; charts; illus. **Indexed:** Per.Islam. (1990-). **Document type:** trade publication.
 Description: Focuses on regular rankings of world's top selling brands, drinking trends around the globe, and new product performance.

IMPACT WORLD DIRECTORY; leading spirits, wine & beer companies; who's who of industry executives. see BUSINESS AND ECONOMICS — Trade And Industrial Directories

338.47 US
IMPACT WORLDWIDE DISTILLED SPIRITS REPORT. 1991. a. $2360. M. Shanken Communications, Inc., 387 Park Ave. S., New York, NY 10016. TEL 212-684-4224. FAX 212-684-5424. TELEX 422687 MSHANK UI. Ed. Marvin R. Shanken. charts. **Document type:** trade publication.
 Formerly: International Spirits Market Report (ISSN 1061-4923)
 Description: Utilizing the IMPACT Databank, the report analyzes all segments of the U.S. and international distilled spirits market.

663.2 US
IMPACT WORLDWIDE WINE REPORT. 1991. a. $1560. M. Shanken Communications, Inc., 387 Park Ave. S., New York, NY 10016. TEL 212-684-4224. FAX 212-684-5424. TELEX 422687 MSHANK UI. Ed. Marvin R. Shanken. charts. **Document type:** trade publication.
 Formerly: International Wine Market Report (ISSN 1061-9305)
 Description: Analyzes all segments of the U.S. and international wine market.

663.4 US
IMPORT - SPECIALTY INSIGHTS. 1984. a. $525. Beer Marketer's Insights, Inc., Box 264, West Nyack, NY 10994. TEL 914-624-2337. Ed. Jerry Steinman. charts. (back issues avail.) **Document type:** trade publication.
 Formerly: Import Insights.
 Description: Statistical overview of import and specialty market in US, with written analysis. Provides statistics for total import shipments in 19 states by major importers.

663.1 340 US
INDIANA ALCOHOLIC BEVERAGE LAWS AND RULES. a. $17. Michie, A Division of Reed Elsevier Inc., Box 7587, Charlottesville, VA 22906-7587. TEL 804-972-7566; 800-562-1197. FAX 800-643-1280. E-mail: custserv@michie.com; URL: http://www.michie.com. Ed. George Harley. pp./issue: 364.
 Description: Provides all the statutes and rules governing Indiana's alcoholic beverage industry.

663.3 US ISSN 0274-547X
INDIANA BEVERAGE JOURNAL. 1945. m. $20. Indiana Beverage Life, Box 5067, Zionsville, IN 46077. TEL 317-733-0527. FAX 317-733-0528. E-mail: sntsb19@indy.net. (Affiliate: Associated Beverage Publications) Ed. Stewart Baxter. adv. circ. 2,700. **Document type:** trade publication.

663 IT ISSN 0390-0541
CODEN: INBEEW
INDUSTRIE DELLE BEVANDE. (Text in Italian; summaries in English) 1971. bi-m. L.100000($70) (effective 1997). Chiriotti Editori, Viale Rimembranza 60, P.O. Box 66, 10064 Pinerolo, Italy. TEL 39-121-393127. FAX 39-121-794480. Ed. Giovanni Chiriotti. adv.: B&W page L.1800000, color page L.2200000; adv. contact: Giuseppe Chiriotti. bk.rev. circ. 4,700. **Indexed:** Chem.Abstr., Food Sci.& Tech.Abstr., Int.Packag.Abstr., Nutr.Abstr., Packag.Sci.Tech., Sugar Ind.Abstr. **Document type:** trade publication.
 —BLDSC (4464.900000); CASDDS; Linda Hall; UMI. **CCC**.
 Description: Covers all branches of the beverage industry; mineral waters, wines, soft drinks, aperitifs, beers, spirits, and fruit juices.

338.47 658 US
INDUSTRY WORLD. (Former name of issuing body: National Women's Association of Allied Beverage Industries) bi-m. World Association of Alcohol Beverage Industries, Inc., 1250 Eye St. N.W., Ste. 900, Washington, DC 20005. TEL 202-628-3544.
 Formerly: Industry Woman.
 Description: Features developments in the industry. Includes association news.

663.2 FR
INSTITUT NATIONAL DES APPELLATIONS D'ORIGINE. BULLETIN. (Special nos. avail.) 1938. q. 130 F. (outside Europe 185 F.). Institut National des Appellations d'Origine, 138 av. des Champs Elysees, 75008 Paris, France. TEL 1-45-62-54-75. bk.rev. circ. 450.
 Formerly: Institut National des Appellations d'Origine des Vins et Eaux-de-Vie. Bulletin (ISSN 0020-2401)
 Description: Covers texts, data and statistics of the wine industry.

663.4 UK ISSN 0046-9750
CODEN: JINBAL
INSTITUTE OF BREWING. JOURNAL. 1904. bi-m. £195. Institute of Brewing, 33 Clarges St., London W1Y 8EE, England. TEL 44-171-499-8144. FAX 44-171-499-1156. Ed. C.M. Brown. adv. contact: F. Bolton. bk.rev.; illus. circ. 4,200. **Indexed:** Anal.Abstr., ASCA, Biol.Abstr., Biotech.Abstr., Br.Tech.Ind., C.I.S. Abstr., Chem.Abstr., Curr.Adv.Ecol.Sci., Curr.Biotech.Abstr., Curr.Cont., Dairy Sci.Abstr., Field Crop Abstr., Food Sci.& Tech.Abstr., Herb.Abstr., Hort.Abstr., Nutr.Abstr., Plant Breed.Abstr., Sci.Cit.Ind., Sugar Ind.Abstr., VITIS. **Document type:** academic/scholarly publication.
 —BLDSC (4771.000000); CASDDS; CISTI; Genuine Article; SWETS; UnCover.
 Description: Features original research articles on all aspects of brewing science. Also contains Institute news and abstracts of research from other publications.

663 UK
INTERNATIONAL BOTTLER AND PACKER. 1927. m. £41($94) Binsted Publications Ltd., Walton House, 90 London Rd., Hook, Hants. RG27 9LF, England. TEL 01253-764180. FAX 01256-766102. Ed. Edward C. Binsted; Pub. Edward C. Binsted. adv.; illus. circ. 6,000. **Indexed:** Dairy Sci.Abstr., Food Sci.& Tech.Abstr., Int.Packag.Abstr., Key to Econ.Sci. **Document type:** trade publication.
 —BLDSC (4537.500000); SWETS.
 Incorporating: International Beverage News (ISSN 0020-6199); Which incorporated: Wine and Spirit Chronicle.

663 SZ
INTERNATIONAL BREWER'S DIRECTORY. DISTILLERS AND SOFT DRINK GUIDE. (Text in English, French, German) 1928. every 7 yrs., 10th ed., 1994. 600 SFr. Verlag fuer Internationale Wirtschaftsliteratur Ltd., Postfach 28, CH-8047 Zurich, Switzerland. TEL 41-1-4926130. FAX 41-1-4010545. Ed. Walter Hirt. **Document type:** directory.
 Former titles: International Brewer's Directory (ISSN 0074-9796); Internationales Firmenregister der Brauindustrie, Malzerien, Brennereien, Mineralwasser und Erfrischungsgetraenke.

663 UK
INTERNATIONAL DRINKS BULLETIN. fortn. Reed Business Information (Subsidiary of: Reed Elsevier group), Quadrant House, The Quadrant, Sutton, Surrey SM2 5AS, England. TEL 44-181-652-4800. FAX 44-181-652-4748.

663.2 UK ISSN 0954-7541
HD9370.1
INTERNATIONAL JOURNAL OF WINE MARKETING. 1989. 3/yr. £599($899) (foreign Aus.$449) (effective 1998). (University of Surrey, Department of Management Studies) Patrington Press Ltd., Enholmes Hall, Patrington, Hull HU12 0PR, England. TEL 44-1964-630033. FAX 44-1274-547143. (Dist. by: M C B University Press Ltd., 60-62 Toller Ln., Bradford, W. Yorks BD8 9BY, England. TEL 44-1274-777700. FAX 44-1274-785200) Ed. Michael Howley. R&P contact: B.O. Pettman. circ. 100 (paid). (reprint service avail. from SWZ) **Indexed:** Art.Hosp.& Tour. **Document type:** consumer publication, trade publication.
 —BLDSC (4542.701300); UMI.
 Description: Provides in-depth information on all aspects of marketing wine from international sources.

INTERNATIONAL PRODUCT ALERT. see BUSINESS AND ECONOMICS — Marketing And Purchasing

663.2 IT ISSN 0374-5791
ISTITUTO SPERIMENTALE PER L'ENOLOGIA ASTI. ANNALI. (Text in Italian; summaries in English, German and French) 1970. a. L.100000. Istituto Sperimentale per l'Enologia, Via P. Micca 35, 14100 Asti, Italy. FAX 141-436829. circ. 500. (back issues avail.) **Indexed:** Biol.Abstr.

663.2 IT
ITALIAN WINES & SPIRITS (U S AND CANADA EDITION). (Text in English) 1977. q. $23. Editoriale Lariana s.r.l., Via Ciro Menotti 11-D, 20129 Milan, Italy. TEL 392-76110303. FAX 39-2-713847. Ed. Pino Khail. adv. contact: Antonella Khail. circ. 50,000. **Document type:** consumer publication, trade publication.

663.2 IT
ITALIAN WINES & SPIRITS (UK EDITION). (Text in English) 1979. q. $23. Editoriale Lariana s.r.l., Via Ciro Menotti 11-D, 20129 Milan, Italy. TEL 39-2-76110303. FAX 39-2-713847. Ed. Pino Khail. adv. contact: Antonella Khail. circ. 25,000. **Document type:** consumer publication, trade publication.
 Description: Covers Italian wines and food.

663 330 US ISSN 0738-8853
JESSE MEYERS' BEVERAGE DIGEST.* (Supplement avail.: Green Sheet) 1982. s-m. (22/yr.) $525 (foreign $595) (includes supplement). Beverage Digest Compay, LLC, Box 621, Bedford Hills, NY 10507-0621. E-mail: BerDigest@col.com. Ed. John Sicher; Pub. John Sicher. bk.rev.; stat.; circ. controlled. (back issues avail.) **Document type:** newsletter.
 Description: Covers the soft drink industry and related markets, focusing on marketing and statistics.

663.3 BE
LE JOURNAL DU BRASSEUR. Dutch edition: Brouwersblad. (Text in French) 1893. 4/yr. 1200 BEF (foreign 2000 BEF). Confederation des Brasseries de Belgique, Maison des Brasseurs, Grand'Place 10, 1000 Brussels, Belgium. TEL 32-2-511-49-87. FAX 32-2-511-32-59. adv.: B&W page 35000 BEF, color page 58000 BEF; trim 275 x 190. bk.rev.; bibl.; charts; illus.; mkt.; pat.; tr.lit.; index. circ. 4,000. **Indexed:** Biol.Abstr., Chem.Abstr., Food Sci.& Tech.Abstr., Nutr.Abstr. **Document type:** trade publication.
 Formerly: Petit Journal du Brasseur (ISSN 0031-6253)
 Description: Covers production and marketing of Belgian beers.

663 US ISSN 0747-7368
JOURNAL OF GASTRONOMY. 1984. irreg. membership only. American Institute of Wine and Food, 1550 Bryant St., San Francisco, CA 94103. TEL 415-255-3000. Ed. Nancy Jenkins. bk.rev.; illus. circ. 6,000. (back issues avail.) **Indexed:** Hospit.Ind.
 —BLDSC (4987.630000).

JOURNAL OF WINE RESEARCH. see AGRICULTURE — Crop Production And Soil

BEVERAGES 523

663.2   FR   ISSN 0151-4393
JOURNEE VINICOLE. (Text in English, French) 1927. d. 1170 F. (foreign 1920 F.). Promovin, B.P. 1064, 34007 Montpellier Cedex 1, France.
TEL 04-67-07-91-01. FAX 04-67-47-93-63. Ed. J.C. Causse. R&P contact: Jean-Christophe Causse. adv. contact: Stephane Gardere. bk.rev.; illus.; stat.; circ. 15,900 (controlled). **Document type:** newspaper, trade publication.
Description: Daily international newspaper on wine and spirits.

663.2   YU   ISSN 0022-6130
CODEN: JVIVAB
JUGOSLOVENSKO VINOGRADARSTVO I VINARSTVO. 1967. m. $80. Institut za Spoljnu Trgovinu, Mose Pijade 8, Belgrade, Serbia, Yugoslavia. TELEX YU IST 12214. Ed. Vojislav Stankovic. adv.; stat. **Indexed:** Chem.Abstr.
—CASDDS.

663   GW   ISSN 0173-6981
K T B L ARBEITSBLAETTER WEINBAU. irreg., no.71, 1993. DM.8. Kuratorium fuer Technik und Bauwesen in der Landwirtschaft e.V., Bartningstr. 49, 64289 Darmstadt, Germany.
TEL 06151-7001-0. FAX 06151-7001123. **Document type:** monographic series.

663   US   ISSN 0882-2573
KANE'S BEVERAGE WEEK; the newsletter of beverage marketing. 1939. w. (bi-w. in July, Aug.). $429 (foreign $404). Whitaker Newsletters Inc., 313 South Ave., Box 192, Fanwood, NJ 07023. TEL 908-889-6336. FAX 908-889-6339. Ed. Joel Whitaker. bk.rev. (back issues avail.) **Document type:** newsletter.
●Also available online. Vendor(s): NewsNet (FB06).
—CCC.
Description: Covers the news of the beverage industry, with particular emphasis on beer, wine and spirits. Includes new products, federal and state regulations, market trends and advertising research.

663.3   GW
KENNZAHLEN ZUR BETRIEBSKONTROLLE UND QUALITAETSBESCHREIBUNG IN DER BRAUWIRTSCHAFT. irreg. DM.149. B. Behr's Verlag GmbH, Averhoffstr. 10, 22085 Hamburg, Germany. TEL 49-40-2270080. FAX 49-40-2201091. E-mail: behrs@behrs.de; URL: http://www.behrs.de. **Document type:** trade publication.

663   US   ISSN 0023-0138
KENTUCKY BEVERAGE JOURNAL. 1949. m. $24 (effective 1997). Midway Publications, Box 346, Midway, KY 40347-0346. Ed. John D. Meyers. adv. contact: Gene McLean. illus.; mkt. circ. 1,800.
Document type: trade publication.

663   UK
KEY NOTE MARKET REPORT: AFTER DINNER DRINKS. Variant title: After Dinner Drinks. irreg., no.8, 1994. £205. Key Note Ltd., Field House, 72 Oldfield Rd., Hampton, Middlesex TW12 2HQ, England. TEL 44-181-783-0755. FAX 44-181-783-0049. **Document type:** trade publication.
●Also available online.
Also available on CD-ROM.
Formerly: Key Note Report: After Dinner Drinks (ISSN 0954-4542)

663   UK
KEY NOTE MARKET REPORT: BOTTLED WATERS. irreg., no.3, 1995. £205. Key Note Ltd., Field House, 72 Oldfield Rd., Hampton, Middlesex TW12 2HQ, England. TEL 44-181-783-0755. FAX 44-181-783-0049. Ed. Phillippa Smith. **Document type:** trade publication.
●Also available online.
Also available on CD-ROM.
Former titles: Key Note Report: Bottled Waters; Key Note Report: Mineral Water (ISSN 0957-7386)

663.4   UK
KEY NOTE MARKET REPORT: BREWERIES & THE BEER MARKET. Variant title: Breweries & the Beer Market. 1991. irreg., no.14, 1995. £205. Key Note Ltd., Field House, 72 Oldfield Rd., Hampton, Middlesex TW12 2HQ, England. TEL 44-181-783-0755. FAX 44-181-783-0049. Ed. Simon Howitt. **Document type:** trade publication.
●Also available online.
Also available on CD-ROM.
Formerly: Key Note Report: Breweries and the Beer Market (ISSN 1352-5492)

663   UK
KEY NOTE MARKET REPORT: CIDER. Variant title: Cider. 1993. irreg. £205. Key Note Ltd., Field House, 72 Oldfield Rd., Hampton, Middlesex TW12 2HQ, England. TEL 44-181-783-0755. FAX 44-181-783-0049. **Document type:** trade publication.
●Also available online.
Also available on CD-ROM.
Formerly: Key Note Report: Cider (ISSN 0951-9122)

663.52   UK
KEY NOTE MARKET REPORT: DISTILLERS (WHISKY). Variant title: Distillers (Whisky). irreg., no.10, 1994. £205. Key Note Ltd., Field House, 72 Oldfield Rd., Hampton, Middlesex TW12 2HQ, England. TEL 44-181-783-0755. FAX 44-181-783-0049. **Document type:** trade publication.
●Also available online.
Also available on CD-ROM.
Formerly: Key Note Report: Distillers (Whisky) (ISSN 0954-4569)

663.52   UK
KEY NOTE MARKET REPORT: DISTILLERS (WHITE SPIRITS). Variant title: Distillers (White Spirits). irreg., no.7, 1990. £185. Key Note Ltd., Field House, 72 Oldfield Rd., Hampton, Middlesex TW12 2HQ, England. TEL 44-181-783-0755. FAX 44-181-783-1940. **Document type:** trade publication.

663   UK
KEY NOTE MARKET REPORT: FRUIT JUICES & HEALTH DRINKS. Variant title: Fruit Juices & Health Drinks. irreg., no.6, 1994. £205. Key Note Ltd., Field House, 72 Oldfield Rd., Hampton, Middlesex TW12 2HQ, England. TEL 44-181-783-0755. FAX 44-181-783-0049. **Document type:** trade publication.
●Also available online.
Also available on CD-ROM.
Formerly: Key Note Report: Fruit Juices and Health Drinks (ISSN 0954-4666)

663   UK
KEY NOTE MARKET REPORT: HOT DRINKS. Variant title: Hot Drinks. irreg., no.5, 1992. £185. Key Note Ltd., Field House, 72 Oldfield Rd., Hampton, Middlesex TW12 2HQ, England. TEL 44-181-783-0755. FAX 44-181-783-1940. **Document type:** trade publication.
●Also available online.
Also available on CD-ROM.
Formerly: Key Note Report: Hot Drinks.

663   UK
KEY NOTE MARKET REPORT: LOW ALCOHOL DRINKS. Variant title: Low Alcohol Drinks. 1989. irreg., no.3, 1995. £205. Key Note Ltd., Field House, 72 Oldfield Rd., Hampton, Middlesex TW12 2HQ, England. TEL 44-181-783-0755. FAX 44-181-783-0049. **Document type:** trade publication.
●Also available online.
Also available on CD-ROM.
Formerly: Key Note Report: Low Alcohol Drinks (ISSN 0957-736X)

663.4 658.8   UK
KEY NOTE MARKET REPORT: PREMIUM LAGERS, BEERS AND CIDERS. Variant title: Premium Lagers, Beers and Ciders. 1992. irreg., no.2, 1993. £285. Key Note Ltd., Field House, 72 Oldfield Rd., Hampton, Middlesex TW12 2HQ, England. TEL 44-181-783-0755. FAX 44-181-783-0049. **Document type:** trade publication.
●Also available online.
Also available on CD-ROM.
Formerly: Key Note Report: Premium Lagers, Beers and Ciders (ISSN 1352-6944)

663   UK
KEY NOTE MARKET REPORT: SOFT DRINKS (CARBONATES & CONCENTRATES). Variant title: Soft Drinks (Carbonates & Concentrates). irreg., no.11, 1993. £285. Key Note Ltd., Field House, 72 Oldfield Rd., Hampton, Middlesex TW12 2HQ, England. TEL 44-181-783-0755. FAX 44-181-783-0049. **Document type:** trade publication.
●Also available online.
Also available on CD-ROM.
Formerly: Key Note Report: Soft Drinks (Carbonates and Concentrates) (ISSN 0954-450X)

663.2   UK
KEY NOTE MARKET REPORT: WINE. Variant title: Wine. irreg., no.12, 1996. £205. Key Note Ltd., Field House, 72 Oldfield Rd., Hampton, Middlesex TW12 2HQ, England. TEL 44-181-783-0755. FAX 44-181-783-0049. **Document type:** trade publication.
●Also available online.
Also available on CD-ROM.
Formerly: Key Note Report: Wine (ISSN 0954-5034)

663   UK
KEY NOTE MARKET REVIEW: U K DRINKS MARKET. irreg., no.8, 1995. £410. Key Note Ltd., Field House, 72 Oldfield Rd., Hampton, Middlesex TW12 2HQ, England. TEL 44-181-783-0755. FAX 44-181-783-0049. **Document type:** trade publication.
●Also available online.
Also available on CD-ROM.
Formerly: Key Note Market Review: U K Drinking Habits.

663   UK   ISSN 1356-6199
KEY NOTE MARKET REVIEW: U K SOFT DRINKS. Variant title: U K Soft Drinks. 1992. irreg., no.2, 1994. £410. Key Note Ltd., Field House, 72 Oldfield Rd., Hampton, Middlesex TW12 2HQ, England. TEL 44-181-783-0755. FAX 44-181-783-0049. **Document type:** trade publication.
●Also available online.
Also available on CD-ROM.

663.3   JA
KIRIN BREWERY COMPANY. ANNUAL REPORT. 1956. a. Kirin Brewery Co. Ltd., Technology Development Department - Kirin Biru K.K., 26-1, Jingumae 6-chome, Shibuya-ku, Tokyo 150, Japan.
TEL 03-3499-6111. FAX 03-3499-6151.

KOMPASS AGRIBUSINESSS AND FOOD AND BEVERAGE. see BUSINESS AND ECONOMICS — Trade And Industrial Directories

KOMPASS PROFESSIONNEL. AGRICULTURE, ALIMENTATION. see BUSINESS AND ECONOMICS — Trade And Industrial Directories

663   UK
▼**LATIN AMERICAN DRINKS BUYER.** (Text in Spanish and Portuguese) 1996. q. $50 (effective 1997). Crier Publications Ltd., Artic House, Rye Ln., Dunton Green, Sevenoaks, Kent TN14 5HB, England.
TEL 01732-451515. FAX 01732-451383. E-mail: antk@crier.demon.co.uk. Ed. Heather Buckle; Pub. John Whitbread. adv. contact: Philip McLean. circ. 14,000. **Document type:** trade publication.
Description: Discusses matters of interest to major purchasing companies of drinks in all Latin American nations.

663.1 340   US
LAWS AND REGULATIONS OF THE STATE OF MARYLAND RELATING TO ALCOHOLIC BEVERAGES AND TOBACCO TAX. (YEAR) CUMULATIVE SUPPLEMENT. a. $25. Michie, A Reed Elsevier Inc., Box 7587, Charlottesville, VA 22906-7587.
TEL 804-972-7566; 800-562-1197.
FAX 800-643-1280. E-mail: custserv@michie.com; URL: http://www.michie.com. Ed. George Harley.

663.6   US   ISSN 1040-3736
LEISURE BEVERAGE INSIDER NEWSLETTER. 1968. bi-w. $299 (foreign $310). Whitaker Newsletters Inc., 313 South Ave., Box 192, Fanwood, NJ 07023.
TEL 908-889-6336. FAX 908-889-6339. Ed. Fred Rossi. bk.rev.; charts; tr.lit. circ. 409. (reprint service avail. from UMI) **Document type:** newsletter.
—CCC.
Formerly: Soft Drink "Insider" Newsletter (ISSN 0038-0555)
Description: Covers the news of the beverage industry, with particular emphasis on soft drinks, mixers and bottled water. Includes new products, federal and state regulations, marketing trends and advertising research.

B

BEVERAGES

663.2 — FR — ISSN 1010-3074
LA LETTRE DE L'O I V. English edition (ISSN 1010-3066) (Supplement avail.: La lettre Vin, Nutrition et Sante) 11/yr. 190 F. (foreign 250 F.) (effective 1997); newsstand price: 20 F. Office International de la Vigne et du Vin, 18 rue d'Aguesseau, 75008 Paris, France. TEL 33-1-44948080. FAX 33-1-42669063. E-mail: OIV101675.2013@compuserve.com. Ed. Yann Juban. **Document type:** newsletter.
Description: Covers the activities of the organization, the introduction of vineyards and the publication of new journals.

663.2 — FR — ISSN 1024-3119
LETTRE NUTRITION ET SANTE. English edition: Nutrition and Health (ISSN 1024-3100) 11/yr. 190 F. (foreign 250 F.) (effective 1996). Office International de la Vigne et du Vin, 18 rue d'Aguesseau, 75008 Paris, France. TEL 33-1-44948080. FAX 33-1-42669063.
Description: Covers the activities of the vineyards and the publication of new journals.

338.47 — UK
LICENSED AND CATERING NEWS. 1944. m. £25. Ulster Magazines Ltd., 58 Rugby Rd., Belfast BT7 1PT, N. Ireland. TEL 44-1232-230425. FAX 44-1232-243595. Ed. Larry Nixon. circ. 4,500. **Document type:** trade publication.
Formerly: Ulster Licensed Trade News.

642.5 — UK — ISSN 1356-0034
THE LICENSEE AND MORNING ADVERTISER. 1794. 2/wk. £98.80 (foreign £182) (effective 1997). Society of Licensed Victuallers, Elvian House, Nixey Close, Slough, Berkshire SL1 1NQ, England. TEL 44-1753-811911. FAX 44-1753-810503. E-mail: 100656.106@compuserve.com. Ed. John Tomlin. adv. contact: Brian Ayling. bk.rev.; charts; illus.; circ. 14,755 (paid). **Document type:** trade publication.

LICENSING LAWS N S W: LIQUOR ACT & REGULATIONS. see LAW

LIQUOR CONTROL LAW REPORTS; federal and all states. see BUSINESS AND ECONOMICS — Public Finance, Taxation

LIQUOR LAWS VICTORIA. see LAW

338.47 — AT
LIQUOR RETAILING HANDBOOK. 1987. a. Aus.$95. Thomson Business Publishing, 47 Chippen St., Chippendale, N.S.W. 2008, Australia. TEL 02-699-2411. FAX 02-698-3920. Ed. Glynis Macri. adv. circ. 852.
Formerly: Liquor Marketing Yearbook (ISSN 1031-4857)

663.4 — UK — ISSN 0144-7866
LONDON DRINKER. 1979. m. £7 (foreign £10). Campaign for Real Ale, London Branches, 122 Manor Way, Uxbridge, Mddx., England. I.H. Amy. R&P contact: I.H. Amy. TEL 44-181-398-4556. adv. contact: B. Tillbrook. bk.rev. circ. 5,000. **Document type:** consumer publication.
Description: Covers real ale, in and around London.

663.3 — US — ISSN 0024-7960
M B A A TECHNICAL QUARTERLY. 1964. q. $100 (effective 1997). Master Brewers Association of the Americas, 2421 N. Mayfair Rd., Ste. 310, Wauwatosa, WI 53226-1407. TEL 414-774-8558. Ed. Harold Broderick. adv.; abstr.; charts; illus.; index. circ. 4,200. (processed) **Indexed:** Chem.Abstr., Food Sci.& Tech.Abstr., Nutr.Abstr.
—BLDSC (8710.740100).

641.21 — US — ISSN 1086-4199
MALT ADVOCATE; beer and whisky magazine. 1994. q. $12.95 (effective 1995); newsstand price: $3.50. Malt Society, 3416 Oak Hill Rd., Emmaus, PA 18049. TEL 610-967-1083. E-mail: maltman999@aol.com. (Subscr. to: I P D, 674 Via de la Valle, Ste. 200, Solana Beach, CA 92075. TEL 800-610-MALT) Ed. John Hansell. adv.: B&W page $1700; trim 8 1/2 x 11. bk.rev. circ. 25,000. (back issues avail.) **Document type:** consumer publication.
●Also available online.

663 — SP
MARCO REAL; periodico economico de vinos, cervezas y espirituosos. 1987. s-m. (except Aug.) 9911 ptas. Ediciones Marco Real S.A., Valentin Beato 11, 28037 Madrid, Spain. TEL 327-00-44. FAX 204-12-08. TELEX 42677 EMR. Ed. J.J. Delgado. bk.rev. circ. 15,000. **Document type:** trade publication.
Description: Provides the latest news on the companies and products in the world of wine, beer, and spirits. Includes restaurant and drink critiques, results of wine tasting events, opinions on fairs and congresses, and editorials on legislation.

663.2 — US — ISSN 0277-9277
HD9350.1
MARKET WATCH (NEW YORK). 1981. m. $60. Marvin R. Shanken Communications, Inc., 387 Park Ave. S., New York, NY 10016. TEL 212-684-4224. FAX 212-684-5424. TELEX 422687 MSHANK UI. Ed. Marvin R. Shanken. adv. **Indexed:** PROMT. **Document type:** trade publication.
Description: Provides market intelligence on the wine, spirit, and beer businesses.

663 — GW
MARKETING JAHRBUCH WEIN. 1984. a. DM.115. Meininger Verlag GmbH, Maximilianstr. 7-17, 67433 Neustadt, Germany. TEL 49-6321-8908-0. FAX 49-6321-8908-73. **Document type:** trade publication.
Formerly (until 1991): Weinjahr.

MARMITE. see FOOD AND FOOD INDUSTRIES

663.1 — US — ISSN 1058-9341
MARYLAND - WASHINGTON BEVERAGE JOURNAL. 1938. m. $31.50. Beverage Journal, Inc., 7451 Race Rd., Box 1002, Hanover, MD 21076-4002. TEL 410-796-5455. FAX 410-796-5511. E-mail: beujrnl@ix.netcom.com. Ed. Lee Murray. adv. contact: Stephen Patten. bk.rev.; charts; illus.; mkt. circ. 9,000. **Document type:** trade publication.
Former titles: Maryland - Washington - Delaware Beverage Journal (ISSN 0037-0045); Seaboard Beverage Journal.
Description: Covers the beer, wine, and liquor industry in Maryland and Washington, DC.

663 — US
MASSACHUSETTS BEVERAGE BUSINESS. 1944. m. $52. New Beverage Publications, Inc., Box 932, Boston, MA 02117-0932. TEL 617-423-7200. FAX 617-482-7163. Ed. Peter Stone; Pub. S.I. Stone. adv. circ. 7,800. **Document type:** trade publication.
Former titles: Massachusetts Beverage Price Journal (ISSN 1084-1113); Massachusetts Beverage Journal.
Description: Contains wholesale prices for spirits, wine and malt beverages, news and reports of trade events.
Refereed Serial

663.3 — US
MASTER BREWERS ASSOCIATION OF AMERICA. COMMUNICATIONS. 1940. q. $55. Master Brewers Association of America, 2421 N. Mayfair Rd., Ste. 310, Wauwatosa, WI 53226-1407. TEL 414-774-8558. charts; illus. **Document type:** newsletter.
Description: Acts as an internal newsletter.

663 658.8 — UK
MINERAL WATER: THE INTERNATIONAL MARKET. (Subseries of: Market Direction reports) a. £2500($5000) (effective 1997). Euromonitor, 60-61 Britton St., London EC1M 5NA, England. TEL 44-171-251-8024. FAX 44-171-608-3149. E-mail: info@euromonitor.com; URL: http://www.euromonitor.com. (Addr. in N. America: Euromonitor International, 122 S. Michigan Ave., Ste. 1200, Chicago, IL 60603. TEL 800-577-3876. FAX 312-922-1157) (looseleaf format) **Document type:** trade publication.
●Also available online. Vendor(s): Data-Star, Knight-Ridder Information, Inc.
Description: Analyzes the mineral-water markets in France, Germany, Italy, Spain, the U.K., the U.S., Canada and Japan.

663.61 — GW — ISSN 0171-5720
DER MINERALBRUNNEN. 1951. m. DM.36. Gesellschaft der Freunde und Foerderer der deutschen Mineralbrunnen e.V., Kennedyallee 28, 53175 Bonn, Germany. TEL 49-228-959900. FAX 49-228-373453. Eds. Andreas Rottke, Wolfgang Stubbe. adv. contact: Ulrich Wermke. bk.rev.; illus. circ. 2,800. **Indexed:** Food Sci.& Tech.Abstr., Nutr.Abstr. **Document type:** trade publication.
Formerly: Naturbrunnen (ISSN 0028-0828)
Description: Communicates views on all issues affecting the mineral water industry.

663 — IT
MIXER. 1976. 10/yr. L.60000 (foreign L.120000). (Associazione Italiana Barmen e Sostenitori - Italian Bartenders Association) Gruppo E.S. s.r.l., Via Solari, 19, 20144 Milan, Italy. TEL 02-58102128. FAX 02-89406970. Ed. Franca Borga. adv.; bk.rev.; illus. circ. 128,000. **Document type:** trade publication.
Former titles (until 1983): Mixer il Barman; Barman.

663.1 — IT
MIXER INTERNATIONAL. (Text in English, German) 1994. q. L.80000 (effective 1994). Gruppo E.S. s.r.l., Via Solari 19, 20144 Milan, Italy. TEL 02-58102128. FAX 02-89406970. Ed. Paolo Borgio. circ. 48,386. **Document type:** trade publication.

664 — US
MIXIN'. 1983. m. $38. American Bartenders' Association, Box D, Plant City, FL 33564. TEL 800-935-3232. FAX 813-752-2768. circ. 5,000. **Document type:** newsletter.
Description: Bartending, wine and spirit information. Includes bar product news and editorials.

663.3 — US — ISSN 0026-7538
TP500
MODERN BREWERY AGE. (Annual supplement avail.: Blue Book) 1933. bi-m. $85. Business Journals, 50 Day St., Box 5550, Norwalk, CT 06856. TEL 203-853-6015. Ed. Peter Reid. adv.; bk.rev.; charts; illus.; stat.; tr.lit. circ. 5,000. **Indexed:** Biol.Abstr., PROMT. **Document type:** trade publication.
●Also available online. Vendor(s): Information Access Co., Lexis-Nexis.
—BLDSC (5883.750000); UMI.

663.3 — US — ISSN 0076-9932
MODERN BREWERY AGE BLUE BOOK. (Supplement to: Modern Brewery Age) 1941. a. $175. Business Journals, 50 Day St., Box 5550, Norwalk, CT 06856. TEL 203-853-6015. Ed. Peter Reid. **Document type:** academic/scholarly publication.

663.3 — US
MODERN BREWERY AGE: TABLOID EDITION. 1958. w. $85. Business Journals, 50 Day St., Box 5550, Norwalk, CT 06856. TEL 203-853-6015. adv. circ. 1,944. **Document type:** trade publication.

663.4 — IT — ISSN 1121-1598
IL MONDO DELLA BIRRA; mensile d'informazione, attualita e costume della birra. 1982. m. L.90000 (foreign L.110000). Tuttopress Editrice s.r.l., Via Cagliero 21, 20125 Milan, Italy. TEL 39-2-6682834. FAX 39-2-6072185. Ed. Silvano Rusmini. adv.; bk.rev. circ. 44,000. **Document type:** trade publication.
Description: Covers beer for pubs, bars, pizzerias, discos, restaurants, hotels, breweries, importers, distributors, wholesalers, and supermarkets.

663 634.8 — FR — ISSN 1148-4330
MONITEUR VINICOLE. Variant title: Moniteur Vinicole International. (Text in French) 1856. m. 175 F. (foreign 275 F.). Societe Nouvelle Meridionale d'Imprimerie et d'Edition (S N M I E), Centre d'Affaires CAP SUD, Immeuble Orion, Route de Marseille, 84000 Avignon, France. TEL 90-86-03-33. FAX 90-27-05-67. Ed. Marie-Claire Forcina. adv.: B&W page 8300 F., color page 16600 F.; trim 373 x 243; adv. contact: Christian Hodapp. circ. 10,000.

MONTHLY BREWING INDUSTRY COMMENTARY. see BUSINESS AND ECONOMICS — Economic Situation And Conditions

BEVERAGES

663   AT
MORGAN INDEX ON BEVERAGES DRUNK (AUSTRALIA). 1973. m. Roy Morgan Research, Box 2282U, Melbourne, Vic. 3001, Australia. TEL 61-3-96296888. FAX 61-3-96291250.

663   AU
MOSTVIERTLER. m. Eggersdorferstr. 51, Postfach 12, A-3302 Amstetten, Austria. TEL 7472-337536. circ. 12,000.

663.2   SW   ISSN 0345-8202
MUNSKAENKEN. Variant title: Tidskriften Munskaenken. 1958. q. SEK 160. Foereningen Munskaenkarna, Furusangsvaegen 32, S-161 28 Broma, Sweden. TEL 46-8-30-10-43. FAX 46-8-30-11-52. Ed. Bruno Kjellen. adv. contact: Catarina Hiort af Ornaas. bk.rev. circ. 6,000. (back issues avail.) Document type: bulletin.

338.47 658   US
N B W A HANDBOOK.* a. membership only. National Beer Wholesalers Association, 1100 S. Washington St., Alexandria, VA 22314-4408. TEL 703-578-4300.

338.47 658   US
N B W A LEGISLATIVE AND REGULATORY ISSUES ALERT.* q. membership only. National Beer Wholesalers Association, 1100 S. Washington St., Alexandria, VA 22314-4408. TEL 703-578-4300.

N C S L A MINUTES OF ANNUAL MEETING. (National Conference of State Liquor Administrators) see *PUBLIC ADMINISTRATION*

N C S L A OFFICIAL DIRECTORY. (National Conference of State Liquor Administrators) see *PUBLIC ADMINISTRATION*

663   FR   ISSN 0984-1695
N E I D.* Variant title: N E I D Informations. no.113, 1980. 10/yr. 434 F. Negociants Exportateurs Importateurs Distributeurs, 116 bd. Haussmann, 75008 Paris, France. TEL 42-94-96-50. FAX 42-94-14-46. TELEX 280054F. Ed. Luc E. Reutenauer. adv. circ. 10,446.
    Former titles (until 1986): Information Internationale des Vins et Spiritueux (ISSN 1169-0399); (until 1982): Information des Vins et Spiritueux (ISSN 0150-2972); (until 1977): N E E E I D Informations Liaisons (ISSN 0150-2980); (until 1971): Informations Liaisons - S N E D (ISSN 1169-0380)

N W PALATE MAGAZINE; wine, food, & travel of the Pacific Northwest. see *TRAVEL AND TOURISM*

338.47 663   US
NATIONAL ASSOCIATION OF BEVERAGE IMPORTERS. BULLETIN. irreg. National Association of Beverage Importers, 1025 Vermont Ave., N.W., Ste. 1205, Washington, DC 20005. TEL 202-638-1617. FAX 202-638-3122.

338.47 663   US
NATIONAL ASSOCIATION OF BEVERAGE IMPORTERS. IMPORT REPORT. irreg. membership only. National Association of Beverage Importers, 1025 Vermont Ave., N.W., Ste. 1205, Washington, DC 20005. TEL 202-638-1617. FAX 202-638-3122.

338.47 658   US
NATIONAL ASSOCIATION OF BEVERAGE RETAILERS. NEWS AND VIEWS. (Former name of issuing body: National Liquor Stores Association) q. membership only. National Association of Beverage Retailers, 5101 River Rd., Ste. 108, Bethesda, MD 20816. TEL 301-656-1494. FAX 301-656-7539. Ed. Stephen Kay. circ. 15,000 (controlled). Document type: newsletter.
    Formerly: National Liquor Stores Association. News and Views.

338.47 658   US   ISSN 1062-0990
NATIONAL BEER WHOLESALERS ASSOCIATION. BEER PERSPECTIVES NEWSLETTER.* Key Title: Beer Perspectives. w. membership only. National Beer Wholesalers Association, 1100 S. Washington St., Alexandria, VA 22314-4408. TEL 703-578-4300.

338.47 658   US
NATIONAL BEER WHOLESALERS ASSOCIATION. DISTRIBUTOR PRODUCTIVITY REPORT. biennial. National Beer Wholesalers Association, 5205 Leesburg Pike, Ste. 1600, Falls Church, VA 22041. TEL 703-578-4300.

663.1 640.73   AT   ISSN 0816-0430
NATIONAL LIQUOR NEWS. 1984. m. Aus.$65. Thomson Business Publishing, 47 Chippen St., Chippendale, N.S.W. 2008, Australia. TEL 02-699-2411. FAX 02-698-3920. Ed. Glynis Macri. adv.; cum.index. circ. 9,735.
    Formerly: National Thomson's Liquor Guide (ISSN 0812-3705)
    Description: Covers only trade aspects around all liquor brands sold in Australia.

663   US   ISSN 0028-1808
NEBRASKA BEVERAGE ANALYST. 1936. m. $12. Bell Publications, Beverage Analyst Group, 2403 Champa St., Denver, CO 80205. TEL 303-296-1600. FAX 303-295-2159. Ed. Sherry Smith. R&P contact: Larry Bell. adv.; illus.; mkt.; stat. circ. 3,000. Document type: trade publication.

663   US   ISSN 1053-6345
NEVADA BEVERAGE ANALYST. m. Bell Publications, Beverage Analyst Group, 2403 Champa St., Denver, CO 80205. TEL 303-296-1600. FAX 303-295-2159. Ed. Sherry Smith; Pub. Larry Bell. adv. Document type: trade publication.
    Formerly: Nevada Beverage Index (ISSN 0191-4723)

663.3   US   ISSN 0741-0506
NEW BREWER; the magazine for micro and pub brewers. 1983. bi-m. $55 (foreign $65) (effective 1997). (Association of Brewers) Institute for Brewing Studies, 736 Pearl St., Box 1769, Boulder, CO 80306. TEL 303-447-0816. FAX 303-447-2825. Ed. Richard Backus. R&P contact: Richard Backus. adv. contact: Linda Stark. bk.rev.; cum.index: 1983-1996. circ. 6,000. (back issues avail.) Document type: trade publication.
    Description: For those interested in the business of operating small breweries, including restaurateurs, and entrepreneurs. Includes all aspects of brewing.

663.1   US   ISSN 0028-5552
NEW JERSEY BEVERAGE JOURNAL. 1949. m. $25. Gem Publishers, Inc., 2414 Morris Ave., Union, NJ 07083-5708. TEL 908-964-5060. FAX 908-964-1472. Ed. Harry Slone. adv.; bk.rev.; illus.; mkt. circ. 9,342. Document type: trade publication.
    Description: News and information on the alcoholic beverage industry in the state, including package stores, restaurants, bars, grills, taverns, hotels, clubs, seasonal bars, and distributor salespersons.

663.1   US   ISSN 0194-813X
NEW MEXICO BEVERAGE ANALYST. 1947. m. $10. Bell Publications, Beverage Analyst Group, 2403 Champa St., Denver, CO 80205. TEL 303-296-1600. FAX 303-295-2159. Ed. Sherry Smith. adv.; bk.rev.; illus. circ. 1,000. Document type: trade publication.
    Formerly: New Mexico Beverage Journal (ISSN 0028-6141)

663.3   CC   ISSN 1001-9286
NIANGJIU KEJI. (Text in Chinese) 1980. bi-m. Y28.80 (foreign $30) (effective 1997 & 1998). Niangjiu Keji Zazhishe, 45 Shachong Zhonglu, Guiyang, Guizhou 550002, People's Republic of China. TEL 86-851-5796163. (Dist. overseas by: China International Book Trading Corp, P.O. Box 399, Beijing 100044, P.R. China) Eds. Yuncheng Ding, Ping Huang. R&P contact: Yuncheng Ding. adv.: B&W page $400, color page $2000. circ. 16,000 (paid). pp./issue: 112. Document type: trade publication.
    Description: Covers spirits, bears, wines, liqueurs, foreign research trends, cultures of alcoholic beverages, and new products.
    Refereed Serial

663.1   US   ISSN 1065-9846
OBSERVER (PHILADELPHIA). 1936. m. $29. Observer Corp., 531 E. Front St., Berwick, PA 18603-4915. TEL 717-752-0711. FAX 717-752-0722. Ed. Julianne Crispin; Pub. James Curran. R&P contact: Julianne Crispin. adv. contact: Gina Curran. circ. 8,000. Document type: trade publication.
    Description: Covers Pennsylvania'a alcoholic beverage industry.

663 630 614.7   SZ   ISSN 1023-2958
                                  CODEN: SZOWAZ
OBST- UND WEINBAU. 1864. 27/yr. 62 SFr. (Europe 88 SFr.; elsewhere 113 SFr.). Eidgenoessische Forschungsanstalt, Postfach 185, CH-8820 Waedenswil, Switzerland. TEL 01-7836111. FAX 01-7806341. Ed. Walter Mueller. adv.; bk.rev. circ. 4,500. **Indexed:** Biol.Abstr., Biotech.Abstr., Chem.Abstr., Crop Physiol.Abstr., Excerp.Med., Food Sci.& Tech.Abstr., Hort.Abstr., Seed Abstr., Sugar Ind.Abstr., VITIS, Weed Abstr. Document type: trade publication.
    —BLDSC (6208.116000); CASDDS.
    Formerly: Schweizerische Zeitschrift fuer Obst und Weinbau (ISSN 0371-4942)

663   AU
OESTERREICHISCHE SPIRITUOSEN ZEITUNG. m. Fachzeitschriftenverlag GmbH, Schwarzenbergplatz 6, A-1030 Vienna, Austria. TEL 43-1-7153193. FAX 43-1-7154819. Ed. Bruno Mayer. adv. contact: Andreas Lugauer. circ. 2,000. Document type: trade publication.

663.1   AU
OESTERREICHISCHES GETRAENKE INSTITUT. MITTEILUNGEN. 1947. 6/yr. S.670. Oesterreichisches Getraenke Institut, Michaelerstr. 25, A-1182 Vienna, Austria. TEL 43-1-47969240. FAX 43-1-479692411. Ed. Helmuth Schwarz. adv.; bk.rev.; charts; illus.; stat. circ. 1,000. **Indexed:** Biol.Abstr., Food Sci.& Tech.Abstr. Document type: trade publication.
    Formerly: Versuchsstation fuer das Gaerungsgewerbe in Wien. Mitteilungen (ISSN 0042-4390)

663.1   UK   ISSN 0043-5775
OFF-LICENCE NEWS. 1970. w. £55 (Europe £95; elsewhere £150). William Reed Publishing Ltd., Broadfield Park, Crawley, W. Sussex RH11 9RT, England. TEL 44-1293-613400. FAX 44-1293-610320. Ed. Sandy Guthrie. adv. contact: Tony Hankes. illus.; stat. circ. 25,071. **Indexed:** Art.Hosp.& Tour. Document type: trade publication.
    —BLDSC (6236.510000).
    Description: Aimed at buyers and retailers of alcoholic drinks.

338.47   FR
OFFICE INTERNATIONAL DE LA VIGNE ET DU VIN. REGLEMENTS DE LA C E E. (Editions in English, French, Spanish) irreg. 250 F. (foreign 350 F.) (effective 1997). Office International de la Vigne et du Vin, 18 rue d'Aguesseau, 75008 Paris, France. TEL 33-1-44948080. FAX 33-1-42669063. E-mail: OIV101675.2013@compuserve.com.
    Formerly: Office International de la Vigne et du Vin. Reglements.

641   US   ISSN 0740-1361
OHIO BEVERAGE JOURNAL; first trade journal of Ohio's beverage, restaurant and hotel industry. 1938. m. $12 (effective 1997). Midwest Beverage Publications, Inc., 3 12th St., Wheeling, WV 26003. TEL 304-232-7620. FAX 304-233-1236. Ed. Arnold Lazarus. adv.; bk.rev.; illus.; mkt.; tr.lit.; circ. 7,125 (controlled). Document type: trade publication.
    Former titles: Buckeye Beverage Journal (ISSN 0007-2826); Buckeye Tavern.
    Description: Covers the alcohol and restaurant industries, with state, national and international news.

641   US   ISSN 0030-1183
OHIO TAVERN NEWS. 1939. s-m. $15. Daily Reporter Inc., 329 S. Front St., Columbus, OH 43215. TEL 614-224-4835. FAX 614-224-8649. Ed. Chris Bailey. R&P contact: Dan Shillingburg. adv. contact: J. Thomas Weeks. bk.rev.; illus. circ. 8,000. Document type: trade publication.
    Description: Serves Ohio's on- and off-premise liquor permit holders, beverage alcohol manufacturers, distributors and wholesalers, related industry associations, and other representatives of the state's hospitality industry. Covers industry trends and local, state and federal legislation as it pertains to the alcoholic beverage and hospitality industries.

BEVERAGES

663 US ISSN 1051-4562
ON PREMISE. bi-m. $200 membership. Tavern League of Wisconsin, 103 N. Hamilton, Madison, WI 53703. TEL 608-251-1133. **Document type:** trade publication.
   Formerly (until 1990): TopShelf (ISSN 0749-2022)

ONTARIO GRAPE GROWER. see *AGRICULTURE — Crop Production And Soil*

663.2 UK ISSN 1352-1195
OZ CLARK'S WINE GUIDE (YEAR). 1984. a. £9.99. Websters Wine Guide Ltd., Axe & Bottle Ct., 70 Newcomen St., London SE1 1YT, England. TEL 44-171-407-5956. FAX 44-171-407-6437. Ed. Claire Harcup. R&P contact: Adrian Webster. adv.: B&W page £1100; trim 198 x 130; adv. contact: Tim Bradshaw. circ. 40,000 (paid). (back issues avail.) **Document type:** consumer publication.
   Formerly (until 1992): Websters Wine Guide (ISSN 0957-7777)
   Refereed Serial

663 US
PERISCOPE (GREAT NECK); news and views of the beverage world. 1982. m. included with Beverage World. Stragegic Business Co., 226 W. 26th St., 10th FL., New York, NY 10001. TEL 212-822-5930. Ed. Shirley Alvarez. stat. circ. 29,000. **Document type:** trade publication.
   ●Also available online. Vendor(s): Information Access Co.

663.4 NE ISSN 1380-6084
PINT - NIEUWS. 1980. bi-m. fl.35. Pint, P.O. Box 3757, 1001 AN Amsterdam, Netherlands. TEL 31-252-522909. FAX 31-10-4112879. E-mail: msjansen@stud.let.ruu.nl. Ed. Jos Brouwer. adv. contact: W. Verboom. bk.rev.; software rev.; illus.; stat.; tr.lit.; index; circ. 6,500 (controlled). (back issues avail.) **Document type:** consumer publication, newsletter.

663 UK
PINTPOT. 1960. q. free. Manners PR, 20 Grove Pl., Bedford MK40 3JJ, England. TEL 44-1234-357274. FAX 44-1234-210282. Ed. Jacquie Manners. circ. 10,000. **Document type:** trade publication.

663 641.2 YU ISSN 0554-2308
PIVARSTVO. (Text in Serbo-Croatian; summaries in English and German) 1967. q. 9000 din.($12) Poslovna Zajednica Industrije Piva i Slada Jugoslavije - Beer and Malt Industry of Yugoslavia Business Association, Deligradska 18, 11000 Belgrade, Serbia, Yugoslavia. TEL 011-644-953. adv.; index, cum.index: 1967-1977, 1978-1987. circ. 1,000. (back issues avail.)

PLAISIRS DE LA TABLE. see *FOOD AND FOOD INDUSTRIES*

PODRAVKA; znanstveno-strucni casopis. see *AGRICULTURE*

663 XR ISSN 0862-2159
POTRAVINARSKE AKTUALITY. NAPOJOVY PRUMYSL. 1958. 10/yr. Ustav Zemedelskych a Potravinarskych Informaci, Potravinarske Aktuality - Institute of Agricultural and Food Information, Londynska 55, 120 00 Prague 2, Czech Republic. TEL 420-2-250051. FAX 420-2-66312812. E-mail: insav@login.cz. adv. contact: L. Masakova. **Document type:** consumer publication.
   Formerly (until 1983): Potravinarske Aktuality. Rada G (ISSN 0139-5785)

663.2 US ISSN 0739-8077
TP544
PRACTICAL WINERY & VINEYARD; in-depth coverage from vine to market. 1980. bi-m. $29. Don Neel and Associates, 15 Grande Paseo, San Rafael, CA 94903. TEL 415-479-5819. Ed. Don Neel. adv. contact: Lauren Macfarlane. bk.rev.; index; circ. 2,500 (paid). (back issues avail.) **Document type:** trade publication.
   Formerly: Practical Winery.

663 FR ISSN 1150-6709
PREFERENCES. 1990. 4/yr. 175 Chemin de la Roseraie, B.P. 57, 84202 Carpentras Cedex, France. FAX 90-67-18-86. Ed. Robert Roux-Guerraz. circ. 23,000.
   Description: Aimed at restaurant owners, wine waiters, buyers.

663.2 SP
PRENSA DEL RIOJA. (2 issues in English, 8 in Spanish each year) 1985. 10/yr. 6200 ptas. (effective 1996). Chile 9, 1o, 26005 Logrono, Spain. TEL 34-41-221968. FAX 34-41-223110. Ed. Javier Pascual Corral. adv. contact: Estibaliz Aguado Moreno. bk.rev.; circ. 7,500 (paid). **Document type:** consumer publication.
   Description: Covers wine, gastronomy, tourism and the wine-growing region of Rioja.
   Refereed Serial

663.2 FR ISSN 0221-301X
PRESSE DU VIN-VINETEC. (Text in French; summaries in English) 1978. m. S.F.P. Vinitec, 79 rue Raymond Poincare, 33110 Le Bouscat, France. Ed. Philippe Dourthe. adv.; bk.rev.; charts; illus.; stat. circ. 10,000.

PROCESSED FOODS & BEVERAGES DIRECTORY (YEAR). see *BUSINESS AND ECONOMICS — Trade And Industrial Directories*

PRODUCT ALERT. see *FOOD AND FOOD INDUSTRIES*

663.1 UK
THE PUBLICAN NEWSPAPER. w. £60 (effective 1996). Quantum Publishing Ltd., 29-31 Lower Coombe St., Croydon, Surrey CR9 1LX, England. TEL 44-181-681-2099. FAX 44-181-680-8828. Ed. Kate Oppenheimer; Pub. Sarah Jones. adv. contact: David Wilson. illus. circ. 32,251. (tabloid format; also avail. in microfilm from UMI; reprint service avail. from UMI) **Document type:** newspaper, trade publication.
   —CCC.
   Formerly: Publican (ISSN 0142-0755)

663.2 US ISSN 0740-1248
QUARTERLY REVIEW OF WINES. 1977. q. $14.95 (Canada $22.95; Europe $34.95). Q R W, Inc., 24 Garfield Ave., Winchester, MA 01890. TEL 617-729-7132. FAX 617-721-0572. E-mail: qrwinc@tiac.net; URL: http://www.tiac.net/users/qrwinc. (Subscr. to: Box 591, Winchester, MA 01890) Ed. Richard L. Elia. R&P contact: Ms. Harley MacKenzie. adv. contact: Jack Lynch. bk.rev. circ. 80,000. (back issues avail.) **Document type:** trade publication.
   —UnCover.
   Description: Articles on wines, food and travel.
   Refereed Serial

663.2 SP
R I V E. (Revista Internacional de Vinos Espanoles) 10/yr. Baeza 6, 28002 Madrid, Spain. TEL 1-415-90-72. Ed. Jose L. Dorado.

634.8 663.2 GW ISSN 0034-1118
REBE UND WEIN. 1947. m. DM.60. Jahrbuch Verlag, Schwabstr. 20, 74189 Weinsberg, Germany. Ed. Hans Roeck. adv.; bk.rev.; charts; illus.; index. circ. 6,600. **Document type:** bulletin.

663 JA ISSN 0389-9136
RESEARCH INSTITUTE OF BREWING. REPORT. 1905. a. free or exchange basis. Research Institute of Brewing, 3-7-1 Kagamiyama, Higashi - Hiroshima 739, Japan. TEL 81-824-20-0800. FAX 81-824-20-0802. **Document type:** academic/scholarly publication.

RESTAURANT WINE; buying - selling - serving: the full-service guide to on sale beverage profits. see *HOTELS AND RESTAURANTS*

REVISTA DE GASTRONOMIA Y ENOLOGIA. see *HOTELS AND RESTAURANTS*

634.8 FR ISSN 0760-9868
REVUE D'OENOLOGUES ET DES TECHNIQUES VITI-VINICOLES ET OENOLOGIQUES. 1974. 5/yr. 245 F. (foreign 310 F.) (effective 1997). Bourgogne Publications, Chateau de Chaintre, 71570 Chaintre, France. TEL 33-03-85374321. FAX 33-03-85371983. E-mail: oenee@club-internet.fr. Ed. M. Gautier; Pub. H.L. Arnould. adv.: B&W page 8900 F., color page 12460 F.; adv. contact: H.L. Arnould. bk.rev. circ. 15,000. **Document type:** academic/scholarly publication, trade publication.

663 US ISSN 0035-4562
RHODE ISLAND BEVERAGE JOURNAL. 1944. m. $25. Rhode Island Beverage Journal, Inc., 2508 Whitney Ave., Box 5157, Hamden, CT 06518. TEL 203-288-3375. FAX 203-288-2693. Ed. Gerald P. Slone. adv.; illus.; mkt. circ. 1,274. **Document type:** trade publication.

RIVISTA DI VITICOLTURA E DI ENOLOGIA. see *AGRICULTURE — Crop Production And Soil*

663.3 US
SAKE CONNECTION. 1991. irreg. $8 for 4 issues (foreign $15) (effective 1997). Fred Eckhardt Communications, Box 546, Portland, OR 97207-0546. TEL 503-289-7596. E-mail: eckhardt@pdxnet.com. Ed. Fred Eckhardt. adv.; bk.rev. circ. 1,000. (back issues avail.) **Document type:** newsletter.
   Description: Covers sake and Chinese rice wines, sake breweries in U.S. and Japan.

663.3 DK ISSN 0109-3460
SAMLERNYT. 1984. bi-m. membership. Skandinavisk Bryggerisouvenir Samlerforening, c/o Villy Rasmussen, Hybenvej 3, DK-2690 Karlslunde, Denmark. Ed. Kim Kjelstrup. illus. circ. 500.

SCANDINAVIAN FOOD AND DRINK REPORT. see *FOOD AND FOOD INDUSTRIES*

663.2 SZ ISSN 0036-7796
SCHWEIZERISCHE WEINZEITUNG/JOURNAL VINICOLE SUISSE.* (Text in French, German) 14/yr. 73 SFr. Bahnhofstr. 43, Postfach 1319, CH-8180 Buelach, Switzerland.

663 UK
SCOTTISH LICENSED TRADE GUARDIAN. 1881. m. £36.95 (foreign £42.95) (effective 1996 & 1997). Peebles Publishing Group Ltd., Bergius House, Clifton St., Glasgow G3 7LA, Scotland. TEL 44-141-331-1022. FAX 44-141-331-1395. Ed. Louise O'Neil. adv.; illus.; mkt.; index. circ. 9,800. **Document type:** trade publication.
   Formerly: National Guardian (ISSN 0027-9404)

641 UK ISSN 0036-9322
SCOTTISH LICENSED TRADE NEWS. 1964. 24/yr. £43.95 (foreign £49.95) (effective 1996 & 1997). Peebles Publishing Group Ltd., Bergius House, Clifton St., Glasgow G3 7LA, Scotland. TEL 44-141-331-1022. FAX 44-141-331-1395. Ed. Pat Duffy. adv.; circ. 16,000 (controlled). (tabloid format) **Document type:** trade publication.
   Description: For retailers of liquor in stores, hotels and bars.

663.2 US
▼**SMART WINE;** just drink it! 1997. m. $30 (Canada $45; rest of world $75) (effective 1997); newsstand price: $3.95. SmartWired Inc., 867 W. Napa St., Sonoma, CA 95476. TEL 707-939-0822; 800-895-9463. FAX 707-939-0833. E-mail: gregwalter@smartwine.com; URL: http://smartwine.com. Ed. Gregory S. Walter; Pub. Gregory S. Walter. adv.: B&W page $5500, color page $7500; trim 9 x 10 11/16; adv. contact: Nina Rosenblatt. bk.rev. (back issues avail.) **Document type:** consumer publication.
   ●Also available online.
   Description: Covers wine, food and travel for the value-conscious consumer.

663.1 US ISSN 0887-2783
SOCIAL HISTORY OF ALCOHOL REVIEW.* 1980. s-a. $15 to individuals; institutions $20; foreign $20. Alcohol & Temperance History Group, Southwest Regional Laboratory, 4665 Lampson Ave., Los Alamitos, CA 90720-5139. TEL 904-392-0271. (Subscr. to: c/o Prof. Richard F. Hamm, SHAR Sec.-Treas., Dept. of History, State University of New York at Albany, Social Sciences Bldg. 341, Albany, NY 12222) Ed. W. Scott Haine. bk.rev. circ. 150. **Document type:** academic/scholarly publication.
   Former titles (until 1985): Alcohol in History: A Multidisciplinary Newsletter (ISSN 0749-7989); Alcohol and Temperance History Group Newsletter.
   Description: Provides a forum for the exchange of ideas among scholars in all disciplines who are interested in any aspect of alcohol use, abuse, production, and control within given societies or countries.

BEVERAGES

634.8 US ISSN 0037-9956
SOCIETY OF MEDICAL FRIENDS OF WINE. BULLETIN. 1956. s-a. $10. Society of Medical Friends of Wine, Box 218, Sausalito, CA 94966. TEL 415-331-8313. FAX 415-331-1258. Ed. Albert Alhadeff. bk.rev.; bibl.; illus. circ. 3,000. **Document type:** bulletin.

663.6 UK
CODEN: SDMIE3
SOFT DRINKS INTERNATIONAL. 1888. m. £60 (rest of Europe £70; elsewhere £90) (effective 1997). British Soft Drinks Association Ltd., 20-22 Stukeley St., London WC2B 5LR, England. TEL 44-171-430-0356. FAX 44-171-831-6014. E-mail: bsda@ukbusiness.com; URL: http://www.ukbusiness.com/bsda. Ed. Stewart Farr. R&P contact: Sally Hall. adv.: B&W page £680; color page £1190; adv. contact: Sally Hall. bk.rev.; charts; illus.; pat.; tr.lit.; index. circ. 4,500. **Indexed:** Food Sci.& Tech.Abstr., Int.Packag.Abstr., Key to Econ.Sci. **Document type:** trade publication.
—SWETS.
Former titles (until Jan. 1996): Soft Drinks Management International (ISSN 0953-4776); (until 1988): Soft Drinks; (until 1985): Soft Drinks Trade Journal (ISSN 0038-058X)
Description: Provides in depth coverage on the manufacture, distribution, and marketing of soft drinks, fruit juices, and bottled water throughout Europe and the rest of the world.

663.6 658.8 UK
SOFT DRINKS: THE INTERNATIONAL MARKET. (Subseries of: Market Direction reports) a. £2500($5000) (effective 1997). Euromonitor, 60-61 Britton St., London EC1M 5NA, England. TEL 44-171-251-8024. FAX 44-171-608-3149. E-mail: info@euromonitor.com; URL: http://www.euromonitor.com. (Addr. in N. America: Euromonitor International, 122 S. Michigan Ave., Ste. 1200, Chicago, IL 60603. TEL 800-577-3876. FAX 312-922-1157) (looseleaf format) **Document type:** trade publication.
● Also available online. Vendor(s): Data-Star, Knight-Ridder Information, Inc.
Description: Analyzes the soft drinks market in France, Germany, Italy, Spain, the U.K., the U.S., Canada, and Japan.

663.2 SP
SOMMELIER. 12/yr. Ediciones Sociales S.L., Rosellon 186, 4o 1a, 08008 Barcelona, Spain. TEL 3-323-14-91. FAX 3-454-85-65. Ed. Susana Cayuela. **Document type:** consumer publication.

663 647 FR ISSN 0762-5979
SOMMELIERS.* 6/yr. Intersom, 17 rue Jacques Imbert, 75017 Paris, France. TEL 42-06-48-38. FAX 42-08-46-85. Ed. Christian Saint-Roche. circ. 9,500.

663 US ISSN 0193-0613
SOUTHERN BEVERAGE JOURNAL. 1948. m. $30. S B J Publishing, Inc., Box 561107, Miami, FL 33256-1107. TEL 305-233-7230. FAX 305-252-2580. E-mail: sobevjrnl@aol.com. Ed. Jacqueline N. Preston; Pub. Jacqueline N. Preston. R&P contact: Jacqueline N. Preston. adv. contact: Richard Pierce. circ. 30,000. **Document type:** trade publication.

663.93 US ISSN 1077-3460
SPECIALTY COFFEE RETAILER; the coffee business monthly. 1994. m. $39 (Canada $48; elsewhere $110). R C M Enterprises, Inc., 15500 Wayzata Blvd., Ste. 922, Box 720, Wayzata, MN 55391. TEL 612-473-5088; 800-451-9287. FAX 612-473-7068. Ed. Paul Froiland; Pub. Robert C. Mead. adv.: B&W page $1695; adv. contact: Brian Grau. illus. circ. 7,500. (back issues avail.) **Document type:** trade publication.
Description: Provides owners and managers of coffee houses and coffee retail operations with information on products and equipment, merchandising, retailing trends and management strategies.

663.1 658.8 UK
SPIRITS: THE INTERNATIONAL MARKET. (Subseries of: Market Direction reports) a. £2500($5000) (effective 1997). Euromonitor, 60-61 Britton St., London EC1M 5NA, England. TEL 44-171-251-8024. FAX 44-171-608-3146. E-mail: info@euromonitor.com; URL: http://www.euromonitor.com. (N. American addr.: Euromonitor International, 122 S. Michigan Ave., Ste. 1200, Chicago, IL 60603. TEL 800-577-3876. FAX 312-922-1157) (looseleaf format) **Document type:** trade publication.
● Also available online. Vendor(s): Data-Star, Knight-Ridder Information, Inc.
Description: Covers the spirits markets in France, Germany, Italy, Spain, the U.K., the U.S., Canada, and Japan.

658.8 US ISSN 0747-3206
SPIRITS, WINE & BEER MARKETING IN MINNESOTA, NORTH & SOUTH DAKOTA.* 1934. m. $24. Diamond Publications, Box 398, Hopkins, MN 55343-0398. TEL 612-449-9446. FAX 612-449-9447. Ed. Gary L. Diamond. adv. circ. 11,500. **Document type:** trade publication.
Formerly: Northwest Beverage Journal.

663 US ISSN 0747-3192
SPIRITS, WINE & BEER MARKETING IN MISSOURI.* 1945. m. $24. Diamond Publications, Box 398, Hopkins, MN 55343-0398. TEL 612-449-9446. FAX 612-449-9447. Ed. Gary L. Diamond. adv.; illus. circ. 8,500. **Document type:** trade publication.
Formerly: Missouri Beverage Journal (ISSN 0191-4685)

663.53 GW ISSN 0081-3729
SPIRITUOSEN-JAHRBUCH. 1950. a. DM.79.50. Versuchs- und Lehranstalt fuer Spiritusfabrikation und Fermentationstechnologie, Seestr. 13, 13353 Berlin, Germany. TEL 030-4509-0. FAX 030-4536067. TELEX 184403-VLSF-D. adv. circ. 4,500. **Document type:** trade publication.

663 GW ISSN 0038-7657
SPIRITUOSEN- UND WEINHANDEL. 1966. q. DM.48($6) Zeitungs- und Zeitschriftenverlag Heinrichs, Brueggekamp 1, 30890 Barsinghausen, Germany. TEL 49-5105-2289. Ed. G. Heinrichs. adv.; bk.rev.; charts; stat.; tr.lit. circ. 3,900. (tabloid format) **Document type:** trade publication.

663.2 US
SPOTLIGHT'S WINE COUNTRY GUIDE. 1989. m. $18 free in hotels, wineries and AAA offices. Spotlight Publishing Co., 5 Kenilworth Ct., Novato, CA 94945. TEL 415-898-7908. FAX 415-898-7751. Ed. Reggie Winner; Pub. William Schoen. R&P contact: William Schoen. adv. contact: Dennis Delee. circ. 800,000. **Document type:** consumer publication.
Description: For Northern California's visitors and wineries. Covers wine tasting, dining, entertainment, sights, shopping and sports.

663.2 UK
SPYGLASS; the wine magazine with refreshing acidity. m. newsstand price: £2. N H Publishing, Downside House, Shepton Mallet, Somerset BA4 4JL, England. **Document type:** consumer publication.

STATE CAPITALS. ALCOHOLIC BEVERAGE CONTROL. see PUBLIC ADMINISTRATION

663.3 US ISSN 0279-2133
STATEWAYS. 1972. 6/yr. $20 (Canada and Mexico $25; elsewhere $50) (effective 1997). Hunter Publishing Limited Partnership, 2101 S. Arlington Heights Rd., Ste. 150, Arlington Heights, IL 60005. TEL 847-427-9512. FAX 847-427-2097. Ed. Michael Applehaum; Pub. Seymour Leikind. R&P contact: Michael Applehaum. adv. contact: John Pennacchio. bk.rev. circ. 9,200. **Document type:** trade publication.
Description: Directed to the 19 Alcohol Beverage Control markets.

663.4 US
SUDS 'N STUFF. 1985. bi-m. $10 (Canada & Mexico $20; elsewhere $25). Bosak Publishing Inc., 4764 Galicia Way, Oceanside, CA 92056. TEL 619-724-4447. Ed. Sandra Powers. adv. contact: Mike Bosak. bk.rev. circ. 20,000. **Document type:** consumer publication.
Description: Contains information about beer for the consumer.

663 US ISSN 0081-931X
KF3920
SUMMARY OF STATE LAWS AND REGULATIONS RELATING TO DISTILLED SPIRITS. 1938? biennial. $17. Distilled Spirits Council of the United States, Inc., Legal Division, 1250 Eye St., N.W., Ste. 900, Washington, DC 20005. TEL 202-682-8825. FAX 202-682-8888. Ed.Bd. circ. controlled.

380.141 II
TEA DIRECTORY. (Text in English) 1960. irreg., latest 1982. Rs.35. Tea Board, 14 B.T.M. Sarani (Brabourne Rd.), P.O. Box 2172, Calcutta 700001, India. TEL 26-0210. TELEX 021-4527. Ed. Shri R.N. Mondal.

663.94 II ISSN 0375-3077
TEA RESEARCH ASSOCIATION. ADVISORY BULLETIN. 1971. irreg., no.11, 1986. price varies. Tea Research Association, Tocklai Experimental Station, Jorhat 785008, Assam, India. cum. index every 5 yrs. **Indexed:** Hort.Abstr., Trop.Abstr. **Document type:** bulletin.

663 633 II
TEA RESEARCH ASSOCIATION. MEMORANDUM. 1938. irreg., no.30, 1977. price varies. Tea Research Association, Tocklai Experimental Station, Jorhat 785008, Assam, India. charts. **Indexed:** Hort.Abstr., Trop.Abstr.

663 633 II
TEA RESEARCH ASSOCIATION. OCCASIONAL SCIENTIFIC PAPERS. (Text in English) 1968. irreg., latest no.12. price varies. Tea Research Association, Tocklai Experimental Sta., Jorhat 785008, Assam, India. bibl.; charts. **Indexed:** Hort.Abstr.

663 630 II ISSN 0564-6723
TEA RESEARCH ASSOCIATION. TOCKLAI EXPERIMENTAL STATION. SCIENTIFIC ANNUAL REPORT. (Text in English) a. price varies. Tea Research Association, Tocklai Experimental Station, Jorhat 785008, Assam, India. **Indexed:** Biol.Abstr., Hort.Abstr., Rev.Appl.Entomol., Rev.Plant Path., Trop.Abstr.

663.3 JA ISSN 0916-6491
CODEN: RLKBAD
TECHNICAL REPORT OF KIRIN. (Text in English or German) 1958. a. free or exchange basis. Kirin Brewery Co. Ltd. - Kirin Biru K.K. Gijutsubu, 26-1, Jingumae 6-chome, Shibuya-ku, Tokyo, Japan. Ed. Hiroshi Yokoyama. **Indexed:** Biol.Abstr., Food Sci.& Tech.Abstr. **Document type:** corporate report.
—BLDSC (8716.510000); CASDDS.
Formerly: Kirin Brewery Company, Tokyo. Research Laboratory. Report (ISSN 0075-6229)

663 US ISSN 1048-8200
TEXAS BEVERAGE NEWS.* 1958. s-m. $15. Box 122539, Ft. Worth, TX 76121-2539. TEL 817-244-6988. adv. circ. 3,240. **Document type:** trade publication.

THOMSON'S LIQUOR GUIDE. see CONSUMER EDUCATION AND PROTECTION

663 FR ISSN 0082-5484
TOUTE LA BOISSON. INTERNATIONAL. a. 125 F. S E P Edition, 194-196 rue Marcadet, 75018 Paris, France.

TUTTI AL BAR; mensile di informazione e di aggiornamento per i professionisti del bar. see HOTELS AND RESTAURANTS

664 II ISSN 0496-6201
CODEN: TAABAA
TWO AND A BUD. 1954. s-a. Rs.420 (foreign $18). Tea Research Association, Tocklai Experimental Station, Jorhat 785008, Assam, India. Ed.Bd. adv.; bk.rev.; bibl.; charts; tr.lit. **Indexed:** Biol.Abstr., Chem.Abstr., Food Sci.& Tech.Abstr., Forest.Abstr., Hort.Abstr., Plant Breed.Abstr., Rev.Appl.Entomol., Rev.Plant Path., Rural Recreat.Tour.Abstr., Soils & Fert., Trop.Abstr., Weed Abstr., World Agri.Econ.& Rural Sociol.Abstr.
—CASDDS.

BEVERAGES

663.4 US ISSN 1059-6887
HD9397.U5
THE U S BEER MARKET: IMPACT DATABANK REVIEW AND FORECAST. 1980. a. $845 (foreign $865) (effective 1997). M. Shanken Communications, Inc., 387 Park Ave. S., New York, NY 10016. TEL 212-684-4224. FAX 212-684-5424. TELEX 422687 MSHANK UI. Ed. Marvin R. Shanken. charts. **Document type:** trade publication.
    Formerly: Impact American Beer Market Review and Forecast (ISSN 0198-9952)
    Description: Provides research on the U.S. beer market.

663.1 US
HD9390.U6
THE U S DISTILLED SPIRITS MARKET: IMPACT DATABANK REVIEW AND FORECAST. 1976. a. $845 (foreign $865) (effective 1997). M. Shanken Communications, Inc., 387 Park Ave. S., New York, NY 10016. TEL 212-684-4224. FAX 212-684-5424. TELEX 422687 MSHANK UI. Ed. Marvin R. Shanken. charts. **Document type:** trade publication.
    Formerly: Impact American Distilled Spirits Market Review and Forecast (ISSN 0163-9536)
    Description: Provides research on the U.S. market for distilled spirits.

663.2 US
HD9374
THE U S WINE MARKET: IMPACT DATABANK REVIEW AND FORECAST. 1975. a. $845 (foreign $865) (effective 1997). M. Shanken Communications, Inc., 387 Park Ave. S., New York, NY 10016. TEL 212-684-4224. FAX 212-684-5424. TELEX 422687 MSHANK UI. Ed. Marvin R. Shanken. charts. (back issues avail.) **Document type:** trade publication.
    Formerly: Impact American Wine Market Review and Forecast (ISSN 0163-9544)
    Description: Provides research on the U.S. market for wine.

ULSTER FOOD TRADER. see *FOOD AND FOOD INDUSTRIES*

663.2 US ISSN 1047-6865
TP544
THE UNDERGROUND WINE JOURNAL. 1978. bi-m. $48 (foreign $83). Wine Journal Enterprises, Inc., 1654 Amberwood Dr., Ste. A, South Pasadena, CA 91030. TEL 818-441-6617. FAX 818-441-6765. E-mail: winejne@ix.netcom.com; christi449@aol.com. Ed. Christine R. Graham; Pubs. John Tilson, Christine R. Graham. R&P contact: Edward H. Barker. adv. contact: Edward H. Barker. bk.rev.; illus.; tr.lit.; circ. 10,000 (paid). (back issues avail.) **Document type:** consumer publication, trade publication.
    Incorporates (in 1992): Rarities (ISSN 0279-5612)
    Description: Describes and rates fine U.S. and imported wines, distilled spirits. Provides the history and background data of wineries and regions. Also covers fine dining, special-interest travel, and interviews with wine experts.
    Refereed Serial

663 FR ISSN 1161-3580
UNION FRANCAISE DES OENOLOGUES. ANNUAIRE. (Supplement to: Revue Francaise d'Oenologie (ISSN 0395-899X)) 1969, 2nd ed. a. 800 F. Revue Francaise des Oenologues, Maison des Agriculteurs, Mas de Saporta, 34970 Lattes, France. Ed. Dominique Traxel. adv. contact: Elise Galabert.
    Formerly: Union National des Oenologues. Annuaire (ISSN 1161-3572)

V W D - GETRAENKE. see *BUSINESS AND ECONOMICS — Investments*

VIGNERON CHAMPENOIS; organe de la vigne et du vin de champagne. see *AGRICULTURE — Crop Production And Soil*

VIGNEVINI. see *AGRICULTURE — Crop Production And Soil*

VINEYARD AND WINERY MANAGEMENT; the bottom line resource for grower and vintner. see *AGRICULTURE — Crop Production And Soil*

663.2 IT
VINI E LIQUORI. 1971. m. (10/yr.). L.60000 (foreign L.120000). Gruppo E.S. s.r.l., Via Solari 19, 20144 Milan, Italy. TEL 39-2-58102128. FAX 39-2-89406970. Ed. Franca Borgio. adv.: B&W page L.5900000, color page L.9400000. circ. 100,000. **Document type:** consumer publication.

663.2 IT
VINO. (Text in English) q. L.18000. Vino S.p.A., Via D. Trentacoste 7, 20134 Milan, Italy. TEL 2-21-56-31. FAX 2-26-41-08-47. Ed. Enrico Guagnini. adv. circ. 30,000.

663.2 SP ISSN 1131-5997
VINO Y GASTRONOMIA. 1981. 12/yr. Santa Hortensia 27 bajo, 28002 Madrid, Spain. TEL 34-1-4151662. FAX 34-1-5194887. Ed. Luis Magana Ruiz. R&P contact: Sofia Magana. adv. contact: Sofia Magana. **Document type:** consumer publication.
    Former titles (until 1991): Vina, Vino y Gastronomia (ISSN 1130-2917); (until 1989): Vina y Vino (ISSN 0211-8947)

663.2 RU ISSN 0869-3625
TP559.R8 CODEN: VIVSA6
VINOGRAD I VINO ROSSII.* 1939. bi-m. $110 (effective 1998). Tverckoi-Yamckoi 1-i per. 18-3, kom. 215, 125834 Moscow, Russia. TEL 7-095-2508504. (Dist. by: Mezhdunarodnaya Kniga, B. Yakimanka 39, 117049 Moscow, Russia. TEL 7-095-2384967. FAX 7-095-2384634) illus.; index. **Indexed:** Biol.Abstr., Chem.Abstr., Food Sci.& Tech.Abstr., Hort.Abstr., Nutr.Abstr., Plant Breed.Abstr., Plant Grow.Reg.Abstr., VITIS, Weed Abstr.
    —BLDSC (0038.680000); CASDDS; CISTI; Linda Hall.
    Formerly: Vinodelie i Vinogradarstvo S.S.S.R. (ISSN 0042-6318)

634.8 663.2 FR ISSN 0042-6334
VINS D'ALSACE; revue viticole et vinicole mensuelle. (Text in French, German) 1911. m. 200 F. (foreign 230 F.) (effective 1997). Association des Viticulteurs d'Alsace, Maison des Vins d'Alsace, 12 av. de la Feve-aux-Vins, B.P. 1225, 68012 Colmar Cedex, France. TEL 33-3-89242400. FAX 33-3-89240781. Ed. Keiffer Simone. adv.; bk.rev.; bibl.; stat.; tr.lit.; index. **Document type:** corporate report.

338.4 IE ISSN 0790-2158
VINTNERS WORLD. 1942. m. I£20. (Vintners Federation of Ireland) Jemma Publications Ltd., Marino House, 53 Glasthule Rd., Sandycove, Co. Dublin, Ireland. TEL 2800000. FAX 2801818. Ed. Pat Nolan. adv.: B&W page I£1045, color page I£1375; trim 270 x 180. bk.rev.; index; circ. 7,500 (controlled). **Document type:** trade publication.
    Former titles: Licensing World; Irish Licensing World.

663 SZ ISSN 0177-2570
VINUM. French edition (ISSN 1420-5602) (Editions in French, German, Spanish) 1981. 10/yr. 109 SFr. Vinum Verlags AG, Klosbachstr. 85, CH-8030 Zurich, Switzerland. TEL 41-1-2622618. FAX 41-1-2685240. E-mail: edition@vinum.ch; URL: http://www.vinum.ch. Ed. Rolf Bichsel. R&P contact: Natascha Kriesi. adv. contact: Natascha Kriesi. bk.rev. circ. 50,000. **Document type:** consumer publication.

338.47 658 US
W S G A CHECKOUT. 1972. m. membership only. Wine and Spirits Guild of America, c/o Priscilla Felton, 30 W. 39th Ave., Ste. 106, San Mateo, CA 94403. TEL 612-377-6459. FAX 612-377-6211. **Document type:** newsletter.
    Formerly: W S G A Newsletter.

338.47 US
W S S A GRAPEVINE. 6/yr. membership. Wine and Spirits Shippers Association, 11800 Sunrise Valley Dr., Ste. 332, Reston, VA 22091. TEL 703-860-2300. FAX 703-860-2422. E-mail: info@wssa.ccom. circ. 2,000.
    Description: Summary of transportation rates, regulations, and other developments of interest to beverage importers.

663 US ISSN 1075-5586
HD9377.W2
WASHINGTON WINESTYLE.* 1993. bi-m. $18. Forward Publishing, Inc., 538 Shelton Place N.E., Renton, WA 98056-3984. TEL 206-232-8681. FAX 206-232-0846. E-mail: winestyle@aol.com. Ed. Kathy Ward. adv.: B&W page $895; adv. contact: Bill Ward. circ. 7,500. **Document type:** consumer publication.

663 GW ISSN 0171-5089
DER WEIHENSTEPHANER. 1924. q. DM.109 (effective 1997). (Verband Ehemaliger Weihenstephaner e.V.) Verlag Hans Carl GmbH, Andernacherstr. 33a, 90411 Nuernberg, Germany. TEL 49-911-95285-0. FAX 49-911-9528548. adv.: B&W page DM.2075, color page DM.3695; adv. contact: Korinna Thoenissen. circ. 2,043. **Indexed:** Food Sci.& Tech.Abstr. **Document type:** corporate report, newsletter.
    —BLDSC (9288.280000).

663.2 GW
HD9383.1
WEINWIRTSCHAFT. 1864. 26/yr. DM.258 (foreign DM.310.80) (effective 1997). Meininger Verlag GmbH, Maximilianstr. 7-17, 67433 Neustadt, Germany. TEL 49-6321-8908-0. FAX 49-6321-8908-73. Ed. Hermann Pik. adv.; bk.rev.; charts; illus.; mkt.; pat.; tr.lit.; index. **Indexed:** Biol.Abstr., Chem.Abstr., Excerp.Med., Rural Recreat.Tour.Abstr., VITIS, World Agri.Econ.& Rural Sociol.Abstr. **Document type:** trade publication.
    —CCC.
    Former titles: Weinwirtschaft - Markt (ISSN 0723-1350); Weinwirtschaft - German Wine Review; Allgemeine Deutsche Weinfachzeitung (ISSN 0012-0960)

663 GW ISSN 0375-8818
CODEN: WEWIAW
DIE WEINWISSENSCHAFT; viticulturual and enological sciences. (Text in English, French, German) 1946. 4/yr. DM.90 (effective 1997). Fachverlag Dr. Fraund GmbH, Postfach 1329, 61364 Friedrichsdorf, Germany. TEL 49-6172-7106-0. FAX 49-6172-710610. Ed. K. Schaller. bk.rev. (back issues avail.) **Indexed:** Food Sci.& Tech.Abstr., Hort.Abstr., Plant Grow.Reg.Abstr. **Document type:** academic/scholarly publication.
    —CASDDS. **CCC.**

663 GW ISSN 0171-4457
HD9348.G3
WER UND WAS IN DER DEUTSCHEN GETRAENKE - INDUSTRIE. biennial. DM.249 (effective 1996). B. Behr's Verlag GmbH, Averhoffstr. 10, 22085 Hamburg, Germany. TEL 49-40-2270080. FAX 49-40-2201091. E-mail: behrs@behrs.de; URL: http://www.behrs.de. **Document type:** directory.

663.3 UK
WHAT'S BREWING. 1972. m. £18. (Campaign for Real Ale Ltd.) C A M R A Books, 230 Hatfield Rd., St. Albans, Herts. AL1 4LW, England. TEL 44-1727-867201. FAX 44-1727-867670. E-mail: camra@camra.org.uk; URL: http://www.camra.org.uk. Ed. Roger Protz. adv. contact: Peter Tonge. bk.rev. circ. 40,000. **Document type:** consumer publication.
    Description: Covers beer, brewing and pubs in Britain and worldwide.

663 338 US
WHAT'S BREWING. 10/yr. membership. National Coffee Service Association, 4000 Williamsburg Sq., Fairfax, VA 22032. TEL 703-273-9008. FAX 703-273-9011. circ. 650.

663.2 BE
WIJNKRONIEK; gastronomisch magazine. (Text in Dutch) 1977. 6/yr. 1500 BEF. Vlaamse Wijngilde, Forthoekstr. 12, 8370 Blankenberge, Belgium. TEL 32-50-412003. Ed. A. Aspeslagh.

BEVERAGES

663   UK   ISSN 0269-9443
WINE. 1984. m. £35.95 (Europe £40; rest of world £57) (effective 1996). Quest Magazines Ltd., Publishing House, 652 Victoria Rd., South Ruislip, Mddx. HA4 0SX, England. TEL 44-181-842-1010. FAX 44-181-841-2557. (Subscr. to: Fulham House, Goldsworth Rd., Woking, Surrey GU21 1LY, England. TEL 44-1483-733800. FAX 44-1483-756792) Ed. Susan Lowe; Pub. Marcin Miller. adv. contact: Eva Fiks-Pompe. bk.rev. circ. 35,000. **Document type:** consumer publication.
    Formerly: What Wine? (ISSN 0267-4157)
    Description: Features wine tastings and notes, regional insights and travelogues, the latest wine world news, and advice on food and wine pairings.

663.2   SA   ISSN 1021-1454
WINE; a taste of good living. (Text in English) 1993. m. R.80 (foreign R.125; airmail R.290). Ramsay, Son & Parker (Pty) Ltd., P.O. Box 180, Howard Place 7450, Cape Town, South Africa. TEL 27-21-5311391. FAX 27-21-5312212. E-mail: wine@rsp.co.za. Ed. Mike Froud. adv.: B&W page R.5050, color page R.7510; trim 280 x 210; adv. contact: Andrew Stodel. bk.rev.; circ. 12,084 (paid). **Document type:** consumer publication.
    Description: Presents news and feature articles on South African and other wines, food, wine accessories, retail information and other topics of interest to local wine consumers.

663.2   US   ISSN 0887-8463
WINE ADVOCATE. bi-m. $40 (foreign $70) (effective 1997). Box 311, Monkton, MD 21111-0311. TEL 301-329-6477. FAX 301-357-4504. Ed. Robert M. Parker.

WINE & DINE E-ZINE. see *HOTELS AND RESTAURANTS*

663   UK
WINE & SPIRIT INTERNATIONAL. 1874. m. £90 (Europe £100; U.S. & Canada $135; rest of world £155) (effective 1997). Quest Magazines Ltd., Publishing House, 652 Victoria Rd., South Ruislip, Mddx. HA4 0SX. TEL 44-181-842-1010. FAX 44-181-841-2557. Ed. Barbara Cormie; Pub. Damian Riley-Smith. adv. contact: Matthew Newell. bk.rev.; illus.; stat. circ. 6,622. **Indexed:** Key to Econ.Sci. **Document type:** trade publication.
    Former titles: Wine & Spirit (ISSN 0264-4797); (until 1973): Wine & Spirit Trade International.
    Description: Industry news for commercial wine and spirit makers, importers-exporters and retailers. Features include reviews and profiles, auction results, U.K. and international news and services guide.

663 382   UK
WINE AND SPIRIT INTERNATIONAL YEAR BOOK. 1898. a. £85 (foreign £90) (effective 1997). Quest Magazines Ltd., Publishing House, 652 Victoria Rd., South Ruislip, Mddx. HA4 0SX, England. TEL 44-181-842-1010. FAX 44-181-841-2557. Ed. Chris Losh; Pub. Chris Mitchell. adv. contact: Carole White. **Document type:** directory.
    Formerly: Wine and Spirit Trade International Year Book (ISSN 0306-8846).
    Description: Lists wine producers, their key personnel, brands, and agents worldwide.

663.1   US   ISSN 0890-0299
WINE & SPIRITS. 1981. 8/yr. $22. Winestate Publications, Inc., 818 Brannan St., San Francisco, CA 94103-4937. TEL 415-255-7736. FAX 415-255-9659. (Subscr. to: Box 1548, Princeton, NJ 08542. TEL 609-921-2196) Ed. Joshua Greene; Pub. Joshua Greene. adv. contact: Michael Kinney. bk.rev. circ. 55,000. (back issues avail.) **Document type:** consumer publication.
    Formerly: Wine and Spirits Buying Guide.

663   JA
WINE & SPIRITS. (Text in Japanese) bi-m. Ohta Publications Co. Ltd., Dame Ginza Bldg., 6-7-18 Ginza, Chuo-ku, Tokyo 104, Japan. TEL 81-3-3571-1181. FAX 81-3-3574-1650. (Subscr. in US to: Ken Kamimoto, One Executive Dr., 2F, Fort Lee, NJ 07024) Ed. Kazuhiko Haruguchi; Pub. Tonosuke Ohta. circ. 22,000.

663.2   US
WINE & SPIRITS INDUSTRY MARKETING. 1971. a. $215 (for May 1997 ed.) Adams Trade Press, 2101 S. Arlington, Ste. 150, Arlington Heights, IL 60005. TEL 800-396-3939. **Indexed:** SRI. **Document type:** directory.
    Former titles (until 1996): Jobson's Wine and Spirits Industry Marketing; Jobson's Wine Marketing Handbook; Wine Marketing Handbook.
    Description: Lists individual companies in the wine and spirits industry, along with professional organizations, suppliers, importers, and marketers.

663.2 330   US   ISSN 1057-8544
WINE BUSINESS INSIDER. 1991. w. $192 (effective Jul. 1995). SmartWired Inc., 867 W. Napa St., Sonoma, CA 95476. TEL 707-939-0822. FAX 707-939-0833. E-mail: winebiz@aol.com; URL: http://smartwine.com. Ed. Rich Cartiere; Pub. W. Lewis Perdue. (back issues avail.) **Document type:** newsletter, trade publication.
    Description: Covers the wine business including sales, marketing, who's who in the industry, and more.

338.47   US   ISSN 1075-7058
WINE BUSINESS MONTHLY; & grower and cellar news. 1994. m. $69 (students $24, free to qualified personnel; Canada & Mexico $36; elsewhere $48); newsstand price: $5.95. SmartWired Inc., 867 W. Napa St., Sonoma, CA 95476. TEL 707-939-0822. FAX 707-939-0833. E-mail: winebiz@aol.com; URL: http://smartwine.com. Ed. Rich Cartiere; Pub. W. Lewis Perdue. adv.: page $1725; trim 13 1/2 x 10; adv. contact: Jennifer Popish. circ. 9,000. (tabloid format; back issues avail.) **Document type:** newspaper, trade publication.
    Description: Contains articles on wine production and vineyards as well as information on wine sales, stocks and other aspects of the wine business.

663.2   US   ISSN 0897-8492
TP557
WINE COUNTRY GUIDE TO CALIFORNIA; the complete guide to wineries, restaurants and lodging in California wine country. 1984. a. $6.95. Marvin R. Shanken Communications, Inc., 387 Park Ave. S., New York, NY 10016. TEL 212-684-4224. FAX 212-684-5424. TELEX 422687 MSHANK UI. Ed. Marvin R. Shanken. adv.; index. **Document type:** directory, trade publication.
    Formerly (untl 1989): Wine Spectator Wine Maps (ISSN 0882-7506).
    Description: Covers nine wine growing areas of California.

663   US   ISSN 0892-662X
TP544
WINE EAST. 1974. bi-m. $20 (effective 1997). L & H Photojournalism, 620 N. Pine St., Lancaster, PA 17603. TEL 717-393-0943. FAX 717-393-7398. Eds. Hudson Cattell, Linda Jones McKee. adv.; bk.rev.; illus. circ. 1,500. **Document type:** trade publication.
    Description: Includes features on winemaking, grape growing and marketing.

663.2   US   ISSN 1078-3318
WINE ENTHUSIAST. 1988. 6/yr. $14.95. 8 Saw Mill River Rd., Hawthorne, NY 10532. TEL 914-345-8463. FAX 914-345-3028. Ed. W.R. Tish. adv.; bk.rev. circ. 75,000.
    Formerly (until 1990): Wine Times.
    Description: Covers domestic and world wine regions, cellaring, and wine news.

663   US   ISSN 1059-0234
TP546.5
WINE INDUSTRY PHONE BOOK. 1989. a. $10. Vineyard and Winery Services, Inc., 103 Third St., Box 231, Watkins Glen, NY 14891. TEL 607-535-7133. FAX 607-535-2998. Ed. J. William Moffett. R&P contact: J. William Moffett. adv. contact: Hope Merletti. circ. 1,500. **Document type:** directory.
    Description: Lists phone numbers of all grape- and wine-affiliated wineries and personnel, suppliers, and services available throughout the U.S., Canada, and the world.

663.1   US
WINE LABEL. q. $10. (Wine Label Collectors Club of America) Burt Wuttken, Ed. & Pub., 429 Via de la Paz, Pacific Palisades, CA 90272. TEL 310-454-9331. (back issues avail.) **Document type:** newsletter.
    Description: Examines wine label design and covers contest results, developments, and tips about collecting.

663   UK
WINE LINE. 6/yr. Academy of Wine Service, 40 Foscote Rd., Hendon, London NW4 3SD, England. TEL 081-202-6770. Ed. Ann Satchell. circ. 10,000.

663   US   ISSN 1065-4895
TP544
THE WINE NEWS. (Includes insert: Inside Wine (1065-4909)) 1985. bi-m. $24 (foreign $44) (effective 1995). T.E. Smith, Ed. & Pub., Box 14-2096, Coral Gables, FL 33114. TEL 305-444-7250. FAX 305-444-5706. R&P contact: Kathy Sinnes. adv. contact: Elizabeth Kuehner Smith. bk.rev. circ. 55,000. **Document type:** consumer publication.
    Description: Educates, guides, and entertains readership about wine through interviews, commentary, historical perspectives, as well as food and wine pairing tips for both the novice and collector.

663.2   US   ISSN 1053-4776
WINE ON LINE; food and wine magazine. 1983. w. $100. Enterprises Publishing, 400 E. 59th St., Ste. 9F, New York, NY 10022. TEL 212-755-4363. FAX 212-755-4365. Eds. Jerome Walmon, Mary O'Brien. adv.; bk.rev.; tr.lit. circ. 1,500,000. (also avail. in magnetic tape) **Document type:** consumer publication.
    ●Also available online.
    Also available on CD-ROM.
    Description: Discusses wine and food with reviews and educational articles.

663.2   US   ISSN 0193-497X
                   CODEN: WISPEV
WINE SPECTATOR. 1976. s-m. (20/yr.). $40 (Canada $53; overseas $110); newsstand price: $2.95. M. Shanken Communications, Inc., 387 Park Ave. S., New York, NY 10016. TEL 212-684-4224. FAX 212-684-5424. TELEX 422687 MSHANK UI. (Subscr. to: P.O. Box 50462, Boulder, CO 80322. TEL 800-752-7799. FAX 212-481-0722) Ed. Marvin R. Shanken. adv. (tabloid format; back issues avail.) **Indexed:** Mag.Ind. **Document type:** consumer publication.
    Description: Reports on European and California wines; discusses fine foods and which wines best accompany them.

663.2   US   ISSN 1058-5729
WINE SPECTATOR MAGAZINE'S ULTIMATE GUIDE TO BUYING WINE. 1992-1993; resumed. a. M. Shanken Communications, Inc., 387 Park Ave. S., New York, NY 10016. FAX 212-684-5424. TELEX 422687 MSHANK UI. Ed. Marvin R. Shanken; Pub. Marvin R. Shanken. **Document type:** directory.
    Description: Lists fine wines by type, producer and country.

663.2 658.8   UK
WINE: THE INTERNATIONAL MARKET. (Subseries of: Market Direction reports) a. £2500($5000) (effective 1997). Euromonitor, 60-61 Britton St., London EC1M 5NA, England. TEL 44-171-251-8024. FAX 44-171-608-3149. E-mail: info@euromonitor.com; URL: http://www.euromonitor.com. (N. American addr.: Euromonitor International, 122 S. Michigan Ave., Ste. 1200, Chicago, IL 60603. TEL 800-577-3876. FAX 312-922-1157) (looseleaf format) **Document type:** trade publication.
    ●Also available online. Vendor(s): Data-Star, Knight-Ridder Information, Inc.
    Description: Covers the wine markets in France, Germany, Italy, Spain, the U.K., the U.S., Canada, and Japan.

BEVERAGES — ABSTRACTING, BIBLIOGRAPHIES, STATISTICS

663.2　　　　　　　CN　　ISSN 0228-6157
WINE TIDINGS. 1973. 8/yr. Can.$25.68. Kylix Media Inc., 5165 Sherbrooke St. W., Ste. 414, Montreal, PQ H4A 1T6, Canada. TEL 514-481-5892. FAX 514-481-9699. URL: http://www.cmpa.ca. Ed. Tony Aspler; Pub. Judy Rochester. adv. contact: Judy Rochester. bk.rev.; illus. circ. 13,391. **Document type:** consumer publication.
　　Formerly: Tidings (ISSN 0381-730X)
　　Description: Wine appreciation, food, recipes and travel to wine-producing countries.

663.2 790.13　　　　　US
WINE TRADER. 1977. bi-m. $18; newsstand price: $4. Wine Investigation for Novices and Oenophiles, Box 1598, Carson City, NV 89702. TEL 702-884-2648. FAX 702-884-2484. E-mail: winetrader@aol.com. Ed. Jerry D. Mead; Pub. Jerry D. Mead. adv.; bk.rev. circ. 30,000. **Document type:** consumer publication, trade publication.
　　Incorporates (1968-199?): W I N O Newsletter.
　　Description: Covers wine and other alcoholic beverages of general interest to consumers, collectors, and the trade.

663.2　　　　　　　US
WINE X MAGAZINE; a new voice for a new generation of wine consumers. 1993. bi-m. $14.95 (Canada $30; U.K. $44) (effective 1997). 4184 Sonoma Mountain Rd., Santa Rosa, CA 95404. TEL 707-545-0992; 888-229-4639. FAX 707-545-0992. E-mail: wi@wco.com; URL: http://www.winery.com/winex. Ed. Darryl M. Roberts; Pub. Darryl M. Roberts. R&P contact: Darryl M. Roberts. adv. contact: Dyan Lasch. bk.rev.; circ. 50,000 (paid). **Document type:** consumer publication.
　　Former titles (until 1995): Wines International; (until 1994): Wines International Quarterly.
　　Description: Informs and educates consumers about wine.

634.8 663.2　　　US　　ISSN 0043-583X
WINES AND VINES; the authoritative voice of the grape and wine industry. 1919. m. (s-m. Dec.). $32.50 (Canada & Mexico $39, elsewhere $50) (effective 1997). Hiaring Co., 1800 Lincoln Ave., San Rafael, CA 94901-1298. TEL 415-453-9700. FAX 415-453-2517. Ed. Philip E. Hiaring. adv. contact: Dottie Kubota-Cordery. bk.rev.; bibl.; charts; illus.; mkt.; stat. circ. 3,500. (back issues avail.) **Indexed:** Chem.Abstr., PROMT. **Document type:** trade publication.
—Linda Hall.

WINES AND VINES: DIRECTORY OF THE WINE INDUSTRY IN NORTH AMERICA. see *BUSINESS AND ECONOMICS — Trade And Industrial Directories*

663.1　　　　　　　II
WINES, WHISKY, RUM, GIN, BEER REPORT. 1970. w. Rs.635($75) International Press Cutting Service, P.O. Box 121, Allahabad 211001, India. Ed. N. Khanna. bk.rev.; index. circ. 1,200. (looseleaf format; also avail. in processed) **Document type:** newsletter.
　　Formerly: Fermented Wines, Liqueurs, Brandy, Gin, Rum, Whisky, Beer and Alcoholic Drinks (ISSN 0047-0945)

663.1　　　　　　US　　ISSN 0043-6399
WISCONSIN BEVERAGE JOURNAL. 1942. m. $15. Illinois Beverage Media, Inc., 2260 Bracken Lane, Northfield, IL 60093-2903. TEL 708-441-7776. Ed. Jim O'Brien. adv.; bk.rev.; illus.; mkt.; stat. circ. 6,000. **Document type:** trade publication.
　　Description: Trade publication for the beverage alcohol industry in Wisconsin.

663.2　　　　　　　US
WOMEN ON WINE CHAPTER FLYER. m. Women on Wine, 6110 Sunset Ranch Dr., Riverside, CA 92506. TEL 714-784-3096.

663.2　　　　　　　US
WOMEN ON WINE NATIONAL NEWS. m. $10 to non-members. Women on Wine, 6110 Sunset Ranch Dr., Riverside, CA 92506. TEL 714-784-3096. adv.
　　Description: Includes regional reports and a calendar of events.

663.9 382　　　　　US　　ISSN 0043-8340
HD9195.A1
WORLD COFFEE & TEA. 1960. m. $24 (foreign $30). G C I Publishing Co., Inc., 1801 Rockville Pike, Ste. 330, Rockville, MD 20852. TEL 301-984-7333. Ed. Richard Hanley. index. circ. 8,000. (back issues avail.) **Document type:** trade publication.
—BLDSC (9353.250000); SWETS.

663　　　　　　　UK　　ISSN 0969-8159
WORLD DRINK TRENDS. a. £28. (Produktschap voor Gedistilleerde Dranken, NE) N T C Publications Ltd., Farm Rd., Henley-on-Thames, Oxfordshire RG9 1EJ, England. TEL 01491-411000. FAX 01491-571188. **Document type:** trade publication.
　　Description: Compilation of worldwide statistics describing world trends in alcohol production, country-by-country statistics and charts on drink consumption.

663 358.8　　　　　UK
▼**WORLD DRINKS DATABOOK.** 1995. irreg. £275($550) Euromonitor, 60-61 Turnmill St., London EC1M 5NA, England. TEL 44-171-251-8024. FAX 44-171-608-3149. E-mail: info@euromoney.com; URL: http://www.euromoney.com. (Addr. in N. America: Euromonitor International, 122 S. Michigan Ave., Ste. 1200, Chicago, IL 60603. TEL 800-577-3876. FAX 312-922-1157) charts; stat. **Document type:** directory.
　　Description: Analyzes the European alcoholic and nonalcoholic beverage industries.

663　　　　　　　UK　　ISSN 1360-7995
WORLD DRINKS REPORT. s-m. £275 (rest of Europe £295; elsewhere £320) (effective 1997). Agra Europe (London) Ltd., 25 Frant Rd., Tunbridge Wells, Kent TN2 5JT, England. TEL 44-1892-533813. FAX 44-1892-544895. E-mail: 100637.3460@compuserve.com.

663 330.9　　　　　UK
WORLD MARKET FOR HOT DRINKS. irreg. £3950($7900) Euromonitor, 60-61 Britton St., London EC1M 5NA, England. TEL 44-171-251-8024. FAX 44-171-608-3149. E-mail: info@euromonitor.com; URL: http://www.euromonitor.com. (N. American addr.: Euromonitor International, 122 S. Michigan Ave., Ste. 1200, Chicago, IL 60603. TEL 800-577-3876. FAX 312-922-1157) **Document type:** directory, trade publication.
　　Description: Contains global and regional market analyses, product trends and developments, corporate profiles, and market forecasts.

663.4　　　　　　　IT　　ISSN 1121-158X
THE WORLD OF BEER; news and views on the best of international brewing. (Text in English, French, German or Spanish) 1987. s-a. $21. Tuttopress Editrice s.r.l., Via Cagliero 21, 20125 Milan, Italy. TEL 39-2-6682834. FAX 39-2-6072185. Ed. Silvano Rusmini. R&P contact: Vanda Loda. adv.: color page L.8500000; adv. contact: Alessandra Costanzo. circ. 12,000. **Document type:** trade publication.

663　　　　　　　UK
WORLD'S MAJOR SOFT DRINK COMPANIES. irreg. £495($990) (effective 1997). Euromonitor, 60-61 Britton St., London EC1M 5NA, England. TEL 44-171-251-8024. FAX 44-171-608-3149. E-mail: info@euromonitor.com; URL: http://www.euromonitor.com. (Addr. in N. America: Euromonitor International, 122 S. Michigan Ave., Ste. 1200, Chicago, IL 60603. TEL 800-577-3876. FAX 312-922-1157) **Document type:** directory.

YEAST; a forum for yeast researchers. see *BIOLOGY — Biotechnology*

663.3　　　　　　US　　ISSN 0196-5921
ZYMURGY. 1978. q. $33 (Canada $39; elsewhere $50) (effective 1996). American Homebrewers Association Inc., Box 1679, Boulder, CO 80306-1679. TEL 303-447-0816. FAX 303-447-2825. E-mail: dena@aob.org; URL: http://www.beertown.org. Ed. Dena Niskek. R&P contact: Dena Niskek. adv. contact: Linda Starck. bk.rev.; index; circ. 24,000 (paid). (back issues avail.) **Document type:** consumer publication.
　　Description: For the home brewer and beer enthusiast.
　　Refereed Serial

BEVERAGES — Abstracting, Bibliographies, Statistics

663 630　　　　　　AT　　ISSN 1320-6486
AUSTRALIA. BUREAU OF STATISTICS. AUSTRALIAN WINE AND GRAPE INDUSTRY. 1979. a. Aus.$25. Australian Bureau of Statistics, P.O. Box 10, Belconnen, A.C.T. 2616, Australia. **Document type:** government publication.
　　Formed by the merger of (1979-1993): Viticulture, Australia, Preliminary (ISSN 1031-0800); (1979-1993): Wine Production, Australia and States (ISSN 1031-0827)
　　Description: Covers bearing and non-bearing vines, and production of grapes for winemaking and drying purposes.

663 330　　　　　　AT　　ISSN 0312-925X
AUSTRALIA. BUREAU OF STATISTICS. SALES OF AUSTRALIAN WINE AND BRANDY BY WINEMAKERS. 1975. m. Aus.$10.50 per no. Australian Bureau of Statistics, P.O. Box 10, Belconnen, A.C.T. 2616, Australia. **Document type:** government publication.
　　Description: Provides the quantity of wine sales classified by type and brandy, including seasonally adjusted figures and trend estimates.

663 630　　　　　　AT　　ISSN 0158-9067
AUSTRALIA. BUREAU OF STATISTICS. VITICULTURE, AUSTRALIA. 1978-1994. a. Aus.$21.50. Australian Bureau of Statistics, P.O. Box 10, Belconnen, A.C.T. 2616, Australia. **Document type:** government publication.
　　Description: Features statistics of grapes and grape products, imports, exports, consumption and sales of Australian wine and brandy.

663　　　　　　　UK
B L R A STATISTICAL HANDBOOK; a compilation of drinks industry statistics. 1973. a. Brewers and Licensed Retailers Association, 42 Portman Sq., London W1H OBB, England. **Document type:** trade publication.
　　Formerly: Brewers' Society (ISSN 0306-6002)

663　　　　　　　FR
DATAVIN. 11/yr. 100 F. (effective 1997). Office Internationale de la Vigne et du Vin, 18 rue d'Aguesseau, 75008 Paris, France. TEL 33-1-44948080. FAX 33-1-42669063. E-mail: OIV101675.2013@compuserve.com.
　　Description: World catalogue of vitivinicultural events.

663　　　　　　　UK　　ISSN 0965-5360
DRINK POCKET BOOK (YEAR). 1989. a. £28. N T C Publications Ltd., Farm Rd., Henley-on-Thames, Oxfordshire RG9 1EJ, England. TEL 01491-411000. FAX 01491-571188. **Document type:** trade publication.
　　Description: Provides detailed statistical data for those working in drink manufacturing, retailing, advertising and marketing.

EXTRAKTE: NAHRUNG UND GENUSS. see *FOOD AND FOOD INDUSTRIES — Abstracting, Bibliographies, Statistics*

663　　　　　　　US
FOODS ADLIBRA BEVERAGE EDITION. m. $125 (foreign $150) (effective 1998). (General Mills, Inc.) Foods Adlibra Publications, 9000 Plymouth Ave., N., Minneapolis, MN 55427. TEL 612-540-4759. FAX 612-540-3166. Ed. J.E. O'Connell. **Document type:** abstracting/indexing.
　　●Also available online. Vendor(s): Knight-Ridder Information, Inc. (File no.79).

INFORMATIONSDIENST PRAXISBEZOGENER LITERATUR IM WEINBAU. see *AGRICULTURE — Abstracting, Bibliographies, Statistics*

663.42 016   GW   ISSN 0723-1520
                          CODEN: MOBRDJ
MONATSSCHRIFT FUER BRAUWISSENSCHAFT. (Text in German; summaries in English and German) 1948. bi-m. DM.184 (effective 1997). (Technische Universitaet Muenchen und Berlin) Verlag Hans Carl GmbH, Andernacherstr. 33a, 90411 Nuernberg, Germany. TEL 49-911-95285-0. FAX 49-911-9528548. (Co-publisher: Westkreuz-Verlag) Eds. Karl-Ullrich Heyse, Wolfgang Popp. adv.: B&W page DM.1100, color page DM.1600; adv. contact: Korinna Thoenissen. bk.rev.; abstr.; bibl.; charts; illus.; tr.lit.; index, cum.index. circ. 2,800. (reprint service avail.) Indexed: Anal.Abstr., Biol.Abstr., Chem.Abstr., Curr.Adv.Ecol.Sci., Curr.Adv.Genetics & Molec.Biol., Curr.Cont., Curr.Cont., Curr.Pack.Abstr., Excerp.Med., Food Sci.& Tech.Abstr., IBR, Ind.Sci.Rev., Nutr.Abstr., VITIS. **Document type:** academic/scholarly publication.
—BLDSC (5906.260000); CASDDS; CISTI; Ei; Genuine Article; Linda Hall. **CCC.**
    Formerly: Brauwissenschaft (ISSN 0006-9337)

338.47 663   US
NATIONAL ASSOCIATION OF BEVERAGE IMPORTERS. STATISTICAL REPORT. m. (with q. & a. compilations). $425 to non-members. National Association of Beverage Importers, 1025 Vermont Ave., N.W., Ste. 1205, Washington, DC 20005. TEL 202-638-1617. FAX 202-638-3122.
    Description: Provides statistics on beverage importers arranged by product. Includes a comparison of tax payments.

663   FR
SITUATION ET STATISTIQUES MONDIALES DU SECTEUR VITICOLE. (Text in English, French) 1980. a. 135 F. (effective 1996). Office International de la Vigne et du Vin, 18 rue d'Aguesseau, 75008 Paris, France. TEL 33-01-44-94-80-80. FAX 33-01-42-66-90-63.
    Formerly: Situation de la Viticulture dans le Monde.
    Description: Reports on the previous year's acreage devoted to viticultural production, exports, imports, consumption of wine and grapes, inventories.

SITUATION ET STATISTIQUES MONDIALES DU SECTEUR VITIVINICOLE EN (YEAR). see AGRICULTURE — Abstracting, Bibliographies, Statistics

STATISTICAL RECORD OF BLACK AMERICA. see BIOGRAPHY — Abstracting, Bibliographies, Statistics

663.2 016   GW   ISSN 0042-7500
                          CODEN: VITIAY
VITIS; Berichte ueber Rebenforschung mit Dokumentation der Weinbauforschung. (Text in English, French, German) 1956. q. DM.80. Bundesanstalt fuer Zuechtungsforschung an Kulturpflanzen, Institut fuer Rebenzuechtung Geilweilerhof, 76833 Siebeldingen, Germany. TEL 49-6345-410. FAX 49-6345-41177. E-mail: irz@geilweilerhof.suew.shuttle.de. Eds. H. Duering, M. Klenert. bk.rev.; abstr.; bibl.; charts; illus.; index. circ. 700. Indexed: ASCA, Biol.Abstr., Chem.Abstr., Crop Physiol.Abstr., Curr.Adv.Ecol.Sci., Curr.Cont., Excerp.Med., Food Sci.& Tech.Abstr., Hort.Abstr., Irr.& Drain.Abstr., Plant Breed.Abstr., Plant Grow.Reg.Abstr., Soils & Fert., VITIS. **Document type:** academic/scholarly publication, abstracting/indexing.
—BLDSC (9244.120000); CASDDS; EMDOCS; Genuine Article; Linda Hall.

BIBLIOGRAPHIES

A A B'S BIBLIOGRAPHY OF RARE & OUT-OF-PRINT TITLES FOR SALE. see PUBLISHING AND BOOK TRADE — Abstracting, Bibliographies, Statistics

A B A BOOK BUYER'S HANDBOOK (YEAR). (American Booksellers Association, Inc.) see PUBLISHING AND BOOK TRADE

011   AT   ISSN 0726-1276
A B N AUTHORITIES. (Australian Bibliographic Network) 1982. q. Aus.$145 (effective 1997). National Library of Australia, Publications Section, Cultural and Educational Services Division, Canberra, A.C.T. 2600, Australia. TEL 61-6-262-1365. FAX 61-6-273-4493. circ. 380. (microfiche; reprint service avail. from ISI,UMI) **Document type:** bibliography.
    Description: Lists verified forms of heading that have been established by participants in the Australian Bibliographic Network. Also includes cross-references and scope notes used with headings.

691.3 620.1 016   US   ISSN 0084-6325
A C I BIBLIOGRAPHY. 1955. irreg., no.15, 1989. price varies. American Concrete Institute, Box 19150, Redford Sta., Detroit, MI 48219. TEL 313-532-2600. FAX 313-538-0655. (reprint service avail. from UMI) Indexed: Concr.Abstr. **Document type:** bibliography.
—CISTI.

A I B NOTIZIE. (Associazione Italiana Biblioteche) see LIBRARY AND INFORMATION SCIENCES

016.05   GW
▼**A I D A.** (Articoli Italiani di Periodici Accademici) 1997. a. DM.1200 (effective 1998). Zeller Publications, Postfach 1949, 49009 Osnabrueck, Germany. TEL 49-541-4045914. FAX 49-541-41255. E-mail: zeller@zeller.os.eunet.de. **Document type:** bibliography.
●Available only on CD-ROM.
    Description: Bibliography of Italian academic periodical literature.

A O P BIBLIOGRAFIJA/AUTOMATIC DATA PROCESSING. BIBLIOGRAPHY. (Automatska Obrada Podataka) see COMPUTERS — Abstracting, Bibliographies, Statistics

015   FR   ISSN 1145-3982
Z2169
A PROPOS (PARIS). 1974. m. free. Documentation Francaise, 29-31 quai Voltaire, 75344 Paris Cedex 07, France. TEL 33-1-40157000. FAX 33-1-40157230. TELEX 215 666 DOCFRAN. (Subscr. to: 124 rue Henri Barbusse, 93308 Aubervilliers Cedex, France. TEL 33-1-48395600. FAX 33-1-48395601) Ed. Sophie Seyer. adv. circ. 25,000. (also avail. in microfiche from DFR) Indexed: CERDIC. **Document type:** bulletin.
    Formerly (until 1990): D F Actualites (ISSN 0338-4187); Incorporates: France. Direction de la Documentation. Catalogue des Publications Editees ou Diffusees par la Documentation Francaise; Formerly: France, Direction de la Documentation. Tables de la Documentation Francaise.

A S T I S OCCASIONAL PUBLICATIONS. (Arctic Science & Technology Information System) see EARTH SCIENCES — Abstracting, Bibliographies, Statistics

011   US
A TO ZOO; subject access to children's picture books. irreg., 5th ed., 1996. $65. R.R. Bowker, A Division of Reed Elsevier plc group, 121 Chanlon Rd., New Providence, NJ 07974. TEL 908-464-6800. FAX 908-665-6688. TELEX 138-755. E-mail: info@bowker.com; URL: http://www.bowker.com. (Subscr. to: Order Dept., Box 31, New Providence, NJ 07974-9903. TEL 800-521-8110) Eds. Carolyn W. Lima, John A. Lima. **Document type:** consumer publication.
●Also available on CD-ROM. Producer(s): Bowker Electronic Publishing (Children's Reference PLUS).
    Description: Lists more than 15,000 fiction and nonfiction titles for preschool through the second grade.

ABSTRACTA IRANICA. see HISTORY — Abstracting, Bibliographies, Statistics

011   SP
ACADEMIA ALFONSO X EL SABIO. CUADERNOS BIBLIOGRAFICOS. 1977. irreg., no.10, 1986. Academia Alfonso X el Sabio, Murcia, Spain. **Document type:** bibliography.

ACCOUNTING WRITING; A P W C bibliography series. see BUSINESS AND ECONOMICS — Abstracting, Bibliographies, Statistics

ADOPTION NEWSLETTER DIRECTORY. see CHILDREN AND YOUTH — Abstracting, Bibliographies, Statistics

AFRICA BIBLIOGRAPHY. see HISTORY — History Of Africa

AFRICA GEOSCIENCE REVIEW. see EARTH SCIENCES — Geology

015.6   UK   ISSN 0306-9516
Z3501
AFRICAN BOOKS IN PRINT. (In 2 vols.) 1975. irreg., 4th ed., 1993. £250($400) Hans Zell Publishers (Subsidiary of: Bowker - Saur Ltd.), P.O. Box 56, Oxford OX1 25J, England. TEL 44-1865-511428. FAX 44-1865-311534. (Orders to: Bowker-Saur Ltd., Customer Service, Maypole House, Maypole Rd., E. Grinstead, W. Sussex RH19 1HH, England. TEL 44-1342-330100. FAX 44-1342-330198; US subscr. to: 121 Chanlon Rd., Box 31, New Providence, NJ 07974-9903. TEL 908-464-6800) **Document type:** bibliography.
—BLDSC (0732.365000).
    Description: Provides full bibliographic and acquisition information on some 24,000 books published - in English and in French - in 45 African countries by more than 700 publishers. Includes 4,000 titles in over 120 African languages.

960 016   II   ISSN 0001-9941
AFRICAN BOOKS NEWSLETTER. (Text in English) 1965. m. $52. K.K. Roy (Private) Ltd., 55 Gariahat Rd., P.O. Box 10210, Calcutta 700 019, India. Ed. K.K. Roy. adv.; mkt.; index. circ. 2,300. (looseleaf format; also avail. in microfilm) **Document type:** newsletter.

AFRICAN SPECIAL BIBLIOGRAPHIC SERIES. see HISTORY — Abstracting, Bibliographies, Statistics

960 015   SW   ISSN 0348-8691
AFRICANA IN THE LIBRARY OF THE SCANDINAVIAN INSTITUTE OF AFRICAN STUDIES. (Text in English, French and Swedish) 1963. a. SEK 100 (effective 1997). Nordiska Afrikainstitutet - Scandinavian Institute of African Studies, P.O. Box 1703, S-751 47 Uppsala, Sweden. TEL 18-562270. FAX 18-123775. Ed. Kristina Rylander. circ. 1,800. **Document type:** bibliography.
    Formerly (until no.37, 1976): Africana i Nordiska Vetenskapliga. Bibliotek (ISSN 0044-6645)

960 300   US
Z3503
AFRICANA JOURNAL; a bibliographic library journal and review annual. 1970. a. $65. Holmes & Meier Publishers, Inc., 160 Broadway E. Wing, New York, NY 10038. TEL 212-374-0100. FAX 212-374-1313. (U.K. addr.: Book Representation & Distribution, Ltd., 244 A London Rd., Hadleigh, Essex SS7 2DE, England. TEL 702-552912. FAX 702-556095) Ed. David E. Gardinier; Pub. Miriam Holmes. R&P contact: Julia Vaingurt. adv.; bk.rev. Indexed: Amer.Hist.& Life (1982-), Bibl.Ind., Bibl.Ling., Curr.Cont.Africa, Documentatieblad, Hist.Abstr., Lib.Lit., M.L.A., Mid.East: Abstr.& Ind., MLA Intl.Bibl. **Document type:** academic/scholarly publication.
—KR SourceOne.
    Former titles: Africana Annual (ISSN 1041-1267); Africana Journal (ISSN 0095-1080); (until 1974): Africana Library Journal (ISSN 0002-0303).
    Description: Covers books on Africa in all fields: humanities, social sciences, history, education, fine arts, religion and philosophy.

AGRICULTURAL ENGINEERING INDEX (YEARS). see AGRICULTURE

011   JA
AICHI-KEN KYODO SHIRYO SOGO MOKUROKU. 1964. irreg., latest 1987. 4000 Yen. Aichi Library Association - Aichi Toshokan Kyokai, 1-12-1 Higashisakura, Higashi-ku, Nagoya, Aichi, Japan. bibl.

AIDS BIBLIOGRAPHY (BETHESDA). see MEDICAL SCIENCES — Abstracting, Bibliographies, Statistics

AKADEMIA ROLNICZA WE WROCLAWIU. ZESZYTY NAUKOWE. BIBLIOGRAFIE. see AGRICULTURE — Abstracting, Bibliographies, Statistics

BIBLIOGRAPHIES

011 UK ISSN 0964-3400
Z921.B854
ALPHANUMERIC REPORTS PUBLICATIONS INDEX. 1992. biennial. £27 (foreign £33) (effective 1997). British Library, Document Supply Centre, Boston Spa, Wetherby, W. Yorks. LS23 7BQ, England. TEL 44-1937-546080. FAX 44-1937-546286. TELEX 557381. (Turpin Distribution Services Ltd., Blackhorse Rd., Letchworth, Herts. SG6 1HN, England. TEL 44-1462-672555. FAX 44-1462-480947) **Document type:** abstracting/indexing.

011 US
ALTERNATIVE PUBLISHERS OF BOOKS IN NORTH AMERICA. 1994. biennial. $20. C R I S E S Press, Inc., 1716 S.W. Williston Rd., Gainesville, FL 32608. TEL 352-335-2200. E-mail: willett@afn.org. (Co-sponsors: Alternatives in Print Task Force; Social Responsibilities Round Table; American Library Association) Ed. Byron Anderson. **Document type:** directory.
Description: Lists name, address, ISBN, phone, fax, e-mail, Internet address, previous names, editor, year founded, average number of books published per year, average press run, other materials produced, and a narrative description of 138 alternative presses. Includes bibliography and subject index.

378.3 011 II
ALUMNI PUBLICATIONS: A CATALOGUE. (First Edition covers 1950-1975) (Text in English) 1976. quinquennial. free. United States Educational Foundation in India, Fulbright House, 12 Hailey Rd., New Delhi 110 001, India. Ed. Dr. P.D. Sayal.

AMERICAN BIBLIOGRAPHY OF SLAVIC AND EAST EUROPEAN STUDIES. see HISTORY — Abstracting, Bibliographies, Statistics

AMERICAN BOOK PUBLISHING RECORD; arranged by Dewey Decimal Classification and indexed by author, title and subject. see PUBLISHING AND BOOK TRADE — Abstracting, Bibliographies, Statistics

AMERICAN INDIAN BIBLIOGRAPHIC SERIES. see ETHNIC INTERESTS — Abstracting, Bibliographies, Statistics

AMERICAN SOCIETY OF AGRICULTURAL ENGINEERS. COMPREHENSIVE INDEX OF PUBLICATIONS. see AGRICULTURE

AMSTERDAM STUDIES IN THE THEORY AND HISTORY OF LINGUISTIC SCIENCE. SERIES 5: LIBRARY AND INFORMATION SOURCES IN LINGUISTICS. see LINGUISTICS — Abstracting, Bibliographies, Statistics

016 809 US ISSN 0161-0376
Z1007
ANALYTICAL & ENUMERATIVE BIBLIOGRAPHY. 1977. q. $12 to individuals; institutions $17. Bibliographical Society of Northern Illinois, c/o Department of English, Northern Illinois University, DeKalb, IL 60115. TEL 815-753-6634. FAX 815-753-0606. E-mail: T80WPW1@MVS.CSO.NIU.EDU. Ed. William P. Williams. adv. contact: Craig S. Abbott. bk.rev. circ. 300. (back issues avail.) **Indexed:** Abstr.Engl.Stud., Amer.Hum.Ind., M.L.A., MLA Intl.Bibl. **Document type:** academic/scholarly publication.
—KR SourceOne; SWETS.
Description: Contains articles on bibliography, textual scholarship, and publishing and printing history, especially as these related to English and American literature.
Refereed Serial

ANATOMY OF WONDER; a critical guide to science fiction. see LITERATURE — Abstracting, Bibliographies, Statistics

ANNALES DE NORMANDIE; revue d'etudes regionales. see HISTORY — Abstracting, Bibliographies, Statistics

L'ANNEE PHILOLOGIQUE; bibliographie critique et analytique de l'antiquite greco-latine. see CLASSICAL STUDIES — Abstracting, Bibliographies, Statistics

080 UN
ANNOTATED ACCESSIONS LIST OF STUDIES AND REPORTS IN THE FIELD OF SCIENCE STATISTICS. 1966. a. UNESCO Publishing, Division of Statistics on Science and Technology, 7 Place de Fontenoy, 75352 Paris 07 SP, France. TEL 33-1-45681010. URL: http://www.unesco.org/publications. abstr.; bibl.; stat. circ. 1,000. **Document type:** bibliography.

011 US ISSN 0748-5190
ANNOTATED BIBLIOGRAPHIES OF SERIALS: A SUBJECT APPROACH. no.5, 1986. irreg. price varies. Greenwood Press, Inc. (Subsidiary of: Greenwood Publishing Group Inc.), 88 Post Rd. W., Box 5007, Westport, CT 06881-5007. TEL 203-226-3571. FAX 203-226-1502. **Document type:** bibliography.

ANNOTATED BIBLIOGRAPHY OF ENGLISH STUDIES. see LITERATURE — Abstracting, Bibliographies, Statistics

334 011 II
ANNOTATED BIBLIOGRAPHY OF LITERATURE ON COOPERATIVE MOVEMENTS IN SOUTH-EAST ASIA. (Text in English) 1963. s-a. Rs.15($2) International Cooperative Alliance, Regional Office and Education Centre for South-East Asia, Box 3312, 43 Friends Colony, New Delhi 110014, India. (Publications of regional offices can also be ordered from: International Cooperative Alliance, World Headquarters, 11 Upper Grosvenor St., London WIX 9PA, England) Ed. B.D. Pandey. abstr. circ. 500. (processed) **Document type:** bibliography.
Formerly: Annotated Bibliography of Literature Produced by the Cooperative Movements in South-East Asia (ISSN 0003-5084)

016.05 US
▼**ANNOTATIONS (YEAR)**; a directory of periodicals listed in the Alternative Press Index. 1996. a. $15. Alternative Press Center, Inc., Box 33109, Baltimore, MD 21218. TEL 410-243-2471. FAX 410-235-5323. E-mail: altpress@igc.apc.org; URL: http://www.igc.apc.org/altpress.
Description: Presents critical and descriptive annotations that complement the bibliographic entries of 220 journals.

ANNUAL BIBLIOGRAPHY OF MODERN ART. see ART

ANNUAL BIBLIOGRAPHY OF THE HISTORY OF THE PRINTED BOOK AND LIBRARY. see PRINTING — Abstracting, Bibliographies, Statistics

ANNUAL BIBLIOGRAPHY OF VICTORIAN STUDIES. see LITERATURE — Abstracting, Bibliographies, Statistics

ANNUAL EGYPTOLOGICAL BIBLIOGRAPHY/BIBLIOGRAPHIE EGYPTOLOGIQUE ANNUELLE/JAEHRLICHE AEGYPTOLOGISCHE BIBLIOGRAPHIE. see HISTORY — Abstracting, Bibliographies, Statistics

ANTARCTIC BIBLIOGRAPHY. see SCIENCES: COMPREHENSIVE WORKS — Abstracting, Bibliographies, Statistics

011 CK ISSN 0570-393X
Z1731
ANUARIO BIBLIOGRAFICO COLOMBIANO. 1951. irreg. no.24, 1995. price varies. Instituto Caro y Cuervo, Seccion de Publicaciones, Apdo. Aereo 51502, Bogota, Colombia. E-mail: carocuer@apenway.cam.co.

015 CR ISSN 0066-5010
Z1453
ANUARIO BIBLIOGRAFICO COSTARRICENSE. 1956. irreg. free. Asociacion Costarricense de Bibliotecarios, Apdo. 3308, San Jose, Costa Rica. circ. 500.

015 DR
ANUARIO BIBLIOGRAFICO DOMINICANO.* a. Biblioteca Nacional, Cesar Nicolas Penson, Santo Domingo, Dominican Republic.

011 EC ISSN 0252-8649
ANUARIO BIBLIOGRAFICO ECUATORIANO. (Published as the 6th issue each year of Bibliografia Ecuatoriana) 1975. a. Universidad Central del Ecuador, Biblioteca General, Apdo. 3291, Quito, Ecuador.

011 UY ISSN 0304-8861
Z1881
ANUARIO BIBLIOGRAFICO URUGUAYO. 1946-1949; resumed 1968. a. donation or exchange basis. Biblioteca Nacional de Uruguay, Director General, Av. 18 de Julio 1790, Montevideo, Uruguay. TEL 598-2-485030. FAX 598-2-496902. circ. 600.

015 US ISSN 0084-893X
ANUARIO - C B A - YEARBOOK.* (Text in English, Spanish) 1968. a. $62. E. Darino, Ed. & Pub., 222 Park Ave. S., Apt. 2A, New York, NY 10003. adv.; bk.rev. circ. 3,000.

011 US
APPALACHIAN BIBLIOGRAPHY. (Supplement avail.: Appalachian Outlook) 1980. irreg., latest 1980. $15. West Virginia University, Charles C. Wise, Jr. Library, Main Office, Box 6069, Morgantown, WV 26506-6069. TEL 304-293-3640. Ed. J.B. Brown. **Document type:** bibliography.
Description: Covers all aspects of Appalachian regional culture.

ARBITRIUM; Zeitschrift fuer Rezensionen zur germanistischen Literaturwissenschaft. see LITERARY AND POLITICAL REVIEWS

011 US ISSN 0195-7163
ARCADIA BIBLIOGRAPHICA VIRORUM ERUDITORUM. 1979. irreg., vol.16, 1997. Eurolingua, Box 101, Bloomington, IN 47402-0101. TEL 812-332-8918. **Document type:** bibliography.
Description: Biobibliographical monographs of scholars whose work is of international significance in the area of humanities.

011 IT ISSN 0390-1009
DG655.6
ARCHIVIO STORICO CIVICO E BIBLIOTECA TRIVULZIANA. LIBRI & DOCUMENTI. 1975. 3/yr. exchange basis only. Archivio Storico Civico e Biblioteca Trivulziana, Castello Sforzesco, 20121 Milan, Italy. TEL 39-2-86454638. FAX 39-2-875926. Ed. Giovanni Piazza. bk.rev.; bibl.; illus.; cum.index: 1975-1994. circ. 500. (back issues avail.) **Document type:** academic/scholarly publication.
—BLDSC (5207.320000).
Description: Featuring articles in history, literature and philology.

015 MX ISSN 0187-5817
Z1425
ARCHIVO GENERAL DE LA NACION. BOLETIN BIBLIOGRAFICO. (The last print ed. was no.21, Apr.-June 1991; subsequent issues avail. on diskette only) 1987. bi-m. Archivo General de la Nacion, Direccion de Informacion y Documentacion, Eduardo Molina y Albaniles, Col. Penitenciaria Ampliacion s-n, 15350 Mexico DF, Mexico. TEL 7-95-73-11. FAX 7-89-52-96. (diskette format) **Document type:** bibliography.

982 015 AG
ARGENTINA. CONGRESO DE LA NACION. BIBLIOTECA. BOLETIN. 1918-1990 (no.117); resumed 1995. a. exchange basis. Congreso de la Nacion, Biblioteca, Rivadavia 1850, 1033 Capital Federal, Buenos Aires, Argentina. TEL 541-371-5595. bibl. circ. 1,500. **Document type:** bulletin.
Formerly: Argentina. Congreso. Biblioteca. Boletin (ISSN 0004-1009)

ASIAN AND PACIFIC COCONUT COMMUNITY. BIBLIOGRAPHY SERIES. see AGRICULTURE — Abstracting, Bibliographies, Statistics

890 015 II ISSN 0004-4547
ASIAN BOOKS NEWSLETTER. (Text in English) 1966. m. $48. K.K. Roy (Private) Ltd., 55 Gariahat Rd., P.O. Box 10210, Calcutta 700 019, India. Ed. K.K. Roy. adv.; index. circ. 2,300. (also avail. in microfilm)

ASLIB BOOK GUIDE; a monthly list of recommended scientific and technical books. see SCIENCES: COMPREHENSIVE WORKS — Abstracting, Bibliographies, Statistics

ASSOCIATION FOR GERONTOLOGY IN HIGHER EDUCATION. BRIEF BIBLIOGRAPHY. see GERONTOLOGY AND GERIATRICS — Abstracting, Bibliographies, Statistics

BIBLIOGRAPHIES 533

011   GH
ASSOCIATION OF AFRICAN UNIVERSITIES. NEW ACQUISITIONS LIST. irreg. free. Association of African Universities, P.O. Box 5744, Accra, Ghana. **Document type:** bibliography.

011   IT   ISSN 0392-4270
ASSOCIAZIONE CENTRO DI DOCUMENTAZIONE. NOTIZIARIO. Key Title: Notiziario del Centro di Documentazione. 1970. m. Lit.40000($15) (effective 1997). Associazione Centro di Documentazione, Via Orafi 29, C.P. 347, 51100 Pistoia, Italy. TEL 39-573-977353. FAX 39-573-997353.
     Formerly: Cooperativa Centro di Documentazione. Notiziario.

011   US
ATHENAEUM BOOKSHELF. 1976. bi-m. membership. Athenaeum of Philadelphia, 219 S. Sixth St., Philadelphia, PA 19106-3794. TEL 215-925-2688. bk.rev. circ. 1,400. **Document type:** bibliography.

AUS DEM ANTIQUARIAT. see *PUBLISHING AND BOOK TRADE*

011   AT   ISSN 0067-172X
AUSTRALIAN BOOKS IN PRINT; including information on book trade associations. 1956. a. Aus.$130($115) D.W. Thorpe, A member of the Reed Elsevier plc group, 18 Salmon St., Port Melbourne, Vic. 3207, Australia. TEL 61-3-92457370. FAX 61-3-92457395. E-mail: customer.service@thorpe.com.au; URL: http://www.reed-elsevier.com. Ed. Victoria Matthews. bk.rev.; bibl.; index. circ. 4,000. **Document type:** bibliography.
—BLDSC (1798.020000). **CCC.**
     Description: Provides bibliographic information on over 150,000 in-print books published in - or about - Australia or written by Australian authors. Details more than 4,000 publishers and distributors whose titles are represented, plus information on Australian representation, associations, and book series.

015
AUSTRALIAN BOOKS IN PRINT ON MICROFICHE. 1980. m. (11/yr.). Aus.$320($150) D.W. Thorpe, A member of the Reed Elsevier plc group, 18 Salmon St., Port Melbourne, Vic. 3207, Australia. TEL 61-3-92457370. FAX 61-3-92457395. E-mail: customer.service@thorpe.com.au; URL: http://www.reed-elsevier.com. (microfiche) **Document type:** bibliography.
     Description: Updates of all in-print and advised forthcoming Australian books, together with separate series, distributors and Australian publishers' fiche.

010   AT   ISSN 0067-1878
Z4019
AUSTRALIAN GOVERNMENT PUBLICATIONS. 1961. a. Aus.$75 (effective 1997). National Library of Australia, Publications Section, Cultural and Educational Services Division, Canberra, A.C.T. 2600, Australia. TEL 61-6-262-1365. FAX 61-6-273-4493. circ. 600. (microfiche; reprint service avail. from ISI,UMI) **Indexed:** AESIS. **Document type:** bibliography.
●Also available online.
—CISTI; Linda Hall.

AUSTRALIAN INSTITUTE OF ABORIGINAL AND TORRES STRAIT ISLANDER STUDIES. ANNUAL BIBLIOGRAPHY. see *ANTHROPOLOGY — Abstracting, Bibliographies, Statistics*

AUSTRALIAN NINETEENTH CENTURY LITERATURE IN PRINT. see *LITERATURE — Abstracting, Bibliographies, Statistics*

015   SP
▼**AUTORIDADES DE LA BIBLIOTECA NACIONAL DE ESPANA EN C D - R O M.** 1996. s-a. $1189. Biblioteca Nacional de Espana, Paeo de Recoletos 20, 28001 Madrid, Spain. E-mail: editor@chadwyck.es; URL: http://www.chadwyck.com. (Dist. in Spain and Latin America by: Chadwyck-Healey Espana S.L., Juan Bravo 18, 2o C, 28006 Madrid, Spain. TEL 34-1-5755597. FAX 34-1-575-9885; In N. America: Chadwyck-Healey Inc., 1101 King St., Alexandria, VA 22314. TEL 800-752-0515. FAX 703-683-7589)
●Available only on CD-ROM. Producer(s): Chadwyck-Healey Inc.
     Description: Provides the bibliographic authority database of the National Library.

028.5   US   ISSN 1055-792X
Z1037
AWARD-WINNING BOOKS FOR CHILDREN AND YOUNG ADULTS. 1989. irreg. Scarecrow Press, Inc., 4720 Boston Way, Ste. A, Lanham, MD 20706-4310. TEL 800-462-6420. **Document type:** bibliography.

015   MX   ISSN 0188-901X
AZTECA BOLETIN BIBLIOGRAFICO INTERNACIONAL. 1990. q. free. Fondo de Cultura Economica, Carretera Picacho Ajusco 227, Col. Bosques del Pedregal, 14200 Mexico, D.F., Mexico. TEL 52-5-2274662. FAX 52-5-2274659. Ed. Ali Chumacero. circ. 10,000. **Document type:** bibliography.

015.942   UK   ISSN 0968-3097
B N B ON C D - R O M. (British National Bibliography) (Colleges edition avail. (bi-m.); Schools edition avail. (3/yr.)) 1950. m. £950 (foreign £1,090) (Colleges ed. £475; Schoosd ed £295) (effective 1997). British Library, National Bibliographic Service, Boston Spa, Wetherby, W. Yorks. LS23 7BQ, England. TEL 44-1937-546585. FAX 44-1937-546586. E-mail: http://portico.bl.uk. (Subscr. to: Turpin Distribution Services, Blackhorse Rd., Letchworth, Herts. SB6 1HN, England. TEL 44-1462-672555. FAX 44-1462-480947; Dist. in US by: Chadwyck-Healey Inc., 1101 King St., Alexandria, VA 22314. TEL 800-752-0515. FAX 703-683-7589) cum. files (1950-1985; 1986-). (back issues avail.) **Document type:** bibliography.
●Available only on CD-ROM. Producer(s): Chadwyck-Healey Inc.
     Description: Lists more than 1.5 million books and serials published in the UK and Ireland since 1950.

011   BA
BAHRAIN BIBLIOGRAPHY. a. Ministry of Education, Manama Central Library, P.O. Box 43, Manama, Bahrain. TEL 258550. FAX 274036. TELEX 9094. **Document type:** bibliography.

001.3 015   CK   ISSN 0006-6184
BANCO DE LA REPUBLICA. BIBLIOTECA LUIS ANGEL ARANGO. BOLETIN CULTURAL Y BIBLIOGRAFICO. 1958-1973; resumed 1978. 3/yr. Col.$15000($30) Banco de la Republica, Biblioteca Luis Angel Arango, Barrio de la Candelaria, Calle 11 no. 4-14, Bogota, Colombia. Dir. Dario Jaramillo Agudelo. bk.rev.; bibl.; charts; illus. circ. 4,000. **Indexed:** Amer.Hist.& Life, Hisp.Amer.Per.Ind. (1970), Hist.Abstr., M.L.A.

015   II
BANGIYA SAHITYAKOSHA/SAHITYIK BARSAPANJER. (Text in Bengali) 1970. a. price varies. Bangla Bhasa Sahitya-o-Samskriti Gabesane Samastha, c/o Little Magazine Stall & Bektigata Prakashani, 6B Ramanath Mazumder St., Calcutta 700 009, India. Ed. Asok Kumar Kundu. bk.rev.; bibl. circ. 1,100. **Document type:** bibliography.

015   BG
BANGLADESH NATIONAL BIBLIOGRAPHY. (Text in Bengali, English) 1972. a. National Library of Bangladesh, Directorate of Archives and Libraries, Sher.-&-Bangla Nagar(agargaon), Dhaka 1207, Bangladesh. Ed.Bd. circ. 2,000. **Document type:** abstracting/indexing.
     Description: Index of articles published in the daily newspaper.

490 016   GW   ISSN 0173-6388
Z7043
BAYERISCHE STAATSBIBLIOTHEK. NEW CONTENTS SLAVISTICS. (Text in Slavic and European languages) 1976. q. DM.60. (Staatsbibliothek) Verlag Otto Sagner, Postfach 340108, 80328 Munich, Germany. TEL 49-89-54218-0. FAX 49-89-54218218. TELEX 5. E-mail: postmaster@kubon-sagner.de; URL: http://www.kubon-sagner.de/ksinfo/verlag. circ. 200. (processed; back issues avail.) **Document type:** academic/scholarly publication.
     Former titles: Bayerische Staatsbibliothek. Inhaltsverzeichnisse Slavistischer Zeitschriften (ISSN 0173-6442); Bayerische Staatsbibliothek. Inhaltsverzeichnisse Slavischer Zeitschriften.
     Description: Tables of contents of Slavistic periodicals.

016 940   GW
BAYERISCHE STAATSBIBLIOTHEK. OSTEUROPA-KATALOG AUF C D - R O M. 1972. s-a. DM.890 (effective 1997). Bayerische Staatsbibliothek, Ludwigstr. 16, 80539 Munich, Germany. TEL 49-89-286380. FAX 49-89-28638293. E-mail: dir@bib-bvb.d400.de. Ed. Hermann Leskien. **Document type:** government publication.
●Available only on CD-ROM.
     Formerly (until 1997): Bayerische Staatsbibliotek. Osteuropa-Neuerwerbungen.

BELGIUM. INSTITUT NATIONAL DE STATISTIQUE. CATALOGUE DES PRODUITS ET SERVICES. see *STATISTICS*

330 011   BE
BELGIUM. MINISTERE DES AFFAIRES ECONOMIQUES. BIBLIOTHEQUE FONDS QUETELET. ACCROISSEMENTS. Dutch edition: Belgium. Ministerie van Economische Zaken. Bestuur Economische Informatie. (Text in French) 1948. m. 250 BEF (foreign 375 BEF). Ministere des Affaires Economiques, Administration de l'Information Economique - Ministerie van Economische Zaken, Rue de l'Industrie 6, B-1000 Brussels, Belgium. TEL 32-2-5066054. FAX 32-2-5028425. bk.rev.; bibl. **Document type:** bibliography.
     Formerly: Belgium. Ministere des Affaires Economiques. Bibliotheque Centrale (Fonds Quetelet). Accroissements (ISSN 0005-8521)

016.972   BM   ISSN 0255-0067
Z1591
BERMUDA NATIONAL BIBLIOGRAPHY. 1984. q. (plus a. cum.). B.$10 (foreign $14) to individuals; institutions B.$12.50 (foreign $17) (effective 1997). Bermuda Library, Technical Services, Par-la-Ville, 13 Queen St., Hamilton HM 11, Bermuda. TEL 441-295-2905. FAX 441-292-8443. Ed. Patrice A. Carvell. circ. 100. **Document type:** bibliography.
     Description: Lists all new materials added to the Bermudiana collection.

011   US
BEST BOOK CATALOG IN THE WORLD. 1975. a. (plus q. supplements). $5 (effective 1997). Loompanics Unlimited, Box 1197, Port Townsend, WA 98368. TEL 360-385-5087. FAX 360-385-7785. E-mail: loompanx@olympus.net; URL: http://loompanics.com. Ed. Michael Hoy. adv. contact: Audrey Lee. circ. 30,000. **Document type:** catalog.
     Formerly: Loompanics Book Catalog.
     Description: Source for anarchists, survivalists, iconoclasts, self-liberators, mercenaries, investigators, drop outs, and researchers.
Refereed Serial

BEST BOOKS FOR CHILDREN; preschool through grade 6. see *CHILDREN AND YOUTH — About*

015   IO   ISSN 0523-1639
BIBLIOGRAFI NASIONAL INDONESIA/INDONESIAN NATIONAL BIBLIOGRAPHY. 1953. q. (with a. cumulation). free. Perpustakaan Nasional R.I. - National Library of Indonesia, P.O. Box 3624, Jakarta 1000s, Indonesia. TEL 021-310-3553. FAX 021-310-3554. Ed. Dady P. Rachmananta. adv.; bk.rev. circ. 1,000.

015.489   DK   ISSN 0067-6543
Z2569
BIBLIOGRAFI OVER DANMARKS OFFENTLIGE PUBLIKATIONER. (Text in Danish and English) 1949. a. DKK 325. Det Kongelige Bibliotek, Danske Afdeling, Chr. Brygge 8, DK-1219 Copenhagen K, Denmark. (Dist. by: Dansk BiblioteksCenter, Tempovej 7-11, DK-2750 Ballerup, Denmark) Ed. Gertrud Nielsen. index. circ. 3,200. **Document type:** government publication, bibliography.
—CISTI.
     Formerly (until 1961): Bibliografisk Fortegnelse Over Statens Tryksager og Statsunderstoettede Publikationer (ISSN 0902-7920)
     Description: Annual bibliography of Danish official publications issued at state level.

BIBLIOGRAFIA AGRICOLA. see *AGRICULTURE — Abstracting, Bibliographies, Statistics*

BIBLIOGRAFIA ANALITYCZNA BIBLIOTEKOZNAWSTWA I INFORMACJI NAUKOWEJ. see *LIBRARY AND INFORMATION SCIENCES — Abstracting, Bibliographies, Statistics*

BIBLIOGRAPHIES

011   PL   ISSN 0860-6579
BIBLIOGRAFIA BIBLIOGRAFII POLSKICH/BIBLIOGRAPHY OF POLISH BIBLIOGRAPHIES. 1937. a. Biblioteka Narodowa, Instytut Bibliograficzny, Al. Niepodleglosci 213, 00-973 Warsaw, Poland. TEL 48-2-6082412. FAX 48-22-255251. TELEX 813702 BN PL. **Document type:** bibliography.
—BLDSC (1948.010000); Linda Hall.
Formerly (until 1981): Bibliografia Bibliografii i Nauki o Ksiazce. Cz. 1: Bibliografia Bibliografii Polskich (ISSN 0860-8385); Which supersedes in part (in 1969): Bibliografia Bibliografii i Nauki o Ksiazce (ISSN 0509-6413)

BIBLIOGRAFIA BRASILEIRA DE EDUCACAO. see EDUCATION — Abstracting, Bibliographies, Statistics

BIBLIOGRAFIA BRASILEIRA DE ODONTOLOGIA. see MEDICAL SCIENCES — Abstracting, Bibliographies, Statistics

015   CL   ISSN 0716-176X
BIBLIOGRAFIA CHILENA. 1877. irreg. Esc.1000($10) Direccion de Bibliotecas, Archivos y Museos, Biblioteca Nacional, Alameda 651, Santiago, Chile. TEL 6380461. FAX 6381975. bibl. circ. 1,000. **Document type:** bibliography.
Formerly (until 1981): Anuario de la Prensa Chilena.
Description: Provides a listing of publications issued in Chile.

011   BL   ISSN 0006-0992
BIBLIOGRAFIA CLASSIFICADA.* 1968. bi-m. Centro de Investigacao e Documentacao, Caixa Postal 23, Petropolis, Rio de Janeiro, Brazil. Ed. Arcangelo Raimundo Buzzi.

015.7291   CU   ISSN 0574-6086
Z1511
BIBLIOGRAFIA CUBANA. 1959. a. $35. Biblioteca Nacional Jose Marti, Plaza de la Revolucion, Havana, Cuba. TEL 70-5092. FAX 53-7-335072. TELEX 511963 CU. circ. 500. (also avail. in microfilm from OMN)
Description: Compiles all books, magazines, postals, catalogues of expositions, and programs of musical reference.

BIBLIOGRAFIA DE LA LITERATURA HISPANICA. see LITERATURE — Abstracting, Bibliographies, Statistics

011   SP   ISSN 1133-9519
Z6027.S72
BIBLIOGRAFIA ESPANOLA. CARTOGRAFIA. 1980. a. 2000 ptas. Biblioteca Nacional de Espana, Paseo de Recoletos 20, 28001 Madrid, Spain. TEL 1-5447443. (Co-sponsor: Ministerio de Cultura, Direccion General del Libro y Bibliotecas) circ. 1,000.
Formerly (until 1991): Bibliografia Espanola. Suplemento de Cartografia (ISSN 0214-4441)

015   SP   ISSN 1133-858X
Z2685
BIBLIOGRAFIA ESPANOLA. MONOGRAFIAS. 1969. m. 18000 ptas. (foreign 20000 ptas.) (effective 1994). Biblioteca Nacional de Espana, Paseo de Recoletos 20, 28001 Madrid, Spain. TEL 1-5447443. FAX 34-1-5774054. (Co-sponsor: Ministerio de Cultura, Direccion General del Libro y Bibliotecas) adv. circ. 1,000. **Document type:** bibliography, monographic series.
—BLDSC (1949.340000).
Former titles (until 1994): Bibliografia Espanola (ISSN 0525-3675); Boletin del Deposito Legal de Obras Impresas (ISSN 0006-6362)

011   SP   ISSN 1133-8563
Z2685
BIBLIOGRAFIA ESPANOLA. MONOGRAFIAS. INDICES ACUMULATIVOS. 1958. a. 6000 ptas. Biblioteca Nacional de Espana, Paseo de Recoletos 20, 28001 Madrid, Spain. TEL 1-5447443. (Co-sponsor: Ministerio de Cultura, Direccion General del Libro y Bibliotecas) circ. 1,000. (also avail. in microfiche from BHP; reprint service avail. from KTO) **Document type:** bibliography.
Formerly (until 1993): Bibliografia Espanola. Anual (ISSN 0523-1760)

011   SP
BIBLIOGRAFIA ESPANOLA. MUSICA IMPRESA. 1985. a. Biblioteca Nacional de Espana, Paseo de Recoletos 20, 28001 Madrid, Spain. TEL 1-5447443. (Co-sponsor: Ministerio de Cultura, Direccion General del Libro y Bibliotecas) Ed.Bd. circ. 1,000. **Document type:** bibliography.
Formerly: Bibliografia Espanola. Suplemento de Musica Impresa (ISSN 1130-1392)

011   SP   ISSN 0210-8372
Z6956.S7
BIBLIOGRAFIA ESPANOLA. SUPLEMENTO DE PUBLICACIONES PERIODICAS. 1979. a. 2000 ptas. Biblioteca Nacional de Espana, Plaza del Rey, 1, 28004 Madrid, Spain. TEL 1-5447443. (Dist. by: Distribuidora de Publicaciones, Calle Fernando el Catolico, 77, 28015 Madrid, Spain) (Co-sponsor: Ministerio de Cultura, Direccion General del Libro y Bibliotecas) circ. 1,000.

015   SP
BIBLIOGRAFIA ESPANOLA DESDE 1976 EN C D - R O M. 1993. q. $1449 (effective 1996). Biblioteca Nacional de Espana, Paseo de Recoletos 20, 28001 Madrid, Spain. (Dist. in Spain and Latin America by: Chadwyck-Healey Espana S.L., Juan Bravo 18, 2o C, 28006 Madrid, Spain. TEL 34-1-575-5597. FAX 34-1-575-9885; In N. America: Chadwyck-Healey Inc., 1101 King St., Alexandria, VA 22314. TEL 800-752-0515. FAX 703-683-7589) **Document type:** bibliography.
●Available only on CD-ROM. Producer(s): Chadwyck-Healey Inc.

BIBLIOGRAFIA FILOSOFICA ITALIANA. see PHILOSOPHY — Abstracting, Bibliographies, Statistics

015 850   IT   ISSN 1122-2220
Z2355.A2
BIBLIOGRAFIA GENERALE DELLA LINGUA E DELLA LETTERATURA ITALIANA. 1991. a. L.290000 (foreign L.350000) (effective Sep. 1995). (Centro Pio Rajna) Salerno Editrice, Via di Donna Olimpia 20, 00152 Rome, Italy. TEL 39-6-58205688. FAX 39-6-58238241. (Edit. addr.: Via della Nocetta 77-5A, 00164 Rome, Italy. TEL 39-6-66162127) Ed. Enrico Malato. adv.; bk.rev. circ. 1,000. **Indexed:** MLA Intl.Bibl. **Document type:** bibliography.
●Also available on CD-ROM.

BIBLIOGRAFIA GEOGRAFICA DELLA REGIONE ITALIANA. see GEOGRAPHY — Abstracting, Bibliographies, Statistics

BIBLIOGRAFIA GEOGRAFII POLSKIEJ. see GEOGRAPHY — Abstracting, Bibliographies, Statistics

BIBLIOGRAFIA GEOLOGICA SI GEOFIZICA A ROMANIEI/GEOLOGICAL AND GEOPHYSICAL BIBLIOGRAPHY OF ROMANIA. see EARTH SCIENCES — Abstracting, Bibliographies, Statistics

BIBLIOGRAFIA GEOLOGICZNA POLSKI. see EARTH SCIENCES — Abstracting, Bibliographies, Statistics

BIBLIOGRAFIA GOSPODARKI I INZYNIERII WODNEJ/BIBLIOGRAPHY OF WATER MANAGEMENT AND ENGINEERING. see WATER RESOURCES — Abstracting, Bibliographies, Statistics

BIBLIOGRAFIA HISTORII POLSKIEJ. see HISTORY — Abstracting, Bibliographies, Statistics

BIBLIOGRAFIA HYDROLOGII I OCEANOLOGII/BIBLIOGRAPHY OF HYDROLOGY AND OCEANOLOGY. see EARTH SCIENCES — Abstracting, Bibliographies, Statistics

BIBLIOGRAFIA ITALIANA DI STORIA DELLA SCIENZA. see SCIENCES: COMPREHENSIVE WORKS — Abstracting, Bibliographies, Statistics

015   AA
BIBLIOGRAFIA KOMBETARE E LIBRIT QE BOTOHET NE REPUBLIKEN E SHQIPERISE. 1960. q. $16 (effective 1997). Biblioteka Kombetare, Tirana, Albania. Ed. Maksim Gjinaj. R&P contact: Nermin Basha. adv. contact: Ardian Basha. **Document type:** bibliography.
Former titles (until 1991): Bibliografia Kombetare e Libritqe Botohet ne Republiken Popullore Socialiste te Shqiperise; (until 1985): Bibliografia Kombetare e Republikes Popullore Socialiste te Shqiperise. Libri Shqip (ISSN 0250-5053); (until 1976): Bibliografia Kombetare e Repulikes Popullore te Shqiperise. Libri Shqip (ISSN 0523-1841); (until 1964): Bibliografia e Republikes Popullore te Shqiperise. Vepra Orijjinale dhe Perkthime.
Description: Lists books and other non-periodical publications of Albania.

015   AA
BIBLIOGRAFIA KOMBETARE E REPUBLIKES SE SHQIPERISE. ARTIKUJT E PERIODIKUT SHQIPTAR. 1961. m. $72 (effective 1997). Biblioteka Kombetare, Tirana, Albania. TEL 355-42-238-43. Ed. Maksim Gjinaj. R&P contact: Nermin Basha. adv. contact: Adrian Basha. **Document type:** bibliography.
Former titles (until 1991): Bibliografia Kombetare e Republikes Popullore Socialiste te Shqiperise. Artikujt e Periodikut Shqiptar; (until 1985): Bibliografia Kombetare e Republikes Popullore Socialiste te Shqiperise. Artikujt e Periodikut Shqip (ISSN 0250-5061); (until 1976): Bibliografia Kombetare e Republikes Popullore te Shqiperise. Artikujt e Periodikut Shqip (ISSN 0523-1833); (until 1964): Bibliografia e Periodikut te Republikes Popullore te Shqiperise.
Description: Lists articles published in Albanian periodicals.

015   MX   ISSN 0185-2884
BIBLIOGRAFIA LATINOAMERICANA; trabajos publicados por latinoamericanos en revistas extranjeras. (Text in English) 1980. s-a. Mex.$150($190) (effective 1997). Universidad Nacional Autonoma de Mexico, Direccion General de Bibliotecas, Centro de Informacion Cientifica y Humanistica, Apdo. Postal 70-392, Circuito Exterior, Ciudad Universitaria, 04510 Mexico, D.F., Mexico. TEL 52-5-6223958. FAX 52-5-6162557. E-mail: biblat@selene.cichcu.unam.mx; URL: http://www.cichcu.unam.mx. Ed. Octavio Alonso Gamboa. R&P contact: Octavio Alonso-Gamboa. **Document type:** bibliography.
●Also available online.
Also available on CD-ROM.
—BLDSC (1954.625000).
Description: Bibliographic index that covers 3,000 serials on social sciences and the humanities written by Latin American authors.

015   MX   ISSN 0185-2930
BIBLIOGRAFIA LATINOAMERICANA: PART II; trabajos sobre America Latina publicados en revistas extranjeras. s-a. $190 (includes parts I, II). Universidad Nacional Autonoma de Mexico, Direccion eneral de Bibliotecas, Centro de Informacion Cientifica y Humanistica, Apdo. Postal 70-392, C.P. 04510 Mexico, D.F., Mexico. TEL 52-5-6223958. FAX 52-5-6162557. E-mail: biblat@selene.cichu.unam.mx; URL: http://www.cichu.unam.mx. Ed. Octavio Alonso-Gamboa. R&P contact: Octavio Alonso-Gamboa. **Document type:** bibliography.
●Also available online.
Also available on CD-ROM.
—BLDSC (1954.626000).

BIBLIOGRAFIA METEOROLOGII/BIBLIOGRAPHY OF METEOROLOGY. see METEOROLOGY — Abstracting, Bibliographies, Statistics

015   MX   ISSN 0006-1069
Z1411
BIBLIOGRAFIA MEXICANA. 1967. a. $200 (effective 1997). Universidad Nacional Autonoma de Mexico, Instituto de Investigaciones Bibliograficas, Ciudad Universitaria, Coyoacan, 04510 Mexico D.F., Mexico. TEL 52-5-6226807. FAX 52-5-6650951. E-mail: libros@biblonal.biblioq.unam.mx. (Co-sponsor: Biblioteca Nacional) Ed. Jose G. Moreno de Alba. circ. 1,000.

BIBLIOGRAPHIES 535

015 020   BU   ISSN 0204-7373
BIBLIOGRAFIA NA BULGARSKATA BIBLIOGRAFIIA/BIBLIOGRAPHY OF BULGARIAN BIBLIOGRAPHIES. 1965. a. $50. Narodna Biblioteka Sv.sv. Kiril i Metodii - Cyril and Methodius National Library, 88, V. Levski Blvd., 1504 Sofia, Bulgaria. TEL 359-2-882811. FAX 359-2-435495. Ed. K. Stavrev. R&P contact: K. Stavrev. circ. 350. **Document type:** bibliography.

015   UK
BIBLIOGRAFIA NACIONAL PORTUGUESA EM C D - R O M. s-a. $450 (effective 1996). (Biblioteca Nacional Portuguesa) Chadwyck-Healey Ltd., The Quorum, Barnwell Rd., Cambridge CB5 8SW, England. TEL 44-1223-215512. FAX 44-1223-215514. E-mail: marketing@chadwyck.co.uk; URL: http://www.chadwyck.com. (In N. America: Chadwyck-Healey Inc. 1101 King St., Alexandria, VA 22314. TEL 800-752-0515. FAX 703-683-7589) **Document type:** bibliography.
●Available only on CD-ROM. Producer(s): Chadwyck-Healey Inc.

015   RM   ISSN 1221-9126
Z2923
BIBLIOGRAFIA NATIONALA ROMANA. CARTI, ALBUME, HARTI. 1957. s-m. 72000 lei (effective 1997). Biblioteca Nationala a Romaniei, Str. Ion Ghica 4, Sec. 3 Bucharest 79708, Rumania. TEL 401-6142434. FAX 401-3123381. E-mail: bnr@ul.ici.ro. Ed. Florentina Vasile. **Document type:** bibliography.
Former titles (until 1990): Bibliografia Romaniei. Carti, Albume, Harti (ISSN 1220-5842); (until 1989): Bibliografia Republicii Socialiste. Carti, Albume, Harti (ISSN 1220-5834); Supersedes in part (in 1967): Bibliografia Republicii Socialiste Romania. Carti, Albume, Harti, Note Muzicale (ISSN 0254-6035); Which was formerly (until 1965): Bibliografia Republicii Populare Romane. Carti, Albume, Harti, Note Muzicale (ISSN 0254-6027)

015   RM   ISSN 1221-9134
BIBLIOGRAFIA NATIONALA ROMANA. NOTE MUZICALE, DISCURI, CASETE. 1957. q. 7200 lei (effective 1997). Biblioteca Nationala a Romaniei, Str. Ion Ghica 4, Sec. 3, 79708 Bucharest, Rumania. TEL 40-1-6142434. FAX 40-1-3123381. E-mail: bnr@ul.ici.ro. Ed. Doina Nemes. **Document type:** bibliography.
Former titles (until 1990): Bibliografia Romaniei. Note Muzicale, Discuri, Casete (ISSN 1220-5877); (until 1989): Bibliografia Republicii Socialiste Romania. Note Muzicale, Discuri, Casete (ISSN 1220-5869); (until 1979): Bibliografia Republicii Socialiste Romania. Note Muzicale, Discuri (ISSN 1220-5850); Supersedes in part (in 1967): Bibliografia Republicii Socialiste Romania. Carti, Albume, Harti, Note Muzicale (ISSN 0254-6035); Which was formerly (until 1965): Bibliografia Republicii Populare Romane. Carti, Albume, Harti, Note Muzicale (ISSN 0254-6027).

015   RM   ISSN 1221-5309
Z2925
BIBLIOGRAFIA NATIONALA ROMANA. PUBLICATII OFICIALE. 1992. s-a. 10200 lei (effective 1997). Biblioteca Nationala a Romaniei, Str. Ion Ghica 4, Sec. 3, 79708 Bucharest, Rumania. TEL 401-6142434. FAX 401-3123381. E-mail: bnr@ul.ici.ro. Ed. Maria Oprea. **Document type:** bibliography.
Formerly (until 1992): Bibliografia Romaniei. Publicatii Oficiale (ISSN 1221-1826)

016.05   RM   ISSN 1221-180X
AI19.R8
BIBLIOGRAFIA NATIONALA ROMANA. PUBLICATII SERIALE. 1992. a. 4000 lei (effective 1997). Biblioteca Nationala a Romaniei, Str. Ion Ghica 4, Sec. 3, 79708 Bucharest, Rumania. TEL 401-6142434. FAX 401-3123381. E-mail: bnr@ul.ici.ro. Ed. Cecilia Haraga. **Document type:** bibliography.

015   RM   ISSN 1453-0465
BIBLIOGRAFIA NATIONALA ROMANA. ROMANICA. 1993. a. 13200 lei (effective 1997). Biblioteca Nationala a Romaniei, Str. Ion Ghica 4, Sec. 3, 79708 Bucharest, Rumania. TEL 401-6142434. FAX 401-3123381. E-mail: bnr@ul.ici.ro. Ed. Actarian Emanuel Hrant. **Document type:** bibliography.
Formerly (until 1993): Bibliografia Nationala Romana. Lucrari Aparute in Strainatate (ISSN 1221-4515)

015   RM   ISSN 1223-7485
▼**BIBLIOGRAFIA NATIONALA ROMANA. TEZE DE DOCTORAT.** 1995. a. 3000 lei (effective 1997). Biblioteca Nationala a Romaniei, Str. Ion Ghica 4, Sec. 3, 79708 Bucharest, Rumania. TEL 401-6142434. FAX 401-3123381. E-mail: bnr@ul.ici.ro. Ed. Florentina Vasile. **Document type:** bibliography.

015   IT   ISSN 0006-1077
Z2341
BIBLIOGRAFIA NAZIONALE ITALIANA. (N.S. of Bollettino delle Pubblicazioni Italiane Ricevute per Diritto di Stampa 1886-1957) 1958. m. (plus a. cumulation). L.200000 (effective 1995). (Biblioteca Nazionale Centrale di Firenze) Istituto Centrale per il Catalogo Unico delle Biblioteche Italiane e per le Informazioni Bibliografiche, Viale del Castro Pretorio, 105, 00185 Rome, Italy. TEL 39-06-4959217. FAX 39-06-4959302. (Subcr. to: Editrice Bibliografica, Viale Vittorio Veneto 24, 20124 Milan, Italy. TEL 39-06-29006965. FAX 39-06-654624) Ed. Dr. Carla Guiducci Bonanni. bk.rev.; index. circ. 1,100. (also avail. in microfilm) **Document type:** bibliography.
●Also available online.
Also available on CD-ROM. Producer(s): Chadwyck-Healey Inc.
—Linda Hall.

015 943.8   PL   ISSN 0409-3453
Z2527.P65
BIBLIOGRAFIA POMORZA ZACHODNIEGO. PISMIENNICTWO POLSKIE/BIBLIOGRAPHY OF WEST POMERANIA. POLISH LITERATURE. (Text in Polish; summaries in English and Russian) 1963. irreg. price varies. Ksiaznica Pomorska im. Stanislawa Staszica, Podgorna 15, 70-205 Szczecin, Poland. TEL 48-91-341662. FAX 48-91-344831. Ed. Stanislaw Krzywicki. (also avail. in microfilm) **Document type:** bibliography.
Description: Compiles the literature of western Pomerania.

015   PL   ISSN 0138-0702
BIBLIOGRAFIA POMORZA ZACHODNIEGO. PISMIENNICTWO ZAGRANICZNE/BIBLIOGRAPHY OF WEST POMERANIA. FOREIGN LITERATURE. 1978. irreg. price varies. Ksiaznica Pomorska im. Stanislawa Staszica, Podgorna 15, 70-205 Szczecin, Poland. TEL 48-91-341662. FAX 48-91-344831. Ed. Stanislaw Krzywicki. bk.rev. (also avail. in microfilm) **Document type:** bibliography.
Description: Includes foreign literature of western Pomerania in original languages.

BIBLIOGRAFIA PUBLIKACJI PRACOWNIKOW NAUKOWYCH AKADEMII EKONOMICZNEJ W KRAKOWIE. see BUSINESS AND ECONOMICS — Abstracting, Bibliographies, Statistics

015   PL   ISSN 0523-1930
BIBLIOGRAFIA SLASKA. 1963. a. 15 Zl. Biblioteka Slaska, Ul. Francuska 12, 40-956 Katowice, Poland. TEL 48-32-1564953. FAX 48-32-1564953. bk.rev. circ. 500. **Document type:** bibliography.

BIBLIOGRAFIA TEMATICA SOBRE JUDAISMO ARGENTINO. see RELIGIONS AND THEOLOGY — Judaic

BIBLIOGRAFIA TEOLOGICA COMENTADA DEL AREA IBEROAMERICANA. see RELIGIONS AND THEOLOGY — Abstracting, Bibliographies, Statistics

011   PL   ISSN 0239-4421
Z6956.P7
BIBLIOGRAFIA WYDAWNICTW CIAGLYCH/BIBLIOGRAPHY OF POLISH SERIALS. 1957-1974; resumed 1981. a. 30000 Zl.($15) Biblioteka Narodowa, Instytut Bibliograficzny, Al. Niepodleglosci 213, 00-973 Warsaw, Poland. TEL 48-2-6082409. FAX 48-22-255251. TELEX 813702 BN PL. (Dist. by: P.P. CHZ Ars Polona, ul. Krakowskie Przedmiescie 7, 00-068 Warsaw, Poland) Ed. Anna Potuszynska. index. circ. 450. **Document type:** bibliography.
Formerly: Bibliografia Czasopism i Wydawnictw Zbiorowych (ISSN 0523-1736)

011   PL   ISSN 0239-5606
BIBLIOGRAFIA WYDAWNICTW CIAGLYCH NOWYCH, ZAWIESZONYCH I ZMIENIAJACYCH TYTUL. (Supplement to: Przewodnik Bibliograficzny (ISSN 0033-2518)) 1976. q. price varies. Biblioteka Narodowa, Instytut Bibliograficzny, Al. Niepodleglosci 213, 00-973 Warsaw, Poland. TEL 48-2-6082409. FAX 48-2-6082409. TELEX 813702 BN PL. (Dist. by: P.P. CHZ Ars Polona, ul. Krakowskie Przemiescie 7, 00-068 Warsaw, Poland) Ed. Anna Potuszynska. index. **Document type:** bibliography.

011   PL   ISSN 0006-1093
AI15
BIBLIOGRAFIA ZAWARTOSCI CZASOPISM. 1947. m. price varies. Biblioteka Narodowa, Instytut Bibliograficzny, Al. Niepodleglosci 213, 00-973 Warsaw, Poland. TEL 48-2-6082435. FAX 48-2-6082435. TELEX 813702 BN PL. (Dist. by: P.P. CHZ Ars Polona, ul. Krakowskie Przedmiescie 7, 00-068 Warsaw, Poland) index. circ. 1,600. **Document type:** bibliography.

BIBLIOGRAFICA FOLCLORICA. see FOLKLORE — Abstracting, Bibliographies, Statistics

010   XO   ISSN 0067-6780
BIBLIOGRAFICKY ZBORNIK. (Text in Slovak) 1957. a. price varies. Matica Slovenska, Slovenska Narodna Kniznica, Ul. L. Novomeskeho 32, 036 52 Martin, Slovakia. TEL 0842-313-71. FAX 0842-324-54. TELEX 075-331. Ed. Milos Kovacka. bk.rev. **Document type:** bibliography.

BIBLIOGRAFIE BOTANICZNE/BOTANICAL BIBLIOGRAPHIES. see BIOLOGY — Abstracting, Bibliographies, Statistics

011   XR   ISSN 0139-8539
BIBLIOGRAFIE CESKEHO KNIHOVNICTVI, BIBLIOGRAFIE A VEDECKO-TECHNICKYCH INFORMACI. (Print edition ceased 1995) 1977. a. 60 Kc.($6) Narodni Knihovna Ceske Republiky - National Library of the Czech Republic, Klementinum 190, 110 01 Prague 1, Czech Republic. TEL 420-2-24229500. FAX 420-2-24227796. (Dist. by: Narodni Knihovna Ceske Republiky, Oddeleni Prodeje a Expedice, Centralni Depozitar NK CR, Sterboholska 55, 100 00 Prague 10, Czech Republic. TEL 420-2-7026200) Ed. Jana Sodomkova. circ. 450. (diskette format) **Document type:** bibliography.
Formerly: Bibliograficky Katalog C S S R: Ceske Knihy. Zvlastni Sesit. Bibliografie a V T I (ISSN 0323-1666)
Description: Cumulative bibliography covering Czech literature in librarianship, bibliography and scientific and technical information.

BIBLIOGRAFIE NEDERLANDSE SOCIALE WETENSCHAPPEN; vakbibliografie voor nederland en Nederlandstalig Belgie. see SOCIAL SCIENCES: COMPREHENSIVE WORKS — Abstracting, Bibliographies, Statistics

BIBLIOGRAFIJA JUGOSLAVIJE. CLANCI I PRILOZI U SERIJSKIM PUBLIKACIJAMA. SERIJA A: DRUSTVENE NAUKE. see SOCIAL SCIENCES: COMPREHENSIVE WORKS — Abstracting, Bibliographies, Statistics

BIBLIOGRAFIJA JUGOSLAVIJE. CLANCI I PRILOZI U SERIJSKIM PUBLIKACIJAMA. SERIJA B: PRIRODNE, PRIMENJENE, MEDICINSKE I TEHNICKE NAUKE. see SCIENCES: COMPREHENSIVE WORKS — Abstracting, Bibliographies, Statistics

016   YU   ISSN 0352-5996
AI15
BIBLIOGRAFIJA JUGOSLAVIJE. CLANCI I PRILOZI U SERIJSKIM PUBLIKACIJAMA. SERIJA C: UMETNOST, SPORT, FILOLOGIJA, KNJIZEVNOST. 1950. m. $662 or exchange basis. Jugoslovenski Bibliografsko-Informacijski Institut (YUBIN) - Yugoslav Institute for Bibliography and Information, Terazije 26, Belgrade, Yugoslavia. FAX 11-687-760. Ed. Radomir Glavicki.
●Also available online.
Formerly (until 1985): Bibliografija Jugoslavije. Serija C: Umetnost, Sport, Filologija, Knjizevnost i Muzikalije (ISSN 0373-6377)

BIBLIOGRAPHIES

015　　　　　　YU　　ISSN 0523-2201
Z2951
BIBLIOGRAFIJA JUGOSLAVIJE. KNJIGE, BROSURE I MUZIKALIJE. 1950. s-m. $906 or exchange basis. Jugoslovenski Bibliografsko-Informacijski Institut (YUBIN) - Yugoslav Institute for Bibliography and Information, Terazije 26, Belgrade, Yugoslavia. FAX 11-687-760. Ed. Radomir Glavicki.
●Also available online.

079 015　　　　YU　　ISSN 0350-0349
Z6956.Y9
BIBLIOGRAFIJA JUGOSLAVIJE. SERIJSKE PUBLIKACIJE. 1959. a. $557 or exchange basis. Jugoslovenski Bibliografsko-Informacijski Institut (YUBIN) - Yugoslav Institute for Bibliography and Information, Terazije 26, Belgrade, Yugoslavia. FAX 11-687-760. Ed. Radomir Glavicki. index.
Formerly (until 1975): Bibliografia Jugoslovenske Periodike (ISSN 0006-1158)

015　　　　　　YU　　ISSN 0354-6551
BIBLIOGRAFIJA KNJIGA U VOJVODINI. 1983. a. Matica Srpska, Matice Srpske 1, 21000 Novi Sad, Yugoslavia. Ed. Miro Vuksanovic.
Formerly (until 1992): Bibligrafija Vojvodine. Serija 1. Monografske Publikacije (ISSN 0352-3241)

015　　　　　　YU　　ISSN 0354-4710
Z6514.T7
BIBLIOGRAFIJA PREVODA U S R J. 1969. a. $206 or exchange basis. Jugoslovenski Bibliografsko-Informacijski Institut (YUBIN) - Yugoslav Institute for Bibliography and Information, Terazije 26, Belgrade, Yugoslavia. FAX 11-687-760. Ed. Radomir Glavicki.
●Also available online.
Formerly: Bibliografija Prevoda u S F R J (ISSN 0350-9974)

BIBLIOGRAFIJA ROTO STAMPE I STRIPOVA. see LITERATURE — Abstracting, Bibliographies, Statistics

015　　　　　　YU　　ISSN 0354-4761
Z2953
BIBLIOGRAFIJA ZVANICNIH PUBLIKACIJA S R J. KNJIGE, SERIJSKE PUBLIKACIJE. 1972. a. $137 or exchange basis. Jugoslovenski Bibliografsko-Informacijski Institut (YUBIN) - Yugoslav Institute for Bibliography and Information, Terazije 26, Belgrade, Yugoslavia. TEL 381-11-687760. FAX 381-11-687760. E-mail: yubin@jbi.jbi.bg.ac.yu. Ed. Radomir Glavicki.
Formerly: Bibliografija Zvanicnih Publikacija S F R J (ISSN 0351-2843)

015　　　　　　RU　　ISSN 0869-6020
BIBLIOGRAFIYA. 1929. bi-m. 15000 Rub. Izdatel'stvo Knizhnaya Palata, Sushchevskii val, 64, 129272 Moscow, Russia. TEL 7-095-2888643. FAX 7-095-2889238. Ed. Galina Alekseeva; Pub. Kurilko Aleksey. adv.: page $150; adv. contact: Liliya Kulaeva. bk.rev.; illus.; index. circ. 4,000. **Indexed:** Lib.Lit.
—BLDSC (0015.760000); KR SourceOne.
Formerly (until no.3, 1992): Sovetskaya Bibliografiya (ISSN 0131-6265)

960 015　　　　II　　ISSN 0006-1190
BIBLIOGRAPHIA AFRICANA. 1970. m. Rs.2200.($300) K.K. Roy (Private) Ltd., 55 Gariahat Road, P.O. Box 10210, Calcutta 700 019, India. Ed. K.K. Roy. abstr.; index. circ. 2,000. (tabloid format; also avail. in microform)

011　　　　　　BE　　ISSN 0409-3747
BIBLIOGRAPHIA BELGICA. (Text in Dutch, English, French) 1952. irreg. Commission Belge de Bibliographie et de Bibliologie, 4, Boulevard de l'Empereur, 1000 Brussels, Belgium. FAX 32-80-510465. Ed. Christian F. Verbecke. R&P contact: Mireille M. Vanlaecken. circ. 350. **Document type:** bibliography.
—Linda Hall.

BIBLIOGRAPHIA CARTOGRAPHICA; international documentation of cartographical literature. see GEOGRAPHY — Abstracting, Bibliographies, Statistics

BIBLIOGRAPHIA DE INTERLINGUA. see LINGUISTICS — Abstracting, Bibliographies, Statistics

BIBLIOGRAPHIA MEDICA CECHOSLOVACA. see MEDICAL SCIENCES — Abstracting, Bibliographies, Statistics

BIBLIOGRAPHIC GUIDE TO ANTHROPOLOGY AND ARCHAEOLOGY. see ANTHROPOLOGY — Abstracting, Bibliographies, Statistics

BIBLIOGRAPHIC GUIDE TO ART AND ARCHITECTURE. see ARCHITECTURE — Abstracting, Bibliographies, Statistics

BIBLIOGRAPHIC GUIDE TO BLACK STUDIES. see ETHNIC INTERESTS — Abstracting, Bibliographies, Statistics

011　　　　　　US　　ISSN 0360-2729
Z5051
BIBLIOGRAPHIC GUIDE TO CONFERENCE PUBLICATIONS. (Text in various languages) 1974. a. $410 (effective 1997). G.K. Hall & Co., MacMillan Library Reference USA, Box 159, Thorndike, ME 04986. TEL 212-654-8452; 800-223-6121. FAX 207-948-2863. URL: http://www.mir.com/thordike. (Subscr. to: Simon & Schuster, Library Reference Order Processing, 200 Old Tappan Rd., Old Tappan, NJ 07675. TEL 800-223-2336). **Document type:** bibliography, abstracting/indexing.
—BLDSC (1964.890000); CISTI.
Formerly: Conference Publications Guide (ISSN 0091-7907)
Description: Indexes approximately 26,000 private and government conference publications including proceedings, reports, and summaries of conferences, meetings, and symposia in all fields.

BIBLIOGRAPHIC GUIDE TO DANCE. see DANCE — Abstracting, Bibliographies, Statistics

BIBLIOGRAPHIC GUIDE TO EAST ASIAN STUDIES. see ORIENTAL STUDIES — Abstracting, Bibliographies, Statistics

BIBLIOGRAPHIC GUIDE TO EDUCATION. see EDUCATION — Abstracting, Bibliographies, Statistics

015　　　　　　US　　ISSN 0360-280X
Z7164.G7
BIBLIOGRAPHIC GUIDE TO GOVERNMENT PUBLICATIONS - FOREIGN. 1980. a. $720 (effective 1997). G.K. Hall & Co., MacMillan Library Reference USA, Box 159, Thorndike, ME 04986. TEL 212-654-8452; 800-223-6121. FAX 207-948-2863. URL: http://www.mir.com/thorndike. (Subscr. to: Simon & Schuster, Library Reference Order Processing, 200 Old Tappan Rd., Old Tappan, NJ 07675. TEL 800-223-2336). **Document type:** bibliography, abstracting/indexing.
—BLDSC (1964.893300).
Description: Lists materials catalogued during the past year by the New York Public Library, including additional entries from LC MARC tapes.

011　　　　　　US　　ISSN 0360-2796
Z7164.G7
BIBLIOGRAPHIC GUIDE TO GOVERNMENT PUBLICATIONS - U S. (Text in various languages) 1982. a. $620 (effective 1997). G.K. Hall & Co., MacMillan Library Reference USA, Box 159, Thorndike, ME 04986. TEL 212-654-8452; 800-223-6121. FAX 207-948-2863. URL: http://www.mir.com/thorndike. (Subscr. to: Simon & Schuster, Library Reference Order Processing, 200 Old Tappan Rd., Old Tappan, NJ 07675. TEL 800-223-2336). **Document type:** bibliography, abstracting/indexing.
Formerly: Government Publications Guide (ISSN 0091-7915)
Description: Covers all state, regional and federal government literature.

015　　　　　　US　　ISSN 0162-5314
Z1610
BIBLIOGRAPHIC GUIDE TO LATIN AMERICAN STUDIES. 1978. a. $665 (effective 1997). G.K. Hall & Co., MacMillan Library Reference USA, Box 159, Thorndike, ME 04986. TEL 212-654-8452; 800-223-6121. FAX 207-948-2863. URL: http://www.mir.com/thorndike. (Subscr. to: Simon & Schuster, Library Reference Order Processing, 200 Old Tappan Rd., Old Tappan, NJ 07675. TEL 800-223-2336) **Document type:** bibliography, abstracting/indexing.
Description: Includes 31,000 new acquisitions by the Nettie Lee Benson Latin American Collection in the Texas Library, Austin, and the Library of Congress. Covers all library materials written by Latin American authors, materials published anywhere in the world pertaining to Latin America, and materials in any language, including Indian dialects of Latin America.

BIBLIOGRAPHIC GUIDE TO LAW. see LAW — Abstracting, Bibliographies, Statistics

BIBLIOGRAPHIC GUIDE TO MAPS AND ATLASES. see GEOGRAPHY — Abstracting, Bibliographies, Statistics

BIBLIOGRAPHIC GUIDE TO MIDDLE EASTERN STUDIES. see ORIENTAL STUDIES — Abstracting, Bibliographies, Statistics

BIBLIOGRAPHIC GUIDE TO MUSIC. see MUSIC — Abstracting, Bibliographies, Statistics

BIBLIOGRAPHIC GUIDE TO NORTH AMERICAN HISTORY. see HISTORY — Abstracting, Bibliographies, Statistics

BIBLIOGRAPHIC GUIDE TO PSYCHOLOGY. see PSYCHOLOGY — Abstracting, Bibliographies, Statistics

BIBLIOGRAPHIC GUIDE TO SLAVIC, BALTIC, AND EURASIAN STUDIES. see HISTORY — Abstracting, Bibliographies, Statistics

600 016　　　　US　　ISSN 0360-2761
Z5854
BIBLIOGRAPHIC GUIDE TO TECHNOLOGY. 1974. a. $410 (effective 1997). G.K. Hall & Co., MacMillan Library Reference USA, Box 159, Thorndike, ME 04986. TEL 212-654-8452; 800-223-6121. FAX 207-948-2863. TELEX 94-0037. URL: http://www.mir.com/thorndike. (Subscr. to: Simon & Schuster, Library Reference Order Processing, 200 Old Tappan Rd., Old Tappan, NJ 07675. TEL 800-223-2336) **Document type:** bibliography, abstracting/indexing.
—CISTI.
Formerly: Technology Book Guide (ISSN 0091-7885)
Description: Covers all aspects of technology.

011　　　　　　US　　ISSN 0006-1255
Z1002
BIBLIOGRAPHIC INDEX; a subject list of bibliographies in English and foreign languages. 1937. 3/yr. (3rd issue cumulates all three issues). service basis. H.W. Wilson Co., 950 University Ave., Bronx, NY 10452. TEL 718-588-8400; 800-367-6770. FAX 718-590-1617. TELEX 4990003HWILSON. Ed. Laurel Cooley. **Document type:** abstracting/indexing.
●Also available online. Vendor(s): Wilsonline (BIB).
—BLDSC (1965.000000).
Description: Lists bibliographies with 50 or more citations published in books, pamphlets, or periodicals.

010　　　　　　CN　　ISSN 0709-3756
BIBLIOGRAPHICAL SOCIETY OF CANADA. BULLETIN. 1973. s-a. membership. Bibliographical Society of Canada - La Societe Bibliographique du Canada, P.O. Box 575, Sta. "P", Toronto, ON M5S 2T1, Canada. E-mail: dondertman@library.utoronto.ca; URL: http://www.library.utoronto.ca/-bsc. Ed. Merrill Distad. circ. 400 (controlled). (back issues avail.) **Document type:** newsletter.
●Also available on CD-ROM.
Description: Provides news of the Society and its members as well as information about lectures, exhibitions, research and publication.

010　　　　　　CN　　ISSN 0067-687X
BIBLIOGRAPHICAL SOCIETY OF CANADA. FACSIMILE SERIES. 1951. irreg. price varies. Bibliographical Society of Canada - La Societe Bibliographique du Canada, P.O. Box 575, Sta. "P", Toronto, ON M5S 2T1, Canada. E-mail: dondertman@library.utoronto.ca; URL: http://www.library.utoronto.ca/-bsc. circ. 400. **Document type:** monographic series.
●Also available on CD-ROM.

010　　　　　　CN　　ISSN 0067-6888
BIBLIOGRAPHICAL SOCIETY OF CANADA. MONOGRAPHS. 1957. irreg. price varies. Bibliographical Society of Canada - La Societe Bibliographique du Canada, P.O. Box 575, Sta. "P", Toronto, ON M5S 2T1, Canada. E-mail: dondertman@library.utoronto.ca; URL: http://www.library.utoronto.ca/-bsc. circ. 400. **Document type:** monographic series.
●Also available on CD-ROM.

BIBLIOGRAPHIES

010 CN ISSN 0067-6896
BIBLIOGRAPHICAL SOCIETY OF CANADA. PAPERS. (Text in English and French) 1962. s-a. Can.$35 to individuals; institutions Can.$50 (effective 1998). Bibliographical Society of Canada - La Societe Bibliographique du Canada, P.O. Box 575, Sta. "P", Toronto, ON M5S 2T1, Canada. E-mail: dondertman@library.utoronto.ca; URL: http://www.library.utoronto.ca/~bsc. Ed. Michel Brisebois. bk.rev. circ. 400. **Document type:** academic/scholarly publication.
●Also available on CD-ROM.
—KR SourceOne.
Supersedes: Bibliographical Society of Canada. Newsletter.
Description: Offers scholarly articles and book reviews on all aspects of bibliography including printing and publishing history and textual studies.
Refereed Serial

015 MG ISSN 0067-6926
BIBLIOGRAPHIE ANNUELLE DE MADAGASCAR. 1964. a. 500 Fr.($2) Universite de Madagascar, Bibliotheque Universitaire, B.P. 908, Antananarivo, Madagascar. index. circ. 1,500.

011 SZ ISSN 1012-1331
BIBLIOGRAPHIE ANNUELLE DES LETTRES ROMANDES. (Text in French) 1979. a. 30 SFr. Schweizerische Landesbibliothek - Bibliotheque Nationale Suisse, Hallwylstr. 15, CH-3003 Bern, Switzerland. TEL 41-31-3228911. FAX 41-31-3228463. E-mail: illizch@slb.admin.ch; URL: http://www.snl.ch/. Ed. Marie-Therese Lathion. **Document type:** bibliography.

BIBLIOGRAPHIE ANNUELLE DU MOYEN AGE TARDIF; auteurs et textes latins, vers 1300-1500. see *HISTORY — Abstracting, Bibliographies, Statistics*

015 BE ISSN 0006-1336
Z2405 CODEN: BIBEBJ
BIBLIOGRAPHIE DE BELGIQUE/BELGISCHE BIBLIOGRAFIE. (Former name of issuing body: Bibliotheque Royale de Belgique) (Text in Dutch, French) 1875. m. 6000 BEF. Bibliotheque Royale Albert 1er - Koninklijke Bibliotheek Albert I, 4 bd. de l'Empereur, 1000 Brussels, Belgium. Ed. W. Vanderpijpen. index. (reprint service avail. from KTO) **Document type:** bibliography.
—KNAW.

BIBLIOGRAPHIE DE L'AFRIQUE SUD-SAHARIENNE; sciences humaines et sociales. see *SOCIAL SCIENCES: COMPREHENSIVE WORKS — Abstracting, Bibliographies, Statistics*

011 016 AE ISSN 0523-2392
BIBLIOGRAPHIE DE L'ALGERIE/AL-BIBLIYUGRAFYA AL-DJAZAIRIYAH. (Text in Arabic, French) 1964. s-a. 40 din.($20) Bibliotheque Nationale, Service du Depot Legal, 1 Ave. Frantz Fanon, 16000 Algiers, Algeria. TEL 63-06-32. Ed.Bd. adv. circ. 1,500. (back issues avail.) **Document type:** bibliography.
Description: Lists Algerian publications deposited at the National Library.

015 966 IV ISSN 0084-7860
Z3689
BIBLIOGRAPHIE DE LA COTE D'IVOIRE. 1969. a. 3000 Fr.CFA. Bibliotheque Nationale, B.P. V 180, Abidjan, Ivory Coast. (processed)

BIBLIOGRAPHIE DER BERNER GESCHICHTE/BIBLIOGRAPHIE DE L'HISTOIRE BERNOISE. see *HISTORY — Abstracting, Bibliographies, Statistics*

BIBLIOGRAPHIE DER BUCH- UND BIBLIOTHEKSGESCHICHTE. see *LIBRARY AND INFORMATION SCIENCES — Abstracting, Bibliographies, Statistics*

011 900 SZ ISSN 0378-4584
BIBLIOGRAPHIE DER SCHWEIZERGESCHICHTE/BIBLIOGRAPHIE DE L'HISTOIRE SUISSE. (Text in French, German) 1913. a. 30 SFr. Schweizerische Landesbibliothek - Bibliotheque Nationale Suisse, Hallwylstr. 15, CH-3003 Bern, Switzerland. TEL 41-31-3228911. FAX 41-31-3228463. E-mail: illizch@slb.admin.ch; URL: http://www.snl.ch/. Ed. Pierre-Louis Surchat. **Document type:** bibliography.

011 GW ISSN 0340-6121
BIBLIOGRAPHIE DER WIRTSCHAFTSWISSENSCHAFTEN. 1905. s-a. price varies. Vandenhoeck und Ruprecht, Robert-Bosch-Breite 6, 37079 Goettingen, Germany. TEL 49-551-6959-26. FAX 49-551-695917. (Subscr. to: 37070 Goettingen, Germany) **Document type:** bibliography.
—CCC.

BIBLIOGRAPHIE DES SCHWEIZERISCHEN RECHTS. see *LAW — Abstracting, Bibliographies, Statistics*

015.7 CN ISSN 0006-1441
Z1392.Q3
BIBLIOGRAPHIE DU QUEBEC. 1968. m. Can.$140. Bibliotheque Nationale du Quebec, Section de l'Edition, 2275 rue Holt, Montreal, PQ H2G 3H1, Canada. TEL 514-873-1100. FAX 514-873-9932. index. **Document type:** bibliography.
—CISTI.

016.966 SG ISSN 0378-9942
BIBLIOGRAPHIE DU SENEGAL. (Supplements avail.) (Text in French) 1962. s-a. Secretariat General du Gouvernement, Direction des Archives, Immeuble Administratif, Dakar, Senegal. TEL 221-23-10-88. FAX 221-22-55-78. **Document type:** bibliography.

BIBLIOGRAPHIE GEOGRAPHIQUE INTERNATIONALE. F R A N C I S. 531. see *GEOGRAPHY — Abstracting, Bibliographies, Statistics*

949.3 011 LU ISSN 0253-1631
BIBLIOGRAPHIE LUXEMBOURGEOISE. 1944. a. 450 Fr. Bibliotheque Nationale, 37 Boulevard F.D. Roosevelt, L-2450 Luxembourg, Luxembourg. TEL 22-62-55. FAX 475672. (back issues avail.) **Document type:** bibliography.
Description: Official current Luxembourg bibliography. Lists publications printed in Luxembourg or concerning Luxembourg and those published by Luxembourgers.

BIBLIOGRAPHIE NATIONALE FRANCAISE. ATLAS, CARTES ET PLANS. see *GEOGRAPHY — Abstracting, Bibliographies, Statistics*

015 070.5 FR ISSN 1142-3250
Z2165 CODEN: BIFRA9
BIBLIOGRAPHIE NATIONALE FRANCAISE. LIVRES. 1811. 26/yr. (CD-ROM q.). 2850 F. (foreign 3165 F.) (effective 1997). Bibliotheque Nationale de France, Quai Francois Mauriac, 75706 Paris Cedex 13, France. TEL 33-1-47038610.
FAX 33-1-47038586. adv.; bk.rev.; index. circ. 600. (also avail. in microfilm from PMC; reprint service avail. from KTO) **Document type:** bibliography.
●Also available on CD-ROM. Producer(s): Chadwyck-Healey Inc.
—CISTI; Linda Hall.
Former titles (until 1990): Bibliographie de la France. Livres (ISSN 0150-1402); (until 1977): Bibliographie de la France. 1ere Partie, Bibliographie Officielle (ISSN 0335-5667); Supersedes in part (in 1979): Bibliographie de la France. Biblio (ISSN 0335-5675); Which was formed by the merger of (1933-1971): Biblio (Mensuel) (ISSN 1147-6710); (1814-1971): Bibliographie de la France (ISSN 0006-1344); Which was formerly: Bibliographie de l'Empire Francais (ISSN 1147-6680); (until 1811): Journal General de l'Imprimerie et de la Librairie (ISSN 1147-6672); (1797-1810): Journal Typographique et Bibliographique (ISSN 1147-6664).

BIBLIOGRAPHIE NATIONALE FRANCAISE. MUSIQUE. see *MUSIC — Abstracting, Bibliographies, Statistics*

015 FR ISSN 1142-3269
Z2161
BIBLIOGRAPHIE NATIONALE FRANCAISE. PUBLICATIONS EN SERIE. 1946. 12/yr. 1430 F. (foreign 1630 F.) (effective 1997). Bibliotheque Nationale de France, Quai Francois Mauriac, 75706 Paris Cedex 13, France. TEL 33-1-47038610.
FAX 33-1-47038586. Ed. P.-A. Berend. index. **Document type:** bibliography.
●Also available on CD-ROM. Producer(s): Chadwyck-Healey Inc.
—Linda Hall.
Former titles (until 1990): Bibliographie de la France. Supplement 1. Publications en Serie (ISSN 0150-1399); (until 1977): Bibliographie de la France. 1ere Partie, Bibliographie Officielle. Supplement 1, Publications en Serie (ISSN 1147-6869); (until 1975): Bibliographie de la France. Supplement A, Periodiques (ISSN 1147-6850); Supersedes in part (in 1946): Bibliographie de la France (ISSN 0006-1344)

015 FR ISSN 1142-3277
Z2161
BIBLIOGRAPHIE NATIONALE FRANCAISE. PUBLICATIONS OFFICIELLES. 1857. 6/yr. 1040 F. (foreign 1170 F.) (effective 1997). Bibliotheque Nationale de France, Quai Francois Mauriac, 75706 Paris Cedex 13, France. TEL 33-1-47038610.
FAX 33-1-47038586. Ed. P.-A. Berend. index. **Document type:** bibliography.
●Also available on CD-ROM. Producer(s): Chadwyck-Healey Inc.
—Linda Hall.
Former titles (until 1990): Bibliographie de la France. Supplement 2. Publications Officielles (ISSN 0150-5955); (until 1977): Bibliographie de la France. 1ere Partie, Bibliographie Officielle. Supplement 2. Publications Officielles (ISSN 1149-6932); (until 1975): Bibliographie de la France. Supplement F. Publications Officielles (ISSN 1147-6990); Supersedes in part (in 1946): Bibliographie de la France (ISSN 0006-1344)

370 016 GW ISSN 0947-5524
Z5813
BIBLIOGRAPHIE PAEDAGOGIK/EDUCATIONAL BIBLIOGRAPHY. (Text in English, German) 1967. a. (in 2 vols.). DM.308 (foreign DM.318) (effective 1998). (Fachinformationssystem Bildung) V W B - Verlag fuer Wissenschaft und Bildung, Markgrafenstr. 67, 10969 Berlin, Germany. TEL 49-30-2510415. FAX 49-30-2510412. E-mail: 100615.1565@compuserve.com. (Co-sponsor: Gesellschaft Information Bildung) circ. 300. (back issues avail.) **Document type:** bibliography.
Formed by the 1991 merger of: Bibliographie Paedagogik. Reihe A: Zeitschriftenaufsaetze (ISSN 0176-2567); Bibliographie Paedagogik. Reihe B: Buecher - Sondersammelgebiet Bildungsforschung in Erlangen (ISSN 0176-2575); Which were formerly: Bibliographie Paedagogik (ISSN 0523-2678); Which incorporated: Bibliographie Programmierter Unterricht (ISSN 0067-7027).
Description: Contains 13,000 to 16,000 literature references pertaining to all educational subjects.

BIBLIOGRAPHIE PAPYROLOGIQUE. see *ARCHAEOLOGY — Abstracting, Bibliographies, Statistics*

BIBLIOGRAPHIE ZUR EUROPAEISCHEN DIMENSION DES BILDUNGSWESEN/BIBLIOGRAPHY ON THE EUROPEAN DIMENSION OF EDUCATION. see *EDUCATION — Abstracting, Bibliographies, Statistics*

BIBLIOGRAPHIE ZUR SYMBOLIK, IKONOGRAPHIE UND MYTHOLOGIE. see *ANTHROPOLOGY — Abstracting, Bibliographies, Statistics*

BIBLIOGRAPHIEN ZUR PHILOSOPHIE. see *PHILOSOPHY*

BIBLIOGRAPHIES AND INDEXES IN ECONOMICS AND ECONOMIC HISTORY. see *BUSINESS AND ECONOMICS — Abstracting, Bibliographies, Statistics*

BIBLIOGRAPHIES AND INDEXES IN ETHNIC STUDIES. see *ETHNIC INTERESTS — Abstracting, Bibliographies, Statistics*

BIBLIOGRAPHIES AND INDEXES IN LATIN AMERICAN AND CARIBBEAN STUDIES. see *HISTORY — Abstracting, Bibliographies, Statistics*

BIBLIOGRAPHIES

BIBLIOGRAPHIES AND INDEXES IN SCIENCE FICTION, FANTASY, AND HORROR. see *LITERATURE — Abstracting, Bibliographies, Statistics*

BIBLIOGRAPHIES AND INDEXES IN WOMEN'S STUDIES. see *WOMEN'S STUDIES — Abstracting, Bibliographies, Statistics*

BIBLIOGRAPHIES IN TECHNOLOGY AND SOCIAL CHANGE. see *TECHNOLOGY: COMPREHENSIVE WORKS — Abstracting, Bibliographies, Statistics*

011 US
BIBLIOGRAPHIES OF AMERICAN NOTABLES. 1990. irreg. price varies. Praeger Publishers (Subsidiary of: Greenwood Publishing Group Inc.), 88 Post Rd. W., Box 5007, Westport, CT 06881-5007. TEL 203-226-3571. FAX 203-222-1502. **Document type:** bibliography, monographic series.

BIBLIOGRAPHIES OF BATTLES AND LEADERS. see *MILITARY — Abstracting, Bibliographies, Statistics*

011 800 US ISSN 0749-470X
BIBLIOGRAPHIES OF MODERN AUTHORS. 1984. irreg., no.29, 1994 (approx. 5/yr.). price varies. Borgo Press, Box 2845, San Bernardino, CA 92406. TEL 909-884-5813. FAX 909-888-4942. E-mail: borgopr@gte.net; URL: http://www.borgopress.com. Ed. Boden Clarke; Pub. Robert Reginald. **Document type:** bibliography.
Description: Comprehensive annotated primary and secondary bibliographies of writers of our times, with complete listings of all appearances of the author's books, short fiction, nonfiction, interviews, juvenilia, editorial credits, drama, verse, and screen work.

BIBLIOGRAPHISCHE INFORMATIONEN ZU MIGRATION UND ETHNIZITAET. see *SOCIOLOGY — Abstracting, Bibliographies, Statistics*

BIBLIOGRAPHISCHE INFORMATIONEN ZUR ITALIENISCHEN GESCHICHTE IM 19. UND 20. JAHRHUNDERT. see *HISTORY — Abstracting, Bibliographies, Statistics*

BIBLIOGRAPHY AND INDEX OF GEOLOGY. see *EARTH SCIENCES — Abstracting, Bibliographies, Statistics*

BIBLIOGRAPHY AND SUBJECT INDEX OF SOUTH AFRICAN GEOLOGY. see *EARTH SCIENCES — Abstracting, Bibliographies, Statistics*

BIBLIOGRAPHY OF AGRICULTURE. see *AGRICULTURE — Abstracting, Bibliographies, Statistics*

BIBLIOGRAPHY OF AGRICULTURE. ANNUAL CUMULATIVE INDEX. see *AGRICULTURE — Abstracting, Bibliographies, Statistics*

BIBLIOGRAPHY OF BUSINESS - COMPETITIVE AND BENCHMARKING LITERATURE. see *BUSINESS AND ECONOMICS — Abstracting, Bibliographies, Statistics*

011 GW ISSN 0724-8415
Z3106
BIBLIOGRAPHY OF CHINESE STUDIES; selected articles on China in Chinese, English and German. (Text in Chinese, English, German) 1983. a. DM.18. Deutsches Uebersee-Institut, Uebersee-Dokumentation, Neuer Jungfernstieg 21, 20354 Hamburg, Germany. TEL 49-40-3562-598. FAX 49-40-3562512. E-mail: duei-dok@hwwa.uni-hamburg.de; URL: http://www.rrz.uni-hamburg.de/duei-dok. Ed. Yu-hsi Nieh. bibl. circ. 100. (back issues avail.) **Document type:** bibliography.

BIBLIOGRAPHY OF COMPOSITES MANUFACTURING TECHNICAL RESOURCES. see *ENGINEERING — Abstracting, Bibliographies, Statistics*

BIBLIOGRAPHY OF COMPUTER AND AUTOMATED SYSTEMS TECHNICAL RESOURCES. see *COMPUTERS — Abstracting, Bibliographies, Statistics*

BIBLIOGRAPHY OF DOCTORAL DISSERTATIONS: NATURAL AND APPLIED SCIENCES. see *SCIENCES: COMPREHENSIVE WORKS — Abstracting, Bibliographies, Statistics*

BIBLIOGRAPHY OF DOCTORAL DISSERTATIONS: SOCIAL SCIENCES AND HUMANITIES. see *SOCIAL SCIENCES: COMPREHENSIVE WORKS — Abstracting, Bibliographies, Statistics*

BIBLIOGRAPHY OF ECONOMIC AND SOCIAL DEVELOPMENT SRI LANKA. see *BUSINESS AND ECONOMICS — Abstracting, Bibliographies, Statistics*

BIBLIOGRAPHY OF ECONOMIC AND STATISTICAL PUBLICATIONS ON TANZANIA. see *BUSINESS AND ECONOMICS — Abstracting, Bibliographies, Statistics*

BIBLIOGRAPHY OF ECONOMIC GEOLOGY. see *EARTH SCIENCES — Abstracting, Bibliographies, Statistics*

BIBLIOGRAPHY OF ELECTRONICS MANUFACTURING TECHNICAL RESOURCES. see *ELECTRONICS — Abstracting, Bibliographies, Statistics*

BIBLIOGRAPHY OF MACHINE VISION TECHNICAL RESOURCES. see *ENGINEERING — Abstracting, Bibliographies, Statistics*

BIBLIOGRAPHY OF MACHINING TECHNOLOGY TECHNICAL RESOURCES. see *ENGINEERING — Abstracting, Bibliographies, Statistics*

BIBLIOGRAPHY OF MATERIAL FORMING TECHNICAL RESOURCES. see *ENGINEERING — Abstracting, Bibliographies, Statistics*

011 410 US
BIBLIOGRAPHY OF MEDIAEVAL LATIN LEXICOLOGY. irreg., latest no.3. $69.95 per no. Edwin Mellen Press, 415 Ridge St., Box 450, Lewiston, NY 14092. TEL 716-754-2788. FAX 716-754-4056. **Document type:** monographic series.

BIBLIOGRAPHY OF NORTH WEST ENGLAND. see *HISTORY — History Of Europe*

BIBLIOGRAPHY OF RAPID PROTOTYPING RESOURCES. see *COMPUTERS — Abstracting, Bibliographies, Statistics*

BIBLIOGRAPHY OF ROBOTIC TECHNICAL RESOURCES. see *COMPUTERS — Abstracting, Bibliographies, Statistics*

BIBLIOGRAPHY OF SEISMOLOGY. see *EARTH SCIENCES — Abstracting, Bibliographies, Statistics*

BIBLIOGRAPHY OF SKIING STUDIES. see *SPORTS AND GAMES — Abstracting, Bibliographies, Statistics*

BIBLIOGRAPHY OF TECHNICAL RESOURCES ON PLASTICS IN THE 90'S. see *PLASTICS — Abstracting, Bibliographies, Statistics*

BIBLIOGRAPHY OF THE HISTORY OF MEDICINE. see *MEDICAL SCIENCES — Abstracting, Bibliographies, Statistics*

016 SY ISSN 0067-7302
BIBLIOGRAPHY OF THE MIDDLE EAST.* (Subseries of Syrian Documentation Papers) a. $25. Syrian Documentation Papers, P.O. Box 2712, Damascus, Syria.

015 UK ISSN 0968-0748
Z2071
BIBLIOGRAPHY OF WALES. Key Title: Llyfryddriaeth Cymru. 1909. irreg. (approx. biennial), latest 1997 (for 1993). £40. National Library of Wales - Llyfrgell Genedlaethol Cymru, Aberystwyth, Ceredigion SY23 3BU, Wales. FAX 44-1970-615709. E-mail: holi@llgc.org.uk; URL: http://www.llgc.org.uk. R&P contact: Mari Wyn. index. circ. 450. **Indexed:** Br.Archaeol.Abstr. **Document type:** bibliography. —BLDSC (2015.123000).
Formed by the 1992 merger of: Bibliotheca Celtica (ISSN 0067-7914); (1978-199?): Subject Index to Welsh Periodicals.

BIBLIOGRAPHY ON CABLE TELEVISION. see *COMMUNICATIONS — Abstracting, Bibliographies, Statistics*

BIBLIOGRAPHY ON COLD REGIONS SCIENCE & TECHNOLOGY. see *ENGINEERING — Abstracting, Bibliographies, Statistics*

BIBLIOGRAPHY ON FOREIGN AND COMPARATIVE LAW: BOOKS AND ARTICLES IN ENGLISH. see *LAW — Abstracting, Bibliographies, Statistics*

BIBLIOGRAPHY ON SOILLESS CULTURE. see *AGRICULTURE — Abstracting, Bibliographies, Statistics*

011 UK
▼**BIBLIOLOG;** the spoken word directory. 1995. m. £114. Trade Service Information Ltd., Cherryholt Rd., Stamford, Lincs. PE9 2HI, England. TEL 44-1780-764331. FAX 44-1780-482067. E-mail: info@tsi-ltd.co.uk; URL: http://www.tsi-ltd.co.uk. Ed. Christine Morris. R&P contact: Russell Jackson. adv. contact: Tracey Armstrong. circ. 500 (paid). **Document type:** directory.
Description: Directory of currently available spoken word recordings in the U.K.

BIBLIONEWS AND AUSTRALIAN NOTES AND QUERIES; journal for book collectors. see *PUBLISHING AND BOOK TRADE*

011 US ISSN 0148-9011
BIBLIOSCAN H-L.* 1975. m. $70. Elsim Co., c/o Chivers, 89 Turner St., Ste. 1, Brighton, MA 02135-2525.

011 US ISSN 0148-8996
BIBLIOSCAN Q-Z.* 1974. m. $70. Elsim Co., c/o Chivers, 89 Turner St., Ste. 1, Brighton, MA 02135-2525.

BIBLIOTECA AMADEU AMARAL. SERIE REFERENCIA. see *FOLKLORE — Abstracting, Bibliographies, Statistics*

015 IT ISSN 0067-7418
BIBLIOTECA DI BIBLIOGRAFIA ITALIANA. 1923. irreg., vol.147, 1996. price varies. Casa Editrice Leo S. Olschki, Casella Postale 66, 50100 Florence, Italy. TEL 39-55-6530684. FAX 39-55-6530214. E-mail: celso@olschki.it. circ. 1,000. **Document type:** monographic series.

020 011 UY ISSN 0006-1697
F2781.A2
BIBLIOTECA "JOSE ARTIGAS". BOLETIN - JUNTA DE VECINOS. 1969. q. free. Biblioteca "Jose Artigas", 25 de Mayo 609, Montevideo, Uruguay. abstr.; bibl.; circ. 300 (controlled). (processed) **Document type:** bulletin.
Formerly (until 1974): Junta Departamental de Montevideo. Boletin (ISSN 0797-1745)

015 PE
BIBLIOTECA NACIONAL DE PERU. BIBLIOGRAFIA PERUANA. 1943. irreg., latest 1987-1990 (1 vol.). $35. Biblioteca Nacional de Peru, Apdo. 2335, Lima, Peru. TEL 51-14-287690. FAX 51-14-277331. E-mail: FS___bnp@binape.gob.pe. Ed. Hugo Alvarez. R&P contact: Martha Fernandez de Lopez. bk.rev.; bibl.; illus. circ. 500. **Document type:** bibliography.
Formerly (until 1976): Biblioteca Nacional de Peru. Anuario Bibliografico Peruano.
Description: Peruvian bibliographic compilation

011 IT
BIBLIOTECA STATALE. FONTI E SUSSIDI. 1979. irreg., no.4, 1992. price varies. Biblioteca Statale di Cremona, Via Ugolani Dati 4, 26100 Cremona, Italy. Ed. Emilia Bricchi Piccioni. **Document type:** monographic series.
Description: Lists bibliographic resources available at the Library.

011 IT
BIBLIOTECA STATALE E LIBRERIA CIVICA DI CREMONA. MOSTRE. 1978. irreg., no.19, 1996. exchange basis. Biblioteca Statale e Libreria Civica di Cremona, Via Ugolani Dati 4, Cremona, Italy. Ed. Emilia Brichi Piccioni. circ. 1,780.
Description: Covers historical biographies of various artists.

010 IT ISSN 0067-7531
BIBLIOTECONOMIA E BIBLIOGRAFIA. SAGGI E STUDI. 1964. irreg., vol.27, 1994. price varies. Casa Editrice Leo S. Olschki, Casella Postale 66, 50100 Florence, Italy. TEL 39-55-6530684. FAX 39-55-6530214. E-mail: celso@olschki.it. Ed. Piero Innocenti. circ. 1,000. **Document type:** bibliography.

BIBLIOTEKA CHEMII. see *CHEMISTRY — Abstracting, Bibliographies, Statistics*

011 YU ISSN 0354-7655
BIBLIOTEKA MATICE SRPSKE. BILTEN PRINOVLJENIH KNJIGA ZA STRANIM JEZICIMA. a.? Biblioteka Matice Srpske, Matice Srpske 1, Novi Sad, Yugoslavia. Ed. Miro Vuksanovic.
Formerly: Biblioteka Matice Srpske. Bilten Prinovljenih Stranih Knjiga (ISSN 0354-5717)

BIBLIOTHECA ASCETICO-MYSTICA. see *RELIGIONS AND THEOLOGY — Abstracting, Bibliographies, Statistics*

016   GW   ISSN 0067-7884
BIBLIOTHECA BIBLIOGRAPHICA AURELIANA. (Text in English, French, German, Latin) 1959. irreg., vol.157, 1997. price varies. Verlag Valentin Koerner GmbH, Postfach 100164, 76482 Baden-Baden, Germany. TEL 49-7221-22423. FAX 49-7221-38697. index. **Document type:** monographic series.
    Description: Bibliographies and monographs dealing with Renaissance, humanism and Reformation studies.

011   NE
BIBLIOTHECA BIBLIOGRAPHICA NEERLANDICA. 1968. irreg., no. 34, 1997. price varies. De Graaf Publishers, P.O. Box 6, 2420 AA Nieuwkoop, Netherlands. TEL 31-1725-71461. **Document type:** monographic series, bibliography.

011 200   GW   ISSN 0931-3346
BIBLIOTHECA DISSIDENTIUM. (Subseries of: Bibliotheca Bibliographica Aureliana (ISSN 0067-7884)) (Text in English, French, German and Italian) 1980. irreg., vol.19, 1997. price varies. Verlag Valentin Koerner GmbH, Postfach 100164, 76482 Baden-Baden, Germany. TEL 49-7221-22423. FAX 49-7221-38697. Ed.Bd. circ. 1,000. **Document type:** monographic series.
    Description: Bibliographies and monographs of 16th and 17th century religious dissidents.

011   UK   ISSN 0006-193X
THE BIBLIOTHECK; a Scottish journal of bibliography and allied topics. 1956. 3/yr. Library Association, Scottish Group, George IV Bridge, Edinburgh EH1 1EW, Scotland. Ed. W. Kelly. adv.; bk.rev.; bibl.; cum.index: 1956-1970. circ. 300. **Indexed:** Abstr.Engl.Stud., IBR, LISA, M.L.A., MLA Intl.Bibl. —BLDSC (2019.680000); KR SourceOne.

960 016   BE   ISSN 0774-8353
BIBLIOTHEQUE AFRICAINE. LISTE DES ACQUISITIONS. 1983. q. free. Bibliotheque Africaine, 19 rue des petits Carmes, 1000 Brussels, Belgium. TEL 32-2-5013544. FAX 32-2-5013669. TELEX 25731. Ed.Bd. circ. 1,000. **Document type:** bibliography.
    ●Also available online. Vendor(s): BELINDIS (AFLI).
    Description: Lists recent acquisitions in the field of African studies.

011   CG
BIBLIOTHEQUE NATIONALE. BIBLIOGRAPHIE NATIONALE. (Text in French) 1971. irreg., latest 1975. Bibliotheque Nationale, B.P. 3090, Kinshasa-Gombe, Democratic Republic of the Congo.

015   BO
BIO-BIBLIOGRAFIA BOLIVIANA. 1962. a. $170. Los Amigos del Libro, Casilla 450, Cochabamba, Bolivia. TEL 591-42-54114. FAX 591-411-5128. Ed. Werner Guttentag. R&P contact: Werner Guttentag. adv.; bk.rev.; index. circ. 500. **Document type:** bibliography.
    Formerly: Bibliografia Boliviana (ISSN 0067-6578)

BIO-BIBLIOGRAPHIES IN AFRO-AMERICAN AND AFRICAN STUDIES. see *ETHNIC INTERESTS — Abstracting, Bibliographies, Statistics*

BIOBIBLIOGRAPHIES ET EXPOSES. see *LINGUISTICS — Abstracting, Bibliographies, Statistics*

BIULETIN ZA NOVONABAVENI KNIGI NA CHUZHDI EZITZI. SERIIA B: ESTESTVENI I PRILOZHNI NAUKI. see *BIOLOGY — Abstracting, Bibliographies, Statistics*

BIULETIN ZA NOVONABAVENI KNIGI NA CHUZHDI ETZIZI. SERIIA A: OBSHTESTVENI I HUMANITARNI NAUKI. see *SOCIAL SCIENCES: COMPREHENSIVE WORKS — Abstracting, Bibliographies, Statistics*

011.62   DK   ISSN 0106-9713
BOERNEBIBLIOTEKSKATALOG. BOEGER & TIDSSKRIFTER. EMNEKATALOG. (Not avail. in printed format) 1975. a. (plus supplements). Dansk BiblioteksCenter as, Tempovej 7-11, DK-2750 Ballerup, Denmark. TEL 45-44-867777. FAX 45-44-867892. E-mail: dbc@dan.bib.dk. **Document type:** catalog.
    ●Also available online.
    Also available on CD-ROM.

011.62   DK   ISSN 0106-9691
BOERNEBIBLIOTEKSKATALOG. BOEGER & TIDSSKRIFTER. FORFATTERKATALOG. (Not avail. in printed format) 1975. a. (plus supplements). Dansk BiblioteksCenter as, Tempovej 7-11, DK-2750 Ballerup, Denmark. TEL 45-44-867777. FAX 45-44-867892. E-mail: dbc@dan.bib.dk. **Document type:** catalog.
    ●Also available online.
    Also available on CD-ROM.

011.62   DK   ISSN 0106-9705
BOERNEBIBLIOTEKSKATALOG. BOEGER & TIDSSKRIFTER. TITELKATALOG. 1975. a. (plus supplements). DKK 657.60 (effective 1996). Dansk BiblioteksCenter as, Tempovej 7-11, DK-2750 Ballerup, Denmark. TEL 45-44-867777. FAX 45-44-867892. E-mail: dbc@dan.bib.dk. **Document type:** catalog.
    ●Also available online.
    Also available on CD-ROM.

011   GW   ISSN 0940-0044
Z2225
BOERSENBLATT FUER DEN DEUTSCHEN BUCHHANDEL. 1945. s-w. DM.64.10 per mo. (Boersenverein des Deutschen Buchhandels) Buchhaendler-Vereinigung GmbH, Postfach 100442, 60004 Frankfurt a.M., Germany. TEL 49-69-13060. FAX 49-69-1306201. adv. contact: Etta Nolte. bk.rev.; index. circ. 12,500. **Indexed:** Bibl.Cart., IBR. **Document type:** trade publication.
—SWETS. **CCC.**
    Formed by the merger of (1945-1991): Boersenblatt fuer den Deutschen Buchhandel. Frankfurter Ausgabe (ISSN 0340-7373); Boersenblatt fuer den Deutschen Buchhandel. Leipziger Ausgabe.

011   BO   ISSN 0006-6141
BOLETIN BIBLIOGRAFICO BOLIVIANO.* (Text in Spanish; summaries in English, Spanish) 1955. m. Bol.$80($10) Av. Manco Kapac 269, Dept. 3F, La Paz 30, Bolivia. Ed. Antonio Paredes-Candia. adv.; bk.rev.; bibl.; mkt.; index. circ. 500.

015   CK   ISSN 0121-2400
BOLETIN BIBLIOGRAFICO I S B N. (International Standard Book Number) 1989. s-a. free. Camara Colombiana del Libro, Carrera 17A, No. 37-27, Bogota, Colombia. TEL 2886188. FAX 2873320. Ed. Miguel Laverde Espejo. **Document type:** bibliography.
    Description: Lists Colombian books registered under their ISBN system.

011 015   MX   ISSN 0185-2027
Z1415
BOLETIN BIBLIOGRAFICO MEXICANO. 1940. bi-m. $15. Libreria de Porrua Hermanos y Cia., S.A., A. Rep. de Argentina, 15, 06020 Mexico, D.F., Mexico. TEL 52-5-7025467. FAX 52-5-7024574. URL: http://www.luit.com/porrua/home.html. (Subscr. to: Apdo. M7990, Delegacion Cuauhtemoc, 06020 Mexico D.F., Mexico) Ed. Jose Antonio Perez Porrua. adv.; bk.rev.; bibl.; illus. circ. 25,000. (also avail. in microform from UMI; reprint service avail. from UMI) **Indexed:** Amer.Hist.& Life, Hist.Abstr. **Document type:** bulletin.
—UMI.
    Description: Lists books and other printed material.

BOLLETTINO DELLA BIBLIOGRAFIA FORESTALE ITALIANA. see *FORESTS AND FORESTRY — Abstracting, Bibliographies, Statistics*

011   IT   ISSN 0006-6680
BOLLETTINO DELLE ACCESSIONI DI PERIODICI E LIBRI.* 1959. s-a. $4 to non-members. Vilmy Ricerche, Via C. Cavour 24, 42013 Casalgrande, Italy. Ed. Mirko A. Montanari. bk.rev.; bibl.; charts; stat. circ. 2,450.

BOOKPLATE JOURNAL. see *PUBLISHING AND BOOK TRADE*

025.0634   US   ISSN 0951-838X
Z7164.C81   CODEN: BPONER
BOOKS & PERIODICALS ONLINE. 1987. a. $325 (effective 1997). Library Technology Alliance, Inc., Box 77232, Washington, DC 20013-8232. TEL 202-789-2099. FAX 202-789-2474. Ed. Nuchine S. Nobari; Pub. Nuchine S. Nobari. circ. 1,050. **Document type:** bibliography, directory.
—BLDSC (2250.136000); CISTI.
    Incorporates (1985-1991): Directory of Periodicals Online - Law and Business (ISSN 0884-089X); (1989-1994): Directory of Periodicals Online - Science and Technology (ISSN 0884-0911); (in 1991): Directory of Periodicals Online - Medical and Humanities.
    Description: An international directory of publications available online and on CD-ROM database, full-text, indexed and abstracted.

011   UK   ISSN 0268-6538
BOOKS AT BOSTON SPA. a. £167 (outside the EU £173) (effective 1997). British Library, Document Supply Centre, Boston Spa, Wetherby, W. Yorks. LS23 7BQ, England. TEL 44-1937-546080. FAX 44-1937-546286. TELEX 557381. (Subscr. to: Turpin Distribution Services Ltd., Blackhorse Rd., Letchworth, Herts. SG6 1HN, England. TEL 44-1462-672555. FAX 44-1462-480947) (microfiche) **Document type:** bibliography.

011   US   ISSN 0147-0787
Z733.P958
BOOKS AT BROWN. 1938. a. $10. Brown University Library, Friends of the Library, Box A, Providence, RI 02912. TEL 401-863-2146. Ed. John Stanley. circ. 400. **Indexed:** M.L.A., MLA Intl.Bibl.

015   KO
BOOKS FROM KOREA. (Text in English) 1971. irreg. free. Korean Publishers Association, 105-2 Sagan-dong, Chongno-ku, Seoul 110-190, S. Korea. TEL 82-2-735-2702. FAX 82-2-738-5414. E-mail: kpasibt@soback.kornet.nm.kr. Ed. Sung Taek Lim; Pub. Choon-Ho Na. R&P contact: Yong Tae Chang. adv. contact: Mi Hyun Lim. bk.rev. circ. 2,000.

010   PK   ISSN 0068-0206
BOOKS FROM PAKISTAN. (Text in English) 1967. a. Rs.15. National Book Council of Pakistan, Theosophical Hall, M.A. Jinnah Rd., Karachi, Pakistan.
    Formerly: English Language Publications from Pakistan.

015.942   UK   ISSN 0045-2572
BOOKS IN ENGLISH; a bibliography compiled from UK and US MARC sources. 1970. bi-m. £525 (foreign £695) (effective 1997). British Library, National Bibliographic Service, Boston Spa, Wetherby, W. Yorks. LS23 7BQ, England. TEL 44-1937-546585. FAX 44-1937-546586. URL: http://portico.bl.uk. (Subscr. to: Turpin Distribution Services, Blackhorse Rd., Letchworth, Herts. SG6 1HN, England. TEL 44-1462-672555. FAX 44-1462-480947) cum. index (1971-1980; 1981-1992). circ. 200. (microfiche) **Document type:** bibliography.
    Description: Author/title listing of English-language books published worldwide.

015   US   ISSN 0068-0214
Z1215
BOOKS IN PRINT. (Issued in 9 vols.: Vols.1-4: Authors; Vols. 5-8: Titles; Vol. 9: Publishers & Distributors) 1947. a. (q. microfiche issue.) $525 for 1997-98 ed. R.R. Bowker, A Division of Reed Elsevier Inc., 121 Chanlon Rd., New Providence, NJ 07974. TEL 908-464-6800. FAX 908-665-3502. TELEX 138 755. E-mail: info@bowker.com; URL: http://www.bowker.com. (Subscr. to: Order Dept., Box 31, New Providence, NJ 07974. TEL 800-521-8110) (also avail. in microfiche; magnetic tape) **Document type:** bibliography, directory.
    ●Also available online. Vendor(s): Knight-Ridder Information, Inc. (File no.470), Lexis-Nexis (BIP), Ovid Technologies, Inc. (BBIP).
    Also available on CD-ROM. Producer(s): Bowker Electronic Publishing (Books in Print PLUS).
—BLDSC (2250.210000); CISTI; Linda Hall. **CCC.**
    Description: Lists all currently published books, with price, ISBN and publisher information.

BIBLIOGRAPHIES

011 US
Z1215
BOOKS IN PRINT ON DISC. 1986. m. $1095. R.R. Bowker, A Division of Reed Elsevier Inc., 121 Chanlon Rd., New Providence, NJ 07974. TEL 908-665-2866; 800-521-8110. FAX 908-665-3528. TELEX 138 755. E-mail: info@bowker.com; URL: http://www.reedref.com. (Subscr. to: Electronic Publishing, 121 Chanlon Rd., New Providence, NJ 07974-1154. TEL 800-323-3288) (avail. for MS-DOS, Windows, or Macintosh) **Document type:** bibliography, directory.
●Available only on CD-ROM. Producer(s): Bowker Electronic Publishing (Books in Print PLUS).
Formerly (until Sep. 1997): Books in Print Plus (ISSN 1062-5100)

070.5 011 US
BOOKS IN PRINT ON MICROFICHE. 1982. q. $795 (effective 1995). R.R. Bowker, A Division of Reed Elsevier Inc., 121 Chanlon Rd., New Providence, NJ 07974. TEL 908-464-6800. FAX 908-665-6688. TELEX 138 755. E-mail: info@bowker.com; URL: http://www.reed-elsevier.com. (Subscr. to: Order Dept., Box 31, New Providence, NJ 07974-9903. TEL 800-521-8110) (microfiche) **Document type:** bibliography, directory.
Description: Provides author and title listings. Each quarterly set cumulates and completely updates Books in Print and Forthcoming Books.

015 US ISSN 0000-0310
Z1215
BOOKS IN PRINT SUPPLEMENT; a mid-year updating service listing new and forthcoming books, price changes, and out-of-print titles. (Supplement to: Books in Print (ISSN 0068-0214)) 1973. a. $260 for 3-vol. set (effective 1996-97). R.R. Bowker, A Division of Reed Elsevier Inc., 121 Chanlon Rd., New Providence, NJ 07974. TEL 908-464-6800. FAX 908-665-3502. TELEX 138 755. E-mail: info@bowker.com; URL: http://www.reedref.com. (Subscr. to: Order Dept., Box 31, New Providence, NJ 07974-9903. TEL 800-521-8110) (also avail. in microfiche; magnetic tape) **Document type:** bibliography, directory.
●Also available online. Vendor(s): Knight-Ridder Information, Inc. (File no.470), Ovid Technologies, Inc. (BBIP).
Also available on CD-ROM. Producer(s): Bowker Electronic Publishing (Books in Print PLUS).
—CISTI. **CCC.**
Description: Covers the six months since publication of current Books in Print volumes. Includes publisher address and phone number changes.

011 US
BOOKS IN PRINT WITH BOOK REVIEWS ON DISC. 1987. m. $1595. R.R. Bowker, A Division of Reed Elsevier Inc., 121 Chanlon Rd., New Providence, NJ 07974. TEL 800-521-8110. FAX 908-665-3528. TELEX 138 755. E-mail: info@bowker.com; URL: http://www.reedref.com. (Subscr. to: Order Dept., Box 31, New Providence, NJ 07974-1154. TEL 800-323-3288) (avail. for MS-DOS or Macintosh or Windows)
●Available only on CD-ROM. Producer(s): Bowker Electronic Publishing (Books in Print PLUS).
Formerly (until Sep. 1997): Books in Print with Book Reviews Plus.
Description: Books in Print Plus with more than 225,000 current, full-text book reviews from Library Journal, Publishers Weekly, School Library Journal, Choice, Booklist, Reference and Research Book News, Sci-Tech Book News, University Press Book News, Kirkus Reviews, and BIOSIS.

551 016 UK ISSN 0140-7805
BOOKS IN THE EARTH SCIENCES; and related topics. 1977. q. £50($75) Bibliographic Press, 52 Little Paddocks, Ferring, Worthing, W. Sussex BN12 5NH, England. TEL 44-1903-504019. FAX 44-1903-503545. Ed. N. Edwards. circ. 70. **Document type:** abstracting/indexing.
Description: Continuing bibliography and index of nonserial titles published in the Roman alphabet.

011 US ISSN 0000-0736
Z1000.5
BOOKS OUT-OF-PRINT. irreg., latest edition 1984-88. $110. R.R. Bowker, A Division of Reed Elsevier Inc., 121 Chanlon Rd., New Providence, NJ 07974. TEL 908-464-6800. FAX 908-665-3502. TELEX 138 755. E-mail: info@bowker.com; URL: http://www.reedref.com. (Subscr. to: Order Dept., Box 31, New Providence, NJ 07974-9903. TEL 800-521-8110) (also avail. in magnetic tape; microfiche) **Document type:** bibliography, directory.
●Also available online. Vendor(s): Knight-Ridder Information, Inc. (File no.470), Ovid Technologies, Inc. (BBIP).
Also available on CD-ROM. Producer(s): Bowker Electronic Publishing (Books Out-of-Print PLUS).
Description: Contains publisher-verified entries for out-of-print titles with full bibliographic information. Lists remainder dealers, out-of-print retailers, search services and on-demand publishers.

011 US ISSN 1064-7082
Z1000.5
BOOKS OUT-OF-PRINT PLUS. q. $195. R.R. Bowker, A Division of Reed Elsevier Inc., 121 Chanlon Rd., New Providence, NJ 07974. TEL 800-521-8110. FAX 908-665-3528. TELEX 138 755. E-mail: info@bowker.com; URL: http://www.reedref.com. (Subscr. to: Electronic Publishing, 121 Chanlon Rd., New Providence, NJ 07974-1154. TEL 800-323-3288) (avail. for MS-DOS & Windows) **Document type:** bibliography, directory.
●Also available online.
Also available on CD-ROM. Producer(s): Bowker Electronic Publishing (Books Out-of-Print PLUS).
Description: Lists more than 680,000 titles declared out-of-print (O.P.) or out-of-stock (O.S.I.) since 1979.

011 US
BOOKS OUT-OF-PRINT WITH BOOK REVIEWS PLUS. q. $395. R.R. Bowker, A Division of Reed Elsevier Inc., 121 Chanlon Rd., New Providence, NJ 07974. TEL 800-521-8110. FAX 908-665-3528. TELEX 138 755. E-mail: info@bowker.com; URL: http://www.reedref.com. (avail. for MS-DOS & Windows)
●Also available online.
Also available on CD-ROM. Producer(s): Bowker Electronic Publishing (Books Out-of-Print with Book Reviews PLUS).
Description: Contains more than 680,000 titles declared out-of-print (O.P.) or out-of-stock (O.S.I.) since 1979. Includes reviews from Library Journal, Publishers Weekly, School Library Journal, ALA Booklist, Kirkus Reviews, Bookstore Journal, Reference and Research Books News, Sci-Tech Books News, University Press Book News, BIOSIS, and VOYA.

011 US ISSN 0896-4521
THE BOOKWATCH. 1981. m. $12 (effective 1997). Midwest Book Review, 12424 Mill St., Petaluma, CA 94952. TEL 415-437-5731. Eds. James A. Cox, Diane C. Donovan. adv.; bk.rev. circ. 50,000. **Indexed:** Bk.Rev.Ind. (1988-), Child.Bk.Rev.Ind. (1988-). **Document type:** newsletter.
Formerly: Midwest Bookwatch.
Description: Capsule reviews of quality publications from large and small presses throughout the United States, targeted toward acquisitions librarians and subscribers.

BORCLAR - TICARET VE BANKA HUKUKU BIBLIYOGRAFYASI. see *LAW — Abstracting, Bibliographies, Statistics*

BORGO REFERENCE GUIDES. see *HISTORY*

011 UK
BOSTON SPA CONFERENCES ON C D - R O M. 1992. q. £325 (effective 1997). British Library, Document Supply Centre, Boston Spa, Wetherby, W. Yorks. LS23 7BQ, England. TEL 44-1937-546080. FAX 44-1937-546286. TELEX 557381. (Subscr. to: Turpin Distribution Services Ltd., Blackhorse Rd., Letchworth, Herts. SG6 1HN, England. TEL 44-1462-672555. FAX 44-1462-480947) **Document type:** proceedings.
●Available only on CD-ROM.

011 020 UK
BOSTON SPA SERIALS ON C D - R O M. s-a. £350 (effective 1997). British Library, Document Supply Centre, Boston Spa, Wetherby, W. Yorks. LS23 7BQ, England. TEL 44-1937-546061. FAX 44-1937-546286. TELEX 557381. (Subscr. to: Turpin Distribution Services Ltd., Blackhorse Rd., Letchworth, Herts. SG6 1HN, England. TEL 44-1462-672555. FAX 44-1462-480947) **Document type:** bibliography.
●Available only on CD-ROM.

011 US
BOWKER BUYING GUIDE SERIES. 1988. irreg., latest 1995. price varies. R.R. Bowker, A Division of Reed Elsevier Inc., 121 Chanlon Rd., New Providence, NJ 07974. TEL 908-464-6800. FAX 908-665-6688. TELEX 138 755. E-mail: info@bowker.com; URL: http://www.bowker.com. (Subscr. to: Box 31, New Providence, NJ 07974-9903. TEL 800-521-8110) **Document type:** directory.
Description: Guides to the best reference books in print, including encyclopedias, atlases, dictionaries, and topical references.

011 US
BOWKER - WHITAKER GLOBAL BOOKS IN PRINT ON DISC. 1993. m. $1995. R.R. Bowker, A Division of Reed Elsevier Inc., 121 Chanlon Rd., New Providence, NJ 07974. TEL 908-665-2866; 800-521-8110. FAX 908-665-3528. E-mail: info@bowker.com; URL: http://www.reedref.com. (Subscr. to: Electronic Publishing, 121 Chanlon Rd., New Providence, NJ 07974-1154. TEL 800-323-3288) (Co-publisher: J. Whitaker & Sons) (avail. for MS-DOS & Windows)
●Also available online.
Also available on CD-ROM. Producer(s): Bowker Electronic Publishing (Books In Print PLUS).
Formerly (until Sep. 1997): Bowker - Whitaker Global Books in Print Plus.
Description: Contains more than two million English-language book entries from Bowker's Books in Print Plus and Whitaker's Bookbank.

BOWKER'S LAW BOOKS AND SERIALS IN PRINT; a multimedia sourcebook. see *LAW — Abstracting, Bibliographies, Statistics*

BOWKER'S LAW BOOKS AND SERIALS IN PRINT SUPPLEMENT; materials on law and law related topics recently published and to be published. see *LAW — Abstracting, Bibliographies, Statistics*

BRAILLE BOOKS (LARGE PRINT EDITION). see *HANDICAPPED — Abstracting, Bibliographies, Statistics*

910 016 UK ISSN 0268-2400
Z1601.B7
BRITISH BULLETIN OF PUBLICATIONS ON LATIN AMERICA, THE CARIBBEAN, PORTUGAL AND SPAIN. 1949. s-a. £15. Hispanic and Luso-Brazilian Council, Canning House, 2 Belgrave Sq., London SW1X 8PJ, England. TEL 44-171-235-2303. FAX 44-171-235-3587. (Subscr. to: World Wide Subscription Service Ltd., Unit 4, Gibbs Reed Farm, Ticehurst, E. Sussex TN5 7HE, England. TEL 44-1580-200657. FAX 44-1580-200616) Eds. Carmen Suarez, Philip Davies. adv. contact: Carmen Suarez. bk.rev.; bibl. circ. 1,000. (also avail. in microfilm) **Document type:** bibliography.
Formerly: British Bulletin of Publications on Latin America, the West Indies, Portugal and Spain (ISSN 0007-036X).
Description: Contains information about recently published books and periodical articles in English about Latin America, the Caribbean, Portugal and Spain.

BRITISH GENEALOGICAL BIBLIOGRAPHIES. see *GENEALOGY AND HERALDRY — Abstracting, Bibliographies, Statistics*

016.05　　　　　UK　ISSN 0959-4914
BRITISH LIBRARY. DOCUMENT SUPPLY CENTRE. SCIENCE REFERENCE AND INFORMATION SERVICE. CURRENT SERIALS RECEIVED (YEAR). 1965. a. £64 (foreign £70) (effective 1997). British Library, Document Supply Centre, Boston Spa, Wetherby, W. Yorks. LS23 7BQ, England. TEL 44-1937-546080. FAX 44-1937-546286. TELEX 557381. (Subscr. to: Turpin Distribution Services Ltd., Blackhorse Rd., Letchworth, Herts. SG6 1HN, England. TEL 44-1462-672555. FAX 44-1462-480947) circ. 2,500. **Document type:** bibliography.
—BLDSC (3504.025000); CISTI; KNAW.
　　Formerly (until 1986): British Library. Lending Division. Current Serials Received (ISSN 0309-0655)

015.942　　　　　UK　ISSN 0007-1544
Z2001　　　　　CODEN: BRNBBV
BRITISH NATIONAL BIBLIOGRAPHY. 1950. w. (plus a. & interim cumulations). £595 for full-service print edition (foreign £695); full-service microfiche edition £475 (foreign £575) (effective 1997). British Library, National Bibliographic Service, Boston Spa, Wetherby, W. Yorks. LS23 7BQ, England. TEL 44-1937-546613. FAX 44-1937-546586. URL: http://portico.bl.uk. (Subscr. to: Turpin Distribution Services Ltd., Blackhorse Rd., Letchworth, Herts. SG6 1HN, England. TEL 44-1462-672555. FAX 44-1462-480947) cum.index on microfiche (1950-1980, 1981-1992). circ. 2,500. (also avail. in microfiche from BNB; back issues avail.) **Indexed:** Bibl.Engl.Lang.& Lit. **Document type:** bibliography.
●Also available online.
Also available on CD-ROM.
—BLDSC (2330.995000); CASDDS; CISTI.
　　Description: Lists new books and first issues of serial titles received by the Legal Deposit Office of the British Library. All subjects are covered, including fiction and children's literature.

659.1 016　　　　UK　ISSN 0263-3515
BRITISH RATE AND DATA. 1954. m. £440 (foreign £550) (effective 1996). E M A P Media (Subsidiary of: E M A P Business Communications), 33-39 Bowling Green Ln., London EC1R ODA, England. TEL 44-171-505-8265. FAX 44-171-505-8264. E-mail: andreww@media.emap.co.uk. Ed. David Mahoney. adv. contact: Tom Glenister. circ. 3,010 (paid). **Document type:** trade publication.
●Also available online.
—BLDSC (2265.900000).
　　Incorporates (1961-1988): B R A D Directories and Annuals (ISSN 0263-1040)

011　　　　　　　UK
BRITISH WORDS ON CASSETTE. 1992. irreg. $45. Bowker - Saur Ltd., A member of the Reed Elsevier plc group, Maypole House, Maypole Rd., E. Grinstead, W. Sussex RH19 1HU, England. TEL 44-1342-330100. FAX 44-1342-330191. E-mail: custserv@bowker-saur.co.uk; URL: http://www.reed-elsevier.com. **Document type:** directory.
　　Formerly (until 1992): British Words on Tape (ISSN 1052-3375)
　　Description: Covers more than 6,500 books on tape, educational materials, and works commissioned for tape publication. Entries include author, title, reader, purchase price, rental price, number of cassettes, running time, order number, and publisher's contact information.

BUDAPESTI KOZGAZDASAGTUDOMANYI EGYETEM OKTATOINAK SZAKIRODALMI MUNKASSAGA. see BUSINESS AND ECONOMICS — Abstracting, Bibliographies, Statistics

015 940　　　　BU　ISSN 0323-9969
BULGARIA V CHUZHDATA LITERATURA/BULGARIA IN FOREIGN LITERATURE. 1966. a. $50. Narodna Biblioteka Sv.sv. Kiril i Metodii, 88, V. Levski Blvd., 1504 Sofia, Bulgaria. TEL 359-2-882811. FAX 359-2-435495. Ed. G. Sredkova. R&P contact: G. Sredkova. bibl. circ. 350. **Document type:** bibliography.
—BLDSC (0018.630300).

015　　　　　　　BU
BULGARIAN ACADEMIC BOOKS. (Editions in Bulgarian, English, Russian) 1969. a. free. (Bulgarska Akademiia na Naukite) Publishing House of the Bulgarian Academy of Sciences, Acad. G. Bonchev St., Bldg. 6, 1113 Sofia, Bulgaria. bibl. circ. 1,000. (reprint service avail. from IRC)

015　　　　　　　BU　ISSN 0323-9411
Z5055.B87
BULGARSKI DISERTACII. 1974. a. $64. Narodna Biblioteka Sv.sv. Kiril i Metodii, 88, V. Levski Blvd., 1504 Sofia, Bulgaria. TEL 359-2-882811. FAX 359-2-435495. Ed. S. Pencheva. bibl.; index. circ. 400. **Document type:** bibliography.

BULGARSKI GRAMOFONNI PLOCHI. see MUSIC — Abstracting, Bibliographies, Statistics

015　　　　　　　BU　ISSN 0323-9713
BULGARSKI KNIGOPIS. KUMULATZIA. 1969. a. $70. Narodna Biblioteka Sv.sv. Kiril i Metodii, 88, V. Levski Blvd., 1504 Sofia, Bulgaria. TEL 359-2-882811. FAX 359-2-435495. Ed. S. Pencheva. R&P contact: S. Pencheva. circ. 570. **Document type:** bibliography.

015　　　　　　　BU　ISSN 0323-9616
BULGARSKI KNIGOPIS. SERIIA 1: KNIGI, NOTNI, GRAFICHESKI I KARTOGRAFSKI. 1897. s-m. 1330 lv.($58) (floppy disks 889 lv. ($90)). Narodna Biblioteka Sv.sv. Kiril i Metodii, 88, V. Levski Blvd., 1504 Sofia, Bulgaria. TEL 359-2-882811. FAX 359-2-435495. (Dist. by: Hemus, 6, Rouski Blvd., 1000 Sofia, Bulgaria) Ed. G. Vanchurova. index. circ. 500. (also avail. in diskette format) **Document type:** bibliography.
　　Supersedes in part: Bulgarski Knigopis (ISSN 0007-3997)

016　　　　　　　BU　ISSN 0323-9667
Z2893
BULGARSKI KNIGOPIS. SERIIA 2: SLUZHEBNI IZDANIIA I DISERTATSII. 1897. m. 180 lv.($35) Narodna Biblioteka Sv.sv. Kiril i Metodii, 88, V. Levski Blvd., 1504 Sofia, Bulgaria. TEL 359-2-882811. FAX 359-2-435495. Ed. S. Pencheva. bibl.; index. circ. 430. **Document type:** bibliography.
—BLDSC (0018.634200).
　　Supersedes in part: Bulgarski Knigopis (ISSN 0007-3997)

070 015　　　　　BU　ISSN 0323-9764
BULGARSKI PERIODICHEN PECHAT/BULGARIAN PERIODICALS; vestnitsi, spisaniia, biuletini i periodichni sbornitsi. 1967. a. 40 lv.($60) Narodna Biblioteka Sv.sv. Kiril i Metodii, 88, V. Levski Blvd., 1504 Sofia, Bulgaria. TEL 359-2-882811. FAX 359-2-435495. Ed. I. Kaloyanova. bibl. circ. 580. **Document type:** bibliography.

BULLETIN D'ARABE CHRETIEN. BIBLIOGRAPHIE DES AUTEURS ARABES CHRETIENS. see HISTORY — Abstracting, Bibliographies, Statistics

BULLETIN FOR CONTEXTUAL THEOLOGY IN AFRICA. see RELIGIONS AND THEOLOGY — Abstracting, Bibliographies, Statistics

010 809　　　　US　ISSN 0190-745X
Z1007
BULLETIN OF BIBLIOGRAPHY. 1897. q. $105 (foreign $125). Greenwood Press, Inc., Subscription Publications (Subsidiary of: Greenwood Publishing Group Inc.), 88 Post Rd., W., Box 5007, Westport, CT 06881-5007. TEL 203-226-3571. FAX 203-222-1502. URL: http://www.greenwood.com/bob.html. Ed. Bernard McTigue. bk.rev.; index, cum.index: 1897-1975, 1976-1980. circ. 1,000. **Indexed:** Abstr.Engl.Stud., Amer.Bibl.Slavic & E.Eur.Stud., Amer.Hist.& Life (1974-), Bibl.Engl.Lang.& Lit., Bibl.Ind., Biog.Ind., CERDIC, Geo.Abstr.H.G., Hist.Abstr. (1974-), IBR, Ind.Bk.Rev.Hum., M.L.A., MLA Intl.Bibl., Rel.Ind.One. **Document type:** academic/scholarly publication.
—BLDSC (2834.957000); KR SourceOne; Linda Hall; SWETS; UMI; UnCover.
　　Formerly: Bulletin of Bibliography and Magazine Notes (ISSN 0007-4780)
　　Description: Publishes bibliographies on a wide range of topics in the humanities, social sciences and the fine arts.

011　　　　　　　US
LA BUSCA. 1964. s-a. $25 (foreign $30) (includes El Clarin de la Busca). Taurine Bibliophiles America, 2567 Military Rd., Arlington, VA 22207. (Subscr. to: c/o Donald K. Conover, Treasurer, 2171 Twining Rd., Newton, PA 18940. TEL 610-968-0608) Ed. H. Ray Turner. adv.; bk.rev. circ. 165. **Document type:** bibliography.
　　Description: Forum for exchange of information on the literature of La Fiesta Brava through book reviews, criticism, and commentary.

BIBLIOGRAPHIES   541

BUSINESS PUBLICATION ADVERTISING SOURCE. see ADVERTISING AND PUBLIC RELATIONS — Abstracting, Bibliographies, Statistics

C A SELECTS. AIR POLLUTION (BOOKS & REVIEWS). see ENVIRONMENTAL STUDIES — Abstracting, Bibliographies, Statistics

C A SELECTS. NEW BOOKS IN CHEMISTRY. see CHEMISTRY — Abstracting, Bibliographies, Statistics

C C C C BIBLIOGRAPHY OF COMPOSITION AND RHETORIC. (Conference on College Composition and Communication) see EDUCATION — Abstracting, Bibliographies, Statistics

C C L R C LIBRARY AND INFORMATION SERVICES. RECENT ADDITIONS LIST; book and reports. see LIBRARY AND INFORMATION SCIENCES — Abstracting, Bibliographies, Statistics

C D - R O MS IN PRINT. see COMPUTERS — Abstracting, Bibliographies, Statistics

C M E I S OCCASIONAL PAPERS. (Centre for Middle Eastern and Islamic Studies) see ORIENTAL STUDIES

011 070.5　　　　MX　ISSN 0185-2493
KGF1572
C N I D A INFORMA; boletin bimestral de informacion autoral. 1982. q. free. Secretaria de Educacion Publica, Centro Nacional de Informacion - Direccion General del Derecho de Autor, Agencia Nacional ISBN, Mariano Escobedo 438 - 3o piso, Col. Nueva Anzures, 11590 Mexico, DF, Mexico. TEL 203-16-38. bk.rev. circ. 500.

016.05　　　　　CN　ISSN 0707-3747
C O N S E R MICROFICHE. (Cooperative Online Serials); a computer-output-microfiche listing of serial records in the CONSER database and authenticated by the National Library of Canada and the Library of Congress. (Text in English and French) 1979. a. National Library of Canada, Canadiana Editorial Division, Acquisitions and Bibliographic Services Branch, 395 Wellington St., Ottawa, ON K1A 0N4, Canada. TEL 819-994-6912. FAX 819-953-0291. circ. 150. (microfiche; also avail. in magnetic tape) **Document type:** bibliography.
●Also available online.
—BLDSC (3417.890000).

CAB INTERNATIONAL. ABSTRACT JOURNAL. see FORESTS AND FORESTRY — Abstracting, Bibliographies, Statistics

CAHIERS HENRI BOSCO. see LITERATURE — Abstracting, Bibliographies, Statistics

011 800 700　　　IT
CALABRIA LIBRI; panorama bibliografico e di vita culturale. 1982. q. L.24000($14) Rubbettino Editore, Viale dei Pini 10, 88049 Soveria Mannelli (CA), Italy. TEL 39-968-662034. Ed. Agostino Cajati. (back issues avail.)

CALGARY UNION LIST OF PERIODICALS. see LIBRARY AND INFORMATION SCIENCES — Abstracting, Bibliographies, Statistics

011　　　　　　　US
CALIFORNIA PERIODICALS ON MICROFILM. 1978. a. $345 price includes California Periodicals Index. Gabriel Micrographics, Box 611, Dekalb, IL 60115. TEL 815-895-6842. Ed. Marcia Gabriel. bk.rev. (microfilm)

015　　　　　　　US　ISSN 0008-1574
CALIFORNIA STATE PUBLICATIONS. 1947. m. (with a. cumulation). free to libraries. State Library, Box 942837, Sacramento, CA 94237-0001. TEL 916-653-0085. Ed. Carla Mazzini. bibl. circ. 1,500. (also avail. in microfiche) **Document type:** bibliography.
—Linda Hall.
　　Description: Lists official California state documents received by the Government Publication Section, California State Library.

BIBLIOGRAPHIES

011   US   ISSN 0095-8034
Z6945
CALIFORNIA UNION LIST OF PERIODICALS.* Short title: C U L P. a. $240 to non-members; members $155. C L A S S: Cooperative Library Agency for Systems and Services, 315 Washington St., Ste. 130, Oakland, CA 94607-3810. TEL 408-453-0444. FAX 408-453-5379. (microfiche)
    Description: Contains periodicals holdings information from 703 California libraries and includes over 79,000 unique titles.

015   AG   ISSN 0327-9189
CAMARA ARGENTINA DEL LIBRO. BOLETIN BIBLIOGRAFICO BIMESTRAL. 1993. bi-m. $72. Camara Argentina del Libro, Av. Belgrano 1580, 6o piso, 1093 Buenos Aires, Argentina. TEL 54-1-3819277. FAX 54-1-3819253. **Document type:** bibliography.
    Description: Presents information on Argentine books registered with the ISBN commission.

010   UK   ISSN 0068-6611
CAMBRIDGE BIBLIOGRAPHICAL SOCIETY. TRANSACTIONS. 1949. a. £8($18) Cambridge Bibliographical Society, c/o Cambridge University Library, West Rd., Cambridge CB3 9DR, England. E-mail: nt@ula.cam.ac.uk. Ed. Elisabeth Leedham-Green. circ. 500. **Indexed:** Abstr.Engl.Stud., Amer.Hist.& Life (1964-), Br.Hum.Ind., Hist.Abstr. (1964-), IBR. **Document type:** bibliography.
—BLDSC (8909.550000); UnCover.

016   UK   ISSN 0575-6782
CAMBRIDGE BIBLIOGRAPHICAL SOCIETY. TRANSACTIONS. MONOGRAPH SUPPLEMENTS. 1951. irreg. membership. Cambridge Bibliographical Society, c/o Cambridge University Library, West Rd., Cambridge CB3 9DR, England. E-mail: nt@ula.cam.ac.uk. **Indexed:** Bibl.Engl.Lang.& Lit. **Document type:** bibliography.
—BLDSC (5914.435000).

016   UK
CAMBRIDGE UNIVERSITY LIBRARY. GENIZAH SERIES. irreg. price varies. Cambridge University Press, Edinburgh Bldg., Shaftesbury Rd., Cambridge CB2 2RU, England. TEL 44-1223-312393. FAX 44-1223-315052. TELEX 851817256. E-mail: information@cup.cam.ac.uk; URL: http://www.cup.cam.ac.uk. (N. American addr.: Cambridge University Press, Journals Dept., 40 W. 20th St., New York, NY 10011. TEL 212-924-3900. FAX 212-691-3239) R&P contact: Linda Nicol. **Document type:** bibliography.

900 016   UK
CAMBRIDGE UNIVERSITY LIBRARY. HISTORICAL BIBLIOGRAPHY SERIES. irreg. price varies. Cambridge University Press, Edinburgh Bldg., Shaftesbury Rd., Cambridge CB2 2RU, England. TEL 44-1223-312393. FAX 44-1223-315052. TELEX 851817256. E-mail: information@cup.cam.ac.uk; URL: http://www.cup.cam.ac.uk. (N. American addr.: Cambridge University Press, Journals Dept., 40 W. 20th St., New York, NY 10011. TEL 212-924-3900. FAX 212-691-3239) R&P contact: Linda Nicol. **Document type:** bibliography.

CANADIAN ADVERTISING RATES AND DATA. see ADVERTISING AND PUBLIC RELATIONS — Abstracting, Bibliographies, Statistics

CANADIAN BOOKS FOR YOUNG PEOPLE/LIVRES CANADIENS POUR LA JEUNESSE. see CHILDREN AND YOUTH — Abstracting, Bibliographies, Statistics

015   CN   ISSN 0068-8398
Z1365
CANADIAN BOOKS IN PRINT. (Includes: Author & Title Index & Companion Subject Index) 1967. q. (cloth Jan.; microfiche Apr., Jul., Oct.). price varies. University of Toronto Press, Directories Departement, 10 St. Mary St., Ste. 700, Toronto, ON M4Y 2W8, Canada. TEL 416-978-2239. FAX 416-978-4738. E-mail: utpbooks@gpu.utcc.utoronto.ca. (U.S. addr.: 340 Nagel Dr., Cheektowaga, NY 14225) Ed. M. Butler. circ. 3,500. **Document type:** bibliography.
—CISTI.

016 378   CN   ISSN 0068-9874
CANADIAN THESES/THESES CANADIENNES. (Print edition ceased 1983; microfiche edition began 1984.) (Text in English and French) 1962. s-a. price varies. National Library of Canada, 395 Wellington St., Ottawa, ON K1A 0N4, Canada. TEL 819-994-6912. FAX 819-953-0291. (Dist. by: Canadiana Editorial Division, National Library of Canada, 395 Wellington St., Ottawa, ON K1A 0N4, Canada) Ed. Margot Wiper. index. circ. 1,000. (microfiche; back issues avail. from UMI) **Document type:** bibliography.
    ●Also available online. Vendor(s): CISTI.
    Incorporates: Canadian Theses on Microfiche (Supplement).
    Description: Lists graduate dissertations accepted by Canadian universities.

015.71 015   CN   ISSN 0008-5391
CANADIANA. Microfiche edition: Canadiana on Microfiche (ISSN 0225-3216) (Text in English and French) 1950. m. (plus a. cumulations). price varies. National Library of Canada, 395 Wellington St., Ottawa, ON K1A 0N4, Canada. TEL 819-956-4800. FAX 819-994-1498. (Subscr. to: Canada Communication Group, Publishing, Ottawa, ON K1A 0S9, Canada) Ed. Margot Wiper. index. (also avail. in microform) **Document type:** bibliography.
    ●Also available online.
—CISTI; Linda Hall.
    Description: Comprehensive bibliography which documents, collects, conserves and describes a wide variety of Canadian publications and sound recordings.

015   CN   ISSN 0225-3216
CANADIANA ON MICROFICHE. (Text in English, French) 1978. m. (plus a. quinquennial cumulation). price varies. National Library of Canada, 395 Wellington St., Ottawa, ON K1A 0N4, Canada. TEL 819-994-6912; 819-994-6912. FAX 819-953-0291. (Subscr. to: Canada Communication Group, Publishing, Ottawa, ON K1A 0S9, Canada) Ed. Margot Wiper. **Document type:** bibliography.
    ●Also available online. Vendor(s): CISTI.

015   CN   ISSN 1183-6849
CANADIANA PRE-1901. (Text in English, French) 1980. biennial. price varies. National Library of Canada, 395 Wellington St., Ottawa, ON K1A 0N4, Canada. TEL 819-994-6912. FAX 819-996-0291. (Subscr. to: Canada Communication Group, Publishing, Ottawa, ON K1A 0S9, Canada) Ed. Margot Wiper. **Document type:** bibliography.
    ●Also available online. Vendor(s): CISTI.
    Formerly (until 1991): Canadiana 1867-1900: Monographs (Microfiche Edition).

CANDLELIGHTERS CHILDHOOD CANCER FOUNDATION BIBLIOGRAPHY AND RESOURCE GUIDE. see MEDICAL SCIENCES — Abstracting, Bibliographies, Statistics

011   UN   ISSN 0251-9089
CARIBBEAN DOCUMENTATION CENTRE. CURRENT AWARENESS BULLETIN. 1978. m. free. (U N Economic Commission for Latin America and the Caribbean, Subregional Headquarters for the Caribbean) Caribbean Documentation Center, 22-24 St. Vincent St., P.O. Box 1113, Port-of-Spain, Trinidad & Tobago, W.I. FAX 809-623-8485. TELEX 623 8485. circ. 600. **Document type:** bulletin.
    Description: Alerts readers to highlights of recent acquisitions received at the center.

011   RM
CARTI IN CURS DE APARITIE. q. Centrala Editoriala, Piata Scinteii 1, 79715 Bucharest, Rumania.

Y CASGLWR. see PUBLISHING AND BOOK TRADE — Abstracting, Bibliographies, Statistics

CATALOG OF CURRENT LAW TITLES (ANN ARBOR). see LAW — Abstracting, Bibliographies, Statistics

011   MX
CATALOGO COLECTIVO DE PUBLICACIONES PERIODICAS EXISTENTES EN LAS BIBLIOTECAS DE LA UNIVERSIDAD. 1976. biennial. Mex.$40 (or exchange basis). Universidad Nacional Autonoma de Mexico, Direccion General de Bibliotecas, Villa Obregon, Ciudad Universitaria, Mexico 20, D.F., Mexico.

011   BL
CATALOGO COLETIVO NACIONAL DE PUBLICACOES PERIODICAS (IN MICROFICHES). irreg. $16.57. Instituto Brasileiro de Informacao em Ciencia e Tecnologia, SAS Quadra 5, Lote 6, Bloco H, 70070-000 Brasilia D.F., Brazil. TEL 55-61-2176161. FAX 55-61-2262677. (microfiche)
    ●Also available on CD-ROM.
    Formerly: Catalogo Coletivo de Publicacoes Periodicas (in Microfiches).

CATALOGO DE PUBLICACIONES LATINOAMERICANAS SOBRE FORMACION PROFESIONAL. see EDUCATION — Teaching Methods And Curriculum

011   IT
CATALOGO DEI LIBRI IN COMMERCIO/ITALIAN BOOKS IN PRINT. (In 3 vols., 2 parts; Part 1: Autori, Titoli-Bibliografica - Author-Title (2 vols.); Part 2: Soggetti-Bibliografica - Subject (1 vol.)) 1970. a. L.800000 for 3-vol. set; L.530000 for Author-Title vols.; L.270000 for Subject vol. (effective 1997). (Associazione Italiana Editori) Editrice Bibliografica S.p.A., Viale Vittorio Veneto 24, 20124 Milan, Italy. TEL 02-29006965. FAX 02-654624. (N. America subscr. to: K.G. Saur, A Reed Reference Publishing Company, Part of the Reed Elsevier group, 121 Chanlon Rd., Box 31, New Providence, NJ 07974-9903. TEL 908-665-3576) circ. 2,500. (back issues avail.) **Document type:** bibliography, directory.
    ●Also available on CD-ROM.
    Formerly (until 1975): Catalogo dei Libri Italiani in Commercio (ISSN 0069-1054)
    Description: Provides current bibliographic information for 25,000 Italian-language titles in print; 3,000 publishers represented, and a subject guide organized according to more than 30,000 catchwords.

011   IT
CATALOGO DEI LIBRI IN COMMERCIO - C D - R O M/ITALIAN BOOKS IN PRINT ON C D - R O M. Short title: A L I C E - C D. bi-m. £1125. Informazioni Editoriale, Via Carlo Poma 1, 20129 Milan, Italy. TEL 49-2-70129293. FAX 49-2-70129424. (Europe subscr. to: K.G. Saur Verlag KG, A member of the Reed Elsevier plc group, Ortlerstr. 8, 81373 Munich, Germany. TEL 49-89-76902-2. FAX 49-89-76902150; N. America subscr. to: K.G. Saur, Reed Elsevier New Providence, 121 Chanlon Rd., Box 31, New Providence, NJ 07974. TEL 908-464-6800) (avail. for MS-DOS version)
    ●Available only on CD-ROM. Producer(s): K.G. Saur Verlag.
    Description: Provides access to more than 320,000 Italian-language titles in print, and profiles 3,000 publishers.

015   IT
CATALOGO DEI PERIODICI ITALIANI. 1983. a. L.290000 (effective 1997). Editrice Bibliografica S.p.A., Viale Vittorio Veneto 24, 20124 Milan, Italy. TEL 02-29006965. FAX 02-654624. Ed. Roberto Maini. circ. 1,000. **Document type:** bibliography.
    Description: Reference guide to 14,000 Italian serials in print.

011   JA
CATALOGUE OF BOOKS RECOMMENDED FOR LIBRARIES/SENTEI TOSHO SOMOKUROKU. a. 6500 Yen. Japan Library Association - Nihon Toshokan Kyokai, 1-1-10 Taishido, Setagaya-ku, Tokyo 154, Japan. FAX 81-3-3421-7588. **Document type:** catalog.

015.41053   UK   ISSN 0260-5619
Z2009
CATALOGUE OF BRITISH OFFICIAL PUBLICATIONS NOT PUBLISHED BY H.M.S.O. 1980. bi-m. (plus a. cumulation). £295. Chadwyck-Healey Ltd., The Quorum, Barnwell Rd., Cambridge CB5 8SW, England. TEL 01223-215512. FAX 01223-215513. TELEX 93121 02281 CH G. E-mail: mail@chadwyck.co.uk. (U.S. subscr. to: Chadwyck-Healey Inc., 1101 King St., Alexandria, VA 22314. TEL 800-752-0515) Ed. Alison Moss. **Document type:** catalog.
    ●Also available on CD-ROM. Producer(s): Chadwyck-Healey Inc.
—CISTI.
    Description: Catalogs 11,000 publications from more than 500 official organizations.

015   UK   ISSN 0591-0986
CATALOGUE OF LITTLE PRESS BOOKS IN PRINT PUBLISHED IN THE UK. 1970. biennial. 75p. Association of Little Presses, 86 Lytton Rd., Oxford OX4 2NZ, England. TEL 44-1865-718266. Eds. Bob Cobbing, Gilbert Adair. bibl. circ. 1,000. **Document type:** catalog.

282 011   US   ISSN 0008-8307
Z6951
CATHOLIC PRESS DIRECTORY; official media reference guide to Catholic newspapers, magazines, newsletters, general publishers, and diocesan directors of the United States and Canada. 1923. a. $45. Catholic Press Association, 3555 Veterans Memorial Hwy., Unit O, Ronkonkoma, NY 11779-7637. TEL 516-471-4730. E-mail: cathjourn@aol.com; URL: http://www.catholicpress.org/index.htm. Ed. Christopher F. DeFilippis. adv.; index. circ. 1,400. **Document type:** trade publication.

011 025.3   US   ISSN 1054-3996
CD - MARC BIBLIOGRAPHIC. (Text primarily in English) 1991. q. $1380 (outside N. America $1470). U.S. Library of Congress, Cataloging Distribution Service, Customer Services Section, Washington, DC 20541-5017. TEL 202-707-6100; 800-255-2666. FAX 202-707-1334. E-mail: cdsinfo@mail.loc.gov. **Document type:** government publication, bibliography.
●Available only on CD-ROM.
    Description: Lists nearly 4.8 million USMARC bibliographic records for books, serials, maps, music recordings, and visual aids catalogued by the US Library of Congress.

011 025.3   US   ISSN 1068-8714
Z663
CD - MARC BIBLIOGRAPHIC. ENGLISH ONLY. 1994. q. $580 (outside N. America $680). U.S. Library of Congress, Cataloging Distribution Service, Customer Services Section, Washington, DC 20541-5017. TEL 202-707-6100; 800-255-3666. FAX 202-707-1334. E-mail: cdsinfo@mail.loc.gov. **Document type:** government publication, bibliography.
●Available only on CD-ROM.
    Description: Compiles nearly 3 million English-language USMARC bibliographic records for books, serials, musical recordings, visual materials, and maps.

011 025.3   US   ISSN 1068-8706
Z663
CD - MARC BIBLIOGRAPHIC. ENGLISH ONLY. CURRENT YEARS.. 1994. q. $405 (outside N. America $475). U.S. Library of Congress, Cataloging Distribution Service, Customer Services Section, Washington, DC 20541-5017. TEL 202-707-6100; 800-255-2666. FAX 202-707-1334. E-mail: cdsinfo@mail.loc.gov. **Document type:** bibliography, government publication.
●Available only on CD-ROM.
    Description: Provides current six years US Library of Congress USMARC bibliographic records for books, serials, maps, music recordings, and visual materials.

011 025.3   US   ISSN 1041-2964
Z699.3.A88
CD - MARC NAMES. 1990. q. (on 4 discs). $505 (outside N. America $550). U.S. Library of Congress, Cataloging Distribution Service, Customer Services Section, Washington, DC 20541-5017. TEL 202-707-6100; 800-255-3666. FAX 202-707-1334. E-mail: cdsinfo@mail.loc.gov. **Document type:** government publication.
●Available only on CD-ROM.
    Description: Allows users access to the entire US Library of Congress name authority file of 3.1 million records.

011 025.3   US   ISSN 1063-8784
Z699.4.C25
CD - MARC SERIALS. 1992. q. $435 (outside N. America $480). U.S. Library of Congress, Cataloging Distribution Service, Customer Services Section, Washington, DC 20541-5017. TEL 202-707-6100; 800-255-3666. FAX 202-707-1334. E-mail: cdsinfo@mail.loc.gov. **Document type:** government publication, bibliography.
●Available only on CD-ROM.
—BLDSC (3096.520500).
    Description: Lists nearly 700,000 USMARC serials records, including those from the U.S. newspaper program.

011 025.3   US   ISSN 1041-2956
Z695
CD - MARC SUBJECTS. 1988. q. $385 (outside N. America $425). U.S. Library of Congress, Cataloging Distribution Service, Customer Services Section, Washington, DC 20541-5017. TEL 202-707-6100; 800-255-3666. FAX 202-707-1334. E-mail: cdsinfo@mail.loc.gov. **Document type:** government publication.
●Available only on CD-ROM.
    Description: Contains the 206,300 USMARC bibliographic subject headings records of the four-volume Library of Subject Headings on a single CD-ROM disc.

CELEBRITY BIRTHDAY DIRECTORY. see MOTION PICTURES — Abstracting, Bibliographies, Statistics

028.5 011   US   ISSN 0008-9036
Z1037.A1
CENTER FOR CHILDREN'S BOOKS. BULLETIN. 1947. m. (except Aug.). $35 (foreign $42); institutions $40 (foreign $47) (effective 1997). (University of Illinois at Urbana-Champaign, Graduate School of Library and Information Science, Publications Office) University of Illinois Press, 1325 S. Oak St., Champaign, IL 61820. TEL 217-244-0324. FAX 217-333-5603. E-mail: puboff@alexia.lis.uiuc.edu; URL: http://edfu.lis.uiuc.edu/puboff/bccb. (Co-sponsor: Center for Children's Books) Ed. Janice Del Negro. adv.; B&W page $325; adv. contact: Ann Lowry. bk.rev.; abstr.; tr.lit.; index. circ. 5,000. (also avail. in microform from UMI; reprint service avail. from UMI,ISI) **Indexed:** Bk.Rev.Dig., Bk.Rev.Ind. (1965-), Child.Bk.Rev.Ind. (1965-). **Document type:** bibliography, trade publication.
—KR SourceOne; UMI. CCC.
    Description: Reviews of newly published and forthcoming books for children.
    Refereed Serial

011   PL   ISSN 0239-8931
Z6945
CENTRALNY KATALOG ZAGRANICZNYCH WYDAWNICTW CIAGLYCH W BIBLIOTEKACH POLSKICH. 1971. a. Biblioteka Narodowa, Instytut Bibliograficzny, Zaklad Katalogow Centralnych, Al. Niepodleglosci 213, 00-973 Warsaw, Poland. TEL 48-2-6082435. FAX 48-2-6082435. TELEX 813702 BN PL. (Dist. by: P.P. CHZ Ars Polona, ul. Krakowskie Przedmiescie 7, 00-068 Warsaw, Poland) Ed. Hanna Zawado. index. circ. 400. **Document type:** catalog.
    Formerly (until 1983): Centralny Katalog Biezacych Czasopism Zagranicznych w Bibliotekach Polskich.

944 015   FR   ISSN 0756-3442
CENTRE INTERNATIONAL DE DOCUMENTATION OCCITANE. SERIE BIBLIOGRAPHIQUE. 1977. irreg., latest no.9. price varies. Centre International de Documentation Occitane, Boite Postale 4202, 34544 Beziers Cedex, France.

CENTRO DI CULTURA E STORIA AMALFITANA. RASSEGNA. see ART

057.86 015   XR   ISSN 1210-8952
CESKA NARODNI BIBLIOGRAFIE. CLANKY V NOVINACH A CASOPISECH. (Print edition ceased 1994) 1953. m. Narodni Knihovna Ceske Republiky, Klementinum 190, 110 01 Prague 1, Czech Republic. TEL 420-2-24229500. FAX 420-2-24227796. TELEX 121207 STKN C. (Subscr. to: Albertina Icome Praha, Revolucni 13, 110 00 Prague 1, Czech Republic. TEL 420-2-4803303) Ed. Bohdana Stoklasova. adv.; index. circ. 850. (also avail. in diskette format) **Document type:** bibliography.
●Also available on CD-ROM.
    Former titles (until 1994): Bibliograficky Katalog C S F R: Clanky v Ceskych Casopisech (ISSN 0862-9269); (until 1990): Bibliograficky Katalog C S S R: Clanky v Ceskych Casopisech (ISSN 0006-1115); (until 1954): Bibliograficky Katalog C S S R. Ceske Casopisy; Supersedes: Ceske Casopisy.
    Description: Bibliography of articles in Czech journals and newspapers.

057.86 015   XR   ISSN 1210-8863
Z5055.C917
CESKA NARODNI BIBLIOGRAFIE. DISERTACE A AUTOREFERATY. 1964. irreg. price varies. Narodni Knihovna Ceske Republiky, Klementinum 190, 110 01 Prague 1, Czech Republic. TEL 420-2-24229500. FAX 420-2-24227796. E-mail: mirosovsky.ivo@cdh.nkp.cz. (Dist. by: Albertina Icome Praha, Revolucni 13, 110 00 Prague 1, Czech Republic. TEL 420-2-4803303) Ed. Bohdana Stoklasova. R&P contact: Adolf Knoll. (diskette format) **Document type:** bibliography.
    Former titles (until 1993): Bibliograficky Katalog C S F R: Ceske Knihy. Ceske Disertace a Autoreferaty (ISSN 0862-8599); (until 1990): Bibliograficky Katalog C S S R: Ceske Knihy. Ceske Disertace (ISSN 0232-041X); (until 1979): Bibliograficky Katalog C S S R: Ceske Knihy. Ceskoslovenske Disertace (ISSN 0323-1763)
    Description: Bibliography of Czech dissertation theses and author's abstracts.

CESKA NARODNI BIBLIOGRAFIE. HUDEBNINY. see MUSIC — Abstracting, Bibliographies, Statistics

057.86 015   XR   ISSN 1210-8898
Z2131
CESKA NARODNI BIBLIOGRAFIE. KNIHY. Online edition (XR ISSN 1210-8928) (Includes: Register) 1922. m. 1000 Kc.($30) Narodni Knihovna Ceske Republiky, Klementinum 190, 110 01 Prague 1, Czech Republic. TEL 42-2-24229500. FAX 42-2-24227796. (Dist. by: Narodni Knihovna Ceske Republiky, Odd. Prodeje a Expedice, Centralni Depozitar NK CR, Sterboholska 55, 100 00 Prague, Czech Republic. TEL 42-2-702600) Ed. Bohdana Stoklasova. index. circ. 600. (also avail. in diskette format (ISSN 1210-8901)) **Document type:** bibliography.
●Also available online.
Also available on CD-ROM.
    Former titles (until 1994): Narodni Bibliografie Ceske Republiky. Knihy (ISSN 1210-888X); (until 1993): Bibliograficky Katalog C S F R: Ceske Knihy (ISSN 0862-9218); (until 1990): Bibliograficky Katalog C S S R: Ceske Knihy (ISSN 0323-1615); (until 1955): Ceska Kniha; Supersedes: Bibliograficky Katalog Ceskoslovenske Republiky. Pt. A: Knihy Ceske 1922-1950.
    Description: Bibliography of Czech books.

015.437   XR   ISSN 1211-1325
Z2131.A1
CESKA NARODNI BIBLIOGRAFIE. SOUPIS CESKYCH BIBLIOGRAFII. 1956. a. 27 Kc. Narodni Knihovna Ceske Republiky, Klementinum 190, 110 01 Prague 1, Czech Republic. TEL 420-2-24229500. FAX 420-2-24227796. (Dist. by: Narodni Knihovna Ceske Republiky, Odd. Prodeje a Expedice, Centralni Depozitar NK CR, Sterboholska 55, 100 00 Prague 10, Czech Republic. TEL 420-2-702600) Ed. Bohdana Stoklasova. circ. 300. **Document type:** bibliography.
    Former titles (until 1994): Narodni Bibliografie Ceske Republiky. Soupis Ceskych Bibliografii (ISSN 1210-8944); (until 1993): Bibliograficky Katalog C S F R: Ceske Knihy. Soupis Ceskych Bibliografii (ISSN 0862-9234); (until 1990): Bibliograficky Katalog C S S R: Ceske Knihy. Soupis Ceskych Bibliografii (ISSN 0323-1860)
    Description: Lists Czech bibliographies.

015   XR   ISSN 1211-4375
CESKA NARODNI BIBLIOGRAFIE. ZAHRANICNI BOHEMIKA. 1956. a. 75 Kc. (foreign $6). Narodni Knihovna Ceske Republiky, Klementinum 1990, 110 01 Prague 1, Czech Republic. TEL 420-2024229500. FAX 420-2024227796. Ed. Bohdana Stoklasova. circ. 300. **Document type:** bibliography.
    Former titles (until 1994): Narodna Bibliografie Ceske Republiky. Zakranicni Bohemika (ISSN 1210-8987); (until 1993): Bibliograficky Katalog C S F R Zaharanicni Bohemika (ISSN 1210-4523); (until 1990): Bibliograficky Katalog C S S R. Ceske Knihy, Zakhranicni Bohemika a Slovacika v Roce (ISSN 0323-1917)
    Description: Bibliography of foreign Bohemica deposited or sent to the Czech National Library.

CESKA NARODNI BIBLIOGRAFIE. ZVUKOVE DOKUMENTY. see MUSIC — Abstracting, Bibliographies, Statistics

CESKA ZEMEDELSKA BIBLIOGRAFIE/CZECH AGRICULTURAL BIBLIOGRAPHY. see AGRICULTURE — Abstracting, Bibliographies, Statistics

BIBLIOGRAPHIES

CHECKLIST OF OFFICIAL NEW JERSEY PUBLICATIONS. see *PUBLIC ADMINISTRATION — Abstracting, Bibliographies, Statistics*

CHICANO DATABASE ON C D - R O M. see *ETHNIC INTERESTS*

CHICANO INDEX. see *ETHNIC INTERESTS — Abstracting, Bibliographies, Statistics*

011 US
CHICOREL INDEX SERIES. 1970. irreg., vol.26, 1986. $125 per vol. American Library Publishing Co., Box 4272, Sedona, AZ 86340-4272. TEL 520-282-4922. Ed. Marietta S. Chicorel. R&P contact: Marietta S. Chicorel. bk.rev. (also avail. in microform from UMI) **Document type:** abstracting/indexing, bibliography.
Description: Series of subject guides to various fields in the humanities and social sciences, such as indexes to plays, poetry and short stories in anthologies, on audio and video. Abstracting services for reading and learning disabilities, and the mental health fields.

028.5 370 US ISSN 0069-3480
Z1037.A1
CHILDREN'S BOOKS IN PRINT; an author, title, and illustrator index to books for children and young adults. (Issued in 2 vols.) 1962. a. $159 (effective 1998). R.R. Bowker, A Division of Reed Elsevier Inc., 121 Chanlon Rd., New Providence, NJ 07974. TEL 908-464-6800. FAX 908-665-6688. TELEX 138 755. E-mail: info@bowker.com; URL: http://www.reedref.com. (Subscr. to: Order Dept., Box 31, New Providence, NJ 07974-9903. TEL 800-521-8110) (also avail. in magnetic tape) **Document type:** bibliography, directory.
●Also available online. Vendor(s): Knight-Ridder Information, Inc. (File no.470), Ovid Technologies, Inc. (BBIP).
Also available on CD-ROM. Producer(s): Bowker Electronic Publishing (Books in Print PLUS).
Formerly: Children's Book for Schools and Libraries.
Description: Lists current children's books, fiction and nonfiction, listed by title, author, and illustrator. Features an index of major book awards for the past ten years; includes publisher information.

CHILDREN'S CATALOG. see *CHILDREN AND YOUTH — Abstracting, Bibliographies, Statistics*

CHILDREN'S FICTION ON FICHE. see *CHILDREN AND YOUTH — Abstracting, Bibliographies, Statistics*

011 US
CHRISTIAN BOOKS IN PRINT ON DISC. m. £830. R.R. Bowker, A Division of Reed Elsevier Inc., 121 Chanlon Rd., New Providence, NJ 07974. TEL 908-464-6800; 800-521-8110. FAX 908-665-3528. E-mail: info@bowker.com; URL: http://www.reedref.com. (Subscr. to: Order Dept., Box 31, New Providence, NJ 07974. TEL 800-323-3288) (avail. for MS-DOS or Windows)
●Available only on CD-ROM.
Formerly: (until Sep. 1997): Christian Books in Print Plus.
Description: Carries listings of all kinds of Christian publications, including books, Bibles, audiocassettes, CDs, videos, and religious merchandise and gifts, as well as U.S. publisher and distributor information.

CH'ULPAN MOONWHA/KOREAN PUBLISHING JOURNAL. see *PUBLISHING AND BOOK TRADE*

CHUZHDESTRANNI PERIODICHNI IZDANIIA V PO-GOLEMITE NAUCHNI BIBLIOTEKI. see *SCIENCES: COMPREHENSIVE WORKS — Abstracting, Bibliographies, Statistics*

011 US
EL CLARIN DE LA BUSCA. 1994. q. $25 (foreign $30) (includes La Busca). Taurine Bibliophiles America, 2647 Hidden Valley Ln., Napa, CA 94558. (Subscr. to: Donald K. Conover, Treasurer, 2171 Twining Rd., Newton, PA 18940. TEL 610-968-0608) Ed. Jane Hurwitz. adv.; bk.rev. **Document type:** bibliography.
Description: Provides a forum for ideas on the literature of La Fiesta Brava through book reviews, criticism, and commentary.

011 US ISSN 1053-0460
Z674.5.U5
CLEARINGHOUSE DIRECTORY; a guide to information clearinghouses and their resources, services, and publications. 1990. biennial. $89.50. Gale Research, 835 Penobscot Bldg., 645 Griswold St., Detroit, MI 48226-4094. TEL 313-961-2242; 800-877-4253. FAX 800-414-5043. E-mail: daniel_snyder@gale.com. Ed. Donna Batten. —CISTI.
Description: Describes over 600 information clearinghouses that specialize in providing more precise or current information.

010 NE ISSN 0169-8672
CODICES MANUSCRIPTI BIBLIOTHECAE UNIVERSITATIS LEIDENSIS. 1910. irreg., vol.26, 1989. price varies. E.J. Brill, P.O. Box 9000, 2300 PA Leiden, Netherlands. TEL 31-71-5353500. FAX 31-71-5317532. TELEX 39296 BRILL NL. E-mail: ejbrill@brill.nl. (In N. America: E.J. Brill, 24 Hudson St., Kinderhook, NY 12106. TEL 800-962-4406. FAX 518-758-1959) (Co-publisher: Leiden University Press) R&P contact: Elizabeth Vennekamp. (back issues avail.) **Document type:** monographic series, bibliography.
Description: Descriptive catalogues of manuscript holdings at Leiden University and other collections in the Netherlands, including Arabic, Hebrew, Balinese and Latin manuscripts.

015 BL
COLECCAO RODOLFO GARCIA. 1966. irreg. Biblioteca Nacional de Brasil, Av. Rio Branco, 219, 20042 Rio de Janeiro, Brazil. TEL 021-262-8255. FAX 021-220-4173. TELEX 21-22941. circ. 1,000.
Formerly: (until vol.20, 1983): Biblioteca Nacional. Colecao Rodolfo Garcia. Serie B. Catalogos e Bibliografias.

011 900 IT ISSN 0394-7777
COLLECTANEA BIBLIOGRAPHICA CARMELITANA. (Text in English, French, German, Italian, Latin and Spanish) 1958. irreg. price varies. (Order of Carmelites) Edizioni Carmelitane, Via Sforza Pallavicini 10, 00193 Rome, Italy. TEL 06-66803513. FAX 06-68307200. adv. circ. 500. **Document type:** bibliography.
Description: Forum includes bibliographic studies relevant to Carmelite order.

016.05 378.1 US ISSN 1046-4255
Z6944.S8
COLLEGE MEDIA DIRECTORY. 1965. irreg., 9th ed, 1996. $195. Oxbridge Communications, Inc., 150 Fifth Ave., New York, NY 10011. TEL 212-741-0231. FAX 212-633-2938. **Document type:** directory.
●Also available online.
Also available on CD-ROM.
Formerly: Directory of the College Student Press in America (ISSN 0085-0020)
Description: Covers North American colleges and universities with information on their student and alumni publications.

016 BE
COMMISSION BELGE DE BIBLIOGRAPHIE ET DE BIBLIOLOGIE. BULLETIN. 1957. a. 450 BEF. Commission Belge de Bibliographie et de Bibliologie, 4, Boulevard de l'Empereur, 1000 Brussels, Belgium. FAX 32-80-510465. Ed. Christian F. Verbecke. R&P contact: Mireille M. Vanlaecken. bk.rev.; index. circ. 300. **Document type:** bulletin.
Formerly: Commission Belge de Bibliographie. Bulletin (ISSN 0408-9006)

COMMUNITY PUBLICATION ADVERTISING SOURCE. see *ADVERTISING AND PUBLIC RELATIONS — Abstracting, Bibliographies, Statistics*

COMPENDIUM OF TOURISM STATISTICS. see *TRAVEL AND TOURISM — Abstracting, Bibliographies, Statistics*

THE COMPLETE DIRECTORY OF LARGE PRINT BOOKS AND SERIALS. see *HANDICAPPED — Abstracting, Bibliographies, Statistics*

011 US
CONGRESSIONAL RESEARCH REPORT. 1986. m. $140. Penny Hill Press, 6440 Wiscasset Rd., Bethesda, MD 20816. TEL 301-229-8229. FAX 301-229-6988. Ed. Walt Seager. (back issues avail.) **Document type:** directory.
●Also available online. Vendor(s): Information Access Co.
Formerly: New Products from C R S.
Description: Includes descriptions and ordering information for all publications of U.S. Congressional Research Service of U.S. Congress.

CONSORTIUM ON REVOLUTIONARY EUROPE. SELECTED PAPERS. see *HISTORY — History Of Europe*

640 US
CONSUMER INFORMATION CATALOG. 1971. q. free. U.S. General Services Administration, Consumer Information Center, 18th and F Sts., N.W., Rm. G-142, Washington, DC 20405. TEL 202-501-1794; 888-8PU-EBLO. FAX 202-501-4281. URL: http://www.pueblo.gsa.gov. (Avail. from: Consumer Information Catalog, Pueblo, CO 81009. TEL 719-948-4000) Ed. Christine Antonio. R&P contact: Christine Antonio. bibl. circ. 12,000,000. **Indexed:** MEDOC. **Document type:** government publication, catalog.
●Also available online.
Formerly: Consumer Information.
Description: Lists more than 200 federal consumer publications available free or at low cost.

CONSUMER MAGAZINE AND ADVERTISING SOURCE. see *ADVERTISING AND PUBLIC RELATIONS — Abstracting, Bibliographies, Statistics*

016 301 US ISSN 0887-3569
CONTEMPORARY SOCIAL ISSUES: A BIBLIOGRAPHIC SERIES. 1986. q. $55. Reference and Research Services, 511 Lincoln St., Santa Cruz, CA 95060. TEL 408-426-4479. Ed. Joan Nordquist. (back issues avail.) **Document type:** monographic series, bibliography.
—BLDSC (3425.302700).
Description: Series of bibliographies on current social issues and problems.

CONTENTSDIRECT. see *SCIENCES: COMPREHENSIVE WORKS — Abstracting, Bibliographies, Statistics*

015 IT
COPTIC BIBLIOGRAPHY. 1982. a., plus s-a. supplement. $40. Centro Italiano Microfiches, Pzale. di Ponte Milvio 28, 00191 Rome, Italy. FAX 6-3333457. Ed. Tito Orlandi. circ. 150. **Document type:** bibliography.

015.942 025.3 US
COPYRIGHT CATALOGING: MONOGRAPHS AND DOCUMENTS. (Retrospective cumulation avail.) 1978. w. $31500 (outside N. America $32710) (effective 1994-1996). U.S. Library of Congress, Copyright Office, First St., N.E., Washington, DC 20559. E-mail: cdsinfo@mail.loc.gov. (Dist. by: U.S. Library of Congress, Cataloging Distribution Service, Customer Services Section, Washington, DC 20541-5017. TEL 202-707-6100. FAX 202-707-1334) (processed)
Description: Compiles MARC data on such copyright information as author, title, copyright claimant name, and registration number.

015.942 025.3 US
COPYRIGHT CATALOGING: SERIALS. (Retrospective cumulation avail.) 1994. s-a. $2000 (outside N. America $2025) (effective 1994-1996). U.S. Library of Congress, Copyright Office, First St., N.E., Washington, DC 20559. E-mail: cdsinfo@mail.loc.gov. (Dist. by: U.S. Library of Congress, Cataloging Distribution Service, Customer Services Section, Washington, DC 20541-5017. TEL 202-707-6100. FAX 202-707-1334) (processed) **Document type:** bibliography.
Description: Provides U.S. Copyright Office cataloging data for registrations of copyright since 1978.

CORNELL MODERN INDONESIA PROJECT PUBLICATIONS. see *ORIENTAL STUDIES*

011   US   ISSN 0000-1392
THE CORNERSTONE (NEW PROVIDENCE). 1988. q. (free with subscr. to Ulrich's International Periodicals Directory). R.R. Bowker, A Division of Reed Elsevier Inc., 121 Chanlon Rd., New Providence, NJ 07974. TEL 888-269-5372. FAX 908-665-6688. TELEX 138 755. E-mail: info@bowker.com; URL: http://www.reedref.com. (Subscr. to: Order Dept., Box 31, New Providence, NJ 07974) Ed. Nan Hudes. —BLDSC (4337.084000). **CCC.**
Supersedes (in 1992): Ulrich's News (ISSN 0000-1163); Incorporates (1987-1992): Plus (ISSN 0000-1341)
Description: Provides updates on information technology, serials publishing, and new products and programs from R.R. Bowker. Also represented are Bowker-Saur, K.G. Saur, and D.W. Thorpe.

COSTUME SOCIETY OF AMERICA. SYMPOSIA ABSTRACTS. see *CLOTHING TRADE — Abstracting, Bibliographies, Statistics*

COSTUME SOCIETY OF AMERICA BIBLIOGRAPHY. see *CLOTHING TRADE — Abstracting, Bibliographies, Statistics*

COTTON AND TROPICAL FIBRES. see *AGRICULTURE — Abstracting, Bibliographies, Statistics*

COUNTY GENEALOGICAL BIBLIOGRAPHIES. see *GENEALOGY AND HERALDRY — Abstracting, Bibliographies, Statistics*

COURTENAY REFORMATION FACSIMILES. see *RELIGIONS AND THEOLOGY — Protestant*

COURTENAY STUDIES IN REFORMATION THEOLOGY. see *RELIGIONS AND THEOLOGY — Protestant*

CRITICAL BIBLIOGRAPHY OF FRENCH LITERATURE. see *LITERATURE — Abstracting, Bibliographies, Statistics*

CUADERNOS DE INFORMACION EDUCACIONAL. see *EDUCATION — Abstracting, Bibliographies, Statistics*

CUADERNOS RAYUELA; bibliografia sobre America Latina. see *HISTORY — Abstracting, Bibliographies, Statistics*

CULTURE WATCH; a monthly annotated bibliography on culture, art, and political affairs. see *LITERARY AND POLITICAL REVIEWS — Abstracting, Bibliographies, Statistics*

011   US   ISSN 0011-300X
Z1219
CUMULATIVE BOOK INDEX. CD-ROM edition (US ISSN 1076-7061) 1898. m. (11/yr.) (q. and a. cumulations). service basis. H.W. Wilson Co., 950 University Ave., Bronx, NY 10452. TEL 718-588-8400; 800-367-6770. FAX 718-590-1617. TELEX 4990003HWILSON. Ed. Nancy Wong. (also avail. in magnetic tape) **Document type:** abstracting/indexing.
●Also available online. Vendor(s): Ovid Technologies, Inc., Wilsonline (File CBI).
Also available on CD-ROM. Producer(s): SilverPlatter Information, Inc., H.W. Wilson.
—BLDSC (3492.000000); CISTI; Linda Hall.
Description: World list of books published in the English language.

016   FR   ISSN 0398-8074
Z282
CURIOSPRESS INTERNATIONAL; annuaire international des editeurs de publications etranges et curieuses. (Text in English, French, German, Italian, Spanish) 1974. biennial. 45 F. c/o Ed. Pierre Birukoff, INFOS al International, B.P. 127, 75563 Paris 12, France. illus.

CURRENT BASEBALL PUBLICATIONS. see *SPORTS AND GAMES — Abstracting, Bibliographies, Statistics*

CURRENT BIBLIOGRAPHY ON AFRICAN AFFAIRS. see *POLITICAL SCIENCE — Abstracting, Bibliographies, Statistics*

CURRENT BIBLIOGRAPHY ON SCIENCE AND TECHNOLOGY: ENERGY/KAGAKU GIJUTSU BUNKEN SOKUHO. ENERUGI-HEN. see *ENERGY — Abstracting, Bibliographies, Statistics*

CURRENT BIBLIOGRAPHY ON SCIENCE AND TECHNOLOGY: LIFE SCIENCES/KAGAKU GIJUTSU BUNKEN SOKUHO. RAIFUSAIENSU HEN. see *BIOLOGY — Abstracting, Bibliographies, Statistics*

CURRENT CONTENTS: ARTS & HUMANITIES. see *HUMANITIES: COMPREHENSIVE WORKS — Abstracting, Bibliographies, Statistics*

011   JA   ISSN 0386-7293
AI19.J3
CURRENT CONTENTS OF ACADEMIC JOURNALS IN JAPAN. (Text in English) 1971. a. $85. 2-14-6 Yayoi, Bunkyo-ku, Tokyo 113, Japan, Japan. TEL 3817-5825. FAX 3817-5830. (Dist. by: Business Center for Academic Societies Japan, 5-16-19, Honkomagome, Bunkyo-ku, Tokyo 113, Japan; Dist. in U.S. by: International Specialized Book Services, Inc., 5602 N.E. Hassalo St., Portland, OR 97213) circ. 1,000. **Document type:** abstracting/indexing.

CURRENT GENEALOGICAL PUBLICATIONS. see *GENEALOGY AND HERALDRY — Abstracting, Bibliographies, Statistics*

CURRENT JAPANESE PERIODICALS FOR (YEAR). see *PUBLISHING AND BOOK TRADE — Abstracting, Bibliographies, Statistics*

CURRENT MATHEMATICAL PUBLICATIONS. see *MATHEMATICS — Abstracting, Bibliographies, Statistics*

CURRENT PUBLICATIONS IN LEGAL AND RELATED FIELDS. see *LAW — Abstracting, Bibliographies, Statistics*

CURRENT RESEARCH IN FRENCH STUDIES AT UNIVERSITIES IN THE UNITED KINGDOM AND IRELAND. see *LINGUISTICS — Abstracting, Bibliographies, Statistics*

CURRENT WORK IN THE HISTORY OF MEDICINE; an international bibliography. see *MEDICAL SCIENCES — Abstracting, Bibliographies, Statistics*

CURRENT WORLD AFFAIRS; a quarterly bibliography. see *CIVIL DEFENSE — Abstracting, Bibliographies, Statistics*

016.05 004.6   US
▼**CYBERHOUND'S GUIDE TO PUBLICATIONS ON THE INTERNET.** 1996. irreg. $79. Gale Research, 835 Penobscot Bldg., 645 Griswold St., Detroit, MI 48226-4094. TEL 313-961-6083; 800-877-4253. FAX 800-414-5043. E-mail: daniel__snyder@gale.com. **Document type:** directory.
Description: Provides information on more than 3700 internet publications.

015   XR
CZECH BOOKS FOR YOU.* 1974. 4/yr. free. Artia Pegass Press Co. Ltd., Narodni tr. 25, P.O. Box 825, 111 21 Prague, Czech Republic. FAX 42-2-2137-555. TELEX 121065 ARTA C. adv.; bk.rev.
Formerly (until 1991): Czech Books in Print (ISSN 0862-447X)

025.309   DK
D A N B I B; union catalogue of acquisitions of foreign literature in Danish research libraries, special libraries and public libraries, from 1980 also including Danish national bibliography. 1901. a. DKK 1.18 per command. Dansk BiblioteksCenter as, Tempovej 7-11, DK-2750 Ballerup, Denmark. TEL 45-44-86-77-77. FAX 45-44-97-14-85. E-mail: dbc@dan.bib.dk. Dir. Mogens Brabrand Jensen.
●Available only online.
Former titles: Dansk BiblioteksCenter. A L B A - Accessionskatalogen; Statens Bibliotekstjeneste. ALBA - Accessionskatalogen; Rigsbibliotekarembedet. ALBA - Accessionskatalogen (ISSN 0109-9256); Rigsbibliotekarembedet. Accessionskatalog (ISSN 0084-9715)

011   II   ISSN 0971-4448
D K NEWSLETTER; a journal of news and reviews of Indian publications in English. 1975. q. Rs.20($10) (effective 1995-96). D. K. Agencies (P) Ltd., A-15-17, Mohan Garden, Najafgarh Road, New Delhi 110 059, India. TEL 91-11-559-8899. FAX 91-11-559-8898. E-mail: indbook.dka@axcess.net.in. Ed. J. Rai Mittal. adv.; bk.rev. circ. 3,100. **Document type:** newsletter.

D L A P S. (Defense Logistics Agency Publishing System) see *PUBLIC ADMINISTRATION — Abstracting, Bibliographies, Statistics*

016.05   TS
DALIL AD-DAWRIAT LI-DAWLAT AL-IMARAT AL-ARABIYYAH AL-MUTTAHIDAH/DIRECTORY OF THE PERIODICALS IN THE UNITED ARAB EMIRATES. (Text in Arabic, English) 1990. biennial. dh.20. Cultural Foundation, National Library, P.O. Box 2380, Abu Dhabi, United Arab Emirates. TELEX 22414 CULCEN EM. Ed. Jumaa al-Qubaisi. **Document type:** bibliography.
Description: Comprehensive bibliographic information on all periodicals published in the U.A.E. since 1961.

DANCE RESEARCH. see *DANCE — Abstracting, Bibliographies, Statistics*

DANIA POLYGLOTTA; literature on Denmark in languages other than Danish and books of Danish interest published abroad. see *LITERATURE — Abstracting, Bibliographies, Statistics*

015   DK   ISSN 0070-282X
DANSKE FORLAEGGERFORENING. FAELLESLAGERKATALOG. 1970. s-a. DKK 180. Danske Forlaeggerforening, Koebmagergade 11, 3, DK-1150 Copenhagen K, Denmark. (Co-sponsor: Danske Boghandlerforening) circ. 750.

DAVISON'S TEXTILE BLUE BOOK EUROPE. see *TEXTILE INDUSTRIES AND FABRICS — Abstracting, Bibliographies, Statistics*

DAVISON'S TEXTILE BUYER'S GUIDE. see *TEXTILE INDUSTRIES AND FABRICS — Abstracting, Bibliographies, Statistics*

015   GW
DEUTSCHE NATIONALBIBLIOGRAPHIE (C D - R O M AKTUELL). 1989. bi-m. DM.3000($1950) (effective 1997). (Deutsche Bibliothek) Buchhaendler-Vereinigung GmbH, Postfach 100442, 60004 Frankfurt a.M., Germany. TEL 49-69-1306-243. FAX 49-69-1306201. E-mail: weber@bhv.de. **Document type:** bibliography.
●Available only on CD-ROM. Producer(s): Chadwyck-Healey Inc.
Formerly: Deutsche Bibliographie (C D - R O M Edition).

015.43   GW   ISSN 0939-0421
Z2221
DEUTSCHE NATIONALBIBLIOGRAPHIE. REIHE A, MONOGRAPHIEN UND PERIODIKA DES VERLAGSBUCHHANDELS. 1947. w. DM.2340. (Deutsche Bibliothek) Buchhaendler-Vereinigung GmbH, Postfach 100442, 60004 Frankfurt a.M., Germany. TEL 49-69-13060. FAX 49-69-1306201. E-mail: weber@bhv.de. bibl.; index. **Document type:** bibliography.
—Linda Hall.
Former titles: Deutsche Nationalbibliographie. Wochentliches Verzeichnis. Ausgabe 1 Amtsblatt der Deutschen Bibliothek; Deutsche Bibliographie. Woechentliches Verzeichnis. Ausgabe 1 Amtsblatt der Deutschen Bibliothek (ISSN 0170-1037)

015.431   GW   ISSN 0940-2721
Z2221
DEUTSCHE NATIONALBIBLIOGRAPHIE. REIHE D, MONOGRAPHIEN UND PERIODIKA. HALBJAHRES-VERZEICHNIS. 1951. s-a. (Deutsche Bibliothek) Buchhaendler-Vereinigung GmbH, Postfach 100442, 60004 Frankfurt a.M., Germany. TEL 49-69-13060. FAX 49-69-1306201. E-mail: weber@bhv.de. bibl.; index. **Document type:** bibliography.
—Linda Hall.
Formerly: Deutsche Bibliographie. Halbjahres-Verzeichnis (ISSN 0532-5854)

015.43   GW   ISSN 0942-4318
Z2221
DEUTSCHE NATIONALBIBLIOGRAPHIE. REIHE E, MONOGRAPHIEN UND PERIODIKA. FUENFJAHRES-VERZEICHNIS. 1945. irreg. price varies. (Deutsche Bibliothek) Buchhaendler-Vereinigung GmbH, Postfach 100442, 60004 Frankfurt a.M., Germany. TEL 49-69-13060. FAX 49-69-1306201. E-mail: weber@bhv.de. bibl.; index. **Document type:** bibliography.
—Linda Hall.
Formerly: Deutsche Bibliographie. Fuenfjahres-Verzeichnis (ISSN 0418-8233)

BIBLIOGRAPHIES

015.43   GW   ISSN 0939-057X
Z2221
DEUTSCHE NATIONALBIBLIOGRAPHIE. REIHE G, FREMDSPRACHIGER GERMANICA UND UEBERSETZUNGEN DEUTSCHSPRACHIGER WERKE. 1954. q. DM.712. (Deutsche Buecherei Leipzig) Buchhaendler-Vereinigung GmbH, Postfach 100442, 60004 Frankfurt a.M., Germany. TEL 49-69-13060. FAX 49-69-1306201. E-mail: weber@bhv.de. (Co-sponsor: Deutsche Bibliothek) bibl.; cum.index: 1954-1963. **Document type:** bibliography.
  Formed by 1992 merger of: Bibliographie der Uebersetzungen Deutschsprachiger Werke (ISSN 0006-1409); Bibliographie Fremdsprachiger Germanica (ISSN 0323-3154)
  Description: Covers works in all fields and subjects. Includes a systematic author and publisher index.

DEUTSCHE NATIONALBIBLIOGRAPHIE. REIHE M, MUSIKALIEN UND MUSIKSCHRIFTEN. see *MUSIC — Abstracting, Bibliographies, Statistics*

015   GW
DEUTSCHE NATIONALBIBLIOGRAPHIE. REIHE N, VORANKUENDIGUNGEN, MONOGRAPHIEN UND PERIODIKA (CIP). 1975. w. DM.720. (Deutsche Bibliothek) Buchhaendler-Vereinigung GmbH, Postfach 100442, 60004 Frankfurt a.M., Germany. TEL 49-69-1306-0. FAX 49-69-1306201. E-mail: weber@bhv.de. **Document type:** bibliography. —Linda Hall.
  Formerly: Deutsche Nationalbibliographie: Vorankuendigungen, Monographien und Periodika; **Incorporates:** Deutsche Nationalbibliographie. Reihe A: Neuerscheinungen des Buchhandels (ISSN 0323-3596); Deutsche Bibliographie: Neuerscheinungen-Sofortdienst (ISSN 0340-3416)
  Description: Bibliography of new publications.

DEUTSCHER WETTERDIENST. BIBLIOGRAPHIEN. see *METEOROLOGY — Abstracting, Bibliographies, Statistics*

053 015   GW
CODEN: DEZEDX
DEUTSCHSPRACHIGE ZEITSCHRIFTEN. 1956. a. DM.146 (effective 1997). Verlag der Schillerbuchhandlung Hans Banger, Guldenbachstr. 1, 50935 Cologne, Germany. TEL 49-221-431641. FAX 49-221-4303271. **Document type:** directory.
—BLDSC (3578.510000); CASDDS; Linda Hall.
  Former titles: Deutschsprachige Zeitschriften Deutschland - Oesterreich - Schweiz (ISSN 0419-005X); Anschriften Deutschsprachiger Zeitschriften (ISSN 0066-460X)

A DIFFERENT LIGHT REVIEW; a catalog of gay and lesbian literature. see *HOMOSEXUALITY*

011   US   ISSN 0899-353X
Z5771   CODEN: DIPREH
DIRECTORIES IN PRINT; an annotated guide to business and industrial directories, professional and scientific rosters, and other lists and guides of all kinds. (Supplement avail.: Directory Information Service) 1980. irreg., 9th ed., 1991. $260. Gale Research, 835 Penobscot Bldg., 645 Griswold St., Detroit, MI 48226-4094. TEL 313-961-2242; 800-877-4253. FAX 800-414-5043. E-mail: daniel_snyder@gale.com. Eds. Charles B. Montney, Julie E. Towell.
●Also available online. Vendor(s): Knight-Ridder Information, Inc.
—BLDSC (3590.533500); CISTI; Linda Hall.
  Formerly (until 1988): Directory of Directories (ISSN 0275-5580)
  Description: Details of current projects and associated literature worldwide, with information on funding agencies and the communications infrastructure.

DIRECTORIO DE REVISTAS ESPANOLAS DE CIENCIAS SOCIALES Y HUMANAS. see *SOCIAL SCIENCES: COMPREHENSIVE WORKS — Abstracting, Bibliographies, Statistics*

DIRECTORIO M P M - MEDIOS AUDIOVISUALES/M P M - MEXICAN AUDIOVISUAL MEDIA RATES & DATA; tarifas y datos-cine, radio y television. (Medios Publicitarios Mexicanos, S.A.) see *ADVERTISING AND PUBLIC RELATIONS — Abstracting, Bibliographies, Statistics*

DIRECTORIO M P M - MEDIOS IMPRESOS/M P M - MEXICAN PRINT MEDIA RATES & DATA; tarifas y datos-anuncio exterior, periodicos y revistas. (Medios Publicitarios Mexicanos, S.A.) see *ADVERTISING AND PUBLIC RELATIONS — Abstracting, Bibliographies, Statistics*

DIRECTORY MARKETPLACE. see *PUBLISHING AND BOOK TRADE*

011   UK
DIRECTORY OF ACRONYMS. 1993. biennial. £27 (foreign £33) (effective 1997). British Library, Document Supply Centre, Boston Spa, Wetherby, W. Yorks LS23 7BQ, England. TEL 44-1937-546080. FAX 44-1937-546286. TELEX 557381. (Subscr. to: Turpin Distribution Services Ltd., Blackhorse Rd., Letchworth, Herts. SG6 1HN, England. TEL 44-1462-672555. FAX 44-1462-480947). **Document type:** bibliography.
  Description: Provides details of more than 8,000 acronyms present in the Document Supply Centre's Conference Index database of over 300,000 records.

DIRECTORY OF AUSTRALIAN ASSOCIATIONS. see *BUSINESS AND ECONOMICS — Trade And Industrial Directories*

016.05   US   ISSN 1057-1337
Z6951
DIRECTORY OF ELECTRONIC JOURNALS, NEWSLETTERS AND ACADEMIC DISCUSSION LISTS. 1991. a. $79 to non-members; members $55. Association of Research Libraries, 21 Dupont Circle, Ste. 800, Washington, DC 20036. TEL 202-296-2296. FAX 202-872-0884. E-mail: pubs@cni.org; URL: http://arl.cni.org/scomm/edir/index.html. Ed. Dru Mogge. **Document type:** directory.
●Also available online.
—BLDSC (3593.495500); CISTI; Linda Hall.
  Description: Aims to be a tool for assisting individuals in locating Internet resources as well as assisting librarians in building electronic collections.

DIRECTORY OF GRANTS IN THE HUMANITIES. see *EDUCATION — Abstracting, Bibliographies, Statistics*

011 808.87   US
DIRECTORY OF HUMOR MAGAZINES & HUMOR ORGANIZATIONS IN AMERICA (AND CANADA). 1985. triennial. $34.95. Wry-Bred Press, Inc., Box 1454, Madison Sq. Sta., New York, NY 10159-1454. TEL 212-689-5473. FAX 212-689-6859. Ed. Glenn Ellenbogen. **Document type:** directory.
  Description: Covers humor and anything related to it.

015   IR
Z6958.I65
DIRECTORY OF IRANIAN PERIODICALS AND NEWSPAPERS/RAHNAMAY-I MAJALLAH-HA VA RUZNAMEHA-YI IRAN. (Text in Persian) 1974. a. $30. National Library of Iran, Shahid Bahonar St., Tehran 19548, Iran. TEL 98-21-2280937. FAX 98-21-2288680. Eds. Poori Soltani, Reza Eqtedar. circ. 1,000. **Document type:** bibliography.
  Incorporates: Directory of Iranian Newspapers; **Former titles:** Rahnamay-i Majallah-ha-yi Iran (ISSN 0378-7443); Directory of Iranian Periodicals (ISSN 0084-9960)
  Description: Bibliographic information on all periodicals and newspapers published in Iran.

DIRECTORY OF PERIODICALS PUBLISHED IN INDIA. see *PUBLISHING AND BOOK TRADE*

DIRECTORY OF POLITICAL NEWSLETTERS. see *POLITICAL SCIENCE — Abstracting, Bibliographies, Statistics*

DIRECTORY OF SMALL MAGAZINE - PRESS EDITORS AND PUBLISHERS. see *PUBLISHING AND BOOK TRADE — Abstracting, Bibliographies, Statistics*

011   CH
DIRECTORY OF TAIWAN. (Text in Chinese, English) 1950. a. $15.40 (foreign $41.30) (effective Apr. 1993). China News, 110 Yenping S. Rd., 11F, Taipei, Taiwan 106, Republic of China. TEL 02-388-7931. FAX 02-381-5987. Ed. Daisy C.H. Liao. adv. contact: Chiu Chi-sen. **Document type:** directory.
  Description: Lists phone numbers and names of chief executives for government, embassies, banks, business organizations, associations, airlines, insurance companies and more.

DIVIDENDS FROM WOOD RESEARCH; recent publications of the Forest Products Laboratory. see *FORESTS AND FORESTRY — Abstracting, Bibliographies, Statistics*

016.33   BL   ISSN 0101-4854
DOCUMENTACAO AMAZONICA; catalogo coletivo. 1974. irreg. free. Superintendencia do Desenvolvimento da Amazonia, Travessa Antonio Baena 1113, Cx. Postal 874, Belem, Para, Brazil. (Prepared by: Rede de Bibliotecas da Amazonia) stat.
  Description: Economic conditions in the Amazon valley.

334 011   II
DOCUMENTATION BULLETIN FOR SOUTH-EAST ASIA.* (Text in English) 1969. q. Rs.30($4) International Cooperative Alliance, Regional Office and Education Centre for South-East Asia, P.O. Box 3312, 43 Friends Colony, New Delhi 110014, India. Ed. B.D. Pandey. circ. 500. (processed)
  Formerly: International Cooperative Alliance. Regional Office and Education Centre for South-East Asia. Documentation Bulletin (ISSN 0012-4591)

016   IT   ISSN 0070-6906
DOCUMENTI SULLE ARTI DEL LIBRO. 1962. irreg., latest 1995. price varies. Edizioni Il Polifilo, Via Borgonuovo 2, 20121 Milan, Italy. Ed. Alberto Vigevani.

E FOR ENVIRONMENT; an annotated bibliography of children's books with environmental themes. see *ENVIRONMENTAL STUDIES*

015   UK   ISSN 0046-0958
EAST ANGLIAN BIBLIOGRAPHY. 1960. q. £30 (foreign £44) (effective 1997). East Anglian Librarians Consultative Committee, County Library, Northgate St., Ipswich, Suffolk IP1 3DE, England. TEL 44-1473-232041. FAX 44-1473-232041. (Subscr. and adv. addr.: c/o Alan Leventhal, Kings Lynn Library, London Rd., Kings Lynn, Norfolk PE30 5EZ England. TEL 44-1553-772568) Ed. Ed Button. R&P contact: Ed Button. adv. contact: Alan Leventhal. circ. 65. **Document type:** bibliography.
  Description: Lists all local material added to public library collections in East Anglia.

EAST ASIA BIBLIOGRAPHY; a review of new publications on China & the Far East. see *BUSINESS AND ECONOMICS — Abstracting, Bibliographies, Statistics*

EBSCO BULLETIN OF SERIALS CHANGES. see *LIBRARY AND INFORMATION SCIENCES*

015   UK   ISSN 0140-7082
EDINBURGH BIBLIOGRAPHICAL SOCIETY TRANSACTIONS. 1938. biennial. £10 membership (students £5). Edinburgh Bibliographical Society, c/o National Library of Scotland, George IV Bridge, Edinburgh EH1 1EW, Scotland. TEL 44-131-226-4531. FAX 44-131-220-6662. TELEX 72638 NLSEDI G. E-mail: library@admin.nls. uk. Ed. K.J. Dunn. R&P contact: K.J. Dunn. circ. 200. **Document type:** academic/scholarly publication.
  Formerly: Edinburgh Bibliographical Society. Publications.

THE EFFICIENT HOUSE SOURCEBOOK; an annotated bibliography and directory of helpful organizations. see *BUILDING AND CONSTRUCTION*

EGYPTIAN MUSEUM. LIBRARY. CATALOGUE. see *ARCHAEOLOGY — Abstracting, Bibliographies, Statistics*

011 800   US   ISSN 0161-0996
Z5579.6
EIGHTEENTH CENTURY: A CURRENT BIBLIOGRAPHY. 1975. a. $92.50. A M S Press, Inc., 56 E. 13th St., New York, NY 10003. TEL 212-777-4700. FAX 212-995-5413. Ed. Jim Springer Brock. bk.rev index. (back issues avail.)
  Description: Bibliography of books and articles in literature, art, history, philosophy and science from or about the eighteenth century.

011　　　　　　　FR　　ISSN 1021-6928
ELEMENTS DE BIBLIOGRAPHIE SUR LES PAYS DU SAHEL/ELEMENTS FOR A BIBLIOGRAPHY ON THE SAHELIAN COUNTRIES. 1976. a. free. Organization for Economic Cooperation and Development, 2 rue Andre-Pascal, 75775 Paris Cedex 16, France. (U.S. orders to: O.E.C.D. Publication & Information Center, 2001 L St., N.W., Ste. 650, Washington, DC 20036-4922. TEL 202-785-6323) (also avail. in microfiche from OEC)

EL-HI TEXTBOOKS AND SERIALS IN PRINT; including related teaching materials K-12. see EDUCATION — Abstracting, Bibliographies, Statistics

ENERGY INFORMATION DIRECTORY. see ENERGY

EOTVOS LORAND TUDOMANYEGYETEM. TUDOMANYOS TAJEKOZTATO. see SCIENCES: COMPREHENSIVE WORKS — Abstracting, Bibliographies, Statistics

ERLANGER BAUSTEINE ZUR FRAENKISCHEN HEIMATFORSCHUNG. see HISTORY

016　　　　　　　UK　　ISSN 0305-3679
ESSEX UNION LIST OF SERIALS. 1971. s-a. £5. Essex Libraries, Goldlay Gardens, Chelmsford, Essex CM2 0EW, England. Ed.Bd. bibl. circ. 200. (microfiche) **Document type:** bibliography.

ESTUARIES AND COASTAL WATERS OF THE BRITISH ISLES; an annual bibliography of recent scientific papers. see ENVIRONMENTAL STUDIES — Abstracting, Bibliographies, Statistics

015　　　　　　　ET　　ISSN 0071-1772
Z3521
ETHIOPIAN PUBLICATIONS: BOOKS, PAMPHLETS, ANNUALS AND PERIODICAL ARTICLES. 1963. irreg. $5. Addis Ababa University, Institute of Ethiopian Studies, P.O. Box 1176, Addis Ababa, Ethiopia. TEL 251-1-119469. FAX 251-1-552688. E-mail: IES@padis.gn.apc.org. Ed. Abdussamad H. Ahmad. circ. 1,000. (back issues avail.) **Indexed:** A.I.C.P. **Document type:** academic/scholarly publication.

ETUDES STRATEGIQUES ET MILITAIRES (COLLECTION). see LINGUISTICS — Abstracting, Bibliographies, Statistics

EUDORA WELTY NEWSLETTER. see LITERATURE

011　　　　　　　GW　　ISSN 1011-1077
EUROPAEISCHE INTEGRATION - AUSWAHLBIBLIOGRAPHIE. 1974. 2/yr. free. Arbeitskreis Europaeische Integration e.V., Bachstr. 32, 53115 Bonn, Germany. FAX 49-228-698437. (Co-sponsor: Vertretung der Europaeischen Kommission) Ed.Bd. circ. 2,100. **Indexed:** P.A.I.S.For.Lang.Ind. **Document type:** bibliography.

EUROPEAN BIBLIOGRAPHY OF SLAVIC AND EAST EUROPEAN STUDIES/BIBLIOGRAPHIE EUROPEENE DES TRAVAUX SUR L'EX-URSS ET L'EUROPE DE L'EST/EUROPAEISCHE BIBLIOGRAPHIE OESTEUROPASTUDIEN. see HISTORY — Abstracting, Bibliographies, Statistics

EUROPEAN ORGANIZATION FOR NUCLEAR RESEARCH. LIST OF SCIENTIFIC PUBLICATIONS/CONSEIL EUROPEEN POUR LA RECHERCHE NUCLEAIRE. LISTE DES PUBLICATIONS SCIENTIFIQUES. see PHYSICS — Abstracting, Bibliographies, Statistics

EX LIBRIS; Aktueller Buchdienst fuer Studenten und Dozenten der Rechts, Wirtschafts, und Informatik. see PUBLISHING AND BOOK TRADE

EXTENSION BIBLIOGRAFICA. see SOCIAL SCIENCES: COMPREHENSIVE WORKS — Abstracting, Bibliographies, Statistics

016.05　　　　　　　US　　ISSN 1059-6852
Z6941
FAXON GUIDE TO SERIALS. 1931. a. $25 (free to qualified personnel). Faxon Company, Inc., 15 Southwest Park, Westwood, MA 02090. TEL 617-329-3350. FAX 617-320-0141. TELEX 681-7238. adv.; illus. circ. 10,000. **Document type:** catalog.
—Linda Hall.
Former titles: Faxon Librarians' Guide to Serials (ISSN 0275-8466); Faxon Librarians' Guide (ISSN 0146-2660); Faxon Librarians' Guide to Periodicals (ISSN 0092-0487); Faxon Indexed Periodicals.

011　　　　　　　PR　　ISSN 0015-0592
Z1201　　　　　　　　　　CODEN: FBHIDO
FICHERO BIBLIOGRAFICO HISPANOAMERICANO. 1961. 11/yr. $75. Melcher Ediciones, c/o Margaret Melcher, Box 6000, San Juan, PR 00906. TEL 787-724-1352. FAX 787-724-2886. adv.; bk.rev.; index. (also avail. in microfilm from UMI; reprint service avail. from UMI) **Document type:** bibliography.
—CASDDS; Linda Hall; UMI.
Description: Lists new books in Spanish published in the Americas and Spain.

FICTION ON FICHE. see LITERATURE — Abstracting, Bibliographies, Statistics

011 956 011　　　　　　LE　　ISSN 0257-439X
FIHRIST; index to Arabic periodical literature. (Text in Arabic; occasionally in English, French, German, Spanish) 1981. q. £L500($200) Al-Fihrist Academic Research Institute, Abu Hishmah Bldg., Farabi St., Watwat (al-zarif), P.O. Box 14-5968, Beirut, Lebanon. (Subscr. to: Syrian Lebanese Commercial Bank (Account no. for Al-Fihrist 20195), Hamra Branch, P.O. Box 118701, Beirut, Lebanon) Ed. Samir Shaykh. adv.; bk.rev.; index. circ. 1,500.

FILMATISEREDE BOEGER. see MOTION PICTURES

FINE ARTS PERIODICALS; an international directory of the visual arts. see ART — Abstracting, Bibliographies, Statistics

015　　　　　　　FI　　ISSN 0356-178X
FINUC-S. (Text in English, Finnish, Swedish) 1974. a. FIM 300. Helsingin Yliopiston Kirjasto - Helsinki University Library, Box 15, Unioninkatu 36, SF-00014, University of Helsinki, Finland.
Formerly: Fink-S.
Description: Finnish Union Catalog of Serials on microfiche.

FOCUS ON BRITISH BIOLOGICAL AND MEDICAL SCIENCES RESEARCH. see BIOLOGY

011 330　　　　　　UK　　ISSN 1350-4959
FOCUS ON BRITISH BUSINESS AND MANAGEMENT SCIENCES RESEARCH. 1994. m. £28 (foreign £34) (effective 1997). British Library, Document Supply Centre, Boston Spa, Wetherby, W. Yorks LS23 7BQ, England. TEL 44-1937-546080. FAX 44-1937-546286. TELEX 557381. (Subscr. to Turpin Distribution Services Ltd., Blackhorse Rd., Letchworth, Herts. SG6 1HN, England. TEL 44-1462-672555. FAX 44-1462-480947) adv.; index. **Document type:** bibliography.
—BLDSC (3964.203854).

011 004　　　　　　UK　　ISSN 1350-4967
FOCUS ON BRITISH ENGINEERING AND COMPUTER SCIENCES RESEARCH. 1994. m. £26 (foreign £31) (effective 1996). British Library, Document Supply Centre, Boston Spa, Wetherby, W. Yorks LS23 7BQ, England. TEL 44-1937-546080. FAX 44-1937-546286. TELEX 557381. (Subscr. to: Turpin Distribution Services Ltd., Blackhorse Rd., Letchworth, Herts. SG6 1HN, England. TEL 44-1462-672555. FAX 44-1462-480947) adv.; index. **Document type:** bibliography.
—BLDSC (3964.203855).

FOCUS ON BRITISH ENVIRONMENTAL SCIENCES RESEARCH. see ENVIRONMENTAL STUDIES

FOR YOUNGER READERS, BRAILLE AND TALKING BOOKS (LARGE PRINT EDITION). see HANDICAPPED — Abstracting, Bibliographies, Statistics

011　　　　　　　US　　ISSN 0015-8119
Z1219
FORTHCOMING BOOKS. (Supplement to: Books in Print) 1966. bi-m. (issues cumulate; q. microfiche avail.). $265. R.R. Bowker, A Division of Reed Elsevier Inc., 121 Chanlon Rd., New Providence, NJ 07974. TEL 908-464-6800. FAX 908-665-3502. TELEX 138 755. E-mail: info@boker.com; URL: http://www.reedref.com. (Subscr. to: Order Dept., Box 31, New Providence, NJ 07974-9903. TEL 800-521-8110) (also avail. in magnetic tape; microfiche) **Document type:** bibliography, directory.
●Also available online. Vendor(s): Knight-Ridder Information, Inc. (File no.470); Ovid Technologies, Inc. (BBIP).
Also available on CD-ROM. Producer(s): Bowker Electronic Publishing (Books in Print PLUS).
—Linda Hall. **CCC**.
Incorporates (1967-1986): Subject Guide to Forthcoming Books (ISSN 0000-0264)
Description: Lists just-published and to-be-published books, with ISBNs and U.S. Library of Congress numbers.

016 614　　　　　　FR　　ISSN 0992-8235
FRANCE. MINISTERE DE LA SOLIDARITE, DE LA SANTE ET DE LA PROTECTION SOCIALE. BULLETIN OFFICIEL. 1957. w. 396 F. Ministere des Affaires Sociales et de la Solidarite Nationale, Service de l'Information et de la Communication, 1 place Fontenoy, 75700 Paris, France. TEL 40-56-60-00. (Subscr. to: Journaux Officiels, 26 rue Desaix, 75015 Paris, France) (Co-sponsor: France. Ministere du Travail et de la Participation) bk.rev. circ. 13,500.
Former titles: France. Ministere des Affaires Sociales et Solidarite National. Bulletin Officiel; France. Ministere de la Sante et de la Famille. Bulletin Officiel; France. Ministere de la Sante et de la Securite Sociale. Bulletin Officiel.

FRANCE. SECRETARIAT D'ETAT CHARGE DE L'ENVIRONNEMENT ET DE LA QUALITE DE LA VIE. BULLETIN DE DOCUMENTATION DE L'ENVIRONNEMENT. see ENVIRONMENTAL STUDIES — Abstracting, Bibliographies, Statistics

DIE FRAUENFRAGE IN DEUTSCHLAND. BIBLIOGRAPHIE. see WOMEN'S STUDIES — Abstracting, Bibliographies, Statistics

FRENCH 20 BIBLIOGRAPHY; critical and biographical references for the study of French literature since 1885. see LINGUISTICS — Abstracting, Bibliographies, Statistics

011　　　　　　　US　　ISSN 1040-8258
Z6941　　　　　　　　　　CODEN: FSONEO
FULLTEXT SOURCES ONLINE. 1989. s-a. $116 per issue (foreign $131). BiblioData, Box 61, Needham Heights, MA 02194. TEL 617-444-1154. FAX 617-449-4584. E-mail: ina@bibliodata.com; URL: http://www.bibliodata.com. **Document type:** directory.
—BLDSC (4055.564500); CISTI.
Description: Focuses on periodicals, journals, newspapers, newsletters and newswires that are available online in fulltext. Also lists URLs as well as dates of coverage for each title.

FUNDHEFT FUER ARBEITS- UND SOZIALRECHT; systematischer Nachweis der Gesetzgebung, Rechtsprechung, Buecher und Aufsaetze. see LAW — Abstracting, Bibliographies, Statistics

FUTURES RESEARCH QUARTERLY. see SCIENCES: COMPREHENSIVE WORKS

011 020　　　　　　US
G P O SALES PUBLICATIONS REFERENCE FILE: MAGNETIC TAPE. bi-w. $850 (foreign $1062.50). U.S. Government Printing Office, Superintendent of Documents, Washington, DC 20402. (Subscr. to: Box 371954, Pittsburgh, PA 15250-7954. TEL 202-512-1800. FAX 202-512-2250) (magnetic tape) **Document type:** bibliography, government publication.
Description: Lists current publications offered for sale by the Superintendent of Documents.

BIBLIOGRAPHIES

011 020   US
G P O SALES PUBLICATIONS REFERENCE FILE: MICROFICHE EDITION. bi-m. (plus m. supplements). $125 (foreign $156.25). U.S. Government Printing Office, Superintendent of Documents, Washington, DC 20402. (Subscr. to: Box 371954, Pittsburgh, PA 15250-7954. TEL 202-512-1800. FAX 202-512-2250) (microfiche; back issues avail.) **Document type:** government publication, bibliography.
    Description: Lists current publications offered for sale by the Superintendent of Documents, arranged by several elements.

011 800   UK
GALACTIC CENTRAL BIBLIOGRAPHIES. 1990. irreg., no.46, 1996. price varies. Galactic Central Publications, c/o Phil Stephensen-Payne, Ed., 25A Copgrove Rd., Leeds, W. Yorks. LS8 2SP, England. E-mail: 73212.16@compuserve.com. (Outside UK orders to: Chris Drumm, Box 445, Polk City, Iowa, 50226, U.S.) Pub. Phil Stephensen-Payne. R&P contact: Phil Stephensen-Payne. **Document type:** bibliography.
    Description: Provides current bibliographies of science fiction and fantasy writers. Includes all of the authors stories, books, poems, edited works, nonfiction works.

016.05   US   ISSN 1048-7972
Z6951
GALE DIRECTORY OF PUBLICATIONS AND BROADCAST MEDIA. (In 3 vols. plus Update) 1869. a. $425 (includes Gale Directory of Publications and Broadcast Media Update). Gale Research, 835 Penobscot Bldg., 645 Griswold St., Detroit, MI 48226-4094. TEL 313-961-2242; 800-877-4253. FAX 800-414-5043. E-mail: daniel_snyder@gale.com. Eds. Karen Troshynski-Thomas and Deborah M. Burek. circ. 11,000.
    ●Also available online. Vendor(s): Knight-Ridder Information, Inc.
    —BLDSC (4066.776000); CISTI.
    Former titles (until 1989): Gale Directory of Publications (ISSN 0892-1636); (until 1987): I M S Directory of Publications; (until 1982): Ayer Directory of Publications (ISSN 0145-1642); Ayer Directory of Newspapers, Magazines, and Trade Publications (ISSN 0067-2696)
    Description: Bibliography of newspapers, magazines and trade publications.

011   US
GALE DIRECTORY OF PUBLICATIONS AND BROADCAST MEDIA UPDATE. a. included in Gale Directory of Publications and Broadcast Media. Gale Research, 835 Penobscot Bldg., 645 Griswold St., Detroit, MI 48226-4094. TEL 313-961-2242; 800-877-4253. FAX 800-414-5043. E-mail: daniel_snydet@gale.com. Ed. Julie Winklepleck.
    Description: Interedition service providing more than 2,500 updates to listings in the main volume and nearly 1,500 new listings.

011   US   ISSN 1040-9351
Z6941
GALE INTERNATIONAL DIRECTORY OF PUBLICATIONS; an international guide to more than 4,800 newspapers, magazines, and other periodicals circulating primarily outside the United States and Canada. 1989. irreg. $100. Gale Research, 835 Penobscot Bldg., 645 Griswold St., Detroit, MI 48226-4094. TEL 313-961-2242; 800-877-4253. FAX 800-414-5043. E-mail: daniel_snyder@gale.com. Eds. Kay Gill, Darren L. Smith.
    Description: Provides access in a geographic arrangement to basic information about newspapers, magazines, and similar publications circulating primarily outside the United States and Canada.

GARDEN LITERATURE; an index to periodical articles and book reviews. see GARDENING AND HORTICULTURE — Abstracting, Bibliographies, Statistics

GEORGE ELIOT - GEORGE HENRY LEWES STUDIES. see LITERARY AND POLITICAL REVIEWS

GEOSOURCES. see EARTH SCIENCES — Abstracting, Bibliographies, Statistics

GEOTITLES; geoscience bibliography. see EARTH SCIENCES — Abstracting, Bibliographies, Statistics

011   GW
▼**GERMAN AND EAST EUROPEAN BOOKS IN PRINT.** (Text in English, German; summaries in Czech, Hungarian, Polish) 1996. s-a. DM.395. Buchhaendler-Vereinigung GmbH, Postfach 100442, 60004 Frankfurt a.M., Germany. TEL 49-69-1306-0. FAX 49-69-1306201. E-mail: weber@bhv.de. **Document type:** bibliography.
    ●Available only on CD-ROM.
    Description: Offers a comprehensive survey of books in print and publishers in Germany, the Czech Republic, Hungary and Poland.

015   GW
GERMAN BOOKS OUT OF PRINT ON C D - R O M. (Supplement to: German Books in Print on C D - R O M) (Text in English, German) a. £275. K.G. Saur Verlag KG, A member of the Reed Elsevier plc group, Ortlerstr. 8, 81373 Munich, Germany. TEL 49-89-76902-0. FAX 49-89-76901250. E-mail: 100730.1341@compuserve.com; URL: http://www.reed-elsevier.com. (avail. for MS-DOS) **Document type:** bibliography.
    ●Available only on CD-ROM.
    Description: Includes 380,000 titles dating back to 1987 from over 9,000 publishers.

015   GW
GERMANY. DEUTSCHER BUNDESTAG. WISSENSCHAFTLICHE DIENSTE. AKTUELLE BIBLIOGRAPHIEN DER BIBLIOTHEK. 1962. irreg. free. Deutscher Bundestag, Abteilung Wissenschaftliche Dienste, Bundeshaus, 53113 Bonn, Germany. TEL 49-228-1622967. **Document type:** government publication.
    Formerly (until 1996): Germany. Deutscher Bundestag. Wissenschaftliche Dienste. Bibliographien.

015   GW   ISSN 0344-9130
GERMANY. DEUTSCHER BUNDESTAG. WISSENSCHAFTLICHE DIENSTE. MATERIALIEN. 1965. irreg. free. Deutscher Bundestag, Abteilung Wissenschaftliche Dienste, Bundeshaus, 53113 Bonn, Germany. TEL 49-228-1622967. **Document type:** academic/scholarly publication, government publication.

GERMANY. DEUTSCHER BUNDESTAG. WISSENSCHAFTLICHE DIENSTE. NEUE AUFSAETZE IN DER BIBLIOTHEK. see SCIENCES: COMPREHENSIVE WORKS — Abstracting, Bibliographies, Statistics

011   GW   ISSN 0931-3397
GERMANY. DEUTSCHER BUNDESTAG. WISSENSCHAFTLICHE DIENSTE. NEUERWERBUNGEN DER BIBLIOTHEK. 1961. 6/yr. free. Deutscher Bundestag, Abteilung Wissenschaftliche Dienste, Bundeshaus, 53113 Bonn, Germany. TEL 49-228-1622967. FAX 49-228-1626257. TELEX 886529-BTHT-D. circ. 1,350. **Document type:** government publication.
    Formerly: Germany (Federal Republic, 1949-). Deutscher Bundestag Wissenschaftliche Dienste. Neuerwerbungen.

015   GH   ISSN 0855-0093
GHANA NATIONAL BIBLIOGRAPHY. 1967. bi-m. $60. Ghana Library Board, George Padmore Research Library of African Affairs, P.O. Box 2970, Accra, Ghana. TEL 233-21-223526. bibl. circ. 200. **Document type:** bibliography.
    —BLDSC (4166.315000).
    Formerly: Ghana: A Current Bibliography (ISSN 0072-4378)
    Description: Covers material published in Ghana, including new serials, books by Ghanaians about Ghana published abroad, theses and dissertations, periodical articles about Ghana, and a list of publishers whose publications are listed in particular issues and their addresses.

015   IT
GIUNTA REGIONALE DI VENETO. NOTIZIARIO BIBLIOGRAFICO. 3/yr. free. Giunta Regionale di Veneto, Dipartimento per l'Informazione, Palazzo Sceriman, Cannaregio Lista di Spagna, 30121 Venice, Italy. TEL 39-41-792616. Ed. Anelio Pellizzon. circ. 15,000.

GOOD READING; a guide for serious readers. see PUBLISHING AND BOOK TRADE

354 015   CN   ISSN 0709-0412
Z1373
GOVERNMENT OF CANADA PUBLICATIONS QUARTERLY CATALOGUE; a comprehensive listing of all Government publications with index. (Catalog no. IC6-1) (Text in English and French) 1953. q. Can.$76 (foreign $91.20). Canada Communication Group, Publishing Division, 45 Sacre-Coeur Blvd., Rm. A2411 E, Hull, PQ K1A OS9, Canada. TEL 819-956-5365. FAX 819-956-5134. index. circ. 2,800. **Indexed:** Popul.Ind.
    —CISTI; Linda Hall.
    Formerly: Canadian Government Publications Monthly Catalogue (ISSN 0008-3690)

015.73   US   ISSN 0072-5188
Z1223.Z7
GOVERNMENT REFERENCE BOOKS; a biennial guide to U.S. government publications. 1968. biennial. $67.50 (effective 1997). Libraries Unlimited, Inc., Box 6633, Englewood, CO 80155-6633. TEL 800-237-6124. FAX 303-220-8843. Ed. Leroy C. Schwarzkopf.
    —CISTI.
    Description: Identifies key information resources from the printed matter issued by U.S. government agencies. Arranged in four sections: general references, social sciences, science and technology, and humanities.

361.73   US   ISSN 0145-8302
GRANTECHS. 1974. bi-w. $100. Grantechs, 3240 N. Webster Rd., Tucson, AZ 85715. Ed. Warren Smith. circ. 1,000.
    Formerly (until Jan. 1977): Grants Newsletter.
    Description: Lists grant programs.

011   US   ISSN 0898-8277
GREAT AMERICAN ORATORS. 1989. irreg. price varies. Greenwood Press, Inc. (Subsidiary of: Greenwood Publishing Group Inc.), 88 Post Rd. W., Box 5007, Westport, CT 06881-5007. TEL 203-226-3571. FAX 203-222-1502. **Document type:** monographic series.
    —BLDSC (4214.439700).

GREAT BRITAIN. CIVIL AVIATION AUTHORITY. LIBRARY BULLETIN. see TRANSPORTATION — Air Transport

011   UK   ISSN 0267-1727
GREAT BRITAIN. H.M.S.O. BOOKS IN PRINT. Variant title: H.M.S.O. in Print. 1985. bi-m. H.M.S.O. Books, 51 Nine Elms Ln., London SW8 5DR, England. TEL 44-171-873-0011. FAX 44-171-873-8247. (Subscr. to: H.M.S.O. Books, P.O. Box 276, London SW8 5DT, England. TEL 44-171-873-8499. FAX 44-171-873-8222) (microfiche) **Document type:** catalog, government publication.
    ●Also available online. Vendor(s): Knight-Ridder Information, Inc.
    Description: Lists all H.M.S.O. publications in print and available from the Publications Centre.

011   UK   ISSN 0951-8843
GREAT BRITAIN. H.M.S.O. DAILY LIST. d. (5/w.). H.M.S.O. Books, 51 Nine Elms Ln., London SW8 5DR, England. TEL 44-171-873-0011. TELEX 297138. (Subscr. to: H.M.S.O. Books, P.O. Box 276, London SW8 5DT, England. TEL 44-171-873-8499 FAX 44-171-873-8222) **Document type:** catalog, government publication.
    ●Also available online. Vendor(s): Knight-Ridder Information, Inc.
    Formerly (until 1986): Daily List of Government Publications (ISSN 0263-743X)
    Description: Lists all U.K. government publications published or sold by H.M.S.O., including Parliamentary and non-Parliamentary publications, Statutory Instruments, and agency and Northern Ireland publications.

011   UK   ISSN 0263-7197
Z2009
GREAT BRITAIN. H.M.S.O. MONTHLY CATALOGUE. Variant title: Great Britain. H.M.S.O. Government Publications (Monthly). m. H.M.S.O. Books, 51 Nine Elms Ln., London SW8 5DR, England. TEL 44-171-873-0011. FAX 44-171-873-8247. (Subscr. to: H.M.S.O. Books, P.O. Box 276, London SW8 5DT, England. TEL 44-171-873-8499. FAX 44-171-873-8222) **Document type:** catalog, government publication.
● Also available online. Vendor(s): Knight-Ridder Information, Inc.
—CISTI.
Description: Lists all titles published by H.M.S.O. during the previous month, excluding Statutory Instruments.

011   UK   ISSN 0955-7601
GREAT BRITAIN. H.M.S.O. PUBLICATIONS CATALOGUE. a. H.M.S.O. Books, 51 Nine Elms Ln., London SW8 5DR, England. TEL 44-171-873-0011. FAX 44-171-873-8247. (Subscr. to: H.M.S.O. Books, P.O. Box 276, London SW8 5DT, England. TEL 44-171-873-8499. FAX 44-171-873-8222) **Document type:** catalog, government publication.
● Also available online. Vendor(s): Knight-Ridder Information, Inc.
—BLDSC (4319.424000).
Description: Lists all the publications received at H.M.S.O. during the calendar year from the British, European and international organizations for which H.M.S.O. is an agent.

011   UK
GREAT BRITAIN. H.M.S.O. STATUTORY INSTRUMENTS LIST. m. H.M.S.O. Books, 51 Nine Elms Ln., London SW8 5DR, England. TEL 44-171-873-0011. FAX 44-171-873-8247. (Subscr. to: H.M.S.O. Books, P.O. Box 276, London SW8 5DT, England. TEL 44-171-873-8499. FAX 44-171-873-8222) **Document type:** catalog, government publication.
● Also available online. Vendor(s): Knight-Ridder Information, Inc.
Description: Lists H.M.S.O. Statutory Instruments, which are not included in the monthly and annual catalogs. Includes Northern Ireland Statuatory Rules.

011   UK
Z2009
GREAT BRITAIN. STATIONERY OFFICE. ANNUAL CATALOGUE. a. price varies. Stationery Office, 51 Nine Elms Ln., London SW8 5DR, England. TEL 44-171-873-0011. (Subscr. to: Stationery Office, Publications Centre, P.O. Box 276, London SW8 5DT, England. TEL 44-171-873-8466. FAX 44-171-873-8222) circ. 6,600. **Document type:** government publication, catalog.
● Also available online. Vendor(s): Knight-Ridder Information, Inc.
—BLDSC (4319.425000); CISTI; Linda Hall.
Former titles (until 1996): Great Britain. H.M.S.O. Annual Catalogue (ISSN 0951-8584); (until 1986): Great Britain. H.M.S.O. Government Publications (ISSN 0143-9499); (until 1973): Great Britain. H.M.S.O. Catalogue of Government Publications.
Description: Lists the publications that the Stationery Office received during the calendar year, except for Statutory Instruments.

011   UK   ISSN 0267-2146
GREAT BRITAIN. H.M.S.O. COMMITTEE REPORTS INDEX. 1985. q. H.M.S.O. Books, Subscriptions, 51 Nine Elms Ln., London SW8 5DR, England. TEL 071-873-8499. TELEX 297138. (Subscr. to: H.M.S.O. Books, Box 276, London SW8 5DR, England. TEL 071-873-9090. FAX 071-873-8200) **Document type:** catalog, government publication.
● Also available online. Vendor(s): Knight-Ridder Information, Inc.
—BLDSC (3337.852000).
Description: Lists the chairmen of committee reports published by H.M.S.O.

015.68   SA
GREY BIBLIOGRAPHIES. 1946. irreg., no.19, 1991. price varies. South African Library, P.O. Box 496, Cape Town 8000, South Africa. TEL 27-21-246320. FAX 27-21-244848. TELEX 5-22604 SA. **Document type:** bibliography.
Description: Bibliographies of subjects of South African interest.

053.1   GW   ISSN 0017-4599
GROSS WARTENBERGER HEIMATBLATT. 1955. m. Verlag Helmut Preussler, Dagmarstr. 8, 90482 Nuernberg, Germany. Ed. Karl-Heinz Eisert. adv.; bk.rev. **Document type:** newsletter.

050   IT
GUIDA DELLA STAMPA PERIODICA ITALIANA. 1969. biennial. L.100000. Unione della Stampa Periodica Italiana, Viale Battista Bardanzellu 95, 00155 Rome, Italy. TEL 40-65-941. FAX 40-66-859. adv. circ. 10,000. **Document type:** directory.
Description: Lists periodical publishers in Italy. Includes the statutes and organs of the union and legislation.

015   IT
GUIDA RAGIONATA AI PERIODICI ITALIANI. irreg. Strumenti Editoriali s.r.l., Via Verona 9, 20135 Milan, Italy. TEL 02-58301054. FAX 02-58320473. Ed. Bea Marin.
Formerly: Catalogo Ragionato dei Periodici Italiani.

GUIDE DES BANQUES DE DONNEES FACTUELLES FRANCAISES SUR LES MATERIAUX. see ENGINEERING — Computer Applications

016 658.8   US   ISSN 0533-5248
Z5771
GUIDE TO AMERICAN DIRECTORIES. 1954. biennial. $85. B. Klein Publications, Box 6578, Delray Beach, FL 33482. TEL 407-496-3316. FAX 407-496-5546. Ed. Bernard Klein.
Description: Covers over 200 classifications of business, industry and the professions.

GUIDE TO AMERICAN SCIENTIFIC AND TECHNICAL DIRECTORIES. see TECHNOLOGY: COMPREHENSIVE WORKS — Abstracting, Bibliographies, Statistics

GUIDE TO COLLECTIONS OF MANUSCRIPTS RELATING TO AUSTRALIA; a selective union list. see HISTORY — Abstracting, Bibliographies, Statistics

614.7 016   II   ISSN 0252-7979
GUIDE TO CURRENT LITERATURE IN ENVIRONMENTAL HEALTH ENGINEERING AND SCIENCE. (Text in English) 1970. m. Rs.20 to individuals; institutions Rs.60. National Environmental Engineering Research Institute, Documentation and Library Services, Nehru Marg, Nagpur 440020, India. (Affiliate: Council of Scientific and Industrial Research) (processed)

011   JA
GUIDE TO EXHIBITIONS IN THE WORLD. (Text in English) s-a. Convention Forum, c/o C.N.T. Inc. Hamaso Building, 1-11 Kanda Ogawamachi, Chiyoda-ku, Tokyo 101, Japan. TEL 03-3293-2757. FAX 03-3293-3520.
Description: Lists the schedules of major world exhibitions, trade fairs, international conferences and scientific conferences.

050 015   II   ISSN 0017-5285
Z6958.I4
GUIDE TO INDIAN PERIODICAL LITERATURE. (Text in English) 1964. q. (plus a. cumulation). Rs.12000($200) (effective 1996). Indian Documentation Service, Patal Nagar, Post Box No. 13, Gurgaon 122 001, Haryana, India. (Dist. by: Scientific Distribution Service, 5-A, Bhagat-ki-kothi Box No. 33, Jodhpur, Rajasthan 342 001, India. FAX 91-291-49093) Ed. V.K. Jain. adv.
—BLDSC (4229.300000).

011   UK
GUIDE TO INTERNATIONAL JOURNALS & PERIODICALS. 1887. a. free. Dawson UK Ltd., Cannon House, Folkestone, Kent CT19 5EE, England. TEL 44-1303-850101. FAX 44-1303-850440. TELEX 96392. URL: http://www.dawson.co.uk. Ed. Reinhild Coles. adv. contact: Marion Watts. circ. 6,000. **Document type:** directory.
Former titles: Little Red Book (ISSN 0265-5810); Guide to the Press of the World (ISSN 0072-8748)
Description: Lists 8,500 journals and other periodicals in all major subject areas.

011 020 070.5   GW   ISSN 0164-0747
Z1033.M5
GUIDE TO MICROFORMS IN PRINT. AUTHOR - TITLE. 1975. a. DM.596($285) K.G. Saur Verlag KG, A member of the Reed Elsevier plc group, Ortlerstr. 8, 81373 Munich, Germany. TEL 49-89-76902-0. FAX 49-89-76902150. E-mail: 100730.1341@ compuserve.com; URL: http://www.reed-elsevier. com. (Subscr. to: Postfach 701620, 81316 Munich, Germany; N. America subscr. to: K.G. Saur, 121 Chanlon Rd., New Providence, NJ 07974-9903. TEL 908-665-3576) adv. circ. 2,000. **Document type:** bibliography, directory.
—BLDSC (4229.700000); CISTI; Linda Hall.
Supersedes in part: Guide to Microforms in Print (ISSN 0017-5293); Incorporates: International Microforms in Print.
Description: Covers domestic and foreign publications issued by non-commercial and commercial sources and all genres of published material - books, journals, newspapers, government publications, archival material, collections. Entries are listed in alphabetical sequence and consist of author, title, volume, date, price, publisher, type of microform and ordering information.

017   GW   ISSN 0163-8386
Z1033.M5
GUIDE TO MICROFORMS IN PRINT. SUBJECT. 1975. a. DM.596($285) K.G. Saur Verlag KG, A member of the Reed Elsevier plc group, Ortlerstr. 8, 81373 Munich, Germany. TEL 49-89-76902-0. FAX 49-89-76902150. E-mail: 100730.1341@ compuserve.com; URL: http://www.reed-elsevier. com. (Subscr. to: Postfach 701620, 81316 Munich, Germany; N. America subscr. to: K.G. Saur, 121 Chanlon Rd., New Providence, NJ 07974-9903, USA. TEL 908-665-3576) index. circ. 1,500. **Document type:** directory.
Incorporates: International Microforms in Print.
Description: Subject access to all the microform publications listed in Guide to Microform in Print. Titles are categorized under subject headings based on the Dewey Decimal System.

011   GW   ISSN 0164-0739
Z1033.M5
GUIDE TO MICROFORMS IN PRINT. SUPPLEMENT. 1979. a. DM.248($155) K.G. Saur Verlag KG, A member of the Reed Elsevier plc group, Ortlerstr. 8, 81373 Munich, Germany. TEL 49-89-76902-0. FAX 49-89-76902150. E-mail: 100730.1341@ compuserve.com; URL: http://www.reed-elsevier. com. (Subscr. to: Postfach 701620, 81316 Munich, Germany; N. America subscr. to: K.G. Saur, A Reed Reference Publishing Company, 121 Chanlon Rd., New Providence, NJ 07974-9903, USA. TEL 908-665-3576) Ed. Barbara Hopkinson. adv.; bibl. circ. 1,000. (back issues avail.) **Document type:** bibliography, directory.
—CISTI.
Former titles: Microforms in Print. Supplement; Microlist (ISSN 0362-1014)
Description: Provides both author-title and subject listings of new titles published since the previous edition of the two main volumes.

011   AT   ISSN 1035-5391
GUIDE TO NEW AUSTRALIAN BOOKS. 1990. bi-m. Aus.$57. (Monash University, National Centre for Australian Studies) D.W. Thorpe, A member of the Reed Elsevier plc group, 18 Salmon St., Port Melbourne, Vic. 3207, Australia. TEL 61-3-92457370. FAX 61-3-92457395. E-mail: customer.service@thorpe.com.au; URL: http://www. reed-elsevier.com. (Subscr. to: P.O. Box 146, Port Melbourne, Vic. 3207, Australia) circ. 5,000. **Document type:** bibliography, directory.
● Also available on CD-ROM.
Description: Provides a complete listing of new books, along with bibliographic details and descriptive annotations.

016 070   CN   ISSN 0315-7288
GUIDE TO PERIODICALS AND NEWSPAPERS IN THE PUBLIC LIBRARIES OF METROPOLITAN TORONTO. 1970. a. Can.$59. Metropolitan Toronto Library Board, 789 Yonge St., Toronto, ON M4W 2G8, Canada. TEL 416-393-7018. FAX 416-393-7229. Ed.Pat Burchell. adv. contact: Mario Bernardi. **Document type:** catalog.
Formerly: Toronto. Public Libraries. Guide to Serials Currently Received in the Public Libraries of Metropolitan Toronto.

550 BIBLIOGRAPHIES

011.02   US   ISSN 0072-8624
GUIDE TO REFERENCE BOOKS (YEAR). 1902. irreg., latest 11th ed. $275. American Library Association, 50 E. Huron St., Chicago, IL 60611-2795. TEL 312-944-6780; 800-545-2433. FAX 312-440-9374. Ed. Robert Balay.
—CCC.
Description: Comprehensive coverage of reference books in all fields.

GUIDE TO REFERENCE BOOKS FOR SCHOOL MEDIA CENTERS. see LIBRARY AND INFORMATION SCIENCES — Abstracting, Bibliographies, Statistics

011 Z1000.5   US   ISSN 0072-8667
GUIDE TO REPRINTS. (Text in English, French, German, Italian, Latin, Spanish) 1967. a. $170. Guide to Reprints, Inc., Box 249, Kent, CT 06757. Ed. Ann S. Davis. adv. circ. 2,000. **Document type:** bibliography.
—CISTI; Linda Hall.

011.53   US
A GUIDE TO U.S. GOVERNMENT INFORMATION; subject bibliography index. a. free. U.S. Government Printing Office, Superintendent of Documents, Sales Management Division (SSMB), Washington, DC 20402. (Orders to: Superintendent of Documents, U.S. Government Printing Office, Box 371954, Pittsburgh, PA 15250-7954. TEL 202-512-1800. FAX 202-512-2250) **Document type:** bibliography.
Description: Lists individual subject bibliographies available from the U.S. Government Printing Office

GUOWAI KEJI ZILIAO MULU - CEHUIXUE/FOREIGN SCIENCE AND TECHNOLOGY LITERATURE CATALOGUE - SURVEY. see GEOGRAPHY — Abstracting, Bibliographies, Statistics

015 Z1791   GY   ISSN 0376-5202
GUYANESE NATIONAL BIBLIOGRAPHY. (Text in English) 1973. q. G.$100($30) (effective 1995). National Library, 76-77 Main and Church Sts., Box 10240, Georgetown, Guyana. TEL 592-2-62690. FAX 592-2-62699. Ed. Karen Sills. index. circ. 250. **Document type:** bibliography.

H C I M A QUARTERLY CURRENT AWARENESS BULLETIN FOR HOSPITALITY MANAGEMENT. (Hotel and Catering International Management Association) see HOTELS AND RESTAURANTS — Abstracting, Bibliographies, Statistics

011   GW
▼**HAMBURG-BIBLIOGRAPHIE**. 1995. a. (Staats- und Universitaetsbibliothek Hamburg) K.G. Saur Verlag KG, A member of the Reed Elsevier plc group, Ortlerstr. 8, 81373 Munich, Germany. TEL 49-89-76902-0. FAX 49-89-76902150. E-mail: 100730.1341@compuserve.com; URL: http://www.reed-elsevier.com. **Document type:** bibliography.

HANDBUCH DER UNIVERSITAETEN UND FACHHOCHSCHULEN BUNDESREPUBLIK DEUTSCHLAND, OESTERREICH, SCHWEIZ. see EDUCATION — Higher Education

016 300   IS
HARRY S. TRUMAN RESEARCH INSTITUTE FOR THE ADVANCEMENT OF PEACE. REPRINT SERIES. (Text in English) 1971. irreg. exchange basis. Hebrew University of Jerusalem, Harry S. Truman Research Institute for the Advancement of Peace, Mount Scopus, Jerusalem, Israel. TEL 972-2-882300. FAX 972-2-828076. TELEX 26458-IL. Ed. Chaia Beckerman. bibl. circ. 500. **Document type:** academic/scholarly publication.
Formerly: Harry S. Truman Research Institute, Jerusalem. Occasional Papers.

026 059.992   US
HARVARD - YENCHING LIBRARY BIBLIOGRAPHICAL SERIES. 1970. irreg., approx. every 4 or 5 yrs., latest vol.4. price varies. Harvard - Yenching Library, 2 Divinity Ave., Cambridge, MA 02138. TEL 617-495-3327. FAX 617-496-6008. Ed.Bd. circ. 200. **Document type:** academic/scholarly publication.

500 016   UK   ISSN 0144-6053
HARWELL INFORMATION BULLETIN. w. £200 (effective 1995). A E A Technology (Harwell), Harwell, Didcot, Oxon. OX11 0RB, England. TEL 44-1235-432907. FAX 44-1235-432859. A. Tompkins. **Document type:** bulletin.
Formerly: Great Britain. Atomic Energy Research Establishment. Harwell Information Bulletin.

015   US
HAWAIIAN ACQUISITION LIST; a quarterly bibliography. 1944. q. free. University of Hawaii Library, Hawaiian Collection, 2550 the Mall, Honolulu, HI 96822. TEL 808-956-7923. FAX 808-956-5968. URL: htp://www2.hawaii.edu/~speccoll/h.html/. Ed. Chieko Tachihata. circ. 180 (controlled). (processed) **Document type:** bibliography.
Supersedes (from vol.41, no.4, 1985): Current Hawaiiana (ISSN 0011-3522)

HEALTH INDUSTRY QUICKSOURCE; a complete descriptive reference to healthcare information resources. see MEDICAL SCIENCES — Abstracting, Bibliographies, Statistics

015 Z2244.H5   GW   ISSN 0171-1423
HESSISCHE BIBLIOGRAPHIE. 1977. a. price varies. (Stadt- und Universitatsbibliothek Frankfurt am Main) K.G. Saur Verlag KG, A member of the Reed Elsevier plc group, Ortlerstr. 8, 81373 Munich, Germany. TEL 49-89-76902-0. FAX 49-89-76902150. E-mail: 100730.1341@compuserve.com; URL: http://www.reed-elsevier.com. (Subscr. to: Postfach 701620, 81316 Munich, Germany) **Document type:** bibliography.
●Also available online.

015   GW   ISSN 0170-2408
HIERSEMANNS BIBLIOGRAPHISCHE HANDBUECHER. 1979. irreg., vol.12, 1996. price varies. Anton Hiersemann Verlag, Rosenbergstr. 113, 70193 Stuttgart, Germany. TEL 49-711-638265. FAX 49-711-6369010. (Subscr. to: Postfach 140155, 70071 Stutttgart, Germany) **Document type:** bibliography.

HIGHER EDUCATION ABSTRACTS; abstracts of periodical literature, monographs and conference papers on college students, faculty and administration. see EDUCATION — Higher Education

015   AT
HISTORICAL SOCIETY OF SOUTH AUSTRALIA. GUIDESHEET. 1978. irreg. free. Historical Society of South Australia Inc., Institute Bldg., 122 Kintore Ave., Adelaide, S.A. 5000, Australia. TEL 61-8-82264000. Ed. Brian Samuels. circ. 2,000. (back issues avail.) **Document type:** monographic series.

011   AG   ISSN 0073-327X
HONTANAR.* irreg. Editorial Universitaria de Buenos Aires, Riva Davia 1571-1573, Buenos Aires, Argentina.

HORIZON. BULLETIN BIBLIOGRAPHIQUE O R S T O M. see EARTH SCIENCES — Abstracting, Bibliographies, Statistics

HUMAN REPRODUCTION UPDATE. see BIOLOGY — Abstracting, Bibliographies, Statistics

HUMAN RIGHTS ORGANIZATIONS & PERIODICALS DIRECTORY. see POLITICAL SCIENCE — Civil Rights

850 011   GW   ISSN 0177-9478
HUMANISTISCHE BIBLIOTHEK. REIHE I: ABHANDLUNGEN. 1967. irreg., vol.47. DM.98. Wilhelm Fink Verlag, Ohmstr. 5, 80802 Munich, Germany. TEL 49-89-348017. FAX 49-89-341378. URL: http://www.fink.de. R&P contact: Marlene Braun. **Document type:** monographic series.

850 011   GW   ISSN 0177-9486
HUMANISTISCHE BIBLIOTHEK. REIHE II: TEXTE. 1968. irreg., vol.32, 1997. DM.128. Wilhelm Fink Verlag, Ohmstr. 5, 80802 Munich, Germany. TEL 49-89-348017. FAX 49-89-341378. URL: http://www.fink.de. R&P contact: Marlene Braun. adv. contact: Axel Korlendick. **Document type:** monographic series.

850 011   GW   ISSN 0177-9494
HUMANISTISCHE BIBLIOTHEK. REIHE III: SKRIPTEN. 1972. irreg., vol.4. DM.28. Wilhelm Fink Verlag, Ohmstr. 5, 80802 Munich, Germany. TEL 49-89-348017. FAX 49-89-341378. URL: http://www.fink.de. R&P contact: Marlene Braun. **Document type:** monographic series.

HUMANS & OTHER SPECIES; the quarterly journal of resources on their relationship. see PSYCHOLOGY — Abstracting, Bibliographies, Statistics

HYDROTITLES; hydroscience bibliography. see EARTH SCIENCES — Abstracting, Bibliographies, Statistics

I C S S R UNION CATALOGUE OF SOCIAL SCIENCE PERIODICALS. (Indian Council of Social Science Research) see SOCIAL SCIENCES: COMPREHENSIVE WORKS — Abstracting, Bibliographies, Statistics

011   NE
I D C PUBLISHERS. CATALOGUE OF CATALOGUES. (Text in English) 1993. biennial. free. I D C Publishers bv, P.O. Box 11205, 2301 EE Leiden, Netherlands. TEL 31-71-5142700. FAX 31-71-5131521. E-mail: info@idc.nl; URL: http://www.idc.nl. illus. **Document type:** catalog.
Formerly: Inter Documentation Company. Catalogue of Catalogues.
Description: Provides a comprehensive guide to 271 available microform collections of historical and current materials, grouped by general subject areas in the arts, history, religion, law and sciences, with brief synopses describing the scope of each individual collection. Also includes information on CD-ROM publications.

I E C CATALOGUE OF PUBLICATIONS. (International Electrotechnical Commission) see ELECTRONICS

016   II   ISSN 0073-6627
I N S D O C UNION CATALOGUE SERIES. irreg. Rs.1200. Indian National Scientific Documentation Centre, 14 Statsang Vihar Marg, New Delhi 110 067, India. Ed. S.N. Dutta.

016.05   FR   ISSN 1018-4783
                CODEN: ILSAEN
I S S N COMPACT. (International Standard Serial Number); CD-ROM edition of the ISSN Register. (Not avail. in printed format) (Text in English, French) 1992. q. International Centre for the Registration of Serials, I S S N International Centre - Centre International d'Enregistrement des Publications en Serie, 20 rue Bachaumont, 75002 Paris, France. TEL 33-1-44-88-22-20. FAX 33-1-40-26-32-43. TELEX 219 847 F. E-mail: issnic@issn.org; URL: http://www.issn.org. (Dist. in the U.S. by: Chadwyck-Healy Inc., 1101 King St., Alexandria, VA 22314. TEL 800-752-0515) (also avail. in microfiche; magnetic tape; back issues avail.) **Document type:** bibliography.
●Available only on CD-ROM.
—BLDSC (4583.976200).
Description: Bibliographic information for all serial publications that have been assigned an ISSN, with a listing of abbreviations used as key words.

016.05   FR   ISSN 1022-100X
I S S N REGISTER (MICROFICHE EDITION)/REGISTRE DE L'I S S N (EDITION SUR MICROFICHE). (International Standard Serial Number) (Not avail. in printed format) 1974. q. 2400 F. International Centre for the Registration of Serials, I S S N International Centre - Centre International d'Enregistrement des Publications en Serie, 20 rue Bachaumont, 75002 Paris, France. TEL 33-1-44-88-22-20. FAX 33-1-40-26-32-43. TELEX 219 847 F. E-mail: issnic@issn.org; URL: http://www.issn.org. index. circ. 1,000. (also avail. in magnetic tape; back issues avail.)
●Also available on CD-ROM.
—Linda Hall.
Formerly (until 1993): I S D S Register (Microfiche Edition) (ISSN 0257-2222); Incorporates: I S D S Bulletin (ISSN 0300-3000)

011   FR   ISSN 1021-500X
I S S N REGISTER (TAPE EDITION)/REGISTRE DE L I S S N (EDITION SUR BANDE MAGNETIQUE). (International Standard Serial Number) (Not avail. in printed format) 1974. q. International Centre for the Registration of Serials, I S S N International Center - Centre International d'Enregistrement des Publications en Serie, 20 rue Bachaumont, 75002 Paris, France. TEL 33-1-44-88-22-20. FAX 33-1-40-26-32-43. E-mail: issnic@issn.org; URL: http://www.issn.org. circ. 50. (also avail. in microfiche; back issues avail.)
● Also available on CD-ROM.
   Formerly (until 1993): I S D S Register (Tape Edition) (ISSN 0256-8888)

IMPRESSUM BULLETIN. see *JOURNALISM — Abstracting, Bibliographies, Statistics*

IMPRESSUM 1 - SCHWEIZERISCHES MEDIENHANDBUCH. see *JOURNALISM — Abstracting, Bibliographies, Statistics*

INACTIVE OR DISCONTINUED ITEMS FROM THE 1950 REVISION OF THE CLASSIFIED LIST. see *LIBRARY AND INFORMATION SCIENCES — Abstracting, Bibliographies, Statistics*

297 016   UK   ISSN 1360-0982
Z3013
INDEX ISLAMICUS. (Text in all languages) 1958. q. £250($375) (effective 1997). (Royal Academy for Islamic Civilization, Aaman, Jordan and University Library, Cambridge) Bowker - Saur Ltd., A member of the Reed Elsevier plc group, Maypole House, Maypole Rd., E. Grinstead, W. Sussex RH19 1HU, England. TEL 44-1342-330100. FAX 44-1342-330191. E-mail: custserv@bowker-saur.co.uk; URL: http://www.reed-elsevier.com. Eds. G.J. Roper, C.H. Bleaney. Document type: abstracting/indexing.
● Also available on CD-ROM.
—BLDSC (4380.465000).
   Former titles (until 1995): Quarterly Index Islamicus (ISSN 0308-7395); (until 1976): Index Islamicus (ISSN 0306-9524)
   Description: Lists, in a detailed subject arrangement, books, articles and papers on Islamic subjects.

050 016.5   IO   ISSN 0216-6216
AI19.I55
INDEX OF INDONESIAN LEARNED PERIODICALS/INDEKS MADJALAH ILMIAH INDONESIA. (Text in English, Indonesian) 1960. s-a. Rps.12000($40) Indonesian Institute of Sciences, Centre for Scientific Documentation and Information - Lembaga Ilmu Pengetahuan Indonesia, P.O. Box 4298, Jakarta 12042, Indonesia. TEL 62-21-5733465. FAX 62-21-5733467. (Subscr. to: Yayasan Memajukan Jasa Informasi (YASMIN), Jln. Widya Chandra XI/3, Kompleks LIPI, P.O. Box 4509, Jakarta 12045, Indonesia) Ed. Endang Sri Rusmiyati Rahayu. circ. 500. Indexed: E.I.

011   LY
INDEX OF LIBYAN PERIODICALS. a. Libyan Studies Center, P.O. Box 5070, Sidi Munaider, Tripoli, Libya. TEL 33996. FAX 31616. TELEX 20424. Document type: abstracting/indexing.

016 059.924   IS
INDEX TO HEBREW PERIODICALS (C D - R O M EDITION). (Text in Hebrew) 6/yr. (with a. cumulation). $320 (effective 1993). University of Haifa Library, Haifa 31905, Israel. FAX 972-4-257753. (Subscr. to: C D I Systems, P.O. Box 45064, Jerusalem, Israel. TEL 972-2-870122) Ed. Mrs. Amira Kehat. Document type: abstracting/indexing.
● Available only on CD-ROM.
   Supersedes: Index to Hebrew Periodicals (Microfiche Edition).

016 059   PH   ISSN 0073-599X
AI3
INDEX TO PHILIPPINE PERIODICALS. 1946. q. $60. University of the Philippines Diliman, University Library, Gonzalez Hall, Diliman, Quezon City 1101, Philippines. TEL 632-9205301. FAX 632-9292180. circ. 93 (controlled). Document type: abstracting/indexing.
—BLDSC (4385.220000).
   Formerly (until 1960): Index to Philippine Periodical Literature.
   Description: Author subject index to periodicals published in the Philippines.

015   II
INDIA. DEPARTMENT OF PUBLICATION. PUBLICATIONS. (Text in English) 1932. m. free. Government of India, Department of Publications, Controller of Publications, Civil Lines, Delhi 110 054, India. circ. 300.
   Description: Government publications catalog.

950   II   ISSN 0073-6090
DS405
INDIA: A REFERENCE ANNUAL. (Text in English) 1953. a. $23. Ministry of Information & Broadcasting, Publications Division, Patiala House, Tilak Marg, New Delhi 110001, India. (Subscr. in U.S. to: M-S Inter Culture Associates, Thompson, CT 06277) circ. 20,000. Document type: government publication, bibliography.
—BLDSC (4391.228000).

011   II   ISSN 0971-1589
Z3201
INDIAN BOOKS IN PRINT. (Text in English) 1969. a. Rs.6000 for 1996 ed.; Rs.7200 for 1997 ed. Indian Bibliographies Bureau, 219, 'Kadambari', 19 - IX Rohini, New Delhi 110 085, India. TEL 91-11-7257523. FAX 91-11-7256502. Ed. Sher Singh. Document type: bibliography.
—BLDSC (4393.150000).
   Description: Contains complete bibliographical details of about 125,000 Indian books in print.

015   II   ISSN 0019-6002
Z3201.A2
INDIAN NATIONAL BIBLIOGRAPHY. (Sanskrit fascicule in Devanagari script available for 1958-62, 1963-67) (Editions in Assamese, Bengali, English, Oriya, Sanskrit, Tamil, Hindi, and Malayalam) 1957. m. (plus a. cumulation). Rs.540($144) price varies for annual cums. Central Reference Library, Belvedere, Calcutta 700 027, India. TEL 91-479-1721-22. circ. 500. Document type: bibliography.
—Linda Hall.
   Description: Bibliographical record of current India publications in 14 major languages of India, received by the National Library under the Delivery of Books Act.

015   II   ISSN 0073-6708
INDIAN STATISTICAL INSTITUTE. LIBRARY. BIBLIOGRAPHIC SERIES.* (Text in English) 1959. irreg. price varies. Indian Statistical Institute, 203 Barrackpore Trunk Rd., Calcutta 700035, India.

L'INDICE; dei libri del mese. see *PUBLISHING AND BOOK TRADE*

011   AT   ISSN 0310-6659
Z3279
INDONESIAN ACQUISITIONS LIST/DAFTAR PENGADAAN BAHAN INDONESIA. 1971. irreg. free. National Library of Australia, Publications Section, Cultural and Educational Services Division, Canberra, A.C.T. 2600, Australia. TEL 61-6-262-1365. FAX 61-6-273-4493. circ. 300. (reprint service avail. from ISI,UMI) Document type: bibliography.

INDUSTRIAL LITERATURE REVIEW. see *BUSINESS AND ECONOMICS — Abstracting, Bibliographies, Statistics*

011   FR
INDUSTRIATHEQUE. m. Ministere de l'Industrie et de l'Amenagement du Territoire, 101, rue de Grenelle, 75700 Paris Cedex, France.

INFOLINGUA. see *COMPUTERS — Abstracting, Bibliographies, Statistics*

INFORMATION ALERTS. see *EDUCATION — Abstracting, Bibliographies, Statistics*

658   US   ISSN 0733-8961
                         CODEN: IRPTD4
THE INFORMATION REPORT. 1974. m. $160 (effective 1997). Washington Researchers, Ltd., Box 19005, 20th St. Sta., Washington, DC 20036-9005. TEL 202-333-3499. FAX 202-625-0656. E-mail: research@researchers.com; URL: http://www.researchers.com/pub/businetl/researchers.html. Ed. Walt Seager. R&P contact: Ellen O'Kane. bk.rev.; bibl.; s-a. index. (back issues avail.) Indexed: Alloys Ind., Eng.Mat.Abstr., Lib.Lit., Met.Abstr.Ind., Met.Abstr., Nonfer.Met.Alert, PCC Alert, Steels Alert, World Alum.Abstr. Document type: newsletter, bibliography.
● Also available online. Vendor(s): NewsNet (IT08).
   Description: Informs managers about studies, surveys, reports, directories, and periodicals. Provides full ordering information.

INFORMATION TECHNOLOGY AND THE LAW; an international bibliography. see *LAW — Abstracting, Bibliographies, Statistics*

010   IT   ISSN 0391-6812
INFORMAZIONE BIBLIOGRAFICA; trimestrale di analisi delle produzione literaria italiana e di informazione culturale. 1975. 4/yr. Lit.80000 (foreign Lit.14000) (effective 1997). Societa Editrice il Mulino, Strada Maggiore, 37, 40125 Bologna, Italy. TEL 39-51-256011. FAX 39-51-256034. E-mail: riviste@mulino.it. Eds. Pasquale Petrucci, Giuseppe Ulianich. adv.: B&W page Lit.275000. index. circ. 4,000. (back issues avail.)

011   US
INGRAM - BOOKS IN PRINT PLUS. w. $1300. R.R. Bowker, A Division of Reed Elsevier Inc., 121 Chanlon Rd., New Providence, NJ 07974. TEL 800-521-8110; 800-323-3288. FAX 908-665-3528. TELEX 138 755. E-mail: info@bowker.com; URL: http://www.reedref.com. (avail. for MS-DOS version) Document type: bibliography, directory.
● Available only on CD-ROM. Producer(s): Bowker Electronic Publishing (Books In Print PLUS).
   Description: Contains all the features and information found on Books in Print Plus, along with weekly title-by-title update of the Ingram book and audio inventories, and Ingram Flash-Back electronic ordering capabilities.

011   US
INGRAM - BOOKS IN PRINT PLUS WITH BOOK REVIEWS PLUS. w. $1800. R.R. Bowker, A Division of Reed Elsevier Inc., 121 Chanlon Rd., New Providence, NJ 07974. TEL 800-521-8110; 800-323-3288. FAX 908-665-3528. TELEX 138 755. E-mail: info@bowker.com; URL: http://www.reedref.com. (avail. for MS-DOS version) Document type: bibliography, directory.
● Available only on CD-ROM. Producer(s): Bowker Electronic Publishing (Books In Print PLUS).
   Description: Contains features similar to Books in Print with Book Reviews Plus, along with Ingram weekly updates.

011 020   UK
INSIDE CONFERENCES ON C D - R O M. 1994. q. £500 (effective 1997). British Library, Document Supply Centre, Boston Spa, Weatherby, W. Yorks. LS23 7BQ, England. TEL 44-1937-546080. FAX 44-1937-546286. TELEX 557381. (Subscr. to: Turpin Distribution Services Ltd., Blackhorse Rd., Letchworth, Herts. SG6 1HN, England. TEL 44-1462-672755. FAX 44-1432-480947) Document type: bibliography.
● Available only on CD-ROM.
   Description: Details the contents pages of 20,000 conference proceedings received at the British Library Document Supply Centre each year.

011 020   UK
INSIDE INFORMATION ON C D - R O M. m. £600 (effective 1996). British Library, Document Supply Centre, Boston Spa, Wetherby, W. Yorks. LS23 7BQ, England. TEL 44-1937-546080. FAX 44-1937-546080. TELEX 557381. (Subscr. to: Turpin Distribution Services Ltd., Blackhorse Rd., Letchworth, Herts. SG6 1HN, England. TEL 44-1462-627555. FAX 44-1462-480947) Document type: bibliography.
● Available only on CD-ROM.
   Description: Gives access to the contents pages to more than 10,000 of the most frequently held titles at the British Library Document Supply Centre.

BIBLIOGRAPHIES

011 020 BE
INSTITUT PROVINCIAL D'ETUDES ET RECHERCHES BIBLIOTHECONOMIQUES. MEMOIRES. 1978. irreg. Institut Provincial d'Etudes et Recherches Bibliotheconomiques, 15 rue des Croisiers, B-4000 Leige, Belgium. bk.rev.; abstr.; bibl. circ. 1,000. (back issues avail.)

INSTITUT ZA NUKLEARNE NAUKE, VINCA. BIBLIOGARIJA RADOVA. see ENERGY — Abstracting, Bibliographies, Statistics

INSTITUTE OF DEVELOPMENT STUDIES. DEVELOPMENT BIBLIOGRAPHY SERIES. see BUSINESS AND ECONOMICS — Abstracting, Bibliographies, Statistics

011 II
INSTITUTE OF ECONOMIC GROWTH. BOOK REVIEW LIST. m. Institute of Economic Growth, University Enclave, New Delhi 110007, India. TEL 7257101. **Document type:** bibliography.

011 II
INSTITUTE OF ECONOMIC GROWTH. LIST OF PERIODICAL HOLDING IN THE I E G LIBRARY. irreg. Institute of Economic Growth, University Enclave, New Delhi 110007, India. TEL 7257101. **Document type:** bibliography.

011 II
INSTITUTE OF ECONOMIC GROWTH. LIST OF PERIODICALS CURRENTLY RECEIVED IN THE I E G LIBRARY. irreg. Institute of Economic Growth, University Enclave, New Delhi 110007, India. TEL 7257101. **Document type:** bibliography.

011 II
INSTITUTE OF ECONOMIC GROWTH. MICRO DOCUMENT LIST. m. Institute of Economic Growth, University Enclave, New Delhi 110007, India. TEL 7257101. **Document type:** bibliography.

011 II
INSTITUTE OF ECONOMIC GROWTH. SELECTIVE LIST OF BOOKS AND DOCUMENTS ADDED TO THE LIBRARY. m. Institute of Economic Growth, University Enclave, New Delhi 110007, India. TEL 7257101. **Document type:** bibliography.

015 CK ISSN 0073-991X
INSTITUTO CARO Y CUERVO. SERIE BIBLIOGRAFICA. 1960. irreg., no.15, 1995. price varies. Instituto Caro y Cuervo, Seccion de Publicaciones, Apdo. Aereo 51502, Bogota, Colombia. E-mail: carocuer@apenway.cam.co.

011 DR
INSTITUTO TECNOLOGICO DE SANTO DOMINGO. BIBLIOTECA. BOLETIN DE ADQUISICIONES. q. Instituto Tecnologico de Santo Domingo, Biblioteca, Apdo. Postal 342-9, Santo Domingo, Dominican Republic. **Document type:** bibliography.

800 015 SP ISSN 0020-4536
Z1007
INSULA; revista de letras y ciencias humanas. 1946. m. 5250 ptas. (Europe 7000 ptas.; America 8450 ptas.; elsewhere 9550 ptas.). Insula: Libreria Ediciones y Publicaciones, S.A., Carretera de Irun, Km. 12200 (Var. de Fuencarral), 28049 Madrid, Spain. TEL 91-3589689. FAX 91-3589364. Ed. Carlos Alvarez-Ude. adv.; bk.rev.; bibl.; illus.; cum.index: 1946-1980. circ. 6,000. (also avail. in microfilm from BHP,UMI; back issues avail.; reprint service avail. from UMI) **Indexed:** Amer.Hist.& Life (1959-1964), Arts & Hum.Cit.Ind., Arts & Hum.Cit.Ind., ASCA, Biol.Abstr., Chic.Per.Ind., Curr.Cont., Hisp.Amer.Per.Ind. (1990-1994), Hist.Abstr. (1959-1964), IBR, M.L.A., MLA Intl.Bibl., SSCI.
—CINDOC; KR SourceOne; UMI.

011 US ISSN 0250-6262
Z1007
INTER-AMERICAN REVIEW OF BIBLIOGRAPHY/REVISTA INTERAMERICANA DE BIBLIOGRAFIA. (Text in English, French, Portuguese and Spanish) 1951. s-a. $20 (foreign $32). (Inter-American Committee on Bibliography) Organization of American States, General Secretariat, Department of Publications, 1889 F St., N.W., Washington, DC 20006-4499. TEL 202-458-3527. FAX 202-458-3534. bk.rev.; bibl.; illus.; index. circ. 3,000. (also avail. in microform from UMI; reprint service avail. from UMI) **Indexed:** Amer.Hist.& Life (1955-), Arts & Hum.Cit.Ind., Curr.Cont., Hisp.Amer.Per.Ind. (1970-), Hist.Abstr. (until 1995), IBR, Ind.Bk.Rev.Hum., Lib.Lit., MLA Intl.Bibl. **Document type:** bibliography.
—BLDSC (4531.894000); SWETS.

960 015 UK ISSN 0020-5877
Z3501
INTERNATIONAL AFRICAN BIBLIOGRAPHY; current books, articles and papers in African studies. 1971. q. £125($215) (effective 1997). (Centre of African Studies, University of London, School of Oriental and African Studies) Bowker - Saur Ltd., A member of the Reed Elsevier plc group, Maypole House, Maypole Rd., E. Grinstead, W. Sussex RH19 1HU, England. TEL 44-1342-330100. FAX 44-1342-330191. E-mail: custserv@boker-saur.co.uk; URL: http://www.reed-elsevier.com. (Subscr. to: Worldwide subscriptions, Unit 6, Gibbs Reed Farm, Ticehurst, E. Sussex TN5 7HE, England. TEL 44-1342-850501) Ed. David Hall. index. **Indexed:** A.I.C.P., Bibl.Ind., Curr.Cont.Africa, Popul.Ind. **Document type:** bibliography.
  Description: Indexes the latest periodical articles, books and papers published internationally on Africa. Details more than 4000 publications, and articles from 1150 periodicals, 250 of which are African.

011 GW ISSN 0724-2298
INTERNATIONAL ANNUAL BIBLIOGRAPHY OF FESTSCHRIFTEN. Short title: I J B F. (Text in English, German) 1980. a. (in 4 vols.). DM.1400 (CD-ROM DM.1400 (DM.700 with printed ed.)) (effective 1998). Zeller Publications, Postfach 1949, 49009 Osnabrueck, Germany. TEL 49-541-4045914. FAX 49-541-41255. E-mail: zeller@zeller.os.eunet.de. Ed. Wolfram Zeller. R&P contact: Ivon Illmer. **Document type:** bibliography.
●Also available on CD-ROM.

INTERNATIONAL BIBLIOGRAPHY OF AUSTRIAN PHILOSOPHY/INTERNATIONALE BIBLIOGRAPHIE ZUR OESTERREICHISCHEN PHILOSOPHIE. see PHILOSOPHY — Abstracting, Bibliographies, Statistics

INTERNATIONAL BIBLIOGRAPHY OF HISTORICAL DEMOGRAPHY/BIBLIOGRAPHIE INTERNATIONALE DE LA DEMOGRAPHIE HISTORIQUE. see POPULATION STUDIES — Abstracting, Bibliographies, Statistics

INTERNATIONAL BIBLIOGRAPHY OF THE SOCIAL SCIENCES. POLITICAL SCIENCE. see POLITICAL SCIENCE — Abstracting, Bibliographies, Statistics

INTERNATIONAL BIBLIOGRAPHY OF THE SOCIAL SCIENCES. SOCIAL AND CULTURAL ANTHROPOLOGY. see ANTHROPOLOGY — Abstracting, Bibliographies, Statistics

016 327 US ISSN 0000-0477
Z6482
INTERNATIONAL BIBLIOGRAPHY: PUBLICATIONS OF INTERGOVERNMENTAL ORGANIZATIONS. 1973. q. $100. Marsten Book Services Ltd., P.O. Box 87, Oxford OX2 ODT, England, OX2 ODT. adv.; index. circ. 1,200. **Document type:** bibliography.
  Formerly: (until 1983): I B I D (International Bibliography, Information, Documentation) (ISSN 0000-0329).
  Description: Current coverage of specialized information published by the United Nations system and related governmental organizations.

011 GW ISSN 0170-9348
Z2005
INTERNATIONAL BOOKS IN PRINT; a listing of English-language titles published in Africa, Asia, Australia, Canada, Continental Europe, Latin America, New Zealand, Oceania, and the Republic of Ireland. (In 4 vols., 2 parts; Part One: Author-Title List; Part Two: Subject Guide) 1979. a., 16th ed., 1997. DM.598($385) for each part; 2-part set $695. K.G. Saur Verlag KG, A member of the Reed Elsevier plc group, Ortlerstr. 8, 81373 Munich, Germany. TEL 49-89-76902-0. FAX 49-89-76902150. E-mail: 100730.1341@compuserve.com; URL: http://www.reed-elsevier.com. (Subscr. to: Postfach 701620, 81316 Munich, Germany; N. America subscr. to: K.G. Saur, 121 Chanlon Rd., New Providence, NJ 07974-9903. TEL 908-665-2830) **Document type:** bibliography, directory.
●Also available on CD-ROM. Producer(s): K.G. Saur Verlag.
—BLDSC (4537.390000); CISTI.
  Description: Covers English-language fiction and nonfiction books, pamphlets and microforms. Provides prices and detailed publisher and distributor information.

011 GW
INTERNATIONAL BOOKS IN PRINT PLUS. a. $995. K.G. Saur Verlag KG, A member of the Reed Elsevier plc group, Ortlerstr. 8, 81373 Munich, Germany. TEL 49-89-76902-0. FAX 49-89-76902150. E-mail: 100730.1341@compuserve.com; URL: http://www.reed-elsevier.com. (Subscr. to: Postfach 701620, 81316 Munich, Germany; N. America subscr. to: K.G. Saur, 121 Chanlon Rd., Box 31, New Providence, NJ 07974-9903, USA. TEL 908-464-6800) (avail. for MS-DOS version) **Document type:** directory.
●Available only on CD-ROM. Producer(s): K.G. Saur Verlag.
  Formerly: International Books in Print on C D - R O M.
  Description: Provides access to over 250,000 English-language titles published outside the US and the UK.

INTERNATIONAL COURT OF JUSTICE. BIBLIOGRAPHY/COUR INTERNATIONALE DE JUSTICE. BIBLIOGRAPHIE. (International Court of Justice) see LAW — Abstracting, Bibliographies, Statistics

INTERNATIONAL DIRECTORY OF LITTLE MAGAZINES AND SMALL PRESSES. see PUBLISHING AND BOOK TRADE — Abstracting, Bibliographies, Statistics

016 GW
INTERNATIONAL GUIDE TO MICROFORM MASTERS. a. £1625. K.G. Saur Verlag KG, A member of the Reed Elsevier plc group, Ortlerstr. 8, 81373 Munich, Germany. TEL 49-89-76901250. FAX 49-89-76901250. E-mail: 100730.1341@compuserve.com; URL: http://www.reed-elsevier.com. (N. America subscr. to: K.G. Saur, 121 Chanlon Rd., New Providence, NJ 07974-9903. TEL 908-464-6800)
●Available only on CD-ROM.
  Description: Provides access to the microform collections of over 200 libraries and research institutes in the US, Canada and Europe.

011 US ISSN 0748-206X
THE INTERNATIONAL INFORMATION REPORT; the international industry dossier. 1985. m. $160 (effective 1995). Washington Researchers, Ltd., Box 19005, 20th St. Sta., Washington, DC 20036-9005. TEL 202-333-3499. FAX 202-625-0656. E-mail: research@researchers.com; URL: http://www.researchers.com/pub/busintel/researchers.html. Ed. Walter Seager. R&P contact: Ellen O'Kane. bk.rev.; s-a index, cum.index. (looseleaf format; back issues avail.) **Indexed:** Alloys Ind., Eng.Mat.Abstr., Met.Abstr., Met.Abstr.Ind., Nonfer.Met.Alert, PCC Alert, Steels Alert, World Alum.Abstr. **Document type:** newsletter.
●Also available online. Vendor(s): NewsNet (IT75).
  Description: Keeps managers current on the best sources of critical data and analysis on such topics as the strong overseas competition, political risks, export markets, and global demographics.

BIBLIOGRAPHIES

011 341   UK
INTERNATIONAL LEGAL BOOKS IN PRINT. (In 2 vols.) 1991. irreg., 2nd ed., 1993-1994. £235. Bowker - Saur Ltd., A member of the Reed Elsevier plc group, Maypole House, Maypole Rd., E. Grinstead, W. Sussex RH19 1HH, England.
TEL 44-1342-330100. FAX 44-1342-330191.
E-mail: custserv@bowker-saur.co.uk; URL: http//www.reed-elsevier.com. **Document type:** bibliography, directory.
    Description: Provides a comprehensive bibliography of more than 20,000 English-language legal texts and treaties published or distributed in the U.K., Western Europe, and and current or former British Commonwealth countries.

INTERNATIONAL MEDIEVAL BIBLIOGRAPHY. see HISTORY — Abstracting, Bibliographies, Statistics

001 016   GW   ISSN 0020-9201
INTERNATIONALE BIBLIOGRAPHIE DER ZEITSCHRIFTENLITERATUR AUS ALLEN GEBIETEN DES WISSENS/INTERNATIONAL BIBLIOGRAPHY OF PERIODICAL LITERATURE FROM ALL FIELDS OF KNOWLEDGE. Short title: I B Z. N.S. 1965. 12/yr. (in 2 vols., 6 nos./vol.). DM.5400 (CD-ROM DM.2500 with printed edition) (effective 1998). Zeller Publications, Postfach 1949, 49009 Osnabrueck, Germany. TEL 49-541-4045914.
FAX 49-541-41255. E-mail: zeller@zeller.os.eunet.de; URL: http://www.brzn.de. Ed. Wolfram Zeller. R&P contact: Ivon Illmer. index. **Document type:** bibliography.
● Also available online.
Also available on CD-ROM.
—BLDSC (4554.100000); Linda Hall.

011   GW   ISSN 0323-5734
Z2233
INTERNATIONALE BIBLIOGRAPHIE ZUR DEUTSCHEN KLASSIK 1750-1850. 1960. a. DM.278. K.G. Saur Verlag KG, A member of the Reed Elsevier plc group, Ortlerstr. 8, 8173 Munich, Germany.
TEL 49-89-76902464. FAX 49-89-76902150. Ed. Heidi Zeilinger. adv. contact: Romana Kimmel. bk.rev.; index. (back issues avail.) **Document type:** bibliography.
    Description: Covers German literature and literary criticism, both books and articles. Includes index of reviews. In 2 sections: collections and general works; and individual writers.

INTERNATIONALE JAHRESBIBLIOGRAPHIE DER KONGRESSBERICHTE/INTERNATIONAL ANNUAL BIBLIOGRAPHY OF CONGRESS PROCEEDINGS. see MEETINGS AND CONGRESSES — Abstracting, Bibliographies, Statistics

016 020   GW   ISSN 0535-5079
INVENTARE NICHTSTAATLICHER ARCHIVE. 1952. irreg., no.38, 1996. price varies. (Landschaftsverband Rheinland, Rheinisches Archiv- und Museumsamt) Rheinland Verlag GmbH, Abtei Brauweiler, Postfach 2140, 50250 Pulheim, Germany.
TEL 49-2234-9854265. FAX 49-2234-82503.
(Dist. by: Dr. Rudolf Habelt GmbH, Am Buchenhang 1, 53115 Bonn, Germany. TEL 49-228-9238322.
FAX 49-228-232017) **Document type:** monographic series.

011 332.6   II
INVESTMENT PLANNING AND PROJECT EVALUATION BIBLIOGRAPHY. irreg. Institute of Economic Growth, University Enclave, New Delhi 110007, India.
TEL 7257101. **Document type:** bibliography.

015   IR   ISSN 0075-0522
Z3366
IRANIAN NATIONAL BIBLIOGRAPHY/KETAB SHENASI-YE MELLI-YE IRAN. 1963. q. price varies. National Library of Iran, Shahid Bahonar St., Tehran 19548, Iran. TEL 98-21-2280937. FAX 98-21-2288680.
Ed.Bd. circ. 2,000. **Document type:** bibliography.
    Description: Bibliographic information on all books, pamphlets and talking books (sound recordings) published in Iran.

015   IQ
IRAQI NATIONAL BIBLIOGRAPHY. (Text in Arabic, English, French, German, Kurdish and Old Turkish) 1971. 3/yr. free. National Library, Bab al-Moadham, Baghdad, Iraq. Ed. Y.M. Qazanchi. circ. 3,000.
    Formerly: Bulletin of Iraq Publications Depository.

ISRAEL. CENTRAL BUREAU OF STATISTICS. NEW STATISTICAL PROJECTS AND PUBLICATIONS IN ISRAEL. see STATISTICS

ISRAEL. GEOLOGICAL SURVEY. BIBLIOGRAPHY SERIES. see EARTH SCIENCES — Abstracting, Bibliographies, Statistics

ISTORIYA SIBIRI I DAL'NEGO VOSTOKA; tekushchii ukazatel' literatury. see HISTORY — Abstracting, Bibliographies, Statistics

J A E R I REPORT. (Japan Atomic Energy Research Institute) see ENERGY — Nuclear Energy

011   US   ISSN 1066-8454
J I S COMPUTERIZED BIBLIOGRAPHY. 1991. a. $15 (diskette $30). Institute for Interdisciplinary Research, 2828 Third St., Ste. 11, Santa Monica, CA 90405-4150. TEL 310-396-0517. (also avail. in diskette format) **Document type:** bibliography.

JAHRBUCH FUER WIRTSCHAFTSWISSENSCHAFTEN; review of economics. see BUSINESS AND ECONOMICS — Abstracting, Bibliographies, Statistics

015   JM   ISSN 0075-2991
JAMAICAN NATIONAL BIBLIOGRAPHY. (Fourth no. is a. cumulation) 1964. q. $20. National Library of Jamaica, 12 East St., P.O. Box 823, Kingston, Jamaica, W.I. TEL 809-92-20620.
FAX 809-92-25567. TELEX 596. E-mail: natlibjm@uwimona.edu.jm. Ed. June Vernon. circ. 200. (reprint service avail. from UMI) **Document type:** bibliography.
    Formerly: Institute of Jamaica, Kingston. West Indian Reference Library. Jamaica Accessions.

011   JA   ISSN 0910-7908
Z3301
JAPAN ENGLISH PUBLICATIONS IN PRINT. (Text in English) 1985. irreg., 2nd ed., 1993.
27000 Yen($270) Japan Publications Guide Service, 5-5-13 Matsushiro, Tsukuba-shi, Ibaraki-ken 305, Japan. FAX 81-3-3667-9646. (Subscr. to: Intercontinental Marketing Corp., IPO Box 5056, Tokyo 100-31, Japan. TEL 81-3-3661-7458) Ed. W.E. Ball. adv.; bibl. circ. 1,000. (also avail. in diskette format) **Document type:** directory.
—CCC.
    Incorporates (1987-1993): Japan Publishers Directory; Formed by the merger of: Japan English Magazine Directory (ISSN 0387-3935); Japan English Books in Print (ISSN 0388-4201)
    Description: Provides a complete listing of useful directories and information sources.

015   JA
JAPANESE BOOKS IN PRINT (YEAR). 1977. a. 57750 Yen. Japan Book Publishers Association - Nihon Shoseki Shuppan Kyokai, 6 Fukuro-machi, Shinjuku-ku, Tokyo 162, Japan.
TEL 81-3-3268-1301. FAX 81-3-3268-1196. Ed. Takao Watanabe. circ. 5,700. **Document type:** bibliography.

JAPANESE MILITARY AIRCRAFT SERIALS. see AERONAUTICS AND SPACE FLIGHT — Abstracting, Bibliographies, Statistics

015.52   JA   ISSN 0389-4002
Z3301
JAPANESE NATIONAL BIBLIOGRAPHY WEEKLY LIST/NIHON ZENKOKU SHOSHI. (Text in Japanese) 1955. w. 600 Yen per no. National Diet Library - Kokuritsu Kokkai Toshokan, 1-10-1 Nagata-cho, Chiyoda-ku, Tokyo 100, Japan.
TEL 81-3-3581-2331. FAX 81-3-3597-9104.
E-mail: kokusai@ndlmail.ndl.go.jp; URL: http://www.ndl.go.jp. circ. 600. **Document type:** bibliography.
● Also available on CD-ROM.
    Formerly (until 1981): Current Publications-Nohon Shuho (ISSN 0385-3292)

956.96 016   JO
JORDANIAN NATIONAL BIBLIOGRAPHY; annual register of book production in Jordan. (Text in Arabic, English) 1979. a. $20. Jordan Library Association, P.O. Box 6289, Amman, Jordan. TEL 629-412.

016.05   NE   ISSN 1380-5673
Z6415.T7
JOURNALS IN TRANSLATION (DISKETTE VERSION). 1976-1991; resumed N.S. 1996. s-a. fl.75 includes printed version (effective 1996 & 1997). International Translations Centre (ITC), Schuttersveld 2, 2611 WE Delft, Netherlands.
TEL 31-15-2142242. FAX 31-15-2158535. E-mail: itc@library.tudelft.nl. (diskette format) **Document type:** bibliography.
    Supersedes (in 1996): Journals in Translation (ISSN 0950-9747)
    Description: Lists current and noncurrent journals published in translated form. Covers all subject areas; includes publisher information; lists source journals; and indicates whether translated full-text or selectively.

016.3   US   ISSN 0075-4951
KANSAS STATE UNIVERSITY. LIBRARY BIBLIOGRAPHY SERIES. 1964. irreg., no.15, 1982. price varies. Kansas State University, Farrell Library - Serials Rec'g. Unit, Manhattan, KS 66506.
TEL 913-532-6516. (Subscr. to: Chief Accountant's Office, Kansas State University Libraries, Manhattan, KS 66506)
—Linda Hall.

011   PL   ISSN 0324-8003
KARTKOWY KATALOG NOWOSCI. 1951. w. 15600 Zl.($33.80) Panstwowe Przedsiebiorstwo "Skladnica Ksiegarska", Ul. Mazowiecka 9, Warsaw, Poland. (Dist. by: Ars Polona-Ruch, Krakowskie Przedmiescie 7, Warsaw, Poland) Ed. Barbara Napierzynska. bk.rev.; bibl. circ. 5,000.

011.62 370   DK
KATALOG FOR SKOLEBIBLIOTEKER. SKOLEBIBLIOTEKARENS. 1975. a. DKK 1996.80 (includes Emnekatalog, Forfatterkatalog) (effective 1996). Dansk BiblioteksCenter as, Tempovej 7-11, DK-2750 Ballerup, Denmark. TEL 45-44-867777. FAX 45-44-867892. E-mail: dbc@dan.bib.dk.
● Also available online.
Also available on CD-ROM.
    Former titles: Katalog for Skolebiblioteker. Emnekatalog (ISSN 0106-7591); Katalog for Skolebiblioteker. Forfatterkatalog (ISSN 0106-7575)

011 370   DK   ISSN 0106-7583
KATALOG FOR SKOLEBIBLIOTEKER. TITELKATALOG. (Supplements avail.) 1975. a. DKK 278.40 (includes supplements) (effective 1996). Dansk BiblioteksCenter as, Tempovej 7-11, DK-2750 Ballerup, Denmark. TEL 45-44-867777.
FAX 45-44-867892. E-mail: dbc@dan.bib.dk. **Document type:** catalog.
● Also available online.
Also available on CD-ROM.
    Supersedes in part: Katalog for Boerne- og Skolebiblioteker.

015   YU
KATALOG KNJIGA JUGOSLAVENSKIH IZDAVACA. 1955. a. $80. Udruzenje Izdavaca i Kinjizara Jugoslavije - Association of Yugoslav Publishers and Booksellers, Kneza Milosa 25, 11000 Belgrade, Yugoslavia.
TEL 3811-642-533. FAX 3811-646-339. Ed. Ognjen Lakicevic. adv. circ. 1,800. (back issues avail.)
    Description: List of available domestic book titles.

015   YU   ISSN 0352-132X
Z6945
KATALOG STRANIH SERIJSKIH PUBLIKACIJA U BIBLIOTEKAMA JUGOSLAVIJE. (In 2 vols.) (Text in Serbo-Croatian) 1957. a. $583 or exchange basis. Jugoslovenski Bibliografsko-Informacijski Institut (YUBIN) - Yugoslav Institute for Bibliography and Information, Terazije 26, Belgrade, Yugoslavia.
TEL 011 333-013. FAX 011-687-760. Ed. Radomir Glavicki. circ. 350. (back issues avail.)
    Formerly (until 1978): Katalog Tekucih Stranih Publikacija u Bibliotekama Jugoslavije (ISSN 0350-0411)
    Description: Catalogue of foreign periodicals in the libraries of Yugoslavia.

015   US   ISSN 1054-2841
Z1223.5.K4
KENTUCKY CHECKLIST OF STATE PUBLICATIONS. 1962. q. free. Department for Libraries and Archives, Public Records Division, Box 537, Frankfort, KY 40602-0537. TEL 502-875-7000. FAX 502-564-5773. Ed. William C. Richardson. circ. 500. (processed; also avail. in microfiche)
 Former titles: Kentucky Monthly Checklist; Monthly Checklist of Kentucky State Publications (ISSN 0091-5653)
 Description: A list of publications generated through the Public Records Division by the departments, commissions, societies, councils, and cabinets of the state.

015   KE
KENYA. GOVERNMENT PRINTING AND STATIONERY DEPARTMENT. CATALOGUE OF GOVERNMENT PUBLICATIONS. irreg. (approx. a.). Government Printing and Stationery Department, P.O. Box 30128, Nairobi, Kenya. **Document type:** government publication.

011   SJ
KHARTOUM UNIVERSITY PRESS. CLASSIFIED LIST OF PUBLICATIONS. (Text in Arabic, English) a. free. Khartoum University Press, P.O. Box 321, Khartoum, Sudan. TEL 80558. TELEX 22738 KUP SD.
 Description: Lists all publications available from Khartoum University Press.

016.968   SA
KILLIE CAMPBELL AFRICANA LIBRARY. BIBLIOGRAPHIC SERIES. 1993. irreg., vol.2, 1994. Killie Campbell Africana Library, 220 Marriott Rd., Durban 4001, South Africa. (back issues avail.) **Document type:** bibliography.

296 011   IS   ISSN 0023-1851
Z6367
KIRYAT SEFER; bibliographical quarterly. (Text in various languages) 1924. q. $60. Jewish National and University Library, P.O. Box 34165, Jerusalem 91341, Israel. TEL 972-2-585039. FAX 972-2-527741. TELEX 25367. E-mail: JNL@RAM1.HUJI.AC.IL. Ed. Avigdor Shinan. bk.rev.; index. circ. 1,000. **Document type:** bibliography.
 —BLDSC (5097.650000).
 Description: Annotated bibliography of all publications in Israel, and of Judaism published abroad.

840 011   GW   ISSN 0453-9834
KLASSISCHE TEXTE DES ROMANISCHEN MITTELALTERSZWEISPRACHIGEN AUSGABEN. 1962. irreg., vol.30. DM.98. Wilhelm Fink Verlag, Ohmstr. 5, 80802 Munich, Germany. TEL 49-89-348017. FAX 49-89-341378. URL: http://www.fink.de. R&P contact: Marlene Braun. **Document type:** monographic series.

011   GW   ISSN 0941-6617
KLEINE BIBLIOGRAPHISCHE REIHE. irreg. Laurentius, Kirchroederstr. 44H, 30625 Hannover, Germany. TEL 49-511-5353374. FAX 49-511-5323346. E-mail: dehmlow.raimund@mh-hannover.de; URL: http://www.germany.net/teilnehmer/100/115158/laurent.htm. (Subscr. to: Laurentius Vertrieb, Bonhoefferstr. 19, 30926 Seelze, Germany. TEL 49-5137-5653) Ed. Raimund Dehmlow. **Document type:** bibliography.

015   BW
KNIGI BELARUSI/BYELORUSSIAN BOOKS. (Text in Byelorussian, Russian) 1984. a. 60 Rub. Nationalnaya Knizhnaya Palata Belarusi, Pr. Masherava, 11, 220600 Minsk, Belarus. TEL 23-08-39. Ed. L.N. Nekhaichik. circ. 250.
 Formerly: Knigi Belorusskoi S.S.R. (ISSN 0235-3393)
 Description: State bibliographical directory containing information on books in all fields.

KOKUTRITSU KOKKAI TOSHOKAN. SANKO SHOSI KENKYU/NATIONAL DIET LIBRARY. REFERENCE SERVICE AND BIBLIOGRAPHY. see *LIBRARY AND INFORMATION SCIENCES*

016.01   DK   ISSN 0105-5046
KONGELIGE BIBLIOTEK. FAGBIBLIOGRAFIER. 1975. irreg., no.16, 1985. Kongelige Bibliotek - Royal Library, Christians Brygge 8, DK-1219 Copenhagen K, Denmark.

020   DK   ISSN 0105-8215
KONGELIGE BIBLIOTEK. SPECIALHJAELPEMIDLER. 1978. irreg., no.33, 1997. Kongelige Bibliotek - Royal Library, Christians Brygge 8, DK-1219 Copenhagen K, Denmark.

KONINKLIJK INSTITUUT VOOR TAAL-, LAND- EN VOLKENKUNDE. BIBLIOGRAPHICAL SERIES. see *LINGUISTICS* — *Abstracting, Bibliographies, Statistics*

KONINKLIJK INSTITUUT VOOR TAAL-, LAND- EN VOLKENKUNDE. LIBRARY. ACCESSIONS LIST. see *ANTHROPOLOGY* — *Abstracting, Bibliographies, Statistics*

KONINKLIJK INSTITUUT VOR DE TROPEN. ANNOTATED BIBLIOGRAPHIES SERIES. see *AGRICULTURE* — *Abstracting, Bibliographies, Statistics*

KONINKLIJK NEDERLANDS HISTORISCH GENOOTSCHAP. KRONIEK; lijst van de voornaamste in...verschenen boeken en artikelen op het van de Nederlandse geschiedenis. see *HISTORY* — *History Of Europe*

010   II   ISSN 0075-6970
KOTHARI'S WORLD OF REFERENCE WORKS. 1963. irreg. $10. Kothari Publications, 12 India Exchange Place, Calcutta 700 001, India. TEL 91-33-220-9563. Ed. H. Kothari. adv.
 Description: Lists international reference works and directories worldwide. Names of publishers, addresses and prices.

011   SW   ISSN 0280-0799
Z2646.C55
KULTURTIDSKRIFTEN (YEAR); katalog oever kulturtidskrifter i Sverige. 1981. a. free. Statens Kulturraad, P.O. Box 31003, S-400 32 Goeteborg, Sweden. TEL 46-31-24-34-20. FAX 46-31-24-38-10. E-mail: progek@postbox.postnet.se; URL: http://sunsite.kth.se/DS/. Ed. Erik Oestling. **Indexed:** MLA Intl.Bibl. **Document type:** bibliography.

LILACS-CD-ROM. (Literatura Latinoamericana y del Caribe en Ciencias de la Salud) see *MEDICAL SCIENCES* — *Abstracting, Bibliographies, Statistics*

LATIN AMERICAN AND CARIBBEAN STUDIES IN THE HUMANITIES AND SOCIAL SCIENCES IN THE UNIVERSITIES OF THE UNITED KINGDOM. see *HISTORY* — *Abstracting, Bibliographies, Statistics*

015   LV   ISSN 1407-0030
LATVIJAS JAUNAKAS GRAMATAS. 1983. w. $108 (effective 1998). Latvijas Nacionalas Bibliotekas, Bibliografijas Instituts, Anglikanu iela 5, 1816 Riga, Latvia. TEL 7-0132-7220588. (Dist. by: Mezhdunarodnaya Kniga, B. Yakimanka 39, 117049 Moscow, Russia. TEL 7-095-2384967. FAX 7-095-2384634) Ed. Gundega Bligzne; Pub. Gundega Bligzne. circ. 500. **Document type:** bibliography.

016.05   LV   ISSN 1407-0049
LATVIJAS PRESE (YEAR). 1957. a. 2 Ls.($3) Latvijas Nacionalas Bibliotekas, Bibliografijas Instituts, Anglikanu iela 5, 1816 Riga, Latvia. TEL 7-0132-7212668. Ed. S. Rozenbaha; Pub. Leva Vecvagare. circ. 200. **Document type:** bibliography.

016.05   LV   ISSN 1017-7604
LATVIJAS PRESES HRONIKA. 1957. m. $53 (effective 1998). Latvijas Nacionalas Bibliotekas, Bibliografijas Instituts, Anglikanu iele 5, 1816 Riga, Latvia. TEL 7-0132-223181. (Dist. by: Mezhdunarodnaya Kniga, B. Yakimanka 39, 117049 Moscow, Russia. TEL 7-095-2384967. FAX 7-095-2384634) Ed.Bd.; Pub. Gundega Bligzne. circ. 270. **Indexed:** Forest.Abstr. **Document type:** bibliography.
 —BLDSC (0097.488500).
 Formerly (until 1990): Latvijas P.S.R. Preses Hronika (ISSN 0130-9226)

LAW BOOKS IN PRINT; law books in English published throughout the world. see *LAW* — *Abstracting, Bibliographies, Statistics*

LAW BOOKS PUBLISHED. see *LAW* — *Abstracting, Bibliographies, Statistics*

860 015   CK
LEA. 1976. irreg. Carrera 44 no. 47-49, Apdo. Aereo 4307, Medellin, Colombia. Eds. Luis Amadeo Perez, German Suescun.

015   AT   ISSN 0814-9631
LEGAL DEPOSIT PUBLICATIONS IN WESTERN AUSTRALIA. (Print edition ceased) 1984. 2/yr. Aus.$30. Library and Information Service of Western Australia, Alexander Library Bldg., Perth Cultural Centre, Perth, W.A. 6000, Australia. TEL 61-9-4273111. FAX 61-9-4273256. URL: http://www.liswa.wa.gov.au. R&P contact: J.S. Battye. circ. 50. (back issues avail.) **Document type:** bibliography.
 ●Available only online.
 Description: Alphabetical list by author, title and subject of new Western Australian monographs and serials in the J.S. Battye Library of West Australian history.

LEGAL LOOSELEAFS IN PRINT. see *LAW* — *Abstracting, Bibliographies, Statistics*

LEGAL NEWSLETTERS IN PRINT. see *LAW* — *Abstracting, Bibliographies, Statistics*

LEGAL PUBLISHER. see *LAW*

015   RU   ISSN 0024-1172
AI15
LETOPIS' GAZETNYKH STATEI. 1936. 52/yr. $414 (effective 1998). (Komitet po Pechati Soveta Ministrov) Izdatel'stvo Kniga, 50, Gorky St., 125047 Moscow, Russia. circ. 3,000.

057 016   BU   ISSN 0324-0398
AI15
LETOPIS NA STATIITE OT BULGARSKITE SPISANIIA I SBORNITSI/ARTICLES FROM BULGARIAN JOURNALS AND COLLECTIONS. 1952. s-m. 1480 lv.($58) Narodna Biblioteka Sv.sv. Kiril i Metodii, 88, V. Levski Blvd., 1504 Sofia, Bulgaria. TEL 359-2-882811. FAX 359-2-435495. Ed. R. Strumina. bk.rev. circ. 420. **Document type:** bibliography.
 —BLDSC (0097.530000).
 Supersedes in part: Letopis na Periodichna Pechat (ISSN 0024-1180)

016 276   BU   ISSN 0324-0347
AI15
LETOPIS NA STATIITE OT BULGARSKITE VESTNITSI/ARTICLES FROM BULGARIAN NEWSPAPERS; mesechen bibliografski biuletin. 1952. m. 680 lv.($35) Narodna Biblioteka Sv.sv. Kiril i Metodii, 88, V. Levski Blvd., 1504 Sofia, Bulgaria. TEL 359-2-882811. FAX 359-2-435495. Ed. M. Gavrilova. R&P contact: M. Gavrilova. illus.; stat. circ. 375. **Document type:** bibliography.
 Supersedes in part: Letopis na Periodichna Pechat (ISSN 0024-1180)

011   BW
Z2514.W5
LETOPIS' PECHATI BELARUSI/LETAPIS DRUKU BELARUSI. (Text in Byelorussian, Russian) 1924. m. $194 (effective 1998). Nationalnaya Knizhnaya Palata Belarusi - National Book Chamber of Belarus, Pr. Masherava, 11, 220600 Minsk, Belarus. TEL 230839. (Dist. by: Mezhdunarodnaya Kniga, B. Yakimanka 39, 117049 Moscow, Russia. TEL 7-095-2384967. FAX 7-095-2384634) Ed. K.V. Bazarboyeva. circ. 380.
 —BLDSC (0097.300000).
 Formerly: Latopis' Pechati B.S.S.R. (ISSN 0130-9218); Incorporates (in 1992): Belaruskaya S.S.R. v Pechati S.S.S.R. i Zarubezhnykh Stran (ISSN 0868-524X); Which was formerly (1946-1990): Belaruskaya S.S.R. v Pechati S.S.S.R. i Zarubezhnykh Socialisticheskikh Stran (ISSN 0207-9003)
 Description: State bibliographical guide, containing information on all types of publications: books, periodicals, newspapers.

050 015   RU   ISSN 0024-1202
AI15
LETOPIS' ZHURNAL'NYKH STATEI. 1926. 52/yr. $715 (effective 1998). Rossiiskaya Gosudarstvennaya Biblioteka - Russian State Library, Vozdizhenka, 3, 101000 Moscow, Russia. FAX 7-95-2002255. TELEX 411167 GBL SU. circ. 3,980. (reprint service avail. from KTO)
 —BLDSC (0097.400000).

LETTERA; percorsi bibliografici in psichiatria. see *PSYCHOLOGY* — *Abstracting, Bibliographies, Statistics*

BIBLIOGRAPHIES

015 301.16   IT   ISSN 0024-144X
AS221
LETTURE; mensile di informazione culturale, letteratura e spettacolo. 1946. 10/yr. foreign L.102000 (effective 1997). Periodici San Paolo, Via Liberazione 4, 12051 Alba (CN), Italy. TEL 39-2-48071. FAX 39-2-48072515. E-mail: letture@stpauls.it. Ed. Giusto Truglia; Pub. Giuseppe Proietti. R&P contact: Mauro Broggi. TEL 39-2-48008838. adv. contact: Corrado Minnella. bk.rev.; film rev.; music rev.; play rev.; bibl.; illus.; index, cum.index. circ. 8,000. **Indexed:** MLA Intl.Bibl. —KR SourceOne.
 Description: Contains articles on cultural events and trends, reviews and essays on film directors, writers and poets.

015   IT   ISSN 1122-5521
I LIBRI; bimestrale di bibliografia italiana. 1994. bi-m. L.120000 (effective 1997). Casalini Libri, Via Benedetto da Maiano 3, 50014 Fiesole (Florence), Italy. TEL 39-55-5018181. FAX 39-55-5018201. E-mail: libri@casalini.it; URL: http://www.casalini.it. Ed. Reinoud Boeks; Pub. Barbara Casalini. R&P contact: Carla De Jager. TEL 39-55-6481184. adv. contact: Eunice Miles. index. **Indexed:** Arts & Hum.Cit.Ind., Compumath. **Document type:** trade publication.
 Description: Contains complete bibliographical records for works which have appeared in Italy in the previous 2 months. Covers all subject areas and includes indices.

015   CL
LIBRO CHILENO EN VENTA. 1975. biennial. $108. Servicio de Extension de Cultura Chilena, Portugal 12, Depto. 45, Casilla 58-22, Santiago, Chile. FAX 562-2223695. E-mail: serec@reuna.cl. Dir. Marta Dominguez Diaz. **Document type:** bibliography.

011   PR
LIBROS EN VENTA EN HISPANOAMERICA Y ESPANA/SPANISH BOOKS IN PRINT; guia bibliografica de libros disponibles en espanol. (In 3 vols.: author, title, subject) 1964. a. $395. Melcher Ediciones, c/o Margaret Melcher, Box 6000, San Juan, PR 00906. TEL 787-724-1352. FAX 787-724-2886. (Alt. addr.: Sol 9, Old San Juan, PR 00901) **Document type:** bibliography, directory.
 ●Also available on CD-ROM. Producer(s): K.G. Saur Verlag.
 Description: Lists Spanish-language books in print in 36 countries.

011   US
LIBROS EN VENTA EN HISPANOAMERICA Y ESPANA PLUS/SPANISH BOOKS IN PRINT PLUS. s-a. $995. R.R. Bowker, A Division of Reed Elsevier plc group, 121 Chanlon Rd., New Providence, NJ 07974. TEL 908-665-2866; 800-323-3288. FAX 908-665-3528. TELEX 138 755. E-mail: info@bowker.com; URL: http://www.reedref.com. (MS-DOS version) **Document type:** bibliography.
 ●Available only on CD-ROM. Producer(s): Bowker Electronic Publishing.
 Description: Provides information on more than 150,000 Spanish-language books from more than 5,000 publishers in 36 countries, including Central and South America, Cuba, Mexico, Puerto Rico, and Spain, as well as books in Spanish from the United States, France, Germany, Italy, Sweden, Switzerland, Israel, and the People's Republic of China. Each entry provides the author, title, edition, language of original, translator, publisher, year of publication, number of pages, and price.

011   SP   ISSN 0214-6304
Z2683
LIBROS ESPANOLES EN VENTA. 1973. m. 30000 ptas. (CD-ROM ed. 55000 ptas.). Ministerio de Cultura, Centro del Libro y de la Lectura, Agencia Espanol I S B N, C. Santiago Rusinol, 8, 28040 Madrid, Spain. TEL 536-88-30. FAX 553-99-90. circ. 1,000 (paid). **Document type:** bibliography.
 ●Also available online.
 Also available on CD-ROM.
 —Linda Hall.
 Former titles (until 1986): Libros Espanoles en Venta I S B N (ISSN 0213-1099); (until 1982): Libros Espanoles I S B N (ISSN 0377-0974); (until 1973): Libros Espanoles. Catalogo I S B N (ISSN 0302-4652)

LIFE SCIENCE BOOK REVIEW. see BIOLOGY — Abstracting, Bibliographies, Statistics

LIGHT'S LIST OF LITERARY MAGAZINES (YEAR). see LITERARY AND POLITICAL REVIEWS — Abstracting, Bibliographies, Statistics

LINGUISTIC BIBLIOGRAPHY/BIBLIOGRAPHIE LINGUISTIQUE. see LINGUISTICS — Abstracting, Bibliographies, Statistics

LIST OF CLASSES OF UNITED STATES GOVERNMENT PUBLICATIONS AVAILABLE FOR SELECTION BY DEPOSITORY LIBRARIES. see LIBRARY AND INFORMATION SCIENCES — Abstracting, Bibliographies, Statistics

011   FR   ISSN 0259-000X
Z6945.A2
LIST OF SERIAL TITLE WORD ABBREVIATIONS. 1991. irreg. 980 F. International Centre for the Registration of Serials, I S S N International Centre - Centre International d'Enregistrement des Publications en Serie, 20 rue Bachaumont, 75002 Paris, France. TEL 33-1-44-88-22-20. FAX 33-1-40-26-32-43. TELEX 219 847 F. E-mail: issnic@issn.org; URL: http://www.issn.org. (also avail. in diskette format (ISSN 1018-810X))
 —KNAW.
 Description: Contains the key words of the titles of serials processed by the ISSN network and their abbreviations.

015   RU
LITERATURA O SAKHALINSKOI OBLASTI. 1968. a. 0.30 Rub. (Sakhalinskaya Oblastnaya Biblioteka) Dal'nevostochnoe Knizhnoe Izdatel'stvo, Sakhalinskoe Otdelenie, Ul. Dzerzhinskogo, 34, Yuzhno-Sakhalinsk, Russia.

LITERATURA PIEKNA. ADNOTOWANY ROCZNIK BIBLIOGRAFICZNY. see LITERATURE — Abstracting, Bibliographies, Statistics

016   KR   ISSN 0130-917X
AI15
LITOPIS GAZETNYKH STATEI; derzhavnyi bibliografichnii pokazhchik Ukrainy. 1937. m. $120 (effective 1997). (Ministerstvo Informatsii Ukrainy - Information Ministry of Ukraine) Knizhkova Palata Ukrainy - Book Chamber of Ukraine, Prosp. Gagarina 27, 253094 Kiev, Ukraine. TEL 380-44-5520134. FAX 380-44-5520184. Ed. V.L. Stupak. **Document type:** bibliography.
 —BLDSC (0098.259000).

011   KR   ISSN 0130-9196
LITOPIS KNIG; derzhavnii bibliografichnii pokazhchik Ukrainy. 1924. m. $120 (effective 1997). (Ministerstvo Informatsii Ukrainy - Information Ministry of Ukraine) Knizhkova Palata Ukrainy - Book Chamber of Ukraine, Prosp. Gagarina 27, 253094 Kiev, Ukraine. TEL 380-44-5520134. FAX 380-44-5520184. Ed. O.B. Zubareva. **Document type:** bibliography.
 —BLDSC (0098.260150).

015   KR   ISSN 0130-9250
LITOPIS RETSENZII. (Text in Ukrainian) 1936. a. $10 (effective 1997). (Ministerstvo Informatsii Ukrainy - Information Ministry of Ukraine) Knizhkova Palata Ukrainy - Book Chamber of Ukraine, Prosp. Gagarina 27, 253094 Kiev, Ukraine. TEL 380-44-5520134. FAX 380-44-5520184. Ed. O.B. Zubareva. **Document type:** bibliography.

016   KR   ISSN 0130-9188
LITOPIS ZHURNAL'NYKH STATEI; derzhavnii bibliografichnii pokazhchik Ukrainy. 1936. m. $120 (effective 1997). (Ministerstvo Informatskii Ukrainy - Information Ministry of Ukraine) Knizhkova Palata Ukrainy - Book Chamber of Ukraine, Prosp. Gagarina 27, 253094 Kiev, Ukraine. TEL 380-44-5520134. FAX 380-44-5520184. **Document type:** bibliography.
 —BLDSC (0098.260050).

016   FR
LIVRES DISPONIBLES. (In 6 vols.) 1972. a. 3990 F. Electre, 35 rue Gregoire-de-Tours, 75006 Paris Cedex 06, France. Ed. Pascal Fouche. (also avail. in microfiche) **Document type:** bibliography.
 ●Also available on CD-ROM.
 —CISTI; Linda Hall.
 Formed by the merger of: Catalogue de l'Edition Francaise (ISSN 0069-1089); Repertoire des Livres de Langue Francaise Disponibles (ISSN 0080-1003)

015   FR
LIVRES ET PUBLICATIONS EN SERIE. 6/yr. $1835. Bibliotheque Nationale de France, Quai Francois Mauriac, 75706 Paris Cedex 13, France. TEL 33-1-47038610. FAX 33-1-47038586. E-mail: contact@chadwyck.fr. (Dist. by: Chadwyck-Healey France, 50 rue de Paradis, 75010 Paris, France. TEL 33-1-44838181. FAX 33-1-44838183; In N. America: Chadwyck-Healey Inc., 1101 King St., Alexandria, VA 22314. TEL 800-752-0515. FAX 703-683-7589) **Document type:** bibliography.
 Formerly: Bibliographie Nationale Francaise depuis 1970 sur C D - R O M.

LIVRES HEBDO. see PUBLISHING AND BOOK TRADE — Abstracting, Bibliographies, Statistics

015   PO   ISSN 0870-6093
Z2715
LIVROS DISPONIVEIS (YEAR). a. Associacao Portuguesa de Editores e Livreiros, Av. Estados Unidos da America, 97 6o Esq., 1700 Lisbon, Portugal. TEL 351-1-8489136. FAX 351-1-8489377. Ed. Jose Manuel Lello. **Document type:** catalog.
 Formerly (until 1987): Catalogo dos Livros Disponiveis (ISSN 0871-0503)

M L A INTERNATIONAL BIBLIOGRAPHY OF BOOKS AND ARTICLES ON THE MODERN LANGUAGES AND LITERATURES. (Modern Language Association of America) see LITERATURE — Abstracting, Bibliographies, Statistics

M L B D NEWSLETTER; monthly of indological bibliography. (Motilal Banarsidass (Delhi)) see ORIENTAL STUDIES — Abstracting, Bibliographies, Statistics

MABUA/FOUNTAIN; religious creation in literature, society and thought. see LITERATURE

011   MH
MACAO. DIRECCAO DOS SERVICOS DE ESTATISTICA E CENSOS. BOLETIM BIBLIOGRAFICO/MACAO. CENSUS AND STATISTICS DEPARTMENT. BIBLIOGRAPHY BULLETIN. (Text in Portuguese) 1984. m. free. Direccao dos Servicos de Estatistica e Censos, Rua Inacio Baptista, No. 4-6, P.O. Box 3022, Macao. TEL 853-3995311. FAX 853-307825. **Document type:** government publication.
 Description: Contains the information of publications received from external sources.

MADHYA PRADESH WHO'S WHO. see BIOGRAPHY

011   US   ISSN 0000-0914
Z6941
MAGAZINES FOR LIBRARIES; for the general reader and school, junior college, university and public libraries. 3rd ed. 1978. irreg., 9th ed., 1997. $170. R.R. Bowker, A Division of Reed Elsevier Inc., 121 Chanlon Rd., New Providence, NJ 07974. TEL 908-464-6800. FAX 908-665-6688. TELEX 138 755. E-mail: info@bowker.com; URL: http://www.reedref.com. (Subscr. to: Order Dept., Box 31, New Providence, NJ 07974-9903. TEL 800-521-8110) Eds. Bill Katz, Linda Sternberg Katz. **Indexed:** Bk.Rev.Ind. (1988-1989), Child.Bk.Rev.Ind. (1988-1989). **Document type:** bibliography, directory.
 Description: Describes and evaluates magazines organized by subject area. Indicates magazine content and editorial policies.

011 020   US   ISSN 0000-1368
Z6944.C5
MAGAZINES FOR YOUNG PEOPLE; a Children's Magazine Guide companion volume. 1987. irreg., 2nd edition, 1992. $38. R.R. Bowker, A Division of Reed Elsevier Inc., 121 Chanlon Rd., New Providence, NJ 07974. TEL 908-464-6800. FAX 908-665-6688. TELEX 138 755. E-mail: info@bowker.com; URL: http://www.reedref.com. (Subscr. to: Order Dept., Box 31, New Providence, NJ 07974-9903. TEL 800-521-8110) Eds. Bill Katz, Linda Sternberg Katz. **Document type:** consumer publication.
 Formerly (until 1991): Magazines for School Libraries (ISSN 0000-0957)
 Description: Describes and evaluates more than 1,100 magazines in 74 subject areas. Covers both curriculum-related and general-interest periodicals, as well as journals and newsletters for children, young adults, and librarians.

MAGAZINES IN SPECIAL MEDIA. see HANDICAPPED — Abstracting, Bibliographies, Statistics

556 BIBLIOGRAPHIES

016   HU   ISSN 0134-1464
Z2148.L5
MAGYAR IRODALOM ES IRODALOMTUDOMANY BIBLIOGRAFIAJA. (Print ed. ceased 1989) 1976. a. Orszagos Szechenyi Konyvtar - National Szechenyi Library, Budavari Palota F epulet, 1827 Budapest, Hungary. TEL 36-1-155-6967. FAX 36-1-202-0804. E-mail: vili@oszk.hu. (Subscr. to: Nemzetkozi es Kulturalis Kapcsolatok Irodaja - Public Relations and Cultural Affairs, Budavari Palota F epulet, 1827 Budapest, Hungary) (Co-sponsor: Orszagos Tudomanyos Kutatasi Alap) Ed. Katalin Velich. bk.rev. circ. 500. (diskette format) **Document type:** bibliography.
   Description: Lists books, studies, and articles on Hungarian literature and theory of literature published in Hungary and abroad.

015   HU   ISSN 1218-5604
MAGYAR KONYVESZET. (Print ed. ceased 1991) 1994. a. $150. Orszagos Szechenyi Konyvtar - National Szechenyi Library, Budavari Palota F epulet, 1827 Budapest, Hungary. TEL 36-1-1556967. FAX 36-1-202-0804. E-mail: vili@oszk.hu. (Subscr. to: Nemzetkozi es Kulturalis Kapcsolatok Irodaja - Public Relations and Cultural Affairs, Budavari Palota F epulet, 1827 Budapest, Hungary) (microfiche) **Indexed:** Amer.Hist.& Life (1972-), Hist.Abstr. (1972-). **Document type:** bibliography.
●Also available on CD-ROM.
   Description: Lists books, brochures, official publications, first issues and title changes of serials published in Hungary from 1976 and officially deposited in the library.

016   HU   ISSN 0231-4592
Z6956.H8
MAGYAR NEMZETI BIBLIOGRAFIA. IDOSZAKI KIADVANYOK BIBLIOGRAFIAJA. (Print ed. ceased 1990) (Text in Hungarian; introduction in English and Russian) 1946. a. price varies. Orszagos Szechenyi Konyvtar - National Szechenyi Library, Budavari Palota F epulet, 1827 Budapest, Hungary. TEL 36-1-156-9378. FAX 36-1-202-0804. E-mail: vili@oszk.hu. (Subscr. to: Nemzetkozi es Kulturalis Kapcsolatok Irodaja, Public Relations and Cultural Affairs, Budavari Palota F epulet, 1827 Budapest, Hungary) Ed. Aniko Nagy. circ. 620. **Document type:** bibliography.
●Available only on CD-ROM.
   Formerly (until 1980): Kurrens Idoszaki Kiadvanyok (ISSN 0134-0247); Which supersedes in part (in 1977): Magyar Nemzeti Bibliografia (ISSN 0373-1766)
   Description: Bibliography of Hungarian periodicals officially deposited in the National Szechenyi Library.

MAGYAR NEMZETI BIBLIOGRAFIA. IDOSZAKI KIADVANYOK REPERTORIUMA; tarsadalomtudomanyok, termeszettudomanyok. see *SOCIAL SCIENCES: COMPREHENSIVE WORKS — Abstracting, Bibliographies, Statistics*

015   HU   ISSN 1218-2192
MAGYAR NEMZETI BIBLIOGRAFIA. KONYVEK/HUNGARIAN NATIONAL BIBLIOGRAPHY. BOOKS. 1994. s-a. $700 (multiusers $800). Orszagos Szechenyi Konyvtar - National Szechenyi Library, Budavari Palota F epulet, 1827 Budapest, Hungary. TEL 36-1-1556967. FAX 36-1-2020804. E-mail: vili@oszk.hu. (Subscr. to: Nemzetkozi es Kulturalis Kapcsolatok Irodaja - Public Relations and Cultural Affairs, Budavari Palota F epulet, 1827 Budapest, Hungary) **Document type:** bibliography.
●Available only on CD-ROM.
   Description: Lists books, brochures, official publications, first issues and title changes of serials published in Hungary from 1976 deposited in the library.

016   HU   ISSN 0133-6843
Z2141
MAGYAR NEMZETI BIBLIOGRAFIA. KONYVEK BIBLIOGRAFIAJA. (Annual Cumulation: Magyar Konyveszet (HU 0133-3496)) (Text in Hungarian; introduction in English, German) 1946. s-m. 2640 Ft.($60) Orszagos Szechenyi Konyvtar - National Szechenyi Library, Budavari Palota F epulet, 1827 Budapest, Hungary. TEL 36-1-156-8497. FAX 36-1-202-0804. E-mail: vili@oszk.hu. (Subscr. to: Nemzetkozi es Kulturalis Kapcsolatok Irodaja, Public Relations and Cultural Affairs, Budavari Palota F epulet, 1827 Budapest, Hungary) Ed. Eva Balogh. circ. 800. (also avail. in microfiche) **Document type:** bibliography.
●Also available on CD-ROM.
  —BLDSC (5345.003500).
   Supersedes in part (in 1977): Magyar Nemzeti Bibliografia (ISSN 0373-1766)
   Description: Bibliography of books, brochures, official publications, first issues and title changes of serials published in Hungary and officially deposited in the National Szechenyi Library.

015   HU   ISSN 1416-5414
▼**MAGYAR NEMZETI BIBLIOGRAFIA. PERIODIKUMOK/HUNGARIAN NATIONAL BIBLIOGRAPHY. SERIALS.** 1996. s-a. $700. Orszagos Szechenyi Konyvtar - National Szechenyi Library, Budavari Palota F epulet, 1827 Budapest, Hungary. TEL 36-1-1556967. FAX 36-1-2020804. E-mail: vili@oszk.hu. (Subscr. to: Nemzetkozi es Kulturalis Kapcsolatok Irodaja - Public Relations and Cultural Affairs, Budavari Palota F epulet, 1827 Budapest, Hungary) **Document type:** bibliography.
●Available only on CD-ROM.
   Description: Lists periodicals, first issues and title changes, published in Hungary and officially deposited in the library from 1986.

MAGYAR NEMZETI BIBLIOGRAFIA. ZENEMUVEK BIBLIOGRAFIAJA. see *MUSIC — Abstracting, Bibliographies, Statistics*

015   HU   ISSN 0541-9492
MAGYAR TUDOMANYOS AKADEMIA KONYVTARA KEZIRATTARANAK KATALOGUSAI/CATALOGI COLLECTIONIS MANUSCRIPTORUM BIBLIOTHECAE ACADEMIAE SCIENTIARUM HUNGARICAE. (Text in Hungarian; summaries in English, French, German) 1966. irreg. price varies; also avail. on exchange basis. Magyar Tudomanyos Akademia Konyvtara, Arany Janos u.1, P.O. Box 1002, 1245 Budapest 5, Hungary. Ed. D. Csanak. **Document type:** bibliography.
   Description: Information on the library's manuscripts, with catalogues of outstanding bequests.

027 011   UG   ISSN 0047-3138
MAKERERE UNIVERSITY. LIBRARY. LIBRARY BULLETIN AND ACCESSIONS LIST. 1954. q. S.70($10.) Makerere University, Library, Box 16002, Kampala, Uganda. Ed. Margaret M. Barlow. circ. 300. (tabloid format)

011   MW
MALAWI NATIONAL BIBLIOGRAPHY; list of publications deposited in the library of the National Archives. 1963-1983; resumed 1994. irreg. K.50 (foreign £10($20)). National Archives of Malawi, Library, Mkulichi Rd., P.O. Box 62, Zomba, Malawi. TEL 265-50-522-184. FAX 265-522-148. Ed. D.W. Ambali. circ. 200 (controlled). **Document type:** bibliography, government publication.
   Formerly (until 1967): Malawi. List of Publications Deposited in the Library of the National Archives.
   Description: Lists Malawian imprints at the National Archives Library.

015   MM   ISSN 0258-669X
MALTA NATIONAL BIBLIOGRAPHY/BIBLIOGRAFIJA NAZZJONALITA MALTA. 1984. a. $9. National Library of Malta, 36 Old Treasury St., Valletta, Malta. TEL 356-236585. FAX 356-235992. Ed. John B. Sultana. circ. 500. **Document type:** bibliography.
  —BLDSC (5356.347000).
   Refereed Serial

MANAGEMENT (BALTIMORE); a bibliography for N A S A managers. see *BUSINESS AND ECONOMICS — Abstracting, Bibliographies, Statistics*

MANAGEMENT BIBLIOGRAPHIES AND REVIEWS. see *BUSINESS AND ECONOMICS — Abstracting, Bibliographies, Statistics*

MARINE AFFAIRS BIBLIOGRAPHY; a comprehensive index to marine law and policy literature. see *LAW — Abstracting, Bibliographies, Statistics*

MARKAZ AL-MALIK FAISAL LIL-BUHUTH WAL-DIRASAT AL-ISLAMIYYAH. FIHRIS AL-MAKHTUTAT/KING FAISAL CENTER FOR RESEARCH AND ISLAMIC STUDIES. MANUSCRIPT CATALOGUE. see *ORIENTAL STUDIES — Abstracting, Bibliographies, Statistics*

MARKETSEARCH. see *BUSINESS AND ECONOMICS — Abstracting, Bibliographies, Statistics*

MARXISM AND THE MASS MEDIA; towards a basic bibliography. see *COMMUNICATIONS*

015.52   JA   ISSN 0913-025X
MATERIALS ON ASIA - ACCESSION LIST AND REVIEW/AJIA SHIRYO TSUHO. (Text mainly in Japanese, sometimes in English) 1963. bi-m. 1960 Yen. National Diet Library - Kokuritsu Kokkai Toshokan, 1-10-1 Nagata-cho, Chiyoda-ku, Tokyo 100, Japan. TEL 81-3-3581-2331. FAX 81-3-3597-9104. E-mail: kokusai@ndlmai.ndl.go.jp; URL: http://www.ndl.go.jp. bk.rev.: bibl.; circ. 490 (controlled). **Document type:** bibliography.
   Formerly: Materials on Asia and Africa - Accession List and Review/Ajia Afurika Shiryo Tsuho (ISSN 0025-536X)

A MATTER OF FACT: STATEMENTS CONTAINING STATISTICS ON CURRENT SOCIAL, ECONOMIC AND POLITICAL ISSUES. see *HISTORY*

MEDIABOOK SPECIALIZZATI. see *SCIENCES: COMPREHENSIVE WORKS — Abstracting, Bibliographies, Statistics*

MEDICAL AND HEALTH CARE BOOKS AND SERIALS IN PRINT; an index to literature in health sciences. see *MEDICAL SCIENCES — Abstracting, Bibliographies, Statistics*

MEDICINAL AND AROMATIC PLANTS. see *MEDICAL SCIENCES — Abstracting, Bibliographies, Statistics*

011 940   US
MEDIEVAL BOOK. 1993. irreg. University of Notre Dame Press, Notre Dame, IN 46556. TEL 219-631-6346. FAX 219-631-8148. (Subscr. in US to: 11030 S. Langley Ave., Chicago, IL 60628. TEL 800-621-2736; Overseas subscr. to: Eurospan University Press Group, 3 Henrietta St., London WC2E 8LU, England) R&P contact: Ann Bromley. TEL 219-631-6346. **Document type:** monographic series.

011   MF
MEMORANDUM OF BOOKS PRINTED IN MAURITIUS AND REGISTERED IN THE ARCHIVES OFFICE. (Text in English; summaries in English, French) 1894. q. free. Archives Department, Development Bank of Mauritius Complex, Petite Riviere, Mauritius.

011   MX
MEXICO. CENTRO DE INFORMACION TECNICA Y DOCUMENTACION. INDICE BIBLIOGRAFICO. 1972. a. Mex.$80($5) Instituto Nacional de Productividad, Calzada Atzcapotzalco-la Villa 209, Col. Santa Catarina, 02250 Mexico DF, Mexico. Ed. Marco A. Tapia. cum.index. circ. 2,500. (also avail. in microfilm)

353 015   US   ISSN 0026-2110
Z1223.5.M5
MICHIGAN DOCUMENTS. 1952. q. free. Library of Michigan, Box 30007, Lansing, MI 48909. TEL 517-373-1580. URL: http://libofmich.lib.mi.us. index. circ. 500. **Document type:** bibliography, directory.
   Description: A bibliographic listing of Michigan governmental publications received by the Library of Michigan.

016   US   ISSN 0147-0604
MICHIGAN STATE UNIVERSITY. LIBRARY. AFRICANA: SELECT RECENT ACQUISITIONS. (Text in English, French, Italian, Portuguese, Russian, Spanish and Swahili) 1965. q. free. Michigan State University Libraries, Africana Section, East Lansing, MI 48824-1048. TEL 517-355-2366. FAX 517-432-1445. E-mail: lauer@pilot.msu.edu. Ed. Joseph J. Lauer. circ. 200 (controlled). (processed) **Document type:** bibliography.

BIBLIOGRAPHIES

011 US ISSN 0270-8523
Z1033.M5
MICROFORMS ANNUAL.* 1973. biennial. $15 (free to libraries). Microforms International (Subsidiary of: Pergamon Press, Inc.), 1345 Avenue of the Americas, NO 1036C, New York, NY 10105-0302. TEL 914-592-7700. adv. circ. 15,000.
Formerly: M I M C Microforms Annual (ISSN 0362-4552)

011 US ISSN 0361-2635
Z1033.M5
MICROPUBLISHERS' TRADE LIST ANNUAL. Cover title: M T L A, the Micropublishers' Trade List Annual. 1978. a. $375. Chadwyck-Healey Inc., 1101 King St., Ste. 380, Alexandria, VA 22314-2944. TEL 703-683-4890. FAX 703-683-7589. TELEX 9312102282 SS G. (U.K. addr.: Chadwyck-Healey Ltd., The Quorum, Barnwell Rd., Cambridge CB2 1NR, England. TEL 44-223-215512. FAX 44-223-215513) index. circ. 300. (microfiche) —BLDSC (5759.800000).
Description: Microfiche lists and indexes of publications from more than 1,700 publishers, for large public and academic libraries.

015 RU
MOSKOVSKII UNIVERSITET. BIBLIOTEKA. RUKOPISNAYA I PECHATNAYA KNIGA V FONDAKH. 1973. irreg. 0.76 Rub. Moskovskii Universitet, Ul. Gertsena 5-7, 103009 Moscow, Russia. illus.

016 BE ISSN 0773-8560
MUSEE ROYAL DE L'AFRIQUE CENTRALE. CATALOGUE DES EDITIONS/KONINKLIJK MUSEUM VOOR MIDDEN-AFRIKA. CATALOGUS DER UITGAVEN. (Text in Dutch, French) 1965. a. Musee Royal de l'Afrique Centrale - Koninklijk Museum voor Midden-Afrika, 13 Steenweg op Leuven, B-3080 Tervuren, Belgium. TEL 32-2-7695299. FAX 32-2-7670242. Document type: catalog.
Formerly (until 1970): Musee Royal de l'Afrique Centrale. Publications (ISSN 0082-2906)

MUSIC & MUSICIANS: BRAILLE SCORES CATALOG - CHORAL (LARGE PRINT EDITION). see HANDICAPPED — Abstracting, Bibliographies, Statistics

MUSIC & MUSICIANS: BRAILLE SCORES CATALOG - INSTRUMENTAL (LARGE PRINT EDITION). see HANDICAPPED — Abstracting, Bibliographies, Statistics

MUSIC & MUSICIANS: BRAILLE SCORES CATALOG - ORGAN (LARGE PRINT EDITION). see HANDICAPPED — Abstracting, Bibliographies, Statistics

MUSIC & MUSICIANS: BRAILLE SCORES CATALOG - PIANO (LARGE PRINT EDITION). see HANDICAPPED — Abstracting, Bibliographies, Statistics

MUSIC & MUSICIANS: BRAILLE SCORES CATALOG - VOCAL. PART I: CLASSICAL (LARGE PRINT EDITION). see HANDICAPPED — Abstracting, Bibliographies, Statistics

MUSIC & MUSICIANS: BRAILLE SCORES CATALOG - VOCAL. PART II: POPULAR (LARGE PRINT EDITION). see HANDICAPPED — Abstracting, Bibliographies, Statistics

MUSIC & MUSICIANS: INSTRUCTIONAL CASSETTE RECORDINGS CATALOG (LARGE PRINT EDITION). see HANDICAPPED — Abstracting, Bibliographies, Statistics

MUSIC & MUSICIANS: INSTRUCTIONAL DISC RECORDINGS CATALOG (LARGE PRINT EDITION). see HANDICAPPED — Abstracting, Bibliographies, Statistics

MUSIC & MUSICIANS: LARGE PRINT SCORES AND BOOKS CATALOG (LARGE PRINT EDITION). see HANDICAPPED — Abstracting, Bibliographies, Statistics

011 II
N A S S D O C RESEARCH INFORMATION SERIES. BIBLIOGRAPHIC REPRINTS. (Text in English) irreg. Rs.25. Indian Council of Social Science Research, National Social Science Documentation Centre, 35 Ferozshah Rd., New Delhi 110 001, India. TEL 91-11-338-3091. FAX 91-11-338-8037. TELEX 31-61083-ISSR-IN. Ed. K.G. Tyagi. circ. 100. Document type: bibliography.
Description: Contains bibliographies compiled for scholars on different social science topics.

017 NO ISSN 0357-1955
N O S P - MIKRO. (Nordisk Samkatalog foer Periodika) Key Title: N O S P - Mikro (Mikrofilmkort). CD-ROM edition: N O S P (C D - R O M) (NO ISSN 0805-4770) (Not avail. in printed format) 1978. s-a. $300 (CD-ROM $480) (effective 1997). University of Oslo Library, N O S P - Centre, N-0242 Oslo, Norway. TEL 47-22-859110. FAX 47-22-859050. E-mail: nosp@ub.uio.no; URL: http://www.nbo.uio.no/nosp/. Ed. Elisabeth Lindboe. circ. 400. (microfiche) Document type: catalog.
●Also available on CD-ROM.
Description: Catalogues over 135,000 serial publications from 600 research libraries throughout Scandinavia.

015 PP
N R I BIBLIOGRAPHIES. 1976. irreg. price varies. National Research Institute, P.O. Box 5854, Boroko, NCD, Papua New Guinea. TEL 675-26-0300. FAX 675-26-0213.

011 AT
N U C O M 6. (National Union Catalogue of Monographs) 1982. s-a. Aus.$140 (effective 1997). National Library of Australia, Publications Section, Cultural and Educational Services Division, Canberra, A.C.T. 2600, Australia. TEL 61-6-262-1365. FAX 61-6-273-4493. circ. 100. (also avail. in microfiche)
●Also available online.
Former titles: N U C O M 5 (ISSN 1035-0667); (until 1990): N U C O M 4 (ISSN 1032-8645); Which superseded in part (in 1989): A B N Catalogue (ISSN 0815-0303); Which was formerly (until 1985): A B N Union Catalogue (ISSN 0729-2562)
Description: Lists all records except serial and non-book records on the ABN database.

057.86 015 XR ISSN 1210-8936
Z5949.C9
NARODNI BIBLIOGRAFIE CESKE REPUBLIKY. GRAFIKA A MAPY. 1958. a. 55 Kc. (foreign $9). Narodni Knihovna Ceske Republiky, Klementinum 190, 110 01 Prague 1, Czech Republic. TEL 42-2-24229500. FAX 42-2-24227769. (Dist. by: Narodni Knihovna Ceske Republiky, Odd. Prodeje a Expedice, Centralni Depozitar NK CR, Sterboholska 55, 100 00 Prague 10, Czech Republic. TEL 42-2-702600) Ed. Bohdana Stoklasova. R&P contact: Adolf Knoll. circ. 300. Document type: bibliography.
Former titles (until 1993): Bibliograficky Katalog C S F R: Ceske Knihy. Ceska Grafika a Mapy za Rok (Year) (ISSN 0862-9226); (until 1990): Bibliograficky Katalog C S S R: Ceske Knihy. Ceska Grafika a Mapy za Rok (Year) (ISSN 0323-1712)
Description: Bibliography of Czech plans and maps.

NATIONAL AERONAUTICAL LABORATORY. BIBLIOGRAPHY SERIES. see AERONAUTICS AND SPACE FLIGHT — Abstracting, Bibliographies, Statistics

NATIONAL ASSOCIATION OF ELEMENTARY SCHOOL PRINCIPALS. PROFESSIONAL RESOURCES CATALOG. see EDUCATION — School Organization And Administration

015 BB ISSN 0256-7709
NATIONAL BIBLIOGRAPHY OF BARBADOS. 1975. s-a. $10. National Library Service, Culloden Farm, Culloden Rd., St. Michael, Barbados, W.I. TEL 246-429-5716. FAX 246-436-1501. TELEX WB 2222. Ed.Bd. circ. 100. Document type: bibliography.
●Also available online.
Description: Lists works deposited with the National Library Service in compliance with the Publications Act and works of Barbadian authorship printed abroad.

011 BS ISSN 0027-8777
Z3559
NATIONAL BIBLIOGRAPHY OF BOTSWANA. 1969. 3/yr. $6. National Library Service, Private Bag 0036, Gaborone, Botswana. TEL 267-352397. FAX 267-301149. Ed. Gertrude Kayaga Mulindwa; Pub. Basiamang Garebakwena. index. circ. 300. Document type: bibliography, government publication.
Description: Lists publications issued in Botswana and deposited at the National Library Service under terms of the legal deposit law.

015 NR ISSN 0331-0019
Z3553.N5
NATIONAL BIBLIOGRAPHY OF NIGERIA. 1951. m. with s-a. and a. cumulations. National Library of Nigeria, 4 Wesley St., P.M.B. 12626, Lagos, Nigeria. TEL 234-1-634704. Document type: bibliography. —Linda Hall.
Former titles: Nigerian Publications; Nigerian publications: Current National Bibliography (ISSN 0078-0812)

011 ZA ISSN 0377-1636
Z3573.Z3
NATIONAL BIBLIOGRAPHY OF ZAMBIA. a. K.500. National Archives, P.O. Box RW 50010, Ridgeway, Lusaka, Zambia. Ed. Christine Kamwana. circ. 500. (looseleaf format; back issues avail.) Document type: bibliography, government publication.

011 JA ISSN 1341-4623
NATIONAL DIET LIBRARY. BOOKS ON JAPAN IN WESTERN LANGUAGES RECENTLY ACQUIRED. (Text in English) 1993. s-a. National Diet Library - Kokuritsu Kokkai Toshokan, 1-10-1 Nagata-cho, Chiyoda-ku, Tokyo 100, Japan. TEL 81-3-3581-2331. FAX 81-3-3597-9104. E-mail: kokusai@ndlmail.ndl.go.jp; URL: http://www.ndl.go.jp. circ. 800 (controlled). Document type: bibliography.

015 US ISSN 1050-5830
HF5466
NATIONAL DIRECTORY OF CATALOGS. 1990. a. $395. Oxbridge Communications, Inc., 150 Fifth Ave., Ste. 302, New York, NY 10011. TEL 212-741-0231. FAX 212-633-2938. (also avail. in diskette format) Document type: directory.
●Also available online.
Also available on CD-ROM.
Description: Lists more than 9000 mail order catalogs with comprehensive business information.

011 US
Z6951
NATIONAL DIRECTORY OF COMMUNITY NEWSPAPERS. 1923. a. $95. American Newspaper Representatives, Inc., 1700 W. Big Beaver Rd., Ste. 200, Troy, MI 48084-3543. TEL 800-550-7557. FAX 248-643-0606. E-mail: amnspreps@aol.com. Ed. Robert Sontag. R&P contact: Robert Sontag. adv. circ. 1,000. Document type: directory.
Formerly: Directory of Community Newspapers (ISSN 1045-1102)

016.05 US ISSN 0895-4321
Z6941
NATIONAL DIRECTORY OF MAGAZINES. 1987. a. $495. Oxbridge Communications, Inc., 150 Fifth Ave., New York, NY 10011. TEL 212-741-0231. FAX 212-633-2938. (also avail. in diskette format) Document type: directory.
●Also available online.
Also available on CD-ROM.
—CISTI.
Description: Provides publishers with comprehensive information on the state of the magazine industry with more than 25,000 listings.

NATIONAL ENGLISH LITERARY MUSEUM. BIBLIOGRAPHIC SERIES. see LITERATURE — Abstracting, Bibliographies, Statistics

NATIONAL ENGLISH LITERARY MUSEUM. INTRODUCTION SERIES. see LITERATURE — Abstracting, Bibliographies, Statistics

NATIONAL RESEARCH COUNCIL. TRANSPORTATION RESEARCH BOARD. BIBLIOGRAPHY. see TRANSPORTATION — Abstracting, Bibliographies, Statistics

BIBLIOGRAPHIES

011 025.3 371.3   US   ISSN 0734-7669
NATIONAL UNION CATALOG. AUDIOVISUAL MATERIALS. 1953. q. $115 to N. American libraries (overseas libraries $130). (U.S. Library of Congress, Cataloging Distribution Service, Customer Services Section) Advanced Library Systems, Inc., 100 Brickstone Sq., Box 246, Andover, MA 01810. TEL 508-470-0610. FAX 508-475-1072. (Subscr. also to: Superintendent of Documents, Box 371954, Pittsburgh, PA 15250-7954. TEL 202-512-1800. FAX 202-512-2250; Or: U.S. Library of Congress, Cataloging Distribution Service, Customer Services Section, Washington, DC 20541-5017. TEL 202-707-6100. FAX 202-707-1334) circ. 2,501. (also avail. in microfiche from ADL; back issues avail.) **Document type:** catalog, government publication.
—CISTI; Linda Hall.
   Former titles: Audiovisual Materials (ISSN 0190-9827); Films and Other Materials for Projection (ISSN 0091-3294); Library of Congress Catalog. Motion Pictures and Filmstrips (ISSN 0041-7807)
   Description: Compiles bibliographic records for motion pictures, filmstrips, transparency and slide sets, videotape recordings, and kits cataloged by the US Library of Congress since 1983.

025.3 655 011   US   ISSN 0734-7650
NATIONAL UNION CATALOG. BOOKS. 1956. m. $680 to N. American libraries (overseas libraries $790). (U.S. Library of Congress, Cataloging Distribution Service, Customer Services Section) Advanced Library Systems, Inc., 100 Brickstone Sq., Box 246, Andover, MA 01810. TEL 508-470-0610; 800-255-3666. FAX 508-475-1072. E-mail: cdsinfo@mail.loc.gov. (Subscr. also to: Superintendent of Documents, U.S. Government Printing Office, Box 371954, Pittsburgh, PA 15250-7954. TEL 202-512-1800. FAX 202-512-2250; Or: U.S. Library of Congress, Cataloging Distribution Service, Customer Services Section, Washington, DC 20541-5017. TEL 202-707-6100. FAX 202-707-1334) circ. 2,093. (also avail. in microfiche from ADL; back issues avail.) **Document type:** catalog, government publication.
—BLDSC (6033.240000).
   Formerly (until 1983): National Union Catalog (ISSN 0028-0348)
   Description: Lists bibliographic records for books, pamphlets, manuscripts, map atlases, microform masters, and US and international monographic government publications.

011 025.3 526   US   ISSN 0734-7634
NATIONAL UNION CATALOG. CARTOGRAPHIC MATERIALS. 1983. q. $210 to N. American libraries (foreign libraries $235). (U.S. Library of Congress, Cataloging Distribution Service, Customer Services Section) Advanced Library Systems, Inc., 100 Brickstone Sq., Box 246, Andover, MA 01810-0005. TEL 508-470-0610. FAX 508-475-1072. (Subscr. also to: Superintendent of Documents, U.S. Government Printing Office, Box 371954, Pittsburgh, PA 15250-7954. TEL 202-512-1800. FAX 202-512-2250; Or: U.S. Library of Congress, Cataloging Distribution Service, Customer Services Section, Washington, DC 20541-5017. TEL 202-707-6100. FAX 202-707-1334) (microform; back issues avail.) **Document type:** catalog, government publication.
   Description: Compiles bibliographic records of single-sheet maps, map sets, atlases, and maps treated as serials cataloged by the US Library Congress.

NATIONAL UNION CATALOGUE OF LIBRARY MATERIALS FOR PEOPLE WITH DISABILITIES. see HANDICAPPED — Abstracting, Bibliographies, Statistics

011   AT   ISSN 0812-9258
NATIONAL UNION CATALOGUE OF SERIALS. Short title: N U C U S. 1984. s-a. Aus.$80 (effective 1997). National Library of Australia, Publications Section, Cultural and Educational Services Division, Canberra, A.C.T. 2600, Australia. TEL 61-6-262-1535. FAX 61-6-273-4493. circ. 1,300. (microfiche; reprint service avail. from ISI,UMI)
—Linda Hall.

NESTOR. see ARCHAEOLOGY — Abstracting, Bibliographies, Statistics

011   UN   ISSN 0255-5190
NEW ACQUISITIONS IN THE U N E C A LIBRARY. 1962. bi-m. exchange basis. United Nations Economic Commission for Africa - Commission Economique pour l'Afrique, P.O. Box 3001, Addis Ababa, Ethiopia. (processed)

NEW LITERATURE ON OLD AGE. see GERONTOLOGY AND GERIATRICS — Abstracting, Bibliographies, Statistics

011   IS   ISSN 0334-5262
NEW REFERENCE BOOKS. (Text in English and Hebrew) 1973. s-a. free. Jewish National and University Library, Reference Department, P.O. Box 34165, Jerusalem 91341, Israel. TEL 972-2-6585027. FAX 972-2-6511771. TELEX 25367. E-mail: libby@vms.huji.ac.il. Ed. Libby Kahane. bibl. circ. 600. **Document type:** bibliography.
   Description: Listing of new reference books in libraries of the Hebrew University and the National Library.

011 350   US
NEW RESOURCES. 1970. bi-m. State Library, 1500 Senate St., Box 11469, Columbia, SC 29211. TEL 803-734-8666. FAX 803-734-8676. Ed. Curtis Rogers. circ. 575 (controlled). (processed) **Document type:** bibliography.
   Formerly (until 1988): New Resources for State Government and Agencies (ISSN 0883-5853)
   Description: Lists recent state library acquisitions of interest to state employees.

011   US
NEW SCHOLARLY BOOKS IN AMERICA.* 1972. q. $8 (free to qualified personnel). Beverly Books Inc., 29 Race St., Frenchtown, NJ 08825-1011. Ed. Norman Perle. bk.rev. circ. 10,000.

NEW TECHNICAL BOOKS; a selective list with descriptive annotations. see SCIENCES: COMPREHENSIVE WORKS — Abstracting, Bibliographies, Statistics

011   US
THE NEW YORK TIMES SCHOOL MICROFILM COLLECTION INDEX. irreg. (New York Times Company) U M I (Subsidiary of: Bell & Howell Company), 300 N. Zeeb Rd., Ann Arbor, MI 48106. TEL 313-761-4700; 800-521-0600. FAX 800-864-0019. illus. **Document type:** abstracting/indexing.
   Formerly: New York Times School Microfilm Collection Index by Reels (ISSN 0095-5663)

011   AT   ISSN 0157-7662
NEW ZEALAND BOOKS IN PRINT. 1964. a. Aus.$75($70) D.W. Thorpe, A member of the Reed Elsevier plc group, 18 Salmon St., Port Melbourne, Vic. 3207, Australia. TEL 61-3-92457370. FAX 61-3-92457395. E-mail: customer.service@thorpe.com.au; URL: http://www.reed-elsevier.com. (N. America subscr. to: K.G. Saur, A Reed Reference Publishing Company, 121 Chanlon Rd., New Providence, NJ 07974-9903. TEL 908-665-3576) Ed. Victoria Mathews; Pub. Michael Webster. R&P contact: D. Morris. adv. contact: Oriana Ruffini. circ. 2,000. **Indexed:** Bibl.Engl.Lang.& Lit. **Document type:** bibliography, directory.
—CCC.
   Description: Provides bibliographic information on over 6,000 titles. Entries are indexed by title, publishers and subject; includes a book trade fax directory and directory of New Zealand libraries.

015   NZ   ISSN 0028-8497
NEW ZEALAND NATIONAL BIBLIOGRAPHY. 1966. m. NZ.$270 (foreign NZ.$810); microfiche NZ.$198 (foreign NZ.$270) (effective 1997). National Library of New Zealand, P.O. Box 1467, Wellington, New Zealand. TEL 64-4-4743067. FAX 64-4-4743124. E-mail: shop@natlib.govt.nz. Ed. K. Rollitt. circ. 650. (also avail. in microfiche; back issues avail.) **Document type:** bibliography.
•Also available online.
—BLDSC (6096.300000). **CCC.**
   Description: Bibliographic citations for New Zealand publications (including non-books) published in the current and preceding five years. Includes works written by New Zealanders or about New Zealand published overseas.

015   NZ   ISSN 1171-4018
NEW ZEALAND SERIALS. 1992. irreg. NZ.$170. National Library of New Zealand, P.O. Box 1467, Wellington, New Zealand. TEL 64-4-7473067. FAX 64-4-4743124. E-mail: shop@natlib.govt.nz. (microform) **Document type:** bibliography.
•Also available online.
   Description: Bibliographic citations for all New Zealand serials contained in the New Zealand National Bibliography from 1982 as well as those catalogued retrospectively during that time.

011   US   ISSN 0899-0425
Z6941
NEWSLETTERS IN PRINT; a descriptive guide to more than 11,500 subscription, membership, and free newsletters, bulletins, digests, updates, and similar serial publications issued in the United States or Canada and available in print or online. 1966. a. $225. Gale Research, 835 Penobscot Bldg., 645 Griswold St., Detroit, MI 48226-4094. TEL 313-961-2242; 800-877-4253. FAX 800-414-5043. E-mail: daniel_snyder@gale.com. Ed. Carolyn Fischer.
•Also available online. Vendor(s): Knight-Ridder Information, Inc. (File no.469).
Also available on CD-ROM.
   Former titles: Newsletter Directory (ISSN 0893-7656); National Directory of Newsletters and Reporting Services (ISSN 0547-6232)
   Description: Updating on newsletters available in the U.S. and Canada.

NEWSPAPER ADVERTISING SOURCE. see ADVERTISING AND PUBLIC RELATIONS — Abstracting, Bibliographies, Statistics

015   NR   ISSN 0078-0693
NIGERIAN BOOKS IN PRINT. 1968. a. $5. National Library of Nigeria, 4 Wesley St., P.M.B. 12626, Lagos, Nigeria. TEL 234-1-634704. **Document type:** bibliography.

NIGERIAN INSTITUTE OF SOCIAL AND ECONOMIC RESEARCH. LIBRARY. LIST OF ACCESSIONS. see SOCIAL SCIENCES: COMPREHENSIVE WORKS — Abstracting, Bibliographies, Statistics

016   JA
NIHON HAKUSHIROKU. 1955. irreg. 5800 Yen. Kojunsha, 2-9 Kitakarasuyama, Setagaya-ku, Tokyo, Japan. bibl.

NIJHOFF INFORMATION, NEW PUBLICATIONS FROM GERMANY, AUSTRIA AND SWITZERLAND. see PUBLISHING AND BOOK TRADE — Abstracting, Bibliographies, Statistics

NIJHOFF INFORMATION, NEW PUBLICATIONS FROM THE NETHERLANDS. see PUBLISHING AND BOOK TRADE — Abstracting, Bibliographies, Statistics

016.8   UK   ISSN 1353-1980
AP4
NINETEENTH CENTURY BIBLIOGRAPHIC RECORDS. 1994. a. Chadwyck-Healey Ltd., The Quorum, Barnwell Rd., Cambridge CB5 8SW, England. TEL 44-1223-215512. FAX 44-1223-215514. E-mail: marketing@chadwyck.co.uk; URL: http://www.chadwyck.com. (In N. America: Chadwyck-Healey Inc., 1101 King St., Alexandria, VA 22314. TEL 800-752-0515. FAX 703-683-7589) (also avail. in microfiche from CHL) **Document type:** bibliography.
•Available only on CD-ROM. Producer(s): Chadwyck-Healey Inc.
   Description: Presents bibliographic data on English language books and pamphlets of permanent research value republished in the Nineteenth Century microfiche program.

015.481   NO   ISSN 0029-1870
Z2591
NORSK BOKFORTEGNELSE. AARSKATALOG. 1903. a (in 3 vols.). NOK 900 (effective 1996). University of Oslo Library, Bibliographic Services Department, N-0242 Oslo, Norway. FAX 47-22-85-90-50. E-mail: a.h.langballe@ub.uio.no; URL: http://www.nbo.vio.no/norbok.html. Ed. Oeivind Berg. (also avail. in microfiche) **Indexed:** Bibl.Engl.Lang.& Lit. **Document type:** bibliography.
•Also available on CD-ROM.
   Former titles (until 1952): Aarskatalog over Norsk Litteratur (ISSN 0805-7001); (until 1903): Kvartalskatalog over Norsk Litteratur (ISSN 0805-9357)

015.481   NO   ISSN 0805-6978
Z2595
NORSK BOKFORTEGNELSE. NYHETSLISTE/NORWEGIAN NATIONAL BIBLIOGRAPHY. LIST OF NEW BOOKS. 1972. fortn. NOK 900 (effective 1997). University of Oslo Library, Bibliographic Services Department, N-0242 Oslo, Norway. FAX 47-22-85-90-50. E-mail: a.h.langballe@ub.uio.no; URL: http://www2.nbo.uio.no/ubobok/uboboknor.html. Ed. Oeivind Berg. **Document type:** bibliography.
 Formerly (until 1994): Norsk Bokfortegnelse (ISSN 0805-6986).

NORSK MUSIKKFORTEGNELSE. LYDFESTINGER/NORWEGIAN NATIONAL DISCOGRAPHY. see *MUSIC — Abstracting, Bibliographies, Statistics*

NORSK MUSIKKFORTEGNELSE. NOTETRYKK/NORWEGIAN NATIONAL BIBLIOGRAPHY OF PRINTED MUSIC. see *MUSIC — Abstracting, Bibliographies, Statistics*

015.481   NO   ISSN 0805-3340
▼**NORSK PERIODIKAFORTEGNELSE/NORWEGIAN LIST OF SERIALS.** 1995. a. NOK 240 (effective 1997). University of Oslo Library, Bibliographic Services Department, N-242 Oslo, Norway. FAX 47-22-85-90-50. E-mail: a.h.langballe@ub.uio.no; URL: http://www.nbo.uio.no/baser/norper.html. Ed. Oeivind Berg. **Document type:** bibliography.
 ●Also available on CD-ROM.

011.34   NO   ISSN 0332-978X
NORSKE TIDSSKRIFTARTIKLER/NORWEGIAN INDEX TO PERIODICAL ARTICLES. 1981. a. NOK 660 (effective 1997). University of Oslo Library, Bibliographic Services Department, N-0242 Oslo, Norway. FAX 47-22-85-90-50. E-mail: a.h.langballe@ub.uio.no; URL: http://www.nbo.uio.no/baser/norart.html. Ed. Oeivind Berg. **Document type:** bibliography.
 ●Also available on CD-ROM.

NORTH AMERICAN RELIGION. see *RELIGIONS AND THEOLOGY*

NOSTRA TRIBUNA. see *LAW — Abstracting, Bibliographies, Statistics*

NOTABLE CHILDREN'S TRADE BOOKS IN THE FIELD OF SOCIAL STUDIES. see *SOCIAL SCIENCES: COMPREHENSIVE WORKS — Abstracting, Bibliographies, Statistics*

NOTICIAS DEL PUERTO DE MONTEREY. see *HISTORY — History Of North And South America*

NOTIZIARIO BIBLIOGRAFICO DI AUDIOLOGIA O R L E FONIATRIA. see *MEDICAL SCIENCES — Abstracting, Bibliographies, Statistics*

NOVAYA LITERATURA PO SOTSIAL'NYM I GUMANITARNYM NAUKAM. EKONOMIKA; bibliograficheskii ukazatel' see *BUSINESS AND ECONOMICS — Abstracting, Bibliographies, Statistics*

NOVAYA LITERATURA PO SOTSIAL'NYM I GUMANITARNYM NAUKAM. FILOSOFIYA I SOTSIOLOGIYA; bibliograficheskii ukazatel' see *PHILOSOPHY — Abstracting, Bibliographies, Statistics*

NOVAYA LITERATURA PO SOTSIAL'NYM I GUMANITARNYM NAUKAM. GOSUDARSTVO I PRAVO; bibliograficheskii ukazatel' see *LAW — Abstracting, Bibliographies, Statistics*

◂**NOVAYA LITERATURA PO SOTSIAL'NYM I GUMANITARNYM NAUKAM. ISTORIYA - ARKHEOLOGIYA - ETNOGRAFIYA;** bibliograficheskii ukazatel' see *HISTORY — Abstracting, Bibliographies, Statistics*

◂**NOVAYA LITERATURA PO SOTSIAL'NYM I GUMANITARNYM NAUKAM. LITERATUROVEDENIE;** bibliograficheskii ukazatel' see *LITERATURE — Abstracting, Bibliographies, Statistics*

◂**NOVAYA LITERATURA PO SOTSIAL'NYM I GUMANITARNYM NAUKAM. NAUKOVEDENIE;** bibliograficheskii ukazatel' see *POLITICAL SCIENCE — Abstracting, Bibliographies, Statistics*

NOVAYA LITERATURA PO SOTSIAL'NYM I GUMANITARNYM NAUKAM. RELIGIOVEDENIE; bibliograficheskii ukazatel' see *RELIGIONS AND THEOLOGY — Abstracting, Bibliographies, Statistics*

NOVAYA LITERATURA PO SOTSIAL'NYM I GUMANITARNYM NAUKAM. YAZYKOZNANIE; bibliograficheskii ukazatel' see *LINGUISTICS — Abstracting, Bibliographies, Statistics*

011   SP
NOVEDADES; servicio de informacion bibliografica. m. Editorial Planeta S.A., Corcega 273-277, 08008 Barcelona, Spain. illus.

015   AG   ISSN 0327-9979
NOVEDADES BIBLIOGRAFICAS. 1993. 3/yr. exchange basis. Congreso de la Nacion, Biblioteca, Rivadavia 1850, 1033 Capital Federal, Argentina. **Document type:** catalog.

011   DK   ISSN 0106-035X
Z5917.S5
NOVELLEREGISTER; titel- og forfatterindeks til novellesamlinger og antologier. 1971. a. DKK 596 (effective 1996). Dansk BiblioteksCenter as, Tempovej 7-11, DK-2750 Ballerup, Denmark. TEL 45-44-867777. FAX 45-44-867892. E-mail: dbc@dan.bib.dk.

NOVINKY LITERATURY: ZDRAVOTNICTVI. see *MEDICAL SCIENCES — Abstracting, Bibliographies, Statistics*

NUMISMATIC BOOKS IN PRINT. see *NUMISMATICS — Abstracting, Bibliographies, Statistics*

NUOVO BOLLETTINO BIBLIOGRAFICO SARDO; archivio tradizioni popolari. see *PUBLISHING AND BOOK TRADE — Abstracting, Bibliographies, Statistics*

NY LITTERATUR OM KVINNOR/NEW LITERATURE ON WOMEN; en bibliografi. see *WOMEN'S STUDIES — Abstracting, Bibliographies, Statistics*

011   DK   ISSN 0907-1709
NYE LYDBOEGER. a. Dansk BiblioteksCenter as, Tempovej 7-11, DK-2750 Ballerup, Denmark. TEL 45-44-867777. FAX 45-44-867892. E-mail: dbc@dan.bib.dk. illus.
 Former titles (until 1992): Gode Lydboeger (ISSN 0107-5209); (until 1981): Lydbogskatalog.

015.489   DK   ISSN 0900-1166
NYERE DANSK FAGLITTERATUR. (Printed format ceased in 1995) 1967. a. DKK 978.80. Dansk BiblioteksCenter as, Tempovej 7-11, DK-2750 Ballerup, Denmark. TEL 45-44-867777. FAX 45-44-867892. E-mail: dbc@dan.bib.dk.
 ●Also available online.
 Also available on CD-ROM.

330 016   FR   ISSN 0474-5086
O E C D CATALOGUE OF PUBLICATIONS. a. free. Organization for Economic Cooperation and Development, 2 rue Andre-Pascal, 75775 Paris Cedex 16, France. (Subscr. in U.S. to: O.E.C.D. Publications and Information Center, 2001 L St., N.W., Ste. 650, Washington, D.C. 20036-4922. TEL 202-785-6323)

O E C D LIBRARY SPECIAL ANNOTATED BIBLIOGRAPHY: AUTOMATION/O C D E BIBLIOTHEQUE BIBLIOGRAPHIE SPECIALE ANALYTIQUE: AUTOMATION. see *COMPUTERS — Abstracting, Bibliographies, Statistics*

O E C S SELECT BIBLIOGRAPHY. (Organisation of Eastern Caribbean States) see *BUSINESS AND ECONOMICS — Economic Situation And Conditions*

OCCULT PUBLICATIONS DIRECTORY. see *PARAPSYCHOLOGY AND OCCULTISM — Abstracting, Bibliographies, Statistics*

OESTERREICHISCHE VOLKSKUNDLICHE BIBLIOGRAPHIE. see *FOLKLORE — Abstracting, Bibliographies, Statistics*

011   US   ISSN 0147-2542
OHIO DOCUMENTS. 1971. q. Ohio State Library Board, 65 S. Front St., Columbus, OH 43215-4163. TEL 614-644-7051. FAX 614-752-9178. URL: http://winslo.ohio.gov. Ed. Clyde Hordusky. **Document type:** government publication.

015   XR   ISSN 1210-4566
Z2133
OHLASENE KNIHY. Short title: O.K. 1993. bi-m. 240 Kc. (foreign $14). Narodni Knihovna Ceske Republiky - National Library of the Czech Republic, Klementinum 190, 110 01 Prague 1, Czech Republic. TEL 420-2-21663306. FAX 420-2-21663306. (Dist. by: Narodni Knihovna Ceske Republiky, Oddeleni Prodeje a Expedice, Centralni Depozitar NK CR, Sterboholska 55, 100 00 Prague 10, Czech Republic. TEL 420-2-702600) Ed. Antonin Jerabek. R&P contact: Adolf Knoll. bk.rev.; index. **Document type:** bibliography.
 ●Also available online.
 Description: Lists Czech books to be published.

011   US
OMNIBUS. 1990. 3/yr. King County Library System, 300 Eighth Ave. N., Seattle, WA 98109-5191. TEL 206-684-6650. FAX 206-684-6690. Ed. Marcia Iverson. bk.rev. circ. 10,000. **Document type:** bibliography.
 Description: Reviews of books, videos, cassettes, compact discs, government documents, and periodicals in the KCLS collection for all ages.

ONGOING CURRENT BIBLIOGRAPHY OF PLASTIC & RECONSTRUCTIVE SURGERY. see *MEDICAL SCIENCES — Abstracting, Bibliographies, Statistics*

011   CN   ISSN 0316-1617
ONTARIO GOVERNMENT PUBLICATIONS, MONTHLY CHECKLIST/PUBLICATIONS DU GOUVERNEMENT DE L'ONTARIO, LISTE MENSUELLE. 1971. m. Can.$12. (Checklist and Catalogue Service) Ministry of Government Services, Publications Ontario, 880 Bay St., 1st Fl., Toronto, ON M7A 1N8, Canada. TEL 416-326-5300. adv. circ. 3,000.

010   US   ISSN 0078-5768
OREGON STATE MONOGRAPHS. BIBLIOGRAPHIC SERIES. 1938. irreg., latest no.23. price varies. Oregon State University Press, 101 Waldo Hall, Corvallis, OR 97331. TEL 541-737-3166. (back issues avail.; reprint service avail. from UMI) **Document type:** monographic series, bibliography.

540 016   NE
ORGANIC AND ORGANOMETALLIC CRYSTAL STRUCTURES; BIBLIOGRAPHY. (Subseries of: Molecular Structures and Dimensions) 1971. irreg. Kluwer Academic Publishers, Postbus 17, 3300 AA Dordrecht, Netherlands. TEL 31-78-6392392. FAX 31-78-6392254. E-mail: services@wkap.nl; URL: http://www.wkap.nl. (Dist. by: Kluwer Academic Publishers Group, P.O. Box 322, 3300 AH Dordrecht, Netherlands. TEL 31-78-6392392. FAX 31-78-6546474; N. America dist. addr.: Box 358, Accord Sta., Hingham, MA 02018-0358. TEL 617-871-6600) **Document type:** bibliography.

OUTSTANDING SCIENCE TRADE BOOKS FOR CHILDREN. see *CHILDREN AND YOUTH — Abstracting, Bibliographies, Statistics*

010   UK   ISSN 0078-7124
OVERSEAS DIRECTORIES, WHO'S WHO, PRESS GUIDES, YEAR BOOKS AND OVERSEAS PERIODICAL SUBSCRIPTIONS. 1947. biennial. £18($55) New Product Newsletter Co. Ltd., 1A Chesterfield St., London W.1., England. Ed. H.R. Vaughan. adv. circ. 5,000. (also avail. in microfilm from UMI)

016.05   US   ISSN 0163-7010
Z6944.N44
OXBRIDGE DIRECTORY OF NEWSLETTERS. 1979. a. $495. Oxbridge Communications, Inc., 150 Fifth Ave., New York, NY 10011. TEL 212-741-0231. FAX 212-633-2938. **Document type:** directory.
 ●Also available online.
 Also available on CD-ROM.
 —BLDSC (6320.582700).
 Description: Lists over 20,000 newsletters published in the U.S. and Canada, arranged by major subject categories.

P A I S INTERNATIONAL - JOURNALS INDEXED IN (YEAR). (Public Affairs Information Service, Inc.) see *SOCIAL SCIENCES: COMPREHENSIVE WORKS*

P I E. (Publications Indexed for Engineering) see *ENGINEERING — Abstracting, Bibliographies, Statistics*

BIBLIOGRAPHIES

011 II
PACIFIC ISLANDS BOOKS NEWS LETTERS. (Text in English) 1981. m. Rs.352($71) K.K. Roy (Private) Ltd., 55 Gariahat Rd., P.O. Box 10210, Calcutta 700 019, India. Ed. Dr. K.K. Roy.

015.45 IT
PAGINE APERTE; mensile bibliografico. 1962. m. free. Diffusione San Paolo srl, Corso Regina Margherita, 2, 10153 Turin, Italy. TEL 011-83-67-44. FAX 011-888831. Dir. Antonio Tarzia. adv.: bk.rev. circ. 80,000. **Document type:** bibliography.
Formerly: Edizioni Nostre (ISSN 0013-0982)
Description: Reviews books.

PAKISTAN'S BOOKS & LIBRARIES; the only monthly magazine of its kind. see PUBLISHING AND BOOK TRADE

011 572 011 070.5 PP ISSN 0252-8347
Z4811
PAPUA NEW GUINEA NATIONAL BIBLIOGRAPHY. (Text in English, Hiri Motu, Tok Pisin) 1981. s-a. K.36 (effective 1996). National Library Service, Office of Libraries and Archives, P.O. Box 734, Waigani, N.C.D., Papua New Guinea. FAX 675-3251331. Ed. Karina Sereva. index; circ. 280 (controlled). (back issues avail.) **Document type:** bibliography.
—BLDSC (6404.514500).

011 PY ISSN 0257-7070
Z1821
PARAGUAY; uno ano de bibliografia. 1980. a. $25. Distribuidor Internacional Publicaciones Paraguayas, P.O. Box 2507, Ayoreos e-4a y 5a, Asuncion, Paraguay. TEL 595-21-495367. FAX 595-21-447460. Ed. Margarita Kallsen. bk.rev.; bibl. circ. 1,000.

011 II
PATRIKAPANJEE. (Text in Bengali) 1982. a. Rs.50. Bangla Bhasa Shitya-o-Samaskriti Gabesana Samastha, c/o Little Magazine Stall & Bektigata Prakashani, 6B Ramanath Mazumder St., Calcutta 700 009, India. Ed. Asok Kumar Kundu. bibl. circ. 1,100. **Document type:** bibliography.

PEDAGOGY AND CULTURAL PRACTICE. see EDUCATION — Abstracting, Bibliographies, Statistics

011 AT
Z6961
PERIODICALS IN PRINT: AUSTRALIA, NEW ZEALAND & PAPUA NEW GUINEA. 1981. a., 13th ed., 1996. Aus.$85($155) D.W. Thorpe, A member of the Reed Elsevier plc group, 18 Salmon St., Port Melbourne, Vic. 3207, Australia. TEL 61-3-92457370. FAX 61-92457395. URL: http://www.reed-elsevier.com. (Subscr. to: P.O. Box 146, Port Melbourne, Vic. 3207, Australia) circ. 2,000. **Document type:** bibliography, directory.
—CCC.
Former titles: Australian Periodicals in Print (ISSN 1030-2476); Australian Serials in Print (ISSN 0725-5462)
Description: Lists some 13,000 periodicals published in Australia, New Zealand and the Pacific Islands; includes magazines, directories, yearbooks carrying ISSNs, newspapers, proceedings, and trade publications. Government publications - with the exception of major serials - are excluded. Entries are indexed by title, publisher, and subject.

011 SA ISSN 0379-4482
CODEN: SABINET
PERIODICALS IN SOUTHERN AFRICAN LIBRARIES. Short title: P I S A L. 1986. 2/yr. R.250. State Library, P.O. Box 397, Pretoria 0001, South Africa. TEL 27-12-21-8931. FAX 27-12-325-5984. E-mail: tienie@statelib.pwv.gov.za. (also avail. in microfiche) **Document type:** catalog.
● Also available online.
Description: Union catalogue of serials in Southern Africa.

015.599 PH ISSN 0303-190X
Z3296 CODEN: PNBIDI
PHILIPPINE NATIONAL BIBLIOGRAPHY. (Supplement avail.: Philippine National Bibliography. Part 2: Theses and Dissertations (ISSN 0116-2705)) (Text in English) 1974. q. (with a. cumulations). price varies. National Library, T.M. Kalaw St., Manila, Philippines. TEL 02-524-1011. FAX 02-524-2329. Ed. Leonila D. Tominez. circ. 2,500. **Document type:** bibliography.
—CASDDS.
Description: Lists current works of research value published or printed in the Philippines by Filipino authors, or about the Philippines.

015.599 PH ISSN 0116-2705
PHILIPPINE NATIONAL BIBLIOGRAPHY. PART 2: THESES AND DISSERTATIONS. (Supplement to: Philippine National Bibliography (ISSN 0303-190X)) (Text in English) 1985. a. price varies. National Library, T.M. Kalaw St., Manila, Philippines. TEL 63-2-524-1011. FAX 63-2-524-2329. Ed. Leonila D. Tominez. **Document type:** bibliography.

015 PH ISSN 0115-7213
PHILIPPINES. NATIONAL LIBRARY. T N L RESEARCH GUIDE SERIES. Short title: T N L Research Guide Series. 1971. irreg., approx. 2/yr. exchange basis. National Library, Bibliography Division, T.M. Kalaw St., Manila, Philippines. TEL 63-2-524-1011. FAX 63-2-524-2329. Ed. Leonila D. Tominez. circ. 300. (processed)

PHONOLOG REPORTER; all-in-one-reporter. see MUSIC — Abstracting, Bibliographies, Statistics

PHOTOSYNTHESIS BIBLIOGRAPHY. see BIOLOGY — Abstracting, Bibliographies, Statistics

011 070 UK ISSN 0957-6916
PIMS EUROPEAN CONSUMER DIRECTORY. 1989. s-a. £185 (effective 1997). PIMS (UK) Ltd., PIMS House, Mildmay Ave., London N1 4RS, England. TEL 44-171-226-1000. FAX 44-171-354-7053. (Subscr. to: 1133 Broadway, New York, NY 10010) **Document type:** directory.
Description: Consumer publications listed by subject area - country.

011 070 UK ISSN 0955-1581
PIMS EUROPEAN NEWSPAPERS DIRECTORY. 1989. 2/yr. £185 (effective 1997). PIMS (UK) Ltd., PIMS House, Mildmay Ave., London N1 4RS, England. TEL 44-171-226-1000. FAX 44-171-354-7053. (Subscr. to: 1133 Broadway, New York, NY 10010, U.S.A.) **Document type:** directory.
Description: Contacts in 80 subject areas for major European daily and Sunday newspapers.

011 070 UK ISSN 0957-6908
PIMS U S A CONSUMER DIRECTORY. 1989. 2/yr. £179 (effective 1997). PIMS (UK) Ltd., PIMS House, Mildmay Ave., London N1 4RS, England. TEL 44-171-226-1000. FAX 44-171-354-7053. (Subscr. to: 1133 Broadway, New York, NY 10010, U.S.A.) **Document type:** directory.
Description: Consumer publications listed by subject area.

011 070 UK ISSN 0955-8675
PIMS U S A NEWSPAPER DIRECTORY. 1989. s-a. £179 (effective 1997). PIMS (UK) Ltd., PIMS House, Mildmay Ave., London N1 4RS, England. TEL 44-171-226-1000. FAX 44-171-354-7053. (Subscr. to: 1133 Broadway, New York, NY 10010, U.S.A.) **Document type:** directory.
Description: Contacts in over 30 subject areas for US daily newspapers.

011 070 UK ISSN 0954-6138
PIMS U S A TRADE & TECHNICAL DIRECTORY. 1988. 2/yr. £179 (effective 1997). PIMS (UK) Ltd., PIMS House, Mildmay Ave., London N1 4RS, England. TEL 44-171-226-1000. FAX 44-171-354-7053. (Subscr. to: 1133 Broadway, New York, NY 10010, U.S.A.) **Document type:** directory.
Description: Trade and technical publications listed by subject area.

PIMSLEUR'S CHECKLIST OF BASIC AMERICAN LEGAL PUBLICATIONS. see LAW — Abstracting, Bibliographies, Statistics

PLAYWRIGHTS UNION OF CANADA CATALOGUE OF CANADIAN PLAYS. see THEATER — Abstracting, Bibliographies, Statistics

011 PL ISSN 0554-5625
POLONICA ZAGRANICZNE; bibliografia. 1960. a. 8.50 Zl.($4) Biblioteka Narodowa, Instytut Bibliograficzny, Al. Niepodleglosci 213, 00-973 Warsaw, Poland. TEL 48-2-6082408. FAX 48-22-255251. TELEX 813702 BN PL. (Dist. by: P.P. CHZ Ars Polona, ul. Krakowskie Przemiescie 7, 00-068 Warsaw, Poland) Ed. Danuta Bilikiewicz-Blanc. circ. 3,000. **Document type:** bibliography.
Description: Covers books, maps and printed music, etchings, and first issues of foreign serials in Polish language or fully devoted to Poland and Poles.

POLSKA AKADEMIA NAUK. ODDZIAL W KRAKOWIE. KOMISJA HISTORYCZNA. PRACE. see HISTORY — Abstracting, Bibliographies, Statistics

POLSKA BIBLIOGRAFIA BIBLIOLOGICZNA/POLISH BIBLIOGRAPHY OF LIBRARY SCIENCE. see LIBRARY AND INFORMATION SCIENCES — Abstracting, Bibliographies, Statistics

PREHLED PEDAGOGICKE LITERATURY. see EDUCATION — Abstracting, Bibliographies, Statistics

070 015 II ISSN 0445-6653
PRESS IN INDIA. (Issued in two parts) (Text in English) 1957. a., latest 1990. $95.40 (or £32.06). Controller of Publications, Government of India, Civil Lines, Delhi 110054, India. title index. circ. 1,000.

011 070.5 GW ISSN 0176-5248
PRESSE-PORTRAETS; das Angebot des Pressehandels. (Supplement to: Presse Report) 1978. a. DM.45. Presse Fachverlag, Eidelstedter Weg 22, 20255 Hamburg, Germany. TEL 49-40-565031. FAX 49-40-5602920. URL: http://www.presse.de/pfv/pfv.htm. index. circ. 73,000.
Description: Catalog for the trade and the consumer of newspapers, magazines, comic books, and paperback books, with publishing information and short descriptions.

013 UK ISSN 0079-5402
PRIVATE PRESS BOOKS; a checklist of books issued by private presses in the past year. 1960. a. £20($40) to non-members. Private Libraries Association, Ravelston, South View Rd., Pinner, Middlesex HA5 3YD, England. Ed. David Chambers. R&P contact: David Chambers. adv. contact: David Chambers. index. cum.index. circ. 400. **Document type:** bibliography.
—BLDSC (6617.067800).

016 947 RU ISSN 0555-2982
CODEN: PBYSA8
PROBLEMY SEVERA; tekushchii ukazatel' literatury. 1968. m. $90. Rossiiskaya Akademiya Nauk, Sibirskoe Otdelenie, Gosudarstvennaya Publichnaya Nauchno-tekhnicheskaya Biblioteka, Voskhod 15, 630200 Novosibirsk, Russia. TEL 3832-66-13-67. FAX 3832-66-03-08. TELEX 133220 LIBRO SU. Eds. S.V. Vasiliev, S.S. Guzner.
—CISTI; Linda Hall.

PROCEEDINGS IN PRINT. see MEETINGS AND CONGRESSES — Abstracting, Bibliographies, Statistics

011 US
PROGRESSIVE PERIODICALS DIRECTORY UPDATE. 1981. a. $16. Progressive Education, Box 120574, Nashville, TN 37212. Ed. Craig T. Canan. circ. 1,500. **Document type:** bibliography.
Formerly: U S Progressive Periodicals Update.

011 PL ISSN 0033-2518
Z2523 CODEN: PRBIBA
PRZEWODNIK BIBLIOGRAFICZNY; urzedowy wykaz drukow wydanych w Rzeczypospolitej Polskiej. (Quarterly supplement avail.: Bibliografia Wydawnictw Ciaglych Nowych, Zawieszonych i Zmieniajacych Tytul (ISSN 0239-5606)) 1944. w. 29 Zl.($145) (price changes every quarter). Biblioteka Narodowa, Instytut Bibliograficzny, Al. Niepodleglosci 213, 00-973 Warsaw, Poland. TEL 48-22-255976. FAX 48-22-255976. TELEX 813702 BN PL. (Dist. by: P.P. CHZ Ars Polona, ul. Krakowskie Przedmiescie 7, 00-068 Warsaw, Poland) index. circ. 3,000. **Document type:** bibliography.
—CASDDS.
Description: Covers books, maps and printed music, in classified order by UDC.

BIBLIOGRAPHIES

PUBLIC INTERNATIONAL LAW; a current bibliography of books and articles. see *LAW — Abstracting, Bibliographies, Statistics*

015   RM
PUBLICATII DIN ROMANIA. s-a. Agentia Nationala de Presa Rompres, Piata Presei Libere Nr. 1, Bucharest, Rumania. TEL 17-60-10. FAX 17-04-87.

PUBLICATIONS IN EDUCATION AND THE SOCIAL SCIENCES IN ISRAEL. see *SOCIOLOGY — Abstracting, Bibliographies, Statistics*

070.5   US   ISSN 0079-7855
Z1215
PUBLISHERS TRADE LIST ANNUAL; a buying and reference guide to books and related products. 1872. a. £275. R.R. Bowker, A Division of Reed Elsevier Inc., 121 Chanlon Rd., New Providence, NJ 07974. TEL 908-464-6800. FAX 908-665-3502. TELEX 138 755. E-mail: info@bowker.com; URL: http://www.reedref.com. (Subscr. to: Order Dept., Box 31, New Providence, NJ 07974-9903. TEL 800-521-8110) index. **Document type**: bibliography, directory.
—Linda Hall. **CCC**.
  Description: Binds the catalogs and booklists of leading U.S. and Canadian publishers, as well as a small press guide.

015   CC   ISSN 0578-073X
QUANGUO XIN SHUMU/NEW BOOKS CATALOG OF P R C. (Text in Chinese) m. Y21.60($72) Zhongguo Banben Tushuguan, Shukan Fuwu Bu, 32 Beizongbu Hutong, Dong Cheng Qu, Beijing 100735, People's Republic of China. (Dist. outside China by: China International Book Trading Corp., P.O. Box 2820, Beijing, P.R.C.; Dist. in US by: China Books & Periodicals, Inc., 2929 24th St., San Francisco, CA 94110. TEL 415-282-2994) bibl.
  Description: Lists new books published in the People's Republic of China. Entries are arranged by subject, and include publisher, publication date, price, pages, and ISBN.

011.37   CN
QUEBEC (PROVINCE). SERVICES DOCUMENTAIRES MULTIMEDIA. CHOIX: DOCUMENTATION AUDIOVISUELLE. (Text in French) 1978. 6/yr. (plus a. cumulation). Can.$46($58) Services Documentaires Multimedia Inc., 75 Port-Royal E., bureau 300, Montreal, PQ H3L 3T1, Canada. TEL 514-382-0895. FAX 514-384-9139. E-mail: info@sdm.qc.ca; URL: http://www.sdm.qc.ca. circ. 400. (also avail. in microfiche)
●Also available online.
Also available on CD-ROM.
  Former titles: Quebec (Province). Centrale des Bibliotheques. Choix: Documentation Audiovisuelle (ISSN 0706-2257); Quebec (Province). Centrale des Bibliotheques. Choix Jeunesse: Documentation Audiovisuelle (ISSN 0706-2273)

011   CN
QUEBEC (PROVINCE). SERVICES DOCUMENTAIRES MULTIMEDIA. CHOIX: DOCUMENTATION IMPRIMEE. (Text in French) 1978. 20/yr. (plus a. cumulation). Can.$140($165) Services Documentaires Multimedia Inc., 75 Port-Royal E., bureau 300, Montreal, PQ H3L 3T1, Canada. TEL 514-382-0895. FAX 514-384-9139. E-mail: info@sdm.qc.ca; URL: http://www.sdm.qc.ca. circ. 800. (also avail. in microfiche)
●Also available online.
Also available on CD-ROM.
  Formerly: Quebec (Province). Centrale des Bibliotheques. Choix: Documentation Imprimee (ISSN 0706-2249)

011.62   CN
QUEBEC (PROVINCE). SERVICES DOCUMENTATION MULTIMEDIA. CHOIX JEUNESSE: DOCUMENTATION IMPRIMEE. (Text in French) 1978. 10/yr. Can.$41($51) Services Documentaires Multimedia Inc., 75 Port-Royal E., bureau 300, Montreal, PQ H3L 3T1, Canada. TEL 514-382-0895. FAX 514-384-9139. E-mail: info@sdm.qc.ca; URL: http://www.sdm.qc.ca. (also avail. in microfiche)
●Also available online.
Also available on CD-ROM.
  Formerly: Quebec (Province). Centrale des Bibliotheques. Choix Jeunesse: Documentation Imprimee (ISSN 0706-2265)

015   AT   ISSN 0313-7813
QUEENSLAND GOVERNMENT PUBLICATIONS. 1977. bi-m. free. Library Board of Queensland, Queensland Cultural Centre, Southbank, South Brisbane, Qld. 4101, Australia. TEL 61-7-38407893. FAX 61-7-38462421. TELEX AA 100200. Ed. Kathy Szokolay. circ. 200. **Document type**: bibliography, government publication.
  Description: Listing of government publications received in State Library of Queensland.

016.05   US   ISSN 1057-8188
R S A P NEWSLETTER. 1991. 2/yr. $5. Research Society for American Periodicals, Box 5096 - Univ. of North Texas, Denton, TX 76203. TEL 817-565-2134. Ed. James T.F. Tanner. R&P contact: James T.F. Tanner. adv. contact: James T.F. Tanner. circ. 300. (looseleaf format) **Document type**: newsletter.
  Description: Covers the Society's activities and conferences, and recent publications in the field of periodicals research.

015   II
RECENT INDIAN BOOKS. (Text in English) 1975. q. free. Federation of Publishers & Booksellers Associations in India, 4833-24 Govind Lane, Ansari Rd., New Delhi 110002, India. Ed. J.C. Mehta. adv.; bk.rev.; index. circ. 2,000.

011 910   FR   ISSN 0293-311X
RECHERCHES PYRENEENNES. 1980. irreg. 140 F. Centre Regional d'Information sur les Pyrenees, c/o Universite de Toulouse le Mirail, 5 Allees Antonio Machado, 31058 Toulouse, France. TEL 61-50-43-97. FAX 61-50-49-10.

015   SP   ISSN 1132-6840
RED DE BIBLIOTECAS UNIVERSITARIAS; catalogo colectivo. Short title: Rebiun. 1992. s-a. 125000 ptas. (effective 1997). D O C 6 S.A., Mallorca 272, 08007 Barcelona, Spain. TEL 34-3-2154313. FAX 34-3-4883621. E-mail: mail@doc6.es. **Document type**: bibliography.

020   US   ISSN 0887-3763
Z1035.1
REFERENCE AND RESEARCH BOOK NEWS; annotations and reviews of new books for libraries. 1986. q. $80 to individuals (foreign $95); institutions $100 (foreign $115). Book News, Inc. (Portland), 5739 N.E. Sumner St., Portland, OR 97218. TEL 503-281-9230. FAX 503-287-4485. E-mail: BookNews@BookNews.com; URL: http://www.books.com.booknews. Ed. Jane Erskine; Pub. Fred Gullette. adv.; bk.rev. circ. 1,700. (back issues avail.) **Indexed**: Bk.Rev.Ind. (1987-), Child.Bk.Rev.Ind. (1987-).
●Also available online.
Also available on CD-ROM.
—Linda Hall.
  Incorporates (1989-1992): University Press Book News (ISSN 1040-8991)
  Description: Concise, subject-arranged reviews of new scholarly and reference books appropriate for academic and public libraries and librarians.

011   US   ISSN 0272-1988
Z1035.1
REFERENCE BOOK REVIEW. 1976. 2/yr. $11. Box 190954, Dallas, TX 75219. FAX 214-479-1038. Eds. Cameron Northouse, Donna Northouse. bk.rev.; index. circ. 1,000. (back issues avail.) **Indexed**: Bk.Rev.Ind. (1984-), Child.Bk.Rev.Ind. (1984-). **Document type**: bibliography, academic/scholarly publication.

015   CL   ISSN 0716-1778
REFERENCIAS CRITICAS SOBRE AUTORES CHILENOS. 1968. a., latest 1987. Direccion de Bibliotecas, Archivos y Museos, Biblioteca Nacional, Alameda 651, Santiago, Chile. TEL 6380461. FAX 6381975. **Document type**: bibliography.
  Description: Contains data on literary criticism of Chilean authors and some coverage of Spanish and Ibero-American authors.

016   UK   ISSN 0305-960X
RELIGIOUS BOOKS IN PRINT. 1974. a. £60. J. Whitaker & Sons Ltd., 12 Dyott St., London WC1A 1DF, England. TEL 44-171-420-6000. FAX 44-171-836-2909. adv. **Document type**: bibliography.

610 016   MX   ISSN 0304-1840
REMEDIA. Variant title: Referencias Medicas de Informacion Actualizada. 1974. bi-m. Instituto Mexicano del Seguro Social, Division de Bibliotecas y Documentacion Biomedica, Apdo. Postal 12976, 03001 Mexico D.F., Mexico. circ. 2,000.

REPERTOIRE BIBLIOGRAPHIQUE DE LA PHILOSOPHIE/INTERNATIONAL PHILOSOPHICAL BIBLIOGRAPHY/BIBLIOGRAFISCH REPERTORIUM VAN DE WIJSBEGEERTE. see *PHILOSOPHY — Abstracting, Bibliographies, Statistics*

016   GW   ISSN 0085-5499
REPERTOIRE BIBLIOGRAPHIQUE DES LIVRES IMPRIMES EN FRANCE. 1968. irreg., vol.23, 1997. price varies. Verlag Valentin Koerner GmbH, Postfach 100164, 76482 Baden-Baden, Germany. TEL 49-7221-22423. FAX 49-7221-38697. **Document type**: monographic series.
  Description: Bibliography of all books printed in France during the 16th, 17th and 18th centuries.

010   FR
REPERTOIRE DES ANNUAIRES. 1936. a. 250 F. Syndicat Professionnel Annuaire, Telematique, Communication (ATC), 35 rue Gregoire de Tours, 75006 Paris, France. adv. contact: Jean-Raoul Guillerot. **Document type**: directory.
  Formerly: Annuaire des Annuaires (ISSN 0066-2720)

REPERTOIRE INTERNATIONAL DES BANQUES DE DONNEES BIOMEDICALES. see *MEDICAL SCIENCES — Computer Applications*

REPERTOIRE INTERNATIONAL DES BANQUES DE DONNEES JURIDIQUES. see *LAW — Computer Applications*

016.362   US   ISSN 1047-1286
Z7164.C4
RESOURCES (NEW YORK); a directory of New York City directories. 1988. biennial, latest 1996. $9. Community Service Society, Office of Information, 105 E. 22nd St., New York, NY 10010. TEL 212-254-8900. Eds. Patricia Friedland, Rabina Naraine. **Document type**: directory.

THE REVIEW OF EDUCATION - PEDAGOGY - CULTURAL STUDIES. see *EDUCATION — Abstracting, Bibliographies, Statistics*

REVISTA BRASILEIRA DE INFORMACAO BIBLIOGRAFICA EM CIENCIAS SOCIAIS. see *SOCIAL SCIENCES: COMPREHENSIVE WORKS — Abstracting, Bibliographies, Statistics*

015   CL
REVISTA CHILENA EN VENTA. 1974. irreg. $80. Servicio de Extension de Cultura Chilena, Portugal 12, Depto. 45, Casilla 58-22, Santiago, Chile. FAX 562-2223695. E-mail: serec@reuna.cl. Dir. Marta Dominguez Diaz. (processed) **Document type**: bibliography.

011   MX
REVISTA DE REVISTAS. w. $85. Editorial Excelsior S.C.L., Revista de Revistas, Reforma 18, Mexico 1 D.F., Mexico. Ed. Gustavo Duran de Huerta. adv. circ. 30,000.

015   SP   ISSN 0211-1993
REVISTAS ESPANOLAS CON I S S N. 1981. irreg. 3500 ptas. Ministerio de Cultura, Direccion General del Libros y Bibliotecas, Plaza del Rey, 1, 28004 Madrid, Spain. TEL 1-5447443. (Dist. by: Distribuidora de Publicaciones, Calle Fernando el Catolico, 77, 28015 Madrid, Spain) Ed.Bd. bibl. circ. 1,000.

015   US   ISSN 0085-5642
Z6953.8
REVISTERO;* el mas completo informe sobre las publicaciones periodicas de America Latina. 1972. a. $60. E. Darino, Ed. & Pub. 222 Park Ave. S., Apt. 2A, New York, NY 10003. circ. 1,000.

REVUE BIBLIOGRAPHIQUE DE SINOLOGIE. see *SOCIAL SCIENCES: COMPREHENSIVE WORKS — Abstracting, Bibliographies, Statistics*

BIBLIOGRAPHIES

011.34　　　　　　NE　ISSN 0980-2797
PN4832
LA REVUE DES REVUES; revue internationale d'histoire de bibliographie. (Text in French; summaries in English) 1986. 2/yr. fl.185 (effective 1998). (Association Ent'revues, FR) John Benjamins Publishing Co., Amsteldijk 44, P.O. Box 75577, 1070 AN Amsterdam, Netherlands. TEL 31-20-6738156. FAX 31-20-6792956. URL: http://www.benjamins.nl. (In N. America: Box 27519, Philadelphia, PA 19118-0519. TEL 215-836-1200. FAX 215-836-1204) (Co-sponsor: Centre National des Lettres, FR) Ed. Olivier Corpet. (back issues avail.) **Document type**: academic/scholarly publication.
　Description: Devoted to the cultivation, study and bibliographical description of periodicals as a genre, from the 17th to 20th centuries.

015　　　　　　　　BL
RIO DE JANEIRO, BRAZIL (STATE). INSTITUTO ESTADUAL DO LIVRO. DIVISAO DE BIBLIOTECAS. BOLETIM BIBLIOGRAFICO. 1977. irreg. Instituto Estadual do Livro, Divisao de Bibliotecas, Av. Presidente Vargas 1261, Rio de Janeiro, Brazil. circ. 1,000.

011　　　　　　　　RU
ROSSIISKAYA AKADEMIYA NAUK. BIBLIOGRAFIYA IZDANII. Cover title: Bibliografiya Izdanii Akademii Nauk. 1982. a. Rossiiskaya Akademiya Nauk, Biblioteka, Birzhevaya liniya 1, 199034 St. Petersburg, Russia. Ed. V.P. Leonov.
　Formerly (until 1992): Bibliografiya Izdanii Akademii Nauk S.S.S.R. (ISSN 0234-4343)

RUDOLF STEINER PUBLICATIONS. see PHILOSOPHY — Abstracting, Bibliographies, Statistics

011　　　　　　　　IS
RUPPIN INSTITUTE LIBRARY. LIBRARY'S ACCESSION LIST. (Text in English and Hebrew) 1981. s-a. free. Ruppin Institute Library, Emek Hefer 40250, Israel. TEL 972-9-8983086. FAX 972-9-8981307. E-mail: library@ruppin.ac.il. Ed. Janet Hilman. circ. 100. **Document type**: bibliography.

057.1　　　　　　UK　ISSN 1350-7230
RUSSIAN BOOKS IN PRINT ON C D - R O M. (Text in English, French, German, Russian) 1993. q. $995. Bowker - Saur Ltd., A member of the Reed Elsevier plc group, Maypole House, Maypole Rd., E. Grinstead, W. Sussex RH19 1HU, England. TEL 44-1342-330100. FAX 44-1342-330191. E-mail: custserv@bowker-saur.co.uk; URL: http://www.reed-elsevier.com. **Document type**: directory.
●Available only on CD-ROM. Producer(s): Bowker - Saur Ltd.
　Description: Provides access to information on all books published in Russia from 1989 to mid-1993, as well as all planned titles from 1993-1997. Includes books published in the Baltics, Ukraine, and other ex-Soviet States - more than 150.000 in all with 50,000 annotations.

S A L A L M BIBLIOGRAPHY AND REFERENCE SERIES. (Seminar on the Acquisition of Latin American Library Materials) see LIBRARY AND INFORMATION SCIENCES — Abstracting, Bibliographies, Statistics

020 016　　　　　US　ISSN 0098-6275
Z689
S A L A L M NEWSLETTER. 1973. bi-m. $25 to non-members. Seminar on the Acquisition of Latin American Library Materials, Benson Latin American Collection, University of Texas at Austin, Sid Richardson Hall 1.109, Austin, TX 78713. TEL 512-495-4471. FAX 512-495-4488. Ed. Nancy Hallock. bk.rev.; bibl. Indexed: CALL. **Document type**: newsletter.
—BLDSC (8070.557000).

S A L G NEWSLETTER. (South Asia Library Group) see LIBRARY AND INFORMATION SCIENCES — Abstracting, Bibliographies, Statistics

005.3　　　　　　US
THE S I G C A T FOUNDATION COMPENDIUM OF C D - R O M S. a. $30. Special Interest Group on C D - R O M Applications & Technology, 11343 Sunset Hills Rd., Reston, VA 22090. TEL 202-512-1265. FAX 703-435-5553. (Alt. addr.: P.O. Box 3706, Reston, VA 22090) (Co-sponsors: U.S. Government Printing Office - Office of Electronic Dissemination Services; U.S. Geological Survey Library) Ed. Jerry McFaul. **Document type**: directory, government publication, bibliography.
●Available only on CD-ROM.
　Description: Descibes more than 500 CD-ROM publications containing U.S. government information.

S I L - A A I B BIBLIOGRAPHY. (Summer Institute of Linguistics, Australian Aborigines and Islanders Branch) see LINGUISTICS — Abstracting, Bibliographies, Statistics

S I O REFERENCE SERIES. BIBLIOGRAPHY. (Scripps Institution of Oceanography) see EARTH SCIENCES — Oceanography

011　　　　　　　GW　ISSN 0419-7305
SAECHSISCHE BIBLIOGRAPHIE. (Text in German) 1961. a. DM.75. Saechsische Landesbibliothek, Marienalle 12, 01099 Dresden, Germany. TEL 49-351-8130-0. FAX 49-351-8130200. Ed. Ulrich Voigt. **Document type**: bibliography.

011　　　　　　　BL　ISSN 0104-0863
SAO PAULO. BIBLIOTECA MARIO DE ANDRADE. REVISTA. 1943. a. free. Departamento de Bibliotecas Publicas, Divisao de Documentacao e Comunicacao, c/o Helena Gomes de Oliveira, R. Frei Caneca, 1402, 01307-002 Sao Paulo, Brazil. TEL 55-11-2532331 ext. 270. FAX 55-11-2894645. bk.rev.; illus. circ. 2,000.
　Formerly (until vol.49, 1988): Sao Paulo. Biblioteca Mario de Andrade. Boletim Bibliografico (ISSN 0100-4948)

SARDIUS; bibliography of southern African politics and economics. see POLITICAL SCIENCE — Abstracting, Bibliographies, Statistics

011　　　　　　　　US
SCARECROW AUTHOR BIBLIOGRAPHIES. 1969. irreg., latest no.89. price varies. Scarecrow Press, Inc., 4720 Boston Way, Ste. A, Lanham, MD 20706-4310. TEL 800-462-6420. **Document type**: bibliography.

SCHWANN BEST RATED C DS - CLASSICAL. see MUSIC — Abstracting, Bibliographies, Statistics

SCHWANN BEST RATED C DS - JAZZ, POPULAR, ETC. see MUSIC — Abstracting, Bibliographies, Statistics

SCIENCE AND TECHNOLOGY (PITTSBURGH); a purchase guide for libraries. see SCIENCES: COMPREHENSIVE WORKS — Abstracting, Bibliographies, Statistics

SCIENCE FICTION, FANTASY, & HORROR; comprehensive bibliography of books and short fiction published in the English language. see LITERATURE — Abstracting, Bibliographies, Statistics

SCIENTIFIC SERIALS IN THAI LIBRARIES. see SCIENCES: COMPREHENSIVE WORKS — Abstracting, Bibliographies, Statistics

011 300 600　　　US　ISSN 0196-6006
SCITECH BOOK NEWS; an annotated bibliography of new books in science, technology, & medicine. 1977. q. $80 to individuals (foreign $95); institutions $100 (foreign $115). Book News, Inc. (Portland), 5739 N.E. Sumner St., Portland, OR 97218. TEL 503-281-9230. FAX 503-287-4485. URL: http://www.books.com/booknews. Ed. Jane Erskine. adv. contact: Jane Erskine. bk.rev.; abstr.; bibl. circ. 2,400. (back issues avail.) Indexed: Bk.Rev.Ind. (1984-), Child.Bk.Rev.Ind. (1984-). **Document type**: bibliography.
●Also available online.
Also available on CD-ROM.
—Linda Hall.
　Description: Concise reviews of high-level books in science, technology, medicine, agriculture and engineering.

015　　　　　　　　FR　ISSN 0769-0509
Z7552
SCRIBECO. 1986. 6/yr. 657 F. (foreign 892 F.) (effective 1997). Institut National de la Statistique et des Etudes Economiques, 18 bd. Adolphe Pinard, 75675 Paris Cedex 14, France. TEL 33-1-41175050. FAX 33-1-41176666.

011　　　　　　　SA　ISSN 1018-9599
SECOND SUPPLEMENT TO THE S A JOINT CATALOGUE OF MONOGRAPHS ON MICROFICHE. AUTHOR INDEX. (1992-1994) 1971. irreg. R.718.20. State Library, P.O. Box 397, Pretoria 0001, South Africa. TEL 27-12-21-8931. FAX 27-12-325-5984. TELEX 322171 SA. E-mail: susan__o@statelib.pwv.gov.za. **Document type**: catalog.
　Formerly (until 1992): S A Joint Catalogue of Monographs of Microfiche, Series 2, Author Index (ISSN 0379-0606); Supersedes in part: S A Joint Catalogue of Monographs on Microfiche.

011　　　　　　　SA　ISSN 1018-9602
SECOND SUPPLEMENT TO THE S A JOINT CATALOGUE OF MONOGRAPHS ON MICROFICHE. TITLE INDEX. (1992-1994) (Text in English) 1971. biannual. R.513. State Library, P.O. Box 397, Pretoria 0001, South Africa. TEL 27-12-21-8931. FAX 27-12-325-5984. E-mail: susan__o@statelib.pwv.gov.za. **Document type**: catalog.
　Formerly (until 1992): S A Joint Catalogue of Monographs on Microfiche, Series 1, Title Index (ISSN 0379-0592); Supersedes in part: S A Joint Catalogue of Monographs on Microfiche.

SEED PATHOLOGY AND MICROBIOLOGY. see AGRICULTURE — Abstracting, Bibliographies, Statistics

SELECT: NATIONAL BIBLIOGRAPHIC SERVICE NEWSLETTER. see LIBRARY AND INFORMATION SCIENCES

SELECTED ANNOTATED BIBLIOGRAPHY OF POPULATION STUDIES IN THE NETHERLANDS. see POPULATION STUDIES — Abstracting, Bibliographies, Statistics

SELECTED BIBLIOGRAPHIES ON AGEING. see GERONTOLOGY AND GERIATRICS — Abstracting, Bibliographies, Statistics

011　　　　　　　　US　ISSN 0886-4179
Z6941
SERIALS DIRECTORY; an international reference book. 1986. a. $339 (Canada & Mexico $369; elsewhere $389); CD-ROM $529 (Canada & Mexico $535; elsewhere $575). EBSCO Industries, Inc., Title Information Department, 5724 Hwy. 280 East, Birmingham, AL 35242. TEL 205-991-6600. FAX 205-995-1582. (Subscr. to: EBSCO Subscription Services, Box 2543, Birmingham, AL 35201. TEL 800-826-3024) **Document type**: directory.
●Also available on CD-ROM.
—BLDSC (8242.737980); CISTI.
　Description: Includes information on over 150,000 international titles (journals, newspapers and monograph series).

016.05　　　　　CN　ISSN 0709-0536
SERIALS HOLDINGS IN NEWFOUNDLAND LIBRARIES. 1974. irreg. price varies. Memorial University of Newfoundland Library, Periodicals Division, St. John's, NF A1C 5S7, Canada. TEL 709-753-8425. FAX 709-737-4569. TELEX 016-4101. Ed. S. Ellison. circ. controlled. (also avail. in microfiche).
　Former titles (until 1979): Serials Holdings in the Libraries of Memorial University of Newfoundland, St. John's Public Library and College of Trades and Technology (ISSN 0316-6597); Memorial University of Newfoundland. Library. Serials Holdings in the Libraries of Memorial University of Newfoundland and St. John's Public Library (ISSN 0316-6600)

SERIALS IN THE BRITISH LIBRARY. see LIBRARY AND INFORMATION SCIENCES — Abstracting, Bibliographies, Statistics

BIBLIOGRAPHIES

016   NE
SERIALS IN WESTERN LANGUAGES; research collections on microfiche. (Text in English) irreg., 3rd ed., 1993. free. I D C Publishers bv, P.O. Box 11205, 2301 EE Leiden, Netherlands. TEL 31-71-5142700. FAX 31-71-5131721. E-mail: info@idc.nl; URL: http://www.idc.nl. illus. **Document type**: catalog.
   Description: Presents information on microform availability of more than 1900 serials and newspapers in Western languages.

011   RH   ISSN 0037-3494
Z858.N348
SHELFMARK. 1966. q. Z.$1. National Library and Documentation Service, P.O. Box 1773, Bulawayo, Zimbabwe. bk.rev.; abstr.; bibl. circ. 300.

SIERRA LEONE PUBLICATIONS. see *LIBRARY AND INFORMATION SCIENCES — Abstracting, Bibliographies, Statistics*

070.5 011   BL   ISSN 0103-8834
SINDICATO NACIONAL DOS EDITORES DE LIVROS. INFORMATIVO BIBLIOGRAFICO. 1968. a. Sindicato Nacional dos Editores de Livros, Centro de Bibliotecnia, Av. Rio Branco 37, 15o andar, s-1503-06, 20090-003 Rio de Janeiro, RJ, Brazil. TEL 021-233-6481. FAX 021-253-8502. TELEX 21-37063. Ed. Nilson Lopes da Silva. bibl.; stat. **Document type**: bibliography.
   Former titles (until 1976): Sindicato Nacional dos Editores de Livros. Centro de Bibliotecnia. Resumo Bibliografica; (until 1972): Sindicato Nacional dos Editores de Livros. Centro de Bibliotecnia. Resenha Bibliografica.

011   SW   ISSN 0037-6469
SKOLANS ARTIKELSERVICE; register och kopior av tidningsartiklar valda i anslutning till laeroplanerna foer grundskolans hoegstadium och gymnasieskolan. 1961. 12/yr. SEK 8600. Bibliotekstjaenst AB, P.O. Box 200, S-221 00 Lund, Sweden. TEL 46-18-00-00. FAX 46-18-04-41. Ed. Irja Heino. bibl.; index. **Document type**: bibliography.
   Formerly (until 1961): Skolans Artikelregister.

011   XV   ISSN 0353-1716
Z2957.S6
SLOVENSKA BIBLIOGRAFIJA. KNJIGE. 1948. q. Narodna in Univerzitetna Knjiznica, Turjaska 1, 61001 Ljubljana, Slovenia. TEL 061-150-141. FAX 38-61-150-134. TELEX 32285 NUK-LJB-SLO.
   Formerly (until 1985): Slovenska Bibliografija (ISSN 0350-3585)

016   XO
SLOVENSKA NARODNA BIBLIOGRAFIJA. ROZPISOVY RAD CLANKY. 1954. 14/yr. $49. Matica Slovenska, Slovenska Narodna Kniznica, Ul. L. Novomeskeho 32, 036 52 Martin, Slovakia. TEL 0842-313-71. FAX 0842-324-54. TELEX 075331. Ed. Ludmila Rokosova. index. **Document type**: bibliography.
   Former titles: Slovenska Narodna Bibliografia Seria C: Clanky (ISSN 0231-9748); Clanky v Slovenskych Casopisoch (ISSN 0578-4131); Slovenske Casopisy.

016   XO   ISSN 0231-9780
SLOVENSKA NARODNA BIBLIOGRAFIA SERIA A: KNIHY. 1949. 13/yr. $78. Matica Slovenska, Slovenska Narodna Kniznica, Ul. L. Novomeskeho 32, 036 52 Martin, Slovakia. TEL 0842-313-71. FAX 0842-324-54. TELEX 075 331. Ed. Maria Okalova. **Document type**: bibliography.
   —BLDSC (8309.760000).
   Former titles (until 1970): Bibliograficky Katalog C S S R. Slovenske Knihy (ISSN 0583-6204); (until 1955): Bibliograficky Katalog C S R. Slovenska Kniha (ISSN 0231-5459)

016   XO
SLOVENSKA NARODNA BIBLIOGRAFIA SERIA B: PERIODIKA. (Text in Hungarian, Russian, Slovak; summaries in English, French, German, Slovak) 1981. every 5 yrs. Matica Slovenska, Slovenska Narodna Kniznica, Ul. L. Novomeskeho 32, 036 52 Martin, Slovakia. TEL 0842-313-71. FAX 0842-324-54. TELEX 075 331. Ed. Anna Kucianova. bibl. (back issues avail.)

015   XO
SLOVENSKA NARODNA BIBLIOGRAFIA SERIA C: MAPY. (Text in English and Slovak; summaries in English, French, German, Slovak) 1976. every 5 yrs. Matica Slovenska, Slovenska Narodna Kniznica, Ul. L. Novomeskeho 32, 036 52 Martin, Slovakia. TEL 0842-313-71. FAX 0842-324-54. TELEX 075 331. Ed. Anna Kucianova. **Document type**: bibliography.

016   XO
SLOVENSKA NARODNA BIBLIOGRAFIA SERIA D: DIZERTACNE PRACE. (Text in Czech, English, Russian, Slovak; summaries in English, French, German, Slovak) 1978. a. Matica Slovenska, Slovenska Narodna Kniznica, Ul. L. Novomeskeho 32, 036 52 Martin, Slovakia. TEL 0842-313-71. FAX 0842-324-54. TELEX 075 331. Ed. Anna Kucianova. (back issues avail.) **Document type**: bibliography.

016   XO
SLOVENSKA NARODNA BIBLIOGRAFIA SERIA E: SPECIALNE TLACE. (Text in English, French, German, Hungarian, Slovak; summaries in English, French, German, Slovak) 1980. a. Matica Slovenska, Slovenska Narodna Kniznica, Ul. L. Novomeskeho 32, 036 52 Martin, Slovakia. TEL 0842-313-71. FAX 0842-324-54. TELEX 085 331. Ed. Anna Kucianova. film rev. (back issues avail.) **Document type**: bibliography.

016   XO
SLOVENSKA NARODNA BIBLIOGRAFIA SERIA F: FIREMNA LITERATURA. (Text in Czech, English, French, German, Hungarian, Russian, Slovak, Spanish; summaries in English, French, German, Slovak) 1986. biennial. Matica Slovenska, Slovenska Narodna Kniznica, Ul. L. Novomeskeho 32, 036 52 Martin, Slovakia. TEL 0842-313-71. FAX 0842-324054. TELEX 075 331. Ed. Anna Kucianova. tr.lit. (back issues avail.) **Document type**: bibliography.

SLOVENSKA NARODNA BIBLIOGRAFIA SERIA G: GRAFIKA. see *ART — Abstracting, Bibliographies, Statistics*

016   XO
SLOVENSKA NARODNA BIBLIOGRAFIA SERIA I: OFICIALNE DOKUMENTY. (Text in Russian, Slovak; summaries in English, French, German, Slovak) 1980. biennial. Matica Slovenska, Slovenska Narodna Kniznica, Ul. L. Novomeskeho 32, 036 52 Martin, Slovakia. TEL 0842-313-71. FAX 0842-324-54. TELEX 075 331. Ed. Anna Kucianova. (back issues avail.) **Document type**: bibliography.

016   XO
SLOVENSKA NARODNA BIBLIOGRAFIA SERIA J: AUDIOVIZUALNE DOKUMENTY. (Text in English, French, Slovak; summaries in English, French, German, Slovak) 1981. a. Matica Slovenska, Slovenska Narodna Kniznica, Ul. L. Novomeskeho 32, 036 52 Martin, Slovakia. TEL 0842-313-71. FAX 0842-324-54. TELEX 075 331. Ed. Anna Kucianova. (back issues avail.) **Document type**: bibliography.

015   XO   ISSN 0231-973X
SLOVENSKA NARODNA BIBLIOGRAFIA: SERIE B-J. (Text in Czech, English, French, German, Hungarian, Russian, Slovak, Spanish; summaries in English, French, German, Slovak) 1981. q. Matica Slovenska, Slovenska Narodna Kniznica, Ul. L. Novomeskeho 32, 036 52 Martin, Slovakia. TEL 0842-313-71. FAX 0842-324-54. TELEX 075 331. (Subscr. to: Ustredna Expedicia a Dovoz Tlace, Nam. Slobody 6, 813 81 Bratislava, Slovakia) Ed. Anna Kucianova. (back issues avail.) **Document type**: bibliography.

016   US   ISSN 0148-9720
Z1033.L73
SMALL PRESS RECORD OF BOOKS IN PRINT. 1969. a. $55 (for 26th ed.). Dustbooks, Box 100, Paradise, CA 95967. TEL 916-877-6110; 800-477-6110. FAX 916-877-0222. Ed. Len Fulton. adv. **Document type**: bibliography.
   ●Available only on CD-ROM.
   Former titles (until 1975): Small Press Record of Books (ISSN 0361-364X); (until 1972): Small Press Record of Non-periodical Publications (ISSN 0081-0185)
   Description: Lists books in print by small publishers worldwide.

016.3   US   ISSN 0887-3577
SOCIAL THEORY: A BIBLIOGRAPHIC SERIES. 1986. q. $55. Reference and Research Services, 511 Lincoln St., Santa Cruz, CA 95060. TEL 408-426-4479. Ed. Joan Nordquist. (back issues avail.) **Document type**: monographic series, bibliography.
   Description: Series of bibliographies on and about the work of social theorists.

SOCIETE D'ARCHEOLOGIE COPTE. BIBLIOTHEQUE DE MANUSCRITS. see *ARCHAEOLOGY*

SOFTWARE ENCYCLOPEDIA; a guide for personal, professional, and business users. see *COMPUTERS — Software*

015   PL   ISSN 0239-0345
Z2523   CODEN: SOAPE7
SOON TO APPEAR...; forthcoming Polish books. German edition: In Kuerze Erscheinen (ISSN 0209-0376); Russian edition: Vykhodiat iz Pechati (ISSN 0239-0299) (Text in English) 1953. m. $14.30. AGPOL - Polexportpress, Ul. Kerbedzia 4, 00-957 Warsaw, Poland. (Dist. by: Ars Polona, Krakowskie Przedmiescie 7, Warsaw, Poland) Ed. Ryszard Salinger. adv.; bk.rev.; illus.; index. circ. 6,000.
   Formerly: New Polish Publications (ISSN 0028-6486)

SOUTH AFRICAN INSTITUTE OF INTERNATIONAL AFFAIRS. BIBLIOGRAPHICAL SERIES/SUID-AFRIKAANSE INSTITUUT VAN INTERNASIONALE AANGELEENTHEDE. BIBLIOGRAFIESE REEKS. see *POLITICAL SCIENCE — Abstracting, Bibliographies, Statistics*

015.68   SA   ISSN 0036-0864
Z3603   CODEN: SANBAU
SOUTH AFRICAN NATIONAL BIBLIOGRAPHY. Short title: S A N B. (Text in Afrikaans, English, indigenous languages) 1959. q. (with a. cumulation). R.243.96 (overseas $160). State Library, P.O. Box 397, Pretoria 0001, South Africa. TEL 27-12-21-8931. FAX 27-12-325-5984. E-mail: kellbc@statelib.pwv.gov.za. bibl. circ. 440. (also avail. in microfiche (ISSN 1024-6045) from PSL; back issues avail.) **Document type**: bibliography.
   —BLDSC (8343.300000); CASDDS; KNAW.
   Formerly (until 1959): South Africa. State Library. Publications Received.
   Description: Comprehensive classified listing of monographic and serial publications received by the State Library.

015.96   FJ   ISSN 0257-9146
SOUTH PACIFIC BIBLIOGRAPHY. 1981. biennial. F.$24. Pacific Information Centre, University of the South Pacific, G.P.O. Box 1168, Suva, Fiji. TEL 313900. FAX 300830. E-mail: mamtora_j@usp.ac.fj. Ed. Jayshree Mamtora. circ. 400. (also avail. in microform) **Document type**: bibliography.
   Supersedes: University of the South Pacific. Library. Pacific Collection. Accession List; Incorporates: University of the South Pacific. Library. Legal Deposit Accessions.
   Description: Lists works published in the South Pacific and overseas relating wholly or in part to the region.

996   FJ   ISSN 1011-5145
SOUTH PACIFIC RESEARCH REGISTER. 1982. biennial. F.$10. Pacific Information Centre, University of the South Pacific, G.P.O. Box 1168, Suva, Fiji. TEL 313900. FAX 300830. E-mail: mamtora_j@usp.ac.fj. Ed. Jayshree Mamtora. (also avail. in microform) **Document type**: bibliography.
   Supersedes: Fiji Register of Research and Investigations.
   Description: Directory of international researchers on subjects with a direct South Pacific interest.

370 016   MY   ISSN 0126-7590
SOUTHEAST ASIAN MINISTERS OF EDUCATION ORGANISATION. REGIONAL CENTRE FOR EDUCATION IN SCIENCE AND MATHEMATICS. LIBRARY ACCESSION LIST. (Text in English) s-a. free. Southeast Asian Ministers of Education Organisation, Regional Centre for Education in Science and Mathematics, 11700 Glugor, Penang, Malaysia. TEL 604-6583266. FAX 604-6572541. circ. 100. (reprint service avail.)

015   SA
SOUTHERN AFRICAN BOOKS IN PRINT. CD-ROM edition: Southern African Books in Print on C D - R O M (SA ISSN 1024-039X) 1993. a. (microfiche s-a.; CD-ROM q.). R.650 ($187 in US; £120 in UK) for print or microfiche; CD-ROM R.1300 ($375 in US; £242 in UK) (effective 1996). Books in Print Information Services, P.O. Box 15129, Vlaeberg 8018, South Africa. FAX 27-21-4615467. (also avail. in microfiche) **Document type:** bibliography.
●Also available on CD-ROM.
Description: Lists more than 31000 books in 31 languages published and sold in Southern Africa.

010   US
SOUTHERN ILLINOIS UNIVERSITY AT CARBONDALE. LIBRARY. BIBLIOGRAPHIC CONTRIBUTIONS. 1964. irreg. price varies. Southern Illinois University at Carbondale, Library Affairs, Library Affairs, IL 62901. TEL 618-453-2522. Ed. Carolyn A. Snyder. circ. 600. **Document type:** bibliography.
Formerly: Southern Illinois University, Carbondale. University Libraries. Bibliographic Contributions (ISSN 0073-4977)

SPRINGER BOOKS ON PROFESSIONAL COMPUTING. see *COMPUTERS*

SPROUT. see *GARDENING AND HORTICULTURE — Abstracting, Bibliographies, Statistics*

016   GW   ISSN 0942-3869
Z6956.G3
STAMM; Presse- und Medien Handbuch. 1947. a. DM.194. Stamm Verlag GmbH, Goldammerweg 16, 45134 Essen, Germany. TEL 49-201-843000. FAX 49-201-472590. Ed. Ulrich Tewes. circ. 8,000. **Document type:** directory.
Former titles (until 1991): Stamm. Leitfaden Durch Presse und Werbung (ISSN 0341-7093); (until 1972): Leitfaden fuer Presse und Werbung (ISSN 0075-8728)

050   US   ISSN 0085-6630
Z6951
STANDARD PERIODICAL DIRECTORY. 1963. a. $695. Oxbridge Communications, Inc., 150 Fifth Ave., New York, NY 10011. TEL 212-741-0231. FAX 212-633-2938. (Dist. by: Gale Research Inc., Dept. 77748, Detroit, MI 48277-0748)
●Also available online.
Also available on CD-ROM.
—BLDSC (8430.276000); CISTI; Linda Hall.

STATE REFERENCE PUBLICATIONS; a bibliographic guide to state blue books, legislative manuals and other general reference sources. see *LAW — Abstracting, Bibliographies, Statistics*

011 310   II
STATISTICAL ANNUALS: LIST OF I E G LIBRARY HOLDINGS. a. Institute of Economic Growth, University Enclave, New Delhi 110007, India. TEL 7257101. **Document type:** bibliography.

STIFTUNG LESEN. LESE-EMPFEHLUNGEN. see *CHILDREN AND YOUTH — For*

STORIES: A LIST OF STORIES TO TELL AND TO READ ALOUD. see *CHILDREN AND YOUTH — Abstracting, Bibliographies, Statistics*

010   US   ISSN 0081-7600
Z1008
STUDIES IN BIBLIOGRAPHY. 1948. a. $40. (Bibliographical Society of the University of Virginia) University Press of Virginia, Box 3608, University Sta., Charlottesville, VA 22903. TEL 804-924-3468. FAX 804-982-2655. E-mail: dlv8g@virginia.edu; webmaster@www.upress. virginia.edu; URL: http://etext.lib.virginai.edu/bsuva. html; http://www.upress.virginia.edu. Ed. D. Vander Meulen. circ. 2,000. **Indexed:** ASCA, IBR, M.L.A, MLA Intl.Bibl. **Document type:** academic/scholarly publication, bibliography.
●Also available online.
—Linda Hall.
Description: Scholarly articles on bibliographic topics.

016   US   ISSN 0000-0159
Z1215
SUBJECT GUIDE TO BOOKS IN PRINT. (Issued in 5 vols.) 1956. a. $369.95. R.R. Bowker, A Division of Reed Elsevier Inc., 121 Chanlon Rd., New Providence, NJ 07974. TEL 908-464-6800. FAX 908-665-3502. TELEX 138 755. E-mail: info@bowker.com; URL: http://www.reedref.com. (Subscr. to: Order Dept., Box 31, New Providence, NJ 07974-9903). TEL 800-521-8110) (also avail. in microfiche; magnetic tape) **Document type:** bibliography, directory.
●Also available online. Vendor(s): Knight-Ridder Information, Inc. (File no.470), Ovid Technologies, Inc. (BBIP).
Also available on CD-ROM. Producer(s): Bowker Electronic Publishing (Books In Print PLUS).
—CISTI; Linda Hall. **CCC.**
Description: Indexes all nonfiction titles in Books in Print, using U.S. Library of Congress subject headings. Includes a subject thesaurus and publisher information.

011   US
SUBJECT GUIDE TO BOOKS IN PRINT ON MICROFICHE. q. $475. R.R. Bowker, A Division of Reed Elsevier Inc., 121 Chanlon Rd., New Providence, NJ 07974. TEL 800-521-8110. FAX 908-665-6688. TELEX 138 755. E-mail: info@bowker.com; URL: http://www.reedref.com. (Subscr. to: Order Dept., Box 31, New Providence, NJ 07974-9903) (microfiche) **Document type:** bibliography, directory.
Description: Updates Subject Guide to Books in Print, including more than 725,000 in-print and forthcoming titles under 66,000 U.S. Library of Congress subject headings.

011   CN   ISSN 0318-8493
Z1365
SUBJECT GUIDE TO CANADIAN BOOKS IN PRINT. 1973. a. University of Toronto Press, Directories Departement, 10 St. Mary St., Ste. 700, Toronto, ON M4Y 2W8, Canada. TEL 416-978-2239. FAX 416-978-4738. E-mail: utpbooks@gpu.utcc.utoronto.ca. (U.S. addr.: 340 Nagel Dr., Cheektowaga, NY 41225) **Document type:** bibliography.
—CISTI.

016   US   ISSN 0000-0167
Z1037.A1
SUBJECT GUIDE TO CHILDREN'S BOOKS IN PRINT. 1971. a. $159 (effective 1998). R.R. Bowker, A Division of Reed Elsevier Inc., 121 Chanlon Rd., New Providence, NJ 07974. TEL 908-464-6800. FAX 908-665-3502. TELEX 138 755. E-mail: info@bowker.com; URL: http://www.reedref.com. (Subscr. to: Order Dept., Box 31, New Providence, NJ 07974-9903. TEL 800-521-8110) (also avail. in magnetic tape) **Document type:** bibliography, directory.
●Also available online.
Also available on CD-ROM. Producer(s): Bowker Electronic Publishing.
—CCC.
Description: Indexes children's fiction and nonfiction books under Sears and U.S. Library of Congress headings. Includes publisher information.

948.5 016   SW   ISSN 0039-4599
Z2633.3
SUECANA EXTRANEA; boecker om Sverige och svensk skoenlitteratur paa fraemmande spraak. (Text in English & Swedish) 1968. a. SEK 80 (effective 1996). Kungliga Biblioteket - Royal Library, P.O. Box 5039, S-102 41 Stockholm, Sweden. TEL 46-8-463-40-90. FAX 46-8-463-40-04. E-mail: marianne.thorell@kb.se. Ed. Ylva/Tjeder. bibl. circ. 700. **Document type:** bibliography.

016 949.6   GW   ISSN 0081-9131
SUEDOSTEUROPA - BIBLIOGRAPHIE. (Text in European languages) 1956. irreg. price varies. (Suedost-Institut) R. Oldenbourg Verlag GmbH, Rosenheimerstr. 145, 81671 Munich, Germany. TEL 49-89-45051-0. FAX 49-89-45051266. (Subscr. to: Postfach 801360, 81613 Munich, Germany) Ed. Gerhard Seewann. **Document type:** bibliography.

015.4891   FI   ISSN 0355-001X
SUOMEN KIRJALLISUUS/FINNISH NATIONAL BIBLIOGRAPHY/FINLANDS LITTERATUR. Annual edition: Suomen Kirjallisuus Vuosiluettelo (ISSN 0355-0001) (Text in English, Finnish, Swedish) 1972. m. (with a. cumulation). in EU countries; in other European countries FIM 1000; elsewhere FIM 1145 (effective 1996). Helsingin Yliopiston Kirjasto - Helsinki University Library, Unioninkatu 36, FIN-00014 Helsinki, University of Helsinki, Finland. FAX 358-0-70844341. (Dist. by: Valtion Painatuskeskus, Box 516, FIN-00101 Helsinki, Finland) bibl. circ. 900. (also avail. in microfiche) **Document type:** bibliography.
●Also available on CD-ROM.
—BLDSC (8543.550000); Linda Hall.
Description: Contains books published in Finland.

SUOMEN SANOMALEHTIEN MIKROFILMIT/MICROFILMED NEWSPAPERS OF FINLAND. see *JOURNALISM — Abstracting, Bibliographies, Statistics*

015.485   SW   ISSN 0039-6443
Z2625
SVENSK BOKFOERTECKNING/SWEDISH NATIONAL BIBLIOGRAPHY. (Annual cumulation avail.) 1953. 6/yr. SEK 2200 (effective Jan. 1995). (Kungliga Biblioteket, Bibliografiska Avdelningen - Royal Library) Tidnings AB Svensk Bokhandel, P.O. Box 6888, S-113 86 Stockholm, Sweden. TEL 46-8-736-1950. FAX 46-8-736-1955. (Dist. by: AB Seelig & Co., P.O. Box 1308, S-17125 Solna, Sweden) Eds. Gunilla Evers, Eva Tedenmyr. circ. 1,350 (2,200 annual). (back issues avail.) **Indexed:** Bibl.Engl.Lang.& Lit. **Document type:** bibliography.
—KNAW; Linda Hall.
Supersedes: Aarskatalog foer Svenska Bokhandeln; **Incorporates** (in 1986): Svensk Kartfoertckning.

015.485   SW   ISSN 1104-1102
Z2625
SVENSK PERIODICAFOERTECKNING/CURRENT SWEDISH PERIODICALS; tidskrifter, aarsboecker, dagstidningar och rapportserier. 1953. triennial. SEK 860 (effective Jan. 1994). (Kungliga Biblioteket, Bibliografiska Avdelningen - Royal Library) Tidnings AB Svensk Bokhandel, P.O. Box 6888, S-113 86 Stockholm, Sweden. TEL 46-8-736-1950. FAX 46-8-736-1955. (Subscr. to: AB Seelig and Co., P.O. Box 1308, S-171 25 Solna, Sweden) Ed. Ingrid Stroem. circ. 1,000. **Document type:** bibliography.
—BLDSC (8562.200000); KNAW.
Formerly (until 1994): Svensk Tidskriftsfoertckning (ISSN 0586-0431)
Description: Lists the most important periodical publications in Sweden. Publications of local and private character, such as parish magazines and school magazines, are not listed.

011   SW   ISSN 0039-6907
SVENSKA TIDNINGSARTIKLAR. 1953. m. (with a. cumulation). SEK 3800. Bibliotekstjaenst AB, P.O. Box 200, S-221 00 Lund, Sweden. TEL 46-18-00-00. FAX 46-18-04-41. bibl.; index. circ. 300. **Document type:** bibliography.
Formerly (until 1961): Svensk Tidningsindex.

011   SW   ISSN 0039-6915
SVENSKA TIDSKRIFTSARTIKLAR. 1952. m. (with a. cumulation). SEK 4100 (effective 1996). Bibliotekstjaenst AB, P.O. Box 200, S-221 00 Lund, Sweden. TEL 46-18-00-00. FAX 46-18-04-41. index. circ. 700. **Indexed:** Bibl.Engl.Lang.& Lit. **Document type:** bibliography.
Formerly (until 1961): Svensk Tidskriftsindex.

011 070.5   SQ   ISSN 0378-7710
SWAZILAND NATIONAL BIBLIOGRAPHY. 1974. irreg. latest 1988-1993. $12.50. University of Swaziland, Private Bag 4, Kwaluseni, Swaziland. TEL 268-85108. FAX 268-85276. TELEX 2087 WD. Ed.Bd. circ. 300. (back issues avail.) **Document type:** bibliography.
Description: Lists publications issued in Swaziland or received at the University.

SWEDEN. STATISTISKA CENTRALBYRAANS BIBLIOTEK. STATISTIK FRAAN INTERNATIONELLA ORGAN. see *STATISTICS*

015.678 TZ ISSN 0856-003X
Z3588
TANZANIA NATIONAL BIBLIOGRAPHY. 1970. a. Sh.9520 foreign $90. Library Services Board, National Bibliographic Agency, P.O. Box 9283, Dar es Salaam, Tanzania. TEL 255-51-150048. Ed. Lina Lengaki. circ. 250. **Document type:** bibliography.
—BLDSC (8602.704500).
Formerly (until 1982): Printed in Tanzania.
Description: Lists new books and other publications produced in Tanzania and depostied at the National Bibliographic Agency. Includes books, reports, dissertations, other mimeographed documents, and the first issue of new serial titles.

011 GW
TASCHENBUCH DER AUKTIONSPREISE ALTER BUECHER. 1975. a. DM.130. Verlag fuer Buechersammler, Postfach 101756, 52019 Aachen, Germany. FAX 0241-601912. Ed. F. Radtke. adv. **Document type:** catalog.

TASCHENBUCH DES OEFFENTLICHEN LEBENS; Deutschland. see PUBLIC ADMINISTRATION

TECHNICAL RESOURCES ON COATING PROCESSES. see PAINTS AND PROTECTIVE COATINGS — Abstracting, Bibliographies, Statistics

620 016 HU ISSN 0040-1110
TECHNIKA. (Annual editions in English, German, Russian) 1957. m. $30.50. (Hungarian Technical Information Center and Library) Nepszava Lapkiado Vallalat, Rakoczi ut 54, 1964 Budapest 7, Hungary. TEL 224-810. (Subscr. to: Kultura, Box 149, H-1389 Budapest, Hungary) Ed. Emil Szluka. adv.; bk.rev.; abstr.; charts; illus.; pat.; stat.; tr.mk. circ. 15,000. (tabloid format)

620.16 NE ISSN 0929-0567
TECHNISCHE UNIVERSITEIT TE DELFT. BIBLIOTHEEK. LIJST VAN LOPENDE SERIELE PUBLIKATIES. Cover title: Lijst van Lopende Seriele Publikaties - List of Current Serial Publications. 1967. a. fl.65 (effective 1997). Technische Universiteit te Delft, Bibliotheek, P.O. Box 98, 2600 MG Delft, Netherlands. TEL 31-15-782854. FAX 31-15-158759. index. circ. 1,000. **Document type:** bibliography.
—KNAW.
Former titles (until 1993): Technische Universiteit te Delft. Bibliotheek. Lijst van Lopende Tijdschriftabonnementen (ISSN 0923-8689); Technische Hogeschool te Delft. Bibliotheek. Lijst van Lopende Tijdschriftabonnementen.
Description: Lists current serial and periodical subscriptions of the library.

011 US ISSN 0739-3202
F381
TEXAS BOOKS IN REVIEW. vol.7, 1987. q. $10 (foreign $16) (effective 1997). Ctr. for Southwest S W T S U, San Marcos, TX 78666. TEL 512-245-2232. FAX 512-245-7462. E-mail: MBB@SWT.edu; URL: http://www.english.swt.edu/css/cssindex.htm. Eds. Mark Busby, Dick Heaberlin. R&P contact: Dick Heaberlin. adv. contact: Mark Busby. bk.rev. circ. 500. **Indexed:** Amer.Hum.Ind. **Document type:** academic/scholarly publication.
Description: Publishes reviews of books by and about Texans or Texas. Includes regional articles about the literary scene around the state.

011 SW ISSN 0345-0112
TEXT; svensk tidskrift foer bibliografi. (Text in English, Swedish) 1974. irreg. (approx. 1/yr.). SEK 280 per vol. (4 issues). (Center for Bibliographical Studies, Uppsala) Dahlia Books, International Publishers and Booksellers, P.O. Box 1025, S-751 40 Uppsala, Sweden. TEL 46-18-10-10-98. FAX 46-8-100525. Ed. Rolf E. Du Rietz. adv.; bk.rev. circ. 200.

THAILAND. NATIONAL STATISTICAL OFFICE. ANNOTATED STATISTICAL BIBLIOGRAPHY. see STATISTICS

011.7 DK ISSN 0900-2278
Z5055.D3
THESES AND OTHER PUBLICATIONS OF THE UNIVERSITY OF COPENHAGEN. (Text in English) 19?? a. exchange basis. Danish National Library of Science and Medicine, Noerre Alle 49, DK-2200 Copenhagen N, Denmark. TEL 45-31-39-65-23.
FAX 45-31-39-85-33. E-mail: HF@dnlb.dk. Dir. Henriette Fog. adv. contact: Henriette Fog. circ. controlled. (processed) **Document type:** academic/scholarly publication.
Formerly (until 1974): Theses Accepted for the Doctorate and Other Publications Issued by the University.
Description: Provides a checklist of material available for exchange.

011 AT ISSN 1038-3395
THORPE - R O M; Australian & New Zealand books in print, plus annotations, on CD-ROM. 1992. m. Aus.$895 per mo. D.W. Thorpe, A member of the Reed Elsevier plc group, 18 Salmon St., Port Melbourne, Vic. 3207, Australia. TEL 61-3-92457370. FAX 61-3-92457395. E-mail: customer.service@thorpe.com.au; URL: http://www.reed-elsevier.com.
●Available only on CD-ROM.
Description: Includes more than 100,000 Australian, New Zealand and Pacific Island books in print (all Australian titles published since 1990 fully annotated), over 4,000 publishers and distributors, as well as full agency and imprint information.

015.489 DK ISSN 0105-4090
TIDSSKRIFTINDEKS FOR SKOLEBIBLIOTEKER. (Supplements avail.) 1972. a. DKK 300 (includes supplements) (effective 1996). Dansk BiblioteksCenter as, Tempovej 7-11, DK-2750 Ballerup, Denmark. TEL 45-44-867777. FAX 45-44-867892. E-mail: dbc@dan.bib.dk. **Document type:** abstracting/indexing.
●Also available online.

015 NZ ISSN 1170-800X
Z4124.T65
TOKELAU NATIONAL BIBLIOGRAPHY. 1992. irreg. NZ.$48. National Library of New Zealand, P.O. Box 1467, Wellington, New Zealand. TEL 64-4-4743067. FAX 64-4-4743124. E-mail: shop@natlib.govt.nz. **Document type:** bibliography.
●Also available online.
Description: Provides a comprehensive list of Tokelau publications, including non-books.

TRAVAUX. see ENGINEERING — Abstracting, Bibliographies, Statistics

TRAVEL BOOKS WORLDWIDE; the travel book review. see TRAVEL AND TOURISM

015 TR ISSN 1018-7871
TRINIDAD AND TOBAGO NATIONAL BIBLIOGRAPHY. 1975. q. $25. University of the West Indies, Main Library, St. Augustine, Trinidad & Tobago, W.I. TEL 809-662-2002. FAX 809-662-9238. TELEX 24-520-UWI-WG. (Dist by: Central Library of Trinidad and Tobago, P.O. Box 547, Port-of-Spain, Trinidad & Tobago, W.I.) (Co-sponsor: Central Library of Trinidad and Tobago) Ed. Ann Clarke. bk.rev. circ. 172.
—BLDSC (9050.659500).
Supersedes (since 1975, no.5): Recent Acquisitions of Trinidad and Tobago Imprints, Books and Pamphlets.
Description: Provides a listing of works published and printed locally. Excludes most periodicals and government legislation publications.

015.561 TU ISSN 0041-4328
TURKISH NATIONAL BIBLIOGRAPHY/TURKIYE BIBLIYOGRAFYASI. (Text in Turkish) 1928. m. $48. Milli Kutuphane Baskanligi, Bibliografya Hazirlama Sube Mudurlugu - National Library, Bibliography Preparation Department, Bahcelievler, 06490 Ankara, Turkey. TEL 90-312-2224768. FAX 90-312-2230451. E-mail: bibli@kitap.mkutup.gov.tr; URL: http://www.mkutup.gov.tr. (Subscr. to: Kultur Bakanligi, Doner sermaye Isletmeleri Merkez Mudurlugu, Adakale sok. No. 18, Kizilay-Ankara, Turkey.. TEL 90-31-4335171) bibl.; index. circ. 2,000. **Document type:** bibliography.
Description: Contains annual indexes of personal authors, titles of books and periodicals.

015.561 TU ISSN 0041-4344
TURKIYE MAKALELER BIBLIYOGRAFYASI/BIBLIOGRAPHY OF ARTICLES IN TURKISH PERIODICALS. (Text in Turkish) 1952. 12/yr. $48. Milli Kutuphane Baskanligi, Bibliografya Hazirlama Sube Mudurlugu - National Library, Bibliography Preparation Department, Bahcelievler, 06490 Ankara, Turkey. TEL 90-312-2223812. FAX 90-312-2230451. E-mail: bibli@kitap.mkutup.gov.tr; URL: http://www.mkutup.gov.tr. (Subscr. to: Kultur Bakanligi, Doner sermaye Isletmeleri Merkez Mudurlugu, Adakale sok. No. 18, Kizilay-Ankara, Turkey.. TEL 990-312-4335171) index. circ. 2,000. **Document type:** bibliography.
Description: Contains bibliographic entries of articles and reviews appearing in periodicals, as well as congress, conference and seminar papers that have been acquired by the National Library. Includes a separate section covering all agreements, laws, decrees, standards and statutes published in the Official Gazette since January 1992.

015 HU ISSN 0049-5069
UJ KONYVEK. 1964. s-m. 300 Ft.($8) (Orszagos Szechenyi Konyvtar, Konyvtartudomanyi es Modszertani Kozpont - National Szechenyi Library, Center for Library Science and Methodology) Konyvertekesito Vallalat, Vaci u. 19, 1134 Budapest, Hungary. FAX 36-1-20-20-804. TELEX 224226 BIBLN H. (Subscr. to: Kultura, Box 149, H-1389 Budapest, Hungary) Ed. E. Gyori. bk.rev.; bibl. circ. 8,500.
Description: Lists Hungarian books commercially available in the country.

015 HU ISSN 0864-8786
UJ PERIODIKUMOK. 1989. m. 600 Ft. (effective 1997). Orszagos Szechenyi Konyvtar, Konyvtartudomanyi es Modszertani Kozpont - Centre for Library and Information Science at the National Szechenyi Library, Budavari Palota F epulet, 1827 Budapest, Hungary. TEL 36-1-1556967. FAX 36-1-2020804. E-mail: vili@oszk.hu. Ed. Aniko Nagy. circ. 500. **Document type:** bibliography.
●Also available on CD-ROM.
—BLDSC (9082.451000).
Description: Lists new periodicals and title changes officially recorded in the library.

015 BW
UKAZATEL BIBLIOGRAFICHESKIKH POSOBYI. (Text in Byelorussian and Russian) 1978. a. 45 Rub. Nationalnaya Knizhnaya Palata Belarusi, Pr. Masherava, 11, 220600 Minsk, Belarus. TEL 23-08-396. Ed. L.N. Nekhaichik. circ. 300.
Formerly: Bibliograficheskie Posobiya Belorusskoi S.S.R. (ISSN 0203-3941)
Description: Contains bibliographies on books in all fields.

016.05 US ISSN 0000-0175
CODEN: UIPDAM
ULRICH'S INTERNATIONAL PERIODICALS DIRECTORY. (Supplement avail.: Ulrich's Update (ISSN 0000-1074)) 1932. a. since 1980; previously biennial. $459.95 (includes 2/yr. Ulrich's Update) (CD-ROM version $595) (effective 1998). R.R. Bowker, A Division of Reed Elsevier Inc., 121 Chanlon Rd., New Providence, NJ 07974. TEL 908-665-2847; 888-268-5372. FAX 908-771-7725. TELEX 138 755. E-mail: ulrichs@reedref.com; URL: http://www.bowker.com. (U.S. & Canada subscr. to: Order Dept., Box 31, New Providence, NJ 07974. TEL 800-521-8110. FAX 908-665-6688; Elsewhere: Bowker-Saur, Customer Services Dept., Maypole House, Maypole Rd., East Grinstead, W. Sussex RH19 1HU, England. TEL 44-1342-330100. FAX 44-1342-330198) Ed. Edvika Popilskis; Pub. Judy Salk. index. (magnetic tape) **Document type:** bibliography, directory.
●Also available online. Vendor(s): Knight-Ridder Information, Inc. (File no.480), Lexis-Nexis (ULRICHS), Ovid Technologies, Inc. (ULRI).
Also available on CD-ROM. Producer(s): Bowker Electronic Publishing (Ulrich's PLUS), SilverPlatter Information, Inc. (ERL).
—BLDSC (9082.737000); CASDDS; CISTI; Linda Hall. **CCC**.
Incorporates (1967-1987): Irregular Serials and Annuals (ISSN 0000-0043)
Description: Arranged by subject classification, includes magazines, journals, newsletters, newspapers, annuals and irregular serials published worldwide. Separate indices list refereed serials, controlled circulation serials, serials available on CD-ROM, CD-ROM producers, serials available online, online vendors, cessations, publications of international organizations, International Standard Serial Numbers, cumulated title changes, and titles. Entries include title, circulation, frequency, complete publisher address, telephone, fax and telex, description, subscription price, with subscription and distribution addresses, telephone and fax information. Also includes bibliographic classification (LC, DDC and CODEN), abstracting and indexing information, document type notations, document delivery service availability, advertising rates and contact name, among other data.

011 US ISSN 0000-1724
Z6941
ULRICH'S ON DISC; the complete International Serials database on compact laser disc. q. £450. R.R. Bowker Electronic Publishing, 121 Chanlon Rd., New Providence, NJ 07974. TEL 800-323-3288. FAX 908-665-3528. TELEX 138 755. E-mail: info@reedref.com; URL: http://www.reedref.com. (U.S. and Canada subscr. addr.: Electronic Sales Dept., 121 Chanlon Rd., New Providence, NJ 0797-1154. TEL 800-323-3288; Elsewhere: Bowker-Saur, Customer Services Dept., Maypole House, Maypole Rd., East Grinstead, W. Sussex RH19 1HU, England. TEL 44-13423-330100. FAX 44-1342-110198) **Document type:** bibliography, directory.
●Available only on CD-ROM. Producer(s): Bowker Electronic Publishing (Ulrich's PLUS).
—KNAW.
Formerly (until Sep. 1997): Ulrich's Plus (ISSN 1068-0500)

011 US ISSN 0000-1074
CODEN: ULUPE6
ULRICH'S UPDATE. (Supplement to: Ulrich's International Periodicals Directory (ISSN 0000-0175)) 1988. 2/yr. $150 (free with subscription to Ulrich's International Periodicals Directory). R.R. Bowker, A Division of Reed Elsevier Inc., 121 Chanlon Rd., New Providence, NJ 07974. TEL 908-665-2847; 800-346-6049. FAX 908-771-7725. TELEX 138 755. E-mail: ulrichs@reedref.com; URL: http://www.reedref.com. (Subscr. in N. America to: Order Dept., Box 31, New Providence, NJ 07974. TEL 800-521-8110. FAX 908-665-6688; Elsewhere: Bowker-Saur, Customer Services Dept., Maypole House, Maypole Rd., East Grinstead, W. Sussex RH19 1HU, England. TEL 44-1342-330100. FAX 44-1342-330198) Ed. Edvika Popilskis; Pub. Judy Salk. **Document type:** bibliography, directory.
●Also available online. Vendor(s): Knight-Ridder Information, Inc. (File no.480), Lexis-Nexis (ULRICHS), Ovid Technologies, Inc. (ULRI).
Also available on CD-ROM. Producer(s): Bowker Electronic Publishing (Ulrich's PLUS).
—BLDSC (9082.738400); CASDDS; CISTI; Genuine Article; Linda Hall. **CCC**.
Supersedes (in 1988): Bowker International Serials Database Update (ISSN 0000-0892); Which was formerly (until 1985): Ulrich's Quarterly (ISSN 0000-0507); (until 1977): Bowker Serials Bibliography Supplement (ISSN 0000-0094)
Description: Lists information on new periodicals and irregular serials, title changes and cessations received after publication of the base volumes. Cumulates title index and title change index.

UNESCO. PRINCIPAL REGIONAL OFFICE FOR ASIA AND THE PACIFIC. ABSTRACT BIBLIOGRAPHY SERIES ON POPULATION EDUCATION. see EDUCATION — Abstracting, Bibliographies, Statistics

016.912 UN
UNESCO. SCIENTIFIC MAPS AND ATLASES AND OTHER RELATED PUBLICATIONS. irreg. UNESCO Publishing, 7 Place de Fontenoy, 75352 Paris 07 SP, France. TEL 33-1-45684300. FAX 33-1-45685741. URL: http://www.unesco.org/publications. (Dist. in the U.S. by: Bernan Associates, 4611-F Assembly Dr., Lanham, MD 20706-4391. TEL 800-274-4888. FAX 800-865-3450) bibl.; illus.

011 FR
UNESCO DATABASES. (Text in English, French, Spanish) a. 490 F. (effective 1997). UNESCO Publishing, 1 rue Miollis, 75732 Paris Cedex 15, France. TEL 33-1-45684300. FAX 33-1-45685741. TELEX 204461 PARIS. URL: http://www.unesco.org/publications. (Dist. in U.S. by: Bernan Associates, 4611 Assembly Dr., Lanham, MD 20706-4391. TEL 800-274-4888. FAX 800-865-3450)
●Available only on CD-ROM.
Description: Bibliographical references of all UNESCO documents and publications. International specialized bibliographies in every area of education, museums, monuments and sites. Names, addresses and activities of 10,000 research, training and documentation institutions in the social sciences. Also includes the UNESCO and the International Bureau of Education thesauri.

011 500 ZA
UNION LIST OF SCIENTIFIC AND TECHNICAL PERIODICALS IN ZAMBIA. 1980. irreg. K.4.50. National Council for Scientific Research, Box CH 158, Chelston, Lusaka, Zambia. Eds. W.C. Muship, J.C. Michello.

500 016.05 IS ISSN 0333-5321
Z6945
UNION LIST OF SERIALS IN ISRAEL LIBRARIES. Key Title: U L S - Israel. (Not avail. in printed format) 1955. a. $85. Jewish National and University Library, P.O.Box 34165, Jerusalem 91341, Israel. TEL 972-2-585028. FAX 972-511771. Ed. Simona Anner. circ. 120. (microfiche) **Document type:** bibliography.
●Available only online.
Formerly (until 1980): Union List of Serials in Israel Libraries (ISSN 0082-7665)

016 US
UNITED NATIONS DOCUMENTS AND PUBLICATIONS. 1946. q. (plus a. cumulation). NewsBank, Inc., 58 Pine St., New Canaan, CT 06840-5426. TEL 800-752-4650. FAX 203-966-6254. index. circ. 6,975. (also avail. in microfiche)
●Also available on CD-ROM.
Former titles: United Nations Documents and Publications. Checklist; United Nations Documents (ISSN 0191-8087); Readex Microprint Publications (ISSN 0079-984X)

UNITED NATIONS LIBRARY. MONTHLY BIBLIOGRAPHY. PART 1: BOOKS, OFFICIAL DOCUMENTS, SERIALS. see POLITICAL SCIENCE — Abstracting, Bibliographies, Statistics

UNITED NATIONS LIBRARY. MONTHLY BIBLIOGRAPHY. PART 2: SELECTED ARTICLES. see POLITICAL SCIENCE — Abstracting, Bibliographies, Statistics

U.S. DEPARTMENT OF STATE. LIBRARY. COMMERCIAL LIBRARY PROGRAM. PUBLICATIONS LIST. see LIBRARY AND INFORMATION SCIENCES — Abstracting, Bibliographies, Statistics

U.S. ENVIRONMENTAL PROTECTION AGENCY. JOURNAL HOLDINGS REPORT. see ENVIRONMENTAL STUDIES — Abstracting, Bibliographies, Statistics

011 332 US ISSN 0145-0301
Z7164.F5
U.S. FEDERAL RESERVE SYSTEM. RESEARCH LIBRARY - RECENT ACQUISITIONS. m. free. U.S. Federal Reserve System, Board of Governors, Publications Services, Rm. MS-123, Washington, DC 20551. TEL 202-452-3244. FAX 202-728-5886. **Document type:** government publication.

070.5 US ISSN 0734-2764
Z1223.A19
U.S. GOVERNMENT BOOKS; publications for sale by the Government Printing Office. q.? free. U.S. Government Printing Office, Superintendent of Documents, Washington, DC 20402. (Avail. from: Box 37000, Washington, DC 20013-7000) **Document type:** catalog, government publication.
Description: Lists new and popular books sold by the U.S. government on a very wide variety of topics, including agriculture, business, children, energy, health, history, and vacations.

015.942 025.3 US
U.S. GOVERNMENT PRINTING OFFICE. CATALOGING FILE. (Retrospective cumulation avail.) m. $1920 (outside N. America $2270) (effective 1996). U.S. Library of Congress, Cataloging Distribution Service, Washington, DC 20541-5017. TEL 202-707-6100; 800-255-3666. FAX 202-707-1334. E-mail: cdsinfo@mail.loc.gov. (processed) **Document type:** bibliography.
Description: Compiles MARC records for books, serials, maps, audiovisual materials, and computer files cataloged by the U.S. Government Printing Office on OCLC.

011 US
U.S. GOVERNMENT SUBSCRIPTIONS. q. free. U.S. Government Printing Office, Superintendent of Documents, Mail Stop SSMB, Washington, DC 20402. (Avail. from: Superintendent of Documents, U.S. Government Printing Office, Box 371954, Pittsburgh, PA 15250-7954. TEL 202-512-1800. FAX 202-512-2250) **Document type:** catalog.
Formerly: Government Periodicals and Subscription Services.
Description: Provides a comprehensive listing of periodicals published by U.S. government agencies that are available to the public; materials cover a very wide variety of interests.

BIBLIOGRAPHIES

015   KE   ISSN 1070-2717
Z3516   CODEN: ALEAEZ
U.S. LIBRARY OF CONGRESS. ACCESSIONS LIST: EASTERN AND SOUTHERN AFRICA. (Supplements avail.: Serial Supplement and Annual Publishers Directory (ISSN 1074-3839)) 1968. bi-m. free to libraries. U.S. Library of Congress Office, Embassy of the United States of America, P.O. Box 30598, Nairobi, Kenya. TEL 254-2-225484. FAX 254-2-217646. E-mail: loc-nbo@tt.sasa.unon.org. Indexed: Popul.Ind. **Document type:** government publication, bibliography.
  Formerly: U.S. Library of Congress. Accessions List: Eastern Africa (ISSN 0090-371X)
  Description: Lists monographs and serials acquired for the Library of Congress from commercial publishers, governmental, nongovernmental and international organizations throughout the countries of eastern and southern Africa and the Indian Ocean.

020   KE
Z6959.Z9
U.S. LIBRARY OF CONGRESS. ACCESSIONS LIST: EASTERN AND SOUTHERN AFRICA. SERIAL SUPPLEMENT. (Supplement to: U.S. Library of Congress. Accessions List: Eastern and Southern Africa (ISSN 1070-2717)) 1968. bi-a. U.S. Library of Congress Office, Embassy of the United States of America, P.O. Box 30598, Nairobi, Kenya. TEL 254-2-225484. FAX 254-2-217646. E-mail: loc-nbo@tt.sasa.unon.org. **Document type:** government publication, bibliography.
  Formerly (until 1995): U.S. Library of Congress. Annual Serial Supplement (ISSN 1074-3820)
  Description: Lists all serial titles currently received by the Nairobi Office, covering countries in eastern and southern Africa and the Indian Ocean.

015.73 025.3   US
U.S. LIBRARY OF CONGRESS. AUTHORITY FILES - NAME AUTHORITIES. (Retrospective cumulation avail.) 1977. w. $12595 (outside N. America $12660) (effective 1996). U.S. Library of Congress, Cataloging Distribution Service, Customer Services Section, Washington, DC 20541-5017. TEL 202-707-6100; 800-255-3666. FAX 202-707-1334. E-mail: cdsinfo@mail.loc.gov. (processed) **Document type:** bibliography.
  Description: Compiles MARC records for personal, corporate, conference, and geographical name headings, uniform titles, and series.

011.295   US
U.S. LIBRARY OF CONGRESS. BOOKS C J K. (Chinese, Japanese, Korean) (Retrospective cumulation avail.) 1987. every 4 wks. $1555 (outside N. America $1865) (effective 1996). U.S. Library of Congress, Cataloging Distribution Service, Customer Services Section, Washington, DC 20541-5017. TEL 202-707-6100; 800-255-3666. FAX 202-707-1334. E-mail: cdsinfo@mail.loc.gov. (processed) **Document type:** bibliography.
  Description: Compiles MARC records for Chinese-, Japanese-, and Korean-language monographs cataloged by the US Library of Congress.

011 025.3   US   ISSN 1073-4929
Z693
U.S. LIBRARY OF CONGRESS. CATALOGER'S DESKTOP. 1994. q. $870 (outside N. America $875). U.S. Library of Congress, Cataloging Distribution Service, Customer Services Section, Washington, DC 20541-5017. TEL 202-707-6100; 800-255-3666. FAX 202-707-1334. E-mail: cdsinfo@mail.loc.gov. (diskette format) **Document type:** government publication.
●Available only on CD-ROM.
  Description: Comprises the most popular US Library of Congress cataloging publications, including LOC Rule Interpretations; Subject Cataloging Manual: Subject Headings; Subject Cataloging Manual: Classification; USMARC Concise Formats; USMARC Format for Bibliographic Data; USMARC Format for Authority Data; and the entire set of USMARC Code Lists.

011.1 025.3   US
U.S. LIBRARY OF CONGRESS. CATALOGING FILES - BOOKS ALL. (Also avail. in CANMARC and UKMARC file conversions; retrospective cumulation avail.) 1968. w. $15280 (outside N. America $16410); in CANMARC format $15280; in UKMARC format $15280) (effective 1996). U.S. Library of Congress, Cataloging Distribution Service, Customer Services Section, Washington, DC 20541-5017. TEL 202-707-6100; 800-255-3666. FAX 202-707-1334. E-mail: cdsinfo@mail.loc.gov. (processed) **Document type:** bibliography.
  Description: Compiles the entire U.S. Library of Congress MARC bibliography for books in all languages.

015.942 025.3   US
U.S. LIBRARY OF CONGRESS. CATALOGING FILES - BOOKS ENGLISH. (Retrospective cumulation avail.) 1968. w. $13525 (outside N. America $14405) (effective 1997). U.S. Library of Congress, Cataloging Distribution Service, Customer Services Section, Washington, DC 20541-5017. TEL 202-707-6100; 800-255-3666. FAX 202-707-1334. E-mail: cdsinfo@mail.loc.gov. (processed) **Document type:** bibliography.
  Description: Compiles the entire U.S. Library of Congress MARC database for all books published in English.

015.73 025.3   US
U.S. LIBRARY OF CONGRESS. CATALOGING FILES - BOOKS U S. (Retrospective cumulation avail.) 1968. w. $8410 (outside N. America $9125) (effective 1996). U.S. Library of Congress, Cataloging Distribution Service, Customer Services Section, Washington, DC 20541-5017. TEL 202-707-6100; 800-255-3666. FAX 202-707-1334. E-mail: cdsinfo@mail.loc.gov. (processed) **Document type:** bibliography.
  Description: Compiles all U.S. Library of Congress MARC bibliographic records for books printed in the US.

011.1 025.3   US
U.S. LIBRARY OF CONGRESS. CATALOGING FILES - COMPLETE SERVICE. (Retrospective cumulation avail.) 1968. w. $21025 (outside N. America $22420) (effective 1996). U.S. Library of Congress, Cataloging Distribution Service, Customer Services Section, Washington, DC 20541-5017. TEL 202-707-6100; 800-255-3666. FAX 202-707-1334. E-mail: cdsinfo@mail.loc.gov. (processed) **Document type:** bibliography.
  Description: Compiles the entire U.S. Library of Congress MARC bibliography.

016.912 025.3   US
U.S. LIBRARY OF CONGRESS. CATALOGING FILES - MAPS. (Retrospective cumulation avail.) 1973. every 4 wks. $1280 (outside N. America $1550) (effective 1996). U.S. Library of Congress, Cataloging Distribution Service, Customer Services Section, Washington, DC 20541-5017. TEL 202-707-6100; 800-255-3666. FAX 202-707-1334. E-mail: cdsinfo@mail.loc.gov. **Document type:** bibliography.
  Description: Compiles U.S. Library of Congress MARC bibliographic records for all single- and multi-sheet maps, map sets, and maps treated as serials.

016.78   US
U.S. LIBRARY OF CONGRESS. CATALOGING FILES - MUSIC. (Retrospective cumulation avail.) 1984. every 4 wks. $1280 (outside N. America $1550) (effective 1996). U.S. Library of Congress, Cataloging Distribution Service, Customer Services Section, Washington, DC 20541-5017. TEL 202-707-6100; 800-255-3666. FAX 202-707-1334. E-mail: cdsinfo@mail.loc.gov. (processed) **Document type:** bibliography.
  Description: Compiles U.S. Library of Congress MARC bibliographic records for printed and manuscript music and for music and nonmusic sound recordings.

016.05   US
U.S. LIBRARY OF CONGRESS. CATALOGING FILES - SERIALS. (Retrospective cumulation avail.) 1973. every 4 wks. $5200 (outside N. America $5565) (effective 1996). U.S. Library of Congress, Cataloging Distribution Service, Customer Services Section, Washington, DC 20541-5017. TEL 202-707-1334. E-mail: cdsinfo@mail.loc.gov. (processed) **Document type:** bibliography.
  Description: Compiles U.S. Library of Congress MARC records for serial publications cataloged or processed by the Cooperative Online Serials Program (CONSER).

011.37   US
U.S. LIBRARY OF CONGRESS. CATALOGING FILES - VISUAL MATERIALS. (Retrospective cumulation avail.) 1972. every 4 wks. $1280 (outside N. America $1550) (effective 1996). U.S. Library of Congress, Cataloging Distribution Service, Customer Services Section, Washington, DC 20541-5017. TEL 202-707-6100; 800-255-3666. FAX 202-707-1334. E-mail: cdsinfo@mail.loc.gov. (processed) **Document type:** bibliography.
  Description: Compiles all U.S. Library of Congress MARC bibliographic records for motion pictures, video recordings, filmstrips, transparencies, slides, and nonprojectable graphics.

011 025.3   US   ISSN 0041-7912
Z696   CODEN: LCCCAH
U.S. LIBRARY OF CONGRESS. CLASSIFICATION - ADDITIONS AND CHANGES. 1928. q. $105 (outside N. America $115). U.S. Library of Congress, Cataloging Distribution Service, Customer Services Section, Washington, DC 20541-5017. TEL 202-707-6100; 800-255-3666. FAX 202-707-1334. E-mail: cdsinfo@mail.loc.gov. circ. 1,500. (back issues avail.) **Document type:** government publication.
—CASDDS.
  Description: Provides updates of schedules made to LC Classification Schedules. Notifies of new and changed class numbers that may soon appear on Library of Congress records.

011 025.3   US   ISSN 1058-5257
Z733.U58
U.S. LIBRARY OF CONGRESS. COMPLETE CATALOG OF BIBLIOGRAPHIC PRODUCTS AND SERVICES. a. free. U.S. Library of Congress, Cataloging Distribution Service, Customer Services Section, Washington, DC 20541-5017. TEL 202-707-6100; 800-255-3666. FAX 202-707-1334. E-mail: cdsinfo@mail.loc.gov. (Also avail. through: Superintendent of Documents, U.S. Government Printing Office, Box 371954, Pittsburgh, PA 15250-7954. TEL 202-512-1800. FAX 202-512-2250) **Document type:** government publication, catalog.
  Former titles (until 1991): Access C D S (ISSN 1058-5249); (until 1990): Library of Congress. Catalogs and Technical Publications (ISSN 0743-6181)
  Description: Provides lists and annotations of all Cataloging Distribution Service serials, books, and databases available.

011 025.3   US   ISSN 1052-1445
Z696.U4
U.S. LIBRARY OF CONGRESS. FREE - FLOATING SUBDIVISIONS: AN ALPHABETIC INDEX. 1989? a. (8th ed., 1996). $25 (outside N. America $30). U.S. Library of Congress, Cataloging Distribution Service, Customer Services Section, Washington, DC 20541-5017. TEL 202-707-6100; 800-255-3666. FAX 202-707-1334. E-mail: cdsinfo@mail.loc.gov. **Document type:** government publication, abstracting/indexing.
  Description: Lists US Library of Congress subject subdivisions assigned by the subject cataloger under designated subjects without the usage being established editorially and, therefore, without the usage appearing in the subject authority file under each individual subject heading.

BIBLIOGRAPHIES

016.780266   US   ISSN 1074-0414
U.S. LIBRARY OF CONGRESS. MUSIC CATALOG ON C D - R O M. (Not avail. in printed format) 1993. s-a. $170 (outside N. America $180). U.S. Library of Congress, Cataloging Distribution Service, Customer Services Section, Washington, DC 20541-5017. TEL 202-707-6100; 800-255-3666. FAX 202-707-1334. E-mail: cdsinfo@mail.loc.gov. **Document type:** government publication.
●Available only on CD-ROM.
  Description: Compiles more than 180,000 USMARC bibliographic records and 19 indexes for music recordings, scores, and librettos.

U.S. LIBRARY OF CONGRESS. MUSIC CATALOG ON MICROFICHE. see *MUSIC — Abstracting, Bibliographies, Statistics*

016.05   US   ISSN 0028-6680
Z6945.U5
U.S. LIBRARY OF CONGRESS. NEW SERIAL TITLES. (Supplement avail.: Union List of Serials, 3rd ed.) 1953. m. with q. and a. cumulations. $470 (outside N. America $530). U.S. Library of Congress, Cataloging Distribution Service, Customer Services Section, Washington, DC 20541-5017. TEL 202-707-6100; 800-255-3666. FAX 202-707-1334. E-mail: cdsinfo@mail.loc.gov. circ. 2,250. (back issues avail.) **Document type:** catalog, government publication.
●Also available on CD-ROM.
—BLDSC (6088.000000); CISTI; Linda Hall; UnCover. **CCC.**
  Supersedes: National Register of Microform Masters (ISSN 0090-3299)
  Description: Provides an authoritative source for serials bibliographic information in print today.

011.24927   US
U.S. LIBRARY OF CONGRESS. NON-ROMAN CATALOGING FILES - BOOKS. ARABIC. (Retrospective cumulation avail.) 1991. q. $4060 (outside N. America $4100) (effective 1996). U.S. Library of Congress, Cataloging Distribution Service, Customer Services Section, Washington, DC 20541-5017. TEL 202-707-6100; 800-255-3666. FAX 202-707-1334. E-mail: cdsinfo@mail.loc.gov. (processed) **Document type:** bibliography.
  Description: Compiles MARC records for Arabic- and Persian-language monographs cataloged by the US Library of Congress.

015.942 025.3   US
U.S. LIBRARY OF CONGRESS. NON-ROMAN CATALOGING FILES. HEBREW. (Retrospective cumulation avail.) 1989. q. $1050 (outside N. America $1185) (effective 1994-1996). U.S. Library of Congress, Cataloging and Distribution Service, Customer Services Section, Washington, DC 20541-5017. TEL 202-707-6100; 800-255-3666. FAX 202-707-1334. E-mail: cdsinfo@mail.loc.gov. (processed) **Document type:** bibliography.
  Description: Compiles MARC records for Hebrew- and Yiddish-language monographs cataloged by the US Library of Congress.

U.S. LIBRARY OF CONGRESS. PERIOD SUBDIVISIONS UNDER NAMES OF PLACES. (U.S. Library of Congress) see *LIBRARY AND INFORMATION SCIENCES*

016.328   US
U.S. LIBRARY OF CONGRESS. REFERENCE FILES - INDEX TO HISPANIC LEGISLATION. (Retrospective cumulation avail.) 1976. q. $3500 (outside N. America $3600) (effective 1996). U.S. Library of Congress, Cataloging Distribution Service, Customer Services Section, Washington, DC 20541-5017. TEL 202-707-6100; 800-255-3666. FAX 202-707-1334. E-mail: cdsinfo@mail.loc.gov. (processed) **Document type:** bibliography, abstracting/indexing.
  Description: Provides hard-to-find information on the legislation of countries studied by the US Library of Congress Hispanic Law Division Law Library.

011.31   US
U.S. LIBRARY OF CONGRESS. REFERENCE FILES - NATIONAL UNION CATALOG OF MANUSCRIPT COLLECTIONS. (Retrospective cumulation avail.) 1989. q. $1050 (outside N. America $1185) (effective 1996). U.S. Library of Congress, Cataloging Distribution Service, Customer Services Section, Washington, DC 20541-5017. TEL 202-707-6100; 800-255-3666. FAX 202-707-1334. E-mail: cdsinfo@mail.loc.gov. (processed) **Document type:** bibliography.
  Description: Compiles MARC records for collections of personal and family papers, business records, and other manuscripts of historical and research importance.

011.37 778.53   US
U.S. LIBRARY OF CONGRESS. REFERENCE FILES - NITRATE FILM. 1994. a. $4125 (outside N. America $4200) (effective 1996). U.S. Library of Congress, Cataloging Distribution Service, Customer Services Section, Washington, DC 20541-5017. TEL 202-707-6100; 800-255-3666. FAX 202-707-1334. E-mail: cdsinfo@mail.loc.gov. (processed) **Document type:** abstracting/indexing.
  Description: Contains MARC bibliographic records for historic film preservation.

011.295   US
U.S. LIBRARY OF CONGRESS. SERIALS C J K. (Chinese, Japanese, Korean) 1994. every 4 wks. $2040 (outside N. America $2070) (effective 1996). U.S. Library of Congress, Cataloging Distribution Service, Customer Services Section, Washington, DC 20541-5017. TEL 202-707-6100; 800-255-3666. FAX 202-707-1334. E-mail: cdsinfo@mail.loc.gov. (processed) **Document type:** bibliography.
  Description: Compiles MARC records for Chinese-, Japanese-, and Korean-language serial publications cataloged by the US Library of Congress and other Cooperative Online Serials Program participants.

025.3   US   ISSN 0361-5243
U.S. LIBRARY OF CONGRESS. SUBJECT HEADINGS CUMULATIVE MICROFORM EDITION. Key Title: Subject Headings in Microform. q. $100 (outside N. America $115). U.S. Library of Congress, Cataloging Distribution Service, Customer Services Section, Washington, DC 20541-5017. TEL 202-707-6100; 800-255-3666. FAX 202-707-1334. E-mail: cdsinfo@mail.loc.gov. (Subscr. also to: Superintendent of Documents, U.S. Government Printing Office, Box 317954, Pittsburgh, PA 15250-7954. TEL 202-512-1800. FAX 202-512-2250) (microform) **Document type:** government publication.
  Description: Provides a cumulation of the US Library of Congress subject heading classification.

U.S. NUCLEAR REGULATORY COMMISSION. TITLE LIST OF DOCUMENTS MADE PUBLICLY AVAILABLE. see *ENERGY — Abstracting, Bibliographies, Statistics*

011   US
UNITED STATES GOVERNMENT INFORMATION; publications - periodicals - electronic products. Short title: U.S. Government Information. s-a. free. U.S. Government Printing Office, Superintendent of Documents, Mail Stop: SM, Washington, DC 20402. (Orders to: Superintendent of Documents, U.S. Government Printing Office, Box 371954, Pittsburgh, PA 15250-7954. TEL 202-512-1800. FAX 202-512-2250) **Document type:** catalog, government publication.
  Description: Lists books, serial publications, and electronic products spanning all topics for sale from the U.S. government.

015   DR   ISSN 0041-8277
UNIVERSIDAD AUTONOMA DE SANTO DOMINGO. BIBLIOTECA CENTRAL. BOLETIN DE ADQUISICIONES.* 1969. bi-m. free. Universidad Autonoma de Santo Domingo, Biblioteca Central, Santo Domingo, Dominican Republic. bk.rev.; bibl.; circ. controlled.

015   EC
UNIVERSIDAD CENTRAL DEL ECUADOR. BIBLIOTECA GENERAL. BIBLIOGRAFIA ECUATORIANA. (The sixth issue of the year is a compilation) 1975. bi-m. Universidad Central del Ecuador, Biblioteca General, Apdo. 3291, Quito, Ecuador.

011   VE
UNIVERSIDAD DE LOS ANDES. INSTITUTO DE INVESTIGACIONES LITERARIAS. SERIE ENSAYO Y CRITICA LITERARIA.* 1981. irreg. free. Universidad de Los Andes, Instituto de Investigaciones Literarias, Via los Chorras de Milla, Merida 5101, Venezuela. circ. 500.
  Supersedes (1977-1978): Universidad de Los Andes. Instituto de Investigaciones Literarias. Serie Bibliografico; Which was formerly (1971-1977): Universidad de Los Andes. Centro de Investigaciones Literarias. Serie Bibliografico.

011   SP
UNIVERSIDAD DE NAVARRA. COLECCION BIBLIOGRAFIA. 1977. irreg. 11788 ptas. Ediciones Universidad de Navarra, S.A., Apdo. 396, 31080 Pamplona, Spain. TEL 94 825 6850.

011   SP
UNIVERSIDAD DE SEVILLA. SERIE: BIBLIOTECA UNIVERSITARIA. irreg., latest no.9. Universidad de Sevilla, Servicio de Publicaciones, Calle Porvenir 2, 41013 Seville, Spain. TEL 34-5-4231958. FAX 34-5-4232245.

011 370   SP
UNIVERSIDAD DE SEVILLA. SERIE: TESTIMONIO UNIVERSITARIO. irreg., latest no.5. Universidad de Sevilla, Servicio de Publicaciones, Calle Porvenir 27, 41013 Seville, Spain. TEL 34-5-4231958. FAX 34-5-4232245.

020 011   MX   ISSN 0006-1719
Z1007
UNIVERSIDAD NACIONAL AUTONOMA DE MEXICO. INSTITUTO DE INVESTIGACIONES BIBLIOGRAFICAS. BOLETIN. 1969. s-a. $80 (effective 1997). Universidad Nacional Autonoma de Mexico, Instituto de Investigaciones Bibliograficas, Ciudad Universitaria, Coyoacan, 04510 Mexico D.F., Mexico. TEL 52-5-6226807. FAX 52-5-6650951. E-mail: libros@biblional.bibliog.unam.mx. (Co-sponsor: Biblioteca Nacional) Ed. Jose G. Moreno de Alba. bibl.; illus. **Indexed:** Hisp.Amer.Per.Ind. (1969-1978).
  Supersedes: Biblioteca Nacional. Boletin.

010   MX   ISSN 0076-7468
UNIVERSIDAD NACIONAL AUTONOMA DE MEXICO. SEMINARIO DE INVESTIGACIONES BIBLIOTECOLOGICA. PUBLICACIONES. SERIE B. BIBLIOGRAFIA.* 1960. irreg., no.4, 1967. Universidad Nacional Autonoma de Mexico, Seminario de Investigaciones Bibliotecologicas, Ciudad Universitaria, 04510 Mexico D.F., Mexico. Ed. Dr. Alicia Perales de Mercado. circ. controlled.

UNIVERSIDADE DE SAO PAULO. DEPARTAMENTO DE SOCIOLOGIA. SERIE BIBLIOGRAFIA. see *SOCIOLOGY — Abstracting, Bibliographies, Statistics*

010   BL
UNIVERSIDADE DE SAO PAULO. FACULDADE DE ECONOMIA E ADMINISTRACAO. BIBLIOTECA. BOLETIM. 1965. irreg. exchange basis. Universidade de Sao Paulo, Faculdade de Economia e Administracao, Biblioteca, Cidade Universitaria Armando de Salles Oliveira, C.P. 11498, 01000 Sao Paulo, Brazil. bk.rev. circ. 250.
  Formerly: Universidade de Sao Paulo. Faculdade de Ciencias Economicas e Administrativas. Biblioteca. Boletim.

013   GW   ISSN 0080-5173
UNIVERSITAET DES SAARLANDES. JAHRESBIBLIOGRAPHIE. 1968. a. exchange basis. Universitaet des Saarlandes, Universitaetsbibliothek, 66123 Saarbruecken, Germany. TEL 49-681-3023010. FAX 49-681-3022796. E-mail: ubswk@rz.uni-sb.de; URL: http://www.uni-sb.de/z-einr/ub/uni-veroeff/jbpub.html. Ed. Wolfgang Kowalk. **Document type:** bibliography.
●Also available online.

011   GW
UNIVERSITAETSBIBLIOTHEK GIESSEN. HANDSCHRIFTENKATALOGE. (Text in German, Latin) 1979. irreg. Universitaetsbibliothek Giessen, Otto-Behaghel-Str. 8, 35394 Giessen, Germany. TEL 49-641-9914001. FAX 49-641-9914009. circ. 500. **Document type:** monographic series.

BIBLIOGRAPHIES

011.31 011.44 NO ISSN 0801-9908
UNIVERSITETSBIBLIOTEKET I TRONDHEIM. SPESIALSAMLINGENE. KATALOG. 1977. irreg. price varies (also exchange basis). Universitetsbiblioteket i Trondheim, Spesialsamlingene, N-7004 Trondheim, Norway. TEL 47-73-59-21-88. FAX 47-73-59-09-60. URL: http://www.ubt.ntnu.no/ubt/. Dir. Monica Aase. circ. 200. **Document type:** bibliography.
—KNAW.
 Formerly (until 1984): Universitetsbiblioteket i Trondheim. Avdeling B. Spesialsamlingene. Katalog (ISSN 0800-1375)

010 NZ ISSN 0067-0499
UNIVERSITY OF AUCKLAND LIBRARY. BIBLIOGRAPHICAL BULLETIN. 1964. irreg., no.19, 1993. exchange basis. University of Auckland Library, Serials Unit, Private Bag 92019, Auckland, New Zealand. TEL 64-9-3737999. FAX 64-9-3737401. E-mail: n.heinz@auckland.ac.nz. R&P contact: Neil Heinz. circ. 93. **Document type:** monographic series.

011 US
UNIVERSITY OF CALIFORNIA PUBLICATIONS IN CATALOGS & BIBLIOGRAPHIES. 1986. irreg., vol.11, 1994. price varies. University of California Press, 2120 Berkeley Way, Berkeley, CA 94720. TEL 510-642-4247. FAX 510-643-7127. (Orders to: California-Princeton Fulfillment Services, 1445 Lower Ferry Rd., Ewing, NJ 08618. TEL 800-777-4726. FAX 800-999-1958) (back issues avail.) **Document type:** bibliography.
 Description: Lists publications and catalogs available in the University of California libraries.

UNIVERSITY OF GUELPH LIBRARY. COLLECTION UPDATE. see *LIBRARY AND INFORMATION SCIENCES*

016 430 UK ISSN 0260-5929
Z5055.G69
UNIVERSITY OF LONDON. INSTITUTE OF GERMANIC STUDIES. RESEARCH IN GERMANIC STUDIES. 1968. a. price varies. University of London, Institute of Germanic Studies, 29 Russell Sq., London WC1B 5DP, England. TEL 44-171-580-2711. FAX 44-171-436-3497. E-mail: igs@sas.ac.uk. circ. 1,000. **Document type:** bibliography.
 Formerly (until 1981): University of London. Institute of Germanic Studies. Theses in Progress at British Universities (ISSN 0082-4127)
 Description: Bulletin of recently published work in German studies in British and Irish universities.

011 US
UNIVERSITY OF MAINE. COOPERATIVE EXTENSION. PUBLICATIONS CATALOG. a. free. University of Maine, Cooperative Extension, 5741 Libby Hall, Orono, ME 04469-5741. TEL 207-581-3185; 800-287-0274. FAX 207-581-1387. E-mail: mspencer@umce.umext.maine.edu; URL: http://www.umext.maine.edu. Ed. Melanie Spencer. R&P contact: Melanie Spencer. **Document type:** government publication, catalog.
 Description: Lists a wide variety of general-interest titles available to the public.

011 AT ISSN 0814-9704
UNIVERSITY OF NEW ENGLAND. LIBRARY PUBLICATIONS. a. University of New England, Dixson Library, Armidale, N.S.W. 2351, Australia. TEL 61-67-732165. FAX 61-67-733273. E-mail: kschmude@metz.une.edu.au.

996 FJ ISSN 1011-5129
UNIVERSITY OF THE SOUTH PACIFIC. PUBLICATIONS. 1981. a. F.$10. Pacific Information Centre, University of the South Pacific, G.P.O. Box 1168, Suva, Fiji. TEL 313900. E-mail: mamtora_j@usp.ac.fj. Ed. Jayshree Mamtora. **Document type:** bibliography.
 Description: Includes works written, published, authorized and sponsored by the University of the South Pacific or individuals associated with it.

011 SA
UNIVERSITY OF THE WITWATERSRAND, JOHANNESBURG. LIBRARY. BIBLIOGRAPHICAL SERIES. 1958. irreg. (unnumbered). University of the Witwatersrand, Johannesburg, Library, Private Bag XI, Wits 2050, South Africa. TEL 27-11-716-2330. FAX 27-11-403-1421. **Document type:** bibliography.

UNIVERSITY OF TORONTO. CENTRE OF CRIMINOLOGY LIBRARY. ACQUISITIONS LIST. see *CRIMINOLOGY AND LAW ENFORCEMENT — Abstracting, Bibliographies, Statistics*

UTANO - ZIMBABWE; an annotated health information bibliography. see *MEDICAL SCIENCES — Abstracting, Bibliographies, Statistics*

011 SW ISSN 0347-6820
UTLAENDSKA NYFOERVAERV TILL STOERRE SVENSKA FOLKBIBLIOTEK. 1948. q. (plus a. update). SEK 8625 (effective 1993). Bibliotekstjaenst AB, P.O. Box 200, S-221 00 Lund, Sweden. TEL 46-18-00-00. FAX 46-18-04-41. Ed. Diana Gerlach. circ. 150. **Document type:** bibliography.

011 GW
V V B - VERZEICHNIS VERGRIFFENER BUECHER C D - R O M. a. DM.490. Buchhaendler-Vereinigung GmbH, Postfach 100442, 60004 Frankfurt a.M., Germany. TEL 49-69-1306-0. FAX 49-69-1306201. E-mail: weber@bhv.de. (Dist. by: K.G. Saur Verlag KG, Ortlerstr. 8, 81373 Munich, Germany. TEL 49-89-76902-0. FAX 49-89-76901250) **Document type:** bibliography.
 ●Available only on CD-ROM.

016 SW ISSN 0042-2150
VAESTGOETALITTERATUR. 1963. a. SEK 100 (effective 1994). Foereningen foer Vaestgoetalitteratur, P.O. Box 325, 532 24 Skara, Sweden. Ed. W. Aengermark. bk.rev.; bibl.; illus. circ. 1,700.

VARIETY'S DIRECTORY OF MAJOR U S SHOW BUSINESS AWARDS. see *THEATER*

015 GW ISSN 0945-473X
Z317
VERLAGSAUSLIEFERUNGEN. 1994. a. DM.46 (effective 1997). Verlag der Schillerbuchhandlung Hans Banger, Guldenbachstr. 1, 50935 Cologne, Germany. TEL 49-221-431641. FAX 49-221-4303271. **Document type:** bibliography, directory.

015 GW ISSN 0944-3754
Z317
VERLAGSVERTRETUNGEN. 1993. a. DM.68 (effective 1997). Verlag der Schillerbuchhandlung Hans Banger, Guldenbachstr. 1, 50935 Cologne, Germany. TEL 49-221-431641. FAX 49-221-4303271. **Document type:** bibliography, directory.

011 800 SZ ISSN 1019-3537
VERZEICHNIS AUSLAENDISCHER ZEITSCHRIFTEN IN SCHWEIZERISCHEN BIBLIOTHEKEN/REPERTOIRE DES PERIODIQUES ETRANGERS RECUS PAR LES BIBLIOTHEQUES SUISSES/REPERTORIO DEI PERIODICI STRANIERI NELLE BIBLIOTECHE SVIZZERE. (Text in French, German, Italian) 1904. irreg. 600 SFr. Schweizerische Landesbibliothek - Bibliotheque Nationale Suisse, Hallwylstr. 15, CH-3003 Bern, Switzerland. TEL 41-31-3228911. FAX 41-31-3228463. E-mail: illizch@slb.admin.ch; URL: http://www.snl.ch/. **Document type:** bibliography.
 ●Also available online.
 Also available on CD-ROM.
 Formerly (until 1925): Zeitschriften-Verzeichnis der Schweizerischen Bibliotheken (ISSN 1421-3001)

015 GW ISSN 0067-8899
Z2221
VERZEICHNIS LIEFERBARER BUECHER/GERMAN BOOKS IN PRINT. Short title: V L B. (Consists of five sections: Authors-Titles-Catchword (in seven vols., 26th ed., 1996-97); ISBN Index to German Books in Print (in one vol., 26th ed., 1996-97); Subject Guide to German Books in Print (in six vols., 19th ed., 1996-97); Supplement (in one vol., 26th ed., 1997); ISBN Index to Supplement (in one vol., 26th ed., 1997)) 1971. a. DM.898 for Author-Title-Catchword; DM.468 for ISBN Index; DM.666 for Subject Guide; DM.226 for Supplement; DM.115 for ISBN Index to Supplement. (Buchhaendler-Vereinigung GmbH) K.G. Saur Verlag KG, A member of the Reed Elsevier plc group, Ortlerstr. 8, 81373 Munich, Germany. TEL 49-89-76902-0. FAX 49-89-76902150. E-mail: 100730.1341@compuserve.com; URL: http://www.reed-elsevier.com. (Subscr. to: Postfach 701620, 81316 Munich, Germany; N. America subscr. to: K.G. Saur, 121 Chanlon Rd., New Providence, NJ 07974. TEL 908-665-3576) index. **Document type:** bibliography, directory.
 ●Also available on CD-ROM. Producer(s): K.G. Saur Verlag.
 —BLDSC (9218.260000); CISTI; Linda Hall.
 Description: Lists every book available in the German language. Includes listings of series, publishers, and ISBNs.

015 GW
VERZEICHNIS LIEFERBARER BUECHER - C D - R O M/GERMAN BOOKS IN PRINT ON C D - R O M. (Supplement avail.: German Books Out of Print on C D - R O M) (Text in English, French, German) 12/yr. $1295. (Buchhaendler-Vereinigung GmbH) K.G. Saur Verlag KG, A member of the Reed Elsevier plc group, Ortlerstr. 8, 81373 Munich, Germany. TEL 49-89-76902-0. FAX 49-89-76901250. E-mail: 100730.1341@compuserve.com; URL: http://www.reed-elsevier.com. (N. America subscr. to: K.G. Saur, 121 Chanlon Rd., New Providence, NJ 07974-9903, USA. TEL 908-464-6800) (avail. for MS-DOS version) **Document type:** bibliography.
 ●Available only on CD-ROM. Producer(s): K.G. Saur Verlag.
 Description: Contains more than 600,000 books, audiocassettes, videos, software, and bibles found in the hardcopy edition of German Books in Print. Features the complete contents of L.I.B.R.I. (the database of wholesalers in Hamburg and Frankfurt) and S.B.Z. (the database of the Swiss Book Center).

VICTORIAN FICTION RESEARCH GUIDES. see *LITERATURE — Abstracting, Bibliographies, Statistics*

011 AT ISSN 0313-2463
VICTORIAN GOVERNMENT PUBLICATIONS. 1976. m. Aus.$50 (effective 1997). Government Publications Librarian, State Library of Victoria, 328 Swanston St., Melbourne, Vic. 3000, Australia. TEL 61-3-96699920. FAX 61-3-96631480. E-mail: dianneb@slv.vic.gov.au; URL: http://banyule.vicnet.net.au/vgb. Ed. Dianne Beaumont. adv.; circ. 70 (paid). (back issues avail) **Document type:** government publication.
 Description: Comprehensive record of Victorian government publishing from both state and local government sources.

015 US
VIRGINIA STATE DOCUMENTS. 1991. a. $5. Library of Virginia, 800 E. IBroad St., Richmond, VA 23219-1905. TEL 804-692-3999. FAX 804-692-3736. circ. 700. **Document type:** bibliography.
 Formed by the merger of (1926-1988): Check-List of Virginia State Publications (ISSN 0364-7293) & Virginia State Publications in Print (ISSN 0507-102X)
 Description: Comprehensive bibliography of all publications issued by Virginia state government agencies within a given year.

BIBLIOGRAPHIES

015   RU
VOLOGODSKAYA BIBLIOTEKA IM. BABUSHKINA. LITERATURA O VOLOGODSKOI OBLASTI. 1961. a. 2000 Rub. Vologodskaya Oblastnaya Universalnaya Nauchnaya Biblioteka, Otdel Kraevedcheskoi Bibliografii, Ul. Ul'yanovoi, 1, 160000 Vologda, Russia. TEL 7-8172-721103. FAX 7-8172-251769. E-mail: bibln@vcom.ru. E.A. Volkova. circ. 500. **Document type:** bibliography.
Description: Publishes brief annotated bibliographical list of books and articles from local and center press.

011   UK
WALFORD'S GUIDE TO REFERENCE MATERIAL. (In 3 vols.) 1959. triennial. price varies. Library Association Publishing Ltd., 7 Ridgmount St., London WC1E 7AE, England. TEL 44-171-636-7543. FAX 44-171-636-3627. TELEX 9312134504-LAG. (Dist. in U.S. by: Bernan Associates, 4611-F Assembly Dr., Lanham, MD 20706-4391. TEL 800-274-4447. FAX 800-865-3450) Ed. A.J. Walford. index. **Document type:** bibliography.
Formerly: Guide to Reference Material (ISSN 0072-8640)

011   US   ISSN 0083-7393
F192.5
WASHINGTON (YEAR); a comprehensive directory of the Nation's Capital, its people and institutions. 1966. a. $85. Columbia Books, Inc., 1212 New York Ave., N.W., Ste. 330, Washington, DC 20005. TEL 202-898-0662. FAX 202-898-0775. E-mail: cbibooks@worldnet.att.net; URL: http://www.d-net.com/columbia/. Ed. R. Wilson Hardy. index. (back issues avail.) **Document type:** directory.
—CISTI.
Formerly: Washington.
Description: Compilation of the 4,400 key public and private institutions in the Washington area and the 18,000 personnel who are responsible for directing them, broken down into 17 subject areas. Includes combined alphabetical index of organizations and individuals.

WELLCOME UNIT FOR THE HISTORY OF MEDICINE. RESEARCH PUBLICATIONS. see MEDICAL SCIENCES

015 029.7   CC   ISSN 1000-0437
AP95.C4
WENXIAN/DOCUMENTS. (Text in Chinese) 1979. q. Y13.80($31.20) (effective 1992). (Beijing Tushuguan - Beijing Library) Shumu Wenxian Chubanshe, c/o Branch of Beijing Library, 7 Wenjin Jie, Beijing 100802, People's Republic of China. TEL 601-6633-378. (Dist. outside China by: China International Book Trading Corp., P.O. Box 399, Beijing, P.R.C.; Dist. in US by: China Books & Periodicals, Inc., 2929 24th St., San Francisco, CA 94110) Ed. Chen Xianghua. circ. 6,000. **Indexed:** Amer.Hist.& Life (1990-), (1992-1993), Hist.Abstr. (1990-), (1992-1993). **Document type:** academic/scholarly publication.
Description: Covers documents and research results on ancient and contemporary Chinese literature and history from the collections of Beijing Library and other libraries at home and abroad.

010   US   ISSN 0512-4743
Z6945
WEST VIRGINIA UNION LIST OF SERIALS. 1962. a. $62. West Virginia University, Wise Library, Box 6069, Morgantown, WV 26506-6069. TEL 304-293-5395. FAX 304-293-6638. Ed. Mildred Moyers. **Document type:** bibliography.
Description: Computer-based listing of major serials for forty-five libraries in West Virginia as well as all of the West Virginia University libraries.

011   US   ISSN 1052-2212
PN3427
WHAT DO I READ NEXT? 1991. a. $82. Gale Research, 835 Penobscot Bldg., 645 Griswold St., Detroit, MI 48226-4094. TEL 313-961-2242; 800-877-4253. FAX 800-414-5043. E-mail: aniel_snyder@gale.com. Ed.Bd.
Description: Points out the similarities between various works of fiction to help readers make on-the-spot decisions about the fiction they want to read next.

WHAT WORKS: AN ANNOTATED BIBLIOGRAPHY OF CASE STUDIES OF SUSTAINABLE DEVELOPMENT. see ENVIRONMENTAL STUDIES — Abstracting, Bibliographies, Statistics

015   UK   ISSN 0953-0398
Z2001
WHITAKER'S BOOKS IN PRINT. 1874. a. £410($426) J. Whitaker & Sons Ltd., 12 Dyott St., London WC1A 1DF, England. TEL 44-171-420-6000. FAX 44-171-836-2909. (Dist. in US by: R.R. Bowker Co., A Reed Reference Publishing Company, 121 Chanlon Rd., Box 31, New Providence, NJ 07974-9903, USA. TEL 908-464-6800) (also avail. in microfiche) **Document type:** bibliography.
●Also available online. Vendor(s): Knight-Ridder Information, Inc. (File no.430).
Also available on CD-ROM. Producer(s): Bowker Electronic Publishing.
—BLDSC (9311.000580); CISTI; Linda Hall.
Formerly: British Books in Print (ISSN 0068-1350)
Description: Bibliographic guide to identify and order any of the more than 850,000 titles available from some 30,000 publishers and distributors in the UK. Books are listed in one alphabetical sequence of authors, titles, and subjects. Includes a publishers ISBN prefix listing, a directory of publishers, and a book trade bibliography.

WHO'S WHO AMONG AMERICA'S TEACHERS. see EDUCATION — Abstracting, Bibliographies, Statistics

016   UK   ISSN 0000-0213
Z6956.E5
WILLINGS PRESS GUIDE; a guide to the press of the United Kingdom and to the principal publications of Europe, the Americas, Australasia, Asia, Africa and the Middle East. (In 2 vols.: Vol.1 UK Edition; Vol.2 Overseas Edition) 1874. a. £179 (£136 for individual vols.) (effective 1997). Hollis Directories Ltd., Harlequin House, 7 High St., Teddington, Middlesex TW11 8EH, England.
TEL 44-181-977-7711. FAX 44-181-977-1133. E-mail: willings@hollis-pr.demon.co.uk; hollis@hollis-pr.demon.co.uk. Ed. Nesta Hollis. adv.: B&W page £800, color page £1750; 275 x 185. subject index. circ. 4,500. **Document type:** directory.
—BLDSC (9319.000000); Linda Hall.
Description: Information on publications in the UK and overseas. Includes information on publishers and services to the publishing industry.

016   US
WORDS ON CASSETTE (YEAR). Variant title: Books on Tape. 1985. a., 13th ed., 1998. $149.95 (effective 1998). R.R. Bowker, A Division of Reed Elsevier Inc., 121 Chanlon Rd., New Providence, NJ 07974. TEL 908-464-6800. FAX 908-665-6688. TELEX 138 755. E-mail: info@bowker.com; URL: http://www.bowker.com. (Subscr. to: Order Dept., Box 31, New Providence, NJ 07974-9903. TEL 800-521-8110) (also avail. in magnetic tape) **Document type:** bibliography, directory.
—CCC.
Incorporates (in 1992): On Cassette (ISSN 0000-1260); (1984-1992): Words on Tape (ISSN 8755-3759)
Description: Covers more than 60,000 audiocassettes, and features more than 6,000 new releases, with title, authors-readers-performers, and producer-distributor indexes.

WORK IN AMERICA INSTITUTE: HIGHLIGHTS OF THE LITERATURE. see BUSINESS AND ECONOMICS — Abstracting, Bibliographies, Statistics

WORLD BANK. PUBLICATIONS UPDATE. see BUSINESS AND ECONOMICS — International Development And Assistance

011   AT
WORLD BIBLIOGRAPHY OF BIBLIOGRAPHIES OF BIBLIOGRAPHIES. 1987. irreg. Noyce Publishing, G.P.O. Box 2222T, Melbourne, Vic. 3001, Australia. (back issues avail.)

WORLD GUIDE TO SCIENTIFIC ASSOCIATIONS AND LEARNED SOCIETIES. see SCIENCES: COMPREHENSIVE WORKS

WORLD GUIDE TO SPECIAL LIBRARIES. see LIBRARY AND INFORMATION SCIENCES

WORLD SURVEY OF ISLAMIC MANUSCRIPTS. see RELIGIONS AND THEOLOGY — Islamic

WRITERS DIRECTORY. see BUSINESS AND ECONOMICS — Trade And Industrial Directories

015.43 016.0531   GW   ISSN 0934-1897
Z D; Nachweis von Aufsaetzen aus 200 deutschen Zeitschriften. (Not avail. in print format) 1964. m. DM.70. Deutsches Bibliotheksinstitut, Abt. 1 - Publikationen, Alt-Moabit 101A, 10559 Berlin, Germany. TEL 49-30-39077-0. FAX 49-30-39077100. circ. 450. (microfiche; diskette format) **Document type:** abstracting/indexing.
●Also available on CD-ROM.
Formerly (until 1988): Zeitschriftendienst (ISSN 0417-2957)

Z G A BIBLIOGRAPHIC SERIES. (Zambia Geographical Association) see GEOGRAPHY — Abstracting, Bibliographies, Statistics

ZAMBIA. NATIONAL COUNCIL FOR SCIENTIFIC RESEARCH. N C S R BIBLIOGRAPHY. see SCIENCES: COMPREHENSIVE WORKS — Abstracting, Bibliographies, Statistics

015   PL   ISSN 0044-1813
ZAPOWIEDZI WYDAWNICZE. 1951. w. 2600 Zl. Panstwowe Przedsiebiorstwo "Skladnica Ksiegarska", Ul. Mazowiecka 9, Warsaw, Poland. (Dist. by: Ars Polona-Ruch, Krakowskie Przedmiescie 7, Warsaw, Poland) Ed. Krystyna Babska. bk.rev.; bibl. circ. 2,300. (processed)
Description: Contains announcements of books.

ZEITSCHRIFTENBIBLIOGRAPHIE GERONTOLOGIE. see GERONTOLOGY AND GERIATRICS — Abstracting, Bibliographies, Statistics

780 016   GW   ISSN 0044-3824
ML118
ZEITSCHRIFTENDIENST MUSIK. 1965. bi-m. DM.85. Deutsches Bibliotheksinstitut, Abt. 1 - Publikationen, Alt-Moabit 101A, 10559 Berlin, Germany. TEL 49-30-39077-0. FAX 49-30-39077100. circ. 200. (also avail. in microfiche) **Document type:** abstracting/indexing.

ZHONGGUO SHEHUI KEXUE WENXIAN TILU/CHINESE SOCIAL SCIENCE DOCUMENTATIONS INDEX. see SOCIAL SCIENCES: COMPREHENSIVE WORKS — Abstracting, Bibliographies, Statistics

015   RH
ZIMBABWE NATIONAL BIBLIOGRAPHY. 1961. a. Z.$40. National Archives, Private Bag 7729, Causeway, Harare, Zimbabwe. Eds. Bertha Mugwise, D. Sbanda. index. circ. 400. **Document type:** government publication, bibliography.
Former titles (until 1978): Rhodesia National Bibliography (ISSN 0085-5677); (until 1966): Publications Deposited in the National Archives.

015   RH
ZIMBABWEAN PERIODICALS; a bibliographical. 1988. irreg. Z.$30. National Archives, Private Bag 7729, Causeway, Harare, Zimbabwe. Ed. Bertha Mugwise. **Document type:** bibliography, government publication.

016.05   GW
ZIMPEL. TEIL 2: PUBLIKUMSZEITSCHRIFTEN. base vol. (plus m. updates). DM.380 for base vol. (DM.610 with m. updates) (effective 1996). Verlag Dieter Zimpel, Angererstr. 36, 80796 Munich, Germany. TEL 49-89-3073445. FAX 49-89-302409. Ed. Ingrid Finsterwald. **Document type:** directory.
Former titles: Zimpel. Teil 2: Zeitschriften (ISSN 0179-7638); (until 1986): Deutschen Vollredaktionen. Teil 2. Zeitschriften (ISSN 0173-1041)

ZIONIST LITERATURE. see PUBLISHING AND BOOK TRADE — Abstracting, Bibliographies, Statistics

BICYCLES AND MOTORCYCLES

see Sports and Games—Bicycles and Motorcycles

BIOENGINEERING

see Biology—Bioengineering

BIOGRAPHY

920 US ISSN 0898-9575
CT25
A - B: AUTO - BIOGRAPHY STUDIES. 1986. s-a. $15 to individuals; institutions $30 (effective 1997). University of Kansas, Joyce & Elizabeth Hall Center for the Humanities, Lawrence, KS 66045-2967. TEL 913-864-4798. FAX 913-864-3884. E-mail: autobiog@kuhub.cc.ukans.edu; hallentr@kansas.edu; URL: http://www.kansas.edu/~hallcntr/. Eds. Rebecca & Joseph Hogan. adv. contact: Lori Askeland. bk.rev.; bibl.; cum.index: 1985-1996. **Document type:** academic/scholarly publication.
—BLDSC (0537.005900); KR SourceOne; UnCover.
Description: Devoted to autobiography, biography, diaries, letters and relations between lifewriting and other discourse.
Refereed Serial

A B M S MEDICAL SPECIALIST PLUS. see *MEDICAL SCIENCES*

920 FR
A LA PREMIERE PERSONNE.* 1980. irreg. price varies. Editions Syros, 9 bis, rue Abel-Lovelacque, 75013 Paris, France.

A P S A BIOGRAPHICAL DIRECTORY. (American Political Science Association) see *POLITICAL SCIENCE*

A S C A P BIOGRAPHICAL DICTIONARY. (American Society of Composers, Authors and Publishers) see *MUSIC*

920 BE ISSN 0065-0609
ACADEMIE ROYALE DES SCIENCES, DES LETTRES ET DES BEAUX ARTS DE BELGIQUE. INDEX BIOGRAPHIQUE DES MEMBRES, CORRESPONDANTS ET ASSOCIES. 1948. irreg., 3rd ed., 1984. 500 BEF. Academie Royale des Sciences, des Lettres et des Beaux-Arts de Belgique, Palais des Academies, 1 rue Ducale, 1000 Brussels, Belgium. (Subscr. to: Altera Diffusion, rue Rodenbach 98, 1190 Brussels, Belgium) circ. 350. **Document type:** directory.

AFRICAN-AMERICAN BIOGRAPHIES. see *CHILDREN AND YOUTH — For*

920 US ISSN 1040-127X
CT104
ALMANAC OF FAMOUS PEOPLE; a comprehensive reference guide to more than 30,000 famous and infamous newsmakers from biblical times to the present. 1981. irreg. 6th ed., 1998. $115 for 2 vol. set. Gale Research, 835 Penobscot Bldg., 645 Griswold St., Detroit, MI 48226-4094. TEL 313-961-2242; 800-877-4253. FAX 800-414-5043. E-mail: daniel_snyder@gale.com. Ed. Frank V. Castronova.
•Also available online. Vendor(s): Lexis-Nexis.
Formerly: Biography Almanac (ISSN 0738-0097)
Description: Brief biographical data with citations to over 30,000 biographical sketches appearing in over 960 sources.

ALMANACH DU PEUPLE. see *ENCYCLOPEDIAS AND GENERAL ALMANACS*

509.2 US ISSN 0000-1287
Q141
AMERICAN MEN AND WOMEN OF SCIENCE; a biographical directory of today's leaders in physical, biological and related sciences. (In 8 vols.) 1906. triennial, 20th ed., 1997. $900 (effective 1998). R.R. Bowker, A Division of Reed Elsevier Inc., 121 Chanlon Rd., New Providence, NJ 07974. TEL 908-464-6800. FAX 908-665-6688. TELEX 138 755. E-mail: info@bowker.com; URL: http://www.reedref.com. (Subscr. to: Order Dept., Box 31, New Providence, NJ 07974-9903. TEL 888-269-5372) (also avail. in magnetic tape) **Indexed:** Child.Auth.& Illus. **Document type:** directory.
•Also available online. Vendor(s): Knight-Ridder Information, Inc. (File no.236).
Also available on CD-ROM. Producer(s): Bowker Electronic Publishing.
—CISTI. CCC.
Former titles (until 1990): American Men and Women of Science. The Physical and Biological Sciences (ISSN 0192-8570); Which supersedes in part (in 1971): American Men of Science (ISSN 0192-7647)
Description: Capsule biographies of prominent Americans and Canadians, including birthplace and date, scientific field, education, experience, research focus and mailing address. Includes an index by discipline and geographic location.

150 920 US ISSN 0196-6545
BF11
AMERICAN PSYCHOLOGICAL ASSOCIATION. DIRECTORY. 1916. quadrennial. $70 to non-members; members $50 (effective 1997). American Psychological Association, 750 First St., N.E., Washington, DC 20002. TEL 202-336-5500. FAX 202-336-5502. Ed. John A. Lazo. circ. 8,000. **Document type:** directory.
Formerly: American Psychological Association. Biographical Directory (ISSN 0090-9076)

AMIS DE RAMUZ. BULLETIN. see *LITERATURE*

920 FR
ANNUAIRE MONDIAL DES CORSES. biennial. 350 F. Association Mondiale des Corses, 100 rue Saint-Lazare, 75009 Paris, France.
TEL 45-26-61-54. Ed. X. Moreschi. adv.; illus.
Description: Presents data and photos of a wide range of prominent Corsicans.

ARGENTINA. DEPARTAMENTO DE ESTUDIOS HISTORICOS NAVALES. SERIE C: BIOGRAFIAS NAVALES ARGENTINAS. see *MILITARY*

AUSTIN GENEALOGICAL SOCIETY QUARTERLY. see *GENEALOGY AND HERALDRY*

AUSTRALIAN ART AUCTION RECORDS. see *ART*

AUSTRALIAN CHURCHES OF CHRIST HISTORICAL SOCIETY. DIGEST. see *HISTORY — History Of Australasia And Other Areas*

AUSTRALIAN DIRECTORY OF ACADEMICS; who's who in Australian universities. see *EDUCATION — Higher Education*

920 AT
AUSTRALIAN MEN AND WOMEN OF SCIENCE, ENGINEERING AND TECHNOLOGY. irreg., 12th ed., 1995. £95. (Australian Academy of Science) D.W. Thorpe, A member of the Reed Elsevier plc group, 18 Salmon St., Port Melbourne, Vic. 3207, Australia. TEL 61-3-92457370. FAX 61-3-92457395. E-mail: customer.service@thorpe.com.au; URL: http://www.reed-elsevier.com. (Co-sponsor: Australian Academy of Technological Sciences and Engineering) pp./issue: 396.
Description: Biographical directory profiles 3,500 living scientists and engineers at work in Australia and overseas.

AUSTRALIAN PLAYWRIGHTS; a series of monographs and video programmes. see *LITERATURE*

920 US ISSN 0741-8655
Z5304.A8
AUTHOR BIOGRAPHIES MASTER INDEX. 1978. irreg., 5th ed., 1997. $260. Gale Research, 835 Penobscot Bldg., 645 Griswold St., Detroit, MI 48226-4094. TEL 800-877-4253. FAX 800-414-5043. E-mail: geri_speace@gale.com. Ed. Geri Speace.
Description: Indexes biographies of literary figures.

920 301 UK ISSN 0967-5507
AUTO-BIOGRAPHY. 1992. s-a. £20 membership. British Sociological Association Study Group on Auto-Biography, c/o Michael Erben, University of Southampton, School of Education, Southampton SO17 1BJ, England. TEL 44-161-275-2496. FAX 44-1703-593939. Ed. Lizbeth Stanley. R&P contact: Michael Erben. TEL 44-1703-595000. adv. contact: Michael Erben. bk.rev. **Document type:** academic/scholarly publication.
Description: Provides scholarly discussion of biography and autobiography.
Refereed Serial

920 GW
BADEN-WUERTTEMBERGISCHE BIOGRAPHIEN. 1994. irreg. DM.48. Kommission fuer Geschichtliche Landeskunde in Baden-Wuerttemberg, Eugenstr. 7, 70182 Stuttgart, Germany. Ed. Bernd Ottnad. circ. 800. **Document type:** bulletin.
Description: Short biographies of people connected with the state of Baden-Wuerttemberg who died after 1952.

BEAN HOME NEWSLETTER. see *LITERATURE*

BELCHER BULLETIN. see *GENEALOGY AND HERALDRY*

920 XO ISSN 0067-8724
BIOGRAFICKE STUDIE. (Text in Slovak; summaries in German, occasionally in English, Russian) 1970. a. price varies. Matica Slovenska, Slovenska Narodna Kniznica, Biograficky Ustav, Ul. L. Novomesheho 32, 036 52 Martin, Slovakia. TEL 42-842-38706. FAX 42-842-32454. Ed. Augustin Matovcik. bk.rev. **Document type:** proceedings.

920 IT
BIOGRAFIE. 1994. irreg., no.2, 1996. price varies. Liguori Editore s.r.l., Via Posillipo 394, 80123 Naples, Italy. TEL 39-81-7206111. FAX 39-81-7206244. Pub. Guido Liguori. adv. contact: Maria Liguori. **Document type:** monographic series.

920 GW
BIOGRAPHICAL DICTIONARY OF THE FORMER SOVIET UNION. irreg., 2nd ed., 1992. $275. K.G. Saur Verlag KG, A member of the Reed Elsevier plc group, Ortlerstr. 8, 81373 Munich, Germany. TEL 49-89-769020. FAX 49-89-76902150. E-mail: 100730.1341@compuserve.com; URL: http://www.reed-elsevier.com. (U.S. subscr. to: K.G. Saur, 121 Chanlon Rd., New Providence, NJ 07974-9903. TEL 908-665-3576) Eds. Vladimir Chuguev, Jeanne Vronskaya. **Document type:** monographic series.
Formerly: Biographical Dictionary of the Soviet Union.
Description: Profiles 6500 figures who shaped Soviet history. Includes index by profession.

920 US ISSN 0162-4962
CT100 CODEN: BGPYE2
BIOGRAPHY (HONOLULU); an interdisciplinary quarterly. 1978. q. $28 to individuals (foreign $36); institutions $36 (foreign $48). (Biographical Research Center) University of Hawaii Press, Journals Department, 2840 Kolowalu St., Honolulu, HI 96822. TEL 808-956-8833.
FAX 808-988-6052. E-mail: uphjourn@hawaii.edu; biograph@hawaii.edu; URL: http://www2.hawaii.edu/uhpress/journals/bi/bihome.html. Ed. Craig Howes. R&P contact: K. Leber. TEL 808-956-8834. adv. contact: Ann Ludeman. bk.rev.; abstr.; bibl.; index, cum.index. circ. 450. (back issues avail.; reprint service avail. from UMI,ISI) **Indexed:** Amer.Hist.& Life (1978-), Arts & Hum.Cit.Ind., ASCA, Bk.Rev.Ind. (1981-), Child.Bk.Rev.Ind. (1981-), Curr.Cont., G.Soc.Sci.& Rel.Per.Lit., Hist.Abstr. (1978-), Ind.Bk.Rev.Hum., M.L.A., MLA Intl.Bibl., SSCI. **Document type:** academic/scholarly publication.
—BLDSC (2072.329000); Genuine Article; KR SourceOne; SWETS; UMI; UnCover.
Description: Focuses on life-writing and biographical theory.
Refereed Serial

BIOGRAPHY

920 US ISSN 1081-4973
CT107
BIOGRAPHY FOR BEGINNERS. 2/yr. $40. Omnigraphics, Inc., 2500 Penobscot Bldg., Detroit, MI 48226. TEL 313-961-1383; 800-234-1340. FAX 313-961-1340. Ed. Laurie Lanzen Harris; Pub. Frederick G. Ruffner, Jr. R&P contact: Laurie Lanzen Harris. illus.; index. circ. 1,500.
    Description: Includes 15 biographies of notable world figures, authors, artists, cartoonists, TV and film stars and sports stars. For ages 6-9.

920 US ISSN 1058-2347
CT107
BIOGRAPHY TODAY; profiles of people of interest to young readers. 1992. 3/yr. $49 (effective 1997). Omnigraphics, Inc., 2500 Penobscot Bldg., Detroit, MI 48226. TEL 313-961-1340; 800-234-1340. FAX 313-961-1340. Ed. Laurie Lanzen Harris; Pub. Frederick G. Ruffner, Jr. R&P contact: Laurie Lanzen Harris. illus.; index. circ. 2,500.
    —KR SourceOne.
    Description: Each issue contains 15-20 biographies of persons of interest to young readers, with the individual's full name and birth date, and a narrative sketch highlighting information on birth, growing up, education, family, career highlights, honors and awards. For ages 9 and up.

920 GW ISSN 0933-5315
CT21
BIOS; Zeitschrift fuer Biographieforschung und Oral History. 1988. 2/yr. DM.72.50 (foreign DM.75) (effective 1997). Verlag Leske und Budrich GmbH, Postfach 300551, 51334 Leverkusen, Germany. TEL 49-2171-2079. FAX 49-2171-41209.
    Document type: academic/scholarly publication.
    —KR SourceOne.

920 UK
BIRMINGHAM POST AND MAIL YEAR BOOK AND WHO'S WHO. 1949. a. £30. Kingslea Press Ltd., 137 Newhall St., Birmingham B3 1SF, England. TEL 44-121-236-8112. FAX 44-121-200-1480. adv. circ. 1,700. **Document type:** directory.
    Former titles: Birmingham Post Year Book and Who's Who; Birmingham Post and Mail Year Book and Who's Who; (until 1985): Birmingham Post Year Book and Who's Who.

920 910.03 US ISSN 1060-9148
BLACK AUTHORS & PUBLISHED WRITERS DIRECTORY. (Supplement avail.: Black Literary Players Newsletter) 1993. a. $49.95 (effective 1997). Grace Publishing Co., 829 Langdon Ct., Rochester, MI 48307-2921. TEL 248-556-7335. Ed. Grace Adams. adv. **Document type:** directory.
    Description: For free-lance writers, established authors, and groups interested in Black talent, Black literature, marketplace. Includes profiles of writers, authors, agents, print and broadcast media and libraries.

920 910.03 US ISSN 1066-9396
BLACK LITERARY PLAYERS. (Supplement to: Black Authors and Published Writers Directory) 1993. m. $36 (effective 1997). Grace Publishing Co., 829 Langdon Ct., Rochester, MN 48307-2921. TEL 248-556-7335. Ed. Grace Adams. adv.; B&W page $225. bk.rev.; circ. 1,400 (paid). (back issues avail.) **Document type:** newsletter.
    Description: Contains Black publishing and entertainment industry news, reviews and subscriber views.

920 US ISSN 1040-7405
BOOTBLACK; the Horatio Alger magazine. 1989. 7/yr. $35. 1001 S.W. 5th Court, Boynton Beach, FL 33426. TEL 407-736-2340. bk.rev.

920 800 US ISSN 0743-9628
BORGO BIOVIEWS. 1983. irreg., no.9, 1997 (approx. 4/yr.). price varies. Borgo Press, Box 2845, San Bernardino, CA 92406. TEL 909-884-5813. FAX 909-888-4942. E-mail: borgopr@gte.net; URL: http://www.borgopress.com. Pub. Robert Reginald.
    Description: Biographies and autobiographies of prominent men and women of our time.

920 FR
BOTTIN MONDAIN; Tout Paris-Toute la France. 1903. a. $100. Societe Bottin Mondain, 15 Place de la Madeleine, 75008 Paris, France. TEL 33-1-44511313. FAX 33-1-42666901. Ed. Blanche de Kersaint; Pub. Antoine Roche de la Rigodiere. adv. contact: Mrs. Acker. **Document type:** directory.

BUILDERS OF INDIAN ANTHROPOLOGY. see SOCIAL SCIENCES: COMPREHENSIVE WORKS

920 CN ISSN 1189-4709
JL111.E93
CANADIAN FEDERAL GOVERNMENT HANDBOOK. 1985. a. Can.$59.95. Globe Information Services, 444 Front St. W., Toronto, ON M5V 2S9, Canada. TEL 416-585-5250. FAX 416-585-5249. Ed. Mary Ferguson.
    ● Also available online.
    —CISTI.
    Formerly (until 1992): Ottawa's Senior Executives Guide (ISSN 0826-8355).
    Description: Authoritative handbook providing comprehensive information on the Canadian Federal Government.

CANADIAN PLAINS REFERENCE WORKS. see SCIENCES: COMPREHENSIVE WORKS

920 CN ISSN 0068-9963
CANADIAN WHO'S WHO. 1910. a. Can.$160. University of Toronto Press, Directories Departement, 10 St. Mary St., Ste. 700, Toronto, ON M3H 5T8, Canada. TEL 416-978-2239. FAX 416-978-4738. E-mail: utpbooks@gpu.utcc.utoronto.ca. (US addr.: 340 Nagel Dr., Cheektowaga, NY 14225) Ed. Kieran Simpson. circ. 5,000. **Indexed:** Child.Auth.& Illus. **Document type:** directory.
    ● Also available online.
    —CISTI. CCC.
    Formerly: Who's Who, The Canadian.

920 800 US ISSN 1074-2670
PR4432
CARLYLE STUDIES ANNUAL; essays on Thomas and Jane Carlyle and their circle. 1979. a. $15 (effective 1997). c/o Rodger L. Tarr, Ed., Department of English, Illinois State University, Normal, IL 61790. R&P contact: Rodger L. Tarr. circ. 250. (back issues avail.) **Indexed:** M.L.A. **Document type:** academic/scholarly publication.
    —UnCover.
    Former titles (until 1993): Carlyle Annual (ISSN 1050-3099); (until 1989): Carlyle Newsletter (ISSN 0269-8226)

CARPATHO-RUSYN AMERICAN. see ETHNIC INTERESTS

CATALOGUE OF PUBLICATIONS BY AARDVARK ENTREPRISES. see LITERATURE

920 UK ISSN 0045-6020
CELEBRITY BULLETIN. 1952. s-w. £720. Celebrity Service Ltd., 93-97 Regent St., London W1R 7TA, England. TEL 44-171-439-9840. FAX 44-171-494-3500. Ed. Diane F. Oliver. **Document type:** bulletin.

920 US
CENTRUM JANA PAWLA II BIULETYN. English edition: Pope John Paul II Center Newsletter. (Text in Polish) 1979. 5/yr. $5. Pope John Paul II Center, Orchard Lake Schools, Orchard Lake, MI 48324. TEL 313-683-0408. Ed. Rev. Roman Nir. bk.rev. circ. 328. (back issues avail.) **Document type:** newsletter.
    Description: Biographical information, memoirs, publications and activities.

CHEMISTS AND CHEMISTRY. see CHEMISTRY

920 IT
CHI,SONO.* bi-m. L.15000. Gruppo Editoriale Suono s.r.l., Via Capo Peloro, 30, 00141 Rome, Italy. TEL 893608. circ. 60,000.

CHINA DIRECTORY (YEAR)/ZHONGGUO ZUZHIBIE RENMINGBU/CHUGOKU SOSHIKIBETSU JINMEIBO. see POLITICAL SCIENCE — International Relations

CHIROPRACTIC HISTORY. see MEDICAL SCIENCES — Chiropractic, Homeopathy, Osteopathy

920 VE ISSN 0069-5033
COLECCION "ANIVERSARIOS CULTURALES". 1965. irreg., no.4, 1968. Universidad Central de Venezuela, Direccion de Cultura, Biblioteca, Piso 10, Ciudad Universitaria, Caracas, Venezuela.

COLLECTION MONOGRAPHIQUE RODOPI EN LITTERATURE FRANCAISE CONTEMPORAINE. see LITERATURE

COLLECTIVE BIOGRAPHIES. see CHILDREN AND YOUTH — For

920 US
THE COMPLETE MARQUIS WHO'S WHO ON C D - R O M. a. (plus s-a. updates). £995. Marquis Who's Who, A Division of Reed Elsevier Inc., 121 Chanlon Rd., New Providence, NJ 07974. TEL 908-464-6800; 800-621-9669. FAX 908-665-6688. E-mail: info@reedref.com; URL: http://www.reedref.com. (avail. for Windows and Macintosh)
    Description: Includes all the entries from the renowned Who's Who in America, and Who's Who in the World, as well as 16 other Marquis print volumes, covering the whole range of human endeavour and achievement - from the arts to business, from government to religion, and law to science.

COMPOSERS OF THE AMERICAS/COMPOSITORES DE AMERICA. see MUSIC

CONFLUENCE (WENATCHEE). see MUSEUMS AND ART GALLERIES

CONGRESSIONAL YELLOW BOOK; who's who in Congress, including committees and key staff. see PUBLIC ADMINISTRATION

CONSORTIUM ON REVOLUTIONARY EUROPE. SELECTED PAPERS. see HISTORY — History Of Europe

928 US ISSN 0010-7468
Z1224
CONTEMPORARY AUTHORS. 1962. irreg., vol.134, 1991. $108. Gale Research, 835 Penobscot Bldg., 645 Griswold St., Detroit, MI 48226-4094. TEL 313-961-2242; 800-877-4253. FAX 800-441-5043. E-mail: daniel_snyder@gale.com. Ed. Hal May. bibl.; cum.index. **Indexed:** Child.Auth.& Illus. **Document type:** academic/scholarly publication.
    —CISTI.
    Description: Biographies and descriptions of contemporary authors.

928 US ISSN 0748-0636
PN453
CONTEMPORARY AUTHORS AUTOBIOGRAPHY SERIES. 1984. a. $108. Gale Research, 835 Penobscot Bldg., 645 Griswold St., Detroit, MI 48226-4094. TEL 313-961-2242; 800-877-4253. FAX 800-414-5043. E-mail: daniel_snyder@gale.com. Ed. Joyce Nakamura. circ. 1,500. (back issues avail.) **Document type:** academic/scholarly publication.
    Description: Self-descriptions of contemporary authors.

920 910.03 US ISSN 1058-1316
E185.96
CONTEMPORARY BLACK BIOGRAPHY. 1991. s-a. $39.95 per no. Gale Research, 835 Penobscot Bldg., 645 Griswold St., Detroit, MI 48266-4094. TEL 313-961-2242; 800-877-4253. FAX 800-414-5043. E-mail: daniel_snyder@gale.com. Ed. Michael L. LaBlanc.
    Description: Provides about 70 biographical entries per volume about prominent black individuals.

920 686.2 US ISSN 0885-8462
NC999.2
CONTEMPORARY GRAPHIC ARTISTS; a biographical, bibliographical, and critical guide to current illustrators, animators, cartoonists, designers, and other graphic artists. irreg., vol.3, 1988. $108 per vol. Gale Research, 835 Penobscot Bldg., 645 Griswold St., Detroit, MI 48226-2094. TEL 313-961-2242; 800-877-4253. FAX 800-414-5043. E-mail: daniel_snyder@gale.com. Ed. Maurice Horn.
    Description: Biographies and bibliographies of commercial artists.

CONTEMPORARY MUSICIANS. see MUSIC

927 US ISSN 0749-064X
PN2285
CONTEMPORARY THEATRE, FILM & TELEVISION. 1984. irreg., vol.10, 1992. $115. Gale Research, 835 Penobscot Bldg., 645 Griswold St., Detroit, MI 48226-4094. TEL 313-961-2242; 800-877-4253. FAX 800-414-5043. E-mail: daniel__snyder@gale.com. (Subscr. to: Box 33477, Detriot, MI 48232-5477) Ed. Emily J. McMurray. cum.index. (back issues avail.) **Indexed:** Child.Auth.& Illus., Perf.Arts Biog.Master Ind. **Document type:** directory.
—BLDSC (3425.307700).
Incorporating (1912-1981): Who's Who in the Theatre (ISSN 0083-9833)
Description: Biographies of workers in theatre, film and television industries.

CONTEMPORARY WOMEN. see *CHILDREN AND YOUTH — For*

COOPER SOCIETY NEWSLETTER. see *LITERATURE*

930.1 US ISSN 0361-4735
CC110
CURRENT BIOGRAPHIES OF LEADING ARCHAEOLOGISTS. 1975. irreg. $7.95. Institute for Human History, Box 648, Gloucester, VA 22061-0648. TEL 804-642-2851. Ed. Christine W. Dragoo. **Document type:** monographic series.

920 US ISSN 0011-3344
CT100
CURRENT BIOGRAPHY. 1940. m. (except Dec.). $69. H.W. Wilson Co., 950 University Ave., Bronx, NY 10452. TEL 718-588-8400; 800-367-6770. FAX 718-590-1617. TELEX 4990003 HWILSON. E-mail: cbmail.wlb.hwilson.com; URL: http://www.hwilson.com/curbio.html. Ed. J. Graham. bibl.; index, cum.index 1940-1995. **Indexed:** Acad.Ind., DAAI, Ind.Per.Art.Relat.Law, Lib.Lit., Mag.Ind., TOM.
—CISTI; KR SourceOne.

920 US ISSN 0084-9499
CT100
CURRENT BIOGRAPHY YEARBOOK. 1940. a. $69. H.W. Wilson Co., 950 University Ave., Bronx, NY 10452. TEL 718-588-8400; 800-367-6770. FAX 718-590-1716. TELEX 4990003HWILSON. Ed. J. Graham. bibl.; index, cum.index: 1940-1995. **Indexed:** Amer.Bibl.Slavic & E.Eur.Stud., Child.Auth.& Illus.
●Also available on CD-ROM. Producer(s): H.W. Wilson (WILSONDISC).
—CISTI.

929.72 UK ISSN 1356-7802
CT770
DEBRETT'S PEOPLE OF TODAY. Key Title: People of Today. 1982. a. £100 (foreign £113)(CD-ROM edition £129) (effective 1997). Debrett's Peerage Ltd., 73-77 Britannia Rd., P.O. Box 357, Fulham, London SW6 2JY, England. TEL 44-171-736-6524. FAX 44-171-731-7768. E-mail: people@debretts.co.uk; URL: http://www.debrett's.co.uk. Ed. Jonathan Parker. **Document type:** directory.
Former titles (until 1991): Debrett's Distinguished People of Today (ISSN 0957-0284); (until 1988): Debrett's Handbook (ISSN 0264-2581)

920 GW ISSN 0341-6771
DEIKE GEDENKTAGE. 1923. m. 45 SFr. Verlag Horst Deike KG, Postfach 100452, 78404 Konstanz, Germany. TEL 07531-8155-0. FAX 07531-815581. **Document type:** bulletin.
—CCC.

DEPUTADOS BRASILEIROS: REPERTORIO BIOGRAFICO. see *PUBLIC ADMINISTRATION*

920 CN ISSN 0070-4717
F1005
DICTIONARY OF CANADIAN BIOGRAPHY. 1966. irreg. University of Toronto Press, Directories Departement, 10 St. Mary St., Ste. 700, Toronto, ON M4Y 2W8, Canada. TEL 416-978-2239. FAX 416-978-4738. (U.S. addr.: 340 Nagel Dr., Cheektowaga, NY 14225) Ed. Ramsay Cook. **Document type:** academic/scholarly publication.

DICTIONARY OF CONTEMPORARY AMERICAN ARTISTS. see *ART*

920 UK ISSN 0419-1137
CT101
DICTIONARY OF INTERNATIONAL BIOGRAPHY. 1963. a. £115($195) Melrose Press Ltd., 3 Regal Ln., Soham, Ely, Cambridgeshire CB7 5BA, England. TEL 44-1353-721091. FAX 44-1353-721839. (Dist. in US by: Taylor & Francis Inc., 1900 Frost Rd., Ste. 101, Bristol, PA 19007-1598) Ed. Jocelyn Timothy; Pub. Nicholas Law. adv. contact: Jean Pearson. **Document type:** directory.
—BLDSC (3580.295000); CISTI.
Description: Contains approximately 5,000 biographical entries of leaders in all fields.

920 800 US
DICTIONARY OF LITERARY BIOGRAPHY. 1978. irreg., vol.99, 1990. $112. Gale Research, 835 Penobscot Bldg., 645 Griswold St., Detroit, MI 48226-4094. TEL 313-961-2242; 800-977-4253. FAX 800-414-5043. E-mail: daniel__snyder@gale.com. Eds. Matthew J. Bruccoli, Richard Layman. **Indexed:** Child.Auth.& Illus., M.L.A., MLA Intl.Bibl., Perf.Arts Biog.Master Ind.
Description: Reference on works of literary biography.

920 800 US
DICTIONARY OF LITERARY BIOGRAPHY: DOCUMENTARY SERIES. irreg., vol.8, 1991. $108. Gale Research, 835 Penobscot Bldg., 645 Griswold St., Detroit, MI 48266-4094. TEL 313-961-2242; 800-877-4253. FAX 800-414-5043. E-mail: daniel__snyder@gale.com.
Description: Concentrates on the major figures of a particular literary period, movement or genre in each volume.

920 800 US ISSN 0731-7867
PS221
DICTIONARY OF LITERARY BIOGRAPHY YEARBOOK. 1981. a. $112. Gale Research, 835 Penobscot Bldg., 645 Griswold St., Detroit, MI 48226-4094. TEL 313-961-2242; 800-877-4253. FAX 800-414-5043. E-mail: daniel__snyder@gale.com.
Description: Annual reference on works of literary biography.

920 967 MF ISSN 1025-367X
DICTIONNAIRE DE BIOGRAPHIE MAURICIENNE/DICTIONARY OF MAURITIAN BIOGRAPHY. (Text in English or French) 1941. irreg. $8. Societe de l'Historie de l'Ile Maurice, Rue de Froberville, Curepipe Road, Mauritius.

920 658 II ISSN 0070-542X
DIRECTORY OF DIRECTORS. (Text in English) 1966. irreg. Rs.30($9) Kothari Publications, 12 India Exchange Place, Calcutta 700 001, India. TEL 91-33-220-9563. Ed. H. Kothari. adv. **Document type:** directory.
Description: Lists about 2500 names, addresses and ages of leading Indian company directors.

DOCUMENTATIEBLAD NADERE REFORMATIE. see *RELIGIONS AND THEOLOGY — Protestant*

920 942 UK ISSN 0070-7120
DORSET WORTHIES. 1962. irreg., no. 20, 1993. Dorset County Museum, Dorchester, Dorset, England. TEL 44-1305-262735. Ed. Jo Draper. R&P contact: R. de Peyer. **Document type:** monographic series.

920 US
EARL BLACKWELL'S CELEBRITY REGISTER. a. (Celebrity Service International, Inc.) Gale Research, 835 Penobscot Bldg., 645 Griswold St., Detroit, MI 48226-4094. TEL 313-961-2242; 800-877-4253. FAX 800-414-5043. E-mail: daniel__snyder@gale.com. Ed. Patsy Maharam.

920 949.2 NE ISSN 0929-9807
EGODOCUMENTEN. 1988. 2/yr. price varies. (Stichting Egodocument) Uitgeverij Verloren, Larenseweg 123, 1221 CL Hilversum, Netherlands. TEL 31-35-6859856. FAX 31-35-6836557. Ed. R.M. Dekker. illus. (back issues avail.) **Document type:** monographic series.
Description: Publishes scholarly editions of autobiographies, journals and correspondence from the period 1500 to 1850.

920 382 BE
EURO - WHO'S WHO; who is who in the institutions of the European Union and in the other European Organizations. (Text in English, French, German) 1978. triennial, 5th ed. 1996. 4500 BEF. Editions Delta, Rue Scailquin 55, B-1210 Brussels, Belgium. TEL 32-2-217-55-55. FAX 32-2-217-93-93. (Dist. in US by: Bernan, 4611-F Assembly Dr., Lanham, MD 20706-4391) Ed. Georges-Francis Seingry. adv. circ. 6,000. **Document type:** directory.
Formerly: European Communities and Other European Organizations Who's Who (ISSN 0771-7911)
Description: Includes the biographies of the senior civil servants currently working within the institutions of the European Union and within more than twenty other European organizations, and the chairmen and secretaries of more than 1500 non-governmental organizations.

EUROPEAN JOYCE STUDIES. see *LITERATURE*

920 600 UK
EUROPEAN RESEARCH AND DEVELOPMENT DATABASE (YEAR). (In 2 vols.) a. £995. Bowker - Saur Ltd., A member of the Reed Elsevier plc group, Maypole House, Maypole Rd., E. Grinstead, W. Sussex RH19 1HU, England. TEL 44-1342-330100. FAX 44-1342-330191. E-mail: custserv@bowker-saur.co.uk; URL: http://www.bowker-saur.co.uk/service/. **Document type:** bibliography.
●Also available on CD-ROM.
Description: Reference tool for research and development throughout Europe. Lists over 21,000 organizations and 85,000 individuals in the field.

920 540 560 AG ISSN 0325-4216
QH113 CODEN: FACEDE
F A C E N A. (Text in Spanish; summaries in English) 1978. biennial. Arg.$200. Facultad de Ciencias Exactas y Naturales y Agrimensura, 9 de Julio 1449, 3400 Corrientes, Argentina. Ed.Bd. bk.rev.; index. (back issues avail.) **Indexed:** Biol.Abstr., Chem.Abstr.
—CASDDS.

FAULKNER NEWSLETTER & YOKNAPATAWPHA REVIEW. see *LITERATURE*

FEDERAL REGIONAL YELLOW BOOK; who's who in the federal government's departments, agencies, courts, military installations and service academies outside of Washington, DC. see *PUBLIC ADMINISTRATION*

FIGURES DE WALLONIE. see *HISTORY — History Of Europe*

FINEST HOUR. see *HISTORY*

920 831 282 360 GW ISSN 0173-5543
FRAENKISCHER HAUSKALENDER UND CARITASKALENDER. 1949. a. DM.6.50. Echter Wuerzburg, Fraenkische Gesellschaftsdruckerei und Verlag GmbH, Postfach 5560, 97005 Wuerzburg, Germany. TEL 49-931-6671-0. Ed. Hans Kufner. circ. 18,000. **Document type:** bulletin.

920 US ISSN 1060-5312
FRANKLIN PIERCE TIMES. 1992. a. $11.50 (effective 1996). 79 Elm St., Springfield, VT 05156. TEL 802-885-3151. Ed. Irving Bell. bk.rev.; circ. 200 (paid). (back issues avail.) **Document type:** newsletter.
Description: Biography of the 14th U.S. president, including all his available letters. Contains commentary and news of efforts to obtain greater interest in the life and achievements of Franklin Pierce.

920 943 GW ISSN 0341-0749
GEDENKTAGE DES MITTELDEUTSCHEN RAUMES. 1958. a. DM.19.80. (Stiftung Mitteldeutscher Kulturrat) Ferd. Duemmlers Verlag, Kaiserstr. 31-37, 53113 Bonn, Germany. (Subscr. to: Postfach 1480, 53004 Bonn, Germany) Ed.Bd. (back issues avail.)

GOUVERNEMENT ET LES CABINETS MINISTERIELS. see *PUBLIC ADMINISTRATION*

BIOGRAPHY

920   US   ISSN 1065-9552
JK2447
GOVERNORS OF AMERICAN STATES, COMMONWEALTHS, AND TERRITORIES. a. $8.95. National Governors' Association, 444 N. Capitol St., Ste. 250, Washington, DC 20001. TEL 202-624-5330. Ed. Alicia Albergold. **Document type:** directory.
  Former titles (until 1991): Directory of Governors of the American States, Commonwealths, and Territories (ISSN 0898-3291); (until 1988): Governors of the American States, Commonwealths, and Territories (ISSN 0196-4348)
  Description: Biographical information of American governors.

920 968   SA
GRAHAM'S TOWN SERIES. 1971. irreg. no.7, 1984. price varies. (Rhodes University) Grahamstown Publicity Association, 63 High St., Grahamstown 6140, South Africa. Eds. Guy Butler, Winnie Maxwell. **Document type:** monographic series.
  Description: Publishes historical material relating to the Eastern Cape in the nineteenth century, including diaries and collections of letters.

920   FR
GRANDS NOTABLES DU PREMIER EMPIRE. price varies. C N R S Editions, 20-22 rue St. Amand, 75015 Paris, France. TEL 45-33-16-00. FAX 45-33-92-13. TELEX 200 356 F. adv.; bk.rev.; index; circ. 1,500 (controlled).

GREAT AFRICAN AMERICANS. see *CHILDREN AND YOUTH — For*

GREAT MINDS OF SCIENCE. see *CHILDREN AND YOUTH — For*

920   CC   ISSN 1003-7225
GUO MORUO XUEKAN. (Text in Chinese) 1987. q. Y5.60. (Sichuan Guo Moruo Study Institute) Guo Moruo Xuekan Qikanshe, Dafo Si Nei, Leshan, Sichuan 614003, People's Republic of China. TEL 86-833-2139721. (Dist. overseas by: Jiangsu Publications Import & Export Corp., 56 Gao Yun Ling, Nanjing, Jiangsu, P.R.C.) Eds. Zhang Hao, Wang Jinhou. adv. contact: Anna Tang. circ. 3,000. **Document type:** academic/scholarly publication.
  Description: Studies the literary life, theory and works of Guo Moruo, a distinguished writer, scientist and social activist in modern Chinese history.
  Refereed Serial

HANS - PFITZNER - GESELLSCHAFT. MITTEILUNGEN. see *MUSIC*

HAYDN - STUDIEN. see *MUSIC*

920 820   AT   ISSN 0729-2449
HERMIT PRESS PAMPHLETS. 1982. irreg. Pioneer Books, P.O. Box 57, Oaklands Park, S.A. 5046, Australia. TEL 61-8-82984645. FAX 61-8-83772355. (Hermit Press) Ed. Paul Depasquale. **Document type:** academic/scholarly publication, monographic series.
  Description: Presents biographical studies of neglected writers for academic and general readership.

HILLARY CLINTON QUARTERLY. see *LITERARY AND POLITICAL REVIEWS*

HISPANIC BIOGRAPHIES. see *CHILDREN AND YOUTH — For*

920   FR   ISSN 1251-5132
HISTOIRE ECONOMIQUE ET FINANCIERE DE LA FRANCE. MEMOIRE. 1990. irreg. Ministere de l'Economie et des Finances, Comite pour l'Histoire Economique et Financiere de la France, 6 av. de l'Opera, 2eme Etage, 75001 Paris, France. TEL 33-1-44775264. FAX 33-1-44775298. URL: http://www.finances.gouv.fr/dicom/cheff. (Subscr. to: Imprimerie Nationale - Editions DACF, 27 rue de la Convention, 75015 Paris Cedex 15, France)

HISTORIC GUELPH; the royal city. see *HISTORY — History Of North And South America*

920   US
HUAXIA MINGREN/CHINA'S FAMOUS PEOPLE. (Text in Chinese) bi-m. $18.50. China Books & Periodicals, Inc., 2929 24th St., San Francisco, CA 94110. TEL 415-282-2994. FAX 415-282-0994.

920   US   ISSN 0899-1138
IMAGES OF EXCELLENCE. 1986. bi-m. $6. Images of Excellence Foundation, Box 11311, Boiling Springs, NC 28017. Ed. Robert Detjen.

920 954   II   ISSN 0073-6244
INDIA WHO'S WHO. (Text in English) 1969. a. $100. (India News and Feature Alliance) I N F A Publications, Jeevan Deep Bldg., Parliament St., New Delhi 110 001, India. TEL 91-11-3733330. FAX 91-11-3746788. Ed. Inder Jit; Pub. Poonam I. Kaushishi. adv. circ. 5,000. **Document type:** directory.
  Description: Profiles of 5,000 influential men and women.

920   II
INDIAN BIOGRAPHY. 1976-19??; resumed 1990. irreg. Rs.25. Centre for Asian Dokumentation, K-15, CIT Bldg., Christopher Rd., Calcutta 700 014, India. (Dist. by: Punthi Pustak, 136-4B Bidhan Sarani, Calcutta 700004, India) Ed. S. Chaudhuri.
  Description: Presents concise biographical notices of eminent people in South Asia and Indologists throughout the world.

509   II
INDIAN NATIONAL SCIENCE ACADEMY. BIOGRAPHICAL MEMOIRS OF FELLOWS. (Text in English) irreg. price varies. Indian National Science Academy, 1 Bahadur Shah Zafar Marg, New Delhi 110002, India. TEL 91-11-3232066. FAX 91-11-3235648. TELEX 31-61835 INSA IN. E-mail: insa@gias101.vsnl.net.in; insa@delnet.ren.nic.in. bibl.
  Formerly: National Institute of Sciences of India. Biographical Memoirs of Fellows (ISSN 0547-7557)

920   FR   ISSN 0020-0492
INFORMATIONS RAPIDES DE L'ADMINISTRATION FRANCAISE.* (In 6 Sections) 1960. frequency varies per section. 296.60 F. for all 6 sections. Tour Gramma A, 195 rue de Bercy, 75582 Paris Cedex 12, France. Ed. Marie Saulgeot. (looseleaf format)

920 780   IT   ISSN 0393-2915
ML410.V82
INFORMAZIONI E STUDI VIVALDIANI. (Text in English, French, German and Italian; summaries in English and Italian) 1980. a. L.24000 (effective Jan. 1996). (Istituto Italiano Antonio Vivaldi) B M G Ricordi S.p.A., Via Berchet 2, 20100 Milan, Italy. TEL 39-2-8881. FAX 39-2-88812270. TELEX 325217 RICOR I. Ed. Antonio Fanna. bk.rev.; illus. circ. 1,300. **Indexed:** RILM. **Document type:** bulletin.
—BLDSC (4496.957000).

800   UK   ISSN 0143-8263
Z1010
INTERNATIONAL AUTHORS AND WRITERS WHO'S WHO. 1934. biennial. £95($155) Melrose Press Ltd., 3 Regal Ln., Soham, Ely, Cambridgeshire CB7 5BA, England. TEL 44-1353-721091. FAX 44-1353-721839. (Dist. in U.S. by: International Publication Services, Taylor & Francis, Inc., 1900 Frost Rd., Ste.101, Bristol, PA 19007-1598) Eds. David Cummings, Dennis McIntire; Pub. Nicholas Law. adv. contact: Jean Pearson. **Indexed:** Child.Auth.& Illus. **Document type:** directory.
  Formerly: Author's and Writer's Who's Who (ISSN 0067-2386)
  Description: Biographical profiles on leading authors, novelists, playwrights, journalists, editors, critics and columnists worldwide.

920 200   GW
INTERNATIONAL BIOGRAPHICAL DICTIONARY OF RELIGION; an encyclopedia of more than 4000 leading personalities. (Text in English) a. $250. (Union of International Associations, BE) K.G. Saur Verlag KG, A member of the Reed Elsevier plc group, Ortlerstr. 8, 81373 Munich, Germany. TEL 49-89-769020. FAX 49-89-76902150. E-mail: 100730.1341@compuserve.com; URL: http://www.reed-elsevier.com. (N. America subscr. to: K.G. Saur, 121 Chanlon Rd., Box 31, New Providence, NJ 07974-9903. TEL 908-665-3576; Alt. addr.: Postfach 701620, 81316 Munich, Germany) Eds. Jon C. Jenkins, Cecile Vanden Bloock. **Document type:** directory.
  Formerly: International Biographical Dictionary of the Religious World (Year).
  Description: Lists over 4,000 key religious leaders of the major religions of the world, including hierarchies from Christianity, Islam, Buddhism, Hinduism, Sikhism, Baha'i, Confucianism, Jainism, Shintoism, and Judaism. Theologians and other academics, spiritual leaders, administrators, pastors, priests, rabbis, imams, monks, and nuns are included.

012   US
INTERNATIONAL DIRECTORY OF DISTINGUISHED LEADERSHIP. 1986. a. $165 (effective 1997). American Biographical Institute, Inc., Governing Board of Editors, 5126 Bur Oak Circle, Box 31226, Raleigh, NC 27622. TEL 919-781-8710. FAX 919-781-8712. Ed. Janet M. Evans; Pub. Janet M. Evans. circ. 5,000. **Document type:** directory.
  Former titles (until 1985): Community Leaders of America; Community Leaders and Noteworthy Americans (ISSN 0094-5587)
  Refereed Serial

920 020   US
▼**INTERNATIONAL DIRECTORY OF SERIALS SPECIALISTS.** 1995. irreg. $24.95. Haworth Press, Inc., 10 Alice St., Binghamton, NY 13904-1580. TEL 800-342-9678. FAX 607-722-6362. E-mail: subscribe@haworth.com. Ed. Jean Whiffin. **Document type:** directory.

920   UK   ISSN 0074-9613
CT120
INTERNATIONAL WHO'S WHO (YEARS). 1935. a. £170($310) (effective 1997-98). Europa Publications Ltd., 18 Bedford Sq., London WC1B 3JN, England. TEL 44-171-580-8236. FAX 44-171-636-1664. TELEX 21540 EUROPA G. E-mail: edit@europapublications.co.uk. (Orders to: Sales and Publicity, 43 Gower St., London WC1E 6HH, England. TEL 44-171-631-3361. FAX 44-171-637-0922) Ed. Richard Fitzwilliams. circ. 5,500. **Indexed:** Child.Auth.& Illus. **Document type:** directory.
—BLDSC (4552.100000); CISTI. **CCC.**
  Description: Covers the world's leading men and women, both the famous and the less well known. Bibliographical information about important figures from a wide variety of fields. Each entry gives nationality, date and place of birth, education, career details, present position, honours, awards, publications, current address, and, wherever possible, personal interests.

920   UK   ISSN 0952-3839
INTERNATIONAL WHO'S WHO IN MEDICINE. 1986. irreg. £115($195) Melrose Press Ltd., 3 Regal Ln., Soham, Ely, Cambridgeshire CB7 5BA, England. TEL 44-1353-721091. FAX 44-1353-721839. (Dist. in U.S. by: Taylor and Francis Inc., 1900 Frost Rd., Ste. 101, Bristol, PA 19007-1598) Ed. Jocelyn Timothy; Pub. Nicholas Law. adv. contact: Jean Pearson. **Document type:** directory.
  Description: Details the careers and achievements of approximately 5,000 leading exponents of medicine.

BIOGRAPHY

520　　　　　　　UK
PS324
INTERNATIONAL WHO'S WHO IN POETRY AND POETS' ENCYCLOPAEDIA. 1957. biennial. £95($155) Melrose Press Ltd., 3 Regal Ln., Soham, Ely, Cambridgeshire CB7 5BA, England. TEL 44-1353-721091. FAX 44-1353-721839. (Dist. in US by: Taylor & Francis Inc., 1900 Frost Rd., Ste. 101, Bristol, PA 19007-1598) Eds. David Cummings, Dennis McIntire; Pub. Nicholas Law. **Document type**: directory.
　　Formerly: International Who's Who in Poetry (ISSN 0539-1342)
　　Description: Biographies and bibliographies of approximately 4,000 established and emerging poets from around the world.

920　　　　　　　UK
INTERNATIONAL WHO'S WHO OF INTELLECTUALS. 1978. biennial. £175($295) (effective 1997). Melrose Press Ltd., 3 Regal Ln., Soham, Ely, Cambridgeshire CB7 5BA, England. TEL 44-1353-721091. FAX 44-1353-721839. (Dist. in US by: Taylor & Francis Inc., 1900 Frost Rd., Ste. 101, Bristol, PA 19007-1598) Ed. Jocelyn Timothy; Pub. Nicholas Law. (back issues avail.) **Document type**: directory.
　　Description: Contains essays detailing the lives and achievements of approximately 1,500 men and women.

INTERNATIONAL WHO'S WHO OF WOMEN (YEAR). see WOMEN'S STUDIES

920 320　　UK　　ISSN 0074-9621
JA51
INTERNATIONAL YEAR BOOK AND STATESMEN'S WHO'S WHO. 1953. a. £195. Reed Information Services (Subsidiary of: Reed Elsevier group), Windsor Court, E. Grinstead House, E. Grinstead, W. Sussex RH19 1XA, England. TEL 01342-335832. FAX 01342-335948. TELEX 95127-INFSER-G. circ. 1,700. pp./issue: 1400. **Document type**: directory. —CISTI.
　　Description: Provides information on the structure and function of the world's major international and national organizations. Also contains career details of politicians - the attainments of leading diplomats, heads of state, judges, bankers, influential industrialists.

920　　　　　　　GW
INTERNATIONALES BIOGRAPHISCHES ARCHIV - PERSONEN AKTUELL. 1913. w. DM.128.70 per quarter. Munzinger Archiv GmbH, Albersfelderstr. 34, 88213 Ravensburg, Germany. TEL 49-751-76931-0. FAX 49-751-652424. Ed. Dr. Ludwig Munzinger. circ. 1,000. **Document type**: newsletter.
　　Formerly: Internationales Biographisches Archiv (ISSN 0020-9457)

011　　　　　　　JA
J I C S T HOLDING LIST OF SERIALS: A LIST. (Japan Information Center for Science and Technology) triennial. Japan Science and Technology Corporation, Information Center for Science and Technology - Kagaku Gijutsu Shinko Gigyodan, 5-3, Yonbancho, Chiyoda-ku, Tokyo 102, Japan. TEL 81-3-5214-8413. FAX 81-3-5214-8410.
　　Formerly: J I C S T Holding List of Serials and Proceedings: A List.

JAMES DICKEY NEWSLETTER. see LITERATURE

920 610　　UK　　ISSN 0967-7720
R134
JOURNAL OF MEDICAL BIOGRAPHY. 1993. 4/yr. £36($67) to individuals; institutions £47($88). Royal Society of Medicine Press Ltd., 1 Wimpole St., London W1M 8AE, England. TEL 44-171-290-2900. FAX 44-171-290-2929. Ed. J.M.H. Moll. **Indexed**: Amer.Hist.& Life (1993-), Hist.Abstr. (1993-) **Document type**: academic/scholarly publication.
　　—BLDSC (5017.049000).
　　Refereed Serial

JOYCE STUDIES ANNUAL. see LITERATURE

920 808.068　　　　US
JUNIOR AUTHORS AND ILLUSTRATORS SERIES. 1951. irreg., vol.7, 1996. price varies. H.W. Wilson Co., 950 University Ave., Bronx, NY 10452. TEL 718-588-8400; 800-367-6770. FAX 718-590-1617. TELEX 4990003 HWILSON. Ed. Sally Holmes Holtze. index. **Document type**: monographic series.
　　Description: Contains biographical sketches of outstanding creators of children's literature.

JUSTICES OF THE SUPREME COURT. see CHILDREN AND YOUTH — For

KATERI; Lily of the Mohawks. see RELIGIONS AND THEOLOGY — Roman Catholic

920　　　　　　　UK　　ISSN 0075-6083
KINGS OF TOMORROW SERIES. 1967. irreg. price varies. Monarchist Press Association, 7 Sutherland Rd., West Ealing, London W13 0DX, England. circ. 3,500.

920　　　　　　　GW　　ISSN 0454-1383
KOEPFE DES 20. JAHRHUNDERTS. 1957. irreg. DM.12.80. Colloquium Verlag, Luetzowstr. 105, 10785 Berlin, Germany. circ. 3,000.

920　　　　　　　FI　　ISSN 1237-7570
KUKA KUKIN ON/WHO'S WHO IN FINLAND. 1909. quadrennial, latest 1994. FIM 785 (effective 1997). Kustannusosakeyhtio Otava, Uudenmaankatu 7R 8-12, SF-00120 Helsinki, Finland. TEL 358-9-19961. FAX 358-9-1996477. Ed. Irja Hamalainen. circ. 7,000. **Document type**: directory.
　●Also available online.

KULTUUR JA ELU/CULTURE AND LIFE. see ETHNIC INTERESTS

920 980　　NE　　ISSN 1384-5799
LATINOAMERICANISTAS EN EUROPA (YEAR); registro bio-bibliografico. (Text in Spanish) 7th ed., 1995. irreg. fl.60($40) Centrum voor Studie en Documentatie van Latijns Amerika - Center for Latin American Research and Documentation - Centro de Estudios y Documentacion Latinoamericanos, Keizersgracht 395-397, 1016 EK Amsterdam, Netherlands. TEL 31-20-5253498. FAX 31-20-6255127. **Document type**: directory.
　　Description: Contains biographical and bibliographical information on some 500 researchers in Latin American studies (social sciences and humanities) who are resident in Europe.

920 943　　　　GW
LEBENSBILDER AUS BADEN-WUERTTEMBERG. (Vols. 1-6: Schwaebische Lebensbilder) 1940. irreg. DM.54. Kommission fuer Geschichtliche Landeskunde in Baden-Wuerttemberg, Eugenstr. 7, 70182 Stuttgart, Germany. Eds. Gerhard Taddey, Joachim Fischer. **Document type**: monographic series.
　　Formerly: Lebensbilder aus Schwaben und Franken.
　　Description: Essays on important men and women in the history of ancient Bade and Wuerttemberg.

LEGENDARY HEROES OF THE WILD WEST. see CHILDREN AND YOUTH — For

LEITENDE MAENNER UND FRAUEN DER WIRTSCHAFT. see BUSINESS AND ECONOMICS — Management

920 800 100 530　　GW　　ISSN 0936-4242
B2681.L44
LICHTENBERG-JAHRBUCH. 1979. a. DM.98. (Lichtenberg-Gesellschaft e.V.) Saarbruecker Druckerei und Verlag GmbH, Halbergstr. 3, 66121 Saarbruecken, Germany. TEL 49-681-66501-0. FAX 49-681-6650110. adv.; bk.rev.; bibl.; illus. circ. 500. (back issues avail.) **Document type**: academic/scholarly publication.
　　Formerly: Photorin (ISSN 0172-0015)

LINCOLN MEMORIAL ASSOCIATION NEWSLETTER. see HISTORY — History Of North And South America

920 895.1　　CC　　ISSN 1003-0638
LU XUN YANJIU YUEKAN/LU XUN STUDIES MONTHLY. (Text in Chinese) 1984. m. $49.50. Beijing Lu Xun Bowuguan, Beijing 100034, People's Republic of China. TEL 6060478. (Dist. in US by: China Books & Periodicals, Inc., 2929 24th St., San Francisco, CA 94110. TEL 415-282-2994) Eds. Shi Yuhua, Chen Shuyu. adv. contact: Qiaosheng Huang. circ. 2,000. **Document type**: academic/scholarly publication.

MABUA/FOUNTAIN; religious creation in literature, society and thought. see LITERATURE

920　　　　　　　US　　ISSN 1083-2327
MCCALLUM OBSERVER. 1985. q. $11 (foreign $13) (effective 1997). Box 313, Lansing, IL 60438-0313. TEL 708-895-0736. Ed. Lynda Mendoza. adv.; bk.rev. contact: 200. **Document type**: newsletter.
　　Description: Focuses on the acting career of David McCallum.
　　Refereed Serial

015　　　　　　　II
MADHYA PRADESH WHO'S WHO. (Text in English) 1978. a. Rs.30. New Era Publication, S.N.6, Char Bungalow Rd., Professor Colony, Bhopal 462001, India.

340　　　　　　　US
MARTINDALE-HUBBELL PREMIER ACCOUNT NEWS. 1992. 4/yr. free to qualified personnel. Martindale-Hubbell, A Division of Reed Elsevier Inc., 121 Chanlon Rd., New Providence, NJ 07974. TEL 800-526-4902. FAX 908-464-3553. TELEX 138755. E-mail: info@martindale.com; URL: http://www.martindale.com. (Subscr. to: Box 1001, Summit, NJ 07902-1001) **Document type**: consumer publication.

920 610　　　　　UK
MEDICAL SCIENCES INTERNATIONAL WHO'S WHO. 1980. irreg., 5th ed., 1992. £340. Longman Group UK Ltd., Westgate House, 6th Fl., The High, Harlow, Essex CM20 1YR, England. TEL 44-1279-442601. FAX 44-1279-444501. (Subscr. to: Pearson Professional, P.O. Box 77, Fourth Ave., Harlow, Essex CM19 5BQ, England. TEL 44-1279-623924. FAX 44-1279-639609; Dist. in U.S. and Canada by: Gale Research Inc., 835 Penobscot Bldg., Detroit, MI 48226) **Document type**: directory.
　　Formerly: International Medical Who's Who.

012　　　　　　　US　　ISSN 0461-7398
MEN AND WOMEN OF HAWAII.* Variant title: Who's Who in Hawaii. 1918. every 7-10 yrs; 9th ed., 1972. $25. S B Printers, Inc., Box 100, Honolulu, HI 96810-0100. TEL 808-537-5353. Ed. Betty Buker. circ. 3,000.

920　　　　　　　UK　　ISSN 0306-3666
CT120
MEN OF ACHIEVEMENT. 1974. a. £115($195) Melrose Press Ltd., 3 Regal Ln., Soham, Ely, Cambridgeshire CB7 5BA, England. TEL 44-1353-721091. FAX 44-1353-721839. (Dist. in U.S. by: Taylor and Francis Inc., 1900 Frost Rd., Ste. 101, Bristol, PA 19007-1598) Ed. Jocelyn Timothy; Pub. Nicholas Law. adv. contact: Jean Pearson. **Document type**: directory.
　　—BLDSC (5678.413000); CISTI.
　　Description: Contains approximately 5,000 biographical profiles of contemporary male achievers from all fields of influence.

920　　　　　　　CC　　ISSN 1002-6282
MINGREN ZHUANJI. (Text in Chinese) 1985. m. Y36 (effective 1994). Henan People's Publishing House, Mingren Zhuanji Editorial Department, No. 73, Nongye Lu, Zhengzhou, Henan 450002, People's Republic of China. TEL 5951756. FAX 544757. (Dist. overseas by: China International Book Trading Corp., P.O. Box 399, Beijing, People's Republic of China) Ed. Deng Zhigang. adv.: page Y.10000; adv. contact: Ruixiang Song. circ. 190,000. **Document type**: bibliography.
　　Description: Provides literary biographies of great names in all times all over the world.

MODERN ARTS CRITICISM. see ART

MULTICULTURAL JUNIOR BIOGRAPHIES. see CHILDREN AND YOUTH — For

BIOGRAPHY

925 500 US ISSN 0077-2933
Q141 CODEN: BMNSAC
NATIONAL ACADEMY OF SCIENCES. BIOGRAPHICAL MEMOIRS. 1953. irreg. price varies. National Academy Press, 2101 Constitution Ave., N.W., Washington, DC 20418. TEL 800-624-6242. FAX 202-334-2451. **Indexed:** Biol.Abstr., GeoRef. **Document type:** monographic series.
—CASDDS; CISTI; Linda Hall. **CCC**.

NATIONAL CONFERENCE OF LIEUTENANT GOVERNORS. BIOGRAPHICAL SKETCHES AND PORTRAITS. see *PUBLIC ADMINISTRATION*

920 US ISSN 0077-5371
NATIONAL REGISTER OF PROMINENT AMERICANS AND INTERNATIONAL NOTABLES. 1966. biennial. $125. National Register of Prominent Americans, Drawer 1375, Washington, DC 20013-1375. Ed. William Smith. bk.rev. (also avail. in microform from UMI; reprint service avail. from UMI)

NATIVE AMERICAN LEADERS OF THE WILD WEST. see *CHILDREN AND YOUTH — For*

NEW YORK GENEALOGICAL AND BIOGRAPHICAL RECORD. see *GENEALOGY AND HERALDRY*

920 US ISSN 0161-2433
CT120
THE NEW YORK TIMES BIOGRAPHICAL SERVICE. 1969. m. (New York Times Company) U M I (Subsidiary of: Bell & Howell Company), 300 N. Zeeb Rd., Ann Arbor, MI 48106. TEL 313-761-4700; 800-521-0600. FAX 800-864-0019. index. circ. 750. (looseleaf format) **Indexed:** Child.Auth.& Illus. **Document type:** bibliography.
—CISTI; KR SourceOne.
Formerly: New York Times Biographical Edition (ISSN 0048-0088)

NEW ZEALAND BUSINESS WHO'S WHO. see *BUSINESS AND ECONOMICS — Trade And Industrial Directories*

920 US ISSN 0028-9396
PS1029.A3
NEWSBOY.* 1962. 6/yr. $20 (effective 1991). Horatio Alger Society, 23726 N. Overhill Dr., Lake Zurich, IL 60047-8044. TEL 517-882-3203. Ed. William R. Gowen; Pub. William R. Gowen. R&P contact: William R. Gowen. adv. contact: William Gowen. bk.rev.; index. circ. 300. (back issues avail.) **Indexed:** M.L.A. **Document type:** newsletter.
Formerly: Horatio Alger Newsboy (ISSN 0018-4918)
Description: Contains organization news.

920 US ISSN 0899-0417
CT120
NEWSMAKERS. 1990. q. (plus a. cumulation). $93 (effective 1994). Gale Research, 835 Penobscot Bldg., 645 Griswold St., Detroit, MI 48226-4094. TEL 313-961-2242; 800-877-4253. FAX 800-414-5043. E-mail: daniel_snyder@gale.com. Ed. Louise Mooney. (also avail. in diskette format; magnetic tape)
●Also available online. Vendor(s): Lexis-Nexis. Also available on CD-ROM.
Description: Contains biographical facts on about 50 prominent personalities in each issue.

NORTH KOREA DIRECTORY (YEAR); comprehensive guide to North Korean organizations and leadership. see *POLITICAL SCIENCE — International Relations*

NOTABLE HISPANIC AMERICAN WOMEN. see *WOMEN'S STUDIES*

NOUVELLE BIBLIOTHEQUE NERVALIENNE. see *LITERATURE*

OESTERREICHISCHE KOMPONISTEN DES 20. JAHRHUNDERTS. see *MUSIC*

OFFICIAL A B M S DIRECTORY OF BOARD CERTIFIED MEDICAL SPECIALISTS. see *MEDICAL SCIENCES*

920.4 976 US
OKLAHOMA WESTERN BIOGRAPHIES. 1988. irreg. price varies. University of Oklahoma Press, 1005 Asp Ave., Norman, OK 73019. TEL 405-325-5111. FAX 405-325-4000. **Document type:** academic/scholarly publication.

OLD NEWS. see *HISTORY — History Of North And South America*

PENNSYLVANIA MAGAZINE OF HISTORY AND BIOGRAPHY. see *HISTORY — History Of North And South America*

920 800 US ISSN 0890-1465
Z1003.3.P4
PENNSYLVANIA PORTFOLIO;* a literary review about Pennsylvania authors, books & libraries. 1983. s-a. $9. Plank's Suburban Press, 2321 Market St., Camp Hill, PA 17011. TEL 717-234-4961. FAX 717-234-7479. Ed. Anthony Arms. adv.; bk.rev.; illus.; tr.lit.; cum.index: 1983-1986. circ. 1,200. (back issues avail.)

920 UK ISSN 0079-0729
PEOPLE FROM THE PAST SERIES. 1964. irreg., no.15, 1977. £4.95. Dobson Books Ltd., 80 Kensington Church St., London W8 4BZ, England. Ed. Egon Larsen. **Document type:** monographic series.

PEOPLE TO KNOW. see *CHILDREN AND YOUTH — For*

920 AG
PERFILES CONTEMPORANEOS. no.2, 1976. irreg. Editorial Plus Ultra, Callao 575, 1022 Buenos Aires, Argentina. Ed. Jose Isaacson.

PERSONALHISTORISK TIDSSKRIFT. see *GENEALOGY AND HERALDRY*

920 DR
PERSONALIDADES DOMINICANAS. a. Molina Morillo y Asociados, c/o Editora de Colores, C. Juan Tomas Mejia y Cotes 8, Arroyo Hondo, Santo Domingo, Dominican Republic. TEL 567-3214.

929 SW ISSN 0031-5699
CT1310
PERSONHISTORISK TIDSKRIFT. 1898. s-a. SEK 120 in Nordic countries; elsewhere SEK 140. Personhistoriska Samfundet - Swedish Society for Personal History Research, c/o L. Aanimmer, Riksarkivet, Box 12541, S-102 29 Stockholm, Sweden. TEL 46-8-737-64-12. FAX 46-8-737-64-74. E-mail: lena.animmer@riksarkivet.ra.se. Eds. Erik Norberg, Gunnar Aaselius. bk.rev.; charts; illus.; index. circ. 500. **Indexed:** Amer.Hist.& Life (1954-), Hist.Abstr. (1954-), M.L.A., MLA Intl.Bibl. **Document type:** academic/scholarly publication.
Description: Constitutes an important tool for biographical and genealogical research, especially concerning Sweden from 1200 AD to the present.

920 PE
PERU REPORT'S GUIDE TO TOP PEOPLE IN PERU; quien es quien? (Text in Spanish; headings in English, Spanish) 1992. irreg., latest 1997. $65. Peru Reporting E.I.R.L., Francisco Grana 319, Magdalena, Lima 17, Peru. TEL 5114-617416. FAX 5114-634466. E-mail: postmast@perurep.com.pe. Ed. Jonathan Cavanagh. adv.; circ. 1,500 (paid).
Description: Guide to the top professionals in 70 areas.
Refereed Serial

PLANTAGENET PRODUCTIONS; libraries of spoken word recordings, of stagescripts, and of family papers. see *LITERATURE*

920 UK
POLITICAL PORTRAITS. 1987. irreg. price varies. University of Wales Press, 6 Gwennyth St., Cathays, Cardiff CF2 4YD, Wales. TEL 44-1222-231919. FAX 44-1222-230908. E-mail: orders@press.wales.ac.uk; URL: http://www.swan.ac.uk/uwp/home.htm. Ed. Kenneth O. Morgan. **Document type:** academic/scholarly publication.
Description: Contains lively essays on several of the decisive figures in the making of British politics over the past 200 years.

920 282 US
POPE JOHN PAUL II CENTER NEWSLETTER. Polish edition: Centrum Jana Pawla II Biuletyn. 1979. 5/yr. $5. Pope John Paul II Center, Orchard Lake Schools, Orchard Lake, MI 48234. TEL 313-683-0408. Ed. Alfred H. Jantz. **Document type:** newsletter.
Description: Includes biographical information, memoirs, publications and activities.

920 IT
POPOLI E PERSONE;* testimonianze e personaggi. 1980. m. L.50000($55) Citta Armoniosa, Casella Postale 411, 42100 Reggio Emilia, Italy.

PRICE WATERHOUSE CORPORATE REGISTER. see *BUSINESS AND ECONOMICS*

920 US ISSN 0898-9745
E872
THE REAL CALVIN COOLIDGE. 1983. a. $2.95 to non-members; free to members. Calvin Coolidge Memorial Foundation, Inc., Box 97, Plymouth, VT 05056. TEL 802-672-3389. Ed. Robert H. Ferrell. bk.rev. circ. 700. (back issues avail.) **Document type:** newsletter.
Description: Articles of original Coolidge research of interest to Coolidge buffs, researchers, and historians.

920 US ISSN 1040-9335
REAL PEOPLE. 1988. bi-m. $24 (effective 1997). Main Street Publishing Co., Inc., 450 Fashion Ave., Ste. 1701, New York, NY 10123-1799. TEL 212-244-2351. FAX 212-244-2367. (Subscr. to: Box 7851, Red Oak, IA 51591-0581) Ed. Alex Polner. R&P contact: Suzanne Hochman. adv. contact: Bob Millar. bk.rev.; illus. circ. 100,000. **Document type:** consumer publication.
Formerly (until 1988): Family Digest (ISSN 0894-5586)
Description: Covers celebrities and other interesting people.

RELIGIOUS LEADERS OF AMERICA. see *RELIGIONS AND THEOLOGY*

920 951 CC
RENMIN/PEOPLE. (Text in Chinese) 1980. bi-m. Y2.40. Renmin Chubanshe, Qikan Bu - People's Publishing House, 166 Chaonei Dajie, Beijing 100706, People's Republic of China. TEL 550415. Ed. Wu Chengwan. bk.rev.; index. circ. 70,000. (back issues avail.)
Description: Introduces Chinese and other personalities in modern history.

920 CC ISSN 1001-6635
DS778.A1
RENWU. (Text in Chinese; table of contents in English) bi-m. Y1.80($33.80) Renmin Chubanshe, Qikan Bu - People's Publishing House, 166 Chaonei Dajie, Beijing 100706, People's Republic of China. TEL 55-0415. (Dist. outside China by: China International Book Trading Corp., P.O. Box 399, Beijing, P.R.C.; Dist. in US by: China Books & Periodicals, Inc., 2929 24th St., San Francisco, CA 94110. TEL 415-282-2994) Ed. Wu Chengwan.
—UnCover.
Description: Contains biographies and reminiscences of Chinese and other personalities in modern history.

920 362.4 US
RESOURCE DIRECTORY OF SCIENTISTS AND ENGINEERS WITH DISABILITIES. 1982. irreg., 3rd ed., 1995. $20. American Association for the Advancement of Science, Project on Science, Technology and Disability, 1200 New York Ave., N.W., Washington, DC 20005. TEL 202-326-6649. FAX 202-371-9849. E-mail: 1summers@aaas.org. Eds. Virginia W. Stern, Laureen Summers. R&P contact: Virginia W. Stern.
Description: Source of role models for disabled youth and mid-career scientists and engineers. Lists 950 scientists and engineers with an address, phone number, discipline and degree(s), position, nature of and age of disability.

920 943 GW ISSN 0080-2670
RHEINISCHE LEBENSBILDER. 1961. irreg., vol.15, 1995. price varies. (Gesellschaft fuer Rheinische Geschichtskunde) Rheinland Verlag GmbH, Abtei Brauweiler, Postfach 2140, 50250 Pulheim, Germany. TEL 49-2234-9854265. FAX 49-2234-82503. (Dist. by: Dr. Rudolf Habelt GmbH, Am Buchenhang 1, 53115 Bonn, Germany. TEL 49-228-9238322. FAX 49-228-232017) **Document type:** monographic series.

RICHARD STRAUSS BLAETTER; neue Folge. see *MUSIC*

RICHARD WAGNER BLAETTER. see *MUSIC*

RIVISTA DALMATICA. see *HISTORY — History Of Europe*

ROMANSERIER OG SELVBIOGRAFISKE SERIER. see *LITERATURE*

BIOGRAPHY

920   US
ROYAL BOOK NEWS. 1984. bi-m. $17. 5590 Jowett Ct., Alexandria, VA 22315-5542. TEL 703-836-0213. E-mail: makoenig@delphi.com. Ed. Marlene Koenig. adv.; bk.rev. **Document type:** newsletter.
    Description: News and reviews of books on British and European royalty from the U.S. and around the world.

920 500   UK   ISSN 0080-4606
Q41   CODEN: BMFRA3
ROYAL SOCIETY OF LONDON. BIOGRAPHICAL MEMOIRS OF FELLOWS OF THE ROYAL SOCIETY. 1932. a. £115 in Europe; U.S. and Canada £121 (effective 1997). Royal Society of London, 6 Carlton House Terrace, London SW1Y 5AG, England. TEL 44-171-839-5561. FAX 44-171-976-1837. E-mail: sales@roysocp2.demon.co.uk; URL: http://www.pubs.royalsoc.ac.uk. R&P contact: Phil Hurst. bibl.; illus.; index. circ. 1,348. (reprint service avail. from ISI) **Document type:** academic/scholarly publication.
    —BLDSC (2072.300000); CASDDS; CISTI.
    Supersedes (in 1954): Obituary Notices of Fellows of the Royal Society.

920 780   GW
SCHUBERT DURCH DIE BRILLE. 1991. s-a. (Internationales Franz Schubert Institut) Verlag Dr. Hans Schneider GmbH, Mozartstr. 6, 82323 Tutzing, Germany. TEL 08158-3050. FAX 08158-7636. **Indexed:** RILM. **Document type:** academic/scholarly publication.

SEVENTEENTH - CENTURY MUSIC. see *MUSIC*

920 780   AT   ISSN 0810-5200
SINATRA INTERNATIONAL. 1974. q. Aus.$15($15) International Sinatra Society, 4 Warwick Court, North Dandenong, Vic. 3175, Australia. Ed. G. Hawkins. bk.rev.; film rev.; stat. circ. 2,000. (back issues avail.)

SLOWNIK BIOGRAFICZNY POLSKICH NAUK MEDYCZNYCH 20 WIEKU. see *MEDICAL SCIENCES*

012 305.5   US   ISSN 1071-3905
SOCIAL REGISTER. Variant title: S.R. (Supplement avail.: Social Register Observer) 1886. s-a. $105 to non-members; members $96. Social Register Association, 381 Park Ave. S, New York, NY 10016. TEL 212-685-2634. Ed.Bd. **Document type:** directory.

920   BL   ISSN 0301-6994
SOCIEDADE BRASILEIRA. 1974. a. Livraria Francisco Alves Editora, Rua Sete de Setembro 177, 20050 Rio de Janeiro RJ, Brazil. adv.

SOMETHING ABOUT THE AUTHOR. see *LITERATURE*

920   US   ISSN 0885-6842
PN497
SOMETHING ABOUT THE AUTHOR. AUTOBIOGRAPHY SERIES. 1986. s-a. $79. Gale Research, 835 Penobscot Bldg., 645 Griswold St., Detroit, MI 48226-4094. TEL 313-961-2242; 800-877-4253. FAX 800-414-5043. E-mail: daniel_snyder@gale.com. Ed. Joyce Nakamura. illus.
    Description: Contains autobiographical essays written especially for the series by authors and illustrators of books for young people.

920 968   SA   ISSN 0085-6363
SOUTH AFRICAN BIOGRAPHICAL AND HISTORICAL STUDIES. 1970. irreg., no.27, 1984. price varies. A.A. Balkema Ltd., P.O. Box 3117, Cape Town 8000, South Africa. (And: P.O. Box 1675, 3000 BR Rotterdam, Netherlands) **Document type:** monographic series.

SOUTHWESTERN STUDIES. MONOGRAPHS. see *HISTORY — History Of North And South America*

920 914.706   US
SOVIET BIOGRAPHICAL SERVICE. 1985. q. $100 (effective 1997 & 1998). J.L. Scherer, Ed. & Pub., 4900 18th Ave. S., Minneapolis, MN 55417. TEL 612-722-1947. index. (looseleaf format) **Document type:** academic/scholarly publication.
    Description: Provides biographies of leaders in the former Soviet republics.

STARS. see *MOTION PICTURES*

920 778.5   IT
STELLE FILANTI. 1978. irreg. Gremese Editore S.r.l., 88 Via Virginia Agnelli, 00151 Rome, Italy. Eds. Claudio G. Fava, Orio Caldiron.

SUZI DEVERAUX INTERNATIONAL FAN CLUB. see *MUSIC*

SVERIGES FOERFATTARFOERBUND. MEDLEMSFOERTECKNING/SWEDISH WRITERS ASSOCIATION. MEMBERSHIP ROLL. see *LITERATURE*

920   SW
SWEDEN. RIKSMARSKALKSAAMBETET. KUNGLIGA HOVSTATERNA. a. A W I International AB, P.O. Box 4627, S-116 91 Stockholm, Sweden. TEL 46-8-7282500. FAX 46-8-338707.

920   SZ
SWISS BIOGRAPHICAL INDEX OF PROMINENT PERSONS/ANNUAIRE SUISSE DU MONDE ET DES AFFAIRES/WER IST WER IN DER SCHWEIZ UND IM FUERSTENTUM LICHTENSTEIN/CHI E CHI IN SVIZZERA?. 1972. biennial. 200 SFr.($150) Editions International Registry of Who's Who S.A., 23, Chemin du Levant, CH-1005 Lausanne, Switzerland. TEL 41-21-3114470. FAX 41-21-3114470. Ed. Louis-Marc Servien. adv. circ. 3,000. **Document type:** directory.

920   PL   ISSN 1230-4328
SYLWETKI LODZKICH UCZONYCH. 1992. 5/yr. $9 (effective 1996 & 1997). Lodzkie Towarzystwo Naukowe, Ul. Piotrkowska 179, 90-447 Lodz, Poland. TEL 48-42-361026. FAX 48-42-361995. (Dist. by: Ars Polona, Krakowskie Przedmiescie 7, 00-068 Warsaw, Poland) Ed. Edward Karasinski. **Document type:** bulletin.

920 970   US   ISSN 0161-8423
E757.2
THEODORE ROOSEVELT ASSOCIATION JOURNAL. 1975. q. $35. Theodore Roosevelt Association, Box 719, Oyster Bay, NY 11771. TEL 516-921-6319. FAX 516-921-6481. Ed. John A. Gable. adv.; bk.rev.; bibl.; illus.; circ. 2,000 (paid). **Indexed:** Amer.Hist.& Life (1989-), Hist.Abstr. (1989-). **Document type:** academic/scholarly publication.
    Description: Contains historical articles and reviews on the life and works of Theodore Roosevelt.

TONIC. see *MUSIC*

TOP MANAGEMENT BELGIUM - LUXEMBURG. see *BUSINESS AND ECONOMICS — Management*

920   GW
TUDUV-STUDIEN. REIHE BAYERN PRIVAT. 1984. irreg. price varies. Tuduv Verlagsgesellschaft mbH, Gabelsbergerstr. 15, 80333 Munich, Germany.

TWAYNE'S UNITED STATES AUTHORS SERIES. see *LITERATURE*

920 792   US
VARIETY'S WHO'S WHO IN SHOW BUSINESS. irreg., latest 1989. $59.95. R.R. Bowker, A Division of Reed Elsevier Inc., 121 Chanlon Rd., New Providence, NJ 07974. TEL 908-464-6800. FAX 908-665-6688. TELEX 138 755. E-mail: info@bowker.com; URL: http://www.reedref.com. (Subscr. to: Order Dept., Box 31, New Providence, NJ 07974-9903. TEL 800-521-8110) **Document type:** bibliography, directory.
    Description: Profiles more than 6,500 industry figures - studio heads, stars, producers, directors, scriptwriters, cinematographers, and many other creative and technical personnel - at work in all facets of film, television, and theatre today.

VERDI NEWSLETTER. see *MUSIC*

920 945   IT
LA VETTA D'ITALIA; mensile di politica e di cultura dell'Alto Adige. 1960. m. L.15000. Tipografia Presel, Via Roma 69, 39100 Bolzano, Italy. TEL 0471 932037. Ed. Andrea Mitolo. (back issues avail.)

920 914.3   NE   ISSN 0924-624X
VIENNA CIRCLE COLLECTION. 1973. irreg., vol.21, 1994. price varies. Kluwer Academic Publishers, Postbus 17, 3300 AA Dordrecht, Netherlands. TEL 31-78-6392392. FAX 31-78-6392254. TELEX 29245 KAPG NL. E-mail: services@wkap.nl; URL: http://www.wkap.nl. (Dist. by: Kluwer Academic Publishers Group, P.O. Box 322, 3300 AH Dordrecht, Netherlands. TEL 31-78-6392392. FAX 31-78-6546474; N. America dist. addr.: Box 358, Accord Sta., Hingham, MA 02018-0358. TEL 617-871-6600. FAX 617-871-6528) Ed.Bd. **Document type:** monographic series.
    —BLDSC (9235.585000).
    Refereed Serial

VIRGINIA MAGAZINE OF HISTORY AND BIOGRAPHY. see *HISTORY — History Of North And South America*

920   US   ISSN 0735-1909
VITAE SCHOLASTICAE. 1982. s-a. $40 to individuals (foreign $50); institutions $60 (foreign $80). (International Society for Educational Biography) Caddo Gap Press, 317 S. Division St., Ste. 2, Ann Arbor, MI 48104. TEL 313-662-0886. FAX 313-668-7672. E-mail: caddogap@aol.com. Ed. Lucy F. Townsend; Pub. Alan H. Jones. R&P contact: Alan H. Jones. adv.; bk.rev.; bibl. circ. 150. **Indexed:** Amer.Hist.& Life (1983-), Hist.Abstr. (1983-). **Document type:** academic/scholarly publication.

VOODOO CHILD. see *MUSIC*

VSPOMOGATEL'NYE ISTORICHESKIE DISTSIPLINY. see *HISTORY — History Of Europe*

WAGNER. see *MUSIC*

WAGNER NEWS. see *MUSIC*

920   GW   ISSN 0172-911X
WER IST WER?; das deutsche who's who. 1948. a. DM.350. Schmidt-Roemhild Verlag, Mengstr. 16, 23552 Luebeck, Germany. TEL 49-451-703101. FAX 49-451-7031253. **Document type:** directory.

920   US   ISSN 0146-8081
E176
WHO WAS WHO IN AMERICA. 1896. irreg., latest 1996. $999.95 for 13-vol. set. Marquis Who's Who, A Division of Reed Elsevier Inc., 121 Chanlon Rd., New Providence, NJ 07974. TEL 908-464-6800. FAX 908-665-6688. TELEX 138 755. E-mail: info@reedref.com; URL: http://www.reedref.com. (Subscr. to: Order Dept., Box 31, New Providence, NJ 07974-9903NJ 07974-9903. TEL 800-521-8110) (also avail. in magnetic tape) **Document type:** directory.
    ●Also available on CD-ROM. Producer(s): Bowker Electronic Publishing.
    —CISTI. **CCC.**
    Description: Profiles over 127,000 notable figures in American history, from the first Jamestown settlement to current times.

920.01   UK   ISSN 0083-937X
DA28
WHO'S WHO (YEAR); an annual biographical dictionary. 1849. a. £95 (effective 1996). A. & C. Black (Publishers) Ltd., Howard Rd., Eaton Socon, Huntingdon, Cambs. PE19 3EZ, England. TEL 44-1480-212666. FAX 44-1480-405014. (Dist. in the U.S. by: St. Martin's Press, 175 Fifth Ave., New York, NY 10010. TEL 800-221-7945) **Document type:** directory.
    —CISTI. **CCC.**
    Description: With more than 29,000 entries, provides an overview of international people from all walks of life.

920   US
WHO'S WHO (YEAR); an annual biographical dictionary. a. $210 (effective 1997). St. Martins Press, Scholarly and Reference Division, 175 Fifth Ave., New York, NY 10010. TEL 212-982-3900. FAX 212-777-6359. **Document type:** academic/scholarly publication.

920 305.895   US   ISSN 1075-7104
▼**WHO'S WHO AMONG ASIAN AMERICANS.** 1995. biennial. Gale Research, 835 Penobscot Bldg., 645 Griswold St., Detroit, MI 48226-4094. TEL 313-961-2242; 800-877-4253. FAX 800-414-5043. E-mail: daniel_snyder@gale.com. Ed. Amy Unterburger.

BIOGRAPHY

920   US   ISSN 0362-5753
E185.96
WHO'S WHO AMONG BLACK AMERICANS. 1976. biennial. $115. Gale Research, 835 Penobscot Bldg., 645 Griswold St., Detroit, MI 48226-4094. TEL 313-961-2242; 800-877-4253. FAX 800-414-5043. E-mail: daniel_snyder@gale.com.
●Also available online. Vendor(s): Lexis-Nexis.
Description: Documents the lives of over 17,000 American blacks who have emerged as leaders and policymakers in their chosen fields.

920   US   ISSN 1052-7354
E184.S75
WHO'S WHO AMONG HISPANIC AMERICANS. 1990. biennial. $89.95. Gale Research, 835 Penobscot Bldg., 645 Griswold St., Detroit, MI 48226-4094. TEL 313-961-2242; 800-877-4253. FAX 800-414-5043. E-mail: daniel_snyder@gale.com. Eds. Amy L. Unterburger, Jane L. Delgado.
●Also available online. Vendor(s): Lexis-Nexis.
Description: Contains biographical data on over 9600 contemporary Hispanic Americans. Arranged alphabetically, with occupation, geographic location, and country of descent indexes.

378 920   US   ISSN 0511-8891
WHO'S WHO AMONG STUDENTS IN AMERICAN JUNIOR COLLEGES. 1966. a. $49.95. Randall Publishing Co., Box 2029, Tuscaloosa, AL 35401. TEL 205-349-2990.

920 379   US
WHO'S WHO AMONG STUDENTS IN AMERICAN UNIVERSITIES AND COLLEGES. a., 62nd ed., 1996. $49.95. Randall Publishing Co., Box 2029, Tuscaloosa, AL 35401. TEL 205-349-2990.

920   US   ISSN 0083-9396
E176
WHO'S WHO IN AMERICA. (In 3 vols.) 1899. a., 52nd ed., 1997. $509.95 (effective Sep. 1997). Marquis Who's Who, A Division of Reed Elsevier Inc., 121 Chanlon Rd., New Providence, NJ 07974. TEL 908-464-6800. FAX 908-665-6688. TELEX 138 755. E-mail: info@reedref.com; URL: http://www.reedref.com. (Subscr. to: Order Dept, Box 31, New Providence, NJ 07974-9903. TEL 800-521-8110) Ed. Harriet L. Tiger; Pub. Sandra S. Barnes. (magnetic tape; microfiche from BHP) **Indexed:** Child.Auth.& Illus. **Document type:** directory.
●Also available online. Vendor(s): Knight-Ridder Information, Inc. (File no.234).
Also available on CD-ROM. Producer(s): Bowker Electronic Publishing.
—BLDSC (9312.050000); CISTI. **CCC.**
Description: Biographical resource on leading and influential Americans. Lists over 92,000 leaders, decision-makers, and innovators from every important field, along with more than 15,000 emerging figures profiled for the first time.

927 700   US   ISSN 0000-0191
N6536
WHO'S WHO IN AMERICAN ART. 1936. biennial, 23rd ed., 1997-1998. $210. R.R. Bowker, A Division of Reed Elsevier Inc., 121 Chanlon Rd., New Providence, NJ 07974. TEL 908-464-6800. FAX 908-665-6688. TELEX 138 755. E-mail: info@bowker.com; URL: http://www.reedref.com. (Subscr. to: Order Dept, Box 31, New Providence, NJ 07974-9903. TEL 800-521-8110) Ed. Liz Kizar. index. (also avail. in magnetic tape) **Indexed:** Child.Auth.& Illus. **Document type:** directory.
●Also available online. Vendor(s): Knight-Ridder Information, Inc. (File no.236).
—CCC.
Description: Profiles artists, critics, curators, collectors, dealers, administrators involved in the visual arts in the U.S. and Canada, with brief biographies and mailing addresses.

920 370   US   ISSN 1046-7203
LA2311
WHO'S WHO IN AMERICAN EDUCATION. 1988. biennial, 5th ed., 1995. $159.95. Marquis Who's Who, A Division of Reed Elsevier Inc., 121 Chanlon Rd., New Providence, NJ 07974. TEL 908-464-6800. FAX 908-665-6688. TELEX 138 755. E-mail: info@reedref.com; URL: http://www.reedref.com. (Subscr. to: Order Dept, Box 31, New Providence, NJ 07974-9903. TEL 800-521-8110) (also avail. in magnetic tape) **Document type:** directory.
●Also available on CD-ROM. Producer(s): Bowker Electronic Publishing.
—CCC.
Description: Provides information on over 27,000 achievers in the field of education - from elementary school teachers to university professors, and from local school board members to US Department of Education administrators.

WHO'S WHO IN AMERICAN LAW. see *LAW*

WHO'S WHO IN AMERICAN NURSING. see *MEDICAL SCIENCES — Nurses And Nursing*

923.2   US   ISSN 0000-0205
E176
WHO'S WHO IN AMERICAN POLITICS. 1967. biennial, 16th ed., 1997-1998. $259.95 for 2-vol. set. R.R. Bowker, A Division of Reed Elsevier Inc., 121 Chanlon Rd., New Providence, NJ 07974. TEL 908-464-6800. FAX 908-665-6688. TELEX 138 755. E-mail: info@bowker.com; URL: http://www.reedref.com. (Subscr. to: Order Dept, Box 31, New Providence, NJ 07974-9903. TEL 800-521-8110) Ed. Beberly McDonough; Pub. Andrew Meyer. index. (also avail. in magnetic tape) **Document type:** directory.
●Also available online. Vendor(s): Knight-Ridder Information, Inc. (File no.236).
—CCC.
Description: Comprises capsule biographies of political decision-makers from President to local town officials.

920 700   UK
WHO'S WHO IN ART. 1927. biennial, latest 27th ed., May 1996. £39.50. Art Trade Press, 9 Brockhampton Rd., Havant, Hants. PO9 1NU, England. TEL 44-1705-484943. (Dist. in N. America by: Gale Research Inc., 835 Penobscot Bldg., Detroit, MI 48266) **Document type:** directory.
Description: Lists prominent persons in the art world.

920 320   UK
WHO'S WHO IN ASIAN AND AUSTRALASIAN POLITICS. irreg., latest 1991. £128($175) Bowker - Saur Ltd., A member of the Reed Elsevier plc group, Maypole House, Maypole Rd., E. Grinstead, W. Sussex RH19 1HU, England. TEL 44-1342-330100. FAX 44-1342-330191. E-mail: custserv@bowker-saur.co.uk; URL: http://www.reed-elsevier.com. **Document type:** directory.
Description: Contains biographical information on more than 3,000 figures who dictate the political climate in this existing region. Covers the political spectrum - politicians, opposition political figures, party activities and trade unionists.

WHO'S WHO IN ASSOCIATION PUBLISHING. see *PUBLISHING AND BOOK TRADE*

920   UK
WHO'S WHO IN AUSTRALASIA AND THE PACIFIC NATIONS. 1989. irreg., 2nd Edn., 1991. £95($165) Melrose Press Ltd., 3 Regal Ln., Soham, Ely, Cambridgeshire CB7 5BA, England. TEL 44-1353-721091. FAX 44-1353-721839. (Dist. in US by: Taylor & Francis Inc., 1900 Frost Rd., Ste. 101, Bristol, PA 19007-1598) **Document type:** directory.
Formerly: Who's Who in Australasia and the Far East.
Description: Contains 8,000 biographical profiles detailing the achievements of leading figures in all areas of interest.

920   US   ISSN 0511-8948
F860
WHO'S WHO IN CALIFORNIA. 1928. a. $205. Who's Who Historical Society, 2533 N. Carson St., Ste. 1147, Carson City, NV 89706. TEL 702-883-2384. Dir. Edna L. Barrett. circ. 4,500. **Document type:** directory.
Supersedes (1950-1952): Who's Who in Los Angeles County.
Description: Lists the biographies of over 4,000 eminent Californians from the arts, science, medicine, education, religion, business, law, and government.

920   CN   ISSN 0083-9450
F1033
WHO'S WHO IN CANADA. 1911. a. $130 (effective 1997). International Press Publications Inc., 90 Nolan Ct., Ste. 21, Markham, ON L3R 4L9, Canada. TEL 905-946-9588. FAX 905-946-9590. E-mail: ipp@interlog.com; URL: http://www.interlog.com/~ipp. Ed. Jack Kohane. **Indexed:** Child.Auth.& Illus. **Document type:** directory.
—CISTI.

920   CN   ISSN 0831-6309
PN1998.A1
WHO'S WHO IN CANADIAN FILM AND TELEVISION (YEAR)/QUI EST QUI AU CINEMA ET A LA TELEVISION AU CANADA. (Text in English, French) 1985. irreg. Can.$39.95. Academy of Canadian Cinema & Television - Academie Canadienne du Cinema et de la Television, 158 Pearl St., Toronto, ON M5H 1L3, Canada. TEL 416-591-2040. FAX 416-591-2157. adv. circ. 3,000. **Document type:** directory.
Description: Guide to industry members working behind the scenes in Canadian film and television.

920   US   ISSN 0147-8265
RZ231
WHO'S WHO IN CHIROPRACTIC, INTERNATIONAL. * 1977. biennial. $49.50. Who's Who in Chiropractic, International Publishing Co., Inc., 7945 Coventry Dr., Castle Rock, CO 80104-9259. Ed. Fern L. Dzaman.
—CISTI.

WHO'S WHO IN COMPUTING. see *COMPUTERS*

920 328   US   ISSN 1054-9234
JK1010
WHO'S WHO IN CONGRESS. 1992. biennial. Congressional Quarterly Inc., 1414 22nd St., N.W., Washington, DC 20037. TEL 202-887-8500. FAX 202-887-6706.

920 330.9   US
WHO'S WHO IN ECONOMIC DEVELOPMENT. a. American Economic Development Council, 9801 W. Higgins, Ste. 540, Rosemont, IL 60018-4726. TEL 847-692-9944. FAX 847-696-2990. E-mail: aedc@interacess.com; URL: http://www.aedc.org/hqtrs. Ed. Marion Morgan. R&P contact: Marion Morgan. adv.: page $800; trim 8 3/8 x 10 7/8; adv. contact: Marion Morgan. circ. 2,700 (controlled). **Document type:** directory.

620   US   ISSN 0149-7537
TA139
WHO'S WHO IN ENGINEERING. 1970. triennial, 9th ed., 1995. $225 to non-members; members $140. American Association of Engineering Societies, 1111 19th St. N.W., Ste. 406, Washington, DC 20036-3690. TEL 202-296-2237. FAX 202-296-1151. E-mail: aaes@access.digex.net. (Dist. in UK by: Bowker-Saur Ltd., Order Processing Dept., Butterworth Services, Borough Green, Sevenoaks, Kent TN15 8PH, England. TEL 0732-884567) **Document type:** directory.
—CISTI; Linda Hall.
Formerly: Engineers of Distinction (ISSN 0149-7545)
Description: Lists more than 14,000 of the world's top engineers, who, because of their distinguished achievements, honors, and awards, have been selected for professional recognition.

BIOGRAPHY

920 330 UK
WHO'S WHO IN EUROPEAN BUSINESS. 1993. irreg. £110. Bowker - Saur Ltd., A member of the Reed Elsevier plc group, Maypole House, Maypole Rd., E. Grinstead, W. Sussex RH19 1HU, England. TEL 44-1342-330100. FAX 44-1342-330191. E-mail: custserv@bowker-saur.co.uk; URL: http://www.reed-elsevier.com. **Document type:** directory.
  Description: Biographies of the top 5,000 business leaders in both Eastern and Western Europe. Profiles the leading executives from Europe's top companies, as well as from the largest companies in each country.

920 320 UK
WHO'S WHO IN EUROPEAN POLITICS. 1990. irreg., 3rd ed., 1997. £189. Bowker - Saur Ltd., A member of the Reed Elsevier plc group, Maypole House, Maypole Rd., E. Grinstead, W. Sussex RH19 1HU, England. TEL 44-1342-330100. FAX 44-1342-330191. E-mail: custserv@bowker-saur.co.uk; URL: http://www.reed-elsevier.com. pp./issue: 880. **Document type:** directory.
  Description: Provides biographical information on more than 9,000 national and international politicians in Eastern and Western Europe.

920 600 UK
WHO'S WHO IN EUROPEAN RESEARCH AND DEVELOPMENT. a. £275. Bowker - Saur Ltd., A member of the Reed Elsevier plc group, Maypole House, Maypole Rd., E. Grinstead, W. Sussex RH19 1HU, England. TEL 44-1342-330100. FAX 44-1342-330191. E-mail: custserv@bowker-saur.co.uk; URL: http://www.bowker-saur.co.uk/service/. Ed. Yolanda Dolling. pp./issue: 1150. **Document type:** directory.
  ●Also available on CD-ROM.
  Formerly: Who's Who in Research and Development.
  Description: Contains detailed biographies of 13,000 senior research professionals, indexed by field of research and country.

920 330 US ISSN 0083-9523
HF3023.A2
WHO'S WHO IN FINANCE AND INDUSTRY. 1936. biennial, 30th ed., 1997. $279.95. Marquis Who's Who, A Division of Reed Elsevier Inc., 121 Chanlon Rd., New Providence, NJ 07974. TEL 908-464-6800. FAX 908-665-6688. TELEX 138 755. E-mail: info@reedref.com; URL: http://www.reedref.com. (Subscr. to: Order Dept., Box 31, New Providence, NJ 07974-9903. TEL 800-521-8110) (also avail. in magnetic tape) **Document type:** directory.
  ●Also available on CD-ROM. Producer(s): Bowker Electronic Publishing.
  —CISTI. **CCC.**
  Formerly: World Who's Who in Commerce and Industry.
  Description: Provides biographical coverage of more than 21,300 principal decision-makers and leaders in the industrial and financial markets.

920 FR ISSN 0083-9531
WHO'S WHO IN FRANCE/QUI EST QUI EN FRANCE. 1953. a. 2222 F.($445) (effective 1996). Editions Jacques Lafitte, 16 rue Camille Pelleton, 92300 Levallois, France. FAX 33-1-41-27-28-40. Ed. Eleonore de Dampierre. adv. circ. 10,000. **Document type:** directory.

920 II ISSN 0301-5106
WHO'S WHO IN INDIA (CALCUTTA). (Text in English) 1973. irreg. Rs.50($15) Kothari Publications, 12 India Exchange Place, Calcutta 700 001, India. TEL 91-33-220-9563. Ed. H. Kothari. adv. **Document type:** directory.
  Description: Biographical roster of leading personalities in India.

920 600 II ISSN 0083-9558
WHO'S WHO IN INDIAN ENGINEERING AND INDUSTRY. 1962. irreg. Rs.30($9) Kothari Publications, 12 India Exchange Place, Calcutta 700 001, India. TEL 91-33-220-9563. Ed. H. Kothari. adv. **Document type:** directory.
  Description: Guide to prominent people and organizations in all branches of Indian engineering and industry.

500 II ISSN 0083-9566
WHO'S WHO IN INDIAN SCIENCE. (Text in English) 1964. irreg., latest 1969. Rs.20($20) Kothari Publications, 12 India Exchange Place, Calcutta 700 001, India. TEL 91-33-220-9563. Ed. H. Kothari. adv. **Document type:** directory.
  Description: Lists biographical information about leading Indian scientists, doctors, engineers and scientific organizations.

920 327 UK ISSN 0956-7984
WHO'S WHO IN INTERNATIONAL AFFAIRS. 1990. irreg., 1st ed. $295. Europa Publications, 18 Bedford Sq., London WC1B 3JN, England. TEL 44-171-580-8236. FAX 44-171-636-1664. TELEX 21540 EUROPA G. **Document type:** directory.
  Description: Profiles 7,000 leading diplomats, politicians, government ministers, heads of state, professors, and journalists.

920 332 UK ISSN 0958-7357
WHO'S WHO IN INTERNATIONAL BANKING. irreg., 6th ed., 1992. £152. Bowker - Saur Ltd., A member of Reed Elsevier plc group, Maypole House, Maypole Rd., E. Grinstead, W. Sussex RH19 1HU, England. TEL 44-1342-330100. FAX 44-1342-3301991. E-mail: custserv@bowker-saur.co.uk; URL: http://www.reed-elsevier.com. **Document type:** directory.
  Description: Provides concise biographical and contact information on some 4,000 of today's leading bankers, including details about the entrant's education, career, civic interests, business and professional memberships, honors and awards, publications.

920 GW
WHO'S WHO IN INTERNATIONAL ORGANIZATIONS. irreg., 2nd ed., 1995. DM.620. (Union of International Associations, BE) K.G. Saur Verlag KG, A member of the Reed Elsevier plc group, Ortlerstr. 8, 81373 Munich, Germany. TEL 49-89-769020. FAX 49-89-76902150. E-mail: 100730@compuserve.com; URL: http://www.reed-elsevier.com. (Subscr. to: Postfach 701620, 81316 Munich, Germany; N. America subscr. to: K.G. Saur, 121 Chanlon Rd., Box 31, New Providence, NJ 07974-9903, USA. TEL 908-665-3576) Eds. Jon J. Jenkins, Jacqueline Nebel. **Document type:** directory.
  Description: Contains 12,000 biographies covering prominent individuals in 7,000 organizations, focusing on every field of human endeavor.

920 GW ISSN 0083-9612
DS80.75
WHO'S WHO IN LEBANON. (Text in English) 1963. biennial, 14th ed., 1996. £190. K.G. Saur Verlag KG, Ortlerstr. 8, 81373 Munich, Germany. E-mail: 100730.1341@compuserve.com; URL: http://www.reed-elsevier.com. (Dist in N. America by: K.G. Saur, 121 Chanlon Rd., New Providence, NJ 07974-9903. TEL 908-464-6800) Ed. Charles G. Gedeon. adv. circ. 3,000. pp./issue: 498.

WHO'S WHO IN MEDICINE AND HEALTHCARE. see MEDICAL SCIENCES

659.2 920 US ISSN 0511-9022
HM263
WHO'S WHO IN PUBLIC RELATIONS (INTERNATIONAL). 1959. irreg., 6th ed., 1992. P R Publishing Co., Inc., Box 600, Exeter, NH 03833. TEL 603-778-0514. FAX 603-778-1741. E-mail: prr@nh.ultranet.com. **Document type:** directory.

920 790.1 US
WHO'S WHO IN RECREATION. 1989. a. $59.95 membership. Society of Recreation Executives, Box 520, Gonzale, FL 32560-0520. TEL 904-477-7992. FAX 904-479-8393. Ed. Hugh C. McDaniel. adv. contact: Hugh C. McDaniel. circ. 4,100 (controlled). **Document type:** directory.

920 US ISSN 1063-5599
Q141
WHO'S WHO IN SCIENCE AND ENGINEERING. 1992. biennial, 4th ed., 1997. $272.95. Marquis Who's Who, A Division of Reed Elsevier Inc., 121 Chanlon Rd., New Providence, NJ 07974. TEL 908-464-6800. FAX 908-665-6688. TELEX 038 755. E-mail: info@reedref.com; URL: http://www.reedref.com. (Subscr. to: Order Dept., Box 31, New Providence, NJ 07974-9903. TEL 800-521-8110) (also avail. in magnetic tape) **Document type:** directory.
  ●Also available on CD-ROM. Producer(s): Bowker Electronic Publishing.
  —CISTI; Linda Hall. **CCC.**
  Description: Profiles 26,000 leading international figures, each selected for achievements in aerospace, microcircuitry, lasers, genetics, biotechnology, and all disciplines of science and engineering.

920 500 UK ISSN 0083-968X
Q141
WHO'S WHO IN SCIENCE IN EUROPE. a. $545. Longman Group UK Ltd., Westgate House, 6th Fl., The High, Harlow, Essex CM20 1YR, England. TEL 44-1279-442601. FAX 44-1279-444501. (Subscr. to: Pearson Professional, P.O. Box 77, Fourth Ave., Harlow, Essex CM19 5BQ, England. TEL 44-1279-623924. FAX 44-1279-639609) **Document type:** directory.
  —BLDSC (9312.541000); CISTI. **CCC.**
  Description: Profiles over 21000 senior research scientists, engineers, agriculturalists, and medical scientists.

920 UK ISSN 0269-1736
WHO'S WHO IN SCOTLAND. 1986. biennial. £35 (effective 1997). Carrick Media, 2-7 Galt House, 31 Bank St., Irvine, Ayrshire KA12 0LL, Scotland. TEL 44-1294-311322. FAX 44-1294-311322. E-mail: carrickmedia.demon.co.uk. **Document type:** directory.
  Description: Biographies of approximately 5,000 people prominent in Scottish public life.

920 320 UK
WHO'S WHO IN SOUTH AFRICAN POLITICS. irreg., 4th ed., 1993. £65. Bowker - Saur Ltd., A Reed Reference Publishing Company, Part of the Reed Elsevier group, Maypole House, Maypole Rd., E. Grinstead, W. Sussex RH19 1HH, England. TEL 0342-330-100. FAX 0342-330-191. (Subscr. to: c/o Butterworths Service Co., Borough Green, Sevenoaks, Kent TN15 8PH, England. TEL 0732-884567) **Document type:** directory.
  Description: Provides biographies on over 150 prominent political figures.

WHO'S WHO IN SUPER SITES. see COMPUTERS — Computer Industry Directories

920 SZ ISSN 0083-9736
DQ52
WHO'S WHO IN SWITZERLAND. 1951. biennial. 178 SFr. (effective 1997). Orell Fuessli Verlag, Dietzingerstr. 3, CH-8036 Zurich, Switzerland. TEL 41-1-4667711. FAX 41-1-4667412. circ. 10,000. **Document type:** directory.

920 600 US ISSN 0887-5901
T39
WHO'S WHO IN TECHNOLOGY. 1979. biennial. $380 (Biography $95; Index $285). Gale Research, 835 Penobscot Bldg., 645 Griswold St., Detroit, MI 48226-4094. TEL 313-961-2242; 800-877-4253. FAX 800-414-5043. E-mail: daniel_snyder@gale.co. Ed. Amy L. Unterburger.
  ●Also available online. Vendor(s): Lexis-Nexis, Questel Orbit Inc. (WHOTECH).
  —CISTI.
  Description: Profiles of the nation's leading scientists and engineers.

920.0593 TH ISSN 0125-1694
WHO'S WHO IN THAILAND.* 1973. m. $6.92. International Publishing and Marketing Co., B.O.A.C. Bldg., 5th Fl., Rajaprasong Corner, Bangkok, Thailand. illus.

BIOGRAPHY

920   LE   ISSN 0083-9752
D198.3
WHO'S WHO IN THE ARAB WORLD. (Text in English) 1965. biennial, 11th, 1992. $280. Publitec Publications, Gedeon House, 135-137 John F. Kennedy St., Jisr el Bacha, P.O. Box 5936, Beirut, Lebanon. (Dist. in N. America by: Gale Research Inc., 835 Penobscot Bldg., Detroit, MI 48226-4094. TEL 313-961-2242) Ed. Charles G. Gedeon. circ. 5,000.

920   US   ISSN 0083-9760
E176
WHO'S WHO IN THE EAST. 1945. biennial, 26th ed., 1996. $279.95. Marquis Who's Who, A Division of Reed Elsevier Inc., 121 Chanlon Rd., New Providence, NJ 07974. TEL 908-464-6800. FAX 908-665-6688. TELEX 138 755. E-mail: info@reedref.com; URL: http://www.reedref.com. (Subscr. to: Order Dept., Box 31, New Providence, NJ 07974-9903. TEL 800-521-8110) (also avail. in magnetic tape) **Document type:** directory.
●Also available on CD-ROM. Producer(s): Bowker Electronic Publishing.
—CCC.
Description: Lists over 22,000 biographies of prominent people living in Connecticut, Delaware, District of Columbia, Maine, Maryland, Massachusetts, New Hampshire, New Jersey, New York, Pennsylvania, Rhode Island, and Vermont, as well as New Brunswick, Newfoundland, Nova Scotia, Prince Edward Island, Quebec, and eastern Ontario in Canada.

WHO'S WHO IN THE EGG AND POULTRY INDUSTRIES. see AGRICULTURE — Abstracting, Bibliographies, Statistics

920   US   ISSN 0083-9787
E176
WHO'S WHO IN THE MIDWEST. 1946. biennial, 25th ed., 1996. $259.95. Marquis Who's Who, A Division of Reed Elsevier Inc., 121 Chanlon Rd., New Providence, NJ 07974. TEL 908-464-6800. FAX 908-665-6688. TELEX 138 755. E-mail: info@reedref.com; URL: http://www.reedref.com. (Subscr. to: Order Dept., Box 31, New Providence, NJ 07974-9903. TEL 800-521-8110) (also avail. in magnetic tape) **Indexed:** Child.Auth.& Illus. **Document type:** directory.
●Also available on CD-ROM. Producer(s): Bowker Electronic Publishing.
—CCC.
Description: Lists some 24,000 biographies of prominent people living in Illinois, Indiana, Iowa, Kansas, Michigan, Minnesota, Missouri, Nebraska, North Dakota, Ohio, South Dakota, and Wisconsin, as well as Manitoba, and western Ontario in Canada.

920   GW
WHO'S WHO IN THE PEOPLE'S REPUBLIC OF CHINA. irreg., 3rd ed., 1991. DM.498($325) for 2-vol. set. K.G. Saur Verlag KG, A member of the Reed Elsevier plc group, Ortlerstr. 8, 81373 Munich, Germany. TEL 49-89-76902-0. FAX 49-89-76902150. E-mail: 100730.1341@compuserve.com; URL: http://www.reed-elsevier.com. (Subscr. to: Bowker-Saur Ltd., Order Processing Dept., Butterworth Services, Borough Green, Sevenoaks, Kent TN15 8PH, England. TEL 01732-884567; N. America subscr. to: K.G. Saur, 121 Chanlon Rd., New Providence, NJ 07974. TEL 908-665-3576) Ed. Wolfgang Bartke. illus. **Document type:** directory.
Description: Profiles more than 4,100 of China's most influential current and political leaders.

920   US   ISSN 0083-9809
E176
WHO'S WHO IN THE SOUTH AND SOUTHWEST. 1946. biennial, 25th ed., 1997. $249.95. Marquis Who's Who, A Division of Reed Elsevier Inc., 121 Chanlon Rd., New Providence, NJ 07974. TEL 908-464-6800. FAX 908-665-6688. TELEX 138 755. E-mail: info@reedref.com; URL: http://www.reedref.com. (Subscr. to: Order Dept., Box 31, New Providence, NJ 07974-9903. TEL 800-521-8110) (also avail. in magnetic tape) **Indexed:** Child.Auth.& Illus. **Document type:** directory.
●Also available on CD-ROM. Producer(s): Bowker Electronic Publishing.
Description: Lists nearly 23,000 biographies of prominent people living in Alabama, Arkansas, Florida, Georgia, Kentucky, Louisiana, Mississippi, North Carolina, Oklahoma, South Carolina, Tennessee, Texas, Virginia, West Virginia, Puerto Rico, the Virgin Islands, and Mexico.

WHO'S WHO IN THE U K INFORMATION WORLD. see LIBRARY AND INFORMATION SCIENCES

920   US   ISSN 0083-9817
E176
WHO'S WHO IN THE WEST. 1946. biennial, 26th ed., 1997. $272.95. Marquis Who's Who, A Division of Reed Elsevier Inc., 121 Chanlon Rd., New Providence, NJ 07974. TEL 908-464-6800. FAX 908-665-6688. TELEX 138 755. E-mail: info@reedref.com; URL: http://www.reedref.com. (Subscr. to: Order Dept., Box 31, New Providence, NJ 07974-9903. TEL 800-521-8110) (also avail. in magnetic tape) **Document type:** directory.
●Also available on CD-ROM. Producer(s): Bowker Electronic Publishing.
—CCC.
Description: Lists over 23,000 biographies of prominent people living in Alaska, Arizona, California, Colorado, Hawaii, Idaho, Montana, Nevada, New Mexico, Oregon, Utah, Washington, and Wyoming, as well as Alberta, British Columbia, and Saskatchewan in Canada.

920   US   ISSN 0083-9825
CT120
WHO'S WHO IN THE WORLD. 1971. a., 15th ed., 1998. $369.95. Marquis Who's Who, A Division of Reed Elsevier Inc., 121 Chanlon Rd., New Providence, NJ 07974. TEL 908-464-6800. FAX 908-665-6688. TELEX 138 755. E-mail: info@reedref.com; URL: http://www.reedref.com. (Subscr. to: Order Dept., Box 31, New Providence, NJ 07974-9903. TEL 800-521-8110) (also avail. in magnetic tape) **Document type:** directory.
●Also available on CD-ROM. Producer(s): Bowker Electronic Publishing.
—BLDSC (9312.558500); CISTI. **CCC.**
Description: Profiles 36,000 individual biographies of the people whose activities are shaping today's world. Includes prominent government figures, high-ranking military officers, leaders of the largest corporations in each country, heads of religious organizations, pioneers in science and the arts, and more.

WHO'S WHO IN TRAINING AND DEVELOPMENT. see BUSINESS AND ECONOMICS — Management

920 360   US   ISSN 1076-4755
WHO'S WHO IN WASHINGTON NONPROFIT GROUPS. 1994. a. Congressional Quarterly Inc., 1414 22nd St., N.W., Washington, DC 20037. TEL 202-887-8500. FAX 202-728-1863. Ed. Jerry A. Orvedahl.

920   US   ISSN 0083-9841
E176
WHO'S WHO OF AMERICAN WOMEN. 1958. biennial, 20th ed., 1996. $249. Marquis Who's Who, A Division of Reed Elsevier Inc., 121 Chanlon Rd., New Providence, NJ 07974. TEL 908-464-6800. FAX 908-665-6688. TELEX 138 755. E-mail: info@reedref.com; URL: http://www.reedref.com. (Subscr. to: Order Dept., Box 31, New Providence, NJ 07974-9903. TEL 800-521-8110) (also avail. in magnetic tape) **Document type:** directory.
●Also available on CD-ROM. Producer(s): Bowker Electronic Publishing.
—CCC.
Description: Contains vital and insightful biographical facts on more than 24,000 achievers. Covers a wide range of disciplines and professions including government, business, the arts, and medicine.

920 808.02   UK
WHO'S WHO OF AUSTRALIAN WRITERS. irreg., 2nd ed., 1995. £48. (Australia Council, AT) Bowker - Saur Ltd., A member of the Reed Elsevier plc group, Maypole House, Maypole Rd., E. Grinstead, W. Sussex RH19 1HU, England. TEL 44-1342-330100. FAX 44-1342-330191. E-mail: custserv@bowker-saur.co.uk; URL: http://www.reed-elsevier.com. (Co-sponsor: National Center for Australian Studies, Monash University) **Document type:** directory.
Description: Includes approximately 5,000 entries on living writers of fiction, poetry, plays, radio and TV scripts.

920   SA
WHO'S WHO OF SOUTHERN AFRICA INCLUDING MAURITIUS, NAMIBIA, ZIMBABWE, BOTSWANA, SWAZILAND AND NEIGHBORING COUNTRIES. (Text in English) 1907. a. R.320 (for 1996-1997 edition). Jonathan Ball Publishers, P.O. Box 411697, Craighall 2024, South Africa. TEL 27-11-8802406. FAX 27-11-8802366. Ed. S.V. Hayes. adv. **Document type:** directory.
Former titles: Who's Who of Southern Africa Including Mauritius, South West Africa, Zimbabwe and Neighboring Countries; Who's Who of Southern Africa Including Mauritius, South West Africa, Zimbabwe-Rhodesia and Neighboring Countries; Who's Who of Southern Africa Including Mauritius, South West Africa, Rhodesia and Neighboring Countries; Who's Who of Southern Africa (ISSN 0083-9876); Incorporates: Who's Who of Rhodesia, Mauritius, Central and East Africa (ISSN 0083-9868)
Refereed Serial

WHO'S WHO OF VICE-CHANCELLORS, PRESIDENTS AND RECTORS OF COMMONWEALTH UNIVERSITIES. see EDUCATION — Higher Education

920 320   UK
WHO'S WHO OF WOMEN IN WORLD POLITICS; biographies of women currently in government legislatures worldwide. 1991. irreg. £78. Bowker - Saur Ltd., A member of the Reed Elsevier plc group, Maypole House, Maypole Rd., E. Grinstead, W. Sussex RH19 1HU, England. TEL 44-1342-330100. FAX 44-1342-330191. E-mail: custserv@bowker-saur.co.uk; URL: http://www.reed-elsevier.com. **Document type:** directory.
Description: Features more than 1,500 biographies organized by country, and in alphabetical order, of prominent female politicians from over 100 countries.

920   UK
WHO'S WHO ON THE SCREEN. 1983. irreg. £6.95($21.35) Madeleine Productions, 15 Wallace Ave., Worthing BN11 5RA, England. Ed. John Walter Skinner. bibl.; illus.; stat. circ. 5,000.

920   UK   ISSN 0084-0254
AS122
WILLIAM MORRIS SOCIETY. JOURNAL. 1962. 2/yr. £13.50($20) membership. William Morris Society, Kelmscott House, 26 Upper Mall, Hammersmith, London W6 9TA, England. TEL 44-181-741-3735. Ed. Nicholas Salmon. adv.; bk.rev. circ. 2,200. (back issues avail.) **Indexed:** DAAI, Ind.Bk.Rev.Hum. **Document type:** bulletin.
—KR SourceOne; UnCover.

WINE PRESS. see GENEALOGY AND HERALDRY

WINESBURG EAGLE. see LITERATURE

WOMEN OF ACHIEVEMENT AND HERSTORY. see WOMEN'S INTERESTS

WORLD LEADER UPDATE. see POLITICAL SCIENCE

920   US   ISSN 1041-3529
AS8
WORLD OF WINNERS; a current and historical perspective on awards and their winners. 1989. irreg., 2nd ed. 1991. $80. Gale Research, 835 Penobscot Bldg., 645 Griswold St., Detroit, MI 48226-4094. TEL 313-961-2242; 800-877-4253. FAX 800-414-5043. E-mail: daniel__snyder@gale.com. Ed. Gita Siegman.

WORLD WHO'S WHO OF WOMEN. see WOMEN'S INTERESTS

WRITERS DIRECTORY. see BUSINESS AND ECONOMICS — Trade And Industrial Directories

ZHONGGUO ZUOJIA; daxing wenxue shuangyuekan. see LITERATURE

920   CC   ISSN 1003-0557
ZHONGHUA ERNU. (Text in Chinese) 1988. bi-m. (Zhonghua Quanguo Qingnian Lianhehui) Zhongguo Qingnian Chubanshe, 10 Dong Dajie, Qianmen, Beijing 100051, People's Republic of China. TEL 86-10-7012288. **Document type:** consumer publication.
Description: Contains biographies of Chinese officials, entrepreneurs, artists, writers and other prominent figures.

920   CC   ISSN 1005-2151
ZHONGHUA ERNU (HAIWAIBAN). (Text in Chinese) m. (Zhonghua Quanguo Qingnian Lianhehui) Zhongguo Qingnian Chubanshe, 10 Dong Dajie, Qianmen, Beijing 100051, People's Republic of China. TEL 86-10-7012288. (Dist. overseas by: China Book Trading Corp., P.O. Box 399, Beijing 100044, P.R. China) pp./issue: 80. **Document type:** consumer publication.
   Description: For overseas Chinese. Contains biographies of Chinese officials, entrepreneurs, writers, artists and other prominent features.

BIOGRAPHY — Abstracting, Bibliographies, Statistics

920   US   ISSN 1042-9778
ANNUAL OBITUARY (YEAR). 1980. a. $92. Gale Research, 835 Penobscot Bldg., 645 Griswold St., Detroit, MI 48226-4094. TEL 313-961-2242; 800-877-4253. FAX 800-414-5043. E-mail: daniel__snyder@gale.com. index, cum.index.
   Description: Features information about recently deceased internationally prominent people. Most entries include selected reading list.

BIBLIOGRAPHIA FRANCISCANA. see RELIGIONS AND THEOLOGY — Abstracting, Bibliographies, Statistics

920 016   US   ISSN 0730-1316
Z5305.U5
BIOGRAPHY AND GENEALOGY MASTER INDEX. (Microfiche ed. is titled: Bio-Base) 1975. a. $320 for annual update; 5 yr. cum. $950 (microfiche $250) (CD-ROM single user $450) (effective 1997). Gale Research, 835 Penobscot Bldg., 645 Griswold St., Detroit, MI 48226-4094. TEL 313-961-2242; 800-877-4253. FAX 800-414-5043. E-mail: geri__speace@gale.com. Ed. Geri Speace. (also avail. in microfiche (ISSN 0742-2318))
   ●Also available online. Vendor(s): Knight-Ridder Information, Inc. (File nos.287,288).
   Also available on CD-ROM.
   —CISTI.
   Formerly: Biographical Dictionaries Master Index.
   Description: Index to biographical and genealogical information found in biographical dictionaries and Who's Whos.

016.92 920   US   ISSN 0006-3053
Z5301
BIOGRAPHY INDEX. 1946. q. (with a. and biennial cumulations). $190. H.W. Wilson Co., 950 University Ave., Bronx, NY 10452. TEL 718-588-8400; 800-367-6770. FAX 718-590-1617. TELEX 4990003HWILSON. Ed. Charles Cornell. (also avail. in magnetic tape) **Indexed:** Child.Auth.& Illus. **Document type:** abstracting/indexing.
   ●Also available online. Vendor(s): Knight-Ridder Information, Inc., OCLC, Wilsonline (File BIO).
   Also available on CD-ROM. Producer(s): SilverPlatter Information, Inc., H.W. Wilson (WILSONDISC).
   —BLDSC (2072.330000); CISTI; Linda Hall.
   Description: Quarterly index to biographical material in books and magazines.

920   US
CHILDREN'S AUTHORS AND ILLUSTRATORS; an index to biographical dictionaries. 1977. biennial, 4th ed., 1987. $150. Gale Research, 835 Penobscot Bldg., 645 Griswold St., Detroit, MI 48226-4094. TEL 313-961-2242; 800-877-4253. FAX 800-414-5043. E-mail: daniel_snyder@gale.com. Ed. Joyce Nakamura.
   Description: Primary sources of biographical information on authors and illustrators of books for children.

920 944   FR
DICTIONNAIRE DE BIOGRAPHIE FRANCAISE. irreg., vol.19, 1998. Letouzey et Ane Editeurs, 87 bd. Raspail, 75006 Paris, France. TEL 33-1-45488014. FAX 33-1-45490343. Ed.Bd. (back issues avail.)
   Description: Provides biographies on the men and women who played an important role in French history.

920 071   US   ISSN 1058-5648
F614.C8
OBITUARIES INDEX. 1989. irreg. University of Minnesota at Crookston, Crookston, MN 56716.

PEOPLE IN POWER. see POLITICAL SCIENCE — Abstracting, Bibliographies, Statistics

920   US   ISSN 1051-8002
E185.5
STATISTICAL RECORD OF BLACK AMERICA. 1990. biennial. $95. Gale Research, 835 Penobscot Bldg., 645 Griswold St., Detroit, MI 48226-4094. TEL 313-961-2242; 800-877-4253. FAX 800-414-5043. E-mail: daniel__snyder@gale.com. Ed. Carrell P. Horton. charts.
   Description: Provides answers to questions on a wide range of related topics, from population and social services to income, spending and wealth. Includes subject index and bibliography.

BIOLOGICAL CHEMISTRY

see Biology–Biological Chemistry

BIOLOGY

see also Biology–Bioengineering; Biology–Biological Chemistry; Biology–Biophysics; Biology–Biotechnology; Biology–Botany; Biology–Computer Applications; Biology–Cytology and Histology; Biology–Entomology; Biology–Genetics; Biology–Microbiology; Biology–Microscopy; Biology–Ornithology; Biology–Physiology; Biology–Zoology; Medical Sciences; Pharmacy and Pharmacology

571.9 610   DK   ISSN 0903-4641
CODEN: APMSEL
A P M I S. (Supplements avail.) (Text and summaries in English) 1926. m. DKK 2780 in Europe (US, Canada and Japan DKK 2800) (includes supplements) (effective 1997). Munksgaard International Publishers Ltd., 35 Noerre Soegade, P.O. Box 2148, DK-1016 Copenhagen K, Denmark. TEL 45-33-127030. FAX 45-33-129387. E-mail: fsub@mail.munksgaard.dk. (In N. America: Commerce Place, 350 Main St., Malden, MA 02148-5018. TEL 617-388-8273. FAX 617-388-8274) Ed. Joergen Rygaard. bk.rev. circ. 1,500. (reprint service avail. from ISI) **Indexed:** Abstr.Hyg., ASCA, Biol.Abstr., Biotech.Abstr., Chem.Abstr., Curr.Adv.Ecol.Sci., Curr.Adv.Genetics & Molec.Biol., Curr.Cont., Dairy Sci.Abstr., Dent.Ind., Excerp.Med., Helminthol.Abstr., Ind.Med., Ind.Sci.Rev., Ind.Vet., INIS Atomind., Med.& Surg.Dermat., Nutr.Abstr., Pig News & Info., Rev.Plant Path., Sci.Cit.Ind., Small Anim.Abstr., Vet.Bull. **Document type:** academic/scholarly publication.
   —BLDSC (1568.740000); ADONIS; CASDDS; CISTI; Genuine Article; KNAW; SWETS; UnCover. CCC.
   Formed by the merger of: Acta Pathologica, Microbiologica et Immunologica Scandinavica. Section A: Pathology (ISSN 0108-0164); Acta Pathologica, Microbiologica et Immunologica Scandinavica. Section B: Microbiology (ISSN 0108-0180); Acta Pathologica, Microbiologica et Immunologica Scandinavica. Section C: Immunology (ISSN 0108-0202); **Formerly:** Acta Pathologica et Microbiologica Scandinavica. Section A: Pathology (ISSN 0365-4184); From 1970, supersedes in part and continues numbering of: Acta Pathologica et Microbiologica Scandinavica (ISSN 0001-6624); Section B continued in part (from 1975): Acta Pathologica et Microbiologica Scandinavica. Section B: Microbiology and Immunology (ISSN: 0365-5571); From 1970, superseded in part and continued numbering of: Acta Pathologica et Microbiologica Scandinavica (ISSN: 0365-5563); Section C was formerly (until 1982): Acta Pathologica et Microbiologica Scandinavica. Section C: Immunology (ISSN: 0304-1328); From 1975, also continued in part: Acta Pathologica et Microbiologica Scandinavica. Section B: Microbiology and Immunology.
   Refereed Serial

610 576   DK   ISSN 0903-465X
R81   CODEN: AISSE2
A P M I S SUPPLEMENTUM. 1926. irreg. free to subscribers. Munksgaard International Publishers Ltd., P.O. Box 2148, DK-1016 Copenhagen K, Denmark. TEL 45-33-127030. FAX 45-33-129387. E-mail: fsub@mail.munksgaard.dk. (In N. America: Commerce Place, 350 Main St., Malden, MA 02148-50018. TEL 617-338-8273. FAX 617-388-8274) Ed. Joergen Rygaard. (also avail. in microfilm from PMC; reprint service avail. from ISI) **Indexed:** Biol.Abstr., Chem.Abstr., Curr.Cont., Dent.Ind., Helminthol.Abstr., Ind.Med., Ind.Sci.Rev., Int.Abstr.Biol.Sci., Trop.Dis.Bull. **Document type:** academic/scholarly publication.
   —BLDSC (1568.750000); ADONIS; CASDDS; CISTI; EMDOCS; KNAW; SWETS; UnCover. CCC.
   Formed by the 1988 merger of: Acta Pathologica, Microbiologica et Immunologica Scandinavica. Section A. Supplement (ISSN 0108-0172); Which was formerly (until 1982): Acta Pathologica et Microbiologica Scandinavica. Section A. Supplement (ISSN 0365-5571) & Acta Pathologica, Microbiologica et Immunologica Scandinavica. Section C. Supplement (ISSN 0108-0210); Which was formerly (until 1981): Acta Pathologica et Microbiologica Scandinavica. Section C. Supplement (ISSN 0105-8703); Superseded in part (in 1970): Acta Pathologica et Microbiologica Scandinavica. Supplementum (ISSN 0065-1486)

570   US   ISSN 0001-2386
A S B BULLETIN. 1953. q. $20 (effective through 1996). Association of Southeastern Biologists, Inc., Appalachian University, Dept. of Biology, Boone, NC 26608. TEL 919-726-6841. FAX 919-726-2426. Ed. Ken Shull. bk.rev.; abstr.; charts; illus.; stat. circ. 1,300. (also avail. in microform from UMI; reprint service avail. from UMI) **Indexed:** Biol.Abstr., Deep Sea Res.& Oceanogr.Abstr. **Document type:** bulletin, academic/scholarly publication.
   —CISTI; Linda Hall.

577 613.1   UK   ISSN 0951-5674
ABERDEEN LETTERS IN ECOLOGY. 1987. a. £10. University of Aberdeen, Department of Agriculture, MacRobert Bldg., 581 King St., Aberdeen AB24 5UA; Scotland. TEL 44-1224-274122. FAX 44-1224-273731. E-mail: agrisec@aberdeen.ac.uk. Ed. Robert Naylor. circ. 250 (paid). **Document type:** academic/scholarly publication.
   Description: Brief reports of current research work.
   Refereed Serial

570 540   MV   ISSN 1019-5289
CODEN: IMBKB6
ACADEMIA DE STIINTE A REPUBLICII MOLDOVA. BULETINUL. STIINTE BIOLOGICE SI CHIMICE/AKADEMIYA NAUK RESPUBLIKI MOLDOVA. IZVESTIYA. BIOLOGICHESKIE I KHIMICHESKIE NAUKI. (Text in Rumanian, Russian) bi-m. $50. Academia de Stiinte a Republicii Moldova, Bibliotaca Stiintifica Centrala, Bd. Stefan cel Mare, 1, 2001 Kishinev, Moldova. TEL 383-2-264023. **Indexed:** Biol.Abstr., Chem.Abstr., Crop Physiol.Abstr., Field Crop Abstr., GeoRef., Hort.Abstr., Plant Grow.Reg.Abstr., Seed Abstr., Soyabean Abstr., Triticale Abstr.
   —BLDSC (0073.777050); CASDDS; CISTI; KNAW; Linda Hall.
   Formerly: Akademiya Nauk Moldovskoi S.S.R. Izvestiya. Biologicheskie i Khimicheskie Nauki (ISSN 0568-5192)

BIOLOGY

570   **FR**   ISSN 0764-4469
Q2   CODEN: CRASEV
ACADEMIE DES SCIENCES. COMPTES RENDUS. SERIE 3: SCIENCES DE LA VIE. (Text and summaries in English and French) 1835. 12/yr. 2933 F.($561) (foreign 4170 F.) (effective 1998). John Libbey Eurotext, 127 av. de la Republique, 92120 Montrouge, France. TEL 33-1-46730660.
FAX 33-1-40840999. E-mail: marketing@jle.com. (Subscr. to: A T E I, 3 av. Pierre Kerautret, 92230 Romainville, France. TEL 33-1-48408686. FAX 33-1-48400731) Ed. Francois Gros. charts; illus.; index. circ. 3,200. (also avail. in microform from PMC) **Indexed:** Anim.Breed.Abstr., Appl.Mech.Rev., ASCA, Bio-Contr.News & Info., Biol.Abstr., Biotech.Abstr., Br.Geol.Lit., Chem.Abstr., Crop Physiol.Abstr., Curr.Adv.Biochem., Curr.Adv.Cell & Devel.Biol., Curr.Adv.Genetics & Molec.Biol., Curr.Cont., Dairy Sci.Abstr., Deep Sea Res.& Oceanogr.Abstr., Ecol.Abstr., Eng.Ind., Excerp.Med., Field Crop Abstr., Food Sci.& Tech.Abstr., Forest. Prod.Abstr., Forest.Abstr., Geo.Abstr.H.G., Geo.Abstr.P.G., Geol.Abstr., Helminthol.Abstr., Herb.Abstr., Hort.Abstr., Ind.Med., Ind.Sci.Rev., Ind.Vet., INIS Atomind., Irr.& Drain.Abstr., Math.R., Met.Abstr., Meteor.& Geoastrophys.Abstr., Nutr.Abstr., Ocean.Abstr., Ornam.Hort., Pig News & Info., Plant Breed Abstr., Plant Grow.Reg.Abstr., Pollut.Abstr., Potato Abstr., Poult.Abstr., Protozool.Abstr., Rev.Appl.Entomol., Rev.Med.& Vet.Mycol., Rev.Plant Path., Seed Abstr., Sel.Water Res.Abstr., So.Pac.Per.Ind., Soils & Fert., Soyabean Abstr., Sport Fish.Abstr., Triticale Abstr., Vet.Bull., Weed Abstr., Wild.Rev., Zoo.Rec. **Document type:** academic/scholarly publication.
—BLDSC (3370.042200); CASDDS; CISTI; Ei; EMDOCS; Genuine Article; KNAW; KR SourceOne; Linda Hall; SWETS. **CCC.**
Former titles (until 1984): Academie des Sciences. Comptes Rendus des Seances. Serie 3: Sciences de la Vie (ISSN 0249-6313); (until 1981): Academie des Sciences. Comptes Rendus Hebdomadaires des Seances. Series D: Sciences Naturelles (ISSN 0567-655X)
Description: Contains information on theoretical biology, molecular biology, genetics, marine biology, general ecology, anthropology, animal nutrition and botany.
Refereed Serial

ACADEMIE SERBE DES SCIENCES ET DES ARTS. CLASSE DES SCIENCES MATHEMATIQUES ET NATURELLES. BULLETIN. SCIENCES NATURELLES. see *SCIENCES: COMPREHENSIVE WORKS*

578.77   **XR**
ACADEMY OF SCIENCES OF THE CZECH REPUBLIC. HYDROBIOLOGICAL INSTITUTE. ANNUAL REPORT. (Text in English) 1960. a. exchange basis only. Academy of Sciences of the Czech Republic, Hydrobiological Institute, Na Sadkach 7, 370 05 Ceske Budejovice, Czech Republic.
TEL 004238-45484. FAX 42-38-45718. TELEX 144 406 CSAC C. Eds. Z. Brandl, V. Straskrabova. circ. 750. (back issues avail.) **Indexed:** Biol.Abstr. **Document type:** academic/scholarly publication.
Former titles: Czechoslovak Academy of Sciences. Hydrobiological Institute. Annual Report; Czechoslovak Academy of Sciences. Institute of Landscape Ecology. Section of Hydrobiology. Annual Report (ISSN 0232-0533); Czechoslovakia. Academy of Sciences. Hydrobiological Laboratory. Annual Report.
Description: Contains brief description of scientific results and other activities of the institute during a given year.

ACTA ALBERTINA RATISBONENSIA. see *EARTH SCIENCES*

571.3 611   **JA**   ISSN 0022-7722
                        CODEN: KAIZAN
ACTA ANATOMICA NIPPONICA/KAIBOGAKU ZASSHI. (Text in English or Japanese; summaries in English or German) 1893. bi-m. 15000 Yen. (Japanese Association of Anatomists) Business Center for Academic Societies Japan, 5-16-9 Honkomagome, Bunkyo-ku, Tokyo 113, Japan. TEL 03-5814-5811. FAX 03-5814-5822. TELEX 2722268 BCJSP J. adv.; bk.rev.; abstr.; bibl.; index. circ. 1,950. **Indexed:** Biol.Abstr., Chem.Abstr., Dent.Ind., Excerp.Med., Ind.Med., Ind.Vet., INIS Atomind., Vet.Bull. **Document type:** academic/scholarly publication.
—CISTI. **CCC.**

570   **CI**   ISSN 0448-0147
QH178.Y8   CODEN: ACBLDN
ACTA BIOLOGICA. (Text and summaries in Croatian, English, French, German and Russian) 1913. biennial. $10. Hrvatska Akademija Znanosti i Umjetnosti - Croatian Academy of Sciences and Arts, Zrinski trg 11, 41000 Zagreb, Croatia.
TEL 48-41-433-661. FAX 48-41-433-383. Eds. Z. Lorkovic, Z. Devide. circ. 800. (back issues avail.) **Indexed:** Biol.Abstr.
—KNAW; Linda Hall.

615.532   **GW**   ISSN 0722-4192
ACTA BIOLOGICA; Zeitschrift fuer angewandte Homoeo-Phytotherapie, Ganzheitsbehandlungen und Sondermethoden der Medizin. 1962. s-a. Pascoe Pharmazeutische Praeparate GmbH, Schiffenberger Weg 55, 35394 Giessen, Germany.
TEL 0641-7960-0. FAX 0641-77333. circ. 7,500. **Document type:** academic/scholarly publication.

570 610   **PL**   ISSN 0065-1087
QH301   CODEN: ACBMAN
ACTA BIOLOGICA ET MEDICA. 1957. irreg. Gdanskie Towarzystwo Naukowe, Ul. Grodzka 12, 80-841 Gdansk, Poland. TEL 48-58-312124.
FAX 48-58-314282. **Indexed:** AgroLibrex.
—BLDSC (0602.700000); CISTI.

570   **HU**   ISSN 0236-5383
QH301   CODEN: ABAHAU
ACTA BIOLOGICA HUNGARICA. (Text in English) 1948-198?; resumed 1990. q. $136 (effective 1998). (Magyar Tudomanyos Akademia) Akademiai Kiado Rt., P.O. Box 245, H-1519 Budapest, Hungary. TEL 36-1-2043976. FAX 36-1-2043973. Ed. Janos Salanki. adv.; bk.rev.; bibl.; charts; illus.; index. **Indexed:** Apic.Abstr., ASCA, Biol.Abstr., Chem.Abstr., Curr.Cont., Dairy Sci.Abstr., Excerp.Med., GeoRef., Ind.Med., Neurosci.Cit.Ind. **Document type:** academic/scholarly publication.
—BLDSC (0602.874000); CASDDS; CISTI; Genuine Article; KNAW; Linda Hall. **CCC.**
Former titles (until 1983): Academiae Scientiarum Hungaricae. Acta Biologica (ISSN 0001-5288); (until 1950): Hungarica Acta Biologica (ISSN 0367-6390)
Description: Provides a forum for original research in the field of experimental biology. Covers cytology, morphology, embryology, genetics, endocrinology, radiation biology, cellular level of biological regulation, ethology and environmental biology.

570   **YU**   ISSN 0514-6658
S590   CODEN: ZMBLAP
ACTA BIOLOGICA IUGOSLAVICA. SERIJA I BILJKA. 1952. 3/yr. $78. Unija Bioloskih Naucnih Drustava Jugoslavije - Yugoslav Union of Biological Sciences, Nemanjina 6, fah 127, 11080 Belgrade Zemun, Yugoslavia. Ed. Gligorije Antonovic. **Indexed:** Field Crop Abstr., Herb.Abstr., Plant Grow.Reg.Abstr., Soils & Fert.
—BLDSC (9500.400000); CASDDS.

570 615   **YU**   ISSN 0021-3225
QP509   CODEN: IPPABX
ACTA BIOLOGICA IUGOSLAVICA. SERIJA C: IUGOSLAVICA PHYSIOLOGICA ET PHARMACOLOGICA ACTA. (Text in English; summaries in Serbo-Croatian) 1965. 3/yr. $78. Unija Bioloskih Naucnih Drustava Jugoslavije - Yugoslav Union of Biological Sciences, Nemanjina 6, fah 127, 11080 Belgrade Zemun, Yugoslavia. Ed. Vladislav V. Varagic. index. circ. 1,000. **Indexed:** Biol.Abstr., Chem.Abstr., Curr.Cont., Dairy Sci.Abstr., Excerp.Med., Ind.Sci.Rev., INIS Atomind., Sci.Cit.Ind.
—BLDSC (4588.895000); CASDDS; CISTI; Linda Hall.

577   **YU**   ISSN 0531-9110
ACTA BIOLOGICA IUGOSLAVICA. SERIJA D: EKOLOGIJA. 1966. s-a. $72. Unija Bioloskih Naucnih Drustava Jugoslavije - Yugoslav Union of Biological Sciences, Nemanjina 6, fah 127, 11080 Belgrade Zemun, Yugoslavia. Ed. Milorad Jankkovic.
—Linda Hall.
Description: Focuses on ecological issues.

570   **YU**   ISSN 0350-2643
ACTA BIOLOGICA IUGOSLAVICA. SERIJA G: BIOSISTEMATIKA. 1975. s-a. $72. Unija Bioloskih Naucnih Drustava Jugoslavije - Yugoslav Union of Biological Sciences, Nemanjina 6, fah 127, 11080 Belgrade Zemun, Yugoslavia. Ed. Beatrica Djulic.

570   **BL**   ISSN 0101-5354
QH301   CODEN: ABLEEC
ACTA BIOLOGICA LEOPOLDENSIA. 1979. 2/yr. $24 or exchange basis. (Universidade do Vale do Rio dos Sinos) Unisinos, Av. Unisinos, 950, 93022-000 Sao Leopoldo RS, Brazil. TEL 55-51-5903333 ext. 1951. FAX 55-51-592-1035. Ed. Elena Diehl Fleig. bibl.; charts; illus. **Document type:** academic/scholarly publication.
—CISTI.

570   **BL**   ISSN 0301-2123
QH301   CODEN: ACBPAW
ACTA BIOLOGICA PARANAENSE. (Text in Portuguese; summaries in English and French) 1960. a. free. Universidade Federal do Parana, Setor de Ciencias Biologicas, Cx. Postal 19020, 81531-990 Curitiba, Parana, Brazil. TEL 55-41-3663144 ext. 165. FAX 55-41-2662042. TELEX 415100. Ed. Dr. Sebastiao Laroca. bk.rev.; index. circ. 1,000. **Indexed:** Biol.Abstr., Curr.Cont., Deep Sea Res.& Oceanogr.Abstr., GeoRef. **Document type:** academic/scholarly publication.
—CASDDS; CISTI; KNAW; UMI.
Supersedes in part: Universidade Federal do Parana. Departamento de Botanica. Boletim; Zoologia (ISSN 0044-5053); Formerly: Universidade do Parana. Departamento de Botanica e Farmacognosia. Boletim (ISSN 0041-8900)
Refereed Serial

570   **VE**   ISSN 0001-5326
QH7   CODEN: ABVEAO
ACTA BIOLOGICA VENEZUELICA. (Text in English, Portuguese, Spanish) 1951. 2/yr. $4 per no. Universidad Central de Venezuela, Instituto de Zoologia Tropical, Facultad de Ciencias, Apdo. 47058, Caracas 1041-A, Venezuela.
FAX 58-2-6052136. TELEX 29452 UCVFCVC. E-mail: lmorales@conicit.ve. Ed. Dr. Antonio Machado. R&P contact: Dr. Antonio Machado. bk.rev.; bibl.; charts; illus.; index; circ. 1,500 (controlled). **Indexed:** Biol.Abstr., Chem.Abstr., Deep Sea Res.& Oceanogr.Abstr., Rev.Appl.Entomol., Sport Fish.Abstr., Wild.Rev., Zoo.Rec. **Document type:** academic/scholarly publication.
—Linda Hall.
Description: Publishes original contributions to systematics, ecology, physiology, parasitology and related biological disciplines. Includes short notes on methodological innovations and recent advances.
Refereed Serial

570   **NE**   ISSN 0001-5342
QH301   CODEN: ABIOAN
ACTA BIOTHEORETICA. (Text in English) 1935. q. fl.440 to institutions; $226 to institutions in U.S. (effective 1998). (Prof. Dr. Jan van der Hoeven Foundation for Theoretical Biology) Kluwer Academic Publishers, Postbus 17, 3300 AA Dordrecht, Netherlands. TEL 31-78-6392392.
FAX 31-78-6392254. TELEX 29245 KAPG NL. E-mail: services@wkap.nl; URL: http://www.wkap.nl. (Dist. by: Kluwer Academic Publishers Group, P.O. Box 322, 3300 AH Dordrecht, Netherlands. TEL 31-78-6392392. FAX 31-78-6546474; N. America dist. addr.: Box 358, Accord Sta., Hingham, MA 02018-0358. TEL 617-871-6600. FAX 617-871-6528) Ed.Bd. bibl.; charts; illus. (also avail. in microform from UMI; back issues avail.) **Indexed:** Arts & Hum.Cit.Ind., ASCA, Biol.Abstr., Chem.Abstr., Curr.Adv.Ecol.Sci., Curr.Cont., Deep Sea Res.& Oceanogr.Abstr., Excerp.Med., Ind.Med., Ind.Sci.Rev., Int.Abstr.Biol.Sci., Plant Breed.Abstr., Sci.Cit.Ind. **Document type:** academic/scholarly publication.
—BLDSC (0604.000000); CASDDS; CISTI; EMDOCS; Genuine Article; Linda Hall; SWETS; UMI; UnCover. **CCC.**
Refereed Serial

570   **BU**   ISSN 0861-0509
                        CODEN: ACYME6
ACTA CYTOBIOLOGICA ET MORPHOLOGICA. (In 2 parts) (Text in English) 1977. a. (Bulgarska Akademiia na Naukite, Institut po Klet'chna Biologiia i Morfologiia) Publishing House of the Bulgarian Academy of Sciences, Acad. G. Bonchev St., Bldg. 6, 1113 Sofia, Bulgaria. Ed.Bd.
—CASDDS; CISTI; KNAW; Linda Hall.
Formerly (until 1989): Acta Morphologica (ISSN 0204-9139)

ACTA FACULTATIS MEDICAE UNIVERSITATIS BRUNENSIS. see *MEDICAL SCIENCES*

BIOLOGY 583

570   PL   ISSN 0065-132X
QH301.P63   CODEN: AHBPAX
ACTA HYDROBIOLOGICA. (Text in English; abstracts in Polish) 1959. q. $120 (effective 1996 & 1997). Polska Akademia Nauk, Zaklad Biologii Wod im. Karola Starmacha - Polish Academy of Sciences, Karol Starmach Institute of Freshwater Biology, Ul. Slawkowska 17, 31-016 Krakow, Poland. TEL 48-12-215082. FAX 48-12-222115. Ed. Antoni Amirowicz. R&P contact: Janush Starmach. illus. circ. 650. **Indexed:** AgroLibrex, Biol.Abstr., Chem.Abstr., Curr.Adv.Ecol.Sci., Deep Sea Res.& Oceanogr.Abstr., Ecol.Abstr., Geo.Abstr.P.G., Geol.Abstr., GeoRef., IBR, Pollut.Abstr., Sel.J.Water, Sel.Water Res.Abstr., Sport Fish.Abstr., Vet.Bull., Wild.Rev., Zoo.Rec. **Document type:** academic/scholarly publication.
—BLDSC (0624.485000); CASDDS; CISTI; UnCover.
Description: Devoted to the study of biology of inland water. The scope includes ecology, physiology, taxonomy and methodology.
Refereed Serial

ACTA MEDICA ET BIOLOGICA/IGAKU SEIBUTSUGAKU KENKYU KIYO. see *MEDICAL SCIENCES*

ACTA MEDICA ROMANA. see *MEDICAL SCIENCES*

571.3 611   BU
ACTA MORFOLOGICA. (Text in various languages) 1976. s-a. 4 lv. (Bulgarska Akademiia na Naukite) Publishing House of the Bulgarian Academy of Sciences, Acad. G. Bonchev St., Bldg. 6, 1113 Sofia, Bulgaria. circ. 484. (reprint service avail. from IRC) **Indexed:** Biol.Abstr.

570   PL   ISSN 0065-1400
QP351   CODEN: ANEXAC
ACTA NEUROBIOLOGIAE EXPERIMENTALIS. (Text in English) 1928. q. $220 (effective 1998). Polska Akademia Nauk, Instytut Biologii Doswiadczalnej im. M. Nenckiego - Polish Academy of Sciences, M. Nencki Institute of Experimental Biology, Ul. Pasteura 3, 02-093 Warsaw, Poland. TEL 48-22-659-8571. FAX 48-22-225342. E-mail: wrobel@nencki.gov.pl. (Dist. by: Ars Polona, Krakowskie Przedmiescie 7, 00-068 Warsaw, Poland; Dist. also by: Mezhdunarodnaya Kniga, B. Yakimanka 39, 117049 Moscow, Russia. TEL 7-095-2384967. FAX 7-095-2384634) Ed. A. Wrobel. index. (reprint service avail. from ISI) **Indexed:** AgroAgen, ASCA, Biol.Abstr., Chem.Abstr., Curr.Adv.Ecol.Sci., Curr.Cont., Dent.Ind., Excerp.Med., Ind.Med., Ind.Sci.Rev., Neurosci.Cit.Ind., Psychol.Abstr. (1952-), Rev.Plant Path., Sci.Cit.Ind., SSCI. **Document type:** academic/scholarly publication.
—BLDSC (0639.800000); CASDDS; CISTI; EMDOCS; Genuine Article; KNAW; SWETS; UnCover.
Formerly: Acta Biologiae Experimentalis.

577   FR   ISSN 1146-609X
QH540   CODEN: ACOEEY
ACTA OECOLOGICA; international journal of ecology. (Text in English) 1980. 6/yr. 1250 F. (foreign 1580 F.) (effective 1997). Gauthier-Villars, 5 rue Laromiguiere, 75005 Paris, France. TEL 33-1-40466200. FAX 33-1-40466201. E-mail: gauthier.villars.publisher@mail.sgip.fr; URL: http://www.gauthier-villars.fr. (Subscr. to: Societe de Periodiques Specialises, B.P. 22, 41354 Vineuil Cedex, France. TEL 33-2-54504612. FAX 33-2-54504611) (Co-sponsors: INRA, CNRS, ORSTOM) Ed. Michael Hochberg. bk.rev.; charts. circ. 1,000. (also avail. in microform from MIM,UMI) **Indexed:** Agri.Eng.Abstr., Agroforest.Abstr., ASCA, Biol.Abstr., Bull.Signal., Chem.Abstr., Crop Physiol.Abstr., Curr.Adv.Ecol.Sci., Curr.Cont., Ecol.Abstr., Excerp.Med., Field Crop Abstr., Forest.Abstr., Forest Prod.Abstr., Geo.Abstr.H.G., Herb.Abstr., Hort.Abstr., IBR, Ind.Sci.Rev., Irr.& Drain.Abstr., Key Word Ind.Wildl.Res., Ornam.Hort., Plant Breed.Abstr., Plant Grow.Reg.Abstr., Rev.Appl.Entomol., Sci.Cit.Ind., Seed Abstr., Sel.Water Res.Abstr., Soils & Fert., Sport Fish.Abstr., SSCI, Weed Abstr., Wild.Rev., Zoo.Rec. **Document type:** academic/scholarly publication.
—BLDSC (0641.655000); CASDDS; CISTI; EMDOCS; Genuine Article; Linda Hall; SWETS; UnCover. **CCC.**
Incorporates (1980-1990): Oecologia Applicata (ISSN 0243-7678); (1980-1990): Oecologia Generalis (ISSN 0243-766X); (1980-1990): Oecologica Plantarum (ISSN 0243-7651)
Description: Devoted to fundamental ecology and its applications. Articles cover basic aspects of structure, functioning and changes in populations and ecosystems; the dynamics of populations and ecophysiology and the applications of this research.

570   PL   ISSN 0065-1583
    CODEN: ACPZAU
ACTA PROTOZOOLOGICA. (Text in English) 1963. q. $120 to individuals; institutions $180. Polska Akademia Nauk, Instytut Biologii Doswiadczalnej im. M. Nenckiego - Polish Academy of Sciences, M. Nencki Institute of Experimental Biology, Ul. Pasteura 3, 02-093 Warsaw, Poland. TEL 48-22-659-8571. FAX 48-22-225342. E-mail: jurek@nencki.gov.pl. (Dist. by: Ars Polona, Krakowskie Przedmiescie 7, 00-068 Warsaw, Poland) Ed. Jerzy Sikora. illus. circ. 460. (reprint service avail. from ISI) **Indexed:** AgroAgen, ASCA, Bio-Contr.News & Info., Biol.Abstr., Chem.Abstr., Curr.Adv.Ecol.Sci., Curr.Cont., Deep Sea Res.& Oceanogr.Abstr., Excerp.Med., Helminthol.Abstr., Ind.Sci.Rev., Ind.Vet., Protozool.Abstr., Sci.Cit.Ind., Vet.Bull. **Document type:** academic/scholarly publication.
—BLDSC (0661.370000); CASDDS; CISTI; EMDOCS; Genuine Article; Linda Hall; SWETS; UnCover.

570 610   SW   ISSN 1101-8429
ACTA REGIAE SOCIETATIS SCIENTIARUM ET LITTERARUM GOTHOBURGENSIS. BIOMEDICA. (Text in English) 1991. irreg. SEK 100. Kungl. Vetenskaps-och Vitterhets-Samhaellet i Goeteborg - Royal Society of Arts and Science in Gothenburg, c/o Goeteborgs Universitetsbibliotek, P.O. Box 5096, S-402 22 Goeteborg, Sweden.

581   PL   ISSN 0001-6977
QK1   CODEN: ASBNA2
ACTA SOCIETATIS BOTANICORUM POLONIAE. (Text in English; summaries in Polish) 1923. q. $44. Polskie Towarzystwo Botaniczne, Al. Ujazdowskie 4, 00-478 Warsaw, Poland. (Dist. by: Ars Polona, Krakowskie Przedmiescie 7, 00-068 Warsaw, Poland) Ed. B. Rodkiewicz. bibl. circ. 660. **Indexed:** AgroLibrex, ASCA, Biol.Abstr., Chem.Abstr., Crop Physiol.Abstr., Curr.Adv.Ecol.Sci., Curr.Cont., Energy Ind., Energy Info.Abstr., Field Crop Abstr., Forest.Abstr., Forest Prod.Abstr., Geo.Abstr., Herb.Abstr., Hort.Abstr., INIS Atomind., Irr.& Drain.Abstr., Plant Grow.Reg.Abstr., Seed Abstr., Soils & Fert., Triticale Abstr., Trop.Oil Seeds Abstr., Weed Abstr.
—BLDSC (0583.000000); CASDDS; CISTI; Genuine Article; UnCover.
Description: Publishes original papers, short communications, and critical reviews in all fields of botany.

570 510   XV   ISSN 0351-580X
    CODEN: ASTLDL
ACTA STEREOLOGICA. (Text in English) 1982. s-a. $60. Institute of Histology and Embryology, Medical Faculty, Korytkova 2, 61105 Ljubljana, Slovenia. TEL 386-61-441121. FAX 386-61-1401294. (Co-sponsor: International Society for Stereology) Ed. Miroslav Kalisnik. adv.; bk.rev.; index. circ. 500. **Indexed:** Alloys Ind., Biol.Abstr., Chem.Abstr., Eng.Mat.Abstr., Excerp.Med., Met.Abstr., Met.Abstr.Ind., Nonfer.Met.Alert, PCC Alert, Steels Alert, World Alum.Abstr., Zent.Math. **Document type:** proceedings.
—BLDSC (0663.375000); CASDDS; CISTI; Linda Hall.
Refereed Serial

570   XR   ISSN 0001-7124
    CODEN: ACBIBC
ACTA UNIVERSITATIS CAROLINAE: BIOLOGICA. (Text in English) 1954. 4/yr. $80. (Univerzita Karlova, Prirodovedecka Fakulta) Karolinum - Nakladatelstvi Univerzity Karlovy, Ovocny trh 5, 116 36 Prague 1, Czech Republic. TEL 420-2-24491111. FAX 420-2-24491451. E-mail: edice@cuni.cz. Ed. Milan Chvala. bibl.; charts; illus.; stat.; index. circ. 650. **Indexed:** Apic.Abstr., Biol.Abstr., Curr.Adv.Ecol.Sci., Excerp.Med., Plant Breed.Abstr., Soils & Fert., Sport Fish.Abstr., VITIS, Wild.Rev., Zoo.Rec. **Document type:** academic/scholarly publication.
—BLDSC (0584.500000); CASDDS; CISTI; Linda Hall.
Description: Covers cooperative research projects in the field of zoology, anthrology and botany.

570   HU   ISSN 0563-0592
QH7   CODEN: AUSGAC
ACTA UNIVERSITATIS DE ATTILA JOZSEF NOMINATAE. ACTA BIOLOGICA. (Text in English) 1947; N.S. 1955. a. exchange basis. Attila Jozsef University, c/o E. Szabo, Exchange Librarian, Dugonics ter 13, P.O. Box 393, 6701 Szeged, Hungary. (Subscr. to: Kultura, Box 149, 1389 Budapest, Hungary) Ed. Gyula Farkas. circ. 400. **Indexed:** Anthropol.Lit.
—CASDDS; CISTI; Linda Hall.
Description: Journal of animal and plant taxonomy and physiology, physical anthropology and ecology.

570   PL   ISSN 0208-4449
ACTA UNIVERSITATIS NICOLAI COPERNICI. BIOLOGIA. 1956. irreg. price varies. Uniwersytet Mikolaja Kopernika, Wydawnictwo, Ul. Gagarina 11, 87-100 Torun, Poland. TEL 48-56-14295. TELEX 21224. (Dist. by: Osrodek Rozpowszechniania Wydanictw Naukowych PAN, Palac Kultury i Nauki, 00-901 Warsaw, Poland) **Indexed:** AgroLibrex, Biol.Abstr., Curr.Adv.Ecol.Sci. **Document type:** academic/scholarly publication.
Formerly: Uniwersytet Mikolaja Kopernika, Torun. Nauki Matematyczno-Przyrodnicze. Biologia (ISSN 0083-4521)

570   CK   ISSN 0304-3584
QH301   CODEN: ACBIEF
ACTUALIDADES BIOLOGICAS. (Summaries in English) 1972-1993; resumed 1997 (vol.20, no.68). q. free. Universidad de Antioquia, Departamento de Biologia, Apdo. Aereo 1226, Medellin, Colombia. TEL 57-4-2105622. FAX 57-4-2638282. E-mail: actubiol@matematicas.ude.edu.co. Ed. Gabriel Roldan Perez. bk.rev.; illus. circ. 1,500. **Indexed:** Biol.Abstr., Chem.Abstr.
—CASDDS.
Description: Presents results of investigations in all fields of biology, most of which take place in Colombia.

570   FR   ISSN 0753-3918
ACTUALITES BIOLOGIQUES. (Supplement avail.: Cahier Technique de la Biologie) m. 900 F. (effective 1997). Centre National des Biologistes, 80 av. du Maine, 75014 Paris, France. TEL 33-1-43229770. FAX 33-1-43217312. Ed.Bd.; Pub. Gerard Cazalet. adv. contact: Jeanne Berga. **Document type:** trade publication.
Description: For professionals and administrators of biological analysis laboratories.

570   YU   ISSN 0354-5547
ADRIATICO. (Text in English) 1994. s-a.? Center for Mediterranean Studies, Stanka Dragojevica 2, Podgorica, Yugoslavia. Ed. Sanja Elezovic.

ADVANCED DRUG DELIVERY REVIEWS. see *PHARMACY AND PHARMACOLOGY*

BIOLOGY

570   **US**   ISSN 0301-5556
QL801
ADVANCES IN ANATOMY, EMBRYOLOGY AND CELL BIOLOGY. 1966. irreg., vol.118, 1990. Springer-Verlag, 175 Fifth Ave., New York, NY 10010. TEL 212-460-1500. FAX 212-473-6272. (Also: Berlin, Heidelberg, Tokyo and Vienna) (reprint service avail. from ISI) **Indexed:** ASCA, Biol.Abstr., Ind.Med., Ind.Sci.Rev., Ind.Vet., Sci.Cit.Ind., Vet.Bull. **Document type:** monographic series.
—BLDSC (0698.800000); CISTI; KNAW.
Refereed Serial

ADVANCES IN BEHAVIORAL BIOLOGY. see *PSYCHOLOGY*

ADVANCES IN BIOCLIMATOLOGY. see *METEOROLOGY*

ADVANCES IN COLLOID AND INTERFACE SCIENCE; an international journal devoted to experimental and theoretical developments in interfacial and colloidal phenomena and their implications in biology, chemistry, physics and technology. see *CHEMISTRY — Physical Chemistry*

570   **US**
ADVANCES IN DEVELOPMENTAL BIOLOGY. irreg. $109.50 per vol. (effective 1997). J A I Press Inc., 55 Old Post Rd., No. 2, Greenwich, CT 06836-1678. TEL 203-661-7602. FAX 203-661-0792. E-mail: 102062.2525@compuserve.com. (Addr. in Europe: J A I Press Ltd., The Courtyard, 28 High St., Hampton Hill, Mddx. TW12 1PD, England. TEL 44-181-943-9296. FAX 44-181-943-9317) Ed. Paul M. Wassarman. (back issues avail.)

ADVANCES IN ECOLOGICAL RESEARCH. see *ENVIRONMENTAL STUDIES*

570 619   **US**   ISSN 0065-2598
                              CODEN: AEMBAP
ADVANCES IN EXPERIMENTAL MEDICINE AND BIOLOGY. 1967. irreg., vol.412, 1997. price varies. Plenum Publishing Corp., 233 Spring St., New York, NY 10013-1578. TEL 212-620-8000. FAX 212-463-0742. TELEX 23-421139. E-mail: books@plenum.com. Ed.Bd. **Indexed:** ASCA, Bibl.Agri., Biol.Abstr., Chem.Abstr., Curr.Adv.Ecol.Sci., Dent.Ind., Excerp.Med., Ind.Med., Ind.Sci.Rev., INIS Atomind., Sci.Cit.Ind. **Document type:** monographic series.
—BLDSC (0706.050000); ADONIS; CASDDS; CISTI; Genuine Article; KNAW; SWETS; UnCover. **CCC**.
Refereed Serial

ADVANCES IN FISH BIOLOGY AND FISHERIES. see *FISH AND FISHERIES*

ADVANCES IN LIMNOLOGY/ERGEBNISSE DER LIMNOLOGIE. see *EARTH SCIENCES — Hydrology*

578.77   **US**   ISSN 0065-2881
QH91.A1   CODEN: AMBYAR
ADVANCES IN MARINE BIOLOGY. 1963. irreg., vol.31, 1997. Academic Press, Inc., 525 B St., Ste. 1900, San Diego, CA 92101-4495. TEL 619-231-0926. FAX 619-699-6715. (Subscr. to: Order Dept., 6277 Sea Harbor Dr., 4th Fl., Orlando, FL 32887. TEL 800-321-5068) Eds. J.H.S. Blaxter, F.S. Russell. index. (reprint service avail. from ISI) **Indexed:** ASCA, Biol.Abstr., Biol.& Agr.Ind., Chem.Abstr., Curr.Adv.Ecol.Sci., Deep Sea Res.& Oceanogr.Abstr., Geo.Abstr., Helminthol.Abstr., Ind.Sci.Rev., Sci.Cit.Ind, Sport Fish.Abstr., Wild.Rev., Zoo.Rec. **Document type:** monographic series.
—BLDSC (0709.340000); CASDDS; CISTI; KNAW; KR SourceOne; Linda Hall; SWETS; UnCover. **CCC**.
Refereed Serial

571.6   **US**   ISSN 1053-9506
                              CODEN: ARCGEH
ADVANCES IN REGULATION OF CELL GROWTH SERIES. 1989. irreg. price varies. Lippincott - Raven Publishers (Subsidiary of: Wolters Kluwer N.V.), 227 E. Washington Sq., Philadelphia, PA 19106. TEL 215-238-4200. FAX 215-238-4227. URL: http://www.lrpub.com. (Subscr. to: Box 1600, Hagerstown, MD 21741-1600. TEL 800-777-2295. FAX 301-824-7390) R&P contact: Alice McElhinney. (reprint service avail. from UMI) **Document type:** monographic series.
—CASDDS; CISTI.
Refereed Serial

570 614   **IE**   ISSN 0393-5965
QR101   CODEN: AROBFT
AEROBIOLOGIA; international journal of aerobiology. (Text in English) 1985. q. fl.393($242) (effective 1997). (Italian Association for Aerobiology) Elsevier Science Ireland Ltd., P.O. Box 85, Limerick, Ireland. TEL 353-61-471944. FAX 353-61-472144. URL: http://www.elsevier.nl/. (Subscr. to: Elsevier Science, Regional Sales Office, P.O. Box 211, 1000 AE Amsterdam, Netherlands. TEL 31-20-4853757. FAX 31-20-4853432; Subscr. in the Americas to: Elsevier Science, Regional Sales Office, Box 945, New York, NY 10159-0945. TEL 212-633-3730. FAX 212-633-3680; Subscr. in Australasia and the Far East to: Elsevier Science (Singapore) Pte Ltd, No.1 Temasek Ave., No.17-01 Millenia Tower, Singapore 039192, Singapore. TEL 65-434-3727. FAX 65-337-2230) Ed. P. Mandrioli. R&P contact: Annette Moloney. **Document type:** academic/scholarly publication.
—BLDSC (0721.350000); CISTI.
Formerly (until 1994): European Journal of Aerobiology.
Description: Publishes original research and review papers in the interdisciplinary fields of aerobiology and biosphere-atmosphere interaction, including airborne microbiology, biometeorology, climatology, and related issues such as respiratory allergology, indoor air quality and biological weathering.
Refereed Serial

AEROSPACE MEDICINE AND BIOLOGY; a continuing bibliography. see *MEDICAL SCIENCES — Abstracting, Bibliographies, Statistics*

AFRICAN JOURNAL OF TROPICAL HYDROBIOLOGY AND FISHERIES. see *FISH AND FISHERIES*

THE AG BIOETHICS FORUM. see *AGRICULTURE*

570   **JA**
AGEHA/SWALLOW-TAIL. (Text in Japanese) 1949. biennial. Aichi Kenritsu Kariya Koto Gakko, Seibutsu Kurabu O B Agehakai - Aichi Prefectural Kariya Senior High School, Agehakai in Alumnus of Biological Club, c/o Mr. Masami Sugiura, 5-25, Yahatamachi, Kariya-shi, Aichi-ken 448, Japan.

AGRICULTURAL AND BIOLOGICAL RESEARCH. see *AGRICULTURE*

AGRO SUR. see *AGRICULTURE*

AIDS WEEKLY PLUS. see *MEDICAL SCIENCES — Communicable Diseases*

577   **IT**
AIRONE. 1981. m. L.70000 (foreign L.160000) (effective 1997). Editoriale Giorgio Mondadori S.p.A., Via A. Ponti, 10, 20143 Milan, Italy. TEL 02-891661. FAX 02-89125888. Ed. Nicoletta Salvatori. adv.: B&W page L.20300000, color page L.31300000. bk.rev.; charts; illus. circ. 100,000.
Description: Features items on ecology, nature and civilization.

570   **JA**   ISSN 0912-5949
AIZU SEIBUTSU DOKOKAISHI/AIZU BIOLOGICAL CIRCLE. JOURNAL. (Text in Japanese) 1962. a. Aizu Seibutsu Dokokai - Aizu Biological Circle, 8-1 Hanaharumachi, Aizuwakamatsu-shi, Fukushima-ken 965, Japan.

570   **AJ**
                            CODEN: IABLAQ
AKADEMIYA NAUK AZERBAIJANA. IZVESTIYA. SERIYA BIOLOGICHESKIKH NAUK. (Text in Azerbaijani and Russian) 1958. bi-m. 22.20 Rub. Izdatel'stvo Elm, Ul. Narimanova, 37, 370073 Baku, Azerbaijan. (Subscr. to: Mezhdunarodnaya Kniga, Moscow, G-200, Russia) Ed. V. Volubaev. charts; illus.; index. circ. 820. **Indexed:** Bio-Contr.News & Info., Biol.Abstr., Chem.Abstr., Crop Physiol.Abstr., Field Crop Abstr., Hort.Abstr., Ind.Vet., INIS Atomind., Nutr.Abstr., Poult.Abstr., Protozool.Abstr., Small Anim.Abstr., Triticale Abstr., Vet.Bull.
—CASDDS; CISTI; Linda Hall.
Formerly: Akademiya Nauk Azerbaidzhanskoi S.S.R. Izvestiya. Seriya Biologicheskikh Nauk (ISSN 0132-6112)

570   **GS**
AKADEMIYA NAUK GRUZINSKOI S.S.R. IZVESTIYA. SERIYA BIOLOGICHESKAYA. (Text in Georgian and Russian) bi-m. 23.70 Rub. Akademiya Nauk Gruzinskoi S.S.R., Ul. Dzerzhinskogo 8, Tbilisi, Georgia. **Indexed:** Biol.Abstr., Chem.Abstr., Field Crop Abstr., INIS Atomind., Maize Abstr., Triticale Abstr.

570   **KZ**
QH301   CODEN: IKABAR
AKADEMIYA NAUK KAZAKHSTANA. IZVESTIYA. SERIYA BIOLOGICHESKAYA. (Text in Russian) 1955. bi-m. Gylym, Ul. Pushkina 111-113, 480100 Alma-Ata, Kazakhstan. TEL 3272-611877. (Subscr. to: G.R. Kondubayeva, ul. Shevchenko 28, 480021 Alma-Ata, Kazakhstan) Ed. K.T. Tashenov. charts; illus.; index. **Indexed:** Anim.Breed.Abstr., Biol.Abstr., Chem.Abstr., Crop Physiol.Abstr., Dairy Sci.Abstr., Field Crop Abstr., Helminthol.Abstr., Herb.Abstr., Hort.Abstr., Ind.Vet., Plant Breed.Abstr., Protozool.Abstr., Rev.Plant Path., Seed Abstr., Sel.Water Res.Abstr., Soils & Fert., Triticale Abstr., Vet.Bull., Weed Abstr. **Document type:** academic/scholarly publication.
—CASDDS; CISTI; Linda Hall.
Formerly (until 1992): Akademiya Nauk Kazakhskoi S.S.R. Izvestiya. Seriya Biologicheskaya (ISSN 0002-3183)

AKADEMIYA NAUK RESPUBLIKI KYRGYZSTAN. IZVESTIYA. KHIMIKO-TEKHNOLOGICHESKIE I BIOLOGICHESKIE NAUKI. see *CHEMISTRY*

AKADEMIYA NAUK TAJIKISTANA. DOKLADY. see *MATHEMATICS*

570   **TA**
                            CODEN: ITOBAO
AKADEMIYA NAUK TAJIKISTANA. IZVESTIYA. OTDELENIE BIOLOGICHESKIKH NAUK. (Text in Russian) 1966. q. 12.40 Rub. Akademiya Nauk Tajikistana, Pr. Rudaki 33, 734025 Dushanbe, Tajikistan. TEL 22-50-83. charts; illus. **Indexed:** Bio-Contr.News & Info., Biol.Abstr., Chem.Abstr., Cott.& Trop.Fibr.Abstr., Crop Physiol.Abstr., Field Crop Abstr., GeoRef., Helminthol.Abstr., Hort.Abstr., Ind.Vet., INIS Atomind., Plant Grow.Reg.Abstr., Soyabean Abstr., Triticale Abstr.
—CASDDS; CISTI.
Formerly (until 1992): Akademiya Nauk Tadzhikskoi S.S.R. Izvestiya. Otdelenie Biologicheskikh Nauk (ISSN 0002-3477)

570   **TK**
                            CODEN: ITUBAK
AKADEMIYA NAUK TURKMENISTANA. IZVESTIYA. SERIYA BIOLOGICHESKIKH NAUK. 1960. bi-m. 13.50 Rub. (effective Jan. 1992). Akademiya Nauk Turkmenistana, Ul. Gogolya, 15, 744000 Ashkhabad, Turkmenistan. charts; illus.; index. circ. 500. **Indexed:** Bio-Contr.News & Info., Biol.Abstr., Chem.Abstr., Helminthol.Abstr., Hort.Abstr., Ornam.Hort., Vet.Bull., Weed Abstr.
—CASDDS; CISTI.
Formerly (until 1992): Akademiya Nauk Turkmenskoi S.S.R. Izvestiya. Seriya Biologicheskikh Nauk (ISSN 0321-1746)

570   **BW**
                            CODEN: VABBA3
AKADEMIYA NAVUK BELARUSI. VESTSI. SERIYA BIYALAGICHNKYKH NAVUK/NATIONAL ACADEMY OF SCIENCES OF BELARUS. PROCEEDINGS. BIOLOGICAL SERIES. (Text in Byelorussian, Russian; summaries in English) 1956. bi-m. 30000 Rub.($65) (effective 1998). Vydavetstvo Belaruskaya Navuka, Zhodzinskaya, 18, 220141 Minsk 67, Belarus. TEL 268-58-19. TELEX 252277 NAUKA. (Dist. by: Mezhdunarodnaya Kniga, B. Yakimanka 39, 117049 Moscow, Russia. TEL 7-095-2384967. FAX 7-095-2384634) Ed. A.G. Lobanok. bibl.; charts; illus.; index. circ. 300. **Indexed:** Biol.Abstr., Crop Physiol.Abstr., Field Crop Abstr., Herb.Abstr., Nutr.Abstr., Plant Grow.Reg.Abstr., Potato Abstr., Seed Abstr., Triticale Abstr. **Document type:** academic/scholarly publication.
—CASDDS; CISTI; KNAW; Linda Hall.
Formerly: Akademiya Navuk Belarusskai S.S.R. Vestsi. Seriya Biologichnykh Navuk (ISSN 0002-3558)
Description: Presents results of experimental research on a wide range of biological sciences from biomolecules to biosphere. Analytical reviews of the advances in science and technology, science chronicles and various other materials are also presented.

ALBERTA NATURALIST. see *CONSERVATION*

578.77　　　　　GW　ISSN 0342-1120
QK564
ALGOLOGICAL STUDIES; Archiv fuer Hydrobiologie, Supplementbaende. (Text in English, French and German) 1970. irreg. price varies. E. Schweizerbart'sche Verlagsbuchhandlung, Johannesstr. 3A, 70176 Stuttgart, Germany. TEL 49-711-625001. FAX 49-711-625005. Ed. O. Lhotsky. bk.rev. **Indexed:** Biol.Abstr., Sport Fish.Abstr., Wild.Rev., Zoo.Rec. **Document type:** academic/scholarly publication.
—CISTI; KNAW; Linda Hall; UnCover. **CCC**.

ALMANAK NUKLIR BIOLOGI DAN KIMIA. see ENERGY — Nuclear Energy

570　　　　　IS　ISSN 0333-9815
ALON LEMOREH HABIOLOGIA/PAMPHLET FOR BIOLOGY TEACHERS. (Text in Hebrew) 1969. 4/yr. $20. Hebrew University of Jerusalem, Amos De Shalit Science Teaching Centre, Jerusalem, Israel. TEL 972-2-585365. Ed. Talmona Oryan. bk.rev.; index. circ. 700. (back issues avail.) **Indexed:** Ind.Heb.Per.
 Description: Provides biology teachers with ideas and activities for classroom enrichment. Discusses current information in the biological sciences and problems and issues in biology education.

570　　　　　GW　ISSN 0232-5381
ALTENBURGER NATURWISSENSCHAFTLICHE FORSCHUNGEN. (Text in German; summaries in English and German) 1981. biennial. Naturkundliches Museum Mauritianum, Postfach 1644, 04590 Altenburg, Germany. TEL 49-3447-2589. Ed. Norbert Hoeser. circ. 1,600. **Document type:** academic/scholarly publication.

570　　　　　JA　ISSN 0065-6682
QH91.A1　　　　　CODEN: ARJPB8
AMAKUSA MARINE BIOLOGICAL LABORATORY. PUBLICATIONS. (Text and summaries in English) 1966. a. exchange basis. Kyushu University, Amakusa Marine Biological Laboratory - Kyushu Daigaku Amakusa Rinkai Jikkensho, 2231 Tomioka, Reihoku-cho, Amakuga-gun, Kumamoto-ken 863-25, Japan. TEL 81-969-35-0003. FAX 81-969-35-2413. Ed. Taiji Kikuchi. R&P contact: Taiji Kikuchi. adv. contact: Taiji Kikuchi. circ. 450. **Indexed:** Biol.Abstr., Curr.Adv.Ecol.Sci., Ecol.Abstr., Zoo.Rec. **Document type:** academic/scholarly publication.
—BLDSC (7024.765000); Linda Hall.
 Description: Publishes mainly achievements of laboratory staff and visiting scientists. Also contains ecological and taxonomic studies of benthic invertebrates in the littoral and shallow sea.

577　　　　　GW　ISSN 0065-6755
QH117　　　　　CODEN: AMAZAP
AMAZONIANA; LIMNOLOGIA ET OECOLOGIA REGIONALIS SYSTEMAE FLUMINIS AMAZONAS. (Text and summaries in English) 1965. a. (2 nos./vol.). DM.88. Universitaetsbuchhandlung Muehlau, Holtenauer Str. 116, 24100 Kiel, Germany. TEL 49-431-8009-0. FAX 49-431-800950. Eds. Djalma Batista, Harald Sioli. **Indexed:** ASCA, Biol.Abstr., Curr.Adv.Ecol.Sci., Curr.Cont., Ecol.Abstr., Forest.Abstr., Forest Prod.Abstr., Geo.Abstr.H.G., Geo.Abstr.P.G., GeoRef., Soils & Fert. **Document type:** academic/scholarly publication.
—Genuine Article; UnCover.

570　　　　　US　ISSN 0002-7685
QH1
THE AMERICAN BIOLOGY TEACHER. 1938. m. (during school year). $60 (foreign $75) (effective 1997). National Association of Biology Teachers, Inc., 11250 Roger Bacon Dr., Ste. 19, Reston, VA 22090. TEL 703-471-1134. FAX 703-435-5582. E-mail: NABTer@aol.com; URL: http://www.nabt.org. Ed. Randy Moore. adv. contact: Michele Bedsaul. bk.rev.; film rev.; software rev.; charts; illus.; stat.; index. circ. 12,000. (also avail. in microfilm from UMI; back issues avail.) **Indexed:** ASCA, Biol.Abstr., Biol.Dig., C.I.J.E., Cont.Pg.Educ., Curr.Adv.Ecol.Sci., Curr.Adv.Genetics & Molec.Biol., Curr.Cont., Educ.Ind., Environ.Abstr., Gen.Sci.Ind., Helminthol.Abstr., Media Rev.Dig., SSCI, Telegen. **Document type:** academic/scholarly publication.
—BLDSC (0810.800000); CIS; CISTI; Genuine Article; KR SourceOne; Linda Hall; SWETS; UMI; UnCover.
 Description: Includes updates on biological research, educational strategies and technologies, suggestions for laboratory and classroom exercises, book reviews and audio-visual reviews.
 Refereed Serial

572.8 610　　　　　US
AMERICAN BLOOD RESOURCES ASSOCIATION. JOURNAL. 1979. q. $80 (foreign $105). American Blood Resources Association, Box 669, Annapolis, MD 21404-0669. TEL 410-263-8296. FAX 410-263-2298. URL: 463.3276@compuserve.com. Ed. Robert W. Reilly. adv.; tr.lit. circ. 4,000. (back issues avail.) **Document type:** trade publication.
 Former titles (until 1992): Plasmapheresis (ISSN 0894-6779); (until 1987): Plasma Quarterly (ISSN 0739-8751)

AMERICAN JOURNAL OF CLINICAL PATHOLOGY. see MEDICAL SCIENCES

570　　　　　US　ISSN 1042-0533
QP1　　　　　CODEN: AJHUES
AMERICAN JOURNAL OF HUMAN BIOLOGY. 1989. bi-m. $610 (foreign $715) (effective 1998). (Human Biology Council) John Wiley & Sons, Inc., Journals, 605 Third Ave., New York, NY 10158. TEL 212-850-6645. FAX 212-850-6021. TELEX 12-7063. E-mail: SUBINFO@JWILEY.COM; URL: http://www.wiley.co.uk. (Subscr. outside the Americas to: John Wiley & Sons Ltd., Baffins Ln., Chichester, W. Sussex PO19 1UD, England. TEL 44-1243-779777. FAX 44-1243-776128) Ed. Robert M. Malina. adv.: B&W page £640, color page £1515; trim 254 x 174. circ. 800. (also avail. in microform from UMI; back issues avail.) **Indexed:** Anthropol.Lit., Arts & Hum.Cit.Ind., ASCA, Curr.Cont., Fam.Ind., Popul.Ind., SSCI. **Document type:** academic/scholarly publication.
—BLDSC (0824.900000); CISTI; Genuine Article; KNAW; SWETS; UnCover. **CCC**.
 Formerly: Human Biology (New York).
 Description: Provides a forum for research in human biology. For scientists and professionals interested in understanding individual and population variations in health and disease. Covers a wide range of topics in such areas as genetic variation, anatomy and physiology, growth and aging, physical performance and evolution.
 Refereed Serial

BIOLOGY 585

570　　　　　US　ISSN 0003-0147
QH1　　　　　CODEN: AMNTA4
THE AMERICAN NATURALIST; devoted to the advancement and correlation of the biological sciences. 1867. m. $67 to individuals (Canada $89.69; elsewhere $85); institutions $237 (Canada $271.59; elsewhere $255); students $47 (Canada $68.29; elsewhere $65) (effective 1998). (American Society of Naturalists) University of Chicago Press, Journals Division, Box 37005, Chicago, IL 60637. TEL 773-753-3347. FAX 773-753-0811. E-mail: subscriptions@journals.uchicago.edu; URL: http://www.journals.uchicago.edu/AN/. Ed. Joel G. Kingsolver. adv.: page $410; trim 6 5/8 x 9 1/2. bk.rev.; index. circ. 3,800. (also avail. in microform from UMI,PMC; microfiche from IDC; reprint service avail.) **Indexed:** Acid Pre.Dig., Anim.Breed.Abstr., Apic.Abstr., ASCA, Bio-Contr.News & Info., Biol.Abstr., Biol.& Agr.Ind., Chem.Abstr., Curr.Adv.Ecol.Sci., Curr.Adv.Genetics & Molec.Biol., Curr.Cont., Curr.Ref.Fish Res., Dairy Sci.Abstr., Deep Sea Res.& Oceanogr.Abstr., Ecol.Abstr., Environ.Per.Bibl. (1989-), Field Crop.Abstr., Gen.Sci.Ind., Geo.Abstr., Helminthol.Abstr., Herb.Abstr., Ind.Sci.Rev., INIS Atomind., Int.Abstr.Biol.Sci., Key Word Ind.Wildl.Res., Math.R., Nutr.Abstr., Ornam.Hort., Plant Breed.Abstr., Protozool.Abstr., Rev.Plant Path., Risk Abstr., Sci.Cit.Ind., Seed Abstr., Sel.Water Res.Abstr., Sport Fish.Abstr., SSCI, Weed Abstr., Wild.Rev., Zoo.Rec. **Document type:** academic/scholarly publication.
—BLDSC (0846.000000); CASDDS; CISTI; Ei; EMDOCS; Genuine Article; KR SourceOne; Linda Hall; SWETS; UMI; UnCover. **CCC**.
 Refereed Serial

372.357　　　　　NE　ISSN 0926-3543
AMOEBA. (Text in Dutch) 1926. 6/yr. fl.50. Nederlands Jeugdbond voor Natuurstudie - Netherlands Youth Organization for Natural Studies, Noordereinde 60, 1243 JJ 's Gravenland, Netherlands. TEL 31-5700-18351. Eds. Hajo Molegraaf, Liesbeth Bakker. charts; illus.; stat. **Document type:** bulletin.
 Description: Presents environmental studies to young people as well as botany, entomology, ornithology, zoology and conservation. Includes lists of local, regional and national events of relevance to members.

571.3 611　　　　　US　ISSN 0003-276X
QL801　　　　　CODEN: ANREAK
THE ANATOMICAL RECORD. 1906. 18/yr. $2995 (foreign $3310) (effective 1998). (American Association of Anatomists) John Wiley & Sons, Inc., Journals, 605 Third Ave., New York, NY 10158. TEL 212-850-6645. FAX 212-850-6021. TELEX 12-7063. E-mail: SUBINFO@JWILEY.COM; URL: http://www.wiley.uk.co. (Subscr. outside the Americas to: John Wiley & Sons Ltd., Baffins Ln., Chichester, W. Sussex PO19 1UD, England. TEL 44-1243-779777. FAX 44-1243-776128) Ed. Aaron J. Ladman. adv.: B&W page $640, color page $1515; trim 279 x 210. bk.rev.; abstr.; bibl.; charts; illus.; index. circ. 1,200. (also avail. in microform from UMI; microfilm from PMC; back issues avail.; reprint service avail. from SWZ) **Indexed:** Abstr.Anthropol., Anim.Breed.Abstr., ASCA, Biol.Abstr., Biol.& Agr.Ind., Chem.Abstr., Curr.Adv.Cell & Devel.Biol., Curr.Adv.Ecol.Sci., Curr.Cont., Curr.Tit.Dent., Dent.Ind., Excerp.Med., Ind.Med., Ind.Sci.Rev., Ind.Vet., INIS Atomind., Neurosci.Cit.Ind., Nutr.Abstr., Sci.Cit.Ind., Sport Fish.Abstr., THA, Vet.Bull., Wild.Rev., Zoo.Rec. **Document type:** academic/scholarly publication.
•Also available online.
—BLDSC (0898.000000); CASDDS; EMDOCS; Genuine Article; KNAW; KR SourceOne; Linda Hall; SWETS; UnCover. **CCC**.
 Refereed Serial

571.3 611　　　　　II　ISSN 0003-2778
QM1　　　　　CODEN: JAINAA
ANATOMICAL SOCIETY OF INDIA. JOURNAL. (Text in English) 1951. s-a. Rs.200($45) Anatomical Society of India, Department of Anatomy, M.L.B. Medical College, Jhansi 284128 (U.P.), India. TEL 0517-442032. Ed. G.S. Longia. adv.: page Rs.1200. bk.rev.; charts; illus.; index. circ. 550. **Indexed:** Biol.Abstr., Chem.Abstr., Excerp.Med., Ind.Vet., Nutr.Abstr., Vet.Bull. **Document type:** academic/scholarly publication.
—CASDDS; CISTI.
 Description: Covers anatomy, anthropology, cytology, histology, genetics and clinical applied medicine.
 Refereed Serial

BIOLOGY

ANGEIOLOGIE. see *MEDICAL SCIENCES — Cardiovascular Diseases*

571.86   IT   ISSN 1121-1431
QL1   CODEN: AIBOE7
ANIMAL BIOLOGY. (Text and summaries in English) 1980. 3/yr. L.150000 (foreign L.200000) (effective 1996). Halocynthia Association, Istituto di Zoologia, Universita di Palermo, Via Archirafi 18, 90123 Palermo, Italy. TEL 39-91-6621020. FAX 39-91-6172009. Ed. Giacomo De Leo. index. circ. 400. (reprint service avail. from ISI) **Indexed**: Biol.Abstr., Curr.Adv.Ecol.Sci., Curr.Cont., Excerp.Med., Helminthol.Abstr., Ind.Med., Zoo.Rec. —BLDSC (0902.972000); CASDDS; CISTI; Linda Hall; UnCover.
Former titles (until 1991): Acta Embryologiae et Morphologiae Experimentalis (ISSN 0391-9706); (until 1980): Acta Embryologiae Experimentalis (ISSN 0065-1184); (until 1968): Acta Embryologiae et Morphologiae Experimentalis (ISSN 0567-7416)

570 610   FR   ISSN 0003-3898
RB1   CODEN: ABCLAI
ANNALES DE BIOLOGIE CLINIQUE. (Text in English or French; summaries in English, French) 1943. 11/yr. 2895 F.($565) (effective 1997). (Societe Francaise de Biologie Clinique) John Libbey Eurotext, 127 av. de la Republique, 92120 Montrouge, France. TEL 33-1-46730660. FAX 33-1-40840999. E-mail: marketing@jle.com. (Subscr. to: A T E I, 3 av. Pierre Kerautret, 92230 Romainville, France. TEL 33-1-48408686. FAX 33-1-48400731) Ed. P. Kamoun. adv.; bk.rev.; charts; illus.; index. circ. 3,000. **Indexed**: ASCA, Biol.Abstr., C.I.S. Abstr., Chem.Abstr., Chem.Cit.Ind., Curr.Adv.Ecol.Sci., Curr.Cont., Excerp.Med., Food Sci.& Tech.Abstr., Helminthol.Abstr., Ind.Med., Ind.Sci.Rev., Ind.Vet., INIS Atomind., Nutr.Abstr., Pig News & Info., Protozool.Abstr., Rev.Med.& Vet.Mycol., Sci.Cit.Ind., Vet.Bull. **Document type**: academic/scholarly publication.
—BLDSC (0967.730000); CASDDS; CISTI; EMDOCS; Genuine Article; KNAW; SWETS. **CCC**.
Description: Covers all aspects of clinical biology, from instrumentation and methodology to laboratory applications, clinical investigations, animal experimentation, human pathology and evaluations of apparatus or reagents.
Refereed Serial

571.9 616.07   FR   ISSN 0242-6498
CODEN: ASPAD2
ANNALES DE PATHOLOGIE. (Text in French; summaries in English, French) 1924. 6/yr. 1228 F. (foreign 1477 F.) (effective 1997). (Societe Francaise de Pathologie) Masson - Periodiques, 120 bd. St. Germain, 75006 Paris, France. TEL 33-1-40466200. FAX 33-1-404662011. (Subscr. to: Societe de Periodiques Specialises, B.P. 22-F, 41354 Vineuil Cedex, France. TEL 33-2-54504612. FAX 33-2-54504611) Ed. D. Henin. bk.rev.; bibl.; illus.; index. circ. 1,400. (also avail. in microform from UMI; reprint service avail. from ISI) **Indexed**: ASCA, Biol.Abstr., Chem.Abstr., Curr.Adv.Cancer Res., Curr.Adv.Ecol.Sci., Curr.Cont., Dent.Ind., Excerp.Med., Ind.Med., Ind.Sci.Rev., Rev.Med.& Vet.Mycol., Sci.Cit.Ind. **Document type**: academic/scholarly publication.
—BLDSC (0991.300000); CASDDS; CISTI; EMDOCS; Genuine Article; KNAW; SWETS; UMI. **CCC**.
Formerly (until 1981): Annales d'Anatomie Pathologique (ISSN 0003-3871)
Description: Publishes observations and works of a morphological order, reflecting the achievements of French-speaking anatomopathologists.

570   PL   ISSN 0066-2232
QH301.L8   CODEN: AUCBAJ
ANNALES UNIVERSITATIS MARIAE CURIE-SKLODOWSKA. SECTIO C. BIOLOGIA. (Text in English or Polish; summaries in English, French, German) 1946. a. price varies. Uniwersytet Marii Curie-Sklodowskiej, Wydawnictwo, Pl. M. Curie-Sklodowskiej 5, 20-031 Lublin, Poland. TEL 48-31-375304. FAX 48-81-354966. TELEX 0643223. Ed. Zbigniew Lorkiewicz. circ. 950. **Indexed**: Biol.Abstr., Chem.Abstr., Curr.Adv.Ecol.Sci., Field Crop Abstr., Forest.Abstr., Forest Prod.Abstr., Herb.Abstr., Hort.Abstr., Int.Abstr.Biol.Sci., Plant Breed.Abstr., Rev.Appl.Entomol. **Document type**: academic/scholarly publication.
—CASDDS; CISTI.

ANNALS OF AGRI BIO RESEARCH; an international journal of basic and applied agriculture and biology. see *AGRICULTURE*

ANNALS OF ANATOMY; Zentralblatt fuer die gesamte wissenschaftliche Anatomie. see *MEDICAL SCIENCES*

570   UK   ISSN 0003-4746
QH301   CODEN: AABIAV
ANNALS OF APPLIED BIOLOGY. 1914. 6/yr. (in 2 vols., 3 nos./vol.) £189($390) Association of Applied Biologists, Horticultural Research International, Wellesbourne, Warwickshire CV35 9EF, England. TEL 44-1789-470382. FAX 44-1789-470234. Ed. E. Griffiths. adv.; illus.; cum.index: 1914-1978, 1979-1985. circ. 3,000. **Indexed**: Agri.Eng.Abstr., ASCA, Bio-Contr.News & Info., Biodet.Abstr., Biol.Abstr., Biol.& Agr.Ind., Biotech.Abstr., Chem.Abstr., Crop Physiol.Abstr., Curr.Adv.Ecol.Sci., Curr.Biotech.Abstr., Curr.Cont., Ecol.Abstr., Excerp.Med., Fababean Abstr., Field Crop Abstr., Food Sci.& Tech.Abstr., Forest Abstr., Forest Prod.Abstr., Geo.Abstr., Helminthol.Abstr., Herb.Abstr., Hort.Abstr., Ind.Med., Ind.Sci.Rev., INIS Atomind., Irr.& Drain.Abstr., Maize Abstr., Nutr.Abstr., Ornam.Hort., Plant Breed.Abstr., Plant Grow.Reg.Abstr., Potato Abstr., Rev.Appl.Entomol., Rev.Plant Path., Rice Abstr., Sci.Cit.Ind, Soils & Fert., Sorghum & Millets Abstr., Soyabean Abstr., Sport Fish.Abstr., Triticale Abstr., Trop.Oil Seeds Abstr., Weed Abstr., Wild.Rev., Zoo.Rec. **Document type**: academic/scholarly publication.
—BLDSC (1038.000000); CASDDS; CISTI; EMDOCS; KR SourceOne; Linda Hall; SWETS; UnCover.

570   II   ISSN 0970-0153
CODEN: ANBIEO
ANNALS OF BIOLOGY; an international journal of basic and applied biology. (Text in English) 1985. s-a. Rs.500($60) (effective 1997). Agri Bio Research Publishers, 121 Mohalla Chaudharian, Hisar 125 001, India. TEL 91-1662-37530. Eds. Dr. R.K. Behl, Dr. Manjit S. Dhindsa. adv.; bk.rev. circ. 500. **Indexed**: Agrindex, Biol.Abstr., Crop Physiol.Abstr., Curr.Adv.Ecol.Sci., Ecol.Abstr., Field Crop Abstr., Forest.Abstr., Geo.Abstr.P.G., Herb.Abstr., Hort.Abstr., Indian Sci.Abstr., Irr.& Drain.Abstr., Plant Grow.Reg.Abstr., Seed Abstr., Soils & Fert., Sorghum & Millets Abstr., Soyabean Abstr., Triticale Abstr., Trop.Oil Seeds Abstr., Weed Abstr., Zoo.Rec. **Document type**: academic/scholarly publication.
—BLDSC (1039.300000); CASDDS; CISTI.

570   UK   ISSN 0301-4460
QP34.5   CODEN: AHUBBJ
ANNALS OF HUMAN BIOLOGY. (Text in English; summaries in French and German) 1974. bi-m. £294($485) to institutions (effective 1998). (Society for the Study of Human Biology) Taylor & Francis Ltd., 1 Gunpowder Sq., London EC4A 3DE, England. TEL 44-171-583-0490. FAX 44-171-583-0585. TELEX 858840. E-mail: info@tandf.co.uk; URL: http://www.tandf.co.uk/. (Subscr. in N. America to: Taylor & Francis Inc., 1900 Frost Rd., Ste. 101, Bristol, PA 19007-1598. TEL 800-821-8312. FAX 215-785-5515) Ed.Bd. adv.; bk.rev.; bibl.; charts; stat.; index. (also avail. in microform) **Indexed**: A.I.C.P., Abstr.Anthropol., Abstr.Hyg., Anthropol.Lit., ASCA, Bibl.Dev.Med.& Child Neur., Biol.Abstr., Chem.Abstr., Curr.Adv.Ecol.Sci., Curr.Adv.Genetics & Molec.Biol., Curr.Cont., Dairy Sci.Abstr., Dent.Ind., Ergon.Abstr., Excerp.Med., Geo.Abstr., IDA, Ind.Med., Ind.Sci.Rev., NRN, Nutr.Abstr., Popul.Ind., Risk Abstr., SSCI, Trop.Dis.Bull. **Document type**: academic/scholarly publication.
—BLDSC (1040.900000); CASDDS; CISTI; Genuine Article; KNAW; Linda Hall; SWETS; UnCover. **CCC**.
Description: Publishes papers concerning research into biological aspects of human populations with regard to their ecology, demography, genetics, evolution, and the growth, physiology, disease patterns and behavior of the individuals composing them.
Refereed Serial

570   FR   ISSN 0003-5017
CODEN: ANBLAT
L'ANNEE BIOLOGIQUE. 1895. 4/yr. 880 F. (foreign 1150 F.) (effective 1997). Masson - Periodiques, 120 bd. St. Germain, 75006 Paris, France. TEL 33-1-40466200. FAX 33-1-40466201. (Subscr. to: Societe de Periodiques Specialises, B.P. 22-F, 41354 Vineuil Cedex, France. TEL 33-2-54504612. FAX 33-2-54504611) Ed. P. de Puytorac. adv.; bk.rev.; bibl.; charts; illus.; index. circ. 1,000. (reprint service avail. from ISI) **Indexed**: ASCA, Biol.Abstr., Chem.Abstr., Curr.Adv.Ecol.Sci., Curr.Cont., Curr.Ref.Fish Res., Deep Sea Res.& Oceanogr.Abstr., GeoRef., Helminthol.Abstr., Ind.Med., Ind.Sci.Rev., Sci.Cit.Ind. **Document type**: academic/scholarly publication.
—BLDSC (1048.000000); CASDDS; CISTI; Genuine Article; Linda Hall; SWETS. **CCC**.
Description: Contains articles on all topics: general biology, biochemistry, molecular biology, zoology, botany, ecology, animal and vegetal physiology, psychophysiology, paleontology.

570   FR   ISSN 1157-4135
ANNUAIRE DE LA RECHERCHE BIO-MEDICALE. Short title: A R B M. 1989. a., 5th ed., 1995. $149. Editions Scientifiques Elsevier, 141 rue de Javel, 75747 Paris Cedex 15, France. TEL 33-1-45599063. (Subscr. in U.S. and Canada to: Elsevier Science Inc., Box 882, Madison Sq. Sta., New York, NY 10159-0882. TEL 212-989-5800) **Document type**: directory.
Description: Covers all public and semi-public biomedical research centers in France, including INSERM, CEA, CNRS, ORSTOM, medical schools, science faculties, Pasteur Institutes, and centers for cancer research.

573.6 306.7   US
ANNUAL EDITIONS: HUMAN SEXUALITY. 1975. a. $12.95. Dushkin Publishing Group, Sluice Dock, Guilford, CT 06437-9989. TEL 203-453-4351. FAX 203-453-6000. Ed. Ollie Pocs; Pub. Ian Nielsen. illus. **Document type**: academic/scholarly publication.
Former titles: Annual Editions: Readings in Human Sexuality (ISSN 0163-836X); Focus: Human Sexuality (ISSN 0147-0655)
Refereed Serial

570   US
ANNUAL EDITIONS: LIFE MANAGEMENT. 1992. a. $12. Dushkin Publishing Group, Sluice Dock, Guilford, CT 06437-9989. TEL 203-453-4351. FAX 203-453-6000. Ed. Ann Daluiso; Pub. Ian Nielsen. illus. **Document type**: academic/scholarly publication.

ANNUAL STUDENT SYMPOSIUM ON MARINE AFFAIRS. PROCEEDINGS. see *EDUCATION*

559.89 570   UK   ISSN 0954-1020
Q127.A48   CODEN: ANTSE8
ANTARCTIC SCIENCE. q. £176($322) (foreign £194) (effective 1998). (British Antarctic Survey) Blackwell Science Ltd., Osney Mead, Oxford OX2 0EL, England. TEL 44-1865-206206. FAX 44-1865-721205. E-mail: journals.cs@blacksci.co.uk; URL: http://www.black.co.uk. Ed.Bd.; Pub. Allen Stevens. R&P contact: Sarah Pollard. adv. contact: Martine Cariou-Keen. bk.rev.; illus.; index. circ. 455. (also avail. in microform from UMI; back issues avail.) **Indexed**: ASCA, Curr.Cont., Ecol.Abstr., Environ.Per.Bibl. (1990-), Geo.Abstr.P.G., Geol.Abstr., Ind.Sci.Rev., Meteor.& Geoastrophys.Abstr., Mineral.Abstr., Sport Fish.Abstr., Wild.Rev., Zoo.Rec. **Document type**: academic/scholarly publication.
—BLDSC (1542.130500); CISTI; Ei; EMDOCS; Genuine Article; Linda Hall; SWETS; UMI; UnCover. **CCC**.
Refereed Serial

570   JA   ISSN 0286-4444
AOMORIKEN SEIBUTSU GAKKAISHI/AOMORIKEN BIOLOGICAL SOCIETY. JOURNAL. (Text in Japanese; summaries in English) 1956. a. Aomoriken Seibutsu Gakkai - Aomoriken Biological Society, Hirosaki Daigaku Rigakubu Seibutsugaku Kyoshitsu, 3 Bunkyocho, Hirosaki-shi, Aomori-ken 036, Japan.

APPLIED SOIL ECOLOGY. see *AGRICULTURE — Crop Production And Soil*

AQUATIC CONSERVATION: MARINE AND FRESHWATER ECOSYSTEMS. see *CONSERVATION*

BIOLOGY 587

578.77 GW ISSN 0003-9136
QH301 CODEN: AHYBA4
ARCHIV FUER HYDROBIOLOGIE. (Supplements avail.) (Text in English, French and German) 1906. 12/yr. (in 3 vols., 4 nos./vol.). DM.138 per no. (effective 1997). (International Association for Theoretical and Applied Limnology) E. Schweizerbart'sche Verlagsbuchhandlung, Johannesstr. 3A, 70176 Stuttgart, Germany. TEL 49-711-625001. FAX 49-711-625005. Ed. W. Lampert. adv.; bk.rev.; bibl.; charts; illus. (reprint service avail. from SWZ) **Indexed:** ASCA, Biol.Abstr., Chem.Abstr., Curr.Adv.Ecol.Sci., Curr.Adv.Genetics & Molec.Biol., Curr.Cont., Deep Sea Res.& Oceanogr.Abstr., Excerpt.Med., Geo.Abstr., Helminthol.Abstr., IBR, Ind.Sci.Rev., INIS Atomind., Sci.Cit.Ind., Sel.Water Res.Abstr., So.Pac.Per.Ind., Soils & Fert., Sport Fish.Abstr., SSCI, W.R.C.Inf., Wild.Rev., Zoo.Rec. **Document type:** academic/scholarly publication.
—BLDSC (1613.000000); CASDDS; CISTI; EMDOCS; Genuine Article; KNAW; Linda Hall; SWETS; UnCover. **CCC.**

578.77 GW ISSN 0930-4681
ARCHIV FUER HYDROBIOLOGIE. SUPPLEMENT-BAND: ARBEITEN AUS DEM LIMNOLOGISCHEN INSTITUT DER UNIVERSITAET KONSTANZ. irreg. price varies. (Universitaet Konstanz, Limnologische Institut) E. Schweizerbart'sche Verlagsbuchhandlung, Johannesstr. 3A, 70176 Stuttgart, Germany. TEL 49-711-625001. FAX 49-711-625005. **Document type:** monographic series.
—KNAW.
 Former titles (until 1980): Archiv fuer Hydrobiologie. Supplement-Band: Arbeiten aus dem Limnologischen Institut der Universitaet Freiburg (ISSN 0342-1112); (until 1961): Archiv fuer Hydrobiologie. Supplement-Band: Schriften der Hydrobiologische Station Falkau - Schwarzwald (ISSN 0425-6581)

578.77 GW ISSN 0945-3784
ARCHIV FUER HYDROBIOLOGIE. SUPPLEMENT-BAND: LARGE RIVERS. irreg. price varies. E. Schweizerbart'sche Verlagsbuchhandlung, Johannesstr. 3A, 70176 Stuttgart, Germany. TEL 49-711-625001. FAX 49-711-625005. **Document type:** monographic series.
—KNAW.

578.77 GW ISSN 0341-2881
CODEN: AHBSA8
ARCHIV FUER HYDROBIOLOGIE. SUPPLEMENT-BAND: MONOGRAPHIC STUDIES. 1911. irreg. price varies. E. Schweizerbart'sche Verlagsbuchhandlung, Johannesstr. 3A, 70176 Stuttgart, Germany. TEL 49-711-625001. FAX 49-711-625005. **Document type:** monographic series.
—CASDDS; CISTI; KNAW; UnCover. **CCC.**
 Former titles (until 1967): Archiv fuer Hydrobiologie. Supplement-Band (ISSN 0365-284X); Archiv fuer Hydrobiologie und Planktonkunde. Supplement-Band (ISSN 0931-6256)

578.77 GW ISSN 0342-1066
ARCHIV FUER HYDROBIOLOGIE. SUPPLEMENT-BAND: UNTERSUCHUNGEN DES ELBE-AESTUARS. 1961. irreg. price varies. E. Schweizerbart'sche Verlagsbuchhandlung, Johannesstr. 3A, 70176 Stuttgart, Germany. TEL 49-711-625001. FAX 49-711-625005. **Document type:** monographic series.
—BLDSC (1613.001000); KNAW.

570 GW ISSN 0003-9365
QL366 CODEN: APRKAI
ARCHIV FUER PROTISTENKUNDE. (Text in English, French and German; summaries in English) 1902. q. DM.574 (foreign DM.582) (effective 1996). Gustav Fischer Verlag Jena, Villengang 2, 07745 Jena, Germany. TEL 49-3641-626444. FAX 49-3641-626500. (Subscr. to: Postfach 100537, 07705 Jena, Germany) Ed. S.J. Casper. adv.: page DM.550; trim 210 x 280. bk.rev.; bibl.; charts; illus.; index. cum.index: vols.1-50, 1902-1918 (in 2 vols.). circ. 350. (also avail. in microfilm from BHP; reprint service avail. from ISI) **Indexed:** Abstr.Hyg., ASCA, Bio-Contr.News & Info., Biol.Abstr., Chem.Abstr., Curr.Adv.Ecol.Sci., Curr.Cont., Deep Sea Res.& Oceanogr.Abstr., Excerp.Med., Helminthol.Abstr., Ind.Sci.Rev., Ind.Vet., Protozool.Abstr., Ref.Zh., Sci.Cit.Ind, Trop.Dis.Bull., Vet.Bull. **Document type:** academic/scholarly publication.
—BLDSC (1623.400000); CISTI; Genuine Article; Linda Hall; SWETS; UnCover. **CCC.**

570 YU ISSN 0354-4664
ARCHIVES OF BIOLOGICAL SCIENCES. (Text in English) 1949. q.? Srpsko Biolosko Drustvo, Institut za Bioloska Istrazivanja "Sinisa Stankovic", Kneza Milosa 101, Belgrade, Yugoslavia. Ed. Maksim Todorovic.
—CISTI.
 Formerly: Arhiv Bioloskih Nauka (ISSN 0375-8575)

570 611 IT ISSN 0004-0223
CODEN: AIAEA2
ARCHIVIO ITALIANO DI ANATOMIA E DI EMBRIOLOGIA/ITALIAN JOURNAL OF ANATOMY AND EMBRYOLOGY. (Text in Italian; summaries in English, French, German) 1902. q. L.150000 (foreign L.200000). Editrice Sedicesimo, Via Mannelli 29r, 50136 Florence, Italy. TEL 055-2476781. FAX 055-2478568. Ed. Enzo Brizzi. adv.; bk.rev.; charts; illus.; index. circ. 600. **Indexed:** Biol.Abstr., Chem.Abstr., Curr.Adv.Ecol.Sci., Dent.Ind., Excerp.Med., Ind.Med., Ind.Vet., Vet.Bull.
—CASDDS; CISTI; KNAW.

570 AG ISSN 0004-0401
ARCHIVO DE CIENCIAS BIOLOGICAS Y NATURALES, TEORICAS Y APLICADAS.* 1956. 2/yr. $1 per no. (approx.). Librart s.r.l., Casilla Correo 5047, Buenos Aires, Argentina. Ed. A. Silvia Colla.
—Linda Hall.

571.3 SP ISSN 0004-0436
ARCHIVO ESPANOL DE MORFOLOGIA. (Text in English, Spanish) 1941; N.S. 1996. 3/yr. 18000 ptas.($150) to individuals; institutions 25000 ptas.($210) (effective 1997 & 1998). Morphos Ediciones, S.L., Apdo. 12093, 46080 Valencia, Spain. FAX 34-6-3608442. E-mail: andres.martinez-almagro@uv.es. Ed. Andres Martinez-Almagro. **Document type:** monographic series.

570 PE ISSN 0250-5037
QP82.2.A4 CODEN: ABANDH
ARCHIVOS DE BIOLOGIA ANDINA. (Text in Spanish and sometimes English: summaries in English) 1965. s-a. free. Universidad Nacional Mayor de San Marcos, Instituto de Biologia Andina, Centro de Investigacion, Apdo. 5073, Lima, Peru. Ed. Dr. E. Picon-Reategui. abstr.; bibl.; charts; stat. circ. 1,000. **Indexed:** A.I.C.P., Biol.Abstr., Chem.Abstr., Ind.Med., Rev.Plant Path, Sci.Cit.Ind.
—CASDDS.
 Formerly (until 1977): Universidad Nacional Mayor de San Marcos. Instituto de Biologia Andina. Archivos (ISSN 0020-3750)

ARCTIC AND ALPINE RESEARCH. see *SCIENCES: COMPREHENSIVE WORKS*

570 560 AG ISSN 0325-3856
ARGENTINA. MUSEO PROVINCIAL DE CIENCIAS NATURALES. COMUNICACIONES. (Text in Spanish; summaries in English) 1967; N.S 1983. irreg. exchange basis. Ministerio de Educacion y Cultura, Museo Provincial de Ciencias Naturales, Florentino Amechino, Primera Junta 2859, 3000 Santa Fe, Argentina. TEL 54-42-523843. FAX 54-42-523843. E-mail: ameghino@santafe.com.ar; URL: http://www.unl.edu.ar/SantaFe/museo__cn__html. Ed. Carlos Alberto Virasoro. circ. 1,000. (back issues avail.) **Document type:** academic/scholarly publication, government publication, monographic series.
—Linda Hall.
 Description: Covers natural resources of the Santa Fe region, with emphasis on how to care for them within the ecological balance of nature.
 Refereed Serial

570 RH ISSN 0250-6386
AS622 CODEN: AZIMDI
ARNOLDIA ZIMBABWE. 1964. irreg. price varies. National Museums and Monuments of Zimbabwe, P.O. Box 240, Bulawayo, Zimbabwe. TEL 60045. Ed. A. Kumirai. illus.; index. circ. 400. **Indexed:** Biol.Abstr., GeoRef., P.L.E.S.A. (1990-), Rev.Appl.Entomol., Sport Fish.Abstr., Wild.Rev., Zoo.Rec. **Document type:** academic/scholarly publication.
—BLDSC (1684.105000).
 Former titles: Arnoldia Zimbabwe Rhodesia; Arnoldia Rhodesia (ISSN 0066-7781)
 Description: Results of research in the natural sciences in southern Africa.

570 660 BL ISSN 0365-0979
QH301 CODEN: ABTTAP
ARQUIVOS DE BIOLOGIA E TECNOLOGIA. (Text mainly in Portuguese; abstracts in English) 1946. q. R.130 (foreign $130) (effective 1997-98). Instituto de Tecnologia do Parana, Rua Prof. Algacyr Munhoz Mader, 3775, 81350-010 Curitiba PR, Brazil. TEL 55-41-33463141. FAX 55-41-2476788. E-mail: tecpar@tecpar.br; URL: http://www.tecpar.br/tecpar/tecpar.html. Ed. Carlos R. Soccol; Pub. Graca Maria Simoes Luz. R&P contact: Graca Maria Simoes Luz. adv. contact: Graca Maria Simoes Luz. abstr.; bibl.; charts; illus.; stat. circ. 300. (also avail. in microform from UMI; back issues avail.) **Indexed:** ASCA, Biodet.Abstr., Biol.Abstr., Chem.Abstr., Curr.Adv.Ecol.Sci., Curr.Cont., Dairy Sci.Abstr., Excerp.Med., Field Crop Abstr., Forest.Abstr., Herb.Abstr., Hort.Abstr., Ind.Med., Ind.Vet., INIS Atomind., Irr.& Drain.Abstr., Maize Abstr., Ornam.Hort., Poult.Abstr., Rev.Med. & Vet.Mycol., Seed Abstr., Sel.Water Res.Abstr., Soils & Fert., Soyabean Abstr., Sugar Ind.Abstr., Vet.Bull. **Document type:** academic/scholarly publication.
—BLDSC (1695.000000); CASDDS; Genuine Article; KNAW; UMI.
 Description: Presents original research on biological sciences, agriculture and food technology.
 Refereed Serial

570 GW ISSN 0171-4090
ARTICULATA; Zeitschrift fuer Biologie, Systematik und Neubeschreibung von Orthopteren. (Text in English, French and German) 1975. s-a. DM.40. Deutsche Gesellschaft fuer Orthopterologie e.V., c/o Dr. Peter Detzel, Ed., Turnierstr. 9, 70599 Stuttgart, Germany. bk.rev.; index. circ. 650. (back issues avail.) **Indexed:** Entomol.Abstr. **Document type:** academic/scholarly publication.

570 PH ISSN 0117-3375
CODEN: ALSCE9
ASIA LIFE SCIENCES; the Asian international journal of life sciences. (Text in English) 1992. s-a. P.300 to individuals (foreign $40); institutions P.500 (foreign $50) (effective 1997). (University of the Philippines Los Banos) Rushing Water Publishers Ltd., No. 81 Diamond Jubileeville, Masaya, Bay, Laguna 4033, Philippines. TEL 9-63-49-3368. FAX 9-63-49-2721. (Subscr. to: Asia Life Sciences, D-206 Biological Sciences Bldg., University of the Philippines Los Banos, College, Laguna 4031, Philippines) Ed. William Sm. Gruezo. R&P contact: William Sm. Gruezo. bk.rev.; illus.; index. circ. 1,000. **Document type:** academic/scholarly publication.
—BLDSC (1742.249300).
 Refereed Serial

578.77 CC ISSN 1011-4041
QH179 CODEN: AMABEP
ASIAN MARINE BIOLOGY. 1985. a., vol.13, 1996. $29. Marine Biological Association of Hong Kong, c/o The Swire Institute of Marine Science, Cape d'Aguilar Rd., Shek O, Hong Kong, People's Republic of China. (Dist. in Europe by: Universal Book Services, Warmonderweg 80, 2341 KZ Oegstgeest, Netherlands. TEL 31-71-170208. FAX 31-71-171856; People's Republic of China; Dist. in rest of the world by: Hong Kong University Press, 139 Pokfulam Rd., Hong Kong. TEL 852-2550-2703. FAX 852-2875-0734) illus. **Indexed:** Zoo.Rec. **Document type:** academic/scholarly publication.

ASSOCIATION DES ANATOMISTES. BULLETIN. see *MEDICAL SCIENCES*

ASSOCIATION OF MARINE LABORATORIES OF THE CARIBBEAN. NEWSLETTER. see *EARTH SCIENCES — Oceanography*

ASSOCIATION OF MARINE LABORATORIES OF THE CARIBBEAN. PROCEEDINGS. see *EARTH SCIENCES — Oceanography*

ATELIERS. see *CHILDREN AND YOUTH. — For*

ATENEO PARMENSE. ACTA BIO-MEDICA. see *MEDICAL SCIENCES*

ATLANTIDE REPORT. SCIENTIFIC RESULTS OF THE DANISH EXPEDITION TO THE COASTS OF TROPICAL WEST AFRICA. see *ENVIRONMENTAL STUDIES*

BIOLOGY

577   AT   ISSN 0307-692X
QH197   CODEN: AJECDQ
AUSTRALIAN JOURNAL OF ECOLOGY. 1976. q. Aus.$403($606) (effective 1997). (Ecological Society of Australia) Blackwell Science Pty Ltd, P.O. Box 378, Carlton South, Vic. 3053, Australia. TEL 61-3-93470300. FAX 61-3-93493016. Ed.Bd. adv.: B&W page $790, color page $1650. index. circ. 1,300. (back issues avail.; reprint service avail. from UMI) **Indexed:** Agroforest.Abstr., Apic.Abstr., ASCA, Bibl.Agri., Bio-Contr.News & Info., Biol.Abstr., Chem.Abstr., Crop Physiol.Abstr., Curr.Adv.Ecol.Sci., Curr.Cont., Curr.Ref.Fish Res., Deep Sea Res.& Oceanogr.Abstr., Ecol.Abstr., Environ.Per.Bibl (1981-), Field Crop Abstr., Forest.Abstr., Forest Prod.Abstr., Geo.Abstr.H.G., Geo.Abstr.P.G., Helminthol.Abstr., Herb.Abstr., Ind.Sci.Rev., Ind.Vet., Irr.& Drain.Abstr., Key Word Ind.Wldl.Res., Rev.Appl.Entomol., Sci.Cit.Ind., Seed Abstr., Soils & Fert., SSCI, Weed Abstr. **Document type:** academic/scholarly publication.
—BLDSC (1807.580000); CASDDS; CISTI; Ei; EMDOCS; Genuine Article; Linda Hall; SWETS; UMI; UnCover. **CCC.**
     Description: Publishes original papers describing experimental, comprehensive, observational or theoretical studies on terrestrial, marine or freshwater systems.

570   JA   ISSN 0917-866X
AZABU DAIGAKU SEIBUTSU KAGAKU SOGO KENKYUJO KIYO/AZABU UNIVERSITY. RESEARCH INSTITUTE OF BIOSCIENCES. REPORT. (Text in Japanese) 1991. a. Azabu Daigaku, Seibutsu Kagaku Sogo Kenkyujo - Azabu University, Research Institute of Biosciences, 17-71 Fuchinobe 1-chome, Sagamihara-shi, Kanagawa-ken 229, Japan.

570   SP   ISSN 1131-5628
AZARA. 1989. a. 1000 ptas. Universidad de Zaragoza, Facultad de Veterinaria, Departamento de Biologia, Miguel Servet, 177, 50013 Zaragoza, Spain. **Indexed:** Ind.SST.

B A B A TRADE ASSOCIATION FOR THE BRITISH BIOMASS INDUSTRIES. THE DIGEST. see ENERGY

B B A - BIOENERGETICS. (Biochimica et Biophysica Acta) see BIOLOGY — Botany

570   US
QH315
B S C S: THE NATURAL SELECTION; innovative science education. 1958. 2/yr. free. Biological Sciences Curriculum Study, Pikes Peak Research Park, 5415 Mark Dabling Blvd., Colorado Springs, CO 80918. TEL 719-531-5550. FAX 719-531-9104. Ed. Cathrine M. Monson. R&P contact: Cathrine M. Monson. adv.; bk.rev.; bibl.; illus. circ. 10,000. (also avail. in microform from UMI) **Document type:** newsletter.
—CISTI; UMI.
     Former titles (until vol.4, no.1, 1981): B S C S Journal (ISSN 0162-3613); (until 1979): Biological Sciences Curriculum Study Journal; Supersedes (1959-1978): B S C S Newsletter (ISSN 0005-3295)
     Description: Prepares and implements innovative K-12 science programs. Informs educators about BSCS programs and other advances in science education.

570   GW   ISSN 0067-2858
BADISCHER LANDESVEREIN FUER NATURKUNDE UND NATURSCHUTZ, FREIBURG. MITTEILUNGEN. NEUE FOLGE. 1919. a. DM.50. Badischer Landesverein fuer Naturkunde und Naturschutz e.V., Gerberau 32, 79098 Freiburg, Germany. TEL 49-761-2012561. FAX 49-761-2012563. Ed. H. Koerner. bk.rev. circ. 2,500. **Indexed:** Biol.Abstr. **Document type:** academic/scholarly publication.
     Description: Publications on biology, geology and mineralogy.

570   JA
BAIORISACHI SHINPOJUMU KOEN YOSHISHU/BIO RESEARCH SYMPOSIUM. (Text in English, Japanese) 1989. a. Nihon Miripoa Rimiteddo - Nihon Millipore Ltd., 3-12 Kitashinagawa 1-chome, Shinagawa-ku, Tokyo 140, Japan.

570   JA   ISSN 0915-4531
BAIOTORENDO/BIOTRENDS. (Text in Japanese) 1989. q. 2400 Yen per no. Maruzen Co., Ltd., 3-10 Nihonbashi 2-chome, Chuo-ku, Tokyo 103, Japan.

570   US   ISSN 0198-0068
                            CODEN: BANRDU
BANBURY REPORTS. Variant title: Banbury Reports Series. 1979. irreg., vol.35, 1991. price varies. Cold Spring Harbor Laboratory Press, Publications Department, Box 100, Cold Spring Harbor, NY 11724. TEL 800-843-4388. FAX 516-349-1946. E-mail: cshpress@cshl.org; URL: http://www.cshl.org. Ed. John Inglis. **Indexed:** Biol.Abstr., Chem.Abstr. **Document type:** monographic series.
—CASDDS; CISTI; KNAW. **CCC.**
     Description: Devoted to risk assessments including topics pertaining to human diseases.

570 630   BG   ISSN 1016-4057
BANGLADESH JOURNAL OF BIOLOGICAL SCIENCES. (Text in English) 1955. s-a. Tk.30($5) Bangladesh Society for Biological and Agricultural Sciences, Dept. of Biochemistry, University of Dhaka, Ramna, Dhaka 2, Bangladesh. Ed. Kamaluddin Ahmad. bk.rev. circ. 500. (back issues avail.) **Indexed:** Biol.Abstr., Chem.Abstr., Dairy Sci.Abstr., Field Crop Abstr., Herb.Abstr., Plant Breed.Abstr.
—Linda Hall.
     Former titles: Bangladesh Journal of Biological and Agricultural Sciences (ISSN 0045-1428); Pakistan Journal of Biological and Agricultural Sciences (ISSN 0078-8244)

BANGLADESH JOURNAL OF SOIL SCIENCE. see AGRICULTURE — Crop Production And Soil

570 598.2   UK   ISSN 0408-5655
BARDSEY OBSERVATORY REPORT. 1953. a. £5. Bardsey Bird & Field Observatory, c/o L. Richardson, 33 Doveridge Rd., Hall Green, Birmingham B28 OLT. TEL 44-121-745-8881. FAX 44-121-200-2454. Ed. P. Hope Jones. circ. 300. (back issues avail.) **Indexed:** Biol.Abstr. **Document type:** academic/scholarly publication.
     Description: Reports on activities and research concerning Bardsey Island, a national nature reserve off the northwestern coast of Wales.

611.018   IT   ISSN 1120-9992
BASIC AND APPLIED MYOLOGY. Short title: B A M. 1991. 6/yr. (in 1 vol.). L.15000($150) (effective 1996). Unipress s.a.s., 231 Via C. Battisti, 35123 Padova, Italy. FAX 39-49-8752542. (Edit. addr.: Ugo Carrera, Department of Biomedical Sciences, Universita di Padua, Via Trieste 75, 35131 Padova, Italy. FAX 39-49-8276049) Ed. Ugo Carraro. circ. 100. (back issues avail.) **Document type:** academic/scholarly publication.
—BLDSC (1861.468000).

570   US   ISSN 0090-5542
                            CODEN: BLFSBY
BASIC LIFE SCIENCES. 1973. irreg., latest vol.64. price varies. Plenum Publishing Corp., 233 Spring St., New York, NY 10013-1578. TEL 212-620-8000. FAX 212-463-0742. TELEX 23-421139. E-mail: books@plenum.com. Ed. Ernest H.Y. Chu. **Indexed:** Biol.Abstr., Chem.Abstr., Ind.Med., INIS Atomind. **Document type:** monographic series.
—BLDSC (1863.980000); CASDDS; CISTI; KNAW. **CCC.**
     Refereed Serial

BASLER VEROEFFENTLICHUNGEN ZUR GESCHICHTE DER MEDIZIN UND DER BIOLOGIE. NEUE FOLGE. see MEDICAL SCIENCES

BEHAVIORAL AND BRAIN SCIENCES; an international journal of current research and theory with open peer commentary. see PSYCHOLOGY

591.7   US   ISSN 1045-2249
QL750   CODEN: BEECE3
BEHAVIORAL ECOLOGY. 1990. bi-m. £36($55) to individuals; institutions £170($265); students £20($32.50) (effective 1998). (International Society for Behavioral Ecology) Oxford University Press, Journals, 2001 Evans Rd., Cary, NC 27513. TEL 919-677-0977; 800-852-7323. FAX 919-677-1714. E-mail: jnlorders@oup-usa.org; URL: http://www.oup-usa.org/. (Subscr. outside N. America to: Oxford University Press, Journals, Great Clarendon St., Oxford OX2 6DP, England. TEL 44-1865-267907. FAX 44-1865-267485) Ed.Bd. adv. circ. 1,366. (back issues avail.) **Indexed:** Apic.Abstr., ASCA, Curr.Cont., Ecol.Abstr., Environ.Per.Bibl. (1993-), Key Word Ind.Wldl.Res., Sport Fish.Abstr., Wild.Rev., Zoo.Rec. **Document type:** academic/scholarly publication.
—BLDSC (1877.390000); EMDOCS; Genuine Article; SWETS; UMI; UnCover. **CCC.**
     Description: Publishes research on environmental influences on the evolution and adaptation of animal behavior.
     Refereed Serial

570   GW   ISSN 0721-3468
BEITRAEGE ZUR NATURKUNDE DER WETTERAU.* (Text in German; summaries in English and German) 1981. a. DM.12. Naturkundlicher Arbeitskreis Wetterau, Fuhrstr. 5, 61191 Rosbach, Germany. adv.; bk.rev. circ. 800. (also avail. in microfiche; back issues avail.)

570 550   GW   ISSN 0342-5452
BEITRAEGE ZUR NATURKUNDE IN OSTHESSEN. 1969. irreg., no.32, 1996. DM.30. (Verein fuer Naturkunde in Osthessen e.V.) Verlag Parzeller GmbH & Co. KG, Postfach 409, 36004 Fulda, Germany. TEL 49-661-280-0. FAX 49-661-280-285. bk.rev. circ. 500. **Document type:** monographic series.

500.9   GW   ISSN 0340-4277
QH5   CODEN: BNNIDQ
BEITRAEGE ZUR NATURKUNDE NIEDERSACHSENS. 1948. q. DM.33. Kastanienallee 13, 31224 Peine, Germany. TEL 49-5171-12233. FAX 49-5171-48283. (Subscr. to: J. Streichert, Stettiner Str. 3, 31241 Gr. Ilsede, Germany) Ed. Dr. Hans Oelke; Pub. Dr. Hans Oelke. adv.; bk.rev.; abstr.; charts; illus.; stat.; index. circ. 800. **Indexed:** Biol.Abstr., Forest.Abstr., Key Word Ind.Wldl.Res. **Document type:** academic/scholarly publication.
—BLDSC (1886.000000).
     Formerly (1965-1971): Natur, Kultur und Jagd (ISSN 0028-0577)

BEITRAEGE ZUR RHEINKUNDE. see HISTORY — History Of Europe

570 610   AU
BERICHTE NATURWISSENSCHAFTLICH - MEDIZINISCHEN VEREINS IN INNSBRUCK. (Text in English, French and German; summaries in English, French, German and Italian) 1870. a. S.500. Naturwissenschaftlich - Medizinischer Verein in Innsbruck, Technikerstr. 25, A-6020 Innsbruck, Austria. TEL 43-512-5076142. FAX 43-512-2185358. E-mail: erwin.meyer@uibk.ac.at. Ed. Dr. Erwin Meyer. bk.rev. circ. 500. **Indexed:** Biol.Abstr. **Document type:** academic/scholarly publication.
     Description: Covers biological, faunistic, floristic, environmental and medical sciences. Accentuates the problems of the Alps, other high mountain groups and the Mediterranean basin.
     Refereed Serial

577 614.7   GW   ISSN 0173-7074
BERLINER NATURSCHUTZBLAETTER; Zeitschrift fuer Berlin und Brandenburg. 1922. q. DM.50($37) Volksbund Naturschutz e.V., Abbestr. 13, 10587 Berlin, Germany. Ed. K. Andreas Bley. adv.; bk.rev.; index. circ. 1,200. (back issues avail.) **Indexed:** IBR. **Document type:** academic/scholarly publication.
     Description: Publication covering pollution, preservation and protection of nature in and around Berlin. Features forests, land, wildlife, and plant vegetation. Includes association news and events.

BIOLOGY

570 581   JA   ISSN 0286-9306
QR171.I6   CODEN: BIMIDK
BIFIDOBACTERIA AND MICROFLORA. s-a. $65. (Japan Bifidus Foundation) Business Center for Academic Societies Japan, 5-16-9 Honkomagome, Bunkyo-ku, Tokyo 113, Japan. TEL 03-5814-5811. FAX 03-5814-5822. TELEX 2722268 BCJSP J. **Indexed:** Sugar Ind.Abstr.
—CASDDS; CISTI.

570 581   JA   ISSN 0914-2509
Z5185.B53
BIFIZUSU/BIFIDUS FLORES, FRUCTUS ET SEMINA. 1987. s-a. 5150 Yen. (Nihon Bifizusukin Senta - Japan Bifidus Foundation) Business Center for Academic Societies Japan, 16-9, Honkomagome 5-chome, Bunkyo-ku, Tokyo 113, Japan. **Document type:** academic/scholarly publication.
—CISTI.
     Formed by the merger of (1981-1987): Bifidus: Bibliography of Bifidobacteria and Microflora (ISSN 0285-7006); (1985-1987): Bifidus, Fructus et Semina (ISSN 0911-7636); (1984-1987): Nihon Bifizusukin Senta Nyusu (ISSN 0914-3262)

DIE BINNENGEWAESSER; Einzeldarstellungen aus der Limnologie und ihren Grenzgebieten. see EARTH SCIENCES — Hydrology

BIO MED. see MEDICAL SCIENCES

570 610   DK   ISSN 0107-4415
BIO-NYT/BIO-NEWS; biologi, medicin, natur, miljoe. 1981. irreg. (4-6/yr.) DKK 225. Foreningen af Yngre Biologer, Falkonergaardsvej 4, DK-1959 Frederiksberg C, Denmark. TEL 45-35-37-64-08. FAX 45-35-37-12-51. E-mail: ole_terney@online.pol.dk. Ed. Ole Terney. bk.rev.; index, cum index: 1981-1993. circ. 1,000. (back issues avail.) **Document type:** newsletter.
     Description: Contains popular reviews and news of international research in biology, medicine and environment with literature references and list of new books in Danish categorized according to subject.

570   II   ISSN 0970-0889
                               CODEN: BSRB
BIO-SCIENCE RESEARCH BULLETIN. 1985. 2/yr. Rs.300($50) Dr. A.K. Sharma, Ed. & Pub., 140 (RPS) D.D.A. Flats, Mansarovar Park, Shahdara, New Delhi 110 032, India. TEL 91-11-2117408. R&P contact: A.K. Sharma. adv. contact: A.K. Sharma. bk.rev. circ. 600. **Document type:** academic/scholarly publication, bulletin.
—CCC.

572.8   NE   ISSN 0921-0687
                               CODEN: BMOLEY
BIOACTIVE MOLECULES. (Text in English) 1986. irreg., vol.12, 1990. price varies. Elsevier Science B.V., Books Division, P.O. Box 211, 1000 AE Amsterdam, Netherlands. TEL 31-20-4853911. FAX 31-20-4853705. TELEX 18582 ESPA NL. E-mail: nlinfo-f@elsevier.nl; usinfo-f@elsevier.com; forinfo-kyf04035@niftyserve.or.jp; URL: http://www.elsevier.nl/. (Subscr. in the Americas to: Elsevier Science, Regional Sales Office, Box 945, New York, NY 10159-0945; Subscr. in Australasia and the Far East to: Elsevier Science (Singapore) Pte Ltd, No.1 Temasek Ave., No.17-01 Millenia Tower, Singapore 039192, Singapore; Subscr. in Japan to: Elsevier Science Japan, 9-15 Higashi-Azabu 1-chome, Minato-ku, Tokyo 106, Japan. TEL 212-989-5800) (back issues avail.) **Document type:** monographic series.
—CASDDS; CISTI. **CCC.**
     Refereed Serial

570 630   UK   ISSN 0143-1404
BIOCONTROL NEWS AND INFORMATION. 1980. q. £160($180) (effective 1997). CAB International, Wallingford, Oxon. OX10 8DE, England. TEL 44-1491-832111. FAX 44-1491-826090. TELEX 847964 COMAGG G. E-mail: cabi@cabi.org; URL: http://www.cabi.org. (U.S. subscr. to: CAB International, North American Office, 198 Madison Ave., New York, NY 10016. TEL 212-726-6490. FAX 212-686-7993) (reprint service avail.) **Indexed:** Weed Abstr. **Document type:** abstracting/indexing.
●Also available online. Vendor(s): DIMDI, European Space Agency, Knight-Ridder Information, Inc., STN International.
—BLDSC (2071.100000).

570   JA   ISSN 1342-4815
                               CODEN: BISCFY
▼**BIOCONTROL SCIENCE.** (Text in English) 1996. a. 6500 Yen (effective 1998). Nihon Bokin Bobai Gakkai - Society for Antibacterial and Antifungal Agents, 3rd Fl., Shin-Kousan Bldg., 13-38, Nishimotocho 1-chome, Nishi-ku, Osaka 550, Japan. Ed. Tetsuaki Tsuchido. R&P contact: Iwao Yamamoto.
—CASDDS.

570   SP
BIODATOS BASICOS. (Supplement to: Universidad de Oviedo. Revista de Biologia) 1989. irreg., vol.5, 1992. price varies. Universidad de Oviedo, Facultad de Biologia, Jesus Arias de Velasco, s-n, 33005 Oviedo, Spain. Ed. Julian Rubio Cardiel.

BIODEGRADATION. see ENVIRONMENTAL STUDIES — Waste Management

BIODIVERSITY AND CONSERVATION. see CONSERVATION

577   UK   ISSN 0967-9952
QH75.A1   CODEN: BDLTEE
BIODIVERSITY LETTERS. 1993. bi-m. Blackwell Science Ltd., Osney Mead, Oxford OX2 0EL, England. TEL 44-1865-206206. FAX 44-1865-721205. E-mail: journals.cs@blacksci.co.uk; URL: http://www.black.co.uk. Ed. R. Hengeveld; Pub. Allen Stevens. R&P contact: Sarah Pollard. adv. contact: Martine Cariou-Keen. **Indexed:** Ecol.Abstr., Environ.Per.Bibl., IDA. **Document type:** academic/scholarly publication.
—BLDSC (2071.800000); CISTI; Linda Hall; SWETS; UnCover.

570   UK   ISSN 0265-9247
                               CODEN: BIOEEJ
BIOESSAYS. 1984. m. £73($120) to individuals; institutions £235($395) (effective 1997). Company of Biologists Ltd., Bidder Bldg., 140 Cowley Rd., Cambridge CB4 4DL, England. TEL 44-1223-426164. FAX 44-1223-423353. E-mail: cob@cambridge.cityscape.co.uk; URL: http://www.cityscape.co.uk/users/ag64. Ed. Adam S. Wilkins. adv. contact: Richard Skaer. **Indexed:** ASCA, Curr.Adv.Biochem., Curr.Adv.Cancer Res., Curr.Adv.Cell & Devel.Biol., Curr.Adv.Ecol.Sci., Curr.Adv.Genetics & Molec.Biol., Curr.Biotech.Abstr., Curr.Cont., Ind.Sci.Rev., Maize Abstr., Neurosci.Cit.Ind., Potato Abstr., Protozool.Abstr., Sci.Cit.Ind., Soyabean Abstr., Sport Fish.Abstr., Telegen, Triticale Abstr., Wild.Rev., Zoo.Rec. **Document type:** academic/scholarly publication.
—BLDSC (2072.118000); CASDDS; CISTI; EMDOCS; Linda Hall; SWETS; UMI; UnCover.
     Description: Current-awareness journal reviewing advances in molecular, cellular and developmental biology.

171.7   US   ISSN 1063-3596
BIOETHICS BULLETIN.* 1992. 2/yr. free. American Bar Association, Coordinating Group on Bioethics and the Law, 740 15th St., N.W., Washington, DC 20005-1009. TEL 202-331-2278. FAX 202-331-2220. Ed. Richard Mondelbaum. **Document type:** newsletter.

174.957   IT   ISSN 1122-2344
BIOETICA. 1993. s-a. L.48000 (foreign L.68000) (effective 1993). (Consulta di Bioetica) Franco Angeli Editore, Viale Monza 106, 20127 Milan, Italy. TEL 02-28-27-651.

570   US   ISSN 1060-2488
BIOFEEDBACK (CINCINNATI). q. $105 with S.L.A. membership (students & retired members $25). Special Libraries Association, Biological Sciences Division, c/o John Tebo, Ed., Chemistry-Biology Laboratory, University of Cincinnati, 503 Rieveschel Hall, Mail Location 0151, Cincinnati, OH 45221-0151. TEL 513-556-1494. FAX 513-556-1103. E-mail: tebo@ucbeh.san.uc.edu. (Subscr. to: 1700 18th St., N.W., Washington, DC 20009-2508) R&P contact: Adam Schiff. adv. contact: Lawrence Kelland. bk.rev.; bibl.; circ. 600 (paid). **Document type:** newsletter.
     Description: Contains Division news, announcements, and information of interest to biological science librarians.

572.8   GW   ISSN 0940-0079
                               CODEN: BFRME3
BIOFORUM. 1978. 10/yr. DM.160 (effective 1996). G I T Verlag GmbH, Roesslerstr. 90, 64293 Darmstadt, Germany. TEL 49-6151-8090-0. FAX 49-6151-8090133. E-mail: gitverlag@t-online.de; URL: http://www.gitverlag.com. Ed. J.P. Matthes. adv.: B&W page DM.5820, color page DM.8730; trim 185 x 260; adv. contact: Anna Seidinger. circ. 10,000. **Indexed:** VITIS. **Document type:** trade publication.
—CASDDS.
     Formerly: Forum Mikrobiologie.

572.8   GW
▼**BIOFORUM INTERNATIONAL**; bioresearch plus biotechnology. (Text in English) 1997. s-a. G I T Verlag GmbH, Roesslerstr. 90, 64293 Darmstadt, Germany. TEL 49-6151-8090-0. FAX 49-6151-8090133. E-mail: gitverlaggmbh@gitverlag.com; URL: http://www.gitverlag.com. Ed. Joerg-Peter Matthes. adv.: B&W page DM.7845, color page DM.10755; trim 185 x 260; adv. contact: Anna Seidinger. circ. 20,000 (paid). **Document type:** trade publication.

570   FR   ISSN 1165-6638
BIOGEOGRAPHICA. (Text in English, French, Spanish) 1924. q. 330 F. to non-members (foreign 375 F.); members 260 F. (foreign 290 F.) (effective 1997). Societe de Biogeographie, 57 rue Cuvier, 75231 Paris, France. Ed. W.R. Lourenco. bk.rev.; charts; illus. circ. 550. **Indexed:** Biol.Abstr., Bull.Signal., Deep Sea Res.& Oceanogr.Abstr., Ind.Med. **Document type:** bulletin.
—BLDSC (2072.169000).
     Former titles (until 1992): Societe de Biogeographe. Compte Rendu des Seances (ISSN 0037-9018); (until 1969): Societe de Biogeographie. Compte-Rendu Sommaire des Seances (ISSN 1153-320X)

570.9   JA   ISSN 0067-8716
BIOGEOGRAPHICAL SOCIETY OF JAPAN. BULLETIN/NIHON SEIBUTSU CHIRI GAKKAI KAIHO. (Text in English, Japanese; summaries in English) 1928. a. 6000 Yen($47) Biogeographical Society of Japan - Nippon Seibutsu Chiri Gakkai, No. 2-26-12 Sendagi, Bunkyo-ku, Tokyo 113, Japan. TEL 81-3-3828-0445. Ed. Seiroku Sakai. index. **Indexed:** Apic.Abstr., Biol.Abstr. **Document type:** bulletin.
—CCC.

BIOIMAGING. see PHYSICS

570   SW   ISSN 0345-1127
BIOLOGEN. 1933. q. SEK 100 (effective through 1998). Biologilaerarnas Foerening, c/o L. Vide, Blekingev. 22, S-186 45 Vallentuna, Sweden. Ed. Lars Ljunggren; Vega Otterland. adv. contact: Magnus von Krusenstierna. **Document type:** academic/scholarly publication.
     Formerly (until 1965): Medlemsblad foer Biologilaerarnas Foerening.

570   IT   ISSN 0392-2510
BIOLOGI ITALIANI. 1971. m. L.30000($14.98) to non-members. Ordine Nazionale dei Biologi, Via Icilio 7, 00153 Rome, Italy. TEL 39-6-571061. FAX 39-6-57106235. Ed. Ernesto Landi. adv.: B&W page L.1850000, color page L.2400000. bk.rev. circ. 35,000. **Document type:** academic/scholarly publication.
—BLDSC (2072.680000).
     Description: Covers clinical biology, environment, biotechnology, didactic of biology.

570   PK   ISSN 0006-3096
QH301   CODEN: BILGA6
BIOLOGIA. (Supplement avail.) (Text in English, French, German) 1955. s-a. Rs.400($50) or exchange basis. Biological Society of Pakistan, Biological Laboratories, Government College, Lahore, Pakistan. Ed. Dr. M.S. Mahoon. bk.rev.; bibl.; charts; illus.; index. circ. 200. **Indexed:** Biol.Abstr., Chem.Abstr., Curr.Adv.Ecol.Sci., Deep Sea Res.& Oceanogr.Abstr., Field Crop Abstr., Herb.Abstr., Hort.Abstr., Rev.Plant Path., Sci.Cit.Ind., Soils & Fert. **Document type:** academic/scholarly publication.
—BLDSC (2072.750000); CASDDS; KNAW; Linda Hall. **CCC.**

590 BIOLOGY

570   MX   ISSN 0185-2000
BIOLOGIA. 1970. q. price varies. Consejo Nacional para la Ensenanza de la Biologia, Calejon de Pino 18, C.P. 01070, Chimalistac San Angel, Mexico 20 D.F., Mexico. Ed. Lopez de la Rosa. adv.; bk.rev.; charts; bibl.; illus.; cum.index: 1970-1975. circ. 1,500.

578.7   AG   ISSN 0326-1638
CODEN: BIACEB
BIOLOGIA ACUATICA. (Text in English or Spanish, summaries in English and Spanish) 1981. irreg. (1-2/yr.) $10 (foreign $15). Instituto de Limnologia, Casilla de Correo 712, 1900 La Plata, Argentina. TEL 54-1-2375864. FAX 54-1-2377799. E-mail: postmaster@ilpla.edu.ar. Ed. Hugo L. Lopez. **Indexed:** Sport Fish.Abstr., Wild.Rev., Zoo.Rec.
—BLDSC (2072.780000).
   Description: Includes papers and research on freshwater biology.
   Refereed Serial

570   IT
BIOLOGIA E ETOLOGIA. 1986. irreg., no.5, 1992. price varies. Liguori Editore s.r.l., Via Posillipo 394, 80123 Naples, Italy. TEL 39-81-7206111. FAX 39-81-7206244. Ed. Bruno D'Udine; Pub. Guido Liguori. adv. contact: Maria Liguori. **Document type:** monographic series.

570   GR   ISSN 0750-7321
QH151   CODEN: BGAHA8
BIOLOGIA GALLO-HELLENICA. 1967. irreg., 1-2/yr. 200 F. per no. to individuals; institutions 250 F. Greek-French Society of Biological Sciences, University of Athens, Section of Ecology, Dept. of Biology, Panepistimioupolis, 157 71 Athens, Greece. (Co-sponsor: Hellenic Zoological Society) Ed.Bd. circ. 500. **Indexed:** Biol.Abstr., Bull.Signal., Ref.Zh., Zoo.Rec. **Document type:** academic/scholarly publication.
—BLDSC (2072.815000).
   Supersedes: Acta Biologica Hellenica (ISSN 0065-1095)

570   IT   ISSN 0394-9060
BIOLOGIA OGGI. (Text in English, French, Italian) 1972. q. Lit.50000 membership in Italy; elsewhere $110 journal only (effective 1997). Associazione Nazionale Laureati in Scienze Biologiche, Via Guglielmo degli Ubertini, 64, 00176 Rome, Italy. TEL 39-6-21707494. bk.rev.; circ. 1,000 (controlled). **Indexed:** Biol.Abstr. **Document type:** academic/scholarly publication.
—BLDSC (2072.825000); CISTI; Linda Hall.
   Former titles (until 1987): Biologia Contemporanea (ISSN 0392-1298); (until 1974): Minerva Biologica (ISSN 0374-8952)
   Refereed Serial

570   PL   ISSN 0137-8031
BIOLOGIA W SZKOLE. 1948. 5/yr. $10. (Ministerstwo Edukacji Narodowej) Wydawnictwa Szkolne i Pedagogiczne, Ul. Dabrowskiego 8, 00-950 Warsaw, Poland. TEL 48-22-265451. FAX 48-22-268971. (Dist. by: Ars Polona, Krakowskie Przedmiescie 7, 00-068 Warsaw, Poland) Ed. Danuta Cichy. circ. 8,000. **Indexed:** AgroLibrex.
   Description: For biology teachers at all levels and for students in teacher training colleges and universities. Discusses developments in the biological sciences and recent achievements in the methodology of teaching biology, with articles to improve teachers' knowledge, and comments on teaching syllabi and school textbooks.

BIOLOGICAL ABSTRACTS; references, abstracts, and indexes to the world's life sciences research literature. see BIOLOGY — *Abstracting, Bibliographies, Statistics*

BIOLOGICAL ABSTRACTS - R R M CUMULATIVE INDEX. see BIOLOGY — *Abstracting, Bibliographies, Statistics*

570   CC   ISSN 0006-3193
QH301   CODEN: SWHTA4
BIOLOGICAL BULLETIN/SHENGWUXUE TONGBAO. Variant English title: Bulletin of Biology. Variant spelling: Sheng Wu Hsueh T'ung Pao. (Text in Chinese and English) bi-m. (Chinese Society of Zoology) Science Press, Marketing and Sales Department, 16 Donghuangchenggen North St., Beijing 100717, People's Republic of China. TEL 4010642. FAX 4012180. TELEX 210247-SPBJ-CN. (US office: Science Press New York, Ltd., 63-117 Alderton St., Rego Park, NY 11374. TEL 718-459-4638) (Co-sponsor: Chinese Botanical Society) charts; illus.
—CASDDS; Linda Hall.
   Refereed Serial

570   US   ISSN 0006-3185
QH301   CODEN: BIBUBX
BIOLOGICAL BULLETIN. 1897. bi-m. (2 vols./yr.) $100 to individuals; institutions @195 (effective 1997). Marine Biological Laboratory, Woods Hole, MA 02543. TEL 508-289-7428. FAX 508-457-1924. E-mail: vgibson@MBL.EDU; URL: http://www.mbl.edu:80/html/bb/bb.home.html. Ed. Michael J. Greenberg. R&P contact: Pamela Clapp. adv. contact: Suean Pennington. s-a. index, cum.index (approx. every 10 yrs.). circ. 2,100. (also avail. in microfilm from UMI,PMC; back issues avail.) **Indexed:** Anim.Breed.Abstr., Biol.Abstr., Biol.& Agr.Ind., Chem.Abstr., Curr.Adv.Ecol.Sci., Curr.Cont., Deep Sea Res.& Oceanogr.Abstr., Ecol.Abstr., Gen.Sci.Ind., Geo.Abstr., GeoRef., Helminthol.Abstr., Ind.Med. (1994-), Ind.Sci.Rev., Int.Aerosp.Abstr., Neurosci.Cit.Ind., Nutr.Abstr., Ocean.Abstr., Pollut.Abstr., Psychol.Abstr., Rev.Appl.Entomol., Sci.Cit.Ind., Sel.Water Res.Abstr., Sport Fish.Abstr., Wild.Rev., Zoo.Rec. **Document type:** academic/scholarly publication.
●Also available online. Vendor(s): Information Access Co., UMI.
—BLDSC (2075.000000); CASDDS; CISTI; Genuine Article; KR SourceOne; Linda Hall; SWETS; UMI; UnCover.
   Description: Original research reports of general interest to biologists worldwide.
   Refereed Serial

570   PL
QH301   CODEN: BSPDAJ
BIOLOGICAL BULLETIN OF POZNAN. (Text in English, French and German) 1960. a. price varies. Poznanskie Towarzystwo Przyjaciol Nauk, Ul. Mielzynskiego 27-29, 61-725 Poznan, Poland. (Dist. by: Ars Polona-Ruch, Krakowskie Przedmiescie 7, Warsaw, Poland) Ed. Jozef Bielawski. bibl.; charts; illus. **Indexed:** Biol.Abstr., Chem.Abstr., GeoRef. **Document type:** bulletin.
—CASDDS; CISTI.
   Formerly: Societe des Amis des Sciences et des Lettres de Panan. Bulletin. Serie D: Sciences Biologiques (ISSN 0079-4570)

BIOLOGICAL CONSERVATION. see CONSERVATION

570   US   ISSN 1049-9644
SB925   CODEN: BCIOEB
BIOLOGICAL CONTROL; theory and application in pest management. 1991. 9/yr. $265 (foreign $295) (effective 1997). Academic Press, Inc., Journal Division, 525 B Ste., Ste. 1900, San Diego, CA 92101-4495. TEL 619-230-1840. FAX 619-699-6800. E-mail: apsubs@acad.com; URL: http://www.apnet.com/journal/bc.htm; http://www.idealibrary.com/. (Subscr. to: Box 861213, Orlando, FL 32886-1213. TEL 407-374-4040. FAX 407-363-9661) Ed.Bd. **Indexed:** ASCA, Bibl.Agri., Curr.Cont., Ind.Sci.Rev., Sci.Cit.Ind. **Document type:** academic/scholarly publication.
●Also available online.
—BLDSC (2075.130000); EMDOCS; Genuine Article; SWETS; UnCover. CCC.
   Description: Promotes the science and technology of biological control and includes articles on entomology, plant pathology, nematology, and weed science.

BIOLOGICAL PSYCHIATRY; a journal of psychiatric research. see MEDICAL SCIENCES — *Psychiatry And Neurology*

BIOLOGICAL PSYCHOLOGY. see PSYCHOLOGY

570   619   CL   ISSN 0716-9760
QH301   CODEN: ABMXA2
BIOLOGICAL RESEARCH. (Text in English) 1964. q. $100 (effective 1997). Sociedad de Biologia de Chile, Casilla 16164, Santiago 9, Chile. TEL 56-2-6862850. FAX 56-2-2225515. E-mail: pzapata@genes.bio.puc.cl. Ed. Patricio Zapata. adv.; bk.rev. circ. 1,250. (also avail. in microfiche from UMI) **Indexed:** Biol.Abstr., Chem.Abstr., Curr.Adv.Ecol.Sci., Curr.Cont., Excerp.Med., Helminthol.Abstr., Ind.Med., Ind.Sci.Rev., Sci.Cit.Ind. **Document type:** academic/scholarly publication.
—BLDSC (2077.675000); CASDDS; EMDOCS; KNAW; Linda Hall; UMI.
   Formerly (until 1992): Archivos de Biologia y Medicina Experimentales (ISSN 0004-0533)
   Description: Publishes original works in the different fields of the biological sciences.
   Refereed Serial

570   FI   ISSN 0356-1062
QH301
BIOLOGICAL RESEARCH REPORTS FROM THE UNIVERSITY OF JYVASKYLA. 1975. irreg. exchange basis. Jyvaskylan Yliopisto - University of Jyvaskyla, Publications Center, PL 35, 40100 Jyvaskyla 10, Finland. TEL 941-601-211. FAX 603-371. TELEX 28219 JYK SF. Eds. Jukka Saerkkae, Markku Kuitunen. circ. 450. **Document type:** monographic series.

570   NE   ISSN 0929-1016
QH527   CODEN: BRHREI
BIOLOGICAL RHYTHM RESEARCH. (Text in English) 1970. q. fl.615($373) (effective 1997). (European Society for Chronobiology) Swets & Zeitlinger bv, P.O. Box 825, 2160 SZ Lisse, Netherlands. TEL 31-252-435111. FAX 31-252-415888. TELEX 41325. E-mail: orders@swets.nl; URL: http://www.swets.nl. (Dist. in N. America by: Swets & Zeitlinger, Box 613, Royersford, PA 19468. TEL 800-447-9387. FAX 610-524-5366) Ed. W.J. Rietveld. R&P contact: J.v.d. Valk. adv. contact: Patrick Kleian. bk.rev.; charts; illus. circ. 600. (also avail. in microform from SWZ; reprint service avail. from SWZ) **Indexed:** ASCA, Biol.Abstr., Chem.Abstr., Curr.Adv.Ecol.Sci., Curr.Cont., Dairy Sci.Abstr., Ecol.Abstr., Excerp.Med., GeoRef., Helminthol.Abstr., Ind.Sci.Rev., Ind.Vet., Neurosci.Cit.Ind., Sci.Cit.Ind., Small Anim.Abstr., Sport Fish.Abstr., SSCI, Vet.Bull., Wild.Rev., Zoo.Rec. **Document type:** academic/scholarly publication.
●Also available online.
—BLDSC (2079.590000); CASDDS; CISTI; EMDOCS; Genuine Article; KNAW; Linda Hall; SWETS; UnCover. CCC.
   Formerly: Journal of Interdisciplinary Cycle Research (ISSN 0022-1945)
   Description: Publishes original scientific research results and reviews of biological rhythm research.

570   UK   ISSN 0142-8004
BIOLOGICAL RHYTHMS. 1970. s-m. (diskette m.). £110 (diskette £120; both £180) (effective 1997). S U B I S, Mansion House, 19 Kingfield Rd., Sheffield S11 9AS, England. TEL 44-114-2554433. FAX 44-114-2554626. E-mail: subis@sheffac.demon.co.uk; URL: http://www.shef.ac.uk/uni/companies/shap. (also avail. in diskette format) **Document type:** abstracting/indexing.
—CCC.
   Formerly: Circadian Rhythms.
   Description: Current awareness service for researchers in clinical and life sciences.

570   JA   ISSN 0045-2033
CODEN: SBTKAQ
BIOLOGICAL SCIENCE/SEIBUTSU KAGAKU. (Text in Japanese) 1949. q. 950 Yen per no. (Japanese Society of Biological Scientists - Nihon Seibutsu Kagakusha Kyokai) Iwanami Shoten Publishers, 2-5-5 Hitotsubashi, Chiyoda-ku, Tokyo 101-02, Japan. FAX 03-239-9618. (Dist. overseas by: Japan Publications Trading Co., Ltd., Box 5030, Tokyo International, Tokyo 100-31, Japan; Or: 1255 Howard St., San Francisco, CA 94103) Ed. K. Nagano. **Indexed:** Chem.Abstr., INIS Atomind., Jap.Per.Ind.
—Linda Hall.

570   US   ISSN 1081-292X
                CODEN: USFODA
▼BIOLOGICAL SCIENCE REPORT. (Subseries of:
Technical Report Series) 1995. irreg. U.S. National
Biological Service, Information Transfer Center,
1201 Oak Ridge Dr., Ste. 200, Ft. Collins, CO
80525-5589. TEL 970-226-9401.
FAX 970-226-9455. (Orders to: U.S. Fish and
Wildlife Service, Publications Unit, Mail Stop 130,
Webb Bldg., 4401 N. Fairfax Dr., Arlington, VA
22203) (also avail. in microform from NTI) **Indexed:**
Ecol.Abstr., Geo.Abstr.H.G., Geo.Abstr.P.G., Zoo.Rec.
Document type: government publication, monographic
series, academic/scholarly publication.
●Also available online.
—CASDDS; CISTI.
   Supersedes: U.S. Fish and Wildlife Service.
Biological Report (ISSN 0895-1926); Which was
formerly (1976-1984): F W S - O B S (ISSN
0197-6087)
   Description: Publishes original scientific research,
reviews, inventories and reports.
   Refereed Serial

570   UK   ISSN 0953-5365
BIOLOGICAL SCIENCES REVIEW. 5/yr. (Sep.-May).
£20.95 (Europe £29.50; rest of world £34.50)
(effective 1997 & 1998). (University of Manchester,
School of Biology) Philip Allan Publishers Ltd.,
Market Pl., Deddington, Oxon. OX15 0SE, England.
TEL 44-1869-338652. FAX 44-1869-338803. Ed.
Liz Sheffield. R&P contact: Ceri Jenkins. adv.
contact: Ceri Jenkins. illus. circ. 23,000. (back
issues avail.) **Document type:** academic/scholarly
publication.
—BLDSC (2080.455000).
   Refereed Serial

570   US   ISSN 0006-324X
QH1   CODEN: PBSWAO
BIOLOGICAL SOCIETY OF WASHINGTON. PROCEEDINGS.
1880. q. $25 to individuals ; institutions $40
(effective 1997). Biological Society of Washington,
National Museum of Natural History, Smithsonian
Institution, Washington, DC 20560.
TEL 202-786-2550. (Subscr. to: Allen Press, Inc.,
Box 1897, Lawrence, KS 66044. TEL
913-843-1234) Ed. Brian Robbins. charts; illus.;
index, cum.index: 1881-1922, 1923-1961. circ.
900. (back issues avail.) **Indexed:** Aqua.Sci.&
Fish.Abstr., Art & Archaeol.Tech.Abstr., ASCA,
Biol.Abstr., Curr.Adv.Ecol.Sci., Curr.Cont., Deep Sea
Res.& Oceanogr.Abstr., Ecol.Abstr., Geol.Abstr.,
GeoRef., Ind.Sci.Rev., So.Pac.Per.Ind., Sport
Fish.Abstr., Wild.Rev., Zoo.Rec. **Document type:**
academic/scholarly publication.
—BLDSC (6661.000000); CISTI; Genuine Article;
Linda Hall; UnCover.
   Description: Journal of international scope for
publication of papers bearing on systematics in the
biological sciences (both botany and zoology,
including paleontology).
   Refereed Serial

570   UK   ISSN 1045-1056
RA401.A1   CODEN: BILSEC
BIOLOGICALS. 1973. q. £171 (effective 1998).
(International Association of Biological
Standardization) Academic Press Ltd. (Subsidiary of:
Harcourt Brace & Company Ltd.), 24-28 Oval Rd.,
London NW1 7DX, England. TEL 44-171-267-4466.
FAX 44-171-482-2293. TELEX 25775 ACPRES G.
E-mail: apsubs@acad.com; URL: http://www.hbuk.
co.uk/ap/biologicals; http://www.europe.idealibrary.
com/. (Subscr. to: Harcourt Brace & Company Ltd.,
Foots Cray High St., Sidcup, Kent DA14 5HP,
England. TEL 44-171-300-3322. FAX
44-181-309-0807) Eds. F. Horaud, Elwyn Griffiths.
R&P contact: Catherine John. adv. contact: Nik
Screen. (reprint service avail. from SWZ) **Indexed:**
Abstr.Hyg., ASCA, Biol.Abstr., Biotech.Abstr.,
Chem.Abstr., Curr.Cont., Diar.Dis.Res.,
Dok.Arbeitsmed., Excerp.Med., Ind.Sci.Rev., Ind.Vet.,
INIS Atomind., Rev.Med.& Vet.Mycol., Sci.Cit.Ind.,
Trop.Dis.Bull., Vet.Bull. **Document type:**
academic/scholarly publication.
●Also available online.
—BLDSC (2081.670000); CASDDS; CISTI;
EMDOCS; Genuine Article; KNAW; Linda Hall; SWETS.
CCC.
   Formerly: Journal of Biological Standardization
(ISSN 0092-1157)
   Description: Devoted to the timely publication of
broad ranging reports relevant to the development,
preparation, and quality control of biologicals used in
human and veterinary medicine.

570   KZ   ISSN 0136-2100
BIOLOGICHESKIE NAUKI.* 1971. irreg. 1.20 Rub.
Kazakhskii Gosudarstvennyi Universitet, Ul. Lenina
18, Alma-Ata, Kazakhstan. bk.rev.; bibl.; illus.
Indexed: Biol.Abstr., Chem.Abstr., Cott.&
Trop.Fibr.Abstr., Excerp.Med., Field Crop Abstr.,
Forest.Abstr., Forest Prod.Abstr., Helminthol.Abstr.,
Ind.Med., Ind.Vet., INIS Atomind., Plant
Grow.Reg.Abstr., Potato Abstr., Small Anim.Abstr.,
Sport Fish.Abstr., Weed Abstr., Wild.Rev.

570   XR   ISSN 0366-0486
QH301   CODEN: BILIAC
BIOLOGICKE LISTY/BIOLOGICAL REVIEW. (Text in Czech
or Slovak; summaries in English) 1912. q. DM.173.
(Ceska Akademie Ved, Ustav Molekularni Genetiky)
S K Press, v.o.s., Masarykovo nam. 35, 251 01
Ricany, Czech Republic. TEL 53-83-06. (Dist. in
Western countries by: Kubon & Sagner, P.O. Box 34
01 08, 8000 Munich, Germany) illus. **Indexed:**
Anim.Breed.Abstr., Biol.Abstr., Chem.Abstr.,
Curr.Tit.Ocean, Deep Sea Res.& Oceanogr.Abstr.,
INIS Atomind.
—BLDSC (2081.700000); CASDDS; CISTI.
   Description: Papers and reviews dealing with
general biology and all branches of modern
experimental biology; discussions on analogous
subjects; reports on Czechoslovak biology.

570   GW   ISSN 0406-3317
BIOLOGIE IN DER SCHULE. 1951. 6/yr. DM.82.60
(effective 1997); newsstand price: DM.13.90.
Paedagogischer Zeitschriftenverlag, Postfach 269,
10107 Berlin, Germany. TEL 49-30-20183592.
FAX 49-30-20183593. (Subscr. to: CVK Cornelsen
Verlagskontor, Postfach 100271, 33502 Bielefeld,
Germany) Ed. Bernd Golle. circ. 2,400. **Indexed:** IBR.
Document type: academic/scholarly publication.
—CISTI.

570   GW   ISSN 0045-205X
                CODEN: BLUZAR
BIOLOGIE IN UNSERER ZEIT. 1971. 6/yr. DM.110
(foreign DM.122) to individuals; institutions DM.160
(foreign DM.172); students DM.75 (foreign DM.87)
(effective 1997). Wiley - V C H, Postfach 101161,
69451 Weinheim, Germany.
TEL 49-6201-606-147. FAX 49-6201-606117.
TELEX 465516-VCHWH-D. E-mail: subservice@
vchgroup.de; URL: http://www.vchgroup.de. (Subscr.
in the Americas to: John Wiley & Sons, Inc., 605
Third Ave., New York, NY 10158. TEL
212-850-6645. FAX 212-850-6021) Ed. K. Kuehl.
adv. contact: R. Roth. bk.rev.; index. circ. 9,610.
(reprint service avail. from ISI) **Indexed:** Biol.Abstr.,
Chem.Abstr., Excerp.Med., INIS Atomind. **Document
type:** academic/scholarly publication.
—CASDDS; CISTI; Linda Hall; SWETS. CCC.
   Description: Presents current developments in all
areas of biology.

570   LI   ISSN 1392-0146
QH301   CODEN: BOLOE8
BIOLOGIJA. 1993. q. foreign $12 (effective 1998).
(Lietuvos Mokslu Akademija) Leidykla Academia, A.
Gostauto 12, 2600 Vilnius, Lithuania.
TEL 370-2-626851. (Co-sponsor: Lietuvos
Aukstosios Mokyklos) Ed. A. Merkys. R&P contact: A.
Garliauskas. adv. contact: A. Garliauskas. **Document
type:** academic/scholarly publication.
—BLDSC (2082.490000); CASDDS; CISTI; KNAW.
   Formed by the merger of (1961-1993): Lietuvos
T.S.R. Aukstuju Mokyklu Mokslu Darbai. Biologija
(ISSN 0459-3383); (1990-1993): Lietuvos Mokslu
Akademija. Eksperimentine Biologija (ISSN
0235-7232); Which superseded in part (in 1990):
Lietuvos T.S.R. Mokslu Akademijos Darbai. C Serija.
Biologijos Mosklai (ISSN 0131-3851)

570   GW   ISSN 0006-3282
BIOLOGISCHE ABHANDLUNGEN. (Text in German;
summaries in English, French, German, Russian)
1949. irreg. DM.5 per. no. Biologie-Verlag,
Schlossallee 10a, 65388 Schlangenbad, Germany.
Ed. Herbert Bruns. charts; illus.; index. **Indexed:**
Biol.Abstr. **Document type:** monograph series.

BIOLOGISCHE TIERMEDIZIN. see *VETERINARY SCIENCE*

570   GW   ISSN 0006-3304
                CODEN: BIZNAT
BIOLOGISCHES ZENTRALBLATT; an international journal
of cell biology, genetics, evolution and developmental
biology. (Text and summaries in English and
German) 1881. 4/yr. DM.286 (foreign DM.294)
(effective 1996). Gustav Fischer Verlag Jena,
Villengang 2, 07745 Jena, Germany.
TEL 49-3641-626444. FAX 49-3641-626500.
(Subscr. to: Postfach 100537, 07705 Jena,
Germany) Eds. H. Boehme, R. Rieger. adv.: page
DM.550; trim 170 x 240. bk.rev.; charts; illus. circ.
350. (also avail. in microform from UMI,PMC;
reprint service avail. from UMI) **Indexed:**
Anim.Breed.Abstr., ASCA, Biol.Abstr., Chem.Abstr.,
Curr.Adv.Ecol.Sci., Curr.Cont., Deep Sea Res.&
Oceanogr.Abstr., Ecol.Abstr., Excerp.Med., Fababean
Abstr., Field Crop Abstr., Helminthol.Abstr.,
Herb.Abstr., Hort.Abstr., Ind.Sci.Rev., INIS Atomind.,
Key Word Ind.Wildl.Res., Plant Breed.Abstr., Rev.Plant
Path., Sci.Cit.Ind., SSCI, Weed Abstr., Wild.Rev.,
Zoo.Rec. **Document type:** academic/scholarly
publication.
—BLDSC (2084.000000); CASDDS; CISTI;
EMDOCS; Genuine Article; Linda Hall; UMI; UnCover.
CCC.

570   UK   ISSN 0006-3347
QH1   CODEN: BLGTB8
BIOLOGIST. 1953. 5/yr. £27 in the U.K.; N. and S.
America $60; elsewhere £33 (effective 1997).
Institute of Biology, 20-22 Queensberry Pl., London
SW7 2DZ, England. TEL 44-171-581-8333.
FAX 44-171-823-9409. E-mail: info@job.primex.co.
uk; URL: http://www.primex.co.uk/iob. Ed. Dr. S.
Silver. adv.; bk.rev.; illus. circ. 15,500. **Indexed:**
Curr.Adv.Ecol.Sci., Dairy Sci.Abstr., Ecol.Abstr.,
Environ.Abstr., Field Crop Abstr., Food Sci.&
Tech.Abstr., Geo.Abstr.H.G., Helminthol.Abstr., IDA,
Ind.Vet., Nutr.Abstr., Plant Breed.Abstr., Seed Abstr.,
Sport Fish.Abstr., Vet.Bull., Weed Abstr., Wild.Rev.,
Zoo.Rec. **Document type:** academic/scholarly
publication.
—BLDSC (2086.200000); CASDDS; CISTI; Linda
Hall; UnCover. CCC.
   Description: Overview articles, news, reviews for
professional biologists in the areas of biomedical,
environmental, agricultural, and educational biology.

578.77 551.46   RU   ISSN 0134-3475
QH91.A1   CODEN: BIMOD4
BIOLOGIYA MORYA/MARINE BIOLOGY. English
translation: Russian Journal of Marine Biology (US
ISSN 1063-0740) (Text in Russian; summaries in
English) 1975. bi-m. $170 (effective 1998).
(Rossiiskaya Akademiya Nauk, Otdelenie Obshchei
Biologii) Izdatel'stvo Nauka, 90 Profsoyuznaya ul.,
117864 Moscow, Russia. (Co-sponsor: Rossiiskaya
Akademiya Nauk, Dal'nevostochnyi Nauchnyi Tsentr)
Ed. Dr. Vladimir L. Kasyanov. illus. circ. 1,200.
Indexed: Anim.Breed.Abstr., Biol.Abstr., Chem.Abstr.,
Curr.Cont., Deep Sea Res.& Oceanogr.Abstr.,
Ecol.Abstr., Geo.Abstr., Helminthol.Abstr.,
Ind.Sci.Rev., Ref.Zh., Sci.Cit.Ind., Sel.Water Res.Abstr.,
Sport Fish.Abstr., Wild.Rev., Zoo.Rec. **Document type:**
academic/scholarly publication.
—BLDSC (0017.945000); CASDDS; CISTI; Genuine
Article; KNAW. CCC.
   Description: Publishes papers on marine
organisms and their activities, various biological
studies conducted on marine objects; practical
problems of preservation, rational utilization of
biological resources of the sea and limitation of
activity of some harmful sea organisms.

570   IT   ISSN 0392-7393
IL BIOLOGO. (Text in English, French, Italian) 1961.
bi-m. Lit.50000 membership in Italy (effective
1997). Associazione Nazionale Laureati in Scienze
Biologiche, Via Guglielmo degli Ubertini 64, 00176
Rome, Italy. TEL 39-6-21707494. circ. 1,000
(controlled). **Document type:** bulletin.

BIOLOGY

570   IE   ISSN 0791-7945
QH301   CODEN: BENVE3
BIOLOGY AND ENVIRONMENT; proceedings of the Royal Irish Academy. 1836. 3/yr. I£25 to individuals; institutions I£90 (effective 1997). Royal Irish Academy, 19 Dawson St., Dublin 2, Ireland. TEL 353-1-6762570. FAX 353-1-6762346. Eds. Martin Steer, Paul Giller. charts; illus.; index, cum.index. circ. 600. (also avail. in microform from PMC) **Indexed:** Aqua.Sci.& Fish.Abstr., ASCA, Biol.Abstr., Br.Geol.Lit., Chem.Abstr., Curr.Adv.Ecol.Sci., Curr.Cont., Deep Sea Res.& Oceanogr.Abstr., Excerp.Med., Geo.Abstr., GeoRef., Ind.Med., Ind.Vet., INSPEC, Phys.Ber., RILA, Sci.Cit.Ind., Vet.Bull. **Document type:** academic/scholarly publication, proceedings.
—BLDSC (2086.996500); CASDDS; CISTI; KNAW; Linda Hall.
Formerly (until 1993): Royal Irish Academy. Proceedings. Section B: Biological, Geological and Chemical Sciences (ISSN 0035-8983)

BIOLOGY AND FERTILITY OF SOILS. see *AGRICULTURE — Crop Production And Soil*

570   NE   ISSN 0169-3867
QH331   CODEN: BIOPEI
BIOLOGY AND PHILOSOPHY. (Text in English) 1986. q. fl.485 to institutions; $249 to institutions in U.S. (effective 1998). Kluwer Academic Publishers, Postbus 17, 3300 AA Dordrecht, Netherlands. TEL 31-78-6392392. FAX 31-78-6392254. TELEX 29245 KAPG NL. E-mail: services@wkap.nl; URL: http://www.wkap.nl. (Dist. by: Kluwer Academic Publishers Group, P.O. Box 322, 3300 AH Dordrecht, Netherlands. TEL 31-78-6392392. FAX 31-78-6546474; N. America dist. addr.: Box 358, Accord Sta., Hingham, MA 02018-0358. TEL 617-871-6600. FAX 617-871-6528) Ed. Michael Ruse. adv.; bk.rev.; illus.; index. circ. 500. (also avail. in microform from UMI; back issues avail.; reprint service avail. from SWZ) **Indexed:** Arts & Hum.Cit.Ind., ASCA, Biol.Abstr., Bull.Signal., Curr.Adv.Ecol.Sci., Curr.Cont., Ecol.Abstr., Geo.Abstr., Ind.Med., Phil.Ind., Ref.Zh., Sport Fish.Abstr., SSCI, Wild.Rev., Zoo.Rec. **Document type:** academic/scholarly publication.
—BLDSC (2087.002000); CISTI; Genuine Article; Linda Hall; SWETS; UMI; UnCover. **CCC.**
Description: Publishes discussions of the philosophical implications of biological research, as well as the social implications of recent advances and developments in the biological sciences.
Refereed Serial

578.074   UK   ISSN 1355-8331
THE BIOLOGY CURATOR. m. membership. Biology Curators Group, c/o Ms. K. Way, Natural History Museum, Zoology Department, Cromwell Rd., London SW7 5BD, England. TEL 0171-938-8892. (Editorial addr.: c/o Biology Curator, Natural History Section, Bolton Museum & Art Gallery, Le Mans Crescent, Bolton BL1 1SE, England) Eds. K. Berry, P. Francis. **Document type:** academic/scholarly publication.
—BLDSC (2087.052000).
Formed by the merger of (1989-1994): Journal of Biological Curation (ISSN 0958-7608); (1975-1994): B C G Newsletter (ISSN 0144-588X)
Description: Provides a forum for persons concerned with the collection of biological specimens and records, along with their interpretation and conservation.

570.7   II   ISSN 0970-5961
BIOLOGY EDUCATION. (Text in English) 1984. q. Rs.120($40) (University Grants Commission) New Age International Pvt. Ltd., Journals Division, 4835-24 Ansari Rd., Daryaganj, New Delhi 110 002, India. TEL 91-11-3261487. FAX 91-11-3267437. TELEX 031-66507-WELIN. circ. 1,000. **Document type:** academic/scholarly publication.
—BLDSC (2087.064000).

BIOLOGY FOR THE FUTURE (YEAR); higher education courses in biology and related sciences. see *EDUCATION — Guides To Schools And Colleges*

570   FR   ISSN 0253-2069
QH301   CODEN: BYILDJ
BIOLOGY INTERNATIONAL: I U B S NEWSMAGAZINE. s-a. $40. International Union of Biological Sciences, 51 bd de Montmorency, 75016 Paris, France. TEL 45-25-00-09. **Indexed:** Biol.Abstr. **Document type:** newsletter, academic/scholarly publication.
—CASDDS; CISTI.
Former titles: I U B S Newsmagazine; I U B S Newsletter.

573.6   US   ISSN 0523-6754
CODEN: BIRSB5
BIOLOGY OF REPRODUCTION. SUPPLEMENT. 1969. a. $15. Society for the Study of Reproduction, 1603 Monrow St., Madison, WI 53711-2021. TEL 608-256-2777. FAX 608-256-4610. URL: http://www.ssr.org/bor. (back issues avail.) **Indexed:** Biol.Abstr. **Document type:** academic/scholarly publication.
—KNAW; SWETS.

573.6   US
▼**BIOLOGY OF REPRODUCTION MONOGRAPH SERIES.** (Has subseries: Equine Reproduction (No.6-)) 1995. irreg. price varies. Society for the Study of Reproduction, 1603 Monroe St., Madison, WI 53711-2021. TEL 608-256-2777. FAX 608-256-4610. **Document type:** monographic series.
Description: Covers various aspects of the biology of reproduction.

BIOLOGY OF THE NEONATE; foetal and neonatal research. see *MEDICAL SCIENCES — Obstetrics And Gynecology*

BIOMARKERS. see *MEDICAL SCIENCES*

570   US   ISSN 0067-8821
CODEN: BMATBJ
BIOMATHEMATICS. (Text in English) 1970. irreg. price varies. Springer-Verlag, 175 Fifth Ave., New York, NY 10010. TEL 212-460-1500. FAX 212-473-6272. (Also: Berlin, Heidelberg, Tokyo and Vienna) (reprint service avail. from ISI) **Indexed:** Math.R., Sci.Cit.Ind, Zent.Math. **Document type:** academic/scholarly publication.
—BLDSC (2087.730000); CISTI.

570   UK   ISSN 0961-088X
QR1   CODEN: BILEE4
BIOMEDICAL LETTERS; a prestige international biomedical journal for the rapid publication of biomedical communications. 1976. £150. Faculty Press, 88 Regent St., Cambridge CB2 1DP, England. Ed.Bd. adv.; bk.rev.; abstr.; bibl.; charts; illus.; index. **Indexed:** ASCA, Biol.Dig., Chem.Abstr., Curr.Adv.Ecol.Sci., Curr.Biotech.Abstr., Curr.Cont., Excerp.Med., Ind.Vet., Microbiol.Abstr., Ref.Zh., Rev.Med.& Vet.Mycol., Rev.Plant Path., Sugar Ind.Abstr., Vet.Bull.
—BLDSC (2087.833000); CASDDS; CISTI; KNAW; SWETS. **CCC.**
Formerly: Microbios Letters (ISSN 0307-5494)
Description: Explores chemical microbiology, cellular pharmacology, virology, bacteriology, biochemistry, immunology, hematology, molecular biology, biochemical genetics and biophysics, radiation biology and cancer research.

BIOMEDICAL PERSPECTIVES. see *MEDICAL SCIENCES*

BIOMEDICAL RESEARCH TECHNOLOGY RESOURCES; a research resources directory. see *BIOLOGY — Abstracting, Bibliographies, Statistics*

BIOMEDIZINSCHE FORSCHUNG - INFORMATIONEN. see *MEDICAL SCIENCES*

BIOMETEOROLOGY; proceedings of the International Congress of Biometeorology. see *METEOROLOGY*

BIOMETEOROLOGY BULLETIN. see *METEOROLOGY*

BIOMETRIC BULLETIN. see *STATISTICS*

570   GW   ISSN 0323-3847
QH323.5   CODEN: BIJODN
BIOMETRICAL JOURNAL; journal of mathematical methods in biosciences. (Text in English) 1959. 8/yr. DM.195 (foreign DM.211) to individuals; institutions DM.945 (foreign DM.985) (effective 1997). Akademie Verlag GmbH, Muehlenstr. 33-34, 13187 Berlin, Germany. TEL 49-30-47889348. FAX 49-30-47889357. E-mail: info@akademie-verlag.de. (Subscr. in the Americas to: John Wiley & Sons, Inc., 605 Third Ave., New York, NY 10158. TEL 212-850-6645. FAX 212-850-6021) Ed. J. Laeuter. adv.; bk.rev.; abstr.; bibl.; charts; illus.; stat.; index. **Indexed:** Anim.Breed.Abstr., ASCA, Biol.Abstr., Biostat., Compumath, Curr.Cont.(1973-), Curr.Ind.Stat., Excerp.Med., INIS Atomind., J.Cont.Quant.Meth., Math.R., Oper.Res.Manage.Sci., Plant Breed.Abstr., Qual.Contr.Appl.Stat., Rice Abstr., Sport Fish.Abstr., SSCI, Stat.Theor.Meth.Abstr. (1973-), Wild.Rev., Zent.Math., Zoo.Rec. **Document type:** academic/scholarly publication.
—BLDSC (2087.990000); CISTI; Genuine Article; Linda Hall; SWETS; UnCover. **CCC.**
Formerly: Biometrische Zeitschrift.

BIOMETRICS. see *STATISTICS*

BIOMETRIKA. see *BIOLOGY — Abstracting, Bibliographies, Statistics*

570   II   ISSN 0970-9835
BIONATURE. (Text in English) 1981. s-a. (Society of Bionaturalists) Hindustan Publishing Corp., 4805-24, 1st Fl., Bharat Ram Rd., Darya Ganj, New Delhi 110 002, India. TEL 91-11-3254401. FAX 91-11-6863511. E-mail: hpcpd@giasdl01.vsnl.net.in.

572.8   KR   ISSN 0233-7657
QP801.P69   CODEN: BIKLEK
BIOPOLIMERY I KLETKA. (Text and summaries in English, Russian, Ukrainian) 1985. bi-m. $249 (effective 1998). Akademiya Nauk Ukrainy, Institut Molekulyarnoi Biologii i Genetiki, Vul. Akad. Zabolotnogo, 150, 252627 Kiev 143, Ukraine. TEL 38-44-2660789. FAX 38-44-2660759. E-mail: kornelyuk@imbg.kiev.ua. (Dist. by: Mezhdunarodnaya Kniga, B. Yakimanka 39, 117049 Moscow, Russia; Dist. in U.S. by: Victor Kamkin Inc., 4956 Boiling Brook Pkwy, Rockville, MD 20852. TEL 301-881-5973. FAX 301-881-1637) Ed. Alexander I. Kornelyuk. circ. 300. **Indexed:** Djerelo, Triticale Abstr.
—BLDSC (0017.994000); CASDDS; Linda Hall.

570 600   US   ISSN 0888-7470
CODEN: BPTEEP
BIOPROCESS TECHNOLOGY SERIES. 1986. irreg., vol.23, 1996. price varies. Marcel Dekker, Inc., 270 Madison Ave., New York, NY 10016. TEL 212-696-9000. FAX 212-685-4540. TELEX 421419. Ed. Russell Dekker; Pub. Graham Garratt. R&P contact: Julia Mulligan.
—BLDSC (2089.474250); CASDDS; CISTI; Ei; KNAW. **CCC.**
Refereed Serial

570   US   ISSN 0005-3155
ML549.8   CODEN: BIOSAN
BIOS; a quarterly journal of biology. 1930. q. $15 (Canada and Mexico $17; elsewhere $23) (effective 1997). (National Biological Society) Beta Beta Beta, Box 670, Madison, NJ 07940-0670. TEL 201-377-8407. Ed. Dr. James J. Nagle. adv.; bk.rev.; charts; illus. circ. 10,500. (also avail. in microfilm from UMI) **Indexed:** Biol.Abstr., Biol.Dig, Biotech.Abstr., Chem.Abstr., Curr.Adv.Ecol.Sci., Deep Sea Res.& Oceanogr.Abstr., Sport Fish.Abstr., Wild.Rev., Zoo.Rec. **Document type:** academic/scholarly publication.
●Also available online.
—BLDSC (2089.600000); CASDDS; CISTI; Linda Hall; UMI; UnCover.
Description: Covers biology news reports, juried undergraduate research, graduate reviews, and Society news. Includes calendar of events.

570   UK
▼**BIOSAFETY.** 1995. irreg. (updates approx. q.). £34($50) (effective 1997 & 1998). Science Reviews Ltd., P.O. Box 81, Northwood, Middlesex HA6 3DY, England. TEL 44-1923-823586. FAX 44-1923-825006. E-mail: scilet@scilet.com; URL: http://www.scilet.com/scilet.htm. **Document type:** academic/scholarly publication.
●Available only online.
Refereed Serial

BIOLOGY

570 US ISSN 0006-3568
QH1 CODEN: BISNAS
BIOSCIENCE. 1951. m. $60 to members; institutions $165 (foreign institutions $193. American Institute of Biological Sciences, 1444 Eye St., N.W., Ste. 200, Washington, DC 20005. TEL 202-628-1500. FAX 202-628-1509. E-mail: bioscience@aibs.org; URL: http://www.aibs.rog/bioscience.html. Ed. Rebecca Chasan; Pub. Clifford J. Gabriel. R&P contact: Rebecca Chasan. adv. contact: John Waler. bk.rev.; bibl.; illus.; index. circ. 12,000. (also avail. in microform from UMI; back issues avail.; reprint service avail. from UMI) **Indexed:** Abstr.Bull.Inst.Pap.Chem., Acad.Ind., Acid Pre.Dig., Acid Rain Abstr., Acid Rain Ind., Anim.Breed.Abstr., Bibl.Agri., Bio-Contr.News & Info., Biol.Abstr., Biol.& Agr.Ind., Biol.Dig., Bk.Rev.Ind. (1991-), C.I.J.E., C.I.J.E., Chem.Abstr., Child.Bk.Rev.Ind. (1991-), Curr.Adv.Ecol.Sci., Curr.Biotech.Abstr., Curr.Cont., Curr.Lit.Fam.Plan., Curr.Tit.Ocean., Cyb.Abstr., Dairy Sci.Abstr., Deep Sea Res.& Oceanogr.Abstr., Environ.Abstr., Environ.Per Bibl. (1991-), Field Crop Abstr., Forest.Abstr., Fut.Surv., Gard.Lit. (1992-), Gen.Sci.Ind., GeoRef., Helminthol.Abstr., Hlth.Ind., Hort.Abstr., Ind.Sci.Rev., Ind.Vet., INIS Atomind., Key Word Ind.Wildl.Res., Mag.Ind., Ocean.Abstr., PMR, Pollut.Abstr., R.G.Abstr., R.G., Ref.Sour., Rev.Appl.Entomol., Rev.Plant.Path., Risk Abstr., Sci.Cit.Ind., Sel.Water Res.Abstr., Small Anim.Abstr., Soils & Fert., Sport Fish.Abstr., SSCI, Telegen, Triticale Abstr., Weed Abstr., Wild.Rev., Zoo.Rec. **Document type:** academic/scholarly publication. ●Also available online. Vendor(s): Information Access Co., UMI.
—BLDSC (2089.611400); CASDDS; CIS; CISTI; EMDOCS; Genuine Article; KNAW; KR SourceOne; Linda Hall; SWETS; UMI; UnCover. **CCC.**
Description: Contains articles from all areas of biological sciences, including animals, humans, plants, and the environment.
Refereed Serial

660.6 572 JA ISSN 0916-8451
QH345 CODEN: BBBIEJ
BIOSCIENCE, BIOTECHNOLOGY, AND BIOCHEMISTRY. (Text in English) 1924. m. $360 to non-members; members $100 (effective 1996). Japan Society for Bioscience, Biotechnology, and Agrochemistry - Nippon Nogeikagaku Kai, 2-4-16 Yayoi, Bunkyo-ku, Tokyo 113, Japan. TEL 03-3811-8789. FAX 81-3-3815-1920. Ed. Hajime Iwamura. adv. circ. 3,300. **Indexed:** Anal.Abstr., Apic.Abstr., ASCA, Biodet.Abstr., Biol.Abstr., Biol.& Agr.Ind., Chem.Abstr., Chem.Cit.Ind., Cott.& Trop.Fibr.Abstr., Crop Physiol.Abstr., Curr.Adv.Biochem., Curr.Adv.Ecol.Sci., Curr.Adv.Genetics & Molec.Biol., Curr.Biotech.Abstr., Curr.Cont., Dairy Sci.Abstr., Energy Ind., Energy Info.Abstr., Environ.Abstr., Excerp.Med., Fababean Abstr., Field Crop Abstr., Food Sci.& Tech.Abstr., Geo.Abstr., Helminthol.Abstr., Ind.Sci.Rev., Ind.Vet., INIS Atomind., Irr.& Drain.Abstr., Maize Abstr., Mass Spectr.Bull., Neurosci.Cit.Ind., Nutr.Abstr., Ornam.Hort., Pig News & Info., Plant Grow.Reg.Abstr., Potato Abstr., Protozool.Abstr., Rev.Med.& Vet.Mycol., Rice Abstr., Rural Recreat.Tour.Abstr., Sci.Cit.Ind., Seed Abstr., Sel.Water Res.Abstr., Soils & Fert., Sorghum & Millets Abstr., Sport Fish.Abstr., SSCI, Sugar Ind.Abstr., Telegen, Triticale Abstr., Vet.Bull., VITIS, Weed Abstr., Wild.Rev., World Agri.Econ.& Rural Sociol.Abstr. **Document type:** academic/scholarly publication.
—BLDSC (2089.611470); CASDDS; CISTI; Genuine Article; KNAW; KR SourceOne; Linda Hall; SWETS; UnCover. **CCC.**
Formerly (until 1992): Agricultural and Biological Chemistry (ISSN 0002-1369)
Description: Publishes original papers and reviews in the fields of bioscience, biotechnology and biochemistry.
Refereed Serial

570 II
BIOSCIENCE RESEARCH BULLETIN. (Text in English) s-a. $50. Hindustan Publishing Corp., 4805-24, 1st Fl., Bharat Ram Rd., Darya Ganj, New Delhi 110 002, India. TEL 91-11-3254401. FAX 91-11-6863511. E-mail: hpcpd@giasdl01.vsnl.net.in.

570 575.1 FR ISSN 1158-467X
CODEN: BIOSER
BIOSCIENCES. Variant title: Biosciences Appliquees. (Text and summaries in English and French) 1982. 4/yr. 450 F.($50) Dunod, 15 rue Gossin, 92543 Montrouge Cedex, France. TEL 33-39-56-52-10. Ed. Christian Doinel. adv.; bk.rev.; index. circ. 1,000. **Indexed:** Apic.Abstr., Biodet.Abstr., Curr.Biotech.Abstr. **Document type:** academic/scholarly publication.
—CASDDS; CISTI.
Formerly (until 1990): Bio-Sciences (Chateaufort) (ISSN 0292-8418)

BIOSIS SERIAL SOURCES. see *BIOLOGY — Abstracting, Bibliographies, Statistics*

570 GW ISSN 0947-0867
CODEN: BOSPFD
▼**BIOSPEKTRUM.** 1995. bi-m. DM.98 to individuals; institutions DM.198; students DM.40 (effective 1996). (Vereinigung fuer Allgemeine und Angewandte Mikrobiologie) Spektrum Akademischer Verlag GmbH, Vangerowstr. 20, 69115 Heidelberg, Germany. TEL 49-6221-9126-0. FAX 49-6221-912638. E-mail: kaschura@spektrum-verlag.com; URL: http://www.spektrum-verlag.com. (Co-sponsor: Gesellschaft fuer Biologische Chemie) Ed. Andreas Mietzsch. **Document type:** academic/scholarly publication.
—BLDSC (2089.616800); CASDDS; SWETS. **CCC.**

570 AU ISSN 1026-4949
BIOSYSTEMATICS AND ECOLOGY. (Text in English) irreg., vol.13, 1997. Verlag der Oesterreichischen Akademie der Wissenschaften, Postfach 471, A-1011 Vienna, Austria. TEL 43-1-51581401. FAX 43-1-51581400. E-mail: verlag@oeaw.ac.at; URL: http://www.ac.at/einheiten/verlag. Ed. Wilfried Morawetz. **Document type:** academic/scholarly publication, monographic series.

570 IE ISSN 0303-2647
QH301 CODEN: BSYMBO
BIOSYSTEMS. 1967. 15/yr. fl.2380($1368) (effective 1998). Elsevier Science Ireland Ltd., P.O. Box 85, Limerick, Ireland. TEL 353-61-471944. FAX 353-61-472144. (Subscr. to: Elsevier Science, Regional Sales Office, P.O. Box 211, 1000 AE Amsterdam, Netherlands. TEL 31-20-4853757. FAX 31-20-4853432; Subscr. in the Americas to: Elsevier Science, Regional Sales Office, Box 945, New York, NY 10159-0945. TEL 212-633-3730. FAX 212-633-3680; Subscr. in Australasia and the Far East to: Elsevier Science (Singapore) Pte Ltd, No.1 Temasek Ave., No.17-01 Millenia Tower, Singapore 039192, Singapore. TEL 65-434-3727. FAX 65-337-2230) Ed. A.W. Schwartz. R&P contact: Annette Moloney. charts; illus.; index. (also avail. in microform from UMI) **Indexed:** ASCA, Biol.Abstr., Chem.Abstr., Compumath, Curr.Adv.Ecol.Sci., Curr.Cont., Ecol.Abstr., Excerp.Med., Ind.Med., Ind.Sci.Rev., Sport Fish.Abstr., Wild.Rev., Zoo.Rec. **Document type:** academic/scholarly publication.
—BLDSC (2089.670000); CASDDS; CISTI; EMDOCS; Genuine Article; KR SourceOne; Linda Hall; SWETS; UnCover. **CCC.**
Formerly (until 1974): Currents in Modern Biology (ISSN 0011-4014)
Description: Devoted to achieving an improved understanding of biological origins and evolution by means of the analysis and modeling of complex biological systems.
Refereed Serial

571.3 UK ISSN 1352-2396
BIOTRANSFORMATIONS. 1989. irreg. The Royal Society of Chemistry, Thomas Graham House, Science Park, Milton Rd., Cambridge CB4 4WF, England. TEL 44-1223-420066. FAX 44-1223-423429. E-mail: sales@rsc.org; URL: http://chemistry.rsc.org/rsc/. (Dist. by: Turpin Distribution Services Ltd., Blackhorse Rd., Letchworth, Herts. SG6 1HN, England. TEL 44-1462-672555. FAX 44-1462-480947; Subscr. in N. America to: ACS, 1155 Sixteenth St., N.W., Washington, DC 22036. TEL 202-776-8100. FAX 202-872-6067) **Document type:** monographic series.
Description: Surveys the literature on biotransformations in animals.

570 IO ISSN 0216-5023
SD235.S67 CODEN: BITREF
BIOTROPIA. (Text in English) a. $10. Seameo Biotrop - Southeast Asian Regional Centre for Tropical Biology, P.O. Box 116, Bogor 16001, Indonesia. TEL 62-251-323848. FAX 62-251-326851. Ed. Gloria L. Enriquez. **Document type:** academic/scholarly publication.
Formed by the merger of: Seameo Biotrop Newsletter & Biotrop Bulletin in Tropical Biology & Biotrop Technical Bulletin.
Description: Contains scientific articles on research findings in the fields of tropical forest biology, tropical agricultural pest biology and tropical aquatic biology.

578.0913 US ISSN 0006-3606
QH1 CODEN: BTROAZ
BIOTROPICA. 1969. 4/yr. $95 (effective 1997). Association for Tropical Biology, Inc., c/o Dr. Julie S. Denslow, Exec. Dir., Dept. of Plant Biology, Louisiana State University, Baton Rouge, LA 70803. TEL 504-388-8411. FAX 504-388-8459. URL: http://ecology.umsl.edu/atb/. Ed. Robert Marquis. circ. 1,600. (also avail. in microform from UMI; reprint service avail. from UMI) **Indexed:** Agroforest.Abstr., Apic.Abstr., ASCA, Ber.Biochem.Biol., Biol.Abstr., Curr.Adv.Ecol.Sci., Curr.Cont., Deep Sea Res.& Oceanogr.Abstr., Ecol.Abstr., Excerp.Med., Forest.Abstr., Forest Prod.Abstr., Geo.Abstr.P.G., Geol.Abstr., Helminthol.Abstr., Hort.Abstr., IDA, Ind.Sci.Rev., Key Word Ind.Wildl.Res., Plant Breed.Abstr., Sci.Cit.Ind., Seed Abstr., Sel.Water Res.Abstr., So.Pac.Per.Ind., Soils & Fert., Sport Fish.Abstr., Weed Abstr., Wild.Rev., Zoo.Rec. **Document type:** academic/scholarly publication.
—BLDSC (2089.900000); CISTI; Genuine Article; Linda Hall; SWETS; UMI; UnCover.
Formerly: Association for Tropical Biology. Bulletin.
Refereed Serial

570 II
ISSN 0971-0108
CODEN: BIOVED
BIOVED. (Text in English) 1990. s-a. Rs.100 to individuals (foreign $50); institutions Rs.500 (foreign $125). Bioved Research Society, c/o Brijesh K. Dwivedi, General Secretary, 252A-4A Om Gayatri Nagar, Teliarganj, Allahabad 211 004, U.P., India. TEL 91-532-644069. FAX 91-532-640429. Ed. B.K. Dwivedi. **Document type:** academic/scholarly publication.
—BLDSC (2090.050000); CASDDS. **CCC.**
Description: Concerns with researches in life sciences.

577 332 US
BIOWORLD FINANCIAL WATCH. w. $710. American Health Consultants, BioWorld Publishing Group, Box 740021, Atlanta, GA 30374. TEL 404-262-7436. FAX 404-814-0759. URL: http://www.ahcpub.com. Pub. Donald R. Johnston. (only avail. by fax) **Document type:** newsletter.

570 US
BIOWORLD INTERNATIONAL. w. $699. American Health Consultants, BioWorld Publishing Group, Box 740021, Atlanta, GA 30374. TEL 404-262-7436. FAX 404-814-0759. URL: http://www.ahcpub.com. Pub. Donald R. Johnston. (only avail. by fax) **Document type:** newsletter.

570 US
BIOWORLD TODAY. d. $1350. American Health Consultants, BioWorld Publishing Group, Box 740021, Atlanta, GA 30374. TEL 404-262-7436. FAX 404-814-0759. URL: http://www.ahcpub.com. Pub. Donald R. Johnston. (only avail. by fax) **Document type:** newsletter.

577 US
BIOWORLD WEEK. w. $495. American Health Consultants, BioWorld Publishing Group, Box 740021, Atlanta, GA 30374. TEL 404-262-7436. FAX 404-814-0759. URL: http://www.ahcpub.com. Pub. Donald R. Johnston. **Document type:** newsletter.

570 JA ISSN 0913-5219
BIRDER/BADA. (Text in Japanese) 1987. m. 9960 Yen. Bun'ichi Sogo Shuppan Co., Ltd., 13-10, Nishigokencho, Shinjuku-ku, Tokyo 162, Japan. TEL 81-3-3235-7341. FAX 81-3-3269-1402. Ed. Masayuki Harada; Pub. Takeshi Okumura. R&P contact: Masayuki Harada. bk.rev. circ. 36,000. **Document type:** trade publication.

BOLETIN DE AGRICULTURA BIOLOGICO-DINAMICA. see *AGRICULTURE*

570   SP   ISSN 0211-0326
BOLETIN DE CIENCIAS DE LA NATURALEZA. 1960. s-a. 500 ptas. Instituto de Estudios Asturianos, Plaza de Porlier 5, Apdo. 9, 33003 Oviedo, Spain. **Indexed:** Ind.SST.
Formerly (until 1979): Instituto de Estudios Asturianos. Boletin. Suplemento de Ciencias (ISSN 0561-3566)

BOTANISCHER VEREIN VON BERLIN UND BRANDENBURG. VERHANDLUNGEN. see *BIOLOGY — Botany*

BOUNDARY-LAYER METEOROLOGY; an international journal of physical and biological processes in the atmospheric boundary layer. see *METEOROLOGY*

BRAGANTIA. see *AGRICULTURE*

570 628   UK
BRITISH ECOLOGICAL SOCIETY. ECOLOGICAL ISSUES SERIES. irreg., no.5, 1994. price varies. British Ecological Society, 26 Blades Ct., Deodar Rd., Putney, London SW15 2NU, England. **Document type:** monographic series.

570   UK
BRITISH SOCIETY FOR DEVELOPMENTAL BIOLOGY. SYMPOSIA. 1973. irreg., no.18, 1986. price varies. Cambridge University Press, Edinburgh Bldg., Shaftesbury Rd., Cambridge CB2 2RU, England. TEL 44-1223-312393. FAX 44-1223-315052. TELEX 851817256. E-mail: information@cup.cam.ac.uk; URL: http://www.cup.cam.ac.uk. (N. American addr.: Cambridge University Press, Journals Dept., 40 W. 20th St., New York, NY 10011. TEL 212-924-3900. FAX 212-691-3239) R&P contact: Linda Nicol. **Indexed:** Biol.Abstr. **Document type:** proceedings.

570   US   ISSN 0068-2799
     CODEN: BSBIAW
BROOKHAVEN SYMPOSIA IN BIOLOGY. irreg., no.36, 1991. (Brookhaven National Laboratory) Plenum Publishing Corp., 233 Spring St., New York, NY 10013-1578. TEL 212-620-8000. FAX 212-463-0742. TELEX 23-421139. E-mail: books@plenum.com. (Dist. by: National Technical Information Service, 5285 Port Royal Rd., Springfield, VA 22151) **Indexed:** Anim.Breed.Abstr., Biol.Abstr., Dairy Sci.Abstr., Deep Sea Res.& Oceanogr.Abstr., Excerp.Med., Helminthol.Abstr., Ind.Med., Plant Breed.Abstr. **Document type:** proceedings.
—CASDDS; CISTI.
Refereed Serial

BUFFALO SOCIETY OF NATURAL SCIENCES. BULLETIN. see *SCIENCES: COMPREHENSIVE WORKS*

570 610   US   ISSN 0007-4888
R850   CODEN: BEXBAN
BULLETIN OF EXPERIMENTAL BIOLOGY AND MEDICINE. English translation of: Byulleten' Eksperimental'noi Biologii i Meditsiny (RU ISSN 0365-9615) 1956. m. $1815 (foreign $2125) (effective 1998). (Rossiiskaya Akademiya Meditsinskikh Nauk, RU) Plenum Publishing Corp., Consultants Bureau, 233 Spring St., New York, NY 10013-1578. TEL 212-620-8468. FAX 212-463-0742. TELEX 23-421139. Ed. D.S. Sarkisov. (also avail. in microfilm from UMI; back issues avail.) **Indexed:** ASCA, Biol.Abstr., Chem.Titles, Curr.Adv.Biochem., Curr.Adv.Ecol.Sci., Curr.Adv.Genetics & Molec.Biol., Curr.Cont., Excerp.Med., Ind.Med., Ind.Sci.Rev., INIS Atomind., Int.Abstr.Biol.Sci., Neurosci.Cit.Ind., Sci.Cit.Ind., SSCI. **Document type:** academic/scholarly publication.
—BLDSC (0409.500000); CISTI; Genuine Article; SWETS; UMI; UnCover. CCC.
Refereed Serial

BULLETIN OF MARINE SCIENCE. see *EARTH SCIENCES — Oceanography*

570   US   ISSN 0092-8240
QH505.A1   CODEN: BMTBAP
BULLETIN OF MATHEMATICAL BIOLOGY; a journal devoted to research at the interface of theoretical and experimental biology. 1939. bi-m. fl.1247($770) (effective 1997). (Society for Mathematical Biology) Elsevier Science Inc., Box 945, New York, NY 10159-0945. TEL 212-633-3730. FAX 212-633-3680. E-mail: nlinfo-f@elsevier.nl; usinfo-f@elsevier.com; forinfo-kyf04035@niftyserve.or.jp; URL: http://www.elsevier.nl/. (Subscr. outside the Americas to: Elsevier Science, Regional Sales Office, P.O. Box 211, 1000 AE Amsterdam, Netherlands. TEL 31-20-4853757. FAX 31-20-4853432; Subscr. in Australasia and the Far East to: Elsevier Science (Singapore) Pte Ltd, No.1 Temasek Ave., No.17-01 Millenia Tower, Singapore 039192, Singapore. TEL 65-434-3727. FAX 65-337-2230; Subscr. in Japan to: Elsevier Science Japan, 9-15 Higashi-Azabu 1-chome, Minato-ku, Tokyo 106, Japan. TEL 81-3-5561-5033. FAX 81-3-5561-5047) Ed. Lee A. Segel. adv.; bk.rev.; software rev. circ. 1,250. (also avail. in microfilm from UMI; reprint service avail. from SWZ) **Indexed:** Acoust.Abstr., Anim.Breed.Abstr., Appl.Mech.Rev., ASCA, Bibl.Agri., Biol.Abstr., Biostat., Chem.Abstr., Compumath, Curr.Adv.Ecol.Sci., Curr.Cont., Deep Sea Res.& Oceanogr.Abstr., Excerp.Med., Helminthol.Abstr., Ind.Med., Ind.Sci.Rev., INIS Atomind., INSPEC (1974-1985), Math.R., Risk Abstr., Sci.Cit.Ind., Sport Fish.Abstr., Wild.Rev., Zent.Math. **Document type:** academic/scholarly publication, bulletin.
—BLDSC (2867.970000); CASDDS; CISTI; EMDOCS; Genuine Article; Linda Hall; SWETS; UMI; UnCover. CCC.
Formerly: Bulletin of Mathematical Biophysics (ISSN 0007-4985)
Description: Rapid communication forum for experimental and theoretical biologists.
Refereed Serial

611.01816   IT   ISSN 0391-481X
     CODEN: BMBMD5
BULLETIN OF MOLECULAR BIOLOGY AND MEDICINE; a journal for the rapid publication of reports in the field of biochemical sciences. (Text in English) 1975. q. L.90000($150) (effective 1997). (Dipartimento Biochimica e Biologia Molecolare, Bari and Dipartimento Biochimica e Biotecnologie Mediche, Napoli, Universita degli Studi) Casa Editrice Idelson, Via A. De Gasperi, 55, 80133 Naples, Italy. TEL 39-81-5524733. FAX 39-81-5518295. Eds. Francesco Salvatore, Ernesto Quagliariello. abstr.; charts; stat. **Indexed:** Excerp.Med. (1994-).
—BLDSC (2881.370000); CASDDS; CISTI; EMDOCS.
Description: Contains topics about molecular biology and medicine.

570 370   NE   ISSN 0166-512X
BULLETIN VOOR HET ONDERWIJS IN DE BIOLOGIE. 1969. bi-m. fl.42.50. N I B I, Postbus 8616, 3503 RP Utrecht, Netherlands. TEL 31-30-369244. Ed. P.A.M. Oor. adv. **Document type:** bulletin.
Formerly (until 1979): Bulletin voor Docenten in de Biologie (ISSN 0921-5530)

C A L M SCIENCE. (Conservation and Land Management) see *CONSERVATION*

C B E VIEWS. (Council of Biology Editors Inc.) see *PUBLISHING AND BOOK TRADE*

570   JA   ISSN 0915-4353
C E L S S JOURNAL/C E L S S GAKKAISHI. (Text in Japanese; summaries in English) 1989. s-a. 5000 Yen. Japan Society for Controlled Ecological and Life Support Systems, Institute for Future Technology, 2-6-11, Tomiokabashi Bldg., Fukagawa, Kohtoh-ku, Tokyo 135, Japan. FAX 81-3-5245-1061. **Document type:** proceedings.

000   JA   ISSN 0917-4869
C E L S S NEWS. (Text in Japanese) 1988. 4/yr. Japan Society for Controlled Ecological and Life Support Systems, Institute for Future Technology, 2-6-11, Tomiokabashi Bldg., Fukagawa, Kohtoh-ku, Tokyo 135, Japan. FAX 81-3-5245-1061. **Document type:** newsletter.

C F S. (Courier Forschungsinstitut Senckenberg) see *SCIENCES: COMPREHENSIVE WORKS*

C M A S BULLETIN D'INFORMATION/C M A S NEWSLETTER. (Confederation Mondiale des Activites) see *EARTH SCIENCES — Oceanography*

570   SP   ISSN 0214-848X
CADERNOS DA AREA DE CIENCIAS BIOLOXICAS. INVENTARIOS. 1988. irreg. Seminario de Estudos Galegos, El Castro, 15168 Sada (La Coruna), Spain. **Indexed:** Ind.SST. **Document type:** monographic series.

570   FR
CAHIER TECHNIQUE DU BIOLOGISTE. (Supplement to: Actualites Biologiques) q. 500 F. (foreign 550 F.) (effective 1996). Centre National des Biologistes, 80, Av. du Maine, 75014 Paris, France. TEL 43-22-97-70. FAX 43-21-73-12. **Document type:** academic/scholarly publication.
Description: Features original biological research reports for doctors, pharmacists, laboratory directors and technicians.
Refereed Serial

578.77   FR   ISSN 0007-9723
QH90   CODEN: CBIMA5
CAHIERS DE BIOLOGIE MARINE. (Text in English, French) 1960. 4/yr. 950 F. Station Biologique de Roscoff, B.P. 74, 29682 Roscoff Cedex, France. TEL 33-2-98292302. FAX 33-2-98292324. E-mail: jouin@sb-roscoff.fr; URL: http://www.sb-roscoff.fr/services.html. Ed. Claude Jouin-Toulmond; Pub. Andre Toulmond. adv.; bk.rev.; bibl.; charts; illus. circ. 400. (back issues avail.) **Indexed:** ASCA, Biol.Abstr., Bull.Signal., Chem.Abstr., Curr.Adv.Ecol.Sci., Curr.Adv.Genetics & Molec.Biol., Curr.Cont., Deep Sea Res.& Oceanogr.Abstr., Ecol.Abstr., Geo.Abstr.P.G., GeoRef., Helminthol.Abstr., Ind.Sci.Rev., Ocean.Abstr., Pollut.Abstr., Sci.Cit.Ind., Sel.Water Res.Abstr., Soils & Fert., Sport Fish.Abstr., Wild.Rev., Zoo.Rec. **Document type:** academic/scholarly publication.
—BLDSC (2948.650000); CASDDS; CISTI; Genuine Article; Linda Hall; SWETS; UMI; UnCover.
Description: Contains papers and short notes concerning marine biology, reproduction, life cycles, developmental biology, morphogenesis, genetics, population dynamics, ecophysiology, plankton, benthos and algology.
Refereed Serial

570 551.46   JA   ISSN 0288-6243
CALANUS. (Text in English, Japanese; summaries in Japanese) 1968. a. Kumamoto Daigaku, Rigakubu, Fuzoku Aitsu Rinkai Jikkenjo - Kumamoto University, Faculty of Science, Aitsu Marine Biological Station, Aitsu, Matsushimacho, Amakusa-gun, Kumamotoken 861-61, Japan.

570   US   ISSN 0885-4629
Q11   CODEN: CFAMBS
CALIFORNIA ACADEMY OF SCIENCES. MEMOIRS. 1868. irreg., vol.21, 1996. price varies. California Academy of Sciences, Golden Gate Park, San Francisco, CA 94118. TEL 415-750-7243. Ed. Alan E. Leviton. **Document type:** monographic series.
—Linda Hall.
Refereed Serial

570   US   ISSN 0068-547X
Q11   CODEN: PCASAV
CALIFORNIA ACADEMY OF SCIENCES. PROCEEDINGS. 1854. irreg., vol.49, 1995. $35 (effective 1997). California Academy of Sciences, Golden Gate Park, San Francisco, CA 94118. TEL 415-750-7243. Ed. Alan E. Leviton. index. circ. 1,000. (also avail. in microform from UMI) **Indexed:** Biol.Abstr., Curr.Adv.Ecol.Sci., Deep Sea Res.& Oceanogr.Abstr., GeoRef., Key Word Ind.Wildl.Res., Ocean.Abstr., Rev.Appl.Entomol., Sport Fish.Abstr., Wild.Rev., Zoo.Rec. **Document type:** proceedings.
—BLDSC (6671.000000); CISTI; KNAW.
Refereed Serial

570   US
CALIFORNIA EDUCATIONAL LINKAGES IN THE LIFE SCIENCES. Abbreviated title: C E L L S. Insert in: California Science Teachers Association Newspaper. 1990. s-a. free. University of California at Berkeley, Lawrence Hall of Science, Berkeley, CA 94720. TEL 510-643-5537. FAX 510-642-1055. circ. 25,000. **Document type:** newsletter.
Description: Aims to promote development of collaborative programs for bringing recent biological science advances into the classroom through various resources.

BIOLOGY

570.9 US ISSN 0068-5755
CALIFORNIA NATURAL HISTORY GUIDES. no.4, 1959. irreg., no.58, 1994. price varies. University of California Press, 2120 Berkeley Way, Berkeley, CA 94720. TEL 510-642-4247. FAX 510-643-7127. (Orders to: California-Princeton Fulfillment Services, 1445 Lower Ferry Rd., Ewing, NJ 08619. TEL 800-777-4726. FAX 800-999-1958) (back issues avail.) **Document type:** monographic series.
—BLDSC (3015.080000).
   Description: Describes the fauna, flora, and geology of various regions of California.
   Refereed Serial

570 UK ISSN 0068-6697
CAMBRIDGE MONOGRAPHS IN EXPERIMENTAL BIOLOGY. 1954. irreg., no.24, 1985. price varies. Cambridge University Press, Edinburgh Bldg., Shaftesbury Rd., Cambridge CB2 2RU, England. TEL 44-1223-312393. FAX 44-1223-315052. TELEX 851817256. E-mail: information@cup.cam.ac.uk; URL: http://www.cup.cam.ac.uk. (N. American addr.: Cambridge University Press, Journals Dept., 40 W. 20th St., New York, NY 10011. TEL 212-924-3900. FAX 212-691-3239) R&P contact: Linda Nicol. **Indexed:** Biol.Abstr. **Document type:** monographic series.
—CISTI.

570 UK ISSN 0006-3231
QH301 CODEN: BRCPAH
CAMBRIDGE PHILOSOPHICAL SOCIETY. BIOLOGICAL REVIEWS. Key Title: Biological Reviews of the Cambridge Philosophical Society. 1923. q. £88($162) (effective 1998). Cambridge University Press, Edinburgh Bldg., Shaftesbury Rd., Cambridge CB2 2RU, England. TEL 44-1223-312393. FAX 44-1223-315052. TELEX 851817256. E-mail: information@cup.cam.ac.uk; URL: http://www.cup.org/journals/CUPJNS.html. (N. American addr.: Cambridge University Press, Journals Dept., 40 W. 20th St., New York, NY 10011. TEL 212-924-3900. FAX 212-691-3239) Ed. W.A. Foster. R&P contact: Linda Nicol. bibl.; charts; illus.; index. (also avail. in microform from UMI; microfiche from IDC; back issues avail.) **Indexed:** Anim.Breed.Abstr., ASCA, Biol.Abstr., Biol.& Agr.Ind., Chem.Abstr., Curr.Adv.Ecol.Sci., Curr.Cont., Ecol.Abstr., Excerp.Med., Field Crop Abstr., Gen.Sci.Ind., Geo.Abstr., Geol.Abstr., GeoRef., Helminthol.Abstr., Herb.Abstr., Hort.Abstr., Ind.Med., Ind.Sci.Rev., Ind.Vet., Nutr.Abstr., Protozool.Abstr., Sci.Cit.Ind., Soils & Fert., Sport Fish.Abstr., SSCI, Vet.Bull., Weed Abstr., Wild.Rev., Zoo.Rec. **Document type:** monographic series.
—BLDSC (2079.000000); CASDDS; CISTI; EMDOCS; Genuine Article; KR SourceOne; SWETS; UMI; UnCover. **CCC.**
   Description: Covers all aspects of biological science.

CAMBRIDGE STUDIES IN BIOLOGICAL ANTHROPOLOGY. see *ANTHROPOLOGY*

570 510 UK ISSN 0263-9424
CODEN: CSMBDK
CAMBRIDGE STUDIES IN MATHEMATICAL BIOLOGY. 1980. irreg., no.6, 1987. price varies. Cambridge University Press, Edinburgh Bldg., Shaftesbury Rd., Cambridge CB2 2RU, England. TEL 44-1223-312393. FAX 44-1223-315052. TELEX 851817256. E-mail: information@cup.cam.ac.uk; URL: http://www.cup.cam.ac.uk. (N. American addr.: Cambridge University Press, Journals Dept., 40 W. 20th St., New York, NY 10011. TEL 212-924-3900. FAX 212-691-3239) Ed.Bd. R&P contact: Linda Nicol. **Indexed:** Biol.Abstr., Math.R. **Document type:** monographic series.
—BLDSC (3015.994600); CISTI.

CANADIAN BULLETIN OF FISHERIES AND AQUATIC SCIENCES. see *FISH AND FISHERIES*

570 CN ISSN 0845-5066
QH301.C246
CANADIAN FEDERATION OF BIOLOGICAL SOCIETIES. ANNUAL MEETING. PROGRAMME, PROCEEDINGS. 1987. a. $10. Canadian Federation of Biological Societies, 104 - 1750 Courtwood Cres., Ottawa, ON K2C 2B5, Canada. TEL 613-225-8889. FAX 613-225-9621. R&P contact: Paul Hough. adv. contact: Natalie Lamarche. author index. **Indexed:** Biol.Abstr. **Document type:** proceedings.
   Formed by the 1987 merger of: Programme - Canadian Federation of Biological Societies. Annual Meeting (ISSN 0845-5058); Canadian Federation of Biological Societies. Annual Meeting. Proceedings (ISSN 0714-8577); Which continues in part: Canadian Federation of Biological Societies. Programme and Proceedings of the Annual Meeting (ISSN 0709-1265); Which was formed by the merger of: Canadian Federation of Biological Societies. Programme of the Annual Meeting (ISSN 0068-8703); Canadian Federation of Biological Societies. Annual Meeting. Proceedings (ISSN 0068-869X).
   Description: Contains summaries and descriptions of papers, posters and symposia presented at the annual meeting of the federation.

570 CN ISSN 0068-8681
CANADIAN FEDERATION OF BIOLOGICAL SOCIETIES. NEWSLETTER. (Text in English, French) 1959. s-a. Canadian Federation of Biological Societies, 104 - 1750 Courtwood Cres., Ottawa, ON K2C 2B5, Canada. TEL 613-225-8889. FAX 613-225-9621. URL: http://www.fermentas.com/cfbs. Ed.Bd. R&P contact: Paul Hough. adv. contact: Natalie Lamarche. **Document type:** newspaper.
●Also available online.
—CISTI.
   Description: Reports about science projects, funding, and new developments in biological sciences.

CANADIAN SPECIAL PUBLICATION OF FISHERIES AND AQUATIC SCIENCES. see *FISH AND FISHERIES*

CANADIAN TECHNICAL REPORT OF FISHERIES AND AQUATIC SCIENCES. see *FISH AND FISHERIES*

570 PR ISSN 0008-6452
Q1 CODEN: CRJSA4
CARIBBEAN JOURNAL OF SCIENCE. 1961. s-a. $20 to individuals; institutions $35; students $13 (effective 1997 & 1998). University of Puerto Rico, College of Arts and Science, Box 5000, Mayaguez, PR 00681-5000. TEL 787-265-3809. FAX 787-265-1225. E-mail: j_mari@rvmac.upr.clu.edu; URL: http://mayaweb.upr.clu.edu/artssciences/cjs/cjs.htm. Ed. Jose A. Mari Mutt. adv. contact: Eloy Morales. bk.rev.; cum.index: vol.1-15, vol.16-27. circ. 500. **Indexed:** Biol.Abstr., Deep Sea Res.& Oceanogr.Abstr., Ecol.Abstr., Geo.Abstr.P.G., Geol.Abstr., Sport Fish.Abstr., Wild.Rev., Zoo.Rec. **Document type:** academic/scholarly publication.
—BLDSC (3053.100000); CISTI; Linda Hall; UnCover.
   Description: Publishes original articles in all areas of Caribbean natural science.
   Refereed Serial

CARIBBEAN RESEARCH INSTITUTE. REPORT. see *HISTORY — History Of North And South America*

CARNEGIE MUSEUM OF NATURAL HISTORY. ANNALS. see *SCIENCES: COMPREHENSIVE WORKS*

CARNEGIE MUSEUM OF NATURAL HISTORY. BULLETIN. see *SCIENCES: COMPREHENSIVE WORKS*

599.7 US ISSN 0190-5724
CODEN: CRNVD2
CARNIVORE; interfacing biology, anthropology and environmental studies. (Text in English; summaries in German, Russian or Spanish) 1978. q. $35. Carnivore Research Institute, Box 1246, Crystal Bay, NV 89402. Ed. Randall Eaton. adv.; bk.rev.; abstr.; bibl.; charts; illus.; index. circ. 700. (back issues avail.; reprint service avail. from ISI) **Indexed:** Anim.Breed.Abstr., Biol.Abstr., Curr.Adv.Ecol.Sci., Curr.Cont., Deep Sea Res.& Oceanogr.Abstr., GeoRef., Helminthol.Abstr.
—CISTI; Linda Hall.

570 US ISSN 0045-5865
CAROLINA TIPS. 1938. 4/yr. free to qualified personnel. Carolina Biological Supply Co., 2700 York Rd., Burlington, NC 27215. TEL 910-584-0381. FAX 910-584-3399. E-mail: tips@caroscicom. Ed. Phillip Owens. R&P contact: Gwen W. Oakley. adv. contact: Harry Shoffner. bk.rev.; illus.; index. circ. 100,000. (processed) **Indexed:** Biol.Abstr. **Document type:** newsletter.
●Also available online.

CEIBA. see *AGRICULTURE*

570 NE ISSN 1061-5385
CODEN: CADCEF
CELL ADHESION AND COMMUNICATION. 1993. 6/yr. $177 (effective 1998). Gordon and Breach - Harwood Academic, Amsteldisk 166, 1st Fl., 1079 LH Amsterdam, Netherlands. URL: http://www.gbhap.com/Cell_Adhesion_Communication/. (Subscr. to: International Publishers Distributor, Box 32160, Newark, NJ 07102. TEL 800-545-8398. FAX 215-750-6343) Eds. Clayton Buck, Jean-Paul Thiery. (also avail. in microform) **Indexed:** ASCA, Curr.Cont., Excerp.Med. (1994-), Ind.Med. (1994-), Ind.Sci.Rev.
●Also available online.
Also available on CD-ROM.
—BLDSC (3097.655000); CASDDS; CISTI; EMDOCS; SWETS. **CCC.**
   Description: Presents research, short communications, and reviews on all families of adhesion receptors and counterreceptors from diverse biological systems.

570 US ISSN 0740-784X
QH601 CODEN: CEMBDG
CELL MEMBRANES, METHODS AND REVIEWS. 1974. irreg., vol.3, 1987. price varies. Plenum Publishing Corp., 233 Spring St., New York, NY 10013-1578. TEL 212-620-8000. FAX 212-463-0742. TELEX 23-421139. E-mail: books@plenum.com. Ed. Bd. **Indexed:** ASCA, Biol.Abstr., Chem.Abstr., Excerp.Med., Ind.Sci.Rev. **Document type:** monographic series.
—BLDSC (3097.798000); CASDDS; CISTI; Linda Hall.
   Supersedes (in 1983): Methods in Membrane Biology (ISSN 0093-4771)
   Refereed Serial

570 CC ISSN 1001-0602
CELL RESEARCH/XIBAO YANJIU. (Text in English) 1990. s-a. $60 to individuals (foreign $70); institutions $125 (foreign $135) (effective 1996). (Shanghai Xibao Shengwusuo) Science Press, Marketing and Sales Department, 16 Donghuangchenggen North St., Beijing 100717, People's Republic of China. TEL 4010642. FAX 4019810. (Overseas dist. by: Science Press New York, Ltd., 84-04 58th Ave., Elmhurst, NY 11373. TEL 718-476-0238. FAX 718-476-0273) Ed. Zheng Yao. pp./issue: 104. **Document type:** academic/scholarly publication.
—BLDSC (3097.858000); CISTI.
   Description: Features research work in the field of animal and plant cell biology.
   Refereed Serial

CELL STRESS & CHAPERONES. see *MEDICAL SCIENCES*

570 611 US ISSN 1073-1180
QH611 CODEN: CEVIEF
CELL VISION; journal of analytical morphology. 1994. bi-m. $125 in US & Canada; S. America & Europe $145; elsewhere $150. Eaton Publishing Co., 154 E. Central St., Natick, MA 01760. TEL 508-655-8282. FAX 508-655-9910. Ed. Jiang Gu; Pub. Francis Eaton. R&P contact: Jiang Gu. adv.: B&W page $2200, color page $2900; trim 8 1/4 x 10 7/8; adv. contact: Christine McAndrews. circ. 5,000. (back issues avail.) **Indexed:** Chem.Abstr. **Document type:** academic/scholarly publication.
—BLDSC (3097.877500); CASDDS; Ei; EMDOCS; KNAW; SWETS. **CCC.**
   Refereed Serial

BIOLOGY

572.8   FR   ISSN 0145-5680
QH611   CODEN: CMBID4
CELLULAR AND MOLECULAR BIOLOGY. (Supplements avail.) (Text in English) 1977. 8/yr. 2950 F.($590) (supplements 400 F. per no.) (effective 1998). C M B Association, 1 av. du Pave Neuf, 93160 Noisy-le-Grand, France. TEL 33-1-45923719. FAX 33-1-43042030. Ed. Raymond J. Wegmann. R&P contact: Raymond Wegmann. adv. contact: Mieke Wegmann. bk.rev.; index. circ. 750. (back issues avail.) **Indexed:** ASCA, Biol.Abstr., Bull.Signal., Chem.Abstr., Curr.Cont., Excerp.Med., Ind.Med., Ind.Sci.Rev., Sci.Cit.Ind. **Document type:** academic/scholarly publication, monographic series.
—BLDSC (3097.921000); CASDDS; CISTI; KNAW; Linda Hall; SWETS; UMI; UnCover. **CCC.**
Formerly (until 1977): Annales d'Histochimie (ISSN 0003-4355); Incorporates: Cyto-Enzymology.
Description: Covers all relevant areas of the life sciences. Analyzes the relationship between structure and chemical and/or physical content.
Refereed Serial

509   SZ   ISSN 1420-682X
Q1.A1   CODEN: CMLSFI
CELLULAR AND MOLECULAR LIFE SCIENCES. (Text in English) 1945. m. 1054.50 SFr. (foreign 1086 SFr.) (effective 1997). Birkhaeuser Verlag, P.O. Box 133, CH-4010 Basel, Switzerland. TEL 41-61-2050730. FAX 41-61-2050791. E-mail: cmlsedit@birkhauser.ch; URL: http://www.birkhauser.ch. (Dist. in N. America by: Springer-Verlag, Mercedes Distribution Center, 160 Imlay St., Brooklyn, NY 11231, USA) Ed. P. Solles. adv.; charts; illus.; index. **Indexed:** Anim.Breed.Abstr., Apic.Abstr., Arts & Hum.Cit.Ind., ASCA, Bio-Contr.News & Info., Biodet.Abstr., Biol.Abstr., Biotech.Abstr., Chem.Abstr., Chem.Cit.Ind., Chem.Infd., Cott.& Trop.Fibr.Abstr., Crop Physiol.Abstr., Curr.Adv.Biochem., Curr.Adv.Cancer Res., Curr.Adv.Cell & Devel.Biol., Curr.Adv.Ecol.Sci., Curr.Cont., Dairy Sci.Abstr., Deep Sea Res.& Oceanogr.Abstr., Dent.Ind., Dok.Arbeitsmed., Excerp.Med., Field Crop Abstr., Food Sci.& Tech.Abstr., Forest Abstr., Forest Prod.Abstr., Helminthol.Abstr., Herb.Abstr., Hort.Abstr., Ind.Chem., Ind.Med., Ind.Sci.Rev., Ind.Vet., INSPEC, Irr.& Drain.Abstr., Lab.Haz.Bull., Maize Abstr., Mass Spectr.Bull., Met.Abstr., Neurosci.Cit.Ind., Nutr.Abstr., Ocean.Abstr., Pig News & Info., Plant Breed Abstr., Plant Grow.Reg.Abstr., Pollut.Abstr., Poult.Abstr., Psychol.Abstr., Rev.Appl.Entomol., Rev.Med.& Vet.Mycol., Sci.Cit.Ind., Seed Abstr., Sel.Water Res.Abstr., Soils & Fert., Soyabean Abstr., Sport Fish.Abstr., SSCI, Sugar Ind.Abstr., THA, Triticale Abstr., Vet.Bull., VITIS, W.R.C.Inf., Weed Abstr., Wild.Rev., Zoo.Rec. **Document type:** academic/scholarly publication.
●Also available online.
—BLDSC (3097.923800); CASDDS; CISTI; EMDOCS; Genuine Article; KNAW; Linda Hall; SWETS; UMI; UnCover. **CCC.**
Formerly (until 1997): Experientia (ISSN 0014-4754)
Refereed Serial

617.22 570.22   US   ISSN 1052-5882
    CODEN: CMMIEQ
CELLULAR AND MOLECULAR MECHANISMS OF INFLAMMATION; receptors of inflammatory cells: structure-function relationships. 1990. irreg., vol.5, 1998. Academic Press, Inc., 525 B St., Ste. 1900, San Diego, CA 92101-4495. TEL 619-231-0926. FAX 619-699-6715. (Subscr. to: Order Dept., 6277 Sea Harbor Dr., 4th Fl., Orlando, FL 32887. TEL 800-321-5068) Eds. Charles G. Cochrane, Michael A. Gimbrone, Jr.
—BLDSC (3097.924000); CASDDS; CISTI; KNAW. **CCC.**

570   MG
CENTRE D'INFORMATION ET DE DOCUMENTATION SCIENTIFIQUE ET TECHNIQUE. RECHERCHES POUR LE DEVELOPPEMENT. SERIE SCIENCES BIOLOGIQUE. (Text in French; summaries in English, French) 1985. s-a. 60 F.($10) Centre d'Information et de Documentation Scientifique et Technique, B.P. 6224, Antananarivo 101, Madagascar. TEL 261-2-33288. abstr.; bibl.; charts; illus.; stat. circ. 1,000. (back issues avail.)

570   SP
CENTRO DE INVESTIGACIONES BIOLOGICAS. MEMORIA CIENTIFICA. 1963. biennial. free. Centro de Investigaciones Biologicas, Velazquez 144, 28006 Madrid, Spain. TEL 34-91-5611800. FAX 34-91-5627518. **Document type:** academic/scholarly publication.
Formerly: Centro de Investigaciones Biologicas. Memoria.
Description: Reports on the current projects of the institution, as well as on the scientific production of the different groups.

CESKO-SLOVENSKA PATOLOGIE A SOUNDI LEKARSTVI. see *MEDICAL SCIENCES*

570   CE   ISSN 0069-2379
    CODEN: CYJBA2
CEYLON JOURNAL OF SCIENCE. BIOLOGICAL SCIENCES. (Text in English) 1957. s-a. Rs.150($16) University of Peradeniya, P.O. Box 35, Peradeniya, Sri Lanka. Ed. W.R. Breckenridge. bk.rev.; charts; illus. circ. 500. **Indexed:** Biol.Abstr., Curr.Adv.Ecol.Sci., Helminthol.Abstr., IBR, Nutr.Abstr., Ornam.Hort., Plant Breed Abstr., Rev.Appl.Entomol., Sri Lanka Sci.Ind., Weed Abstr. **Document type:** academic/scholarly publication.
—BLDSC (3125.500000); CISTI; Linda Hall; UnCover.

CHEMICO-BIOLOGICAL INTERACTIONS; a journal of molecular and biochemical toxicology. see *ENVIRONMENTAL STUDIES — Toxicology And Environmental Safety*

CHEMISTRY AND ECOLOGY. see *CHEMISTRY*

CHIBA DAIGAKU RIGAKUBU KAIYO SEITAIKEI KENKYU SENTA NENPO/CHIBA UNIVERSITY. MARINE ECOSYSTEM RESEARCH CENTER. ANNUAL REPORT. see *EARTH SCIENCES — Oceanography*

570   JA   ISSN 0385-0986
CHIBA SEIBUTSUSHI/BIOLOGICAL SOCIETY OF CHIBA. BULLETIN. (Text in Japanese; summaries in English, Japanese) 1948. s-a. Chibaken Seibutsu Gakkai - Biological Society of Chiba, Chiba Daigaku Rigakubu, 1-33 Yayoicho, Inage-ku, Chiba-shi, Chiba-ken 263, Japan.

CHIHUAHUAN DESERT DISCOVERY. see *EARTH SCIENCES*

CHIHUAHUAN DESERT NEWSBRIEFS. see *EARTH SCIENCES*

CHINESE MEDICAL SCIENCES JOURNAL. see *MEDICAL SCIENCES*

570   IT   ISSN 0390-0037
QP84.6   CODEN: CBLGA2
CHRONOBIOLOGIA. (Text in English) 1974. q. L.250000($180) (International Society for Chronobiology) Casa Editrice Il Ponte, Casella Postale 1071, 20101 Milan, Italy. TEL (0039)-2 31072676. bk.rev.; abstr.; bibl.; illus.; index. circ. 6,000. (also avail. in microfiche from UMI) **Indexed:** Apic.Abstr., Biol.Abstr., Bull.Signal., Chem.Abstr., Curr.Adv.Ecol.Sci., Curr.Cont., Excerp.Med., Ind.Med., Psychol.Abstr. (1977-), Ref.Zh.
—BLDSC (3188.300000); CASDDS; EMDOCS; KNAW; SWETS; UMI; UnCover.

570   US   ISSN 0742-0528
    CODEN: CHBIE4
CHRONOBIOLOGY INTERNATIONAL; the journal of biological and medical rhythm research. 1984. bi-m. $395 (foreign $417.50) (effective 1998). (International Society of Chronobiology) Marcel Dekker Journals, 270 Madison Ave., New York, NY 10016. TEL 212-696-9000. FAX 212-685-4540. (Subscr. to: Box 5107, Monticello, NY 12701-5176) Eds. Ludger Rensing, Michael Smolensky. adv.; charts; illus. (reprint service avail. from UMI) **Indexed:** ASCA, Curr.Adv.Cancer Res., Curr.Adv.Ecol.Sci., Curr.Cont., Excerp.Med., Ind.Sci.Rev., Psychol.Abstr. (1984-), SSCI. **Document type:** academic/scholarly publication.
—BLDSC (3188.320000); CASDDS; CISTI; EMDOCS; Genuine Article; KNAW; SWETS; UMI. **CCC.**
Incorporates: Annual Review of Chronopharmacology (ISSN 0743-9539)
Description: Publishes original research investigations, short communications, and commentaries in chronobiology and related disciplines.
Refereed Serial

570   CU   ISSN 0138-7154
QH301   CODEN: CIBIDA
CIENCIAS BIOLOGICAS. (Text in Spanish; summaries in English) 1977. s-a. $24 in S. America; N. America $26; elsewhere $30 (or on exchange basis). Academia de Ciencias de Cuba, Instituto de Ecologia y Sistematica, Industria 452, Havana 2, Cuba. Ed.Bd. charts; illus. circ. 2,000. **Indexed:** Apic.Abstr., Biol.Abstr., Curr.Adv.Ecol.Sci., Forest Prod.Abstr., Plant Breed.Abstr.
—BLDSC (3198.202700); CISTI.

CIMBEBASIA. MEMOIR. see *SCIENCES: COMPREHENSIVE WORKS*

578.77   IT
CIVICA STAZIONE IDROBIOLOGICA DI MILANO. QUADERNI. (Text in Italian; summaries in English) 1970. irreg. free to researchers. Civica Stazione Idrobiologica di Milano, Viale Gadio, 2, 20121 Milan, Italy. TEL 02-86462051. FAX 39-2-8690719. R&P contact: Cristina Gilardi. bibl.; charts; illus. **Document type:** academic/scholarly publication.

CLINICAL ANATOMY. see *MEDICAL SCIENCES*

CLINICAL INVESTIGATOR NEWS. see *PHARMACY AND PHARMACOLOGY*

CLINICAL SCIENCE. see *MEDICAL SCIENCES*

016.574   US   ISSN 0084-8824
COLD SPRING HARBOR LABORATORY. ABSTRACTS OF PAPERS PRESENTED AT MEETINGS. irreg. (8-13/yr.) Cold Spring Harbor Laboratory Press, Publications Department, Box 100, Cold Spring Harbor, NY 11724. TEL 800-843-4388. FAX 516-349-1946. E-mail: cshpress@cshl.org; URL: http://www.cshl.org. circ. controlled. (processed) **Document type:** abstracting/indexing.

570   US   ISSN 0069-5009
COLD SPRING HARBOR LABORATORY. ANNUAL REPORT. 1924. a. Cold Spring Harbor Laboratory Press, Publications Department, Box 100, Cold Spring Harbor, NY 11724. TEL 800-843-4388. FAX 516-349-1946. E-mail: cshpress@cshl.org; URL: http://www.cshl.org. circ. controlled. **Indexed:** Environ.Abstr. **Document type:** corporate report.

570   US   ISSN 0091-7451
QH301   CODEN: CSHSAZ
COLD SPRING HARBOR LABORATORY. SYMPOSIA ON QUANTITATIVE BIOLOGY. 1933. a. price varies. Cold Spring Harbor Laboratory Press, Publications Department, Box 100, Cold Spring Harbor, NY 11724. TEL 800-843-4388. FAX 516-349-1946. E-mail: cshpress@cshl.org; URL: http://www.cshl.org. (back issues avail.) **Indexed:** ASCA, Biol.Abstr., Biol.& Agr.Ind., Curr.Cont., Dent.Ind., Excerp.Med., Ind.Med., Ind.Sci.Rev., INIS Atomind., Maize Abstr., Sci.Cit.Ind. **Document type:** proceedings.
—BLDSC (3296.000000); CASDDS; CISTI; EMDOCS; Genuine Article; KNAW; KR SourceOne; Linda Hall; SWETS; UMI; UnCover. **CCC.**

570   US   ISSN 0270-1847
    CODEN: CHMSDK
COLD SPRING HARBOR MONOGRAPH SERIES. 1970. irreg. price varies. Cold Spring Harbor Laboratory Press, Publications Department, Box 100, Cold Spring Harbor, NY 11724. TEL 800-843-4388. FAX 516-349-1946. E-mail: cshpress@cshl.org; URL: http://www.cshl.org. illus.; index. **Indexed:** Biol.Abstr., Chem.Abstr., Sci.Cit.Ind. **Document type:** monographic series.
—BLDSC (3295.855000); CASDDS; CISTI; KNAW. **CCC.**

570   SP
COLECCION CIENCIAS BIOLOGICAS. 1974. irreg., no.14 1983. price varies. (Universidad de Navarra, Facultad de Ciencias) Ediciones Universidad de Navarra, S.A., Apdo. 396, 31080 Pamplona, Spain. TEL 94 825 6850.

570   US   ISSN 0069-6285
COLUMBIA BIOLOGICAL SERIES. 1910. irreg., no.24, 1968. Columbia University Press, 562 W. 113th St., New York, NY 10025. TEL 212-666-1000. Ed. Kate Witterberg. R&P contact: Lisa Simmars. **Document type:** monographic series.
Refereed Serial

BIOLOGY

572.8   US
COLUMBIA SERIES IN MOLECULAR BIOLOGY. irreg., latest 1976. price varies. Columbia University Press, 562 W. 113th St., New York, NY 10025. TEL 212-666-1000. Ed. Kate Witterberg. R&P contact: Lisa Simmars. **Document type:** monographic series.
Refereed Serial

570   NE   ISSN 0894-8550
QH301
COMMENTS ON THEORETICAL BIOLOGY. 1988. 4/yr. (in 1 vol., 4 nos./vol.). $197 (effective 1998). Gordon and Breach - Harwood Academic, Amsteldisk 166, 1st Fl., 1079 LH Amsterdam, Netherlands. (Subscr. to: International Publishers Distributor, Box 32160, Newark, NJ 07102. TEL 800-545-8398. FAX 215-750-6343) Ed.Bd. (also avail. in microform)
—BLDSC (3336.042000); CISTI. **CCC.**

COMPARATIVE BRAIN RESEARCH IN MAMMALS. see *MEDICAL SCIENCES — Psychiatry And Neurology*

571.3 577   II   ISSN 0379-0436
QH540   CODEN: CPECDM
COMPARATIVE PHYSIOLOGY AND ECOLOGY. 1976. q. $28. Impex India, M-S Premier Publication, 863 Sadarpura, Behind Syndicate Bank Building, Chopasani Rd., Jodhpur 342 003, India. **Indexed:** Bio-Contr.News & Info., Biol.Abstr., Chem.Abstr., Curr.Adv.Ecol.Sci., Curr.Cont., Curr.Ref.Fish Res., Excerp.Med., Field Crop Abstr., Helminthol.Abstr., Hort.Abstr., Ind.Sci.Rev., Ind.Vet., Poult.Abstr., Rice Abstr., Sci.Cit.Ind., Soils & Fert., Vet.Bull., Weed Abstr.
—BLDSC (3363.793400); CASDDS; CISTI; Genuine Article; Linda Hall; UMI. **CCC.**

570   AG   ISSN 0326-1956
                           CODEN: COBIEJ
COMUNICACIONES BIOLOGICAS. (Text in English, Spanish) 1982. q. Arg.$25 (foreign $30). Instituto de Biologia Celular, Facultad de Medicina, Paraguay 2155, 1121 Buenos Aires, Argentina. TEL 54-1-9615010. FAX 54-1-112541. Ed. Dr. Amanda Pellegrino de Iraldi. irreg. circ. 1,000. (back issues avail.) **Indexed:** Biol.Abstr., Chem.Abstr., Ind.Med.
—BLDSC (3395.600000); CASDDS; CISTI; KNAW.
Description: Includes original papers and clinical work cases on biology.

CONSERVATION BIOLOGY. see *CONSERVATION*

CONTEMPORARY TOPICS IN IMMUNOBIOLOGY. see *MEDICAL SCIENCES — Allergology And Immunology*

570   US   ISSN 0160-5313
QH301   CODEN: CBGMDW
CONTRIBUTIONS IN BIOLOGY AND GEOLOGY. 1974. irreg. (approx. 3/yr.). Milwaukee Public Museum, 800 W. Wells St., Milwaukee, WI 53233. TEL 414-278-2710. FAX 414-223-1396. Ed. Rodney M. Watkins. circ. 1,500. **Indexed:** GeoRef., Sport Fish.Abstr., Wild.Rev., Zoo.Rec.
—CISTI; Linda Hall.

578.77   US
                      CODEN: CMSCAY
CONTRIBUTIONS IN MARINE SCIENCE - MONOGRAPHIC SERIES.* 1945. irreg. price varies. University of Texas at Austin, Marine Science Institute, 750 Channelview Dr., Port Aransas, TX 78373. TEL 512-749-6723. FAX 512-749-6725. Eds. Ruth Grundy, Terry Whitledge. circ. 1,200. **Indexed:** Biol.Abstr., Biol.& Agr.Ind., Chem.Abstr., Curr.Adv.Ecol.Sci., Deep Sea Res.& Oceanogr.Abstr., Ecol.Abstr., Excerp.Med., Geo.Abstr., Geol.Abstr., GeoRef., Ind.Sci.Rev., Nutr.Abstr., Ocean.Ind., Sci.Cit.Ind., Sport Fish.Abstr., Wild.Rev., Zoo.Rec. **Document type:** monographic series.
—CASDDS; CISTI; Linda Hall; UnCover.
Former titles (until 1992): Contribution in Marine Science; University of Texas. Institute of Marine Science. Contributions (ISSN 0082-3449); University of Texas. Institute of Marine Science. Publications.
Refereed Serial

CORNELL FOCUS. see *AGRICULTURE*

570.15195   US
CORNELL UNIVERSITY. NEW YORK STATE COLLEGE OF AGRICULTURE AND LIFE SCIENCES. BIOMETRICS UNIT. ANNUAL REPORT. 1949. a. free. New York State College of Agriculture and Life Sciences, Department of Plant Breeding and Biometry, Cornell University, 436 Warren Hall, Ithaca, NY 14853. TEL 607-255-5488. FAX 607-255-4698. E-mail: biometrics@cornell.edu. Ed. Laurie L. Coon. bk.rev.; circ. controlled. **Document type:** corporate report.

CRITICAL REVIEWS IN NEUROBIOLOGY. see *MEDICAL SCIENCES — Psychiatry And Neurology*

570   SP   ISSN 0211-5700
QH301
CUADERNOS DE INVESTIGACION BIOLOGICA. irreg. Universidad del Pais Vasco, Facultad de Ciencias, Laboratorio de Citologia e Histologia, Apdo. 6444, 48080 Bilbao, Spain. **Indexed:** Ind.SST.
—CISTI.

578.77   US   ISSN 0889-5546
CURRENT (PACIFIC GROVE); the journal of marine education. 1976. q. $40 (effective Mar. 1995). National Marine Education Association, Box 51215, Pacific Grove, CA 93950. TEL 408-648-4841. FAX 408-648-7960. Ed. Nora L. Deans. adv. contact: Lisa Tooker. bk.rev.; bibl.; charts; illus.; stat. circ. 1,500. (back issues avail.) **Indexed:** G.Soc.Sci.& Rel.Per.Lit.
Description: Features in-depth articles about marine, physical, earth, and life sciences and marine education and research
Refereed Serial

CURRENT AWARENESS. S D I SERVICE. see *MEDICAL SCIENCES*

CURRENT AWARENESS IN BIOLOGICAL SCIENCES. see *BIOLOGY — Abstracting, Bibliographies, Statistics*

CURRENT COMMENTS; the newsletter of discovery and innovation. see *MEDICAL SCIENCES — Experimental Medicine, Laboratory Technique*

CURRENT CONTENTS: LIFE SCIENCES. see *BIOLOGY — Abstracting, Bibliographies, Statistics*

572.8   US
CURRENT PROTOCOLS IN MOLECULAR BIOLOGY. base vol. plus q. updates. $440 (Canada $470.80); update service $172 (Canada $184.04); CD-ROM version $396 (Canada $520.02) (effective 1995). John Wiley & Sons, Inc., Journals, 605 Third Ave., New York, NY 10158. TEL 212-850-6645. FAX 212-850-6021. (Subscr. to: Box 2535, Secaucus, NJ 07096-2535) **Document type:** academic/scholarly publication.
● Also available on CD-ROM.

570   US   ISSN 0070-2137
QH573   CODEN: CTCRAE
CURRENT TOPICS IN CELLULAR REGULATION. 1969. irreg., vol.35, 1997. Academic Press, Inc. (Subsidiary of: Harcourt Brace Jovanovich), 525 B St., Ste. 1900, San Diego, CA 92101-4495. TEL 619-231-0926. FAX 619-699-6715. (Subscr. to: Order Dept., 6277 Sea Harbor Dr., 4th Fl., Orlando, FL 32887. TEL 800-321-5068) Eds. Bernard L. Horecker, Earl R. Stadtman. (reprint service avail. from ISI) **Indexed:** ASCA, Biol.Abstr., Chem.Abstr., Curr.Adv.Ecol.Sci., Ind.Med., Ind.Sci.Rev., Sci.Cit.Ind.
—BLDSC (3504.875000); CASDDS; CISTI; Linda Hall; UnCover. **CCC.**
Refereed Serial

570   NE   ISSN 0732-4413
QH301   CODEN: CDBID9
CURRENT TOPICS IN CHINESE SCIENCE. SECTION D: BIOLOGY. 1982. irreg., vol.3, 1985. Gordon and Breach - Harwood Academic, Amsteldisk 166, 1st Fl., 1079 LH Amsterdam, Netherlands. (Subscr. to: International Publishers Distributor, Box 32160, Newark, NJ 07102. TEL 800-545-8398. FAX 215-750-6343) (also avail. in microfilm) **Document type:** monographic series.
—**CCC.**
Refereed Serial

570   US   ISSN 0070-2153
QL951   CODEN: CTDBA5
CURRENT TOPICS IN DEVELOPMENTAL BIOLOGY. 1966. irreg., vol.36, 1997. Academic Press, Inc., 525 B St., Ste. 1900, San Diego, CA 92101-4495. TEL 619-231-0926. FAX 619-699-6715. (Subscr. to: Order Dept., 6277 Sea Harbor Dr., 4th Fl., Orlando, FL 32887. TEL 800-321-5068) Ed. A.A. Moscona. (reprint service avail. from ISI) **Indexed:** Anim.Breed.Abstr., ASCA, Biol.Abstr., Chem.Abstr., Curr.Adv.Ecol.Sci., Ind.Med., Ind.Sci.Rev., Nutr.Abstr., Poult.Abstr., Sci.Cit.Ind., Sport Flsh.Abstr., Wild.Rev., Zoo.Rec. **Document type:** monographic series.
—BLDSC (3504.880000); CASDDS; CISTI; Linda Hall; SWETS; UnCover. **CCC.**
Refereed Serial

CURRENT TOPICS IN MEMBRANES AND TRANSPORT. see *BIOLOGY — Cytology And Histology*

CURRENT TOPICS IN PATHOLOGY. see *MEDICAL SCIENCES*

570   II   ISSN 0378-7540
                     CODEN: CTSCDI
CURRENT TRENDS IN LIFE SCIENCES; recent researches in cold water fisheries. irreg., vol.21, 1996. price varies. Today and Tomorrow's Printers and Publishers, 24B-5 Desh Badhu Gupta Rd., Karol Bagh, New Delhi 110 005, India. TEL 5721928. (Dist. in U.S. by: Scholarly Publications, 2825 Wilcrest Dr., Ste. 255, Houston, TX 77042. TEL 713-781-0070. FAX 713-781-2112) Ed. K.L. Sehgal. **Indexed:** Biol.Abstr., Chem.Abstr., Curr.Adv.Ecol.Sci., Curr.Cont. **Document type:** monographic series.
—BLDSC (3504.945000); CASDDS; CISTI. **CCC.**

577   AT
CURTIN UNIVERSITY. SCHOOL OF ENVIRONMENTAL BIOLOGY. BULLETIN. 1980. irreg., no.16, 1995. free. Curtin University, School of Environmental Biology, Bentley, W.A., Australia. TEL 61-9-3517964. FAX 61-9-3512495. E-mail: imajerj@info.curtis.edu.au. Ed. J.D. Majer. circ. 150. (back issues avail.)
Former titles: Curtin University. School of Biology. Bulletin; Western Australian Institute of Technology. Department of Biology. Bulletin (ISSN 0158-3301)
Refereed Serial

570   US   ISSN 0340-8132
                     CODEN: LSRPD8
DAHLEM WORKSHOP REPORTS. LIFE SCIENCES RESEARCH REPORT. 1976. irreg., vol.36, 1986. price varies. Springer-Verlag, 175 Fifth Ave., New York, NY 10010. TEL 212-460-1500. FAX 212-473-6272. (Also: Berlin, Heidelberg, Tokyo and Vienna) **Document type:** monographic series.
—BLDSC (5208.961000); CASDDS; CISTI; KNAW.

DANA-REPORT. see *EARTH SCIENCES — Oceanography*

570 550   GW   ISSN 0416-833X
                     CODEN: DEBEAC
DECHENIANA-BEIHEFTE (BONN). (Text in German; summaries in English) 1955. irreg. DM.25. Naturhistorischer Verein, Nussallee 15a, 53115 Bonn, Germany. TEL 0228-692377. Ed. Bodo Moeseler. (back issues avail.) **Indexed:** Curr.Adv.Ecol.Sci. **Document type:** monographic series.
—Linda Hall.

DEEP-SEA RESEARCH. PART 1: OCEANOGRAPHIC RESEARCH PAPERS. see *EARTH SCIENCES — Oceanography*

570   IT   ISSN 0416-928X
                     CODEN: DLPNAM
DELPINOA. (Text in Italian; summaries in English) 1959. irreg. exchange basis. Universita degli Studi di Napoli, Dipartimento di Biologia Vegetale, Via Foria 223, 80139 Naples, Italy. Ed. Giuseppe Caputo. bibl.; charts; illus. circ. 650. **Indexed:** Biol.Abstr.

DENMARK. FISKERIMINISTERIET. FORSOEGSLABORATORIUM. AARSBERETNING. see *FISH AND FISHERIES*

BIOLOGY

500 US ISSN 0070-3753
DENVER MUSEUM OF NATURAL HISTORY. PROCEEDINGS. 1955-1966 (no.16); resumed 1991. irreg., ser.3, no.1, 1991. $5 per no. Denver Museum of Natural History, 2001 Colorado Blvd., Denver, CO 80205-5798. TEL 303-370-6442. FAX 303-331-6492. R&P contact: Richard S. Peigler. **Indexed:** GeoRef.
Formerly: Colorado Museum of Natural History.

571.9 UK ISSN 0009-9716
CODEN: CMIFAR
DESCRIPTIONS OF PATHOGENIC FUNGI AND BACTERIA. (Former name of issuing body: Commonwealth Mycological Institute (C M I)) 1964. q. £80($140) (effective 1997). (International Mycological Institute) CAB International, Wallingford, Oxon. OX10 8DE, England. TEL 44-1491-832111. FAX 44-1491-826090. TELEX 847964 COMAGG G. E-mail: cabi@cabi.org; URL: http://www.cabi.org. (Alt. addr.: International Mycological Institute, Bakeham Ln., Egham, Surrey TW20 9TY, England; U.S. subscr. to: Oxford University Press, Customer Services Dept., 2001 Evans Rd., Cary, NC 27513. TEL 800-445-9714. FAX 919-677-1303) charts; illus.; cum.index. (looseleaf format) **Indexed:** Biol.Abstr., Forest.Abstr., Forest Prod.Abstr., Rev.Appl.Entomol., Rev.Plant Path. **Document type:** academic/scholarly publication.
 Description: Provides descriptions of pathogens for use by plant pathologists and medical mycologists.

DEUTSCHE GESELLSCHAFT FUER PATHOLOGIE. VERHANDLUNGEN. see *MEDICAL SCIENCES*

571.3 UK ISSN 0950-1991
QL951 CODEN: DEVPED
DEVELOPMENT (CAMBRIDGE). 1953. s-m. £970 (U.S. & Canada $1682; elsewhere £995) (effective 1998). Company of Biologists Ltd., Bidder Bldg., 140 Cowley Rd., Cambridge CB4 4DL, England. TEL 44-1223-426164. FAX 44-1223-423353. E-mail: cob@cambridge.cityscape.co.uk; URL: http://www.cityscape.co.uk/ag64/devindex.htm. Ed. C.C. Wylie. adv. contact: Richard Skaer. abstr.; bibl.; illus.; index. circ. 2,600. (back issues avail.) **Indexed:** Anim.Breed.Abstr., Biol.Abstr., Biol.& Agr.Ind., Chem.Abstr., Curr.Cont., Dairy Sci.Abstr., Dent.Ind., Excerp.Med., Geo.Abstr.H.G., Helminthol.Abstr., Ind.Med., Ind.Sci.Rev., Ind.Vet., INIS Atomind., Sci.Cit.Ind., Sport Fish.Abstr., Vet.Bull., Wild.Rev., Zoo.Rec. **Document type:** academic/scholarly publication.
 —BLDSC (3578.598000); CASDDS; CISTI; EMDOCS; KNAW; KR SourceOne; Linda Hall; SWETS; UMI; UnCover.
Formerly: Journal of Embryology and Experimental Morphology (ISSN 0022-0752)
 Description: Publishes primary research providing an insight into mechanisms of plant and animal development from the molecular and cellular to the tissue levels.

571.3 GW ISSN 0949-944X
QL951 CODEN: WRABDT
DEVELOPMENT, GENES AND EVOLUTION. Online edition (GW ISSN 1432-041X) (Text in English) 1894. 10/yr. DM.1035.50 (foreign DM.1060) (effective 1998). (European Developmental Biology Organization, Executive Board) Springer-Verlag, Heidelberger Platz 3, 14197 Berlin, Germany. TEL 49-30-82787-0. FAX 49-30-82787448. E-mail: subscriptions@springer.de; URL: http://link.springer.de. (Subscr. in N. America to: Springer-Verlag New York, Inc., 333 Meadowlands Pkwy., Secaucus, NJ 07094. TEL 212-460-1500. FAX 212-473-6272) Ed. D. Tautz. adv. contact: Edda Lueckermann. bibl.; charts; illus.; index. (also avail. in microform from UMI; back issues avail.; reprint service avail. from ISI) **Indexed:** ASCA, Biol.Abstr., Chem.Abstr., Curr.Adv.Ecol.Sci., Curr.Cont., Excerp.Med., Ind.Sci.Rev., Neurosci.Cit.Ind., Sci.Cit.Ind., Sport Fish.Abstr., Wild.Rev., Zoo.Rec. **Document type:** academic/scholarly publication.
 ●Also available online.
 —CASDDS; CISTI; EMDOCS; Genuine Article; Linda Hall; UMI; UnCover. **CCC**.
Former titles: Roux's Archives of Developmental Biology (ISSN 0930-035X); (until 1986): Wilhelm Roux's Archives of Developmental Biology (ISSN 0340-0794); Roux' Archiv fuer Entwicklungsmechanik der Organismen (ISSN 0043-5546)
 Description: Reports on experimental work at the systemic, cellular and molecular levels in the field of animal and plant systems.
 Refereed Serial

570 AT ISSN 0012-1592
CODEN: DGDFA5
DEVELOPMENT, GROWTH AND DIFFERENTIATION/HASSEI, SEICHO, BUNKA. (Text in English) 1950. bi-m. Aus.$507 (foreign Aus.$569) (effective 1997). (Japanese Society of Developmental Biologists, JA – Nihon Hassei Seibutsu Gakkai) Blackwell Science Pty Ltd, P.O. Box 378, Carlton South, Vic. 3053, Australia. TEL 61-3-93470300. FAX 61-3-93493016. Ed. Chiaki Katagiri. adv.; bibl.; charts; illus. circ. 1,500. (back issues avail.) **Indexed:** ASCA, Biol.Abstr., Chem.Abstr., Curr.Adv.Ecol.Sci., Curr.Cont., Dairy Sci.Abstr., Excerp.Med., Ind.Sci.Rev., INIS Atomind., Sci.Cit.Ind. **Document type:** academic/scholarly publication.
 —BLDSC (3579.035000); CASDDS; CISTI; Genuine Article; KNAW; Linda Hall; SWETS; UnCover. **CCC**.
Formerly (until 1959): Embryologia.
 Description: Covers developmental phenomena for all types of organisms, including plants and microorganisms. Focus is biochemical and analytical.
 Refereed Serial

570 US ISSN 0012-1606
CODEN: DEBIAO
DEVELOPMENTAL BIOLOGY; an international journal. 1959. 24/yr. $2350 (foreign $2850) (effective 1997). Academic Press, Inc., Journal Division, 525 B St., Ste. 1900, San Diego, CA 92101-4495. TEL 619-230-1840. FAX 619-699-6800. E-mail: apsubs@acad.com; URL: http://www.apnet.com/www/journal/db.htm; http://www.idealibrary.com/. (Subscr. to: Box 861213, Orlando, FL 32886-1213. TEL 407-347-4040. FAX 407-363-9661) Ed. Eric N. Olson. adv.; charts; illus.; index every 6 mos. (back issues avail.) **Indexed:** Anim.Breed.Abstr., ASCA, Bibl.Agri., Biol.Abstr., Biol.& Agr.Ind., Chem.Abstr., Curr.Adv.Biochem., Curr.Adv.Cell & Devel.Biol., Curr.Adv.Ecol.Sci., Curr.Adv.Genetics & Molec.Biol., Curr.Cont., Dairy Sci.Abstr., Dent.Ind., Excerp.Med., Gen.Sci.Ind., Helminthol.Abstr., Ind.Med., Ind.Sci.Rev., INIS Atomind., Neurosci.Cit.Ind., Nutr.Abstr., Poult.Abstr., Sci.Cit.Ind., Sport Fish.Abstr., Wild.Rev., Zoo.Rec. **Document type:** academic/scholarly publication.
 ●Also available online.
 —BLDSC (3579.051900); ADONIS; CASDDS; CISTI; Genuine Article; KR SourceOne; Linda Hall; SWETS; UnCover. **CCC**.
 Description: Publishes original analytical research on mechanisms of development, differentiation, growth, regulation, and tissue repair in plants and animals at the molecular, cellular, and genetic levels.
 Refereed Serial

571.8 611 US ISSN 1058-8388
QL801 CODEN: DEDYEI
DEVELOPMENTAL DYNAMICS. 1901. m. $1997 (foreign $2207) (effective 1998). John Wiley & Sons, Inc., Journals, 605 Third Ave., New York, NY 10158. TEL 212-850-6645. FAX 212-850-6021. TELEX 12-7063. E-mail: SUBINFO@JWILEY.COM; URL: http://www.wiley.co.uk. (Subscr. outside N. America to: John Wiley & Sons Ltd., Baffins Ln., Chichester, W. Sussex PO19 1UD, England. TEL 44-1243-779777. FAX 44-1243-776128) Ed. Paul F. Goetinck. adv.: B&W page £640, color page £1515; trim 279 x 210. bk.rev.; abstr.; bibl.; charts; illus. circ. 1,250. (also avail. in microform from PMC,SWZ,UMI; microfiche from IDC; back issues avail.; reprint service avail. from SWZ) **Indexed:** Abstr.Anthropol., Anim.Breed.Abstr., ASCA, Biol.Abstr., Chem.Abstr., Curr.Adv.Ecol.Sci., Curr.Cont., Dent.Ind., Excerp.Med., Ind.Med., Ind.Sci.Rev., Ind.Vet., INIS Atomind., Neurosci.Cit.Ind., Nutr.Abstr., Poult.Abstr., Sci.Cit.Ind., Small Anim.Abstr., Sport Fish.Abstr., Vet.Bull., Wild.Rev., Zoo.Rec. **Document type:** academic/scholarly publication.
 ●Also available online.
 —BLDSC (3579.054470); CASDDS; CISTI; EMDOCS; Genuine Article; KNAW; Linda Hall; SWETS; UnCover. **CCC**.
Formerly: American Journal of Anatomy (ISSN 0002-9106)
 Description: Provides a focus for communication among developmental biologists who study the emergence of form during animal development.
 Refereed Serial

573.8 612.8 US ISSN 0012-1630
QL750 CODEN: DEPBA5
DEVELOPMENTAL PSYCHOBIOLOGY. 1967. 8/yr. $825 (foreign $965) (effective 1998). (International Society for Developmental Psychology) John Wiley & Sons, Inc., Journals, 605 Third Ave, New York, NY 10158-0012. TEL 212-850-6645. FAX 212-850-6021. TELEX 12-7063. E-mail: SUBINFO@JWILEY.COM; URL: http://www.wiley.co.uk. (Subscr. outside the Americas to: John Wiley & Sons Ltd., Baffins Ln., Chichester, W. Sussex PO19 1UD, England. TEL 44-1243-779777. FAX 44-1243-776128) Ed. William P. Smotherman. adv.: B&W page £640, color page £1515; trim 254 x 165. bk.rev.; index. circ. 800. (also avail. in microform from UMI; reprint service avail. from UMI; back issues avail.) **Indexed:** ASCA, Biol.Abstr., Chem.Abstr., Child Devel.Abstr., Curr.Adv.Ecol.Sci., Curr.Cont., Dairy Sci.Abstr., Excerp.Med., Fam.Ind., Ind.Med., Ind.Sci.Rev., Neurosci.Cit.Ind., Psychol.Abstr. (1969-), Psychol.R.G., Sci.Cit.Ind., SSCI. **Document type:** academic/scholarly publication.
 —BLDSC (3579.058000); CASDDS; CISTI; Genuine Article; KR SourceOne; SWETS; UMI; UnCover. **CCC**.
 Description: Presents original research reports that contribute to the understanding of behaviorally related processes, whether in the embryo, fetus, neonate, or juvenile.
 Refereed Serial

DEVELOPMENTS IN BIOGEOCHEMISTRY. see *EARTH SCIENCES*

DEVELOPMENTS IN BIOLOGICAL STANDARDIZATION. see *METROLOGY AND STANDARDIZATION*

578.77 551.4 NE ISSN 0167-8418
CODEN: DHIMDR
DEVELOPMENTS IN HYDROBIOLOGY. (Text in English) 1981. irreg., vol.86, 1993. price varies. Kluwer Academic Publishers, Postbus 17, 3300 AA Dordrecht, Netherlands. TEL 31-78-6392392. FAX 31-78-6392254. TELEX 29245 KAPG NL. E-mail: services@wkap.nl; URL: http://www.wkap.nl. (Dist. by: Kluwer Academic Publishers Group, P.O. Box 322, 3300 AH Dordrecht, Netherlands. TEL 31-78-6392392. FAX 31-78-6546474; N. America dist. addr.: Box 358, Accord Sta., Hingham, MA 02018-0358. TEL 617-871-6600. FAX 617-871-6528) Ed. H.J. Dumont. **Indexed:** Biol.Abstr., Chem.Abstr. **Document type:** monographic series.
 —CASDDS; CISTI.
 Refereed Serial

DEVELOPMENTS IN IMMUNOLOGY. see *MEDICAL SCIENCES — Allergology And Immunology*

DEVELOPMENTS IN MARINE BIOLOGY. see *EARTH SCIENCES — Oceanography*

BIOLOGY

570   GW   ISSN 0301-4681
QH573   CODEN: DFFNAW
DIFFERENTIATION; ontogeny, neoplasia and differentiation therapy. Online edition (GW ISSN 1432-0436) (Text in English) 1973. 10/yr. DM.1805.50 (foreign DM.1830) (effective 1998). (International Society of Differentiation) Springer-Verlag, Heidelberger Platz 3, 14197 Berlin, Germany. TEL 49-30-82787-0. FAX 49-30-82787448. E-mail: subscriptions@springer.de; URL: http://link.springer.de. (Subscr. in N. America to: Springer-Verlag New York, Inc., 333 Meadowlands Pkwy., Secaucus, NJ 07094. TEL 212-460-1500. FAX 212-473-6272) Ed. W.W. Franke. (also avail. in microform from UMI; back issues avail.; reprint service avail. from ISI) Indexed: ASCA, Biol.Abstr., Chem.Abstr., Curr.Adv.Cell & Devel.Biol., Curr.Cont., Dairy Sci.Abstr., Dent.Ind., Excerp.Med., Helminthol.Abstr., Ind.Med., Ind.Sci.Rev., Plant Grow.Reg.Abstr., Sci.Cit.Ind. Document type: academic/scholarly publication. ●Also available online.
—BLDSC (3584.240000); ADONIS; CASDDS; CISTI; EMDOCS; Genuine Article; KNAW; Linda Hall; SWETS; UMI; UnCover. CCC.
    Description: Reports on the most up-to-date research results on problems of biological diversification in plants and animals.

DIRASAT. MEDICAL AND BIOLOGICAL SCIENCES. see *MEDICAL SCIENCES*

DIRASAT. NATURAL AND ENGINEERING SCIENCES. see *SCIENCES: COMPREHENSIVE WORKS*

DIRECTORY OF PATHOLOGY TRAINING PROGRAMS (YEAR). see *MEDICAL SCIENCES*

DISCOVERY. see *SCIENCES: COMPREHENSIVE WORKS*

570 028.5   IT
DO DO. 1990. m. L.60000 (foreign L.90000) (effective 1997). Editoriale Giorgio Mondadori S.p.A., Via A. Ponti, 10, 20143 Milan, Italy. TEL 02-891661. FAX 02-89125888. Ed. Nicoletta Salvaroti. adv.: B&W page L.8150000, color page L.12500000. circ. 75,000.
    Formerly: Airone Junio.

595   RU   ISSN 0012-4966
QH505   CODEN: DKBSAS
DOKLADY BIOLOGICAL SCIENCES. English translation of: Rossiiskaya Akademiya Nauk. Doklady. 1962. bi-m. $1270 in US; elsewhere $1485 (effective 1998). (Russian Academy of Sciences, Biology Section) Maik Nauka - Interperiodica, Mezhdunarodnyi Otdel, Ul. Profsoyuznaya, 90, 117864 Moscow, Russia. TEL 7-095-3360066. FAX 7-095-3360666. (Dist. by: Plenum Publishing Corp., 233 Spring St., New York, NY 10013-1578, U.S.A. TEL 212-620-8468. FAX 212-463-0742) Ed. V.A. Kabanov. index. (also avail. in microfilm from UMI; back issues avail.) Indexed: Anim.Breed.Abstr., Bio-Contr.News & Info., Biol.Abstr., Chem.Titles, Curr.Adv.Ecol.Sci., Deep Sea Res.& Oceanogr.Abstr., Energy Res.Abstr., Excerp.Med., Forest.Abstr., Ind.Med., INIS Atomind., Int.Abstr.Biol.Sci., Potato Abstr., Protozool.Abstr., Sel.Water Res.Abstr., Soils & Fert., Sport Fish.Abstr., Triticale Abstr., Weed Abstr., Wild.Rev., Zoo.Rec. Document type: academic/scholarly publication.
—BLDSC (0411.200000); CISTI; SWETS; UMI; UnCover. CCC.
    Refereed Serial

OKLADY BOTANICAL SCIENCES. see *BIOLOGY — Botany*

577 550   GW   ISSN 0340-3947
ORTMUNDER BEITRAEGE ZUR LANDESKUNDE. (Text in English, German) 1967. a. DM.15. Museum fuer Naturkunde, Muensterstr. 271, 44122 Dortmund, Germany. TEL 49-231-5024850. FAX 49-231-5024852. Ed.Bd. bk.rev. circ. 600. (back issues avail.) Document type: academic/scholarly publication.

570   GW   ISSN 0341-406X
    CODEN: DRSRDQ
DROSERA; Naturkundliche Mitteilungen aus Nordwestdeutschland. (Text in German; summaries in English) 1976. s-a. DM.60. Staatliches Museum fuer Naturkunde und Vorgeschichte, Damm 40-44, 26135 Oldenburg, Germany. TEL 49-441-9244300. FAX 49-441-2489164. Ed. Ulf Beichle. R&P contact: Ulf Beichle. Indexed: Biol.Abstr. Document type: academic/scholarly publication.
—BLDSC (3627.399800). CCC.

570   KE   ISSN 0374-7387
QH195.A23   CODEN: EANHAU
E A N H S BULLETIN. (Text in English) 1971. 3/yr. membership. East Africa Natural History Society, P.O. Box 44486, Nairobi, Kenya. TEL 254-2-742161. FAX 254-2-741424. E-mail: kipepeo@form-net.com. Ed. Edward Vanden Berge. R&P contact: Lorna Depew. TEL 254-125-22078. bk.rev.; bibl. Indexed: A.I.C.P., Biol.Abstr., Key Word Ind.Wildl.Res., Sport Fish.Abstr., Wild.Rev., Zoo.Rec. Document type: bulletin.
—Linda Hall.
    Description: Contains information about natural history subjects and related correspondence.

ECOGRAPHY; pattern and diversity in ecology. see *ENVIRONMENTAL STUDIES*

577   SP   ISSN 0214-0896
QH171   CODEN: ECOLEV
ECOLOGIA. (Text in English, Spanish; summaries in English) 1972. a. 1500 ptas. (foreign 1900 ptas.) (effective 1997). Direccion General de Conservacion de la Naturaleza, Gran Via de San Francisco, 4, 28005 Madrid, Spain. TEL 34-1-3476008. FAX 34-1-3476303. Ed. Ramon Montoya. bk.rev.; bibl.; charts; illus.; stat. circ. 3,000. (back issues avail.) Indexed: Aqua.Sci.& Fish.Abstr., Bio-Contr.News & Info., Biol.Abstr., Chem.Abstr., Curr.Adv.Ecol.Sci., Curr.Cont., Forest.Abstr., Forest Prod.Abstr., Herb.Abstr., Ind.SST, Ind.Vet., Rev.Appl.Entomol., Seed Abstr., Sport Fish.Abstr., Weed Abstr., Wild Life Rev., Wild.Rev., Zoo.Rec. Document type: academic/scholarly publication.
    Formerly (until 1987): Estacion Central de Ecologia. Boletin (ISSN 0210-2536)

577 550   BO
    CODEN: ECBOE9
ECOLOGIA EN BOLIVIA. (Text in Spanish; abstracts in English, German) 1982. 3/yr. $30 (effective 1996 & 1997). Instituto de Ecologia, Casilla 10077, La Paz, Bolivia. TEL 591-2-792582. FAX 591-2-797511. Ed. Cecile de Morales. bk.rev. circ. 1,000. (back issues avail.) Indexed: Curr.Adv.Ecol.Sci., Sport Fish.Abstr., Wild.Rev., Zoo.Rec. Document type: academic/scholarly publication, bulletin.
    Description: Publishes scientific work on ecology and biodiversity in Bolivia.
    Refereed Serial

577   PE
ECOLOGIA Y DESARROLLO. 1985. irreg., no.6003, 1993. price varies. Centro de Estudios Regionales Andinos "Bartolome de Las Casas", Apdo. 14087, Lima 14, Peru. TEL 511-4429992. FAX 511-4427894. Document type: monographic series.

ECOLOGICAL ABSTRACTS. see *BIOLOGY — Abstracting, Bibliographies, Statistics*

ECOLOGICAL APPLICATIONS. see *ENVIRONMENTAL STUDIES*

577   AT   ISSN 0912-3814
QH540   CODEN: ECRSEX
ECOLOGICAL RESEARCH. (Text in English) 1986. 3/yr. Aus.$283($283) (23850 Yen) (effective 1997). (Ecological Society of Japan, JA) Blackwell Science Pty Ltd, P.O. Box 378, Carlton South, Vic. 3053, Australia. TEL 61-3-93470300. FAX 61-3-93493016. Ed. Koichi Fujii. adv.: page $790; trim 275 x 210. Indexed: ASCA, Curr.Cont., Ecol.Abstr., Geo.Abstr.P.G., Geol.Abstr., Rice Abstr., Sci.Cit.Ind., Sport Fish.Abstr., Wild.Rev., Zoo.Rec. Document type: academic/scholarly publication.
—BLDSC (3649.100000); CASDDS; CISTI; EMDOCS; Genuine Article; Linda Hall; UMI; UnCover. CCC.
    Description: Contains research papers on all aspects of ecology: aquatic, terrestrial, and marine.

570   JA   ISSN 0371-0548
QK900
ECOLOGICAL REVIEW/SEITAIGAKU KENKYU. (Text in English) 1935. a. Tohoku University, Mt. Hakkoda Botanical Laboratory - Tohoku Daigaku Hakkodasan Shokubutsu Jikkenjo, c/o Botanical Garden, Tohoku University, Kawauchi, Aoba-ku, Sendai 908, Japan. TEL 81-22-217-6765. FAX 81-22-217-6766. E-mail: 050842@cctu.cc.tohoku.ac.jp. Ed. Tadaki Hirose. Document type: academic/scholarly publication.
—BLDSC (3649.250000); Linda Hall.

ECOLOGICAL SOCIETY OF AMERICA. BULLETIN. see *ENVIRONMENTAL STUDIES*

577   US   ISSN 0070-8356
    CODEN: ESASAM
ECOLOGICAL STUDIES: ANALYSIS AND SYNTHESIS. 1970. irreg., vol.119, 1996. price varies. Springer-Verlag, 175 Fifth Ave., New York, NY 10010. TEL 212-460-1500. FAX 212-473-6272. (Also: Berlin, Heidelberg, Tokyo and Vienna) (reprint service avail. from ISI) Indexed: Bibl.Agri., Biol.Abstr., Chem.Abstr., Forest.Abstr. Document type: monographic series.
—CASDDS; CISTI; Ei.

577   II
THE ECOLOGISTS. (Text in English) 6/yr. $12. Hindustan Publishing Corp., 4805-24, 1st Fl., Bharat Ram Rd., Darya Ganj, New Delhi 110 002, India. TEL 91-11-3254401. FAX 91-11-6863511. E-mail: hpcpd@giasdl01.vsnl.net.in.

ECOLOGY. see *ENVIRONMENTAL STUDIES*

ECOLOGY & ENVIRONMENT. see *ENVIRONMENTAL STUDIES*

577 613.1   II
▼**ECOLOGY, ENVIRONMENT AND CONSERVATION.** (Text in English) 1995. q. Rs.200($50) to individuals; institutions Rs.300($150). Enviro Media, 2nd Fl., Rohan Heights, P.O. Box 90, Karad 415 110, India. Ed. R.K. Trivedy. R&P contact: R.K. Trivedy. bk.rev. Document type: academic/scholarly publication.
    Description: Contains research papers, technical articles, news and other relevant information on all aspects of ecology, environment, pollution and nature conservation.

ECOTROPICA. ECOSISTEMAS TROPICALES. see *EARTH SCIENCES — Oceanography*

570 610   US   ISSN 0724-6706
    CODEN: EQJMD4
THE EINSTEIN QUARTERLY; journal of biology and medicine. 1982. q. $138 (effective 1998). (Albert Einstein College of Medicine) Springer-Verlag, Medical Journals, 175 Fifth Ave., New York, NY 10010. TEL 212-460-1500. FAX 212-473-6272. E-mail: orders@springer-ny.com; URL: http://www.springer-ny.com. (N. American subscr. to: Journal Fulfillment Services, Box 2485, Secaucus, NJ 07096-2485. TEL 800-777-4643. FAX 201-348-4505; Subscr. outside N. America to: Heidelberger Platz 3, D-14197 Berlin, Germany. TEL 49-30-8207-0. FAX 49-30-8207448) Eds. A. Shah, R. Katz-Sidlow. R&P contact: Ian Gross. adv. contact: Robert Vrooman. (also avail. in microform from ISI; reprint service avail. from ISI) Indexed: Chem.Abstr., Excerp.Med. Document type: academic/scholarly publication.
—BLDSC (3665.635000); CASDDS; CISTI. CCC.
    Description: Provides a forum for the discussion of the interface of medicine and the social sciences.
    Refereed Serial

577   XO
EKOLOGIA. (Text in English) 1982. q. $148 in US (effective 1996). (Slovenska Akademia Vied, Ustav Experimentalnej Biologie a Ekologie) Vydavatel'stvo S A P, s.r.o. - Slovak Academic Press Ltd., P.O. Box 57, Nam. Slobody 6, 810 05 Bratislava, Slovakia. TEL 42-7-211728. (Dist. by: Slovart, Nam. Slobody 6, 817 64 Bratislava, Slovakia) Ed. Milan Rucicka. Indexed: ASCA, Bio-Contr.News & Info., Biol.Abstr., Curr.Cont., Curr.Dig.Sov.Press, Excerp.Med., Forest.Abstr., Geo.Abstr.H.G., Geo.Abstr.P.G., Herb.Abstr., SSCI, Weed Abstr.

BIOLOGY

577 PL ISSN 0420-9036
QH162 CODEN: ELPLBS
EKOLOGIA POLSKA/POLISH JOURNAL OF ECOLOGY. (Text in English; summaries in Polish) 1953. q. $132 (effective 1998). Polska Akademia Nauk, Instytut Ekologii, Dziekanow Lesny k-Warszawy, 05-092 Lomianki, Poland. TEL 48-22-7513046. FAX 48-22-7513100. (Dist. by: Ars Polona, Krakowskie Przedmiescie 7, 00-068 Warsaw, Poland; Dist. also by: Mezhdunarodnaya Kniga, B. Yakimanka 39, 117049 Moscow, Russia. TEL 7-095-2384967. FAX 7-095-2384634) Ed. Leszek Grum. R&P contact: Anna Hillbricht-Ilkowska. adv. contact: Anna Hillbricht-Ilkowska. bk.rev.; bibl.; illus. circ. 980. **Indexed:** AgroLibrex, Bio-Contr.News & Info., Biol.Abstr., Chem.Abstr., Curr.Adv.Ecol.Sci., Curr.Cont., Curr.Ref.Fish Res., Deep Sea Res.& Oceanogr.Abstr., Ecol.Abstr., Excerp.Med., Field Crop Abstr., Forest.Abstr., Forest Prod.Abstr., Geo.Abstr.P.G., Herb.Abstr., Hort.Abstr., Key Word Ind.Wildl.Res., Plant Breed.Abstr., Rev.Appl.Entomol., Sel.Water Res.Abstr., Soils & Fert., Sport Fish.Abstr., Triticale Abstr., Wild.Rev., Zoo.Rec. **Document type:** academic/scholarly publication.
—BLDSC (3668.900000); CASDDS; CISTI; Linda Hall; SWETS; UnCover.
Formerly (until 1970): Ekologia Polska. Seria A (ISSN 0070-9557); (until 1955): Ekologia Polska.
Description: Publishes original research papers concerning various ecological fields.

577 BU ISSN 0204-7675
QH540 CODEN: EKOLDI
EKOLOGIIA. (Text in various languages) 1975. irreg. price varies. (Bulgarska Akademiia na Naukite) Publishing House of the Bulgarian Academy of Sciences, Acad. G. Bonchev St., Bldg. 6, 1113 Sofia, Bulgaria. circ. 430. (reprint service avail. from IRC) **Indexed:** Chem.Abstr, Helminthol.Abstr., Sel.Water Res.Abstr., Soils & Fert., Weed Abstr.
—BLDSC (0057.040000); CASDDS; CISTI; KNAW; Linda Hall.

577 KR ISSN 0203-4646
QH541.5.S3 CODEN: EKMODH
EKOLOGIYA MORYA; respublikanskii mezhvedomstvennyi sbornik nauchnykh trudov. (Text in Russian; summaries in English and Russian) 1980. 4/yr. (Akademiya Nauk Ukrainy, Institut Biologii Yuzhnykh Morei im. A.O. Kovalevskogo) Vidavnitstvo Naukova Dumka, Vul. Tereshchenkivska 3, 252601 Kiev, Ukraine. TEL 044-224-4068. FAX 044-224-7060. (Dist. by: Mezhdunarodnaya Kniga, B. Yakimanka 39, 117049 Moscow, Russia) Ed. V.E. Zaika. **Indexed:** Chem.Abstr., Curr.Adv.Ecol.Sci., Deep Sea Res.& Oceanogr.Abstr., Helminthol.Abstr., Sel.Water Res.Abstr., So.Pac.Per.Ind.
—CASDDS; CISTI; Linda Hall.
Formerly: Biologiya Morya (ISSN 0320-9695)

EKOTEKNIK. see ENVIRONMENTAL STUDIES

570 550 FR
ELECTRICITE DE FRANCE. DIRECTION DES ETUDES ET RECHERCHES. COLLECTION DE NOTES INTERNES. BIOLOGIE, SCIENCES DE LA TERRE ET ENVIRONNEMENT. 1992. irreg. 1500 F. Electricite de France (EDF), Direction des Etudes et Recherches, 1 av. du General de Gaulle, 92140 Clamart, France. TEL 1-47-65-43-21. FAX 1-47-65-31-24. TELEX 204 347 F.

ENDANGERED SPECIES UPDATE. see CONSERVATION

570 NE ISSN 1062-3329
CODEN: ENDTE9
ENDOTHELIUM. 1993. q. $129 (effective 1998). Gordon and Breach - Harwood Academic, Amsteldisk 166, 1st Fl., 1079 LH Amsterdam, Netherlands. URL: http://www.gbhap.com/Endothelium. (Subscr. to: International Publishers Distributor, Box 32160, Newark, NJ 07102. TEL 800-545-8398. FAX 215-750-6343) (also avail. in microform) **Indexed:** Excerp.Med. (1994-). **Document type:** academic/scholarly publication.
●Also available online.
Also available on CD-ROM.
—BLDSC (3743.651000); CASDDS; CISTI; EMDOCS; KNAW; SWETS. **CCC.**
Description: Reports on endothelial cell research.

ENVIRONMENTAL & NUTRITIONAL INTERACTIONS. see NUTRITION AND DIETETICS

ENVIRONMENTAL BIOLOGY. see ENVIRONMENTAL STUDIES

ENVIRONMENTAL SCIENCE RESEARCH. see ENVIRONMENTAL STUDIES

ESCUELA TECNICA SUPERIOR DE INGENIEROS DE MONTES. BIBLIOTECA. BOLETIN BIBLIOGRAFICO Y DOCUMENTAL. INFORMACION FORESTAL. SERIE A: MONOGRAFIAS. see FORESTS AND FORESTRY — Abstracting, Bibliographies, Statistics

ESCUELA TECNICA SUPERIOR DE INGENIEROS DE MONTES. BIBLIOTECA. BOLETIN BIBLIOGRAFICO Y DOCUMENTAL. INFORMACION FORESTAL. SERIE B: PUBLICACIONES PERIODICAS. see FORESTS AND FORESTRY — Abstracting, Bibliographies, Statistics

570 UK ISSN 0071-1489
ESSEX NATURALIST. 1887; N.S. 1977. a. price varies. Essex Field Club, Passmore Edwards Museum, Romford Rd., Stratford, London E15, England. Ed. M.W. Hanson. adv. circ. 1,000. **Indexed:** Biol.Abstr., Br.Archaeol.Abstr., Br.Geol.Lit., Br.Hum.Ind., Geo.Abstr., Zoo.Rec. **Document type:** academic/scholarly publication.
—BLDSC (3812.000000).

577 ER ISSN 1406-0914
QH301 CODEN: EATBEC
ESTONIAN ACADEMY OF SCIENCES. PROCEEDINGS. BIOLOGY - ECOLOGY/EESTI TEADUSTE AKADEEMIA. TOIMETIED. BIOLOOGIA - OKOLOOGIA. (Text in English; summaries in English and Estonian) 1997. q. $106 (effective 1998). Teaduste Akadeemia Kirjastus, Estonia pst.7, EE-0100 Tallinn, Estonia. TEL 372-2-454156. FAX 372-6-466026. E-mail: virve@kirj.ee. (Dist. by: Mezhdunarodnaya Kniga, B. Yakimanka 39, 117049 Moscow, Russia. TEL 7-095-2384967. FAX 7-095-2384634; Subscr. to: Akateeminen Kirjakauppa 128 SF, 00101 Helsinki, Finland. Or: Bibliteksjanst AB 200, S22100 Lund, Sweden) Ed. Prof. Juri Martin. illus. circ. 550. **Indexed:** Anim.Breed.Abstr., Biol.Abstr., Chem.Abstr., Dairy Sci.Abstr., Field Crop Abstr., Forest.Abstr., GeoRef., Helminthol.Abstr., Ind.Vet., INIS Atomind., Int.Aerosp.Abstr., NAA, Plant Breed.Abstr., Potato Abstr., Rev.Plant Path., Sel.Water Res.Abstr., Soils & Fert., Vet.Bull., Weed Abstr. **Document type:** academic/scholarly publication, proceedings.
—CASDDS; CISTI; KNAW; Linda Hall.
Formed by the merger of (1991-1997): Eesti Teaduste Akadeemia. Toimetised. Okoloogia (ISSN 0868-5894); (1990-1997): Eesti Teaduste Akadeemia. Toimetised. Bioloogia (ISSN 1018-7642); Which was formerly (1956-1990): Akademiya Nauk Estonskoi S.S.R. Izvestiya. Biologiya (ISSN 0013-2144)

551.4609 614.7 US ISSN 0160-8347
S932.C47 CODEN: ESTUDO
ESTUARIES; a journal of research on any aspect of natural science and management applied to estuaries. 1978. q. $75 to individuals; institutions $230 (foreign $245) (effective 1997). Estuarine Research Federation, 490 Chippingwood Dr., No. 2, Port Republic, MD 20676-2140. TEL 318-475-5443. FAX 318-475-5675. Eds. Scott Nixon, Gilles Billen. R&P contact: Harold Stevenson. adv. contact: Joy Bartholonnew. bk.rev.; abstr.; bibl.; charts; illus.; maps; stat.; index. circ. 1,800. (also avail. in microform from MIM,UMI,PMC; back issues avail.; reprint service avail. from UMI) **Indexed:** Abstr.Bull.Inst.Pap.Chem., ASCA, Biodet.Abstr., Biol.Abstr., Chem.Abstr., Curr.Adv.Ecol.Sci., Curr.Cont., Curr.Tit.Ocean, Deep Sea Res.& Oceanogr.Abstr., Ecol.Abstr., Environ.Per.Bibl., Excerp.Med., Geo.Abstr.P.G., Geol.Abstr., GeoRef., Ind.Sci.Rev., INIS Atomind., Ocean.Abstr., Pollut.Abstr., Sci.Cit.Ind., Sel.Water Res.Abstr., Sport Fish.Abstr., W.R.C.Inf., Weed Abstr., Wild.Rev., Zoo.Rec. **Document type:** academic/scholarly publication.
—BLDSC (3812.593700); CASDDS; CISTI; EMDOCS; Genuine Article; KR SourceOne; Linda Hall; SWETS; UMI; UnCover. **CCC.**
Formerly: Chesapeake Science (ISSN 0009-3262)
Refereed Serial

ESTUARINE, COASTAL AND SHELF SCIENCE. see EARTH SCIENCES — Oceanography

ESTUDIOS DE ANTROPOLOGIA BIOLOGICA. see ANTHROPOLOGY

570 NE ISSN 0896-4343
CODEN: EMLSE5
ETTORE MAJORANA INTERNATIONAL SCIENCE SERIES. LIFE SCIENCES. irreg., latest vol.14. price varies. Gordon and Breach - Harwood Academic, Amsteldisk 166, 1st Fl., 1079 LH Amsterdam, Netherlands. (Subscr. to: International Publishers Distributor, Box 32160, Newark, NJ 07102. TEL 800-545-8398. FAX 215-750-6343) Ed. Antonino Zichichi. bibl.; index. **Indexed:** Chem.Abstr. **Document type:** monographic series.
—CISTI.

570 FR ISSN 0999-5749
RB37.A1 CODEN: BIOLE6
EUROBIOLOGISTE. 1955. bi-m. 680 F. (foreign 750 F.) (effective 1997). Centre National des Biologistes, 80 av. du Maine, 75014 Paris, France. TEL 33-1-43229770. FAX 33-1-43217312. Ed.Bd; Pub. Gerard Cazalet. adv. contact: Jeanne Berga. bk.rev. circ. 3,200. **Indexed:** Biol.Abstr., Chem.Abstr., Excerp.Med., I.P.A. **Document type:** academic/scholarly publication.
●Also available online.
—CASDDS; Linda Hall. **CCC.**
Former titles: Biologiste (ISSN 0981-6003) & Pharmacien Biologiste (ISSN 0553-9323)
Description: Scholarly articles focusing on research findings in the biological sciences.
Refereed Serial

EUROPEAN JOURNAL OF MORPHOLOGY. see BIOLOGY — Physiology

577 FR ISSN 1164-5563
QH84.8 CODEN: EJSBE2
EUROPEAN JOURNAL OF SOIL BIOLOGY. (Text and summaries in English, French) 1964. 4/yr. 840 F. (foreign 1050 F.) (effective 1997). Gauthier-Villars, 5 rue Laromiguiere, 75005 Paris, France. TEL 33-1-40466200. FAX 33-1-40466201. TELEX 634 916 F. E-mail: gauthier.villars.publisher@mail.sgip.fr; URL: http://www.gauthier-villars.fr. (Subscr. to: Societe de Periodiques Specialises, B.P. 22-F, 41354 Vineuil Cedex, France. TEL 33-2-54504612. FAX 33-2-54504611) Ed. P. Trehen. adv.; bk.rev.; bibl.; charts; illus.; index. circ. 1,000. (also avail. in microform from UMI) **Indexed:** ASCA, Biol.Abstr., Chem.Abstr., Curr.Adv.Ecol.Sci., Curr.Cont., Curr.Cont.Abstr., Energy Ind., Energy Info.Abstr., Excerp.Med., Forest.Abstr., Forest Prod.Abstr., Geo.Abstr., Helminthol.Abstr., Herb.Abstr., Rev.Appl.Entomol., Sci.Cit.Ind., Soils & Fert., Sport Fish.Abstr., Weed Abstr., Wild.Rev., Zoo.Rec. **Document type:** academic/scholarly publication.
—BLDSC (3829.741000); CASDDS; CISTI; Ei; Genuine Article; Linda Hall; SWETS; UnCover. **CCC.**
Formerly: Revue d'Ecologie et de Biologie du Sol (ISSN 0035-1822)
Description: Examines biology and ecology of the soil; also focuses on interactions of soil organisms and the ecosystem balance.

EUROPEAN JOURNAL OF ULTRASOUND. see MEDICAL SCIENCES — Radiology And Nuclear Medicine

EVOLUTION & HUMAN BEHAVIOR. see SOCIAL SCIENCES: COMPREHENSIVE WORKS

570 573 US ISSN 0272-0809
EVOLUTIONARY MONOGRAPHS. 1979. irreg. price varies. University of Chicago, Department of Ecology and Evolution, 1101 E. 57th St., Chicago, IL 60637. TEL 312-702-9475. Ed. Leigh M. Van Valen. circ. 200 (paid). **Indexed:** Biol.Abstr., Deep Sea Res.& Oceanogr.Abstr., GeoRef. **Document type:** academic/scholarly publication, monographic series
—BLDSC (3834.452000).
Description: Publishes long papers and other nonstandard items in the evolutionary half of biology and historical geology.
Refereed Serial

570   US   ISSN 0093-4755
QH359   CODEN: EVTHB4
EVOLUTIONARY THEORY; an international journal of fact and interpretation. 1973. irreg. $28. University of Chicago, Department of Ecology and Evolution, 1101 E. 57th St., Chicago, IL 60637. TEL 312-702-9475. Eds. Leigh M. Van Valen, Virginia C. Maiorana. bk.rev.; circ. 650 (paid). **Indexed:** Anim.Breed.Abstr., Biol.Abstr., Biostat., Bull.Signal., Curr.Adv.Ecol.Sci., Curr.Cont., Deep Sea Res.& Oceanogr.Abstr., GeoRef. **Document type:** academic/scholarly publication.
—BLDSC (3834.455200); Linda Hall; UnCover.
Description: Publishes factual and theoretical papers and reviews on topics in evolutionary biology.
Refereed Serial

570 610   SZ   ISSN 0071-335X
                        CODEN: EXPSAU
EXPERIENTIA. SUPPLEMENTUM. (Text in English, French and German) 1953. irreg., latest 1996. price varies. Birkhaeuser Verlag, P.O. Box 133, CH-4010 Basel, Switzerland. TEL 41-61-7217784. FAX 41-61-7217950. E-mail: orders@birkhauser. ch. **Indexed:** Biol.Abstr., Chem.Abstr., Ind.Med. **Document type:** academic/scholarly publication.
—CASDDS; CISTI; KNAW. **CCC.**
Description: Covers new research in medical biology.

595.72   UK   ISSN 0168-8162
                        CODEN: EAACEM
EXPERIMENTAL & APPLIED ACAROLOGY. (Text and summaries in English) 1985. m. £225 (foreign $375) to individuals; institutions £535 (foreign $890) (effective 1998). Thomson Science (Subsidiary of: International Thomson Publishing Group), 2-6 Boundary Row, London SE1 8HN, England. TEL 44-171-8560066. FAX 44-171-5229623. TELEX 290164 CHAPMA G. E-mail: jhelp@chall.co.uk; URL: http://www.thomsonscience.com. (Subscr. to: International Thomson Publishing Services Ltd., Cheriton House, North Way, Andover. Hants. SP10 5BE, England. TEL 44-1264-342713. FAX 44-1264-342807; Subscr. in US & Canada to: 400 Market St., Philadelphia, PA 19106. TEL 800-552-5866) Eds. F. Jongeman, L.P.S. van der Geest. adv.; bk.rev.; illus.; index. circ. 1,000. (back issues avail.; reprint service avail. from ISI) **Indexed:** Apic.Abstr., ASCA, Bio-Contr.News & Info., Biol.Abstr., Curr.Cont., Ecol.Abstr., Entomol.Abstr., Environ.Per.Bibl. (1991-1994), Excerp.Med., Fababean Abstr., Hort.Abstr., IDA, Ind.Vet., Poult.Abstr., Rev.Appl.Entomol., Rev.Med.& Vet.Mycol., Soils & Fert., Sport Fish.Abstr., Vet.Bull., Wild.Rev., Zoo.Rec. **Document type:** academic/scholarly publication.
●Also available online.
—BLDSC (3838.620000); CASDDS; CISTI; EMDOCS; Genuine Article; Linda Hall; SWETS; UMI; UnCover. **CCC.**
Description: Brings together basic and applied research on various acarine groups, so that acarologists may more easily keep abreast of developments in related fields.
Refereed Serial

570   GW   ISSN 1430-3418
▼**EXPERIMENTAL BIOLOGY ONLINE.** 1996. irreg. free. (Society for Experimental Biology) Springer-Verlag, Heidelberger Platz 3, 14197 Berlin, Germany. TEL 49-30-82787-0. FAX 49-30-82787448. E-mail: subscriptions@springer.de; URL: http://link.springer.de. Ed.Bd. **Document type:** academic/scholarly publication.
●Available only online.
—**CCC.**
Description: Specializes in short, topical research papers in experimental biology organized in three sections: animal biology, plant biology, and cell biology.
Refereed Serial

EXPERIMENTAL PARASITOLOGY. see *MEDICAL SCIENCES — Communicable Diseases*

570   US   ISSN 0892-6638
QH301   CODEN: FAJOEC
F A S E B JOURNAL. 1942. m. $95 to non-members (foreign $148); institutions $225 (foreign $273). Federation of American Societies for Experimental Biology, 9650 Rockville Pike, Bethesda, MD 20814. TEL 301-530-7100. FAX 301-571-1855. Ed. William J. Whelan. adv.; abstr.; charts; illus.; index. circ. 24,000. (also avail. in microform; back issues avail.; reprint service avail. from UMI) **Indexed:** Anim.Breed.Abstr., ASCA, Bibl.Agri., Biol.Abstr., Biotech.Abstr., Chem.Abstr., Chem.Cit.Ind., Curr.Adv.Cancer Res., Curr.Adv.Ecol.Sci., Curr.Cont., Dairy Sci.Abstr., Excerp.Med., Food Sci.& Tech.Abstr., Helminthol.Abstr., Ind.Med., Ind.Sci.Rev., INIS Atomind., Med.& Surg.Dermat., NRN, Sci.Cit.Ind., Sport Fish.Abstr., SSCI, THA, Trop.Dis.Bull., Wild.Rev., Zoo.Rec. **Document type:** academic/scholarly publication.
—BLDSC (3896.579700); CASDDS; CISTI; EMDOCS; Genuine Article; KNAW; KR SourceOne; Linda Hall; SWETS; UMI; UnCover. **CCC.**
Supersedes: Federation of American Societies for Experimental Biology. Federation Proceedings (ISSN 0014-9446)
Description: Presents scholarly papers on and reviews of research in experimental biology, encompassing physiology, biological chemistry, pharmacology, experimental therapeutics, immunology, nutrition, and cell biology.
Refereed Serial

FACULTAD NACIONAL DE AGRONOMIA MEDELLIN. REVISTA. see *AGRICULTURE*

FAELTBIOLOGEN. see *ENVIRONMENTAL STUDIES*

FAUNA ENTOMOLOGICA SCANDINAVICA. see *BIOLOGY — Entomology*

570   FR   ISSN 0428-2779
                        CODEN: FBIOAA
FEUILLETS DE BIOLOGIE; le repertoire medical pratique. 1960. bi-m. 740 F. (effective 1997). Editions Orion, 9 av. du Bel Air, 95870 Bezons, France. TEL 33-1-39472260. FAX 33-1-30762212. Ed. Dr. Bernard Bousquet. adv.; bk.rev.; bibl.; charts; illus. circ. 4,000. **Indexed:** Biol.Abstr., Chem.Abstr., Excerp.Med., Rev.Med.& Vet.Mycol.
—BLDSC (3913.600000); CASDDS; EMDOCS; SWETS.

570   JA   ISSN 0917-4850
FIRUDO BAIOROJISUTO/FIELD BIOLOGIST. (Text in Japanese) 1991. s-a. 5000 Yen. Gunma Yagai Seibutsu Gakkai - Field Biologist's Society of Gunma, c/o Mr. S. Saito, Gunma Pref. Women's University, 1395 Kaminote, Tamamuramachi, Sawa-gun, Gunma-ken 370-11, Japan. TEL 0270-65-8511. FAX 0270-65-9538. Ed. Yukio Shishida. bk.rev.; circ. 500 (controlled). **Document type:** academic/scholarly publication.
Description: Covers ecology, systematics, biogeography, and natural environment.
Refereed Serial

578.77   UK   ISSN 1050-4648
QL638.97   CODEN: FSIMEP
FISH AND SHELLFISH IMMUNOLOGY. 1991. 8/yr. £214 (effective 1998). Academic Press Ltd. (Subsidiary of: Harcourt Brace & Company Ltd.), 24-28 Oval Rd., London NW1 7DX, England. TEL 44-171-267-4466. FAX 44-171-482-2293. TELEX 25775 ACPRES G. E-mail: apsubs@acad.com; URL: http://www.hbuk.co.uk./ap/fsi; http://www.europe.idealibrary.com/. (Subscr. to: Harcourt Brace & Company Ltd., Foots Cray High St., Sidcup, Kent DA14 5HP, England. TEL 44-181-300-3322. FAX 44-180-309-0807) Eds. A.E. Ellis, C. Secombes. R&P contact: Catherine John. adv. contact: Nik Screen. (reprint service avail. from SWZ) **Indexed:** ASCA, Curr.Cont., Sport Fish.Abstr., Wild.Rev., Zoo.Rec. **Document type:** academic/scholarly publication.
●Also available online.
—BLDSC (3934.880000); CISTI; Genuine Article; SWETS; UnCover. **CCC.**
Description: Presents studies on the basic mechanisms of both the specific and nonspecific defense systems, the cells, tissues, and hormonal factors involved, their dependence on environmental and intrinsic factors, response to pathogens, response to vaccination, and applied studies on the development of specific vaccines for use in the aquaculture industry.
Refereed Serial

578.77   US   ISSN 0095-0157
                        CODEN: FMPUA4
FLORIDA MARINE RESEARCH PUBLICATIONS. 1973. irreg. exchange basis. Florida Marine Research Institute, Department of Environmental Protection, 100 8th Ave. S.E., St. Petersburg, FL 33701. FAX 813-823-0166. Ed. K.A. Steidinger. charts; illus. circ. 1,000. **Indexed:** Aqua.Sci.& Fish.Abstr., Biol.Abstr., Curr.Adv.Ecol.Sci., Deep Sea Res.& Oceanogr.Abstr., Ocean.Abstr., Sport Fish.Abstr., Wild.Rev., Zoo.Rec.
—BLDSC (3956.070000); CISTI; Linda Hall.
Supersedes its: Educational Series, Leaflet Series, Professional Papers, Saltwater Fishery Leaflets, Special Scientific Report, and Technical Series.

508   US
QH1   CODEN: BFMSEU
FLORIDA MUSEUM OF NATURAL HISTORY. BULLETIN. 1956. irreg. price varies. Florida Museum of Natural History, University of Florida, Museum Rd., Box 117800, Gainesville, FL 32611-7800. TEL 352-392-1721. FAX 352-846-0267. E-mail: rjbryant@flmnh.ufl.edu; URL: http://www.flmnh.edu/admin/bulletin.htm. Eds. John F. Eisenberg, Richard Franz. R&P contact: Rhoda J. Bryant. cum.index. circ. 700. **Indexed:** Biol.Abstr., Curr.Adv.Ecol.Sci., Deep Sea Res.& Oceanogr.Abstr., GeoRef., Sport Fish.Abstr., Wild.Rev., Zoo.Rec. **Document type:** monographic series, academic/scholarly publication.
—CISTI; Linda Hall.
Former titles: Florida Museum of Natural History. Bulletin. Biological Sciences (ISSN 1052-3669); (until 1990): Florida State Museum. Bulletin. Biological Sciences (ISSN 0071-6154)
Description: Presents the results of research in the natural sciences, emphasizing the circum-Caribbean region.

570 610   UK   ISSN 1350-4975
FOCUS ON BRITISH BIOLOGICAL AND MEDICAL SCIENCES RESEARCH. 1994. m. £28 (foreign £33) (effective 1997). British Library, Document Supply Centre, Boston Spa, Wetherby, W. Yorks LS23 7BQ, England. TEL 44-1937-546080. FAX 44-1937-546286. TELEX 557381. (Subscr. to: Turpin Distribution Services Ltd., Blackhorse Rd., Letchworth, Herts. SG6 1HN, England. TEL 44-1462-672555. FAX 44-1462-480947) adv.; index. **Document type:** bibliography.
—BLDSC (3964.203853).

FOLIA BIOCHIMICA ET BIOLOGICA GRAECA. see *BIOLOGY — Biological Chemistry*

570   XR   ISSN 0015-5500
QH301   CODEN: FOBLAN
FOLIA BIOLOGICA. (Text and summaries in English) 1955. bi-m. £124 (effective 1997). Ceska Akademie Ved, Ustav Molekularni Genetiky - Czech Academy of Sciences, Institute of Molecular Genetics, Flemingovo nam. 2, 166-37 Prague, Czech Republic. TEL 44-171-267-4466. FAX 44-171-482-2293. TELEX 25775 ACPRES G. (Dist. by: Harcourt Brace & Company Ltd., Foots Cray High St., Sidcup, Kent DA14 5HP, England. TEL 44-181-300-3322. FAX 44-181-309-0807) Eds. J. Rlman, I. Hlozanek. R&P contact: Catherine John. adv. contact: Nik Screen. bk.rev.; abstr.; charts; illus.; index. circ. 950. **Indexed:** Anim.Breed.Abstr., Biol.Abstr., C.I.S. Abstr., Chem.Abstr., Curr.Adv.Cancer Res., Curr.Adv.Ecol.Sci., Curr.Cont., Dairy Sci.Abstr., Excerp.Med., Helminthol.Abstr., Ind.Med., Ind.Sci.Rev., Ind.Vet., INIS Atomind., Sci.Cit.Ind., Vet.Bull. **Document type:** academic/scholarly publication.
—BLDSC (3967.000000); CASDDS; CISTI; Genuine Article; KNAW; Linda Hall; SWETS; UnCover. **CCC.**
Description: Publishes reports on the results of original research in the field of molecular and cellular biology.

BIOLOGY

570   PL   ISSN 0015-5497
CODEN: FOBGA8
FOLIA BIOLOGICA; international journal of biological research. (Text and summaries in English) 1953. q. $40. Polska Akademia Nauk, Instytut Systematyki i Ewolucji Zwierzat - Polish Academy of Sciences, Institute of Systematics and Evolution of Animals, Ul. Slawkowska 17, 31-016 Krakow, Poland. TEL 48-12-227006. FAX 48-12-224294. TELEX 0322414 PAN PL. (Dist. by: Ars Polona, Krakowskie Przedmiescie 7, 00-068 Warsaw, Poland) Ed. Halina Kosciuszko. R&P contact: Halina Kosciuszko. adv. contact: Ewa Zychowska. bk.rev.; abstr.; bibl.; charts; illus.; index; circ. 500 (paid). **Indexed:** AgroAgen, Anim.Breed.Abstr., Biol.Abstr., Chem.Abstr., Curr.Adv.Ecol.Sci., Curr.Cont., Dent.Ind., Excerp.Med., Ind.Med., Ind.Sci.Rev., INIS Atomind., Plant Breed.Abstr. **Document type:** academic/scholarly publication.
—BLDSC (3966.900000); CASDDS; CISTI; Genuine Article; Linda Hall.
Description: Publishes papers concerning various aspects of experimental zoology, nuclear and chromosome research and ultrastructural studies.
Refereed Serial

570   NE   ISSN 0920-2676
FOLIA BIOTHEORETICA. 1936. irreg. price varies. Kluwer Academic Publishers, Postbus 17, 3300 AA Dordrecht, Netherlands. TEL 31-78-6392255. FAX 31-78-6392254. TELEX 29245 KAPG NL. E-mail: services@wkap.nl; URL: http://www.wkap.nl. (Dist. by: Kluwer Academic Publishers Group, P.O. Box 322, 3300 AH Dordrecht, Netherlands. TEL 31-78-6392392. FAX 31-78-6546474; N. America dist. addr.: Box 358, Accord Sta., Hingham, MA 02018-0358. TEL 617-871-6600. FAX 617-871-6528) **Document type:** monographic series.
Refereed Serial

FOLIA DENDROLOGICA. see *FORESTS AND FORESTRY*

570   XR
CODEN: FFUBAP
FOLIA FACULTATIS SCIENTIARUM NATURALIUM UNIVERSITATIS MASARYKIANAE BRUNENSIS: BIOLOGIA. a. price varies. Masarykova Universita, Prirodovedecka Fakulta - Masaryk University, Faculty of Sciences, Kotlarska 2, 611 37 Brno, Czech Republic. **Indexed:** Biol.Abstr., Chem.Abstr., Helminthol.Abstr. **Document type:** academic/scholarly publication, monographic series.
—BLDSC (3965.862000); CASDDS; CISTI; Linda Hall.
Formerly: Folia Facultatis Scientiarum Naturalium Universitatis Purkynianae Brunensis: Biologia (ISSN 0323-0082)

571.3   PL   ISSN 0015-5659
QL799   CODEN: FOMOAJ
FOLIA MORPHOLOGICA. (Text in English) 1929. q. 60 Zl. Polskie Towarzystwo Anatomiczne - Polish Anatomical Society, c/o Akademia Medyczna w Poznaniu, Zaklad Anatomii, Ul. Swieckiego 6, 60-781 Poznan, Poland. TEL 48-61-699181. FAX 48-61-658985. Ed. Prof. Witold Wozniak. adv.; bk.rev.; charts; illus.; index. circ. 870. **Indexed:** Biol.Abstr., Chem.Abstr., Dent.Ind., Excerp.Med., Ind.Med., INIS Atomind., Vet.Bull. **Document type:** bulletin.
—BLDSC (3971.610000); CASDDS; CISTI; KNAW; Linda Hall.
Refereed Serial

616.079   UK   ISSN 0954-0105
CODEN: FAIMEZ
FOOD AND AGRICULTURAL IMMUNOLOGY. 1989. q. £116($198) to individuals; institutions £348 ($572) (effective 1997). Carfax Publishing Co., P.O. Box 25, Abingdon, Oxon. OX14 3UE, England. TEL 44-1235-401000. FAX 44-1235-401550. E-mail: enquiries@carfax.co.uk. (Subscr. in N. America to: Carfax Publishing Co., 875-81 Massachusetts Ave., Cambridge, MA 02139) Ed. M.R.A. Morgan. **Indexed:** ASCA, Biodet.Abstr., Food Sci.& Tech.Abstr. **Document type:** academic/scholarly publication.
—BLDSC (3977.004500); CASDDS; CISTI; EMDOCS; Genuine Article; SWETS; UMI. **CCC.**
Description: Features original immunological research with food, agricultural, environmental and veterinary applications.
Refereed Serial

FOREST ECOLOGY AND MANAGEMENT; an international journal. see *FORESTS AND FORESTRY*

570 550   NE   ISSN 1381-2491
QH7
FOUNDATION FOR SCIENTIFIC RESEARCH IN THE CARIBBEAN REGION. PUBLICATION. (Text in English) 1946. irreg. no.137, 1996. price varies. Foundation for Scientific Research in the Caribbean Region - Natuurwetenschappelijke Studiekring voor het Caraibische Gebied, Instituut voor Taxonomische Zoologie, Plantage Middenlaan 45, 1018 DC Amsterdam, Netherlands. TEL 31-20-5255926. FAX 31-20-5256612. Ed. Louise J. van der Steen. R&P contact: Louise J. Westermann. (back issues avail.) **Indexed:** Biol.Abstr., GeoRef. **Document type:** monographic series.
Formerly (until 1990): Natuurwetenschappelijke Studiekring voor Suriname en de Nederlandse Antillen. Uitgaven (ISSN 0300-5534)

FRANC - VERT. see *CONSERVATION*

570   US   ISSN 0891-5849
QP527   CODEN: FRBMEH
FREE RADICAL BIOLOGY & MEDICINE. 1985. 14/yr. fl.2272($1306) (effective 1998). (Oxygen Society) Elsevier Science Inc., Box 945, New York, NY 10159-0945. TEL 212-633-3730. FAX 212-633-3680. E-mail: nlinfo-f@elsevier.nl; usinfo-f@elsevier.com; forinfo-kyf04035@niftyserve.or.jp; URL: http://www.elsevier.nl/. (Subscr. outside the Americas to: Elsevier Science, Regional Sales Office, P.O. Box 211, 1000 AE Amsterdam, Netherlands. TEL 31-20-4853757. FAX 31-20-4853432; Subscr. in Australasia and the Far East to: Elsevier Science (Singapore) Pte Ltd, No.1 Temasek Ave., No.17-01 Millenia Tower, Singapore 039192, Singapore. TEL 65-434-3727. FAX 65-337-2230; Subscr. in Japan to: Elsevier Science Japan, 9-15 Higashi-Azabu 1-chome, Minato-ku, Tokyo 106, Japan. TEL 81-3-5561-5033. FAX 81-3-5561-5047) Eds. K.J.A. Davies, W.A. Pryor. (also avail. in microform from UMI; back issues avail.) **Indexed:** ASCA, Chem.Cit.Ind., Curr.Adv.Biochem., Curr.Adv.Cell & Devel.Biol., Curr.Adv.Ecol.Sci., Curr.Cont., Excerp.Med., Ind.Sci.Rev., INIS Atomind., Neurosci.Cit.Ind., Sci.Cit.Ind., THA. **Document type:** academic/scholarly publication.
—BLDSC (4033.326480); ADONIS; CASDDS; CISTI; EMDOCS; Genuine Article; KNAW; SWETS; UMI; UnCover. **CCC.**
Formed by the merger of: Advances in Free Radical Biology and Medicine (ISSN 8755-9668); Journal of Free Radicals in Biology and Medicine; Which was formerly: Journal of Free Radicals in Biology (ISSN 0748-5514)
Refereed Serial

577 333.7   II
▼**FRENCH INSTITUTE, PONDICHERRY. PONDY PAPERS IN ECOLOGY**. (Text in English; summaries in French) 1997. irreg. (approx. 3/yr.). price varies. Institut Francais de Pondichery, P.O. Box 33, Pondichery 605 001, India. TEL 91-413-34-170. FAX 91-413-39-534. E-mail: instran@giasmd01.vsnl.net.in. Ed. F. Houllier. circ. 250.

578.77   UK   ISSN 0308-6739
CODEN: OPFAEI
FRESHWATER BIOLOGICAL ASSOCIATION. OCCASIONAL PUBLICATIONS. 1976. irreg. price varies. Freshwater Biological Association, The Ferry House, Ambleside, Cumbria LA22 0LP, England. Ed. D.W. Sutcliffe. circ. 400. (also avail. in microfiche; back issues avail.) **Indexed:** Curr.Adv.Ecol.Sci., Forest.Abstr., Math.R., Soils & Fert. **Document type:** academic/scholarly publication, monographic series.
—BLDSC (6225.650000).

578.77   UK   ISSN 0367-1887
CODEN: FBSPAT
FRESHWATER BIOLOGICAL ASSOCIATION. SCIENTIFIC PUBLICATIONS. a. price varies. Freshwater Biological Association, The Ferry House, Ambleside, Cumbria LA22 0LP, England. Eds. J.M. Elliott, D.W. Sutcliffe. circ. 2,500. (also avail. in microfiche; back issues avail.) **Indexed:** Biol.Abstr., Curr.Adv.Ecol.Sci., Deep Sea Res.& Oceanogr.Abstr., Sport Fish.Abstr., Wild.Rev., Zoo.Rec. **Document type:** academic/scholarly publication.
—BLDSC (8191.000000); CISTI.

578.77   UK   ISSN 0046-5070
QH96.A1   CODEN: FWBLAB
FRESHWATER BIOLOGY. 1971. 8/yr. £728($1329.50) (foreign £801) (effective 1998). Blackwell Science Ltd., Osney Mead, Oxford OX2 OEL, England. TEL 44-1865-206206. FAX 44-1865-721205. E-mail: journals.cs@blacksci.co.uk; URL: http://www.black.co.uk. Eds. C.R. Townsend, A.G. Hildrew; Pub. Allen Stevens. R&P contact: Sarah Pollard. adv. contact: Martine Cariou-Keen. abstr.; charts; illus.; stat.; index. circ. 805. (also avail. in microform from UMI; back issues avail.; reprint service avail. from ISI) **Indexed:** Abstr.Bull.Inst.Pap.Chem., Acid Pre.Dig., ASCA, Bio-Contr.News & Info., Biol.Abstr., Biol.& Agr.Ind., Chem.Abstr., Curr.Adv.Ecol.Sci., Curr.Cont., Curr.Ref.Fish Res., Deep Sea Res.& Oceanogr.Abstr., Ecol.Abstr., Environ.Per.Bibl. (1990-), Excerp.Med., Geo.Abstr.P.G., Geol.Abstr., Helminthol.Abstr., Ind.Sci.Rev., Rev.Appl.Entomol., Sci.Cit.Ind., Sel.J.Water, Sel.Water Res.Abstr., Sport Fish.Abstr., W.R.C.Inf., Weed Abstr., Wild.Rev., Zoo.Rec. **Document type:** academic/scholarly publication.
—BLDSC (4037.200000); CASDDS; CISTI; EMDOCS; Genuine Article; KR SourceOne; Linda Hall; SWETS; UMI; UnCover. **CCC.**
Refereed Serial

FUCHAKU SEIBUTSU KENKYU/MARINE FOULING. see *EARTH SCIENCES — Oceanography*

570   JA   ISSN 0910-8750
FUJI KEIZAI FUZOKU ABE KENKYUJO KENKYU HOKOKU/FUJI KEIZAI. ABE RESEARCH LABORATORY. INVESTIGATION AND RESEARCH REPORT. (Text in Japanese) 1979. bi-m. 18000 Yen. Fuji Keizai, Fuzoku Abe Kenkyujo - Fuji Keizai, Abe Research Laboratory, F.K. Bldg., 2-5 Kodenmacho, Nihonbashi, Chuo-ku, Tokyo 103, Japan. TEL 03-3664-5820. FAX 03661-6920. Ed. Hideo Abe. adv.: page $2000; adv. contact: Masakazu Nagamine. circ. 3,000.
Description: Covers taxonomy, physiology, ecology and more.

570   JA   ISSN 0917-4362
FUJI WOMEN'S COLLEGE. BIOLOGICAL LABORATORY. OCCASIONAL PUBLICATIONS/FUJI JOSHI DAIGAKU. FUJI JOSHI TANKI DAIGAKU. SEIBUTSUGAKU KENKYUSHITSU. KACHURUI SHUISHU. (Text in English) 1970. irreg. exchange basis. Fuji Joshi Daigaku, Seibutsu Kenkyushitsu - Fuji Women's College, Biological Laboratory, Kita-16, Nishi-2, Kita-ku, Sapporo, Hokkaido 001, Japan. TEL 81-11-736-0311. FAX 81-11-709-8541. Ed. Masaharu Kawakatsu. **Document type:** academic/scholarly publication.

570   JA   ISSN 0912-0300
FUKUSHIMA SEIBUTSU/FUKUSHIMA BIOLOGICAL SOCIETY. JOURNAL. (Text in Japanese) 1958. a. Fukushimaken Seibutsu Dokokai - Fukushima Biological Society, Fukushima Daigaku Kyoikugakubu Seibutsugaku Kyoshitsu, 2 Naomichi, Asakawa, Matsukawamachi, Fukushima-shi, Fukushima-ken 960-12, Japan.

FUKUYAMA DAIGAKU FUZOKU NAIKAI SEIBUTSU SHIGEN KENKYUJO HOKOKU/FUKUYAMA UNIVERSITY. RESEARCH INSTITUTE OF MARINE BIORESOURCES. REPORT. see *EARTH SCIENCES — Oceanography*

573.6   US   ISSN 0895-1942
QK623.S73   CODEN: FGNEEA
FUNGAL GENETICS NEWSLETTER. 1962. a. $15 (online free) (effective 1997). Fungal Genetics Stock Center, University of Kansas Medical School, Department of Microbiology, Kansas City, KS 66160-7420. TEL 913-588-7044. FAX 913-588-7295. E-mail: fgsc@kuhub.cc.ukans.edu; URL: http://www.kumc.edu/*fgsc. Ed. Peter J. Russell. R&P contact: Kevin McCluskey. TEL 913-588-7044. circ. 1,000. (back issues avail.) **Indexed:** Biol.Abstr., Rev.Plant Path. **Document type:** newsletter.
●Also available online.
—BLDSC (4056.650000).
Formerly: Neurospora Newsletter (ISSN 0028-3975)
Description: Publishes articles, bibliographies and addresses for researches in fungal genetics.

578.77   DK   ISSN 0416-704X
GALATHEA REPORT; scientific results of the Danish expedition to the coast of Tropical West Africa 1950-52. (Text in English) 1956. irreg., vol. 17. price varies. Apollo Books Aps., Kirkeby Sand 19, DK-5771 Stenstrup, Denmark. TEL 45-62-26-37-37. FAX 45-62-26-37-80.

GALAXEA. see *EARTH SCIENCES — Oceanography*

GAME BIRD AND CONSERVATIONISTS GAZETTE. see *CONSERVATION*

GARCIA DE ORTA: SERIE DE ANTROPOBIOLOGIA. see *ANTHROPOLOGY*

578.77   CL   ISSN 0716-9655
GAYANA: OCEANOLOGIA. (Text in English or Spanish) 1971. s-a. Universidad de Concepcion, Facultad de Ciencias Naturales y Oceanograficas, Casilla 2407, Concepcion, Chile. FAX 56-41-240280. (Subscr. to: Editorial Universidad de Concepcion, Depto. Ventas, Cas. 1557, Concepcion, Chile) Ed. Andres O. Angulo. adv. contact: Alejandro Wittker. **Indexed:** Biol.Abstr. **Document type:** abstracting/indexing, directory.
    Formerly: Gayana: Miscelanea (ISSN 0374-7999)

GENERAL AND DIAGNOSTIC PATHOLOGY. see *MEDICAL SCIENCES*

570 550   II   ISSN 0251-1223
QH301   CODEN: GBOSBU
GEOBIOS; an international journal of life sciences on earth. (Text in English) 1974. q. $40 to individuals; institutions $80. Geobios, Zion, Box 14, Zion, 41B-B1-A, P.W.D. Colony, Jodhpur 342 001, India. Ed. D.N. Sen. adv./ bk.rev. (reprint service avail.) **Indexed:** Biol.Abstr., Br.Geol.Lit., Curr.Adv.Ecol.Sci., Excerp.Med., Geo.Abstr.P.G., Hort.Abstr., INIS Atomind. **Document type:** academic/scholarly publication.
    —BLDSC (4116.901500); CASDDS; CISTI; Linda Hall.

570 550   II   ISSN 0253-3340
QH301
GEOBIOS NEW REPORTS. (Text in English) 1982. biennial. $35 to individuals; institutions $70. Geobios, Zion, Box 14, Zion, 41B-B1-A, P.W.D. Colony, Jodhpur 342 001, India. Ed. David N. Sen. bk.rev. (reprint service avail.) **Indexed:** Curr.Adv.Ecol.Sci.

570   GW   ISSN 0368-2307
QH5   CODEN: JGNWA2
GESELLSCHAFT FUER NATURKUNDE IN WUERTTEMBERG. JAHRESHEFTE. 1845. a. DM.35 price varies. Gesellschaft fuer Naturkunde in Wuerttemberg e.V., Rosenstein 1, 70191 Stuttgart, Germany. TEL 0711-89360. Ed. Siegmund Seybold. circ. 1,100. **Indexed:** Biol.Abstr., GeoRef. **Document type:** proceedings.
    —Linda Hall.
    Formerly: Verein fuer Vaterlaendische Naturkunde in Wuerttemberg. Jahresheft.

570   KR   ISSN 0375-8990
                   CODEN: GBZUAM
GIDROBIOLOGICHESKII ZHURNAL = nauchnyi zhurnal. English translation: Hydrobiological Journal (US ISSN 0018-8166) (Text in Russian; summaries in English) 1965. bi-m. $410 (effective 1998). (Akademiya Nauk Ukrainy, Otdelenie Obshchei Biologii) Izdatel'stvo Naukova Dumka, c/o Yu.A. Khramov, Dir., Ul. Repina, 3, Kiev 252 601, Ukraine. TEL 418-60-04. (Subscr. to: Mezhdunarodnaya Kniga, ul. Dimitrova 39, Moscow G-200, Russia) Ed. V.D. Romanenko. **Indexed:** Biol.Abstr., Chem.Abstr., Deep Sea Res.& Oceanogr.Abstr., Helminthol.Abstr., INIS Atomind., Ocean.Abstr., Pollut.Abstr., Protozool.Abstr., Sel.Water Res.Abstr., Sport Fish.Abstr., Wild.Rev., Zoo.Rec. **Document type:** academic/scholarly publication.
    —BLDSC (0048.350000); CASDDS; CISTI; KNAW.

577   IT   ISSN 1121-8487
GIORNALE DELLA NATURA; mensile delle alternative del vivere ecologico. Key Title: Giornale della Natura Illustrato. 1986. m. L.40000($40) (effective Jan. 1997). Stampa Natura Solidarieta s.p.a., Via Bezzini 4, 20131 Milan, Italy. TEL 39-2-26680654. FAX 39-2-26680664. adv.; circ. 30,000 (paid). **Document type:** consumer publication.
    Description: Covers ecology-friendly products, organic agriculture and environment-conscious ways of living.

570 500   UK   ISSN 0373-241X
                 CODEN: GGNTAS
GLASGOW NATURALIST. 1908. a. £6. Glasgow Natural History Society, c/o Dr. J.R. Downie, Ed., Graham Kerr (Zoology) Bldg., University of Glasgow, Glasgow G12 8QQ, Scotland. TEL 44-141-330-5157. FAX 44-141-330-5971. E-mail: j.downie@bio.gla.ac.uk. R&P contact: Dr. J.R. Downie. adv.; bk.rev.; charts; illus.; cum.index every 5 yrs. circ. 500. (also avail. in microfilm from PMC) **Indexed:** Biol.Abstr., Curr.Adv.Ecol.Sci., Deep Sea Res.& Oceanogr.Abstr. **Document type:** academic/scholarly publication.
    —BLDSC (4184.000000).
    Description: Contains general articles, papers, and short notes on natural history of Scotland.
    Refereed Serial

577   CN
GLOBAL BIODIVERSITY MAGAZINE. French edition: Biodiversite Mondiale (ISSN 1195-311X) 1991. q. $26.75 to individuals; institutions $53.50 (effective 1997). Canadian Museum of Nature, Publishing Division, P.O. Box 3443, Stn. D, Ottawa, ON K1P 6P4, Canada. TEL 613-566-4209. FAX 613-566-4763. E-mail: biodiv@mus-nature.ca. Ed. Don E. McAllister. R&P contact: Susan Swan. adv. contact: Dory Cameron. bk.rev.; illus. **Indexed:** Can.B.P.I. **Document type:** academic/scholarly publication.
    —BLDSC (4195.351500). **CCC.**
    Former titles: Global Biodiversity Newsletter (ISSN 1195-3101); Canadian Biodiversity Newsletter.

570 170   IT
GLOBAL BIOETHICS. (Text in English) q. $90 to individuals; institutions $115 (effective 1995-96). (International Institute for the Study of Man) Angelo Pontecorboli Editore, c/o Inst. d'Antropologia, Universita di Firenze, Via del Proconsolo 12, 50122 Florence, Italy. TEL 39-55-2398065. FAX 39-55-283358. E-mail: antropos@cesit1.unifi.it. Ed. A.B. Chiarelli. bk.rev.; abstr. circ. 400. **Document type:** academic/scholarly publication.
    Formerly (until 1991): Problemi di Bioetica.
    Description: Forum for reflection and debate on all questions inherent in the generally-defined boundaries of bio-ethics, medical ethics and environmental ethics.

570   UK   ISSN 1354-1013
QC981.8.C5
▼**GLOBAL CHANGE BIOLOGY.** 1995. 8/yr. £290($530) (foreign £319) (effective 1998). Blackwell Science Ltd., Osney Mead, Oxford OX2 0EL, England. TEL 44-1865-206206. FAX 44-1865-721205. E-mail: journals.cs@blacksci.co.uk; URL: http://www.black.co.uk. Eds. S. Long, H. Smith; Pub. Allen Stevens. R&P contact: Sarah Pollard. adv. contact: Martine Cariou-Keen. circ. 255. (back issues avail.) **Indexed:** ASCA, Curr.Cont., Environ.Per.Bibl. **Document type:** academic/scholarly publication.
    —BLDSC (4195.358330); CISTI; Genuine Article. **CCC.**
    Description: Disseminates the latest research on the connection between current environmental change and biological systems.
    Refereed Serial

GORTANIA; atti del Museo Friulano di Storia Naturale. see *EARTH SCIENCES*

570   FR   ISSN 0154-0238
GROUPE D'ETUDE DES RYTHMES BIOLOGIQUES. BULLETIN. 1969. q. 100 F. Groupe d'Etude des Rythmes Biologiques, c/o Institut de Physiologie, Universite Louis Pasteur, 4 rue Kirschleger, 67085 Strasbourg Cedex, France. TEL 33-3-88358768. FAX 33-3-88243334. Ed. Bernard Canguilhem; Pub. Bernard Canguilhem. R&P contact: Bernard Canguilhem. adv. contact: Bernard Buisson. **Document type:** newsletter, bulletin.
    Refereed Serial

612.6   US   ISSN 1041-1232
QH511.A1   CODEN: GDAGE9
GROWTH, DEVELOPMENT & AGING. 1937. q. $90 to non-members (foreign $110); members $40 (foreign $50) (effective 1997). Growth Publishing Co., Inc., Box 42, Bar Harbor, ME 04609-0042. TEL 207-288-3533. FAX 207-288-6079. Ed. Dr. David E. Harrison. R&P contact: Dr. David E. Harrison. bk.rev.; bibl.; charts; illus.; index. circ. 625. (also avail. in microform from UMI,PMC; reprint service avail. from UMI,ISI) **Indexed:** Abstr.Anthropol., Anim.Breed.Abstr., ASCA, Biol.Abstr., Biol.& Agr.Ind., Chem.Abstr., Curr.Adv.Ecol.Sci., Curr.Cont., Dairy Sci.Abstr., Dent.Ind., Excerp.Med., Ind.Med., Ind.Sci.Rev., Ind.Vet., INIS Atomind., Mid.East: Abstr.& Ind., Nutr.Abstr., Sci.Cit.Ind., THA, Vet.Bull., W.R.C.Inf. **Document type:** academic/scholarly publication.
    —BLDSC (4223.032500); CASDDS; CISTI; Genuine Article; KNAW; KR SourceOne; Linda Hall; SWETS; UMI; UnCover.
    Formerly (until 1987): Growth (ISSN 0017-4793)
    Description: Devoted to problems of normal and abnormal growth patterns; relationship among growth, development and aging; and mathematical models related to these areas.
    Refereed Serial

GRUENSTIFT (BERLIN); das Umweltmagazin fuer Berlin und Brandenburg. see *CONSERVATION*

GUNNERIA. see *ARCHAEOLOGY*

570   TU   ISSN 0072-9221
                   CODEN: HFMBDA
HACETTEPE FEN VE MUHENDISLIK BILIMLERI DERGISI. SERI A: BIYOLOJI/HACETTEPE BULLETIN OF NATURAL SCIENCES AND ENGINEERING. SERIES A: BIOLOGY. (Text and summaries in English, Turkish) 1971. a. free. Hacettepe Universitesi, Fen Fakultesi - Hacettepe University, Faculty of Science, 06532 Beytepe, Ankara, Turkey. FAX 90-312-2352531. Ed. Hulya Cingi. adv.; illus. **Indexed:** INIS Atomind., Zoo.Rec. **Document type:** academic/scholarly publication.
    —CASDDS.
    Description: Publishes short to medium length research papers.
    Refereed Serial

HANDBOOK OF BEHAVIORAL NEUROBIOLOGY. see *MEDICAL SCIENCES — Psychiatry And Neurology*

HASTINGS CENTER REPORT. see *MEDICAL SCIENCES*

570   US   ISSN 0073-1331
QH91.A1
HAWAII INSTITUTE OF MARINE BIOLOGY. TECHNICAL REPORTS. 1964. irreg., no.39, 1988. price varies. Hawaii Institute of Marine Biology, University of Hawaii, Box 1346, Kaneohe, HI 96744. TEL 808-237-7401. FAX 808-247-6634. Ed. Philip Helfrich. circ. 200. **Indexed:** Deep Sea Res.& Oceanogr.Abstr., Ocean.Abstr. **Document type:** academic/scholarly publication.
    Refereed Serial

570   AI   ISSN 0002-2918
QH301   CODEN: BZARAZ
HAYASTANY KENSABANAKAN ANDES/BIOLOGICHESKII ZHURNAL ARMENII. (Text in Armenian, Russian; summaries in English) 1948. 4/yr. 400 dram. Akademiya Nauk Armenii, Pr. Marshala Bagramayana, 24, 375019 Erevan, Armenia. TEL 78852-524580. TELEX 243344. Ed. G.G. Batikian. abstr.; illus. **Indexed:** Anim.Breed.Abstr., Biodet.Abstr., Biol.Abstr., Chem.Abstr., Crop Physiol.Abstr., Dairy Sci.Abstr., Field Crop Abstr., Food Sci.& Tech.Abstr., Forest.Abstr., Herb.Abstr., Hort.Abstr., INIS Atomind., Maize Abstr., Plant Breed.Abstr., Poult.Abstr., Rev.Plant Path., Seed Abstr., Sel.Water Res.Abstr., Soils & Fert., Triticale Abstr., Vet.Bull., VITIS. **Document type:** academic/scholarly publication.
    —CISTI.

570   JA   ISSN 0910-6855
HEKICHI SEITAI KAGAKU KENKYUJO KENKYU KIYO/INSTITUTE FOR ECOLOGICAL SCIENCE IN REMOTE DISTRICT. BULLETIN. (Text in English, Japanese) 1974. a. Hekichi Seitai Kagaku Kenkyujo, 3311-1, Yakushiji, Minamikawachimachi, Kawachi-gun, Tochigi-ken 329-04, Japan. **Document type:** bulletin.

BIOLOGY

HELICITE; journal of Australasian cave research. see EARTH SCIENCES — Geology

HIROSAKI DAIGAKU RIGAKUBU FUZOKU FUKAURA RINKAI JISSHUJO HOKOKU/HIROSAKI UNIVERSITY. FUKAURA MARINE BIOLOGICAL LABORATORY. REPORT. see EARTH SCIENCES — Oceanography

HIROSAKI IGAKU/HIROSAKI MEDICAL JOURNAL. see MEDICAL SCIENCES

570   JA   ISSN 0367-5912
QH301   CODEN: HIRKAC
HIROSHIMA DAIGAKU SEIBUTSU GAKKAISHI/BIOLOGICAL SOCIETY OF HIROSHIMA UNIVERSITY. BULLETIN. (Text in English, Japanese) 1934. a. Hiroshima Daigaku Seibutsu Gakkai - Biological Society of Hiroshima University, Hiroshima Daigaku Rigakubu, 1-89 Higashisendacho 1-chome, Naka-ku, Hiroshima-shi, Hiroshima-ken 730. **Indexed:** Jap.Per.Ind.
—CASDDS.

HIROSHIMA UNIVERSITY. LABORATORY FOR AMPHIBIAN BIOLOGY. SCIENTIFIC REPORT. see BIOLOGY — Zoology

HIROSHIMA UNIVERSITY. MUKAISHIMA MARINE BIOLOGICAL STATION. CONTRIBUTIONS. see EARTH SCIENCES — Oceanography

HISTORIA NATURAL. see SCIENCES: COMPREHENSIVE WORKS

HISTORICAL BIOLOGY; an international journal of paleobiology. see PALEONTOLOGY

570 550   UK
HISTORICAL STUDIES IN THE LIFE AND EARTH SCIENCES. irreg., no.2, 1994. Natural History Museum, Cromwell Rd., London SW7 5BD, England. TEL 44-171-938-8761. FAX 44-171-938-8709. **Document type:** monographic series.

HISTORICAL STUDIES IN THE PHYSICAL AND BIOLOGICAL SCIENCES. see SCIENCES: COMPREHENSIVE WORKS

570   UK   ISSN 0391-9714
QH305   CODEN: HPLSDO
HISTORY AND PHILOSOPHY OF THE LIFE SCIENCES. 1916. 3/yr. £121($199) to institutions (effective 1998). (Stazione Zoologica di Napoli, IT) Taylor & Francis Ltd., 1 Gunpowder Sq., London EC4A 3DE, England. TEL 44-171-583-0490. FAX 44-171-583-0585. TELEX 858540. E-mail: info@tandf.co.uk; URL: http://www.tandf.co.uk/. (Subscr. in N. America to: Taylor & Francis Inc., 1900 Frost Rd., Ste. 101, Bristol, PA 19007-1598. TEL 800-821-8312. FAX 215-785-5515) Ed. M.D. Grmek. bk.rev. (back issues avail.) **Indexed:** Amer.Hist.& Life (1983-1994), Arts & Hum.Cit.Ind., ASCA, Hist.Abstr. (1983-1994), Ind.Med., SSCI. **Document type:** academic/scholarly publication.
—BLDSC (4317.820000); CISTI; Genuine Article; SWETS; UnCover. **CCC.**
Supersedes in part (in 1979): Stazione Zoologica di Napoli. Pubblicazioni (ISSN 0039-081X)
Description: Explores the historical development of the life sciences and the social and epistemological implications.
Refereed Serial

570   JA   ISSN 0018-3393
QH301   CODEN: HKDSBF
HOKKAIDO KYOIKU DAIGAKU KIYO. DAI-2-BU, B. SEIBUTSUGAKU, CHIGAKU, NOGAKU-HEN/HOKKAIDO UNIVERSITY OF EDUCATION. JOURNAL. SECTION 2 B. BIOLOGY, GEOLOGY, AND AGRICULTURE. (Text in English, French, Japanese; summaries in English) vol.32, 1982. s-a. exchange basis. Hokkaido University of Education - Hokkaido Kyoiku Daigaku, Ainosato 5-jo, 3-chome, Kita-ku, Sapporo-shi, Hokkaido 002, Japan. circ. 500. **Indexed:** Biol.Abstr., Chem.Abstr. **Document type:** bulletin.

570   II   ISSN 0441-2370
HORNBILL. (Text in English) 1976. q. £15($30) Bombay Natural History Society, Hornbill House, Shaheed Bhagat Singh Rd., Bombay 400 023, India. TEL 244085. Ed.Bd. adv.; bk.rev. circ. 3,000. (back issues avail.) **Indexed:** Biol.Abstr., Curr.Adv.Ecol.Sci., Forest.Abstr., Key Word Ind.Wildl.Res.

HRVATSKA AKADEMIJA ZNANOSTI I UMJETNOSTI. RAZRED ZA PRIRODNE ZNANOSTI. RAD. see EARTH SCIENCES — Geology

HUAXI YIKE DAXUE XUEBAO/WEST CHINA UNIVERSITY OF MEDICAL SCIENCES. JOURNAL. see MEDICAL SCIENCES

570   US   ISSN 0018-7143
GN1   CODEN: HUBIAA
HUMAN BIOLOGY (DETROIT). 1929. bi-m. $70 to individuals; institutions $132 (effective 1997). Wayne State University Press, 4809 Woodward Ave., Detroit, MI 48201-1309. TEL 313-577-6120. FAX 313-577-6131. Ed. Michael Crawford. R&P contact: Mary Garcia. bk.rev.; charts; index. circ. 1,654. (also avail. in microform from UMI; back issues avail.; reprint service avail. from KTO,UMI) **Indexed:** A.I.C.P., Abstr.Anthropol., Amer.Bibl.Slavic & E.Eur.Stud., Anthropol.Lit., Art & Archaeol.Tech.Abstr., Behav.Med.Abstr., Bibl.Dev.Med.& Child Neur., Biol.Abstr., Biol.& Agr.Ind., Biol.Dig., Chem.Abstr., Curr.Adv.Ecol.Sci., Curr.Cont., Dairy Sci.Abstr., Dok.Arbeitsmed., Excerp.Med., Gen.Sci.Ind., Helminthol.Abstr., Ind.Med., Ind.Sci.Rev., INIS Atomind., Lang.& Lang.Behav.Abstr., Mid.East: Abstr.& Ind., Nutr.Abstr., Popul.Ind., Psychol.Abstr., Sci.Cit.Ind., So.Pac.Per.Ind., Sp.Ed.Needs Abstr., SSCI, Trop.Dis.Bull. **Document type:** academic/scholarly publication.
●Also available online. Vendor(s): Information Access Co., UMI.
—BLDSC (4336.000000); CASDDS; CISTI; EMDOCS; Genuine Article; KNAW; KR SourceOne; Linda Hall; SWETS; UMI; UnCover. **CCC.**
Description: Focuses on genetics; population genetics, evolutionary and genetic demography, quantitative genetics, genetic epidemiology, behavioral genetics, molecular genetics; growth and physiological parameters of genetic and environmental interactions.
Refereed Serial

HUMAN ETHOLOGY BULLETIN. see ANTHROPOLOGY

HUMAN EVOLUTION; international journal. see ANTHROPOLOGY

HUMAN NATURE; an interdisciplinary biosocial perspective. see SOCIAL SCIENCES: COMPREHENSIVE WORKS

HUMBOLDT SOCIETY NEWSLETTER. see HOMOSEXUALITY

578.77   NE   ISSN 0018-8158
QH90   CODEN: HYDRB8
HYDROBIOLOGIA. (Supplement avail.: Journal of Applied Phycology (ISSN 0921-8971)) (Text in English) 1948. 25 volumes/yr. fl.11925 to institutions; $6125 to institutions in U.S. (effective 1998). Kluwer Academic Publishers, Postbus 17, 3300 AA Dordrecht, Netherlands. TEL 31-78-6392392. FAX 31-78-6392254. TELEX 29245 KAPG NL. E-mail: services@wkap.nl; URL: http://www.wkap.nl. (Dist. by: Kluwer Academic Publishers Group, P.O. Box 322, 3300 AH Dordrecht, Netherlands. TEL 31-78-6392392. FAX 31-78-6546474; N. America dist. addr.: Box 358, Accord Sta., Hingham, MA 02018-0358. TEL 617-871-6600. FAX 617-871-6528) Ed. H.J. Dumont. adv.; bk.rev.; bibl. circ. 1,000. (also avail. in microform from UMI; reprint service avail. from SWZ) **Indexed:** Acid Pre.Dig., Acid Rain Abstr., Acid Rain Ind., ASCA, Bio-Contr.News & Info., Biol.Abstr., Cadscan, Chem.Abstr., Chem.Cit.Ind., Curr.Adv.Ecol.Sci., Curr.Cont., Curr.Ref.Fish Res., Deep Sea Res.& Oceanogr.Abstr., Ecol.Abstr., Environ.Abstr., Environ.Per.Bibl. (1993-), Excerp.Med., Food Sci.& Tech.Abstr., Geo.Abstr.H.G., Geo.Abstr.P.G., Geol.Abstr., Helminthol.Abstr., IDA, Ind.Sci.Rev., Lead Abstr., Nutr.Abstr., Ocean.Abstr., Pollut.Abstr., Rev.Plant Path., Sci.Cit.Ind., Sel.J.Water, Sel.Water Res.Abstr., So.Pac.Per.Ind., Soils & Fert., Sport Fish.Abstr., SSCI, W.R.C.Inf., Weed Abstr., Wild.Rev., Zincscan, Zoo.Rec. **Document type:** academic/scholarly publication.
—BLDSC (4343.000000); CASDDS; CIS; CISTI; Ei; EMDOCS; Genuine Article; KR SourceOne; Linda Hall; SWETS; UMI; UnCover. **CCC.**
Description: Publishes original articles in the fields of fundamental limnology and marine biology.
Refereed Serial

578.77 551.48   US   ISSN 0018-8166
QH91.A1   CODEN: HYBJA
HYDROBIOLOGICAL JOURNAL. English translation of: Gidrobiologicheskii Zhurnal (KR ISSN 0375-8990) 1970. 7/yr. $1192 (foreign $1300.50) (effective 1997). Begell House Inc., 79 Madison Ave., Ste. 1205, New York, NY 10016-7892. TEL 212-725-1999. FAX 212-213-8368. E-mail: begellhouse@worldnet.att.net. (Co-sponsors: Ukrainian Academy of Science; Russian Academy of Science) Ed. Robert J. Behnke. adv.; bk.rev.; charts; illus.; index. circ. 325. (also avail. in microform from UMI) **Indexed:** Biol.Abstr., Curr.Adv.Ecol.Sci., Curr.Tit.Ocean., Deep Sea Res.& Oceanogr.Abstr., Ecol.Abstr., Excerp.Med., Fuel & Energy Abstr., Geo.Abstr.P.G., Geol.Abstr., INIS Atomind., Sel.J.Water, Sel.Water Res.Abstr., Sport Fish.Abstr., W.R.C.Inf., Weed Abstr., Wild.Rev., Zoo.Rec. **Document type:** academic/scholarly publication.
—BLDSC (0412.088600); CISTI; Ei; SWETS; UMI; UnCover. **CCC.**
Description: Focuses on freshwater and marine biology.

578.77   BU   ISSN 0324-0924
QH90.A1   CODEN: KHIDD9
HYDROBIOLOGY. (Text in Bulgarian, English, French and Russian) 1975. irreg. 1.32 lv. per no. (Bulgarska Akademiia na Naukite) Publishing House of the Bulgarian Academy of Sciences, Acad. G. Bonchev St., Bldg. 6, 1113 Sofia, Bulgaria. (Dist. by: Hemus, 6, Rouski Blvd., 1000 Sofia, Bulgaria) bibl.; illus. circ. 430. (reprint service avail. from IRC) **Indexed:** Sel.Water Res.Abstr.
—BLDSC (0391.865000); CASDDS; CISTI; KNAW; Linda Hall.

570   JA   ISSN 0914-6660
HYOGO RIKUSUI SEIBUTSU/HYOGO FRESH-WATER BIOLOGY. (Text in Japanese) 1981. 3/yr. Hyogo Rikusui Seibutsu Kenkyukai - Hyogo Fresh-Water Biological Society, c/o Mr. Noboru Nishimura, 1841 Sekinomiya, Sekinomiyacho, Yabu-gun, Hyogo-ken 667-11, Japan.

570   JA
HYOGO SEIBUTSU/HYOGO BIOLOGY. (Text in Japanese) a. Hyogoken Seibutsu Gakkai - Hyogo Biological Society, c/o Mr. Nakanishi, Kenritsu Hyogo Koto Gakko, 1 Teraikecho, Nagata-ku, Kobe-shi, Hyogo-ken 653, Japan.

570   JA   ISSN 0915-8987
HYUMAN SAIENSU/HUMAN SCIENCE.* (Text in Japanese) 1990. bi-m. 800 Yen per no. Hyuman Saiensu Shinko Zaidan - Japan Health Science Foundation, c/o Japan Public Health Association, Koei Bldg., 29-8 Shinjuku 1-chome, Shinjuku-ku, Tokyo, Japan.

I-BUNPI KENKYUKAISHI/JAPANESE SOCIETY OF GASTRIC SECRETION RESEARCH. PROCEEDINGS. see MEDICAL SCIENCES — Endocrinology

I C E S IDENTIFICATION LEAFLETS FOR PLANKTON/FICHES D'IDENTIFICATION DU PLANCTON. see ENVIRONMENTAL STUDIES

578.77   DK   ISSN 0903-2606
GC1080   CODEN: TMESEX
I C E S TECHNIQUES IN MARINE ENVIRONMENTAL SCIENCES. (Text in English) 1987. irreg., no.16, 1991. DKK 40 per issue. International Council for the Exploration of the Sea, Palaegade 2-4, DK-1261 Copenhagen K, Denmark. FAX 33-93-4215. E-mail: postmaster@server.ices.inst.dk; URL: http://www. ices.inst.dk. Ed. J. Pawlak. circ. 500. (back issues avail.) **Document type:** monographic series.
—CASDDS.

I M A JOURNAL OF MATHEMATICS APPLIED IN MEDICINE & BIOLOGY. (Institute of Mathematics and Its Applications) see MATHEMATICS

I M S NEWSLETTER. (International Marine Science) see EARTH SCIENCES — Oceanography

570   UK   ISSN 0952-2204
                  CODEN: IMSEE8
I U B S MONOGRAPH SERIES. 1985. irreg., latest no.8, 1992. price varies. (International Union of Biological Sciences, FR) I R L Press Ltd. (Subsidiary of: Oxford University Press), Pinkhill House, Southfield Rd., Eynsham, Oxford OX8 1JJ, England. TEL 44-865-882283. FAX 44-865-882890. (Subscr. to: IUBS Secretariat, 51 bd. de Montmorency, 75016 Paris, France; U.S. subscr. to: I R L Press, Box Q, McLean, VA 22101) **Indexed:** Biol.Abstr. (1986-). **Document type:** monographic series.
—BLDSC (4588.827000).

IGAKU TO SEIBUTSUGAKU/MEDICINE AND BIOLOGY. see *MEDICAL SCIENCES*

570   US   ISSN 0073-490X
QH9   CODEN: INHNAH
ILLINOIS. NATURAL HISTORY SURVEY. BIOLOGICAL NOTES. 1933. irreg., no.140, 1997. $4 per no. Department of Natural Resources, Natural History Survey, Natural Resources Bldg., 607 E. Peabody Dr., Champaign, IL 61820. TEL 217-244-2115. FAX 217-333-4949. Ed. Charles Warwick. circ. 1,500. (back issues avail.) **Indexed:** Biol.Abstr., Rev.Plant Path., Sport Fish.Abstr., Wild Life Rev., Wild.Rev., Zoo.Rec. **Document type:** government publication.
—Linda Hall.
Description: Reports of research results and techniques; faunistic surveys with emphasis on Illinois species.
Refereed Serial

570   US   ISSN 0073-4918
QH1   CODEN: INHBAF
ILLINOIS. NATURAL HISTORY SURVEY. BULLETIN. 1876. irreg., vol.35, no.4, 1997. $10 per no. Department of Natural Resources, Natural History Survey Division, Natural Resources Bldg., 607 E. Peabody Dr., Champaign, IL 61820. TEL 217-244-2115. FAX 217-333-4949. Ed. Charles Warwick. R&P contact: Charles Warwick. bibl.; illus. **Indexed:** Biol.Abstr., Rev.Plant Path., Sport Fish.Abstr., Wild Life Rev., Wild.Rev., Zoo.Rec. **Document type:** academic/scholarly publication.
—BLDSC (2558.000000); Linda Hall; UnCover.
Description: Reports of research results and biological data with emphasis on Illinois.
Refereed Serial

508   US   ISSN 0888-9546
QH105.I3
ILLINOIS. NATURAL HISTORY SURVEY. SPECIAL PUBLICATION. 1976. irreg., no.19, 1997. price varies. Department of Natural Resources, Natural History Survey Division, Natural Resources Bldg., 607 E. Peabody Dr., Champaign, IL 61820. TEL 217-244-2115. FAX 217-333-4949. Ed. Charles Warwick. R&P contact: Charles Warwick. bibl.; illus. **Indexed:** Biol.Abstr., Rev.Plant Path., Sport Fish.Abstr., Wild Life Rev., Wild.Rev., Zoo.Rec. **Document type:** government publication.
—BLDSC (4365.423000); Linda Hall.
Description: Covers a range of topics related to the biological resources of Illinois.

ILLINOIS. STATE MUSEUM. SCIENTIFIC PAPERS SERIES. see *SCIENCES: COMPREHENSIVE WORKS*

570   US   ISSN 0073-4748
                  CODEN: ILBMA4
ILLINOIS BIOLOGICAL MONOGRAPHS. 1914. irreg. University of Illinois Press, 1325 S. Oak St., Champaign, IL 61820. TEL 217-333-0950. FAX 217-244-8082. (also avail. in microform from UMI,JOH; reprint service avail. from UMI) **Indexed:** Biol.Abstr., Rev.Appl.Entomol. **Document type:** monographic series.
—CISTI; Linda Hall.
Refereed Serial

ILLINOIS STEWARD. see *CONSERVATION*

571.974   FR   ISSN 0923-2532
                   CODEN: IBSPE
IMMUNO-ANALYSE ET BIOLOGIE SPECIALISEE. 1986. bi-m. 1224 F. to institutions (US $234; elsewhere 1410 F.) (effective 1998). (Societe Francaise de Biophysique et de Medecine Nucleaire) Editions Scientifiques et Medicales Elsevier, 141 rue de Javel, 75747 Paris, France. TEL 33-1-45589068. FAX 33-1-45589421. URL: http://www.elsevier.nl/. (Subscr. in U.S. and Canada to: Elsevier Science Inc., Box 945, Madison Sq. Sta., New York, NY 10159-0945. TEL 212-633-3730. FAX 212-633-3680) Ed. J. Ingrand. adv.; bk.rev. circ. 2,000. **Indexed:** Excerp.Med. **Document type:** academic/scholarly publication.
—BLDSC (4369.654800); CISTI; EMDOCS; SWETS. CCC.
Formerly: Trait-d'Union.
Description: Covers research and application of clinical biology as in immunology, molecular biology, cell biology, analyses involving probes and receptors.

IMMUNOLOGY AND CELL BIOLOGY. see *MEDICAL SCIENCES* — *Allergology And Immunology*

570   UK
INDEX FILICUM. 1906. irreg. price varies. (Royal Botanic Gardens) Oxford University Press, Oxford Journals, Walton St., Oxford OX2 6DP, England. TEL 01865-267907. FAX 01865-267773. TELEX 837330-OXPRES-G. E-mail: jnlorders@oup.co.uk. (U.S. subscr. to: Oxford University Press Inc., 2001 Evans Rd., Cary, NC 27513. TEL 919-677-0977. FAX 919-677-1714) Ed. B.S. Parris. **Document type:** academic/scholarly publication.

570   UK
INDEX KEWENSIS. 1896. every 5 yrs. (Royal Botanic Gardens, Herbarium) Oxford University Press, Oxford Journals, Walton St., Oxford OX2 6DP, England. TEL 01865-267907. FAX 01865-267773. TELEX 837330-OXPRES-G. E-mail: jnlorders@oup.co.uk. (U.S. subscr. to: Oxford University Press Inc., 2001 Evans Rd., Cary, NC 27513. TEL 919-677-0977. FAX 919-677-1714) (also avail. in microfilm from BHP) **Document type:** academic/scholarly publication.

570   II   ISSN 0302-7554
QH301   CODEN: INBID9
INDIAN BIOLOGIST. (Text in English) 1968. s-a. $30. Indian Association of Biological Sciences, c/o Life Science Centre, University of Calcutta, 35 Ballygunge Circular Rd., Calcutta 19, India. Eds. T.M. Das, S.P. Raychaudhuri. adv.; bk.rev. circ. 1,000. **Indexed:** Biol.Abstr., Chem.Abstr, Curr.Cont., Excerp.Med., INIS Atomind.
—CASDDS; CISTI; Linda Hall; UnCover.

570   II   ISSN 0019-5189
QH301   CODEN: IJEBA6
INDIAN JOURNAL OF EXPERIMENTAL BIOLOGY. (Text in English) 1963. m. Rs.500($240) (Council of Scientific and Industrial Research, Publications & Information Directorate) Scientific Publishers, P.O. Box 91, 5A, New Pali Rd., Jodhpur 342 001, India. TEL 91-291-33323. Ed. K. Satayanarayana. bibl.; charts; illus.; index. circ. 1,200. (back issues avail.) **Indexed:** Abstr.Anthropol., Abstr.Hyg., Anal.Abstr., Bio-Contr.News & Info., Biol.Abstr., Biotech.Abstr., Chem.Abstr., Crop Physiol.Abstr., Curr.Adv.Ecol.Sci., Curr.Cont., Curr.Leather Lit., Dairy Sci.Abstr., Diar.Dis.Res., Excerp.Med., Field Crop Abstr., Food Sci.& Tech.Abstr., Helminthol.Abstr., Hort.Abstr., Ind.Med., Ind.Sci.Rev., INIS Atomind., INSPEC, Irr.& Drain.Abstr., Maize Abstr., Nutr.Abstr., Ornam.Hort., Plant Grow.Reg.Abstr., Poult.Abstr., Protozool.Abstr., Rev.Appl.Entomol., Rev.Med.& Vet.Mycol., Rice Abstr., Sci.Cit.Ind., Seed Abstr., Soils & Fert., Sport Fish.Abstr., Sugar Ind.Abstr., Triticale Abstr., Trop.Dis.Bull., Vet.Bull., Weed Abstr., Wild.Rev., Zoo.Rec. **Document type:** academic/scholarly publication.
—BLDSC (4412.200000); CASDDS; CISTI; Ei; Genuine Article; KNAW; Linda Hall; SWETS; UnCover.

INDIAN JOURNAL OF MARINE SCIENCES. see *EARTH SCIENCES* — *Oceanography*

INDIAN JOURNAL OF MEDICAL PHOTOGRAPHY. see *PHOTOGRAPHY*

INDIAN JOURNAL OF MEDICAL RESEARCH. SECTION B: BIOMEDICAL RESEARCH OTHER THAN INFECTIOUS DISEASES. see *MEDICAL SCIENCES*

570   II   ISSN 0253-4436
QH301   CODEN: IRLSEG
INDIAN REVIEW OF LIFE SCIENCES. (Text in English) 1981. a. $80. Geobios, Zion, P.O. Box 14, Zion, 41B-B1-A, P.W.D. Colony, Jodhpur 342 001, India. Ed. David N. Sen. (reprint service avail.) **Indexed:** Chem.Abstr., Crop Physiol.Abstr., Curr.Adv.Ecol.Sci., Field Crop Abstr., Herb.Abstr., Plant Grow.Reg.Abstr., Triticale Abstr., Weed Abstr.
—CASDDS; CISTI; Linda Hall.

INDONESIAN JOURNAL OF BIOANTHROPOLOGY/BERKALA BIOANTHROPOLOGI INDONESIA. see *ANTHROPOLOGY*

INFORMATIK, BIOMETRIE UND EPIDEMIOLOGIE. see *MEDICAL SCIENCES*

INFORMATION DU TECHNICIEN BIOLOGISTE. see *MEDICAL SCIENCES* — *Experimental Medicine, Laboratory Technique*

INFORMATION TECHNOLOGY REPORT. see *BIOLOGY* — *Computer Applications*

570   GW
INFORMATIONEN FUER DEN BIOLOGIEUNTERRICHT; aktuelle Informationen, Lehrmittel und Materialien, bibliographische Hilfen. 1968. s-a. DM.10($8) Paedagogisches Zentrum Berlin, Uhlandstr. 96-97, 33617 Berlin, Germany. FAX 49-30-8687266. bk.rev. circ. 1,000.

500.75   FR   ISSN 0248-3807
INSTITUT D'ETHNOLOGIE. ARCHIVES ET DOCUMENTS, MICRO EDITION. SCIENCES NATURELLES. a. Musee de l'Homme, Institut d'Ethnologie, Palais de Chaillot, Place du Tracadero, France.

INSTITUT FUER DEN WISSENSCHAFTLICHEN FILM. PUBLIKATIONEN ZU WISSENSCHAFTLICHEN FILMEN. SEKTION BIOLOGIE. see *MOTION PICTURES*

INSTITUT PASTEUR DE TUNIS. ARCHIVES. see *MEDICAL SCIENCES*

570 614,7   BE   ISSN 0374-6429
QH301   CODEN: BNBBAA
INSTITUT ROYAL DES SCIENCES NATURELLES DE BELGIQUE. BULLETIN. SERIE BIOLOGIE. 1930. a. 1500 BEF($25) (foreign 1750 BEF). Koninklijk Belgisch Instituut voor Natuurwetenschappen - Institut Royal des Sciences Naturelles de Belgique, Vautierstraat 29, 1000 Brussels, Belgium. abstr.; bibl.; charts; illus.; cum.index. circ. 1,500. (back issues avail.) **Indexed:** Biol.Abstr., Bull.Signal., Ref.Zh., Sport Fish.Abstr., Wild.Rev., Zoo.Rec. **Document type:** academic/scholarly publication.

INSTITUTE OF ENVIRONMENTAL SCIENCES. ANNUAL MEETING. PROCEEDINGS. see *ENVIRONMENTAL STUDIES*

INSTITUTE OF ENVIRONMENTAL SCIENCES. TUTORIAL SERIES. see *ENVIRONMENTAL STUDIES*

570   BL   ISSN 0020-3661
                  CODEN: BBIBAT
INSTITUTO BIOLOGICO DA BAHIA. BOLETIM. (Summaries in English and Portuguese) 1954. irreg. Instituto Biologico da Bahia, Av. Adhemar de Barros-Ondina, Caixa Postal 553, 40000 Salvador, Bahia, Brazil. Dir. Antonio A.J. da Silva. bibl.; charts; illus. **Indexed:** Biol.Abstr., Chem.Abstr.
—CASDDS.

INSTITUTO COLOMBIANO AGROPECUARIO. REVISTA I C A. see *AGRICULTURE*

578.0913   PO   ISSN 0871-1755
INSTITUTO DE INVESTIGACAO CIENTIFICA TROPICAL. COMUNICACOES. SERIE DE CIENCIAS BIOLOGICAS. 1989. irreg. price varies. Instituto de Investigacao Cientifica Tropical, Rua da Junqueira 30, 1300 Lisbon, Portugal. TEL 351-1-3622621. FAX 351-1-3631460. E-mail: cdi@iict.pt; URL: http://www.iict.pt. (Subscr. to: Centro de Documentacao e Informacao, Rua Jau 47, 1300 Lisbon, Portugal) circ. 1,000. **Document type:** monographic series.

INSTITUTO DE LA PATAGONIA. ANALES. CIENCIAS SOCIALES. see *HISTORY* — *History Of North And South America*

BIOLOGY

570 610 BL ISSN 0074-0276
CODEN: MIOCAS
INSTITUTO OSWALDO CRUZ, RIO DE JANEIRO. MEMORIAS. (Text in English) 1909. bi-m. $70 (Latin America, Africa, Asia $80; elsewhere $120) or exchange basis (effective 1997). Fundacao Oswaldo Cruz, Avda. Brasil 4365, 21045-900 Rio de Janeiro, Brazil. TEL 55-21-5984335. FAX 55-21-2805048. Ed. Hooman Momen. adv. contact: Luciane de C.B. Soares. bk.rev. circ. 1,400. (also avail. in microform from PMC) **Indexed:** Abstr.Hyg., ASCA, Bio-Contr.News & Info., Biol.Abstr., Helminthol.Abstr., Ind.Med., Ind.Sci.Rev., Ind.Vet., Poult.Abstr., Protozool.Abstr., Rev.Appl.Entomol., Rev.Med.& Vet.Mycol., Sport Fish.Abstr., Trop.Dis.Bull., Vet.Bull., Wild.Rev., Zoo.Rec. **Document type:** academic/scholarly publication.
—BLDSC (5661.000000); CISTI; Genuine Article; KNAW; Linda Hall; SWETS; UnCover. **CCC**.

570 SP
INSTITUTO PIRENAICO DE ECOLOGIA. MONOGRAFIAS. 1987. irreg., no.6, 1992. price varies. Consejo Superior de Investigaciones Cientificas (C.S.I.C.), Instituto Pirenaico de Ecologia, Avda. Regimiento de Galicia, s-n, 22700 Jaca (Huesca), Spain. TEL 974-361441. E-mail: ipjaca@pinar1.csic.es. Ed. Juan Pablo Martinez Rica. **Document type:** monographic series.

570 MX ISSN 0365-1932
QH301 CODEN: AENBAU
INSTITUTO POLITECNICO NACIONAL. ESCUELA NACIONAL DE CIENCIAS BIOLOGICAS. ANALES. Key Title: Anales de la Escuela Nacional de Ciencias Biologicas (Mexico). (Text in Spanish; summaries in English, Spanish) 1938. a. Mex.$150($50) (effective 1997). Instituto Politecnico Nacional, Escuela Nacional de Ciencias Biologicas, Carpio y Plan de Ayala, Col. Santo Tomas, Apdo. Postal 42-186, 11340, Mexico, D.F., Mexico. FAX 52-5-3963503. Dr. Fernando de la Jara Alcocer; Pub. Paul Vallejo de Aquino. charts; illus.; stat.; circ. 1,000 (controlled). **Indexed:** Sport Fish.Abstr., Wild.Rev., Zoo.Rec. **Document type:** academic/scholarly publication.
—BLDSC (0873.000000); CISTI; Linda Hall.
Description: Presents original research in the biological sciences: zoology, botany, morphology, ecology.
Refereed Serial

570 RM
INSTITUTUL DE SUBINGINERI ORADEA. LUCRARI STIINTIFICE: SERIA BIOLOGIC. (Text in Rumanian, occasionally in English or French; summaries in English, French, German or Rumanian) 1967. a. Institutul de Subingineri Oradea, Calea Armatei Rosii Nr. 5, 3700 Oradea, Rumania.
Formerly: Institutul Pedagogic Oradea. Lucrari Stiintifice Seria Biologic; which continued in part (in 1973): Institutul Pedagogic Oradea. Lucrari Stiintifice: Seria Educatie Fizica, Biologie, Stiinte Medicale; which superseded in part (in 1971): Institutul Pedagogic Oradea. Lucraria Stiintifice: Seria A and Seria B; which was formerly (until 1969): Institutul Pedagogic Oradea. Lucrari Stiintifice.

INTERMOUNTAIN JOURNAL OF SCIENCES. see *SCIENCES: COMPREHENSIVE WORKS*

INTERNATIONAL ASSOCIATION OF THEORETICAL AND APPLIED LIMNOLOGY. COMMUNICATIONS/INTERNATIONALE VEREINIGUNG FUER THEORETISCHE UND ANGEWANDTE LIMNOLOGIE. MITTEILUNGEN. see *EARTH SCIENCES — Hydrology*

INTERNATIONAL ASSOCIATION OF THEORETICAL AND APPLIED LIMNOLOGY. PROCEEDINGS/INTERNATIONALE VEREINIGUNG FUER THEORETISCHE UND ANGEWANDTE LIMNOLOGIE. VERHANDLUNGEN. see *EARTH SCIENCES — Hydrology*

570 UK ISSN 0962-5968
INTERNATIONAL BIOLOGICAL PROGRAMME SERIES. 1975. irreg., no.26, 1981. price varies. Cambridge University Press, Edinburgh Bldg., Shaftesbury Rd., Cambridge CB2 2RU, England. TEL 44-1223-312393. FAX 44-1223-315052. TELEX 851817256. E-mail: information@cup.cam.ac.uk; URL: http://www.cup.cam.ac.uk. (N. American addr.: Cambridge University Press, Journals Dept., 40 W. 20th St., New York, NY 10011. TEL 212-924-3900. FAX 212-691-3239) R&P contact: Linda Nicol. **Indexed:** Biol.Abstr. **Document type:** monographic series.

570 UK
INTERNATIONAL INSTITUTE OF BIOLOGICAL CONTROL. ANNUAL REPORT. a. CAB International, Wallingford, Oxon OX10 8DE, England. TEL 44-1344-872999. FAX 44-1344-875007. E-mail: cabi-iibc-hq@cabi.org. (Alt. addr.: Institute of Biological Control, Silwood Park, Buckhurst Rd., Ascot, Berks SL5 7TA, England)

616 IT ISSN 0393-6155
CODEN: IBMAEP
INTERNATIONAL JOURNAL OF BIOLOGICAL MARKERS. 1986. 4/yr. L.160000 (Europe $160) (effective 1997). Wichtig Editore s.r.l., Via Friuli, 72-74, 20135 Milan, Italy. TEL 39-2-55195971. **Indexed:** ASCA.
—BLDSC (4542.151100); CASDDS; CISTI; EMDOCS; Genuine Article; KNAW; SWETS; UnCover. **CCC**.

INTERNATIONAL JOURNAL OF BIOMETEOROLOGY. see *METEOROLOGY*

570 SP ISSN 0214-6282
QH491 CODEN: IJDBE5
INTERNATIONAL JOURNAL OF DEVELOPMENTAL BIOLOGY. (Text in English) 1960. bi-m. 11000 ptas. in Europe; US $100; elsewhere 16500 ptas. to individuals; institutions in Europe 26400 ptas.; US $280; elsewhere 36300 ptas. (effective 1998). (Universidad del Pais Vasco, Facultad de Medicina) U B C Press, Casilla 1397, 48080 Bilbao, Spain. TEL 34-4-4648800 ext. 2153. FAX 34-4-4648966. E-mail: gcparmaj@lg.ehu.es; URL: http://www.lg.ehu.es/ijdb. Ed. Nuria G. de Ubieta. R&P contact: Juan J. Rodriguez. adv.: B&W page 75000 ptas., color page 150000 ptas.; adv. contact: Juan Jose Rodriguez. bk.rev. circ. 1,000. **Indexed:** ASCA, Biol.Abstr., Curr.Cont., Excerp.Med., Ind.Med.Esp., Ind.Sci.Rev., Ind.SST, Sci.Cit.Ind. **Document type:** academic/scholarly publication.
—BLDSC (4542.185090); CASDDS; EMDOCS; Genuine Article; KNAW; SWETS; UnCover. **CCC**.
Formerly (until 1989): Anales del Desarrollo (ISSN 0569-9908)
Description: Reports substantial and original findings in biological development. Covers all animal or vegetable organisms.
Refereed Serial

INTERNATIONAL JOURNAL OF FERTILITY AND WOMEN'S MEDICINE. see *MEDICAL SCIENCES*

INTERNATIONAL JOURNAL OF MEDICAL AND BIOLOGICAL FRONTIERS. see *MEDICAL SCIENCES*

570 II ISSN 0379-8097
CODEN: BMEMDK
INTERNATIONAL SOCIETY OF APPLIED BIOLOGY. BIOLOGICAL MEMOIRS. 1977. s-a. Rs.500($60) International Society of Applied Biology, Division of Biochemistry, Central Drug Research Institute, Lucknow (U.P.) 226 001, India. FAX 91-5222-293405. E-mail: root@ren.nic.in. Ed. O.P. Shkula. R&P contact: Anil Roy Chowdhury. bk.rev. **Indexed:** Biol.Abstr., Curr.Adv.Ecol.Sci.
—CASDDS; CISTI; KNAW; Linda Hall; UnCover. **CCC**.
Description: Covers various classical and applied aspects of life sciences.

535 570 NE ISSN 0929-7138
INTERNATIONAL SOCIETY ON OPTICS WITHIN LIFE SCIENCES. SERIES (PROCEEDINGS). Abbreviated title: O W L S. (Text in English) 1993. irreg., vol.2, 1993. price varies. Elsevier Science B.V., Books Division, P.O. Box 211, 1000 AE Amsterdam, Netherlands. TEL 31-20-4853911. FAX 31-20-4853705. E-mail: nlinfo-f@elsevier.nl; usinfo-f@elsevier.com; forinfo-kyf04035@niftyserve.or.jp; URL: http://www.elsevier.nl/. (Subscr. in the Americas to: Elsevier Science, Regional Sales Office, Box 945, New York, NY 10159-0945. TEL 212-633-3730. FAX 212-633-3680; Subscr. in Australasia and the Far East to: Elsevier Science (Singapore) Pte Ltd, No.1 Temasek Ave., No.17-01 Millenia Tower, Singapore 039192, Singapore. TEL 65-434-3727. FAX 65-337-2230; Subscr. in Japan to: Elsevier Science Japan, 9-15 Higashi-Azabu 1-chome, Minato-ku, Tokyo 106, Japan. TEL 81-3-5561-5033. FAX 81-3-5561-5047) Ed. Gert von Bally. **Document type:** proceedings.
—BLDSC (6273.800000).
Refereed Serial

570 615 US ISSN 0731-0358
INTERNATIONAL SYMPOSIUM ON QUANTUM BIOLOGY AND QUANTUM PHARMACOLOGY. PROCEEDINGS. Represents: International Journal of Quantum Chemistry. Symposium. Variant title: Lowdin Symposia. 1974. a. price varies. John Wiley & Sons, Inc., 605 Third Ave., New York, NY 10158. TEL 212-850-6000. FAX 212-850-6088. TELEX 12-7063. Ed. Per-Olov Lowdin. **Indexed:** INSPEC (1980-). **Document type:** proceedings.
Refereed Serial

570 FR ISSN 0445-1333
INTERNATIONAL UNION OF BIOLOGICAL SCIENCES. GENERAL ASSEMBLIES. PROCEEDINGS. triennial. International Union of Biological Sciences, 51 bd. E. Montmorency, 75016 Paris, France. TEL 45-25-00-09. **Document type:** proceedings.
Formerly: International Union of Biological Sciences. Reports of General Assemblies (ISSN 0074-9362)

578.77 GW ISSN 0020-9309
CODEN: IGHYAZ
INTERNATIONALE REVUE DER GESAMTEN HYDROBIOLOGIE. (Text in English, French and German) 1908. 4/yr. DM.195 (foreign DM.203) to individuals; institutions DM.795 (foreign DM.815) (effective 1997). Akademie Verlag GmbH, Muehlenstr. 33-34, 13187 Berlin, Germany. TEL 49-30-47889348. FAX 49-30-47889357. E-mail: info@akademie-verlag.de. (Subscr. in the Americas to: John Wiley & Sons, Inc., 605 Third Ave., New York, NY 10158. TEL 212-850-6645. FAX 212-850-6021) Ed.Bd. adv.; charts; illus.; index. **Indexed:** ASCA, Biol.Abstr., Chem.Abstr., Curr.Adv.Ecol.Sci., Curr.Cont., Excerp.Med., Geo.Abstr., Helminthol.Abstr, Ind.Sci.Rev., INIS Atomind., Sci.Cit.Ind., Sel.Water Res.Abstr., W.R.C.Inf. **Document type:** academic/scholarly publication.
—BLDSC (4554.600000); CASDDS; CISTI; EMDOCS; Genuine Article; Linda Hall; SWETS; UnCover. **CCC**.
Description: Covers the analysis and assessment of biological structures in water in their interconnection with the internal and external cycle of materials.

571.3 AT ISSN 0818-0164
QL362.5 CODEN: ITAXEO
INVERTEBRATE TAXONOMY; Australian journal of scientific research. 1971. bi-m. Aus.$450($450) (effective 1998). (C.S.I.R.O. Australia) C.S.I.R.O. Publishing, 150 Oxford St., Collingwood, Vic. 3066, Australia. TEL 61-3-96627622. FAX 61-3-96627611. E-mail: dwm@publish.csiro.au; URL: http://www.publish.csiro.au/journals/it. (Co-sponsor: Australian Academy of Science) Eds. D.W. Morton, S.L. Farrer. adv.; index. circ. 500. (also avail. in microfiche from UMI; back issues avail.) **Indexed:** Bio-Contr.News & Info., Biol.Abstr., Curr.Cont., Ecol.Abstr., Forest Prod.Abstr., Geol.Abstr., Zoo.Rec. **Document type:** academic/scholarly publication.
●Also available online.
—BLDSC (4557.703700); CISTI; Genuine Article; Linda Hall; UMI; UnCover. **CCC**.
Formerly (until 1987): Australian Journal of Zoology, Supplementary Series (ISSN 0310-9089)
Description: Covers taxonomy and systematics of invertebrates of the Indo-Pacific Region.

BIOLOGY

IRISH FISHERIES INVESTIGATIONS. SERIES A: FRESHWATER. see *FISH AND FISHERIES*

IRISH FISHERIES INVESTIGATIONS. SERIES B: MARINE. see *FISH AND FISHERIES*

570   IS
ISRAEL INSTITUTE FOR BIOLOGICAL RESEARCH. SCIENTIFIC ACTIVITIES. 1970. a. free. Israel Institute for Biological Research, P.O. Box 19, 74100 Ness-Ziona, Israel. TEL 972-8-381595. FAX 972-8-401404. E-mail: wxiibr@weizmann. weizmann.ac.il. Document type: bibliography.

578.77   IT   ISSN 0374-9118
QH96   CODEN: MIIMAS
ISTITUTO ITALIANO DI IDROBIOLOGIA. MEMORIE. (Text in English) 1942. a. exchange basis. Istituto Italiano di Idrobiologia, 28048 Verbania Pallanza (VB), Italy. FAX 39-323-556513. Ed. Riccardo de Bernardi. circ. 800. **Indexed:** Aqua.Sci.& Fish.Abstr., Biol.Abstr., Curr.Adv.Ecol.Sci., Deep Sea Res.& Oceanogr.Abstr., Ecol.Abstr., Geo.Abstr.H.G., Geo.Abstr.P.G., Sport Fish.Abstr., Water Resour.Abstr., Wild.Rev., Zoo.Rec. Document type: academic/scholarly publication.
—BLDSC (5673.950000); CASDDS; CISTI; EMDOCS; KR SourceOne; Linda Hall; UnCover.

572.8   RU   ISSN 0202-7070
QH506   CODEN: ITMBCG
ITOGI NAUKI I TEKHNIKI: MOLEKULYARNAYA BIOLOGIYA. irreg., latest vols.27-28, 1989. 6.60 Rub. Vsesoyuznyi Institut Nauchno-Tekhnicheskoi Informatsii (VINITI), Ul. Baltiiskaya 14, Moscow A-219, Russia. (Subscr. to: Mezhdunarodnaya Kniga, Dimitrova ul. 39, 113095 Moscow, Russia) **Indexed:** Chem.Abstr.

570   RU   ISSN 0203-5405
QH301
ITOGI NAUKI I TEKHNIKI: OBSHCHIE PROBLEMY BIOLOGII. 1982. irreg., latest vol.6, 1987. price varies. Vsesoyuznyi Institut Nauchno-Tekhnicheskoi Informatsii (VINITI), Ul. Baltiiskaya 14, Moscow A-219, Russia. (Subscr. to: Mezhdunarodnaya Kniga, Dimitrova ul. 39, 113095 Moscow, Russia)
—Linda Hall.

ITOGI NAUKI I TEKHNIKI: ONKOLOGIYA. see *MEDICAL SCIENCES — Oncology*

570   GW   ISSN 0944-3266
QH305
JAHRBUCH FUER GESCHICHTE UND THEORIE DER BIOLOGIE. a. DM.40.20 (foreign DM.42) (effective 1998). (Deutsche Gesellschaft fuer Geschichte und Theorie der Biologie) V W B - Verlag fuer Wissenschaft und Bildung, Markgrafenstr. 67, 10969 Berlin, Germany. TEL 49-30-2510415. FAX 49-30-2510412. E-mail: 100615.1565@ compuserve.com. Eds. Hans-Joerg Rheinberger, Michael Weingarten. (back issues avail.) Document type: academic/scholarly publication.
Description: Presents articles about various themes of the history of biology.

JAPAN SOCIETY FOR COMPARATIVE ENDOCRINOLOGY. PROCEEDINGS. see *MEDICAL SCIENCES — Endocrinology*

750   JA   ISSN 0918-4430
JAPANESE JOURNAL OF BIOMETRICS. (Text in English, Japanese) 1980. s-a. 10000 Yen. Nihon Keiryo Seibutsu Gakkai - Biometric Society of Japan, c/o Prof. T. Komazawa, Institute of Statistical Mathematics, Minami-Azabu 4-6-7, Minato-ku, Tokyo 106, Japan. TEL 81-3-5421-8764. FAX 81-3-5421-8796. Ed. Hiroyuki Uesaka. adv. contact: Takatoshi Sato. **Indexed:** Curr.cont.(1992-), Stat.Theor.Meth.Abstr. (1992-). Document type: academic/scholarly publication.

JAPANESE JOURNAL OF ECOLOGY/NIPPON SEITAI GAKKAISHI. see *ENVIRONMENTAL STUDIES*

615 577   JA   ISSN 0368-9395
JAPANESE JOURNAL OF HEALTH AND HUMAN ECOLOGY. (Text and summaries in English, Japanese) 1935. bi-m. 17000 Yen. Kyorin Shoin, 4-2-1 Yushima, Bunkyo-ku, Tokyo 113, Japan. TEL 03-811-4887. (Subscr. to: 5-21-16 Omori-Nishi, Ota-ku, Tokyo 143, Japan) Ed. M. Uematsu.

JAPANESE JOURNAL OF MEDICAL SCIENCE AND BIOLOGY. see *MEDICAL SCIENCES*

JAPANESE MATRIX (COLLAGEN) CLUB. PROCEEDINGS OF THE ANNUAL MEETING. see *MEDICAL SCIENCES*

JAPANESE PELAGIC INVESTIGATION ON FUR SEALS. see *BIOLOGY — Zoology*

570   JA
JAPANESE SOCIETY OF DEVELOPMENTAL BIOLOGISTS. PROCEEDINGS OF ANNUAL MEETING/NIHON HASSEI SEIBUTSU GAKKAI TAIKAI HAPPYO YOSHISHU. (Text in Japanese) a. Japanese Society of Developmental Biologists - Nihon Hassei Seibutsu Gakkai, Tokyo Daigaku Rigakubu Dobutsugaku Kyoshitsu, 3-1 Hongo 7-chome, Bunkyo-ku, Tokyo 113, Japan. Document type: proceedings.

570   CC   ISSN 1001-1633
JIEPOUXUE ZAZHI/JOURNAL OF ANATOMY. (Text in Chinese) q. Di 2 Junyi Daxue - No.2 Military University of Medical Science, 594 Xiangyin Lu, Shanghai 200433, People's Republic of China. TEL 488706. (Co-sponsor: Chinese Society of Anatomy) Ed. Huang Ying.

JINRUI DOTAI GAKKAI KAIHO/HUMAN ERGOLOGY SOCIETY. NEWSLETTER. see *PHYSICS*

JOURNAL EPIDEMIOLOGY AND BIOSTATISTICS. see *PUBLIC HEALTH AND SAFETY*

JOURNAL INTERNATIONAL DE BIOETHIQUE/INTERNATIONAL JOURNAL OF BIOETHICS. see *PHILOSOPHY*

570   II
JOURNAL OF ADVANCES IN BIOSCIENCE. (Text in English) s-a. $10. Hindustan Publishing Corp., 5805-24, 1st Fl., Bharat Ram Rd., Darya Ganj, New Delhi 110 002, India. TEL 91-11-3254401. FAX 91-11-6863511. E-mail: hpcpd@giasdl01.vsnl. net.in.

571.3 611   UK   ISSN 0021-8782
QL801   CODEN: JOANAY
JOURNAL OF ANATOMY. 8/yr. £456($776) (effective 1998). (Anatomical Society of Great Britain and Ireland) Cambridge University Press, Edinburgh Bldg., Shaftesbury Rd., Cambridge CB2 2RU, England. TEL 44-1223-312393. FAX 44-1223-315052. TELEX 851817256. E-mail: information@cup.cam.ac.uk; URL: http://www.cup. cam.ac.uk. (N. American addr.: Cambridge University Press, Journals Dept., 40 W. 20th St., New York, NY 10011. TEL 212-924-3900. FAX 212-691-3239) Ed. P.K. Thomas. R&P contact: Linda Nicol. adv. contact: Rebecca Symons. bk.rev.; bibl.; charts; illus.; index. cum.index: 1866-1966. (also avail. in microform from UMI; microfilm from BHP; back issues avail.; reprint service avail. from SWZ) **Indexed:** Abstr.Anthropol., Anim.Breed.Abstr., ASCA, Biol.Abstr., Chem.Abstr., Curr.Cont, Dairy Sci.Abstr., Dent.Ind., Excerp.Med., GeoRef., Ind.Med., Ind.Sci.Rev., Ind.Vet., INIS Atomind., Int.Abstr.Biol.Sci, Neurosci.Cit.Ind., Nutr.Abstr., Poult.Abstr., Sci.Cit.Ind., Sport Fish.Abstr., Vet.Bull., Wild.Rev., Zoo.Rec. Document type: academic/scholarly publication.
—BLDSC (4929.000000); CASDDS; CISTI; Genuine Article; KNAW; Linda Hall; SWETS; UMI; UnCover. CCC.
Description: Presents articles and reviews covering normal human and comparative anatomy, including applied anatomy, physical anthropology, neurology, endocrinology, embryology.

591.7   UK   ISSN 0021-8790
QL750   CODEN: JAECAP
JOURNAL OF ANIMAL ECOLOGY. 1932. bi-m. £255($465) (foreign £280) (effective 1998). (British Ecological Society) Blackwell Science Ltd., Osney Mead, Oxford OX2 0EL, England. TEL 44-1865-206206. FAX 44-1865-721205. E-mail: journals.cs@blacksci.co.uk; URL: http://www.black.co.uk. Eds. B. Shorrocks, S. Albon; Pub. Allen Stevens. R&P contact: Sarah Pollard. adv. contact: Martine Cariou-Keen. bk.rev.; bibl.; illus.; index. circ. 2,845. (also avail. in microform from UMI; back issues avail.; reprint service avail. from ISI) **Indexed:** Abstr.Anthropol., Abstr.Hyg., Anim.Breed.Abstr., ASCA, Bio-Contr.News & Info., Biol.Abstr., Biol.& Agr.Ind., Chem.Abstr., Curr.Cont., Curr.Ref.Fish Res., Deep Sea Res.& Oceanogr.Abstr., Ecol.Abstr., Environ.Per.Bibl. (1974-), Field Crop Abstr., Forest.Abstr., Geo.Abstr.P.G., Helminthol.Abstr., Herb.Abstr., Ind.Sci.Rev., Ind.Vet., Key Word Ind.Wildl.Res., Math.R., Nutr.Abstr., Poult.Abstr., Rev.Appl.Entomol., Sci.Cit.Ind., Soils & Fert., Sport Fish.Abstr., Trop.Dis.Bull., Vet.Bull., W.R.C.Inf., Wild.Rev., Zoo.Rec. Document type: academic/scholarly publication.
—BLDSC (4936.000000); CISTI; EMDOCS; Genuine Article; KR SourceOne; Linda Hall; SWETS; UMI; UnCover. CCC.
Refereed Serial

JOURNAL OF APPLIED AQUACULTURE. see *FISH AND FISHERIES*

577   UK   ISSN 0021-8901
S3   CODEN: JAPEAI
JOURNAL OF APPLIED ECOLOGY. 1964. bi-m. £255($465) (foreign £280) (effective 1998). (British Ecological Society) Blackwell Science Ltd., Osney Mead, Oxford OX2 0EL, England. TEL 44-1865-206206. FAX 44-1865-721205. E-mail: journals.cs@blacksci.co.uk; URL: http://www.black.co.uk. Ed.Bd.; Pub. Allen Stevens. R&P contact: Sarah Pollard. adv. contact: Martine Cariou-Keen. bk.rev.; bibl.; charts; illus.; index. circ. 2,720. (also avail. in microform from UMI; back issues avail.; reprint service avail. from ISI) **Indexed:** Agroforest.Abstr., ASCA, Bio-Contr.News & Info., Biol.Abstr., Biol.& Agr.Ind., Biostat., Biotech.Abstr., Chem.Abstr., Cott.& Trop.Fibr.Abstr., Crop Physiol.Abstr., Curr.Cont., Deep Sea Res.& Oceanogr.Abstr., Ecol.Abstr., Energy Ind., Energy Info.Abstr., Environ.Abstr., Environ.Per.Bibl. (1989-), Excerp.Med., Field Crop Abstr., Forest.Abstr., Forest Prod.Abstr., Geo.Abstr.P.G., GeoRef., Helminthol.Abstr., Herb.Abstr., Hort.Abstr., IDA, Ind.Sci.Rev., Ind.Vet., Irr.& Drain.Abstr., Key Word Ind.Wildl.Res., Nutr.Abstr., Pig News & Info., Plant Breed.Abstr., Protozool.Abstr., Rev.Appl.Entomol., Rural Recreat.Tour.Abstr., Sci.Cit.Ind., Seed Abstr., Sel.Water Res.Abstr., Small Anim.Abstr., Soils & Fert., Sport Fish.Abstr., Triticale Abstr., Vet.Bull., W.R.C.Inf., Weed Abstr., Wild.Rev., World Agri.Econ.& Rural Sociol.Abstr., Zoo.Rec. Document type: academic/scholarly publication.
—BLDSC (4942.500000); CASDDS; CISTI; Ei; EMDOCS; Genuine Article; KR SourceOne; Linda Hall; SWETS; UMI; UnCover. CCC.
Description: Publishes papers that discuss the application of ecological ideas, theories, and methods to the use of biological resources in the widest sense.
Refereed Serial

JOURNAL OF APPLIED PHYCOLOGY. see *BIOLOGY — Botany*

BIOLOGY

578.77 333.91   US   ISSN 0733-2076
SH151   CODEN: JAQSDY
JOURNAL OF AQUACULTURE AND AQUATIC SCIENCES. 1980. irreg. $70 for 4 issues to individuals in N. America (overseas $85); libraries in N. America $140 (overseas $170). The Written Word, 7601 E. Forest Lake Dr., N.W., Parkville, MO 64152. TEL 816-842-5936. FAX 816-474-5597. E-mail: 76702,447@compuserve.com. Ed. John Farrell Kuhns; Pub. John Farrell Kuhns. adv. contact: Carol L. Kuhns. bk.rev.; abstr.; bibl.; charts; illus.; index; circ. 800 (paid). (back issues avail.) **Indexed:** Aqua.Sci.& Fish.Abstr., Aquacult.Abstr., Biol.Abstr., Curr.Cont., Deep Sea Res.& Oceanogr.Abstr., Sport Fish.Abstr., Wild.Rev., Zoo.Rec. **Document type:** academic/scholarly publication.
●Also available online. Vendor(s): CompuServe, Inc.
—CASDDS; Linda Hall. **CCC.**
Formerly (until 1982): Journal of Aquaculture.
Description: Publishes original scientific research and correspondence pertaining to the art or science of cultivating aquatic plants and animals in artificial tanks or ponds.
Refereed Serial

571.95   US   ISSN 0887-2082
           CODEN: JBTOEB
JOURNAL OF BIOCHEMICAL TOXICOLOGY. 1986. bi-m. $356 (foreign $455) (effective 1998). John Wiley & Sons, Inc., Journals, 605 Third Ave., New York, NY 10158-0012. TEL 212-850-6645. FAX 212-850-6021. TELEX 12-7063. E-mail: subinfo@jwiley.com; URL: http://www.wiley.co.uk. (Subscr. outside the Americas to: John Wiley & Sons Ltd., Bafins Ln., Chichester, W. Sussex PO19 1UD, England. TEL 44-1243-779777. FAX 44-1243-776128) Ed. E. Hodgson. adv.: B&W page £640, color page £1515; trim 279 x 210. circ. 855. (also avail. in microform) **Indexed:** ASCA, Curr.Cont., Sci.Cit.Ind. **Document type:** academic/scholarly publication.
—BLDSC (4951.800000); CASDDS; CISTI; Genuine Article; KNAW; SWETS; UnCover. **CCC.**
Description: Focuses on the molecular mechanism of action and detoxication of exogenous and endogenous chemical toxic agents. Includes effects on the organisms at all stages of development.

JOURNAL OF BIOGEOGRAPHY. see *GEOGRAPHY*

JOURNAL OF BIOLOGICAL CONTROL. see *AGRICULTURE — Crop Production And Soil*

570   UK   ISSN 0021-9266
QH315   CODEN: JBIEAO
JOURNAL OF BIOLOGICAL EDUCATION. 1966. q. £52 (N. & S. America $112; elsewhere £61) (effective 1997). Institute of Biology, 20-22 Queensberry Pl., London SW7 2DZ, England. TEL 44-171-581-8333. FAX 44-171-823-9409. URL: http://www.primex.co.uk/iob. Ed. John A. Barker. adv. contact: Clare P. Chatham. bk.rev.; illus.; index; circ. 2,300 (paid). (back issues avail.) **Indexed:** ASCA, Biol.Abstr., Br.Educ.Ind., C.I.J.E., Chem.Abstr, Cont.Pg.Educ., Curr.Cont., Dairy Sci.Abstr., Ecol.Abstr., Educ.Ind., Educ.Tech.Abstr., Environ.Abstr., Geo.Abstr., High.Educ.Curr.Aware.Bull., IBR, India Rev.Dig., Mult.Ed.Abstr., Res.High.Educ.Abstr., Rural Recreat.Tour.Abstr., SSCI, Tech.Educ.Abstr., Telegen, World Agri.Econ.& Rural Sociol.Abstr. **Document type:** academic/scholarly publication.
—BLDSC (4953.100000); CIS; Genuine Article; KR SourceOne; Linda Hall; SWETS; UnCover. **CCC.**
Description: Presents articles on practical work, curricular matters, and teaching methods in biology.
Refereed Serial

570   US   ISSN 0274-497X
TR1   CODEN: JBPHD3
JOURNAL OF BIOLOGICAL PHOTOGRAPHY. 1933. q. $65 (foreign $75) (effective 1996). Biological Photographic Association, Inc., 1819 Peachtree St., N.E., Ste. 620, Atlanta, GA 30309-1849. TEL 404-351-6300. FAX 404-351-3348. E-mail: assnhq@atl.mindspring.com. Ed. Joseph Ogrodnick. bk.rev.; bibl.; illus.; index. circ. 1,875. (also avail. in microform from UMI; reprint service avail. from UMI) **Indexed:** Biol.Abstr., Chem.Abstr., Deep Sea Res.& Oceanogr.Abstr., GeoRef., Ind.Med., Ind.Vet., INIS Atomind. **Document type:** academic/scholarly publication.
—BLDSC (4953.135000); CISTI; Linda Hall; SWETS; UMI; UnCover.
Formerly: Biological Photographic Association. Journal (ISSN 0006-3215)
Refereed Serial

570   IT   ISSN 0393-974X
           CODEN: JBRAER
JOURNAL OF BIOLOGICAL REGULATORS AND HOMEOSTATIC AGENTS. (Text in Italian; summaries in English) 1987. q. L.160000 (Europe $160) (effective 1997). Wichtig Editore s.r.l., Via Friuli 72-74, 20135 Milan, Italy. TEL 39-2-55195443. FAX 39-2-55195971. **Indexed:** ASCA, Curr.Cont. —BLDSC (4953.220000); CASDDS; EMDOCS; Genuine Article; KNAW; SWETS; UnCover. **CCC.**

570   IQ   ISSN 1012-344X
           CODEN: JBSREF
JOURNAL OF BIOLOGICAL SCIENCE RESEARCH. (Text in English; summaries in Arabic, English) 1965. 3/yr. ID.5($15) to individuals; institutions $50. Scientific Research Council of Iraq, Biological Research Centre, Jadiriyah, P.O. Box 2371, Baghdad, Iraq. TEL 7765116. TELEX 213976 SRC 112. Ed. Azwar N. Khalaf. circ. 750. **Indexed:** Biol.Abstr., Chem.Abstr., Curr.Cont., Food Sci.& Tech.Abstr., Pollut.Abstr., Rev.Appl.Entomol., Rev.Med.& Vet.Mycol., Sport Fish.Abstr., Wild.Rev., Zoo.Rec. **Document type:** academic/scholarly publication.
—CASDDS.
Formerly (until 1982): Scientific Research Council of Iraq. Biological Science Research Centre. Journal (ISSN 0067-2890)

570   II   ISSN 0021-9282
QH1   CODEN: JBSBAV
JOURNAL OF BIOLOGICAL SCIENCES. (Text in English) 1958. s-a. Rs.30($8) Bombay Biological Association, c/o Biology Dept., R. J. College, Ghatkopar, Bombay 400086, India. Eds. S.M. Karmarkar, K.P. Dhage. adv.; bk.rev.; charts; illus.; index. circ. 250. (also avail. in microfilm from UMI; reprint service avail. from UMI) **Indexed:** Biol.Abstr., Chem.Abstr., Indian Sci.Abstr., Seed Abstr., Vet.Bull.
—CASDDS; CISTI; Linda Hall.

570   SI   ISSN 0218-3390
JOURNAL OF BIOLOGICAL SYSTEMS. 1993. q. $90 to individuals; institutions $224 (developing countries $135). World Scientific Publishing Co. Pte. Ltd., Farrer Rd., P.O. Box 128, Singapore 9128, Singapore. TEL 65-3825663. FAX 65-3825919. TELEX RS-28561-WSPC. E-mail: wspcsl@singnet.com.sg; sales@wspc2.demon.co.uk; wspc@wspc.com; URL: http://www.singnet.com.sg/~wspclib/. (UK addr.: 57 Shelton St., Covent Garden, London WC2H 9HE, England. TEL 44-171-836-0888. FAX 44-171-836-2020; US addr.: 1060 Main St., Ste. 1B, River Edge, NJ 07661. TEL 800-227-7562. FAX 201-487-9656) Eds. P.M. Auger, R.V. Jean. **Document type:** academic/scholarly publication.
—BLDSC (4953.420000); CISTI.
Description: Promotes interdisciplinary approaches in biology and in medicine, including mathematical methods and general systems theory as they contribute to the study of biological situations.

JOURNAL OF BIOMEDICAL OPTICS. see *PHYSICS — Optics*

JOURNAL OF BIOMEDICAL SCIENCE. see *MEDICAL SCIENCES*

570   II   ISSN 0250-5991
           CODEN: JOBSDN
JOURNAL OF BIOSCIENCES. (Text in English) 1979. q. Rs.150($100) (effective 1997). Indian Academy of Sciences, C.V. Raman Avenue, P.B 8005, Bangalore 560 080, India. TEL 91-80-3342546. FAX 91-80-3346094. TELEX 0845-2178-ACAD-IN. E-mail: jbiosci@ias.ernet.in. Ed. M.K. Chandrashekaran. circ. 1,250. (back issues avail.; reprint service avail. from ISI) **Indexed:** Apic.Abstr., ASCA, Chem.Abstr., Curr.Cont., Dairy Sci.Abstr., Ecol.Abstr., Environ.Abstr., Excerp.Med., Field Crop Abstr., Helminthol.Abstr., Ind.Sci.Rev., Ind.Vet., INIS Atomind., Protozool.Abstr., Rev.Med.& Vet.Mycol., Sci.Cit.Ind., Soils & Fert., Sorghum & Millets Abstr., Telegen, Trop.Oil Seeds Abstr., Weed Abstr. **Document type:** academic/scholarly publication.
—BLDSC (4954.070000); CASDDS; CIS; CISTI; EMDOCS; Genuine Article; KNAW; Linda Hall; SWETS; UMI; UnCover.
Incorporates (1934-1991): Indian Academy of Sciences. Proceedings. Animal Sciences (ISSN 0253-4118) & Indian Academy of Sciences. Proceedings. Plant Sciences (ISSN 0253-410X)

570.285   US   ISSN 1066-5277
           CODEN: JCOBEM
JOURNAL OF COMPUTATIONAL BIOLOGY; a journal of computational molecular cell biology. 1994. q. $111 to individuals (foreign $174); institutions $257 (foreign $300) (effective through 1998). Mary Ann Liebert, Inc. Publishers, 2 Madison Ave., Larchmont, NY 10538. TEL 914-834-3100. FAX 914-834-3688. E-mail: liebert@pipeline.com. Eds. David T. Kingsbury, Michael S. Waterman. adv. (back issues avail.) **Indexed:** Curr.Cont., Excerp.Med. (1996-), Ind.Med. (1995-). **Document type:** academic/scholarly publication.
—BLDSC (4963.455000); CASDDS; Genuine Article; SWETS.
Description: Provides a forum for scientific and technical issues associated with the analysis and management of biological information at the molecular level.
Refereed Serial

508.676   KE
QH1
JOURNAL OF EAST AFRICAN NATURAL HISTORY. (Text in English) 1910. s-a. $30. East Africa Natural History Society, P.O. Box 44486, Nairobi, Kenya. TEL 254-2-749957. FAX 254-2-741049. E-mail: kipepeo@form-net.com. (Co-sponsor: National Museums of Kenya) Ed. Edward Vanden Berghe. R&P contact: Lorna Depew. TEL 254-125-22078. bk.rev. circ. 1,035. **Indexed:** Weed Abstr., Zoo.Rec. **Document type:** academic/scholarly publication.
—CISTI; Linda Hall.
Formerly (until 1994): Journal of the East Africa Natural History Society and National Museum (ISSN 0012-8317)
Description: Contains information about natural history or conservation of the natural environment.
Refereed Serial

570   II   ISSN 0970-9037
QH183   CODEN: JECBEA
JOURNAL OF ECOBIOLOGY; international journal of scientific research on environmental biology and inter-relations. (Text in English) 1989. q. $200 (effective 1996). Palani Paramount Publications, 69D, Anna Nagar, Palani 624 602, India. TEL 91-4545-42332. FAX 91-4545-42199. Ed. S. Palanichamy. R&P contact: S. Palanichamy. adv.: page $125. bk.rev.; charts; illus. circ. 400. (reprint service avail.) **Document type:** academic/scholarly publication.
—BLDSC (4971.850000).
Refereed Serial

577   UK   ISSN 0022-0477
           CODEN: JECOAB
JOURNAL OF ECOLOGY. 1913. bi-m. £255($465) (foreign £280) (effective 1998). (British Ecological Society) Blackwell Science Ltd., Osney Mead, Oxford OX2 OEL, England. TEL 44-1865-206206. FAX 44-1865-721205. E-mail: journals.cs@blacksci.co.uk; URL: http://www.black.co.uk. Ed. J. Silvertown; Pub. Allen Stevens. R&P contact: Sarah Pollard. adv. contact: Martine Cariou-Keen. bk.rev.; abstr.; bibl.; charts; illus.; maps; index, cum.index: vols.1-20 (1913-1932), vols.21-50 (1933-1982). circ. 3,420. (also avail. in microform from UMI; back issues avail.; reprint service avail. from ISI) **Indexed:** Agroforest.Abstr., ASCA, Bibl.Agri., Bio-Contr.News & Info., Biol.Abstr., Biol.& Agr.Ind., Biostat., Br.Archaeol.Abstr., Br.Geol.Lit., Chem.Abstr., Crop Physiol.Abstr., Curr.Cont., Curr.Ref.Fish Res., Deep Sea Res.& Oceanogr.Abstr., Ecol.Abstr., Energy Rev., Environ.Abstr., Environ.Per.Bibl. (1982-), Excerp.Med., Field Crop Abstr., Forest.Abstr., Forest Prod.Abstr., Gen.Sci.Ind., Geo.Abstr.H.G., Geol.Abstr., GeoRef., Helminthol.Abstr., Herb.Abstr., IBR, Ind.Sci.Rev., Key Word Ind.Wildl.Res., Plant Breed.Abstr., Rev.Appl.Entomol., Rev.Plant Path., Sci.Cit.Ind., Seed Abstr., Sel.Water Res.Abstr., Soils & Fert., Sport Fish.Abstr., Triticale Abstr., Weed Abstr., Wild.Rev., Zoo.Rec. **Document type:** academic/scholarly publication.
—BLDSC (4972.000000); CASDDS; CISTI; EMDOCS; Genuine Article; KR SourceOne; Linda Hall; SWETS; UMI; UnCover. **CCC.**
Refereed Serial

570 572 US ISSN 0278-0771
GN476.7 CODEN: JOUEE9
JOURNAL OF ETHNOBIOLOGY. (Abstracts in English, French, Spanish) 1981. s-a. $35 to individuals; students $25; institutions $60. Society of Ethnobiology, c/o Gayle Fritz, Anthropology - CB1114, Washington University, St. Louis, MO 63130-4899. TEL 314-935-8588. FAX 314-935-8535. Ed. Eugene Hunn. adv.; bk.rev. circ. 400. (back issues avail.) **Indexed:** Abstr.Anthropol., Anthropol.Lit., Biol.Abstr., Sport Fish.Abstr., Wild.Rev., Zoo.Rec. **Document type:** academic/scholarly publication.
—BLDSC (4979.602350); UnCover.
Description: Features articles about the uses of plants and animals by native peoples worldwide, both prehistorically and historically. Covers ethnozoology, paleoethnobotany, paleozoology, and ethnobotany.
Refereed Serial

570 UK ISSN 0022-0949
QH301 CODEN: JEBIAM
JOURNAL OF EXPERIMENTAL BIOLOGY. 1923. m. £829 (U.S. & Canada $1437; elsewhere £850) (effective 1998). Company of Biologists Ltd., Bidder Bldg., 140 Cowley Rd., Cambridge CB4 4DL, England. TEL 44-1223-426164. FAX 44-1223-423353. E-mail: cob@cambridge.cityscape.co.uk; URL: http://www.cityscape.co.uk/users/ag64. Ed. R.G. Boutilier. adv. contact: Richard Skaer. charts; illus.; index; cum.index vols. 16-46. circ. 1,700. (back issues avail.) **Indexed:** Apic.Abstr., ASCA, Biol.Abstr., Biol.& Agr.Ind., Chem.Abstr., Chem.Cit.Ind., Curr.Adv.Cell & Devel.Biol., Curr.Cont., Curr.Ref.Fish Res., Dairy Sci.Abstr., Deep Sea Res.& Oceanogr.Abstr., Dent.Ind., Excerp.Med., Gen.Sci.Ind., Geo.Abstr., Helminthol.Abstr., Hort.Abstr., Ind.Med., Ind.Sci.Rev., Ind.Vet., Key Word Ind.Wildl.Res., Med.& Surg.Dermat., Neurosci.Cit.Ind., Nutr.Abstr., Ocean.Abstr., Pollut.Abstr., Psychol.Abstr., Rev.Appl.Entomol., Soils & Fert., Sport Fish.Abstr., SSCI, Trop.Dis.Bull., Vet.Bull., W.R.C.Inf., Weed Abstr., Wild.Rev., Zoo.Rec. **Document type:** academic/scholarly publication.
—BLDSC (4980.000000); CASDDS; CISTI; EMDOCS; KNAW; KR SourceOne; Linda Hall; SWETS; UMI; UnCover.
Formerly (until 1929): British Journal of Experimental Biology (ISSN 0366-0788)
Description: Covers integrative biology from molecular to whole animal.
Refereed Serial

578.77 NE ISSN 0022-0981
QH91.A1 CODEN: JEMBAM
JOURNAL OF EXPERIMENTAL MARINE BIOLOGY AND ECOLOGY. 1967. 22/yr. fl.5100($2931) (effective 1998). Elsevier Science B.V., P.O. Box 211, 1000 AE Amsterdam, Netherlands. TEL 31-20-4853911. FAX 31-20-4853598. TELEX 18582 ESPA NL. E-mail: nlinfo-f@elsevier.nl; usinfo-f@elsevier.com; forinfo-kyf04035@niftyserve.or.jp; URL: http://www.elsevier.nl/. (Subscr. in the Americas to: Elsevier Science, Regional Sales Office, Box 945, New York, NY 10159-0945. TEL 212-633-3730. FAX 212-633-3680; Subscr. in Australasia and the Far East to: Elsevier Science (Singapore) Pte Ltd, No.1 Temasek Ave., No.17-01 Millenia Tower, Singapore 039192, Singapore. TEL 65-434-3727. FAX 65-337-2230; Subscr. in Japan to: Elsevier Science Japan, 9-15 Higashi-Azabu 1-chome, Minato-ku, Tokyo 106, Japan. TEL 81-3-5561-5033. FAX 81-3-5561-5047) Ed.Bd. (also avail. in microform from UMI; reprint service avail. from ISI,SWZ) **Indexed:** Aqua.Sci.& Fish.Abstr., ASCA, Biol.Abstr., Biol.& Agr.Ind., Chem.Abstr., Curr.Cont., Curr.Ref.Fish Res., Deep Sea Res.& Oceanogr.Abstr., Ecol.Abstr., Energy Ind., Energy Info.Abstr., Environ.Abstr., Environ.Per.Bibl. (1990-1993), Excerp.Med., Geo.Abstr.H.G., GeoRef., Helminthol.Abstr., Ind.Sci.Rev., Mar.Sci.Cont.Tab., Nutr.Abstr., Ocean.Abstr., Pollut.Abstr., Sci.Cit.Ind., Sel.Water Res.Abstr., Sport Fish.Abstr., SSCI, W.R.C.Inf., Wild.Rev., Zoo.Rec. **Document type:** academic/scholarly publication.
—BLDSC (4981.600000); CASDDS; CISTI; EMDOCS; Genuine Article; Linda Hall; SWETS; UnCover. **CCC**.
Description: Provides a forum for work in the biochemistry, physiology, behavior, and genetics of marine plants and animals in relation to their ecology.
Refereed Serial

578.7 II ISSN 0970-3594
QH90.A1 CODEN: JOHYE4
JOURNAL OF HYDROBIOLOGY. 1985. s-a. Rs.750($20) Vikram University, School of Studies in Zoology, Box 233, Ujjain 456 010, India. Ed. K.S. Rao. adv.; bk.rev. **Indexed:** Biol.Abstr., Zoo.Rec.
—CISTI; UnCover.

570 US ISSN 0883-1394
CODEN: JIDBE9
JOURNAL OF INFERENTIAL AND DEDUCTIVE BIOLOGY.* 1985. irreg. $188. Danielli Associates, c/o Richard F. Danielli, 7 Marston Way, No. 7, Worcester, MA 01609-2176. Eds. Roger V. Jean, Alejandro B. Engel. adv.; bk.rev.
—CASDDS.

JOURNAL OF MAMMALOGY. see *BIOLOGY — Zoology*

570 GW ISSN 0303-6812
QH323.5 CODEN: JMBLAJ
JOURNAL OF MATHEMATICAL BIOLOGY. Online edition (GW ISSN 1432-1416) (Text in English) m. DM.1430 (foreign DM.1441.60) (effective 1998). Springer-Verlag, Heidelberger Platz 3, 14197 Berlin, Germany. TEL 49-30-82787-0. FAX 49-30-82787448. E-mail: subscriptions@springer.de; URL: http://link.springer.de. (Subscr. in N. America to: Springer-Verlag New York, Inc., 333 Meadowlands Pkwy., Secaucus, NJ 07094. TEL 212-460-1500. FAX 212-473-6272) Eds. K.P. Hadeler, A. Hastings. (also avail. in microform from UMI; reprint service avail. from ISI) **Indexed:** Anim.Breed.Abstr., ASCA, Biostat., Compumath, Comput.Abstr., Curr.Adv.Biochem., Curr.Adv.Ecol.Sci., Curr.Adv.Genetics & Molec.Biol., Curr.Cont. (1990-), Deep Sea Res.& Oceanogr.Abstr., Excerp.Med., Helminthol.Abstr., Ind.Med., Ind.Sci.Rev., INSPEC, Math.R., Plant Breed.Abstr., Sci.Cit.Ind., Sport Fish.Abstr., Stat.Theor.Meth.Abstr. (1990-), Wild.Rev., Zent.Math., Zoo.Rec. **Document type:** academic/scholarly publication.
•Also available online.
—BLDSC (5012.375000); AskIEEE; CISTI; Genuine Article; KR SourceOne; Linda Hall; SWETS; UMI; UnCover. **CCC**.
Description: Includes the fields of genetics, demography, ecology, neurobiology, epidemiology, morphogenesis, and cell biology.
Refereed Serial

571.3 US ISSN 0362-2525
QL801 CODEN: JOMOAT
JOURNAL OF MORPHOLOGY. 1887. m. $1995 (foreign $2205) (effective 1998). John Wiley & Sons, Inc., Journals, 605 Third Ave., New York, NY 10158. TEL 212-850-6645. FAX 212-850-6021. TELEX 12-7063. E-mail: SUBINFO@JWILEY.COM; URL: http://www.wiley.co.uk. (Subscr. outside the Americas to: John Wiley & Sons Ltd., Baffins Ln., Chichester, W. Sussex PO19 1UD, England. TEL 44-1243-779777. FAX 44-1243-776128) Ed. Frederick W. Harrison. adv.: B&W page £640, color page £1515; trim 254 x 174. abstr.; bibl.; charts; illus.; index. circ. 900. (also avail. in microform from SWZ,PMC,UMI; back issues avail.; reprint service avail. from SWZ) **Indexed:** Anim.Breed.Abstr., ASCA, Biol.Abstr., Chem.Abstr., Curr.Adv.Cell & Devel.Biol., Curr.Adv.Ecol.Sci., Curr.Cont., Deep Sea Res.& Oceanogr.Abstr., Dent.Ind., Excerp.Med., Helminthol.Abstr., Ind.Med., Ind.Sci.Rev., Ind.Vet., INIS Atomind., Neurosci.Cit.Ind., Poult.Abstr., Rev.Appl.Entomol., Sci.Cit.Ind., Sport Fish.Abstr., SSCI, Vet.Bull., Wild.Rev., Zoo.Rec. **Document type:** academic/scholarly publication.
—BLDSC (5021.000000); CASDDS; CISTI; EMDOCS; Genuine Article; KNAW; Linda Hall; SWETS; UnCover. **CCC**.
Former titles (until 1930): Journal of Morphology and Physiology (ISSN 0095-9626); (until 1923): Journal of Morphology (ISSN 0022-2887)
Description: Publishes original research in morphology including cytology, protozoology, developmental biology, and general and functional morphology.
Refereed Serial

570 II ISSN 0970-3799
JOURNAL OF NATURAL & PHYSICAL SCIENCES. 1987. s-a. Rs.100($50) Gurukul Kangri University, Department of Mathematics, Hardwar 249 404, India. Ed. S.L. Singh. bk.rev. circ. 200. **Indexed:** Zent.Math.
Description: Covers biology, chemistry, physics, and mathematics.

570 UK ISSN 0022-2933
QH1 CODEN: JNAHA9
JOURNAL OF NATURAL HISTORY. 1841. m. £740($1220) (effective 1997). Taylor & Francis Ltd., 1 Gunpowder Sq., London EC4A 3DE, England. TEL 44-171-583-0490. FAX 44-171-583-0585. TELEX 858540. E-mail: info@tandf.co.uk; URL: http://www.tandf.co.uk/. (Subscr. in N. America to: Taylor & Francis Inc., 1900 Frost Rd., Ste. 101, Bristol, PA 19007-1598. TEL 800-821-8312. FAX 215-785-5515) Eds. P.G. Moore, A. Polaszek. adv.; bk.rev. (also avail. in microform) **Indexed:** Apic.Abstr., ASCA, Bio-Contr.News & Info., Biol.Abstr., Curr.Adv.Ecol.Sci., Curr.Cont., Curr.Ref.Fish Res., Curr.Tit.Ocean, Deep Sea Res.& Oceanogr.Abstr., Ecol.Abstr., Environ.Per.Bibl. (1991-), Geol.Abstr., GeoRef., Helminthol.Abstr., IBR, Ind.Sci.Rev., Ind.Vet., Ref.Sour., Rev.Appl.Entomol., Sci.Cit.Ind., So.Pac.Per.Ind., Soils & Fert., Sport Fish.Abstr., Weed Abstr., Wild.Rev., Zoo.Rec. **Document type:** academic/scholarly publication.
—BLDSC (5021.200000); CISTI; EMDOCS; Genuine Article; Linda Hall; SWETS; UnCover. **CCC**.
Formerly (until 1967): Annals and Magazine of Natural History.
Description: Contains original research and reviews in systematics and evolutionary and general biology.
Refereed Serial

B

JOURNAL OF NUCLEAR AGRICULTURE AND BIOLOGY. see *AGRICULTURE — Crop Production And Soil*

JOURNAL OF PALEOLIMNOLOGY. see *PALEONTOLOGY*

578.77 UK ISSN 0142-7873
QH90.8.P5 CODEN: JPLRD9
JOURNAL OF PLANKTON RESEARCH. 1979. m. £270 (foreign $450) (effective 1998). Oxford University Press, Academic Division, Great Clarendon St., Oxford OX2 6DP, England. TEL 44-1865-267907. FAX 44-1865-267485. TELEX 837330-OXPRES-G. E-mail: jnl.info@oup.co.uk; URL: http://www.oup.co.uk/journals. (U.S. subscr. to: Oxford University Press Inc., 2001 Evans Rd., Cary, NC 27513. TEL 800-852-7323. FAX 919-677-1714) Ed. D.H. Cushing; Pub. Steven Johnson. R&P contact: Joolz Longley. adv.; index. circ. 800. (back issues avail.; reprint service avail. from SWZ) **Indexed:** Arts & Hum.Cit.Ind., ASCA, Chem.Abstr., Curr.Adv.Ecol.Sci., Curr.Cont., Deep Sea Res.& Oceanogr.Abstr., Ecol.Abstr., Geo.Abstr.H.G., Geol.Abstr., Sci.Cit.Ind., Sel.Water Res.Abstr., W.R.C.Inf. **Document type:** academic/scholarly publication.
—BLDSC (5040.350000); CASDDS; CISTI; EMDOCS; Genuine Article; Linda Hall; SWETS; UMI; UnCover. **CCC**.
Description: A forum for international papers covering zooplankton and phytoplankton in three main areas: ecology (including model studies); physiology; distribution, life and taxonomy.

JOURNAL OF QUATERNARY SCIENCE. see *EARTH SCIENCES — Geology*

636.0845 US ISSN 0022-409X
SF85 CODEN: JRMGAQ
JOURNAL OF RANGE MANAGEMENT; covering the study, management, and use of rangeland ecosystems and range resources. 1948. bi-m. $95 (foreign $112); with Rangelands $140 (foreign $158) (effective 1995-1997). Society for Range Management, 1839 York St., Denver, CO 80206-1213. TEL 303-355-7070. Ed. Gary Frasier. adv. contact: Patty Rich. bk.rev.; bibl.; charts; illus.; index. circ. 6,000. (also avail. in microfilm from UMI; reprint service avail. from UMI) **Indexed:** Agri.Eng.Abstr., Agroforest.Abstr., ASCA, Biol.Abstr., Biol.& Agr.Ind., Biol.Dig., Biotech.Abstr., Chem.Abstr., Crop Physiol.Abstr., Curr.Adv.Ecol.Sci., Curr.Cont., Dairy Sci.Abstr., Ecol.Abstr., Energy Ind., Energy Info.Abstr., Environ.Per.Bibl. (1972-), Farm & Garden Ind., Field Crop Abstr., Forest.Abstr., Forest Prod.Abstr., Geo.Abstr.H.G., Geo.Abstr.P.G., GeoRef., Herb.Abstr., IDA, Ind.Sci.Rev., Ind.Vet., INIS Atomind., Int.Abstr.Oper.Res., Irr.& Drain.Abstr., Plant Breed.Abstr., Plant Grow.Reg.Abstr., Sci.Cit.Ind., Seed Abstr., Soils & Fert., Sport Fish.Abstr., SSCI, Triticale Abstr., Vet.Bull., Weed Abstr., Wild.Rev., World Agri.Econ.& Rural Sociol.Abstr., Zoo.Rec. **Document type:** trade publication.
—BLDSC (5046.000000); CASDDS; EMDOCS; Genuine Article; KR SourceOne; Linda Hall; SWETS; UMI; UnCover.
Description: Offers a forum of technical articles about research in range science and range management.
Refereed Serial

BIOLOGY

570 US ISSN 1079-9893
QH603.C43 CODEN: JRETET
JOURNAL OF RECEPTOR AND SIGNAL TRANSDUCTION RESEARCH. 1995. bi-m. $750 (foreign $772.50) (effective 1998). Marcel Dekker Journals, 270 Madison Ave., New York, NY 10016. TEL 212-696-9000. TELEX 421419 MARDEEK. (Subscr. to: Box 5017, Monticello, NY 12701. TEL 800-228-1160) Eds. Ross B. Mikkelsen, Vladimir K. Pliska. adv. contact: Lourdes Barroso. bk.rev.; charts; illus.; index. (also avail. in microform from RPI; back issues avail.) **Indexed:** ASCA, Biol.Abstr., Chem.Abstr., Curr.Adv.Biochem., Curr.Adv.Cell & Devel.Biol., Curr.Adv.Ecol.Sci., Curr.Cont., Dairy Sci.Abstr., Excerp.Med., Ind.Med., Ind.Sci.Rev., Protozool.Abstr., Sci.Cit.Ind. **Document type:** academic/scholarly publication.
—BLDSC (5047.849000); CASDDS; CISTI; EMDOCS; Genuine Article; KNAW; Linda Hall; SWETS; UMI; UnCover. **CCC.**
   Formed by the merger of (1980-1995): Journal of Receptor Research (ISSN 0197-5110) & Second Messengers and Phosphoproteins (ISSN 0895-7479): Which was formerly titled (until 1988): Journal of Cyclic Nucleotide and Protein Phosphorylation Research; Journal of Cyclic Nucleotide Research (ISSN 0095-1544)
   Refereed Serial

612 573.6 II
JOURNAL OF REPRODUCTION AND FERTILITY. q. Indian Society for the Study of Reproduction and Endocrinology, c/o Department of Zoology, University of Delhi, Delhi 110007, India. (also avail. in microfilm from PMC) **Indexed:** Biol.Abstr., Biol.& Agr.Ind., Curr.Cont., Small Anim.Abstr., Vet.Bull.

573.6 UK ISSN 0449-3087
CODEN: JRFSAR
JOURNAL OF REPRODUCTION AND FERTILITY. SUPPLEMENT. 1966. irreg. price varies. Journals of Reproduction & Fertility Ltd., 22 Newmarket Rd., Cambridge CB5 8DT, England. TEL 44-1223-351809. FAX 44-1223-359754. E-mail: jrf@cityscape.co.uk. (Dist. by: Portland Press, P.O. Box 32, Commerce Way, Colchester, Essex CO2 8HP, England. TEL 44-1206-796351) Ed. Dr. C. Doberska. (back issues avail.) **Indexed:** Biol.Abstr., Ind.Med., Sport Fish.Abstr., Wild.Rev., Zoo.Rec. **Document type:** academic/scholarly publication, monographic series.
—BLDSC (5049.601000); CASDDS; CISTI; KNAW; Linda Hall; SWETS. **CCC.**

573.6 II ISSN 0254-3583
CODEN: JRBED2
JOURNAL OF REPRODUCTIVE BIOLOGY AND COMPARATIVE ENDOCRINOLOGY. (Text in English) 1981. s-a. $75. (Society for Reproductive Biology and Comparative Endocrinology) Hindustan Publishing Corp., 4805-24, 1st Fl., Bharat Ram Rd., Darya Ganj, New Delhi 110 002, India. TEL 91-11-3254401. FAX 91-11-6863511. E-mail: hpcpd@giasdl01.vsnl.net.in.
—CASDDS.

JOURNAL OF SEA RESEARCH. see EARTH SCIENCES — Oceanography

JOURNAL OF SOCIAL AND EVOLUTIONARY SYSTEMS. see PSYCHOLOGY

577 591 595.7 II ISSN 0970-1370
JOURNAL OF SOIL BIOLOGY AND ECOLOGY. (Text and summaries in English) 1981. s-a. Rs.400($60) (effective 1997). Indian Society of Soil Biology and Ecology, University of Agricultural Sciences, Department of Entomology, Hebbal, Bangalore 560 024, India. TEL 91-80-3330153. FAX 91-80-3330277. Ed. G.K. Veeresh. adv. circ 350. (back issues avail.) **Indexed:** Biol.Abstr., Soils & Fert., Sorghum & Millets Abstr.
●Also available on CD-ROM.
—BLDSC (5064.955000); CISTI.
   Refereed Serial

570 US ISSN 1047-8477
QH573 CODEN: JSBIEM
JOURNAL OF STRUCTURAL BIOLOGY. (Text in various languages) 1957. 9/yr. $395 (foreign $495) (effective 1997). Academic Press, Inc., Journal Division, 525 B St., Ste. 1900, San Diego, CA 92101-4495. TEL 619-230-1840. FAX 619-699-6859. E-mail: apsubs@acad.com; URL: http://www.apnet.com/www/journal/sb.htm; http://www.idealibrary.com/. (Subscr. to: Box 861213, Orlando, FL 32886-1213. TEL 407-347-4040. FAX 407-363-9661) Ed. Alasdair C. Steven. adv.; bibl.; charts; illus.; index. **Indexed:** Abstr.Bull.Inst.Pap.Chem., Abstr.Hyg., Anim.Breed.Abstr., ASCA, Bibl.Agri., Biol.Abstr., Chem.Abstr., Curr.Adv.Ecol.Sci., Curr.Cont., Dairy Sci.Abstr., Excerp.Med., Field Crop Abstr., GeoRef., Helminthol.Abstr., Herb.Abstr., Ind.Med., Ind.Sci.Rev., Ind.Vet., Nutr.Abstr., Pig News & Info., Poult.Abstr., Protozool.Abstr., Rev.Plant Path., Sci.Cit.Ind., Soils & Fert., Sport Fish.Abstr., Trop.Dis.Bull., Vet.Bull., Wild.Rev., Zoo.Rec. **Document type:** academic/scholarly publication.
●Also available online.
—BLDSC (5066.874500); ADONIS; CASDDS; CISTI; EMDOCS; Genuine Article; Linda Hall; SWETS; UnCover. **CCC.**
   Former titles: Journal of Ultrastructure and Molecular Structure Research (ISSN 0889-1605); Journal of Ultrastructure Research (ISSN 0022-5320)
   Description: Deals with the structural analysis of biological matter at all levels of organization by means of light and electron microscopy, x-ray diffraction, nuclear magnetic resonance, as well as other imaging, diffraction, spectroscopic, or scanning probe techniques yielding structural information.
   Refereed Serial

570 NE ISSN 0022-5010
QH305 CODEN: JHBIA9
JOURNAL OF THE HISTORY OF BIOLOGY. 1968. 3/yr. fl.445 to institutions; $228.50 to institutions in U.S. (effective 1998). Kluwer Academic Publishers, Postbus 17, 3300 AA Dordrecht, Netherlands. TEL 31-78-6392392. FAX 31-78-6392254. TELEX 29245 KAPG NL. E-mail: services@wkap.nl; URL: http://www.wkap.nl. (Dist. by: Kluwer Academic Publishers Group, P.O. Box 322, 3300 AH Dordrecht, Netherlands. TEL 31-78-6392392. FAX 31-78-6546474; N. America dist. addr.: Box 358, Accord Sta., Hingham, MA 02018-0358. TEL 617-871-6600) Eds. Everett Mendelsohn, Shirley A. Roe. adv.; bk.rev.; charts; illus.; index. (also avail. in microform from UMI; reprint service avail. from SWZ) **Indexed:** Amer.Hist.& Life (1968-), Arts & Hum.Cit.Ind., ASCA, Biol.Abstr., Biol.& Agr.Ind., Curr.Adv.Ecol.Sci., Curr.Cont., Deep Sea Res.& Oceanogr.Abstr., Hist.Abstr. (1968-), IBR, Ind.Med., Ind.Sci.Rev., Plant Breed.Abstr., Ref.Zh., Sci.Cit.Ind. **Document type:** academic/scholarly publication.
—BLDSC (5000.700000); CISTI; Genuine Article; KR SourceOne; Linda Hall; SWETS; UMI; UnCover. **CCC.**
   Description: Publishes research on the history of the biological sciences, with particular emphasis on developments of the 19th and 20th centuries, including philosophical issues.
   Refereed Serial

JOURNAL OF THE PERIPHERAL NERVOUS SYSTEM. see MEDICAL SCIENCES — Psychiatry And Neurology

570 UK ISSN 0022-5193
QH301 CODEN: JTBIAP
JOURNAL OF THEORETICAL BIOLOGY; an international multidisciplinary journal. 1961. 24/yr. £1655 (effective 1998). Academic Press Ltd. (Subsidiary of: Harcourt Brace & Company Ltd.), 24-28 Oval Rd., London NW1 7DX, England. TEL 44-171-267-4466. FAX 44-171-482-2293. TELEX 25775 ACPRES G. E-mail: apsubs@acad.com; URL: http://www.hbuk.co.uk/ap/jtb; http://www.europe.idealibrary.com/. (Subscr. to: Harcourt Brace & Company Ltd., Foots Cray High St., Sidcup, Kent DA14 5HP, England. TEL 44-181-300-3322. FAX 44-181-309-0807) Eds. J. Tuson, L. Wolpert. R&P contact: Catherine John. adv. contact: Nik Screen. bibl.; charts; illus.; index. **Indexed:** Abstr.Anthropol., Apic.Abstr., ASCA, Bibl.Agri., Biol.Abstr., Biostat., Chem.Abstr., Chem.Cit.Ind., Compumath, Curr.Adv.Biochem., Curr.Adv.Cell & Devel.Biol., Curr.Adv.Ecol.Sci., Curr.Adv.Genetics & Molec.Biol., Curr.Cont., Dairy Sci.Abstr., Deep Sea Res.& Oceanogr.Abstr., Dent.Ind., Ecol.Abstr., Excerp.Med., Field Crop Abstr., Geo.Abstr.H.G., Geol.Abstr., GeoRef., Helminthol.Abstr., Herb.Abstr., Ind.Med., Ind.Sci.Rev., Ind.Vet., INIS Atomind., Int.Aerosp.Abstr., Key Word Ind.Wildl.Res., Math.R., Neurosci.Cit.Ind., Nutr.Abstr., Protozool.Abstr., Risk Abstr., Sci.Cit.Ind., Sport Fish.Abstr., SSCI, Vet.Bull., Weed Abstr., Wild.Rev., Zoo.Rec. **Document type:** academic/scholarly publication.
●Also available online.
—BLDSC (5069.075000); ADONIS; CASDDS; CISTI; EMDOCS; Genuine Article; KR SourceOne; Linda Hall; SWETS; UnCover. **CCC.**
   Description: Provides a forum for theoretical papers that give insight into biological processes.

THE JOURNAL OF TRACE ELEMENTS IN EXPERIMENTAL MEDICINE. see MEDICAL SCIENCES — Experimental Medicine, Laboratory Technique

570 GW ISSN 0946-672X
CODEN: JTEBFO
JOURNAL OF TRACE ELEMENTS IN MEDICINE AND BIOLOGY. (Text in English) 1987. q. DM.506 (foreign £223) (effective 1997). (Society for Minerals and Trace Elements) Gustav Fischer Verlag, Villengang 2, 07745 Jena, Germany. TEL 49-3641-626430. FAX 49-3641-626421. E-mail: office.j@gfischer.de. (Subscr. to: Stockton Press, Subscription Dept., Houndmills, Basingstoke, Hants RG21 6XS, England) Ed.Bd. index. (back issues avail.) **Indexed:** ASCA, Chem.Abstr., Curr.Cont., Excerp.Med., Ind.Med. (1992-), Sci.Cit.Ind. **Document type:** academic/scholarly publication.
—BLDSC (5069.744400); CASDDS; CISTI; EMDOCS; Genuine Article; KNAW; SWETS; UnCover. **CCC.**
   Formerly (until 1994): Journal of Trace Elements and Electrolytes in Health and Disease (ISSN 0931-2838)
   Refereed Serial

590 636.89 US ISSN 1071-2232
SF996.45
JOURNAL OF WILDLIFE REHABILITATION. 1977. q. $38 to individuals (Canada and Mexico $44; elsewhere $46); libraries $28 (effective 1997). International Wildlife Rehabilitation Council, 4437 Central Pl., Ste. B4, Suisun, CA 94585-1669. TEL 707-864-1761. FAX 707-864-3106. E-mail: iwrc@inreach.com; URL: http://www.iwrc-online.org. Ed. Jan White. R&P contact: Mary Reynolds. bk.rev. circ. 2,000. (back issues avail.) **Indexed:** ASCA, Sport Fish.Abstr., Wild.Rev. **Document type:** trade publication.
—BLDSC (5072.630500); Genuine Article; UnCover.
   Formerly: Wildlife Journal (ISSN 0893-6560)
   Description: Dedicated to the dissemination of information related to the field of wildlife rehabilitation.
   Refereed Serial

570 JA ISSN 0287-6531
KAGAWA SEIBUTSU/BIOLOGICAL SOCIETY OF KAGAWA. BULLETIN. (Text in Japanese; summaries in English, Japanese) 1953. a. 2000 Yen. Kagawa Seibutsu Gakkai - Biological Society of Kagawa, Kagawa Daigaku Kyoikugakubu Seibutsugaku Kyoshitsu, 1-? Saiwaicho, Takamatsu-shi, Kgawa-ken 760, Japan.

BIOLOGY 611

570 551.46   JA
KAIYO SEIBUTSU KANKYO KENKYUJO KENKYU HOKOKU/MARINE ECOLOGY RESEARCH INSTITUTE. REPORT. (Text in Japanese; summaries in English, Japanese) irreg. Kaiyo Seibutsu Kankyo Kenkyujo, Chuo Kenkyuta - Marine Ecology Research Institute, Central Laboratory, 300, Iwawada, Onjukumachi, Isumi-gun, Chiba-ken 299-51, Japan.

570   PH   ISSN 0115-0553
QH301   CODEN: KPJBAR
KALIKASAN; the Philippine journal of biology. 1972. 3/yr. P.50($15) to individuals; P.200 ($30) to institutions. Kalikasan Press, Box 361, University of the Philippines at Los Banos Post Office, College, Laguna 3720, Philippines. Ed. I.J. Dogma, Jr. bk.rev.; illus.; index. circ. 1,000. **Indexed:** Biol.Abstr., Biol.& Agr.Ind., Chem.Abstr., Curr.Adv.Ecol.Sci., Curr.Cont., Dairy Sci.Abstr., Entomol.Abstr., Helminthol.Abstr., Hort.Abstr., Microbiol.Abstr., Rev.Plant Path., Soils & Fert., Weed Abstr.
—CASDDS; CISTI; Linda Hall. **CCC.**

KANAZAWA DAIGAKU RIGAKUBU FUZOKU NOTO RINKAI JIKKENJO KENKYU GAIYO NENJI HOKOKU/KANAZAWA UNIVERSITY. NOTO MARINE LABORATORY. ANNUAL PROGRESS REPORTS. see *EARTH SCIENCES — Oceanography*

570 370   US   ISSN 1064-105X
KANSAS BIOLOGY TEACHER. 1991. irreg. (1-2/yr.). $10 membership. (Emporia State University, Division of Biology) Emporia State University Press, 1200 Commercial, Emporia, KS 66801-5087. TEL 316-341-5614. (Co-sponsor: Kansas Association of Biology Teachers) Ed. John Richard Schrock. circ. 200. (back issues avail.)
Description: Covers biology education, science education and teacher training.
Refereed Serial

570   JA   ISSN 0915-6089
KATACHI NO KAGAKKAIHO/SOCIETY FOR SCIENCE ON FORM. CIRCULAR. (Text in Japanese) 1987. 3/yr. Katachi no Kagakkai - Society for Science on Form, Japan, Tokyo University of Agriculture & Technology, Dept. of Mechanical Engineering, 24-16 Nakamachi 2-chome, Koganei-shi, Tokyo 184, Japan. TEL 81-423-67-5607. FAX 81-423-67-5607. E-mail: takaki@tansei.cc.u-tokyo.ac.jp. Ed. Ryuji Takaki. **Document type:** academic/scholarly publication.
Refereed Serial

570   KE
KENYA JOURNAL OF SCIENCES. SERIES B: BIOLOGICAL SCIENCES. (Text in English) 1980. s-a. $40 in Africa, Asia, and Europe; N. and S. America, Australia, and N. Zealand $45 (effective 1997 & 1998). Kenya National Academy of Sciences, P.O. Box 39450, Nairobi, Kenya. **Indexed:** Biol.Abstr., Chem.Abstr., Dairy Sci.Abstr., Field Crop Abstr., Food Sci.& Tech.Abstr., Herb.Abstr. **Document type:** academic/scholarly publication.
—Linda Hall.
Formerly: Kenya Journal of Science and Technology. Series B: Biological Sciences (ISSN 0250-8257)

570   II   ISSN 0374-860X
KERALA ACADEMY OF BIOLOGY. JOURNAL.* (Text in Malayalam; summaries in English) s-a. Rs.15. Kerala Academy of Biology, Trivandrum, India. **Indexed:** Biol.Abstr.

570 910 550 614.7   FI   ISSN 0453-7831
AS262.T84
KEVO SUBARCTIC RESEARCH INSTITUTE. REPORTS. (Text in English, German; summaries in English) 1964. irreg. price varies. University of Turku, Kevo Subarctic Research Institute, FIN-20500 Turku, Finland. FAX 358-21-331167. (Dist. by: The Academic Bookstore, Keskuskatu 1, SF-00100 Helsinki, Finland) Ed. Seppo Neuvonen. circ. 400. **Indexed:** Biol.Abstr., Curr.Adv.Ecol.Sci., Curr.Adv.Plant.Sci., Curr.Cont., Entomol.Abstr., Forest.Abstr., Geo.Abstr., Rev.Appl.Entomol., Zoo.Rec.
—CISTI.

578.77   SU   ISSN 1012-8840
GC1   CODEN: JFMSDF
KING ABDUL AZIZ UNIVERSITY. FACULTY OF MARINE SCIENCE. JOURNAL. (Text in Arabic, English) 1981. a. $5. King Abdul Aziz University, Faculty of Marine Science, P.O. Box 1540, Jeddah 21441, Saudi Arabia. TEL 6952386. FAX 6952381. TELEX 601141 KAUNI SJ. Ed. A.K. Behairy. illus. **Indexed:** Deep Sea Res.& Oceanogr.Abstr.
Description: Promotes research in the field of marine science.

570   JA
KINKI DAIGAKU RAIFU SAIENSU KENKYU HOKOKU/KINKI UNIVERSITY. LIFE SCIENCE INSTITUTE. REPORT OF STUDIES. (Text in Japanese) 1976. a. Kinki Daigaku, Raifu Saiensu Kenkyujo - Kinki University, Life Science Institute, 377-2, Ono Higashi, Osaka Sayama-shi, Osaka 589, Japan.

570   JA   ISSN 0287-4970
KISHU SEIBUTSU/KISHU BIOLOGICAL NEWS. (Text in Japanese) 1962. a. Wakayamaken Seibutsu Dokokai - Wakayama Biological Society, c/o Mr. Nakamura, 838 Mikuzu, Wakayama-shi, Wakayama-ken 641, Japan.

570   JA   ISSN 0023-1924
R850.A1   CODEN: KAEMAW
KITASATO ARCHIVES OF EXPERIMENTAL MEDICINE. (Text in English, French and German) 1917. q. $3. Kitasato Institute, 5-9-1 Shirokane, Minato-ku, Tokyo 108, Japan. Ed. Hiroshi Anzai. bibl.; charts; illus. (also avail. in microfilm from PMC) **Indexed:** Biol.Abstr., Chem.Abstr., Excerp.Med., Ind.Med., Ind.Vet., INIS Atomind., Pig News & Info., Protozool.Abstr., Rev.Appl.Entomol., Small Anim.Abstr., Vet.Bull.
—CASDDS; CISTI.

KOBE UNIVERSITY. FACULTY OF AGRICULTURE. SCIENCE REPORTS. see *AGRICULTURE*

KOCHI UNIVERSITY. AGRICULTURAL SCIENCE. RESEARCH REPORTS. see *AGRICULTURE*

570   JA   ISSN 0389-0287
KOCHI UNIVERSITY. FACULTY OF SCIENCE. MEMOIRS. SERIES D, BIOLOGY/KOCHI DAIGAKU RIGAKUBU KIYO. SEIBUTSUGAKU. (Text in English) 1980. a. Kochi University, Faculty of Science - Kochi Daigaku Rigakubu, 5-1, Akebonocho 2-chome, Kochi-shi, Koshi-ken 780, Japan. **Indexed:** Biol.Abstr.
—BLDSC (5597.836000); CISTI.

570   AU   ISSN 0075-6547
QL571   CODEN: KLRUAS
KOLEOPTEROLOGISCHE RUNDSCHAU. 1912. a. S.300. Zoologisch-Botanische Gesellschaft in Oesterreich, Althanstr. 14, Postfach 287, A-1091 Vienna, Austria. TEL 0222-313361465. FAX 0222-31336700. circ. 180. **Indexed:** Biol.Abstr., IBR, Rev.Appl.Entomol.
—Linda Hall.

570   DK   ISSN 0366-3612
QH7   CODEN: BSVSAQ
KONGELIGE DANSKE VIDENSKABERNES SELSKAB. BIOLOGISKE SKRIFTER. (Text mostly in English) 1941. irreg., vol.47, 1997. price varies. Kongelige Danske Videnskabernes Selskab - Royal Danish Academy of Sciences and Letters, H.C. Andersens Blvd. 35, DK-1553 Copenhagen V, Denmark. TEL 45-33-113240. FAX 45-33-910736. E-mail: pg@royalacademy.dk. (Orders to: Munksgaard Export and Subscription Service, P.O. Box 2148, Noerre Soegade 35, DK-1370 Copenhagen K, Denmark) Ed. Poul Lindegaard Hjorth. bibl.; illus. **Indexed:** Biol.Abstr., Curr.Adv.Ecol.Sci., Seed Abstr. **Document type:** academic/scholarly publication, monographic series.
—BLDSC (2086.000000); CISTI; KNAW; Linda Hall.

570 591   BE   ISSN 0777-0111
KONINKLIJK BELGISCH INSTITUUT VOOR NATUURWETENSCHAPPEN. STUDIEDOCUMENTEN/INSTITUT ROYAL DES SCIENCES NATURELLES DE BELGIQUE. DOCUMENTS DE TRAVAIL. (Text in Dutch, English, French) 1963. irreg. price varies. Koninklijk Belgisch Instituut voor Natuurwetenschappen - Institut Royal des Sciences Naturelles de Belgique, Vautierstraat 29, 1000 Brussels, Belgium. bibl.; charts; illus. (back issues avail.)

570   PL
   CODEN: KOSMEY
KOSMOS. (Text in Polish; contents page in English) 1876. q. 34 Zl. (foreign $72) (effective 1997). Polskie Towarzystwo Przyrodnikow im. Kopernika, Ul. Pawinskiego 5a, 02-106 Warsaw, Poland. TEL 48-22-6584729. E-mail: klw@ibbrain.ibb.waw.pl. (Subscr. to: AMOS, ul. Zuga 12, 01-806 Warsaw, Poland. TEL 48-22-3465211) Ed. K.L. Wierzchowski. R&P contact: K.L. Wierzchowski. bk.rev.; charts; illus.; index. circ. 1,000. **Indexed:** AgroLibrex, Biol.Abstr., Chem.Abstr., Field Crop Abstr., Herb.Abstr., Protozool.Abstr. **Document type:** academic/scholarly publication.
—CASDDS; CISTI; Linda Hall.
Formerly: Kosmos. Series A. Biologia (ISSN 0023-4249)
Description: Devoted to dissemination of knowledge in biological sciences, addressed to scientists, university and middle school teachers, and students.
Refereed Serial

KOTAIGUN SEITAI GAKKAI KAIHO/SOCIETY OF POPULATION ECOLOGY. REPORT. see *POPULATION STUDIES*

570   NO   ISSN 0333-3124
KRISTIANSAND MUSEUM. AARBOK. 1965. a. NOK 50. Kristiansand Museum, P.O. Box 1018 Lundsiden, N-4602 Kristiansand, Norway. TEL 47-38-09-23-88. FAX 47-38-09-23-78. Dir. Per Arvid Aasen. circ. 900. **Document type:** academic/scholarly publication.

KUWAIT BULLETIN OF MARINE SCIENCE. see *FISH AND FISHERIES*

KYOTO DAIGAKU. REICHORUI KENKYUJO NENPO/KYOTO UNIVERSITY. PRIMATE RESEARCH INSTITUTE. ANNUAL REPORT. see *ANTHROPOLOGY*

570   JA   ISSN 0452-9987
   CODEN: CBLKAE
KYOTO UNIVERSITY. BIOLOGICAL LABORATORY. CONTRIBUTIONS. (Text in English) 1955. a. Kyoto University, Faculty of General Education, Biological Laboratory - Kyoto Daigaku Kyoyobu Seibutsugaku Kyoshitsu, Yoshida Nihonmatsucho, Sakyo-ku, Kyoto 606, Japan. TEL 81-75-753-6849. FAX 81-75-753-6864. Ed. Makoto Kato. R&P contact: Makoto Kato. adv. contact: Makoto Kato. **Indexed:** Apic.Abstr. **Document type:** proceedings.
—BLDSC (3431.520000).
Refereed Serial

570   JA   ISSN 0454-7802
QH301   CODEN: MFKBBJ
KYOTO UNIVERSITY. FACULTY OF SCIENCE. MEMOIRS. SERIES OF BIOLOGY. (Text in English) 1924; N.S. 1967. s-a. exchange basis. Kyoto University, Faculty of Science - Kyoto Daigaku Rigakubu, Kitashirakawa Oiwake-cho, Sakyo-ku, Kyoto 606, Japan. (back issues avail.) **Indexed:** Biol.Abstr., Chem.Abstr., Curr.Adv.Ecol.Sci., Deep Sea Res.& Oceanogr.Abstr., Field Crop Abstr., Herb.Abstr., INIS Atomind.
—BLDSC (5597.850000); CISTI; KNAW; Linda Hall.

570 551.48   JA
KYOTO UNIVERSITY. OTSU HYDROBIOLOGICAL STATION. COLLECTED PAPERS. (Text in Chinese, English; summaries in Chinese, English, Japanese) a. Kyoto University, Faculty of Science, Otsu Hydrobiological Station - Kyoto Daigaku Rigakubu Fuzoku Otsu Rinko Jikkenjo, Shimosakamotocho, Otsu-shi, Shiga-ken 520-01, Japan.

LABORATORY TECHNIQUES IN BIOCHEMISTRY AND MOLECULAR BIOLOGY. see *BIOLOGY — Biological Chemistry*

LASERS IN THE LIFE SCIENCES. see *PHYSICS — Optics*

LATVIJAS ZINATNU AKADEMIJAS VESTIS/LATVIAN ACADEMY OF SCIENCES. PROCEEDINGS. see *SCIENCES: COMPREHENSIVE WORKS*

570   JA
LEBEN/KAGOSHIMA DAIGAKU SEIBUTSU KENKYUKAI KAISHI. (Text in Japanese) a. Kagoshima Daigaku, Seibutsu Kenkyukai - Biological Society of Kagoshima University, Kagoshima Daigaku Gakuyukai, 21-24 Korimoto 1-chome, Kagoshima-shi, Kagoshima-ken 890, Japan.

LEBENDIGE ERDE; Zeitschrift fuer Biologisch-Dynamische Wirtschaftsweise. see *AGRICULTURE*

LECTURE NOTES IN BIOMATHEMATICS. see *MATHEMATICS*

LECTURES ON MATHEMATICS IN THE LIFE SCIENCES. see *MATHEMATICS*

580 590   LH
LIECHTENSTEIN. BOTANISCH-ZOOLOGISCHE GESELLSCHAFT LIECHTENSTEIN SARGANS-WERDENBERG. BERICHT. 1972. a. $30. Botanisch-Zoologische Gesellschaft Liechtenstein-Sargans-Werdenberg, Im Bretscha 22, FL-9494 Schaan, Liechtenstein. Ed. Mario Broggi. R&P contact: F. Flueck-Wirth. adv.; bk.rev.; bibl.; illus. circ. 1,000. **Document type:** proceedings.

577   LI   ISSN 0235-7224
CODEN: EKOLEJ
LIETUVOS MOKSLU AKADEMIJA. EKOLOGIJA. (Text in English, Lithuanian, Russian; summaries in Lithuanian, Russian) 1955. q. foreign $12 (effective 1998). Leidykla Academia, A. Gostauto 12, 2600 Vilnius, Lithuania. TEL 370-2-626851. Ed. T. Eitminaviciute. R&P contact: A. Garliauskas. adv. contact: A. Garliauskas. circ. 680. **Indexed:** Chem.Abstr., Forest.Abstr., Forest Prod.Abstr., Helminthol.Abstr., Herb.Abstr., Hort.Abstr., INIS Atomind., Vet.Bull., Zoo.Rec. **Document type:** academic/scholarly publication.
—BLDSC (0397.597950); CASDDS; CISTI; KNAW.
Supersedes in part (in 1990): Lietuvos T.S.R. Mokslu Akademijos Darbai. C Serija. Biologijos Mokslai (ISSN 0131-3851)

570   US   ISSN 0885-1573
LIFE SCIENCE. (Subseries of: S I R S Science (ISSN 0885-1530)) 1985. a. $85. Social Issues Resources Series, Box 2348, Boca Raton, FL 33427-2348. TEL 561-994-0079; 800-232-SIRS. FAX 561-994-4704. E-mail: custserve@sirs.com; URL: http://www.sirs.com. Ed. Trudy Collins; Pub. Bonnie Milnes. R&P contact: Bonnie Milnes. (looseleaf format) **Document type:** academic/scholarly publication.
Description: Reprints 70 articles that examine the universal instincts of self-preservation and protection of the young.

570   US   ISSN 1069-9422
CODEN: LSBSF7
LIFE SUPPORT AND BIOSPHERE SCIENCE. 1994. q. $160 (foreign $185) (effective 1998). Cognizant Communication Corporation, 3 Hartsdale Rd., Elmsford, NY 10523-3701. TEL 914-592-7720. FAX 914-592-8981. Ed. Winston Huff; Pub. Robert N. Miranda. R&P contact: Robert N. Miranda. adv. contact: Lori Miranda. **Document type:** academic/scholarly publication.
Description: Study of habitat, food production, and waste recycling.
Refereed Serial

570   UK   ISSN 0024-4066
QH1   CODEN: BJLSBG
LINNEAN SOCIETY. BIOLOGICAL JOURNAL; a journal of evolution. 1791. m. £695 (effective 1998). Academic Press Ltd. (Subsidiary of: Harcourt Brace & Company Ltd.), 24-28 Oval Rd., London NW1 7DX, England. TEL 44-171-267-4466. FAX 44-171-482-2293. TELEX 25775 ACPRES G. E-mail: apsubs@acad.com; URL: http://www.hbuk.co.uk/ap/biojls; http://www.europe.idealibrary.com/. (Subscr. to: Harcourt Brace & Company Ltd., Foots Cray High St., Sidcup, Kent DA14 5HP, England. TEL 44-181-300-3322. FAX 44-181-309-0807) Ed. Andy Richford. R&P contact: Catherine John. adv. contact: Nik Screen. bk.rev.; bibl.; illus.; index per vol. (also avail. in microfilm from BHP; reprint service avail. from SWZ) **Indexed:** Anim.Breed.Abstr., Apic.Abstr., ASCA, Bibl.Agri., Bio-Contr.News & Info., Biol.Abstr., Curr.Adv.Genetics & Molec.Biol., Curr.Cont., Deep Sea Res.& Oceanogr.Abstr., Ecol.Abstr., Field Crop Abstr., Forest.Abstr., Geo.Abstr., Geol.Abstr., GeoRef., Helminthol.Abstr., Herb.Abstr., Ind.Sci.Rev., Key Word Ind.Wildl.Res., Nutr.Abstr., Plant Breed.Abstr., Potato Abstr., Rev.Appl.Entomol., Rev.Plant Path., Sci.Cit.Ind., Seed Abstr., Soils & Fert., Sport Fish.Abstr., Weed Abstr., Wild.Rev., Zoo.Rec. **Document type:** academic/scholarly publication.
● Also available online.
—BLDSC (2075.460000); CISTI; EMDOCS; Genuine Article; KNAW; Linda Hall; SWETS; UnCover. **CCC.**
Formerly (until 1969): Linnean Society of London. Proceedings.
Description: Examines the process of organic evolution, with particular emphasis on theoretical and empirical contributions illustrating unifying concepts of evolutionary biology.

570   US   ISSN 0161-6366
CODEN: LSSSDM
LINNEAN SOCIETY. SYMPOSIA SERIES. 1976. irreg., no.12, 1986. Academic Press, Inc., 525 B St., Ste. 1900, San Diego, CA 92101-4495. TEL 619-231-0926. FAX 619-699-6715. (Subscr. to: Order Department, 6277 Sea Harbor Dr., 4th Fl., Orlando, FL 32887. TEL 800-321-5068) (reprint service avail. from ISI) **Indexed:** Biol.Abstr., Chem.Abstr., GeoRef. **Document type:** proceedings.
—BLDSC (5221.493000); CASDDS; CISTI.

572.8   US
LIPPINCOTT-RAVEN PRESS SERIES ON MOLECULAR AND CELLULAR BIOLOGY. 1992. irreg. price varies. Lippincott - Raven Publishers (Subsidiary of: Wolters Kluwer N.V.), 227 E. Washington Sq., Philadelphia, PA 19106. TEL 215-238-4200. FAX 215-238-4227. URL: http://www.lrpub.com. (Subscr. to: Box 1600, Hagerstown, MD 21741-1600. TEL 800-777-2295. FAX 301-824-7390) Ed. Fred C. Fox. R&P contact: Alice McElhinney. **Document type:** proceedings.
—BLDSC (7296.539450); CISTI.
Formerly: Raven Press Series on Molecular and Cellular Biology (ISSN 1066-8330)

570.15195   PL   ISSN 0458-0036
LISTY BIOMETRYCZNE/BIOMETRICAL LETTERS. 1964. 2/yr. Polskie Towarzystwo Biometryczne - Polish Biometric Society, Ul. Przesmyckiego 20, 51-151 Wroclaw, Poland. TEL 48-71-251271. FAX 48-71-251271. Ed. Z. Kaczmarek.

LIVING HEALTHY; learning to live with digestive disease. see *MEDICAL SCIENCES — Gastroenterology*

570.9   UK   ISSN 0076-0579
CODEN: LONAAE
LONDON NATURALIST. 1915. a. £5. London Natural History Society, 5 Temple Close, Cassiobury, Watford, Herts WD1 3DR, England. TEL 44-1923-233706. FAX 44-1923-226095. Ed. K.H. Hyatt. R&P contact: K.H. Hyatt. bk.rev. circ. 1,200. (back issues avail.) **Indexed:** Geo.Abstr., GeoRef. **Document type:** bulletin.
—BLDSC (5294.000000).

570   SP   ISSN 0214-8315
LUCAS MALLADA; revista de Ciencias. 1989. a. 750 ptas. Instituto de Estudos Altoaragoneses, Diputacion Provincial de Huesca, Avda. del Parque 10, 22002 Huesca, Spain. **Indexed:** Ind.SST.
—CINDOC.

910   SW   ISSN 1400-1144
LUND STUDIES IN GEOGRAPHY. (Text in English) 1949. irreg. price varies. Lund University Press, P.O. Box 141, S-221 00 Lund, Sweden. TEL 46-46-31-20-00. FAX 46-46-30-53-38. E-mail: order@studl.se. B. Lenntorp. index. cum.index every 4 yrs. **Indexed:** Geo.Abstr.P.G., IDA, IDA. **Document type:** academic/scholarly publication.
—CISTI.
Formerly (until 1994): Lund Studies in Geography. Series B. Human Geography (ISSN 0076-1478)

570   FI   ISSN 0024-7383
QH7   CODEN: LUTUAA
LUONNON TUTKIJA. (Text in Finnish; summaries in English) 1897. 5/yr. FIM 120. Societas Biologica Fennica Vanamo, c/o Dept. of Ecology and Systematics, P.O. Box 7, FIN-00014 University of Helsinki, Finland. Ed. Juhani Manttari. adv.; bk.rev.; charts; illus.; index, cum.index. circ. 2,200. **Indexed:** Biol.Abstr., Curr.Adv.Ecol.Sci., Deep Sea Res.& Oceanogr.Abstr. **Document type:** academic/scholarly publication.
—BLDSC (5307.350000).

571.9 616.07   NE
LYSOSOMES IN BIOLOGY AND PATHOLOGY. 1973. irreg., vol.7, 1984. price varies. Elsevier Science B.V., Book Division, P.O. Box 211, 1000 AE Amsterdam, Netherlands. TEL 31-20-4853911. FAX 31-20-4853705. TELEX 18582 ESPA NL. E-mail: nlinfo-f@elsevier.nl; usinfo-f@elsevier.com; forinfo-kyf04035@niftyserve.or.jp; URL: http://www.elsevier.nl/. (Subscr. in the Americas to: Elsevier Science, Regional Sales Office, Box 945, New York, NY 10159-0945. TEL 212-633-3730. FAX 212-633-3680; Subscr. in Australasia and the Far East to: Elsevier Science (Singapore) Pte Ltd, No.1 Temasek Ave., No.17-01 Millenia Tower, Singapore 039192, Singapore. TEL 65-434-3727. FAX 65-337-2230; Subscr. in Japan to: Elsevier Science Japan, 9-15 Higashi-Azabu 1-chome, Minato-ku, Tokyo 106, Japan. TEL 81-3-5561-5033. FAX 81-3-5561-5047) **Document type:** monographic series.
Refereed Serial

M B I. (Medico-Biologic Information) see *MEDICAL SCIENCES*

570   US   ISSN 0275-8679
CODEN: MLBID5
M B L LECTURES IN BIOLOGY. 1981. irreg., vol.10, 1990. price varies. (Marine Biological Laboratory) John Wiley & Sons, Inc., Journals, 605 Third Ave., New York, NY 10158. TEL 212-475-7700. Eds. Harlyn O. Halvorson, K.E. van Holde. **Indexed:** Biol.Abstr., Chem.Abstr.
—BLDSC (5413.408000); CASDDS; CISTI; KNAW. **CCC.**

MADOQUA; journal of arid zone biology and nature conservation research. see *CONSERVATION*

MAINE AGRICULTURAL AND FOREST EXPERIMENT STATION. ANNUAL REPORT. see *AGRICULTURE*

570 610   XN   ISSN 0351-3254
CODEN: PANND2
MAKEDONSKA AKADEMIJA NA NAUKITE I UMETNOSTITE. ODDELENIE ZA BIOLOSKI I MEDICINSKI NAUKI. PRILOZI/MACEDONIAN ACADEMY OF SCIENCES AND ARTS. SECTION OF BIOLOGICAL AND MEDICAL SCIENCES. CONTRIBUTIONS. 1980. s-a. Makedonska Akademija na Naukite i Umetnostite, Oddelenie za Bioloski i Medicinski Nauki, Bulevar Krste Misrkov bb, P.O. Box 428, Skopje, Macedonia. TEL 235-506. Ed. Kiril Micevski. **Indexed:** Chem.Abstr.
—BLDSC (0132.071000); CASDDS; KNAW; Linda Hall.
Description: Presents research reports in botany, zoology, biochemistry, medicine and pharmacology.

MALAYSIAN APPLIED BIOLOGY JOURNAL. see *AGRICULTURE*

BIOLOGY

570   Q1   MY   ISSN 1394-1712   CODEN: MLJSA4
MALAYSIAN JOURNAL OF SCIENCE SERIES A: LIFE SCIENCES. (Text in English) 1971. 2/yr. University of Malaya, Faculty of Science, Lembah Pantai, 59100 Kuala Lumpur, Malaysia. TEL 565000. TELEX UNIMAL-MA-37453. Ed. Dr. Yong Hoi-Sen. adv.; bk.rev. circ. 1,000. **Indexed:** Biol.Abstr., Chem.Abstr., Deep Sea Res.& Oceanogr.Abstr. —BLDSC (5356.069020); CASDDS.
     Supersedes in part (in 1994): Malaysian Journal of Science - Jernal Sains Malaysia (ISSN 0126-7906)
     Description: Covers original research, communications, and reviews in the field of life sciences.
     Refereed Serial

MANAB MON; a journal depicting the modern trends in psychology, biology, and sociology. see *PSYCHOLOGY*

578.77   QL121   NE   CODEN: MBPHAX
MARINE AND FRESHWATER BEHAVIOUR AND PHYSIOLOGY. 1973. 12/yr. (in 3 vols., 4 nos./vol.). $376 (effective 1998). Gordon and Breach - Harwood Academic, Amsteldisk 166, 1st Fl., 1079 LH Amsterdam, Netherlands. URL: http://www.gbhap.com/Marine_Freshwater_Behaviour_Physiology_A_B/. (Subscr. to: International Publishers Distributor, Box 32160, Newark, NJ 07102. TEL 800-545-8398. FAX 215-750-6343) Ed. David L. Macmillan. adv.; bk.rev.; charts; illus.; index. (also avail. in microform) **Indexed:** ASCA, Biol.Abstr., Chem.Abstr., Curr.Adv.Ecol.Sci., Curr.Cont., Curr.Ref.Fish Res., Deep Sea Res.& Oceanogr.Abstr., Ecol.Abstr., Environ.Per.Bibl. (1991-1993), Food Sci.& Tech.Abstr., GeoRef., Ind.Sci.Rev., INSPEC, Ocean.Abstr., Pollut.Abstr., Psychol.Abstr. (1972-). **Document type:** academic/scholarly publication.
● Also available online.
Also available on CD-ROM.
—CASDDS; CISTI; Linda Hall; SWETS; UnCover. **CCC.**
     Formerly (until vol.25): Marine Behaviour and Physiology (ISSN 0091-181X)
     Refereed Serial

MARINE AND FRESHWATER RESEARCH. see *EARTH SCIENCES — Oceanography*

578.77   II   ISSN 0025-3146   CODEN: JMBIAA
MARINE BIOLOGICAL ASSOCIATION OF INDIA. JOURNAL. (Text mainly in English; occasionally in French, German or Spanish) 1959. a. $15 to individuals; institutions $30. Marine Biological Association of India, Post Box No. 2673, Ernakulam, Cochin 682-031, Kerala, India. Ed. K. Rengarajan. adv.; bk.rev.; charts; illus.; index. circ. 700. **Indexed:** Biol.Abstr., Curr.Adv.Ecol.Sci., Deep Sea Res.& Oceanogr.Abstr., Geo.Abstr., Helminthol.Abstr., W.R.C.Inf.
—CASDDS; CISTI; UnCover.
     Description: Contains original contributions about marine biology. Covers plankton, coral, ecosystems, population dynamics, propagation of cultivable species, biology of fishes, marine reptiles, sea birds, mammals and pollution.

578.77   QH301   UK   ISSN 0025-3154   CODEN: JMBAAK
MARINE BIOLOGICAL ASSOCIATION OF THE UNITED KINGDOM. JOURNAL. Key Title: Journal of the Marine Biological Association of the United Kingdom. Short title: J M B A. 1887. q. £237($415) (effective 1998). Cambridge University Press, Edinburgh Bldg., Shaftesbury Rd., Cambridge CB2 2RU, England. TEL 44-1223-312393. FAX 44-1223-315052. TELEX 851817256. E-mail: information@cup.cam.ac.uk; URL: http://www.cup.cam.ac.uk. (N. American addr.: Cambridge University Press, Journals Dept., 40 W. 20th St., New York, NY 10011. TEL 212-924-3900. FAX 212-691-3239) Eds. Michael Whitfield, Ann Pulsford. R&P contact: Linda Nicol. adv. contact: Rebecca Symons. bk.rev. (also avail. in microform from UMI; microfilm from BHP; back issues avail.; reprint service avail. from SWZ) **Indexed:** Anim.Breed.Abstr., ASCA, Biol.Abstr., Biol.& Agr.Ind., Cadscan, Chem.Abstr., Curr.Adv.Ecol.Sci., Curr.Cont., Curr.Tit.Ocean, Deep Sea Res.& Oceanogr.Abstr., Ecol.Abstr., Environ.Per.Bibl. (1990-1994), Geo.Abstr, GeoRef., Helminthol.Abstr., Int.Abstr.Biol.Sci., Lead Abstr., Nutr.Abstr., Ocean.Abstr., Sci.Cit.Ind., Sel.Water Res.Abstr., Sport Fish.Abstr., W.R.C.Inf., Wild.Rev., Zincscan, Zoo.Rec. **Document type:** academic/scholarly publication.
—BLDSC (4821.000000); CASDDS; CISTI; EMDOCS; Genuine Article; KR SourceOne; Linda Hall; SWETS; UMI. **CCC.**
     Description: Publishes original research on all aspects of marine biology
     Refereed Serial

578.77   UK   ISSN 0260-2784
MARINE BIOLOGICAL ASSOCIATION OF THE UNITED KINGDOM. OCCASIONAL PUBLICATIONS. 1980. irreg. price varies. Marine Biological Association of the United Kingdom, Citadel Hill, Plymouth PL1 2PB, England. TEL 44-1752-633334. FAX 44-1752-633102. Ed. Ann Pulsford. bk.rev. circ. 500. **Indexed:** Aqua.Sci.& Fish.Abstr., Deep Sea Res.& Oceanogr.Abstr. **Document type:** academic/scholarly publication, monographic series.
—CISTI.
     Refereed Serial

578.77   JA   ISSN 0366-4481   CODEN: BUMVA4
MARINE BIOLOGICAL STATION OF ASAMUSHI. BULLETIN/TOHOKU DAIGAKU ASAMUSHI RINKAI JIKKENJO HOKOKU. 1946. a. exchange basis. Tohoku University, Faculty of Science, Marine Biological Station - Tohoku Daigaku rigakubu Fuzoku Rinkai Jikkenjo, 9 Sakamoto, Asamushi, Aomori 039-34, Japan. illus.; index. **Indexed:** Agrindex, Biol.Abstr., Curr.Adv.Ecol.Sci., Deep Sea Res.& Oceanogr.Abstr. **Document type:** bulletin.
—BLDSC (2609.750000).

578.77   QH91.A1   GW   ISSN 0025-3162   CODEN: MBIOAJ
MARINE BIOLOGY; international journal on life in oceans and coastal waters. Online edition (GW ISSN 1432-1793) (Text in English) 1967. m. DM.5034 (foreign DM.5063.40) (effective 1998). Springer-Verlag, Heidelberger Platz 3, 14197 Berlin, Germany. TEL 49-30-82787-0. FAX 49-30-82787448. E-mail: subscriptions@springer.de; URL: http://link.springer.de. (Subscr. in N. America to: Springer-Verlag New York, Inc., 333 Meadowlands Pkwy., Secaucus, NJ 07094. TEL 212-460-1500. FAX 212-473-6272) Ed. O. Kinne. adv.; charts; illus. (also avail. in microform from UMI; back issues avail.; reprint service avail. from ISI) **Indexed:** Biol.Abstr., Biol.& Agr.Ind., Cadscan, Curr.Adv.Biochem., Curr.Adv.Cell & Devel.Biol., Curr.Adv.Ecol.Sci., Curr.Cont., Curr.Ref.Fish Res., Deep Sea Res.& Oceanogr.Abstr., Ecol.Abstr., Environ.Abstr., Environ.Per.Bibl. (1974-), Excerp.Med., Food Sci.& Tech.Abstr., Fuel & Energy Abstr., Geo.Abstr.H.G., Geol.Abstr., Helminthol.Abstr., IBR, Ind.Sci.Rev., INIS Atomind., Lead Abstr., Nutr.Abstr., Ocean.Abstr., Pollut.Abstr., Sci.Cit.Ind., Sel.Water Res.Abstr., Soils & Fert., W.R.C.Inf., Zincscan, Zoo.Rec. **Document type:** academic/scholarly publication.
● Also available online.
—BLDSC (5373.700000); CASDDS; CISTI; EMDOCS; Genuine Article; KR SourceOne; Linda Hall; SWETS; UMI; UnCover. **CCC.**
     Description: Reports on plankton research, theoretical biology related to the marine environment, apparatus and techniques, and underwater exploration and experimentation.

578.77 333.72   UK   ISSN 0268-7666
MARINE CONSERVATION. q. £15 (overseas £20) (effective 1996). Marine Conservation Society, 9 Gloucester Rd., Ross-on-Wye, Herefordshire HR9 5BU, England. TEL 44-1989-566017. FAX 44-1989-567815. Ed. Samantha Pollard. circ. 6,000 (paid). **Document type:** newsletter.
     Formerly (until 1985): Sea.
     Description: Provides current information and articles on marine biology and conservation.

577.7   GW   ISSN 0173-9565   CODEN: MAECDR
MARINE ECOLOGY. (Text in English) 1916. 4/yr. DM.673 in Europe; rest of world DM.679 (effective 1998). (Stazione Zoologica di Napoli, IT) Blackwell Wissenschaft, Kurfuerstendamm 57, 10707 Berlin, Germany. TEL 49-30-32790679. FAX 49-30-32790610. E-mail: aboverwalt@blackwis.de; URL: http://www.blackwis.de. Eds. Joerg Ott, Rupert Riedl. adv.: B&W page DM.560; trim 196 x 122. circ. 560. **Indexed:** Biol.Abstr., Curr.Adv.Ecol.Sci., Curr.Cont., Curr.Tit.Ocean, Ecol.Abstr., Environ.Per.Bibl. (1972-), Geo.Abstr.H.G., IBR, Ocean.Abstr., Sci.Cit.Ind., Sel.Water Res.Abstr., Sport Fish.Abstr., Wild.Rev., Zoo.Rec. **Document type:** academic/scholarly publication.
—BLDSC (5373.850000); CASDDS; CISTI; Genuine Article; Linda Hall; SWETS; UnCover. **CCC.**
     Supersedes in part (in 1979): Stazione Zoologica di Napoli. Pubblicazioni (ISSN 0039-081X)
     Description: Covers biological and ecological topics regarding the Mediterranean and other seas.

MARINE ENVIRONMENTAL RESEARCH. see *ENVIRONMENTAL STUDIES — Pollution*

578.77 591   QL128   NO   ISSN 0542-6987   CODEN: MAISBP
MARINE INVERTEBRATES OF SCANDINAVIA. (Text in English) irreg. price varies. Scandinavian University Press, P.O. Box 2959 Toeyen, N-0608 Oslo, Norway. TEL 47-22-57-54-00. FAX 47-22-57-53-53. E-mail: mail@scup.no; URL: http://www.scup.no. (US addr.: 875 Massachusetts Ave., Ste. 84, Cambridge, MA 02139. TEL 617-497-6515. FAX 617-354-6875) **Document type:** academic/scholarly publication, monographic series.

570   XR
MASARYK UNIVERSITY. FACULTY OF SCIENCES. SCRIPTA BIOLOGICA/SCRIPTA FACULTATIS SCIENTIARUM NATURALIUM UNIVERSITATIS MASARYKIANAE BRUNENSIS. BRIOLOGIA. (Text in English, French and Russian) a. price varies. Masarykova Universita, Prirodovedecka Fakulta - Masaryk University, Faculty of Sciences, Kotlarska 2, 611 37 Brno, Czech Republic. Ed. Jiri Gaisler. bibl. **Indexed:** Biol.Abstr., Chem.Abstr., Field Crop Abstr., Herb.Abstr., Plant Grow.Reg.Abstr. **Document type:** academic/scholarly publication.
—CISTI.
     Former titles: Scripta Facultatis Scientiarum Naturalium Universitatis Purkynianae Brunensis. Biologia (ISSN 0231-5777); Supersedes in part (in 1970): Universita J.E. Purkyne. Prirodovedecka Fakulta. Spisy.

MASSACHUSETTS WILDLIFE. see *CONSERVATION*

MATHEMATICAL BIOSCIENCES; an international journal. see *MATHEMATICS*

570 617.6   JA   ISSN 0385-1613   CODEN: MATSDE
MATSUMOTO SHIGAKU/MATSUMOTO DENTAL COLLEGE SOCIETY. JOURNAL. (Text in Japanese; summaries in English) 1975. 3/yr. 3500 Yen($35) Matsumoto Dental College Society - Matsumoto Shika Daigaku Gakkai, 1780 Gobara, Hiroka, Shojiri-shi 399-07, Japan. FAX 81-263-53-3456. Ed. Minoru Yamaoka. adv.; bk.rev. circ. 2,000. **Document type:** academic/scholarly publication.
—BLDSC (5413.245000); CASDDS.

BIOLOGY

570   DK   ISSN 0106-1054
QH132.G73
MEDDELELSER OM GROENLAND, BIOSCIENCE. 1878. irreg. price varies. (Kommissionen for Videnskabelige Undersoegelser i Groenland, GL - Commission for Scientific Research in Greenland) Geografforlaget ApS, Fruerhoejvej 43, DK-5464 Brenderup, Denmark. Eds. Gert Steen Mogensen, G. Hoepner Petersen. charts; illus. **Indexed:** Biol.Abstr., Chem.Abstr., Curr.Adv.Ecol.Sci. **Document type:** academic/scholarly publication.
—CISTI; Linda Hall.
     Formerly: Greenland Biosciences; Supersedes in part (in 1979): Meddelelser om Groenland (ISSN 0025-6676)

MEDICINAL CHEMISTRY RESEARCH; an international journal for rapid communications on design and mechanisms of action of biologically active agents. see *MEDICAL SCIENCES*

MEDICINSKI RAZGLEDI. see *MEDICAL SCIENCES*

551.46   US   ISSN 0085-0683
QH92.3   CODEN: MHGCBG
MEMOIRS OF THE HOURGLASS CRUISES. 1969. irreg. exchange basis. Florida Marine Research Institute, Department of Environmental Protection, 100 8th Ave. S.E., St. Petersburg, FL 33701.
FAX 813-823-0166. Ed. K.A. Steidinger. charts; illus. circ. 1,000. (tabloid format; back issues avail.) **Indexed:** Aqua.Sci.& Fish.Abstr., Biol.Abstr., Deep Sea Res.& Oceanogr.Abstr., Ocean.Abstr., Sport Fish.Abstr., Wild.Rev., Zoo.Rec.

570   II
MEMOIRS ON INDIAN ANIMAL TYPES. (Text in English) 1983. irreg., latest 1995. price varies. Hindustan Publishing Corp., 4805-24, Bharat Ram Rd., Flat Nos. 1&2, 1st Fl., Daryaganj, New Delhi 110002. TEL 91-11-3254402. FAX 91-11-6863511. E-mail: hpcpd@giasdl01.vsnl.net.in. Ed. M.L. Bhatia. **Document type:** academic/scholarly publication, monographic series.

570   CN   ISSN 0702-0007
     CODEN: OPBIDL
MEMORIAL UNIVERSITY OF NEWFOUNDLAND. OCCASIONAL PAPERS IN BIOLOGY. (Text in English; summaries in English and French) 1978. irreg., vol.12, 1988. price varies. Memorial University of Newfoundland, Department of Biology, St. John's, NF A1C 5S7, Canada. TEL 709-737-7498.
FAX 709-737-3018. E-mail: pscott@plato.ucs.mun.ca. Eds. P.J. Scott, A. Whittick. R&P contact: P.J. Scott. (back issues avail.) **Indexed:** Biol.Abstr. **Document type:** academic/scholarly publication.
—CISTI.
Refereed Serial

MEMORIE DI BIOLOGIA MARINA E DI OCEANOGRAFIA. see *EARTH SCIENCES — Oceanography*

METABOLISM: CLINICAL AND EXPERIMENTAL. see *MEDICAL SCIENCES — Endocrinology*

572.8   US   ISSN 1064-3745
     CODEN: MMBIED
METHODS IN MOLECULAR BIOLOGY. 1984. irreg., vol.32, 1994. price varies. Humana Press Inc., 999 Riverside Dr., Ste. 208, Totowa, NJ 07512-1165. TEL 973-256-1699. FAX 973-256-8341. E-mail: humana@mindspring.com; URL: http://humanapress.com. Ed. John Walker. R&P contact: Richard Hruska. (back issues avail.) **Indexed:** Ind.Med. (1993-).
—BLDSC (5748.201800); CASDDS; CISTI. **CCC**.
     Description: Offers the latest molecular biology and biochemistry laboratory methods and protocols.

570   US   ISSN 0076-8227
QH1   CODEN: PMUBAE
MICHIGAN STATE UNIVERSITY. MUSEUM PUBLICATIONS. BIOLOGICAL SERIES. (Text in English; summaries occasionally in German) 1957. irreg. (approx. 1-2/yr.). price varies. Michigan State University, Museum, East Lansing, MI 48824.
TEL 517-355-2370. circ. 1,850. **Indexed:** Biol.Abstr., GeoRef. **Document type:** academic/scholarly publication, monographic series.
—Linda Hall.

578.77   GW   ISSN 0176-3296
QL121   CODEN: MMAREZ
MICROFAUNA MARINA. 1970. irreg. price varies. (Akademie der Wissenschaften und der Literatur, Mainz, Mathematisch-Naturwissenschaftliche Klasse) Gustav Fischer Verlag, Wollgrasweg 49, 70599 Stuttgart, Germany. TEL 49-711-458030.
FAX 49-711-4580334. TELEX 7111788-FIBUCH. (Subscr. to: Postfach 720143, 70577 Stuttgart, Germany) Ed. Peter Ax. **Indexed:** Biol.Abstr., Deep Sea Res.& Oceanogr.Abstr. **Document type:** monographic series.
—BLDSC (5759.025000); CISTI; Linda Hall. **CCC**.
     Supersedes (in 1984): Mikrofauna des Meeresbodens (ISSN 0342-3247)

MICRONESICA. see *ANTHROPOLOGY*

570   JA   ISSN 0914-7357
MIE SEIBUTSU/MIE BIOLOGICAL SOCIETY. JOURNAL. (Text in Japanese) 1950. a. Mie Seibutsu Kyoikukai - Mie Biological Society, c/o Mr. Akira Aoyama, Mie Kenritsu Yokkaichi Koto Gakko, Tomida, Yokkaichi-shi, Mie-ken 510, Japan.

570   JA   ISSN 0910-2523
MITSUBISHI KASEI INSTITUTE OF LIFE SCIENCES. ANNUAL REPORT. (Text in English) 1971. a. Mitsubishi Kasei Institute of Life Sciences - Mitsubishi Kagaku Seimei Kagaku Kenkyujo, 11 Minamioya, Machida-shi, Tokyo 194, Japan.
—KNAW.

MODELING OF GEO-BIOSPHERE PROCESS. see *EARTH SCIENCES*

570   US
MODERN BIOLOGY SERIES.★ irreg. price varies. Holt, Rinehart and Winston, Inc., c/o Harcourt Brace Jovanovich, 6277 Sea Harbor Dr., Orlando, FL 32887. TEL 407-345-2500.
Refereed Serial

MODERN PATHOLOGY. see *MEDICAL SCIENCES*

572.8   US   ISSN 0737-4038
QH506   CODEN: MBEVEO
MOLECULAR BIOLOGY AND EVOLUTION. 1983. bi-m. $335 (effective 1997). University of Chicago Press, Journals Division, 5702 S. Woodlawn Ave., Chicago, IL 60637. TEL 773-753-3347.
FAX 773-753-0811. TELEX 25-4603. (Subscr. to: Box 37005, Chicago, IL 60637) Ed. Barry G. Hall. adv. circ. 1,000. (also avail. in microform from UMI,PMC; reprint service avail. from ISI,UMI) **Indexed:** Abstr.Anthropol., Anim.Breed.Abstr., ASCA, Biol.Abstr., Curr.Adv.Biochem., Curr.Adv.Cell & Devel.Biol., Curr.Adv.Ecol.Sci., Curr.Adv.Genetics & Molec.Biol., Curr.Cont., Curr.Cont., Dairy Sci.Abstr., Excerp.Med., Ind.Sci.Rev., Sci.Cit.Ind., Sport Fish.Abstr., Wild.Rev., Zoo.Rec. **Document type:** academic/scholarly publication.
—BLDSC (5900.782000); CASDDS; CISTI; EMDOCS; Genuine Article; KNAW; Linda Hall; SWETS; UMI; UnCover. **CCC**.
Refereed Serial

572.8   UK   ISSN 1356-1324
▼**MOLECULAR BIOLOGY TECHNIQUES.** 1995. s-m. (diskette m.). £110 (diskette £120; both £180) (effective 1997). S U B I S, Mansion House, 19 Kingfield Rd., Sheffield S11 9AS, England.
TEL 44-114-255-4433. FAX 44-114-255-4626. E-mail: subis@sheffac.demon.co.uk; URL: http://www.shef.ac.uk/uni/companies/shap. (also avail. in diskette format) **Document type:** abstracting/indexing.
     Description: Current awareness service for researchers in clinical and life sciences.

MOLECULAR BRAIN RESEARCH. see *MEDICAL SCIENCES — Psychiatry And Neurology*

MOLECULAR DIAGNOSIS; a journal devoted to the understanding of human disease through the clinical application of molecular biology. see *MEDICAL SCIENCES*

MOLECULAR HUMAN REPRODUCTION. see *MEDICAL SCIENCES — Obstetrics And Gynecology*

MOLECULAR PSYCHIATRY. see *MEDICAL SCIENCES — Psychiatry And Neurology*

570   KO   ISSN 1016-8478
     CODEN: MOCEEK
MOLECULES AND CELLS. (Text in English) q. 30000 Won membership. Korean Society of Molecular Biology, c/o Institute for Molecular Biology and Genetics, Seoul National University, Sinlim-dong, Kwanak-gu, Seoul 151-742, S. Korea.
TEL 02-884-4490. FAX 02-266-9083. Ed. Sung-Ki Lee. **Indexed:** ASCA, Curr.Cont., Ind.Sci.Rev.
—BLDSC (5900.857500); CASDDS; Genuine Article.

570.9   NE   ISSN 0077-0639
QH301   CODEN: MOBIAN
MONOGRAPHIAE BIOLOGICAE. (Text in English) 1957. irreg., vol.73, 1995. price varies. Kluwer Academic Publishers, Postbus 17, 3300 AA Dordrecht, Netherlands. TEL 31-78-6392392.
FAX 31-78-6392254. TELEX 29245 KAPG NL. E-mail: services@wkap.nl; URL: http://www.wkap.nl. (Dist. by: Kluwer Academic Publishers Group, P.O. Box 322, 3300 AH Dordrecht, Netherlands. TEL 31-78-6392392. FAX 31-78-6546474; N. America dist. addr.: Box 358, Accord Sta., Hingham, MA 02018-0358. TEL 617-871-6600. FAX 617-871-6528) Ed. M. Dumont. **Indexed:** Biol.Abstr., Deep Sea Res.& Oceanogr.Abstr., Sport Fish.Abstr., Wild.Rev., Zoo.Rec. **Document type:** monographic series.
—BLDSC (5917.783000); CASDDS; CISTI.
Refereed Serial

MONOGRAPHS IN EPIDEMIOLOGY AND BIOSTATISTICS. see *PUBLIC HEALTH AND SAFETY*

MONOGRAPHS IN PSYCHOBIOLOGY. see *PSYCHOLOGY*

571.3 611   RU
     CODEN: AAGEAA
MORFOLOGIYA. 1916. m. $37.80. (Rossiiskaya Akademiya Meditsinskikh Nauk) Morfologiya, Park Lenina 5a, 197046 St. Petersburg, Russia. (Co-sponsor: Vsesoyuznoe Nauchnoe Obshchestvo Anatomov, Gistologov i Embriologov) Ed. F.V. Sudzilovskii. bk.rev.; bibl.; index. **Indexed:** Biol.Abstr., Chem.Abstr., Dent.Ind., Ind.Med., INIS Atomind.
—CASDDS; CISTI; KNAW.
     Formerly (until 1992): Arkhiv Anatomii, Gistologii i Embriologii (ISSN 0004-1947)
     Description: Carries original investigations; reviews and discussion of papers on cytology, histology, embryology (normal and topographic), and comparative anatomy and anthropology; methods of morphological investigation; history of morphology; reports on the latest achievements in morphological sciences.

570   US   ISSN 0096-3925
QH301   CODEN: MUBBDD
MOSCOW UNIVERSITY BIOLOGICAL SCIENCES BULLETIN. English translation in part of: Moskovskii Universitet. Vestnik. Seriya 16: Biologiya (RU ISSN 0137-0944) 1974. q. $950 (effective 1998). (Moskovskii Universitet, RU) Allerton Press, Inc., 150 Fifth Ave., New York, NY 10011. TEL 212-924-3950.
FAX 212-463-9684. Ed. M.V. Gusev. bibl.; charts; illus.; index. **Indexed:** Biol.Abstr., Crop Physiol.Abstr., Excerp.Med., Field Crop Abstr., Forest.Abstr., Herb.Abstr., Hort.Abstr., Sport Fish.Abstr., Weed Abstr., Wild.Rev., Zoo.Rec. **Document type:** academic/scholarly publication.
—BLDSC (0416.237000); CISTI; UnCover. **CCC**.
     Description: Covers human, animal and plant physiology, genetics, flora and fauna, biochemistry and biophysics, cell physiology.

570   RU   ISSN 0137-0952
QH301   CODEN: VMUBDF
MOSKOVSKII UNIVERSITET. VESTNIK. SERIYA 16: BIOLOGIYA. (English translation: Moscow University Biological Sciences Bulletin (ISSN 0096-3925), and Soil Sciences Bulletin (ISSN 0147-6874).) (Text in Russian; contents page in English) 1960. q. $38 (effective 1998). Moskovskii Universitet, Ul. Gertsena 5-7, 103009 Moscow, Russia. bk.rev.; bibl.; index. **Indexed:** Biol.Abstr., Field Crop Abstr., Plant Grow.Reg.Abstr.
—BLDSC (0032.697300); CASDDS; CISTI; Linda Hall.
     Formerly (until 1977): Moskovskii Universitet. Vestnik. Seriya 6: Biologiya, Pochvovedenie (ISSN 0579-9422)

BIOLOGY 615

570   RU   ISSN 0027-1403
Q60   CODEN: BYMOAB
MOSKOVSKOE OBSHCHESTVO ISPYTATELEI PRIRODY. BIOLOGICHESKII OTDEL. BYULLETEN/MOSCOW SOCIETY OF NATURALISTS. BIOLOGICAL SERIES. BULLETIN. (Text in Russian; summaries in English) 1829; N.S. 1917. bi-m. $104 (effective 1998). Moskovskii Universitet, Moskovskoe Obshchestvo Ispytatelei Prirody, Ul. Gertsena 5-7, 103009 Moscow, Russia. Ed. T.A. Rabotnov. bk.rev.; abstr.; bibl.; charts; illus. circ 1,635. (also avail. in microfiche from IDC) **Indexed:** Bio-Contr.News & Info., Biol.Abstr., Deep Sea Res.& Oceanogr.Abstr., Forest.Abstr., GeoRef., Herb.Abstr., INIS Atomind., Key Word Ind.Wildl.Res., Rev.Appl.Entomol., Triticale Abstr. **Document type:** bulletin.
—BLDSC (0022.000000); CISTI; KNAW; Linda Hall.

570   US   ISSN 0097-0883
QH323   CODEN: BMDIAY
MOUNT DESERT ISLAND BIOLOGICAL LABORATORY. BULLETIN. 1960. a. $10 to non-members. Mount Desert Island Biological Laboratory, Salsbury Cove, ME 04672. TEL 207-288-3605. Ed. Gregg Kormanik. charts; illus.; index. circ. 1,000. **Indexed:** Biol.Abstr., Curr.Cont., Deep Sea Res.& Oceanogr.Abstr., Sport Fish.Abstr., Wild.Rev., Zoo.Rec. **Document type:** academic/scholarly publication.
—Linda Hall.

570   JA   ISSN 0910-0903
MUKIN SEIBUTSU/JOURNAL OF GERMFREE LIFE AND GNOTOBIOLOGY. (Text in English, Japanese) 1971. s-a. Nihon Mukin Seibutsu Noto Baioroji Gakkai - Japanese Association of Germfree Life and Gnotobiology, c/o Ms. Kazuko Adachi, Kobe Gakuin Daigaku Eiyogakubu, Arise, Ikawadanicho, Nishi-ku, Kobe-shi, Hyogo-ken 673, Japan.

570   AG   ISSN 0524-9481
                               CODEN: RANCEQ
MUSEO ARGENTINO DE CIENCIAS NATURALES "BERNARDINO RIVADAVIA." INSTITUTO NACIONAL DE INVESTIGACION DE LAS CIENCIAS NATURALES. REVISTA. ECOLOGIA. 1963. irreg., vol.3, no.4, 1991. Museo Argentino de Ciencias Naturales "Bernardino Rivadavia", Instituto Nacional de Investigacion de las Ciencias Naturales, Avda. Angel Gallardo 470, Casilla de Correo 220-Sucursal 5, Buenos Aires, Argentina. **Indexed:** GeoRef., Zoo.Rec. **Document type:** academic/scholarly publication.
—CISTI; Linda Hall.

578.77   AG   ISSN 0524-9503
QH91.A1   CODEN: RNBHD3
MUSEO ARGENTINO DE CIENCIAS NATURALES "BERNARDINO RIVADAVIA." INSTITUTO NACIONAL DE INVESTIGACION DE LAS CIENCIAS NATURALES. REVISTA. HIDROBIOLOGIA. 1963. irreg., vol.6, no.9, 1987. Museo Argentino de Ciencias Naturales "Bernardino Rivadavia", Instituto Nacional de Investigacion de las Ciencias Naturales, Avda. Angel Gallardo 470, Casilla de Correo 220-Sucursal 5, Buenos Aires, Argentina. **Indexed:** BSL Biol., GeoRef.
—CISTI; Linda Hall.

570 550   IT   ISSN 0505-205X
                               CODEN: BMSNA
MUSEO CIVICO DI STORIA NATURALE DI VENEZIA. BOLLETTINO. (Text in English, French, German, Italian, Spanish; summaries in English, Italian) 1932. a. exchange basis. Museo Civico di Storia Naturale di Venezia, Fontego dei Turchi, S. Croce 1730, 30135 Venice, Italy. TEL 39-41-721852. FAX 39-41-5242592. index; circ. 1,000 (controlled). **Indexed:** Biol.Abstr., Entomol.Abstr., Zoo.Rec. **Document type:** bulletin.
—CISTI.
     Former titles (until 1954): Bollettino della Societa Veneziana di Storia Naturale del Museo Civico di Storia Naturale; (until 1940): Societa Veneziana di Storia Naturale. Bollettino.
     Description: Covers taxonomy, biogeography, ecology, and the flora and fauna of the lagoon of Venice.
     Refereed Serial

570   IT
MUSEO CIVICO DI STORIA NATURALE DI VERONA. MEMORIE. SERIE 2, SEZIONE A: SCIENZE DELLA VITA. 1977. irreg., vol.11, 1994. price varies. Museo Civico di Storia Naturale di Verona, Lungadige Porta Vittoria, 9, 37129 Verona, Italy. TEL 39-45-8079400. FAX 39-45-8035639. **Document type:** monographic series.
     Formerly: Museo Civico di Storia Naturale di Verona. Memorie. Serie 2, Part 1: Biologia.

570   IT   ISSN 0392-758X
MUSEO REGIONALE DI SCIENZE NATURALI, TORINO. BOLLETTINO. 1983. s-a. L.50000. Museo Regionale di Scienze Naturali Torino, Redazione, Via Giolitti 36, 10123 Torino, Italy. TELEX 220685 REGPIE I. Ed. Olindo Bortesi. adv. contact: Olindo Bortesi. (back issues avail.) **Document type:** bulletin.
—BLDSC (2227.600000).
     Description: Features readings on natural sciences, including paleontology, botany, mineralogy, geology and zoology.

MUSEU MUNICIPAL DO FUNCHAL. BOLETIM. see *BIOLOGY — Zoology*

570   RM   ISSN 0068-3078
QH1   CODEN: TMNAAK
MUSEUM D'HISTOIRE NATURELLE "GRIGORE ANTIPA". TRAVAUX. (Text in English, French, German; summaries in Rumanian; abstracts in English and French) 1957. a. price varies. Muzeul de Istorie Naturala "Grigore Antipa", Soseaua Kiseleff Nr. 1, 79744 Bucharest, Rumania. TEL 40-1-6504710. FAX 40-1-6505250. Ed. Dumitru Murariu. R&P contact: Dumitru Murariu. TEL 40-1-6505250. bk.rev.; index. circ. 900. **Indexed:** Ocean.Abstr. **Document type:** academic/scholarly publication.
—CISTI; Linda Hall.
     Formerly: Muzeul de Istoria Naturala "Grigore Antipa." Travaux.

MUSEUM NATIONAL D'HISTOIRE NATURELLE, PARIS. MEMOIRES. see *SCIENCES: COMPREHENSIVE WORKS*

570   PL   ISSN 0068-466X
                               CODEN: ASMHE9
MUZEUM GORNOSLASKIE W BYTOMIU. ROCZNIK. SERIA PRZYRODA. (Text and summaries in English and Polish) 1962. irreg. $15. Muzeum Gornoslaskie, Pl. Sobieskiego 2, 41-902 Bytom, Poland. TEL 48-32-81-34-01. **Document type:** proceedings.
—BLDSC (1035.005000).

570   SP   ISSN 1130-9717
QH301
N A C C BIOLOXIA. (Nova Acta Cientifica Compostelana) 1990. a. price varies. Universidade de Santiago de Compostela, Servicio de Publicacions e Intercambio Cientifico, Campus Universitario, 15706 Santiago de Compostela, Spain. TEL 34-81-593500. FAX 34-81-593963. E-mail: spub1@usc.es; URL: http://www.usc.es/~spub1/. Ed. Jose Luis Perez-Cirera. charts; illus. circ. 500. **Indexed:** Ind.SST. **Document type:** academic/scholarly publication.
     Supersedes (1971-1986): Trabajos Compostelanos de Biologia (ISSN 0211-0733)

570   US   ISSN 0258-1213
                               CODEN: NALSDJ
N A T O ADVANCED SCIENCE INSTITUTES SERIES A: LIFE SCIENCES. irreg., vol.290, 1997. price varies. (North Atlantic Treaty Organization, Scientific Affairs Division, BE) Plenum Publishing Corp., 233 Spring St., New York, NY 10013-1578. TEL 212-620-8000. FAX 212-463-0742. TELEX 23-421139. E-mail: books@plenum.com. (back issues avail.) **Document type:** monographic series, proceedings.
●Also available online. Vendor(s): European Space Agency (File no.128).
—BLDSC (6033.648690); CASDDS; CISTI; KNAW. CCC.
     Formerly (until 1984): N A T O Advanced Study Institutes Series. Series A. Life Sciences (ISSN 0161-0449)
     Refereed Serial

N B I A NEWSLETTER. (New Brunswick Institute of Agrologists) see *AGRICULTURE*

N C R R REPORTER. (National Center for Research Resources) see *MEDICAL SCIENCES*

570.11   JA   ISSN 0914-563X
QH95.58   CODEN: PNSBEF
N I P R SYMPOSIUM ON POLAR BIOLOGY. PROCEEDINGS. (Text in English) 1967. a., no.10, 1997. exchange basis. National Institute of Polar Research - Kokuritsu Kyokuchi Kenkyujo, Library, 9-10, Kaga 1-chome, Itabashi-ku, Tokyo 173, Japan. TEL 81-3-3962-2214. FAX 81-3-3962-2225. TELEX 272-3515 POLRSCJ. E-mail: hasegawa@nipr.ac.jp. Ed Takeo Hirasawa. circ. 1,000. **Indexed:** Geo.Abstr., GeoRef., Sport Fish.Abstr., Wild.Rev., Zoo.Rec. **Document type:** proceedings.
—BLDSC (6848.270550); CASDDS; CISTI; KNAW; UnCover.
     Supersedes in part (in 1987): National Institute of Polar Research. Memoirs. Special Issue (ISSN 0386-0744); Which was formerly (until 1972): Japanese Antarctic Research Expedition Scientific Reports. Special Issue (ISSN 0386-5452)
     Refereed Serial

N T I S ALERTS: MEDICINE & BIOLOGY. (U.S. National Technical Information Service) see *BIOLOGY — Abstracting, Bibliographies, Statistics*

570   JA   ISSN 0387-4249
NAGASAKIKEN SEIBUTSU GAKKAISHI/NAGASAKI BIOLOGICAL SOCIETY. TRANSACTIONS. (Text in English, Japanese) 1971. s-a. 2000 Yen per no. Nagasakiken Seibutsu Gakkai - Nagasaki Biological Society, Nagasaki Daigaku Kyoyobu Seibutsugaku Kyoshitsu, 1-14 Bunkyomachi, Nagasaki-shi, Nagasaki-ken 852, Japan.

570   JA   ISSN 0912-0114
NAN'YO SEIBUTSU/NAN'YO BIOLOGICAL SOCIETY. REPORTS. (Text in Japanese) 1985. a. Nan'yo Seibutsu Kenkyukai - Nan'yo Biological Society, c/o Mr. Kiyokazu Hashigoe, Sunokawa, Uchiumimura, Minamiuwa-gun, Ehimeken 798-37, Japan.

570   II   ISSN 0369-8211
Q73   CODEN: PAIBA6
NATIONAL ACADEMY OF SCIENCES, INDIA. PROCEEDINGS. SECTION B. BIOLOGICAL SCIENCES. (Text in English) 1931-32. q. Rs.150($50) National Academy of Sciences, 5 Lajpatra Rd., Allahabad 211002, Uttar Pradesh, India. Ed. H.C. Khare. bk.rev.; bibl.; charts; illus.; stat. circ. 500. **Indexed:** Biol.Abstr., Chem.Abstr., Curr.Adv.Ecol.Sci., Curr.Cont., Helminthol.Abstr., Plant Breed.Abstr., Sorghum & Millets Abstr. **Document type:** proceedings.
—BLDSC (6761.901000); CASDDS; CISTI.

570 371.3   US
NATIONAL ASSOCIATION OF BIOLOGY TEACHERS. NEWS AND VIEWS; issues, events, professional development for biology teachers. 5/yr. membership. National Association of Biology Teachers, Inc., 11250 Roger Bacon Dr., Ste. 19, Reston, VA 22090. TEL 703-471-1134. FAX 703-435-5582. E-mail: NABTer@aol.com; URL: http://www.nabt.org. Ed. Cheryl Merrill. circ. 8,000. (looseleaf format) **Document type:** newsletter.

578.77 540 639.2   KO   ISSN 1225-2751
                               CODEN: PTHPD9
NATIONAL FISHERIES UNIVERSITY OF PUSAN. INSTITUTE OF MARINE SCIENCES. CONTRIBUTIONS. (Text in Korean; summaries in English) 1968. a. 12000 Won($16) National Fisheries University of Pusan, Institute of Marine Sciences, Haewundae, Pusan 612-021, S. Korea. TEL 51-742-0475. Ed. Chung-Gil Park. circ. 800. (back issues avail.) **Indexed:** Curr.Adv.Ecol.Sci.
—CASDDS; Linda Hall.
     Formerly (until 1983): National Fisheries University of Pusan. Institute of Marine Sciences. Publications (ISSN 0250-3387)
     Description: Covers physical oceanography, chemical oceanography, marine geology, and marine biology.

570   JA   ISSN 0912-1315
S494.5.B563
NATIONAL INSTITUTE OF AGROBIOLOGICAL RESOURCES. ANNUAL REPORT. (Text in English) 1985. a. Ministry of Agriculture, Forestry and Fisheries, National Institute of Agrobiological Resources - Norin Suisansho Nogyo Seibutsu Shigen Kenkyujo, 1-2 Kannondai 2-chome, Tsukuba-shi, Ibaraki-ken 305, Japan.
—BLDSC (1364.620000); Linda Hall.

BIOLOGY

570 610   JA   ISSN 0386-5541
NATIONAL INSTITUTE OF POLAR RESEARCH. MEMOIRS. SERIES E: BIOLOGY AND MEDICAL SCIENCE. (Text and summaries in English) 1959. irreg., no.39, 1996. exchange basis. National Institute of Polar Research - Kokuritsu Kyokuchi Kenkyujo, Library, 9-10, Kaga 1-chome, Itabashi-ku, Tokyo 173, Japan. TEL 81-3-3962-2214. FAX 81-3-3962-2225. TELEX 272-2515 POLRSCJ. E-mail: hasegawa@nipr.ac.jp. Ed. Takeo Hirasawa. circ. 1,000. **Indexed:** Biol.Abstr. **Document type:** monographic series.
—BLDSC (5626.812000).
 Supersedes: Japanese Antarctic Research Expedition, 1956-1962. Scientific Reports. Series E. Biology (ISSN 0075-3394)

570 930   GW   ISSN 0077-6025
NATUR UND MENSCH: JAHRESMITTEILUNGEN DER NATURHISTORISCHEN GESELLSCHAFT NUERNBERG. 1965. a. price varies. Naturhistorische Gesellschaft Nuernberg e.V., Gewerbemuseumsplatz 4, Luitpoldhaus, 90403 Nuernberg, Germany. TEL 0911-227970. circ. 2,500. **Indexed:** Biol.Abstr., Key Word Ind.Wildl.Res. **Document type:** bulletin.
 Formerly (until 1969): Naturhistorische Gesellschaft Nuernberg. Mitteilungen und Jahresbericht.

570   BL
NATURA. 1975. s-a. free. Universidade Federal da Bahia, Instituto de Biologia, Rua Barao de Geremoabo-Ondina, 40000 Salvador, Bahia, Brazil. (Co-sponsor: Instituto de Ciencias da Saude) Ed. Antonio Pedreira. circ. 1,500.

500 550 634.9 614.7   IT   ISSN 0028-0658
NATURA & MONTAGNA; magazine for divulgation in natural sciences. 1954. s-a. L.70000 (effective 1997). (Societa Emiliana pro Montibus et Silvis) Patron Editore, Via Badini 12, 40050 Quarto Inferiere (BO), Italy. TEL 39-51-767003. FAX 39-51-768252. Ed. Carlo Ferrari. adv.; bk.rev. circ. 2,500. (back issues avail.)

570   DK   ISSN 0077-6033
QH7   CODEN: NAJUAC
NATURA JUTLANDICA. (Text in English) 1947. irreg. DKK 100($17) per vol. or exchange basis. Naturhistorisk Museum - Natural History Museum, Bygning 210, Universitetsparken, DK-8000 Aarhus C, Denmark. TEL 86-12-97-77. FAX 86-13-08-82. Ed. Anders Holm Joensen. illus. circ. 1,000. **Indexed:** Biol.Abstr., Curr.Adv.Ecol.Sci., Ecol.Abstr., Key Word Ind.Wildl.Res., Sport Fish.Abstr, Wild.Rev., Zoo.Rec.
—BLDSC (6036.500000); Linda Hall.

570 560   CN   ISSN 0707-3887
NATURAL HISTORY CONTRIBUTIONS. 1978. irreg., latest vol.11, 1992. free. Saskatchewan Museum Royal, 2340 Albert St., Regina, Sask. S4P 3V7, Canada. TEL 306-787-2801. FAX 306-787-2645. Ed. Keith Roney. circ. 300. (back issues avail.) **Document type:** monographic series.

570 550   JA   ISSN 1340-2684
NATURAL HISTORY MUSEUM AND INSTITUTE, CHIBA. JOURNAL. SPECIAL ISSUE. (Text in English, Japanese) 1994. irreg. exchange basis. Natural History Museum and Institute, Chiba, 955-2 Aoba-cho, Chuo-ku, Chiba 260, Japan. TEL 81-43-265-3111. FAX 81-43-266-2481. Ed.Bd. circ. 1,500 (controlled). (back issues avail.) **Document type:** monographic series.
 Description: Contains original articles and reviews on natural history.
 Refereed Serial

570 550   JA   ISSN 1340-2692
NATURAL HISTORY RESEARCH. SPECIAL ISSUE. (Text in English) 1994. irreg. exchange basis. Natural History Museum and Institute, Chiba, 955-2 Aoba-cho, Chuo-ku, Chiba 260, Japan. TEL 81-43-265-3111. FAX 81-43-266-2481. Ed.Bd. circ. 1,500 (controlled). (back issues avail.) **Document type:** monographic series.
 Description: Contain original articles and reviews on natural history.
 Refereed Serial

NATURAL HISTORY RESEARCH CENTER. PUBLICATION. see *SCIENCES: COMPREHENSIVE WORKS*

570   BL   ISSN 0101-1944
QH7   CODEN: NTRLDP
NATURALIA. (Text in Portuguese; summaries in English, Portuguese) 1975; N.S. 1980. a. $30 or exchange basis. Universidade Estadual Paulista, Av. Vicente Ferreira 1278, Caixa Postal 71, 17515-901 Marilia SP, Brazil. TEL 55-144-222504. FAX 55-144-222504. Ed.Bd. charts; illus.; stat. circ. 1,000. **Indexed:** Abstr.Anthropol., Apic.Abstr., Biol.Abstr., Curr.Adv.Cell & Devel.Biol., Curr.Adv.Ecol.Sci., Curr.Adv.Genetics & Molec.Biol., GeoRef, Math.R., Sociol.Abstr., Zoo.Rec. **Document type:** academic/scholarly publication.
—BLDSC (6041.910000); CASDDS; CISTI; Linda Hall.

570   UK   ISSN 0028-0771
QH1   CODEN: NTRLAM
NATURALIST. 1875. q. £20. Yorkshire Naturalists' Union, University of Bradford, Bradford, W. Yorks BD7 1DP, England. TEL 44-1274-384212. FAX 44-1274-384231. E-mail: m.r.d.seaward@ bradford.ac.uk. Ed. M.R.D. Seaward. adv.; bk.rev.; index. circ. 3,600. (also avail. in microfilm from UMI; reprint service avail. from UMI) **Indexed:** Biol.Abstr., Chem.Abstr., Curr.Adv.Ecol.Sci., GeoRef., IBR, Rev.Plant Path. **Document type:** academic/scholarly publication.
—BLDSC (6042.000000); UMI. **CCC.**

500.9   BE   ISSN 0028-0801
QH3   CODEN: NTUBA7
LES NATURALISTES BELGES. 1920. q. 750 BEF membership (foreign 800 BEF) (effective 1996). Naturalistes Belges a.s.b.l., Rue Vautier 29, 1040 Brussels, Belgium. TEL 32-2-6480475. Ed. Alain Quintart. bk.rev.; charts; illus.; index. **Indexed:** Biol.Abstr., Geo.Abstr., Zoo.Rec. **Document type:** bulletin.

570   US   ISSN 0277-609X
NATURALISTS' DIRECTORY AND ALMANAC INTERNATIONAL. 1877. irreg., 46th ed., 1993. fl.76. Box 382595, Cambridge, MA 02238-2595. TEL 904-371-9858. FAX 904-371-0962. (Dist. by: Backhuys Publishers - Universal Book Services, P.O. Box 321, 2300 AH Leiden, Netherlands. TEL 31-71-171200. FAX 31-71-171856) Eds. R.H. Arnett, M.E. Arnett. adv.; bk.rev.; bibl. circ. 5,000. (back issues avail.) **Document type:** directory.
—CISTI.
 Formerly: Naturalists' Directory International.

NATURE MEDICINE. see *MEDICAL SCIENCES*

570   US   ISSN 1072-8368
QH506   CODEN: NSBIEW
NATURE STRUCTURAL BIOLOGY. 1994. m. $530 (Canada $567; Central & South America $675) (effective 1998). MacMillan Magazines Ltd., 1234 National Press Bldg., Washington, DC 20045. TEL 202-626-2513. FAX 202-628-1609. URL: http://www.structbio.nature.com. (Subcr. to: Nature, 345 Park Ave. S., New York, NY 10160-1743. TEL 212-726-9244) Ed. Guy Riddihough. adv.; illus.; index. **Indexed:** ASCA, Curr.Cont., Excerp.Med. (1995-), Food Sci.& Tech.Abstr., Ind.Med. (1995-), Ind.Sci.Rev. **Document type:** academic/scholarly publication.
—BLDSC (6047.375000); CASDDS; CISTI; Genuine Article; KNAW; SWETS; UnCover. **CCC.**
 Description: Publishes biomedical research results in structural biology, including applications of new technologies and techniques.
 Refereed Serial

570 550   GW   ISSN 0374-6054
QH5   CODEN: BBNGAZ
NATURHISTORISCHE GESELLSCHAFT HANNOVER. BEIHEFTE ZU DEN BERICHTEN. (Text in German; summaries in English and German) 1928. irreg. DM.40. Naturhistorische Gesellschaft Hannover, Postfach 510153, 30631 Hannover, Germany. FAX 49-511-6432304. bibl.; charts; illus. circ. 850. **Document type:** monographic series.

NATURHISTORISCHE GESELLSCHAFT NUERNBERG. ABHANDLUNGEN. see *ARCHAEOLOGY*

570 550   GW   ISSN 0932-9447
NATURWISSENSCHAFTLICHE ZEITSCHRIFT FUER NIEDERBAYERN. 1864. triennial. DM.20. Naturwissenschaftlicher Verein fuer Niederbayern, Altstadt 79, 84028 Landshut, Germany. TEL 49-871-881218. FAX 49-871-881218. Ed. Georg Spitzlberger. bk.rev. **Document type:** proceedings.

570   GW   ISSN 0720-3705
NATURWISSENSCHAFTLICHER VEREIN FUER SCHWABEN. BERICHTE. 1848. q. DM.40 (effective 1996). Naturwissenschaftlicher Verein fuer Schwaben e.V., Im Thaele 3, 86152 Augsburg, Germany. TEL 49-821-3246730. FAX 49-821-3246780. Eds. Hermann Oblinger, Otto Mair. bk.rev. circ. 1,000. (back issues avail.) **Indexed:** IBR. **Document type:** academic/scholarly publication.
 Formerly (until 1885): Naturhistorischer Verein Augsburg. Bericht (ISSN 0340-3734)

570 560   NE   ISSN 0374-955X
NATUURHISTORISCH GENOOTSCHAP IN LIMBURG. PUBLICATIES. (Text in Dutch and English; summaries in English) 1948. irreg. (1-2/yr.), vol.40, 1995. price varies. (Natuurhistorisch Genootschap in Limburg) Publicatie Bureau N H G, Groenstraat 106, 6074 EL Melick, Netherlands. TEL 31-475-532351. Ed. Jo van der Coelen. R&P contact: A. Lenders. circ. 1,000. (back issues avail.) **Indexed:** Biol.Abstr., GeoRef., Rev.Appl.Entomol., Zoo.Rec. **Document type:** academic/scholarly publication.
—CISTI.
 Description: Covers the biological, geological, and paleontological research of Limburg.

NAUKOVE TOVARYSTVO IMENI SHEVCHENKA. PROCEEDINGS OF THE SECTION OF CHEMISTRY, BIOLOGY AND MEDICINE. see *CHEMISTRY*

570   NE   ISSN 1380-8427
     CODEN: NJAEEK
NETHERLANDS JOURNAL OF AQUATIC ECOLOGY. (Text in English) vol.9, 1975. 4/yr. fl.210. Netherlands Society of Aquatic Ecology, Department of Aquatic Ecotoxicology, University of Amsterdam, Kruislaan 320, 1098 SM Amsterdam, Netherlands. TEL 31-20-5257891. FAX 31-20-6659125. Ed. Jaap Dorgelo. adv.; bk.rev. **Indexed:** Aqua.Sci.& Fish.Abstr., Biol.Abstr., Chem.Abstr., Curr.Adv.Ecol.Sci., Ecol.Abstr., Excerp.Med., Geo.Abstr.H.G., Sel.Water Res.Abstr., W.R.C.Inf. **Document type:** academic/scholarly publication.
—BLDSC (6077.000200); CASDDS; CISTI; EMDOCS; KR SourceOne; Linda Hall; SWETS; UnCover.
 Former titles (until 1992): Hydrobiological Bulletin (ISSN 0165-1404); Hydrobiologische Vereniging. Mededelingen.

NEUE DENKSCHRIFTEN DES NATURHISTORISCHEN MUSEUMS IN WIEN. see *EARTH SCIENCES*

NEUROBIOLOGICAL RESEARCH. see *MEDICAL SCIENCES — Psychiatry And Neurology*

NEUROBIOLOGY OF LEARNING AND MEMORY. see *MEDICAL SCIENCES — Psychiatry And Neurology*

NEURON. see *MEDICAL SCIENCES — Psychiatry And Neurology*

NEW DEVELOPMENTS IN BIOSCIENCES. see *MEDICAL SCIENCES*

570   UN   ISSN 0077-8877
QH315
NEW TRENDS IN BIOLOGY TEACHING SERIES. (Text in English and French; summaries in Spanish) 1966. irreg., vol.5, 1987. $20. UNESCO Publishing, 7 Place de Fontenoy, 75352 Paris 07 SP, France. TEL 33-1-45684300. FAX 33-1-45685741. URL: http://www.unesco.org/publications. (Dist. in U.S. by: Bernan Associates, 4611-F Assembly Dr., Lanham, MD 20706-4391. TEL 800-274-4888. FAX 800-865-3450)

577 NZ ISSN 0110-6465
QH540 CODEN: NZJED6
NEW ZEALAND JOURNAL OF ECOLOGY. 1953. 2/yr. NZ.$100 to institutions (foreign $110). New Zealand Ecological Society, Inc., P.O. Box 25-178, Christchurch, New Zealand. TEL 64-3-3256701. FAX 64-3-3252418. E-mail: sheppars@lincoln.ac.nz. Ed. Grabor Lovei. bk.rev.; 21 year cum.index. circ. 700. (also avail. in microfiche from IDC) **Indexed:** Apic.Abstr., ASCA, Biol.Abstr., Chem.Abstr., Curr.Adv.Ecol.Sci., Curr.Cont., Curr.Ref.Fish Res., Ecol.Abstr., Excerp.Med., Field Crop Abstr., Forest.Abstr., Forest Prod.Abstr., Geo.Abstr., Herb.Abstr., Ind.Sci.Rev., Ind.Vet., Sci.Cit.Ind., Seed Abstr., Sel.Water Res.Abstr., Sport Fish.Abstr., Vet.Bull., Weed Abstr., Wild.Rev., Zoo.Rec. **Document type:** academic/scholarly publication.
—BLDSC (6093.530000); CASDDS; Genuine Article.
Formerly: New Zealand Ecological Society. Proceedings (ISSN 0077-9946)
Description: Publishes scientific studies of ecology in, or relevant to, New Zealand.
Refereed Serial

NEW ZEALAND JOURNAL OF MARINE AND FRESHWATER RESEARCH. see EARTH SCIENCES — Oceanography

578.77 NZ
NEW ZEALAND MARINE SCIENCES SOCIETY REVIEW. 1961. a. NZ.$25 (effective 1993). New Zealand Marine Sciences Society, P.O. Box 434, Cambridge, New Zealand. TEL 64-7-8567026. FAX 64-7-8560151. adv.; bk.rev.; bibl.; circ. 300 (controlled). (processed) **Document type:** newsletter, proceedings.
Former titles (until no.33, 1991): New Zealand Marine Sciences Society News (ISSN 0112-8396); New Zealand Marine Sciences Newsletter (ISSN 0028-842X)

570 NZ ISSN 0113-7492
CODEN: NZNSEZ
NEW ZEALAND NATURAL SCIENCES. 1973. a. NZ.$18 to individuals; libraries NZ.$25. University of Canterbury, Zoology Department, Private Bag 4800, Christchurch 1, New Zealand. TEL 64-3-364-2860. FAX 64-3-364-2024. Ed. Mark D. Sanders. bk.rev. circ. 260. **Indexed:** Biol.Abstr., Curr.Adv.Ecol.Sci., Ecol.Abstr., Excerp.Med., Geo.Abstr., Geol.Abstr., Mineral.Abstr., Ref.Zh., Sport Fish.Abstr., Wild.Rev., Zoo.Rec. **Document type:** academic/scholarly publication.
—BLDSC (6096.315000); CASDDS; CISTI; Linda Hall.
Formerly (until 1988): Mauri Ora (ISSN 0302-086X)
Description: Documents scientific research in the earth, life and environmental sciences relevant to New Zealand or Antarctica.
Refereed Serial

NEWS FROM HUDSONIA. see ENVIRONMENTAL STUDIES

570 JA
NICHII SEIBUTSUGAKU KYOKAI KAIHO/ASSOCIAZIONE BIOLOGICA ITALO-GIAPPONESE BOLLETTINO. (Text in English, Japanese) 1979. a. Nichii Seibutsugaku Kyokai - Associazione Biologica Italo-Giapponese, Nagoya Daigaku Rigakubu Rinkai Jikkenjo, Furocho, Chikusa-ku, Nagoya-shi, Aichi-ken 464, Japan.

570 JA ISSN 0289-4548
NIHON BENTOSU GAKKAISHI/BENTHOS RESEARCH. (Text in English, Japanese; summaries in English) 1970. s-a. 4000 Yen to individuals; institutions 8000 Yen. Nihon Bentosu Gakkai - Japanese Association of Benthology, Ocean Research Institute, University of Tokyo, Minami-Dai, Nakano-ku, Tokyo 164, Japan. TEL 81-3-5351-6469. FAX 81-3-3375-6716. E-mail: sirayama@ori.u-tokyo.ac.jp. circ. 500 (paid).
—BLDSC (1892.075000).
Description: Contains research articles related to benthic biologies, such as ecology, taxonomy, fisheries and conservation biology.
Refereed Serial

570.88 JA
NIHON BUNSHI SEIBUTSU GAKKAI KAIHO/BIOLOGY MOLECULAR SOCIETY OF JAPAN. REPORT. (Text in Japanese) 3/yr. Nihon Bunshi Seibutsu Gakkai - Biology Molecular Society of Japan, Nihon Gakkai Jimu Senta, 16-9, Honkomagome 5-chome, Bunkyo-ku, Tokyo 113, Japan.

570 JA ISSN 0289-2421
NIHON SEITAI GAKKAI KANTO CHIKUKAI KAIHO/ECOLOGICAL SOCIETY OF JAPAN. KANTO BRANCH. NEWS. (Text in Japanese) 1961. a. Nihon Seitai Gakkai, Kanto Chikukai - Ecological Society of Japan, Kanto Branch, P.O. Box 16, Tukuba Norin Kenkyu, Danchinai Yubinkyoku Shishobako, Norin Suisansho 305, Japan.

570 JA
NIHON SEITAI GAKKAI KYUSHU CHIKUKAI KAIHO/ECOLOGICAL SOCIETY OF JAPAN. KYUSHU BRANCH. BULLETIN. (Text in Japanese) q. Nihon Seitai Gakkai Kyushu Chikukai - Ecological Society of Japan, Kyushu Branch, Nihon Daigaku Rigakubu Fuzoku Amakusa Rinkai Jikkenjo, 2331 Tomioka, Reihokumachi, Amakusa-gun, Kumamoto-ken 863-25, Japan.

570 JA
NIHON SEITAI GAKKAI TOHOKU CHIKUKAI KAIHO/ECOLOGICAL SOCIETY OF JAPAN. TOHOKU BRANCH. NEWS. (Text in Japanese) a. Nihon Seitai Gakkai, Tohoku Chikukai - Ecological Society of Japan, Tohoku Branch, Tohoku Daigaku Rigakubu Seibutsugaku Kyoshitsu, Aoba, Aramaki, Aoba-ku, Sendai-shi, Miyagi-ken 980, Japan.

570 JA ISSN 0387-8236
CODEN: NDRHE4
NIIGATA DAIGAKU RIGAKUBU FUZOKU SADO RINKAI JIKKENJO TOKUBETSU HOKOKU/NIIGATA UNIVERSITY. SADO MARINE BIOLOGICAL STATION. SPECIAL PUBLICATION. (Text in Japanese; summaries in English, Japanese) 1978. irreg. Niigata Daigaku, Rigakubu, Fuzoku Sado Rinkai Jikkenjo - Niigata University, Faculty of Science, Sado Marine Biological Station, 8050 Igarashi Ninocho, Niigata-shi, Niigata-ken 950-21, Japan.
—BLDSC (8380.640000).

570 JA ISSN 0371-2672
QH301 CODEN: SRNBAD
NIIGATA UNIVERSITY. FACULTY OF SCIENCE. SCIENCE REPORTS. SERIES D: BIOLOGY/NIIGATA DAIGAKU RIGAKUBU KENKYU HOKOKU. D-RUI, SEIBUTSUGAKU. (Text in English) 1952. a. exchange basis. Niigata Daigaku, Rigakubu - Niigata University, Faculty of Science, 8050 Igarashi Nino-cho, Niigata-shi, Niigata-ken 950-21, Japan. **Indexed:** Biol.Abstr., Soils & Fert.
—CASDDS; CISTI; UnCover.
Supersedes in part (in 1964): Niigata University. Faculty of Science. Journal. Series 2: Biology, Geology, and Mineralogy (ISSN 0549-4842)

570 JA ISSN 0388-7154
NIIGATAKEN SEIBUTSU KYOIKU KENKYUKAISHI/NIIGATA PREFECTURAL BIOLOGICAL SOCIETY FOR EDUCATION. BULLETIN. (Text in Japanese) 1964. a. membership. Niigataken Seibutsu Kyoiku Kenkyukai, c/o Mr. Akiyama, Niigata Kenritsu Niigata Chuo Koto Gakko, 5314-1, Gakkocho Dori Nibancho, Niigata-shi, Niigata-ken 951, Japan.

570 JA ISSN 0911-6788
NIPPON BISEIBUTSU KABU HOZON RENMEI KAISHI/JAPAN FEDERATION FOR CULTURE COLLECTIONS. BULLETIN. (Text in English, Japanese) 1985. s-a. Nippon Biseibutsu Kabu Hozon Renmei - Japan Federation for Culture Collections, Tokyo Nogyo Daigaku Sogo Kenkyujo, Kinkabu Hozonshitsu, 1-1, Sakuragaoka 1-chome, Setagaya-ku, Tokyo 156, Japan. TEL 03-420-2131.
—BLDSC (2593.590000).

570 JA ISSN 0029-0750
NISSEIKEN TAYORI/NIPPON INSTITUTE FOR BIOLOGICAL SCIENCE. JOURNAL. (Text in Japanese) 1955. m. free. Nippon Seibutsu Kagaku Kenkyujo - Nippon Institute for Biological Science, 2221-1 Shin-machi, Ome, Tokyo 198, Japan. TEL 81-428-33-1001. FAX 81-428-31-6166. TELEX 2852077-NIBSJ. Ed. Hiromasa Tanaka. bk.rev.; charts; illus.; cum.index. circ. 1,600. (looseleaf format) **Document type:** newsletter.
Description: Summary of research activities in the institute; articles for technical extension; and records of the semi-annual seminar held by the Pathology Division of the Japanese Society for Veterinary Science.

NOGYO KANKYO GIJUTSU KENKYUSHO HOKOKU/NATIONAL INSTITUTE OF AGRO-ENVIRONMENTAL SCIENCES. BULLETIN. see AGRICULTURE

570 JA ISSN 0911-6575
CODEN: NSSHEC
NOGYO SEIBUTSU SHIGEN KENKYUJO KENKYU HOKOKU/NATIONAL INSTITUTE OF AGROBIOLOGICAL RESOURCES. BULLETIN. (Text in English, Japanese) 1985. a. exchange basis. Norin Suisansho, Nogyo Seibutsu Shigen Kenkyujo - Ministry of Agriculture, Forestry and Fisheries, National Institute of Agrobiological Resources, 2-1-2, Kannondai, Tsukuba-shi, Ibaraki-ken 305, Japan. TEL 0298-38-7004. FAX 0298-38-7408. Ed. Kenji Takayanagi. **Indexed:** Agrindex, Biol.Abstr., Chem.Abstr., Crop Physiol.Abstr., Fababean Abstr., Field Crop Abstr., Rice Abstr., Seed Abstr., Soyabean Abstr. **Document type:** bulletin.
—BLDSC (2640.010000); CASDDS; Linda Hall.

570 JA ISSN 0915-6836
S494.5.B563
NOGYO SEIBUTSU SHIGEN KENKYUJO KENKYU SHIRYO/NATIONAL INSTITUTE OF AGROBIOLOGICAL RESOURCES. MISCELLANEOUS PUBLICATION. (Text in English, Japanese) 1989. irreg. Norin Suisansho, Nogyo Seibutsu Shigen Kenkyujo - Ministry of Agriculture, Forestry and Fisheries, National Institute of Agrobiological Resources, 1-2 Kannondai 2-chome, Tsukuba-shi, Ibaraki-ken 305, Japan.

570 JA ISSN 0911-9590
NOGYO SEIBUTSU SHIGEN KENKYUJO NENPO/NATIONAL INSTITUTE OF AGROBIOLOGICAL RESOURCES. ANNUAL REPORT. (Text in Japanese) a. Norin Suisansho, Nogyo Seibutsu Shigen Kenkyujo - Ministry of Agriculture, Forestry and Fisheries, National Institute of Agrobiological Resources, 1-2 Kannondai 2-chome, Tsukuba-shi, Ibaraki-ken 305, Japan.

570 JA ISSN 0289-9248
NOGYO SEIBUTSU SHIGEN KENKYUJO NYUSU/NATIONAL INSTITUTE OF AGROBIOLOGICAL RESOURCES. NEWS. (Text in Japanese) 1984. q. Norin Suisansho, Nogyo Seibutsu Shigen Kenkyujo - Ministry of Agriculture, Forestry and Fisheries, National Institute of Agrobiological Resources, 1-2 Kannondai 2-chome, Tsukuba-shi, Ibaraki-ken 305, Japan.

NONLINEAR DYNAMICS, PSYCHOLOGY, AND LIFE SCIENCES. see PSYCHOLOGY

570 910 FI ISSN 0356-0910
AS262
NORDENSKIOLD-SAMFUNDETS TIDSKRIFT. (Text in Swedish) 1941. a. FIM 120 (effective 1997). Nordenskiold-Samfundet i Finland, c/o Department of Ecology and Systematics, P.O. Box 7, Unionsgatan 44, FIN-00014 University of Helsinki, Finland. TEL 358-9-191-86-01. FAX 358-9-191-86-56. E-mail: carl-adam.haeggsrom@helsinki.fi. Ed. Carl-Adam Haeggstrom. bk.rev. circ. 500. **Document type:** academic/scholarly publication.
Description: Deals with the natural sciences regarding the coastal areas and archipelagoes of Finland, the Baltic Sea and the arctic areas.

570 AT ISSN 0078-1630
CODEN: NQNAAG
NORTH QUEENSLAND NATURALIST. 1932. irreg., no.189, 1989. Aus.$10 membership (effective Sep. 1993). North Queensland Naturalists Club, P.O. Box 991, Cairns, N. Queensland 4870, Australia. Ed.Bd. bk.rev. circ. 220. **Indexed:** Biol.Abstr.

NOTICIAS DE GALAPAGOS. see SCIENCES: COMPREHENSIVE WORKS

570 CU
NOTICIERO CIENTIFICO. SERIE: BIOLOGIA. fortn. Academia de Ciencias, Instituto de Documentacion e Informacion Cientifico-Tecnica (I D I C T), Capitolio Nacional, Prado y San Jose, Havana 2, Cuba.

570 NE ISSN 0166-6584
CODEN: NOODDJ
NOTULAE ODONATOLOGICAE. (Text in English, French, German, Italian, Spanish) 1978. s-a. fl.40. Societas Internationalis Odonatologica, S.I.O. Central Office, P.O. Box 256, 3720 AG Bilthoven, Netherlands. Ed.Bd. bk.rev.; charts. circ. 500. **Indexed:** Biol.Abstr., Entomol.Abstr., Genet.Abstr., Ref.Zh., Zoo.Rec. **Document type:** bulletin.

570 FR ISSN 0181-3684
NOUVEAU BIOLOGISTE. 10/yr. 550 F. 4 rue Pasquier, 75008 Paris, France. TEL 42-65-15-97. FAX 42-65-58-05. Ed. A. Bedossa. circ. 3,500.

BIOLOGY

NUCLEAR MEDICINE AND BIOLOGY. see *MEDICAL SCIENCES — Radiology And Nuclear Medicine*

NUKADA INSTITUTE FOR MEDICAL AND BIOLOGICAL RESEARCH. REPORTS. see *MEDICAL SCIENCES*

NUTRITION AND THE BRAIN. see *NUTRITION AND DIETETICS*

571.9   BU   ISSN 0324-1998
CODEN: OSPADK
OBSTA I SRAVNITELNA PATOLOGIIA. (Text in various languages) 1976. s-a. price varies. (Bulgarska Akademiia na Naukite) Publishing House of the Bulgarian Academy of Sciences, Acad. G. Bonchev St., Bldg. 6, 1113 Sofia, Bulgaria. circ. 500. (reprint service avail. from IRC) **Indexed:** Abstr.Bulg.Sci.Med.Lit., Biol.Abstr., BSL Biol., Chem.Abstr., Excerp.Med., Ind.Vet., Poult.Abstr., Vet.Bull.
—BLDSC (0126.705200); CASDDS; KNAW.

OCEAN BIOCOENOSIS SERIES. see *EARTH SCIENCES — Oceanography*

OCEANOGRAPHY AND MARINE BIOLOGY: AN ANNUAL REVIEW. see *EARTH SCIENCES — Oceanography*

OCHANOMIZU UNIVERSITY. TATEYAMA MARINE LABORATORY. CONTRIBUTIONS. see *EARTH SCIENCES — Oceanography*

OCROTIREA NATURII SI A MEDIULUI INCONJURATOR. see *SCIENCES: COMPREHENSIVE WORKS*

570   NE   ISSN 0375-0183
CODEN: ODTGAI
ODONATOLOGICA. (Text in English, French, German) 1972. q. fl.220. Societas Internationalis Odonatologica, S.I.O. Central Office, P.O. Box 256, 3720 AG Bilthoven, Netherlands. Ed.Bd. bk.rev.; charts. circ. 500. **Indexed:** Biol.Abstr., Entomol.Abstr., Genet.Abstr., Ref.Zh., Zoo.Rec. **Document type:** academic/scholarly publication, abstracting/indexing.
—UnCover.

577   GW   ISSN 0029-8549
QH540   CODEN: OECOBX
OECOLOGIA. Online edition (GW ISSN 1432-1939) (Text in English) 1924. 16/yr. DM.4950 (foreign DM.4989.20) (effective 1998). (International Association for Ecology, (Intecol), NE) Springer-Verlag, Heidelberger Platz 3, 14197 Berlin, Germany. TEL 49-30-82787-0. FAX 49-30-82787448. E-mail: subscriptions@springer.de; URL: http://link.springer.de. (Subscr. in N. America to: Springer-Verlag New York, Inc., 333 Meadowlands Pkwy., Secaucus, NJ 07094. TEL 212-460-1500. FAX 212-473-6272) Ed.Bd. adv.; bibl.; illus.; index. (also avail. in microform from UMI; back issues avail.; reprint service avail. from ISI) **Indexed:** Apic.Abstr., ASCA, Bibl.Agri., Bio-Contr.News & Info., Biol.Abstr., Biol.& Agr.Ind., Crop Physiol.Abstr., Curr.Adv.Ecol.Sci., Curr.Cont., Curr.Ref.Fish Res., Deep Sea Res.& Oceanogr.Abstr., Ecol.Abstr., Excerp.Med., Field Crop Abstr., Forest.Abstr., Forest Prod.Abstr., Geo.Abstr.H.G., GeoRef., Helminthol.Abstr., Herb.Abstr., Hort.Abstr., Ind.Sci.Rev., Ind.Vet., Irr.& Drain.Abstr., Key Word Ind.Wildl.Res., Ocean.Abstr., Poult.Abstr., Rev.Appl.Entomol., Rice Abstr., Sci.Cit.Ind., Seed Abstr., Soils & Fert., Sport Fish.Abstr., Triticale Abstr., Weed Abstr., Wild.Rev., Zoo.Rec. **Document type:** academic/scholarly publication.
● Also available online.
—BLDSC (6235.262600); CISTI; EMDOCS; Genuine Article; KR SourceOne; Linda Hall; SWETS; UMI; UnCover. CCC.
Formerly: Zeitschrift fuer Morphologie und Oekologie der Tiere.
Description: Presents articles on research developments in the functional relationships between plant and animal organisms and their environment.

OEKOWERKMAGAZIN; Naturschutz in Berlin und Brandenburg. see *CONSERVATION*

570   US   ISSN 0078-3994
QH105.03   CODEN: BOBNAJ
OHIO BIOLOGICAL SURVEY. BULLETIN. NEW SERIES. 1913; N.S. 1959. irreg., vol.11, no.3, 1996. price varies. Ohio Biological Survey, 1315 Kinnear Rd., Columbus, OH 43212. TEL 614-292-9645. FAX 614-688-4322. Ed. Veda M. Cafazzo. circ. 1,000. **Indexed:** Biol.Abstr., Sport Fish.Abstr., Wild.Rev., Zoo.Rec. **Document type:** academic/scholarly publication, bulletin.
—CISTI.
Refereed Serial

570   US   ISSN 1074-9233
OHIO BIOLOGICAL SURVEY. MISCELLANEOUS CONTRIBUTIONS. 1994. irreg. price varies. Ohio Biological Survey, 1315 Kinnear Rd., Columbus, OH 43212. TEL 614-292-9645. FAX 614-688-4322. Ed. Veda M. Cafazzo. circ. 1,000. **Document type:** academic/scholarly publication.
Refereed Serial

OIKOS; a journal of ecology. see *ENVIRONMENTAL STUDIES*

570   JA   ISSN 0030-154X
CODEN: OFAJAE
OKAJIMA'S FOLIA ANATOMICA JAPONICA/OKAJIMA FORIA ANATOMIKA YAPONIKA. (Text in English) 1922. bi-m. 18000 Yen. Okajima Foria Anatomica Yaponika Henshubu, c/o Keio University, School of Medicine, Dept. of Anatomy, 35, Shinano-machi, Shinjuku-ku, Tokyo 160, Japan. TEL 81-3-3353-1211. FAX 81-3-5379-1977. (Subscr. to: Japan Publications Trading Co., Ltd., P.O. Box 5030, Tokyo International Post Office, Tokyo, Japan) Ed. Sadakazu Aiso. bk.rev.; bibl.; illus.; index. circ. 400. **Indexed:** Biol.Abstr., Chem.Abstr., Dent.Ind., Excerp.Med., Ind.Med. **Document type:** academic/scholarly publication.
—BLDSC (6252.800000); CASDDS; Linda Hall.
Description: Publishes original papers in all the fields of anatomical science, macroscopic anatomy, embryology, experimental morphology, physical anthropology, and macroscopic research methods.
Refereed Serial

570   JA   ISSN 0916-930X
QH301   CODEN: OSSHEN
OKAYAMA DAIGAKU SHIGEN SEIBUTSU KAGAKU KENKYUJO HOKOKU/OKAYAMA UNIVERSITY. RESEARCH INSTITUTE FOR BIORESOURCES. BULLETIN. (Text in English, Japanese) 1990. q. exchange basis. Okayama Daigaku, Shigen Seibutsu Kagaku Kenkyujo - Okayama University, Research Institute for Bioresources, 20-1 Chuo 2-chome, Kurashiki 710, Japan. Ed. Isao Aoyama. circ. 875. **Indexed:** Biol.Abstr., Chem.Abstr., GeoRef., Plant Breed.Abstr., Rev.Plant Path.
—BLDSC (2668.520000); CASDDS; Linda Hall; UnCover.
Formed by the merger of (1916-1990): Okayama Universitaet. Berichte des Ohara Instituts fuer Landwirtschaftliche Biologie (ISSN 0365-9860); Which was formerly (until 1954): Okayama Universitaet. Berichte des Ohara Instituts fuer Landwirtschaftliche Forschungen (ISSN 0365-9879); (1924-1990): Nogaku Kenkyu - Ohara Institute for Agricultural Biology. Report (ISSN 0029-0874); Which was formerly: Nogaku Koenshu.

570   JA   ISSN 0917-5911
OKAZAKI KOKURITSU KYODO KENKYU KIKO KISO SEIBUTSUGAKU KENKYUJO KYODO KENKYU HOKOKUSHO/NATIONAL INSTITUTE FOR BASIC BIOLOGY, OKAZAKI NATIONAL RESEARCH INSTITUTES. JOINT RESEARCH REPORT. (Text in Japanese) 1988. biennial. Okazaki Kokuritsu Kyodo Kenkyu Kiko Kiso Seibutsugaku Kenkyujo - National Institute for Basic Biology, Okazaki National Research Institutes, 38 Saigonaka, Myodaijicho, Okazaki-shi, Aichi-ken 444, Japan.

570   JA
OKINAWA SEIBUTSU GAKKAI TSUSHIN/BIOLOGICAL SOCIETY OF OKINAWA NEWS. (Text in Japanese) 1967. 2/yr. Okinawa Seibutsu Gakkai - Biological Society of Okinawa, Ryukyu Daigaku Rigakubu, 1 Senbaru, Nishiharacho, Nakagami-gun, Okinawa-ken 903-01, Japan. FAX 81-98-895-5376. Ed. Michio Hidaka. **Document type:** newsletter.

570   JA   ISSN 0474-0394
OKINAWA SEIBUTSU GAKKAISHI/BIOLOGICAL MAGAZINE OKINAWA. (Text in English, Japanese) 1964. a. 4000 Yen. Okinawa Seibutsu Gakkai, Ryukyu Daigaku Rigakubu, 1 Senbaru, Nishiharacho, Nakagami-gun, Okinawa-ken 903-01, Japan. FAX 81-98-895-5376. Ed. Eishin Isa. circ. 600. **Indexed:** Jap.Per.Ind. **Document type:** bulletin.
Refereed Serial

OKINAWA TOSHO KENKYU/ISLAND STUDIES IN OKINAWA. see *EARTH SCIENCES*

578.77   DK   ISSN 0078-5326
QH91.A1   CODEN: OPHLAN
OPHELIA; an international journal of marine biology. (Supplement avail. (ISSN 0107-5896)) (Text in English) 1964. 6/yr. DKK 1280 (effective through 1998). (Marine Biological Laboratory) Apollo Books Aps, Kirkeby Sand 19, DK-5771 Stenstrup, Denmark. TEL 45-62-26-37-37. FAX 45-62-26-37-80. Ed. Kirsten Muus. adv. circ. 600. (back issues avail.) **Indexed:** ASCA, Bibl.Agri., Biol.Abstr., Chem.Abstr., Curr.Adv.Biochem., Curr.Adv.Cell & Devel.Biol., Curr.Adv.Ecol.Sci., Curr.Cont., Deep Sea Res.& Oceanogr.Abstr., Helminthol.Abstr., IBR, Ind.Sci.Rev., Mar.Sci.Cont.Tab., Nutr.Abstr., Ocean.Abstr., Pollut.Abstr., Sci.Cit.Ind., Sel.Water Res.Abstr., Sport Fish.Abstr., Wild.Rev., Zoo.Rec. **Document type:** academic/scholarly publication.
—BLDSC (6270.800000); CISTI; EMDOCS; Linda Hall; SWETS; UMI; UnCover.

578.77   DK   ISSN 0107-5896
CODEN: OPSUD6
OPHELIA. SUPPLEMENTUM. (Supplement to: Ophelia (ISSN 0078-5326)) (Text in English) 1980. irreg. (Marine Biological Laboratory) Apollo Books Aps, Kirkeby Sand 19, DK-5771 Stenstrup, Denmark. TEL 45-62-26-37-37. FAX 45-62-26-37-80. **Indexed:** Biol.Abstr., Zoo.Rec. **Document type:** academic/scholarly publication.
—BLDSC (6270.810000); CASDDS; CISTI; Linda Hall; SWETS.

570 610   FR   ISSN 0992-5945
OPTION - BIO; le journal de l'analyse medicale et de la biologie clinique. 1989. 22/yr. 578 F. (institutions in Americas $111; elsewhere 670 F.) (effective 1998). Editions Scientifiques et Medicales Elsevier, 141 rue de Javel, 75747 Paris, France. TEL 33-1-45589068. FAX 33-1-45589421. URL: http://www.elsevier.nl/. (Subscr. in U.S. and Canada to: Elsevier Science Inc., Box 945, Madison Sq. Sta., New York, NY 10159-0945. TEL 212-633-3730. FAX 212-633-3680) Ed. F. Mauriat. adv. circ. 6,800. **Document type:** academic/scholarly publication.
—CCC.
Description: Provides day-to-day news, scientific information in the medical and biological areas, diagnostic approaches and technical viewpoints.

570   US   ISSN 0553-0342
ORGANIZATION OF AMERICAN STATES. DEPARTMENT OF SCIENTIFIC AFFAIRS. SERIE DE BIOLOGIA: MONOGRAFIAS. (Text in Spanish) 1965. irreg., no.20, 1978. $3.50 per no. Organization of American States, 1889 F St., N.W., Washington, DC 20006. TEL 703-941-1617. circ. 3,000. **Document type:** monographic series.

BIOLOGY

572.38 578   NE   ISSN 0169-6149
QH325   CODEN: OLEBEM
ORIGINS OF LIFE AND EVOLUTION OF THE BIOSPHERE.
1968. bi-m. fl.690 to institutions; $354 to institutions in U.S. (effective 1998). (International Society for the Study of the Origins of Life) Kluwer Academic Publishers, Postbus 17, 3300 AA Dordrecht, Netherlands. TEL 31-78-6392392. FAX 31-78-6392254. TELEX 29245 KAPG NL. E-mail: services@wkap.nl; URL: http://www.wkap.nl. (Dist. by: Kluwer Academic Publishers Group, P.O. Box 322, 3300 AH Dordrecht, Netherlands. TEL 31-78-6392392. FAX 31-78-6546474; N. America dist. addr.: Box 358, Accord Station, Hingham, MA 02018-0358. TEL 617-871-6600. FAX 617-871-6528) Ed. James P. Ferris. adv.; bk.rev.; bibl.; illus. (also avail. in microform from UMI) **Indexed:** Appl.Mech.Rev., ASCA, Astron.& Astrophys.Abstr., Biol.Abstr., Chem.Abstr., Curr.Adv.Ecol.Sci., Curr.Cont., Deep Sea Res.& Oceanogr.Abstr., Environ.Per.Bibl. (1985-), Excerp.Med., Geo.Abstr., Geol.Abstr., GeoRef., IBR, IBZ, Ind.Med., Ind.Sci.Rev., INIS Atomind., INSPEC (1970-), Int.Aerosp.Abstr., Phys.Ber., Ref.Zh., Sci.Cit.Ind. **Document type:** academic/scholarly publication.
—BLDSC (6291.265100); AskIEEE; CASDDS; CISTI; Genuine Article; KR SourceOne; Linda Hall; SWETS; UMI; UnCover. **CCC.**
    Former titles: Origins of Life (ISSN 0302-1688); (until 1974): Space Life Sciences (ISSN 0038-6286)
    Description: Publishes experimental and theoretical studies of chemical evolution, including evolution of planetary atmospheres, prebiotic chemistry and biochemical evolution.
    Refereed Serial

570   SP   ISSN 0213-4039
ORSIS. Variant title: Organismes i Sistemes. (Text in Catalan, English, French, Spanish) 1985. a. 1300 ptas.($12) or exchange basis. Universitat Autonoma de Barcelona, Departament de Biologia Animal, de Biologia Vegetal i d'Ecologia, Servei de Publicacions, Apartat Postal 20, 08193 Bellaterra (Barcelona), Spain. TEL 3-581-11-93. **Indexed:** Ind.SST. **Document type:** academic/scholarly publication.
—BLDSC (6293.839500); KNAW.
    Description: Publishes original works and review articles on botany, zoology and ecology.

570   JA   ISSN 0915-1052
OSAKA BAIOSAIENSU KENKYUJO NENPO. English edition: Osaka Bioscience Institute. Annual Report (ISSN 0915-3373) (Text in Japanese) 1987. a. Osaka Baiosaiensu Kenkyujo, 2-4 Furuedai 6-chome, Suita-shi, Osaka 565, Japan.

570 581   JA   ISSN 0389-9047
OSAKA-SHIRITSU SHIZENSHI HAKUBUTSUKAN SHUZO SHIRYO MOKUROKU/OSAKA MUSEUM OF NATURAL HISTORY. SPECIAL PUBLICATIONS. (Text in Japanese) 1969. a. price varies; also avail. on exchange basis. Osaka-shiritsu Shizenshi Hakubutsukan - Osaka Museum of Natural History, 1-23 Nagai Koen, Higashi-sumiyoshi-ku, Osaka-shi, Osaka-fu 546, Japan. TEL 81-6-697-6221. FAX 81-6-697-6225. Ed. Yorio Miyatake. circ. 1,000.
—BLDSC (8379.670000).

OSSA; international journal of skeletal research. see
MEDICAL SCIENCES

570   UK   ISSN 0958-6601
    CODEN: OMBIEZ
OXFORD MONOGRAPHS ON BIOGEOGRAPHY. 1981. irreg., no.9, 1994. price varies. Oxford University Press, Walton St., Oxford OX2 6UP, England. TEL 44-1865-56767. FAX 44-1865-56646. (US subscr. to: Oxford University Press Inc., 2001 Evans Rd., Cary, NC 27513. TEL 919-677-0977. FAX 919-677-1714) Ed.Bd. **Indexed:** Sport Fish.Abstr., Wild.Rev., Zoo.Rec. **Document type:** monographic series.
    Refereed Serial

570   UK
OXFORD SERIES IN ECOLOGY AND EVOLUTION. irreg. Oxford University Press, Walton St., Oxford OX2 6DP, England. TEL 44-1865-56767. FAX 44-1865-56646. (Subscr. in US to: Oxford University Press Inc., 2001 Evans Rd., Cary, NC 27513. TEL 919-677-0977. FAX 919-677-1714) **Document type:** monographic series.

P A S C A L T 215: BIOTECHNOLOGIES. see *MEDICAL SCIENCES — Abstracting, Bibliographies, Statistics*

PALAEOHISTORIA; acta et communicationes instituti bioarchaeologici universitatis groninganae. see
ARCHAEOLOGY

PARASITE IMMUNOLOGY. see *MEDICAL SCIENCES — Communicable Diseases*

577   BE   ISSN 0031-1812
    CODEN: PARGAW
PARASITICA. (Text in Dutch, English, French, German) 1945. q. 8100 BEF. Association pour les Etudes et Recherches de Zoologie Appliquee et de Phytopathologie, 11 rue du Bordia, 5030 Gembloux, Belgium. FAX 32-81-625272. TELEX CENTRAGRO 59165. Ed. R. Moens. adv.; bk.rev.; charts; illus.; index. circ. 550. (also avail. in microform from PMC) **Indexed:** Bio-Contr.News & Info., Biol.Abstr., Biotech.Abstr., Chem.Abstr., Curr.Adv.Ecol.Sci., Curr.Cont., Forest.Abstr., Helminthol.Abstr., Hort.Abstr., Potato Abstr., Rev.Appl.Entomol., Rev.Plant Path., Rice Abstr., Soils & Fert., Triticale Abstr., Weed Abstr., Zoo.Rec. **Document type:** academic/scholarly publication.
—CASDDS; CISTI; Linda Hall.

PATHOLOGIE BIOLOGIE. see *MEDICAL SCIENCES*

PATHOLOGY. see *MEDICAL SCIENCES*

PATHOLOGY PATTERNS. see *MEDICAL SCIENCES*

PATOLOGIA. see *MEDICAL SCIENCES*

571.9   MX   ISSN 0185-4305
PATOLOGIA; revista latinoamericana. (Text in Spanish; summaries in English, Portuguese) 1992. q. Mex.$300($70) (effective 1996 & 1997). (Asociacion Latinoamericana de Patologia) Obsidiana Editores, S.A., Czda. de Tlalpan 2365, Col. Ciudad Jardin, 04370 Mexico DF, Mexico. TEL 6899133. (Dist. by: Distribuidora Editorial de Mexico SA de CV, P.O. Box 76-026, 04201 Mexico DF, Mexico. TEL 525-5447953. FAX 525-6896545) (Co-sponsor: Asociacion Mexicana de Patologos) Ed. Dr. Luis Benitez-Bribiesca; Pub. Jorge Godoy-Gutierrez. adv.; bk.rev.; charts; illus.; index; circ. 630 (paid); 1,370 (controlled). (back issues avail.) **Indexed:** Biol.Abstr., Curr.Cont., Excerp.Med., Helminthol.Abstr., Sci.Cit.Ind. **Document type:** academic/scholarly publication.
●Also available on CD-ROM.
    Formerly (until 1970): Asociacion Mexicana de Patologos. Boletin.
    Description: Contains original articles, research reports, review articles, clinical cases and notices related to anatomical pathology.
    Refereed Serial

PATOLOGICHESKAYA FIZIOLOGIYA I EKSPERIMENTAL'NAYA TERAPIYA/PATHOLOGICAL PHYSIOLOGY AND EXPERIMENTAL THERAPY. see *MEDICAL SCIENCES*

PEDOBIOLOGIA. see *AGRICULTURE — Crop Production And Soil*

PELAGOS. see *EARTH SCIENCES — Oceanography*

PENNSYLVANIA ACADEMY OF SCIENCE. JOURNAL. see *SCIENCES: COMPREHENSIVE WORKS*

570 610   CI   ISSN 0031-5362
QH301   CODEN: PDBIAD
PERIODICUM BIOLOGORUM. (Text in English; summaries in Croatian and English) 1886. q. $25. Hrvatsko Prirodoslovno Drustvo - Croatian Society of Natural Sciences, Ilica 16-3, 41000 Zagreb, Croatia. TEL 041-425-288. FAX 041-425-288. Ed. Vlatko Silobrcic. bk.rev.; index. circ. 900. (back issues avail.) **Indexed:** Biol.Abstr., Chem.Abstr., Curr.Adv.Biochem., Curr.Adv.Cell & Devel.Biol., Curr.Adv.Ecol.Sci., Curr.Adv.Genetics & Molec.Biol., Curr.Cont., Dairy Sci.Abstr., Excerp.Med., Field Crop Abstr., Helminthol.Abstr., Herb.Abstr., Maize Abstr., Nutr.Abstr., Plant Breed.Abstr., Rev.Med.& Vet.Mycol., Sci.Cit.Ind., Soils & Fert., Sport Fish.Abstr., Wild.Rev., Zoo.Rec. **Document type:** academic/scholarly publication.
—BLDSC (6426.240000); CASDDS; CISTI; Genuine Article; Linda Hall; UnCover.

PERSPECTIVES IN BIOLOGY AND MEDICINE. see *MEDICAL SCIENCES*

571.43   NE   ISSN 0272-6327
PERSPECTIVES IN BIOMECHANICS. irreg. Gordon and Breach - Harwood Academic, Amsteldisk 166, 1st Fl., 1079 LH Amsterdam, Netherlands. (Subscr. to: International Publishers Distributor, Box 32160, Newark, NJ 07102. TEL 800-545-8398. FAX 215-750-6343) Ed. D.N. Ghista. (also avail. in microform) **Document type:** monographic series.
    Refereed Serial

570 301   AT   ISSN 1038-5762
PERSPECTIVES IN HUMAN BIOLOGY. 1992. a. Aus.$30($24) (effective 1997). Centre for Human Biology, Dept. of Anatomy & Human Biology, Univ. of Western Australia, Nedlands, W.A. 6907, Australia. TEL 61-9-3803491. FAX 61-9-3801051. E-mail: rpervan@anhb.uwa.edu.au; URL: http://www.wspc.com.sq. Ed.Bd. bk.rev. circ. 200. **Document type:** academic/scholarly publication.
—BLDSC (6428.143180).
    Description: Publishes research papers and reviews which foster a primarily biological understanding of humans, with emphasis on the integration of the constituent disciplines.
    Refereed Serial

PETERSON'S GRADUATE AND PROFESSIONAL PROGRAMS: THE BIOLOGICAL SCIENCES (YEAR) (BOOK 3). see *EDUCATION — Guides To Schools And Colleges*

PHILIPPIA. see *MUSEUMS AND ART GALLERIES*

570   UK   ISSN 0268-487X
    CODEN: PHOEEU
PHOENIX (SOMERSHAM). 1985. a. £18. 1 Warners Farm, Warners Drove, Somersham, Cambs PE17 3HW, England. TEL 01487-841733. FAX 01487-843270. Ed. Michael Jennings. adv.; abstr.; bibl.; illus.; stat.; tr.lit.; index. circ. 750. (back issues avail.) **Indexed:** Sport Fish.Abstr., Wild.Rev., Zoo.Rec. **Document type:** academic/scholarly publication, newsletter.

PHOTOCHEMICAL & PHOTOBIOLOGICAL REVIEWS. see *CHEMISTRY*

PHOTOCHEMISTRY AND PHOTOBIOLOGY. see *CHEMISTRY*

578.77   TH   ISSN 0858-1088
QH193.T46   CODEN: RBPCE9
PHUKET MARINE BIOLOGICAL CENTER. RESEARCH BULLETIN. (Text in English) 1973. irreg. (1-2/yr.) $10 (effective 1993). Phuket Marine Biological Center, P.O. Box 60, Phuket 83000, Thailand. TEL 076-391128. FAX 076-391127. Ed. Samsak Chullasorn. illus. circ. 500. (back issues avail.) **Document type:** bulletin.
    Description: Examines research results carried out at the center; in cooperation with the center; or independent research performed in Thailand and adjacent areas.
    Refereed Serial

570   TH   ISSN 0858-3633
PHUKET MARINE BIOLOGICAL CENTER. SPECIAL PUBLICATIONS. (Text in English) 1983. irreg. price varies. Phuket Marine Biological Center, P.O. Box 60, Phuket 83000, Thailand. TEL 076-391128. FAX 66-76-391127. Ed. Somsak Chullasorn. illus. circ. 500. **Document type:** proceedings.
    Description: Contains papers from the Tropical Marine Mollusc Programme.

573.4 616.48   II
▼**PINEAL GLAND: ITS MOLECULAR SIGNALS.** (Text in English) 1996. irreg. $30 per no. Hindustan Publishing Corp, 4805-24 Bharat Ram Rd., Flat Nos. 1 & 2, 1st Fl., Daryaganj, New Delhi 110002, India. TEL 91-11-3254401. FAX 91-11-6863511. E-mail: hpcpd@giasdl01.vsnl.net.in. Ed. Chandana Haldar. **Document type:** monographic series.

PIRINEOS; a journal on mountain ecology. see *GEOGRAPHY*

BIOLOGY

578.77   JA
PLANKTON BIOLOGY AND ECOLOGY. (Text in English) s-a. 9000 Yen (effective 1998). Plankton Society of Japan - Nihon Purankuton Gakkai, c/o Laboratory of Aquatic Ecology, Faculty of Agriculture, Tohoku University, 1-1 Amamiya-machi, Tsutsumi-dori, Aoba-ku, Sendai 981, Japan. TEL 81-22-717-8734. FAX 81-22-717-8734. E-mail: yendo@bios.tohoku.ac.jp. Ed. Shuhei Nishida. R&P contact: Yoshinari Endo. adv. contact: Yoshinari Endo. circ. 700.
Description: Publishes papers, reviews and notes dealing with all aspects of biology and ecology of marine and freshwater plankton, and their interactions with the environments in any aquatic systems.
Refereed Serial

578.77   JA   ISSN 0387-8961
THE PLANKTON SOCIETY OF JAPAN. BULLETIN/NIHON PURANKUTON GAKKAIHO. (Text in English, Japanese) 1953. s-a. 9000 Yen (effective 1998). Plankton Society of Japan - Nihon Purankuton Gakkai, c/o Laboratory of Aquatic Ecology, Faculty of Agriculture, Tohoku University, 1-1 Amamiya-machi, Tsutsumi-dori, Aoba-ku, Sendai 981, Japan. TEL 81-22-717-8734. FAX 81-22-717-8734. E-mail: yendo@bios.tohoku.ac.jp. Ed. Shuhei Nishida. R&P contact: Yoshinari Endo. adv. contact: Yoshinari Endo. bk.rev. circ. 700. **Indexed:** Agrindex, Biol.Abstr., Curr.Adv.Ecol.Sci., Deep Sea Res.& Oceanogr.Abstr., Jap.Per.Ind. **Document type:** bulletin.
—CISTI.
Description: Covers all aspects of zoo- and phytoplankton in marine, freshwater, brackish and airborne environments.

PLANT BREEDING AND SEED SCIENCE/HODOWLA ROSLIN I NASIENNICTWO. see *AGRICULTURE*

581.7   UK   ISSN 0140-7791
CODEN: PLCEDV
PLANT, CELL AND ENVIRONMENT. 1978. m. £840($1555) (foreign £925) (effective 1998). Blackwell Science Ltd., Osney Mead, Oxford OX2 0EL, England. TEL 44-1865-206206. FAX 44-1865-721205. E-mail: journals.cs@blacksci.co.uk; URL: http://www.black.co.uk. Eds. H. Smith, E. Billett; Pub. Allen Stevens. R&P contact: Sarah Pollard. adv. contact: Martine Cariou-Keen. bk.rev.; bibl.; illus.; index. circ. 760. (also avail. in microform from UMI; back issues avail.; reprint service avail. from ISI) **Indexed:** ASCA, Bibl.Agri., Biol.Abstr., Biotech.Abstr., Chem.Abstr., Chem.Cit.Ind., Cott.& Trop.Fibr.Abstr., Crop Physiol.Abstr., Curr.Adv.Ecol.Sci., Curr.Cont., Ecol.Abstr., Environ.Abstr., Environ.Per.Bibl. (1989-), Excerp.Med., Fababean Abstr., Field Crop Abstr., Forest.Abstr., Forest Prod.Abstr., Herb.Abstr., Hort.Abstr., IBR, Ind.Sci.Rev., Irr.& Drain.Abstr., Maize Abstr., Meteor.& Geoastrophys.Abstr., Ornam.Hort., Plant Breed.Abstr., Plant.Grow.Reg.Abstr., Potato Abstr., Rice Abstr., Sci.Cit.Ind., Soils & Fert., Soyabean Abstr., Triticale Abstr., Weed Abstr. **Document type:** academic/scholarly publication.
—BLDSC (6514.200000); CASDDS; CISTI; EMDOCS; Genuine Article; Linda Hall; SWETS; UMI; UnCover. **CCC.**
Refereed Serial

572.8   NE   ISSN 0167-4412
CODEN: PMBIDB
PLANT MOLECULAR BIOLOGY; an international journal on molecular biology, biochemistry and genetic engineering. (Text in English) 1981. 18/yr. fl.3339 to institutions; $1713 to institutions in U.S. (effective 1998). (International Society for Plant Molecular Biology) Kluwer Academic Publishers, Postbus 17, 3300 AA Dordrecht, Netherlands. TEL 31-78-6392392. FAX 31-78-6392254. TELEX 29245 KAPG NL. E-mail: services@wkap.nl; URL: http://www.wkap.nl. (Dist. by: Kluwer Academic Publishing Group, P.O. Box 332, 3300 AH Dordrecht, Netherlands. TEL 31-78-6392392. FAX 31-78-6546474; N. America dist. addr.: Box 358, Accord Sta., Hingham, MA 02018-0358. TEL 617-871-6600. FAX 617-871-6528) Ed. Rob A. Schilperoort. adv.; bk.rev. (also avail. in microform from UMI; back issues avail.; reprint service avail. from SWZ) **Indexed:** ASCA, Bibl.Agri., Biol.Abstr., Biotech.Abstr., Chem.Abstr., Cott.& Trop.Fibr.Abstr., Crop Physiol.Abstr., Curr.Adv.Biochem., Curr.Adv.Ecol.Sci., Curr.Adv.Genetics & Molec.Biol., Curr.Biotech.Abstr., Curr.Cont., Fababean Abstr., Field Crop Abstr., Food Sci.& Tech.Abstr., Hort.Abstr., Ind.Sci.Rev., Int.Abstr.Biol.Sci., Maize Abstr., Ornam.Hort., Rice Abstr., Sci.Cit.Ind., Seed Abstr., Soyabean Abstr., Telegen. **Document type:** academic/scholarly publication.
—BLDSC (6520.350000); CASDDS; CISTI; EMDOCS; Genuine Article; Linda Hall; SWETS; UMI; UnCover. **CCC.**
Description: Publishes research concerned with plant molecular biology, biochemistry and plant molecular genetics, including cyanobacteria and algae.
Refereed Serial

570   US   ISSN 0147-619X
QH452   CODEN: PLSMDX
PLASMID; a journal focused on extrachromosomal gene systems and mobile genetic elements in prokaryotes and eukaryotes. 1977. bi-m. $295 (foreign $365) (effective 1997). Academic Press, Inc., Journal Division, 525 B St., Ste. 1900, San Diego, CA 92101-4495. TEL 619-230-1840. FAX 619-699-6800. E-mail: apsubs@acad.com; URL: http://www.apnet.com/www/journal/pl.htm. (Subscr. to: Box 620000, Orlando, FL 32891-8340. TEL 800-543-9534) Eds. Richard Kolodner, Francis Macrina. adv.; index. (back issues avail.) **Indexed:** ASCA, Bibl.Agri., Biotech.Abstr., Chem.Abstr., Curr.Adv.Ecol.Sci., Curr.Biotech.Abstr., Curr.Cont., Dairy Sci.Abstr., Food Sci.& Tech.Abstr., Hort.Abstr., Ind.Med., Ind.Sci.Rev., Plant Breed.Abstr., Rev.Plant Path., Sci.Cit.Ind., Telegen. **Document type:** academic/scholarly publication.
•Also available online.
—BLDSC (6528.790000); ADONIS; CASDDS; CISTI; Genuine Article; Linda Hall; SWETS; UnCover. **CCC.**
Description: Focuses on the biology of extrachromosomal genetic elements in both prokaryotic and eukaryotic systems, including their biological behavior, molecular structure and genetic function, their gene products and their use as genetic tools.
Refereed Serial

571.3   UK   ISSN 0953-7104
CODEN: PLTEEF
PLATELETS (ABINGDON). 1990. bi-m. £84($140) to individuals; institutions £262 ($428) (effective 1997). Carfax Publishing Co., P.O. Box 25, Abingdon, Oxon OX14 3UE, England. TEL 44-1235-401000. FAX 44-1235-401550. E-mail: enquiries@carfax.co.uk. (N. American subscr. to: Carfax Publishing Co., 875-81 Massachusetts Ave., Cambridge, MA 02139) circ. 200. **Indexed:** Curr.Cont., Ind.Sci.Rev., Sci.Cit.Ind. **Document type:** academic/scholarly publication.
—BLDSC (6537.844500); CASDDS; CISTI; EMDOCS; Genuine Article; KNAW; SWETS. **CCC.**
Description: Publishes articles on all aspects of platelet-related research, including vascular disease, cerebral and myocardial ischaemia, asthma, inflammation, growth factors, pathology and morphology of platelets, and comparison with other cells and clinical trials of antiplatelet agents.

570   GW   ISSN 0722-4060
QL104   CODEN: POBIDP
POLAR BIOLOGY. Online edition (GW ISSN 1432-2056) (Text in English) 1982. m. DM.2024.80 (foreign DM.2040.40) (effective 1998). Springer-Verlag, Heidelberger Platz 3, 14197 Berlin, Germany. TEL 49-30-82787-0. FAX 49-30-82787448. E-mail: subscriptions@springer.de; URL: http://link.springer.de. (Subscr. in N. America to: Springer-Verlag New York, Inc., 333 Meadowlands Pkwy., Secaucus, NJ 07094. TEL 212-460-1500. FAX 212-473-6272) Ed. G. Hempel. (also avail. in microfiche from UMI; reprint service avail. from ISI) **Indexed:** ASCA, Chem.Abstr., Curr.Adv.Ecol.Sci., Curr.Cont., Deep Sea Res.& Oceanogr.Abstr., Ecol.Abstr., Geo.Abstr.H.G., Geol.Abstr., Ind.Sci.Rev., Sci.Cit.Ind., Soils & Fert. **Document type:** academic/scholarly publication.
•Also available online.
—BLDSC (6541.936500); CASDDS; CISTI; EMDOCS; Genuine Article; Linda Hall; SWETS; UMI; UnCover. **CCC.**
Description: Presents results of all kinds of studies in plants, animals, and microorganisms of marine, limnic and terrestrial habitats of Arctic and Antarctic regions.

570   PL   ISSN 0867-1656
QH301   CODEN: BPABEN
POLISH ACADEMY OF SCIENCES. BULLETIN. BIOLOGICAL SCIENCES. (Text in English, French, German) 1953. q. $100. Polska Akademia Nauk, Centrum Upowszechniania Nauki, Palac Kultury i Nauki, Pietro XXIII, pok.23-10, 00-901 Warsaw, Poland. (Dist. by: Ars Polona, Krakowskie Przedmiescie 7, 00-068 Warsaw, Poland) R&P contact: Irmina Grodzka-Autoszkiewicz. adv. contact: Ewa Bartkowiak. bibl.; charts; illus. circ. 180. **Indexed:** Abstr.Hyg., AgroAgen, Anim.Breed.Abstr., Biol.Abstr., Chem.Abstr., Curr.Adv.Ecol.Sci., Dairy Sci.Abstr., Deep Sea Res.& Oceanogr.Abstr., Excerp.Med., Fababean Abstr., Field Crop Abstr., Food Sci.& Tech.Abstr., GeoRef., Helminthol.Abstr., Herb.Abstr., Hort.Abstr., Ind.Med., Ind.Vet., INIS Atomind., Nutr.Abstr., Ornam.Hort., Plant Breed.Abstr., Sci.Cit.Ind., Seed Abstr., Soils & Fert., Sport Fish.Abstr., Trop.Dis.Bull., Vet.Bull., Weed.Abstr., Wild.Rev., Zoo.Rec. **Document type:** academic/scholarly publication, bulletin.
—CASDDS; CISTI; Linda Hall.
Formerly (until 1983): Academie Polonaise des Sciences. Bulletin. Serie des Sciences Biologiques (ISSN 0001-4087)
Refereed Serial

577   PL   ISSN 0324-8763
QH540   CODEN: PECTDR
POLISH ECOLOGICAL STUDIES. (Text in English; summaries in Polish) 1975. q. $108 (effective 1997). Polska Akademia Nauk, Instytut Ekologii, Dziekanow Lesny k-Warszawy, 05-092 Lomianki, Poland. TEL 48-22-7513046. FAX 48-22-7513100. (Dist. by: Ars Polona, Krakowskie Przedmiescie 7, 00-068 Warsaw, Poland) Ed. Gabriela Bujalska. R&P contact: Gabriela Bujalska. adv. contact: Gabriela Bujalska. bibl. circ. 430. **Indexed:** Biol.Abstr., Chem.Abstr., Curr.Adv.Ecol.Sci., Ecol.Abstr., Excerp.Med., Geo.Abstr.H.G., GeoRef., Plant Breed.Abstr., Sport Fish.Abstr., Wild.Rev., Zoo.Rec. **Document type:** academic/scholarly publication.
—BLDSC (6543.583000); CASDDS; CISTI; Linda Hall. **CCC.**
Description: Publishes original papers from the range of the experimental, descriptive and theoretical ecology and other branches of sciences closely connected with broad ecological and environmental aspects.

POLLICHIA. MITTEILUNGEN. see *EARTH SCIENCES*

BIOLOGY

578.77   PL   ISSN 0032-3764
QH301   CODEN: PAHYA2
POLSKIE ARCHIWUM HYDROBIOLOGII/POLISH ARCHIVES OF HYDROBIOLOGY. (Text in English, French or German) 1926. q. $108 (effective 1997). Polska Akademia Nauk, Miedzynarodowe Cetrum Ekologiczne - Polish Academy of Sciences, International Centre of Ecology, Dziekanow Lesny k-Warszawy, 05-092 Lomianki, Poland. TEL 48-22-7513046. FAX 48-22-7513100. (Dist. by: Ars Polona, Krakowskie Przedmiescie 7, 00-068 Warsaw, Poland) Ed. Romuald Z. Klekowski. R&P contact: Ewa Kamler. abstr.; illus.; index. circ. 590. **Indexed:** AgroAgen, AgroLibrex, Biol.Abstr., Bull.Signal., Chem.Abstr., Curr.Ref.Fish Res., Deep Sea Res.& Oceanogr.Abstr., Ecol.Abstr., Geo.Abstr.H.G., Geol.Abstr., Ref.Zh., Sel.Water Res.Abstr., Sport Fish.Abstr., Weed Abstr., Wild.Rev., World Fish.Abstr., Zoo.Rec. **Document type:** academic/scholarly publication.
—BLDSC (6546.450000); CASDDS; CISTI; Linda Hall; SWETS.
    Formerly (until 1953): Archiwum Hydrobiologii i Rybactwa.
    Description: Publishes reports of original research in every field of hydrobiology, as well as theoretical papers, review articles and complete bibliographies.

570   PO
         CODEN: PABAA2
PORTUGALIAE ACTA BIOLOGICA. SERIE A. MORFOLOGIA, FISIOLOGIA, GENETICA E BIOLOGIA GERAL. (Text in English, French, German, Portuguese) 1944. irreg. price varies. Universidade de Lisboa, Museu, Laboratorio e Jardim Botanico, Rua da Escola Politecnica, 58, 1294 Lisbon Codex, Portugal. TEL 351-1-3961521. Ed. F.M. Catarino. R&P contact: F.M. Catarino. adv. contact: Manuel dos Santos Lopes. bk.rev. circ. 250. **Indexed:** Biol.Abstr., Chem.Abstr., Field Crop Abstr., Herb.Abstr., Hort.Abstr., Rev.Plant Path. **Document type:** academic/scholarly publication.
—CASDDS; CISTI; Linda Hall.
    Supersedes in part: Portugaliae Acta Biologica (ISSN 0032-5147)

570   PO   ISSN 0375-0280
QK1   CODEN: PABBA5
PORTUGALIAE ACTA BIOLOGICA. SERIE B. SISTEMATICA, ECOLOGIA, BIOGEOGRAFIA E PALEONTOLOGIA. (Text in English, French, German, Portuguese) 1945. irreg. price varies. Universidade de Lisboa, Museu, Laboratorio e Jardim Botanico, Rua da Escola Politecnica, 58, 1294 Lisbon Codex, Portugal. TEL 351-1-3961521. Ed. F.M. Catarino. R&P contact: F.M. Catarino. adv. contact: Manuel dos Santos Lopes. circ. 250. **Indexed:** Field Crop Abstr., Herb.Abstr. **Document type:** academic/scholarly publication.
—BLDSC (6556.100000); CASDDS; CISTI; Linda Hall.
    Supersedes in part: Portugaliae Acta Biologica (ISSN 0032-5147)

570   PL   ISSN 0079-4619
QH7   CODEN: PTPRAI
POZNANSKIE TOWARZYSTWO PRZYJACIOL NAUK. KOMISJA BIOLOGICZNA. PRACE. (Text in English, Polish; summaries in English) 1921. irreg. vol.74, 1994. price varies. Poznanskie Towarzystwo Przyjaciol Nauk, Komisja Biologiczna, Ul. Mielzynskiego 27-29, 61-725 Poznan, Poland. (Dist. by Ars Polona-Ruch, Krakowskie Przedmiescie 7, 00-068 Warsaw, Poland) Ed.Bd. **Indexed:** Biol.Abstr., Chem.Abstr. **Document type:** academic/scholarly publication.
—BLDSC (6586.000000); Linda Hall.

DER PRAEPARATOR. see CONSERVATION

577   US   ISSN 0091-0376
QH540   CODEN: PRNTBZ
PRAIRIE NATURALIST. 1968. q. $15 to individuals; institutions $20; students $10. Noth Dakota Natural Science Society, Division of Biological Sciences, Box 4050, Emporia State University, Emporia, KS 66801. TEL 316-341-5612. E-mail: finkelm@esumail.emporia.edu. Ed. Elmer J. Finck. R&P contact: Cindy Moore. adv. contact: Cindy Moore. bk.rev.; circ. 600 (paid). **Indexed:** Biol.Abstr., Key Word Ind.Wildl.Res., Sport Fish.Abstr., Wild Life Rev., Wild.Rev., Zoo.Rec. **Document type:** academic/scholarly publication.
—BLDSC (6598.551000); UnCover.
    Description: Presents research on the North American grasslands and their biota.
    Refereed Serial

570.07 370   GW   ISSN 0177-8382
         CODEN: PNWBAV
PRAXIS DER NATURWISSENSCHAFTEN. BIOLOGIE. 1951. 8/yr. DM.112 (foreign DM.128) (effective 1997). Aulis-Verlag Deubner und Co. KG, Antwerpener Str. 6-12, 50672 Cologne, Germany. TEL 49-221-951454-0. FAX 49-221-518443. Ed.Bd. R&P contact: Wolfgang Deubner. adv. contact: Ulrike Lennertz. bk.rev.; abstr.; illus.; index. **Indexed:** Chem.Abstr., IBR. **Document type:** academic/scholarly publication.
—CISTI.
    Formerly: Praxis der Naturwissenschaften. Biologie im Unterricht der Schulen (ISSN 0341-8510)

570   CI   ISSN 0351-0662
QH7
PRIRODA. 1911. 10/yr. (Hrvatsko Prirodosovno Drustvo) Vjesnik, Avenija Bratstva i Jedinstva 4, 41000 Zagreb, Croatia. TEL 041-515-555. Ed. Tomislav Krcmar. circ. 10,000.
—BLDSC (6615.800000).

570   YU   ISSN 0373-2134
PRIRODNJACKI MUZEJ U BEOGRADU. GLASNIK. SERIJA B: BIOLOSKE NAUKE. 1949. irreg. Prirodnjacki Muzej u Beogradu, Njegoseva 51, Belgrade, Yugoslavia. Ed. Vojislav Vasic. **Indexed:** GeoRef.
—BLDSC (0050.240000).

570   KR   ISSN 0555-2656
Q300   CODEN: PBNKAV
PROBLEMY BIONIKI. 1968. s-a. 1.40 Rub. (Khar'kovskii Institut Radioelektroniki) Izdatel'stvo Vysshaya Shkola, Khar'kovskoe Otdelenie, Universitetskaya 16, 310003 Kharkov, Ukraine. Ed. Yu. Shabanov-Kushnarenko. circ. 700. **Indexed:** Biol.Abstr., Chem.Abstr., INSPEC, Zent.Math.
—CASDDS; CISTI; KNAW; Linda Hall.
    Description: Presents articles on the problems of the mathematical and physical simulation of man's intellectual activity; and the result of bionic researches.

570   US   ISSN 0172-6625
         CODEN: PRLSEP
PROCEEDINGS IN LIFE SCIENCES. 1976. irreg. price varies. Springer-Verlag, 175 Fifth Ave., New York, NY 10010. TEL 212-460-1500. FAX 212-473-6272. (Also: Berlin, Heidelberg, Tokyo and Vienna) Eds. D.G. Weiss, A. Gorio. **Document type:** proceedings.
—CCC.

PROGRESS IN CLINICAL AND BIOLOGICAL RESEARCH. see MEDICAL SCIENCES

578.77   US   ISSN 0079-6603
QP551   CODEN: PNMBAF
PROGRESS IN NUCLEIC ACID RESEARCH AND MOLECULAR BIOLOGY. 1963. irreg., vol.58, 1997. Academic Press, Inc., 525 B St., Ste. 1900, San Diego, CA 92101-4495. TEL 619-231-0926. FAX 619-699-6715. (Subscr. to: Order Dept., 6277 Sea Harbor Dr., 4th Fl., Orlando, FL 32887. TEL 800-321-5068) Eds. J.N. Davidson, Waldo E. Cohn. (reprint service avail. from ISI) **Indexed:** ASCA, Biol.Abstr., Chem.Abstr., Chem.Cit.Ind., Curr.Adv.Ecol.Sci., Dok.Arbeitsmed., Ind.Med., Ind.Sci.Rev, Sci.Cit.Ind.
—BLDSC (6871.210000); CASDDS; CISTI; Linda Hall; SWETS; UnCover. **CCC.**
    Formerly (until vol.2): Progress in Nucleic Acid Research.
    Refereed Serial

PROTECTA; protezione civile, ecologia, ambiente. see ENVIRONMENTAL STUDIES

570   US
PROTEIN INFORMATION RESOURCE NEWSLETTER. 1985. irreg., no.12, 1992. free to qualified personnel. National Biomedical Research Foundation, 3900 Reservoir Rd., N.W., Washington, DC 20007. TEL 202-687-2121. FAX 202-687-1662. Ed. Kathryn E. Sidman. bk.rev.; circ. 1,000. **Document type:** newsletter.
    Formerly: Protein Identification Resource Newsletter.

570 333.9   PL   ISSN 1230-509X
PRZEGLAD PRZYRODNICZY. 1990. q. 16 Zl. (in US $16). Lubuski Klub Przyrodnikow, Ul. 1 Maja 22, 66-200 Swiebodzin, Poland. TEL 48-688-28236. Eds. A. Jermaczek, P. Pawlaczyk. bk.rev.; index; circ. 1,000 (paid). **Indexed:** AgroLibrex. **Document type:** academic/scholarly publication, monographic series.
—BLDSC (6944.693000).
    Formerly (until 1993): Lubuski Przeglad Przyrodniczy (ISSN 0867-0331)
    Description: Regional forum on nature protection and ecology.

PSIQUIATRIA BIOLOGICA. see MEDICAL SCIENCES — Psychiatry And Neurology

PUERTO RICO HEALTH SCIENCES JOURNAL. see MEDICAL SCIENCES

571.3 611   IT   ISSN 0390-7139
QUADERNI DI ANATOMIA PRATICA. 1945. q. L.90000($125) (effective 1997). Piccin Editore, Via Altinate 107, 35100 Padua, Italy. TEL 39-49-655566. FAX 39-49-8750693. adv.; bk.rev. (reprint service avail. from UMI) **Indexed:** Biol.Abstr., Excerp.Med.

THE QUARTERLY JOURNAL OF NUCLEAR MEDICINE. see MEDICAL SCIENCES — Radiology And Nuclear Medicine

570   US   ISSN 0033-5770
QH301   CODEN: QRBIAK
QUARTERLY REVIEW OF BIOLOGY. 1926. q. $37 to individuals (Canada $44.59; elsewhere $42); institutions $126 (Canada $139.82; elsewhere $131); students $25 (Canada $31.75; elsewhere $30) (effective 1998). University of Chicago Press, Journals Division, 5720 S. Woodlawn Ave., Chicago, IL 60637. TEL 773-753-3347.
    FAX 773-753-0811. E-mail: subscriptions@journals.uchicago.edu; URL: http://www.journals.uchicago.edu/QPB/. (Subscr. to: Box 37005, Chicago, IL 60637) Eds. Frank C. Erk, George C. Williams. adv.: page $475; trim 6 3/4 x 10. bk.rev.; bibl.; charts; illus.; software rev.; index. circ. 3,200. (also avail. in microform from KTO,UMI) **Indexed:** Abstr.Anthropol., Acad.Ind., ASCA, Biol.Abstr., Biol.& Agr.Ind., Biol.Dig., Bk.Rev.Ind. (1989-), Chem.Abstr., Child.Bk.Rev.Ind. (1989-), Curr.Adv.Ecol.Sci., Curr.Cont., Deep Sea Res.& Oceanogr.Abstr., Ecol.Abstr., Excerp.Med., Gen.Sci.Ind., Geo.Abstr., Geol.Abstr., Helminth.Abstr., Hort.Abstr., Ind.Med., Ind.Sci.Rev., Key Word Ind.Wildl.Res., Nutr.Abstr., Plant Breed.Abstr., Ref.Sour., Rev.Plant Path., Sci.Cit.Ind., Sel.Water Res.Abstr., Sport Fish.Abstr., Weed Abstr., Wild.Rev., Zoo.Rec. **Document type:** academic/scholarly publication.
—BLDSC (7206.000000); CASDDS; CISTI; Genuine Article; KR SourceOne; Linda Hall; SWETS; UMI; UnCover. **CCC.**
    Description: Features recent research and software reviews in the various fields of the biological sciences.
    Refereed Serial

QUARTERLY REVIEWS OF BIOPHYSICS. see BIOLOGY — Biophysics

QUATERNARY OF SOUTH AMERICAN AND ANTARCTIC PENINSULA. see EARTH SCIENCES — Geology

578.77   CN
QUEBEC (PROVINCE). DIRECTION DE LA RECHERCHE SCIENTIFIQUE ET TECHNIQUE. ACTIVITES (YEAR). (Text in French) 1953-1979; N.S. 1988. a. free. Ministere de l'Agriculture, des Pecheries et de l'Alimentation, Direction de la Recherche Scientifique et Technique, Secretariat d'Edition, 96 Montee Sandy-Beach, C.P. 1070, Gaspe, PQ G0C 1R0, Canada. TEL 418-368-7616. FAX 418-368-8400. **Indexed:** Biol.Abstr., Ocean.Ind. **Document type:** government publication.
—CISTI.
    Supersedes (in 1988): Quebec (Province). Direction Generale des Peches Maritimes. Direction de la Recherche. Rapport Annuel (ISSN 0318-8779); (in 1969): Quebec (Province). Marine Biological Station, Grande-Riviere. Rapport (ISSN 0079-8754)

BIOLOGY

578.77   CN   ISSN 0712-0613
CODEN: CIQTDG
QUEBEC (PROVINCE). DIRECTION DE LA RECHERCHE SCIENTIFIQUE ET TECHNIQUE. CAHIER D'INFORMATION. 1960. irreg., no.130, 1992. free or exchange basis. Ministere de l'Agriculture, des Pecheries et de l'Alimentation, Direction de la Recherche Scientifique et Technique, Secretariat d'Edition, 96 Montee Sandy-Beach, C.P. 1070, Gaspe, PQ G0C 1R0, Canada. TEL 418-368-7616. FAX 418-368-8400. circ. 600. **Indexed:** Biol.Abstr., Ocean.Ind., Sport Fish.Abstr., Wild.Rev., Zoo.Rec. **Document type:** government publication.
   Former titles: Quebec (Province). Direction Generale des Peches Maritimes. Cahier d'Information; Quebec (Province). Marine Biological Station, Grande-Riviere. Cahiers d'Information (ISSN 0079-8762)

509   AT   ISSN 0079-8843
CODEN: QLNAAE
QUEENSLAND NATURALIST. 1908. s-a. Aus.$4 per no. Queensland Naturalists' Club Inc., G.P.O. Box 5663, West End, Brisbane, Qld. 4101, Australia. Ed. Peter Woodall. circ. 600. **Indexed:** Biol.Abstr., GeoRef., Sport Fish.Abstr., Wild.Rev., Zoo.Rec. **Document type:** academic/scholarly publication.
  —CISTI; Linda Hall; UnCover.
   Description: Covers natural history and natural science.

QUETICO-SUPERIOR WILDERNESS RESEARCH CENTER, ELY, MINNESOTA. ANNUAL REPORT. see *CONSERVATION*

570   JA   ISSN 0288-3473
RAIFU SAIENSU/LIFE SCIENCE. (Text in Japanese) 1974. m. 800 Yen per no. Seimei Kagaku Shinkokai - Life Science Promotion Association, 9-20, Kitasonomachi, Takatsuki-shi, Osaka 569, Japan.

570   JA
RAIFU SAIENSU SHINKO ZAIDAN NENPO/LIFE SCIENCE FOUNDATION OF JAPAN. ANNUALS. (Text in Japanese) 1986. a. Raifu Saiensu Shinko Zaidan - Life Science Foundation of Japan, 203 Hanzomon Asai Biru, 2-18 Hayabusacho, Chiyoda-ku, Tokyo 102, Japan.

570   SP   ISSN 0583-7499
REAL SOCIEDAD ESPANOLA DE HISTORIA NATURAL. BOLETIN. ACTAS. (Text in Spanish; summaries in English, French) 1872. a. 7000 ptas. individual membership; institutions 10000 ptas.; foreign 12000 ptas. (or exchange basis). Real Sociedad Espanola de Historia Natural, Facultades de Biologia y Geologia, Ciudad Universitaria, 28040 Madrid, Spain. TEL 34-1-3945000. FAX 34-1-3945000. E-mail: rsehno@eucmax.sim.ucm.es; URL: http://www.ucm.es/info/rsehn/. Ed. Antonio Perejon Rincon. bk.rev. circ. 900. (reprint service avail.) **Indexed:** Biol.Abstr., Curr.Adv.Ecol.Sci., Deep Sea Res.& Oceanogr.Abstr., Ind.SST. **Document type:** bulletin.
  —CISTI.
   Supersedes in part (in 1950): Real Sociedad Espanola de Historia Natural. Boletin (ISSN 0365-9755); Which superseded in part (in 1901): Sociedad Espanola de Historia Natural. Anales (ISSN 0210-5160).

570   SP   ISSN 0366-3272
QH301   CODEN: BSHBA7
REAL SOCIEDAD ESPANOLA DE HISTORIA NATURAL. BOLETIN. SECCION BIOLOGICA. (Text in Spanish; summaries in English, French) 1901. a. 7000 ptas. individual membership; institutions 10000 ptas.; foreign 12000 ptas. (or exchange basis). Real Sociedad Espanola de Historia Natural, Facultades de Biologia y Geologia, Ciudad Universitaria, 28040 Madrid, Spain. TEL 34-1-3945000. FAX 34-1-3945000. E-mail: rsehno@eucmax.sim.ucm.es; URL: http://www.ucm.es/info/rsehn/. Ed. Antonio Perejon Rincon. (reprint service avail.) **Indexed:** Ecol.Abstr., Ind.SST. **Document type:** bulletin.
  —BLDSC (2188.100000); CASDDS; CISTI.
   Supersedes in part (in 1950): Real Sociedad Espanola de Historia Natural. Boletin (ISSN 0365-9755)

RECENT ADVANCES IN HISTOPATHOLOGY. see *MEDICAL SCIENCES*

577   II   ISSN 0971-1708
CODEN: PGECDY
RECENT RESEARCHES IN ECOLOGY, ENVIRONMENT AND POLLUTION. 1988. irreg., vol.10, 1993. price varies. Today and Tomorrow's Printers & Publishers, 24B-5 Desh Badhu Gupta Rd., Karol Bagh, New Delhi 110 005, India. TEL 5721928. (Dist. in U.S. by: Scholarly Publications, 2825 Wilcrest Dr., Ste. 255, Houston, TX 77042. TEL 713-781-0070. FAX 713-781-2112) Ed. Malabika Ray. **Indexed:** Biol.Abstr., Chem.Abstr., Curr.Cont. **Document type:** monographic series.
  —BLDSC (7305.087900); CASDDS; CISTI. **CCC.**
   Formerly (until 1988): Progress in Ecology (ISSN 0253-665X)

REFERATIVNYI ZHURNAL. OBSHCHIE VOPROSY PATOLOGICHESKOI ANATOMII. see *BIOLOGY — Abstracting, Bibliographies, Statistics*

570   AT   ISSN 1031-3613
QH251   CODEN: RFDEEH
REPRODUCTION, FERTILITY AND DEVELOPMENT. 1989. 8/yr. Aus.$420($420) (effective 1998). (C.S.I.R.O. Australia) C.S.I.R.O. Publishing, 150 Oxford St., Collingwood, Vic. 3066, Australia. TEL 61-3-96627618. FAX 61-3-96627611. E-mail: agrant@publish.csiro.au; URL: http://www.publish.csiro.au/journals/rfd. Ed. A. Grant. adv.; charts; illus.; index. circ. 700. (also avail. in microform from UMI; back issues avail.) **Indexed:** Abstr.Hyg., Anim.Breed.Abstr., ASCA, Biol.Abstr., Biol.& Agr.Ind., Biotech.Abstr., Chem.Abstr., Curr.Adv.Ecol.Sci., Curr.Biotech.Abstr., Curr.Cont., Curr.Leather Lit., Curr.Ref.Fish Res., Dairy Sci.Abstr., Deep Sea Res.& Oceanogr.Abstr., Environ.Per.Bibl., Excerp.Med., Field Crop.Abstr., Food Sci.& Tech.Abstr., Forest.Abstr., Forest.Prod.Abstr., GeoRef., Helminthol.Abstr., Hort.Abstr., Ind.Med., Ind.Sci.Rev., Ind.Sci.Rev., Ind.Vet., INIS Atomind., Nutr.Abstr., Plant Breed.Abstr., Poult.Abstr., Rev.Appl.Entomol., Rev.Med.& Vet.Mycol., Rev.Plant Path., Sci.Cit.Ind., Soils & Fert., Sport Fish.Abstr., SSCI, Triticale Abstr., Trop.Dis.Bull., Vet.Bull., Weed Abstr., Wild.Rev., Zoo.Rec. **Document type:** academic/scholarly publication.
  —BLDSC (7713.603000); CASDDS; CISTI; EMDOCS; Genuine Article; KNAW; KR SourceOne; Linda Hall; SWETS; UMI; UnCover. **CCC.**
   Formed by the merger of (1982-1989): Clinical Reproduction and Fertility (ISSN 0725-556X); (1948-1989): Australian Journal of Biological Sciences (ISSN 0004-9417)
   Description: Covers reproductive biology, reproductive endocrinology and developmental biology.

573.6   FR   ISSN 0926-5287
SF768   CODEN: RNDEE5
REPRODUCTION, NUTRITION, DEVELOPMENT. (Supplement avail. (ISSN 0926-5309)) (Text mainly in English; abstracts in English, French) 1961. bi-m. 1802 F. (institutions in Americas $345; elsewhere 2260 F.) (effective 1998). (Institut National de la Recherche Agronomique) Editions Scientifiques et Medicales Elsevier, 141 rue de Javel, 75747 Paris, France. TEL 33-1-45589022. FAX 33-1-45589421. URL: http://www.elsevier.nl/. (Subscr. in U.S. and Canada to: Elsevier Science Inc., Box 945, Madison Sq. Sta., New York, NY 10159-0945. TEL 212-633-3730. FAX 212-633-3680) Eds. M.A. Driancourt, L. Gueguen, J.E. Flechon. adv.; charts; illus.; index. circ. 2,000. (also avail. in microform) **Indexed:** Anal.Abstr., Anim.Breed.Abstr., ASCA, Biol.Abstr., Biotech.Abstr., Chem.Abstr., Curr.Adv.Cell & Devel.Biol., Curr.Adv.Ecol.Sci., Curr.Adv.Genetics & Molec.Biol., Curr.Cont., Dairy Sci.Abstr., Deep Sea Res.& Oceanogr.Abstr., Dent.Ind., Excerp.Med., Field Crop Abstr., Food Sci.& Tech.Abstr., Genet.Abstr., Helminthol.Abstr., Herb.Abstr., Ind.Med., Ind.Sci.Rev., Ind.Vet., Nutr.Abstr., Pig News & Info., Poult.Abstr., Protozool.Abstr., Sci.Cit.Ind., Soyabean Abstr., Triticale Abstr., Vet.Bull. **Document type:** academic/scholarly publication.
  —BLDSC (7713.630000); CASDDS; CISTI; EMDOCS; Genuine Article; KNAW; Linda Hall; SWETS; UnCover. **CCC.**
   Former titles (until 1989): Reproduction, Nutrition, Developpement (ISSN 0181-1916); (until 1989): Annales de Biologie Animale, Biochimie, Biophysique (ISSN 0003-388X)
   Description: Presents papers about reproduction, development and nutrition in animals.
  Refereed Serial

573.6   PH
REPRODUCTIONS. (Text in English) 1970. irreg. (15-20/yr.). P.5($4) University of Santo Tomas, Institute for the Study of Human Reproduction, Faculty of Medicine, Espana St., Sampaloc, Manila, Philippines. Ed. Dr. Vicente J.A. Rosales. bk.rev. circ. 5,000. (looseleaf format)

REPUBLIC OF CHINA. NATIONAL SCIENCE COUNCIL. PROCEEDINGS. PART B: LIFE SCIENCES. see *MEDICAL SCIENCES*

570   JA
RESEARCH INSTITUTE OF EVOLUTIONARY BIOLOGY. PUBLICATIONS. (Text in English, French) 1978. irreg. Research Institute of Evolutionary Biology - Shinka Seibutsugaku Kenkyujo, 4-28 Kamiyoga 2-chome, Setagaya-ku, Tokyo 158, Japan. **Document type:** academic/scholarly publication, monographic series.

RESONANCE (SUMTERVILLE). see *PHYSICS*

577 628   US   ISSN 1070-4868
S494.5.P47
THE RESOURCES OF INTERNATIONAL PERMACULTURE. Variant title: T R I P. 1986. irreg. $25. Yankee Permaculture, Hemenway - Permaculture, Box 2052, Ocala, FL 34478-2052. Ed. Dan Hemenway. R&P contact: Dan Hemenway. (also avail. in diskette format) **Document type:** directory.
   Supersedes in part (in 1990): T I P S Y: International Permaculture Species Yearbook (ISSN 0896-5781)
   Description: Lists groups allied to the permaculture movement worldwide.

RESTORATION AND MANAGEMENT NOTES. see *CONSERVATION*

573.6   UK   ISSN 1359-6004
CODEN: REREFD
▼**REVIEWS OF REPRODUCTION.** 1996. 3/yr. £50($80) (effective 1997 & 1998). Journals of Reproduction & Fertility Ltd., 22 Newmarket Rd., Cambridge CB5 8DT, England. TEL 44-1223-351809. FAX 44-1223-359754. E-mail: jrf@cityscape.co.uk. (Dist. by: Portland Press, P.O. Box 32, Commerce Way, Colchester, Essex CO2 8HP, England. TEL 44-1206-796351. FAX 44-1206-799331) Ed. Dr. C.A. Doberska. adv.: page £352; trim 170 x 240. **Document type:** academic/scholarly publication.
  —BLDSC (7794.260000); CASDDS; CISTI.
   Description: Illustrated reviews on recent developments in the field of basic mechanisms in reproductive biology.
  Refereed Serial

570   BL   ISSN 0034-7108
QH301   CODEN: RBBIAL
REVISTA BRASILEIRA DE BIOLOGIA. (Text in English, French, German, Italian, Portuguese and Spanish) 1941. q. $45. Academia Brasileira de Ciencias, Rua Anfilofio de Carvalho 29, Caixa Postal 229, 20000 Rio de Janeiro, Brazil. bk.rev.; bibl.; charts; illus.; index. **Indexed:** Biol.Abstr., Chem.Abstr., Curr.Adv.Biochem., Curr.Adv.Cell & Devel.Biol., Dent.Ind., Helminthol.Abstr., Ind.Med., Ind.Vet., Plant Breed Abstr., Rev.Appl.Entomol., Vet.Bull.
  —BLDSC (7844.000000); CASDDS; Linda Hall; UnCover.

REVISTA BRASILEIRA DE PARASITOLOGIA VETERINARIA/BRAZILIAN JOURNAL OF VETERINARY PARASITOLOGY. see *VETERINARY SCIENCE*

REVISTA BRASILEIRA DE PESQUISAS MEDICAS E BIOLOGICAS/BRAZILIAN JOURNAL OF MEDICAL AND BIOLOGICAL RESEARCH. see *MEDICAL SCIENCES*

BIOLOGY

570   CU   ISSN 0253-5688
QH301   CODEN: RCNCD5
REVISTA C E N I C. CIENCIAS BIOLOGICAS. (Text and summaries in English, Spanish) 1969. 3/yr. $60 in N. America and S. America; elsewhere $90) (effective 1997). (Ministerio de Educacon Superior) Centro Nacional de Investigaciones Científicas, Ave. 25 y 158, Apdo. 6880 y 6990, Havana 10600, Cuba. TEL 537-218066. FAX 537-330497. TELEX 51-1582 CNIC CU. E-mail: cnic@reduniv.edu.cu. Ed. Juan J. Meitin Casas. adv.; bk.rev.; bibl.; charts. circ. 750. (back issues avail.) **Indexed:** Biol.Abstr., Chem.Abstr.
—BLDSC (7804.760000); CASDDS; CISTI.
Formerly (until 1986): Revista de Ciencias Biologicas (ISSN 0258-6002)
Description: Presents national and international articles in the biological sciences; covers biotechnology, bioengineering, environmental pollution and pharmacology.

611.01816 610   CU   ISSN 0864-0300
REVISTA CUBANA DE INVESTIGACIONES BIOMEDICAS. (Text in Spanish; summaries in English, Spanish) s-a. $30 in S. America; N. America $32; elsewhere $34. Ministerio de Salud Publica, Centro Nacional de Informacion de Ciencias Medicas, Calle E No. 452, e-19 y 21, Plaza de la Revolucion, Apdo. 6520, Havana, Cuba. TEL 809-32-5338. (Dist. by: Ediciones Cubanas, Obispo No. 527, Apdo. 605, Havana, Cuba) Ed. Maura Diaz. bibl.; charts; illus.; index. circ. 1,300. **Indexed:** I.P.A.
—BLDSC (7852.109200); EMDOCS.

573.6   CU   ISSN 0138-6700
REVISTA CUBANA DE REPRODUCCION ANIMAL. (Table of contents and abstracts in English) 1975. 2/yr. $14 in N. America; S. America $15; Europe $19. Centro de Informacion y Documentacion Agropecuario, Gaveta Postal 4149, Havana 4, Cuba. (Dist. by: Ediciones Cubanas, Obispo No. 527, Apdo. 605, Havana, Cuba) Dir. J.R. Morales. bibl.; charts; illus. **Indexed:** Agrindex, Anim.Breed.Abstr., Biol.Abstr., Ind.Vet., Poult.Abstr.

570   PO   ISSN 0034-7736
QH301   CODEN: RVBIAP
REVISTA DE BIOLOGIA. (Text in English, French, German, Portuguese) 1957. irreg. price varies. Universidade de Lisboa, Museu, Laboratorio e Jardim Botanico, Rua da Escola Politecnica, 58, 1294 Lisbon Codex, Portugal. TEL 351-1-3961521. Ed. F.M. Catarino. R&P contact: F.M. Catarino. adv. contact: Manuel dos Santos Lopes. bk.rev.; charts; illus. circ. 250. (also avail. in microform from UMI; reprint service avail. from UMI) **Indexed:** Biol.Abstr., Chem.Abstr., Crop Physiol.Abstr., Curr.Adv.Ecol.Sci., Field Crop Abstr., Herb.Abstr., Plant Grow.Reg.Abstr., Triticale Abstr., W.R.C.Inf. **Document type:** academic/scholarly publication.
—BLDSC (7842.750000); CASDDS; CISTI; UMI.

570   UY   ISSN 0304-971X
QH305.2.U8   CODEN: RBURDA
REVISTA DE BIOLOGIA DEL URUGUAY. (Text in Spanish; summaries in English) 1973. a. $20. Fernando Mane-Garzon, Ed. & Pub., Casilla de Correo 157, Montevideo, Uruguay. illus.; index. circ. 1,500. (back issues avail.) **Indexed:** Biol.Abstr., Deep Sea Res.& Oceanogr.Abstr. **Document type:** academic/scholarly publication.
—CISTI; Linda Hall.

578.77   CL
QH91.A1   CODEN: RBIMAY
REVISTA DE BIOLOGIA MARINA Y OCEANOGRAFIA. (Text in English, Spanish; summaries in English, Spanish) 1948. s-a. $30 (foreign $50) or exchange basis (effective 1997). Universidad de Valparaiso, Instituto de Oceanologia, Casilla 13-D, Vina del Mar, Chile. TEL 56-32-832702. FAX 56-32-833214. E-mail: fbalbon@uv.cl. Ed. Fernando Balbontin. R&P contact: Fernando Balbontin. TEL 56-32-832702. cum.index. circ. 700. **Indexed:** Biol.Abstr., Curr.Adv.Ecol.Sci., Curr.Adv.Plant.Sci., Deep Sea Res.& Oceanogr.Abstr., Ecol.Abstr., Geo.Abstr.H.G., Helminthol.Abstr., Mar.Sci.Cont.Tab., Ocean.Abstr., Sel.Water Res.Abstr., Sport Fish.Abstr., Wild.Rev., Zoo.Rec. **Document type:** academic/scholarly publication.
—BLDSC (7843.000000); CISTI.
Formerly (until 1997): Revista de Biologia Marina (ISSN 0080-2115)
Description: Papers on marine biology, ecology, physical, chemical and biological oceanography, marine geology, and estuarine environment.
Refereed Serial

570.909   CR   ISSN 0034-7744
RC960   CODEN: RBTCAP
REVISTA DE BIOLOGIA TROPICAL. (Text in English, Spanish) 1953. 3/yr. (with supplements). $30. Editorial de la Universidad de Costa Rica, Apdo. 75-2060, Ciudad Univ. R. Facio, 2050 San Pedro de Montes de Oca, San Jose, Costa Rica. TEL 506-25-3133. FAX 506-24-9367. TELEX UNICORI 2544. Ed. Julian Monge-Najera. charts; illus.; index. circ. 1,800. (also avail. in microform from UMI; microfilm from OMN; reprint service avail. from UMI; back issues avail.) **Indexed:** Abstr.Hyg., Apic.Abstr., Aqua.Sci.& Fish.Abstr., ASCA, Biol.Abstr., Bull.Signal., Chem.Abstr., Curr.Adv.Ecol.Sci., Curr.Cont., Deep Sea Res.& Oceanogr.Abstr., Ecol.Abstr., Field Crop Abstr., Helminthol.Abstr., Herb.Abstr., Hort.Abstr., Ind.Med., Ind.Vet., Nutr.Abstr., Rev.Appl.Entomol., Sel.Water Res.Abstr., Soils & Fert., Sport Fish.Abstr., Trop.Dis.Bull., Vet.Bull., Wild.Rev., Zoo.Rec. **Document type:** academic/scholarly publication.
—BLDSC (7843.200000); CASDDS; Genuine Article; Linda Hall; UMI; UnCover.

570   VE   ISSN 1012-2494
QH106.5   CODEN: RECLEQ
REVISTA DE ECOLOGIA LATINOAMERICANA. (Text in English, Portuguese, Spanish; abstracts in English) 1983. 3/yr. $650. Centro de Investigacion y Reproduccion de Especies Silvestres, Apdo. Postal 397, Merida 5101, Venezuela. TEL 58-74-712939. E-mail: cires@ciens.ula.ve. Ed. Hector Fernando Aguilar. adv. contact: Lieselotte Hoeger de Aguilar. bk.rev. circ. 1,500. **Indexed:** Biol.Abstr.
Refereed Serial

578.77   CU   ISSN 0252-1962
QH109.C9   CODEN: RIMAD2
REVISTA DE INVESTIGACIONES MARINAS. (Text in Spanish; summaries in English and Spanish) 1980. 3/yr. C.$4.50($24) in N. America; S. America $25; Europe $26. (Universidad de La Habana, Direccion de Informacion Cientifico Tecnica) Ediciones Cubanas, Obispo No. 527, Apdo. 605, Havana, Cuba. **Indexed:** Deep Sea Res.& Oceanogr.Abstr.
—BLDSC (7862.053000); CISTI; KNAW; Linda Hall.

REVISTA ECUATORIANA DE MEDICINA Y CIENCIAS BIOLOGICAS. see *MEDICAL SCIENCES*

570   BL   ISSN 0104-7264
REVISTA UNIVERSIDADE RURAL; serie ciencias da vida. 1971. s-a. R.24. Universidade Federal Rural do Rio de Janeiro, Ed. Suzana Bencke Amato.
Formerly (until 1995): Universidade Federal Rural do Rio de Janeiro. Arquivos (ISSN 0100-2481)
Description: Publishes original works on basic and applied research.

577   FR   ISSN 1166-9632
QH541.5.M66   CODEN: REALEG
REVUE D'ECOLOGIE ALPINE. (Text in English, French, German and Italian) 1963. irreg. 200 F.($15) Universite de Grenoble I (Universite Scientifique et Medicale de Grenoble), Centre de Biologie Alpine, Universite Joseph Fourier, B.P. 53X, 38041 Grenoble Cedex 1, France. Ed. B. Souchier. adv.; bk.rev.; illus.; maps. circ. 900. (back issues avail.) **Indexed:** Bibl.Cart., Biol.Abstr., Bull.Signal. **Document type:** academic/scholarly publication.
—BLDSC (7898.720000); CISTI.
Former titles (until 1988): Documents de Cartographie Ecologique (ISSN 0335-5330); Documents pour la Carte de la Vegetation des Alpes (ISSN 0419-5728)
Description: Features original articles addressing methods in map-making and applications in ecological studies.

578.77   FR   ISSN 0240-8783
QH96.A1   CODEN: RHTRDD
REVUE D'HYDROBIOLOGIE TROPICALE. (Text in French; summaries in English) 1967. q. 390 F. (Institut Francais de Recherche Scientifique pour le Developpement en Cooperation) O R S T O M Editions - Diffusion, 32 Av. Henri Varagnat, 93143 Bondy Cedex, France. TEL 33-1-48025500. FAX 33-1-48473088. E-mail: lopes@bondy.orstom. fr. circ. 500. (back issues avail.) **Indexed:** Curr.Adv.Ecol.Sci., Curr.Tit.Ocean., Deep Sea Res.& Oceanogr.Abstr., Helminthol.Abstr., IBR, Sport Fish.Abstr., Wild.Rev., Zoo.Rec. **Document type:** academic/scholarly publication.
—BLDSC (7921.280000); CISTI; Linda Hall.
Supersedes: Cahiers O R S T O M Serie Hydrobiologie (ISSN 0029-7240)

570   FR   ISSN 0373-2851
   CODEN: RSNAA6
REVUE DES SCIENCES NATURELLES D'AUVERGNE. 1921. a. 70 F. Societe d'Histoire Naturelle d'Auvergne, Faculte de Botanique, 2 rue Ledru, 63000 Clermont-Ferrand, France. (back issues avail.)
—BLDSC (7948.200000).

570   FR   ISSN 0338-9898
REVUE FRANCAISE DES LABORATOIRES. 1972. s-m. 730 F. Labo-France, 7 rue Godot de Mauroy, 75009 Paris, France. adv. circ. 7,000.
Formerly: Revue Francaise des Fournisseurs de Laboratoires.

570   BE   ISSN 0375-1465
REVUE VERVIETOISE D'HISTOIRE NATURELLE; bulletin trimestriel des Naturalistes Vervietois. (Text in French) 1944. q. 400 BEF. Imprimerie Hamers J.C., Hameau de Husquet, 119, B-4820 Dison, Belgium. (Subscr. to: M.L. Phillipe, 89 rue de Jehanster, B-4800 Verviers, Belgium) Ed. J. Lambert. circ. 300.
Formerly (until 1949): Naturaliste Amateur (ISSN 0770-0709)

570   JA   ISSN 0286-8172
RIKUSUI SEIBUTSUGAKUHO/BIOLOGY OF INLAND WATERS. (Text in English or Japanese) 1980. irreg. 3500 Yen membership. Nara Rikusui Seibutsu Kenkyukai - Nara Scientific Research Society of Inland Water Biology, c/o Nara Joshi Daigaku Rigakubu, Seibutsugaku Kyoshitsu, Kitauoyanish-machi, Nara-shi, Nara-ken 630, Japan. TEL 0742-20-3424. E-mail: ape@cc.nara-wu.ac.jp. Ed. Makoto Nagoshi. circ. 300. **Document type:** academic/scholarly publication.
Description: Includes observation notes, comments, and original papers on biology of inland waters, e.g. ecology, taxonomy, physiology and ethology.
Refereed Serial

570   IT   ISSN 0035-6050
QH301   CODEN: RBILAV
RIVISTA DI BIOLOGIA/BIOLOGY FORUM. (Text in Italian; English edition also avail.) 1919. 3/yr. L.80000 for bilingual ed. (foreign L.120000); English only ed. $50 (effective 1997). (Universita degli Studi di Perugia) Tilgher-Genova s.a.s., Via Assarotti 31-15, 16122 Genova GE, Italy. TEL 39-6-5810789. FAX 39-6-5894742. TELEX 662078 UNIPGI. Ed. Giuseppe Sermonti. adv.; bk.rev.; charts; illus.; index. circ. 750. (also avail. in microform from UMI; reprint service avail. from UMI) **Indexed:** Arts & Hum.Cit.Ind., ASCA, Biol.Abstr., Chem.Abstr., Curr.Adv.Ecol.Sci., Curr.Cont., Deep Sea Res.& Oceanogr.Abstr., Environ.Per.Bibl. (1989-1994), Excerp.Med., Ind.Med., INSPEC, Nutr.Abstr., Plant Breed.Abstr.
—BLDSC (7982.100000); CASDDS; CISTI; Genuine Article; KNAW; Linda Hall; SWETS; UMI.
Description: Features essays, reviews, critiques and comments on biological topics.

571.9   IT   ISSN 0391-1551
   CODEN: RBNPD3
RIVISTA DI BIOLOGIA NORMALE E PATOLOGICA. (Text and summaries in English and Italian) 1975. bi-m. L.10000. Universita degli Studi di Messina, Centro Universitario di Ricerca sui Tumori, Via G. Venezian, Messina 98100, Italy. Ed. Carmelo Cavallaro. bk.rev. circ. 300. (back issues avail.) **Indexed:** Abstr.Hyg., Biol.Abstr., Chem.Abstr., Excerp.Med., Ind.Vet., Vet.Bull.
—CASDDS. CCC.

578.77   IT   ISSN 0048-8399
QH96.25.I8   CODEN: RIIDBN
RIVISTA DI IDROBIOLOGIA. (Text in Italian; summaries in English) 1960. q. exchange basis. Universita degli Studi di Perugia, Istituto di Idrobiologia, Via Elce di Sotto, 06100 Perugia, Italy. TEL 39-75-5855705. FAX 39-75-5855709. Ed. Giampaolo Moretti. bk.rev.; illus.; cum.index. circ. 300. **Indexed:** Biol.Abstr., Chem.Abstr., Sel.Water Res.Abstr. **Document type:** monographic series.
—BLDSC (7986.650000); CASDDS; CISTI.

RIVISTA DI NEUROBIOLOGIA. see *MEDICAL SCIENCES — Psychiatry And Neurology*

RIVISTA ITALIANA DI BIOLOGIA E MEDICINA. see *MEDICAL SCIENCES*

BIOLOGY

570   BL   ISSN 0370-6583
QH301   CODEN: RODRAD
RODRIGUESIA. 1935; N.S. Sep. 1939. s-a. $36 (effective 1997). Ministerio do Meio Ambiente, dos Recursos Hidricos e da Amazonia Legal, Jardim Botanico do Rio de Janeiro, Biblioteca Barbosa Rodrigues, Rua Jardim Botanico 1008, 22460-000 Gavea, Rio de Janeiro, Brazil. TEL 55-21-2748246. FAX 55-21-2744897. TELEX 021-33623. **Indexed:** Biol.Abstr., Forest.Abstr., Forest Prod.Abstr., Rev.Plant Path.
—Linda Hall.

571.86 612.64
612.64   RM   ISSN 1220-0522
CODEN: RRMEEA
ROMANIAN JOURNAL OF MORPHOLOGY AND EMBRYOLOGY/REVUE ROUMAINE DE MORPHOLOGIE ET EMBRYOLOGIE. (Text in English, French, German, Russian and Spanish) 1964. q. (Academia de Stiinte Medicale) Editura Academiei Romane, Calea 13 Septembrie 13, 76117 Bucharest, Rumania. (Dist. by: Rodipet SA, Piata Presei Libere 1, Sec. 1, PO Box 33-57, Bucharest, Rumania. TEL 401-6185103. FAX 401-226407) Ed. V.D. Marza. bk.rev.; charts; illus.; index. **Indexed:** Biol.Abstr., Chem.Abstr., Curr.Adv.Cancer Res., Curr.Adv.Ecol.Sci., Excerp.Med., Ind.Med., Nutr.Abstr. **Document type:** academic/scholarly publication.
—BLDSC (8019.636500); CASDDS; CISTI; KNAW; Linda Hall.
Formerly (until 1990): Morphologie et Embryologie (ISSN 0377-5038); Which supersedes in part (in 1975): Revue Roumaine de Morphologie et de Physiologie (ISSN 0377-4953); Which was formed by the 1974 merger of: Revue Roumaine de Physiologie (ISSN 0035-399X); Revue Roumaine de Morphologie et d'Embryologie (ISSN 0377-4945); Which was formed by the 1973 merger of: Morfologia Normala si Patologica (ISSN 0027-1063) & Revue Roumaine d'Embryologie et de Cytologie. Serie de Cytologie (ISSN 0556-8056) & Revue Roumaine d'Embryologie (0300-063X); Which was formerly titled (1964-1972): Revue Roumaine d'Embryologie et de Cytologie. Serie d'Embryologie (ISSN 0035-4007).

570   RU
CODEN: IANBAM
ROSSIISKAYA AKADEMIYA NAUK. IZVESTIYA. SERIYA BIOLOGICHESKAYA. English translation: Russian Academy of Sciences. Biology Bulletin (US ISSN 1062-3590) (Text in Russian; summaries in English) 1936. bi-m. 39.90 Rub. Izdatel'stvo Nauka, 90 Profsoyuznaya ul., 117864 Moscow, Russia. (Dist. by: Mezhdunarodnaya Kniga, B. Yakimanka 39, 117049 Moscow, Russia) Ed. E.N. Mishustin. bk.rev.; index. (tabloid format) **Indexed:** Biol.Abstr., Chem.Abstr., Crop Physiol.Abstr., Deep Sea Res.& Oceanogr.Abstr., Field Crop Abstr., Geo.Abstr., Helminthol.Abstr., Ind.Med., Ind.Sci.Rev., INIS Atomind., Protozool.Abstr., Rev.Appl.Entomol., Rice Abstr., Soyabean Abstr., Triticale Abstr. **Document type:** academic/scholarly publication.
—CASDDS; CISTI; Genuine Article; Linda Hall. **CCC.**
Formerly: Akademiya Nauk S.S.S.R. Izvestiya. Seriya Biologicheskaya (ISSN 0002-3329)

ROYAL COLLEGE OF PATHOLOGISTS OF AUSTRALASIA. BROADSHEETS. see *MEDICAL SCIENCES*

ROYAL COLLEGE OF PATHOLOGISTS OF AUSTRALASIA. BULLETIN. see *MEDICAL SCIENCES*

ROYAL NETHERLANDS ACADEMY OF SCIENCES. PROCEEDINGS; biological, chemical, geological, physical and medical sciences. see *SCIENCES: COMPREHENSIVE WORKS*

570   CN   ISSN 0384-8159
QL1   CODEN: ROMCAD
ROYAL ONTARIO MUSEUM. LIFE SCIENCES. CONTRIBUTIONS. 1928. irreg. price varies. Royal Ontario Museum, Publications, 100 Queen's Park, Toronto, ON M5S 2C6, Canada. TEL 416-586-5581. FAX 416-586-5887. E-mail: sandras@rom.on.ca. (Subscr. to: University of Toronto Press, Order Fulfilment Division, 5201 Dufferin St. Downsview, ON M3H 5T8, Canada. TEL 416-667-7791) Ed. Sandra Shaul. R&P contact: Glen Ellis. TEL 416-586-5582. bibl. **Indexed:** Biol.Abstr., Curr.Adv.Ecol.Sci., Deep Sea Res.& Oceanogr.Abstr., GeoRef., Sport Fish.Abstr., Wild.Rev., Zoo.Rec. **Document type:** monographic series, academic/scholarly publication.
—BLDSC (5208.955000); CISTI; Linda Hall.

570   CN   ISSN 0082-5093
CODEN: ROLMB5
ROYAL ONTARIO MUSEUM. LIFE SCIENCES. MISCELLANEOUS PUBLICATIONS. 1963. irreg. price varies. Royal Ontario Museum, Publications, 100 Queen's Park, Toronto, ON M5S 2C6, Canada. TEL 416-586-5581. FAX 416-586-5887. E-mail: sandras@rom.on.ca. (Subscr. to: University of Toronto Press, Order Fulfilment Division, 5201 Dufferin St. Downsview, ON M3H 5T8, Canada. TEL 416-667-7791) Ed. Sandra Shaul. R&P contact: Glen Ellis. TEL 416-586-5582. bibl. **Indexed:** Biol.Abstr., GeoRef., Zoo.Rec. **Document type:** academic/scholarly publication.

570 591   CN   ISSN 0082-5107
QL1.   CODEN: ROLOAA
ROYAL ONTARIO MUSEUM. LIFE SCIENCES. OCCASIONAL PAPERS. 1935. irreg. price varies. Royal Ontario Museum, Publications, 100 Queen's Park, Toronto, ON M5S 2C6, Canada. TEL 416-586-5581. FAX 416-586-5887. E-mail: sandras@rom.on.ca. (Subscr. to: University of Toronto Press, Order Fulfilment Division, 5201 Dufferin St. Downsview, Ont. M3H 5T8, Canada. TEL 416-667-7791) Ed. Sandra Shaul. R&P contact: Glen Ellis. TEL 416-586-5582. bibl. **Indexed:** Biol.Abstr., GeoRef., Sport Fish.Abstr., Wild.Rev., Zoo.Rec. **Document type:** academic/scholarly publication.
—CISTI; Linda Hall.

570   UK   ISSN 0962-8436
QH301   CODEN: PTRBAE
ROYAL SOCIETY OF LONDON. PHILOSOPHICAL TRANSACTIONS. SERIES B. BIOLOGICAL SCIENCES. m. £705 in Europe; U.S. and Canada £740; elsewhere £760 (effective 1998). Royal Society of London, 6 Carlton House Terrace, London SW1Y 5AG, England. TEL 44-171-839-5561. FAX 44-171-976-1837. E-mail: sales@roysocp2.demon.co.uk; URL: http://www.pubs.royalsoc.ac.uk. Ed. Semir Zeki. R&P contact: Phil Hurst. adv. contact: John Taylor. circ. 630. (also avail. in microform from PMC; microfiche from IDC; reprint service avail. from ISI) **Indexed:** Acid Rain Abstr., Acid Rain Ind., Apic.Abstr., ASCA, Bio-Contr.News & Info., Biol.Abstr., Br.Archaeol.Abstr., Br.Geol.Lit., Chem.Abstr., Compumath, Curr.Adv.Ecol.Sci., Curr.Biotech.Abstr., Dairy Sci.Abstr., Dent.Ind., Ecol.Abstr., Excerp.Med., Field Crop Abstr., Forest.Abstr., Forest Prod.Abstr., Geo.Abstr.H.G., Geol.Abstr., GeoRef., Helminthol.Abstr., Herb.Abstr., Ind.Med., Ind.Sci.Rev., Ind.Vet., Maize Abstr., Nutr.Abstr., Ocean.Abstr., Petrol.Abstr., Plant Breed.Abstr., Rev.Plant Path. So.Pac.Per.Ind., Soils & Fert., Sorghum & Millets Abstr., Sport Fish.Abstr., Vet.Bull., Wild.Rev., Zoo.Rec. **Document type:** academic/scholarly publication.
—BLDSC (6464.000000); ADONIS; CASDDS; CISTI; EMDOCS; Genuine Article; SWETS. **CCC.**
Description: Original papers on biological subjects. *Refereed Serial*

570   UK   ISSN 0962-8452
QH301   CODEN: PRLBA4
ROYAL SOCIETY OF LONDON. PROCEEDINGS. SERIES B. BIOLOGICAL SCIENCES. 1832. m. £380 in Europe; U.S. and Canada £394 (effective 1997). Royal Society of London, 6 Carlton House Terrace, London SW1Y 5AG, England. TEL 44-171-839-5561. FAX 44-171-976-1837. E-mail: sales@roysocp2.demon.co.uk; URL: http://www.pubs.royalsoc.ac.uk. Ed. J.L. Harper. R&P contact: Phil Hurst. adv. contact: John Taylor. circ. 1,226. (also avail. in microform from PMC; reprint serv. avail. from ISI) **Indexed:** Anim.Breed.Abstr., ASCA, Bibl.Agri., Bio-Contr.News & Info., Biol.Abstr., Br.Archaeol.Abstr., Br.Geol.Lit., Chem.Abstr., Compumath, Comput.Abstr., Curr.Adv.Ecol.Sci., Curr.Cont., Dairy Sci.Abstr., Deep Sea Res.& Oceanogr.Abstr., Dent.Ind., Eng.Ind., Excerp.Med., Field Crop Abstr., Forest.Abstr., Geo.Abstr., Geol.Abstr., Helminthol.Abstr., Ind.Med., Ind.Sci.Rev., Ind.Vet., Nutr.Abstr., Plant Breed.Abstr., Protozool.Abstr., Rev.Appl.Entomol., Soils & Fert., Sport Fish.Abstr., SSCI, Weed Abstr., Wild.Rev., Zoo.Rec. **Document type:** academic/scholarly publication.
●Also available online.
—BLDSC (6804.600000); ADONIS; CASDDS; CISTI; EMDOCS; Genuine Article; KR SourceOne; SWETS. **CCC.**
Description: Original papers on any aspect of biological science at the postgraduate level or above. *Refereed Serial*

570   RU   ISSN 1062-3590
QH301   CODEN: BRASEK
RUSSIAN ACADEMY OF SCIENCES. BIOLOGY BULLETIN. Key Title: Biology Bulletin of the Russian Academy of Sciences. English translation of: Rossiiskaya Akademiya Nauk. Izvestiya. Seriya Biologicheskaya. 1975. bi-m. $1195 in US; elsewhere $1400 (effective 1998). (Rossiiskaya Akademiya Nauk) Maik Nauka - Interperiodica, Mezhdunarodnyi Otdel, Ul. Prosoyuznaya, 90, 117864 Moscow, Russia. TEL 7-095-3360066. FAX 7-095-3360666. (Dist. by: Plenum Publishing Corp., 233 Spring St., New York, NY 10013-1578, U.S.A.. TEL 212-620-8468. FAX 212-463-0742) Ed. N.G. Krushchov. bibl.; charts; illus.; index. (back issues avail.) **Indexed:** Biodet.Abstr., Biol.Abstr., Chem.Titles, Curr.Adv.Ecol.Sci., Curr.Ref.Fish Res., Excerp.Med., Field Crop Abstr., Forest.Abstr., Ind.Med., INIS Atomind., Int.Abstr.Biol.Sci., Maize Abstr., Rice Abstr., Seed Abstr., Triticale Abstr., Weed Abstr. **Document type:** academic/scholarly publication.
—BLDSC (0406.045000); CISTI; UMI; UnCover. **CCC.**
Formerly (until 1992): Academy of Sciences of the U S S R. Biology Bulletin (ISSN 0098-2164)
Refereed Serial

RUSSIAN JOURNAL OF ECOLOGY. see *ENVIRONMENTAL STUDIES*

578.77   RU   ISSN 1063-0740
QH91.A1   CODEN: RJMBED
RUSSIAN JOURNAL OF MARINE BIOLOGY. English translation of: Biologiya Morya (RU ISSN 0134-3475) 1975. bi-m. $915 in US; elsewhere $1070 (effective 1998). (Russian Academy of Sciences) Maik Nauka - Interperiodica, Mezhdunarodnyi Otdel, Ul. Profsoyuznaya, 90, 117864 Moscow, Russia. TEL 7-095-3360066. FAX 7-095-3360666. (Dist. by: Plenum Publishing Corp., 233 Spring St., New York, NY 10013-1578, U.S.A.. TEL 212-620-8468. FAX 212-463-0742) Ed. Vladimir L. Kasyanov. (also avail. in microfilm from UMI; back issues avail.) **Indexed:** Biol.Abstr., Curr.Adv.Ecol.Sci., Curr.Cont., Deep Sea Res.& Oceanogr.Abstr., Geo.Abstr., Int.Abstr.Biol.Sci., Ocean.Abstr. **Document type:** academic/scholarly publication.
—BLDSC (0420.761500); CISTI; SWETS; UMI; UnCover. **CCC.**
Formerly (until 1993): Soviet Journal of Marine Biology (ISSN 0145-1456)
Refereed Serial

570   JA   ISSN 0289-6389
QH91.A1   CODEN: NRFHE8
SADO MARINE BIOLOGICAL STATION. REPORT/NIIGATA DAIGAKU RIGAKUBU FUZOKU SADO RINKAI JIKKENJO KENKYU HOKOKU. (Text and summaries in English) 1971. a. exchange basis. Niigata Daigaku, Rigakubu Fuzoku Sado Rinkai Jikkenjo - Niigata University, Sado Marine Biological Station, 2-8050 Igarashi, Niigata 950-21, Japan. TEL 0259-75-2012. FAX 0259-75-2012. Ed. Yoshiharu Honma. bibl.; circ. 600 (controlled). **Indexed:** Biol.Abstr. **Document type:** academic/scholarly publication.
●Also available online.
Also available on CD-ROM.
—BLDSC (7601.230000).
Formerly: Sado Marine Biological Station. Annual Report (ISSN 0388-0117)
Refereed Serial

570   KN
SAENGMULHAK/BIOLOGY. (Text in Korean) q. Science and Encyclopaedia Publishing House, Pyongyang, N. Korea.

570   JA
SAITAMA SEIBUTSU/SAITAMA BIOLOGICAL SOCIETY OF HIGH SCHOOL TEACHERS. (Text in Japanese) 1959. a. Saitamaken Koto Gakko Seibutsu Kenkyukai - Saitama Biological Society of High School Teachers, Fukaya Dai 1 Koko, 21, Tokiwacho, Fukaya-shi, Saitama-ken 366, Japan.

BIOLOGY

570   AS262   RU   CODEN: VLUBB6
SANKT-PETERBURGSKII UNIVERSITET. VESTNIK. SERIYA BIOLOGIYA. (Text in Russian; contents page and summaries in English) 1946. q. 18.60 Rub. Sankt-Peterburgskii Universitet, Universitetskaya Nab. 7-9, St. Petersburg V-164, Russia. (Subscr. to: Mezhdunarodnaya Kniga, ul. Dimitrova 39, Moscow G-200, Russia) Ed. S.P. Merkur'ev. bk.rev.; charts; illus.; index. circ. 1,330. **Indexed:** Bio-Contr.News & Info., Biol.Abstr., Chem.Abstr., Crop Physiol.Abstr., Field Crop Abstr., Forest.Abstr., Helminthol.Abstr., Herb.Abstr., Hort.Abstr., Int.Aerosp.Abstr., Plant Breed.Abstr., Plant Grow.Reg.Abstr. **Document type:** academic/scholarly publication.
—CASDDS; CISTI; KNAW; Linda Hall.
    Formerly (until 1992): Leningradskii Universitet. Vestnik. Seriya Biologiya (ISSN 0321-186X)

570   JA
SANKYO SEIMEI KAGAKU KENKYU SHINKO ZAIDAN KENKYU HOKOKUSHU/REPORT OF STUDIES SUPPORTED BY SANKYO FOUNDATION OF LIFE SCIENCE. (Text in Japanese) 1988. a. Sankyo Seimei Kagaku Kenkyu Shinko Zaidan - Sankyo Foundation of Life Science, 12-5 Akasaka 3-chome, Minato-ku, Tokyo 105, Japan.

570   QH91.A1   NO   ISSN 0036-4827   CODEN: SARIA3
SARSIA; Nordic journal of marine biology. (Text in English) 1961. q. NOK 700 in Europe; elsewhere NOK 800 (effective 1997). University of Bergen, Department of Fisheries and Marine Biology, Bergen High Technology Center, N-5020 Bergen, Norway. TEL 47-55-584400. FAX 47-55-584450. E-mail: sarsia@ifm.uib.no; URL: http://www.ifm.uib.no/sarsia/sarsia.htm. (Co-sponsor: Nordic Publishing Board (NOP-N)) Ed. Ulf Baamstedt. circ. 700. (reprint service avail.) **Indexed:** Biol.Abstr., Chem.Abstr., Curr.Adv.Ecol.Sci., Curr.Cont., Deep Sea Res.& Oceanogr.Abstr., Ecol.Abstr., Excerp.Med., Geo.Abstr.H.G., Helminthol.Abstr., IBR, Ind.Sci.Rev., Ocean.Abstr., Sci.Cit.Ind., Sport Fish.Abstr., Wild.Rev., Zoo.Rec. **Document type:** academic/scholarly publication.
—BLDSC (8076.100000); CASDDS; Genuine Article; Linda Hall; UnCover.
    Description: Publishes original articles and review articles on all aspects of marine biology and ecology, particularly papers on the North and North Atlantic, including the Arctic. Also publishes special issues on marine topics and proceedings of symposia.
    Refereed Serial

333.7   FI   ISSN 0356-276X
SAVON LUONTO. 1969. a. FIM 30 (effective 1996). Kuopion Luonnon Ystavain Yhdistys - Kuopio Naturalists' Society, Kuopio Museum, Kauppak 23, FIN-70100 Kuopio, Finland. charts; illus.; stat. (back issues avail.) **Document type:** academic/scholarly publication.
    Description: Contains non-scientific reviews on nature, nature conservation, and natural history mainly in eastern Finland.

570   FI   ISSN 0356-3189
SAVONIA. (Text in English) 1972. irreg. exchange basis. Kuopion Luonnon Ystavain Yhdistys - Kuopio Naturalists' Society, Kuopio Museum, Kauppak. 23, FIN-70100 Kuopio, Finland. charts; illus.; stat. (back issues avail.) **Indexed:** Curr.Adv.Ecol.Sci. **Document type:** monographic series.
    Description: Contains mainly dissertations and proceedings of symposia.

570   NE   ISSN 1006-9305   CODEN: SCCLFO
SCIENCE IN CHINA. SERIES C: LIFE SCIENCES. (Text in English) 1952. 12/yr. $250 (effective 1998). (Chinese Academy of Sciences) Gordon and Breach - Harwood Academic, Amsteldisk 166, 1st Fl., 1079 LH Amsterdam, Netherlands. (Subscr. to: International Publishers Distributor, Box 32160, Newark, NJ 07102. TEL 800-545-8398. FAX 215-750-6343) Ed. Dongsheng Yan. **Document type:** academic/scholarly publication.
—BLDSC (8141.670130); CASDDS; CISTI; Genuine Article; KNAW; Linda Hall; UnCover.
    Supersedes in part (in 1996): Science in China. Series B.: Chemistry, Life Sciences and Earth Sciences (ISSN 1001-652X); Which was formerly (until 1989): Scientia Sinica. Series B: Chemistry, Life Sciences and Earth Sciences (ISSN 0253-5823); Which superseded in part: Scientia Sinica.
    Description: Contains academic papers on scientific work in the field of life sciences.

570 615.8 531.6   FR   ISSN 0767-6891
SCIENCES ORGONOMIQUES; revue des lois de la vie. 1986. q. 150 F. (foreign 308 F.). Societe d'Edition pour la Diffusion de l'Orgonomie (S.E.DIF.OR.), Alle du Chene Vert-Parc Liserb, 06000 Nice, France. Ed.Bd. illus. circ. 1,800. (back issues avail.)
    Description: Deals with biology, physics and medicine from an energetic or orgonomic perspective; discusses applications of the theories and works of Wilhelm Reich.

578.77   US
SEARS FOUNDATION FOR MARINE RESEARCH. MEMOIRS. 1948. irreg., no.1, pt 9, 1989. price varies. Sears Foundation for Marine Research, Kline Geology Laboratory, Yale University, Box 208109, New Haven, CT 06520-8109. TEL 203-432-3760. Ed. Keith S. Thomson. (back issues avail.) **Indexed:** Deep Sea Res.& Oceanogr.Abstr. **Document type:** monographic series.

570   JA   ISSN 0286-7761
SEIBUTSU FUKUOKA/BIOLOGIA FUKUOKA. (Text in Japanese; summaries in English) 1961. a. membership. Fukuokaken Koto Gakko Seibutsu Bukai - Biological Society of Fukuokaken High School Teachers, Fukuoka Daigaku Fuzoku Ohori Koto Gakko, 12-1 Ropponmatsu 1-chome, Chuo-ku, Fukuoka-shi, Fukuoka-ken 810, Japan.

570   JA   ISSN 0385-5996
SEIBUTSU KAGAKU NYUSU/BIOLOGICAL SCIENCE NEWS. (Text in Japanese) 1971. m. Zoological Society of Japan, Toshin Bldg., 2-27-2 Hongo, Bunkyo-ku, Tokyo 113, Japan. TEL 81-3-3814-5461. FAX 81-3-3814-5352. **Document type:** newsletter.

570   JA   ISSN 0582-4087
SEIBUTSU KANKYO CHOSETSU/ENVIRONMENT CONTROL IN BIOLOGY. (Text in English, Japanese) 1963. q. 2000 Yen per no. Nihon Seibutsu Kankyo Chosetsu Gakkai - Japanese Society of Environment Control in Biology, Tokyo Daigaku Nogakubu, Nogyo Kogakka Kankyo Chosetsu Kogaku Kenkyushitsu, 1-1 Yayoi 1-chome, Bunkyo-ku, Tokyo 113. TEL 81-3-3812-2111. FAX 81-3-3813-2437. bk.rev. circ. 1,500. **Indexed:** Agrindex, Biol.Abstr., Jap.Per.Ind.
    Refereed Serial

570   JA
SEIBUTSU KENKYU/JAPAN ASSOCIATION OF BIOLOGY EDUCATION. RESEARCH REPORT. (Text in Japanese) a. Nihon Seibutsu Kyoikukai - Japan Association of Biology Education, c/o Mr. Shinpei Ono, Tokyo Toritsu Fukagawa Koto Gakko, 32-19 Toyo 5-chome, Koto-ku, Tokyo 135, Japan.

570 370   JA   ISSN 0287-119X
SEIBUTSU KYOIKU/JAPANESE JOURNAL OF BIOLOGICAL EDUCATION. (Text in Japanese; summaries in English, Japanese) q. 1500 Yen per no. Nihon Seibutsu Kyoiku Gakkai - Society of Biological Sciences Education of Japan, Tokyo Gakugei Daigaku Seibutsugaku Kyoshitsu, 1-1 Nukui Kitamachi 4-chome, Koganei-shi, Tokyo 184, Japan. Ed. Nobuyasu Katayama. circ. 1,100. **Document type:** academic/scholarly publication.
    Refereed Serial

570   JA   ISSN 0917-1606
SEIBUTSU SHIIKU KENKYUKAI KAISHI/AQUARIUM AND TERRARIUM ANIMALS. (Text in Japanese) 1989. 4/yr. 1300 Yen per no. Seibutsu Shiiku Kenkyukai - Aquarium and Terrarium Animals, 31-7 Machiya 4-chome, Arakawa-ku, Tokyo 116, Japan.

570   JA   ISSN 0386-9539
QH305
SEIBUTSUGAKUSHI KENKYU/JAPANESE JOURNAL OF THE HISTORY OF BIOLOGY. (Text in Japanese) 1955. s-a. 1500 Yen per no. Nihon Kagakushi Gakkai, Seibutsugakushi Bunkakai - History of Science Society of Japan, Biology Division, Osaka Kyoiku Daigaku, Kankyo Kagaku Kyoiku Kenkyushitsu, 4-698-1 Asahigaoka, Kashiwara-shi, Osaka 582, Japan. **Indexed:** Jap.Per.Ind. **Document type:** academic/scholarly publication.

570   JA   ISSN 0287-7775
SEICHO/JOURNAL OF GROWTH. (Text in Japanese; summaries in English) 1962. s-a. 5000 Yen. Aichi-Gakuin University, Department of Anatomy, 1-100 Kusumoto-cho, Chikusaku-ku, Nagoya 464, Japan. TEL 052-751-2561. FAX 052-752-5988. Ed. Takeo Miyao. bk.rev.; index. circ. 250. (back issues avail.)
    ●Also available online. Vendor(s): JICST.
—Linda Hall.

570   JA   ISSN 0386-7617   CODEN: KNSKDK
SEICHO KAGAKU KYOKAI KENKYU NENPO/FOUNDATION FOR GROWTH SCIENCE. ANNUAL RESEARCH REPORTS. (Text in English, Japanese; summaries in English) 1977. a. Seicho Kagaku Kyokai, 15-2, Yoyogi 2-chome, Shibuya-ku, Tokyo 151, Japan. **Indexed:** Chem.Abstr.
—CASDDS.

570   JA   ISSN 0288-1578
SEIMEI KAGAKU KENKYUJO KIYO/SOPHIA LIFE SCIENCE BULLETIN. (Text in Japanese; summaries in English) 1982. a. Jochi Daigaku, Seimei Kagaku Kenkyujo - Sophia University, Life Science Institute, 7-1 Kioicho, Chiyoda-ku, Tokyo 102, Japan.

570   JA   ISSN 0286-0198   CODEN: SEIKDT
SEITAIGAKUTEKI EIYOGAKU KENKYU/JAPANESE ASSOCIATION FOR ECOLOGICAL NUTRITION RESEARCH. ANNALS. (Text in Japanese; summaries in English, Japanese) 1977. a. Seitaigakuteki Eiyogaku Kenkyukai, Matsui Byoin, 7-10, Ikegami 1-chome, Ota-ku, Tokyo 146, Japan.

570   RU
S13   CODEN: SSBLAO
SEL'SKOKHOZYAISTVENNAYA BIOLOGIYA. SERIYA BIOLOGIYA RASTENII. (Text in Russian; summaries in English) 1966. bi-m. $72. Rossiiskaya Akademiya Sel'skokhozyaistvennykh Nauk, c/o Tsentral'naya Nauchnaya Sel'skokhozyaistvennaya Biblioteka, Orlikov per. 3, 107804 Moscow. TEL 7-095-2078972. FAX 7-095-2075662. Ed. Valeriya M. Anan'ina. circ. 100. **Indexed:** Agri.Eng.Abstr., Anim.Breed.Abstr., Biol.Abstr., Chem.Abstr., Cott.& Trop.Fibr.Abstr., Crop Physiol.Abstr., Dairy Sci.Abstr., Excerp.Med., Field Crop Abstr., Herb.Abstr., Hort.Abstr., Ind.Vet., Maize Abstr., Nutr.Abstr., Pig News & Info., Plant Breed.Abstr., Plant Grow.Reg.Abstr., Poult.Abstr., Rev.Plant Path., Rice Abstr., Seed Abstr., Sorghum & Millets Abstr., Soyabean Abstr., Triticale Abstr., Trop.Oil Seeds Abstr., Vet.Bull., Weed Abstr.
—BLDSC (0163.140000); CASDDS; CISTI.
    Supersedes in part (in 1989): Sel'skohozyaistvennaya Biologiya (ISSN 0131-6397)

570   RU   CODEN: SSBLAO
SEL'SKOKHOZYAISTVENNAYA BIOLOGIYA. SERIYA BIOLOGIYA ZHIVOTNYKH. 1966. bi-m. $72. Rossiiskaya Akademiya Sel'skokhozyaistvennykh Nauk, c/o Tsentral'naya Nauchnaya Sel'skokhozyaistvennaya Biblioteka, Orlikov per. 3, 107804 Moscow, Russia. TEL 7-095-2078972. FAX 7-095-2075662. Ed. Valeriya M. Anan'ina. circ. 100.
—BLDSC (0163.140000); CASDDS; CISTI.
    Supersedes in part (in 1989): Sel'skohozyaistvennaya Biologiya (ISSN 0131-6397)

SEMINARS IN CELL AND DEVELOPMENTAL BIOLOGY. see *BIOLOGY — Cytology And Histology*

SENCKENBERGIANA MARITIMA. see *EARTH SCIENCES — Oceanography*

570 551   GW   ISSN 0365-7000
QH5   CODEN: ASNGA7
SENCKENBERGISCHE NATURFORSCHENDE GESELLSCHAFT. ABHANDLUNGEN. 1884. irreg., no.547, 1994. Senckenbergische Naturforschende Gesellschaft, Senckenberganlage 25, 60325 Frankfurt a.M., Germany. TEL 49-69-7542-0. FAX 49-69-746238. E-mail: sjessel@sng.uni-frankfurt.de. Ed. Willi Ziegler. **Indexed:** Biol.Abstr., Deep Sea Res.& Oceanogr.Abstr., GeoRef., Sport Fish.Abstr., Wild.Rev. **Document type:** academic/scholarly publication.
—Linda Hall. **CCC.**

SENEGAL. CENTRE DE RECHERCHE OCEANOGRAPHIQUE. DOCUMENT SCIENTIFIQUE. see *EARTH SCIENCES — Oceanography*

SENSORY SYSTEMS. see *PSYCHOLOGY*

570   KO   ISSN 0377-5232
QH301   CODEN: SNBAAO
SEOUL NATIONAL UNIVERSITY. FACULTY PAPERS. BIOLOGY AND AGRICULTURE SERIES. (Text in English) 1971. a. Seoul National University, San 56-1, Sinlim-dong, Kwanak-ku, Seoul 151-742, S. Korea. **Indexed:** Excerp.Med. **Document type:** monographic series.

639.967827   TZ
SERENGETI WILDLIFE RESEARCH CENTRE. REPORT. 1985. biennial. Serengeti Wildlife Research Centre, P.O. Box 661, Arusha, Tanzania. circ. 500. **Description:** Presents scientific results of research projects.

570   JA   ISSN 0913-6002
SETO MARINE BIOLOGICAL LABORATORY. ANNUAL REPORT/SETO RINKAI JIKKENJO NENPO. (Text in Japanese) 1987. a. Kyoto University, Faculty of Science, Seto Marine Biological Laboratory - Kyoto Daigaku Rigakubu Fuzoku Seto Rinkai Jikkenjo, Shirahamacho, Nishimuro-gun, Wakayama-ken 649-22, Japan.

578.77   JA   ISSN 0037-2870
SETO MARINE BIOLOGICAL LABORATORY. PUBLICATIONS/SETO RINKAI JIKKENJO KIYO. (Text in English) 1949. s-a. exchange basis. Kyoto University, Faculty of Science, Seto Marine Biological Laboratory - Kyoto Daigaku Rigakubu Fuzoku Seto Rinkai Jikkenjo, Shirahama-cho, Nishimuro-gun, Wakayama-ken 649-22, Japan. TEL 81-739-42-3515. FAX 81-739-42-4518. Ed. Shin Kubota. charts; illus.; index. circ. 460. **Indexed:** Curr.Adv.Ecol.Sci., Deep Sea Res.& Oceanogr.Abstr., GeoRef., Sel.Water Res.Abstr. **Document type:** academic/scholarly publication.
—BLDSC (7112.000000).
Description: Publishes scientific papers on marine biology related to Japanese and Indo-Pacific waters, especially those on taxonomy, morphology and biology.
Refereed Serial

578.77   JA   ISSN 0389-6609
SETO MARINE BIOLOGICAL LABORATORY. SPECIAL PUBLICATION SERIES. (Text in English) 1959. irreg. exchange basis. Kyoto University, Faculty of Science, Seto Marine Biological Laboratory - Kyoto Daigaku Rigakubu Fuzoku Seto Rinkai Jikkenjo, Shirahama-cho, Nishimuro-gun, Wakayama-ken 649-22, Japan. TEL 81-739-42-3515. FAX 81-739-42-4518. Ed. Shin Kubota. circ. 460. **Indexed:** Biol.Abstr., Deep Sea Res.& Oceanogr.Abstr. **Document type:** academic/scholarly publication, monographic series.
Formerly: Seto Marine Biological Laboratory. Special Publications (ISSN 0080-9098)

570   CC   ISSN 1001-9426
SHENGWU SHUXUE XUEBAO. (Text in Chinese) s-a. $1 per issue. Anhui Nongxueyuan - Anhui Institute of Agriculture, Hefei, Anhui 230061, People's Republic of China. TEL 240759. Ed. Shih Tsehua. **Document type:** academic/scholarly publication.

570 370   CC   ISSN 1004-7549
SHENGWUXUE JIAOXUE/BIOLOGY TEACHING. (Text in Chinese) 1958. m. $19.80. Huadong Shifan Daxue, Shengwu Xi - East China Normal University, Biology Department, 3663 Zhongshan Beilu, Shanghai 200062, People's Republic of China. TEL 2577577. FAX 021-2576217. TELEX 33328 ECNU CN. (Subscr. overseas to: China National Publishing Industry Co., Shanghai Branch, 380 Bei Suzhou Lu, Shanghai, P.R. China) Ed. Ma Weiliang. adv.: page $1000. circ. 30,000. **Document type:** academic/scholarly publication.
Description: Introduces modern biological science and biology teaching experiences.

578.77 591 551.46
639.2   JA   ISSN 0385-1109
SHIMA MARINELAND. SCIENCE REPORT. (Text in English, Japanese) 1972. irreg. exchange basis. Shima Marineland Foundation, Kashikojima, Ago-cho, Shima-gun, Mie 517-05, Japan. TEL 81-5994-3-1225. FAX 81-5994-3-1224. Ed. T. Tsujii. R&P contact: Tadashi Tsujii. adv. contact: Shuzo Okubo. circ. 1,500. **Indexed:** Biol.Abstr., Deep Sea Res.& Oceanogr.Abstr. **Document type:** academic/scholarly publication.

SHINSHU DAIGAKU RIGAKUBU FUZOKU SUWA RINKO JIKKENJO HOKOKU/SHINSHU UNIVERSITY. SUWA HYDROBIOLOGICAL STATION. REPORT. see *EARTH SCIENCES — Hydrology*

570   CC   ISSN 0001-5334
CODEN: SYSWAE
SHIYAN SHENGWU XUEBAO/ACTA BIOLOGICAE EXPERIMENTALIS SINICA. Variant spelling: Shih Yen Sheng Wu Hsueh Pao. (Text in Chinese; summaries in English) 1936. q. $33.20 (effective 1997). Shanghai Xibao Shengwu Yanjiusuo - Shanghai Institute of Cell Biology, 320 Yueyang Lu, Shanghai 200031, People's Republic of China. TEL 4315030. (Dist. overseas by: Guoji Shudian - China International Book Trading Corporation, P.O. Box 399, Beijing 100044, P.R. China) Ed. Yahui Wang. charts; illus. **Indexed:** Biol.Abstr., Chem.Abstr., Curr.Adv.Ecol.Sci., Ind.Vet., Pig News & Info. **Document type:** academic/scholarly publication.
—BLDSC (0601.700000); CASDDS; CISTI; Linda Hall.

570   CC   ISSN 1000-3207
CODEN: SSXUET
SHUISHENG SHENGWU XUEBAO/ACTA HYDROBIOLOGICA SINICA. (Text in Chinese; summaries in English) 1955. q. $63.60. (Chinese Academy of Sciences, Institute of Hydrobiology) Science Press, Marketing and Sales Department, 16 Donghuangchengen North St., Beijing 100717, People's Republic of China. TEL 4010642. FAX 4019810. adv. circ. 6,000. **Document type:** academic/scholarly publication.
—BLDSC (0624.500000); CASDDS.
Description: Directed to college instructors, students, and researchers; contains research articles, brief reports and reviews about taxonomy, ecology, physiology, pathology, toxicology, disease prevention; genetics and breeding of freshwater fish, algae, and other organisms.
Refereed Serial

577   RU   ISSN 0869-8627
QH540   CODEN: ISBNBN
SIBIRSKII EKOLOGICHESKII ZHURNAL. English edition: Siberian Journal of Ecology. (Text in Russian) 1963. 3/yr. $87 (effective 1998). Rossiiskaya Akademiya Nauk, Sibirskoe Otdelenie, Morskoi pr. 2, 630090 Novosibirsk, Russia. TEL 3832-350570. FAX 3832-356002. (Dist. by: Mezhdunarodnaya Kniga, B. Yakimanka 39, 117049 Moscow, Russia. TEL 7-095-2384967. FAX 7-095-2384634) Ed. I.Yu. Koropachinskii. bk.rev.; illus.; index. circ. 800. **Indexed:** Biol.Abstr., Chem.Abstr., Field Crop Abstr., Forest.Abstr., Forest Prod.Abstr., Irr.& Drain.Abstr., Seed Abstr., Soils & Fert. **Document type:** academic/scholarly publication.
—BLDSC (0164.139000); CASDDS; CISTI; Linda Hall.
Former titles (until 1994): Sibirskii Biologicheskii Zhurnal (ISSN 0869-1347); (until 1990): Akademiya Nauk S.S.S.R. Sibirskoe Otdelenie. Izvestiya. Seriya Biologicheskikh Nauk (ISSN 0568-6547)

570   NE   ISSN 0165-2656
SIBOGA EXPEDITION. 1902. irreg., vol.148, 1986. price varies. (Nederlandse Maatschappij voor Natuurwetenschappelijk Onderzoek van Oost- en West-Indie) E.J. Brill, P.O. Box 9000, 2300 PA Leiden, Netherlands. TEL 31-71-5353500. FAX 31-71-5317532. TELEX 39296 BRILL NL. E-mail: ejbrill@brill.nl. (In N. America: E.J. Brill, 24 Hudson St., Kinderhook, NY 12106. TEL 800-962-4406. FAX 518-758-1959) (Co-sponsor: Maatschappij voor Wetenschappelijk Onderzoek in de Tropen) R&P contact: Elizabeth Vennekamp. **Indexed:** Zoo.Rec. **Document type:** monographic series.
Refereed Serial

570   JA   ISSN 0559-9822
CODEN: SIEBA7
SIEBOLDIA ACTA BIOLOGICA/SHIBORUDIA. (Text in English, Japanese) 1952. irreg. exchange basis. Kyushu University, College of General Education, Biological Laboratory - Kyushu Daigaku Kyoyobu Seibutsugaku Kyoshitsu, 4-2-1 Ropponmatsu, Chuo-ku, Fukuoka 810, Japan. TEL 81-92-731-8745. FAX 81-92-771-4161. (reprint service avail. from UMI) **Indexed:** Biol.Abstr.
—CASDDS.

570   XO   ISSN 0037-6930
QH7   CODEN: BLGPAT
SLOVENSKA AKADEMIA VIED. BIOLOGICKE PRACE/SLOVAK ACADEMY OF SCIENCES. TREATISES ON BIOLOGY. (Text in English or Slovak; summaries in English, German, Russian) 1955. irreg. $5. Veda, Publishing House of the Slovak Academy of Sciences, Bradacova 7, 852 86 Bratislava, Slovakia. (Dist. by: Slovart, Nam. Slobody 6, 817 64 Bratislava, Slovakia) charts; illus. circ. 500. **Indexed:** Biol.Abstr.
—CISTI; Linda Hall.

SMITH MEDICAL FUNDING REPORT; the quarterly guide to research - project grant opportunities for hospitals & medical centers. see *MEDICAL SCIENCES*

570   BO
SOCIEDAD BOLIVIANA DE HISTORIA NATURAL. REVISTA. (Text in Spanish; summaries occasionally in English) 1974. irreg. Sociedad Boliviana de Historia Natural, Casilla de Correo 538, Cochabamba, Bolivia. illus. **Indexed:** Biol.Abstr.

570   CL   ISSN 0037-850X
QH301   CODEN: BOBCAK
SOCIEDAD DE BIOLOGIA DE CONCEPCION. BOLETIN. (Summaries in English) 1927. s-a. exchange basis. Sociedad de Biologia de Concepcion, Casilla 4006, Concepcion, Chile. Ed. Hugo I. Moyano. charts; illus.; index. circ. 1,000. **Indexed:** Biol.Abstr., Chem.Abstr., Deep Sea Res.& Oceanogr.Abstr., GeoRef. **Document type:** academic/scholarly publication, bulletin.
—Linda Hall.

570   PO   ISSN 0081-0665
QK1
SOCIEDADE BROTERIANA. MEMORIAS. (Text in European languages; summaries in English, French and Portuguese) 1930-199?; suspended. irreg. (approx. 1/yr.) Esc.8500($55) Sociedade Broteriana, Arcos do Jardim, 3049 Coimbra, Portugal. TEL 351-39-22897. FAX 351-39-20780. (Co-sponsor: Universidade de Coimbra. Instituto Botanico) Eds. J.F. Mesquita, J.A.R. Paiva. circ. 1,000. **Indexed:** Biol.Abstr., Excerp.Bot., Forest.Abstr., Forest Prod.Abstr. **Document type:** proceedings.
—CISTI; KNAW; Linda Hall.
Description: Covers research on floristic studies, plant phytosociology and phytogeography.

570   IT   ISSN 0366-2047
CODEN: BONNAB
SOCIETA DEI NATURALISTI IN NAPOLI. BOLLETTINO. (Text in Italian; summaries in English) 1887. a. L.50000. Giannini Editore, Via Cisterna dell'Olio, 80134 Naples, Italy. TEL 39-81-5513928. **Indexed:** Biol.Abstr., Chem.Abstr., Deep Sea Res.& Oceanogr.Abstr. **Document type:** academic/scholarly publication, bulletin.
—CASDDS.

BIOLOGY

570　　　　　IT　　ISSN 0037-8771
QH301　　　　　　CODEN: BSIBAC
SOCIETA ITALIANA DI BIOLOGIA SPERIMENTALE. BOLLETTINO/JOURNAL OF BIOLOGICAL RESEARCH. (Text in English and Italian) 1924. bi-m. L.130000($200) (effective 1997). Casa Editrice Idelson, Via Alcide de Gasperi 55, 80133 Naples, Italy. TEL 39-81-5524733. FAX 39-81-5518295. Ed. Pietro de Franciscis. adv.; charts; illus.; stat.; index. (also avail. in microform from PMC) **Indexed:** Anal.Abstr., Anim.Breed.Abstr., Biol.Abstr., Biotech.Abstr., Chem.Abstr., Curr.Adv.Ecol.Sci., Dairy Sci.Abstr., Deep Sea Res.& Oceanogr.Abstr., Dent.Ind., Excerp.Med., Ind.Med., Ind.Vet., INIS Atomind., Nutr.Abstr., Poult.Abstr., Vet.Bull.
—BLDSC (2231.000000); CASDDS; CISTI; KNAW; Linda Hall; SWETS; UMI.
   Description: Features articles and research papers covering a wide variety of topics in experimental biology; includes anatomy, molecular biology, botany, cardiology and clinical chemistry.

570 550 592　　IT　　ISSN 0392-6710
　　　　　　　　　　　CODEN: BSNTDQ
SOCIETA SARDA DI SCIENZE NATURALI. BOLLETTINO. (Text in English, French, Italian; summaries in English and Italian) 1967. a. L.40000 (effective 1997). Societa Sarda di Scienze Naturali, c/o Dipto. di Botanica ed Ecologia Vegetale dell'Universita, Via Muroni 25, 07100 Sassari, Italy. TEL 39-79-237087. FAX 39-79-233600. E-mail: ssmain.uniss.it. Ed. Bruno Corrias. R&P contact: Bruno Corrias. adv. circ.: Bruno Corrias. bk.rev.; index. circ. 700. (back issues avail.) **Indexed:** Biol.Abstr. **Document type:** bulletin.

570　　　　　NE　　ISSN 0926-3551
SOCIETAS INTERNATIONALIS ODONATOLOGICA. RAPID COMMUNICATIONS. 1980. irreg. price varies. Societas Internationalis Odonatologica, S.I.O. Central Office, P.O. Box 256, 3720 AG Bilthoven, Netherlands. Ed.Bd. bk.rev.; charts. circ. 500. **Indexed:** Biol.Abstr., Entomol.Abstr., Genet.Abstr., Ref.Zh., Zoo.Rec. **Document type:** academic/scholarly publication.
—BLDSC (8318.550000).

581 591　　　FI　　ISSN 0373-6873
QH7　　　　　　　CODEN: MSFFAS
SOCIETAS PRO FAUNA ET FLORA FENNICA. MEMORANDA. (Text in English, Finnish, German and Swedish; summaries in English) 1927. 4/yr. FIM 75 or exchange basis. Societas pro Fauna et Flora Fennica, P.O. Box 17, FIN-00014 University of Helsinki, Finland. Ed. Olof Bistrom. adv.; bk.rev. circ. 1,550. (back issues avail.) **Indexed:** Biol.Abstr., IBR, Ref.Zh., Rev.Appl.Entomol., Sport Fish.Abstr., Weed Abstr., Wild.Rev., Zoo.Rec.
—BLDSC (5645.000000); CISTI; KNAW; Linda Hall; UnCover.
Refereed Serial

570　　　　　SP　　ISSN 0212-3037
SOCIETAT CATALANA DE BIOLOGIA. TREBALLS. 1963. a. 1500 ptas. Societat Catalana de Biologia, Carme 47, 08001 Barcelona, Spain. **Indexed:** Ind.SST.

570 551　　　SP
SOCIETAT D'HISTORIA NATURAL DE LES BALEARS. MONOGRAFIE. 1991. irreg. no.5, 1996. price varies. Societat d'Historia Natural de les Balears, Sant Roc, 4, 07001 Palma de Mallorca, Spain. TEL 34-71-719667. FAX 34-71-719667. Ed. Guillem Pons i Buades. **Document type:** monographic series.

570　　　　　FR　　ISSN 0037-9026
　　　　　　　　　　　CODEN: CRSBAW
SOCIETE DE BIOLOGIE ET DE SES FILIALES. COMPTES RENDUS DES SEANCES. 1849. bi-m. 960 F. (foreign 1066 F.) (effective 1997). Masson - Periodiques, 120 bd. St. Germain, 75006 Paris, France. TEL 33-1-40466200. FAX 33-1-40466201. (Subscr. to: Societe de Periodiques Specialises, B.P. 22-F, 41354 Vineuil Cedex, France. TEL 33-2-54504612. FAX 33-2-54504611) Ed. Miss Faibie. adv.; index. circ. 1,300. (also avail. in microform from PMC; reprint service avail. from ISI) **Indexed:** Anim.Breed.Abstr., Apic.Abstr., Biol.Abstr., Biotech.Abstr., Chem.Abstr., Crop Physiol.Abstr., Curr.Adv.Biochem., Curr.Adv.Cell & Devel.Biol., Curr.Adv.Genetics & Molec.Biol., Dairy Sci.Abstr., Deep Sea Res.& Oceanogr.Abstr., Excerp.Med., Food Sci.& Tech.Abstr., Forest.Abstr., Forest Prod.Abstr., Helminthol.Abstr., Herb.Abstr., Hort.Abstr., Ind.Med., Ind.Vet., INIS Atomind., Nutr.Abstr., Ornam.Hort., Poult.Abstr., Protozool.Abstr., Rev.Appl.Entomol., Rev.Plant Path., Seed Abstr., Sport Fish.Abstr., Trop.Dis.Bull., Vet.Bull., Wild.Rev., Zoo.Rec. **Document type:** academic/scholarly publication.
—BLDSC (3387.000000); CASDDS; CISTI; Genuine Article; KNAW; SWETS; UnCover. CCC.
   Description: Accounts of meetings of the society and its branches.

570 550　　　LU　　ISSN 0304-9620
　　　　　　　　　　　CODEN: BNLXAO
SOCIETE DES NATURALISTES LUXEMBOURGEOIS. BULLETIN. (Text and summaries in English, French, German) 1890. a. 500 Fr.($8) Societe des Naturalistes Luxembourgeois, B.P. 327, L-2013 Luxembourg, Luxembourg. FAX 0352-31-38-19. Ed. Paul Diederich. bk.rev. circ. 850. (back issues avail.) **Document type:** bulletin.
—BLDSC (2747.000000); Linda Hall.

570　　　　　JA　　ISSN 0081-1106
SOCIETE FRANCO-JAPONAISE DE BIOLOGIE. BULLETIN/NICHIFUTSU SEIBUTSU GAKKAISHI. (Text in English, French or Japanese) 1955. a. Societe Franco-Japonaise de Biologie - Nichifutsu Seibutsu Gakkai, c/o Mr. Sadao Yasugi, Tokyo Toritsu Daigaku Rigakubu Seibutsugakka, 1-1 Minamiosawa, Hachioji-shi, Tokyo 192-03, Japan.

570　　　　　FR　　ISSN 0366-1326
　　　　　　　　　　　CODEN: BMSLAG
SOCIETE LINNEENNE DE LYON. BULLETIN MENSUEL. (Text in French; summaries in English) 1822. 200. 200 F. Societe Linneenne de Lyon, 33 rue Bossuet, 69006 Lyon, France. Ed. P. Berthet. adv.; bk.rev.; index. circ. 1,600. (back issues avail.) **Indexed:** A.I.C.P., Biol.Abstr., GeoRef., Rev.Plant Path. **Document type:** bulletin.
—BLDSC (2875.300000); Linda Hall.

571.4645　　　US　　ISSN 1069-3610
SOCIETY FOR CRYOBIOLOGY. NEWS NOTES. 1979. q. membership only. Society for Cryobiology, 8650 Rockville Pike, Bethesda, MD 20814. TEL 706-721-4173. FAX 706-721-2347. Ed. A.M. Karow. bk.rev. circ. 500. **Document type:** newsletter.
   Description: News of interest about the society.

570　　　　　US　　ISSN 0583-9009
　　　　　　　　　　　CODEN: SBSYAT
SOCIETY FOR DEVELOPMENTAL BIOLOGY. SYMPOSIUM. (Since 1967 issued as supplement to Journal of Developmental Biology) no.39, 1981. irreg. no.47, 1989. price varies. John Wiley & Sons, Inc., Journals, 605 Third Ave., New York, NY 10158. TEL 212-475-7700. **Indexed:** Biol.Abstr., Chem.Abstr., Ind.Med.
—BLDSC (8584.950000); CASDDS. CCC.

570　　　　　UK　　ISSN 0309-6831
　　　　　　　　　　　CODEN: SEBSDI
SOCIETY FOR EXPERIMENTAL BIOLOGY. SEMINAR SERIES. 1976? irreg. no.32, 1987. price varies. Cambridge University Press, Edinburgh Bldg., Shaftesbury Rd., Cambridge CB2 2RU, England. TEL 44-1223-312393. FAX 44-1223-315052. TELEX 851817256. E-mail: information@cup.cam. ac.uk; URL: http://www.cup.cam.ac.uk. (N. American addr.: Cambridge University Press, Journals Dept., 40 W. 20th St., New York, NY 10011. TEL 212-924-3900. FAX 212-691-3239) R&P contact: Linda Nicol. adv. **Indexed:** Biol.Abstr. **Document type:** proceedings.
—BLDSC (8239.429500); CASDDS; CISTI; KNAW.

570　　　　　UK　　ISSN 0081-1386
　　　　　　　　　　　CODEN: SSEBA9
SOCIETY FOR EXPERIMENTAL BIOLOGY. SYMPOSIA. 1947. irreg., no.50, 1996. £70($115) Portland Press Ltd., 59 Portland Pl., London W1N 3AJ, England. TEL 44-171-580-5530. FAX 44-171-323-1136. E-mail: sales@portlandpress.co.uk; URL: http://www.portlandpress.co.uk. (Subscr. to: Commerce Way, P.O. Box 32, Colchester, Essex CO2 8HP, England. TEL 44-1206-796351. FAX 44-1206-779331) Ed. K. Bowler. R&P contact: Adam Marshall. **Indexed:** ASCA, Biol.Abstr., Chem.Abstr., Curr.Adv.Ecol.Sci., Ind.Med. **Document type:** proceedings.
—BLDSC (8585.000000); CASDDS; CISTI; KNAW; SWETS; UnCover.

570 610　　　US　　ISSN 0037-9727
QP1　　　　　　　CODEN: PSEBAA
SOCIETY FOR EXPERIMENTAL BIOLOGY AND MEDICINE. PROCEEDINGS. 1903. 11/yr. $135 to individuals (foreign $165); institutions $245 (foreign $270) (effective 1996). Blackwell Science Inc., 350 Main St., Malden, MA 02148. TEL 617-876-7000; 800-759-6102. FAX 617-388-8255. Ed. Dr. Gregory W. Siskind. adv.; abstr.; bibl.; illus.; index. circ. 3,200. (also avail. in microfilm from PMC,WWS) **Indexed:** Abstr.Hyg., Anim.Breed.Abstr., ASCA, Biol.Abstr., Biotech.Abstr., Chem.Abstr., Curr.Adv.Biochem., Curr.Adv.Cell & Devel.Biol., Curr.Adv.Ecol.Sci., Curr.Cont., Dairy Sci.Abstr., Dent.Ind., Excerp.Med., Food Sci.& Tech.Abstr., Helminthol.Abstr., Ind.Med., Ind.Sci.Rev., Ind.Vet., Nutr.Abstr., Pig News & Info., Poult.Abstr., Protozool.Abstr., Rev.Med.& Vet.Mycol., Rev.Plant Path., Small Anim.Abstr., Sport Fish.Abstr., THA, Trop.Dis.Bull., Vet.Bull., W.R.C.Inf., Wild.Rev., Zoo.Rec. **Document type:** academic/scholarly publication.
—BLDSC (6814.000000); CASDDS; CISTI; Genuine Article; KNAW; Linda Hall; SWETS; UnCover. CCC.
   Description: Attempts to promote investigation in the biomedical sciences by encouraging and facilitating the interchange of scientific information among disciplines. Presents original articles, minireviews, and symposia.
Refereed Serial

570　　　　　US　　ISSN 0361-6525
QH301　　　　　　CODEN: SOCIDT
SOCIOBIOLOGY. 1976. irreg. (approx. a.). $50 (effective 1997). California State University, Chico, Department of Biological Sciences, Chico, CA 95926. TEL 916-898-5116. FAX 916-898-4363. E-mail: dkistner@oavax.csuchico.edu. Ed. David H. Kistner. adv.; bk.rev.; illus.; index. circ. 400. (back issues avail.) **Indexed:** ASCA, Bibl.Agri., Biol.Abstr., Bull.Signal., Curr.Adv.Ecol.Sci., Curr.Cont., Forest Prod.Abstr., Sci.Cit.Ind., Sport Fish.Abstr., Wild.Rev., Zoo.Rec. **Document type:** academic/scholarly publication.
—BLDSC (8319.562000); CISTI; Genuine Article; UnCover. CCC.
   Description: Provides research articles and translations of classic papers on various aspects of the biology of social animals.
Refereed Serial

570　　　　　BU　　ISSN 0081-1823
SOFIISKI UNIVERSITET. BIOLOGICHESKI FAKULTET. GODISHNIK. irreg., vol.71, 1977. price varies. Publishing House of the Bulgarian Academy of Sciences, Acad. G. Bonchev St., Bldg. 6, 1113 Sofia, Bulgaria. Ed. I. Penev. circ. 550. (reprint service avail. from IRC) **Indexed:** Biol.Abstr., Chem.Abstr., Field Crop Abstr.

BIOLOGY

631.417 578.757 UK ISSN 0038-0717
S590 CODEN: SBIOAH
SOIL BIOLOGY & BIOCHEMISTRY. 1969. m. fl.2709($1557) (effective 1998). (Council of Biological and Medical Abstracts) Elsevier Science Ltd., Pergamon, P.O. Box 800, Kidlington, Oxford OX5 1DX, England. TEL 44-1865-843000. FAX 44-1865-843010. E-mail: nlinfo-f@elsevier.nl; usinfo-f@elsevier.com; forinfo-kyf04035@niftyserve.or.jp; URL: http://www.elsevier.nl/. (Subscr. to: Elsevier Science, Regional Sales Office, P.O. Box 211, 1000 AE Amsterdam, Netherlands. TEL 31-20-4853757. FAX 31-20-4853432; Subscr. in the Americas to: Elsevier Science, Regional Sales Office, Box 945, New York, NY 10159-0945. TEL 212-633-3730. FAX 212-633-3680; Subscr. in Australasia and the Far East to: Elsevier Science (Singapore) Pte Ltd, No.1 Temasek Ave., No.17-01 Millenia Tower, Singapore 039192, Singapore. TEL 65-434-3727. FAX 65-337-2230) Ed. J.S. Waid. adv.; bk.rev.; charts; stat. circ. 1,250. (also avail. in microfiche from MIM; microfilm from UMI; back issues avail.) **Indexed:** ASCA, Bibl.Agri., Bio-Contr.News & Info., Biol.Abstr., Biol.& Agr.Ind., Biol.Dig., Biotech.Abstr., Chem.Abstr., Curr.Adv.Ecol.Sci., Curr.Biotech.Abstr., Curr.Cont., Deep Sea Res.& Oceanogr.Abstr., Ecol.Abstr., Energy Ind., Energy Info.Abstr., Environ.Per.Bibl. (1972-1994), Excerp.Med., Field Crop.Abstr., Forest.Abstr., Forest Prod.Abstr., Geo.Abstr.H.G., Helminthol.Abstr., Herb.Abstr., Hort.Abstr., IDA, Ind.Sci.Rev., Irr.& Drain.Abstr., Maize Abstr., Plant Breed.Abstr., Plant Grow.Reg.Abstr., Rev.Plant Path., Rice Abstr., Sci.Cit.Ind., Seed Abstr., Sel.Water Res.Abstr., Soils & Fert., Sorghum & Millets Abstr., Soyabean Abstr., Sugar Ind.Abstr., W.R.C.Inf., Weed Abstr. **Document type:** academic/scholarly publication.
—BLDSC (8321.820100); CASDDS; CISTI; EMDOCS; Genuine Article; KR SourceOne; Linda Hall; SWETS; UMI; UnCover. **CCC.**
Description: Provides a forum for research on soil organisms, their biochemical activities, and the influence on the soil environment and plant growth.
Refereed Serial

578.77 SA ISSN 0259-0050
CODEN: SMBBBL
SOUTH AFRICAN ASSOCIATION FOR MARINE BIOLOGICAL RESEARCH. BULLETIN. 1960. a., latest no.22, 1996. free. South African Association for Marine Biological Research, P.O. Box 10712, Marine Parade 4056, South Africa. TEL 27-31-373536. FAX 27-31-372132. Ed. Tania Smith. R&P contact: Tania Smith. circ. 450 (controlled). **Indexed:** Aqua.Sci.& Fish.Abstr., Deep Sea Res.& Oceanogr.Abstr., Ocean.Abstr. **Document type:** academic/scholarly publication, bulletin.
—BLDSC (2758.900000).
Description: Reviews the research of the Oceanographic Research Institute and curatorial activities of Sea World, Durban, for a general audience.
Refereed Serial

SOUTH AFRICAN INSTITUTE FOR MEDICAL RESEARCH. PUBLICATION. see *MEDICAL SCIENCES*

570 333.7 SA
SOUTH AFRICAN INSTITUTE OF ECOLOGISTS AND ENVIRONMENTAL SCIENTISTS. BULLETIN. 1982. 3/yr. South African Institute of Ecologists and Environmental Scientists, P.O. Box 37618, Valyland 7978, South Africa. illus. **Document type:** academic/scholarly publication, bulletin.
Formerly (until vol.12, no.3, 1993): South African Institute of Ecologists. Bulletin (ISSN 0257-8638)

570 572 916.8 SA ISSN 0303-2515
QH1 CODEN: ASAMAS
SOUTH AFRICAN MUSEUM. ANNALS/SUID-AFRIKAANSE MUSEUM. ANNALE. (Text in English) 1898. irreg. price varies. South African Museum, P.O. Box 61, Cape Town 8000, South Africa. TEL 27-21-243330. FAX 27-21-246716. E-mail: elouw@nv1.samuseum.ac.za. Ed. Elizabeth Louw. R&P contact: M.A. Cluver. illus.; circ. 450 (controlled). (back issues avail.) **Indexed:** Abstr.Anthropol., Aqua.Sci.& Fish.Abstr., Biol.Abstr., Deep Sea Res.& Oceanogr.Abstr., GeoRef., Ind.S.A.Per., Ocean.Abstr., Sel.Water Res.Abstr., Sport Fish.Abstr., Wild.Rev., Zoo.Rec. **Document type:** academic/scholarly publication, monographic series.
—BLDSC (1032.000000); CISTI; UnCover.
Description: Publishes research and review articles in the fields of anthropology, archeology, geology, paleontology, entomology, and vertebrate and invertebrate zoology.
Refereed Serial

SOUTHEASTERN ASSOCIATION OF FISH AND WILDLIFE AGENCIES. PROCEEDINGS. see *FISH AND FISHERIES*

551.48 551.48 SA ISSN 1018-3469
QH90.A1 CODEN: SAASEK
SOUTHERN AFRICAN JOURNAL OF AQUATIC SCIENCES. (Text and summaries in English) 1964. 2/yr. R.120($40) (effective through 1994). Southern African Society of Aquatic Scientists, c/o F.C. de Moor, Albany Museum, Somerset St., Grahamstown 6140. TEL 27-461-22318. FAX 27-461-22398. E-mail: amfd@warthog.ru.ac.za. Ed. B.R. Allanson. adv.; bk.rev.; charts; illus.; cum.index: 1975-1985. circ. 400. (also avail. in microfiche) **Indexed:** Biol.Abstr., Chem.Abstr., Curr.Adv.Ecol.Sci., Curr.Tit.Ocean, Ind.S.A.Per., INIS Atomind., S.A.Wateraabstr., Sci.Cit.Ind., Sel.J.Water, Sel.Water Res.Abstr., Sport Fish.Abstr., W.R.C.Inf., Wild.Rev., Zoo.Rec. **Document type:** academic/scholarly publication.
—BLDSC (8352.591000); CASDDS; CISTI; Linda Hall; UnCover. **CCC.**
Former titles: Limnological Society of Southern Africa. Journal (ISSN 0377-9688); Limnological Society of Southern Africa. Newsletter (ISSN 0024-3582)
Description: Research papers on the aquatic sciences, with emphasis on Southern African issues and circumstances.
Refereed Serial

570 610 FR ISSN 0295-1967
CODEN: SPEBEQ
SPECTRA BIOLOGIE. 1982. 8/yr. 390 F. (foreign 560 F.) (effective 1997). P C I, 24 rue de Dunkerque, 75010 Paris, France. TEL 33-1-45267865. FAX 33-1-42806436. Ed. Monique Chevalier. adv. contact: Catherine Leclerq-Bourdon. bk.rev. circ. 5,000. **Document type:** academic/scholarly publication.
—BLDSC (8408.690000); CASDDS.
Description: Focuses on analytical techniques and instruments routinely used in clinical laboratories. Disseminates information on the growth of the profession and on new concepts, which are expected to greatly affect clinical laboratory practice.

SPEZIELLE PATHOLOGISCHE ANATOMIE. see *MEDICAL SCIENCES*

572.8 US ISSN 1066-5099
QH442.2 CODEN: STCEEJ
STEM CELLS; reporting on clinical and experimental research in the field of progenitor cell differentiation and proliferation. 1983. bi-m. $115 to individuals (foreign $135); institutions $195 (foreign $215) (effective 1997). AlphaMed Press, Inc., One Prestige Pl., Ste. 290, Miamisburg, OH 45342-3758. TEL 937-291-2355. FAX 937-291-4229. E-mail: alphamedpress@alphamedpress.com. Ed. Dr. Martin J. Murphy, Jr. R&P contact: Christina Martin. adv. contact: Mark Mlyniec. bk.rev. (back issues avail.) **Indexed:** ASCA, Chem.Abstr., Curr.Adv.Cancer Res., Curr.Adv.Cell & Devel.Biol., Curr.Adv.Ecol.Sci., Curr.Cont., Excerp.Med., Ind.Med., Ind.Sci.Rev., Sci.Cit.Ind., Telegen. **Document type:** academic/scholarly publication.
—BLDSC (8464.133510); CASDDS; CISTI; EMDOCS; Genuine Article; KNAW; Linda Hall; SWETS; UnCover. **CCC.**
Formerly (until 1992): International Journal of Cell Cloning (ISSN 0737-1454)
Refereed Serial

577.7 US ISSN 0969-2126
QH506 CODEN: STRUE6
STRUCTURE. 1993. m. $235 to individuals (outside N. America £150); institutions $695 (outside N. America £450) (effective 1997). Current Biology Ltd., 400 Market St., Ste. 700, Philadelphia, PA 19106. TEL 800-552-5866. FAX 215-574-2270. E-mail: info@hugo.curbio.com; biomednet@cursci.co.uk; URL: http://BioMednet.com/cgi-bin/members1/titles.pl. (Dist. by: Turpin Distribution Services Ltd., Blackhorse Rd., Letchworth, Herts. SG6 1HN, England. TEL 44-1462-672555. FAX 44-1462-480947; Addr. in UK: Current Biology Ltd., 34-42 Cleveland St., London W1P 6LB, England. TEL 44-171-323-0323. FAX 44-171-636-6911) Eds. Wayne A. Hendrickson, Carl-Ivar Braenden. adv.: B&W page $660, color page $1510; trim 8 1/2 x 11. circ. 600. (reprint service avail.) **Indexed:** Food Sci.& Tech.Abstr., Ind.Med. (1994-). **Document type:** academic/scholarly publication.
●Also available online.
Also available on CD-ROM.
—BLDSC (8478.687000); ADONIS; CASDDS; CISTI; EMDOCS; Genuine Article; KNAW; SWETS.
Description: Directed toward researchers, educators and students of biology. Features original research and reviews.
Refereed Serial

570 614.7 SP ISSN 0211-4623
QH171 CODEN: STOEEB
STUDIA OECOLOGICA. 1981. a. 1500 ptas. (effective 1995). Ediciones Universidad de Salamanca, Apdo. 325, 37080 Salamanca, Spain. TEL 34-23-294598. Dir. Jose Manuel Gomez Gutierrez. **Indexed:** Apic.Abstr., Ind.SST. **Document type:** academic/scholarly publication.

570 RM ISSN 1221-8103
QH301 CODEN: SUBBA8
STUDIA UNIVERSITATIS "BABES-BOLYAI". BIOLOGIA. (Text in English, French, German, Rumanian) 1958. s-a. exchange basis. Universitatea "Babes-Bolyai", Biblioteca Centrala Universitara, Str. Clinicilor Nr. 2, Cluj-Napoca 3400, Rumania. TEL 36-64-197092. FAX 36-64-197633. Ed. A. Marga. bk.rev.; abstr.; charts; illus. **Indexed:** Biol.Abstr., Chem.Abstr., Excerp.Med., Field Crop Abstr., Herb.Abstr., Maize Abstr., Rev.Plant Path., Soils & Fert., VITIS. **Document type:** academic/scholarly publication.

573.6 NE
STUDIES IN FERTILITY AND STERILITY. (Text in English) irreg. price varies. Kluwer Academic Publishers, Postbus 17, 3300 AA Dordrecht, Netherlands. TEL 31-78-6392392. FAX 31-78-6392254. TELEX 29245 KAPG NL. E-mail: services@wkap.nl; URL: http://www.wkap.nl. (Dist. by: Kluwer Academic Publishers Group, P.O. Box 322, 3300 AH Dordrecht, Netherlands. TEL 31-78-6392392. FAX 31-78-6546474; N. America dist. addr.: Box 358, Accord Sta., Hingham, MA 02018-0358. TEL 617-871-6600. FAX 617-871-6528) **Document type:** monographic series.
Refereed Serial

STUDIES IN HUMAN ECOLOGY. see *ENVIRONMENTAL STUDIES*

STUDIES ON THE NATURAL HISTORY OF THE CARIBBEAN REGION. see *BIOLOGY — Zoology*

STUDII SI CERCETARI DE BIOLOGIE. SERIA BIOLOGIE ANIMALA. see *BIOLOGY — Zoology*

SURFACTANT SCIENCE SERIES. see *CHEMISTRY*

BIOLOGY

577.85   IS   ISSN 0334-5114
CODEN: SYMBER
SYMBIOSIS. (Text in English) 1985. bi-m. (2 vols./yr.) $295. Balaban Publishers, International Science Services, P.O. Box 2039, Rehovot 76120, Israel. TEL 972-8-9476216. FAX 972-8-9467632. (And: Mario Negri Sud Research Institute, School for Scientific Communication, 66030 S. Maria Imbaro, Italy. TEL 39-872-570316. FAX 39-872-578240) Ed. Margalith Galun. (reprint service avail. from UMI) **Indexed:** ASCA, Curr.Cont., Fababean Abstr., Field Crop Abstr., Forest.Abstr., Herb.Abstr., Ind.Sci.Rev., Plant Grow.Reg.Abstr., Sci.Cit.Ind., Soils & Fert. **Document type:** academic/scholarly publication.
—BLDSC (8581.640000); CASDDS; CISTI; EMDOCS; Genuine Article; Linda Hall; SWETS; UnCover.
Description: Contains original research in symbiotic interactions at the molecular, cellular and organismic levels.

570   NE   ISSN 0165-5752
QL757   CODEN: SYPAD4
SYSTEMATIC PARASITOLOGY; an international journal. (Text in English) 1979. 9/yr. fl.1386 to institutions; $711 to institutions in U.S. (effective 1998). Kluwer Academic Publishers, Postbus 17, 3300 AA Dordrecht, Netherlands. TEL 31-78-6392254. FAX 31-78-6392254. TELEX 29245 KAPG NL. E-mail: services@wkap.nl; URL: http://www.wkap.nl. (Dist. by: Kluwer Academic Publishers Group, P.O. Box 322, 3300 AH Dordrecht, Netherlands. TEL 31-78-6392392. FAX 31-78-6546474; N. America dist. addr.: Box 358, Accord Sta., Hingham, MA 02018-0358. TEL 617-871-6600. FAX 617-871-6528) Ed. D.I. Gibson. adv. (also avail. in microform from UMI; reprint service avail. from SWZ) **Indexed:** Abstr.Hyg., ASCA, Bio-Contr.News & Info., Biol.Abstr., Curr.Adv.Ecol.Sci., Curr.Cont., Helminthol.Abstr., Ind.Med., Ind.Sci.Rev., Ind.Vet., Protozool.Abstr., Sci.Cit.Ind., Soils & Fert., Trop.Dis.Bull., Vet.Bull. **Document type:** academic/scholarly publication.
—BLDSC (8589.188000); CISTI; EMDOCS; Genuine Article; Linda Hall; SWETS; UMI; UnCover. **CCC.**
Description: Publishes original papers on the systematics, taxonomy and nomenclature of parasites, including nematodes, arthropods, and other parasitic groups.
Refereed Serial

570 540   JA   ISSN 0371-5167
CODEN: TAKHAA
TAKEDA RESEARCH LABORATORIES. JOURNAL. (Text in Japanese or English; summaries in English) 1936. a. 2000 Yen. Takeda Chemical Industries, Ltd., Pharmaceutical Research Division, 17-85 Jusohonmachi 2-chome, Yodogawa-ku, Osaka 532, Japan. Ed. Kanji Meguro. circ. 1,400. (back issues avail.) **Indexed:** Biol.Abstr., Chem.Abstr., Excerp.Med. **Document type:** academic/scholarly publication.
—CASDDS; EMDOCS.

570   JA
TAKEDA SCIENCE FOUNDATION SYMPOSIUM ON BIOSCIENCE. PROCEEDINGS. (Text in English) 1983. biennial. Takeda Kagaku Shinko Zaidan - Takeda Science Foundation, 17-85, Juso Honmachi 2-chome, Yodogawa-ku, Osaka 532, Japan. **Document type:** proceedings.

570   AT   ISSN 0819-6826
TASMANIAN NATURALIST. 1904. a. Aus.$15 to individuals (foreign Aus.$18); libraries Aus.$18 (foreign Aus.$23) (effective 1996). Tasmanian Field Naturalist Club, Inc., G.P.O. Box 68A, Hobart, Tas. 7001, Australia. TEL 61-3-62337870. FAX 61-3-62337594. Ed. Robert Taylor. R&P contact: G. Gates. bk.rev.; bibl.; illus.; maps; circ. 200 (paid). (back issues avail.) **Document type:** academic/scholarly publication.
Description: Covers natural history of Tasmania, including views on management of natural areas and values.
Refereed Serial

TAUCHEN; internationales Unterwasser-Magazin. see *SPORTS AND GAMES*

540 570   US   ISSN 1043-4658
QH506   CODEN: TCHNEV
TECHNIQUE (SAN DIEGO). 1989. bi-m. Academic Press, Inc., Journal Division, 525 B St., Ste. 1900, San Diego, CA 92101-4995. TEL 619-230-1840. FAX 619-699-6800. TELEX 181726. URL: http://www.apnet.com. (Subscr. to: Box 620000, Orlando, FL 32891-8340. TEL 800-543-9534) **Indexed:** Biol.Abstr., Chem.Abstr. **Document type:** academic/scholarly publication.
—CASDDS. **CCC.**

TECHNIQUE ET BIOLOGIE; revue de documentation scientifique et d'information professionnelle. see *MEDICAL SCIENCES — Experimental Medicine, Laboratory Technique*

TECHNIQUES IN DIAGNOSTIC PATHOLOGY. see *MEDICAL SCIENCES*

571.976   US   ISSN 0040-3709
QM691   CODEN: TJADAB
TERATOLOGY; the international journal of abnormal development. 1968. m. $1740 (foreign $1950) (effective 1998). (Teratology Society) John Wiley & Sons, Inc., Journals, 605 Third Ave., New York, NY 10158. TEL 212-850-6645. FAX 212-850-6021. TELEX 12-7063. E-mail: SUBINFO@JWILEY.COM; URL: http://www.wiley.co.uk. (Subscr. outside the Americas to: John Wiley & Sons Ltd., Baffins Ln., Chichester, W. Sussex PO19 1UD, England. TEL 44-1243-779777. FAX 44-1243-776128) Ed. Thomas W. Sadler. adv. B&W page £400, color page £1515; trim 279 x 210. bk.rev.; bibl.; charts; illus.; index. circ. 1,600. (also avail. in microform from SWZ,UMI; back issues avail.; reprint service avail. from SWZ) **Indexed:** Anim.Breed.Abstr., Art & Archaeol.Tech.Abstr., ASCA, Bibl.Dev.Med.& Child Neur., Biol.Abstr., Biotech.Abstr., Chem.Abstr., Curr.Adv.Cell & Devel.Biol., Curr.Adv.Ecol.Sci., Curr.Adv.Genetics & Molec.Biol., Curr.Cont., Dent.Ind., Excerp.Med., Helminthol.Abstr., I.P.A., Ind.Med., Ind.Sci.Rev., Ind.Vet., Neurosci.Cit.Ind., Nutr.Abstr., Poult.Abstr., Sci.Cit.Ind., Sport Fish.Abstr., THA, Vet.Bull., Wild.Rev., Zoo.Rec. **Document type:** academic/scholarly publication.
● Also available online.
—BLDSC (8792.180000); ADONIS; CASDDS; CISTI; Genuine Article; KNAW; Linda Hall; SWETS; UnCover. **CCC.**
Description: Investigates abnormal fetal development in humans and in experimental animal models.
Refereed Serial

570 551.46   SP   ISSN 0212-5919
CODEN: THALEP
THALASSAS; revista de ciencias del mar. (Text and summaries in English and Spanish) 1983. a. 3000 ptas. (effective 1996). Universidade de Santiago de Compostela, Servicio de Publicacions e Intercambio Científico, Campus Universitario, 15704 Santiago de Compostela, Spain. TEL 34-81-593500. FAX 34-81-593963. E-mail: spub1ic@usc.es; URL: http://www.usc.es/~spub1/. Ed. Federico Vilas Martin. charts; illus. circ. 400. (back issues avail.) **Indexed:** Ind.SST, Sport Fish.Abstr., Wild.Rev., Zoo.Rec. **Document type:** academic/scholarly publication.
—**CCC.**

570   CI   ISSN 0495-4025
QL1   CODEN: THJUAP
THALASSIA JUGOSLAVICA. 1956. q. exchange basis. Rudier Boskovic Institute, Center for Marine Research, P.O. Box 1016, 41001 Zagreb, Croatia. Ed. Tomo Gamulin. illus. **Indexed:** Deep Sea Res.& Oceanogr.Abstr. **Document type:** academic/scholarly publication.
—CASDDS.

570   US   ISSN 0082-3945
THEORETICAL AND EXPERIMENTAL BIOLOGY; an international series of monographs. 1961. irreg., vol.6, 1967. Academic Press, Inc., 525 B St., Ste. 1900, San Diego, CA 92101-4995. TEL 619-231-0962. FAX 619-699-6715. (Subscr. to: Order Dept., 6277 Sea Harbor Dr., 4th Fl., Orlando, FL 32887. TEL 800-321-5068) Ed. J.F. Danielli. (reprint service avail. from ISI) **Indexed:** Biol.Abstr. **Document type:** monographic series.
Refereed Serial

570   US   ISSN 0040-5809
QH301   CODEN: TLPBAQ
THEORETICAL POPULATION BIOLOGY; an international journal. 1970. bi-m. $490 (foreign $590) (effective 1997). Academic Press, Inc., Journal Division, 525 B St., Ste. 1900, San Diego, CA 92101-4995. TEL 619-230-1840. FAX 619-699-6800. URL: http://www.apnet.com/www/journal/tp.htm; http://www.idealibrary.com/. (Subscr. to: Box 861213, Orlando, FL 32886-1213. TEL 407-347-4040. FAX 407-363-9661) Ed.Bd. (back issues avail.) **Indexed:** Abstr.Hyg., Anim.Breed.Abstr., ASCA, Bio-Contr.News & Info., Biol.Abstr., Curr.Adv.Ecol.Sci., Curr.Adv.Genetics & Molec.Biol., Curr.Cont., Dairy Sci.Abstr., Deep Sea Res.& Oceanogr.Abstr., Ecol.Abstr., Environ.Per.Bibl., Helminthol.Abstr., Ind.Med., Ind.Sci.Rev., Math.R., Popul.Ind., Protozool.Abstr. **Document type:** academic/scholarly publication.
—BLDSC (8814.566000); CISTI; EMDOCS; Genuine Article; Linda Hall; SWETS; UnCover. **CCC.**
Description: Covers the theoretical aspects of the biology of populations, particularly in the areas of ecology, genetics, demography, and epidemiology.
Refereed Serial

577   HU   ISSN 0563-587X
QH178.H8   CODEN: TSCAB8
TISCIA; dissertationes biologiae a collegio exploratorum fluminis Tisciae editae. (Text in English) 1965. a. exchange basis. Attila Jozsef University, c/o E. Szabo, Exchange Librarian, Dugonics ter 13, P.O. Box 393, 6701 Szeged, Hungary. (Subscr. to: Kultura, P.O. Box 149, 1389 Budapest, Hungary) (Co-sponsor: Tisza Kutato Bizottsag) Ed. Gyorgy Bodrogkozi. charts; illus. circ. 300. **Indexed:** Aqua.Sci.& Fish.Abstr., Biol.Abstr., Chem.Abstr., Entomol.Abstr., GeoRef., Microbiol.Abstr., Sel.Water Res.Abstr. **Document type:** academic/scholarly publication.
—BLDSC (8858.430000); CASDDS.
Description: Covers the biology and ecology of ecosystems and their pollution in and around the Tisza River.

TISSUE ANTIGENS. see *MEDICAL SCIENCES*

570   JA
TOHO DAIGAKU RIGAKUBU SEIBUTSU GAKKA GYOSEKI HOKOKU/TOHO UNIVERSITY. FACULTY OF SCIENCE. DEPARTMENT OF BIOLOGY. RESEARCH REPORT. (Text in Japanese) triennial. Toho Daigaku, Rigakubu, Seibutsugakka - Toho University, Faculty of Science, Department of Biology, 2-1 Miyama 2-chome, Funabashi-shi, Chiba-ken 274, Japan.

576.58   JA   ISSN 0915-5228
TOHOKU DAIGAKU IDEN SEITAI KENKYU SENTA NENPON/TOHOKU UNIVERSITY. INSTITUTE OF GENETIC ECOLOGY. ANNUAL REPORT. (Text in English, Japanese) 1989. a. Tohoku Daigaku, Iden Seitai Kenkyu Senta - Tohoku University, Institute of Genetic Ecology, 1-1 Katahira 2-chome, Aoba-ku, Sendai-shi, Miyagi-ken 980-77, Japan. TEL 81-22-2276200. FAX 81-22-217-5692. **Document type:** bulletin.

576.58   JA   ISSN 0919-7303
TOHOKU UNIVERSITY. INSTITUTE OF GENETIC ECOLOGY. NEWSLETTER. (Text in English) 1989. a. Tohoku Daigaku, Iden Seitai Kenkyu Senta - Tohoku University, Institute of Genetic Ecology; 1-1 Katahira 2-chome, Aoba-ku, Sendai-shi, Miyagi-ken 980-77, Japan. TEL 81-22-217-5692. FAX 81-22-263-9845. **Document type:** newsletter.

570   JA   ISSN 0040-8786
CODEN: STUBAS
TOHOKU UNIVERSITY. SCIENCE REPORTS. SERIES 4: BIOLOGY/TOHOKU DAIGAKU RIKA HOKOKU. DAI-4-SHU, SEIBUTSUGAKU. (Text in English) 1924. a. exchange basis. Tohoku Daigaku, Rigakubu - Tohoku University, Faculty of Science, Aoba, Aramaki, Aoba-ku, Sendai-shi, Miyagi-ken 980, Japan. Ed. Dr. K. Sohma. bibl.; charts; illus.; index. circ. 700. (also avail. in microform from PMC) **Indexed:** Agrindex, Biol.Abstr., Chem.Abstr., Deep Sea Res.& Oceanogr.Abstr., Excerp.Med., GeoRef., Met.Abstr.
—BLDSC (8158.500000); CASDDS.

TOKYO DAIGAKU RIGAKUBU FUZOKU RINKAI JIKKENJO NENPO/UNIVERSITY OF TOKYO. MISAKI MARINE BIOLOGICAL STATION. ANNUAL REPORT. see *EARTH SCIENCES — Oceanography*

BIOLOGY

577 614.7 NE ISSN 0166-2082
CODEN: TEHEDH
TOPICS IN ENVIRONMENTAL HEALTH. (Text in English) 1978. irreg., vol. 7, 1985. price varies. Elsevier Science B.V., Books Division, P.O. Box 211, 1000 AE Amsterdam, Netherlands. TEL 31-20-4853911. FAX 31-20-4853705. TELEX 18582 ESPA NL. E-mail: nlinfo-f@elsevier.nl; usinfo-f@elsevier.com; forinfo-kyf04035@niftyserve.or.jp; URL: http://www.elsevier.nl/. (Subscr. in the Americas to: Elsevier Science, Regional Sales Office, Box 945, New York, NY 10159-0945. TEL 212-633-3730. FAX 212-633-3680; Subscr. in Australasia and the Far East to: Elsevier Science (Singapore) Pte Ltd, No.1 Temasek Ave., No.17-01 Millenia Tower, Singapore 039192, Singapore. TEL 65-434-3727. FAX 65-337-2230; Subscr. in Japan to: Elsevier Science Japan, 9-15 Higashi-Azabu 1-chome, Minato-ku, Tokyo 106, Japan. TEL 81-3-5561-5033. FAX 81-3-5561-5047) Ed. J.O. Nriagu. (back issues avail.) **Indexed:** Chem.Abstr. **Document type:** monographic series.
—CASDDS; CISTI.
Refereed Serial

TOPICS IN GEOBIOLOGY. see *EARTH SCIENCES — Geology*

570 NE ISSN 0378-6099
CODEN: TOPHDY
TOPICS IN PHOTOSYNTHESIS. (Text in English) 1976. irreg., vol.11, 1992. price varies. Elsevier Science B.V., Books Division, P.O. Box 211, 1000 AE Amsterdam, Netherlands. TEL 31-20-4853911. FAX 31-20-4853705. TELEX 18582 ESPA NL. E-mail: nlinfo-f@elsevier.nl; usinfo-f@elsevier.com; forinfo-kyf04035@niftyserve.or.jp; URL: http://www.elsevier.nl/. (Subscr. in the Americas to: Elsevier Science, Regional Sales Office, Box 945, New York, NY 10159-0945. TEL 212-633-3730. FAX 212-633-3680; Subscr. in Australasia and the Far East to: Elsevier Science (Singapore) Pte Ltd, No.1 Temasek Ave., No.17-01 Millenia Tower, Singapore 039192, Singapore. TEL 65-434-3727. FAX 65-337-2230; Subscr. in Japan to: Elsevier Science Japan, 9-15 Higashi-Azabu 1-chome, Minato-ku, Tokyo 106, Japan. TEL 81-3-5561-5033. FAX 81-3-5561-5047) Ed. J. Barber. (back issues avail.) **Indexed:** Biol.Abstr., Chem.Abstr. **Document type:** monographic series.
—BLDSC (8867.485000); CASDDS; CISTI.
Refereed Serial

616.3 NE ISSN 0928-3935
TOPICS IN SECONDARY METABOLISM. (Text in English) 1989. irreg., vol.3, 1992. price varies. Elsevier Science B.V., Books Division, P.O. Box 211, 1000 AE Amsterdam, Netherlands. TEL 31-20-4853911. FAX 31-20-4853705. E-mail: nlinfo-f@elsevier.nl; usinfo-f@elsevier.com; forinfo-kyf04035@niftyserve.or.jp; URL: http://www.elsevier.nl/. (Subscr. in the Americas to: Elsevier Science, Regional Sales Office, Box 945, New York, NY 10159-0945. TEL 212-633-3730. FAX 212-633-3680; Subscr. in Australasia and the Far East to: Elsevier Science (Singapore) Pte Ltd, No.1 Temasek Ave., No.17-01 Millenia Tower, Singapore 039192, Singapore. TEL 65-434-3727. FAX 65-337-2230; Subscr. in Japan to: Elsevier Science Japan, 9-15 Higashi-Azabu 1-chome, Minato-ku, Tokyo 106, Japan. TEL 81-3-5561-5033. FAX 81-3-5561-5047) (back issues avail.) **Document type:** academic/scholarly publication.
—BLDSC (8867.487500).

570 CN ISSN 0820-683X
TORONTO FIELD NATURALIST. 1938. 8/yr. Can.$25. 14 College St., No. 605, Toronto, ON M5G 1K2, Canada. TEL 416-968-6255. Ed. Helen Juhola. bk.rev.; cum.index: 1938-92. circ. 1,500. **Document type:** newsletter.
Description: Stimulates public interest in natural history and encourages the preservation of Canada's natural heritage through conservation.

570 JA ISSN 0287-5632
TOTTORI SEIBUTSU/TOTTORI BIOLOGICAL SOCIETY. JOURNAL. (Text in Japanese) 1966. a. membership. Tottoriken Seibutsu Gakkai - Tottori Biological Society, Tottori Kenritsu Hakubutsukan, 2-124, Higashimachi, Tottori-shi, Tottori-ken 680, Japan.

570 JA ISSN 0389-7494
TOYAMA-KEN SEIBUTSU GAKKAI KAISHI/BIOLOGICAL SOCIETY OF TOYAMA. JOURNAL. (Text in Japanese) a. Toyamaken Seibutsu Gakkai - Biological Society of Toyama, c/o Mr. Honda, 3687 Mitsukaichi, Kurobe-shi, Toyama-ken 938, Japan.

570 JA ISSN 0917-2033
TOYAMAKEN KOTO GAKKO KYOIKU KENKYUKAI SEIBUTSU BUNKAIHO/TOYAMA BIOLOGICAL EDUCATION SOCIETY. REPORT. (Text in Japanese) a. Toyamaken Koto Gakko Kyoiku Kenkyukai Seibutsu Bukai - Toyama Biological Education Society, Toyama Kenritsu Kureha Koto Gakko, 2070-5 Kurehamachi, Toyama-shi, Toyama-ken 930-01, Japan.

TRANSYLVANIA UNIVERSITY OF BRASOV. BULLETIN. SERIES B. see *MATHEMATICS*

577 UK ISSN 0169-5347
QH540 CODEN: TREEEQ
TRENDS IN ECOLOGY AND EVOLUTION. Library compendium: Trends in Ecology and Evolution (Reference Edition) (ISSN 0968-0012) 1986. m. fl.1349($775) to institutions (effective 1998). Elsevier Science Ltd., P.O. Box 800, Kidlington, Oxford OX5 1DX, England. TEL 44-1865-843000. FAX 44-1865-843010. E-mail: nlinfo-f@elsevier.nl; usinfo-f@elsevier.com; forinfo-kyf04035@niftyserve.or.jp; URL: http://www.elsevier.nl/. (Subscr. to: Elsevier Science, Regional Sales Office, P.O. Box 211, 1000 AE Amsterdam, Netherlands. TEL 31-20-4853757. FAX 31-20-4853432; Subscr. in the Americas to: Elsevier Science, Regional Sales Office, Box 945, New York, NY 10159-0945. TEL 212-633-3730. FAX 212-633-3680; Subscr. in Australasia and the Far East to: Elsevier Science (Singapore) Pte Ltd, No.1 Temasek Ave., No.17-01 Millenia Tower, Singapore 039192, Singapore. TEL 65-434-3727. FAX 65-337-2230) Ed. Andrew M. Sugden. adv.; index. circ. 1,649. (back issues avail.) **Indexed:** Anim.Breed.Abstr., Apic.Abstr., Arts & Hum.Cit.Ind., ASCA, Bio-Contr.News & Info., Biol.Abstr., Curr.Cont., Ecol.Abstr., Environ.Per.Bibl (1989-), Geo.Abstr.H.G., Geo.Abstr.P.G., Geol.Abstr., Herb.Abstr., Hort.Abstr., IBR, Ind.Sci.Rev., Sci.Cit.Ind., Soils & Fert., Sport Fish.Abstr., SSCI, Weed Abstr., Wild.Rev., Zoo.Rec. **Document type:** academic/scholarly publication.
—BLDSC (9049.569000); ADONIS; CISTI; Genuine Article; Linda Hall; SWETS; UnCover. **CCC.**
Description: Contains reviews, commentaries, discussions and letters in all areas of ecology and evolutionary science.
Refereed Serial

531.62 IO ISSN 0854-1566
TROPICAL BIODIVERSITY. (Text in English) 1992. 3/yr. Rps.30000($50) to individuals (developing countries $25; developed countries $50); institutions Rps.45000 (developing countries $60; developed countries $200) (effective 1997 & 1998). Indonesian Foundation for the Advancement of Biological Sciences, P.O. Box 103, Depok 16401, Indonesia. FAX 62-21-775-1837. E-mail: 62-21-775-1837. Ed. Jatna Supriatna. bk.rev. circ. 250. **Document type:** academic/scholarly publication.
—BLDSC (9054.359300).
Refereed Serial

TROPICAL FRESHWATER BIOLOGY. see *FISH AND FISHERIES*

570 JA ISSN 0917-415X
TROPICS/NETTAI KENKYU. (Text in English, Japanese) 1991. q. Nihon Nettai Seiti Gakkai - Japan Society of Tropical Ecology, c/o Mr. Hotta, Kagoshima Daigaku Rigakubu Seibutsugakka, 21-35 Korimoto 1-chome, Kagoshima-shi, Kagoshima-ken 890, Japan. **Indexed:** Apic.Abstr.
—BLDSC (9057.027000).

570 TU ISSN 1300-0152
CODEN: TJBIEZ
TURKISH JOURNAL OF BIOLOGY/TURK BIYOLOJI DERGISI. (Text in English, Turkish) 1976. 4/yr. $100 (effective 1996 & 1997). Scientific and Technical Research Council of Turkey - TUBITAK - Turkiye Bilimsel ve Teknik Arastirma Kurumu, Ataturk Bulvari, No. 221, Kavaklidere, 06100 Ankara, Turkey. TEL 90-312-4685300. FAX 90-312-4271336. TELEX 43186 BTAK TR. E-mail: bdym@tubitak.gov.tr. Ed. Dr. Ahmet Noyan. **Indexed:** Apic.Abstr., Biol.Abstr., Dairy Sci.Abstr., Food Sci.& Tech.Abstr., Hort.Abstr., Seed Abstr., Zoo.Rec. **Document type:** academic/scholarly publication.
—CASDDS.
Formerly (until 1994): Doga Turkish Journal of Biology - Doga Turk Biyoloji Dergisi (ISSN 1010-7576)
Refereed Serial

TURKISH JOURNAL OF MEDICAL & BIOLOGICAL RESEARCH. see *MEDICAL SCIENCES*

570 FI ISSN 0082-6979
CODEN: ATYBAK
TURUN YLIOPISTO. JULKAISUJA. SARJA A. II. BIOLOGICA - GEOGRAPHICA - GEOLOGICA. (Latin title: Annales Universitatis Turkuensis) (Text in English, Finnish, French and German) 1957. irreg. price varies. Turun Yliopisto - University of Turku, FIN-20500 Turku, Finland. FAX 358-21-3335050. TELEX 62123 TYK SF. URL: http://www.utu.fi/kirjasto. **Indexed:** INIS Atomind. **Document type:** monographic series, academic/scholarly publication.
—CASDDS; CISTI; EMDOCS; KR SourceOne; Linda Hall.
Description: Studies biology, genetics, geography and geology.

572.8 US ISSN 0735-9543
CODEN: USMBD6
U C L A SYMPOSIUM SERIES ON MOLECULAR AND CELLULAR BIOLOGY. N.S., 1982. irreg., vol.106, 1989. price varies. (University of California at Los Angeles) John Wiley & Sons, Inc., Journals, 605 Third Ave., New York, NY 10158. TEL 212-475-7700. **Indexed:** Biol.Abstr., Chem.Abstr., Ornam.Hort. **Document type:** monographic series.
—CASDDS; CISTI. **CCC.**
Refereed Serial

570 JA ISSN 0914-9201
UCHU SEIBUTSU KAGAKU/BIOLOGICAL SCIENCE IN SPACE. (Text in English, Japanese; summaries in English) 1987. q. Nihon Uchu Seibutsu Kagakkai - Japanese Society for Biological Science in Space, Uchu Kagaku Kenkyujo, 1-1 Yoshinodai 3-chome, Sagamihara-shi, Kanagawa-ken 229, Japan.

570 US ISSN 0301-5629
RM862.7 CODEN: USMBA3
ULTRASOUND IN MEDICINE & BIOLOGY. 1974. 9/yr. fl.1427($820) to institutions (effective 1998). (World Federation for Ultrasound in Medicine and Biology) Elsevier Science Inc., Box 945, New York, NY 10159-0945. TEL 212-633-3730. FAX 212-633-3680. E-mail: nlinfo-f@elsevier.nl; usinfo-f@elsevier.com; forinfo-kyf04035@niftyserve.or.jp; URL: http://www.elsevier.nl/. (Subscr. outside the Americas to: Elsevier Science, Regional Sales Office, P.O. Box 211, 1000 AE Amsterdam, Netherlands. TEL 31-20-4853757. FAX 31-20-4853432; Subscr. in Australasia and the Far East to: Elsevier Science (Singapore) Pte Ltd, No.1 Temasek Ave., No.17-01 Millenia Tower, Singapore 039192, Singapore. TEL 65-434-3727. FAX 65-337-2230; Subscr. in Japan to: Elsevier Science Japan, 9-15 Higashi-Azabu 1-chome, Minato-ku, Tokyo 106, Japan. TEL 81-3-5561-5033. FAX 81-3-5561-5047) Ed. P.N.T. Wells. adv.; charts; illus.; index. circ. 2,000. (also avail. in microfilm from UMI) **Indexed:** Appl.Mech.Rev., ASCA, Biol.Abstr., Curr.Adv.Ecol.Sci., Curr.Cont., Dent.Ind., Excerp.Med., Ind.Med., Ind.Sci.Rev., INSPEC, Sci.Cit.Ind. **Document type:** academic/scholarly publication.
—BLDSC (9082.815000); AskIEEE; CISTI; Ei; EMDOCS; Genuine Article; KNAW; KR SourceOne; Linda Hall; SWETS; UMI; UnCover. **CCC.**
Refereed Serial

BIOLOGY

578.77   UN   ISSN 0253-0112
CODEN: URMSEH
UNESCO REPORTS IN MARINE SCIENCE. Russian edition: Doklady yunesko po Morskim Naukam (ISSN 0257-6600); Spanish edition: Informes de la UNESCO sobre Ciencias del Mar (ISSN 0257-6597); Chinese edition: Jiaokewen Zuzhi Haiyang Kexue Baogao (ISSN 0257-6619); French edition: Rapports de l'UNESCO sur les Sciences de la Mer (ISSN 0257-6589); Arabic edition: Taqarir al-Yunasku fi 'Ulum al-Bihar (ISSN 0257-6627) 1974. irreg. (3-5/yr.). free to qualified personnel. UNESCO, SC-IOC-MRI, 1 rue Miollis, 75732 Paris Cedex 15, France. TEL 33-1-45681010. E-mail: g.wright@unesco.org; URL: http://www.unesco.org/publications. Ed. Gary Wright. **Indexed:** Curr.Adv.Ecol.Sci., Deep Sea Res.& Oceanogr.Abstr., Geo.Abstr., IDA, Meteor.& Geoastrophys.Abstr., Sport Fish.Abstr., Wild.Rev., Zoo.Rec.
—BLDSC (9090.208000); CISTI.

570   US
U.S. NATIONAL BIOLOGICAL SERVICE. RESEARCH PUBLICATIONS. irreg. (approx. q.). U.S. National Biological Service, Information Transfer Center, Publications Management Officer, 1201 Oak Ridge Dr., Ste. 200, Fort Collins, CO 80525-5589. TEL 970-226-9401. FAX 970-226-9455. **Document type:** government publication.
Supersedes (in 1995): U.S. Fish and Wildlife Service. New Publications.
Description: Provides a comprehensive listing of all publications of the U.S. National Biological Service.

570   CK   ISSN 0120-8063
UNIVERSIDAD DE BOGOTA JORGE TADEO LOZANO. MUSEO DEL MAR. INFORME. (Text in Spanish; summaries in English) 1971. irreg. price varies. Universidad de Bogota Jorge Tadeo Lozano, Museo del Mar, Carrera 4, No. 22-61, Bogota, Colombia. TEL 57-1-3426581. FAX 57-1-2826197. Dir. Elvira Maria Alvarado-Chacon. bibl. **Document type:** monographic series.

570   UY   ISSN 0250-653X
QH301
UNIVERSIDAD DE LA REPUBLICA. FACULTAD DE HUMANIDADES Y CIENCIAS. REVISTA. SERIE CIENCIAS BIOLOGICAS. N.S. 1978. irreg. exchange basis. Universidad de la Republica, Facultad de Humanidades y Ciencias, Seccion Revista, Tristan Narvaja 1674, Montevideo, Uruguay. Dir. Beatriz Martinez Osorio.
Formerly: Universidad de la Republica. Facultad de Humanidades y Ciencias. Revista. Serie Ciencias; Supersedes in part: Universidad de la Republica. Facultad de Humanidades y Ciencias. Revista.

570   SP
UNIVERSIDAD DE MURCIA. ANALES DE BIOLOGIA. (Consists of 4 subseries, also numbered individually) (Text mainly in English and Spanish; occasionally in other European languages) 1984. a. 2000 ptas. (effective 1997). Universidad de Murcia, Servicio de Publicaciones, Santo Cristo 1, 30080 Murcia, Spain. TEL 34-68-363014. FAX 34-68-363414. E-mail: vgm@pas.um.es; URL: http://www.um.es/~spumweb. Ed. Diego Rivera Nunez. bk.rev. circ. 500. (back issues avail.) **Indexed:** Ind.SST, Rev.Med.& Vet.Mycol. **Document type:** academic/scholarly publication.
Description: Contains original advances in the field of the biological sciences.

570 614.7   SP   ISSN 0213-4004
QH540   CODEN: ABSAEZ
UNIVERSIDAD DE MURCIA. ANALES DE BIOLOGIA. SECCION BIOLOGIA AMBIENTAL. (Subseries of: Anales de Biologia) (Text mainly in English and Spanish; occasionally in other European languages) 1984. a. 2000 ptas. (effective 1997). Universidad de Murcia, Servicio de Publicaciones, Santo Cristo 1, 30080 Murcia, Spain. TEL 34-68-363014. FAX 34-68-363414. E-mail: vgm@pas.um.es; URL: http://www.um.es/~spumweb. Ed. Diego Rivera Nunez. bk.rev. circ. 500. (back issues avail.) **Indexed:** Ind.SST. **Document type:** academic/scholarly publication.
—CISTI.

572.8   SP
UNIVERSIDAD DE MURCIA. ANALES DE BIOLOGIA. SECCION BIOLOGIA MOLECULAR Y MICROBIANA. (Subseries of: Anales de Biologia) (Text mainly in English and Spanish; occasionally in other European languages) 1984. irreg., vol.16, 1990. 2000 ptas. (effective 1997). Universidad de Murcia, Servicio de Publicaciones, Santo Cristo 1, 30080 Murcia, Spain. TEL 34-68-363014. FAX 34-68-363414. E-mail: vgm@pas.um.es; URL: http://www.um.es/~spumweb. Ed. Diego Rivera Nunez. bk.rev. circ. 500. (back issues avail.) **Indexed:** Field Crop Abstr., Herb.Abstr., Plant Grow.Reg.Abstr. **Document type:** academic/scholarly publication.
—CISTI
Formerly: Universidad de Murcia. Anales de Biologia. Seccion Biologia General (ISSN 0213-5442)

570   SP   ISSN 0212-8977
CODEN: RBUOE2
UNIVERSIDAD DE OVIEDO. REVISTA DE BIOLOGIA. (Text in Spanish; abstracts in English and Spanish) 1942. a. 2500 ptas. Universidad de Oviedo, Facultad de Biologia, c/o Carlos Lastra, Redactor, Departamento de Zoologia, 33071 Oviedo, Spain. (Subscr. to: Servicio de Publicaciones, Univ. de Oviedo, Arguelles, 19, 33071 Oviedo, Spain. TEL 34-85-104486. FAX 34-85-104488) circ. 750. **Indexed:** Biol.Abstr., Curr.Adv.Ecol.Sci., Ind.SST. **Document type:** academic/scholarly publication.
—BLDSC (7842.760000); CASDDS; CISTI.
Formerly (until 1981): Universidad de Oviedo. Facultad de Ciencias, Revista. Serie Biologia (ISSN 0473-6303)

578.77   BL   ISSN 0374-0412
QH91.A1   CODEN: URTBAV
UNIVERSIDADE FEDERAL DE PERNAMBUCO. DEPARTAMENTO DE OCEANOGRAFIA. CENTRO DE TECNOLOGIA. TRABALHOS OCEANOGRAFICOS.* (Text in English, French and Portuguese; summaries in English) 1959. irreg. exchange basis. Universidade Federal de Pernambuco, Departamento de Oceanografia, Centro de Tecnologia, Av. Prof. Moraes Rego, Campus Universitario, 50739 Recife, PE, Brazil. TEL 081-271-3128. FAX 081-271-8090. TELEX 811267. circ. 900. **Indexed:** Biol.Abstr., Deep Sea Res.& Oceanogr.Abstr.
Former titles (until 1966): Universidade Federal de Pernambuco. Instituto Oceanografico. Trabalhos (ISSN 0080-0236); (until 1963): Universidade do Recife. Instituto Oceanografico. Trabalhos; (until 1960): Instituto de Biologia Marinha e Oceanografia. Trabalhos.

578.77   BL   ISSN 0100-7068
UNIVERSIDADE FEDERAL DO RIO GRANDE DO NORTE. CENTRO DE BIOCIENCIAS. DEPARTAMENTO DE OCEANOGRAFIA E LIMNOLOGIA. BOLETIM. 1964. irreg., vol.8, 1991. exchange basis. (Universidade Federal do Rio Grande do Norte, Departamento de Oceanografia e Limnologia) Conselho Editorial, Praia de Mae Luiza, s-n, 59020 Natal RN, Brazil. FAX 842296. Ed. Francisca de Assis de Sousa. circ. 1,000. **Indexed:** Biol.Abstr. **Document type:** bulletin.
Formerly (until vol.5, 1971): Universidade Federal do Rio Grande do Norte. Instituto de Biologia Marinha. Boletim (ISSN 0041-8927)
Description: Covers hydrology, marine biology, and aquaculture.

570   BL   ISSN 0102-597X
QH117   CODEN: BOIBEM
UNIVERSIDADE FEDERAL DO RIO GRANDE DO SUL. INSTITUTO DE BIOCIENCIAS. BOLETIM. (Text in Portuguese; summaries in English) 1954. irreg., no.45, 1989. $7 per no. (effective 1997). Universidade Federal do Rio Grande do Sul, Instituto de Biociencias, Biblioteca, R. Sarmento, Lote 500, S-114, 90050-170 Porto Alegre - RS, Brazil. TEL 55-512-3163256. FAX 55-512-3163121. E-mail: bibbio@vortex.ufres.br. Ed.Bd. charts; illus.; index. circ. 1,000. **Indexed:** Biol.Abstr., Chem.Abstr. **Document type:** academic/scholarly publication, monographic series.
Former titles (until 1977): Universidade Federal do Rio Grande do Sul. Instituto Central de Biociencias. Boletim (ISSN 0101-0972); (until 1970): Universidade do Rio Grande do Sul. Instituto de Ciencias Naturais. Boletim (ISSN 0079-4058)

570   IT   ISSN 0085-0950
UNIVERSITA DEGLI STUDI DI GENOVA. MUSEI E ISTITUTI BIOLOGICI. BOLLETTINO. Key Title: Bollettino dei Musei e degli Istituti Biologici dell'Universita di Genova. (Text in English or Italian; summaries in English) 1891. a. exchange basis. Universita degli Studi di Genova, Istituto di Zoologia, Via Balbi 5, 16126 Genoa, Italy. TEL 39-10-2099454. FAX 39-10-2099323. E-mail: zoologia@unige.it. Ed. Silvio Spano. circ. 500. **Indexed:** Biol.Abstr., Deep Sea Res.& Oceanogr.Abstr. **Document type:** academic/scholarly publication.

570   AU   ISSN 0587-484X
UNIVERSITAET INNSBRUCK. ALPIN-BIOLOGISCHE STUDIEN. (Subseries of: Universitaet Innsbruck. Veroeffentlichungen) 1970. irreg., vol.6, 1974. price varies. Oesterreichische Kommissionsbuchhandlung, Maximilianstr. 17, A-6020 Innsbruck, Austria. Ed. Heinz Janetschek.

570   RM   ISSN 0041-9133
QH301   CODEN: AUIBAF
UNIVERSITATEA "AL. I. CUZA" DIN IASI. ANALELE STIINTIFICE. SECTIUNEA 2A: BIOLOGIE. (Text in French, German, Rumanian or Russian) 1955. a. 35 lei. Universitatea "Al. I. Cuza" din Iasi, Calea M. Eminescu 11, Jassy, Rumania. (Subscr. to: ILEXIM, Str. 13 Decembrie Nr. 3, P.O. Box 136-137, Bucharest, Rumania) Ed. C. Toma. bk.rev.; abstr.; charts; illus. circ. 550. **Indexed:** Biol.Abstr., Chem.Abstr., Hort.Abstr., Math.R.
—BLDSC (0869.621000); CASDDS; CISTI; Linda Hall.
Description: Contains information on genetics, microbiology, plant anatomy, vegetal taxonomy, entomology, ecology and cellular biology.

570 630   RM   ISSN 0254-7236
CODEN: AUCHD6
UNIVERSITATEA DIN CRAIOVA. ANALE. SERIA: BIOLOGIE, AGRONOMIE, HORTICULTURA. (Text in Rumanian; summaries in English, French and German) 1972. a. 80 lei($15) Universitatea din Craiova, Str. A.I. Cuza nr. 13, 1100 Craiova, Rumania. circ. 300.
—CASDDS.

570 581   TU   ISSN 0256-7865
CODEN: CFABEW
UNIVERSITE D'ANKARA. FACULTE DES SCIENCES. COMMUNICATIONS. SERIE C. BIOLOGIE. (Text in English, French, German) 1983. a. exchange basis. Ankara Universitesi, Fen Fakultesi, Besevler, Ankara, Turkey. index. circ. 250. (back issues avail.) **Document type:** academic/scholarly publication.

570   TG   ISSN 1016-9210
UNIVERSITE DU BENIN. ANNALES. SERIE SCIENCE. (Text in French; summaries in English, French) 1975. a. 2000 F.($5) Universite du Benin, B.P. 1515, Lome, Togo. TEL 25-48-44. FAX 25-87-84. TELEX 52-58 UBTO. Ed. Messanvi Gbeassor. bk.rev. **Document type:** academic/scholarly publication.

570   US   ISSN 0568-8604
QH1
UNIVERSITY OF ALASKA. BIOLOGICAL PAPERS. 1955. irreg., no.25, 1996. $30. University of Alaska at Fairbanks, Institute of Arctic Biology, Library, Box 75700, 308 Irving I, Fairbanks, AK 99775-7000. TEL 907-474-7658. FAX 907-474-7666. Ed. Jean James. R&P contact: Jean James. bibl.; illus. circ. 500. (back issues avail.) **Indexed:** Biol.Abstr., Sport Fish.Abstr., Wild.Rev., Zoo.Rec. **Document type:** monographic series.
—CISTI; Linda Hall.
Refereed Serial

570   US   ISSN 0161-3243
CODEN: BPURDY
UNIVERSITY OF ALASKA. BIOLOGICAL PAPERS. SPECIAL REPORTS. 1975. irreg., no.5, 1992. $30. University of Alaska at Fairbanks, Institute of Arctic Biology, Library, Box 757000, 308 Irving I, Fairbanks, AK 99775-7000. TEL 907-474-7658. FAX 907-474-7666. Ed. Jean James. R&P contact: Jean James. **Document type:** monographic series.
—CASDDS; CISTI.

570   US   ISSN 0272-9075
UNIVERSITY OF CALIFORNIA. LAWRENCE BERKELEY LABORATORY. BIOLOGY AND MEDICINE DIVISION. ANNUAL REPORT. a. (University of California, Lawrence Berkeley Laboratory, Biology and Medicine Division) U.S. National Technical Information Service, 5285 Port Royal Rd., Springfield, VA 22161. TEL 703-487-4600.

BIOLOGY

UNIVERSITY OF COLORADO. INSTITUTE OF ARCTIC AND ALPINE RESEARCH. OCCASIONAL PAPERS. see *SCIENCES: COMPREHENSIVE WORKS*

570 500.9 US ISSN 0272-2658
UNIVERSITY OF KANSAS. MUSEUM OF NATURAL HISTORY. PUBLIC EDUCATION SERIES. 1974. irreg., no.12, 1992. price varies. University of Kansas, Museum of Natural History, 602 Dyche Hall, Lawrence, KS 66045-2454. Ed. Joseph T. Collins. (reprint service avail.)
—Linda Hall.

570 500.9 US ISSN 0193-7766
UNIVERSITY OF KANSAS. MUSEUM OF NATURAL HISTORY. SPECIAL PUBLICATIONS. 1946. irreg., no.19, 1991. price varies. University of Kansas, Natural History Museum, 602 Dyche Hall, Lawrence, KS 66045-2454. TEL 785-654-4450. FAX 785-864-5335. E-mail: huerterb@falcon.cc.ukans.edu. Ed. Joseph T. Collins. (reprint service avail.) **Document type:** academic/scholarly publication.
—Linda Hall.
Refereed Serial

578.77 SJ ISSN 0379-9611
CODEN: AUKUDH
UNIVERSITY OF KHARTOUM. HYDROBIOLOGICAL RESEARCH UNIT. ANNUAL REPORT. (Text in English) a. University of Khartoum, Hydrobiological Research Unit, Box 321, Khartoum, Sudan.

UNIVERSITY OF OSAKA PREFECTURE. BULLETIN. SERIES B: AGRICULTURE AND LIFE SCIENCES. see *AGRICULTURE*

UNIVERSITY OF SANTO TOMAS. GRADUATE SCHOOL. JOURNAL OF GRADUATE RESEARCH. see *SOCIAL SCIENCES: COMPREHENSIVE WORKS*

611.01816 US
UNIVERSITY OF SOUTH FLORIDA. INTERNATIONAL BIOMEDICAL SYMPOSIA SERIES. 1986. irreg., vol.3, 1987. price varies. Plenum Publishing Corp., 233 Spring St., New York, NY 10013-1578. TEL 212-620-8000. FAX 212-463-0742. TELEX 23-421139. E-mail: books@plenum.com. Ed. Andor Szentivanyi. charts; illus. **Document type:** proceedings.
Refereed Serial

UNIVERSITY OF TSUKUBA. SHIMODA MARINE RESEARCH CENTER. CONTRIBUTIONS. see *EARTH SCIENCES — Oceanography*

UNIVERSITY OF WAIKATO. ANTARCTIC RESEARCH UNIT. REPORT. see *EARTH SCIENCES — Geology*

570 CN ISSN 0317-3348
UNIVERSITY OF WATERLOO BIOLOGY SERIES. 1971. irreg. price varies. University of Waterloo, Department of Biology, Waterloo, ON N2L 3G1, Canada. TEL 519-885-1211. FAX 519-746-0614. Ed. J.C. Semple. **Document type:** academic/scholarly publication.
—BLDSC (9120.133000); CISTI.

570 550 US
UNIVERSITY OF WISCONSIN-MILWAUKEE. FIELD STATION BULLETIN. 1968. s-a. free. University of Wisconsin-Milwaukee, Field Sta., 3095 Blue Goose Rd., Saukville, WI 53080. TEL 414-675-6844. Ed. Millicent S. Ficken. circ. 400. (back issues avail.) **Indexed:** Biol.Abstr. **Document type:** academic/scholarly publication.

570 PL ISSN 1230-6088
UNIWERSYTET GDANSKI. ZESZYTY NAUKOWE. BIOLOGIA. (Text in Polish; summaries in English) 1979. irreg., latest no.10. price varies. Uniwersytet Gdanski, Wydzial Biologii, Geografii i Oceanologii, c/o Biblioteka Glowna, Ul. Armii Krajowej 110, 81-824 Sopot, Poland. TEL 51-0061. TELEX 051-2247 BMOR PL. (Dist. by: Ars Polona-Ruch, Krakowskie Przedmiescie 7, 00-680 Warsaw, Poland) Ed. Hanna Piotrowska. **Indexed:** AgroLibrex. **Document type:** academic/scholarly publication.
Former titles (until 1991): Uniwersytet Gdanski. Wydzial Biologii, Geografii i Oceanologii. Zeszyty Naukowe. Biologia (ISSN 0867-3357); (until 1984): Uniwersytet Gdanski. Wydzial Biologii i Nauk o Ziemi. Zeszyty Naukowe. Biologia (ISSN 0208-4961).
Description: Covers the botany (phytosociology, floristical investigations, lichenology, and cytology) as well as the zoology (animal physiology and ornithology) of northern Poland.

570 PL ISSN 0554-811X
UNIWERSYTET IM. ADAMA MICKIEWICZA. BIOLOGIA. (Text in Polish; summaries in English) 1961. irreg., no.57, 1996. price varies. Adam Mickiewicz University Press, Nowowiejskiego 55, 61-734 Poznan, Poland. TEL 48-61-527380. FAX 48-61-527701. TELEX 413260 UAMPL. Pub. Maria Jankowska. R&P contact: Malgorzata Bis. circ. 400. **Indexed:** AgroLibrex. **Document type:** academic/scholarly publication, monographic series.
—BLDSC (9120.440000); CISTI.
Formerly: Uniwersytet im. Adama Mickiewicza w Poznaniu. Wydzial Biologii i Nauk o Ziemi. Seria Biologia.
Description: Contains current research results of the university's biologists, their Ph.D. works, monographs and other scientific works. Each volume is devoted to the work of one author.

572.8 PL ISSN 0137-2351
QH506 CODEN: ZNUMDV
UNIWERSYTET JAGIELLONSKI. ZESZYTY NAUKOWE. PRACE Z BIOLOGII MOLEKULARNEJ. (Text in Polish; summaries in English) 1974. irreg., 1984. 42 Zl. per no. Uniwersytet Jagiellonski, Instytut Biologii Molekularnej, Ul. Golegia 24, 31-007 Krakow, Poland. (Dist. by: Ars Polona, Krakowskie Przedmiescie 7, 00-068 Warsaw, Poland) Ed. Z. Zak. bibl.; illus. circ. 420. **Indexed:** Chem.Abstr.
—CASDDS; CISTI.

570 PL ISSN 0860-2441
UNIWERSYTET SLASKI W KATOWICACH. PRACE NAUKOWE. ACTA BIOLOGICA SILESIANA. (Text in English, Polish; summaries in English, Polish and Russian) 1975. irreg. price varies. Wydawnictwo Uniwersytetu Slaskiego, Ul. Bankowa 12B, 40-007 Katowice, Poland. TEL 48-32-596-915. FAX 48-32-599-605. TELEX 0315584 USKPL. (Dist. by: CHZ Ars Polona, P.O. Box 1001, 00-950 Warsaw, Poland) **Indexed:** AgroLibrex, Triticale Abstr. **Document type:** academic/scholarly publication.
Formerly (until 1985): Acta Biologica (ISSN 0208-5046)
Description: Covers biochemistry, botany, histology, microbiology, physiology, zoology, morphology, systematics, environmental protection.

570 GW ISSN 0341-5260
UNTERRICHT BIOLOGIE; Beitraege zu seiner Gestaltung. 1965. 10/yr. DM.143.60 (foreign DM.153.60). Erhard Friedrich Verlag GmbH, Im Brande 17, 30926 Seelze, Germany. TEL 49-511-40004-0. FAX 49-511-40004170. (Subscr. to: Postfach 100150, 30917 Seelze, Germany) Ed. Barbara Dulitz. abstr.; cum.index. circ. 15,000. **Indexed:** Biol.Abstr., IBR. **Document type:** academic/scholarly publication.
—BLDSC (9121.285000); CISTI. CCC.
Incorporates: Naturwissenschaften im Unterricht Biologie (ISSN 0342-5487); Formerly: Biologieunterricht (ISSN 0006-3274)

577 US ISSN 0882-584X
URBAN WILDLIFE MANAGER'S NOTEBOOK.* (Supplement to: Urban Wildlife News) 1983. q. $25. National Institute for Urban Wildlife, 5130 West Running Brook Rd., Columbia, MD 21044-1523. Ed. Louise E. Dove. bk.rev. circ. 1,000. (looseleaf format; back issues avail.) **Indexed:** Sport Fish.Abstr., Wild.Rev.
Description: Series of conservation leaflets that explore a single in-depth topic in each issue.

572.8 BU ISSN 0205-0625
QH506 CODEN: UMBIEX
USPEHI NA MOLECULIARNATA BIOLOGIA/ADVANCES IN MOLECULAR BIOLOGY. 1975. s-a. 1.36 lv. per no. (Bulgarska Akademiia na Naukite) Publishing House of the Bulgarian Academy of Sciences, Acad. G. Bonchev St., Bldg. 6, 1113 Sofia, Bulgaria. circ. 450. (reprint service avail. from IRC)
—CASDDS; Linda Hall.
Supersedes: Molekulna Biologiia.

570 RU ISSN 0042-1324
QH301 CODEN: USBIA3
USPEKHI SOVREMENNOI BIOLOGII. 1932. bi-m. $119 (effective 1998). (Rossiiskaya Akademiya Nauk) Izdatel'stvo Nauka, 90 Profsoyuznaya ul., 117864 Moscow, Russia. TEL 095-336-0266. FAX 095-420-222- (Dist. in U.S. by: Victor Kamkin Inc., 4956 Boiling Brook Pkwy., Rockville, MD 20852. TEL 301-881-5973. FAX 301-881-1673) Ed. A.N. Belozerskii. bk.rev. **Indexed:** Anim.Breed.Abstr., Biol.Abstr., Chem.Abstr., Crop Physiol.Abstr., Deep Sea Res.& Oceanogr.Abstr., Field Crop Abstr., Herb.Abstr., Ind.Med., Int.Aerosp.Abstr., Plant Breed.Abstr., Protozool.Abstr., Triticale Abstr., Trop.Oil Seeds Abstr.
—BLDSC (0386.000000); CASDDS; CISTI; KNAW; Linda Hall.

570 UZ ISSN 0042-1685
QH301.A3652 CODEN: UZBZAZ
UZBEKSKII BIOLOGICHESKII ZHURNAL. (Text in Russian) 1957. bi-m. 11.10 Rub. (Akademiya Nauk Uzbekistana) Izdatel'stvo Fan, Ul. Gogolya 70, k. 105, 700000 Tashkent, Uzbekistan. charts; illus. **Indexed:** Bio-Contr.News & Info., Biol.Abstr., Chem.Abstr., Crop Physiol.Abstr., Dairy Sci.Abstr., Field Crop Abstr., Helminthol.Abstr., Herb.Abstr., Hort.Abstr., Ind.Vet., Pig News & Info., Plant Grow.Reg.Abstr., Rev.Plant Path., Sorghum & Millets Abstr., Vet.Bull., Weed Abstr.
—BLDSC (0384.030000); CASDDS; CISTI; Linda Hall.

577 FR ISSN 0240-8759
CODEN: VIMID2
VIE ET MILIEU/LIFE AND ENVIRONMENT; periodique d'ecologie generale. (Text in English, French) 1950. q. 740 F. (foreign 920 F.) (effective 1997). Universite de Paris VI (Pierre et Marie Curie), Laboratoire Arago, 66650 Banyuls sur Mer, France. TEL 33-4-68887327. FAX 33-4-68881699. E-mail: vimilieu@arago.univ.perp.fr. Ed. Alain Guille. R&P contact: Nicole Coineau. adv. contact: Nicole Coineau. bk.rev.; charts; illus.; index. **Indexed:** Agri.Ind., Anim.Behav.Abstr., Aqua.Sci. & Fish.Abstr., Biol.Abstr., Bull.Signal., Curr.Adv.Ecol.Sci., Deep Sea Res.& Oceanogr.Abstr., Ecol.Abstr., Excerp.Med., Geo.Abstr.H.G., Geol.Abstr., GeoRef., Helminthol.Abstr., Ocean.Abstr., Pollut.Abstr., Soils & Fert., Sport Fish.Abstr., Wild.Rev., Zoo.Rec. **Document type:** academic/scholarly publication.
—BLDSC (9235.000000); CISTI; SWETS; UnCover.
Description: Journal of general ecology: Organisms, communities and ecosystems biology and ecology; trophic webs, energetics; benthic ecology; pollution; numerical ecology, modelings; evolutionary biology and phylogeny, with emphasis on marine, lagoonar and terrestrial milieus. Includes one special topic issue each year.
Refereed Serial

570 SP ISSN 0210-945X
VIERAEA. 1970. a. 2500 ptas.($30) (effective 1996). Museo de Ciencias Naturales de Tenerife, Apdo. 853, 38080 Santa Cruz de Tenerife, Spain. FAX 34-22-228753. Ed. Juan Jose Bacallado Aranega. bk.rev. **Indexed:** Biol.Abstr., Ind.SST, Zoo.Rec. **Document type:** bulletin.

BIOLOGY

571.9 616.07 GW ISSN 0945-6317
RB1 CODEN: VARCEM
VIRCHOWS ARCHIV. Online edition (GW ISSN 1432-2307) (Text in English) 1847. m. DM.2832.80 (foreign DM.2848.40) (effective 1998). Springer-Verlag, Heidelberger Platz 3, 14197 Berlin, Germany. TEL 49-30-82787-0. FAX 49-30-82787448. E-mail: subscriptions@springer.de; URL: http://link.springer.de. (Subscr. in N. America to: Springer-Verlag New York, Inc., 333 Meadowlands Pkwy., Secaucus, NJ 07094. TEL 212-460-1500. FAX 212-473-6272) Ed.Bd. adv.; bibl.; charts; illus.; index, cum.index: vols.301-325, vols.326-343. (also avail. in microform from UMI,PMC; back issues avail.; reprint service avail. from ISI) **Indexed:** ASCA, Biol.Abstr., Chem.Abstr., Curr.Adv.Cancer Res., Curr.Adv.Cell & Devel.Biol., Curr.Adv.Ecol.Sci., Curr.Adv.Genetics & Molec.Biol., Curr.Cont., Dairy Sci.Abstr., Dent.Ind., Excerp.Med., Helminthol.Abstr., Ind.Med., Ind.Sci.Rev., Ind.Vet., Med.& Surg.Dermat., Neurosci.Cit.Ind., Protozool.Abstr., Sci.Cit.Ind., Vet.Bull. **Document type:** academic/scholarly publication.
●Also available online.
—BLDSC (9238.000000); ADONIS; CASDDS; CISTI; EMDOCS; Genuine Article; KNAW; SWETS; UMI; UnCover. **CCC**.
Formed by the 1994 merger of: Virchows Archiv. Section B: Cell Pathology (ISSN 0340-6075); Virchows Archiv. Section A: Pathological Anatomy and Histopathology (ISSN 0174-7398); Which was formerly: Virchows Archiv. Section A: Pathological Anatomy and Histology. (ISSN 0340-1227); Virchows Archiv. Abteilung A: Pathologische Anatomie (ISSN 0042-6423)
Description: Provides fundamental research on disease and on human pathological anatomy and histology in particular.

578.77 US ISSN 0083-6427
VIRGINIA INSTITUTE OF MARINE SCIENCE, GLOUCESTER POINT. EDUCATIONAL SERIES. 1943. irreg., latest 1994. price varies. Virginia Institute of Marine Science, Gloucester Point, VA 23062. TEL 804-642-7170. FAX 804-642-7097. **Document type:** monographic series.

578.77 US ISSN 0083-6435
VIRGINIA INSTITUTE OF MARINE SCIENCE, GLOUCESTER POINT. MARINE RESOURCES ADVISORY SERIES. 1970. irreg., latest 1995. price varies. Virginia Institute of Marine Science, Gloucester Point, VA 23062. TEL 804-642-7170. FAX 804-642-7097. **Document type:** monographic series.

578.77 US ISSN 0083-6443
VIRGINIA INSTITUTE OF MARINE SCIENCE, GLOUCESTER POINT. SPECIAL SCIENTIFIC REPORT. 1948. irreg., no.122, 1988. price varies. Virginia Institute of Marine Science, Gloucester Point, VA 23062. TEL 804-642-7170. FAX 804-642-7097. (also avail. in microfiche) **Indexed:** Biol.Abstr., Ocean.Abstr.

570 JA
VITAE. (Text in Japanese) 1957. a. Kyushu Daigaku, Seibutsu Kenkyubu - Kyushu University, Bio Researching Club, Kyushu Daigaku Kyoyobu, Kagai Katsudo Kyoyo Shisetsu, Ropponmatsu, Chuo-ku, Fukuoka-shi, Fukuoka-ken 810, Japan.

570 JA ISSN 0910-4003
 CODEN: VIORE6
VIVA ORIGINO. (Text in English, Japanese) 1971. 3/yr. 4000 Yen. Seimei no Kigen Oyobi Shinka Gakkai - Society for the Study of the Origin and Evolution of Life, Osaka Furitsu Daigaku Sogo Kagakubu, Seimei Kagaku Koza, Mozu Umemachi, Sakai-shi, Osaka 591, Japan.
—BLDSC (9244.320000); CASDDS.

VOPROSY RADIOBIOLOGII I BIOLOGICHESKOGO DEISTVIYA TSITOSTATICHESKIKH PREPARATOV. see MEDICAL SCIENCES — Radiology And Nuclear Medicine

570 550 JA ISSN 0913-0187
WASEDA DAIGAKU KYOIKUGAKUBU GAKUJUTSU KENKYU. SEIBUTSUGAKU, CHIGAKU HEN/WASEDA UNIVERSITY. SCHOOL OF EDUCATION. SCIENTIFIC RESEARCHES: BIOLOGY, GEOLOGY. (Text and summaries in English and Japanese) 1952. a. membership. Waseda Daigaku, Kyoikugakubu - Waseda University, School of Education, Shinjuku-ku, Tokyo 169-50, Japan. TEL 03-3203-4141. FAX 03-3208-1032. **Indexed:** Jap.Per.Ind.

570 631 JA ISSN 0511-1978
WASEDA SEIBUTSU/WASEDA BIOLOGY. (Text in Japanese) 1953. irreg. Waseda Daigaku Seibutsu Dokokai - Waseda Biological Circle, c/o Waseda Daigaku, Ippan Kyoiku Seibutsugaku Kyoshitsu, 6-1 Nishiwaseda 1-chome, Shinjuku-ku, Tokyo 160, Japan.

570 US ISSN 0043-0927
QH1 CODEN: WMJBA2
WASMANN JOURNAL OF BIOLOGY. 1937. s-a. $6.50. University of San Francisco, Biology Department, San Francisco, CA 94117. TEL 415-666-6381. Ed. Gary L. Stevens. abstr.; bibl.; charts; illus.; index. circ. 400. **Indexed:** Biol.Abstr., Biol.Dig., Chem.Abstr., Curr.Adv.Ecol.Sci., Deep Sea Res.& Oceanogr.Abstr., Geo.Abstr., Nutr.Abstr., Soils & Fert., Sport Fish.Abstr., Wild.Rev., Zoo.Rec. **Document type:** academic/scholarly publication.
—BLDSC (9264.000000); CISTI; Linda Hall; UnCover.
Refereed Serial

WENNER GREN CENTER INTERNATIONAL SYMPOSIUM SERIES. see SCIENCES: COMPREHENSIVE WORKS

WHALEWATCHER. see CONSERVATION

577 PL ISSN 0013-2969
 CODEN: WEKLAF
WIADOMOSCI EKOLOGICZNE. (Text in Polish; summaries in English) 1955. q. $36 (effective 1995). Polska Akademia Nauk, Instytut Ekologii, Dziekanow Lesny, 05-150 Lomianki, Poland. TEL 48-22-7513046. FAX 48-22-7513100. (Dist. by: Ars Polona, Krakowskie Przedmiescie 7, 00-068 Warsaw, Poland) Ed. Eligiusz Pieczynski. R&P contact: Eligiusz Pieczynski. adv. contact: Eligiusz Pieczynski. bk.rev.; bibl. circ. 860. **Indexed:** AgroLibrex, Biol.Abstr., Field Crop Abstr., GeoRef., Herb.Abstr., Sel.Water Res.Abstr.
—BLDSC (9313.100000).
Formerly: Ekologia Polska. Seria B.
Description: Publishes various articles, reports from conferences as well as information on activities of ecological institutions in Poland and other countries.

616.96 PL ISSN 0043-5163
 CODEN: WIPAAZ
WIADOMOSCI PARAZYTOLOGICZNE. (Text in Polish or English; summaries English) 1955. bi-m. $33. Polskie Towarzystwo Parazytologiczne - Polish Parasitological Society, Ul. C.K. Norwida 29, 50-375 Wroclaw, Poland. Ed. Izabela Zlotorzycka. bk.rev.; bibl.; charts; illus.; tr.lit.; index. circ. 1,150. **Indexed:** Abstr.Hyg., AgroAgen, AgroLibrex, Apic.Abstr., Biol.Abstr., Chem.Abstr., Curr.Adv.Ecol.Sci., Excerp.Med., Helminthol.Abstr., Ind.Med., Ind.Vet., Rev.Appl.Entomol., Rev.Plant Path., Trop.Dis.Bull., Vet.Bull.
—CASDDS; CISTI.

577 US ISSN 0084-0122
WILDLIFE BEHAVIOR AND ECOLOGY. 1971. irreg., latest 1995. price varies. University of Chicago Press, 5801 S. Ellis Ave., Chicago, IL 60637. TEL 773-702-7899. E-mail: sales@press.uchicago.edu; URL: http://www.press.uchicago.edu. (Subscr. to: 11030 S. Langley, Chicago, IL 60628. TEL 800-621-2736. FAX 800-621-8471) Ed. George B. Schaller. (reprint service avail. from ISI,UMI)
Refereed Serial

572.8 615 UK ISSN 0963-5823
WILEY SERIES ON MOLECULAR PHARMACOLOGY OF CELL REGULATION. irreg. John Wiley & Sons Ltd., Journals, Baffins Ln., Chichester, W. Sussex PO19 1UD, England. TEL 44-1243-779777. FAX 44-1243-843232. E-mail: cs-journals@wiley.co.uk; URL: http://www.wiley.co.uk. **Document type:** academic/scholarly publication, monographic series.
—BLDSC (9317.877900).

WOHNUNG & GESUNDHEIT; Fachzeitschrift fuer oekologisches Bauen & Leben. see ARCHITECTURE

WOOLHOPE NATURALISTS' FIELD CLUB, HEREFORDSHIRE. TRANSACTIONS. see ARCHAEOLOGY

571.864 FR ISSN 0084-1641
RC889
WORLD CONGRESS ON FERTILITY AND STERILITY. PROCEEDINGS. (Format and publisher of Proceedings vary) (Text in English) 1953. triennial, 15th, 1995, Montpellier. International Federation of Fertility Societies, c/o Prof. Bernard Hedon, 337 rue de al Combe Caude, 34090 Montpellier, France. TEL 33-4-67635340. FAX 33-4-67419427. E-mail: algcsi@mnet.fr; bhiffs@mnet.fr. circ. 3,000. **Indexed:** Anim.Breed.Abstr., Biol.Abstr. **Document type:** proceedings.

570 CC ISSN 1001-4276
QH7 CODEN: WUKEE8
WUYI KEXUE/WUYI SCIENCE. (Text in Chinese, English) a. Y4.20. (Fujian Science Commission) Wuyi Kexue Bianjibu, Shengfangsuo, Fujian Nongxueyuan, Jinshan, Fuzhou, Fujian 350002, People's Republic of China. (Dist. overseas by: Jiangsu Publications Import & Export Corp., 56 Gao Yun Ling, Nanjing, Jiangsu, P.R.C.) **Indexed:** Biol.Abstr.
Description: Covers the new research results in botany, zoology and environmental ecology.

570 PL
WYZSZA SZKOLA PEDAGOGICZNA IM. KOMISJI EDUKACJI NARODOWEJ W KRAKOWIE. ROCZNIK NAUKOWO-DYDAKTYCZNY. PRACE Z DYDAKTYKI BIOLOGII. 1964. irreg., no.4, 1990. price varies. Wydawnictwo Naukowe W S P, Ul. Karmelicka 41, 31-128 Krakow, Poland. TEL 33-78-20. (Co-sponsor: Ministerstwo Edukacji Narodowej)

YALE JOURNAL OF BIOLOGY AND MEDICINE. see MEDICAL SCIENCES

570 JA ISSN 0910-7053
YAMAGUCHI SEIBUTSU/YAMAGUCHI SOCIETY OF BIOLOGY. BULLETIN. (Text in Japanese) a. Yamaguchi Seibutsu Gakkai - Yamaguchi Society of Biology, c/o Mr. Kazumi Hoshiide, Yamaguchi Daigaku Kyoikugakubu Seibutsugakka, 1677-1 Yoshida, Yamaguchi-shi, Yamaguchi-ken 753, Japan.

570 JA ISSN 0914-0085
YAMANASHI SEIBUTSU/YAMANASHI BIOLOGICAL AMATEUR SOCIETY. BULLETIN. (Text in Japanese) 1955. a. Yamanashi Seibutsu Dokokai - Yamanashi Biological Amateur Society, c/o Mr. Shiro Nakagome, 246 Nagatsuka, Shikishimacho, Nakakoma-gun, Yamanashi-ken 400-01, Japan.

YOKOHAMA MEDICAL JOURNAL. see MEDICAL SCIENCES

570 JA
YOKOHAMA NATIONAL UNIVERSITY. SCIENCE REPORTS. SECTION 2: BIOLOGICAL AND GEOLOGICAL SCIENCES/YOKOHAMA KOKURITSU DAIGAKU RIKA KIYO. DAI-2-RUI. SEIBUTSUGAKU, CHIGAKU. (Text in European languages and Japanese) 1952. a. exchange basis only. Yokohama Kokuritsu Daigaku, Kyoikugakubu - Yokohama National University, Faculty of Education, 156 Tokiwadai, Hodogaya-ku, Yokohama-shi, Kanagawa-ken 240, Japan. illus. **Indexed:** Biol.Abstr., Forest.Abstr., Forest Prod.Abstr., GeoRef., Jap.Per.Ind., JTA, Rev.Plant Path. **Document type:** academic/scholarly publication.
—BLDSC (8163.000000); Linda Hall.
Formerly: Yokohama National University. Science Reports. Section 2: Biological Sciences (ISSN 0513-5613)

570 JA ISSN 0912-151X
YOKOHAMA SHIRITSU DAIGAKU KIHARA SEIBUTSUGAKU KENKYUJO NENPO/YOKOHAMA CITY UNIVERSITY. KIHARA INSTITUTE FOR BIOLOGICAL RESEARCH. ANNUAL REPORT. (Text in Japanese) 1984. a. Yokohama Shiritsu Daigaku, Kihara Seibutsugaku Kenkyujo - Yokohama City University, Kihara Institute for Biological Research, 122-20 Mutsukawa 3-chome, Minami-ku, Yokohama-shi, Kanagawa-ken 232, Japan.

YUNYI NATURALIST. see CHILDREN AND YOUTH — For

ZEITSCHRIFT FUER MORPHOLOGIE UND ANTHROPOLOGIE. see ANTHROPOLOGY

BIOLOGY — ABSTRACTING, BIBLIOGRAPHIES, STATISTICS

570   GW   ISSN 0939-5075
QH301   CODEN: ZNCBDA
ZEITSCHRIFT FUER NATURFORSCHUNG. SECTION C: A JOURNAL OF BIOSCIENCES. (Text in English) 1946. bi-m. DM.694 (effective 1998). Verlag der Zeitschrift fuer Naturforschung, Postfach 2645, 72016 Tuebingen, Germany. TEL 49-7071-31555. FAX 49-7071-360571. Ed. H. Hausen. R&P contact: Tamina Greifeld. bk.rev.; bibl.; charts; illus.; index. **Indexed:** Agroforest.Abstr., Apic.Abstr., ASCA, Biol.Abstr., Biotech.Abstr., Chem.Abstr., Chem.Cit.Ind., Crop Physiol.Abstr., Curr.Adv.Ecol.Sci., Curr.Cont., Dairy Sci.Abstr., Deep Sea Res.& Oceanogr.Abstr., Dent.Ind., Excerp.Med., Fababean Abstr., Field Crop Abstr., Forest.Abstr., Forest Prod.Abstr., Helminthol.Abstr., Herb.Abstr., Hort.Abstr., Ind.Med., Ind.Sci.Rev., Ind.Vet., Maize Abstr., Mass Spectr.Bull., Ornam.Hort., Plant Breed.Abstr., Plant Grow.Reg.Abstr., Potato Abstr., Rev.Med.& Vet.Mycol., Rev.Plant Path., Rice Abstr., Seed Abstr., Soils & Fert., Soyabean Abstr., Sport Fish.Abstr., Vet.Bull., Weed Rev., Zoo.Rec. **Document type:** academic/scholarly publication.
—BLDSC (9475.010000); CASDDS; CISTI; EMDOCS; Genuine Article; Linda Hall; SWETS; UnCover. **CCC.**
     Formerly (until 1986): Zeitschrift fuer Naturforschung. Section C: Biosciences (ISSN 0341-0382)
     Refereed Serial

570   CC
ZHONGGUO SHENGWU FANGZHI/CHINESE JOURNAL OF BIOLOGICAL CONTROL. (Text in Chinese) q. Zhongguo Nongye Kexueyuan, Shengwu Fangzi Yanjiusuo, 30 Baishiqiao Lu, Beijing 100081, People's Republic of China. TEL 86-10-8314433. FAX 86-10-8323182. Ed. Qiu Shibang. pp./issue: 48. **Indexed:** Biodet.Abstr. **Document type:** academic/scholarly publication.
—BLDSC (3180.296000).
     Formerly (until 1995): Shengwu Fangzhi Tongbao (ISSN 1000-1034)
     Description: Covers research reports and experiments in the field of biological control.
     Refereed Serial

570   RU   ISSN 0044-4596
                CODEN: ZOBIAU
ZHURNAL OBSHCHEI BIOLOGII. (Text in Russian; summaries in English) 1940. bi-m. $175 (effective 1998). (Rossiiskaya Akademiya Nauk, Otdelenie Obshchei Biologii) Izdatel'stvo Nauka, 90 Profsoyuznaya ul., 117864 Moscow, Russia. TEL 095-336-0266. FAX 095-420-2220. (Dist. in U.S. by: Victor Kamkin Inc., 4956 Boiling Brook Pkwy., Rockville, MD 20852. TEL 301-881-5973. FAX 301-881-1637) Ed. N.I. Nuzhdin. index. (tabloid format) **Indexed:** Abstr.Hyg., Anim.Breed.Abstr., ASCA, Biol.Abstr., Chem.Abstr., Curr.Adv.Ecol.Sci., Curr.Cont., Dairy Sci.Abstr., Deep Sea Res.& Oceanogr.Abstr., Excerp.Med., Helminthol.Abstr., Ind.Med., Ind.Sci.Rev., Ind.Vet., Int.Aerosp.Abstr., Protozool.Abstr., Sci.Cit.Ind., Soils & Fert., Trop.Dis.Bull., Vet.Bull.
—BLDSC (0063.000000); CASDDS; CISTI; Genuine Article; KNAW; Linda Hall. **CCC.**

570   XR   ISSN 0044-4812
ZIVA; casopis pro biologickou praci. (Text in Czech and Slovak) 1953. bi-m. DM.65. (Ceska Akademie Ved) Academia, Publishing House of the Czech Academy of Sciences, Vodickova 40, 112 29 Prague 1, Czech Republic. TEL 235-17-92. (Subscr. to: Artia, Ve Smeckach 30, 111 27 Prague 1, Czech Republic) Ed. Slavomil Hejny. bk.rev.; illus.; index. circ. 22,000. **Indexed:** Biol.Abstr., Chem.Abstr., Curr.Cont.
—CISTI; Linda Hall.
     Description: Devoted to the popularization of natural sciences, botany, zoology, nature conservation; information about recent research into biology and new trends in research work.

571.3   GW   ISSN 0720-213X
QL1   CODEN: ZMPHDI
ZOOMORPHOLOGY; an international journal of comparative and functional morphology. Online edition (GW ISSN 1432-234X) (Text in English) 1924. q. DM.1501.60 (foreign DM.1506.80) (effective 1998). Springer-Verlag, Heidelberger Platz 3, 14197 Berlin, Germany. TEL 49-30-82787-0. FAX 49-30-82787448. E-mail: subscriptions@springer.de; URL: http://link.springer.de. (Subscr. in N. America to: Springer-Verlag New York, Inc., 333 Meadowlands Pkwy., Secaucus, NJ 07094. TEL 212-460-1500. FAX 212-473-6272) Ed. O. Kraus. adv.; bibl.; illus. (also avail. in microform from UMI; back issues avail.; reprint service avail. from ISI) **Indexed:** ASCA, Biol.Abstr., Curr.Adv.Ecol.Sci., Curr.Cont., Curr.Ref.Fish Res., Deep Sea Res.& Oceanogr.Abstr., Helminthol.Abstr., Ind.Sci.Rev., Sci.Cit.Ind., Sport Fish.Abstr., Wild.Rev., Zoo.Rec. **Document type:** academic/scholarly publication.
● Also available online.
—BLDSC (9530.310000); ADONIS; CISTI; Genuine Article; Linda Hall; SWETS; UMI; UnCover. **CCC.**
     Former titles: Zoomorphologie (ISSN 0340-6725); Zeitschrift fuer Morphologie der Tiere (ISSN 0044-3131)
     Description: Reviews research on animal morphology at all levels of ontogeny and organization, including ultrastructure of invertebrates and vertebrates.

577   US   ISSN 0720-1842
                CODEN: ZOOPDH
ZOOPHYSIOLOGY. (Text in English) 1971. irreg., vol.33, 1995. price varies. Springer-Verlag, 175 Fifth Ave., New York, NY 10010. TEL 212-460-1500. FAX 212-473-6272. (Also: Berlin, Heidelberg, Tokyo and Vienna) Ed. D.S. Farne. (reprint service avail. from ISI) **Indexed:** Biol.Abstr. **Document type:** monographic series.
—BLDSC (9531.259000); CISTI; KNAW.
     Formerly (until 1977): Zoophysiology and Ecology (ISSN 0084-5663)

BIOLOGY — Abstracting, Bibliographies, Statistics

016.58   BE   ISSN 0066-9784
A E T F A T INDEX; releve des travaux de phanerogamie systematique et des taxons nouveaux concernant l'Afrique au sud du Sahara et Madagascar. (Text in English, French) 1953. a. $8.50. Association pour l'Etude Taxonomique de la Flore d'Afrique Tropicale, 136 rue de la Hulpe, 1331 Rossieres, Belgium. Ed. J. Lejoly. cum.index: 1953-1985.

551.46 660   US   ISSN 1043-8971
TP248.27.M37
A S F A MARINE BIOTECHNOLOGY ABSTRACTS. (Aquatic Sciences & Fisheries Abstracts) 1989. q. $335 (foreign $360). Cambridge Scientific Abstracts, 7200 Wisconsin Ave., 6th Fl., Bethesda, MD 20814. TEL 301-961-6750. FAX 301-961-6720. E-mail: market@csa.com; URL: http://www.csa.com. Ed.Bd.; Pub. Ted Caris. abstr.; index. (also avail. in magnetic tape; back issues avail.) **Document type:** abstracting/indexing.
● Also available online. Vendor(s): European Space Agency, Knight-Ridder Information, Inc. (File nos.44 and 76), STN International.
Also available on CD-ROM. Producer(s): Knight-Ridder, Inc., NISC, SilverPlatter Information, Inc.
—BLDSC (1740.620000).
     Formerly: Marine Biotechnology Abstracts.
     Description: Covers the application of molecular biology and genetics to marine and aquatic organisms.

016.57   CN   ISSN 0226-1685
A S T I S BIBLIOGRAPHY. (Not avail. in printed format) 1979. a. Can.$120 (foreign $120) (effective 1997). Arctic Science & Technology Information System, Arctic Institute of North America, University of Calgary, 2500 University Dr. N.W., Calgary, AB T2N 1N4, Canada. TEL 403-220-4036. FAX 403-282-4609. E-mail: rgoodwin@acs.ucalgary.ca. Ed. C. Ross Goodwin. circ. 100. **Document type:** bibliography.
● Also available online. Vendor(s): QL Systems Ltd. Also available on CD-ROM.
—BLDSC (1747.067100); CISTI.
     Description: Contains the complete contents of the ASTIS database on a CD-ROM.

ABSTRACTS: CELLULAR PATHOLOGY. see *MEDICAL SCIENCES — Abstracting, Bibliographies, Statistics*

660 330   UK   ISSN 0263-6778
ABSTRACTS IN BIOCOMMERCE. (Sub-series avail.: BioCommerce Financial Abstracts (ISSN 1354-280X)) 1982. s-m. (diskette s-m; CD-ROM q.). £459($878) (diskette £830 ($1500); CD-ROM £1500 ($2400)) (effective 1 996). BioCommerce Data Ltd., Prudential Bldgs., 95 High St., Slough, Berks. SL1 1DH, England. TEL 44-1753-511777. FAX 44-1753-512239. E-mail: biocom@dial.pipex.com; URL: www.biospace.com/biocommerce. Ed. A. Crafts-Lighty. q. cum. and index. (also avail. in diskette format; back issues avail.) **Document type:** abstracting/indexing.
● Also available online. Vendor(s): Data-Star (CELL), Knight-Ridder Information, Inc. (file no.286).
Also available on CD-ROM.
—CISTI. **CCC.**
     Description: Abstracts articles in newsletters, magazines, scientific journals, and newspapers on commercial applications of biotechnology.

595.7 016   US   ISSN 0001-3579
Z5856   CODEN: AEMYA
ABSTRACTS OF ENTOMOLOGY. 1970. m. $290 (effective 1997). BIOSIS, 2100 Arch St., Philadelphia, PA 19103-1399. TEL 215-587-4847; 800-523-4806. FAX 215-587-2016. E-mail: info@mail.biosis.org; URL: http://www.biosis.org. bk.rev.; abstr.; bibl.; index, cum.index. **Indexed:** Rev.Appl.Entomol. **Document type:** abstracting/indexing.
—BLDSC (0564.230000).
     Description: Current awareness journal containing abstracts and content summaries in English of pure and applied research involving insects, arachnids and insecticides.

589.2 016   US   ISSN 0001-3617
QK600   CODEN: ABMYA5
ABSTRACTS OF MYCOLOGY. 1967. m. $290 (effective 1997). BIOSIS, 2100 Arch St., Philadelphia, PA 19103-1399. TEL 215-587-4847; 800-523-4806. FAX 215-587-2016. E-mail: info@mail.biosis.org; URL: http://www.biosis.org. bk.rev.; abstr.; bibl.; index, cum.index. **Indexed:** Rev.Plant Path. **Document type:** abstracting/indexing.
—BLDSC (0565.430000); CASDDS.
     Description: Contains abstracts in English about research involving fungi, lichens, and fungicides.

660   UK   ISSN 0954-9897
S494.5.B563
AGBIOTECH NEWS AND INFORMATION. 1989. m. £895($690) (effective 1997). CAB International, Wallingford, Oxon. OX10 8DE, England. TEL 44-1491-832111. FAX 44-1491-826090. TELEX 847964 COMAGG G. E-mail: cabi@cabi.org; URL: http://www.cabi.org. (U.S. subscr. to: CAB International, North American Office, 198 Madison Ave., New York, NY 10016. TEL 212-726-6490. FAX 212-686-7993) (back issues avail.) **Indexed:** Food Sci.& Tech.Abstr. **Document type:** abstracting/indexing.
—BLDSC (0736.034000).
     Description: Contains a comprehensive selection of abstracts of the world's literature on agricultural biotechnology and some human applications of biotechnology. Focuses on the impact of biotechnology in agriculture and policy issues, as well as the purely scientific ones.

AGRO-AGEN; bibliographic database. see *AGRICULTURE — Abstracting, Bibliographies, Statistics*

AGRO-LIBREX; bibliographic database. see *AGRICULTURE — Abstracting, Bibliographies, Statistics*

AGROFORESTRY ABSTRACTS. see *FORESTS AND FORESTRY — Abstracting, Bibliographies, Statistics*

BIOLOGY — ABSTRACTING, BIBLIOGRAPHIES, STATISTICS

591.5 016   US   ISSN 0301-8695
QL750
ANIMAL BEHAVIOR ABSTRACTS. 1972. q. $615 (foreign $655). Cambridge Scientific Abstracts, 7200 Wisconsin Ave., 6th Fl., Bethesda, MD 20814. TEL 301-961-6750. FAX 301-961-6720. E-mail: market@csa.com; URL: http://www.csa.com. Ed. R. Hilton; Pub. Ted Caris. adv.; bk.rev.; abstr.; index. (also avail. in magnetic tape; back issues avail.) **Indexed:** Agri.Eng.Abstr., Cal.Tiss.Abstr., Chemorec.Abstr., Comput.& Info.Sys., Oncol.Abstr., Pollut.Abstr. **Document type:** abstracting/indexing.
●Also available online. Vendor(s): Knight-Ridder Information, Inc. (File no.76/LIFE SCIENCES COLLECTION), STN International (LIFESCI). Also available on CD-ROM. Producer(s): NISC, SilverPlatter Information, Inc.
—BLDSC (0902.960000).
    Formerly: Behavioural Biology Abstracts, Section A: Animal Behaviour (ISSN 0300-5852)
    Description: Covers field and laboratory studies of all aspects of animal behavior.

591.15 016   UK   ISSN 0003-3499
SF1
ANIMAL BREEDING ABSTRACTS; a monthly abstract of world literature. 1933. m. £460($805) (effective 1997). CAB International, Wallingford, Oxon. OX10 8DE, England. TEL 44-1491-832111. FAX 44-1491-826090. TELEX 847964 COMAGG G. E-mail: cabi@cabi.org; URL: http://www.cabi.org. (U.S. subscr. to: CAB International, North American Office, 198 Madison Ave., New York, NY 10016. TEL 212-726-6490. FAX 212-686-7993) adv.; bk.rev.; abstr.; index. circ. 1,400. (also avail. in diskette format; back issues avail.; reprint service avail.) **Indexed:** Anim.Breed.Abstr., Dairy Sci.Abstr., Field Crop Abstr., Herb.Abstr., Nutr.Abstr., Pig News & Info., Rural Recreat.Tour.Abstr., Vet.Bull., World Agri.Econ.& Rural Sociol.Abstr. **Document type:** abstracting/indexing.
●Also available online. Vendor(s): DIMDI, European Space Agency, Knight-Ridder Information, Inc.
—BLDSC (0903.000000); Linda Hall.
    Description: Covers animal breeding, genetics, reproduction, and production; includes research about immunogenetics, genetic engineering, and fertility improvement.

016.57   UK   ISSN 1350-4541
APOPTOSIS (SHEFFIELD). 1993. s-m. (diskette m.) £90 (diskette £120; both £180) (effective 1997). S U B I S, Mansion House, 19 Kingfield Rd., Sheffield S11 9AS, England. TEL 44-114-255-4433. FAX 44-114-255-4626. E-mail: subis@sheffac.demon.co.uk; URL: http://www.shef.ac.uk/uni/companies/shap. (also avail. in diskette format) **Document type:** abstracting/indexing.
    Description: Current awareness service for researchers in clinical and life sciences.

581   II   ISSN 0970-2377
APPLIED BOTANY ABSTRACTS. (Text in English) 1981. q. $150. National Botanical Research Institute, Economic Botany Information Service, Rana Prata Marg, Lucknow 226 001, India. FAX 0522-244330. TELEX 0535-315. (Dist. overseas by: HPC Publishers' Distributors Pvt. Ltd., 4805-24, 1st Fl., Bharat Ram Rd., Darya Ganj, New Delhi 110 002. TEL 91-11-3254401. FAX 91-11-6863511) Eds. A.K. Srivastava, R. Mitra. circ. 300.
    Formerly (until 1980): Current Literature in Plant Science.

016.597 639.2   US   ISSN 1083-883X
▼**AQUATIC BIOLOGY, AQUACULTURE & FISHERIES RESOURCES.** 1995. q. $2895. National Information Services Corporation (NISC), 3100 St. Paul St., Ste. 806, Baltimore, MD 21218. TEL 410-243-0797. FAX 410-243-0982. **Document type:** abstracting/indexing.
●Available only on CD-ROM. Producer(s): NISC.
    Description: Provides access to comprehensive information on the science and management of aquatic organisms and environments.

B S B I ABSTRACTS; abstracts from literature relating to the vascular plants of the British Isles. (Botanical Society of the British Isles) see BIOLOGY — Botany

016.58   PL   ISSN 0860-4509
BIBLIOGRAFIE BOTANICZNE/BOTANICAL BIBLIOGRAPHIES. 1983. irreg. price varies. Polska Akademia Nauk, Instytut Botaniki im. W. Szafera - Polish Academy of Sciences, W. Szafer Institute of Botany, Ul. Lubicz 46, 31-512 Krakow, Poland. TEL 48-12-215144. FAX 48-12-219790. E-mail: wysocki@ib-pn.krakow.pl. Ed. Jadwiga Sieminska. adv. contact: Jacek Wieser. circ. 300 0 (paid). **Document type:** academic/scholarly publication.
    Description: Presents a list of publications dealing with all plant groups by Polish botanists as well publications covering territory of Poland by foreign authors.

016 581   GW
BIBLIOGRAPHIA PHYTOSOCIOLOGICA SYNTAXONOMICA. 1971. irreg. price varies. J. Cramer in der Gebrueder Borntraeger Verlagsbuchhandlung, Johannesstr. 3A, 70176 Stuttgart, Germany. TEL 49-711-625001. FAX 49-711-625005. **Indexed:** Biol.Abstr. **Document type:** academic/scholarly publication, bibliography.

016 589.1   UK   ISSN 0006-1573
Z5356.F97
BIBLIOGRAPHY OF SYSTEMATIC MYCOLOGY. CD-ROM edition: B S M on C D - R O M. 1947. s-a. £60($105) to member countries; non-members £75($125); Japan $125 (CD-ROM £850($1495)) (effective 1997). International Mycological Institute, Bakeham Lane, Egham, Surrey TW20 9TV, England. URL: http://www.cabi.org/. (N. American addr.: 198 Madison Ave., New York, NY 10016-4314. FAX 212-686-7993) Ed. Ken Hudson. bk.rev. (also avail. in diskette format; reprint service avail.) **Indexed:** Plant Breed.Abstr., Rev.Plant Path. **Document type:** bibliography, abstracting/indexing.
●Also available on CD-ROM.
—CISTI
    Description: Lists papers and books on all aspects of the taxonomy of fungi each year.

BILTEN DOKUMENTACIJE. POLJOPRIVREDA. BILJNA PROIZVODNJA/BULLETIN OF DOCUMENTATION. AGRICULTURAL-PLANT PRODUCTION. see AGRICULTURE — Abstracting, Bibliographies, Statistics

016.57   SW   ISSN 0284-9321
BIO SCIENCE ABSTRACTS. (Text in English) 1988. irreg. price varies. Lund University Press, P.O. Box 141, S-221 00 Lund, Sweden. TEL 46-46-31-20-00. FAX 46-46-30-53-38. E-mail: order@studli.se. Eds. B. Klinge, C. Owman. **Document type:** academic/scholarly publication.

016.57   US   ISSN 0898-5227
BIOBUSINESS SEARCH GUIDE. 1986. biennial. BIOSIS, 2100 Arch St., Philadelphia, PA 19103-1399. TEL 215-587-4847. FAX 215-587-2016. **Document type:** monographic series.
—CISTI.

016.572   US   ISSN 1065-7509
BIOCHEMISTRY AND BIOPHYSICS CITATION INDEX. bi-m. $1170 for CD-ROM. Institute for Scientific Information, 3501 Market St., Philadelphia, PA 19104. TEL 215-386-0100. FAX 215-386-2911. (UK addr.: Brunel Science Park, Brunel University, Uxbridge UB6 3PG, England) (also avail. in magnetic tape) **Document type:** academic/scholarly publication, bibliography.
●Also available on CD-ROM.
    Description: Provides bibliographic data, cited references, related records and English-language author abstracts for international scholarly research journals and conference proceedings.

660 330   UK   ISSN 1354-280X
BIOCOMMERCE FINANCIAL ABSTRACTS. (Subseries of: Abstracts in BioCommerce (ISSN 0263-6778)) 1994. s-m. £195($340) BioCommerce Data Ltd., Prudential Bldgs., 95 High St., Slough, Berks. SL1 1DH, England. TEL 44-1753-511777. FAX 44-1753-512239. E-mail: biocom@dial.pipex.com; URL: http://www.biospace.com/biocommerce. Ed. A. Crafts-Lighty. **Document type:** abstracting/indexing.
●Also available online. Vendor(s): Data-Star (CELL), Knight-Ridder Information, Inc. (File no.286).
    Description: Abstracts articles on the financial aspects of biotechnology company development from newsletters, magazines, journals, and other periodicals.

016.66606   US   ISSN 1068-5693
R856.A1
BIOENGINEERING ABSTRACTS. 1974. m. $665 (foreign $785). Cambridge Scientific Abstracts, 7200 Wisconsin Ave., 6th Fl., Bethesda, MD 20814-4823. TEL 301-961-6700. FAX 301-961-6720. E-mail: market@csa.com; URL: http://www.csa.com. (Co-publisher: Engineering Information, Inc.) Ed. Evelyn Beck; Pub. Ted Caris. bk.rev.; abstr.; index. (back issues avail.; reprint service avail.) **Document type:** abstracting/indexing.
●Also available online.
Also available on CD-ROM. Producer(s): Knight-Ridder, Inc. (Biotechnology & Bioengineering).
—CCC.
    Former titles (until 1992): Bioengineering and Biotechnology Abstracts (ISSN 1041-2913); Bioengineering Abstracts (ISSN 0736-6213)
    Description: Covers the world's technological literature in the area of bioengineering and biomedical engineering.

016.57   US   ISSN 0006-3169
QH301   CODEN: BIABA4
BIOLOGICAL ABSTRACTS; references, abstracts, and indexes to the world's life sciences research literature. CD-ROM edition (US ISSN 1058-4129) 1926. s-m. $7000 (universities $6200) (effective 1997). BIOSIS, 2100 Arch St., Philadelphia, PA 19103-1399. TEL 215-587-4847; 800-253-4806. FAX 215-587-2016. E-mail: info@mail.biosis.org; URL: http://www.biosis.org. abstr.; index, cum.index. (also avail. in microfilm from BIO) **Indexed:** Anim.Breed.Abstr., Ind.Vet., JAMA, Popul.Ind., Rev.Plant Path., Vet.Bull., VITIS, Weed Abstr. **Document type:** abstracting/indexing.
●Also available online. Vendor(s): DIMDI, Data-Star, Knight-Ridder Information, Inc. (File nos.5 & 55), Ovid Technologies, Inc. (BIOL), STN International (BIOSIS).
Also available on CD-ROM. Producer: SilverPlatter Information, Inc.
—BLDSC (2074.000000); CASDDS; CISTI; Linda Hall.
    Formed by the 1926 merger of: Abstracts of Bacteriology (ISSN 0096-5340) & Botanical Abstracts (ISSN 0096-526X)
    Description: Provides references to current published research from the biological and biomedical journal literature. Abstracts are categorized in each issue under broad subject headings.

016   US   ISSN 0006-3169
BIOLOGICAL ABSTRACTS CUMULATIVE INDEXES. 1927. s-a. $2820 (universities $2700). BIOSIS, 2100 Arch St., Philadelphia, PA 19103-1399. TEL 215-587-4847; 800-523-4806. FAX 215-587-2016. E-mail: info@mail.biosis.org; URL: http://www.biosis.org. (also avail. in microform from BIO) **Document type:** abstracting/indexing.
—Linda Hall.

016.574   US   ISSN 0192-6985
Z5321   CODEN: BARRDG
BIOLOGICAL ABSTRACTS - R R M. (Reports, Reviews, Meetings); references and indexes to the world's life science reports, reviews, and meeting literature. CD-ROM edition (US ISSN 1058-4137) 1965. s-m. $3500 (universities $3100) (effective 1997). BIOSIS, 2100 Arch St., Philadelphia, PA 19103-1399. TEL 215-587-4847; 800-523-4806. FAX 215-587-2016. E-mail: info@mail.biosis.org; URL: http://www.biosis.org. bk.rev.; bibl.; index. (also avail. in microfiche) **Document type:** abstracting/indexing.
●Also available online. Vendor(s): DIMDI, Data-Star, Knight-Ridder Information, Inc. (File nos.5 & 55), Ovid Technologies, Inc. (BIOL), STN International (BIOSIS).
Also available on CD-ROM. Producer(s): SilverPlatter Information, Inc.
—BLDSC (2074.100000); CASDDS; CISTI; Linda Hall.
    Formerly (until 1980): BioResearch Index (ISSN 0006-3541)
    Description: Provides indexed and classified bibliographic entries for research reports, reviews; books on biology and biomedicine; conference literature.

BIOLOGY — ABSTRACTING, BIBLIOGRAPHIES, STATISTICS

016.57 US
BIOLOGICAL ABSTRACTS - R R M CUMULATIVE INDEX. (Reports, Reviews, and Meetings) 1970. s-a. $1400 (US degree-granting institutions $1370). BIOSIS, 2100 Arch St., Philadelphia, PA 19103-1399. TEL 215-587-4847; 800-523-4806. FAX 215-587-2016. E-mail: info@mail.biosis.org; URL: http://www.biosis.org. bk.rev. (also avail. in microfiche from BIO) **Document type:** abstracting/indexing.
    Former titles: Cumulative Index to Biological Abstracts R R M; Cumulative Index to Bioresearch Index; Annual Cumulative Index to Bioresearch Index.

016.574 016.63
630 US ISSN 0006-3177
Z5073
BIOLOGICAL & AGRICULTURAL INDEX. CD-ROM edition (US ISSN 1076-7037) 1964. m. (except Aug.) with q. and a. cumulations. H.W. Wilson Co., 950 University Ave., Bronx, NY 10452. TEL 718-588-8400; 800-367-6770. FAX 718-590-1617. TELEX 4990003HWILSON. Ed. Syed Shah. (also avail. in magnetic tape) **Document type:** abstracting/indexing.
●Also available online. Vendor(s): Knight-Ridder Information, Inc., OCLC, Ovid Technologies, Inc., Wilsonline.
Also available on CD-ROM. Producer(s): SilverPlatter Information, Inc., H.W. Wilson (WILSONDISC).
    —CISTI; Linda Hall.
    Formerly: Agricultural Index.
    Description: Provides a cumulative subject index to periodicals in the fields of biology, agriculture and related sciences.

016.574 US ISSN 0095-2958
QH301
BIOLOGY DIGEST. 1974. m. (Sep.-May). $129. Plexus Publishing, Inc., 143 Old Marlton Pike, Medford, NJ 08055. TEL 609-654-6500. FAX 609-654-4309. Ed. Thomas H. Hogan. adv.; bk.rev.; abstr.; bibl.; illus.; cum.index; circ. 2,000 (paid). (also avail. in microfiche from UMI) **Document type:** abstracting/indexing.
●Also available online. Vendor(s): OCLC.
Also available on CD-ROM.
    —BLDSC (2087.058000); UMI.
    Incorporates: Environmental Quality Abstracts (ISSN 0095-0149)
    Description: Contains abstracts of current life science articles and research reports for high school and college students.

570 US ISSN 0891-740X
BIOMEDICAL RESEARCH TECHNOLOGY RESOURCES; a research resources directory. 1977. biennial. free. U.S. National Institutes of Health, National Center for Research Resources, Westwood Bldg., Rm. 10A15, 5333 Westbard Ave., Bethesda, MD 20892. TEL 301-594-7938. circ. 9,000. **Document type:** government publication, directory.
    Former titles (until 1984): Biomedical Research Technology Program; Biotechnology Resources.
    Description: Directory of biomedical research technology centers.

570.15195 UK ISSN 0006-3444
QH301 CODEN: BIOKAX
BIOMETRIKA. 1901. q. £75 (foreign $130) (effective 1998). (Biometrika Trust) Oxford University Press, Academic Division, Great Clarendon St., Oxford OX2 6DP, England. TEL 44-1865-267907. FAX 44-1865-267485. E-mail: jnl.info@oup.co.uk; URL: http://www.oup.co.uk/journals. (Subscr. in U.S. to: Oxford University Press Inc., 2001 Evans Rd., Cary, NC 27513. TEL 800-852-7323. FAX 919-677-1714) Ed. A.P. Dawid; Pub. Steven Johnson. R&P contact: Joolz Longley. charts; illus.; author index: vols.1-78, 1901-1991; subject index: vols.1-37, 1901-1950. circ. 3,700. (also avail. in microform from UMI,PMC; back issues avail.; reprint service avail. from UMI) **Indexed:** Anim.Breed.Abstr., ASCA, Biol.Abstr., Biol.& Agr.Ind., Biostat., C.I.S. Abstr., Chem.Abstr., Compumath, Curr.Adv.Ecol.Sci., Curr.Cont.(1964-), Curr.Ind.Stat., Dairy Sci.Abstr., Excerp.Med., Helminthol.Abstr., Hort.Abstr., Ind.Sci.Rev., INSPEC (1977-1986), J.Cont.Quant.Meth., Math.R., Nutr.Abstr., Oper.Res.Manage.Sci., Plant Breed.Abstr., Qual.Contr.Appl.Stat., Risk Abstr., Sci.Cit.Ind., Sport Fish.Abstr., SSCI, Stat.Theor.Meth.Abstr. (1964-), W.R.C.Inf., Wild.Rev., Zent.Math., Zoo.Rec. **Document type:** academic/scholarly publication.
    —BLDSC (2089.000000); CISTI; KR SourceOne; Linda Hall; SWETS; UMI; UnCover.
    Description: Contains statistics with theoretical papers of direct or potential value in applications.

016.5714 US ISSN 0523-6800
QH505.A1
BIOPHYSICAL SOCIETY. ANNUAL MEETING. ABSTRACTS. 1958. a. $770 includes Biophysical Journal ($820 outside the Americas) (effective 1997). Biophysical Society, 9650 Rockville Pike, Bethesda, MD 20814-3998. TEL 301-571-8338. FAX 301-530-7133. URL: http://www.biophysics.saseb.com. Ed. Peter Moore. R&P contact: Betty Kirkland. adv. contact: Betty Kirkland. **Indexed:** Biol.Abstr. **Document type:** academic/scholarly publication, proceedings.
    Formerly: Biophysical Society. Abstracts (ISSN 0067-8910); **Supersedes:** Biophysical Society. Symposium Proceedings (ISSN 0520-1985)
    Refereed Serial

016.57 US ISSN 1081-8669
CODEN: BISCDW
BIOSIS EVOLUTIONS. 1994. 4/yr. free. BIOSIS, Marketing and Sales Department, 2100 Arch St., Philadelphia, PA 19103-1399. TEL 215-587-4847; 800-523-4806. FAX 215-587-2016. E-mail: info@mail.biosis.org; URL: http://www.biosis.org/htmls/evol/. Ed. Sharon F. Suer. circ. 10,000. **Indexed:** Biol.Dig., C.I.J.E. **Document type:** newsletter.
    —Linda Hall.
    Formed by the merger of (1970-1994): BioScene (ISSN 0090-3337); (1983-1994): BioSearch (ISSN 1041-8946)
    Description: Reports information on BIOSIS' products and services as well as items of current interest to the user of biological and biomedical information.

016.57 US
BIOSIS SEARCH GUIDE (YEAR). 1977. biennial. $135 (effective 1997). BIOSIS, 2100 Arch St., Philadelphia, PA 19103-1399. TEL 215-587-4847; 800-523-4806. FAX 215-587-2016. E-mail: info@mail.biosis.org; URL: http://www.biosis.org. **Document type:** abstracting/indexing.
    —CISTI.
    Former titles: BIOSIS Previews Search Guide (Year) (ISSN 0898-2414); BIOSIS Search Guide.

016.57 US
Z5321 CODEN: SSBDE4
BIOSIS SERIAL SOURCES. 1938. a. $85 worldwide (effective 1997). BIOSIS, 2100 Arch St., Philadelphia, PA 19103-1399. TEL 215-587-4847. FAX 215-587-2016. E-mail: info@mail.biosis.org; URL: http://www.biosis.org. (Addr. in the UK: BIOSIS, U.K., 54 Micklegate, York YO1 1LF, England. TEL 44-1904-644269. FAX 44-1904-612793) **Document type:** abstracting/indexing.
●Also available on CD-ROM.
    —CASDDS; CISTI; Linda Hall.
    Former titles (until 1996): Serial Sources for the BIOSIS Previews Database (ISSN 1044-4297); (until 1989): Serial Sources for the BIOSIS Database (ISSN 0162-2048); (until 1978): BIOSIS: List of Serials with Coden, Title Abbreviations, New, Changed and Ceased Titles (ISSN 0067-8937); (until 1969): Biological Abstracts List of Serials with Title Abbreviations (ISSN 0523-6568)

570.15195 510 US ISSN 1041-7648
QH323.5
BIOSTATISTICA. 1989. q. $125 (foreign $149) (effective 1998). Executive Sciences Institute, 1005 Mississippi Ave., Davenport, IA 52803. TEL 319-324-4463. FAX 319-322-3725. Ed. Bruce Brocka. adv.; bk.rev. **Document type:** abstracting/indexing.
    Description: Includes mathematical biological abstracts, a calendar, and current book contents.

660 UK ISSN 0953-2226
BIOTECH KNOWLEDGE SOURCES. 1988. m. £166($315) (effective 1996). BioCommerce Data Ltd., Prudential Bldgs., 95 High St., Slough, Berks. SL1 1DH, England. TEL 44-1753-511777. FAX 44-1753-512239. E-mail: biocom@dial.pipex.com; URL: www.biospace.com/biocommerce. Ed. A. Crafts-Lighty. index. (back issues avail.) **Document type:** abstracting/indexing.
    —BLDSC (2089.739500); CISTI. CCC.
    Description: Contains details of new information sources in biotechnology (e.g., books, journals, market surveys, and reports), forthcoming conferences, and announcements and reviews of new database services.

016.660 UK ISSN 0262-5318
TP248.13
BIOTECHNOLOGY ABSTRACTS. Key Title: Derwent Biotechnology Abstracts. CD-ROM edition (UK ISSN 1358-6009) 1982. fortn. $1750. Derwent Publications Ltd., Derwent House, 14 Great Queen St., London WC2B 5DF, England. TEL 44-171-3442800. (U.S. subscr. to: Derwent Inc., 1313 Dolley Madison Blvd., Suite 303, McLean, VA 22101. TEL 703-790-0400)
●Also available online. Vendor(s): Knight-Ridder Information, Inc. (File no.357), Questel Orbit Inc. (BIOT).
Also available on CD-ROM.
    —BLDSC (3555.360000); CISTI.
    Description: Covers broad range of technical aspects of biotechnology: from genetic manipulation and biochemical engineering to fermentation and downstream processing.

660 US ISSN 1057-607X
TP248.13
BIOTECHNOLOGY CITATION INDEX. bi-m. $1540. Institute for Scientific Information, 3501 Market St., Philadelphia, PA 19104. TEL 215-386-0100. FAX 215-386-2911. (UK addr.: Brunel Science Park, Brunel University, Uxbridge UB6 3PQ, England) (also avail. in magnetic tape) **Document type:** abstracting/indexing.
●Also available on CD-ROM.
    Description: Provides bibliographic data, cited references, related records and English-language author abstracts from international scholarly research journals and conference proceedings.

660 HU ISSN 0237-0115
BIOTECHNOLOGY INFORMATION. Variant title: Biotech-Info. 1984. m. 3600 Ft. Orszagos Muszaki Informacios Kozpont es Konyvtar (O.M.I.K.K.) - National Technical Information Centre and Library, Muzeum u. 17, P.O. Box 12, 1428 Budapest, Hungary. Ed. Fazekasne Zsuzsanna Horvath. abstr. circ. 420.

576 574.192   JA
BISEIBUTSU KAGAKU BUNRUI KENKYUKAI KOEN YOSHISHU/ABSTRACTS OF ANNUAL MEETING ON MICROBIAL CHEMOTAXONOMY. (Text in English, Japanese) 1988. a. Biseibutsu Kagaku Bunrui Kenkyukai - Society of Microbial Chemotaxonomy, Tokyo Daigaku Oyo Biseibutsu Kenkyujo, 1-1 Yayoi 1-chome, Bunkyo-ku, Tokyo 113, Japan. **Document type:** abstracting/indexing.

016.57   BU   ISSN 0861-5691
BIULETIN ZA NOVONABAVENI KNIGI NA CHUZHDI EZITZI. SERIIA B: ESTESTVENI I PRILOZHNI NAUKI. 1960. m. 250 lv.($41) Narodna Biblioteka Sv.sv. Kiril i Metodii, 88, V. Levski Blvd., 1504 Sofia, Bulgaria. TEL 359-2-882811. FAX 359-2-435495. **Document type:** bulletin.
Description: Lists newly acquired foreign-language books in the natural sciences.

016.58   DK   ISSN 0900-2367
BOTANISK CENTRALBIBLIOTEK. FORTEGNELSE OVER LOEBENDE PERIODICA. 1977. irreg. free. Botanisk Centralbibliotek, Soelvgade 83, OPG.S, DK-1307 Copenhagen K, Denmark. E-mail: bcb@bot.ku.dk. Ed. Annelise Hartmann.

C A S BIOTECH UPDATES. AGRICULTURE. (Chemical Abstracts Service) see AGRICULTURE — Abstracting, Bibliographies, Statistics

C A S BIOTECH UPDATES. BIOCHEMICAL IMMOBILIZATION & BIOCATALYTIC REACTORS. see CHEMISTRY — Abstracting, Bibliographies, Statistics

612.015   US   ISSN 0884-7479
              CODEN: CBUBE2
C A S BIOTECH UPDATES. BIOSENSORS. s-w. $240 (effective 1998). Chemical Abstracts Service (Subsidiary of: American Chemical Society), 2540 Olentangy River Rd., Box 3012, Columbus, OH 43210-0012. TEL 614-447-3600. FAX 614-447-3713. TELEX 6842086. **Document type:** abstracting/indexing.
Description: Covers use of immobilized enzymes, immunological components, and cell fractions or whole cells for biochemical analysis, body fluid monitoring, and diagnostics; electrodes, thermistors, transistors, and light-detection-type biosensors in the detection and determination of sample components.

016.5716   US   ISSN 1040-709X
              CODEN: CUCCEE
C A S BIOTECH UPDATES. CELL & TISSUE CULTURE. s-w. $240 (effective 1998). Chemical Abstracts Service (Subsidiary of: American Chemical Society), 2540 Olentangy River Rd., Box 3012, Columbus, OH 43210-0012. TEL 614-447-3600. FAX 614-447-3713. TELEX 6842086. **Document type:** abstracting/indexing.
Description: Covers methods and applications of culturing animal and plant cells; studies of organism metabolism and physiology as well as processes for the laboratory or commercial-scale production of cell metabolites.

C A S BIOTECH UPDATES. COMMERCIAL FERMENTATION. see CHEMISTRY — Abstracting, Bibliographies, Statistics

575.1 540   US   ISSN 1045-8581
              CODEN: CBDPER
C A S BIOTECH UPDATES. D N A & R N A PROBES. s-w. $240 (effective 1998). Chemical Abstracts Service (Subsidiary of: American Chemical Society), 2540 Olentangy River Rd., Box 3012, Columbus, OH 43210-0012. TEL 614-447-3600. FAX 614-447-3713. TELEX 6842086. **Document type:** abstracting/indexing.
Description: Covers DNA and RNA probes and their applications - such as detection of biological species or strains; taxonomy; clinical diagnosis of microbial infections and genetic diseases.

575.1   US   ISSN 0895-6618
              CODEN: CUDREU
C A S BIOTECH UPDATES. D N A FORMATION & REPAIR. s-w. $240 (effective 1998). Chemical Abstracts Service (Subsidiary of: American Chemical Society), 2540 Olentangy River Rd., Box 3012, Columbus, OH 43210-0012. TEL 614-447-3600. FAX 614-447-3713. TELEX 6842086. **Document type:** abstracting/indexing.
Description: Covers aspects of the biosynthesis and repair of DNA; enzyme studies of the various DNA polymerases and factors involved in DNA formation.

612.015   US   ISSN 1040-7081
              CODEN: CUEBEL
C A S BIOTECH UPDATES. ENZYMES IN BIOTECHNOLOGY. s-w. $240 (effective 1997). Chemical Abstracts Service (Subsidiary of: American Chemical Society), 2540 Olentangy River Rd., Box 3012, Columbus, OH 43210-0012. TEL 614-447-3600. FAX 614-447-3713. TELEX 6842086. **Document type:** abstracting/indexing.
Description: Covers laboratory, commercial, and industrial uses as well as applications of enzymes in genetics, medicine, organic synthesis, electrochemistry, and clinical and medical analysis.

575.1   US   ISSN 0884-7460
              CODEN: CBUEEB
C A S BIOTECH UPDATES. GENETIC ENGINEERING. s-w. $240 (effective 1998). Chemical Abstracts Service (Subsidiary of: American Chemical Society), 2540 Olentangy River Rd., Box 3012, Columbus, OH 43210-0012. TEL 614-447-3600. FAX 614-447-3713. TELEX 6842086. **Document type:** abstracting/indexing.
Description: Covers various aspects of genetic manipulation and genetic engineering in animals, plants, microorganisms, and viruses; recombinant DNA technology, gene splicing, molecular cloning, and plasmid and cosmid vector methodology.

575.1   US   ISSN 1045-859X
              CODEN: CBNSEI
C A S BIOTECH UPDATES. NUCLEIC ACID & PROTEIN SEQUENCES. s-w. $240 (effective 1998). Chemical Abstracts Service (Subsidiary of: American Chemical Society), 2540 Olentangy River Rd., Box 3012, Columbus, OH 43210-0012. TEL 614-447-3600. FAX 614-447-3713. TELEX 6842086. **Document type:** abstracting/indexing.
Formerly (until Jan. 1990): Biopolymer Sequences.
Description: Covers newly determined biopolymer sequences, including the nucleotide sequences of DNA and RNA and the amino acid sequences of proteins (enzymes, hormones); partial and complete sequences; database management and computerized manipulation of sequence information.

C A S BIOTECH UPDATES. PHARMACEUTICAL APPLICATIONS. see CHEMISTRY — Abstracting, Bibliographies, Statistics

C A SELECTS. ALKOXYLATED OLEOCHEMICALS. see CHEMISTRY — Abstracting, Bibliographies, Statistics

016.57   US   ISSN 0162-7694
              CODEN: CSLAD4
C A SELECTS. ANIMAL LONGEVITY AND AGING. s-w. $240 to non-members; members $70 (effective 1998). Chemical Abstracts Service (Subsidiary of: American Chemical Society), 2540 Olentangy River Rd., Box 3012, Columbus, OH 43210-0012. TEL 614-447-3600; 800-333-9511. FAX 614-447-3713. TELEX 6842086. **Document type:** abstracting/indexing.
Description: Covers animal longevity and senescence, senility, limb regeneration, geriatrics, and gerontology.

016.579   US   ISSN 1047-8167
              CODEN: CSATE7
C A SELECTS. ANTIFUNGAL & ANTIMYCOTIC AGENTS. 1988. s-w. $240 to non-members; members $70 (effective 1998). Chemical Abstracts Service (Subsidiary of: American Chemical Society), 2540 Olentangy River Rd., Box 3012, Columbus, OH 43210-0012. TEL 614-447-3600. FAX 614-447-3713. TELEX 6842086. **Document type:** abstracting/indexing.
Formerly (until 1989): BIOSIS CAS Selects: Antifungal Agents.
Description: Covers the antifungal and antimycotic activities of both established and developmental drugs. Includes synthesis, mechanism(s) of action, formulation, and structure-activity relationships.

C A SELECTS. DRUG ANALYSIS BIOLOGICAL FLUIDS & TISSUES. see PHARMACY AND PHARMACOLOGY — Abstracting, Bibliographies, Statistics

C A SELECTS. FREE RADICALS (BIOCHEMICAL ASPECTS). see CHEMISTRY — Abstracting, Bibliographies, Statistics

C A SELECTS. LEUKOTRIENES. see CHEMISTRY — Abstracting, Bibliographies, Statistics

C A SELECTS. MONOCLONAL ANTIBODIES. see MEDICAL SCIENCES — Abstracting, Bibliographies, Statistics

C A SELECTS. OLEOCHEMICALS CONTAINING NITROGEN. see CHEMISTRY — Abstracting, Bibliographies, Statistics

C A SELECTS. OMEGA-3 FATTY ACIDS & FISH OIL. see CHEMISTRY — Abstracting, Bibliographies, Statistics

595.7 011   US   ISSN 1047-8140
              CODEN: CSAYEM
C A SELECTS. PESTICIDE ANALYSIS. 1988. s-w. $240 to non-members; members $70 (effective 1998). Chemical Abstracts Service (Subsidiary of: American Chemical Society), 2540 Olentangy River Rd., Box 3012, Columbus, OH 43210-0012. TEL 614-447-3600. FAX 614-447-3713. TELEX 6842086. **Document type:** abstracting/indexing.
Formerly (until 1989): BIOSIS CAS Selects: Pesticide Analysis.
Description: Covers the analysis of pesticides (insecticides, herbicides, and fungicides). Includes chemical and physical analysis of preparations used for controlling plant and animal pests.

016.57   US   ISSN 1051-3930
              CODEN: CAPSEL
C A SELECTS. PHOSPHOLIPIDS (CHEMICAL ASPECTS). 1990. s-w. $240 to non-members; members $70 (effective 1998). Chemical Abstracts Service (Subsidiary of: American Chemical Society), 2540 Olentangy River Rd., Box 3012, Columbus, OH 43210-0012. TEL 614-447-3600. FAX 614-447-3713. TELEX 6842086. **Document type:** abstracting/indexing.
Description: Covers analysis, properties, preparation, reactions, and uses in food, feed, pharmaceuticals, cosmetics, and membrane models of phospholipids.

612.015   US   ISSN 0362-9848
              CODEN: CASPDQ
C A SELECTS. PSYCHOBIOCHEMISTRY. s-w. $240 to non-members; members $70 (effective 1998). Chemical Abstracts Service (Subsidiary of: American Chemical Society), 2540 Olentangy River Rd., Box 3012, Columbus, OH 43210-0012. TEL 614-447-3600. FAX 614-447-3713. TELEX 6842086. **Document type:** abstracting/indexing.
Description: Covers the pathological and pharmacological aspects of mental function, including human and animal behavior, and emotions.

C A SELECTS. STEROIDS (BIOCHEMICAL ASPECTS). see PHARMACY AND PHARMACOLOGY — Abstracting, Bibliographies, Statistics

016.579   US   ISSN 1047-8078
              CODEN: CSVVEG
C A SELECTS. VIRUCIDES & VIRUSTATS. 1986. s-w. $240 to non-members; members $70 (effective 1998). Chemical Abstracts Service (Subsidiary of: American Chemical Society), 2540 Olentangy River Rd., Box 3012, Columbus, OH 43210-0012. TEL 614-447-3600; 800-333-9511. FAX 614-447-3713. TELEX 6842086. **Indexed:** Chem.Abstr. **Document type:** abstracting/indexing.
Formerly (until 1989): BIOSIS CAS Selects: Antiviral Agents (ISSN 0885-6990)
Description: Covers the antiviral activity of both established and developmental drugs; includes synthesis, mechanism(s) of action, formulation, and structure-activity relationships.

016.57265   US   ISSN 1083-2750
              CODEN: CSPPF3
C A SELECTS PLUS. AMINO ACIDS, PEPTIDES AND PROTEINS. s-w. $250 to non-members; members $75 (effective 1998). Chemical Abstracts Service (Subsidiary of: American Chemical Society), 2540 Olentangy River Rd., Box 3012, Columbus, OH 43210-0012. TEL 614-447-3600; 800-333-9511. FAX 614-447-3713. TELEX 6842086. **Document type:** abstracting/indexing.
Formerly: C A Selects. Amino Acids, Peptides and Proteins (ISSN 0275-701X)
Description: Covers chemistry and synthesis of amino acids, peptides, and proteins.

C A SELECTS PLUS. HERBICIDES. see CHEMISTRY — Abstracting, Bibliographies, Statistics

BIOLOGY — ABSTRACTING, BIBLIOGRAPHIES, STATISTICS

632.95 US ISSN 1084-2373
CODEN: CSPIFG
C A SELECTS PLUS. INSECTICIDES. s-w. $250 to non-members; members $75 (effective 1998). Chemical Abstracts Service (Subsidiary of: American Chemical Society), 2540 Olentangy River Rd., Box 3012, Columbus, OH 43210-0012. TEL 614-447-3600. FAX 614-447-3713. TELEX 6842086. **Document type:** abstracting/indexing.
 Formerly (until 1996): C A Selects. Insecticides (ISSN 0160-9092)
 Description: Covers preparation, mechanism of action, and effects of insecticides; insect control and repellants.

016.612 US ISSN 1069-5540
QP88.2
CALCIUM AND CALCIFIED TISSUE ABSTRACTS. 1969. q. $550 (foreign $625). Cambridge Scientific Abstracts, 7200 Wisconsin Ave., 6th Fl., Bethesda, MD 20814. TEL 301-961-6750. FAX 301-961-6720. E-mail: market@csa.com; URL: http://www.csa.com. Pub. Ted Caris. adv.; bk.rev.; abstr.; index. (also avail. in magnetic tape) **Indexed:** Cal.Tiss.Abstr., Chemorec.Abstr., Comput.& Info.Sys., NRN, Oncol.Abstr., Pollut.Abstr. **Document type:** abstracting/indexing.
 ●Also available online. Vendor(s): Knight-Ridder Information, Inc. (File no.76/LIFE SCIENCES COLLECTION), STN International (LIFESCI).
 Also available on CD-ROM. Producer(s): SilverPlatter Information, Inc.
 Formerly (until 1994): Calcified Tissue Abstracts (ISSN 0008-0586)
 Description: Covers the role of calcium metabolism in maintaining body function, including bone structure and diseases.

571.6 UK ISSN 0263-7251
CELL CYCLE. m. £80 (effective 1997). S U B I S, Mansion House, 19 Kingfield Rd., Sheffield S11 9AS, England. TEL 44-114-2554433. FAX 44-114-2554626. E-mail: subis@sheffac.demon.co.uk; URL: http://www.shef.ac.uk/uni/companies/shap. (looseleaf format; back issues avail.) **Document type:** abstracting/indexing.
 —CCC.
 Description: Current awareness service for researchers in clinical and life sciences.

595.7 011 FR ISSN 0295-060X
CENTRE INTERNATIONAL DE DOCUMENTATION ARACHNOLOGIQUE. LISTE DES TRAVAUX ARACHNOLOGIQUES. 1968. a. 100 F. Centre International de Documentation Arachnologique, 61 rue de Buffon, 75005 Paris, France. FAX 40-79-3863. E-mail: arachne@mnhn.fr. Ed. Jacqueline Heurtault. adv.; bibl.; index. (also avail. in record)
 Description: Presents a listing of publications covering arachnology. Includes author's name, title of work, and year first published.

CHEMICAL ABSTRACTS - BIOCHEMISTRY SECTIONS. see CHEMISTRY — Abstracting, Bibliographies, Statistics

595.7 591 JA
CHOJU KANKEI TOKEI/ANNUAL STATISTICS OF BIRDS AND ANIMALS. (Text in Japanese) a. Kankyocho, Shizen Hogokyoku - Environment Agency, Nature Conservation Bureau, 2-2 Kasumigaseki 1-chome, Chiyoda-ku, Tokyo 100, Japan.

591 BL
CONGRESSO BRAILEIRO DE ZOOLOGIA E CONGRESSO LATINO-AMERICANO DE ZOOLOGIA. RESUMOS. irreg., 12th, 1992, Belem. (Conselho Nacional de Desenvolvimento Cientifico e Tecnologico) Museu Paraense Milio Goeldi, Caixa Postal 399, 66017-970 Belem, Para, Brazil. TEL 091-228-2341. FAX 091-929-1412. (Co-sponsors: Sociedade Brasileira de Zoologia; Universidade Federal do Para) **Document type:** abstracting/indexing.

CORNELL UNIVERSITY. NEW YORK STATE COLLEGE OF AGRICULTURE AND LIFE SCIENCES. BIOMETRICS UNIT. ANNUAL REPORT. see BIOLOGY

570.15195 SP ISSN 0212-4203
CUADERNOS DE BIOESTADISTICA Y SUS APLICACIONES INFORMATICAS. (Text mainly in Spanish, occasionally in English; summaries in English, Spanish) 1982. a. 2100 ptas. (foreign 2500 ptas.) (effective 1996). Universidad de Zaragoza, Facultad de Medicina, Departamento de Bioestadistica, Domingo Miral, s-n, 50009 Zaragoza, Spain. TEL 34-76-761703. FAX 34-76-761704. Ed. E. Rubio Calvo. circ. 250. **Indexed:** Ind.SST. **Document type:** academic/scholarly publication.
 Description: Includes articles on original research, applications, and reviews.
 Refereed Serial

576 UK ISSN 0964-8712
Z5180
CURRENT ADVANCES IN APPLIED MICROBIOLOGY & BIOTECHNOLOGY. 1984. m. fl.1945($1118) (effective 1998). Elsevier Science B.V., P.O. Box 211, 1000 AE Amsterdam, Netherlands. TEL 31-20-4853911. FAX 31-20-4853598. TELEX 18582 ESPA NL. E-mail: nlinfo-f@elsevier.nl; forinfo-f@elsevier.com; forinfo-kyf04035@niftyserve.or.jp; URL: http://www.elsevier.nl/. (Subscr. in the Americas to: Elsevier Science, Regional Sales Office, Box 945, New York, NY 10159-0945. TEL 212-633-3730. FAX 212-633-3680; Subscr. in Australasia and the Far East to: Elsevier Science (singapore) Pte Ltd, No.1 Temasek Ave., No.17-01 Millenia Tower, Singapore 039192, Singapore. TEL 65-434-3727. FAX 65-337-2230; Subscr. in Japan to: Elsevier Science Japan, 9-15 Higashi-Azabu 1-chome, Minto-ku, Tokyo 106, Japan. TEL 81-3-5561-5033. FAX 81-3-5561-5047) adv. (also avail. in diskette format; microfilm from UMI) **Indexed:** Curr.Cont. **Document type:** abstracting/indexing.
 ●Also available online. Vendor(s): Ovid Technologies, Inc. (CABS).
 —BLDSC (3494.060900); UMI. **CCC.**
 Formerly (until 1992): Current Advances in Microbiology (ISSN 0741-1669)
 Description: Provides current awareness service in the sphere of applied microbiology and biotechnology. Gives listings of titles of microbiological papers published throughout the world classified into 149 main areas and provides a comprehensive listing of review articles.

016.5716 UK ISSN 0741-1626
Z5322.C3
CURRENT ADVANCES IN CELL & DEVELOPMENTAL BIOLOGY. 1984. m. fl.2225($1279) (effective 1998). Elsevier Science B.V., P.O. Box 211, 1000 AE Amsterdam, Netherlands. TEL 31-20-4853911. FAX 31-20-4853598. TELEX 18582 ESPA NL. E-mail: nlinfo-f@elsevier.nl; usinfo-f@elsevier.com; forinfo-kyf04035@niftyserve.or.jp; URL: http://www.elsevier.nl/. (Subscr. in the Americas to: Elsevier Science, Regional Sales Office, Box 945, New York, NY 10159-0945. TEL 212-633-3730. FAX 212-633-3680; Subscr. in Australasia and the Far East to: Elsevier Science (Singapore) Pte Ltd, No.1 Temasek Ave., No.17-01 Millenia Tower, Singapore 039192, Singapore. TEL 65-434-3727. FAX 65-337-2230; Subscr. in Japan to: Elsevier Science Japan, 9-15 Higashi-Azabu 1-chome, Minto-ku, Tokyo 106, Japan. TEL 81-3-5561-5033. FAX 81-3-5561-5047) (also avail. in diskette format; microfilm from UMI) **Indexed:** Curr.Cont. **Document type:** abstracting/indexing.
 ●Also available online. Vendor(s): Ovid Technologies, Inc. (CABS).
 —BLDSC (3494.062000); UMI. **CCC.**
 Description: Provides a current awareness service in the sphere of cell and developmental biology. Gives listings of titles of cell and developmental biology papers published throughout the world classified into 76 main areas and provides a comprehensive listing of review articles.

575.1 UK ISSN 0741-1642
Z5322.G4
CURRENT ADVANCES IN GENETICS AND MOLECULAR BIOLOGY. 1984. m. fl.3070($1764) (effective 1998). Elsevier Science B.V., P.O. Box 211, 1000 AE Amsterdam, Netherlands. TEL 31-20-485-3911. FAX 31-20-4853598. TELEX 18582 ESPA NL. E-mail: nlinfo-f@elsevier.nl; usinfo-f@elsevier.com; forinfo-kyf04035@niftyserve.or.jp; URL: http://www.elsevier.nl/. (Subscr. in the Americas to: Elsevier Science, Regional Sales Office, Box 945, New York, NY 10159-0945. TEL 212-633-3730. FAX 212-633-3680; Subscr. in Australasia and the Far East to: Elsevier Science (Singapore) Pte Ltd, No.1 Temasek Ave., No.17-01 Millenia Tower, Singapore 039192, Singapore. TEL 65-434-3727. FAX 65-337-2230; Subscr. in Japan to: Elsevier Science Japan, 9-15 Higashi-Azabu 1-chome, Minato-ku, Tokyo 106, Japan. TEL 81-3-5561-5033. FAX 81-3-5561-5047) adv. (also avail. in diskette format; microfilm from UMI) **Indexed:** Curr.Cont. **Document type:** abstracting/indexing.
 ●Also available online. Vendor(s): Ovid Technologies, Inc. (CABS).
 —BLDSC (3494.064100); CISTI; UMI. **CCC.**
 Description: Provides current awareness service for biologists, ecologists and environmental scientists. Gives listings of titles of ecological papers published throughout the world classified into 61 main areas and provides a comprehensive listing of review articles.

581 016 UK ISSN 0306-4484
Z5353 CODEN: CAPSCJ
CURRENT ADVANCES IN PLANT SCIENCE. 1972. m. fl.2725($1566) (effective 1998). Elsevier Science B.V., P.O. Box 211, 1000 AE Amsterdam, Netherlands. TEL 31-20-4853911. FAX 31-20-48535988. TELEX 18582 ESPA NL. E-mail: nlinfo-f@elsevier.nl; usinfo-f@elsevier.com; forinfo-kyf04035@niftyserve.or.jp; URL: http://www.elsevier.nl/. (Subscr. in the Americas to: Elsevier Science, Regional Sales Office, Box 945, New York, NY 10159-0945. TEL 212-633-3730. FAX 212-633-3680; Subscr. in Australasia and the Far East to: Elsevier Science (Singapore) Pte Ltd, No.1 Temask Ave., No.17-01 Millenia Tower, Singapore 039192, Singapore. TEL 65-434-3727. FAX 65-337-2230; Subscr. in Japan to: Elsevier Science Japan, 9-15 Higashi-Azabu 1-chome, Minato-ku, Tokyo 106, Japan. TEL 81-3-5561-5033. FAX 81-3-5561-5047) adv.; bk.rev. circ. 1,200. (also avail. in diskette format (ISSN 1350-6536); microfilm from UMI; back issues avail.) **Indexed:** Weed Abstr. **Document type:** abstracting/indexing.
 ●Also available online. Vendor(s): Ovid Technologies, Inc. (CABS).
 —BLDSC (3494.065000); Linda Hall; UMI. **CCC.**
 Description: Provides current awareness service in the sphere of plant science. Gives listings of titles of plant science papers published throughout the world classified into 48 main areas and provides a comprehensive listing of review articles.

BIOLOGY — ABSTRACTING, BIBLIOGRAPHIES, STATISTICS

016.572 UK ISSN 0965-0504
Z5524.B54
CURRENT ADVANCES IN PROTEIN BIOCHEMISTRY. 1984. m. fl.1860($1069) (effective 1998). Elsevier Science B.V., P.O. Box 211, 1000 AE Amsterdam, Netherlands. TEL 31-20-4853911. FAX 31-20-4853598. TELEX 18582 ESPA NL. E-mail: nlinfo-f@elsevier.nl; usinfo-f@elsevier.com; forinfo-kyf04035@niftyserve.or.jp; URL: http://www.elsevier.nl/. (Subscr. in the Americas to: Elsevier Science, Regional Sales Office, Box 945, New York, NY 10159-0945. TEL 212-633-3730. FAX 212-633-3680; Subscr. in Australasia and the Far East to: Elsevier Science (Singapore) Pte Ltd, No.1 Temaesk Ave., No.17-01 Millenia Tower, Singapore 039192, Singapore. TEL 65-434-3727. FAX 65-337-2230; Subscr. in Japan to: Elsevier Science Japan, 9-15 Higashi-Azabu 1-chome, Minato-ku, Tokyo 106, Japan. TEL 81-3-5561-5033. FAX 81-3-5561-5047) adv. (also avail. in diskette format; microform from UMI) **Indexed:** Curr.Cont. **Document type:** abstracting/indexing.
●Also available online. Vendor(s): Ovid Technologies, Inc. (CABS).
—BLDSC (3494.067000); UMI. **CCC.**
Formerly (until 1992): Current Advances in Biochemistry (ISSN 0741-1618)
Description: Lists titles of protein biochemistry papers published throughout the world classified into 141 main areas; and provides a comprehensive listing of review articles.

016.57 NE ISSN 0733-4443
QH301
CURRENT AWARENESS IN BIOLOGICAL SCIENCES. (Consists of 12 sections, Current Advances in: Applied Microbiology & Biotechnology; Cancer Research; Cell & Developmental Biology; Clinical Chemistry; Ecological & Environmental Sciences; Endocrinology & Metabolism; Genetics & Molecular Biology; Immunology & Infectious Diseases; Neuroscience; Plant Science; Protein Biochemistry; Toxicology) 1954. m. fl.11700($7222) (effective 1997). Elsevier Science B.V., P.O. Box 211, 1000 AE Amsterdam, Netherlands. TEL 31-20-4853757. FAX 31-20-4853432. E-mail: nlinfo-f@elsevier.nl; usinfo-f@elsevier.com; forinfo-kyf04035@niftyserve.or.jp; URL: http://www.elsevier.nl/. (Subscr. in the Americas to: Elsevier Science, Regional Sales Office, Box 945, New York, NY 10159-0945. TEL 212-633-3730. FAX 212-633-3680; Subscr. in Australasia and the Far East to: Elsevier Science (Singapore) Pte Ltd, No.1 Temasek Ave., No.17-01 Millenia Tower, Singapore 039192, Singapore. TEL 65-434-3727. FAX 65-337-2230; Subscr. in Japan to: Elsevier Science Japan, 9-15 Higashi-Azabu 1-chome, Minato-ku, Tokyo 106, Japan. TEL 81-3-5561-5033. FAX 81-3-5561-5047) adv. circ. 1,000. (also avail. in microfilm from UMI; back issues avail.) **Indexed:** Biol.Abstr., Chem.Abstr., Ind.Vet., Nutr.Abstr., Vet.Bull. **Document type:** abstracting/indexing.
●Also available online. Vendor(s): Ovid Technologies, Inc. (CABS).
—BLDSC (3494.315000); CISTI; Linda Hall. **CCC.**
Formerly (until 1983): International Abstracts of Biological Sciences (ISSN 0020-5818)
Description: Provides comprehensive coverage of recent publications in the entire spectrum of biological sciences, including relevant work in toxicology and the biomedical and environmental sciences.

574 630 615 016 KO
CURRENT BIBLIOGRAPHIES ON SCIENCE AND TECHNOLOGY: BIOLOGY, PHARMACY AND FOOD SCIENCE. 1962. m. $107. Korea Institute for Economics and Technology, P.O. Box 205, 206-9 Cheongryangri-Dong, Dongdaimun-Ku, Seoul, S. Korea. circ. 300. (reprint service avail. from UMI)
Formerly: Current Index to Journals in Science and Technology: Biology, Agriculture, Pharmacy; Which superseded in part: Current Bibliography on Science and Technology.

016.57 JA ISSN 0285-5100
CURRENT BIBLIOGRAPHY ON SCIENCE AND TECHNOLOGY: LIFE SCIENCES/KAGAKU GIJUTSU BUNKEN SOKUHO. RAIFUSAIENSU HEN. (Text in Japanese) 1981. 3/m. $2500. Japan Science and Technology Corporation, Information Center for Science and Technology - Kagaku Gijutsu Shinko Jigyodan, 5-3, Yonbancho, Chiyoda-ku, Tokyo 102, Japan. TEL 81-3-5214-8413.
FAX 81-3-5214-8410. index. circ. 600. **Document type:** bibliography.
●Also available online. Vendor(s): JICST.
Also available on CD-ROM.

016.57 US ISSN 0960-9822
QH301 CODEN: CUBLE2
CURRENT BIOLOGY. 1991. m. $175 to individuals (outside N. America £105); institutions $495 (outside N. America £295) (effective 1997). Current Biology Ltd., 800 Market St., Ste. 700, Philadelphia, PA 19106. TEL 800-552-5866. FAX 215-574-2270. E-mail: info@hugo.curbio.com; biomednet@cursci.co.uk; URL: http://BioMedNet.com/cbiology/. (Dist. by: Turpin Distribution Services Ltd., Blackhorse Rd., Letchworth, Herts. SG6 1HN, England. TEL 44-1462-672555. FAX 44-1462-480947; Addr in UK: Current Biology Ltd., 34-42 Cleveland St., London W1P 6LB, England. TEL 0171-323-0323. FAX 0171-636-6911) Ed. Peter Newmark. adv.: B&W page $860, color page $1855; trim 8 1/2 x 11. illus. circ. 9,100. (also avail. in diskette format) **Indexed:** ASCA, Curr.Cont., Ind.Med. (1994-), Neurosci.Cit.Ind., Sport Fish.Abstr., SSCI, Wild.Rev. **Document type:** academic/scholarly publication.
●Also available online.
—BLDSC (3494.651300); ADONIS; CASDDS; CISTI; EMDOCS; Genuine Article; KNAW; SWETS; UnCover. **CCC.**
Description: Directed toward researchers, educators and students of biology. Features original research and reviews of the latest developments in the different specializations within the field.
Refereed Serial

016.6606 UK ISSN 0960-5037
TP248.2 CODEN: CUBIER
CURRENT BIOTECHNOLOGY. 1983. m. £523($940) (effective 1997). The Royal Society of Chemistry, Thomas Graham House, Science Park, Milton Rd., Cambridge CB4 4WF, England.
TEL 44-1223-420066. FAX 44-1223-423429. E-mail: sales@rsc.org; URL: http://chemistry.rsc.org/rsc/. (Subscr. to: Turpin Distribution Services Ltd., Blackhorse Rd., Letchworth, Herts. SG6 1HN, England. TEL 44-1462-672555. FAX 44-1462-480947; U.S. addr.: Publications Expediting, Inc., 200 Meacham Ave., Elmont, NY 11003) Ed. Keith Pimley. adv. **Document type:** abstracting/indexing, bulletin.
●Also available online. Vendor(s): Data-Star (CUBI), Knight-Ridder Information, Inc. (File no.358). Also available on CD-ROM. Producer(s): Knight-Ridder, Inc.
—BLDSC (3494.651500); CISTI.
Formerly (until 1990): Current Biotechnology Abstracts (ISSN 0264-3391)
Description: Reports on the latest scientific, technical and techno-commercial advances in the broad field of biotechnology.

016.57 US ISSN 0011-3409
Z5321 CODEN: CCLSBC
CURRENT CONTENTS: LIFE SCIENCES. Short title: C C: L S. (Includes Author Index and Address Directory, Current Book Contents and Title Word Index) 1958. w. $1015. Institute for Scientific Information, 3501 Market St., Philadelphia, PA 19104.
TEL 215-386-0100. FAX 215-386-2211. (And: Brunel Science Park, Brunel University, Uxbridge UB8 3PQ, England) (also avail. in magnetic tape; diskette format) **Indexed:** Abstr.Bull.Inst.Pap.Chem., Abstr.Hyg., Compumath, Ind.Sci.Rev., Ind.Vet., Sci.Cit.Ind., SSCI. **Document type:** academic/scholarly publication, bibliography. (CTOC,CBIB,LIFE).
●Also available online. Vendor(s): Knight-Ridder Information, Inc. (File no.440), Ovid Technologies, Inc.
Also available on CD-ROM.
—BLDSC (3496.170000); CASDDS; CISTI; KNAW.
Formerly: Current Contents, Chemical, Pharmaco-Medical and Life Sciences.
Description: Lists the tables of contents of the world's leading scientific publications in life sciences including biochemistry, biomedical research, experimental medicine, immunology, microbiology, neuroscience, physiology and toxicology.

016.6606 US ISSN 0958-1669
TP248.13 CODEN: CUOBE3
CURRENT OPINION IN BIOTECHNOLOGY. 1990. bi-m. $350 to individuals (outside N. America £210); institutions $895 (outside N. America £530) (effective 1997). Current Biology Ltd., 400 Market St., Ste. 700, Philadelphia, PA 19106. TEL 800-552-5866. FAX 215-574-2270. E-mail: info@hugo.curbio.com; biomednet@cursci.co.uk. (Dist. by: Turpin Distribution Services Ltd., Blackhorse Rd., Letchworth, Herts. SG6 1HN, England. TEL 44-1462-672555. FAX 44-1462-480947; Addr. in UK: Current Biology Ltd., 34-42 Cleveland St., London W1P 6LB, England. TEL 44-171-323-0323. FAX 44-171-636-6911) Eds. J. Davies, M. Rosenberg. adv.; illus.; pat. circ. 1,000. (also avail. in diskette format) **Indexed:** ASCA, Biol.Abstr., Chem.Abstr., Chem.Cit.Ind., Excerp.Med. (1993-), Ind.Med. (1995-), Int.Abstr.Biol.Sci. **Document type:** academic/scholarly publication.
●Also available online. Vendor(s): OCLC.
Also available on CD-ROM.
—BLDSC (3500.772500); ADONIS; CASDDS; CISTI; Ei; EMDOCS; Genuine Article; SWETS. **CCC.**
Description: Presents review articles followed by annotated bibliographies for researchers and educators in biotechnology. Includes a bibliography of the current world literature published during the previous year.

575.8 US ISSN 0955-0674
QH573 CODEN: COCBE3
CURRENT OPINION IN CELL BIOLOGY. 1989. bi-m. $195 to individuals (outside N. America £110); institutions $595 (outside N. America £350) (effective 1997). Current Biology Ltd., 400 Market St., Ste. 700, Philadelphia, PA 19106. TEL 800-552-5866. FAX 215-574-2270. E-mail: info@hugo.curbio.com; biomednet@cursci.co.uk; URL: http://BioMedNet.com/cig-bin/members1/titles.pl. (Dist. by: Turpin Distribution Services Ltd., Blackhorse Rd., Letchworth, Herts. SG6 1HN, England. TEL 44-1462-672555. FAX 44-1462-480947; Addr. in UK: Current Biology Ltd., 34-42 Cleveland St., London W1P 6LB, England. TEL 44-171-323-0323. FAX 44-171-636-6911) Eds. M. Kirschner, K. Simons. adv.; bibl.; illus. circ. 3,200. (also avail. in diskette format) **Indexed:** ASCA, Chem.Abstr., Curr.Cont., Excerp.Med., Ind.Med., Ind.Sci.Rev., Int.Abstr.Biol.Sci. **Document type:** academic/scholarly publication.
●Also available online. Vendor(s): OCLC.
Also available on CD-ROM.
—BLDSC (3500.773500); ADONIS; CASDDS; CISTI; EMDOCS; Genuine Article; KNAW; SWETS. **CCC.**
Description: Directed toward researchers, educators and students in cell biology. Presents review articles, followed by annotated bibliographies of references consulted. Includes a bibliography of the current world literature published during the previous year.

575.1 US ISSN 0959-437X
QH426 CODEN: COGDET
CURRENT OPINION IN GENETICS & DEVELOPMENT. 1991. bi-m. $195 to individuals (outside N. America £110); institutions $595 (outside N. America £350) (effective 1997). Current Biology Ltd., 400 Market St., Ste. 700, Philadelphia, PA 19106. TEL 800-552-5866. FAX 215-574-2270. E-mail: info@hugo.curbio.com; biomednet@cursci.co.uk; URL: http://BioMedNet.com/cgi-bin/members1/titles.pl. (Dist. by: Turpin Distribution Services Ltd., Blackhorse Rd., Letchworth, Herts. SG6 1HN, England. TEL 44-1462-672555. FAX 44-1462-480947; Addr. in UK: Current Biology Ltd., 34-42 Cleveland St., London W1P 6LB, England. TEL 44-171-323-0323. FAX 44-171-636-6911) Eds. R.A. Laskey, M.P. Scott. adv.; illus. circ. 20,000. (also avail. in diskette format) **Indexed:** ASCA, Curr.Cont., Excerp.Med. (1993-), Ind.Med. (1992-), Ind.Sci.Rev., Int.Abstr.Biol.Sci. **Document type:** academic/scholarly publication.
●Also available online. Vendor(s): OCLC.
Also available on CD-ROM.
—BLDSC (3500.775100); ADONIS; CASDDS; CISTI; EMDOCS; Genuine Article; KNAW; SWETS; UnCover. **CCC.**
Description: Directed toward researchers, educators and students of genetics and development. Presents review articles, followed by annotated bibliographies of references consulted. Includes a bibliography of the current world literature published during the previous year.

BIOLOGY — ABSTRACTING, BIBLIOGRAPHIES, STATISTICS

616.8   US   ISSN 0959-4388
QP351   CODEN: COPUEN
CURRENT OPINION IN NEUROBIOLOGY. 1991. bi-m. $195 to individuals (outside N. America £110); institutions $595 (outside N. America £350) (effective 1997). Current Biology, Ltd., 400 Market St., Ste. 700, Philadelphia, PA 19106. TEL 800-552-5866. FAX 215-574-2270. E-mail: info@hugo.curbio.com; biomednet@cursci.co.uk; URL: http://BioMedNet.com/cgi-bin/members1/titles.pl. (Dist. by: Turpin Distribution Services Ltd., Blackhorse Rd., Letchworth, Herts. SG6 1HN, England. TEL 44-1462-672555. FAX 44-1462-480947; Addr. in UK: Current Biology Ltd., 34-42 Cleveland St., London W1P 6LB, England. TEL 44-171-323-0323. FAX 44-171-636-6911) Eds. A.J. Aguayo, M.C. Raff. adv.; illus. circ. 2,400. (also avail. in diskette format) **Indexed:** ASCA, Compumath, Excerp.Med. (1993-), Ind.Med. (1992-), Neurosci.Cit.Ind., SSCI. **Document type:** academic/scholarly publication.
● Also available online. Vendor(s): OCLC. Also available on CD-ROM.
— BLDSC (3500.775850); ADONIS; CASDDS; EMDOCS; Genuine Article; KNAW; SWETS; UnCover. **CCC.**
    Description: Directed toward researchers, educators and students of neurobiology. Presents review articles, followed by annotated bibliographies of references consulted. Includes a bibliography of the current world literature published during the previous year.

612.015   US   ISSN 0959-440X
QH506   CODEN: COSBEF
CURRENT OPINION IN STRUCTURAL BIOLOGY. 1991. bi-m. $195 to individuals (outside N. America £110); institutions $595 (outside N. America £350) (effective 1997). Current Biology Ltd., 400 Market St., Ste. 700, Philadelphia, PA 19106. TEL 800-552-5866. FAX 215-574-2270. E-mail: info@hugo.curbio.com; biomednet@cursci.co.uk; URL: http://BioMedNet.com/cgi-bin/members1/titles.pl. (Dist. by: Turpin Distribution Services Ltd., Blackhorse Rd., Letchworth, Herts. SG6 1HN, England. TEL 44-1462-672555. FAX 44-1462-480947; Addr. in UK: Current Biology Ltd., 34-32 Cleveland St., London W1P 6LB, England. TEL 44-171-323-0323. FAX 44-171-636-6911) Eds. W.A. Hendrickson, Aaron Klug. adv.; illus. circ. 1,800. (also avail. in diskette format) **Indexed:** ASCA, Chem.Cit.Ind., Curr.Cont., Excerp.Med. (1993-), Food Sci.& Tech.Abstr., Ind.Med. (1995-), Ind.Sci.Rev. **Document type:** academic/scholarly publication.
● Also available online. Vendor(s): OCLC. Also available on CD-ROM.
— BLDSC (3500.779000); ADONIS; CASDDS; CISTI; EMDOCS; Genuine Article; SWETS; UnCover. **CCC.**
    Description: Presents review articles, followed by annotated bibliographies of references consulted; includes a bibliography of the current world literature published during the previous year for researchers, educators and students of structural biology.

011   US   ISSN 0590-4102
CURRENT PRIMATE REFERENCES. 1964. m. $55 to individuals (foreign $77); institutions $66 (foreign $88) (effective 1996). Primate Information Center, University of Washington, 1101 Westlake Ave. N., Seattle, WA 98109. TEL 206-543-4376. FAX 206-616-1540. E-mail: pic@bart.rprc.washington.edu. Ed. Jackie L. Pritchard. adv. circ. 500. **Document type:** abstracting/indexing.
    Description: Indexes all scholarly publications concerned with nonhuman primates. Includes citations to journal articles, books, book chapters, technical reports, and dissertations.

016.57   UK   ISSN 0267-1956
QH320.G7
CURRENT RESEARCH IN BRITAIN. BIOLOGICAL SCIENCES. (Other vols. avail.: Physical Sciences, Social Sciences, Humanities) 1980. a. £90 (foreign £95). Longman Cartermill Ltd., Technology Centre, St. Andrews, Fife KY16 9EA, Scotland. TEL 44-1937-843434. FAX 44-1937-546333. TELEX 557381. Ed. Mike Bale. **Document type:** abstracting/indexing.
● Also available online. Vendor(s): Questel Orbit Inc. (CRIB).
— BLDSC (3501.952500).
    Formerly (until 1985): Research in British Universities, Polytechnics and Colleges. Vol.2: Biological Sciences (ISSN 0143-0734)
    Description: Research guide for those who work in higher education, industry, technology, medicine, science, social sciences, government. Compiles information submitted by over 4,000 departments representing more than 500 institutions.

DIABETES MELLITUS. see *MEDICAL SCIENCES — Abstracting, Bibliographies, Statistics*

576   JA
DOJO BISEIBUTSU KENKYUKAI KOEN YOSHISHU/SOIL MICROBIOLOGICAL SOCIETY OF JAPAN. ABSTRACTS OF THE MEETING. (Text in Japanese) a. 1000 Yen (effective 1997). Dojo Biseibutsu Kenkyukai - Soil Microbiological Society of Japan, Nogyo Kankyo Gijutsu Kenkyujo, 1-1 Kannondai 3-chome, Tsukuba-shi, Ibaraki-ken 305, Japan. Ed. Masanori Saito. **Document type:** proceedings.

016.577   UK   ISSN 0305-196X
QH540
ECOLOGICAL ABSTRACTS. 1974. m. fl.2485($1428) (effective 1998). Elsevier - Geo Abstracts (Subsidiary of: Elsevier Science Ltd.), Regency House, 34 Duke St., Norwich NR3 3AP, England. TEL 44-1603-626327. FAX 44-1603-667934. (Subscr. to: Elsevier Science, Regional Sales Office, P.O. Box 1000 AE Amsterdam, Netherlands. TEL 31-20-4853757. FAX 31-20-4853432; Subscr. in the Americas to: Elsevier Science, Regional Sales Office, Box 945, New York, NY 10159-0945. TEL 212-633-3730. FAX 212-633-3680; Subscr in Australasia and the Far East to: Elsevier Science (Singapore) Pte Ltd, No.1 Temasek Ave., No.17-01 Millenia Tower, Singapore 039192, Singapore. TEL 65-434-3727. FAX 65-337-2230) Ed. P.J. Jarvis. index. circ. 600. (also avail. in microform from UMI; back issues avail.) **Indexed:** Field Crop Abstr., Forest.Abstr., Forest Prod.Abstr., Herb.Abstr., Sport Fish.Abstr., Wild.Rev. **Document type:** abstracting/indexing.
● Also available online. Vendor(s): Knight-Ridder Information, Inc. (File no.292), Questel Orbit Inc. (GEOB).
— BLDSC (3648.850000); CISTI; Linda Hall. **CCC.**
    Description: International abstracting service for ecologists and biologists.

016.57   UK
ECONOMY BULLETINS; a series of current awareness bulletins for researchers in biology and medicine. 1967. m. £80. S U B I S, Mansion House, 19 Kingfield Rd., Sheffield S11 9AS, England. TEL 44-114-2554433. FAX 44-114-2554626. E-mail: subis@sheffac.demon.co.uk; URL: http://www.shef.ac.uk/uni/companies/shap. **Document type:** abstracting/indexing.

EMBASE LIST OF JOURNALS INDEXED (YEAR). see *MEDICAL SCIENCES — Abstracting, Bibliographies, Statistics*

016.57155   UK   ISSN 0957-3518
ENDOTHELIUM. 1990. s-m. (diskette m.). £115 (diskette £120; both £180) (effective 1997). S U B I S, Mansion House, 19 Kingfield Rd., Sheffield S11 9AS, England. TEL 44-114-2554433. FAX 44-114-2554626. E-mail: subis@sheffac.demon.co.uk; URL: http://www.shef.ac.uk/uni/companies/shap. (also avail. in diskette format) **Document type:** abstracting/indexing.
    Description: Current awareness service for researchers. Covers all aspects of endothelial structure and function, including endothelins and EDRF.

595.7 016   US   ISSN 0013-8924
QL461
ENTOMOLOGY ABSTRACTS. 1969. m. $985 (foreign $1095). Cambridge Scientific Abstracts, 7200 Wisconsin Ave., 6th Fl., Bethesda, MD 20814. TEL 301-961-6750. FAX 301-961-6720. E-mail: market@csa.com; URL: http://www.csa.com. Ed. Robert Hilton; Pub. Ted Caris. adv.; index. (also avail. in magnetic tape; back issues avail.) **Indexed:** Cal.Tiss.Abstr., Chemorec.Abstr., Comput.& Info.Sys., Oncol.Abstr., Pollut.Abstr. **Document type:** abstracting/indexing.
● Also available online. Vendor(s): Knight-Ridder Information, Inc. (File no.76/LIFE SCIENCES COLLECTION); STN International (LIFESCI). Also available on CD-ROM. Producer(s): NISC, SilverPlatter Information, Inc.
— BLDSC (3789.550000); CISTI.
    Description: Covers insects, arachnids, myriapods, onychophorans, and terrestrial isopods.

ENTREZ DOCUMENT RETRIEVAL SYSTEM. see *MEDICAL SCIENCES — Abstracting, Bibliographies, Statistics*

ENVIROFICHE. see *ENVIRONMENTAL STUDIES — Abstracting, Bibliographies, Statistics*

ENVIRONMENT ABSTRACTS. see *ENVIRONMENTAL STUDIES — Abstracting, Bibliographies, Statistics*

016.574 016.3337   US
▼**ESSENTIAL ECOLOGY, ZOOLOGY & PLANT SCIENCE ABSTRACTS.** 1995. s-a. $479. National Information Services Corporation (NISC), 3100 St. Paul St., Ste. 806, Baltimore, MD 21218. TEL 410-243-0797. FAX 410-243-0982. **Document type:** abstracting/indexing.
● Available only on CD-ROM. Producer(s): NISC.
    Description: Provides citations and abstracts of papers from major journals in the fields of ecology, zoology and plant science.

ESSENTIAL FISHERIES ABSTRACTS. see *FISH AND FISHERIES — Abstracting, Bibliographies, Statistics*

016.5982   US
▼**ESSENTIAL ORNITHOLOGICAL ABSTRACTS.** 1995. s-a. $479. National Information Services Corporation (NISC), 3100 St. Paul St., Ste. 806, Baltimore, MD 21218. TEL 410-243-0797. FAX 410-243-0982. **Document type:** abstracting/indexing.
● Available only on CD-ROM. Producer(s): NISC.
    Description: Presents full citations and abstracts of research from notable ornithological journals.

016.574   US
▼**ESSENTIAL WILDLIFE & CONSERVATION BIOLOGY ABSTRACTS.** 1995. s-a. $479. National Information Services Corporation (NISC), 3100 St. PAul St., Ste. 806, Baltimore, MD 21218. TEL 410-243-0797. FAX 410-243-0982. **Document type:** abstracting/indexing.
● Available only on CD-ROM. Producer(s): NISC.
    Description: Provides full citations and abstracts from notable journals in the fields of wildlife and conservation biology.

EXCERPTA MEDICA ABSTRACT JOURNALS. see *MEDICAL SCIENCES — Abstracting, Bibliographies, Statistics*

EXCERPTA MEDICA. SECTION 1: ANATOMY, ANTHROPOLOGY, EMBRYOLOGY & HISTOLOGY. see *MEDICAL SCIENCES — Abstracting, Bibliographies, Statistics*

EXCERPTA MEDICA. SECTION 2: PHYSIOLOGY. see *MEDICAL SCIENCES — Abstracting, Bibliographies, Statistics*

EXCERPTA MEDICA. SECTION 4: MICROBIOLOGY: BACTERIOLOGY, MYCOLOGY, PARASITOLOGY AND VIROLOGY. see *MEDICAL SCIENCES — Abstracting, Bibliographies, Statistics*

EXCERPTA MEDICA. SECTION 5: GENERAL PATHOLOGY AND PATHOLOGICAL ANATOMY. see *MEDICAL SCIENCES — Abstracting, Bibliographies, Statistics*

BIOLOGY — ABSTRACTING, BIBLIOGRAPHIES, STATISTICS

016.57   NE   ISSN 0014-4258
                   CODEN: DBITA
EXCERPTA MEDICA. SECTION 21: DEVELOPMENTAL BIOLOGY AND TERATOLOGY. 1961. m. fl.2915($1675) (effective 1998). Elsevier Science B.V., P.O. Box 211, 1000 AE Amsterdam, Netherlands. TEL 31-20-4853757. FAX 31-20-4853432. TELEX 18582 ESPA NL. E-mail: nlinfo-f@elsevier.nl; URL: http://www.elsevier.nl/. (Subscr. in the Americas to: Elsevier Science, Regional Sales Office, Box 945, New York, NY 10159-0945. TEL 212-633-3730. FAX 212-633-3680; Subscr. in Australasia and the Far East to: Elsevier Science (Singapore) Pte Ltd, No.1 Temasek Ave., No.17-01 Millenia Tower, Singapore 039192, Singapore. TEL 65-434-3727. FAX 65-337-2230; Subscr. in Japan to: Elsevier Science Japan, 9-15 Higashi-Azabu 1-chome, Minato-ku Tokyo 106, Japan. TEL 81-3-5561-5033. FAX 81-3-5561-5047) adv.; index, cum.index. **Document type:** abstracting/indexing.
● Also available online. Vendor(s): DIMDI, Data-Star, JICST, Knight-Ridder Information, Inc., Ovid Technologies, Inc.
     Also available on CD-ROM. Producer(s): SilverPlatter Information, Inc.
     —BLDSC (3835.828000); CISTI; Linda Hall. **CCC**.
     Description: Covers both experimental and clinical aspects of embryology and fetal, neonatal development.

573.21 016   NE   ISSN 0014-4266
QH431   CODEN: HUGEA
EXCERPTA MEDICA. SECTION 22: HUMAN GENETICS. 1963. 20/yr. fl.4730($2718) (effective 1998). Elsevier Science B.V., P.O. Box 211, 1000 AE Amsterdam, Netherlands. TEL 31-20-4853757. FAX 31-20-4853432. TELEX 18582 ESPA NL. E-mail: nlinfo-f@elsevier.nl; URL: http://www.elsevier.nl. (Subscr. in the Americas to: Elsevier Science, Regional Sales Office, Box 945, New York, NY 10159-0945. TEL 212-633-3730. FAX 212-633-3680; Subscr. in Australasia and the Far East to: Elsevier Science (Singapore) Pte Ltd, No.1 Temasek Ave., No.17-01 Millenia Tower, Singapore 039192, Singapore. TEL 65-434-3727. FAX 65-337-2230; Subscr. in Japan to: Elsevier Science Japan, 9-15 Higashi-Azabu 1-chome, Minato-ku Tokyo 106, Japan. TEL 81-3-5561-5033. FAX 81-3-5561-5047) adv.; index, cum.index. **Indexed:** A.I.C.P. **Document type:** abstracting/indexing.
● Also available online. Vendor(s): DIMDI, Data-Star, JICST, Knight-Ridder Information, Inc., Ovid Technologies, Inc.
     Also available on CD-ROM. Producer(s): SilverPlatter Information, Inc.
     —BLDSC (3835.838000); CISTI; Linda Hall. **CCC**.
     Description: Covers both clinical and experimental aspects of human genetics; includes genetics of lower animals when potentially relevant to human medicine; congenital defects and malformations; basic genetics such as DNA synthesis, gene structure and regulation, genetics recombination and mutagenesis.

EXCERPTA MEDICA. SECTION 23: NUCLEAR MEDICINE. see *MEDICAL SCIENCES — Abstracting, Bibliographies, Statistics*

EXCERPTA MEDICA. SECTION 27: BIOPHYSICS, BIO-ENGINEERING AND MEDICAL INSTRUMENTATION. see *MEDICAL SCIENCES — Abstracting, Bibliographies, Statistics*

016.572   NE   ISSN 0927-278X
EXCERPTA MEDICA. SECTION 29: CLINICAL AND EXPERIMENTAL BIOCHEMISTRY. 1948. 40/yr. fl.4770($2741) (effective 1998). Elsevier Science B.V., P.O. Box 211, 1000 AE Amsterdam, Netherlands. TEL 31-20-4853757. FAX 31-20-4853432. TELEX 18582 ESPA NL. E-mail: nlinfo-f@elsevier.nl; URL: http://www.elsevier.nl/. (Subscr. in the Americas to: Elsevier Science, Regional Sales Office, Box 945, New York, NY 10159-0945. TEL 212-633-3730. FAX 212-633-3680 57765-337-2230; Subscr. in Australasia and the Far East to: Elsevier Science (Singapore) Pte Ltd, No.1 Temasek Ave., No.17-01 Millenia Tower, Singapore 039192, Singapore. TEL 65-434-3727; Subscr. in Japan to: Elsevier Science Japan, 9-15 Higashi-Azabu 1-chome, Minato-ku Tokyo 106, Japan. TEL 81-3-5561-5033. FAX 81-3-5561-5047) adv./ bk.rev.; charts; index, cum.index. **Indexed:** Chem.Abstr. **Document type:** abstracting/indexing.
● Also available online. Vendor(s): DIMDI, Data-Star, JICST, Knight-Ridder Information, Inc., Ovid Technologies, Inc.
     Also available on CD-ROM. Producer(s): SilverPlatter Information, Inc.
     —BLDSC (3835.824200); CISTI; Linda Hall. **CCC**.
     Former titles (until 1992): Excerpta Medica. Section 29. Clinical Biochemistry (ISSN 0300-5372); Excerpta Medica. Section 29: Biochemistry (ISSN 0014-4339); Which supersedes in part (in 1964): Excerpta Medica. Section 2: Physiology, Biochemistry and Pharmacology (ISSN 0014-4061)
     Description: Covers both clinical chemistry and general biochemistry and includes analytical methods, chemical function tests, enzyme assay, enzyme mode of action studies, biochemical roles in disease, metabolic biochemistry, nutritional analysis and molecular transport.

016.57   UK
EXPRESS BULLETINS; a series of current awareness bulletins for researchers in biology and medicine. 1967. s-m. £105 (diskette £120) (effective 1997). S U B I S, Mansion House, 19 Kingfield Rd., Sheffield S11 9AS, England. TEL 44-114-2554433. FAX 44-114-2554626. E-mail: subis@sheffac.demon.co.uk. **Document type:** abstracting/indexing.

581 635   US   ISSN 1061-9011
Z5353
F P I: FLOWERING PLANT INDEX. 1991. s-a. $120. Andersen Horticultural Library, 3675 Arboretum Dr., Box 39, Chanhassen, MN 55317. TEL 612-442-2440. Ed. Richard T. Isaacson. circ. 45. (back issues avail.)
     Description: Index of plant illustrations.

GAYANA: BOTANICA. see *BIOLOGY — Botany*

GAYANA: OCEANOLOGIA. see *BIOLOGY*

GAYANA: ZOOLOGIA. see *BIOLOGY — Zoology*

GENBANK. see *BIOLOGY — Computer Applications*

575.1   UK   ISSN 0957-3526
GENE EXPRESSION. 1990. m. £80 (effective 1997). S U B I S, Mansion House, 19 Kingfield Rd., Sheffield S11 9AS, England. TEL 44-114-2554433. FAX 44-114-2554626. E-mail: subis@sheffac.demon.co.uk; URL: http://www.shef.ac.uk/uni/companies/shap. **Indexed:** ASCA. **Document type:** abstracting/indexing.
—CCC.
     Description: Current awareness service for researchers. Covers molecular control of gene expression in prokaryotes and eukaryotes.

GENE THERAPY (SHEFFIELD). see *MEDICAL SCIENCES — Abstracting, Bibliographies, Statistics*

575.1 016   US   ISSN 0016-674X
QH431
GENETICS ABSTRACTS. 1968. m. $1035 (foreign $1095). Cambridge Scientific Abstracts, 7200 Wisconsin Ave., 6th Fl., Bethesda, MD 20814. TEL 301-961-6750. FAX 301-961-6720. E-mail: market@csa.com; URL: http://www.csa.com. Ed. Wilma Ek; Pub. Ted Caris. adv.; bk.rev.; abstr.; index. (also avail. in magnetic tape; back issues avail.) **Indexed:** Anim.Breed.Abstr., Cal.Tiss.Abstr., Chemorec.Abstr., Comput.& Info.Sys., Oncol.Abstr., Pollut.Abstr., Weed Abstr. **Document type:** abstracting/indexing.
● Also available online. Vendor(s): Knight-Ridder Information, Inc. (File no.76/LIFE SCIENCES COLLECTION), STN International (LIFESCI).
     Also available on CD-ROM. Producer(s): SilverPlatter Information, Inc.
     —BLDSC (4115.050000); CISTI.
     Description: Covers all aspects of genetics in humans, animals, and plants, with emphasis on molecular genetics.

016.57   UK   ISSN 1351-5284
HELICOBACTER. 1994. s-m. (diskette m.). £90 (diskette £120; both £180) (effective 1997). S U B I S, Mansion House, 19 Kingfield Rd., Sheffield S11 9AS, England. TEL 44-114-255-4433. FAX 44-114-255-4626. E-mail: subis@sheffac.demon.co.uk; URL: http://www.shef.ac.uk/uni/companies/shap. (also avail. in diskette format) **Document type:** abstracting/indexing.
     Description: Current awareness service for researchers in clinical and life sciences.

HELMINTHOLOGICAL ABSTRACTS. see *AGRICULTURE — Abstracting, Bibliographies, Statistics*

016.612   UK   ISSN 1355-4786
Z6663.R4   CODEN: HRUPF8
HUMAN REPRODUCTION UPDATE. 1963. bi-m. £360 (foreign $660) (includes 3 CD-ROMs) (effective 1998). (Reproduction Research Information Service Ltd.) Oxford University Press, Academic Division, Great Clarendon St., Oxford OX2 6DP, England. TEL 44-1865-267907. FAX 44-1865-267485. TELEX 837330-OXPRES-G. E-mail: jnl.info@oup.co.uk; URL: http://www.oup.co.uk/journals. (U.S. subscr. to: Oxford University Press Inc., 2001 Evans Rd., Cary, NC 27513. TEL 800-852-7323. FAX 919-677-1714) Ed. R.G. Edwards; Pub. Julie Hoare. R&P contact: Joolz Longley. adv.; bibl.; s-a. index. circ. 900. **Indexed:** ASCA, Excerp.Med. (1996-), Popul.Ind., Vet.Bull. **Document type:** bibliography.
● Also available online.
     —BLDSC (4336.431500); CISTI; EMDOCS; Genuine Article; Linda Hall; SWETS; UnCover. **CCC**.
     Formed by the 1995 merger of: Oxford Review of Reproductive Biology (ISSN 0955-8713) & Bibliography of Reproduction (ISSN 0006-1565)
     Description: Comprehensive review service of research within the field of human reproduction.

581 011   GW   ISSN 0073-5787
INDEX HEPATICARUM. (Text in English) 1962. irreg. price varies. J. Cramer in der Gebrueder Borntraeger Verlagsbuchhandlung, Johannesstr. 3A, 70176 Stuttgart, Germany. TEL 49-711-625001. FAX 49-711-625005. Eds. P. Geissler, H. Bischler. **Document type:** academic/scholarly publication, abstracting/indexing.

589.2 016   UK   ISSN 0019-3895
SB599
INDEX OF FUNGI. 1940. s-a. £70($125) (effective 1997). CAB International, Wallingford, Oxon. OX10 8DE, England. TEL 44-1491-432111. FAX 44-1491-826090. TELEX 847964 COMAGG G. E-mail: cabi@cabi.org; URL: http://www.cabi.org. (U.S. subscr. to: CAB International, North American Office, 198 Madison Ave., New York, NY 10016. TEL 800-528-4841. FAX 212-686-7993) cum.index every 10 yrs. **Indexed:** Rev.Plant Path. **Document type:** abstracting/indexing.
● Also available online. Vendor(s): DIMDI, European Space Agency, Knight-Ridder Information, Inc., STN International.
     —CISTI; Linda Hall.

INDONESIAN BIOLOGICAL AND AGRICULTURAL INDEX/INDEKS BIOLOGI DAN PERTANIAN DE INDONESIA. see *AGRICULTURE — Abstracting, Bibliographies, Statistics*

BIOLOGY — ABSTRACTING, BIBLIOGRAPHIES, STATISTICS

016.5714   US
INTERNATIONAL BIOPHYSICS CONGRESS. ABSTRACTS. 1961. irreg. $10. Massachusetts Institute of Technology, International Biophysics Congress, Cambridge, MA 02139. Ed. Walter Rosenelith.

016.5736   UK   ISSN 0954-0725
QP251
JOURNAL OF REPRODUCTION AND FERTILITY. ABSTRACT SERIES. 1988. irreg. price varies. Journals of Reproduction & Fertility Ltd., 22 Newmarket Rd., Cambridge CB5 8DT, England. TEL 44-1223-351809. FAX 44-1223-359754. E-mail: jrf@cityscape.co.uk. (Dist. by: Portland Press, P.O. Box 32, Commerce Way, Colchester, Essex CO2 8HP, England. TEL 44-1206-796351) adv. contact: C.H. Clarke. (back issues avail.) **Indexed:** Ind.Med., Sport Fish.Abstr., Wild.Rev. **Document type:** proceedings.
—BLDSC (5049.600500); CISTI; KNAW; Linda Hall.

612   JA
KARUSHUMU SHINPOJUMU KOEN YOSHI/ABSTRACTS OF CALCIUM SYMPOSIUM. (Text in Japanese) 1989. s-a. Karushumu Shinpojumu Un'ei Iinkai - Management Committee of Calcium Symposium, Shokuseikatsu Kenkyukai, 12-19, Nishihonmachi 1-chome, Nishi-ku, Osaka 550, Japan. **Document type:** abstracting/indexing.

KEW RECORD OF TAXONOMIC LITERATURE RELATING TO VASCULAR PLANTS. see *BIOLOGY — Botany*

575
KIKAN KEISEI KENKYUKAI KOEN YOSHISHU/JAPANESE SOCIETY FOR BASIC AND APPLIED ORGAN RESEARCH. ABSTRACTS OF THE MEETING. (Text in Japanese) s-a. Kikan Keisei Kenkyukai - Japanese Society for Basic and Applied Organ Research, Nagoya Daigaku Igakubu, Koku Gekagaku Kyoshitsu, 65 Tsurumaicho, Showa-ku, Nagoya-shi, Aichi-ken 466, Japan.

016.57   JA
KYOKUIKI SEIBUTSU SHINPOJUMU KOEN YOSHISHU/ABSTRACTS OF THE SYMPOSIUM ON POLAR BIOLOGY. (Text in English, Japanese) a. Kokuritsu Kyokuchi Kenkyujo - National Institute of Polar Research, 9-10 Kaga 1-chome, Itabashi-ku, Tokyo 173, Japan. **Document type:** abstracting/indexing.

016.57   US
LIFE SCIENCE BOOK REVIEW. 1991. bi-m. $24. Carolina Press, Box 24906, Winston-Salem, NC 27114. TEL 919-768-9180. Ed. Andrew Goliszek. **Description:** Covers all areas of the life sciences.

016.576   US   ISSN 0300-838X
QR53
MICROBIOLOGY ABSTRACTS: SECTION A. INDUSTRIAL & APPLIED MICROBIOLOGY. 1965. m. $975 (foreign $1085). Cambridge Scientific Abstracts, 7200 Wisconsin Ave., 6th Fl., Bethesda, MD 20814. TEL 301-961-6750. FAX 301-961-6720. E-mail: market@csa.com; URL: http://www.csa.com. Ed.Bd.; Pub. Ted Caris. adv.; bk.rev. (also avail. in magnetic tape; back issues avail.) **Indexed:** Cal.Tiss.Abstr., Chemorec.Abstr., Comput.& Info.Sys., Oncol.Abstr., Pollut.Abstr. **Document type:** abstracting/indexing.
●Also available online. Vendor(s): Knight-Ridder Information, Inc. (File no.76/LIFE SCIENCES COLLECTION), STN International (LIFESCI). Also available on CD-ROM. Producer(s): NISC, SilverPlatter Information, Inc.
—BLDSC (5757.770000); CISTI.
Description: Covers scientific research and practical applications in pharmaceuticals, foods, and agriculture.

589.9   US   ISSN 0300-8398
QR1
MICROBIOLOGY ABSTRACTS: SECTION B. BACTERIOLOGY. 1966. m. $1045 (foreign $1085). Cambridge Scientific Abstracts, 7200 Wisconsin Ave., 6th Fl., Bethesda, MD 20814. TEL 301-961-6750. FAX 301-961-6720. E-mail: market@csa.com; URL: http://www.csa.com. Ed.Bd.; Pub. Ted Caris. adv.; bk.rev.; abstr. (also avail. in magnetic tape; back issues avail.) **Indexed:** Cal.Tiss.Abstr., Chemorec.Abstr., Comput.& Info.Sys., Oncol.Abstr., Pollut.Abstr. **Document type:** abstracting/indexing.
●Also available online. Vendor(s): Knight-Ridder Information, Inc. (File no.76/LIFE SCIENCES COLLECTION), STN International (LIFESCI). Also available on CD-ROM. Producer(s): SilverPlatter Information, Inc.
—BLDSC (5757.780000); CISTI.
Description: Covers clinical applications and pure research in all aspects of bacteriology.

016.576   US   ISSN 0301-2328
QK564
MICROBIOLOGY ABSTRACTS: SECTION C. ALGOLOGY, MYCOLOGY AND PROTOZOOLOGY. 1972. m. $975 (foreign $1085). Cambridge Scientific Abstracts, 7200 Wisconsin Ave., 6th Fl., Bethesda, MD 20814. TEL 301-961-6750. FAX 301-961-6720. E-mail: market@csa.com; URL: http://www.csa.com. Ed.Bd.; Pub. Ted Caris. adv.; bk.rev.; abstr. (also avail. in magnetic tape; back issues avail.) **Indexed:** Cal.Tiss.Abstr., Chemorec.Abstr., Comput.& Info.Sys., Helminthol.Abstr., Oncol.Abstr., Pollut.Abstr., Rev.Plant Path. **Document type:** abstracting/indexing.
●Also available online. Vendor(s): Knight-Ridder Information, Inc. (File no.76/LIFE SCIENCES COLLECTION), STN International (LIFESCI). Also available on CD-ROM. Producer(s): NISC, SilverPlatter Information, Inc.
—BLDSC (5757.790000).
Description: Covers life cycles of algae, fungi, and protozoa, and their interactions with animals and plants.

016.5795   UK   ISSN 1351-5292
MYCOBACTERIA. 1994. s-m. (diskette m.). £90 (diskette £120; both £180) (effective 1997). S U B I S, Mansion House, 19 Kingfield Rd., Sheffield S11 9AS, England. TEL 44-114-255-4433. FAX 44-114-255-4626. E-mail: subis@sheffac. demon.co.uk; URL: http://www.shef.ac.uk/uni/ companies/shap. (also avail. in diskette format) **Document type:** abstracting/indexing.
Description: Current awareness service for researchers in clinical and life sciences.

016.5728   US   ISSN 1060-8788
N C B I NEWS. 1991. 3/yr. free. U.S. National Center for Biotechnology Information, National Library of Medicine, Bldg. 38A, Rm. 8N-803, 8600 Rockville Pike, Bethesda, MD 20894. TEL 301-496-2475. FAX 301-480-9241. E-mail: info@ncbi.nlm.nih.gov. circ. 25,000. **Document type:** newsletter, government publication.
Description: Informs the biomedical community about N.C.B.I. research activities and the availability of molecular biology database and software services.

016.57   US
N T I S ALERTS: MEDICINE & BIOLOGY. w. $140 (foreign $195). U.S. National Technical Information Service, 5285 Port Royal Rd., Springfield, VA 22161. TEL 703-487-4630. FAX 703-321-8547. TELEX 64617. index. (back issues avail.)
Former titles: Abstract Newsletter: Medicine and Biology; Weekly Abstract Newsletter: Medicine and Biology; Weekly Government Abstracts. Medicine and Biology (ISSN 0364-6432)

NEMATOLOGICAL ABSTRACTS. see *AGRICULTURE — Abstracting, Bibliographies, Statistics*

589.9   JA
NIHON ARCHAEBACTERIA KENKYUKAI KOENKAI YOSHISHU/JAPAN SOCIETY FOR ARCHAEBACTERIOLOGY. ABSTRACTS OF ANNUAL MEETING. (Text in Japanese) 1988. a. Nihon Archaebacteria Kenkyukai - Japan Society for Archaebacteriology, Noda Sangyo Kagaku Kenkyujo, 399, Noda, Noda-shi, Chiba-ken 278, Japan. **Document type:** abstracting/indexing.

016.57   JA
NIHON BAIOREOROJI GAKKAI NENKAI SHOROKUSHU/JAPANESE SOCIETY OF BIORHEOLOGY. ABSTRACTS OF THE ANNUAL MEETING. (Text in Japanese) a. Nihon Baioreoroji Gakkai - Japanese Society of Biorheology, Gunma Prefectural Cardiovascular Center, Kho 3-12, Kameizumi-machi, Maebashi, Gunma 371, Japan. Ed. Makoto Kaibara; Pub. Khoichi Taniguchi. **Document type:** academic/scholarly publication.

016.57   JA
NIHON BENTOSU GAKKAI TAIKAI/JAPANESE ASSOCIATION OF BENTHOLOGY. ABSTRACTS OF ANNUAL MEETING. (Text in English, Japanese) 1987. a. Nihon Bentosu Gakkai - Japanese Association of Benthology, Ocean Research Institute, University of Tokyo, Minami-dai, Nakano-ku, Tokyo 164, Japan. TEL 81-3-5351-6469. FAX 81-3-3375-6716. E-mail: sirayama@ori.u-tokyo.ac.jp. **Document type:** abstracting/indexing.

589.9   JA
NIHON BOKIN BOBAI GAKKAI. NENJI TAIKAI YOSHISHU/SOCIETY FOR ANTIBACTERIAL AND ANTIFUNGAL AGENTS, JAPAN. ABSTRACTS OF THE MEETING. (Text in Japanese) a. 3000 Yen (effective 1998). Nihon Bokin Bobai Gakkai - Society for Antibacterial and Antifungal Agents, Japan, 3rd Fl., Shin-Kousan Bldg., 13-38, Nishimotocho 1-chome, Nishi-ku, Osaka 550, Japan. Ed. Tetsuaki Tsuchido; Pub. Hajime Masago. R&P contact: Iwao Yamamoto. adv. contact: Iwao Yamamoto. **Document type:** academic/scholarly publication.

597   JA
NIHON GYORUI GAKKAI NENKAI KOEN YOSHI/ICHTHYOLOGY SOCIETY OF JAPAN. ADVANCE ABSTRACTS FOR THE ANNUAL MEETING. (Text in English, Japanese) a. Nihon Gyorui Gakkai - Ichthyology Society of Japan, Tokyo Suisan Daigaku, 5-7 Konan 4-chome, Minato-ku, Tokyo 108, Japan. **Document type:** abstracting/indexing.

575.1   JA
NIHON IDEN GAKKAI TAIKAI PUROGURAMU YOKOSHU/GENETICS SOCIETY OF JAPAN. ABSTRACTS OF THE ANNUAL MEETING. (Text in English) a. 10000 Yen($130) Nihon Iden Gakkai - Genetics Society of Japan, Kokuritsu Idengaku Kenkyujo, 111 Yata, Mishima-shi, Shizuoka-ken 411, Japan. E-mail: nakata@fupharm.fukuyama-u.ac.jp. (Dist. outside Japan by: Business Center for Academic Societies Japan, 16-9 Honkomagome 5-chome, Bunkyo-ku, Tokyo 113, Japan. TEL 81-3-5814-5811. FAX 81-3-5814-5822) Ed. Atsuo Nakata. R&P contact: Atsuo Nakata. bk.rev. **Document type:** abstracting/indexing, academic/scholarly publication.
Refereed Serial

573.21   JA
NIHON JINRUI IDEN GAKKAI TAIKAI SHOROKUSHU/JAPAN SOCIETY OF HUMAN GENETICS. ABSTRACTS OF THE ANNUAL MEETING. (Text in English, Japanese) a. Nihon Jinrui Iden Gakkai - Japan Society of Human Genetics, Tokyo Ika Shika Daigaku Jinrui Idengaku Kenkyushitsu, 5-45 Yushima 1-chome, Bunkyo-ku, Tokyo 113, Japan. **Document type:** abstracting/indexing.

595.7   JA
NIHON KONCHU GAKKAI TAIKAI KOEN YOSHI/ENTOMOLOGICAL SOCIETY OF JAPAN. ABSTRACTS OF ANNUAL MEETING. (Text in Japanese) a. 5000 Yen membership only. Entomological Society of Japan - Nihon Konchu Gakkai, Kokuritsu Kagaku Hakubutsukan Dobutsu Kenkyubu, 23-1 Hyakuninicho 3-chome, Shinjuku-ku, Tokyo 160, Japan. TEL 03-3364-7129. FAX 03-3364-7104. Ed. Masataka Sato. adv. contact: Hiroshi Kajita. **Document type:** proceedings.
●Also available online.

016.57   JA
NIHON MUKIN SEIBUTSU NOTO BAIOROJI GAKKAI SOKAI NITTEI TO SHOROKU/JAPANESE ASSOCIATION OF GERMFREE LIFE AND GNOTOBIOLOGY. ABSTRACTS OF MEETING. (Text in Japanese) a. Nihon Mukin Seibutsu Noto Baioroji Gakkai - Japanese Association of Germfree Life and Gnotobiology, c/o Ms. Kazuko Adachi, Kobe Gakuin Daigaku Eiyogakubu, Arise, Ikawadanicho, Nishi-ku, Kobe-shi, Hyogo-ken 673, Japan. **Document type:** abstracting/indexing.

BIOLOGY — ABSTRACTING, BIBLIOGRAPHIES, STATISTICS

016.5716   JA
NIHON SAIBO SEIBUTSU GAKKAI TAIKAI KOEN YOSHISHU/JAPAN SOCIETY FOR CELL BIOLOGY. ABSTRACTS OF THE MEETING. (Text in Japanese) a. 4000 Yen. Nihon Saibo Seibutsu Gakkai - Japan Society for Cell Biology, Ogawa Higashi Iru, Shimodachuri Dori, Kamigyi-ku, Kyoto 602, Japan. **Document type:** abstracting/indexing.

612 301   JA
NIHON SEIRI JINRUI GAKKAI TAIKAI SHOROKUSHU/JAPAN SOCIETY OF PHYSIOLOGICAL ANTHROPOLOGY. ABSTRACTS OF THE MEETING. (Text in Japanese) a. Nihon Seiri Jinrui Gakkai, c/o Business Center for Academic Societies Japan, 5-16-9 Honkomagome, Bunkyo-ku, Tokyo 113, Japan. TEL 81-3-5814--5801. FAX 81-3-5814-5820. E-mail: iwanaga@design.ti.chiba.u.ac.jp. **Document type:** abstracting/indexing.

575.1
NIHON SENSHOKUTAI KENSA GAKKAI SHOROKUSHU/JAPANESE ASSOCIATION FOR CHROMOSOME ANALYSIS. ABSTRACT OF ANNUAL MEETING. (Text in English, Japanese) 1988. a. Nihon Senshokutai Kensa Gakkai, c/o Nihon Gene Research Lab's Inc., 3-36, Ohgimachi 2-chome, Miyagino-ku, Sendai-shi 983, Japan. TEL 81-22-238-070. E-mail: kgg0250@niftyserve.or.jp. **Document type:** abstracting/indexing.

581.2 595.7   JA   ISSN 0916-958X
NIHON SHOKUBUTSU BYORI GAKKAI BAIOKONTOROURU KENKYUKAI KOEN YOSHI/PHYTOPATHOLOGICAL SOCIETY OF JAPAN. ABSTRACTS OF THE MEETING OF BIOCONTROL. (Text in Japanese) 1989. a. 1000 Yen. Nihon Shokubutsu Byori Gakkai, Baiokontororu Kenkyukai - Phytopathological Society of Japan, Research Group for Biocontrol, c/o Shokubo Bldg., Komagome 1-43-11, Toshima-ku, Tokyo 170, Japan. TEL 03-3943-6021. circ. 400. **Document type:** abstracting/indexing.

591   ISSN 0917-5725
NIPPON DOBUTSU KODO GAKKAI TAIKAI HAPPYO YOSHISHU/JAPAN ETHOLOGICAL SOCIETY. ABSTRACTS OF MEETING. (Text in Japanese) 1983. a. Nippon Dobutsu Kodo Gakkai - Japan Ethological Society, Kyoto Daigaku Rigakubu Dobutsugaku Kyoshitsu, Kitashirakawa Oiwakecho, Sakyo-ku, Kyoto 606-01, Japan. **Document type:** abstracting/indexing.

612   JA
NO NO IGAKU SEIBUTSUGAKU KONWAKAI SHOROKU/ABSTRACTS OF CONFERENCE ON MEDICINE AND BIOLOGY OF THE BRAIN. (Text in Japanese) 1986. s-a. No no Igaku Seibutsugaku Konwakai, Fujita Gakuen Hoken Eisei Daigaku, Igakubu Seirigaku Kyoshitsu, 1-98, Dengakugakubo, Kutsukakecho, Toyoake-shi, Aichi-ken 470-11, Japan. **Document type:** abstracting/indexing.

612   JA   ISSN 0387-2351
NOVA ANGIOLOGICAE/NOVA ANGIOROJI. (Text in Japanese, English) 1963. bi-m. Japanese College of Angiology - Nihon Myakkan Gakkai, c/o Tokyo Ika Shika Daigaku, Igakubu Dai 2 Geka, 5-45, Yushima 1-chome, Bunkyo-ku, Tokyo 113, Japan. **Document type:** abstracting/indexing.

016.572   US   ISSN 1070-2466
QP551
NUCLEIC ACIDS ABSTRACTS. 1971. m. $885 (foreign $945). Cambridge Scientific Abstracts, 7200 Wisconsin Ave., 6th Fl., Bethesda, MD 20814. TEL 301-961-6750. FAX 301-961-6720. E-mail: market@csa.com; URL: http://www.csa.com. Ed. Wilma Ek; Pub. Ted Caris. adv.; bk.rev.; abstr.; index. (also avail. in magnetic tape) **Indexed:** Comput.& Info.Sys. **Document type:** abstracting/indexing.
●Also available online. Vendor(s): Knight-Ridder Information, Inc. (File no.76/LIFE SCIENCES COLLECTION), STN International (LIFESCI).
Also available on CD-ROM. Producer(s): SilverPlatter Information, Inc.
Former titles (until 1994): Cambridge Scientific Biochemistry Abstracts: Part 2. Nucleic Acids (ISSN 8756-7512); Biochemistry Abstracts: Part 2. Nucleic Acids (ISSN 0143-3318); Nucleic Acids Abstracts (ISSN 0048-1041)
Description: Covers physical, chemical, and biological aspects of nucleic acids and nucleoproteins.

OCEANOGRAPHIC LITERATURE REVIEW. see *EARTH SCIENCES — Abstracting, Bibliographies, Statistics*

OXYTOCIN AND VASOPRESSIN. see *MEDICAL SCIENCES — Abstracting, Bibliographies, Statistics*

578 535 016   FR   ISSN 1146-5395
P A S C A L E 30: MICROSCOPIE ELECTRONIQUE ET DIFFRACTION ELECTRONIQUE. (Printed format ceased Jan. 1995) (Text in English, French) 1984. 10/yr. Centre National de la Recherche Scientifique, Institut de l'Information Scientifique et Technique, 2 allee du Parc de Brabois, 54514 Vandoeuvre-Les-Nancy Cedex, France. TEL 83-50-46-00. FAX 83-50-46-50. (Co-sponsor: Institut de Soudure) adv. contact: Veronique Guinvarc'h. abstr. (also avail. in microfiche) **Document type:** bibliography.
●Also available online. Vendor(s): European Space Agency (File no.14), Knight-Ridder Information, Inc. (File no.144), Telesystemes - Questel.
Also available on CD-ROM.
—CISTI; Linda Hall.
Former titles: P A S C A L Explore. E 30: Microscopie Electronique et Diffraction Electronique (ISSN 0761-2028); P A S C A L Explore. Part 30: Microscopie Electronique et Diffraction Electronique; Which superseded: Bulletin Signaletique. Part 761: Microscopie Electronique. Diffraction Electronique (ISSN 0007-5663)

575.1 016   FR   ISSN 1146-5484
P A S C A L E 58: GENETIQUE. (Printed format ceased Jan. 1995) (Text in English, French) 1984. 10/yr. Centre National de la Recherche Scientifique, Institut de l'Information Scientifique et Technique, 2 allee du Parc de Brabois, 54514 Vandoeuvre-Les-Nancy Cedex, France. TEL 83-50-46-00. FAX 83-50-46-50. adv. contact: Veronique Guinvarc'h. abstr.; index, cum.index. (also avail. in microfiche) **Document type:** bibliography.
●Also available online. Vendor(s): European Space Agency (File no.14), Knight-Ridder Information, Inc. (File no.144), Telesystemes - Questel.
Also available on CD-ROM.
—Linda Hall.
Former titles: P A S C A L Explore. E 58: Genetique (ISSN 0246-1447); P A S C A L Explore. Part 60: Genetique; Which superseded: Bulletin Signaletique. Part 363: Genetique (ISSN 0301-3464)

576.64 615.37 016   FR   ISSN 1146-5492
P A S C A L E 61: MICROBIOLOGIE: BACTERIOLOGIE, VIROLOGIE, MYCOLOGIE, PROTOZOAIRES PATHOGENES. (Printed format ceased Jan. 1995) (Text in French, English) 1961. 10/yr. Centre National de la Recherche Scientifique, Institut de l'Information Scientifique et Technique, 2 allee du Parc de Brabois, 54514 Vandoeuvre-Les-Nancy Cedex, France. TEL 83-50-46-00. FAX 83-50-46-50. adv. contact: Veronique Guinvarc'h. abstr.; index, cum.index. (also avail. in microfiche) **Document type:** bibliography.
●Also available online. Vendor(s): European Space Agency (File no.14), Knight-Ridder Information, Inc. (File no.144), Telesystemes - Questel.
Also available on CD-ROM.
—Linda Hall.
Former titles: P A S C A L Explore. E 61: Microbiologie: Bacteriologie, Virologie, Mycologie, Protozoaires Pathogenes (ISSN 0761-2133); P A S C A L Explore. Part 61: Microbiologie: Bacteriologie, Virologie, Mycologie, Protozoaires Pathogenes; Which superseded in part (in 1984): Bulletin Signaletique. Part 340: Microbiologie - Virologie - Immunologie (ISSN 0007-5450)

613.37   FR   ISSN 1146-5506
P A S C A L E 62: IMMUNOLOGIE. (Printed format ceased Jan. 1995) (Text in French, English) 1961. 10/yr. Centre National de la Recherche Scientifique, Institut de l'Information Scientifique et Technique, 2 allee du Parc de Brabois, 54514 Vandoeuvre-Les-Nancy Cedex, France. TEL 83-50-46-00. FAX 83-50-46-50. adv. contact: Veronique Guinvarc'h. index, cum.index. (also avail. in microfiche) **Document type:** bibliography.
●Also available online. Vendor(s): European Space Agency (File no.14), Knight-Ridder Information, Inc. (File no.144), Telesystemes - Questel.
Also available on CD-ROM.
—Linda Hall.
Former titles: P A S C A L Explore. E 62: Immunologie (ISSN 0761-2141); P A S C A L Explore. Part 62: Immunologie; Which superseded in part (in 1984): Bulletin Signaletique. Part 340: Microbiologie - Virologie - Immunologie (ISSN 0007-5450)

575.1 016   FR   ISSN 1146-5549
P A S C A L E 68: GENETIQUE HUMAINE. (Printed format ceased Jan. 1995) (Text in English, French) 1961. 10/yr. Centre National de la Recherche Scientifique, Institut de l'Information Scientifique et Technique, 2 allee du Parc de Brabois, 54514 Vandoeuvre-les-Nancy Cedex, France. TEL 83-50-46-00. FAX 83-50-46-50. adv. contact: Veronique Guinvarc'h. (also avail. in microfiche) **Document type:** bibliography.
●Also available online. Vendor(s): European Space Agency, Knight-Ridder Information, Inc., Telesystemes - Questel.
Also available on CD-ROM.
Formerly: P A S C A L Explore. E 68: Genetique Humaine (ISSN 0246-1455); Which supersedes in part: P A S C A L Explore. E 60: Genetique (ISSN 0761-2125)

P A S C A L E 84: GENIE BIOMEDICAL. INFORMATIQUE BIOMEDICALE. see *MEDICAL SCIENCES — Abstracting, Bibliographies, Statistics*

016.572   FR   ISSN 1146-5255
P A S C A L F 52: BIOCHIMIE - BIOPHYSIQUE - MOLECULAIRE - BIOLOGIE MOLECULAIRE ET CELLULAIRE. (Printed format ceased Jan. 1995) (Text in English, French) 1984. 10/yr. Centre National de la Recherche Scientifique, Institut de l'Information Scientifique et Technique, 2 allee du Parc de Brabois, 54514 Vandoeuvre-les-Nancy Cedex, France. TEL 83-50-46-00. FAX 83-50-46-50. adv. contact: Veronique Guinvarc'h. index, cum.index. **Document type:** bibliography.
●Also available online. Vendor(s): European Space Agency (File no.14), Knight-Ridder Information, Inc. (File no.144), Telesystemes - Questel.
Also available on CD-ROM.
—Linda Hall.
Former titles: P A S C A L Folio. F 52: Biochimie. Biophysique Moleculaire. Biologie Moleculaire et Cellulaire (ISSN 0761-1897); P A S C A L Folio. Part 52. Biochimie. Biologie Moleculaire et Cellulaire; Which superseded: Bulletin Signaletique. Part 320: Biochimie. Biologie Moleculaire et Cellulaire; Bulletin Signaletique. Part 320: Biochimie. Biophysique Moleculaire (ISSN 0301-0295)

016.571   FR   ISSN 1146-5263
P A S C A L F 53: ANATOMIE ET PHYSIOLOGIE DES VERTEBRES. (Printed format ceased Jan. 1995) (Text in English, French) 1984. 10/yr. Centre National de la Recherche Scientifique, Institut de l'Information Scientifique et Technique, 2 allee du Parc de Brabois, 54514 Vandoeuvre-les-Nancy Cedex, France. TEL 83-50-46-00. FAX 83-50-46-50. adv. contact: Veronique Guinvarc'h. index, cum.index. (also avail. in microfiche) **Document type:** bibliography.
●Also available online. Vendor(s): European Space Agency (File no.14), Knight-Ridder Information, Inc. (File no.144), Telesystemes - Questel.
Also available on CD-ROM.
Former titles: P A S C A L Folio. F 53: Anatomie et Physiologie des Vertebres (ISSN 0761-1900); P A S C A L Folio. Part 64: Anatomie et Physiologie des Vertebres; Which superseded in part: Bulletin Signaletique. Part 365: Zoologie des Vertebres. Ecologie Animale. Physiologie Appliquee Humaine (ISSN 0181-0014); Which was formerly: Bulletin Signaletique. Part 365: Physiologie des Vertebres (ISSN 0301-3472); Which superseded in part: Bulletin Signaletique. Part 360. Biologie et Physiologie Animales.

BIOLOGY — ABSTRACTING, BIBLIOGRAPHIES, STATISTICS

581 016 · FR · ISSN 1146-528X
P A S C A L. F 55: BIOLOGIE VEGETALE. (Printed format ceased Jan. 1995) (Text in English, French) 1984. 10/yr. Centre National de la Recherche Scientifique, Institut de l'Information Scientifique et Technique, 2 allee du Parc de Brabois, 54514 Vandoeuvre-Les-Nancy Cedex, France. TEL 83-50-46-00. FAX 83-50-46-50. adv. contact: Veronique Guinvarc'h. index, cum.index. (also avail. in microfiche) **Document type:** bibliography.
●Also available online. Vendor(s): European Space Agency (File no.14), Knight-Ridder Information, Inc. (File no.144), Telesystemes - Questel.
Also available on CD-ROM.
—Linda Hall.
Former titles: P A S C A L Folio. F 55: Biologie Vegetale (ISSN 0761-1927); P A S C A L Folio. Part 55: Biologie Vegetale; Which superseded in part: Bulletin Signaletique. Part 370: Biologie et Physiologie Vegetales. Sylviculture (ISSN 0240-8546); Bulletin Signaletique. Part 370. Biologie et Physiologie Vegetales (ISSN 0007-5515)

016.577 · FR · ISSN 1146-5298
P A S C A L F 56: ECOLOGIE ANIMALE, VEGETALE ET MICROBIENNE. ETHOLOGIE ANIMALE. (Printed format ceased Jan. 1995) (Text in English, French) 1984. 10/yr. Centre National de la Recherche Scientifique, Institut de l'Information Scientifique et Technique, 2 allee du Parc de Brabois, 54514 Vandoeuvre-Les-Nancy Cedex, France. TEL 83-50-46-00. FAX 83-50-46-50. adv. contact: Veronique Guinvarc'h. (also avail. in microfiche) **Document type:** bibliography.
●Also available online. Vendor(s): European Space Agency (File no.14), Knight-Ridder Information, Inc. (File no.144), Telesystemes - Questel.
Also available on CD-ROM.
—Linda Hall.
Former titles: P A S C A L Folio. F 56: Ecologie Animale et Vegetale (ISSN 0246-1153); P A S C A L Folio. Part 56: Ecologie Animale et Vegetale; Which superseded in part: Bulletin Signaletique. Part 370: Biologie et Physiologie Vegetales; Bulletin Signaletique. Part 365: Zoologie des Vertebres. Ecologie Animale. Physiologie Appliquee Humaine (ISSN 0181-0014)

591 016 · FR · ISSN 1146-5077
P A S C A L. T 260: ZOOLOGIE FONDAMENTALE ET APPLIQUEE DES INVERTEBRES. (Printed format ceased Jan. 1995) (Text in English, French) 10/yr. Centre National de la Recherche Scientifique, Institut de l'Information Scientifique et Technique, 2 allee du Parc de Brabois, 54514 Vandoeuvre-Les-Nancy Cedex, France. TEL 83-50-46-00. FAX 83-50-46-50. (Co-sponsor: Institut National de la Recherche Agronomique) (also avail. in microfiche) **Document type:** bibliography.
●Also available online. Vendor(s): European Space Agency (File no.14), Knight-Ridder Information, Inc. (File no.144), Telesystemes - Questel.
Also available on CD-ROM.
Former titles: P A S C A L Thema. T 260: Zoologie Fondamentale et Appliquee des Invertebres (Milieu Terrestre, Eaux Douces) (ISSN 0761-1714); P A S C A L Thema. Part 260: Zoologie Fondamentale et Appliquee des Invertebres (Milieu Terrestre, Eaux Douces); Which superseded: Bulletin Signaletique. Part 364: Protozoaires et des Invertebres. Zoologie Generale et Appliquee (ISSN 0181-0006); Which superseded: Bulletin Signaletique. Part 360: Biologie Animale. Physiologie et Pathologie des Protozoaires et des Invertebres; Bulletin Signaletique. Part 360. Biologie Animale. Physiologie - Pathologie des Invertebres. Ecologie (ISSN 0301-3456); Bulletin Signaletique. Part 360. Biologie Animale. Physiologie des Invertebres; Bulletin Signaletique. Part 360. Biologie et Physiologie Animale (ISSN 0007-5485).

PARASITOLOGY (SHEFFIELD). see *MEDICAL SCIENCES — Abstracting, Bibliographies, Statistics*

PEPTIDE HORMONE RECEPTORS. see *MEDICAL SCIENCES — Abstracting, Bibliographies, Statistics*

581.133 016 · XR · ISSN 0924-1906
PHOTOSYNTHESIS BIBLIOGRAPHY. (Text in English, French or German) 1974. a. price varies. c/o Zdanek Sestak, Ed., Czech Academy of Sciences, Institute of Experimental Botany, Na Karlovce 1A, 160 00 Prague 6, Czech Republic.
TEL 420-2-3111032. FAX 420-2-24310113. E-mail: sestak@site.cas.cz. cum.index every 5 yrs. circ. 150. (back issues avail.) **Indexed:** Biol.Abstr. **Document type:** bibliography.
Refereed Serial

PLANT BREEDING ABSTRACTS. see *GARDENING AND HORTICULTURE — Abstracting, Bibliographies, Statistics*

581.1505 016 · UK · ISSN 0966-0100
PLANT GENETIC RESOURCES ABSTRACTS. 1992. q. £195($340) (effective 1997). (Commonwealth Agricultural Bureaux, International Board for Plant Genetic Resources) CAB International, Wallingford, Oxon OX10 8DE, England. TEL 44-1491-832111. FAX 44-1491-826090. E-mail: cabi@cabi.org; URL: http://www.cabi.org. (U.S. subscr. to: CAB International, North American Office, 198 Madison Ave., New York 10016. TEL 212-726-6490. FAX 212-686-7993) (also avail. in diskette format; back issues avail.) **Document type:** abstracting/indexing.
●Also available online.

581 016 · RU · ISSN 0208-1547
Z7408.S65
POCHVY, RASTITEL'NYI I ZHIVOTNY MIR SIBIRI I DAL'NEGO VOSTOKA; tekushchii ukazatel' literatury. 1963. bi-m. $60. Rossiiskaya Akademiya Nauk, Sibirskoe Otdelenie, Gosudarstvennaya Publichnaya Nauchno-tekhnicheskaya Biblioteka, 15 Voskhod St., 630200 Novosibirsk, Russia. TEL 3832-66-13-67. FAX 3832-66-03-08. TELEX 133220 LIBRO SU. Ed.Bd.
Formerly (until 1983): Rastitel'nyi Mir Sibiri i Dal'nego Vostoka (ISSN 0320-4316)
Description: Offers an index of books, articles, summaries of reports from conferences and symposia on agronomy, forestry, vegetation of Siberia and Far East.

POLISH JOURNAL OF PATHOLOGY. see *MEDICAL SCIENCES — Abstracting, Bibliographies, Statistics*

PROLACTIN. see *MEDICAL SCIENCES — Abstracting, Bibliographies, Statistics*

PROTOZOOLOGICAL ABSTRACTS. see *MEDICAL SCIENCES — Abstracting, Bibliographies, Statistics*

570 016 · RU · ISSN 0034-2300
QH7 · CODEN: RZBLAS
REFERATIVNYI ZHURNAL. BIOLOGIYA. 1958. m. 619.50 Rub. (861 Rub. including index). Vsesoyuznyi Institut Nauchno-Tekhnicheskoi Informatsii (VINITI), Moscow A-219, Russia. (Subscr. to: Mezhdunarodnaya Kniga, Dimitrova ul. 39, 113095 Moscow, Russia) abstr.; bibl.; index. circ. 2,930. **Indexed:** Apic.Abstr., Biol.Abstr., Chem.Abstr., Helminthol.Abstr. **Document type:** abstracting/indexing.
—CASDDS; Linda Hall.
Formerly: Referativnyi Zhurnal. Biologicheskaya Khimiya (ISSN 0486-2260)

REFERATIVNYI ZHURNAL. BIOLOGIYA SEL'SKOKHOZYAISTVENNYKH ZHIVOTNYKH. see *AGRICULTURE — Abstracting, Bibliographies, Statistics*

016.5714 · RU · ISSN 0202-912X
REFERATIVNYI ZHURNAL. BIONIKA - BIOKIBERNETIKA - BIOINZHENERIYA. 1975. m. 63 Rub. (75.60 Rub. with index). Vsesoyuznyi Institut Nauchno-Tekhnicheskoi Informatsii (VINITI), Baltiiskaya ul. 14, Moscow A-219, Russia. (Subscr. to: Mezhdunarodnaya Kniga, Dimitrova ul. 39, 113095 Moscow, Russia) **Document type:** abstracting/indexing.

016.577 · RU · ISSN 0202-5140
REFERATIVNYI ZHURNAL. EKOLOGIYA CHELOVEKA. 1987. m. $320 (effective 1998). Vsesoyuznyi Institut Nauchno-Tekhnicheskoi Informatsii (VINITI), Baltiiskaya ul. 14, A-219 Moscow, Russia. (Subscr. to: Mezhdunarodnaya Kniga, Dimitrova ul. 39, 113095 Moscow, Russia)

581 016 · RU · ISSN 0202-9235
REFERATIVNYI ZHURNAL. FITOPATOLOGIYA. 1978. m. $171 (effective 1998). Vsesoyuznyi Institut Nauchno-Tekhnicheskoi Informatsii (VINITI), Baltiiskaya ul. 14, Moscow A-219, Russia. (Subscr. to: Mezhdunarodnaya Kniga, Dimitrova ul. 39, 113095 Moscow, Russia) **Document type:** abstracting/indexing.

016.571 · RU · ISSN 0207-141X
REFERATIVNYI ZHURNAL. FIZIOLOGIYA I MORFOLOGIYA CHELOVEKA I ZHIVOTNYKH. 1959. m. 281.40 Rub. (315 Rub. with index). Vsesoyuznyi Institut Nauchno-Tekhnicheskoi Informatsii (VINITI), Baltiiskaya ul. 14, Moscow A-219, Russia. (Subscr. to: Mezhdunarodnaya Kniga, Dimitrova ul. 39, 113095 Moscoe, Russia) **Document type:** abstracting/indexing.

573.21 016 · RU · ISSN 0202-9146
REFERATIVNYI ZHURNAL. GENETIKA CHELOVEKA. 1969. m. $462 (effective 1998). Vsesoyuznyi Institut Nauchno-Tekhnicheskoi Informatsii (VINITI), Baltiiskaya ul. 14, Moscow A-219, Russia. (Subscr. to: Mezhdunarodnaya Kniga, Dimitrova ul. 39, 113095 Moscow, Russia) **Document type:** abstracting/indexing.

575.1 016 · RU · ISSN 0202-9138
REFERATIVNYI ZHURNAL. GENETIKA I SELEKTSIYA VOZDELYVAEMYKH RASTENII. 1978. m. $261 (effective 1998). Vsesoyuznyi Institut Nauchno-Tekhnicheskoi Informatsii (VINITI), Baltiiskaya ul. 14, Moscow A-219, Russia. (Subscr. to: Mezhdunarodnaya Kniga, Dimitrova ul. 39, 113095 Moscow, Russia) **Document type:** abstracting/indexing.

016.5719 · RU
REFERATIVNYI ZHURNAL. OBSHCHIE VOPROSY PATOLOGICHESKOI ANATOMII. 1976. m. 53.80 Rub. (54.60 Rub. including index). Vsesoyuznyi Institut Nauchno-Tekhnicheskoi Informatsii (VINITI), Baltiiskaya ul., 14, Moscow A-219, Russia. (Subscr. to: Mezhdunarodnaya Kniga, Dimitrova ul. 39, 113095 Moscow, Russia) **Document type:** abstracting/indexing.
Formerly: Referativnyi Zhurnal. Obshchie Voprosy Patologii (ISSN 0202-9189)

016.5714 016 · RU · ISSN 0131-355X
QH652.A1 · CODEN: RZRBDD
REFERATIVNYI ZHURNAL. RADIATSIONNAYA BIOLOGIYA. 1973. m. 56 Rub. (60 Rub. including index). Vsesoyuznyi Institut Nauchno-Tekhnicheskoi Informatsii (VINITI), Baltiiskaya ul., 14, Moscow A-219, Russia. (Subscr. to: Mezhdunarodnaya Kniga, Dimitrova ul. 39, 113095 Moscow, Russia) **Indexed:** Chem.Abstr. **Document type:** abstracting/indexing.
—CASDDS; Linda Hall.

REFERATIVNYI ZHURNAL. RASTENIEVODSTVO (BIOLOGICHESKIE OSNOVY). see *AGRICULTURE — Abstracting, Bibliographies, Statistics*

REVIEW OF AROMATIC AND MEDICINAL PLANTS. see *MEDICAL SCIENCES — Abstracting, Bibliographies, Statistics*

616.969 636.089 016 · UK · ISSN 0034-6624
REVIEW OF MEDICAL AND VETERINARY MYCOLOGY. 1943. q. £210($370) (effective 1997). CAB International, Wallingford, Oxon. OX10 8DE, England. TEL 44-1491-832111. FAX 44-1491-826090. TELEX 847964 COMAGG G. E-mail: cabi@cabi.org; URL: http://www.cabi.org. (U.S. subscr. to: CAB International, North American Office, 198 Madison Ave., New York, NY 10016. TEL 212-726-6490. FAX 212-686-7993) circ. 650. (also avail. in diskette format) **Indexed:** Abstr.Hyg., Biol.Abstr., Ind.Vet., Trop.Dis.Bull., Vet.Bull. **Document type:** academic/scholarly publication, abstracting/indexing.
●Also available online. Vendor(s): DIMDI, European Space Agency, Knight-Ridder Information, Inc., STN International.
—BLDSC (7792.000000).
Description: Covers mycoses of man and domestic, farm, and wild animals, along with allergic disorders associated with fungi and poisoning by fungi or mold-contaminated foods.

589.2 UK ISSN 0034-6438
SB599
REVIEW OF PLANT PATHOLOGY; consisting of abstracts and reviews of current literature on plant pathology. 1922. m. £445($780) (effective 1997). CAB International, Wallingford, Oxon. OX10 8DE, England. TEL 44-1491-832111.
FAX 44-1491-826090. TELEX 847964 COMAGG G. E-mail: cabi@cabi.org; URL: http://www.cabi.org. (U.S. subscr. to: CAB International, North American Office, 198 Madison Ave., New York, NY 10016. TEL 212-726-6490. FAX 212-686-7993) adv.; bk.rev.; abstr.; index. circ. 1,950. (also avail. in diskette format) **Indexed:** Abstr.Hyg., Biol.Abstr., Field Crop Abstr., Forest.Abstr., Forest Prod.Abstr., Helminthol.Abstr., Herb.Abstr., Plant Breed.Abstr., Rev.Appl.Entomol., Trop.Dis.Bull., Weed Abstr. **Document type:** academic/scholarly publication, abstracting/indexing.
●Also available online. Vendor(s): DIMDI, European Space Agency, Knight-Ridder Information, Inc., STN International.
—CISTI; Linda Hall.
Formerly: Review of Applied Mycology.
Description: Covers diseases of crop plants, ornamental plants and forest trees caused by fungi, bacteria, viruses, mycoplasma-like organisms, and nonparasitic factors and their control.

SEA GRANT ABSTRACTS; publications from the nation's Sea Grant programs. see EARTH SCIENCES — Abstracting, Bibliographies, Statistics

SEED ABSTRACTS. see AGRICULTURE — Abstracting, Bibliographies, Statistics

SEQUENCES OF PROTEINS OF IMMUNOLOGICAL INTEREST. see MEDICAL SCIENCES — Abstracting, Bibliographies, Statistics

581 JA
SHIDA SHOKUBUTSU BUNKEN MOKUROKU/BIBLIOGRAPHY OF PTERIDOPHYTES BY JAPANESE FERNISTS. (Text in Japanese) a. Nippon Shida no Kai - Nippon Fernist Club, Tokyo Nogyo Daigaku Seibutsugaku Kenkyushitsu, 1-1 Sakuragaika 1-chome, Setagaya-ku, Tokyo 157, Japan. **Document type:** bibliography.

581 574.82 JA
SHOKUBUTSU SOSHIKI SAIBOU BUNSHISEIBUTSU GAKKAI TAIKAI SHINPOJUMU KOEN YOSHISHU/JAPANESE SOCIETY FOR PLANT CELL AND MOLECULAR BIOLOGY. ABSTRACTS OF THE MEETING AND SYMPOSIUM. (Text in English, Japanese) biennial. Nihon Shokubutsu Saibou Bunshiseibutsu Gakkai - Japanese Society for Plant Cell and Molecular Biology, 30-15 Hongo 5-chome, Bunkyo-ku, Tokyo 113-91, Japan. **Document type:** abstracting/indexing.
Formerly: Shokubutsu Soshiki Baiyo Gakkai Taikai Shinpojumu Koen Yoshishu - Japanese Association for Plant Tissue Culture. Abstracts of the Meeting and Symposium.

016.5727 RU ISSN 0202-8980
SIGNAL'NAYA INFORMATSIYA. ENZIMOLOGIYA. 1984. m. 27.80 Rub. Vsesoyuznyi Institut Nauchno-Tekhnicheskoi Informatsii (VINITI), Baltiiskaya ul. 14, Moscow A-219, Russia. (Subscr. to: Mezhdunarodnaya Kniga, Dimitrova ul. 39, 113095 Moscow, Russia) **Document type:** abstracting/indexing.

016.5713 RU ISSN 0233-6618
SIGNAL'NAYA INFORMATSIYA. FIZIOLOGIYA I MORFOLOGIYA CHELOVEKA I ZHIVOTNYKH: KROV' I LIMFA. 1985. m. 9.60 Rub. Vsesoyuznyi Institut Nauchno-Tekhnicheskoi Informatsii (VINITI), Baltiiskaya ul. 14, Moscow A-219, Russia. (Subscr. to: Mezhdunarodnaya Kniga, Dimitrova ul. 39, 113095 Moscow, Russia) **Document type:** abstracting/indexing.
Formerly: Signal'naya Informatsiya. Fiziologiya Cheloveka i Zhivotnykh: Krov' i Limfa (ISSN 0131-6559)

595.7 576 FR
STATION BIOLOGIQUE DE BESSE EN CHANDESSE. ANNALES. (Text in English, French and German) 1966. a. 100 F.($15) Universite Clermont II, Station Biologique Besse, BP 45, 63170 Aubiere, France. Ed.Bd. (back issues avail.) **Indexed:** Biol.Abstr., Bull.Signal, Curr.Adv.Ecol.Sci.

612 JA
TOKYO SHIKA DAIGAKU SEIRIGAKU KYOSHITSU GYOSEKISHU/TOKYO DENTAL COLLEGE. DEPARTMENT OF PHYSIOLOGY. BIBLIOGRAPHY. (Text in English, Japanese) 1964. irreg. Tokyo Shika Daigaku, Seirigaku Kyoshitsu, 2-2, Masago 1-chome, Mihama-ku, Chiba-shi, Chiba-ken 261, Japan. **Document type:** bibliography.

595.7 632.9 016 UN ISSN 0142-193X
TSETSE AND TRYPANOSOMIASIS INFORMATION QUARTERLY. Short title: T T I Q. (Editions in English and French) 1978. q. Food and Agriculture Organization of the United Nations (Rome), Via delle Terme de Caracalla, 00100 Rome, Italy. TEL 57974350. FAX 57975155. abstr.; bibl. **Indexed:** Helminthol.Abstr., Ind.Vet., Rev.Appl.Entomol., Vet.Bull. **Document type:** abstracting/indexing.
Description: Includes abstracts of scientific articles about tsetse and trypanosomiasis.

575.1 US ISSN 0092-5594
RG627
U.S. CENTERS FOR DISEASE CONTROL. CONGENITAL MALFORMATIONS SURVEILLANCE. Key Title: Congenital Malformations Surveillance. q. U.S. Centers for Disease Control, 1600 Clifton Rd., Atlanta, GA 30333. TEL 404-639-3311. stat. **Indexed:** Curr.Lit.Fam.Plan. **Document type:** government publication.
—CISTI.

576 JA ISSN 0082-481X
QR1
UNIVERSITY OF TOKYO. INSTITUTE OF APPLIED MICROBIOLOGY. REPORTS. (Text in English) 1961. a. free. University of Tokyo, Institute of Applied Microbiology - Tokyo Daigaku Oyo Biseibutsu Kenkyujo, 1-1-1 Yayoi, Bunkyo-ku, Tokyo 113, Japan. Ed. Shoji Mizushima. author index; circ. controlled. **Indexed:** JTA.
—KNAW.
Description: Contains abstracts of original papers.

VIROLOGY AND AIDS ABSTRACTS. see MEDICAL SCIENCES — Abstracting, Bibliographies, Statistics

016.3337 574 US ISSN 1070-5007
SK351
WILDLIFE WORLDWIDE. 1992. q. $895. National Information Services Corporation (NISC), 3100 St. Paul St., Ste. 806, Baltimore, MD 21218. TEL 410-243-0797. FAX 410-243-0982. **Document type:** abstracting/indexing.
●Available only on CD-ROM. Producer(s): NISC.
Supersedes in part: Wildlife and Fish Worldwide (ISSN 1046-6479)

581 631.4 016 GW ISSN 0044-3263
QK867 CODEN: ZPBOAL
ZEITSCHRIFT FUER PFLANZENERNAEHRUNG UND BODENKUNDE/JOURNAL OF PLANT NUTRITION AND SOIL SCIENCE. (Text in English and German) 1922. bi-m. DM.595 (foreign DM.625) (effective 1997). (Deutsche Bodenkundliche Gesellschaft, GW) Wiley - V C H, Postfach 101161, 69451 Weinheim, Germany. TEL 49-6201-606147.
FAX 49-6201-606117. TELEX 465516-VCHWH-D. E-mail: subservice@vchgroup.de; URL: http://www.vchgroup.de. (Subscr. in the Americas to: John Wiley & Sons, Inc., 605 Third Ave., New York, NY 10158. TEL 212-850-6645. FAX 212-850-6021) (Co-sponsor: Deutsche Gesellschaft fuer Pflanzenernaehrung) Ed. H. Beringer, W. Fischer. adv.; bk.rev.; abstr.; charts; illus. circ. 900. (also avail. in microfiche from VCI; reprint service avail. from ISI) **Indexed:** ASCA, Biol.Abstr., Chem.Abstr., Crop Physiol.Abstr., Curr.Adv.Ecol.Sci., Curr.Cont., Field Crop Abstr., Food Sci.& Tech.Abstr., Forest.Abstr., Herb.Abstr., Hort.Abstr., Ind.Sci.Rev., Nutr.Abstr., Plant Breed.Abstr., Plant Grow.Reg.Abstr., Sci.Cit.Ind., Sel.Water Res.Abstr., Soils & Fert., Sorghum & Millets Abstr., VITIS, Weed Abstr. **Document type:** academic/scholarly publication.
—BLDSC (9478.500000); CASDDS; CISTI; Genuine Article; Linda Hall; SWETS; UnCover. **CCC**.
Formerly: Zeitschrift fuer Pflanzenernaehrung, Duengung, Bodenkunde.
Description: Covers the entire spectrum of plant nutrition and soil science.

016.57 CC ISSN 1001-1900
ZHONGGUO SHENGWUXUE WENZHAI/CHINESE BIOLOGICAL ABSTRACTS. (Text in Chinese) 1987. m. $100 (annual index $15). Zhongguo Kexueyuan, Shanghai Wenxian Qingbao Zhongxin - Chinese Academy of Sciences, Shanghai Documentation and Information Center, 319 Yueyang Lu, Shanghai 200031, People's Republic of China.
TEL 0086-021-4336650.
FAX 0086-021-4718906. (Co-sponsor: Biology Documentation and Information Network, Chinese Academy of Sciences) Ed. Shen Jingyan. index. circ. 1,500. **Document type:** abstracting/indexing.
●Also available online.

590 016.05 US ISSN 0144-3607
Z7991 CODEN: ZOREAU
ZOOLOGICAL RECORD. (Consists of 27 sections and subsections avail. separately) 1864. a. $3250 (effective 1997). BIOSIS, 2100 Arch St., Philadelphia, PA 19103-1399. TEL 215-587-4847; 800-523-4806. FAX 215-587-2016. E-mail: info@mail.biosis.org; URL: http://www.biosis.org. (And: BIOSIS UK, Garforth House, 54 Micklegate, York, North Yorkshire YO1 1LF, England. TEL 0904-644269. FAX 0904-612793) (Co-publisher: Zoological Society of London, UK) Ed. Marcia Edwards. index. (also avail. in microfilm from UMI; microfiche from BHP; back issues avail.) **Indexed:** Bio-Contr.News & Info., Helminthol.Abstr. **Document type:** abstracting/indexing.
●Also available online. Vendor(s): Knight-Ridder Information, Inc. (File no.185).
Also available on CD-ROM. Producer(s): SilverPlatter Information, Inc.
—BLDSC (9520.000000); CISTI; Linda Hall; SWETS.
Description: Contains a comprehensive index to publications of zoological interest containing material on the biology of an animal, including anatomy, behavior, communication, development, distribution, ecology, evolution, nutrition, systematics and related areas.

590 025 US ISSN 1053-802X
Z699.5.Z66
ZOOLOGICAL RECORD SEARCH GUIDE. 1985. irreg., latest 1997. $85 (effective 1997). BIOSIS, 2100 Arch St., Philadelphia, PA 19103-1399.
TEL 215-587-4847; 800-523-4806.
FAX 215-587-2016. E-mail: info@mail.biosis.org; URL: http://www.biosis.org. (And: BIOSIS UK, Garforth House, 54 Micklegate, York, North Yorkshire YO1 1LF, England. TEL 0904-644269. FAX 0904-612793) **Document type:** abstracting/indexing.
—CISTI; Linda Hall.
Description: Presents an overview of the editorial policies of the Zoological Record, discusses criteria for inclusion of materials, and lists subjects, key words and terms.

590 016.05 US ISSN 1041-4657
Z7991 CODEN: ZRSSEY
ZOOLOGICAL RECORD SERIAL SOURCES. 1988. a., 6th ed., 1996. $60 (effective 1997). BIOSIS, 2100 Arch St., Philadelphia, PA 19103-1399.
TEL 215-587-4847; 800-523-4806.
FAX 215-587-2016. E-mail: info@mail.biosis.org; URL: http://www.biosis.org. (And: BIOSIS UK, Garforth House, 54 Micklegate, York YO1 1LF, England. TEL 0904-644269. FAX 0904-612793) **Document type:** abstracting/indexing.
—BLDSC (9520.030000); Linda Hall.
Description: Comprehensive list of serial publications scanned for Zoological Record. Includes bibliographic details and a list of publishers with their addresses.

BIOLOGY — Bioengineering

A I U M REPORTER. (American Institute of Ultrasound in Medicine) see MEDICAL SCIENCES — Radiology And Nuclear Medicine

ADVANCES IN BIOCHEMICAL ENGINEERING - BIOTECHNOLOGY. see BIOLOGY — Biotechnology

571.43 US ISSN 0360-9960
R856.A1 CODEN: ADBIDL
ADVANCES IN BIOENGINEERING. (Represents Proceedings of annual meetings) a. $40 to non-members; members $20. American Society of Mechanical Engineers, 22 Law Dr., Fairfield, NJ 07007-2300. TEL 800-843-2763. Ed. L. Thibault. illus. **Indexed:** Biol.Abstr., Chem.Abstr.
—CASDDS; Linda Hall. **CCC**.
Refereed Serial

BIOLOGY — BIOENGINEERING

610.28 537 US
ADVANCES IN ELECTROMAGNETIC FIELDS IN LIVING SYSTEMS. 1994. irreg., vol.2, 1997. price varies. Plenum Publishing Corp., 233 Spring St., New York, NY 10013-1578. TEL 212-620-8000. FAX 212-463-0742. TELEX 23-421139. E-mail: books@plenum.com. Ed. James C. Lin. **Document type:** monographic series.
 Description: Presents research on the theory, interactions and applications of electromagnetic fields in biology and medicine.
 Refereed Serial

610.28 US
ALTERNATIVES TO THE USE OF LIVE VERTEBRATES IN BIOMEDICAL RESEARCH AND TESTING. q. National Library of Medicine, Toxicology and Environmental Health Information Program, E-mail: sidney_siegel@occshost.nlm.nih.gov; URL: gopher://gopher.nlm.nih.gov:70/00/teh/animals/.abtehalt.txt. **Document type:** academic/scholarly publication, bibliography.
 ●Available only online.
 Description: Assists in identifying methods and procedures helpful in supporting the development, testing, application, and validation of alternatives to the use of vertebrates in biomedical research and toxicology testing.

ANNALS OF BIOMEDICAL ENGINEERING. see *MEDICAL SCIENCES*

618.178 US ISSN 1064-5462
QH324.2   CODEN: ARLIEY
ARTIFICIAL LIFE. 1994. q. $50 to individuals (foreign $66); institutions $140 (foreign $156); students, retirees $25 (foreign $41) (effective 1997). M I T Press, 5 Cambridge Center, Cambridge, MA 02142-1493. TEL 617-253-2889. FAX 617-577-1545. E-mail: journals-orders@mit.edu; URL: http://www-mitpress.mit.edu. Ed.Bd. R&P contact: Paul Dzug. circ. 1,000 (paid). (also avail. in microfiche from UMI) **Document type:** academic/scholarly publication.
 —BLDSC (1735.045000); CISTI; SWETS; UMI.
 Description: Acts as a primary forum for international scientific and engineering research in the new discipline of synthetic biological work. Covers topics from the origin of life, through self-reproduction, to evolution, growth and development all the way to the dynamics of whole ecosystems. Presents articles and reviews on synthetic approaches to the spectrum of biological phenomena.

610.28 JA ISSN 0913-7556
     CODEN: BMEEEV
B M E: BIO MEDICAL ENGINEERING. (Text in Japanese) 1987. m. 1500 Yen per no. Nihon M E Gakkai - Japan Society of Medical Electronics and Biological Engineering, c/o Nihon Gakkai Jimu Senta, 16-0, Honkomagome 5-chome, Bunkyo-ku, Tokyo 113, Japan. **Indexed:** Chem.Abstr.
 —CASDDS; CISTI.

610.28 JA
BAIOENJINIARINGU SHINPOJUMU RONBUNJU/BIOENGINEERING SYMPOSIUM. (Text in Japanese; summaries in English) 1989. a. 5000 Yen. Nihon Kikai Gakkai - Japan Society of Mechanical Engineers, 4-9 Yoyogi 2-chome, Shibuya-ku, Tokyo 151, Japan.

610.28 574 NE ISSN 0959-2989
R857.M3   CODEN: BMENEO
BIO-MEDICAL MATERIALS AND ENGINEERING; an international journal. 1991. bi-m. fl.740($424) (effective 1997). I O S Press, Van Diemenstraat 94, 1013 CN Amsterdam, Netherlands. TEL 31-20-6382189. FAX 31-20-6203419. E-mail: market@iospress.nl; URL: http://www.iospress.nl/iospress. (Subscr. in U.S. and Canada to: Box 10558, Burke, VA 22009-0558. TEL 703-323-5534. FAX 703-250-4705) Ed. T. Yokobori. (also avail. in microform from UMI; back issues avail.) **Indexed:** Alloys Ind., ASCA, Eng.Mat.Abstr.,Ind.Med. (1992-), Met.Abstr., Met.Abstr.Ind., Nonfer.Met.Alert, PCC Alert, Steels Alert, World Alum.Abstr. **Document type:** academic/scholarly publication.
 —BLDSC (2087.839000); CASDDS; CISTI; Genuine Article; KNAW; UMI. CCC.
 Description: Covers materials and engineering for biological and medical systems.
 Refereed Serial

610.28 PL ISSN 0208-5216
BIOCYBERNETICS AND BIOMEDICAL ENGINEERING. (Text in English; summaries in Polish) 1981. irreg., vol.14, 1994. price varies. (Polska Akademia Nauk, Instytut Biocybernetyki i Inzynierii Biomedycznej) Wydawnictwo Naukow P W N - Polish Scientific Publishers P W N Ltd., Ul. Miodowa 10, 00-251 Warsaw, Poland. TEL 48-22-260207. FAX 48-22-6954288. (Dist. by: Ars Polona, Krakowskie Przedmiescie 7, 00-251 Warsaw, Poland) Ed. Maciej Nalecz. bibl.; illus. circ. 300.
 —BLDSC (2071.225000).
 Description: Publishes original papers on biocybernetics and biomedical engineering.

344 610.28 174 US
BIOLAW: A LEGAL AND ETHICAL REPORTER ON MEDICINE, HEALTH CARE, AND BIOENGINEERING. base vol. (plus m. updates). $415 for Resource Manual, Monthly Updates, & Special Sections; Microfiche Research Supplement $730; combined $865 (back issues per yr. $950). University Publications of America (Subsidiary of: Congressional Information Service), 4520 East-West Hwy., Ste. 800, Bethesda, MD 20814-3389. TEL 301-657-3200; 800-692-6300. FAX 301-657-3203. Ed.Bd. (looseleaf format; also avail. in microfiche; back issues avail.) **Document type:** academic/scholarly publication.
 Incorporates (in 1986): Bioethics Reporter.
 Description: Covers the most recent developments in case law concerning bioethics.

572.43 NE ISSN 0194-2778
BIOMEDICAL ENGINEERING AND COMPUTATION SERIES. 1980. irreg., vol.2, 1980. price varies. Gordon and Breach - Harwood Academic, Amsteldisk 166, 1st Fl., 1079 LH Amsterdam, Netherlands. (Subscr. to: International Publishers Distributor, Box 32160, Newark, NJ 07102. TEL 800-545-8398. FAX 215-750-6343) Ed. D.N. Ghista. (also avail. in microform) **Document type:** monographic series.
 —CCC.
 Refereed Serial

610.28 UK ISSN 1352-7673
BIOMEDICAL SCIENTIST. 1951. m. £48 (effective 1997). I B M S, 12 Coldbath Sq., London EC1R 5HL, England. TEL 44-171-636-8192. E-mail: 101771.3572@compuserve.com. Ed. Roy Owen. circ. 14,000. **Indexed:** CINAHL. **Document type:** academic/scholarly publication.
 —BLDSC (2087.880150).
 Former titles (until 1994): I M L S Gazette (ISSN 0267-2928); Institute of Medical Laboratory Science. Gazette (ISSN 0307-5656); Institute of Medical Laboratory Technology. Gazette (ISSN 0020-2959)
 Description: Provides professional information for biomedical laboratory scientists.

572.43 US ISSN 1059-0153
QP517.B56   CODEN: BIMIEL
BIOMIMETICS. 1992. q. $165 (foreign $195) (effective 1997). Plenum Publishing Corp., 233 Spring St., New York, NY 10013-1578. TEL 212-620-8000. FAX 212-463-0742. TELEX 23-421139. Eds. J.F. Vincent, A.V. Srinivasan. bk.rev. **Indexed:** Alloys Ind., Eng.Mat.Abstr., INSPEC (1992-), Met.Abstr.Ind., Met.Abstr., Nonfer.Met.Alert, PCC Alert, Steels Alert, World Alum.Abstr. **Document type:** academic/scholarly publication.
 —BLDSC (2089.213000); AskIEEE; CASDDS; CISTI; Ei; KR SourceOne; SWETS; UMI. CCC.
 Description: Covers research in the morphology and mechanics of non-medical structural biological materials, including mechanical and chemical analysis of materials, development and production of materials based on direct biomimicry, and designing of novel synthetic materials.
 Refereed Serial

BIOTECHNOLOGY ADVANCES; research reviews and patent abstracts. see *BIOLOGY — Biotechnology*

BIOTECHNOLOGY AND BIOENGINEERING. see *BIOLOGY — Biotechnology*

BIOTECHNOLOGY AND GENETIC ENGINEERING REVIEWS. see *BIOLOGY — Biotechnology*

BIOTEKHNOLOGIYA. see *BIOLOGY — Biotechnology*

BIOTRONICS; environment control and environmental biology. see *BIOLOGY — Biotechnology*

C A S BIOTECH UPDATES. D N A & R N A PROBES. see *BIOLOGY — Abstracting, Bibliographies, Statistics*

C A S BIOTECH UPDATES. D N A FORMATION & REPAIR. see *BIOLOGY — Abstracting, Bibliographies, Statistics*

C A S BIOTECH UPDATES. GENETIC ENGINEERING. see *BIOLOGY — Abstracting, Bibliographies, Statistics*

C A S BIOTECH UPDATES. NUCLEIC ACID & PROTEIN SEQUENCES. see *BIOLOGY — Abstracting, Bibliographies, Statistics*

610.28 US
C R I S P: BIOMEDICAL RESEARCH INFORMATION ON C D - R O M. 1994. q. $87 (foreign $108.75). (U.S. Department of Health and Human Services) U.S. Government Printing Office, c/o Superintendent of Documents, Washington, DC 20242. (Subscr. to: Superintendent of Documents, U.S. Government Printing Office, Box 371954, Pittsburgh, PA 15250-7954. TEL 202-512-1800. FAX 202-512-2250) (back issues avail.) **Document type:** government publication.
 ●Available only on CD-ROM.
 Description: Presents project and administrative information on current N.I.H. biomedical research projects.

660 UK ISSN 1357-5481
     CODEN: JCEEFG
▼**CELLULAR ENGINEERING.** 1995. q. £205 (effective 1997). INSPEC, I.E.E., Michael Faraday House, Six Hills Way, Stevenage, Herts SG1 2AY, England. TEL 44-1438-767266. FAX 44-1438-742792. E-mail: inspec@iee.org.uk; URL: http://www.iee.org.uk. (Subscr. to: Publications Sales Dept., P.O. Box 96, Stevenage, Herts SG1 2SD, England. TEL 44-1438-313311; Subscr. in U.S. to: INSPEC Dept., IEEE, 445 Hoes Ln., Box 1331, Piscataway, NJ 08855-1331. TEL 908-562-5553. FAX 908-562-8737) (Co-sponsor: International Federation for Medical and Biological Engineering) Ed. Peter Rolfe. (back issues avail.) **Document type:** academic/scholarly publication.
 —AskIEEE; CASDDS; CISTI; KR SourceOne.
 Previously announced as: Journal of Cellular Engineering (Incorporating Molecular Engineering).

662 CI ISSN 0352-9568
     CODEN: CBEQEZ
CHEMICAL AND BIOCHEMICAL ENGINEERING QUARTERLY. (Text in English; summaries in Croatian and English) 1987. q. $40. Savez Kemicara i Tehnologa Hrvatske, Berislaviceva 6-1, P.O. Box 697, 41000 Zagreb, Croatia. Ed. Egon Bauman. adv.; bk.rev.; charts; illus. circ. 1,500. **Indexed:** ASCA, Curr.Biotech.Abstr., T.C.E.A.
 —BLDSC (3137.530500); CASDDS; CISTI; Ei; Genuine Article; UnCover.

CHEMICAL AND BIOLOGICAL DEFENSE INFORMATION ANALYSIS CENTER. NEWSLETTER. see *ENGINEERING — Chemical Engineering*

CHEMICAL ENGINEERING JOURNAL AND BIOCHEMICAL ENGINEERING JOURNAL; an international journal of research and development. see *ENGINEERING — Chemical Engineering*

572.43 NE ISSN 1025-5842
▼**COMPUTER METHODS IN BIOMECHANICS AND BIOMEDICAL ENGINEERING.** 1997. q. $80 (effective 1998). Gordon and Breach - Harwood Academic, Amsteldisk 166, 1st Fl., 1079 LH Amsterdam, Netherlands. (Subscr. to: International Publishers Distributor, Box 32160, Newark, NJ 07102. TEL 800-545-8398. FAX 215-750-6343) Eds. John Middleton, Nigel Shrive.
 Description: Focuses on the importance of integrating the disciplines of engineering with medical technology and clinical expertise.

BIOLOGY — BIOENGINEERING

610.28 US
R856.A1 CODEN: CRBEDR
CRITICAL REVIEWS IN BIOMEDICAL ENGINEERING. 1974. bi-m. $99.95 to individuals; institutions $540 (effective 1997). Begell House Inc., 79 Madison Ave., Ste. 1205, New York, NY 10016-7892. TEL 212-725-1999. FAX 212-213-8368. E-mail: begellhouse@worldnet.att.net. Ed. John R. Bourne. R&P contact: Jim Kelly. adv. contact: Jm Kelly. bibl.; charts; illus. circ. 680. (back issues avail.) **Indexed:** ASCA, Bioeng.Abstr., Biol.Abstr., Curr.Adv.Ecol.Sci., Curr.Cont., Excerp.Med., Ind.Med., Ind.Sci.Rev., INSPEC. **Document type:** academic/scholarly publication.
—BLDSC (3487.472300); AskIEEE; CISTI; EMDOCS; Genuine Article; KNAW; KR SourceOne; Linda Hall; SWETS; UnCover. **CCC.**
Former titles: C R C Critical Reviews in Biomedical Engineering (ISSN 0278-940X); Critical Reviews in Bioengineering (ISSN 0731-6984); C R C Critical Reviews in Bioengineering (ISSN 0045-642X)
Description: Critically surveys the wide range of research and applied activities in this field.
Refereed Serial

CRITICAL REVIEWS IN CLINICAL LABORATORY SCIENCES. see *MEDICAL SCIENCES*

572.43 NE **ISSN 0166-0861**
CODEN: DBBID6
DEVELOPMENTS IN BIOENERGETICS AND BIOMEMBRANES. (Text in English) 1977. irreg., vol.7, 1988. price varies. Elsevier Science B.V., Books Division, P.O. Box 211, 1000 AE Amsterdam, Netherlands. TEL 31-20-4853911. FAX 31-20-4853705. TELEX 18582 ESPA NL. E-mail: nlinfo-f@elsevier.nl; usinfo-f@elsevier.com; forinfo-kyf04035@niftyserve.or.jp; URL: http://www.elsevier.nl/. (Subscr. in the Americas to: Elsevier Science, Regional Sales Office, Box 945, New York, NY 10159-0945. TEL 212-633-3730. FAX 212-633-3680; Subscr. in Australasia and the Far East to: Elsevier Science (Singapore) Pte Ltd, No.1 Temasek Ave., No.17-01 Millenia Tower, Singapore 039192, Singapore. TEL 65-434-3727. FAX 65-337-2230; Subscr. in Japan to: Elsevier Science Japan, 9-15 Higashi-Azabu 1-chome, Minato-ku, Tokyo 106, Japan. TEL 81-3-5561-5033. FAX 81-3-5561-5047) (back issues avail.) **Indexed:** Chem.Abstr. **Document type:** monograph series.
—CASDDS; CISTI. **CCC.**
Refereed Serial

EUROPEAN SYMPOSIUM ON BIOCHEMICAL ENGINEERING SCIENCE. PROCEEDINGS. see *ENGINEERING — Chemical Engineering*

610.28 US
FOUNDATION FOR BIOMEDICAL RESEARCH. NEWS. 1984. bi-m. $25. Foundation for Biomedical Research, 818 Connecticut Ave. N.W., 3rd Fl., Washington, DC 20006. TEL 202-457-0654. FAX 202-457-0659. circ. 1,800. (looseleaf format; back issues avail.) **Document type:** newsletter.
Formerly (until May 1993): Foundation for Biomedical Research. Newsletter.

610.28 NE **ISSN 0921-3775**
CODEN: FMBEEQ
FRONTIERS OF MEDICAL AND BIOLOGICAL ENGINEERING. (Text in English) 1988. q. DM.420 (effective 1997). (Japan Society of Medical Electronics and Biomedical Engineering, JA) V S P, P.O. Box 346, 3700 AH Zeist, Netherlands. TEL 31-30-6925790. FAX 31-30-6932081. E-mail: 100341.2372@compuserve.com. Ed. T. Togawa. (back issues avail.) **Document type:** academic/scholarly publication.
—BLDSC (4042.037000); KNAW.
Description: Covers the field of medical and biological engineering in the broadest sense, including clinical, industrial and technical data and applications.

660 574 UK **ISSN 0959-020X**
TP248.13 CODEN: GEBIER
THE GENETIC ENGINEER AND BIOTECHNOLOGIST. (Free supplement avail.: European Bio Patent Watch) 1981. q. £52($104) to individuals; institutions £228 ($436) (effective 1997). (G B Biotechnology Ltd.) Carfax Publishing Co., P.O. Box 25, Abingdon, Oxon. OX14 3UE, England. TEL 44-1235-401000. FAX 44-1235-401550. E-mail: enquiries@carfax.co.uk. (Subscr. in N. America to: Carfax Publishing Co., 875-81 Massachusetts Ave., Cambridge, MA 02139. TEL 800-354-1420. FAX 617-354-6875) Ed. Caroline MacDonald. adv.; bk.rev. **Indexed:** Agri.Eng.Abstr., ASCA, Curr.Adv.Biochem., Curr.Biotech.Abstr., Food Sci.& Tech.Abstr., SSCI, Telegen. **Document type:** academic/scholarly publication.
—BLDSC (4111.845500); ADONIS; CASDDS; CISTI; Ei; Genuine Article; UMI. **CCC.**
Former titles (until 1990): International Industrial Biotechnology (ISSN 0269-7815); (until 1986): Industrial Biotechnology (ISSN 0268-3024); (until 1985): Industrial Biotechnology Wales (ISSN 0266-9854)
Description: Contains news, articles and original papers on developments and research in biotechnology and genetic engineering.
Refereed Serial

610.28 600 US **ISSN 0739-5175**
R856.A1 CODEN: IEMBDE
I E E E ENGINEERING IN MEDICINE AND BIOLOGY MAGAZINE. bi-m. $145 to non-members (effective 1998). (I E E E, Engineering in Medicine and Biology Society) Institute of Electrical and Electronics Engineers, Inc., 345 E. 47th St., New York, NY 10017-2394. TEL 732-981-0060; 800-678-4333. FAX 732-981-9667. E-mail: customer.service@ieee.org; URL: http://www.ieee.org. (Subscr. to: 445 Hoes Ln., Box 1331, Piscataway, NJ 08855-1331) Ed. Dr. A.S. Wald. adv.; bk.rev.; charts; illus.; pat.; index. (also avail. in microform; back issues avail.) **Indexed:** Bioeng.Abstr., Curr.Cont., Excerp.Med., INSPEC, SSCI.
—BLDSC (4362.927800); AskIEEE; CISTI; Ei; EMDOCS; Genuine Article; KNAW; KR SourceOne; SWETS; UMI; UnCover. **CCC.**
Formerly (until June 1982): Engineering in Medicine and Biology; Supersedes (1962-19??): I E E E - E M B S Newsletter.
Description: Technical, short items on current technologies and methods used in biomedical and clinical engineering. Includes news items and correspondence.

610.28 US **ISSN 0018-9294**
R895.A1 CODEN: IEBEAX
I E E E TRANSACTIONS ON BIOMEDICAL ENGINEERING. 1953. m. $450 to non-members (effective 1998). (I E E E, Engineering in Medicine and Biology Society) Institute of Electrical and Electronics Engineers, Inc., 345 E. 47th St., New York, NY 10017-2394. TEL 732-981-0060; 800-678-4333. FAX 732-981-9667. E-mail: customer.service@ieee.org; URL: http://www.ieee.org. (Subscr. to: Box 1331, 445 Hoes Lane, Piscataway, NJ 08855-1331) Ed. Michael R. Neuman. bk.rev.; abstr.; illus.; index. (also avail. in microform) **Indexed:** A.S.& T.Ind., Appl.Mech.Rev., ASCA, Bioeng.Abstr., Biol.Abstr., Biostat., Chem.Abstr., Compumath, Curr.Adv.Ecol.Sci., Curr.Cont., Deep Sea Res.& Oceanogr.Abstr., Dent.Ind., Eng.Ind., Ergon.Abstr., Excerp.Med., Ind.Med., Ind.Sci.Rev., INIS Atomind., INSPEC, Int.Aerosp.Abstr., Math.R., Neurosci.Cit.Ind., Psychol.Abstr., Sci.Cit.Ind., SSCI.
—BLDSC (4363.152000); AskIEEE; CASDDS; CISTI; Ei; Genuine Article; KNAW; KR SourceOne; Linda Hall; SWETS; UMI; UnCover. **CCC.**
Former titles (until 1963): I E E E Transactions on Bio-Medical Electronics; (until 1962): I R E Transactions on Bio-Medical Electronics; (until 1960): I R E Transactions on Medical Electronics; (until 1955): Professional Group on Medical Electronics. Transactions.
Description: Focuses on concepts and methods of the physical and engineering sciences applied in biology and medicine.

572.43 US **ISSN 1063-6528**
RM950 CODEN: IEEREN
I E E E TRANSACTIONS ON REHABILITATION ENGINEERING. 1993. q. $180 to non-members (effective 1998). Institute of Electrical and Electronics Engineers, Inc., 345 E. 47th St., New York, NY 10017-2394. TEL 732-981-0060; 800-678-4333. FAX 732-981-9667. E-mail: customer.service@ieee.org; URL: http://www.ieee.org. (Subscr. to: Box 1331, 445 Hoes Lane, Piscataway, NJ 08855-1331) Ed. Charles J. Robinson. adv. **Indexed:** ASCA, Excerpt.Med. (1996-).
—BLDSC (4363.218500); AskIEEE; CISTI; Ei; Genuine Article; KR SourceOne; SWETS; UMI; UnCover. **CCC.**
Description: Covers human performance measurement and analysis, nerve stimulation, motor control and simulation, biomechanics, signal processing, hardware and software for rehabilitation engineering applications.

610 574 UK
I F M B E NEWS. (Supplement to: Medical and Biological Engineering and Computing (ISSN 0140-0118)) 1977. bi-m. (International Federation for Medical and Biological Engineering) INSPEC, I.E.E., Michael Faraday House, Six Hills Way, Stevenage, Herts SG1 2AY, England. TEL 44-1438-767266. FAX 44-1438-742849. E-mail: inspec@iee.org.uk; URL: http://www.iee.org.uk. Ed. Peter Rolfe. **Document type:** academic/scholarly publication.
—KNAW.
Formerly (until 1995): M B E C News (ISSN 0140-0134)

610.28 UK **ISSN 0954-4119**
R856.A1 CODEN: PIHMEQ
INSTITUTION OF MECHANICAL ENGINEERS. PROCEEDINGS. PART H: JOURNAL OF ENGINEERING IN MEDICINE. 1971. bi-m. $471 in the Americas (rest of world £269) for Part H; $3483 in the Americas (rest of the world £1990) for parts A-J (effective 1997). Mechanical Engineering Publications Ltd., Northgate Ave., Bury St. Edmunds, Suffolk IP32 6BW, England. TEL 44-1284-763277. FAX 44-1284-704006. E-mail: sales@imeche.org.uk. Ed. A. Unsworth. adv.; illus. circ. 668. (also avail. in microform from UMI; reprint service avail. from UMI) **Indexed:** Alloys Ind., ASCA, Bioeng.Abstr., Dent.Ind., Eng.Ind., Eng.Mat.Abstr., Excerp.Med., Fluidex, Ind.Med., INSPEC, ISMEC, Met.Abstr.Ind., Met.Abstr., Nonfer.Met.Alert, PCC Alert, Steels Alert, World Alum.Abstr. **Document type:** academic/scholarly publication, proceedings.
—BLDSC (6724.900900); AskIEEE; CISTI; Ei; EMDOCS; Genuine Article; KNAW; KR SourceOne; Linda Hall; SWETS; UMI. **CCC.**
Formerly: Engineering in Medicine (ISSN 0046-2039)
Description: Publishes scholarly research articles on theoretical and experimental application in joint and bone replacement prosthetics, mechanical coupling, and ambulatory design; with reviews of supplies and medical equipment; and announcements of conferences, seminars, and exhibitions.

610.28 JA **ISSN 0910-1705**
IYO KOGAKU KENKYU SHISETSU HOKOKU/TOKYO WOMEN'S MEDICAL COLLEGE. INSTITUTE OF BIOMEDICAL ENGINEERING. REPORTS. (Text in English, Japanese) 1976. a. Tokyo Joshi Ika Daigaku, Iyo Kogaku Kenkyu Shisetsu, 10, Kawadacho, Shinjuku-ku, Tokyo 162, Japan.
—BLDSC (7520.276000).

JOURNAL OF BIOMECHANICS. see *MEDICAL SCIENCES*

BIOLOGY — BIOLOGICAL CHEMISTRY

610.28 US ISSN 0363-8855
R856.A1 CODEN: JCEND7
JOURNAL OF CLINICAL ENGINEERING. 1976. bi-m. $185 to individuals (foreign $225); institutions $225 (foreign $245) (effective 1998); newsstand price: $41. Lippincott - Raven Publishers (Subsidiary of: Wolters Kluwer N.V.), 227 E. Washington Sq., Philadelphia, PA 19106-3780. TEL 215-238-4200. URL: http://www.lrpub.com/jce. Ed. Timothy Baker; Pub. Michael Randers-Pehrson. adv. contact: Ray Thibodeau. bk.rev.; charts; illus.; tr.lit.; index. circ. 2,526. (also avail. in microform from UMI; back issues avail.) **Indexed:** Abstr.Health Care Manage.Stud., Bioeng.Abstr., Biol.Abstr., Excerp.Med., Hosp.Lit.Ind., INSPEC (1979-). **Document type:** academic/scholarly publication, newsletter.
●Also available online.
—BLDSC (4958.420000); AskIEEE; CISTI; Ei; EMDOCS; KNAW; KR SourceOne; Linda Hall; SWETS; UMI; UnCover. **CCC.**
Description: Publishes professional papers covering advances in, and practical aspects of, clinical and biomedical engineering.
Refereed Serial

660 JA ISSN 0922-338X
QR151 CODEN: JFBIEX
JOURNAL OF FERMENTATION AND BIOENGINEERING. (Text in English) 1925. m. fl.1713($984) (effective 1998). Society of Fermentation and Bioengineering, Japan, c/o Osaka Daigaku Kogakubu, 2-1 Yamadaoka, Suita-shi, Osaka-fu 565, Japan. TEL 81-6-877-5111. FAX 81-6-879-2034. E-mail: sfbj@iijnet.or.jp. (Dist. outside Japan by: Elsevier Science B.V., P.O. Box 2227, 1000 CE Amsterdam, Netherlands. TEL 31-20-4853642. FAX 31-20-4853598; Subscr. in U.S. and Canada to: Elsevier Science Inc., Journal Information Center, 655 Ave. of the Americas, New York, NY 10010. TEL 212-633-3750. FAX 212-633-3990) Ed. Itaru Urabe; Pub. Shiro Nagai. adv. contact: Takekuma Kuroki. index. **Indexed:** ASCA, Biol.Abstr., Biotech.Abstr., Chem.Abstr., Chem.Cit.Ind., Compumath, Curr.Adv.Biochem., Curr.Adv.Genetics & Molec.Biol., Curr.Biotech.Abstr., Curr.Cont., Dairy Sci.Abstr., Energy Ind., Energy Info.Abstr., Excerp.Med., Food Sci.& Tech.Abstr., Ind.Sci.Rev., INIS Atomind., JTA, Potato Abstr., Rice Abstr., Sci.Cit.Ind., Sel.Water Res.Abstr., Soils & Fert., Sugar Ind.Abstr. **Document type:** academic/scholarly publication.
—BLDSC (4983.997000); ADONIS; CASDDS; CISTI; Ei; EMDOCS; Genuine Article; Linda Hall; SWETS; UnCover. **CCC.**
Formerly: Journal of Fermentation Technology (ISSN 0385-6380)
Description: Publishes original research papers, review articles and letters concerning fermentation technology, biochemical technology, food technology and microbiology.
Refereed Serial

610 574 UK ISSN 0140-0118
R895.A1 CODEN: MBECDY
MEDICAL & BIOLOGICAL ENGINEERING & COMPUTING. (Supplement avail.: M B E C News (ISSN 0140-0134)) 1962. bi-m. £330 (effective 1997). (International Federation for Medical and Biological Engineering) INSPEC, I.E.E., Michael Faraday House, Six Hills Way, Stevenage, Herts SG1 2AY, England. TEL 44-1438-767266. FAX 44-1438-742849. E-mail: inspec@iee.org.uk; URL: http://www.iee.org.uk. (Subscr. to: Box 96, Stevenage, Herts. SG1 2SD, England. TEL 44-1438-3133311. FAX 44-1438-742792; US addr.: IEEE, 445 Hoes Ln., Box 1331, Piscataway, NJ 08855-1331. TEL 908-562-5553. FAX 908-562-8737) Ed. Peter Rolfe. adv.; bk.rev.; abstr.; bibl.; charts; illus.; index. circ. 1,300. (also avail. in microform from UMI) **Indexed:** A.S.& T.Ind., Appl.Mech.Rev., ASCA, Bioeng.Abstr., Biol.Abstr., Chem.Abstr., Chem.Cit.Ind., Compumath, Comput.Cont., Curr.Adv.Ecol.Sci., Curr.Cont., Cyb.Abstr., Eng.Ind., Ergon.Abstr., Excerp.Med., Ind.Med., Ind.Sci.Rev., INSPEC, Mass Spectr.Bull., Neurosci.Cit.Ind., Sci.Cit.Ind., SSCI, Vet.Bull. **Document type:** academic/scholarly publication.
—BLDSC (5525.770000); AskIEEE; CASDDS; CISTI; Ei; Genuine Article; KNAW; KR SourceOne; Linda Hall; SWETS; UMI; UnCover. **CCC.**
Former titles: Medical and Biological Engineering (ISSN 0025-696X); Biological Engineering; Medical Electronics.
Description: Contains technical papers on subjects such as medical electronics, biomechanics, medical computing, patient monitoring, nuclear medicine, imaging, rehabilitation and biosensors.

MEDICAL PROGRESS THROUGH TECHNOLOGY; signal processing - imaging systems - assist systems - implants - sensors and instrumentation - computers. see *BIOLOGY — Biotechnology*

610.28 US ISSN 0277-1063
CODEN: BENYDB
NORTHEAST BIOENGINEERING CONFERENCE. PROCEEDINGS. Key Title: Bioengineering. (Conferences prior to 1982 published by Pergamon Press plc; conferences not held 1983-1984) 1973. a. price varies. Institute of Electrical and Electronics Engineers, Inc., 345 E. 47th St., New York, NY 10017-2394. TEL 732-981-0060; 800-678-4333. FAX 732-981-9667. E-mail: customer.service@ieee.org; URL: http://www.ieee.org. (Subscr. to: 445 Hoes Lane, Box 1331, Piscataway, NJ 08855-1331) **Indexed:** ASCA.
—BLDSC (6842.154400); CASDDS; UMI.
Former titles (until 1979): New England (Northeast) Bioengineering Conference. Proceedings (ISSN 0270-1820); (until 1978): New England Bioengineering Conference. Proceedings (ISSN 0163-1896)
Description: Forum for the exchange of technical and scientific information among engineers, physicians and other scientists interested in research, development and education.

OF VALUE. see *PHILOSOPHY*

610.28 NE ISSN 0920-5438
CODEN: PRBEEZ
PROGRESS IN BIOMEDICAL ENGINEERING. 1987. irreg., vol.7, 1989. price varies. Elsevier Science B.V., Books Division, P.O. Box 211, 1000 AE Amsterdam, Netherlands. TEL 31-20-4853705. TELEX 18582 ESPA NL. E-mail: nlinfo-f@elsevier.nl; usinfo-f@elsevier.com; forinfo-kyf04035@niftyserve.or.jp; URL: http://www.elsevier.nl/. (Subscr. in the Americas to: Elsevier Science, Regional Sales Office, Box 945, New York, NY 10159-0945. TEL 212-633-3730. FAX 212-633-3680; Subscr. in Australasia and the Far East to: Elsevier Science (Singapore) Pte Ltd, No.1 Temasek Ave., No.17-01 Millenia Tower, Singapore 039192, Singapore. TEL 65-434-3727. FAX 65-337-2230; Subscr. in Japan to: Elsevier Science Japan, 9-15 Higashi-Azabu 1-chome, Minato-ku, Tokyo 106, Japan. TEL 81-3-5561-5033. FAX 81-3-5561-5047) (back issues avail.) **Document type:** monographic series.
—CASDDS; CISTI; Ei; KNAW. **CCC.**
Refereed Serial

610.28 JA
RAIOENJINIARINGU BUMON GAKUJUTSU KOENKAI KOEN RONBUNSHU/JAPANESE SOCIETY OF MECHANICAL ENGINEERS. BIOENGINEERING DIVISION CONFERENCE. (Text in Japanese; summaries in English) 1989. a. 6000 Yen. Nihon Kikai Gakkai - Japan Society of Mechanical Engineers, 4-9 Yoyogi 2-chome, Shibuya-ku, Tokyo 151, Japan.

TECHNOLOGY AND HEALTH CARE. see *MEDICAL SCIENCES*

TISSUE ENGINEERING. see *BIOLOGY — Cytology And Histology*

TRANSGENIC RESEARCH. see *BIOLOGY — Genetics*

TRANSGENICS. see *BIOLOGY — Genetics*

ZHONGGUO SHENGWU YIXUE GONGCHENG XUEBAO/CHINESE JOURNAL OF BIOMEDICAL ENGINEERING. see *MEDICAL SCIENCES*

BIOLOGY — Biological Chemistry

572.06 UK ISSN 0959-860X
A C B NATIONAL MEETING HANDBOOK. 1985. a. (Association of Clinical Biochemists) P R C Associates, The Annexe, Fitznells Manor, Chessington Rd., Ewell Village, Surrey KT17 1TF, England. TEL 081-786-7376. FAX 081-786-7262. Ed. J.D. Berg. adv. circ. 4,500. (back issues avail.) **Document type:** bulletin.
—CCC.

572.06 UK ISSN 0959-9029
A C B NATIONAL MEETING PROCEEDINGS. 1987. a. (Association of Clinical Biochemists) P R C Associates, The Annexe, Fitznells Manor, Chessington Rd., Ewell Village, Surrey KT17 1TF, England. TEL 081-786-7376. FAX 081-786-7262. Ed. S.P. Halloran. adv. circ. 2,500. (back issues avail.) **Document type:** bulletin.
—CCC.

612.015 UK ISSN 0261-4553
A T PASES. (Adenosine Triphosphatases) s-m. (diskette m.). £90 (diskette £120; both £180) (effective 1997). S U B I S, Mansion House, 19 Kingfield Rd., Sheffield S11 9AS, England. TEL 44-114-2554433. FAX 44-114-2554626. E-mail: subis@sheffac.demon.co.uk; URL: http://www.shef.ac.uk/uni/companies/shap. (also avail. in diskette format; looseleaf format; back issues avail.) **Document type:** abstracting/indexing.
—CCC.
Description: Current awareness service for researchers in clinical and life sciences.

ABSTRACTS OF SYMPOSIUM ON PEPTIDE CHEMISTRY/PEPUCHIDO KAGAKU TORONKAI KOEN YOSHISHU. see *FISH AND FISHERIES — Abstracting, Bibliographies, Statistics*

572 PL ISSN 0001-527X
QP501 CODEN: ABPLAF
ACTA BIOCHIMICA POLONICA. (Text and summaries in English) 1954. q. $80. Polskie Towarzystwo Biochemiczne, Ul. Pasteura 3, 02-093 Warsaw, Poland. FAX 48-22-225342. TELEX 814892. E-mail: abp@neucki.gov.pl. (Dist. by: Ars Polona, Krakowskie Przedmiescie 7, 00-068 Warsaw, Poland) Ed. K. Raczynska-Bojanowska. adv.: B&W page $40, color page $80. bk.rev.; charts; illus.; index. circ. 1,500. **Indexed:** AgroAgen, AgroLibrex, ASCA, Biol.Abstr., Chem.Abstr., Curr.Adv.Ecol.Sci., Curr.Cont., Dairy Sci.Abstr., Dent.Ind., Excerp.Med., Field Crop Abstr., Food Sci.& Tech.Abstr., Helminthol.Abstr., Herb.Abstr., Ind.Med., Ind.Sci.Rev Int.Abstr.Biol.Sci., Nutr.Abstr., Sci.Cit.Ind. **Document type:** academic/scholarly publication.
—BLDSC (0600.990000); CASDDS; CISTI; Genuin Article; Linda Hall; UnCover.

BIOLOGY — BIOLOGICAL CHEMISTRY

572   AG   ISSN 0325-2957
CODEN: ABCLDL
ACTA BIOQUIMICA CLINICA LATINOAMERICANA. (Text in Spanish; summaries in English, Spanish) 1966. q. $70. Federacion Bioquimica de la Provincia de Buenos Aires, Calle 6, No. 1344, 1900 La Plata, Buenos Aires, Argentina. TEL 021-38821-42797. FAX 54-21-254224. Ed. Juan M. Castagnino. adv.; bk.rev.; abstr.; bibl.; charts; illus.; index; circ. 3,000 (controlled). Indexed: ASCA, Biol.Abstr., Chem.Abstr., Curr.Adv.Ecol.Sci., Excerp.Med., Ind.Med., INIS Atomind.
—BLDSC (0603.500000); CASDDS; CISTI; Genuine Article; KNAW.
Formerly: Bioquimica Clinica (ISSN 0006-3533)

ACTA CRYSTALLOGRAPHICA. SECTION D: BIOLOGICAL CRYSTALLOGRAPHY. see CHEMISTRY — Crystallography

572   GW   ISSN 0065-1281
CODEN: AHISA9
ACTA HISTOCHEMICA; international journal of structural biochemistry. (Text in English, French, German; summaries in English) 1954. 4/yr. DM.556 (foreign DM.564) (effective 1996). Gustav Fischer Verlag Jena, Villengang 2, 07745 Jena, Germany. TEL 49-3641-626444. FAX 49-3641-6266500. (Subscr. to: Postfach 100537, 07705 Jena, Germany) Ed. R. Grossrau. adv.: page DM.750; trim 170 x 240. bk.rev.; bibl.; charts; illus.; index. circ. 450. (also avail. in microform from PMC,SWZ; reprint service avail. from ISI) Indexed: ASCA, Biol.Abstr., Chem.Abstr., Curr.Adv.Ecol.Sci., Curr.Cont., Dairy Sci.Abstr., Dent.Ind., Excerp.Med., Helminthol.Abstr., Ind.Med., Ind.Sci.Rev., Ind.Vet., INIS Atomind., Neurosci.Cit.Ind., Nutr.Abstr., Ref.Zh., Sci.Cit.Ind., Sport Fish.Abstr., Vet.Bull., Wild.Rev., Zoo.Rec. **Document type:** academic/scholarly publication.
—BLDSC (0624.000000); CASDDS; CISTI; Ei; EMDOCS; Genuine Article; KNAW; Linda Hall; SWETS; UnCover. **CCC.**

ACTA HISTOCHEMICA ET CYTOCHEMICA/NIHON SOSHIKI SAIBO KAGAKKAI GAKKAISHI. see BIOLOGY — Cytology And Histology

ACTA PHYSIOLOGICA HUNGARICA. see BIOLOGY — Physiology

572   PL   ISSN 0208-614X
QP501   CODEN: AUFBD3
ACTA UNIVERSITATIS LODZIENSIS: FOLIA BIOCHIMICA ET BIOPHYSICA. (Text in Polish; summaries in various languages) 1955; N.S. 1981. irreg. Wydawnictwo Uniwersytetu Lodzkiego, Ul. Jaracza 34, Lodz, Poland. TEL 331671. (Dist. by: Ars Polona-Ruch, Krakowskie Przedmiescie 7, Warsaw, Poland) Indexed: INIS Atomind. **Document type:** academic/scholarly publication.
—BLDSC (0585.205500); CASDDS; CISTI; KNAW; Linda Hall.
Supersedes in part: Uniwersytet Lodzki. Zeszyty Naukowe. Seria 2: Nauki Matematyczno-Przyrodnicze (ISSN 0076-0366)
Description: Publishes articles devoted to the studies on biochemistry and biophysics.

574.192   US
▼**ADVANCES IN AMINO ACID MIMETICS AND PEPTIDOMIMETICS.** 1997. irreg. $109.50. J A I Press Inc., 55 Old Post Rd., No.2, Box 1678, Greenwich, CT 06830-1678. TEL 203-661-7602. FAX 203-661-0792. E-mail: jai@jaipress.com. (In Europe to: JAI Press Ltd., 38 Tavistock St., Covent Garden, London WC2E 7PB, England. TEL 44-171-379-8834. FAX 44-171-379-8835) Ed. Andrew Abell. **Document type:** academic/scholarly publication, monographic series.

ADVANCES IN ANTIVIRAL DRUG DESIGN. see PHARMACY AND PHARMACOLOGY

572.57   US
ADVANCES IN APPLIED LIPID RESEARCH. 1992. irreg., vol.3, 1997. $109.50. J A I Press Inc., 55 Old Post Rd., No.2, Box 1678, Greenwich, CT 06830-1678. TEL 203-661-7602. FAX 203-661-0792. E-mail: jai@jaipress.com. (In Europe: JAI Press Ltd., 38 Tavistock St., Covent Garden, London WC2E 7PB, England. TEL 44-171-379-8834. FAX 44-171-379-8835) Ed. Fred Padley. **Document type:** monographic series, academic/scholarly publication.

ADVANCES IN BIOCHEMICAL ENGINEERING - BIOTECHNOLOGY. see BIOLOGY — Biotechnology

572   NE   ISSN 0272-3840
CODEN: ABIODQ
ADVANCES IN BIOMATERIALS. 1983. irreg., vol.10, 1992. price varies. (European Society for Biomaterials) Elsevier Science B.V., Books Division, P.O. Box 211, 1000 AE Amsterdam, Netherlands. TEL 31-20-4853911. FAX 31-20-4853705. TELEX 18582 ESPA NL. E-mail: nlinfo-f@elsevier.nl; usinfo-f@elsevier.com; forinfo-kyf04035@niftyserve.or.jp; URL: http://www.elsevier.nl/. (Subscr. in the Americas to: Elsevier Science, Regional Sales Office, Box 945, New York, NY 10159-0945. TEL 212-633-3730. FAX 212-633-3680; Subscr. in Australasia and the Far East to: Elsevier Science (Singapore) Pte Ltd, No.1 Temasek Ave., No.17-01 Millenia Tower, Singapore 039192, Singapore. TEL 65-434-3727. FAX 65-337-2230; Subscr. in Japan to: Elsevier Science Japan, 9-15 Higashi-Azabu 1-chome, Minato-ku, Tokyo 106, Japan. TEL 81-3-5561-5033. FAX 81-3-5561-5047) **Document type:** monographic series.
—BLDSC (0700.220000); CASDDS; CISTI; KNAW. **CCC.**
Refereed Serial

ADVANCES IN BIOPHYSICAL CHEMISTRY. see CHEMISTRY — Physical Chemistry

ADVANCES IN BIOPHYSICS. see BIOLOGY — Biophysics

ADVANCES IN CARBOHYDRATE CHEMISTRY AND BIOCHEMISTRY. see CHEMISTRY — Organic Chemistry

572   US   ISSN 0065-2423
RB1   CODEN: ACLCA9
ADVANCES IN CLINICAL CHEMISTRY. 1958. irreg., vol.32, 1996. Academic Press, Inc., 525 B St., Ste. 1900, San Diego, CA 92101-4495. TEL 619-231-0926. FAX 619-699-6715. (Subscr. to: Order Dept., 6277 Sea Harbor Dr., 4th Fl., Orlando, FL 32887. TEL 800-321-5068) Ed. Herbert E. Spiegel. index, cum.index: vols.1-5 (1958-1962). (reprint service avail. from ISI) Indexed: ASCA, Biol.Abstr., Curr.Adv.Ecol.Sci., Diar.Dis.Res., Ind.Med., Ind.Sci.Rev., Sci.Cit.Ind
—BLDSC (0703.900000); CASDDS; CISTI; Linda Hall; SWETS. **CCC.**
Refereed Serial

572   US   ISSN 1064-2722
QP501   CODEN: ADEBEG
ADVANCES IN DEVELOPMENTAL BIOCHEMISTRY. 1992. irreg., vol.5, 1997. $109.50. J A I Press Inc., 55 Old Post Rd., No. 2, Box 1678, Greenwich, CT 06830-1678. TEL 203-661-7602. FAX 203-661-0792. E-mail: jai@jaipress.com. (Addr. in Europe: J A I Press Ltd., 38 Tavistock St., Covent Garden, London WC2E 7PB, England. TEL 44-171-379-8834. FAX 44-171-379-8835) Ed. Paul Wassarman. **Document type:** academic/scholarly publication.
—BLDSC (0704.243600); CISTI. **CCC.**

577   NE   ISSN 0924-8137
ADVANCES IN EICOSANOID RESEARCH. (Text in English) 1988. irreg. price varies. Kluwer Academic Publishers, Postbus 17, 3300 AA Dordrecht, Netherlands. TEL 31-78-6392392. FAX 31-78-6392254. TELEX 29245 KAPG NL. E-mail: services@wkap.nl; URL: http://www.wkap.nl. (Dist. by: Kluwer Academic Publishers Group, P.o. Box 322, 3300 AH Dordrecht, Netherlands. TEL 31-78-6392392. FAX 31-78-6546474; N. America dist. addr.: Box 358, Accord Sta., Hingham, MA 02018-0358. TEL 617-871-6600. FAX 617-871-6528) (back issues avail.) **Document type:** monographic series.
Refereed Serial

572.7   US   ISSN 0065-258X
QP601.A1   CODEN: AERAAD
ADVANCES IN ENZYMOLOGY AND RELATED AREAS OF MOLECULAR BIOLOGY. 1942. irreg., vol.64, 1990. price varies. John Wiley & Sons, Inc. (Subsidiary of: Wiley Interscience Journals), 605 Third Ave., New York, NY 10158-0012. TEL 212-850-6800. Ed. F.F. Nord. Indexed: ASCA, Biol.Abstr., Chem.Abstr., Curr.Adv.Ecol.Sci., Curr.Biotech.Abstr., Dairy Sci.Abstr., Ind.Med., Ind.Sci.Rev., Sci.Cit.Ind., Trop.Dis.Bull. **Document type:** academic/scholarly publication.
—BLDSC (0705.970000); CASDDS; CISTI; Genuine Article; Linda Hall; SWETS; UnCover. **CCC.**
Formerly: Advances in Enzymology and Related Subjects of Biochemistry.
Refereed Serial

572   US   ISSN 0941-3472
ADVANCES IN LECTIN RESEARCH. 1988. irreg. Springer-Verlag, 175 Fifth Ave., New York, NY 10010. TEL 212-460-1500. FAX 212-473-6272. **Document type:** monographic series.

573.8   US
▼**ADVANCES IN LIPOBIOLOGY.** 1996. irreg., vol.2, 1997. $128.50. J A I Press Inc., 55 Old Post Rd., No.2, Box 1678, Greenwich, CT 06830-1678. TEL 203-661-7602. FAX 203-661-0792. E-mail: jai@jaipress.com. (Subscr. in UK to: JAI Press Ltd., 38 Tavistock St., Covent Garden, London WC2E 7PB, England. TEL 44-171-379-8834. FAX 44-171-3798835) Ed. Richard Gross. **Document type:** academic/scholarly publication, monographic series.

ADVANCES IN MODERN ENVIRONMENTAL TOXICOLOGY. see ENVIRONMENTAL STUDIES — Toxicology And Environmental Safety

612.8   US   ISSN 0098-6089
QP356.3   CODEN: ADNEDZ
ADVANCES IN NEUROCHEMISTRY. 1975. irreg., latest vol.8. price varies. Plenum Publishing Corp., 233 Spring St., New York, NY 10013-1578. TEL 212-620-8000. FAX 212-463-0742. TELEX 23-421119. E-mail: books@plenum.com. Eds. B.W. Agranoff, M.H. Aprison. Indexed: Biol.Abstr., Chem.Abstr., Curr.Adv.Ecol.Sci. **Document type:** monographic series.
—BLDSC (0709.476000); CASDDS; CISTI; KNAW. **CCC.**
Refereed Serial

572   US   ISSN 0065-3233
QD431   CODEN: APCHA2
ADVANCES IN PROTEIN CHEMISTRY. 1944. irreg., vol.49, 1996. Academic Press, Inc., 525 B St., Ste. 1900, San Diego, CA 92101-4495. TEL 619-231-0926. FAX 619-699-6715. (Subscr. to: Order Dept., 6277 Sea Harbor Dr., 4th Fl., Orlando, FL 32887. TEL 800-321-5068) Eds. M.L. Anson, John T. Edsall. (reprint service avail. from ISI) Indexed: Abstr.Hyg., ASCA, Biol.Abstr., Chem.Abstr., Chem.Cit.Ind., Curr.Adv.Ecol.Sci., Dairy Sci.Abstr., Excerp.Med., Food Sci.& Tech.Abstr., Ind.Med., Ind.Sci.Rev., Nutr.Abstr., Sci.Cit.Ind., Trop.Dis.Bull. **Document type:** monographic series.
—BLDSC (0711.000000); CASDDS; CISTI; EMDOCS; KNAW; Linda Hall; SWETS; UnCover. **CCC.**
Refereed Serial

572   US   ISSN 1040-7952
QP625.N89   CODEN: ASMRE5
ADVANCES IN SECOND MESSENGER AND PHOSPHOPROTEIN RESEARCH. 1972. irreg. price varies. Lippincott - Raven Publishers (Subsidiary of: Wolters Kluwer N.V.), 227 E. Washington Sq., Philadelphia, PA 19106. TEL 215-238-4200. FAX 215-238-4227. URL: http://www.lrpub.com. (Subscr. to: Box 1600, Hagerstown, MD 21741-1600. TEL 800-777-2295. FAX 301-824-7390) Eds. Paul Greengard, G. Alan Robison. R&P contact: Alice McElhinney. (reprint service avail. from UMI) Indexed: ASCA, Biol.Abstr., Chem.Abstr., Curr.Adv.Ecol.Sci., Curr.Cont., Ind.Med., Ind.Sci.Rev., Sci.Cit.Ind. **Document type:** proceedings.
—BLDSC (0711.383350); CASDDS; CISTI; Genuine Article; Linda Hall; SWETS; UnCover.
Former titles (until 1988): Advances in Cyclic Nucleotide Research and Protein Phosphorylation Research (ISSN 0747-7767); (until 1984): Advances in Cyclic Nucleotide Research (ISSN 0084-5930)
Refereed Serial

ADVENTURES WITH SCIENCE. see CHILDREN AND YOUTH — For

572   RU   ISSN 0869-8481
AGROKHIM BIZNES. (Text in English and Russian) 1991. bi-m. 210000 Rub. (foreign $55) (effective 1997). Interchim, Dostoevskogo ul., 2, 103030 Moscow, Russia. TEL 7-095-2813716. FAX 7-095-2815988. E-mail: ahbmag@aha.ru. Ed. Anatoli Pekhov. adv.: B&W page $1200, color $1700. charts; pat.; stat.; tr.lit.; circ. 5,000 (paid). (also avail. in diskette format; back issues avail.) **Document type:** consumer publication.
Description: Presents activities of chemical enterprises in Russia and C.I.S. and their relations with world market.

BIOLOGY — BIOLOGICAL CHEMISTRY

AMERICAN SOCIETY FOR NEUROCHEMISTRY. TRANSACTIONS. see *MEDICAL SCIENCES — Psychiatry And Neurology*

572.65   AU   ISSN 0939-4451
QD431.A1   CODEN: AACIE6
AMINO ACIDS. (Text in English) 1991. 8/yr. DM.1016 (effective 1998). Springer-Verlag, Sachsenplatz 4-6, P.O. Box 89, A-1201 Vienna, Austria. TEL 43-1-3302415. FAX 43-1-3302426. E-mail: springer@springer.co.at. (Subscr. in N. America to: Springer-Verlag New York, Inc., 175 Fifth Ave., New York, NY 10010. TEL 212-460-1500. FAX 212-473-6272) Ed.Bd. **Indexed:** ASCA, Chem.Cit.Ind., Compumath, Curr.Cont., Excerp.Med. (1993-), Ind.Sci.Rev., Sci.Cit.Ind. **Document type:** academic/scholarly publication.
—BLDSC (0859.152000); ADONIS; CASDDS; CISTI; EMDOCS; Genuine Article; KNAW; SWETS; UMI. **CCC.**

572.65   UK   ISSN 0269-7521
QD431.A1   CODEN: AACPER
AMINO ACIDS, PEPTIDES AND PROTEINS. 1968. a. £139.50 (effective 1997). The Royal Society of Chemistry, Thomas Graham House, Science Park, Milton Rd., Cambridge CB4 4WF, England. TEL 44-1223-420066. FAX 44-1223-423429. E-mail: sales@rsc.org; URL: http://chemistry.rsc.org/rsc/. (Subscr. to: Turpin Distribution Services Ltd., Blackhorse Rd., Letchworth, Herts. SG6 1HN, England. TEL 44-1462-480947. FAX 44-1462-480947; Subscr. in N. America to: ACS, 1155 Sixteenth St., N.W., Washington, DC 22036, USA. TEL 202-776-8100. FAX 202-872-6067) charts; illus.; index. (back issues avail.) **Indexed:** Chem.Abstr., Food Sci.& Tech.Abstr. **Document type:** academic/scholarly publication.
—BLDSC (0859.155000); CASDDS; CISTI; Linda Hall. **CCC.**
Formerly: Amino Acids and Peptides (ISSN 0306-0004)

572   US   ISSN 0003-2697
QP501   CODEN: ANBCA2
ANALYTICAL BIOCHEMISTRY; methods in the biological sciences. 1960. 22/yr. $2100 (foreign $2500) (effective 1997). Academic Press, Inc., Journal Division, 525 B. St., Ste. 1900, San Diego, CA 92101-4495. TEL 619-230-1840. FAX 619-699-6800. E-mail: apsubs@acad.com; URL: http://www.apnet.com/www/journal/ab.htm; http://www.idealibrary.com/. (Subscr. to: Box 861213, Orlando, FL 32886-1213. TEL 407-347-4040. FAX 407-363-9661) Ed. William B. Jakoby. adv.; charts; illus.; index. (back issues avail.) **Indexed:** Abstr.Bull.Inst.Pap.Chem., Anal.Abstr., Apic.Abstr., ASCA, Biol.Abstr., Biotech.Abstr., Chem.Abstr., Chem.Cit.Ind., Crop Physiol.Abstr., Curr.Adv.Biochem., Curr.Adv.Cell & Devel.Biol., Curr.Adv.Genetics & Molec.Biol., Curr.Cont., Curr.Leather Lit., Dairy Sci.Abstr., Deep Sea Res.& Oceanogr.Abstr., Dent.Ind., Excerp.Med., Field Crop Abstr., Food Sci.& Tech.Abstr., Helminthol.Abstr., Herb.Abstr., Hort.Abstr., Ind.Med., Ind.Sci.Rev., Ind.Vet., INIS Atomind., Maize Abstr., Mass Spectr.Bull., Neurosci.Cit.Ind., Nutr.Abstr., Rev.Appl.Entomol., Rev.Med.& Vet.Mycol., Sci.Cit.Ind., Soils & Fert., THA, Vet.Bull. **Document type:** academic/scholarly publication.
● Also available online.
—BLDSC (0896.500000); ADONIS; CASDDS; CISTI; EMDOCS; Genuine Article; Linda Hall; SWETS; UnCover. **CCC.**
Description: Emphasizes methods in the biological and biochemical sciences and all related fields.
Refereed Serial

572.8   NE   ISSN 1358-6122
   CODEN: ANBIFP
▼**ANCIENT BIOMOLECULES.** 1996. 4/yr. $70 (effective 1998). Gordon and Breach - Harwood Academic, Amsteldisk 166, 1st Fl., 1079 LH Amsterdam, Netherlands. (Subscr. to: International Publishers Distributor, Box 32160, Newark, NJ 07102. TEL 800-545-8398. FAX 215-750-6343) **Document type:** academic/scholarly publication.
—CASDDS. **CCC.**

ANNALI DI MICROBIOLOGIA ED ENZIMOLOGIA. see *BIOLOGY — Microbiology*

612.015   UK   ISSN 0004-5632
   CODEN: ACBOBU
ANNALS OF CLINICAL BIOCHEMISTRY. bi-m. £93 (foreign £97). (Association of Clinical Biochemists) Royal Society of Medicine Press Ltd., 1 Wimpole St., London W1M 8AE, England. TEL 44-171-290-2900. FAX 44-171-290-2929. Ed. S.P. Halloran. adv.; bk.rev.; illus.; index. circ 3,650. (back issues avail.) **Indexed:** Anal.Abstr., ASCA, Biol.Abstr., Chem.Abstr., Curr.Adv.Ecol.Sci., Curr.Cont., Dent.Ind., Excerp.Med., Ind.Med., Ind.Sci.Rev., INIS Atomind., Kidney, Nutr.Abstr., Rev.Med.& Vet.Mycol., Sci.Cit.Ind, SSCI, THA, Vet.Bull. **Document type:** academic/scholarly publication.
—BLDSC (1040.230000); ADONIS; CASDDS; CISTI; EMDOCS; Genuine Article; KNAW; SWETS; UMI; UnCover. **CCC.**
Description: Presents international papers about clinical biochemistry, especially for the understanding, diagnosis and treatment of human disease.
Refereed Serial

572   US   ISSN 0066-4154
QP501   CODEN: ARBOAW
ANNUAL REVIEW OF BIOCHEMISTRY. 1932. a. $68 to individuals (foreign $74); institutions $136 (foreign $148) (effective 1998). Annual Reviews Inc., 4139 El Camino Way, Box 10139, Palo Alto, CA 94303-0139. TEL 650-493-4400; 800-523-8635. FAX 650-424-0910. E-mail: service@annurev.org; URL: http://www.annurev.org. Ed. Charles C. Richardson. R&P contact: Jeanne Kunz. bibl.; index, cum.index. (also avail. in microfilm from UMI; back issues avail.; reprint service avail.) **Indexed:** Abstr.Bull.Inst.Pap.Chem., Anim.Breed.Abstr., ASCA, Biol.Abstr., Biol.& Agr.Ind., Biotech.Abstr., Chem.Abstr., Chem.Cit.Ind., Curr.Adv.Ecol.Sci., Curr.Cont., Dairy Sci.Abstr., Diar.Dis.Res., Excerp.Med., Field Crop Abstr., Food Sci.& Tech.Abstr., Helminthol.Abstr., Hort.Abstr., Ind.Med., Ind.Sci.Rev., INIS Atomind., M.M.R.I., Nutr.Abstr., Plant Breed.Abstr., Soils & Fert., SSCI, THA, Trop.Dis.Bull., VITIS, Weed Abstr. **Document type:** academic/scholarly publication.
—BLDSC (1522.000000); ADONIS; CASDDS; CISTI; EMDOCS; Genuine Article; KNAW; KR SourceOne; Linda Hall; SWETS; UMI; UnCover. **CCC.**
Description: Original critical reviews of the significant primary literature and current developments in biochemistry.

ANNUAL REVIEW OF BIOPHYSICS AND BIOMOLECULAR STRUCTURE. see *BIOLOGY — Biophysics*

ANTI-CANCER DRUG DESIGN. see *MEDICAL SCIENCES — Oncology*

ANTIINFECTIVE DRUGS AND CHEMOTHERAPY. see *MEDICAL SCIENCES — Oncology*

ANTISENSE AND NUCLEIC ACID DRUG DEVELOPMENT. see *BIOLOGY — Genetics*

572   US   ISSN 0273-2289
TP248.3   CODEN: ABIBDL
APPLIED BIOCHEMISTRY AND BIOTECHNOLOGY. (Consists of: Part A, Enzyme Engineering and Biotechnology; Part B, Molecular Biotechnology (ISSN 1073-6085)) 1976. 27/yr. $950 (foreign $996) (effective 1998). Humana Press Inc., 999 Riverview Dr., Ste. 208, Totowa, NJ 07512-1165. TEL 201-256-1699. FAX 201-256-8341. E-mail: humana@mindspring.com; URL: http://lbin.com/humana.html. (Dist. in Japan by: Maruzen Co. Ltd., Journals Div., P.O. Box 5050, Tokyo 100-31, Japan. TEL 03-3275-8591. FAX 03-3278-1937) Ed. David Walt. R&P contact: Richard Hruska. adv. contact: Thomas B. Lanigan, Jr. bk.rev.; bibl.; charts; illus. **Indexed:** ASCA, Biodet.Abstr., Biol.Abstr., Chem.Abstr., Chem.Cit.Ind., Curr.Adv.Ecol.Sci., Curr.Biotech.Abstr., Curr.Cont., Excerp.Med., Food Sci.& Tech.Abstr., Ind.Med., Ind.Sci.Rev., Mat.Sci.Cit.Ind., Sci.Cit.Ind, SSCI, Sugar Ind.Abstr., Telegen, Triticale Abstr. **Document type:** academic/scholarly publication.
—BLDSC (1571.880000); ADONIS; CASDDS; CISTI; Ei; Genuine Article; Linda Hall; SWETS; UnCover. **CCC.**
Formerly (until vol.5, 1980): Journal of Solid-Phase Biochemistry (ISSN 0146-0641)
Description: Presents innovative, practically-oriented research articles in the applications of biotechnology covering genetic engineering, enzyme engineering, fermentation technology, proteins and nucleic acids.
Refereed Serial

572   RU   ISSN 0003-6838
QH345   CODEN: APBMAC
APPLIED BIOCHEMISTRY AND MICROBIOLOGY. English translation of: Prikladnaya Biokhimiya i Mikrobiologiya (RU ISSN 0555-1099) 1965. bi-m. $1535 in US; elsewhere $1795 (effective 1998). (Russian Academy of Sciences) Maik Nauka - Interperiodica, Mezhdunarodnyi Otdel, Ul. Profsoyuznaya, 90, 117864 Moscow, Russia. TEL 7-095-3360066. FAX 7-095-3360666. (Dist. by: Plenum Publishing Corp., 233 Spring St., New York, NY 10013-1578, U.S.A.. TEL 212-620-8468. FAX 212-463-0742) Ed. B.F. Poglazov. (also avail. in microfilm from UMI; back issues avail.) **Indexed:** ASCA, Biol.Abstr., Chem.Cit.Ind., Chem.Titles, Curr.Biotech.Abstr., Excerp.Med., Food Sci.& Tech.Abstr., Ind.Med., INIS Atomind., Pollut.Abstr. **Document type:** academic/scholarly publication.
—BLDSC (0404.670000); CISTI; Genuine Article; SWETS; UMI; UnCover. **CCC.**
Refereed Serial

AQUATIC TOXICOLOGY. see *ENVIRONMENTAL STUDIES — Toxicology And Environmental Safety*

BIOLOGY — BIOLOGICAL CHEMISTRY

572 US ISSN 0003-9861
QP501 CODEN: ABBIA4
ARCHIVES OF BIOCHEMISTRY AND BIOPHYSICS. 1942. 24/yr. $2295 (foreign $2750) (effective 1997). Academic Press, Inc., Journal Division, 525 B St., Ste. 1900, San Diego, CA 92101-4495. TEL 619-230-1840. FAX 619-699-6800. E-mail: apsubs@acad.com; URL: http://www.apnet.com/www/journal/bb.htm; http://www.idealibrary.com/. (Subscr. to: Box 861213, Orlando, FL 32886-1213. TEL 407-347-4040. FAX 407-363-9661) Ed. J. Thomas August. adv.; bibl.; illus.; index. (back issues avail.) **Indexed:** Abstr.Bull.Inst.Pap.Chem., AIDS Abstr., Appl.Mech.Rev., ASCA, Bibl.Agri., Biodet.Abstr., Biol.Abstr., Biotech.Abstr., C.I.S.Abstr., Chem.Abstr., Chem.Cit.Ind., Crop Physiol.Abstr., Curr.Adv.Biochem., Curr.Adv.Cell & Devel.Biol., Curr.Adv.Ecol.Sci., Curr.Adv.Genetics & Molec.Biol., Curr.Cont., Dairy Sci.Abstr., Deep Sea Res.& Oceanogr.Abstr., Dent.Ind., Environ.Abstr., Excerp.Med., Field Crop.Abstr., Food Sci.& Tech.Abstr., Helminthol.Abstr., Herb.Abstr., Hort.Abstr., Ind.Med., Ind.Sci.Rev., Ind.Vet., INIS Atomind., Maize Abstr., Mass Spectr.Bull., Neurosci.Cit.Ind., Nutr.Abstr., Ornam.Hort., Pig News & Info., Plant Breed.Abstr., Potato Abstr., Protozool.Abstr., Rev.Appl.Entomol., Rev.Med.& Vet.Mycol., Rev.Plant Path., Sci.Cit.Ind, Seed Abstr., Soils & Fert., Sorghum & Millets Abstr., Soyabean Abstr., Sport Fish.Abstr., Triticale Abstr., Trop.Dis.Bull., Trop.Oil Seeds Abstr., Vet.Bull., Weed Abstr., Wild.Rev., Zoo.Rec. **Document type:** academic/scholarly publication.
●Also available online.
—BLDSC (1633.000000); ADONIS; CASDDS; CISTI; Ei; EMDOCS; Genuine Article; Linda Hall; SWETS; UnCover. **CCC.**
Description: Presents articles in the areas of biochemistry and biophysics, especially those related to molecular biology, cell biology, and developmental biology.
Refereed Serial

ARCHIVES OF PHYSIOLOGY AND BIOCHEMISTRY. see *BIOLOGY — Physiology*

572 AG ISSN 0004-4768
QP501 CODEN: RABAAO
ASOCIACION BIOQUIMICA ARGENTINA. REVISTA. 1934. q. $60. Asociacion Bioquimica Argentina, Venezuela 1823-3er. Piso, Buenos Aires 1096, Argentina. Ed. Raul G. Coronato. adv.; bk.rev.; abstr.; charts; illus.; index. circ. 3,000. **Indexed:** Biol.Abstr., Chem.Abstr.
—CASDDS; CISTI; Linda Hall.

612.015 UK ISSN 0141-8912
ASSOCIATION OF CLINICAL BIOCHEMISTS. NEWS SHEET. Key Title: News Sheet - Association of Biochemists Limited. Cover title: A C B News Sheet. 1951. m. membership. Association of Clinical Biochemists, c/o Dr. Jonathan D. Berg, Ed., Department of Clinical Biochemistry, Sandwell District General Hospital, West Bromwich, W. Midlands B71 4HJ, England. TEL 44-1836-635771. FAX 44-121-745-7929. Pub. Peter Carpenter. adv.; bk.rev. circ. 3,600.
—**CCC.**
Description: Focuses on information about developments in laboratory health care in the U.K. and abroad.

572 AT
CODEN: CBREEU
AUSTRALIAN ASSOCIATION OF CLINICAL BIOCHEMISTS. NEWSLETTER.* 1979. q. Aus.$50 (membership). (Australian Association of Clinical Biochemists) Associated Business Publications Pty. Ltd., P.O. Box 440, Broadway, N.S.W. 2007, Australia. TEL 61-2-2122780. FAX 61-2-2814594. Ed. Richard Ryall. adv.; bk.rev. circ. 1,300. **Document type:** newsletter.

572 AT ISSN 0067-1703
QD415.A1 CODEN: ABIPBR
AUSTRALIAN BIOCHEMICAL SOCIETY. PROCEEDINGS. 1968. a. Aus.$45. (Australian Biochemical Society, CSIRO-Division of Human Nutrition) D A Information Services, 648 Whitehorse Rd., Mitcham, Vic. 3132, Australia. TEL 61-3-92107777. FAX 61-3-92107788. E-mail: service@dadirect.com.au; URL: http://www.dadirect.com.au. Ed. M.G. Clark. adv. circ. 1,400. **Indexed:** Biol.Abstr., Curr.Adv.Ecol.Sci., Curr.Cont., Dairy Sci.Abstr., Helminthol.Abstr., Nutr.Abstr. **Document type:** monographic series.
—CASDDS; CISTI; Linda Hall.
Formerly: Australian Biochemical Society. Programme and Abstracts.

AUTOIMMUNE DISEASES. see *MEDICAL SCIENCES — Allergology And Immunology*

572 NE ISSN 0304-4165
B B A - GENERAL SUBJECTS. (Section of: Biochimica et Biophysica Acta (ISSN 0006-3002)) 1947. 9/yr. fl.1709($982) (effective 1998). Elsevier Science B.V., P.O. Box 211, 1000 AE Amsterdam, Netherlands. TEL 31-20-4853911. FAX 31-20-4853598. TELEX 18582 ESPA NL. E-mail: nlinfo-f@elsevier.nl; usinfo-f@elsevier.com; forinfo-kyf04035@niftyserve.or.jp; URL: http://www.elsevier.nl/. (Subscr. in the Americas to: Elsevier Science, Regional Sales Office, Box 945, New York, NY 10159-0945. TEL 212-633-3730. FAX 212-633-3680; Subscr. in Australasia and the Far East to: Elsevier Science (Singapore) Pte Ltd, No.1 Temasek Ave., No.17-01 Millenia Tower, Singapore 039192, Singapore. TEL 65-434-3727. FAX 65-337-2230; Subscr. in Japan to: Elsevier Science Japan, 9-15 Higashi-Azabu 1-chome, Minato-ku, Tokyo 106, Japan. TEL 81-3-5561-5033. FAX 81-3-5561-5047) Ed.Bd. (also avail. in microform from UMI) **Indexed:** ASCA, Biodet.Abstr., Curr.Leather Lit., Dairy Sci.Abstr., Field Crop Abstr., INIS Atomind., Phys.Ber., Soils & Fert. **Document type:** academic/scholarly publication.
—ADONIS; CISTI; EMDOCS; Genuine Article; SWETS; UnCover. **CCC.**
Description: Contains a collection of diverse, authoritative papers which complete BBA's comprehensive coverage of the fields of biochemistry and biophysics.
Refereed Serial

572.57 NE ISSN 0005-2760
QD1
B B A - LIPIDS & LIPID METABOLISM. (Section of: Biochimica et Biophysica Acta (ISSN 0006-3002)) 18/yr. fl.3418($1964) (effective 1998). Elsevier Science B.V., P.O. Box 211, 1000 AE Amsterdam, Netherlands. TEL 31-20-4853911. FAX 31-20-4853598. TELEX 18582 ESPA NL. E-mail: nlinfo-f@elsevier.nl; usinfo-f@elsevier.com; forinfo-kyf04035@niftyserve.or.jp; URL: http://www.elsevier.nl/. (Subscr. in the Americas to: Elsevier Science, Regional Sales Office, Box 945, New York, NY 10159-0945. TEL 212-633-3730. FAX 212-633-3680; Subscr. in Australasia and the Far East to: Elsevier Science (Singapore) Pte Ltd, No.1 Temasek Ave., No.17-01 Millenia Tower, Singapore 039192, Singapore. TEL 65-434-3727. FAX 65-337-2230; Subscr. in Japan to: Elsevier Science Japan, 9-15 Higashi-Azabu 1-chome, Minato-ku, Tokyo 106, Japan. TEL 81-3-5561-5033. FAX 81-3-5561-5047) Ed.Bd. (also avail. in microform from UMI) **Indexed:** ASCA, Crop Physiol.Abstr., Curr.Adv.Ecol.Sci., Excerp.Med., Field Crop Abstr., Hort.Abstr., Ind.Vet., Maize Abstr., Poult.Abstr., Protozool.Abstr., Rev.Med.& Vet.Mycol., Seed Abstr. **Document type:** academic/scholarly publication.
—ADONIS; CISTI; EMDOCS; Genuine Article; SWETS; UnCover. **CCC.**
Description: Focuses on lipid isolation and characterization, lipid biosynthesis and metabolism, phospholipids and phospholipases, glycolipids, fatty acid metabolism, prostaglandins and related substances, sterols and bile acids, functions of lipids in health and disease.
Refereed Serial

B B A - MOLECULAR BASIS OF DISEASE. see *MEDICAL SCIENCES*

572 NE ISSN 0167-4838
QD1
B B A - PROTEIN STRUCTURE AND MOLECULAR ENZYMOLOGY. (Section of: Biochimica et Biophysica Acta (ISSN 0006-3002)) 1967. 14/yr. fl.3987($2292) (effective 1998). Elsevier Science B.V., P.O. Box 211, 1000 AE Amsterdam, Netherlands. TEL 31-20-4853911. FAX 31-20-4853598. TELEX 18582 ESPA NL. E-mail: nlinfo-f@elsevier.nl; usinfo-f@elsevier.com; forinfo-kyf04035@niftyserve.or.jp; URL: http://www.elsevier.nl/. (Subscr. in the Americas to: Elsevier Science, Regional Sales Office, Box 945, New York, NY 10159-0945. TEL 212-633-3730. FAX 212-633-3680; Subscr. in Australasia and the Far East to: Elsevier Science (Singapore) Pte Ltd, No.1 Temasek Ave., No.17-01 Millenia Tower, Singapore 039192, Singapore. TEL 65-434-3727. FAX 65-337-2230; Subscr. in Japan to: Elsevier Science Japan, 9-15 Higashi-Azabu 1-chome, Minato-ku, Tokyo 106, Japan. TEL 81-3-5561-5033. FAX 81-3-5561-5047) Ed.Bd. (also avail. in microform from UMI; back issues avail.) **Indexed:** ASCA, Biol.Abstr., Chem.Abstr., Curr.Adv.Ecol.Sci., Curr.Cont., Dairy Sci.Abstr., Excerp.Med., Field Crop Abstr., Hort.Abstr., Ind.Chem., Rev.Med.& Vet.Mycol., Seed Abstr., Vet.Bull. **Document type:** academic/scholarly publication.
—ADONIS; CISTI; Genuine Article; SWETS. **CCC.**
Formerly (until 1982): B B A - Protein Structure (ISSN 0005-2795)
Description: Focuses on protein structure, protein conformation, metalloproteins. protein spectroscopy, structure in solution, and protein dynamics.
Refereed Serial

BABRAHAM INSTITUTE. REPORT. see *BIOLOGY — Physiology*

672 BG ISSN 0253-5432
CODEN: BJSRDG
BANGLADESH JOURNAL OF SCIENTIFIC RESEARCH. (Text in English) 1978. 2/yr. Tk.80($10) Bangladesh Association for the Advancement of Science, Department of Biochemistry, University of Dhaka, Ramna, Dhaka 2, Bangladesh. Ed. Abdul Mannan. adv.; bk.rev. circ. 2,500. **Indexed:** Biol.Abstr., Chem.Abstr., Diar.Dis.Res., Field Crop Abstr., Herb.Abstr., Plant Grow.Reg.Abstr.
—CASDDS; CISTI; Linda Hall.

572.973 BE
BELGIUM. STATION DE RECHERCHES FORESTIERES ET HYDROBIOLOGIQUES. TRAVAUX. SERIE D. HYDROBIOLOGIE. (Text in Dutch and French) 1941. irreg. Station de Recherches Forestieres et Hydrobiologiques, Duboislaan 14, Groenendaal, B-1990 Hoeilaart, Belgium.
Formerly: Belgium. Administration des Eaux et Forets. Station de Recherche des Eaux et Forets. Travaux. Serie D. Hydrobiologie (ISSN 0067-5369)

BIO OPTIONS. see *AGRICULTURE*

BIOCATALYSIS AND BIOTRANSFORMATION. see *BIOLOGY — Biotechnology*

572 GW ISSN 0946-1310
CODEN: BIOCFE
BIOCHEMICA. (Text in English) 1994. q. free. Boehringer Mannheim GmbH, Sandhofer Str. 116, 68298 Mannheim, Germany. TEL 49-621-759-8555. FAX 49-621-759-8830. E-mail: burkhard__zieboIz@bmg.boehringer-mannheim.com; URL: http://biochem.boehringer-mannheim.com. (Addr. in the US: 9115 Hague Rd., Box 50414, Indianapolis, IN 46250-0414. TEL 800-428-5433) Ed. Dr. Burkhard Ziebolz. **Document type:** academic/scholarly publication.
—BLDSC (2066.821000); CASDDS.
Formed by the merger of (1993-1994): Colloquium (ISSN 0945-1110); (1993-1994): Biochemica - Information (Internationale Ausgabe) (ISSN 0945-1102)
Description: Disseminates information of interest to the research community.

BIOLOGY — BIOLOGICAL CHEMISTRY

572   US   ISSN 0006-291X
QH301   CODEN: BBRCA9
BIOCHEMICAL AND BIOPHYSICAL RESEARCH COMMUNICATIONS. 1959. 36/yr. $2100 (foreign $2550) (effective 1997). Academic Press, Inc., Journal Division, 525 B St., Ste. 1900, San Diego, CA 92101-4495. TEL 619-230-1840. FAX 619-699-6800. E-mail: apsubs@acad.com; URL: http://www.apnet.com/www/journal/rc.htm; http://www.idealibrary.com. (Subscr. to: Box 861213, Orlando, FL 32886-1213. TEL 407-347-4040. FAX 407-363-9661) Ed.Bd. adv.; bibl.; charts; illus.; index. cum.index. (back issues avail.) **Indexed:** Abstr.Bull.Inst.Pap.Chem., AIDS Abstr., AIDS Abstr., Anim.Breed.Abstr., Apic.Abstr., ASCA, Bibl.Agri., Biodet.Abstr., Biol.Abstr., Biotech.Abstr., Chem.Abstr., Chem.Cit.Ind., Crop Physiol.Abstr., Curr.Adv.Biochem., Curr.Adv.Cancer Res., Curr.Adv.Cell & Devel.Biol., Curr.Adv.Ecol.Sci., Curr.Adv.Genetics & Molec.Biol., Curr.Cont., Dairy Sci.Abstr., Dent.Ind., Excerp.Med., Field Crop.Abstr., Food Sci.& Tech.Abstr., Forest.Abstr., Forest Prod.Abstr., Helminthol.Abstr., Herb.Abstr., Hort.Abstr., Ind.Med., Ind.Sci.Rev., Ind.Vet., INIS Atomind., Mass Spectr.Bull., Neurosci.Cit.Ind., Nutr.Abstr., Pig News & Info., Plant Grow.Reg.Abstr., Poult.Abstr., Rev.Med.& Vet.Mycol., Rev.Plant Path., Sci.Cit.Ind, Sport Fish.Abstr., Sugar Ind.Abstr., THA, Weed Abstr., Wild.Rev., Zoo.Rec. **Document type:** academic/scholarly publication.
●Also available online.
—BLDSC (2066.900000); ADONIS; CASDDS; CISTI; EMDOCS; Genuine Article; Linda Hall; SWETS; UnCover. **CCC.**
   Description: Devoted to the rapid dissemination of timely and significant experimental results in the diverse fields of modern biology.
Refereed Serial

612.015   US   ISSN 1077-3150
QP501   CODEN: BMMEF4
BIOCHEMICAL AND MOLECULAR MEDICINE; an international journal. 1969. bi-m. $499 (foreign $575) (effective 1997). Academic Press, Inc., Journal Division, 525 B St., Ste. 1900, San Diego, CA 92101-4495. TEL 619-230-1840. FAX 619-699-6800. E-mail: apsubs@acad.com; URL: http://www.apnet.com/www/journal/mm.htm; http://www.idealibrary.com/. (Subscr. to: Box 861213, Orlando, FL 32886-1213. TEL 407-347-4040. FAX 407-363-9661) Ed. Edward R.B. McCabe. adv.; index. (back issues avail.) **Indexed:** Anal.Abstr., ASCA, Biol.Abstr., Biotech.Abstr., Chem.Abstr., Curr.Adv.Ecol.Sci., Curr.Cont., Dairy Sci.Abstr., Dent.Ind., Excerp.Med., Helminthol.Abstr., Ind.Med., Ind.Sci.Rev., INIS Atomind., Mass Spectr.Bull., Nutr.Abstr., Poult.Abstr., Rev.Med.& Vet.Mycol., Sci.Cit.Ind., SSCI, Trop.Oil Seeds Abstr. **Document type:** academic/scholarly publication.
●Also available online.
—BLDSC (2066.934000); ADONIS; CASDDS; CISTI; EMDOCS; Genuine Article; Linda Hall; SWETS; UnCover. **CCC.**
   Former titles (until 1995): Biochemical Medicine and Metabolic Biology (ISSN 0885-4505); Biochemical Medicine (ISSN 0006-2944)
   Description: Publishes papers describing original research in biochemistry, physiological chemistry, and metabolic biology. Emphasis is on the determination of the interrelations among reactions, sequences, and formed elements of the cell.
Refereed Serial

572.3071   UK   ISSN 0307-4412
QP518   CODEN: BIEDDX
BIOCHEMICAL EDUCATION. 1972. q. fl.378($217) (effective 1998). (International Union of Biochemistry) Elsevier Science Ltd., Pergamon, P.O. Box 800, Kidlington, Oxford OX5 1DX, England. TEL 44-1865-843000. FAX 44-1865-843010. E-mail: nlinfo-f@elsevier.nl; usinfo-f@elsevier.com; forinfo-kyf04035@niftyserve.or.jp; URL: http://www.elsevier.nl/. (Subscr. to: Elsevier Science, Regional Sales Office, P.O. Box 211, 1000 AE Amsterdam, Netherlands. TEL 31-20-4853757. FAX 31-20-4853432; Subscr. in the Americas to: Elsevier Science, Regional Sales Office, Box 945, New York, NY 10159-0945. TEL 212-633-3730. FAX 212-633-3680; Subscr. in Australasia and the Far East to: Elsevier Science (Singapore) Pte Ltd, No.1 Temasek Ave., No.17-01 Millenia Tower, Singapore 039192, Singapore. TEL 65-434-3727. FAX 65-337-2230) Ed. Edward J. Wood. adv.; bk.rev. circ. 5,000. (also avail. in microfilm from UMI; reprint service avail. from UMI) **Indexed:** ASCA, C.I.J.E., Chem.Abstr., Cont.Pg.Educ., Curr.Adv.Ecol.Sci., Educ.Ind., Educ.Tech.Abstr., Excerp.Med., Helminthol.Abstr., Ind.Sci.Rev., Res.High.Educ.Abstr., SSCI. **Document type:** academic/scholarly publication.
—BLDSC (2066.960000); CASDDS; CISTI; Genuine Article; KR SourceOne; SWETS; UMI; UnCover. **CCC.**
   Description: Assists in the teaching of biochemistry to science and medical students throughout the world.
Refereed Serial

575.1 574.192   US   ISSN 0006-2928
QH431   CODEN: BIGEBA
BIOCHEMICAL GENETICS. 1967. m. $695 (foreign $815) (effective 1998). Plenum Publishing Corp., 233 Spring St., New York, NY 10013-1578. TEL 212-620-8000. FAX 212-463-0742. TELEX 23-421139. Ed. Hugh S. Forrest. adv. (also avail. in microfilm from UMI; back issues avail.) **Indexed:** Anim.Breed.Abstr., ASCA, Bibl.Agri., Biol.Abstr., Biol.& Agr.Ind., Biotech.Abstr., Chem.Abstr., Curr.Adv.Ecol.Sci., Curr.Cont., Dairy Sci.Abstr., Dent.Ind., Excerp.Med., Helminthol.Abstr., Hort.Abstr., Ind.Med., Ind.Sci.Rev., INIS Atomind., Maize Abstr., Ornam.Hort., Plant Breed.Abstr., Plant Grow.Reg.Abstr., Poult.Abstr., Psychol.Abstr., Sci.Cit.Ind, Sorghum & Millets Abstr., Soyabean.Abstr., Sport Fish.Abstr., Triticale Abstr., Wild.Rev., Zoo.Rec. **Document type:** academic/scholarly publication.
●Also available online.
—BLDSC (2066.980000); CASDDS; CISTI; EMDOCS; Genuine Article; KNAW; KR SourceOne; Linda Hall; SWETS; UMI; UnCover. **CCC.**
   Description: Publishes original research results in biochemical genetics.
Refereed Serial

572   UK   ISSN 0264-6021
QP501   CODEN: BIJOAK
BIOCHEMICAL JOURNAL. 1906. s-m. (8 vols. of 3 parts per year). £965($1715) (Biochemical Society) Portland Press Ltd., 59 Portland Pl., London W1N 3AJ, England. TEL 44-171-580-5530. FAX 44-171-323-1136. E-mail: sales@portlandpress.co.uk; URL: http://bj.portlandpress.co.uk. (Subscr. to: Commerce Way, P.O. Box 32, Colchester, Essex CO2 8HP, England. TEL 44-1206-796351. FAX 44-1206-799331) Ed. K. Siddle. Pub. Rhonda Oliver. R&P contact: Adam Marshall. adv. contact: Adam Marshall. index. circ. 2,600. (also avail. in microfilm from UMI,PMC; microfiche; back issues avail.) **Indexed:** Abstr.Bull.Inst.Pap.Chem., Abstr.Hyg., Anal.Abstr., Anim.Breed.Abstr., ASCA, Bibl.Agri., Biol.Abstr., Biotech.Abstr., C.I.S. Abstr., Chem.Abstr., Chem.Cit.Ind., Crop Physiol.Abstr., Curr.Adv.Biochem., Curr.Adv.Cancer Res., Curr.Adv.Ecol.Sci., Curr.Adv.Genetics & Molec.Biol., Curr.Cont., Dairy Sci.Abstr., Dent.Ind., Excerp.Med., Fababean Abstr., Field Crop Abstr., Food Sci.& Tech.Abstr., Helminthol.Abstr., Herb.Abstr., Hort.Abstr., Ind.Med., Ind.Sci.Rev., Ind.Vet., INIS Atomind., Maize Abstr., Mass Spectr.Bull., Neurosci.Cit.Ind., Nutr.Abstr., Poult.Abstr., Protozool.Abstr., Rev.Appl.Entomol., Rev.Med.& Vet.Mycol., Sci.Cit.Ind., Seed Abstr., Small Anim.Abstr., So.Pac.Per.Ind., Soils & Fert., Soyabean Abstr., Triticale Abstr., Trop.Dis.Bull., Vet.Bull., Weed Abstr. **Document type:** academic/scholarly publication.
●Also available online.
—BLDSC (2067.000000); CASDDS; CISTI; EMDOCS; Genuine Article; KNAW; SWETS; UnCover. **CCC.**
   Formed by the merger of: Biochemical Journal. Part 1: Cellular Aspects (ISSN 0306-3283); Biochemical Journal. Part 2: Molecular Aspects (ISSN 0306-3275)
   Description: Contains original refereed papers about all aspects of biochemistry.
Refereed Serial

BIOCHEMICAL PHARMACOLOGY. see *PHARMACY AND PHARMACOLOGY*

572   II   ISSN 0365-9429
   CODEN: BCRVA5
BIOCHEMICAL REVIEWS. (Text in English) vol.43, 1972. a. Society of Biological Chemists, Dept. of Biochemistry, Indian Institute of Science, Bangalore 560012, India. **Indexed:** Biol.Abstr., Chem.Abstr. —CASDDS; CISTI; Linda Hall.

572   UK   ISSN 0067-8694
QH345   CODEN: BSSYAT
BIOCHEMICAL SOCIETY SYMPOSIUM. 1948. a. £65($110.50) (effective 1997). Portland Press Ltd., 59 Portland Pl., London W1N 3AJ, England. TEL 44-171-580-5530. FAX 44-171-323-1136. E-mail: sales@portlandpress.co.uk; URL: http://www.portlandpress.co.uk. (Subscr. to: Commerce Way, P.O. Box 32, Colchester, Essex CO2 8HP, England. TEL 44-1206-796351. FAX 44-1206-799331) R&P contact: Adam Marshall. (back issues avail.) **Indexed:** ASCA. **Document type:** proceedings.
—BLDSC (2068.150000); CASDDS; CISTI; Genuine Article; KNAW; Linda Hall. **CCC.**
Refereed Serial

572　　　　　　UK　　ISSN 0300-5127
QH345　　　　　　　　　CODEN: BCSTBS
BIOCHEMICAL SOCIETY TRANSACTIONS. 1973. 4/yr. £156($264) (effective 1997). Portland Press Ltd., 59 Portland Pl., London W1N 3AJ, England. TEL 44-171-580-5530. FAX 44-171-323-1136. E-mail: sales@portlandpress.co.uk; URL: http://www.portlandpress.co.uk. (Subscr. to: Commerce Way, P.O. Box 32, Colchester, Essex CO2 8HP, England. TEL 44-1206-796351. FAX 44-1206-799331) Ed. K. Snell. adv. contact: Adam Marshall. bk.rev.; adv.; bibl.; charts; index. circ. 1,500. (back issues avail.) **Indexed:** Abstr.Hyg., Anal.Abstr., Anim.Breed.Abstr., Apic.Abstr., ASCA, Biol.Abstr., Chem.Abstr., Chem.Cit.Ind., Crop Physiol.Abstr., Curr.Adv.Biochem., Curr.Adv.Cell & Devel.Biol., Curr.Adv.Ecol.Sci., Curr.Adv.Genetics & Molec.Biol., Curr.Cont., Dairy Sci.Abstr., Diar.Dis.Res., Excerp.Med., Field Crop Abstr., Food Sci.& Tech.Abstr., Helminthol.Abstr., Herb.Abstr., Hort.Abstr., Ind.Med., Ind.Sci.Rev., Ind.Vet., INIS Atomind., Maize Abstr., Neurosci.Cit.Ind., Nutr.Abstr., Plant Grow.Reg.Abstr., Poult.Abstr., Protozool.Abstr., Rev.Appl.Entomol., Rev.Med.& Vet.Mycol., Sci.Cit.Ind., Seed Abstr., Sel.Water Res.Abstr., Soils & Fert., Trop.Dis.Bull., Vet.Bull. **Document type:** academic/scholarly publication.
—BLDSC (2068.155000); ADONIS; CASDDS; CISTI; EMDOCS; Genuine Article; KNAW; Linda Hall; SWETS; UnCover. **CCC.**
Description: Contains short reviews from colloquia sponsored by the society.
Refereed Serial

572　　　　　　UK　　ISSN 0305-1978
QH83　　　　　　　　　CODEN: BSECBU
BIOCHEMICAL SYSTEMATICS AND ECOLOGY. 1973. 8/yr. fl.1690($971) (effective 1998). Elsevier Science Ltd., Pergamon, P.O. Box 800, Kidlington, Oxford OX5 1DX, England. TEL 44-1865-843000. FAX 44-1865-843010. E-mail: nlinfo-f@elsevier.nl; usinfo-f@elsevier.com; forinfo-kyf04035@niftyserve.or.jp; URL: http://www.elsevier.nl/. (Subscr. to: Elsevier Science, Regional Sales Office, P.O. Box 211, 1000 AE Amsterdam, Netherlands. TEL 31-20-4853757. FAX 31-20-4853432; Subscr. in the Americas to: Elsevier Science, Regional Sales Office, Box 945, New York, NY 10159-0945. TEL 212-633-3730. FAX 212-633-3680; Subscr. in Australasia and the Far East to: Elsevier Science (Singapore) Pte Ltd, No.1 Temasek Ave., No.17-01 Millenia Tower, Singapore 039192, Singapore Singapore 039192, Singapore. TEL 914-524-9200. FAX 914-333-2444) Eds. Mick Richardson, Peter Waterman. adv.; bk.rev. circ. 1,000. (also avail. in microfilm from UMI; back issues avail.) **Indexed:** Anim.Breed.Abstr., Apic.Abstr., ASCA, Biodet.Abstr., Biol.Abstr., Chem.Abstr., Curr.Adv.Biochem., Curr.Adv.Ecol.Sci., Curr.Cont., Deep Sea Res.& Oceanogr.Abstr., Excerp.Med., Fababean Abstr., Field Crop Abstr., Forest.Abstr., Forest Prod.Abstr., Helminthol.Abstr., Herb.Abstr., Hort.Abstr., Ind.Sci.Rev., Ocean.Abstr., Plant Breed.Abstr., Plant Grow.Reg.Abstr., Rev.Plant Path., Sci.Cit.Ind., Seed Abstr., Sel.Water Res.Abstr., Soils & Fert., Sorghum & Millets Abstr., Soyabean Abstr., Sport Fish.Abstr., Triticale Abstr., Weed Abstr., Wild.Rev., Zoo.Rec. **Document type:** academic/scholarly publication.
—BLDSC (2068.162000); CASDDS; CISTI; EMDOCS; Genuine Article; Linda Hall; SWETS; UMI; UnCover. **CCC.**
Formerly (until 1974): Biochemical Systematics (ISSN 0045-2025)
Description: Publishes papers on the application of biochemistry and chemistry to systematic problems in biology, and on the role of biochemistry in interactions between organisms or between organisms and their environments.
Refereed Serial

610.28　　　　　US　　ISSN 1044-4203
TP202
BIOCHEMICALS ORGANIC COMPOUNDS FOR RESEARCH AND DIAGNOSTIC REAGENTS. a. Sigma Chemical Co., Box 14508, St. Louis, MO 63178.
—CISTI.

572　　　　　　US　　ISSN 0006-2960
QP501　　　　　　　　　CODEN: BICHAW
BIOCHEMISTRY. 1964. w. $1870 to institutional non-members; members $137 (effective 1997). American Chemical Society, 1155 16th St., N.W., Washington, DC 20036. TEL 800-335-9511. FAX 614-447-3671. (Subscr. to: Membership and Subscription Services, Box 3337, Columbus, OH 43210. TEL 614-447-3776) Ed. Dr. Gordon G. Hammes. adv.; charts; index. circ. 6,200. (also avail. in microform from UMI; back issues avail.; reprint service avail. from ISI) **Indexed:** Abstr.Bull.Inst.Pap.Chem., Abstr.Hyg., AIDS Abstr., Anim.Breed.Abstr., ASCA, Bibl.Agri., Biol.Abstr., Biol.& Agr.Ind., Biotech.Abstr., Biwk.Pap.Rad.Chem.& Photochem., Chem.Abstr., Chem.Cit.Ind., Crop Physiol.Abstr., Curr.Adv.Biochem., Curr.Adv.Cancer Res., Curr.Adv.Cell & Devel.Biol., Curr.Adv.Ecol.Sci., Curr.Adv.Genetics & Molec.Biol., Curr.Cont., Curr.Leather Lit., Dairy Sci.Abstr., Deep Sea Res.& Oceanogr.Abstr., Dent.Ind., Excerp.Med., Field Crop Abstr., Food Sci.& Tech.Abstr., Gen.Sci.Ind., Helminthol.Abstr., Hort.Abstr., Ind.Med., Ind.Sci.Rev., Ind.Vet., INIS Atomind., Maize Abstr., Mass Spectr.Bull., Mat.Sci.Cit.Ind., Neurosci.Cit.Ind., Nutr.Abstr., Protozool.Abstr., Rev.Med.& Vet.Mycol., Sci.Cit.Ind, Soils & Fert., Sport Fish.Abstr., Telegen, Trop.Dis.Bull., Vet.Bull., Wild.Rev., Zoo.Rec. **Document type:** academic/scholarly publication.
●Also available online. Vendor(s): STN International (CJACS).
—BLDSC (2069.200000); CASDDS; CISTI; EMDOCS; Genuine Article; KNAW; KR SourceOne; Linda Hall; SWETS; UMI; UnCover. **CCC.**
Description: Contains papers on the most current results of original research in all areas of biochemistry. Emphasis is given to the close relationship of chemistry, biochemistry, molecular and cell biology.

572　　　　　　RU　　ISSN 0006-2979
QH301　　　　　　　　　CODEN: BIORAK
BIOCHEMISTRY (MOSCOW). English translation of: Biokhimiya (RU ISSN 0320-9725) 1936. m. $1835 in US; elesewhere $2145 (effective 1998). (Russian Academy of Sciences) Maik Nauka - Interperiodica, Mezhdunarodnyi Otdel, Ul. Profsoyuznaya, 90, 117864 Moscow, Russia. TEL 7-095-3360060. FAX 212-463-0742. (Dist. by: Plenum Publishing Corp., 233 Spring St., New York, NY 10013-1578. TEL 212-620-8468) Ed. V.P. Skulachev. (back issues avail.) **Indexed:** Apic.Abstr., Biol.Abstr., Chem.Abstr., Chem.Titles, Curr.Adv.Biochem., Curr.Adv.Cancer Res., Curr.Adv.Cell & Devel.Biol., Curr.Adv.Ecol.Sci., Curr.Adv.Genetics & Molec.Biol., Curr.Cont., Curr.Leather Lit., Excerp.Med., Food Sci.& Tech.Abstr., Ind.Sci.Rev., INIS Atomind., Int.Abstr.Biol.Sci., Mass Spectr.Bull., Protozool.Abstr. **Document type:** academic/scholarly publication.
—BLDSC (0406.000000); CASDDS; CISTI; Genuine Article; Linda Hall; SWETS; UMI; UnCover. **CCC.**
Refereed Serial

BIOCHEMISTRY AND BIOPHYSICS CITATION INDEX. see *BIOLOGY — Abstracting, Bibliographies, Statistics*

572　　　　　　CN　　ISSN 0829-8211
QP501　　　　　　　　　CODEN: BCBIEQ
BIOCHEMISTRY AND CELL BIOLOGY/BIOCHIMIE ET BIOLOGIE CELLULAIRE. (Text mainly in English, occasionally in French) 1944. m. Can.$98 to individuals (foreign $108); institutions Can.$265 (foreign $265) (effective 1996). National Research Council of Canada, Research Journals, Ottawa, ON K1A 0R6, Canada. TEL 613-993-9084. FAX 613-952-7656. URL: http://www.cisti.nrc.ca/cisti/journals/. Eds. Drs. David L. Brown, Martin Tenniswood. adv.; B&W page Can.$600; trim 8 1/2 x 11; adv. contact: Hoda Jabbour. bibl.; illus.; index. circ. 2,000. (also avail. in microform from UMI,PMC; reprint service avail. from UMI) **Indexed:** Abstr.Bull.Inst.Pap.Chem., Abstr.Hyg., Anal.Abstr., Anim.Breed.Abstr., Apic.Abstr., ASCA, Biol.Abstr., Biol.& Agr.Ind., Biotech.Abstr., Chem.Abstr., Crop Physiol.Abstr., Curr.Adv.Ecol.Sci., Curr.Cont., Dairy Sci.Abstr., Dent.Ind., Excerp.Med., Field Crop Abstr., Food Sci.& Tech.Abstr., Helminthol.Abstr., Herb.Abstr., Hort.Abstr., Ind.Med., Ind.Sci.Rev., Ind.Vet., INIS Atomind., Maize Abstr., Nucl.Sci.Abstr., Nutr.Abstr., Pig News & Info., Plant Breed.Abstr., Rev.Med.& Vet.Mycol., Sci.Cit.Ind., Seed Abstr., Soils & Fert., Soyabean Abstr., Sport Fish.Abstr., Triticale Abstr., Trop.Dis.Bull., Vet.Bull., Weed Abstr., Wild.Rev., World Text.Abstr., Zoo.Rec. **Document type:** academic/scholarly publication.
—BLDSC (2069.474000); ADONIS; CASDDS; CISTI; Genuine Article; KNAW; KR SourceOne; Linda Hall; SWETS; UMI; UnCover. **CCC.**
Former titles (until 1986): Canadian Journal of Biochemistry and Cell Biology - Revue Canadien de Biochimie et Biologie Cellulaire (ISSN 0714-7511); (until 1983): Canadian Journal of Biochemistry (ISSN 0008-4018); Which supersedes in part (in 1963): Canadian Journal of Biochemistry and Physiology (ISSN 0576-5544); Which was formerly (until 1954): Canadian Journal of Medical Sciences (ISSN 0316-4403); (until 1950): Canadian Journal of Research. Section E: Medical Sciences (ISSN 0366-743X).
Refereed Serial

572　　　　　　AT　　ISSN 1039-9712
QP501　　　　　　　　　CODEN: BMBIES
BIOCHEMISTRY AND MOLECULAR BIOLOGY INTERNATIONAL. 1980. 18/yr. $750 (foreign $750) (effective 1997). (International Union of Biochemistry and Molecular Biology) Australian Academic Press Pty. Ltd., 31 Jeays St., Bowen Hills, Qld. 4006, Australia. TEL 61-7-3257176. FAX 61-7-32525908. E-mail: 100355.3122@compuserve.com; URL: http://www.apnet.com/www/journal/bm.htm; http://www.idealibrary.com/. (Dist. by: Harcourt Brace & Company Australia, Locked Bag 16, Marrickville, N.S.W. 2204, Australia; Dist. in US by: Academic Press, Box 861213, Orlando, FL 32886-1213. TEL 407-347-4040. FAX 407-363-9661) Ed. A.W. Linnane. R&P contact: A.W. Linnane. circ. 1,000. **Indexed:** ASCA, Biotech.Abstr., Chem.Abstr., Chem.Cit.Ind., Curr.Adv.Biochem., Curr.Adv.Cancer Res., Curr.Adv.Cell & Devel.Biol., Curr.Adv.Ecol.Sci., Curr.Adv.Genetics & Molec.Biol., Curr.Cont., Dairy Sci.Abstr., Excerp.Med., Helminthol.Abstr., Ind.Med., Ind.Sci.Rev., Ind.Vet., Neurosci.Cit.Ind., Protozool.Abstr., Rev.Med.& Vet.Mycol., Sci.Cit.Ind, Sport Fish.Abstr., Vet.Bull., Wild.Rev., Zoo.Rec. **Document type:** academic/scholarly publication.
●Also available online.
—BLDSC (2069.540000); CASDDS; CISTI; EMDOCS; Genuine Article; KNAW; Linda Hall; SWETS; UnCover.
Formerly (until 1993): Biochemistry International (ISSN 0158-5231)
Description: Devoted to the dissemination of original research findings among the scientific communities of the forty nations represented by the International Union of Biochemistry.

572　　　　　　US　　ISSN 0887-6495
　　　　　　　　　　　　　CODEN: BIELEO
BIOCHEMISTRY OF THE ELEMENTS. 1980. irreg., vol.12, 1994. price varies. Plenum Publishing Corp., 233 Spring St., New York, NY 10013-1578. TEL 212-620-8000. FAX 212-463-0742. TELEX 23-421139. E-mail: books@plenum.com. Ed. Earl Frieden. (back issues avail.) **Document type:** monographic series.
—BLDSC (2069.720000); CASDDS; CISTI; KNAW.
Refereed Serial

BIOLOGY — BIOLOGICAL CHEMISTRY

572 US ISSN 0194-0538
BIOCHEMISTRY: SERIES OF MONOGRAPHS. 1980. irreg., latest 1985. price varies. John Wiley & Sons, Inc., Journals, 605 Third Ave., New York, NY 10158-0012. TEL 212-850-6000. Ed. Alton Meister.
—CISTI. **CCC.**
Refereed Serial

572 NE ISSN 0006-3002
QD1 CODEN: BBACAQ
BIOCHIMICA ET BIOPHYSICA ACTA; international journal of biochemistry and biophysics. Short title: B B A. (In 10 sections: Bioenergetics, Biomembranes, Gene Stucture and Expression, General Subjects, Lipids and Lipid Metabolism, Molecular Basis of Disease, Molecular Cell Research, Protein Structure and Molecular Enzymology, Reviews on Biomembranes, Reviews on Cancer) (Text in English) 1947. m. fl.18860($10839) (effective 1998). Elsevier Science B.V., P.O. Box 211, 1000 AE Amsterdam, Netherlands. TEL 31-20-4853911. FAX 31-20-4853598. TELEX 18582 ESPA NL. E-mail: nlinfo-f@elsevier.nl; usinfo-f@elsevier.com; forinfo-kyf04035@niftyserve.or.jp; URL: http://www.elsevier.nl/. (Subscr. in the Americas to: Elsevier Science, Regional Sales Office, Box 945, New York, NY 10159-0945. TEL 212-633-3730. FAX 212-633-3680; Subscr. in Australasia and the Far East to: Elsevier Science (Singapore) Pte Ltd, No.1 Temasek Ave., No.17-01 Millenia Tower, Singapore 039192, Singapore. TEL 65-434-3727. FAX 65-337-2230; Subscr. in Japan to: Elsevier Science Japan, 9-15 Higashi-Azabu 1-chome, Minato-ku, Tokyo 106, Japan. TEL 81-3-5561-5033. FAX 81-3-5561-5047) Ed.Bd. adv.; charts; illus.; index, cum.index. circ. 4,500. (also avail. in microform from UMI; reprint service avail. from ISI) **Indexed:** Anal.Abstr., Anim.Breed.Abstr., Apic.Abstr., Bibl.Agri., Biol.Abstr., Biwk.Pap.Rad.Chem.& Photochem., Chem.Abstr., Chem.Cit.Ind., Curr.Adv.Biochem., Curr.Adv.Cancer Res., Curr.Adv.Genetics & Molec.Biol., Curr.Cont., Dent.Ind., Excerp.Med., Fababean Abstr., Field Crop Abstr., Food Sci.& Tech.Abstr., Helminthol.Abstr., Herb.Abstr., Ind.Med., INIS Atomind., Kidney, Maize Abstr., Mass Spectr.Bull., Mat.Sci.Cit.Ind., Neurosci.Cit.Ind., Nutr.Abstr., Rev.Plant Path., Telegen, Vet.Bull., Weed Abstr. **Document type:** academic/scholarly publication.
—CASDDS; CISTI; Genuine Article; Linda Hall; UnCover. **CCC.**
Refereed Serial

572 FR ISSN 0300-9084
CODEN: BICMBE
BIOCHIMIE. (Text and summaries in English) 1914. 10/yr. 3124 F. to institutions (US $597; outside the Americas 3830 F) (effective 1998). (Societe Francaise de Biochimie et Biologie Moleculaire) Editions Scientifiques et Medicales Elsevier, 141 rue de Javel, 75747 Paris, France. TEL 33-1-45589022. FAX 33-1-45589421. URL: http://www.elsevier.nl/. (Subscr. in N. America to: Elsevier Science Inc., Box 945, Madison Sq. Sta., New York, NY 10159-0945. TEL 212-633-3730. FAX 212-633-3680) Ed. M. Grunberg-Manago. adv.; bk.rev.; bibl.; charts; illus. circ. 3,000. (also avail. in microform from UMI; reprint service avail. from ISI) **Indexed:** Anal.Abstr., ASCA, Biol.Abstr., Biotech.Abstr., Chem.Abstr., Chem.Cit.Ind., Curr.Adv.Ecol.Sci., Curr.Cont., Dairy Sci.Abstr., Excerp.Med., Food Sci.& Tech.Abstr., Helminthol.Abstr., Ind.Med., Ind.Sci.Rev., Ind.Vet., INIS Atomind., Nutr.Abstr., Rev.Med.& Vet.Mycol., Sci.Cit.Ind., Sugar Ind.Abstr., Trop.Dis.Bull., Vet.Bull. **Document type:** academic/scholarly publication.
—BLDSC (2070.500000); CASDDS; CISTI; EMDOCS; Genuine Article; KNAW; Linda Hall; SWETS; UnCover. **CCC.**
Formerly: Societe de Chimie Biologique. Bulletin (ISSN 0037-9042)
Description: Publishes original work, review articles and mini-reviews in enzymology, genetics, immunology, microbiology, structure of macromolecules.
Refereed Serial

572 US ISSN 1043-1802
QP517.B49 CODEN: BCCHES
BIOCONJUGATE CHEMISTRY. 1990. 6/yr. $344 to institutional non-members; members $35 (effective 1997). American Chemical Society, 1155 16th St., N.W., Washington, DC 20036. TEL 800-333-9511. FAX 614-447-3671. (Subscr. to: Membership and Subscription Services, Box 3337, Columbus, OH 43210. TEL 614-447-3776) Ed. Claude F. Meares. (back issues avail.) **Indexed:** ASCA, Chem.Cit.Ind., Curr.Cont., Ind.Sci.Rev., Mat.Sci.Cit.Ind., Sci.Cit.Ind. **Document type:** academic/scholarly publication.
—BLDSC (2071.080000); CASDDS; CISTI; EMDOCS; Genuine Article; KNAW; Linda Hall; SWETS; UMI; UnCover. **CCC.**
Description: Emphasizes the joining of two different molecular functions by chemical or biological means.

572 SZ ISSN 0302-4598
QP341 CODEN: BEBEBP
BIOELECTROCHEMISTRY AND BIOENERGETICS; an international journal devoted to electrochemical aspects of biology and biological aspects of electrochemistry. (Text in English) 1974. bi-m. fl.2341($1345) (effective 1998). Elsevier Science S.A., P.O. Box 564, CH-1001 Lausanne 1, Switzerland. TEL 41-21-3207381. FAX 41-21-3235444. TELEX 450620-ELSA-CH. (Subscr. to: Elsevier Science, Regional Sales Office, P.O. Box 211, 1000 AE Amsterdam, Netherlands. TEL 31-20-4853757. FAX 31-20-4853432; Subscr. in the Americas to: Elsevier Science, Regional Sales Office, Box 945, New York, NY 10159-0954. TEL 212-633-3730. FAX 212-633-3680; Subscr. in Australasia to: Elsevier Science (Singapore) Pte. Ltd., No. 1 Temasek Ave., No. 17-01 Millenia Tower, Singapore 039192, Singapore. TEL 65-434-3727. FAX 65-434-2230) Ed. Hermann Berg. adv.; bk.rev. (also avail. in microform from UMI; back issues avail.) **Indexed:** ASCA, Biol.Abstr., Chem.Abstr., Chem.Cit.Ind., Curr.Adv.Ecol.Sci., Curr.Cont., Electroanal.Abstr, Excerp.Med., Ind.Sci.Rev. **Document type:** academic/scholarly publication.
—BLDSC (2072.008000); CASDDS; CISTI; Ei; EMDOCS; Genuine Article; Linda Hall; SWETS; UnCover. **CCC.**
Description: Publishes papers on electrochemical aspects of biology and biological aspects of electrochemistry.
Refereed Serial

572 SZ
BIOELECTROCHEMISTRY: PRINCIPLES AND PRACTICE. (Text in English) 1994. irreg. 148 SFr. Birkhaeuser Verlag, P.O. Box 133, CH-4010 Basel, Switzerland. TEL 41-61-7217784. FAX 41-61-7217950. E-mail: orders@birkhauser.ch. (Dist. in N. America by: Springer-Verlag, Mercedes Distribution Center, 160 Imlay St., Brooklyn, NY 11231, USA) Ed.Bd. **Document type:** monographic series.
Description: Compiles information on all the physiochemical aspects of the different biochemical and physiological processes.

575.192 NE ISSN 0951-6433
QP771 CODEN: BIFAEU
BIOFACTORS; vitamins, trace elements, growth factors, autoregulatory substances. (Text in English) 1988. 4/yr. fl.400($239) (effective 1996). (International Union of Biochemistry and Molecular Biology) I O S Press, Van Diemenstraat 94, 1013 CN Amsterdam, Netherlands. TEL 31-20-6382189. FAX 31-20-6203419. E-mail: market@iospress.nl; URL: http://www.iospress.nl/iospress. (In N. America: Box 10558, Burke, VA 22009-0558. TEL 703-323-5554. FAX 703-250-4705) Ed.Bd. adv.; bk.rev.; illus.; index. (back issues avail.; reprint service avail. from SWZ) **Indexed:** Biol.Abstr., Chem.Abstr., Curr.Adv.Biochem., Curr.Adv.Cell & Devel.Biol., Curr.Adv.Genetics & Molec.Biol., Curr.Cont., Excerp.Med. (until 1993; 1996-), Ind.Med., Sci.Cit.Ind. **Document type:** academic/scholarly publication.
—BLDSC (2072.123000); CASDDS; CISTI; EMDOCS; Genuine Article; Linda Hall; UMI; UnCover. **CCC.**
Description: Contains papers and short communications aimed at identifying and investigating effects and roles of trace substances required by organisms.
Refereed Serial

612.015 NE ISSN 0168-8561
QP801.B66 CODEN: BIAME7
BIOGENIC AMINES. 1984. bi-m. DM.540 (effective 1997). V S P, P.O. Box 346, 3700 AH Zeist, Netherlands. TEL 31-30-6925790. FAX 31-30-6932081. E-mail: 100341.2372@compuserve.com. Eds. S.H. Parvez, T. Nagatsu. (back issues avail.) **Indexed:** ASCA, Curr.Cont., Excerp.Med., Ind.Sci.Rev., Neurosci.Cit.Ind., Sci.Cit.Ind. **Document type:** academic/scholarly publication.
—BLDSC (2072.149000); CASDDS; CISTI; KNAW; SWETS. **CCC.**
Description: Publishes research on all aspects of biogenic amines and amino acid transmitters, related compounds, and interactions.
Refereed Serial

572 NE ISSN 0168-2563
QH343.7 CODEN: BIOGEP
BIOGEOCHEMISTRY; an international journal. (Text and summaries in English) 1984. m. fl.1704 to institutions; $874 to institutions in U.S. (effective 1998). Kluwer Academic Publishers, Postbus 17, 3300 AA Dordrecht, Netherlands. TEL 31-78-6392392. FAX 31-78-6392254. TELEX 29245 KAPG NL. E-mail: services@wkap.nl; URL: http://www.wkap.nl. (Dist. by: Kluwer Academic Publishers Group, P.O. Box 322, 3300 AH Dordrecht, Netherlands. TEL 31-78-6392392. FAX 31-78-6546474; N. America dist. addr.: Box 358, Accord Sta., Hingham, MA 02018-0358. TEL 617-871-6600. FAX 617-871-6528) Ed. Robert W. Howarth. adv.; bk.rev. (also avail. in microform from UMI; reprint service avail. from SWZ) **Indexed:** ASCA, Bibl.Agri., Biol.Abstr., Bull.Signal., Chem.Abstr., Curr.Adv.Ecol.Sci., Curr.Cont., Deep Sea Res.& Oceanogr.Abstr., Ecol.Abstr., Environ.Per.Bibl. (1993-), Excerp.Med. (until 19??), Geo.Abstr.P.G., Geol.Abstr., Ind.Sci.Rev., Int.Abstr.Biol.Sci., Irr.& Drain.Abstr., Rice Abstr., Sci.Cit.Ind., Sel.Water Res.Abstr., Soils & Fert. **Document type:** academic/scholarly publication.
—BLDSC (2072.163000); CASDDS; CISTI; EMDOCS; Genuine Article; Linda Hall; SWETS; UMI; UnCover. **CCC.**
Description: Publishes original papers dealing with biotic controls on the chemistry of the environment or the geochemical control of the structure and function of ecosystems.
Refereed Serial

572 RU ISSN 0320-9725
CODEN: BIOHAO
BIOKHIMIYA. English translation: Biochemistry (Moscow) (US ISSN 0006-2979) (Text in Russian; summaries in English) 1936. m. $288 (effective 1998). (Rossiiskaya Akademiya Nauk) Izdatel'stvo Nauka, 90 Profsoyuznaya ul., 117864 Moscow, Russia. Ed. S.E. Sevezin. adv.; bk.rev.; illus.; index, cum.index: 1946-1955. circ. 4,230. **Indexed:** Abstr.Bull.Inst.Pap.Chem., Anal.Abstr., Biol.Abstr., Biotech.Abstr., Chem.Abstr., Dairy Sci.Abstr., Excerp.Med., Food Sci.& Tech.Abstr., Helminthol.Abstr., Ind.Med., INIS Atomind., Nutr.Abstr., Soils & Fert.
—BLDSC (0018.100000); CASDDS; CISTI; KNAW. **CCC.**

591.192 612.015 KR ISSN 0136-9377
QP1 CODEN: BZCHDI
BIOKHIMIYA ZHIVOTNYKH I CHELOVEKA; respublikanski mezhvedomstvennyi sbornik nauchnykh trudov. (Text in Russian) 1977. a. (Akademiya Nauk Ukrainy, Institut Biokhimii im. A.V. Palladina) Vidavnitstvo Naukova Dumka, Vul. Tereshchenivska 3, 252601 Kiev, Ukraine. TEL 044-224-4060. (Dist. by: Mezhdunarodnaya Kniga,B. Yakimanka 39, 117049 Moscow, Russia) Ed. B.K. Lishko. **Indexed:** Chem.Abstr.
—CASDDS; Linda Hall.

572.8   XO
                       CODEN: BLOAAO
BIOLOGIA. SECTION: CELLULAR AND MOLECULAR BIOLOGY. (Two other sections avail.: Botany; Zoology) (Text in English) 1946. s-a. $50 ($138 for 3 sections). Slovak Academy of Sciences, Institute of Ecolbiology, Stefanikova 3, 814 34 Bratislava, Slovakia. TEL 42-7-494845. FAX 42-7-493824. E-mail: st@savba.savba.sk. (Dist. by: Slovak Academic Press, Ltd., P.O. Box 57, Nam. Slobody 6, 810 05 Bratislava, Slovakia) Ed. Dezider Toth. adv.; bk.rev.; charts, illus.; index. **Indexed:** Biodet.Abstr., Biol.Abstr., Chem.Abstr., Ind.Med., INIS Atomind., Soyabean Abstr., Sport Fish.Abstr., Triticale Abstr., Wild.Rev., Zoo.Rec. **Document type:** academic/scholarly publication.
—BLDSC (2072.700000); CASDDS; CISTI; Genuine Article; KNAW; Linda Hall.
     Formerly (until 1994): Biologia. D: Biochemia a Molekularna Biologia (ISSN 0862-1152); Supersedes in part (in 1969): Biologia (ISSN 0006-3088)
     Description: Covers original experimental and descriptive works in basic biological research from molecular biology and biochemistry.

BIOLOGICAL & PHARMACEUTICAL BULLETIN. see PHARMACY AND PHARMACOLOGY

572   GW   ISSN 1431-6730
QP501   CODEN: BICHF3
BIOLOGICAL CHEMISTRY. (Text and summaries in English and German) 1877. m. DM.1206 to institutions; individuals DM.236 (effective 1998). Walter de Gruyter und Co., Genthiner Str. 13, 10785 Berlin, Germany. TEL 49-30-26005-0. FAX 49-30-26005251. E-mail: wdg-info@degruyter.de; URL: http://www.degruyter.de. (U.S. addr.: Walter de Gruyter, Inc., 200 Saw Mill River Rd., Hawthorne, NY 10532. TEL 914-747-0110) Ed. Hans-Joachim Fritz. adv.; abstr.; bibl.; charts; illus.; stat.; index. circ. 1,000. (also avail. in microform from UMI,PMC) **Indexed:** Anim.Breed.Abstr., ASCA, Biodet.Abstr., Biol.Abstr., Biotech.Abstr., Chem.Abstr., Chem.Cit.Ind., Chem.Infd., Curr.Adv.Biochem., Curr.Adv.Cancer Res., Curr.Adv.Cell & Devel.Biol., Curr.Adv.Ecol.Sci., Curr.Adv.Genetics & Molec.Biol., Curr.Cont., Dairy Sci.Abstr., Dent.Ind., Excerp.Med., Food Sci.& Tech.Abstr., Ind.Med., Ind.Sci.Rev., Mass Spectr.Bull., Nutr.Abstr., Sci.Cit.Ind., Sport Fish.Abstr., THA, Vet.Bull., Wild.Rev., Zoo.Rec. **Document type:** academic/scholarly publication.
—BLDSC (2075.080000); CASDDS; CISTI; EMDOCS; Genuine Article; KNAW; Linda Hall; SWETS; UMI; UnCover. **CCC.**
     Former titles: Biological Chemistry Hoppe-Seyler (ISSN 0177-3593); Hoppe-Seyler's Zeitschrift fuer Physiologische Chemie (ISSN 0018-4888)

BIOLOGICAL MAGNETIC RESONANCE. see PHYSICS

BIOLOGICAL PSYCHIATRY; a journal of psychiatric research. see MEDICAL SCIENCES — Psychiatry And Neurology

612.015   US   ISSN 0271-9355
                       CODEN: BRDEDQ
BIOLOGICAL REGULATION & DEVELOPMENT. 1979. irreg., vol.3B, 1984. price varies. Plenum Publishing Corp., 233 Spring St., New York, NY 10013-1578. TEL 212-620-8000. FAX 212-463-0742. TELEX 23-421139. E-mail: books@plenum.com. Ed. Robert F. Goldberger. **Indexed:** Chem.Abstr. **Document type:** monographic series.
—CASDDS; CISTI.
     Refereed Serial

572   SZ   ISSN 1016-0922
                       CODEN: BISIEH
BIOLOGICAL SIGNALS. (Text in English) 1992. bi-m. 167.30 SFr.($130.60) to individuals; institutions 478 SFr.($373) (effective 1998). S. Karger AG, Allschwilerstr. 10, P.O. Box, CH-4009 Basel, Switzerland. TEL 41-61-3061111. FAX 41-61-3061234. E-mail: karger@karger.ch; URL: http://www.karger.ch. Ed.Bd. (also avail. in microform from UMI) **Indexed:** ASCA, Excerp.Med. (1993-), Ind.Med. (1993-). **Document type:** academic/scholarly publication.
—BLDSC (2080.710000); CASDDS; CISTI; EMDOCS; Genuine Article; KNAW; SWETS; UnCover. **CCC.**
     Refereed Serial

540   US   ISSN 0163-4984
QP534   CODEN: BTERDG
BIOLOGICAL TRACE ELEMENT RESEARCH. 1979. 15/yr. $775 (foreign $825) (effective 1998). (International Association of Bioinorganic Scientists) Humana Press Inc., 999 Riverview Dr., Ste. 208, Totowa, NJ 07512. TEL 973-256-1699. FAX 973-256-8341. E-mail: humana@mindspring.com; URL: http://www.humanapress.com. (Dist. in Japan by: Maruzen Co. Ltd., Journals Div., P.O. Box 5050, Tokyo 100-31, Japan. TEL 03-3275-8591. FAX 03-3278-1937) Ed. Gerhard N. Schrauzer. R&P contact: Richard Hruska. adv. contact: Thomas B. Lanigan, Jr. bk.rev.; bibl.; charts; illus. **Indexed:** ASCA, Biol.Abstr., Chem.Abstr., Chem.Cit.Ind., Curr.Adv.Ecol.Sci., Curr.Cont., Dairy Sci.Abstr., Excerp.Med., Ind.Med., Ind.Sci.Rev., Poult.Abstr., Sci.Cit.Ind., Sel.Water Res.Abstr., Soyabean Abstr., Sport Fish.Abstr., Wild.Rev. **Document type:** academic/scholarly publication.
—BLDSC (2081.600000); ADONIS; CASDDS; CISTI; EMDOCS; Genuine Article; KNAW; Linda Hall; SWETS; UnCover. **CCC.**
     Description: A forum for original papers in biological, environmental and biomedical research on trace elements. Stresses the integrative aspects of trace element research in all relevant fields, especially focusing on nutritional studies in humans and in animal models.
     Refereed Serial

591.192   US   ISSN 0730-7918
                       CODEN: BICADE
BIOLOGY OF CARBOHYDRATES. 1981. irreg., vol.3. J A I Press Inc., 55 Old Post Rd., No. 2, Box 1678, Greenwich, CT 06836-1678. TEL 203-661-7602. FAX 203-661-0792. (In Europe: J A I Press Ltd., The Courtyard, 28 High St., Hampton Hill, Mddx. TW12 1PD, England. TEL 44-181-943-9296. FAX 44-181-943-9317) **Document type:** monographic series.
—BLDSC (2087.040000); CASDDS; CISTI.

BIOMATERIALS. see MEDICAL SCIENCES

572   US
BIOMATERIALS FORUM; the torch. 6/yr. $45 ($50 foreign). Society for Biomaterials, 6518 Walker St., Ste. 150, Minneapolis, MN 55426-4215. TEL 612-927-8108. FAX 612-927-6707. Ed. Rosealee M. Lee. adv.; bk.rev. circ. 2,000. **Document type:** consumer publication.

572.65   UK   ISSN 1353-8616
                       CODEN: BPPAFS
BIOMEDICAL PEPTIDES, PROTEINS & NUCLEIC ACIDS; structure, synthesis & biological activity. 1994. q. £95 to individuals; institutions £125 (effective 1996). Mayflower Worldwide Ltd., P.O. Box 13, Kingswinford, W. Midlands DY6 0HQ, England. TEL 44-1384-279324. FAX 44-1384-294463. Ed. Roger Epton. R&P contact: Roger Epton. **Document type:** academic/scholarly publication.
—BLDSC (2087.854000); CASDDS.
     Refereed Serial

572   JA   ISSN 0916-717X
                       CODEN: BRTEE5
BIOMEDICAL RESEARCH ON TRACE ELEMENTS. (Text in English, Japanese; summaries in English) 1990. irreg. 75000 Yen. Japan Society for Biomedical Research on Trace Elements - Nihon Biryo Genso Gakkai, Nihon Daigaku Igakubu Kagaku Kyoshitsu, 30-1, Oyaguchi Kamicho, Itabashi-ku, Tokyo 173, Japan. TEL 03-3972-8111. FAX 03-5995-6956. Ed. Yasuyuki Arakawa. **Document type:** academic/scholarly publication.
—BLDSC (2087.875000); CASDDS.

572   UK   ISSN 0966-0844
QP532   CODEN: BOMEEH
BIOMETALS. 1988. 4/yr. £425 (foreign $705) (effective 1998). Thomson Science (Subsidiary of: International Thomson Publishing Group), 2-6 Boundary Row, London SE1 8HN, England. TEL 44-171-865-0198. FAX 44-171-410-6600. E-mail: rapid@rapidcom.co.uk; URL: http://www.thomsonscience.com. (Subscr. in US to: 400 Market St., Ste. 750, Philadelphia, PA 19106. TEL 215-574-2266. FAX 215-574-2292) Ed. G. Winkelmann. adv. contact: Julie Gribben. **Indexed:** ASCA, Biodet.Abstr., Chem.Cit.Ind., Curr.Cont., Excerp.Med. (1994-), Ind.Sci.Rev., Sci.Cit.Ind. **Document type:** academic/scholarly publication.
●Also available online.
Also available on CD-ROM.
—BLDSC (2087.940000); ADONIS; CASDDS; CISTI; EMDOCS; Genuine Article; SWETS; UMI. **CCC.**
     Formerly: Biology of Metals (ISSN 0933-5854)
     Description: Provides an international, multidisciplinary forum for new research and clinical results concerning the role of metal ions in biology, biochemistry and medicine.

BIOORGANICHESKAYA KHIMIYA. see CHEMISTRY — Organic Chemistry

BIOPHYSICAL CHEMISTRY; an international journal devoted to the physics and chemistry of biological phenomena. see BIOLOGY — Biophysics

BIOSCIENCE, BIOTECHNOLOGY, AND BIOCHEMISTRY. see BIOLOGY

BIOSCIENCE REPORTS; molecular and cellular biology of the cell surface. see BIOLOGY — Cytology And Histology

BIOTECHNOLOGY AND APPLIED BIOCHEMISTRY. see BIOLOGY — Biotechnology

BIOTECHNOLOGY AND BIOENGINEERING. see BIOLOGY — Biotechnology

BIOTECHNOLOGY: APPARATUS, PLANT, AND EQUIPMENT. see BIOLOGY — Biotechnology

BISEIBUTSU KAGAKU BUNRUI KENKYUKAI KOEN YOSHISHU/ABSTRACTS OF ANNUAL MEETING ON MICROBIAL CHEMOTAXONOMY. see BIOLOGY — Abstracting, Bibliographies, Statistics

BLOOD. see MEDICAL SCIENCES — Hematology

C A SELECTS. CALCIUM CHANNEL BLOCKERS. see CHEMISTRY — Abstracting, Bibliographies, Statistics

C A SELECTS. HYPERTENSION & ANTIHYPERTENSIVES. see MEDICAL SCIENCES — Abstracting, Bibliographies, Statistics

C A SELECTS. LEUKOTRIENES. see CHEMISTRY — Abstracting, Bibliographies, Statistics

C A SELECTS. OLEOCHEMICALS CONTAINING NITROGEN. see CHEMISTRY — Abstracting, Bibliographies, Statistics

C A SELECTS. OMEGA-3 FATTY ACIDS & FISH OIL. see CHEMISTRY — Abstracting, Bibliographies, Statistics

C A SELECTS. PHOSPHOLIPIDS (CHEMICAL ASPECTS). see BIOLOGY — Abstracting, Bibliographies, Statistics

C A SELECTS. PHOTOBIOCHEMISTRY. see CHEMISTRY — Abstracting, Bibliographies, Statistics

C A SELECTS PLUS. AMINO ACIDS, PEPTIDES AND PROTEINS. see BIOLOGY — Abstracting, Bibliographies, Statistics

BIOLOGY — BIOLOGICAL CHEMISTRY

612.015   CN   CODEN: CBCBBB
CANADIAN SOCIETY OF BIOCHEMISTRY AND MOLECULAR BIOLOGY. BULLETIN. (Text mainly in English; occasionally in French) s-a. Can.$10($10) Canadian Society of Biochemistry and Molecular Biology, c/o Dr. E.R. Tustanoff, Sec., Dept. of Biochemistry, University of Western Ontario, London, ON N6A 5C1, Canada. TEL 519-661-3060. FAX 519-661-3175. Ed. David Evans. adv.; bk.rev. circ. 750. **Document type:** bulletin.
—CASDDS; CISTI.
    Formerly: Canadian Biochemical Society. Bulletin (ISSN 0008-302X)
    Description: Covers news and meetings in Canada's biochemistry field.

CANCER BIOCHEMISTRY BIOPHYSICS. see *MEDICAL SCIENCES — Oncology*

572   NE   ISSN 1073-5070   CODEN: CLETEC
CARBOHYDRATE LETTERS. 1994. q. $77 (effective 1998). Gordon and Breach - Harwood Academic, Amsteldisk 166, 1st Fl., 1079 LH Amsterdam, Netherlands. URL: http://www.gbhap.com/Carbohydrate__Letters/. (Subscr. to: International Publishers Distributor, Box 32160, Newark, NJ 07102. TEL 800-545-8398. FAX 215-750-6343) Ed. Pierre G. Sinay. (back issues avail.) **Indexed:** Food Sci.& Tech.Abstr. **Document type:** academic/scholarly publication.
●Also available online.
Also available on CD-ROM.
—BLDSC (3050.990150); CASDDS; EMDOCS. **CCC.**
    Description: Promotes the understanding of the precise biological role of sugars, as defined through developments in the chemistry of carbohydrates.
Refereed Serial

572   US   ISSN 0069-0732
CAROTENOIDS OTHER THAN VITAMIN A. (Subseries of: I U P A C Chemical Data Series (ISSN 0275-0910)) (Text in English) 1967. irreg., 3rd, 1972, Cluj, Rumania. price varies. (International Union of Pure and Applied Chemistry) C R C Press, Inc., 2000 Corporate Blvd., N.W., Boca Raton, FL 33431. TEL 561-994-0555; 800-272-7737. FAX 561-998-9784. TELEX 568689-CRC PRESS. **Document type:** monographic series.

CELL BIOCHEMISTRY AND BIOPHYSICS. see *BIOLOGY — Cytology And Histology*

612.015 610   UK   ISSN 0263-6484
QH611   CODEN: CBFUDH
CELL BIOCHEMISTRY AND FUNCTION. 1983. q. $925 (foreign $925) (effective 1998). John Wiley & Sons Ltd., Journals, Baffins Ln., Chichester, W. Sussex PO19 1UD, England. TEL 44-1243-779777. FAX 44-1243-775878. E-mail: info-assets@wiley.co.uk; URL: http://www.wiley.co.uk. (Subscr. in the Americas to: John Wiley & Sons, Inc., 605 Third Ave., New York, NY 10158. TEL 212-850-6645. FAX 212-850-6021) Ed. J. Chayen. adv.; B&W page £595, color page £1495; trim 260 x 200; adv. contact: Bob Kern. bk.rev.; abstr.; illus.; index. circ. 300. (also avail. in microform from UMI; back issues avail.; reprint service avail. from SWZ) **Indexed:** ASCA, Chem.Abstr., Curr.Adv.Ecol.Sci., Curr.Cont., Excerp.Med., Ind.Med., Ind.Sci.Rev., Sci.Cit.Ind. **Document type:** academic/scholarly publication.
—BLDSC (3097.702000); CASDDS; CISTI; EMDOCS; Genuine Article; KNAW; SWETS; UMI; UnCover. **CCC.**
    Description: Provides a forum for reporting and discussing the biochemistry of whole cells and of the link between the biochemistry and the functioning of cells in isolation, in assemblies, and in tissues.

612.015   UK   ISSN 0142-8020
CELL CALCIUM (SHEFFIELD). 1976. s-m. (diskette m.). £125 (diskette £120; both £180) (effective 1997). S U B I S, Mansion House, 19 Kingfield Rd., Sheffield S11 9AS, England. TEL 44-114-2554433. FAX 44-114-2554626. E-mail: subis@sheffac.demon.co.uk; URL: http://www.shef.ac.uk/uni/companies/shap. (also avail. in diskette format) **Indexed:** Curr.Adv.Biochem., Curr.Adv.Cell & Devel.Biol., Curr.Adv.Ecol.Sci., Vet.Bull. **Document type:** abstracting/indexing.
—**CCC.**
    Description: Current awareness service for researchers in clinical and life sciences. Covers calcium in signal transduction, calcium transport, calcium-binding proteins, muscle and nerve cell calcium.

572   UK   ISSN 0142-8047
CELL MEMBRANES. 1970. s-m. (diskette m.). £125 (diskette £120; both £180) (effective 1997). S U B I S, Mansion House, 19 Kingfield Rd., Sheffield S11 9AS, England. TEL 44-114-2554433. FAX 44-114-2554626. E-mail: subis@sheffac.demon.co.uk; URL: http://www.shef.ac.uk/uni/companies/shap. (also avail. in diskette format) **Indexed:** Chem.Abstr., Sci.Cit.Ind. **Document type:** abstracting/indexing.
—**CCC.**
    Description: Current awareness service for researchers in clinical and life sciences. Covers membrane transport, protein transport, channels, electrical properties, lipids and model systems.

572   SZ   ISSN 1015-8987   CODEN: CEPBEW
CELLULAR PHYSIOLOGY AND BIOCHEMISTRY. 1991. 6/yr. 161 SFr.($123.20) to individuals; institutions 460 SFr.($352) (effective 1998). S. Karger AG, Allschwilerstr. 10, P.O. Box, CH-4009 Basel, Switzerland. TEL 41-61-3061111. FAX 41-61-3061234. E-mail: karger@karger.ch; URL: http://www.karger.ch. Ed. F. Lang. (also avail. in microform from UMI) **Indexed:** ASCA, Curr.Cont., Excerp.Med. (1993-). **Document type:** academic/scholarly publication.
—BLDSC (3097.934000); CASDDS; CISTI; EMDOCS; Genuine Article; KNAW; Linda Hall; UnCover. **CCC.**
    Description: Covers mechanisms of intracellular transmission; cellular pharmacology; maintenance, regulation, and disturbance of cell volume; regulation of cell growth and differentiation; control of cellular metabolism; and molecular biology and function of ion carriers.
Refereed Serial

572   US   ISSN 0093-6855   CODEN: CMMUAO
CHEMICAL MUTAGENS. 1971. irreg., vol.10, 1986. Plenum Publishing Corp., 233 Spring St., New York, NY 10013-1578. TEL 212-620-8000. FAX 212-463-0742. **Document type:** monographic series.
—CASDDS; CISTI. **CCC.**

CHEMICAL SENSES. see *BIOLOGY — Physiology*

CHEMICO-BIOLOGICAL INTERACTIONS; a journal of molecular and biochemical toxicology. see *ENVIRONMENTAL STUDIES — Toxicology And Environmental Safety*

572   US   ISSN 0069-3111
QP551   CODEN: CBCAB8
CHEMISTRY AND BIOCHEMISTRY OF AMINO ACIDS, PEPTIDES, AND PROTEINS. 1971. irreg., vol.7, 1983. price varies. Marcel Dekker, Inc., 270 Madison Ave., New York, NY 10016. TEL 212-696-9000. FAX 212-685-4540. TELEX 421419. Ed. Russell Dekker; Pub. Graham Garratt. R&P contact: Julia Mulligan. **Indexed:** Chem.Abstr. **Document type:** monographic series.
—CASDDS; CISTI; Linda Hall. **CCC.**
Refereed Serial

CHEMISTRY & BIOLOGY. see *BIOLOGY — Biotechnology*

CHEMISTRY AND ECOLOGY. see *CHEMISTRY*

572   IE   ISSN 0009-3084   CODEN: CPLIA4
CHEMISTRY AND PHYSICS OF LIPIDS. 1966. m. fl.3472($1995) (effective 1998). Elsevier Science Ireland Ltd., P.O. Box 85, Limerick, Ireland. TEL 353-61-471944. FAX 353-61-472144. (Subscr. to: Elsevier Science, Regional Sales Office, P.O. Box 211, 1000 AE Amsterdam, Netherlands. TEL 31-20-4853757. FAX 31-20-4853432; Subscr. in the Americas to: Elsevier Science, Regional Sales Office, Box 945, New York, NY 10159-0945. TEL 212-633-3730. FAX 212-633-3680; Subscr. in Australasia and the Far East to: Elsevier Science (Singapore) Pte Ltd, No.1 Temasek Ave., No.17-01 Millenia Tower, Singapore 039192, Singapore. TEL 65-434-3727. FAX 65-337-2230) Eds. F. Paltauf, H.H.O. Schmid. R&P contact: Annette Moloney. illus.; index. (also avail. in microform from UMI) **Indexed:** Apic.Abstr., ASCA, Biol.Abstr., Chem.Abstr., Chem.Cit.Ind., Curr.Adv.Biochem., Curr.Adv.Cell & Devel.Biol., Curr.Adv.Ecol.Sci., Curr.Cont., Excerp.Med., Ind.Med., Ind.Sci.Rev., Mass Spectr.Bull., Nutr.Abstr., Sci.Cit.Ind. **Document type:** academic/scholarly publication.
—BLDSC (3170.100000); ADONIS; CASDDS; CISTI; Ei; EMDOCS; Genuine Article; Linda Hall; SWETS; UnCover. **CCC.**
    Description: Publishes papers and review articles in the field of molecular biology which emphasize chemical and biophysical aspects of lipids.
Refereed Serial

CHLOROPLASTS. see *BIOLOGY — Botany*

572.57   UK   ISSN 0964-7597
CHOLESTEROL & LIPOPROTEINS. 1992. s-m. (diskette m.). £90 (diskette £120; both £180) (effective 1997). S U B I S, Mansion House, 19 Kingfield Rd., Sheffield S11 9AS, England. TEL 44-114-2554433. FAX 44-114-2554626. E-mail: subis@sheffac.demon.co.uk; URL: http://www.shef.ac.uk/uni/companies/shap. (also avail. in diskette format) **Document type:** abstracting/indexing.
    Description: Current awareness service for researchers in life sciences.

572   US   ISSN 0095-4861   CODEN: CBAND5
CLINICAL AND BIOCHEMICAL ANALYSIS. 1974. irreg., vol.24, 1988. price varies. Marcel Dekker, Inc., 270 Madison Ave., New York, NY 10016. TEL 212-696-9000. FAX 212-685-4540. TELEX 421419. Ed. M.K. Schwartz; Pub. Graham Garratt. R&P contact: Julia Mulligan. **Indexed:** Biol.Abstr., Chem.Abstr. **Document type:** monographic series.
—CASDDS; CISTI; KNAW.
Refereed Serial

572   AT   ISSN 0159-8090   CODEN: CBREEU
CLINICAL BIOCHEMIST REVIEWS.* 1980. q. Aus.$50. Associated Business Publications Pty. Ltd., P.O. Box 440, Broadway, N.S.W. 2007, Australia. TEL 61-2-2122780. FAX 61-2-2814594. Ed. Robert A.J. Conyers. circ. 1,600. **Document type:** bulletin.
—BLDSC (3286.260800); CASDDS; CISTI.

BIOLOGY — BIOLOGICAL CHEMISTRY

572   US   ISSN 0009-9120
RB112.5   CODEN: CLBIAS
CLINICAL BIOCHEMISTRY. (Text in English, French) 1967. 8/yr. fl.643($369) (effective 1998). (Canadian Society of Clinical Chemists, CN) Elsevier Science Inc., Box 945, New York, NY 10159-0945. TEL 212-633-3730. FAX 212-633-3680. E-mail: nlinfo-f@elsevier.nl; usinfo-f@elsevier.com; forinfo-kyf04035@niftyserve.or.jp; URL: http://www.elsevier.nl/. (Subscr. outside the Americas to: Elsevier Science, Regional Sales Office, P.O. Box 211, 1000 AE Amsterdam, Netherlands. TEL 31-20-4853757. FAX 31-20-4853432; Subscr. in Australasia and the Far East to: Elsevier Science (Singapore) Pte Ltd, No.1 Temasek Ave., No.17-01 Millenia Tower, Singapore 039192, Singapore. TEL 65-434-3727. FAX 65-337-2230; Subscr. in Japan to: Elsevier Science Japan, 9-15 Higashi-Azabu 1-chome, Minato-ku, Tokyo 106, Japan. TEL 81-3-5561-5033. FAX 81-3-5561-5047) (Co-sponsor: National Academy of Biochemistry) Ed. R. Yatscoff. adv.; charts; illus.; stat. circ. 1,500. (also avail. in microfilm from UMI; back issues avail.) **Indexed:** Biol.Abstr., Biotech.Abstr., Chem.Abstr. Compumath, Curr.Adv.Biochem., Curr.Cont., Dairy Sci.Abstr., Excerp.Med., Helminthol.Abstr., Ind.Med., Ind.Sci.Rev., INIS Atomind., Mass Spectr.Bull., Nutr.Abstr., Rev.Plant Path. **Document type:** academic/scholarly publication.
—BLDSC (3286.262000); ADONIS; CASDDS; CISTI; EMDOCS; Genuine Article; KNAW; Linda Hall; SWETS; UMI; UnCover. **CCC.**
    Description: Publishes articles relating to the applications of molecular biology, biochemistry, chemistry and immunology to clinical investigation and to the diagnosis, therapy, and monitoring of human diseases.
    Refereed Serial

612.015   NE   ISSN 0892-2187
CODEN: CCECEY
CLINICAL CHEMISTRY AND ENZYMOLOGY COMMUNICATIONS. 1988. 6/yr. (in 1 vol., 6 nos./vol.). $131 (effective 1998). Gordon and Breach - Harwood Academic, Amsteldisk 166, 1st Fl., 1079 LH Amsterdam, Netherlands. URL: http://www.gbhap.com/Clinical_Chemistry_Enzymology_Communications/. (Subscr. to: International Publishers Distributor, Box 32160, Newark, NJ 07102. TEL 800-545-8398. FAX 215-750-6343) Ed. Giorgio Federici. (also avail. in microform)
● Also available online.
Also available on CD-ROM.
—BLDSC (3286.268050); CASDDS; CISTI; Ei; EMDOCS; SWETS; UnCover. **CCC.**
    Refereed Serial

591.192   UK   ISSN 0885-7431
CLINICAL NEUROCHEMISTRY. 1986. irreg. Academic Press Ltd. (Subsidiary of: Harcourt Brace & Company Ltd.), 24-28 Oval Rd., London NW1 7DX, England. TEL 44-171-267-4466. FAX 44-171-482-2293. **Document type:** academic/scholarly publication, monographic series.
—CISTI.

572   US   ISSN 0366-5887
CODEN: CGBCA9
COLLOQUIUM MOSBACH. Variant title: Gesellschaft fuer Biologische Chemie, Mosbach. Colloquium. (Contributions in English, French and German) 1951. irreg., vol.45, 1995. price varies. Springer-Verlag, 175 Fifth Ave., New York, NY 10010. TEL 212-460-1500. FAX 212-473-6272. (Also: Berlin, Heidelberg, Tokyo and Vienna) (reprint service avail. from ISI) **Indexed:** Biol.Abstr. **Document type:** academic/scholarly publication.
—CASDDS; KNAW.
    Formerly: Gesellschaft fuer Physiologische Chemie, Mosbach. Colloquium (ISSN 0072-4246)

572   US   ISSN 0300-9629
QP33   CODEN: CBPAB5
COMPARATIVE BIOCHEMISTRY AND PHYSIOLOGY. PART A: COMPARATIVE PHYSIOLOGY. (Text and summaries in English, French and German) 1961. m. fl.5701($3276) (effective 1998). Elsevier Science Inc., Box 945, New York, NY 10159-0945. TEL 212-633-3730. FAX 212-633-3680. E-mail: nlinfo-f@elsevier.nl; usinfo-f@elsevier.com; forinfo-kyf04035@niftyserve.or.jp; URL: http://www.elsevier.nl/. (Subscr. outside the Americas to: Elsevier Science, Regional Sales Office, P.O. Box 211, 1000 AE Amsterdam, Netherlands. TEL 31-20-4853757. FAX 31-20-4853432; Subscr. in Australasia and the Far East to: Elsevier Science (Singapore) Pte Ltd, No.1 Temasek Ave., No.17-01 Millenia Tower, Singapore 039192, Singapore. TEL 65-434-3727. FAX 65-337-2230; Subscr. in Japan to: Elsevier Science Japan, 9-15 Higashi-Azabu 1-chome, Minato-ku, Tokyo 106, Japan. TEL 81-3-5561-5033. FAX 81-3-5561-5047) Eds. P.W. Hochachka, T.P. Mommsen. adv.: B&W page $550, color page $1350. bk.rev.; bibl.; charts; illus. circ. 2,000. (also avail. in microfiche from MIM; microfilm from UMI; back issues avail.) **Indexed:** Anim.Breed.Abstr., Apic.Abstr., ASCA, Bibl.Agri., Bio-Contr.News & Info., Biol.Abstr., Chem.Abstr., Curr.Adv.Cancer Res., Curr.Adv.Ecol.Sci., Curr.Cont., Curr.Ref.Fish Res., Dairy Sci.Abstr., Deep Sea Res.& Oceanogr.Abstr., Dent.Ind., Excerp.Med., Helminthol.Abstr., Herb.Abstr., Ind.Med., Ind.Sci.Rev., Ind.Vet., Key Word Ind.Wildl.Res., Maize Abstr., Neurosci.Cit.Ind., Nutr.Abstr., Ocean.Abstr., Pig News & Info., Pollut.Abstr., Poult.Abstr., Sci.Cit.Ind., Sel.Water Res.Abstr., Small Anim.Abstr., Sport Fish.Abstr., Vet.Bull., Wild.Rev., Zoo.Rec. **Document type:** academic/scholarly publication.
—BLDSC (3363.751000); ADONIS; CASDDS; CISTI; EMDOCS; Genuine Article; Linda Hall; SWETS; UMI. **CCC.**
    Description: Original research on the biochemistry and physiology of animals.
    Refereed Serial

572   US   ISSN 0305-0491
QP33   CODEN: CBPBB8
COMPARATIVE BIOCHEMISTRY AND PHYSIOLOGY. PART B: COMPARATIVE BIOCHEMISTRY. (Text and summaries in English, French and German) 1961. m. fl.5570($3201) (effective 1998). Elsevier Science Inc., Box 945, New York, NY 10159-0945. TEL 212-633-3730. FAX 212-633-3680. E-mail: nlinfo-f@elsevier.nl; usinfo-f@elsevier.com; forinfo-kyf04035@niftyserve.or.jp; URL: http://www.elsevier.nl/. (Subscr. outside the Americas to: Elsevier Science, Regional Sales Office, P.O. Box 211, 1000 AE Amsterdam, Netherlands. TEL 31-20-4853757. FAX 31-20-4853432; Subscr. in Australasia and the Far East to: Elsevier Science (Singapore) Pte Ltd, No.1 Temasek Ave., No.17-01 Millenia Tower, Singapore 039192, Singapore. TEL 65-434-3727. FAX 65-337-2230; Subscr. in Japan to: Elsevier Science Japan, 9-15 Higashi-Azabu 1-chome, Minato-ku, Tokyo 106, Japan. TEL 81-3-5561-5033. FAX 81-3-5561-5047) Eds. P.W. Hochachka, T.P. Mommsen. adv.: B&W page $550, color page $1350. bk.rev.; bibl.; charts; illus. circ. 2,000. (also avail. in microfiche from MIM; microfilm from UMI; back issues avail.) **Indexed:** Anim.Breed.Abstr., Apic.Abstr., ASCA, Bio-Contr.News & Info., Biodet.Abstr., Biol.Abstr., Chem.Abstr., Chem.Cit.Ind., Curr.Adv.Biochem., Curr.Adv.Cell & Devel.Biol., Curr.Adv.Ecol.Sci., Curr.Adv.Genetics & Molec.Biol., Curr.Cont., Dairy Sci.Abstr., Deep Sea Res.& Oceanogr.Abstr., Dent.Ind., Excerp.Med., Helminthol.Abstr., Ind.Med., Ind.Sci.Rev., Ind.Vet., Neurosci.Cit.Ind., Nutr.Abstr., Ocean.Abstr., Pig News & Info., Pollut.Abstr., Poult.Abstr., Protozool.Abstr., Sci.Cit.Ind., Small Anim.Abstr., Soyabean Abstr., Sport Fish.Abstr., SSCI, Vet.Bull., Wild.Rev., Zoo.Rec. **Document type:** academic/scholarly publication.
—BLDSC (3363.752000); ADONIS; CASDDS; CISTI; EMDOCS; Genuine Article; SWETS; UMI; UnCover. **CCC.**
    Description: Original research on the biochemistry and physiology of animals.
    Refereed Serial

615   US   ISSN 0742-8413
QP33   CODEN: CBPCEE
COMPARATIVE BIOCHEMISTRY AND PHYSIOLOGY. PART C: COMPARATIVE PHARMACOLOGY & TOXICOLOGY. (Text in English and French) 1975. 9/yr. fl.4054($2330) (effective 1998). Elsevier Science Inc., Box 945, New York, NY 10159-0945. TEL 212-989-5800. FAX 212-633-3990. E-mail: nlinfo-f@elsevier.nl; usinfo-f@elsevier.com; forinfo-kyf04035@niftyserve.or.jp; URL: http://www.elsevier.nl/. (Subscr. outside the Americas to: Elsevier Science, Regional Sales Office, P.O. Box 211, 1000 AE Amsterdam, Netherlands. TEL 31-20-4853757; Subscr. in Australasia and the Far East to: Elsevier Science (Singapore) Pte Ltd, No.1 Temasek Ave., No.17-01 Millenia Tower, Singapore 039192, Singapore. TEL 65-434-3727; Subscr. in Japan to: Elsevier Science Japan, 9-15 Higashi-Azabu 1-chome, Minato-ku, Tokyo 106, Japan) Eds. P.W. Hochachka, T.P. Mommsen. adv.: B&W page $550, color page $1350. bk.rev.; abstr.; charts; illus.; index. circ. 1,500. (also avail. in microfiche from MIM; microfilm from UMI) **Indexed:** Apic.Abstr., ASCA, Biol.Abstr., Chem.Abstr., Curr.Adv.Ecol.Sci., Curr.Cont., Dairy Sci.Abstr., Deep Sea Res.& Oceanogr.Abstr., Excerp.Med., Helminthol.Abstr., Ind.Med., Ind.Sci.Rev., Ind.Vet., Neurosci.Cit.Ind., Nutr.Abstr., Ocean.Abstr., Poult.Abstr., Protozool.Abstr., Rev.Med.& Vet.Mycol., Sci.Cit.Ind., Sel.Water Res.Abstr., Sport Fish.Abstr., Vet.Bull., Weed Abstr., Wild.Rev., Zoo.Rec. **Document type:** academic/scholarly publication.
—BLDSC (3363.752500); ADONIS; CASDDS; CISTI; EMDOCS; Genuine Article; Linda Hall; SWETS; UMI. **CCC.**
    Formerly: Comparative Biochemistry and Physiology. Part C: Comparative Pharmacology (ISSN 0306-4492)
    Description: Publishes research studying the actions of drugs and chemicals on cells, tissues, and whole animals.
    Refereed Serial

572   NE   ISSN 0069-8032
COMPREHENSIVE BIOCHEMISTRY. 1962. irreg., vol.37, 1990. price varies. Elsevier Science B.V., Books Division, P.O. Box 211, 1000 AE Amsterdam, Netherlands. TEL 31-20-4853911. FAX 31-20-4853705. TELEX 18582 ESPA NL. E-mail: nlinfo-f@elsevier.nl; usinfo-f@elsevier.com; forinfo-kyf04035@niftyserve.or.jp; URL: http://www.elsevier.nl/. (Subscr. in the Americas to: Elsevier Science, Regional Sales Office, Box 945, New York, NY 10159-0945. TEL 212-633-3730. FAX 212-633-3680; Subscr. in Australasia and the Far East to: Elsevier Science (Singapore) Pte Ltd, No.1 Temasek Ave., No.17-01 Millenia Tower, Singapore 039192, Singapore. TEL 65-434-3727. FAX 65-337-2230; Subscr. in Japan to: Elsevier Science Japan, 9-15 Higashi-Azabu 1-chome, Minato-ku, Tokyo 106, Japan. TEL 81-3-5561-5033. FAX 81-3-5561-5047) Eds. M. Florkin, E.H. Stotz. **Indexed:** Ind.Sci.Rev., Sci.Cit.Ind. **Document type:** monographic series.
—CCC.
    Refereed Serial

COMPUTERS & CHEMISTRY. see *CHEMISTRY — Computer Applications*

572   CL   ISSN 0069-8784
CONFERENCIAS DE BIOQUIMICA.* 1967. a. Universidad de Chile, Instituto de Quimica Fisiologica y Patologica, Av. Bernardo O'Higgins 1058, Casilla 10-D, Santiago, Chile.

CONTEMPORARY NEUROSCIENCE. see *MEDICAL SCIENCES — Psychiatry And Neurology*

BIOLOGY — BIOLOGICAL CHEMISTRY

572　　　　　US　　ISSN 1040-9238
QP501　　　　　　　CODEN: CRBBEJ
CRITICAL REVIEWS IN BIOCHEMISTRY AND MOLECULAR BIOLOGY. 1971. bi-m. $495 (effective 1998). C R C Press, Inc., 2000 Corporate Blvd., N.W., Boca Raton, FL 33431. TEL 561-994-0555; 800-272-7737. FAX 561-998-9784. TELEX 568689-CRC PRESS. Ed. Gerald D. Fasman. bibl.; charts; illus. circ. 570. (back issues avail.) Indexed: ASCA, Biol.Abstr., Chem.Abstr., Curr.Adv.Ecol.Sci., Curr.Cont., Food Sci.& Tech.Abstr., Helminthol.Abstr., Ind.Med., Ind.Sci.Rev., INIS Atomind., Sci.Cit.Ind. Document type: academic/scholarly publication.
—BLDSC (3487.471500); ADONIS; CASDDS; CISTI; EMDOCS; Genuine Article; KNAW; Linda Hall; SWETS; UnCover. **CCC.**
Formerly: C R C Critical Reviews in Biochemistry (ISSN 0045-6411)
Description: Includes, in each issue, several critical surveys on specific topics of current interest.
Refereed Serial

CRYO - LETTERS. see BIOLOGY — Physiology

CURRENT ADVANCES IN PROTEIN BIOCHEMISTRY. see BIOLOGY — Abstracting, Bibliographies, Statistics

CURRENT OPINION IN STRUCTURAL BIOLOGY. see BIOLOGY — Abstracting, Bibliographies, Statistics

572　　　　　US
CURRENT PROTOCOLS IN PROTEIN SCIENCE. a. (with q. updates). $390 (CD-ROM $490) (effective 1997). John Wiley & Sons, Inc., Journals, 605 Third Ave., New York, NY 10158. TEL 212-850-6645. FAX 212-850-6021. E-mail: subinfo@jwiley.com. Ed.Bd. Document type: academic/scholarly publication, monographic series.
●Also available on CD-ROM.
Description: Covers both basic and advanced methods used in protein purification, characterization, and analysis.

573.8 612.8　　US　　ISSN 0093-4747
CURRENT TOPICS IN NEUROBIOLOGY. 1973. irreg. Plenum Publishing Corp., 233 Spring St., New York, NY 10013-1578. TEL 212-620-8000. FAX 212-463-0742. Document type: monographic series.
—CISTI.

572.65　　　　UK　　ISSN 1359-6101
QP552.G76　　　　　　CODEN: CGFRFB
CYTOKINE AND GROWTH FACTOR REVIEWS. 1989. q. fl.722($415) (effective 1997). Elsevier Science Ltd., Pergamon, P.O. Box 800, Kidlington, Oxford OX5 1DX, England. TEL 44-1865-843000. FAX 44-1865-843010. E-mail: nlinfo-f@elsevier.nl; usinfo-f@elsevier.com; forinfo-kyf04035@niftyserve.or.jp; URL: http://www.elsevier.nl/. (Subscr. to: Elsevier Science, Regional Sales Office, P.O. Box 211, 1000 AE Amsterdam, Netherlands. TEL 31-20-4853757. FAX 31-20-4853432; Subscr. in the Americas to: Elsevier Science, Regional Sales Office, Box 945, New York, NY 10159-0945. TEL 212-633-3730. FAX 212-633-3680; Subscr. in Australasia and the Far East to: Elsevier Science (Singapore) Pte Ltd, No.1 Temasek Ave., No.17-01 Millenia Tower, Singapore 039192, Singapore. TEL 65-434-3727. FAX 65-337-2230) Ed. John K. Heath. (also avail. in microfilm from UMI; back issues avail.) Document type: academic/scholarly publication.
—BLDSC (3506.778500); CASDDS; CISTI; KNAW; SWETS; UMI; UnCover. **CCC.**
Formerly (until vol.7): Progress in Growth Factor Research (ISSN 0955-2235)
Description: Features reviews of current research and applications on cytokines, growth factors and related regulatory peptides.
Refereed Serial

616.0791 571.9644　NE　ISSN 1384-1238
▼**CYTOKINE YEARBOOK.** (Text in English) 1996. a. fl.130. (International Society for Interferon and Cytokine Research) Kluwer Academic Publishers, Postbus 17, 3300 AA Dordrecht, Netherlands. TEL 31-78-6392392. FAX 31-78-6392254. E-mail: services@wkap.nl; URL: http://www.wkap.nl. (Dist. by: Kluwer Academic Publishers Group, P.O. Box 322, 3300 AH Dordrecht, Netherlands. TEL 31-78-6392392. FAX 31-78-6546474; N. America dist. addr.: Box 358, Accord Sta., Hingham, MA 02018-0358. TEL 617-871-6600. FAX 617-871-6528) Ed.Bd. Document type: academic/scholarly publication.
—CISTI.
Description: Discusses current developments in cytokine and interferon research.

D N A. (Deoxyribonucleic Acid) see BIOLOGY — Genetics

571.6 572.86
611.018　　　US　　ISSN 1044-5498
QH442　　　　　　　CODEN: DCEBE8
D N A AND CELL BIOLOGY. 1981. m. $187 to individuals (foreign $271); institutions $666 (foreign $706) (effective through 1998). Mary Ann Liebert, Inc. Publishers, 2 Madison Ave., Larchmont, NY 10538. TEL 914-834-3100. FAX 914-834-3688. E-mail: liebert@pipeline.com. Ed. Mark I. Greene. adv.; bk.rev. circ. 1,200. Indexed: Anim.Breed.Abstr., ASCA, Biol.Abstr., Chem.Abstr., Curr.Adv.Biochem., Curr.Adv.Ecol.Sci., Curr.Adv.Genetics & Molec.Biol., Curr.Biotech.Abstr., Curr.Cont., Excerp.Med., Ind.Med., Ind.Sci.Rev., Int.Abstr.Biol.Sci., Sci.Cit.Ind., Telegen. Document type: academic/scholarly publication.
—BLDSC (3605.721420); CASDDS; CISTI; EMDOCS; Genuine Article; KNAW; SWETS; UnCover.
Former titles: D N A (ISSN 0198-0238); Recombinant D N A.
Description: Covers eukaryotic or prokaryotic gene structure, organization, expressions, and evolution. Publishes papers, short communications, reviews, and editorials. Includes papers studying genetics at RNA or protein levels.
Refereed Serial

572.43　　　　NE　　ISSN 0165-1714
　　　　　　　　　　　CODEN: DEBIDR
DEVELOPMENTS IN BIOCHEMISTRY. 1978. irreg., vol.29, 1992. price varies. Elsevier Science B.V., Books Division, P.O. Box 211, 1000 AE Amsterdam, Netherlands. TEL 31-20-4853911. FAX 31-20-4853705. TELEX 18582 ESPA NL. E-mail: nlinfo-f@elsevier.nl; usinfo-f@elsevier.com; forinfo-kyf04035@niftyserve.or.jp; URL: http://www.elsevier.nl/. (Subscr. in the Americas to: Elsevier Science, Regional Sales Office, Box 945, New York, NY 10159-0945. TEL 212-633-3730. FAX 212-633-3680; Subscr. in Australasia and the Far East to: Elsevier Science (Singapore) Pte Ltd, No.1 Temasek Ave., No.17-01 Millenia Tower, Singapore 039192, Singapore. TEL 65-434-3727. FAX 65-337-2230; Subscr. in Japan to: Elsevier Science Japan, 9-15 Higashi-Azabu 1-chome, Minato-ku, Tokyo 106, Japan. TEL 81-3-5561-5033. FAX 81-3-5561-5047) (back issues avail.) Indexed: Biol.Abstr., Chem.Abstr. Document type: monographic series.
—CASDDS; CISTI; KNAW. **CCC.**
Refereed Serial

572　　　　　NE　　ISSN 0167-4978
　　　　　　　　　　　CODEN: DLCBDQ
DEVELOPMENTS IN CLINICAL BIOCHEMISTRY. (Text in English) 1980. irreg. price varies. (Commission of the European Communities) Kluwer Academic Publishers, Postbus 17, 3300 AA Dordrecht, Netherlands. TEL 31-78-6392392. FAX 31-78-6392254. TELEX 29245 KAPG NL. E-mail: services@wkap.nl; URL: http://www.wkap.nl. (Dist. by: Kluwer Academic Publishers Group, P.O. Box 322, 3300 AH Dordrecht, Netherlands. TEL 31-78-6392392. FAX 31-78-6546474; N. America dist. addr.: Box 358, Accord Sta., Hingham, MA 02018-0358. TEL 617-871-6600. FAX 617-871-6528) Document type: monographic series.
—CASDDS.
Refereed Serial

572.8　　　　NE　　ISSN 0167-9023
　　　　　　　　　　　CODEN: DMCBDX
DEVELOPMENTS IN MOLECULAR AND CELLULAR BIOCHEMISTRY. (Text in English) 1981. irreg., vol.11, 1993. price varies. Kluwer Academic Publishers, Postbus 17, 3300 AA Dordrecht, Netherlands. TEL 31-78-6392392. FAX 31-78-6392254. TELEX 29245 KAPG NL. E-mail: services@wkap.nl; URL: http://www.wkap.nl. (Dist. by: Kluwer Academic Publishers Group, P.O. Box 322, 3300 AH Dordrecht, Netherlands. TEL 31-78-6392392. FAX 31-78-6546474; N. America dist. addr.: Box 358, Accord Sta., Hingham, MA 02018-0358. TEL 617-871-6600. FAX 617-871-6528) Indexed: Biol.Abstr., Biotech.Abstr., Curr.Adv.Cancer Res. Document type: monographic series.
—CISTI.
Refereed Serial

019　　　　　MX
DICCIONARIO DE ESPECIALIDADES BIOQUIMICAS. 1984. a. Mex.$200($100) Ediciones P L M, S.A. de C.V., San Bernadino 17, Col. del Valle, 03100 Mexico, D.F., Mexico. TEL 687-1766. FAX 536-5027. Ed. Federico Garcia Ortega. adv.; bk.rev. circ. 6,000.

572　　　　　KE　　ISSN 1015-079X
Q85.2　　　　　　　CODEN: DIINE4
DISCOVERY AND INNOVATION. 1989. q. KShs.1000 to individuals (rest of Africa $60; elsewhere $80); institutions KShs.1500 (rest of Africa $70; elsewhere $90) (effective 1995). (African Academy of Sciences) Academy Science Publishers, P.O. Box 14798, Nairobi, Kenya. TEL 254-2-884401. FAX 254-2-884406. TELEX 25446 AFACS. E-mail: aas@arcc.kacct.kenya-net.org; abc@dial.pipex.com. (Third World Academy of Sciences) Ed. Keto E. Mshigeni. adv.: B&W page KShs.20000 ($500), color page $1500; adv. contact: Serah W. Mwanycky. index. Indexed: ASCA, Biol.Abstr., Chem.Abstr., Curr.Cont., Documentatieblad, P.L.E.S.A. (1990-), SSCI. Document type: academic/scholarly publication.
—BLDSC (3596.330000); CASDDS; CISTI; Genuine Article; SWETS.
Description: Takes a multidisciplinary approach to covering progress in scientific research, technological innovation, and issues that affect these two areas.
Refereed Serial

DOJIN NYUSU/DOJIN NEWS. see CHEMISTRY — Analytical Chemistry

572　　　　　RU　　ISSN 0012-4958
　　　　　　　　　　　CODEN: DBIOAM
DOKLADY BIOCHEMISTRY. English translation of: Rossiiskaya Akademiya Nauk. Doklady. 1964. bi-m. $1160 in US; elsewhere $1355 (effective 1998). (Russian Academy of Sciences, Biochemistry Section) Maik Nauka - Interperiodica, Mezhdunarodnyi Otdel, Ul. Profsoyuznaya, 90, 117864 Moscow, Russia. TEL 7-095-3360066. FAX 7-095-3360666. (Dist. by: Plenum Publishing Corp., 233 Spring St., New York, NY 10013-1578, U.S.A.. TEL 212-620-8468. FAX 212-463-0742) Ed. V.A. Kabanov. index. (also avail. in microfilm from UMI; back issues avail.) Indexed: Anim.Breed.Abstr., Biol.Abstr., Chem.Titles, Curr.Adv.Ecol.Sci., Energy Res.Abstr., Excerp.Med., Field Crop Abstr., Ind.Med., INIS Atomind., Int.Abstr.Biol.Sci., Mass Spectr.Bull., Plant Grow.Reg.Abstr., Potato Abstr., Poult.Abstr., Seed Abstr., Soils & Fert., Triticale Abstr. Document type: academic/scholarly publication.
—BLDSC (0411.099000); CISTI; SWETS; UMI; UnCover. **CCC.**
Refereed Serial

DONJINDO NEWSLETTER. see CHEMISTRY — Analytical Chemistry

DRUG TARGETING. see PHARMACY AND PHARMACOLOGY

572   UK   ISSN 0261-4189
QH506   CODEN: EMJODG
THE E M B O JOURNAL. 1982. 24/yr. £695 (foreign $1090) (effective 1998). (European Molecular Biology Organization) Oxford University Press, Academic Division, Great Clarendon St., Oxford OX2 6DP, England. TEL 44-1865-267907. FAX 44-1865-267485. TELEX 837330-OXPRES-G. E-mail: jnl.info@oup.co.uk; URL: http://www.oup.co.uk/journals. (U.S. subscr. to: Oxford University Press Inc., 2001 Evans Rd., Cary, NC 27513. TEL 800-852-7323. FAX 919-677-1714) Ed. C.J. Leaver; Pub. Martin Richardson. R&P contact: Joolz Longley. adv.; illus.; index. circ. 4,800. (back issues avail.; reprint service avail. from SWZ) **Indexed:** Anim.Breed.Abstr., ASCA, Bibl.Agri., Biol.& Agr.Ind., Chem.Cit.Ind., Curr.Adv.Biochem., Curr.Adv.Cancer Res., Curr.Adv.Cell & Devel.Biol., Curr.Adv.Ecol.Sci., Curr.Adv.Genetics & Molec.Biol., Curr.Biotech.Abstr., Curr.Cont., Dairy Sci.Abstr., Food Sci.& Tech.Abstr., Ind.Sci.Rev., Ind.Vet., INIS Atomind., Maize Abstr., Neurosci.Cit.Ind., Potato Abstr., Protozool.Abstr., Sci.Cit.Ind., Seed Abstr., Soyabean Abstr., Telegen, Triticale Abstr., Weed Abstr. **Document type:** academic/scholarly publication.
● Also available online.
—BLDSC (3733.085000); CASDDS; CISTI; EMDOCS; Genuine Article; KNAW; KR SourceOne; Linda Hall; SWETS; UMI; UnCover. **CCC.**
   Description: Covers all areas of molecular biology, including immunology, cell biology, molecular genetics, expression, neurobiology, virology, and plant science.

572   SZ
                      CODEN: ENENDT
EMERGING BIOCHEMICAL AND BIOPHYSICAL TECHNIQUES. 1994. irreg. 148 SFr. Birkhaeuser Verlag, P.O. Box 133, CH-4010 Basel, Switzerland. TEL 41-61-7217784. FAX 41-61-7217950. E-mail: orders@birkhauser.ch. (Dist. in N. America by: Springer-Verlag, Mercedes Distribution Center, 160 Imlay St., Brooklyn, NY 11231, USA) Eds. T.M. Schuctor, T.M. Laue. **Document type:** academic/scholarly publication.

ENDOCYTOBIOSIS AND CELL RESEARCH. see *BIOLOGY — Genetics*

ENVIRONMENTAL TOXICOLOGY AND CHEMISTRY. see *ENVIRONMENTAL STUDIES — Toxicology And Environmental Safety*

572.7   US   ISSN 0094-8500
TP248.E5   CODEN: ENENDT
ENZYME ENGINEERING. irreg., vol.13, 1996. New York Academy of Sciences, 2 E. 63rd St., New York, NY 10021. TEL 212-838-0230. Ed.Bd. **Indexed:** Curr.Biotech.Abstr.
—CASDDS; CISTI. **CCC.**
   Refereed Serial

591 612   UK   ISSN 0142-8071
ENZYME REGULATION. 1971. m. £80 (effective 1997). S U B I S, Mansion House, 19 Kingfield Rd., Sheffield S11 9AS, England. TEL 44-114-2554433. FAX 44-114-2554626. E-mail: subis@sheffac.demon.co.uk; URL: http://www.shef.ac.uk/uni/companies/shap. **Document type:** abstracting/indexing.
—**CCC.**
   Description: Current awareness service for researchers in life sciences.

572   GW
                      CODEN: SFWOEH
ERNST SCHERING RESEARCH FOUNDATION WORKSHOP. irreg., no.7, 1993. (Schering Research Foundation) Springer-Verlag, Heidelberger Platz 3, 14197 Berlin, Germany. TEL 49-30-82787-0. FAX 49-30-82787448. E-mail: subscriptions@springer.de. Eds. K. Chwalisz, R. Garfield. **Document type:** monographic series.
—CASDDS.
   Formerly: Schering Foundation Workshop (ISSN 0945-246X)

572   UK   ISSN 0071-1365
QH345   CODEN: ESBIAV
ESSAYS IN BIOCHEMISTRY. 1965. a. £17.50($30) (Biochemical Society) Portland Press Ltd., 59 Portland Pl., London W1N 3AJ, England. TEL 44-171-580-5530. FAX 44-171-323-1136. E-mail: sales@portlandpress.co.uk; URL: http://www.portlandpress.co.uk. (Subscr. to: Commerce Way, P.O. Box 32, Colchester, Essex CO2 8HP, England. TEL 44-1206-796351. FAX 44-1206-799331) Ed. D.K. Apps. R&P contact: Adam Marshall. (reprint service avail. from ISI) **Indexed:** Anim.Breed.Abstr., ASCA, Biol.Abstr., Chem.Abstr., Curr.Adv.Ecol.Sci., Ind.Med., Ind.Sci.Rev., Nutr.Abstr., Sci.Cit.Ind. **Document type:** academic/scholarly publication.
—BLDSC (3811.676000); CASDDS; CISTI; Linda Hall; SWETS; UnCover.
   Refereed Serial

572   GW   ISSN 0014-2956
QP501   CODEN: EJBCAI
EUROPEAN JOURNAL OF BIOCHEMISTRY. Online edition (GW ISSN 1432-1033) (Text in English) 1967. 24/yr. DM.3928 (foreign DM.3988) (effective 1998). (Federation of European Biochemical Societies) Springer-Verlag, Heidelberger Platz 3, 14197 Berlin, Germany. TEL 49-30-82787-0. FAX 49-30-82787448. E-mail: subscriptions@springer.de; URL: http://link.springer.de. (Subscr. in N. America to: Springer-Verlag New York, Inc., 333 Meadowlands Pkwy., Secaucus, NJ 07094. TEL 212-460-1500. FAX 212-473-6272) Ed.Bd. adv.; bibl., charts, illus., index. (also avail. in microform from UMI; back issues avail.; reprint service avail. from ISI) **Indexed:** Anim.Breed.Abstr., Apic.Abstr., ASCA, Bibl.Agri., Biol.Abstr., Biol.& Agr.Ind., Biotech.Abstr., Chem.Abstr., Chem.Cit.Ind., Crop Physiol.Abstr., Curr.Adv.Biochem., Curr.Adv.Cancer Res., Curr.Adv.Cell & Devel.Biol., Curr.Adv.Ecol.Sci., Curr.Adv.Genetics & Molec.Biol., Curr.Cont., Curr.Ref.Fish Res., Dairy Sci.Abstr., Dent.Ind., Excerp.Med., Field Crop Abstr., Food Sci.& Tech.Abstr., Forest.Abstr., Helminthol.Abstr., Herb.Abstr., Hort.Abstr., Ind.Med., Ind.Sci.Rev., Ind.Vet., INIS Atomind., Maize Abstr., Mass Spectr.Bull., Neurosci.Cit.Ind., Nutr.Abstr., Poult.Abstr., Protozool.Abstr., Rev.Plant Path Abstr., Sci.Cit.Ind, Seed Abstr., Soils & Fert., Sport Fish.Abstr., Triticale Abstr., Trop.Dis.Bull., Vet.Bull., Weed Abstr., Wild.Rec., Zoo.Rec., Zoo.Rec. **Document type:** academic/scholarly publication.
● Also available online.
—BLDSC (3829.723000); ADONIS; CASDDS; CISTI; Ei; Genuine Article; KNAW; KR SourceOne; Linda Hall; SWETS; UMI; UnCover. **CCC.**
   Description: Covers the entire basic biomedical sciences community, including molecular genetics, enzymology, physical and inorganic chemistry, metabolic regulation, molecular neurobiology, and developmental biochemistry and immunology.

572   GW   ISSN 0945-5795
EUROPEAN JOURNAL OF BIOCHEMISTRY (C D - R O M). a. DM.3009 (effective 1997). (Federation of European Biological Societies) Springer-Verlag, Heidelberger Platz 3, 14197 Berlin, Germany. TEL 49-30-82787-0. FAX 49-30-82787448. E-mail: subscriptions@springer.de; URL: http://link.springer.de. (Subscr. in N. America to: Springer-Verlag New York, Inc., 333 Meadowlands Pkwy., Secaucus, NJ 07094. TEL 212-460-1500. FAX 212-473-6272) **Indexed:** Curr.Cont.
● Available only on CD-ROM.

612   GW   ISSN 0939-4974
RB40.A1   CODEN: EJCBEO
EUROPEAN JOURNAL OF CLINICAL CHEMISTRY AND CLINICAL BIOCHEMISTRY. (Text in English, French and German) 1963. m. DM.423.60 (foreign DM.438) to individuals; institutions DM.1157.60 (foreign DM.1172) (effective 1998). (Deutsche Gesellschaft fuer Klinische Chemie) Walter de Gruyter und Co., Genthiner Str. 13, 10785 Berlin, Germany. TEL 49-30-26005-0. FAX 49-30-26005251. E-mail: wdg-info@degruyter.de; URL: http://www.degruyter.de. (U.S. addr.: Walter de Gruyter, Inc., 200 Saw Mill River Rd., Hawthorne, NY 10532. TEL 914-747-0110) Ed. G. Buettner. adv.; bk.rev.; charts; illus.; index. circ. 1,100. **Indexed:** Anal.Abstr., ASCA, Biol.Abstr., Chem.Abstr., Curr.Adv.Biochem., Curr.Cont., Dairy Sci.Abstr., Dent.Ind., Excerp.Med., Helminthol.Abstr., Ind.Med., Ind.Sci.Rev., Ind.Sci.Rev., Ind.Vet., INIS Atomind., Nutr.Abstr., Protozool.Abstr., Rev.Med.& Vet.Mycol., Sci.Cit.Ind. **Document type:** academic/scholarly publication.
—BLDSC (3829.726600); CASDDS; CISTI; EMDOCS; Genuine Article; KNAW; Linda Hall; SWETS; UnCover. **CCC.**
   Formerly: Zeitschrift fuer Klinische Chemie und Klinische Biochemie (ISSN 0340-076X)

572   IT   ISSN 1121-760X
                      CODEN: EJHIE2
EUROPEAN JOURNAL OF HISTOCHEMISTRY. Cover title: E J H. (Text in English) 1954. q. $200. (Societa Italiana di Istochimica) Luigi Ponzio e Figlio Editori, Via D. da Catalogna 1-3, 27100 Pavia, Italy. TEL 382-35000. FAX 382-304435. Ed. Maria G.M. Romanini. adv.; bk.rev. circ. 500. **Indexed:** ASCA, Chem.Abstr., Curr.Adv.Cell & Devel.Biol., Curr.Adv.Ecol.Sci., Curr.Cont., Dairy Sci.Abstr., Excerp.Med., Ind.Med., Ind.Sci.Rev., Ind.Vet., Neurosci.Cit.Ind., Risk Abstr., Sci.Cit.Ind., Vet.Bull. **Document type:** academic/scholarly publication.
—BLDSC (3829.729900); CASDDS; CISTI; EMDOCS; Genuine Article; KNAW; SWETS.
   Former titles (until 1991): European Journal of Basic and Applied Histochemistry (ISSN 1121-4201); (until 1990): Basic and Applied Histochemistry (ISSN 0391-7258); (until 1979): Rivista di Istochimica Normale e Patologica (ISSN 0485-2400)

615   FR   ISSN 0223-5234
                      CODEN: EJMCA5
EUROPEAN JOURNAL OF MEDICINAL CHEMISTRY. (Text and summaries in English) 1965. m. 2791 F.($621) to institutions (US $534; elsewhere 3420 F.) (effective 1998). (Societe Francaise de Chimie Therapeutique) Editions Scientifiques et Medicales Elsevier, 141 rue de Javel, 75747 Paris, France. TEL 33-1-45589022. FAX 33-1-45589421. URL: http://www.elsevier.nl/. (Subscr. in U.S. and Canada to: Elsevier Science Inc., Box 945, Madison Sq. Sta., New York, NY 10159-0945. TEL 212-633-3730. FAX 212-633-3680) (Co-sponsor: European Federation of Medicinal Chemistry) Eds. C. Combet Farnoux, O. Lafont. adv.; bk.rev.; bibl.; charts; index. circ. 3,000. (also avail. in microform from UMI) **Indexed:** ASCA, Biol.Abstr., Biotech.Abstr., Chem.Abstr., Chem.Cit.Ind., Curr.Adv.Ecol.Sci., Curr.Chem.React., Curr.Cont., Excerp.Med., Helminthol.Abstr., I.P.A., Ind.Chem., Ind.Sci.Rev., INIS Atomind., Neurosci.Cit.Ind., Protozool.Abstr., Rev.Med.& Vet.Mycol., Sci.Cit.Ind. **Document type:** academic/scholarly publication.
—BLDSC (3829.731500); ADONIS; CASDDS; CISTI; EMDOCS; Genuine Article; KNAW; Linda Hall; SWETS; UMI. **CCC.**
   Formerly (until 1973): Chimica Therapeutica (ISSN 0009-4374)
   Description: Publishes original papers, laboratory notes, short or preliminary communications, new products.
   Refereed Serial

EUROPEAN JOURNAL OF NEUROSCIENCE. see *MEDICAL SCIENCES — Psychiatry And Neurology*

EXCERPTA MEDICA. SECTION 29: CLINICAL AND EXPERIMENTAL BIOCHEMISTRY. see *BIOLOGY — Abstracting, Bibliographies, Statistics*

BIOLOGY — BIOLOGICAL CHEMISTRY

572   KO   CODEN: KJBID3
EXPERIMENTAL AND MOLECULAR MEDICINE. (Text and summaries in English) 1964. q. 30000 Won($40) Korean Society of Medical Biochemistry and Molecular Biology, No. 12 KOFST, 635-4 Yeoksam-dong, Kangnam-gu, Seoul 135-703, S. Korea. TEL 82-2-565-1621. FAX 82-2-565-1622. (Co-sponsor: Korean Federation of Science and Technology Societies) Ed. Tong-Ho Lee. adv.; bk.rev. circ. 500. **Indexed:** ASCA, Biol.Abstr., Chem.Abstr., Excerp.Med., Ind.Med. **Document type:** academic/scholarly publication.
—CASDDS; CISTI; Genuine Article.
Formerly (until 1996): Korean Journal of Biochemistry (ISSN 0378-8512)
Description: Publishes research papers and mini-reviews in the fields of basic and applied molecular biology, and experimental biochemistry in medicine.
Refereed Serial

EXTREMOPHILES; life under extreme conditions. see BIOLOGY — Biotechnology

572   NE   ISSN 0014-5793
QP501   CODEN: FEBLAL
F E B S LETTERS; for the rapid publication of short, complete and essentially final reports of immediate importance to investigators in biochemistry, biophysics and molecular biology. (Text in English, French and German; summaries in English) 1968. 63/yr. fl.6321($3633) (effective 1998). (Federation of European Biochemical Societies) Elsevier Science B.V., P.O. Box 211, 1000 AE Amsterdam, Netherlands. TEL 31-20-4853911. FAX 31-20-4853598. TELEX 18582 ESPA NL. E-mail: nlinfo-f@elsevier.nl; usinfo-f@elsevier.com; forinfo-kyf04035@niftyserve.or.jp; URL: http://www.elsevier.nl/. (Subscr. in the Americas to: Elsevier Science, Regional Sales Office, Box 945, New York, NY 10159-0945. TEL 212-633-3730. FAX 212-633-3680; Subscr. in Australasia and the Far East to: Elsevier Science (Singapore) Pte Ltd, No.1 Temasek Ave., No.17-01 Millenia Tower, Singapore 039192, Singapore. TEL 65-434-3727. FAX 65-337-2230; Subscr. in Japan to: Elsevier Science Japan, 9-15 Higashi-Azabu 1-chome, Minato-ku, Tokyo 106, Japan. TEL 81-3-5561-5033. FAX 81-3-5561-5047) Ed. G. Semenza. adv.; bk.rev.; charts; illus.; stat.; cum.index; circ. controlled. (also avail. in microform from UMI; reprint service avail. from ISI) **Indexed:** AIDS Abstr., Anim.Breed.Abstr., Apic.Abstr., ASCA, Bio-Contr.News & Info., Biol.Abstr., Biotech.Abstr., Biwk.Pap.Rad.Chem.& Photochem., Chem.Abstr., Chem.Cit.Ind., Crop Physiol.Abstr., Curr.Adv.Biochem., Curr.Adv.Cancer Res., Curr.Adv.Cell & Devel.Biol., Curr.Adv.Ecol.Sci., Curr.Adv.Genetics & Molec.Biol., Curr.Cont., Dairy Sci.Abstr., Dent.Ind., Excerp.Med., Field Crop Abstr., Food Sci.& Tech.Abstr., Forest.Abstr., Helminthol.Abstr., Herb.Abstr., Hort.Abstr., Ind.Med., Ind.Sci.Rev., Ind.Vet., INIS Atomind., Mass Spectr.Bull., Neurosci.Cit.Ind., Nutr.Abstr., Ornam.Hort., Pig News & Info., Poult.Abstr., Protozool.Abstr., Sci.Cit.Ind., Seed Abstr., Soils & Fert., Sorghum & Millets Abstr., Soyab Soyabean Abstr., Telegen, THA, Triticale Abstr., Trop.Oil Seeds Abstr., Weed Abstr. **Document type:** academic/scholarly publication.
—BLDSC (3901.600000); ADONIS; CASDDS; CISTI; Genuine Article; Linda Hall; SWETS; UnCover. **CCC.**

FIZIOLOGIYA I BIOKHIMIYA KUL'TURNYKH RASTENII/PHYSIOLOGY AND BIOCHEMISTRY OF CULTIVATED PLANTS; nauchno-teoreticheskii zhurnal. see BIOLOGY — Physiology

FOCUS ON BIOPESTICIDES PLUS. see AGRICULTURE — Crop Production And Soil

572   US   ISSN 1359-0278
QP551   CODEN: FODEFH
▼**FOLDING AND DESIGN.** 1996. bi-m. Current Biology Ltd., 400 Market St., Ste. 700, Philadelphia, PA 19106-2514. TEL 800-427-1796; 215-574-2225. E-mail: biomednet@cursci.co.uk; info@hugo.curbio.com; URL: http://www.cursci.co.uk/biomed.html. (Addr. in UK: Middlesex House, 34-42 Cleveland St., London W1P 6LB, England. TEL 44-171-580-8377. FAX 44-171-5808428) Eds. Alan Fersht, Fred Cohen. adv. contact: Daryl Rayner. index. (back issues avail.) **Document type:** academic/scholarly publication.
●Also available online.
—BLDSC (3964.565000); ADONIS; CASDDS; CISTI; Genuine Article. **CCC.**
Description: Presents research papers and reviews on protein and RNA folding and design for research graduates and upwards.
Refereed Serial

572   GR   ISSN 0015-5489
    CODEN: FBBGAJ
FOLIA BIOCHIMICA ET BIOLOGICA GRAECA. (Text in English, French, German and Greek) 1964. irreg. (3-4/yr.). exchange basis. (Hellenic Society of Marine Molecular Biology) Institute of Marine Molecular Biology, 2 Lampsaku St., Athens 611, Greece. Ed. A. Christomanos. **Indexed:** Biol.Abstr., Chem.Abstr., Excerp.Med.
—CASDDS; CISTI.

FOUNDATIONS OF PHYSICS; an international journal devoted to the conceptual and fundamental theories of modern physics, biophysics, and cosmology. see PHYSICS

572   NE   ISSN 1071-5762
RB170   CODEN: FRARER
FREE RADICAL RESEARCH. 12/yr. (in 2 vols., 6 nos./vol.). $243 (effective 1998). Gordon and Breach - Harwood Academic, Amsteldijk 166, 1st Fl., 1079 LH Amsterdam, Netherlands. URL: http://www.gbhap.com/Free_Radical_Research/. (Subscr. to: International Publishers Distributor, Box 32160, Newark, NJ 07102. TEL 800-545-8398. FAX 215-750-6343) Eds. Barry Halliwell, Helmut Sies. (also avail. in microform) **Indexed:** ASCA, Chem.Cit.Ind., Curr.Cont., Excerp.Med., Food Sci.& Tech.Abstr., Ind.Sci.Rev., Sci.Cit.Ind. **Document type:** academic/scholarly publication.
●Also available online.
Also available on CD-ROM.
—BLDSC (4033.326495); CASDDS; CISTI; EMDOCS; SWETS; UnCover. **CCC.**
Formerly: Free Radical Research Communications (ISSN 8755-0199)
Refereed Serial

572   UK   ISSN 1353-6516
▼**FRONTIERS IN METABOLISM.** 1996. irreg. £18.95($32.20) Portland Press Ltd., 59 Portland Pl., London W1N 3AJ, England. TEL 44-171-580-5530. FAX 44-171-323-1136. E-mail: sales@portlandpress.co.uk; URL: http://www.portlandpress.co.uk. (Subscr. to: Commerce Way, P.O. Box 32, Colchester, Essex CO2 8HP, England. TEL 44-1206-796351. FAX 44-1206-799331) Ed. K. Snell. R&P contact: Adam Marshall. **Document type:** monographic series.
Refereed Serial

572   US
G W U M C. DEPARTMENT OF BIOCHEMISTRY. ANNUAL SPRING SYMPOSIA SERIES. 1982. irreg. latest 1996. price varies. (George Washington University Medical Center) Plenum Publishing Corp., 233 Spring St., New York, NY 10013-1578. TEL 212-620-8000. FAX 212-463-0742. TELEX 23-421139. E-mail: books@plenum.com. Ed.Bd. **Document type:** proceedings.
Refereed Serial

GEOMICROBIOLOGY JOURNAL; an international journal of geomicrobiology and microbial biogeochemistry. see BIOLOGY — Microbiology

612.015   IT   ISSN 0392-2227
    CODEN: GICCD7
GIORNALE ITALIANO DI CHIMICA CLINICA. 1976. bi-m. L.150000($125) Piccin Editore, Via Altinate 107, 35100 Padua, Italy. TEL 39-49-655566. FAX 39-49-8750693. adv. circ. 8,450. (reprint service avail. from UMI) **Indexed:** Chem.Abstr., Curr.Adv.Ecol.Sci., Excerp.Med.
—CASDDS; CISTI; EMDOCS.

612.015   UK   ISSN 0959-6658
    CODEN: GLYCE3
GLYCOBIOLOGY. 1991. m. £140 (foreign £232) to individuals; institutions £375 (foreign £595) (effective 1998). Oxford University Press, Academic Division, Great Clarendon St., Oxford OX2 6DP, England. TEL 44-1865-267907. FAX 44-1865-267485. TELEX 837330-OXPRES-G. E-mail: jnl.info@oup.co.uk; URL: http://www.oup.co.uk/journals. (U.S. subscr. to: Oxford University Press Inc., 2001 Evans Rd., Cary, NC 27513. TEL 800-852-7323. FAX 919-677-1714) Ed.Bd. R&P contact: Joolz Longley. adv.; bk.rev. circ. 720. (reprint service avail. from SWZ) **Indexed:** ASCA, Curr.Cont., Ind.Med. (1993-), Ind.Sci.Rev., Sci.Cit.Ind. **Document type:** academic/scholarly publication.
—BLDSC (4196.303000); CASDDS; CISTI; EMDOCS; Genuine Article; KNAW; Linda Hall; SWETS; UMI; UnCover. **CCC.**
Description: Provides a forum for the publication of original research papers on any aspect of the structure and functions of glycobiology or any aspect of proteins that specifically interact with saccharides.

612.015   UK   ISSN 1356-1316
▼**GLYCOBIOLOGY RESEARCH.** 1995. s-m. (diskette m.). £120 (diskette £120; both £180) (effective 1997). S U B I S, Mansion House, 19 Kingfield Rd., Sheffield S11 9AS, England. TEL 44-114-2554433. FAX 44-114-2554626. E-mail: subis@sheffac.demon.co.uk; URL: http://www.shef.ac.uk/uni/companies/shap. (also avail. in diskette format) **Document type:** abstracting/indexing.
Description: Current awareness service for researchers in clinical and life sciences.

572   UK   ISSN 0282-0080
    CODEN: GLJOEW
GLYCOCONJUGATE JOURNAL. 1984. bi-m. £110 to institutions (effective 1998). (International Glyconjugate Organization) Chapman & Hall, Journals Department (Subsidiary of: International Thomson Publishing Group), 2-6 Boundary Row, London SE1 8HN, England. TEL 44-171-8650066. FAX 44-171-5229623. TELEX 290164 CHAPMA G. E-mail: jhelp@chall.co.uk; URL: http://www.chaphall.com/chaphall/journals.html. (Dist. by: International Thomson Publishing Services Ltd., Cheriton House, North Way, Andover, Hants. SP10 5BE, England. TEL 44-1264-342713. FAX 44-1264-342807; Subscr. in US & Canada to: 400 Market St., Philadelphia, PA 19106. TEL 800-552-5866) Ed. H. Schachter. adv. (back issues avail.; reprint service avail.) **Indexed:** ASCA, Chem.Abstr., Chem.Cit.Ind., Curr.Adv.Biochem., Curr.Adv.Cancer Res., Curr.Adv.Ecol.Sci., Curr.Cont., Excerp.Med., Ind.Med. (1992-), Ind.Sci.Rev., Neurosci.Cit.Ind., Sci.Cit.Ind. **Document type:** academic/scholarly publication.
●Also available online.
—BLDSC (4196.305000); ADONIS; CASDDS; CISTI; EMDOCS; Genuine Article; KNAW; SWETS. **CCC.**
Incorporates (1994-1996): Glycosylation and Disease (ISSN 0969-3653)
Description: Examines the metabolism and functions of the glycolipids, glycoproteins, oligo- and polysaccharides, and proteoglycans.
Refereed Serial

HANDBOOK ON SYNCHROTRON RADIATION. see INSTRUMENTS

572   US   ISSN 1043-9811
QP514
HARPER'S BIOCHEMISTRY. 1939. biennial. $36.95. Appleton & Lange (Subsidiary of: Simon & Schuster Company), Box 120041, Stamford, CT 06912-0041. TEL 203-406-4500. bk.rev.
—BLDSC (4264.885500); CISTI. **CCC.**
Former titles (until 1988): Harper's Review of Biochemistry (ISSN 0734-9866); (until 1979): Review of Physiological Chemistry (ISSN 0080-1976)

612.015   UK   ISSN 0950-0510
HEAT SHOCK PROTEINS. m. £80 (effective 1997). S U B I S, Mansion House, 19 Kingfield Rd., Sheffield S11 9AS, England. TEL 44-114-2554433. FAX 44-114-2554626. E-mail: subis@sheffac.demon.co.uk; URL: http://www.shef.ac.uk/uni/companies/shap. (looseleaf format; back issues avail.) **Document type:** abstracting/indexing.
—CCC.
Description: Current awareness service for researchers in clinical and life sciences.

HIKAKU SEIRI SEIKAGAKU/COMPARATIVE PHYSIOLOGY AND BIOCHEMISTRY. see *BIOLOGY — Physiology*

THE HISTOCHEMICAL JOURNAL. see *BIOLOGY — Cytology And Histology*

HISTOCHEMISTRY AND CELL BIOLOGY. see *BIOLOGY — Cytology And Histology*

HOKKAIDORITSU SUISAN SHIKENJO KENKYU HOKOKU/HOKKAIDO FISHERIES EXPERIMENTAL STATION. SCIENTIFIC REPORTS. see *FISH AND FISHERIES*

572.8   US   ISSN 0272-457X
QR185.8.H93   CODEN: HYBRDY
HYBRIDOMA; a journal of molecular immunology and experimental and clinical immunotherapy. 1981. bi-m. $171 to individuals (foreign $224); institutions $376 (foreign $439) (effective through 1998). Mary Ann Liebert, Inc. Publishers, 2 Madison Ave., Larchmont, NY 10538. TEL 914-834-3100. FAX 914-834-3688. E-mail: liebert@pipeline.com. Ed. Dr. Zenon Steplewski. adv. circ. 800. **Indexed:** ASCA, Biol.Abstr., Biotech.Abstr., Chem.Abstr., Curr.Adv.Cancer Res., Curr.Adv.Ecol.Sci., Curr.Biotech.Abstr., Curr.Cont., Dairy Sci.Abstr., Excerp.Med., Ind.Med., Ind.Sci.Rev., Ind.Vet., Poult.Abstr., Sci.Cit.Ind., Telegen, Vet.Bull. **Document type:** academic/scholarly publication.
—BLDSC (4340.385000); CASDDS; CISTI; EMDOCS; Genuine Article; KNAW; SWETS; UnCover.
 Incorporates (in 1990): Monoclonal Antibodies (ISSN 1047-871X); **Formerly** (until 1990): Monoclonal Antibody News (ISSN 0272-4588)
 Description: Publishes research in molecular immunology and experimental and clinical immunotherapy. Includes papers on the application of monoclonal antibodies for diagnostics and therapy, and original articles on various aspects of hybridoma research.
 Refereed Serial

540   US   ISSN 0275-0910
   CODEN: IDSEDC
I U P A C CHEMICAL DATA SERIES. (Includes subseries: Carotenoids Other Than Vitamin A (ISSN 0069-0732); Chemistry of Natural Products (ISSN 0069-3162); Coordination in Chemistry (ISSN 0069-3162); Photochemistry (ISSN 0079-1806); Macromolecular Chemistry (ISSN 0079-2075); Experimental Thermodynamics Series.) irreg., no.39, 1994. price varies. (International Union of Pure and Applied Chemistry) C R C Press, Inc., 2000 Corporate Blvd., N.W., Boca Raton, FL 33431. TEL 561-994-0555; 800-272-7737. FAX 561-998-9784. TELEX 568689-CRC PRESS. **Document type:** monographic series.
—BLDSC (4588.957000); CISTI.

572   II   ISSN 0970-6399
   CODEN: IJBIEG
INDIAN JOURNAL OF AGRICULTURAL BIOCHEMISTRY. (Text in English) 1988. s-a. Rs.200($50) Indian Society of Agricultural Biochemists, c/o Dept. of Agricultural Technology, Kanpur 208 002, India. Ed. G.G. Sanwal; Pub. G.P. Srivastava. R&P contact: G.P. Srivastava. **Document type:** academic/scholarly publication.
—BLDSC (4409.915000); CASDDS.
 Description: Publishes original papers and reviews on all aspects of agricultural biochemistry.

572   II   ISSN 0301-1208
QP501   CODEN: IJBBBQ
INDIAN JOURNAL OF BIOCHEMISTRY AND BIOPHYSICS. (Published in two sections: A and B) (Text in English) 1963. bi-m. Rs.250($120) (Council of Scientific and Industrial Research, Publications and Information Directorate) Scientific Publishers, P.O. Box 91, 5A, New Pali Rd., Jodhpur 342 001, India. TEL 91-291-33323. (Co-sponsor: Society of Biological Chemists) Ed. B.S. Janqi. adv. circ. 1,000. (back issues avail.) **Indexed:** Abstr.Hyg., Anal.Abstr., Anim.Breed.Abstr., ASCA, Biol.Abstr., Biotech.Abstr., Chem.Abstr., Crop Physiol.Abstr., Curr.Adv.Ecol.Sci., Curr.Cont., Dairy Sci.Abstr., Dent.Ind., Excerp.Med., Food Sci.& Tech.Abstr., Helminthol.Abstr., Hort.Abstr., Ind.Med., Ind.Sci.Rev., INIS Atomind., Nutr.Abstr., Protozool.Abstr., Rev.Appl.Entomol., Rev.Med.& Vet.Mycol., Rev.Plant Path., Sci.Cit.Ind., SSCI, Trop.Dis.Bull., Vet.Bull. **Document type:** academic/scholarly publication.
—BLDSC (4410.420000); CASDDS; CISTI; Genuine Article; KNAW; Linda Hall; SWETS; UnCover.
 Formerly: Indian Journal of Biochemistry (ISSN 0019-5081)

INSECT BIOCHEMISTRY AND MOLECULAR BIOLOGY. see *BIOLOGY — Entomology*

INSTITUT PASTEUR. ANNALES. ACTUALITES. see *BIOLOGY — Microbiology*

572   FI   ISSN 0074-3690
INTERNATIONAL CONGRESS OF HISTOCHEMISTRY AND CYTOCHEMISTRY. PROCEEDINGS. (Proceedings published in host country) 1960. quadrennial, latest 1984, Helsinki. price varies. University of Helsinki, Department of Anatomy, c/o Dr. Pertti Panula, Siltavuorenpenger 20A, FIN-00170 Helsinki, Finland. adv. circ. 1,000.

572   UK   ISSN 1357-2725
QP501   CODEN: IJBBFU
INTERNATIONAL JOURNAL OF BIOCHEMISTRY & CELL BIOLOGY. 1970. m. fl.3376($1940) (effective 1998). Elsevier Science Ltd., Pergamon, P.O. Box 800, Kidlington, Oxford OX5 1DX, England. TEL 44-1865-843000. FAX 44-1865-843010. E-mail: nlinfo-f@elsevier.nl; usinfo-f@elsevier.com; forinfo-kyf04035@niftyserve.or.jp; URL: http://www.elsevier.nl/. (Subscr. to: Elsevier Science, Regional Sales Office, P.O. Box 211, 1000 AE Amsterdam, Netherlands. TEL 31-20-4853757. FAX 31-20-4853432; Subscr. in the Americas to: Elsevier Science, Regional Sales Office, Box 945, New York, NY 10159-0945. TEL 212-633-3730. FAX 212-633-3680; Subscr. in Australasia and the Far East to: Elsevier Science (Singapore) Pte Ltd, No.1 Temasek Ave., No.17-01 Millenia Tower, Singapore 039192, Singapore. TEL 65-434-3727. FAX 65-337-2230) Ed. G.A. Kerkut. adv.; charts; illus.; stat.; index. circ. 1,000. (also avail. in microfilm from UMI; back issues avail.; reprint service avail. from UMI) **Indexed:** ASCA, Biol.Abstr., Chem.Abstr., Chem.Cit.Ind., Curr.Adv.Biochem., Curr.Adv.Cancer Res., Curr.Adv.Ecol.Sci., Curr.Adv.Genetics & Molec.Biol., Curr.Cont., Dairy Sci.Abstr., Dent.Ind., Excerp.Med., Helminthol.Abstr., Ind.Med., Ind.Sci.Rev., Ind.Vet., Neurosci.Cit.Ind., Nutr.Abstr., Poult.Abstr., Protozool.Abstr., Rev.Med.& Vet.Mycol., Sci.Cit.Ind., Sport Fish.Abstr., SSCI, Vet.Bull., Wild.Rev., Zoo.Rec. **Document type:** academic/scholarly publication.
—BLDSC (4542.135000); ADONIS; CASDDS; CISTI; Ei; Genuine Article; Linda Hall; SWETS; UMI; UnCover. **CCC.**
 Formerly (until 1995): International Journal of Biochemistry (ISSN 0020-711X)
 Description: Provides comprehensive coverage of new research in growth areas of biochemistry.
 Refereed Serial

INTERNATIONAL JOURNAL OF BIOCHROMATOGRAPHY. see *CHEMISTRY — Analytical Chemistry*

572.8   NE   ISSN 0141-8130
QP801.P64   CODEN: IJBMDR
INTERNATIONAL JOURNAL OF BIOLOGICAL MACROMOLECULES; structure, function and interactions. (Text in English) 1979. 8/yr. fl.2112($1214) (effective 1998). Elsevier Science B.V., P.O. Box 211, 1000 AE Amsterdam, Netherlands. TEL 31-20-4853911. FAX 31-20-4853598. (Subscr. in the Americas to: Elsevier Science, Regional Sales Office, Box 945, New York, NY 10159-0945. TEL 212-633-3730. FAX 212-633-3680; Subscr. in Australasia and the Far East to: Elsevier Science (Singapore) Pte Ltd, No.1 Temasek Ave., No.17-01 Millenia Tower, Singapore 039192, Singapore. TEL 65-434-3727. FAX 65-337-2230; Subscr. in Japan to: Elsevier Science Japan, 9-15 Higashi-Azabu 1-chome, Minato-ku, Tokyo 106, Japan. TEL 81-3-5561-5033. FAX 81-3-5561-5047) Eds. Edward Atkins, Ian Wilson. adv.; bk.rev.; abstr.; illus.; index. (also avail. in microfilm from UMI; back issues avail.) **Indexed:** Abstr.Bull.Inst.Pap.Chem., ASCA, Biol.Abstr., Chem.Abstr., Chem.Cit.Ind., Curr.Adv.Biochem., Curr.Adv.Cell & Devel.Biol., Curr.Adv.Genetics & Molec.Biol., Curr.Cont., Dairy Sci.Abstr., Excerp.Med., Food Sci.& Tech.Abstr., Ind.Sci.Rev., Int.Abstr.Biol.Sci, Mat.Sci.Cit.Ind., Sci.Cit.Ind., Telegen. **Document type:** academic/scholarly publication.
—BLDSC (4542.151000); CASDDS; CISTI; Genuine Article; KNAW; Linda Hall; SWETS; UMI; UnCover. **CCC.**
 Description: Reports research into the structure of natural macromolecules: proteins, carbohydrates, nucleic acids, viruses and membranes.
 Refereed Serial

INTERNATIONAL JOURNAL OF NEUROSCIENCE. see *MEDICAL SCIENCES — Psychiatry And Neurology*

INTERNATIONAL JOURNAL OF OCCUPATIONAL MEDICINE, IMMUNOLOGY AND TOXICOLOGY. see *OCCUPATIONAL HEALTH AND SAFETY*

INTERNATIONAL LABORATORY BUYERS' GUIDE. see *BIOLOGY — Biotechnology*

612.015 612.3   UK   ISSN 0142-8152
IRON METABOLISM. s-m. (diskette m.). £90 (diskette £120; both £180) (effective 1997). S U B I S, Mansion House, 19 Kingfield Rd., Sheffield S11 9AS, England. TEL 44-114-2554433. FAX 44-114-2554626. E-mail: subis@sheffac.demon.co.uk; URL: http://www.shef.ac.uk/uni/companies/shap. (also avail. in diskette format; looseleaf format; back issues avail.) **Document type:** abstracting/indexing.
—**CCC.**
 Description: Current awareness service for researchers in clinical and life sciences.

572.7   UK   ISSN 0197-887X
   CODEN: ISBLEK
ISOZYME BULLETIN. 1967. a. $9 to individuals (foreign $10); institutions $11. c/o W.R. Chegwidden, Ed., Sheffield Hallam University, City Campus, Pond St., Sheffield S1 1WB, England. TEL 44-114-253-3042. FAX 44-114-253-2020. E-mail: w.r.chegwidden@shu.ac.uk. adv.; bk.rev.; circ. 150 (paid). **Indexed:** Sport Fish.Abstr., Wild.Rev., Zoo.Rec. **Document type:** bulletin.
—BLDSC (4583.539000).

572   RU   ISSN 0202-795X
QP501   CODEN: INBKBD
ITOGI NAUKI I TEKHNIKI: BIOLOGICHESKAYA KHIMIYA. irreg., vol.32, 1989. 6.60 Rub. Vsesoyuznyi Institut Nauchno-Tekhnicheskoi Informatsii (VINITI), Ul. Baltiiskaya 14, Moscow A-219, Russia. (Subscr. to: Mezhdunarodnaya Kniga, Dimitrova ul. 39, 113095 Moscow, Russia) **Indexed:** Chem.Abstr.
—CASDDS; Linda Hall.

IYAKU ANZENSEI KENKYUKAI KAIHO/JAPANESE SOCIETY FOR BIOPHARMACEUTICAL STATISTICS. BULLETIN. see *PHARMACY AND PHARMACOLOGY*

IYAKU ANZENSEI KENKYUKAI TEIREIKAI SHIRYO/PROCEEDINGS OF REGULAR MEETINGS ON BIOPHARMACEUTICAL STATISTICS. see *PHARMACY AND PHARMACOLOGY*

JOURNAL DE CHIMIE PHYSIQUE ET DE PHYSICO-CHIMIE BIOLOGIQUE; an international journal of physical chemistry, chemical physics and biophysics. see *CHEMISTRY — Physical Chemistry*

BIOLOGY — BIOLOGICAL CHEMISTRY

572.33 — US — ISSN 0883-9115
CODEN: JBCPEV
JOURNAL OF BIOACTIVE AND COMPATIBLE POLYMERS. 1986. q. $345 (foreign $393) (effective 1997); $360 (foreign $415) (effective 1998). Technomic Publishing Co., Inc., 851 New Holland Ave., Box 3535, Lancaster, PA 17604. TEL 717-291-5609. FAX 717-295-4538. TELEX 230 753565 (TECHNOMIC UD). E-mail: marketing@techpub.com; URL: http://www.techpub.com. Ed. Raphael M. Ottenbrite. circ. 225. (back issues avail.) **Indexed:** Alloys Ind., ASCA, Chem.Cit.Ind., Curr.Cont., Eng.Mat.Abstr., Excerp.Med., Intl.Polym.Sci.& Tech., Mat.Sci.Cit.Ind., Met.Abstr.Ind., Met.Abstr., Nonfer.Met.Alert, PCC Alert, RAPRA, Steels Alert, World Alum.Abstr. **Document type:** academic/scholarly publication.
—BLDSC (4951.567000); CASDDS; CISTI; Ei; EMDOCS; Genuine Article; KNAW; Linda Hall; SWETS; UMI. **CCC.**
Refereed Serial

612.015 574.191 — NE — ISSN 0165-022X
QP519.7 — CODEN: JBBMDG
JOURNAL OF BIOCHEMICAL AND BIOPHYSICAL METHODS. 1979. 9/yr. fl.1827($1050) (effective 1998). Elsevier Science B.V., P.O. Box 211, 1000 AE Amsterdam, Netherlands. TEL 31-20-4853911. FAX 31-20-4853598. TELEX 18582 ESPA NL. E-mail: nlinfo-f@elsevier.nl; usinfo-f@elsevier.com; forinfo-kyf04035@niftyserve.or.jp; URL: http://www.elsevier.nl/. (Subscr. in the Americas to: Elsevier Science, Regional Sales Office, Box 945, New York, NY 10159-0945. TEL 212-633-3730. FAX 212-633-3680; Subscr. in Australasia and the Far East to: Elsevier Science (Singapore) Pte Ltd, No.1 Temasek Ave., No.17-01 Millenia Tower, Singapore 039192, Singapore. TEL 65-434-3727. FAX 65-337-2230; Subscr. in U.S. and Canada to: Elsevier Science Inc., Box 882, Madison Sq. Sta., New York, NY 10159. TEL 81-3-5561-5033. FAX 81-3-5561-5047) Eds. C.F. Chignell, S. Hjerten. adv.; bk.rev. (also avail. in microform from UMI; reprint service avail. from ISI,SWZ) **Indexed:** ASCA, Biol.Abstr., Chem.Abstr., Chem.Cit.Ind., Curr.Adv.Biochem., Curr.Adv.Cell & Devel.Biol., Curr.Adv.Genetics & Molec.Biol., Curr.Cont., Dairy Sci.Abstr., Excerp.Med., Food Sci.& Tech.Abstr., Ind.Med., Ind.Sci.Rev., INIS Atomind., INSPEC, Sci.Cit.Ind., Sugar Ind.Abstr. **Document type:** academic/scholarly publication.
—BLDSC (4951.570000); ADONIS; AskIEEE; CASDDS; CISTI; Genuine Article; KR SourceOne; Linda Hall; SWETS; UnCover. **CCC.**
Description: Publishes research papers dealing with the development of new methods or the significant modification of existing techniques to solve biological problems.
Refereed Serial

572 — US — ISSN 1065-9668
QP501 — CODEN: JOBOEC
JOURNAL OF BIOCHEMICAL ORGANIZATION. 1993. q. $295 (effective 1996). Nova Science Publishers, Inc., 6080 Jericho Tpke., Ste. 207, Commack, NY 11725-3401. TEL 516-499-3103. FAX 516-499-3146. E-mail: novasci1@aol.com. Eds. Boris Kurganov, Boris Poglazov. **Document type:** academic/scholarly publication.
—CASDDS; CISTI.
Description: Devoted to the problems of organization, functioning, and regulation of biochemical systems.

572 — JA — ISSN 0021-924X
QP501 — CODEN: JOBIAO
JOURNAL OF BIOCHEMISTRY. (Text in English) 1922. m. $240. Japanese Biochemical Society - Nihon Seikagakkai, c/o Ishikawa Bldg., 3F, 5-25-15 Hongo, Bunkyo-ku, Tokyo 113, Japan. TEL 3817-5811. FAX 3817-5815. TELEX 2722268 BCJSP J. (Dist. by: Business Center for Academic Societies Japan, 5-16-9 Honkomagome, Bunkyo-ku, Tokyo 113, Japan. TEL 5814-5811) adv.; abstr.; bibl.; charts; illus.; stat.; index. circ. 2,650. (also avail. in microfilm from PMC) **Indexed:** Apic.Abstr., ASCA, Biol.Abstr., Chem.Abstr., Chem.Cit.Ind., Curr.Adv.Biochem., Curr.Adv.Cancer Res., Curr.Adv.Cell & Devel.Biol., Curr.Adv.Genetics & Molec.Biol., Curr.Cont., Curr.Ref.Fish Res., Dairy Sci.Abstr., Deep Sea Res.& Oceanogr.Abstr., Dent.Ind., Excerp.Med., Food Sci.& Tech.Abstr., Helminthol.Abstr., Ind.Med., Ind.Sci.Rev., INIS Atomind., Mass Spectr.Bull., Neurosci.Cit.Ind., Nutr.Abstr., Rev.Med.& Vet.Mycol., Sci.Cit.Ind.
—BLDSC (4952.000000); CASDDS; CISTI; Ei; Genuine Article; KNAW; Linda Hall; SWETS; UnCover. **CCC.**

572 — US — ISSN 1025-8140
▼**JOURNAL OF BIOCHEMISTRY, MOLECULAR BIOLOGY AND BIOPHYSICS.** 1997. q. $90 (effective 1998). Harwood Academic Publishers, c/o International Publishers Distributor, P.O. Box 3054, Langhorne, PA 19047-3054. TEL 215-750-2642. FAX 215-750-6343. (Subscr. to: International Publishers Distributor, P.O. Box 90, Reading, Berkshire RG1 8JL, England. TEL 44-173-456-8316) **Indexed:** ASCA.

572.43 — US — ISSN 0145-479X
QH511.A1 — CODEN: JBBID4
JOURNAL OF BIOENERGETICS AND BIOMEMBRANES. 1970. bi-m. $395 (foreign $460) (effective 1998). Plenum Publishing Corp., 233 Spring St., New York, NY 10013-1578. TEL 212-620-8000. FAX 212-463-0742. TELEX 23-421139. Ed. Peter L. Pedersen. adv.; bibl.; charts; illus. (also avail. in microfilm from UMI; back issues avail.) **Indexed:** Abstr.Bull.Inst.Pap.Chem., ASCA, Biol.Abstr., Chem.Abstr., Chem.Cit.Ind., Curr.Adv.Biochem., Curr.Cont., Excerp.Med., Ind.Med., Ind.Sci.Rev., INIS Atomind., INSPEC, Sci.Cit.Ind. **Document type:** academic/scholarly publication.
—BLDSC (4952.820000); AskIEEE; CASDDS; CISTI; Genuine Article; KR SourceOne; Linda Hall; SWETS; UMI; UnCover. **CCC.**
Formerly: Journal of Bioenergetics (ISSN 0449-5705)
Description: Publishes original research contributions in the areas of bioenergetics, biomembranes and transport, including muscle contraction, electron transport, ATP synthesis, and membrane transport.
Refereed Serial

572 — US — ISSN 0021-9258
QP501 — CODEN: JBCHA3
JOURNAL OF BIOLOGICAL CHEMISTRY. (CD-ROM version ceased in 1997) 1905. w. $1600 (foreign $1590); online $1100. American Society for Biochemistry and Molecular Biology, Inc., Box 630591, Baltimore, MD 21263. URL: http://www.highwire.stanford.edu/jbc/. Ed. Herbert Tabor. adv.; index. circ. 7,200. (also avail. in microform from UMI,PMC; reprint service avail. from UMI) **Indexed:** Abstr.Bull.Inst.Pap.Chem., Abstr.Hyg., AIDS Abstr., Anim.Breed.Abstr., ASCA, Biol.Abstr., Biol.& Agr.Ind., Biotech.Abstr., Biwk.Pap.Rad.Chem.& Photochem., Chem.Abstr., Chem.Cit.Ind., Crop Physiol.Abstr., Curr.Adv.Biochem., Curr.Adv.Cancer Res., Curr.Adv.Cell & Devel.Biol., Curr.Adv.Genetics & Molec.Biol., Curr.Cont., Curr.Ref.Fish Res., Dairy Sci.Abstr., Deep Sea Res.& Oceanogr.Abstr., Dent.Ind., Excerp.Med., Field Crop Abstr., Food Sci.& Tech.Abstr., Helminthol.Abstr., Herb.Abstr., Hort.Abstr., Ind.Med., Ind.Sci.Rev., Ind.Vet., INIS Atomind., Maize Abstr., Mass Spectr.Bull., Neurosci.Cit.Ind., Nutr.Abstr., Pig News & Info., Plant Grow.Reg.Abstr., Poult.Abstr., Protozool.Abstr., Rev.Appl.Entomol., Rev.Med.& Vet.Mycol., Sci.Cit.Ind., Seed Abstr., Soils & Fert., Soyabean Abstr., Sport Fish.Abstr., Telegen, Triticale Abstr., Trop.Dis.Bull., Vet.Bull., Weed Abstr., Wild.Rev., Zoo.Rec. **Document type:** academic/scholarly publication.
●Also available online.
—BLDSC (4953.000000); CASDDS; CISTI; Genuine Article; KNAW; KR SourceOne; Linda Hall; SWETS; UMI; UnCover. **CCC.**
Refereed Serial

546 — GW — ISSN 0949-8257
QP531 — CODEN: JJBCFA
▼**JOURNAL OF BIOLOGICAL INORGANIC CHEMISTRY.** Online edition (GW ISSN 1432-1327) (Text in English) 1996. bi-m. DM.687 (foreign DM.726.90) (effective 1998). (Society of Biological Inorganic Chemistry) Springer-Verlag, Heidelberger Platz 3, 14197 Berlin, Germany. TEL 49-30-82787-0. FAX 49-30-82787488. E-mail: subscriptions@springer.de; URL: http://link.springer.de. (Subscr. in N. America to: Springer-Verlag New York, Inc., 333 Meadowlands Pkwy., Secaucus, NJ 07094. TEL 212-460-1500. FAX 212-473-6272) Ed.Bd. **Document type:** academic/scholarly publication.
●Also available online.
—BLDSC (4663.436500); CASDDS; Genuine Article. **CCC.**
Description: Covers aspects of chemistry related biological systems, including enzyme catalysis transport and toxicity, synthetic chemistry, and analytical methods.

JOURNAL OF BIOLUMINESCENCE AND CHEMILUMINESCENCE. see *CHEMISTRY — Physical Chemistry*

616.07 — NE — ISSN 0925-2738
QP519.9.N83 — CODEN: JBNME9
JOURNAL OF BIOMOLECULAR N M R. (Nuclear Magnetic Resonance) 1991. 8/yr. fl.1408 to institutions; $723 to institutions in U.S. (effective 1998). E S C O M Science Publishers BV, P.O. Box 214, 2300 AL Leiden, Netherlands. TEL 31-78-127052. FAX 31-71-121772. Ed. Kurt Wuthrich. **Indexed:** ASCA, Chem.Cit.Ind., Curr.Cont., Ind.Med. (1992-), Ind.Sci.Rev., Sci.Cit.Ind. **Document type:** academic/scholarly publication.
—BLDSC (4953.830000); CASDDS; CISTI; Genuine Article; SWETS; UnCover. **CCC.**
Description: Publishes research on technical developments and innovative applications of nuclear magnetic resonance spectroscopy for the study of the structure and dynamic properties of biopolymers in solution, liquid crystals, solids and in mixed environments such as membranes.

572.65 — US — ISSN 0739-1102
CODEN: JBSDD6
JOURNAL OF BIOMOLECULAR STRUCTURE & DYNAMICS. 1983. bi-m. $109 to individuals; institutions $830; commercial $990. Adenine Press, Box 340, Guilderland, NY 12084. TEL 518-456-0784. FAX 518-452-4955. E-mail: rhs07@cns.vax.albany.edu; URL: http://www.albany.edu/chemistry/sarma/contents.html. Ed. Ramaswamy H. Sarma.
—BLDSC (4953.850000); CASDDS; CISTI; EMDOCS; Genuine Article; KNAW; Linda Hall; SWETS; UnCover. **CCC.**
Description: Covers both experimental and theoretical investigations in the area of nucleic acids, nucleotides, proteins, peptides, membranes, polysacharides and all their components, metal complexes and model systems.

JOURNAL OF BRAIN SCIENCE. see *MEDICAL SCIENCES — Psychiatry And Neurology*

BIOLOGY — BIOLOGICAL CHEMISTRY

572 US ISSN 0730-2312
QH506 CODEN: JCEBD5
JOURNAL OF CELLULAR BIOCHEMISTRY. (Supplement avail. (ISSN 0733-1959)) 1972. 19/yr. $3150 (foreign $3465) (effective 1998). John Wiley & Sons, Inc., Journals, 605 Third Ave., New York, NY 10158. TEL 212-850-6645. FAX 212-850-6021. TELEX 12-7063. E-mail: SUBINFO@JWILEY.COM; URL: http://www.wiley.co.uk. (Subscr. outside the Americas to: John Wiley & Sons Ltd., Baffins Ln., Chichester, W. Sussex PO19 1UD, England. TEL 44-01243-449777. FAX 44-1243-776128) Ed.Bd. adv.: B&W page £640, color page £1515; trim 254 x 174. bk.rev.; charts; illus.; stat. circ. 850. (also avail. in microform from UMI; back issues avail.; reprint service avail. from ISI) **Indexed:** ASCA, Biol.Abstr., Biotech.Abstr., Chem.Abstr., Curr.Adv.Biochem., Curr.Adv.Cell & Devel.Biol., Curr.Adv.Ecol.Sci., Curr.Adv.Genetics & Molec.Biol., Curr.Cont., Excerp.Med., Ind.Med., Ind.Sci.Rev., INIS Atomind., Mat.Sci.Cit.Ind., Neurosci.Cit.Ind., Protozool.Abstr., Sci.Cit.Ind., Sport Fish.Abstr., SSCI, Wild.Rev., Zoo.Rec. **Document type:** academic/scholarly publication.
●Also available online.
—BLDSC (4955.010000); ADONIS; CASDDS; CISTI; EMDOCS; Genuine Article; KNAW; Linda Hall; SWETS; UnCover. **CCC.**
Former titles (until 1982): Journal of Supramolecular Structure and Cellular Biochemistry (ISSN 0275-3723); (until 1981): Journal of Supramolecular Structure (ISSN 0091-7419)
Description: Publishes timely reviews, commentaries, and descriptions of original research in areas where complex cellular, photogenic, clinical, or animal model systems are studied by biochemical, genetic or quantitative ultrastructural approaches.
Refereed Serial

JOURNAL OF CELLULAR BIOCHEMISTRY. SUPPLEMENT. see *BIOLOGY — Cytology And Histology*

JOURNAL OF CEREBRAL BLOOD FLOW AND METABOLISM. see *MEDICAL SCIENCES — Psychiatry And Neurology*

JOURNAL OF CHEMICAL AND BIOCHEMICAL KINETICS. see *CHEMISTRY*

JOURNAL OF CHEMICAL NEUROANATOMY. see *MEDICAL SCIENCES — Psychiatry And Neurology*

JOURNAL OF CHROMATOGRAPHY - BIOMEDICAL APPLICATIONS; an international journal devoted to new developments and advances in biomedical applications of chromatography and electrophoresis. see *CHEMISTRY*

JOURNAL OF COMPARATIVE PHYSIOLOGY. B: BIOCHEMICAL, SYSTEMATIC, AND ENVIRONMENTAL PHYSIOLOGY. see *BIOLOGY — Physiology*

572.33 US ISSN 1064-7546
QP801.P64 CODEN: JEPDED
JOURNAL OF ENVIRONMENTAL POLYMER DEGRADATION. 1994. q. $195 (foreign $230) (effective 1997). Plenum Publishing Corp., 233 Spring St., New York, NY 10013-1578. TEL 212-620-8000. FAX 212-463-0742. TELEX 23-421139. Eds. Richard A. Gross, Stephen P. McCarthy. adv. **Indexed:** Alloys Ind., ASCA, Curr.Cont., Eng.Mat.Abstr., Environ.Per.Bibl., Intl.Polym.Sci.& Tech., Met.Abstr.Ind., Met.Abstr., Nonfer.Met.Alert, RAPRA, Steels Alert, World Alum.Abstr. **Document type:** academic/scholarly publication.
—CASDDS; CISTI; Genuine Article; SWETS; UMI; UnCover. **CCC.**
Description: Provides interdisciplinary coverage of the science of polymer degradation, including new materials, natural origin polymers, degradable blends and composites, processing, material property elucidation, and degradation testing.
Refereed Serial

612.015 NE ISSN 8755-5093
CODEN: ENINEG
JOURNAL OF ENZYME INHIBITION. 4/yr. (in 1 vol., 4 nos./vol.). $218 (effective 1998). Gordon and Breach - Harwood Academic, Amsteldisk 166, 1st Fl., 1079 LH Amsterdam, Netherlands. URL: http://www.gbhap.com/Enzyme__Inhibition/. (Subscr. to: International Publishers Distributor, Box 32160, Newark, NJ 07102. TEL 800-545-8398. FAX 215-750-6343) Ed. H.J. Smith. (also avail. in microform) **Indexed:** ASCA, Chem.Cit.Ind., Curr.Cont., Food Sci.& Tech.Abstr., Sci.Cit.Ind.
●Also available online.
Also available on CD-ROM.
—BLDSC (4979.460000); CASDDS; CISTI; EMDOCS; SWETS; UnCover. **CCC.**
Refereed Serial

572 RU ISSN 0022-0930
QP1 CODEN: JEBPA9
JOURNAL OF EVOLUTIONARY BIOCHEMISTRY AND PHYSIOLOGY. English translation of: Zhurnal Evolyutsionnoi Biokhimii i Fiziologii (RU ISSN 0044-4529) 1969. bi-m. $1495 in US; elsewhere $1750 (effective 1998). (Russian Academy of Sciences, RU) Maik Nauka - Interperiodica, Mezhdunarodnyi Otdel, Ul. Profsoyuznaya, 90, 117864 Moscow, Russia. TEL 7-095-3360066. FAX 7-095-3360666. (Dist. by: Plenum Publishing Corp., 233 Spring St., New York, NY 10013-1578. TEL 212-620-8000. FAX 212-463-0742) Ed. V.L. Sviderskii. (also avail. in microfilm from UMI; back issues avail.) **Indexed:** ASCA, Biol.Abstr., Excerp.Med., Ind.Med., Int.Abstr.Biol.Sci., Neurosci.Cit.Ind. **Document type:** academic/scholarly publication.
—BLDSC (0414.450000); CASDDS; CISTI; Genuine Article; UMI; UnCover. **CCC.**
Refereed Serial

JOURNAL OF HISTOTECHNOLOGY. see *BIOLOGY — Cytology And Histology*

572 US ISSN 0162-0134
QP501 CODEN: JIBIDJ
JOURNAL OF INORGANIC BIOCHEMISTRY; an interdisciplinary journal. 1971. 16/yr. fl.2130($1224) (effective 1998). Elsevier Science Inc., Box 945, New York, NY 10159-0945. TEL 212-633-3730. FAX 212-633-3680. TELEX 420643 AEP UI. E-mail: usinfo-f@elsevier.nl; URL: http://www.elsevier.nl/. (Subscr. outside the Americas to: Elsevier Science, Regional Sales Office, P.O. Box 211, 1000 AE Amsterdam, Netherlands. TEL 31-20-4853757. FAX 31-20-4853432; Subscr. in Australasia and the Far East to: Elsevier Science (Singapore) Pte Ltd, No.1 Temasek Ave., No.17-01 Millenia Tower, Singapore 039192, Singapore. TEL 65-434-3727. FAX 65-337-2230; Subscr. in Japan to: Elsevier Science Japan, 9-15 Higashi-Azabu 1-chome, Minato-ku, Tokyo 106, Japan. TEL 81-3-5561-5033. FAX 81-3-5561-5047) Ed. H.A.O. Hill, J.F. Riordan. adv.; bk.rev.; charts; illus.; index. (also avail. in microform from UMI) **Indexed:** Apic.Abstr., ASCA, Bibl.Agri., Biol.Abstr., Cadscan, Chem.Abstr., Chem.Cit.Ind., Curr.Adv.Biochem., Curr.Adv.Ecol.Sci., Curr.Cont., Excerp.Med., Ind.Med., Ind.Sci.Rev., Int.Abstr.Biol.Sci., Lead Abstr., Mass Spectr.Bull., Sci.Cit.Ind., Zincscan. **Document type:** academic/scholarly publication.
—BLDSC (5007.150000); CASDDS; CISTI; Genuine Article; KNAW; Linda Hall; SWETS; UnCover. **CCC.**
Formerly (until vol.10): Bioinorganic Chemistry (ISSN 0006-3061)
Description: Publishes research papers and short communications in the areas of inorganic biochemistry.
Refereed Serial

572.57 NE ISSN 0929-7855
CODEN: JLMSEO
JOURNAL OF LIPID MEDIATORS AND CELL SIGNALING. (Text in English) 1989. 9/yr. fl.2040($1172) (effective 1998). Elsevier Science B.V., P.O. Box 211, 1000 AE Amsterdam, Netherlands. TEL 31-20-4853911. FAX 31-20-4853598. TELEX 18582 ESPA NL. E-mail: nlinfo-f@elsevier.nl; usinfo-f@elsevier.com; forinfo-kyf04035@niftyserve.or.jp; URL: http://www.elsevier.nl/. (Subscr. in the Americas to: Elsevier Science, Regional Sales Office, Box 945, New York, NY 10159-0945. TEL 212-633-3730. FAX 212-633-3680; Subscr. in Australasia and the Far East to: Elsevier Science (Singapore) Pte Ltd, No.1 Temasek Ave., No.17-01 Millenia Tower, Singapore 039192, Singapore. TEL 65-434-3727. FAX 65-337-2230; Subscr. in Japan to: Elsevier Science Japan, 9-15 Higashi-Azabu 1-chome, Minato-ku, Tokyo 106, Japan. TEL 81-3-5561-5033. FAX 3113-5561-5047) Ed. B.B. Vargaftig. (also avail. in microform from UMI; back issues avail.) **Indexed:** ASCA, Curr.Cont., Excerp.Med., Ind.Sci.Rev., Neurosci.Cit.Ind., Sci.Cit.Ind. **Document type:** academic/scholarly publication.
—BLDSC (5010.497000); ADONIS; CASDDS; CISTI; EMDOCS; Genuine Article; KNAW; SWETS; UnCover. **CCC.**
Formerly (until vol.9, no.2, 1994): Journal of Lipid Mediators (ISSN 0921-8319)
Description: Publishes articles on the chemistry, biophysics, pharmacology, toxicology, pathology, immunology and clinical aspects of lipid mediators in general.
Refereed Serial

572 US ISSN 0022-2275
QP751 CODEN: JLPRAW
JOURNAL OF LIPID RESEARCH. 1959. m. $80 to individuals (foreign $115); institutions $240 (foreign $275). Federation of American Societies for Experimental Biology, 9650 Rockville Pike, Bethesda, MD 20814. TEL 301-530-7100. FAX 301-571-1855. Ed. Lewis I. Gidez. bibl.; illus.; index. circ. 2,100. (also avail. in microform from UMI; reprint service avail. from UMI) **Indexed:** Anal.Abstr., ASCA, Bibl.Agri., Biol.Abstr., Biol.Dig., Biotech.Abstr., Chem.Abstr., Chem.Cit.Ind., Curr.Adv.Biochem., Curr.Adv.Cell & Devel.Biol., Curr.Adv.Ecol.Sci., Curr.Adv.Genetics & Molec.Biol., Curr.Chem.React, Curr.Cont., Dairy Sci.Abstr., Dent.Ind., Excerp.Med., Food Sci.& Tech.Abstr., Helminthol.Abstr., Ind.Chem., Ind.Med., Ind.Sci.Rev., Ind.Vet., INIS Atomind., Maize Abstr., Mass Spectr.Bull., Nutr.Abstr., Sci.Cit.Ind, Sport Fish.Abstr., Telegen, THA, Vet.Bull., Wild.Rev., Zoo.Rec. **Document type:** academic/scholarly publication.
—BLDSC (5010.500000); CASDDS; CISTI; Genuine Article; KNAW; Linda Hall; SWETS; UMI; UnCover. **CCC.**
Refereed Serial

JOURNAL OF MEMBRANE SCIENCE. see *CHEMISTRY — Physical Chemistry*

BIOLOGY — BIOLOGICAL CHEMISTRY

572 **UK** ISSN 0022-2836
QH301 CODEN: JMOBAK
JOURNAL OF MOLECULAR BIOLOGY. 1959. 50/yr. £320($475) to individuals; institutions £2495 (effective 1998). Academic Press Ltd. (Subsidiary of: Harcourt Brace & Company Ltd.), 24-28 Oval Rd., London NW1 7DX, England. TEL 44-171-2674466. FAX 44-171-4822293. TELEX 25775-ACPRES-G. E-mail: apsubs@acad.com; URL: http://www.hbuk.co.uk/ap/jmb; http://www.europe.idealibrary.com/. (Subscr. to: Harcourt Brace & Company Ltd., Foots Cray High St., Sidcup, Kent DA14 5HP, England. TEL 44-181-3003322. FAX 44-181-3090807) Ed. P. Wright. R&P contact: Catherine John. adv. contact: Nik Screen. bibl.; charts; illus.; index,cum.index. **Indexed:** Abstr.Hyg., Anim.Breed.Abstr., ASCA, Bibl.Agri., Biol.Abstr., Biol.& Agr.Ind., Biostat., Biotech.Abstr., Chem.Abstr., Chem.Cit.Ind., Compumath, Curr.Adv.Biochem., Curr.Adv.Cancer Res., Curr.Adv.Cell & Devel.Biol., Curr.Adv.Ecol.Sci., Curr.Adv.Genetics & Molec.Biol., Curr.Cont., Dairy Sci.Abstr., Excerp.Med., Food Sci.& Tech.Abstr., Helminthol.Abstr., Ind.Med., Ind.Sci.Rev., Ind.Vet., INIS Atomind., Plant Breed.Abstr., Poult.Abstr., Protozool.Abstr., Sci.Cit.Ind., Soils & Fert., Sport Fish.Abstr., Triticale Abstr., Trop.Dis.Bull., Vet.Bull., Wild.Rev., Zoo.Rec. **Document type:** academic/scholarly publication.
●Also available online.
—BLDSC (5020.700000); ADONIS; CASDDS; CISTI; Genuine Article; KR SourceOne; Linda Hall; SWETS; UnCover. **CCC.**
Description: Presents original scientific research concerning studies of organisms or their components at the molecular level.

JOURNAL OF MOLECULAR CATALYSIS A: CHEMICAL. see CHEMISTRY — Physical Chemistry

JOURNAL OF MOLECULAR CATALYSIS B: ENZYMATIC. see CHEMISTRY — Physical Chemistry

572 **UK** ISSN 0952-3499
QP517.M67 CODEN: JMORE4
JOURNAL OF MOLECULAR RECOGNITION. 1988. 7/yr. $755 (foreign $755) (effective 1998). John Wiley & Sons Ltd., Journals, Baffins Ln., Chichester, W. Sussex PO19 1UD, England. TEL 44-1243-779777. FAX 44-1243-775878. E-mail: info-assets@wiley.co.uk; URL: http://www.wiley.co.uk. (Subscr. in the Americas to: John Wiley & Sons, Inc., 605 Third Ave., New York, NY 10158. TEL 212-850-6645. FAX 212-850-6021) Ed. Irwin M. Chaiken. adv.: B&W page £595, color page £1495; trim 279 x 210; adv. contact: Bob Kern. bk.rev. (also avail. in microform from UMI; back issues avail.) **Indexed:** ASCA, Chem.Abstr. **Document type:** academic/scholarly publication.
—BLDSC (5020.725000); CASDDS; CISTI; Ei; EMDOCS; Genuine Article; KNAW; SWETS; UMI; UnCover. **CCC.**
Description: Devoted to research on the basic principles, characterization, and application of specific molecular interactions in chemistry, biology, biotechnology and medicine.
Refereed Serial

616.8 574.192 **US** ISSN 0022-3042
QP351 CODEN: JONRA9
JOURNAL OF NEUROCHEMISTRY. 1956. m. $479 to individuals (foreign $479); institutions $1838 (foreign $1838) (effective 1998); newsstand price: $137. (International Society for Neurochemistry) Lippincott - Raven Publishers (Subsidiary of: Wolters Kluwer N.V.), 227 E. Washington Sq., Philadelphia, PA 19106. TEL 215-238-4200. FAX 215-238-4227. URL: http://www.lrpub.com. (Subscr. to: Box 1600, Hagerstown, MD 21741-1600. TEL 800-777-2295. FAX 301-824-7390) Eds. Dr. B. Collier, Dr. G. Lunt; Pub. Nancy Megley. R&P contact: Alice McElhinney. adv. contact: Ray Thibodeau. bk.rev.; bibl.; charts; illus.; index; circ. 1,347 (paid). (also avail. in microform from UMI; back issues avail.; reprint service avail. from UMI) **Indexed:** AIDS Abstr., ASCA, Biol.Abstr., Biotech.Abstr., Chem.Abstr., Chem.Cit.Ind., Curr.Adv.Biochem., Curr.Adv.Ecol.Sci., Curr.Cont., Dairy Sci.Abstr., Dent.Ind., Excerp.Med., Ind.Med., Ind.Sci.Rev., Ind.Vet., INIS Atomind., Mass Spectr.Bull., Neurosci.Cit.Ind., Nutr.Abstr., Sci.Cit.Ind., SSCI, THA, Trop.Dis.Bull., Vet.Bull. **Document type:** academic/scholarly publication.
●Also available online.
—BLDSC (5021.500000); CASDDS; CISTI; Genuine Article; KNAW; Linda Hall; SWETS; UMI; UnCover. **CCC.**
Description: Provides complete coverage of the biochemical aspects of behavior and brain function.
Refereed Serial

JOURNAL OF NUTRITIONAL BIOCHEMISTRY. see NUTRITION AND DIETETICS

572.65 **US**
CODEN: IJPPC3
JOURNAL OF PEPTIDE RESEARCH. (Text in English) 1997. m. DKK 3780 in Europe; US, Canada and Japan DKK 3900 (effective 1997). (American Peptide Society, US) Munksgaard International Publishers Ltd., 35 Noerre Soegade, P.O. Box 2148, DK-1016 Copenhagen K, Denmark. TEL 45-33-127030. FAX 45-33-129387. E-mail: fsub@mail.munksgaard.dk. (In N. America: Commerce Place, 350 Main St., Malden, MA 02148-6018. TEL 617-388-8273. FAX 617-388-8274) Ed. Victor J. Hruby. adv.; charts; illus.; index. circ. 1,400. (reprint service avail. from ISI,SWZ) **Indexed:** Abstr.Hyg., ASCA, Biol.Abstr., Biotech.Abstr., Chem.Abstr., Chem.Cit.Ind., Curr.Adv.Biochem., Curr.Adv.Genetics & Molec.Biol., Curr.Chem.React, Curr.Cont., Dairy Sci.Abstr., Dent.Ind., Ind.Chem., Ind.Med., Ind.Sci.Rev., Ind.Vet., INIS Atomind., Mat.Sci.Cit.Ind., Sci.Cit.Ind, Trop.Dis.Bull., Vet.Bull. **Document type:** academic/scholarly publication.
—ADONIS; CASDDS; CISTI; Ei; EMDOCS; Genuine Article; KNAW; SWETS; UnCover. **CCC.**
Formed by the merger of (1968-1997): International Journal of Peptide and Protein Research (ISSN 0367-8377); (1988-1997): Peptide Research (ISSN 1040-5704)
Refereed Serial

612.015 **UK** ISSN 1075-2617
CODEN: JPSIEI
JOURNAL OF PEPTIDE SCIENCE. 1994. 8/yr. $445 (foreign $445) (effective 1998). (European Peptide Society) John Wiley & Sons Ltd., Journals, Baffins Ln., Chichester, W. Sussex PO19 1UD, England. TEL 44-1243-779777. FAX 44-1243-775878. E-mail: info-assets@wiley.co.uk; URL: http://www.wiley.co.uk. (Subscr. in N. America to: John Wiley & Sons, Inc., 605 Third Ave., New York, NY 10158) Ed. Conrad Schneider. adv.: B&W page £595, color page £1495; trim 279 x 210; adv. contact: Bob Kern. (also avail. in microform from UMI; back issues avail.) **Document type:** academic/scholarly publication.
—BLDSC (5030.530000); CASDDS; CISTI; SWETS. **CCC.**
Refereed Serial

JOURNAL OF PHARMACOLOGICAL AND TOXICOLOGICAL METHODS. see ENVIRONMENTAL STUDIES — Toxicology And Environmental Safety

572 **SZ** ISSN 1011-1344
QH515 CODEN: JPPBEG
JOURNAL OF PHOTOCHEMISTRY AND PHOTOBIOLOGY, B: BIOLOGY. (Text in English) 1987. 15/yr. fl.3564($2048) (effective 1998). (European Society for Photobiology) Elsevier Science S.A., P.O. Box 564, CH-1001 Lausanne 1, Switzerland. TEL 41-21-3207381. FAX 41-21-3235444. TELEX 450620-ELSA-CH. (Subscr. to: Elsevier Science, Regional Sales Office, P.O. Box 211, 1000 AE Amsterdam, Netherlands. TEL 31-20-4853757. FAX 31-20-4853432; Subscr. in the Americas to: Elsevier Science, Regional Sales Office, Box 945, New York, NY 10159-0945. TEL 212-633-3730. FAX 212-633-3680; Subscr. in Australasia to: Elsevier Science (Singapore) Pte. Ltd., No. 1 Temasek Ave., No. 17-01 Millenia Tower, Singapore 039192, Singapore. TEL 65-434-3727. FAX 65-337-2230) Ed. G. Jori. bk.rev. (also avail. in microform from UMI) **Indexed:** ASCA, Chem.Abstr., Chem.Cit.Ind., Curr.Adv.Biochem., Curr.Adv.Cancer Res., Curr.Cont., Eng.Ind., Excerp.Med. (1993-), Ind.Sci.Rev., Met.Abstr., Photo.Abstr., Phys.Ber., Sci.Cit.Ind. **Document type:** academic/scholarly publication.
—BLDSC (5034.850000); CASDDS; CISTI; EMDOCS; Genuine Article; KNAW; Linda Hall; SWETS. **CCC.**
Description: Publishes papers for scientists who seek to understand light and its interactions with the processes of life. Also includes technological developments, forthcoming events, conference reports, and reports on current areas of research.
Refereed Serial

572 **II** ISSN 0971-7811
JOURNAL OF PLANT BIOCHEMISTRY AND BIOTECHNOLOGY. (Text in English) 1992. s-a. Rs.400 (foreign $100) to non-members. Society for Plant Biochemistry and Biotechnology, Division of Biochemistry, Indian Agricultural Research Institute, New Delhi 110 012, India. TEL 91-11-5750932. FAX 91-11-5750932. Ed. R.P. Sharma; Pub. S.L. Mehta. circ. 1,000 (paid). **Indexed:** ASCA, Curr.Cont., Food Sci.& Tech.Abstr.
—Genuine Article.
Refereed Serial

JOURNAL OF PROTEIN CHEMISTRY. see CHEMISTRY — Organic Chemistry

572 **UK** ISSN 0022-4251
QP251 CODEN: JRPFA4
JOURNAL OF REPRODUCTION AND FERTILITY. (Supplement avail.: ISSN 0449-3087) 1960. bi-m. £270($460) (effective 1998). Journals of Reproduction & Fertility Ltd., 22 Newmarket Rd., Cambridge CB5 8DT, England. TEL 44-1223-351809. FAX 44-1223-359754. E-mail: jrf@cityscape.co.uk. (Dist. by: Portland Press, P.O. Box 32, Commerce Way, Colchester, Essex CO2 8HP, England. TEL 44-1206-796351) Ed. Dr. C. Doberska. R&P contact: C.A. Doberska. adv.: page £352; trim 170 x 240; adv. contact: C.H. Clarke. bibl.; charts; illus.; index. circ. 2,200. (back issues avail.) **Indexed:** Abstr.Anthropol., Anim.Breed.Abstr., ASCA, Bibl.Repro., Biol.Abstr., Biol.& Agr.Ind., Biotech.Abstr., Chem.Abstr., Curr.Adv.Ecol.Sci., Dairy Sci.Abstr., Excerp.Med., Ind.Med., Ind.Sci.Rev., Ind.Vet., INIS Atomind., Key Word Ind.Wildl.Res., Neurosci.Cit.Ind., Nutr.Abstr., Poult.Abstr., Sci.Cit.Ind., Sport Fish.Abstr., Vet.Bull., Wild.Rev., Zoo.Rec. **Document type:** academic/scholarly publication.
—BLDSC (5049.600000); CASDDS; CISTI; Genuine Article; KNAW; KR SourceOne; Linda Hall; SWETS; UnCover. **CCC.**
Description: Molecular biology, biochemistry and physiology of reproduction and early embryogenesis in man and other animals.
Refereed Serial

612 **UK** ISSN 1350-7702
CODEN: JSRRER
JOURNAL OF SEROTONIN RESEARCH. 1994. q. £65($120) to individuals; institutions £95 ($170) (effective 1996). Euroscience Press, P.O. Box 3405, London N1 0NZ, England. TEL 44-171-601-8138. FAX 44-171-601-7969. (Dist. by: Royal Society of Medicine Press Ltd., P.O. Box 9002, London W1A 0ZA, England. TEL 44-171-290-2900. FAX 44-171-290-2929) Ed. Dr. Ted Dinan. bk.rev. **Indexed:** Excerp.Med. (1995-). **Document type:** academic/scholarly publication.
—BLDSC (5064.010300); CASDDS; KNAW.
Refereed Serial

BIOLOGY — BIOLOGICAL CHEMISTRY

572 UK ISSN 0960-0760
QP801.S6 CODEN: JSBBEZ
JOURNAL OF STEROID BIOCHEMISTRY AND MOLECULAR BIOLOGY. 1970. 24/yr. fl.4844($2784) (effective 1998). Elsevier Science Ltd., Pergamon, P.O. Box 800, Kidlington, Oxford OX5 1DX, England. TEL 44-1865-843000. FAX 44-1865-843010. (Subscr. to: Elsevier Science, Regional Sales Office, P.O. Box 211, 1000 AE Amsterdam, Netherlands. TEL 31-20-4853757. FAX 31-20-4853432; Subscr. in the Americas to: Elsevier Science, Regional Sales Office, Box 945, New York, NY 10159-0945. TEL 212-633-3730. FAX 212-633-3680; Subscr. in Australasia and the Far East to: Elsevier Science (Singapore) Pte Ltd, No.1 Temasek Ave., No.17-01 Millenia Tower, Singapore 039192, Singapore. TEL 65-434-3727. FAX 65-337-2230) Eds. J.R. Pasqualini, R. Scholler. adv.; bk.rev. circ. 1,250. (also avail. in microfilm from UMI; back issues avail.) **Indexed:** Anal.Abstr., Anim.Breed.Abstr., ASCA, Biol.Abstr., Chem.Abstr., Chem.Cit.Ind., Curr.Adv.Biochem., Curr.Adv.Cancer Res., Curr.Adv.Ecol.Sci., Curr.Adv.Genetics & Molec.Biol., Curr.Cont., Dairy Sci.Abstr., Excerp.Med., Ind.Med., Ind.Sci.Rev., Ind.Vet., INIS Atomind., Mass Spectr.Bull., Neurosci.Cit.Ind., Nutr.Abstr., Pig News & Info., Sci.Cit.Ind., SSCI. **Document type:** academic/scholarly publication.
—BLDSC (5066.850010); ADONIS; CASDDS; CISTI; EMDOCS; Genuine Article; Linda Hall; SWETS; UMI; UnCover. **CCC.**
Formerly (until 1991): Journal of Steroid Biochemistry (ISSN 0022-4731)
Description: Covers recent experimental and theoretical developments in disciplines related to steroids.
Refereed Serial

612.015 SZ ISSN 1018-1172
RC691 CODEN: JVREE9
JOURNAL OF VASCULAR RESEARCH. (Text in English) 1964. bi-m. 94.50 SFr.($72.60) to individuals; institutions 696 SFr.($548) (effective 1998). S. Karger AG, Allschwilerstr. 10, P.O. Box, CH-4009 Basel, Switzerland. TEL 41-61-3061111. FAX 41-61-3061234. E-mail: karger@karger.ch; URL: http://www.karger.ch. Ed. M.J. Mulvany. adv.; bibl.; charts; illus.; index. circ. 1,000. (also avail. in microform from RPI) **Indexed:** ASCA, Biol.Abstr., Chem.Abstr., Curr.Adv.Ecol.Sci., Curr.Cont., Excerp.Med., Ind.Med., Ind.Sci.Rev., Kidney, Med.& Surg.Dermat., Nutr.Abstr., Sci.Cit.Ind., THA. **Document type:** academic/scholarly publication.
—BLDSC (5072.269000); CASDDS; CISTI; EMDOCS; Genuine Article; KNAW; SWETS; UnCover. **CCC.**
Incorporates (1982-1997): International Journal of Microcirculation: Clinical & Experimental (ISSN 0167-6865); *Former titles* (until 1991): Blood Vessels (ISSN 0303-6847); Angiologica (ISSN 0003-3189)
Refereed Serial

572 IT ISSN 0075-4447
JOURNEES BIOCHIMIQUES LATINES. RAPPORTS.* (Text in French and Italian) irreg. (every 2-3 yrs.) 9th, 1968, Monaco. Inquire: Prof. A. Bonsignore, University of Genoa, Italy.

572 JA ISSN 0453-073X
QD415.A1 CODEN: KASEAA
KAGAKU TO SEIBUTSU/CHEMISTRY AND BIOLOGY. (Text in Japanese) 1962. m. 1030 Yen per no. (Nippon Nogei Kagakkai - Japan Society for Bioscience, Biotechnology and Agrochemistry) Gakkai Shuppan Senta - Japan Scientific Societies Press, 2-10, Hongo 6-chome, Bunkyo-ku, Tokyo 113, Japan. **Indexed:** Chem.Abstr., INIS Atomind., Jap.Per.Ind.
—CASDDS.

572 JA ISSN 0911-8691
KANSANKA SHISHITSU KENKYU/LIPID PEROXIDE AND RESEARCH. (Text in Japanese) a. 4000 Yen. Nihon Kasanka Shishitsu Furi Rajikaru Gakkai - Japanese Society of Lipid Peroxide and Free Radical Research, c/o Mr. Kunio Yagi, Oyo Seikgaku Kenkyujo, Mitakecho, Kani-gun, Gifu-ken 505-01, Japan.

KISO ROKA GAKKAI SAKYURA/BIOMEDICAL GERONTOLOGY CIRCULAR. see *GERONTOLOGY AND GERIATRICS*

KISO ROKA KENKYU/BIOMEDICAL GERONTOLOGY. see *GERONTOLOGY AND GERIATRICS*

572 BU ISSN 0204-9716
KLINICHNA LABORATORIIA. (Text in Bulgarian) 1970. q. 2000 lv.($18) (effective 1997). Tsentar za Informatsiia po Meditsina, 1, Sv. Georgi Sofiiski St., 1431 Sofia, Bulgaria. TEL 359-2-522342. FAX 359-2-522393. E-mail: mutafov@medun.acad.bg; URL: http://www.medun.acad.bg. Ed. S. Danev. adv.: B&W page $50, color page $150; trim 110 x 160. bk.rev.; index. circ. 200. (back issues avail.) **Document type:** academic/scholarly publication, abstracting/indexing.
Description: Abstracts of foreign publications in the field of medical laboratory, includes methods, techniques and equipment.

612.015 XR ISSN 1210-7921
CODEN: KBMEF
KLINICKA BIOCHEMIE A METABOLISMUS. (Text in Czech or Slovak; summaries in Czech and English) 1972. 4/yr. $76 (effective 1997 & 1998). (Ceska Lekarska Spolecnost J.E. Purkyne - Czech Medical Association) Nakladatelske Stredisko C L S J.E. Purkyne, Sokolska 31, 120 26 Prague 2, Czech Republic. TEL 420-2-24911420. FAX 420-2-24911420. (Dist. by: Abont s.r.o., Chlumova 17, 130 00 Prague 3, Czech Republic) Ed. A. Kazda. bk.rev. circ. 750. **Indexed:** Chem.Abstr., Curr.Adv.Ecol.Sci., Excerp.Med. (until 1992; 1996-). **Document type:** academic/scholarly publication.
—BLDSC (5099.284790); CASDDS; EMDOCS. **CCC.**
Formerly (until Aug. 1993): Biochemia Clinica Bohemoslovaca (ISSN 0139-9608)
Refereed Serial

616.075 615.19 SW ISSN 0282-440X
KLINISK KEMI; medlemsblad foer S F K K. 1975. bi-m. SEK 200 membership (effective 1993). Svensk Foerening foer Klinisk Kemi, c/o K. Hellsing, Avdeling foer Klinisk Kemi, Akademiska Sjukhuset, S-751 85 Uppsala, Sweden.
Formerly (until vol.4, 1985): Svensk Foerening foer Klinisk Kemi - Medlemsblad.

616.0756 615.19 SW ISSN 1101-2013
KLINISK KEMI I NORDEN. 1989. 3-4/yr. Nordisk Foerening foer Klinisk Kemi, c/o K. Hellsing, Avdelingen foer Klinisk Kemi, Akademiska Sjukhuset, S-751 85 Uppsala, Sweden.

KOGYO GIJUTSUIN. BISEIBUTSU KOGYO GIJUTSU KENKYUJO. KENKYU HOKOKU/FERMENTATION RESEARCH INSTITUTE. REPORT. see *BIOLOGY — Microbiology*

572.8 NE ISSN 0075-7535
QP519 CODEN: LTBBDT
LABORATORY TECHNIQUES IN BIOCHEMISTRY AND MOLECULAR BIOLOGY. (Text in English) 1968. irreg., vol. 25, 1993. price varies. Elsevier Science B.V., Books Division, P.O. Box 211, 1000 AE Amsterdam, Netherlands. TEL 31-20-4853911. FAX 31-20-4853705. TELEX 18582 ESPA NL. E-mail: nlinfo-f@elsevier.nl; usinfo-f@elsevier.com; forinfo-kyf04035@niftyserve.or.jp; URL: http://www.elsevier.nl/. (Subscr. in the Americas to: Elsevier Science, Regional Sales Office, Box 945, New York, NY 10159-0945. TEL 212-633-3730. FAX 212-633-3680; Subscr. in Australasia and the Far East to: Elsevier Science (Singapore) Pte Ltd, No.1 Temasek Ave., No.17-01 Millenia Tower, Singapore 039192, Singapore. TEL 65-434-3727. FAX 65-337-2230; Subscr. in Japan to: Elsevier Science Japan, 9-15 Higashi-Azabu 1-chome, Minato-ku, Tokyo 106, Japan. TEL 81-3-5561-5033. FAX 81-3-5561-5047) Eds. P.C van der Vliet, A.J. Levine. (back issues avail.) **Document type:** monographic series.
—BLDSC (5141.915000); CISTI; Ei; KNAW; SWETS. **CCC.**
Refereed Serial

612.015 581 UK ISSN 0143-4217
LECTINS. s-m. (diskette m.). £90 (diskette £120; both £180) (effective 1997). S U B I S, Mansion House, 19 Kingfield Rd., Sheffield S11 9AS, England. TEL 44-114-2554433. FAX 44-114-2554626. E-mail: subis@sheffac.demon.co.uk; URL: http://www.shef.ac.uk/uni/companies/shap. (also avail. in diskette format; looseleaf format; back issues avail.) **Document type:** abstracting/indexing.
—**CCC.**
Description: Current awareness service for researchers in clinical and life sciences.

572.65 NE ISSN 0929-5666
CODEN: LPSCEM
LETTERS IN PEPTIDE SCIENCE. (Text in English) 1994. bi-m. fl.1125 to institutions; $934 to institutions in U.S. (effective 1998). E S C O M Science Publishers BV, P.O. Box 214, 2300 AE Leiden, Netherlands. TEL 31-71-127052. FAX 31-71-121772. (back issues avail.) **Indexed:** ASCA. **Document type:** academic/scholarly publication.
—BLDSC (5185.170180); CASDDS; CISTI; Genuine Article; SWETS. **CCC.**
Description: Concerned with the isolation, structural characterization, synthesis and biological activity of peptides.

572.57 UK ISSN 1357-7166
CODEN: LITEEI
LIPID TECHNOLOGY NEWSLETTER. 1989. bi-m. P.J. Barnes & Associates, P.O. Box 345, High Wycombe HP10 9HL, England. Ed. P.J. Barnes. (also avail. in microform from UMI; back issues avail.) **Indexed:** Food Sci.& Tech.Abstr. **Document type:** trade publication, newsletter.
—BLDSC (5221.798000).
Formerly (until 1995): Lipid Technology (ISSN 0956-666X)
Description: Presents recent international developments in oils, fats and lipids in food technology, biotechnology, nutrition and pharmaceuticals.
Refereed Serial

572.57 US ISSN 0024-4201
QP501 CODEN: LPDSAP
LIPIDS. 1966. m. $95 to individuals (foreign $110); institutions $215 (foreign $230). (American Oil Chemists' Society) A O C S Press, 1608 Broadmoor Dr., Box 3489, Champaign, IL 61821-0489. TEL 217-359-2344. FAX 217-351-8091. E-mail: publications@aocs.org; URL: http://www.aocs.org. Ed. Howard R. Knapp; Pub. Mary Lane. R&P contact: Connie Winslow. TEL 217-359-5401. circ. 1,600 (paid). (also avail. in microfilm from UMI; reprint service avail. from UMI) **Indexed:** ASCA, Bibl.Agri., Biol.Abstr., Chem.Abstr., Chem.Cit.Ind., Curr.Adv.Biochem., Curr.Adv.Cell & Devel.Biol., Curr.Adv.Ecol.Sci., Curr.Cont., Dairy Sci.Abstr., Deep Sea Res.& Oceanogr.Abstr., Excerp.Med., Field Crop Abstr., Food Sci.& Tech.Abstr., Helminthol.Abstr., Hort.Abstr., Ind.Med., Ind.Sci.Rev., Ind.Vet., INIS Atomind., Maize Abstr., Mass Spectr.Bull., Neurosci.Cit.Ind., Nutr.Abstr., Poult.Abstr., Rev.Med.& Vet.Mycol., Rice Abstr., Sci.Cit.Ind., Seed Abstr., Soils & Fert., Soyabean Abstr., Sport Fish.Abstr., SSCI, THA, Trop.Oil Seeds Abstr., Vet.Bull., Wild.Rev., Zoo.Rec. **Document type:** academic/scholarly publication.
—BLDSC (5221.850000); CASDDS; CISTI; Ei; Genuine Article; KNAW; Linda Hall; SWETS; UMI; UnCover. **CCC.**
Description: Contains original research on lipids, biochemistry, and related biomedical subjects.
Refereed Serial

572.57 UK ISSN 0264-9659
LIPOSOMES. 1984. s-m. (diskette m.). £110 (diskette £120; both £180) (effective 1997). S U B I S, Mansion House, 19 Kingfield Rd., Sheffield S11 9AS, England. TEL 44-114-2554433. FAX 44-114-2554626. E-mail: subis@sheffac.demon.co.uk; URL: http://www.shef.ac.uk/uni/companies/shap. (also avail. in diskette format) **Document type:** abstracting/indexing.
—**CCC.**
Description: Current awareness service for researchers. Offers information on the structure and pharmacology of liposomes and natural membrane vesicles.

612.015 618.92 UK ISSN 1351-5322
LYSOSOMES AND ENDOCYTOSIS. s-m. (diskette m.). £90 (diskette £120; both £180) (effective 1997). S U B I S, Mansion House, 19 Kingfield Rd., Sheffield S11 9AS, England. TEL 44-114-2554433. FAX 44-114-2554626. E-mail: subis@sheffac.demon.co.uk; URL: http://www.shef.ac.uk/uni/companies/shap. (also avail. in diskette format; looseleaf format; back issues avail.) **Document type:** abstracting/indexing.
—**CCC.**
Formerly (until 1993): Lysosomes (ISSN 0142-8187)
Description: Current awareness service for researchers in clinical and life sciences.

BIOLOGY — BIOLOGICAL CHEMISTRY

MATERIAL UND ORGANISMEN/MATERIALS AND ORGANISMS/MATERIAU ET ORGANISMES. see CHEMISTRY — Analytical Chemistry

MEDICAL ENGINEERING AND PHYSICS. see MEDICAL SCIENCES

612.015   UK   ISSN 0952-0422
MEMBRANE LIPIDS. m. £80 (effective 1997). S U B I S, Mansion House, 19 Kingfield Rd., Sheffield S11 9AS, England. TEL 44-114-2554433. FAX 44-114-2554626. E-mail: subis@sheffac.demon.co.uk; URL: http://www.shef.ac.uk/uni/companies/shap. (looseleaf format; back issues avail.) Document type: abstracting/indexing.
—CCC.
Description: Current awareness service for researchers in clinical and life sciences.

612.015 610   UK   ISSN 0143-4233
MEMBRANE PROTEINS. 1981. m. £80 (effective 1997). S U B I S, Mansion House, 19 Kingfield Rd., Sheffield S11 9AS, England. TEL 44-114-2554433. FAX 44-114-2554626. E-mail: subis@sheffac.demon.co.uk; URL: http://www.shef.ac.uk/uni/companies/shap. Document type: abstracting/indexing.
—CCC.
Description: Current awareness service for researchers which covers antigens and band 3 proteins.

METHODOLOGICAL SURVEYS IN BIOANALYSIS OF DRUGS. see PHARMACY AND PHARMACOLOGY

572.7   US   ISSN 1046-2023
QP519.7   CODEN: MTHDE9
METHODS: A COMPANION TO METHODS IN ENZYMOLOGY. Key Title: Methods (San Diego). (In 3 sections: Genomethods; Immunomethods; Neuroprotocols) 1990. m. $195 (foreign $225) (effective 1997). Academic Press, Inc., Journal Division, 525 B St., Ste. 1900, San Diego, CA 92101-4495. TEL 619-230-1840. FAX 619-699-6800. E-mail: apsubs@acad.com; URL: http://www.apnet.com/www/journal/me.htm; http://www.idealibrary.com/. (Subscr. to: Box 861213, Orlando, FL 32886-1213. TEL 407-347-4040. FAX 407-363-9661) Eds. John N. Abelson, Kenneth W. Adolph. (back issues avail.) Indexed: ASCA, Chem.Abstr., Excerp.Med. (1994-), Ind.Med., Neurosci.Cit.Ind. Document type: academic/scholarly publication.
●Also available online.
—BLDSC (5746.575000); CASDDS; CISTI; EMDOCS; Genuine Article; KNAW; Linda Hall; SWETS; UnCover. CCC.
Incorporates (in 1995): Methods - GenoMethods (ISSN 1078-1501); (1992-1995): NeuroProtocols (ISSN 1058-6741); (in 1995): Methods - Immunomethods (ISSN 1078-151X); Which was formerly (1992-1994): Immunomethods (ISSN 1058-6687)
Description: Contains topic-oriented articles that cover new methods applicable to a number of disciplines.
Refereed Serial

612.015   GW
METHODS AND PRINCIPLES IN MEDICINAL CHEMISTRY. 1993. irreg., vol.3, 1994. DM.158. V C H Verlagsgesellschaft mbH, Postfach 101161, 69451 Weinheim, Germany. TEL 06201-606147. FAX 06201-606117. TELEX 465516-VCHWH-D. Ed.Bd. Document type: monographic series.

572.7   US   ISSN 0076-6879
QP601   CODEN: MENZAU
METHODS IN ENZYMOLOGY. 1955. irreg., vol.275, 1996. price varies. Academic Press, Inc., 525 B St., Ste. 1900, San Diego, CA 92101-4495. TEL 619-231-0926. FAX 619-699-6715. E-mail: ap@acad.com; URL: http://www.apnet.com. (Subscr. to: Order Dept., 6277 Sea Harbor Dr., 4th Fl., Orlando, FL 32887. TEL 800-321-5068) Eds. S.P. Colowick, N.O. Kaplan. (reprint service avail. from ISI) Indexed: Abstr.Hyg., ASCA, Biol.Abstr., Chem.Abstr., Chem.Cit.Ind., Dairy Sci.Abstr., Dent.Ind., Excerp.Med., Ind.Med., Ind.Sci.Rev., Nutr.Abstr., Protozool.Abstr., Rev.Med.& Vet.Mycol., Sci.Cit.Ind., Sugar Ind.Abstr. Document type: monographic series.
—BLDSC (5748.060000); CASDDS; CISTI; KNAW; SWETS; UnCover. CCC.
Refereed Serial

547.1223   GW   ISSN 0899-4536
METHODS IN STEREOCHEMICAL ANALYSIS. (Text in English) 1982. irreg. DM.139.60. V C H Verlagsgesellschaft mbH, Postfach 101161, 69451 Weinheim, Germany. TEL 49-6201-606-0. FAX 49-6201-606328. E-mail: subservice@vchgroup.de. (Subscr. in N. America to: John Wiley & Sons, Inc., 605 Third Ave., New York, NY 10158. TEL 212-850-6645. FAX 212-850-6021) Document type: academic/scholarly publication, monographic series.

572   US   ISSN 0076-6941
QD271   CODEN: MBANAA
METHODS OF BIOCHEMICAL ANALYSIS. 1954. irreg., vol.34, 1990. price varies. John Wiley & Sons, Inc., 605 Third Ave., New York, NY 10158-0012. TEL 212-850-6000. Ed. David Glick. Indexed: Abstr.Hyg., ASCA, Biol.Abstr., Biotech.Abstr., Chem.Abstr., Comput.Rev., Curr.Adv.Ecol.Sci., Ind.Med., Ind.Sci.Rev., Math.R., Nutr.Abstr. Document type: monographic series.
—BLDSC (5747.000000); CASDDS; CISTI; Linda Hall; SWETS. CCC.
Refereed Serial

MICROCIRCULATION, ENDOTHELIUM AND LYMPHATICS. see MEDICAL SCIENCES — Hematology

MITTEILUNGEN AUS DEM GEBIETE DER LEBENSMITTELUNTERSUCHUNG UND HYGIENE/TRAVAUX DE CHIMIE ALIMENTAIRE ET D'HYGIENE. see NUTRITION AND DIETETICS

572   NE   ISSN 0166-6851
    CODEN: MBIPDP
MOLECULAR AND BIOCHEMICAL PARASITOLOGY. 1980. 14/yr. fl.5222($3001) (effective 1998). Elsevier Science B.V., P.O. Box 211, 1000 AE Amsterdam, Netherlands. TEL 31-20-4853911. FAX 31-20-4853598. TELEX 18582 ESPA NL. E-mail: nlinfo-f@elsevier.nl; usinfo-f@elsevier.com; forinfo-kyf04035@niftyserve.or.jp; URL: http://www.elsevier.nl/. (Subscr. in the Americas to: Elsevier Science, Regional Sales Office, Box 945, New York, NY 10159-0945. TEL 212-633-3730. FAX 212-633-3680; Subscr. in Australasia and the Far East to: Elsevier Science (Singapore) Pte Ltd, No.1 Temasek Ave., No.17-01 Millenia Tower, Singapore 039192, Singapore. TEL 65-434-3727. FAX 65-337-2230; Subscr. in Japan to: Elsevier Science Japan, 9-15 Higashi-Azabu 1-chome, Minato-ku, Tokyo 106, Japan. TEL 81-3-5561-5033. FAX 81-3-5561-5047) Ed.Bd. adv. (also avail. in microform from UMI; back issues avail.) Indexed: Abstr.Hyg., ASCA, Biol.Abstr., Biotech.Abstr., Chem.Abstr., Curr.Adv.Biochem., Curr.Adv.Cell & Devel.Biol., Curr.Adv.Ecol.Sci., Curr.Adv.Genetics & Molec.Biol., Curr.Cont., Curr.Cont., Excerp.Med., Helminthol.Abstr., Ind.Med., Ind.Sci.Rev., Protozool.Abstr., Sci.Cit.Ind., Trop.Dis.Bull. Document type: academic/scholarly publication.
—BLDSC (5900.753000); ADONIS; CASDDS; CISTI; Genuine Article; SWETS; UnCover. CCC.
Description: Provides a medium for the rapid publication of investigations of the molecular biology, molecular immunology and biochemistry of parasitic protozoa and helminths and their interactions with the host.
Refereed Serial

572   US   ISSN 0300-8177
QR151   CODEN: MCBIB8
MOLECULAR AND CELLULAR BIOCHEMISTRY; an international journal for chemical biology in health and disease. (Text in English) 1973. 24/yr. fl.6240 to institutions; $3204 to institutions in U.S. (effective 1998). Kluwer Academic Publishers Boston, Box 358, Accord Sta., Hingham, MA 02018-0358. TEL 617-871-6600. FAX 617-871-6528. TELEX 200190. E-mail: services@wkap.nl; URL: http://www.wkap.nl. (Dist. outside N. America by: Kluwer Academic Publishers Group, P.O. Box 322, 3300 AH Dordrecht, Netherlands. TEL 31-78-6392392. FAX 31-78-6546474) Ed. Naranjan S. Dhalla. adv.; bk.rev.; bibl.; illus. circ. 1,000. (also avail. in microform from UMI,PMC; back issues avail.; reprint service avail. from SWZ,UMI) Indexed: Abstr.Hyg., Anal.Abstr., ASCA, Bibl.Agri., Biol.Abstr., Chem.Abstr., Curr.Adv.Cancer Res., Curr.Adv.Ecol.Sci., Curr.Cont., Dairy Sci.Abstr., Dent.Ind., Excerp.Med., Food Sci.& Tech.Abstr., Helminthol.Abstr., Ind.Med., Ind.Sci.Rev., Neurosci.Cit.Ind., Nutr.Abstr., Sci.Cit.Ind., Trop.Dis.Bull. Document type: academic/scholarly publication.
—BLDSC (5900.756000); CASDDS; CISTI; EMDOCS; Genuine Article; Linda Hall; SWETS; UMI; UnCover. CCC.
Supersedes: Enzymologia (ISSN 0013-9424)
Refereed Serial

572   RU   ISSN 0026-8933
QH506   CODEN: MOLBBJ
MOLECULAR BIOLOGY (NEW YORK). English translation of: Molekulyarnaya Biologiya (RU ISSN 0026-8984) 1967. bi-m. $1745 in US; elsewhere $2040 (effective 1998). (Russian Academy of Sciences, RU) Maik Nauka - Interperiodica, Ul. Profsoyuznaya 90, Moscow 117864, Russia. TEL 7-095-3360066. FAX 7-095-3360666. Ed. L.L. Kiselev. (also avail. in microfilm from UMI; back issues avail.) Indexed: Anim.Breed.Abstr., ASCA, Biol.Abstr., Chem.Cit.Ind., Chem.Titles, Curr.Adv.Ecol.Sci., Curr.Cont., Curr.Cont., Excerp.Med., Ind.Med., Ind.Sci.Rev., Int.Abstr.Biol.Sci. Document type: academic/scholarly publication.
—BLDSC (0416.235000); CASDDS; CISTI; Genuine Article; KR SourceOne; SWETS; UMI; UnCover. CCC.
Refereed Serial

572   US   ISSN 0077-0221
    CODEN: MBBBAD
MOLECULAR BIOLOGY, BIOCHEMISTRY AND BIOPHYSICS. 1967. irreg. price varies. Springer-Verlag, 175 Fifth Ave., New York, NY 10010. TEL 212-460-1500. FAX 212-473-6272. (Also: Berlin, Heidelberg, Tokyo and Vienna) (reprint service avail. from ISI) Indexed: Biol.Abstr., Chem.Abstr., Curr.Adv.Ecol.Sci., Ind.Med. Document type: academic/scholarly publication.
—CASDDS; CISTI; KNAW; Linda Hall.

572   NE   ISSN 0301-4851
QH506   CODEN: MLBRBU
MOLECULAR BIOLOGY REPORTS; an international journal on molecular and cellular biology. 1973. q. fl.582 to institutions; $298.50 to institutions in U.S. (effective 1998). Kluwer Academic Publishers, Postbus 17, 3300 AA Dordrecht, Netherlands. TEL 31-78-6392392. FAX 31-78-6392254. TELEX 29245 KAPG NL. E-mail: services@wkap.nl; URL: http://www.wkap.nl. (Dist. by: Kluwer Academic Publishers Group, P.O. Box 322, 3300 AH Dordrecht, Netherlands. TEL 31-78-6392392. FAX 31-78-6546474; N. America dist. addr.: Box 358, Accord Sta., Hingham, MA 02018-0358. TEL 617-871-6600. FAX 617-871-6528) Eds. H. Bloemendal, W.H. Reeves. adv.; bk.rev. (also avail. in microform from UMI; reprint service avail. from SWZ) Indexed: ASCA, Biol.Abstr., Biotech.Abstr., Chem.Abstr., Curr.Adv.Ecol.Sci., Curr.Cont., Helminthol.Abstr., Ind.Med., Ind.Sci.Rev., Int.Abstr.Biol.Sci., Sci.Cit.Ind., Telegen. Document type: academic/scholarly publication.
—BLDSC (5900.798000); CASDDS; CISTI; EMDOCS; Genuine Article; KNAW; Linda Hall; SWETS; UMI; UnCover. CCC.
Description: Publishes original research papers on molecular and cellular biology, including DNA replication, protein biosynthesis and related subjects.
Refereed Serial

BIOLOGY — BIOLOGICAL CHEMISTRY

572   **UK**   **ISSN 0161-5890**
QR180   **CODEN: MOIMD5**
MOLECULAR IMMUNOLOGY. (Text in English, French, German or Spanish) 1964. 18/yr. fl.3388($1947) (effective 1998). Elsevier Science Ltd., Pergamon, P.O. Box 800, Kidlington, Oxford OX5 1DX, England. TEL 44-1865-843000. FAX 44-1865-843010. E-mail: nlinfo-f@elsevier.nl; usinfo-f@elsevier.com; forinfo-kyf04035@niftyserve.or.jp; URL: http://www.elsevier.nl/. (Subscr. to: Elsevier Science, Regional Sales Office, P.O. Box 211, 1000 AE Amsterdam, Netherlands. TEL 31-20-4853757. FAX 31-20-4853432; Subscr. in the Americas to: Elsevier Science, Regional Sales Office, Box 945, New York, NY 10159-0945. TEL 212-633-3730. FAX 212-633-3680; Subscr. in Australasia and the Far East to: Elsevier Science (Singapore) Pte Ltd, No.1 Temasek Ave., No.17-01 Millenia Tower, Singapore 039192, Singapore. TEL 65-434-3727. FAX 65-337-2230) Ed. Michel Fougereau. adv.; bk.rev.; charts; illus.; index. circ 2,100. (also avail. in microfilm from UMI; back issues avail.) **Indexed:** Abstr.Hyg., Anim.Breed.Abstr., Apic.Abstr., ASCA, Biol.Abstr., Biotech.Abstr., Chem.Abstr., Curr.Adv.Cancer Res., Curr.Adv.Ecol.Sci., Curr.Cont., Curr.Cont., Dairy Sci.Abstr., Dent.Ind., Excerp.Med., Helminthol.Abstr., Ind.Med., Ind.Sci.Rev., Ind.Vet., Protozool.Abstr., Sci.Cit.Ind., Trop.Dis.Bull., Vet.Bull. **Document type:** academic/scholarly publication.
—BLDSC (5900.817700); ADONIS; CASDDS; Genuine Article; KNAW; Linda Hall; SWETS; UMI; UnCover. **CCC.**
Formerly: Immunochemistry (ISSN 0019-2791)
Description: Communicates immunological knowledge which can be delineated at the molecular level.
Refereed Serial

572.8   **UK**   **ISSN 0968-7688**
QH601   **CODEN: MMEBE7**
MOLECULAR MEMBRANE BIOLOGY. 1978. q. £127($210) to institutions (effective 1998). Taylor & Francis Ltd., 1 Gunpowder Sq., London EC4A 3DE, England. TEL 44-171-583-0490. FAX 44-171-583-0585. E-mail: info@tandf.co.uk; URL: http://www.tandf.co.uk/. (Subscr. in N. America to: Taylor & Francis, Inc., 1900 Frost Rd., Ste. 101, Bristol, PA 19007-1598. TEL 800-821-8312. FAX 215-785-5515) Ed. J.A. Lucy. adv.; abstr.; index. **Indexed:** A.A.P.P.Abstr., ASCA, Biol.Abstr., Chem.Abstr., Curr.Adv.Ecol.Sci., Curr.Cont., Excerp.Med., Ind.Med., Ind.Sci.Rev., Sci.Cit.Ind. **Document type:** academic/scholarly publication.
—BLDSC (5900.817955); CASDDS; CISTI; Genuine Article; KNAW; Linda Hall; SWETS; UnCover. **CCC.**
Formerly (until 1994): Membrane Biochemistry (ISSN 0149-046X)
Description: Provides specialists in physiology, biochemistry, biophysics and medicine, with a forum for research in the study of membranes.
Refereed Serial

MOLECULAR NEUROBIOLOGY; a review journal. see *MEDICAL SCIENCES — Psychiatry And Neurology*

572.8   **RU**   **ISSN 0026-8984**
QH506   **CODEN: MOBIBO**
MOLEKULYARNAYA BIOLOGIYA. English translation: Molecular Biology (New York) (US ISSN 0026-8933) 1967. bi-m. $197. (Rossiiskaya Akademiya Nauk) Izdatel'stvo Nauka, 90 Profsoyuznaya ul., 117864 Moscow, Russia. TEL 095-336-0266. FAX 095-240-2220. (Dist. in U.S. by: Victor Kamkin Inc., 4956 Boiling Brook Pkwy., Rockville, MD 20852. TEL 301-881-5973. FAX 301-881-1637) charts; index. **Indexed:** Biol.Abstr., Biotech.Abstr., Chem.Abstr., Excerp.Med., Ind.Med.
—BLDSC (0115.926000); CASDDS; CISTI; KNAW; Linda Hall. **CCC.**

572   **PL**   **ISSN 0077-0485**
   CODEN: MOBCA5
MONOGRAFIE BIOCHEMICZNE. 1962. irreg., vol.40, 1995. price varies. Polskie Towarzystwo Biochemiczne, Ul. Pasteura 3, 02-093 Warsaw, Poland. FAX 48-22-225342. TELEX 814892. E-mail: konarska@neucki.gov.pl. (Dist by: Ars Polona, Krakowskie Przedmiescie 7, 00-068 Warsaw, Poland) Ed. Liliana Konarska. bibl. **Document type:** academic/scholarly publication, monographic series.
—CASDDS.

572   **ISSN 0309-0698**
MONOGRAPHS ON PHYSICAL BIOCHEMISTRY. irreg. price varies. Oxford University Press, Walton St., Oxford OX2 6DP, England. TEL 44-1865-56767. FAX 44-1865-56646. (Subscr. in US to: Oxford University Press Inc., 2001 Evans Rd., Cary, NC 27513. TEL 919-677-0977. FAX 919-677-1714) Eds. W.F. Harrington, A.R. Peacocke. **Document type:** monographic series.
Refereed Serial

MUTAGENESIS. see *BIOLOGY — Genetics*

MUTATION RESEARCH; international journal on mutagenesis, chromosome breakage and related subjects. see *BIOLOGY — Genetics*

MUTATION RESEARCH - D N A REPAIR. see *BIOLOGY — Genetics*

MUTATION RESEARCH - FUNDAMENTAL AND MOLECULAR MECHANISMS OF MUTAGENESIS. see *BIOLOGY — Genetics*

MUTATION RESEARCH - GENETIC TOXICOLOGY AND ENVIRONMENTAL MUTAGENESIS. see *BIOLOGY — Genetics*

MUTATION RESEARCH LETTERS. see *BIOLOGY — Genetics*

MUTATION RESEARCH - MUTATION RESEARCH GENOMICS. see *BIOLOGY — Genetics*

MUTATION RESEARCH - REVIEWS IN GENETIC TOXICOLOGY. see *BIOLOGY — Genetics*

MYCOTOXIN RESEARCH. see *BIOLOGY — Microbiology*

NATURAL PRODUCT LETTERS. see *CHEMISTRY*

612.015 616.8   **UK**   **ISSN 0142-8403**
NEUROCHEMISTRY. m. £80 (effective 1997). S U B I S, Mansion House, 19 Kingfield Rd., Sheffield S11 9AS, England. TEL 44-114-2554433. FAX 44-114-2554626. E-mail: subis@sheffac.demon.co.uk; URL: http://www.shef.ac.uk/uni/companies/shap. (looseleaf format; back issues avail.) **Document type:** abstracting/indexing.
—CCC.
Description: Current awareness service for researchers in clinical and life sciences.

591.192   **US**
NEUROMETHODS. 1985. s-a. $99.50 (foreign $129) (effective 1997). Humana Press Inc., 999 Riverview Dr., Ste. 208, Totowa, NJ 07512. TEL 973-256-1699. FAX 973-256-8341. E-mail: humana@mindspring.com; URL: http://humanapress.com. **Document type:** monographic series.
Formerly: Neuromethods. Series 1: Neurochemistry (ISSN 1048-6089)
Description: Presents detailed methods and techniques for neuroscientists.

NEUROSCIENCE COMMUNICATIONS. see *MEDICAL SCIENCES — Abstracting, Bibliographies, Statistics*

NEUROTOXICOLOGY AND TERATOLOGY. see *MEDICAL SCIENCES — Psychiatry And Neurology*

577.1   **NE**   **ISSN 0167-7306**
   CODEN: NCBIDL
NEW COMPREHENSIVE BIOCHEMISTRY. (Text in English) 1979. irreg., vol.26, 1993. price varies. Elsevier Science B.V., Books Division, P.O. Box 211, 1000 AE Amsterdam, Netherlands. TEL 31-20-4853911. FAX 31-20-4853705. TELEX 18582 ESPA NL. E-mail: nlinfo@elsevier.nl; usinfo-f@elsevier.com; forinfo-kyf04035@niftyserve.or.jp; URL: http://www.elsevier.nl/. (Subscr. in the Americas to: Elsevier Science, Regional Sales Office, Box 945, New York, NY 10159-0945. TEL 212-633-3730. FAX 212-633-3680; Subscr. in Australasia and the Far East to: Elsevier Science (Singapore) Pte Ltd, No.1 Temasek Ave., No.17-01 Millenia Tower, Singapore 039192, Singapore. TEL 65-434-3727. FAX 65-337-2230; Subscr. in Japan to: Elsevier Science Japan, 9-15 Higashi-Azabu 1-chome, Minato-ku, Tokyo 106, Japan. TEL 81-3-5561-5033. FAX 81-3-5561-5047) Eds. A. Neuberger, L.L.M. van Deenen. **Document type:** monographic series.
—BLDSC (6082.890000); CASDDS. **CCC.**
Refereed Serial

572   **JA**   **ISSN 0913-3348**
   CODEN: NOKKEL
NIHON OYO KOSO KYOKAISHI/JAPAN FOUNDATION FOR APPLIED ENZYMOLOGY. JOURNAL. (Text in Japanese) a. Nihon Oyo Koso Kyokai - Japan Foundation of Applied Enzymology, 16-89 Kashima 3-chome, Yodogawa-ku, Osaka 532, Japan. **Indexed:** Chem.Abstr.
—BLDSC (6112.915600); CASDDS.

NIHON SEIKAGAKKAI KINKI SHIBU REIKAI YOSHISHU/JAPANESE BIOCHEMICAL SOCIETY. KINKI BRANCH OFFICE. ABSTRACTS OF MEETING. see *FISH AND FISHERIES — Abstracting, Bibliographies, Statistics*

NIHON TANPAKU KOGAKKAI NENKAI PUROGURAMU YOSHISHU/PROTEIN ENGINEERING SOCIETY OF JAPAN. ABSTRACTS OF THE MEETING. see *FISH AND FISHERIES — Abstracting, Bibliographies, Statistics*

572   **JA**
NIHON TANPAKU KOGAKKAI NYUZURETA/PROTEIN ENGINEERING SOCIETY OF JAPAN. NEWSLETTER. (Text in Japanese) 1988. 4/yr. Nihon Tanpaku Kogakkai - Protein Engineering Society of Japan, Tokyo Rika Daigaku Seimei Kagaku Kenkyujo, Tsugita Kenkyushitsu, 2669 Yamazaki, Noda-shi, Chiba-ken 278, Japan.

573.8   **UK**   **ISSN 1351-525X**
NITRIC OXIDE. 1994. s-m. (diskette m.). £110 (diskette £120; both £180) (effective 1997). S U B I S, Mansion House, 19 Kingfield Rd., Sheffield S11 9AS, England. TEL 44-114-255-4433. FAX 44-114-255-4626. E-mail: subis@sheffac.demon.co.uk; apsubs@acad.com; URL: http://www.apnet.com/www/journal/no.htm. (also avail. in diskette format) **Document type:** abstracting/indexing.
●Also available online.
Description: Current awareness service for researchers in clinical and life sciences.

NUCLEIC ACIDS ABSTRACTS. see *BIOLOGY — Abstracting, Bibliographies, Statistics*

572.65   **US**   **ISSN 0933-1891**
   CODEN: NAMBE8
NUCLEIC ACIDS AND MOLECULAR BIOLOGY. 1987. irreg., vol.9. Springer-Verlag, 175 Fifth Ave., New York, NY 10010. TEL 212-460-1500. FAX 212-473-6272. **Document type:** monographic series.
—BLDSC (6183.745000); CASDDS; CISTI; KNAW; UnCover. **CCC.**

572   **UK**   **ISSN 0305-1048**
QP620   **CODEN: NARHAD**
NUCLEIC ACIDS RESEARCH. (Supplement avail.: Nucleic Acids Symposia Series (ISSN 0261-3166)) 1974. 24/yr. £940 (foreign $1595) (effective 1998). Oxford University Press, Academic Division, Great Clarendon St., Oxford OX2 6DP, England. TEL 44-1865-267907. FAX 44-1865-267485. TELEX 837330-OXPRES-G. E-mail: jnl.info@oup.co.uk; URL: http://www.oup.co.uk/journals. (Subscr. in U.S. to: Oxford University Press Inc., 2001 Evans Rd., Cary, NC 27513. TEL 800-852-7323. FAX 919-677-1714) Ed.Bd.; Pub. Julie Hoare. R&P contact: Joolz Longley. adv.; index. circ. 3,100. (back issues avail.; reprint service avail. from SWZ) **Indexed:** Anim.Breed.Abstr., ASCA, Bibl.Agri., Bio-Contr.News & Info., Chem.Abstr., Chem.Cit.Ind., Curr.Adv.Biochem., Curr.Adv.Cell & Devel.Biol., Curr.Adv.Ecol.Sci., Curr.Adv.Genetics & Molec.Biol., Curr.Biotech.Abstr., Curr.Cont., Fababean Abstr., Food Sci.& Tech.Abstr., Ind.Sci.Rev., Ind.Vet., Maize Abstr., Neurosci.Cit.Ind., Plant Grow.Reg.Abstr., Potato Abstr., Poult.Abstr., Rev.Med.& Vet.Mycol., Rice Abstr., Sci.Cit.Ind., Soils & Fert., Soyabean Abstr. **Document type:** academic/scholarly publication.
●Also available online.
Also available on CD-ROM.
—BLDSC (6183.850000); CASDDS; CISTI; EMDOCS; Genuine Article; KNAW; SWETS; UMI; UnCover. **CCC.**
Description: International rapid-publication journal on nucleic acids, constituents and analogues. Publishing RFLP sequence reprints, sequence data, NMR assignment data and methods.

BIOLOGY — BIOLOGICAL CHEMISTRY

572.65   UK   ISSN 0261-3166
CODEN: NACSD8
NUCLEIC ACIDS SYMPOSIUM SERIES. 1975. s-a. £80 (foreign $140) (effective 1998). Oxford University Press, Academic Division, Great Clarendon St., Oxford OX2 6DP, England. TEL 44-1865-267907. FAX 44-1865-267485. E-mail: jnl.info@oup.co.uk; URL: http://www.oup.co.uk/journals. (Subscr. in US to: Oxford University Press Inc., 2001 Evans Rd., Cary, NC 27513. TEL 800-852-7323. FAX 919-677-1714) Pub. Julie Hoare. R&P contact: Joolz Longley. **Document type:** proceedings.
—BLDSC (6183.860000); CASDDS; CISTI; KNAW; Linda Hall; SWETS. **CCC.**
Formerly (until 1978): Nucleic Acids Research. Special Publication (ISSN 0309-1872)

591.192   US   ISSN 0732-8311
QD320   CODEN: NUNUD5
NUCLEOSIDES & NUCLEOTIDES; an international journal for rapid communication. 1974. m. $1195 (foreign $1240) (effective 1998). Marcel Dekker Journals, 270 Madison Ave., New York, NY 10016. TEL 212-696-6000. FAX 212-685-4540. TELEX 421419 MARDEEK. (Subscr. to: Box 5017, Monticello, NY 12701) Ed. John A. Secrist, III. adv. contact: Lourdes Barroso. bibl.; charts; illus. (also avail. in microform from RPI) **Indexed:** Abstr.Bull.Inst.Pap.Chem., ASCA, Biol.Abstr., Chem.Cit.Ind., Curr.Adv.Biochem., Curr.Adv.Ecol.Sci., Curr.Adv.Genetics & Molec.Biol., Curr.Chem.React., Curr.Cont., Excerp.Med., Ind.Chem., Ind.Sci.Rev., Nutr.Abstr., Sci.Cit.Ind.
—BLDSC (6184.080000); CASDDS; CISTI; Ei; EMDOCS; Genuine Article; Linda Hall; SWETS; UMI; UnCover. **CCC.**
Supersedes in part (in 1982): Journal of Carbohydrates, Nucleosides, Nucleotides (ISSN 0094-0585)

OLD HERBORN UNIVERSITY SEMINAR MONOGRAPHS.
see *BIOLOGY — Microbiology*

ONCOGENE. see *MEDICAL SCIENCES — Oncology*

572   JA
OSAKA SHIKA DAIGAKU SEIKAGAKU KYOSHITSU GYOSEKISHU/OSAKA DENTAL UNIVERSITY. DEPARTMENT OF BIOCHEMISTRY. ACHIEVEMENT. (Text in English, Japanese) 1961. irreg. Osaka Shika Daigaku, Seikagaku Kyoshitsu, 1-47, Kyobashi, Higashi-ku, Osaka 540, Japan.

572.6   JA   ISSN 0078-6705
QP551
OSAKA UNIVERSITY. INSTITUTE FOR PROTEIN RESEARCH. MEMOIRS/OSAKA DAIGAKU TANPAKUSHITSU KENKYUSHO KIYO. (Text in English) 1959. a. exchange basis. Osaka Daigaku, Tanpakushitsu Kenkyusho - Osaka University, Institute for Protein Research, 3-2 Yamadaoka, Suita, Osaka 565, Japan. TEL 06-877-5111. FAX 06-876-2533. Ed. Toshio Takagi. circ. 300. **Indexed:** Nutr.Abstr. **Document type:** abstracting/indexing.
—CISTI; Linda Hall.

OXIDATION COMMUNICATIONS. see *CHEMISTRY — Organic Chemistry*

572   UK   ISSN 0950-057X
OXYGEN RADICALS. s-m. (diskette m.). £120 (diskette £120; both £180) (effective 1997). S U B I S, Mansion House, 19 Kingfield Rd., Sheffield S11 9AS, England. TEL 44-114-2554433. FAX 44-114-2554626. E-mail: subis@sheffac.demon.co.uk; URL: http://www.shef.ac.uk/uni/companies/shap. bk.rev. (also avail. in diskette format; looseleaf format; back issues avail.) **Document type:** abstracting/indexing.
—CCC.
Description: Current awareness service for researchers in clinical and life sciences.

P A S C A L. F 52: BIOCHIMIE - BIOPHYSIQUE - MOLECULAIRE - BIOLOGIE MOLECULAIRE ET CELLULAIRE. see *BIOLOGY — Abstracting, Bibliographies, Statistics*

572   PH   ISSN 0115-6403
CODEN: BPBSDA
P B S BULLETIN. 1978. a. P.50($10) Philippine Biochemical Society, c/o Dept. of Biochemistry, University of the Philippines College of Medicine, Box 593, Manila, Philippines. FAX 63-2-50-17-06. Ed. E.M.T. Mendoza. adv.; bk.rev. circ. 200.
—CASDDS.

572   PK   ISSN 0300-8185
QP501   CODEN: PJBIAL
PAKISTAN JOURNAL OF BIOCHEMISTRY. (Text in English) 1968. s-a. Rs.100($50) Pakistan Society of Biochemists, Institute of Chemistry, University of Punjab, Lahore 54590, Pakistan. Ed. Prof. Nazar-ul-Hasnain. adv. circ. 400. **Indexed:** Biol.Abstr., Chem.Abstr., Curr.Adv.Ecol.Sci., ExtraMED. **Document type:** academic/scholarly publication.
●Also available on CD-ROM.
—BLDSC (6340.897000); CASDDS; CISTI; Linda Hall; UnCover.

PAKISTAN JOURNAL OF PHARMACEUTICAL SCIENCES.
see *PHARMACY AND PHARMACOLOGY*

PATHOPHYSIOLOGY. see *BIOLOGY — Physiology*

572.65   JA   ISSN 0388-3698
QP552.P4   CODEN: PECHDP
PEPTIDE CHEMISTRY. (Text in English) 1962. a. Protein Research Foundation, Peptide Institute - Tanpakushitsu Kenkyu Shoreikai Pepuchido Kenkyujo, 476, Ina, Minoo-shi, Osaka 562, Japan. **Indexed:** Apic.Abstr., Chem.Cit.Ind.
—BLDSC (6422.953400); CASDDS.

572.65   JA   ISSN 0385-8847
PEPTIDE INFORMATION. (Text in English) 1975. 3/w. Protein Research Foundation, Peptide Institute - Tanpakushitsu Kenkyu Shoreikai Pepuchido Kenkyujo, 476, Ina, Minoo-shi, Osaka 562, Japan.

572.65   US   ISSN 0196-9781
QP552.P4   CODEN: PPTDD5
PEPTIDES; an international journal. 1980. 10/yr. fl.2979($1712) (effective 1998). Elsevier Science Inc., Box 945, New York, NY 10159-0945. TEL 212-633-3730. FAX 212-633-3680. E-mail: nlinfo-f@elsevier.nl; usinfo-f@elsevier.com; forinfo-kyf04035@niftyserve.or.jp; URL: http://www.elsevier.nl/. (Subscr. outside the Americas to: Elsevier Science, Regional Sales Office, P.O. Box 211, 1000 AE Amsterdam, Netherlands. TEL 31-20-4853757. FAX 31-20-4853432; Subscr. in Australasia and the Far East to: Elsevier Science (Singapore) Pte Ltd, No.1 Temasek Ave., No.17-01 Millenia Tower, Singapore 039192, Singapore. TEL 65-434-3727. FAX 65-337-2230; Subscr. in Japan to: Elsevier Science Japan, 9-15 Higashi-Azabu 1-chome, Minato-ku, Tokyo 106, Japan. TEL 81-3-5561-5033. FAX 81-3-5561-5047) Ed. Abba J. Kastin. adv.; illus.; index. (also avail. in microfilm from UMI; reprint service avail. from ISI,UMI) **Indexed:** Anim.Breed.Abstr., Biol.Abstr., Chem.Abstr., Chem.Cit.Ind., Curr.Adv.Ecol.Sci., Curr.Cont., Dent.Ind., Excerp.Med., Ind.Med., Ind.Sci.Rev., Ind.Vet., Neurosci.Cit.Ind., Poult.Abstr., Psychol.Abstr. (1981-), Sci.Cit.Ind., Small Anim.Abstr., Vet.Bull. **Document type:** academic/scholarly publication.
—BLDSC (6422.954000); ADONIS; CASDDS; CISTI; Genuine Article; KNAW; Linda Hall; SWETS; UMI; UnCover. **CCC.**
Description: Original contributions on the chemistry, biochemistry, endocrinology, gastroenterology, physiology and pharmacology of peptides and their neurological, psychological and behavioral effects.
Refereed Serial

PESTICIDE BIOCHEMISTRY AND PHYSIOLOGY; an international journal. see *AGRICULTURE — Crop Production And Soil*

615   US   ISSN 0091-3057
QP901   CODEN: PBBHAU
PHARMACOLOGY, BIOCHEMISTRY AND BEHAVIOR. 1973. m. fl.4385($2520) (effective 1998). Elsevier Science Inc., Box 945, New York, NY 10159-0945. TEL 212-633-3730. FAX 212-633-3680. E-mail: nlinfo-f@elsevier.nl; usinfo-f@elsevier.com; forinfo-kyf04035@niftyserve.or.jp; URL: http://www.elsevier.nl/. (Subscr. outside the Americas to: Elsevier Science, Regional Sales Office, P.O. Box 211, 1000 AE Amsterdam, Netherlands. TEL 31-20-4853757. FAX 31-20-4853432; Subscr. in Australasia and the Far East to: Elsevier Science (Singapore) Pte Ltd, No.1 Temasek Ave., No.17-01 Millenia Tower, Singapore 039192, Singapore. TEL 65-434-3727. FAX 65-337-2230; Subscr. in Japan to: Elsevier Science Japan, 9-15 Higashi-Azabu 1-chome, Minato-ku, Tokyo 106, Japan. TEL 81-3-5561-5033. FAX 81-3-5561-5047) Eds. George F. Koob, Sandra E. File. adv.; illus.; index. (also avail. in microform from UMI; reprint service avail. from UMI,ISI) **Indexed:** Anim.Behav.Abstr., ASCA, Biol.Abstr., Biotech.Abstr., Chem.Abstr., Curr.Adv.Ecol.Sci., Curr.Cont., Dairy Sci.Abstr., Dent.Ind., Excerp.Med., Ind.Med., Ind.Sci.Rev., Neurosci.Cit.Ind., Psychol.Abstr. (1973-), Risk Abstr., Sci.Cit.Ind., Sci.Cit.Ind., Sport Fish.Abstr., SSCI, THA, Wild.Rev. **Document type:** academic/scholarly publication.
—BLDSC (6447.078000); ADONIS; CASDDS; CISTI; Genuine Article; KNAW; SWETS; UMI; UnCover. **CCC.**
Description: Original reports of systematic studies in the areas of pharmacology, biochemistry, toxicology and behavior, in which the primary emphasis and theoretical context are behavioral.
Refereed Serial

612.015   UK   ISSN 0264-9624
PHOSPHOLIPIDS. m. £80 (effective 1997). S U B I S, Mansion House, 19 Kingfield Rd., Sheffield S11 9AS, England. TEL 44-114-2554433. FAX 44-114-2554626. E-mail: subis@sheffac.demon.co.uk; URL: http://www.shef.ac.uk/uni/companies/shap. (looseleaf format; back issues avail.) **Indexed:** Chem.Cit.Ind. **Document type:** abstracting/indexing.
—CCC.
Description: Current awareness service for researchers in clinical and life sciences.

572.43   NE   ISSN 0166-8595
CODEN: PHRSDI
PHOTOSYNTHESIS RESEARCH; an international journal. (Text in English) 1980. m. fl.2000 to institutions; $1026 to institutions in U.S. (effective 1998). Kluwer Academic Publishers, Postbus 17, 3300 AA Dordrecht, Netherlands. TEL 31-78-6392392. FAX 31-78-6392254. TELEX 29245 KAPG NL. E-mail: services@wkap.nl; URL: http://www.wkap.nl. (Dist. by: Kluwer Academic Publishers Group, P.O. Box 322, 3300 AH Dordrecht, Netherlands. TEL 31-78-6392392. FAX 31-78-6546474; N. America dist. addr.: Box 358, Accord Sta., Hingham, MA 02018-0358. TEL 617-871-6600. FAX 617-871-6528) Ed. R.E. Blankenship. adv.; bk.rev. (also avail. in microform from UMI; back issues avail.; reprint service avail. from SWZ) **Indexed:** ASCA, Biol.Abstr., Chem.Abstr., Chem.Cit.Ind., Crop Physiol.Abstr., Curr.Adv.Ecol.Sci., Curr.Cont., Field Crop Abstr., Forest.Abstr., Herb.Abstr., Hort.Abstr., Ind.Sci.Rev., INSPEC (1988-), Int.Abstr.Biol.Sci., Maize Abstr., Ornam.Hort., Plant Breed.Abstr., Plant Grow.Reg.Abstr., Sci.Cit.Ind., Soils & Fert., Soyabean Abstr., Triticale Abstr., Weed Abstr. **Document type:** academic/scholarly publication.
—BLDSC (6474.365000); AskIEEE; CASDDS; CISTI; Ei; EMDOCS; Genuine Article; KR SourceOne; Linda Hall; SWETS; UMI; UnCover. **CCC.**
Description: Publishes papers dealing with basic and applied aspects of photosynthesis, including light absorption and emission, primary photochemistry, photorespiration, molecular biology, environmental and ecological aspects, and bacterial and algal photosynthesis.
Refereed Serial

BIOLOGY — BIOLOGICAL CHEMISTRY

572 — JA — ISSN 0031-9082
QP501 — CODEN: SBBKA4
PHYSICO-CHEMICAL BIOLOGY/SEIBUTSU BUTSURI KAGAKU. (Text English, Japanese) 1951. bi-m. 1200 Yen per no. Society of Electrophoresis - Denki Eido Gakkai, Azabu Daigaku Juigakubu Kachiku Eiseigaku Kyoshitsu, 17-71, Fuchinobe 1-chome, Sagamihara-shi, Kanagawa-ken 229, Japan. Ed. Toshitsugu Oda. adv.; bk.rev.; illus.; index. circ. 1,600. **Indexed:** Biol.Abstr., Chem.Abstr., INIS Atomind.
—CASDDS; CISTI. **CCC**.

PHYSIOLOGICAL CHEMISTRY AND PHYSICS AND MEDICAL N M R. see *BIOLOGY — Biophysics*

PHYTOCHEMICAL ANALYSIS. see *BIOLOGY — Botany*

572 — UK — ISSN 0197-8969
CODEN: APPEDR
PHYTOCHEMICAL SOCIETY OF EUROPE. ANNUAL PROCEEDINGS. a. Oxford University Press, Oxford Journals, Walton St., Oxford OX2 6DP, England. TEL 01865-267907. FAX 01865-267773. TELEX 837330-OXPRES-G. E-mail: jnlorders@oup.co.uk. (U.S. subscr. to: Oxford University Press Inc., 2001 Evans Rd., Cary, NC 27513. TEL 919-677-0977. FAX 919-677-1714) Ed. Peter J. Lea. adv. **Indexed:** Chem.Abstr. **Document type:** proceedings.
—BLDSC (6787.560000); CISTI.

PIVARSTVO. see *BEVERAGES*

572 — II — ISSN 0379-5578
QK861 — CODEN: PBJODQ
PLANT BIOCHEMICAL JOURNAL. (Text in English) 1974. s-a. Rs.15($5) Plant Biochemical Society, c/o Y.P. Abrol, Nuclear Research Laboratory, Agricultural Research Institute, New Delhi 110012, India. Ed. Prof. S.P. Sen Kalyani. bibl.; charts. (also avail. in microfiche from NTI) **Indexed:** Abstr.Bull.Inst.Pap.Chem., Biol.Abstr., Chem.Abstr., Curr.Cont., Hort.Abstr.
—CASDDS; CISTI; Linda Hall.

PLANT MOLECULAR BIOLOGY MANUAL. see *BIOLOGY — Biotechnology*

PLATELETS (SHEFFIELD). see *BIOLOGY — Physiology*

612.015 — UK — ISSN 0143-4225
POLYPEPTIDES. m. £80 (effective 1997). S U B I S, Mansion House, 19 Kingfield Rd., Sheffield S11 9AS, England. TEL 44-114-2554433. FAX 44-114-2554626. E-mail: subis@sheffac.demon.co.uk; URL: http://www.shef.ac.uk/uni/companies/shap. **Document type:** abstracting/indexing.
—**CCC**.
Description: Current awareness service for researchers.

572 — UK — ISSN 0964-5845
CODEN: PPRMEN
PORTLAND PRESS RESEARCH MONOGRAPH. 1992. irreg., vol.10, 1996. Portland Press Ltd., 59 Portland Pl., London W1N 3AJ, England. TEL 44-171-580-5530. FAX 44-171-323-1136. E-mail: sales@portlandpress.co.uk; URL: http://www.portlandpress.co.uk. (Subscr. to: Commerce Way, P.O. Box 32, Colchester, Essex CO2 8HP, England. TEL 44-1206-796351. FAX 44-1206-799331) R&P contact: Adam Marshall. (back issues avail.) **Document type:** monographic series.
—BLDSC (6555.660000); CASDDS; CISTI.
Refereed Serial

572 — PL — ISSN 0032-5422
QP501 — CODEN: PSTBAH
POSTEPY BIOCHEMII. (Text in Polish; summaries in English) 1953. q. $80. Polskie Towarzystwo Biochemiczne, Ul. Pasteura 3, 02-093 Warsaw, Poland. FAX 48-22-225342. TELEX 814892. E-mail: postepy@neucki.gov.pl. (Dist. by: Ars Polona, Krakowskie Przedmiescie 7, 00-068 Warsaw, Poland) Ed. Zofia Zielinska. bk.rev.; charts; illus.; index. circ. 1,810. **Indexed:** AgroLibrex, Anim.Breed.Abstr., Biol.Abstr., Chem.Abstr., Curr.Adv.Ecol.Sci., Dairy Sci.Abstr., Ind.Med. **Document type:** academic/scholarly publication.
—CASDDS; CISTI; Linda Hall.

572 — US — ISSN 1082-6068
QH324 — CODEN: PBBIF4
PREPARATIVE BIOCHEMISTRY AND BIOTECHNOLOGY. 1971. q. $575 (foreign $590) (effective 1998). Marcel Dekker Journals, 270 Madison Ave., New York, NY 10016. TEL 212-696-9000. FAX 212-685-4540. TELEX 421419 MARDEEK. (Subscr. to: Box 5017, Monticello, NY 12701. TEL 800-228-1160) Ed. Carel J. van Oss. adv. (also avail. in microform from RPI) **Indexed:** ASCA, Biol.Abstr., Biotech.Abstr., Chem.Abstr., Curr.Adv.Ecol.Sci., Curr.Cont., Dairy Sci.Abstr., Excerp.Med., Helminthol.Abstr., Ind.Med., Ind.Sci.Rev., Int.Aerosp.Abstr., Sci.Cit.Ind. **Document type:** academic/scholarly publication.
—BLDSC (6607.841000); CASDDS; CISTI; Genuine Article; KNAW; Linda Hall; SWETS; UMI; UnCover. **CCC**.
Formerly: Preparative Biochemistry (ISSN 0032-7484)
Refereed Serial

576 — RU — ISSN 0555-1099
QH345 — CODEN: PBMIAK
PRIKLADNAYA BIOKHIMIYA I MIKROBIOLOGIYA. English translation: Applied Biochemistry and Microbiology (US ISSN 0003-6838) bi-m. $174 (effective 1998). Izdatel'stvo Nauka, 90 Profsoyuznaya ul., 117864 Moscow, Russia. TEL 234-05-84. **Indexed:** Abstr.Bull.Inst.Pap.Chem., Crop Physiol.Abstr., Curr.Biotech.Abstr., Field Crop Abstr., Food Sci.& Tech.Abstr., Herb.Abstr., Hort.Abstr., Seed Abstr.
—BLDSC (0131.920000); CASDDS; CISTI; KNAW; Linda Hall.

PROCESS BIOCHEMISTRY. see *BIOLOGY — Biotechnology*

572 — US
PROGRESS IN BIOCHEMISTRY, BIOTECHNOLOGY, AND NONLINEAR BIOLOGY. 1990. q. $295 (effective 1996). Nova Science Publishers, Inc., 6080 Jericho Tpke., Ste. 207, Commack, NY 11725-2808. TEL 516-499-3103. FAX 516-499-3146. E-mail: novasci1@aol.com. Ed. E.I. Volkov. **Document type:** academic/scholarly publication.
—KNAW.
Former titles: Progress in Biochemistry and Biotechnology; Journal of Nonlinear Biology (ISSN 1047-1200)

572 — US — ISSN 0177-8757
RB112.5 — CODEN: PCBMEM
PROGRESS IN CLINICAL BIOCHEMISTRY AND MEDICINE. 1984. irreg. price varies. Springer-Verlag, 175 Fifth Ave., New York, NY 10010. TEL 212-460-1500. FAX 212-473-6272. (Also: Berlin, Heidelberg, Tokyo and Vienna) (reprint service avail. from ISI) **Indexed:** Curr.Adv.Ecol.Sci. **Document type:** monographic series.
—CASDDS; CISTI; KNAW; Linda Hall.

572 — GW — ISSN 0079-6336
QH611 — CODEN: PHCCAS
PROGRESS IN HISTOCHEMISTRY AND CYTOCHEMISTRY. (Text in English, French, German) 1970. irreg. price varies. Gustav Fischer Verlag, Wollgrasweg 49, 70599 Stuttgart, Germany. TEL 49-711-458030. FAX 49-711-4580334. (U.S. address: Lubrecht & Cramer Ltd., 38 Rte. 48, Forestburgh, NY 12777-6400) **Indexed:** ASCA, Biol.Abstr., Chem.Abstr., Curr.Adv.Biochem., Curr.Adv.Cancer Res., Curr.Adv.Cell & Devel.Biol., Curr.Adv.Ecol.Sci., Excerp.Med., Ind.Med., Ind.Sci.Rev., Sci.Cit.Ind. **Document type:** monographic series.
—BLDSC (6868.437000); CASDDS; CISTI; EMDOCS; SWETS; UMI. **CCC**.

571.74 — NE
PROGRESS IN HORMONE BIOCHEMISTRY. (Text in English) irreg. price varies. Kluwer Academic Publishers, Postbus 17, 3300 AA Dordrecht, Netherlands. TEL 31-78-6392392. FAX 31-78-6392254. TELEX 29245 KAPG NL. E-mail: services@wkap.nl; URL: http://www.wkap.nl. (Dist. by: Kluwer Academic Publishers Group, P.O. Box 322, 3300 AH Dordrecht, Netherlands. TEL 31-78-6392392. FAX 31-78-6546474; N. America dist. to: Box 358, Accord Sta., Hingham, MA 02018-0358. TEL 617-871-6600. FAX 617-871-6528) **Document type:** monographic series.
Refereed Serial

PROGRESS IN MOLECULAR AND SUBCELLULAR BIOLOGY. see *BIOLOGY — Cytology And Histology*

572.57 — NE — ISSN 0168-9614
QP552.L5 — CODEN: PPLIEF
PROGRESS IN PROTEIN - LIPID INTERACTIONS. (Text in English) 1985. irreg., vol.2, 1986. price varies. Elsevier Science B.V., P.O. Box 211, 1000 AE Amsterdam, Netherlands. TEL 31-20-4853911. FAX 31-20-4853598. E-mail: nlinfo-f@elsevier.nl; usinfo-f@elsevier.com; forinfo-kyf04035@niftyserve.or.jp; URL: http://www.elsevier.nl/. (Subscr. in the Americas to: Elsevier Science, Regional Sales Office, Box 945, New York, NY 10159-0945. TEL 212-633-3730. FAX 212-633-3680; Subscr. in Australasia and the Far East to: Elsevier Science (Singapore) Pte Ltd, No.1 Temasek Ave., No.17-01 Millenia Tower, Singapore 039192, Singapore. TEL 65-434-3727. FAX 65-337-2230; Subscr. in Japan to: Elsevier Science Japan, 9-15 Higashi-Azabu 1-chome, Minato-ku, Tokyo 106, Japan. TEL 81-3-5561-5033. FAX 81-3-5561-5047) Eds. A. Watts, J.J.H.H.M. De Pont. (back issues avail.) **Document type:** monographic series.
—CASDDS; CISTI; Linda Hall.

PROLACTIN. see *MEDICAL SCIENCES — Abstracting, Bibliographies, Statistics*

PROSTAGLANDINS - BIOLOGY. see *MEDICAL SCIENCES — Endocrinology*

PROSTAGLANDINS, LEUKOTRIENES AND CANCER. see *MEDICAL SCIENCES — Oncology*

612.015 — UK — ISSN 0950-0588
PROTEASES AND INHIBITORS. m. £80 (effective 1997). S U B I S, Mansion House, 19 Kingfield Rd., Sheffield S11 9AS, England. TEL 44-114-2554433. FAX 44-114-2554626. E-mail: subis@sheffac.demon.co.uk; URL: http://www.shef.ac.uk/uni/companies/shap. (looseleaf format; back issues avail.) **Indexed:** Neurosci.Cit.Ind. **Document type:** abstracting/indexing.
—**CCC**.
Description: Current awareness service for researchers in clinical and life sciences.

572.65 — US — ISSN 0929-8665
QP551 — CODEN: PPELEN
PROTEIN AND PEPTIDE LETTERS; international journal for rapid publication of short papers in protein and peptide science. (Text in English) 1994. 6/yr. fl.356 to individuals (outside Europe $162); institutions fl.1012 (outside Europe $460) (effective 1998). Bentham Science Publishers, 7436 S.W. 117 Ave., Box 130, Miami, FL 33183. FAX 305-596-5120. Ed. Ben M. Dunn. adv. contact: T. Lucas. **Indexed:** ASCA, Chem.Abstr., Int.Abstr.Biol.Sci. **Document type:** academic/scholarly publication.
—BLDSC (6935.935000); CASDDS; CISTI; Genuine Article; SWETS. **CCC**.
Description: Features short reviews, communications and crystallization reports.
Refereed Serial

572 — UK — ISSN 0269-2139
TP248.P77 — CODEN: PRENE9
PROTEIN ENGINEERING. 1986. m. £360 (foreign $590) (effective 1998). Oxford University Press, Academic Division, Great Clarendon St., Oxford OX2 6DP, England. TEL 44-1865-267907. FAX 44-1865-267485. TELEX 837330-OXPRES-G. E-mail: jnl.info@oup.co.uk; URL: http://www.oup.co.uk/journals. (U.S. subscr. to: Oxford University Press Inc., 2001 Evans Rd., Cary, NC 27513. TEL 800-852-7323. FAX 919-677-1714) Eds. A.R. Rees, G. Petsko; Pub. Steven Johnson. R&P contact: Joolz Longley. adv.; bk.rev.; illus.; index. circ. 1,000. (back issues avail.; reprint service avail. from SWZ) **Indexed:** ASCA, Biol.Abstr., Chem.Abstr., Chem.Cit.Ind., Curr.Adv.Biochem., Curr.Adv.Genetics & Molec.Biol., Curr.Biotech.Abstr., Curr.Cont., Excerp.Med., Food Sci.& Tech.Abstr., Ind.Sci.Rev., Sci.Cit.Ind., Telegen. **Document type:** academic/scholarly publication.
●Also available online.
—BLDSC (6936.050000); CASDDS; CISTI; Ei; EMDOCS; Genuine Article; Linda Hall; SWETS; UMI; UnCover. **CCC**.
Description: International research results advancing the understanding of the structural and biochemical basis of protein function.
Refereed Serial

BIOLOGY — BIOLOGICAL CHEMISTRY

572.8 US ISSN 1046-5928
QP551 CODEN: PEXPEJ
PROTEIN EXPRESSION AND PURIFICATION. 1990. 9/yr. $245 (foreign $280) (effective 1997). Academic Press, Inc., Journal Division, 525 B St., Ste. 1900, San Diego, CA 92101-4495. TEL 619-230-1840. FAX 619-699-6800. E-mail: apsubs@acad.com; URL: http://www.apnet.com/www/journal/pt.htm. (Subscr. to: Box 620000, Orlando, FL 32891-8340. TEL 800-543-9534) Ed. Owen W. Griffith. (back issues avail.) Indexed: ASCA, Chem.Cit.Ind., Curr.Cont., Food Sci.& Tech.Abstr., Ind.Med. (1992-), Sci.Cit.Ind. Document type: academic/scholarly publication.
●Also available online.
—BLDSC (6936.060000); CASDDS; CISTI; EMDOCS; Genuine Article; KNAW; Linda Hall; SWETS; UnCover. **CCC.**
Description: Presents papers on protein isolations based on conventional fractionation techniques as well as those employing the variety of molecular biological procedures used in the expression of proteins.
Refereed Serial

574.192 UK ISSN 1369-4804
▼**PROTEIN PROFILE ONLINE.** Announced for publication in 1998. irreg. Oxford University Press, Academic Division, Great Clarendon St., Oxford OX2 6DP, England. TEL 44-1865-267907. FAX 44-1865-267485. E-mail: jnl.info@oup.co.uk; URL: http://www.oup.co.uk. (Subscr. in the Americas to: Oxford University Press, 2001 Evans Rd., Cary, NC 27513, USA. TEL 919-677-0977. FAX 919-677-1714) Document type: academic/scholarly publication.
●Available only online.

572 UK ISSN 0961-8368
QP551 CODEN: PRCIEI
PROTEIN SCIENCE. 1992. m. £530($895) (effective 1998). (Protein Society) Cambridge University Press, Edinburgh Bldg., Shaftesbury Rd., Cambridge CB2 2RU, England. TEL 44-1223-312393. FAX 44-1223-315052. TELEX 851817256. E-mail: information@cup.cam.ac.uk; URL: http://www.cup.cam.ac.uk. (N. American addr.: Cambridge University Press, Journals Dept., 40 W. 20th St., New York, NY 10011. TEL 212-924-3900. FAX 212-691-3239) Ed. Hans Neurath. R&P contact: Linda Nicol. adv. contact: Rebecca Symons. bk.rev. (back issues avail.) Indexed: ASCA, Chem.Cit.Ind., Curr.Cont., Excerp.Med. (1993-), Food Sci.& Tech.Abstr., Ind.Med. (1992-), Ind.Sci.Rev., Sci.Cit.Ind., SSCI. Document type: academic/scholarly publication.
●Also available online.
—BLDSC (6936.105500); CASDDS; CISTI; EMDOCS; Genuine Article; KNAW; SWETS; UMI; UnCover. **CCC.**
Description: Publishes papers on protein structure, function, and biochemical significance.
Refereed Serial

572 UK ISSN 0952-0406
PROTEINS: POST-TRANSLATIONAL PROCESSING. s-m. (diskette m.) £125 (diskette £120; both £180) (effective 1997). S U B I S, Mansion House, 19 Kingfield Rd., Sheffield S11 9AS, England. TEL 44-114-2554433. FAX 44-114-2554626. E-mail: subis@sheffac.demon.co.uk; URL: http://www.shef.ac.uk/uni/companies/shap. (also avail. in diskette format) Document type: abstracting/indexing.
—**CCC.**
Formerly (until 1987): Protein Phosphorylation (ISSN 0142-8292)
Description: Current awareness service for researchers. Covers phosphorylation, methylation, acetylation, amidation, sulphation, hydroxylation and glycoslation as well as transport of proteins.

572 US ISSN 0887-3585
QP551 CODEN: PSFGEY
PROTEINS: STRUCTURE, FUNCTION, AND GENETICS. 1987. 17/yr. $1295 (foreign $1592.5) (effective 1998). John Wiley & Sons, Inc., Journals, 605 Third Ave., New York, NY 10158. TEL 212-850-6645. FAX 212-850-6021. TELEX 12-7063. E-mail: SUBINFO@JWILEY.COM; URL: http://www.wiley.co.uk. (Subscr. outside the Americas to: John Wiley & Sons Ltd., Baffins Ln., Chichester, W. Sussex PO19 1UD, England. TEL 44-1243-779777. FAX 44-1243-776128) Ed. E.E. Lattman. adv.: B&W page £640, color page £1515; trim 279 x 210. bk.rev. circ. 1,200. (also avail. in microform from UMI; back issues avail.) Indexed: Apic.Abstr., ASCA, Biol.Abstr., Chem.Abstr., Chem.Cit.Ind., Curr.Cont., Excerp.Med., Food Sci.& Tech.Abstr., Ind.Sci.Rev., Sci.Cit.Ind. Document type: academic/scholarly publication.
—BLDSC (6936.164000); CASDDS; CISTI; EMDOCS; Genuine Article; KNAW; Linda Hall; SWETS; UnCover. **CCC.**
Description: Concentrates on advances in all areas of biochemistry: structure, function, genetics, computation, and design.
Refereed Serial

572 UK ISSN 0933-4807
CODEN: PTRDEO
PTERIDINES. (Text in English) 1989. 4/yr. International Society of Pteridinology, Portsmouth PO3 6AD, England. TEL 44-1705-822331. Ed.Bd. adv.; bk.rev.; index. Indexed: ASCA, Chem.Cit.Ind., Excerp.Med. (1994-). Document type: academic/scholarly publication.
—BLDSC (6946.579300); CASDDS; CISTI; EMDOCS; Genuine Article; Linda Hall. **CCC.**
Description: Multi-disciplinary study of pteridines and related materials.

668 KE ISSN 0048-6043
SB952.P9 CODEN: PYRPAN
PYRETHRUM POST. (Text in English) 1948. s-a. $30. Pyrethrum Bureau, Pyrethrum Board of Kenya, P.O. Box 420, Nakuru, Kenya. TEL 254-37-211567. FAX 254-37-45274. TELEX 33080 PYBOARD KE. (Alt. addr.: Kenya Pyrethrum Centre, 5411 Oberralm 807, Salzburg, Austria. TEL 43-645-3381. FAX 43-645-82356) Ed. R.M. Kuria. bk.rev.; abstr.; charts; stat.; biennial index; circ. KE. (tabloid format) Indexed: Anal.Abstr., Biol.Abstr., Biotech.Abstr., Chem.Abstr, Excerp.Med., Hort.Abstr., Ind.Vet., Plant Breed.Abstr., Rev.Appl.Entomol., Small Anim.Abstr., Vet.Bull. Document type: academic/scholarly publication.
—BLDSC (7162.000000); CASDDS; Linda Hall.
Description: Provides a vehicle to disseminate scientific research findings about pyrethrum and related products.

547.873 575.1 UK ISSN 1355-8382
QP623 CODEN: RNARFU
▼**R N A.** (Ribonucleic Acid) 1995. m. £315($415) (effective 1998). (R N A Society) Cambridge University Press, Edinburgh Bldg., Shaftesbury Rd., Cambridge CB2 2RU, England. TEL 44-1223-312393. FAX 44-1223-315052. TELEX 851817256. E-mail: information@cup.cam.ac.uk; URL: http://www.cup.cam.ac.uk. (N. American addr.: Cambridge University Press, Journals Dept., 40 W. 20th St., New York, NY 10011. TEL 212-924-3900. FAX 212-691-3239) Ed. Timothy W. Nilsen. R&P contact: Linda Nicol. adv. contact: Rebecca Symons. bk.rev. Indexed: ASCA, Ind.Med. (1995-). Document type: academic/scholarly publication.
—BLDSC (7993.990800); CASDDS; CISTI; Genuine Article; KNAW. **CCC.**
Description: Surveys original research in all areas of R.N.A. structure and function in eukaryotic, prokaryotic, and viral systems.
Refereed Serial

572 UK ISSN 0143-6767
CODEN: RACBDZ
RECENT ADVANCES IN CLINICAL BIOCHEMISTRY. 1978. irreg., vol.3. Churchill Livingstone (Subsidiary of: Pearson Professional), Robert Stevenson House, 1-3 Baxter's Pl., Leith Walk, Edinburgh EH1 3AF, Scotland. TEL 44-131-556-2424. FAX 44-131-459-1177. URL: http://www.churchillmed.com. (US subscr. to: Churchill Livingstone, 650 Ave. of the Americas, New York, NY 10011. TEL 212-206-5000) Document type: academic/scholarly publication, monographic series.
—CASDDS.

610 US ISSN 1087-8475
QH603.C43 CODEN: RSTRFO
RECEPTORS AND SIGNAL TRANSDUCTION. 1990. q. $240 (foreign $260) (effective 1998). Humana Press Inc., 999 Riverview Dr., Ste. 208, Totowa, NJ 07512. TEL 973-256-1699. FAX 973-256-8341. E-mail: humana@mindspring.com; URL: http://humanapress.com. (Dist. in Japan by: Maruzen Co. Ltd., Journals Div., P.O. Box 5050, Tokyo 100-31, Japan. TEL 03-32758591. FAX 03-32781937) Ed. Gerald Litwack. R&P contact: Richard Hruska. adv. contact: Thomas B. Lanigan, Jr. bk.rev.; abstr.; bibl.; charts; illus.; index. Indexed: ASCA, Biol.Abstr., Chem.Abstr., Curr.Cont., Excerp.Med., Ind.Med. (1992-), Neurosci.Cit.Ind., Sci.Cit.Ind. Document type: academic/scholarly publication.
—ADONIS; CASDDS; CISTI; Genuine Article; KNAW; SWETS. **CCC.**
Formerly (until 1996): Receptor (ISSN 1052-8040)
Description: Focuses on all phases of modern research on receptors and signal transduction involving every class of organism, in every field of research including neuroscience, endocrinology, pharmacology and oncology.
Refereed Serial

572 UK
REDOX REPORT; communications in free radical research. 1994. bi-m. £120($180) to individuals; institutions £260 ($395) (effective 1998). Churchill Livingstone (Subsidiary of: Pearson Professional), Robert Stevenson House, 1-3 Baxter's Pl., Leith Walk, Edinburgh EH1 3AF, Scotland. TEL 44-131-556-2424. FAX 44-131-535-1704. URL: http://www.churchillmed.com. (Subscr. to: Pearson Professional Ltd., P.O. Box 77, Fourth Ave., Harlow, Essex CM19 5BQ, England. TEL 44-1279-623924. FAX 44-1279-639609; U.S. subscr. to: Churchill Livingstone, Box 3217, Secaucus, NJ 07096-3217. TEL 800-553-5426. FAX 201-319-9659) Eds. J.W. Eaton, N.H. Hunt. adv. contact: David Dunnachie. bk.rev. Indexed: ASCA, Curr.Cont., Excerp.Med., Int.Abstr.Biol.Sci., Zoo.Rec. Document type: academic/scholarly publication.
Description: Publishes reviews, research articles, hypotheses, debates, and correspondence on the role of free radicals, oxidative stress, activated oxygen, peroxidative, and redox processes, primarily in human biology and pathology.

REGULATORY PEPTIDES. see CHEMISTRY — Organic Chemistry

RELAZIONI CLINICO SCIENTIFICHE. see MEDICAL SCIENCES

REPRODUCTION, NUTRITION, DEVELOPMENT. see BIOLOGY

REPRODUCTIVE TOXICOLOGY. see ENVIRONMENTAL STUDIES — Toxicology And Environmental Safety

572.65 JA ISSN 0387-4141
CODEN: HAMKE3
RESEARCH COMMITTEE OF ESSENTIAL AMINO ACIDS. REPORTS/HISSU AMINOSAN KENKYU. (Text in Japanese) 1958. bi-m. Research Committee of Essential Amino Acids - Hissu Aminosan Kenkyu Iinkai, Kyoritsu Joshi Daigaku Kasei Gakubu Shokumotsu Gakka, 2-1 Hitotsubashi 2-chome, Chiyoda-ku, Tokyo 101, Japan. charts. Indexed: Chem.Abstr.
—CASDDS.
Description: Contains research reports focusing on nutrition and its physiological effects.

591.192 US ISSN 0096-2902
QP356.3 CODEN: RMNUBP
RESEARCH METHODS IN NEUROCHEMISTRY. 1972. irreg., vol.6, 1985. price varies. Plenum Publishing Corp., 233 Spring St., New York, NY 10013-1578. TEL 212-620-8000. FAX 212-463-0742. TELEX 23-421139. E-mail: books@plenum.com. Eds. Neville Marks, Richard Rodnight. Indexed: Biol.Abstr., Chem.Abstr. Document type: monographic series.
—CASDDS; CISTI; Linda Hall. **CCC.**
Refereed Serial

RESEARCHES ASSISTED BY THE ASAHI GLASS FOUNDATION. REPORTS. see CHEMISTRY

REVIEWS OF HEMATOLOGY. see MEDICAL SCIENCES — Hematology

BIOLOGY — BIOLOGICAL CHEMISTRY

REVIEWS OF PHYSIOLOGY, BIOCHEMISTRY AND PHARMACOLOGY. see *BIOLOGY — Physiology*

572   RM   ISSN 0001-4214
QP501   CODEN: RRBCAD
REVUE ROUMAINE DE BIOCHIMIE. (Text and summaries in English, French, German or Russian) 1964. 4/yr. (Academia Romana) Editura Academiei Romane, Calea 13 Septembrie 13, 76117 Bucharest, Rumania. (Dist. by: Rodipet SA, Piata Presei Libere 1, Sec. 1, Box 33-57, Bucharest, Rumania. TEL 401-6185103. FAX 401-2226407) Ed. Mihai Serban. charts; illus.; index. circ. 1,000. **Indexed:** Anal.Abstr., Biol.Abstr., Biotech.Abstr., Chem.Abstr., Curr.Adv.Cancer Res., Curr.Adv.Ecol.Sci., Curr.Cont., Dairy Sci.Abstr., Excerp.Med., Nutr.Abstr., Plant Breed.Abstr.
—BLDSC (7946.050000); CASDDS; CISTI; KNAW; Linda Hall.

RIBOSOMES AND TRANSLATION. see *BIOLOGY — Cytology And Histology*

ROYAL SOCIETY OF CHEMISTRY. JOURNAL: PERKIN TRANSACTIONS 1; a journal of organic and bio-organic chemistry. see *CHEMISTRY — Organic Chemistry*

RUSSIAN JOURNAL OF BIOORGANIC CHEMISTRY. see *CHEMISTRY — Organic Chemistry*

572   II
S B C NEWSLETTER. 3/yr. Society of Biological Chemists, Department of Biochemistry, Indian Institute of Science, Bangalore 560012, India.

THE SCIENCE OF THE TOTAL ENVIRONMENT; an international journal for scientific research into the environment and its relationship with man. see *ENVIRONMENTAL STUDIES*

572   JA
SEIBUTSU KINO KANKEI SHIRYOSHU/FINDINGS OF BIOFUNCTIONAL CHEMISTRY. (Text in Japanese) 1990. a. Norin Suisansho, Norin Suisan Gijutsu Kaigi Jimukyoku - Ministry of Agriculture, Forestry and Fisheries; Agriculture, Forestry and Fisheries Research Council, 2-1 Kasumigaseki 1-chome, Chiyoda-ku, Tokyo 100, Japan.

572   JA   ISSN 0037-1017
CODEN: SEIKAQ
SEIKAGAKU/JAPANESE BIOCHEMICAL SOCIETY. JOURNAL. (Text in Japanese) 1925. m. 18000 Yen. Nihon Seikagakkai - Japanese Biochemical Society, c/o Ishikawa Bldg. 3F, 25-16, Hongo 5-chome, Bunkyo-ku, Tokyo 113, Japan. FAX 03-3815-1934. Ed. Y. Nagai. adv.; bk.rev.; charts; illus.; index. circ. 20,709. **Indexed:** ASCA, Biol.Abstr., Chem.Abstr., Curr.Adv.Biochem., Curr.Adv.Cancer Res., Curr.Adv.Cell & Devel.Biol., Curr.Adv.Ecol.Sci., Curr.Adv.Genetics & Molec.Biol., Curr.Cont., Ind.Med., JTA, Sci.Cit.Ind.
—BLDSC (8219.700000); CASDDS; CISTI; Genuine Article; UnCover. **CCC.**

SELECTED METHODS OF CLINICAL CHEMISTRY. see *PHARMACY AND PHARMACOLOGY*

SEMINARS IN ARTHRITIS & RHEUMATISM. see *MEDICAL SCIENCES — Rheumatology*

SEMINARS IN CANCER BIOLOGY. see *MEDICAL SCIENCES — Oncology*

572   GW
SERVA MAIN CATALOG (YEAR). a. Serva Feinbiochemica GmbH und Co. KG, Carl-Benz-Str. 7, 69115 Heidelberg, Germany. TEL 06221-502-0. FAX 06221-502113. **Document type:** catalog.

SEXUAL PLANT REPRODUCTION. see *BIOLOGY — Botany*

572   CC   ISSN 1000-3282
CODEN: SHYCD4
SHENGWU HUAXUE YU SHENGWU WULI JINZHAN/PROGRESS IN BIOCHEMISTRY AND BIOPHYSICS. (Text in Chinese) 1973. bi-m. $85.20. (Chinese Academy of Sciences, Institute of Biophysics) Science Press, Marketing and Sales Department, 16 Donghuangchenggen North St., Beijing 100717, People's Republic of China. TEL 4010642. FAX 4019810. adv. circ. 11,000. **Indexed:** ASCA. **Document type:** academic/scholarly publication.
—BLDSC (6865.968000); CASDDS; Genuine Article.
Description: Covers the latest scientific developments in biochemistry, biophysics, molecular biology, and neuroscience. Includes review articles, research papers, short communications, and lectures on basic theories and applied knowledge.
Refereed Serial

572   CC   ISSN 0582-9879
CODEN: SHWPAU
SHENGWU HUAXUE YU SHENGWU WULI XUEBAO/ACTA BIOCHEMICA ET BIOPHYSICA SINICA. English translation: Chinese Journal of Biochemistry and Biophysics (US ISSN 0898-512X) (Text in Chinese) 1958. bi-m. $3.20 per no. (Zhongguo Kexueyuan, Shengwu Huaxue Yanjiusuo - Chinese Academy of Sciences, Institute of Biochemistry) Shanghai Scientific and Technical Publishers, 450 Ruijin Er (2) Rd., Shanghai 200020, People's Republic of China. TEL 86-21-6473-6055. FAX 86-21-6473-0679. (Dist. overseas by: Guoji Shudian - China International Book Trading Corporation, P.O. Box 399, Beijing 100044, P.R.C.; Sponsor addr.: 320 Yueyang Lu, Shanghai 200031, P.R. China. TEL 86-21-6437-4430. FAX 86-21-6433-8357) Ed. De-Bao Wang; Pub. Lian-Kang Shen. R&P contact: Shi-Long Yuan. adv. contact: Lian-Kang Shen. **Indexed:** Biol.Abstr., Chem.Abstr, Curr.Adv.Ecol.Sci., Field Crop Abstr., Hort.Abstr., Ind.Sci.Rev., Rice Abstr. **Document type:** academic/scholarly publication.
—BLDSC (0600.800000); CASDDS; CISTI; Linda Hall.

572   CC   ISSN 1000-8543
CODEN: SHZAE4
SHENGWU HUAXUE ZAZHI/CHINESE BIOCHEMICAL JOURNAL. (Text in Chinese) 1985. bi-m. $30 (effective 1996). Beijing Yike Daxue, Shengwu Huaxue yu Fenzi Shengwuxue Xi - Beijing Medical University, Department of Biochemistry and Molecular Biology, No. 38, Xueyuan Lu, Beijing 100083, People's Republic of China. TEL 8610-2091416. FAX 8610-2015681. TELEX 222782 BMU CN. (Overseas subscr. to: Guoji Shudian - China International Book Trading Corp., P.O. Box 399, Beijing, P.R.C.) (Co-sponsor: Chinese Biochemical Society) Ed. Zhang Naiheng. adv.; bk.rev. circ. 3,000. **Document type:** academic/scholarly publication.
—BLDSC (3180.273500); CASDDS.
Description: Contains research reports and short communications on biochemistry and molecular biology.
Refereed Serial

572   JA   ISSN 0285-1520
SHISHITSU SEIKAGAKU KENKYU/JAPANESE CONFERENCE ON THE BIOCHEMISTRY OF LIPIDS. PROCEEDINGS. (Text in English, Japanese) 1961. a. Nihon Shishitsu Seikagaku Kenkyukai - Japanese Conference on the Biochemistry of Lipids, c/o Teikyo Daigaku Igakubu Dai 1 Seikagaku Kyoshitsu, 11-1, Kaga 2-chome, Itabashi-ku, Tokyo 173, Japan. **Document type:** proceedings.

572   JA
SHISHITSU SEIKAGAKU KENKYU CIRCULAR/JAPANESE CONFERENCE ON THE BIOCHEMISTRY OF LIPIDS CIRCULAR. (Text in Japanese) 1964. a. Nihon Shishitsu Seikagaku Kenkyukai - Japanese Conference on the Biochemistry of Lipids, c/o Teikyo Daigaku Igakubu Dai 1 Seikagaku Kyoshitsu, 11-1 Kaga 2-chome, Itabashi-ku, Tokyo 173, Japan.

572   UK   ISSN 0964-7589
SIGNAL TRANSDUCTION & CYCLIC NUCLEOTIDES. 1970. s-m. (diskette m.). £120 (diskette £120; both £180) (effective 1997). S U B I S, Mansion House, 19 Kingfield Rd., Sheffield S11 9AS, England. TEL 44-114-2554433. FAX 44-114-2554626. E-mail: subis@sheffac.demon.co.uk; URL: http://www.shef.ac.uk/uni/companies/shap. (also avail. in diskette format) **Document type:** abstracting/indexing.
—CCC.
Supersedes: Signal Transduction (ISSN 0952-0392); Cyclic A M P (ISSN 0142-8055)
Description: Current awareness service for researchers in clinical and life sciences.

SIGNAL'NAYA INFORMATSIYA. ENZIMOLOGIYA. see *BIOLOGY — Abstracting, Bibliographies, Statistics*

SOCIETY FOR NEUROSCIENCE. ABSTRACTS. see *MEDICAL SCIENCES — Psychiatry And Neurology*

572   II   ISSN 0300-0486
CODEN: PSBCAW
SOCIETY OF BIOLOGICAL CHEMISTS. PROCEEDINGS. (Text in English) a. Society of Biological Chemists, Department of Biochemistry, Indian Institute of Science, Bangalore 560012, India. **Indexed:** Biol.Abstr.

SOIL BIOLOGY & BIOCHEMISTRY. see *BIOLOGY*

SOSHIKI BAIYO KENKYU/TISSUE CULTURE RESEARCH COMMUNICATIONS. see *BIOLOGY — Cytology And Histology*

572   NE
SOVIET SCIENTIFIC REVIEWS SUPPLEMENT SERIES. SECTION C: PHYSICOCHEMICAL BIOLOGY. irreg., latest vol.8. price varies. Gordon and Breach - Harwood Academic, Amsteldisk 166, 1st Fl., 1079 LH Amsterdam, Netherlands. (Subscr. to: International Publishers Distributor, Box 32160, Newark, NJ 07102. TEL 800-545-8398. FAX 215-750-6343) Ed.Bd. (also avail. in microform) **Indexed:** Zent.Math. **Document type:** monographic series.
Refereed Serial

540   NE   ISSN 0712-4813
CODEN: SPIJDZ
SPECTROSCOPY; an international journal. (Text in English and French) 1982. 4/yr. fl.406($226) (effective 1996). I O S Press, Van Diemenstraat 94, 1013 CN Amsterdam, Netherlands. TEL 31-20-6382189. FAX 31-20-6203419. E-mail: market@iospress.nl; URL: http://www.iospress.nl/iospress. (Subscr. in U.S. and Canada to: Box 10558, Burke, VA 22009-0558. TEL 703-323-5554. FAX 703-250-4705) Ed.Bd. bk.rev. (also avail. in microform from UMI) **Indexed:** Biol.Abstr., Chem.Abstr., Chem.Titles, Curr.Cont., Mass Spectr.Bull., Met.Abstr., Sci.Cit.Ind. **Document type:** academic/scholarly publication.
—BLDSC (8411.113800); CASDDS; CISTI; Ei; Genuine Article; SWETS; UMI. **CCC.**
Incorporates (1980-1983): European Journal of Mass Spectrometry in Biochemistry, Medicine and Environmental Research (ISSN 0379-8399)
Description: Covers all aspects of spectroscopy in chemistry.
Refereed Serial

572   US   ISSN 1077-3444
STEREOCHEMICAL TECHNOLOGY NEWS. 1994. m. $395. Business Communications Co., Inc. (Norwalk), 25 Van Zant St., Ste. 13, Norwalk, CT 06855. TEL 203-853-4266. FAX 203-853-0348. Ed. Philip Rotheim. **Document type:** newsletter.

572.579   UK   ISSN 0142-8330
STEROID RECEPTORS. 1976. s-m. (diskette m.). £110 (diskette £120; both £180) (effective 1997). S U B I S, Mansion House, 19 Kingfield Rd., Sheffield S11 9AS, England. TEL 44-114-2554433. FAX 44-114-2554626. E-mail: subis@sheffac.demon.co.uk; URL: http://www.shef.ac.uk/uni/companies/shap. (also avail. in diskette format) **Document type:** abstracting/indexing.
—CCC.
Description: Current awareness service for researchers. Covers receptors for androgens, vitamin D, estrogens, progesterone, corticosteroids.

BIOLOGY — BIOLOGICAL CHEMISTRY

572 — RM — ISSN 0049-2396
CODEN: SCBIA5
STUDII SI CERCETARI DE BIOCHIMIE. (Text in Rumanian; summaries in English and Rumanian) vol.19, 1976. 2/yr. (Academia Romana, Institutul de Biochimie) Editura Academiei Romane, Calea 13 Septembrie 13, 76117 Bucharest, Rumania. (Dist. by: Rodipet SA, Piata Presei Libere 1, Sec.1, P.O. Box 33-57, Bucharest, Rumania. TEL 401-6185103. FAX 401-2226407) Ed. Mihai Serban. bk.rev.; bibl.; charts; illus. Indexed: Apic.Abstr., Biol.Abstr., Chem.Abstr, Dairy Sci.Abstr.
—BLDSC (8492.670000); CASDDS; CISTI; Linda Hall.

572 — US — ISSN 0306-0225
QH611 — CODEN: SBCBAG
SUBCELLULAR BIOCHEMISTRY. 1971. irreg., vol.26, 1996. price varies. Plenum Publishing Corp., 233 Spring St., New York, NY 10013-1578. TEL 212-620-8000. FAX 212-463-0742. TELEX 23-421139. E-mail: books@plenum.com. Eds. D.B. Roodyn, J.R. Harris. adv.; bk.rev.; charts; illus.; index. Indexed: Biol.Abstr., Chem.Abstr., Curr.Cont., Excerp.Med., Ind.Med. **Document type:** monographic series.
—BLDSC (8501.890000); CISTI. **CCC.**
Supersedes (1972-1975): Journal of Sub-Cellular Biochemistry.
Refereed Serial

572 — JA
SYMPOSIUM ON BIO-HYBRID. (Text in Japanese) 1986. a. 1000 Yen. Tanpakushitsu Haiburiddo Kenkyukai - Protein-Hybrid Society, Toin Gakuen Yokohama Daigaku, Kogakubu Zairyo Kogakka, 1614, Kurogenecho, Aoba-ku, Yokohama-shi, Kanagawa-ken 225, Japan. TEL 81-45-974-5060. FAX 81-45-972-5972. Ed. Yuji Inada. R&P contact: Yuji Inada. circ. 500 (paid). **Document type:** proceedings.
Formerly: Tanpakushitsu Haiburiddo Kenkyukai - Symposium on Protein-Hybrid.

572 660 — UK — ISSN 1355-7912
▼**SYNTHETIC BIOTRANSFORMATIONS.** 1996. q. £48 to individuals; institutions £154 (effective 1996). Carfax Publishing Co., P.O. Box 25, Abingdon, Oxon. OX14 3UE, England. TEL 44-1235-555335. FAX 44-1235-553559. (Subscr. to: Elsevier Science BV, Customer Service Dept., PO Box 330, 1000 AH Amsterdam, Netherlands. TEL 31-20-485-3757. FAX 31-20-485-3432) **Document type:** academic/scholarly publication.
—**CCC.**

572 — JA — ISSN 0039-9450
QP501 — CODEN: TAKKAJ
TANPAKUSHITSU KAKUSAN KOSO/PROTEIN, NUCLEIC ACID, ENZYME. (Text in Japanese) 1956. m. 13200 Yen. Kyoritsu Shuppan Co., Ltd., 4-6-19 Kohinata, Bunkyo-ku, Tokyo 112, Japan. Ed. Koichi Nobusawa. adv.; bk.rev.; bibl.; charts; illus.; s-a. index. circ. 6,000. Indexed: Chem.Abstr., Dent.Ind., Ind.Med., INIS Atomind., Jap.Per.Ind., JTA.
—CASDDS; CISTI; Linda Hall.

572 660 — JA — ISSN 0916-1554
QD431.A1 — CODEN: TKKDE4
TANPAKUSHITSU KOGAKU KISO KENKYU SENTA DAYORI/RESEARCH CENTER FOR PROTEIN ENGINEERING. NEWS. (Text in Japanese) 1989. a. Osaka Daigaku, Tanpakushitsu Kenkyujo, Fuzoku Tanpakushitsu Kogaku Kiso Kenkyu Senta - Osaka University, Institute for Protein Research, Research Center for Protein Engineering, 3-2, Yamadaoka, Suita-shi, Osaka 565, Japan. TEL 81-6-879-8634. FAX 81-6-879-8636. E-mail: kusunoki@protein.osaka-u.ac.jp/; URL: http://www.protein.osaka-u.ac.jp/ Ed. Masami Kusunoki. **Document type:** academic/scholarly publication.
—BLDSC (8602.651000).

612 — JA
TETSU TAISHA KENKYUKAI PUROGURAMU SHOROKUSHU/CONFERENCE ON CURRENT TOPICS FOR IRON METABOLISM. PROGRAM AND ABSTRACTS. (Text in Japanese) 1977. a. Tetsu Taisha Kenkyukai - Iron Metabolism Research, Shigei Igaku Kenkyujo, 2117, Yamada, Okayama-shi, Okayama-ken 701-02, Japan.

615 — US — ISSN 0888-7519
CODEN: TCMUE9
TOPICS IN CHEMICAL MUTAGENESIS. 1984. irreg., latest vol.2. price varies. Plenum Publishing Corp., 233 Spring St., New York, NY 10013-1578. TEL 212-620-8000. FAX 212-463-0742. TELEX 23-421139. E-mail: books@plenum.com. Ed. Frederick J. de Serres. (back issues avail.) **Document type:** monographic series.
—CASDDS; CISTI.
Refereed Serial

TOXICOLOGY IN VITRO. see ENVIRONMENTAL STUDIES — Toxicology And Environmental Safety

572 — UK — ISSN 0968-0004
QH345 — CODEN: TBSCDB
TRENDS IN BIOCHEMICAL SCIENCES. Library compendium: Trends in Biochemical Sciences (Reference Edition) (ISSN 0376-5067) 1976. m. fl.1349($775) (effective 1998). (International Union of Biochemistry) Elsevier Science Ltd., P.O. Box 800, Kidlington, Oxford OX5 1DX, England. TEL 44-1865-843000. FAX 44-1865-843010. E-mail: nlinfo-f@elsevier.nl; usinfo-f@elsevier.com; forinfo-kyf04035@niftyserve.or.jp; URL: http://www.elsevier.nl/. (Subscr. to: Elsevier Science, Regional Sales Office, P.O. Box 211, 1000 AE Amsterdam, Netherlands. TEL 31-20-4853757. FAX 31-20-4853432; Subscr. in the Americas to: Elsevier Science, Regional Sales Office, Box 945, New York, NY 10159-0945. TEL 212-633-3730. FAX 212-633-3680; Subscr. in Australasia and the Far East to: Elsevier Science (Singapore) Pte Ltd, No.1 Temasek Ave., No.17-01 Millenia Tower, Singapore 039192, Singapore. TEL 65-434-3727. FAX 65-337-2230) Ed. Jo McEntyre. adv.; bk.rev.; illus.; index. (also avail. in microfilm from UMI; reprint service avail. from SWZ) Indexed: Abstr.Hyg., ASCA, Biol.Abstr., Biotech.Abstr., Chem.Abstr., Chem.Cit.Ind., Curr.Adv.Biochem., Curr.Adv.Cell & Devel.Biol., Curr.Adv.Ecol.Sci., Curr.Adv.Genetics & Molec.Biol., Curr.Cont., Dairy Sci.Abstr., Deep Sea Res.& Oceanogr.Abstr., Excerp.Med., Food Sci.& Tech.Abstr., Helminthol.Abstr., Hort.Abstr., Ind.Sci.Rev., Nutr.Abstr., Sci.Cit.Ind., Soils & Fert., Sport Fish.Abstr., SSCI, Wild.Rev. **Document type:** academic/scholarly publication.
—BLDSC (9049.546000); ADONIS; CISTI; EMDOCS; Genuine Article; SWETS. **CCC.**
Description: Provides students and researchers with information on recent developments in a wide range of biochemically based sciences.
Refereed Serial

572 — UK — ISSN 0376-5067
CODEN: TBSCDB
TRENDS IN BIOCHEMICAL SCIENCES (REFERENCE EDITION). 1976. a. £645($514) includes m. Trends in Biochemical Sciences (effective 1995). (International Union of Biochemistry) Elsevier Science Ltd., P.O. Box 800, Kidlington, Oxford OX5 1DX, England. TEL 44-1865-843000. FAX 44-1865-843010. E-mail: nlinfo-f@elsevier.nl; usinfo-f@elsevier.com; forinfo-kyf04035@niftyserve.or.jp; URL: http://www.elsevier.nl/. (Subscr. to: Elsevier Science, Regional Sales Office, P.O. Box 211, 1000 AE Amsterdam, Netherlands. TEL 31-20-4853757. FAX 31-20-4853432; Subscr. in the Americas to: Elsevier Science, Regional Sales Office, Box 945, New York, NY 10159-0945. TEL 212-633-3730. FAX 212-633-3680; Subscr. in Australasia and the Far East to: Elsevier Science (Singapore) Pte Ltd, No.1 Temasek Ave., No.17-01 Millenia Tower, Singapore 039192, Singapore. TEL 65-434-3727. FAX 65-337-2230) Ed. Jo McEntyre. index. Indexed: Chem.Cit.Ind., Excerp.Med. **Document type:** academic/scholarly publication.
—BLDSC (9049.546200); CASDDS; CISTI; Linda Hall; SWETS; UnCover. **CCC.**
Description: Compendium of archival material from Trends in Biochemical Sciences.
Refereed Serial

TRENDS IN BIOTECHNOLOGY. see BIOLOGY — Biotechnology

TRENDS IN BIOTECHNOLOGY (REFERENCE EDITION). see BIOLOGY — Biotechnology

TUMOR BIOLOGY. see MEDICAL SCIENCES — Oncology

572 — UK — ISSN 0968-6797
U K PRODUCT REVIEW. 1986. bi-m. free. Macmillan Magazines Ltd., Porters South, 4-6 Crinan St., London N1 9XW, England. TEL 44-171-833-4000. FAX 44-171-843-4640. Ed. Charles Wenz. adv.: B&W page £1170; adv. contact: Karen O'Neill. software rev, tr.lit.; circ. 15,000. (back issues avail.) **Document type:** trade publication.

572 — KR — ISSN 0201-8470
QP501 — CODEN: UBZHD4
UKRAIN'SKYI BIOKHIMICHNYI ZHURNAL/UKRAINIAN BIOCHEMICAL JOURNAL/UKRAINSKII BIOKHIMICHESKII ZHURNAL; nauchno-teoreticheskii zhurnal. (Text in Russian; summaries in English and Russian) 1926. bi-m. $123 (effective 1998). Akademiya Nauk Ukrainy, Institut Biokhimii im. A.V. Palladina, Vul. Deontovicha, 9, 252601 Kiev 30, Ukraine. TEL 38-44-2241181. Ed. V.K. Lishko. adv.; bk.rev.; abstr.; bibl.; charts; illus.; index. circ. 1,496. Indexed: Apic.Abstr., ASCA, Biol.Abstr., Biotech.Abstr., Chem.Abstr., Curr.Adv.Ecol.Sci., Dairy Sci.Abstr., Djerelo, Ind.Med., Ind.Vet., Nutr.Abstr., Vet.Bull.
—BLDSC (0384.180000); CASDDS; CISTI; Genuine Article; KNAW; Linda Hall. **CCC.**

UNIVERSIDAD NACIONAL MAYOR DE SAN MARCOS. FACULTAD DE FARMACIA Y BIOQUIMICA. REVISTA. see PHARMACY AND PHARMACOLOGY

WALTER AND ANDREE DE NOTTBECK FOUNDATION SCIENTIFIC REPORTS. see BIOLOGY — Microbiology

572 — NR — ISSN 0043-2989
CODEN: WAJBAK
WEST AFRICAN JOURNAL OF BIOLOGICAL AND APPLIED CHEMISTRY. 1957. q. £N40. P.O.Box 4021, U.I. Post Office, University of Ibadan, Ibadan, Oyo State, Nigeria. TEL 234-22-410247. Ed. Olumbe Bassir. adv.; bk.rev.; charts. circ. 1,000. Indexed: Biol.Abstr., Chem.Abstr., Field Crop Abstr., Herb.Abstr., Nutr.Abstr. **Document type:** academic/scholarly publication.
—BLDSC (9298.690000); CASDDS; CISTI; Linda Hall.

WUHAN LIANGSHI GONGYE XUEYUAN XUEBAO/WUHAN FOOD INDUSTRY COLLEGE. JOURNAL. see AGRICULTURE — Feed, Flour And Grain

572 — UK — ISSN 0049-8254
CODEN: XENOBH
XENOBIOTICA; the fate of foreign compounds in biological systems. 1971. m. £664($1095) to institutions (£796($1314) with online ed.) (effective 1998). Taylor & Francis Ltd., 1 Gunpowder Sq., London EC4A 3DE, England. TEL 44-171-583-0490. FAX 44-171-583-0585. TELEX 858540. E-mail: info@tandf.co.uk; URL: http://www.tandf.co.uk/. (Subscr. in N. America to: Taylor & Francis Inc., 1900 Frost Rd., Ste. 101, Bristol, PA 19007-1598. TEL 800-821-8312. FAX 215-785-5515) Ed. G.G. Gibson. adv.; bk.rev.; charts; stat.; index. Indexed: ASCA, Biol.Abstr., Biotech.Abstr., Chem.Abstr., Chem.Cit.Ind., Curr.Adv.Biochem., Curr.Adv.Ecol.Sci., Curr.Cont., Dairy Sci.Abstr., Deep Sea Res.& Oceanogr.Abstr., Dent.Ind., Environ.Per.Bibl. (1979-), Excerp.Med., Helminthol.Abstr., Ind.Med., Ind.Sci.Rev., Ind.Vet., Lab.Haz.Bull., Mass Spectr.Bull., Pig News & Info., Poult.Abstr., Rev.Med.& Vet.Mycol., Sci.Cit.Ind., Small Anim.Abstr., Vet.Bull., Weed Abstr. **Document type:** academic/scholarly publication.
—BLDSC (9367.020000); ADONIS; CASDDS; CISTI; Genuine Article; Linda Hall; SWETS; UnCover. **CCC.**
Description: Covers three main areas: general xenobiochemistry, molecular toxicology, and clinical pharmacokinetics and metabolism.
Refereed Serial

YEAST; a forum for yeast researchers. see BIOLOGY — Biotechnology

| 572 | RU | ISSN 0044-4529 |
QH345.Z5 | | CODEN: ZEBFAJ
ZHURNAL EVOLYUTSIONNOI BIOKHIMII I FIZIOLOGII. (Text in Russian; summaries in English) 1965. bi-m. $152 (effective 1998). (Rossiiskaya Akademiya Nauk) Izdatel'stvo Nauka, 90 Profsoyuznaya ul., 117864 Moscow, Russia. TEL 095-336-0266. FAX 095-420-2220. (Dist. in U.S. by: Victor Kamkin Inc., 4956 Boiling Brook Pkwy., Rockville, MD 20852. TEL 301-881-5973. FAX 301-881-1637) bk.rev.; charts; illus.; index. **Indexed:** Anim.Breed.Abstr., Biol.Abstr., Chem.Abstr., Excerp.Med., Field Crop Abstr., Ind.Med., Int.Aerosp.Abstr., Seed Abstr., Soyabean Abstr. —BLDSC (0067.700000); CASDDS; CISTI; KNAW; Linda Hall. **CCC.**

BIOLOGY — Biophysics

ACTA PHYSIOLOGICA HUNGARICA. see BIOLOGY — Physiology

ACTA UNIVERSITATIS LODZIENSIS: FOLIA BIOCHIMICA ET BIOPHYSICA. see BIOLOGY — Biological Chemistry

| 571.4 | IE | ISSN 0065-227X |
QH505.A1 | | CODEN: ADVBAT
ADVANCES IN BIOPHYSICS. (Text in English) 1968. a. fl.478($275) (effective 1998). (Biophysical Society of Japan, JA) Elsevier Science Ireland Ltd., P.O. Box 85, Limerick, Ireland. TEL 353-61-471944. FAX 353-61-472144. TELEX 72191 ENH EI. (Subscr. to: Elsevier Science, Regional Sales Office, P.O. Box 211, 1000 AE Amsterdam, Netherlands. TEL 31-20-4853757. FAX 31-20-4853432; Subscr. in the Americas to: Elsevier Science, Regional Sales Office, Box 945, New York, NY 10159-0945. TEL 212-633-3730. FAX 212-633-3680; Subscr. in Australasia and the Far East to: Elsevier Science (Singapore) Pte Ltd, No.1 Temasek Ave., No.17-01 Millenia Tower, Singapore 039192, Singapore. TEL 65-434-3727. FAX 65-337-2230) (Co-publisher: Japan Scientific Societies Press) Ed. Masao Kotani. R&P contact: Annette Moloney. circ. 1,400. **Indexed:** ASCA, Biol.Abstr., Chem.Abstr., Curr.Adv.Ecol.Sci., Excerp.Med, Ind.Med., Ind.Sci.Rev., Sci.Cit.Ind. **Document type:** academic/scholarly publication. —BLDSC (0700.260000); CASDDS; CISTI; EMDOCS; Linda Hall; SWETS; UnCover. **CCC.**
Description: For researchers and teachers in biophysics, biochemistry and related disciplines such as molecular genetics and cellular biology, medicine, physics, chemistry, and bio-engineering.
Refereed Serial

| 571.464 | | UK |
ADVANCES IN LOW - TEMPERATURE BIOLOGY. irreg. $109.50 per vol. J A I Press Ltd., The Courtyard, 28 High St., Hampton Hill, Mddx. TW12 1PD, England. TEL 44-181-943-9296. FAX 44-181-943-9317. E-mail: jai@cix.compulink.co.uk. (Addr. in the US: J A I Press Inc., 55 Old Post Rd., No. 2, Greenwich, CT 06836-1678. TEL 203-661-7602. FAX 203-661-0792) Ed. Peter L. Steponkus. (back issues avail.) **Document type:** academic/scholarly publication.

| 571.4 | JA | ISSN 0385-213X |
AMIRAZE SHINPOJUMU/PROCEEDINGS OF THE SYMPOSIUM ON AMYLASE. (Text in English, Japanese) 1965. a. Amiraze Kenkyukai - Amylase Research Society, Osaka Shiritsu Kogyo Kenkyujo, 6-50 Morinomiya 1-chome, Joto-ku, Osaka 536, Japan. **Document type:** proceedings.

| 571.4 | US | ISSN 1056-8700 |
QH505 | | CODEN: ABBSE4
ANNUAL REVIEW OF BIOPHYSICS AND BIOMOLECULAR STRUCTURE. 1972. a. $70 to individuals (foreign $75); institutions $140 (foreign $150) (effective 1998). Annual Reviews Inc., 4139 El Camino Way, Box 10139, Palo Alto, CA 94303-0139. TEL 650-493-4400; 800-523-8635. FAX 650-424-0910. E-mail: service@annurev.org; URL: http://www.annurev.org. Ed. Robert M. Stroud. R&P contact: Jeanne Kunz. bibl.; index, cum.index every 5 yrs. (also avail. in microfilm from UMI; back issues avail.; reprint service avail.) **Indexed:** ASCA, Biol.Abstr., Chem.Abstr., Chem.Cit.Ind., Curr.Adv.Ecol.Sci., Curr.Cont., Deep Sea Res.& Oceanogr.Abstr., Ind.Med., Ind.Sci.Rev., INIS Atomind., INSPEC, Nucl.Sci.Abstr., Sci.Cit.Ind. **Document type:** academic/scholarly publication. —BLDSC (1522.060000); ADONIS; CASDDS; CISTI; EMDOCS; Genuine Article; KNAW; Linda Hall; SWETS; UMI; UnCover. **CCC.**
Former titles (until vol.20, 1991): Annual Review of Biophysics and Biophysical Chemistry (ISSN 0883-9182); (until vol.14, 1985): Annual Review of Biophysics and Bioengineering (ISSN 0084-6589)
Description: Original reviews of critical literature and current developments in biophysics and biomolecular structure.
Refereed Serial

ARCHIVES OF BIOCHEMISTRY AND BIOPHYSICS. see BIOLOGY — Biological Chemistry

B B A - GENERAL SUBJECTS. see BIOLOGY — Biological Chemistry

B B A - LIPIDS & LIPID METABOLISM. see BIOLOGY — Biological Chemistry

B B A - PROTEIN STRUCTURE AND MOLECULAR ENZYMOLOGY. see BIOLOGY — Biological Chemistry

| 577 | | JA |
BAIOMEKANIZUMU/BIOMECHANISMS. (Text in Japanese; summaries in English) 1972. biennial. 18000 Yen per no. Baiomekanizumu Gakkai - Society of Biomechanisms Japan, S. Sugano Lab., Dept. of Mech. Eng., Waseda University, 3-4-1 Okubo, Shinjuku-ku, Tokyo 169, Japan. —**CCC.**

| 577 | JA | ISSN 0285-0885 |
QH513 | | |
BAIOMEKANIZUMU GAKKAISHI/SOCIETY OF BIOMECHANISMS. JOURNAL. (Text in Japanese; summaries in English) 1969. q. Baiomekanizumu Gakkai - Society of Biomechanisms Japan, Sugano Lab., Dept. of Mech. Eng., Waseda University, 3-4-1 Okubo, Shinjuku-ku, Tokyo 169, Japan. —**CCC.**

| 571.4 | | JA |
BAIOMEKANIZUMU GAKUJUTSU KOENKAI YOKOSHU/SOCIETY OF BIOMECHANISMS. PROCEEDINGS OF THE ANNUAL MEETING. (Text in English, Japanese) 1980. a. 4000 Yen. Baiomekanizumu Gakkai - Society of Biomechanisms Japan, Sugano Lab., Dept. of Mech. Eng., Waseda University, 4-1 Okubo 3-chome, Shinjuku-ku, Tokyo 169, Japan.

BIOCHEMICAL AND BIOPHYSICAL RESEARCH COMMUNICATIONS. see BIOLOGY — Biological Chemistry

BIOCHEMISTRY AND BIOPHYSICS CITATION INDEX. see BIOLOGY — Abstracting, Bibliographies, Statistics

BIOCHIMICA ET BIOPHYSICA ACTA; international journal of biochemistry and biophysics. see BIOLOGY — Biological Chemistry

BIOELECTROCHEMISTRY AND BIOENERGETICS; an international journal devoted to electrochemical aspects of biology and biological aspects of electrochemistry. see BIOLOGY — Biological Chemistry

| 570 | US | ISSN 0197-8462 |
QP82.2.E43 | | CODEN: BLCTDO
BIOELECTROMAGNETICS. 1980. 8/yr. $670 (foreign $810) (effective 1998). (Bioelectromagnetics Society) John Wiley & Sons, Inc., Journals, 605 Third Ave., New York, NY 10158. TEL 212-850-6645. FAX 212-850-6021. TELEX 12-7063. E-mail: SUBINFO@JWILEY.COM; URL: http://www.wiley.co.uk. (Subscr. outside the Americas to: John Wiley & Sons Ltd., Baffins Ln., Chichester, W. Sussex PO19 1UD, England. TEL 44-1243-779777. FAX 44-1243-776128) Ed. Ben Greenebaum. adv.: B&W page £640, color page £1515; trim 279 x 210. bk.rev.; bibl.; charts; illus.; index. circ. 950. (also avail. in microform from UMI; back issues avail.) **Indexed:** ASCA, Biol.Abstr., Chem.Abstr., Curr.Adv.Ecol.Sci., Curr.Cont., Dent.Ind., Excerp.Med, Ind.Med., Ind.Sci.Rev., INIS Atomind., INSPEC (1982-), Neurosci.Cit.Ind., Sci.Cit.Ind., SSCI. **Document type:** academic/scholarly publication. ●Also available online. —BLDSC (2072.009000); AskIEEE; CASDDS; CISTI; Genuine Article; KR SourceOne; Linda Hall; SWETS; UnCover. **CCC.**
Description: Devoted to research on biological systems as they are influenced by natural or manufactured electric and-or magnetic fields at frequencies from D.C. to visible light.
Refereed Serial

| 571.4 | US | ISSN 0889-4191 |
BIOELECTROMAGNETICS SOCIETY NEWSLETTER. 1978. 6/yr. $65 to non-members (foreign $75). Bioelectromagnetics Society, 7519 Ridge Rd., Frederick, MD 21702-3519. TEL 301-663-4252. FAX 301-371-8955. Ed. Mary Ellen O'Connor. bk.rev. circ. 800. (back issues avail.) **Document type:** newsletter.

| 571.4 | UK | ISSN 0952-0384 |
BIOELECTRONICS AND BIOSENSORS. 1986. s-m. (diskette m.). £110 (diskette £120; both £180) (effective 1997). S U B I S, Mansion House, 19 Kingfield Rd., Sheffield S11 9AS, England. TEL 44-114-2554433. FAX 44-114-2554626. E-mail: subis@sheffac.demon.co.uk; URL: http://www.shef.ac.uk/uni/companies/shap. (also avail. in diskette format) **Document type:** abstracting/indexing. —**CCC.**
Formerly (until 1987): Bioelectronics (ISSN 0268-1633)
Description: Current awareness service for researchers in clinical and life sciences. Covers bioelectricity, biochips, enzyme electrodes and in vivo NMR.

| 571.4 | RU | ISSN 0006-3029 |
QH505.A1 | | CODEN: BIOFAI
BIOFIZIKA. (Text in Russian; summaries in English) 1956. bi-m. $232 (effective 1998). (Rossiiskaya Akademiya Nauk) Izdatel'stvo Nauka, 90 Profsoyuznaya ul., 117864 Moscow, Russia. (Dist. by: Mezhdunarodnaya Kniga, B. Yakimanka 39, 117049 Moscow, Russia; Dist. in U.S. by: Victor Kamkin Inc., 4956 Boiling Brook Pkwy., Rockville, MD 20852. TEL 301-881-5973. FAX 301-881-1637) Ed. A.A. Krasnovskii. index. (tabloid format) **Indexed:** Apic.Abstr., ASCA, Biol.Abstr., Biotech.Abstr., Chem.Abstr., Curr.Adv.Ecol.Sci., Curr.Cont., Dairy Sci.Abstr., Dent.Ind., Excerp.Med., Ind.Med., Ind.Sci.Rev., INIS Atomind., INSPEC (1973-), Int.Aerosp.Abstr., Neurosci.Cit.Ind., Phys.Ber., Psychol.Abstr., Sci.Cit.Ind. —BLDSC (0018.030000); AskIEEE; CASDDS; CISTI; Genuine Article; KNAW; KR SourceOne; Linda Hall; SWETS. **CCC.**

| 571.4 | RU | ISSN 0233-4755 |
 | | CODEN: BIMEE9
BIOLOGICHESKIE MEMBRANY. English translation: Membrane and Cell Biology (US ISSN 1023-6597) (Text in Russian) 1984. bi-m. $216 (effective 1998). (Rossiiskaya Akademiya Nauk) Biologicheskie Membrany, Vavilova ul., 34, komn.335, 117990 Moscow, Russia. TEL 7-095-1359886. FAX 7-095-1359886. E-mail: biomemb@imb.ac.ru. Ed. Yu.A. Chizmadzhev. adv.: page $100; adv. contact: Yuri Ermakov. bk.rev.; index. **Document type:** academic/scholarly publication. —BLDSC (0017.845000); CASDDS; CISTI; Genuine Article; Linda Hall. **CCC.**
Description: Presents experimental and theoretical work on the physics, chemistry and biology of membranes at the molecular and cellular levels.
Refereed Serial

BIOLOGY — BIOPHYSICS

BIOMEKHANIKA/BIOMECHANICS. see *PHYSICS — Mechanics*

571.4   KR   ISSN 0374-6569
CODEN: BNKABJ
BIONIKA; respublikanskii mezhvedomstvennyi sbornik nauchnykh trudov. (Text in Russian) 1965. a. $199. (Akademiya Nauk Ukrainy, Institut Gidromekhaniki) Vidavnitstvo Naukova Dumka, Vul. Tereshchenkivska 3, 252601 Kiev, Ukraine. TEL 044-224-4068. FAX 044-224-7060. (Dist. by: Mezhdunarodnaya Kniga, B. Yakimanka 39, 117049 Moscow, Russia) Ed. G.V. Logvinovich. **Indexed:** INSPEC (1972-).
—AskIEEE; CISTI; KR SourceOne; Linda Hall. **CCC.**

571.4   NE   ISSN 0301-4622
QH345   CODEN: BICIAZ
BIOPHYSICAL CHEMISTRY; an international journal devoted to the physics and chemistry of biological phenomena. 1974. 21/yr. fl.3955($2273) (effective 1998). Elsevier Science B.V., P.O. Box 211, 1000 AE Amsterdam, Netherlands. TEL 31-20-4853911. FAX 31-20-4853598. TELEX 18582 ESPA NL. E-mail: nlinfo-f@elsevier.nl; usinfo-f@elsevier.nl; forinfo-kyf04035@niftyserve.or.jp; URL: http://www.elsevier.nl/. (Subscr. in the Americas to: Elsevier Science, Regional Sales Office, Box 945, New York, NY 10159-0945. TEL 212-633-3730. FAX 212-633-3680; Subscr. in Australasia and the Far East to: Elsevier Science (Singapore) Pte Ltd, No.1 Temasek Ave., No.17-01 Millenia Tower, Singapore 039192, Singapore. TEL 65-434-3727. FAX 65-337-2230; Subscr. in Japan to: Elsevier Science Japan, 9-15 Higashi-Azabu 1-chome, Minato-ku, Tokyo 106, Japan. TEL 81-3-5561-5033. FAX 81-3-5561-5047) Ed.Bd. adv.; bk.rev.; index. (also avail. in microform from UMI; reprint service avail. from ISI,SWZ) **Indexed:** Apic.Abstr., ASCA, Biol.Abstr., Chem.Abstr., Chem.Cit.Ind., Curr.Adv.Biochem., Curr.Adv.Cell & Devel.Biol., Curr.Adv.Ecol.Sci., Curr.Adv.Genetics & Molec.Biol., Curr.Cont., Dairy Sci.Abstr., Excerp.Med., Ind.Med., Ind.Sci.Rev., INIS Atomind., Sci.Cit.Ind. **Document type:** academic/scholarly publication.
—BLDSC (2089.380000); CASDDS; CISTI; EMDOCS; Genuine Article; KNAW; Linda Hall; SWETS; UnCover. **CCC.**
Description: Devoted to the interpretation of biological phenomena in terms of the principles and methods of physics and chemistry.
Refereed Serial

571.4   US   ISSN 0006-3495
QH505.A1   CODEN: BIOJAU
BIOPHYSICAL JOURNAL. 1960. m. (in 2 vols., 6 nos./vol.). $770 includes Biophysical Society. Annual Meeting. Abstracts ($820 outside the Americas) (effective 1997). Biophysical Society, 9650 Rockville Pike, Bethesda, MD 20814-3998. TEL 301-571-8338. FAX 301-530-7133. Ed. Peter Moore. R&P contact: Betty Kirkland. adv. contact: Betty Kirkland. bibl.; charts; illus.; index. circ. 5,200. (also avail. in microform from UMI; microfiche from UMI) **Indexed:** Anim.Breed.Abstr., Apic.Abstr., Appl.Mech.Rev., ASCA, Biol.Abstr., Biwk.Pap.Rad.Chem.& Photochem., Chem.Abstr., Chem.Cit.Ind., Curr.Adv.Biochem., Curr.Adv.Cell & Devel.Biol., Curr.Adv.Ecol.Sci., Curr.Adv.Genetics & Molec.Biol., Curr.Cont., Dairy Sci.Abstr., Deep Sea Res.& Oceanogr.Abstr., Excerp.Med., Field Crop Abstr., Food Sci.& Tech.Abstr., Ind.Med., Ind.Sci.Rev., INIS Atomind., INSPEC (1974-), Mat.Sci.Cit.Ind., Neurosci.Cit.Ind., Phys.Ber., Protozool.Abstr., Sci.Cit.Ind, Triticale Abstr. **Document type:** academic/scholarly publication.
—BLDSC (2089.400000); AskIEEE; CASDDS; CISTI; Ei; EMDOCS; Genuine Article; KR SourceOne; Linda Hall; SWETS; UMI; UnCover. **CCC.**
Description: Reports on the latest theoretical and experimental developments in biophysical research.
Refereed Serial

BIOPHYSICAL SOCIETY. ANNUAL MEETING. ABSTRACTS. see *BIOLOGY — Abstracting, Bibliographies, Statistics*

571.4   UK   ISSN 0006-3509
QH505.A1   CODEN: BIOPAE
BIOPHYSICS. English translation of: Biofizika (RU ISSN 0006-3029) 1957. bi-m. fl.4029($2315) (effective 1998). Elsevier Science Ltd., Pergamon, P.O. Box 800, Kidlington, Oxford OX5 1DX, England. TEL 44-1865-843000. FAX 44-1865-843010. E-mail: nlinfo-f@elsevier.nl; usinfo-f@elsevier.nl; forinfo-kyf04035@niftyserve.or.jp; URL: http://www.elsevier.nl/. (Subscr. to: Elsevier Science, Regional Sales Office, P.O. Box 211, 1000 AE Amsterdam, Netherlands. TEL 31-20-4853757. FAX 31-20-4853432; Subscr. in the Americas to: Elsevier Science, Regional Sales Office, Box 945, New York, NY 10159-0945. TEL 212-633-3730. FAX 212-633-3680; Subscr. in Australasia and the Far East to: Elsevier Science (Singapore) Pte Ltd, No.1 Temasek Ave., No.17-01 Millenia Tower, Singapore 039192, Singapore. TEL 65-434-3727. FAX 65-337-2230) Ed. K.B. Dawson. adv.; abstr.; charts; index. circ. 1,000. (also avail. in microfilm from UMI; back issues avail.; reprint service avail. from UMI) **Indexed:** Appl.Mech.Rev., Biol.Abstr., Curr.Adv.Ecol.Sci., Excerp.Med., Ind.Med., INSPEC (1972-). **Document type:** academic/scholarly publication.
—BLDSC (0406.100000); AskIEEE; CISTI; KR SourceOne; Linda Hall; SWETS; UMI; UnCover. **CCC.**
Description: Russian scientific journal devoted entirely to biophysics.
Refereed Serial

532 574.191   UK   ISSN 0006-355X
QH505   CODEN: BRHLAU
BIORHEOLOGY; an international journal. (Text in English, French or German) 1962. bi-m. fl.1306($751) (effective 1998). (International Society of Biorheology) Elsevier Science Ltd., Pergamon, P.O. Box 800, Kidlington, Oxford OX5 1DX, England. TEL 44-1865-843000. FAX 44-1865-843010. E-mail: nlinfo-f@elsevier.nl; usinfo-f@elsevier.nl; forinfo-kyf04035@niftyserve.or.jp; URL: http://www.elsevier.nl/. (Subscr. to: Elsevier Science, Regional Sales Office, P.O. Box 211, 1000 AE Amsterdam, Netherlands. TEL 31-20-4853757. FAX 31-20-4853432; Subscr. in the Americas to: Elsevier Science, Regional Sales Office, Box 945, New York, NY 10159-0945. TEL 212-633-3730. FAX 212-633-3680; Subscr. in Australasia and the Far East to: Elsevier Science (Singapore) Pte Ltd, No.1 Temasek Ave., No.17-01 Millenia Tower, Singapore 039192, Singapore. TEL 65-434-3727. FAX 65-337-2230) Eds. Alex Silberberg, Dr. Pedro Verdugo. adv.; bk.rev.; charts; illus. circ. 1,150. (also avail. in microfilm from UMI; back issues avail.) **Indexed:** Appl.Mech.Rev., ASCA, Biol.Abstr., Chem.Abstr., Curr.Adv.Ecol.Sci., Curr.Cont., Dairy Sci.Abstr., Excerp.Med., Ind.Med., Ind.Sci.Rev., INSPEC (1978-), Mat.Sci.Cit.Ind., Sci.Cit.Ind. **Document type:** academic/scholarly publication.
—BLDSC (2089.500000); ADONIS; AskIEEE; CASDDS; CISTI; EMDOCS; Genuine Article; KR SourceOne; Linda Hall; SWETS; UMI; UnCover. **CCC.**
Description: Features articles on deformation and flow-related processes, in vivo and extra vivum, on biological systems under physiological and pathological conditions.
Refereed Serial

BIOSENSORS AND BIOELECTRONICS. see *BIOLOGY — Biotechnology*

BIOSPECTROSCOPY; an international interdisciplinary journal. see *CHEMISTRY — Analytical Chemistry*

CANCER BIOCHEMISTRY BIOPHYSICS. see *MEDICAL SCIENCES — Oncology*

CELL BIOCHEMISTRY AND BIOPHYSICS. see *BIOLOGY — Cytology And Histology*

COGNITIVE SYSTEMS. see *PSYCHOLOGY*

571.4   NE   ISSN 0143-8123
QH506   CODEN: CMCBDM
COMMENTS ON MOLECULAR AND CELLULAR BIOPHYSICS. 6/yr. $250 (effective 1998). Gordon and Breach - Harwood Academic, Amsteldisk 166, 1st Fl., 1079 LH Amsterdam, Netherlands. (Subscr. to: International Publishers Distributor, Box 32160, Newark, NJ 07102. TEL 800-545-8398. FAX 215-750-6343) Eds. David M. Jameson, Dinu Georgescauld. bk.rev. (also avail. in microform) **Indexed:** Chem.Abstr., INSPEC (1980-), Phys.Ber.
—BLDSC (3336.029300); AskIEEE; CASDDS; CISTI; KR SourceOne; UnCover. **CCC.**

371.464   US   ISSN 0011-2240
QH324   CODEN: CRYBAS
CRYOBIOLOGY; international journal of low temperature biology. 1964. 8/yr. (Society for Cryobiology) Academic Press, Inc., Journal Division, 525 B St., Ste. 1900, San Diego, CA 92101-4495. TEL 619-230-1840. FAX 619-699-6800. E-mail: apsubs@acad.com; URL: http://www.apnet.com/www/journal/cy.htm; http://www.idealibrary.com/. (Subscr. to: Box 861213, Orlando, FL 32886-1213. TEL 407-347-4040. FAX 407-363-9661) Ed. David E. Pegg. adv.; index. **Indexed:** Anim.Breed.Abstr., ASCA, Biol.Abstr., Chem.Abstr., Curr.Adv.Cell & Devel.Biol., Curr.Adv.Ecol.Sci., Curr.Cont., Dairy Sci.Abstr., Deep Sea Res.& Oceanogr.Abstr., Helminthol.Abstr., Hort.Abstr., Ind.Med., Ind.Sci.Rev., Ind.Vet., INIS Atomind., Nutr.Abstr., Sci.Cit.Ind., Sport Fish.Abstr., Sugar Ind.Abstr., Vet.Bull., Wild.Rev., Zoo.Rec. **Document type:** academic/scholarly publication.
●Also available online.
—BLDSC (3490.135000); CASDDS; CISTI; Genuine Article; KNAW; Linda Hall; SWETS; UnCover. **CCC.**
Description: Publishes research articles on all aspects of low temperature biology.
Refereed Serial

571.4   US   ISSN 0070-2129
QH511.A1   CODEN: CUTBAO
CURRENT TOPICS IN BIOENERGETICS. 1966. irreg., vol.17, 1994. Academic Press, Inc., 525 B St., Ste. 1900, San Diego, CA 92101-4495. TEL 619-231-0926. FAX 619-699-6715. (Subscr. to: Order Dept., 6277 Sea Harbor Dr., 4th Fl., Orlando, FL 32887. TEL 800-321-5068) Ed. C.P. Lee. (reprint service avail. from ISI) **Indexed:** ASCA, Biol.Abstr., Curr.Adv.Ecol.Sci., Ind.Sci.Rev., Nutr.Abstr., Sci.Cit.Ind.
—BLDSC (3504.870000); CASDDS; CISTI; Linda Hall; SWETS; UnCover. **CCC.**
Refereed Serial

CURRENT TOPICS IN NEUROBIOLOGY. see *BIOLOGY — Biological Chemistry*

571.4   RU   ISSN 0012-4974
QH505   CODEN: DOKBAG
DOKLADY BIOPHYSICS. English translation of: Rossiiskaya Akademiya Nauk. Doklady. 1964. s-a. $565 in US; elsewhere $660 (effective 1998). (Russian Academy of Sciences, Biophysics Section) Maik Nauka - Interperiodica, Mezhdunarodnyi Otdel, Ul. Profsoyuznaya, 90, 117864 Moscow, Russia. TEL 7-095-3360066. FAX 7-095-3360666. TELEX 23-421139. (Dist. by: Plenum Publishing Corp., 233 Spring St., New York, NY 10013-1578, U.S.A. TEL 212-620-8468. FAX 212-463-0742) Ed. V.A. Kabanov. (also avail. in microform from UMI; back issues avail.) **Indexed:** Biol.Abstr., Curr.Adv.Ecol.Sci., Energy Res.Abstr., Excerp.Med., Ind.Med., INIS Atomind., INSPEC, Int.Abstr.Biol.Sci. **Document type:** academic/scholarly publication.
—BLDSC (0411.250000); CISTI; SWETS; UMI; UnCover. **CCC.**
Refereed Serial

ELECTRICAL SENSITIVITY NEWS. see *ENVIRONMENTAL STUDIES — Toxicology And Environmental Safety*

571.4   US   ISSN 1061-9526
QP341   CODEN: ELAGE9
ELECTRO- AND MAGNETOBIOLOGY. 1982. 3/yr. $635 (foreign $646.25) (effective 1998). (International Society for Bioelectricity) Marcel Dekker Journals, 270 Madison Ave., New York, NY 10016. TEL 212-696-9000. FAX 212-685-4540. TELEX 421419. (Subscr. to: Box 5017, Monticello, NY 12701) Ed. Stephen D. Smith. R&P contact: Julia Mulligan. adv. contact: Lourdes Barroso. (also avail. in microform from RPI) **Indexed:** ASCA, Biol.Abstr., Chem.Abstr., Curr.Cont., Excerp.Med., Ind.Sci.Rev., INSPEC, Sci.Cit.Ind. **Document type:** academic/scholarly publication.
—BLDSC (3698.187000); AskIEEE; CASDDS; CISTI; Genuine Article; KR SourceOne; SWETS; UMI; UnCover. **CCC.**
Formerly: Journal of Bioelectricity (ISSN 0730-823X)
Refereed Serial

EMERGING BIOCHEMICAL AND BIOPHYSICAL TECHNIQUES. see *BIOLOGY — Biological Chemistry*

EURO COURSES. HEALTH PHYSICS AND RADIATION PROTECTION. see *ENERGY — Nuclear Energy*

BIOLOGY — BIOPHYSICS

571.4   GW   ISSN 0175-7571
QH505   CODEN: EBJOE8
EUROPEAN BIOPHYSICS JOURNAL. Online edition (GW ISSN 1432-1017) (Text in English) bi-m. DM.1392.40 (foreign DM.1792.80) (effective 1998). Springer-Verlag, Heidelberger Platz 3, 14197 Berlin, Germany. TEL 49-30-82787-0. FAX 49-30-82787448. E-mail: subscriptions@springer.de; URL: http://link.springer.de. (Subscr. in N. America to: Springer-Verlag New York, Inc., 333 Meadowlands Pkwy., Secaucus, NJ 07094. TEL 212-460-1500. FAX 212-473-6272) Ed. P.M. Bayley. adv. (also avail. in microform from UMI; reprint service avail. from ISI) **Indexed:** ASCA, Chem.Cit.Ind., Curr.Adv.Ecol.Sci., Curr.Cont., Dairy Sci.Abstr., Excerp.Med., Ind.Med., Ind.Sci.Rev., INIS Atomind., INSPEC, Phys.Ber., Sci.Cit.Ind., SSCI. **Document type:** academic/scholarly publication.
●Also available online.
—BLDSC (3829.489400); AskIEEE; CASDDS; CISTI; Ei; Genuine Article; KR SourceOne; Linda Hall; SWETS; UMI; UnCover. **CCC.**
     Former titles: European Biophysical Journal; (until 1984): Biophysics of Structure and Mechanism (ISSN 0340-1057); Supersedes in part (in 1974): Biophysik (ISSN 0006-3517)
     Description: Topics covered include molecular and structural interactions, membrane and receptor biophysics, thermodynamics, and energetics of biological processes.

EXTRACELLULAR MATRIX. see BIOLOGY — Cytology And Histology

F E B S LETTERS; for the rapid publication of short, complete and essentially final reports of immediate importance to investigators in biochemistry, biophysics and molecular biology. (Federation of European Biochemical Societies) see BIOLOGY — Biological Chemistry

FARMACEVTSKI VESTNIK; strokovno glasilo slovenske farmacije. see PHARMACY AND PHARMACOLOGY

GENERAL PHYSIOLOGY AND BIOPHYSICS. see BIOLOGY — Physiology

571.4   NE   ISSN 1383-8121
                 CODEN: HBPHFH
▼**HANDBOOK OF BIOLOGICAL PHYSICS.** (Text in English) 1995. irreg. price varies. Elsevier Science B.V., Books Division, P.O. Box 211, 1000 AE Amsterdam, Netherlands. TEL 31-20-4853911. FAX 31-20-5803705. URL: http://www.elsevier.nl/. (Subscr. in the Americas to: Elsevier Science, Regional Sales Office, Box 945, New York, NY 10159-0945. TEL 212-633-3730. FAX 212-633-3680; Subscr. in Australasia and the Far East to: Elsevier Science (Singapore) Pte Ltd, No.17-01 Millenia Tower, Singapore 039192, Singapore. TEL 65-434-3727. FAX 65-337-2230; Subscr. in Japan to: Elsevier Science Japan, 9-15 Higashi-Azabu 1-chome, Minato-ku, Tokyo 106, Japan. TEL 81-3-5561-5033. FAX 81-3-5561-5047) Ed. A.J. Hoff. **Document type:** academic/scholarly publication, monographic series.
—CASDDS; CISTI.

571.4   US   ISSN 0073-0475
                 CODEN: HBBIAD
HARVARD BOOKS IN BIOPHYSICS. 1965. irreg., no.3, 1983. price varies. (Harvard University Medical School, Department of Biophysics) Harvard University Press, 79 Garden St., Cambridge, MA 02138. TEL 617-495-2600. FAX 617-495-5898. URL: http://www.hup.harvard.edu. R&P contact: Mindy Koyanis. TEL 617-495-2619. adv. contact: Denise Waddington. **Indexed:** Biol.Abstr., Chem.Abstr. **Document type:** monographic series.
—CASDDS.
     Refereed Serial

571.4   JA
HOSEIKEN NYUSU/RADIATION BIOLOGY CENTER NEWS. (Text in Japanese) 1977. q. membership. Kyoto Daigaku, Hoshasen Seibutsu Kenkyu Senta - Kyoto University, Radiation Biology Center, Yoshida Konoecho, Sakyo-ku, Kyoto 606-01, Japan.

571.4   JA   ISSN 0441-747X
                 CODEN: HSKEAT
HOSHASEN SEIBUTSU KENKYU/RADIATION BIOLOGY RESEARCH COMMUNICATION. (Text in Japanese) 1965. q. 3000 Yen (foreign $45) (effective 1997). Hoshasen Seibutsu Kenkyukai - Society of Radiation Biology Research, c/o Research Reactor Institute, Kyoto University, Kumatori-cho, Sennan-gun, Osaka 590-04, Japan. TEL 81-724-51-2628. FAX 81-724-51-2628. E-mail: akahon@rri.kyoto-u.ac.jp. Ed. Takeo Ohnishi. R&P contact: Hiroshi Utsumi. adv. contact: Hiroshi Utsumi. bk.rev. **Indexed:** Chem.Abstr., INIS Atomind. **Document type:** academic/scholarly publication.
—BLDSC (7227.945000); CASDDS.
     Refereed Serial

571.4   II
INDIAN BIOPHYSICAL SOCIETY. PROCEEDINGS. irreg. Indian Biophysical Society, c/o Saha Institute of Nuclear Physics, 92 Acharya Prafulla Chandra Rd., Calcutta 700009, India.

INTERNATIONAL AGROPHYSICS; a quarterly journal on physical properties and processes affecting plant production. see AGRICULTURE — Crop Production And Soil

INTERNATIONAL BIOPHYSICS CONGRESS. ABSTRACTS. see BIOLOGY — Abstracting, Bibliographies, Statistics

INTERNATIONAL JOURNAL OF RADIATION BIOLOGY. see MEDICAL SCIENCES — Oncology

JOURNAL OF BIOCHEMICAL AND BIOPHYSICAL METHODS. see BIOLOGY — Biological Chemistry

JOURNAL OF BIOCHEMISTRY, MOLECULAR BIOLOGY AND BIOPHYSICS. see BIOLOGY — Biological Chemistry

571.4   FR   ISSN 0092-0606
QH505   CODEN: JBPHBZ
JOURNAL OF BIOLOGICAL PHYSICS; an international journal for the formulation and application of physical and mathematical models in the biological sciences. (Text in English) 1973. q. fl.460 to institutions; $236 to institutions in U.S. (effective 1998). European Physical Society, 34 rue Marc Seguin, B.P. 2136, 68060 Mulhouse Cedex, France. TEL 33-3-89329440. FAX 33-3-89329449. TELEX 29245 KAPG NL. E-mail: g.thomas@univ-mulhouse.fr; URL: http://www.wkap.nl. (Dist. by: Kluwer Academic Publishing Group, P.O. Box 322, 3300 AH Dordrecht, Netherlands. TEL 31-78-6392392. FAX 31-78-6546474; N. America dist. addr.: Box 358, Accord Sta., Hingham, MA 02018-0358. TEL 617-871-6600. FAX 617-871-6528) Ed. Terrence W. Barrett. bk.rev. (also avail. in microform from UMI; reprint service avail. from SWZ) **Indexed:** ASCA, Biol.Abstr., Chem.Abstr., Excerp.Med., INSPEC. **Document type:** academic/scholarly publication.
—BLDSC (4953.150000); AskIEEE; CASDDS; CISTI; Genuine Article; KR SourceOne; Linda Hall; SWETS; UMI; UnCover. **CCC.**
     Description: Devoted to the physical understanding of fundamental principles of biological and medical systems.
     Refereed Serial

JOURNAL OF BIOMOLECULAR N M R. see BIOLOGY — Biological Chemistry

571.4   UK   ISSN 1050-6411
QP321   CODEN: JEKIE3
JOURNAL OF ELECTROMYOGRAPHY AND KINESIOLOGY. 1991. q. fl.625($359) (effective 1998). Elsevier Science Ltd., P.O. BOx 800, Kidlington, Oxford OX2 8DP, England. TEL 44-1865-843000. FAX 44-1865-843010. E-mail: nlinfo-f@elsevier.nl; usinfo-f@elsevier.com; forinfo-kyf04035@niftyserve.or.jp; URL: http://www.elsevier.nl/. (Subscr. to: Elsevier Science, Regional Sales Office, P.O. Box 211, 1000 AE Amsterdam, Netherlands. TEL 31-20-4853757. FAX 31-20-4853432; Subscr. in the Americas to: Elsevier Science, Regional Sales Office, Box 945, New York, NY 10159-0945. TEL 212-633-3730. FAX 212-633-3680; Subscr. in Australasia and the Far East to: Elsevier Science (Singapore) Pte Ltd, No.1 Temasek Ave., No.17-01 Millenia Tower, Singapore 039192, Singapore. TEL 65-434-3727. FAX 65-377-2230) Ed.Bd. adv.; charts; illus. circ. 1,000. (also avail. in microform from UMI; reprint service avail. from UMI) **Indexed:** ASCA, Curr.Cont., Excerp.Med. (1992-), Neurosci.Cit.Ind., SSCI. **Document type:** academic/scholarly publication.
—BLDSC (4974.855000); CISTI; EMDOCS; Genuine Article; KNAW; SWETS; UMI; UnCover. **CCC.**
     Description: Presents original articles on the study of muscle interaction and motion, using both mechanical and electrical detection techniques.
     Refereed Serial

JOURNAL OF ENVIRONMENTAL RADIOACTIVITY. see ENVIRONMENTAL STUDIES

JOURNAL OF LUMINESCENCE; an interdisciplinary journal of research on excited state processes in condensed matter. see PHYSICS — Optics

JOURNAL OF PURE AND APPLIED ULTRASONICS. see PHYSICS — Sound

JOURNAL OF SUBMICROSCOPIC CYTOLOGY AND PATHOLOGY. see BIOLOGY — Cytology And Histology

571.4   UK   ISSN 0306-4565
QH516   CODEN: JTBIDS
JOURNAL OF THERMAL BIOLOGY. 1976. bi-m. fl.1221($702) (effective 1998). Elsevier Science Ltd., Pergamon, P.O. Box 800, Kidlington, Oxford, England. TEL 44-1865-843000. FAX 44-1865-843010. E-mail: nlinfo-f@elsevier.nl; usinfo-f@elsevier.com; forinfo-kyf04035@niftyserve.or.jp; URL: http://www.elsevier.nl/. (Subscr. to: Elsevier Science, Regional Sales Office, P.O. Box 211, 1000 AE Amsterdam, Netherlands. TEL 31-20-4853757. FAX 31-20-4853432; Subscr. in the Americas to: Elsevier Science, Regional Sales Office, Box 945, New York, NY 10159-0945. TEL 212-633-3730. FAX 212-633-3680; Subscr. in Australasia and the Far East to: Elsevier Science (Singapore) Pte Ltd, No.1 Temasek Ave., No.17-01 Millenia Tower, Singapore 039192, Singapore. TEL 65-434-3727. FAX 65-337-2230) Eds. K. Bowler, James E. Heath. adv.; bk.rev.; illus.; stat.; index. circ. 1,000. (also avail. in microfilm from UMI) **Indexed:** Agri.Eng.Abstr., Apic.Abstr., ASCA, Chem.Abstr., Curr.Adv.Ecol.Sci., Curr.Cont., Curr.Ref.Fish Res., Dairy Sci.Abstr., Deep Sea Res.& Oceanogr.Abstr., Excerp.Med., Helminthol.Abstr., Ind.Sci.Rev., Ind.Vet., INSPEC, Pig News & Info., Poult.Abstr., Sci.Cit.Ind., Sport Fish.Abstr., Vet.Bull., Wild.Rev., Zoo.Rec. **Document type:** academic/scholarly publication.
—BLDSC (5069.095000); AskIEEE; CASDDS; CISTI; EMDOCS; Genuine Article; KNAW; KR SourceOne; Linda Hall; SWETS; UMI; UnCover. **CCC.**
     Description: Covers research into the mechanisms by which living organisms respond to temperature change.

MEDECINE NUCLEAIRE; imagerie fonctionelle et metabolique. see MEDICAL SCIENCES — Radiology And Nuclear Medicine

MEMBRANE PROTEINS. see BIOLOGY — Biological Chemistry

MERIDIAN; Zeitschrift fuer Kosmobiologie, Astrologie und angewandte Psychologie. see NEW AGE PUBLICATIONS

MOLECULAR BIOLOGY, BIOCHEMISTRY AND BIOPHYSICS. see BIOLOGY — Biological Chemistry

BIOLOGY — BIOPHYSICS

541 RU ISSN 0134-8485
CODEN: MFBVAX
MOLEKULYARNAYA FIZIKA I BIOFIZIKA VODNYKH SISTEM. (Text in Russian) 1973. irreg. 1.03 Rub. per issue. Sankt-Peterburgskii Universitet, Universitetskaya Nab. 7-9, St. Petersburg V-164, Russia. illus. **Indexed:** Chem.Abstr.
—CASDDS.
Supersedes: Struktura i Rol' Vody v Zhivom Organizme (ISSN 0585-4393)

NEUROBIOLOGY OF DISEASE. see *MEDICAL SCIENCES — Psychiatry And Neurology*

571.4 JA ISSN 0913-4778
NIHON BAIOREOROJI GAKKAISHI/JAPANESE SOCIETY OF BIORHEOLOGY. JOURNAL. Variant title: B & R. (Text in Japanese; summaries in English) 1987. q. 2000 Yen. Nihon Baioreoroji Gakkai - Japanese Society of Biorheology, Gunma Prefectural Cardiovascular Center, Kho 3-12, Kameizumi-machi, Maebashi, Gunma 371, Japan. Ed. Makoto Kaibara; Pub. Khoichi Taniguchi. **Document type:** academic/scholarly publication.

571.4 JA ISSN 0915-0374
NIHON SEITAI JIKI GAKKAISHI/JAPAN BIOMAGNETISM AND BIOELECTROMAGNETICS SOCIETY. JOURNAL. (Text in English, Japanese) 1988. s-a. Nihon Seitai Jiki Gakkai, Tokyo Daigaku Igakubu, Iyo Denshi Kenkyu Shisetsu, 3-1 Hongo 7-chome, Bunkyo-ku, Tokyo 113, Japan.

P A S C A L. F 52: BIOCHIMIE - BIOPHYSIQUE - MOLECULAIRE - BIOLOGIE MOLECULAIRE ET CELLULAIRE. see *BIOLOGY — Abstracting, Bibliographies, Statistics*

PHYSICO-CHEMICAL BIOLOGY/SEIBUTSU BUTSURI KAGAKU. see *BIOLOGY — Biological Chemistry*

571.45 UK ISSN 0031-9155
QH505 CODEN: PHMBA7
PHYSICS IN MEDICINE AND BIOLOGY. (Text in English; abstracts in English, French, German) 1956. m. £630($1160) to institutions (microfiche edition £472); students in the EU £28 (elsewhere £37) (effective 1997). (Institute of Physics) I O P Publishing Ltd., Dirac House, Temple Back, Bristol BS1 6BE, England. TEL 44-117-929-7481. FAX 44-117-929-4318. E-mail: custserv. ioppublishing.co.uk; URL: http://www.iop.org. (US subscr. to: American Institute of Physics, Member and Subscriber Services, 500 Sunnyside Blvd., Woodbury, NY 11797-2900. TEL 516-349-7800) (Co-sponsors: Hospital Physicists Association, UK; International Organization for Medical Physics; European Federation of Organizations for Medical Physics) Ed. M.O. Leach. adv. contact: John Irish. bk.rev.; bibl.; charts; illus.; index. circ. 769. (also avail. in microfilm from AIP; microfiche from AIP; back issues avail.; reprint service avail. from IRC) **Indexed:** ASCA, Biol.Abstr., Chem.Abstr., Curr.Adv.Ecol.Sci., Curr.Cont., Dairy Sci.Abstr., Dok.Arbeitsmed., Excerp.Med., Ind.Med., Ind.Sci.Rev., INSPEC, Nutr.Abstr., Sci.Cit.Ind. **Document type:** academic/scholarly publication.
●Also available online.
—BLDSC (6478.800000); AskIEEE; CASDDS; CISTI; Ei; Genuine Article; KR SourceOne; Linda Hall; SWETS; UnCover. **CCC**.
Description: Covers the use of physical agents such as ionizing and non-ionizing radiation, electromagnetic fields and ultrasound in diagnosis, therapy and radiobiology; corresponding physical methods of dosimetry; associated hazards and protection requirements.

453 US ISSN 0748-6642
QP501 CODEN: PCPNER
PHYSIOLOGICAL CHEMISTRY AND PHYSICS AND MEDICAL N M R. (Nuclear Magnetic Resonance) 1969. s.a. $80 (outside US $87). Pacific Press, Box 1452 Melville, NY 11747. TEL 516-694-2929. FAX 516-249-3734. Ed. Gilbert N. Ling; Pub. Gilbert N. Ling. adv.; bk.rev.; index; circ. 351 (paid). (back issues avail.) **Indexed:** Apic.Abstr., ASCA, Biol.Abstr., Chem.Abstr., Chem.Cit.Ind., Curr.Adv.Ecol.Sci., Curr.Cont., Ind.Med., Sci.Cit.Ind. **Document type:** academic/scholarly publication.
—BLDSC (6484.710000); CASDDS; CISTI; Genuine Article; KNAW; Linda Hall; SWETS; UnCover.
Formerly (until 1983): Physiological Chemistry and Physics (ISSN 0031-9325)
Description: Reviews of and reports on original research in biophysics, biochemistry, cellular physiology, nuclear magnetic resonance and related areas.
Refereed Serial

571.46 KR ISSN 0869-2327
CODEN: KRBIEQ
PROBLEMY KRIOBIOLOGII/PROBLEMS OF CRYOBIOLOGY. (Text in Russian; summaries in English) 1985. q. $60 (effective 1998). Ukrainian Academy of Sciences, Institute of Problems of Criobiology and Criomedicine, Ul. Pereyaslavskaya 23, 310015 Kharkov, Ukraine. TEL 724143. FAX 720084. Ed. V.I. Grishchenko.
—CASDDS; Linda Hall.
Formerly: Kriobiologiya (ISSN 0233-7673)
Description: Provides basic information to researchers investigating the various phenomena involved in the interaction between low temperatures and living cells or tissue, as well as to clinicians who are undertaking trials of hypothermia.

571.4 UK ISSN 0079-6107
QH505.A1 CODEN: PBIMAC
PROGRESS IN BIOPHYSICS & MOLECULAR BIOLOGY. 1950. bi-m. fl.1655($951) (effective 1998). Elsevier Science Ltd., Pergamon, P.O. Box 800, Kidlington, Oxford OX5 1DX, England. TEL 44-1865-843000. FAX 44-1865-843010. E-mail: nlinfo-f@elsevier.nl; usinfo-f@elsevier.com; forinfo-kyf04035@niftyserve.or.jp; URL: http://www.elsevier.nl/. (Subscr. to: Elsevier Science, Regional Sales Office, P.O. Box 211, 1000 AE Amsterdam, Netherlands. TEL 31-20-4853757. FAX 31-20-4853432; Subscr. in the Americas to: Elsevier Science, Regional Sales Office, Box 945, New York, NY 10159-0945. TEL 212-633-3730. FAX 212-633-3680; Subscr. in Australasia and the Far East to: Elsevier Science (Singapore) Pte Ltd, No.1 Temasek Ave., No.17-01 Millenia Tower, Singapore 039192, Singapore. TEL 65-434-3727. FAX 65-337-2230) Eds. T.L. Blundell, D. Noble. index. (also avail. in microfilm from UMI) **Indexed:** Appl.Mech.Rev., ASCA, Biol.Abstr., Chem.Abstr., Chem.Cit.Ind., Curr.Adv.Ecol.Sci., Curr.Cont., Excerp.Med., Ind.Med., Ind.Sci.Rev., INSPEC, Plant Breed.Abstr., Sci.Cit.Ind. **Document type:** academic/scholarly publication.
—BLDSC (6866.100000); ADONIS; AskIEEE; CASDDS; CISTI; Genuine Article; KR SourceOne; Linda Hall; SWETS; UMI; UnCover. **CCC**.
Description: Integrates developments in the physical and biological sciences.
Refereed Serial

571.4 UK ISSN 0033-5835
QH505.A1 CODEN: QURBAW
QUARTERLY REVIEWS OF BIOPHYSICS. (Text in English, French or German) 1968. q. £162($285) (effective 1998). (International Union for Pure and Applied Biophysics) Cambridge University Press, Edinburgh Bldg., Shaftesbury Rd., Cambridge CB2 2RU, England. TEL 44-1223-312393. FAX 44-1223-315052. TELEX 851817256. E-mail: information@cup.cam.ac.uk; URL: http://www.cup.cam.ac.uk. (N. American addr.: Cambridge University Press, Journals Dept., 40 W. 20th St., New York, NY 10011. TEL 212-924-3239. FAX 212-691-3239) Ed.Bd. R&P contact: Linda Nicol. adv. contact: Rebecca Symons. bibl.; charts; illus.; index. (also avail. in microform from UMI; back issues avail.; reprint service avail. from SWZ) **Indexed:** Appl.Mech.Rev., ASCA, Biol.Abstr., Chem.Abstr., Curr.Adv.Biochem., Curr.Adv.Cancer Res., Curr.Cont, Dairy Sci.Abstr., Excerp.Med., Ind.Med., Ind.Sci.Rev. **Document type:** academic/scholarly publication.
—BLDSC (7206.300000); CASDDS; CISTI; Genuine Article; Linda Hall; SWETS; UMI; UnCover. **CCC**.
Description: Reviews recent progress and problems in biophysics and molecular biology.

571.4 GW ISSN 0301-634X
QH505.A1 CODEN: REBPAT
RADIATION AND ENVIRONMENTAL BIOPHYSICS. Online edition (GW ISSN 1432-2099) (Text in English) 1963. q. DM.1409.60 (foreign DM.1413.20) (effective 1998). Springer-Verlag, Heidelberger Platz 3, 14197 Berlin, Germany. TEL 49-30-82787-0. FAX 49-30-82787448. E-mail: subscriptions@springer.de; URL: http://link.springer.de. (Subscr. in N. America to: Springer-Verlag New York, Inc., 333 Meadowlands Pkwy., Secaucus, NJ 07094. TEL 212-460-1500. FAX 212-473-6272) Eds. U. Hagen, A. Kellerer. adv.; charts; illus.; index. (also avail. in microform from UMI; back issues avail.; reprint service avail. from ISI) **Indexed:** ASCA, Biol.Abstr., Chem.Abstr., Curr.Adv.Biochem., Curr.Adv.Cell & Devel.Biol., Curr.Adv.Ecol.Sci., Curr.Adv.Genetics & Molec.Biol., Curr.Cont., Deep Sea Res.& Oceanogr.Abstr., Excerp.Med., Ind.Med., INSPEC, Risk Abstr., Sci.Cit.Ind. **Document type:** academic/scholarly publication.
●Also available online.
—BLDSC (7227.930000); AskIEEE; CASDDS; CISTI; EMDOCS; Genuine Article; KNAW; KR SourceOne; Linda Hall; SWETS; UMI; UnCover. **CCC**.
Supersedes in part (in 1974): Biophysik (ISSN 0006-3517)
Description: Covers the biophysics of ionizing and non-ionizing radiation. Examines the biological effects of temperature, pressure, gravitational forces, electricity, and magnetism, and the biophysical aspects of environmental and space influence.

RADIATION RESEARCH; an international journal. see *PHYSICS — Nuclear Physics*

RADIATSIONNAYA BIOLOGIYA, RADIOEKOLOGIYA. see *MEDICAL SCIENCES — Radiology And Nuclear Medicine*

REFERATIVNYJ ZHURNAL. BIONIKA - BIOKIBERNETIKA - BIOINZHENERIYA. see *BIOLOGY — Abstracting, Bibliographies, Statistics*

REFERATIVNYI ZHURNAL. RADIATSIONNAYA BIOLOGIYA. see *BIOLOGY — Abstracting, Bibliographies, Statistics*

REPRODUCTION, NUTRITION, DEVELOPMENT. see *BIOLOGY*

571.4 RM ISSN 1220-515X
CODEN: RJBEEZ
ROMANIAN JOURNAL OF BIOPHYSICS. (Text in English, French, German; summaries in English) 1991. q. (Societatea Nationala de Biofizica Pura si Aplicata) Editura Academiei Romane, Calea 13 Septembrie 13, 76117 Bucharest, Rumania. (Dist. by: Rodipet SA, Piata Presei Libere 1, Sec.1, PO Box 33-57, Bucharest, Rumania. TEL 401-6185103. FAX 401-2226407) Ed. C. Dimoftache.
—BLDSC (8019.628000); CASDDS; CISTI.

571.6 JA ISSN 0582-4052
CODEN: SEBUAL
SEIBUTSU BUTSURI/BIOPHYSICS. (Text in English, Japanese) 1961. bi-m. 12000 Yen. Nihon Seibutsu Butsuri Gakkai - Biophysical Society of Japan, Realize Inc., 4-1-4 Hongo, Bunkyo-ku, Tokyo 133, Japan. TEL 81-3-3815-8511. FAX 81-3-3815-8529. E-mail: rlz@ppp.bekkoame.or.jp; URL: http://www.soc.nacsis.ac.jp/. Ed. Yutaka Kirino. adv. contact: Shinichi Kojima. circ. 3,500. **Indexed:** Chem.Abstr., INIS Atomind., Jap.Per.Ind. **Document type:** academic/scholarly publication.
—CASDDS.
Description: Contains review articles covering all fields of biophysics plus business news of the society and various other information.
Refereed Serial

SHENGWU HUAXUE YU SHENGWU WULI JINZHAN/PROGRESS IN BIOCHEMISTRY AND BIOPHYSICS. see *BIOLOGY — Biological Chemistry*

SHENGWU HUAXUE YU SHENGWU WULI XUEBAO/ACTA BIOCHEMICA ET BIOPHYSICA SINICA. see *BIOLOGY — Biological Chemistry*

BIOLOGY — BIOTECHNOLOGY

571.4 US ISSN 0932-2353
CODEN: SSBIEJ
SPRINGER SERIES IN BIOPHYSICS. 1986. irreg. price varies. Springer-Verlag, 175 Fifth Ave., New York, NY 10010. TEL 212-460-1500.
FAX 212-473-6272. (Also: Berlin, Heidelberg, Tokyo and Vienna) (reprint service avail. from ISI) **Document type:** monographic series.
—CASDDS; CISTI; KNAW. **CCC.**

BIOLOGY — Biotechnology

A S F A MARINE BIOTECHNOLOGY ABSTRACTS. (Aquatic Sciences & Fisheries Abstracts) see *BIOLOGY — Abstracting, Bibliographies, Statistics*

ABSTRACTS IN BIOCOMMERCE. see *BIOLOGY — Abstracting, Bibliographies, Statistics*

660 GW ISSN 0138-4988
TA164 CODEN: ACBTDD
ACTA BIOTECHNOLOGICA. (Text in English) 1981. q. DM.195 (foreign DM.203) to individuals; institutions DM.595 (foreign DM.615) (effective 1997). Akademie Verlag GmbH, Muehlenstr. 33-34, 13187 Berlin, Germany. TEL 49-30-47889348.
FAX 49-30-47889357. E-mail: info@akademie-verlag.de. Ed. W. Babel. bk.rev. circ. 300. (tabloid format) **Indexed:** ASCA, Biodet.Abstr., Biotech.Abstr., Chem.Abstr., Curr.Adv.Ecol.Sci., Curr.Biotech.Abstr., Curr.Cont., Dairy Sci.Abstr., Excerp.Med., Food Sci.& Tech.Abstr., Ind.Sci.Rev., Sci.Cit.Ind., Sugar Ind.Abstr., Telegen. **Document type:** academic/scholarly publication.
—BLDSC (0603.700000); CASDDS; CISTI; Ei; EMDOCS; Genuine Article; KNAW; Linda Hall; SWETS; UnCover. **CCC.**
Description: Interdisciplinary forum for environmental, industrial, and agricultural biotechnology.

660 630 NE ISSN 0169-0566
ADVANCES IN AGRICULTURAL BIOTECHNOLOGY. (Text in English) 1983. irreg., vol.26, 1989. price varies. Kluwer Academic Publishers, Postbus 17, 3300 AA Dordrecht, Netherlands. TEL 31-78-6392392.
FAX 31-78-6392254. TELEX 29245 KAPG NL. E-mail: services@wkap.nl; URL: http://www.wkap.nl. (Dist. by: Kluwer Academic Publishers Group, P.O. Box 322, 3300 AH Dordrecht, Netherlands. TEL 31-78-6392392. FAX 31-78-6546474; N. America dist. addr.: Box 358, Accord Sta., Hingham, MA 02018-0358. TEL 617-871-6600. FAX 617-871-6528) (back issues avail.) **Document type:** monographic series.
Refereed Serial

660.63 US ISSN 0724-6145
TP248.3 CODEN: ABEBDZ
ADVANCES IN BIOCHEMICAL ENGINEERING - BIOTECHNOLOGY. 1972. irreg., vol.54, 1996. price varies. Springer-Verlag, 175 Fifth Ave., New York, NY 10010. TEL 212-460-1500.
FAX 212-473-6272. E-mail: orders@springer-ny.com; URL: http://springer-ny.com. (Also: Berlin, Heidelberg, Tokyo and Vienna) Eds. T.K Ghose, A. Fiechter. (reprint service avail. from ISI) **Indexed:** Bibl.Agri., Biotech.Abstr., Chem.Abstr., Curr.Biotech.Abstr., Food Sci.& Tech.Abstr., Ind.Med. **Document type:** monographic series.
—BLDSC (0699.925500); CASDDS; CISTI; Ei; KNAW; Linda Hall; SWETS; UnCover. **CCC.**
Formerly: Advances in Biochemical Engineering (ISSN 0065-2210)
Description: Publishes new research in biochemical engineering and other areas of biotechnology.

660.6 US ISSN 1061-8945
R857.B54 CODEN: ABIOER
ADVANCES IN BIOSENSORS. irreg., vol.4, 1997. $109.50. J A I Press Inc., 55 Old Post Rd., No.2, Box 1678, Greenwich, CT 06830-1678.
TEL 203-661-7602. FAX 203-661-0792. E-mail: jai@jaipress.com. (Subscr. in UK and Europe to: JAI PRess Ltd., 38 Tavistock St., Covent Garden, London WC2E 7PB, England. TEL 44-171-379-8834. FAX 44-171-379-8835) Ed. A.P.F. Turner. **Document type:** monographic series.
—BLDSC (0700.275000); CASDDS; CISTI.

AGBIOTECH NEWS AND INFORMATION. see *BIOLOGY — Abstracting, Bibliographies, Statistics*

AGRICULTURAL & ENVIRONMENTAL BIOTECHNOLOGY ABSTRACTS. see *AGRICULTURE — Abstracting, Bibliographies, Statistics*

AGRICULTURAL RESEARCH. see *AGRICULTURE — Crop Production And Soil*

660 542 US ISSN 0749-3223
CODEN: ABLAEY
AMERICAN BIOTECHNOLOGY LABORATORY. (Includes a. Buyers' Guide) 1983. 13/yr. $145 (foreign $175). International Scientific Communications, Inc., 30 Controls Dr., Box 870, Shelton, CT 06484-0870. TEL 203-926-9300. FAX 203-926-9310. (U.K. subscr. to: I.S.C. House, Progress Business Centre, 5 Whittle Pkwy., Slough, Berks. SL1 6DQ, England. TEL 44-1628-668881. FAX 44-1628-669199) Ed. Brian Howard. adv.; charts; illus.; stat.; tr.lit.; circ. 70,016 (controlled). **Indexed:** ASCA, Curr.Biotech.Abstr., Curr.Cont., Telegen. **Document type:** academic/scholarly publication.
—BLDSC (0810.806000); CASDDS; CISTI; Ei; Genuine Article; KNAW; SWETS.

660 636 US ISSN 1049-5398
SF140.B54 CODEN: ANBTEN
ANIMAL BIOTECHNOLOGY. 1990. 3/yr. $495 (foreign $506.25) (effective 1998). Marcel Dekker Journals, 270 Madison Ave., New York, NY 10016.
TEL 212-696-9000. FAX 212-685-4540. TELEX 42149 MARDEEK. (Subscr. to: Box 10018, Church St. Sta., New York, NY 10249) Ed. Lawrence B. Schook. adv. contact: Eridania Perez. **Indexed:** ASCA, Environ.Per.Bibl. (1992-1993), Food Sci.& Tech.Abstr. **Document type:** academic/scholarly publication.
—BLDSC (0902.975000); CASDDS; Genuine Article; SWETS; UMI. **CCC.**
Description: Covers the identification and manipulation of genes and their products in domesticated animals.
Refereed Serial

660 JA ISSN 0912-6686
ANNUAL REPORT OF I C BIOTECH. (Text in English) 1978. a. Osaka University, International Center for Biotechnology - Osaka Daigaku Seibutsu Kogaku Kokusai Koryu Senta, 2-1 Yamadaoka, Suita-shi, Osaka 565, Japan. TEL 81-6-879-7455.
FAX 81-6-879-7474. E-mail: toshida@icb.osaka-u.ac.jp. Ed. Toshiomi Yoshida.
Formerly (until 1985): International Center of Cooperative Research and Development in Microbial Engineering (ISSN 0387-5377)

ANTIVIRAL AGENTS BULLETIN; antiviral drug and vaccine development information. see *PHARMACY AND PHARMACOLOGY*

APPLIED BIOCHEMISTRY AND BIOTECHNOLOGY. see *BIOLOGY — Biological Chemistry*

APPLIED CYTOGENETICS. see *BIOLOGY — Genetics*

576 660 GW ISSN 0175-7598
QR53 CODEN: AMBIDG
APPLIED MICROBIOLOGY AND BIOTECHNOLOGY. Online edition (GW ISSN 1432-0614) (Text in English) 1975. m. DM.3935 (foreign DM.3964.40) (effective 1998). Springer-Verlag, Heidelberger Platz 3, 14197 Berlin, Germany. TEL 49-30-82787-0. FAX 49-30-82787448. E-mail: subscriptions@springer.de; URL: http://link.springer.de. (Subscr. in N. America to: Springer-Verlag New York, Inc., 333 Meadowlands Pkwy., Secaucus, NJ 07094. TEL 212-460-1500. FAX 212-473-6272) Ed. A. Steinbuchel. (also avail. in microform from UMI; reprint service avail. from ISI) **Indexed:** Abstr.Hyg., ASCA, Bio-Contr.News & Info., Biodet.Abstr., Biol.& Agr.Ind., Biotech.Abstr., Chem.Abstr., Chem.Cit.Ind., Curr.Adv.Biochem., Curr.Adv.Ecol.Sci., Curr.Adv.Genetics & Molec.Biol., Curr.Biotech.Abstr., Curr.Cont., Dairy Sci.Abstr., Deep Sea Res.& Oceanogr.Abstr., Excerp.Med., Food Sci.& Tech.Abstr., Helminthol.Abstr., Ind.Sci.Rev., Ind.Vet., INIS Atomind., Mat.Sci.Cit.Ind., Nutr.Abstr., Pig News & Info., Potato Abstr., Rev.Med.& Vet.Mycol., Rev.Plant Path., Sci.Cit.Ind., Sel.Water Res.Abstr., Soils & Fert., Sugar Ind.Abstr., Triticale Abstr., Vet.Bull., W.R.C.Inf., Weed Abstr. **Document type:** academic/scholarly publication.
●Also available online.
—BLDSC (1576.100000); ADONIS; CASDDS; CISTI; EMDOCS; Genuine Article; KR SourceOne; Linda Hall; SWETS; UMI; UnCover. **CCC.**
Former titles (until 1984): European Journal of Applied Microbiology and Biotechnology (ISSN 0171-1741); European Journal of Applied Microbiology (ISSN 0340-2118)
Description: Covers the following areas: biotechnology, biochemical engineering, applied genetics and regulation, applied microbial and cell physiology, food biotechnology, and environmental biotechnology.

ARQUIVOS DE BIOLOGIA E TECNOLOGIA. see *BIOLOGY*

ARTIFICIAL CELLS, BLOOD SUBSTITUTES, AND IMMOBILIZATION BIOTECHNOLOGY. see *MEDICAL SCIENCES — Experimental Medicine, Laboratory Technique*

660 US ISSN 0219-0303
▼**ASIA-PACIFIC BIOTECH NEWS.** (Editions in Chinese, English) 1997. w. $375 for English ed. (print & online eds. $450); Chinese ed. $200 (print & online eds. $450). World Scientific Publishing Co. Pte. Ltd., K H Biotech Services Pte. Ltd., Farrer Rd., P.O. Box 128, Singapore 912805, Singapore.
TEL 65-382-5663. FAX 65-382-5919. E-mail: sales@wspc.com; URL: http://www.wspc.com.sg. (US addr.: 1060 Main St., River Edge, NJ 07661. TEL 800-227-7562. FAX 888-977-2665; UK addr.: 57 Shelton St., Covent Garden, London WC2H 9HE, England. TEL 44-171-836-0888. FAX 44-171-836-2020) Ed. Ham-Hai Chua.
●Also available online.
Description: Offers coverage of news mainly in the fields of food, agriculture, pharmaceuticals and health care. Contains new government policies and regulations, company profiles, corporate deals, industry trends, new product developments and patents, new biotech techniques, technological updates and new drugs.

ASIAN - AUSTRALASIAN JOURNAL OF ANIMAL SCIENCES. see *AGRICULTURE — Poultry And Livestock*

660 AT ISSN 1036-7128
CODEN: AUBIE5
AUSTRALASIAN BIOTECHNOLOGY. 1987. bi-m. Aus.$72 (foreign Aus.$96). Australian Biotechnology Association Ltd., P.O. Box 4, Gardenvale, Vic. 3185, Australia. TEL 61-3-95968879.
FAX 61-3-95968874. E-mail: aba@netspace.net.au; URL: http://www.aba.asn.au/. Eds. M. Palyne, D. Tribe. R&P contact: Barbara Arnold. adv. contact: Gary Dolder. bk.rev.; index; circ. 1,200 (paid). (back issues avail.) **Indexed:** Arts & Hum.Cit.Ind., ASCA, Curr.Biotech.Abstr., Food Sci.& Tech.Abstr., SSCI. **Document type:** newsletter.
—BLDSC (1793.610000); CASDDS; CISTI; EMDOCS; Genuine Article; UnCover.
Formerly (until Aug. 1991): Australian Journal of Biotechnology (ISSN 0819-3355)

BIOLOGY — BIOTECHNOLOGY

660   UK
B B S R C BUSINESS. 1967. q. free. Biotechnology and Biological Sciences Research Council, Polaris House, North Star Ave., Swindon, Wilts. SN2 1UH, England. TEL 44-1793-413200. FAX 44-1793-413201. Ed. Monica Winstanley. charts; illus. **Indexed:** Environ.Abstr. **Document type:** newsletter.
    Supersedes in part (in Apr. 1994): A F R C News (ISSN 0267-8489)
    Description: Presents research in biology and biotechnology, agriculture, food, chemicals, and pharmaceuticals.

660   664   UK
B B S R C SCIENCE BRIEF. 1967. s-a. free. Biotechnology and Biological Sciences Research Council, Polaris House, North Star Ave., Swindon, Wilts. SN2 1UH, England. TEL 44-1793-413200. FAX 44-1793-413201. Ed. Monica Winstanley. circ. 2,500.
    Supersedes in part (in Apr. 1994): A F R C News (ISSN 0267-8489)

660   US
B I O'S EDITORS' AND REPORTERS' GUIDE TO BIOTECHNOLOGY. a. free. Biotechnology Industry Organization, 1625 K St., N.W., Ste. 1100, Washington, DC 20006-1604. TEL 202-857-0244. FAX 202-857-0237. E-mail: info@bio.org; URL: http://www.bio.org.
    Description: Source of facts, figures, and ideas for coverage of biotechnology.

660   JA
BAIOINDASUTORI NENKAN/YEARBOOK OF BIOINDUSTRY. (Text in Japanese) 1985. a. 55000 Yen. C M C Co., Ltd., 5-4, Uchikanda 1-chome, Chiyoda-ku, Tokyo 101, Japan.

660   JA
BAIOTEKUNOROJI JOHO/BIOTECHNOLOGY INFORMATION. (Text in Japanese) irreg. Norin Suisansho, Norin Suisan Gijutsu Kaigi Jimukyoku - Ministry of Agriculture, Forestry and Fisheries; Agriculture, Forestry and Fisheries Research Council, 2-1 Kasumigaseki 1-chome, Chiyoda-ku, Tokyo 100, Japan.

660   JA
BAIOTEKUNOROJI REBYU/BIOTECHNOLOGY REVIEW. (Text in Japanese) 1988. a. 80000 Yen. C M C Co., Ltd., 5-4 Uchikanda 1-chome, Chiyoda-ku, Tokyo 101, Japan.

BEN-GURION UNIVERSITY OF THE NEGEV. INSTITUTES FOR APPLIED RESEARCH. SCIENTIFIC ACTIVITIES. see *AGRICULTURE*

660.6   FR   ISSN 0291-2430
BIO; lettre des biotechnologies. (Text in English, French) 1981. 18/yr. 2200 F. A Jour, 11 rue du Marche St. Honore, 75001 Paris, France. TEL 42-61-45-17. FAX 40-20-07-75. TELEX 214 341 F AJOUR. Ed. Patrice Dacquin. adv.; bk.rev. circ. 1,500. (back issues avail.)
    —CISTI. **CCC**.

660   JA   ISSN 0910-6545
    CODEN: BIINEG
BIO INDASUTORI/BAIO INDASUTORI. (Text in Japanese) 1984. m. 4500 Yen per no. C M C Co., Ltd., 5-4, Uchikanda 1-chome, Chiyoda-ku, Tokyo 101, Japan. **Indexed:** Chem.Abstr.
    —BLDSC (2066.656900); CASDDS.

660   US
BIO NEWS; news & events from the biotechnology industry. bi-m. Biotechnology Industry Organization, 1625 K St., N.W., Ste. 1100, Washington, DC 20006-1604. TEL 202-857-0244. FAX 202-857-0237. E-mail: info@bio.org; URL: http://www.bio.org. Ed. Eric Christensen. **Document type:** newsletter.

660   NE   ISSN 1024-2422
TP248.65.E59   CODEN: BOBOEQ
BIOCATALYSIS AND BIOTRANSFORMATION. 4/yr. (in 1 vol., 4 nos./vol.). $209 (effective 1998). Gordon and Breach - Harwood Academic, Amsteldisk 166, 1st Fl., 1079 LH Amsterdam, Netherlands. URL: http://www.gbhap.com/Biocatalysis_Biotransformation/. (Subscr. to: International Publishers Distributor, Box 32160, Newark, NJ 07102. TEL 800-545-8398. FAX 215-750-6343) Ed. Dr. David Leak. adv.; bk.rev. (also avail. in microform; back issues avail.) **Indexed:** ASCA, Chem.Abstr., Chem.Cit.Ind., Curr.Cont., Food Sci.& Tech.Abstr., Int.Abstr.Biol.Sci. **Document type:** academic/scholarly publication.
    ●Also available online.
    Also available on CD-ROM.
    —BLDSC (2066.809100); CASDDS; CISTI; Ei; SWETS. **CCC**.
    Formerly: Biocatalysis (ISSN 0886-4454)
    Description: International journal covering the industrial exploitation of biological catalysts for the interconversion of chemical species.
    Refereed Serial

BIOCHIMIE. see *BIOLOGY — Biological Chemistry*

BIOCOMMERCE FINANCIAL ABSTRACTS. see *BIOLOGY — Abstracting, Bibliographies, Statistics*

660   US
BIOCONNECTION. 1986. 3/yr. Michigan Biotechnology Institute, 3900 Collins Rd., Box 27609, Lansing, MI 48909. TEL 517-337-3181. FAX 517-337-2122. Ed. Gretchen Smith. circ. 2,500. (back issues avail.) **Document type:** academic/scholarly publication.

BIOENGINEERING ABSTRACTS. see *BIOLOGY — Abstracting, Bibliographies, Statistics*

BIOFORUM INTERNATIONAL; bioresearch plus biotechnology. see *BIOLOGY*

660.6   FR   ISSN 0294-3506
TP248.13   CODEN: BIOFEM
BIOFUTUR; mensuel Europeen de biotechnologie. (Supplement avail.: Le Technoscope) (Text mainly in French) 1982. 11/yr. 877 F. to institutions (US $210; outside N. America 1050 F) (effective 1998). Editions Scientifiques et Medicales Elsevier, 141 rue de Javel, 75747 Paris, France. TEL 33-1-45589049. FAX 33-1-45589421. URL: http://www.elsevier.nl/. (Subscr. in U.S. and Canada to: Elsevier Science Inc., Box 945, New York, NY 10159-0945. TEL 212-633-3630. FAX 212-633-3680) Ed. Annette Nillet. adv.; bk.rev. circ. 10,000. (also avail. in microform from UMI; back issues avail.) **Indexed:** Anim.Breed.Abstr., ASCA, Biol.Abstr., Chem.Abstr., Curr.Adv.Ecol.Sci., Curr.Biotech.Abstr., Curr.Cont., Dairy Sci.Abstr., Excerp.Med., Ind.Med., Paper & Bd.Abstr., Sci.Cit.Ind., SSCI, Telegen. **Document type:** academic/scholarly publication.
    —BLDSC (2072.147000); CASDDS; CISTI; EMDOCS; Genuine Article; SWETS. **CCC**.
    Description: Provides a comprehensive picture of the world of biotechnology and its application in all relevant sectors such as health, agro-food, agriculture, the environment.

BIOMATERIALS. see *MEDICAL SCIENCES*

BIOMIMETICS. see *BIOLOGY — Bioengineering*

660   US   ISSN 1065-612X
HD9999.B443   CODEN: BOPEEW
BIOPEOPLE. 1992. q. $48 (outside US & Canada $68); newsstand price: 14. Bioventure Publishing, 2555 Flores St., Ste. 555, San Mateo, CA 94403-2342. TEL 415-574-7128. FAX 415-574-8319. E-mail: biogodess@aol.com. Ed. Cynthia Robbins-Roth; Pub. Patty Fox. R&P contact: Patty Fox. adv. contact: Bill Stanley.
    Description: Features the personalities behind the business and science of biotechnology.

BIOPHOTONICS INTERNATIONAL; photonic solutions for biotechnology and medicine. see *MEDICAL SCIENCES*

620   GW   ISSN 0178-515X
    CODEN: BIENEU
BIOPROCESS ENGINEERING; bioreactors, upstream and downstream processes, measurement and control. Online edition (GW ISSN 1432-0797) (Text in English) 1986. m. DM.2594.80 (foreign DM.2605.60) (effective 1998). Springer-Verlag, Heidelberger Platz 3, 14197 Berlin, Germany. TEL 49-30-82787-0. FAX 49-30-82787448. E-mail: subscriptions@springer.de; URL: http://link.springer.de. (Subscr. in N. America to: Springer-Verlag New York, Inc., 333 Meadowlands Pkwy., Secaucus, NJ 07094. TEL 212-460-1500. FAX 212-473-6272) Ed. H. Brauer. **Indexed:** ASCA, Biodet.Abstr., Compumath, Curr.Adv.Biochem., Curr.Adv.Ecol.Sci., Curr.Biotech.Abstr., Curr.Cont., Excerp.Med., Telegen. **Document type:** academic/scholarly publication.
    ●Also available online.
    —BLDSC (2089.474200); ADONIS; CASDDS; CISTI; Ei; EMDOCS; Genuine Article; SWETS; UMI; UnCover. **CCC**.
    Description: Devoted to engineering closely related to biotechnology and all technical and economic aspects of the processes in which natural or derived biological substances are the basic material.

660   CN   ISSN 1195-8162
BIOQUAL NEWSLETTER/BULLETIN BIOQUAL. q. membership. Environment Canada, Technology Development Directorate - Environnement Canada, Direction du Developpement Technologique, Ottawa, ON K1A 0H3, Canada. TEL 819-953-9399. FAX 819-953-7253. **Document type:** newsletter.
    Description: Informs members of new developments in biotechnology as they relate to the preservation of the environment.

333.8   UK   ISSN 0960-8524
TP360   CODEN: BIRTEB
BIORESOURCE TECHNOLOGY. 1991. m. fl.2752($1582) (effective 1998). Elsevier Science Ltd., P.O. Box 800, Kidlington, Oxford OX5 1DX, England. TEL 44-1865-843000. FAX 44-1865-843010. E-mail: nlinfo-f@elsevier.nl; usinfo-f@elsevier.com; forinfo-kyf04035@niftyserve.or.jp; URL: http://www.elsevier.nl/. (Subscr. to: Elsevier Science, Regional Sales Office, P.O. Box 211, 1000 AE Amsterdam, Netherlands. TEL 31-20-4853757. FAX 31-20-4853432; Subscr. in the Americas to: Elsevier Science, Regional Sales Office, Box 945, New York, NY 10159-0945. TEL 212-633-3730. FAX 212-633-3680; Subscr. in Australasia and the Far East to: Elsevier Science (Singapore) Pte Ltd, No.1 Temasek Ave., No.17-01 Millenia Tower, Singapore 039192, Singapore. TEL 65-434-3727. FAX 65-337-2230) (Co-sponsors: Biomass and Biofuels Association, UK; Biomass Energy Research Association, US) Ed.Bd. adv.; bk.rev.; charts; illus. (back issues avail.) **Indexed:** Abstr.Bull.Inst.Pap.Chem., AESIS, Agri.Eng.Abstr., Agroforest.Abstr., AIT Reports, ASCA, Bibl.Agri., Biodet.Abstr., Biol.Abstr., Biotech.Abstr., Chem.Abstr., Cott.& Trop.Fibr.Abstr., Curr.Adv.Ecol.Sci., Curr.Adv.Plant Sci., Curr.Biotech.Abstr., Curr.Cont., Dairy Sci.Abstr., Ecol.Abstr., Energy Ind., Energy Info.Abstr., Energy Rev., Eng.Ind., Environ.Abstr., Environ.Per.Bibl. (1985-), Excerp.Med., Field Crop Abstr., Food Sci.& Tech. Abstr., Forest.Abstr., Forest Prod.Abstr., Gas Abstr., Geo.Abstr.H.G., Geo.Abstr.P.G., Herb.Abstr., Hort.Abstr., IDA, Ind.Sci.Rev., INIS Atomind., INSPEC, Irr.& Drain.Abstr., Maize Abstr., Mat.Sci.Cit.Ind., Nutr.Abstr., Ocean.Abstr., Pig News & Info., Pollut.Abstr., Potato Abstr., Poult.Abstr., Protozool.Abstr., Rice Abstr., Rural Recreat.Tour.Abstr., Sci.Cit.Ind., Sel.Water Res.Abstr., Soils & Fert., Sorghum & Millets Abstr., Soyabean Abstr., Sport Fish.Abstr., SSCI, Sugar Ind.Abstr., Triticale Abstr., Trop.Oil Seeds Abstr., Vet.Bull., W.R.C.Inf., Inf., Weed Abstr., Wild.Rev., World Agri.Econ.& Rural Sociol.Abstr., Zoo.Rec. **Document type:** academic/scholarly publication.
    —BLDSC (2089.495000); CASDDS; CISTI; Ei; EMDOCS; Genuine Article; KR SourceOne; Linda Hall; SWETS; UnCover. **CCC**.
    Incorporates (in 1991): Biological Wastes (ISSN 0269-7483); (1981-1991): Biomass (ISSN 0144-4565); Which incorporated (in 1988): Energy in Agriculture (ISSN 0167-5826); Biological Wastes was formerly titled (1979-1987): Agricultural Wastes (ISSN 0141-4607).
    Description: Publishes original papers, review articles, case studies and other material for the professional in the fundamentals, applications and management of bioresource technology.
    Refereed Serial

BIOLOGY — BIOTECHNOLOGY

660   US   ISSN 0887-6207
HD9999.B44
BIOSCAN; the worldwide biotech industry reporting service. 1986. bi-m. $975 (foreign $1145). American Health Consultants Inc., 3525 Piedmont Rd., N.E. Bldg. 6, Ste. 400, Atlanta, GA 30305. TEL 800-668-2421. Pub. Phyllis Steckler. R&P contact: Betsy Durkin. (looseleaf format; also avail. in diskette format) **Document type:** directory.
●Also available online.
—CISTI.
Description: Provides information on more than 1000 biotechnology companies worldwide. Includes company name, address, phone numbers and names of officers, research & development activities, joint ventures, products, information on corporate financial history, investments, and mergers.

BIOSCIENCE, BIOTECHNOLOGY, AND BIOCHEMISTRY. see BIOLOGY

660.6   UK   ISSN 0956-5663
R857.B54   CODEN: BBIOE4
BIOSENSORS AND BIOELECTRONICS. 1985. m. fl.1593($916) (effective 1998). Elsevier Science Ltd., P.O. Box 800, Kidlington, Oxford OX5 1DX, England. TEL 44-1865-843000. FAX 44-1865-843010. E-mail: nlinfo-f@elsevier.nl; usinfo-f@elsevier.com; forinfo-kyf04035@niftyserve.or.jp; URL: http://www.elsevier.nl/. (Subscr. to: Elsevier Science, Regional Sales Office, P.O. Box 211, 1000 AE Amsterdam, Netherlands. TEL 31-20-4853757. FAX 31-20-4853432; Subscr. in the Americas to: Elsevier Science, Regional Sales Office, Box 945, New York, NY 10159-0945. TEL 212-633-3730. FAX 212-633-3680; Subscr. in Australasia and the Far East to: Elsevier Science (Singapore) Pte Ltd, No.1 Temasek Ave., No.17-01 Millenia Tower, Singapore 039192, Singapore. TEL 65-434-3727. FAX 65-337-2230) Ed.Bd. adv.; bk.rev.; charts; illus.; index. **Indexed:** ASCA, Biol.Abstr., Biotech.Abstr., Chem.Abstr., Chem.Cit.Ind., Curr.Adv.Ecol.Sci., Curr.Biotech.Abstr., Curr.Cont., Environ.Abstr., Excerp.Med., Ind.Sci.Rev., INSPEC (1990-), Pollut.Abstr., Sci.Cit.Ind., Telegen, W.R.C.Inf. **Document type:** academic/scholarly publication.
—BLDSC (2089.611910); ADONIS; AskIEEE; CASDDS; CISTI; Ei; EMDOCS; Genuine Article; KR SourceOne; Linda Hall; SWETS; UnCover. **CCC.**
Formerly (until 1989): Biosensors (ISSN 0265-928X)
Description: Covers research, technology and applications of biosensors and the exploitation of biochemicals in electronic devices.
Refereed Serial

660   NE   ISSN 0923-179X
TP248.25.S47   CODEN: BISPE4
BIOSEPARATION; international journal of separation science in biotechnology. (Text in English) 1990. bi-m. fl.814 to institutions; $417.50 to institutions in U.S. (effective 1998). Kluwer Academic Publishers, Postbus 17, 3300 AA Dordrecht, Netherlands. TEL 31-78-6392294. FAX 31-78-6392254. TELEX 29245 KAPG NL. E-mail: services@wkap.nl; URL: http://www.wkap.nl. (Dist. by: Kluwer Academic Publishers Group, P.O. Box 322, 3300 AH Dordrecht, Netherlands. TEL 31-78-6392392. FAX 31-78-6546474; N. America dist. addr.: Box 358, Accord Sta., Hingham, MA 02018-0358. TEL 617-871-6600. FAX 617-871-6528) Ed. Tony Atkinson. (also avail. in microform from UMI; back issues avail.; reprint service avail. from SWZ) **Indexed:** ASCA, Biol.Abstr., Chem.Abstr., Chem.Cit.Ind., Food Sci.& Tech.Abstr. **Document type:** academic/scholarly publication.
—BLDSC (2089.611950); CASDDS; CISTI; Ei; EMDOCS; Genuine Article; SWETS; UMI; UnCover. **CCC.**
Description: Presents papers on all aspects of separation science applicable or potentially applicable to commercial-scale biotechnological process.
Refereed Serial

660 574.28   US   ISSN 1067-2818
HD9706.65.B55   CODEN: BBGUEC
BIOTECH BUYER'S GUIDE. 1989. a. $50 (free to qualified personnel). American Chemical Society, 1155 16th St., N.W., Washington, DC 20036. TEL 800-227-5558. FAX 202-872-4615. (Subscr. to: Membership and Subscription Services: Box 3337, Columbus, OH 43210. TEL 614-447-3776) adv.; circ. 65,000 (controlled). **Document type:** academic/scholarly publication, directory.
—CISTI.
Description: For scientists involved in recombinant DNA, monoclonal antibody techniques and bioprocessing.

BIOTECH KNOWLEDGE SOURCES. see BIOLOGY — Abstracting, Bibliographies, Statistics

330 660 340   US
BIOTECH MARKET NEWS & LEGAL STRATEGIES. 1985. m. $322. Chandler Publishing Ltd., Box 11155, Ft. Lauderdale, FL 33339. TEL 954-522-4344. FAX 954-522-7750. Ed. Edward J. Chandler. circ. 15,000. **Document type:** newsletter.
Formerly: BioTech Market News and Strategies (ISSN 0740-1221)

660   UK   ISSN 0263-8029
                           CODEN: BTNEEN
BIOTECH NEWS. 1982. m. £82.50 (foreign £90.50). Springfield Information Services, P.O. Box 31, Peterborough, Cambs. PE1 1SD, England. TEL 01733-267272. Ed. John Franks. bk.rev.; abstr.; tr.lit. (back issues avail.) **Indexed:** Curr.Biotech.Abstr. **Document type:** academic/scholarly publication.
—BLDSC (2089.740000); CASDDS; CISTI.

660   BE
BIOTECH PRODUCTS INTERNATIONAL. (Text in English) 1989. 7/yr. 3000 BEF($95) (free to qualified personnel). Pan European Publishing Co. (Subsidiary of: Reed Elsevier plc), Rue Verte 216, 1030 Brussels, Belgium. TEL 32-2-2402611. FAX 32-2-2427111. Ed. S. Soukias. adv.; illus.; tr.lit.; circ. 30,020 (controlled). (tabloid format) **Document type:** trade publication.
Description: Provides information on new products and services of interest to professionals in all branches of the biotechnology field.

660 574.192
636.089   US   ISSN 1069-4773
                           CODEN: BRPOEF
BIOTECH REPORTER; agricultural research - business. 1984. m. $135 (foreign $165); university and government individuals $65 (effective 1997). Freiberg Publishing Company, Inc., Box 7, 2302 W. First, Cedar Falls, IA 50613. TEL 319-277-3599. FAX 319-277-3783. Ed. Karol Cutler; Pub. Bill Freiberg. adv. contact: Kathy Freiberg. tr.lit. circ. 1,500. (back issues avail.; reprint service avail.) **Indexed:** ASCA, Curr.Biotech.Abstr., Telegen.
—BLDSC (2089.760000); CISTI.
Former titles (until 1993): AgBiotechnology News (ISSN 0899-3998); Agricultural Biotechnology News (ISSN 0748-822X); Agricultural Biotechnology.
Description: Current scientific and business news in field of agricultural biotechnology.

BIOTECHNIC AND HISTOCHEMISTRY; a journal for microtechnic and histochemistry. see BIOLOGY — Microscopy

660.6   US   ISSN 0736-6205
                         CODEN: BTNQDO
BIOTECHNIQUES; the journal of laboratory technology for bioresearch. (Euro Edition avail.) 1983. 12/yr. $105 (foreign $135). Eaton Publishing Co., 154 E. Central St., Natick, MA 01760. TEL 508-655-8282. FAX 508-655-9910. Ed. James Ellingboe. R&P contact: James Ellingboe. adv. contact: Esta Warshofsky. bk.rev. circ. 60,000. **Indexed:** ASCA, Chem.Cit.Ind., Curr.Adv.Biochem., Curr.Adv.Ecol.Sci., Curr.Adv.Genetics & Molec.Biol., Curr.Cont., Excerp.Med., Food Sci.& Tech.Abstr., Ind.Sci.Rev., Sci.Cit.Ind., Telegen.
—BLDSC (2089.820000); CASDDS; CISTI; Ei; EMDOCS; Genuine Article; KNAW; Linda Hall; SWETS; UnCover. **CCC.**

BIOTECHNOLOGY ABSTRACTS. see BIOLOGY — Abstracting, Bibliographies, Statistics

660 610.28   US   ISSN 0734-9750
TP248.2   CODEN: BIADDD
BIOTECHNOLOGY ADVANCES; research reviews and patent abstracts. 1983. bi-m. fl.1670($960) (effective 1998). Elsevier Science, Box 945, New York, NY 10159-0945. TEL 212-633-3730. FAX 212-633-3680. E-mail: nlinfo-f@elsevier.nl; usinfo-f@elsevier.com; forinfo-kyf04035@niftyserve.or.jp; URL: http://www.elsevier.nl/. (Subscr. outside the Americas to: Elsevier Science, Regional Sales Office, P.O. Box 211, 1000 AE Amsterdam, Netherlands. TEL 31-20-4853757. FAX 31-20-4853432; Subscr. in Australasia and the Far East to: Elsevier Science (Singapore) Pte Ltd, No.1 Temasek Ave., No.17-01 Millenia Tower, Singapore 039192, Singapore. TEL 65-434-3727. FAX 65-337-2230; Subscr. in Japan to: Elsevier Science Japan, 9-15 Higashi-Azabu 1-chome, Minato-ku, Tokyo 106, Japan. TEL 81-3-5561-5033. FAX 81-3-5561-5047) Ed. M. Moo-Young. pat. (also avail. in microfilm from UMI) **Indexed:** ASCA, Bibl.Agri., Biodet.Abstr., Chem.Cit.Ind., Curr.Adv.Ecol.Sci., Curr.Biotech.Abstr., Curr.Cont., Ind.Sci.Rev., Paper & Bd.Abstr., Sci.Cit.Ind., Soils & Fert., Telegen. **Document type:** academic/scholarly publication.
—BLDSC (2089.845000); ADONIS; CASDDS; CISTI; Ei; EMDOCS; Genuine Article; Linda Hall; SWETS; UMI; UnCover. **CCC.**
Description: Covers all aspects of biotechnology including relevant developments in related disciplines of biology, chemistry, and engineering.
Refereed Serial

660 612.015   UK   ISSN 0885-4513
QP501   CODEN: BABIEC
BIOTECHNOLOGY AND APPLIED BIOCHEMISTRY. 1979. bi-m. £120($210) (effective 1997). (International Union of Biochemistry) Portland Press Ltd., 59 Portland Pl., London W1N 3AJ, England. TEL 44-171-580-5530. FAX 44-171-323-1136. E-mail: sales@portlandpress.co.uk; URL: http://www.portlandpress.co.uk. (Subscr. to: Commerce Way, P.O. Box 32, Colchester, Essex CO2 8HP, England. TEL 44-1206-796351. FAX 44-1206-799331) Ed. R.L. Lundblad. adv. contact: Adam Marshall. index. circ. 500. (back issues avail.) **Indexed:** Abstr.Bull.Inst.Pap.Chem., ASCA, Biodet.Abstr., Biotech.Abstr., Chem.Abstr., Chem.Cit.Ind., Curr.Biotech.Abstr., Curr.Cont., Curr.Leather Lit., Dairy Sci.Abstr., Excerp.Med., Food Sci.& Tech.Abstr., Ind.Med., INIS Atomind., Sci.Cit.Ind., Sugar Ind.Abstr. **Document type:** academic/scholarly publication.
—BLDSC (2089.848000); ADONIS; CASDDS; CISTI; Ei; EMDOCS; Genuine Article; KNAW; Linda Hall; SWETS; UnCover. **CCC.**
Formerly: Journal of Applied Biochemistry (ISSN 0161-7354)
Description: Publication of articles concerning expression, purification, characterization and application of biological macromolecules in therapeutics and diagnostics with medical, dental and veterinary applications.
Refereed Serial

BIOLOGY — BIOTECHNOLOGY

660   574.28   US   ISSN 0006-3592
QH324   CODEN: BIBIAU
BIOTECHNOLOGY AND BIOENGINEERING. 1958. 28/yr. $2635 (foreign $3125) (effective 1998). John Wiley & Sons, Inc., Journals, 605 Third Ave., New York, NY 10158-0012. TEL 212-850-6645. FAX 212-850-6021. TELEX 12-7063. E-mail: SUBINFO@JWILEY.COM; URL: http://www.wiley.com/0006-3592. (Overseas subscr. to: John Wiley & Sons Ltd., Baffins Ln., Chichester, W. Sussex PO19 1UD, England. TEL 44-1243-779777. FAX 44-1243-776128) Ed. Douglas S. Clark. adv.: B&W page £640, color page £1515. bibl.; charts; illus.; index. circ. 1,700. (also avail. in microform from UMI; back issues avail.) **Indexed:** Abstr.Bull.Inst.Pap.Chem., ASCA, Biodet.Abstr., Biol.Abstr., Biol.& Agr.Ind., Biotech.Abstr., Chem.Abstr., Chem.Cit.Ind., Chem.Eng.Abstr., Chem.Titles, Curr.Adv.Biochem., Curr.Adv.Cancer Res., Curr.Adv.Cell & Devel.Biol., Curr.Adv.Ecol.Sci., Curr.Adv.Genetics & Molec.Biol, Curr.Biotech.Abstr., Curr.Cont., Dairy Sci.Abstr., Deep Sea Res.& Oceanogr.Abstr., Energy Ind., Energy Info.Abstr., Excerp.Med., Food Sci.& Tech.Abstr., Forest Prod.Abstr., Gas Abstr., Helminthol.Abstr., Herb.Abstr., Hort.Abstr., Ind.Sci.Rev., Ind.Vet., INIS Atomind., Maize Abstr., Mat.Sci.Cit.Ind., Nutr.Abstr., Ocean.Abstr., Pig News & Info., Rev.Med.& Vet.Mycol., Sci.Cit.Ind., Sel.J.Water, Sel.Water Res.Abstr., Sorghum & Millets Abstr., Sugar Ind.Abstr., T.C.E.A., Triticale Abstr., Vet.Bull., W.R.C.Inf. **Document type:** academic/scholarly publication, proceedings.
—BLDSC (2089.850000); ADONIS; CASDDS; CISTI; Ei; EMDOCS; Genuine Article; KR SourceOne; Linda Hall; SWETS; UMI; UnCover. **CCC.**
Description: Presents original research on all aspects of biochemical and microbial technology.
Refereed Serial

660   574.28 610   UK   ISSN 0264-8725
TP248.13   CODEN: BGERES
BIOTECHNOLOGY AND GENETIC ENGINEERING REVIEWS. 1984. a. £99.50. Intercept Ltd., P.O. Box 716, Andover, Hants. SP10 1YG, England. TEL 01264-334748. FAX 01264-334058. Ed. Michael P. Tombs. index. circ. 300. (back issues avail.) **Indexed:** ASCA, Biol.Abstr., Biol.& Agr.Ind., Curr.Adv.Ecol.Sci., Curr.Biotech.Abstr., Curr.Cont., Ind.Sci.Rev., Ind.Vet., Maize Abstr., Potato Abstr., Telegen, Vet.Bull. **Document type:** academic/scholarly publication.
—BLDSC (2089.860500); CASDDS; CISTI; Ei; KNAW; KR SourceOne; Linda Hall; SWETS; UnCover. **CCC.**

660   NE
▼**BIOTECHNOLOGY ANNUAL REVIEW.** (Text in English) 1995. a. fl.425($265.75) Elsevier Science B.V., P.O. Box 211, 1000 AE Amsterdam, Netherlands. TEL 31-20-4853911. FAX 31-20-4853705. E-mail: nl-info-f@elsevier.nl; usinfo-f@elsevier.com; forinfo-kyf04035@niftyserve.or.jp; URL: http://www.elsevier.nl/. (Subscr. in the Americas to: Elsevier Science, Regional Sales Office, Box 945, New York, NY 10159-0945. TEL 212-633-3730. FAX 212-633-3680; Subscr. in Australasia and the Far East to: Elsevier Science (Singapore) Pte Ltd, No.1 Temasek Ave., No.17-01 Millenia Tower, Singapore 039192, Singapore. TEL 65-434-3727. FAX 65-337-2230; Subscr. in Japan to: Elsevier Science Japan, 9-15 Higashi-Azabu 1-chome, Minato-ku, Tokyo 106, Japan. TEL 81-3-5561-5033. FAX 81-3-5561-5047) Ed. M. Raafat El-Gewely. illus. **Document type:** academic/scholarly publication.
Description: Reviews developments in biotechnology, including technical advances and applications in medicine, agriculture, marine biology, industry, bioremediation and the environment.
Refereed Serial

660   574.192   UK   ISSN 0938-5584
BIOTECHNOLOGY: APPARATUS, PLANT, AND EQUIPMENT. 1985. m. £145($261) (effective 1997). The Royal Society of Chemistry, Thomas Graham House, Science Park, Milton Rd., Cambridge CB4 4WF, England. TEL 44-1223-420066. FAX 44-1223-423623. E-mail: sales@rsc.org; URL: http://chemistry.rsc.org/rsc/. (Subscr. to: Turpin Distribution Services Ltd., Blackhorse Rd., Letchworth, Herts. SG6 1HN, England. TEL 44-1462-672555. FAX 44-1462-480947) **Indexed:** W.R.C.Inf. **Document type:** abstracting/indexing.
Formerly: Biotechnologie (ISSN 0178-8108)
Description: Summarizes articles on the practical methods and hardware used by biotechnologists.

660   US
BIOTECHNOLOGY AT WORK SERIES. irreg., no.10, 1992. free up to 5 copies. Biotechnology Industry Organization, 1625 K St., N.W., Ste. 1100, Washington, DC 20006. TEL 202-857-0244. FAX 202-857-0237. E-mail: info@bio.org; URL: http://www.bio.org. R&P contact: Eric Christensen. **Document type:** monographic series.
Description: Covers the latest development of biotechnology in environmental, agricultural and medical fields.

BIOTECHNOLOGY DIRECTORY (YEAR). see *BUSINESS AND ECONOMICS — Trade And Industrial Directories*

660   370   UK   ISSN 0955-6621
TP248.13   CODEN: BIEDEY
BIOTECHNOLOGY EDUCATION. 1990. 4/yr. £75 (effective 1993). Helix Publishing, 1 Howard Ct., 94-96 Blackheath Hill, Greenwich, London SE10 8AF, England. Ed. Paul Wymer. (also avail. in microfilm from UMI; back issues avail.) **Document type:** academic/scholarly publication.
—BLDSC (2089.861540); CASDDS; UMI.
Description: Resource for teachers and students in the biological sciences.
Refereed Serial

660   US   ISSN 1052-6153
CODEN: BHANE3
BIOTECHNOLOGY HANDBOOKS. 1987. irreg., latest vol.9. Plenum Publishing Corp., 233 Spring St., New York, NY 10013-1578. TEL 212-620-8000. FAX 212-463-0742. **Document type:** academic/scholarly publication, monographic series.
—BLDSC (2089.861590); CASDDS; CISTI. **CCC.**

660   630   US   ISSN 0934-943X
CODEN: BAFOEG
BIOTECHNOLOGY IN AGRICULTURE AND FORESTRY. 1986. irreg., vol.34, 1995. price varies. Springer-Verlag, 175 Fifth Ave., New York, NY 10010. TEL 212-460-1500. FAX 212-473-6272. (Also: Berlin, Heidelberg, Tokyo, Vienna) (reprint service avail. from ISI) **Document type:** academic/scholarly publication.
—BLDSC (2089.847000); CASDDS. **CCC.**

BIOTECHNOLOGY INFORMATION. see *BIOLOGY — Abstracting, Bibliographies, Statistics*

343.0786606   US   ISSN 0730-031X
KF3827.G4   CODEN: BLREEL
BIOTECHNOLOGY LAW REPORT. 1982. bi-m. $706 to libraries (foreign $759) (effective 1998). Mary Ann Liebert, Inc. Publishers, 2 Madison Ave., Larchmont, NY 10538. TEL 914-834-3100. FAX 914-834-3688. E-mail: liebert@pipeline.com. Ed. Gerry J. Elman. **Indexed:** ABC, Arts & Hum.Cit.Ind., ASCA, Curr.Biotech.Abstr., SSCI, Telegen. **Document type:** academic/scholarly publication.
—CISTI.
Description: Examines the evolving body of law governing biotechnology, particularly in the pharmaceutical, chemical, agriculture, food processing, energy, mineral recovery, and waste treatment industries.

660   UK   ISSN 0141-5492
QR53   CODEN: BILED3
BIOTECHNOLOGY LETTERS. 1979. m. £80($160) to individuals; institutions £270 (N. America $540) (effective 1995). Chapman & Hall, Journals Department (Subsidiary of: International Thomson Publishing Group), 2-6 Boundary Row, London SE1 8HN, England. TEL 44-171-8560066. FAX 44-171-5229623. TELEX 290164 CHAPMA G. E-mail: jhelp@chall.co.uk; URL: http://www.chaphall.com/chaphall/journals.html. (Subscr. to: International Thomson Publishing Services Ltd., Cheriton House, North Way, Andover, Hants. SP10 5BE, England. TEL 44-1264-342713. FAX 44-1264-342807; Subscr. in US & Canada to: 400 Market St., Philadelphia, PA 19106. TEL 800-552-5866) Ed. John D. Bu'Lock. adv.; abstr.; bibl.; charts; illus. (reprint service avail.) **Indexed:** ASCA, Bibl.Agri., Biodet.Abstr., Biol.Abstr., Biotech.Abstr., Chem.Abstr., Chem.Cit.Ind., Cott.& Trop.Fibr.Abstr., Curr.Adv.Biochem., Curr.Adv.Ecol.Sci., Curr.Adv.Genetics & Molec.Biol, Curr.Biotech.Abstr., Curr.Cont., Dairy Sci.Abstr., Energy Info.Abstr., Excerp.Med., Field Crop Abstr., Food Sci.& Tech.Abstr., Food Sci.& Tech.Abstr., Hort.Abstr., Ind.Sci.Rev., Maize Abstr., Rice Abstr., Sci.Cit.Ind., Sel.Water Res.Abstr., Sugar Ind.Abstr., Telegen, Triticale Abstr. **Document type:** academic/scholarly publication.
—BLDSC (2089.863000); CASDDS; CIS; CISTI; Genuine Article; SWETS; UMI; UnCover. **CCC.**
Description: Covers topics relating to actual or potential applications of biological reactions effected by microbial, plant, or animal cells and derived bio-catalysts.
Refereed Serial

660   US   ISSN 0930-8938
CODEN: BIMOE5
BIOTECHNOLOGY MONOGRAPHS. 1985. irreg., vol.5. Springer-Verlag, 175 Fifth Ave., New York, NY 10010. TEL 212-460-1500. FAX 212-473-6272. **Document type:** academic/scholarly publication, monographic series.
—CASDDS; CISTI; KNAW.

660   US   ISSN 0273-3226
CODEN: BINWEY
BIOTECHNOLOGY NEWS. 1981. 30/yr. $564 (foreign $584). C T B International Publishing Inc., Box 218, Maplewood, NJ 07040-0218. TEL 201-379-7749. FAX 201-379-1158. Ed. Christopher Brogna. Pub. Oykue Brogna. R&P contact: Christopher Brogna. bk.rev.; index. (back issues avail.) **Indexed:** Curr.Biotech.Abstr. **Document type:** newsletter.
—BLDSC (2089.867000); CASDDS; CISTI. **CCC.**
Description: Written for executives in the biotechnology industry. Covers company news, regulatory changes, financial trends, technical developments, market analyses and patents.

660   US
BIOTECHNOLOGY NEWS' BIOINDUSTRY DIRECTORY. a. C T B International Publishing Inc., Box 218, Maplewood, NJ 07040-0218. TEL 201-379-7749. FAX 201-379-1158. **Document type:** directory.

660   US   ISSN 8756-7938
TP248.13   CODEN: BIPRET
BIOTECHNOLOGY PROGRESS. 1985. bi-m. $445 (Canada & Mexico $453; Europe $463; elsewhere $470). American Institute of Chemical Engineers, 345 E. 47th St., New York, DC 20036. TEL 212-705-8100; 800-242-4363. FAX 212-705-8400. (Subscr. to: American Chemical Society, Subscription Services, Box 3337, Columbus, OH 43210) Ed. Jerome S. Schultz. adv.; bibl.; charts; index. circ. 2,800. (also avail. in microform from UMI; back issues avail.; reprint service avail. from UMI) **Indexed:** A.S.& T.Ind., ASCA, Biol.Abstr., Chem.Abstr., Chem.Cit.Ind., Curr.Adv.Ecol.Sci., Curr.Biotech.Abstr., Curr.Cont., Eng.Ind., Food Sci.& Tech.Abstr., Ind.Sci.Rev., Sel.Water Res.Abstr., Telegen. **Document type:** trade publication.
—BLDSC (2089.868330); CASDDS; CISTI; Ei; EMDOCS; Genuine Article; KR SourceOne; Linda Hall; SWETS; UMI; UnCover. **CCC.**
Description: Reports developments and research results impacting the food, pharmaceutical and bioengineering fields.
Refereed Serial

660 US ISSN 1088-4270
TP248.25.A96 CODEN: BSIJF7
BIOTECHNOLOGY SOFTWARE & INTERNET JOURNAL; the computer software journal for scientists. 1984. bi-m. $166 (foreign $194) (effective 1998). Mary Ann Liebert, Inc. Publishers, 2 Madison Ave., Larchmont, NY 10538. TEL 914-834-3100. FAX 914-834-3688. E-mail: liebert@pipeline.com. Ed. Kevin Ahern. adv.; bk.rev. (back issues avail.) **Indexed**: Telegen. **Document type**: academic/scholarly publication.
—BLDSC (2089.868552); CASDDS; CISTI; Genuine Article; SWETS.
 Former titles (until 1996): Biotechnology Software Journal (ISSN 1077-4890); (until 1994): Biotechnology Software (ISSN 0749-0372)
 Description: Contains news and reviews of all areas of scientific computing, including software, hardware and network products. Expanded coverage to include rapidly expanding base of Internet applications available to researchers.

660 UK ISSN 0951-208X
CODEN: BTECE6
BIOTECHNOLOGY TECHNIQUES. 1987. m. £64($128) to individuals; institutions £216 (N. America £432) (effective 1995). Chapman & Hall, Journals Department (Subsidiary of: International Thomson Publishing Group), 2-6 Boundary Row, London SE1 8HN, England. TEL 44-171-8560066. FAX 44-171-5229323. E-mail: jhelp@chall.co.uk; URL: http://www.chaphall.com/chaphall/journals.html. (Subscr. to: International Thomson Publishing Services Ltd., Cheriton House, North Way, Andover, Hants. SP10 5BE, England. TEL 44-1264-342713. FAX 44-1264-342807; Subscr. in US & Canada to: 400 Market St., Philadelphia, PA 19106. TEL 800-552-5866) Ed. Colin Ratledge. index. circ. 500. (also avail. in microfilm; back issues avail.; reprint service avail.) **Indexed**: ASCA, Biodet.Abstr., Biotech.Abstr., Chem.Abstr., Chem.Cit.Ind., Curr.Adv.Biochem., Curr.Adv.Cell & Devel.Biol., Curr.Biotech.Abstr., Curr.Cont., Dairy Sci.Abstr., Environ.Abstr., Excerp.Med., Food Sci.& Tech.Abstr., Ind.Sci.Rev., Mat.Sci.Cit.Ind., Rev.Med.& Vet.Mycol., Sci.Cit.Ind., Sel.Water Res.Abstr., Sugar Ind.Abstr., Telegen. **Document type**: academic/scholarly publication.
—BLDSC (2089.868600); CASDDS; CISTI; EMDOCS; Genuine Article; Linda Hall; SWETS; UMI; UnCover. **CCC**.
 Description: Provides rapid publication and permanent record for new techniques in biotechnology.
 Refereed Serial

660 UK
BIOTECHNOLOGY TODAY; Web's daily biotechnology news. d. Society of Chemical Industry, 14 Belgrave Sq., London SW1X 8PS, England. TEL 44-171-235-3681. FAX 44-171-235-9410. E-mail: webmaster@chemind.co.uk; URL: http://biotech.mond.org.
●Available only online.
 Description: Covers the latest news in biotechnology, as well as science job opportunities.

660 610.28 RU ISSN 0234-2758
CODEN: BTKNEZ
BIOTEKHNOLOGIYA. English translation: Russian Biotechnology (US ISSN 1068-3682) (Text in Russian) 1985. m. $186 (effective 1998). (State Scientific Research Institute for Genetics and Selection of Industrial Microorganisms) G N I I Genetika, Dorozhnyi 1-i pr., 1, 113545 Moscow, Russia. TEL 7-095-3150801. FAX 7-095-3150501. E-mail: boss@vnigen.msk.su. (Dist. by: Mezhnunarodnaya Kniga, B. Yakimanka 39, 117049 Moscow, Russia. TEL 7-095-2384967. FAX 7-095-2384634) adv.: page 1500000 Rub. ($500); trim 220 x 160; adv. contact: Gordon Irina. cum.index: 1985-1995. circ. 600. (also avail. in diskette format; back issues avail.) **Document type**: academic/scholarly publication.
—BLDSC (0017.999000); CASDDS. **CCC**.
 Description: Presents papers and reviews on biotechnology and bioengineering.

610.28 574 NE ISSN 0921-299X
CODEN: BTHREW
BIOTHERAPY; an international journal on biological agents. (Text in English) 1988. q. fl.523 to institutions; $268.50 to institutions in U.S. (effective 1998). Kluwer Academic Publishers, Postbus 17, 3300 AA Dordrecht, Netherlands. TEL 31-78-6392392. FAX 31-78-6392254. TELEX 29245 KAPG NL. E-mail: services@wkap.nl; URL: http://www.wkap.nl. (Dist. by: Kluwer Academic Publishers Group, P.O. Box 322, 3300 AH Dordrecht, Netherlands. TEL 31-78-6392392. FAX 31-78-6546474; N. America dist. addr.: Box 358, Accord Sta., Hingham, MA 02018-0358. TEL 617-871-6600. FAX 617-871-6528) Ed. Huub Schellekens. (also avail. in microform from UMI; back issues avail.; reprint service avail. from SWZ) **Indexed**: ASCA, Biol.Abstr., Bull.Signal., Chem.Abstr., Curr.Cont., Excerp.Med., Ind.Med., Ind.Sci.Rev., Inpharma, Int.Abstr.Biol.Sci., Reac., Sci.Cit.Ind. **Document type**: academic/scholarly publication.
—BLDSC (2089.873800); CASDDS; CISTI; EMDOCS; Genuine Article; KNAW; SWETS; UMI; UnCover. **CCC**.
 Description: Publishes papers in all disciplines of biological research relating to the use of biological agents in the treatment of disease.
 Refereed Serial

616 JA ISSN 0914-2223
CODEN: BITPE9
BIOTHERAPY. (Text in Japanese; summaries in English) 1987. m. 2000 Yen per no. Cancer and Chemotherapy Publishers, Inc., Russhu Bldg., 2-2-3 Nihonbashi, Tokyo 103, Japan. TEL 81-3-3278-0052. FAX 81-3-3281-0435. Ed. Tetsuo Taguchi. adv.; bk.rev.; circ. 3,500 (paid). (also avail. in microfilm) **Indexed**: Biol.Abstr.
—BLDSC (2089.873900).
 Description: Covers immunology, molecular biology, cytology and gene therapy.
 Refereed Serial

660 614.7 JA ISSN 0289-0011
BIOTRONICS; environment control and environmental biology. (Text in English) 1972. a. free. (Ministry of Education) Kyushu University, Biotron Institute, Kyushu University 12, Fukuoka 812-81, Japan. TEL 81-92-651-7913. FAX 81-92-651-7913. Ed. Hiromi Eguchi. charts. circ. 1,000. **Indexed**: Agri.Eng.Abstr., Biol.Abstr., Curr.Adv.Ecol.Sci., Curr.Adv.Plant Sci., Hort.Abstr. **Document type**: academic/scholarly publication.
—CISTI; UnCover.
 Description: Contains original contributions, information on environment control and environmental biology for biological researchers, and news.

660 US ISSN 0892-1903
CODEN: BIVIEW
BIOVENTURE VIEW. 1986. m. $550 (outside US and Canada $699); newsstand price: $50. BioVenture Publishing, Inc., 2555 Flores St., Ste. 555, San Mateo, CA 94403-2342. TEL 415-574-7128. FAX 415-574-8319. E-mail: biogodess@aol.com. Ed. Cynthia Robbins-Roth; Pub. Patty Fox. R&P contact: Patty Fox. adv. contact: Bill Stanley. circ. 950 (paid). **Document type**: newsletter.
●Also available online. Vendor(s): CompuServe, Inc., Data-Star, Dow Jones News Retrieval, European Space Agency, Information Access Co., Knight-Ridder Information, Inc. (File no.636).
—BLDSC (2090.100000). **CCC**.
 Description: Offers analysis of the companies, products, and events that drive the multibillion-dollar biotechnology industry.

660 610.28 CR ISSN 0255-7924
BOLETIN DE BIOTECNOLOGIA. 1984. q. free. Consejo Nacional para Investigaciones Cientificas y Tecnologicas, Departamento de Informacion y Documentacion, Apdo. 10318, San Jose, Costa Rica. Ed.Bd. bk.rev. circ. 1,500.

C A S BIOTECH UPDATES. BIOCHEMICAL IMMOBILIZATION & BIOCATALYTIC REACTORS. see *CHEMISTRY — Abstracting, Bibliographies, Statistics*

C A S BIOTECH UPDATES. BIOSENSORS. see *BIOLOGY — Abstracting, Bibliographies, Statistics*

C A S BIOTECH UPDATES. ENVIRONMENTAL BIOTECHNOLOGY. see *ENVIRONMENTAL STUDIES — Abstracting, Bibliographies, Statistics*

C A S BIOTECH UPDATES. ENZYMES IN BIOTECHNOLOGY. see *BIOLOGY — Abstracting, Bibliographies, Statistics*

660 UK ISSN 0957-0330
CODEN: CSBIED
CAMBRIDGE STUDIES IN BIOTECHNOLOGY. 1985. irreg. Cambridge University Press, Edinburgh Bldg., Shaftesbury Rd., Cambridge CB2 2RU, England. TEL 44-1223-312393. FAX 44-1223-315052. TELEX 817256. E-mail: information@cup.cam.ac.uk; URL: http://www.cup.cam.ac.uk. (N. American addr.: Cambridge University Press, 40 W. 20th St., New York, NY 10011. TEL 212-924-3900. FAX 212-691-3239) R&P contact: Linda Nicol. **Indexed**: Food Sci.& Tech.Abstr. **Document type**: monographic series.
—BLDSC (3015.992500); CISTI.

660.6 CN ISSN 1188-455X
CANADIAN BIOTECH NEWS. 1988. 52/yr. Can.$500($425) Canadian Biotechnology News Service, 20 Stonepark Lane, Nepean, ON K2H 9P4, Canada. TEL 613-726-0115. FAX 613-726-7344. Ed. Peter Winter. adv.; bk.rev. circ. 3,000. (also avail. in microfiche from MML; back issues avail.) **Indexed**: Can.B.P.I. **Document type**: newsletter.
—CISTI.
 Formerly (until vol.4, no.10): New Biotech Business (ISSN 0838-5777)
 Description: Covers economics and finance in biotechnology. Includes information on company developments, patents and technology transfer.

660.6 CN
▼**CANADIAN BIOTECH RESEARCH**. 1996. m. Can.$120($180) (effective Jun. 1996). Canadian Biotechnology News Service, 20 Stone Park Lane, Nepean, ON K2H 9P4, Canada. TEL 613-726-0115. FAX 613-726-7344. E-mail: pwinter@hookup.net. Ed. Peter Winter. circ. 3,000 (controlled). **Document type**: trade publication.
 Description: Provides articles and news on the application of biotech research to various sections. Principle focus is the health care, but applications of biotechnology to agriculture and the environment are also covered.

CELL TRANSPLANTATION. see *BIOLOGY — Cytology And Histology*

CELLULAR ENGINEERING. see *BIOLOGY — Bioengineering*

CENTRE FOR PLANT BREEDING AND REPRODUCTION RESEARCH. ANNUAL REPORT. see *AGRICULTURE — Crop Production And Soil*

CEREVISIA; Belgian journal of Brewing and Biotechnology. see *BEVERAGES*

660 574.192 547 US ISSN 1074-5521
QP501 CODEN: CBOLE2
CHEMISTRY & BIOLOGY. 1994. m. $190 to individuals (outside N. America £120); institutions $695 (outside N. America £450) (effective 1997). Current Biology Ltd., 400 Market St., Ste. 700, Philadelphia, PA 19106. TEL 800-552-5866. FAX 215-574-2270. E-mail: info@hugo.curbio.com; biomednet@cursci.co.uk; URL: http://BioMedNet.com/cgi-bin/members/titles.pl. (Dist. by: Turpin Distribution Services Ltd., Blackhorse Rd., Letchworth, Herts. SG6 1HN, England. TEL 44-1462-672555. FAX 44-1462-480947; Addr. in UK: Current Biology Ltd., 34-42 Cleveland St., London W1P 6LB, England) Eds. S.L. Schreiber, K.C. Nicolaou. adv.: B&W page $600, color page $1510; trim 8 1/2 x 11. illus. circ. 4,700. **Indexed**: ASCA, Curr.Cont., Ind.Sci.Rev. **Document type**: academic/scholarly publication.
●Also available online.
Also available on CD-ROM.
—BLDSC (3168.890000); ADONIS; CASDDS; CISTI; EMDOCS; Genuine Article; SWETS. **CCC**.
 Description: Directed toward researchers, educators and students of signaling, molecular recognition and structure-based design. Features original research and reviews.
 Refereed Serial

BIOLOGY — BIOTECHNOLOGY

660 US ISSN 1042-749X
TP248.13
CHINESE JOURNAL OF BIOTECHNOLOGY. Selective English translation of: Shengwu Gongcheng Xuebao (CC ISSN 1000-3061) 1989. q. $555 (effective 1998). Allerton Press, Inc., 150 Fifth Ave., New York, NY 10011. TEL 212-924-3950. FAX 212-463-9684. Ed. Jiao Ruishen. **Indexed:** Food Sci.& Tech.Abstr. **Document type:** academic/scholarly publication.
—CISTI. **CCC.**
Description: Covers cell biology, monoclonal antibodies, genetic engineering, cloning and gene expression, biosynthesis, etc.
Refereed Serial

CLINICAL ASPECTS OF BIOMEDICINE. see *MEDICAL SCIENCES*

COMPUTING IN BIOMEDICINE. see *MEDICAL SCIENCES — Computer Applications*

660 US
CONFERENCE ON COMMERCIAL BIOTECHNOLOGY (YEAR). a. $175. Business Communications Co., Inc. (Norwalk), 25 Van Zant St., Ste. 13, Norwalk, CT 06855. TEL 203-853-4266. FAX 203-853-0348. TELEX 6502934929 WUI.

660 US
TP248.13 CODEN: CRBTE5
CRITICAL REVIEWS IN BIOTECHNOLOGY. 1983. q. $375 (effective 1998). C R C Press, Inc., 2000 Corporate Blvd., N.W., Boca Raton, FL 33431. TEL 561-994-0555; 800-272-7737. FAX 561-998-9784. TELEX 568689-CRC PRESS. Eds. Graham G. Stewart, Inge Russell. **Indexed:** ASCA, Curr.Adv.Ecol.Sci., Curr.Biotech.Abstr., Curr.Cont., Food Sci.& Tech.Abstr., Helminthol.Abstr., Ind.Sci.Rev., Sci.Cit.Ind., Sport Fish.Abstr., Wild.Rev. **Document type:** academic/scholarly publication.
—BLDSC (3487.472400); ADONIS; CASDDS; CISTI; Genuine Article; Linda Hall; SWETS; UnCover. **CCC.**
Formerly: C R C Critical Reviews in Biotechnology (ISSN 0738-8551)
Description: Presents state-of-the-art review articles covering the spectrum of technologies involving the use of living organisms and biological processes in a wide range of industrial, agricultural, and medical applications.
Refereed Serial

CURRENT ADVANCES IN APPLIED MICROBIOLOGY & BIOTECHNOLOGY. see *BIOLOGY — Abstracting, Bibliographies, Statistics*

CURRENT BIOTECHNOLOGY. see *BIOLOGY — Abstracting, Bibliographies, Statistics*

CURRENT OPINION IN BIOTECHNOLOGY. see *BIOLOGY — Abstracting, Bibliographies, Statistics*

581.2 NE ISSN 0924-1949
CODEN: CPBAE2
CURRENT PLANT SCIENCE AND BIOTECHNOLOGY IN AGRICULTURE. 1985. irreg., vol.18, 1993. price varies. Kluwer Academic Publishers, Postbus 17, 3300 AA Dordrecht, Netherlands. TEL 31-78-6392392. FAX 31-78-6392254. TELEX 29245 KAPG NL. E-mail: services@wkap.nl; URL: http://www.wkap.nl. (Dist. by: Kluwer Academic Publishers Group, P.O. Box 322, 3300 AH Dordrecht, Netherlands. TEL 31-78-6392392. FAX 31-78-6546474; N. America dist. addr.: Box 358, Accord Sta., Hingham, MA 02018-0358. TEL 617-871-6600. FAX 617-871-6528) (back issues avail.) **Document type:** monographic series, proceedings.
—BLDSC (3501.284300); CASDDS; CISTI.
Description: Scholarly monographs and conference papers reporting state of the art research findings and techniques in plant science and biotechnology, with particular emphasis on agricultural applications.
Refereed Serial

CYTOTECHNOLOGY; international journal of cell culture and biotechnology. see *BIOLOGY — Cytology And Histology*

DEVELOPMENTS IN BIOLOGICAL STANDARDIZATION. see *METROLOGY AND STANDARDIZATION*

610.285 660 NE
DEVELOPMENTS IN BIOTHERAPY. 1991. irreg. price varies. Kluwer Academic Publishers, Postbus 17, 3300 AA Dordrecht, Netherlands. TEL 31-78-6392392. FAX 31-78-6392254. E-mail: services@wkap.nl; URL: http://www.wkap.nl. (Dist. by: Kluwer Academic Publishers Group, P.O. Box 322, 3300 AH Dordrecht, Netherlands. TEL 31-78-6392392. FAX 31-78-6546474; N. America dist. addr.: Box 358, Accord Sta., Hingham, MA 02018-0358. TEL 617-871-6600. FAX 617-871-6528) **Document type:** monographic series.

660 170 FR
▼**DICTIONNAIRE PERMANENT: BIOETHIQUE ET BIOTECHNOLOGIES.** 1995. base vol. (plus m. updates). 1860 F. for base vol. (updates 400 F.). Editions Legislatives et Administratives, 80 ave. de la Marne, 92546 Montrouge Cedex, France. TEL 40-92-68-68. FAX 46-56-00-15. TELEX 632 855 F. Ed. Daniel Vigneau. (looseleaf format)
Description: Covers legal and business issues in bioethics and biotechnology.

DIRECTORY OF BRITISH BIOTECHNOLOGY. see *BUSINESS AND ECONOMICS — Trade And Industrial Directories*

DRUG DISCOVERY TODAY. see *PHARMACY AND PHARMACOLOGY*

ECOLOGICAL ENGINEERING; the journal of ecotechnology. see *ENVIRONMENTAL STUDIES*

660 US
ELECTRONICS AND BIOTECHNOLOGY ADVANCED. FORUM SERIES. irreg., latest vol.4. (Electronics and Biotechnology Advanced) Plenum Publishing Corp., 233 Spring St., New York, NY 10013. TEL 212-620-8000. FAX 212-463-0742.

591 636.089 US
EMBRYO TRANSFER NEWSLETTER. 1978. q. $70 membership (effective 1997). International Embryo Transfer Society, 1111 N. Dunlap Ave., Savoy, IL 61874. TEL 217-356-3182. FAX 217-398-4119. Ed.Bd. R&P contact: Vicki R. Smith. adv. contact: Vicki R. Smith. bk.rev.; abstr.; circ. 750 (paid). **Document type:** newsletter.
Description: Features articles and announcements related to embryo transfer.

660 US ISSN 0141-0229
TP248.E5 CODEN: EMTED2
ENZYME AND MICROBIAL TECHNOLOGY; biotechnology research and reviews. 1979. 16/yr. fl.2279($1310) (effective 1998). Elsevier Science Inc., Box 945, New York, NY 10159-0945. TEL 212-633-3730. FAX 212-633-3680. E-mail: usinfo-f@elsevier.com; URL: http://www.elsevier.nl/. (Subscr. outside the Americas to: Elsevier Science, Regional Sales Office, P.O. Box 211, 1000 AE Amsterdam, Netherlands. TEL 31-20-4853757. FAX 31-20-4853432; Subscr. in Australasia and the Far East to: Elsevier Science (Singapore) Pte Ltd, No.1 Temasek Ave., No.17-01 Millenia Tower, Singapore 039192, Singapore. TEL 65-434-3727. FAX 65-337-2230; Subscr. in Japan to: Elsevier Science Japan, 9-15 Higashi-Azabu 1-chome, Minato-ku, Tokyo 106, Japan. TEL 81-3-5561-5033. FAX 81-3-5561-5047) Eds. Sheldon W. May, Raymond E. Spier. adv.; bk.rev.; illus.; index. (also avail. in microform from UMI; back issues avail.) **Indexed:** Anal.Abstr., ASCA, Biodet.Abstr., Biol.Abstr., Biotech.Abstr., Chem.Abstr., Chem.Cit.Ind., Cott.& Trop.Fibr.Abstr., Curr.Adv.Biochem., Curr.Adv.Ecol.Sci., Curr.Biotech.Abstr., Curr.Cont., Dairy Sci.Abstr., Eng.Ind., Excerpt.Med., Food Sci.& Tech.Abstr., Ind.Sci.Rev., Mat.Sci.Cit.Ind., Paper & Bd.Abstr., Risk Abstr., Sci.Cit.Ind., Sugar Ind.Abstr., Telegen, Triticale Abstr. **Document type:** academic/scholarly publication.
—BLDSC (3791.933000); ADONIS; CASDDS; CISTI; Ei; Genuine Article; Linda Hall; SWETS; UMI; UnCover. **CCC.**
Description: Encompasses basic and applied aspects of the use of enzymes, microbes and cells of mammalian or plant origin. Also covers economic and legal issues bearing on the 'new' biotechnology.
Refereed Serial

660 FR ISSN 0765-2046
CODEN: EBNWEI
EUROPEAN BIOTECHNOLOGY NEWSLETTER. (Text in English) 1986. 22/yr. 3428 F. to institutions (US $655; elsewhere 3500 F.) (effective 1998). Editions Scientifiques et Medicales Elsevier, 141 rue de Javel, 75747 Paris, France. TEL 33-1-45589049. FAX 33-1-45589421. URL: http://www.elsevier.nl/. (Subscr. in U.S. and Canada to: Elsevier Science Inc., Box 945, Madison Sq. Sta., New York, NY 10159-0945. TEL 212-633-3730. FAX 212-633-3680) Ed. O. Revelant. (also avail. in microform from UMI) **Document type:** academic/scholarly publication, newsletter.
—BLDSC (3829.489450); CASDDS; CISTI; SWETS. **CCC.**
Description: Publishes full-length articles and short communications on various aspects of biotechnology.

EUROPEAN MATERIALS RESEARCH SOCIETY. MONOGRAPHS. see *ENGINEERING — Engineering Mechanics And Materials*

EUROPEAN MATERIALS RESEARCH SOCIETY. SYMPOSIA PROCEEDINGS. see *ENGINEERING — Engineering Mechanics And Materials*

660 576 JA ISSN 1431-0651
▼**EXTREMOPHILES;** life under extreme conditions. Online edition (JA ISSN 1433-4909) 1997. q. DM.380 (effective 1998). Springer-Verlag Tokyo, 3-13, Hongo 3-chome, Bunkyo-ku, Tokyo 113, Japan. TEL 81-3-38120331. FAX 81-3-38120719. E-mail: svt-ebs@ppp.bekkoame.or.jp. (Dist. outside Japan by: Springer-Verlag, Heidelberger Platz 3, 14197 Berlin, Germany. TEL 49-30-82787-0. FAX 49-30-82787448; Subscr. in N. America to: Springer-Verlag New York, Inc., 333 Meadowlands Pkwy., Secaucus, NJ 07094. TEL 212-460-1500. FAX 212-473-6272) Ed. K. Horikoshi. adv.: B&W page 70000 Yen. **Document type:** academic/scholarly publication.
●Also available online.
—BLDSC (3854.505650). **CCC.**
Description: International journal for both basic and applied research on microorganisms living under extreme conditions.
Refereed Serial

F E M S. IMMUNOLOGY AND MEDICAL MICROBIOLOGY. (Federation of European Microbiological Societies) see *BIOLOGY — Microbiology*

F E M S. MICROBIOLOGY; international journal providing for the rapid publication of reports on microbiological research. (Federation of European Microbiological Societies) see *BIOLOGY — Microbiology*

F E M S. MICROBIOLOGY ECOLOGY. (Federation of European Microbiological Societies) see *BIOLOGY — Microbiology*

F E M S. MICROBIOLOGY LETTERS; an international journal providing for the rapid publication of short reports on microbiological research. (Federation of European Microbiological Societies) see *BIOLOGY — Microbiology*

F E M S. MICROBIOLOGY REVIEWS. (Federation of European Microbiological Societies) see *BIOLOGY — Microbiology*

660 608.7 US
FEDERAL BIO-TECHNOLOGY TRANSFER DIRECTORY. 1994. a. Biotechnology Information Institute, 1700 Rockville Pike, Ste. 400, Rockville, MD 20852. TEL 301-424-0255. FAX 301-424-0257. Ed. Ronald A. Rader. R&P contact: Ronald A. Rader. **Document type:** directory.
Description: Catalogs all federal government inventions and technology transfer in the biomedical and basic biotechnology fields from 1980 to present.

660　　　　　　　FR　　ISSN 0985-2662
FLASH ETATS-UNIS. 1984. 11/yr. 2000 F.($399) 1890F. in France; 2042F. to institutions in Europe (effective 1997). Editions Scientifiques et Medicales Elsevier, 141 rue de Javel, 75747 Paris, France. TEL 33-1-45589049. (Subscr. in U.S. and Canada to: Elsevier Science Inc., Box 945, Madison Sq. Sta., New York, NY 10159-0945. TEL 212-633-3730. FAX 212-633-3680) (also avail. in microform from UMI; back issues avail.) **Document type:** newsletter.
—CCC.
Description: Scientific, technological and economic information about biotechnology in the U.S.

660.6　　　　　　FR　　ISSN 0985-2654
FLASH JAPON. 1984. 11/yr. 2000 F.($399) 1890F. in France; 2042F. to institutions in Europe (effective 1997). Editions Scientifiques et Medicales Elsevier, 141 rue de Javel, 75747 Paris, France. TEL 33-1-45589049. FAX 33-1-45589421. URL: http://www.elsevier.nl/. (Subscr. in U.S. and Canada to: Elsevier Science Inc., Box 945, Madison Sq. Sta., New York, NY 10159-0945. TEL 212-633-3730. FAX 212-633-3680) (also avail. in microform from UMI) **Document type:** newsletter.
—CCC.
Description: Scientific, economic and technological information about biotechnology in Japan.

660 664　　　　　UK　　ISSN 0960-3085
TP368　　　　　　　　　　　CODEN: FBPREO
FOOD AND BIOPRODUCTS PROCESSING; transactions: part c. 1991. q. £191 (foreign $315) (effective 1998). Institution of Chemical Engineers, George E. Davis Bldg., 165-189 Railway Terr., Rugby, Warks. CV21 3HQ, England. TEL 44-1788-78214. FAX 44-1788-578214. URL http://www.icheme.org/. **Indexed:** ASCA, Br.Tech.Ind., Compumath, Food Sci.& Tech.Abstr. **Document type:** academic/scholarly publication.
●Also available online.
—BLDSC (3977.026870); CASDDS; CISTI; Ei; Genuine Article; SWETS; UnCover. CCC.
Description: Presents papers on processing aspects of food - drink and biochemical engineering.
Refereed Serial

660 664　　　　　US　　ISSN 0890-5436
TP248.65.F66　　　　　　　CODEN: FBIOEE
FOOD BIOTECHNOLOGY. 1987. 3/yr. $595 (foreign $606.25) (effective 1998). Marcel Dekker Journals, 270 Madison Ave., New York, NY 10016. TEL 212-969-9000. FAX 212-685-4540. TELEX 421419. (Subscr. to: Box 5017, Monticello, NY 12701) Ed. Dietrich Knorr. R&P contact: Julia Mulligan. adv. contact: Lourdes Barroso. (microfiche) **Indexed:** ASCA, Curr.Biotech.Abstr., Curr.Cont., Dairy Sci.Abstr., Environ.Abstr., Food Sci.& Tech.Abstr. **Document type:** academic/scholarly publication.
—BLDSC (3977.071000); CASDDS; CISTI; Ei; Genuine Article; Linda Hall; SWETS. CCC.
Refereed Serial

660 547　　　　　FI　　ISSN 0780-6655
　　　　　　　　　　　　　　CODEN: FBIREN
FOUNDATION FOR BIOTECHNICAL AND INDUSTRIAL FERMENTATION RESEARCH. (Text in various languages) 1983. a. Foundation for Biotechnical and Industrial Fermentation Research, P.O. Box 350, FIN-00101 Helsinki, Finland. (Dist. by: Akateeminen Kirjakauppa, Keskuskatu, FIN-00101 Helsinki, Finland) Eds. Matti Korhola, Viveka Backstroem. **Document type:** proceedings.
—BLDSC (4024.890000); CASDDS; CISTI.

577.1　　　　　　GW　　ISSN 0930-4320
　　　　　　　　　　　　　　CODEN: GBMOEB
G B F - MONOGRAPHIEN. 1987. irreg. (Gesellschaft fuer Biotechnologische Forschung) V C H Verlagsgesellschaft mbH, Postfach 101161, 69451 Weinheim, Germany. TEL 06201-606-147. FAX 06201-606117. TELEX 465516 VCHVW-D. (U.S. addr.: V C H Publishers Inc., 220 E. 23rd St., New York, NY 10010-4066. TEL 212-683-8333) **Indexed:** Chem.Abstr. (1987-), I.M.M.Abstr. **Document type:** monographic series.
—BLDSC (4095.326000); CASDDS; CISTI; KNAW. CCC.
Supersedes (1975-1984): Schriftenreihe der G B F (ISSN 0930-4312)

G E N GUIDES TO BIOTECHNOLOGY COMPANIES. (Genetic Engineering News) see *BUSINESS AND ECONOMICS — Trade And Industrial Directories*

GENE; an international journal focusing on gene cloning and gene structure and function. see *BIOLOGY — Genetics*

GENES TO CELLS. see *BIOLOGY — Microbiology*

660 575　　　　　NE
QH426　　　　　　　　　　CODEN: GANTDN
GENETIC ANALYSIS, BIOMOLECULAR ENGINEERING. 1984. bi-m. fl.704($404) (effective 1998). Elsevier Science B.V., P.O. Box 211, 1000 AE Amsterdam, Netherlands. TEL 31-20-4853911.
FAX 31-20-4853598. TELEX 18582 ESP NL. E-mail: nlinfo-f@elsevier.nl; usinfo-f@elsevier.com; forinfo-kyf04035@niftyserve.or.jp; URL: http://www.elsevier.nl/. (Subscr. in the Americas to: Elsevier Science, Regional Sales Office, Box 945, New York, NY 10159-0945; Subscr. in Australasia and the Far East to: Elsevier Science (Singapore) Pte Ltd, No.1 Temasek Ave., No.17-01 Millenia Tower, Singapore 039192, Singapore; Subscr. in Japan to: Elsevier Science Japan, 9-15 Higashi-Azabu 1-chome, Minato-ku, Tokyo 106, Japan. TEL 212-989-5800. FAX 212-633-3990) Ed.Bd. abstr.; bibl. (also avail. in microform from UMI; reprint service avail. from SWZ) **Indexed:** ASCA, Biol.Abstr., Curr.Adv.Ecol.Sci., Curr.Cont., Excerpt.Med., Ind.Med., Sci.Cit.Ind., Telegen. **Document type:** academic/scholarly publication.
—BLDSC (4111.843800); CASDDS; CISTI; EMDOCS; Genuine Article; KNAW; SWETS; UnCover. CCC.
Former titles (until vol.12): Genetic Analysis Techniques and Applications (ISSN 1050-3862); (until 1989): Genetic Analysis Techniques (ISSN 0735-0651)
Description: Publishes papers on new methods, materials and instruments for biomolecular engineering, molecular biology, cell biology, biochemistry, and genetics.
Refereed Serial

THE GENETIC ENGINEER AND BIOTECHNOLOGIST. see *BIOLOGY — Bioengineering*

GENETIC ENGINEERING. see *BIOLOGY — Genetics*

GENETIC ENGINEERING AND BIOTECHNOLOGY: MONITOR. see *BIOLOGY — Genetics*

GENETIC ENGINEERING AND BIOTECHNOLOGY YEARBOOK. see *BIOLOGY — Genetics*

GENETIC ENGINEERING NEWS; the information source of the biotechnology industry. see *BIOLOGY — Genetics*

GENOME RESEARCH. see *BIOLOGY — Microbiology*

HANGUK NONGHWAHAKHOECHI/AGRICULTURAL CHEMISTRY AND BIOTECHNOLOGY. see *AGRICULTURE — Crop Production And Soil*

660　　　　　　JA　　ISSN 0915-3411
HYOGO BAIOTEKUNOROJI KONWAKAI KAIHO/HYOGO BIOTECHNOLOGY ASSOCIATION. ANNUAL REPORT. (Text in Japanese) 1987. a. 3500 Yen. Hyogo Baiotekunoroji Konwakai - Hyogo Biotechnology Association, Hyogo Kenritsu Sangyo Kaikan, 28-33 Nakayamate Dori 7-chome, Chuo-ku, Kobe-shi, Hyogo-ken 650, Japan.

IMMUNOTECHNOLOGY; an international journal of immunological engineering. see *MEDICAL SCIENCES — Allergology And Immunology*

INDIAN LITERATURE IN ENVIRONMENTAL ENGINEERING; a bibliographic review. see *ENVIRONMENTAL STUDIES — Abstracting, Bibliographies, Statistics*

660　　　　　　UK　　ISSN 0964-8305
QP517.B5　　　　　　　　　CODEN: IBBIES
INTERNATIONAL BIODETERIORATION & BIODEGRADATION. 1965. 8/yr. fl.1482($852) (effective 1998). (Biodeterioration Society) Elsevier Science Ltd., P.O. Box 800, Kidlington, Oxford OX5 1DX, England. TEL 44-1865-843000.
FAX 44-1865-843010. E-mail: nlinfo-f@elsevier.nl; usinfo-f@elsevier.com; forinfo-kyf04035@niftyserve.or.jp; URL: http://www.elsevier.nl/. (Subscr. to: Elsevier Science, Regional Sales Office, P.O. Box 211, 1000 AE Amsterdam, Netherlands. TEL 31-20-4853757. FAX 31-20-4853432; Subscr. in the Americas to: Elsevier Science, Regional Sales Office, Box 945, New York, NY 10159-0945. TEL 212-633-3730. FAX 212-633-3680; Subscr. in Australasia and the Far East to: Elsevier Science (Singapore) Pte Ltd, No.1 Temasek Ave., No.17-01 Millenia Tower, Singapore 039192, Singapore. TEL 65-434-3727. FAX 65-337-2230) (Co-sponsor: Pan-American Biodeterioration Society) Ed.Bd. adv.; bk.rev.; bibl.; charts; illus.; index; circ. controlled. (back issues avail.) **Indexed:**
Abstr.Bull.Inst.Pap.Chem., Alloys Ind., ASCA, Biol.Abstr., Br.Ceram.Abstr., Cadscan, Chem.Abstr., Corros.Abstr., Curr.Adv.Biochem., Curr.Adv.Ecol.Sci., Curr.Cont., Deep Sea Res.& Oceanogr.Abstr., Ecol.Abstr., Eng.Mat.Abstr., Environ.Abstr., Environ.Per.Bibl. (1990-), Excerpt.Med., Food Sci.& Tech.Abstr., Forest.Abstr., Forest Prod.Abstr., Ind.Vet., Lead Abstr., Met.Abstr., Met.Abstr.Ind., Nonfer.Met.Alert, Nutr.Abstr., PCC Alert, Poult.Abstr., Ref.Zh., Rev.Appl.Entomol., Rev.Med.& Vet.Mycol., Rev.Plant Path., Sci.Cit.Ind., Soils & Fert., Steels Alert, Vet.Bull., World Alum.Abstr., World Surf.Coat., World Text.Abstr., Zincscan. **Document type:** academic/scholarly publication.
●Also available online. Vendor(s): CISTI, DIMDI, European Space Agency (File nos.16 & 124/CAB), Knight-Ridder Information, Inc., Ovid Technologies, Inc.
—BLDSC (4537.147000); CASDDS; CISTI; Ei; EMDOCS; Genuine Article; KR SourceOne; Linda Hall; SWETS; UnCover. CCC.
Formerly (until 1992): International Biodeterioration (ISSN 0265-3036); Which was formed by the merger of (1965-1983): International Biodeterioration Bulletin (ISSN 0020-6164); (1974-1983): Waste Materials Biodegradation Research Titles (ISSN 0305-0262); (1972-1983): Biodeterioration Research Titles; Which was formerly (1967-1971): I B B R I S. International Biodeterioration Bulletin Reference Index Supplement (ISSN 0018-8573)
Description: Presents original research papers and reviews on the biological causes of deterioration or advantageous biological upgrading of all types of materials.
Refereed Serial

620.1　　　　　　UK
QH530.5.I56
INTERNATIONAL BIODETERIORATION SYMPOSIUM. PROCEEDINGS. Running title: Biodeterioration and Biodegradation. biennial, 8th 1990, Windsor, Canada. £135. Elsevier Science Ltd., Books Division, P.O. Box 800, Kidlington, Oxford OX5 1DX, England. TEL 44-1865-843000. FAX 44-1865-843010.
E-mail: nlinfo-f@elsevier.nl; usinfo-f@elsevier.com; forinfo-kyf04035@niftyserve.or.jp; URL: http://www.elsevier.nl/. (Subscr. to: Elsevier Science, Regional Sales Office, P.O. Box 211, 1000 AE Amsterdam, Netherlands. TEL 31-20-4853757. FAX 31-20-4853432; Subscr. in the Americas to: Elsevier Science, Regional Sales Office, Box 945, New York, NY 10159-0945. TEL 212-633-3730. FAX 212-633-3680; Subscr. in Australasia and the Far East to: Elsevier Science (Singapore) Pte Ltd, No.1 Temasek Ave., No.17-01 Millenia Tower, Singapore 039192, Singapore. TEL 65-434-3727. FAX 65-337-2230) Ed. H.W. Rossmore. bibl.; illus. **Document type:** proceedings.
Refereed Serial

BIOLOGY — BIOTECHNOLOGY

660 542   US   ISSN 0888-7225
TP248.13
INTERNATIONAL BIOTECHNOLOGY LABORATORY.
(Includes a. Buyers' Guide) 1983. 7/yr. $135 (foreign $165). International Scientific Communications, Inc., 30 Controls Dr., Box 870, Shelton, CT 06484-0870. TEL 203-926-9300. FAX 203-926-9310. TELEX 964292. (U.K. subscr. to: I.S.C. House, Progress Business Centre, 5 Whittle Pkwy., Slough, Berks. SL1 6DQ, England. TEL 44-1628-668881. FAX 44-1628-669199) Ed. Brian Howard. bk.rev.; charts; illus.; stat.; tr.lit.; circ. 37,000 (controlled). **Indexed:** Curr.Adv.Ecol.Sci., Curr.Biotech.Abstr., Mass Spectr.Bull. **Document type:** trade publication.
—BLDSC (4537.195100).

INTERNATIONAL JOURNAL OF ANIMAL SCIENCES. see *AGRICULTURE — Poultry And Livestock*

660   CN   ISSN 1206-7865
▼**INTERNATIONAL JOURNAL OF ENVIRONMENTAL & BIODIVERSITY AWARENESS.** (Text in Arabic, English) 1997. q. Can.$400. P.O. Box 98029, S. Common Post, 2150 Burnhamthorpe Rd., Mississagua, ON L5L 3A0, Canada. FAX 416-277-2875. (And: P.O. Box 38552, Abdulla Al-Salem, Kuwait City 72256, Kuwait. FAX 965-489-1179) Ed. M.I. Ismail.
Description: Designed for concise, cooperative publication of simple accelerated and creative ideas for awareness of environmental monitoring and control.
Refereed Serial

660 544 574.192   US
INTERNATIONAL LABORATORY BUYERS' GUIDE. 1972. a. International Scientific Communications, Inc., 30 Controls Dr., Shelton, CT 06484. TEL 203-926-9300. FAX 203-926-9310. (U.K. subscr. to: ISC House, Progress Business Centre, 5 Whittle Pky., Slough, Berks SL1 6DQ, UK. TEL 44-1628-668881. FAX 44-1625-669199) Ed. Brian Howard; Pub. William N. Wham. adv.: page $7605; trim 8 1/4 x 10 7/8. circ. 90,000. (also avail. in microfiche; back issues avail.) **Document type:** trade publication.
●Also available online.

660   CN
INTRON - CANADIAN MOLECULAR BIOLOGY. 1993. bi-m. Can.$60 (effective Sep. 1996). Canadian Biotechnology News Service, 340 Richmond Rd., Box 67039, Ottawa, ON K2A 0E8, Canada. TEL 613-726-0115. FAX 613-726-7344. Ed. Peter Winter. circ. 6,000 (controlled). **Document type:** trade publication.
Description: Examines the application of molecular biology to the life sciences.

ISOTOPES IN THE PHYSICAL AND BIOMEDICAL SCIENCES. see *CHEMISTRY*

ISRAEL AGRITECHNOLOGY FOCUS. see *AGRICULTURE*

660   JA
JAPAN BIOINDUSTRY LETTERS. 4/yr. Bioindustry Development Center, Dowa Bldg. 7F, 5-10-5 Shinbashi, Minato-ku, Tokyo 105, Japan. TEL 03-4333545. FAX 03-4591440.

660   NE   ISSN 1058-7330
JAPANESE TECHNOLOGY REVIEWS: BIOTECHNOLOGY (SECTION E). 1989. irreg. 60 ECU (effective 1993). Gordon and Breach - Harwood Academic, Amsteldisk 166, 1st Fl., 1079 LH Amsterdam, Netherlands. (Subscr. to: International Publishers Distributor, Box 32160, Newark, NJ 07102. TEL 800-545-8398. FAX 215-750-6343) Ed. Toshiaki Ikoma. (also avail. in microform) **Document type:** monographic series.
—BLDSC (4662.120455); CISTI. **CCC.**
Supersedes in part: Japanese Technology Review (ISSN 0898-5693)

660.284   NE   ISSN 0920-5063
R857.P6   CODEN: JBSEEA
JOURNAL OF BIOMATERIALS SCIENCE. POLYMER EDITION. (Text in English) 1989. m. DM.1100 (effective 1997). V S P, P.O. Box 346, 3700 AH Zeist, Netherlands. TEL 31-30-6925790. FAX 31-30-6932081. E-mail: 100341.2372@compuserve.com. Ed.Bd. **Indexed:** Alloys Ind., ASCA, Chem.Cit.Ind., Curr.Cont., Eng.Mat.Abstr., Excerp.Med. (1996-), Ind.Sci.Rev., Intl.Polym.Sci.& Tech., Mat.Sci.Cit.Ind., Met.Abstr., Met.Abstr.Ind., Nonfer.Met.Alert, PCC Alert, RAPRA, Sci.Cit.Ind., SSCI, Steels Alert, World Alum.Abstr. **Document type:** academic/scholarly publication.
—BLDSC (4953.517000); CASDDS; CISTI; EMDOCS; Linda Hall; SWETS; UnCover.
Description: Explores research on the mechanisms of interactions between biomaterials and living organisms, focusing at the molecular and cellular levels.
Refereed Serial

660 610   US   ISSN 0021-9304
R856   CODEN: JBMRBG
JOURNAL OF BIOMEDICAL MATERIALS RESEARCH. (Includes q. section: Applied Biomaterials) 1966. 20/yr. $2995 (foreign $3345) (effective 1998). (Society for Biomaterials) John Wiley & Sons, Inc., Journals, 605 Third Ave., New York, NY 10158. TEL 212-850-6645. FAX 212-850-6021. TELEX 12-7063. E-mail: subinfo@jwiley.com; URL: http://www.wiley.com/0021-9304/. (Subscr. outside the Americas to: John Wiley & Sons Ltd., Baffins Ln., Chichester, W. Sussex PO19 1UD, England. TEL 44-1243-779777. FAX 44-1243-776128) (Co-sponsor: European Society for Biomaterials) Ed. James Anderson. adv.: B&W page £640, color page £1515; trimm 279 x 210. illus. circ. 2,500. (also avail. in microform from UMI; back issues avail.; reprint service avail. from UMI) **Indexed:** Alloys Ind., Appl.Mech.Rev., ASCA, Bioeng.Abstr., Biol.Abstr., Biol.& Agr.Ind., Chem.Abstr., Chem.Cit.Ind., Curr.Adv.Cell & Devel.Biol., Curr.Cont., Dent.Ind., Eng.Ind., Eng.Mat.Abstr., Eng.Mat.Abstr., Excerp.Med., Ind.Med., Ind.Sci.Rev., INIS Atomind., Intl.Polym.Sci.& Tech., Mat.Sci.Cit.Ind., Met.Abstr., Met.Abstr.Ind., Nonfer.Met.Alert, PCC Alert, RAPRA, Sci.Cit.Ind., Steels Alert, World Alum.Abstr. **Document type:** academic/scholarly publication.
—BLDSC (4953.700000); CASDDS; CISTI; Ei; Genuine Article; KNAW; SWETS; UMI; UnCover. **CCC.**
Incorporates (1990-1995): Journal of Applied Biomaterials (ISSN 1045-4861)
Description: Covers topics ranging from alloys, polymers and ceramics to surgery, dentistry and implanted devices.
Refereed Serial

660   NE   ISSN 0168-1656
CODEN: JBITD4
JOURNAL OF BIOTECHNOLOGY. (Text and summaries in English) 1984. 21/yr. fl.3948($2269) (effective 1998). Elsevier Science B.V., P.O. Box 211, 1000 AE Amsterdam, Netherlands. TEL 31-20-4853911. FAX 31-20-4853598. TELEX 18582 ESPA NL. E-mail: nlinfo-f@elsevier.nl; usinfo-f@elsevier.com; forinfo-kyf04035@niftyserve.or.jp; URL: http://www.elsevier.nl/. (Subscr. in the Americas to: Elsevier Science, Regional Sales Office, Box 945, New York, NY 10159-0945. TEL 212-633-3730. FAX 212-633-3680; Subscr. in Australasia and the Far East to: Elsevier Science (Singapore) Pte Ltd, No.1 Temasek Ave., No.17-01 Millenia Tower, Singapore 039192, Singapore. TEL 65-434-3727. FAX 65-337-2230; Subscr. in Japan to: Elsevier Science Japan, 9-15 Higashi-Azabu 1-chome, Minato-ku, Tokyo 106, Japan. TEL 81-3-5561-5033. FAX 81-3-5561-5047) Ed. A. Fiechter. adv.: bk.rev.; abstr. (also avail. in microform from UMI; back issues avail.; reprint service avail. from ISI,SWZ) **Indexed:** ASCA, Bibl.Agri., Biodet.Abstr., Biol.& Agr.Ind., Chem.Cit.Ind., Curr.Adv.Biochem., Curr.Adv.Cell & Devel.Biol., Curr.Biotech.Abstr., Curr.Cont., Cyb.Abstr., Excerp.Med., Food Sci.& Tech.Abstr., Ind.Sci.Rev., Ind.Vet., Mat.Sci.Cit.Ind., Sci.Cit.Ind., Sugar Ind.Abstr., Telegen. **Document type:** academic/scholarly publication.
—BLDSC (4954.120000); ADONIS; CASDDS; CISTI; Ei; Genuine Article; KR SourceOne; Linda Hall; SWETS; UnCover. **CCC.**
Description: Provides a medium for full-length and short articles on various aspects of biotechnology.
Refereed Serial

660 610   UK   ISSN 1353-3010
JOURNAL OF BIOTECHNOLOGY IN HEALTHCARE; research and regulation. 1994. q. £265($395) (outside Europe £280) (effective 1996). Henry Stewart Publications, Russell House, 28-30 Little Russell St., London WC1A 2HN, England. TEL 44-171-404-3040. FAX 44-171-486-7083. (Addr. in N. America: Henry Stewart Publications, North American Office, 810 E. 10th St., Box 1897, Lawrence, KS 66044-8897. TEL 913-843-1221. FAX 913-843-1274) Ed.Bd. bk.rev. (back issues avail.) **Document type:** academic/scholarly publication.
—BLDSC (4954.140000); CISTI.
Description: Contains research articles and reviews on the diagnostic and therapeutic efficacy of biologicals and genetically manipulated organisms.
Refereed Serial

660   UK   ISSN 0268-2575
TP248.13   CODEN: JCTBED
JOURNAL OF CHEMICAL TECHNOLOGY AND BIOTECHNOLOGY. 1951. m. $1075 (foreign $1075) (effective 1998). (Society of Chemical Industry) John Wiley & Sons Ltd., Journals, Baffins Ln., Chichester, W. Sussex PO19 1UD, England. TEL 44-1243-779777. FAX 44-1243-775878. E-mail: info-assets@wiley.co.uk; URL: http://www.wiley.co.uk. (Subscr. in the Americas to: John Wiley & Sons, Inc., 605 Third Ave., New York, NY 10158. TEL 212-850-6645. FAX 212-850-6021) Ed. J. Melling; Pub. Ernest Kirkwood. adv.: B&W page £595, color page £1495; trim 297 x 210; adv. contact: Bob Kern. illus.; index. circ. 950. (also avail. in microform from PMC,UMI; back issues avail.; reprint service avail. from ISI) **Indexed:** A.S.& T.Ind., AESIS, Anal.Abstr., API Abstr., API Catal., API Hlth.& Environ., API Oil., API Pet.Ref., API Pet.Subst., API Transport., ASCA, Bibl.Agri., Biol.Abstr., Biotech.Abstr., Br.Ceram.Abstr., Br.Tech.Ind., C.I.S. Abstr., Cadscan, Chem.Abstr., Chem.Cit.Ind., Chem.Eng.Abstr., Chem.Infd., Curr.Biotech.Abstr., Curr.Cont., Curr.Leather Lit., Dairy Sci.Abstr., Deep Sea Res.& Oceanogr.Abstr., Energy Info.Abstr., Eng.Ind., Environ.Abstr., Excerp.Med., Fluidex, Food Sci.& Tech.Abstr., Gas Abstr., I.M.M.Abstr., Ind.Sci.Rev., INIS Atomind., INSPEC, Irr.& Drain.Abstr., Lead Abstr., Met.Abstr., RAPRA, Risk Abstr., Sci.Cit.Ind., Sel.Water Res.Abstr., Soils & Fert., Sport Fish.Abstr., Sugar Ind.Abstr., T.C.E.A., Telegen, W.R.C.Inf., Wild.Rev., World Alum.Abstr., World Surf.Coat., World Text.Abstr., Zincscan. **Document type:** academic/scholarly publication.
—BLDSC (4957.089000); CASDDS; CISTI; Ei; EMDOCS; Genuine Article; KR SourceOne; Linda Hall; SWETS; UnCover. **CCC.**
Supersedes (as of 1986): Journal of Chemical Technology and Biotechnology. Part A: Chemical Technology (ISSN 0264-3413); Journal of Chemical Technology and Biotechnology. Part B: Biotechnology (ISSN 0264-3421); Which supersedes in part (with vol.33, 1983): Journal of Chemical Technology and Biotechnology (ISSN 0142-0356); Journal of Applied Chemistry and Biotechnology (ISSN 0375-9210); Which was formerly: Journal of Applied Chemistry (ISSN 0021-8871)
Description: Covers studies related to the conversion of scientific discovery into products and processes in the areas of biotechnology and chemical technology, especially where these two areas interact.
Refereed Serial

JOURNAL OF FERMENTATION AND BIOENGINEERING. see *BIOLOGY — Bioengineering*

BIOLOGY — BIOTECHNOLOGY

660 576   UK   ISSN 1367-5435
QR53   CODEN: JIMIE7
JOURNAL OF INDUSTRIAL MICROBIOLOGY AND BIOTECHNOLOGY. 1986. bi-m. £501($775) to institutions (effective 1997). (Society for Industrial Microbiology, US) Stockton Press (Subsidiary of: Macmillan Press Ltd.), Houndmills, Basingstoke, Hants. RG21 6XS, England. TEL 44-1256-351898. FAX 44-1256-328339. URL: http://www.stockton-press.co.uk. Ed. J.J. Cooney; Pub. Harry Holt. adv. contact: Robert Sloan. illus.; cum.index. (also avail. in microfilm from UMI; back issues avail.) Indexed: ASCA, Biodet.Abstr., Curr.Adv.Biochem., Curr.Adv.Ecol.Sci., Curr.Adv.Genetics & Molec.Biol., Curr.Biotech.Abstr., Curr.Cont., Excerp.Med. (until 1993), Food Sci.& Tech.Abstr., Rev.Med.& Vet.Mycol., Sugar Ind.Abstr. **Document type:** academic/scholarly publication.
—BLDSC (5006.330500); CASDDS; CISTI; Ei; Genuine Article; Linda Hall; SWETS; UnCover. **CCC.**
Formerly: Journal of Industrial Microbiology (ISSN 0169-4146)
Description: Publishes original research articles, short communications, critical reviews in the fields of biotechnology, fermentation, environmental microbiology, biodegradation, biodeterioration, quality control, and other areas of applied microbiology.
Refereed Serial

660   US   ISSN 0941-2905
TP248.27.M37   CODEN: JMBOEW
JOURNAL OF MARINE BIOTECHNOLOGY. Online edition (US ISSN 1432-1408) 1993. q. $181 (effective 1998). (Japanese Society of Marine Biotechnology) Springer-Verlag, Life Science Journals, 175 Fifth Ave., New York, NY 10010. TEL 212-460-1500. FAX 212-473-6272. E-mail: orders@springer-ny.com; URL: http://www.springer-ny.com. (N. American subscr. to: Journal Fulfillment Services, Box 2485, Secaucus, NJ 07096-2485. TEL 800-777-4643. FAX 201-348-4505; Elsewhere: Heidelberger Platz 3, 1000 Berlin 33, Germany. TEL 49-30-8207-0. FAX 49-30-8207448) Ed. T. Matsunaga. R&P contact: Ian Gross. adv. contact: Robert Vrooman. (also avail. in microfilm from UMI; reprint service avail. from ISI) **Document type:** academic/scholarly publication.
●Also available online.
—BLDSC (5011.720000); CISTI; UMI. **CCC.**
Description: Provides a forum for advances in the field.
Refereed Serial

JOURNAL OF MICROBIOLOGICAL METHODS. see BIOLOGY — Microbiology

JOURNAL OF PLANT BIOCHEMISTRY AND BIOTECHNOLOGY. see BIOLOGY — Biological Chemistry

660 658.8   UK
KEY NOTE MARKET REPORT: BIOTECHNOLOGY. Variant title: Biotechnology. irreg., no.4, 1991. Key Note Ltd., Field House, 72 Oldfield Rd., Hampton, Middlesex TW12 2HQ, England. TEL 44-181-783-0755. FAX 44-181-783-1940. **Indexed:** Bibl.Agri. **Document type:** trade publication.
Former titles: Key Note Report: Biotechnology; (until 1988) Key Note Report. Biotechnology Products (ISSN 0268-4497)

660   JA
KINKI BIO-INDUSTRY CONFERENCE. BIO INDUSTRY. (Text in Japanese) bi-m. Kinki Baioindasutori Shinko Kaigi - Kinki Bio-Industry Conference, Osaka Kagaku Gijutsu Senta, 8-4 Utsubohonmachi 1-chome, Nishi-ku, Osaka 550, Japan.

663 641   GW   ISSN 0341-2067
KLEINBRENNEREI. 1949. m. DM.63.60. Verlag Eugen Ulmer GmbH, Wollgrasweg 41, 70599 Stuttgart, Germany. TEL 49-711-4507-0. FAX 49-711-4507-120. (Subscr. to: Postfach 700561, 70574 Stuttgart, Germany) Ed. H.-J. Pieper. R&P contact: G. Friedrich. adv. contact: F. Mueller. bk.rev. circ. 6,900. **Indexed:** Food Sci.& Tech.Abstr. **Document type:** trade publication.
—BLDSC (5099.083000). **CCC.**

660   US   ISSN 1081-7972
▼**LIFE SCIENCES & BIOTECHNOLOGY UPDATE.** 1995. m. $289 (Canada $329; elsewhere $359) (effective 1997). Infoteam Inc., Box 15640, Plantation, FL 33318-5640. TEL 954-473-9560. FAX 954-473-0544. Ed. Kevin Hamilton. E-mail: infoteamma@aol.com; URL: http://home.aol.com/infoteamma. **Document type:** newsletter.
●Also available online. Vendor(s): Data-Star, Dow Jones News Retrieval, Information Access Co., Knight-Ridder Information, Inc., Lexis-Nexis, NewsNet, UMI.
Description: Covers research and development, technology, applications, products, processes, and other kinds of activities.

660   US   ISSN 0275-3685
McGRAW-HILL'S BIOTECHNOLOGY NEWSWATCH. s-m. $825 (foreign $865). McGraw-Hill Companies, Energy & Business Newsletters, 1221 Ave. of the Americas, 36th Fl., New York, NY 10020. TEL 212-512-6410. Ed. Kevin Hamilton. (looseleaf format; reprint service avail. from UMI)
●Also available online. Vendor(s): Dow Jones News Retrieval (BIO), Knight-Ridder Information, Inc. (File no.624/McGRAW-HILL PUBLICATIONS ONLINE), Lexis-Nexis (BIOTEC), NewsNet (BT08).
—BLDSC (2089.868000); CISTI; SWETS.

MATERIALS SCIENCE AND ENGINEERING C: BIOMIMETIC MATERIALS, SENSORS AND SYSTEMS. see ENGINEERING — Engineering Mechanics And Materials

MEALEY'S LITIGATION REPORT: BIOTECHNOLOGY. see LAW

MEDICAL & PHARMACEUTICAL BIOTECHNOLOGY ABSTRACTS. see MEDICAL SCIENCES — Abstracting, Bibliographies, Statistics

610   NE   ISSN 0047-6552
   CODEN: MDPTBG
MEDICAL PROGRESS THROUGH TECHNOLOGY; signal processing - imaging systems - assist systems - implants - sensors and instrumentation - computers. (Text in English) 1972. q. fl.464 to institutions; $276 to institutions in U.S. (effective 1997). Kluwer Academic Publishers, Postbus 17, 3300 AA Dordrecht, Netherlands. TEL 31-78-6392392. FAX 31-78-6392254. TELEX 29245 KAPG NL. E-mail: services@wkap.nl; URL: http://www.wkap.nl. (Dist. by: Kluwer Academic Publishers Group, P.O. Box 322, 3300 AH Dordrecht, Netherlands. TEL 31-78-6392392. FAX 31-78-6546474; N. America dist. addr.: Box 358, Accord Sta., Hingham, MA 02018-0358. TEL 617-871-6600. FAX 617-871-6528) Ed. Dr. H. Hutten. adv.; bk.rev. (also avail. in microfilm from UMI; back issues avail.; reprint service avail. from SWZ) **Indexed:** ASCA, Bioeng.Abstr., Chem.Abstr., CINAHL, Curr.Cont., Excerp.Med., Ind.Med., Ind.Sci.Rev., INSPEC (1974-), Nutr.Abstr., Sci.Cit.Ind. **Document type:** academic/scholarly publication.
—BLDSC (5531.350000); AskIEEE; CISTI; Ei; Genuine Article; KNAW; KR SourceOne; Linda Hall; SWETS; UMI; UnCover. **CCC.**
Refereed Serial

660   US   ISSN 0737-8483
MEMBRANE & SEPARATION TECHNOLOGY NEWS. 1982. m. $399. Business Communications Co., Inc. (Norwalk), 25 Van Zant St., Norwalk, CT 06855. TEL 203-853-4266. FAX 203-853-0348. TELEX 6502934929 WUI. Ed. Karen Lindsey. circ. 375.
●Also available online. Vendor(s): Data-Star, Information Access Co., Knight-Ridder Information, Inc., NewsNet (BT05).
—**CCC.**

660   US   ISSN 1054-4984
TP159.M4
MEMBRANE TECHNOLOGY REVIEWS. 1986. irreg., no. 6, 1995. Business Communications Co., Inc. (Norwalk), 25 Van Zant St., Norwalk, CT 06855. TEL 203-853-4266. FAX 203-853-0348. TELEX 6502934929 WUI. **Document type:** academic/scholarly publication.
Description: For academic and industrial scientists and engineers who are participating in new areas of membrane research and development. Covers oil and water separations, downstream processing of biologicals, wastewater treatment and the synthesis of specialties based on new vegetable oils.

MICROBIAL & COMPARATIVE GENOMICS. see BIOLOGY — Genetics

660   JA
MICROBIAL UTILIZATION OF RENEWABLE RESOURCES. (Text in English) 1980. biennial. Osaka University, International Center for Biotechnology - Osaka Daigaku Kogaku Kokusai Koryu Senta, 2-1 Yamadaoka, Suita-shi, Osaka 565, Japan. TEL 81-6-879-7455. FAX 81-79-7454. Ed. Toshiomi Yoshida. **Document type:** proceedings.

660   IT   ISSN 1120-4826
   CODEN: MIBIFK
MINERVA BIOTECNOLOGICA; a journal on biotechnology and molecular biology. (Text in English) 1989. q. $105 to individuals; institutions $155 (effective 1997). Edizioni Minerva Medica, Corso Bramante 83-85, 10126 Turin, Italy. TEL 39-11-678282. FAX 39-11-674502. Ed.Bd.; Pub. Alberto Oliaro. adv.: B&W page $1200, color page $2000; trim 215 x 280; adv. contact: F. Filippo. circ. 5,000 (paid). (also avail. in microfilm from UMI) **Indexed:** ASCA. **Document type:** academic/scholarly publication.
—BLDSC (5794.053000); Genuine Article; UMI.
Description: Covers biotechnology and molecular biology.
Refereed Serial

660 610   US   ISSN 1073-6085
TP248.13   CODEN: MLBOEO
MOLECULAR BIOTECHNOLOGY. (Part B of Applied Biochemistry and Biotechnology (ISSN 0273-2289)) 1994. 6/yr. (in 2 vols., 3 nos./vol.). $270 (foreign $290) (effective 1998). Humana Press, Inc., 999 Riverview Dr., Ste. 208, Totowa, NJ 07512-1165. TEL 973-256-1699. FAX 973-256-8341. E-mail: humana@mindspring.com; URL: http://humanapress.com. (Dist. in Japan by: Maruzen Co. Ltd., Journals Div., P.O. Box 5050, Tokyo 100-31, Japan. TEL 03-3275-8591. FAX 03-3278-1937) Ed. John M. Walker. R&P contact: Richard Hruska. adv. contact: Thomas B. Lanigan, Jr. bk.rev.; software rev. circ. 500. **Indexed:** ASCA, Bibl.Agri., Biol.Abstr., Chem.Abstr., Curr.Cont., Excerp.Med., Food Sci.& Tech.Abstr., Ind.Med. (1995-). **Document type:** academic/scholarly publication.
—BLDSC (5900.798400); ADONIS; CASDDS; CISTI; Genuine Article; Linda Hall; SWETS. **CCC.**
Description: Provides detailed laboratory protocols and methods for molecular biology techniques, and publishes review articles and critical research results on the application of these techniques in basic and applied research in biotechnology.
Refereed Serial

MOLECULAR BREEDING; new strategies in plant improvement. see BIOLOGY — Botany

660 338.025   US   ISSN 1074-9942
HD9999.B443
NATIONAL BIOTECH REGISTER. 1992. a. $79.50. Barry Inc., Box 551, Wilmington, MA 01887-0551. TEL 508-658-0442. FAX 508-657-8691. E-mail: natbio@barryinc.com; URL: http://www.barryinc.com/bio. Ed. Joan Carrns. **Document type:** directory, trade publication.
Description: Provides current, comprehensive coverage of material on research and development activity in the biotechnology industry. Outlines the focus of 1,900 leading companies and classifies them by research activity.

BIOLOGY — BIOTECHNOLOGY

660.6 US ISSN 1087-0156
TP248.3 CODEN: NABIF9
NATURE BIOTECHNOLOGY. 1983. m. $530 (Canada $5567; Central & South America $675) (effective 1998). Nature Publishing Co. (Subsidiary of: Macmillan Magazines, Ltd.), 345 Park Ave. S., 10th Fl., New York, NY 10010-1707. TEL 212-726-9200. FAX 212-696-9006. URL: http://www.biotech.nature.com. (Subscr. to: Nature Biotechnology, Box 5054, Brentwood, TN 37024-5054. TEL 800-524-0328; Subscr. outside N. America to: Macmillan Magazines, Ltd., Brunel Rd., Basingstoke, Hants RG21 2XS, England. TEL 44-1256-29242) Ed. Susan Hassler; Pub. James Skowrenski. adv. contact: Bill Moran. bk.rev.; charts; illus.; tr.lit. circ. 15,000. (also avail. in microfilm from UMI; back issues avail.) **Indexed:** Abstr.Bull.Inst.Pap.Chem., Anim.Breed.Abstr., ASCA, Bio-Contr.News & Info., Biotech.Abstr., C.I.J.E., Chem.Abstr., Curr.Adv.Biochem., Curr.Adv.Cell & Devel.Biol., Curr.Adv.Ecol.Sci., Curr.Adv.Genetics & Molec.Biol., Curr.Biotech.Abstr., Curr.Cont., Dairy Sci.Abstr., Deep Sea Res.& Oceanogr.Abstr., Excerp.Med., Food Sci.& Tech.Abstr., Ind.Sci.Rev., Ind.Vet., INIS Atomind., Maize Abstr., Potato Abstr., Rice Abstr., Sci.Cit.Ind., Seed Abstr., Soils & Fert., SSCI, Telegen, Vet.Bull., W.R.C.Inf. **Document type:** academic/scholarly publication.
—BLDSC (6046.257000); CASDDS; CISTI; Ei; EMDOCS; KNAW; KR SourceOne; Linda Hall; SWETS; UMI; UnCover. **CCC.**
Formerly (until vol.14, no.3, Mar. 1996): Bio-Technology (ISSN 0733-222X)
Refereed Serial

660 JA ISSN 0285-4600
NIKKEI BIOTECHNOLOGY/NIKKEI BAIOTEKU. (Text in Japanese) 1981. fortn. 148320 Yen. Nikkei Business Publications, Inc. (Subsidiary of: Nihon Keizai Shimbun, Inc.), 2-7-6 Hirakawa-cho, Chiyoda-ku, Tokyo 102, Japan. TEL 81-3-5210-8117. FAX 81-3-5210-8119. URL: http://www.nikkeibp.co.jp/. (Subscr. to: Nikkei Business Pub. Inc., Reader Service Center, P.O. Box 20, Kasai Post Office, Tokyo 134-70, Japan) Ed. Takao Kawata; Pub. Hitoshi Sawai. **Document type:** trade publication, newsletter.
Description: Covers biotechnology developments.

660 630.24 JA
CODEN: NNKKAA
NIPPON NOGEIKAGAKU KAISHI/JAPAN SOCIETY FOR BIOSCIENCE, BIOTECHNOLOGY, AND AGROCHEMISTRY. JOURNAL. (Text in Japanese; title and contents page in English) 1924. m. $200 to non-members; members $80. Nippon Nogeikagaku Kai - Japan Society for Bioscience, Biotechnology and Agrochemistry, c/o Japan Academic Societies Centre Bldg., 2-4-16 Yayoi, Bunkyo-ku, Tokyo 113, Japan. FAX 03-3815-1920. Ed. Eiji Ichishma. adv.; bk.rev. circ. 13,300. **Indexed:** ASCA, Biol.Abstr., Chem.Abstr., Curr.Adv.Biochem., Curr.Adv.Genetics & Molec.Biol., Curr.Biotech.Abstr., Curr.Chem.React., Curr.Cont., Dairy Sci.Abstr., Field Crop Abstr., Food Sci.& Tech.Abstr., Helminthol.Abstr., Herb.Abstr., Hort.Abstr., Ind.Chem., JTA, Maize Abstr., Mass Spectr.Bull., Nutr.Abstr., Potato Abstr., Seed Abstr., Soyabean Abstr., Sugar Ind.Abstr. **Document type:** academic/scholarly publication.
—BLDSC (6113.431500); CASDDS; CISTI; Genuine Article; Linda Hall; UnCover. **CCC.**
Formerly: Agricultural Chemical Society of Japan. Journal (ISSN 0002-1407)
Description: Contains original and review papers in the fields of bioscience, biotechnology and biochemistry.

660 JA ISSN 0912-7550
OKAYAMAKEN BAIOTEKUNOROJI KENKYUJO KENKYU NENPO/OKAYAMA PREFECTURAL RESEARCH INSTITUTE OF BIOTECHNOLOGY. ANNUAL REPORT. (Text in Japanese) 1986. a. Okayamaken Baiotekunoroji Kenkyujo - Okayama Prefectural Research Institute of Biotechnology, 1174-1 Kodaoki, San'yocho, Akaiwa-gun, Okayama-ken 709-08, Japan. TEL 08695-5-0271. FAX 08695-5-1914. Dir. Nobutomo Takagi.

P A S C A L T 215: BIOTECHNOLOGIES. see *MEDICAL SCIENCES — Abstracting, Bibliographies, Statistics*

615.285 US
PHARMACEUTICAL BIOTECHNOLOGY. 1992. irreg., vol.10, 1997. price varies. Plenum Publishing Corp., 233 Spring St., New York, NY 10013-1578. TEL 212-620-8000. FAX 212-463-0742. TELEX 23-421139. E-mail: books@plenum.com. Ed. Ronald T. Borchardt. (back issues avail.) **Indexed:** Ind.Med. (1993-). **Document type:** monographic series.
Description: Scholarly monographs on theoretical and practical advances in the pharmaceutical sciences, focusing on biotechnology applications and developments in drug dosage design.

660 PH ISSN 0117-0503
PHILIPPINE JOURNAL OF BIOTECHNOLOGY. (Text in English) 1990. s-a. P.100 (overseas $40). Philippine Council for Advanced Science and Technology Research and Development, Department of Science and Technology, Taguig, Metro Manila, Philippines. (Co-sponsors: National Institute of Molecular Biology and Biotechnology; University of Philippines Los Banos) 6455.0800000.
—BLDSC (6455.080000).

PIRTFERM PAPERS. see *ENVIRONMENTAL STUDIES — Waste Management*

660 UK
PLANT AND MICROBIAL BIOTECHNOLOGY RESEARCH SERIES. 1992. irreg., no.2, 1992. Cambridge University Press, Edinburgh Bldg., Shaftesbury Rd., Cambridge CB2 2RU, England. TEL 44-1223-312393. FAX 44-1223-315052. TELEX 851817256. E-mail: information@cup.cam.ac.uk; URL: http://www.cup.cam.ac.uk. (N. American addr.: 40 W. 20th St., New York, NY 10011-4211. TEL 212-924-3900. FAX 212-391-3239) R&P contact: Linda Nicol. **Document type:** monographic series.

PLANT BIOTECHNOLOGY. see *BIOLOGY — Botany*

581.88 660 NE
PLANT MOLECULAR BIOLOGY MANUAL. (Text in English) 2nd ed., 1994. base vol. (plus irreg. supplement). $94.50 (effective 1994). Kluwer Academic Publishers, Postbus 17, 3300 AA Dordrecht, Netherlands. TEL 31-78-6392392. FAX 31-78-6392254. TELEX 29245 KAPG NL. E-mail: services@wkap.nl; URL: http://www.wkap.nl. (Dist. by: Kluwer Academic Publishers Group, P.O. Box 322, 3300 AH Dordrecht, Netherlands. TEL 31-78-6392392. FAX 31-78-6546474; N. America dist. addr.: Box 358, Accord Sta., Hingham, MA 02018-0358. TEL 617-871-6600. FAX 617-871-6528) Ed.Bd. bibl. (looseleaf format) **Document type:** academic/scholarly publication.
Description: Presents comprehensive coverage of the molecular aspects of plant molecular biology, including such topics as the introduction of genes into plants, nucleic acid extraction, the use of markers in transgenic plants.

PLANT TISSUE CULTURE AND BIOTECHNOLOGY. see *BIOLOGY — Botany*

581.0724 660 NE
PLANT TISSUE CULTURE MANUAL; fundamentals and applications. (Text in English) base vol. (plus irreg. supplement). Kluwer Academic Publishers, Postbus 17, 3300 AA Dordrecht, Netherlands. TEL 31-78-6392392. FAX 31-78-6392254. TELEX 29245 KAPG NL. E-mail: services@wkap.nl; URL: http://www.wkap.nl. (Dist. by: Kluwer Academic Publishers Group, P.O. Box 322, 3300 AH Dordrecht, Netherlands. TEL 31-78-6392392. FAX 31-78-6546474; N. America dist. addr.: Box 358, Accord Sta., Hingham, MA 02018-0358. TEL 617-871-6600. FAX 617-871-6528) Ed. K. Lindsey. (looseleaf format) **Document type:** academic/scholarly publication.
Description: Presents a broad range of techniques for research workers in the fields of cell and molecular biology, physiology, plant breeding and propagation and genetic engineering.

PLASMAS AND POLYMERS. see *CHEMISTRY — Organic Chemistry*

POLYMER THERAPEUTICS. see *PHARMACY AND PHARMACOLOGY*

POLYTECHNISCH TIJDSCHRIFT - PROCESTECHNIEK; vakblad voor de ingenieur. see *ENGINEERING*

660 630 NE ISSN 0925-5214
SB129 CODEN: PBTEED
POSTHARVEST BIOLOGY AND TECHNOLOGY. (Text in English) 1991. 9/yr. fl.1335($767) (effective 1998). Elsevier Science B.V., P.O. Box 211, 1000 AE Amsterdam, Netherlands. TEL 31-20-4853911. FAX 31-20-4853598. TELEX 18582 ESPA NL. E-mail: nlinfo-f@elsevier.nl; usinfo-f@elsevier.com; forinfo-kyf04035@niftyserve.or.jp; URL: http://www.elsevier.nl/. (Subscr. in the Americas to: Elsevier Science, Regional Sales Office, Box 945, New York, NY 10159-0945. TEL 212-633-3730. FAX 212-633-3680; Subscr. in Australasia and the Far East to: Elsevier Science (Singapore) Pte Ltd, No.1 Temasek Ave., No.17-01 Millenia Tower, Singapore 039192, Singapore. TEL 65-434-3727. FAX 65-337-2230; Subscr. in Japan to: Elsevier Science Japan, 9-15 Higashi-Azabu 1-chome, Minato-ku, Tokyo 106, Japan. TEL 81-3-5561-5033. FAX 81-3-5561-5047) Eds. Graeme E. Hobson, Alley E. Watada. adv.; bk.rev. (also avail. in microform from UMI; back issues avail.) **Indexed:** ASCA, Curr.Cont., Food Sci.& Tech.Abstr. **Document type:** academic/scholarly publication.
—BLDSC (6563.921500); CASDDS; EMDOCS; Genuine Article; SWETS; UnCover. **CCC.**
Description: Devoted exclusively to original papers and review articles on biological and technological research on postharvest handling or treatment, quality evaluation, packaging, storage and distribution - transportation of agronomic (including forage) and horticultural crops.
Refereed Serial

664 CI ISSN 0352-9193
CODEN: PTBREK
PREHRAMBENO-TEHNOLOSKA I BIOTEHNOLOSKA REVIJA/FOOD TECHNOLOGY AND BIOTECHNOLOGY REVIEW. (Text in Croatian, Macedonian, Serbian, Slovenian; abstract in English) 1963. q. $80. Sveuciliste u Zagrebu, Prehrambeno-Biotechnoloski Fakultet - University of Zagreb, Faculty of Food Technology and Biotechnology, Kaciceva 23, 41000 Zagreb, Croatia. TEL 385-41-411039. FAX 385-41-418230. Ed. Pavao Mildner. adv.; bk.rev. circ. 600. **Indexed:** ASCA, Biotech.Abstr., Chem.Abstr., Food Sci.& Tech.Abstr., Ref.Zh.
—CASDDS; Genuine Article.
Description: Covers all aspects of food science and biotechnology.

PREPARATIVE BIOCHEMISTRY AND BIOTECHNOLOGY. see *BIOLOGY — Biological Chemistry*

660 574.192 UK ISSN 0032-9592
TP500 CODEN: PRBCAP
PROCESS BIOCHEMISTRY. 1966. 8/yr. fl.1068($614) (effective 1998). Elsevier Science Ltd., P.O. Box 800, Kidlington, Oxford OX5 1DX, England. TEL 44-1865-843000. FAX 44-1865-843010. E-mail: nlinfo-f@elsevier.nl; usinfo-f@elsevier.com; forinfo-kyf04035@niftyserve.or.jp; URL: http://www.elsevier.nl/. (Subscr. to: Elsevier Science, Regional Sales Office, P.O. Box 211, 1000 AE Amsterdam, Netherlands. TEL 31-20-4853757. FAX 31-20-4853432; Subscr. in the Americas to: Elsevier Science, Regional Sales Office, Box 945, New York, NY 10159-0945. TEL 212-633-3730. FAX 212-633-3680; Subscr. in Australasia and the Far East to: Elsevier Science (Singapore) Pte Ltd, No.1 Temasek Ave., No.17-01 Millenia Tower, Singapore 039192, Singapore. TEL 65-434-3727. FAX 65-337-2230) Ed. C.M. Brown. adv.; bk.rev.; charts; illus.; tr.lit.; index. circ. 3,750. (also avail. in microform from UMI) **Indexed:** Agri.Eng.Abstr., ASCA, Bibl.Agri., Biol.Abstr., Biotech.Abstr., Chem.Abstr., Chem.Cit.Ind., Chem.Eng.Abstr., Curr.Adv.Ecol.Sci., Curr.Biotech.Abstr., Curr.Cont., Dairy Sci.Abstr., Energy Ind., Energy Info.Abstr., Excerp.Med., Food Sci.& Tech.Abstr., Ind.Sci.Rev., Maize Abstr., Nutr.Abstr., Potato Abstr., Sci.Cit.Ind., Sel.Water Res.Abstr., Sugar Ind.Abstr., T.C.E.A., Telegen, W.R.C.Inf. **Document type:** academic/scholarly publication.
—BLDSC (6849.983500); CASDDS; CISTI; Ei; EMDOCS; Genuine Article; Linda Hall; SWETS; UMI; UnCover. **CCC.**
Formerly (until 1991): Process Biochemistry International.
Description: Reports advances in the science and technology of the application of living organisms to processing and production methods in the food, beverage and pharmaceutical industries, and the energy, waste and water treatment industries.
Refereed Serial

BIOLOGY — BIOTECHNOLOGY

PROGRESS IN BIOCHEMISTRY, BIOTECHNOLOGY, AND NONLINEAR BIOLOGY. see *BIOLOGY — Biological Chemistry*

PROGRESS IN BIOMEDICAL ENGINEERING. see *BIOLOGY — Bioengineering*

663.1 NE ISSN 0921-0423
CODEN: PBITE3
PROGRESS IN BIOTECHNOLOGY. (Text in English) 1985. irreg., vol.9, 1994. price varies. Elsevier Science B.V., Books Division, P.O. Box 211, 1000 AE Amsterdam, Netherlands. TEL 31-20-4853911. FAX 31-20-4853705. TELEX 18582 ESPA NL. E-mail: nlinfo-f@elsevier.nl; usinfo-f@elsevier.com; forinfo-kyf04035@niftyserve.or.jp; URL: http://www.elsevier.nl/. (Subscr. in the Americas to: Elsevier Science, Regional Sales Office, Box 945, New York, NY 10159-0945. TEL 212-633-3730. FAX 212-633-3680; Subscr. in Australasia and the Far East to: Elsevier Science (Singapore) Pte Ltd, No.1 Temasek Ave., No.17-01 Millenia Tower, Singapore 039192, Singapore. TEL 65-434-3727. FAX 65-337-2230; Subscr. in Japan to: Elsevier Science Japan, 9-15 Higashi-Azabu 1-chome, Minato-ku, Tokyo 106, Japan. TEL 81-3-5561-5033. FAX 81-3-5561-5047) (back issues avail.) **Document type:** monographic series, proceedings.
—BLDSC (6866.160000); CASDDS; CISTI; KNAW. **CCC.**
Refereed Serial

610.285 FR ISSN 0222-0776
R B M - REVUE EUROPEENNE DE TECHNOLOGIE BIOMEDICALE. (Text in English or French; summaries in English and French) 1979. 8/yr. 744 F. (institutions in US $142; elsewhere 860 F.) (effective 1998). Editions Scientifiques et Medicales Elsevier, 141 rue de Javel, 75747 Paris, France. TEL 33-1-45589067. FAX 33-1-45589421. URL: http://www.elsevier.nl/. (Subscr. in U.S. and Canada to: Elsevier Science Inc., Box 945, Madison Sq. Sta., New York, NY 10159-0945. TEL 212-633-3730. FAX 212-633-3680) Ed. C.A. Cuenod. circ. 6,000. **Indexed:** Bull.Signal., Excerp.Med. (1993-). **Document type:** academic/scholarly publication.
—CISTI; EMDOCS. **CCC.**
Description: Publishes objective, scientific medical and technical information on all aspects of biomedical technology involved in cardiology, radiology, NMR, surgery, intensive care and emergency medicine, resuscitation and clinical chemistry equipment.
Refereed Serial

RESOURCE AND ENVIRONMENTAL BIOTECHNOLOGY. see *METALLURGY*

660 US ISSN 1068-3682
TP248.19.S65
RUSSIAN BIOTECHNOLOGY. English translation of: Biotekhnologiya (RU ISSN 0234-2758) 1986. m. $885 (effective 1998). (State Scientific Research Institute for Genetics and Selection of Industrial Microorganisms, RU) Allerton Press, Inc., 150 Fifth Ave., New York, NY 10011. TEL 212-924-3950. FAX 212-463-9684. Ed. V.G. Debabov. **Indexed:** Sugar Ind.Abstr. **Document type:** academic/scholarly publication.
—BLDSC (0420.752500); CISTI. **CCC.**
Formerly: Soviet Biotechnology (ISSN 0890-734X)
Description: Covers industrial microbiology, genetic engineering, biosynthesis of antibiotics, immunomodulators and immunoassays, monoclonal antibodies, etc.

660 574.87 JA ISSN 0287-3796
CODEN: SAKOEO
SAIBO KOGAKU/CELL TECHNOLOGY. (Text in Japanese) 1982. m. 1650 Yen per no. Shujunsha Co., Ltd., 6th Kowa Bldg., 4-15-21, Nishi-Azabu, Minato-ku, Tokyo 106, Japan. Ed. Yayoi Tanaka. **Indexed:** Chem.Abstr. **Document type:** academic/scholarly publication.
—CASDDS; CISTI.

660 574.87 JA ISSN 0912-3628
SAIBO KOGAKU, BESSATSU/CELL TECHNOLOGY, SPECIAL ISSUE. (Text in Japanese) 1986. irreg. 3700 Yen. Shujunsha Co., Ltd., 6th Kowa Bldg., 4-15-21, Nishi-Azabu, Minato-ku, Tokyo 106, Japan. Ed. Yayoi Tanaka. **Document type:** academic/scholarly publication.

660 CC ISSN 1003-3505
SHENGWU GONGCHENG JINZHAN/PROGRESS IN BIOTECHNOLOGY. 1976. bi-m. $30. Zhongguo Kexueyuan, Wenxian Qingbao Zhongxin - Chinese Academy of Sciences, Documentation and Information Center, 8 Kexueyuan Nanlu, Zhongguancun, Beijing 100080, People's Republic of China. TEL 86-10-6256-2548. FAX 86-10-6256-7325. Ed. Zhang Shuyong. R&P contact: Ziyi Chen. adv.: page $500. circ. 5,000. **Document type:** academic/scholarly publication.
●Also available on CD-ROM.
Description: Reports the new developments in the field of biotechnology all over the world.

660 CC ISSN 1000-3061
TP248.13 CODEN: SGXUED
SHENGWU GONGCHENG XUEBAO/BIOTECHNOLOGY.
English translation: Chinese Journal of Biotechnology (US ISSN 1042-749X) (Text in Chinese; summaries in English) 1985. q. $66.80. (Chinese Academy of Sciences, Institute of Microbiology) Science Press, Marketing and Sales Department, 16 Donghuangchenggen North St., Beijing 100717, People's Republic of China. TEL 4010642. FAX 4019810. adv.; abstr. circ. 6,000. **Document type:** academic/scholarly publication.
—CASDDS.
Description: Contains research papers on genetic, fermentation, cell and enzyme engineering. Includes new methods for strain breeding, kinetics, regulation of biosynthesis; biochemical engineering unit operations and processes, resource development and environmental protection.
Refereed Serial

SOSHIKI BAIYO KENKYU/TISSUE CULTURE RESEARCH COMMUNICATIONS. see *BIOLOGY — Cytology And Histology*

660 631 SA
SOUTH AFRICAN SUGAR ASSOCIATION EXPERIMENT STATION. BIOTECHNOLOGY DEPARTMENT. ANNUAL REVIEW. 1994. a. South African Sugar Association Experiment Station, Biotechnology Department, Private Bag X02, Mount Edgecombe 4300, South Africa. TEL 27-31-593205. FAX 27-31-595406. TELEX 6-23020. adv. **Document type:** corporate report.

660 US ISSN 1057-705X
HD9999.B443
STATE-BY-STATE BIOTECHNOLOGY DIRECTORY; centers, companies, and contacts. 1990. a. $149. Institute for Biotechnology Information, c/o Mark Dibner, Pres., Box 14569, Research Triangle Park, NC 27709. TEL 919-544-5111. **Document type:** directory.
—**CCC.**
Description: Lists the state contacts, biotechnology centers, and biotechnology companies in all 50 states.

SYNTHETIC BIOTRANSFORMATIONS. see *BIOLOGY — Biological Chemistry*

660 UK ISSN 0167-7799
TP248.13 CODEN: TRBIDM
TRENDS IN BIOTECHNOLOGY. Library compendium: Trends in Biotechnology (Reference Edition) (ISSN 0167-9430) 1983. m. fl.1349($775) (effective 1998). Elsevier Science Ltd., P.O. Box 800, Kidlington, Oxford OX5 1DX, England. TEL 44-1865-843000. FAX 44-1865-843010. E-mail: nlinfo-f@elsevier.nl; forinfo-kyf04035@niftyserve.or.jp; URL: http://www.elsevier.nl/. (Subscr. to: Elsevier Science, Regional Sales Office, P.O. Box 211, 1000 AE Amsterdam, Netherlands. TEL 31-20-4853757. FAX 31-20-4853432; Subscr. in the Americas to: Elsevier Science, Regional Sales Office, Box 945, New York, NY 10159-0945. TEL 212-633-3730. FAX 212-633-3680; Subscr. in Australasia and the Far East to: Elsevier Science (Singapore) Pte Ltd, No.1 Temasek Ave., No.17-01 Millenia Tower, Singapore 039192, Singapore. TEL 65-434-3727. FAX 65-337-2230) Ed. Clare Robinson. adv.; bk.rev.; illus.; index. (back issues avail.) **Indexed:** ASCA, Biol.Abstr., Chem.Abstr., Chem.Cit.Ind., Curr.Adv.Ecol.Sci., Curr.Biotech.Abstr., Curr.Cont., Dairy Sci.Abstr., Excerp.Med., Food Sci.& Tech.Abstr., Hort.Abstr., Ind.Sci.Rev., Ornam.Hort., Rice Abstr., Sci.Cit.Ind., Telegen. **Document type:** academic/scholarly publication.
—BLDSC (9049.547000); ADONIS; CASDDS; CISTI; Genuine Article; SWETS; UnCover. **CCC.**
Description: Covers all aspects of applied biosciences, including microbiology, molecular biology, immunology, plant and animal cell culture, agriculture and medicine.
Refereed Serial

660 UK ISSN 0167-9430
TP248.13
TRENDS IN BIOTECHNOLOGY (REFERENCE EDITION). 1983. a. £345($514) includes m. Trends in Biotechnology (effective 1995). Elsevier Science Ltd., P.O. Box 800, Kidlington, Oxford OX5 1DX, England. TEL 44-1865-843000. FAX 44-1865-843010. E-mail: nlinfo-f@elsevier.nl; usinfo-f@elsevier.com; forinfo-kyf04035@niftyserve.or.jp; URL: http://www.elsevier.nl/. (Subscr. to: Elsevier Science, Regional Sales Office, P.O. Box 211, 1000 AE Amsterdam, Netherlands. TEL 31-20-4853757. FAX 31-20-4853432; Subscr. in the Americas to: Elsevier Science, Regional Sales Office, Box 945, New York, NY 10159-0945. TEL 212-633-3730. FAX 212-633-3680; Subscr. in Australasia and the Far East to: Elsevier Science (Singapore) Pte Ltd, No.1 Temasek Ave., No.17-01 Millenia Tower, Singapore 039192, Singapore. TEL 65-434-3727. FAX 65-337-2230) Ed. Clare Robinson. (back issues avail.) **Document type:** academic/scholarly publication.
—CISTI; Ei; SWETS. **CCC.**
Description: Compendium of archival material from Trends in Biotechnology.
Refereed Serial

TRENDS IN PLANT SCIENCE. see *BIOLOGY — Botany*

660 UK
THE U K BIOTECHNOLOGY HANDBOOK. 1988. a. £115($185) (1995 edition). (BioIndustry Association) BioCommerce Data Ltd., Prudential Bldgs., 95 High St., Slough, Berks. SL1 1DH, England. TEL 44-1753-511777. FAX 44-1753-512239. E-mail: biocom@dial.pipex.com; URL: http://www.biospace.com/biocommerce. Ed.Bd. **Document type:** directory.
Description: Profiles more than 720 U.K. organizations involved in biotechnology. Contains review articles.

BIOLOGY — BOTANY

660   BE
CODEN: MFLRA3
UNIVERSITEIT GENT. FACULTEIT VAN DE LANDBOUWKUNDIGE EN TOEGEPASTE BIOLOGISCHE WETENSCHAPPEN. MEDEDELINGEN. (Text and summaries in Dutch, English, French or German) 1933. 4/yr. 4000 BEF. Universiteit Gent, Faculteit van de Landbouwkundige en Toegepaste Biologische Wetenschappen, Coupure Links 653, 9000 Ghent, Belgium. TEL 32-9-2645902. FAX 32-9-2646245. Ed. A. Huyghebaert. circ. 300. **Indexed:** Agrindex, Bio-Contr.News & Info., Biol.Abstr., Biotech.Abstr., Chem.Abstr., Cott.& Trop.Fibr.Abstr., Dairy Sci.Abstr., Excerp.Med., Field Crop Abstr., Food Sci.& Tech.Abstr., Herb.Abstr., Hort.Abstr., Ind.Vet., Nutr.Abstr., Ornam.Hort., Plant Breed.Abstr., Potato Abstr., Rev.Appl.Entomol., Rice Abstr., Seed Abstr., Soils & Fert., Sorghum & Millets Abstr., Sugar Ind.Abstr., Triticale Abstr., Vet.Bull., Weed Abstr. **Document type:** academic/scholarly publication, bulletin.
—CASDDS; Linda Hall.
    Former titles: Rijksuniversiteit Gent. Faculteit Landbouwwetenschappen. Mededelingen (ISSN 0368-9697); (until 1970): Rijksfaculteit Landbouwwetenschappen te Gent. Mededelingen (ISSN 0369-1721); (until 1966): Mededelingen van de Landbouwhogeschool en de Opzoekingsstations van de Staat te Gent (ISSN 0369-0695); Incorporates (1949-1962): Rijkslandbouwhogeschool Gent. Laboratorium voor Houttechnologie. Mededelingen (ISSN 0369-0660).

VETERINARY BIOTECHNOLOGY NEWSLETTER. see *VETERINARY SCIENCE*

WORLD JOURNAL OF MICROBIOLOGY AND BIOTECHNOLOGY. see *BIOLOGY — Microbiology*

660   615.19   US
WORLDWIDE BIOTECH. 1989. m. $150 (outside N. America $165). Worldwide Videotex, Box 3273, Boynton Beach, FL 33424-3273. TEL 407-738-2276. Ed. Mark Wright; Pub. Mark Wright. bk.rev. (back issues avail.) **Document type:** newsletter.
● Also available online. Vendor(s): Data-Star, Information Access Co., Knight-Ridder Information, Inc.
    Description: Provides news and information on biotechnology as an international industry, reporting on the deals between US biotechnology companies and both US and international pharmaceutical corporations. Monitors the emerging EC marketplace and the growing Japanese interest.

660   641.3   UK   ISSN 0749-503X
CODEN: YESTE3
YEAST; a forum for yeast researchers. 1985. 16/yr. $1155 (foreign $1155) (effective 1998). John Wiley & Sons Ltd., Journals, Baffins Ln., Chichester, W. Sussex PO19 1UD, England. TEL 44-1243-779777. FAX 44-1243-775878. E-mail: info-assets@wiley.co.uk; URL: http://www.wiley.co.uk. (Subscr. in the Americas to: John Wiley & Sons, Inc., 605 Third Ave., New York, NY 10158. TEL 212-850-6645. FAX 212-850-6021) Ed. S.G. Oliver. adv.: B&W page £595, color page £1495; trim 260 x 200; adv. contact: Bob Kern. (also avail. in microform from UMI; back issues avail.; reprint service avail. from SWZ) **Indexed:** Curr.Adv.Ecol.Sci., Curr.Cont., Excerp.Med. (1992-), Food Sci.& Tech.Abstr., Ind.Sci.Rev., Sci.Cit.Ind., Telegen. **Document type:** academic/scholarly publication.
—BLDSC (9417.976000); ADONIS; CASDDS; CISTI; EMDOCS; Genuine Article; Linda Hall; SWETS; UMI; UnCover. **CCC.**
    Description: Contains original research articles along with major and minor reviews and short communications on all aspects of saccharomyces and other yeast genera.
Refereed Serial

BIOLOGY — Botany

see also Agriculture–Crop Production and Soil; Forests and Forestry; Gardening and Horticulture

580   DK   ISSN 0904-6453
CODEN: AAUREL
A A U REPORTS. Variant title: Aarhus University Reports. 1976. irreg. DKK 80 (effective 1997). (University of Aarhus, Botanical Institute - Aarhus Universitet) Aarhus University Press, Bldg. 170, DK-800 Aarhus C, Denmark. FAX 86-19-84-33. Ed. H. Balslev. illus. circ. 300.
—BLDSC (0537.695100).
    Formerly (until 1988): Aarhus University. Botanical Institute. Reports (ISSN 0105-4236)

A S C NEWSLETTER (WASHINGTON). (Association of Systematics Collections) see *MUSEUMS AND ART GALLERIES*

581   US   ISSN 0279-9936
A S P P NEWSLETTER. bi-m. $30 to non-members; members $2. American Society of Plant Physiologists, 15501 Monona Dr., Rockville, MD 20855. TEL 301-257-0560. FAX 301-279-2996. Ed. Jody Carlson. circ. 4,500.
    Description: For society members to keep them informed on items of personal or professional interest.

581   CH   ISSN 0006-8063
QK1   CODEN: BBASA6
ACADEMIA SINICA. BOTANICAL BULLETIN. Key Title: Zhongyang Yanjiuyuan Zhiwuxue Huikan. (Text in English; summaries in Chinese) 1960. q. $60 to individuals; libraries $100. Academia Sinica, Institute of Botany - Chung Yang Yen Chiu Yuan Chih Wu Hsueh Yen Chiu So, Nankang, Taipei, Taiwan 11529, Republic of China. TEL 886-2-789-9590. FAX 886-2-7827954. E-mail: dtyler@gate.sinica.edu.tw; URL: http://www.botany.sinica.edu.tw/bulletin. (Dist. by: Lily Journal and Book Co. & Ltd., 4F-3, No. 125, Roosevelt Rd., Sec.3, Taipei, Taiwan, Republic of China) Ed. Yaw-Huei Lin; Pub. Jei-Fu Shaw. adv.; bibl.; charts; illus.; stat.; index, cum.index. circ. 450. (also avail. in microfilm) **Indexed:** ASCA, Biol.Abstr., Cadscan, Chem.Abstr., Crop Physiol.Abstr., Curr.Adv.Ecol.Sci., Curr.Cont., Curr.Cont., Field Crop Abstr., Food Sci.& Tech.Abstr., Genet.Abstr., Helminthol.Abstr., Herb Abstr., Hort.Abstr., Lead Abstr., Maize Abstr., Ornam.Hort., Plant Breed.Abstr., Plant Grow.Reg.Abstr., Rev.Plant Path., Rice Abstr., Sci.Cit.Ind., Seed Abstr., Soils & Fert., Triticale Abstr., Virol.Abstr., Weed Abstr., Zincscan. **Document type:** academic/scholarly publication, bulletin.
● Also available on CD-ROM.
—BLDSC (2253.000000); CASDDS; CISTI; EMDOCS; Genuine Article; KNAW; Linda Hall; UMI; UnCover.
    Description: Publishes papers on all aspects of botany.

581   PL   ISSN 0065-0951
SB13   CODEN: AAGWAU
ACTA AGROBOTANICA. (Text in Polish and English; summaries in English, French or Polish) 1953. irreg., vol.41, no.2, 1990. price varies. Polskie Towarzystwo Botaniczne, Al. Ujazdowskie 4, 00-478 Warsaw, Poland. (Dist. by: Ars Polona, Krakowskie Przedmiescie 7, 00-068 Warsaw, Poland) Ed. M. Saniewski. illus. circ. 300. **Indexed:** AgroLibrex, Biol.Abstr., Chem.Abstr., Crop Physiol.Abstr., Excerp.Med., Field Crop Abstr., Helminthol.Abstr., Herb.Abstr., Hort.Abstr., INIS Atomind., Irr.& Drain.Abstr., Maize Abstr., Rev.Plant Path., Seed Abstr., Soils & Fert., Soyabean Abstr., Triticale Abstr., Weed Abstr.
—BLDSC (0589.500000); CASDDS; Linda Hall.

581   PL   ISSN 0001-5296
CODEN: ABCBAM
ACTA BIOLOGICA CRACOVIENSIA. BOTANICA. (Text in English) 1958. s-a. price varies. (Polska Akademia Nauk, Oddzial w Krakowie, Komisja Biologiczna) Ossolineum, Publishing House of the Polish Academy of Sciences, Pl. Slony 14a, 50-062 Wroclaw, Poland. TEL 48-71-3436961. FAX 48-71-448103. TELEX 0712771 OSS PL. Ed. Helena Wcislo. charts; illus.; index. circ. 950. **Indexed:** AgroAgen, Biol.Abstr., Bull.Signal, Chem.Abstr., Curr.Adv.Ecol.Sci., Curr.Cont., Field Crop Abstr., Helminthol.Abstr., Herb.Abstr., IBR, Key Word Ind.Wildl.Res., Sci.Cit.Ind. **Document type:** academic/scholarly publication.
—BLDSC (0602.400000); CASDDS; CISTI; KNAW; Linda Hall; UnCover.
    Description: Problems of karyology, cytotaxonomy and embryology of Cormophyta; plant-derived active substances; and physiology and morphogenesis of lower plants.

581   SP   ISSN 0210-7597
ACTA BOTANICA BARCINONENSIA. (Text in various languages) 1964. irreg., latest no.43. price varies or on exchange basis. Universitat de Barcelona, Facultat de Biologia, Departament de Biologia Vegetal, Avda. Diagonal, 615, 08028 Barcelona, Spain. TEL 34-3-4021472. FAX 34-3-4112842. Ed. Xavier Llimona. circ. 1,000. **Indexed:** Biol.Abstr., Ind.SST, Rice Abstr. **Document type:** academic/scholarly publication, monographic series.
    Supersedes (since 1978): Acta Geobotanica Barcinonensia (ISSN 0065-1222)
    Description: Covers a single work mainly on plant taxonomy and phytocenology, vascular plants and cryptogams of the Western Mediterranean area.
Refereed Serial

581   576   CI   ISSN 0365-0588
CODEN: ABCRA2
ACTA BOTANICA CROATICA. (Text and summaries in Croatian, English, French and German) 1925. a. $30. Sveuciliste u Zagrebu, Prirodoslovno-Matematicki Fakultet, Bioloski Odjel - University of Zagreb, Faculty of Natural Sciences, Division of Biology, Marulicev trg 20-II, 41000 Zagreb, Croatia. (Subscr. to: RO "Mladost", Sektor Vanjska Trgovina, Poslovnica Uvoz-Izvoz, Ilica 30, Zagreb, Croatia. TEL 38-41-453-222) Ed. Ljudevit Ilijanic. bk.rev.; index, cum.index. circ. 500. (back issues avail.) **Indexed:** Biol.Abstr., Chem.Abstr., Crop Physiol.Abstr., Forest.Abstr., Hort.Abstr., Plant Grow.Reg.Abstr., Ref.Zh., Weed Abstr., Zoo.Rec.
—CASDDS; Linda Hall.
    Description: Publishes original scientific papers on various fields of botany.

581   CU   ISSN 0138-6824
ACTA BOTANICA CUBANA. 1980. irreg., no.84, 1989. Academia de Ciencias de Cuba, Instituto de Ecologia y Sistematica, Industria 452, Havana 2, Cuba. bibl.; charts; illus. circ. 2,000. **Indexed:** Biol.Abstr.
    Formerly: Acta Botanica Cuba.

581   FI   ISSN 0001-5369
QH7   CODEN: ABFEAC
ACTA BOTANICA FENNICA. (Text in English) 1925. irreg. (1-4/yr.). price varies. Finnish Zoological and Botanical Publishing Board, P.O. Box 17, P. Rautatiekatu 13, FIN-00014 University of Helsinki, Finland. TEL 358-9-191-74-05. FAX 358-9-191-20-07. E-mail: elmor__kr@cc.helsinki.fi; URL: http://www.helsinki.fi/elmo__kr/sekj.htm. (Subscr. to: Tiedkirja OY, Kirkkokatu 14, FIN-00170 Helsinki, Finland. TEL 358-0-635177) (Co-sponsors: Finnish Academy of Sciences and Letters; Societas Scientiarum Fennica; Societas pro Fauna et Flora Fennica and Societas Biologica Fennica Vanamo) Ed. Krzysztof Raciborski. illus.; cum.index: nos.1-40, 41-100, 100-125, 125-137, 138-142. circ. 1,025. (also avail. in microfiche from IDC) **Indexed:** Biol.Abstr., Chem.Abstr., Curr.Adv.Ecol.Sci., Deep Sea Res.& Oceanogr.Abstr., Ecol.Abstr., Geo.Abstr., Geol.Abstr., GeoRef, Ref.Zh., Soils & Fert., VITIS. **Document type:** academic/scholarly publication.
—CASDDS; CISTI; KNAW; Linda Hall; UnCover.
    Description: Original botanical monographs by Finnish and foreign botanists.

BIOLOGY — BOTANY

581   **FR**   ISSN 1253-8078
QK1   CODEN: ABGAE9
ACTA BOTANICA GALLICA. 1854. irreg. (6-7/yr.). 900 F. Societe Botanique de France, Rue J.B. Clement, 92296 Chatenay-Malabry Cedex, France. TEL 46-83-55-20. FAX 46-83-13-03. Ed. J.L. Guignard. bk.rev.; index. circ. 1,300. **Indexed:** Apic.Abstr., ASCA, Biol.Abstr., Chem.Abstr., Curr.Adv.Ecol.Sci., Curr.Adv.Genetics & Molec.Biol., Curr.Cont., Ecol.Abstr., Field Crop.Abstr., Forest.Abstr., Forest Prod.Abstr., Geol.Abstr., Helminthol.Abstr., Herb.Abstr., Hort.Abstr., Plant Breed.Abstr., Plant Grow.Reg.Abstr., Rev.Plant Path., Triticale Abstr., Weed Abstr. **Document type:** academic/scholarly publication.
—BLDSC (0606.200000); CASDDS; CISTI; Genuine Article; Linda Hall; SWETS; UnCover.
Formerly: Actualites Botaniques (ISSN 0181-1789); Supersedes (in 1978): Societe Botanique de France. Colloques.
Description: Focuses on all aspects of botany.

ACTA BOTANICA HORTI BUCURESTIENSIS. see *GARDENING AND HORTICULTURE*

581   **HU**   ISSN 0236-6495
QK1   CODEN: ABOHE2
ACTA BOTANICA HUNGARICA. (Text in English, French, German, Russian, Spanish) 1954. q. $128 (effective 1998). Magyar Tudomanyos Akademia) Akademiai Kiado Rt., P.O. Box 245, H-1519 Budapest, Hungary. TEL 36-1-2043976. FAX 36-1-2043973. Ed. Attila Borhidi. adv.; bk.rev.; charts; illus.; index. **Indexed:** Anim.Breed.Abstr., ASCA, Biol.Abstr., Chem.Abstr., Crop Physiol.Abstr., Curr.Adv.Ecol.Sci., Curr.Cont., Excerp.Med., Excerp.Bot., Field Crop Abstr., Forest.Abstr., Forest Prod.Abstr., Herb.Abstr., Hort.Abstr., Plant Grow.Reg.Abstr., Seed Abstr., Soils & Fert., Triticale Abstr., Weed Abstr. **Document type:** academic/scholarly publication.
—CASDDS; CISTI; KNAW; Linda Hall; UnCover. **CCC.**
Formerly (until 1982): Academiae Scientiarum Hungaricae. Acta Botanica (ISSN 0001-5350).
Description: Publishes papers by Hungarian botanists. Covers ecology, cytology, phytology, algology, mycology, bryology, taxonomy, paleobotany and more.

581   **II**   ISSN 0379-508X
QK1   CODEN: ABOIB2
ACTA BOTANICA INDICA. (Text in English) 1973. s-a. Rs.75 to individuals; institutions Rs.150; foreign £50. Society for the Advancement of Botany, Department of Botany, Meerut College, Meerut 250006, India. (Dist. overseas by: HPC Publishers' Distributors Pvt. Ltd., 4805-24, 1st Fl., Bharat Ram Rd., Darya Ganj, New Delhi 110 002, India. TEL 91-11-3254401. FAX 91-11-6863511) Ed. Dr. V. Singh. adv.; bk.rev.; bibl.; illus.; cum.index. circ. 1,000. (reprint service avail. from ISI) **Indexed:** Agroforest.Abstr., Apic.Abstr., Biol.Abstr., Crop Physiol.Abstr., Curr.Adv.Ecol.Sci., Curr.Cont., Excerp.Med., Field Crop Abstr., Helminthol.Abstr., Herb.Abstr., Hort.Abstr., INIS Atomind., Rev.Plant Path., Rice Abstr., Soils & Fert., Triticale Abstr., Weed Abstr. **Document type:** academic/scholarly publication.
—BLDSC (0606.750000); CISTI; Linda Hall; UMI; UnCover.
Refereed Serial

581   **IC**   ISSN 0374-5066
QK325.5
ACTA BOTANICA ISLANDICA. (Text in English, French, German; summaries in English) 1972. irreg. $20 (effective 1997). Icelandic Institute of Natural History - Akureyri Division, P.O. Box 180, IS-602 Akureyri, Iceland. TEL 354-462-2983. FAX 354-461-1296. E-mail: hkris@nattfs.is. Ed. Hoerdur Kristinsson. bk.rev.; bibl.; illus. circ. 190. **Indexed:** Biol.Abstr., Curr.Adv.Ecol.Sci. **Document type:** academic/scholarly publication.
—BLDSC (0606.800000); CISTI; Linda Hall.
Supersedes (1963-1968): Flora.
Description: Original research in the flora and vegetation of Iceland with emphasis on floristics, plant sociology, taxonomy, ecology.

581 633   **SP**   ISSN 0210-9506
                        CODEN: ABMAE5
ACTA BOTANICA MALACITANA. (Text in English, French, Italian, Spanish) 1975. a. 3500 ptas.($25) (effective 1998). Universidad de Malaga, Facultad de Ciencias, Departamento de Biologia Vegetal, Apdo. 59, 29080 Malaga, Spain. TEL 34-5-2133342. FAX 34-52-131944. Dir. B. Cabezudo. bk.rev.; bibl.; charts; illus.; index. circ. 500. (back issues avail.) **Indexed:** Apic.Abstr., Ind.SST, Ornam.Hort. **Document type:** academic/scholarly publication.
Description: Disseminates results of original works relating to any aspect of botany; including systematic botany, chorology, taxonomy and ecology.
Refereed Serial

581   **MX**   ISSN 0187-7151
ACTA BOTANICA MEXICANA. 1988. q. $15. Instituto de Ecologia, Apdo. Postal 63, 91000 Xalapa, Veracruz, Mexico. FAX 52-28-187809. (back issues avail.) **Indexed:** Apic.Abstr. **Document type:** academic/scholarly publication.

581   **UK**   ISSN 0044-5983
QK1   CODEN: ABNRAN
ACTA BOTANICA NEERLANDICA. (Text in English) 1952. q. £150($274) (foreign £165) (effective 1998). (Koninklijke Nederlandse Botanische Vereniging, NE - Royal Botanical Society of the Netherlands) Blackwell Science Ltd., Osney Mead, Oxford OX2 0EL, England. TEL 44-1865-206206. FAX 44-1865-721205. E-mail: journals.cs@blacksci.co.uk; URL: http://www.black.co.uk. Ed. J. van Andel; Pub. Allen Stevens. R&P contact: Sarah Pollard. adv. contact: Martine Cariou-Keen. bk.rev.; illus. circ. 725. (also avail. in microform from UMI; back issues avail.) **Indexed:** ASCA, Biol.Abstr., Chem.Abstr., Crop Physiol.Abstr., Curr.Adv.Ecol.Sci., Curr.Cont., Deep Sea Res.& Oceanogr.Abstr., Ecol.Abstr., Excerp.Med., Field Crop Abstr., Forest.Abstr., Forest Prod.Abstr., Geo.Abstr.P.G., Helminthol.Abstr., Herb.Abstr., Hort.Abstr., Ind.Sci.Rev., Maize Abstr., Plant Breed.Abstr., Plant Grow.Reg.Abstr., Potato Abstr., Rev.Plant Path, Sci.Cit.Ind., Sci.Cit.Ind, Soils & Fert., Weed Abstr. **Document type:** academic/scholarly publication.
—BLDSC (0607.000000); CASDDS; CISTI; EMDOCS; Genuine Article; Linda Hall; SWETS; UMI; UnCover. **CCC.**
Incorporates (1846-1951): Nederlandsch Kruidkundig Archief; (1904-1951): Recueil des Travaux Botaniques Neerlandais.
Description: Presents research in all aspects of plant science. Includes phytopathology, cytotaxonomy, algology, and morphology, cell biology, physiology, cytology, and cell and tissue culture.
Refereed Serial

581   **XO**
ACTA BOTANICA SLOVACA. (Text in Slovak; summaries in English, German and Russian) irreg. price varies. (Slovenska Akademia Vied) Veda, Publishing House of the Slovak Academy of Sciences, Bradacova 7, 852 86 Bratislava, Slovakia. (Dist. by: Slovart, Nam. Slobody 6, 817 64 Bratislava, Slovakia)
Former titles: Acta Botanica; Acta Instituti Botanici.

581   **VE**   ISSN 0084-5906
                        CODEN: ABOVA6
ACTA BOTANICA VENEZUELICA. (Text and summaries in English and Spanish) 1965. irreg. price varies. Fundacion Instituto Botanico de Venezuela, Jardin Botanico de Caracas, Av. Salvador Allende, Apdo. 2156, Caracas 1010A, Venezuela. TEL 02-6629254. FAX 02-6629081. Eds. Gilberto Morillo, Alberto Rodriguez. charts; illus. circ. 1,000. (processed) **Indexed:** Biol.Abstr., Field Crop Abstr., Forest.Abstr., Herb.Abstr.

589.2   **PL**   ISSN 0001-625X
QK600   CODEN: ACMYAC
ACTA MYCOLOGICA. (Text and summaries in English, French, German, Polish) 1965. irreg., vol.25, no.2, 1990. price varies. Polskie Towarzystwo Botaniczne - Polish Botanical Society, Al. Ujazdowskie 4, 00-478 Warsaw, Poland. Ed. Alina Skirgiello. bk.rev.; bibl.; charts; illus. circ. 320. **Indexed:** AgroAgen, Bio-Contr.News & Info., Biodet.Abstr., Biol.Abstr., Chem.Abstr., Excerp.Bot., Forest.Abstr., Maize Abstr., Rev.Med.& Vet.Mycol., Rev.Plant Path, Seed Abstr., Soils & Fert., Soyabean Abstr., Triticale Abstr.
—BLDSC (0639.300000); CASDDS; Linda Hall.
Description: Examines research in botany.

561   **PL**   ISSN 0001-6594
QE901   CODEN: APBCAG
ACTA PALAEOBOTANICA. (Text in English, occasionally in French and German; summaries in English) 1960. s-a. $47.50 (effective 1997). Polska Akademia Nauk, Instytut Botaniki im. W. Szafera, Ul. Lubicz 46, 31-512 Krakow, Poland. TEL 48-12-215144. FAX 48-12-219790. E-mail: nhwysock@cyf-kr.edu. pl. Ed. Leon Stuchlik. bk.rev.; bibl.; charts; illus. circ. 500. **Indexed:** AgroAgen, AgroLibrex, Biol.Abstr., Curr.Adv.Ecol.Sci., Ecol.Abstr., Excerp.Bot., Geo.Abstr., Geol.Abstr., GeoRef., IBR, Plant Breed.Abstr. **Document type:** academic/scholarly publication.
—BLDSC (0642.480000); CISTI.
Description: Contains original papers concerned with all topics of paleobotany, palaeoecology and palynology.
Refereed Serial

581   **PL**   ISSN 0137-5881
                        CODEN: APPLDE
ACTA PHYSIOLOGIAE PLANTARUM. (Text in English) 1978. q. 20 Zl.($50) (Polish Academy of Sciences, Department of Plant Physiology in Krakow) Agencja Wydawnicza ARIES, Ul. Zorzy 22, 40-639 Warsaw, Poland. TEL 48-22-153162. FAX 48-22-153162. Ed. Grzegorz Marszalkowski. R&P contact: Grzegorz Marszalkowski. TEL 48-22-499476. adv. contact: Grzegorz Marszalkowski. bk.rev.; illus. circ. 400. **Indexed:** AgroAgen, ASCA, Biol.Abstr., Chem.Abstr., Crop Physiol.Abstr., Curr.Adv.Ecol.Sci., Curr.Cont., Excerp.Med., Field Crop Abstr., Herb.Abstr., Hort.Abstr., Irr.& Drain.Abstr., Plant Grow.Reg.Abstr., Seed Abstr., Soils & Fert. **Document type:** academic/scholarly publication.
—BLDSC (0650.700000); CASDDS; EMDOCS; Genuine Article; Linda Hall.
Description: Publishes papers, reviews and short communications covering theoretical as well as practical aspects of plant physiology and related sciences.
Refereed Serial

581.9   **SW**   ISSN 0084-5914
                        CODEN: APGSAL
ACTA PHYTOGEOGRAPHICA SUECICA. (Text and summaries in English) 1929. a. SEK 125 membership (effective 1997). (Svenska Vaextgeografiska Saellskapet - Swedish Phytogeographical Society) Opulus Press AB, P.O. Box 25137, S-750 25 Uppsala, Sweden. TEL 46-18-32-06-62. FAX 46-18-32-13-68. Ed. Erik Sjoegren. adv. contact: Elisabet Olsson. circ. 300. (reprint service avail.) **Indexed:** Biol.Abstr., Curr.Adv.Ecol.Sci., Field Crop Abstr., Forest.Abstr., Forest Prod.Abstr., Geo.Abstr., Herb.Abstr., Plant Breed.Abstr., Seed Abstr., Soils & Fert. **Document type:** academic/scholarly publication.
—BLDSC (0656.000000); KNAW; Linda Hall; UnCover.
Refereed Serial

632 581   **HU**   ISSN 0238-1249
                        CODEN: APEHEG
ACTA PHYTOPATHOLOGICA ET ENTOMOLOGICA HUNGARICA. (Text in English) 1966. q. $156 (effective 1998). (Magyar Tudomanyos Akademia) Akademiai Kiado Rt., P.O. Box 245, H-1519 Budapest, Hungary. TEL 36-1-2043976. FAX 36-1-2043973. Ed. Zoltan Kiraly. adv.; bk.rev.; bibl.; charts; illus. **Indexed:** Bio-Contr.News & Info., Biol.Abstr., Chem.Abstr., Curr.Adv.Ecol.Sci., Curr.Cont., Excerp.Bot., Field Crop Abstr., Forest.Abstr., Helminthol.Abstr., Hort.Abstr., Plant Breed.Abstr., Plant Grow.Reg.Abstr., Potato Abstr., Rev.Appl.Entomol., Rev.Plant Path., Seed Abstr., Soils & Fert. **Document type:** academic/scholarly publication.
—BLDSC (0656.450000); CASDDS; Genuine Article; KNAW; Linda Hall; UnCover. **CCC.**
Formerly (until 1985): Academiae Scientiarum Hungaricae. Acta Phytopathologica (ISSN 0001-6780).
Description: Publishes papers on the infectious diseases of plants, damages caused by insects and investigates the basic aspects of chemical and biological protection.

BIOLOGY — BOTANY

581 JA ISSN 0001-6799
CODEN: SHBCAM
ACTA PHYTOTAXONOMICA ET GEOBOTANICA/SHOKUBUTSU BUNRUI CHIRI. (Text in English and Japanese) 1932. 2/yr. 8000 Yen. Phytogeographical Society - Shokubutsu Bunrui Chiri Gakkai, c/o Faculty of Integrated Human Studies, Kyoto University, Sakyo-ku, Kyoto 606-01, Japan. (Subscr.to: Japan Publications Trading Co., Ltd., P.O. Box 5030 Tokyo International, Tokyo 100-31, Japan.) Ed. Hiroshi Tobe. R&P contact: Hidetoshi Nagamasu. bk.rev.; index. circ. 750. (also avail. in microform) **Indexed:** Biol.Abstr., Chem.Abstr., Field Crop Abstr., Herb.Abstr., Jap.Per.Ind., Rev.Plant Path. **Document type:** academic/scholarly publication.
—CASDDS; Linda Hall.

581 SW ISSN 0347-4917
ACTA REGIAE SOCIETATIS SCIENTIARUM ET LITTERARUM GOTHOBURGENSIS. BOTANICA. 1972. irreg., no.4, 1995. price varies: also exchange basis. Kungliga Vetenskaps- och Vitterhets-Samhaelle, c/o Goeteborgs Universitetsbibliotek, P.O. Box 5096, S-402 22 Goeteborg, Sweden. **Document type:** monographic series.
—Linda Hall.
Supersedes in part: Goeteborgs Kungliga Vetenskaps- och Vitterhets- Samhaelle. Handlingar.

ACTA SOCIETATIS BOTANICORUM POLONIAE. see BIOLOGY

581 370 PL ISSN 0208-6174
QK322
ACTA UNIVERSITATIS LODZIENSIS: FOLIA BOTANICA. (Text in Polish; summaries in various languages) 1955-1974; N.S. 1981. irreg. Wydawnictwo Uniwersytetu Lodzkiego, Ul. Jaracza 34, Lodz, Poland. TEL 331671. (Dist. by: Ars Polona-Ruch, Krakowskie Przedmiescie 7, Warsaw, Poland) **Document type:** academic/scholarly publication.
—BLDSC (0585.206000); CISTI; KNAW; Linda Hall.
Supersedes in part: Uniwersytet Lodzki. Zeszyty Naukowe. Seria 2: Nauki Matematyczno-Przyrodnicze (ISSN 0076-0366)
Description: Articles and notices on flora and vegetation of Poland with special attention to the studies on plant cover synanthropization.

581 PL ISSN 0860-3111
ACTA UNIVERSITATIS LODZIENSIS: FOLIA PHYSIOLOGICA CYTOLOGICA ET GENETICA. (Text and abstracts in English, Polish) 1955-1974; N.S. 1986. irreg. Wydawnictwo Uniwersytetu Lodzkiego, Ul. S. Jaracza 34, Lodz, Poland. TEL 331671. (Dist. by: Ars Polona-Ruch, Krakowskie Przedmiescie 7, Warsaw, Poland) Ed.Bd. **Document type:** academic/scholarly publication.
—CISTI; Linda Hall.
Supersedes in part: Uniwersytet Lodzki. Zeszyty Naukowe. Seria 2: Nauki Matematyczno-Przyrodnicze (ISSN 0076-0366)
Description: Articles on plant sciences, especially plant physiology and biochemistry, plant cytology and cytochemistry, plant cytogenetics, and plant biotechnology including cultures in vitro and micropropagation of plants.

581 PL ISSN 0524-451X
QK1
ACTA UNIVERSITATIS WRATISLAVIENSIS. PRACE BOTANICZNE. (Text and summaries in English or Polish) 1964. irreg. price varies. (Uniwersytet Wroclawski) Wydawnictwo Uniwersytetu Wroclawskiego, Spolka z o.o., Pl. Uniwersytetcki 9-13, 50-137 Wroclaw, Poland. TEL 48-71-441006. FAX 48-71-402735. Ed. Jadwiga Aniol-Kwiatkowska. charts; illus. circ. 250. **Indexed:** AgroLibrex. **Document type:** academic/scholarly publication.
—KNAW; Linda Hall.

580 635.9 AT ISSN 0313-4083
QK431 CODEN: JABGDP
ADELAIDE BOTANIC GARDEN. JOURNAL. 1976. irreg. price varies. Adelaide Botanic Garden, North Terrace, Adelaide, S.A. 5000, Australia. TEL 08-228-2308. FAX 08-223-1809. Ed. H.R. Toelken. bk.rev. circ. 200. (back issues avail.) **Indexed:** Biol.Abstr., Hort.Abstr., Ornam.Hort., Plant Breed.Abstr.
—Linda Hall; UnCover.

580.74 635 333.7 AT ISSN 0728-7704
ADELAIDE BOTANIC GARDEN BOARD. ANNUAL REPORT. Key Title: Annual Report of the Board of the Botanic Gardens of Adelaide. 1857. a. free. Adelaide Botanic Garden Board, North Terrace, Adelide, S.A. 5000, Australia. TEL 61-8-2282320. FAX 61-8-2231809. Ed. Brian Morley. R&P contact: Brian Morley. bibl.; charts; stat. circ. 300. (back issues avail.) **Document type:** corporate report.

581 II
ADVANCE IN FRONTIERS OF PLANT SCIENCES. (Text in English) irreg., latest no. 30. $10. Hindustan Publishing Corp., 4805-24, 1st Fl., Bharat Ram Rd., Darya Ganj, New Delhi 110 002, India. TEL 91-11-3254401. FAX 91-11-6863511. E-mail: hpcpd@giasdl01.vsnl.net.in.

581 US ISSN 0065-2296
QK1 CODEN: ABTRAJ
ADVANCES IN BOTANICAL RESEARCH. 1963. irreg., vol.27, 1997. Academic Press, Inc., 525 B St., Ste. 1900, San Diego, CA 92101-4495. TEL 619-231-0926. FAX 619-699-6715. (Subscr. to: Order Dept., 6277 Sea Harbor Dr., 4th Fl., Orlando, FL 32887. TEL 800-321-5068) Ed. R.D. Preston. (reprint service avail. from ISI) **Indexed:** ASCA, Biol.Abstr., Biol.& Agr.Ind., Chem.Abstr., Curr.Adv.Ecol.Sci., Deep Sea Res.& Oceanogr.Abstr., Field Crop.Abstr., Forest.Abstr., Forest Prod.Abstr., Herb.Abstr., Ind.Sci.Rev., Plant Breed.Abstr., Sci.Cit.Ind., Sci.Cit.Ind., Soils & Fert., Weed Abstr.
—BLDSC (0700.500000); CASDDS; CISTI; KR SourceOne; Linda Hall; SWETS; UnCover.
Refereed Serial

581 GW ISSN 0253-6226
QK532.4 CODEN: ABRYDX
ADVANCES IN BRYOLOGY. (Text in English) 1981. irreg. price varies. J. Cramer in der Gruebeder Borntraeger Verlagsbuchhandlung, Johannesstr. 3A, 70176 Stuttgart, Germany. TEL 49-711-625001. FAX 49-711-625005. Ed. N. Miller. **Document type:** academic/scholarly publication.
—BLDSC (0700.700000); CASDDS; Linda Hall.

581 US ISSN 0741-8280
ADVANCES IN ECONOMIC BOTANY. 1983. irreg., latest no.12. price varies. New York Botanical Garden, Scientific Publications Department, Bronx, NY 10458-5126. TEL 718-817-8721. FAX 718-817-8842. TELEX 5106015451 BOTGARD NYK UG. Ed. C. Peters. (back issues avail.) **Indexed:** Apic.Abstr., Curr.Adv.Ecol.Sci. **Document type:** monographic series.
—BLDSC (0704.550000); CISTI; Linda Hall; UnCover. **CCC.**
Description: Original research and symposia dealing with the uses and management of plants.
Refereed Serial

581 NE ISSN 1382-4252
CODEN: ADPHFM
▼**ADVANCES IN PHOTOSYNTHESIS.** (Text in English) 1995. irreg., vol.4, 1995. price varies. Kluwer Academic Publishers, Postbus 17, 3300 AA Dordrecht, Netherlands. TEL 31-78-6392392. FAX 31-78-6392254. E-mail: services@wkap.nl; URL: http://www.wkap.nl. (Dist. by: Kluwer Academic Publishers Group, P.O. Box 322, 3300 AH Dordrecht, Netherlands. TEL 31-78-6392392. FAX 31-78-6546474; N. America dist. addr.: Box 358, Accord Sta., Hingham, MA 02018-0358. TEL 617-871-6600. FAX 617-871-6528) (back issues avail.) **Document type:** monographic series.
—BLDSC (0709.785000); CASDDS. **CCC.**
Refereed Serial

ADVANCES IN PLANT BREEDING/FORTSCHRITTE DER PFLANZENZUECHTUNG. see AGRICULTURE — Crop Production And Soil

581 US ISSN 0736-4539
SB599 CODEN: APLPD6
ADVANCES IN PLANT PATHOLOGY. 1982. irreg., vol.11, 1995. Academic Press, Inc., 525 B St., Ste. 1900, San Diego, CA 92101-4495. TEL 305-345-2000. FAX 619-699-6715. (Subscr. to: Order Dept., 6277 Sea Harbor Dr., 4th Fl., Orlando, FL 32887. TEL 800-321-5068) Eds. D.S. Ingram, P.H. Williams. (reprint service avail. from ISI) **Indexed:** Chem.Abstr.
—CASDDS; CISTI; Linda Hall; UnCover.
Refereed Serial

581 II ISSN 0970-3586
ADVANCES IN PLANT SCIENCES. (Text in English) 1988. s-a. $50. (Academy of Plant Sciences, India) Hindustan Publishing Corp., 4805-24, 1st Fl., Bharat Ram Rd., Darya Ganj, New Delhi 110 002, India. TEL 91-11-3254401. FAX 91-11-6863511. E-mail: hpcpd@giasdl01.vsnl.net.in.
—BLDSC (0710.170000); Linda Hall.

581 II ISSN 0376-480X
QK658 CODEN: APSRDD
ADVANCES IN POLLEN SPORE RESEARCH. 1976. a., vol.21, 1996. $65. Today and Tomorrow's Printers and Publishers, 24B-5 Desh Bandhu Gupta Rd., Karol Bagh, New Delhi 110 005, India. TEL 91-11-572-1928. (Dist. in U.S. by: Scholarly Publications, 2825 Wilcrest Dr., Ste. 255, Houston, TX 77042. TEL 713-781-0070. FAX 713-781-2112) Ed. C.P. Malik. **Indexed:** Biol.Abstr., Curr.Cont. **Document type:** monographic series.
—CASDDS; CISTI; Linda Hall. **CCC.**
Description: Reports, interprets and evaluates progress in the field of pollen spore research.

581 NE ISSN 0168-8022
CODEN: AVSCDA
ADVANCES IN VEGETATION SCIENCE. (Text in English) 1980. irreg., vol.16, 1995. price varies. Kluwer Academic Publishers, Postbus 17, 3300 AA Dordrecht, Netherlands. TEL 31-78-6392392. FAX 31-78-6392254. E-mail: services@wkap.nl; URL: http://www.wkap.nl. (Dist. by: Kluwer Academic Publishers Group, P.O. Box 322, 3300 AH Dordrecht, Netherlands. TEL 31-78-6392392. FAX 31-78-6546474; N. America dist. addr.: Box 358, Accord Sta., Hingham, MA 02018-0358. TEL 617-871-6600. FAX 617-871-6528) (back issues avail.) **Indexed:** Biol.Abstr. **Document type:** monographic series.
—CISTI.
Refereed Serial

AFRICAN JOURNAL OF RANGE & FORAGE SCIENCE. see AGRICULTURE — Crop Production And Soil

581 SA ISSN 1023-3121
▼**AFRICAN PLANT PROTECTION.** (Text in English) 1995. s-a. R.90 to individuals (foreign $50); institutions R.125 (foreign $60) (effective 1997). Box 26320, Arcadia 0007, South Africa. TEL 27-12-6672016. FAX 27-12-6672494. Ed. F.C. Wehner. **Indexed:** Ind.S.A.Per. **Document type:** academic/scholarly publication.
—BLDSC (0732.907000).
Description: Publishes research articles and short communications relating to the protection of plants and crops.

AFRICAN VIOLET MAGAZINE. see GARDENING AND HORTICULTURE

581 US ISSN 0735-8652
AGAVE. 1983. irreg. $35 membership. Desert Botanical Garden, 1201 N. Galvin Pkwy., Phoenix, AZ 85008. TEL 602-941-1225. bk.rev.; illus. circ. 6,000.
Description: Covers botany, plant conservation, landscaping, ecology, ethnobotany, and desert horticulture.

AGROCIENCIA. see AGRICULTURE

AGRONOMIA MOCAMBICANA. see AGRICULTURE

581 JA
AKASAWA SHOKUBUTSU JIKKENSHITSU SHOKUBUTSU BUNRUI KENKYU HOKOKU/AKASAWA BOTANICAL LABORATORY. PHYTOTAXONOMIC REPORTS. (Text in Japanese) 1987. a. 200 Yen. Akasawa Shokubutsu Hyohonko - Akasawa Botanical Laboratory and Herbarium, 11-13, Kawahara, Nakamura, Kitajimacho, Itano-gun, Tokushima-ken 771-02, Japan.

AKITA PREFECTURAL COLLEGE OF AGRICULTURE. BULLETIN. see AGRICULTURE

ALEXANDRIA JOURNAL OF AGRICULTURAL RESEARCH. see AGRICULTURE

ALGOLOGICAL STUDIES; Archiv fuer Hydrobiologie, Supplementbaende. see BIOLOGY

BIOLOGY — BOTANY

581 KR
AL'GOLOGIYA. 1991. q. $150. Akademiya Nauk Ukrainy, Institut Botaniki im. N.G. Kholodnogo, Ul. Tereshchenkovskaya, 2, 252601 Kiev, Ukraine. TEL 38-44-2251311. Ed. S.P. Wasser. adv.; bk.rev.; bibl.; charts; illus. circ. 500. (back issues avail.) **Indexed:** Djerelo. **Document type:** academic/scholarly publication.

581 US ISSN 0065-6275
QK149 CODEN: ALSOA7
ALISO. 1948. s-a. $40 (foreign $44) (effective 1998). Rancho Santa Ana Botanic Garden, 1500 N. College Ave., Claremont, CA 91711. TEL 909-625-8767. FAX 909-626-7670. E-mail: joslin@cgs.edu; URL: http://www.cgs.edu.isnt/rsa. Ed. R.K. Benjamin. R&P contact: Roy L. Taylor. adv. contact: Janet R. Taylor. bk.rev.; s-a. index; circ. 350 (paid). (back issues avail.) **Indexed:** Biol.Abstr., Ecol.Abstr., Excerp.Bot., Field Crop Abstr., Plant Breed.Abstr. **Document type:** academic/scholarly publication.
—Linda Hall; UnCover.
Description: Publishes original papers dealing with botanical systematics and evolution, including related studies in cytology, ecology, cladistics, genetics, biogeography, morphology, anatomy and physiology.
Refereed Serial

581 II ISSN 0971-4693
ALLELOPATHY JOURNAL. (Text in English) 1994. s-a. Rs.200($40) to individuals; institutions Rs.500($80) (effective 1997); individuals Rs.300($50); institutions Rs.600($80) (effective 1998). International Allelopathy Foundation, 10-67, Haryana Agricultural University, Hisar 125 004, India. TEL 91-1662-78083. FAX 91-1662-34952. adv.: page $200. bk.rev.; circ. 300 (paid). **Indexed:** Agroforest.Abstr., Bio-Contr.News & Info., Biol.Abstr., Chem.Abstr., Crop Physiol.Abstr., Field Crop Abstr., Forest.Abstr., Herb.Abstr., Hort.Abstr., Indian Sci.Abstr., Plant Breed Abstr., Plant Grow.Reg.Abstr., Rev.Plant Path., Seed Abstr., Weed Abstr. **Document type:** academic/scholarly publication.
—BLDSC (0789.896000). CCC.
Description: Contains research papers and reviews on the current developments of agriculture. Also includes biographies of eminent scientists.
Refereed Serial

581 US ISSN 0735-8032
QK1 CODEN: LLRTD5
ALLERTONIA; a series of occasional papers. 1975. irreg., vol.7, no.4, 1997. price varies. National Tropical Botanical Garden, Box 340, Lawai, Kauai, HI 96765. TEL 808-332-7324. FAX 808-332-9765. Ed. David H. Lorence. R&P contact: David Lorence. index. circ. 300. (back issues avail.) **Indexed:** Biol.Abstr., Chem.Abstr., Curr.Adv.Ecol.Sci., So.Pac.Per.Ind. **Document type:** academic/scholarly publication, monographic series.
—CASDDS; Linda Hall.
Description: Presents results of original botanical or horticultural research.
Refereed Serial

580 IT ISSN 0065-6429
CODEN: ALLIAM
ALLIONIA. (Text in English, French, Italian) 1952. a. exchange basis. Universita degli Studi di Torino, Dipartimento di Biologia Vegetale, Viale P.A. Mattioli 25, 10125 Turin, Italy. TEL 39-11-6699884. FAX 39-11-655839. Ed. Arturo Ceruti. circ. 500. **Indexed:** Biol.Abstr., Chem.Abstr., Field Crop Abstr. Forest.Abstr., Forest Prod.Abstr., Herb.Abstr., Hort.Abstr., Mycol.Abstr., Rev.Med.& Vet.Mycol., Soils & Fert. **Document type:** academic/scholarly publication.
—CASDDS.
Description: Contains articles on plant sciences, especially mycology, taxonomy of flowering plants, phytogeography, phytosociology and lichenology.
Refereed Serial

635.9 SA ISSN 0002-6301
ALOE. (Text in English) 1963. q. R.85($33) (foreign R.130) (effective 1997). Succulent Society of South Africa - Vetplantvereniging van Suid-Afrika, Private Bag X10, Brooklyn 0011, South Africa. TEL 27-12-983588. FAX 27-12-983588. Ed. F.E. Steffens. adv.; bk.rev.; charts; illus.; index, cum.index: 1963-1990 (vols.1-27). circ. 1,500. **Indexed:** Ind.S.A.Per., Ornam.Hort. **Document type:** academic/scholarly publication.
Description: Contains popular accounts of individual species, field trips, detailed growing tips, plant locations, and plant ecology.

582.14 635.955 RH ISSN 1016-524X
ALOE, CACTUS & SUCCULENT SOCIETY OF ZIMBABWE. INGENS BULLETIN. 1989. 2/yr. Aloe, Cactus & Succulent Society of Zimbabwe, P.O. Box CY 300, Causeway, Harare, Zimbabwe. TEL 263-4-39175. Ed. Michael J. Kimberley. R&P contact: Michael J. Kimberley. circ. 1,000. **Document type:** bulletin.

581 635 US ISSN 0197-3789
AMERICAN BAMBOO SOCIETY. JOURNAL. 1980. irreg. $30 includes Newsletter. American Bamboo Society, Inc., 750 Krumkill Rd., Albany, NY 12203-5976. TEL 518-458-7618. FAX 518-458-7625. URL: http://www.halcyon.com/p1rabbit/bamboo/abs.html. Ed. Kenneth Brennecke. circ. 1,000 (paid). (back issues avail.)
Description: Information on the biology, culture and history of bamboo, including its many uses.

635 581 US
AMERICAN BAMBOO SOCIETY NEWSLETTER. 1980. bi-m. $30 includes Journal. American Bamboo Society, Inc., 750 Krumkill Rd., Albany, NY 12203-5976. TEL 518-458-7618. FAX 518-458-7625. URL: http://www.halcyon.com/p1rabbit/bamboo/abs.html. Ed. Michael Bartholomew. circ. 1,000 (paid). (back issues avail.) **Document type:** newsletter.
Description: Information on the biology, culture, uses and history of bamboo, and information on activities of the A B S.

587.31 US ISSN 0002-8444
QK520 CODEN: AMFJA2
AMERICAN FERN JOURNAL. 1910. q. $20 (foreign $27) (effective 1997). American Fern Society, Inc., c/o Dr. David B. Lellinger, 326 West St., N.W., Vienna, VA 22180-4151. URL: http://www.visuallink.com/fern. Ed. George Yatskievych. bk.rev.; illus.; index, cum.index: vols.1-25; circ. 1,000 (paid). (also avail. in microfilm from PMC; microfiche from IDC) **Indexed:** ASCA, Biol.Abstr., Chem.Abstr., Curr.Adv.Ecol.Sci., Curr.Cont., Excerp.Bot., GeoRef, Hort.Abstr., Ind.Sci.Rev., Sci.Cit.Ind., Soils & Fert. **Document type:** academic/scholarly publication.
—BLDSC (0815.000000); Genuine Article; Linda Hall; SWETS; UnCover.
Description: Technical reports on all aspects of the biology of ferns.
Refereed Serial

581 US ISSN 0002-9122
QK1 CODEN: AJBOAA
AMERICAN JOURNAL OF BOTANY; devoted to all branches of plant sciences. 1914. m. $165 (Canada and Mexico $175; elsewhere $190) (effective 1998). Botanical Society of America, Inc. (Columbus), Business Office, 1735 Neil Ave., Columbus, OH 43210. TEL 614-292-3519. Ed. Karl V. Niklas. R&P contact: Kimberly Hiser. adv.; bibl.; charts; illus.; index. circ. 5,000. (also avail. in microfilm from PMC; microfiche from IDC; back issues avail.) **Indexed:** Agri.Ind., Apic.Abstr., ASCA, Biol.Abstr., Biol.& Agr.Ind., Biol.Dig., Biotech.Abstr., Chem.Abstr., Cott.& Trop.Fibr.Abstr., Crop Physiol.Abstr., Curr.Adv.Ecol.Sci., Curr.Cont., Deep Sea Res.& Oceanogr.Abstr., Ecol.Abstr., Excerp.Med., Field Crop.Abstr., Forest.Abstr., Forest Prod.Abstr., Gen.Sci.Ind., Geo.Abstr., Geol.Abstr., Helminthol.Abstr., Herb.Abstr., Hort.Abstr., Ind.Sci.Rev., INIS Atomind., Irr.& Drain.Abstr., Maize Abstr., Ocean.Abstr., Ornam.Hort., Plant Breed.Abstr., Plant Grow.Reg.Abstr., Potato Abstr., Rev.Plant Path, Sci.Cit.Ind., Seed Abstr., Sel.Water Res.Abstr., Soils & Fert., Soyabean Abstr., Triticale Abstr., VITIS, Weed Abstr. **Document type:** academic/scholarly publication.
—BLDSC (0822.000000); CASDDS; CISTI; EMDOCS; Genuine Article; KR SourceOne; Linda Hall; SWETS; UnCover.
Description: Devoted to every aspect of scientific botany. Provides researchers and the public with the current work in all areas of the botanical sciences.
Refereed Serial

581 632 US ISSN 0569-6992
AMERICAN PHYTOPATHOLOGICAL SOCIETY. MONOGRAPHS. 1961. irreg. latest 1986. price varies. A P S Press, 3340 Pilot Knob Rd., St. Paul, MN 55121-2097. TEL 612-454-7250. FAX 612-454-0766. TELEX 6502439657 (MCI UW). E-mail: aps@scisoc.org; URL: http://www.scisoc.org. (back issues avail.) **Indexed:** Biol.Abstr., Plant Breed.Abstr., Rev.Plant Path. **Document type:** monographic series.
—CISTI.
Description: Explores current topics and research in plant diseases.

AMERICAN SOCIETY FOR HORTICULTURAL SCIENCE. JOURNAL. see *GARDENING AND HORTICULTURE*

581 US ISSN 1048-7794
AMERICAN SOCIETY OF PLANT TAXONOMISTS NEWSLETTER. Abbreviated title: A S P T Newsletter. 1987. q. American Society of Plant Taxonomists (Delaware), c/o David M. Johnson, Sec., Dept. of Botany - Microbiology, Ohio Wesleyan University, Delaware, OH 43015. E-mail: krrobert@uiuc.edu. Ed. Ken Robertson. R&P contact: Ken Robertson. TEL 217-244-2171. adv. contact: Gregory Brown. **Document type:** newsletter.

581 GW ISSN 0721-6513
ANDRIAS. (Text mainly in German; summaries in English) 1981. irreg. Staatliches Museum fuer Naturkunde Karlsruhe, Erbprinzenstr. 13, 76133 Karlsruhe, Germany. TEL 49-721-1752111. FAX 49-721-1752110. Ed. Siegfried Rietschel. (back issues avail.) **Document type:** academic/scholarly publication.

582.13 II
ANGIOSPERM TAXONOMY. (Text in English) s-a. Hindustan Publishing Corp., 4805-24, 1st Fl., Bharat Ram Rd., Darya Ganj, New Delhi 110 002, India. TEL 91-11-3254401. FAX 91-11-6863511. E-mail: hpcpd@giasdl01.vsnl.net.in.

581 FI ISSN 0003-3847
QK1 CODEN: ABOFAQ
ANNALES BOTANICI FENNICI. (Text in English) 1964. q. FIM 500($96) (Academy of Finland) Finnish Zoological and Botanical Publishing Board, P.O. Box 17, P. Rautatiekatu 13, FIN-00014 University of Helsinki, Finland. TEL 358-9-1917405. FAX 358-9-1917443. E-mail: elmor_kr@cc.helsinki.fi; URL: http://sekj.pc.helsinki.fi/journals. (Dist. by: Tiedekirja OY, Kirkkokatu 14, FIN-00014 Helsinki, Finland) (Co-sponsors: Finnish Academy of Sciences and Letters; Societas Scientarum Fennica, Societas pro Fauna et Flora Fennica, Societas Biologica Fennica Vanamo) Ed. Krzysztof Raciborski. charts; illus.; stat.; index. circ. 750. **Indexed:** Arct.Bibl., ASCA, Biol.Abstr., Chem.Abstr., Curr.Adv.Ecol.Sci., Curr.Cont., Deep Sea Res.& Oceanogr.Abstr., Ecol.Abstr., Excerp.Med., Field Crop Abstr., Forest.Abstr., Forest Prod.Abstr., Geo.Abstr., GeoRef, Hort.Abstr., IBR, Ind.Sci.Rev., Ocean.Abstr., Plant Breed.Abstr., Pollut.Abstr., Ref.Zh., Rev.Plant Path, Sci.Cit.Ind, Sel.Water Res.Abstr., Soils & Fert., Weed Abstr. **Document type:** academic/scholarly publication.
—BLDSC (0969.210000); CASDDS; CISTI; EMDOCS; Genuine Article; Linda Hall; SWETS; UMI.
Description: Short, original botanical papers by Finnish and foreign botanists. Terrestrial and aquatic ecology, phytogeography and palaeoecology of Boreal zone, plant taxonomy, effect of air pollution on plants, and cryptogamic botany.

581 IT ISSN 0365-0812
CODEN: ABORAS
ANNALI DI BOTANICA. (Text in various European languages; summaries in English & Italian) 1885. a. exchange basis only. Universita degli Studi "La Sapienza", Dipartimento di Biologia Vegetale, Biblioteca, Piazzale Aldo Moro 5, 00185 Rome, Italy. TEL 39-6-49912445. FAX 39-6-4463865. E-mail: pignatti@axrma.uniroma1.it. Ed. Sandro Pignatti. R&P contact: Ubrizsy Savoia. bk.rev.; charts; illus.; index. circ. 500. **Indexed:** Biol.Abstr., Chem.Abstr., Deep Sea Res.& Oceanogr.Abstr., Rev.Med.& Vet.Mycol. **Document type:** bulletin.
—CASDDS; CISTI; Linda Hall.
Supersedes (in 1902): Istituto Botanico di Roma. Annuario.
Description: Deals with problems on ecology and the European vegetation survey program.

BIOLOGY — BOTANY

581   UK   ISSN 0305-7364
QK1   CODEN: ANBOA4
ANNALS OF BOTANY. 1887. m. £322 (effective 1998). Academic Press Ltd. (Subsidiary of: Harcourt Brace & Company Ltd.), 24-28 Oval Rd., London NW1 7DX, England. TEL 44-171-267-4466. FAX 44-171-482-2293. TELEX 25775 ACPRES G. E-mail: apsubs@acad.com; URL: http://www.hbuk.co.uk/ap/aob; URL: http://www.europe.idealibrary.com/. (Subscr. to: Harcourt Brace & Company Ltd., Foots Cray High St., Sidcup, Kent, DA14 5HP, England. TEL 44-181-300-3322. FAX 44-181-306-0807) (Co-sponsor: Annals of Botany Company) Ed. M. Jackson. R&P contact: Catherine John. adv. contact: Nik Screen. bk.rev.; bibl.; charts; illus.; index, cum.index. vols.1-25 (present series). (also avail. in microfilm from PMC; microfiche from IDC; reprint service avail. from SWZ) **Indexed:** ASCA, Biodet.Abstr., Biol.Abstr., Biol.& Agr.Ind., Chem.Abstr., Cott.& Trop.Fibr.Abstr., Crop Physiol.Abstr., Curr.Adv.Ecol.Sci., Curr.Cont., Ecol.Abstr., Excerp.Med., Fababean Abstr., Field Crop Abstr., Food Sci.& Tech.Abstr., Forest.Abstr., Forest Prod.Abstr., Geo.Abstr., GeoRef., Herb.Abstr., Hort.Abstr., Ind.Sci.Rev., Irr.& Drain.Abstr., Maize Abstr., Ornam.Hort., Plant Breed.Abstr., Plant Grow.Reg.Abstr., Potato Abstr., Rev.Plant Path., Rice Abstr., Sci.Cit.Ind, Seed Abstr., Sel.Water Res.Abstr., Soils & Fert., Sorghum & Millets Abstr., Soyabean Abstr., Sport Fish.Abstr., Triticale Abstr., Trop.Oil Seeds Abstr., Weed Abstr., Wild.Rev. **Document type:** academic/scholarly publication.
●Also available online.
—BLDSC (1040.000000); CASDDS; EMDOCS; Genuine Article; KR SourceOne; SWETS; UnCover. **CCC.**
Description: Emphasizes current research in growth, mathematical models of physiological processes, and plant ultrastructure.

581   II   ISSN 0971-3573
ANNALS OF PLANT PROTECTION SCIENCES. (Text in English) 1993. s-a. $30. (Society of Plant Protection Sciences) Hindustan Publishing Corp., 4805-24, 1st Fl., Bharat Ram Rd., Darya Ganj, New Delhi 110 002, India. TEL 91-11-3254401. FAX 91-11-6863511. E-mail: hpcpd@giasdl01.vsnl.net.in.
—BLDSC (1043.523000).

581 632   US   ISSN 0066-4286
SB599   CODEN: APPYAG
ANNUAL REVIEW OF PHYTOPATHOLOGY. 1963. a. $62 to individuals (foreign $67); institutions $124 (foreign $134) (effective 1998). Annual Reviews Inc., 4139 El Camino Way, Box 10139, Palo Alto, CA 94303-0139. TEL 650-493-4400; 800-523-8635. FAX 650-855-9815. E-mail: service@annurev.org; URL: http://www.annurev.org. Ed. Robert K. Webster; Pub. John McNeil. R&P contact: Jeanne Kunz. bibl.; index, cum.index. (also avail. in microfilm from UMI; back issues avail.; reprint service avail.) **Indexed:** Acid Rain Abstr., Acid Rain Ind., ASCA, Bibl.Agri., Biodet.Abstr., Biol.Abstr., Biol.& Agr.Ind., Biotech.Abstr., Chem.Abstr., Curr.Adv.Ecol.Sci., Curr.Cont., Environ.Abstr., Excerp.Med., Field Crop Abstr., Forest.Abstr., Forest Prod.Abstr., Helminthol.Abstr., Herb.Abstr., Hort.Abstr., Ind.Sci.Rev., M.M.R.I., Plant Breed.Abstr., Rev.Plant Path., Sci.Cit.Ind, Soils & Fert., VITIS, Weed Abstr. **Document type:** academic/scholarly publication.
—BLDSC (1527.200000); CASDDS; CISTI; EMDOCS; Genuine Article; KR SourceOne; Linda Hall; SWETS; UMI; UnCover. **CCC.**
Description: Original critical reviews of the significant primary literature and current developments in phytopathology.

581   US   ISSN 1040-2519
    CODEN: ARPBEX
ANNUAL REVIEW OF PLANT PHYSIOLOGY AND PLANT MOLECULAR BIOLOGY. 1950. a. $60 to individuals (foreign $65); institutions $120 (foreign $130) (effective 1998). Annual Reviews Inc., 4139 El Camino Way, Box 10139, Palo Alto, CA 94303-0139. TEL 650-493-4400; 800-523-8635. FAX 650-855-9815. E-mail: service@annurev.org; URL: http://www.annurev.org. Ed. Russell L. Jones; Pub. John McNeil. R&P contact: Jeanne Kunz. bibl.; index, cum.index. (also avail. in microfilm from UMI; back issues avail.; reprint service avail.) **Indexed:** Abstr.Bull.Inst.Pap.Chem., ASCA, Biol.Abstr., Biol.& Agr.Ind., Biotech.Abstr., Chem.Abstr., Curr.Adv.Ecol.Sci., Curr.Cont., Field Crop Abstr., Forest.Abstr., Forest Prod.Abstr., Helminthol.Abstr., Herb.Abstr., Hort.Abstr., Ind.Sci.Rev., INIS Atomind., M.M.R.I., Maize Abstr., Psychol.Abstr., Rev.Plant Path., Sci.Cit.Ind., Soils & Fert., Triticale Abstr., Vet.Bull., VITIS, Weed Abstr. **Document type:** academic/scholarly publication.
—BLDSC (1528.050000); CASDDS; CISTI; Genuine Article; KR SourceOne; Linda Hall; SWETS; UMI; UnCover. **CCC.**
Formerly: (until vol.38, 1987): Annual Review of Plant Physiology (ISSN 0066-4294)
Description: Original critical reviews of the significant primary literature and current developments in plant physiology and plant molecular biology.

APPLIED BOTANY ABSTRACTS. see *BIOLOGY — Abstracting, Bibliographies, Statistics*

581   US   ISSN 0893-7702
AQUAPHYTE. 1981. s-a. free. (Center for Aquatic Plants, Aquatic Plant Information Retrieval System (APIRS)) University of Florida, Center for Aquatic Plants, 7922 N.W. 71st St., Gainesville, FL 32653. TEL 352-392-1799. FAX 352-392-3462. E-mail: varamey@nervm.nerdc.ufl.edu; URL: http://aquat1.ifas.ufl.edu/. Ed. Victor Ramey. R&P contact: Victor Ramey. bk.rev.; abstr.; bibl. circ. 5,500. (back issues avail.) **Document type:** newsletter.
Description: Publishes items of interest to aquatic plant managers, researchers, and regulators, including literature reviews, meeting announcements, and articles.

581.92 551.46   NE   ISSN 0304-3770
QK916   CODEN: AQBODS
AQUATIC BOTANY; an international scientific journal dealing with applied and fundamental research on submerged, floating and emergent plants in marine and freshwater ecosystems. (Text in English) 1975. m. fl.1575($905) (effective 1998). Elsevier Science B.V., P.O. Box 211, 1000 AE Amsterdam, Netherlands. TEL 31-20-4853911. FAX 31-20-4853598. TELEX 18582 ESPA NL. E-mail: nlinfo-f@elsevier.nl; usinfo-f@elsevier.com; forinfo-kyf04035@niftyserve.or.jp; URL: http://www.elsevier.nl/. (Subscr. in the Americas to: Elsevier Science, Regional Sales Office, Box 945, New York, NY 10159-0945. TEL 212-633-3730. FAX 212-633-3680; Subscr. in Australasia and the Far East to: Elsevier Science (Singapore) Pte Ltd, No.1 Temasek Ave., No.17-01 Millenia Tower, Singapore 039192, Singapore. TEL 65-434-3727. FAX 65-337-2230; Subscr. in Japan to: Elsevier Science Japan, 9-15 Higashi-Azabu 1-chome, Minato-ku, Tokyo 106, Japan. TEL 212-989-5800. FAX 212-633-3990) Eds. C. den Hartog, J.M.A. Brown. adv.; bk.rev.; bibl.; illus.; index. (also avail. in microfilm from UMI; reprint service avail. from SWZ) **Indexed:** Acid Pre.Dig., Acid Rain Abstr., Acid Rain Ind., Appl.Ecol.Abstr., Aqua.Sci.& Fish.Abstr., ASCA, Biol.Abstr., Cadscan, Chem.Abstr., Curr.Adv.Ecol.Sci., Curr.Cont., Excerp.Med., Forest.Abstr., Geo.Abstr.P.G., IDA, Ind.Sci.Rev., Irr.& Drain.Abstr., Lead Abstr., Mar.Sci.Cont.Tab., Ocean.Abstr., Plant Grow.Reg.Abstr., Sci.Cit.Ind., Seed Abstr., Sel.Water Res.Abstr., So.Pac.Per.Ind., Sport Fish.Abstr., W.R.C.Inf., Weed Abstr., Wild.Rev., Zincscan, Zoo.Rec. **Document type:** academic/scholarly publication.
—BLDSC (1582.370000); CASDDS; CISTI; EMDOCS; Genuine Article; SWETS; UnCover. **CCC.**
Description: Concerned with fundamental studies on structure, function, dynamics and classification of plant-dominated aquatic ecosystems.
Refereed Serial

THE AQUATIC GARDENER. see *GARDENING AND HORTICULTURE*

581 635   US   ISSN 1046-9397
AQUATIC PLANT NEWS. 1986. q. $35 to individuals; students $5. Aquatic Plant Management Society, Inc., Box 121086, Clermont, FL 34712-1086. TEL 352-392-9613. Ed. Wendy Andrew. R&P contact: William T. Haller. **Document type:** newsletter.

581.9   NE   ISSN 0921-8572
AQUATIC PLANT STUDIES. 1987. irreg., vol.2, 1989. price varies. Elsevier Science B.V., Books Division, P.O. Box 211, 1000 AE Amsterdam, Netherlands. TEL 31-20-4853911. FAX 31-20-4853705. TELEX 18582 ESPA NL. E-mail: nlinfo-f@elsevier.nl; usinfo-f@elsevier.com; forinfo-kyf04035@niftyserve.or.jp; URL: http://www.elsevier.nl/. (Subscr. in the Americas to: Elsevier Science, Regional Sales Office, Box 945, New York, NY 10159-0945; Subscr. in Australasia and the Far East to: Elsevier Science (Singapore) Pte Ltd, No.1 Temasek Ave., No.17-01 Millenia Tower, Singapore 039192, Singapore; Subscr. in Japan to: Elsevier Science Japan, 9-15 Higashi-Azabu 1-chome, Minato-ku, Tokyo 106, Japan. TEL 212-989-5800) (back issues avail.) **Document type:** monographic series.
Refereed Serial

AQUILEGIA. see *CONSERVATION*

581 574.1   FI   ISSN 0570-5169
    CODEN: ASBOD8
AQUILO. SERIE BOTANICA. (Text in English, German) 1963. s-a. price varies. Societas Amicorum Naturae Ouluensis, Department of Botany, University of Oulu, Linnanmaa, FIN-90570 Oulu, Finland. TEL 358-8-553-1546. FAX 358-981-553-1500. E-mail: pekka.lahdesmaki@oulu.fi. Ed. Pekka Lahdesmaki. circ. 305. (back issues avail.) **Indexed:** Biol.Abstr., Chem.Abstr., Curr.Adv.Ecol.Sci., Deep Sea Res.& Oceanogr.Abstr., Ecol.Abstr., Geo.Abstr., Geol.Abstr., Sel.Water Res.Abstr. **Document type:** academic/scholarly publication.
—BLDSC (1583.100000); CASDDS.
Description: Covers botany, ecology, pollution and plant physiology.
Refereed Serial

581   GW   ISSN 1434-1662
ARBEITSGEMEINSCHAFT SAECHSISCHER BOTANIKER. BERICHTE. 1959. a. DM.40. Technische Universitaet Dresden, Institut fuer Botanik, Mommsenstr. 13, 01062 Dresden, Germany. bk.rev.; illus. circ. 800. **Indexed:** Biol.Abstr. **Document type:** academic/scholarly publication.
Description: Contains studies in botany, geobotany, and taxonomy.

581   GW   ISSN 0172-875X
ARBEITSKREIS FUER MAMMILLARIENFREUNDE. MITTEILUNGSBLATT. (Summaries in English.) 1977. 4/yr. DM.70. Arbeitskreis fuer Mammillarienfreunde e.V., Knietschstr. 21, 67227 Frankenthal, Germany. TEL 49-6233-9486. Ed. Othmar Appenzeller. R&P contact: Othmar Appenzeller. adv. contact: Guenter Ellenberg. bk.rev. circ. 650. **Document type:** newsletter.

634.9 581   US   ISSN 0279-0106
ARBOR AGE. 1981. m. $40 (foreign $65) (effective 1997). Hunter Publishing Limited Partnership, 2101 S. Arlington Heights Rd., Ste. 150, Arlington Heights, IL 60005. TEL 847-427-9512. FAX 847-427-2097. Ed. Helen Stone; Pub. Colleen Long. adv. contact: Melissa Barrasso. tr.lit. circ. 15,500. **Document type:** trade publication.
—BLDSC (1593.530000).
Description: Directed to the urban tree industry.

582   PL   ISSN 0066-5878
QK1   CODEN: ARKOA9
ARBORETUM KORNICKIE. (Text in English and Polish; summaries in English and Russian) 1955. a. price varies. Polska Akademia Nauk, Instytut Dendrologii, Ul. Parkowa 5, 62-035 Kornik, Poland. TEL 48-61-170033. FAX 48-61-170166. E-mail: idkornik@pozn1v.put.poznan.pl. (Co-sponsor: Arboretum Kornickie) Ed Tadeusz Przybylski. adv. contact: Tadeusz Przybylski. bibl.; charts; illus. circ. 540. **Indexed:** AgroLibrex, Biol.Abstr., Chem.Abstr., Forest.Abstr., Forest Prod.Abstr., Hort.Abstr., Soils & Fert. **Document type:** academic/scholarly publication.
—CASDDS.
Formerly: Kornik, Poland. Instytut Dendrologii i Pomologii. Prace.

ARBORETUM LEAVES. see *GARDENING AND HORTICULTURE*

BIOLOGY — BOTANY

ARCHIV FUER HYDROBIOLOGIE. see *BIOLOGY*

ARCHIV FUER HYDROBIOLOGIE. SUPPLEMENT-BAND: ARBEITEN AUS DEM LIMNOLOGISCHEN INSTITUT DER UNIVERSITAET KONSTANZ. see *BIOLOGY*

ARCHIV FUER HYDROBIOLOGIE. SUPPLEMENT-BAND: LARGE RIVERS. see *BIOLOGY*

ARCHIV FUER HYDROBIOLOGIE. SUPPLEMENT-BAND: MONOGRAPHIC STUDIES. see *BIOLOGY*

ARCHIV FUER HYDROBIOLOGIE. SUPPLEMENT-BAND: UNTERSUCHUNGEN DES ELBE-AESTUARS. see *BIOLOGY*

581   IT   ISSN 1122-7214
QK101
ARCHIVIO GEOBOTANICO; international journal of geobotany, plant ecology and taxonomy. (Text in English, French, Italian; summaries in English, French) 1995. s-a. L.90000($58) (effective 1997 & 1998). Universita di Pavia, Dipartimento di Ecologia del Territorio, Via S. Epifanio 14, 27100 Pavia, Italy. TEL 39-382-23069. FAX 39-382-34240. E-mail: botanici@ipv36.unipv.it. (Subscr. to: A. Delfino Editore, Via Lucca 33, 00161 Rome, Italy. TEL 39-6-44231327) Ed. Augusto Pirola. R&P contact: Graziano Rossi. bk.rev.; charts; illus.; index. circ. 600. **Indexed:** Biol.Abstr., Field Crop Abstr., Herb.Abstr. **Document type:** academic/scholarly publication.
—Linda Hall.
   Formed by the merger of (1925-1992): Archivio Botanico Italiano (ISSN 1121-2101); Which was formerly (until 1988): Archivio Botanico e Biogeografico Italiano (ISSN 0004-0053); (until 1955): Archivio Botanico (ISSN 1121-225X); (until 1935): Archivio Botanico per la Sistematica, Fitogeografia e Genetica (ISSN 1120-5482); And (1888-1992): Atti dell'Istituto Botanico e del Laboratorio Crittogamico dell'Universita di Pavia (ISSN 0373-3947); Which was formerly (until 1981): Atti dell'Istituto Botanico dell'Universita e del Laboratorio Crittogamico di Pavia (ISSN 0367-6951); (until 1941): Atti dell'Istituto Botanico Giovanni Briosi e del Laboratorio Crittogamico Italiano (ISSN 1122-8121); (until 1929): Universita di Pavia. Istituto Botanico. Atti (ISSN 0365-298X).
Refereed Serial

581   SP   ISSN 1131-5199
ARCHIVOS DE FLORA IBERICA. 1991. irreg. price varies. Real Jardin Botanico de Madrid, Plaza de Murillo 2, 28014 Madrid, Spain. (Co-sponsor: Consejo Superior de Investigaciones Cientificas) **Indexed:** Ind.SST.

ARNOLDIA. see *GARDENING AND HORTICULTURE — Florist Trade*

581   FR   ISSN 0066-8184
ARVERNIA BIOLOGICA: BOTANIQUE; recueil des travaux des laboratoires de botanique de l'U.F.R. de recherche scientifique et technique. 1930. irreg. exchange basis only. Universite de Clermont II, Laboratoire de Biologie Vegetale, 4, rue Ledru, F-63038 Clermont-Ferrand Cedex 1, France. Ed.Bd. **Indexed:** VITIS. **Document type:** academic/scholarly publication.

581   II   ISSN 0971-2402
CODEN: ASCIEU
ASIAN JOURNAL OF PLANT SCIENCE. (Text in English) 1989. s-a. Rs.100($20) Ranjana Malvey, Pub., 6-4-361 26A Anjarieya Swamy Colony, Bholakpur, Secunderabad 500 380, India. Eds. M. Prabhakar, K. Vaidyanath. bk.rev. (also avail. in diskette format; back issues avail.). **Indexed:** Apic.Abstr., Biol.Abstr., Indian Sci.Abstr. **Document type:** academic/scholarly publication.
   Description: Contains research papers and review articles covering all fields of plant science.
Refereed Serial

581   II   ISSN 0971-1678
ASPECT OF PLANT SCIENCES. 1976. vol. 14. irreg., vol.15, 1996. Rs.495($65) Today and Tomorrow's Printers and Publishers, 24B-5 Desh Bandhu Gupta Road, Karol Bagh, New Delhi 110 005, India. TEL 91-11-572-1928. (Dist. in U.S. by: Scholarly Publications, 2825 Wilcrest Dr., Ste. 255, Houston, TX 77042. TEL 713-781-0070. FAX 713-781-2112) Eds. T.N. Bhardwaja, C.B. Gena. **Document type:** academic/scholarly publication.
—CCC.
   Description: Contains articles of theoretical and methodological interest, as well as studies based on empirical research in the field of plant sciences.

581   US   ISSN 0004-5764
ASSOCIATION OF OFFICIAL SEED ANALYSTS. NEWS LETTER. 1927. 3/yr. $20 (foreign $40). Association of Official Seed Analysts, Inc., Box 81152, Lincoln, NE 68501-1152. TEL 402-476-3852. FAX 402-476-6547. Ed. Jan Ferguson Spears. R&P contact: Larry Prenticl. TEL 402-472-1444. abstr.; cum.index: 1927-1940, 1941-1970. circ. 500. **Indexed:** Field Crop Abstr., Herb.Abstr., Maize Abstr., Seed Abstr., Soyabean Abstr., Trop.Oil Seeds Abstr. **Document type:** newsletter.

551.5   FI
ATLAS FLORAE EUROPAEAE. (Text in English) 1972. irreg., vol.10, 1994. price varies. Societas Biologica Fennica Vanamo, c/o Dept. of Ecology and Systematics, P.O. Box 7, FIN-00014 University of Helsinki, Finland. (Dist. by: Akateeminen Kirjakauppa (Academic Bookstore), Keskuskatu 1, SF-00100 Helsinki, Finland) (Co-sponsor: Committee for Mapping the Flora of Europe) Eds. Jaakko Jalas, Juha Suominen. **Indexed:** Bibl.Agri., Biol.Abstr., Bull.Signal., Chem.Abstr., Curr.Cont., Pollut.Abstr. **Document type:** academic/scholarly publication.

581   PL   ISSN 0067-0294
ATLAS FLORY POLSKIEJ I ZIEM OSCIENNYCH/FLORAE POLONICAE TERRARUNIQUE ADIACENTIUM SCONOGRAPHIA. (Text in Latin and Polish) 1960. irreg., vol.6, 1983. price varies. Polska Akademia Nauk, Instytut Botaniki im. W. Szafera, Ul. Lubicz 46, 31-512 Krakow, Poland. TEL 48-12-215144. FAX 48-12-219790. Ed. J. Madalski. **Indexed:** Biol.Abstr.

588.2   PL
ATLAS ROZMIESZCZENIA GEOGRAFICZNEGO MCHOW W POLSCE/ATLAS OF THE GEOGRAPHICAL DISTRIBUTION OF MOSSES IN POLAND. (Text in English and Polish) 1962. irreg. price varies. Akademia Nauk, Instytut Botaniki im. W. Szafera, Ul. Lubicz 46, 31-512 Krakow, Poland. TEL 48-12-215144. FAX 48-12-219790. E-mail: wysocki@ib-pan.krakow.pl. Ed. Ryszard Ochyra. circ. 500 (paid).
   Description: Presents distribution maps for all varieties of mosses known to occur in Poland. The text describes the history of the species, its ecology, and reviews in detail its world distribution.

579.7   PL
ATLAS ROZMIESZCZENIA GEOGRAFICZNEGO POROSTOW W POLSCE/ATLAS OF THE GEOGRAPHICAL DISTRIBUTION OF LICHENS IN POLAND. (Text in English and Polish) 1993. irreg. price varies. Polska Akademia Nauk, Instytut Botaniki im. W. Szafera, Ul. Lubicz 46, 31-512 Krakow, Poland. TEL 48-12-215144. FAX 48-12-219790. E-mail: nhwysock@cyf-kr.edu.pl. Ed. Stanislaw Cieslinski. circ. 300 (paid). **Document type:** academic/scholarly publication.
   Description: Presents lichens distribution maps in Poland. Provides description of each species and full list of localities.

581.2   AT   ISSN 0815-3191
CODEN: AAPPDN
AUSTRALASIAN PLANT PATHOLOGY. 1972. q. Aus.$75 (libraries Aus.$90) (effective 1997). (Australasian Plant Pathology Society) J & B Desktop Publishing Pty. Ltd., 32 Range St., Toowoomba, Qld. 4350, Australia. TEL 61-76-325654. FAX 61-76-325685. E-mail: dodmanb@tmba.design.net.au; URL: http://www.csu.edu.au/special/apps/aapshp/htm. Ed. R.L. Dodman. R&P contact: R.L. Dodman. adv.; bk.rev. circ. 550. (back issues avail.). **Indexed:** ASCA, Bio-Contr.News & Info., Curr.Cont., Forest.Abstr., Helminthol.Abstr., Hort.Abstr., Rev.Med.& Vet.Mycol., Rev.Plant Path., Seed Abstr., Soyabean Abstr., Triticale Abstr., Weed Abstr. **Document type:** academic/scholarly publication.
—BLDSC (1796.095000); CASDDS; Genuine Article.
   Formerly (until 1978): Australian Plant Pathology Society. Newsletter (ISSN 0156-0972)
   Description: Publishes research papers, short research notes, general articles, review articles, and disease notes or new records.
Refereed Serial

581   AT   ISSN 0067-1924
QK1   CODEN: AJBTAP
AUSTRALIAN JOURNAL OF BOTANY. 1953. bi-m. Aus.$320($320) (effective 1998). (C.S.I.R.O. Australia) C.S.I.R.O. Publishing, 150 Oxford St., Collingwood, Vic. 3066, Australia. TEL 61-3-96627624. FAX 61-3-96627611. E-mail: deborah.penrose@publish.csiro.au; URL: http://www.publish.csiro.au/journals/ajb/electronic.html. Ed. D.L. Penrose. adv.; index. circ. 800. (also avail. in microform from UMI; back issues avail.) **Indexed:** ASCA, Biol.Abstr., Biol.& Agr.Ind., Chem.Abstr., Crop Physiol.Abstr., Curr.Adv.Ecol.Sci., Curr.Cont., Deep Sea Res.& Oceanogr.Abstr., Ecol.Abstr., Environ.Per.Bibl. (1975-1993), Field Crop Abstr., Food Sci.& Tech.Abstr., Forest.Abstr., Forest Prod.Abstr., Geo.Abstr.H.G., Geo.Abstr.P.G., Geol.Abstr., Helminthol.Abstr., Herb.Abstr., Hort.Abstr., Ind.Sci.Rev., Ornam.Hort., Plant Breed.Abstr., Plant Grow.Reg.Abstr., Rev.Med.& Vet.Mycol., Rev.Plant Path, Sci.Cit.Ind., Sel.Water Res.Abstr., So.Pac.Per.Ind., Soils & Fert., VITIS, Weed Abstr. **Document type:** academic/scholarly publication.
●Also available online.
—BLDSC (1805.000000); CASDDS; CISTI; EMDOCS; Genuine Article; KR SourceOne; Linda Hall; SWETS; UMI; UnCover. CCC.
   Description: Publishes original research in plant sciences: ecology and ecophysiology, conservation biology and biodiversity, forest biology and management, cell biology and tissue culture, palaeobotany, reproductive biology and genetics, mycology and pathology, and structure and development.

581 635   AT   ISSN 0005-0008
CODEN: ANPLAV
AUSTRALIAN PLANTS. 1959. q. Aus.$30. Society for Growing Australian Plants, 860 Henry Lawson Dr., Picnic Point, N.S.W. 2213, Australia. TEL 61-2-773-9866. E-mail: sgap@ozemail.com.au; URL: http://www.ozemail.com.au/~sgap/apoline.html. Ed. W.H. Payne. adv.; bk.rev.; charts; illus.; index every 2 yrs.; circ. 10,000 (paid). (also avail. in microfilm from UMI; reprint service avail. from UMI) **Indexed:** Biol.Abstr., Hort.Abstr., Ornam.Hort., Pinpointer, Soils & Fert. **Document type:** academic/scholarly publication.
●Also available online.
—UMI.
   Description: Examines the Australian flora for horticultural development and its conservation. Provides a link between the academic scientist and the general public by representing current scientific research in a popular manner.

BIOLOGY — BOTANY

581   AT   ISSN 1030-1887
CODEN: ASBOE9
AUSTRALIAN SYSTEMATIC BOTANY. 1972. bi-m. Aus.$380($380) (effective 1998). (C.S.I.R.O. Australia) C.S.I.R.O. Publishing, 150 Oxford St., Collingwood, Vic. 3066, Australia. TEL 61-3-96627624. FAX 61-3-96627611. E-mail: deborah.penrose@publish.csiro.au; URL: http://www.publish.csiro.au/journals/asb. Ed. D.L. Penrose. circ. 500. (also avail. in microform from UMI; back issues avail.) **Indexed:** ASCA, Biol.Abstr., Curr.Adv.Ecol.Sci., Curr.Cont., Ecol.Abstr., Geol.Abstr., Ind.Sci.Rev. **Document type:** academic/scholarly publication.
—BLDSC (1822.350000); CISTI; Genuine Article; Linda Hall; UMI; UnCover. **CCC.**
   Supersedes (in 1988): Brunonia (ISSN 0313-4245); Which was formerly: Commonwealth Scientific and Industrial Research Organization. Herbarium Australiense. Brunonia; Commonwealth Scientific and Industrial Research Organization. Herbarium Australiense. Contributions from Herbarium Australiense.
   Description: Devoted to the taxonomy, biogeography and evolution of all plant groups.

580   NE   ISSN 0005-2728
QD1
B B A - BIOENERGETICS. (Biochimica et Biophysica Acta) (Section of: Biochimica et Biophysica Acta (ISSN 0006-3002)) 1970. 15/yr. fl.2848($1637) (effective 1998). Elsevier Science B.V., P.O. Box 211, 1000 AE Amsterdam, Netherlands. TEL 31-20-4853911. FAX 31-20-4853598. TELEX 18582 ESP NL. E-mail: nlinfo-f@elsevier.nl; usinfo-f@elsevier.com; forinfo-kyf04035@niftyserve.or.jp; URL: http://www.elsevier.nl/. (Subscr. in the Americas to: Elsevier Science, Regional Sales Office, Box 945, New York, NY 10159-0945. TEL 212-633-3730. FAX 212-633-3680; Subscr. in Australasia and the Far East to: Elsevier Science (Singapore) Pte Ltd, No.1 Temasek Ave., No.17-01 Millenia Tower, Singapore 039192, Singapore. TEL 65-434-3727. FAX 65-337-2230; Subscr. in Japan to: Elsevier Science Japan, 9-15 Higashi-Azabu 1-chome, Minato-ku, Tokyo 106, Japan. TEL 81-3-5561-5033. FAX 81-3-5561-5047) Ed.Bd. (also avail. in microform from UMI) **Indexed:** ASCA, Biotech.Abstr., Crop Physiol.Abstr., Curr.Adv.Ecol.Sci., Curr.Cont., Dairy Sci.Abstr., Excerp.Med., Field Crop Abstr., Hort.Abstr., Ind.Sci.Rev., Ind.Vet., Sci.Cit.Ind., Weed Abstr. **Document type:** academic/scholarly publication.
—ADONIS; CISTI; EMDOCS; Genuine Article; SWETS; UnCover. **CCC.**
   Description: Provides full coverage of both plants and animals.
   Refereed Serial

581 580   UK   ISSN 0307-2657
B S B I ABSTRACTS; abstracts from literature relating to the vascular plants of the British Isles. 1971. a. £18 (foreign £20) membership. Botanical Society of the British Isles, c/o Department of Botany, The Natural History Museum, Cromwell Rd., London SW7 5BD, England. Ed. D.H. Kent. circ. 3,000. **Indexed:** Weed Abstr. **Document type:** abstracting/indexing.
—BLDSC (2354.101800); CISTI; Linda Hall.
   Description: Contains full details of publication, often with summaries, of books and research papers relating to the distribution and taxonomic classification of U.K. plants.

581   UK   ISSN 0309-930X
B S B I NEWS. 1972. 3/yr. £18 (foreign £20) membership. Botanical Society of the British Isles, c/o Department of Botany, The Natural History Museum, Cromwell Rd., London SW7 5BD, England. —Linda Hall.
   Description: Contains topical information of the society's activities and meetings, as well as other features of interest to persons studying the botany of the British Isles.

581   PL   ISSN 0067-2815
BADANIA FIZJOGRAFICZNE NAD POLSKA ZACHODNIA. SERIA B. BOTANIKA. (Text in Polish; summaries in English, French or German) 1948. irreg., vol.43, 1994. price varies. Poznanskie Towarzystwo Przyjaciol Nauk, Ul. Sew. Mielzynskiego 27-29, 61-725 Poznan, Poland. TEL 48-61-527-441. illus.; charts. circ. 300. **Indexed:** AgroLibrex. **Document type:** bulletin.
—BLDSC (1856.206000).
   Supersedes in part (in 1974): Badania Fizjograficzne nad Polska Zachodnia. Seria B. Biologia (ISSN 0373-7497)

581 635   US   ISSN 0005-4003
SB1   CODEN: BAILAI
BAILEYA; a journal of horticultural taxonomy. 1953. irreg., vol.23, 1989. $25 (foreign $30) per vol. L. H. Bailey Hortorium, Cornell University, Ithaca, NY 14853. TEL 607-255-2131. FAX 607-255-7979. E-mail: pf13@cornell.edu. Ed. Jerold I. Davis. R&P contact: Jerold I. Davis. bk.rev.; bibl.; charts; illus.; index. circ. 650. (also avail. in microform from UMI; reprint service avail. from UMI) **Indexed:** Biol.Abstr., Curr.Adv.Ecol.Sci., Hort.Abstr., Ornam.Hort., Plant Breed.Abstr. **Document type:** academic/scholarly publication.
—SWETS; UMI; UnCover.
   Refereed Serial

581 635   JA   ISSN 0289-2111
CODEN: BAJOE2
BAMBOO JOURNAL. (Text in English, Japanese) 1981. a. Japan Society of Bamboo Development and Protection - Nihon no Take o Mamoru Kai, Kyoto Dento Sangyo Kaikan, 9-2 Okazaki Seishojimachi, Sakyo-ku, Kyoto 606, Japan.
—CASDDS.

581   BG   ISSN 0253-5416
QK358.7   CODEN: BJBTB3
BANGLADESH JOURNAL OF BOTANY. (Text in English) 1972. 2/yr. $66. Bangladesh Botanical Society, c/o Department of Botany, University of Dhaka, Dhaka 1000, Bangladesh. TEL 505848. Ed. Syed Hadiuzzaman. adv.; bk.rev. circ. 700. (back issues avail.) **Indexed:** ASCA, Biol.Abstr., Chem.Abstr., Curr.Adv.Ecol.Sci., Curr.Cont., ExtraMED, Field Crop Abstr., Food Sci.& Tech.Abstr., Herb.Abstr., Plant Breed.Abstr., Sel.Water Res.Abstr., Soils & Fert. **Document type:** academic/scholarly publication.
•Also available on CD-ROM.
—BLDSC (1861.670000); CASDDS; CISTI; Genuine Article; Linda Hall; UnCover.

581   US   ISSN 0198-7356
BARTONIA. 1909. a. $17.50. Philadelphia Botanical Club, c/o Academy of Natural Sciences of Philadelphia, 1900 Benjamin Franklin Pkwy., Philadelphia, PA 19103. TEL 215-299-1000. Ed. Alfred E. Schuyler. bk.rev. circ. 350. **Indexed:** Biol.Abstr., Curr.Adv.Ecol.Sci. **Document type:** academic/scholarly publication.
—BLDSC (1863.830000); UnCover.
   Refereed Serial

581   SZ   ISSN 0067-4605
QK1   CODEN: BAUHBX
BAUHINIA. (Text mainly in German; occasionally in English, French and Italian) 1955. irreg. (approx. 1/yr.). 25 SFr. (Basler Botanische Gesellschaft) Verlag Wepf und Co., Eisengasse 5, CH-4001 Basel, Switzerland. TEL 41-61-3119576. FAX 41-61-3119576. Ed. R. Leuschner. circ. 500. **Indexed:** Biol.Abstr., GeoRef., Plant Breed.Abstr. **Document type:** monographic series.
—BLDSC (1866.900000).

581   GW   ISSN 0341-3624
BAUM-ZEITUNG; fuer Baumfreunde, Natur und Umwelt. 1966. q. DM.25. Stiftsallee 29b, 32425 Minden, Germany. TELEX 97857 SDL. Ed. Wilhelm Scheidler. adv.; bk.rev. circ. 2,500. (back issues avail.)

581   GW   ISSN 0373-7640
BAYERISCHE BOTANISCHE GESELLSCHAFT. BERICHTE. (Text in German; summaries in English, German) 1890. a. DM.50. Bayerische Botanische Gesellschaft, Menzingerstr. 67, 80638 Munich, Germany. TEL 49-89-17861264. FAX 49-89-17861193. Ed. Wolfgang Lippert. R&P contact: Wolfgang Lippert. bk.rev.; index. circ. 1,200. (back issues avail.) **Indexed:** Biol.Abstr., Curr.Adv.Ecol.Sci., Excerp.Bot., IBR. **Document type:** bulletin.
—CISTI.

BEGONIAN. see *GARDENING AND HORTICULTURE*

581   GW   ISSN 0005-8041
QK1   CODEN: BEPFAT
BEITRAEGE ZUR BIOLOGIE DER PFLANZEN. (Text in English and German) 1870. 3/yr. price varies. Duncker und Humblot GmbH, Postfach 410329, 12113 Berlin, Germany. TEL 49-30-7900060. FAX 49-30-79000631. E-mail: duh-werbung@t-online.de. Ed.Bd. charts; illus.; index. **Indexed:** Biol.Abstr., Chem.Abstr., Curr.Adv.Ecol.Sci., Excerp.Med., Field Crop Abstr., Herb.Abstr., INIS Atomind., Rev.Plant Path., Weed Abstr. **Document type:** academic/scholarly publication.
—BLDSC (1878.800000); CISTI; Linda Hall; SWETS. **CCC.**

581   BE   ISSN 0778-4031
QK1   CODEN: BJBOEP
BELGIAN JOURNAL OF BOTANY. (Text in English French; occasional articles in Flemish or German) 1862. 2/yr. 2000 BEF (effective 1996). Societe Royale de Botanique de Belgique, Chaussee de Wavre 1850, B-1160 Brussels, Belgium. TEL 32-2-2693905. FAX 32-2-2701567. Ed. P. Compere. bk.rev.; bibl.; charts; illus.; cum.index: vols. 1-25, 26-49, 51-75, 76-100. circ. 700. (also avail. in microform from PMC; microfiche from IDC) **Indexed:** ASCA, Biol.Abstr., Bull.Signal., Crop Physiol.Abstr., Curr.Adv.Ecol.Sci., Curr.Cont., Excerp.Med., Field Crop Abstr., Forest.Abstr., Forest Prod.Abstr., Geo.Abstr, Helminthol.Abstr., Herb.Abstr., Hort.Abstr., Rev.Plant Path., Rural Recreat.Tour.Abstr., Seed Abstr., Soils & Fert., Weed Abstr., World Agri.Econ.& Rural Sociol.Abstr. **Document type:** academic/scholarly publication.
—BLDSC (1888.023240); CASDDS; CISTI; Linda Hall; UnCover.
   Formerly (until 1990): Societe Royale de Botanique de Belgique. Bulletin (ISSN 0037-9557)
   Refereed Serial

581.08   NE   ISSN 0169-4375
QK1
BELMONTIA. 1974. irreg., vol. 21, 1989. exchange basis. Agricultural University, Department of Plant Taxonomy, Generaal Foulkesweg 37, P.O. Box 8010, 6700 ED Wageningen, Netherlands. Ed.Bd.
   Description: Covers various research in botany.

BIBLIOGRAFIE BOTANICZNE/BOTANICAL BIBLIOGRAPHIES. see *BIOLOGY — Abstracting, Bibliographies, Statistics*

BIBLIOGRAPHIA PHYTOSOCIOLOGICA SYNTAXONOMICA. see *BIOLOGY — Abstracting, Bibliographies, Statistics*

BIBLIOGRAPHY OF SYSTEMATIC MYCOLOGY. see *BIOLOGY — Abstracting, Bibliographies, Statistics*

581   GW   ISSN 0067-7892
BIBLIOTHECA BOTANICA. Originalabhandlungen aus dem Gesamtgebiet der Botanik. 1886. irreg. price varies. E. Schweizerbart'sche Verlagsbuchhandlung, Johannesstr. 3A, 70176 Stuttgart, Germany. TEL 49-711-625001. FAX 49-711-625005. Ed.Bd. **Document type:** monographic series.
—CISTI; Linda Hall. **CCC.**

581   GW
BIBLIOTHECA DIATOMOLOGICA. (Text in English and German) 1983. irreg. price varies. J. Cramer in der Gebrueder Borntraeger Verlagsbuchhandlung, Johannesstr. 3A, 70176 Stuttgart, Germany. TEL 49-711-625001. FAX 49-711-625005. Ed. H. Lange-Bertalot. **Document type:** academic/scholarly publication, bibliography.

581   GW
BIBLIOTHECA LICHENOLOGICA. (Text in English, French, German) 1973. irreg. price varies. J. Cramer in der Gebrueder Borntraeger Verlagsbuchhandlung, Johannesstr. 3A, 70176 Stuttgart, Germany. TEL 49-711-625001. FAX 49-711-625005. Ed. V. Wirth. **Document type:** academic/scholarly publication, bibliography.

589.2   GW   ISSN 0067-8066
QK600   CODEN: BIMYDY
BIBLIOTHECA MYCOLOGICA. 1967. irreg. price varies. J. Cramer in der Gebrueder Borntraeger Verlagsbuchhandlung, Johannesstr. 3A, 70176 Stuttgart, Germany. TEL 49-711-625001. FAX 49-711-625005. Eds. A. Bresinsky, H. Butin, H.-O. Schwantes. **Indexed:** Biol.Abstr. **Document type:** academic/scholarly publication, bibliography.
—CISTI.

581 GW ISSN 0067-8112
BIBLIOTHECA PHYCOLOGICA. 1967. irreg. price varies.
J. Cramer in der Gebrueder Borntraeger
Verlagsbuchhandlung, Johannsstr. 3A, 70176
Stuttgart, Germany. TEL 49-711-625001.
FAX 49-711-625005. Eds. L. Kies, R. Schnetter.
Indexed: Biol.Abstr. **Document type:**
academic/scholarly publication, bibliography.
—BLDSC (2019.330000); CISTI.

BIFIDOBACTERIA AND MICROFLORA. see *BIOLOGY*

BIFIZUSU/BIFIDUS FLORES, FRUCTUS ET SEMINA. see *BIOLOGY*

BILTEN ZA HMELJ, SIRAK I LEKOVITO BILJE. see *AGRICULTURE — Agricultural Economics*

581 XO
CODEN: BLOAAO
BIOLOGIA. SECTION: BOTANY. (Two other sections avail.:
Zoology; Cellular and Molecular Biology) (Text in
English) 1946. s-a. $50 ($138 for 3 sections).
Slovak Academy of Sciences, Institute of Botany,
Dubravska cesta 14, 842 23 Bratislava, Slovakia.
TEL 421-7-373507. FAX 421-7-371948. E-mail:
botuinst@savba.savba.sk. (Dist. by: Slovak Academic
Press, Ltd., P.O. Box 57, Nam. Slobody 6, 810 05
Bratislava, Slovakia) Ed. Igor Mistrik. adv.; bk.rev.;
charts; illus.; index. **Indexed:** Biodet.Abstr., Biol.Abstr.,
Chem.Abstr., Excerp.Med., Forest.Abstr., Forest
Prod.Abstr., GeoRef., Helminthol.Abstr., Ind.Med.,
INIS Atomind., Irr.& Drain.Abstr., Plant Breed.Abstr.,
Seed Abstr., Soyabean Abstr., Sport Fish.Abstr.,
Triticale Abstr., Wild.Rev., Zoo.Rec. **Document type:**
academic/scholarly publication.
—BLDSC (2072.700000); CASDDS; CISTI; Genuine
Article; KNAW; Linda Hall.
Formerly (until 1994): Biologia. A: Botanika (ISSN
0862-1128); Supersedes in part (in 1969): Biologia
(ISSN 0006-3088)
Description: Brings original experimental and
descriptive works in basic biological research from
taxonomy, phytocenology, physiology and cytology.

581 NE ISSN 0006-3134
QK1 CODEN: BPABAJ
BIOLOGIA PLANTARUM; journal for experimental botany.
(Text in English, French, German; summaries in
Czech, English) 1959. 8/yr. fl.1418 to institutions;
$728 to institutions in U.S. (effective 1998).
(Czechoslovak Academy of Sciences, Institute of
Experimental Botany) Kluwer Academic Publishers,
Postbus 17, 3300 AA Dordrecht, Netherlands.
TEL 31-78-6392392. FAX 31-78-6392254. TELEX
29245 KAPG NL. E-mail: services@wkap.nl; URL:
http://www.wkap.nl. (Dist. by: Kluwer Academic
Publishers Group, P.O. Box 322, 3300 AH
Dordrecht, Netherlands. TEL 31-78-6392392. FAX
31-78-6546474; N. America dist. addr.: Box 358,
Accord Sta., Hingham, MA 02018-0358. TEL
617-871-6600. FAX 617-871-6528)
(Co-publisher: Academia, XR) Ed. J. Catsky. bk.rev.;
abstr.; bibl.; charts; illus.; index. (also avail. in
microform from UMI) **Indexed:** ASCA, Biol.Abstr.,
Bull.Signal., Chem.Abstr., Crop Physiol.Abstr.,
Curr.Adv.Ecol.Sci., Curr.Adv.Genetics & Molec.Biol.,
Curr.Cont., Deep Sea Res.& Oceanogr.Abstr.,
Excerp.Med., Fababean Abstr., Field Crop Abstr.,
Forest.Abstr., Forest Prod.Abstr., Herb.Abstr.,
Hort.Abstr., Ind.Sci.Rev., INIS Atomind., Irr.&
Drain.Abstr., Maize Abstr., Ornam.Hort., Plant
Breed.Abstr., Plant Grow.Reg.Abstr., Ref.Zh.,
Sci.Cit.Ind., Seed Abstr., Sel.Water Res.Abstr., Soils &
Fert., Sorghum & Millets Abstr., SSCI, Triticale Abstr.,
Trop.Oil Seeds Abstr., VITIS, Weed Abstr., Zoo.Rec.
Document type: academic/scholarly publication.
—BLDSC (2072.850000); CASDDS; CISTI;
EMDOCS; Genuine Article; Linda Hall; SWETS;
UnCover. **CCC.**
Description: Original papers and brief
communications in the fields of plant physiology,
experimental ecology, experimental morphology,
genetics, cytology, biochemistry and pathology.
Refereed Serial

581 US ISSN 0887-2236
SB732.6
BIOLOGICAL AND CULTURAL TESTS FOR CONTROL OF PLANT DISEASES. Short title: B and C Tests. 1986.
a. $30 (foreign $37). (American Phytopathological
Society) A P S Press, 3340 Pilot Knob Rd., St. Paul,
MN 55121-2097. TEL 612-454-7250;
800-328-7560. FAX 612-454-0766. TELEX
6502439657 (MCI UW). E-mail: aps@scisoc.org;
URL: http://www.scisoc.org. Ed. Craig H. Canaday.
circ. 1,453. (back issues avail.)
—CISTI; Linda Hall.
Description: Reviews current experiments in
disease control. Also includes short guidelines on
how to prepare reports and how to convert US units
of measurement to the metric system.

BIOLOGICAL SOCIETY OF WASHINGTON. PROCEEDINGS.
see *BIOLOGY*

581 US ISSN 0893-3138
BISHOP MUSEUM BULLETINS IN BOTANY. 1922. irreg.,
no.3, 1993. price varies. (Bernice Pauahi Bishop
Museum) Bishop Museum Press, 1525 Bernice St.,
Box 19000-A, Honolulu, HI 96817.
TEL 808-847-3511. FAX 808-841-8968. circ. 300.
(reprint service avail. from UMI)
—CISTI; Linda Hall.
Supersedes in part (in 1987): Bernice P. Bishop
Museum Bulletin (ISSN 0005-9439)
Description: Covers botany of Hawaii and the
Pacific Basin.

581 SP ISSN 0212-8314
QK329
BLANCOANA. 1983. a. 500 ptas. (effective 1997).
Universidad de Jaen, Facultad de Ciencias
Experimentales, Herbario Jaen, 23071 Jaen, Spain.
TEL 34-953-212159. FAX 34-953-212141. (Dist.
by: Libreria Agricola, Fernando VI, 2, 28004 Madrid,
Spain. TEL 34-91-4190940) Ed. Carlos
Fernandez-Lopez. **Indexed:** Ind.SST. **Document type:**
newspaper.
Description: Information on vascular plants.

BLUE BILL. see *BIOLOGY — Ornithology*

582 NE ISSN 0006-5196
QK1 CODEN: BLMAAE
BLUMEA; a journal of plant-taxonomy and
plant-geography. (Supplement avail. (ISSN
0373-4293)) 1934. 2/yr. fl.100 (effective 1994).
Rijksherbarium - Hortus Botanicus, Publications
Department, P.O. Box 9514, 2300 RA Leiden,
Netherlands. E-mail: adema@rulrhb.leidenuniv.nl.
Ed.Bd. charts; illus.; index. circ. 600. (also avail. in
microfiche from IDC; back issues avail.) **Indexed:**
ASCA, Biol.Abstr., Curr.Adv.Ecol.Sci., Curr.Cont.,
Excerp.Bot., Field Crop Abstr., Forest.Abstr., Forest
Prod.Abstr., Herb.Abstr., Plant Breed.Abstr.,
So.Pac.Per.Ind. **Document type:** academic/scholarly
publication.
—CISTI; EMDOCS; Linda Hall; SWETS; UnCover.
Description: International journal on descriptive
botany of Phanerogams and well as Cryptogams,
excluding fungi, with emphasis on the Malesian area.
Coverage includes taxonomy, plant geography,
morphology and anatomy.
Refereed Serial

581 NE ISSN 0373-4293
CODEN: BLSUE6
BLUMEA. SUPPLEMENT. (Supplement to: Blumea (ISSN
0006-5196)) 1937. irreg., vol.9, 1995. price
varies. Rijksherbarium - Hortus Botanicus,
Publications Department, P.O. Box 9514, 2300 RA
Leiden, Netherlands. illus. (back issues avail.)
Indexed: Biol.Abstr., Zoo.Rec. **Document type:**
monographic series.
—CISTI; Linda Hall.
Supersedes (after vol.15, 1991): Leiden Botanical
Series (ISSN 0169-8508)
Description: Taxonomic monographs and extensive
studies in comparative botany.
Refereed Serial

581 NO ISSN 0006-5269
QK1 CODEN: BLYTAT
BLYTTIA; Norsk Botanisk Forenings tidsskrift. (Text in
Norwegian; summaries in English) 1943. q.
NOK 490 in Nordic countries; elsewhere $93
(effective 1997). (Norwegian Botanical Association)
Scandinavian University Press, P.O. Box
2959-Toeyen, N-0608 Oslo, Norway.
TEL 47-22-57-54-00. FAX 47-22-57-53-53. E-mail:
mail@scup.no; URL: http://www.scup.no. (US addr.:
875 Massachusetts Ave., Ste. 84, Cambridge, MA
02139. TEL 617-497-6515. FAX 617-354-6875)
Ed. Klaus Hoeiland. adv.; bk.rev.; bibl.; charts; illus.;
index. circ. 1,400. (back issues avail.; reprint service
avail. from ISI) **Indexed:** Bibl.Agri., Biol.Abstr.,
Curr.Adv.Ecol.Sci., Ecol.Abstr., Excerp.Bot, Field Crop
Abstr., Herb.Abstr., Plant Breed.Abstr., Rev.Plant
Path., Sel.Water Res.Abstr., Soyabean Abstr., Weed
Abstr. **Document type:** academic/scholarly
publication.
—BLDSC (2116.000000). **CCC.**
Description: Covers all aspects of botany with
emphasis on investigation of the Norwegian flora.

BOCAGIANA. see *BIOLOGY — Zoology*

581 CK
BOLETIN BOTANICO LATINOAMERICANO. 1978. s-a.
$10. Asociacion Latinoamericana de Botanica,
Instituto de Ciencias Nacionales, Universidad
Nacional, Apdo. 7495, Bogota, Colombia.
TEL 57-1-3681380. FAX 57-1-3681345. E-mail:
eforero@ciencias.ciencias.unal.edu.co. Ed. Enrique
Forero. bk.rev.; bibl. circ. 1,000. **Document type:**
bulletin.
Description: Devoted to bibliographies in some
issues, directories in others, but in most cases to
miscellaneous botany news.

589.2 CL ISSN 0716-114X
BOLETIN MICOLOGICO. (Text in English, Italian,
Portuguese, Spanish; summaries English, Spanish)
1982. s-a. $25. Universidad de Valparaiso, Facultad
de Medicina, Casilla 92-V, Valparaiso, Chile.
FAX 56-32-217612. Ed. Dr. Eduardo Piontelli. R&P
contact: Eduardo Piontelli. TEL 56-32-217612.
—BLDSC (2212.060000).
Description: Publishes research papers, notes,
commentaries, reviews and conference proceedings
on general mycology.

581 AG ISSN 0524-0476
BONPLANDIA. (Text in Spanish) 1960. irreg. exchange
basis. Instituto de Botanica del Nordeste, Sargento
Cabral 2131, Casilla de Correo 209, 3400
Corrientes, Argentina. TEL 0783-27309.
FAX 0783-27131. Ed. Carmen L. Cristobal. circ.
700. (looseleaf format; back issues avail.) **Indexed:**
VITIS. **Document type:** academic/scholarly publication.

581 US ISSN 0006-7180
BONSAI BULLETIN. 1963. q. $12. Bonsai Society of
Greater New York, Inc., 71 Milbar Blvd., E.
Farmingdale, NY 11735. Ed. Carlos Silva. adv.;
bk.rev.; charts; illus.; cum.index. circ. 800.

581 US
BOREALIS. 1982. 8/yr. $12 (foreign $30) (effective
1998). Alaska Native Plant Society, Box 141613,
Anchorage, AK 99514. TEL 907-333-8212. Ed.
Julia Richetts. R&P contact: Verna Pratt. adv.; B&W
page $25; adv. contact: Verna Pratt. bk.rev. circ.
180. **Document type:** newsletter.
Formerly: Alaska Native Plant Society. Newsletter.

581 II ISSN 0045-2629
QH301 CODEN: BTNCAD
THE BOTANICA. (Text in English) 1950. a. Rs.75($7.5)
Delhi University Botanical Society, Department of
Botany, University of Delhi, Delhi 110007, India.
(Dist. by: HPC Publisher's Distributors (Pvt.) Ltd.,
4805-24, 1st Fl., Bharat Ram Rd., Darya Ganj, New
Delhi 110 002, India. TEL 91-11-3254402. FAX
91-11-6863511) Ed. M.R. Vajayaraghavan. adv.;
bk.rev.; bibl.; index; circ. 500 (controlled). **Indexed:**
Biol.Abstr., Environ.Abstr., Field Crop Abstr.,
Herb.Abstr. **Document type:** academic/scholarly
publication.
—CASDDS; CISTI.

BIOLOGY — BOTANY

581   GW   ISSN 0932-8629
QK1   CODEN: BOACEJ
BOTANICA ACTA. (Text and summaries in English, German) 1882. 6/yr. DM.423. Georg Thieme Verlag, Ruedigerstr. 14, 70469 Stuttgart, Germany. TEL 0711-8931-0. FAX 0711-8931298. (Subscr. to: Postfach 104853, 70042 Stuttgart, Germany) Ed. U. Luettge. bibl.; charts; illus.; index. circ. 2,000. (also avail. in microfiche from IDC) **Indexed:** Apic.Abstr., ASCA, Biol.Abstr., Chem.Abstr., Curr.Adv.Ecol.Sci., Curr.Cont., Deep Sea Res.& Oceanogr.Abstr., Ecol.Abstr., Excerp.Med., Forest.Abstr., Forest Prod.Abstr., Ind.Sci.Rev., INIS Atomind., Potato Abstr., Sci.Cit.Ind. **Document type:** academic/scholarly publication.
—BLDSC (2251.980000); CASDDS; CISTI; EMDOCS; Genuine Article; SWETS; UMI; UnCover. **CCC.**
    Formerly (until 1987): Deutsche Botanische Gesellschaft. Berichte (ISSN 0365-9631)

581   SP   ISSN 0214-4565
QK329   CODEN: TDBCD8
BOTANICA COMPLUTENSIS. 1968. a. 2000 ptas.($22) (effective 1997). Universidad Complutense de Madrid, Facultad de Ciencias Biologicas, Departamento de Biologia Vegetal I, Servicio de Publicaciones, Ciudad Universitaria, 28040 Madrid, 28040 Madrid, Spain. TEL 34-1-3944402. FAX 34-1-3945034. E-mail: spajbot@eucmax.sim.ucm.es. Ed. Santiago Pajaron. adv.; bk.rev.; bibl.; illus. circ. 500. **Indexed:** Biodet.Abstr., Ind.SST. **Document type:** academic/scholarly publication.
—CASDDS.
    Former titles (until 1986): Universidad Complutense. Departamento de Botanica. Trabajos (ISSN 0212-4890); (until 1982): Universidad Complutense. Departamento de Botanica y Fisiologia Vegetal. Trabajos (ISSN 0210-5179); (until 1975): Universidad Complutense. Departamento de Botanica. Trabajos (ISSN 0377-8371); (until 1974): Universidad de Madrid. Departamento de Botanica y Fisiologia Vegetal. Trabajos (ISSN 0580-468X)
    Refereed Serial

581   SW   ISSN 0068-0370
BOTANICA GOTHOBURGENSIA. (Subseries of Acta Universitatis Gothoburgensis) (Text in English, German, Norwegian, Swedish) 1963. irreg., no.7, 1978. price varies; also exchange basis. Acta Universitatis Gothoburgensis, P.O. Box 5096, S-402 22 Goeteborg, Sweden. TEL 46-31-7731733. FAX 46-31163797. Ed.Bd. **Document type:** monographic series.

581   SZ   ISSN 0253-1453
QK1   CODEN: BOHEDP
BOTANICA HELVETICA. (Text in English, French, German, Italian) 1891. 2/yr. 300 SFr. (foreign 304 SFr.) (effective 1997). (Schweizerische Botanische Gesellschaft) Birkhaeuser Verlag, P.O. Box 133, CH-4010 Basel, Switzerland. TEL 41-61-2050730. FAX 41-61-2050791. E-mail: subscriptions@birkhauser.ch. (Dist. in N. America by: Springer-Verlag, Mercedes Distribution Center, 160 Imlay St., Brooklyn, NY 11231, USA) Ed. H.P. Ruffner. charts; illus.; index. circ. 1,100. (back issues avail.) **Indexed:** ASCA, Biol.Abstr., Bull.Signal., Crop Physiol.Abstr., Curr.Adv.Ecol.Sci., Curr.Cont., Ecol.Abstr., Forest.Abstr., Geo.Abstr.P.G., Hort.Abstr., Rev.Plant Path., VITIS. **Document type:** academic/scholarly publication.
—BLDSC (2252.008000); CISTI; Genuine Article; KNAW; Linda Hall; UMI; UnCover. **CCC.**
    Formerly (until 1981): Schweizerische Botanische Gesellschaft. Berichte (ISSN 0080-7281)

580   SP   ISSN 0211-7150
BOTANICA MACARONESICA. 1976. s-a. exchange basis. Jardin Botanico Canario Viera y Clavijo, Apartado de Correo 14 de Tarifa Alta s-n, 35017 Las Palmas de Gran Canaria, Spain. TEL 34-28-353604. FAX 34-28-352250. E-mail: jadcan@ext.step.es. circ. 300. **Indexed:** Ind.SST. **Document type:** academic/scholarly publication.
    Description: Provides articles on botany, conservation and nature in the Macaronesian floristic area.
    Refereed Serial

589.45   GW   ISSN 0006-8055
QK564   CODEN: BOTNA7
BOTANICA MARINA. (Text in English) 1957. bi-m. DM.1338.80 to institutions; individuals DM.211.80 (effective 1998). Walter de Gruyter und Co., Genthiner Str. 13, 10785 Berlin, Germany. TEL 49-30-26005-0. FAX 49-30-26005251. E-mail: wdg-info@degruyter.de; URL: http://www.degruyter.de. (U.S. addr.: Walter de Gruyter, 200 Saw Mill River Rd., Hawthorne, NY 10532. TEL 914-747-0110) Ed.Bd. adv.; charts; illus.; index. circ. 450. **Indexed:** ASCA, Biol.Abstr., Biotech.Abstr., Chem.Abstr., Curr.Adv.Ecol.Sci., Curr.Cont., Curr.Tit.Ocean, Deep Sea Res.& Oceanogr.Abstr., Ind.Sci.Rev., Ocean.Abstr., Pollut.Abstr., Sci.Cit.Ind., Sel.Water Res.Abstr., So.Pac.Per.Ind., W.R.C.Inf. **Document type:** academic/scholarly publication.
—BLDSC (2252.100000); CASDDS; CISTI; EMDOCS; Genuine Article; Linda Hall; SWETS; UnCover. **CCC.**

581   UK   ISSN 1359-4869
QK1   CODEN: BJSCE6
BOTANICAL JOURNAL OF SCOTLAND. 1836. s-a. £19 to individuals (outside the E.U. £21 ($33.50)); institutions £38 (outside the E.U. elsewhere £42 ($67)) (effective 1996). (Botanical Society of Scotland) Edinburgh University Press, 22 George Sq., Edinburgh EH8 9LF, Scotland. TEL 44-131-650-4213. FAX 44-131-662-0053. TELEX 727442 UNIVED G. Ed. J.H. Leonard; Pub. Vivian C. Bone. adv. contact: Kathryn MacLean. bk.rev.; bibl.; charts; illus. circ. 650. **Indexed:** Biol.Abstr., Curr.Adv.Ecol.Sci., Deep Sea Res.& Oceanogr.Abstr., Forest.Abstr., Geo.Abstr., Herb.Abstr., Hort.Abstr., Rev.Plant Path., Sel.Water Res.Abstr., Soils & Fert., Weed Abstr. **Document type:** academic/scholarly publication.
—BLDSC (2254.600000); Linda Hall. **CCC.**
    Former titles (until 1991): Botanical Society of Edinburgh Transactions (ISSN 0374-6607); (until 1970): Botanical Society of Edinburgh. Transactions and Proceedings (ISSN 0372-0578)

581   US   ISSN 0006-8101
QK1   CODEN: BOREA4
THE BOTANICAL REVIEW; interpreting botanical progress. 1935. q. $82 (foreign $89) (effective 1997). New York Botanical Garden, Scientific Publications Department, Bronx, NY 10458-5126. TEL 718-817-8721. FAX 718-817-8842. Ed. Dennis W. Stevenson. adv.; bibl.; index. circ. 2,000. (also avail. in microform from UMI,PMC; microfiche from IDC; back issues avail.) **Indexed:** Acid Rain Abstr., Acid Rain Ind., ASCA, Bibl.Agri., Biol.Abstr., Biol.& Agr.Ind., Chem.Abstr., Crop Physiol.Abstr., Curr.Adv.Ecol.Sci., Curr.Cont., Deep Sea Res.& Oceanogr.Abstr., Ecol.Abstr., Environ.Abstr., Environ.Per.Bibl. (1989-1994), Field Crop Abstr., Forest.Abstr., Forest Prod.Abstr., Gen.Sci.Ind., Geo.Abstr., Helminthol.Abstr., Herb.Abstr., Hort.Abstr., Ind.Sci.Rev., INIS Atomind., Ornam.Hort., Plant Breed.Abstr., Rev.Plant Path., Seed Abstr., Soils & Fert., SSCI. **Document type:** academic/scholarly publication.
• Also available online. Vendor(s): Information Access Co.
—BLDSC (2256.000000); CASDDS; CIS; CISTI; Genuine Article; KR SourceOne; Linda Hall; SWETS; UMI; UnCover. **CCC.**
    Description: Review and synthesis of articles in all fields of plant science. Includes list of books received.
    Refereed Serial

581   II   ISSN 0006-8128
    CODEN: BBSUAY
BOTANICAL SURVEY OF INDIA. BULLETIN. (Text in English) 1959. q. price varies. Botanical Survey of India, c/o Ministry of the Environment and Forests, Paryavaran Bhavan, C G O Complex Phase II, Lodi Rd., New Delhi 110 002, India. TEL 436-3951. Ed. A.R.K Sastry. bk.rev.; charts; illus.; index; circ. 250 (controlled). (tabloid format; back issues avail.) **Indexed:** Biol.Abstr., Field Crop Abstr., Forest.Abstr., Forest Prod.Abstr., Herb.Abstr., Indian Sci.Abstr.
—CISTI; Linda Hall.

581
BOTANICAL SURVEY OF INDIA. OCCASIONAL PUBLICATIONS. irreg. price varies. Botanical Survey of India, c/o Ministry of the Environment and Forests, Paryavaran Bhavan, C G O Complex Phase II, Lodi Rd., New Delhi 110 002, India. TEL 436-3951.

581   RU   ISSN 0006-8136
    CODEN: BOTZA9
BOTANICHESKII ZHURNAL. (Text in Russian; summaries in English) 1916. m. $294 (effective 1998). (Rossiiskaya Akademiya Nauk, Vsesoyuznoe Botanicheskoe Obshchestvo, S.-Peterburgskoe Otdelenie) Izdatel'stvo Nauka, S.-Peterburgskoe Otdelenie, Mendeleevskaya liniya, 1, 199034 St. Petersburg B-34, Russia. (Dist. by: Victor Kamkin Inc., 4956 Boiling Brook Pkwy, Rockville, MD 20852. TEL 301-881-5973) Ed. A.L. Takhtayan. adv.; bk.rev.; index. (tabloid format) **Indexed:** Biol.Abstr., Chem.Abstr., Crop Physiol.Abstr., Curr.Adv.Ecol.Sci., Deep Sea Res.& Oceanogr.Abstr., Excerp.Med., Field Crop Abstr., Forest.Abstr., Forest Prod.Abstr., Geo.Abstr., Herb.Abstr., Hort.Abstr., Int.Aerosp.Abstr., Maize Abstr., Ornam.Hort., Plant Breed.Abstr., Rev.Plant Path., Seed Abstr., Soils & Fert., Triticale Abstr., Weed Abstr. **Document type:** academic/scholarly publication.
—BLDSC (0019.000000); CASDDS; CISTI; KNAW. **CCC.**

581   UK   ISSN 0956-3237
THE BOTANICS. q. Royal Botanic Garden Edinburgh, Inverleith Row, Edinburgh EH3 5LR, Scotland. TEL 0131-552-7171. FAX 0131-552-0382. Eds. Norma Gregory, Jackie Roberts. **Document type:** newsletter.

581   GW   ISSN 0938-1759
BOTANICUS BRIEF; info for plant lovers around the world. 1977. m. DM.41. Grethenweg 84, 60598 Frankfurt a.M., Germany. TEL 069-683621. FAX 069-681479. Ed. Dieter Frank. bk.rev.; index. circ. 1,000. (back issues avail.) **Document type:** newsletter.

581   HU   ISSN 0006-8144
    CODEN: BOKOAX
BOTANIKAI KOZLEMENYEK/BOTANICAL PROCEEDINGS. (Text in Hungarian; summaries in English, German) 1901. q. $26.50. Magyar Biologiai Tarsasag, Fo u. 68, 1027 Budapest, Hungary. Eds. G. Fekete (Section A); F. Zsoldos (Section B). adv.; bk.rev.; charts; illus.; index. **Indexed:** Biol.Abstr., Chem.Abstr., Crop Physiol.Abstr., Curr.Adv.Ecol.Sci., Curr.Cont., Field Crop Abstr., GeoRef., Herb.Abstr., Ornam.Hort., Plant Grow.Reg.Abstr., Rev.Plant Path, Seed Abstr., Weed Abstr.
—BLDSC (2257.500000); CASDDS; CISTI.
    Formerly (until 1908): Noventyani Kozlemenyek (ISSN 0200-299X)

581   GW   ISSN 0006-8152
    CODEN: BJPPAQ
BOTANISCHE JAHRBUECHER FUER SYSTEMATIK, PFLANZENGESCHICHTE UND PFLANZENGEOGRAPHIE. (Text in English, French, German) 1880. 4/yr. DM.174 per no. (foreign $120.20) (effective 1997). E. Schweizerbart'sche Verlagsbuchhandlung, Johannesstr. 3A, 70176 Stuttgart, Germany. TEL 49-711-625001. FAX 49-711-625005. Ed.Bd adv.; bk.rev.; bibl.; charts; illus. **Indexed:** Biol.Abstr., Curr.Adv.Ecol.Sci., Field Crop Abstr., Herb.Abstr., IBR Plant Breed.Abstr., Triticale Abstr. **Document type:** academic/scholarly publication.
—CISTI; Linda Hall; SWETS; UnCover. **CCC.**

581 570   GW   ISSN 0945-4292
BOTANISCHER VEREIN VON BERLIN UND BRANDENBURG. VERHANDLUNGEN. 1859. a. DM.30 Botanischer Verein von Berlin und Brandenburg e.V. Koenigin-Luise-Str. 6-8, 14195 Berlin, Germany. Ed G. Klemm. bk.rev. **Indexed:** Biol.Abstr. **Document type** proceedings.
    Formerly: Berliner Botanischer Verein. Verhandlun (ISSN 0724-3111)

581   JA   ISSN 0287-9794
BOTANY. (Text in Japanese) 1951. a. Kumamoto Kine Shokubutsu Saishukai - Kumamoto Herbalists Association, Kumamoto Hakubutsukan, 3-2 Furukyomachi, Kumamoto-shi, Kumamoto-ken 860 Japan.

BIOLOGY — BOTANY

581   SA   ISSN 0006-8241
QK1   CODEN: BTHLAA
BOTHALIA. 1921. 2/yr. R.134.80 (effective 1997). National Botanical Institute, Private Bag X101, Pretoria 0001, South Africa. TEL 27-12-804-3200. FAX 27-12-804-3211. Ed. O.A. Leistner. R&P contact: H. du Plessis. illus.; index. circ. 400. (also avail. in microfiche from IDC; reprint service avail. from ISI) **Indexed:** ASCA, Biodet.Abstr., Biol.Abstr., Curr.Adv.Ecol.Sci., Curr.Cont., Excerpt.Bot., Field Crop Abstr., Forest.Abstr., Forest Prod.Abstr., Geo.Abstr., Herb.Abstr., Ind.S.A.Per., INIS Atomind., Rev.Plant Path., Soils & Fert. **Document type:** academic/scholarly publication.
—BLDSC (2261.000000); EMDOCS; Genuine Article; SWETS.
    Description: Main fields covered include taxonomy, ecology, anatomy, and cytology.

581   US
BOYCE THOMPSON INSTITUTE FOR PLANT RESEARCH. ANNUAL REPORT. no.48, 1971. a. free. Boyce Thompson Institute for Plant Research, Inc., Tower Rd., Cornell University, Ithaca, NY 14853. TEL 607-254-1234. FAX 607-254-1242. Ed. G.M. Colavito. charts; illus. circ. 1,000. **Indexed:** Rev.Plant Path. **Document type:** corporate report.

581   BL   ISSN 0084-800X
QK1   CODEN: BRADD8
BRADEA; boletin do herbarium bradeanum. (Text in Portuguese; summaries in English) 1969. irreg. R.35 (foreign R.40) (effective 1996). Herbarium Bradeanum, C.P. 15005, 20031-040 Rio de Janeiro, RJ, Brazil. Ed. Margarth Emmerich. R&P contact: Miriam Cristina Alvarez Pereira. abstr.; bibl.; charts; illus.; index; circ. 400 (controlled). **Indexed:** Ash.G.Bot.Per., Biol.Abstr. **Document type:** bulletin.
—BLDSC (2265.920000).
    Description: Presents original papers in botany, with emphasis on the flora of Brazil.

581 635.933   UK   ISSN 0265-086X
BRADLEYA. (Text in English, German) 1983. a. £12($20) (effective 1997). British Cactus & Succulent Society, 71 Lakes Ln., Newport Pagnell, Bucks. MK16 8HT, England. TEL 44-1908-611650. (Subscr. to: Miss W. Dunn, 43 Dewar Dr., Sheffield 572GR. TEL 44-1904-410512; Alt addr: c/o D.V. Slade 15 Brentwood Crescent, Hull Rd., York YO1 5HU. TEL 44-1742-361649) Ed. Gordon Rowley. bk.rev.; illus.; index. circ. 1,300. (back issues avail.) **Indexed:** Ornam.Hort. **Document type:** academic/scholarly publication.
    Formerly: Cactus and Succulent Journal of Great Britain (ISSN 0007-9375)
    Description: Presents current research and papers on cacti and other succulent plants. Serves as yearbook of the society.
    Refereed Serial

BRAUNSCHWEIGER NATURKUNDLICHE SCHRIFTEN. see *BIOLOGY — Zoology*

583.56   UK   ISSN 0264-3405
BRITISH CACTUS & SUCCULENT JOURNAL. 1945. q. £12 outside the E.U. £13 ($28) (effective 1996 & 1997). British Cactus & Succulent Society, 71 Lakes Ln., Newport Pagnell, Bucks. MK16 8HT, England. TEL 44-1908-611650. Ed. G.E. Cheetham. adv.; bk.rev.; illus.; index; circ. 5,600 (controlled). (back issues avail.) **Indexed:** Biol.Abstr., Hort.Abstr., Ornam.Hort. **Document type:** academic/scholarly publication.
—BLDSC (2292.250000); UnCover.
    Formerly (until 1982): National Cactus and Succulent Journal (ISSN 0027-8858)
    Description: Contains scholarly and popular discussions of classification, history of succulents, geographic and travel articles, and descriptions of collections.

BRITISH JOURNAL OF PHYTOTHERAPY. see *ALTERNATIVE MEDICINE*

581   UK   ISSN 0300-4562
BRITISH LICHEN SOCIETY BULLETIN. 1958. 2/yr. £15($30) to institutions; individuals £18.50($37). University of Nottingham, Department of Life Science, Nottingham NG7 2RD, England. TEL 44-115-9513211. FAX 44-115-9513251. E-mail: pdc@nottingham.ac.uk; URL: http://www.argonet.co.uk/users/jmgray/. (Subscr. to: J.M. Gray, Penmore, Perranuthnoe, Penzance, Cornwall TR20 9NF, England) Ed. P.D. Crittenden. adv.; bk.rev.; bibl.; charts; illus.; stat.; cum.index. circ. 600. (processed) **Document type:** bulletin.
    Description: Contains topical items, historical material, and recent reviews about lichens.

581   UK   ISSN 0301-9195
QK520   CODEN: BPSBA7
BRITISH PTERIDOLOGICAL SOCIETY. BULLETIN. Short title: B P S Bulletin. 1973. a. £25 (includes Fern Gazette and Pteridologist) (effective 1996 & 1997). British Pteridological Society, c/o Botany Department, Natural History Museum, Cromwell Rd., London SW7 5BD, England. TEL 44-171-938-9497. Ed. A.M. Paul. circ. 800. **Indexed:** Biol.Abstr., Curr.Adv.Ecol.Sci. **Document type:** bulletin.
—BLDSC (2423.650000).
    Supersedes: British Pteridological Society. Newsletter (ISSN 0068-2403)
    Description: Reports on activities and meetings of the society.

BRITISH SOCIETY FOR PLANT GROWTH REGULATION. MONOGRAPHS. see *AGRICULTURE — Crop Production And Soil*

582   US   ISSN 0007-196X
QK1   CODEN: BRTAAN
BRITTONIA. 1931. q. $76 (foreign $84) (effective 1997). New York Botanical Garden, Scientific Publications Department, Bronx, NY 10458-5126. TEL 718-871-8721. FAX 718-817-8842. Ed. Andrew Henderson. adv.; bk.rev.; abstr.; bibl.; illus.; index. circ. 900. (also avail. in microfiche from UMI; back issues avail.) **Indexed:** ASCA, Biol.Abstr., Chem.Abstr., Curr.Adv.Ecol.Sci., Curr.Cont., Deep Sea Res.& Oceanogr.Abstr., Field Crop Abstr., Forest.Abstr., Forest Prod.Abstr., Herb.Abstr., Hort.Abstr., Ind.Sci.Rev., Rev.Plant Path., Sci.Cit.Ind., So.Pac.Per.Ind., Weed Abstr. **Document type:** academic/scholarly publication.
—BLDSC (2348.250000); CASDDS; CISTI; EMDOCS; Genuine Article; Linda Hall; UMI; UnCover. CCC.
    Description: Original research articles on subjects encompassing the field of systematic botany.
    Refereed Serial

584.22   US   ISSN 0090-8738
QK495.B76
BROMELIAD SOCIETY. JOURNAL. Key Title: Journal of the Bromeliad Society. 1951. bi-m. $25 (foreign $30). Bromeliad Society, Inc., 720 Millertown Rd., Auburn, CA 95603. TEL 916-885-0201. (Subscr. to: Carolyn Schoenau, Box 12981, Gainesville, FL 32604) Ed. Chet Blackburn. R&P contact: Chet Blackburn. adv. contact: Chet Blackburn. bk.rev.; illus.; index; circ. 1,700 (paid). **Document type:** academic/scholarly publication.
—UnCover.
    Formerly: Bromeliad Society Bulletin (ISSN 0007-2184)
    Description: Promotes and maintains general and scientific interest in research and preservation of the bromeliad plant family.
    Refereed Serial

581   GW   ISSN 0724-0155
DIE BROMELIE. 1980. 3/yr. DM.55 membership. Deutsche Bromelien-Gesellschaft e.V., Siesmayerstr. 61, 60323 Frankfurt a.M., Germany. TEL 0911-315334. Ed. Wolfgang Tittelbach. adv.; bk.rev. circ. 400. (back issues avail.) **Document type:** academic/scholarly publication.

581   GW   ISSN 0723-2470
BRYOLOGISCHE BEITRAEGE. (Text in English and German) 1982. a. DM.35. I D H - Verlag, Funkenstr. 13, 53902 Bad Muenstereifel, Germany. Ed. Ruprecht Duell. (back issues avail.)
—BLDSC (2353.989000).

588   US   ISSN 0007-2745
CODEN: BRYOAM
BRYOLOGIST. (Text in English, French, German and Spanish; summaries in English) 1898. q. $40 to individuals (foreign $45); institutions $55 (foreign $60); students $35 (effective 1997). American Bryological & Lichenological Society, c/o Robert J. Thomas, Sec.-Treas., Department of Biology, Bates College, Lewiston, ME 04240. TEL 207-786-6105. FAX 207-786-6035. E-mail: dvitt@gpu.srv.ualberta.ca. (Dist. by: Allen Press, Inc., Box 368, Lawrence, KS 66044) Ed. Dale H. Vitt. R&P contact: Dale H. Vitt. TEL 403-492-3390. adv. contact: Dale H. Vitt. bk.rev.; abstr.; bibl.; charts; illus.; stat.; cum.index: 1898-1957, 1958-1972; circ. 1,000 (paid). (also avail. in microform from UMI; microfiche from IDC; reprint service avail. from UMI) **Indexed:** Acid Rain Abstr., Acid Rain Ind., ASCA, Biol.Abstr., Chem.Abstr., Curr.Adv.Ecol.Sci., Curr.Cont., Ecol.Abstr., Geo.Abstr., Ind.Sci.Rev., INIS Atomind., Rev.Plant Path., Sci.Cit.Ind., So.Pac.Per.Ind., Soils & Fert. **Document type:** academic/scholarly publication.
—BLDSC (2354.000000); CASDDS; CISTI; EMDOCS; Genuine Article; Linda Hall; SWETS; UMI; UnCover. CCC.
    Description: Devoted to the study of bryophytes and lichens.
    Refereed Serial

581   GW   ISSN 0258-3348
QK532.4   CODEN: BRBIDS
BRYOPHYTORUM BIBLIOTHECA. (Text in English and German) 1973. irreg. price varies. J. Cramer in der Gebrueder Borntraeger Verlagsbuchhandlung, Johannesstr. 3A, 70176 Stuttgart, Germany. TEL 49-711-625001. FAX 49-711-625005. Eds. J.-P. Frahm, S.R. Gradstein. **Document type:** academic/scholarly publication, bibliography.
—BLDSC (2354.020000); CASDDS.

BULLETIN DE LA MURITHIENNE. see *EARTH SCIENCES*

631.52 581   NE   ISSN 1010-6251
BULLETIN EUCARPIA. 1966. a. fl.40 to non-members (effective 1998). European Association for Research on Plant Breeding, c/o Mrs. Dr.Ir. M.J. de Jeu, Sec.-Gen., P.O. Box 315, 6700 AH Wageningen, Netherlands. circ. 1,250. **Indexed:** Plant.Breed.Abstr. **Document type:** bulletin, proceedings.
    Supersedes: Eucarpia - Bulletin d'Information (ISSN 0071-2221)
    Description: Publishes brief items of news and information relating to plant breeding, including reports of section activities and schedules of conferences and symposia.

BULLETIN OF MEDICO-ETHNO-BOTANICAL RESEARCH. see *ALTERNATIVE MEDICINE*

581   II   ISSN 0970-4612
QK1   CODEN: BPAAS:B
BULLETIN OF PURE & APPLIED SCIENCES. SECTION B: BOTANY. 2/yr. Rs.300($50) Dr. A.K. Sharma, Ed. & Pub., 140 (RPS) D.D.A. Flat, Mansarovar Park, Shahdara, New Delhi 110 032, India. TEL 91-11-2117408. R&P contact: A.K. Sharma. adv. contact: A.K. Sharma. bk.rev. circ. 600. **Document type:** academic/scholarly publication.
—Linda Hall. CCC.

BUNKAZAI NO CHU-KIN-GAI/INSECT & FUNGUS DAMAGE TO CULTURAL PROPERTIES. see *BIOLOGY — Entomology*

581   NE   ISSN 0169-6289
C B S NEWSLETTER. 1983. s-a. free. Centraalbureau voor Schimmelcultures, Postbus 273, 3740 AG Baarn, Netherlands. TEL 31-35-5481240. FAX 31-35-5416142. E-mail: info@cbs.knaw.nl. Ed. R.A. Samson. R&P contact: R.A. Samson. **Document type:** newsletter.
—KNAW.

581 333.7   US
C N P S INVENTORY OF RARE AND ENDANGERED VASCULAR PLANTS OF CALIFORNIA. irreg., 5th ed., 1993. $22.95. California Native Plant Society, 1722 J St., Ste. 17, Sacramento, CA 95814. Eds. Mark W. Skinner, Bruce M. Pavlik.
    Description: Presents information on distribution, rarity, endangerment, legal status, habitat, plant growth form, blooming time, and literature sources for over 1,700 species, subspecies and varieties of California's endangered flora.

BIOLOGY — BOTANY

581 MX ISSN 0526-717X
CACTACEAS Y SUCULENTAS MEXICANAS. 1955. q. Mex.$50($15) (effective 1995). Sociedad Mexicana de Cactologia, A.C., 2da. de Juarez, No. 42, Colonia San Alvaro, 02090 Mexico, D.F., Mexico. TEL 3411796. Ed. Jorge Meyran. cum.index every 4 yrs. circ. 800. (back issues avail.) **Document type:** academic/scholarly publication.
Description: Covers systematic and floristic botany, succulent plants phytogeography, physiology and ecology. For both scientists and amateurs.
Refereed Serial

583.47 US ISSN 0007-9367
SB438
CACTUS AND SUCCULENT JOURNAL. 1929. bi-m. $40 (effective 1995). Cactus & Succulent Society of America, Inc., c/o Seymour Linden, Corresponding Sec., 1535 Reeves St., Los Angeles, CA 90035. TEL 310-556-1923. FAX 310-286-9629. E-mail: U4BIA@aol.com. (Edit. addr.: 5508 N. Astell Ave., Azusa, CA 91702. TEL 818-334-7349. FAX 818-334-0658) Ed. Myron Kimnach; Pub. Jerry Barad. R&P contact: Jerry Barad. adv.; bk.rev.; illus.; index. circ. 5,000. (also avail. in microform from UMI; reprint service avail. from UMI) **Indexed:** Biol.Abstr., Hort.Abstr., Ornam.Hort. **Document type:** academic/scholarly publication.
—UMI; UnCover. **CCC.**
Description: Contains scholarly articles on new species, descriptions of plants, and discussions on horticultural practices, plus popular articles covering geographic localities and collections, and cultivation issues.

635 US
CALIFORNIA NATIVE PLANT SOCIETY. BULLETIN. 1979. 4/yr. membership only. California Native Plant Society, 1722 J St., Ste. 17, Sacramento, CA 95814. TEL 916-447-2677. **Document type:** bulletin.
Former titles: California Native Plant Society. Journal; (until 1992): California Native Plant Society. Bulletin (ISSN 1046-1442)

581 US ISSN 0190-8723
CALIFORNIA NATIVE PLANT SOCIETY. SPECIAL PUBLICATION. 1974. m. California Native Plant Society, 1722 J St., Ste. 17, Sacramento, CA 95814. TEL 916-447-2677.

581 CN ISSN 0008-3046
CANADIAN BOTANICAL ASSOCIATION. BULLETIN. (Text in English and French) 1967. q. Can.$45 to non-members. Canadian Botanical Association, Department of Botany, University of Guelph, Guelph, ON N1G 2W1, Canada. TEL 519-824-4120. FAX 519-767-1991. Ed. J.F. Gerrath. adv.; bk.rev.; circ. 285 (paid). **Document type:** bulletin.
—CISTI. **CCC.**

581 CN ISSN 0008-4026
CODEN: CJBOAW
CANADIAN JOURNAL OF BOTANY/JOURNAL CANADIEN DE BOTANIQUE. (Text mainly in English, occasionally in French) 1929. m. Can.$176 to individuals (foreign $186); institutions Can.$475 (foreign $475) (effective 1996). National Research Council of Canada, Research Journals, Ottawa, ON K1A 0R6, Canada. TEL 613-993-9084. FAX 613-952-7656. URL: http://www.cisti.nrc.ca/cisti/journals/. Ed. I.E.P. Taylor. adv.: B&W page Can.$600; trim 8 1/2 x 11; adv. contact: Hoda Jabbour. bibl.; charts; illus.; index. circ. 1,600. (also avail. in microform from UMI,PMC; back issues avail.; reprint service avail. from UMI) **Indexed:** Abstr.Bull.Inst.Pap.Chem., Acid Pre.Dig., Acid Rain Abstr., Acid Rain Ind., Agroforest.Abstr., Apic.Abstr., ASCA, Bio-Contr.News & Info., Biodet.Abstr., Biol.Abstr., Biol.& Agr.Ind., Biotech.Abstr., Chem.Abstr., Cott.& Trop.Fibr.Abstr., Crop Physiol.Abstr., Curr.Adv.Ecol.Sci., Curr.Cont., Deep Sea Res.& Oceanogr.Abstr., Ecol.Abstr., Environ.Abstr., Environ.Per.Bibl. (1975-1993), Excerp.Med., Fababean Abstr., Field Crop Abstr., Food Sci.& Tech.Abstr., Forest.Abstr., Forest Prod.Abstr., Geo.Abstr.P.G., Geol.Abstr., GeoRef., Helminthol.Abstr., Herb.Abstr., Hort.Abstr., Ind.Sci.Rev., INIS Atomind., Irr.& Drain.Abstr., Maize Abstr., Nutr.Abstr., Ornam.Hort., Plant Breed.Abstr., Plant Grow.Reg.Abstr., Potato Abstr., Rev.Plant.Path., Rice Abstr., Sci.Cit.Ind., Seed Abstr., Sel.Water Res.Abstr., Soils & Fert., Sorghum & Millets Abstr., Soyabean Abstr., Triticale Abstr., Trop.Oil Seeds Abstr., VITIS, W.R.C.Inf., Weed Abstr., World Text.Abstr. **Document type:** academic/scholarly publication.
—BLDSC (3030.000000); CASDDS; CIS; CISTI; EMDOCS; Genuine Article; KR SourceOne; Linda Hall; SWETS; UMI; UnCover. **CCC.**
Formerly (until 1950): Canadian Journal of Research. Section B: Botanical Sciences (ISSN 0366-7391); Which superseded in part (in 1935): Canadian Journal of Research (ISSN 0366-6581)
Refereed Serial

CANADIAN JOURNAL OF HERBALISM. see *ALTERNATIVE MEDICINE*

581 574.8 CN ISSN 0706-0661
CODEN: CJPPD6
CANADIAN JOURNAL OF PLANT PATHOLOGY. (Text in English, French) 1979. q. Can.$75 (foreign $85) (effective 1996). Canadian Phytopathological Society, Dept. of Environmental Biology, University of Guelph, Guelph, ON N1G 2W1, Canada. TEL 519-824-4120. FAX 519-837-0442. (Edit. addr.: Research Centre, Agriculture & Agri-Food Canada, Fredericton, NB E3B 4Z7, Canada) Ed. Dr. R.P. Singh. circ. 900. (back issues avail.) **Indexed:** ASCA, Bio-Contr.News & Info., Biodet.Abstr., Biol.Abstr., Biol.& Agr.Ind., Biotech.Abstr., Chem.Abstr., Cott.& Trop.Fibr.Abstr., Curr.Adv.Ecol.Sci., Curr.Cont., Environ.Abstr., Fababean Abstr., Field Crop Abstr., Forest.Abstr., Forest Prod.Abstr., Herb Abstr., Hort.Abstr., Irr.& Drain.Abstr., Plant Breed Abstr., Potato Abstr., Seed Abstr., Soils & Fert., Soyabean Abstr., Triticale Abstr., Trop.Oil Seeds Abstr., Weed Abstr. **Document type:** academic/scholarly publication.
—BLDSC (3034.400000); CASDDS; CISTI; Genuine Article; KR SourceOne; Linda Hall; SWETS; UnCover. **CCC.**
Description: Publication of original research in plant pathology including technology aspects of plant disease control.

581 CN ISSN 0008-4220
CODEN: CPLSAY
CANADIAN JOURNAL OF PLANT SCIENCE. (Text in English or French) 1921. q. Can.$58 (foreign Can.$62) (effective 1997). Agricultural Institute of Canada, 141 Laurier Ave. W., Ste. 1112, Ottawa, ON K1P 5J3, Canada. TEL 613-232-9459. FAX 613-594-5190. E-mail: journals@aic.ca; URL: http://www.aic.ca. Ed. L. Bailey. R&P contact: T. Fenton. adv. contact: T. Fenton. bibl.; charts; illus.; stat.; index. circ. 1,200. (also avail. in microform from UMI,PMC; reprint service avail. from UMI) **Indexed:** Agri.Eng.Abstr., ASCA, Bio-Contr.News & Info., Biol.Abstr., Biol.& Agr.Ind., Biotech.Abstr., Chem.Abstr., Crop Physiol.Abstr., Curr.Adv.Ecol.Sci., Curr.Cont., Ecol.Abstr., Environ.Abstr., Environ.Per.Bibl. (1972-1993), Excerp.Med., Field Crop.Abstr., Food Sci.& Tech.Abstr., Food Sci.& Tech.Abstr., Forest.Abstr., Forest Prod.Abstr., Geo.Abstr., Helminthol.Abstr., Herb.Abstr., Hort.Abstr., Ind.Sci.Rev., Ind.Vet., INIS Atomind., Irr.& Drain.Abstr., Maize Abstr., Nutr.Abstr., Ocean.Abstr., Ornam.Hort., Plant Breed.Abstr., Plant Grow.Reg.Abstr., Pollut.Abstr., Potato Abstr., Rev.Appl.Entomol., Rev.Med.& Vet.Mycol., Rev.Plant Path., Rice Abstr., Sci.Cit.Ind., Seed Abstr., Sel.Water Res.Abstr., Soils & Fert., Sorghum & Millets Abstr., Soyabean Abstr., Telegen, Triticale Abstr., Vet.Bull., VITIS, W.R.C.Inf., Weed Abstr., World Agri.Econ.& Rural Sociol.Abstr. **Document type:** academic/scholarly publication.
—BLDSC (3034.500000); CASDDS; CIS; CISTI; EMDOCS; Genuine Article; KR SourceOne; Linda Hall; SWETS; UMI; UnCover. **CCC.**
Description: Research on agronomy and horticulture.
Refereed Serial

632 581.2 CN ISSN 0008-476X
CODEN: CPDSAS
CANADIAN PLANT DISEASE SURVEY. (Not avail. in print format) (Text in English and French) 1921. q. free. Agriculture and Agri-Food Canada, Pest Management Research Centre, 1391 Sandford St., London, ON N5V 4T3, Canada. TEL 519-457-1470. FAX 519-457-3997. E-mail: hiltons@em.agr.ca; URL: http://res.agr.ca/lond/pmrc/pmrchome.html. Ed. Stephanie Hilton; Pub. Stephanie Hilton. charts; illus.; index. cum.index: 1954-1994. circ. 800. (also avail. in diskette format; also avail. by e-mail) **Indexed:** ASCA, Biol.Abstr., Curr.Adv.Ecol.Sci., Curr.Cont., Field Crop Abstr., Forest.Abstr., Helminthol.Abstr., Herb.Abstr., Hort.Abstr., Ind.Sci.Rev., Maize Abstr., Plant Breed.Abstr., Ref.Zh., Rev.Plant Path., Seed Abstr., Soils & Fert., Soyabean Abstr., Triticale Abstr. **Document type:** government publication.
—UnCover.
Description: Reports the occurrence and severity of plant diseases in each province of Canada and assesses the losses from disease.

581 574 CN ISSN 1183-9597
CANADIAN SOCIETY OF PLANT PHYSIOLOGISTS. BULLETIN/SOCIETE CANADIENNE DE PHYSIOLOGIE VEGETALE. BULLETIN. (Text in English, French) 1957. q. membership. Canadian Society of Plant Physiologists - Societe Canadienne de Physiologie Vegetale, Agriculture Canada, Research Station, Harrow, ON N0R 1G0, Canada. TEL 514-872-8491. FAX 514-872-9406. Ed. Dr. Lorna Woodrow. adv.; bk.rev. circ. 550. (back issues avail.) **Document type:** bulletin.

581 NZ ISSN 0110-5892
CANTERBURY BOTANICAL SOCIETY. JOURNAL. 1966. a. NZ.$10 to non-members; members free (effective 1996 & 1997). Canterbury Botanical Society (NZ) Inc., P.O. Box 8212, Christchurch, New Zealand. Ed. Colin Burrows. bk.rev. circ. 250. **Document type:** academic/scholarly publication.
Description: Includes articles mailny on indigenous plants and their ecology, especially in the South Island of New Zealand.

CAPSICUM & EGGPLANT NEWSLETTER. see *GARDENING AND HORTICULTURE*

BIOLOGY — BOTANY

581 US
CAREERS IN BOTANY. 1965. irreg., latest 1995. $0.75. Botanical Society of America, Inc. (Columbus), Business Office, 1735 Neil Ave., Columbus, OH 43210. TEL 614-292-3519. Ed.Bd. R&P contact: Kimberly Hiser. **Document type:** academic/scholarly publication.
Former titles: Botany as a Profession (ISSN 0068-0397); Botanical Society of America. Miscellaneous Publications.

581 US ISSN 0190-9215
CARNIVOROUS PLANT NEWSLETTER. 1971. q. $15 (foreign $20) (effective Mar. 1991). (International Carnivorous Plant Society) Fullerton Arboretum, c/o Leo C. Song, Jr., California State University, Fullerton, CA 92634. TEL 714-773-2766. FAX 714-773-3426. E-mail: leosong@fullerton.edu; URL: http://www.hpl.hp.com/bot/cp_home.html. adv.; bk.rev.; film rev.; bibl.; illus. circ. 950. (back issues avail.) **Document type:** newsletter.
Description: Covers anything pertaining to carnivorous plants, natural history, and culture.

CAROLINEA; Beitraege zur Naturkundlichen Forschung in Suedwestdeutschland. see EARTH SCIENCES

581 US ISSN 0008-7475
QK1 CODEN: CSTNAC
CASTANEA. (Former name of issuing body: Southern Appalachian Botanical Club) 1936. q. $25 (effective 1997). Southern Appalachian Botanical Society, Department of Biology, University of North Carolina at Charlotte, Charlotte, NC 28223. TEL 704-547-4065. FAX 704-547-3128. Ed. Audrey Mellichamp. adv.; bk.rev.; bibl.; index, cum.index. circ. 1,000. **Indexed:** Biol.Abstr., Curr.Adv.Ecol.Sci., Curr.Cont., Ecol.Abstr., Forest.Abstr., Forest Prod.Abstr., Geo.Abstr., Ornam.Hort., Soils & Fert. **Document type:** academic/scholarly publication.
—BLDSC (3064.000000); CASDDS; Linda Hall; UnCover.
Description: Considers, reviews, and educates about the botany of the Southeastern United States.
Refereed Serial

635 US
CASTILLEJA. 1981. 4/yr. $5 membership only. Wyoming Native Plant Society, 1604 Grand Ave., Laramie, WY 82070. Ed. Walter Fertig. bk.rev. circ. 200. **Document type:** newsletter.
Formerly: W N P S Newsletter.

581 AU
CATALOGUS FLORAE AUSTRIA. irreg. price varies. Verlag der Oesterreichischen Akademie der Wissenschaften, Dr. Ignaz-Seipel-Platz 2, A-1010 Vienna, Austria. TEL 43-1-51581401. FAX 43-1-51581400. E-mail: verlag@oeaw.ac.at; URL: http://www.ac.at/einheiten/verlag. **Document type:** monographic series.

581 UK ISSN 0969-0239
TS933.C4 CODEN: CELLE8
CELLULOSE. 1994. q. £245 (foreign $405) (effective 1998). (American Chemical Society, Cellulose Division, US) Thomson Science (Subsidiary of: International Thomson Publishing Group), 2-6 Boundary Row, London SE1 8HN, England. TEL 44-171-8650066. FAX 44-171-5229623. TELEX 290164 CHAPMA G. E-mail: journal@rapidcom.co.uk; URL: http://www.thomsonscience.com. (Dist. by: International Thomson Publishing Services Ltd., Cheriton House, North Way, Andover, Hants. SP10 5BE, England. TEL 44-1264-342713. FAX 44-1264-342807; Subscr. in US & Canada to: 400 Market St., Philadelphia, PA 19106. TEL 800-522-5866) (Co-sponsor: Japanese Cellulose Research Society) Ed. John C. Roberts. adv. (reprint service avail.) **Indexed:** ASCA, Paper & Bd.Abstr. **Document type:** academic/scholarly publication.
●Also available online.
—BLDSC (3098.059800); CASDDS; Genuine Article. **CCC.**
Description: Contains research and review papers relating to scientific progress in the field of cellulose, especially the chemistry, biochemistry, physics, and materials science of cellulose and its derivatives.
Refereed Serial

CENTRAL PLANTATION CROPS RESEARCH INSTITUTE. ANNUAL REPORT. see AGRICULTURE

CENTRAL PLANTATION CROPS RESEARCH INSTITUTE. NEWSLETTER. see AGRICULTURE

CENTRAL PLANTATION CROPS RESEARCH INSTITUTE. RESEARCH HIGHLIGHTS. see AGRICULTURE

589.2 IT
CENTRO MICOLOGICO FRIULANO. BOLLETTINO. 1976. a. Centro Micologico Friulano, Via Beato Odorico da Pordenone 3, 33100 Udine, Italy.

CEREAL RUST BULLETIN. see AGRICULTURE — Crop Production And Soil

581 US
CHEMIE DER PFLANZENSCHUTZ- UND SCHAEDLINGS-BEKAEMPFUNGSMITTEL. (Text in German) 1970. irreg. price varies. Springer-Verlag, 175 Fifth Ave., New York, NY 10010. TEL 212-460-1500. FAX 212-473-6272. (Also: Berlin, Heidelberg, Tokyo and Vienna) Ed. R. Wegler. (reprint service avail. from ISI) **Document type:** monographic series.

CHEMISTRY OF PLANT PROTECTION SERIES. see CHEMISTRY

581 CC ISSN 1001-0718
QK1 CODEN: CJBOE2
CHINESE JOURNAL OF BOTANY. Chinese edition: Zhiwu Xuebao (ISSN 0577-7496) (Text in English) 1989. s-a. $49 to individuals (foreign $59); institutions $78 (foreign $88) (effective 1996). (Chinese Academy of Sciences, Chinese Botanical Society) Science Press, Marketing and Sales Department, 16 Donghuangchenggen North St., Beijing 100717, People's Republic of China. TEL 4010642. FAX 4019810. (Overseas dist. by: Science Press New York, Ltd., 84-04 58th Ave., Elmhurst, NY 11373. TEL 718-476-0238) Ed. Wang Fuxiong. adv.; bk.rev. circ. 2,000. pp./issue: 96. **Document type:** academic/scholarly publication.
—BLDSC (3180.297300).
Description: Publishes original articles on all aspects of plant sciences with emphasis on basic research. Includes reviews, notes, short communications, and institution briefs.
Refereed Serial

581 576 UK ISSN 0264-9640
CHLOROPLASTS. s-m. (diskette m.) £90 (diskette £120; both £180) (effective 1997). S U B I S, Mansion House, 19 Kingfield Rd., Sheffield S11 9AS, England. TEL 44-114-2554433. FAX 44-114-2554626. E-mail: subis@sheffac.demon.co.uk; URL: http://www.shef.ac.uk/uni/companies/shap. (also avail. in diskette format; looseleaf format; back issues avail.) **Document type:** abstracting/indexing.
—CCC.
Description: Current awareness service for researchers in life sciences.

581 SP ISSN 1132-7685
CIENCIAS DE LA TIERRA. (In 5 series: Botania, Geografia, Geologia, Paleontologia, Zoologia) 1984. irreg., no.19, 1996. price varies. Instituto de Estudios Riojanos, C. Muro de la Mata, 8 principal, 26071 Logrono, Spain. TEL 34-41-262064. FAX 34-41-246667.

581 UK ISSN 0748-3007
QH83 CODEN: CLADEC
CLADISTICS: THE INTERNATIONAL JOURNAL OF THE WILLI HENNIG SOCIETY. 1986. q. £118 (effective 1998). (Willi Hennig Society) Academic Press Ltd. (Subsidiary of: Harcourt Brace & Company Ltd.), 24-28 Oval Rd., London NW1 7DX, England. TEL 44-171-267-4466. FAX 44-171-482-2293. TELEX 25775 ACPRES G. E-mail: apsubs@acad.com; URL: http://www.hbuk.co.uk/ap/cladistics; http://www.europe.idealibrary.com/. (Subscr. to: Harcourt Brace & Company Ltd., Foots Cray High St., Sidcup, Kent DA14 5HP, England. TEL 44-181-300-3322. FAX 44-181-309-0807) Eds. D. Upscomb, C.J. Humphries. R&P contact: Catherine John. adv. contact: Nik Screen. circ. 800. (reprint service avail. from SWZ) **Indexed:** ASCA, Curr.Cont., Ecol.Abstr., Geol.Abstr., Ind.Sci.Rev., Sci.Cit.Ind. **Document type:** academic/scholarly publication.
●Also available online.
—BLDSC (3274.292500); Genuine Article; Linda Hall; SWETS; UnCover. **CCC.**
Description: Covers theory, method, the philosophical aspects of systematics, and the role of systematic and evolutionary studies in the investigation of biogeographical and other general biological phenomena.

581 SP ISSN 0010-0730
CODEN: COBOAX
COLLECTANEA BOTANICA. (Text in various languages) 1946. a. $15 or exchange basis. Institut Botanic de Barcelona, Parc de Montjuic, Av. dels Montanyans, 08038 Barcelona, Spain. Ed.Bd. bk.rev.; bibl.; charts; illus. circ. 1,050. **Indexed:** Biol.Abstr., Curr.Adv.Ecol.Sci., Field Crop Abstr., Herb.Abstr., Ind.SST, Ref.Zh., Zoo.Rec. **Document type:** bulletin.
—BLDSC (3299.000000); Linda Hall.

581 GW ISSN 1430-0540
COLLOQUES PHYTOSOCIOLOGIQUES. (Text in English, French and German) 1975. irreg. price varies. J. Cramer in der Gebrueder Borntraeger Verlagsbuchhandlung, Johanesstr. 3a, 70176 Stuttgart, Germany. TEL 49-711-625001. FAX 49-711-625005. Ed. J.M. Gehu. charts; illus. (back issues avail.) **Indexed:** Biol.Abstr. **Document type:** academic/scholarly publication.

COMMONWEALTH SCIENTIFIC AND INDUSTRIAL RESEARCH ORGANIZATION. DIVISION OF TROPICAL CROPS AND PASTURES. BIENNIAL RESEARCH REPORT. see AGRICULTURE — Crop Production And Soil

COMMONWEALTH SCIENTIFIC AND INDUSTRIAL RESEARCH ORGANIZATION. DIVISION OF TROPICAL CROPS AND PASTURES. TECHNICAL PAPER. see AGRICULTURE — Crop Production And Soil

581 BL ISSN 0102-3306
QK263
CONGRESSO NACIONAL DE BOTANICA. ANAIS. (Text in Portuguese; summaries in English, Portuguese, Spanish) 1950. a. Sociedade Botanica do Brasil, c/o Museu Paraense Emilio Goeldi, Caixa Postal 399, 60000 Belem, Para, Brazil. FAX 091-229-1412. charts; illus.

581 IS
CONSPECTUS FLORAE ORIENTALIS. (Text in English) 1980. irreg., no.6, 1992. $15 per no. Israel Academy of Sciences and Humanities, 43 Jabotinski St., P.O. Box 4040, Jerusalem 91040, Israel. TEL 972-2-636211. FAX 972-2-666059. Ed. Zofia Lasman. adv. contact: Tami Korman. **Document type:** monographic series.
Description: Annotated catalog of the flora of the Middle East.
Refereed Serial

581 RM ISSN 0069-9616
CODEN: CBGBBV
CONTRIBUTII BOTANICE. 1958. a. exchange basis only. Universitatea Gradina Botanica, Str. Republicii nr. 42, Cluj-Napoca, Rumania. Ed. Onoriu Ratiu. **Indexed:** Chem.Abstr., Rev.Plant Path.
—CASDDS.

581 US ISSN 0736-0509
CODEN: CNYGEJ
CONTRIBUTIONS FROM THE NEW YORK BOTANICAL GARDEN. 1898-1931; resumed 1984. irreg., no.20, 1993. price varies. New York Botanical Garden, Scientific Publications Department, Bronx, NY 10458-5126. TEL 718-817-8721. FAX 718-817-8842. Ed. W. Buck. (back issues avail.) **Document type:** monographic series.
—CCC.
Description: Reprints of classical works, translations and annotated bibliographies on botanical subjects.
Refereed Serial

589 GU
CORAL REEF NEWSLETTER. 1972. 2/yr. $5. University of Guam, Marine Laboratory, Mangilao 96923, Guam. TEL 671-734-2421. FAX 671-734-6767. Ed. C. Birkeland. bk.rev.; abstr.; bibl. circ. 1,300.

CORNELL PLANTATIONS. see COLLEGE AND ALUMNI

CORRIERE FITOPATOLOGICO. see BIOLOGY — Entomology

COTTON AND TROPICAL FIBRES. see AGRICULTURE — Abstracting, Bibliographies, Statistics

BIOLOGY — BOTANY

635   US   ISSN 0891-9100
CROSSOSOMA. 1975. bi-m. $8 to individuals; institutions $15. Southern California Botanists, c/o Alan Romspert, Department of Biology, California State University, Fullerton, CA 92634. TEL 714-773-3614. Ed. Allan Schoenherr. bk.rev. circ. 350. **Document type:** academic/scholarly publication.
    Description: Covers the study, preservation, and conservation of native plants of California.

635   US
CROSSWORDS. 3/yr. membership only. Gesneriad Hybridizers Association, 4115 Pillar Dr., Rt. 1, Whitmore Lake, MI 48189.

581   SZ   ISSN 0257-9421
                             CODEN: CRHEEO
CRYPTOGAMICA HELVETICA. (Text in French, German and Italian) 1898. irreg., vol.15, 1977. price varies. (Schweizerische Naturforschende Gesellschaft) F. Flueck-Wirth, Krypto, P.O. Box, CH-9053 Teufen, Switzerland. FAX 41-71-3331664. bibl.; charts; illus.; index. (back issues avail.) **Indexed:** Biol.Abstr. **Document type:** newsletter.
    Formerly: Beitraege zur Kryptogamenflora der Schweiz.

589.3   FR   ISSN 0181-1568
                             CODEN: CRALD9
CRYPTOGAMIE: ALGOLOGIE. (Text and summaries in English, French, German, Italian, Spanish) 1922. q. 410 F. (effective 1998). (Museum National d'Histoire Naturelle, Laboratoire de Cryptogamie) A.D.A.C., 12 rue Buffon, 75005 Paris, France. E-mail: reviers@mnhn.fr; bury@mnhn.fr. Ed. Denis Lamy. bk.rev.; abstr.; bibl.; charts; illus.; index. circ. 500. (back issues avail.) **Indexed:** ASCA, Biol.Abstr., Bull.Signal., Chem.Abstr., Curr.Adv.Ecol.Sci., Curr.Cont., Deep Sea Res.& Oceanogr.Abstr., Ecol.Abstr., GeoRef., Helminthol.Abstr., Mar.Sci.Cont.Tab., So.Pac.Per.Ind., W.R.C.Inf. **Document type:** academic/scholarly publication.
—CASDDS; CISTI; Genuine Article; Linda Hall; SWETS; UnCover.
    Supersedes (in 1980): Revue Algologique (ISSN 0035-0702); Incorporates (in 1978): Societe Phycologique de France. Bulletin (ISSN 0081-122X)
    Description: Publishes papers concerning all aspects of research on marine and freshwater algae.

588.2   FR   ISSN 0181-1576
QK532.4   CODEN: CBLIDB
CRYPTOGAMIE: BRYOLOGIE ET LICHENOLOGIE. (Text and summaries in English, French, German, Italian, Spanish) 1874. q. 410 F. (effective 1998). (Museum National d'Histoire Naturelle, Laboratoire de Cryptogamie) A.D.A.C., 12 rue Buffon, 75005 Paris, France. E-mail: lamy@mnhn.fr; bury@mnhn.fr. Ed. Denis Lamy. bk.rev.; abstr.; bibl.; index. circ. 450. (also avail. in microfiche from IDC; back issues avail.) **Indexed:** ASCA, Biol.Abstr., Bull.Signal., Chem.Abstr., Curr.Adv.Ecol.Sci., Curr.Cont., Ecol.Abstr., Excerp.Med., Geo.Abstr., Rev.Plant Path. **Document type:** academic/scholarly publication.
—BLDSC (3490.155400); CASDDS; CISTI; Genuine Article; Linda Hall; SWETS; UnCover.
    Supersedes (in 1980): Revue Bryologique et Lichenologique (ISSN 0399-0575)
    Description: Publishes research results from all fields of bryology and lichenology.

589.2   FR   ISSN 0181-1584
                             CODEN: CRMYD6
CRYPTOGAMIE: MYCOLOGIE. (Text and summaries in English, French, German, Italian, Spanish) 1936. q. 410 F. (effective 1998). (Museum National d'Histoire Naturelle, Laboratoire de Cryptogamie) A.D.A.C., 12 rue Buffon, 75005 Paris, France. E-mail: cryplich@mnhn.fr; bury@mnhn.fr. Ed. Denis Lamy. bk.rev.; bibl.; index. circ. 450. (back issues avail.) **Indexed:** ASCA, Bio-Contr.News & Info., Biol.Abstr., Bull.Signal., Curr.Adv.Ecol.Sci., Curr.Cont., Ecol.Abstr., Forest.Abstr., Forest Prod.Abstr., Hort.Abstr., Maize Abstr., Mycol.Abstr., Plant Breed.Abstr., Rev.Med.& Vet.Mycol., Rev.Plant Path., Seed Abstr., Soils & Fert., Trop.Oil Seeds Abstr. **Document type:** academic/scholarly publication.
—BLDSC (3490.155450); CASDDS; CISTI; Genuine Article; Linda Hall; SWETS; UnCover.
    Supersedes (in 1980): Revue de Mycologie (ISSN 0484-8578)
    Description: Publishes results and synthesis papers concerning the biology of fungi.

CUADERNOS DE FITOPATOLOGIA; revista de fitopatologia terapeutica. see FORESTS AND FORESTRY

589.2   SP   ISSN 1132-0605
CUADERNOS DE TRABAJO DE FLORA MICOLOGICA IBERICA. 1990. irreg. price varies. Real Jardin Botanico de Madrid, Plaza de Murillo 2, 28014 Madrid, Spain. (Co-sponsor: Consejo Superior de Investigaciones Cientificas) **Indexed:** Ind.SST.

581 615   CU   ISSN 0138-8037
CUBA. CENTRO DE INFORMACION Y DOCUMENTACION AGROPECUARIO. BOLETIN DE RESENAS. SERIE: PLANTAS MEDICINALES. (Abstracts in English) 1983. irreg. C.$1 or exchange basis. Centro de Informacion y Documentacion Agropecuario, Gaveta Postal 4149, Havana 4, Cuba. TEL 301672. TELEX 0511007. (Dist. by: Ediciones Cubanas, Obispo No. 461, Apdo. 605, Havana, Cuba) charts; stat. **Indexed:** Agrindex.
    Formerly: Cuba. Centro de Informacion y Divulgacion Agropecuario. Boletin de Resenas. Serie: Plantas Medicinales.

581   AT   ISSN 0727-9620
QK445   CODEN: CUNNEY
CUNNINGHAMIA. 1981. 2/yr. Aus.$60 to individuals; institutions Aus.$90; foreign Aus.$105. National Herbarium of New South Wales, Royal Botanic Gardens Sydney, Mrs Macquaries Rd., Sydney, N.S.W. 2000, Australia. FAX 61-2-251-7231. URL: http://www.rbgsyd.gov.au. Eds. Doug Benson, Gary Bridle. R&P contact: Gary Bridle. circ. 1,000. **Indexed:** Biol.Abstr., Curr.Adv.Ecol.Sci. **Document type:** academic/scholarly publication, government publication.
—UnCover.
    Description: Provides papers on ecological research in NSW, including vegetation maps.

CURRENT ADVANCES IN PLANT SCIENCE. see BIOLOGY — Abstracting, Bibliographies, Statistics

581   II   ISSN 0253-7125
                             CODEN: CRMPDD
CURRENT RESEARCH ON MEDICINAL AND AROMATIC PLANTS. (Text in English) 1979. q. $300 (effective Jan. 1995). Central Institute of Medicinal and Aromatic Plants, Council of Scientific & Industrial Research, P.O. Box 1, P.O. CIMAP, Lucknow 226015, India. TEL 91-522-387520. FAX 91-522-385554. TELEX 0535-298 CIMAP IN. E-mail: root@cimap.sirnetd.ernet.in. Ed. Sushil Kumar. adv.; bk.rev. circ. 250. **Indexed:** Hort.Abstr. **Document type:** academic/scholarly publication.
—CASDDS; CISTI.
    Formerly: Central Indian Medicinal Plants Organisation. Newsletter.

CURRENT TOPICS IN MEDICAL MYCOLOGY. see MEDICAL SCIENCES — Communicable Diseases

581 635   US
CYCAD SOCIETY NEWSLETTER. 1976. q. $15. Cycad Society, c/o David S. Mayo, Sec.Treas., 1161 Phyllis Ct., Mountain View, CA 94040. Ed. Garrie P. Landry. circ. 450. (back issues avail.)

589.2   XR
QK600
CZECH MYCOLOGY. (Text in English) 1947. q. DM.124. Ceska Vedecka Spolecnost pro Mukologii, P.O. Box 106, 111 21 Prague 1, Czech Republic. TEL 26-94-51. (Dist. in Western countries by: Kubon & Sagner, P.O. Box 34 01 08, 8000 Munich 34, Germany) Ed.Bd. bk.rev.; abstr.; charts; illus.; index. circ. 850. **Indexed:** Bio-Contr.News & Info., Biol.Abstr., Chem.Abstr., Excerp.Med., Ind.Vet., Rev.Med.& Vet.Mycol., Rev.Plant Path., Vet.Bull. —CISTI.
    Formerly (until 1993): Ceska Mykologie (ISSN 0009-0476)
    Description: Devoted to all aspects of mycology, especially to taxonomy (systematics); physiology, the genetics of fungi, mycological toxicology, phytopathology, etc.

581   DK   ISSN 0109-3142
DANSKE PLANTEVAERNSKONFERENCE. 1984. a. DKK 50. Danish Institute of Agricultural Sciences, Research Centre Foulum, P.O. Box 23, DK-8830 Tjele, Denmark. FAX 45-89-99-16-99. illus. circ. 800.

581   SW   ISSN 1101-5527
DAPHNE; tidskrift foer botanik i Stockholms och Soedermanlands laen. 1990. s-a. SEK 90 membership (effective 1994). Stockholm Universitaet, Botaniska Institutionen, S-106 91 Stockholm, Sweden. Ed. Raoul Iseborg. circ. 500. **Document type:** bulletin.
    Description: Publishes local botanical reports for botanists in the Stockholm area.

500.9   AG   ISSN 0011-6793
QK1   CODEN: DARWAG
DARWINIANA. (Text in English, Spanish; summaries in English) 1922. s-a. $75 (effective 1996 & 1997). (Academia Nacional de Ciencias Exactas, Fisicas y Naturales de Buenos Aires) Instituto de Botanica Darwinion, Labarden y del Campo, Casilla de Correo 22, San Isidro 1642, Buenos Aires, Argentina. TEL 742-8534. FAX 541-747-4748. E-mail: postmaster@darwin.edu.ar. (Co-sponsor: Consejo Nacional de Investigaciones Cientificas y Tecnicas) Eds. Juan C. Gamerro, Juan H. Hunziker. bk.rev.; bibl.; illus. circ. 900. **Indexed:** Biol.Abstr., Chem.Abstr., Curr.Adv.Ecol.Sci., Ecol.Abstr., Excerp.Med., Field Crop Abstr., Forest.Abstr., Forest Prod.Abstr., Herb.Abstr., Plant Breed.Abstr., Rev.Plant Path., VITIS. **Document type:** academic/scholarly publication.
—CISTI; KNAW; Linda Hall.
    Description: Botanical research on systematics, anatomy, cytogenetics, embryology, evolution, palynology, ecology, plant geography and floristics. *Refereed Serial*

581 635   US   ISSN 0734-3434
QK938.D4
DESERT PLANTS. 1979. s-a. $15 to individuals; institutions $20. 2120 E. Allen Rd., Tucson, AZ 85719. TEL 520-318-7046. FAX 520-621-1296. E-mail: mnorem@ag.arizona.edu. Ed. Margaret Norem. R&P contact: Margaret Norem. circ. 1,000 (paid). **Indexed:** Abstr.Anthropol., Agroforest.Abstr., Hort.Abstr., Sport Fish.Abstr., Triticale Abstr., Wild.Rev. **Document type:** academic/scholarly publication.
—Linda Hall; UnCover.
    Description: Designed to broaden knowledge of plants indigenous or adaptable to arid and sub-arid regions; contains material of interest to industrial and planning horticulturists and botanists; and covers plant distribution, environment, and economic importance. *Refereed Serial*

DEUTSCHE BAUMSCHULE. see GARDENING AND HORTICULTURE

581 634.9   GW   ISSN 0070-3958
DEUTSCHE DENDROLOGISCHE GESELLSCHAFT. MITTEILUNGEN. 1893. a. free. Deutsche Dendrologische Gesellschaft, Hawstr. 28, 54290 Trier, Germany. TEL (0651)3 30 61. Ed. Horst Bartels. bk.rev.; cum.index. circ. 1,500.

DEVELOPMENTS IN PLANT AND SOIL SCIENCES. see AGRICULTURE — Crop Production And Soil

581   NE
DEVELOPMENTS IN PLANT BREEDING. (Text in English) 1994. irreg. price varies. Kluwer Academic Publishers, Postbus 17, 3300 AA Dordrecht, Netherlands. TEL 31-78-6392392. FAX 31-78-6392254. TELEX 29245 KAPG NL. E-mail: services@wkap.nl; URL: http://www.wkap.nl. (Dist. by: Kluwer Academic Publishers Group, P.O. Box 322, 3300 AH Dordrecht, Netherlands. TEL 31-78-6392392. FAX 31-78-6546474; N. America dist. addr.: Box 358, Accord Sta., Hingham, MA 02018-0358. TEL 617-871-6600. FAX 617-871-6528) **Document type:** monographic series *Refereed Serial*

DEVELOPMENTS IN PLANT GENETICS AND BREEDING. see BIOLOGY — Genetics

581.2 NE
DEVELOPMENTS IN PLANT PATHOLOGY. (Text in English) 1993. irreg., vol.3, 1993. price varies. (British Society for Plant Pathology) Kluwer Academic Publishers, Postbus 17, 3300 AA Dordrecht, Netherlands. TEL 31-78-6392392. FAX 31-78-6392254. TELEX 29245 KAPG NL. E-mail: services@wkap.nl; URL: http://www.wkap.nl. (Dist. by: Kluwer Academic Publishers Group, P.O. Box 322, 3300 AH Dordrecht, Netherlands. TEL 31-78-6392392. FAX 31-78-6546474; N. America dist. addr.: Box 358, Accord Sta., Hingham, MA 02018-0358. TEL 617-871-6600. FAX 617-871-6528) **Document type:** monographic series.
Refereed Serial

581 JA ISSN 0911-9310
DIATOM. (Text in English, Japanese) 1985. a. Nihon Keiso Gakkai - Japanese Society of Diatomology, 8-9-813 Honcho 3-chome, Koganei-shi, Tokyo 184, Japan. **Indexed:** Ecol.Abstr.

589.4 GW ISSN 0269-249X
DIATOM RESEARCH. (Text in English) 2/yr. DM.196 (foreign $142) (effective 1997). Gebrueder Borntraeger Verlagsbuchhandlung, Johannesstr. 3A, 70176 Stuttgart, Germany. TEL 49-711-625001. FAX 49-711-625005. **Indexed:** Geo.Abstr.P.G. **Document type:** academic/scholarly publication.
—BLDSC (3580.235300); Linda Hall; UnCover. **CCC.**

581 SX ISSN 0012-3013
DINTERIA; contributions to the flora and vegetation of Namibia. (Text and summaries in Afrikaans, English, German) 1968. irreg., no.19, 1987. price varies. Namibia Scientific Society, P.O. Box 67, Windhoek, Namibia. TEL 061-225372. Ed. W. Giess. illus.; index. circ. 1,000. (back issues avail.) **Indexed:** Curr.Adv.Ecol.Sci., Forest.Abstr., Forest Prod.Abstr., Ind.S.A.Per. **Document type:** academic/scholarly publication.
—BLDSC (3588.550000).

581 GW ISSN 0070-6728
QK1 CODEN: DIBOD5
DISSERTATIONES BOTANICAE. 1967. irreg. price varies. J. Cramer in der Gebrueder Borntraeger Verlagsbuchhandlung, Johannesstr. 3A, 70176 Stuttgart, Germany. TEL 49-711-625001. FAX 49-711-625005. **Indexed:** Biol.Abstr. **Document type:** academic/scholarly publication.
—CISTI.

589.2 UK ISSN 0012-396X
DISTRIBUTION MAPS OF PLANT DISEASES. (Former name of issuing body: Commonwealth Mycological Institute (C M I)) 1942. s-a. £80($140) (effective 1997). (International Mycological Institute) CAB International, Wallingford, Oxon. OX10 8DE, England. TEL 44-1491-832111. FAX 44-1491-826090. TELEX 847964 COMAGG G. E-mail: cabi@cabi.org; URL: http://www.cabi.org. (Alt. addr.: International Mycological Institute, Bakeham Ln., Egham, Surrey TW20 9TY, England; U.S. subscr. to: Oxford University Press, Customer Services Department, 2001 Evans Rd., Cary, NC 27513. TEL 800-445-9714. FAX 919-677-1303) charts; maps. (reprint service avail.) **Indexed:** Forest.Abstr., Forest Prod.Abstr., Rev.Appl.Entomol., Rev.Plant Path. **Document type:** academic/scholarly publication.
—BLDSC (3604.000000).
Description: Comprises a series of maps giving the world distribution of a plant pathogen, incorporating information from the literature and records of the International Mycological Institute Biosystematic Reference Collection.

581 BE ISSN 0779-1100
DISTRIBUTIONES PLANTARUM AFRICANARUM. 1969. irreg. 220 BEF per no. (foreign 230 BEF) (effective 1993). Jardin Botanique National de Belgique, Domaine de Bouchout, 1860 Meise, Belgium. TEL 32-2-2693905. (back issues avail.) **Document type:** monographic series.

...VERSITY; a news journal for the international genetic resources community. see *BIOLOGY — Genetics*

581 RU ISSN 0012-4982
QK1 CODEN: DKBSBT
DOKLADY BOTANICAL SCIENCES. English translation of: Rossiiskaya Akademiya Nauk. Doklady. 1964. s-a. $565 in US; elsewhere $660 (effective 1998). (Russian Academy of Sciences, Botanical Section) Maik Nauka - Interperiodica, Mezhdunarodnyi Otdel, Ul. Profsoyuznaya, 90, 117864 Moscow, Russia. TEL 7-095-3360066. FAX 7-095-3360666. (Dist. by: Plenum Publishing Corp., 233 Spring St., New York, NY 10013-1578. TEL 212-620-8468. FAX 212-463-0472) Ed. V.A. Kabanov. index. (also avail. in microfilm from UMI; back issues avail.) **Indexed:** Biol.Abstr., Chem.Titles, Cott.& Trop.Fibr.Abstr., Crop Physiol.Abstr., Curr.Adv.Ecol.Sci., Energy Res.Abstr., Field Crop Abstr., Hort.Abstr., INIS Atomind., Int.Abstr.Biol.Sci., Irr.& Drain.Abstr., Maize Abstr., Plant Grow.Reg.Abstr., Soils & Fert., Soyabean Abstr., Triticale Abstr., Weed Abstr. **Document type:** academic/scholarly publication.
—BLDSC (0411.290000); CISTI; SWETS; UMI; UnCover. **CCC.**
Refereed Serial

580 DR
DOMINICAN REPUBLIC. CENTRO NACIONAL DE INVESTIGACIONES AGROPECUARIAS. LABORATORIO DE SANIDAD VEGETAL.* irreg. (5-6/yr.). free. Centro Nacional de Investigaciones Agropecuarias, Laboratorio de Sanidad Vegetal, San Cristobal, Dominican Republic. circ. controlled. (processed)

581 US ISSN 1064-4032
QK1
DOUGLASIA. 1976. q. membership only. Washington Native Plant Society, University of Washington, Department of Botany, Box 28690, Seattle, WA 98118-8690. TEL 206-760-8022. Ed. Karen Hinman. R&P contact: Karen Hinman. **Document type:** academic/scholarly publication, newsletter.

581 II ISSN 0970-2695
DR. H.S. GOUR VISHWAVIDYALAYA, SAGAR BOTANICAL SOCIETY. BULLETIN. 1948. s-a. Rs.30($10) to individuals; institutions Rs.60($25). Dr. H.S. Gour Vishwavidyalaya, Sagar Botanical Society, Department of Botany, Gour Nagar, Sagar 470 003, Madhya Pradesh, India. TEL 91-7582-25452. FAX 91-7582-23236. Ed. Dr. T.R. Sahu. adv.; bk.rev. circ. 300. **Indexed:** Biol.Abstr. **Document type:** bulletin.
—CISTI.
Formerly (until 1983): University of Sagar. Botanical Society. Bulletin (ISSN 0376-1908)
Refereed Serial

581 614.7 BN ISSN 0352-0781
DRUSTVO EKOLOGA BOSNE I HERCEGOVINE. BILTEN. SERIJA A - EKOLOSKE MONOGRAFIJE.* (Text in Serbo-Croatian; summaries in English, German and Russian) 1982. biennial. Oslobodjenje, Dzemala Bijedica 185, 71000 Sarajevo, Bosnia Hercegovina. TEL 071 659-377. (Subscr. to: Drustvo Ekologa BiH, Vojvode R. Putnika 43-a, 71000 Sarajevo, Bosnia Hercegovina) Ed. Radomir Lakusic.

581 614.7 BN ISSN 0352-0811
DRUSTVO EKOLOGA BOSNE I HERCEGOVINE. BILTEN. SERIJA B - NAUCNI SKUPOVI I SAVJETOVANJA.* (Text in Serbo-Croatian; summaries in English, German, Russian) 1982. biennial. 12000 din.($20) Oslobodjenje, Dzemala Bijedica 185, 71000 Sarajevo, Bosnia Hercegovina. TEL 071 659-377. (Subscr. to: Drustvo Ekologa BiH, Vojvode R. Putnika 43-a, 71000 Sarajevo, Bosnia Hercegovina) Ed. Radomir Lakusic. circ. 500.

581 BE ISSN 0251-1134
DUMORTIERA. 1975. 3/yr. 410 BEF (foreign 450 BEF) (effective 1993). Jardin Botanique National de Belgique - Nationale Plantentuin van Belgie, Domaine de Bouchout, 1860 Meise, Belgium. TEL 32-2-3693905. **Document type:** monographic series.

581 US ISSN 0013-0001
SB1 CODEN: ECBOA5
ECONOMIC BOTANY; devoted to applied botany and plant utilization. 1947. q. $88 includes s-a- Plants & People newsletter (foreign $97) (effective 1997). (Society for Economic Botany) New York Botanical Garden, Scientific Publications Department, Bronx, NY 10458-5126. TEL 718-817-8721. FAX 718-817-8842. Ed. Lawrence Kaplan. adv.; bk.rev.; abstr.; bibl.; illus. circ. 2,000. (also avail. in microform from UMI,PMC; back issues avail.) **Indexed:** Agroforest.Abstr., Art & Archaeol.Tech.Abstr., Arts & Hum.Cit.Ind., ASCA, Bibl.Agri., Biodet.Abstr., Biol.Abstr., Biol.& Agr.Ind., Biol.Dig., Biotech.Abstr., Chem.Abstr., Curr.Adv.Ecol.Sci., Curr.Cont., Energy Info.Abstr., Environ.Abstr., Environ.Per.Bibl. (1980-), Excerp.Med., Field Crop Abstr., Food Sci.& Tech.Abstr., Forest.Abstr., Forest Prod.Abstr., Herb.Abstr., Hort.Abstr., Ind.Sci.Rev., Ind.Vet., Ornam.Hort., Plant Breed.Abstr., Rev.Plant Path., Rice Abstr., Rural Recreat.Tour.Abstr., Sci.Cit.Ind., Seed Abstr., Sel.Water Res.Abstr., So.Pac.Per.Ind., Soils & Fert., SSCI, Sugar Ind.Abstr., Vet.Bull., VITIS, Weed Abstr., World Agri.Econ.& Rural Sociol.Abstr. **Document type:** academic/scholarly publication.
—BLDSC (3651.700000); CASDDS; CISTI; EMDOCS; Genuine Article; KR SourceOne; Linda Hall; SWETS; UMI; UnCover. **CCC.**
Description: Original research on the uses of plants by people.
Refereed Serial

581 UK ISSN 0960-4286
QK1
EDINBURGH JOURNAL OF BOTANY. 1900. 3/yr. £96($164) (effective 1998). Cambridge University Press, Edinburgh Bldg., Shaftesbury Rd., Cambridge CB2 2RU, England. TEL 44-1223-312393. FAX 44-1223-315052. TELEX 851817256. E-mail: information@cup.cam.ac.uk; journals___ subscriptions@cup.org; URL: http://www.cup.org/journals/CUPJNLS.html. (N. American addr.: Cambridge University Press, Journals Dept., 40 W. 20th St., New York, NY 10011. TEL 212-924-3900. FAX 212-924-3900) Ed. John A. Raven. R&P contact: Linda Nicol. adv. contact: Rebecca Symons. bk.rev.; illus. circ. 550. (reprint service avail. from UMI) **Indexed:** Biol.Abstr., Curr.Adv.Ecol.Sci., Excerp.Bot, Field Crop Abstr., Herb.Abstr., Hort.Abstr., Ornam.Hort., Triticale Abstr. **Document type:** academic/scholarly publication.
—BLDSC (3660.973000); UMI; UnCover. **CCC.**
Formerly (until 1990): Royal Botanic Garden, Edinburgh. Notes (ISSN 0080-4274)
Description: Covers plant systematics and related areas of biodiversity, conservation, and phytogeography in southwest Asia and the Himalayas, as well as elsewhere throughout the world.

EDITOR & PUBLISHER INTERNATIONAL YEAR BOOK; encyclopedia of the newspaper industry. see *JOURNALISM*

581 UA ISSN 1011-3835
CODEN: EGJBAY
EGYPTIAN JOURNAL OF BOTANY/AL-MAJALLAH AL-MISRIYYAH LIL-NABAT. (Text in English; summaries in English and Arabic) 1958. 2/yr. $57 (effective 1997). (Botanical Society of Egypt, Research Department) National Information and Documentation Centre (NIDOC), Tahrir St., Dokki, Awqaf P.O., Cairo, Egypt. TEL 20-2-3371696. Ed. S. Al-Abyad. charts; illus. circ. 1,000. (reprint service avail. from IRC) **Indexed:** Biol.Abstr., Chem.Abstr., Curr.Adv.Ecol.Sci., Fababean Abstr., Field Crop Abstr., Herb.Abstr., Hort.Abstr., Rev.Plant Path., Rice Abstr., Soils & Fert., Soyabean Abstr., Weed Abstr. **Document type:** academic/scholarly publication.
—BLDSC (3664.300000); CASDDS; CISTI; Linda Hall.
Former titles (until 1972): Journal of Botany of the United Arab Republic (ISSN 0021-9363); (until 1959): Egyptian Journal of Botany (ISSN 0375-9237)

BIOLOGY — BOTANY

581   UA   ISSN 1110-0230
EGYPTIAN JOURNAL OF PHYTOPATHOLOGY. (Text in English; summaries in Arabic and English) 1969. s-a. $57 (effective 1997). (Egyptian Phytopathological Society, Research Department) National Information and Documentation Centre (NIDOC), Tahrir St., Dokki, Awqaf P.O., Cairo, Egypt. TEL 20-2-3371696. Ed. M.M. Ragab. circ. 1,000. (reprint service avail. from IRC) **Indexed:** Bio-Contr.News & Info., Biodet.Abstr., Biol.Abstr., Chem.Abstr, Fababean Abstr., Field Crop Abstr., Food Sci.& Tech.Abstr., Herb.Abstr., Hort.Abstr., Irr.& Drain.Abstr., Potato Abstr., Rev.Plant Path., Seed Abstr. **Document type:** academic/scholarly publication.
—SWETS.

EKOLOGIA. see *BIOLOGY*

581.1   US
ENCYCLOPEDIA OF PLANT PHYSIOLOGY. NEW SERIES. 1975. irreg., vol.20, 1993. price varies. Springer-Verlag, 175 Fifth Ave., New York, NY 10010. TEL 212-460-1500. FAX 212-473-6272. (Also: Berlin, Heidelberg, Tokyo and Vienna) Eds. A. Pirson, M.H. Zimmermann. (reprint service avail. from ISI) **Indexed:** Chem.Abstr. **Document type:** monographic series.

581   GW   ISSN 0170-4818
ENGLERA. (Text and summaries in English, German) 1979. irreg. price varies. Botanischer Garten und Botanisches Museum Berlin-Dahlem, Koenigin-Luise-Str. 6-8, 14191 Berlin, Germany. TEL 49-30-83006194. FAX 49-30-83006186. E-mail: son@zedat.fu-berlin.de; URL: http://www.bgbm.fu-berlin.de/bgbm/library/publikat/publbgbm.htm. Ed. H.W. Lack. circ. 800. (back issues avail.) **Indexed:** Curr.Adv.Ecol.Sci. **Document type:** academic/scholarly publication, monographic series.
—Linda Hall.
     Description: Original papers in the fields of taxonomic and floristic botany.
     Refereed Serial

581.191   UK   ISSN 0098-8472
QK757   CODEN: EEBODM
ENVIRONMENTAL AND EXPERIMENTAL BOTANY; an international journal. 1961. bi-m. fl.1140($655) (effective 1998). Elsevier Science Ltd., Pergamon, P.O. Box 800, Kidlington, Oxford OX5 1DX, England. TEL 44-1865-843000. FAX 44-1865-843010. E-mail: nlinfo-f@elsevier.nl; usinfo-f@elsevier.com; forinfo-kyf04035@niftyserve.or.jp; URL: http://www.elsevier.nl/. (Subscr. to: Elsevier Science, Regional Sales Office, P.O. Box 211, 1000 AE Amsterdam, Netherlands. TEL 31-20-4853757. FAX 31-20-4853432; Subscr. in the Americas to: Elsevier Science, Regional Sales Office, Box 945, New York, NY 10159-0945. TEL 212-633-3730. FAX 212-633-3680; Subscr. in Australasia and the Far East to: Elsevier Science (Singapore) Pte Ltd, No.1 Temasek Ave., No.17-01 Millenia Tower, Singapore 039192, Singapore. TEL 65-434-3727. FAX 65-337-2230) Ed. Morton W. Miller. adv.; bk.rev.; charts; illus.; index. circ. 1,200. (also avail. in microfilm from UMI; back issues avail.) **Indexed:** ASCA, Bibl.Agri., Biol.Abstr., Biol.& Agr.Ind., Chem.Abstr., Cott.& Trop.Fibr.Abstr., Crop Physiol.Abstr., Curr.Adv.Genetics & Molec.Biol., Curr.Cont., Deep Sea Res.& Oceanogr.Abstr., Ecol.Abstr., Environ.Per.Bibl. (1974-), Excerp.Med., Field Crop Abstr., Food Sci.& Tech.Abstr., Forest.Abstr., Forest Prod.Abstr., Herb.Abstr., Hort.Abstr., Ind.Sci.Rev., INSPEC, Irr.& Drain.Abstr., Maize Abstr., Nutr.Abstr., Ornam.Hort., Plant Breed.Abstr., Plant Grow.Reg.Abstr., Pollut.Abstr., Rice Abstr., Sci.Cit.Ind., Seed Abstr., Sel.Water Res.Abstr., Soils & Fert., Soyabean Abstr., Triticale Abstr., Weed Abstr. **Document type:** academic/scholarly publication.
—BLDSC (3791.383000); CASDDS; CISTI; EMDOCS; Genuine Article; KR SourceOne; Linda Hall; SWETS; UMI; UnCover. **CCC.**
     Formerly (until 1976): Radiation Botany (ISSN 0033-7560)
     Description: Publishes research papers on the physical and biological mechanisms that relate to the working of plant systems and their interaction with the environment, including radiation botany, cytogenetics, chemical mutagenesis, pollution effects, phytopathology, and topics in the soil sciences pertaining to plant growth.
     Refereed Serial

580   US
EPIPHYLLUM BULLETIN. Variant title: E S A Bulletin. 1945. q. $15 (Canada & Mexico $20; elsewhere $25). Epiphyllum Society of America, Box 585, Long Beach, CA 90801-0585. TEL 562-438-4554. Ed. Raymond Eden. adv. contact: Raymond Eden. circ. 500. **Indexed:** Tel.Abstr. **Document type:** newsletter.
     Description: Contains Epi Society news plus articles of interest to epicacti enthusiasts.

ERLANGER BAUSTEINE ZUR FRAENKISCHEN HEIMATFORSCHUNG. see *HISTORY*

581   VE   ISSN 0252-8274
                    CODEN: ERNSDF
ERNSTIA. (Text mainly in Spanish; occasionally in French, Portuguese; summaries in English and Spanish) 1981. irreg. (approx. 7/yr.). exchange basis. Universidad Central de Venezuela, Facultad de Agronomia, Instituto de Botanica Agricola, Herbario, Apdo. 4579, Maracay, Edo. Aragua 2101, Venezuela. Ed. Baltasar Trujillo. circ. 200. (back issues avail.) **Indexed:** Potato Abstr.

ESSENTIAL ECOLOGY, ZOOLOGY & PLANT SCIENCE ABSTRACTS. see *BIOLOGY — Abstracting, Bibliographies, Statistics*

ESTACION EXPERIMENTAL DE AULA DEI. ANALES. see *AGRICULTURE — Crop Production And Soil*

581 615   II   ISSN 0971-1252
ETHNOBOTANY. (Text in English) 1989. s-a. Rs.400($50) (Society of Ethnobotanists) Deep Publications, A-3-27A DDA Flats, Paschim Vihar, New Delhi 110063, India. TEL 91-11-5579514. FAX 91-11-5437621. Ed. S.L. Kapoor. bk.rev. (back issues avail.) **Document type:** academic/scholarly publication.
—BLDSC (3814.890000).
     Description: Carries original research papers, review articles, short communications on ethnobotany, ethno-medicine, ethno-chemistry, ethno-pharmacology, ethno-taxonomy, ethno-pharmacognosy.
     Refereed Serial

631.52 581   GW   ISSN 0071-2515
EUROPEAN ASSOCIATION FOR RESEARCH ON PLANT BREEDING. REPORT OF THE CONGRESS. Represents: Proceedings of the Eucarpia Congress. 1956. triennial, 13th, 1992, Angers, France. price varies. Springer-Verlag, Heidelberger Platz 3, 14197 Berlin, Germany. TEL 49-30-82787-0. FAX 49-30-82787448. E-mail: subscriptions@springer.de. (Subscr. in N. America to: Springer-Verlag New York, Inc., 333 Meadowlands Pkwy., Secaucus, NJ 07094. TEL 212-460-1500. FAX 212-473-6272) **Document type:** proceedings.

589.3   UK   ISSN 0967-0262
QK564   CODEN: EJPHE5
EUROPEAN JOURNAL OF PHYCOLOGY. 1953. q. £154($270) (effective 1998). (British Phycological Society) Cambridge University Press, The Edinburgh Bldg., Shaftesbury Rd., Cambridge CB2 2RU, England. TEL 44-1223-312393. FAX 44-1223-315052. TELEX 851817256. E-mail: information@cup.cam.ac.uk; journals-subscriptions@cup.org; URL: http://www.cup.org/journals/CUPJNLS.html. (N. American addr.: Cambridge University Press, Journals Dept., 40 W. 20th St., New York, NY 10011. TEL 212-924-3900. FAX 212-691-3239) Ed. Christine A. Maggs. R&P contact: Linda Nicol. adv. contact: Rebecca Symons. bk.rev.; illus.; index. (back issues avail.) **Indexed:** ASCA, Biol.Abstr., Curr.Adv.Ecol.Sci., Curr.Cont., Deep Sea Res.& Oceanogr.Abstr., Ind.Sci.Rev., Ocean.Abstr., Plant Breed.Abstr., Pollut.Abstr., Risk Abstr., Sci.Cit.Ind. **Document type:** academic/scholarly publication.
—BLDSC (3829.734500); CISTI; Genuine Article; Linda Hall; SWETS; UMI; UnCover. **CCC.**
     Supersedes (in 1993): British Phycological Journal (ISSN 0007-1617); Which was formerly: British Phycological Bulletin.
     Description: Contains scientific research articles on the study of algae.

581.2   NE   ISSN 0929-1873
SB599   CODEN: EPLPEH
EUROPEAN JOURNAL OF PLANT PATHOLOGY. (Text in English) 1895. 9/yr. fl.1186 to institutions; $608.50 to institutions in U.S. (effective 1998). (European Foundation for Plant Pathology) Kluwer Academic Publishers, Postbus 17, 3300 AA Dordrecht, Netherlands. TEL 31-78-6392392. FAX 31-78-6392254. TELEX 29245 KAPG NL. E-mail: services@wkap.nl; URL: http://www.wkap.nl. (Dist. by: Kluwer Academic Publishers Group, P.O. Box 322, 3300 AH Dordrecht, Netherlands. TEL 31-78-6392392. FAX 31-78-6546474; N. America dist. addr.: Box 358, Accord Sta., Hingham, MA 02018-0358. TEL 617-871-6600. FAX 617-871-6528) Ed. Bob Schippers. adv.; bk.rev.; abstr.; bibl.; charts; illus.; index, cum.index every 25 yrs. circ. 1,300. (also avail. in microform from SWZ) **Indexed:** ASCA, Bio-Contr.News & Info., Biol.Abstr., Biotech.Abstr., Bull.Signal., Chem.Abstr., Curr.Cont., Fababean Abstr., Field Crop Abstr., Forest.Abstr., Forest Prod.Abstr., Helminthol.Abstr., Herb.Abstr., Hort.Abstr., Ind.Sci.Rev., Int.Abstr.Biol.Sci., Plant Breed.Abstr., Plant Grow.Reg.Abstr., Potato Abstr., Rev.Appl.Entomol., Rev.Plant Path., Sci.Cit.Ind., Seed Abstr., Soils & Fert., Soyabean Abstr., SSCI, Triticale Abstr., Trop.Oil Seeds Abstr., Weed Abstr. **Document type:** academic/scholarly publication.
—BLDSC (3829.736200); CASDDS; EMDOCS; Genuine Article; Linda Hall; SWETS; UnCover. **CCC.**
     Former titles: Netherlands Journal of Plant Pathology (ISSN 0028-2944); (until 1962): Tijdschrift over Plantenziekte (ISSN 0926-3454)
     Description: Covers the entire field of plant diseases and pests, including mycological and virological topics, entomological, nematological, weed and plant protection problems.
     Refereed Serial

582.14 635.955   RH   ISSN 0301-441X
QK495.L72
EXCELSA. 1971. biennial. $18 to individuals; institutions $25. Aloe, Cactus & Succulent Society of Zimbabwe, P.O. Box CY 300, Causeway, Harare, Zimbabwe. TEL 263-4-39175. Ed. Michael J. Kimberley. R&P contact: Michael J. Kimberly. adv.; bk.rev.; bibl.; charts; illus.; index, cum.index: 1971-1986. circ. 1,000. (back issues avail.) **Document type:** academic/scholarly publication.
     Description: Articles on the succulent flora of Zimbabwe, Africa, and the rest of the world.

582.14   RH   ISSN 1022-5919
EXCELSA TAXONOMIC SERIES. 1978. irreg, latest vol.4. Aloe, Cactus & Succulent Society of Zimbabwe, P.O. Box CY 300, Causeway, Harare, Zimbabwe. TEL 263-4-39175. Ed. Michael J. Kimberley. R&P contact: Michael J. Kimberley. bibl.; charts; illus.; index. circ. 1,000. **Document type:** monographic series.

581   GW   ISSN 0014-4045
Z5354.P7
EXCERPTA BOTANICA. SECTIO B: SOCIOLOGICA. (Text in English, French and German) 1959. irreg. (4 nos./vol.). DM.248 (foreign £128) (effective 1997). Gustav Fischer Verlag, Villengang 2, 07745 Jena, Germany. TEL 49-3641-626430. FAX 49-3641-626421. E-mail: office.j@gfischer.de. (Subscr. to: Stockton Press, Subscriptions Dept., Houndmills, Basingstoke, Hants RG21 6XS, England) Ed. D. Brandes. adv.; bibl.; index. circ. 550. **Indexed:** Curr.Adv.Ecol.Sci., Deep Sea Res.& Oceanogr.Abstr. **Document type:** academic/scholarly publication.
—CISTI; Linda Hall; SWETS. **CCC.**

581   US   ISSN 0071-3392
                    CODEN: EXBOAG
EXPERIMENTAL BOTANY; AN INTERNATIONAL SERIES OF MONOGRAPHS. 1964. irreg., vol.19, 1984. Academic Press, Inc., 525 B St., Ste. 1900, San Diego, CA 92101-4495. TEL 619-231-0926. FAX 619-699-6715. (Subscr. to: Order Dept., 6277 Sea Harbor Dr., 4th Fl., Orlando, FL 32887. TEL 800-321-5068) Eds. J.F. Sutcliffe, J. Cronshaw. (reprint service avail. from ISI) **Indexed:** Biol.Abstr. **Document type:** monographic series.
—CASDDS; CISTI.

EYESPY; the discovery magazine for kids. see *ENVIRONMENTAL STUDIES*

BIOLOGY — BOTANY

632 581   UN   ISSN 0254-9727
CODEN: FAOPA2
F A O PLANT PROTECTION BULLETIN (MULTILINGUAL EDITION); a publication of the world reporting service on plant diseases, pests, and their control. (Text in English, French, Spanish) 1952. q. $24. Food and Agriculture Organization of the United Nations (Rome), Plant Production and Protection Division, Via delle Terme Caracalla, 00100 Rome, Italy. TEL 57974350. FAX 57975155. Ed. K. Zammarano. bibl.; charts; illus.; index. circ. 6,000. (also avail. in microfilm from UMI; reprint service avail. from UMI) **Indexed:** Bio-Contr.News & Info., Biodet.Abstr., Biol.Abstr., Biol.& Agr.Ind., Biotech.Abstr., Chem.Abstr., Curr.Adv.Ecol.Sci., Curr.Cont., Ecol.Abstr., Excerp.Med., Field Crop Abstr., Forest Abstr., Forest Prod.Abstr., Helminthol.Abstr., Herb.Abstr., Hort.Abstr., IDA, Maize Abstr., Ornam.Hort., Plant Breed.Abstr., Potato Abstr., Rev.Appl.Entomol., Rev.Plant Path. Rice Abstr., Seed Abstr., So.Pac.Per.Ind., Sorghum & Millets Abstr., Soyabean Abstr., Triticale Abstr., Trop.Oil Seeds Abstr., Weed Abstr. **Document type:** bulletin.
—KR SourceOne; Linda Hall; UnCover.
Formerly (until 1981): F A O Plant Protection Bulletin (ISSN 0014-5637)
Description: Reports on the incidence and spread of plant diseases and pests, quarantine measures and major operations for prevention and control.

F P I: FLOWERING PLANT INDEX. see BIOLOGY — Abstracting, Bibliographies, Statistics

581   GW   ISSN 0014-8962
QK45   CODEN: FRZBAW
FEDDES REPERTORIUM; Zeitschrift fuer botanische Taxonomie und Geobotanik. (Text in English, German) 1905. 4/yr. DM.195 (foreign DM.203) to individuals; institutions DM.645 (foreign DM.665) (effective 1997). Akademie Verlag GmbH, Muehlenstr. 33-34, 13187 Berlin, Germany. TEL 49-30-47889348. FAX 49-30-47889357. E-mail: info@akademie-verlag.de. (Subscr. in the Americas to: John Wiley & Sons, Inc., 605 Third Ave., New York, NY 10158. TEL 212-850-6645. FAX 212-850-6021) Ed. G. Natho. bibl.; charts; illus.; index. **Indexed:** Biol.Abstr., Curr.Adv.Ecol.Sci., Deep Sea Res.& Oceanogr.Abstr., Field Crop Abstr., Herb.Abstr., Ornam.Hort., Plant Breed.Abstr., Soils & Fert., Weed Abstr. **Document type:** academic/scholarly publication.
—BLDSC (3901.700000); CISTI; EMDOCS; Linda Hall; UnCover.
Formerly: Feddes Repertorium Specierum Novarum Regni Vegetabilis.
Description: Covers all groups of the plant world including extant and fossil.

581   UK   ISSN 0308-0838
QK520   CODEN: FEGADG
FERN GAZETTE. 1909. s-a. £25 (includes Bulletin and Pteridologist) (effective 1996 & 1997). British Pteridological Society, c/o Botany Department, Natural History Museum, Cromwell Rd., London SW7 5BD, England. TEL 44-171-938-9497. Ed. B.A. Thomas. index. circ. 650. (also avail. in microfiche from IDC) **Indexed:** Biol.Abstr., Curr.Adv.Ecol.Sci., Geo.Abstr. **Document type:** academic/scholarly publication.
—BLDSC (3907.300000); UnCover.
Formerly: British Fern Gazette (ISSN 0524-5826)
Description: Focuses on the taxonomy, cytology, ecology, chemistry and morphology of pteridophytes.
Refereed Serial

581   US   ISSN 0015-0746
QK1   CODEN: FLDBAG
FIELDIANA: BOTANY. 1895. irreg. (Field Museum of Natural History, Library - Publications Division) Field Museum Press, Roosevelt Rd. at Lake Shore Dr., Chicago, IL 60605-2498. TEL 312-922-9410. FAX 312-427-7269. bibl.; charts; illus.; index. circ. 550. (back issues avail.; reprint service avail. from UMI) **Indexed:** Biol.Abstr., Chem.Abstr., Curr.Adv.Ecol.Sci., Deep Sea Res.& Oceanogr.Abstr., Ecol.Abstr., Forest.Abstr., Forest Prod.Abstr., GeoRef.
—CISTI; Linda Hall.
Description: Focuses on systematics, geographic distribution studies and floras, chiefly of Central and South America.
Refereed Serial

581   BU   ISSN 0324-0975
QK333   CODEN: FITODF
FITOLOGIJA. (Text in Bulgarian; summaries in English, French, German and Russian) vol.20, 1982. a. Bulgarska Akademiia na Naukite, Institut po Botanika, Acad. G. Bonchev St., Bldg. 23, 1113 Sofia, Bulgaria. Ed. Simeon Vanev. circ. 480. (back issues avail.; reprint service avail. from IRC) **Indexed:** Biol.Abstr., BSL Biol.
—BLDSC (3948.233000); CISTI; KNAW; Linda Hall.

581.2   PE   ISSN 0430-6155
FITOPATOLOGIA. (Text in English, Portuguese, Spanish; summaries in English, Spanish) 1966. 3/yr. $40 (effective 1996 & 1997). Asociacion Latinoamericana de Fitopatologia, Apdo. 1558, Lima 100, Peru. FAX 51-1-4351570. TELEX 25672 PE. E-mail: e.french@cgnet.com. Ed. Teresa Icochea. R&P contact: E. French. adv. contact: E. French. bk.rev. circ. 700. **Indexed:** Bio-Contr.News & Info., Biodet.Abstr., Biol.Abstr., Chem.Abstr., Cott.& Trop.Fibr.Abstr., Field Crop Abstr., Forest.Abstr., Forest Prod.Abstr., Hort.Abstr., Maize Abstr., Potato Abstr., Rev.Plant Path., Seed Abstr., Triticale Abstr., Weed Abstr. **Document type:** academic/scholarly publication.
—BLDSC (3948.235000); Linda Hall.
Description: Covers plant pathology, with an emphasis on Latin America. Includes research papers, methodology, reviews and notes.
Refereed Serial

581   IT
FITOSOCIOLOGIA. (Text in English, French, Italian, Spanish; summaries in English and French) 1964. a. exchange basis only. Societa Italiana di Fitosociologia - Italian Society for Phytosociology, Via Scopoli 22-24, 27100 Pavia, Italy. FAX 39-382-34240. Ed. E. Biondi. adv. contact: Edoardo Biondi. bk.rev.; illus. circ. 350. (back issues avail.) **Indexed:** Biol.Abstr. **Document type:** academic/scholarly publication.
Formerly (until 1989): Societa Italiana di Fitosociologia. Notiziario (ISSN 1120-4605)
Description: Contains original articles in the field of phytosociology, proceedings of scientific meetings, and reports on society activities.
Refereed Serial

581   BL   ISSN 0100-4204
CODEN: FTSSDV
FITOSSANIDADE. 1974. irreg. free. Fitossanitaristas do Ceara, Rua Livreiro Edesio, 612-401, 60135-620 Fortaleza, Ceara, Brazil. TEL 55-85-2571242. FAX 55-85-2438442. E-mail: fmsales@ufc.br. Ed. Fernando Montenegro de Sales. adv.; bibl.; charts; illus. circ. 1,000. **Indexed:** Rev.Appl.Entomol. **Document type:** academic/scholarly publication.
—CASDDS.
Refereed Serial

581.634   IT   ISSN 0367-326X
RS164   CODEN: FTRPAE
FITOTERAPIA; rivista di studi ed applicazioni delle piante medicinali. (Text in English, French and Italian; summaries in English) 1934. bi-m. free to qualified personnel. IdB Holding, Viale Ortles 12, 20139 Milan, Italy. TEL 39-2-57496442. FAX 39-2-57496443. E-mail: indenami@mbox.vol.it. Ed. Romano Vitali. R&P contact: Romano Vitali. adv.; bk.rev.; circ. 4,200 (controlled). (also avail. in microform from UMI; back issues avail.) **Indexed:** Agroforest.Abstr., Apic.Abstr., Biol.Abstr., Biotech.Abstr., Chem.Abstr., Crop Physiol.Abstr., Excerp.Med., Field Crop Abstr., Forest.Abstr., Forest Prod.Abstr., Herb.Abstr., Hort.Abstr., I.P.A., Ind.Vet., Irr.& Drain.Abstr., Ornam.Hort., Plant Breed.Abstr., Plant Grow.Reg.Abstr., Seed Abstr., Soils & Fert. **Document type:** bulletin.
●Also available online.
—BLDSC (3948.250000); CASDDS; CISTI; EMDOCS; KNAW; Linda Hall; UMI.
Description: Publishes articles concerning chemistry, pharmacology and the use of medicinal plants and their derivatives.

FITOTERAPIA. see ALTERNATIVE MEDICINE — Abstracting, Bibliographies, Statistics

580   RU   ISSN 0015-3303
QK710   CODEN: FZRSAV
FIZIOLOGIYA RASTENII. English translation: Russian Journal of Plant Physiology (RU ISSN 1021-4437) (Text in Russian; summaries in English) 1954. bi-m. $240 (effective 1998). (Rossiiskaya Akademiya Nauk) Izdatel'stvo Nauka, 90 Profsoyuznaya ul., 117864 Moscow, Russia. (Dist. by: Mezhdunarodnaya Kniga, ul. Dimitrova D.39, 113095 Moscow, Russia; Dist. in U.S. by: Victor Kamkin Inc., 4956 Boiling Brook Pkwy, Rockville, MD 20852. TEL 301-881-5973) Ed. A.L. Kursanov. bk.rev.; charts; illus.; index. circ. 2,800. **Indexed:** Agri.Eng.Abstr., Biol.Abstr., Chem.Abstr., Crop Physiol.Abstr., Fababean Abstr., Field Crop Abstr., Forest.Abstr., Herb.Abstr., Hort.Abstr., INIS Atomind., Irr.& Drain.Abstr., Maize Abstr., Ornam.Hort., Plant Grow.Reg.Abstr., Potato Abstr., Rice Abstr., Seed Abstr., Sorghum & Millets Abstr., Soyabean Abstr., Triticale Abstr., VITIS, Weed Abstr. **Document type:** academic/scholarly publication.
—BLDSC (0390.500000); CASDDS; CISTI; Linda Hall. **CCC**.

500.9   EC   ISSN 0015-380X
FLORA. (Text in English and Spanish) 1937. irreg. exchange basis. Instituto Ecuatoriano de Ciencias Naturales - Ecuadorian Institute of Natural Sciences, P.O. Box 408, Center, Quito, Ecuador. Ed. M. Acosta-Solis. bk.rev.; abstr.; bibl.; charts; illus. circ. 2,000. **Indexed:** Biol.Abstr., Curr.Cont., Ind.Sci.Rev.

580   GW   ISSN 0367-2530
CODEN: FLRABG
FLORA (JENA); Morphologie, Geobotanik, Oekologie. (Text in English, French and German; summaries in English) 1818. 4/yr. DM.604 (foreign DM.612) (effective 1996). Gustav Fischer Verlag Jena, Villengang 2, 07745 Jena, Germany. TEL 49-3641-626444. FAX 49-3641-626500. (Subscr. to: Postfach 100537, 07705 Jena, Germany) Ed. E.J. Jaeger. adv.: page DM.750; trim 210 x 280. bk.rev.; bibl.; charts; illus.; index. cum.index: vols.26-100. circ. 420. (reprint service avail. from ISI) **Indexed:** Bibl.Agri., Biol.Abstr., Chem.Abstr., Curr.Adv.Ecol.Sci., Curr.Cont., Deep Sea Res.& Oceanogr.Abstr., Ecol.Abstr., Excerp.Med., Forest.Abstr., Forest Prod.Abstr., Geo.Abstr., Geol.Abstr., IBR, Ind.Sci.Rev., Ref.Zh., Triticale Abstr., Weed Abstr. **Document type:** academic/scholarly publication.
—BLDSC (3953.500000); CASDDS; CISTI; EMDOCS; Genuine Article; KR SourceOne; SWETS; UnCover. **CCC**.

589   NE
FLORA AGARICINA NEERLANDICA. (Text in English) 1988. irreg., vol.3, 1995. fl.70 per vol. paperback; hardbound fl.120 per vol. (effective 1996). (Rijksherbarium - Hortus Botanicus) A.A. Balkema, P.O. Box 1675, 3000 BR Rotterdam, Netherlands. TEL 31-10-4145822. FAX 31-10-4135947. E-mail: sales@balkema.nl; URL: http://www.nl/ima/balkema/. (Dist. in U.S by: Ashgate Publishing Co., Old Post Rd., Brookfield, VT 05036. TEL 800-535-9544. FAX 802-276-3837) Ed.Bd. (back issues avail.) **Document type:** monographic series.
Description: Publishes studies on families of agarics and boleti as occurring in the Netherlands and adjacent regions.

581   CK   ISSN 0120-4351
CODEN: FLCOEK
FLORA DE COLOMBIA. 1983. irreg. $30 or exchange basis (effective 1997). Universidad Nacional de Colombia, Instituto de Ciencias Naturales, Apdo. 7495, Bogota, Colombia. TEL 57-1-3165305. Ed. Gary Stiles. R&P contact: Jaime Uribe M. adv. contact: Jaime Uribe M. circ. 2,000. **Document type:** monographic series.
—CISTI; KNAW.

581   VE   ISSN 0798-8613
FLORA DE VENEZUELA. 1964. irreg. price varies. Fundacion Instituto Botanico de Venezuela, Jardin Botanico de Caracas, Av. Salvador Allende, Apdo. 2156, Caracas 1010A, Venezuela. TEL 02-6629254. FAX 02-6629081. Ed. Silvia Llamozas. charts; illus.

BIOLOGY — BOTANY

581 GW ISSN 0071-576X
FLORA ET VEGETATIO MUNDI. (Text in English, French and German) 1960. irreg. price varies. J. Cramer in der Gebrueder Borntraeger Verlagsbuchhandlung, Johannesstr. 3A, 70176 Stuttgart, Germany. TEL 49-711-625001. FAX 49-711-625005. **Indexed:** Biol.Abstr. **Document type:** academic/scholarly publication.

581 NE ISSN 0374-7778
CODEN: FMSPA4
FLORA MALESIANA. SERIES 1: SPERMATOPHYTA. (Vols. 2 & 3 not published) (Text in English) 1950. irreg., vol.12, part 2, 1996. price varies. (Foundation Flora Malesiana) Rijksherbarium - Hortus Botanicus, Publications Department, P.O. Box 9514, 2300 RA Leiden, Netherlands. Eds. W.J.J.O. de Wilde, C. Kalkman. bibl.; illus.; index. (back issues avail.) **Document type:** monographic series.
—BLDSC (3954.500000); Linda Hall.
Description: Systematic account of the seed plants occurring in Malesia.
Refereed Serial

581 NE ISSN 0071-5786
FLORA MALESIANA. SERIES 2: PTERIDOPHYTA. (Text in English) 1959. irreg., vol.2, part 2, 1996. price varies. (Foundation Flora Malesiana) Rijksherbarium - Hortus Botanicus, Publications Department, P.O. Box 9514, 2300 RA Leiden, Netherlands. Eds. H.P. Nooteboom, C. Kalkman. index. circ. 1,300. (back issues avail.) **Indexed:** Biol.Abstr., Forest.Abstr. **Document type:** monographic series.
—Linda Hall.
Description: Systematic account of ferns and fern allies occurring in Malesia.
Refereed Serial

581 NE ISSN 0071-5778
FLORA MALESIANA BULLETIN. (Supplement avail.) a. fl.40 (free to qualified personnel) (effective 1996). Rijksherbarium - Hortus Botanicus, Publications Department, P.O. Box 9514, 2300 RA Leiden, Netherlands. E-mail: veldkamp@rulrhb.leidenuniv.nl. Eds. J.F. Veldkamp, M.A. Rifai. bibl.; cum.index every 4 yrs. (back issues avail.) **Document type:** academic/scholarly publication, bulletin.
Description: Covers progress in Malesian botany, including expeditions, fieldwork, herbaria, and recent publications of interest to botanists with an interest in the botany of the Pacific and Australasian regions.
Refereed Serial

581 US ISSN 0071-5794
QK205 CODEN: FLNMAV
FLORA NEOTROPICA. 1968. irreg., no.73, 1995. price varies. (Organization for Flora Neotropica) New York Botanical Garden, Scientific Publications Department, Bronx, NY 10458-5126. TEL 718-817-8721. FAX 718-817-8842. Eds. James L. Luteyn, Scott A. Mori. (back issues avail.) **Indexed:** Curr.Adv.Ecol.Sci. **Document type:** monographic series.
—KNAW. CCC.
Description: Taxonomic treatments of all plants native to the new world tropics.
Refereed Serial

581 DK ISSN 0347-8742
CODEN: FLECDR
FLORA OF ECUADOR. (Text in English) 1973. irreg. price varies. Nordic Publications in Botany, Gothersgade 130, DK-1123 Copenhagen K, Denmark. Eds. Gunnar Harling, Lennart Andersson. circ. 500. **Indexed:** Biol.Abstr.
Formerly: Opera Botanica. Series B. Flora of Ecuador.
Refereed Serial

581 SA
FLORA OF SOUTHERN AFRICA. 1963. irreg. price varies. National Botanical Institute, Private Bag X101, Pretoria 0001, South Africa. TEL 27-12-804-3200. FAX 27-12-804-3211. Ed. O.A. Leistner. R&P contact: H. du Plessis. illus.; index. circ. 300. **Document type:** academic/scholarly publication, monographic series.
Description: Taxonomic treatises on the flora of Southern Africa (south of Angola, Zambia, Zimbabwe, Mozambique).

581 IS
FLORA OF THE U.S.S.R.. (Text in English) irreg. Israel Program for Scientific Translations, P.o. Box 7145, Jerusalem, Israel.

581 IS
FLORA PALAESTINA. (Supplement avail.) (Text in English) 1966. irreg., no.4, 1986. $60 per no. Israel Academy of Sciences and Humanities, 43 Jabotinsky St., P.O. Box 4040, Jerusalem 91040, Israel. Ed. Zohia Lasman. adv. contact: Tami Korman. **Document type:** monographic series.
Description: Illustrated compendium of the flora of Israel and Jordan.
Refereed Serial

581 PL
FLORA POLSKI: GRZYBY/FLORA OF POLAND: FUNGI. (Text in English, Polish) 1957. irreg., vol.24, 1993. price varies. Polska Akademia Nauk, Instytut Botaniki im. W. Szafera, Ul. Lubicz 46, 31-512 Krakow, Poland. TEL 48-12-215144. FAX 48-12-219790. E-mail: nhwysock@cyf-kr.edu.pl. Ed. Alina Skirgiello. circ. 500 (paid).
Formerly: Flora Polska: Rosliny Zarodnikowe Polski i Ziem Osciennych (ISSN 0071-5824)
Refereed Serial

581 PL
FLORA POLSKI: ROSLINY NACZYNIOWE/FLORA OF POLAND: VASCULAR PLANTS. 1919. irreg. price varies. Polska Akademia Nauk, Instytut Botaniki im. W. Szafera, Ul. Lubicz 46, 31-512 Krakow, Poland. TEL 48-12-215144. FAX 48-12-219790. E-mail: nhwysock@cyf-kr.edu.pl. Ed. Zbigniew Mirek. illus. circ. 800. **Indexed:** Biol.Abstr. **Document type:** academic/scholarly publication.
Formerly: Flora Polska: Rosliny Naczyniowe Polski i Ziem Osciennych (ISSN 0071-5816)

581 PL ISSN 0071-5840
FLORA SLODKOWODNA POLSKI/FRESHWATER FLORA OF POLAND. 1963. irreg., vol.3, 1983. price varies. Polska Akademia Nauk, Instytut Botaniki im. W. Szafera, Ul. Lubicza 46, 31-512 Krakow, Poland. TEL 48-12-215144. FAX 48-12-219790. E-mail: nhwysock@cyf-kr.edu.pl. Ed. Jadwiga Sieminska. circ. 870. **Document type:** academic/scholarly publication.

581 BE ISSN 0779-116X
FLORE D'AFRIQUE CENTRALE (ZAIRE - RWANDA - BURUNDI). 1959. irreg., latest 1993. price varies. Jardin Botanique National de Belgique - Nationale Plantentuin van Belgie, Domaine de Bouchout, 1860 Meise, Belgium. TEL 32-2-2693905. Ed. P. Bamps. (back issues avail.) **Indexed:** Forest.Abstr., Forest Prod.Abstr. **Document type:** monographic series.
Formerly: Flore du Congo, du Rwanda et du Burundi.

581 FR ISSN 0430-666X
FLORE DE LA NOUVELLE CALEDONIE ET DEPENDANCES. 1967. irreg., no.20, 1996. 230 F. Museum National d'Histoire Naturelle, Laboratoire de Phanerogamie, 16 rue Buffon, 75005 Paris, France. TEL 33-1-40793353. FAX 33-1-40793342. E-mail: morat@mnhn.fr. Ed. P. Morat. **Document type:** monographic series.

581 FR
FLORE DE MADAGASCAR ET DES COMORES. 1937. irreg., no.176, 1994. 330 F. Museum National d'Histoire Naturelle, Laboratoire de Phanerogamie, 16 rue de Buffon, 75005 Paris, France. TEL 33-1-40793353. FAX 33-1-40793342. E-mail: morat@mnhn.fr. Ed. P. Morat. **Document type:** monographic series.

581 FR ISSN 0071-5867
FLORE DU CAMBODGE, DU LAOS ET DU VIETNAM. 1960. irreg., no.28, 1996. 328 F. Museum National d'Histoire Naturelle, Laboratoire de Phanerogamie, 16 rue Buffon, 75005 Paris, France. TEL 33-1-40793353. FAX 33-1-40793342. E-mail: morat@mnhn.fr. Ed. P. Morat. **Document type:** monographic series.

581 CM ISSN 0071-5875
FLORE DU CAMEROUN. 1963. irreg., latest 1992. price varies. Ministere de la Recherche Scientifique et Technique, Herbier National, B.P. 1601, Yaounde, Cameroon. TEL 237-314416. FAX 237-201854. Ed. Benoit Satabie; Pub. Benoit Satabie. adv.; bk.rev. circ. 550. (also avail. in microfiche; back issues avail.) **Document type:** academic/scholarly publication, government publication, trade publication.
—SWETS.
Description: Teaches about 7,500 types of plants and flowers from Cameroon.

581 FR ISSN 0071-5883
FLORE DU GABON. 1961. irreg., no.34, 1995. 190 F. Museum National d'Histoire Naturelle, Laboratoire de Phanerogamie, 16 rue Buffon, 75005 Paris, France. TEL 33-1-40793353. FAX 33-1-40793342. E-mail: morat@mnhn.fr. Ed. P. Morat. **Document type:** monographic series.
—BLDSC (3955.280000).

589.2 BE ISSN 0379-1890
CODEN: FICALL
FLORE ILLUSTREE DES CHAMPIGNONS D'AFRIQUE CENTRALE. 1935; N.S. 1970. irreg., latest no.14. price varies. Jardin Botanique National de Belgique - Nationale Plantentuin van Belgie, Domaine de Bouchout, 1860 Meise, Belgium. TEL 32-2-2693905. illus. (back issues avail.) **Document type:** monographic series.
—KNAW.
Formerly (until no.17, 1970): Flore Iconographique des Champignons du Congo (ISSN 0374-7700)

589.3 BE ISSN 0779-1089
FLORE PRATIQUE DES ALGUES D'EAU DOUCE DE BELGIQUE. (Text in French) 1986. irreg., no.4, 1992. price varies. Jardin Botanique National de Belgique - Nationale Plantentuin van Belgie, Domaine de Bouchout, 1860 Meise, Belgium. TEL 32-2-2693905. Ed. P. Compere. (back issues avail.) **Document type:** monographic series.

581 US
FLORIDA. DEPARTMENT OF AGRICULTURE AND CONSUMER SERVICES. BOTANY CIRCULAR. 1976. bi-m. free. Department of Agriculture and Consumer Services, Division of Plant Industry, 1911 S.W. 34th St., Box 147100, Gainesville, FL 32614-7100. TEL 904-372-3505. FAX 904-955-2301. Ed. Maeve McConnell. R&P contact: Maeve McConnell. (looseleaf format) **Document type:** government publication.

581 US ISSN 0428-6294
CODEN: BFACDN
FLORIDA. DEPARTMENT OF AGRICULTURE AND CONSUMER SERVICES. DIVISION OF PLANT INDUSTRY. BULLETIN SERIES. irreg., vol.15, 1993. price varies. Department of Agriculture and Consumer Services, Division of Plant Industry, 1911 S.W. 34th St., Box 147100, Gainesville, FL 32614-7100. TEL 904-372-3505. FAX 904-955-2301. **Document type:** bulletin, government publication.
Formerly: Plant Pathology Bulletins.

581.2 US ISSN 0032-0870
CODEN: FPPCB6
FLORIDA. DEPARTMENT OF AGRICULTURE AND CONSUMER SERVICES. PLANT PATHOLOGY CIRCULAR. 1962. bi-m. free. Department of Agriculture and Consumer Services, Division of Plant Industry, 1911 S.W. 34th St., Box 147100, Gainesville, FL 32614-7100. TEL 904-372-3505. FAX 904-955-2301. Ed. Maeve McConnell. R&P contact: Maeve McConnell. (looseleaf format) **Indexed:** Biol.Abstr., Curr.Cont. **Document type:** government publication.

FLORIDA. DIVISION OF PLANT INDUSTRY. BIENNIAL REPORT. see *AGRICULTURE*

581 GW ISSN 0934-456X
CODEN: FLRUEB
FLORISTISCHE RUNDBRIEFE; Zeitschrift fuer floristische Geobotanik, Populationsoekologie. 1967. irreg. DM.15. Ruhr-Universitaet Bochum, Spezielle Botanik Universitaetsstr. 150, 44801 Bochum, Germany. FAX 49-234-7094284. Ed. H. Haeupler. bk.rev. circ. 1,400. (back issues avail.) **Indexed:** Biol.Abstr. (1990-). **Document type:** academic/scholarly publication.
Formerly (until 1987): Goettinger Floristische Rundbriefe (ISSN 0340-4145)

BIOLOGY — BOTANY

581   SA   ISSN 0015-4504
QK396
THE FLOWERING PLANTS OF AFRICA. 1921. biennial. R.110 (effective 1997). National Botanical Institute, Private Bag X101, Pretoria 0001, South Africa. TEL 27-12-8043200. FAX 27-12-8043211. Ed. O.A. Leistner. R&P contact: H. du Plessis. illus.; index. circ. 500. **Indexed:** Biol.Abstr., Curr.Adv.Ecol.Sci. **Document type:** academic/scholarly publication.
—SWETS.
    Formerly: Flowering Plants of South Africa.
    Description: Presents color plates of African plants with accompanying text.

581   SP   ISSN 0210-6574
FOLIA BOTANICA MISCELLANEA. 1979. irreg. 2352 ptas. Universidad de Barcelona, Facultad de Biologia, Departamento do Botanica, Avda. Diagonal 645, 08017 Barcelona, Spain. **Indexed:** Ind.SST.

581   SW   ISSN 0015-5551
QK1   CODEN: FGPBA7
FOLIA GEOBOTANICA ET PHYTOTAXONOMICA. (Text in English) 1966. q. SEK 1500 (effective 1997). Czechoslovak Academy of Sciences, Botanical Institute, P.O. Box 25137, S-750 25 Uppsala, Sweden. TEL 46-18-320662. FAX 46-18-321368. (Dist. ByOpulus Press AB, Box 25137, S-750 25 Uppsla, Sweden. TEL 46-18-32-06-62) Eds. T. Herben, Z. Skaala. bk.rev.; charts; illus.; index. (also avail. in microform from UMI) **Indexed:** ASCA, Biol.Abstr., Curr.Adv.Ecol.Sci., Curr.Adv.Genetics & Molec.Biol., Curr.Cont., Ecol.Abstr., Field Crop Abstr., Geo.Abstr., GeoRef., Herb.Abstr., Irr.& Drain.Abstr., Plant Breed.Abstr., Rev.Plant Path., Weed Abstr. **Document type:** academic/scholarly publication.
—BLDSC (3969.980000); CISTI; Genuine Article; SWETS; UnCover. **CCC.**
    Formerly: Folia Geobotanica et Phytotaxonomica Bohemoslovaca.
    Description: Devoted to geobotany (plant sociology, synecology and autecology, paleoecology, plant geography), plant taxonomy (algae, fungi, bryophytes, higher plants), nomenclature, and cytotaxonomy.
    Refereed Serial

635   PL   ISSN 0867-1761
FOLIA HORTICULTURAE. 1989. irreg., (2-3/yr.) $10 per issue (effective 1997 & 1998). Polskie Towarzystwo Nauk Ogrodniczych - Polish Society for Horticultural Science, Al. 29 Listopada 54, 31-425 Krakow, Poland. FAX 48-12-111322. E-mail: robrzezi@kinga.cyf-kr.edu.pl. (Co-sponsor: Polska Akademia Nauk, Komitet Badan Naukowych) Ed. Jan Myczkowski. circ. 450. **Document type:** academic/scholarly publication.
—BLDSC (3970.450000).
    Description: Publishes original papers and short communications covering theoretical as well as practical aspects of horticultural sciences.
    Refereed Serial

635   US   ISSN 0532-3215
FOUR SEASONS (BERKELEY). 1964. a. $16 for 4 issues. East Bay Regional Park District, Tilden Regional Park, Botanic Garden, Berkeley, CA 94708-2396. TEL 510-841-8732. FAX 510-848-6025. Ed. Stephen W. Edwards. R&P contact: Stephen W. Edwards. bk.rev. circ. 400.
    Description: Covers all aspects of California native plants. Includes both technical and semi-popular articles.
    Refereed Serial

581   PL   ISSN 0015-931X
QK1   CODEN: FRFGAF
FRAGMENTA FLORISTICA ET GEOBOTANICA. (Text in English, French, German; abstracts in English) 1954. s-a. $67.50 (effective 1997). Polska Akademia Nauk, Instytut Botaniki im. W. Szafera, Ul. Lubicz 46, 31-512 Krakow, Poland. TEL 48-12-215144. FAX 48-12-219790. E-mail: nhwysock@cyf-kr.edu.pl. Ed. Jerzy Wolek. bk.rev.; bibl.; charts; illus.; circ. 600 (paid). **Indexed:** AgroAgen, Biol.Abstr., Ecol.Abstr., Field Crop Abstr., GeoRef., Herb.Abstr., IBR, Plant Breed.Abstr., Rev.Plant Path. **Document type:** academic/scholarly publication.
—BLDSC (4032.100000); CISTI.
    Description: Publishes original papers covering all aspects of botany, espacially vegetation monographs and articles on plant taxonomy and ecology, phytopgeography, cryptogamic botany, plant anatomy, cytology and embryology as well as biosystematics, evolutionary botany and experimental embryology.
    Refereed Serial

581   PL   ISSN 1233-0132
FRAGMENTA FLORISTICA ET GEOBOTANICA. SERIES POLONICA. (Text in Polish; summaries in English) 1994. a. $32 (effective 1997). Polska Akademia Nauk, Instytut Botaniki im. W. Szafera - Polish Academy of Sciences, W. Szafer Institute of Botany, Ul. Lubicz 46, 31-512 Krakow, Poland. TEL 48-12-215144. FAX 48-12-219790. E-mail: nhwysock@cyf-kr.edu.pl. Ed. Ludwik Frey. adv. contact: Jacek Wieser. bk.rev.; circ. 500 (paid). **Indexed:** AgroLibrex. **Document type:** academic/scholarly publication.
    Description: Publishes original papers relevant mainly to the Polish territory, covering all aspects of botany, especially vegetation monographs and articles on plant taxonomy and ecology, phytogeography, cryptogamic botany, plant anatomy, cytology and embryology as well as biosystematics, evolutionary botany and experimental embryology.
    Refereed Serial

FRAGMENTA PHYTOMEDICA ET HERBOLOGICA. see *AGRICULTURE*

581   US   ISSN 0092-1793
QK149
FREMONTIA. 1973. q. $35 (foreign $45). California Native Plant Society, 1722 J St., Ste. 17, Sacramento, CA 95814. TEL 916-447-2677. Ed. Phyllis Faber. adv.; bk.rev.; index. circ. 9,000. (back issues avail.) **Indexed:** Ash.G.Bot.Per., Gard.Lit. (1992-), R.G.
—BLDSC (4033.830000).
    Description: Provides articles of general interest about California's native plants.

581   US   ISSN 0016-2167
SB21   CODEN: FOPSAC
FRONTIERS OF PLANT SCIENCE. 1948. s-a. free. Agricultural Experiment Station, Box 1106, New Haven, CT 06504-1106. TEL 203-789-7223. Ed. Paul Gough. illus. circ. 6,000. **Indexed:** Bibl.Agri., Biol.Abstr., Chem.Abstr., Curr.Adv.Ecol.Sci., Excerp.Med., Field Crop Abstr., Forest.Abstr., Herb.Abstr., Hort.Abstr., Plant Breed.Abstr., VITIS.
—BLDSC (4042.050000); Linda Hall.

FRUITS; fruit and horticultural productions in tropical and Mediterranean regions. see *GARDENING AND HORTICULTURE*

581 635   JA   ISSN 0287-3494
FUJI TAKERUI SHOKUBUTSUEN HOKOKU/FUJI BAMBOO GARDEN. REPORTS. (Text in Japanese; summaries in English, Japanese) 1956. a. Nihon Take Sasa no Kai - Japan Bamboo Society, c/o Fuji Takerui Shokubutsuen, 885 Minamiishiki, Nagaizumicho, Sunto-gun, Shizuoka-ken 411, Japan.

581   JA   ISSN 0913-2546
FUKUOKA NO SHOKUBUTSU/BOTANY OF FUKUOKA. (Text in Japanese) 1974. a. Fukuoka Shokubutsu Kenkyukai - Botanical Society of Fukuokai, c/o Mr. Hijiri Masumura, 76 Yamanoi, Chikugo-shi, Fukuoka-ken 833, Japan.

FUNCTIONAL ECOLOGY. see *CONSERVATION*

581 595   AG   ISSN 0074-025X
FUNDACION MIGUEL LILLO. MISCELANEA. (Text in Spanish; summaries in English, French, German) 1937. irreg., no.88, 1992. (Secretaria de Ciencia y Tecnologia) Fundacion Miguel Lillo, Miguel Lillo 251, 4000 Tucuman, Argentina. Ed. Jose A. Haedo Rossi. charts; illus. circ. 500. (back issues avail. **Indexed:** Anim.Behav.Abstr., Aqua.Sci.& Fish.Abstr., Biol.Abstr., Bull.Signal., Ecol.Abstr., Entomol.Abstr., Ref.Zh., Zoo.Rec.
—BLDSC (5811.728000).

581 333.7   AG
FUNDACION MIGUEL LILLO. SERIE CONSERVACION DE LA NATURALEZA. 1979. irreg., vol.5, 1991. Fundacion Miguel Lillo, Miguel Lillo 251, 4000 Tucuman, Argentina. Ed. Jose A. Haedo Rossi. bibl.; charts; illus. circ. 500.

589.2   US   ISSN 1087-1845
QK600   CODEN: FGBIFV
FUNGAL GENETICS AND BIOLOGY; an international journal. 1977. bi-m. $195 (foreign $249) (effective 1997). Academic Press, Inc., Journal Division, 525 B St., Ste. 1900, San Diego, CA 92101-4495. TEL 619-230-1840. FAX 619-699-6800. E-mail: apsubs@acad.com; URL: http://www.apnet.com/ www.journal/fg.htm; http://www.idealibrary.com/. (Subscr. to: Box 861213, Orlando, FL 32886-2130. TEL 407-347-4040. FAX 407-363-9661) Ed. John E. Hamer. adv.; bk.rev.; index. (back issues avail.) **Indexed:** ASCA, Bio-Contr.News & Info., Biodet.Abstr., Chem.Abstr., Curr.Adv.Ecol.Sci., Curr.Biotech.Abstr., Curr.Cont., Excerp.Med. (1993-), Ind.Med. (1995-), Ind.Sci.Rev., Plant Breed.Abstr., Rev.Med.& Vet.Mycol., Sci.Cit.Ind, Soils & Fert. **Document type:** academic/scholarly publication.
●Also available online.
—BLDSC (4056.630000); ADONIS; CASDDS; CISTI; Genuine Article; SWETS; UnCover. **CCC.**
    Formerly (until vol.20, no.1, 1996): Experimental Mycology (ISSN 0147-5975)
    Description: Publishes experimental investigations that relate structure and function to growth, reproduction, morphogenesis, and differentiation of fungi and their traditional allies.
    Refereed Serial

589.2   SZ
FUNGI AND CONSERVATION NEWSLETTER. a. International Union for Conservation of Nature and Natural Resources, Species Survival Commission - Fungi Specialist Group, Rue Mauverney 28, CH-1196 Gland, Switzerland. TEL 41-22-9990001. FAX 41-22-9990002. TELEX 419624-IUCN-CH. (Subscr. to: T. Laessoe, Dept. of Mycology, Botanical Institute, Oster Farimagsgade 2D, DK-1353 Copenhagen K, Denmark) **Document type:** newsletter.

GAERTNERBOERSE UND GARTENWELT; Gb und Gw. see *GARDENING AND HORTICULTURE*

581   PO   ISSN 0379-9506
QK1   CODEN: GOBTAO
GARCIA DE ORTA: SERIE DE BOTANICA. 1973. 2/yr. price varies. Instituto de Investigacao Cientifica Tropical, Rua da Junqueira 30, 1300 Lisbon, Portugal. TEL 351-1-3622621. FAX 351-1-3631460. E-mail: cdi@iict.pt; URL: http://www.iict.pt. (Subscr. to: Centro de Documentacao e Informacao, Rua Jau 47, 1300 Lisbon, Portugal) circ. 1,000. **Indexed:** Herb.Abstr., Weed Abstr. **Document type:** academic/scholarly publication.

581   SI   ISSN 0072-0178
GARDENS' BULLETIN, SINGAPORE. (Text in English) 1891. s-a. price varies. National Parks Board, Singapore Botanic Gardens, Cluny Rd., Singapore 1025, Singapore. TEL 4741165. FAX 4754295. Ed. Ng Siew Yin. adv.; bk.rev.; index. circ. 400. **Indexed:** Biol.Abstr., Field Crop Abstr., Forest.Abstr., Forest Prod.Abstr., Herb.Abstr., Hort.Abstr., Plant Breed.Abstr., Plant Grow.Reg.Abstr., So.Pac.Per.Ind. **Document type:** academic/scholarly publication.
    Description: Contains articles of botanical and horticultural interests.
    Refereed Serial

BIOLOGY — BOTANY

581   CL   ISSN 0016-5301
QH119   CODEN: GBCZAO
GAYANA: BOTANICA. (Text in English or Spanish) 1961. a. Universidad de Concepcion, Facultad de Ciencias Naturales y Oceanograficas, Casilla 2407, Concepcion, Chile. FAX 56-41-240280. (Subscr. to: Editorial Universidad de Concepcion, Depto. Ventas, Cas. 1557, Concepcion, Chile) Ed. Andres O. Angulo. adv. contact: Alejandro Wittker. circ. 1,000. **Indexed:** Biol.Abstr., Deep Sea Res.& Oceanogr.Abstr. **Document type:** abstracting/indexing, directory.
—BLDSC (4089.550000); UnCover.

581   NE   ISSN 0925-9864
SB123.3   CODEN: GRCEE9
GENETIC RESOURCES AND CROP EVOLUTION; an international journal. Short title: G R A C E. 1953. bi-m. fl.937 to institutions; $481 to institutions in U.S. (effective 1998). Kluwer Academic Publishers, Postbus 17, 3300 AA Dordrecht, Netherlands. TEL 31-78-6392392. FAX 31-78-6392254. TELEX 29245 KAPG NL. E-mail: services@wkap.nl; URL: http://www.wkap.nl. (Dist. by: Kluwer Academic Publishers Group, P.O. Box 322, 3300 AH Dordrecht, Netherlands. TEL 31-78-6392392. FAX 31-78-6546474; N. American dist. addr.: Box 358, Accord Sta., Hingham, MA 02018-0358. TEL 617-871-6600. FAX 617-871-6528) Eds. P. Hanelt, K. Hammer. (also avail. in microform from UMI; back issues avail.) **Indexed:** Apic.Abstr., ASCA, Biol.Abstr., Chem.Abstr., Compumath, Curr.Cont., Field Crop Abstr., Herb.Abstr., Int.Abstr.Biol.Sci., Plant Breed.Abstr., Rev.Plant Path., Rice Abstr., Soils & Fert., VITIS. **Document type:** academic/scholarly publication.
—BLDSC (4111.907000); CASDDS; EMDOCS; Genuine Article; SWETS; UMI; UnCover. **CCC**.
Formerly (until 1992): Kulturpflanze (ISSN 0075-7209)
   Description: Publishes original articles on taxonomical, morphological, cytological, ethnobotanical and biochemical research of genetic resources, including contributions on broader issues in gene-bank management, such as collection, storage, maintenance and documentation.
Refereed Serial

581   SZ   ISSN 1420-6803
QK1   CODEN: BGBIAG
GEOBOTANICAL INSTITUTE E T H. BULLETIN. (Text in English, German) 1928. a. 40 SFr. (effective 1997 & 1998). Eidgenoessische Technische Hochschule Zurich, Geobotanisches Institut, Stiftung Ruebel, Zurichbergstr. 38, CH-8044 Zurich, Switzerland. TEL 41-1-6322756. FAX 41-1-6321215. E-mail: langenau@geobot.umnw.ethz.ch. Eds. Elias Landolt, Peter Edwards. adv. contact: Johannes Kollmann. circ. 1,650. (back issues avail.) **Indexed:** Biol.Abstr., Curr.Cont., IBR. **Document type:** academic/scholarly publication.
Formerly (until 1996): Geobotanisches Institut E T H, Stiftung Ruebel, Zurich. Berichte (ISSN 0373-7896)
   Description: Progress reports and technical articles by the Institute.

581   SZ   ISSN 0254-9433
     CODEN: VGRZAR
GEOBOTANISCHES INSTITUT E T H, STIFTUNG RUEBEL, ZURICH. VEROEFFENTLICHUNGEN. (Text and summaries in German and English) 1923. irreg. vol.127, 1996. 55 SFr. Eidgenoessische Technische Hochschule Zurich, Geobotanisches Institut, Stiftung Ruebel, Zurichbergstr. 38, CH-8044 Zurich, Switzerland. TEL 41-1-6322756. FAX 41-1-6321215. charts; illus.; stat. circ. 550. (back issues avail.) **Indexed:** Biol.Abstr., Curr.Adv.Ecol.Sci., Curr.Adv.Plant Sci., Curr.Cont., Ecol.Abstr., Excerp.Bot., Excerp.Med., Field Crop Abstr., Forest.Abstr., Herb.Abstr., IBR, Plant Grow.Reg.Abstr., Seed Abstr., Soils & Fert., Weed Abstr. **Document type:** academic/scholarly publication, monographic series.
—Linda Hall.

GEOBOTANY. see *EARTH SCIENCES — Geology*

581   JA   ISSN 0911-422X
GIFUKEN SHOKUBUTSU KENKYUKAISHI/GIFU BOTANICAL SOCIETY. BULLETIN. (Text in Japanese) 1984. a. 3000 Yen (effective Apr. 1996). Gifuken Shokubutsu Kenkyukai - Gifu Botanical Society, Gifu Daigaku Kyoikugakubu, Seibutsugaku Kyoshitsu Shokubutsu, Bunrui Kenkyushitsu, Yanagido, Gifu-shi, Gifu-ken 501-11, Japan. TEL 058-293-2258. FAX 058-293-2207. E-mail: takahash@cc.gifu-u.ac.jp. Ed. Hiroshi Takahashi. circ. 300. **Document type:** bulletin.
Refereed Serial

581   IT   ISSN 0017-0070
QK1   CODEN: GBOIAX
GIORNALE BOTANICO ITALIANO. (Text in English, French, German, Italian, Spanish; summaries in English and Italian) 1844. bi-m. L.240000. Societa Botanica Italiana, Via Giorgio La Pira 4, 50121 Florence, Italy. TEL 39-55-2757379. Ed. Giovanni Cristofolini. charts; illus. circ. 1,300. **Indexed:** Biol.Abstr., Chem.Abstr., Crop Physiol.Abstr., Curr.Adv.Ecol.Sci., Excerp.Bot., Field Crop Abstr., Forest.Abstr., Forest Prod.Abstr., Geo.Abstr., Herb.Abstr., Hort.Abstr., INIS Atomind., Maize Abstr., Plant Breed.Abstr., Plant Grow.Reg.Abstr., Rev.Med.& Vet.Mycol., Rev.Plant Path., Seed Abstr., Soils & Fert., Triticale Abstr., Trop.Oil Seeds Abstr., Weed Abstr. **Document type:** academic/scholarly publication, proceedings.
—CASDDS; CISTI; Linda Hall.

581   IE   ISSN 0332-0235
GLASRA. 1976-1987; N.S 1990. a. exchange basis. National Botanic Gardens, Glasnevin, Dublin 9, Ireland. TEL 353-1-8374388. FAX 353-1-8360080. Ed. Donal Synnott. R&P contact: Donal Synnott. bk.rev. circ. 300. **Document type:** academic/scholarly publication, government publication.
—BLDSC (4189.600000).
Formerly: National Botanic Gardens Glasnevin. Contributions.
Refereed Serial

581   GW   ISSN 0323-6862
GLEDITSCHIA; Beitraege zur botanischen Taxonomie und deren Grenzgebiete. (Text and summaries in English, German) 1973. s-a. DM.240 (foreign DM.250) (effective 1997). Akademie Verlag GmbH, Muehlenstr. 33-34, 13187 Berlin, Germany. TEL 49-30-47889348. FAX 49-30-47889357. E-mail: info@akademie-verlag.de. (Subscr. in the Americas to: John Wiley & Sons, Inc., 605 Third Ave., New York, NY 10158. TEL 212-850-6645. FAX 212-850-6021) Eds. G. Natho, D. Benkert. bk.rev.; charts; illus.; index. **Document type:** academic/scholarly publication.
   Description: Covers botanical taxonomy, research results in plant systematics, and related disciplines.

635 583.81   US   ISSN 0017-1352
GLOXINIAN; the magazine for gesneriad growers. 1951. q. $20 (foreign $25). American Gloxinia and Gesneriad Society, Inc., c/o Michael A. Riley, Business Manager, 101 W. 104th St., New York, NY 10025. TEL 212-666-2395. FAX 212-666-5114. E-mail: Riley2362@aol.com; URL: http://www.aggs.org. Ed. Jeanne Katzenstein. adv.; bk.rev.; circ. 3,200 (paid). **Indexed:** Biol.Abstr. **Document type:** consumer publication.
—UnCover.

581.1   NE   ISSN 0017-2294
GORTERIA; tijdschrift voor de floristiek. (Supplement avail. (ISSN 0928-8228)) (Text in Dutch; summaries in English) 1961. bi-m. fl.35 (effective 1994). Rijksherbarium - Hortus Botanicus, Publications Department, P.O. Box 9514, 2300 RA Leiden, Netherlands. E-mail: meijden@rulrhb.leidenuniv.nl. Ed.Bd. bk.rev.; charts; illus.; index. circ. 1,400. (back issues avail.) **Indexed:** Biol.Abstr., Curr.Adv.Ecol.Sci., Ecol.Abstr., Excerp.Bot., Field Crop Abstr., Geo.Abstr.H.G., Herb.Abstr., Plant Breed.Abstr. **Document type:** academic/scholarly publication.
—SWETS.
   Description: Papers on the flora of the Netherlands and adjoining countries.

581   NE   ISSN 0928-8228
GORTERIA. SUPPLEMENT. (Text in English) 1992. irreg., vol.3, 1996. price varies. Rijksherbarium - Hortus Botanicus, Publications Department, P.O. Box 9514, 2300 RA Leiden, Netherlands. Ed.Bd. **Document type:** monographic series.
   Description: Publishes in-depth scholarly studies of topics relating to the flora of the Netherlands.

581   NO   ISSN 0017-3134
QK658   CODEN: GRNABF
GRANA; international journal of palynology and aerobiology. (Text in English) 1954. 6/yr. NOK 1690 in Nordic countries; elsewhere $286 (effective 1997). Scandinavian University Press, P.O. Box 2959 Toeyen, N-0608 Oslo, Norway. TEL 47-22-57-54-00. FAX 47-22-57-53-53. E-mail: mail@scup.no; URL: http://www.scup.no (U.S. addr.: 875 Massachusetts Ave., Ste. 84, Cambridge, MA 02139. TEL 617-497-6515. FAX 617-354-6875) Ed. Siwert Nilsson. adv.; bibl.; illus. circ. 700. **Indexed:** Acid Rain Abstr., Acid Rain Ind., Apic.Abstr., ASCA, Biol.Abstr., Br.Geol.Lit., Curr.Adv.Ecol.Sci., Curr.Cont., Forest.Abstr., Forest Prod.Abstr., Geo.Abstr.H.G., Geo.Abstr.P.G., Geol.Abstr., GeoRef., Ornam.Hort., Plant Breed.Abstr., Rev.Med.& Vet.Mycol. **Document type:** academic/scholarly publication.
—BLDSC (4209.600000); ADONIS; CISTI; EMDOCS; Genuine Article; Linda Hall; SWETS; UnCover. **CCC**.
Formerly (until 1970): Grana Palynologica (ISSN 0374-793X)
   Description: Presents original articles, mainly on theoretical palynology.

581 591   NE   ISSN 0167-2932
GRASDUINEN. 1979. m. fl.7.50 per no. Geillustreerde Pers B.V., Haaksbergweg 75, 1101 BR Amsterdam, Netherlands. TEL 31-20-4300300. FAX 31-20-4300316. Ed. Frans Buissink. circ. 80,000. **Document type:** consumer publication.

581 591   US   ISSN 0017-3614
QH1   CODEN: GRBNAR
GREAT BASIN NATURALIST. 1939. q. $25 to individuals; institutions $50. Brigham Young University, 290 Life Science Museum, Provo, UT 84602. TEL 801-378-5053. Ed. Richard W. Baumann. illus.; index, cum.index: 1939-1990. circ. 550. (back issues avail.) **Indexed:** ASCA, Bio-Contr.News & Info., Biol.Abstr., Curr.Adv.Ecol.Sci., Curr.Cont., Curr.Ref.Fish Res., Excerp.Med. (until 19??), Forest.Abstr., Geo.Abstr., Helminthol.Abstr., INIS Atomind., Protozool.Abstr., Rev.Appl.Entomol., Seed Abstr., Sel.Water Res.Abstr., Soils & Fert., Sport Fish.Abstr., Triticale Abstr., Weed Abstr., Wild.Rev., Zoo.Rec.
—BLDSC (4214.450000); CASDDS; EMDOCS; Genuine Article; Linda Hall; UnCover.

581 591   US   ISSN 0160-239X
     CODEN: GBNMD9
GREAT BASIN NATURALIST MEMOIRS. 1976. irreg., no.7,1982. price varies. Brigham Young University, 290 Life Science Museum, Provo, UT 84602. TEL 801-378-5053. Ed. Richard W. Baumann. circ. 500. (back issues avail.) **Indexed:** Biol.Abstr., Zoo.Rec.
—CASDDS.

581 635   US
GROWING NATIVE. 1990. bi-m. $30 (effective 1997). (Growing Native Research Institute) Louise Lacey, Ed. & Pub., Box 489, Berkeley, CA 94701. TEL 510-232-9865. bk.rev.; bibl.; illus. (back issues avail.) **Document type:** newsletter.
   Description: Describes California native flora and supplies information on propagating and growing plants; interviews gardeners.

581   CC   ISSN 1000-3142
QK355   CODEN: GUZHEI
GUANGXI ZHIWU/GUANGXI PLANTS. (Text in Chinese) 1981. q. Guangxi Zhiwu Yanjiusuo - Guangxi Botanic Institute, Yanshan, Guilin, Guangxi 541006, People's Republic of China. TEL 335103. Ed. Li Shugang.

GUIDE TO GRADUATE STUDY IN BOTANY FOR THE UNITED STATES AND CANADA. see *EDUCATION — Guides To Schools And Colleges*

GUNNERIA. see *ARCHAEOLOGY*

H D R A NEWS. (Henry Doubleday Research Association) see *GARDENING AND HORTICULTURE*

H S I BULLETIN. (Heliconia Society International) see GARDENING AND HORTICULTURE

581   JA   ISSN 0388-2845
HANA NO WA/HIROSHIMA CITY PARK ASSOCIATION. NEWS. (Text in Japanese) 1980. q. Hiroshimashi Koen Kyokai - Hiroshima City Park Association, 3-495 Kurashige, Saeki-ku, Hiroshima-shi, Hiroshima-ken 730, Japan. **Document type:** newsletter.

581   NE   ISSN 0302-3141
QK911   CODEN: HVSCEK
HANDBOOK OF VEGETATION SCIENCE. (Text in English) irreg., no.12, 1994. price varies. Kluwer Academic Publishers, Postbus 17, 3300 AA Dordrecht, Netherlands. TEL 31-78-6392392. FAX 31-78-6392254. TELEX 29245 KAPG NL. E-mail: services@wkap.nl; URL: http://www.wkap.nl. (Dist. by: Kluwer Academic Publishers Group, P.O. Box 322, 3300 AH Dordrecht, Netherlands. TEL 31-78-6392392. FAX 31-78-6546474; N. America dist. addr.: Box 358, Accord Sta., Hingham, MA 02018-0358. TEL 617-871-6600. FAX 617-871-6528) **Document type:** monographic series.

581   US   ISSN 1043-4534
QK1
HARVARD PAPERS IN BOTANY. 1989. irreg. price varies. Harvard University Herbaria, 22 Divinity Ave., Cambridge, MA 02138. TEL 617-495-2360. FAX 617-495-9484. E-mail: gromero@oeb.harvard. edu. Ed. Gustavo Romero. illus. **Indexed:** Biol.Abstr., Chem.Abstr., Field Crop Abstr., Herb.Abstr., Plant Breed.Abstr. **Document type:** academic/scholarly publication.
—BLDSC (4268.375000); Linda Hall; UnCover.
   Formed by the 1989 merger of (1932-1986): Botanical Museum Leaflets (ISSN 0006-8098); (1969-1987): Farlow Herbarium of Cryptogamic Botany. Occasional Papers (ISSN 0090-8754); (1891-1984): Harvard University. Gray Herbarium. Contributions (ISSN 0195-6094)
   Description: Discusses botanical papers
Refereed Serial

581   JA   ISSN 0073-0912
QK533   CODEN: JHBLAI
HATTORI BOTANICAL LABORATORY. JOURNAL/HATTORI SHOKUBUTSU KENKYUJO HOKOKU; devoted to bryology and lichenology. (Text in European languages) 1947. 2/yr. 8000 Yen($72) Hattori Botanical Laboratory - Hattori Shokubutsu Kenkyujo, Obi, Nichinan-shi, Miyazaki-ken 889-25, Japan. TEL 0987-25-0110. Ed. Sinske Hattori. circ. 500. (back issues avail.) **Indexed:** Biol.Abstr., Chem.Abstr., Curr.Adv.Ecol.Sci., Plant Breed.Abstr., Rev.Plant Path. **Document type:** academic/scholarly publication.
—BLDSC (4757.900000); CASDDS; CISTI; Linda Hall; SWETS; UnCover.

HEATHER SOCIETY. YEARBOOK. see GARDENING AND HORTICULTURE

581 615.33   PL   ISSN 0018-0599
   CODEN: HPBIA9
HERBA POLONICA. (Text in English, German, Polish; summaries in English) 1955. q. $30. Instytut Roslin i Przetworow Zielarskich - Research Institute of Medicinal Plants, Libelta 27, 61-707 Poznan, Poland. TEL 48-61-525616. FAX 48-61-527463. TELEX 414367. Ed. Jerzy Lutomski. adv. contact: Anna Krajewska-Patan. bk.rev.; bibl.; charts; illus.; index. circ. 1,000. **Indexed:** AgroLibrex, Anal.Abstr., Bibl.Agri., Biol.Abstr., Biol.& Agr.Ind., Biotech.Abstr., Bull.Signal, Chem.Abstr., Curr.Adv.Ecol.Sci., Curr.Cont., Excerp.Med., Hort.Abstr., I.P.A., Landwirt.Zentralbl., Ref.Zh. **Document type:** academic/scholarly publication.
● Also available online.
—BLDSC (4296.880000); CASDDS; UMI.
   Formerly: Instytut Roslin Leczniczy. Biuletyn.

581 615.89   US   ISSN 0899-5648
HERBALGRAM. 1979. q. $25 (Canada $30; elsewhere $35). American Botanical Council, Box 201660, Austin, TX 78720. TEL 512-331-8868. FAX 512-331-1924. E-mail: custserv@herbalgram.org. Ed. Mark Blumenthal; Pub. Mark Blumenthal. adv. contact: Margaret Wright. bk.rev.; stat.; tr.lit. circ. 50,000. (back issues avail.) **Indexed:** Gard.Lit. (1992-).
—UnCover.
   Description: Covers many of the facets of the Herb movement, both within the U.S. and internationally.

581.63   FR   ISSN 1250-6273
HERBALIA. 1994. q. 150 F. (foreign 215 F.) (effective Feb. 1997). Institut Interprofessionnel des Plantes a Parfum, Medicinales et Aromatiques, ZI des Trois Routes, 49120 Chemille, France.
TEL 33-2-41303079. FAX 33-2-41305948. Ed. Gilles Verniau. adv. contact: Paul Gicquiaud. circ. 400. **Document type:** newsletter.

581   US   ISSN 0731-7824
HERBARIUM NEWS. 1981. irreg. $9 to individuals (foreign $11); institutions $16 (foreign $19) (effective 1997). Missouri Botanical Garden, Box 299, St. Louis, MO 63166-0299.
TEL 314-577-9534. FAX 314-577-9594. Ed. James Solomon. bk.rev. circ. 600. (back issues avail.) **Document type:** newsletter.
   Description: Provides rapid communication of current events in the herbarium community.

588.2   GW   ISSN 0018-0971
QK533.84.E8515   CODEN: HRZGD4
HERZOGIA. (Text in English, French and German) 1969. a. DM.64($37.10) (foreign $38.50) (effective 1997). (Bryologisch-Lichenologische Arbeitsgemeinschaft fuer Mittel-Europa) J. Cramer in der Gebrueder Borntraeger Verlagsbuchhandlung, Johannesstr. 3A, 70176 Stuttgart, Germany.
TEL 49-711-625001. FAX 49-711-625005. Eds. G. Philippi, E. Ruuss. adv.; bk.rev. **Indexed:** Rev.Plant Path. **Document type:** academic/scholarly publication.
—BLDSC (4300.450000); Linda Hall. **CCC.**

581   GW   ISSN 0439-0687
   CODEN: HFBRAY
HESSISCHE FLORISTISCHE BRIEFE. 1952. q. DM.30. Naturwissenschaftlicher Verein Darmstadt, Havelstr. 7, 64295 Darmstadt, Germany.
TEL 49-6151-133288. Ed. Michael Hoellwarth. adv.; bk.rev. circ. 800. **Document type:** academic/scholarly publication.

581   JA   ISSN 0046-7413
QK369   CODEN: HKBAAI
HIKOBIA. (Text and summaries in English, Japanese) 1950. a. 5000 Yen($40) Hikobia Botanical Club - Hikobiakai, c/o Laboratory of Plant Taxonomy & Ecology, Dept. of Biological Science, Faculty of Science, Hiroshima University, 5-1, Kagamiyama 1-chome, Higashi-hiroshima-shi 739, Japan.
TEL 81-824-24-7451. FAX 81-824-24-0734. E-mail: hdeguch@ipc.hiroshima-u.ac.jp. Ed. Hironori Deguchi. bk.rev.; illus.; stat. circ. 400. (back issues avail.) **Indexed:** Biol.Abstr., Field Crop Abstr., Forest.Abstr., Herb.Abstr. **Document type:** academic/scholarly publication.
   Description: Covers the flora, taxonomy and vegetation of Japan.
Refereed Serial

581   JA
HIROSHIMA UNIVERSITY. FACULTY OF SCIENCE. BOTANICAL INSTITUTE. RESEARCH REPORT. (Text in English) a. Hiroshima University, Faculty of Science - Hiroshima Daigaku Rigakubu, 1-3, Kagamiyama, Higashihiroshima-shi, Hiroshima-ken 724, Japan.

581 635   JA   ISSN 0386-5304
HIROSHIMASHI SHOKUBUTSU KOEN KIYO/HIROSHIMA BOTANICAL GARDEN. BULLETIN. (Text in English, Japanese) 1977. a. Hiroshimashi Shokubutsu Koen - Hiroshima Botanical Garden, 3-495 Kurashige, Saiki-ku, Hiroshima-shi, Hiroshima-ken 731-51, Japan. **Document type:** bulletin.

581 635   JA   ISSN 0387-8597
HIROSHIMASHI SHOKUBUTSU KOEN SAIBAI KIROKU/HIROSHIMA BOTANICAL GARDEN. INVESTIGATION. (Text in Japanese) 1979. a. Hiroshimashi Shokubutsu Koen - Hiroshima Botanical Garden, 3-495 Kurashige, Saiki-ku, Hiroshima-shi, Hiroshima-ken 731-51, Japan.

BIOLOGY — BOTANY   707

581   BL   ISSN 0073-2877
QK263   CODEN: HOEHAE
HOEHNEA. (Text and summaries in English, Portuguese) 1971. s-a. price varies. Instituto de Botanica, Caixa Postal 4005, 01061-970 Sao Paulo, SP, Brazil. TEL 55-11-55846300.
FAX 55-11-5773678. Ed. Maria Teresa de Paiva Azevedo. (also avail. in microform; back issues avail.) **Indexed:** Biol.Abstr., Curr.Adv.Ecol.Sci. **Document type:** bulletin.
—CASDDS.
   Supersedes in part: Arquivos de Botanica do Estado de Sao Paulo (ISSN 0374-5031); Incorporates (1962-1987, vol.14): Rickia (ISSN 0080-3014); Which also supersedes in part: Arquivos de Botanica do Estado de Sao Paulo.
Refereed Serial

581   JA
HOKKAIDO DAIGAKU NOGAKUBU FUZOKU SHOKUBUTSUEN NENPO/HOKKAIDO UNIVERSITY. FACULTY OF AGRICULTURE. BOTANIC GARDEN. ANNUAL REPORT. (Text in Japanese) a. Hokkaido Daigaku, Nogakubu, Fuzoku Shokubutsuen - Hokkaido University, Faculty of Agriculture, Botanic Garden, Nishi 8-chome, Kita 3-jo, Chuo-ku, Sapporo-shi, Hokkaido 060, Japan. Ed. Hideki Takahashi. **Document type:** academic/scholarly publication.

HOKKAIDO UNIVERSITY. INSTITUTE OF ALGOLOGICAL RESEARCH. SCIENTIFIC PAPERS/HOKKAIDO DAIGAKU RIGAKUBU KAISO KENKYUJO OBUN HOKOKU. see EARTH SCIENCES — Oceanography

HOKKAIDORITSU SUISAN SHIKENJO KENKYU HOKOKU/HOKKAIDO FISHERIES EXPERIMENTAL STATION. SCIENTIFIC REPORTS. see FISH AND FISHERIES

HOME-GROWN CEREALS AUTHORITY. CEREALS R & D CONFERENCE. PROCEEDINGS. see AGRICULTURE — *Crop Production And Soil*

581   GW   ISSN 0340-4196
QK314
HOPPEA. (Text in German; summaries in English and German) 1815. a. price varies. Regensburgische Botanische Gesellschaft, Institut fuer Botanik, Universitaet Regensburg, 93040 Regensburg, Germany. TEL 49-941-943-3124.
FAX 49-941-943-3106. URL: http://www.biologie.uni-regenburg.de/botanik/schoenfelder/hoppea.html. Ed. P. Schoenfelder. bk.rev.; bibl.; index. (back issues avail.) **Document type:** academic/scholarly publication.
—Linda Hall.
   Description: Studies flora and vegetation of Bavaria.

581 740   US   ISSN 0192-3641
HUNT INSTITUTE FOR BOTANICAL DOCUMENTATION. BULLETIN. 1979. irreg. $4 per vol. Hunt Institute for Botanical Documentation, Carnegie Mellon University, 5000 Forbes Ave., Pittsburgh, PA 15213-3890. TEL 412-268-2434.
FAX 412-268-5677. Ed. Sharon M. Tomasic. circ. 700. **Document type:** bulletin.
—Linda Hall.

581   US   ISSN 0073-4071
HUNTIA; a journal of botanical history. 1963. irreg., latest vol.9, no.2. $60 per vol. Hunt Institute for Botanical Documentation, Carnegie Mellon University, 5000 Forbes Ave., Pittsburgh, PA 15213-3890. TEL 412-268-2434.
FAX 412-268-5677. Ed. R.W. Kiger. bk.rev. circ. 350. **Document type:** academic/scholarly publication.
—BLDSC (4337.280000); Linda Hall. **CCC.**

BIOLOGY — BOTANY

581 674   NE   ISSN 0928-1541
QK647   CODEN: IAJOEB
I A W A JOURNAL. (Text in English) 1931; N.S. 1980. q. fl.100($70) (effective 1998). International Association of Wood Anatomists, P.O. Box 80102, 3508 TC Utrecht, Netherlands. TEL 31-30-2532643. FAX 31-30-2518061. Ed. P. Baas. bk.rev.; index. circ. 800. (back issues avail.) **Indexed:** Abstr.Bull.Inst.Pap.Chem., Art & Archaeol.Tech.Abstr., ASCA, Biol.Abstr., Curr.Adv.Ecol.Sci., Curr.Cont., Forest.Abstr., Forest Prod.Abstr., NAA, Ornam.Hort., Paper & Bd.Abstr. **Document type:** academic/scholarly publication.
—BLDSC (4359.675100); CISTI; EMDOCS; Genuine Article; Linda Hall; SWETS; UnCover. **CCC.**
  Former titles (until 1993): I A W A Bulletin (ISSN 0254-3915); I A W A Publications.
  Description: Devoted to research on the microstructure of wood and bark and related plant products such as bamboo, rattan and palms. Also covers fundamental, systematic and evolutionary botanical aspects and applied forestry.

I E S NEWSLETTER. (Institute of Ecosystem Studies) see ENVIRONMENTAL STUDIES

581   UK
I M I TECHNICAL HANDBOOKS. irreg., no.2, 1994. (International Mycological Institute) CAB International, Wallingford, Oxon. OX10 8DE, England. TEL 44-1491-83211. FAX 44-1491-826090. TELEX 847964 COMAGG G. E-mail: cabi@cabi.org; URL: http://www.cabi.org. (U.S. subscr. to: CAB International, North American Office, 198 Madison Ave., New York, NY 10016. TEL 212-726-6490. FAX 212-686-7993) **Document type:** monographic series.

589.2   UK
I S M S NEWSLETTER. q. International Society for Mushroom Science, c/o Dr. P.B. Flegg, 50 St. Flora's Rd., Littlehampton BN17 6BB, England. TEL 44-903-716469. **Document type:** newsletter.

589.2   BE   ISSN 0779-1070
ICONES MYCOLOGICAE. 1982. irreg., part 7, 1987. price varies. Jardin Botanique National de Belgique - Nationale Plantentuin van Belgie, Domaine de Bouchout, 1860 Meise, Belgium. TEL 32-2-2693905. illus. (back issues avail.) **Document type:** monographic series.

653.934   MX   ISSN 0188-4018
ICONES ORCHIDACEARUM. (Text in English, Spanish) 1990. irreg. $37. Herbarium Amo, Apdo. Postal 53-123, 11320 Mexico D.F., Mexico. TEL 52-5-203-1909. FAX 52-5-531-4349. E-mail: eric@mail.internet.com.mx. Eds. Eric Hagsater, Gerardo A. Salazar. illus.; index. circ. 600. **Document type:** monographic series.
  Description: Contains botanical illustrations dedicated to orchids with descriptions and data on distribution, habitat and conservation.

581   SG   ISSN 0073-4403
ICONES PLANTARUM AFRICANARUM. 1953. irreg. 44 Fr. Institut Fondamental d'Afrique Noire - Cheikh Anta Diop, B.P. 206, Dakar, Senegal.

581   BL   ISSN 0073-4705
QK1   CODEN: IHBOAG
IHERINGIA. SERIE BOTANICA. (Text in Portuguese; summaries in English) 1958. s-a. price varies. Fundacao Zoobotanica do Rio Grande do Sul, Museu de Ciencias Naturais, Caixa Postal 1188, 90690-000 Porto Alegre, RS, Brazil. TEL 55-51-3361511. FAX 55-51-3361778. E-mail: ebib@pampa.tche.br. Ed. Zulanira Meyer Rosa. abstr.; bibl.; illus. circ. 600. **Indexed:** Biol.Abstr., Chem.Abstr.
—BLDSC (4363.520000); CISTI. **CCC.**

IMMERGRUENE BLAETTER. see GARDENING AND HORTICULTURE

INDEX HEPATICARUM. see BIOLOGY — Abstracting, Bibliographies, Statistics

INDEX KEWENSIS. see BIOLOGY

INDEX OF FUNGI. see BIOLOGY — Abstracting, Bibliographies, Statistics

581   IS
INDEX SEMINUM; wild and cultivated plants. (Text in English) a. free. Tel Aviv University, Department of Botany, Ramat Aviv, Tel Aviv 69 978, Israel. TEL 03-420151. Ed. Yeduha Tankus.

581   SA
INDEX SEMINUM; list of plant genetic resources available in South Africa. 1994. a. (Department of Agriculture) Directorate of Plant and Quality Control, National Genebank, Private Bag X258, Pretoria 0001, South Africa. **Document type:** government publication, academic/scholarly publication.

581   NE   ISSN 0073-6007
Z5354.C52
INDEX TO PLANT CHROMOSOME NUMBERS. (Subseries of Regnum Vegetabile) 1956. irreg. price varies. (International Association for Plant Taxonomy) Bohn Stafleu van Loghum B.V. (Subsidiary of: Wolters Kluwer N.V.), Postbus 246, 3990 GA Houten, Netherlands. TEL 31-3403-95711. FAX 31-3403-50903. Ed. R.J. Moore. circ. 1,000.
—CISTI.

581   II   ISSN 0254-4091
QK358   CODEN: IBREDR
INDIAN BOTANICAL REPORTER. (Text in English) s-a. Rs.40($10) to individuals; institutions Rs.75 ($20). Marathwada University, Department of Botany, Executive Editor, Aurangabad 431 004, India. **Indexed:** Biol.Abstr., Chem.Abstr., Excerp.Bot., Field Crop Abstr., Herb.Abstr., Rev.Plant Path.
—CASDDS.

587.31   II   ISSN 0970-2741
QK529.I4   CODEN: IFJOEC
INDIAN FERN JOURNAL. (Text in English) 1984. s-a. $50 (effective 1997). Indian Fern Society, Punjabi University, Department of Botany, Patiala 147 002, India. TEL 91-175-822250. Ed. S.S. Bir. bk.rev. (back issues avail.) **Document type:** abstracting/indexing.
—CISTI; Linda Hall.
  Refereed Serial

581   II   ISSN 0073-6376
INDIAN FOREST RECORDS (NEW SERIES) BOTANY. (Text in English) 1937. irreg., vol.6, no.1, 1980. price varies. Forest Research Institute & Colleges, P.O. New Forest, Dehra Dun, India. circ. 500. **Indexed:** Biol.Abstr., Curr.Adv.Ecol.Sci., Forest.Abstr., Forest Prod.Abstr., Indian Sci.Abstr., Rev.Appl.Entomol.
—CISTI; Linda Hall.

581   II   ISSN 0250-829X
QK358   CODEN: IJBODX
INDIAN JOURNAL OF BOTANY. (Supplement avail.) (Text in English) 1978. s-a. Rs.100($25) S. Krishnamurthy, 6-1-127-2, Khairatabad, Hyderabad 500 004, India. Ed. A. Satyanarayana. adv.; bk.rev. circ. 500. **Indexed:** Biol.Abstr., Chem.Abstr., Curr.Adv.Ecol.Sci., Excerp.Med., Field Crop Abstr., Herb.Abstr., Hort.Abstr., Ind.Vet., INIS Atomind., INSPEC, Maize Abstr., Rev.Med.& Vet.Mycol., Seed Abstr., Sorghum & Millets Abstr., Triticale Abstr., Trop.Oil Seeds Abstr., Weed Abstr. **Document type:** academic/scholarly publication.
—CASDDS; CISTI; Linda Hall.
  Description: Presents original research in plant science.

INDIAN JOURNAL OF GENETICS AND PLANT BREEDING. see BIOLOGY — Genetics

581 575.1   II
INDIAN JOURNAL OF PLANT GENETIC RESOURCES. (Text in English) s-a. Rs.300 (foreign $100). Indian Society of Plant Genetic Resources, NBPGR Campus, Pusa, New Delhi 110 012, India. TEL 91-11-578-5457. Ed. B.B. Singh. R&P contact: B.B. Singh. adv. **Document type:** academic/scholarly publication.
  Description: For botanists, geneticsts, plant breeders, and those concerned with plant genetic resources.

581.1   II   ISSN 0019-5502
QK710   CODEN: IPPYA2
INDIAN JOURNAL OF PLANT PHYSIOLOGY. (Text in English) 1958. 4/yr. $100. Indian Society for Plant Physiology, Division of Plant Physiology, Indian Agricultural Research Institute, New Delhi 110 012, India. (Dist. by: HPC Publisher's Distributors (Pvt.) Ltd., 4805-24, 1st Fl., Bharat Ram Rd., Darya Ganj, New Delhi 110 002, India. TEL 91-11-3254402. FAX 91-11-6863511) Ed. G.C. Srivastava. bk.rev. circ. 1,000. **Indexed:** Biol.Abstr., Chem.Abstr., Cott.& Trop.Fibr.Abstr., Crop Physiol.Abstr., Curr.Adv.Ecol.Sci., Curr.Adv.Genetics & Molec.Biol., Curr.Cont., Field Crop Abstr., Food Sci.& Tech.Abstr., Forest.Abstr., Herb.Abstr., Hort.Abstr., INIS Atomind., Irr.& Drain.Abstr., Maize Abstr., Plant Grow.Reg.Abstr., Potato Abstr., Rice Abstr., Seed Abstr., Soils & Fert., Sorghum & Millets Abstr., Soyabean Abstr., Triticale Abstr., Trop.Oil Seeds Abstr., Weed Abstr. **Document type:** academic/scholarly publication.
—BLDSC (4420.150000); CASDDS; CISTI; Linda Hall; UnCover.

581.2   II   ISSN 0537-2410
INDIAN PHYTOPATHOLOGICAL SOCIETY. BULLETIN. 1963. irreg. Indian Phytological Society, c/o Indian Agricultural Research Institute, Division of Mycology, New Delhi 110012, India. **Indexed:** Biol.Abstr., Rev.Plant Path.
—Linda Hall.

581.2   II   ISSN 0367-973X
SB599   CODEN: IPHYAU
INDIAN PHYTOPATHOLOGY. (Text in English) 1948. q. Rs.800($80) (Indian Phytopathological Society) Malhotra Publishing House, A-38-3, Mayapuri Industrial Area, Phase-I, New Delhi 110 064, India. TEL 91-11-5143928. FAX 91-11-5724135. (Dist. overseas by: HPC Publishers' Distributors Pvt. Ltd., 4805-24, 1st Fl., Bharat Ram Rd., Darya Ganj, New Delhi 110 002, India. TEL 91-11-3254401. FAX 91-11-6863511) Ed. A.K. Sarbhoy. adv.; bk.rev. circ. 2,000. (processed) **Indexed:** Bio-Contr.News & Info., Biol.Abstr., Biotech.Abstr., Chem.Abstr., Cott.& Trop.Fibr.Abstr., Excerp.Med., Fababean Abstr., Field Crop Abstr., Forest.Abstr., Helminthol.Abstr., Irr.& Drain.Abstr., Ornam.Hort., Plant Breed.Abstr., Plant Grow.Reg.Abstr., Potato Abstr., Rev.Med.& Vet.Mycol., Rev.Plant Path., Rice Abstr., Soils & Fert., Sorghum & Millets Abstr., Triticale Abstr., Trop.Oil Seeds Abstr., Weed Abstr. **Document type:** academic/scholarly publication.
—BLDSC (4427.000000); CASDDS; Linda Hall; SWETS; UnCover.

581   CU
INFORMACION EXPRESS. SERIE: PLANTAS MEDICINALES Y FLORES. 1985. a. C.$0,30($3) in N. America; S. America and Europe $6; elsewhere $5; or exchange basis. Centro de Informacion y Documentacion Agropecuario, Gaveta Postal 4149, Havana 4, Cuba. TEL 301672. TELEX 0511007. (Dist. by: Ediciones Cubanas, Obispo No. 527, Apdo. 605, Havana, Cuba) stat. **Indexed:** Agrindex.

581   FR   ISSN 0073-7917
INFORMATIONS ANNUELLES DE CARYOSYSTEMATIQUE ET CYTOGENETIQUE.* 1967. a. price varies. Institut de Botanique, Strasbourg, 8 rue Goethe, Strasbourg, France.

581   IT   ISSN 0020-0697
QK1   CODEN: IBOIBM
INFORMATORE BOTANICO ITALIANO. (Text in English, French, German and Italian; summaries in English and Italian) 1969. 3/yr. L.120000. Societa Botanica Italiana, Via Giorgio La Pira, 4, 50121 Florence, Italy. TEL 39-55-2757379. Ed. Giovanni Cristofolini. charts; illus.; index. circ. 1,300. **Indexed:** Biol.Abstr., Deep Sea Res.& Oceanogr.Abstr., Excerp.Bot. **Document type:** academic/scholarly publication, bulletin.
—BLDSC (4496.760000); CISTI; Linda Hall.

581.2 631　　　　IT　　ISSN 0020-0735
　　　　　　　　　　　CODEN: INFTAP
INFORMATORE FITOPATOLOGICO. Short title: I F. 1951. m. (11/yr.). L.73000 (effective 1996). Edagricole S.p.A., Via Emilia Levante 31, 40139 Bologna, Italy. TEL 39-51-492211. FAX 39-51-493660. Eds. Gabriele Goidanich, Gilberte Govi. adv.: B&W page L.1000000, color page L.14000000; 185 x 247. bk.rev.; illus.; tr.lit.; index. circ. 8,900. **Indexed:** Agri.Eng.Abstr., Bio-Contr.News & Info., Biol.Abstr., Chem.Abstr., Forest.Abstr., Hort.Abstr., Irr.& Drain.Abstr., Plant Breed.Abstr., Potato Abstr., Rev.Appl.Entomol., Rev.Med.& Vet.Mycol., Rev.Plant Path., Rice Abstr., Seed Abstr., Soyabean Abstr., Triticale Abstr., Weed Abstr.
—BLDSC (4496.800000); CASDDS; UMI.
　Description: Examines all aspects and problems of phytopathology.

581　　　　　　SP　　ISSN 0210-6205
INSTITUCIO CATALANA D'HISTORIA NATURAL. BUTLLETI. SECCIO DE BOTANICA. 1974. irreg. 1400 ptas. Institucion Catalana de Historia Natural, Carme 47, 08001 Barcelona, Spain.

581　　　　　　SP　　ISSN 0211-707X
QH7
INSTITUCIO CATALANA D'HISTORIA NATURAL. TREBALLS. 1915. irreg. 2500 ptas. Institucion Catalana de Historia Natural, Carme 47, 08001 Barcelona, Spain. **Indexed:** Ind.SST.

581　　　　　　SP　　ISSN 0210-8062
INSTITUT BOTANIC DE BARCELONA. TREBALLS. (Text in Catalan, English) 1914. irreg., vol.15, 1992. $10 or exchange basis. Institut Botanic de Barcelona, Parc de Montjuic, Av. dels Muntanyans, s-n, 08038 Barcelona, Spain. Ed. A.M. Romo. circ. 1,050. **Indexed:** Biol.Abstr., Field Crop Abstr., Herb.Abstr., Ind.SST, Ref.Zh., Zoo.Rec. **Document type:** monographic series.

581　　　　　　GW　　ISSN 0344-5615
QK1　　　　　　　　　CODEN: MIAHDA
INSTITUT FUER ALLGEMEINE BOTANIK UND BOTANISCHER GARTEN. MITTEILUNGEN. (Text in English and German; summaries in English) 1914. irreg., vol.26, 1996. exchange basis. Universitaet Hamburg, Institut fuer Allgemeine Botanik und Botanischer Garten, Ohnhorststr. 18, 22609 Hamburg, Germany. FAX 49-40-82282254. Ed. M. Engels. R&P contact: D. Lorch. bk.rev.; illus.; circ. 550. **Indexed:** Biol.Abstr., Chem.Abstr, Curr.Adv.Genetics & Molec.Biol., Rev.Plant Path. **Document type:** academic/scholarly publication, bulletin.
—CASDDS; CISTI.
　Refereed Serial

580　　　　　　SZ　　ISSN 0074-7408
INTERNATIONAL ASSOCIATION OF PLANT BREEDERS FOR THE PROTECTION OF PLANT VARIETIES. CONGRESS REPORTS. 1939. a., 39th, Kenya, 1993. International Association of Plant Breeders for the Protection of Plant Varieties, c/o Bernard Le Buanec, Sec.-Gen., Chemin du Reposoir 5-7, CH-1260 Nyon, Switzerland. TEL 022-3619977. FAX 022-3619219. TELEX 419974 SEED CH. **Document type:** proceedings.

581　　　　　　US　　ISSN 1058-5893
QK1　　　　　　　　　CODEN: IPLSE2
INTERNATIONAL JOURNAL OF PLANT SCIENCES; a journal embracing all departments of botanical science. 1875. bi-m. $68 to non-member individuals (Canada $84.76; elsewhere $80); institutions $218 (Canada $245.26; elsewhere $230); members $44 (Canada $59.08; elsewhere $56) (effective 1998). University of Chicago Press, Journals Division, Box 37005, Chicago, IL 60637. TEL 773-753-3347. FAX 773-753-0811. E-mail: subscriptions@journals.uchicago.edu; URL: http://www.journals.uchicago.edu/IJPS/. Eds. Edward D. Garber, Manfred Ruddat. adv.: page $355; trim 8 1/2 x 11. bk.rev.; bibl.; charts; illus.; index. circ. 1,500. (also avail. in microform from UMI,PMC; microfiche from IDC; reprint service avail. from UMI,ISI) **Indexed:** Abstr.Bull.Inst.Pap.Chem., ASCA, Biol.Abstr., Biol.& Agr.Ind., Chem.Abstr., Crop Physiol.Abstr., Curr.Adv.Ecol.Sci., Curr.Cont., Deep Sea Res.& Oceanogr.Abstr., Ecol.Abstr., Excerp.Med., Field Crop Abstr., Forest.Abstr., Forest Prod.Abstr., Gen.Sci.Ind., Geo.Abstr., Geol.Abstr., GeoRef., Herb.Abstr., Hort.Abstr., Ind.Sci.Rev., INIS Atomind., Ornam.Hort., Plant Breed.Abstr., Rev.Plant Path., Sci.Cit.Ind., Seed Abstr., Soils & Fert., Soyabean Abstr., Triticale Abstr., Trop.Oil Seeds Abstr., VITIS, Weed Abstr. **Document type:** academic/scholarly publication.
—BLDSC (4542.468700); CASDDS; CISTI; EMDOCS; Genuine Article; KR SourceOne; Linda Hall; SWETS; UMI; UnCover. CCC.
　Formerly (until Mar. 1992): Botanical Gazette (ISSN 0006-8071)
　Description: Presents the results of original investigations in all areas of plant biology, including development, physiology, reproductive biology, evolution, cell biology, genetics, ecology, systematics, and paleobotany.
　Refereed Serial

581　　　　　　II　　ISSN 0254-0126
SB724　　　　　　　　CODEN: IJTSEY
INTERNATIONAL JOURNAL OF TROPICAL PLANT DISEASES. 1983. s-a. Rs.900($90) Today and Tomorrow's Printers & Publishers, 24B-5 Desh Bandu Gupta Rd., Karol Bagh, New Delhi 110 005, India. TEL 91-11-5721928. (Dist. in U.S. by: Scholarly Publications, 2825 Wilcrest Dr., Ste. 255, Houston, TX 77042. TEL 713-781-0070. FAX 713-781-2112) Eds. S.P. Raychaudhuri, Anupam Varma. (back issues avail.) **Indexed:** Biol.Abstr., Crop Physiol.Abstr., Curr.Cont., Food Sci.& Tech.Abstr., Hort.Abstr., Plant Grow.Reg.Abstr., Potato Abstr., Sorghum & Millets Abstr., Triticale Abstr., Trop.Oil Seeds Abstr. **Document type:** academic/scholarly publication.
—BLDSC (4542.696160); Linda Hall; UnCover. CCC.
　Description: Publishes research findings, new ideas and selected reviews on all aspects of plant pathological problems.

581　　　　　　US　　ISSN 0254-8844
INTERNATIONAL ORGANIZATION OF PLANT BIOSYSTEMATISTS. NEWSLETTER. 1983. s-a. $14. International Organization of Plant Biosystematists, c/o Peter C. Hoch, Missouri Botanical Garden, P.O. Box 299, St. Louis, MO 63166-0299. TEL 314-577-5175. FAX 314-577-9596. E-mail: hoch@mobot.org. (Co-sponsor: Swiss Federal Institute of Technology (ETH)) Ed. K.M. Urbanska. bk.rev. circ. 500. (back issues avail.) **Document type:** newsletter.
　Description: Exchanges personal and scientific developments between students of plant evolutionary processes, mainly on the species level.

589.45　　　　BL　　ISSN 0074-7874
QK564
INTERNATIONAL SEAWEED SYMPOSIUM. PROCEEDINGS. (Published by host country) 1952. triennial. price varies. International Seaweed Symposium, c/o Dr. Eurico Oliveira, Instituto das Biociencias, Univ. de Sao Paulo, Caixa Postal 11461, 05422-970 Sao Paulo SP, Brazil. FAX 11-55-818-7416. (Co-sponsor: International Seaweed Association) adv. circ. 400. **Indexed:** Biol.Abstr., Deep Sea Res.& Oceanogr.Abstr. **Document type:** proceedings.
—Linda Hall. CCC.

589.2　　　　　UK
INTERNATIONAL SOCIETY FOR MUSHROOM SCIENCE. SYMPOSIA PROCEEDINGS. irreg., 4th, 1990, Sydney. International Society for Mushroom Science, c/o Dr. P.B. Flegg, 50 St. Flora's Rd., Littlehampton BN17 6BB, England. TEL 44-903-716469. **Document type:** proceedings.

581　　　　　　II　　ISSN 0539-0346
INTERNATIONAL SOCIETY OF PLANT MORPHOLOGISTS. YEARBOOK. (Text in English) 1951. a. $55. International Society of Plant Morphologists, University of Delhi, Department of Botany, Delhi 110 007, India. bk.rev. circ. 1,200.

581　　　　　　KR　　ISSN 0257-9936
　　　　　　　　　　　CODEN: IAKRBM
INTRODUKTSIYA I AKKLIMATYZATSIYA RASTENII; respublikanskii mezhvedomstvennyi sbornik nauchnykh trudov. (Text in Ukrainian) 1965. s-a. (Akademiya Nauk Ukrainy, Tsentral'nyi Botanicheskii Sad) Vidavnitstvo Naukova Dumka, Vul. Tereshchenkivska 3, 252601 Kiev, Ukraine. TEL 044-244-4068. FAX 044-224-7060. (Dist. by: Mezhdunarodnaya Kniga, B. Yakimanka 39, 117049 Moscow, Russia) (Co-sponsor: Donetskii Botanicheskii Sad) Eds. A.M. Grodzinskii, N.E. Kondratyuk. **Indexed:** Forest.Abstr., Hort.Abstr., Seed Abstr.
—CASDDS; Linda Hall.
　Formerly (until 1984): Introduktsiya ta Akklimatyzatsiya Rozlyn na Ukrayini (ISSN 0579-4005)

581　　　　　　IR　　ISSN 0006-2774
IRANIAN JOURNAL OF PLANT PATHOLOGY/BIMARIHAYE GUIAHI. (Text in English or Persian, summaries in English and Persian) 1963. q. IRl.7000 per no. Iranian Phytopathological Society, Box 19395-1454, Teheran, Iran. TEL 98-21-2400645. FAX 98-21-2400645. Ed.Bd. bibl.; charts; illus. circ. 2,000. **Indexed:** Biol.Abstr., Chem.Abstr., Maize Abstr., Rev.Plant Path., Triticale Abstr., Weed Abstr. **Document type:** academic/scholarly publication.
—BLDSC (4567.529000).
　Description: Publishes original research papers and short reports in the area of plant pathology.
　Refereed Serial

581　　　　　　US
ISELYA; botanical journal. 1979. q. $8 to individuals; institutions $10. X Club, Department of Biological Science, Nicholls State University, Thibodaux, LA 70310. Ed.Bd. circ. 200. (back issues avail.)
　Refereed Serial

581　　　　　　IS　　ISSN 0792-9978
QK1　　　　　　　　　CODEN: IJUPEU
ISRAEL JOURNAL OF PLANT SCIENCES. (Text in English) 1951. 4/yr. $205 (effective 1996). Laser Pages Publishing (1992) Ltd., P.O. Box 52507, Jerusalem 91502, Israel. TEL 972-2-370699. FAX 972-2-370625. Ed. A.M. Mayer. bk.rev.; charts; illus.; index. circ. 600. **Indexed:** Agroforest.Abstr., ASCA, Biol.Abstr., Chem.Abstr., Cott.& Trop.Fibr.Abstr., Crop Physiol.Abstr., Curr.Cont., Deep Sea Res.& Oceanogr.Abstr., Ecol.Abstr., Field Crop Abstr., Food Sci.& Tech.Abstr., Forest.Abstr., Forest Prod.Abstr., Herb.Abstr., Hort.Abstr., IDA, Ind.Sci.Rev., Ornam.Hort., Plant Breed.Abstr., Plant Grow.Reg.Abstr., Rev.Plant Path., Sci.Cit.Ind., Seed Abstr., Soils & Fert., Sorghum & Millets Abstr., Triticale Abstr., Weed Abstr., Zoo.Rec. **Document type:** academic/scholarly publication.
—BLDSC (4583.812800); CASDDS; CISTI; EMDOCS; Genuine Article; Linda Hall; SWETS; UnCover. CCC.
　Formerly (until vol.42, 1994): Israel Journal of Botany (ISSN 0021-213X); Supersedes: Research Council of Israel. Bulletin (Section D); Palestine Journal of Botany.
　Description: Publishes original research covering all aspects of basic and applied plant sciences, including systematics and evolution, plant physiology, geobotany, phytochemistry, and molecular plant biology.
　Refereed Serial

581　　　　　　SP　　ISSN 0213-8530
ITINERA GEOBOTANICA. 1987. a. price varies. Universidad de Leon, Secretariado de Publicaciones, Campus de Verganza, s-n, 24007 Leon, Spain. TEL 34-87-291558. FAX 34-87-291558. E-mail: dbvlhc@unileon.es. Ed. Angel Penas Merino. bk.rev.; circ. 1,000 (controlled). **Indexed:** Ind.SST. **Document type:** bulletin.
　Refereed Serial

BIOLOGY — BOTANY

581   RU   ISSN 0202-716X
SB123
ITOGI NAUKI I TEKHNIKI: RASTENIEVODSTVO. (Text in Russian) irreg., vol.7, 1986. price varies. Vsesoyuznyi Institut Nauchno-Tekhnicheskoi Informatsii (VINITI), Ul. Baltiiskaya 14, Moscow A-219, Russia. (Subscr. to: Mezhdunarodnaya Kniga, Dimitrova ul. 39, 113095 Moscow, Russia)

581.1   JA   ISSN 0912-2214
J S P P NEWSLETTER. (Text in English) 1979. a. membership. Japanese Society of Plant Physiologists - Nihon Shokubutsu Seiri Gakkai, Shimodachuri Ogawa Higashi, Kamigyo-ku, Kyoto 602, Japan. FAX 81-75-415-3662. E-mail: jspp@nacos.com. Ed. Koji Asada. **Document type:** newsletter.

JANGAL VA MARTA'. see *ENVIRONMENTAL STUDIES*

581   JA   ISSN 0911-6052
JAPAN SOCIETY OF PLANT TAXONOMISTS. PROCEEDINGS/NIHON SHOKUBUTSU BUNRUI GAKKAI KAIHO. (Text and summaries in English or Japanese) 1952. s-a. 3000 Yen. Japan Society of Plant Taxonomists, c/o Makino Herbarium, Tokyo Metropolitan University, Minamiosawa, Hachioji, Tokyo 192-03, Japan. Ed. Jin Murata. R&P contact: Masanobu Higuchi. circ. 350. **Document type:** proceedings.

589.3   JA
CODEN: NSOGAJ
JAPANESE JOURNAL OF PHYCOLOGY (JAPANESE EDITION). (Text in Japanese) 1953. 3/yr. Japanese Society of Phycology, JA - Nihon Sorui Gakkai, c/o Division of Biological Sciences, Graduate School of Science, Hokkaido University, Sapporo 060, Japan. TEL 81-11-706-2745. FAX 81-11-746-1512. E-mail: horig@bio.hokudai.ac.jp. Ed. Isao Inouye. adv.; bk.rev.; cum.index: vols.1-10; vols.11-20. circ. 3,000. **Indexed:** Biol.Abstr., Chem.Abstr., Curr.Cont., Deep Sea Res.& Oceanogr.Abstr., Jap.Per.Ind., Sel.Water Res.Abstr., SSCI. **Document type:** academic/scholarly publication.
—BLDSC (4657.200000); CASDDS; CISTI; UnCover.
Supersedes in part (in 1995): Japanese Journal of Phycology (Bilingual Edition); Which was formerly: Sorui - Japanese Society of Phycology. Bulletin (ISSN 0038-1578)
Description: Contains original research articles, research notes, reviews and Society information and activities.
Refereed Serial

581.1   JA
JAPANESE SOCIETY OF PLANT PHYSIOLOGISTS. NEWS/NIHON SHOKUBUTSU SEIRI GAKKAI TSUSHIN. (Text in Japanese) 1968. 3/yr. Japanese Society of Plant Physiologists - Nihon Shokubutsu Seiri Gakkai, Ogawa Higashi Iru, Shimodachuri Dori, Kamigyo-ku, Kyoto 602, Japan. FAX 81-75-415-3662. E-mail: jspp@nacos.com. Ed. Koji Asada.

581.1   JA
JAPANESE SOCIETY OF PLANT PHYSIOLOGISTS. PROCEEDINGS OF THE ANNUAL MEETING AND SYMPOSIUM/NIHON SHOKUBUTSU SEIRI GAKKAI NENKAI OYOBI SHINPOJUMU KEON YOSHISHU. (Text in English, Japanese) 1960. a. Japanese Society of Plant Physiologists - Nihon Shokubutsu Seiri Gakkai, Ogawa Higashi Iru, Shimodachuri Dori, Kamigyo-ku, Kyoto 602, Japan. FAX 81-75-415-3662. E-mail: jspp@nacos.com. Ed. Koji Asada. **Document type:** proceedings.

581   BL   ISSN 0103-2550
JARDIM BOTANICO DO RIO DE JANEIRO. ARQUIVOS. 1915, N.S. 1947. a. Cr.$2905($37) (effective 1997). Ministerio do Meio Ambiente, dos Recursos Hidricos e da Amazonia Legal, Jardim Botanico do Rio de Janeiro, Biblioteca Barbosa Rodrigues, Rua Jardim Botanico 1008, 22460-000 Gavea, Rio de Janeiro, Brazil. TEL 55-21-2748246. FAX 55-21-2744897. TELEX 021-33623. circ. 1,000. (also avail. in microfiche from IDC)
Description: Presents results of research conducted by the botanical garden.

581   SP   ISSN 0211-1322
QK1   CODEN: AJBMD7
JARDIN BOTANICO DE MADRID. ANALES. (Text in English, French, German, Italian, Portuguese, Spanish; summaries in English) 1940. s.a. 3100 ptas. (foreign 5200 ptas.) (effective 1997). Consejo Superior de Investigaciones Cientificas, Real Jardin Botanico de Madrid, Vitruvio 8, 28006 Madrid, Spain. TEL 34-1-4203017. FAX 34-1-4200157. TELEX 42182 CSIC E. Eds. G. Nieto Feliner, M.T. Telleria. bk.rev.; bibl.; charts; illus.; index. circ. 850. (back issues avail.) **Indexed:** Agrindex, Biol.Abstr., Bull.Signal., Curr.Adv.Ecol.Sci., Excerp.Bot., Forest.Abstr., Hort.Abstr., Ind.SST. **Document type:** academic/scholarly publication.
—CISTI.
Formerly (1950-1978): Instituto Botanico A.J. Cavanilles. Anales.
Description: Covers systematic botany and related subjects, particularly plant ecology.
Refereed Serial

581   CU   ISSN 0253-5696
QK227   CODEN: RJBNDR
JARDIN BOTANICO NACIONAL. REVISTA. (Text in Spanish; summaries in English and Spanish) 1980. 3/yr. C.$4.50($24) in N. America; S. America $25; Europe $26. (Universidad de La Habana, Direccion de Informacion Cientifica y Tecnica) Ediciones Cubanas, Obispo No. 527, Apdo. 605, Havana, Cuba. (back issues avail.) **Indexed:** Curr.Adv.Ecol.Sci., Ornam.Hort.
—KNAW.

581   DR
JARDIN BOTANICO NACIONAL "DR. RAFAEL M. MOSCOSO." BOLETIN. (Text in English, Spanish) 1977. irreg., latest 1983. exchange basis. Jardin Botanico Nacional "Dr. Rafael M. Moscoso", Apdo. Postal 21-9, Santo Domingo, Dominican Republic. FAX 809-562-6893. Ed. Jose Amado Rodriguez. illus.; charts; bibl.

581   BE   ISSN 0303-9153
JARDIN BOTANIQUE NATIONAL DE BELGIQUE. BULLETIN/NATIONALE PLANTENTUIN VAN BELGIE. BULLETIN. 1902. q. 3760 BEF (foreign 3880 BEF) (effective 1994). Jardin Botanique National de Belgique - Nationale Plantentuin van Belge, Domaine de Bouchout, 1860 Meise, Belgium. TEL 32-2-2693905. Ed. A. Robyns. bk.rev.; cum.index: vols.26-50. **Indexed:** Agri.Ind., Ash.G.Bot.Per., Biol.Abstr., Field Crop Abstr., Forest.Abstr., Forest Prod.Abstr., GeoRef., Herb.Abstr., Plant Breed.Abstr., Rev.Plant Path. **Document type:** bulletin.
—CISTI; UnCover.
Formerly (until 1967): Jardin Botanique de l'Etat a Bruxelles. Bulletin (ISSN 0374-6313)

580.5   GW   ISSN 0949-5460
QK1   CODEN: ANBTAJ
JOURNAL OF APPLIED BOTANY. (Text in German; summaries in English) 1919. 6/yr. (in 3 vols., 2 nos./vol.). DM.510 in Europe; rest of world DM.514 (effective 1998). Blackwell Wissenschaft, Kurfuerstendamm 57, 10707 Berlin, Germany. TEL 49-30-32790634. FAX 49-30-32790610. E-mail: aboverwalt@blackwis.de; URL: http://www.blackwis.com. Ed. H.J. Jaeger. bk.rev. (also avail. in microform from SWZ; back issues avail.) **Indexed:** Apic.Abstr., ASCA, Biol.Abstr., Biotech.Abstr., Chem.Abstr., Crop Physiol.Abstr., Curr.Cont., Deep Sea Res.& Oceanogr.Abstr., Excerp.Med., Fababean Abstr., Field Crop.Abstr., Forest.Abstr., Forest Prod.Abstr., Herb.Abstr., Hort.Abstr., Ind.Sci.Rev., INIS Atomind., Maize Abstr., Plant Breed.Abstr., Plant Grow.Reg.Abstr., Rev.Plant Path., Risk Abstr., Sci.Cit.Ind, Seed Abstr., Soils & Fert., Triticale Abstr., Weed Abstr. **Document type:** academic/scholarly publication.
—BLDSC (4940.655000); CASDDS; CISTI; EMDOCS; Genuine Article; Linda Hall. **CCC.**
Formerly (until 1995): Angewandte Botanik (ISSN 0066-1759)

JOURNAL OF APPLIED GENETICS; an international journal of genetics. see *BIOLOGY — Genetics*

589.3   NE   ISSN 0921-8971
SH338.7   CODEN: JAPPEL
JOURNAL OF APPLIED PHYCOLOGY. (Supplement to: Hydrobiologia (ISSN 0018-8158)) (Text in English) 1989. bi-m. fl.890 to institutions; $456.50 to institutions in U.S. (effective 1998). Kluwer Academic Publishers, Postbus 17, 3300 AA Dordrecht, Netherlands. TEL 31-78-6392392. FAX 31-78-6392254. TELEX 29245 KAPG NL. E-mail: services@wkap.nl; URL: http://www.wkap.nl. (Dist. by: Kluwer Academic Publishers Group, P.O. Box 322, 3300 AH Dordrecht, Netherlands. TEL 31-78-6392392. FAX 31-78-6546474; N. America dist. addr.: Box 358, Accord Sta., Hingham, MA 02018-0358. TEL 617-871-6600. FAX 617-871-6528) Ed. B.A. Whitton. (also avail. in microform from UMI; back issues avail.; reprint service avail. from SWZ) **Indexed:** Aqu.Sci.Abstr., Chem.Abstr., Curr.Cont., Deep Sea Res.& Oceanogr.Abstr., Ecol.Abstr., Ecol.Abstr., Ind.Sci.Rev., Int.Abstr.Biol.Sci., Mar.Sci.Cont.Tab., Sci.Cit.Ind., Sel.Water Res.Abstr., Soc.Sci.Ind., Sport Fish.Abstr., W.R.C.Inf., Wild.Rev., Zoo.Rec. **Document type:** academic/scholarly publication.
—BLDSC (4943.880000); CASDDS; CISTI; Ei; EMDOCS; Genuine Article; Linda Hall; SWETS; UMI; UnCover. **CCC.**
Description: Publishes work on the commercial use of algae, including fundamental research, techniques and practical applications in biotechnology, genetic engineering, pollution control and monitoring, and other areas.
Refereed Serial

581 635   US   ISSN 0146-6623
SB614   CODEN: JAPMDB
JOURNAL OF AQUATIC PLANT MANAGEMENT. 1961. s-a. $70. Aquatic Plant Management Society, Inc., Box 121086, Clermont, FL 34712-1086. TEL 202-547-5437. FAX 202-547-5645. Ed. William T. Haller. R&P contact: William T. Haller. TEL 352-392-9613. circ. 600. (also avail. in microform from ISI; back issues avail.) **Indexed:** ASCA, Bio-Contr.News & Info., Biol.Abstr., Chem.Abstr., Curr.Cont., Irr.& Drain.Abstr., Ornam.Hort., Rice Abstr., Sci.Cit.Ind., Sel.Water Res.Abstr., Soils & Fert., W.R.C.Inf., Weed Abstr. **Document type:** academic/scholarly publication.
—BLDSC (4947.160000); CASDDS; Genuine Article; Linda Hall; UnCover.
Formerly (until 1976): Hyacinth Control Journal (ISSN 0146-9533)
Description: Encourages scientific research and promotes the control and management of aquatic plants through scientifically sound procedures.
Refereed Serial

588   UK   ISSN 0373-6687
QK534   CODEN: JBRYAR
JOURNAL OF BRYOLOGY. vol.7, 1972. 2/yr. £64 (foreign £72). (British Bryological Society) W.S. Maney & Son Ltd., Hudson Rd., Leeds LS9 7DL, England. TEL 01532-497481. FAX 01532-486983. adv.; bk.rev.; abstr. circ. 760. (back issues avail.; reprint service avail. from ISI) **Indexed:** ASCA, Biol.Abstr., Curr.Cont., Ecol.Abstr., Ind.Sci.Rev., Sci.Cit.Ind. **Document type:** academic/scholarly publication.
—BLDSC (4954.570000); Genuine Article; Linda Hall; SWETS; UMI; UnCover.
Formerly: British Bryological Society. Transactions (ISSN 0068-1385)
Refereed Serial

581 643.9   SA   ISSN 0259-1901
JOURNAL OF DENDROLOGY. (Text and summaries in Afrikaans and English) 1981. s-a. R.12.00. Dendrological Society - Dendrologiese Vereniging, P.O. Box 104, Pretoria 0001, South Africa. TEL 27-12-574009. FAX 27-12-571029. Ed. F. Von Breitenbach. bk.rev. circ. 2,500. (back issues avail.) **Indexed:** Forest.Abstr., Ind.S.A.Per. **Document type:** academic/scholarly publication.
—BLDSC (4968.350000).

581   II   ISSN 0250-9768
CODEN: JETBDQ
JOURNAL OF ECONOMIC AND TAXONOMIC BOTANY. (Text in English) 1976. q. Rs.2550($180) Scientific Publishers, Journals Division, P.O. Box 91, 5A, New Pali Rd., Jodhpur 342 001, India. TEL 91-291-33323. Ed. J.K. Maheshwari. **Indexed:** Forest.Abstr. **Document type:** academic/scholarly publication.
—BLDSC (4972.620000); Linda Hall.

JOURNAL OF EVOLUTIONARY BIOLOGY. see *BIOLOGY — Genetics*

581　　　　UK　　ISSN 0022-0957
QK1　　　　　　　CODEN: JEBOA6
JOURNAL OF EXPERIMENTAL BOTANY. 1950. m. £370($660) (effective 1997). (Society for Experimental Biology) Oxford University Press, Academic Division, Great Clarendon St., Oxford OX2 6DP, England. TEL 44-1865-267907. FAX 44-1865-267485. TELEX 837330-OXPRES-G. E-mail: jnl.info@oup.co.uk; URL: http://www.oup.co.uk/journals. (U.S. subscr. to: Oxford University Press Inc., 2001 Evans Rd., Cary, NC 27513. TEL 800-852-7323. FAX 919-677-1714) Ed. Bill Davies; Pub. Steven Johnson. R&P contact: Joolz Longley. adv.; bk.rev.; index. circ. 1,500. (also avail. in microform from UMI) **Indexed:** Abstr.Bull.Inst.Pap.Chem., ASCA, Bibl.Agri., Biol.Abstr., Biol.& Agr.Ind., Biotech.Abstr., Cadscan, Chem.Abstr., Chem.Cit.Ind., Cott.& Trop.Fibr.Abstr., Crop Physiol.Abstr., Curr.Cont., Deep Sea Res.& Oceanogr.Abstr., Excerp.Med., Fababean Abstr., Field Crop Abstr., Food Sci.& Tech.Abstr., Forest.Abstr., Forest Prod.Abstr., Helminthol.Abstr., Herb.Abstr., Herb.Abstr., Hort.Abstr., Ind.Sci.Rev., Int.Abstr.Biol.Sci., Irr.& Drain.Abstr., Lead Abstr., Maize Abstr., Ornam.Hort., Plant Breed.Abstr., Plant Grow.Reg.Abstr., Potato Abstr., Rev.Plant Path., Rice Abstr., Sci.Cit.Ind., Seed Abstr., Sel.Water Res.Abstr., Soils & Fert., Soyabean Abstr., Triticale Abstr., Trop.Oil Seeds Abstr., VITIS, Weed Abstr., Zincscan. **Document type:** academic/scholarly publication. ●Also available online. —BLDSC (4981.000000); CASDDS; CISTI; EMDOCS; Genuine Article; KR SourceOne; Linda Hall; SWETS; UMI; UnCover. **CCC.**
Description: Presents papers in the fields of plant physiology, biochemistry, biophysics, molecular biology, and related topics.

JOURNAL OF FRUIT AND ORNAMENTAL PLANT RESEARCH. see *GARDENING AND HORTICULTURE*

JOURNAL OF HERBS, SPICES & MEDICINAL PLANTS. see *GARDENING AND HORTICULTURE*

581　　　　JA　　ISSN 0022-2062
JOURNAL OF JAPANESE BOTANY/SHOKUBUTSU KENKYU ZASSHI. 1916. bi-m. 8500 Yen. Tsumura & Co., Tsumura Laboratory, 3586 Yoshiwara Ami-machi, Inashiki-gun, Ibaraki-ken 300-11, Japan. FAX 81-298-89-2158. Ed. Shoji Shibata. adv. contact: Minoru Okada. bk.rev. circ. 1,200. **Indexed:** Biol.Abstr., Curr.Adv.Ecol.Sci., Field Crop Abstr., Herb.Abstr., Ornam.Hort., Rev.Plant Path. **Document type:** bulletin.
—BLDSC (5008.900000); Linda Hall.

JOURNAL OF MEDICAL & VETERINARY MYCOLOGY. see *MEDICAL SCIENCES — Communicable Diseases*

JOURNAL OF MEDICAL AND VETERINARY MYCOLOGY. SUPPLEMENT. see *MEDICAL SCIENCES — Communicable Diseases*

581　　　　II　　ISSN 0971-3719
JOURNAL OF MYCOPATHOLOGICAL RESEARCH. 1955. s-a. $40. Indian Mycological Society, Department of Botany, University of Calcutta, 35 B.C. Rd., Calcutta 700 019, India. TEL 91-33-551-4189. FAX 91-33-475-3681. Ed. Balen Nandi; Pub. A.K. Manna. adv.; pub $200. bk.rev. circ. 500. **Indexed:** Biol.Abstr., Indian Sci.Abstr., Rev.Plant Path. **Document type:** academic/scholarly publication.
—BLDSC (5021.172000); CISTI; Linda Hall; UnCover.
Formerly: Indian Journal of Mycological Research (ISSN 0537-2054)
Description: Covers taxonomy, physiology and biochemistry of microorganisms, molecular basis of host-parasite interactions, industrial microbiology and microbial biotechnology.
Refereed Serial

JOURNAL OF OILSEEDS RESEARCH. see *AGRICULTURE — Crop Production And Soil*

561　　　　II　　ISSN 0022-3379
QE993　　　　　CODEN: JPLYAR
JOURNAL OF PALYNOLOGY. (Text in English) 1966. s-a. Rs.700($60) (Palynological Society of India) Today and Tomorrow's Printers & Publishers, 24B-5 Desh Bandhu Gupta Rd., Karol Bagh, New Dehli 110 005, India. TEL 91-11-5721928. (Dist. in U.S. by: Scholarly Publications, 2825 Wilcrest Dr., Ste. 255, Houston, TX 77042. TEL 713-781-0070) Ed. A.R. Kulkarnj Bir Bahadur. adv.; bk.rev.; cum. index. circ. 400. (back issues avail.) **Indexed:** Biol.Abstr., Chem.Abstr., Chem.Cit.Ind., Curr.Adv.Ecol.Sci., Curr.Cont., GeoRef., Rev.Med.& Vet.Mycol. **Document type:** academic/scholarly publication.
—CASDDS; CISTI; Linda Hall; UnCover. **CCC.**
Formerly (until 1972): Palynological Bulletin (ISSN 0031-0492)
Description: Covers all aspects of pollen spore studies, from algae to angiosperms, from the present day plants to fossil plants.

589.3　　　　US　　ISSN 0022-3646
QK564　　　　　CODEN: JPYLAJ
JOURNAL OF PHYCOLOGY. 1965. 6/yr. $295 (effective 1997). (Phycological Society of America) Allen Press, Inc., 1041 New Hampshire St., Box 1897, Lawrence, KS 66044. TEL 913-843-1221. FAX 913-843-1274. (Co-sponsor: American Association for the Advancement of Science) Ed. Carole A. Lembi. abstr.; bibl.; charts. circ. 2,000. (back issues avail.) **Indexed:** Abstr.Bull.Inst.Pap.Chem., ASCA, Biol.Abstr., Chem.Abstr., Chem.Cit.Ind., Curr.Adv.Cell & Devel.Biol., Curr.Adv.Ecol.Sci., Curr.Cont., Deep Sea Res.& Oceanogr.Abstr., Ecol.Abstr., Geo.Abstr.H.G., GeoRef., Ind.Sci.Rev., INIS Atomind., Ocean.Abstr., Pollut.Abstr., Sci.Cit.Ind., Sel.Water Res.Abstr., W.R.C.Inf. **Document type:** academic/scholarly publication.
—BLDSC (5035.500000); CASDDS; CISTI; EMDOCS; Genuine Article; Linda Hall; SWETS; UnCover.
Refereed Serial

581.2　　　　GW　　ISSN 0931-1785
　　　　　　　　　CODEN: JPHYEB
JOURNAL OF PHYTOPATHOLOGY/PHYTOPATHOLOGISCHE ZEITSCHRIFT. (Text in English or German; summaries in English and German) 1930. 12/yr. DM.1771 in Europe; rest of world DM.1788 (effective 1998). Blackwell Wissenschaft, Kurfuerstendamm 57, 10707 Berlin, Germany. TEL 49-30-32790634. FAX 49-30-32790610. E-mail: aboverwalt@blackwis.de; URL: http://www.blackwis.com. Ed.Bd. adv.: B&W page DM.560; trim 190 x 122. bk.rev.; illus.; stat.; index. circ. 700. (also avail. in microform from PMC; back issues avail.) **Indexed:** ASCA, Bio-Contr.News & Info., Biol.Abstr., Biotech.Abstr., Chem.Abstr., Cott.& Trop.Fibr.Abstr., Crop Physiol.Abstr., Curr.Adv.Ecol.Sci., Curr.Cont., Environ.Per.Bibl. (1972-1993), Excerp.Med., Fababean Abstr., Field Crop Abstr., Forest.Abstr., Helminthol.Abstr., Hort.Abstr., Maize Abstr., Ornam.Hort., Plant Grow.Reg.Abstr., Potato Abstr., Rev.Plant Path., Rice Abstr., Sci.Cit.Ind., Seed Abstr., Soils & Fert., Soyabean Abstr., Triticale Abstr., VITIS. **Document type:** academic/scholarly publication.
—BLDSC (5040.250000); CASDDS; CISTI; Genuine Article; SWETS. **CCC.**
Description: Publishes original scientific articles and short communications on all aspects of phytopathology, and on relevant related subjects.

581　　　　II　　ISSN 0256-436X
QK640　　　　　CODEN: JPMOE6
JOURNAL OF PLANT ANATOMY AND MORPHOLOGY. (Text and summaries in English) 1980. a. Rs.300($70) Scientific Publishers, Journals Division, P.O. Box 91, 5A, New Pali Rd., Jodhpur 342 001, India. TEL 91-291-33323. Ed. J.A. Inamdar. adv.; bk.rev. circ. 450. (back issues avail.) **Indexed:** Biol.Abstr., Excerp.Bot., Forest.Abstr., Forest Prod.Abstr., Hort.Abstr., Weed Abstr. **Document type:** academic/scholarly publication.

581　　　　US　　ISSN 0721-7595
QK745　　　　　CODEN: JPGRDI
JOURNAL OF PLANT GROWTH REGULATION. 1981. q. $269 (effective 1998). Springer-Verlag, Life Science Journals, 175 Fifth Ave., New York, NY 10010. TEL 212-460-1500. FAX 212-473-6272. E-mail: orders@springer-ny.com; URL: http://www.springer-ny.com. (N. American subscr. to: Journal Fulfillment Services, Box 2485, Secaucus, NJ 07096-2485. TEL 800-777-4643. FAX 201-348-4505; Elsewhere: Heidelberger Platz 3, 1000 Berlin 33, Germany. TEL 49-30-8207-0. FAX 49-308207448) (Co-sponsors: International Plant Growth Substances Association; Plant Growth Regulator Society of America) Ed. Thomas C. Moore. R&P contact: Ian Gross. adv. contact: Robert Vrooman. (also avail. in microform from UMI; reprint service avail. from ISI) **Indexed:** Abstr.Bull.Inst.Pap.Chem., ASCA, Bibl.Agri., Biotech.Abstr., Chem.Abstr., Cott.& Trop.Fibr.Abstr., Crop Physiol.Abstr., Curr.Adv.Ecol.Sci., Curr.Cont., Fababean Abstr., Field Crop Abstr., Forest.Abstr., Herb.Abstr., Hort.Abstr., Ind.Sci.Rev., Maize Abstr., Ornam.Hort., Plant Grow.Reg.Abstr., Potato Abstr., Rice Abstr., Sci.Cit.Ind., Seed Abstr., Sel.Water Res.Abstr., Soils & Fert., Soyabean Abstr., Triticale Abstr., VITIS, Weed Abstr. **Document type:** academic/scholarly publication.
—BLDSC (5040.514300); CASDDS; CISTI; Genuine Article; SWETS; UMI; UnCover. **CCC.**
Description: Focuses on natural and synthetic plant growth substances and on their effects on plant growth and development.
Refereed Serial

581　　　　US　　ISSN 0190-4167
QK867　　　　　CODEN: JPNUDS
JOURNAL OF PLANT NUTRITION. 1979. m. $1195 (foreign $1240) (effective 1998). Marcel Dekker Journals, 270 Madison Ave., New York, NY 10016. TEL 212-696-9000. FAX 212-685-4540. TELEX 421419 MARDEEK. (Subscr. to: Box 5017, Monticello, NY 12701) Ed. J. Benton Jones, Jr. (also avail. in microform from RPI) **Indexed:** Acid Rain Abstr., Acid Rain Ind., Agri.Eng.Abstr., ASCA, Bibl.Agri., Biol.Abstr., Biol.& Agr.Ind., Cadscan, Chem.Abstr., Cott.& Trop.Fibr.Abstr., Crop Physiol.Abstr., Curr.Adv.Ecol.Sci., Curr.Cont., Environ.Per.Bibl. (1979-), Field Crop Abstr., Forest.Abstr., Herb.Abstr., Hort.Abstr., Lead Abstr., Maize Abstr., Plant Grow.Reg.Abstr., Rev.Plant Path., Rice Abstr., Sci.Cit.Ind., Seed Abstr., Soils & Fert., Sorghum & Millets Abstr., Soyabean Abstr., Triticale Abstr., Trop.Oil Seeds Abstr., VITIS, Zincscan. **Document type:** academic/scholarly publication.
—BLDSC (5040.515000); CASDDS; CISTI; EMDOCS; Genuine Article; KR SourceOne; SWETS; UMI; UnCover. **CCC.**
Refereed Serial

571.9　　　　IT
　　　　　　　　　CODEN: RPVGA9
JOURNAL OF PLANT PATHOLOGY. (Text in English, Italian; summaries in English) 1892. q. Lit.150000 (foreign $100) (effective 1997). University of Pisa, Via del Borghetto 80, 56124 Pisa, Italy. TEL 39-50-571556. FAX 39-50-543564. E-mail: gvann@agr.unipi.it. (Subscr. to: Editioni ETS, Piazza Torricelli 4, 56126 Pisa, Italy. TEL 39-50-20158. FAX 39-50-29544) Ed. Giovanni Vannacci. adv.; bk.rev.; bibl.; charts; illus.; index. circ. 300. **Indexed:** Biol.Abstr., Chem.Abstr., Curr.Adv.Ecol.Sci., Curr.Cont., Helminthol.Abstr., Mycol.Abstr., Potato Abstr., Rev.Plant Path., VITIS. **Document type:** academic/scholarly publication.
—CASDDS; Linda Hall.
Formerly: Rivista di Patologia Vegetale (ISSN 0035-6441)
Description: Publishes original research papers and short notes on fundamental and applied aspects of plant pathology.
Refereed Serial

BIOLOGY — BOTANY

581.1   **GW**   ISSN 0176-1617
QK1   **CODEN:** JPPHEY
JOURNAL OF PLANT PHYSIOLOGY. (Text in German; summaries in German, English) 1909. irreg. (6 nos./vol.). DM.1666 (foreign £727) (effective 1997). Gustav Fischer Verlag, Villengang 2, 07745 Jena, Germany. TEL 49-3641-626430. FAX 49-3641-626421. E-mail: office.j@gfischer.de. (Subscr. to: Stockton Press, Subscription Dept., Houndmills, Basingstoke, Hants RG21 6XS, England) Ed. M. Bopp. adv.; bk.rev.; abstr.; charts; illus.; index. circ. 850. **Indexed:** Abstr.Bull.Inst.Pap.Chem., ASCA, Biol.Abstr., Biotech.Abstr., Chem.Abstr., Crop Physiol.Abstr., Curr.Adv.Ecol.Sci., Curr.Cont., Field Crop Abstr., Food Sci.& Tech.Abstr., Forest.Abstr., Forest Prod.Abstr., Geo.Abstr, Herb.Abstr., Hort.Abstr., Ind.Sci.Rev., INIS Atomind., Irr.& Drain.Abstr., Maize Abstr., Ornam.Hort., Plant Breed.Abstr., Plant Grow.Reg.Abstr., Potato Abstr., Risk Abstr., Sci.Cit.Ind., Seed Abstr., Sel.Water Res.Abstr., Soils & Fert., Soyabean Abstr., Triticale Abstr., VITIS, Weed Abstr. **Document type:** academic/scholarly publication.
—BLDSC (5040.518500); CASDDS; CISTI; EMDOCS; Genuine Article; Linda Hall; SWETS; UMI; UnCover. **CCC.**
    Incorporates: Biochemie und Physiologie der Pflanzen (B P P) (ISSN 0015-3796); Formerly (until 1984): Zeitschrift fuer Pflanzenphysiologie (ISSN 0044-328X)

581   **JA**   ISSN 0918-9440
QK1   **CODEN:** JPLREA
JOURNAL OF PLANT RESEARCH. (Text in English) 1887. q. 18000 Yen (effective 1997). Botanical Society of Japan, Toshin Bldg., Hongo 2-27-2, Bunkyo-ku, Tokyo 113, Japan. TEL 81-3-3814-5675. FAX 81-3-3814-5352. Ed. Masamitsu Wada. adv. circ. 2,600. (also avail. in microfiche from IDC) **Indexed:** ASCA, Biol.Abstr., Chem.Abstr., Curr.Adv.Ecol.Sci., Curr.Adv.Plant Sci., Curr.Cont., Deep Sea Res.& Oceanogr.Abstr., Fababean Abstr., Field Crop Abstr., Forest.Abstr., Forest Prod.Abstr., Herb.Abstr., Hort.Abstr., Ind.Sci.Rev., INIS Atomind., Plant Breed.Abstr., Rice Abstr., Seed Abstr., So.Pac.Per.Ind. **Document type:** academic/scholarly publication.
—BLDSC (5040.522000); CASDDS; CISTI; Genuine Article; Linda Hall; SWETS; UnCover. **CCC.**
    Formerly: Botanical Magazine, Tokyo (ISSN 0006-808X)
    Description: Publishes original papers and review articles in all fields of plant sciences.
    Refereed Serial

581   **SW**   ISSN 1100-9233
WMLC L   **CODEN:** JVESEK
JOURNAL OF VEGETATION SCIENCE. (Text in English) 1990. bi-m. SEK 3000 (effective 1997). (International Association for Vegetation Science) Opulus Press AB, P.O. Box 25137, S-750 25 Uppsala, Sweden. TEL 46-18-32-06-62. FAX 46-18-32-13-68. Ed. E. van der Maarel. adv. contact: Elisabet Olsson. bk.rev. circ. 1,100. (back issues avail.) **Indexed:** ASCA, Biol.Abstr., Curr.Cont., Ecol.Abstr., Ecol.Zoo.& Plant Sci.Abstr. (1990-), Environ.Per.Bibl. (1990-), Geo.Abstr.H.G. **Document type:** academic/scholarly publication.
—BLDSC (5072.277000); CISTI; EMDOCS; Linda Hall; SWETS; UnCover.
    Description: Publishes original articles, short notes and review articles in the field of vegetation science, both methodological and theoretical studies, and descriptive and experimental studies of plant communities and plant populations.
    Refereed Serial

583.47   **GW**   ISSN 0022-7846
KAKTEEN UND ANDERE SUKKULENTEN. 1957. m. DM.65. Deutsche Kakteen Gesellschaft e.V., Nordstr. 30, 26939 Ovelgoenne, Germany. TEL 04480-1408. FAX 04480-1564. adv.; bibl.; charts; illus. **Indexed:** Biol.Abstr. **Document type:** academic/scholarly publication.
    Description: International in scope, containing original descriptions of new species, plus popular or scholarly articles covering field trips, botanical gardens, horticulture, and geographic sites.

581   **JA**
KAN'AOI KENKYU/KANAOI RESEARCH. (Text in Japanese) 1985. a. Yasuo Koshimizu, Pub., 1190 Shimootsuki, Hatano-shi, Kanagawa-ken 257, Japan.

581   **FI**   ISSN 0453-3402
QK600   **CODEN:** KRSTA4
KARSTENIA; the mycological journal. (Text in English) 1950. s-a. FIM 120($25) per vol. in Nordic countries; elsewhere $30 (effective 1997). Finnish Mycological Society, P.O. Box 7, FIN-00014 University of Helsinki, Finland. TEL 358-9-708-4784. FAX 358-9-708-4830. E-mail: orvo.vitikainen@helsinki.fi. Ed. Orvo Vitikainen. bk.rev.; index. circ. 800. **Indexed:** Biol.Abstr., Chem.Abstr, Curr.Adv.Ecol.Sci., Forest.Abstr., Forest Prod.Abstr., Rev.Plant Path. **Document type:** academic/scholarly publication.
—CASDDS; CISTI.
    Refereed Serial

581   **UK**   ISSN 0075-5974
QK1   **CODEN:** KEWBAF
KEW BULLETIN. 1946. q. £130 (effective 1994). H.M.S.O., 51 Nine Elms Ln., London SW8 5DR, England. TEL 44-171-873-0011. FAX 44-171-873-8247. (Subscr. to: H.M.S.O., Publications Centre, P.O. Box 271, London SW8 5DT, England. TEL 44-171-873-9090. FAX 44-171-873-8200) bk.rev.; illus. circ. 550. (also avail. in microform from UMI; microfilm from BHP; reprint service avail. from KTO) **Indexed:** Apic.Abstr., Biol.Abstr., Curr.Adv.Ecol.Sci., Field Crop Abstr., Forest.Abstr., Forest Prod.Abstr., Herb.Abstr., Hort.Abstr., Ornam.Hort., Plant Breed.Abstr., Rev.Plant Path., Soils & Fert. **Document type:** bulletin, government publication.
—BLDSC (5091.000000); CISTI; EMDOCS; Linda Hall; SWETS; UMI; UnCover.

581   **UK**   ISSN 0075-5982
KEW BULLETIN. ADDITIONAL SERIES. 1958. irreg. £40. H.M.S.O., 51 Nine Elms Ln., London SW8 5DR, England. TEL 44-171-873-0011. FAX 44-171-873-8247. circ. 500. **Indexed:** Biol.Abstr., Forest.Abstr. **Document type:** bulletin, government publication.

581   **UK**
KEW RECORD OF TAXONOMIC LITERATURE (YEAR). a. £70. H.S.M.O., Royal Botanical Gardens, Kew, P.O. Box 276, London SW8 5DT, England. TEL 071-873-9090. FAX 071-870-0011.

581   **UK**   ISSN 0307-2835
KEW RECORD OF TAXONOMIC LITERATURE RELATING TO VASCULAR PLANTS. 1971. q. £110 (effective 1994). H.M.S.O., 51 Nine Elms Ln., London SW8 5DR, England. TEL 44-171-873-0011. FAX 44-171-873-8247. (Subscr. to: H.M.S.O. Publications Centre, P.O. Box 276, London SW8 5DT, England. TEL 44-171-873-9090. FAX 44-171-873-8200) (Co-sponsor: Royal Botanic Gardens) Ed. J.M. Lock. circ. 300. **Indexed:** Forest.Abstr., Forest Prod.Abstr. **Document type:** abstracting/indexing, government publication.
—BLDSC (5091.140000).
    Description: Lists references to all publications on the taxonomy of flowering plants, gymnosperms, and ferns.

581   **JA**   ISSN 0510-3517
KIHARA INSTITUTE FOR BIOLOGICAL RESEARCH. WHEAT INFORMATION SERVICE. (Text in English) 1950. 2/yr. 2000 Yen($25) (donation). Kihara Foundation, 641-12 Maioka-cho, Totsuka-ku, Yokohama 244, Japan. TEL 81-45-825-3487. FAX 81-45-825-3307. E-mail: Tsujimoto@yokohama.cu.ac.jp. Ed. Kozo Nishikawa. R&P contact: Kozo Nishikawa. adv. contact: Kozo Nishikawa. bk.rev. circ. 750. **Indexed:** Biol.Abstr., Field Crop Abstr., Plant Breed.Abstr., Plant Grow.Reg.Abstr., Seed Abstr. **Document type:** academic/scholarly publication.
—UnCover.
    Description: Covers genetics and breeding of wheat (Triticum) and its related genera.

589.2   **JA**   ISSN 0388-8266
    CODEN: KJKKAH
KINJIN KENKYUJO KENKYU HOKOKU/TOTTORI MYCOLOGICAL INSTITUTE. REPORTS. (Text in English, Japanese) 1961. a. 4000 Yen. Nihon Kinoko Senta, Kinjin Kenkyujo - Japan Kinoko Research Centre, Tottori Mycological Institute, 211 Hirohata, Kokoge, Tottori-shi, Tottori-ken 689-11, Japan. TEL 81-857-51-8111. FAX 81-857-53-1986. circ. 700. **Indexed:** Agrindex, Biol.Abstr., INIS Atomind., Jap.Per.Ind.
—BLDSC (7619.600000).
    Description: Covers fungal taxonomy, edology, physiology and genetics, and mushroom cultivation.

581   **JA**   ISSN 0914-3823
KINKI SHOKUBUTSU DOKOKAI KAIHO/KINKI BOTANICAL SOCIETY. NEWS. (Text in Japanese) 1951. 3/yr. Kinki Shokubutsu Dokokai - Kinki Botanical Society, c/o Mr. Kozi Hirano, 36-15 Sayamada 3-chome, Sakai-shi, Osaka 581, Japan.

581   **JA**
KINKI SHOKUBUTSU DOKOKAI KAISHI/KINKI BOTANICAL SOCIETY. BULLETIN. (Text in Japanese) 1950. biennial. membership. Kinki Shokubutsu Dokokai - Kinki Botanical Society, c/o Mr. Kozi Hirano, 36-15, Sayamadai 3-chome, Sakai-shi, Osaka 581, Japan. adv. (back issues avail.)

581.096891   **RH**   ISSN 0451-9930
QK381
KIRKIA; the Zimbabwe journal of botany. 1960. s-a. $20. (Ministry of Lands, Agriculture and Water Development, Research and Specialist Services) R & S S Information Services, P.O. Box CY 594, Causeway, Harare, Zimbabwe. TEL 263-4-725313. FAX 263-4-728317. Eds. M. Heads, J.R. Timberlake. bk.rev. circ. 600. (back issues avail.) **Indexed:** Biol.Abstr., Curr.Adv.Ecol.Sci., Excerp.Bot., Field Crop Abstr., Forest.Abstr., Forest Prod.Abstr., Herb.Abstr., Rev.Plant Path. **Document type:** academic/scholarly publication.
—BLDSC (5097.560000).

581   **JA**   ISSN 0387-7361
KITAKYUSHU SHOKUBUTSU TOMO NO KAI KAIHO/KITAKYUSHU BOTANICAL ASSOCIATION. JOURNAL. (Text in Japanese) 1979. a. Kitakyushu Shokubutsu Tomo no Kai - Kitakyushu Botanical Association, c/o Mr. Shigeru Kobayashi, 13-3 Ihori 3-chome, Kokura Kita-ku, Kitakyushu-shi, Fukuoka-ken 803, Japan.

581   **KO**   ISSN 0583-421X
QK370   **CODEN:** KJBOAI
KOREAN JOURNAL OF BOTANY. Key Title: Singmul Hakhoe Chi. (Text in English, Korean; abstract in English) 1958. q. 24000 Won($30) to individuals; institutions $60. Botanical Society of Korea, c/o Young Myung Kwon, Dept. of Biology, Seoul National University, Seoul 151-742, S. Korea. TEL 02-880-6676. FAX 02-872-6881. (Co-sponsor: Ministry of Education) Ed. Kwang-Woong Lee. circ. 800. (back issues avail.) **Indexed:** Biol.Abstr., Curr.Adv.Ecol.Sci., INIS Atomind. **Document type:** academic/scholarly publication.
—CASDDS; CISTI; Linda Hall.
    Description: Publishes original research and review articles on all aspects of plant science, including information on autotrophic microorganisms.

589.2   **KO**   ISSN 0253-651X
QK600   **CODEN:** HKCHDD
KOREAN JOURNAL OF MYCOLOGY. (Text in English, Korean) 1972. q. 30000 Won($40) membership. Korean Society of Mycology, c/o Myung-Hwan Cho, Secy. Gen., Dept. of Agrobiology, Dongguk University, No. 26, Pil-dong, 3-ga, Chung-gu, Seoul 100-715, S. Korea. Ed. Kwon Sang Yoon. bk.rev. circ. 1,000. (back issues avail.) **Indexed:** Biol.Abstr., Chem.Abstr., Forest.Abstr., Rev.Med.& Vet.Mycol., Rev.Plant Path., Soils & Fert. **Document type:** academic/scholarly publication.
—BLDSC (5113.567000); CASDDS; CISTI.

589.2   **KO**
KOREAN SOCIETY OF MYCOLOGY. NEWSLETTER. (Text in English, Korean) s-a. 15000 Won($40) membership. Korean Society of Mycology, c/o Myung-Hwan Cho, Secy. Gen., Dept. of Agrobiology, Dongguk University, No. 26, Pil-dong, 3-ga, Chung-gu, Seoul 100-715, S. Korea. TEL 82-269-6980. FAX 82-269-6980. Ed. Kwon Sang Yoon. **Document type:** bulletin.

581   **AG**   ISSN 0075-7314
QK1   **CODEN:** KURTAK
KURTZIANA. (Text in English and Spanish; summaries in English) 1961. a. $15. Universidad Nacional de Cordoba, Museo Botanico, Casilla de Correo 495, 5000 Cordoba, Argentina. TEL 54-51-332104. TELEX 51822 BUCOR AR. E-mail: postmaster@imbiv.edu.ar. Ed. Armando T. Hunziker. bk.rev. circ. 400. **Indexed:** Biol.Abstr. **Document type:** academic/scholarly publication.
    Description: Illustrated articles on different branches of botany, with emphasis on embryology, morphology and taxonomy.

BIOLOGY — BOTANY

581 — **JA**
KYOTO SHOKUBUTSU/KYOTO BOTANY. (Text in Japanese) bi-m. Kyoto Shokubutsu Dokokai - Kyoto Botanical Association, c/o Mr. Shin'ichi Nishizawa, Omiya Nishi Iru, Motosenganji, Kamigyo-ku, Kyoto 602, Japan.

581 — **JA**
KYOTO UNIVERSITY. FACULTY OF AGRICULTURE. PLANT GERM-PLASM INSTITUTE. REPORT. (Text in English) 1974. irreg. Kyoto University, Faculty of Agriculture, Plant Germ-Plasm Institute - Kyoto Daigaku Nogakubu Fuzoku Shokubutsu Seishokushitsu Kenkyu Shisetsu, 1 Nakajo, Mozumecho, Muko-shi, Kyoku 617, Japan.

581 — **SP** — **ISSN 1132-2365**
LACTARIUS. 1992. a. 500 ptas. (effective 1998). Universidad de Jaen, Facultad de Ciencias Experimentales, Herbario Jaen, 23071 Jaen, Spain. TEL 34-953-212159. FAX 34-953-212141. (Dist. by: Libreria Agricola, Fernando VI, 2, 28004 Madrid, Spain. TEL 34-91-4190940) (Co-sponsor: Asociacion Micologica Lactarius) **Indexed:** Ind.SST. **Document type:** newspaper.

581 — **AU**
LANDESMUSEUM JOANNEUM. ABTEILUNG FUER BOTANIK. MITTEILUNGEN. (Text in German; summaries in English) 1972. irreg. price varies. Landesmuseum Joanneum, Abteilung fuer Botanik, Raubergasse 10, A-8010 Graz, Austria. TEL 43-316-80174750. FAX 43-316-80174800. TELEX 311838-LRGGRA. (Co-sponsor: Steiermaerkische Landesregierung) Ed. Detlef Ernet. bk.rev.; bibl.; illus. circ. 600. **Document type:** academic/scholarly publication.
Description: Results of research on the flora and vegetation of the province of Styria.

581 — **SP** — **ISSN 0210-9778**
QK329 **CODEN: LAZAEE**
LAZAROA. 1979. a. 3000 ptas.($32) (effective 1997). Universidad Complutense de Madrid, Facultad de Farmacia, Departamento de Biologia Vegetal II, Servicio de Publicaciones, Calle Issac Peral s-n, Ciudad Universitaria, 28040 Madrid, Spain. TEL 34-1-3946934. FAX 34-1-3946954. Ed. Salvador Rivas-Martinez. (back issues avail.) **Indexed:** Ecol.Abstr., Ind.SST. **Document type:** academic/scholarly publication.
Description: Covers taxonomy, flora, plant-sociology, geobotany.

LECTINS. see *BIOLOGY — Biological Chemistry*

581 — **BE** — **ISSN 0457-4184**
LEJEUNIA; revue de botanique. (Text in English or French; summaries in English and French) N.S. 1961. irreg., no.152, 1996. price varies. Botanical Society in Liege, Universite de Liege, Departement de Botanique, Sart Tilman, B-4000 Liege, Belgium. TEL 32-4-3663850. FAX 32-4-3663840. Ed. J. Lambinon. R&P contact: J. Lambinon. (back issues avail.) **Indexed:** Agri.Ind., Biol.Abstr., Bull.Signal, Curr.Adv.Ecol.Sci., Ecol.Abstr., Field Crop Abstr., Herb.Abstr., IDA. **Document type:** academic/scholarly publication, bulletin.
Description: Publishes studies on topics in botany, with particular emphasis on the flora and vegetation of Belgium, France, and Africa.
Refereed Serial

588.2 — **UK** — **ISSN 0024-2829**
QK580.7 **CODEN: LCHNB8**
THE LICHENOLOGIST; an international journal. 1968. bi-m. £229 (effective 1998). (British Lichen Society) Academic Press Ltd. (Subsidiary of: Harcourt Brace & Company Ltd.), 24-28 Oval Rd., London NW1 7DX, England. TEL 44-171-267-4466. FAX 44-171-482-2293. TELEX 25775 ACPRES G. E-mail: apsubs@acad.com; URL: http://www.hbuk.co.uk/ap/lichenol; http://www.europe.idealibrary.com/. (Subscr. to: Harcourt Brace & Company Ltd., Foots Cray High St., Sidcup, Kent DA14 5HP, England. TEL 44-181-300-3322. FAX 44-181-309-0807) Ed. D.H. Brown. R&P contact: Catherine John. adv.: B&W page £300, color page £610; adv. contact: Nik Screen. bk.rev.; charts; illus.; cum.index. circ. 900. (reprint service avail. from SWZ) **Indexed:** ASCA, Biol.Abstr., Chem.Abstr., Curr.Adv.Ecol.Sci., Curr.Cont., Energy Ind., Energy Info.Abstr., Excerp.Med., Geo.Abstr, Ind.Sci.Rev., Rev.Plant Path., Sci.Cit.Ind., Soils & Fert. **Document type:** academic/scholarly publication.
•Also available online.
—BLDSC (5207.850000); CASDDS; CISTI; EMDOCS; Genuine Article; Linda Hall; UnCover. **CCC.**
Description: Devoted to the study of lichen-forming fungi and reports of lichenology worldwide.

579.7 — **VE** — **ISSN 1316-4899**
▼**LICHENS.** (Text in English; summaries in various languages) 1997. s-a. $650 to institutions (effective 1997). Centro de Investigacion y Reproduccion de Especies Silvestres, Apartado Posta 397, Merida 5101, Venezuela. TEL 58-74-712939. FAX 58-74-712939. E-mail: cires@ciens.ula.ve. Ed. Hector Fernando Aguilar; Pub. Hector Fernando Aguilar. adv. contact: Lieselotte Hoeger de Aguilar. bk.rev.; bibl.; illus. circ. 2,500. (reprint service avail. from SWZ)
Refereed Serial

581 — **AG** — **ISSN 0075-9481**
QK1 **CODEN: LLOAAW**
LILLOA; revista de botanica. (Text in Latin, Spanish; summaries in English, French, German, Italian) 1937. irreg., vol.37, no.2, 1990. exchange basis only. Fundacion Miguel Lillo, Centro de Informacion Geo-Biologico, Miguel Lillo 251, 4000 San Miguel de Tucuman, Argentina. Ed. Jose A. Haedo Rossi. charts; illus.; bibl. (back issues avail.) **Indexed:** Biol.Abstr., Bull.Signal., Field Crop Abstr., Forest.Abstr., Forest Prod.Abstr., Herb.Abstr., Hort.Abstr., Plant Breed.Abstr., Ref.Zh., Rev.Plant Path.
—BLDSC (5218.000000); CISTI.

581 — **UK** — **ISSN 0024-4074**
QH1 **CODEN: BJLSAF**
LINNEAN SOCIETY. BOTANICAL JOURNAL. 1855. m. (3 vols./yr.). £504 (effective 1998). (Linnean Society of London) Academic Press Ltd. (Subsidiary of: Harcourt Brace & Company Ltd.), 24-28 Oval Rd., London NW1 7DX, England. TEL 44-171-267-4466. FAX 44-171-482-2293. TELEX 25775 ACPRES G. E-mail: apsubs@acad.com; URL: http://www.hbuk.co.uk/ap/botjls; http://www.europe.idealibrary.com/. (Subscr. to: Harcourt Brace & Company Ltd., Foots Cray High St., Sidcup, Kent DA14 5HP, England. TEL 44-181-300-3322. FAX 44-181-309-0807) Ed. D. Edwards. R&P contact: Catherine John. adv. contact: Nik Screen. bibl.; illus.; index. (also avail. in microform from BHP; reprint service avail. from SWZ) **Indexed:** ASCA, Bibl.Agri., Biol.Abstr., Br.Geol.Lit. (1972-), Chem.Abstr., Crop Physiol.Abstr., Curr.Adv.Ecol.Sci., Curr.Adv.Genetics & Molec.Biol., Curr.Cont., Field Crop Abstr., Forest.Abstr., Forest Prod.Abstr., GeoRef., Herb.Abstr., Hort.Abstr., Ind.Sci.Rev., Maize Abstr., Nutr.Abstr., Ornam.Hort., Plant Breed.Abstr., Rev.Plant Path., Sci.Cit.Ind., Seed Abstr., So.Pac.Per.Ind., Soils & Fert., Sport Fish.Abstr., Triticale Abstr., Weed Abstr., Wild.Rev. **Document type:** academic/scholarly publication.
•Also available online.
—BLDSC (2254.300000); CASDDS; CISTI; EMDOCS; Linda Hall; SWETS; UnCover. **CCC.**
Formerly: Linnean Society of London. Journal.
Description: Vehicle for the publication of original research papers in the plant sciences.

635 580 — **US** — **ISSN 1057-3224**
LONGWOOD GRADUATE PROGRAM SEMINARS. 1969. a. free. (Longwood Graduate Program in Public Horticulture Administration) University of Delaware, College of Agricultural Sciences, 153 Townsend Hall, Newark, DE 19717-1303. TEL 302-451-2517. FAX 302-292-3651. Eds. Lynn Hershey Chesson, James E. Swasey. circ. 800 (controlled).
Formerly (until 1985): Longwood Program Seminars (ISSN 0886-6384)
Description: Articles on issues in public horticulture management, with information on course offerings for the University of Delaware's master's program in public horticulture administration.

581 — **AG** — **ISSN 0076-0897**
QK261 **CODEN: LRTZA4**
LORENTZIA. 1970. irreg. $5. Universidad Nacional de Cordoba, Museo Botanico, Casilla de Correo 495, 5000 Cordoba, Argentina. TEL 54-51-332104. TELEX 51822 BUCOR AR. E-mail: postmaster@imbiv.edu.ar. Ed. Armando T. Hunziker. bk.rev. circ. 400. **Indexed:** Biol.Abstr. **Document type:** academic/scholarly publication.
Description: Original illustrated articles on different branches of botany, mostly morphology and taxonomy.

581 — **US** — **ISSN 0099-8400**
CODEN: MCLVAS
MCILVAINEA; journal of amateur Mycology. 1972. a. membership. North American Mycological Association, 3556 Oakwood, Ann Arbor, MI 48104-5213. TEL 313-971-2552. E-mail: kwcee@umich.edu. Ed. Betty Guttman. circ. 2,000. **Indexed:** Biol.Abstr., Rev.Plant Path. **Document type:** academic/scholarly publication.
Formerly: Journal McIlvanea.
Description: Publishes research articles on mushrooms.
Refereed Serial

581 — **US** — **ISSN 0024-9637**
CODEN: MADRAU
MADRONO; a West American journal of botany. 1916. q. $22 to individuals; institutions $50. California Botanical Society, c/o Margriet Wetherwax, Jepson Herbarium, University of California, Berkeley, CA 94720. TEL 510-643-7008. FAX 510-643-5390. Ed. Bob Patterson. bk.rev.; bibl.; charts; illus.; index. circ. 946. (back issues avail.) **Indexed:** Biol.Abstr., Chem.Abstr., Curr.Adv.Ecol.Sci., Field Crop Abstr., Forest.Abstr., Forest Prod.Abstr., Herb.Abstr., Int.Aerosp.Abstr., Rev.Plant Path., Seed Abstr., Sel.Water Res.Abstr., Soils & Fert., Sport Fish.Abstr., Wild.Rev., Zoo.Rec. **Document type:** monographic series.
—CISTI; Linda Hall; SWETS; UnCover.

581 — **HU** — **ISSN 0076-2482**
QR1
MAGYARORSZAG KULTURFLORAJA. (Text in Latin and Hungarian) 1956. irreg., no.67, 1996. price varies. (Magyar Tudomanyos Akademia) Akademiai Kiado Rt., P.O. Box 245, H-1519 Budapest, Hungary. TEL 36-1-2043976. FAX 36-1-2043973. **Indexed:** Biol.Abstr.

MANITOBA NATURALISTS SOCIETY BULLETIN. see *CONSERVATION*

MARSCHENRAT ZUR FOERDERUNG DER FORSCHUNG IM KUESTENGEBIET DER NORDSEE. NACHRICHTEN. see *SCIENCES: COMPREHENSIVE WORKS*

581 — **DK** — **ISSN 0108-1683**
MEDDELELSER FRA SORTSAFPROEVNINGEN/DANISH GAZETTE FOR PLANT VARIETIES; information om plantenyhedsbeskyttelse og sortslisteoptagelse. (Text in Danish, English, French and German) 1982. 5/yr. DKK 199 to individuals; libraries free. Statens Planteavlsudvalg, Afdeling for Sortsafproevning, Teglvaerksvej 10, Tystofte, DK-4230 Skaelskor, Denmark. TEL 45 53 59 61 41. FAX 45-53-59-01-66. Dir. Jutta Rasmussen. circ. 260. **Document type:** bulletin.
Formerly: Bekendtgoerelser fra Plantenyhedsnaevnet.
Description: Information on variety listing and plant breeders' rights, pertinent legislation and news of the EEC and the International Union for Protection of Plant Varieties.

MEDICINAL AND AROMATIC PLANTS. see *MEDICAL SCIENCES — Abstracting, Bibliographies, Statistics*

BIOLOGY — BOTANY

MEDITERRANEA. SERIE DE ESTUDIOS BIOLOGICOS. see
BIOLOGY — Zoology

581 367 UK ISSN 0955-8276
MESEMB STUDY BULLETIN. (Text in English, Latin) 1986. q. £6 (foreign £9). Mesemb Study Group, Brenfield, Bolney Rd., Ansty, W. Sussex RH17 5AW, England. TEL 44-1444-441193. FAX 44-1444-454061. E-mail: msg@mace.demon.co.uk; URL: http://www.demon.co.uk/mace/msg.html. Ed. Suzanne Mace. adv. contact: Suzanne Mace. bk.rev.; illus.; index every 2 yrs. circ. 500. (back issues avail.) **Document type:** bulletin.
  Description: Contains information about Mesembryanthemaceae plants.

581 US ISSN 0026-203X
QK1 CODEN: MBOTAU
MICHIGAN BOTANIST. 1962. q. $16 (effective 1997). Michigan Botanical Club, Inc., University of Michigan Herbarium, 2001 N. University Bldg., 1205 N. University Ave., Ann Arbor, MI 48109-1057. TEL 313-764-2407. E-mail: bjmadsen@umich.edu; URL: http://www.herb.las.umich.edu/umherb.htm. Ed. Barbara Madsen. adv. contact: Thomas Clough. bk.rev.; bibl.; cum.index every 3 yrs. circ. 800. **Indexed:** Biol.Abstr., Curr.Adv.Ecol.Sci., Curr.Cont., Ecol.Abstr., Excerp.Bot, Geo.Abstr., Mich.Mag.Ind., Rev.Plant Path. **Document type:** academic/scholarly publication.
—BLDSC (5753.650000); CISTI; EMDOCS; KR SourceOne; UnCover.
  Description: Papers of scientific interest on various areas of botany for the Great Lakes region.
  Refereed Serial

581 IT ISSN 0394-2597
MICOLOGIA E VEGETAZIONE MEDITERRANEA. (Text in English, Italian) 1986. s-a. L.25000. Gruppo Edologista Micologico Abruzzese, Casella Postale 307, 67051 Avezzano, Italy. TEL 39-863-23223. bibl.; illus. circ. 1,200.

589.2 IT ISSN 0390-0460
QK600 CODEN: MIITDI
MICOLOGIA ITALIANA. 1972. 3/yr. L.35000 (effective 1996). (Unione Micologica Italiana) Edagricole S.p.A., Via Emilia Levante 31, 40139 Bologna, Italy. TEL 39-51-492211. FAX 39-51-493660. Ed. Gilberto Govi. adv.: B&W page L.700000, color page L.1100000; 140 x 205. bk.rev.; index. circ. 3,900. **Indexed:** Apic.Abstr., Biol.Abstr., Forest.Abstr., Rev.Med.& Vet.Mycol., Rev.Plant Path., Soils & Fert.
—BLDSC (5756.700000); Linda Hall.
  Description: Covers ecology, toxicology, physiology, biochemistry and the production of macro-fungi.

579.5 RU ISSN 0026-3648
CODEN: MIFIB2
MIKOLOGIYA I FITOPATOLOGIYA. 1967. bi-m. $131 (effective 1998). (Rossiiskaya Akademiya Nauk) Izdatel'stvo Nauka, 90 Profsoyuznaya ul., 117864 Moscow, Russia. TEL 095-336-0266. FAX 095-240-2220. (Dist. in U.S. by: Victor Kamkin Inc., 4956 Boiling Brook Pkwy., Rockville, MD 20852. TEL 301-881-5973. FAX 301-881-1637) **Indexed:** ASCA, Biol.Abstr., Biotech.Abstr., Chem.Abstr., Cott.& Trop.Fibr.Abstr., Crop Physiol.Abstr., Curr.Adv.Ecol.Sci., Curr.Cont., Dairy Sci.Abstr., Forest.Abstr., Hort.Abstr., Ind.Sci.Rev., Maize Abstr., Plant Grow.Reg.Abstr., Rev.Med.& Vet.Mycol., Rev.Plant Path., Rice Abstr., Sci.Cit.Ind., Seed Abstr., Soils & Fert., Soyabean Abstr., Triticale Abstr.
—BLDSC (0114.750000); CASDDS; Genuine Article; Linda Hall. **CCC.**

581 US ISSN 0026-6493
QK1 CODEN: AMBGA7
MISSOURI BOTANICAL GARDEN. ANNALS. (Text in English, Spanish, with Latin descriptions) 1914. q. $110 includes Novon (Canada and Mexico $115; elsewhere $135) (effective 1997). Missouri Botanical Garden, Box 299, St. Louis, MO 63166-0299. TEL 314-577-5112. FAX 314-577-9594. E-mail: dept11@mobot.org. Ed. M.H. Grayum. illus.; index. circ. 850. (also avail. in microfiche from IDC; microfilm from UMI; reprint service avail. from UMI) **Indexed:** ASCA, Biol.Abstr., Biol.& Agr.Ind., Chem.Abstr., Curr.Adv.Ecol.Sci., Deep Sea Res.& Oceanogr.Abstr., Field Crop Abstr., Forest.Abstr., Forest Prod.Abstr., Geo.Abstr., GeoRef., Herb.Abstr., Hort.Abstr., Ind.Sci.Rev., Ornam.Hort., Plant Breed.Abstr., Rev.Plant Path., So.Pac.Per.Ind., Soils & Fert., Sport Fish.Abstr., Weed Abstr., Zoo.Rec. **Document type:** academic/scholarly publication.
—BLDSC (1029.000000); CISTI; EMDOCS; KR SourceOne; Linda Hall; SWETS; UnCover.
  Description: Publishes papers in systematic botany with an emphasis on tropical botany.

MISSOURI BOTANICAL GARDEN. BULLETIN. see
GARDENING AND HORTICULTURE

581 US ISSN 0161-1542
CODEN: MSBOE5
MISSOURI BOTANICAL GARDEN. MONOGRAPHS IN SYSTEMATIC BOTANY. Key Title: Monographs in Systematic Botany from the Missouri Botanical Garden. 1978. irreg. Missouri Botanical Garden, Box 299, St. Louis, MO 63166-0299. TEL 314-577-9534. FAX 314-577-9594. Ed. Marshall R. Crosby. **Indexed:** Apic.Abstr.
—BLDSC (5917.740000); CISTI.

580.74 JA ISSN 0917-043X
MIYABEA/ILLUSTRATED FLORA OF HOKKAIDO. (Text in English) 1991. irreg. Hokkaido Daigaku, Nogakubu, Fuzoku Shokubutsuen - Hokkaido University, Faculty of Agriculture, Botanic Garden, Nishi 8-chome, Kita 3-jo, Chuo-ku, Sapporo-shi, Hokkaido 060, Japan. Ed. Hideki Takahashi. **Document type:** academic/scholarly publication.

589.3 JA ISSN 0288-139X
MIZUKUSA KENKYUKAI KAIHO/WATER PLANT SOCIETY. BULLETIN. (Text in Japanese; summaries in English, Japanese) 1980. 3/yr. 1000 Yen per no. Mizukusa Kenkyukai - Water Plant Society, Kobe Daigaku Kyoyogakubu Seibutsugaku Kyoshitsu, 2-1 Tsurukabuto 1-chome, Nada-ku, Kobe-shi, Hyogo-ken 657, Japan. E-mail: kadono@icluna.kobe-u.ac.jp. Ed. Yasuro Kadono. R&P contact: Yasuro Kadono. **Document type:** bulletin.

581 US ISSN 0937-8340
QK865 CODEN: MMPSEB
MODERN METHODS OF PLANT ANALYSIS. 1956. irreg., vol.18, 1996. Springer-Verlag, 175 Fifth Ave., New York, NY 10010. TEL 212-460-1500. FAX 212-473-6272. (U.S. subscr. to: Box 2485, Secaucus, NJ 07096-2491. TEL 201-348-4033; Also: Berlin, Heidelberg, Paris, Tokyo and Vienna) **Indexed:** Bibl.Agri. **Document type:** monographic series.
—BLDSC (5890.000300); CASDDS; CISTI; SWETS. **CCC.**
  Supersedes (in 1985): Moderne Methoden der Pflanzenanalyse (ISSN 0077-0183)

581.88 NE ISSN 1380-3743
QK981.4 CODEN: MOBRFL
▼**MOLECULAR BREEDING**; new strategies in plant improvement. (Text in English) 1995. bi-m. fl.657 to institutions; $337 to institutions in U.S. (effective 1998). Kluwer Academic Publishers, Postbus 17, 3300 AA Dordrecht, Netherlands. TEL 31-78-6392392. FAX 31-78-6392254. E-mail: services@wkap.nl; URL: http://www.wkap.nl. (Dist. by: Kluwer Academic Publishers Group, P.O. Box 322, 3300 AH Dordrecht, Netherlands. TEL 31-78-6392392. FAX 31-78-6546474; N. America dist. addr.: Box 358, Accord Sta., Hingham, MA 02018-0358. TEL 617-871-6600. FAX 617-871-6528) Ed. J.N.M. Mol. (back issues avail.) **Indexed:** ASCA, Curr.Cont. **Document type:** academic/scholarly publication.
—BLDSC (5900.799500); CASDDS; CISTI; Genuine Article; SWETS. **CCC.**
  Description: Publishes papers on all aspects of applied plant molecular biology.
  Refereed Serial

581 576 US ISSN 0894-0282
SB732.6 CODEN: MPMIEL
MOLECULAR PLANT - MICROBE INTERACTIONS. 1988. bi-m. $285 (foreign $310) (effective 1996 & 1997). (American Phytopathological Society) A P S Press, 3340 Pilot Knob Rd., St. Paul, MN 55121-2097. TEL 612-454-7250; 800-328-7560. FAX 612-454-0766. TELEX 6502439657 (MCI UW). (International Society for Molecular Plant - Microbe Interactions) Ed. S. Gelvin; Pub. Steven Nelson. adv. contact: Rhonda Wike. circ. 1,492. (back issues avail.) **Indexed:** ASCA, Curr.Adv.Genetics & Molec.Biol., Curr.Cont., Food Sci.& Tech.Abstr., Ind.Sci.Rev., Maize Abstr., Potato Abstr., Rice Abstr., Sci.Cit.Ind., Soils & Fert., Soyabean Abstr.
—BLDSC (5900.826000); CASDDS; CISTI; EMDOCS; Genuine Article; Linda Hall; SWETS; UMI; UnCover.
  Description: Devoted to significant research on the molecular genetics and molecular biology of pathological, symbiotic, and associative interactions of microbes with plants or microbes that affect such interactions.

581 SP ISSN 0213-6201
MONOGRAFIAS DE FLORA Y VEGETACION BETICAS. 1986. a. donation. Universidad de Granada, Facultad de Ciencias, Fuentenueva, s-n, 18001 Granada, Spain. **Indexed:** Ind.SST. **Document type:** monographic series.

581 PL ISSN 0077-0655
QK1
MONOGRAPHIAE BOTANICAE. (Text in English and Polish; summaries in English and German) 1953. irreg., vol.64, 1983. price varies. Polskie Towarzystwo Botaniczne, Al. Ujazdowskie 4, 00-478 Warsaw, Poland. (Dist. by: Ars Polona, Krakowskie Przedmiescie 7, 00-068 Warsaw, Poland) Ed. M. Kostyniuk. bibl. **Indexed:** AgroLibrex, Biol.Abstr., Field Crop Abstr., Herb.Abstr., Plant Breed.Abstr., Rev.Plant Path. **Document type:** monographic series.
—BLDSC (5917.784100); CISTI.

584 333.95 AT
MOOREANA; journal of the Palmetum. 1991. 3/yr. Aus.$35 (effective 1995 & 1996). Townsville City Council, P.O. Box 1268, Townsville, Qld. 4810, Australia. TEL 61-77-220455. FAX 61-77-253290. Ed. John L. Dowe. bk.rev.; video rev.; abstr.; bibl.; illus.; maps. circ. 300. **Document type:** academic/scholarly publication.
  Description: Covers palm botany, conservation and horticulture, botanic gardens research.
  Refereed Serial

581 AT ISSN 0077-1813
QK431 CODEN: MAJBAC
MUELLERIA. 1955. a. Aus.$30 or exchange basis. National Herbarium of Victoria, Birdwood Ave., South Yarra, Vic. 3141, Australia. TEL 61-3-92522300. FAX 61-3-92522350. Ed. Tim Entwisle. R&P contact: Tim Entwisle. adv. contact: Tim Entwisle. bk.rev.; index. circ. 600. **Indexed:** Biol.Abstr., Curr.Adv.Ecol.Sci., Curr.Adv.Plant Sci., Ecol.Abstr., Field Crop Abstr., Herb.Abstr., Plant Breed.Abstr. **Document type:** academic/scholarly publication.
  Refereed Serial

MUSEE ROYAL DE L'AFRIQUE CENTRALE. ANNALES - SCIENCES ECONOMIQUES. SERIE IN 8/KONINKLIJK MUSEUM VOOR MIDDEN-AFRIKA. ANNALEN - ECONOMISCHE WETENSCHAPPEN. REEKS IN 8. see
AGRICULTURE — Agricultural Economics

581 AG ISSN 0376-2793
QK1
MUSEO ARGENTINO DE CIENCIAS NATURALES "BERNARDINO RIVADAVIA." INSTITUTO NACIONAL DE INVESTIGACION DE LAS CIENCIAS NATURALES. REVISTA. BOTANICA. 1948. irreg., vol.7, no.4, 1991. free. Museo Argentino de Ciencias Naturales "Bernardino Rivadavia", Instituto Nacional de Investigacion de las Ciencias Naturales, Avda. Angel Gallardo 470, Casilla de Correo 220-Sucursal 5, Buenos Aires, Argentina. illus.
—CISTI; Linda Hall.
  Formerly: Buenos Aires. Museo Argentino de Ciencias Naturales Bernardino Rivadavia. Instituto Nacional de Investigacion de las Ciencias Naturales. Revista. Ciencias Botanicas.

MUSEO MUNICIPAL DE HISTORIA NATURAL DE SAN RAFAEL. INSTITUTO DE CIENCIAS NATURALES. NOTAS. see *EARTH SCIENCES — Geology*

581　　　　　　　UY　　ISSN 0027-0121
QK1
**MUSEO NACIONAL DE HISTORIA NATURAL.
COMUNICACIONES BOTANICAS.** (Text in English,
French and Spanish) 1942. irreg. (4-6/yr.).
exchange basis only. Museo Nacional de Historia
Natural, Casilla de Correos 399, 11000
Montevideo, Uruguay. illus.; cum.index. circ. 1,200.

581　　　　　　　BL　　ISSN 0100-008X
QK263　　　　　　　　CODEN: BMBMB3
MUSEU BOTANICO MUNICIPAL. BOLETIM. (Text in
English, German and Portuguese; summaries in
English and German) 1971. irreg. Museu Botanico
Municipal, Caixa Postal 1142, 80000 Curitiba,
Parana, Brazil. circ. 1,000. (back issues avail.)
Indexed: Biol.Abstr. **Document type:** bulletin.

581　　　　　　　BL　　ISSN 0080-3197
QK1　　　　　　　　　CODEN: BMJBA9
**MUSEU NACIONAL, RIO DE JANEIRO. BOLETIM. NOVA
SERIE. BOTANICA.** 1944. irreg., no.89, 1992.
exchange basis. Museu Nacional, Quinta da Boa
Vista, 20941-360 Rio de Janeiro RJ, Brazil.
TEL 55-21-5678676. E-mail: mmbib@acd.ujrj.br.
illus. **Indexed:** Biol.Abstr.
— CISTI; Linda Hall.

581　　　　　　　BL
QK263
**MUSEU PARAENSE EMILIO GOELDI. BOLETIM. SERIE
BOTANICA.** 1957. s-a. Cr.$44000($10) per no.
Conselho Nacional de Desenvolvimento Cientifico e
Tecnologico, Museu Paraense Emilio Goeldi, Caixa
Postal 399, 66017-970 Belem, Para, Brazil.
TEL 091-228-2341. FAX 091-229-1412. TELEX
091-1419. bk.rev.; bibl.; charts; illus.; maps. circ.
1,000. **Indexed:** Aqua.Sci. & Fish.Abstr., Biol.Abstr.,
Curr.Adv.Ecol.Sci., GeoRef.
— BLDSC (2143.410000).
　Formerly (until 1984, no.59): Museu Paraense
Emilio Goeldi. Boletim. Nova Serie: Botanica (ISSN
0077-2216)
　Description: Original papers in botanical research.

581　　　　　　　FR
QK1　　　　　　　　　CODEN: BMNBDW
**MUSEUM NATIONAL D'HISTOIRE NATURELLE.
ADANSONIA.** (Text in French; summaries in English
and French) N.S. 1961. q. 500 F. (effective 1997).
Museum National d'Histoire Naturelle, 57 rue Cuvier,
75005 Paris, France. TEL 33-1-40793000.
FAX 33-1-40793484. TELEX MUSNAHN 202641F.
E-mail: dhenry@mnhn.fr. (Dist. outside of France by:
Universal Book Services, Dr. W. Backhuys,
Warmonderweg 80, NL-2341 KZ Oegstgeest,
Netherlands. TEL 31-71-5170208. FAX
31-71-5171856) Ed. Joel Jeremie. adv.; bk.rev.;
charts; illus.; index. circ. 500. **Indexed:** Biol.Abstr.,
Bull.Signal, Curr.Adv.Ecol.Sci., Curr.Cont., Deep Sea
Res.& Oceanogr.Abstr., Field Crop Abstr., Forest
Prod.Abstr., GeoRef., Helminthol.Abstr., Herb.Abstr.,
So.Pac.Per.Ind.
— BLDSC (2626.141900); CASDDS; CISTI.
　Formerly: Museum National d'Histoire Naturelle.
Bulletin - Section B - Adansonia (Botanique,
Phytochimie) (ISSN 0240-8937)

MUSHROOM JOURNAL. see GARDENING AND
HORTICULTURE

589.2　　　　　　　UK　　ISSN 0077-2364
　　　　　　　　　　　　CODEN: MUSCAU
MUSHROOM SCIENCE. Represents: International
Congress on Mushroom Science. Proceedings. (Text
and summaries in English, French, German) 1950.
quadrennial, 13th, 1991, Dublin. International
Society for Mushroom Science, c/o Dr. P.B. Flegg,
50 St. Flora's Rd., Littlehampton BN17 6BB,
England. TEL 44-903-716469. **Indexed:** Biol.Abstr.,
Food Sci.& Tech.Abstr., Rev.Plant Path. **Document
type:** proceedings.
— BLDSC (5990.170000); CASDDS.
　Description: Focuses on mycological research.

579.52　　　　　　　VE
▼**MYCETEAE.** (Text in English; summaries in various
languages) 1997. s-a. $650 to institutions (effective
1997). Centro de Investigacion y Reproduccion de
Especies Silvestres, Apartado Postal 397, Merida
5101, Venezuela. TEL 58-74-712939.
FAX 58-74-712939. E-mail: cires@ciens.ula.ve. Ed.
Hector Fernando Aguilar. adv. contact: Lieselotte
Hoeger de Aguilar. bk.rev. circ. 2,500. (reprint
service avail. from SWZ) **Document type:**
academic/scholarly publication.
　Refereed Serial

589.2　　　　　　　US　　ISSN 0027-5514
QK600　　　　　　　　CODEN: MYCOAE
MYCOLOGIA. 1909. bi-m. $114 (foreign $125)
(effective 1997). (Mycological Society of America)
New York Botanical Garden, Scientific Publications
Department, Bronx, NY 10458-5126.
TEL 718-817-8721. FAX 718-817-8842. Ed. David
Griffin. adv.; bk.rev.; bibl.; charts; illus.; index. circ.
3,000. (also avail. in microform from UMI,PMC;
back issues avail.) **Indexed:** ASCA, Bio-Contr.News &
Info., Biol.Abstr., Biol.& Agr.Ind., Biotech.Abstr.,
Chem.Abstr., Curr.Adv.Ecol.Sci., Curr.Biotech.Abstr.,
Curr.Cont., Dairy Sci.Abstr., Deep Sea Res.&
Oceanogr.Abstr., Ecol.Abstr., Environ.Abstr., Food
Sci.& Tech.Abstr., Forest.Abstr., Forest Prod.Abstr.,
Geol.Abstr., Helminthol.Abstr., Hort.Abstr.,
Ind.Sci.Rev., Ind.Vet., Nutr.Abstr., Plant Breed.Abstr.,
Rev.Med.& Vet.Mycol., Rev.Plant Path., Sci.Cit.Ind.,
Seed Abstr., So.Pac.Per.Ind., Soils & Fert., Vet.Bull.,
VITIS. **Document type:** academic/scholarly publication.
— BLDSC (5993.000000); CASDDS; CIS; CISTI;
EMDOCS; Genuine Article; KNAW; KR SourceOne;
Linda Hall; SWETS; UMI; UnCover. **CCC.**
　Formed by the merger of: Mycological Bulletin;
Journal of Mycology.
　Description: Original research and review articles
on fungi and occasionally lichens.
　Refereed Serial

589.2　　　　　　　UK　　ISSN 0027-5522
　　　　　　　　　　　　CODEN: CMIMAE
MYCOLOGICAL PAPERS. (Former name of issuing body:
Commonwealth Mycological Institute (C M I)) 1925.
irreg. price varies. (International Mycological
Institute) CAB International, Wallingford, Oxon. OX10
8DE, England. TEL 44-1491-832111.
FAX 44-1491-826090. TELEX 847964 COMAGG
G. E-mail: cabi@cabi.org; URL: http://www.cabi.org.
(Alt. addr.: International Mycological Institute,
Bakeham Ln., Egham, Surrey TW20 9TY, England;
U.S. subscr. to: Oxford University Press, Customer
Services Dept., 2001 Evans Rd., Cary, NC 27513.
TEL 800-445-9714. FAX 919-677-1303) **Indexed:**
Rev.Plant Path. **Document type:** monographic series,
academic/scholarly publication.
— BLDSC (5994.060000); CISTI; Linda Hall.
　Description: Provides authoritative monographic
accounts of taxonomy and systematics of fungi.

589.2　　　　　　　UK　　ISSN 0953-7562
QK600　　　　　　　　CODEN: MYCRER
MYCOLOGICAL RESEARCH. 1896. m. £488($854)
(effective 1998). Cambridge University Press,
Edinburgh Bldg., Shaftesbury Rd., Cambridge CB2
2RU, England. TEL 44-1223-312393.
FAX 44-1223-315052. TELEX 851817256. E-mail:
information@cup.cam.ac.uk; URL: http://www.cup.
cam.ac.uk. (N. American addr.: Cambridge University
Press, Journals Dept., 40 W. 20th St., New York, NY
10011. TEL 212-924-3900. FAX 212-691-3239)
Ed. D. Moore. R&P contact: Linda Nicol. adv. contact:
Rebecca Symons. bk.rev.; bibl.; charts; illus.; index.
(also avail. in microform from UMI; back issues
avail.; reprint service avail. from KTO) **Indexed:** ASCA,
Biol.Abstr., Biol.& Agr.Ind., Biotech.Abstr.,
Chem.Abstr., Curr.Cont., Ecol.Abstr., Forest.Abstr.,
Forest Prod.Abstr., Ind.Sci.Rev., Ind.Vet., Ind.Vet.,
Hort.Abstr., Ind.Sci.Rev., Ind.Vet., Irr.& Drain.Abstr.,
Maize Abstr., Rev.Med.& Vet.Mycol., Sci.Cit.Ind.,
Sel.Water Res.Abstr., So.Pac.Per.Ind., Soils & Fert.,
Sugar Ind.Abstr., Triticale Abstr., Trop.Oil Seeds
Abstr., Vet.Bull., Weed Abstr. **Document type:**
proceedings.
— BLDSC (5994.100000); CASDDS; CISTI;
EMDOCS; Genuine Article; Linda Hall; SWETS; UMI;
UnCover. **CCC.**
　Formerly: British Mycological Society. Transactions
(ISSN 0007-1536)
　Description: Deals with fungal biology.

581　　　　　　　US　　ISSN 0541-4938
QK600
MYCOLOGICAL SOCIETY OF AMERICA NEWSLETTER.
1948. s-a. $25. Mycological Society of America, c/o
Dr. Terrence M. Hammill, Ed., Department of Biology,
State University of New York, College at Oswego,
Oswego, NY 13126. (Subscr. to: c/o Dr. F. Brent
Reeves, Jr., Treas., Dept. of Botany, Colorado State
University, Ft. Collins, CO 80523) Ed. Dr. Terrence
M. Hammill. circ. 1,500. **Indexed:** Rev.Med.&
Vet.Mycol.

589.2　　　　　　　UK　　ISSN 0269-915X
QK600　　　　　　　　CODEN: MYCOEI
MYCOLOGIST. 1967. q. £36($58) (effective 1998).
(British Mycological Society) Cambridge University
Press, Edinburgh Bldg., Shaftesbury Rd., Cambridge
CB2 2RU, England. TEL 44-1223-312393.
FAX 44-1223-315052. TELEX 851817256. E-mail:
information@cup.cam.ac.uk; URL: http://www.cup.
cam.ac.uk. (N. American addr.: Cambridge University
Press, Journals Dept., 40 W. 20th St., New York, NY
10011. TEL 212-924-3900. FAX 212-691-3239)
Ed. Geoff/Hadley. R&P contact: Linda Nicol. adv.;
bk.rev.; abstr. (also avail. in microform from UMI;
back issues avail.) **Indexed:** Bio-Contr.News & Info.,
Biol.Abstr., Biotech.Abstr., Curr.Adv.Ecol.Sci.,
Forest.Abstr., Plant Breed.Abstr., Rev.Plant Path.,
Soils & Fert., Sugar Ind.Abstr. **Document type:**
academic/scholarly publication.
— BLDSC (5995.705000); CISTI; Linda Hall; SWETS;
UMI; UnCover. **CCC.**
　Formerly (until 1987): British Mycological Society.
Bulletin (ISSN 0007-1528)
　Description: Covers all aspects of the study of
fungi.

589.2　　　　　　　US　　ISSN 0730-9597
　　　　　　　　　　　　CODEN: MYSEDX
MYCOLOGY SERIES. 1979. irreg., vol.13, 1996. price
varies. Marcel Dekker, Inc., 270 Madison Ave., New
York, NY 10016. TEL 212-696-9000.
FAX 212-658-4540. TELEX 421419. Pub. Graham
Garratt. R&P contact: Julia Mulligan. **Indexed:**
Chem.Abstr. **Document type:** monographic series.
— BLDSC (5995.710000); CASDDS; CISTI. **CCC.**
　Refereed Serial

MYCOPATHOLOGIA. see BIOLOGY — Microbiology

589.2　　　　　　　US　　ISSN 0027-5549
MYCOPHILE. 1960. 6/yr. membership. North American
Mycological Association, 3556 Oakwood, Ann Arbor,
MI 48104-5213. TEL 313-971-2522. E-mail:
kwcee@umich.edu. Eds. Harold Keller, Philip
McIntosh. bk.rev.; circ. 2,000 (controlled).
(processed) **Document type:** newsletter.

589　　　　　　　GW　　ISSN 0940-6360
QK604.2.M92　　　　　CODEN: MCOREZ
MYCORRHIZA. Online edition (GW ISSN 1432-1890)
(Text in English) 1991. bi-m. DM.1172.50 (foreign
DM.1187.20) (effective 1998). Springer-Verlag,
Heidelberger Platz 3, 14197 Berlin, Germany.
TEL 49-30-82787-0. FAX 49-30-82787448.
E-mail: subscriptions@springer.de; URL: http://link.
springer.de/link/service/journals/00572/index.htm.
(Subscr. in N. America to: Springer-Verlag New York,
Inc., 333 Meadowlands Pkwy., Secaucus, NJ 07094.
TEL 212-460-1500. FAX 212-473-6272) Ed.Bd.
(back issues avail.) **Indexed:** ASCA, Curr.Cont.,
Ecol.Abstr., Ind.Sci.Rev., Sci.Cit.Ind. **Document type:**
academic/scholarly publication.
● Also available online.
— BLDSC (5995.752000); CASDDS; EMDOCS;
Genuine Article; SWETS; UMI. **CCC.**
　Description: Devoted to all aspects of research into
the symbiosis between higher plants and certain
fungi or mushrooms, covering original papers and
reviews on all types of mycorrhizae.

581　　　　　　　II　　ISSN 0970-695X
MYCORRHIZA NEWS. (Text in English) 1989. q.
Rs.75($40) for developed countries; developing
countries $20. Tata Energy Research Institute, India
Habitat Centre, Lodi Rd., New Delhi 110 003, India.
TEL 91-11-4693550. FAX 91-11-4621770. E-mail:
mailbox@teri.ernet.in. circ. 1,200. **Document type:**
newsletter.
— BLDSC (5995.752500).
　Description: Official newsletter of the Mycorrhiza
Network Asia, providing a forum for views and
findings on mycorrhiza.

BIOLOGY — BOTANY

589.2   JA   ISSN 1340-3540
QK600   CODEN: MNCEED
MYCOSCIENCE. (Text in English) 1956. q. $100. (Mycological Society of Japan - Nippon Kin Gakkai) Business Center for Academic Societies Japan, 5-16-9 Honkomagome, Bunkyo-ku, Tokyo 113, Japan. TEL 03-5814-5811. FAX 03-5814-5822. TELEX 2722268 BCJSP J. adv.; bk.rev.; abstr.; charts; illus. circ. 1,500. **Indexed:** Agrindex, Biol.Abstr., Chem.Abstr., Curr.Adv.Ecol.Sci., Curr.Cont., Dairy Sci.Abstr., Forest.Abstr., Jap.Per.Ind., Rev.Med.& Vet.Mycol., Rev.Plant Path., Seed Abstr., Soils & Fert.
—BLDSC (5995.752800); CASDDS; EMDOCS; UMI. CCC.
Formerly (until 1994): Mycological Society of Japan. Transactions (ISSN 0029-0289)

589.2   US   ISSN 0093-4666
QK603.2   CODEN: MYXNAE
MYCOTAXON. (Text in English and French) 1974. q. $30 per vol. to individuals (Canada & Mexico $32); institutions $65 (Canada & Mexico $67) (effective 1997). Mycotaxon Ltd., Box 264, Ithaca, NY 14851. TEL 607-273-4357. FAX 607-273-4357. E-mail: rkorf@innet.com; URL: http://www.mycotaxon.com. Ed. Jean B. Cargill. bk.rev.; illus.; circ. 650. (also avail. in microform from UMI; back issues avail.; reprint service avail. from UMI, ISI) **Indexed:** ASCA, Bibl.Agri., Biol.Abstr., Curr.Adv.Ecol.Sci., Curr.Cont., Deep Sea Res.& Oceanogr.Abstr., Excerp.Bot., Ind.Sci.Rev., Rev.Plant Path., Sci.Cit.Ind. **Document type:** academic/scholarly publication.
—BLDSC (5995.760000); CISTI; Genuine Article; Linda Hall; SWETS; UMI; UnCover.
Description: Covers taxonomy and nomenclature of fungi, including lichens.
Refereed Serial

589.2   US
N A T S CURRENT NEWS. 1983. bi-m. $7 (foreign $10). North American Truffling Society, Inc., Box 296, Corvallis, OR 97339. TEL 541-753-2243. Ed. Carolynn Avery. bk.rev.; circ. 250 (paid). **Document type:** newsletter.
Description: Fosters knowledge of truffles and truffle-like fungi.

NA OKIKA O HAWAII/HAWAII ORCHID JOURNAL. see *GARDENING AND HORTICULTURE*

581   JA   ISSN 0385-9916
NAGANOKEN SHOKUBUTSU KENKYUKAISHI/BOTANICAL SOCIETY OF NAGANO. BULLETIN. (Text in Japanese) 1967. a. 2400 Yen. Naganoken Shokubutsu Kenkyukai - Botanical Society of Nagano, Shinshu Daigaku Kyoyobu, 1-1 Asahi 3-chome, Matsumoto-shi, Nagano-ken 390, Japan.

581   JA   ISSN 0386-7080
NARA SHOKUBUTSU KENKYU/NARA BOTANY. (Text in Japanese) 1978. a. 1000 Yen. Nara Shokubutsu Kenkyukai - Botanical Society of Nara, c/o Mr. Suganuma, 239-41 Tsutsuimachi, Yamato Koriyama-shi, Nara-ken 639-11, Japan.

581   XO   ISSN 0323-2646
NASE LIECIVE RASTLINY. bi-m. $27. Herba, Svabinsheho 4-a, 851 01 Bratislava, Slovakia. **Indexed:** Hort.Abstr., Seed Abstr., Weed Abstr.

581   IE   ISSN 0790-0422
NATIONAL BOTANIC GARDENS. OCCASIONAL PAPERS. 1981. irreg, no.9, 1996. exchange basis. National Botanic Gardens, Glasnevin, Dublin 9, Ireland. TEL 353-1-8374388. FAX 353-18360080. Ed. Donal Synnott. R&P contact: Donal Synnott. circ. 300. **Document type:** academic/scholarly publication, government publication.
—BLDSC (6218.200000).
Refereed Serial

581   II
NATIONAL BOTANIC RESEARCH INSTITUTE, LUCKNOW. PROGRESS REPORT. (Text in English) 1966. a. free. National Botanical Research Institute, Lucknow, Lucknow 226001, India. TEL 91-522-282849. FAX 91-522-282849. TELEX 0535-315. E-mail: manager@nbri.sirnetd.ernet.in. (Affiliate: Council of Scientific and Industrial Research) Eds. M.R. Ahamad, Anil K. Gauniyal. circ. 500 (controlled). **Indexed:** Biol.Abstr., Chem.Abstr. **Document type:** corporate report.
Former titles: National Botanic Gardens, Lucknow. Progress Report; National Botanic Gardens, Lucknow. Annual Report (ISSN 0076-1400)
Description: Covers all branches of botany includng crytoganic botany, angiosperms, plant taxonomy, ethnobotany, biodiversity, seed biology, palynology, pharmacognosy, plant breeding and genetics, and more.
Refereed Serial

581   SA
NATIONAL BOTANICAL INSTITUTE. REVIEW. (Text in Afrikaans, English) 1913. a. free. National Botanical Institute (Claremont), Private Bag X7, Claremont 7735, South Africa. TEL 27-21-762-1166. FAX 27-21-762-3229. Ed. A.B. Low. circ. 500 (controlled). **Document type:** corporate report.
Former titles: National Botanic Gardens. Report; National Botanic Gardens of South Africa. Report.
Description: Annual report of the activities of the institute.
Refereed Serial

581   II   ISSN 0971-2976
QK1   CODEN: BUBPAX
NATIONAL BOTANICAL SOCIETY. JOURNAL. (Text in English) 1947. s-a. Rs.150($40) National Botanical Society, 35 Ballygunge Circular Rd., Calcutta 700 019, India. TEL 91-33-475-3681. (Dist. by: HPC Publisher's Distributors (Pvt.) Ltd., 4805-24, 1st Fl, Bharat Ram Rd., Darya Ganj, New Delhi 110 002, India. TEL 91-11-3254402. FAX 91-11-6863511) Ed. R. Mallick. adv. contact: N. Paria. bk.rev.; charts; illus. circ. 250. (reprint service avail.) **Indexed:** Biol.Abstr., Chem.Abstr., Field Crop Abstr., Herb.Abstr., Soils & Fert. **Document type:** academic/scholarly publication.
—CASDDS; CISTI; Linda Hall.
Formerly (until vol.44, 1990): Botanical Society of Bengal. Bulletin (ISSN 0006-811X)

581   JA   ISSN 0385-2431
QK1   CODEN: BMBBD6
NATIONAL SCIENCE MUSEUM. BULLETIN. SERIES B: BOTANY/KOKURITSU KAGAKU HAKUBUTSUKAN KENKYU HOKOKU. B RUI: SHOKUBUTSUGAKU. (Text in English) 1939. q. exchange basis. Monbusho, Kokuritsu Kagaku Hakubutsukan - Ministry of Education, Science and Culture, National Science Museum, 7-20 Ueno Park, Taito-ku, Tokyo 110, Japan. Ed. Shigeru Fukuda. charts; illus. circ. 1,000. **Indexed:** Biol.Abstr., Chem.Abstr., Curr.Adv.Ecol.Sci., Deep Sea Res.& Oceanogr.Abstr., GeoRef., Herb.Abstr., INIS Atomind., Rev.Plant Path., Weed Abstr.
—BLDSC (2644.030000); CISTI.
Supersedes part (in 1975): National Science Museum. Bulletin (ISSN 0028-0119)

581   US
NATIVE PLANT SOCIETY OF NEW MEXICO. NEWSLETTER. 1976. 6/yr. $12 membership only. Native Plant Society of New Mexico, Box 5917, Santa Fe, NM 87502. Ed. Tim McKimmie. adv.; bk.rev. circ. 520. **Document type:** newsletter.
Description: Provides information on activities of chapters throughout New Mexico, and includes articles on topics relating to native plants, landscaping, plant descriptions, conservation, ethnobotany.

581   GW   ISSN 0723-5038
NATUR; Zeitschrift fuer eine oekologische Zukunft. 1981. m. DM.81.60 (foreign DM.96); newsstand price: DM.8. Natur Media GmbH, Belfortstr. 6-8, 81667 Munich, Germany. Ed. Guenter Haaf. adv.: B&W page DM.10790, color page DM.17960; trim 176 x 250; adv. contact: Raimund Arntzen. bk.rev.; circ. 120,696. **Indexed:** Key Word Ind.Wildl.Res. **Document type:** consumer publication.
Description: Focuses mainly on ecological and environmental subjects. Frequently publishes stories on biology, zoology, and ecology of animals and plants, on medical and psychological topics, consumer information, and articles dealing with chemical and nuclear industries and their dangers.

581 595.7   BE   ISSN 0028-0666
   CODEN: NAMOA9
NATURA MOSANA. 1948. q. 800 BEF. 61 rue de Bruxelles, 5000 Namur, Belgium. Ed. J. Margot. bk.rev.; bibl.; index. **Indexed:** Biol.Abstr., Chem.Abstr. **Document type:** academic/scholarly publication, bulletin.

581   UK   ISSN 0968-0446
QK1
NATURAL HISTORY MUSEUM. BULLETIN. BOTANY. 1951. s-a. £78.75. Intercept Ltd., P.O. Box 716, Andover, Hants. SP10 1YG, England. TEL 01264-334748. FAX 01264-334058. illus.; index. circ. 750. **Indexed:** Bibl.Agri., Biol.Abstr., Curr.Adv.Ecol.Sci., GeoRef. **Document type:** academic/scholarly publication, bulletin.
—BLDSC (2644.268500); CISTI; Linda Hall.
Formerly (until 1992): British Museum (Natural History). Bulletin. Botany (ISSN 0068-2292)

NATURHISTORISCHES MUSEUM IN WIEN. ANNALEN. SERIE B: BOTANIK UND ZOOLOGIE. see *SCIENCES: COMPREHENSIVE WORKS*

581 615.19   NP
NEPAL. DEPARTMENT OF MEDICINAL PLANTS. ANNUAL REPORT. (Text in English) 1969. a. free. Ministry of Forests, Department of Medicinal Plants, Thapathali, Katmandu, Nepal. circ. 500.

581 591   JA
NETTAI DOSHOKUBUTSU TOMO NO KAI KAIHO/NEWS OF THE TROPICAL PLANTS AND ANIMALS. (Text in Japanese) 1972. 4/yr. 2000 Yen. Nettai Doshokubutsu Tomo no Kai - Society of Tropical Plants and Animals, Atagawa Banana Wanien Kenkyushitsu, Atagawa Onsen, Higashiizumachi, Kamo-gun, Shizuoka-ken 413-03, Japan. TEL 81-557-23-1105. FAX 81-557-23-0866. Ed. Hideo Shimizu. adv. contact: Satoshi Kimura. **Document type:** newsletter.

581   JA
NETTAI SHOKUBUTSU CHOSA KENKYU NENPO/ANNUAL BULLETIN OF TROPICAL ARBORETUM. (Text in Japanese) 1977. a. Kaiyo Hakurankai Kinen Koen Kanri Zaidan - Management Foundation of National Ocean Expo Memorial Park, 424 Ishikawa, Motobucho, Kunigami-gun, Okinawa-ken 905-03, Japan.

581   II   ISSN 0377-1741
QK1
NEW BOTANIST; an international quarterly journal of plant science research. (Text in English) 1974. q. Rs.700($60) Today and Tomorrow's Printers & Publishers, 24B-5 Desh Bandhu Gupta Rd., Karol Bagh, New Dehli 110 005, India. TEL 91-11-5721928. (Dist. in U.S. by: Scholarly Publications, 2825 Wilcrest Dr., Ste. 255, Houston, TX 77042. TEL 713-781-0070. FAX 713-781-2212) Ed. J.N. Govil. adv.; cum. index. circ. 437. (back issues avail.) **Indexed:** Biol.Abstr., Curr.Adv.Ecol.Sci., Curr.Cont. **Document type:** academic/scholarly publication.
—BLDSC (6082.370000); Linda Hall. CCC.
Description: Deals with the higher reaches of knowledge in plant sciences.

581   II
NEW GLIMPSES IN PLANT RESEARCH. 1986. a. price varies. Today and Tomorrow's Printers & Publishers, 24B-5 Desh Badhu Gupta Rd., Karol Bagh, New Delhi 110 005, India. TEL 91-11-572-1928. (Dist. in US by: Scholarly Publications, 2825 Wilcrest Dr., Ste. 255, Houston, TX 77042. TEL 713-781-0070. FAX 713-781-2112) Ed. J.N. Govil. **Document type:** monographic series.
Formerly (until 1991): Glimpses in Plant Research (ISSN 0971-1686)

581 UK ISSN 0028-646X
QK1 CODEN: NEPHAV
NEW PHYTOLOGIST. 1902. m. £498($830) (effective 1998). Cambridge University Press, Edinburgh House, Shaftesbury Rd., Cambridge CB2 2RU, England. TEL 44-1223-312393.
FAX 44-1223-315052. TELEX 851817256. E-mail: information@cup.cam.ac.uk; URL: http://www.cup.cam.ac.uk. (N. American addr.: Cambridge University Press, Journals Dept., 40 W. 20th St., New York, NY 10011. TEL 212-92-3900. FAX 212-691-3239) Ed. David P. Stribley. R&P contact: Linda Nicol. adv. contact: Rebecca Symons. bk.rev. (also avail. in microform from UMI,BHP; back issues avail.) **Indexed:** Acid Rain Abstr., Acid Rain Ind., ASCA, Bio-Contr.News & Info., Biol.Abstr., Br.Geol.Lit., Chem.Abstr., Compumath, Crop Physiol.Abstr., Curr.Adv.Biochem., Curr.Adv.Ecol.Sci., Curr.Cont., Deep Sea Res.& Oceanogr.Abstr., Ecol.Abstr., Energy Ind., Energy Info.Abstr., Environ.Abstr., Environ.Per.Bibl. (1990-1994), Fababean Abstr., Field Crop Abstr., Food Sci.& Tech.Abstr., Forest.Abstr., Forest Prod.Abstr., Geo.Abstr.H.G., Geol.Abstr., GeoRef., Herb.Abstr., Hort.Abstr., Ind.Sci.Rev., Irr.& Drain.Abstr., Maize Abstr., Ornam.Hort., Plant Grow.Reg.Abstr., Potato Abstr., Rice Abstr., Sci.Cit.Ind., Seed Abstr., Sel.Water Res.Abstr., Soils & Fert., Sorghum & Millets Abstr., Triticale Abstr., Trop.Oil Seeds Abstr., VITIS, W.R.C.Inf., Weed Abstr. **Document type:** academic/scholarly publication.
—BLDSC (6085.000000); CASDDS; CISTI; Genuine Article; Linda Hall; SWETS; UMI; UnCover. **CCC.**
 Description: Presents research papers, review articles on all aspects of the plant sciences.

581 US ISSN 0077-8931
QK1 CODEN: MYBGAJ
NEW YORK BOTANICAL GARDEN. MEMOIRS. Key Title: Memoirs of the New York Botanical Garden. 1900. irreg. no.79, 1995. price varies. New York Botanical Garden, Scientific Publications Department, Bronx, NY 10458-5126. TEL 718-817-8721.
FAX 718-817-8842. Ed. W. Buck. index. (back issues avail.) **Indexed:** Biol.Abstr., Curr.Adv.Ecol.Sci., Rev.Plant Path. **Document type:** monographic series.
—BLDSC (5628.600000); Linda Hall. **CCC.**
 Description: Publishes full-length manuscripts and original research on plant systematics.
 Refereed Serial

581 NZ ISSN 0028-825X
QK1 CODEN: NZJBAS
NEW ZEALAND JOURNAL OF BOTANY. 1963. q. NZ.$140($200) to individuals; institutions NZ.$300 ($200) (effective 1997). (Royal Society of New Zealand) S I R Publishing, P.O. Box 399, Wellington, New Zealand. TEL 64-4-472-7421.
FAX 64-4-473-1841. E-mail: nzjb@rsnz.govt.nz; URL: http://www.rsnz.govt.nz. (Subscr. addr. in US: SIR Publishing, 810 E. 10th St., Box 1897, Lawrence, KS 66044-8897. TEL 913-843-1221) Ed. F.M. Kell. abstr.; bibl.; charts; illus.; index. circ. 450. (back issues avail.) **Indexed:** ASCA, Biol.Abstr., Chem.Abstr., Curr.Adv.Ecol.Sci., Curr.Cont., Deep Sea Res.& Oceanogr.Abstr., Ecol.Abstr., Environ.Abstr., Field Crop Abstr., Forest.Abstr., Forest Prod.Abstr., Geo.Abstr.H.G., Herb.Abstr., Hort.Abstr., Ind.Sci.Rev., Irr.& Drain.Abstr., Plant Breed.Abstr., Rev.Plant Path., Sci.Cit.Ind., Seed Abstr., Sel.Water Res.Abstr., So.Pac.Per.Ind., Soils & Fert., Triticale Abstr., Weed Abstr. **Document type:** academic/scholarly publication.
—BLDSC (6093.200000); CASDDS; CISTI; EMDOCS; Genuine Article; Linda Hall; UnCover. **CCC.**
 Description: Publishes papers on all fields of botany focusing on the South Pacific region.
 Refereed Serial

581 NR ISSN 0795-8692
SB299.P3
NIGERIAN JOURNAL OF PALMS AND OIL SEEDS. 1953. irreg. $50. Nigerian Institute for Oil Palm Research, P.M.B. 1030, Benin City, Bendel State, Nigeria. TEL 234-52-440130. FAX 234-52-440150. Ed. D.A. Okiy. adv.; bk.rev.; index. circ. 1,000. **Indexed:** Biol.Abstr., Cott.& Trop.Fibr.Abstr., Hort.Abstr., Plant Breed.Abstr., Rev.Plant Path., Soils & Fert. **Document type:** academic/scholarly publication.
 Formerly: Nigerian Institute for Oil Palm Research. Journal (ISSN 0078-0715)
 Refereed Serial

588 JA ISSN 0285-0869
NIHON SENTAIRUI GAKKAI KAIHO/BRYOLOGICAL SOCIETY OF JAPAN. PROCEEDINGS. (Text in Japanese; summaries in English) 1972. 3/yr. 3000 Yen. Nihon Sentairui Gakkai - Bryological Society of Japan, National Institute of Polar Research, 9-10, Kaga 1-chome, Itabashi-ku, Tokyo 173, Japan. Ed. Naoki Nishimura. **Document type:** proceedings.

581 JA
NIHON SHOKUBUTSU BUNRUI GAKKAI TAIKAI HAPPYO YOSHISHU/JAPAN SOCIETY OF PLANT TAXONOMISTS. PROCEEDING OF THE ANNUAL MEETING. (Text in English, Japanese) a. Nihon Shokubutsu Bunrui Gakkai - Japan Society of Plant Taxonomists, Tokyo Toritsu Daigaku Rigakubu, Makino Hyohonkan, 1-1 Minamiosawa, Hachioji-shi, Tokyo 192-03, Japan.

NIHON SHOKUBUTSU BYORI GAKKAI BAIOKONTOROR U KENKYUKAI KOEN YOSHI/PHYTOPATHOLOGICAL SOCIETY OF JAPAN. ABSTRACTS OF THE MEETING OF BIOCONTROL. see *BIOLOGY — Abstracting, Bibliographies, Statistics*

581.2 595.7 JA
NIHON SHOKUBUTSU BYORI GAKKAI SHOKUBUTSU KANSEN SEIRI DANWAKAI/SYMPOSIUM ON PHYSIOLOGICAL PLANT PATHOLOGY IN JAPAN. PROCEEDINGS. (Text in Japanese; summaries in English) a. Nihon Shokubutsu Byori Gakkai, Shokubutsu Kansen Seiri Danwakai - Phytopathological Society of Japan, Symposium on Physiological Plant Pathology, Iwate Daigaku Nogakubu, Shokubutsu Byorigaku Koza, 18-8 Ueda 3-chome, Morioka-shi, Iwate-ken 020, Japan. **Document type:** proceedings.

581 JA
NIHON SHOKUBUTSU GAKKAI TAIKAI KENKYU HAPPYO KIROKU/BOTANICAL SOCIETY OF JAPAN. PROCEEDINGS OF THE ANNUAL MEETING. (Text in Japanese) a. 4000 Yen. Nihon Shokubutsu Gakkai - Botanical Society of Japan, 27-2 Hongo 2-chome, Bunkyo-ku, Tokyo 113, Japan. **Document type:** proceedings.

581 JA
NIHON SHOKUBUTSU SAIBOU BUNSHISEIBUTSU GAKKAI KOROKIAMU/JAPANESE SOCIETY FOR PLANT CELL AND MOLECULAR BIOLOGY. CULTURE COLLOQUIUM. (Text in English, Japanese) 1988. biennial. Nihon Shokubutsu Saibou Bunshiseibutsu Gakkai - Japanese Society for Plant Cell and Molecular Biology, 30-15 Hongo 5-chome, Bunkyo-ku, Tokyo 113-91, Japan.
 Formerly: Nihon Shokubutsu Soshiki Baiyo Gakkai Shokubutsu Soshiki Baiyo Korokiamu - Japanese Association for Plant Tissue Culture. Plant Tissue Culture Colloquium.

581 JA ISSN 0389-5246
NIHON SHOKUBUTSUEN KYOKAISHI/JAPAN ASSOCIATION OF BOTANICAL GARDENS. BULLETIN. (Text in Japanese; summaries in English, Japanese) 1966. a. 3000 Yen to non-members; members 2000 Yen. Nihon Shokubutsuen Kyokai - Japan Association of Botanical Gardens, Tokyo Daigaku Rigakubu Fuzuoku Shokubutsuen, 7-1 Hakusan 3-chome, Bunkyo-ku, Tokyo 112, Japan.
TEL 81-424-83-2300. FAX 81-424-88-5832. Ed. Yasuyuki Ueda.

589.2 JA ISSN 0913-7955
NIPPON KIN GAKKAI NYUSU/MYCOLOGICAL SOCIETY OF JAPAN. NEWS. (Text in Japanese) 1968. s-a. Nippon Kin Gakkai - Mycological Society of Japan, Nihon Gakkai Jimu Senta, 16-9 Honkomagome 5-chome, Bunkyo-ku, Tokyo 113, Japan.

581 JA ISSN 0287-3257
NIPPON SHIDA NO KAI KAIHO/NIPPON FERNIST CLUB. JOURNAL. (Text in Japanese) 1952. 3/yr. Nippon Shida no Kai - Nippon Fernist Club, Tokyo Nogyo Daigaku Seibutsugaku Kenkyushitsu, 1-1 Sakuragaoka 1-chome, Setagaya-ku, Tokyo 157, Japan.

581 DK ISSN 0107-055X
QK1 CODEN: NJBODK
NORDIC JOURNAL OF BOTANY. (Supplements avail.) (Text in English) 1981. bi-m. DKK 1700 (effective 1997). Nordic Publications in Botany, The Secretary, Gothersgade 130, DK-1123 Copenhagen K, Denmark. abstr.; bibl.; illus. circ. 500. (also avail. in microform from UMI; microfiche from BHP; microfiche from IDC; back issues avail.; reprint service avail. from UMI) **Indexed:** Apic.Abstr., ASCA, Bio-Contr.News & Info., Chem.Abstr, Crop Physiol.Abstr., Curr.Adv.Ecol.Sci., Deep Sea Res.& Oceanogr.Abstr., Ecol.Abstr., Excerp.Med., Field Crop Abstr., Forest.Abstr., Forest Prod.Abstr., Geo.Abstr.H.G., GeoRef., Herb.Abstr., Hort.Abstr., Ind.Sci.Rev., Ornam.Hort., Plant Breed.Abstr., Plant Grow.Reg.Abstr., Rev.Plant Path., Sci.Cit.Ind., Seed Abstr., Soils & Fert., Weed Abstr. **Document type:** academic/scholarly publication.
—BLDSC (6117.926000); CASDDS; CISTI; EMDOCS; Genuine Article; Linda Hall; SWETS; UMI; UnCover. **CCC.**
 Formed by the merger of (1866-1981): Botanisk Tidsskrift (ISSN 0006-8107); (1839-1981): Botaniska Notiser (ISSN 0006-8195); (1932-1981): Friesia (ISSN 0016-1403); (1952-1981): Norwegian Journal of Botany (ISSN 0300-1156)
 Refereed Serial

NORFOLK BOTANICAL GARDEN SOCIETY BULLETIN. see *GARDENING AND HORTICULTURE*

580 NO
NORGES TEKNISK-NATURVITENSKAPELIGE UNIVERSITET. VITENSKAPSMUSEET. RAPPORT. BOTANISK SERIE. (Text in English, Norwegian; summaries in English) 1974. irreg. exchange basis. Norwegian University of Science and Technology, Museum of Natural History and Archaeology, N-7004 Trondheim, Norway. TEL 47-73-59-22-60. FAX 47-73-59-22-49. E-mail: inger.growen@vm.ntnu.no. Ed. Eli Fremstad. circ. 275 (controlled). **Indexed:** Biol.Abstr. **Document type:** corporate report.
—BLDSC (7287.649550).
 Former titles (until 1996): Universitetet i Trondheim, Vitenskapsmuseet. Rapport. Botanisk Serie (ISSN 0802-2992); (until 1987): Kongelige Norske Videnskabers Selskab, Museet. Rapport. Botanisk Serie (ISSN 0332-8090)
 Description: Contains reports and other material connected to the botanical activity and the geographical area for which the museum is responsible.

581 US ISSN 0078-1312
QK110 CODEN: NAFLBY
NORTH AMERICAN FLORA. Series 1, 1905-1952; Series 2, 1956. irreg., no.13, 1990. price varies. New York Botanical Garden, Scientific Publications Department, Bronx, NY 10458-5126.
TEL 718-817-8721. FAX 718-817-8842. Ed. W. Buck. (back issues avail.) **Indexed:** Biol.Abstr., Curr.Adv.Ecol.Sci. **Document type:** monographic series.
—Linda Hall. **CCC.**
 Description: Taxonomic treatment of plants native to North America and its geologically related areas.
 Refereed Serial

581 US ISSN 0078-1703
CODEN: PNWSBF
NORTHEASTERN WEED SCIENCE SOCIETY. PROCEEDINGS.* 1946. a. $25 (foreign $30). Northeastern Weed Science Society, 3059 Sound Ave., Riverhead, NY 11901-1115. Ed. B. Morose. index. circ. 700. (back issues avail.) **Indexed:** Biol.Abstr., Chem.Abstr. **Document type:** proceedings.
—BLDSC (6841.865000); CASDDS; Linda Hall.
 Formerly: Northeastern Weed Control Conference.

581 VE ISSN 0085-4387
NOTICIERO TUBEROSAS.* (Text in Spanish; summaries in Spanish, occasionally in English and Portuguese) 1971. irreg. free to members. Sociedad Latinoamericana de Tuberosas, Box 97, Maracay, Venezuela. Ed. Alvaro Montaldo. abstr. circ. 250. (processed; also avail. in cards)

BIOLOGY — BOTANY

581   AU
NOTIZEN ZUR FLORA DER STEIERMARK. 1974. irreg. price varies. Landesmuseum Joanneum, Abteilung fuer Botanik, Raubergasse 10, A-8010 Graz, Austria. TEL 43-316-80174750. FAX 43-316-80174800. TELEX 311838-LRGGR-A. (Co-sponsor: Steiermaerkische Landesregierung) Eds. Detlef Ernet, Arnold Zimmermann. circ. 400. **Document type:** academic/scholarly publication.
    Description: Results of research on the flora of the province of Styria.

581 595.7   IT   ISSN 0468-9291
                          CODEN: NOMPA8
NOTIZIARIO SULLA PROTEZIONE DELLE PIANTE. (Text in English and Italian; summaries in English) 1952. a. Lit.60000 (effective 1997). Associazione Italiana per la Protezione delle Piante, Via Celoria 2, 20133 Milan, Italy. TEL 39-2-2362880. Ed. Giorgio Domenichini. adv.; bk.rev. circ. 80,000. **Indexed:** Biol.Abstr. **Document type:** proceedings.
  —CASDDS.
    Formerly (until 1993): Notiziario sulle Malattie delle Piante.

581   GW   ISSN 0029-5035
QK504   CODEN: NOHEAI
NOVA HEDWIGA; journal of cryptogamic science. (Text in English, French and German) 1959. 2 vols. per yr. DM.328($239.10) per vol. (foreign $242) (effective 1997). J. Cramer in der Gebrueder Borntraeger Verlagsbuchhandlung, Johannesstr. 3A, 70176 Stuttgart, Germany. TEL 49-711-625001. FAX 49-711-625005. Ed.Bd. adv.; bk.rev.; charts; illus.; index every 20 vols. **Indexed:** ASCA, Biol.Abstr., Curr.Adv.Ecol.Sci., Curr.Cont., Deep Sea Res.& Oceanogr.Abstr., Ind.Sci.Rev., Ocean.Abstr., Plant Breed.Abstr., Pollut.Abstr., Rev.Plant Path., Sci.Cit.Ind., Sel.Water Res.Abstr., So.Pac.Per.Ind., Soils & Fert., W.R.C.Inf. **Document type:** academic/scholarly publication.
  —BLDSC (6179.050000); CISTI; EMDOCS; Genuine Article; Linda Hall; SWETS; UnCover. **CCC.**

581   GW   ISSN 0078-2238
QK504   CODEN: NOHBA9
NOVA HEDWIGA, BEIHEFTE. (Text in English, French, German) 1962. irreg. price varies. J. Cramer in der Gebrueder Borntraeger Verlagsbuchhandlung, Johannesstr. 3A, 70176 Stuttgart, Germany. TEL 49-711-625001. FAX 49-711-625005. **Indexed:** Biodet.Abstr., Biol.Abstr., Deep Sea Res.& Oceanogr.Abstr., GeoRef. **Document type:** academic/scholarly publication.
  —BLDSC (6179.070000); Linda Hall.

581   US   ISSN 1055-3177
QK96   CODEN: NOVOEK
NOVON; a journal for botanical nomenclature. 1991. q. $110 includes Annals (Canada & Mexico $115; elsewhere $135) (effective through 1998). Missouri Botanical Garden, Scientific Publications, c/o Amy McPherson, Box 299, St. Louis, MO 63166-0299. TEL 314-577-9534. FAX 314-577-9594. E-mail: novon@mobot.org; URL: http://www.mobot.org. Ed. Marshall R. Crosby. R&P contact: Amy McPherson. illus.; index. circ. 860. (back issues avail.) **Document type:** academic/scholarly publication.
  —BLDSC (6180.429700); CISTI; EMDOCS; Linda Hall; SWETS; UnCover.
    Description: Contains papers discussing the establishment of new nomenclature in vascular plants and bryophytes.
    Refereed Serial

581   AT   ISSN 0085-4417
QK1   CODEN: NUYTDN
NUYTSIA. 1970. irreg. Aus.$10 per issue. Department of Conservation and Land Management, Locke Bag 104, Bentley Delivery Centre, W.A. 6893, Australia. TEL 61-9-334-0333. FAX 61-9-334-0498. circ. 600. **Indexed:** Biol.Abstr., CALL, Curr.Adv.Ecol.Sci., Forest.Abstr., Plant Breed.Abstr.

581   SP   ISSN 0376-5016
O P T I M A NEWSLETTER/INFORMATEUR O P T I M A. 1975. s.a. 25 SFr. membership (effective 1997). Organization for the Phyto-Taxonomic Investigation of the Mediterranean Area, Departamento Biologia Vegetal, Universidad Politecnica de Madrid, Ciudad Universitaria, 28040 Madrid, Spain. TEL 34-15445800. FAX 34-13365656. E-mail: iriondo@ccupm.upm.es; URL: http://www.bgbm.fu-berlin.de/optima/. Ed. J.M. Iriondo. R&P contact: J.M. Iriondo. adv.: page $500. bk.rev.; circ. 900 (controlled). **Document type:** newsletter.
    Description: Includes news about botanical research, reports and announcements of meetings and congresses, news of institutions or societies, list of publications and extensive book and journal reviews.

ON THE FRINGE. see GARDENING AND HORTICULTURE

ONTARIO ROYAL BOTANICAL GARDENS. GARDENS' BULLETIN. see GARDENING AND HORTICULTURE

ONTARIO ROYAL BOTANICAL GARDENS. SPECIAL BULLETIN. see GARDENING AND HORTICULTURE

580 635   CN   ISSN 0072-9655
ONTARIO ROYAL BOTANICAL GARDENS. TECHNICAL BULLETIN. 1957. irreg. price varies. Royal Botanical Gardens, Box 399, Hamilton, ON L8N 3H8, Canada. TEL 905-527-1158. FAX 905-577-0375. Ed. J. Lord. circ. 1,000. (back issues avail.) **Document type:** academic/scholarly publication, bulletin.

581   DK   ISSN 0078-5237
QK1   CODEN: OPBOA2
OPERA BOTANICA. (Supplement to: Nordic Journal of Botany) (Text in English) 1953. irreg. DKK 50 (per 16 published pages) (effective 1997). Nordic Publications in Botany, The Secretary, Gothersgade 130, DK-1123 Copenhagen K, Denmark. adv.; bk.rev.; index. circ. 500. (also avail. in microform from UMI; microfiche from IDC; reprint service avail. from UMI; back issues avail.) **Indexed:** Biol.Abstr., Curr.Adv.Ecol.Sci., Curr.Cont, Field Crop Abstr., Forest.Abstr., Herb.Abstr., Plant Breed.Abstr., Sci.Cit.Ind., Soils & Fert., Weed Abstr.
  —BLDSC (6266.700000); CISTI; Linda Hall; UnCover.
    Incorporates (in 1981): Dansk Botanisk Arkiv (ISSN 0011-6211)
    Refereed Serial

581   BE   ISSN 0775-9592
OPERA BOTANICA BELGICA. (Text in English, French) 1988. a. price varies. Jardin Botanique National de Belgique - Nationale Plantentuin van Belgie, Domaine de Bouchout, 1860 Meise, Belgium. TEL 32-2-2693905. (back issues avail.) **Document type:** monographic series.
  —BLDSC (6266.703000); Linda Hall.

581 591   AG   ISSN 0078-5245
Q33   CODEN: OPLLA9
OPERA LILLOANA. (Text in Spanish; summaries in English, French, German, Italian) 1957. irreg., vol.40, 1992. (Secretaria de Ciencia y Tecnologia) Fundacion Miguel Lillo, Centro de Informacion Geo-Biologico, Miguel Lillo 251, 4000 San Miguel de Tucuman, Argentina. Ed. Jose A. Haedo Rossi. bibl.; illus. circ. 500. (back issues avail.) **Indexed:** Biol.Abstr., Bull.Signal., GeoRef, Ref.Zh.
  —CISTI.

581   NE   ISSN 0920-1998
ORCHID MONOGRAPHS. (Text in English) 1986. irreg., vol.8, 1995. price varies. Rijksherbarium - Hortus Botanicus, Publications Department, P.O. Box 9514, 2300 RA Leiden, Netherlands. E-mail: vogel@rulrhb.leidenuniv.nl. Ed. E.F. de Vogel. illus. (back issues avail.) **Document type:** monographic series.
  —Linda Hall.
    Description: Systematic monographs and revisions of groups of Orchidaceae, with an emphasis on the Malesian area.

584.4   II   ISSN 0971-5371
ORCHID SOCIETY OF INDIA. JOURNAL. (Text in English) 1987. a. $35. Hindustan Publishing Corp., 4805-24, 1st Fl., Bharat Ram Rd., Darya Ganj, New Delhi 110 002, India. TEL 91-11-3254401. FAX 91-11-6863511. E-mail: hpcpd@giasdl01.vsnl.net.in.

584 635.94   NE   ISSN 0030-4484
ORCHIDEEEN. 1934. bi-m. fl.55 (foreign fl.79) (effective 1996). Nederlandse Orchideeen Vereniging, c/o T. van den Heuvel, Westerse Drift 53, 9752 LC Haren, Netherlands. TEL 31-50-5341420. FAX 31-50-5341420. E-mail: rednov@kmowarc.nl. (Subscr. to: c/o L. Kristelijn, Apollostraat 4, 1431 WR Aalsmeer, Netherlands. TEL 31-297-320707) Ed. N.A. van der Cingel. R&P contact: N.A. van der Cingel. adv.: B&W page fl.600; adv. contact: T. van den Heuvel. bk.rev.; bibl.; illus. circ. 2,200. **Indexed:** Hort.Abstr. **Document type:** bulletin.
    Description: Covers biological research in ecology, seeding, cultivation, hybridization, and germination. Includes society news, information, reports as well as lists of events and exhibitions.

ORNITHOLOGISCHER VEREIN ZU HILDESHEIM. MITTEILUNGEN. see BIOLOGY — Ornithology

653.934   MX   ISSN 0300-3701
SB409.A1
ORQUIDEA (MEX). (Text in English, Spanish) 1971. irreg. $37. Herbarium Amo, Apdo. Postal 53-123, 11320 Mexico D.F., Mexico. TEL 52-5-203-1909. FAX 52-5-531-4349. E-mail: eric@mail.internet.com.mx. Ed. Eric Hagsater. adv.; bk.rev.; illus.; index. circ. 1,000. **Indexed:** Ash.G.Bot.Per., Biol.Abstr., Excerp.Bot. **Document type:** academic/scholarly publication.

OSAKA-SHIRITSU SHIZENSHI HAKUBUTSUKAN SHUZO SHIRYO MOKUROKU/OSAKA MUSEUM OF NATURAL HISTORY. SPECIAL PUBLICATIONS. see BIOLOGY

581   UK   ISSN 0264-861X
QK725   CODEN: OSPBEO
OXFORD SURVEYS OF PLANT MOLECULAR AND CELL BIOLOGY. 1984. a. price varies. Oxford University Press, Oxford Journals, Walton St., Oxford OX2 6DP, England. TEL 01865-267907. FAX 01865-267773. TELEX 837330-OXPRES-G. E-mail: jnlorders@oup.co.uk. (U.S. subscr. to: Oxford University Press Inc., 2001 Evans Rd., Cary, NC 27513. TEL 919-677-0977. FAX 919-677-1714) Ed. B.J. Miffin. adv. **Indexed:** Cott.&Trop.Fibr.Abstr., Crop Physiol.Abstr., Curr.Adv.Ecol.Sci., Curr.Adv.Genetics & Molec.Biol., Field Crop Abstr., Herb.Abstr., Plant Grow.Reg.Abstr., Seed Abstr., Soils & Fert., Triticale Abstr. **Document type:** academic/scholarly publication.
  —BLDSC (6321.025280); CASDDS; CISTI; Linda Hall. **CCC.**

681   US   ISSN 1042-3524
                           CODEN: PGQUED
P G R S A QUARTERLY.* 1971. q. $25 (foreign $30). Plant Growth Regulator Society of America, c/o C. David Fritz, Rhone Poulenc AG Company, Box 12014, Research Triangle Park, NC 27709. TEL 607-257-1035. FAX 607-254-1242. Ed. Richard Hodgson. bk.rev. circ. 800. (back issues avail.) **Indexed:** Crop Physiol.Abstr., Field Crop Abstr., Ornam.Hort.
  —CASDDS; CISTI; Linda Hall; UnCover.
    Formerly: P G R Bulletin (ISSN 0163-6367)

581   PK   ISSN 0556-3321
QK1   CODEN: PJBOB6
PAKISTAN JOURNAL OF BOTANY. (Text in English) 1969. s-a. Rps.150($40) (effective 1997). Pakistan Botanical Society, Dept. of Botany, University of Karachi, Karachi 75270, Pakistan. TEL 92-21-447867. FAX 92-21-466896. Ed. Abdul Ghaffar. R&P contact: Abdul Ghaffar. adv.; bk.rev.; circ. 1,000 (controlled). (back issues avail.; reprint service avail. from ISI,UMI) **Indexed:** ASCA, Biol.Abstr., Chem.Abstr., Crop Physiol.Abstr., Curr.Adv.Ecol.Sci., Curr.Cont., Excerp.Med., Field Crop Abstr., Food Sci.& Tech.Abstr., Forest.Abstr., Herb.Abstr., Hort.Abstr., Maize Abstr., Plant Grow.Reg.Abstr., Rev.Plant Path., Seed Abstr., Soils & Fert., Soyabean Abstr., Weed Abstr. **Document type:** academic/scholarly publication.
  —BLDSC (6340.950000); CASDDS; CISTI; Genuine Article; Linda Hall; UMI; UnCover. **CCC.**
    Refereed Serial

PAKISTAN JOURNAL OF NEMATOLOGY. see BIOLOGY — Zoology

BIOLOGY — BOTANY

581   PK   ISSN 1016-0035
PAKPHYTON. (Text in English) 1989. a. $50 (effective 1996). Agriculturalists, Breeders and Botanists' Club of Pakistan, Department of Botany, University of the Punjab, Quaid-e-Azam Campus, Lahore 54590, Pakistan. TEL 92-42-5869939.
FAX 92-42-5868313. Eds. Dr. K.A. Siddiqui, H.M.I. Hafiz. circ. 150. **Document type:** academic/scholarly publication.
—BLDSC (6343.235000).
Refereed Serial

561   II   ISSN 0031-0174
QE901   CODEN: PLBOAJ
PALAEOBOTANIST. 1952. 3/yr. Rs.900($90) per vol. Birbal Sahni Institute of Palaeobotany, 53 University Rd., Lucknow 226 007, India. Ed. B.S. Venkatachala. bk.rev.; charts; illus. circ. 400. (back issues avail.) **Indexed:** Biol.Abstr., GeoRef., IBR, Indian Sci.Abstr.
—BLDSC (6343.400000); CISTI; Linda Hall; UnCover.
Description: Aims to popularize palaeobotanical knowledge all over the world.

589.2   NE   ISSN 0031-5850
QK600
PERSOONIA; a mycological journal. (Supplement avail. (ISSN 0920-895X)) (Text in English, French, German) 1959. s-a. price varies. Rijksherbarium - Hortus Botanicus, Publications Department, P.O. Box 9514, 2300 RA Leiden, Netherlands. E-mail: noordeloos@rulrhb.leidenuniv.nl. Eds. J. van Brummelen, M.E. Noordeloos. illus.; index. circ. 300. (back issues avail.) **Indexed:** ASCA, Biol.Abstr., Curr.Adv.Ecol.Sci., Curr.Cont., Excerp.Bot., Rev.Plant Path. **Document type:** academic/scholarly publication.
—BLDSC (6428.104000); Linda Hall; UnCover.
Description: Devoted to the taxonomy of fungi.
Refereed Serial

589.2   NE   ISSN 0920-895X
PERSOONIA. SUPPLEMENT. (Text in English) 1967. irreg., vol.4, 1994. price varies. Rijksherbarium - Hortus Botanicus, Publications Department, P.O. Box 9514, 2300 RA Leiden, Netherlands. Eds. J. van Brummelen, M.E. Noordeloos. (back issues avail.) **Document type:** monographic series.
Description: Publishes in-depth studies on the taxonomy of specific genera of fungi, with particular emphasis on European examples.

581   BL   ISSN 0373-840X
QK263
PESQUISAS: PUBLICACOES DE BOTANICA. Key Title: Pesquisas. Botanica. (Numbering continues those of articles published in Pesquisas) 1957. irreg. price varies or exchange basis. (Universidade do Vale do Rio dos Sinos, Instituto Anchietano de Pesquisas) Unisinos, Av. Unisinos, 950, 93022-000 Sao Leopoldo RS, Brazil. TEL 55-51-5903333 ext. 1951. FAX 55-51-5921035. **Document type:** academic/scholarly publication.
—CISTI.
Supersedes in part (in 1960): Instituto Anchietano de Pesquisas. Pesquisas (ISSN 0480-1873)

PEST MANAGEMENT RECOMMENDATIONS FOR COMMERCIAL TREE-FRUIT PRODUCTION. see *AGRICULTURE — Crop Production And Soil*

581   AU   ISSN 0031-6733
    CODEN: PFLZAQ
PFLANZENARZT. 1948. 8/yr. S.300 (foreign S.400). Oesterreichischer Agrarverlag GmbH, Inkustr. 1-7, A-3400 Klosterneuburg, Austria.
TEL 02243-333006. FAX 02243-3330056. Ed. M. Walch. adv.; bk.rev.; charts; illus.; index. circ. 7,000. **Indexed:** Biol.Abstr., Biotech.Abstr., Chem.Abstr, Field Crop Abstr., Herb.Abstr., Hort.Abstr., Potato Abstr., Rev.Appl.Entomol., Rev.Plant Path., Rural Recreat.Tour.Abstr., Triticale Abstr., VITIS, World Agri.Econ.& Rural Sociol.Abstr.
—CASDDS. **CCC.**

581   AU   ISSN 0031-675X
SB605.A84
PFLANZENSCHUTZBERICHTE. (Text in German; summaries in English) 1947. 2/yr. S.490. Bundesamt und Forschungszentrum fuer Landwirtschaft, Institut fuer Phytomedizin, Spargelfeldstr. 191, A-1226 Vienna, Austria. Eds. Bruno Zwatz, Gerhard Bedlan. R&P contact: Bruno Zwatz. adv.; bk.rev.; charts; illus.; index. circ. 600. **Indexed:** Bio-Contr.News & Info., Biol.Abstr., Excerp.Med., Field Crop Abstr., Herb.Abstr., Hort.Abstr., Plant Breed.Abstr., Rev.Appl.Entomol., Rev.Plant Path., Triticale Abstr., VITIS, Weed Abstr. **Document type:** government publication.
—BLDSC (6439.050000); Linda Hall.
Description: Original articles about plant protection and welfare.

581   GW   ISSN 0079-1369
PHANEROGAMARUM MONOGRAPHIAE. 1969. irreg. price varies. J. Cramer in der Gebrueder Borntraeger Verlagsbuchhandlung, Johannesstr. 3A, 70176 Stuttgart, Germany. TEL 49-711-625001.
FAX 49-711-625005. **Indexed:** Biol.Abstr. **Document type:** monographic series.

581   PH   ISSN 0115-0804
    CODEN: PHPHD9
PHILIPPINE PHYTOPATHOLOGY. (Text in English) 1965. a. P.50($15) Philippine Phytopathological Society, c/o Department of Plant Pathology, Univ. of Philippines at Los Banos, College 4031, Laguna, Philippines. Ed. Avelino Raymundo. (back issues avail.)
—BLDSC (6456.130000); CASDDS.

581   NE   ISSN 0300-3604
QK882   CODEN: PHSYB5
PHOTOSYNTHETICA; international journal for photosynthesis research. (Text in English, French, German; summaries in English) 1967. q. fl.712 to institutions; $365.50 to institutions in U.S. (effective 1998). (Academy of Sciences, Institute of Experimental Botany, XR) Kluwer Academic Publishers, Postbus 17, 3300 AA Dordrecht, Netherlands. TEL 31-78-6392392.
FAX 31-78-6392254. TELEX 29245 KAPG NL. E-mail: services@wkap.nl; URL: http://www.wkap.nl. (Dist. by: Kluwer Academic Publishers Group, P.O. Box 322, 3300 AH Dordrecht, Netherlands. TEL 31-78-6392392. FAX 31-78-6546474; N. America dist. addr.: Box 358, Accord Sta., Hingham, MA 02018-0358. TEL 617-871-6600. FAX 617-871-6528) Ed. Zdenek Sestak. adv.; bk.rev.; bibl.; illus.; index. (also avail. in microform from UMI) **Indexed:** ASCA, Biol.Abstr., Chem.Abstr., Cott.& Trop.Fibr.Abstr., Crop Physiol.Abstr., Curr.Adv.Biochem., Curr.Adv.Ecol.Sci., Curr.Cont., Deep Sea Res.& Oceanogr.Abstr., Excerp.Med., Field Crop Abstr., Forest.Abstr., Forest Prod.Abstr., Herb.Abstr., Hort.Abstr., Irr.& Drain.Abstr., Ornam.Hort., Plant Breed.Abstr., Plant Grow.Reg.Abstr., Sci.Cit.Ind., Seed Abstr., Soils & Fert., Sorghum & Millets Abstr., Soyabean Abstr., Triticale Abstr., Weed Abstr. **Document type:** academic/scholarly publication.
—BLDSC (6474.370000); CASDDS; CISTI; EMDOCS; Genuine Article; Linda Hall; SWETS; UnCover. **CCC.**
Description: An international journal for photosynthesis research, publishing original papers as well as reviews on special topics, bibliography of reviews and methodological papers, reports on conferences.
Refereed Serial

589.3   US   ISSN 0031-8884
QK564   CODEN: PYCOAD
PHYCOLOGIA. (Text in English and French) 1961. 6/yr. $350 (foreign $350) (effective 1996). International Phycological Society, Box 1897, Lawrence, KS 66044-8897. TEL 913-843-1221.
FAX 913-843-1274. Ed. Ojvind Moestrup. R&P contact: Karen Hickey. adv.; bk.rev.; bibl.; charts; illus.; index. circ. 1,250. (also avail. in microform from UMI,SWZ; back issues avail.; reprint service avail. from ISI) **Indexed:** ASCA, Biol.Abstr., Chem.Abstr., Curr.Adv.Ecol.Sci., Curr.Cont., Deep Sea Res.& Oceanogr.Abstr., Ecol.Abstr., Geo.Abstr., Geol.Abstr., Ind.Sci.Rev., Int.Aerosp.Abstr., Ocean.Abstr., Plant Breed.Abstr., Sci.Cit.Ind., Sel.Water Res.Abstr., So.Pac.Per.Ind., Soils & Fert., W.R.C.Inf. **Document type:** academic/scholarly publication.
—BLDSC (6474.650000); CASDDS; CISTI; SWETS; UMI; UnCover.
Refereed Serial

589.3   US   ISSN 0045-3072
PHYCOLOGICAL NEWSLETTER. 1965. 3/yr. membership. Phycological Society of America, c/o Dr. Richard McCourt, Ed., Dept. of Biological Sciences, DePaul University, 1036 W. Belden, Chicago, IL 60614. TEL 312-362-8171.
FAX 312-362-5689. bk.rev. circ. 1,300. **Document type:** newsletter.
Description: News of scientific interest to biologists who study algae, including conference news, research, travel and employment opportunities.

589.3   AT   ISSN 1322-0829
QK564   CODEN: PHREFC
PHYCOLOGICAL RESEARCH. (Text in English) 1953. q. (Japanese Society of Phycology, JA - Nihon Sorui Gakkai) Blackwell Science Pty Ltd, P.O. Box 378, Carlton South, Vic. 3053, Australia.
TEL 61-3-93470300. FAX 61-3-93493016. E-mail: kawai@gradura.scitec.kobe-u.ac.jp. Ed. Hiroshi Kawai. adv.; bk.rev.; cum.index: vols.1-10; vols.11-20. circ. 1,000. **Document type:** academic/scholarly publication.
—BLDSC (6474.755000); CASDDS; CISTI; UnCover. **CCC.**
Supersedes in part (in 1995): Japanese Journal of Phycology (Bilingual Edition); Which was formerly: Sorui - Japanese Society of Phycology. Bulletin (ISSN 0038-1578)
Description: Contains original research articles, research notes, and reviews on all aspects of phycology.
Refereed Serial

581   II   ISSN 0031-8892
PHYKOS. 1962. s-a. $40. (Phycological Society of India) Today and Tomorrow's Printers and Publishers, 24B-5 Desh Bandhu Gupta Rd., Karol Bagh, New Delhi 110 005, India.
TEL 91-11-5721928. (Dist. in U.S. by: Scholarly Publications, 7310 Elcresta Dr., Houston, TX 77083) Ed. G.S. Venkataraman. abstr. **Indexed:** Biol.Abstr., Chem.Abstr., Curr.Cont., Deep Sea Res.& Oceanogr.Abstr., W.R.C.Inf. **Document type:** academic/scholarly publication.

581.1   DK   ISSN 0031-9317
QK1   CODEN: PHPLAI
PHYSIOLOGIA PLANTARUM. (Text in English, French or German) 1948. m. DKK 3850 in Europe (US, Canada and Japan DKK 3970) (effective 1997). (Scandinavian Society for Plant Physiology) Munksgaard International Publishers Ltd., 35 Noerre Soegade, P.O. Box 2148, DK-1016 Copenhagen K, Denmark. TEL 45-33-127030. FAX 45-33-129387. E-mail: fsub@mail.munksgaard.dk. (In N. America: Commerce Place, 350 Main St., Malden, MA 02148-5018. TEL 617-388-6273. FAX 617-388-8274) (Co-sponsor: European Societies of Plant Physiology) Ed. Chris Bornman. charts; illus. circ. 2,000. (also avail. in microform from SWZ,PMC; reprint service avail. from ISI,SWZ) **Indexed:** Abstr.Bull.Inst.Pap.Chem., Agri.Eng.Abstr., ASCA, Biol.Abstr., Biol.& Agr.Ind., Cadscan, Chem.Abstr, Cott.& Trop.Fibr.Abstr., Crop Physiol.Abstr., Curr.Adv.Biochem., Curr.Adv.Ecol.Sci., Curr.Adv.Genetics & Molec.Biol., Curr.Cont., Deep Sea Res.& Oceanogr.Abstr., Excerp.Med., Fababean Abstr., Field Crop Abstr., Food Sci.& Tech.Abstr., Forest Abstr., Forest Prod.Abstr., Herb.Abstr., Hort.Abstr., Ind.Sci.Rev., Irr.& Drain.Abstr., Lead Abstr., Maize Abstr., Ornam.Hort., Plant Breed.Abstr., Plant Grow.Reg.Abstr., Potato Abstr., Rev.Plant Path., Rice Abstr., Sci.Cit.Ind., Seed Abstr., Sel.Water Res.Abstr., Soils & Fert., Triticale Abstr., VITIS, Weed Abstr., Zincscan. **Document type:** academic/scholarly publication.
—BLDSC (6484.000000); CASDDS; CISTI; Genuine Article; KR SourceOne; Linda Hall; SWETS; UnCover. **CCC.**
Refereed Serial

BIOLOGY — BOTANY

581.2 — UK — ISSN 0885-5765
SB599 — CODEN: PMPPEZ
PHYSIOLOGICAL AND MOLECULAR PLANT PATHOLOGY; an international journal of experimental plant pathology. 1971. m. £380 (effective 1998). Academic Press Ltd. (Subsidiary of: Harcourt Brace & Company Ltd.), 24-28 Oval Rd., London NW1 7DX, England. TEL 44-171-267-4466. FAX 44-171-482-2293. TELEX 25775 ACPRES G. E-mail: apsubs@acad.com; URL: http://www.hbuk.co.uk/ap/pmpp; http://www.europe.idealibrary.com/. (Subscr. to: Harcourt Brace & Company Ltd., Foots Cray High St., Sidcup, Kent DA14 5HP, England. TEL 44-181-300-3322. FAX 44-181-309-0807) Ed. D.D. Clarke. R&P contact: Catherine John. adv. contact: Nik Screen. bk.rev.; charts; illus.; index. (reprint service avail. from SWZ) **Indexed:** ASCA, Bibl.Agri., Biol.Abstr., Biotech.Abstr., Chem.Abstr., Cott.& Trop.Fibr.Abstr., Curr.Adv.Ecol.Sci., Curr.Adv.Genetics & Molec.Biol., Curr.Cont., Field Crop Abstr., Food Sci.& Tech.Abstr., Forest.Abstr., Forest Prod.Abstr., Helminthol.Abstr., Hort.Abstr., Ind.Sci.Rev., Maize Abstr., Plant Breed.Abstr., Plant Grow.Reg.Abstr., Potato Abstr., Rev.Plant Path., Sci.Cit.Ind., So.Pac.Per.Ind., Soils & Fert., Triticale Abstr. **Document type:** academic/scholarly publication.
●Also available online.
—BLDSC (6484.533000); CASDDS; CISTI; EMDOCS; Genuine Article; Linda Hall; SWETS; UnCover. **CCC.**
Formerly: Physiological Plant Pathology (ISSN 0048-4059)
Description: Deals with all aspects of the physiology and biochemistry of the plant host-parasite relationship at all levels of complexity, from the molecular to the whole organism.

PHYSIS. see BIOLOGY — Zoology

580 — UK — ISSN 0958-0344
QK865 — CODEN: PHANEL
PHYTOCHEMICAL ANALYSIS. 1990. bi-m. $675 (foreign $675) (effective 1998). John Wiley & Sons Ltd., Journals, Baffins Ln., Chichester, W. Sussex PO19 1UD, England. TEL 44-1243-779777. FAX 44-1243-775878. E-mail: info-assets@wiley.co.uk; URL: http://www.wiley.co.uk. (Subscr. to: John Wiley & Sons, Inc., 605 Third Ave., New York, NY 10158. TEL 212-850-6645. FAX 212-850-6021) Ed. Barry Charlwood. adv.: B&W page £595, color page £1495; trim 297 x 210; adv. contact: Bob Kern. circ. 161. (also avail. in microform from UMI; back issues avail.; reprint service avail. from SWZ) **Indexed:** ASCA, Chem.Cit.Ind., Curr.Cont., Excerp.Med. (1993-). **Document type:** academic/scholarly publication.
—BLDSC (6489.695000); CASDDS; CISTI; EMDOCS; Genuine Article; SWETS; UMI; UnCover. **CCC.**
Description: Publishes original articles on the application of analytical methodology in the plant sciences.
Refereed Serial

581 — US
PHYTOCHEMICAL SOCIETY. PROCEEDINGS. 1965. irreg., vol.22, 1984. (Phytochemical Society) Academic Press, Inc., 525 B St., Ste. 1900, San Diego, CA 92101-4495. TEL 619-231-0926. FAX 619-699-6715. (Subscr. to: Order Dept., 6277 Sea Harbor Dr., 4th Fl., Orlando, FL 32887. TEL 800-321-5068) (reprint service avail. from ISI) **Indexed:** Biol.Abstr. **Document type:** proceedings.
Formerly: Phytochemical Society Symposia Series. Proceedings.

581.19 — UK — ISSN 0031-9422
QK861 — CODEN: PYTCAS
PHYTOCHEMISTRY; international journal of plant biochemistry. (Text in English, French and German) 1962. 24/yr. fl.4873($2801) (effective 1998). (Phytochemical Society of Europe) Elsevier Science Ltd., Pergamon, P.O. Box 800, Kidlington, Oxford OX5 1DX, England. TEL 44-1865-843000. FAX 44-1865-843010. E-mail: nlinfo-f@elsevier.nl; usinfo-f@elsevier.nl; usinfo-f@elsevier.com; forinfo-kyf04035@niftyserve.or.jp; URL: http://www.elsevier.nl/. (Subscr. to: Elsevier Science, Regional Sales Office, P.O. Box 211, 1000 AE Amsterdam, Netherlands. TEL 31-20-4853757. FAX 31-20-4853432; Subscr. in the Americas to: Elsevier Science, Regional Sales Office, Box 945, New York, NY 10159-0945. TEL 212-633-3730. FAX 212-633-3680; Subscr. in Australasia and the Far East to: Elsevier Science (Singapore) Pte Ltd, No.1 Temasek Ave., No.17-01 Millenia Tower, Singapore 039192, Singapore. TEL 65-434-3727. FAX 65-337-2230) (Co-sponsor: Phytochemical Society of North America) Ed. Jeffrey B. Harborne. adv.; bk.rev.; charts; illus.; index. circ. 2,500. (also avail. in microfiche from MIM; microfilm from UMI; back issues avail.) **Indexed:** Abstr.Bull.Inst.Pap.Chem., Agroforest.Abstr., Apic.Abstr., ASCA, Bibl.Agri., Biol.Abstr., Biol.& Agr.Ind., Biotech.Abstr., Chem.Abstr., Chem.Cit.Ind., Chem.Infd., Cott.& Trop.Fibr.Abstr., Crop Physiol.Abstr., Curr.Adv.Biochem., Curr.Adv.Ecol.Sci., Curr.Adv.Genetics & Molec.Biol., Curr.Chem.React., Curr.Cont., Deep Sea Res.& Oceanogr.Abstr., Environ.Abstr., Excerp.Med., Fababean Abstr., Field Crop Abstr., Food Sci.& Tech.Abstr., Forest.Abstr., Forest Prod.Abstr., Helminthol.Abstr., Herb.Abstr., Hort.Abstr., Ind.Chem, Ind.Sci.Rev., Ind.Vet., Irr.& Drain.Abstr., Maize Abstr., Mass Spectr.Bull., Nutr.Abstr., Ocean.Abstr., Ornam.Hort., Plant Breed.Abstr., Plant Grow.Reg.Abstr., Potato Abstr., Rev.Med.& Vet.Mycol., Rice Abstr., Sci.Cit.Ind., Seed Abstr., So.Pac.Per.Ind., Soils & Fert., Sor., Sorghum & Millets Abstr., Soyabean Abstr., Triticale Abstr., Trop.Oil Seeds Abstr., Vet.Bull., VITIS, Weed Abstr. **Document type:** academic/scholarly publication.
—BLDSC (6489.800000); CASDDS; CISTI; EMDOCS; Genuine Article; KR SourceOne; Linda Hall; SWETS; UMI; UnCover. **CCC.**
Description: Covers research on all aspects of pure and applied plant biochemistry.
Refereed Serial

581 — GW — ISSN 0340-269X
QK911 — CODEN: PYCEBI
PHYTOCOENOLOGIA. (Text in English, French, German, Spanish) 1974. 4/yr. DM.149 per no. (effective 1997). (International Society for Vegetation Science) Gebrueder Borntraeger Verlagsbuchhandlung, Johannesstr. 3A, 70176 Stuttgart, Germany. TEL 49-711-625001. FAX 49-711-625005. Ed.Bd. index. **Indexed:** Biol.Abstr., Curr.Adv.Ecol.Sci., Forest.Abstr., Forest Prod.Abstr., Herb.Abstr., Weed Abstr. **Document type:** academic/scholarly publication.
—BLDSC (6489.900000); SWETS; UnCover. **CCC.**

581 — US — ISSN 0031-9430
QK1 — CODEN: PYTLAL
PHYTOLOGIA; an international journal to expedite botanical publication. 1933. m. (in 2 vols.) $22 (Canada $29.50; elsewhere $31.90) (effective 1996). c/o Michael J. Warnock, Ed., 185 Westridge Dr., Huntsville, TX 77340. TEL 409-295-5410. FAX 409-291-0009. Pub. Michael J. Warnock. bk.rev.; abstr.; bibl.; charts; illus.; s-a. index. circ. 400. **Indexed:** Biol.Abstr., Excerp.Bot., Field Crop Abstr., Forest.Abstr., Herb.Abstr., Hort.Abstr., Plant Breed.Abstr., Potato Abstr., Rev.Plant Path., So.Pac.Per.Ind. **Document type:** academic/scholarly publication.
—Linda Hall; SWETS; UnCover.
Refereed Serial

581.4 — II — ISSN 0031-9449
QK1 — CODEN: PHYMAW
PHYTOMORPHOLOGY; an international journal of plant morphology. (Text in English, German, French) 1951. q. $100. (International Society of Plant Morphologists) Scientific Publishers, P.O. Box 91, 5A, New Pali Rd., Jodhpur 342 001, India. TEL 91-291-33323. FAX 91-291-613480. Ed. N.N. Bhandari. adv.; bk.rev.; bibl.; charts; illus.; stat.; index. circ. 1,200. (back issues avail.) **Indexed:** Abstr.Bull.Inst.Pap.Chem., Biol.Abstr., Biol.& Agr.Ind., Chem.Abstr., Curr.Adv.Ecol.Sci., Field Crop Abstr., GeoRef., Herb.Abstr., Hort.Abstr., Ornam.Hort., Plant Breed.Abstr., Plant Grow.Reg.Abstr., Rev.Plant Path., Sorghum & Millets Abstr., Triticale Abstr., Weed Abstr. **Document type:** academic/scholarly publication.
—Linda Hall; SWETS; UnCover.

581 — AG — ISSN 0031-9457
QK1 — CODEN: PHYBAX
PHYTON; international journal of experimental botany. (Text in English, French, German, Italian, Portuguese, Spanish) 1951. 2/yr. $35 (effective Jan. 1994). Fundacion Romulo Raggio, Gaspar Campos 861, 1638 Vicente Lopez, Argentina. TEL 54-1-791-0868. FAX 54-1-796-1456. (Co-sponsor: Sociedad Latinoamericana de Fisiologia Vegetal) Ed. Miguel Raggio. adv.; bk.rev.; index; circ. 750 (controlled). (also avail. in microform from UMI; reprint service avail. from UMI) **Indexed:** Abstr.Bull.Inst.Pap.Chem., ASCA, Bibl.Agri., Biol.Abstr., Chem.Abstr., Crop Physiol.Abstr., Curr.Adv.Ecol.Sci., Curr.Cont., Field Crop Abstr., Forest.Abstr., Forest Prod.Abstr., Helminthol.Abstr., Herb.Abstr., Hort.Abstr., Irr.& Drain.Abstr., Plant Grow.Reg.Abstr., Potato Abstr., Rev.Plant Path., Sci.Cit.Ind., Seed Abstr., Soils & Fert., Triticale Abstr., VITIS, Weed Abstr. **Document type:** academic/scholarly publication.
—BLDSC (6494.100000); CASDDS; CISTI; Genuine Article; Linda Hall; SWETS; UMI; UnCover.

581 — AU — ISSN 0079-2047
QK1 — CODEN: PHYNAZ
PHYTON. ANNALES REI BOTANICAE. 1949. a. (with 2 updates/yr.). S.590 per upd. Verlag Ferdinand Berger und Soehne GmbH, Wienerstr. 21-23, A-3580 Horn, Austria. TEL 43-2983-4161232. FAX 43-2982-2317235. Eds. D. Grill, H. Teppner. **Indexed:** ASCA, Curr.Cont., Herb.Abstr., Soils & Fert., Soyabean Abstr. **Document type:** academic/scholarly publication.
—BLDSC (6494.000000); CASDDS; CISTI; Genuine Article; Linda Hall; UnCover.

581.876 — PL — ISSN 1230-0462
PHYTOPATHOLOGIA POLONICA. (Text in English) 1974. s-a. 8 Zl.($5) per no. (effective 1996 & 1997). Polskie Towarzystwo Fitopatologiczne - Polish Phytopathological Society, Ul. Wojska Polskiego 71 c, 60-625 Poznan, Poland. TEL 48-61-487713. FAX 48-61-487145. TELEX ARPL 0413322. (Co-sponsor: Komitet Badan Naukowych - Committee for Scientific Research) Ed. Malgorzata Manka. R&P contact: Malgorzata Manka. circ. 400. (back issues avail.) **Indexed:** AgroAgen, AgroLibrex. **Document type:** academic/scholarly publication.
—BLDSC (6494.800000).
Formerly (until 1990): Polska Akademia Nauk. Wydzial Nauk Rolniczych i Lesnych. Zeszyty Problemowe Postepow Nauk Rolniczych. Phytopathologia Polonica (ISSN 1230-0810)
Description: Presents research works on diseases caused by fungi, bacteria and viruses on agricultural, horticultural and forest plants.
Refereed Serial

581 UK ISSN 0069-7141
CODEN: CYMPA
PHYTOPATHOLOGICAL PAPERS. (Former name of issuing body: Commonwealth Mycological Institute (C M I)) 1956. irreg. price varies. (International Mycological Institute) CAB International, Wallingford, Oxon. OX10 8DE, England. TEL 44-1491-832111. FAX 44-1491-826090. TELEX 847964 COMAGG G. E-mail: cabi@cabi.org; URL: http://www.cabi.org. (Alt. addr.: International Mycological Institute, Bakeham Ln., Egham, Surrey TW20 9TY, England; U.S. subscr. to: Oxford University Press, Customer Services Dept., 2001 Evans Rd., Cary, NC 27513. TEL 800-445-9714. FAX 919-677-1303) **Indexed:** Biol.Abstr., Helminthol.Abstr., Hort.Abstr., Rev.Plant Path. **Document type:** monographic series, academic/scholarly publication.
—BLDSC (6495.200000); CISTI; Linda Hall.
Description: Explores plantopathological topics; includes country lists of plant diseases and crop diseases.

630 581.2 JA ISSN 0031-9473
CODEN: NSBGAM
PHYTOPATHOLOGICAL SOCIETY OF JAPAN. ANNALS/NIHON SHOKUBUTSU BYORI GAKKAIHO. (Text in English or Japanese) 1918. 6/yr. $50 to individuals; institutions $115. Phytopathological Society of Japan - Nihon Shokubutsu Byori Gakkai, Shokubo Bldg., 1-43-11 Komagome, Toshima-ku, Tokyo 170, Japan. FAX 81-3-3943-6021. Ed. H. Kunoh. adv. circ. 2,600. **Indexed:** Bio-Contr.News & Info., Biodet.Abstr., Biol.Abstr., Chem.Abstr., Crop Physiol.Abstr., Fababean Abstr., Field Crop Abstr., Food Sci.& Tech.Abstr., Forest.Abstr., Forest Prod.Abstr., Helminthol.Abstr., Herb.Abstr., Hort.Abstr., Irr.& Drain.Abstr., Maize Abstr., Plant Breed.Abstr., Potato Abstr., Rev.Appl.Entomol., Seed Abstr., Sel.Water Res.Abstr., Soils & Fert., Soyabean Abstr., Triticale Abstr.
—BLDSC (1031.300000); CASDDS; SWETS; UnCover. **CCC.**

581.2 US ISSN 0031-949X
SB599 CODEN: PHYTAJ
PHYTOPATHOLOGY; an international journal. 1911. m. $270 (foreign $320) (effective 1997). (American Phytopathological Society) A P S Press, 3340 Pilot Knob Rd., St. Paul, MN 55121-2097. TEL 612-454-7250; 800-328-7560. FAX 612-454-0766. TELEX 6502439657 (MCI UW). E-mail: gross@wsunix.wsu.edu. Ed. Margaret E. Daub; Pub. Steven C. Nelson. bk.rev.; abstr.; bibl.; charts; illus.; index. circ. 3,788. (also avail. in microform from UMI,PMC; back issues avail.) **Indexed:** Acid Rain Abstr., Acid Rain Ind., Apic.Abstr., ASCA, Bibl.Agri., Bibl.Ind., Bio-Contr.News & Info., Biol.Abstr., Biol.& Agr.Ind., Biol.Dig., Biotech.Abstr., Chem.Abstr., Cott.& Trop.Fibr.Abstr., Curr.Adv.Ecol.Sci., Curr.Adv.Genetics & Molec.Biol., Curr.Biotech.Abstr., Curr.Cont., Deep Sea Res.& Oceanogr.Abstr., Environ.Abstr., Excerp.Med., Fababean Abstr., Field Crop Abstr., Food Sci.& Tech.Abstr., Forest.Abstr., Forest Prod.Abstr., Geo.Abstr., Helminthol.Abstr., Herb.Abstr., Hort.Abstr., Ind.Sci.Rev., Irr.& Drain.Abstr., Maize Abstr., Nutr.Abstr., Plant Breed.Abstr., Plant Grow.Reg.Abstr., Potato Abstr., Rev.Appl.Entomol., Rev.Plant Path., Rice Abstr., Sci.Cit.Ind., Seed Abstr., Sel.Water Res.Abstr., Soils & Fert., Sorghum & Millets Abstr., Soyabean Abstr., Telegen, Triticale Abstr., Trop.Oil Seeds Abstr., VITIS, Weed Abstr.
—BLDSC (6497.000000); CASDDS; CIS; CISTI; Genuine Article; KR SourceOne; Linda Hall; SWETS; UnCover. **CCC.**
Description: Original research in the field of plant pathology.
Refereed Serial

581.2 US ISSN 0278-0267
PHYTOPATHOLOGY NEWS. 1967. m. $15. (American Phytopathological Society) A P S Press, 3340 Pilot Knob Rd., St. Paul, MN 55121-2097. TEL 612-454-7250. FAX 612-454-0766. TELEX 6502439657 (MCI UW). Ed. Robert F. Nyvall; Pub. Steven C. Nelson. bk.rev.; illus. circ. 4,634.
Description: News to friends and members of the society.

PHYTOPROTECTION. see *AGRICULTURE — Crop Production And Soil*

610 UK ISSN 0951-418X
CODEN: PHYREH
PHYTOTHERAPY RESEARCH; an international journal devoted to medical and scientific research on plants and plant products. 1987. 8/yr. $925 (foreign $925) (effective 1998). John Wiley & Sons Ltd., Journals, Baffins Ln., Chichester, W. Sussex PO19 1UD, England. TEL 44-1243-779777. FAX 44-1243-775878. E-mail: info-assets@wiley. co.uk; URL: http://www.wiley.co.uk. (Subscr. in the Americas to: John Wiley & Sons, Inc., 605 Third Ave., New York, NY 10158. TEL 212-850-6645. FAX 212-850-6021) Ed. Fred J. Evans; Pub. Michael Davis. adv.: B&W page £595, color page £1495; trim 297 x 210; adv. contact: Bob Kern. circ. 450. (also avail. in microform from UMI; back issues avail.; reprint service avail. from SWZ) **Indexed:** ASCA, Bibl.Agri., Chem.Abstr., Chem.Cit.Ind., Curr.Cont., Excerp.Med., Ind.Sci.Rev., Sci.Cit.Ind., SSCI. **Document type:** academic/scholarly publication.
—BLDSC (6497.060000); ADONIS; CASDDS; EMDOCS; Genuine Article; KNAW; SWETS; UMI. **CCC.**
Description: Publishes original medical plant research, including biochemistry and molecular pharmacology, toxicology, pathology, and the clinical application of herbs and natural products to both human and animal medicine.
Refereed Serial

PLANT ANALYSIS MANUAL. see *AGRICULTURE — Crop Production And Soil*

581 574.8 JA ISSN 0032-0781
QK710 CODEN: PCPHA5
PLANT AND CELL PHYSIOLOGY. (Text in English) 1960. 12/yr. $350 to non-members. Japanese Society of Plant Physiologists - Nihon Shokubutsu Seiri Gakkai, Shimotachiuri Ogawa Higashi, Kamikyo-ku, Kyoto 602, Japan. FAX 81-75-415-3661. E-mail: jspp@nacos.com. Ed. Koji Asada. adv.; index. circ. 2,990. (also avail. in microform from PMC; back issues avail.) **Indexed:** Abstr.Bull.Inst.Pap.Chem., ASCA, Bibl.Agri., Biol.Abstr., Biol.& Agr.Ind., Chem.Abstr., Crop Physiol.Abstr., Curr.Adv.Plant Sci., Curr.Cont., Fababean Abstr., Field Crop Abstr., Food Sci.& Tech.Abstr., Forest.Abstr., Forest Prod.Abstr., Herb.Abstr., Hort.Abstr., Ind.Med. (1994-), Ind.Sci.Rev., Int.Aerosp.Abstr., Irr.& Drain.Abstr., Maize Abstr., Ornam.Hort., Plant Grow.Reg.Abstr., Potato Abstr., Rice Abstr., Sci.Cit.Ind., Seed Abstr., Soyabean Abstr., Triticale Abstr., Weed Abstr. **Document type:** academic/scholarly publication.
—BLDSC (6512.250000); CASDDS; CISTI; EMDOCS; KR SourceOne; Linda Hall; SWETS; UnCover.
Description: Covers broad areas of plant sciences, including physiology, biochemistry, biophysics, chemistry, molecular and cell biology as well as gene engineering of plants and microorganisms.

580 NE ISSN 0032-079X
SB13 CODEN: PLSOA2
PLANT AND SOIL; international journal on plant-soil relationships. (Text in English, French and German) 1949. 20/yr. fl.4930 to institutions; $2530 to institutions in U.S. (effective 1998). (Koninklijk Genootschap voor Landbouwwetenschap - Royal Netherlands Society of Agricultural Science) Kluwer Academic Publishers, Postbus 17, 3300 AA Dordrecht, Netherlands. TEL 31-78-6392392. FAX 31-78-6392254. TELEX 29245 KAPG NL. E-mail: services@wkap.nl; URL: http://www.wkap.nl. (Dist. by: Kluwer Academic Publishers Group, P.O. Box 322, NE-3300 AH Dordrecht, Netherlands. TEL 31-78-6392392. FAX 31-78-6546474; N. America dist. addr.: Box 358, Accord Sta., Hingham, MA 02018-0358. TEL 617-871-6600. FAX 617-871-6528) Ed. H. Lambert. adv.; bibl.; charts; illus.; index. (also avail. in microform from UMI,PMC; reprint service avail. from SWZ) **Indexed:** Acid Rain Abstr., Acid Rain Ind., Agri.Eng.Abstr., Agroforest.Abstr., ASCA, Biol.Abstr., Biol.& Agr.Ind., Bull.Signal., Cadscan, Chem.Abstr., Cott.& Trop.Fibr.Abstr., Crop Physiol.Abstr., Curr.Adv.Ecol.Sci., Curr.Cont., Ecol.Abstr., Energy Ind., Energy Info.Abstr., Environ.Abstr., Environ.Per.Bibl. (1981-), Excerp.Med., Fababean Abstr., Field Crop Abstr., Food Sci.& Tech.Abstr., Forest.Abstr., Forest Prod.Abstr., Geo.Abstr.H.G., GeoRef., Herb.Abstr., Hort.Abstr., IDA, Ind.Sci.Rev., Int.Abstr.Biol.Sci., Irr.& Drain.Abstr., Lead Abstr., Maize Abstr., Nutr.Abstr., Ornam.Hort., Plant Breed Abstr., Plant Grow.Reg.Abstr., Potato Abstr., Rev.Plant Path., Rice Abstr., Sci.Cit.Ind., Seed Abstr., Sel.Water Res.Abstr., Soils & Fert., Sorghum & Millets Abstr., Soyabean Abstr., Triticale Abstr., Trop.Oil Seeds Abstr., Weed Abstr., Zincscan. **Document type:** academic/scholarly publication.
—BLDSC (6513.000000); CASDDS; CISTI; EMDOCS; Genuine Article; KR SourceOne; Linda Hall; SWETS; UMI; UnCover. **CCC.**
Description: Publishes original research articles dealing with fundamental and applied aspects of plant nutrition, soil fertility, plant-microbe associations, soil microbiology, soil-borne diseases, soil and plant ecology, agrochemistry and agrophysics.
Refereed Serial

PLANT BIOCHEMICAL JOURNAL. see *BIOLOGY — Biological Chemistry*

581 660 UK ISSN 0260-5902
PLANT BIOTECHNOLOGY. 1981. s-m. (diskette m.). £120 (diskette £120; both £180) (effective 1997). S U B I S, Mansion House, 19 Kingfield Rd., Sheffield S11 9AS, England. TEL 44-114-2554433. FAX 44-114-2554626. E-mail: subis@sheffac.demon.co.uk; URL: http://www.shef.ac.uk/uni/companies/shap. bk.rev. (also avail. in diskette format) **Indexed:** Abstr.Bull.Inst.Pap.Chem. **Document type:** abstracting/indexing.
—**CCC.**
Description: Current awareness service for researchers. Covers plant tissue culture, protoplasts, recombinant work, chemostat technology, immobilized enzymes and cells, biomass production and production of primary and secondary products.

BIOLOGY — BOTANY

581.16 631.53   GW   ISSN 0179-9541
SB123   CODEN: PLABED
PLANT BREEDING/ZEITSCHRIFT FUER PFLANZENZUECHTUNG. (Supplement avail.: Advances in Plant Breeding) (Text in English and German) 1913. 6/yr. DM.1327 in Europe; rest of world DM.1335 (effective 1998). Blackwell Wissenschaft, Kurfuerstendamm 57, 10707 Berlin, Germany. TEL 49-30-32790634. FAX 49-30-32790610. E-mail: aboverwalt@blackwis.de; URL: http://www.blackwis.com. Eds. W. Weber, G. Roebbelen. adv.: B&W page DM.560; trim 190 x 122. bk.rev.; abstr.; bibl.; illus.; stat.; index. circ. 600. (back issues avail.) **Indexed:** Bibl.Agri., Biol.Abstr., Chem.Abstr., Curr.Adv.Ecol.Sci., Curr.Cont., Fababean Abstr., Field Crop Abstr., Food Sci.& Tech.Abstr., Helminthol.Abstr., Herb.Abstr., Hort.Abstr., Ind.Sci.Rev., INSPEC, Int.Abstr.Biol.Sci., Maize Abstr., Plant Breed.Abstr., Plant Grow.Reg.Abstr., Potato Abstr., Rice Abstr., Sci.Cit.Ind., Seed Abstr., Soils & Fert., Sorghum & Millets Abstr., Soyabean Abstr., Triticale Abstr., VITIS, Weed Abstr. **Document type:** academic/scholarly publication.
—BLDSC (6513.980000); CASDDS; CISTI; EMDOCS; Genuine Article; SWETS; UnCover. CCC.
Formerly: Zeitschrift fuer Pflanzenzuechtung (ISSN 0044-3298)
Description: Covers all areas of plant breeding, including plant genetics, plant physiology, plant pathology, and plant growth and development.

PLANT BREEDING SERIES. see AGRICULTURE — Crop Production And Soil

581   US   ISSN 1040-4651
QK725   CODEN: PLCEEW
PLANT CELL. 1989. m. $375 to non-members; institutions $1300; members $330 (includes Plant Physiology) (effective 1998). American Society of Plant Physiologists, 15501 Monona Dr., Rockville, MD 20855. TEL 301-251-0560. FAX 301-279-2996. (Subscr. to: Fulco, Box 3000, Denville, NJ 07843. TEL 800-875-2997. FAX 201-627-5872) Ed. Robert B. Goldberg. **Indexed:** Abstr.Bull.Inst.Pap.Chem., ASCA, Biol.& Agr.Ind., Curr.Cont., Food Sci.& Tech.Abstr., Ind.Med. (1992-), Ind.Sci.Rev., Ornam.Hort., Rice Abstr., Sci.Cit.Ind.
—BLDSC (6514.180000); CASDDS; CISTI; EMDOCS; Genuine Article; KR SourceOne; Linda Hall; SWETS; UMI; UnCover.
Description: Presents original research articles in the areas of plant cell development and molecular biology.
Refereed Serial

581   GW   ISSN 0721-7714
QK725   CODEN: PCRPD8
PLANT CELL REPORTS. Online edition (GW ISSN 1432-203X) (Text in English) 1981. m. DM.1524.80 (foreign DM.1540.40) (effective 1998). Springer-Verlag, Heidelberger Platz 3, 14197 Berlin, Germany. TEL 49-30-82787-0. FAX 49-30-82787448. E-mail: subscriptions@springer.de; URL: http://link.springer.de. (Subscr. in N. America to: Springer-Verlag New York, Inc., 333 Meadowlands Pkwy., Secaucus, NJ 07094. TEL 212-460-1500. FAX 212-473-6272) Eds. N. Amrhein, O.L. Gamborg. (also avail. in microform from UMI; reprint service avail. from ISI) **Indexed:** Abstr.Bull.Inst.Pap.Chem., ASCA, Biol.Abstr., Chem.Abstr., Cott.&Trop.Fibr.Abstr., Crop Physiol.Abstr., Curr.Adv.Ecol.Sci., Curr.Cont., Fababean Abstr., Field Crop Abstr., Food Sci.& Tech.Abstr., Forest.Abstr., Forest Prod.Abstr., Herb.Abstr., Hort.Abstr., Ornam.Hort., Plant Breed.Abstr., Plant Grow.Reg.Abstr., Potato Abstr., Rice Abstr., Sci.Cit.Ind., Seed Abstr., Triticale Abstr., Weed Abstr. **Document type:** academic/scholarly publication.
●Also available online.
—BLDSC (6514.250000); CASDDS; CISTI; EMDOCS; Genuine Article; SWETS; UMI; UnCover. CCC.
Description: Devoted to all aspects of plant cell and plant cell culture research including physiology, cytology, biochemistry, molecular biology, plant genetics, and phytopathology.

581   II   ISSN 0970-4914
PLANT DISEASE RESEARCH. (Text in English) 1984. s-a. Indian Society of Plant Pathologists, Punjab Agricultural University, Ludhiana 141 004, India. Ed. S.S. Chahal. **Indexed:** Rev.Med.& Vet.Mycol.
—BLDSC (6515.020000).

581   NE   ISSN 1385-0237
QK901   CODEN: VGTOA4
PLANT ECOLOGY. (Text in English) 1949. m. fl.3792 to institutions; $1947 to institutions in U.S. (effective 1998). Kluwer Academic Publishers, Postbus 17, 3300 AA Dordrecht, Netherlands. TEL 31-78-6392392. FAX 31-78-6392254. TELEX 29245. E-mail: services@wkap.nl; URL: http://www.wkap.nl. (Dist. by: Kluwer Academic Publishers Group, P.O. Box 322, 3300 AH Dordrecht, Netherlands. TEL 31-78-6392392. FAX 31-78-6546474; N. America dist. addr.: Box 358, Accord Sta., Hingham, MA 02018-0358. TEL 617-871-6600. FAX 617-871-6528) Ed. A. van der Valk. adv.; bk.rev. (also avail. in microform from UMI; reprint service avail. from SWZ) **Indexed:** ASCA, Biol.Abstr., Br.Archaeol.Abstr., Curr.Adv.Ecol.Sci., Curr.Cont., Ecol.Abstr., Energy Ind., Energy Info.Abstr., Field Crop Abstr., Forest.Abstr., Forest Prod.Abstr., Geo.Abstr.H.G., Herb.Abstr., Hort.Abstr., IBR, IDA, Ind.Sci.Rev., Irr.& Drain.Abstr., Plant Breed.Abstr., Sci.Cit.Ind., Seed Abstr., Sel.Water Res.Abstr., Soils & Fert., Weed Abstr. **Document type:** academic/scholarly publication.
—BLDSC (6515.400000); EMDOCS; Genuine Article; Linda Hall; SWETS; UMI; UnCover. CCC.
Formerly: Vegetatio (ISSN 0042-3106)
Description: Publishes original scientific papers dealing with the ecology of vascular plants and bryophytes in terrestrial, aquatic and wetland ecosystems.
Refereed Serial

PLANT FOR LIFE; the biomass initiative newsletter. see ENVIRONMENTAL STUDIES

PLANT GENETIC RESOURCES ABSTRACTS. see BIOLOGY — Abstracting, Bibliographies, Statistics

PLANT GENETIC RESOURCES NEWSLETTER. see CONSERVATION

580   NE   ISSN 0167-6903
SB128   CODEN: PGRED3
PLANT GROWTH REGULATION; an international journal on plant growth and development. (Text in English) 1981. 9/yr. fl.1017 to institutions; $522 to institutions in U.S. (effective 1998). Kluwer Academic Publishers, Postbus 17, 3300 AA Dordrecht, Netherlands. TEL 31-78-6392392. FAX 31-78-6392254. TELEX 29245 KAPG NL. E-mail: services@wkap.nl; URL: http://www.wkap.nl. (Dist. by: Kluwer Academic Publishers Group, P.O. Box 322, 3300 AH Dordrecht, Netherlands. TEL 31-78-6392392. FAX 31-78-6546474; N. America dist. addr.: Box 358, Accord Sta., Hingham, MA 02018-0358. TEL 617-871-6600. FAX 617-871-6528) Eds. Tudor H. Thomas, Thomas J. Gianfagna. adv. (also avail. in microform from UMI; back issues avail.; reprint service avail. from SWZ) **Indexed:** Abstr.Bull.Inst.Pap.Chem., ASCA, Biol.Abstr., Biotech.Abstr., Chem.Abstr., Crop Physiol.Abstr., Curr.Adv.Ecol.Sci., Curr.Cont., Field Crop Abstr., Food Sci.& Tech.Abstr., Ind.Sci.Rev., Maize Abstr., Ornam.Hort., Plant Grow.Reg.Abstr., Rice Abstr., Sci.Cit.Ind., Sci.Cit.Ind., Soyabean Abstr., Triticale Abstr. **Document type:** academic/scholarly publication.
—BLDSC (6517.845000); CASDDS; CISTI; EMDOCS; Genuine Article; Linda Hall; SWETS; UMI; UnCover. CCC.
Description: Publishes original papers linking fundamental and applied research on the natural hormonal regulation of plant processes and the effects of growth regulating substances on plant growth and development.
Refereed Serial

PLANT GROWTH REGULATOR ABSTRACTS. see AGRICULTURE — Abstracting, Bibliographies, Statistics

581   UK   ISSN 0960-7412
QK728   CODEN: PLJUED
THE PLANT JOURNAL FOR CELL AND MOLECULAR BIOLOGY. 1991. 24/yr. £900($1663) (foreign £990) (effective 1998). (Society for Experimental Biology) Blackwell Science Ltd., Osney Mead, Oxford OX2 0EL, England. TEL 44-1865-206206. FAX 44-1865-721205. E-mail: journals.cs@blacksci.co.uk; URL: http://www.black.co.uk. Ed. D. Bowles; Pub. Allen Stevens. R&P contact: Sarah Pollard. adv. contact: Martine Cariou-Keen. bk.rev.; illus.; index. circ. 1,075. (also avail. in microform from UMI; back issues avail.) **Indexed:** ASCA, Curr.Cont., Ind.Med. (1993-), Ind.Sci.Rev., Sci.Cit.Ind. **Document type:** academic/scholarly publication.
—BLDSC (6519.200000); CASDDS; CISTI; EMDOCS; Genuine Article; SWETS; UMI; UnCover. CCC.
Description: Presents papers on advances in the enabling technologies of molecular biology, cell biology, biochemistry, and genetics, as related to plant cell organization, gene regulation, and protein function in plants.
Refereed Serial

PLANT MOLECULAR BIOLOGY MANUAL. see BIOLOGY — Biotechnology

581   US   ISSN 0735-9640
QK981   CODEN: PMBRD4
PLANT MOLECULAR BIOLOGY REPORTER. 1983. q. fl.373 to institutions; $191.50 to institutions in U.S. (effective 1998). (International Society for Plant Molecular Biology) Transaction Publishers, Transaction Periodicals Consortium, Department 3092, Rutgers University, New Brunswick, NJ 08903. TEL 908-445-2280. FAX 908-445-3138. Ed. C.A. Price. adv.: page $500; 4 1/4 x 7 1/2. circ. 2,500. **Indexed:** ASCA, Bibl.Agri., Food Sci.& Tech.Abstr. **Document type:** academic/scholarly publication.
—BLDSC (6520.360000); CASDDS; CISTI; Genuine Article; UMI; UnCover. CCC.
Description: Includes news and opinions about progress in the developing area of plant molecular biology.

581.2   UK   ISSN 0032-0862
SB599   CODEN: PLPAAD
PLANT PATHOLOGY; a record of current work on plant diseases and pests. 1952. bi-m. £318($581) (foreign £350) (effective 1998). (British Society for Plant Pathology) Blackwell Science Ltd., Osney Mead, Oxford OX2 0EL, England. TEL 44-1865-206206. FAX 44-1865-721205. E-mail: journals.cs@blacksci.co.uk; URL: http://www.black.co.uk. Ed. R. Johnson; Pub. Allen Stevens. R&P contact: Sarah Pollard. adv. contact: Martine Cariou-Keen. bk.rev.; bibl.; charts; illus.; index. circ. 1,385. (also avail. in microform from UMI; reprint service avail. from UMI) **Indexed:** ASCA, Bio-Contr.News & Info., Biol.Abstr., Biol.& Agr.Ind., Biotech.Abstr., Chem.Abstr., Cott.&Trop.Fibr.Abstr., Curr.Adv.Ecol.Sci., Curr.Biotech.Abstr., Curr.Cont., Ecol.Abstr., Environ.Per.Bibl., Field Crop Abstr., Food Sci.& Tech.Abstr., Forest.Abstr., Forest Prod.Abstr., Helminthol.Abstr., Herb.Abstr., Hort.Abstr., Ind.Sci.Rev., Maize Abstr., Ornam.Hort., Plant Breed.Abstr., Plant Grow.Reg.Abstr., Potato Abstr., Rev.Appl.Entomol., Rev.Plant Path., Sci.Cit.Ind., Sci.Cit.Ind., Seed Abstr., Soils & Fert., Triticale Abstr., Trop.Oil Seeds Abstr., Weed Abstr. **Document type:** academic/scholarly publication.
—BLDSC (6521.000000); CASDDS; CISTI; EMDOCS; Genuine Article; KR SourceOne; Linda Hall; SWETS; UMI; UnCover. CCC.
Refereed Serial

581.1　　　　　　US　　ISSN 0032-0889
QK1　　　　　　　　　CODEN: PLPHAY
PLANT PHYSIOLOGY. 1926. m. $375 to non-members; institutions $1300; members $330 (includes Plant Cell) (effective 1998). American Society of Plant Physiologists, 15501 Monona Dr., Rockville, MD 20855. TEL 301-251-0560. FAX 301-279-2996. (Subscr. to: Fulco, Box 3000, Denville, NJ 07843. TEL 800-875-2997. FAX 201-627-5872) Ed. Maarten J. Chrispeels. bibl.; charts; illus.; q. index. circ. 5,400. (also avail. in microform from MIM,UMI,PMC; back issues avail.; reprint service avail. from UMI) **Indexed:** Abstr.Bull.Inst.Pap.Chem., Acid Rain Abstr., Acid Rain Ind., ASCA, Bibl.Agri., Biol.Abstr., Biol.& Agr.Ind., Biotech.Abstr., Chem.Abstr., Cott.& Trop.Fibr.Abstr., Crop Physiol.Abstr., Curr.Adv.Biochem., Curr.Adv.Ecol.Sci., Curr.Adv.Genetics & Molec.Biol., Curr.Cont., Deep Sea Res.& Oceanogr.Abstr., Environ.Abstr., Excerpt.Med., Fababean Abstr., Field Crop Abstr., Food Sci.& Tech.Abstr., Forest.Abstr., Forest Prod.Abstr., Herb.Abstr., Hort.Abstr., Ind.Sci.Rev., Irr.& Drain.Abstr., Maize Abstr., Ocean.Abstr., Ornam.Hort., Plant Breed.Abstr., Plant Grow.Reg.Abstr., Potato Abstr., Rev.Plant Path., Rice Abstr., Sci.Cit.Ind., Seed Abstr., Sel.Water Res.Abstr., Soils & Fert., Sorghum & Millets Abstr., Soyabean Abstr., Sugar Ind.Abstr., Triticale Abstr., Trop.Oil Seeds Abstr., VITIS, Weed Abstr.
●Also available online.
—BLDSC (6521.800000); CASDDS; CISTI; EMDOCS; Genuine Article; KR SourceOne; Linda Hall; SWETS; UMI; UnCover. **CCC.**
Description: International journal devoted to the physiology, biochemistry, cellular and molecular biology, biophysics, and environmental biology of plants.
Refereed Serial

581.1　　　　　　US　　ISSN 0079-2241
PLANT PHYSIOLOGY. SUPPLEMENT ABSTRACTS OF ANNUAL MEETING. Variant title: American Society of Plant Physiologists. Proceedings of Annual Meeting. 1926. a. $5 or with subscr. to Plant Physiology. American Society of Plant Physiologists, 15501 Monona Dr., Rockville, MD 20855. TEL 301-251-0560. FAX 301-279-2996. (Subscr. to: Box 64187, Baltimore, MD 21264-0187) index. circ. 5,400. (also avail. in microform; microfiche; reprint service avail. from UMI) **Indexed:** Biol.Abstr., Chem.Abstr.
Description: Compilation of abstracts submitted for annual meetings of the society.

581.1　　　　　　FR　　ISSN 0981-9428
QK710　　　　　　　　CODEN: PPBIEX
PLANT PHYSIOLOGY AND BIOCHEMISTRY. 12/yr. 2150 F. (foreign 2660 F.) (effective 1997). (Societe Francaise de Physiologie Vegetale) Gauthier-Villars, 5 rue Laromiguiere, 75005 Paris, France. TEL 33-1-40466200. FAX 33-1-40466201. TELEX 634 916 F. E-mail: gauthier.villars.publisher@mail.sgip.fr; URL: http://www.gauthier-villars.fr. (Subscr. to: Societe de Periodiques, B.P. 22-F, 41354 Vineuil Cedex, France. TEL 33-2-54504612. FAX 33-2-54504611) Ed. J.C. Kader. adv.; bk.rev.; charts; illus. circ. 1,000. (also avail. in microform from MIM,UMI) **Indexed:** ASCA, Biol.Abstr., Chem.Abstr., Cott.& Trop.Fibr.Abstr., Crop Physiol.Abstr., Curr.Adv.Biochem., Curr.Adv.Ecol.Sci., Curr.Adv.Genetics & Molec.Biol., Curr.Cont., Excerpt.Med., Field Crop Abstr., Food Sci.& Tech.Abstr., Forest.Abstr., Herb.Abstr., Hort.Abstr., Ind.Sci.Rev., Maize Abstr., Ornam.Hort., Plant Breed.Abstr., Rice Abstr., Sci.Cit.Ind., Sci.Cit.Ind., Seed Abstr., Soils & Fert., VITIS, Weed Abstr. **Document type:** academic/scholarly publication.
—BLDSC (6522.090000); CASDDS; CISTI; Genuine Article; Linda Hall; SWETS; UnCover. **CCC.**
Formerly (1963-1987): Physiologie Vegetale. (ISSN 0031-9368); Incorporates (1965-1969): Societe Francaise de Physiologie Vegetale. Bulletin (ISSN 0375-961X); (1959-1969): Annales de Physiologie Vegetale (ISSN 0570-1643)
Description: Embraces physiology, biochemistry, biophysics, structure and genetics at various levels - from the molecular to the whole plant and environment.

PLANT PRESS. see *GARDENING AND HORTICULTURE*

581　　　　　　　NE
PLANT RESOURCES OF SOUTH-EAST ASIA. Short title: P R O S E A. 1989. irreg., vol.11, 1997. price varies. Backhuys Publishers, P.O. Box 321, 2300 AH Leiden, Netherlands. TEL 31-71-5170208. FAX 31-71-5171856. E-mail: backhuys@euronet.nl; URL: http://www.euronet.nl/users/backhuys/. (back issues avail.) **Document type:** monographic series.

581　　　　　　　IE　　ISSN 0168-9452
QK1　　　　　　　　　CODEN: PLSCE4
PLANT SCIENCE; an international journal of experimental plant biology. 1973. 20/yr. fl.4760($2736) (effective 1998). Elsevier Science Ireland Ltd., P.O. Box 85, Limerick, Ireland. TEL 353-61-471944. FAX 353-61-472144. (Subscr. to: Elsevier Science, Regional Sales Office, P.O. Box 211, 1000 AE Amsterdam, Netherlands. TEL 31-20-4853757. FAX 31-20-4853432; Subscr. in the Americas to: Elsevier Science, Regional Sales Office, Box 945, New York, NY 10159-0945. TEL 212-633-3730. FAX 212-633-3680; Subscr. in Australasia and the Far East to: Elsevier Science (Singapore) Pte Ltd, No.1 Temasek Ave., No.17-01 Millenia Tower, Singapore 039192, Singapore. TEL 65-434-3727. FAX 65-337-2230) Eds. J.A. Schiff, J.H. Weil. R&P contact: Annette Moloney. adv.; bk.rev.; illus.; index. circ. 700. (also avail. in microform from UMI) **Indexed:** A.I.Abstr., Abstr.Bull.Inst.Pap.Chem., ASCA, Biol.Abstr., Chem.Abstr., Crop Physiol.Abstr., Curr.Adv.Biochem., Curr.Adv.Ecol.Sci., Curr.Adv.Genetics & Molec.Biol., Curr.Cont., Excerpt.Med., Fababean Abstr., Field Crop Abstr., Food Sci.& Tech.Abstr., Forest.Abstr., Forest Prod.Abstr., Helminthol.Abstr., Herb.Abstr., Hort.Abstr., Ind.Sci.Rev., Maize Abstr., Nutr.Abstr., Ornam.Hort., Plant Grow.Reg.Abstr., Potato Abstr., Rice Abstr., Sci.Cit.Ind., Seed Abstr., Sorghum & Millets Abstr., Telegen, Triticale Abstr., Weed Abstr. **Document type:** academic/scholarly publication.
—BLDSC (6523.390000); CASDDS; CISTI; EMDOCS; Genuine Article; Linda Hall; SWETS; UnCover. **CCC.**
Formerly (until vol.37, 1984): Plant Science Letters (ISSN 0304-4211)
Description: Publishes papers in all areas of experimental plant biology, under the four major section headings of physiology and biochemistry, genetics and molecular biology, cell and tissue studies in vitro, and general research.
Refereed Serial

581　　　　　　　US　　ISSN 0032-0919
QK1　　　　　　　　　CODEN: PSBLAP
PLANT SCIENCE BULLETIN. 1955. q. $15 membership. Botanical Society of America, Inc. (St. Louis), Department of Biology, St. Louis University, 3507 Laclede Ave., St. Louis, MO 63103-2010. TEL 314-977-3903. FAX 314-977-3658. E-mail: leverich@sluvca.slu.edu. Ed. Joe Leverich. R&P contact: Joe Leverich. adv.; bk.rev. circ. 3,100. (also avail. in microform from UMI; reprint service avail. from UMI) **Indexed:** Biol.Abstr. **Document type:** academic/scholarly publication, newsletter.
—BLDSC (6523.450000); CISTI; Linda Hall; SWETS; UMI; UnCover.

581　　　　　　　JA　　ISSN 0913-557X
　　　　　　　　　　　　CODEN: PSBIEK
PLANT SPECIES BIOLOGY. (Text in English) 1986. s-a. 8000 Yen. Society for the Study of Species Biology - Shu Seibutsu Gakkai, c/o Kyoto Daigaku Rigakubu, Shokubutsugaku Kyoshitsu, Oiwakecho, Kitashirakawa, Sakyo-ku, Kyoto 606, Japan. TEL 81-75-753-4131. FAX 81-75-753-4145. E-mail: k53870@sakura.kudpc.kyoto-u.ac.jp. Ed. Shoichi Kawano. **Indexed:** Apic.Abstr.
—BLDSC (6523.615000). **CCC.**
Refereed Serial

581　　　　　　　AU　　ISSN 0378-2697
QK1　　　　　　　　　CODEN: ESPFBP
PLANT SYSTEMATICS AND EVOLUTION. (Supplement avail. (ISSN 0172-6668)) (Text in English) 1851. 20/yr. DM.2810 (effective 1998). Springer-Verlag, Sachsenplatz 4-6, P.O. Box 89, A-1201 Vienna, Austria. TEL 43-1-330-2415. FAX 43-1-330-2426. E-mail: springer@springer.co.at. (N. American subscr. to: Springer-Verlag New York, Inc., 175 Fifth Ave., New York, NY 10010. TEL 212-460-1500. FAX 212-473-6272) Ed. F. Ehrendorfer. bibl.; charts; illus.; stat. (also avail. in microform from UMI,BHP; back issues avail.; reprint service avail. from ISI) **Indexed:** Apic.Abstr., Apic.Abstr., ASCA, Biol.Abstr., Chem.Abstr., Curr.Adv.Ecol.Sci., Curr.Cont., Field Crop Abstr., Forest.Abstr., Herb.Abstr., Hort.Abstr., Ind.Sci.Rev., Ornam.Hort., Plant Breed Abstr., Rev.Plant Path., Sci.Cit.Ind., Soils & Fert., Triticale Abstr., Trop.Oil Seeds Abstr., Weed Abstr. **Document type:** academic/scholarly publication.
—BLDSC (6523.640000); CASDDS; CISTI; EMDOCS; Genuine Article; Linda Hall; SWETS; UMI; UnCover. **CCC.**
Formerly: Oesterreichische Botanische Zeitschrift.
Description: Publishes original papers on the morphology and systematics of plants.

581 333.7　　　　　　UK　　ISSN 1358-4103
▼**PLANT TALK;** news and views on plant conservation worldwide. 1995. q. £16($27) to individuals; institutions £38 ($65) (effective 1998). Botanical Information Company Ltd., P.O. Box 500, Kingston-upon-Thames, Surrey KT2 5XB, England. FAX 44-181-974-5127. E-mail: plant-talk@dial.pipex.com. (Subscr. in US to: Box 65226, Tucson, AZ 85728-5226) Ed. John Akeroyd; Pub. Hugh Synge. R&P contact: Hugh Synge. TEL 44-181-546-6725. adv. contact: Hugh Synge. bk.rev.; illus.; circ. 1,100 (paid). **Document type:** academic/scholarly publication.
—BLDSC (6523.642000).
Description: Includes regular features such as a notice Board, reports on new Flora, plant checklists and reviews of Red Data Books, the books listing endangered plants. Articles cover conservation techniques, examples of plant conservation in action, and news.

581　　　　　　　BG　　ISSN 1018-8029
PLANT TISSUE CULTURE. 1991. s-a. Tk.300 (foreign $66). Bangladesh Association for Plant Tissue Culture, University of Dhaka, Department of Botany, Dhaka-1000, Bangladesh. TEL 880-2-506378. FAX 880-2-865583. TELEX 632458 MEGNA BJ. E-mail: baptc@drik.bgd.toolnet.org. Ed. A.S. Islam. adv.; bk.rev. circ. 500. **Document type:** academic/scholarly publication.
●Available only on CD-ROM.
—BLDSC (6523.650000).
Description: Publishes original papers on tissue culture related topics including plant transformation and genetic engineering of plant sciences.
Refereed Serial

581 660　　　　　　IS
PLANT TISSUE CULTURE AND BIOTECHNOLOGY. 1971; N.S. 1995. 4/yr. $130 to institutions. (International Association for Plant Tissue Culture) Balaban Publishers, International Services, P.O. Box 2039, Rehovot 76100, Israel. TEL 972-8-476216. FAX 972-8-467632. E-mail: vcwatad@volcani.agri.gov.il. (Editorial addr.: c/o Hebrew University of Jerusalem, Faculty of Agriculture, P.O. Box 12, Rehovot 76100, Israel. TEL 972-8-481915. FAX 972-8-467763) Ed. Meira Ziv. adv.; bk.rev.; bibl. circ. 4,000. **Document type:** newsletter.
Formerly (until 1995): International Association for Plant Tissue and Culture. Newsletter (ISSN 0740-0209)
Description: Publishes reports on novel research activities, protocols, feature articles, research reports, and news in the fields of plant tissue culture and biotechnology.

BIOLOGY — BOTANY

581   JA   ISSN 0289-5773
CODEN: SSBAET
PLANT TISSUE CULTURE LETTERS/SHOKUBUTSU SOSHIKI BAIYO. (Text in English, Japanese) 1984. 3/yr. $70. Japanese Society for Plant Cell and Molecular Biology - Nihon Shokubutsu Saibou Bunshiseibuts Gakkai, 30-15, Hongo 5-chome, Bunkyo-ku, Tokyo 113-91, Japan. (Dist. by: Business Center for Academic Societies Japan, Koshin Bldg., 6-16-3 Hongo, Bunkyo-ku, Tokyo 113, Japan; Dist. in U.S. by: International Specialized Book Services, Inc., 5602 N.E. Hassalo St., Portland, OR 97213) Ed. Yutaka Ebizuka. **Indexed:** Chem.Abstr., Food Sci.& Tech.Abstr., Jap.Per.Ind. **Document type:** academic/scholarly publication.
—BLDSC (6523.660000).

PLANT TISSUE CULTURE MANUAL; fundamentals and applications. see BIOLOGY — Biotechnology

PLANT VARIETY PROTECTION. see AGRICULTURE — Crop Production And Soil

581   GW   ISSN 0032-0935
QK1   CODEN: PLANAB
PLANTA; an international journal of plant biology. Online edition (GW ISSN 1432-2048) (Text in English) 1925. m. DM.4051.80 (foreign DM.4112.40) (effective 1998). Springer-Verlag, Heidelberger Platz 3, 14197 Berlin, Germany. TEL 49-30-82787-0. FAX 49-30-82787448. E-mail: subscriptions@springer.de; URL: http://link.springer.de. (Subscr. in N. America to: Springer-Verlag New York, Inc., 333 Meadowlands Pkwy., Secaucus, NJ 07094. TEL 212-460-1500. FAX 212-473-6272) Ed.Bd. adv.; charts; illus. (also avail. in microform from UMI,PMC; back issues avail.; reprint service avail. from ISI) **Indexed:** Abstr.Bull.Inst.Pap.Chem., Biol.Abstr., Biol.& Agr.Ind., Biotech.Abstr., Chem.Abstr., Chem.Cit.Ind., Cott.&Trop.Fibr.Abstr., Crop Physiol.Abstr., Curr.Adv.Biochem., Curr.Adv.Ecol.Sci., Curr.Cont., Deep Sea Res.& Oceanogr.Abstr., Fababean Abstr., Field Crop Abstr., Food Sci.& Tech.Abstr., Forest.Abstr., Forest Prod.Abstr., Hort.Abstr., Ind.Sci.Rev., Int.Aerosp.Abstr., Irr.& Drain.Abstr., Maize Abstr., Ornam.Hort., Plant Grow.Reg.Abstr., Potato Abstr., Rice Abstr., Sci.Cit.Ind., Soils & Fert., Sorghum & Millets Abstr., Soyabean Abstr., Triticale Abstr., Trop.Oil Seeds Abstr., VITIS, Weed Abstr. **Document type:** academic/scholarly publication.
●Also available online.
—BLDSC (6524.000000); CASDDS; CISTI; EMDOCS; Genuine Article; KR SourceOne; Linda Hall; SWETS; UMI; UnCover. **CCC**.
Description: Original articles on structural and functional botany, covering all aspects of plant biology, from biochemistry, biotechnology, and molecular and cell biology, to studies with tissues, organs, whole plants, and populations (crop physiology and physiological ecology.)

581   US   ISSN 1058-1189
QK750
PLANTS FOR TOXICITY ASSESSMENT. 1990. irreg. American Society for Testing and Materials, 100 Barr Harbor Dr., W. Conshohocken, PA 19428-2959. TEL 610-832-9500. FAX 610-832-9555. E-mail: service@local.ast.org.

581   SP   ISSN 1135-8408
POLEN. 1984. a. 5000 ptas. (effective 1998). (Universidad de Cordoba, Departamento de Biologia Vegetal y Ecologia) Includes original papers on palynology and aerobiology., Avda. de San Alberto Magno s-n, 14004 Cordoba, Spain. TEL 57-218599. FAX 57-218598. E-mail: bv1ingaf@uco.es. Ed. Eugenio Dominguez Vilches; Pub. Jose Luis Ubera Jimenez. bk.rev. **Indexed:** Ind.SST. **Document type:** academic/scholarly publication.
Formerly: Asociacion de Palinologos de Lengua Espanola. Anales (ISSN 0213-1811)
Refereed Serial

581   PL   ISSN 0867-0730
QK322
POLISH BOTANICAL STUDIES. (Text and summaries in English) 1990. irreg. (2-3/yr.) price varies. Polska Akademia Nauk, Instytut Botaniki im. W. Szafera - Polish Academy of Sciences, W. Szafer Institute of Botany, Ul. Lubicz 46, 31-512 Krakow, Poland. TEL 48-12-215144. FAX 48-12-219790. E-mail: nhwysock@cyf-kr.edu.pl. Ed. Zbigniew Mirek. adv. contact: Jacek Wieser. bk.rev.; circ. 500 (paid). **Indexed:** AgroAgen, AgroLibrex. **Document type:** academic/scholarly publication, monographic series.
—BLDSC (6543.575500).
Description: Covers taxonomy, ecology, evolution, morphology, anatomy and cytology of all plant groups as well as palaeobotany.
Refereed Serial

581   PL   ISSN 0867-0749
POLISH BOTANICAL STUDIES. GUIDEBOOK SERIES. (Text in English, Polish; summaries in English) 1990. irreg. price varies. Polska Akademia Nauk, Instytut Botaniki im. W. Szafera - Polish Academy of Sciences, W. Szafer Institute of Botany, Ul. Lubicz 46, 31-512 Krakow, Poland. TEL 48-12-215144. FAX 48-12-219790. E-mail: nhwysock@cyf-kr.edu.pl. Ed. Zbigniew Mirek. adv. contact: Jacek Wieser. circ. 1,000 (paid). **Indexed:** AgroAgen. **Document type:** academic/scholarly publication.
Description: Guides to Polish botanical institutions, collections and collectors, botanical literature and directories as well as botanical field-guides and basic information regarding various branches of botany.
Refereed Serial

632.97   PL
▼**POLISH PHYTOPATHOLOGICAL SOCIETY. PROCEEDINGS**. (Text in English) 1995. irreg. price varies. Polskie Towarzystwo Fitopatologiczne, Ul. Wojska Polskiego 71 c, 60-625 Poznan, Poland. TEL 48-61-487713. FAX 48-61-487145. (Co-sponsor: Komitet Badan Naukowych - Committee for Scientific Research) Ed.Bd. **Document type:** proceedings.
Description: Publishes papers presented at the international conferences on plant pathology.

581   PL   ISSN 0080-357X
QK322   CODEN: RSDPAZ
POLSKIE TOWARZYSTWO BOTANICZNE. SEKCJA DENDROLOGICZNA. ROCZNIK. (Text in English or Polish; summaries in English, German, Polish, Russian) 1926. irreg. price varies. Polskie Towarzystwo Botaniczne, Al. Ujazdowskie 4, 00-478 Warsaw, Poland. (Dist. by: Ars Polona, Krakowskie Przedmiescie 7, 00-068 Warsaw, Poland) Ed. Tadeusz Gorczynski. illus. **Indexed:** Biol.Abstr.

581   XR   ISSN 0032-7786
QK1   CODEN: PRESAK
PRESLIA. (Text in Czech, English, French, German, Slovak; summaries in Czech, English, French, German) 1914. q. DM.146. Ceska Botanicka Spolecnost - Czech Botanical Society, Benatska 2, 128 01 Prague 2, Czech Republic. TEL 29-79-41. (Dist. in Western countries by: Kubon & Sagner, Postfach 340108, 80098 Munich, Germany) Ed. Z. Cernohorsky. bk.rev.; rec.rev.; charts; illus.; index, cum.index. circ. 1,400. **Indexed:** Biol.Abstr., Chem.Abstr., Curr.Adv.Ecol.Sci., Ecol.Abstr., Field Crop Abstr., Forest.Abstr., Forest Prod.Abstr., Geo.Abstr., Geol.Abstr., Herb.Abstr., Hort.Abstr., Plant Breed.Abstr., Rev.Plant Path., Seed Abstr., Soils & Fert., Triticale Abstr., Weed Abstr.
—BLDSC (6611.000000); CISTI; KNAW; Linda Hall; UnCover.

581   US   ISSN 0032-8480
SB299.P3   CODEN: PRNCAH
PRINCIPES. 1956. q. $35 (effective 1997). International Palm Society, Inc., Box 1897, Lawrence, KS 66044. TEL 713-964-6345. FAX 713-964-6555. E-mail: palm-dude@genie.com; URL: http://www.palms.org. Ed. Dr. Natalie Uhl. adv. contact: Natalie Uhl. bk.rev.; illus. circ. 3,000. (also avail. in microfilm from UMI; back issues avail.; reprint service avail. from UMI) **Indexed:** Apic.Abstr., Bibl.Agri., Biol.Abstr., Chem.Abstr., Forest.Abstr., Forest Prod.Abstr., Rural Recreat.Tour.Abstr., World Agri.Econ.& Rural Sociol.Abstr. **Document type:** academic/scholarly publication.
—BLDSC (6612.981000); UMI; UnCover.
Description: Contains scientific and popular articles on taxonomy and horticulture of the Palmae.

581   US   ISSN 0340-4773
QK1   CODEN: PRBODU
PROGRESS IN BOTANY. 1949. irreg., vol.57, 1996. price varies. Springer-Verlag, 175 Fifth Ave., New York, NY 10010. TEL 212-460-1500. FAX 212-473-6272. (Also: Berlin, Heidelberg, Tokyo and Vienna) (reprint service avail. from ISI) **Indexed:** Biol.Abstr., Chem.Abstr., Deep Sea Res.& Oceanogr.Abstr., Field Crop Abstr., GeoRef., Herb.Abstr., Plant Breed.Abstr., Rev.Plant Path., Soils & Fert., VITIS, Weed Abstr. **Document type:** monographic series.
—BLDSC (6866.330000); CASDDS; CISTI; Linda Hall; UnCover.
Formerly: Fortschritte der Botanik (ISSN 0071-7878)

582   NE   ISSN 0167-8574
QK564   CODEN: PPREEX
PROGRESS IN PHYCOLOGICAL RESEARCH. 1982. irreg., latest vol.2, 1983. price varies. Elsevier Science B.V., Books Division, P.O. Box 211, 1000 AE Amsterdam, Netherlands. TEL 31-20-4853911. FAX 31-20-4853705. TELEX 18582 ESPA NL. E-mail: nlinfo-f@elsevier.nl; usinfo-f@elsevier.com; forinfo-kyf04035@niftyserve.or.jp; URL: http://www.elsevier.nl. (Subscr. in the Americas to: Elsevier Science, Regional Sales Office, Box 945, New York, NY 10159-0945. TEL 212-633-3730. FAX 212-633-3680; Subscr. in Australasia and the Far East to: Elsevier Science (Singapore) Pte Ltd, No.1 Temasek Ave., No.17-01 Millenia Tower, Singapore 039192, Singapore. TEL 65-434-3727. FAX 65-337-2230; Subscr. in Japan to: Elsevier Science Japan, 9-15 Higashi-Azabu 1-chome, Minato-ku, Tokyo 106, Japan. TEL 81-3-5561-5033. FAX 81-3-5561-5047) Eds. F.E. Round, D.J. Chapman. **Document type:** monographic series.
—BLDSC (6873.100000); CASDDS; CISTI; Linda Hall; UnCover.
Refereed Serial

581   US   ISSN 0749-7741
CODEN: PTRID4
PTERIDOLOGIA. 1979. irreg. price varies. American Fern Society, Inc., c/o Dr. David B. Lellinger, 326 West St., N.W., Vienna, VA 22180-4151. circ. 300 (paid). (back issues avail.) **Indexed:** Biol.Abstr. **Document type:** monographic series.
Description: Technical monographs on ferns and fern-allies.
Refereed Serial

581 635   UK   ISSN 0266-1640
QK520   CODEN: PTEREZ
PTERIDOLOGIST. 1984. a. £25 (includes Bulletin and Fern Gazette) (effective 1996 & 1997). British Pteridological Society, c/o Botany Department, Natural History Museum, Cromwell Rd., London SW7 5BD, England. TEL 44-171-938-9497. Ed. J. Merryweather. bk.rev. circ. 800. **Indexed:** Curr.Adv.Ecol.Sci. **Document type:** academic/scholarly publication.
—BLDSC (6946.579600); UnCover.
Description: Contains articles about growing ferns, fern varieties and fern history, plus other items of interest concerning ferns and allied plants.

581   JA   ISSN 0915-2059
PURANTA/PLANTA. (Text in Japanese) 1989. bi-m. 520 Yen per no. Kenseisha Inc., 6-4 Kakigaracho 1-chome, Nihonbashi, Chuo-ku, Tokyo 103, Japan.

PYMATUNING SYMPOSIA IN ECOLOGY. see ENVIRONMENTAL STUDIES

581   PE   ISSN 1022-5897
QUEPO. 1987. a. S/15 (foreign $15) (effective 1997 & 1998). Sociedad Peruana de Cactus y Suculentas, Apdo. 3215, Lima 100, Peru. TEL 51-1-4792360. FAX 51-1-4762102. Ed. Carlos Ostolaza. adv.; bk.rev.; illus. circ. 3,000.
Description: Deals with cacti conservancy, knowledge of native genera and species and growing methods.
Refereed Serial

581   JA   ISSN 0285-0850
RAIKEN/LICHEN. (Text in Japanese) 1972. 2/yr. 2000 Yen (effective 1997). Chiirui Kenkyukai - Lichenological Society of Japan, c/o H. Harada, Natural History Museum & Institute, Chiba, Aoba-cho 955-2, Chuo-ku, Chiba 260, Japan. FAX 043-266-2481. Ed. Y. Yamamoto. R&P contact: H. Harada. adv. contact: H. Harada. bk.rev. circ. 250. **Document type:** academic/scholarly publication.

BIOLOGY — BOTANY

632 RU ISSN 0033-9946
CODEN: RRESA8
RASTITEL'NYE RESURSY/VEGETATIVE RESOURCES.
1965. q. $114 (effective 1998). (Rossiiskaya Akademiya Nauk) Izdatel'stvo Nauka, 90 Profsoyuznaya ul., 117864 Moscow, Russia. (Dist. in U.S. by: Victor Kamkin Inc., 4956 Boiling Brook Pkwy, Rockville, MD 20852. TEL 301-881-5973) index. circ. 875. **Indexed:** Biol.Abstr., Chem.Abstr., Field Crop Abstr., Forest.Abstr., Forest Prod.Abstr., Herb.Abstr., Hort.Abstr., Ornam.Hort., Plant Grow.Reg.Abstr., Rice Abstr., Seed Abstr., Soils & Fert.
—BLDSC (0140.340000); CASDDS; KNAW; Linda Hall.

581 SP ISSN 0210-363X
REAL ACADEMIA DE CIENCIAS EXACTAS, FISICAS Y NATURALES. MEMORIA. SERIE CIENCIAS NATURALES.
1931. irreg. price varies. Real Academia de Ciencias Exactas, Fisicas y Naturales, Valverde 22, 28004 Madrid, Spain. **Indexed:** Ind.SST.
—KNAW.

581.1 US ISSN 0079-9920
QK861 CODEN: RAPHBE
RECENT ADVANCES IN PHYTOCHEMISTRY. 1968. irreg., approx a., latest vol.30. price varies. Plenum Publishing Corp., 233 Spring St., New York, NY 10013-1578. TEL 212-620-8000. FAX 212-463-0742. TELEX 23-421139. E-mail: books@plenum.com. Ed. Helen Stafford. (back issues avail.) **Document type:** monographic series.
—BLDSC (7303.900000); CASDDS; CISTI; Linda Hall; SWETS; UnCover. **CCC.**

571 CC ISSN 1000-2561
SB111 CODEN: RZXUEX
REDAI ZUOWU XUEBAO/CHINESE JOURNAL OF TROPICAL CROPS. (Text in Chinese; abstracts in Chinese, English) 1980. s-a. Y6($4) (effective 1995). Zhongguo Redai Nongye Kexueyuan - Chinese Academy of Tropical Agricultural Sciences, Baodao Xincun, Danxian (County), Hainan 571737, People's Republic of China. TEL 0890-73143. FAX 0890-23776. (Huanan Redai Zuowu Xueyuan - South China College of Tropical Crops) Ed. Pan Yanqing. **Document type:** academic/scholarly publication.
—BLDSC (3180.681000).
Description: Contains papers on agronomical, pathological, physiological, genetic, entomological and ecological aspects of various tropical crops.

580 NE ISSN 0080-0694
QK96
REGNUM VEGETABILE; a series of publications for the use of plant taxonomists and plant geographers. irreg. price varies. (International Association for Plant Taxonomy) Bohn Stafleu van Loghum B.V. (Subsidiary of: Wolters Kluwer N.V.), Postbus 246, 3990 GA Houten, Netherlands. TEL 31-3403-95711. FAX 31-3403-50903. Ed. F. A. Stafleu. circ. 1,500. **Indexed:** Bibl.Agri., Biol.Abstr., Excerp.Bot., Ref.Zh. **Document type:** monographic series.
—BLDSC (7345.000000); CISTI.

581 IO ISSN 0034-365X
QK1 CODEN: RNWDAP
REINWARDTIA; a journal on taxonomic botany, plant sociology, physiology and ecology. (Text in English) 1950. irreg. price varies. Indonesian Institute of Sciences, R & D Centre for Biology, Jalan Juanda 18, Bogor, Indonesia. TEL 62-251-321038. FAX 62-251-325854. Ed.Bd. bk.rev.; index. circ. 400. **Indexed:** Biol.Abstr., Curr.Adv.Ecol.Sci., Zoo.Rec. (until 19??). **Document type:** academic/scholarly publication.

582.14 SZ ISSN 0486-4271
QK96
REPERTORIUM PLANTARUM SUCCULENTARUM. 1951. a. $6.50. International Organization for Succulent Plant Study, c/o Staedtische Sukkulentensammlung, Mythenquai 88, CH-8002 Zurich, Switzerland. FAX 41-1-2015540. Ed. U. Eggli. circ. 600 (paid). **Document type:** academic/scholarly publication.
—BLDSC (7366.120000); Linda Hall.
Description: Listing of new names of and new literature on succulent plants, including cacti.

581 550 IC
RESEARCH INSTITUTE NEDRI-AS. BULLETIN. (Text in English, German, Icelandic; summaries in English) 1969. irreg. (free to qualified personnel). Rannsoknarstofnunin Nedri-As - Research Institute Nedri-As, Hveragerdi, Iceland. Ed.Bd. **Indexed:** Biol.Abstr.

581 UK ISSN 0951-6654
RESEARCH STUDIES IN BOTANY AND RELATED APPLIED FIELDS. 1982. irreg., vol.13, 1994. £55. Research Studies Press Ltd., 24 Belvedere Rd., Taunton, Somerset TA1 1HD, England. TEL 44-1823-336197. FAX 44-1823-253252. E-mail: vaw@rspltd.demon.co.uk. (Dist. by: John Wiley & Sons Ltd., Baffins Ln., Chichester, W. Sussex PO19 1UD, England. TEL 44-1243-779777. FAX 44-1243-775878) Ed. P.S. Nutman. **Document type:** monographic series.
—BLDSC (7773.217000).

REVIEW OF AROMATIC AND MEDICINAL PLANTS. see MEDICAL SCIENCES — Abstracting, Bibliographies, Statistics

581 II ISSN 0254-1300
REVIEW OF TROPICAL PLANT PATHOLOGY. (Supplement avail.) 1984. irreg. price varies. Today and Tomorrow's Printers & Publishers, 24B-5 Desh Badhu Gupta Rd., Karol Bagh, New Delhi 110 005, India. TEL 91-11-5721928. (Dist. in U.S. by: Scholarly Publications, 2825 Wilcrest Dr., Ste. 255, Houston, TX 77042. TEL 713-781-0070. FAX 713-781-2112) Eds. S.P. Raychaudhuri, J.P. Varma. **Indexed:** Biol.Abstr., Curr.Adv.Ecol.Sci., Curr.Cont. **Document type:** monographic series.
—**CCC.**

581 BL ISSN 0100-8404
QK263 CODEN: RRBODI
REVISTA BRASILEIRA DE BOTANICA/BRAZILIAN JOURNAL OF BOTANY. (Text in English or Portuguese; summaries in English and Portuguese) 1978. a. $75 (effective 1998). Sociedade Botanica de Sao Paulo, Caixa Postal 11491, 05422-970 Sao Paulo, SP, Brazil. TEL 55-11-55846300. FAX 55-11-5773678. Ed. Dr. Rita de Cassia L.F. Ribeiro. circ. 600. (back issues avail.) **Indexed:** Biol.Abstr., Chem.Abstr., Curr.Adv.Ecol.Sci., Curr.Adv.Plant Sci., Deep Sea Res.& Oceanogr.Abstr. **Document type:** academic/scholarly publication.
—CASDDS; CISTI.
Description: Presents results of original research in botanical science.
Refereed Serial

581 BL ISSN 0103-3131
CODEN: RBFVEG
REVISTA BRASILEIRA DE FISIOLOGIA VEGETAL/BRAZILIAN JOURNAL OF PLANT PHYSIOLOGY. (Text and abstracts in English, Portuguese) 1989. s-a. $60 (effective 1997). Sociedade Brasileira de Fisiologia Vegetal, Cx. Postal 0281, 70359-9700 Brasilis DF, Brazil. FAX 55-61-556744. E-mail: calbo@nutecnet.com.br. Ed Adonai Gimenez Calbo. adv.: page $1000. bk.rev.; abstr.; bibl.; charts; stat. circ. 1,000. (also avail. in microform from UMI; back issues avail.) **Indexed:** Abstr.Trop.Agri., Agrindex.
—BLDSC (7844.776000); CASDDS. **CCC.**
Description: Publishes original articles and scientific reviews in plant physiology and related areas.
Refereed Serial

581 SP ISSN 0210-7708
QK329 CODEN: LAGAEL
REVISTA LAGASCALIA. 1971. s-a. 1800 ptas. Universidad de Sevilla, Facultad de Biologia, Departamento de Botanica, Servicio de Publicaciones, Calle Porvenir 7, 41013 Sevilla, Spain. TEL 34-5-4228071. FAX 34-5-4221315. Ed.Bd. illus. circ. 300. **Indexed:** Curr.Adv.Ecol.Sci., Ind.SST, Ornam.Hort.

581 MX ISSN 0187-3180
CODEN: RMMIEL
REVISTA MEXICANA DE MICOLOGIA.* (Text in Spanish; summaries in English and Spanish) 1968. a. $30 or exchange basis. Sociedad Mexicana de Micologia, Apdo. Postal 26-378, 06400 Mexico, D.F., Mexico. FAX 548-36-03. Eds. Conchita Toriello, Miguel Ulloa-Sosa. adv.; bk.rev.; bibl.; charts; illus.; index. cum.index. circ. 1,000. (processed; also avail. in microform from UMI; reprint service avail. from UMI) **Indexed:** Biol.Abstr., Forest.Abstr., Ind.Vet., Potato Abstr., Rev.Med.& Vet.Mycol., Rev.Plant Path., Seed Abstr., Triticale Abstr., Vet.Bull.
—UMI.
Former titles (until 1985): Sociedad Mexicana de Micologia. Boletin (ISSN 0085-6223); Sociedad Mexicana de Micologia. Boletin Informativo.

581.87 FR ISSN 0181-7582
CODEN: RCBBDA
REVUE DE CYTOLOGIE ET DE BIOLOGIE VEGETALES - LE BOTANISTE. 1934. a. (in 4 parts). 855 F. (foreign 950 F.). Laboratoire de Biologie Vegetale Appliquee, 61 rue de Buffon, 75005 Paris, France. (Subscr. to: SETAG, Service Abonnement, 3 rue des Pliantes, 77140 Nemours, France) Eds. Robert Gorenflot, Jean Claude Labereche. bk.rev.; charts; illus.; index. circ. 11,350. (also avail. in microform from PMC) **Indexed:** Biol.Abstr., Chem.Abstr., Curr.Adv.Ecol.Sci., Field Crop Abstr., Herb.Abstr., Plant Breed.Abstr., Sorghum & Millets Abstr. **Document type:** academic/scholarly publication.
—CASDDS; Linda Hall.
Formed by the merger of: Botaniste (ISSN 0045-2637); Revue de Cytologie et de Biologie Vegetales (ISSN 0035-1067).

REVUE DES SCIENCES NATURELLES D'AUVERGNE. see BIOLOGY

581 RM ISSN 0250-5517
QK1 CODEN: RRBVD5
REVUE ROUMAINE DE BIOLOGIE. SERIE BIOLOGIE VEGETALE. (Text in English, French, German, Russian and English) 1956. s-a. (Academia Romana, Institutul de Stiinte Biologice) Editura Academiei Romane, Calea 13 Septembrie 13, 76117 Bucharest, Rumania. (Dist. by: Rodipet SA, Piata Presei Libere 1, Sec.1, P.O. Box 33-57, Bucharest, Rumania. TEL 401-6185103. FAX 401-2226407) Ed. Micolae Boscaiu. bk.rev.; charts; illus. **Indexed:** Biol.Abstr., Chem.Abstr., Curr.Adv.Ecol.Sci., Deep Sea Res.& Oceanogr.Abstr., Excerp.Med., Field Crop Abstr., Forest.Abstr., Herb.Abstr., Plant Breed.Abstr., Rev.Plant Path., Seed Abstr., Triticale Abstr., Weed Abstr. **Document type:** academic/scholarly publication.
—BLDSC (7946.095000); CASDDS; CISTI; KNAW; Linda Hall.
Supersedes in part (in 1976): Revue Roumaine de Biologie (ISSN 0250-6572); Which was formed by the 1974 merger of: Revue Roumaine de Biologie. Serie Botanique (ISSN 0035-3914); Revue Roumaine de Biologie. Serie Zoologie (ISSN 0035-3922); Both of which supersede (in 1964): Revue de Biologie (ISSN 0484-8462)

582.13 II ISSN 0971-2313
CODEN: RHEEE2
RHEEDEA. (Text in English) 1991. s-a. Rs.150 (foreign $60) (effective 1997). Indian Association for Angiosperm Taxonomy, c/o University of Calicut, Department of Botany, Calicut, India. Ed. K.S. Manilal. **Document type:** academic/scholarly publication.
—BLDSC (7960.100990).
Refereed Serial

BIOLOGY — BOTANY

581   **US**   ISSN 0035-4902
QK1   CODEN: RHODAB
RHODORA. 1899. q. $75. New England Botanical Club, Inc., 22 Divinity Ave., Cambridge, MA 02138. TEL 603-862-3222. FAX 603-862-4757. E-mail: janets@christa.unh.edu; URL: http://www.herbaria.harvard.edu/nebc/. (Subscr. to: Box 1897, Lawrence, KS 66044-8897. TEL 913-843-1221. FAX 913-843-1274) Ed. Janet R. Sullivan. R&P contact: Janet R. Sullivan. bk.rev.; charts; illus.; index. circ. 850. (also avail. in microform from UMI,BHP; microfiche from IDC,BHP; back issues avail.; reprint service avail. from UMI) **Indexed:** Apic.Abstr., ASCA, Bibl.Agri., Biol.Abstr., Chem.Abstr., Curr.Adv.Ecol.Sci., Curr.Cont., Deep Sea Res.& Oceanogr.Abstr., Field Crop Abstr., Forest Abstr., Forest Prod.Abstr., Geo.Abstr., Herb.Abstr., Hort.Abstr., Ornam.Hort., Plant Breed.Abstr., Rev.Plant Path., Weed Abstr. **Document type:** academic/scholarly publication.
—BLDSC (7963.200000); Linda Hall; SWETS; UMI; UnCover.
Refereed Serial

RIJKSSTATION VOOR SIERPLANTENTEELT. ACTIVITEITSVERSLAG. see *GARDENING AND HORTICULTURE*

589.2   **IT**   ISSN 0394-9486
RIVISTA DI MICOLOGIA. (Text in Italian; summaries in English, Italian) 1957. q. L.30000 (effective 1997); L.50000 (effective 1998). Associazione Micologica Bresadola, Via A. Volta 46, 38100 Trento, Italy. TEL 39-461-913960. FAX 39-461-913960. adv.; bk.rev.; bibl.; charts; illus.; index. circ. 10,300. **Document type:** bulletin.
Formerly (until 1986): Gruppo Micologico "G. Bresadola". Bollettino (ISSN 0392-4874)
Description: Covers articles and research papers in the field of mycology.

581   **IS**   ISSN 0333-9904
QK378
ROTEM. (Text in Hebrew; summaries in English) q. IS.40. (Israel Plant Information Center) Society for the Protection of Nature in Israel, 4 Hashefela St., Tel Aviv 66183, Israel. TEL 972-3-375063. Ed. G. Pollack, A. Shmida.
Description: Articles on the plants of Israel.

ROTENBURGER SCHRIFTEN. see *HISTORY — History Of Europe*

501   **SP**   ISSN 0212-9108
RUIZIA; monografias del real jardin botanico. (Text mainly in Spanish; occasionally in English, German) 1984. irregr. price varies or on exchange basis. Real Jardin Botanico de Madrid, Plaza de Murillo, 2, 28014 Madrid, Spain. TEL 34-1-4203017. FAX 34-1-4200157. TELEX 42182 CSIC E. (Subscr. to: Servicio de Publicaciones del C.S.I.C., Vitrubio 8, 28006 Madrid, Spain) (Co-sponsor: Consejo Superior de Investigaciones Cientificas) Dir. Maria Teresa Telleria. bibl.; illus.; index. circ. 1,000. (back issues avail.) **Indexed:** Bull.Signal., Excerp.Bot., Herb.Abstr., Ind.SST. **Document type:** monographic series.
—CISTI.

581.1   **RU**   ISSN 1021-4437
QK1   CODEN: RJPPE2
RUSSIAN JOURNAL OF PLANT PHYSIOLOGY. English translation of: Fiziologiya Rastenii (RU ISSN 0015-3303) 1957. bi-m. $1595 in US; elsewhere $1865 (effective 1998). (Russian Academy of Sciences) Maik Nauka - Interperiodica, Mezhdunarodnyi Otdel, Ul. Profsoyuznaya, 90, 117864 Moscow, Russia. TEL 7-095-3360066. FAX 7-095-3360666. (Dist. by: Plenum Publishing Corp., 233 Spring St., New York, NY 10013-1578, U.S.A. TEL 212-620-8468. FAX 212-463-0742) Ed. A.T. Mokronosov. (also avail. in microfilm from UMI; back issues avail.) **Indexed:** Agri.Eng.Abstr., ASCA, Biol.Abstr., Cott.& Trop.Fibr.Abstr., Crop Physiol.Abstr., Curr.Adv.Ecol.Sci., Curr.Cont., Fababean Abstr., Field Crop Abstr., Herb.Abstr., Hort.Abstr., Ind.Sci.Rev., Int.Abstr.Biol.Sci., Irr.& Drain.Abstr., Maize Abstr., Ornam.Hort., Plant Grow.Reg.Abstr., Potato Abstr., Rice Abstr., Sci.Cit.Ind., Seed Abstr., Sel.Water Res.Abstr., Soils & Fert., Soyabean Abstr., Weed Abstr. **Document type:** academic/scholarly publication.
—BLDSC (0420.763200); CASDDS; CISTI; Genuine Article; Linda Hall; SWETS; UMI; UnCover. **CCC.**
Incorporates: Russian Plant Physiology (ISSN 1070-3292); Which was formerly (until 1994): Soviet Plant Physiology (ISSN 0038-5719)
Refereed Serial

551   **JA**
RYOKKA NI KANSURU CHOSA HOKOKU/RESEARCH REPORT OF REVEGETATION IN TOKYO PREFECTURE. (Text in Japanese) 1973. a. Tokyoto Kensetsukyoku - Tokyo Metropolitan Government, Bureau of Construction, 8-1 Nishishinjuku 2-chome, Shinjuku-ku, Tokyo 163-01, Japan.

581   **JA**   ISSN 0917-2157
SAGA NO SHOKUBUTSU/BOTANY OF SAGA. (Text in Japanese) 1966. a. Saga Shokubutsu Tomo no Kai - Botanical Society of Saga, c/o Mr. Inoue, 4-6 Kono Higashi 3-chome, Saga-shi, Saga-ken 840, Japan.

581   **JA**   ISSN 0917-6470
SAGO KOMYUNIKESHON/SAGO COMMUNICATION. (Text in English, Japanese) 1990. 3/yr. free. Tsukuba Sago Kikin - Tsukuba Sago Fund, c/o Institute of Applied Biochem, Tsukuba University, 791-27 Inaoka, Tsukuba, Ibaraki 305, Japan. TEL 81-298-53-6631. FAX 81-298-53-4605. E-mail: hisajima@sakura.cc.tsukuba.ac.jp. Ed. Shigeru Hisajima. bk.rev. circ. 650. **Document type:** academic/scholarly publication.
Description: Covers sago palm research, industrialization, utilization and other sago palm related subjects.

580   **JA**   ISSN 0910-6863
SAITAMA-KEN HANA UEKI SENTA SHIKEN SEISEKISHO/SAITAMA PREFECTURE GARDEN PLANTS CENTER. TEST RESULTS. (Text in Japanese) a. Saitamaken Hana Ueki Senta - Saitama Prefecture Garden Plants Center, 124 Kushibiki, Fukaya-shi, Saitama-ken 366, Japan.

581   **JA**   ISSN 0915-3845
SAKAI SHOKUBUTSU/BOTANY OF SAKAI. (Text in Japanese) 1960. a. membership. Sakai Shokubutsu Dokokai - Sakai Botanical Association, Sakaishiritsu Kagaku Kyoiku Kenkyujo, 1-3 Akahatamachi, Mozu, Sakai-shi, Osaka 591, Japan.

581.05   **SZ**   ISSN 0373-2525
QK1   CODEN: SAUSDH
SAUSSUREA. (Editions in English, French, German, Italian, Latin, Spanish) 1970. a. 60 SFr. to libraries and institutions. Societe Botanique de Geneve, Case Postale 60, CH-1292 Chambesy-GE, Switzerland. TEL 41-22-4185100. FAX 41-22-4185101. Ed. M.C. Wuest. adv.; illus. circ. 400. **Indexed:** Biol.Abstr. **Document type:** academic/scholarly publication.
—CASDDS; Linda Hall.
Supersedes: Societe Botanique de Geneve. Travaux (ISSN 0583-8177)
Description: Disseminates scientific information in all fields of botany.
Refereed Serial

581   **GW**   ISSN 0085-5960
CODEN: SVGKAX
SCHRIFTENREIHE FUER VEGETATIONSKUNDE. 1966. irreg., no. 25, 1992. price varies. (Bundesforschungsanstalt fuer Naturschutz und Landschaftsoekologie) Landwirtschaftsverlag GmbH, Huelsebrockstr. 2, 48165 Muenster, Germany. TEL 49-2501-801-0. FAX 49-2501-801-204. (Subscr. to: Postfach 480249, 48079 Muenster, Germany) charts; illus.; stat. **Indexed:** Biol.Abstr. **Document type:** government publication, monographic series.

581 576 578   **SZ**   ISSN 0373-2959
CODEN: SZPLA7
SCHWEIZERISCHE ZEITSCHRIFT FUER PILZKUNDE/BULLETIN SUISSE DE MYCOLOGIE/BOLLETTINO SVIZZERO DI MICOLOGIA. (Text in French, German, Italian) 1922. 10/yr. 35 SFr. Association Swiss Societies of Mycology, Rigistr. 23, CH-8912 Obfelden, Switzerland. Ed. Ivan/Cucchi. adv. contact: Ivan Cucchi. bk.rev.; illus. circ. 5,200. (back issues avail.) **Document type:** academic/scholarly publication.
—BLDSC (8123.400000).
Description: Contains comprehensive information on all types of fungi, including special features on mushrooms and a fungus of the month.

581   **BE**   ISSN 0779-2387
SCRIPTA BOTANICA BELGICA. (Text in English) 1992. irreg., no.10, 1994. price varies. Jardin Botanique National de Belgique - Nationale Plantentuin van Belgie, Domaine de Bouchout, 1860 Meise, Belgium. TEL 32-2-2693905. Ed. E. Robbrecht. (back issues avail.) **Document type:** monographic series.
—BLDSC (8212.320000).

590   **GW**   ISSN 0341-3772
CODEN: SCGEDL
SCRIPTA GEOBOTANICA. 1970. irreg. price varies. (Universitaet Goettingen, Lehrstuhl fuer Geobotanik) Verlag Erich Goltze GmbH and Co. KG, Hans-Boeckler-Str. 7, 37079 Goettingen, Germany. TEL 49-551-506760. FAX 49-551-5067622. Ed. Hans Heller. **Document type:** academic/scholarly publication, monographic series.
—CASDDS.

581   **UK**
SEDUM SOCIETY NEWSLETTER. 1987. q. £7.50 (Europe £12.50; U.S. $22; rest of world £15) (effective 1997 & 1998). Sedum Society, c/o Ron Mills, 173 Colchester Rd., W. Bergholt, Colchester, Essex CO6 3JY, England. Ed. Ray Stephenson. bk.rev. **Document type:** newsletter.

SEED ABSTRACTS. see *AGRICULTURE — Abstracting, Bibliographies, Statistics*

SEED PATHOLOGY AND MICROBIOLOGY. see *AGRICULTURE — Abstracting, Bibliographies, Statistics*

581 630   **SZ**   ISSN 0251-0952
SB114.A1   CODEN: SSTCBK
SEED SCIENCE AND TECHNOLOGY. (Text and summaries in English, French or German) 1973. 3/yr. 260 SFr. (effective 1997). International Seed Testing Association, P.O. Box 412, CH-8046 Zurich, Switzerland. TEL 41-1-3713133. FAX 41-1-3713427. E-mail: istach@iprolink.ch. Ed. S.R. Draper. circ. 1,200. (also avail. in microfilm from UMI; back issues avail.) **Indexed:** Agri.Eng.Abstr., Agroforest.Abstr., ASCA, Biol.Abstr., Biotech.Abstr., Chem.Abstr., Curr.Adv.Ecol.Sci., Curr.Cont., Field Crop Abstr., Forest.Abstr., Forest Prod.Abstr., Herb.Abstr., Hort.Abstr., Maize Abstr., Ornam.Hort., Plant Breed.Abstr., Rev.Med.& Vet.Mycol., Rev.Plant Path., Rice Abstr., Seed Abstr., Soils & Fert., Triticale Abstr., Weed Abstr. **Document type:** academic/scholarly publication.
—BLDSC (8218.140000); CASDDS; EMDOCS; Genuine Article; Linda Hall; SWETS; UnCover.
Supersedes (1925-1972): International Seed Testing Association. Proceedings (ISSN 0020-8663)

BIOLOGY — BOTANY

581   UK   ISSN 0960-2585
SB113.2   **CODEN: SESREX**
SEED SCIENCE RESEARCH. 1991. q. £155($270) (effective 1997). CAB International, Wallingford, Oxon. OX10 8DE, England. TEL 44-1491-832111. FAX 44-1491-826090. TELEX 847964 COMAGG G. E-mail: cabi@cabi.org; URL: http://www.cabi.org. (U.S. subscr. to: CAB International, North American Office, 198 Madison Ave., New York, NY 10016. TEL 212-726-6490. FAX 212-686-7993) Ed. M. Black. (back issues avail.) **Indexed:** ASCA, Curr.Cont., Food Sci.& Tech.Abstr. **Document type:** academic/scholarly publication.
—BLDSC (8218.155000); CASDDS; EMDOCS; Genuine Article; SWETS; UnCover.
   Description: Provides a medium for the publication of papers in the field of fundamental scientific research on seeds. The emphasis is on the physiology, biochemistry and molecular biology of seeds, covering seed and embryo development, maturation, dormancy, germination, viability, longevity, vigor, reserve mobilization, and the early stages of establishment.

581 635   US   ISSN 1083-8074
SEEDHEAD NEWS. 1983. q. $20. Native Seeds - Search, 2509 N. Campbell Ave., No. 325, Tucson, AZ 85719. TEL 520-327-9123. FAX 520-327-5821. E-mail: jhosofaz@aol.com; URL: http://www.desert.net/seeds/home.htm. Ed. Brooke Gebow; Pub. Brooke Gebow. R&P contact: Kevin Gaither-Banchoff. bk.rev.; circ. 4,400 (paid). (back issues avail.) **Document type:** newsletter.
   Description: Discusses efforts to conserve seeds of crops grown by Native Americans in the Southwest U.S.

581   JA   ISSN 0911-6931
SEIBU MAIZURU SHOKUBUTSU KENKYUJO HOKOKU/SEIBU MAIZURU BOTANICAL INSTITUTE. BULLETIN. (Text in Japanese; summaries in English, Japanese) 1985. a. Seibu Maizuru Shokubutsu Kenkyujo - Seibu Maizuru Botanical Institute, 27 Oishi, Taneji, Maizuru-shi, Kyoto 625-01, Japan. **Document type:** bulletin.

581   US   ISSN 0361-185X
QK1   **CODEN: SELBDH**
SELBYANA. 1976. a. $35 to individuals; institutions $55. Marie Selby Botanical Gardens, 811 S. Palm Ave., Sarasota, FL 34236. TEL 813-366-5730. FAX 813-366-9807. Ed. Margaret D. Lowman. illus. circ. 400. **Indexed:** Biol.Abstr. **Document type:** academic/scholarly publication.
—BLDSC (8230.480000); Linda Hall; UnCover.
   Description: Publishes original, biological research on tropical plants, especially epiphytes, and canopy biology.

581 631.5   KR
SELEKTSIYA I NASINNITSTVO; respublikanskyi mizhvidomchyi tematichnyi naukovyi zbirnik. (Text in Ukrainian) 1964. irreg.? (Ministerstvo Sel'skogo Gospodarstva Ukrainy) Vidavnitstvo Urozhai, Yaroslavov val 10, 252034 Kiev, Ukraine. TEL 0044-220-1626. Ed. D.P. Korzh.
   Formerly (until 1991): Selektsiya i Semenovodstvo (ISSN 0582-5075)

581   BL   ISSN 0375-1651
SELLOWIA; anais botanicos. (Text and summaries in English and Portuguese) 1949. a. $10 (effective 1997). Herbario "Barbosa Rodrigues", Avda. Marcos Konder 800 Centro, 88301-122 Itajai, Santa Catarina, Brazil. TEL 55-47-344-2725. FAX 55-47-344-2725. Ed. Ademir Reis; Pub. Ademir Reis. R&P contact: Zilda Helena Deschamps Bernardes. adv. contact: Zilda Helena Deschamps Bernardes. circ. 1,000. **Document type:** monographic series.

SENCKENBERGIANA BIOLOGICA. see *BIOLOGY — Zoology*

581   GW   ISSN 0944-0178
QK95   **CODEN: SNDTER**
SENDTNERA. (Text in English, French, German and Spanish; summaries in English) 1950. irreg. (1-2/yr.) exchange basis. Botanische Staatssammlung Muenchen, Menzingerstr. 67, 80638 Munich, Germany. (Co-sponsor: Institut fuer Systematische Botanik) Eds. J. Grau, F. Schuhwerk. charts; illus.; index; circ. controlled. (processed) **Indexed:** Biol.Abstr., Herb.Abstr., Plant Breed.Abstr. **Document type:** bulletin.
   Formerly (until 1991): Botanische Staatssammlung Muenchen. Mitteilungen (ISSN 0006-8179)

581   JA   ISSN 0385-3985
SENNKE/TOHOKU PLANT ASSOCIATION. NEWS. (Text in Japanese) 1973. a. 1000 Yen. Tohoku Shokubutsu Aikokai, c/o Miyakonojo Shiritsu Kyodokan, 7-22, Himegimachi, Miyakonojo-shi, Miyazaki-ken 885, Japan. Ed. Itsuo Ogura. circ. 150.

581   XR   ISSN 0231-9705
SEVEROCESKOU PRIRODOU. 1969. irreg., no.29, 1996. 30 Kc. Okresni Vlastivedne Muzeum, Litomerice, Mirove nam. 171, 412 01 Litomerice, Czech Republic. TEL 420-41-62019. Ed. Karel Kubat. **Document type:** bulletin.

583   GW   ISSN 0934-0882
QK827   **CODEN: SPLRE7**
SEXUAL PLANT REPRODUCTION. Online edition (GW ISSN 1432-2145) (Text in English) 1988. bi-m. DM.897.40 (foreign DM.905.20) (effective 1998). Springer-Verlag, Heidelberger Platz 3, 14197 Berlin, Germany. TEL 49-30-82787-0. FAX 49-30-82787448. E-mail: subscriptions@springer.de; URL: http://link.springer.de. (Subscr. in N. America to: Springer-Verlag New York, Inc., 333 Meadowlands Pkwy., Secaucus, NJ 07094. TEL 212-460-1500. FAX 212-473-6272) Ed. J.P. Mascarenhas. (also avail. in microform from UMI; back issues avail.) **Indexed:** ASCA, Bibl.Agri., Bibl.Agri., Biol.Abstr. (1990-), Curr.Cont., Curr.Cont., Ind.Sci.Rev., Sci.Cit.Ind. **Document type:** academic/scholarly publication.
●Also available online.
—BLDSC (8254.484700); ADONIS; CASDDS; CISTI; EMDOCS; Genuine Article; Linda Hall; SWETS; UMI; UnCover. **CCC.**
   Description: Focuses on experimental approaches to the dynamics and mechanisms of sexual processes in all plant forms.
   Refereed Serial

SHIDA SHOKUBUTSU BUNKEN MOKUROKU/BIBLIOGRAPHY OF PTERIDOPHYTES BY JAPANESE FERNISTS. see *BIOLOGY — Abstracting, Bibliographies, Statistics*

581   JA   ISSN 0917-9798
SHIZUOKA SHOKUBUTSU KENKYU KAISHI/BOTANICAL SOCIETY OF SHIZUOKA. BULLETIN. (Text in Japanese) 1987. every 4 yrs. Shizuoka Shokubutsu Kenkyukai - Botanical Society of Shizuoka, c/o Mr. Takehiko Suzaki, 7-3, Nakanodai 2-chome, Fujikawacho, Ihara-gun, Shizuoka-ken 421-33, Japan.

581   JA   ISSN 0388-6212
SHOKUBUTSU CHIRI BUNRUI KENKYU/JOURNAL OF PHYTOGEOGRAPHY AND TAXONOMY. (Text in English, Japanese) 1952. s-a. membership. Shokubutsu Chiri Bunrui Gakkai - Society for the Study of Phytogeography and Taxonomy, c/o Mr. Tatemi Shimizu, Kanazawa Daigaku Rigakubu, 1-1 Marunouchi, Kanazawa-shi, Ishikawa-ken 920, Japan.

581.19   JA
SHOKUBUTSU KAGAKU CHOSETSU GAKKAI TAIKAI KENKYU HAPPYO KIROKUSHU/SOCIETY FOR CHEMICAL REGULATION OF PLANTS. PROCEEDINGS OF ANNUAL MEETING. (Text in Japanese) 1965. a. Shokubutsu Kagaku Chosetsu Gakkai - Society for Chemical Regulation of Plants, 26-6, Taito 1-chome, Taito-ku, Tokyo 110, Japan. **Document type:** proceedings.

581.19   JA
SHOKUBUTSU KAGAKU SHINPOJUMU/SYMPOSIUM ON PHYTOCHEMISTRY. (Text in Japanese; summaries in English) a. Shokubutsu Kagaku Kenkyukai - Phytochemical Society of Japan, Tokyo Daigaku Yakugakubu, Syoyakugaku Shokubutsu Kagaku Kyoshitsu, 3-1 Hongo 7-chome, Bunkyo-ku, Tokyo 113, Japan.

581   JA   ISSN 0916-443X
SHOKUBUTSU KENKYU SHUROKU/BOTANICAL RECORD. (Text in Japanese) 1952. a. Aichi Shokubutsu Kenkyukai - Botanical Society of Aichi, 18 Kamichibata, Maruyamacho, Okazaki-shi, Aichi-ken 444, Japan.

581.19   JA   ISSN 0388-9130
          CODEN: SKACD7
SHOKUBUTSU NO KAGAKU CHOSETSU/CHEMICAL REGULATION OF PLANTS. (Text in Japanese) 1966. s-a. 1800 Yen. Shokubutsu Kagaku Chosetsu Gakkai - Society for Chemical Regulation of Plants, 26-6 Taito 1-chome, Taito-ku, Tokyo 110, Japan. **Indexed:** Agrindex, Chem.Abstr.
—BLDSC (3150.400000); CASDDS.

581   JA
SHOKUBUTSU NO TOMO/BOTANICAL SOCIETY. JOURNAL. (Text in Japanese) 1953. m. 200 Yen per no. Nihon Shokubutsu Tomo no Kai - Botanical Society, 20-12 Higashicho 5-chome, Koganei-shi, Tokyo 184, Japan.

581   JA   ISSN 0912-1692
SHOKUBUTSU SHUNJU/SEASONAL NEWS ON BOTANY.* (Text in Japanese) m. membership. Tokyoto Koen Kyokai - Tokyo Metropolitan Park Association, 801 Marunouchi 3-chome, Chiyoda-ku, Tokyo 160, Japan.

SHOKUBUTSU SOSHIKI SAIBOU BUNSHISEIBUTSU GAKKAI TAIKAI SHINPOJUMU KOEN YOSHISHU/JAPANESE SOCIETY FOR PLANT CELL AND MOLECULAR BIOLOGY. ABSTRACTS OF THE MEETING AND SYMPOSIUM. see *BIOLOGY — Abstracting, Bibliographies, Statistics*

581   JA   ISSN 0289-8233
SHOKUCHO/PHYTO-REGULATORS RESEARCH. (Text in Japanese) 1967. m. 400 Yen per no. Nihon Shokubutsu Chosetsuzai Kenkyu Kyokai - Japan Association for Advancement of Phyto-Regulators, 26-6, Taito 1-chome, Taito-ku, Tokyo 110, Japan.

581 333.7   JA   ISSN 0286-6102
SHOKUCHU SHOKUBUTSU KENKYUKAI KAISHI/INSECTIVOROUS PLANT SOCIETY. JOURNAL. (Text in Japanese; summaries in English) 1950. q. 4000 Yen($38) Shokuchu Shokubutsu Kenkyukai - Insectivorous Plant Society, c/o Department of Biology, Nippon Dental University, 9-20 Fujimi 1-chome, Chiyoda-ku, Tokyo 102, Japan. FAX 81-3-3264-8399. Ed. Yoshio Toyoda. bk.rev. circ. 600. (back issues avail.) **Document type:** bulletin.

581   JA   ISSN 0915-003X
SHOKUSEISHI KENKYU/JAPANESE JOURNAL OF HISTORICAL BOTANY. (Text in Japanese; summaries in English) 1986. 2/yr. 2000 Yen. Shokuseishi Kenkyukai - Japanese Association of Historical Botany, c/o Osaka Shiritsu Daigaku Rigakubu Seibutsugakka, 3-138 Sugimoto 3-chome, Sumiyoshi-ku, Osaka 558, Japan.
—BLDSC (4655.175000).

581   JA   ISSN 0913-5561
SHU SEIBUTSUGAKU KENKYU/STUDY OF SPECIES BIOLOGY. (Text in Japanese) 1977. a. Shu Seibutsu Gakkai - Society for the Study of Species Biology, c/o Kyoto Daigaku Rigakubu Shokubutsugaku Kyoshitsu, Oiwakecho, Kitashirakawa, Sakyo-ku, Kyoto 606, Japan.

581   JA   ISSN 0389-8865
SHUMI NO SAN'YASO/WILD FLOWERS AND ALPINE PLANTS. (Text in Japanese) 1979. m. 1000 Yen per no. Gekkan Satsuki Kenkyusha - Monthly Magazine of Satsuki Publishing Co., 2005-2 Onaribashicho 1-chome, Kanuma-shi, Tochigi-ken 322, Japan.

581   JA   ISSN 0288-741X
SHUSHI SEITAI/SEED ECOLOGY. (Text in English, Japanese; summaries in English) 1969. a. Shushi Seitai Danwakai - Research Group of Seed Ecology, Tohoku Daigaku Rigakubu Fuzoku Shokubutsuen, Kawauchi, Aoba-ku, Sendai-shi, Miyagi-ken 980, Japan.

BIOLOGY — BOTANY

581 US ISSN 0883-1475
SIDA: BOTANICAL MISCELLANY. 1987. irreg. price varies. Botanical Research Institute of Texas, Inc., 509 Pecan St., Fort Worth, TX 76102-4060. TEL 817-332-4441. Ed. Barney L. Lipscomb. R&P contact: Barney L. Lipscomb. circ. 850. **Document type:** academic/scholarly publication.
—BLDSC (8271.695000); Linda Hall.

581 US ISSN 0036-1488
QK1 CODEN: SCBTA4
SIDA: CONTRIBUTIONS TO BOTANY. 1962. 2/yr. $25 to individuals; libraries $35 (foreign libraries $45). Botanical Research Institute of Texas, Inc., 509 Pecan St., Fort Worth, TX 76102-4060. TEL 817-332-4441. FAX 817-332-4112. Ed. Barney L. Lipscomb. R&P contact: Barney L. Lipscomb. bk.rev.; index. circ. 800. **Indexed:** Ash.G.Bot.Per., Biol.Abstr., Curr.Adv.Ecol.Sci., Curr.Adv.Genetics & Molec.Biol., Excerp.Bot., GeoRef. **Document type:** academic/scholarly publication.
—EMDOCS; UnCover.
Refereed Serial

581 SI ISSN 0129-3729
Q80.S5 CODEN: JSNABL
SINGAPORE NATIONAL ACADEMY OF SCIENCE. JOURNAL. (Text in English) 1977. a. S.32($20) National University of Singapore, Department of Botany, Lower Kent Ridge Road, Singapore 0511, Singapore. Ed. A.N. Rao. circ. 1,500. **Indexed:** Biol.Abstr., INSPEC (1969-), Zent.Math.
—AskIEEE; CISTI; KR SourceOne.

581 BL
SISTEMATICA DE PLANTAS INVASORAS. 1988. biennial. $36.30. Instituto Campineiro de Ensino Agricola, Rua Antonio Lapa 78, Cx. Postal 1148, 13025 Campinas, SP, Brazil. TEL 32-4999. FAX 0192-470443. (Subscr. to: Rua Romualdo Andereazzi 425, CEP 13035 Campinas, SP, Brazil) circ. 3,000.

582.16 634.9 XR ISSN 0323-0724
SLEZSKE ZEMSKE MUZEUM. CASOPIS. SERIE C. DENDROLOGIE. 1952. s-a. Slezske Zemske Muzeum, Masarykova tr. 35, 746 46 Opava, Czech Republic.

581 US ISSN 0081-024X
QK1 CODEN: SCBYAJ
SMITHSONIAN CONTRIBUTIONS TO BOTANY. 1969. irreg., no.83, 1993. free. Smithsonian Institution Press, 470 L'Enfant Plaza, Ste. 7100, Washington, DC 20560. TEL 202-287-3738. FAX 202-287-3637. Ed. Don Fisher. circ. 1,400. (reprint service avail. from UMI) **Indexed:** Biol.Abstr., Ecol.Abstr., Forest.Abstr., Forest Prod.Abstr., Geo.Abstr. **Document type:** monographic series.
—BLDSC (8311.530000); CISTI; Linda Hall.

581 AG ISSN 0373-580X
CODEN: BABOAQ
SOCIEDAD ARGENTINA DE BOTANICA. BOLETIN. (Text in Spanish, occasionally in English; summaries in English) 1945. q. $50. Sociedad Argentina de Botanica, Casilla de Correo 22, 1642 San Isidro, Argentina. (Dist by: Fernando Garcia Cambiero, Box 014 Skyway USA, Suite 100, 7225 NW 25th St., Miami, FL, 33122) Dir. Nilda M. Bacigalupo. bk.rev. circ. 800. (back issues avail.) **Indexed:** Biol.Abstr.
—Linda Hall.

581.6 668.5 AG
SOCIEDAD ARGENTINA PARA LA INVESTIGACION DE PRODUCTOS AROMATICOS. ANALES. (Text in Spanish; summaries in English, Spanish) 1977. irreg. (1-2/yr.). $35. Sociedad Argentina para la Investigacion de Productos Aromaticos, Libertad 1079, 2o piso, 1012 Buenos Aires, Argentina. TEL 54-1-383-2360. E-mail: postmaster@saipa.org.ar. Ed. Arnaldo L. Bandoni. adv.: page $150. circ. 600. **Document type:** proceedings.
Formerly: Sociedad Argentina para la Investigacion de Productos Aromaticos. Boletin.
Description: Devoted to aromatic and medicinal plant research and marketing: agricultural, chemical, analytical, industrial, economic, statistical, ethno-botanical.
Refereed Serial

581 MX ISSN 0185-3619
SOCIEDAD BOTANICA DE MEXICO. BOLETIN. (Text in English, Spanish) 1944. s-a. $30. Sociedad Botanica de Mexico, A.C., Apdo. Postal 70-385, Del. Coyoacan; Ciudad Universitaria, 04510 Mexico D.F., Mexico. E-mail: oyama@servidor.unam.mx. Ed. Ken Oyana. bk.rev.; charts; illus.; cum.index: 1944-1990. circ. 1,000. **Indexed:** Biol.Abstr., Ecol.Abstr., Forest.Abstr., Forest Prod.Abstr., Geo.Abstr.P.G. **Document type:** bulletin.
Description: Presents papers on botanical research.
Refereed Serial

589.2 SP ISSN 0214-140X
QK608.S7
SOCIEDAD MICOLOGICA DE MADRID. BOLETIN. 1976. s-a. 3000 ptas. (foreign 3500 ptas.). Sociedad Micologica de Madrid, c/o Real Jardin Botanico, Claudio Moyano 1, 28014 Madrid, Spain. FAX 34-1-4200157. Ed. Francisco D. Calonge. bk.rev. circ. 600. **Indexed:** Ind.SST. **Document type:** bulletin.
Formerly (until 1985): Sociedad Micologica Castellana (ISSN 0210-7937)
Refereed Serial

581 PO ISSN 0373-4641
SOCIEDADE BROTERIANA. ANUARIO. (Text in European languages; summaries in English, French and Portuguese) 1935. a. Esc.900($5) Sociedade Broteriana, Arcos do Jardim, 3049 Coimbra, Portugal. TEL 351-39-22897. FAX 351-39-20780. (Co-sponsor: Universidade de Coimbra, Departamento de Botanica) Eds. J.F. Mesquita, M.T. Leitao. circ. 750. **Indexed:** Biol.Abstr., Excerp.Bot. **Document type:** corporate report.
—CISTI; KNAW.
Description: Covers research on botanical science and history.

581 PO ISSN 0081-0657
QK1 CODEN: BBRTAQ
SOCIEDADE BROTERIANA. BOLETIM. (Text in European languages; summaries in English, French, and Portuguese) 1880. a. Esc.10000($55) Sociedade Broteriana, Arcos do Jardim, 3049 Coimbra, Portugal. TEL 351-39-22897. FAX 351-39-20780. (Co-sponsor: Universidade de Coimbra, Departamento de Botanica) Eds. M.T. Leitao, J.F. Mesquita. circ. 1,100. **Indexed:** Biol.Abstr., Crop Physiol.Abstr., Curr.Adv.Ecol.Sci., Excerp.Bot., Field Crop Abstr., Herb.Abstr., Hort.Abstr., Plant Grow.Reg.Abstr., Weed Abstr. **Document type:** bulletin.
—BLDSC (2146.000000); CISTI; KNAW; Linda Hall.
Description: Covers research on taxonomic botany, cytotaxonomy, plant physiology, cytology, and electron microscopy.

581 FR ISSN 0037-9034
SOCIETE DE BOTANIQUE DU NORD DE LA FRANCE. BULLETIN. 1947. a. 220 F. (effective 1997). Societe de Botanique du Nord de la France, Tresorerie, 14 les Hirsons, 62800 Lievin, France. (Subscr. to: S B N F, CCP Lille No. 284658 F, Centre de Cheque Postaux de Lille, 59000 Lille, France) Ed.Bd. bk.rev. circ. 500. **Indexed:** Biol.Abstr., Bull.Signal. **Document type:** bulletin.
Description: Studies the flora and vegetation of northern France.

580 FR ISSN 0373-0875
SOCIETE LINNEENNE DE PROVENCE. BULLETIN. (Text in Esperanto, French; summaries in Catalan, English, Esperanto, French, German, Spanish) 1909. a. 90 F. (effective 1997). Societe Linneenne de Provence, Lycee Victor Hugo, 3 Bd Desplaces, 13003 Marseille, France. TEL 33-4-91632832. FAX 33-4-91632832. (Subscr. to: Renee Thomas, La Rosette, 2 rue Berthelot, 13014 Marseille, France) Ed. Claude Roux. adv. contact: Rene Thomas. bk.rev. circ. 350. (back issues avail.) **Document type:** bulletin.
Description: Publishes articles on botany, zoology, geology and prehistoric ecology.
Refereed Serial

581 NO ISSN 0800-6865
SOMMERFELTIA. (Supplement avail.) (Text in English) 1985. irreg. (approx. 2/yr.). price varies. University of Oslo, Botanical Garden and Museum, Trondheimsveien 23B, N-0562 Oslo, Norway. TEL 47-22-85-16-29. FAX 47-22-85-18-35. E-mail: r.h.okland@toyen.uio.no. Ed. Rune Halvorsen Oekland. R&P contact: Rune Halvorsen Oekland. circ. 200. (back issues avail.) **Indexed:** Biol.Abstr. **Document type:** monographic series.
—BLDSC (8327.839000); Linda Hall. **CCC.**
Refereed Serial

582.14 635 US ISSN 1075-1386
SONORAN QUARTERLY. 1947. q. $35 membership. Desert Botanical Garden, 1201 N. Galvin Pkwy., Phoenix, AZ 85008. TEL 602-941-1225. Ed. Chuck Smith. R&P contact: Jane Cole. adv. contact: Chuck Smith. bk.rev.; illus. circ. 6,000. (processed) **Document type:** bulletin.
Formerly: Saguaroland Bulletin (ISSN 0275-6919)
Description: Covers desert gardening, horticulture and desert conservation and restoration.

581 SA ISSN 0254-6299
QK396 CODEN: SAJBDD
SOUTH AFRICAN JOURNAL OF BOTANY/SUID-AFRIKAANSE TYDSKRIF VIR PLANTKUNDE. (Supplement avail.: Kirstenbosch Botanic Gardens. Annals) (Text in English) 1982. bi-m. R.197 to individuals; institutions R.217 (foreign $70) (effective 1997). (South African Association of Botanists) Foundation for Education, Science & Technology, P.O. Box 1758, Pretoria 0001, South Africa. TEL 27-12-3226404. FAX 27-12-3207803. E-mail: buro@shuttle.up.ac.za. (Co-sponsor: National Botanic Gardens of South Africa, Kirstenbosch Botanic Garden) Ed. J.N. Eloff. adv. contact: J.N. Eloff. circ. 900. **Indexed:** Apic.Abstr., ASCA, Biol.Abstr., Crop Physiol.Abstr., Curr.Adv.Ecol.Sci., Curr.Adv.Genetics & Molec.Biol., Curr.Cont., Ecol.Abstr., Field Crop Abstr., Forest.Abstr., Geo.Abstr., Herb.Abstr., Hort.Abstr., IBR, Ind.S.A.Per., INIS Atomind., Maize Abstr., Ornam.Hort., Plant Grow.Reg.Abstr., Seed Abstr., Sel.Water Res.Abstr., Soils & Fert., Weed Abstr. **Document type:** academic/scholarly publication.
—BLDSC (8338.730000); CASDDS; CISTI; EMDOCS; Genuine Article; Linda Hall; UnCover. **CCC.**
Incorporates (in 1985): Journal of South African Botany (ISSN 0022-4618)
Description: Publishes original research work in the field of botany.
Refereed Serial

SOUTH AFRICAN JOURNAL OF PLANT AND SOIL. see AGRICULTURE — Crop Production And Soil

581.2 SA
SOUTHERN AFRICAN PLANT PATHOLOGY. (Text in Afrikaans, English) 1981. s-a. Southern African Society for Plant Pathology, Private Bag X5013, Stellenbosch 7599, South Africa. illus. **Document type:** newsletter.
Formerly (until vol.14): S.A. Plant Pathologist (ISSN 1018-4309)

SOYABEAN ABSTRACTS. see AGRICULTURE — Abstracting, Bibliographies, Statistics

SPAIN. MINISTERIO DE AGRICULTURA, PESCA Y ALIMENTACION. BOLETIN DE SANIDAD VEGETAL: PLAGAS. see AGRICULTURE — Crop Production And Soil

581 595.7 US
STATE BIOLOGICAL SURVEY OF KANSAS. TECHNICAL BULLETIN. 1976. irreg. price varies. Biological Survey, Foley Hall, 2041 Constant Ave., Lawrence, KS 66047. Ed. Ralph E. Brooks. circ. 500.

BIOLOGY — BOTANY

581   SA   ISSN 1025-322X
STRELITZIA. 1994. irreg., no.5, 1997. price varies. National Botanical Institute, Private Bag X101, Pretoria 0001, South Africa. TEL 27-12-804-3200. FAX 27-12-804-3211. R&P contact: H. du Plessis. (back issues avail.) **Indexed:** Biol.Abstr., Curr.Adv.Ecol.Sci., Forest.Abstr., Forest Prod.Abstr., GeoRef., Soils & Fert. **Document type:** monographic series, proceedings.
—Linda Hall.
    Formed by the 1994 merger of: Kirstenbosh Botanic Gardens. Annals (ISSN 0258-3305); Which was formerly: Journal os South African Botany (ISSN 0258-5626) & Botanical Society of South Africa. Memoirs (ISSN 0252-9432); Which was formerly: Botanical Survey of South Africa Memoir (ISSN 0374-2083)
    Description: Publishes proceedings and treatises on ecology, taxonomy and economic botany.

581   SP   ISSN 0211-9714
                     CODEN: STBOEA
STUDIA BOTANICA. 1982. a. 1500 ptas. (effective 1995). (Universidad de Salamanca, Departamento de Biologia Vegetal, Botanica, Facultad de Farmacia) Ediciones Universidad de Salamanca, Apdo. 325, 37080 Salamanca, Spain. TEL 34-23-594598. FAX 34-23-263046. Dir. Miguel Ladero Alvarez. circ. 500. **Indexed:** Excerp.Bot., Herb.Abstr., Hort.Abstr., Ind.SST, Pollut.Abstr., Triticale Abstr. **Document type:** academic/scholarly publication.

581   HU   ISSN 0301-7001
QK311   CODEN: SBHUBV
STUDIA BOTANICA HUNGARICA. (Text in English) 1961-1969; resumed 1973. a. $24 (effective 1998). Magyar Termeszettudomanyi Muzeum - Hungarian Natural History Museum, Baross u. 13, 1088 Budapest, Hungary. TEL 36-1-3130035. FAX 36-1-11171669. Ed. Laszlo Lokos. illus. circ. 350. (back issues avail.) **Document type:** academic/scholarly publication.
—BLDSC (8482.374000).
    Incorporates (1961-1969): Fragmenta Botanica (ISSN 0532-3347)
    Description: Contains papers written by museum staff members or based on material deposited there.

580   PL   ISSN 0082-5557
QK1.T7
STUDIA SOCIETATIS SCIENTIARUM TORUNENSIS. SECTIO D. BOTANICA. (Text in Polish; summaries in English, German) 1951. irreg., vol.12, no.2, 1990. price varies. Towarzystwo Naukowe w Toruniu, Ul. Wysoka 16, 87-100 Torun, Poland. TELEX 552388 FSBH PL. Ed. Klemens Kepczynski. **Indexed:** Biol.Abstr. **Document type:** monographic series.

589.2   NE   ISSN 0166-0616
QK600   CODEN: SMYCA2
STUDIES IN MYCOLOGY. (Text in English) 1972. irreg., vol.40, 1996. price varies. Centraalbureau voor Schimmelcultures, Postbus 273, 3740 AG Baarn, Netherlands. TEL 31-35-5481240. FAX 31-35-5416142. E-mail: info@cbs.knaw.nl. Ed. R.A. Samson. R&P contact: R.A. Samson. (back issues avail.) **Indexed:** ASCA, Biol.Abstr., Chem.Abstr., Curr.Adv.Ecol.Sci., Curr.Cont., Ind.Sci.Rev., Rev.Plant Path. **Document type:** academic/scholarly publication.
—BLDSC (8491.145000); CASDDS; CISTI; Genuine Article; KNAW.
    Description: Publishes studies relating to mycological taxonomy.

581.5   SW   ISSN 0282-8677
                     CODEN: SPLEE2
STUDIES IN PLANT ECOLOGY. (Text and summaries in English, German or Swedish) 1972. irreg., no.19, 1994. price varies. (Svenska Vaextgeografiska Saellskapet - Swedish Phytogeographical Society) Opulus Press AB, P.O. Box 25137, S-750 25 Uppsala, Sweden. Ed. Erik Sjoegren. (reprint service avail.) **Indexed:** Curr.Adv.Ecol.Sci.
—BLDSC (8491.223500).
    Formerly (until 1985): Vaextekologiska Studier (ISSN 0346-735X)

581   NE   ISSN 0928-3420
                     CODEN: SPLCEU
STUDIES IN PLANT SCIENCE. (Text in English) 1991. irreg., vol.3, 1993. Elsevier Science B.V., Books Division, P.O. Box 211, 1000 AE Amsterdam, Netherlands. TEL 31-20-4853911. FAX 31-20-4853705. TELEX 18582 ESPA NL. E-mail: nlinfo-f@elsevier.nl; usinfo-f@elsevier.com; forinfo-kyf04035@niftyserve.or.jp; URL: http://www.elsevier.nl/. (Subscr. in the Americas to: Elsevier Science, Regional Sales Office, Box 945, New York, NY 10159-0945. TEL 212-633-3730. FAX 212-633-3680; Subscr. in Australasia and the Far East to: Elsevier Science (Singapore) Pte Ltd, No.1 Temasek Ave., No.17-01 Millenia Tower, Singapore 039192, Singapore. TEL 65-434-3727. FAX 65-337-2230; Subscr. in Japan to: Elsevier Science Japan,9-15 Higashi-Azabu 1-chome, Minato-ku, Tokyo 106, Japan. TEL 81-3-5561-5033. FAX 81-3-5561-5047) (back issues avail.) **Document type:** monographic series.
—BLDSC (8491.223520); CASDDS; CISTI. **CCC**.
    Refereed Serial

581   RM   ISSN 1220-5001
STUDII SI CERCETARI DE BIOLOGIE. SERIA BIOLOGIE VEGETALA. 1948. 2/yr. (Academia Romana) Editura Academiei Romane, Calea 13 Septembrie 13, 76117 Bucharest, Rumania. (Dist. by: Rodipet SA, Piata Presei Libere 1, Sec. 1, P.O. Box 33-57, Bucharest, Rumania. TEL 401-6185103. FAX 401-2226407) Ed. Nicolae Boscaiu. **Indexed:** Biol.Abstr., Chem.Abstr., Field Crop Abstr., Herb.Abstr., Plant Breed.Abstr., Rev.Plant Path., Triticale Abstr.
—BLDSC (8492.820000); CISTI; Linda Hall.
    Supersedes in part (in 1975): Studii si Cercetari de Biologie (ISSN 1015-2237); Which was formed by the merger of (1958-1973): Studii si Cercetari de Biologie. Serie Botanica (ISSN 0370-8934); Which was formerly (until 1963): Studii si Cercetari de Biologie. Seria Biologie Vegetala (ISSN 0365-5997); And (1958-1973): Studii si Cercetari de Biologie. Serie Zoologie (ISSN 0370-8950); Which was formerly (until 1963): Studii si Cercetari de Biologie. Seria Biologie Animala (ISSN 0365-5962)

SUBTROPICAL PLANT SCIENCE. see *GARDENING AND HORTICULTURE*

581   JA   ISSN 0917-1347
SUGE NO KAI KAIHO/JAPANESE CYPERACEAE NEWSLETTER. (Text in Japanese) 1990. 2/yr. Suge no Kai - Japanese Cyperaceae Association, Okayama Rika Daigaku Rigakubu Seibutsugaku Kyoshitsu, 1-1 Ridaicho, Okayama-shi, Okayama-ken 700, Japan. **Document type:** newsletter.

581   BL   ISSN 0100-5405
                     CODEN: SUPHDV
SUMMA PHYTOPATHOLOGICA. (Text mainly in Portuguese; occasionally in English or Spanish) 1975. q. $40 to non-members. (Grupo Paulista de Fitopatologia, Universidade de Sao Paulo, Rodovia C. Tonanni Km 5, 14870-000 Jaboticabal SP, Brazil. TEL 55-16-3232500. FAX 55-16-3224275. Ed.Bd. adv.; bk.rev.; abstr.; bibl.; charts. circ. 600. (back issues avail.) **Indexed:** Biol.Abstr., Helminthol.Abstr., Hort.Abstr., Maize Abstr., Potato Abstr., Rev.Plant Path., Rice Abstr., Seed Abstr., Trop.Oil Seeds Abstr. **Document type:** academic/scholarly publication.
—CASDDS.
    Description: Covers plant diseases and plant pathogens.
    Refereed Serial

589.2   DK   ISSN 0106-7451
SVAMPE. (Text in Danish; summaries in English) 1980. 2/yr. DKK 120 (effective 1996 & 1997). Foreningen til Svampekundskabens Fremme - Danish Mycological Society, P.O. Box 168, DK-2670 Greve, Denmark. TEL 45-43-69-98-02. FAX 45-43-69-98-02. Ed.Bd. bk.rev.; charts; illus. circ. 2,400. **Indexed:** Forest.Abstr., Soils & Fert.

581   SW   ISSN 0039-646X
QK1   CODEN: SBOTAS
SVENSK BOTANISK TIDSKRIFT. (Text in English, French, German, Latin and Swedish) 1907. bi-m. SEK 265 in Sweden; other Nordic countries SEK 335; rest of Europe SEK 390; elsewhere SEK 445 (effective 1998). (Botanical Museum) Svenska Botaniska Foereningen, Oe. Vallgatan 18, SE-223 61 Lund, Sweden. TEL 46-46-222-89-65. FAX 46-46-222-42-34. URL: Britt.Snogerup@sysbot.lu.se. (Co-sponsor: Svenska Botaniska Foereningen) Ed. Stefan Ericsson. adv. contact: Britt Snogerup. bk.rev.; bibl.; charts; illus.; index, cum.index every 20 yrs. circ. 2,800. (also avail. in microfiche from BHP,IDC; back issues avail.) **Indexed:** Biol.Abstr., Chem.Abstr., Curr.Adv.Ecol.Sci., Deep Sea Res.& Oceanogr.Abstr., Ecol.Abstr., Field Crop Abstr., Forest.Abstr., Forest Prod.Abstr., Geo.Abstr.P.G., Herb.Abstr., Hort.Abstr., Plant Breed.Abstr., Rev.Plant Path., Soils & Fert., Weed Abstr. **Document type:** academic/scholarly publication.
—BLDSC (8556.000000); CISTI; Linda Hall.

581   SW   ISSN 0375-2038
QH44   CODEN: SLARAM
SVENSKA LINNE-SALLSKAPET AARSSKRIFT/SWEDISH LINNEUS SOCIETY. YEARBOOK. (Text in English and Swedish; summaries in English) 1918. a. SEK 100($20) (effective 1997). Linne-Sallskapet, Kungshuset, S-222 22 Lund, Sweden. TEL 46-46-222-75-89. FAX 46-46-222-46-06. E-mail: gunnar.broberg@fil.li.se. Ed. Gunnar Broberg. bk.rev. circ. 800. **Indexed:** Zoo.Rec.
—BLDSC (8565.050000).
    Refereed Serial

581   II   ISSN 0256-9493
SWAMY BOTANICAL CLUB. JOURNAL; a journal of plant sciences. (Text in English) 1984. q. $40 to individuals; institutions $80. Swamy Botanical Club, c/o Dr. K.V. Krishnamurthy, Dept. of Plant Sciences, Bharathidasan University, Tiruchirapalli 620 024, India. TEL 0431-60351. FAX 0431-96245. TELEX 0455-253 BARD IN. R&P contact: K.V. Krishnamurthy. adv.; bk.rev. circ. 250. **Document type:** academic/scholarly publication.
—BLDSC (4905.107000).
    Description: Contains research papers on all aspects of plant sciences.
    Refereed Serial

589.2   AU   ISSN 0082-0598
QK600   CODEN: SYAMAU
SYDOWIA: ANNALES MYCOLOGICI; editii in notitiam scientiae mycologicae universalis. (Supplementavail.: Beihefte zur Sydowia: Annales Mycologici, Ser. II) (Text in English, German and Latin) 1947. a. S.1100. Verlag Ferdinand Berger und Soehne GmbH, Wienerstr. 21-23, A-3580 Horn, Austria. TEL 43-2982-4161232. FAX 43-2982-2317235. Ed. O. Petrini. (also avail. in microfiche from BHP) **Indexed:** Biol.Abstr., Plant Breed.Abstr., Rev.Plant Path. **Document type:** academic/scholarly publication.
—BLDSC (8578.900000); CISTI; Linda Hall; UnCover.

581   SW   ISSN 0082-0644
SYMBOLAE BOTANICAE UPSALIENSES. (Since vol. 20 issued as part of Acta Universitatis Upsaliensis) (Text and summaries in English, French, German) 1932. irreg. price varies. (Botaniske Institutionerna, Uppsala - Botanical Institute, Uppsala) A W I International AB, P.O. Box 4627, S-116 91 Stockholm, Sweden. TEL 46-8-7282500. FAX 46-8-338707. Ed. J. A. Nannfeldt. (back issues avail.) **Indexed:** Biol.Abstr., Field Crop Abstr., Geo.Abstr., Herb.Abstr., Rev.Plant Path., Weed Abstr. **Document type:** academic/scholarly publication.
—KNAW; Linda Hall.

581   JA   ISSN 0918-6999
SYOKUBUTSU BUNRUI GAKKAI NYUSU/J S P T NEWSLETTER. (Text in Japanese) 1971. 4/yr. members only. Nihon Shokututsu Bunrui Gakkai - Japan Society of Plant Taxonomists, c/o Makino Herbarium, Tokyo Metropolitan University, Minamiosawa, Hachioji, Tokyo 192-03, Japan. Ed. Y. Watano. circ. 350. **Document type:** newsletter.

BIOLOGY — BOTANY

589.2 UK ISSN 0280-8331
QK623.A1 CODEN: SYASEI
SYSTEMA ASCOMYCETUM. (Former name of issuing body: Commonwealth Mycological Institute (C M I) 1982. s-a. £58($100) (effective 1997). (International Mycological Institute) CAB International, Wallingford, Oxon. OX10 8DE, England. TEL 44-1491-832111. FAX 44-1491-826090. TELEX 847964 COMAGG G. E-mail: cabi@cabi.org; URL: http://www.cabi.org. (Alt. addr.: International Mycological Institute, Bakeham Ln., Egham, Surrey TW20 9TY, England; U.S. subscr. to: Oxford University Press, Customer Services Dept., 2001 Evans Rd., Cary, NC 27513. TEL 800-445-9714. FAX 919-677-1303) **Document type:** academic/scholarly publication.
—BLDSC (8589.173000); CISTI; Linda Hall; SWETS.

581 US ISSN 0363-6445
QK95
SYSTEMATIC BOTANY. 1976. q. $90 (effective 1997). American Society of Plant Taxonomists (Laramie), University of Wyoming, Dept. of Botany, Laramie, WY 82071-3165. TEL 307-766-2214. FAX 307-766-2851. E-mail: ghbrown@uwyo.edu; URL: http://www.csdt.tamu.edu/Flora/aspt/aspthom1.htm. David Giannasi. R&P contact: Gregory K. Brown. adv. contact: Gregory K. Brown. bk.rev.; illus.; circ. 1,900 (paid). (also avail. in microform from ISI; back issues avail.) **Indexed:** ASCA, Bibl.Agri., Biol.Abstr., Biol.& Agr.Ind., Curr.Adv.Ecol.Sci., Curr.Cont., Deep Sea Res.& Oceanogr.Abstr., Field Crop Abstr., GeoRef., Ind.Sci.Rev., Ornam.Hort., Plant Breed.Abstr., Sci.Cit.Ind., Trop.Oil Seeds Abstr., Weed Abstr. **Document type:** academic/scholarly publication.
—BLDSC (8589.181500); CISTI; EMDOCS; Genuine Article; KR SourceOne; Linda Hall; SWETS; UnCover. **CCC.**
Refereed Serial

581 US ISSN 0737-8211
QK95
SYSTEMATIC BOTANY MONOGRAPHS. 1980. irreg. (4-6/yr.). price varies. American Society of Plant Taxonomists (Ann Arbor), University of Michigan Herbarium, N. University Bldg., Ann Arbor, MI 48109-1057. TEL 313-647-2812. FAX 313-763-0369. E-mail: chra@umich.edu; URL: http://www.csdl.tamu.edu/Flora/aspt/aspthome. htm. Ed. Christiane Anderson. R&P contact: Chrisiane Anderson. bibl.; charts; illus.; circ. 500 (paid). (back issues avail.) **Indexed:** Apic.Abstr., Potato Abstr. **Document type:** monographic series.
—BLDSC (8589.181800).
Description: Monographs in taxonomic botany for professional botanists and ecologists.
Refereed Serial

581 630 PL ISSN 0860-3294
SZCZECINSKIE ROCZNIKI NAUKOWE, NAUKI PRZYRODNICZE I ROLNICZE. Variant title: Annales Scientiarum Stetinenses, Nauki Przyrodnicze i Rolnicze. 1986. a. price varies. (Szczecinskie Towrzystwo Naukowe - Szczecin Scientific Society) Ossolineum, Publishing House of the Polish Academy of Sciences, Rynek 9, 50-106 Wroclaw, Poland. TEL 48-71-386-25. FAX 48-71-448-103. TELEX 0712771 OSS PL. **Indexed:** AgroLibrex.

TAIWAN AGRICULTURAL RESEARCH INSTITUTE. RESEARCH SUMMARY. see *AGRICULTURE*

589.3 JA ISSN 0385-3373
TANSUI SORUI KENKYU/STUDIES OF FRESHWATER ALGAE. (Text in Japanese) 1975. every 5 yrs. Tansui Sorui Kenkyukai - Society of Freshwater Algology, c/o Mr. Ichiro Ito, 1148-7, Inocho, Takasaki-shi, Gunma-ken 370, Japan.

581 NE ISSN 0167-9406
CODEN: TUSCD8
TASKS FOR VEGETATION SCIENCE. (Text in English) 1981. irreg., vol.23, 1993. price varies. Kluwer Academic Publishers, Postbus 17, 3300 AA Dordrecht, Netherlands. TEL 31-78-6392392. FAX 31-78-6392254. TELEX 29245 KAPG NL. E-mail: services@wkap.nl; URL: http://www.wkap.nl. (Dist. by: Kluwer Academic Publishers Group, P.O. Box 322, 3300 AH Dordrecht, Netherlands. TEL 31-78-6392392. FAX 31-78-6546474; N. America dist. addr.: Box 358, Accord Sta., Hingham, MA 02018-0358. TEL 617-871-6600. FAX 617-871-6528) **Document type:** monographic series.
—BLDSC (8606.667400); CASDDS; CISTI. **CCC.**
Refereed Serial

581 GW ISSN 0040-0262
QK1 CODEN: TAXNAP
TAXON. (Text in English) 1951. q. $130 (effective 1998). (International Association for Plant Taxonomy) International Association for Plant Taxonomy, Botanischer Garten & Botanisches Museum, Koenigin-Luise-Str. 6-8, 14191 Berlin, Germany. TEL 49-30-8316010. FAX 49-30-83006218. E-mail: iapt@zedat.fu-berlin. de. Eds. B. Zimmer, W. Greuter. adv.; bk.rev.; index. cum.index: vols.1-30. circ. 2,500. (back issues avail.) **Indexed:** ASCA, Biol.Abstr., Biol.& Agr.Ind., Chem.Abstr., Curr.Adv.Ecol.Sci., Curr.Cont., Excerp.Bot., Field Crop Abstr., Forest.Abstr., Forest Prod.Abstr., Geo.Abstr., GeoRef., Herb.Abstr., Hort.Abstr., Plant Breed.Abstr., Ref.Zh., Rev.Plant Path., Sci.Cit.Ind., Seed Abstr., Soils & Fert., Weed Abstr. **Document type:** academic/scholarly publication.
—BLDSC (8611.820000); CASDDS; CISTI; EMDOCS; Genuine Article; KR SourceOne; Linda Hall; SWETS; UnCover.
Description: Covers systematic and evolutionary biology with emphasis on botany.
Refereed Serial

TELMA. see *EARTH SCIENCES*

581 AT ISSN 0312-9764
CODEN: TELODX
TELOPEA. 1975. s-a. Aus.$50 to individuals; institutions Aus.$80; foreign Aus.$95. National Herbarium of New South Wales, Royal Botanic Gardens Sydney, Mrs Macquaries Rd., Sydney, N.S.W. 2000, Australia. FAX 61-2-251-7231. URL: http://www.rbgsyd.gov.au. Eds. Peter Wilson, Gary Bridle. R&P contact: Gary Bridle. illus. circ. 1,000. **Indexed:** Biol.Abstr., Curr.Adv.Ecol.Sci., Ecol.Abstr., Excerp.Bot., Field Crop Abstr., Herb.Abstr. **Document type:** academic/scholarly publication, government publication.
—CISTI; UnCover.
Supersedes: New South Wales National Herbarium. Contributions (ISSN 0077-8753)
Description: Articles on plant systematics with information on plant anatomy, cytology, botanical history and bibliography.

581 XO ISSN 1210-0420
THAISZIA/JOURNAL OF BOTANY. (Text in English) 1991. s-a. 100 Sk.($30) University of P.J. Safarik, Botanical Garden, Namesova 23, 043 52 Kosice, Slovakia. TEL 42-95-6331555. FAX 42-95-6337353. E-mail: thaiszia@kosice.upjs. sk. adv.: page $330. bk.rev.; index. (back issues avail.) **Document type:** academic/scholarly publication.
—BLDSC (8814.138000).
Description: Publishes scientific papers in all fields of botany.

581 591 333.91 IT ISSN 0563-3745
CODEN: THSAA
THALASSIA SALENTINA. (Text in Italian; summaries in English and French) 1966. a. exchange basis. Universita degli Studi di Lecce, Stazione di Biologia Marina di Porto Cesareo, C.P. 193, 73100 Lecce, Italy. TEL 099 29854. circ. 400. (back issues avail.) **Indexed:** Biol.Abstr.

581 US ISSN 1090-1876
TIPULARIA; a botanical magazine. 1986. a. $10. Georgia Botanical Society, c/o Sally Emory, Bus. Mgr., 7575 Rico Rd., Palmetto, GA 30268. TEL 770-463-4227. bk.rev. circ. 450. **Document type:** academic/scholarly publication.

589.3 JA ISSN 0911-1271
TOCHU KASO/CORDYCEPS. (Text in Japanese) 1981. a. Nihon Tochu Kaso no Kai - Japan Cordyceps Club, c/o Mr. Nobuo Yahagi, 374-1 Kamabuchi, Mamurogawamachi, Mogami-gun, Yamagata-ken 999-56, Japan.

581 JA ISSN 0914-840X
TOHOKU SHOKUBUTSU KENKYU/BOTANICAL SOCIETY OF TOHOKU. BULLETIN. (Text in Japanese) 1983. a. Tohoku Shokubutsu Kenkyukai - Botanical Society of Tohoku, c/o Mr. Ueno, 7-28 Johokucho, Shiroishi-shi, Miyagi-ken 989-02, Japan. **Document type:** bulletin.

581.15 575.1 US
TOMATO GENETICS COOPERATIVE REPORT. 1950. a. $5. Tomato Genetics Cooperative, Cornell University, Departments of Agronomy and Plant Breeding, 1017 Bradfield Hall, Ithaca, NY 14853-1901. TEL 607-255-4573. FAX 607-255-8615. E-mail: cday@cornell.edu; URL: http://rhizo.cit.cornell.edu/tgc/. Ed. Richard W. Zobel. circ. 400. **Document type:** newsletter.

581 US
QK1 CODEN: BTBCAL
TORREY BOTANICAL SOCIETY. JOURNAL. (Included: Torreya) 1870. q. $55 (foreign $60) (effective 1997 & 1998). Torrey Botanical Society, H.H. Lehman College CUNY, Bedford Park Blvd. W., Bronx, NY 10468. TEL 718-960-8800. FAX 804-221-6483. Ed. Stewart Ware. R&P contact: Stewart Ware. adv. contact: M. Basile. bk.rev.; bibl.; charts; illus.; index, cum.index: vols.1-75. circ. 1,304. (also avail. in microform from UMI; reprint service avail. from UMI,ISI) **Indexed:** Acid Rain Abstr., Acid Rain Ind., Biol.Abstr., Biol.& Agr.Ind., Chem.Abstr., Crop Physiol.Abstr., Curr.Adv.Ecol.Sci., Curr.Adv.Genetics & Molec.Biol., Curr.Cont., Deep Sea Res.& Oceanogr.Abstr., Energy Ind., Energy Info.Abstr., Environ.Abstr., Excerp.Med., Field Crop Abstr., Forest.Abstr., Forest Prod.Abstr., Geo.Abstr., GeoRef., Herb.Abstr., Hort.Abstr., Ind.Sci.Rev., Maize Abstr., Plant Breed.Abstr., Rev.Plant Path., Sci.Cit.Ind., Seed Abstr., Sel.Water Res.Abstr., Soils & Fert., Weed Abstr. **Document type:** academic/scholarly publication.
—BLDSC (2782.000000); CASDDS; CISTI; EMDOCS; Genuine Article; Linda Hall; SWETS; UMI; UnCover.
Formerly: Torrey Botanical Club. Bulletin (ISSN 0040-9618)
Description: Provides original research in all aspects of botany, except horticulture.

TOXICON; an international journal specialising in toxins. see *PHARMACY AND PHARMACOLOGY*

581 CN ISSN 0829-318X
CODEN: TRPHEM
TREE PHYSIOLOGY; an international botanical journal. 1986. m. Can.$650($480) (effective 1997). Heron Publishing, 202-3994 Shelbourne St., Victoria, BC V8N 3E2, Canada. TEL 250-721-9921. FAX 250-721-9924. E-mail: publisher@ heronpublishing.com; URL: http://heronpublishing. com/tphome.html. Ed. Rozanne Poulson; Pub. Alfred Burdett. adv. contact: Alfred Burdett. bk.rev.; index. **Indexed:** ASCA, Bibl.Agri., Biol.Abstr., Chem.Abstr., Crop Physiol.Abstr., Curr.Adv.Plant Sci., Curr.Cont., Ecol.Abstr., Field Crop Abstr., Forest.Abstr., Forest Prod.Abstr., Hort.Abstr., Ind.Sci.Rev., Irr.& Drain.Abstr., Plant Grow.Reg.Abstr., Seed Abstr., Soils & Fert. **Document type:** academic/scholarly publication.
●Also available online. Vendor(s): Knight-Ridder Information, Inc.
—BLDSC (9047.625000); CASDDS; CISTI; EMDOCS; Linda Hall; SWETS; UnCover. **CCC.**
Description: International journal devoted to research reports and technical reviews on all aspects of the physiology of trees.
Refereed Serial

581 US ISSN 0041-2198
QK477 CODEN: TRBUAL
TREE - RING BULLETIN. 1935. a. $15 (effective 1997). Tree - Ring Society, University of Arizona, Tree - Ring Laboratory, Tucson, AZ 85721. TEL 520-621-1608. FAX 520-621-8229. Ed. Jeffrey S. Dean. R&P contact: Jeffrey S. Dean. charts; illus.; maps; cum.index; circ. 350 (controlled). **Indexed:** Anthropol.Lit., Biol.Abstr., Br.Archaeol.Abstr., Forest.Abstr., Forest Prod.Abstr., GeoRef. **Document type:** academic/scholarly publication, bulletin.
—BLDSC (9047.750000).
Refereed Serial

581 634.9   GW   ISSN 0931-1890
CODEN: TRESEY
TREES; structure and function. Online edition (GW ISSN 1432-2285) (Text in English) 1987. 8/yr. DM.1120 (foreign DM.1139.60) (effective 1998). Springer-Verlag, Heidelberger Platz 3, 14197 Berlin, Germany. TEL 49-30-82787-0. FAX 49-30-82787448. E-mail: subscriptions@springer.de; URL: http://link.springer.de. (Subscr. in N. America to: Springer-Verlag New York, Inc., 333 Meadowlands Pkwy., Secaucus, NJ 07094. TEL 212-460-1500. FAX 212-473-6272) Ed. H. Ziegler. **Indexed:** Curr.Cont. **Document type:** academic/scholarly publication.
●Also available online.
—BLDSC (9047.910500); CASDDS; CISTI; EMDOCS; Genuine Article; Linda Hall; SWETS; UMI; UnCover. **CCC.**
Description: Features articles treating physiology, biochemistry, functional anatomy, structure and ecology of trees and other woody plants.

581   SA   ISSN 0041-2236
SB435
TREES IN SOUTH AFRICA/BOME IN SUID-AFRIKA. (Text in Afrikaans and English) 1949. s-a. R.40($30) to non-members (effective 1993). Tree Society of Southern Africa - Vereniging van Boomvriende in Suidelike Afrika, Box 4116, Johannesburg 2000, South Africa. FAX 011-782-5169. Ed. J.D. Carr. adv.; bk.rev. circ. 1,000. **Indexed:** Biol.Abstr., Curr.Adv.Ecol.Sci., Forest.Abstr., Forest Prod.Abstr., Ind.S.A.Per. **Document type:** academic/scholarly publication.
—UnCover.
Description: Concerns indigenous trees: description, propagation, cultivation, conservation.

TREEWORKER. see *FORESTS AND FORESTRY*

581 660   UK   ISSN 1360-1385
QK1   CODEN: TPSCF9
▼**TRENDS IN PLANT SCIENCE.** 1996. m. fl.1349($775) to institutions (effective 1998). Elsevier Science Ltd., P.O. Box 800, Kidlington, Oxford OX5 1DX, England. TEL 44-1865-843000. FAX 44-1865-843010. E-mail: nlinfo-f@elsevier.nl; usinfo-f@elsevier.com; URL: http://www.elsevier.nl/. (Subscr. to: Elsevier Science, Regional Sales Office, P.O. Box 211, 1000 AE Amsterdam, Netherlands. TEL 31-20-4853757. FAX 31-20-4853432; Subscr. in the Americas to: Elsevier Science, Regional Sales Office, Box 945, New York, NY 10159-0945. TEL 212-633-3730. FAX 212-633-3680; Subscr. in Australasia and the Far East to: Elsevier Science (Singapore) Pte Ltd, No.1 Temasek Ave., No.17-01 Millenia Tower, Singapore 039192, Singapore. TEL 65-434-3727. FAX 65-337-2230) Ed. Andrew Sugden. adv. **Document type:** academic/scholarly publication, trade publication.
—BLDSC (9049.675450); EMDOCS; Genuine Article; KR SourceOne; SWETS. **CCC.**

581   NP
TRIBHUVAN UNIVERSITY. NATURAL HISTORY MUSEUM. JOURNAL. (Text in English) 1977. irreg. Rs.200 (foreign $10) (effective 1997). Tribhuvan University, Natural History Museum, Swoyambhu, Kathmandu, Nepal. Ed. P.K. Shrestha. R&P contact: Shailesh Chandra Singh. circ. 500. **Document type:** academic/scholarly publication.
Refereed Serial

581   II   ISSN 0564-3295
QH540   CODEN: ISTEBI
TROPICAL ECOLOGY. (Text in English, French, Spanish, Portuguese) 1960. s-a. $20 to individuals in developing countries (developed countries $30); institutions Rs.425 (foreign $60). International Society for Tropical Ecology, Dept. of Botany, Banaras Hindu University, Varanasi 221 005, India. TEL 91-542-317099. FAX 91-542-317074. TELEX 0545-304-BHU-IN. Ed. K.P. Singh. R&P contact: K.P. Singh. adv.; bk.rev. circ. 700. (back issues avail.) **Indexed:** Bio-Contr.News & Info., Biol.Abstr., Chem.Abstr., Cott.& Trop.Fibr.Abstr., Curr.Adv.Ecol.Sci., Curr.Cont., Environ.Per.Bibl. (1991-), Excerp.Med., Field Crop Abstr., Forest.Abstr., Forest Prod.Abstr., Herb.Abstr., Irr.& Drain.Abstr., Plant Breed.Abstr., Soils & Fert., Sport Fish.Abstr., Weed Abstr., Wild.Rev., Zoo.Rec. **Document type:** academic/scholarly publication.
—BLDSC (9056.070000); CASDDS; CISTI; EMDOCS; Linda Hall; SWETS; UnCover. **CCC.**
Refereed Serial

581   GW   ISSN 0302-9417
QK474.5
TROPISCHE UND SUBTROPISCHE PFLANZENWELT. 1973. irreg., vol.97, 1997. price varies. (Akademie der Wissenschaften und der Literatur, Mainz, Mathematisch-Naturwissenschaftliche Klasse) Franz Steiner Verlag Wiesbaden GmbH, Birkenwaldstr. 44, 70191 Stuttgart, Germany. TEL 49-711-2582-0. FAX 49-711-2582390. (Subscr. to: Postfach 101061, 70009 Stuttgart, Germany) Ed. Werner Rauh. R&P contact: Sabine Koerner. **Document type:** monographic series.
—CISTI.

581   JA   ISSN 0289-3568
QK1
TSUKUBA JIKKEN SHOKUBUTSUEN KENKYU HOKOKU/TSUKUBA BOTANICAL GARDEN. ANNUALS. (Text in English, Japanese) 1983. irreg. Monbusho, Kokuritsu Kagaku Hakubutsukan, Tsukuba Jikken Shokubutsuen - Ministry of Education, Science and Culture, National Science Museum, Tsukuba Botanical Garden, 1-1 Amakubo 4-chome, Tsukuba-shi, Ibaraki-ken 305, Japan. **Indexed:** Jap.Per.Ind.
—BLDSC (1034.200000).

TULANE STUDIES IN ZOOLOGY AND BOTANY. see *BIOLOGY — Zoology*

581   TU   ISSN 1300-008X
CODEN: DTBDEG
TURKISH JOURNAL OF BOTANY/TURK BOTANIK DERGISI. (Text in English, Turkish) 1976. 6/yr. $150 (effective 1996 & 1997). Scientific and Technical Research Council of Turkey - TUBITAK - Turkiye Bilimsel ve Teknik Arastirma Kurumu, Ataturk Bulvari, No. 221, Kavaklidere, 06100 Ankara, Turkey. TEL 90-312-4685300. FAX 90-312-4271336. TELEX 43186 BTAK TR. E-mail: bdym@tubitak.gov.tr. Ed. Adil Guner. **Indexed:** Biodet.Abstr., Ecol.Abstr., Geol.Abstr., Ornam.Hort., Sugar Ind.Abstr. **Document type:** academic/scholarly publication.
—CASDDS; CISTI.
Formerly (until 1994): Doga Turkish Journal of Botany - Doga Turk Botanik Dergisi (ISSN 1011-0887)
Refereed Serial

581   KR   ISSN 0372-4123
QK1   CODEN: UKBZAW
UKRAIN'SKYI BOTANICHNYI ZHURNAL; nauchnyi zhurnal. (Text in Ukrainian; summaries in English and Russian) 1921. bi-m. $276 (effective 1998). Akademiya Nauk Ukrainy, Institut Botaniki im. M.G. Kholodnogo, Vul. Tereshenkivs'ka, 2, 252601 Kiev 4, Ukraine. TEL 38-44-2251311. Ed. K.M. Sitnik. bk.rev.; illus.; index. **Indexed:** Biol.Abstr., Chem.Abstr., Djerelo, Field Crop Abstr., Forest.Abstr., Herb.Abstr., Hort.Abstr., Int.Aerosp.Abstr., Maize Abstr., Plant Breed.Abstr., Rev.Plant Path., Seed Abstr., Trop.Oil Seeds Abstr., Weed Abstr.
—BLDSC (0384.195000); CASDDS; CISTI; KNAW.

581   MX
UNIVERSIDAD DE GUADALAJARA. INSTITUTO DE BOTANICA. BOLETIN. (Text and summaries in English and Spanish) 1974-1978; resumed 1991. 3/yr. Mex.$30 (foreign $25) or exchange basis (effective 1997). Universidad de Guadalajara, Instituto de Botanica, Apdo. Postal 139, 45110 Zapopan, Jalisco, Mexico. TEL 52-3-6820003. FAX 52-3-6264635. E-mail: mharker@maiz.cucba.udg.mx. Ed. Roberto Gonzalez Tamayo. adv.; bk.rev.; bibl.; illus. circ. 1,000. **Document type:** bulletin.
Supersedes (in 1978): Universidad de Guadalajara. Instituto de Botanica. Boletin Informativo.
Description: Text in English or Spanish; summaries in English and Spanish
Refereed Serial

589.2   SP
UNIVERSIDAD DE JAEN. FACULTAD DE CIENCIAS EXPERIMENTALES. MONOGRAFIAS. 1990. irreg. price varies. Universidad de Jaen, Facultad de Ciencias Experimentales, Herbario Jaen, 23071 Jaen, Spain. TEL 34-953-212159. FAX 34-953-212141. (Dist. by: Libreria Agricola, Fernando VI, 2, 28004 Madrid, Spain. TEL 34-91-4190940) Ed. Carlos Fernandez-Lopez. **Document type:** monographic series.
Description: Covers mycology.

581   SP   ISSN 0213-5450
UNIVERSIDAD DE MURCIA. ANALES DE BIOLOGIA. SECCION BIOLOGIA VEGETAL. (Subseries of: Anales de Biologia) (Text mainly in English and Spanish; occasionally in other European languages) 1984. a. 2000 ptas. (effective 1997). Universidad de Murcia, Servicio de Publicaciones, Santo Cristo 1, 30080 Murcia, Spain. TEL 34-68-363014. FAX 34-68-363414. E-mail: vgm@pas.um.es; URL: http://www.um.es/~spumweb. Ed. Diego Rivera Nunez. bk.rev. circ. 500. (back issues avail.) **Indexed:** Field Crop Abstr., Ind.SST. **Document type:** academic/scholarly publication.
—CISTI.

581   MX   ISSN 0374-5511
CODEN: AMXSAH
UNIVERSIDAD NACIONAL AUTONOMA DE MEXICO. INSTITUTO DE BIOLOGIA. ANALES: SERIE BOTANICA. (Text in English, French, Spanish; summaries in English, French, Spanish) 1967. s-a. Mex.$100($30) per no. (effective 1998). Universidad Nacional Autonoma de Mexico, Instituto de Biologia, Apdo. Postal 70-233, Ciudad Universitaria, 04510 Mexico DF, Mexico. TEL 52-5-6225690. FAX 52-5-6225687. E-mail: javier@mail.ibiologia.unam.mx; URL: http://www.ibiologia.unam.mx. Ed. Alfonso N. Garcia Aldrete. adv. contact: Javier Domingues Galicia. abstr.; charts; illus.; stat. circ. 1,000. (back issues avail.) **Indexed:** Biodet.Abstr., Ecol.Abstr., Geol.Abstr., Rev.Med.& Vet.Mycol., Triticale Abstr. **Document type:** academic/scholarly publication, monographic series.
—Linda Hall.
Supersedes in part: Universidad Nacional Autonoma de Mexico. Instituto de Biologia. Anales (ISSN 0076-7174)
Description: Covers anatomy, cytology, taxonomy, phytochemistry and other biological areas, with emphasis on Mexican study.

581   PO   ISSN 0066-8079
UNIVERSIDADE DE LISBOA. INSTITUTO BOTANICO. ARTIGO DE DIVULGACAO. 1945. irreg. price varies. Universidade de Lisboa, Instituto Botanico, Museu, Laboratorio e Jardim Botanico, Rua da Escola Politecnica 58, 1294 Lisbon Codex, Portugal. Ed. F.M. Catarino. adv. contact: Manuel dos Santos Lopes. **Document type:** academic/scholarly publication.

581   BL   ISSN 0302-2439
QK263
UNIVERSIDADE DE SAO PAULO. DEPARTAMENTO DE BOTANICA. BOLETIM DE BOTANICA. (Text in English, Portuguese) 1973. irreg., vol.15, 1996. free. Universidade de Sao Paulo, Departamento de Botanica, Caixa Postal 11461, 05421-970 Sao Paulo, Brazil. TEL 55-11-8187595. FAX 55-11-8187547. (Co-sponsor: Instituto de Biociencias) Ed. Nanuza Luiza de Menezes. illus. circ. 800. **Indexed:** Curr.Cont.
Supersedes (1937-1969): Universidade de Sao Paulo. Faculdade de Filosofia, Ciencias y Letras. Botanica.
Description: Publishes original scientific research on botany.
Refereed Serial

UNIVERSITE D'ANKARA. FACULTE DES SCIENCES. COMMUNICATIONS. SERIE C. BIOLOGIE. see *BIOLOGY*

581   UA   ISSN 0068-5313
CODEN: CJHPBW
UNIVERSITY OF CAIRO. HERBARIUM. PUBLICATIONS. (Text in English) 1968. a. free to botanical institutions and interested botanists. University of Cairo, Botany Department, Herbarium, Giza 12613, Egypt. Ed. Vivi Taerkholm. circ. 1,500.
—CASDDS.

BIOLOGY — BOTANY

581　　　　　　　　US　　ISSN 0068-6395
QK1　　　　　　　　　　CODEN: UCPBA8
UNIVERSITY OF CALIFORNIA PUBLICATIONS IN BOTANY. 1902. irreg., vol.78, 1985. price varies. University of California Press, 2120 Berkeley Way, Berkeley, CA 94720. TEL 510-642-4247. FAX 510-643-7127. (Orders to: California-Princeton Fulfillment Services, 1445 Lower Ferry Rd., Ewing, NJ 08618. TEL 800-777-4726. FAX 800-999-1958) Ed.Bd. (also avail. in microfilm from BHP; back issues avail.) **Indexed:** Biol.Abstr., Plant Breed.Abstr. **Document type:** monographic series.
—CISTI; Linda Hall.
　Description: Publishes research on various species of native California flora.
　Refereed Serial

581　　　　　　　　TZ
UNIVERSITY OF DAR ES SALAAM. BOTANY DEPARTMENT. DEPARTMENTAL HERBARIUM PUBLICATIONS. 1971. irreg. $5. University of Dar es Salaam, Botany Department, P.O. Box 35060, Dar es Salaam, Tanzania. Ed. Bob Wingfield Clive. circ. 40.

581　　　　　　　　US　　ISSN 0091-1860
QK1　　　　　　　　　　CODEN: CUMHDA
UNIVERSITY OF MICHIGAN. HERBARIUM. CONTRIBUTIONS. (Text in English and Spanish; summaries in English) 1939. irreg., no.17, 1990. price varies. University of Michigan, Herbarium, North University Building, Ann Arbor, MI 48109-1057. TEL 313-764-2407. FAX 313-763-0369. cum.index: 1939-1942; 1966-1972. circ. 250. **Indexed:** Biol.Abstr., Forest.Abstr.
—CISTI; Linda Hall.
　Refereed Serial

UNIVERSITY OF WAIKATO. ANTARCTIC RESEARCH UNIT. REPORT. see *EARTH SCIENCES — Geology*

580　　　　　　　　YU　　ISSN 0351-1588
UNIVERZITET U BEOGRADU. INSTITUT ZA BOTANIKU I BOTANICKE BASTE. GLASNIK. vol. 10, N.S., 1975. a. Univerzitet u Beogradu, Institut za Botaniku i Botanicke Baste, Takovska 43, Belgrade, Yugoslavia. Ed. Milorad M. Jankovic. **Indexed:** Crop Physiol.Abstr., Field Crop Abstr., Herb.Abstr., Plant Grow.Reg.Abstr., Weed Abstr.

581　　　　　　　　PL　　ISSN 0302-8585
QK322　　　　　　　　　CODEN: ZJPBDD
UNIWERSYTET JAGIELLONSKI. ZESZYTY NAUKOWE. PRACE BOTANICZNE. (Text and summaries in English, Polish) 1973. irreg. price varies. Uniwersytet Jagiellonski, Ul. Golegia 24, 31-007 Krakow, Poland. (Dist. by: Ars Polona, Krakowskie Przedmiescie 7, 00-068 Warsaw, Poland) **Indexed:** AgroLibrex, Biol.Abstr., Chem.Abstr., Ecol.Abstr.
—CASDDS; CISTI; Linda Hall.

581　　　　　　　　SW　　ISSN 0042-2169
SB605.S9
VAEXTSKYDDSNOTISER. (Supplement avail.) (Text in Swedish; summaries in English) 1937. 4/yr. SEK 300 (effective 1997). Sveriges Lantbruksuniversitet - Swedish University of Agricultural Sciences, Department of Entomology, P.O. Box 7044, S-750 07 Uppsala, Sweden. TEL 018-671000. FAX 018-672890. Ed. Jan pettersson. adv. contact: Inger Blomstedt. bk.rev.; bibl.; charts; illus.; index, cum.index. **Indexed:** Biol.Abstr., Chem.Abstr., Field Crop Abstr., Helminthol.Abstr., Herb.Abstr., Hort.Abstr., Maize Abstr., Ornam.Hort., Plant Breed.Abstr., Pollut.Abstr., Potato Abstr., Rev.Appl.Entomol., Rev.Plant Path., Soils & Fert., Triticale Abstr. **Document type:** academic/scholarly publication.
　Description: Provides current information about plant protection; results from experiments and research.

581 561　　　　　　　GW　　ISSN 0939-6314
QK900　　　　　　　　　CODEN: VHAREV
VEGETATION HISTORY AND ARCHAEOBOTANY. (Text in English) 1992. q. DM.409.60 (foreign DM.413.20) (effective 1998). Springer-Verlag, Heidelberger Platz 3, 14197 Berlin, Germany. TEL 49-30-82787-0. FAX 49-30-82787448. E-mail: subscriptions@springer.de. (Subscr. in N. America to: Springer-Verlag New York, Inc., 333 Meadowlands Pkwy., Secaucus, NJ 07094. TEL 212-460-1500. FAX 212-473-6272) Ed. K.-E. Behre. **Indexed:** ASCA, Curr.Cont. **Document type:** academic/scholarly publication.
—BLDSC (9153.130000); Genuine Article; SWETS; UMI; UnCover. **CCC.**
　Description: Encompasses the entire field of vegetation history, mainly flora and vegetation development during the Holocene period.

581　　　　　　　　SA　　ISSN 0042-3203
VELD & FLORA. Variant title: Veld. (Text in English and Afrikaans) 1915. q. R.20 to libraries. Botanical Society of South Africa, Kirstenbosch, Claremont, Cape Town 7735, South Africa. TEL 27-21-7972090. FAX 27-21-7972376. Ed. C. Voget. adv.; bk.rev.; index. circ. 15,000. **Indexed:** Biol.Abstr., Gard.Lit. (1992-), Ind.S.A.Per., Plant Breed.Abstr. **Document type:** consumer publication.
—BLDSC (9154.240000); Linda Hall.
　Formerly: Botanical Society of South Africa. Journal (ISSN 0068-0419)

581 333.7　　　　　　US
VIRGINIA NATIVE PLANT SOCIETY. BULLETIN. 1982. 5/yr. $15 individual membership; institutions $40. Virginia Native Plant Society, Box 844, Annandale, VA 22003. TEL 540-332-7850. FAX 540-332-9989. Ed. Nancy Sorrells. adv. contact: Mark Gatewood. bk.rev.; circ. 1,600 (paid). **Document type:** bulletin.
　Formerly: Virginia Wildflower Preservation Society. Bulletin.
　Description: Promotes the conservation of native flora and plant habitats throughout the state of Virginia.

581　　　　　　　　GW　　ISSN 0723-7812
VORTRAEGE FUER PFLANZENZUECHTUNG. irreg., vol.19, 1991. DM.30. Verband Deutscher Pflanzenzuechter, Kaufmannstr. 71, 53115 Bonn, Germany. **Document type:** monographic series.

635　　　　　　　　US
WASHINGTON NATIVE PLANT SOCIETY. OCCASIONAL PAPERS. irreg. membership only. Washington Native Plant Society, University of Washington, Department of Botany, Box 286900, Seattle, WA 98118-8690. TEL 206-543-8022. Ed. Karen Hinman. **Document type:** academic/scholarly publication, monographic series.

581 604.7 333.7　　　　US　　ISSN 0161-3561
WATER, WOODS & WILDLIFE. 1971. bi-m. $10. Wildwood Publishing, Inc., Box 16074, St. Paul, MN 55116-0074. TEL 612-698-9358. Ed. Dan Hinton. adv.; bk.rev. circ. 4,300. (back issues avail.) **Document type:** consumer publication.

581　　　　　　　　UK　　ISSN 0043-1532
WATSONIA. 1949. s-a. £18 (foreign £20) membership. Botanical Society of the British Isles, c/o Department of Botany, The Natural History Museum, Cromwell Rd., London SW7 5BD, England. Ed. B.S. Rushton. adv.; bk.rev.; charts; illus.; stat.; cum.index. circ. 3,000. **Indexed:** Biol.Abstr., Curr.Adv.Ecol.Sci., Curr.Adv.Genetics & Molec.Biol., Field Crop Abstr., Forest.Abstr., Forest Prod.Abstr., Geo.Abstr., Herb.Abstr., Ornam.Hort., Plant Breed.Abstr., Weed Abstr. **Document type:** academic/scholarly publication.
—BLDSC (9280.000000); CISTI; Linda Hall; SWETS; UnCover.
　Description: Deals with all aspects of the distribution and taxonomic classification of flowering plants and ferns throughout the U.K.

581　　　　　　　　IT　　ISSN 0083-7792
WEBBIA; RACCOLTA DI SCRITTI BOTANICI. (Text in various languages) 1905. a. (in 2 pts.). L.250000. (Universita degli Studi di Firenze, Istituto Botanico) Museo Botanico, Via Giorgio La Pira 4, 50121 Florence, Italy. TEL 39-55-2757460. E-mail: musbot@cesit1.unifi.it. Ed. Guido Moggi. bk.rev.; circ. 250 (paid). (also avail. in microfiche from IDC) **Indexed:** Biol.Abstr., Curr.Adv.Ecol.Sci., Ecol.Abstr., Excerp.Bot., Field Crop Abstr., Geo.Abstr., Geol.Abstr., Herb.Abstr. **Document type:** academic/scholarly publication.
—BLDSC (9284.000000); CISTI; SWETS.
　Refereed Serial

581 595.7　　　　　　JA　　ISSN 0372-798X
**　　　　　　　　　　　CODEN: ZASKAN**
WEED RESEARCH. (Text in English and Japanese) 1962. q. 5000 Yen. Weed Science Society of Japan, Shokucho Bldg., 26-6, Taito 1-chome, Taito-ku, Taito 110, Japan. Ed. Kozo Ishizuka. circ. 2,000. (back issues avail.) **Indexed:** Agroforest.Abstr., Crop Physiol.Abstr., Curr.Cont., Field Crop Abstr., Herb.Abstr., Hort.Abstr., Ind.Vet., Irr.& Drain.Abstr., Maize Abstr., Plant Grow.Reg.Abstr., Rice Abstr., Seed Abstr., Soils & Fert., Soyabean Abstr., Triticale Abstr., Trop.Oil Seeds Abstr., Weed Abstr.
—BLDSC (9284.420000); CASDDS.

632 581　　　　　　　US　　ISSN 0091-4487
SB610　　　　　　　　　CODEN: WSWPAF
WESTERN SOCIETY OF WEED SCIENCE. PROCEEDINGS. 1938. a. $16.50 (foreign $18) (effective 1996). Western Society of Weed Science, c/o Wanda Graves, Bus. Mgr., Box 963, Newark, CA 94560. TEL 510-790-1252. **Indexed:** Biotech.Abstr., Chem.Abstr., Hort.Abstr., Plant Breed.Abstr., Soils & Fert., Weed Abstr. **Document type:** academic/scholarly publication, proceedings.
—BLDSC (6834.300000); CASDDS; Linda Hall.

632 581　　　　　　　US　　ISSN 0090-8142
WESTERN SOCIETY OF WEED SCIENCE. RESEARCH PROGRESS REPORT. 1952. a. $16.50 (foreign $18) (effective 1996). Western Society of Weed Science, c/o Wanda Graves, Bus. Mgr., Box 963, Newark, CA 94560. TEL 510-790-1252. **Indexed:** Biotech.Abstr., Plant Breed.Abstr. **Document type:** academic/scholarly publication.

WHAT'S UP AT CHEEKWOOD. see *ART*

581　　　　　　　　PL　　ISSN 0043-5090
**　　　　　　　　　　　CODEN: WIBOA7**
WIADOMOSCI BOTANICZNE. (Text in Polish; summaries in English) 1957. q. $32 (effective 1997). Polska Akademia Nauk, Instytut Botaniki im. W. Szafera, Ul. Lubicz 46, 31-512 Krakow, Poland. TEL 48-12-215144. FAX 48-12-219790. E-mail: nhwysock@cyf-kr.edu.pl. (Dist. by: Ars Polona, Krakowskie Przedmiescie 7, 00-068 Warsaw, Poland) (Co-sponsor: Polskie Towarzystwo Botaniczne) Ed. Bogdan Zemanek. bk.rev.; bibl.; circ. 800 (paid). **Indexed:** AgroLibrex, Biol.Abstr., Chem.Abstr., Rev.Plant Path.
—CASDDS.
　Description: Offers a wide spectrum of publications summarizing and reviewing problems from different branches of botany as well as current news in Polish and world botany; also provides information on botanical collections, scientific expeditions, symposia and congresses.
　Refereed Serial

581 333.7　　　　　　US
WILD FLOWER NOTES. 1966. a. $35 membership. New England Wild Flower Society, Inc., Garden-in-the-Woods, 180 Hemenway Rd., Framingham, MA 01701. TEL 508-877-7630. FAX 508-877-3658. E-mail: newfs@newfs.org; URL http://www.newfs.org/~newfs/. Ed. Sarah Blair Shonbrun. R&P contact: Sarah Blair Shonbrun. adv. contact: Sarah Blair Shonbrun. cum.index: 1982-1987. circ. 4,500. (back issues avail.) **Indexed:** Gard.Lit. (1992-). **Document type:** academic/scholarly publication.
　Former titles (until 1984): Wild Flower Notes and News; (until 1981): Wild Flower Notes and News; (until 1980): New England Wild Flower Notes.
　Description: Articles on botanical and horticultural subjects concerning native plants and their habitats

BIOLOGY — BOTANY

613.2 **581**   US   ISSN 1083-7299
THE WILD FOODS FORUM. 1990. bi-m. $15 (foreign $16.50); newsstand price: $2. Eco Images, Box 61413, Virginia Beach, VA 23466-1413. TEL 757-421-3929. E-mail: wildfood@infi.net. Ed. Vickie Shufer. adv.: page $85; trim 8 x 10 1/2. bk.rev.; video rev.; index; circ. 600 (paid). (back issues avail.) **Document type:** newsletter.
    Description: Feature stories on wild edible foods and their health benefits, rare or poisonous plants, trip reports, upcoming events and survival skills.

581   CN   ISSN 0842-5132
WILDFLOWER; North America's magazine of wild flora. 1985. q. $30 to individuals; libraries $35 (effective 1997). Canadian Wildflower Society, 90 Wolfrey Ave., Toronto, ON M4K 1K8, Canada. TEL 416-466-6428. FAX 416-466-6428. (Subscr. to: 4981 Hwy. 7 E., Unit 12A, Ste. 228, Markham, ON L3R 1N1, Canada) Ed. James L. Hodgins. adv. contact: Zile Zichmanis. bk.rev.; cum.index: 1984-1994. circ. 4,500. **Indexed:** Gard.Lit. (1992-). **Document type:** consumer publication.
    Description: Offers articles and information to readers across the continent for all levels of botanical knowledge and interest.

581   US   ISSN 0898-8803
WILDFLOWER (AUSTIN, 1984). 1984. bi-m. $25 membership (effective 1996). National Wildflower Research Center, 4801 La Crosse Ave., Austin, TX 78739. TEL 512-292-4200. FAX 512-292-4627. E-mail: nwrc@onr.com; URL: http://www.wildflower.org. Ed. Joshua C. Blumenfeld. R&P contact: Joshua C. Blumenfeld. circ. 22,000. **Indexed:** Gard.Lit. (1992-). **Document type:** newsletter.
    Description: Promotes preservation and reestablishment of native North American plants in natural and planned landscapes.

581   GW   ISSN 0511-9618
QK1
WILLDENOWIA. (Text in English, German) 1953. s-a. DM.120. Botanischer Garten und Botanisches Museum Berlin-Dahlem, Koenigin-Luise-Str. 6-8, 14191 Berlin, Germany. TEL 49-30-83006194. FAX 49-30-83006186. E-mail: son@zedat.fu-berlin.de; URL: http://www.bgbm.fu-berlin.de/bgbm/library/publikat/willdimp.htm. Ed. N. Kilian. bk.rev.; index. circ. 1,000. (back issues avail.) **Indexed:** Biol.Abstr., Curr.Adv.Ecol.Sci., Ecol.Abstr., Field Crop Abstr., Forest.Abstr., Herb.Abstr., IBR, Plant Breed.Abstr., Rev.Plant Path., Triticale Abstr., Weed Abstr. **Document type:** academic/scholarly publication.
    —BLDSC (9318.900000); Linda Hall.
    Description: Original papers in the fields of taxonomic and floristic botany.
    Refereed Serial

581   NO   ISSN 0346-4601
QK658   CODEN: WPSFAC
WORLD POLLEN AND SPORE FLORA. (Text in English) 1973. a. price varies. Scandinavian University Press, P.O. Box 2959 Toeyen, N-0608 Oslo, Norway. TEL 47-22-57-54-00. FAX 47-22-57-53-53. E-mail: mail@scup.no; URL: http://www.scup.no (US addr.: 875 Massachusetts Ave., Ste. 84, Cambridge, MA 02139. TEL 617-497-6515. FAX 617-354-6875) Ed. Siwert Nilsson. **Indexed:** Ecol.Abstr. **Document type:** academic/scholarly publication.
    —BLDSC (9358.080500); CISTI; Linda Hall. **CCC.**
    Description: Contains general descriptions of pollen and spores in different plant families of spermatophytes, pteridophytes and fungi.

581   CC   ISSN 1000-470X
WUHAN ZHIWUXUE YANJIU/JOURNAL OF WUHAN BOTANICAL RESEARCH. (Text in Chinese) 1983. q. Wuhan Zhiwu Yanjiusuo, P.O. Box 74006, Wuhan Zhiwu Yanjiusuo, Moshan, Wuchang, Wuhan, Hubei 430074, People's Republic of China. TEL 86-27-7801126. FAX 86-27-7801251. (Dist. overseas by: China International Book Trading Corp., P.O. Box 399, Beijing 100044, P.R China) Ed. Zheng Zhong. illus. pp./issue: 96. **Document type:** academic/scholarly publication.
    Description: Covers the latest scientific research and reports on new theories, technologies, achievements and trends in all branches of botanical science.

581   JA
YAKKOSO TSUCHITORIMOCHI NO TOMO/PARASITIC PLANTS MAGAZINE. 1976. q. 6000 Yen($35) Yakkoso Tsuchitorimochi o Hogo Suru Kai - Preserving Society of Mitrastemon and Balanophora, c/o Mr. Eitaro Akusawa, 19-4, Mejirodai 3-chome, Bunkyo-ku, Tokyo 112, Japan. Ed. Eitaro Akuzawa. circ. 1,500.

581   JA   ISSN 0914-5036
YAMANASHI SHOKUBUTSU KENKYU/BOTANICAL SOCIETY OF YAMANASHI. BULLETIN. (Text in Japanese) 1987. a. Yamanashi Shokubutsu Kenkyukai - Botanical Society of Yamanashi, c/o Mr. Eiji Okubo, 2800-109 Yamamiya-cho, Kofu-shi, Yamanashi-ken 400, Japan.

581   CC   ISSN 1001-9782
YAREDAI ZHIWU TONGXUN/SUBTROPICAL PLANT RESEARCH COMMUNICATIONS. (Text in Chinese) 1972. s-a. Y3. Fujian Institute of Subtropical Botany - Fujian Yaredai Zhiwu Yanjiusuo, Dianqian, Xiamen, Fujian 361006, People's Republic of China. TEL 621047. (Dist. overseas by: China National Publishing Industry Trading Corporation, P.O. Box 782, Beijing 100011, P.R.C.) Ed. Huang Weinan. **Document type:** bulletin.

381   JA   ISSN 0912-2451
YASO/WILD PLANTS. (Text in Japanese) 1935. bi-m. 3500 Yen. Yagai Shokubutsu Kenkyukai - Wild Plants Lover's Club, c/o Mr. Nobushige Kato, 1-18 Wakaba, Shinjuku-ku, Tokyo 160, Japan. TEL 81-3-3357-9090. Eds. Akira Yamamoto, Nobushige Kato. adv. contact: Bansei Makino. circ. 500. pp./issue: 16. **Document type:** bulletin.
    Refereed Serial

581   JA
YASO NO TOMO/ICHIHARA BOTANICAL ASSOCIATION. JOURNAL. (Text in Japanese) a. Ichihara Shokubutsu Kenkyukai - Ichihara Botanical Association, c/o Mr. Yuji Nemoto, 219 Yamaguchi, Ichihara-shi, Chiba-ken 290-05, Japan.

581   JA
YASO TOMO NO KAI/SOCIETY OF THE WILD GRASS. NEWS. (Text in Japanese) a. Yaso Tomo no Kai - Society of the Wild Grass, c/o Mr. Yoshitaka Takahashi, 9-7 Saikumachi, Shinjuku-ku, Tokyo 162, Japan.

581   JA   ISSN 0912-0815
YOKOHAMA SHOKUBUTSUKAI NENPO/YOKOHAMA BOTANICAL SOCIETY. ANNUAL REPORT. (Text in Japanese) 1971. a. 2000 Yen. Yokohama Shokubutsukai - Yokohama Botanical Society, 251-8, Kajigaya-cho, Sakae-ku, Yokohama-shi, Kanagawa-ken 247, Japan. TEL 045-893-8679. Ed. Hideo Takahashi. circ. 300 (paid). **Document type:** bulletin.

581   CC   ISSN 0253-2700
QK1   CODEN: YCWCDP
YUNNAN ZHIWU YANJIU/ACTA BOTANICA YUNNANICA. (Text in Chinese) 1979. q. $40. Zhongguo Kexueyuan, Kunming Zhiwu Yanjiusuo - Academia Sinica, Kunming Institute of Botany, Heilongtan, Kunming 650204, Yunnan, People's Republic of China. TEL 86-871-5150660. FAX 86-871-5150227. Ed. Zhengyi Wu. R&P contact: Guanj. adv. contact: Guanjun Huang. bk.rev.; abstr. circ. 1,800. **Indexed:** Curr.Adv.Ecol.Sci., Hort.Abstr., Ornam.Hort., Weed Abstr. **Document type:** academic/scholarly publication.
    —BLDSC (0608.1100000); CASDDS; Linda Hall.
    Description: Publishes original papers and notes on various fields of botany, including phytotaxonomy, phytogeography, phytochemistry, plant physiology, morphology, ecology and geobotany, domestication of introduced species, utilization of plant resources, and new techniques and achievements in China and abroad.

581   595.7   GW   ISSN 0044-3271
ZEITSCHRIFT FUER PFLANZENKRANKHEITEN UND PFLANZENSCHUTZ. (Text and summaries in English and German) 1891. bi-m. DM.842.70. Verlag Eugen Ulmer GmbH, Wollgrasweg 41, 70599 Stuttgart, Germany. TEL 49-711-4507-0. FAX 49-711-4507-120. (Subscr. to: Postfach 700561, 70574 Stuttgart, Germany) Ed. H. Buchenauer. R&P contact: G. Friedrich. adv.; bk.rev.; abstr.; bibl.; charts; illus.; index. circ. 400. **Indexed:** Agri.Eng.Abstr., ASCA, Bio-Contr.News & Info., Biol.Abstr., Biotech.Abstr., Chem.Abstr., Crop Physiol.Abstr., Curr.Adv.Ecol.Sci., Curr.Cont., Ecol.Abstr., Fababean Abstr., Field Crop Abstr., Food Sci.& Tech.Abstr., Forest.Abstr., Forest Prod.Abstr., Geo.Abstr.P.G., Helminthol.Abstr., Herb.Abstr., Hort.Abstr., IBR, IDA, Ind.Sci.Rev., Maize Abstr., Plant Breed.Abstr., Plant Grow.Reg.Abstr., Potato Abstr., Rev.Appl.Entomol., Rev.Appl.Mycol., Rev.Plant Path., Rice Abstr., Sci.Cit.Ind., Seed Abstr., Sel.Water Res.Abstr., Soils & Fert., Soyabean Abstr., Triticale Abstr., Trop.Oil Seeds Abstr., VITIS. **Document type:** academic/scholarly publication.

581   GW   ISSN 0722-348X
           CODEN: ZPHYDG
ZEITSCHRIFT FUER PHYTOTHERAPIE. (Text in German; summaries in English) 1979. bi-m. DM.75. (Gesellschaft fuer Phytotherapie e.V.) Hippokrates Verlag GmbH, Postfach 300504, 70445 Stuttgart, Germany. TEL 0711-8931-0. FAX 0711-8931453. Ed. Guenther Buck. adv.; bk.rev. circ. 6,000. (back issues avail.) **Document type:** academic/scholarly publication.
    —BLDSC (9484.130000); CASDDS; EMDOCS; KNAW. **CCC.**

589.2   CC   ISSN 0256-1883
QK609.C6   CODEN: ZHXUET
ZHENJUN XUEBAO/ACTA MYCOLOGICA SINICA. (Text in Chinese; summaries in English) 1982. q. $71.20. (Chinese Academy of Sciences, Institute of Microbiology) Science Press, Marketing and Sales Department, 16 Donghuangchenggen North St., Beijing 100717, People's Republic of China. TEL 4010642. FAX 4109810. adv. circ. 11,000. **Indexed:** Biodet.Abstr., Poult.Abstr., Rev.Med.& Vet.Mycol. **Document type:** academic/scholarly publication.
    —BLDSC (0639.350000); CASDDS.
    Description: Contains academic papers on mycology research, including taxonomy, physiology, biochemistry, ecology, genetics, material resources, and industrial, agricultural, medical, and veterinary mycology. Also contains news briefs and reviews of research work.
    Refereed Serial

581   635   CC   ISSN 0529-1542
SB750
ZHIWU BAOHU/PLANT PROTECTION. (Text in Chinese) 1963. bi-m. newsstand price: $3. Zhongguo Zhiwu Baohu Xuehui, Zhongguo Nongke Yuan, Zhibao Suo, 2 Yuanmingyuan Xilu, Beijing 100094, People's Republic of China. TEL 86-10-6258-1177. FAX 86-10-6258-3080. Ed. Li Guangbo. R&P contact: Yunlu Xie. adv. contact: Hongrong Gao. pp./issue: 56. **Indexed:** Curr.Adv.Ecol.Sci., Protozool.Abstr., Seed Abstr.
    Refereed Serial

581   CC   ISSN 0577-7518
ZHIWU BAOHU XUEBAO/ACTA PHYTOPHYLACTICA SINICA. Variant title: Journal of Plant Protection. (Text in Chinese; abstracts in English) q. Y40. Zhongguo Zhiwu Baohu Xuehui - Chinese Society of Plant Protection, Department of Plant Protection, Beijing University of Agriculture, Beijing 100094, People's Republic of China. TEL 86-10-2582244 extn. 319. Ed. Mingtsang Cheo. **Indexed:** Bio-Contr.News & Info., Biol.Abstr., Cott.& Trop.Fibr.Abstr., Curr.Adv.Ecol.Sci., Field Crop Abstr., Hort.Abstr., Maize Abstr., Potato Abstr., Rice Abstr., Triticale Abstr., Weed Abstr. **Document type:** academic/scholarly publication.
    —BLDSC (0656.700000); Linda Hall.
    Description: Contains research reports in this field of botany.

BIOLOGY — COMPUTER APPLICATIONS

581   CC   ISSN 0412-0914
QK710   CODEN: CWSPDA
ZHIWU BINGLI XUEBAO/ACTA PHYTOPATHOLOGICA SINICA. (Text in Chinese) q. $1.80 per no. Zhongguo Zhiwu Bingli Xuehui - China Phytopathological Society, Department of Plant Protection, Beijing University of Agriculture, Beijing 100094, People's Republic of China. TEL 86-10-2582244. FAX 86-10-2582332. Ed. Qiu Weifan. pp./issue: 96. **Indexed:** Bio-Contr.News & Info., Cott.& Trop.Fibr.Abstr., Crop Physiol.Abstr., Curr.Adv.Ecol.Sci., Forest.Abstr., Hort.Abstr., Maize Abstr., Triticale Abstr. **Document type:** academic/scholarly publication.
—Linda Hall.
Refereed Serial

581   CC   ISSN 0529-1526
QK355
ZHIWU FENLEI XUEBAO/ACTA PHYTOTAXONOMICA SINICA. (Text in Chinese; summaries in English) 1951. bi-m. $92.50. (Chinese Academy of Sciences, Institute of Botany) Science Press, Marketing and Sales Department, 16 Donghuangchenggen North St., Beijing 100717, People's Republic of China. TEL 4010642. FAX 4019810. adv. circ. 6,000. **Indexed:** Biol.Abstr. **Document type:** academic/scholarly publication.
—BLDSC (0657.500000); CISTI; Linda Hall.
Description: Contains original papers on phytotaxonomy, phytogeography, phytosystematics, and biosystematics. Also includes discussions from various schools and activities both in China and abroad.
Refereed Serial

581   CC   ISSN 0257-4829
QK710   CODEN: CWSPDA
ZHIWU SHENGLI XUEBAO/ACTA PHYTOPHYSIOLOGICA SINICA. (Text in Chinese) 1964. q. $68.80. (Chinese Society of Plant Physiology) Science Press, Marketing and Sales Department, 16 Donghuangchenggen North St., Beijing 100717, People's Republic of China. TEL 4010642. FAX 4019810. adv. circ. 7,000. **Indexed:** Cott.& Trop.Fibr.Abstr., Curr.Adv.Ecol.Sci., Excerp.Med., Field Crop Abstr., Herb.Abstr., Irr.& Drain.Abstr., Maize Abstr., Ornam.Hort., Plant Grow.Reg.Abstr., Seed Abstr., Sorghum & Millets Abstr., Triticale Abstr., Weed Abstr. **Document type:** academic/scholarly publication.
—BLDSC (0656.750000); CASDDS; CISTI; Linda Hall.
Description: Contains original papers on plant physiology, including plant cell physiology, whole plant physiology, crop physiology, ecological physiology, plant biochemistry and biophysics.
Refereed Serial

581 574.1   CC   ISSN 0412-0922
    CODEN: CHWSAX
ZHIWU SHENGLIXUE TONGXUN/PLANT PHYSIOLOGY COMMUNICATIONS. (Text in Chinese) 1951. bi-m. $23.40. (Chinese Society of Plant Physiology) Science Press, Marketing and Sales Department, 16 Donghuangchenggen North St., Beijing 100717, People's Republic of China. TEL 4010642. FAX 4019810. adv.; bk.rev. **Indexed:** Hort.Abstr., Irr.& Drain.Abstr., Potato Abstr., Rice Abstr., Seed Abstr. **Document type:** academic/scholarly publication.
—BLDSC (6522.100000); CASDDS; CISTI.
Description: Contains original papers, communications, and review articles on plant physiology, biochemistry, and biophysics, from the molecular level to the community level. Also contains columns on techniques and methods, teaching, and news.

581   CC   ISSN 1005-264X
QK355
ZHIWU SHENGTAI XUEBAO/JOURNAL OF PLANT ECOLOGY/ACTA PHYTOECOLOGICA SINICA. (Text in Chinese, English) 1955. bi-m. $24 (effective 1997). (Zhongguo Kexueyuan, Zhiwu Yanjiusuo - Chinese Academy of Sciences, Institute of Botany) Science Press, Marketing and Sales Department, 16 Donghuangchenggen North St., Beijing 100717, People's Republic of China. TEL 86-10-6401-9815. FAX 86-10-6401-9810. (Subscr. to: Chinese Academy of Sciences, Institute of Botany, 20 Nanxincun, Xiangshan, Beijing 100093, P.R. China. TEL 86-10-6259-1431. FAX 86-10-6259-0348) Eds. Yihui Hu, Yonghong Li. R&P contact: Yihui Hu. adv. contact: Yonghong Li. bk.rev. circ. 1,300. **Document type:** academic/scholarly publication.
Formerly (until 1994): Zhiwu Shengtaixue yu Dizhiwuxue Xuebao - Acta Phytoecologica et Geobotanica Sinica (ISSN 1000-0011)
Description: Contains original research papers on plant ecology, including plant ecophysiology, population ecology, community ecology, vegetation science, landscape ecology, ecosystem ecology, and conservation.
Refereed Serial

581   CC   ISSN 0577-7496
QK1   CODEN: CHWHAY
ZHIWU XUEBAO/ACTA BOTANICA SINICA. English edition: Chinese Journal of Botany (ISSN 1001-0718) (Text in Chinese; summaries in English) 1951. m. $169.50. (Chinese Academy of Sciences, Institute of Botany) Science Press, Marketing and Sales Department, 16 Donghuangchenggen North St., Beijing 100717, People's Republic of China. TEL 4010642. FAX 4019810. (Co-sponsor: Chinese Botanical Society) Ed. Cheng Tsui. adv.; bibl.; charts; illus.; index. circ. 12,000. (back issues avail.) **Indexed:** Biodet.Abstr., Biol.Abstr., Chem.Abstr., Crop Physiol.Abstr., Curr.Adv.Ecol.Sci., Ecol.Abstr., Field Crop Abstr., Food Sci.& Tech.Abstr., Forest.Abstr., Geo.Abstr., Geol.Abstr., GeoRef., Herb.Abstr., Hort.Abstr., Irr.& Drain.Abstr., Maize Abstr., Ornam.Hort., Plant Grow.Reg.Abstr., Rev.Plant Path., Rice Abstr., Seed Abstr., Soils & Fert., Sorghum & Millets Abstr., Soyabean Abstr., Triticale Abstr., Trop.Oil Seeds Abstr., Weed Abstr. **Document type:** academic/scholarly publication.
—BLDSC (0608.000000); CASDDS; CISTI; Linda Hall.
Description: Original papers on the applications and theory of plant morphology, cytology, chemistry, physiology, biochemistry, ecology, geobotany, and paleobotany. Also covers the domestication of spices and plant genetics.
Refereed Serial

581   CC   ISSN 1000-0631
QK355
ZHIWU ZAZHI/PLANTS. Variant English title: Journal of Botany. (Text in Chinese) 1973. bi-m. $23.40. (Chinese Academy of Sciences, Institute of Botany) Science Press, Marketing and Sales Department, 16 Donghuangchenggen North St., Beijing 100717, People's Republic of China. TEL 4010642. FAX 4019810. **Document type:** academic/scholarly publication.
—BLDSC (6527.850000); Linda Hall.
Description: Closely incorporates the production practices of agriculture, forestry, horticulture, and medicinal herbs, and introduces a basic knowledge of botany and of China's rich botanical resources. Helpful for middle school instruction and for amateurs interested in botany.

581 613.1   CC   ISSN 1004-0978
    CODEN: ZZYHEJ
ZHIWU ZIYUAN YU HUANJING/JOURNAL OF PLANT RESOURCES AND ENVIRONMENT. (Text in Chinese) 1992. q. $40 (effective 1998). (Jiangsu Institute of Botany) Zhiwu Ziyuan yu Huanjing Bianjibu, Zhongshan Mengwai, Nanjing, Jiangsu 210014, People's Republic of China. TEL 86-25-443-2128. FAX 86-25-443-2074. E-mail: jsszzzzz@public1.ptt.js.cn. (Dist. overseas by: China National Publications Import & Export Corporation, P.O. Box 88, Beijing, P.R. China) (Co-sponsors: Jiangsu Society of Botany; Chinese Society of Environmental Sciences, Branch of Botanical Gardens Conservation) Ed. Shan-An He; Pub. Ding-Fa Xu. R&P contact: Shan-An He. adv. contact: Ding-Fa Xu. bk.rev. **Document type:** academic/scholarly publication.
—BLDSC (6523.381000); CASDDS.
Description: Publishes original articles, research notes and reviews dealing with basic and applied studies in plant resources and environment.
Refereed Serial

581   CC
ZHIWUXUE TONGBAO/BOTANICAL BULLETIN. (Text in Chinese) q. Zhongguo Kexueyuan, Zhiwu Yanjiusuo - Chinese Academy of Sciences, Botanical Institute, 141 Xizhimenwai Dajie, Beijing 100044, People's Republic of China. TEL 893831. Ed. Zhu Zhiqing.
Refereed Serial

ZIVA; casopis pro biologickou praci. see BIOLOGY

580 590   AU   ISSN 0252-1911
    CODEN: VZGOD7
ZOOLOGISCH-BOTANISCHE GESELLSCHAFT IN OESTERREICH. VERHANDLUNGEN. 1851. a. S.250. Zoologisch-Botanische Gesellschaft in Oesterreich, Althanstr. 14, Postfach 287, A-1091 Vienna, Austria. TEL 0222-313361465. FAX 0222-31336700. bk.rev. circ. 1,000. **Indexed:** Biol.Abstr., Curr.Adv.Ecol.Sci., GeoRef., Rev.Appl.Entomol.
—CISTI; Linda Hall.
Formerly (until 1977): Zoologisch-Botanische Gesellschaft, Vienna. Verhandlungen (ISSN 0084-5647)

580 590   AU   ISSN 0084-5639
QH301
ZOOLOGISCH - BOTANISCHE GESELLSCHAFT, VIENNA. ABHANDLUNGEN. irreg. Zoologisch-Botanische Gesellschaft in Oesterreich, Althanstr. 14, Postfach 287, A-1091 Vienna, Austria. TEL 0222-313361465. FAX 0222-31336700.

BIOLOGY — Computer Applications

570.0285   UK   ISSN 1367-4803
    CODEN: COABER
BIOINFORMATICS. 1985. 10/yr. £295 (foreign $495) (effective 1998). Oxford University Press, Academic Division, Great Clarendon St., Oxford OX2 6DP, England. TEL 44-1865-267907. FAX 44-1865-267485. TELEX 837330-OXPRES-G. E-mail: jnl.info@oup.co.uk; URL: http://www.oup.co.uk/journals. (U.S. subscr. to: Oxford University Press Inc., 2001 Evans Rd., Cary, NC 27513. TEL 800-852-7323. FAX 919-677-1714) Eds. G.N. Stormo, C. Sander; Pub. Steven Johnson. R&P contact: Joolz Longley. adv.; bk.rev.; illus.; tr.lit.; index. circ. 825. (back issues avail.; reprint service avail. from SWZ) **Indexed:** A.I.Abstr., ASCA, Bibl.Agri., Biol.Abstr., CAD CAM Abstr., Chem.Abstr., Compumath, Comput.Abstr., Curr.Adv.Ecol.Sci., Curr.Biotech.Abstr., Curr.Cont., Excerp.Med., Ind.Sci.Rev., Sci.Cit.Ind., Telegen. **Document type:** academic/scholarly publication.
—BLDSC (3393.635000); CASDDS; CISTI; Ei; EMDOCS; Genuine Article; KNAW; Linda Hall; SWETS UMI; UnCover. **CCC.**
Formerly: Computer Applications in the Biosciences (ISSN 0266-7061)
Description: International applications-orientated journal publishing full papers, program reviews, new applications and developments for newcomers and computer-literate bioscientists.

BIOLOGICAL CYBERNETICS; communication and control in organisms and automata. see COMPUTERS — Cybernetics

COMPUTER METHODS IN BIOMECHANICS AND BIOMEDICAL ENGINEERING. see BIOLOGY — Bioengineering

570.0285 610.28 UK ISSN 0010-4825
R858.A1 CODEN: CBMDAW
COMPUTERS IN BIOLOGY AND MEDICINE; an international journal. 1971. bi-m. fl.1645($946) (effective 1998). Elsevier Science Ltd., Pergamon, P.O. Box 800, Kidlington, Oxford OX5 1DX, England. TEL 44-1865-843000. FAX 44-1865-843010. E-mail: nlinfo-f@elsevier.nl; usinfo-f@elsevier.com; forinfo-kyf04035@niftyserve.or.jp; URL: http://www.elsevier.nl/. (Subscr. to: Elsevier Science, Regional Sales Office, P.O. Box 211, 1000 AE Amsterdam, Netherlands. TEL 31-20-4853757. FAX 31-20-4853432; Subscr. in the Americas to: Elsevier Science, Regional Sales Office, Box 945, New York, NY 10159-0945. TEL 212-633-3730. FAX 212-633-3680; Subscr. in Australasia and the Far East to: Elsevier Science (Singapore) Pte Ltd, No.1 Temasek Ave., No.17-01 Millenia Tower, Singapore 039192, Singapore. TEL 65-434-3727. FAX 65-337-2230) Ed. R.S. Ledley. adv.; bk.rev. circ. 1,200. (also avail. in microform from UMI; back issues avail.) **Indexed:** Anim.Breed.Abstr., Appl.Mech.Rev., ASCA, Bioeng.Abstr., Biol.Abstr., Biostat., Chem.Abstr., Compumath, Comput.Abstr., Comput.Cont., Comput.Dtbs., Curr.Adv.Ecol.Sci., Curr.Cont., Eng.Ind., Excerp.Med., Ind.Med., Ind.Sci.Rev., INSPEC, Risk Abstr., Sci.Cit.Ind., Telegen. **Document type:** academic/scholarly publication.
—BLDSC (3394.880000); ADONIS; AskIEEE; CASDDS; CISTI; Ei; EMDOCS; Genuine Article; KNAW; KR SourceOne; Linda Hall; SWETS; UMI; UnCover. CCC.
Description: Provides an international medium for the exchange of research, ideas and information on all aspects of the growing use of computers in the fields of bioscience and medicine.
Refereed Serial

004.3 US ISSN 1063-6560
QA402.5 CODEN: EOCMEO
EVOLUTIONARY COMPUTATION. 1993. q. $48 to individuals (foreign $64); institutions $152 (foreign $168); students and retired $32 (foreign $48) (effective 1997). M I T Press, 5 Cambridge Center, Cambridge, MA 02142. TEL 617-253-2889. FAX 617-577-1545. E-mail: journals-orders@mit.edu; URL: http://www.mitpress.mit.edu. Ed. Darrell Whitley. R&P contact: Paul Dzus. adv. (also avail. in microform from UMI) **Document type:** academic/scholarly publication.
—BLDSC (3834.420000); CISTI; SWETS; UMI. CCC.
Description: International forum for facilitating and enhancing the exchange of information among researchers involved in both the theoretical and practical aspects of computational systems of an evolutionary nature.
Refereed Serial

005 574 US ISSN 1080-742X
GENBANK. (Not avail. in print format.) 1992. bi-m. $192 (foreign $240) (effective 1997). U.S. National Library of Medicine, U.S. National Center for Biotechnology Information, Bldg. 38A, Rm. 8N-803, Bldg. 38A, Rm. 8N-803, 8600 Rockville Pike, Bethesda, MD 20894. TEL 301-496-2475. FAX 301-480-2233. E-mail: info@ncbi.nlm.nih.gov; URL: http://www.ncbi.nlm.nih.gov. (Subscr. to: Superintendent of Documents, U.S. Government Printing Office, Box 371954, Pittsburgh, PA 15250-7954. TEL 202-512-1800. FAX 202-512-2250) **Document type:** academic/scholarly publication, government publication.
●Also available online.
Also available on CD-ROM.
Formerly (until 1993): N C B I - GenBank, Genetic Sequence Databank (Flat File) (ISSN 1080-7411)
Description: Provides DNA sequence data in the traditional GenBank flat file format, including annotation and conceptual translations.

F M B E NEWS. (International Federation for Medical and Biological Engineering) see *BIOLOGY — Bioengineering*

570 US ISSN 1081-2911
▼**INFORMATION TECHNOLOGY REPORT.** (Subseries of: Technical Report Series) 1995. irreg. price varies. U.S. National Biological Service, Information Transfer Center, c/o Managing Editor, 1201 Oak Ridge Dr., Ste. 200, Ft. Collins, CO 80525-5589. TEL 970-226-9401. FAX 970-226-9455. (Orders to: U.S. Fish and Wildlife Service, Publications Unit, MS-130, Webb Bldg., 4401 N. Fairfax Dr., Arlington, VA 22203) bibl. (also avail. in microform from NTI) **Document type:** government publication, academic/scholarly publication, monographic series, bibliography, proceedings.
Description: Publishes conference proceedings, synthesis, annotated bibliographies, and other scholarly reports.
Refereed Serial

INTERNATIONAL JOURNAL OF BIO-MEDICAL COMPUTING. see *MEDICAL SCIENCES — Computer Applications*

MEDICAL & BIOLOGICAL ENGINEERING & COMPUTING. see *BIOLOGY — Bioengineering*

BIOLOGY — Cytology And Histology

A C T INTERNATIONAL CYTOGENETICS LABORATORY DIRECTORY. (Association of Cytogenetic Technologists) see *MEDICAL SCIENCES — Experimental Medicine, Laboratory Technique*

571.6 US ISSN 1060-8982
A S C B NEWSLETTER. 1979. m. membership. American Society for Cell Biology, 9650 Rockville Pike, Bethesda, MD 20814-3992. TEL 301-530-7153. FAX 301-530-7139. E-mail: ascbinfo@ascb.org; URL: http://www.ascb.org. Ed. Elizabeth Marincola. R&P contact: R. Kampman. adv.: page $750; adv. contact: R. Sommer. illus. circ. 10,000. **Document type:** newsletter.

ACTA ANATOMICA; international journal of anatomy, embryology and cell biology. see *MEDICAL SCIENCES*

ACTA ANATOMICA NIPPONICA/KAIBOGAKU ZASSHI. see *BIOLOGY*

571.6 US ISSN 0001-5547
RG1 CODEN: ACYTAN
ACTA CYTOLOGICA; the journal of clinical cytology and cytopathology. 1957. bi-m. $172 to individuals; institutions $249 (effective Jan. 1997). (International Academy of Cytology) Science Printers and Publishers, Inc., 8342 Olive Blvd., St. Louis, MO 63132. TEL 314-991-4440. FAX 314-991-4654. Ed. Donna Kessel. Wied; Pub. Donna Kessel. adv. contact: Donna Kessel. bk.rev.; abstr.; bibl.; illus.; stat.; index. circ. 6,800. (also avail. in microform from PMC; microfilm from WWS; back issues avail.) **Indexed:** AIDS Abstr., ASCA, Biol.Abstr., Chem.Abstr., Curr.Adv.Ecol.Sci., Curr.Cont., Dairy Sci.Abstr., Dent.Ind., Excerp.Med., Helminthol.Abstr., Ind.Med., Ind.Sci.Rev., INIS Atomind., Neurosci.Cit.Ind., Rev.Plant Path., Sci.Cit.Ind. **Document type:** academic/scholarly publication.
—BLDSC (0612.100000); CASDDS; CISTI; EMDOCS; Genuine Article; KNAW; SWETS; UMI; UnCover. CCC.
Refereed Serial

571.6 JA ISSN 0044-5991
QM551 CODEN: ACHCBO
ACTA HISTOCHEMICA ET CYTOCHEMICA/NIHON SOSHIKI SAIBO KAGAKKAI GAKKAISHI. (Text in English) 1960. bi-m. 12000 Yen. Japan Society of Histochemistry and Cytochemistry, c/o Nakanishi Printing Co., Shimotachiuri-Ogawa, Kamikyo-ku, Kyoto 602, Japan. TEL 81-75-415-3661. FAX 81-75-415-3662. E-mail: HBE 02610@niftyserve.or.jp. (Dist. overseas by: Japan Publications Trading Co., Ltd., Box 5030, Tokyo International, Tokyo 100-31, Japan) Ed. Tsukasa Ashihara. adv.; bk.rev.; abstr.; bibl.; charts; illus.; index. circ. 1,800. (also avail. in microform from UMI; reprint service avail. from UMI) **Indexed:** ASCA, Biol.Abstr., Chem.Abstr., Curr.Adv.Ecol.Sci., Curr.Cont., Dairy Sci.Abstr., Helminthol.Abstr., Ind.Sci.Rev., INIS Atomind., Nutr.Abstr., Sci.Cit.Ind. **Document type:** academic/scholarly publication.
—BLDSC (0624.040000); CASDDS; CISTI; EMDOCS; Genuine Article; KNAW; Linda Hall; SWETS; UMI; UnCover. CCC.
Description: Features original articles in all fields of histochemistry and cytochemistry. Contains proceedings of the annual meeting of the society.
Refereed Serial

ADVANCES IN ANATOMY, EMBRYOLOGY AND CELL BIOLOGY. see *BIOLOGY*

571.6 NE ISSN 1381-1932
CODEN: ACMBEF
ADVANCES IN CELLULAR AND MOLECULAR BIOLOGY OF PLANTS. (Text in English) 1994. irreg., vol.3, 1995. price varies. Kluwer Academic Publishers, Postbus 17, 3300 AA Dordrecht, Netherlands. TEL 31-78-6392392. FAX 31-78-6392254. TELEX 29245 KAPG NL. E-mail: services@wkap.nl; URL: http://www.wkap.nl. (Dist. by: Kluwer Academic Publishers Group, P.O. Box 322, 3300 AH Dordrecht, Netherlands. TEL 31-78-6392392. FAX 31-78-6546474; N. America dist. addr.: Box 358, Accord Sta., Hingham, MA 02018-0358. TEL 617-871-6600. FAX 617-871-6528) (back issues avail.) **Document type:** monographic series.
—CASDDS.
Refereed Serial

571.6 US
ADVANCES IN MOLECULAR AND CELL BIOLOGY. 1987. a. $97.50. J A I Press Inc., 55 Old Post Rd., No.2, Box 1678, Greenwich, CT 06836-1678. TEL 203-661-7602. (UK addr.: J A I Press Ltd., The Courtyard, 28 High St., Hampton Hill, Mddx. TW12 1PD, England) **Document type:** monographic series.
—CISTI.
Formerly (until 1990): Advances in Cell Biology (ISSN 0898-8455)

AMERICAN JOURNAL OF KIDNEY DISEASES. see *MEDICAL SCIENCES — Urology And Nephrology*

571.6 US ISSN 0363-6143
QH631
AMERICAN JOURNAL OF PHYSIOLOGY: CELL PHYSIOLOGY. 1977. m. $216 to individual non-members (Canada and Mexico $256; elsewhere $291); institutions $323 (Canada and Mexico $363; elsewhere $398); members $108 (effective 1997). American Physiological Society, 9650 Rockville Pike, Bethesda, MD 20814. TEL 301-530-7164. FAX 301-571-8313. E-mail: info@aps.faseb.org; URL: http://www.faseb.org/aps. Ed. Brenda Rauner. circ. 500. (also avail. in microform from UMI; reprint service avail. from UMI) **Indexed:** Abstr.Hyg., ASCA, Biol.Abstr., Biol.& Agr.Ind., Biotech.Abstr., Chem.Abstr., Curr.Cont., Dent.Ind., Excerp.Med., Helminthol.Abstr., Ind.Med., Ind.Sci.Rev., Ind.Vet., Int.Abstr.Biol.Sci., Key Word Ind.Wildl.Res., Nutr.Abstr., Ref.Zh., Sci.Cit.Ind., Trop.Dis.Bull., Vet.Bull. **Document type:** academic/scholarly publication.
—CISTI; EMDOCS; Genuine Article; SWETS; UMI. CCC.
Description: Dedicated to the promotion of contemporary and innovative approaches to the study of cell and general physiology.
Refereed Serial

AMERICAN JOURNAL OF PHYSIOLOGY: LUNG CELLULAR AND MOLECULAR PHYSIOLOGY. see *BIOLOGY — Physiology*

BIOLOGY — CYTOLOGY AND HISTOLOGY

571.5 — US — ISSN 0884-6812
RB43 — CODEN: AQCHED
ANALYTICAL AND QUANTITATIVE CYTOLOGY AND HISTOLOGY. 1979. bi-m. $250 to individuals; institutions $432 (effective Jan. 1997). (International Academy of Cytology) Science Printers and Publishers, Inc., 8342 Olive Blvd., St. Louis, MO 63132. TEL 314-991-4440. FAX 314-991-4654. (Co-sponsor: American Society of Cytology) Ed. Donna Kessel; Pub. Donna Kessel. adv. contact: Donna Kessel. index. circ. 2,500. (also avail. in microform from UMI,PMC; back issues avail.) **Indexed:** ASCA, Biol.Abstr., Chem.Abstr., Curr.Adv.Ecol.Sci., Curr.Adv.Genetics & Molec.Biol., Curr.Cont., Excerp.Med., Ind.Med., Ind.Sci.Rev., Sci.Cit.Ind., SSCI. **Document type:** academic/scholarly publication.
—BLDSC (0896.380000); CASDDS; CISTI; EMDOCS; Genuine Article; KNAW; Linda Hall; SWETS; UMI; UnCover. **CCC.**
Formerly: Analytical and Quantitative Cytology (ISSN 0190-0471)
Refereed Serial

571.6 — NE — ISSN 0921-8912
CODEN: ACPAER
ANALYTICAL CELLULAR PATHOLOGY. (Includes: Bibliographic Alerting Service) 1989. 9/yr. fl.1020($600) (effective 1997). (European Society for Analytical Cellular Pathology) I O S Press, Van Diemenstraat 94, 1013 CN Amsterdam, Netherlands. TEL 31-20-6382189. FAX 31-20-6203419. E-mail: market@iospress.nl; URL: http://www.iospress.nl/iospress. (Subscr. to: Elsevier Science, Regional Sales Office, P.O. Box 211, 1000 AE Amsterdam, Netherlands. TEL 31-20-4853757. FAX 31-20-4853432; Subscr. in the Americas to: Elsevier Science, Regional Sales Office, Box 945, New York, NY 10159-0945. TEL 212-633-3730. FAX 212-633-3680; Subscr. in Australasia and the Far East to: Elsevier Science (Singapore) Pte Ltd, No.1 Temasek Ave., No.17-01 Millenia Tower, Singapore 039192, Singapore. TEL 65-434-3727. FAX 65-337-2230) Ed. Gerard Brugal. adv.; bibl.; illus.; index. (back issues avail.) **Indexed:** ASCA, Curr.Cont., Excerp.Med., Sci.Cit.Ind. **Document type:** academic/scholarly publication.
—BLDSC (0896.540000); CASDDS; CISTI; EMDOCS; Genuine Article; KNAW; SWETS. **CCC.**
Description: Addresses all aspects of analytical and quantitative approaches to cytology and histology with emphasis on applications to pathology.
Refereed Serial

571.6 — US — ISSN 1081-0706
QH573 — CODEN: ARDBF8
ANNUAL REVIEW OF CELL AND DEVELOPMENTAL BIOLOGY. 1985. a. $64 to individuals (foreign $69); institutions $128 (foreign $138) (effective 1998). Annual Reviews Inc., 4139 El Camino Way, Box 10139, Palo Alto, CA 94303-0139. TEL 650-493-4400; 800-523-8535. FAX 650-424-0910. E-mail: service@annurev.org; URL: http://www.annurev.org. Ed. James A. Spudich. R&P contact: Jeanne Kunz. illus.; index. (also avail. in microfilm from UMI; back issues avail.; reprint service avail.) **Indexed:** ASCA, Biol.& Agr.Ind., Curr.Adv.Ecol.Sci., Curr.Cont., Sci.Cit.Ind. **Document type:** academic/scholarly publication.
—BLDSC (1522.108500); ADONIS; CASDDS; CISTI; EMDOCS; Genuine Article; KNAW; KR SourceOne; Linda Hall; SWETS; UMI; UnCover. **CCC.**
Formerly (until vol.10, 1994): Annual Review of Cell Biology (ISSN 0743-4634)
Description: Original critical reviews of the significant primary literature and current developments in cell biology.

571.6 — JA
ANNUAL REVIEW SAIBO SEIBUTSUGAKU/ANNUAL REVIEW OF CELL BIOLOGY. (Text in Japanese) a. 8700 Yen. Chugai Igakusha, 62 Yaraicho, Shinjuku-ku, Tokyo 162, Japan.

571.6 — UK — ISSN 1360-8185
CODEN: APOPFN
▼**APOPTOSIS (LONDON);** an international journal on programmed cell death. 1996. bi-m. £110 (U.S. & Canada $175; elsewhere £115) to individuals; institutions £180 (U.S. & Canada $295; elsewhere £185) (effective 1997). Rapid Science Publishers (Subsidiary of: International Thomson Journals), 2-6 Boundary Row, London SE1 8HN, England. TEL 44-171-865-0198. FAX 44-171-410-6600. E-mail: rapid@rapidcom.co.uk; URL: http://www.thomsonscience.com. (Subscr. in the Americas to: Sarah Whealan, Rapid Science Publishers - ITP, 400 Market St., Ste. 750, Philadelphia, PA 19106. TEL 215-574-2300. FAX 215-574-3533; Subscr. in Europe and rest of world to: Christine Allingham, Subscription Dept., International Thomson Publishing Services (ITPS), Cheriton House, Northway, Andover, Hampshire SP10 5BE, England. TEL 44-1264-342-773. FAX 44-1264-342-807) Ed. Dr. Mels Sluyser. adv. contact: Anthony Gresford. **Document type:** academic/scholarly publication.
—BLDSC (1568.884400); CASDDS; CISTI.
Refereed Serial

571.5 — JA — ISSN 0914-9465
CODEN: AHCYEZ
ARCHIVES OF HISTOLOGY AND CYTOLOGY/SOSHIKI SAIBOGAKU KIROKU. (Text in English) 1950. 5/yr. $250 (effective 1994). Japan Society of Histological Documentation - Nihon Soshiki Kagakkai, c/o Department of Anatomy, Niigata University School of Medicine, Asahimachi, Niigata, Japan. FAX 025-224-1767. Ed. Tsuneo Fujita. adv.; bk.rev.; charts; illus.; index; circ. 700 (controlled). **Indexed:** Abstr.Anthropol., ASCA, Biol.Abstr., Chem.Abstr., Curr.Adv.Ecol.Sci., Curr.Cont., Dairy Sci.Abstr., Dent.Ind., Excerp.Med., Ind.Med., Ind.Sci.Rev., Neurosci.Cit.Ind., Nutr.Abstr., Sci.Cit.Ind. **Document type:** academic/scholarly publication.
—BLDSC (1634.413000); CASDDS; CISTI; EMDOCS; Genuine Article; KNAW; UnCover.
Formerly (until 1988): Archivum Histologicum Japonicum (ISSN 0004-0681)

571.6 — NE — ISSN 0005-2736
QD1
B B A - BIOMEMBRANES. (Biochimica et Biophysica Acta) (Section of: Biochimica et Biophysica Acta (ISSN 0006-3002)) 1947. m. fl.5127($2946) (effective 1998). Elsevier Science B.V., P.O. Box 211, 1000 AE Amsterdam, Netherlands. TEL 31-20-4853911. FAX 31-20-4853598. TELEX 18582 ESPA NL. E-mail: nlinfo-f@elsevier.nl; usinfo-f@elsevier.com; forinfo-kyf04035@niftyserve.or.jp; URL: http://www.elsevier.nl/. (Subscr. in the Americas to: Elsevier Science, Regional Sales Office, Box 945, New York, NY 10159-0945. TEL 212-633-3730. FAX 212-633-3680; Subscr. in Australasia and the Far East to: Elsevier Science (Singapore) Pte Ltd, No.1 Temasek Ave., Singapore 039192, Singapore. TEL 65-434-3727. FAX 65-337-2230; Subscr. in Japan to: Elsevier Science Japan, 9-15 Higashi-Azabu 1-chome, Minato-ku, Tokyo 106, Japan. TEL 81-3-5561-5033. FAX 81-3-5561-5047) Ed.Bd. (also avail. in microform from UMI) **Indexed:** ASCA, Biotech.Abstr., Crop Physiol.Abstr., Curr.Adv.Ecol.Sci., Curr.Cont., Dairy Sci.Abstr., Excerp.Med., Field Crop Abstr., Ind.Sci.Rev., Ind.Vet., Rev.Med.& Vet.Mycol., Sugar Ind.Abstr. **Document type:** academic/scholarly publication.
—BLDSC (2070.000000); ADONIS; CISTI; Ei; EMDOCS; Genuine Article; SWETS; UnCover. **CCC.**
Description: Focuses on research in membrane structure and organization, membrane fluidity and lipid composition, model membranes, and membrane-protein interactions.
Refereed Serial

571.6 — NE — ISSN 0167-4889
B B A - MOLECULAR CELL RESEARCH. (Section of: Biochimica et Biophysica Acta (ISSN 0006-3002)) 1982. 15/yr. fl.2848($1637) (effective 1998). Elsevier Science B.V., P.O. Box 211, 1000 AE Amsterdam, Netherlands. TEL 31-20-4853911. FAX 31-20-4853598. TELEX 18582 ESPA NL. E-mail: usinfo-f@elsevier.com; forinfo-kyf04035@niftyserve.or.jp; URL: http://www.elsevier.nl/. (Subscr. in the Americas to: Elsevier Science, Regional Sales Office, Box 945, New York, NY 10159-0945. TEL 212-633-3730. FAX 212-633-3680; Subscr. in Australasia and the Far East to: Elsevier Science (Singapore) Pte Ltd, No.1 Temasek Ave., No.17-01 Millenia Tower, Singapore 039192, Singapore. TEL 65-434-3727. FAX 65-337-2230; Subscr. in Japan to: Elsevier Science Japan, 9-15 Higashi-Azabu 1-chome, Minato-ku, Tokyo 106, Japan. TEL 81-3-5561-5033. FAX 81-3-5561-5047) Ed.Bd. (also avail. in microform from UMI; back issues avail.) **Indexed:** ASCA, Biol.Abstr., Chem.Abstr., Curr.Cont., Dairy Sci.Abstr., Excerp.Med., Ind.Chem., Ind.Med. **Document type:** academic/scholarly publication.
—ADONIS; CISTI; Genuine Article; SWETS. **CCC.**
Description: Focuses on intact cellular studies at the molecular level. Includes hormone and neurotransmitter action, molecular endocrinology, cell regulation, as well as whole-cell and whole-tissue spectroscopy.
Refereed Serial

571.64 — NE — ISSN 0304-4157
QD1 — CODEN: RVBMA
B B A - REVIEWS ON BIOMEMBRANES. (Section of: Biochemica et Biophysica Acta (0006-3002)) vol.604, 1974. 3/yr. fl.570($327) (effective 1998). Elsevier Science B.V., P.O. Box 211, 1000 AE Amsterdam, Netherlands. TEL 31-20-4853911. FAX 31-20-4853598. TELEX 18582 ESPA NL. E-mail: nlinfo-f@elsevier.nl; usinfo-f@elsevier.com; forinfo-kyf04035@niftyserve.or.jp; URL: http://www.elsevier.nl/. (Subscr. in the Americas to: Elsevier Science, Regional Sales Office, Box 945, New York, NY 10159-0945. TEL 212-633-3730. FAX 212-633-3680; Subscr. in Australasia and the Far East to: Elsevier Science (Singapore) Pte Ltd, No.1 Temasek Ave., No.17-01 Millenia Tower, Singapore 039192, Singapore. TEL 65-434-3727. FAX 65-337-2230; Subscr. in Japan to: Elsevier Science Japan, 9-15 Higashi-Azabu 1-chome, Minato-ku, Tokyo 106, Japan. TEL 81-3-5561-5033. FAX 81-3-5561-5047) Ed.Bd. (also avail. in microform from UMI) **Indexed:** ASCA, Curr.Adv.Ecol.Sci., Curr.Leather Lit., Excerp.Med. **Document type:** academic/scholarly publication.
—ADONIS; CISTI; EMDOCS; Genuine Article; SWETS. **CCC.**
Description: Publishes critical, up-to-date reviews of new developments in the field of biomembranes.
Refereed Serial

571.5 — US — ISSN 0891-2106
BASIC HISTOLOGY. 1975. triennial. Appleton & Lange (Subsidiary of: Simon & Schuster Company), Box 120041, Stamford, CT 06912-0041. TEL 203-406-4500. **Document type:** monographic series.
—CISTI.

BIOCELL. see BIOLOGY — Microscopy

BIOCHEMISTRY AND CELL BIOLOGY/BIOCHIMIE ET BIOLOGIE CELLULAIRE. see BIOLOGY — Biological Chemistry

571.4 — RU — ISSN 0301-2425
QH573
BIOFIZIKA ZHIVOI KLETKI/BIOPHYSICS OF LIVING CELLS. 1970. irreg. $40. (Rossiiskaya Akademiya Nauk, Institut Biofiziki Kletki - Russian Academy of Sciences, Institute of Cell Biophysics) Radical Enterprise, 142292 Pushchino, P.O. Box 84 (AB 7-67), Moscow Region, Russia. TEL 7-95-238-7940. E-mail: karnaukhov@mars.ibioc.serpukhov.su. Ed. V.N. Kharnaukhov. illus. circ. 1,000. (reprint service avail. from IRC) **Indexed:** Ref.Zh. **Document type:** academic/scholarly publication.
—Linda Hall.

BIOLOGICHESKIE MEMBRANY. see BIOLOGY — Biophysics

BIOLOGY — CYTOLOGY AND HISTOLOGY

571.6   US   ISSN 0887-3224
QP88.23   CODEN: ICOTAR
BIOLOGY OF EXTRACELLULAR MATRIX. 1963. irreg. Academic Press, Inc., 525 B St., Ste. 1900, San Diego, CA 92101-4495. TEL 619-231-0926. FAX 619-699-6715. index. **Indexed:** Biol.Abstr., Dent.Ind., Excerp.Med., Ind.Med., Ind.Sci.Rev., INIS Atomind., Nutr.Abstr., Sci.Cit.Ind. **Document type:** monographic series.
—CASDDS; CISTI; KNAW; Linda Hall.
     Formerly (until 1986): International Review of Connective Tissue Research (ISSN 0074-767X)

571.6 578   FR   ISSN 0248-4900
QH212.E4   CODEN: BCELDF
BIOLOGY OF THE CELL. (Text in English) 1962. 9/yr. 3124 F. to institutions (US $597; outside the Americas 3870 F) (effective 1998). (European Cell Biology Organization) Editions Scientifiques et Medicales Elsevier, 141 rue de Javel, 75747 Paris, France. TEL 33-1-45589022. FAX 33-1-45589421. URL: http://www.elsevier.nl/. (Subscr. in U.S. and Canada to: Elsevier Science Inc., Box 945, Madison Sq. Sta., New York, NY 101590945. TEL 212-633-3730. FAX 212-633-3680) (Co-sponsors: Societe Francaise de Microscopie Electronique; Societe de Biologie Cellulaire de France) Ed. Joseph Schrevel. adv.; charts; illus.; index. circ. 3,000. (also avail. in microform from UMI) **Indexed:** Anim.Breed.Abstr., ASCA, Biol.Abstr., Chem.Abstr., Crop Physiol.Abstr., Curr.Adv.Ecol.Sci., Curr.Cont., Dairy Sci.Abstr., Dent.Ind., Excerp.Med., Field Crop Abstr., Herb.Abstr., Hort.Abstr., Ind.Med., Ind.Sci.Rev., Ind.Vet., Plant Grow.Reg.Abstr., Protozool.Abstr., Rev.Med.& Vet.Mycol., Sci.Cit.Ind., Triticale Abstr. **Document type:** academic/scholarly publication.
—BLDSC (2087.045000); CASDDS; EMDOCS; Genuine Article; KNAW; SWETS; UnCover. **CCC.**
     Former titles (until 1981): Biologie Cellulaire; Journal de Microscopie et Biologie Cellulaire; Journal de Microscopie.
     Description: Presents reports, review articles and rapid communications concerning the structure and function of cells in the context of developmental biology, genetics, immunology and physiology.
     Refereed Serial

571.64   US   ISSN 0067-8864
QH601   CODEN: BOMBB5
BIOMEMBRANES. 1971. irreg., vol.12, 1984. price varies. Plenum Publishing Corp., 233 Spring St., New York, NY 10013-1578. TEL 212-620-8000. FAX 212-463-0742. TELEX 23-421139. E-mail: books@plenum.com. Ed. L. A. Manson. **Indexed:** Chem.Abstr., Ind.Med., INIS Atomind. **Document type:** monographic series.
—CASDDS; CISTI; Linda Hall. **CCC.**
     Refereed Serial

571.6   US   ISSN 0144-8463
QH506   CODEN: BRPTDT
BIOSCIENCE REPORTS; molecular and cellular biology of the cell surface. 1981. bi-m. $460 (foreign $540) (effective 1998). (Biochemical Society, UK) Plenum Publishing Corp., 233 Spring St., New York, NY 10013-1578. TEL 212-620-8000. FAX 212-463-0742. TELEX 23-421139. Ed. Charles A. Pasternak. adv. (also avail. in microfilm from UMI; back issues avail.) **Indexed:** ASCA, Biol.Abstr., Biotech.Abstr., Chem.Abstr., Curr.Adv.Ecol.Sci., Curr.Biotech.Abstr., Curr.Cont., Dairy Sci.Abstr., Excerp.Med., Field Crop Abstr., Ind.Med., Ind.Sci.Rev., Nutr.Abstr., Poult.Abstr., Sci.Cit.Ind. **Document type:** academic/scholarly publication.
—BLDSC (2089.611600); ADONIS; CASDDS; CISTI; EMDOCS; Genuine Article; Linda Hall; SWETS; UMI; UnCover. **CCC.**
     Refereed Serial

BIOTECHNIC AND HISTOCHEMISTRY; a journal for microtechnic and histochemistry. see *BIOLOGY — Microscopy*

BLOOD. see *MEDICAL SCIENCES — Hematology*

BRAZILIAN JOURNAL OF GENETICS/REVISTA BRASILEIRA DE GENETICA. see *BIOLOGY — Genetics*

571.6   UK
BRITISH SOCIETY FOR CELL BIOLOGY. SYMPOSIA. 1976. irreg., no.7, 1983. price varies. Cambridge University Press, Edinburgh Bldg., Shaftesbury Rd., Cambridge CB2 2RU, England. TEL 44-1223-312393. FAX 44-1223-315052. TELEX 8581712256. E-mail: information@cup.cam.ac.uk; URL: http://www.cup.cam.ac.uk. (N. American addr.: Cambridge University Press, Journals Dept., 40 W. 20th St., New York, NY 10011. TEL 212-924-3900. FAX 212-691-3239) R&P contact: Linda Nicol. **Indexed:** Biol.Abstr. **Document type:** proceedings.

C A S BIOTECH UPDATES. CELL & TISSUE CULTURE. see *BIOLOGY — Abstracting, Bibliographies, Statistics*

CANADIAN JOURNAL OF PLANT PATHOLOGY. see *BIOLOGY — Botany*

571.3   IT   ISSN 0008-7114
QH1   CODEN: CARYAB
CARYOLOGIA; international journal of cytology, cytosystematics and cytogenetics. (Text and summaries in English) 1948. 4/yr. L.170000 (effective 1995). Universita degli Studi di Firenze, Orto Botanico, Via P.A. Micheli, 3, 50121 Florence, Italy. TEL 39-55-284696. FAX 39-55-2757438. Ed. Fernando Fabbri. bibl.; charts; illus. **Indexed:** Anim.Breed.Abstr., ASCA, Biol.Abstr., Bull.Signal., Chem.Abstr., Curr.Adv.Ecol.Sci., Curr.Cont., Excerp.Med., Herb.Abstr., Hort.Abstr., Ind.Sci.Rev., INIS Atomind., Ornam.Hort., Plant Breed.Abstr., Rev.Plant Path., Sci.Cit.Ind., Seed Abstr., Soils & Fert. —BLDSC (3057.960000); CASDDS; CISTI; Linda Hall; SWETS; UnCover.

571.6   US   ISSN 0092-8674
QH573   CODEN: CELLB5
CELL. 1974. 26/yr. $105 to individuals (foreign $205); institutions $325 (foreign $465). Cell Press, 1050 Massachusetts Ave., Cambridge, MA 02138. TEL 617-661-7060. Ed. Benjamin Lewin. adv.; bk.rev.; charts; illus. circ. 15,500. (reprint service avail. from ISI,UMI) **Indexed:** Abstr.Hyg., AIDS Abstr., Anim.Breed.Abstr., ASCA, Biol.Abstr., Biol.& Agr.Ind., Biotech.Abstr., Chem.Abstr., Curr.Adv.Biochem., Curr.Adv.Cell & Devel.Biol., Curr.Adv.Ecol.Sci., Curr.Adv.Genetics & Molec.Biol., Curr.Cont., Dairy Sci.Abstr., Dent.Ind., Excerp.Med., Food Sci.& Tech.Abstr., Gen.Sci.Ind., Helminthol.Abstr., Ind.Med., Ind.Sci.Rev., Ind.Vet., INIS Atomind., Med.& Surg.Dermat., Neurosci.Cit.Ind., Poult.Abstr., Protozool.Abstr., Sci.Cit.Ind., Soils & Fert., Sorghum & Millets Abstr., SSCI, Telegen, Trop.Dis.Bull., Vet.Bull.
—BLDSC (3097.600000); CASDDS; CISTI; EMDOCS; KNAW; KR SourceOne; Linda Hall; SWETS; UnCover.
     Refereed Serial

571.6   US   ISSN 0737-1233
CELL ANALYSIS. 1982. irreg. Plenum Publishing Corp., 233 Spring St., New York, NY 10013-1578. TEL 212-620-8000. FAX 212-463-0742. **Document type:** monographic series.

571.6   II   ISSN 0254-2935
         CODEN: CCREE3
CELL AND CHROMOSOME RESEARCH JOURNAL. (Text in English) 1978. 2/yr. Rs.150($20) (Association for Cell and Chromosome Research) University of Calcutta, Centre of Advanced Studies in Botany, 35 Ballygunge Circular Rd., Calcutta 700 019, India. FAX 91-33-4754772. Ed. Sibdas Ghosh. bk.rev. circ. 200. (back issues avail.) **Indexed:** Biol.Abstr., Chem.Abstr. **Document type:** academic/scholarly publication.
—CASDDS; CISTI.
     Formerly (until 1981): Cell and Chromosome Research Association. Newsletter.
     Refereed Serial

016.5716   UK
CELL AND TISSUE CULTURE: LABORATORY PROCEDURES. 1993. 2 base vols. (plus q. updates). £420($650) for new orders; update service £120 ($195) (effective 1996). John Wiley & Sons Ltd., Journals, Baffins Ln., Chichester, W. Sussex PO19 1UD, England. TEL 44-1243-779777. FAX 44-1243-843232. E-mail: cs-journals@wiley.co.uk; URL: http://www.wiley.co.uk. (Subscr. in the Americas to: John Wiley & Sons, Inc., 605 Third Ave., New York, NY 10158-0012. TEL 212-850-6347) (looseleaf format) **Document type:** academic/scholarly publication.

571.6   GW   ISSN 0302-766X
QH301   CODEN: CTSRCS
CELL AND TISSUE RESEARCH. Online edition (GW ISSN 1432-0878) (Text in English) m. DM.6581.80 (foreign DM.6642.40) (effective 1998). Springer-Verlag, Heidelberger Platz 3, 14197 Berlin, Germany. TEL 49-30-82787-0. FAX 49-30-82787448. E-mail: subscriptions@springer.de; URL: http://link.springer.de. (Subscr. in N. America to: Springer-Verlag New York, Inc., 333 Meadowlands Pkwy., Secaucus, NJ 07094. TEL 212-460-1500. FAX 212-473-6272) Ed.Bd. adv. (also avail. in microform from UMI; reprint service avail. from ISI) **Indexed:** Anim.Breed.Abstr., Apic.Abstr., ASCA, Biol.Abstr., Chem.Abstr., Curr.Adv.Biochem., Curr.Adv.Cell & Devel.Biol., Curr.Adv.Ecol.Sci., Curr.Cont., Dairy Sci.Abstr., Dent.Ind., Excerp.Med., Helminthol.Abstr., Ind.Med., Ind.Sci.Rev., Ind.Vet., INIS Atomind., Neurosci.Cit.Ind., Nutr.Abstr., Sci.Cit.Ind., Sport Fish.Abstr., Vet.Bull., Wild.Rev., Zoo.Rec. **Document type:** academic/scholarly publication.
●Also available online.
—BLDSC (3097.700000); ADONIS; CASDDS; CISTI; EMDOCS; Genuine Article; KNAW; Linda Hall; SWETS; UMI; UnCover. **CCC.**
     Continues: Zeitschrift fuer Zellforschung und Mikroskopische Anatomie (ISSN 0044-3794)
     Description: Presents significant advances encompassing the broad field of cell biology and microscopical anatomy, ranging from invertebrates to mammals, including humans.

571.6   US   ISSN 1085-9195
QH573   CODEN: CBBIFV
CELL BIOCHEMISTRY AND BIOPHYSICS. 1979. bi-m. $275 (foreign $310) (effective 1998). Humana Press Inc., 999 Riverview Dr., Ste. 208, Totowa, NJ 07512. TEL 973-256-1699. FAX 973-256-8341. E-mail: humana@mindspring.com; URL: http://humanapress.com. (Dist. in Japan by: Maruzen Co. Ltd., Journals Div., P.O. Box 5050, Tokyo 100-31, Japan. TEL 03-32758591. FAX 03-32781937) Ed. Edward Massaro. R&P contact: Richard Hruska. adv. contact: Thomas B. Lanigan, Jr. bk.rev.; bibl.; charts; illus. **Indexed:** ASCA, Biol.Abstr., Biotech.Abstr., Chem.Abstr., Curr.Adv.Ecol.Sci., Curr.Cont., Excerp.Med., Ind.Med., Ind.Sci.Rev., Sci.Cit.Ind. **Document type:** academic/scholarly publication.
—BLDSC (3097.715000); CASDDS; CISTI; Genuine Article; KNAW; Linda Hall; SWETS; UnCover. **CCC.**
     Formerly: Cell Biophysics (ISSN 0163-4992)
     Description: Publishes original papers covering experimental, methodological and theoretical investigations on cells, tissues, organelles and subfragments with emphasis on the mechanisms of cell behavior.
     Refereed Serial

CELL BIOLOGY AND TOXICOLOGY; an international journal devoted to research at the cellular level. see *ENVIRONMENTAL STUDIES — Toxicology And Environmental Safety*

BIOLOGY — CYTOLOGY AND HISTOLOGY

571.6   UK   ISSN 1065-6995
QH573   CODEN: CBIIEV
CELL BIOLOGY INTERNATIONAL. 1977. m. £315 (effective 1998). (International Federation for Cell Biology) Academic Press Ltd. (Subsidiary of: Harcourt Brace & Company Ltd.), 24-28 Oval Rd., London NW1 7DX, England. TEL 44-171-267-4466. FAX 44-171-482-2293. TELEX 25775 ACPRES G. E-mail: apsubs@acad.com; URL: http://www.hbuk.co.uk/ap/cellbio; http://www.europe.idealibrary.com/. (Subscr. to: Harcourt Brace & Company Ltd., Foots Cray High St., Sidcup, Kent DA14 5HP, England. TEL 44-181-300-3322. FAX 44-181-309-0807) Ed. N. Lane. R&P contact: Catherine John. adv. contact: Nik Screen. bk.rev. (reprint service avail. from SWZ) **Indexed:** ASCA, Curr.Adv.Biochem., Curr.Adv.Cell & Devel.Biol., Curr.Adv.Ecol.Sci., Curr.Adv.Genetics & Molec.Biol., Curr.Cont., Dent.Ind., Excerp.Med., Helminthol.Abstr., Ind.Med., Ind.Sci.Rev., Ornam.Hort., Sci.Cit.Ind., THA, 0190633str. **Document type:** academic/scholarly publication.
●Also available online.
—BLDSC (3097.707000); CASDDS; CISTI; EMDOCS; Genuine Article; KNAW; Linda Hall; SWETS; UnCover. **CCC.**
Formerly (until 1993): Cell Biology International Reports (ISSN 0309-1651)
Description: Offers plant and animal scientists the opportunity to inform their peers of new data within a few weeks whether as full papers, or as short reports; promotes the aims of most cell biologists with papers relating to structure and function, as well as new techniques.

571.6   US   ISSN 0172-4665
CODEN: CBMODY
CELL BIOLOGY MONOGRAPHS. 1977. irreg., vol.12, 1985. price varies. Springer-Verlag, 175 Fifth Ave., New York, NY 10010. TEL 212-460-1500. FAX 212-473-6272. (Also: Berlin, Heidelberg, Tokyo and Vienna) (reprint service avail. from ISI) **Indexed:** Biol.Abstr. **Document type:** monographic series.
Supersedes: Protoplasmologia: Handbuch der Protoplasmaforschung (ISSN 0079-7073)

571.6   UK   ISSN 0143-4160
CODEN: CECADV
CELL CALCIUM (EDINBURGH). 1980. m. £330($495) to individuals; institutions £505 ($755) (effective 1998). Churchill Livingstone (Subsidiary of: Pearson Professional), Robert Stevenson House, 103 Baxter's Pl., Leith Walk, Edinburgh EH1 3AF, Scotland. TEL 44-131-556-2424. FAX 44-131-535-1704. URL: http://www.churchillmed.com. (Subscr. to: Pearson Professional Ltd., P.O. Box 77, Fourth Ave., Harlow, Essex CM19 5BQ, England. TEL 44-1279-623924. FAX 44-1279-639609; U.S. subscr. to: Churchill Livingstone, Box 3217, Secaucus, N.J. 07096-3217. TEL 800-553-5426. FAX 201-319-9659) Eds. R.M. Case, Dr. A. Scarpa. adv. contact: Kathy Crawford. bibl. circ. 495. (also avail. in microform from UMI) **Indexed:** Anim.Breed.Abstr., Chem.Abstr., Curr.Adv.Biochem., Curr.Adv.Ecol.Sci., Curr.Cont., Dent.Ind., Excerp.Med., Ind.Med., Ind.Sci.Rev., Sci.Cit.Ind., Vet.Bull. **Document type:** academic/scholarly publication.
—BLDSC (3097.724000); CASDDS; CISTI; EMDOCS; Genuine Article; KNAW; SWETS; UnCover. **CCC.**

571.6   UK   ISSN 1351-5314
CELL CONTACT AND COMMUNICATION. 1976. s-m. (diskette m.) £125 (diskette £120; both £180) (effective 1997). S U B I S, Mansion House, 19 Kingfield Rd., Sheffield S11 9AS, England. TEL 44-114-2554433. FAX 44-114-2554626. E-mail: subis@sheffac.demon.co.uk; URL: http://www.shef.ac.uk/uni/companies/shap. (also avail. in diskette format) **Document type:** abstracting/indexing.
—**CCC.**
Formerly (until 1993): Cell Contact Phenomena (ISSN 0142-8039)
Description: Current awareness service for researchers in clinical and life sciences. Covers cell adhesion and aggregation, invasion and metastasis, cell fusion, intercellular communication.

CELL CYCLE. see BIOLOGY — Abstracting, Bibliographies, Statistics

571.6   UK   ISSN 1350-9047
CODEN: CDDIEK
CELL DEATH AND DIFFERENTIATION. 1994. q. £42 to individuals (U.S. $76; elsewhere £48); institutions £107 (U.S. $192; elsewhere £115) (effective 1996). Stockton Press (Subsidiary of: Macmillan Press Ltd.), Houndmills, Basingstoke, Hants RG21 6XS, England. TEL 44-1256-329242. FAX 44-1256-328339. E-mail: s.marshall@stockton-press.co.uk; URL: http://www.stockton-press.co.uk. Ed. Gerry Melino. adv. contact: Mary Attree. bk.rev. **Indexed:** ASCA, Curr.Cont., Excerp.Med. (1996-). **Document type:** academic/scholarly publication.
—BLDSC (3097.748600); CASDDS; CISTI; EMDOCS; Genuine Article; KNAW; SWETS. **CCC.**
Description: Aims to provide a forum for high-quality papers on cell death, proliferation, differentiation, and development in various eukaryotic models.

615.7 575.1   UK   ISSN 0263-726X
CELL DIFFERENTIATION. s-m. (diskette m.) £90 (diskette £120; both £180) (effective 1997). S U B I S, Mansion House, 19 Kingfield Rd., Sheffield S11 9AS, England. TEL 44-114-2554433. FAX 44-114-2554626. E-mail: subis@sheffac.demon.co.uk; URL: http://www.shef.ac.uk/uni/companies/shap. (also avail. in diskette format; back issues avail.) **Document type:** abstracting/indexing.
—**CCC.**
Description: Current awareness service for researchers in clinical and life sciences.

CELL MEMBRANES. see BIOLOGY — Biological Chemistry

571.6   US   ISSN 0886-1544
QH647   CODEN: CMCYEO
CELL MOTILITY AND THE CYTOSKELETON. 1980. m. $1995 (foreign $2205) (effective 1998). John Wiley & Sons, Inc., Journals, 605 Third Ave., New York, NY 10158. TEL 212-850-6645. FAX 212-850-6021. TELEX 12-7063. E-mail: SUBINFO@JWILEY.COM; URL: http://www.wiley.co.uk. (Subscr. outside the Americas to: John Wiley & Sons Ltd., Baffins Ln., Chichester, W. Sussex PO19 1UD, England. TEL 44-1243-779777. FAX 44-1243-776128) Ed. B.R. Brinkley. adv.: B&W page £640, color page £1515; trim 279 x 210. bibl.; charts; illus.; index. circ. 700. (also avail. in microform from UMI; back issues avail.) **Indexed:** ASCA, Biol.Abstr., Chem.Abstr., Curr.Adv.Cell & Devel.Biol., Curr.Adv.Ecol.Sci., Curr.Cont., Excerp.Med., Ind.Med., Ind.Sci.Rev., Neurosci.Cit.Ind., Sci.Cit.Ind. **Document type:** academic/scholarly publication.
●Also available online.
—BLDSC (3097.826000); CASDDS; CISTI; Ei; EMDOCS; Genuine Article; KNAW; Linda Hall; SWETS; UnCover. **CCC.**
Formerly: Cell Motility (ISSN 0271-6585)
Description: Specializes in the rapid publication of articles concerning all phenomena related to cell motility, including structural, biochemical, biophysical, and theoretical approaches.
Refereed Serial

571.6   UK   ISSN 0141-299X
CELL NUCLEUS. 1978. s-m. (diskette m.) £90 (diskette £120; both £180) (effective 1997). S U B I S, Mansion House, 19 Kingfield Rd., Sheffield S11 9AS, England. TEL 44-114-2554433. FAX 44-114-2554626. E-mail: subis@sheffac.demon.co.uk; URL: http://www.shef.ac.uk/uni/companies/shap. (also avail. in diskette format) **Indexed:** Ind.Sci.Rev., Sci.Cit.Ind. **Document type:** abstracting/indexing.
—**CCC.**
Description: Current awareness service for researchers. Covers nucleosis, chromosomes, nucleolar-organizing regions, nuclear membranes, histones and nucleoproteins.

571.6   UK   ISSN 0960-7722
QH631   CODEN: CPROEM
CELL PROLIFERATION. 1968. bi-m. £266($463) (foreign £293) (effective 1998). (Cell Kinetics Society) Blackwell Science Ltd., Osney Mead, Oxford OX2 0EL, England. TEL 44-1865-206206. FAX 44-1865-721205. E-mail: journals.cs@blacksci.co.uk; URL: http://www.black.co.uk. (Co-sponsors: European Study Group for Cell Proliferation; International Cell Cycle Society) Ed.Bd.; Pub. Allen Stevens. R&P contact: Sarah Pollard. adv. contact: Martine Cariou-Keen. bk.rev.; charts; illus.; index. circ. 495. (also avail. in microform from UMI; back issues avail.; reprint service avail. from ISI) **Indexed:** Anim.Breed.Abstr., ASCA, Biol.Abstr., Chem.Abstr., Curr.Adv.Ecol.Sci., Curr.Cont., Dairy Sci.Abstr., Dent.Ind., Excerp.Med., Helminthol.Abstr., Ind.Med., Ind.Sci.Rev., Ind.Vet., INIS Atomind., Sci.Cit.Ind., Vet.Bull. **Document type:** academic/scholarly publication.
—BLDSC (3097.854000); CASDDS; CISTI; EMDOCS; Genuine Article; KNAW; Linda Hall; SWETS; UMI; UnCover. **CCC.**
Formerly: Cell and Tissue Kinetics (ISSN 0008-8730)
Refereed Serial

571.6   JA   ISSN 0915-907X
CODEN: CELSET
CELL SCIENCE. (Text in English, Japanese) 1985. m. 16800 Yen. Igaku Shuppan Senta - Medical Publication Center Inc., 25-2 Asakusabashi 1-chome, Taito-ku, Tokyo 111, Japan.
—CASDDS.

571.6   JA   ISSN 0386-7196
QH573   CODEN: CSFUDY
CELL STRUCTURE AND FUNCTION. (Text in English) 1975. bi-m. $136. Japan Society for Cell Biology - Nihon Saibo Seibutsu Gakkai, Ogawa Higashi Iru, Shimodachuri Dori, Kamigyo-ku, Kyoto 602, Japan. FAX 075-441-3159. Ed. Y. Tashiro. bk.rev. circ. 1,600. **Indexed:** ASCA, Biol.Abstr., Chem.Abstr., Curr.Adv.Biochem., Curr.Adv.Ecol.Sci., Curr.Cont., Excerp.Med., Helminthol.Abstr., Ind.Med., Ind.Sci.Rev., Ind.Vet., INSPEC, Sci.Cit.Ind., Vet.Bull.
—BLDSC (3097.870000); CASDDS; CISTI; EMDOCS; Genuine Article; KNAW; Linda Hall; SWETS; UnCover. **CCC.**

571.6   US   ISSN 0963-6897
QP89   CODEN: CTRAE8
CELL TRANSPLANTATION. 1992. bi-m. fl.1001($575) (effective 1998). Elsevier Science Inc., Box 945, New York, NY 10159-0945. TEL 212-633-3730. FAX 212-633-3680. E-mail: nlinfo-f@elsevier.nl; usinfo-f@elsevier.com; forinfo-kyf04035@niftyserve.or.jp; URL: http://www.elsevier.nl/. (Subscr. outside the Americas to: Elsevier Science, Regional Sales Office, P.O. Box 211, 1000 AE Amsterdam, Netherlands. TEL 31-20-4853757. FAX 31-20-4853432; Subscr. in Australasia and the Far East to: Elsevier Science (Singapore) Pte Ltd, No.1 Temasek Ave., No.17-01 Millenia Tower, Singapore 039192, Singapore. TEL 65-434-3727. FAX 65-337-2230; Subscr. in Japan to: Elsevier Science Japan, 9-15 Higashi-Azabu 1-chome, Minato-ku, Tokyo 106, Japan. TEL 81-3-5561-5033. FAX 81-3-5561-5047) Ed. Paul R. Sanberg. index. (also avail. in microform from UMI; back issues avail.) **Indexed:** ASCA, Curr.Cont., Excerp.Med. (1993-), Ind.Med. (1994-), Ind.Sci.Rev., Neurosci.Cit.Ind., Sci.Cit.Ind. **Document type:** academic/scholarly publication.
—BLDSC (3097.877000); CISTI; EMDOCS; Genuine Article; KNAW; SWETS; UMI. **CCC.**
Description: Deals with a wide range of topics including physiological, medical, preclinical, tissue engineering, and device-oriented aspects of transplantation of nervous system, endocrine, growth factor-secreting, bone marrow, epithelial, endothelial and genetically engineered cells.
Refereed Serial

571.6   US   ISSN 1060-9989
CODEN: CMSUEO
CELLS AND MATERIALS SUPPLEMENT. 1991. irreg. price varies. Scanning Microscopy International, Inc. Box 66507, AMF O'Hare, Chicago, IL 60666-0507. TEL 708-529-6677. FAX 708-980-6698. **Document type:** monographic series.
—CASDDS; KNAW. **CCC.**

CELLULAR IMMUNOLOGY. see MEDICAL SCIENCES — Allergology And Immunology

BIOLOGY — CYTOLOGY AND HISTOLOGY

571.6 US ISSN 0892-0346
QP351 CODEN: ADCND7
CELLULAR NEUROBIOLOGY. 1980. irreg. Academic Press, Inc., 525 B St., Ste. 1900, San Diego, CA 92101-4495. TEL 619-231-0926. FAX 619-699-6715. (Subscr. to: Order Dept., 6277 Sea Harbor Dr., 4th Fl., Orlando, FL 32887. TEL 800-321-5068) Ed. Sergey Federoff. (back issues avail.; reprint service avail. from ISI) **Indexed:** Biol.Abstr., Chem.Abstr.
—CASDDS; CISTI; KNAW. **CCC.**
Formerly (until 1984): Advances in Cellular Neurobiology (ISSN 0270-0794)
Refereed Serial

CELLULAR PHARMACOLOGY. see *PHARMACY AND PHARMACOLOGY*

615.7 US ISSN 0898-6568
QH604.2 CODEN: CESIEY
CELLULAR SIGNALLING. 1989. 10/yr. fl.1635($940) (effective 1998). Elsevier Science Inc., Box 945, New York, NY 10159-0945. TEL 212-633-3730. FAX 212-633-3680. E-mail: nlinfo@elsevier.nl; usinfo@elsevier.com; forinfo-kyf04035@niftyserve.or.jp; URL: http://www.elsevier.nl/. (Subscr. outside the Americas to: Elsevier Science, Regional Sales Office, P.O. Box 211, 1000 AE Amsterdam, Netherlands. TEL 31-20-4853757. FAX 31-20-4853432; Subscr. in Australasia and the Far East to: Elsevier Science (Singapore) Pte Ltd, No.1 Temasek Ave., No.17-01 Millenia Tower, Singapore 039192, Singapore. TEL 65-434-3727. FAX 65-337-2230; Subscr. in Japan to: Elsevier Science Japan, 9-15 Higashi-Azabu 1-chome, Minato-ku, Tokyo 106, Japan. TEL 81-3-5561-5033. FAX 81-3-5561-5047) Ed. Miles D. Houslay. (also avail. in microfilm from UMI; back issues avail.) **Indexed:** ASCA, Curr.Cont., Excerp.Med., Ind.Sci.Rev., Neurosci.Cit.Ind., Sci.Cit.Ind. **Document type:** academic/scholarly publication.
—BLDSC (3097.942000); ADONIS; CASDDS; CISTI; EMDOCS; Genuine Article; KNAW; Linda Hall; SWETS; UMI; UnCover. **CCC.**
Description: Publishes original papers on all aspects of the mechanisms, actions and structural components of cellular signalling systems, with emphasis on the production, regulation and action of second messengers, receptors, regulatory proteins, effector systems, and the effect of cellular signalling events.
Refereed Serial

CLINICAL BULLETIN OF MYOFASCIAL THERAPY; the practical journal for the soft-tissue practitioner. see *MEDICAL SCIENCES*

CLINICAL CYTOGENETICS. see *BIOLOGY — Genetics*

COMPARATIVE PATHOBIOLOGY. see *MEDICAL SCIENCES*

571.5 NE ISSN 0300-8207
QP88.23 CODEN: CVTRBC
CONNECTIVE TISSUE RESEARCH; an international journal. 1972. 8/yr. (in 2 vols., 4 nos./vol.). $335 (effective 1998). Gordon and Breach - Harwood Academic, Amsteldisk 166, 1st Fl., 1079 LH Amsterdam, Netherlands. (Subscr. to: International Publishers Distributor, Box 32160, Newark, NJ 07102. TEL 800-545-8398. FAX 215-750-6343) Ed. Arthur Veis. adv.; bk.rev.; charts; illus.; index. (also avail. in microform) **Indexed:** ASCA, Biol.Abstr., Chem.Abstr., Curr.Adv.Ecol.Sci., Curr.Cont., Dent.Ind., Excerp.Med., Ind.Med., Ind.Sci.Rev., Med.& Surg.Dermat., Nutr.Abstr., Sci.Cit.Ind.
—BLDSC (3417.665000); CASDDS; CISTI; EMDOCS; SWETS; UnCover. **CCC.**
Refereed Serial

CURRENT ADVANCES IN CELL & DEVELOPMENTAL BIOLOGY. see *BIOLOGY — Abstracting, Bibliographies, Statistics*

CURRENT OPINION IN CELL BIOLOGY. see *BIOLOGY — Abstracting, Bibliographies, Statistics*

571.6 US
CURRENT PROTOCOLS IN CYTOMETRY. 1997. a. (with q. updates). $345 (CD-ROM $490). (International Society for Analytical Cytology) John Wiley & Sons, Inc., 605 Third Ave., New York, NY 10158. TEL 212-850-6645. E-mail: subinfo@jwiley.com. (Dist. in UK by: John Wiley & Sons Ltd., Baffins Ln., Chichester, W. Sussex PO19 1UD, England. TEL 44-1243-779777. FAX 44-1243-775878) Ed.Bd. (looseleaf format) **Document type:** academic/scholarly publication, monographic series.

591.574 US ISSN 0070-2161
QH601 CODEN: CTMTA2
CURRENT TOPICS IN MEMBRANES AND TRANSPORT. 1970. irreg., vol.44, 1997. Academic Press, Inc., 525 B St., Ste. 1900, San Diego, CA 92101-4495. TEL 619-231-0926. FAX 619-699-6715. Eds. Felix Bronner, Arnest Kleinzeller. (reprint service avail. form ISI) **Indexed:** Biol.Abstr., Chem.Abstr., Curr.Adv.Biochem., Curr.Adv.Cell & Devel.Biol., Curr.Adv.Ecol.Sci., Curr.Adv.Genetics & Molec.Biol., Ind.Sci.Rev., Nutr.Abstr., Sci.Cit.Ind.
—CASDDS; CISTI; Linda Hall. **CCC.**
Refereed Serial

571.6 UK ISSN 0011-4529
QH573 CODEN: CYTBAI
CYTOBIOS; a prestige international biomedical research journal of cell biology. (Text in English) 1969. m. £350 (subscr. includes supplements). Faculty Press, 88 Regent St., Cambridge CB2 1DP, England. FAX 44-553-840695. Ed.Bd. adv.; bk.rev.; abstr.; bibl.; charts; illus.; index. **Indexed:** Anim.Breed.Abstr., ASCA, Bibl.Agri., Biol.Abstr., Biol.Dig., Biotech.Abstr., Chem.Abstr., Curr.Adv.Cell & Devel.Biol., Curr.Adv.Ecol.Sci., Curr.Adv.Genetics & Molec.Biol., Curr.Cont., Dairy Sci.Abstr., Excerp.Med., Helminthol.Abstr., Ind.Med., Ind.Sci.Rev., Microbiol.Abstr., Nutr.Abstr., Ornam.Hort., Ref.Zh., Rev.Med.& Vet.Mycol., Sci.Cit.Ind., Small Anim.Abstr., Soils & Fert.
—BLDSC (3506.750000); CASDDS; CISTI; KNAW; SWETS; UnCover. **CCC.**
Description: Emphasizes work at chemical and molecular levels in cytogenetics, cell division and growth, cell physiology and pathology, immunochemistry and immunobiology.

CYTOKINES. see *BIOLOGY — Microbiology*

571.6 JA ISSN 0011-4545
QH301 CODEN: CYTOAN
CYTOLOGIA/KITOROGIA. (Text in English) 1929. q. 25000 Yen. Japan Mendel Society - Nihon Mendel Kyokai, c/o Toshin Bldg., 2-27-2 Hongo, Bunkyo-ku, Tokyo 113, Japan. FAX 81-3-3814-5352. Ed. T. Kuroiwa. circ. 1,000. (also avail. in microfilm from PMC) **Indexed:** Anim.Breed.Abstr., Biol.Abstr., Chem.Abstr., Cott.& Trop.Fibr.Abstr., Curr.Adv.Ecol.Sci., Curr.Cont., Excerp.Med., Fababean Abstr., Forest.Abstr., Helminthol.Abstr., Herb.Abstr., Ind.Sci.Rev., INIS Atomind., Maize Abstr., Ornam.Hort., Plant Breed Abstr., Plant Grow.Reg.Abstr., Potato Abstr., Rev.Med & Vet.Mycol., Sci.Cit.Ind., Seed Abstr., Soils & Fert., Sorghum & Millets Abstr., Triticale Abstr., Trop.Oil Seeds Abstr., Weed Abstr. **Document type:** academic/scholarly publication.
—BLDSC (3506.800000); CASDDS; CISTI; EMDOCS; Linda Hall; SWETS; UnCover.

571.6 US ISSN 0196-4763
QH573 CODEN: CYTODQ
CYTOMETRY (NEW YORK). 1983. 19/yr. $820 (foreign $1152.5) (effective 1998). John Wiley & Sons, Inc., Journals, 605 Third Ave., New York, NY 10158. TEL 212-850-6645. FAX 212-850-6021. TELEX 12-7063. E-mail: SUBINFO@JWILEY.COM; URL: http://www.wiley.co.uk. (Subscr. outside the Americas to: John Wiley & Sons Ltd., Baffins Ln., Chichester, W. Sussex PO19 1UD, England. TEL 44-1243-779777. FAX 44-1243-776128) Ed. Dr. Brian H. Mayall. adv.: B&W page £640, color page £1515; trim 279 x 210. bk.rev.; bibl.; charts; illus.; index. circ. 3,300. (also avail. in microfilm from WWS; microform from UMI; back issues avail.; reprint service avail. from ISI) **Indexed:** ASCA, Biol.Abstr., Chem.Abstr., Curr.Adv.Ecol.Sci., Curr.Cont., Ind.Med, Ind.Sci.Rev. **Document type:** academic/scholarly publication.
—BLDSC (3506.855000); ADONIS; CASDDS; CISTI; EMDOCS; Genuine Article; KNAW; SWETS; UnCover. **CCC.**
Description: Embraces all aspects of cytology, including image and flow cytometry, flow sorting, and applications of quantitative analytical cytology to basic research and clinical medicine.
Refereed Serial

571.6 UK ISSN 0956-5507
CODEN: CYTPEU
CYTOPATHOLOGY. 1990. bi-m. £187($342) (foreign £206) (effective 1998). (British Society for Clinical Cytology) Blackwell Science Ltd., Osney Mead, Oxford OX2 0EL, England. TEL 44-1865-206206. FAX 44-1865-721205. E-mail: journals.cs@blacksci.co.uk; URL: http://www.black.co.uk. Ed. D.V. Coleman; Pub. Allen Stevens. R&P contact: Sarah Pollard. adv. contact: Martine Cariou-Keen. bk.rev.; bibl.; charts; illus. circ. 935. (also avail. in microform from UMI; back issues avail.) **Indexed:** ASCA, Curr.Cont., Ind.Sci.Rev., Sci.Cit.Ind. **Document type:** academic/scholarly publication.
—BLDSC (3506.856000); ADONIS; CISTI; EMDOCS; Genuine Article; KNAW; SWETS; UMI. **CCC.**
Description: Contains original articles and critical reviews on all aspects of clinical cytology.
Refereed Serial

571.6 UK ISSN 0268-1625
CYTOSKELETON. s-m. (diskette m.). £110 (diskette £120; both £180) (effective 1997). S U B I S, Mansion House, 19 Kingfield Rd., Sheffield S11 9AS, England. TEL 44-114-2554433. FAX 44-114-2554626. E-mail: subis@sheffac.demon.co.uk; URL: http://www.shef.ac.uk/uni/companies/shap. (also avail. in diskette format) **Document type:** abstracting/indexing.
—CCC.
Formerly: Microfilaments and Microtubules (ISSN 0142-8209)
Description: Current awareness service for researchers. Covers tubulin, microtubules, microfilaments, neurofilaments, cell motility, cilia and flagella.

571.6 NE ISSN 0920-9069
CODEN: CYTOER
CYTOTECHNOLOGY; international journal of cell culture and biotechnology. (Text in English) 1988. 9/yr. fl.1626 to institutions; $834 to institutions in U.S. (effective 1998). Kluwer Academic Publishers, Postbus 17, 3300 AA Dordrecht, Netherlands. TEL 31-78-6392392. FAX 31-78-6392254. TELEX 29245 KAPG NL. E-mail: services@wkap.nl; URL: http://www.wkap.nl. (Dist. by: Kluwer Academic Publishers Group, P.O. Box 322, 3300 AH Dordrecht, Netherlands. TEL 31-78-6392392. FAX 31-78-6546474; N. America dist. addr.: Box 358, Accord Sta., Hingham, MA 02018-0358. TEL 617-871-6600. FAX 617-871-6528) Ed.Bd. (also avail. in microform; back issues avail.; reprint service avail. from SWZ) **Indexed:** ASCA, Biol.Abstr., Curr.Cont., Int.Abstr.Biol.Sci., Mat.Sci.Cit.Ind., Neurosci.Cit.Ind., Ref.Zh. **Document type:** academic/scholarly publication.
—BLDSC (3506.882000); CISTI; EMDOCS; Genuine Article; SWETS; UMI; UnCover. **CCC.**
Refereed Serial

571.6 UK ISSN 0951-0818
CODEN: DVCBAP
DEVELOPMENTAL AND CELL BIOLOGY SERIES. irreg., no.19, 1987. price varies. Cambridge University Press, Edinburgh Bldg., Shaftesbury Rd., Cambridge CB2 2RU, England. TEL 44-1223-312393. FAX 44-1223-315052. TELEX 851817256. E-mail: information@cup.cam.ac.uk; URL: http://www.cup.cam.ac.uk. (N. American addr.: Cambridge University Press, Journals Dept., 40 W. 20th St., New York, NY 10011. TEL 212-924-3900. FAX 212-691-3239) Ed.Bd. R&P contact: Linda Nicol. illus. **Document type:** monographic series.
—BLDSC (3579.050100).
Formerly: Developmental and Cell Biology Monographs.

DEVELOPMENTS IN MOLECULAR AND CELLULAR BIOCHEMISTRY. see *BIOLOGY — Biological Chemistry*

BIOLOGY — CYTOLOGY AND HISTOLOGY

571.6 US ISSN 8755-1039
CODEN: DICYE7
DIAGNOSTIC CYTOPATHOLOGY. 1985. m. $849 (foreign $1059) (effective 1998). John Wiley & Sons, Inc., Journals, 605 Third Ave., New York, NY 10158. TEL 212-850-6645. FAX 212-850-6021. TELEX 12-7063. E-mail: SUBINFO@JWILEY.COM; URL: http://www.wiley.co.uk. (Subscr. outside the Americas to: John Wiley & Sons Ltd., Baffins Ln., Chichester, W. Sussex PO19 1UD, England. TEL 44-1243-779777. FAX 44-1243-776128) Ed. Carlos W.M. Bedrossian. adv.: B&W page £640, color page £1515; trim 279 x 210. bk.rev.; abstr.; illus. circ. 1,750. (also avail. in microform from UMI; back issues avail.) Indexed: ASCA, Curr.Cont., Excerp.Med. (1992-), Protozool.Abstr. Document type: academic/scholarly publication.
—BLDSC (3579.656500); CISTI; EMDOCS; Genuine Article; KNAW; SWETS; UnCover. **CCC.**
  Description: International forum for original research and review articles on clinical aspects of cytology, encompassing such areas as flow cytometry, electron microscopy, image analysis, and immunocytochemistry.
  Refereed Serial

THE E M B O JOURNAL. (European Molecular Biology Organization) see *BIOLOGY — Biological Chemistry*

EGYPTIAN JOURNAL OF GENETICS AND CYTOLOGY. see *BIOLOGY — Genetics*

571.6 UK ISSN 0940-9912
CODEN: ECBIEP
EPITHELIAL CELL BIOLOGY. 1987. q. £128($205) (foreign £140.25) (effective 1996). Springer-Verlag London Ltd., Sweetapple House, Catteshall Rd., Godalming, Surrey GU7 3DJ, England. TEL 44-1483-418800. FAX 44-1483-415144. (U.S. subscr. to: Springer-Verlag New York, Inc., Box 2485, Secaucus, NJ 07096-2491. TEL 201-348-4403) Ed. Dr. C.S. Potten. adv. (back issues avail.) Indexed: Chem.Abstr., Curr.Cont., Excerp.Med. (1993-), Ind.Med. (1993-), Sci.Cit.Ind. Document type: academic/scholarly publication.
—BLDSC (3794.273000); CASDDS; CISTI; EMDOCS; Genuine Article; KNAW; SWETS. **CCC.**
  Formerly (until 1991): Epithelia (ISSN 0269-4565)
  Description: Publishes research reports, reviews and commentary on the biology and molecular biology of epithelial cells and tissues.

571.6 GW ISSN 0171-9335
QH573 CODEN: EJCBDN
EUROPEAN JOURNAL OF CELL BIOLOGY. (Text in English) 1969. m. (in 3 vols.) DM.540 per vol. (effective 1997). (European Cell Biology Organization) Wissenschaftliche Verlagsgesellschaft mbH, Postfach 101061, 70009 Stuttgart, Germany. TEL 49-711-2582-0. FAX 49-711-2582-290. (Co-sponsors: Deutsche Gesellschaft fuer Elektronenmikroskopie e.V.; Deutsche Gesellschaft fuer Zellbiologie e.V.) Ed.Bd. circ. 1,400. Indexed: Anim.Breed.Abstr., ASCA, Biol.Abstr., Chem.Abstr., Curr.Adv.Ecol.Sci., Curr.Cont., Dairy Sci.Abstr., Dent.Ind., Excerp.Med., Helminthol.Abstr., Ind.Med., Ind.Sci.Rev., INIS Atomind., Nutr.Abstr., Protozool.Abstr., Sci.Cit.Ind. Document type: academic/scholarly publication.
—BLDSC (3829.725700); CASDDS; CISTI; Genuine Article; KNAW; Linda Hall; SWETS; UnCover. **CCC.**
  Formerly: Cytobiologie (ISSN 0070-2463)

EUROPEAN JOURNAL OF HISTOCHEMISTRY. see *BIOLOGY — Biological Chemistry*

571.6 US ISSN 0014-4827
QH581 CODEN: ECREAL
EXPERIMENTAL CELL RESEARCH. 1950. 16/yr. $2125 (effective 1997). (International Society for Cell Biology) Academic Press, Inc., Journal Division, 525 B St., Ste. 1900, San Diego, CA 92101-4495. TEL 619-230-1840. FAX 619-699-6800. E-mail: apsubs@acad.com; URL: http://www.apnet.com/www/journals/ex.htm; http://www.idealibrary.com/. (Subscr. to: Box 861213, Orlando, FL 32886-1213. TEL 407-347-4040. FAX 407-363-9661) Eds. Nils Ringertz, Renato Baserga. adv.; bibl.; charts; illus.; index. (back issues avail.) Indexed: Abstr.Hyg., Anim.Breed.Abstr., ASCA, Biol.Abstr., Biol.& Agr.Ind., Biotech.Abstr., Chem.Abstr., Curr.Adv.Biochem., Curr.Adv.Cell & Devel.Biol., Curr.Adv.Ecol.Sci., Curr.Adv.Genetics & Molec.Biol., Curr.Cont., Dairy Sci.Abstr., Dent.Ind., Excerp.Med., Helminthol.Abstr., Ind.Med., Ind.Sci.Rev., Ind.Vet., INIS Atomind., Neurosci.Cit.Ind., Nutr.Abstr., Pig News & Info., Protozool.Abstr., Rev.Med.& Vet.Mycol., Sci.Cit.Ind., Trop.Dis.Bull., Vet.Bull. Document type: academic/scholarly publication.
●Also available online.
—BLDSC (3838.980000); ADONIS; CASDDS; CISTI; Genuine Article; KNAW; KR SourceOne; Linda Hall; SWETS; UnCover. **CCC.**
  Description: Promotes the understanding of cell biology by publishing experimental studies on the general organization and activity of cells.
  Refereed Serial

571.6 UK ISSN 0268-1617
EXTRACELLULAR MATRIX. 1986. s-m. (diskette m.) £115 (diskette £120; both £180) (effective 1997). S U B I S, Mansion House, 19 Kingfield Rd., Sheffield S11 9AS, England. TEL 44-114-2554433. FAX 44-114-2554626. E-mail: subis@sheffac.demon.co.uk; URL: http://www.shef.ac.uk/uni/companies/shap. (also avail. in diskette format) Document type: abstracting/indexing.
—CCC.
  Description: Current awareness service for researchers in clinical and life sciences.

571.6 PL ISSN 0239-8508
CODEN: FHCYEM
FOLIA HISTOCHEMICA ET CYTOBIOLOGICA. (Text and summaries in English) 1963. q. $40 to individuals in Europe (overseas $50); institutions in Europe $50 (overseas $65) (effective 1996 & 1997). Polskie Towarzystwo Histochemikow i Cytochemikow - Polish Histochemical and Cytochemical Society, c/o P.O. Box 843, 30-960 Krakow 1, Poland. TEL 48-12-227027. FAX 48-12-227027. Ed. Jan A. Litwin. bk.rev.; charts; illus.; index. circ. 500. Indexed: AgroAgen, Anim.Breed.Abstr., ASCA, Biol.Abstr., Chem.Abstr., Curr.Adv.Biochem., Curr.Adv.Cell & Devel.Biol., Curr.Adv.Ecol.Sci., Curr.Cont., Excerp.Med., Helminthol.Abstr., Ind.Med., Ind.Sci.Rev., INIS Atomind., Int.Abstr.Biol.Sci., Nutr.Abstr., Ref.Zh., Sci.Cit.Ind. Document type: academic/scholarly publication.
—BLDSC (3970.295000); CASDDS; CISTI; Genuine Article; KNAW; Linda Hall. **CCC.**
  Formerly (until 1984): Folia Histochemica et Cytochemica (ISSN 0015-5586)
  Refereed Serial

571.6 JA ISSN 0386-4766
CODEN: SAIBD8
GEKKAN SAIBO/CELL. (Text in Japanese) 1969. m. 2000 Yen per no. Nyu Saiensusha - New Science Co., 1-5-12 Akasaka, Minato-ku, Tokyo 107, Japan. Ed. Hisako Fukuda. Indexed: Chem.Abstr., INIS Atomind. Document type: academic/scholarly publication.
—CASDDS; CISTI.

GENOME. see *BIOLOGY — Genetics*

571.64 UK ISSN 0266-1144
GEOTEXTILES AND GEOMEMBRANES. 1984. bi-m. fl.909($522) (effective 1998). (International Geotextile Society) Elsevier Science Ltd., P.O. Box 800, Kidlington, Oxford OX5 1DX, England. TEL 44-1865-843000. FAX 44-1865-843010. E-mail: nlinfo-f@elsevier.nl; usinfo-f@elsevier.com; forinfo-kyf04035@niftyserve.or.jp; URL: http://www.elsevier.nl/. (Subscr. to: Elsevier Science, Regional Sales Office, P.O. Box 211, 1000 AE Amsterdam, Netherlands. TEL 31-20-4853757. FAX 31-20-4853432; Subscr. in the Americas to: Elsevier Science, Regional Sales Office, Box 945, New York, NY 10159-0945. TEL 212-633-3730. FAX 212-633-3680; Subscr. in Australasia and the Far East to: Elsevier Science (Singapore) Pte Ltd, No.1 Temasek Ave., No.17-01 Millenia Tower, Singapore 039192, Singapore. TEL 65-434-3727. FAX 65-337-2230) Eds. T.S. Ingold, J.P. Giroud. adv.; bk.rev. (back issues avail.) Indexed: Appl.Mech.Rev., ASCA, Curr.Cont., Eng.Ind., Geo.Abstr.P.G., Geol.Abstr., Geotech.Abstr., HRIS, Irr.& Drain.Abstr., Mat.Sci.Cit.Ind., Nonwov.Abstr., Soils & Fert. Document type: academic/scholarly publication.
—BLDSC (4161.010000); CISTI; Ei; EMDOCS; Genuine Article; KR SourceOne; Linda Hall; SWETS; UnCover. **CCC.**
  Description: Covers current technology available to research workers, designers, users and manufacturers of geotextiles and geomembranes.
  Refereed Serial

HEREDITAS; a periodical devoted to the publication of original research in all aspects of genetics and cytology. see *BIOLOGY — Genetics*

571.5 UK ISSN 0018-2214
QH611 CODEN: HISJAE
THE HISTOCHEMICAL JOURNAL. 1969. m. $815 (effective 1996). (Royal Microscopical Society) Chapman & Hall, Journals Department (Subsidiary of: International Thomson Publishing Group), 2-6 Boundary Row, London SE1 8HN, England. TEL 44-171-8650066. FAX 44-171-5229623. TELEX 290164 CHAPMA G. E-mail: jhelp@chall.co.uk; URL: http://www.chaphall.com/chaphall/journals.html. (Dist. by: International Thomson Publishing Services Ltd., Cheriton House, North Way, Andover, Hants. SP10 5BE, England. TEL 44-1264-342713. FAX 44-1264-342807; Subscr. in US & Canada to: 400 Market St., Philadelphia, PA 19106. TEL 800-552-5866) Ed. P.J. Stoward. adv.; bk.rev.; charts; illus.; index. (reprint service avail. from ISI, UMI) Indexed: Abstr.Hyg., ASCA, Biol.Abstr., Chem.Abstr., Curr.Adv.Ecol.Sci., Curr.Cont., Dairy Sci.Abstr., Dent.Ind., Excerp.Med., Helminthol.Abstr., Ind.Med., Ind.Sci.Rev., Ind.Vet., Neurosci.Cit.Ind., Nutr.Abstr., Pig News & Info., Poult.Abstr., Protozool.Abstr., Rev.Med.& Vet.Mycol., Sci.Cit.Ind., Trop.Dis.Bull. Document type: academic/scholarly publication.
●Also available online.
—BLDSC (4315.790000); ADONIS; CASDDS; CIST Genuine Article; Linda Hall; SWETS; UMI; UnCover. **CCC.**
  Description: Covers many areas, including biochemistry, histochemistry, pathology, immunocytochemistry, and cell biology.
  Refereed Serial

BIOLOGY — CYTOLOGY AND HISTOLOGY

571.6   GW   ISSN 0948-6143
QH611   CODEN: HCMYAL
HISTOCHEMISTRY AND CELL BIOLOGY. Online edition (GW ISSN 1432-119X) (Text in English) 1958. 12/yr. (in 2 vols., 6 nos./vol.). DM.3827 (foreign DM.3856.40) (effective 1998). (Society for Histochemistry) Springer-Verlag, Heidelberger Platz 3, 14197 Berlin, Germany. TEL 49-30-82787-08. FAX 49-30-82787448. E-mail: subscriptions@springer.de; URL: http://link.springer.de. (Subscr. in N. America to: Springer-Verlag New York, Inc., 333 Meadowlands Pkwy., Secaucus, NJ 07094. TEL 212-460-1500. FAX 212-473-6272) Eds. D. Drenckhahn, J. Roth. adv.; charts; illus. (also avail. in microform from UMI; back issues avail.; reprint service avail. from ISI) Indexed: ASCA, Biol.Abstr., Chem.Abstr., Curr.Adv.Cancer Res., Curr.Adv.Cell & Devel.Biol., Curr.Adv.Ecol.Sci., Curr.Cont., Dairy Sci.Abstr., Dent.Ind., Excerp.Med., Helminthol.Abstr., Ind.Med., Ind.Sci.Rev., Ind.Vet., INIS Atomind., Kidney, Neurosci.Cit.Ind., Sci.Cit.Ind., Vet.Bull. Document type: academic/scholarly publication.
●Also available online.
—BLDSC (4316.003100); ADONIS; CASDDS; CISTI; EMDOCS; Genuine Article; Linda Hall; SWETS; UMI; UnCover. **CCC**.
Former titles: Histochemistry (ISSN 0301-5564); Histochemie - Histochemistry - Histochimie (ISSN 0018-2222)
Description: Original papers on all areas of cyto- and histochemistry, especially morphology and cell biology. Focus is on theory and methodology (including fractionation, homogenization techniques, autoradiography, polarization optics, and fluorescence microscopy).

571.5   SP   ISSN 0213-3911
           CODEN: HIHIES
HISTOLOGY AND HISTOPATHOLOGY. (Text in English) 1986. q. $200 (effective 1997 & 1998). Plaza Fuensanta 2, 7o C., 30008 Murcia, Spain. TEL 34-68-243694. FAX 34-68-364150. Ed. F. Hernandez. adv. Indexed: ASCA, Chem.Abstr., Curr.Cont., Excerp.Med., Ind.Med. (1992-), Ind.Sci.Rev., Neurosci.Cit.Ind., Sci.Cit.Ind. Document type: academic/scholarly publication.
—BLDSC (4316.023100); CASDDS; CISTI; EMDOCS; Genuine Article; KNAW; SWETS; UnCover. **CCC**.
Description: Publishes original works in anatomy, histology, histopathology and cell biology.

576 574   UK   ISSN 0142-8136
IMMUNOHISTOCHEMISTRY. 1970. s-m. (diskette m.) £125 (diskette £120; both £180) (effective 1997). S U B I S, Mansion House, 19 Kingfield Rd., Sheffield S11 9AS, England. TEL 44-114-2554433. FAX 44-114-2554626. E-mail: subis@sheffac.demon.co.uk; URL: http://www.shef.ac.uk/uni/companies/shap. (also avail. in diskette format) Document type: abstracting/indexing.
—**CCC**.
Formerly: Ferritin.
Description: Current awareness service for researchers. Covers immunocytochemistry, immunohistology and immuno-electron microscopy.

IN VITRO TOXICOLOGY; a journal of molecular and cellular toxicology. see ENVIRONMENTAL STUDIES — Toxicology And Environmental Safety

571.6   UK   ISSN 0957-0799
           CODEN: IINCEH
INTERCELLULAR AND INTRACELLULAR COMMUNICATION. 1986. irreg. Cambridge University Press, Edinburgh Bldg., Shaftesbury Rd., Cambridge CB2 2RU, England. TEL 44-1223-312393. FAX 44-1223-315052. E-mail: information@cup.cam.ac.uk; URL: http://www.cup.cam.ac.uk. (N. American addr.: Cambridge University Press, 40 W. 20th St., New York, NY 10011. TEL 212-924-3900. FAX 212-691-3239) Document type: monographic series.
—CASDDS; CISTI.

INTERNATIONAL CONGRESS OF HISTOCHEMISTRY AND CYTOCHEMISTRY. PROCEEDINGS. see BIOLOGY — Biological Chemistry

INTERNATIONAL JOURNAL OF BIOCHEMISTRY & CELL BIOLOGY. see BIOLOGY — Biological Chemistry

INTERNATIONAL ORGANIZATION OF PLANT BIOSYSTEMATISTS. NEWSLETTER. see BIOLOGY — Botany

571.6   US   ISSN 0074-7696
QH573   CODEN: IRCYAJ
INTERNATIONAL REVIEW OF CYTOLOGY. 1952. irreg., vol.176, 1997. Academic Press, Inc., 525 B St., Ste. 1900, San Diego, CA 92101-4495. TEL 619-231-0926. FAX 619-699-6715. (Subscr. to: Order Dept., 6277 Sea Harbor Dr., 4th Fl., Orlando, FL 32887. TEL 800-321-5068) Eds. G.H. Bourne, J.F. Danielli. index; cum.index: 1952-1960, vols.1-9 in vol.10. (reprint service avail. from ISI) Indexed: Abstr.Hyg., Anim.Breed.Abstr., Biol.Abstr., Chem.Abstr., Crop Physiol.Abstr., Curr.Adv.Biochem., Excerp.Med., Ind.Med., Ind.Sci.Rev., INIS Atomind., Maize Abstr., Neurosci.Cit.Ind., Plant Breed.Abstr., Sci.Cit.Ind., Sport Fish.Abstr., Triticale Abstr., Trop.Dis.Bull., Wild.Rev., Zoo.Rec. Document type: academic/scholarly publication.
—BLDSC (4547.050000); CASDDS; CISTI; KNAW; Linda Hall; SWETS; UnCover. **CCC**.
Refereed Serial

571.6   SZ   ISSN 0251-1789
           CODEN: INVMDJ
INVASION AND METASTASIS; multidisciplinary contributions on non-malignant and malignant phenotypes. (Text in English) 1981. bi-m. 292.50 SFr.($228) to individuals; institutions 585 SFr.($456) (effective 1998). S. Karger AG, Allschwilerstr. 10, P.O. Box, CH-4009 Basel, Switzerland. TEL 41-61-3061111. FAX 41-61-3061234. E-mail: karger@karger.ch; URL: http://www.karger.ch. (U.S. subscr. to: S. Karger Publishers, Inc., 79 Fifth Ave., New York, NY 10011, U.S.A.) Ed. M. Maveel. adv.; bk.rev.; illus. circ. 800. (also avail. in microform from UMI) Indexed: ASCA, Biol.Abstr., Chem.Abstr., Curr.Cont., Excerp.Med., Ind.Med., Ind.Sci.Rev., Sci.Cit.Ind. Document type: academic/scholarly publication.
—BLDSC (4557.494400); CASDDS; CISTI; EMDOCS; Genuine Article; KNAW; SWETS; UnCover. **CCC**.
Refereed Serial

571.64   RU   ISSN 0234-2979
QH601
ITOGI NAUKI I TEKHNIKI: BIOFIZIKA MEMBRAN. irreg., latest vols.6, 1989. price varies. Vsesoyuznyi Institut Nauchno-Tekhnicheskoi Informatsii (VINITI), Ul. Baltiiskaya 14, Moscow A-219, Russia. (Subscr. to: Mezhdunarodnaya Kniga, Dimitrova ul. 39, 113095 Moscow, Russia) Indexed: Crop Physiol.Abstr., Field Crop Abstr., Herb.Abstr.
—**CCC**.
Formerly: Itogi Nauki i Tekhniki: Biofizika (ISSN 0202-7003)

JOURNAL OF BIOCHEMISTRY, MOLECULAR BIOLOGY AND BIOPHYSICS. see BIOLOGY — Biological Chemistry

571.6   US   ISSN 0021-9525
           CODEN: JCLBA3
JOURNAL OF CELL BIOLOGY. 1955. bi-w. $625 to institutions (effective 1997). (American Society for Cell Biology) Rockefeller University Press, 1114 First Ave., 4th Fl., New York, NY 10021. TEL 212-327-8572. FAX 212-327-7944. URL: http://www.jch.org; http://www.rockefeller.edu/rupress. (Subscr. to: Box 5108, GPO, New York, NY 10087-5108) Ed. Norton B. Gilula. adv. contact: Charles E. Lynch. charts; illus. circ. 5,046. (also avail. in microform from UMI; reprint service avail. from ISI, UMI) Indexed: Abstr.Bull.Inst.Pap.Chem., Abstr.Hyg., Anim.Breed.Abstr., ASCA, Bibl.Agri., Biol.Abstr., Biol.& Agr.Ind., Biol.& Agr.Ind., Biotech.Abstr., Chem.Abstr., Curr.Adv.Biochem., Curr.Adv.Cancer Res., Curr.Adv.Cell & Devel.Biol., Curr.Adv.Genetics & Molec.Biol., Curr.Cont., Dairy Sci.Abstr., Dent.Ind., Excerp.Med., Field Crop Abstr., Gen.Sci.Ind., Helminthol.Abstr., Herb.Abstr., Ind.Med., Ind.Sci.Rev., Ind.Vet., Neurosci.Cit.Ind., Nutr.Abstr., Plant Breed.Abstr., Poult.Abstr., Protozool.Abstr., Rev.Med.& Vet.Mycol., Sci.Cit.Ind., Soils & Fert., Trop.Dis.Bull., Vet.Bull. Document type: academic/scholarly publication.
—BLDSC (4954.920000); CASDDS; CISTI; Genuine Article; KNAW; KR SourceOne; Linda Hall; SWETS; UMI; UnCover. **CCC**.
Description: Provides a forum for articles in all branches of contemporary cell biology from the international community.
Refereed Serial

571.6   UK   ISSN 0021-9533
QH573   CODEN: JNCSAI
JOURNAL OF CELL SCIENCE. 1852. s-m. £731 (U.S. & Canada $1268; elsewhere £750) (effective 1998). Company of Biologists Ltd., Bidder Bldg., 140 Cowley Rd., Cambridge CB4 4DL, England. TEL 44-1223-426164. FAX 44-1223-423353. E-mail: cob@cambridge.cityscape.co.uk; URL: http://www.cityscape.co.uk/users/ag64. Ed. Fiona M. Watt. adv. contact: Richard Skaer. charts; illus.; index, cum.index: vols.1-10, 11-20, 21-40. circ. 1,800. (back issues avail.) Indexed: Abstr.Hyg., Anim.Breed.Abstr., ASCA, Bibl.Agri., Biol.Abstr., Biol.& Agr.Ind., Chem.Abstr., Curr.Adv.Biochem., Curr.Adv.Cancer Res., Curr.Adv.Cell & Devel.Biol., Curr.Adv.Genetics & Molec.Biol., Curr.Biotech.Abstr., Curr.Cont., Dairy Sci.Abstr., Dent.Ind., Excerp.Med., Field Crop Abstr., GeoRef., Helminthol.Abstr., Ind.Med., Ind.Sci.Rev., INIS Atomind., Int.Abstr.Biol.Sci., Maize Abstr., Neurosci.Cit.Ind., Nutr.Abstr., Ornam.Hort., Plant Breed.Abstr., Protozool.Abstr., Sci.Cit.Ind., Soils & Fert., Soyabean Abstr., Triticale Abstr., Trop.Dis.Bull., Vet.Bull. Document type: academic/scholarly publication.
●Also available online.
—BLDSC (4954.960000); CASDDS; CISTI; KNAW; KR SourceOne; Linda Hall; SWETS; UMI; UnCover.
Formerly (until 1966): Quarterly Journal of Microscopical Science (ISSN 0370-2952)
Description: Covers all aspects of cell biology in plants and animals.

JOURNAL OF CELLULAR BIOCHEMISTRY. see BIOLOGY — Biological Chemistry

572   US   ISSN 0733-1959
           CODEN: JCBSD7
JOURNAL OF CELLULAR BIOCHEMISTRY. SUPPLEMENT. 1972. irreg., latest no.17. price varies. John Wiley & Sons, Inc., Journals, 605 Third Ave., New York, NY 10158. TEL 212-850-6645. FAX 212-850-6021. E-mail: SUBINFO@JILEY.COM. (Subscr. outside the Americas to: John Wiley & Sons Ltd., Baffins Ln., Chichester, W. Sussex PO19 1UD, England. TEL 44-1243-449777. FAX 44-1243-776128) (back issues avail.) Indexed: Biol.Abstr., Chem.Abstr., Ind.Med., Sport Fish.Abstr., Wild.Rev., Zoo.Rec. Document type: academic/scholarly publication.
—BLDSC (4955.011000); CISTI; KNAW; Linda Hall.
Former titles (until 1982): Journal of Supramolecular Structure and Cellular Biochemistry. Supplement (ISSN 0730-6652); (until 1981): Journal of Supramolecular Structure. Supplement (ISSN 0161-3294)
Refereed Serial

571.6   UK   ISSN 1359-7388
▼**JOURNAL OF CELLULAR PATHOLOGY.** 1996. q. £95 (foreign $165) (effective 1998). Oxford University Press, Academic Division, Great Clarendon St., Oxford OX2 6DP, England. TEL 44-1865-267907. FAX 44-1865-267485. E-mail: jnl.info@oup.co.uk; URL: http://www.oup.co.uk/journals. (Subscr. in U.S. to: Oxford University Press Inc., 2001 Evans Rd., Cary, NC 27513. TEL 800-852-7323. FAX 919-677-1714) R&P contact: Joolz Longley. (back issues avail.) Document type: academic/scholarly publication.
—BLDSC (4955.015000).
Refereed Serial

JOURNAL OF CELLULAR PHYSIOLOGY. see BIOLOGY — Physiology

JOURNAL OF CLINICAL ONCOLOGY. see MEDICAL SCIENCES — Oncology

571.5   US   ISSN 0022-1554
QP501   CODEN: JHCYAS
JOURNAL OF HISTOCHEMISTRY AND CYTOCHEMISTRY.* 1953. m. $180 (effective 1992). Histochemical Society, Box 85630, Seattle, WA 98145-1630. TEL 212-362-1801. FAX 212-874-8313. Ed. Dr. Paul J. Anderson. adv.; bk.rev.; bibl.; charts; illus.; index. circ. 4,000. (also avail. in microform from WWS) Indexed: Anim.Breed.Abstr., ASCA, Biol.Abstr., Chem.Abstr., Curr.Adv.Cell & Devel.Biol., Curr.Adv.Ecol.Sci., Curr.Cont., Dairy Sci.Abstr., Dent.Ind., Excerp.Med., Helminthol.Abstr., Ind.Med., Ind.Sci.Rev., Ind.Vet., INIS Atomind., Neurosci.Cit.Ind., Nutr.Abstr., Pig News & Info., Poult.Abstr., Sci.Cit.Ind., Small Anim.Abstr., Trop.Dis.Bull., Vet.Bull.
—BLDSC (5000.000000); CASDDS; CISTI; Genuine Article; KNAW; Linda Hall; SWETS; UnCover. **CCC**.
Refereed Serial

BIOLOGY — CYTOLOGY AND HISTOLOGY

571.5   US   ISSN 0147-8885
RB43   CODEN: JOHIDN
JOURNAL OF HISTOTECHNOLOGY. 1977. q. $60 (effective 1997). National Society for Histotechnology, 4201 Northview Dr., Ste. 502, Bowie, MD 20716-1073. TEL 301-262-6221. FAX 301-262-9188. Ed. Jules Elias. adv.; bk.rev.; index. circ. 5,000. **Indexed:** ASCA, Biol.Abstr., Chem.Abstr., Curr.Cont., Excerp.Med., Ind.Sci.Rev., Sci.Cit.Ind. **Document type:** trade publication.
—BLDSC (5002.400000); CASDDS; CISTI; Genuine Article; KNAW; SWETS; UnCover.
   Description: Publishes original articles, brief reports, notes on techniques, case studies dealing with anatomy, histochemistry, pathology, microscopy, and immunohistochemistry. Articles on applications and evaluations of commercially prepared kits, continuing education, and medical news.
Refereed Serial

571.6   US   ISSN 0022-2631
QH601   CODEN: JMBBBO
JOURNAL OF MEMBRANE BIOLOGY; an international journal for studies on the structure, function and genesis of biomembranes. US 1432-1424. 1969. 18/yr. $1445 (effective 1998). Springer-Verlag, Life Science Journals, 175 Fifth Ave., New York, NY 10010. TEL 212-460-1500. FAX 212-473-6272. E-mail: orders@springer-ny.com; URL: http://www.springer-ny.com. (N. American subscr. to: Journal Fulfillment Services, Box 2485, Secaucus, NJ 07096-2485. TEL 800-777-4643. FAX 201-348-4505; Subscr. outside N. America: Heidelberger Platz 33, 14197 Berlin, Germany. TEL 49-30-8207-0. FAX 49-30-8207448) Ed. W.R. Loewenstein. R&P contact: Ian Gross. adv. contact: Robert Vrooman. (also avail. in microform from UMI; back issues avail.; reprint service avail. from ISI) **Indexed:** ASCA, Biol.Abstr., Chem.Abstr., Curr.Adv.Biochem., Curr.Adv.Cell & Devel.Biol., Curr.Adv.Ecol.Sci., Curr.Cont., Dairy Sci.Abstr., Excerp.Med., Ind.Med., Ind.Sci.Rev., INIS Atomind., Neurosci.Cit.Ind., Poult.Abstr., Sci.Cit.Ind. **Document type:** academic/scholarly publication.
●Also available online.
—BLDSC (5017.600000); ADONIS; CASDDS; CISTI; Genuine Article; Linda Hall; SWETS; UMI; UnCover. **CCC.**
   Description: Contains articles examining the nature, structure, function, and genesis of biological membranes and the physics and chemistry of artificial membranes as relevant to biomembranes.
Refereed Serial

571.6   UK   ISSN 0300-4864
QP362   CODEN: JNCYA2
JOURNAL OF NEUROCYTOLOGY; a journal of cellular neurobiology. 1972. m. $132 to individuals; institutions $835 (effective 1996). Chapman & Hall, Journals Department (Subsidiary of: International Thomson Publishing Group), 2-6 Boundary Row, London SE1 8HN, England. TEL 44-171-8650066. FAX 44-171-5229623. TELEX 290164 CHAPMA G. E-mail: jhelp@chall.co.uk; URL: http://www.chaphall.com/chaphall/journals.html. (Dist. by: International Thomson Publishing Services Ltd., Cheriton House, North Way, Andover, Hants. SP10 5BE, England. TEL 44-1264-342713. FAX 44-1264-342807; Subscr. in US & Canada to: 400 Market St., Philadelphia, PA 19106. TEL 800-552-5866) Ed. Dr. A.R. Lieberman. adv.; bk.rev.; bibl.; illus.; index. (reprint service avail. from ISI, UMI) **Indexed:** ASCA, Biol.Abstr., Chem.Abstr., Curr.Adv.Cell & Devel.Biol., Curr.Adv.Ecol.Sci., Curr.Cont., Dent.Ind., Excerp.Med., Ind.Med., Ind.Sci.Rev., INIS Atomind., Neurosci.Cit.Ind., Sci.Cit.Ind. **Document type:** academic/scholarly publication.
●Also available online.
—BLDSC (5021.540000); ADONIS; CASDDS; CISTI; EMDOCS; Genuine Article; Linda Hall; SWETS; UMI; UnCover. **CCC.**
   Description: Studies the invertebrate and vertebrate nervous conditions under normal, experimental, and pathological conditions.
Refereed Serial

571.6   IT   ISSN 1122-9497
                   CODEN: JSCPEE
JOURNAL OF SUBMICROSCOPIC CYTOLOGY AND PATHOLOGY. (Text in English) 1969. q. Lit.180000($150) (effective 1997). Editrice Compositori s.r.l., Via Stalingrado 97-2, 40128 Bologna, Italy. TEL 39-51-327811. FAX 39-51-327837. E-mail: 1865@compositori.it; URL: http://www.compositori.it. Ed. Baccio Bacetti. R&P contact: Olga Ruggieri. circ. 500. **Indexed:** ASCA, Biol.Abstr., Chem.Abstr., Curr.Cont., Excerp.Med. (1988-1992), Ind.Med., Ind.Sci.Rev., Sci.Cit.Ind., Zoo.Rec. **Document type:** academic/scholarly publication.
—BLDSC (5066.930500); CASDDS; CISTI; Genuine Article; KNAW; Linda Hall; SWETS; UnCover.
   Formerly (until 1988): Journal of Submicroscopic Cytology (ISSN 0022-4782)
   Description: Presents papers dealing with applications of electronmicroscopy, biology, physiology and experimental and diagnostic pathology.

KLINICHNA I TRANSFUZIONNA HEMATOLOGIIA. see *MEDICAL SCIENCES — Hematology*

LIPPINCOTT-RAVEN PRESS SERIES ON MOLECULAR AND CELLULAR BIOLOGY. see *BIOLOGY*

571.64   JA   ISSN 0385-1036
                   CODEN: MAKUD9
MAKU/MEMBRANE. (Text in Japanese; summaries in English) 1976. bi-m. 2800 Yen. Nihon Maku Gakkai - Membrane Society of Japan, 14-9, Hongo 4-chome, Bunkyo-ku, Tokyo 113, Japan. Ed. Masayuki Nakagaki. adv.; bk.rev. circ. 850. (back issues avail.) **Indexed:** Biol.Abstr., Chem.Abstr., Excerp.Med.
—BLDSC (5548.025000); CASDDS; CISTI. **CCC.**

571   IE   ISSN 0925-4773
QH607   CODEN: MEDVE6
MECHANISMS OF DEVELOPMENT. 1972. 20/yr. fl.4355($2503) (effective 1998). Elsevier Science Ireland Ltd., P.O. Box 85, Limerick, Ireland. TEL 353-61-471944. FAX 353-61-472144. (Subscr. to: Elsevier Science, Regional Sales Office, P.O. Box 211, 1000 AE Amsterdam, Netherlands. TEL 31-20-4853757. FAX 31-20-4853432; Subscr. in the Americas to: Elsevier Science, Regional Sales Office, Box 945, New York, NY 10159-0945. TEL 212-633-3730. FAX 212-633-3680; Subscr. in Australasia and the Far East to: Elsevier Science (Singapore) Pte Ltd, No.1 Temasek Ave., No.17-01 Millenia Tower, Singapore 039192, Singapore. TEL 65-434-3727. FAX 65-337-2230) Ed.Bd. R&P contact: Annette Moloney. charts; illus. (also avail. in microform from UMI) **Indexed:** ASCA, Biol.Abstr., Chem.Abstr., Curr.Adv.Ecol.Sci., Curr.Cont., Excerp.Med., Helminthol.Abstr., Ind.Med., Ind.Sci.Rev., INIS Atomind., Neurosci.Cit.Ind., Sci.Cit.Ind. **Document type:** academic/scholarly publication.
—BLDSC (5424.571280); CASDDS; CISTI; EMDOCS; Genuine Article; KNAW; Linda Hall; SWETS; UnCover. **CCC.**
   Former titles (until 1990): Cell Differentiation and Development (ISSN 0922-3371); (until 1988): Cell Differentiation (ISSN 0045-6039)
   Description: Research on development and cellular differentiation in animals, plants and prokaryotes.
Refereed Serial

571.6   NE   ISSN 1023-6597
QH601   CODEN: MCBIEB
MEMBRANE AND CELL BIOLOGY. English translation of: Biologicheskie Membrany (RU ISSN 0233-4755) 1984. 6/yr. $737 (effective 1998). (Russian Academy of Sciences, RU) Gordon and Breach - Harwood Academic, Amsteldisk 166, 1st Fl., 1079 LH Amsterdam, Netherlands. (Subscr. to: International Publishers Distributor, Box 32160, Newark, NJ 07102. TEL 800-545-8398. FAX 215-750-6343) Ed. Dr. Yu.A. Chizmadzhev. bk.rev. (also avail. in microform) **Document type:** academic/scholarly publication.
—BLDSC (0415.891500); CISTI; EMDOCS. **CCC.**
   Formerly (until vol.8): Biological Membranes (ISSN 0748-8653)
   Description: Presents experimental and theoretical work on the physics, chemistry and biology of membranes at the molecular and cellular levels.
Refereed Serial

571.64   NE   ISSN 0927-5193
                   CODEN: MSSREV
MEMBRANE SCIENCE AND TECHNOLOGY SERIES. (Text in English) 1991. irreg., vol.2, 1995. Elsevier Science B.V., Books Division, P.O. Box 211, 1000 AE Amsterdam, Netherlands. TEL 31-20-4853911. FAX 31-20-4853705. TELEX 18582 ESPA NL. E-mail: nlinfo-f@elsevier.nl; usinfo-f@elsevier.com; forinfo-kyf04035@niftyserve.or.jp; URL: http://www.elsevier.nl/. (Subscr. in the Americas to: Elsevier Science, Regional Sales Office, Box 945, New York, NY 10159-0945. TEL 212-633-3730. FAX 212-633-3680; Subscr. in Australasia and the Far East to: Elsevier Science (Singapore) Pte Ltd, No.1 Temasek Ave., No.17-01 Millenia Tower, Singapore 039192, Singapore. TEL 65-434-3727. FAX 65-337-2230; Subscr. in Japan to: Elsevier Science Japan, 9-15 Higashi-Azabu 1-chome, Minato-ku, Tokyo 106, Japan. TEL 81-3-5561-5033. FAX 81-3-5561-5047) **Indexed:** Chem.Cit.Ind. **Document type:** monographic series.
—BLDSC (5548.026350); CASDDS. **CCC.**
Refereed Serial

571.6   US   ISSN 0091-679X
QH585   CODEN: MCBLAG
METHODS IN CELL BIOLOGY. 1964. irreg., vol.51, 1996. Academic Press, Inc., 525 B St., Ste. 1900, San Diego, CA 92101-4495. TEL 619-231-0926. FAX 619-699-6715. (Subscr. to: Order Dept., 6277 Sea Harbor Dr., 4th Fl., Orlando, FL 32887. TEL 800-321-5068) Ed. Leslie Wilson. illus. (reprint service avail. from ISI) **Indexed:** ASCA, Biol.Abstr., Chem.Abstr., Excerp.Med., Ind.Med., Ind.Sci.Rev., Nutr.Abstr., Rev.Plant Path., Sci.Cit.Ind.
—BLDSC (5747.250000); CASDDS; CISTI; KNAW; SWETS; UnCover. **CCC.**
   Formerly: Methods in Cell Physiology (ISSN 0091-6579)
Refereed Serial

571.6   US   ISSN 0898-7750
QH506   CODEN: MMCBEV
METHODS IN MOLECULAR AND CELLULAR BIOLOGY. 1989. bi-m. $296 (Canada & Mexico $356; elsewhere $395) (effective 1997). John Wiley & Sons, Inc., Journals, 605 Third Ave., New York, NY 10158. TEL 212-850-6645. FAX 212-850-6021. TELEX 12-7063. E-mail: SUBINFO@JWILEY.COM; URL: http://www.wiley.co.uk. (Subscr. outside the Americas to: John Wiley & Sons Ltd., Baffins Ln., Chichester, W. Sussex PO19 1UD, England. TEL 44-1243-779777. FAX 44-1243-776128) Ed.Bd. adv.: B&W page £640, color page £1515; trim 279 x 210. bk.rev. circ. 850. (also avail. in microform from UMI; back issues avail.) **Indexed:** ASCA. **Document type:** academic/scholarly publication.
—BLDSC (5748.201700); ADONIS; CASDDS; CISTI; EMDOCS; Genuine Article; KNAW; Linda Hall; SWETS; UnCover. **CCC.**
Refereed Serial

MICROBIAL & COMPARATIVE GENOMICS. see *BIOLOGY — Genetics*

571.657   UK   ISSN 0142-8217
Z5322.C3
MITOCHONDRIA. 1978. s-m. (diskette m.) £110 (diskette £120; both £180) (effective 1997). S U B I S, Mansion House, 19 Kingfield Rd., Sheffield S11 9AS, England. TEL 44-114-2554433. FAX 44-114-2554626. E-mail: subis@sheffac.demon.co.uk; URL: http://www.shef.ac.uk/uni/companies/shap. (also avail. in diskette format) **Document type:** abstracting/indexing.
—**CCC.**
   Description: Current awareness service for researchers. Covers electron transport, cytochromes, oxidative phosphorylation, TCA cycle, pathology.

571.6   US   ISSN 0745-3000
                   CODEN: MOCBDA
MODERN CELL BIOLOGY. 1983. irreg., vol.15. John Wiley & Sons, Inc., 605 Third Ave., New York, NY 10158. TEL 212-850-6645. FAX 212-850-6021. (Subscr. outside the Americas to: John Wiley & Sons Ltd., Baffins Ln., Chichester, W. Sussex PO19 1UD, England. TEL 44-1243-779777. FAX 44-1243-776128) **Document type:** monographic series.
—BLDSC (5885.410000); CASDDS; CISTI; KNAW.

BIOLOGY — CYTOLOGY AND HISTOLOGY

571.6 — UK
MOLECULAR AND CELL BIOLOGY OF HUMAN DISEASES. a., no.5, 1995. Chapman & Hall, 2-6 Boundary Row, London SE1 8HN, England. TEL 44-171-8650066. FAX 44-171-5229623. (In N. America: 115 Fifth Ave., New York, NY 10003) **Document type:** monographic series.

MOLECULAR AND CELLULAR BIOCHEMISTRY; an international journal for chemical biology in health and disease. see *BIOLOGY — Biological Chemistry*

MOLECULAR & CELLULAR DIFFERENTIATION. see *BIOLOGY — Microbiology*

571.6 — NE — ISSN 0167-6970
CODEN: MACRDS
MOLECULAR ASPECTS OF CELLULAR REGULATION. (Text in English) 1980. irreg., vol.6, 1991. price varies. Elsevier Science B.V., Books Division, P.O. Box 211, 1000 AE Amsterdam, Netherlands. TEL 31-20-4853911. FAX 31-20-4853705. TELEX 18582 ESPA NL. E-mail: nlinfo-f@elsevier.com; usinfo-f@elsevier.com; forinfo-kyf04035@niftyserve.or.jp; URL: http://www.elsevier.nl/. (Subscr. in the Americas to: Elsevier Science, Regional Sales Office, Box 945, New York, NY 10159-0945. TEL 212-633-3730. FAX 212-633-3680; Subscr. in Australasia and the Far East to: Elsevier Science (Singapore) Pte Ltd, No.1 Temasek Ave., No.17-01 Millenia Tower, Singapore 039192, Singapore. TEL 65-434-3727. FAX 65-337-2230; Subscr. in Japan to: Elsevier Science Japan, 9-15 Higashi-Azabu 1-chome, Minato-ku, Tokyo 106, Japan. TEL 81-3-5561-5033. FAX 81-3-5561-5047) Ed. P. Cohen. (back issues avail.) **Document type:** monographic series.
—BLDSC (5900.766000); CASDDS; CISTI.
Refereed Serial

MOLECULAR BIOLOGY (NEW YORK). see *BIOLOGY — Biological Chemistry*

571.6 — US — ISSN 1059-1524
QH604 — CODEN: MBCEEV
MOLECULAR BIOLOGY OF THE CELL. 1990. m. $175 to non-members (foreign $225); institutions $375 (foreign $425) (effective 1998). American Society for Cell Biology, 9650 Rockville Pike, Bethesda, MD 20814-3992. TEL 301-530-7153. FAX 301-571-7139. E-mail: mbc@ascb.org; URL: http://www.ascb.org/ascb. Ed. David Botstein. R&P contact: R. Kampman. adv. contact: R. Sommer. abstr.; bibl.; charts; illus.; index; circ. 10,000 (paid). (back issues avail.) **Indexed:** ASCA, Curr.Cont., Excerp.Med. (1993-), Ind.Med. (1992-), Ind.Sci.Rev., Sci.Cit.Ind., SSCI. **Document type:** academic/scholarly publication.
—BLDSC (5900.788000); CASDDS; CISTI; EMDOCS; Genuine Article; KNAW; Linda Hall; SWETS; UnCover.
Formerly: Cell Regulation (ISSN 1044-2030)
Description: Interdisciplinary approach to molecular aspects of cell biology; publishes complete, scholarly papers.
Refereed Serial

MOLECULAR BIOLOGY REPORTS; an international journal on molecular and cellular biology. see *BIOLOGY — Biological Chemistry*

MOLECULAR MEMBRANE BIOLOGY. see *BIOLOGY — Biological Chemistry*

MONALDI ARCHIVES FOR CHEST DISEASE. see *MEDICAL SCIENCES — Respiratory Diseases*

MONOGRAPHS IN CLINICAL CYTOLOGY. see *MEDICAL SCIENCES*

571.6 — NE — ISSN 1010-8793
CODEN: NASBE4
N A T O ADVANCED SCIENCE INSTITUTES SERIES H: CELL BIOLOGY. 1986. irreg., vol.2, 1986. price varies. (North Atlantic Treaty Organization, Scientific Affairs Division, BE) Kluwer Academic Publishers, Postbus 17, 3300 AA Dordrecht, Netherlands. TEL 31-78-6392392. FAX 31-78-6392254. TELEX 29245 KAPG NL. E-mail: services@wkap.nl; URL: http://www.wkap.nl. (Dist. by: Kluwer Academic Publishers Group, P.O. Box 322, 3300 AH Dordrecht, Netherlands. TEL 31-78-6392392. FAX 31-78-6546474; N. America dist. addr.: Box 358, Accord Sta., Hingham, MA 02018-0358. TEL 617-871-6600) (reprint service avail. from ISI) **Document type:** monographic series.
●Also available online. Vendor(s): European Space Agency (File no.128).
—BLDSC (6033.648830); CASDDS; CISTI; KNAW. **CCC.**
Formerly: N A T O Advanced Study Institute. Series H: Cell Biology.
Refereed Serial

NANOBIOLOGY; journal of research on nanoscale living systems. see *BIOLOGY — Microbiology*

571.6 — UK — ISSN 0142-8225
NERVE CELL BIOLOGY. 1972. s-m. (diskette m.). £125 (diskette £120; both £180) (effective 1997). S U B I S, Mansion House, 19 Kingfield Rd., Sheffield S11 9AS, England. TEL 44-114-2554433. FAX 44-114-2554626. E-mail: subis@sheffac.demon.co.uk; URL: http://www.shef.ac.uk/uni/companies/shap. (also avail. in diskette format) **Document type:** abstracting/indexing.
—CCC.
Description: Current awareness service for researchers. Covers nerve cell biology: development, regeneration, structure, tissue culture, pharmacology, immunology, membranes and sensory receptors.

NIHON SAIBO SEIBUTSU GAKKAI TAIKAI KOEN YOSHISHU/JAPAN SOCIETY FOR CELL BIOLOGY. ABSTRACTS OF THE MEETING. see *BIOLOGY — Abstracting, Bibliographies, Statistics*

571.6 — JA
NIHON SOSHIKI BAIYO GAKKAI KAIIN TSUSHIN/JAPANESE TISSUE CULTURE ASSOCIATION. NEWS. (Text in Japanese) 4/yr. Nihon Soshiki Baiyo Gakkai - Japanese Tissue Culture Association, Kinosei Pepuchido Kenkyujo, 4-3-32 Shimojo-machi, Yamagata-shi, Yamagata-ken 990, Japan. Ed. Hiroyoshi Hoshi. **Document type:** newsletter.

571.6 — IT
NOTIZIARIO DI CITOLOGIA. 1980. 3/yr. Lit.20000 (effective 1996). Pacini Editore s.r.l., Via A. Gherardesca 1, 56121 Ospedaletto (Pisa), Italy. TEL 39-50-982439. FAX 39-50-983906. E-mail: pacini@cibernet.it; URL: http://www.cibernet.it/pacini. Ed. G. Giacomini.

571.6 — II — ISSN 0029-568X
QH573 — CODEN: NULSAK
NUCLEUS; international journal of cytology and allied topics. (Supplements issued separately) 1958. 3/yr. Rs.600($60) University of Calcutta, Department of Botany, Cytogenetics Laboratory, 35 Ballygunj Circular Rd., Calcutta 19, West Bengal, India. TEL 91-33-440-5802. FAX 91-33-478-7603. Ed. A. Sharma; Pub. A.K. Sharma. adv.; bk.rev.; charts; illus.; index. circ. 500. **Indexed:** Biol.Abstr., Chem.Abstr., Curr.Adv.Ecol.Sci., Excerp.Med., Genet.Abstr., Ornam.Hort., Plant Breed.Abstr. **Document type:** academic/scholarly publication.
—BLDSC (6184.202000); CASDDS; CISTI; Linda Hall; SWETS; UnCover.
Refereed Serial

PATHOBIOLOGY; journal of immunopathology, molecular and cellular biology. see *MEDICAL SCIENCES*

PEPTIDE HORMONE RECEPTORS. see *MEDICAL SCIENCES — Abstracting, Bibliographies, Statistics*

571.6 — DK — ISSN 0893-5785
QL767 — CODEN: PCREEA
PIGMENT CELL RESEARCH. (Text in English) bi-m. DKK 1940 in Europe (US, Canada and Japan DKK 1910) (includes supplements) (effective 1997). (International Federation of Pigment Cell Societies) Munksgaard International Publishers Ltd., P.O. Box 2148, DK-1016 Copenhagen K, Denmark. TEL 45-33-127030. FAX 45-33-129387. E-mail: fsub@mail.munksgaard.dk. (In N. America: Consumer Place, 350 Main St., Malden, MA 02148-5018. TEL 617-388-8273. FAX 617-388-8274) Ed. J. Matsumoto. adv.; charts; illus. circ. 600. (reprint service avail.) **Indexed:** ASCA, Biol.Abstr., Chem.Abstr., Curr.Cont., Ind.Med., Med.& Surg.Dermat., Sci.Cit.Ind. **Document type:** academic/scholarly publication.
—BLDSC (6500.148000); CASDDS; CISTI; Genuine Article; KNAW; SWETS. **CCC.**
Refereed Serial

PLANT AND CELL PHYSIOLOGY. see *BIOLOGY — Botany*

571.5 — NE — ISSN 0167-6857
CODEN: PTCEDJ
PLANT CELL, TISSUE AND ORGAN CULTURE; an international journal on in vitro culture of higher plants. (Text in English) 1981. m. fl.2220 to institutions; $1140 to institutions in U.S. (effective 1998). Kluwer Academic Publishers, Postbus 17, 3300 AA Dordrecht, Netherlands. TEL 31-78-6392392. FAX 31-78-6392254. TELEX 29245 KAPG NL. E-mail: services@wkap.nl; URL: http://www.wkap.nl. (Dist. by: Kluwer Academic Publishers Group, P.O. Box 322, 3300 AH Dordrecht, Netherlands. TEL 31-78-6392392. FAX 31-78-6546474; N. America dist. addr.: Box 358, Accord Sta., Hingham, MA 02018-0358. TEL 617-871-6600. FAX 617-871-6528) Eds. R.H. Zimmerman, A.H. Scragg. adv.; bk.rev. (also avail. in microform from UMI; reprint service avail. from SWZ) **Indexed:** Abstr.Bull.Inst.Pap.Chem., ASCA, Biol.Abstr., Bull.Signal., Chem.Abstr., Cott.& Trop.Fibr.Abstr., Crop Physiol.Abstr., Curr.Adv.Ecol.Sci., Curr.Biotech.Abstr., Curr.Cont., Environ.Abstr., Field Crop Abstr., Food Sci.& Tech.Abstr., Forest.Abstr., Herb.Abstr., Hort.Abstr., Ind.Sci.Rev., Int.Abstr.Biol.Sci., Maize Abstr., Plant Breed.Abstr., Plant Grow.Reg.Abstr., Potato Abstr., Rice Abstr., Sci.Cit.Ind., Seed Abstr., Soils & Fert., Soyabean Abstr., Telegen, Triticale Abstr., Weed Abstr. **Document type:** academic/scholarly publication.
—BLDSC (6514.300000); CASDDS; CISTI; Ei; EMDOCS; Genuine Article; Linda Hall; SWETS; UMI; UnCover. **CCC.**
Description: Publishes original results of fundamental research on plant cells, tissues and organs, including plant genetics and biotechnology.
Refereed Serial

571.6 — PL — ISSN 0324-833X
QH573 — CODEN: PBKODV
POSTEPY BIOLOGII KOMORKI. (Text in Polish; summaries in English) 1974. q. 50 Zl. (foreign $20) (effective 1998). (Polskie Towarzystwo Anatomiczne) Fundacja Postepu Biologii Komorki, Ul. Marymoncka 99, 01-813 Warsaw, Poland. TEL 48-22-340344. FAX 48-22-370470. (Co-sponsor: Polskie Towarzystwo Biologii Komorki) Ed. Jerzy Kawiak. R&P contact: Jerzy Kawiak. bk.rev.; bibl.; illus. circ. 640. **Indexed:** AgroLibrex, Biol.Abstr., Chem.Abstr. **Document type:** academic/scholarly publication.
—CASDDS.
Refereed Serial

578 616 — UK
PREPARATIVE BIOTRANSFORMATIONS: WHOLE CELL AND ISOLATED ENZYMES IN ORGANIC SYNTHESIS. 1992. base vol. (plus s-a. updates). £485($730) for new orders; update service £110 ($165); core only £375 ($565) (effective 1997). John Wiley & Sons Ltd., Journals, Baffins Ln., Chichester, W. Sussex PO19 1UD, England. TEL 44-1243-779777. FAX 44-1243-843232. E-mail: cs-journals@wiley.co.uk; URL: http://www.wiley.co.uk. (Subscr. in the Americas to: John Wiley & Sons, Inc., 605 Third Ave., New York, NY 10158-0012. TEL 212-850-6347) (also avail. in looseleaf format) **Document type:** academic/scholarly publication.

BIOLOGY — CYTOLOGY AND HISTOLOGY

571.6   US   ISSN 1087-2957
QH605   CODEN: PCCRF9
PROGRESS IN CELL CYCLE RESEARCH. 1995. a., vol.2, 1996. Plenum Publishing Corp., 233 Spring St., New York, NY 10013. TEL 212-620-8000. FAX 212-463-6742.
—CASDDS. **CCC.**

571.6   NE   ISSN 0924-8315
     CODEN: PRCREB
PROGRESS IN CELL RESEARCH. (Text in English) 1990. irreg., vol.3, 1993. price varies. Elsevier Science B.V., Books Division, P.O. Box 211, 1000 AE Amsterdam, Netherlands. TEL 31-20-4853911. FAX 31-20-4853705. TELEX 18582 ESPA NL. E-mail: nlinfo-f@elsevier.nl; usinfo-f@elsevier.com; forinfo-kyf04035@niftyserve.or.jp; URL: http://www.elsevier.nl/. (Subscr. in the Americas to: Elsevier Science, Regional Sales Office, Box 945, New York, NY 10159-0945. TEL 212-633-3730. FAX 212-633-3680; Subscr. in Australasia and the Far East to: Elsevier Science (Singapore) Pte Ltd, No.1 Temasek Ave., No.17-01 Millenia Tower, Singapore 039192, Singapore. TEL 65-434-3727. FAX 65-337-2230; Subscr. in Japan to: Elsevier Science Japan, 9-15 Higashi-Azabu 1-chome, Minato-ku, Tokyo 106, Japan. TEL 81-3-5561-5033. FAX 81-3-5561-5047) **Document type:** monographic series.
—BLDSC (6866.760000); CASDDS; CISTI. **CCC.**
Refereed Serial

PROGRESS IN HISTOCHEMISTRY AND CYTOCHEMISTRY. see *BIOLOGY — Biological Chemistry*

571.6   US   ISSN 0079-6484
QH506   CODEN: PMSBA4
PROGRESS IN MOLECULAR AND SUBCELLULAR BIOLOGY. 1969. irreg., vol.9, 1985. price varies. Springer-Verlag, 175 Fifth Ave., New York, NY 10010. TEL 212-460-1500. FAX 212-473-6272. (Also: Berlin, Heidelberg, Tokyo and Vienna) Ed. F.E. Hahn. (reprint service avail. from ISI) **Indexed:** Biol.Abstr., Chem.Abstr., Ind.Med. (1993-).
Document type: academic/scholarly publication.
—CASDDS; CISTI; KNAW; Linda Hall; UnCover.
Refereed Serial

571.6   AU   ISSN 0033-183X
QH573   CODEN: PROTA5
PROTOPLASMA; an international journal of cell biology. (Text in English, French and German) 1926. 24/yr. DM.3084 (effective 1998). Springer-Verlag, Sachsenplatz 4-6, P.O. Box 89, A-1201 Vienna, Austria. TEL 43-1-330-2415. FAX 43-1-330-2426. E-mail: springer@springer.co.at; URL: http://www.springer.co.at/. (Subscr. in N. America to: Springer-Verlag New York, Inc., 175 Fifth Ave., New York, NY 10010. TEL 212-460-1500. FAX 212-473-6272) Ed. B.E.S. Gunning. adv.; charts; illus.; index. (also avail. in microform from UMI; reprint service avail. from ISI) **Indexed:** Abstr.Bull.Inst.Pap.Chem., ASCA, ASCA, Bibl.Agri., Biol.Abstr., Chem.Abstr., Crop Physiol.Abstr., Curr.Adv.Cell & Devel.Biol., Curr.Adv.Ecol.Sci., Curr.Cont., Excerp.Med., Field Crop Abstr., Forest.Abstr., Helminthol.Abstr., Hort.Abstr., Ind.Med., Ind.Sci.Rev., Maize Abstr., Ornam.Hort., Plant Grow.Reg.Abstr., Potato Abstr., Rice Abstr., Sci.Cit.Ind., Weed Abstr. **Document type:** academic/scholarly publication.
—BLDSC (6937.000000); ADONIS; CASDDS; EMDOCS; Genuine Article; Linda Hall; SWETS; UMI; UnCover. **CCC.**
Description: Covers all areas of cell biology.

571.6   US   ISSN 0080-1844
QH607   CODEN: RCLDAT
RESULTS AND PROBLEMS IN CELL DIFFERENTIATION. 1968. irreg., vol.20, 1994. price varies. Springer-Verlag, 175 Fifth Ave., New York, NY 10010. TEL 212-460-1500. FAX 212-473-6272. (Also: Berlin, Heidelberg, Tokyo and Vienna) (reprint service avail. from ISI) **Indexed:** Biol.Abstr., Chem.Abstr., Ind.Med. **Document type:** academic/scholarly publication.
—BLDSC (7780.220000); CASDDS; CISTI; KNAW. **CCC.**

571.658   UK   ISSN 0952-0414
RIBOSOMES AND TRANSLATION. 1970. s-m. (diskette m.). £90 (diskette £120; both £180) (effective 1997). S U B I S, Mansion House, 19 Kingfield Rd., Sheffield S11 9AS, England. TEL 44-114-2554433. FAX 44-114-2554626. E-mail: subis@sheffac.demon.co.uk; URL: http://www.shef.ac.uk/uni/companies/shap. (also avail. in diskette format) **Document type:** abstracting/indexing.
—**CCC.**
Formerly (until 1987): Ribosomes (ISSN 0142-8322)
Description: Current awareness service for researchers in clinical and life sciences.

RINBOKU NO IKUSHU/FOREST TREE BREEDING. see *FORESTS AND FORESTRY*

RUSSIAN JOURNAL OF GENETICS. see *BIOLOGY — Genetics*

SAIBO KOGAKU/CELL TECHNOLOGY. see *BIOLOGY — Biotechnology*

SAIBO KOGAKU, BESSATSU/CELL TECHNOLOGY, SPECIAL ISSUE. see *BIOLOGY — Biotechnology*

571.6   JA
SAIBO SEIBUTSU/CELL BIOLOGY. (Text in Japanese) 1990. bi-m. Nihon Saibo Seibutsu Gakkai - Japan Society for Cell Biology, Ogawa Higashi Iru, Shimodachuri Dori, Kamigyo-ku, Kyoto 602, Japan.

570   UK   ISSN 1084-9521
QH573   CODEN: SCDBFX
SEMINARS IN CELL AND DEVELOPMENTAL BIOLOGY. 1996. bi-m. £66($112) to individuals; institutions £175 (effective 1998). Academic Press Ltd. (Subsidiary of: Harcourt Brace & Company Ltd.), 24-28 Oval Rd., London NW1 7DX, England. TEL 44-171-267-4466. FAX 44-171-482-2293. TELEX 25775 ACPRES G. E-mail: apsubs@acad.com; URL: http://www.hbuk.co.uk/ap/semcell/; http://www.europe.idealibrary.com/. (Subscr. to: Harcourt Brace & Company Ltd., Foots Cray High St. Sidcup, Kent DA14 5HP, England. TEL 44-181-300-3322. FAX 44-181-309-0807) Ed. Alan Colman. R&P contact: Catherine John. adv. contact: Nik Screen. (reprint service avail. from SWZ) **Indexed:** ASCA, Chem.Abstr., Curr.Cont., Ind.Med., Ind.Sci.Rev. **Document type:** academic/scholarly publication.
● Also available online.
—BLDSC (8239.448346); CASDDS; CISTI; Genuine Article; KNAW; Linda Hall; SWETS; UnCover. **CCC.**
Formed by the merger of (1990-1996): Seminars in Cell Biology (ISSN 1043-4682); (1990-1996): Seminars in Developmental Biology (ISSN 1044-5781)
Description: Covers the latest advances in molecular cell biology and developmental biology.
Refereed Serial

SEMINARS IN HEMATOLOGY. see *MEDICAL SCIENCES — Hematology*

SEMINARS IN RESPIRATORY INFECTIONS. see *MEDICAL SCIENCES — Respiratory Diseases*

571.6   JA   ISSN 0915-3896
SHINKEI SOSHIKI NO SEICHO SAISEI ISHOKU/NEURAL GROWTH, REGENERATION AND TRANSPLANTATION. (Text in Japanese) 1989. a. (Shinkei Soshiki no Seicho Saisei Ishoku Kenkyukai - Japanese Society for Neural Growth, Regeneration and Transplantation) Nyuronsha, 21-19-305, Higashigotanda 5-chome, Shinagawa-ku, Tokyo 141, Japan. **Document type:** academic/scholarly publication.

SHOKUBUTSU SOSHIKI SAIBOU BUNSHISEIBUTSU GAKKAI TAIKAI SHINPOJUMU KOEN YOSHISHU/JAPANESE SOCIETY FOR PLANT CELL AND MOLECULAR BIOLOGY. ABSTRACTS OF THE MEETING AND SYMPOSIUM. see *BIOLOGY — Abstracting, Bibliographies, Statistics*

SOMATIC CELL AND MOLECULAR GENETICS. see *BIOLOGY — Genetics*

571.6   JA   ISSN 0912-3636
SOSHIKI BAIYO KENKYU/TISSUE CULTURE RESEARCH COMMUNICATIONS. (Text mainly in English, sometimes in Japanese) 1982. 4/yr. 6000 Yen. Nihon Soshiki Baiyo Gakkai - Japanese Tissue Culture Association, Research Institute for Functional Peptides, 4-3-32 Shimojo-machi, Yamagata-shi, Yamagata-ken 990, Japan. TEL 81-236-46-2525. FAX 81-236-46-2526. Ed. Hiroyoshi Hoshi. circ. 1,200. **Document type:** academic/scholarly publication.
Description: Covers cytology and histology, biological chemistry, biotechnology, genetics, physiology, cell biology and molecular biology.
Refereed Serial

571.6   JA
SOSHIKI SAIBO KAGAKU KOSHUKAI/COURSE TEXT OF HISTOCHEMISTRY AND CYTOCHEMISTRY. (Text in Japanese) 1976. a. 6000 Yen. (Nihon Soshiki Saibo Kagakkai - Japan Society of Histochemistry and Cytochemistry) Gakusai Kikaku K.K., 5-24, Mejiro 2-chome, Toshima-ku, Tokyo 171, Japan.

571.6   UK   ISSN 0040-8166
QH573   CODEN: TICEBI
TISSUE & CELL. 1969. bi-m. £370($555) to institutions (effective 1998). Churchill Livingstone (Subsidiary of: Pearson Professional), Robert Stevenson House, 1-3 Baxter's Pl., Leith Walk, Edinburgh EH1 3AF, Scotland. TEL 44-131-556-2424. FAX 44-131-535-1704. URL: http://www.churchillmed.com. (Subscr. to: Pearson Professional Ltd., P.O. Box 77, Fourth Ave., Harlow, Essex CM19 5BQ, England. TEL 44-1279-623924. FAX 44-1279-639609; U.S. subscr. to: Churchill Livingstone, Box 3217, Secaucus, NJ, 07096-3217. TEL 800-553-5426. FAX 201-319-9659) Ed. L.D. Russell. adv. contact: David Dunnachie. abstr.; charts; illus.; index. circ. 660. (also avail. in microform from UMI) **Indexed:** Apic.Abstr., ASCA, Biol.Abstr., Biol.Dig., Chem.Abstr., Curr.Adv.Ecol.Sci., Curr.Cont., Excerp.Med., Helminthol.Abstr., Ind.Med., Ind.Sci.Rev., Ind.Vet., Protozool.Abstr., Rev.Appl.Entomol., Sci.Cit.Ind., Trop.Dis.Bull., Vet.Bull. **Document type:** academic/scholarly publication.
—BLDSC (8858.680000); CASDDS; CISTI; Genuine Article; KNAW; Linda Hall; SWETS; UMI; UnCover. **CCC.**
Description: Presents research papers on the organization of cells, their components and extracellular products.
Refereed Serial

571.6 610   UK   ISSN 0142-8810
TISSUE CULTURE. 1981. s-m. (diskette m.). £120 (diskette £120; both £180) (effective 1997). S U B I S, Mansion House, 19 Kingfield Rd., Sheffield S11 9AS, England. TEL 44-114-2554433. FAX 44-114-2554626. E-mail: subis@sheffac.demon.co.uk; URL: http://www.shef.ac.uk/uni/companies/shap. (also avail. in diskette format) **Document type:** abstracting/indexing.
—**CCC.**
Description: Current awareness service for researchers. Focuses on animal cells, especially growth factors tested in vitro, cell growth in vitro, organ culture.

571.5   US   ISSN 1076-3279
     CODEN: TIENFP
TISSUE ENGINEERING. 1993. q. $101 to individuals (foreign $141); institutions $241 (foreign $280) (effective through 1998). (Tissue Engineering Society) Mary Ann Liebert, Inc. Publishers, 2 Madison Ave., Larchmont, NY 10538. TEL 914-834-3100. FAX 914-834-3688. E-mail: liebert@pipeline.com. Eds. Charles A. Vacanti, Anthony G. Mikos. **Indexed:** Excerp.Med. **Document type:** academic/scholarly publication.
—CASDDS; CISTI.
Description: Provides information on an interdisciplinary field dedicated to engineering new tissue that applies the principles and methods of engineering and the life sciences toward the fundamental understanding of structure-function relationships in normal and pathologic tissue and th development of biological substitutes.
Refereed Serial

571.6 SZ ISSN 0250-0868
CODEN: IJTEDP
TISSUE REACTIONS. bi-m. 290 SFr. Bioscience Ediprint Inc., Rue Alexandre-Gauard 16, CH-1227 Carouhe-Geneva, Switzerland. TEL 022-3003383. FAX 022-3002489. TELEX 423355-BIOS-CH. Ed. A. Bertelli.
—BLDSC (4542.695600); CASDDS; CISTI; EMDOCS; Genuine Article; KNAW; SWETS; UMI; UnCover. **CCC.**
Description: Contains the results of research on problems related to alterations of physiological origin, either experimentally induced or of a pathogenic nature, which occur at cellular or tissue levels.

TRANSPLANTATION PROCEEDINGS. see *MEDICAL SCIENCES — Surgery*

571.6 UK ISSN 0962-8924
QH573 CODEN: TCBIEK
TRENDS IN CELL BIOLOGY. Library compendium: Trends in Cell Biology (Reference Edition) (ISSN 0968-0039) 1991. m. fl.1349($775) (effective 1998). Elsevier Science Ltd., P.O. Box 800, Kidlington, Oxford OX5 1DX, England. TEL 44-1865-843000. FAX 44-1865-843010. E-mail: nlinfo-f@elsevier.nl; usinfo-f@elsevier.com; forinfo-kyf04035@niftyserve.or.jp; URL: http://www.elsevier.nl/. (Subscr. to: Elsevier Science, Regional Sales Office, P.O. Box 211, 1000 AE Amsterdam, Netherlands. TEL 31-20-4853757. FAX 31-20-4853432; Subscr. in the Americas to: Elsevier Science, Regional Sales Office, Box 945, New York, NY 10159-0945. TEL 212-633-3730. FAX 212-633-3680; Subscr. in Australasia and the Far East to: Elsevier Science (Singapore) Pte Ltd, No.1 Temasek Ave., No.17-01 Millenia Tower, Singapore 039192, Singapore. TEL 65-434-3727. FAX 65-337-2230) Ed. Carolyn Ellis. adv.; bk.rev.; illus.; index. **Indexed:** AIDS Abstr., ASCA, Excerp.Med. (1992-), Ind.Sci.Rev. **Document type:** academic/scholarly publication.
—BLDSC (9049.552000); ADONIS; CASDDS; CISTI; EMDOCS; Genuine Article; SWETS; UnCover. **CCC.**
Description: Provides comprehensive coverage of new research developments, methodologies, and theories in all specializations of cell biology.
Refereed Serial

571.6 UK ISSN 0968-0039
QH573
TRENDS IN CELL BIOLOGY (REFERENCE EDITION). 1991. a. £345($514) includes m. Trends in Cell Biology (effective 1995). Elsevier Science Ltd., P.O. Box 800, Kidlington, Oxford OX5 1DX, England. TEL 44-1865-843000. FAX 44-1865-843010. E-mail: nlinfo-f@elsevier.nl; usinfo-f@elsevier.com; forinfo-kyf04035@niftyserve.or.jp; URL: http://www.elsevier.nl/. (Subscr. to: Elsevier Science, Regional Sales Office, P.O. Box 211, 1000 AE Amsterdam, Netherlands. TEL 31-20-4853757. FAX 31-20-4853432; Subscr. in the Americas to: Elsevier Science, Regional Sales Office, Box 945, New York, NY 10159-0945. TEL 212-633-3730. FAX 212-633-3680; Subscr. in Australasia and the Far East to: Elsevier Science (Singapore) Pte Ltd, No.1 Temasek Ave., No.17-01 Millenia Tower, Singapore 039192, Singapore. TEL 65-434-3727. FAX 65-337-2230) Ed. Carolyn Ellis. (back issues avail.) **Indexed:** Curr.Cont. **Document type:** academic/scholarly publication.
—**CCC.**
Description: Compendium of archival material from Trends in Cell Biology.
Refereed Serial

571.6 RU ISSN 0041-3771
QH573 CODEN: TSITAQ
TSITOLOGIYA/CYTOLOGY. (Text in Russian; summaries and contents page in English) 1959. m. $263 (effective 1998). (Rossiiskaya Akademiya Nauk, S.-Peterburgskoe Otdelenie) Izdatel'stvo Nauka, S.-Peterburgskoe Otdelenie, Mendeleevskaya liniya, 1, 199034 St. Petersburg B-34, Russia. (Dist. in U.S. by: Victor Kamkin Inc., 4956 Boiling Brook Pkwy, Rockville, MD 20852. TEL 301-881-5973) Ed. N.N. Nikolskii; Pub. S.V. Valchuk. adv.: page $100; adv. contact: N.Ya. Shubina. bk.rev.; charts; illus.; index. circ. 600. **Indexed:** Anim.Breed.Abstr., Biol.Abstr., Biotech.Abstr., Chem.Abstr., Curr.Adv.Ecol.Sci., Curr.Cont., Dairy Sci.Abstr., Excerp.Med., Ind.Med., Ind.Vet., Maize Abstr., Plant Breed.Abstr., Protozool.Abstr., Rev.Med.& Vet.Mycol., Sci.Cit.Ind., Triticale Abstr.
—BLDSC (0397.020000); CASDDS; CISTI; Genuine Article; KNAW; Linda Hall. **CCC.**
Refereed Serial

571 US ISSN 0191-3123
RB25 CODEN: ULPAD3
ULTRASTRUCTURAL PATHOLOGY. 1980. bi-m. £399($659) to institutions (effective 1998). Taylor & Francis Inc., 1900 Frost Rd., Ste. 101, Bristol, PA 19007-1598. TEL 215-785-5800; 800-821-8312. FAX 215-785-5515. E-mail: info@tandf.co.uk; URL: http://www.tandf.co.uk/. (Subscr. in Europe to: Taylor & Francis Ltd., Rankine Rd., Basingstoke, Hants. RG24 8PR, England. TEL 44-1256-840366. FAX 44-1256-479438) Eds. Jan Vincents Johannessen, Victor E. Gould. adv.; bk.rev.; abstr.; bibl.; illus.; stat.; index. circ. 750. (also avail. in microform from UMI; back issues avail.; reprint service avail. from UMI) **Indexed:** ASCA, Biol.Abstr., Chem.Abstr., Curr.Adv.Ecol.Sci., Curr.Cont., Dent.Ind., Excerp.Med., Helminthol.Abstr., Ind.Med., Ind.Sci.Rev., Med.& Surg.Dermat., Neurosci.Cit.Ind., Sci.Cit.Ind. **Document type:** academic/scholarly publication.
—BLDSC (9082.816000); ADONIS; CASDDS; CISTI; Genuine Article; KNAW; SWETS; UnCover. **CCC.**
Description: Covers electron microscopy, immunohistochemistry, the study and diagnosis of human diseases, EM and oncology, theory, and possible applications.
Refereed Serial

571.6 CC ISSN 0253-9977
QH573 CODEN: XISZD3
XIBAO SHENGWUXUE ZAZHI. English edition: Journal of Cytology. (Text in Chinese) 1979. q. (English ed. s-a.). $4 (effective 1997). Zhongguo Kexueyuan, Shanghai Xibao Shengwu Yanjiusuo - Chinese Academy of Sciences, Shanghai Institute of Cytology, 320 Yueyang Lu, Shanghai 200031, People's Republic of China. TEL 315030. Ed. Jiake Tso. **Document type:** academic/scholarly publication.
—CASDDS.

BIOLOGY — Entomology

see also Agriculture–Crop Production and Soil; Engineering–Chemical Engineering

595.1 US
A M C A NEWSLETTER. 1976. q. membership. American Mosquito Control Association, Box 5416, Lake Charles, LA 70606-5416. TEL 318-474-2723. FAX 318-478-9434. Ed. Dr. Jimmie D. Long. adv. circ. 1,600. **Document type:** newsletter.
Formerly: A M C A Vector Review (ISSN 0195-4180)
Description: Helps members keep informed about association-related activities.

595.7 IT ISSN 0065-0757
ACCADEMIA NAZIONALE ITALIANA DI ENTOMOLOGIA. RENDICONTI. 1952. irreg., vol.43, 1995. price varies. Accademia Nazionale Italiana di Entomologia, Via Lanciola, 12-A, Cascine del Riccio, 50125 Florence, Italy. TEL 39-55-209182.

595.7 FR ISSN 0300-4686
CODEN: ACRDCA
ACRIDA. Issued with Acridological Abstracts. (Text and summaries in English, French and Spanish) 1972. q. 420 F.($105) Association d'Acridologie, 105 Bd. Raspail, 75006 Paris, France. Ed. Frederic O. Albrecht. adv.; bk.rev.; charts; illus. circ. 500. (back issues avail.) **Indexed:** Biol.Abstr., Bull.Signal., Curr.Cont., Entomol.Abstr., Helminthol.Abstr., Ind.Sci.Rev., Rev.Appl.Entomol.
—Linda Hall.

595.7 XR ISSN 0374-1036
CODEN: AEMPBY
ACTA ENTOMOLOGICA. (Supplement avail.: Acta Entomologica. Supplementum (ISSN 0231-8571)) (Text in English, French and German) 1923. irreg. price varies. Narodni Muzeum, Prirodovedecke Muzeum, Vaclavske nam. 68, 115 79 Prague 1, Czech Republic. FAX 42-2-24226488. Ed. Josef Jelinek. **Document type:** academic/scholarly publication.
—Linda Hall.

595.7 CL ISSN 0716-5072
CODEN: AECHEV
ACTA ENTOMOLOGICA CHILENA. 1986. a. $30 (effective 1997-98). Universidad Metropolitana de Ciencias de la Educacion, Instituto de Entomologia, Casilla 147, Santiago, Chile. FAX 56-2-2392067. Ed. Jaime Solervicens A. bk.rev. circ. 350. **Indexed:** Apic.Abstr.
—BLDSC (0614.950000).
Supersedes (1960-1974): Centro de Estudios Entomologicos. Publicaciones (ISSN 0376-2106)
Refereed Serial

595.7 XR ISSN 0554-9264
CODEN: AFAEBG
ACTA FAUNISTICA ENTOMOLOGICA. (Supplement avail.: Acta Faunistica Entomologica. Supplementum (ISSN 0551-7931)) (Text in English, German and Russian) 1956. irreg. price varies. Narodni Muzeum, Prirodovedecke Muzeum, Vaclavske nam. 68, 115 79 Prague 1, Czech Republic. FAX 42-2-24226488. Ed. Josef Jelinek. **Indexed:** Biol.Abstr., Curr.Adv.Ecol.Sci., Rev.Appl.Entomol. **Document type:** academic/scholarly publication.
—Linda Hall.

595.7 US ISSN 0065-2806
QL495 CODEN: AIPYAZ
ADVANCES IN INSECT PHYSIOLOGY. 1963. irreg., vol.26, 1996. Academic Press, Inc., 525 B St., Ste. 1900, San Diego, CA 92101-4495. TEL 619-231-0926. FAX 619-699-6715. (Subscr. to: Order Dept., 6277 Sea Harbor Dr., 4th Fl., Orlando, FL 32887. TEL 800-321-5068) Ed.Bd. (reprint service avail. from ISI) **Indexed:** Abstr.Hyg., ASCA, Biol.Abstr., Biol.& Agr.Ind., Chem.Abstr., Curr.Adv.Cell & Devel.Biol., Curr.Adv.Ecol.Sci., Ind.Sci.Rev., Rev.Appl.Entomol., Sci.Cit.Ind., Trop.Dis.Bull.
—BLDSC (0709.230000); CASDDS; CISTI; KR SourceOne; UnCover. **CCC.**
Refereed Serial

595.7 SA ISSN 1021-3589
QL461 CODEN: AFREE2
AFRICAN ENTOMOLOGY. (Text and summaries in Afrikaans, English) 1937; N.S. 1993. s-a. $85 to institutions (includes all Society publications) (effective 1996 & 1997). Entomological Society of Southern Africa, P.O. Box 103, Pretoria 0001, South Africa. TEL 27-12-2062623. Ed. M. Mansell. R&P contact: M. Mansell. bk.rev.; charts; illus.; index. circ. 600. (back issues avail.) **Indexed:** Apic.Abstr., ASCA, Bio-Contr.News & Info., Biol.Abstr., Curr.Adv.Ecol.Sci., Curr.Cont., Entomol.Abstr., Forest.Abstr., IBR, Ind.S.A.Per., Rev.Appl.Entomol., Triticale Abstr., Weed Abstr., Zoo.Rec. **Document type:** academic/scholarly publication.
—BLDSC (0732.438700); CISTI; EMDOCS; Genuine Article; Linda Hall; UMI; UnCover.
Formerly: Entomological Society of Southern Africa. Journal (ISSN 0013-8789)
Description: Publishes articles on African entomology and arachnology.

AFRICAN JOURNAL OF PLANT PROTECTION/REVUE AFRICAINE DE LA PROTECTION DES VEGETAUX. see *AGRICULTURE — Crop Production And Soil*

BIOLOGY — ENTOMOLOGY

595.7 JA ISSN 0389-2751
AKITU/KYOTO ENTOMOLOGICAL SOCIETY. JOURNAL. (Text in English) 1974. a. membership. Kyoto Konchu Gakkai - Kyoto Entomological Society, Kyoto Furitsu Daigaku Konchugaku Kenkyushitsu, 1-5 Shimogamo Hangicho, Sakyo-ku, Kyoto 606, Japan.

595.7 US ISSN 0065-6143
ALDRICH ENTOMOLOGY CLUB. NEWSLETTER. 1962. irreg., vol.17, 1997. free. University of Idaho, Department of Entomology, Moscow, ID 83843. TEL 208-885-6276. FAX 208-885-7760. Ed. James Johnson. circ. 250. **Document type:** newsletter.
   Description: Reports current research activities of the faculty, staff, students & alumni of the club.

595.78 FR ISSN 0002-5208
    CODEN: ALEXBX
ALEXANOR; revue francaise de lepidopterologie. 1959. q. 250 F. (foreign 260 F.) (effective Jan. 1997). Alexanor, 45 rue de Buffon, 75005 Paris, France. TEL 33-1-40793412. Ed. G.C. Luquet. adv.; bk.rev.; abstr.; charts; illus.; index every 2 yrs. circ. 1,000. **Indexed:** Biol.Abstr., Bull.Signal., Entomol.Abstr., Zoo.Rec.

595.7 UK ISSN 0266-8351
THE AMATEUR ENTOMOLOGIST. 1939. irreg., no.23. price varies. Amateur Entomologists' Society, P.O. Box 8774, London SW7 5ZG, England. (Subscr. to: A.E.S. Publications, The Hawthorns, Frating Road, Great Bromley, Colchester, Essex CO7 7JN, England) (back issues avail.) **Document type:** monographic series.
   —BLDSC (0807.000000).
   Description: Publishes handbooks and papers of interest to nonprofessional entomologists.

595.7 UK ISSN 0266-836X
AMATEUR ENTOMOLOGISTS' SOCIETY. BULLETIN. 1935. bi-m. £10 membership (overseas £12). Amateur Entomologists' Society, P.O. Box 8774, London SW7 5ZG, England. E-mail: Jarvisw@bbsrc.ac.uk. (Subscr to: A.E.S. Registrar, P.O. Box 0776, London SW7 5ZG; back issues from: A.E.S. Publications, The Hawthorns, Frating Rd., Great Bromley, Colchester, Essex CO7 7JN, England) Ed. Wayne Jarvis. adv.; bk.rev.; index. circ. 2,000. (back issues avail.) **Document type:** bulletin.
   —BLDSC (2385.000000).
   Description: Contains articles and notes on entomology and covers society activities and announcements.

595.7 UK
AMATEUR ENTOMOLOGISTS' SOCIETY. LEAFLETS. irreg., no.37. price varies. Amateur Entomologists' Society, P.O. Box 8774, London SW7 5ZG, England. (Orders to: A.E.S. Publications, The Hawthorns, Frating Rd., Great Bromley, Colchester, Essex CO7 7JN, England) (back issues avail.) **Document type:** monographic series.
   Description: Informs persons interested in studying and collecting insects.

595.7 UK
AMATEUR ENTOMOLOGISTS' SOCIETY. PAMPHLETS. irreg., no.14, 1993. price varies. Amateur Entomologists' Society, P.O. Box 8774, London SW7 5ZG, England. (Orders to: A.E.S. Publications, The Hawthorns, Great Bromley, Colchester, Essex CO7 7JN, England) (back issues avail.) **Document type:** monographic series.
   Description: Contains information of interest to persons who like to study insects.

595.7 US ISSN 0065-8170
QL461 CODEN: AESMAK
AMERICAN ENTOMOLOGICAL SOCIETY. MEMOIRS. 1916. irreg., no.42, 1994. price varies. American Entomological Society, Academy of Natural Sciences, 1900 Benjamin Franklin Pkwy., Philadelphia, PA 19103-1195. TEL 215-561-3978. FAX 215-299-1028. E-mail: AES@say.acnatsci.org. index. **Indexed:** Biol.Abstr. **Document type:** academic/scholarly publication.
   —Linda Hall.

595.7 US ISSN 0002-8320
QL461
AMERICAN ENTOMOLOGICAL SOCIETY. TRANSACTIONS. 1867. q. $20 to institutions & libraries (foreign $22) (effective 1998). American Entomological Society, Academy of Natural Sciences, 1900 Benjamin Franklin Pkwy., Philadelphia, PA 19103-1195. TEL 215-561-3978. FAX 215-299-1028. E-mail: AES@say.acnatsci.org. Ed. D. Otte. R&P contact: Daniel Otte. bibl.; illus.; index. (also avail. in microform from UMI; microfiche from IDC; reprint service avail. from UMI) **Indexed:** ASCA, Biol.Abstr., Curr.Adv.Ecol.Sci., GeoRef., Rev.Appl.Entomol. **Document type:** academic/scholarly publication.
   —BLDSC (8886.600000); CISTI; Genuine Article; Linda Hall; SWETS; UMI; UnCover.

595.7 US ISSN 1046-2821
QL461 CODEN: AENUEN
AMERICAN ENTOMOLOGIST; entomological articles of general interest. 1955. q. $30 to individuals (foreign $42); institutions $55 (foreign $67); members $15. Entomological Society of America, 9301 Annapolis Rd., Lanham, MD 20706. TEL 301-731-4535. FAX 301-731-4538. (Subscr. to: Box 17, Hyattsville, MD 20781-0177) Ed. J.E. McPherson. adv.; bk.rev.; index. circ. 5,500. (also avail. in microform from UMI) **Indexed:** Bio-Contr.News & Info., Biol.Abstr., Chem.Abstr., Forest.Abstr., Potato Abstr., Rev.Appl.Entomol., Triticale Abstr., Weed Abstr.
   —BLDSC (0813.940100); CISTI; Linda Hall; SWETS; UMI; UnCover. **CCC.**
   Formerly (until 1990): Entomological Society of America. Bulletin (ISSN 0013-8754)
   Description: Entomological articles of general interest.

595.7 US ISSN 8756-971X
RA640 CODEN: JAMAET
AMERICAN MOSQUITO CONTROL ASSOCIATION. JOURNAL. (Supplement avail. (ISSN 1046-3607)) 1940. q. $50 to individuals; institutions $85. American Mosquito Control Association, Box 5416, Lake Charles, LA 70606. TEL 318-474-2723. FAX 318-478-9434. Ed. Dr. Ronald A. Ward. adv.; bk.rev.; abstr.; bibl.; charts; illus.; index. circ. 2,000. (also avail. in microform from PMC) **Indexed:** Abstr.Hyg., ASCA, Biol.Abstr., Biotech.Abstr., Chem.Abstr., Curr.Adv.Ecol.Sci., Curr.Cont., Geo.Abstr., Helminthol.Abstr., Ind.Sci.Rev., Ind.Vet., Protozool.Abstr., Rev.Appl.Entomol., Rice Abstr., Sel.Water Res.Abstr., So.Pac.Per.Ind., Sport Fish.Abstr., Trop.Dis.Bull., Vet.Bull., Wild.Rev., Zoo.Rec.
   —BLDSC (4689.125000); CASDDS; CISTI; Genuine Article; Linda Hall; SWETS; UMI; UnCover. **CCC.**
   Incorporates (1969-1995): Mosquito Systematics (ISSN 0091-3669); **Supersedes** (in 1985): Mosquito News (ISSN 0027-142X)
   Description: Provides information on the biology and control of mosquitoes and other vectors which affect the health of man and animals; the prevention of vector-borne disease and protection of human and animal health, with concern toward protection of the environment.
   Refereed Serial

595.7 JA ISSN 0288-4402
AMICA. (Text in Japanese) 1953. irreg. membership. Toyamaken Konchu Dokokai - Entomological Society of Toyama Prefecture, c/o Mr. Toru Mizuno, Akada, Unazukimachi, Shimoniikawa-gun, Toyama-ken 938-02, Japan.

595.7 II ISSN 0970-3721
ANNALS OF ENTOMOLOGY. (Text in English) 1983. s-a. $300. Hindustan Publishing Corp., 4805-24, 1st Fl., Bharat Ram Rd., Darya Ganj, New Delhi 110 002, India. TEL 91-11-3254401. FAX 91-11-6863511. E-mail: hpcpd@giasdl01.vsnl.net.in.

595.7 591 FR ISSN 0990-0063
ANNUAIRE DES ARACHNOLOGISTES MONDIAUX; acarologistes exceptes. 1968. triennial. 150 F. Centre International de Documentation Arachnologique, 61 rue de Buffon, 75005 Paris, France. FAX 40-79-38-63. E-mail: arachne@mnhn.fr. Ed. Jacqueline Heurtault. **Document type:** directory.

595.7 US ISSN 0066-4170
QL461 CODEN: ARENAA
ANNUAL REVIEW OF ENTOMOLOGY. 1956. a. $60 to individuals (foreign $65); institutions $120 (foreign $130) (effective 1998). Annual Reviews Inc., 4139 El Camino Way, Box 10139, Palo Alto, CA 94303-0139. TEL 650-493-4400; 800-523-8635. FAX 650-424-0910. E-mail: service@annurev.org; URL: http://www.annurev.org. Ed. May Berenbaum. R&P contact: Jeanne Kunz. bibl.; index; cum.index every 5 yrs. (also avail. in microfilm from UMI; back issues avail.; reprint service avail.) **Indexed:** Abstr.Hyg., Apic.Abstr., ASCA, Bibl.Agri., Biol.Abstr., Biol.& Agr.Ind., Biotech.Abstr., Chem.Abstr., Curr.Adv.Ecol.Sci., Curr.Cont., Environ.Abstr., Excerp.Med., Forest.Abstr., Helminthol.Abstr., Hort.Abstr., Ind.Med., Ind.Sci.Rev. M.M.R.I., Plant Breed.Abstr., Rev.Appl.Entomol., Rev.Plant Path., Sci.Cit.Ind., Soils & Fert., Trop.Dis.Bull., VITIS, Weed Abstr. **Document type:** academic/scholarly publication.
   —BLDSC (1522.500000); CASDDS; CISTI; Genuine Article; KR SourceOne; Linda Hall; SWETS; UMI; UnCover. **CCC.**
   Description: Original critical reviews of the significant primary literature and current developments in entomology.

595.7 UK ISSN 0140-1890
QL461
ANTENNA. 1976. q. £22.50 (outside Europe £23.50) (effective 1996). Royal Entomological Society, 41 Queen's Gate, London SW7 5HR, England. TEL 44-171-584-8361. FAX 44-171-581-8505. E-mail: royenson@demon.co.uk; URL: http://www.demon.co.uk/royensoc. **Indexed:** Bio-Contr.News & Info., Rev.Appl.Entomol. **Document type:** proceedings
   —BLDSC (1542.200000); Linda Hall; UnCover.
   Supersedes: Royal Entomological Society of London. Proceedings (ISSN 0080-4355)

595.7 614.7 GW ISSN 0340-7330
SB599 CODEN: ASUMDT
ANZEIGER FUER SCHAEDLINGSKUNDE, PFLANZENSCHUTZ, UMWELTSCHUTZ. (Text in German; summaries in English and German) 1925 8/yr. DM.438 in Europe; rest of world DM.462 (effective 1998). Blackwell Wissenschaft, Kurfuerstendamm 57, 10707 Berlin, Germany. TEL 49-30-32790634. TELEX 49-30-32790610. E-mail: aboverwalt@blackwis.de; URL: http://www.blackwis.com. Ed. W. Schwenke. adv.; bk.rev.; abstr. illus.; stat.; index. (back issues avail.) **Indexed:** Apic.Abstr., ASCA, Bio-Contr.News & Info., Biodet.Abstr., Biol.Abstr., Biotech.Abstr., Chem.Abstr. Curr.Adv.Ecol.Sci., Curr.Cont., Excerp.Med., Field Crop Abstr., Forest.Abstr., Forest Prod.Abstr., Helminthol.Abstr., Herb.Abstr., Hort.Abstr., Key Word Ind.Wildl.Res., Maize Abstr., Rev.Appl.Entomol., Sorghum & Millets Abstr., Triticale Abstr., Weed Abstr. **Document type:** academic/scholarly publication.
   —BLDSC (1567.651200); CASDDS; CISTI; Genuine Article; Linda Hall; SWETS; UnCover. **CCC.**
   Former titles: Anzeiger fuer Schaedlingskunde, Pflanzen- und Umweltschutz (ISSN 0340-7322); Anzeiger fuer Schaedlingskunde und Pflanzenschutz (ISSN 0003-6307)

L'APICOLTORE MODERNO. see *AGRICULTURE*

BIOLOGY — ENTOMOLOGY

595.7   FR   ISSN 0044-8435
CODEN: APDGB5
APIDOLOGIE. (Text mainly in English; summaries in English, French, German) 1970. bi-m. 1352 F. to institutions (US $259; outside the Americas 1620F) (effective 1998). (Institut National de la Recherche Agronomique) Editions Scientifiques et Medicales Elsevier, 141 rue de Javel, 75747 Paris, France. TEL 33-1-45589022. URL: http://www.elsevier.nl/. (Subscr. in U.S. and Canada to: Elsevier Science Inc., Box 945, Madison Sq. Sta., New York, NY 10159-0945. TEL 212-633-3730. FAX 212-633-3680) Ed.Bd. bk.rev. circ. 2,000. (also avail. in microform from UMI; reprint service avail. from ISI) **Indexed:** Apic.Abstr., ASCA, Bibl.Agri., Biol.Abstr., Chem.Abstr., Curr.Adv.Ecol.Sci., Curr.Cont., Ecol.Abstr., Entomol.Abstr., Excerp.Med., Helminthol.Abstr., Hort.Abstr., Ind.Sci.Rev., Neurosci.Cit.Ind., Sci.Cit.Ind., Sugar Ind.Abstr. **Document type:** academic/scholarly publication.
—BLDSC (1568.563000); CASDDS; EMDOCS; Genuine Article; Linda Hall; SWETS. **CCC**.
    Formed by the merger of (1958-1970): Annales de l'Abeille (ISSN 0570-1597); (1950-1970): Zeitschrift fuer Bienenforschung (ISSN 0044-2399)
    Description: Studies bee behavior, bee-plant interactions, pollination, bee genetics and pathology.
Refereed Serial

595.7   IR
APPLIED ENTOMOLOGY AND PHYTOPATHOLOGY/AFAT VA BIMARIHAY GIYAHI. (Text in Persian; summaries in English) 1946. q. free. Plant Pests and Diseases Research Institute - Mu'assasah Tahqiqat Afat va Bimarihay Giyahi, P.O. Box 1454, Tehran 19395, Iran. TEL 98-21-2403012. Ed. Dr. Ebrahim Behdad. charts; illus.; stat. circ. 1,200. **Indexed:** Biol.Abstr., Chem.Abstr., Ecol.Abstr., Rev.Appl.Entomol., Rev.Plant Path., Rice Abstr., Soils & Fert., Zoo.Rec. **Document type:** academic/scholarly publication.
—BLDSC (1572.380000).
    Formerly (until 1990): Entomologie et Phytopathologie Appliquees (ISSN 0013-8800)
    Description: Publishes original research reports and short communications on insect pests, pesticides, and related topics.
Refereed Serial

595.7 591   JA   ISSN 0003-6862
QL461   CODEN: APEZAW
APPLIED ENTOMOLOGY AND ZOOLOGY. (Text in English) 1966. q. $50. Japanese Society of Applied Entomology and Zoology - Nihon Oyo Dobutsu Konchu Gakkai, c/o Japan Plant Protection Association, 1-43-11 Komagome, Toshima-ku, Tokyo 170, Japan. TEL 81-3-3943-6021. FAX 81-3-3943-6021. (Dist. by: Japan Publication Trading Co. Ltd., P.O. Box 5030, Tokyo International, Tokyo 100-31, Japan) Ed. Masakazu Shiga. R&P contact: Masakazu Shiga. adv. contact: Yoshiaki Kono. bk.rev.; charts; illus. circ. 1,900. **Indexed:** ASCA, Bio-Contr.News & Info., Biodet.Abstr., Biol.Abstr., Biotech.Abstr., Chem.Abstr., Cott.& Trop.Fibr.Abstr., Curr.Adv.Cell & Devel.Biol., Curr.Adv.Ecol.Sci., Curr.Cont., Entomol.Abstr., Forest.Abstr., Helminthol.Abstr., Hort.Abstr., Ind.Sci.Rev., INIS Atomind., Maize Abstr., Protozool.Abstr., Rev.Appl.Entomol., Rice Abstr., Sci.Cit.Ind., Seed Abstr., Sorghum & Millets Abstr. **Document type:** academic/scholarly publication.
—BLDSC (1572.400000); CASDDS; Genuine Article; Linda Hall; SWETS; UnCover.

595.7   NE   ISSN 0165-0424
CODEN: AQINDQ
AQUATIC INSECTS; international journal of freshwater entomology. (Text in English) 1979. q. fl.328($199) to individuals; institutions fl.454($275) (effective 1997). Swets & Zeitlinger bv, P.O. Box 825, 2160 SZ Lisse, Netherlands. TEL 31-252-435111. FAX 31-252-415888. TELEX 41325. E-mail: orders@swets.nl; URL: http://www.swets.nl/. (Dist. in N. America by: Swets & Zeitlinger, Box 613, Royersford, PA 19468. TEL 800-447-9387. FAX 610-524-5366) Ed. P. Zwick. R&P contact: J.v.d. Valk. adv. contact: Patrick Kleian. (reprint service avail. from SWZ) **Indexed:** Abstr.Bull.Inst.Pap.Chem., ASCA, Biol.Abstr., Curr.Adv.Ecol.Sci., Curr.Cont., Ecol.Abstr., Geo.Abstr., Ind.Sci.Rev., Int.Abstr.Biol.Sci., Rev.Appl.Entomol., Sci.Cit.Ind., So.Pac.Per.Ind. **Document type:** academic/scholarly publication.
—BLDSC (1582.386000); CISTI; Genuine Article; Linda Hall; SWETS; UnCover. **CCC**.

595.7   FR   ISSN 0763-1901
ARACHNOLOGIA - BULLETIN D'INFORMATION ET DE LIAISON DU C I D A. Key Title: Arachnologia. 1984. a. 40 F.($7) Centre International de Documentation Arachnologique, 61 rue de Buffon, 75005 Paris, France. FAX 40-79-38-63. E-mail: arachne@mnhn.fr. **Document type:** bulletin.
    Formerly: Centre International de Documentation Arachnologique. Bulletin d'Information et de Liaison.

595.7 576 591   TU
ARASTIRMA ESERLERI SERISI.* (Text in Turkish; summaries in English, French or German) 1952. irreg. free. Ministry of Agriculture, Forest and Rural Affairs, Regional Plant Protection Research Institute, Fatih Caddesi 37, Kalaba, Ankara, Turkey. index. circ. 600. (back issues avail.) **Indexed:** Biol.Abstr.

595.7   AU   ISSN 0375-5223
CODEN: ZAOEAJ
ARBEITSGEMEINSCHAFT OESTERREICHISCHER ENTOMOLOGEN. ZEITSCHRIFT. (Supplement avail.: Entomologisches Nachrichtenblatt) 1949. q. S.540. Arbeitsgemeinschaft Oesterreichischer Entomologen, Ludo-Hartmann-Platz 7, A-1160 Vienna, Austria. Ed. Friedrich Weisert. adv. contact: Alexander Dostal. bk.rev.; bibl.; illus. **Indexed:** Biol.Abstr. **Document type:** academic/scholarly publication.

595.7   US   ISSN 0739-4462
QL495   CODEN: AIBPEA
ARCHIVES OF INSECT BIOCHEMISTRY AND PHYSIOLOGY. 1983. m. $1550 (foreign $1760) (effective 1998). (Entomological Society of America) John Wiley & Sons, Inc., Journals, 605 Third Ave., New York, NY 10158. TEL 212-850-6645. FAX 212-850-6021. TELEX 12-7063. E-mail: SUBINFO@JWILEY.COM; URL: http://www.wiley.co.uk. (Subscr. outside the Americas to: John Wiley & Sons Ltd., Baffins Ln., Chichester, W. Sussex PO19 1UD, England. TEL 44-1243-779777. FAX 44-1243-776128) Ed. A. Krishna Kumaran. adv.: B&W page £640, color page £1515; trim 254 x 174. (also avail. in microform from UMI; back issues avail.) **Indexed:** ASCA, Bibl.Agri., Biol.Abstr., Chem.Abstr., Chem.Cit.Ind., Curr.Adv.Ecol.Sci., Curr.Cont., Ind.Sci.Rev., Neurosci.Cit.Ind., Potato Abstr., Sci.Cit.Ind. **Document type:** academic/scholarly publication.
—BLDSC (1634.650000); CASDDS; CISTI; Genuine Article; Linda Hall; SWETS; UnCover. **CCC**.
    Description: Provides an international forum for scientists interested in the field of insect biochemistry and physiology.
Refereed Serial

595.7   JA
ARI/MYRMECOLOGICAL SOCIETY OF JAPAN. JOURNAL. (Text in Japanese; summaries in English) 1965. a. 1000 Yen membership. Nihon Arirui Kenkyukai - Myrmecological Society of Japan, c/o Shiraume Gakuen Tanki Daigaku, 1-830, Ogawa-cho, Kodaira-shi, Tokyo 187, Japan. TEL 81-423-42-2311. Ed. Fuminori Ito; Pub. Masao Kubota. circ. 140 (controlled). **Document type:** proceedings.

595.7   US
SB951.5
ARTHROPOD MANAGEMENT TESTS. 1976. a. $40 to individuals (foreign $45); institutions $45 (foreign $50); members $25 (foreign $30). Entomological Society of America, 9301 Annapolis Rd., Lanham, MD 20706. TEL 301-731-4535. FAX 301-731-4538. (Subscr. to: Box 177, Hyattsville, MD 20781-0177) Ed. A.K. Burditt. **Indexed:** Rev.Appl.Entomol.
—BLDSC (1733.893500); Linda Hall. **CCC**.
    Formerly (until 1995): Insecticide and Acaricide Tests (ISSN 0276-3656)
    Description: Presents the results of field and laboratory screenings performed with agricultural chemicals on a variety of crops.
Refereed Serial

595.2   US   ISSN 0066-8036
QL434   CODEN: AFNLAX
ARTHROPODS OF FLORIDA AND NEIGHBORING LAND AREAS. 1965. irreg., vol.15, 1993. price varies. Department of Agriculture and Consumer Services, Division of Plant Industry, 1911 S.W. 34th St., Box 147100, Gainesville, FL 32614-7100. TEL 904-372-3505. FAX 904-955-2301. Ed. J.B. Heppner. R&P contact: Maeve McConnell. (back issues avail.) **Indexed:** Bibl.Agri., Biol.Abstr., Zoo.Rec. **Document type:** catalog, government publication.
Refereed Serial

595.7   JA   ISSN 0910-5123
ARUBO/ALBO. (Text in Japanese) s-a. membership. Kagoshima Konchu Dokokai - Kagoshima Entomological Society, Sameshima Hifuka, 8-8 Komatsubara 1-chome, Kagoshima-shi, Kagoshima-ken 891-01, Japan.

595.7   SP   ISSN 0210-8984
QL482.S8   CODEN: BAEEDE
ASOCIACION ESPANOLA DE ENTOMOLOGIA. BOLETIN. (Text in Spanish; abstracts in English, Spanish) 1978. s-a. 7500 ptas. Asociacion Espanola de Entomologia, Fac. de Ciencias Biologicas, Univ. de Valencia, 46100 Burjasot, Spain. TEL 34-6-3864680. Ed. Jose Antonio Barrientos Alfageme. R&P contact: Ricardo Jimenez Peydro. adv. contact: Joaquin Baixeras. bk.rev.; bibl.; charts; illus. **Indexed:** IBR, Ind.SST. **Document type:** bulletin.
Refereed Serial

595.7   IT   ISSN 0004-6000
CODEN: BRETA5
ASSOCIAZIONE ROMANA DI ENTOMOLOGIA. BOLLETTINO. 1946. q. L.40000 (effective 1997). Associazione Romana di Entomologia, c/o Museo Civico di Zoologia, Via Ulisse Aldrovandi, 18, 00197 Rome, Italy. E-mail: aletardi@casaccia.enea.it. Ed. Augusto Vigna Taglianti. R&P contact: Flavia Pinzari. bk.rev.; bibl.; charts; illus.; index. circ. 800. **Indexed:** Biol.Abstr. **Document type:** bulletin.
    Description: Presents entomological papers, mainly about central and southern Italy.
Refereed Serial

595.7   GW   ISSN 0171-0079
CODEN: ATLNDS
ATALANTA. (Text in English, German) 1964. s-a. DM.60. Deutsche Forschungszentrale fuer Schmetterlingswanderungen, Humboldtstr. 13A, 95168 Marktleuthen, Germany. TEL 49-9285-480. FAX 49-9285-8238. Ed. Ulf Eitschberger. adv.; bk.rev.; index. circ. 1,200. (back issues avail.) **Indexed:** Curr.Adv.Ecol.Sci., IBR. **Document type:** academic/scholarly publication.
—Linda Hall.

595.7   AT   ISSN 0004-9050
QL487   CODEN: AESJBC
AUSTRALIAN ENTOMOLOGICAL SOCIETY. JOURNAL. 1962. q. Aus.$90 (foreign Aus.$105). Australian Entomological Society, c/o Entomology Branch, Department of Primary Industries, Meiers Rd., Indooroopilly, Qld. 4068, Australia. Ed. P.G. Allsopp. adv.; bk.rev.; charts; illus.; index. **Indexed:** ASCA, Biol.Abstr., Biotech.Abstr., Chem.Abstr., Curr.Adv.Ecol.Sci., Curr.Cont., Entomol.Abstr., Forest.Abstr., Helminthol.Abstr., Ind.Sci.Rev., Ind.Vet., Protozool.Abstr., Rev.Appl.Entomol., So.Pac.Per.Ind., Vet.Bull., Weed Abstr.
—BLDSC (1807.640000); CASDDS; CISTI; Genuine Article; Linda Hall; UnCover.

595.7   AT   ISSN 0374-5147
AUSTRALIAN ENTOMOLOGICAL SOCIETY. MISCELLANEOUS PUBLICATIONS. irreg. price varies. Australian Entomological Society, c/o Entomology Branch, Department of Primary Industries, Meiers Rd., Indooroopilly, Qld. 4068, Australia. **Indexed:** Apic.Abstr., Biol.Abstr.

595.7   AT
AUSTRALIAN ENTOMOLOGICAL SOCIETY. NEWS BULLETIN. 1965. q. Aus.$10 (foreign Aus.$15). Australian Entomological Society, c/o Entomology Branch, Dept. of Primary Industries, Meiers Rd., Indooroopilly, Qld. 4068, Australia. Ed. G.B. Monteith.

595.7   AT   ISSN 1320-6133
CODEN: AUENEZ
AUSTRALIAN ENTOMOLOGIST. 1972. q. Aus.$16 to individuals (foreign Aus.$20); institutions Aus.$20 (foreign Aus.$22). Entomological Society of Queensland, P.O. Box 537, Indooroopilly, Qld. 4068, Australia. E-mail: a.loch@mailbox.uq.edu.au. Ed. D. Hancock. R&P contact: A. Loch. adv. contact: A. Loch. bk.rev.; circ. 500 (controlled). **Indexed:** Biol.Abstr., Curr.Cont., Entomol.Abstr. **Document type:** academic/scholarly publication.
—Linda Hall; UnCover.
    Formerly: Australian Entomological Magazine (ISSN 0311-1881)
    Description: Devoted to the natural history and systematics of the native insect and related arthropod fauna of the Australian region, including the islands of the South West Pacific.
Refereed Serial

BIOLOGY — ENTOMOLOGY

595.7   CC   ISSN 1001-1285
BAIYI KEJI. (Text in Chinese) 1984. q. $8. Zhongguo Baiyi Fangzhi Yanjiuhui - China Termite Prevention Science and Technology Cooperation Center, No. 693, Moganshan Lu, Hangzhou, Zhejiang 310011, People's Republic of China. TEL 86-571-8071061. FAX 86-571-5151540. Ed. Shuqing Lin. R&P contact: Weiying Xu. bk.rev. circ. 1,200.
   Refereed Serial

595.7   UK   ISSN 0265-8690
BEEKEEPER'S ANNUAL. 1982. a. Northern Bee Books, Scout Bottom Farm, Mytholmroyd, Hebden Bridge, W. Yorks HX7 5JS, England. TEL 01422-882751. FAX 01422-886157. **Document type:** bulletin.

595.7   UK   ISSN 0268-4780
THE BEEKEEPER'S QUARTERLY. 1984. q. £12. Northern Bee Books, Scout Bottom Farm, Mytholmroyd, Hebden Bridge, W. Yorks HX7 5JS, England. TEL 01422-882751. FAX 01422-886157. Ed. John Phipps. adv.: page £175; trim 283 x 195; adv. contact: Jeremy Burbridge. bk.rev.; circ. 2,600 (paid). (back issues avail.) **Document type:** newsletter.

595.7   GW   ISSN 0005-805X
QL461   **CODEN: BEIEAP**
BEITRAEGE ZUR ENTOMOLOGIE/CONTRIBUTIONS TO ENTOMOLOGY. (Text in English, German) 1951. s-a. DM.295 (foreign DM.305) (effective 1997). (Deutsches Entomologisches Institut) Akademie Verlag GmbH, Muehlenstr. 33-34, 13187 Berlin, Germany. TEL 49-30-47889348. FAX 49-30-47889357. E-mail: info@akademie-verlag.de. (Subscr. in the Americas to: John Wiley & Sons, Inc., 605 Third Ave., New York, NY 10158. TEL 212-850-6645. FAX 212-850-6021) Ed. J. Oehlke. bk.rev.; charts; illus.; index. **Indexed:** Biol.Abstr., Chem.Abstr., Hort.Abstr., Rev.Appl.Entomol., Soils & Fert. **Document type:** academic/scholarly publication.
   —BLDSC (1879.000000); CISTI; UnCover.

BIOCONTROL SCIENCE AND TECHNOLOGY. see *AGRICULTURE — Crop Production And Soil*

595.7   GW   ISSN 0179-5295
                     CODEN: BIZEE6
BIOLOGISCHE ZEITSCHRIFT. 1986. irreg. price varies. Research and Consulting Institute, Lister Weg 40, 22117 Hamburg, Germany. Ed. R. Sergel. adv.; bk.rev. **Indexed:** Arts & Hum.Cit.Ind., Zoo.Rec. (until 19??).

595.7   US   ISSN 0893-3146
BISHOP MUSEUM BULLETINS IN ENTOMOLOGY. 1922. irreg., no.5, 1991. price varies. (Bernice Pauahi Bishop Museum) Bishop Museum Press, 1525 Bernice St., Box 19000-A, Honolulu, HI 96817. TEL 808-847-3511. FAX 808-841-8968. circ. 300. (reprint service avail. from UMI)
   —CISTI; Linda Hall.
   Supersedes in part (in 1987): Bernice P. Bishop Museum Bulletin (ISSN 0005-9439)
   Description: Covers insects and other arthropods of Hawaii and the Pacific Basin.

595.7   IT   ISSN 0366-2403
                     CODEN: BOZAAW
BOLLETTINO DI ZOOLOGIA AGRARIA E DI BACHICOLTURA. (Text in English, French, German, Italian; summaries in English and Italian) 1928. 2/yr. Lit.70000 (foreign Lit.80000) (effective 1998). Universita degli Studi di Milano, Istituto di Entomologia Agraria, Via Celoria 2, 20133 Milan, Italy. TEL 39-2-2362880. FAX 39-2-26680320. Ed. Luciano Suss. circ. 160. (back issues avail.) **Indexed:** Bio-Contr.News & Info., Biodet.Abstr., Biol.Abstr., Hort.Abstr. **Document type:** academic/scholarly publication, monographic series.
   Refereed Serial

595.7   GW   ISSN 0724-4223
BOMBUS; faunistische Mitteilungen aus Nordwestdeutschland. 1937. irreg. DM.3 per copy. Verein fuer Naturwissenschaftliche Heimatforschung zu Hamburg e.V., Zoologisches Institut und Museum, Martin-Luther-King-Platz 3, 20146 Hamburg, Germany. Ed. Thomas Tischler. circ. 300 (controlled). (back issues avail.) **Indexed:** Biol.Abstr. **Document type:** academic/scholarly publication.

595.7   JA   ISSN 0917-4893
BOSO NO KONCHU/ENTOMOLOGICAL ASSOCIATION OF CHIBA PREFECTURE. REPORT. (Text in Japanese) 1990. 3/yr. 3000 Yen (effective 1995). Chibaken Konchu Danwakai - Entomological Association of Chiba Prefecture, c/o Mr. Yasutoshi Matsui, 3-102, 427-5 Nedo, Kashiwa-shi, Chiba-ken 277, Japan. Ed. Yoshikazu Iwasaka. circ. 200 (controlled).
   Refereed Serial

595.7   UK   ISSN 0007-4853
QL461   **CODEN: BEREA2**
BULLETIN OF ENTOMOLOGICAL RESEARCH; containing original and review articles on economic entomology. 1910. bi-m. £245($430) (effective 1997). CAB International, Wallingford, Oxon. OX10 8DE, England. TEL 44-1491-832111. FAX 44-1491-826090. TELEX 847964 COMAGG G. E-mail: cabi@cabi.org; URL: http://www.cabi.org. (U.S. subscr. to: CAB International, North American Office, 198 Madison Ave., New York, NY 10016. TEL 212-726-6490. FAX 212-686-7993) Ed.Bd. adv.; bibl.; charts; illus.; index. circ. 1,500. (also avail. in microfiche from BHP,IDC; back issues avail.; reprint service avail.) **Indexed:** Abstr.Hyg., Agroforest.Abstr., ASCA, Bibl.Agri., Bio-Contr.News & Info., Biodet.Abstr., Biol.Abstr., Biol.& Agr.Ind., Biotech.Abstr., Chem.Abstr., Cott.& Trop.Fibr.Abstr., Curr.Adv.Ecol.Sci., Curr.Cont., Ecol.Abstr., Entomol.Abstr., Forest.Abstr., Forest Prod.Abstr., Geo.Abstr.H.G., Helminthol.Abstr., Herb.Abstr., Hort.Abstr., IDA, Ind.Sci.Rev., Ind.Vet., Maize Abstr., Plant Breed.Abstr., Rev.Appl.Entomol., Rice Abstr., Sci.Cit.Ind., So.Pac.Per.Ind., Soils & Fert., Sorghum & Millets Abstr., Triticale Abstr., Trop.Dis.Bull., Trop.Oil Seeds Abstr., Vet.Bull. **Document type:** bulletin.
   ●Also available online. Vendor(s): DIMDI, European Space Agency, Knight-Ridder Information, Inc.
   —BLDSC (2853.000000); CASDDS; CISTI; Genuine Article; KR SourceOne; Linda Hall; SWETS; UnCover.
   Description: Contains original research papers on insects, mites, and ticks of economic importance in the agricultural, medical and veterinary medical fields in all parts of the world.

595.7   589.2   JA   ISSN 0389-729X
BUNKAZAI NO CHU-KIN-GAI/INSECT & FUNGUS DAMAGE TO CULTURAL PROPERTIES. Variant English title: Japan Institute of Insect Damage to Cultural Properties. Journal. (Text in Japanese) 1981. s-a. 7000 Yen to members; non-members 13000 Yen. Institute of Insect Damage to Cultural Properties - Bunkazai Chugai Kenkyujo, Grand Mer Ochiai 203, Kamiochiai 1-9-11, Shinjuku-ku, Tokyo 160, Japan. TEL 03-3362-8298. Ed. Katsuji Yamano. adv. circ. 500. (back issues avail.) **Document type:** academic/scholarly publication.
   Description: Includes damage by insects and fungi, studies on insecticides and fungicides, and effects on the environment.

C A SELECTS. PESTICIDE ANALYSIS. see *BIOLOGY — Abstracting, Bibliographies, Statistics*

595.7   US   ISSN 0068-5631
QL475.C3   **CODEN: BCINA4**
CALIFORNIA INSECT SURVEY. BULLETIN. 1950. irreg., vol.27, 1986. price varies. University of California Press, 2120 Berkeley Way, Berkeley, CA 94720. TEL 510-642-4247. FAX 510-643-7127. (Orders to: California-Princeton Fulfillment Services, 1445 Lower Ferry Rd., Ewing, NJ 08618. TEL 800-777-4726. FAX 800-999-1958) Ed.Bd. **Indexed:** Abstr.Hyg., Biol.Abstr., Rev.Appl.Entomol., Trop.Dis.Bull. **Document type:** monographic series.
   —CISTI; Linda Hall.
   Refereed Serial

595.7   CN   ISSN 0008-347X
QL461   **CODEN: CAENAF**
CANADIAN ENTOMOLOGIST. (Text mainly in English; occasionally in French) 1868. bi-m. Can.$187.25 to non-members (foreign $180) (includes Bulletin and Memoir) (effective 1996-1997). Entomological Society of Canada, 393 Winston Ave., Ottawa, ON K2A 1Y8, Canada. TEL 613-725-2619. FAX 613-725-9349. Ed. P. Kevan. bk.rev.; bibl.; charts; illus.; stat.; index. circ. 1,300. (also avail. in microform from UMI,PMC; microfiche from IDC; reprint service avail. from UMI) **Indexed:** ASCA, Bibl.Agri., Bio-Contr.News & Info., Biol.Abstr., Biol.& Agr.Ind., Biotech.Abstr., Chem.Abstr., Curr.Adv.Ecol.Sci., Curr.Adv.Genetics & Molec.Biol., Curr.Cont., Ecol.Abstr., Energy Ind., Energy Info.Abstr., Excerp.Med., Field Crop Abstr., Forest.Abstr., Forest Prod.Abstr., Geo.Abstr., Geol.Abstr., Helminthol.Abstr., Herb.Abstr., Hort.Abstr., IBR, Ind.Sci.Rev., INIS Atomind., Plant Breed.Abstr., Potato Abstr., Protozool.Abstr., Rev.Appl.Entomol., Sci.Cit.Ind., Soils & Fert., Trop.Oil Seeds Abstr. **Document type:** academic/scholarly publication.
   —BLDSC (3022.000000); CASDDS; CISTI; EMDOCS; Genuine Article; KR SourceOne; Linda Hall; SWETS; UMI; UnCover. **CCC.**
   Refereed Serial

595.7   NE
CATALOGUE OF PALAEARCTIC DIPTERA. 1984. irreg., vol.7, 1991. price varies. Elsevier Science B.V., Books Division, P.O. Box 211, 1000 AE Amsterdam, Netherlands. TEL 31-20-4853911. FAX 31-20-4853705. TELEX 18582 ESPA NL. E-mail: nlinfo-f@elsevier.nl; usinfo-f@elsevier.com; forinfo-kyf04035@niftyserve.or.jp; URL: http://www.elsevier.nl/. (Subscr. in the Americas to: Elsevier Science, Regional Sales Office, Box 945, New York, NY 10159-0945. TEL 212-633-3730. FAX 212-633-3680; Subscr. in Australasia and the Far East to: Elsevier Science (Singapore) Pte Ltd, No.1 Temasek Ave., No.17-01 Millenia Tower, Singapore 039192, Singapore. TEL 65-434-3727. FAX 65-337-2230; Subscr. in Japan to: Elsevier Science Japan, 9-15 Higashi-Azabu 1-chome, Minato-ku, Tokyo 106, Japan. TEL 81-3-5561-5033. FAX 81-3-5561-5047) Eds. A. Soos, L. Papp. **Document type:** monographic series.
   Refereed Serial

595.7   II   ISSN 0008-8676
SB767   **CODEN: CECIAI**
CECIDOLOGIA INTERNATIONALE. (Text in English) 1966. 3/yr. $125. Cecidological Society of India, 14 Park Road, Allahabad 211 002, India. TEL 51958. Ed. Prabha Grover. adv.; bk.rev.; bibl.; charts; illus. circ. 250. (also avail. in microfilm) **Indexed:** Bio-Contr.News & Info., Biol.Abstr., Curr.Adv.Ecol.Sci., Forest.Abstr., Forest Prod.Abstr., Helminthol.Abstr., Hort.Abstr.
   Formed by the merger of: Cecidologia Indica; Marcellia.
   Description: Examines phylogenetic studies on cecimyiid and other cecidozoa; their eco-biology, cecidogenesis, biochemistry, regular and pathological morphogenesis. Includes plant- and cecidozoa-pathogen relationships as well as karyological studies.

595.7   JA   ISSN 0388-6492
CELASTRINA. (Text in Japanese) 1978. s-a. 1400 Yen per no. Tsugaru Konchu Dokokai - Tsugaru Insect Lover's Society, c/o Mr. Tadashi Kudo, 323-1 Doi, Itayanagimachi, Kitatsugaru-gun, Aomori-ken 038-36, Japan.

CHOJU KANKEI TOKEI/ANNUAL STATISTICS OF BIRDS AND ANIMALS. see *BIOLOGY — Abstracting, Bibliographies, Statistics*

595.7   JA   ISSN 0913-8323
CHOKEN FIELD/STUDY OF BUTTERFLY. (Text in Japanese) 1986. m. 1480 Yen($76) per no. Choken Shuppan, 13-27 Sojiji 1-chome, Ibaraki-shi, Osaka 567, Japan. TEL 81-726-27-9828. FAX 81-726-27-4464. E-mail: chouken@po.aianet.or.jp. Ed. Yoshiaki/Shouji.

595.7   US   ISSN 0590-6334
QL596.C56
CICINDELA; a quarterly journal devoted to cicindelidae. 1969. q. $7. 4637 W. 69th Terrace, Prairie Village, KS 66208. TEL 913-236-4043. Ed. Ronald L. Huber. bk.rev.; bibl.; charts; illus.; stat. circ. 160. **Indexed:** Biol.Abstr., Entomol.Abstr., Zoo.Rec.
   —UnCover.

BIOLOGY — ENTOMOLOGY

CLADISTICS: THE INTERNATIONAL JOURNAL OF THE WILLI HENNIG SOCIETY. see BIOLOGY — Botany

595.76 US ISSN 0010-065X
CODEN: COBLAO
COLEOPTERISTS BULLETIN. (Text mainly in English; occasionally in other languages) 1947. q. $30 to individuals; institutions $50 (effective 1997). Coleopterists Society, c/o Terry N. Seeno, 3294 Meadowview Rd., Sacramento, CA 95832-1448. TEL 916-262-1160. FAX 916-262-1190. E-mail: tseeno@macnexus.org. Ed. Dr. Wayne Clark. R&P contact: Wayne E. Clark. adv.; bk.rev.; abstr.; bibl.; illus. circ. 750. (back issues avail.) Indexed: ASCA, Bio-Contr.News & Info., Biodet.Abstr., Biol.Abstr., Curr.Adv.Ecol.Sci., Curr.Cont., Ecol.Abstr., Forest.Abstr., Rev.Appl.Entomol., Zoo.Rec. Document type: bulletin.
—BLDSC (3297.000000); Genuine Article; Linda Hall; UnCover.
Incorporating: Coleopterists Newsletter (ISSN 0045-7337)
Description: Contains papers on all aspects of the study of beetles - living and fossil, including systematics, phylogeny, biogeography, behavior, ecology, and techniques for study.
Refereed Serial

579.76 SP ISSN 1130-7609
CODEN: CMONEH
COLEOPTEROLOGICAL MONOGRAPHS. (Text in English, French, Spanish; summaries in English) 1990. irreg. Asociacion Europea de Coleopterologia - European Association of Coleopterology, Depto. de Biologia Animal, Universidad de Barcelona, Avda. Diagonal 645, 08028 Barcelona, Spain. TEL 3-402-14-43. FAX 3-411-08-87. circ. 600. **Document type:** monographic series.

595.7 636 614.8 US ISSN 8756-7881
COMMON SENSE PEST CONTROL QUARTERLY. 1984. q. $30 to individuals; institutions $50. Bio Integral Resource Center, Box 7414, Berkeley, CA 94707. TEL 510-524-2567. FAX 510-524-1758. Ed. William Quarles. R&P contact: William Quarles. adv.; bk.rev.; index. circ. 1,200. (back issues avail.) **Indexed:** Gard.Lit. (1992-). **Document type:** newsletter.
Description: Covers the least-toxic pest management in layperson's terms.

595.7 AT
SB921
COMMONWEALTH SCIENTIFIC AND INDUSTRIAL RESEARCH ORGANISATION. DIVISION OF ENTOMOLOGY. REPORT OF RESEARCH. 1960. biennial. Aus.$15 exchange basis. Commonwealth Scientific and Industrial Research Organisation, Division of Entomology, G.P.O. Box 1700, Canberra City, A.C.T. 2601, Australia. TEL 61-6-2464001. FAX 61-6-2464000. E-mail: jenny.goldie@ento.csiro.au; URL: http://www.csiro.au:8000/test/ento/index.html. Ed. Jenny Goldie. R&P contact: Kelly Rhodes. TEL 61-6-2464033. circ. 1,500. **Indexed:** Rev.Appl.Entomol., Weed Abstr. **Document type:** corporate report.
—CISTI.
Former titles (until 1987): Commonwealth Scientific and Industrial Research Organisation. Division of Entomology. Report (ISSN 1037-3500); (until 1983): Commonwealth Scientific and Industrial Research Organisation. Division of Entomology. Annual Report (ISSN 0728-5825)
Description: Technical description of work in progress at the largest entomological research institution in Australia.

597.7 BL
CONGRESSO BRASILEIRO DE ENTOMOLOGIA. RESUMOS. irreg., 16th, 1997, Bahia. Ministerio da Agricultura e do Abastecimento, Centro Nacional de Pesquisa de Mandioca e Fruticultura Tropical, Laboratorio de Entomologia Embrapa-Mandioca e Fruticultura, Rua Embrapa s-n Caixa Postal 07, Cruz das Almas, Bahia, CEP 44.380-000, Brazil. TEL 55-75-7212120. FAX 55-75-7211118. TELEX 55-75-2074. (Co-sponsor: Sociedade Entomologica do Brasil)

595.7 IT
CONGRESSO NAZIONALE DI ENTOMOLOGIA. ATTI. 1957. irreg., 17th, 1994, Udine. price varies. Accademia Nazionale Italiana di Entomologia, Via Lanciola, 12-A, Cascine del Riccio, 50125 Florence, Italy. FAX 39-55-209182.

595.7 US ISSN 0097-0905
CONNECTICUT. AGRICULTURAL EXPERIMENT STATION, NEW HAVEN. BULLETIN. 1877. irreg., no.941, 1997. free. Agricultural Experiment Station, 123 Huntington St., Box 1106, New Haven, CT 06504-1106. TEL 203-789-7272. Ed. Paul Gough. circ. 2,000. (back issues avail.) **Indexed:** Biol.Abstr., Chem.Abstr., Curr.Adv.Ecol.Sci., Energy Ind., Energy Info.Abstr., Environ.Abstr., Forest.Abstr., Forest Prod.Abstr., Helminthol.Abstr., Hort.Abstr., Soils & Fert., Sugar Ind.Abstr. **Document type:** monographic series.
—BLDSC (2458.500000); CISTI; Linda Hall.

595.705 US
CONTEMPORARY TOPICS IN ENTOMOLOGY. irreg., no.2, 1994. Chapman & Hall, 115 Fifth Ave., New York, NY 10003. TEL 212-780-6235. FAX 212-260-1363. URL: http://www.chaphall.com/chaphall/. **Document type:** monographic series.

595.7 US ISSN 1084-0745
QL461
CONTRIBUTIONS ON ENTOMOLOGY, INTERNATIONAL. 1964; N.S. 1996. irreg. $55. Associated Publishers, Box 140103, Gainesville, FL 32614-0103. TEL 352-371-4071. FAX 352-371-4071. E-mail: vgupta@gnv.ifas.ufl.edu. Ed. Virendra K. Gupta; Pub. Virendra K. Gupta. circ. 200. (back vols. avail.) **Indexed:** Biol.Abstr., Rev.Appl.Entomol. **Document type:** academic/scholarly publication.
—Linda Hall.
Supersedes (in 1996): American Entomological Institute. Contributions (ISSN 0569-4450)
Description: Publishes articles on entomology.
Refereed Serial

595.7 581 IT ISSN 0010-9258
CORRIERE FITOPATOLOGICO. 1963. s-a. free. Bayer Italia S.p.A., Divisione Agraria, Viale Certosa 126, Milan, Italy. Ed. Loredano P. Lazzarini. illus. circ. 60,000.

595.7 US ISSN 1082-5932
CULTURAL ENTOMOLOGY DIGEST.* 1993. s-a. $12 (foreign $18). Box 796, Kalaheo, HI 96741-0796. E-mail: dexter@alom.net. Ed. Dexter Sear. circ. 350 (paid). **Document type:** newsletter.

595.7 GW ISSN 0931-4873
D G A A E NACHRICHTEN. 1987. irreg. (3-4/yr.). membership. Deutsche Gesellschaft fuer Allgemeine und Angewandte Entomologie, Schwabenheimerstr. 101, 69221 Dossenheim, Germany. TEL 49-621-85238. FAX 49-621-861222. E-mail: ba69ed@genius.embnetdkfz-heidelberg.de. circ. 800 (controlled).

595.7 GW ISSN 0012-0073
QL461 CODEN: DENZAX
DEUTSCHE ENTOMOLOGISCHE ZEITSCHRIFT. (Text in English, German) 1857. 2/yr. DM.295 (foreign DM.305) (effective 1997). Akademie Verlag GmbH, Muehlenstr. 33-34, 13187 Berlin, Germany. TEL 49-30-47889348. FAX 49-30-47889357. E-mail: info@akademie-verlag.de. (Subscr. in the Americas to: John Wiley & Sons, Inc., 605 Third Ave., New York, NY 10158. TEL 212-850-6645. FAX 212-850-6021) Ed. H. Hoch. adv.; abstr.; bibl.; charts; illus.; index. (also avail. in microfiche from BHP,IDC) **Indexed:** ASCA, Biol.Abstr., Curr.Adv.Ecol.Sci., Curr.Cont., Fababean Abstr., Rev.Appl.Entomol. **Document type:** academic/scholarly publication.
—CISTI; Genuine Article; Linda Hall; UnCover.
Formerly (until 1875): Berliner Entomologische Zeitung (ISSN 0323-6145)
Description: Publishes original papers on both scientific and applied entomology as well as arachnology and aracology.

595.7 GW ISSN 0344-9084
QL461
DEUTSCHE GESELLSCHAFT FUER ALLGEMEINE UND ANGEWANDTE ENTOMOLOGIE. MITTEILUNGEN. (Text in English, German) 1978. irreg. (approx. biennial). price varies. Deutsche Gesellschaft fuer Allgemeine und Angewandte Entomologie, Schwabenheimerstr. 101, 69221 Dossenheim, Germany. TEL 49-621-85238. FAX 49-621-861222. E-mail: ba69ed@genius.embnetdkfz-heidelberg.de. (back issues avail.) **Indexed:** Agroforest.Abstr., Fababean Abstr., Forest.Abstr., Forest Prod.Abstr., Potato Abstr. **Document type:** bulletin.
—BLDSC (5839.380000).

DISEASES OF AQUATIC ORGANISMS. see BIOLOGY — Zoology

DISTRIBUTION MAPS OF PESTS. see AGRICULTURE

595.7 JA ISSN 0913-7335
DONACIIST. (Text in Japanese) 1987. a. Nekuihamushi Kenkyukai - Donaciists' Society, Yokohama, Kanagawa Kenritsu Hakubutsukan, 5-60 Minami Nakadori, Naka-ku, Yokohama-shi, Kanagawa-ken 231, Japan.

595.7 KE ISSN 0258-8498
DUDU; quarterly newsletter of the International Centre of Insect Physiology and Ecology. (Text in English) 1974. q. free. (International Centre of Insect Physiology and Ecology) ICIPE Science Press, P.O. Box 72913, Nairobi, Kenya. TEL 802573-9. TELEX 25066-DUDU. Ed. M.H. Bugembe. circ. 2,000. **Document type:** newsletter.

595.7 US ISSN 0273-7353
E S A NEWSLETTER. 1978. m. $18 to individuals (foreign $24); institutions $35 (foreign $41). Entomological Society of America, 9301 Annapolis Rd., Lanham, MD 20706. TEL 301-731-4535. FAX 301-731-4538. (Subscr. to: Box 177, Hyattsville, MD 20781-0177) adv. circ. 9,000. (back issues avail.) **Document type:** newsletter.
Description: Contains feature articles, meeting announcements, listing of employment opportunities, notices of grants and awards, member profiles, and branch and section news.

595.7 UK ISSN 0307-6946
QL461 CODEN: EENTDT
ECOLOGICAL ENTOMOLOGY. 1834. q. £212($387) (foreign £233) (effective 1998). (Royal Entomological Society) Blackwell Science Ltd., Osney Mead, Oxford OX2 0EL, England. TEL 44-1865-206206. FAX 44-1865-721205. E-mail: journals.cs@blacksci.co.uk; URL: http://www.black.co.uk. Ed. S.R. Leather; Pub. Allen Stevens. R&P contact: Sarah Pollard. adv. contact: Martine Cariou-Keen. bk.rev.; charts; illus. circ. 1,080. (also avail. in microfiche from BHP; back issues avail.; reprint service avail.) **Indexed:** Abstr.Hyg., Agroforest.Abstr., Apic.Abstr., ASCA, Bio-Contr.News & Info., Biol.Abstr., Biol.& Agr.Ind., Biotech.Abstr., Curr.Adv.Ecol.Sci., Curr.Cont., Ecol.Abstr., Forest.Abstr., Geo.Abstr., Helminthol.Abstr., Ind.Sci.Rev., Ind.Vet., Protozool.Abstr., Rev.Appl.Entomol., Sci.Cit.Ind., Soils & Fert., THA, Trop.Dis.Bull., Vet Bull., Weed Abstr. **Document type:** academic/scholarly publication.
—BLDSC (3648.870000); CISTI; EMDOCS; Genuine Article; KR SourceOne; Linda Hall; SWETS; UMI; UnCover. CCC.
Formerly (until 1976): Royal Entomological Society of London. Transactions (ISSN 0035-8894)
Refereed Serial

595.7 JA ISSN 0387-5733
ELYTRA. (Text in English, Japanese) 1973. s-a. Nihon Shoshi Gakkai - Japanese Society of Coleopterology, Kokuritsu Kagaku Hakubutsukan Dobutsu Kenkyubu, 23-1, Hyakunincho 3-chome, Shinjuku-ku, Tokyo 169, Japan.

595.7 SP ISSN 0214-1353
CODEN: ELTREZ
ELYTRON. a. 6000 ptas.($65) individual membership (effective 1993). Asociacion Europea de Coleopterologia - European Association of Coleopterology, Dept. de Biologia Animal - Artropodes, Universitat de Barcelona, Avda. Diagonal 645, 08028 Barcelona, Spain. TEL 3-4021443. FAX 3-4110887. **Indexed:** Ind.SST.
—BLDSC (3732.563000). CCC.

595.7 US ISSN 0734-9874
CODEN: ENTMEY
ENTOMOGRAPHY. 1982. a. $50. Entomography Publications, 7451 Albezzia Ln., Sacramento, CA 95828. TEL 916-682-9752. Eds. Charles S. Papp, Thomas D. Eichlin. circ. 750. **Indexed:** Biol.Abstr.
—Linda Hall.
Description: Annual review for biosystematics.

BIOLOGY — ENTOMOLOGY

595.7 NE ISSN 0013-8703
CODEN: ETEAAT
ENTOMOLOGIA EXPERIMENTALIS ET APPLICATA. (Text in English, French and German) 1958. m. fl.2132 to institutions; $1094 to institutions in U.S. (effective 1998). Kluwer Academic Publishers, Postbus 17, 3300 AA Dordrecht, Netherlands. TEL 31-78-6392392. FAX 31-78-6392254. TELEX 29245 KAPG NL. E-mail: services@wkap.nl; URL: http://www.wkap.nl. (Dist. by: Kluwer Academic Publishers Group, P.O. Box 322, 3300 AH Dordrecht, Netherlands. TEL 31-78-6392392. FAX 31-78-6546474; N. America dist. addr.: Box 358, Accord Sta., Hingham, MA 02018-0358. TEL 617-871-6600. FAX 617-871-6528) Ed.Bd. index. (also avail. in microform from UMI; reprint service avail. from SWZ) **Indexed:** ASCA, Bio-Contr.News & Info., Biodet.Abstr., Biol.Abstr., Biotech.Abstr., Bull.Signal., Chem.Abstr., Cott.& Trop.Fibr.Abstr., Curr.Adv.Ecol.Sci., Curr.Cont., Ecol.Abstr., Forest.Abstr., Forest Prod.Abstr., Geo.Abstr., Helminthol.Abstr., Hort.Abstr., Ind.Sci.Rev., Ind.Vet., Maize Abstr., Potato Abstr., Protozool.Abstr., Rev.Appl.Entomol., Sci.Cit.Ind., Soils & Fert., Triticale Abstr., VITIS, Weed Abstr. **Document type:** academic/scholarly publication.
—BLDSC (3776.750000); CASDDS; CISTI; EMDOCS; Genuine Article; Linda Hall; SWETS; UMI; UnCover. **CCC**.
Description: Publishes scientific studies and applications of the experimental biology and ecology of insects and other land arthropods.
Refereed Serial

595.7 GW ISSN 0171-8177
QL461 CODEN: ENGND5
ENTOMOLOGIA GENERALIS; Zeitschrift fuer allgemeine und angewandte Entomologie/journal of general and applied entomology. (Text in German; summaries in English) 1974. 4/yr. DM.398($295.50) (foreign $301.30) (effective 1997). E. Schweizerbart'sche Verlagsbuchhandlung, Johannesstr. 3A, 70176 Stuttgart, Germany. TEL 49-711-625001. FAX 49-711-625005. Ed. A.W. Steffan. **Indexed:** Apic.Abstr., ASCA, Biol.Abstr., Curr.Adv.Ecol.Sci., Curr.Cont., Helminthol.Abstr., IBR, Protozool.Abstr., Rev.Appl.Entomol., Soils & Fert., VITIS, Weed Abstr. **Document type:** academic/scholarly publication.
—BLDSC (3776.820000); Genuine Article; Linda Hall; UnCover. **CCC**.
Formerly: Entomologica Germanica (ISSN 0340-2266)

595.7 CC ISSN 1005-295X
ENTOMOLOGIA SINICA. (Text in English) 1994. q. $228 (effective 1996). (Entomological Society of China) China Ocean Press, International Cooperation Department, Haimao Dalou, 1 Fuxingmenwai Dajie, Beijing 100860, People's Republic of China. TEL 8032211. FAX 8033515. TELEX 22536 NBO CN. Ed. Qin Junde. bk.rev. **Document type:** academic/scholarly publication.
—BLDSC (3776.870000); CISTI.
Description: Publishes papers in all fields of research in insects and other terrestrial arthropods.

595.7 FI ISSN 0785-8760
QL482.F5 CODEN: ENFEE8
ENTOMOLOGICA FENNICA. (Text in English, occasionally in German) 1990. q. FIM 180 (foreign FIM 250) (effective 1997). Entomologica Fennica ry, c/o Institute of Zoology, P.O. Box 17, FIN-00014 University of Helsinki, Finland. FAX 358-0-635017. E-mail: juha.viramo@oulu.fi. (Distr. by: Bookstore Tiedekirja, Kirkkokatu 14, FIN-00170 Helsinki, Finland. FAX 358-0-635017) Ed. Juha Viramo. R&P contact: Juha Viramo. bk.rev. circ. 700. **Indexed:** ASCA, Bio-Contr.News & Info., Biol.Abstr., Curr.Adv.Ecol.Sci., Curr.Cont., Entomol.Abstr., Hort.Abstr., IBR, Rev.Appl.Entomol. **Document type:** academic/scholarly publication.
—BLDSC (3777.130000); CASDDS; Genuine Article; Linda Hall; UMI; UnCover.
Formed by the merger of (1947-1990): Acta Entomologica Fennica (ISSN 0001-561X); (1935-1990): Annales Entomologici Fennici (ISSN 0003-4428); (1921-1990): Notulae Entomologicae (ISSN 0029-4594)
Description: Contains original research reports and reviews on ecology, faunistics, behavior, and systematics of insects and other terrestrial arthropods. Mainly a forum for Finnish and Nordic entomologists, but articles from other countries related to Finnish research or to the boreal region are included.
Refereed Serial

595.7 DK ISSN 0013-8711
QL461 CODEN: ENTSBF
ENTOMOLOGICA SCANDINAVICA; journal on entomological systematics and taxonomy. (Supplement avail. (ISSN 0105-3574) (Text in English) 1970. 4/yr. DKK 1140 (effective through 1998). (Societas entomologica Scandinavica) Apollo Books Aps, Kirkeby Sand 19, DK-5771 Stenstrup, Denmark. TEL 45-62-26-37-37. FAX 46-62-26-37-80. Eds. Nils Moeller Andersen, Verner Michelsen. bibl.; charts; illus. circ. 500. (back issues avail.) **Indexed:** ASCA, Bio-Contr.News & Info., Biodet.Abstr., Biol.Abstr., Curr.Adv.Ecol.Sci., Curr.Cont., Helminthol.Abstr., Rev.Appl.Entomol., Soils & Fert., Zoo.Rec. **Document type:** academic/scholarly publication.
—BLDSC (3777.500000); Linda Hall; SWETS; UnCover.

595.7 US ISSN 0013-872X
CODEN: ETMNA6
ENTOMOLOGICAL NEWS. 1889. 5/yr. $20 to institutions & libraries (foreign $22) (effective 1998). American Entomological Society, Academy of Natural Sciences, 1900 Benjamin Franklin Pkwy., Philadelphia, PA 19103-1195. TEL 215-561-3978. FAX 215-299-1028. E-mail: AES@say.acnatsci.org. Ed. Howard Boyd. R&P contact: Howard Boyd. adv.; bk.rev.; charts; illus.; index. circ. 750. (also avail. in microform from UMI; reprint service avail. from UMI) **Indexed:** ASCA, Bio-Contr.News & Info., Biol.Abstr., Chem.Abstr., Curr.Adv.Ecol.Sci., Curr.Cont., Fababean Abstr., Forest.Abstr., GeoRef., Rev.Appl.Entomol., Soils & Fert., Sport Fish.Abstr., Wild.Rev., Zoo.Rec. **Document type:** academic/scholarly publication.
—BLDSC (3778.500000); EMDOCS; Genuine Article; Linda Hall; SWETS; UMI; UnCover.
Refereed Serial

595.7 RU ISSN 0013-8738
QL461 CODEN: ENREBV
ENTOMOLOGICAL REVIEW. English translation of: Entomologicheskoye Obozreniye. vol.49, 1970. 9/yr. $1647 (foreign $1786.50) (effective 1997). (Russian Academy of Sciences, RU) Maika Nauka - Interperiodica, Ul. Profsoyuznaya, 90, 117864 Moscow, Russia. (Dist. by: Maik Nauka - Interperiodica, Subscription Office, Box 1831, Birmingham, AL 35201-1831, U.S.A.. TEL 205-995-1567. FAX 205-995-1588) (Co-publisher: Entomological Society of America) Ed. G.C. Steyskal. adv.; bk.rev.; bibl.; charts; illus.; index. circ. 425. (also avail. in microform from UMI) **Indexed:** Apic.Abstr., Biol.Abstr., Ecol.Abstr. **Document type:** academic/scholarly publication.
—BLDSC (0411.740000); Linda Hall; SWETS; UMI; UnCover. **CCC**.
Description: Covers all aspects of entomology: systematics, faunistics, ecology, morphology, physiology and biochemistry of insects, as well as biological and chemical control of insect pests.
Refereed Serial

595.7 JA ISSN 0286-9810
ENTOMOLOGICAL REVIEW OF JAPAN/KONCHUGAKU HYORON. (Text in English, Japanese) 1945. s-a. 5000 Yen. Japan Coleopterological Society - Nihon Kochu Gakkai, 202 Residence Kotobuki, 2-16-5, Karita Sumiyoshi, Osaka 558, Japan. TEL 06-698-2964. Ed. Dr. Masao Hayashi. adv.; bk.rev.; index. (back issues avail.) **Indexed:** Bio-Contr.News & Info., Zoo.Rec. **Document type:** academic/scholarly publication.

595.7 CN ISSN 0071-0709
ENTOMOLOGICAL SOCIETY OF ALBERTA. PROCEEDINGS. 1953. a. Can.$10. Entomological Society of Alberta, c/o Dept. Biological Sciences, University of Alberta, Edmonton, AB T6G 2E9, Canada. TEL 403-492-3308. FAX 403-492-9234. E-mail: michelew@gpu.srv.ualberta.ca. Ed. M.L. Williamson. cum.index every 10 yrs. circ. 150. **Document type:** proceedings.

595.7 US ISSN 0013-8746
QL461 CODEN: AESAAI
ENTOMOLOGICAL SOCIETY OF AMERICA. ANNALS; devoted to the interest of classical entomology. 1908. bi-m. $75 to individuals (foreign $95); institutions $150 (foreign $170); members $25 (foreign $40). Entomological Society of America, 9301 Annapolis Rd., Lanham, MD 20706. TEL 301-731-4535. FAX 301-731-4538. (Subscr. to: Box 177, Hyattsville, MD 20781-0177) Eds. Carl W. Schaefer, Leo Lachance. adv.; abstr.; bibl.; charts; illus.; index. circ. 2,800. (also avail. in microform from MIM,UMI,PMC) **Indexed:** Abstr.Hyg., Agri.Eng.Abstr., ASCA, Bio-Contr.News & Info., Biodet.Abstr., Biol.Abstr., Biol.& Agr.Ind., Biotech.Abstr., Chem.Abstr., Cott.& Trop.Fibr.Abstr., Curr.Adv.Cell & Devel.Biol., Curr.Adv.Ecol.Sci., Excerp.Med., Forest.Abstr., Helminthol.Abstr., Hort.Abstr., Ind.Sci.Rev., Ind.Vet., INIS Atomind., Maize Abstr., Potato Abstr., Poult.Abstr., Protozool.Abstr., Rev.Appl.Entomol., Sci.Cit.Ind., Seed Abstr., Soils & Fert., Soyabean Abstr., Sport Fish.Abstr., Trop.Dis.Bull., Vet.Bull., Weed Abstr., Wild.Rev., Zoo.Rec. **Document type:** academic/scholarly publication.
—BLDSC (1025.000000); CASDDS; CISTI; Genuine Article; KR SourceOne; Linda Hall; SWETS; UMI; UnCover. **CCC**.
Description: Devoted to the basic aspects of the biology of insects.
Refereed Serial

595.7 CN ISSN 0071-0733
CODEN: JEBCA4
ENTOMOLOGICAL SOCIETY OF BRITISH COLUMBIA. JOURNAL. 1906. a. Can.$20 (foreign Can.$24) (effective 1997). Entomological Society of British Columbia, c/o R.G. Bennett, Ministry of Forests, Seed Pest Management, 7380 Puckle Rd., Saanichton, BC V8M 1W4, Canada. TEL 604-652-6593. FAX 604-652-4204. E-mail: rgbennett@mfor01.for.gov.bc.ca. Ed. P. Belton. adv.; bk.rev. circ. 250. (also avail. in microform from UMI) **Indexed:** Apic.Abstr. **Document type:** academic/scholarly publication.
—CISTI; Linda Hall; UMI; UnCover. **CCC**.
Refereed Serial

595.7 CN ISSN 0071-0741
QL461
ENTOMOLOGICAL SOCIETY OF CANADA. BULLETIN. 1969. q. included with subscription to Canadian Entomologist. Entomological Society of Canada, 393 Winston Ave., Ottawa, ON K2A 1Y8, Canada. TEL 613-725-2619. FAX 613-725-9349. Ed. H. Barclay. **Indexed:** Apic.Abstr., Curr.Adv.Ecol.Sci., Hort.Abstr., Rev.Appl.Entomol. **Document type:** bulletin.
—BLDSC (2505.150000); CISTI; Linda Hall; SWETS. **CCC**.

595.7 CN ISSN 0071-075X
CODEN: MESCAK
ENTOMOLOGICAL SOCIETY OF CANADA. MEMOIRS. (Text in English or French) 1956. irreg. (1-8/yr.). included with subscription to Canadian Entomologist. Entomological Society of Canada, 393 Winston Ave., Ottawa, ON K2A 1Y8, Canada. TEL 613-725-2619. FAX 613-725-9349. Ed. V. Behan-Pelletier. circ. 1,000. (also avail. in microfilm from PMC) **Indexed:** ASCA, Bio-Contr.News & Info., Biol.Abstr., Curr.Adv.Ecol.Sci., Ecol.Abstr., Entomol.Abstr., Hort.Abstr., Rev.Appl.Entomol. **Document type:** academic/scholarly publication.
—BLDSC (5589.950000); CISTI; Genuine Article; Linda Hall; SWETS. **CCC**.
Refereed Serial

595.7 II ISSN 0013-8762
CODEN: BENTAR
ENTOMOLOGICAL SOCIETY OF INDIA. BULLETIN OF ENTOMOLOGY.* (Text in English) vol.11,1970. s-a. Rs.16($3.50) Entomological Society of India, Division of Entomology, Indian Agricultural Research Institute, Delhi 12, India. Ed. Dr. S.K. Prasad. bibl.; charts; illus. **Indexed:** Potato Abstr., Triticale Abstr.
—BLDSC (2853.100000); CISTI; Linda Hall.

BIOLOGY — ENTOMOLOGY

595.7   CN   ISSN 0315-2146
ENTOMOLOGICAL SOCIETY OF MANITOBA. PROCEEDINGS. 1945. a. Can.$10 (effective 1998). Entomological Society of Manitoba, Inc., 195 Dafoe Rd., Winnipeg, MB R3T 2M9, Canada. TEL 204-945-8444. Ed. Desiree Vanderwil. R&P contact: Desiree Vanderwil. circ. 300. **Indexed:** Bio-Contr.News & Info., Biol.Abstr. **Document type:** academic/scholarly publication, proceedings.
—BLDSC (6697.400000); Linda Hall. **CCC.**
Description: Includes annual meeting details, abstracts of scientific papers from the meeting and original scientific papers of particular interest to prairie and forest entomologists.
Refereed Serial

595.7   NZ   ISSN 0110-4527
CODEN: BESZD5
ENTOMOLOGICAL SOCIETY OF NEW ZEALAND. BULLETIN. 1972. irreg., no.11, 1992. price varies. Entomological Society of New Zealand, Mt Albert Research Centre, Private Bag 92169, Auckland, New Zealand. FAX 64-9-8497093. E-mail: mplmjb@dslak.co.nz. **Indexed:** Biol.Abstr. **Document type:** monographic series.
—BLDSC (2505.160000); CISTI; Linda Hall.
Description: Monographs with original research and directories on New Zealand entomology.

595.7   CN   ISSN 0071-0768
CODEN: PESOAL
ENTOMOLOGICAL SOCIETY OF ONTARIO. PROCEEDINGS; annual publication of entomological research. (Editions in English or French with an English abstract.) 1871. a. Can.$35. Entomological Society of Ontario, Queen's University, Dept. of Biology, Kingston, ON K7L 3N6, Canada. TEL 613-545-6136. FAX 613-545-6617. E-mail: harmsenr@biology.queensu.ca; URL: http://www.utoronto.ca/forest/eso/eso.htm. (Subscr. to: Dr. D.B. Lyons, Natural Resources Canada, Canadian Forest Service, P.O. Box 490, Sault Ste. Marie, ON P6A 5M7) Ed. Dr. R. Harmsen. adv.; bk.rev.; index; circ. 375 (paid). (also avail. in microfilm from UMI) **Indexed:** Apic.Abstr., Bio-Contr.News & Info., Biol.Abstr., Chem.Abstr., Curr.Adv.Ecol.Sci., Curr.Cont., Ecol.Abstr., Helminthol.Abstr., Hort.Abstr., Protozool.Abstr., Rev.Appl.Entomol., Sci.Cit.Ind., Zoo.Rec. **Document type:** proceedings, monographic series.
—BLDSC (6697.700000); CASDDS; CISTI; Genuine Article; Linda Hall. **CCC.**
Description: Covers basic and applied entomology.
Refereed Serial

595.7   US   ISSN 0071-0776
ENTOMOLOGICAL SOCIETY OF PENNSYLVANIA. NEWSLETTER. 1965. 4/yr. membership. Entomological Society of Pennsylvania, Dept. of Entomology, PennState University, 501 AFI Bldg., University Park, PA 16802. TEL 814-863-4640. circ. 90. **Document type:** newsletter.

595.7   SA   ISSN 0373-4242
CODEN: MESAAE
ENTOMOLOGICAL SOCIETY OF SOUTHERN AFRICA. MEMOIRS. (Text in English) 1947. irreg., no.14, 1981. $80 (includes all Society publications). Entomological Society of Southern Africa, P.O. Box 103, Pretoria 0001, South Africa. TEL 27-12-2062623. Ed. M. Mansell. R&P contact: M. Mansell. circ. 600. (back issues avail.) **Indexed:** Biol.Abstr., Curr.Cont., Entomol.Abstr., Herb.Abstr., Ind.S.A.Per., Rev.Appl.Entomol., Soils & Fert., Weed Abstr., Zoo.Rec. **Document type:** monographic series.
—Linda Hall.
Description: Scientific monographs on southern African entomology and arachnology.

595.7   SA
ENTOMOLOGICAL SOCIETY OF SOUTHERN AFRICA. PROCEEDINGS OF THE CONGRESS. 1974. irreg., approx. biennial. $80 (includes all Society publications). Entomological Society of Southern Africa, P.O. Box 103, Pretoria 0001, South Africa. TEL 27-12-2062623. Ed. M. Mansell. R&P contact: M. Mansell. abstr. **Indexed:** Biol.Abstr., Curr.Cont., Entomol.Abstr., Ind.S.A.Per., Zoo.Rec. **Document type:** proceedings.

595.7   US   ISSN 0096-5839
QL461   CODEN: MESWAC
ENTOMOLOGICAL SOCIETY OF WASHINGTON. MEMOIRS. 1939. irreg., vol.19, 1997. Entomological Society of Washington, c/o Dept. of Entomology, Smithsonian Institution NHB 168, Washington, DC 20560. Ed. David R. Smith. (back issues avail.) **Document type:** academic/scholarly publication.
Refereed Serial

595.7   US   ISSN 0013-8797
QL461   CODEN: PESWAB
ENTOMOLOGICAL SOCIETY OF WASHINGTON. PROCEEDINGS. 1884. q. $60 to non-members (foreign $70). Entomological Society of Washington, c/o Dept. of Entomology, Smithsonian Institution NHB 168, Washington, DC 20560. Ed. David R. Smith. bk.rev.; charts; illus.; stat.; index. circ. 840. (back issues avail.) **Indexed:** ASCA, Bio-Contr.News & Info., Biol.Abstr., Chem.Abstr., Curr.Adv.Ecol.Sci., Curr.Cont., Forest.Abstr., Helminthol.Abstr., Rev.Appl.Entomol., Soyabean Abstr., Sport Fish.Abstr., Weed Abstr., Wild.Rev., Zoo.Rec. **Document type:** proceedings.
—BLDSC (6698.000000); CISTI; EMDOCS; Genuine Article; Linda Hall; SWETS; UnCover.
Refereed Serial

595.7   RU   ISSN 0367-1445
CODEN: ETOBAE
ENTOMOLOGICHESKOYE OBOZRENIE. (Text in Russian) 1931. q. $190 (effective 1998). (Vsesoyuznoe Entomologicheskoe Obshchestvo) Izdatel'stvo Nauka, S.-Peterburgskoe Otdelenie, Mendeleevskaya liniya, 1, 199034 St. Petersburg, Russia.
—BLDSC (0399.570000); CISTI; KNAW; Linda Hall.

595.7   XO   ISSN 0071-0792
ENTOMOLOGICKE PROBLEMY. (Text in German or Slovak; summaries in English, German, Russian) 1961. irreg. price varies. (Slovenska Akademia Vied, Slovenska Entomologicka Spolocnost) Veda, Publishing House of the Slovak Academy of Sciences, Bradacova 7, 852 86 Bratislava, Slovakia. (Dist. by: Slovart, Nam. Slobody 6, 817 64 Bratislava, Slovakia) Ed. Ilja Okali. **Indexed:** Biol.Abstr., Rev.Appl.Entomol.

595.7   NE   ISSN 0013-8827
CODEN: ETBRAV
ENTOMOLOGISCHE BERICHTEN. (Text in Dutch, English, French and German) 1901. m. fl.220 (effective 1996 & 1997). Nederlandse Entomologische Vereniging, Plantage Middenlaan 64, 1018 DH Amsterdam, Netherlands. Ed. Dr. J.G.M. Cuppen. bk.rev.; charts; illus.; index. circ. 1,000. **Indexed:** Apic.Abstr., Bio-Contr.News & Info., Biol.Abstr., Ecol.Abstr., Entomol.Abstr., Forest.Abstr., Rev.Appl.Entomol. **Document type:** academic/scholarly publication.
—BLDSC (3781.000000); Linda Hall; UnCover.

595.7   GW   ISSN 0013-8835
CODEN: EBBSAA
ENTOMOLOGISCHE BLAETTER FUER BIOLOGIE UND SYSTEMATIK DER KAEFER. (Text in English, French, German and Spanish) 1905. 3/yr. DM.86. Verlag Goecke und Evers, Duererstr. 13, 47799 Krefeld, Germany. Eds. A.M.J. Evers, G.A. Lohse. adv.; bk.rev.; charts; illus.; index.; maps. circ. 500. (back issues avail.) **Indexed:** Biol.Abstr., Entomol.Abstr., Rev.Appl.Entomol., Zoo.Rec.
—CISTI; SWETS. **CCC.**

595.7   AU
ENTOMOLOGISCHES NACHRICHTENBLATT. (Supplement to: Arbeitsgemeinschaft Oesterreichischer Entomologen. Zeitschrift (ISSN 0375-5223)) 1994. q. S.20 per no. (foreign S.25). Arbeitsgemeinschaft Oesterreichischer Entomologen, Ludo-Hartmann-Platz 7, A-1160 Vienna, Austria. Ed. Friedrich Weisert. **Document type:** academic/scholarly publication.

595.7   SW   ISSN 0013-886X
CODEN: ETTIAQ
ENTOMOLOGISK TIDSKRIFT. (Text in English and Swedish) 1880. 3/yr. SEK 200 to individuals in Nordic countries; institutions SEK 280; non-Nordic countries SEK 380 (effective 1997). Sveriges Entomologiska Foerening - Entomological Society of Sweden, Uppsala Universitet, Genetiska Institutionen, Programmet i Naturvaardsbiologi, Box 7003, S-750 07 Uppsala, Sweden. TEL 46-90-18-65-26. E-mail: ola.atlegrim@szoeek.slu.se. (Subscr. to: Sveriges Entomologiska Foerening, c/o Ola Atlegrim, Snipgraend 9, S-906 24 Umeaa, Sweden. TEL 46-90-18-77-89. FAX 46-90-16-68-17) Ed. Sven-Aake Berglind. adv.; bk.rev.; charts; illus.; index, cum.index: 1880-1959. circ. 1,000. **Indexed:** Apic.Abstr., Bio-Contr.News & Info., Biol.Abstr., Rev.Appl.Entomol. **Document type:** academic/scholarly publication.
—CISTI; Linda Hall.
Description: Covers entomology: faunistics, ecology, conservation biology, taxonomy and reviews.
Refereed Serial

595.709489   DK   ISSN 0013-8851
CODEN: ETMDAA
ENTOMOLOGISKE MEDDELELSER. (Text in Danish and English; summaries in English) 1887. 4/yr. DKK 225 to non-members. Entomologisk Forening - Danish Entomological Society, c/o Zoologisk Museum, Universitetsparken 15, 2100 Copenhagen, Denmark. TEL 35-32-10-00. FAX 35-32-10-10. Ed. Leif Lyneborg. adv.; bk.rev.; charts; illus. circ. 700. **Indexed:** Bio-Contr.News & Info., Biol.Abstr., Entomol.Abstr., Rev.Appl.Entomol., Zoo.Rec.
—BLDSC (3785.000000); CISTI; Linda Hall; UnCover.

595.7   UK   ISSN 0013-8878
THE ENTOMOLOGIST. 1840. q. £30 (outside Europe £30.50) (effective 1996). Royal Entomological Society, 41 Queen's Gate, London SW7 5HR, England. TEL 44-171-584-8361. FAX 44-171-581-8505. E-mail: royenson@demon.co.uk; URL: http://www.demon.co.uk/royensoc. (also avail. in microfiche from IDC) **Document type:** academic/scholarly publication.
—BLDSC (3786.000000); CISTI; EMDOCS; Linda Hall; UnCover.

595.7   FR   ISSN 0013-8886
CODEN: ETMGAJ
ENTOMOLOGISTE; revue d'amateurs. 1944. bi-m. 220 F. (Europe 250 F.; elsewhere 290 F.) (effective 1997). Museum National d'Histoire Naturelle, Laboratoire d'Entomologie, 45 rue de Buffon, 75005 Paris, France. Ed. R.M. Quentin. adv.; bk.rev.; charts; illus. **Indexed:** Biol.Abstr.

595.7   UK   ISSN 0013-8894
CODEN: ETGAA5
ENTOMOLOGIST'S GAZETTE. 1950. q. £27 in U.K. & Europe; rest of world £30($66) (effective 1997). Gem Publishing Co., Brightwood, Bell Ln., Brightwell-cum-Sotwell, Wallingford, Oxon OX10 0QD, England. TEL 44-1491-833882. FAX 44-1491-825161. Ed. W.G. Tremewan. adv.: page £35; trim 176 x 110. bk.rev.; charts; illus. circ. 475. (back issues avail.) **Indexed:** Biol.Abstr., Ind.Vet., Rev.Appl.Entomol., Sport Fish.Abstr., Vet.Bull., Wild.Rev., Zoo.Rec. **Document type:** academic/scholarly publication.
—BLDSC (3787.000000); EMDOCS; Linda Hall; UnCover.
Description: Devoted to Palaearctic entomology. Contains articles and notes on the biology, ecology, distribution, taxonomy and systematics of all orders of insects.

BIOLOGY — ENTOMOLOGY

595.7   UK   ISSN 0013-8908
QL461   CODEN: ENMMAT
ENTOMOLOGIST'S MONTHLY MAGAZINE. 1864. 3/yr. £30 in U.K. & Europe; rest of world £33($72) (effective 1997). Gem Publishing Co., Brightwood, Bell Ln., Brightwell-cum-Sotwell, Wallingford, Oxon OX10 0QD, England. TEL 44-1491-833882. FAX 44-1491-825161. Ed. K.G.V. Smith. adv.: page £35; trim 176 x 110. bk.rev.; bibl.; illus.; index. circ. 500. (also avail. in microfiche from IDC; microfilm from BHP; back issues avail.) **Indexed:** Bio.Contr.News & Info., Biol.Abstr., Curr.Adv.Ecol.Sci., Forest.Abstr., Forest Prod.Abstr., Hort.Abstr., Rev.Appl.Entomol., Rice Abstr., Soils & Fert., Weed Abstr., Zoo.Rec. **Document type:** academic/scholarly publication.
—BLDSC (3788.000000); CISTI; Linda Hall; SWETS; UnCover.
    Description: Contains articles on all orders of insects and terrestrial arthropods, specialising in the British fauna and groups other than lepidoptera.

595.7   UK   ISSN 0013-8916
                                CODEN: ERJVAZ
ENTOMOLOGIST'S RECORD AND JOURNAL OF VARIATION. 1890. bi-m. £25($47) (effective 1996). Entomologist's Record, 31 Oakdene Rd., Brockham, Betchworth, Surrey RH3 7JU, England. Ed. P.A. Sokoloff. adv.; bk.rev.; index. circ. 700. (also avail. in microfiche from IDC) **Indexed:** Biol.Abstr. **Document type:** academic/scholarly publication.
—BLDSC (3789.000000).

595.7   BL   ISSN 0103-975X
ENTOMOLOGY NEWSLETTER. 1974. irreg. free. International Society of Sugar Cane Technologists, c/o IAA-Planalsucar, Caixa Postal 153-158, 13600 Araras SP, Brazil. TELEX 019-1872. Ed. P.S.M. Botelho. circ. 150. **Indexed:** Bio-Contr.News & Info., Biol.Abstr., Hort.Abstr., Rev.Appl.Entomol.

595.7   II   ISSN 0377-9335
QL461   CODEN: ENTOD5
ENTOMON. (Text in English) 1976. q. Rs.400 (foreign $120). Association for Advancement of Entomology, c/o Department of Zoology, University of Kerala, Kariavattom, Trivandrum 695 581, India. TEL 91-471-418906. FAX 91-471-446859. E-mail: murali@univker.ernet.in. Ed. Dr. D. Muraleedharan. adv.; bk.rev. circ. 400. **Indexed:** Agroforest.Abstr., Bio-Contr.News & Info., Biodet.Abstr., Biol.Abstr., Chem.Abstr., Curr.Adv.Ecol.Sci., Curr.Adv.Plant Sci., Curr.Cont., Entomol.Abstr., Forest.Abstr., Ind.Sci.Rev., Ornam.Hort., Protozool.Abstr., Ref.Zh., Rev.Appl.Entomol., Sci.Cit.Ind., Soils & Fert., Soyabean Abstr., Triticale Abstr., Trop.Oil Seeds Abstr., Weed Abstr. **Document type:** academic/scholarly publication.
—BLDSC (3790.300000); CASDDS; CISTI; Linda Hall; UnCover.

595.7   NE   ISSN 0106-2808
ENTOMONOGRAPH. 1978. irreg., vol.12, 1990. price varies. E.J. Brill, P.O. Box 9000, 2300 PA Leiden, Netherlands. TEL 31-71-5353500. FAX 31-71-5317532. TELEX 39296 BRILL NL. E-mail: ejbrill@brill.nl. (In N. America: E.J. Brill, 24 Hudson St., Kinderhook, NY 12106. TEL 800-962-4406. FAX 518-758-1959) R&P contact: Elizabeth Vennekamp. (back issues avail.) **Indexed:** Zoo.Rec. **Document type:** monographic series.
—KNAW.
    Description: Scholarly studies of individual species and families of insects from different regions of the world.
Refereed Serial

595.7   US   ISSN 0046-225X
SB599   CODEN: EVETBX
ENVIRONMENTAL ENTOMOLOGY. 1972. bi-m. $75 to individuals (foreign $95); institutions $150 (foreign $170); members $25 (foreign $40). Entomological Society of America, 9301 Annapolis Rd., Lanham, MD 20706. TEL 301-731-4535. FAX 301-731-4538. (Subscr. to: Box 177, Hyattsville, MD 20781-0177) Eds. R.E. Stinner, Karen M. Clancy. adv.; abstr.; bibl.; charts; illus.; stat.; index. circ. 3,100. (also avail. in microform from MIM,UMI; reprint service avail. from UMI) **Indexed:** Agri.Eng.Abstr., Agri.Ind., Apic.Abstr., ASCA, Bibl.Agri., Bio-Contr.News & Info., Biol.Abstr., Biol.& Agr.Ind., Biotech.Abstr., Chem.Abstr., Cott.& Trop.Fibr.Abstr., Curr.Adv.Ecol.Sci., Curr.Cont., Ecol.Abstr., Energy Info.Abstr., Environ.Abstr., Environ.Per.Bibl. (1972-), Excerp.Med., Fababean Abstr., Field Crop Abstr., Forest.Abstr., Forest Prod.Abstr., Hort.Abstr., Ind.Sci.Rev., Ind.Vet., INIS Atomind., Irr.& Drain.Abstr., Maize Abstr., Pollut.Abstr., Potato Abstr., Poult.Abstr., Protozool.Abstr., Rev.Appl.Entomol., Rice Abstr., Sci.Cit.Ind., Seed Abstr., Soils & Fert., Sorghum & Millets Abstr., Soyabean Abstr., Sport Fish.Abstr., Triticale Abstr., Vet.Bull., Weed Abstr., Wild.Rev., Zoo.Rec. **Document type:** academic/scholarly publication.
—BLDSC (3791.464000); CASDDS; CISTI; EMDOCS; Genuine Article; KR SourceOne; Linda Hall; SWETS; UMI; UnCover. **CCC.**
    Description: Reports of research on the interaction of insects with the biological, chemical, and physical aspects of their environment.
Refereed Serial

595.7   JA   ISSN 0071-1268
ESAKIA. (Text in English, French, German) 1960. irreg. membership. Kyushu University, Faculty of Agriculture, Hikosan Biological Laboratory - Kyushu Daigaku Nogakubu Fuzoku Hikosan Seibutsugaku Jikkenjo, Hikosan, Soedacho, Tagawa-gun, Fukuoka-ken 824-07, Japan. Ed. Katsura Morimoto. bk.rev.; charts; illus. **Indexed:** Biol.Abstr., Curr.Adv.Ecol.Sci., Entomol.Abstr., Rev.Appl.Entomol., Zoo.Rec.
—BLDSC (3810.950000); UnCover.

595.7   JA   ISSN 0289-4289
ESSA KONCHU DOKOKAI KAIHO/ESSA ENTOMOLOGICAL SOCIETY. TRANSACTIONS. (Text in English, Japanese) 1946. s-a. 3000 Yen. Essa Konchu Dokokai - Essa Entomological Society, Kurokawa Byoin, Kurokawamura, Kitakanbara-gun, Niigata-ken 959-28, Japan.

595.7   XR   ISSN 1210-5759
QL461   CODEN: EJENE2
EUROPEAN JOURNAL OF ENTOMOLOGY. (Text and summaries in English) 1904. q. $65 to individuals in Europe (elsewhere $85); institutions in Europe $160 (elsewhere $180) (effective Mar. 1997). Academy of Sciences of the Czech Republic, Institute of Entomology, Branisovska 31, 37005 Ceske Budejovice, Czech Republic. TEL 420-38-817213. FAX 420-38-43624. E-mail: eje@entu.cas.cz; URL: http://www.jcu.cz/~entu/eje.htm. Eds. Petr Svacha, Ivo Hodek. adv.; bk.rev.; bibl.; charts; illus. circ. 500. **Indexed:** Apic.Abstr., ASCA, Biol.Abstr., Chem.Abstr., Curr.Adv.Ecol.Sci., Curr.Adv.Genetics & Molec.Biol., Curr.Cont., Ecol.Abstr., Forest.Abstr., Helminthol.Abstr., Hort.Abstr., IBR, Ref.Zh., Rev.Appl.Entomol., Sci.Cit.Ind., Triticale Abstr., Zoo.Rec. **Document type:** academic/scholarly publication.
—BLDSC (3829.728850); CASDDS; CISTI; Genuine Article; Linda Hall; UnCover.
    Formerly (until vol.90, 1993): Acta Entomologica Bohemoslovaca (ISSN 0001-5601)
    Description: Papers on systematic entomology and arachnology, on physiology, morphology, ecology and all experimental and applied branches of entomology by Czech and foreign authors.
Refereed Serial

595.7   US
EXECUTIVE REPORTS. Cover title: Pest Control Executive Reports. 1991. m. $67. Pinto & Associates, Inc., 29839 Oak Rd., Mechanicsville, MD 20659. TEL 301-884-3020. FAX 301-884-4068. Ed. Sandra Kraft; Pub. Lawrence J. Pinto. bk.rev.; charts; illus.; stat.; tr.lit.; circ. 350 (paid). (looseleaf format; back issues avail.) **Document type:** trade publication, newsletter.
    Description: Provides management information relating to pest control, for owners, managers and supervisors of pest control businesses.

EXPERIMENTAL & APPLIED ACAROLOGY. see *BIOLOGY*

FAUNA D'ITALIA; repertorio generale delle specie animali esistenti in Italia. see *BIOLOGY — Zoology*

595.70948   NE   ISSN 0106-8377
                                   CODEN: FESCDE
FAUNA ENTOMOLOGICA SCANDINAVICA. (Text in English) 1973. irreg., vol.32, 1995. price varies. (Societas Entomologica Scandinavica) E.J. Brill, P.O. Box 9000, 2300 PA Leiden, Netherlands. TEL 31-71-5353500. FAX 31-71-5317532. TELEX 39296 BRILL NL. E-mail: ejbrill@brill.nl. (In N. America: E.J. Brill, 24 Hudson St., Kinderhook, NY 12106. TEL 800-962-4406. FAX 518-758-1959) Ed. N.P. Kristensen. R&P contact: Elizabeth Vennekamp. illus. (back issues avail.) **Indexed:** Biol.Abstr., Zoo.Rec. **Document type:** monographic series.
—BLDSC (3897.945000).
    Description: Scholarly studies aiding in the identification and study of specific insect classes indigenous to Fennoscandia and Denmark.
Refereed Serial

595.7   NO   ISSN 0332-7698
QL461   CODEN: FNSBD6
FAUNA NORVEGICA SERIES B. NORWEGIAN JOURNAL OF ENTOMOLOGY. (Text in English; summaries in Norwegian) 1979. s-a. NOK 120 to non-members; members free; outside Norway NOK 160 (effective 1997). Norsk Institutt for Naturforskning (NINA), c/o Kjetil Bevanger, Tungasletta 2, N-7005 Trondheim, Norway. TEL 47-73-58-05-00. FAX 47-73-91-54-33. E-mail: kjetil.bevanger@nina.nina.no. Ed. John O. Solem. R&P contact: Kjetil Bevanger. adv. contact: Kjetil Bevanger. cum.index every 3 yrs. circ. 850. (back issues avail.) **Indexed:** Bio-Contr.News & Info., Ecol.Abstr., IBR, Key Word Ind.Wildl.Res. **Document type:** academic/scholarly publication.
—BLDSC (3899.259000); CISTI; Linda Hall; UnCover. **CCC.**
    Description: Publishes original new information generally relevant to Norwegian entomology, with emphasis on papers which are mainly faunal or zoogeographical in scope or content.

595.7   US
FLEA NEWS. 1980. 2/yr. free to qualified personnel. Iowa State University, Department of Entomology, Ames, IA 50011-3222. TEL 515-232-7714. FAX 515-233-1851. E-mail: relewis@iastate.edu; URL: http://www.public.iastate.edu/~entomology/FleaNews/AboutFleaNews.html. Ed. Robert Lewis. R&P contact: Robert Lewis. bk.rev. circ. 175. **Document type:** newsletter.
●Also available online.
    Description: Devoted to matters involving insects belonging to the order Siphonaptera (fleas) and related subjects.

595.7   GW
FLIES OF THE NEARCTIC REGION. (Text in English, German) 1980. irreg. E. Schweizerbart'sche Verlagsbuchhandlung, Johannesstr. 3A, 70176 Stuttgart, Germany. TEL 49-711-625001. FAX 49-711-625005. Ed. Graham C.D. Griffiths. **Document type:** monographic series.

595.7   US   ISSN 0013-8932
                                CODEN: FPECAI
FLORIDA. DEPARTMENT OF AGRICULTURE AND CONSUMER SERVICES. ENTOMOLOGY CIRCULAR. 1962. bi-m. free. Department of Agriculture and Consumer Services, Division of Plant Industry, 1911 S.W. 34th St., Box 147100, Gainesville, FL 32614-7100. TEL 904-372-3505. FAX 904-955-2301. Ed. Maeve McConnell. R&P contact: Maeve McConnell. (looseleaf format) **Indexed:** Bio-Contr.News & Info., Biol.Abstr., Hort.Abstr., Ind.Vet., Rev.Appl.Entomol., Zoo.Rec. **Document type:** government publication.
—BLDSC (3789.660000).

BIOLOGY — ENTOMOLOGY

595.7 US ISSN 0015-4040
QL461 CODEN: FETMAC
FLORIDA ENTOMOLOGIST; an international journal for the Americas. 1917. q. $30 to non-members; members $25. Florida Entomological Society, c/o R.M. Baranowski, Ed., 18905 S.W. 280 St., Homestead, FL 33031. TEL 813-324-5502. FAX 904-374-5852. bk.rev.; bibl.; charts; illus.; index. circ. 800. **Indexed:** ASCA, Bibl.Agri., Bio-Contr.News & Info., Biodet.Abstr., Biol.Abstr., Biotech.Abstr., Chem.Abstr., Curr.Adv.Ecol.Sci., Curr.Cont., Entomol.Abstr., Forest.Abstr., Hort.Abstr., Ind.Sci.Rev., Maize Abstr., Protozool.Abstr., Rev.Appl.Entomol., Sci.Cit.Ind., Soils & Fert., Sport Fish.Abstr., SSCI, Triticale Abstr., Weed Abstr., Wild.Rev., Zoo.Rec.
—BLDSC (3956.000000); CASDDS; CISTI; EMDOCS; Genuine Article; Linda Hall; SWETS; UnCover.
Refereed Serial

595.7 US ISSN 0885-5943
QL434.A1 CODEN: OPFADH
FLORIDA STATE COLLECTION OF ARTHROPODS. OCCASIONAL PAPERS. 1981. irreg., vol.8, 1993. price varies. Department of Agriculture and Consumer Services, Division of Plant Industry, 1911 S.W. 34th St., Box 147100, Gainesville, FL 32614-7100. TEL 904-372-3505. FAX 904-336-2300. Ed. J.B. Heppner. R&P contact: Maeve McConnell. (back issues avail.) **Document type:** government publication.

595.7 HU ISSN 0373-9465
CODEN: ROKOA5
FOLIA ENTOMOLOGICA HUNGARICA/ROVARTANI KOZLEMENYEK. (Text in English) 1923. a. $48 (effective 1998). Magyar Termeszettudomanyi Muzeum - Hungarian Natural History Museum, Baross u. 13, 1088 Budapest, Hungary. TEL 36-1-3130035. FAX 36-1-1171669. Ed. S. Mahunka. illus. circ. 350. (back issues avail.) **Indexed:** Biol.Abstr., Curr.Adv.Ecol.Sci., Rev.Appl.Entomol. **Document type:** academic/scholarly publication.
—BLDSC (3969.800000).
Description: Contains papers written by museum staff members or based on materials deposited there.

595.7 MX ISSN 0430-8603
QL477 CODEN: FEMXAA
FOLIA ENTOMOLOGICA MEXICANA. (Text and summaries in English and Spanish) 1961. 3/yr. Mex.$115 (foreign $35) (effective 1997-1998). Sociedad Mexicana de Entomologia, A.C., Consejo Editorial Folia Entomologica Mexicana, Apdo. Postal 63, 91000 Xalapa, Veracruz, Mexico. TEL 52-28-421800. FAX 52-28-187809. E-mail: folia@sun.ieco.conacyt.mx; URL: http://folentmex.ieco.conacyt.mx. Ed. Rodolfo Novelo-Gutierrez. R&P contact: Arturo Bonet-Ceballos. adv. contact: Arturo Bonet-Ceballos. bk.rev.; abstr.; bibl.; charts; illus.; index, cum.index: 1961-1971. circ. 800. (also avail. in microfilm from OMN) **Indexed:** Apic.Abstr., Bio-Contr.News & Info., Biol.Abstr., Entomol.Abstr., Hort.Abstr., Poult.Abstr., Rev.Appl.Entomol. **Document type:** academic/scholarly publication.
—Linda Hall.
Description: Presents papers on physiology, morphology, systematics, ecology, and all experimental and applied branches of entomology, arachnology and acarology.
Refereed Serial

THE FOOD INSECTS NEWSLETTER. see *FOOD AND FOOD INDUSTRIES*

595.7 JA ISSN 0429-2871
FRAGMENTA COLEOPTEROLOGICA. (Text in English) 1961. irreg. (approx. a.). Takehiko Nakane, Pub., 2-19-502, Nirenokidai, 3273, Asahigaokacho, Hanamigawa-ku, Chiba-shi, Chiba-ken 262, Japan. circ. 100. **Indexed:** Biol.Abstr.
—BLDSC (4031.800000).

595.7 IT ISSN 0429-288X
FRAGMENTA ENTOMOLOGICA. (Text in English, French, German, Italian, Spanish; summaries in Italian, English) 1951. s-a. exchange basis only. Universita degli Studi di Roma la Sapienza, Via Catone 34, 00192 Rome, Italy. Ed. A. Vigna-Taglianti. bk.rev. circ. 400. **Indexed:** Bio-Contr.News & Info., Biol.Abstr., Entomol.Abstr., Forest.Abstr., Rev.Appl.Entomol., VITIS, Zoo.Rec.
—BLDSC (4031.900000).

595.7 JA ISSN 0915-0323
FUKUI CHUHO/ENTOMOLOGICAL JOURNAL OF FUKUI. (Text in Japanese; summaries in English, Japanese) 1987. s-a. Fukui Konchu Kenkyukai - Fukui Entomological Society, c/o Mr. Masaru Osada, Fukui Shiritsu Kyodo Shizen Kagaku Hakubutsukan, 147, Asuwa Kamicho, Fukui-shi, Fukui-ken 910, Japan.

595.7 JA
FUKUISHIMA NO MUSHI/INSECTS OF FUKUISHIMA. (Text in Japanese) 1980. a. Fukushima Mushi no Kai - Fukuishima Insect Lovers' Association, c/o Mr. Tadao Saito, 18-5 Sakuradai, Tazawa, Fukuishima-shi, Fukuishima-ken 960, Japan.

FUNDACION MIGUEL LILLO. MISCELANEA. see *BIOLOGY — Botany*

595.7 JA ISSN 0916-1112
FUTAO/INSECTS JOURNAL. (Text in English, Japanese) 1989. irreg. (2-4/yr.). 5000 Yen. Futaokai - Entomologists Association, 688-2, Tashima, Tottori-shi, Tottori-ken 680, Japan. Ed. Hiroto Hanafusa. **Document type:** bulletin.

595.7 JA ISSN 0286-3537
GARUI TSUSHIN/JAPAN HETEROCERISTS' JOURNAL. (Text in English, Japanese) 1953. 6/yr. membership. Nihon Garui Gakkai - Japan Heterocerists' Society, Kokuritsu Kagaku Hakubutsukan Bunkan, Hyakunincho 3-chome, Shinjuku-ku, Tokyo 160, Japan.

595.7 AT ISSN 0158-0760
QL487 CODEN: GAENDS
GENERAL AND APPLIED ENTOMOLOGY. 1964. a. Aus.$20. Entomological Society of New South Wales, Entomology Department, Australian Museum, College St., Sydney N.S.W. 2000, Australia. Ed. D.J. Bickel. adv.; bk.rev. circ. 210. **Indexed:** Aus.Sci.Ind., Biol.Abstr., Chem.Abstr., Ind.Vet., Rev.Appl.Entomol., Vet.Bull.
—CASDDS; Linda Hall; UnCover.
Formerly (until vol. 10, 1978): Entomological Society of Australia (N.S.W.) Journal (ISSN 0071-0725)

595.7 JA ISSN 0433-3950
GENSEI/ENTOMOLOGICAL SOCIETY OF KOCHI. JOURNAL. (Text in Japanese; summaries in English, Japanese) 1952. 2/yr. Kochi Konchu Kenkyukai - Entomological Society of Kochi, Kochi Daigaku Nogakubu, Otsu 200, Monobe, Nankoku-shi, Kochi-ken 783, Japan.
—BLDSC (4116.350000).

595.7 IT ISSN 0392-7296
QL482.I8 CODEN: GIENDG
GIORNALE ITALIANO DI ENTOMOLOGIA. (Text in English, French, Italian, Portuguese, Spanish) 1982. 3/yr. L.75000 to individuals; institutions L.89000 (effective 1996) L.83000 to individuals; institutions L.101000 (effective 1997). Marco Berra, Ed. & Pub., Casella Postale 188, 26100 Cremona, Italy. R&P contact: Marco Berra. adv.; illus.; cum.index. circ. 250. **Indexed:** Bio-Contr.News & Info., Curr.Adv.Ecol.Sci., Entomol.Abstr., Forest.Abstr., Zoo.Rec. **Document type:** bulletin.
—Linda Hall.

595.7 US ISSN 0090-0222
QL461 CODEN: GRLEAG
GREAT LAKES ENTOMOLOGIST. 1966. q. $30 per vol. (effective 1997). Michigan Entomological Society, c/o Dept. of Entomology, Michigan State Univ., East Lansing, MI 48824. TEL 517-321-2192. Ed. Mark F. O'Brien. bk.rev.; bibl.; charts; illus.; cum.index. circ. 650. (also avail. in microfilm from UMI; back issues avail.; reprint service avail. from UMI) **Indexed:** ASCA, Bibl.Agri., Bio-Contr.News & Info., Biol.Abstr., Curr.Adv.Ecol.Sci., Curr.Cont., Forest.Abstr., Helminthol.Abstr., Hort.Abstr., Ind.Sci.Rev., Mich.Mag.Ind., Potato Abstr., Rev.Appl.Entomol., Risk Abstr., Sci.Cit.Ind., Soils & Fert., Sport Fish.Abstr., Triticale Abstr., Weed Abstr., Wild.Rev., Zoo.Rec. **Document type:** academic/scholarly publication.
—BLDSC (4214.530000); EMDOCS; Genuine Article; Linda Hall; UMI; UnCover. CCC.
Formerly: Michigan Entomologist (ISSN 0026-2145)
Refereed Serial

595.7 US
GRESSITT CENTER NEWS. 1989. s-a. free. Bishop Museum, Department of Entomology, Box 19000-A, Honolulu, HI 96817-0916. TEL 808-848-4196. FAX 808-841-8968. Ed. Gordon M. Nishida. circ. 800. (back issues avail.) **Document type:** newsletter.
Description: Covers Pacific entomology and activities of Gressitt Center for research.

595.7 SP ISSN 0213-3873
GRUPO ENTOMOLOGICO DE MADRID. BOLETIN. 1985. a. free. Grupo Entomologico de Madrid, c/o Fac. de Ciencias, Univ. Autonoma de Madrid, 28693 Cantoblanco (Madrid), Spain. **Indexed:** Ind.SST.

595.7 US ISSN 0073-134X
CODEN: PHESAI
HAWAIIAN ENTOMOLOGICAL SOCIETY. PROCEEDINGS. 1906. a. $16 (foreign $16.50) (effective Jan. 1991). Hawaiian Entomological Society, c/o Entomology Dept., Bishop Museum, 1525 Bernice St., Honolulu, HI 96817. TEL 808-956-7076. FAX 808-956-2428. Ed. Neal L. Evenhuis. R&P contact: Neal L. Evenhuis. circ. 600. (reprint service avail. from UMI) **Indexed:** Apic.Abstr., Bio-Contr.News & Info., Biol.Abstr., Curr.Adv.Ecol.Sci., Weed Abstr., Zoo.Rec. **Document type:** academic/scholarly publication.
—BLDSC (6707.000000); CISTI; Linda Hall; UnCover.
Description: Technical items on systematics, biology and control of insects and related organisms. Emphasis is on Hawaii and the Pacific area.
Refereed Serial

HESSISCHE FAUNISTISCHE BRIEFE. see *BIOLOGY — Zoology*

595.7 GW ISSN 0724-1348
HETEROCERA SUMATRANA. (Text in English and German) 1982. irreg., vol. 10, 1996. price varies. Heterocera Sumatrana Society e.V., Kreuzburgerstr. 6, 37085 Goettingen, Germany. TEL 49-551-76786. Ed.Bd. R&P contact: Lutz W.R. Kobes. bibl.; illus. (back issues avail.) **Indexed:** Entomol.Abstr. **Document type:** monographic series.
Description: Discusses entomological research of moths and butterflies.
Refereed Serial

595.7 JA ISSN 0389-827X
HIROSHIMA MUSHI NO KAI KAIHO/ENTOMOLOGICAL SOCIETY OF HIROSHIMA. JOURNAL. (Text in Japanese) 1962. a. Hiroshima Mushi no Kai - Entomological Society of Hiroshima, c/o Mr. Murkami, 6963-2, Numatacho Tomo, Asa Minami-ku, Hiroshima-shi, Hiroshima-ken 732, Japan.

595.7 US ISSN 1070-4140
HOLARCTIC LEPIDOPTERA. 1994. s-a. $40 (effective 1996). Association for Tropical Lepidoptera, Box 141210, Gainsville, FL 32614-1210. Ed. J.B. Heppner. bibl.; illus.; tr.lit.; index, cum.index. circ. 1,250. (back issues avail.) **Document type:** academic/scholarly publication.
Description: General taxonomy and conservation of north temperate species of moths and butterflies from North America and Eurasia.
Refereed Serial

595.7 JA ISSN 0917-3560
HOTARU JOHO KOKAN/STUDY GROUP ON FIREFLY. REPORT. (Text in Japanese) irreg. Zenkoku Hotaru Kenkyukai - Study Group on Firefly, c/o Mr. Murakami, 15-19 Hamasaka 2-chome, Tottori-shi, Tottori-ken 680, Japan.

595.7 JA
HOTARU KENKYU TAIKAI/REPORT OF MEETING ON FIREFLY. (Text in Japanese) a. Zenkoku Hotaru Kenkyukai - Study Group on Firefly, c/o Mr. Murakami, 15-19 Hamasaka 2-chome, Tottori-shi, Tottori-ken 680, Japan.

I B R A CONFERENCE ON TROPICAL BEES. (International Bee Research Association) see *AGRICULTURE*

I P M PRACTITIONER; monitoring the field of pest management. (Integrated Pest Management) see *AGRICULTURE*

INDIAN BEE JOURNAL. see *AGRICULTURE*

BIOLOGY — ENTOMOLOGY

595.7   II   ISSN 0073-6392
QL483   CODEN: IFREAI
INDIAN FOREST RECORDS (NEW SERIES) ENTOMOLOGY. (Text in English) 1935. irreg., vol. 14, no. 2. 1981. price varies. Forest Research Institute & Colleges, P.O. New Forest, Dehra Dun, India. circ. 500. **Indexed:** Biol.Abstr., Curr.Adv.Ecol.Sci., Forest.Abstr., Indian Sci.Abstr., Rev.Appl.Entomol.
—CISTI; Linda Hall.

595.7   II   ISSN 0970-969X
INDIAN ODONATOLOGY. (Text in English) 1988. irreg. price varies. International Odonatological Society, D-f, Saraswati Nagar, Jodhpur 342 005, India. TEL 91-291-40766. Ed. B.K. Tyagi. circ. 200. **Document type:** academic/scholarly publication.
Description: Highlights the various characteristics of the dragonfly fauna from the Oriental region.
Refereed Serial

595.7   UK   ISSN 0965-1748
QL495   CODEN: IBMBES
INSECT BIOCHEMISTRY AND MOLECULAR BIOLOGY. 1971. m. fl.2499($1436) (effective 1998). Elsevier Science Ltd., Pergamon, P.O. Box 800, Kidlington, Oxford OX5 1DX, England. TEL 44-1865-843000. FAX 44-1865-843010. E-mail: nlinfo-f@elsevier.nl; usinfo-f@elsevier.com; forinfo-kyf04035@niftyserve.or.jp; URL: http://www.elsevier.nl/. (Subscr. to: Elsevier Science, Regional Sales Office, P.O. Box 211, 1000 AE Amsterdam, Netherlands. TEL 31-20-4853757. FAX 31-20-4853432; Subscr. in the Americas to: Elsevier Science, Regional Sales Office, Box 945, New York, NY 10159-0945. TEL 212-633-3730. FAX 212-633-3680; Subscr. in Australasia and the Far East to: Elsevier Science (Singapore) Pte Ltd, No.1 Temasek Ave., No.17-01 Millenia Tower, Singapore 039192, Singapore. TEL 65-434-3727. FAX 65-337-2230) Ed. Larry Gilbert. adv. circ. 1,015. (also avail. in microfilm from UMI; reprint service avail. from UMI) **Indexed:** Abstr.Hyg., Apic.Abstr., ASCA, Bio-Contr.News & Info., Biol.Abstr., Biotech.Abstr., Chem.Abstr., Curr.Adv.Ecol.Sci., Curr.Cont., Ind.Med. (1993-), Ind.Sci.Rev., Potato Abstr., Protozool.Abstr., Rev.Appl.Entomol., Sci.Cit.Ind., Trop.Dis.Bull. **Document type:** academic/scholarly publication.
—BLDSC (4516.852000); CASDDS; CISTI; EMDOCS; Genuine Article; SWETS; UMI; UnCover. **CCC.**
Formerly (until 1992): Insect Biochemistry (ISSN 0020-1790)
Description: Topics covered include: neurochemistry, hormone and pheromone biochemistry, enzymes and metabolism, hormone action and gene regulation, gene characterization and structure, pharmacology, immunology and cell and tissue culture.
Refereed Serial

595.7   UK   ISSN 0962-1075
QL493.5   CODEN: IMBIE3
INSECT MOLECULAR BIOLOGY. q. £198($362) (foreign £218) (effective 1998). (Royal Entomological Society) Blackwell Science Ltd., Osney Mead, Oxford OX2 0EL, England. TEL 44-1865-206206. FAX 44-1865-721205. E-mail: journals.cs@blacksci.co.uk; URL: http://www.black.co.uk. Eds. J.M. Crampton, A.A. James; Pub. Allen Stevens. R&P contact: Sarah Pollard. adv. contact: Martine Cariou-Keen. circ. 265. (also avail. in microfilm from UMI; back issues avail.) **Indexed:** ASCA, Ind.Med. (1993-). **Document type:** academic/scholarly publication.
—BLDSC (4516.885000); CASDDS; CISTI; EMDOCS; Genuine Article; SWETS; UMI. **CCC.**
Refereed Serial

595.7   KE   ISSN 0191-9040
SB818   CODEN: ISIADL
INSECT SCIENCE AND ITS APPLICATION; the international journal of tropical insect science. 1980. bi-m. KShs.100 to individuals; institutions Ksh.255 (effective through 1994). (International Center of Insect Physiology and Ecology) ICIPE Science Press, P.O. Box 72913, Nairobi, Kenya. TEL 254-2-802537. TELEX 25066-DUDU. (Co-sponsor: African Association of Insect Scientists) Ed. K.N. Saxena. adv. circ. 200. (also avail. in microfilm from MIM,UMI; reprint service avail. from UMI) **Indexed:** Abstr.Hyg., Agroforest.Abstr., ASCA, Bio-Contr.News & Info., Biol.Abstr., Biotech.Abstr., Chem.Abstr., Cott.& Trop.Fibr.Abstr., Curr.Adv.Ecol.Sci., Curr.Cont., Energy Ind., Energy Info.Abstr., Field Crop Abstr., Forest.Abstr., Helminthol.Abstr., Hort.Abstr., Ind.Vet., Maize Abstr., Potato Abstr., Protozool.Abstr., Rev.Appl.Entomol., Rice Abstr., Sorghum & Millets Abstr., Soyabean Abstr., Triticale Abstr., Weed Abstr. **Document type:** academic/scholarly publication.
—BLDSC (4516.918000); CASDDS; CISTI; Genuine Article; Linda Hall; SWETS; UnCover. **CCC.**

595.7   US   ISSN 1043-6057
INSECT WORLD. 1989. bi-m. $30 (effective 1992). Young Entomologists' Society, Inc., International Headquarters, 1915 Peggy Place, Lansing, MI 48910. TEL 517-887-0499. E-mail: YESbug@aol.com. Ed. Gary Dunn. bk.rev.; illus. **Document type:** newsletter.
Description: Contains information for children and adults with an interest in insects.

595.7   JA   ISSN 0020-1804
QL461   CODEN: IMATAR
INSECTA MATSUMURANA/HOKKAIDO UNIVERSITY. FACULTY OF AGRICULTURE. JOURNAL. SERIES OF ENTOMOLOGY. (Text mainly in English) 1926; N.S. 1973. irreg. exchange basis. Hokkaido University, Faculty of Agriculture, Entomological Institute - Hokkaido Daigaku Nogakubu Konchugaku Kyoshitsu, Nishi-9-chome, Kita-9-jo, Kita-ku, Sapporo 060, Japan. charts; illus. **Indexed:** Biol.Abstr., Curr.Adv.Ecol.Sci., Rev.Appl.Entomol.
—BLDSC (4517.000000); Linda Hall; UnCover.

595.7   US   ISSN 0749-6737
   CODEN: INMUEX
INSECTA MUNDI. 1985. q. $35 (foreign $41). Center for Systematic Entomology, Box 140429, Gainesville, FL 32614. Ed. James E. Lloyd. R&P contact: James E. Lloyd. adv. contact: James E. Lloyd. bk.rev.; bibl.; charts; illus. (back issues avail.) **Indexed:** Biol.Abstr., Zoo.Rec. **Document type:** academic/scholarly publication.
—BLDSC (4517.200000); UnCover.
Refereed Serial

595.7   JA   ISSN 0910-5204
QL461
THE INSECTARIUM/INSEKUTARYUMU. (Text in Japanese) 1964. m. 3300 Yen($61) Tokyo Zoological Park Society - Tokyo Dobutsuen Kyokai, c/o Ueno Zoo, 9-83 Ueno Park, Taito-ku, Tokyo 110, Japan. TEL 03-3828-8235. FAX 03-3828-8237. Ed. Minoru Yajima. adv.; bk.rev.; illus.; index. circ. 3,700. (back issues avail.) **Document type:** academic/scholarly publication.
—BLDSC (4517.500000).

595.7   SZ   ISSN 0020-1812
   CODEN: INSOA7
INSECTES SOCIAUX. (Text in English, French and German) 1952. q. 420 SFr. (foreign 432 SFr.) (effective 1997). (International Union for the Study of Social Insects) Birkhaeuser Verlag, P.O. Box 133, CH-4010 Basel, Switzerland. TEL 41-61-2050730. FAX 41-61-2050791. E-mail: subscriptions@birkhauser.ch. (Dist. in N. America by: Springer-Verlag, Mercedes Distribution Center, 160 Imlay St., Brooklyn, NY 11231, USA) Ed. J. Billen. bibl.; charts; illus. circ. 700. (also avail. in microfilm from UMI; reprint service avail. from ISI) **Indexed:** Apic.Abstr., ASCA, Bio-Contr.News & Info., Biol.Abstr., Chem.Abstr., Curr.Adv.Ecol.Sci., Curr.Cont., Forest.Abstr., Helminthol.Abstr., IBR, Rev.Appl.Entomol., Sci.Cit.Ind., Soils & Fert. **Document type:** academic/scholarly publication.
—BLDSC (4518.000000); EMDOCS; Genuine Article; Linda Hall; SWETS; UMI; UnCover. **CCC.**
Description: Covers the various aspects of the biology and evolution of social insects and other presocial arthropods.

595.7   US
INSECTIMES.* q. Nor-Am Chemical Company, 2711 Centerville Rd., Wilmington, DE 19808-1643. TEL 302-477-3014. FAX 302-477-3013. circ. 19,000. (tabloid format)

595.7   US   ISSN 0073-8115
QL489.M5   CODEN: IMICAG
INSECTS OF MICRONESIA. (Text in English, occasionally in French or German) 1954. irreg. price varies. Bishop Museum Press, 1525 Bernice St., Box 19000-A, Honolulu, HI 96817. TEL 808-947-3511. (reprint service avail. from UMI) **Indexed:** Biol.Abstr.
Description: Systematics of terrestrial arthropods of Micronesia.

595.7   US   ISSN 0098-1222
QL475.V5
INSECTS OF VIRGINIA. (Former subseries of: Virginia Polytechnic Institute and State University. Virginia Agricultural Experiment Station. Bulletins) 1969. irreg. exchange basis. Virginia Museum of Natural History, 1001 Douglas Ave., VA 24112. TEL 540-666-8629. Ed. Richard Hoffman. illus. circ. 1,000. **Document type:** academic/scholarly publication.
Description: Contains results of previously unpublished original research dealing with insects of Virginia.
Refereed Serial

INSTITUT PASTEUR DE DAKAR. RAPPORT SUR LE FONCTIONNEMENT TECHNIQUE. see *BIOLOGY — Microbiology*

595.7   BE   ISSN 0374-6232
   CODEN: BIETBB
INSTITUT ROYAL DES SCIENCES NATURELLES DE BELGIQUE. BULLETIN. SERIE A & SERIE B.* 1930. a. 1500 BEF($30) (foreign 1750 BEF). Koninklijk Belgisch Instituut voor Natuurwetenschappen - Institut Royal des Sciences Naturelles de Belgique, Vautierstraat 29, 1000 Brussels, Belgium. bibl.; charts; illus.; cum.index. circ. 1,500. (back issues avail.) **Indexed:** Biol.Abstr., Bull.Signal., Ref.Zh., Rev.Appl.Entomol., Sport Fish.Abstr., Wild.Rev., Zoo.Rec. **Document type:** academic/scholarly publication.

595.7   BL   ISSN 0020-3629
INSTITUTO AGRONOMICO DO SUL. ESCOLA DE AGRONOMIA ELISEU MACIEL. ARQUIVOS DE ENTOMOLOGIA. SERIE A & SERIE B.* 1959. s-a. $1.50. Universidade Federal de Pelotas, Faculdade de Agronomie "Eliseu Maciel", C.P.15, Pelotas, Rio Grande do Sul, Brazil. Ed. Ceslao Mario De Biezanko. bk.rev.; bibl.; charts; illus. circ. 1,500.

595.7 634.9   MX
INSTITUTO NACIONAL DE INVESTIGACIONES FORESTALES, AGRICOLAS Y PECUARIAS. BOLETIN DIVULGATIVO. (Text in Spanish; summaries in English and Spanish) 1961. irreg., no.80, 1994. price varies. Instituto Nacional de Investigaciones Forestales, Agricolas y Pecuarias, Biblioteca Nacional Forestal Ing. Roberto Villasenor Angeles, Av. Progreso No. 5, Col. Viveros de Coyoacan, Delegacion Coyoacan, 04110 Mexico, D.F., Mexico. TEL 52-5-6584333. FAX 52-5-5548849. E-mail: comef@inifap2.inifap.conacyt.mx. (back issues avail.) **Indexed:** Biol.Abstr., Forest.Abstr., Forest Prod.Abstr.
Formerly (until 1985): Instituto Nacional de Investigaciones Forestales. Boletin Divulgativo (ISSN 0185-2361)

595.7 634.9   MX
SD147
INSTITUTO NACIONAL DE INVESTIGACIONES FORESTALES, AGRICOLAS Y PECUARIAS. BOLETIN TECNICO. (Text in Spanish; summaries in English and Spanish) 1961. irreg., latest no.142. price varies. Instituto Nacional de Investigaciones Forestales, Agricolas y Pecuarias, Biblioteca Nacional Forestal Ing. Roberto Villasenor Angeles, Av. Progreso No. 5, Col. Viveros de Coyoacan, Delegacion Coyoacan, 04110 Mexico, D.F., Mexico. TEL 52-5-6584333. FAX 52-5-5548849. E-mail: comef@inifap2.inifap.conacyt.mx. (back issues avail.) **Indexed:** Agri.Eng.Abstr., Biol.Abstr., Forest.Abstr., Forest Prod.Abstr., Soils & Fert.
Formerly (until 1985): Instituto Nacional de Investigaciones Forestales. Boletin Tecnico (ISSN 0185-2310)

BIOLOGY — ENTOMOLOGY

595.7 634.9   MX
INSTITUTO NACIONAL DE INVESTIGACIONES FORESTALES, AGRICOLAS Y PECUARIAS. PUBLICACION ESPECIAL. (Text in Spanish; summaries in English and Spanish) 1961. irreg., no.65, 1995. price varies. Instituto Nacional de Investigaciones Forestales, Agricolas y Pecuarias, Biblioteca Nacional Forestal Ing. Roberto Villasenor Angeles, Av. Progreso No. 5, Col. Viveros de Coyoacan, Delegacion Coyoacan, 04110 Mexico, D.F., Mexico. TEL 52-5-6584333. FAX 52-5-5548849. E-mail: comef@inifap2.inifap.conacyt.mx. (back issues avail.) **Indexed:** Biol.Abstr., Forest.Abstr., Forest Prod.Abstr.
   Formerly (until 1985): Instituto Nacional de Investigaciones Forestales. Publicacion Especial (ISSN 0185-2566)

INSTITUTUL DE CERCETARI PENTRU PROTECTIA PLANTELOR. ANALELE/RESEARCH INSTITUTE FOR PLANT PROTECTION. ANNALS. see *AGRICULTURE*

595.7   KE
INTERNATIONAL CENTRE OF INSECT PHYSIOLOGY AND ECOLOGY. ANNUAL REPORT. 1973. a. (International Centre of Insect Physiology and Ecology) ICIPE Science Press, P.O. Box 72913, Nairobi, Kenya. TEL 802573-9. TELEX 25066-DUDU. Ed. A.N. Mengech. illus. circ. 1,500. **Document type:** corporate report.

595.7   AT   ISSN 0074-364X
INTERNATIONAL CONGRESS OF ENTOMOLOGY. 1910. quadrennial, 18th, 1988, Vancouver, Canada; 19th, 1992, Beijing, China; 20th , 1996, Florence, Italy. price varies. Council for International Congresses of Entomology, c/o Dr. Whitten, CSIRO, Div. of Entomology, G.P.O. Box 1700, Canberra, ACT 2601, Australia. **Indexed:** Biol.Abstr.

595.7   US
INTERNATIONAL ENTOMOLOGY RESOURCE GUIDE: THE INSECT STUDY SOURCEBOOK. 1986. biennial. $10 (Canada & Mexico $13; other $14). Young Entomologists' Society, Inc., International Headquarters, 1915 Peggy Place, Lansing, MI 48910. TEL 517-887-0499. E-mail: YESbug@aol.com. Ed. Gary A. Dunn. circ. 1,000. **Document type:** directory.
   Formerly: Y E S International Entomology Resource Guide.
   Description: Cross-referenced resource guide to entomological equipment, services, livestock, specimens, books and organizations.

595.7   US   ISSN 0164-7954
                       CODEN: IJOADM
INTERNATIONAL JOURNAL OF ACAROLOGY. 1975. q. $80 to individuals; institutions $450 (effective 1997). Indira Publishing House, Box 250456, West Bloomfield, MI 48325-0456. TEL 810-661-2529. FAX 810-661-4066. E-mail: vprasad@ix.netcom.com. Ed. V. Prasad. adv.; bk.rev. **Indexed:** Bio-Contr.News & Info., Biol.Abstr., Ind.Vet., Rev.Appl.Entomol., Sport Fish.Abstr., Wild.Rev., Zoo.Rec. **Document type:** academic/scholarly publication.
   —SWETS; UnCover.
   Refereed Serial

595.7   UK   ISSN 0020-7322
QL494   CODEN: IJIMBQ
INTERNATIONAL JOURNAL OF INSECT MORPHOLOGY AND EMBRYOLOGY. 1972. q. fl.1448($832) (effective 1998). Elsevier Science Ltd., Pergamon, P.O. Box 800, Kidlington, Oxford OX5 1DX, England. TEL 44-1865-843000. FAX 44-1865-843010. E-mail: nlinfo-f@elsevier.nl; usinfo-f@elsevier.com; forinfo-kyf04035@niftyserve.or.jp; URL: http://www.elsevier.nl/. (Subscr. to: Elsevier Science, Regional Sales Office, P.O. Box 211, 1000 AE Amsterdam, Netherlands. TEL 31-20-4853757. FAX 31-20-4853432; Subscr. in the Americas to: Elsevier Science, Regional Sales Office, Box 945, New York, NY 10159-0945. TEL 212-633-3730. FAX 212-633-3680; Subscr. in Australasia and the Far East to: Elsevier Science (Singapore) Pte Ltd, No.1 Temasek Ave., No.17-01 Millenia Tower, Singapore 039192, Singapore. TEL 65-434-3727. FAX 65-337-2230) Ed. Ayodhya P. Gupta. adv.; bk.rev. circ. 1,000. (also avail. in microfilm from UMI; reprint service avail. from UMI) **Indexed:** ASCA, Bio-Contr.News & Info., Biol.Abstr., Chem.Abstr., Curr.Adv.Ecol.Sci., Curr.Cont., Ind.Sci.Rev., Rev.Appl.Entomol., Sci.Cit.Ind. **Document type:** academic/scholarly publication.
   —BLDSC (4542.307000); CISTI; EMDOCS; Genuine Article; Linda Hall; SWETS; UMI; UnCover. **CCC**.
   Description: Covers topics including gross morphology, paleomorphology, macro- and micro-anatomy, ultrastructure, and embryonic and post-embryonic development.
   Refereed Serial

632.9   UK   ISSN 0020-8256
SB950   CODEN: IPCLBZ
INTERNATIONAL PEST CONTROL; crop protection, public health, wood preservation. 1959. bi-m. £69($125) (effective 1997). Research Information Ltd., 222 Maylands Ave., Hemel Hempstead, Herts. HP2 7TD, England. TEL 44-1442-213222. FAX 44-1442-259395. E-mail: resinf@globalnet.co.uk. Ed. D.P. McDonald. adv.: B&W page £576; adv. contact: J. Kumar Patel. bk.rev.; charts; illus.; tr.lit.; index. circ. 4,800. **Indexed:** Abstr.Hyg., Agri.Eng.Abstr., Biol.Abstr., Biol.& Agr.Ind., Biotech.Abstr., Chem.Abstr., Environ.Per.Bibl. (1972-), Excerp.Med., Field Crop.Abstr., Forest.Abstr., Forest Prod.Abstr., Herb.Abstr., Hort.Abstr., Ind.Vet., Poult.Abstr., PROMT, Rev.Appl.Entomol., Rev.Plant Path., Small Anim.Abstr., Soils & Fert., Sport Fish.Abstr., Triticale Abstr., Trop.Dis.Bull., Vet.Bull., Weed Abstr., Wild.Rev., Zoo.Rec. **Document type:** academic/scholarly publication.
   —BLDSC (4544.910000); CASDDS; KR SourceOne; Linda Hall; SWETS; UnCover.
   Description: Deals with all aspects of pest eradication and prevention.

595.7   TU   ISSN 0256-6672
                       CODEN: IQENER
INTERNATIONAL QUARTERLY OF ENTOMOLOGY. 1985. q. $85. Tahsin Yaziclioglu, P. Kutusu 1318, Sirkeci, Istanbul 34438, Turkey. Eds. W.P. McCafferty, F.M. Carpenter. adv.; bk.rev. **Indexed:** Biol.Abstr., Curr.Cont., Entomol.Abstr., Ref.Zh., Rev.Appl.Entomol., Zoo.Rec.
   —CISTI. **CCC**.

595.7   GW   ISSN 1019-2808
INTERNATIONALER ENTOMOLOGISCHER VEREIN. MITTEILUNGEN. 1969. q. DM.30. Internationaler Entomologischer Verein e.V., c/o Museum Wiesbaden, Friedrich-Ebert-Allee 2, 65185 Wiesbaden, Germany. adv.; bk.rev.; index. (back issues avail.) **Indexed:** Biol.Abstr., Entomol.Abstr., Zoo.Rec. **Document type:** newsletter.

595.1   UK   ISSN 1354-2516
                       CODEN: INNEFP
▼**INVERTEBRATE NEUROSCIENCE.** 1995. q. £70($100) to individuals; institutions £245($350). Sheffield Academic Press Ltd., Mansion House, 19 Kingfield Rd., Sheffield S11 9AS, England. TEL 44-114-255-4433. FAX 44-114-255-4626. E-mail: subis@sheffac.demon.ac.uk; URL: http://www.shef.ac.uk/uni/companies/shap. Ed. Peter Usherwood. R&P contact: Duncan Chambers. adv. contact: Duncan Chambers. **Indexed:** Curr.Cont. **Document type:** academic/scholarly publication.
   —BLDSC (4557.703530); CASDDS; CISTI; Genuine Article.
   Description: Publishes articles on invertebrate neuroscience, including studies of molecular biology, development, neurogenetics, neurotoxicology and neuronal networks.
   Refereed Serial

595.7   IS   ISSN 0792-4259
                       CODEN: IRDEE2
INVERTEBRATE REPRODUCTION AND DEVELOPMENT. (Text in English and French) 1979. bi-m. $395. (International Society for Invertebrate Reproduction) Balaban Publishers, International Science Services, P.O. Box 2039, Rehovot 76120, Israel. TEL 972-8-9476216. FAX 972-8-9467632. (And: Mario Negri Sud Research Institute, School for Scientific Communication, 66030 S. Maria Imbaro, Italy. TEL 39-872-570316. FAX 39-872-578240) (Co-sponsor: Centre National de la Recherche Scientifique, FR) Ed.Bd. adv.; bk.rev.; bibl.; charts; illus.; index. (back issues avail.; reprint service avail. from UMI) **Indexed:** ASCA, Bibl.Agri., Biol.Abstr., Chem.Abstr., Curr.Adv.Ecol.Sci., Curr.Cont., Deep Sea Res.& Oceanogr.Abstr., Excerp.Med., Helminthol.Abstr., Ind.Sci.Rev., Rev.Appl.Entomol., Sci.Cit.Ind, SSCI. **Document type:** academic/scholarly publication.
   —BLDSC (4557.703600); CASDDS; CISTI; EMDOCS; Genuine Article; Linda Hall; SWETS; UMI; UnCover. **CCC**.
   Former titles (until 1988): International Journal of Invertebrate Reproduction and Development (ISSN 0168-8170); (until 1984): International Journal of Invertebrate Reproduction (ISSN 0165-1269)
   Description: Papers on the sexual, reproductive and developmental biology of invertebrates.

IRANIAN JOURNAL OF PLANT PATHOLOGY/BIMARIHAYE GUIAHI. see *BIOLOGY — Botany*

595.7   IS   ISSN 0075-1243
QL461   CODEN: IJENB9
ISRAEL JOURNAL OF ENTOMOLOGY. (Text in English) 1966. a. $40 (effective 1997). Entomological Society of Israel, P.O. Box 6, Bet Dagan 50200, Israel. TEL 972-3-9683520. FAX 972-3-9604180. TELEX 381476-AROVC-IL. Ed. A. Friedberg. adv.; bk.rev. circ. 200. **Indexed:** Biol.Abstr., Biotech.Abstr., Chem.Abstr., Entomol.Abstr., Rev.Appl.Entomol., Zoo.Rec. **Document type:** academic/scholarly publication.
   —BLDSC (4583.803500); CASDDS; Linda Hall; UnCover.
   Description: Publishes original contributions in all areas of entomology.
   Refereed Serial

595.7   JA   ISSN 0448-8628
JAPAN ENTOMOLOGICAL ACADEMY. BULLETIN. (Text in English; summaries in Japanese) 1964. irreg. Japan Entomological Academy - Konchu Akademi, Nanzan Daigaku Seibutsugaku Kenkyushitsu, 18 Yamazatocho, Showa-ku, Nagoya-shi, Aichi-ken 466, Japan.

595.7   JA   ISSN 0916-1058
JAPAN HYMENOPTERISTS ASSOCIATION. SPECIAL PUBLICATIONS. (Text in English) 1976. irreg. 6000 Yen per no. Japan Hymenopterists Association - Nihon Hachirui Kenkyukai, c/o Dr. Tsuneki, 4-15 Asahigaoka, Mishima-shi, Shizuoka-ken 411, Japan.

595.7 591   JA   ISSN 0021-4914
                       CODEN: NIPTAR
JAPANESE JOURNAL OF APPLIED ENTOMOLOGY AND ZOOLOGY/NIHON OYO DOBUTSU KONCHU GAKKAISHI. (Text in Japanese; summaries in English) 1957. q. $50. Japanese Society of Applied Entomology and Zoology - Nihon Oyo Dobutsu Konchu Gakkai, c/o Japan Plant Protection Association, 1-43-11 Komagome, Toshima-ku, Tokyo 170, Japan. TEL 81-3-3943-6021. FAX 81-3-3943-6021. (Subscr. to: Japan Publication Trading Co., Ltd., P.O. Box 5030, Tokyo International, Tokyo 100-31, Japan) Ed. Masakazu Shiga. R&P contact: Masakazu Shiga. adv. contact: Yoshiaki Kono. bk.rev.; abstr.; index. circ. 2,600. **Indexed:** ASCA, Bio-Contr.News & Info., Biol.Abstr., Biotech.Abstr., Chem.Abstr., Curr.Cont., Entomol.Abstr., Excerp.Med., Forest.Abstr., Helminthol.Abstr., Hort.Abstr., Ind.Sci.Rev., Potato Abstr., Protozool.Abstr., Rev.Appl.Entomol., Rice Abstr., Sci.Cit.Ind., Soils & Fert., Soyabean Abstr., Sport Fish.Abstr., Triticale Abstr., Weed Abstr., Wild.Rev., Zoo.Rec. **Document type:** academic/scholarly publication.
   —BLDSC (4650.850000); CASDDS; Genuine Article; Linda Hall.

595.7 JA ISSN 0915-5805
JAPANESE JOURNAL OF ENTOMOLOGY/KONCHU. (Text in English, French, German, Japanese) 1926. q. 10000 Yen to non-members; members 8000Yen. Entomological Society of Japan - Nihon Konchu Gakkai, c/o Dept. of Zoology, National Science Museum (Natl. Hist.), 3-23-1 Hyaknin-cho, Shinjuku-ku, Tokyo 169, Japan. TEL 03-3364-7129. FAX 03-3364-7104. (Dist. by: Business Center for Academic Societies Japan, 5-16-9 Honkomagome, Bunkyo-ku, Tokyo 113, Japan. TEL 03-5814-5811) Ed. Masataka Sato. adv. contact: Hiroshi Kajita. bk.rev.; index. cum.index. circ. 1,550. **Indexed:** Bio-Contr.News & Info., Biol.Abstr., Forest.Abstr., Rev.Appl.Entomol., So.Pac.Per.Ind. **Document type:** bulletin.
—BLDSC (4651.810000); CISTI; Linda Hall; UnCover.
Former titles (until 1989): Kontyu (ISSN 0013-8770); Insect; Entomology.

B

595.7 II
JOURNAL OF ACAROLOGY. 1976. s-a. Rs.100($30) Acarological Society of India, University of Agricultural Sciences, Entomology Division, G.K.V.K., Bangalore 560 065, India. TEL 91-80-330153. TELEX 845-8393 OASK IN. Ed. G.P. Channabasavanna. bk.rev. circ. 250. (back issues avail.) **Indexed:** Biol.Abstr., Rev.Appl.Entomol., Zoo.Rec. **Document type:** academic/scholarly publication.
Formerly: Indian Journal of Acarology (ISSN 0970-1400)
Refereed Serial

595.7 630 US ISSN 0735-939X
SB818 CODEN: JAENES
JOURNAL OF AGRICULTURAL ENTOMOLOGY. 1984. q. $30 (Canada and Mexico $37; elsewhere $44) (effective 1997). South Carolina Entomological Society, Inc., Box 582, Clemson, SC 29633. TEL 864-944-8401. FAX 864-656-5065. E-mail: netlkky@innova.net. Ed. Julie L. Todd. R&P contact: William C. Nettles, Jr. adv.: B&W page $45; trim 6 x 9; adv. contact: William C. Nettles, Jr. bk.rev.; index; circ. 370 (paid). (back issues avail.) **Indexed:** Agri.Eng.Abstr., ASCA, Bio-Contr.News & Info., Biol.Abstr., Chem.Abstr., Curr.Cont., Entomol.Abstr., Hort.Abstr., Ind.Med., Ind.Vet., Maize Abstr., Poult.Abstr., Protozool.Abstr., Rev.Appl.Entomol., Rice Abstr., Sci.Cit.Ind., Soyabean Abstr., Triticale Abstr., Vet.Bull. **Document type:** academic/scholarly publication.
—CASDDS; Genuine Article; Linda Hall; UnCover.
Description: Publishes results of original research on insects and other arthropods of agricultural importance (humans, livestock, poultry, and wildlife included).
Refereed Serial

JOURNAL OF APHIDOLOGY. see *AGRICULTURE — Crop Production And Soil*

595.7 GW ISSN 0931-2048
SB599 CODEN: JOAEEB
JOURNAL OF APPLIED ENTOMOLOGY/ZEITSCHRIFT FUER ANGEWANDTE ENTOMOLOGIE. (Text in English, French, or German; abstracts in English) 1913. 10/yr. DM.1669 in Europe; rest of world DM.1676 (effective 1998). Blackwell Wissenschaft, Kurfuerstendamm 57, 10707 Berlin, Germany. TEL 49-30-32790679. FAX 49-30-32790610. E-mail: aboverwalt@blackwis.de; URL: http://www.blackwis.com. Eds. H.R. Schopf, M. Feemers. adv.: B&W page DM.560; trim 195 x 117. bk.rev.; illus.; stat. circ. 550. (reprint service avail. from ISI; back issues avail.) **Indexed:** Agroforest.Abstr., Apic.Abstr., ASCA, Biol.Abstr., Biotech.Abstr., Chem.Abstr., Cott.& Trop.Fibr.Abstr., Curr.Cont., Environ.Per.Bibl. (1972-), Excerp.Med., Field Crop Abstr., Forest.Abstr., Helminthol.Abstr., Herb.Abstr., Hort.Abstr., Ind.Sci.Rev., Maize Abstr., Protozool.Abstr., Rev.Appl.Entomol., Rice Abstr., Soils & Fert., Soyabean Abstr., Triticale Abstr., VITIS. **Document type:** academic/scholarly publication.
—BLDSC (4942.605000); CASDDS; EMDOCS; Genuine Article; Linda Hall; SWETS; UnCover. **CCC**.
Formerly (until 1986): Zeitschrift fuer Angewandte Entomologie (ISSN 0044-2240)
Description: Presents current research in entomology applied to agriculture, forestry, biomedical areas, food, and feed storage.

595.7 574 US ISSN 0161-8202
QL451 CODEN: JARCDP
JOURNAL OF ARACHNOLOGY. (Text in English, French, Portuguese and Spanish) 1973. 3/yr. $80 (foreign $90) (effective 1997). American Arachnological Society, c/o Norman I. Platnick, Secretary, American Museum of Natural History, Central Park W. at 79th St., New York, NY 10024. TEL 212-769-5612. FAX 212-769-5277. bk.rev.; cum.index: vols.1-10; circ. 600 (paid). (back issues avail.) **Indexed:** ASCA, Bio-Contr.News & Info., Curr.Cont., Ind.Sci.Rev., Sci.Cit.Ind. **Document type:** academic/scholarly publication.
—BLDSC (4947.172000); Genuine Article; Linda Hall.
Refereed Serial

595.7 US ISSN 0022-0493
SB599 CODEN: JEENAI
JOURNAL OF ECONOMIC ENTOMOLOGY. 1908. bi-m. $95 to individuals (foreign $115); institutions $190 (foreign $210); members $25 (foreign $40). Entomological Society of America, 9301 Annapolis Rd., Lanham, MD 20706. TEL 301-731-4535. FAX 301-731-4538. (Subscr. to: Box 177, Hyattsville, MD 20781-0177) Ed.Bd. adv.; bibl.; charts; illus.; index. circ. 4,300. (also avail. in microform from UMI,PMC; back issues avail.) **Indexed:** Abstr.Hyg., Agri.Eng.Abstr., Apic.Abstr., ASCA, Bibl.Agri., Bio-Contr.News & Info., Biol.Abstr., Biol.& Agr.Ind., Biol.Dig., Biotech.Abstr., Chem.Abstr., Cott.& Trop.Fibr.Abstr., Crop Physiol.Abstr., Curr.Adv.Genetics & Molec.Biol., Curr.Cont., Dairy Sci.Abstr., Environ.Per.Bibl. (1972-), Excerp.Med., Field Crop Abstr., Food Sci.& Tech.Abstr., Forest.Abstr., Forest Prod.Abstr., Helminthol.Abstr., Herb.Abstr., Hort.Abstr., Ind.Med., Ind.Sci.Rev., Ind.Vet., INIS Atomind., Irr.& Drain.Abstr., Maize Abstr., Nutr.Abstr., Ornam.Hort., Plant Breed.Abstr., Plant Grow.Reg.Abstr., Poult.Abstr., Protozool.Abstr., Psychol.Abstr., Rev.Appl.Entomol., Rev.Plant Path., Rice Abstr., Risk.Abstr., Rural Recreat.Tour.Abstr., Sci.Cit.Ind., Seed Abstr., Small Anim.Abstr., Soils & Fert., Sorghum & Millets Abstr., Soyabean Abstr., Sport Fish.Abstr., SSCI, THA, Triticale Abstr., Trop.Dis.Bull., Trop.Oil Seeds Abstr., Vet.Bull., VITIS, Weed Abstr., Wild.Rev., World Agri.Econ.& Rural Sociol.Abstr., Zoo.Rec. **Document type:** academic/scholarly publication.
—BLDSC (4973.000000); CASDDS; CISTI; EMDOCS; Genuine Article; KR SourceOne; Linda Hall; SWETS; UMI; UnCover. **CCC**.
Description: Reports on the economic significance of insects.
Refereed Serial

595.7 II ISSN 0378-9519
CODEN: JEREDP
JOURNAL OF ENTOMOLOGICAL RESEARCH. 1977. q. Rs.600($50) Malhotra Publishing House, A-38-3 Mayapuri Industrial Area, New Delhi 110064, India. TEL 11-5143928. FAX 11-5724135. TELEX 31-63206 MEER IN. Ed. Prakash Sarup. adv.; bk.rev. circ. 400. (back issues avail.) **Indexed:** Apic.Abstr., Bio-Contr.News & Info., Biol.Abstr., Chem.Abstr., Cott.& Trop.Fibr.Abstr., Entomol.Abstr., Field Crop Abstr., Forest.Abstr., Forest Prod.Abstr., Hort.Abstr., Maize Abstr., Rev.Appl.Entomol., Seed Abstr., Soils & Fert., Sorghum & Millets Abstr., Triticale Abstr., Trop.Oil Seeds Abstr., Weed Abstr. **Document type:** academic/scholarly publication.
—BLDSC (4979.293000); CASDDS; CISTI; Linda Hall; UnCover.

595.7 US ISSN 0749-8004
SB818 CODEN: JESCEP
JOURNAL OF ENTOMOLOGICAL SCIENCE. 1966. q. $20 to individuals; institutions $30; libraries $35; students $5. Georgia Entomological Society, Inc., c/o G. David Buntin, Department of Entomology, Georgia Experiment Station, Griffin, GA 30223-1797. TEL 404-228-7288. FAX 404-228-7287. Ed. Dr. Wayne A. Gardner. bk.rev.; charts; illus. circ. 786. **Indexed:** ASCA, Bio-Contr.News & Info., Biol.Abstr., Chem.Abstr., Cott.& Trop.Fibr.Abstr., Curr.Cont., Food Sci.& Tech.Abstr., Forest.Abstr., Forest Prod.Abstr., Helminthol.Abstr., Hort.Abstr., Maize Abstr., Plant Grow.Reg.Abstr., Poult.Abstr., Rev.Appl.Entomol., Sci.Cit.Ind., Sorghum & Millets Abstr., Soyabean Abstr., Triticale Abstr., Trop.Oil Seeds Abstr., Weed Abstr., Zoo.Rec. **Document type:** academic/scholarly publication.
—BLDSC (4979.293500); CASDDS; EMDOCS; Genuine Article; Linda Hall; SWETS; UnCover.
Formerly (until Jan. 1985): Georgia Entomological Society. Journal (ISSN 0016-8238)
Refereed Serial

595.7 US ISSN 0892-7553
QL496 CODEN: JIBEE8
JOURNAL OF INSECT BEHAVIOR. 1988. bi-m. $345 (foreign $405) (effective 1998). Plenum Publishing Corp., 233 Spring St., New York, NY 10013-1578. TEL 212-620-8000. FAX 212-463-0742. TELEX 23-421139. Eds. William J. Bell, Thomas L. Payne. adv.; bk.rev.; bibl.; charts; illus.; index. (also avail. in microfilm from UMI; back issues avail.) **Indexed:** Apic.Abstr., ASCA, Curr.Cont., Forest.Abstr., Psychol.Abstr. (1992-), Triticale Abstr. **Document type:** academic/scholarly publication.
—BLDSC (5007.450000); CISTI; EMDOCS; Genuine Article; Linda Hall; SWETS; UMI; UnCover. **CCC**.
Description: Covers the ethology, ecology, neurophysiology, genetics, pharmacology and behavior of insects and terrestrial arthropods.
Refereed Serial

595.7 UK ISSN 0022-1910
QL461 CODEN: JIPHAF
JOURNAL OF INSECT PHYSIOLOGY. (Text in English, French and German) 1957. m. fl.2741($1575) (effective 1998). Elsevier Science Ltd., Pergamon, P.O. Box 800, Kidlington, Oxford OX5 1DX, England. TEL 44-1865-843000. FAX 44-1865-843010. E-mail: nlinfo-f@elsevier.nl; usinfo-f@elsevier.com; forinfo-kyf04035@niftyserve.or.jp; URL: http://www.elsevier.nl/. (Subscr. to: Elsevier Science, Regional Sales Office, P.O. Box 211, 1000 AE Amsterdam, Netherlands. TEL 31-20-4853757. FAX 31-20-4853432; Subscr. in the Americas to: Elsevier Science, Regional Sales Office, Box 945, New York, NY 10159-0945. TEL 212-633-3730. FAX 212-633-3680; Subscr. in Australasia and the Far East to: Elsevier Science (Singapore) Pte Ltd, No.1 Temasek Ave., No.17-01 Millenia Tower, Singapore 039192, Singapore. TEL 65-434-3727. FAX 65-337-2230) Ed. Leslie Strong. adv.; bk.rev.; bibl.; charts; illus.; index. circ. 1,800. (also avail. in microfiche from MIM; microfilm from UMI; reprint service avail. from UMI) **Indexed:** Abstr.Hyg., Apic.Abstr., ASCA, Bibl.Agri., Biol.Abstr., Biol.& Agr.Ind., Biotech.Abstr., Chem.Abstr., Curr.Adv.Biochem., Curr.Adv.Cell & Devel.Biol., Curr.Adv.Ecol.Sci., Curr.Cont., Ecol.Abstr., Ind.Sci.Rev., Ind.Vet., Maize Abstr., Mass Spectr.Bull., Neurosci.Cit.Ind., Nutr.Abstr., Rev.Appl.Entomol., Sci.Cit.Ind., Soils & Fert., Trop.Dis.Bull., Vet.Bull. **Document type:** academic/scholarly publication.
—BLDSC (5007.500000); CASDDS; CISTI; EMDOCS; Genuine Article; KR SourceOne; Linda Hall; SWETS; UMI; UnCover. **CCC**.
Description: Contributions from the fields of endocrinology, pheromones, neurobiology, physiological pharmacology, behavior, nutrition, homeostasis, and reproductive processes of insects.
Refereed Serial

595.7 US ISSN 0022-2011
SB942 CODEN: JIVPAZ
JOURNAL OF INVERTEBRATE PATHOLOGY; devoted to the pathology and microbiology of insects and other invertebrates. 1959. bi-m. $550 (foreign $665) (effective 1997). Academic Press, Inc., Journal Division, 525 B St., Ste. 1900, San Diego, CA 92101-4495. TEL 619-230-1840. FAX 619-699-6800. E-mail: apsubs@acad.com; URL: http://www.apnet.com/www/journal/in.htm; http://www.idealibrary.com/. (Subscr. to: Box 861213, Orlando, FL 32886-1213. TEL 407-347-4040. FAX 407-363-9661) Ed. Carol Reinisch. adv.; bibl.; charts; illus.; index. (back issues avail.) **Indexed:** Abstr.Hyg., Apic.Abstr., ASCA, Bibl.Agri., Bio-Contr.News & Info., Biol.Abstr., Biotech.Abstr., Chem.Abstr., Curr.Adv.Biochem., Curr.Adv.Cancer Res., Curr.Adv.Cell & Devel.Biol., Curr.Adv.Ecol.Sci., Curr.Adv.Genetics & Molec.Biol., Curr.Cont., Excerp.Med., Forest.Abstr., Helminthol.Abstr., Ind.Med., Ind.Sci.Rev., INIS Atomind., Ocean.Abstr., Pollut.Abstr., Potato Abstr., Protozool.Abstr., Rev.Appl.Entomol., Rev.Plant Path., Sci.Cit.Ind., So.Pac.Per.Ind., Soils & Fert., Soyabean Abstr., Trop.Dis.Bull. **Document type:** academic/scholarly publication.
•Also available online.
—BLDSC (5007.950000); CASDDS; CISTI; Genuine Article; Linda Hall; SWETS; UnCover. **CCC**.
Description: Presents original research articles and notes on the induction and pathogenesis of diseases of invertebrates.
Refereed Serial

JOURNAL OF MEDICAL ENTOMOLOGY. see *MEDICAL SCIENCES — Communicable Diseases*

JOURNAL OF OILSEEDS RESEARCH. see
AGRICULTURE — Crop Production And Soil

595.78　　　　US　　ISSN 0022-4324
　　　　　　　　　CODEN: JRLPAE
JOURNAL OF RESEARCH ON THE LEPIDOPTERA. 1962. q. $20 to individuals; institutions $28. Lepidoptera Research Foundation, Inc., 9620 Heather Rd., Beverly Hills, CA 90210. TEL 310-274-1052. FAX 310-275-3290. E-mail: mattoni@ucla.edu. Eds. Rudolf H.T. Mattoni, Scott E. Miller. R&P contact: Leona Mattoni. adv.; bk.rev.; charts; illus.; index, cum.index covering 27 yrs. circ. 550. (back issues avail.) **Indexed:** Biol.Abstr., Chem.Abstr., Zoo.Rec. **Document type:** academic/scholarly publication.
—Linda Hall; UnCover.
　Description: Directed to professionals and serious amateurs in the study of lepidoptera. Particular emphasis is placed on all aspects of butterfly biology including genetics, ecology and conservation biology.

638 595.7　　JA　　ISSN 0037-2455
　　　　　　　　　CODEN: NISZAQ
JOURNAL OF SERICULTURAL SCIENCE OF JAPAN/NIPPON SANSHIGAKU ZASSHI. (Text in English, Japanese) 1930. bi-m. 7500 Yen (effective 1995). Japanese Society of Sericultural Science - Nihon Sanshi Gakkai, National Institute of Sericultural and Entomological Science, 1-2 Owashi, Tsukuba-shi, Ibaraki-ken 305, Japan. TEL 0298-38-6056. FAX 0298-38-6028. Ed. Toshihiko Iizuka. adv. contact: Masanobu Ohura. bk.rev.; index. circ. 1,300. **Indexed:** Art & Archaeol.Tech.Abstr., Biol.Abstr., Chem.Abstr., Ecol.Abstr., Geo.Abstr.P.G., Text.Tech.Dig. **Document type:** academic/scholarly publication.
—CASDDS; CISTI; EMDOCS; KR SourceOne; Linda Hall.
　Description: Contains research articles on sericultural science and insect utilization.
　Refereed Serial

JOURNAL OF SOIL BIOLOGY AND ECOLOGY. see
BIOLOGY

JOURNAL OF STORED PRODUCTS RESEARCH. see
AGRICULTURE — Crop Production And Soil

636.089 613　　US　　ISSN 1081-1710
RA639　　　　　　　CODEN: BSVEDL
JOURNAL OF VECTOR ECOLOGY. 1974. s-a. $50 (effective 1996 & 1997). Society for Vector Ecology, Box 87, Santa Ana, CA 92702. TEL 714-971-2421. FAX 714-971-3940. E-mail: mklowden@marvin.ag.uidaho.edu. Ed. Marc J. Klowden. R&P contact: Gilbert L. Challet. adv. contact: H.B. Munns. bk.rev.; circ. 860 (paid). **Indexed:** Abstr.Hyg., ASCA, Biol.Abstr., Chem.Abstr., Curr.Cont., Rev.Appl.Entomol., Trop.Dis.Bull., Zoo.Rec. **Document type:** proceedings, academic/scholarly publication.
—BLDSC (5072.273000); CASDDS. **CCC.**
　Former titles (until Jun. 1995): Society for Vector Ecology. Bulletin; Society of Vector Ecologists. Bulletin (ISSN 0146-6429)
　Description: Contains public health related research papers and proceedings from national and international conferences. Also provides members and selected nonmembers worldwide with updated information regarding disease vector-control information.
　Refereed Serial

595.7　　　　JA　　ISSN 0287-6477
KAKOCHO/NAGOYA ENTOMOLOGICAL SOCIETY. JOURNAL. (Text in Japanese) 1949. 4/yr. membership. Nagoya Konchu Dokokai - Nagoya Entomological Society, c/o Mr. Ando, 5-24 Otowa 1-chome, Ichinomiya-shi, Aichi-ken 491, Japan.

595.7　　　　JA　　ISSN 0288-3821
KANAGAWA CHUHO/KANAGAWA ENTOMOLOGIST'S ASSOCIATION. JOURNAL. (Text in Japanese) 1954. 2/yr. Kanagawa Konchu Danwakai - Kanagawa Entomologist's Association, Kanagawa Kenritsu Hakubutsukan, 5-10 Minami Nakadori, Naka-ku, Yokohama-shi, Kanagawa-ken 231, Japan.

595.7 591　　JA　　ISSN 0915-4698
KANDOKON/JAPANESE JOURNAL OF ENVIRONMENT ENTOMOLOGY AND ZOOLOGY. (Text in English, Japanese) 1989. 4/yr. membership. Nihon Kankyu Dobutsu Konchu Gakkai - Japanese Society of Environmental Entomology and Zoology, 12-19, Nishihonmachi 1-chome, Nishi-ku, Osaka 550, Japan.
—CCC.

595.7　　　　US　　ISSN 0022-8567
QL461　　　　　　CODEN: JKESA7
KANSAS ENTOMOLOGICAL SOCIETY. JOURNAL. 1928. q. $85 (Canada & Mexico $88; elsewhere $100) (effective 1997). Kansas Entomological Society, Box 1897, Lawrence, KS 66044-8897. TEL 913-843-1221. FAX 913-843-1274. (Co-sponsor: Central States Entomological Society) Ed. Leonard Ferrington. bk.rev.; abstr.; bibl.; charts; illus.; index. circ. 800. (also avail. in microform from UMI; reprint service avail. from UMI) **Indexed:** ASCA, Bio-Contr.News & Info., Biol.Abstr., Chem.Abstr., Curr.Adv.Ecol.Sci., Curr.Cont., Forest.Abstr., Forest Prod.Abstr., Helminthol.Abstr., Maize Abstr., Protozool.Abstr., Rev.Appl.Entomol., Soils & Fert., Sorghum & Millets Abstr., Soyabean Abstr., Sport Fish.Abstr., Triticale Abstr., Wild.Rev., Zoo.Rec. **Document type:** academic/scholarly publication.
—BLDSC (4810.400000); Linda Hall; SWETS; UMI; UnCover.
　Description: Covers research on all aspects of the science of entomology.
　Refereed Serial

595.7　　　　JA　　ISSN 0913-9613
KEICHITSU. (Text in Japanese) 1983. 2/yr. 3000 Yen. Gifuken Konchu Bunpu Kenkyukai - Entomological Distribution Society of Gifu Prefecture, Figu Daigaku Kyoiku Gakubu, 1-1, Yanagito, Gifu-shi, Gifu-ken 501-11, Japan.

595.7　　　　JA　　ISSN 0913-5421
KINOKUNI/WAKAYAMA INSECT SOCIETY. BULLETIN. (Text in Japanese) 1971. s-a. Wakayama Konchu Kenkyukai - Wakayama Insect Society, c/o Mr. Isao Matoba, 1410 Yuasa, Yuasacho, Arida-gun, Wakayama-ken 643, Japan.

595.7　　　　JA　　ISSN 0915-9754
KISHIDAIA/TOKYO SPIDER STUDY GROUP. BULLETIN. Variant title: Tokyo Kumo Danwakai Kaishi. (Text in Japanese) 1969. s-a. 2800 Yen (students 2000 Yen). Tokyo Kumo Danwakai, c/o Dr. Hirotsugu Ono, National Science Museum, 23-1 Hyakunincho 3-chome, Shinjuku-ku, Tokyo 169, Japan. Ed. Tomoyuki Kimura. **Document type:** newsletter.

591　　　　PL　　ISSN 0075-6350
KLUCZE DO OZNACZANIA OWADOW POLSKI. 1954. irreg., no.131, 1984. price varies. (Polskie Towarzystwo Entomologiczne) Panstwowe Wydawnictwo Naukowe, Nowy Swiat 72, 00-330 Warsaw, Poland. Ed. A. Warchalowski. bibl. circ. 800. **Indexed:** Biol.Abstr., Rev.Appl.Entomol.
—CISTI.

595.7　　　　JA　　ISSN 0910-8785
KOCHU NYUSU/COLEOPTERISTS' NEWS. (Text in Japanese) 1968. q. 1500 Yen. Nihon Shoshi Gakkai - Japanese Society of Coleopterology, Kokuritsu Kagaku Hakubutsukan Dobutsu Kenkyubu, 23-1, Hyakunincho 3-chome, Shinjuku-ku, Tokyo 169, Japan.

595.7　　　　JA　　ISSN 0023-3218
KONCHU TO SHIZEN/NATURE AND INSECTS. (Text in Japanese) 1966. m. 1210 Yen per no. Nyu Saiensusha - New Science Co., 1-5-12 Akasaka, Minato-ku, Tokyo 107, Japan. **Document type:** academic/scholarly publication.

595.7　　　　KO
KOREAN JOURNAL OF ENTOMOLOGY.* (Text in English and Korean; summaries in English) 1971. s-a. $10. Entomological Society of Korea, c/o Korean University, Korean Entomological Institute, 1, 5-GA, Anam-dong, Sungbuk-gu, Seoul, S. Korea. Ed. Yoo-Hang Shin. (back issues avail.) **Indexed:** Apic.Abstr., Bio-Contr.News & Info., Biol.Abstr., Forest.Abstr., Rev.Appl.Entomol., Rice Abstr.

595.7　　　　JA　　ISSN 0912-5957
KUMAMOTO KONCHU DOKOKAIHO/KUMAMOTO ENTOMOLOGICAL ASSOCIATION. NEWS. (Text in Japanese) 1955. irreg. membership. Kumamoto Konchu Dokokai - Kumamoto Entomological Association, c/o Mr. Isao Otsuka, 2169 Kengunmachi, Kumamoto-shi, Kumamoto-ken 862, Japan.

595.7　　　　JA　　ISSN 0917-7906
KUMO/CHUBU SPIDER STUDY GROUP. REPORT. (Text in Japanese) a. Chubu Kumo Kondankai - Chubu Spider Study Group, c/o Mr. Ogata, 10-6 Yamayashiki Higashiyama, Chiryu-shi, Aichi-ken 472, Japan.

BIOLOGY — ENTOMOLOGY　　　757

595.7　　　　CC　　ISSN 0454-6296
QL461　　　　　　CODEN: KCHPA2
KUNCHONG XUEBAO/ACTA ENTOMOLOGICA SINICA. (Text in Chinese; summaries in English) 1950. q. $79.60. (Chinese Academy of Sciences, Institute of Zoology) Science Press, Marketing and Sales Department, 16 Donghuangchenggen North St., Beijing 100717, People's Republic of China. TEL 4010642. FAX 4019810. Ed. Qin Junde. adv.; index. circ. 11,000. **Indexed:** Apic.Abstr., ASCA, Bio-Contr.News & Info., Biol.Abstr., Chem.Abstr., Cott.& Trop.Fibr.Abstr., Curr.Adv.Ecol.Sci., Ecol.Abstr., Fababean Abstr., Forest.Abstr., Geol.Abstr., GeoRef., Helminthol.Abstr., Hort.Abstr., Ind.Vet., Rev.Appl.Entomol., Rice Abstr., Sci.Cit.Ind., Trop.Oil Seeds Abstr. **Document type:** academic/scholarly publication.
—BLDSC (0615.500000); CASDDS; CISTI; Linda Hall.
　Description: Contains theses dealing with insect faunistics, systematics, morphology, physiology, ecology, insecticide toxicology, and pathology, especially concerning injurious and beneficial insects in agriculture, forestry, animal husbandry, and medicine.
　Refereed Serial

595.7　　　　CC　　ISSN 0452-8255
QL461　　　　　　CODEN: KCCSAK
KUNCHONG ZHISHI/ENTOMOLOGICAL KNOWLEDGE. (Text in Chinese) 1955. bi-m. $37.20. (Chinese Academy of Sciences, Institute of Zoology) Science Press, Marketing and Sales Department, 16 Donghuangchenggen North St., Beijing 100717, People's Republic of China. TEL 4010642. FAX 4019810. Ed. Liu Youjiao. adv. **Document type:** academic/scholarly publication.
—CASDDS.
　Description: Introduces basic knowledge of entomology. Contains entomological research reports, information on experiment techniques, academic discussions, and articles on specific topics.

595.7　　　　CC　　ISSN 1002-0926
KUNCHONGXUE YANJIU JIKAN/CONTRIBUTIONS FROM SHANGHAI INSTITUTE OF ENTOMOLOGY. (Text in Chinese; table of contents in English) irreg., vol.7, 1987. Y4.50 per no. (Chinese Academy of Sciences, Shanghai Institute of Entomology) Shanghai Scientific and Technical Publishers, Journal Department, 450 Ruijin 2 Lu, Shanghai 200020, People's Republic of China.

595.76　　　　JA　　ISSN 0915-3020
LAMELLICORNIA. (Text in English, Japanese) 1985. a. Ramerikorunia Kenkyukai - Society of Lamellicornians, c/o Mr. Masaaki Ishida, 23-5 Miyama 3-chome, Suginami-ku, Tokyo 168, Japan.

595.78　　　　DK　　ISSN 0075-8787
　　　　　　　　　CODEN: LEPDAV
LEPIDOPTERA. (Text in Danish; summaries in English) 1946-51; N.S. 1965. s-a. DKK 280 (effective 1997). Lepidopterologisk Forening, c/o Flemming Vilhelmsen, Soendervigvej 29, DK-2720 Vanloese, Denmark. Ed. Erik Andersen. cum.index: 1965-70. circ. 600. **Indexed:** Biol.Abstr.

595.78　　　　US　　ISSN 0024-0966
QL541　　　　　　CODEN: JLPSAZ
LEPIDOPTERISTS' SOCIETY. JOURNAL. 1947. a. $50 (effective 1997). Lepidopterists' Society, c/o Ron Leuschner, Publ. Coord., 1900 John St., Manhattan Beach, CA 90266. Ed. Lawrence Gall. bk.rev.; bibl.; charts; illus.; index. circ. 1,800. **Indexed:** Bio-Contr.News & Info., Biol.Abstr., Ecol.Abstr., Maize Abstr.
—BLDSC (4814.200000); UnCover.
　Description: Contains taxonomic descriptions and research findings on all aspects of butterflies and moths (lepidoptera).

595.7　　　　US　　ISSN 0075-8795
LEPIDOPTERISTS' SOCIETY. MEMOIRS. 1964. irreg., latest 1991. Lepidopterists' Society, c/o Ron Leuschner, Publ. Coord., 1900 John St., Manhattan Beach, CA 90266. Ed. William E. Miller. **Document type:** monographic series.

BIOLOGY — ENTOMOLOGY

595.78   JA   ISSN 0024-0974
LEPIDOPTEROLOGICAL SOCIETY OF JAPAN. TRANSACTIONS. (Text in English, Japanese; summaries in English) 1945. q. 10000 Yen (effective 1993). Lepidopterological Society of Japan - Nippon Rinshi Gakkai, c/o Ogata Bldg., 2-17 Imabashi 3 chome, Chuo-ku, Osaka 541, Japan. Ed. Yasunori Kishida. adv.; charts; illus.; maps. circ. 1,500. (back issues avail.) **Indexed:** Jap.Per.Ind. **Document type:** academic/scholarly publication.
—CISTI.
Formerly: Butterflies and Moths - Tyo to Ga.

595.7   BE   ISSN 0024-4090
CODEN: LBRBAE
LINNEANA BELGICA/BELGIAN ENTOMOLOGY JOURNAL. (Text in English, French; summaries in Dutch, English, German) 1958. q. 1700 BEF (effective 1997). c/o R. Leestmans, Ed., Krabbosstraat 179, 1653 Beersel Dworp, Belgium. TEL 32-2-3803979. Ed. R. Leestmans. bk.rev.; bibl.; charts; illus.; stat.; index. (back issues avail.) **Indexed:** Biol.Abstr., Zoo.Rec. **Document type:** bulletin.
—BLDSC (5221.494000).
Refereed Serial

595.7   US
M E S NEWSLETTER. irreg. (3-4/yr.). $5 to non-members (effective 1997). Michigan Entomological Society, c/o Dept. of Entomology, Michigan State University, East Lansing, MI 48824. TEL 517-321-2192. Ed. Robert Haack. (back issues avail.) **Document type:** academic/scholarly publication.

595.7   JA   ISSN 0917-4710
MAKUNAGI/ACTA DIPTEROLOGICA. (Text in English, Japanese) irreg. Soshi Gakkai - Societas Dipterologica, c/o Biosystematics Laboratory, Graduate School of Social & Cultural Studies, Kyushu University, Ropponmatsu, Fukuoka 810, Japan. TEL 81-92-726-4637.
FAX 81-92-712-1587. E-mail: shimarcb@mbox.nc.kyushu-u.ac.jp. Ed. H. Shima. R&P contact: H. Shima. **Document type:** academic/scholarly publication.

595.7   UK   ISSN 0269-283X
CODEN: MVENE4
MEDICAL & VETERINARY ENTOMOLOGY. 1987. q. £185($338.50) (foreign £204) (effective 1998). (Royal Entomological Society) Blackwell Science Ltd., Osney Mead, Oxford OX2 0EL, England. TEL 44-1865-206206. FAX 44-1865-721205. E-mail: journals.cs@blacksci.co.uk; URL: http://www.black.co.uk. Eds. G.B. White, A.R. Walker; Pub. Allen Stevens. R&P contact: Sarah Pollard. adv. contact: Martine Cariou-Keen. bk.rev.; illus.; index. circ. 455. (back issues avail.) **Indexed:** Apic.Abstr., ASCA, Curr.Cont., Ecol.Abstr., IDA, Sci.Cit.Ind., Sport Fish.Abstr., Wild.Rev., Zoo.Rec. **Document type:** academic/scholarly publication.
—BLDSC (5526.085000); EMDOCS; Genuine Article; Linda Hall; SWETS; UMI; UnCover. CCC.

595.7   US   ISSN 1083-6284
MEMOIRS ON ENTOMOLOGY, INTERNATIONAL. 1961. irreg., vol.8, 1996. price varies. Associated Publishers, Box 140103, Gainesville, FL 32614-0103. TEL 352-371-4071.
FAX 352-371-4071. E-mail: vgupta@gnv.ifas.ufl.edu. Ed. Virendra K. Gupta; Pub. Virendra K. Gupta. index. circ. 200. (back issues avail.) **Indexed:** Biol.Abstr., Curr.Cont. **Document type:** academic/scholarly publication, monographic series.
—CISTI.
Supersedes (in 1995): American Entomological Institute. Memoirs (ISSN 0065-8162)
Description: Channel for monographic works on insects in all areas and disciplines.
Refereed Serial

595.78   DK   ISSN 1395-9506
▼**MICROLEPIDOPTERA OF EUROPE.** (Text in English) 1996. irreg., vol.2, 1997. price varies. Apollo Books Aps, Kirkeby Sand 19, DK-5771 Stenstrup, Denmark. TEL 45-62-26-37-37.
FAX 45-62-26-37-80. Ed.Bd. (back issues avail.) **Document type:** monographic series.
Description: Provides brief, concise identification guides to all European Microlepidoptera.

595.7   GW   ISSN 0340-4943
QL461
MUENCHENER ENTOMOLOGISCHE GESELLSCHAFT. MITTEILUNGEN. (Text in English, German) 1910. a. DM.60. (Muenchener Entomologische Gesellschaft) Verlag Dr. Friedrich Pfeil, Postfach 650086, 81214 Munich, Germany. TEL 49-89-742827-0.
FAX 49-89-7242772. bk.rev. circ. 1,200. (back issues avail.) **Indexed:** Biol.Abstr. **Document type:** proceedings.
Description: Articles on insect taxonomy, systematics, phylogeny, evolution and biogeography.

595.7   AG   ISSN 0524-949X
MUSEO ARGENTINO DE CIENCIAS NATURALES "BERNARDINO RIVADAVIA." INSTITUTO NACIONAL DE INVESTIGACION DE LAS CIENCIAS NATURALES. REVISTA. ENTOMOLOGIA. 1964. irreg., vol.6, no.4, 1989. Museo Argentino de Ciencias Naturales "Bernardino Rivadavia", Instituto Nacional de Investigacion de las Ciencias Naturales, Avda. Angel Gallardo 470, Casilla de Correo 220 Sucursal 5, Buenos Aires, Argentina. **Indexed:** Rev.Appl.Entomol., Zoo.Rec. **Document type:** academic/scholarly publication.
—CISTI; Linda Hall.

595.7   JA   ISSN 0388-418X
MUSHI/MONTHLY JOURNAL OF ENTOMOLOGY. (Text in English, Japanese) 1971. m. 980 Yen per no. Mushisha, P.O. Box 10, Nakano Yubinkyo-ku, Tokyo 164, Japan.

595.7   JA   ISSN 0917-9828
MUSHI TO SHIZEN/INSECTS AND NATURE. (Text in Japanese) 1991. irreg. Nihon Konchu Kyokai - Japan Insect Association, 22-8 Shimotakaido 3-chome, Suginami-ku, Tokyo 168, Japan.

595.7   GW   ISSN 0027-7452
NACHRICHTENBLATT DER BAYERISCHEN ENTOMOLOGEN. (Text in English, German) 1952. q. included in subscr. to its Mitteilungen. (Muenchener Entomologische Gesellschaft) Verlag Dr. Friedrich Pfeil, Postfach 650086, 81214 Munich, Germany. TEL 49-89-742827-0. FAX 49-89-7242772. Ed. E.G. Burmeister. (back issues avail.) **Indexed:** Apic.Abstr. **Document type:** bulletin.
—CISTI.
Description: Articles on systematics, faunistics, behaviour and morphology of insects.

595.7   JA
NAGOYA KONCHU DOKOKAI RENRAKU GEPPO/N A P I NEWS. (Text in Japanese) 1953. bi-m. Nagoya Konchu Dokokai - Nagoya Entomological Society, c/o Mr. Ando, 5-24 Otowa 1-chome, Ichinomiya-shi, Aichi-ken 491, Japan.

NATURA MOSANA. see *BIOLOGY — Botany*

595.7   UK   ISSN 0968-0454
QL461
NATURAL HISTORY MUSEUM. BULLETIN. ENTOMOLOGY. 1949. s-a. £78.75. Intercept Ltd., P.O. Box 716, Andover, Hants. SP10 1YG, England.
TEL 01264-334748. FAX 01264-334058. illus.; index. circ. 750. **Indexed:** Biol.Abstr., Cott.&Trop.Fibr.Abstr., Rev.Appl.Entomol. **Document type:** academic/scholarly publication, bulletin.
—BLDSC (2644.268700); CISTI; Linda Hall; UnCover.
Formerly (until 1992): British Museum (Natural History). Bulletin. Entomology (ISSN 0524-6431)

595.7   NE   ISSN 0548-1163
NEDERLANDSE ENTOMOLOGISCHE VERENIGING. MONOGRAPHS. (Text in Dutch and English) 1964. irreg., no.10, 1983. price varies. Nederlandse Entomologische Vereniging, Plantage Middenlaan 64, 1018 DH Amsterdam, Netherlands. illus. **Indexed:** Biol.Abstr. **Document type:** monographic series.

595.7   NE
NETHERLANDS ENTOMOLOGICAL SOCIETY. EXPERIMENTAL AND APPLIED ENTOMOLOGY SECTION. PROCEEDINGS. (Text in English) 1990. a. fl.50 (effective 1996 & 1997). Nederlandse Entomologische Vereniging - Netherlands Entomological Society, Experimental and Applied Entomology Section, Plantage Middenlaan 64, 1018 DH Amsterdam, Netherlands. **Indexed:** Apic.Abstr. **Document type:** proceedings.

595.7   GW   ISSN 0722-3773
QL461   CODEN: NENAD3
NEUE ENTOMOLOGISCHE NACHRICHTEN; Beitraege zur Oekologie, Faunistik und Systematik von Lepidopteren. 1982. irreg. price varies. Entomologisches Museum, Humboldtstr. 13A, 95168 Marktleuthen, Germany. TEL 09285-480. FAX 09285-8238. Ed. Ulf Eitschberger. (back issues avail.) **Indexed:** Entomol.Abstr. **Document type:** monographic series.
—BLDSC (6077.338000). CCC.

595.7   JA   ISSN 0028-4955
CODEN: NENTAN
NEW ENTOMOLOGIST/NYU ENTOMOROJISUTO. (Text in English or Japanese) 1951. s-a. 3000 Yen($14) Entomological Society of Shinshu - Shinshu Konchu Gakkai, Shinshu Daigaku Nogakubu Oyo Konchugaku Kyoshitsu, 8304 Minamiminowamura, Kamiina-gun, Nagano-ken 399-45, Japan. Ed. Nagao Koyama. charts; illus.; index. **Indexed:** Biol.Abstr.

595.7   US
CODEN: PMNADO
NEW JERSEY MOSQUITO CONTROL ASSOCIATION. PROCEEDINGS. Variant title: Annual Mosquito Review. (Supplement avail.: New Jersey Mosquito Control Association. Supplement to the Proceedings, Annual Meeting (ISSN 0190-9614)) 1914. a. $10. New Jersey Mosquito Control Association, Inc., c/o Mrs. A.R. Hajek, Mgr. Ed., Mosquito Research & Control, Cook College, Box 231, New Brunswick, NJ 08903. TEL 201-932-9437. FAX 908-932-9257. Ed. Henry R. Rupp. index. cum.index: 1914-1916. circ. 1,500. (back issues avail.) **Indexed:** Abstr.Hyg., Biol.Abstr., Rev.Appl.Entomol., Trop.Dis.Bull. **Document type:** proceedings.
—Linda Hall.
Formerly (until 1975): New Jersey Mosquito Extermination Association. Proceedings (ISSN 0096-5596)

595.7   US   ISSN 0028-7199
CODEN: JNYEAI
NEW YORK ENTOMOLOGICAL SOCIETY. JOURNAL; devoted to entomology in general. 1893. q. $65 (foreign $75) (effective 1996 & 1997). New York Entomological Society, c/o American Museum of Natural History, Central Park West at 79th St., New York, NY 10024-5192. TEL 212-769-5613.
FAX 212-769-5277. E-mail: sorkin@amnh.org. Ed. James Carpenter. bk.rev.; bibl.; charts; illus.; index. circ. 600. (back issues avail.) **Indexed:** Apic.Abstr., ASCA, Bio-Contr.News & Info., Biol.Abstr., Curr.Adv.Ecol.Sci., Curr.Cont., Helminthol.Abstr., Rev.Appl.Entomol., Soils & Fert., Sport Fish.Abstr., Wild.Rev., Zoo.Rec. **Document type:** academic/scholarly publication.
—BLDSC (4832.900000); CISTI; Linda Hall; SWETS; UnCover.
Description: Presents original contributions to insect biology, including systematics, biogeography and natural history.
Refereed Serial

595.7 179   NZ   ISSN 0110-6325
NEW ZEALAND BEEKEEPER. Short title: N.Z. Beekeeper. q. NZ.$38 (foreign $38) (effective 1997). National Beekeepers Association of New Zealand (Inc.), P.O. Box 3079, Napier, New Zealand.
TEL 64-6-8433446. FAX 64-6-8434845. E-mail: natbeeknz@xtra.co.nz. Ed. Harry Brown. R&P contact: Harry Brown. adv. contact: Harry Brown. bk.rev. circ. 1,250. **Document type:** academic/scholarly publication, newsletter.

595.7   NZ   ISSN 0077-9962
QL487.5   CODEN: NEZEA4
NEW ZEALAND ENTOMOLOGIST. 1951. a. NZ.$38 (foreign $40) (effective 1997). Entomological Society of New Zealand, Mt Albert Research Centre, Private Bag 92169, Auckland, New Zealand. FAX 64-9-8497093. E-mail: mplmjb@dslak.co.nz. Ed. J. Early. bk.rev.; index in vols.1-4. circ. 700. **Indexed:** Bio-Contr.News & Info., Biol.Abstr., Curr.Adv.Ecol.Sci., Forest.Abstr., Ind.Sci.Rev., Ind.Vet., Rev.Appl.Entomol., So.Pac.Per.Ind., Soyabean Abstr., Weed Abstr. **Document type:** academic/scholarly publication.
—Linda Hall; UnCover.
Description: Original research in New Zealand and South Pacific entomology.

595.7   JA   ISSN 0918-1067
NIHON DANI GAKKAISHI/ACAROLOGICAL SOCIETY OF JAPAN. JOURNAL. (Text in English, Japanese) 1974. a. 8000 Yen membership. Nihon Dani Gakkai - Acarological Society of Japan, c/o Dr. Tetsuo Gotoh, Faculty of Agriculture, Ibaraki University, Ami-chuo 3-21-1, Inashiki-gun 300-03, Japan. TEL 81-298-88-8560. Ed. Akio Takafuji. bk.rev. **Document type:** academic/scholarly publication.
—CCC.
 Formerly (until 1992): Danirui Kenkyukai Kaiho - Japanese Association for Acarology. Proceedings (ISSN 0285-4856)

595.7
NIHON KONCHU GAKKAI TAIKAI KOEN YOSHI/ENTOMOLOGICAL SOCIETY OF JAPAN. ABSTRACTS OF ANNUAL MEETING. see *BIOLOGY — Abstracting, Bibliographies, Statistics*

595.7   JA   ISSN 0917-9895
NIHON KONCHU KYOKAI NYUSU RETA/JAPAN INSECT ASSOCIATION. NEWSLETTER. (Text in Japanese) 1991. bi-m. Nihon Konchu Kyokai - Japan Insect Association, 22-8 Shimotakaido 3-chome, Suginami-ku, Tokyo 168, Japan. **Document type:** newsletter.

595.7 591   JA   ISSN 0387-9003
NIHON OYO DOBUTSU KONCHU GAKKAI CHUGOKU SHIBU KAIHO/JAPANESE SOCIETY OF APPLIED ENTOMOLOGY AND ZOOLOGY. CHUGOKU BRANCH. JOURNAL. (Text in Japanese; summaries in English) 1959. a. price varies. Nihon Oyo Dobutsu Konchu Gakkai, Chugoku Shibu - Japanese Society of Applied Entomology and Zoology, Chugoku Branch, Chugoku Nogyo Shikenjo, 12-1, Nishifukatsucho 6-chome, Fukuyama-shi, Hiroshima-ken 721, Japan. TEL 81-0849-23-4100. FAX 81-0849-24-7893. Ed. Kazuki Miura; Pub. Nasahiro Kobayashi. circ. 250. **Document type:** academic/scholarly publication.
 Refereed Serial

NIHON OYO DOBUTSU KONCHU GAKKAI KYUSHU SHIBU KAIHO/DELPHAX. see *BIOLOGY — Zoology*

595.7   JA   ISSN 0915-2067
NIHON SEMI NO KAI KAIHO/CICADA. (Text in Japanese) 1978. 3/yr. membership. Nihon Semi no Kai - Japan Cicada Club, c/o Mr. Hashimoto, 43-11 Eifuku 2-chome, Suginami-ku, Tokyo 168, Japan.

NIHON SHOKUBUTSU BYORI GAKKAI BAIOKONTORORU KENKYUKAI KOEN YOSHI/PHYTOPATHOLOGICAL SOCIETY OF JAPAN. ABSTRACTS OF THE MEETING OF BIOCONTROL. see *BIOLOGY — Abstracting, Bibliographies, Statistics*

NIHON SHOKUBUTSU BYORI GAKKAI SHOKUBUTSU KANSEN SEIRI DANWAKAI/SYMPOSIUM ON PHYSIOLOGICAL PLANT PATHOLOGY IN JAPAN. PROCEEDINGS. see *BIOLOGY — Botany*

595.7   JA
NIHON SHOSHIMOKU GAKKAI TOKUBETSU HOKOKU/JAPANESE SOCIETY OF COLEOPTEROLOGY. SPECIAL BULLETIN. (Text in English, Japanese) irreg. Nihon Shoshi Gakkai - Japanese Society of Coleopterology, Kokuritsu Kagaku Hakubutsukan Dobutsu Kenkyubu, 23-1, Hyakunincho 3-chome, Shinjuku-ku, Tokyo 169, Japan.

595.78   DK
NOCTUIDAE EUROPAEAE. (Text in English, French) 1990. irreg., vol.7, 1995. DKK 680 per no. (effective 1997). Apollo Books Aps, Kirkeby Sand 19, DK-5771 Stenstrup, Denmark. TEL 45-62-26-37-37. FAX 45-62-26-37-80. Ed.Bd. illus. (back issues avail.) **Document type:** monographic series.
 Description: Provides a revision of the European species of the lepidoptera family Noctuidae.

595.78   DK   ISSN 0342-7536
NOTA LEPIDOPTEROLOGICA. (Text in English, French, German) 1977. q. DKK 440 (effective through 1998). (Societas Europaea Lepidopterologica) Apollo Books Aps, Kirkeby Sand 19, DK-5771 Stenstrup, Denmark. TEL 45-62-26-37-37. FAX 45-62-26-37-80. (back issues avail.) **Document type:** academic/scholarly publication.
—BLDSC (6152.826000); EMDOCS.
 Description: Publishes contributions on systematic and faunistic lepidopterology.
 Refereed Serial

NOTIZIARIO SULLA PROTEZIONE DELLE PIANTE. see *BIOLOGY — Botany*

595.7   GW   ISSN 0948-6038
NOVA SUPPLEMENTA ENTOMOLOGICA. a. DM.120($98) (foreign DM.125) (effective 1997). (Deutsches Entomologisches Institut) Akademie Verlag GmbH, Muehlenstr. 33-34, 13187 Berlin, Germany. TEL 49-30-47889349. FAX 49-30-47889357. E-mail: info@akademie-verlag.de. (Subscr. in the Americas to: John Wiley & Sons, Inc., 650 Third Ave., New York, NY 10158. TEL 212-850-6645. FAX 212-850-6021) Ed. H. Dathe. **Document type:** academic/scholarly publication.
 Description: Contains catalogs which provide a systematic look at the collection, archive and library contents of the German Entomological Institute.

595.7   US   ISSN 0362-2622
QL461
OCCASIONAL PAPERS IN ENTOMOLOGY. 1959. irreg. exchange basis. Department of Food and Agriculture, Division of Plant Industry, Analysis & Identification, 1220 N St., Sacramento, CA 95814. TEL 916-445-5421. Ed. Fred G. Andrews. illus.; circ. 200 (controlled). **Indexed:** Biol.Abstr., Zoo.Rec.
—Linda Hall.
 Continues: California. Bureau of Entomology. Occasional Papers.
 Refereed Serial

595.7   JA   ISSN 0912-6155
OKERA/IBARAKI INSECT SOCIETY. NEWS. (Text in Japanese) biennial. Ibaraki Konchu Dokokai, c/o Mr. Katsuyoshi Ichige, 493 Senbacho, Mito-shi, Ibaraki-ken 310, Japan.

OPERA LILLOANA. see *BIOLOGY — Botany*

OPUSCULA ZOOLOGICA FLUMINENSIA. see *BIOLOGY — Zoology*

595.7   US   ISSN 0030-5316
QL461   CODEN: ORINAE
ORIENTAL INSECTS; an international journal of systematic entomology of the old world tropics. (Text in English) 1967. a. $30 to individuals; institutions $60. Associated Publishers, Box 140103, Gainesville, FL 32614-0103. TEL 352-371-4071. FAX 352-371-4071. E-mail: vgupta@gnv.ifas.ufl.edu. Ed. Virendra K. Gupta; Pub. Virendra K. Gupta. adv.; bk.rev.; abstr.; bibl.; charts; illus.; index. circ. 300. (back issues avail.; reprint service avail. from UMI) **Indexed:** ASCA, Bibl.Agri., Bio-Contr.News & Info., Biol.Abstr., Curr.Adv.Ecol.Sci., Curr.Cont., Entomol.Abstr., Indian Sci.Abstr., Rev.Appl.Entomol., Rice Abstr., So.Pac.Per.Ind., Soils & Fert., Zoo.Rec. **Document type:** academic/scholarly publication.
—Linda Hall; UMI; UnCover.
 Description: Provides an outlet to the works of systematic entomologists working on Oriental and old world fauna.
 Refereed Serial

OSAKA-SHIRITSU SHIZENSHI HAKUBUTSUKAN SHUZO SHIRYO MOKUROKU/OSAKA MUSEUM OF NATURAL HISTORY. SPECIAL PUBLICATIONS. see *BIOLOGY*

595.7   US   ISSN 0031-0603
QL461   CODEN: PPETA9
PAN-PACIFIC ENTOMOLOGIST. 1924. q. $40 (effective 1998). Pacific Coast Entomological Society, c/o California Academy of Sciences, Golden Gate Park, San Francisco, CA 94118-4599. TEL 415-750-7227. FAX 415-750-7228. E-mail: vlee@calacademy.org. Ed. Robert V. Dowell. R&P contact: Vincent F. Lee. bk.rev.; bibl.; illus.; index. circ. 750. **Indexed:** Apic.Abstr., ASCA, Bio-Contr.News & Info., Biol.Abstr., Chem.Abstr., Curr.Adv.Ecol.Sci., Curr.Cont., Forest.Abstr., Sport Fish.Abstr., Wild.Rev., Zoo.Rec. **Document type:** academic/scholarly publication.
—BLDSC (6357.427000); CISTI; Genuine Article; Linda Hall; SWETS; UnCover.
 Refereed Serial

595.7   JA
PANORPODES. (Text in Japanese) 1976. a. Choshimoku Danwakai - Study Group of Mecopterologist in Japan, c/o Mr. Nobuo Suzuki, Nihon Joshi Taiiku Tanki Daigaku Kyoyo Dai 2 Kenkyushitsu, 19-1, Kitakarasuyama 8-chome, Setagaya-ku, Tokyo 157, Japan.

595.7   US   ISSN 0744-6357
HD9718.5.P473
PEST MANAGEMENT. 1981. m. $45 to non-members (foreign $58). National Pest Control Association, 8100 Oak St., Dunn Loring, VA 22027. TEL 703-573-8330. FAX 703-573-4116. Ed. Kathleen H. Bova. adv.; bk.rev.; circ. 5,500 (controlled). (back issues avail.) **Indexed:** Cott.& Trop.Fibr.Abstr., Soils & Fert., Sport Fish.Abstr., Weed Abstr., Wild.Rev. **Document type:** trade publication.
 Description: Information related to the pest control industry.

595.7   LI
QL495
PHEROMONES. (Text in Russian; summaries in English) 1971. biennial. price varies. Lithuanian Academy of Sciences, Institute of Ecology, Akademijos 23, 232600 Vilnius, Lithuania. Ed.Bd.
—BLDSC (6449.370000); KNAW; Linda Hall.
 Formerly (until 1988): Khemoretseptsiya Nasekomykh (ISSN 0206-3441)
 Description: Focuses on pheromone communication mechanisms of various insects.

595.7   PH   ISSN 0048-3753
THE PHILIPPINE ENTOMOLOGIST. (Text in English) 1968. s-a. P.600($50) (effective Apr. 1993). Philippine Association of Entomologists, c/o Department of Entomology, University of the Philippines at Los Banos, College, Laguna 4031, Philippines. TEL 49-536-236-2351. FAX 49-536-3527. Ed. Leonila A. Corpuz-Roros. adv. contact: Leonila A. Corpuz-Roros. bk.rev.; charts; illus. circ. 1,000. **Indexed:** Bio-Contr.News & Info., Chem.Abstr., Food Sci.& Tech.Abstr., Hort.Abstr., Maize Abstr., Seed Abstr., Sorghum & Millets Abstr., Triticale Abstr., Trop.Oil Seeds Abstr., Weed Abstr. **Document type:** academic/scholarly publication.
 Refereed Serial

595.7   UK   ISSN 0307-6962
QL495   CODEN: PENTDE
PHYSIOLOGICAL ENTOMOLOGY. 1976. q. £185($338.50) (foreign £204) (effective 1998). (Royal Entomological Society) Blackwell Science Ltd., Osney Mead, Oxford OX2 0EL, England. TEL 44-1865-206206. FAX 44-1865-721205. E-mail: journals.cs@blacksci.co.uk; URL: http://www.black.co.uk. Eds. G.J. Goldsworthy, W.M. Blaney; Pub. Allen Stevens. R&P contact: Sarah Pollard. adv. contact: Martine Cariou-Keen. bk.rev.; bibl.; illus.; index. circ. 680. (also avail. in microform from UMI; back issues avail.; reprint service avail. from ISI) **Indexed:** Abstr.Hyg., Apic.Abstr., ASCA, Bibl.Agri., Biol.Abstr., Chem.Abstr., Curr.Adv.Ecol.Sci., Curr.Cont., Ecol.Abstr., Forest.Abstr., Helminthol.Abstr., Ind.Sci.Rev., Mass Spectr.Bull., Potato Abstr., Rev.Appl.Entomol., Sci.Cit.Ind., Sci.Cit.Ind., Trop.Dis.Bull., Zoo.Rec. **Document type:** academic/scholarly publication.
—BLDSC (6484.720000); CASDDS; CISTI; EMDOCS; Genuine Article; Linda Hall; SWETS; UMI; UnCover. CCC.
 Formerly: Journal of Entomology (A) (ISSN 0047-2409)
 Refereed Serial

595.7   II
PHYTOPHAGA. (Text in English) s-a. Rs.100 to individuals (foreign $25); institutions Rs.250 (foreign $40). S. Viswanathan (Printers & Publishers) Pvt. Ltd., 38, McNichols Rd., Chetput, Madras 600 031, India. Ed. T.N. Ananthakrishnan. **Document type:** academic/scholarly publication.
 Description: Publishes original research articles and reviews on topics of entomological interest, principally relating to insect-plant interactions, and biology of plant feeding insects.

PLANT PROTECTION RESEARCH INSTITUTE. ANNUAL REPORT. see *AGRICULTURE — Crop Production And Soil*

595.7   PL   ISSN 0032-3780
QL461   CODEN: PEBEA8
POLSKIE PISMO ENTOMOLOGICZNE/POLISH JOURNAL OF ENTOMOLOGY. (Text and summaries in English) 1922. q. $54. Polskie Towarzystwo Entomologiczne - Polish Entomological Society, Ul. Sienkiewicza 21, 50-335 Wroclaw, Poland. TEL 48-71-225041. Ed. Ryszrd Szadziewski. bk.rev.; bibl.; charts; illus.; index. circ. 500. **Indexed:** Biol.Abstr., Chem.Abstr., Forest.Abstr., Rev.Appl.Entomol., Soils & Fert., Weed Abstr.
—BLDSC (6547.000000); CASDDS; CISTI.
 Refereed Serial

BIOLOGY — ENTOMOLOGY

595.7 US ISSN 0033-2615
QL461 CODEN: PYCHAQ
PSYCHE; journal of entomology. 1874. q. $30 (foreign $35). Cambridge Entomological Club, 26 Oxford St., Cambridge, MA 02138. TEL 617-495-2464. FAX 617-495-5667. Ed. D.G. Furth. illus.; index. circ. 700. **Indexed:** Biol.Abstr., Chem.Abstr., GeoRef., Rev.Appl.Entomol., RILM, Soils & Fert. **Document type:** academic/scholarly publication.
—BLDSC (6946.110000); CISTI; Linda Hall; SWETS; UnCover.
Refereed Serial

595.7 GW ISSN 0070-7279
CODEN: RCHBA3
REICHENBACHIA; Zeitschrift fuer taxonomische Entomologie. (Text in English, French, German) 1962. a. price varies. Staatliches Museum fuer Tierkunde Dresden, Augustusstr. 2, 01067 Dresden, Germany. TEL 49-351-4952503.
FAX 49-351-4952525. Ed. Rainer Emmrich. bk.rev. circ. 350. (back issues avail.) **Indexed:** Biol.Abstr., Zoo.Rec. **Document type:** academic/scholarly publication.
—BLDSC (7350.350000).
Description: Explores taxonomy and sytematics of insecta and arachnida.

REVIEW OF MEDICAL AND VETERINARY ENTOMOLOGY.
see *VETERINARY SCIENCE — Abstracting, Bibliographies, Statistics*

595.7 BL ISSN 0085-5626
CODEN: RBREAL
REVISTA BRASILEIRA DE ENTOMOLOGIA. (Text in English, Portuguese, Spanish; summaries in English) 1954. q. $80 (effective 1997). Sociedade Brasileira de Entomologia, Caixa Postal 9063, 01065-970 Sao Paulo SP, Brazil. TEL 55-11-274-3455 ext. 260. FAX 55-11-2743690. Ed. Ubirajara Ribeiro Martins de Souza. bk.rev. circ. 600. **Indexed:** Biol.Abstr., Bull.Signal., Entomol.Abstr., Rev.Appl.Entomol., Rice Abstr., Zoo.Rec. **Document type:** academic/scholarly publication.
—Linda Hall.
Description: Publishes original papers in entomology, including groups of arthropoda.
Refereed Serial

595.7 CL ISSN 0034-740X
QL461
REVISTA CHILENA DE ENTOMOLOGIA. (Text in English, Spanish) 1951. a. price varies. Sociedad Chilena de Entomologia, Casilla 21132, Santiago 21, Chile. Ed. Mario Elgueta D. adv.; bk.rev.; bibl.; charts; illus. circ. 500. **Indexed:** Bio-Contr.News & Info., Biol.Abstr., Rev.Appl.Entomol., Trop.Oil Seeds Abstr., Weed Abstr.
—BLDSC (7848.600000).

595.7 PE ISSN 0080-2425
REVISTA PERUANA DE ENTOMOLOGIA. (Text in English and Spanish; summaries in English) 1958. a. S/50000($8) Sociedad Entomologica del Peru, Apdo. 4796, Lima 100, Peru. Ed. Pedro G. Aguilar. adv.; bk.rev. circ. 1,000. **Indexed:** Biol.Abstr., Rev.Appl.Entomol.

595.7 JA ISSN 0910-6839
ROSTRIA/HEMIPTEROLOGICAL SOCIETY OF JAPAN. TRANSACTIONS. (Text in English, Japanese) 1962. a. 2000 Yen. Nihon Hanshirui Gakkai - Hemipterological Society of Japan, Kokuritsu Kagaku Hakubutsukan Dobutsu Kenkyubu, 23-1 Hyakunincho 3-chome, Shinjuku-ku, Tokyo 169, Japan. Ed. Masaaki Tomokuni. adv. circ. 220. **Document type:** academic/scholarly publication.

595.7 UK ISSN 0080-4363
CODEN: RESSBM
ROYAL ENTOMOLOGICAL SOCIETY OF LONDON. SYMPOSIA. 1961. biennial. (Royal Entomological Society) Academic Press Ltd. (Subsidiary of: Harcourt Brace & Company Ltd.), 24-28 Oval Rd., London NW1 7DX, England. TEL 44-171-267-4466. FAX 44-171-482-2293. circ. 2,000. **Indexed:** Biol.Abstr., Rev.Appl.Entomol., Zoo.Rec. **Document type:** monographic series.
—BLDSC (8584.600000); CASDDS; Linda Hall.

595.7 JA ISSN 0910-9889
RYUKYU NO KONCHU/INSECTS OF LOOCHOOS. (Text in Japanese) 1977. irreg. 3500 Yen per no. Okinawa Konchu Dokokai - Okinawa Entomological Society, c/o Mr. Kunio Nagamine, 13-67 Takara 2-chome, Naha-shi, Okinawa-ken 901-01, Japan.

595.76 JA ISSN 0916-1287
SAIKAKU/SOCIETY OF LAMELLICORNIANS. RESEARCH REPORT. (Text in Japanese) 1985. a. Ramerikorunia Kenkyukai - Society of Lamellicornians, c/o Mr. Masaaki Ishida, 23-5 Miyamae 3-chome, Suginami-ku, Tokyo 168, Japan.

595.7 JA ISSN 0915-2679
SF542.75.J3
SANSHI KONCHU NOGYO GIJUTSU KENKYUSHO SHIRYO/NATIONAL INSTITUTE OF SERICULTURAL AND ENTOMOLOGICAL SCIENCE. MISCELLANEOUS PUBLICATION. (Text in Japanese) 1989. irreg. National Institute of Sericultural and Entomological Science, 1-2 Ohwashi Tsukuba, Ibaraki 305, Japan.
—BLDSC (5821.330000).

595.7 JA ISSN 0915-2652
SF542.75.J3 CODEN: SKNHEK
SANSHI KONCHU NOGYO GIJUTSU KENKYUSHO HOKOKU/NATIONAL INSTITUTE OF SERICULTURAL AND ENTOMOLOGICAL SCIENCE. BULLETIN. (Text in Japanese) 1990. 1-2/yr. National Institute of Sericultural and Entomological Science, 1-2 Ohwashi Tsukuba, Ibaraki 305, Japan.
—BLDSC (2640.532000).

595.7 JA ISSN 0910-5131
SATSUMA/KAGOSHIMA ENTOMOLOGICAL SOCIETY. RESEARCH REPORT. (Text in Japanese) 1952. s-a. membership. Kagoshima Konchu Dokokai - Kogoshima Entomological Society, Sameshima Hifuka, 8-8 Komatsubara 1-chome, Kagoshima-shi, Kagoshima-ken 891-01, Japan.

595.7 SZ ISSN 0036-7575
CODEN: MSEGAQ
SCHWEIZERISCHE ENTOMOLOGISCHE GESELLSCHAFT. MITTEILUNGEN/SOCIETE ENTOMOLOGIQUE SUISSE. BULLETIN.. (Text in English, French, German and Italian) vol.45, 1972. q. 50 Fr. Fotorotar AG, Gewerbestr. 18, 8132 Egg, Switzerland. Ed. V. Delucchi. bk.rev.; index; illus.; stat.; index. **Indexed:** Biol.Abstr., Forest.Abstr., IBR, Rev.Appl.Entomol.
—BLDSC (5866.000000); CISTI; UnCover.

595.7 NE ISSN 0080-8954
CODEN: SEENAF
SERIES ENTOMOLOGICA. 1966. irreg., vol.52, 1994. price varies. Kluwer Academic Publishers, Postbus 17, 3300 AA Dordrecht, Netherlands. TEL 31-78-6392392. FAX 31-78-6392254. TELEX 29245 KAPG NL. E-mail: services@wkap.nl; URL: http://www.wkap.nl. (Dist. by: Kluwer Academic Publishers Group, P.O. Box 322, 3300 AH Dordrecht, Netherlands. TEL 31-78-6392392. FAX 31-78-6546474; N. America dist. addr.: Box 358, Accord Sta., Hingham, MA 02018-0358. TEL 617-871-6600. FAX 617-871-6528) Ed. K.A. Spencer. **Indexed:** Biol.Abstr., Zoo.Rec. **Document type:** monographic series.
Refereed Serial

595.7 JA ISSN 0037-3680
QL461 CODEN: TSHEAA
SHIKOKU ENTOMOLOGICAL SOCIETY. TRANSACTIONS/SHIKOKU KONCHU GAKKAI KAIHO. (Text in English) 1950. 2/yr. 3000 Yen. Shikoku Entomological Society - Shikoku Konchu Gakkai, Ehime Daigaku Nogakubu Konchugaku Kyoshitsu, 5-7, Tarumi 3-chome, Matsuyama-shi, Ehime-ken 790, Japan. bibl.; charts; illus. circ. 450. **Indexed:** Biol.Abstr., Rev.Appl.Entomol., So.Pac.Per.Ind.

595.7 SP ISSN 0300-5267
QL541 CODEN: SRLPEF
SHILAP; revista de lepidopterologia. 1973. q. 7000 ptas. Sociedad Hispano-Luso-Americana de Lepidopterologia, Apdo. 331, 28080 Madrid, Spain. FAX 34-1-4475609. E-mail: avives@mad.servicom.es. Ed. Antonio Vives. adv.; bk.rev. circ. 1,000. **Indexed:** Ind.SST. **Document type:** bulletin.
—UnCover.
Refereed Serial

595.7 628.96 JA ISSN 0388-9491
SHIROARI/TERMITE. (Text in Japanese) 1962. q. Nihon Shiroari Taisaku Kyokai - Japan Termite Control Association, 2-9 Shinjuku 1-chome, Shinjuku-ku, Tokyo 160, Japan.

630 BL ISSN 0301-8059
SB935.B7 CODEN: ASENBI
SOCIEDADE ENTOMOLOGICA DO BRASIL. ANAIS. (Text in English, Portuguese, or Spanish; summaries in English) 1972. 3/yr. $40. Sociedade Entomologica do Brasil, EMBRAPA - CNPSo, Caixa Postal 231, 86001-970 Londrina, Parana, Brazil.
TEL 55-43-3204253. FAX 55-43-3204253. E-mail: seb@carpa.ciagri.usp.br; URL: http://www.ciagri.usp.br/~seb. Ed. Antonio Ricardo Panizzi. adv. contact: Rosa Torres. circ. 1,500. **Indexed:** Apic.Abstr., Bio-Contr.News & Info., Biodet.Abstr., Biol.Abstr., Chem.Abstr., Cott.& Trop.Fibr.Abstr., Food Sci.& Tech.Abstr., Forest.Abstr., Hort.Abstr., Plant Breed.Abstr., Poult.Abstr., Protozool.Abstr., Rev.Appl.Entomol., Sorghum & Millets Abstr., Soyabean Abstr., Triticale Abstr., Weed Abstr. **Document type:** academic/scholarly publication.
—BLDSC (0868.285000); CASDDS; Linda Hall.
Description: Publishes scientific articles and short communications in entomology.
Refereed Serial

595.7 IT ISSN 0373-3491
QL461 CODEN: BENIAS
SOCIETA ENTOMOLOGICA ITALIANA. BOLLETTINO. (Text in English, French, German, Italian; summaries in English) 1869. 3/yr. L.50000 (foreign L.75000). Societa Entomologica Italiana, Via Brigata Liguria 9, 16121 Genoa, Italy. bk.rev. **Indexed:** Bio-Contr.News & Info., Biol.Abstr., Rev.Appl.Entomol., Zoo.Rec.
—Linda Hall.
Supersedes in part (in 1922): Societa Entomologica Italiana. Bollettino e Memorie.

595.7 IT ISSN 0037-8747
SOCIETA ENTOMOLOGICA ITALIANA. MEMORIE. 1869. a. L.50000 (foreign L.75000). Societa Entomologica Italiana, Via Brigata Luguria, 9, 16121 Genoa, Italy.
—CISTI; Linda Hall.
Supersedes in part (in 1922): Societa Entomologica Italiana. Bollettino e Memorie.

595.7 UA ISSN 0081-0983
SOCIETE ENTOMOLOGIQUE D'EGYPTE. BULLETIN/ENTOMOLOGICAL SOCIETY OF EGYPT. BULLETIN. 1908. a., vol.60, 1976. £E6($11.66) Entomological Society of Egypt - Societe Entomologique d'Egypte, Box 430, Cairo, Egypt. **Indexed:** Apic.Abstr., Bio-Contr.News & Info., Biodet.Abstr., Biol.Abstr., Forest.Abstr., Forest Prod.Abstr., Potato Abstr., Rev.Appl.Entomol., Triticale Abstr., Weed Abstr.

595.7 UA ISSN 0081-0991
SB950.3.E3 CODEN: BEGEBG
SOCIETE ENTOMOLOGIQUE D'EGYPTE. BULLETIN. ECONOMIC SERIES. 1966. a., latest vol.9, 1975. £E3($5) Entomological Society of Egypt - Societe Entomologique d'Egypte, Box 430, Cairo, Egypt. **Indexed:** Bio-Contr.News & Info., Biodet.Abstr., Biol.Abstr., Maize Abstr.
—CASDDS.

595.7 FR ISSN 0037-9271
CODEN: ASEQAQ
SOCIETE ENTOMOLOGIQUE DE FRANCE. ANNALES. (Text and summaries in English, French, Italian, Spanish) 1832. q. 780 F. (foreign 880 F.) (effective 1996). c/o Societe Entomologique, 45 rue Buffon, 75005 Paris, France. Ed. J.Y. Rasplus. bk.rev.; illus.; index. circ. 800. (also avail. in microfiche from IDC) **Indexed:** Apic.Abstr., ASCA, Bio-Contr.News & Info., Curr.Adv.Cell & Devel.Biol., Curr.Adv.Ecol.Sci., Excerp.Med., Fababean Abstr., GeoRef., IBR, Potato Abstr., Rev.Appl.Entomol., Sci.Cit.Ind., Triticale Abstr. **Document type:** academic/scholarly publication.
—BLDSC (0947.000000); CISTI; Linda Hall; SWETS UnCover.

595.7 FR ISSN 0151-0517
QL461
SOCIETE ENTOMOLOGIQUE DE FRANCE. BULLETIN. (Text in French, summaries in English, French, German) 1896. 5/yr. 379.43 F. (foreign 450 F.). Societe Entomologica de France, 45 rue Buffon, 75005 Paris, France. adv.; bk.rev.; charts; illus. (also avail. in microfiche from BHP) **Indexed:** Bio-Contr.News & Info., Biol.Abstr., Curr.Adv.Ecol.Sci., Fababean Abstr., Forest.Abstr., Rev.Appl.Entomol., So.Pac.Per.Ind. **Document type:** bulletin.

BIOLOGY — ENTOMOLOGY

595.7   FR   ISSN 0373-4544
SOCIETE ENTOMOLOGIQUE DE MULHOUSE. BULLETIN. 1894. q. 200 F. (effective 1997). Societe Entomologique de Mulhouse, 35 pl. de la Reunion, 68100 Mulhouse, France. bk.rev. **Document type:** bulletin.
    Description: Biology, systematics, new descriptions of all orders of insects.

595.7   CN   ISSN 0071-0784
QL461   CODEN: SEQMA4
SOCIETE ENTOMOLOGIQUE DU QUEBEC. MEMOIRES. (Text in French; summaries in English) 1968. irreg. Societe Entomologique du Quebec, Complex Scientifique, D-1-54, 2700 rue Einstein, Ste.-Foy, Quebec, Que. G1P 3W8, Canada. TEL 418-656-2131. illus. **Indexed:** Biol.Abstr., Curr.Adv.Ecol.Sci.
    —Linda Hall.

581 591   FR   ISSN 0750-6848
      CODEN: BSLBBS
SOCIETE LINNEENNE DE BORDEAUX. BULLETIN. (Text in French; summaries in English) 1971. q. 200 F.($17) Societe Linneenne de Bordeaux, 1 place Bardineau, 33000 Bordeaux, France. TEL 33-5-56379782. Ed. Michel Laguerre. bk.rev. circ. 600. (tabloid format; back issues avail.) **Indexed:** Biol.Abstr., GeoRef., Zoo.Rec. **Document type:** bulletin.
    —Linda Hall.

595.7   BE   ISSN 0374-6038
QL461   CODEN: BASEBE
SOCIETE ROYALE BELGE D'ENTOMOLOGIE. BULLETIN ET ANNALES. (Text mainly in French) 1855. q. $32 to individuals,; institutions $47 (effective 1997). Societe Royal Belge d'Entomologie, 29, Rue Vautier, 1000 Brussels, Belgium. TEL 32-2-6274296. FAX 32-2-6274132. E-mail: gcoulon@kbinirsmb.be. Ed. Georges Coulon. bk.rev.; index. **Indexed:** Poult.Abstr., Zoo.Rec. **Document type:** academic/scholarly publication.
    —CISTI; Linda Hall.
    Former titles (until 1972): Societe Royale d'Entomologie de Belgique. Bulletin et Annales (ISSN 0049-1128); (until 1955): Societe Entomologique de Belgique. Bulletin et Annales (ISSN 0774-5923); (until 1925): Societe Entomologique de Belgique. Annales (ISSN 0774-5915); Societe Entomologique Belge. Annales (ISSN 0774-5893)
    Refereed Serial

595.7   FR   ISSN 0249-5805
      CODEN: BSNAD3
SOCIETE SCIENCES NAT. BULLETIN. 1972. q. 275 F.($50) Societe Sciences Nat, 2 rue Andre Mellenne, Venette, 60200 Compiegne, France. TEL 44-83-31-10. FAX 44-83-41-01. Ed. Jacques Rigout. adv. circ. 850. (back issues avail.) **Indexed:** Biol.Abstr., Zoo.Rec.
    —Linda Hall.
    Formerly: Societe des Sciences Naturelles. Bulletin.
    Description: Many descriptions of new insects worldwide.

595.7   JA   ISSN 0917-4745
SOSHI GAKKAI NYUSU/SOCIETAS DIPTEROLOGICA. NEWSLETTER. (Text in Japanese) irreg. Soshi Gakkai - Societas Dipterologica, c/o Biosystematics Laboratory, Graduate School of Social & Cultural Studies, Kyushu University, Ropponmatsu, Fukuoka 810, Japan. TEL 81-92-726-4637. FAX 81-92-712-1587. Ed. H./Shima. R&P contact: H. Shima. **Document type:** newsletter.

595.7   SA   ISSN 0255-0180
      CODEN: RAAEAV
SOUTH AFRICA. DEPARTMENT OF AGRICULTURE. ENTOMOLOGY MEMOIR. 1923. irreg, (approx. 4/yr.) price varies. Department of Agriculture, Private Bag X144, Pretoria 0001, South Africa. TEL 27-12-3197141. FAX 27-12-3232516. Ed. Ronelle Hechter. R&P contact: Ronelle Hechter. charts; illus.; stat. circ. 700. **Indexed:** Bio-Contr.News & Info., Biol.Abstr., Forest.Abstr., Forest Prod.Abstr., Rev.Appl.Entomol. **Document type:** government publication, academic/scholarly publication.
    —Linda Hall.
    Former titles: South Africa. Department of Agriculture and Fisheries. Entomology Memoirs (ISSN 0370-3096); (until 1980): South Africa. Department of Agricultural Technical Services. Entomology Memoirs (ISSN 0013-8940)

595.7   US   ISSN 0147-1724
QL475.S68   CODEN: SENTDD
SOUTHWESTERN ENTOMOLOGIST. (Supplement avail. (ISSN 1055-9799)) (Text in English, Spanish) 1976. q. $10 to individuals; institutions $20 (effective 1997). Southwestern Entomological Society, 17360 Coit Rd., Dallas, TX 75252. TEL 972-952-9222. (Alt. addr.: Texas A&M University, Department of Entomology, College Station, TX 77843-2475) Ed. D. Bay. bibl.; charts; illus.; stat.; index. circ. 471. (back issues avail.) **Indexed:** ASCA, Bio-Contr.News & Info., Biol.Abstr., Biotech.Abstr., Chem.Abstr., Cott.&Trop.Fibr.Abstr., Curr.Adv.Ecol.Sci., Curr.Cont., Ind.Vet., Rev.Appl.Entomol., Sci.Cit.Ind., Soils & Fert., Sorghum & Millets Abstr., Soyabean Abstr., Triticale Abstr., Trop.Oil Seeds Abstr., Vet.Bull., Weed Abstr. **Document type:** academic/scholarly publication.
    —BLDSC (8357.160000); CASDDS; EMDOCS; Genuine Article; SWETS; UnCover.
    Description: Contains scientific research.
    Refereed Serial

595.7   US   ISSN 1055-8799
QL475.S68   CODEN: SSOED3
SOUTHWESTERN ENTOMOLOGIST. SUPPLEMENT. (Supplement to: Southwestern Entomologist (ISSN 0147-1724)) irreg. Southwestern Entomological Society, 17360 Coit Rd., Dallas, TX 75252. TEL 972-952-9222. (Alt. addr.: Texas A&M University, Department of Entomology, College Station, TX 77843-2475) Ed. D. Bay.
    —BLDSC (8357.160100); CASDDS; Linda Hall.
    Formerly (until 1989): Supplement to the Southwestern Entomologist (ISSN 0277-7878)
    Description: Contains scientific research.
    Refereed Serial

595.7   GW   ISSN 0373-8981
QL461   CODEN: SMTEBI
STAATLICHES MUSEUM FUER TIERKUNDE DRESDEN. ENTOMOLOGISCHE ABHANDLUNGEN. (Text in English, French and German) 1961. a. price varies. Staatliches Museum fuer Tierkunde Dresden, Augustusstr. 2, 01067 Dresden, Germany. TEL 49-351-4952503. FAX 49-351-4952525. Ed. Rainer Emmrich. bk.rev.; index. circ. 550. (back issues avail.) **Indexed:** Biol.Abstr., IBR, Ref.Zh., Zoo.Rec. **Document type:** academic/scholarly publication.
    —CISTI.
    Description: Explores taxonomy, systematics, morphology, bionomics, ecology and zoogeography of Insecta and Arachnida.

STATE BIOLOGICAL SURVEY OF KANSAS. TECHNICAL BULLETIN. see *BIOLOGY — Botany*

STATION BIOLOGIQUE DE BESSE EN CHANDESSE. ANNALES. see *BIOLOGY — Abstracting, Bibliographies, Statistics*

595.7   JA   ISSN 0915-7883
SURUGA NO KONCHU/INSECTS IN SURUGA. (Text in Japanese) 1953. q. 3000 Yen (effective 1997 & 1998). Shizuoka Konchu Dokokai - Shizuoka Entomological Society, c/o Mr. Takahashi, 13-11 Kitaando 5-chome, Shizuoka-shi, Shizuoka-ken 420, Japan. TEL 81-54-245-6901. Ed. Mayumi Takahashi. **Document type:** bulletin.

595.7   UK   ISSN 0307-6970
QL461   CODEN: SYENDM
SYSTEMATIC ENTOMOLOGY. 1976. q. £185($338.50) (foreign £204) (effective 1998). (Royal Entomological Society) Blackwell Science Ltd., Osney Mead, Oxford OX2 OEL, England. TEL 44-1865-206206. FAX 44-1865-721205. E-mail: journals.cs@blacksci.co.uk; URL: http://www.black.co.uk. Eds. P. Eggleton, R.E. Harbach; Pub. Allen Stevens. R&P contact: Sarah Pollard. adv. contact: Martine Cariou-Keen. bk.rev. circ. 650. (also avail. in microform from UMI; back issues avail.; reprint service avail. from ISI) **Indexed:** Abstr.Hyg., Apic.Abstr., ASCA, Bio-Contr.News & Info., Biol.Abstr., Curr.Adv.Ecol.Sci., Curr.Cont., Ecol.Abstr., Forest.Abstr., Geol.Abstr., Ind.Sci.Rev., Rev.Appl.Entomol., Rice Abstr., Sci.Cit.Ind., Soils & Fert., Trop.Dis.Bull. **Document type:** academic/scholarly publication.
    —BLDSC (8589.180000); CISTI; Genuine Article; Linda Hall; SWETS; UMI; UnCover. **CCC.**
    Formerly: Journal of Entomology (B) (ISSN 0047-2417)
    Refereed Serial

595.7   JA   ISSN 0917-3102
TATEHAMODOKI/MIYAZAKI ENTOMOLOGICAL SOCIETY. JOURNAL. (Text in Japanese) a. Miyazaki Konchu Dokokai - Miyazaki Entomological Society, Miyazakiken Sogo Hakubutsukan, 4-4 Jingu 2-chome, Miyazaki-shi, Miyazaki-ken 880, Japan.

595.7 338   US   ISSN 0883-8828
TECHLETTER; for pest control technicians. 1985. bi-w. $47. Pinto & Associates, Inc., 29839 Oak Rd., Mechanicsville, MD 20659. TEL 301-884-3020. FAX 301-884-4068. Ed. Sandra Kraft; Pub. Lawrence J. Pinto. bk.rev.; illus.; tr.lit.; index; circ. 1,000 (paid). (looseleaf format) **Document type:** newsletter, trade publication.
    Description: Training information for exterminators.

595.7   NE   ISSN 0040-7496
TIJDSCHRIFT VOOR ENTOMOLOGIE. (Text in Dutch, English, French and German) 1858. s-a. fl.300 (effective 1996 & 1997). Nederlandse Entomologische Vereniging, Plantage Middenlaan 64, 1018 DH Amsterdam, Netherlands. Eds. E.J. van Nieukerken, J.V. Tol. charts; illus. **Indexed:** Bio-Contr.News & Info., Biol.Abstr., Rev.Appl.Entomol. **Document type:** academic/scholarly publication.
    —BLDSC (8841.000000); CISTI; Linda Hall; SWETS.

595.7   JA   ISSN 0493-3168
TINEA. (Text in English; summaries in Japanese) 1953. irreg. Japan Heterocerists' Society - Nihon Garui Gakkai, Kokuritsu Kagaku Hakubutsukan Bunkan, Hyakunincho 3-chome, Shinjuku-ku, Tokyo 160, Japan.

595.7   JA
TOBU/HYAKUMANGOKU BUTTERFLY STUDY GROUP. NEWS. (Text in Japanese) bi-m. Hyakumangoku Chodankai - Hyakumangoku Butterfly Study Group, c/o Mr. Matsui, 871-15 Obamachi Higashi, Kanazawa-shi, Ishikawa-ken 920-01, Japan.

595.7   JA   ISSN 0913-5847
TOHOKU KONCHU/JOURNAL OF ENTOMOLOGY IN TOHOKU DISTRICT. (Text in Japanese) 1964. a. Nihon Konchu Gakkai, Tohoku Shibu - Entomological Society of Japan, Tohoku Branch, Tohoku Gakui Daigaku Kyoyogakubu, Seibutsugaku Kenkyushitsu, 9-1 Tenjinzawa, Ichinazaka, Izumi-ku, Sendai-shi, Miyagi-ken 981-31, Japan.

595.7   JA   ISSN 0495-8314
TOMBO/ACTA ODONATOLOGICA. (Text in English, Japanese) 1958. a. membership. Nihon Tonbo Gakkai - Society of Odonatology, Tokyo, c/o Mr. Shojiro Asahina, 4-24 Takadanobaba 4-chome, Shinjuku-ku, Tokyo 160, Japan.

595.7   US   ISSN 0082-6391
QL596.T2
TRIBOLIUM INFORMATION BULLETIN. 1958. a. $29 to individuals; institutions $31. California State University, San Bernardino, School of Natural Sciences, San Bernardino, CA 92407. TEL 909-880-5305. FAX 909-880-5407. Ed. A. Sokoloff. circ. 85. (also avail. in microfilm) **Document type:** newsletter.
    Description: Contains research, teaching, and technical notes on beetles; covers wild type and mutant stocks in laboratories throughout the world. Includes personal and geographical directories and current bibliography on all aspects of research on Tribolium and other Coleoptera.

595.7   US   ISSN 1048-8138
QL560.6   CODEN: TRLEER
TROPICAL LEPIDOPTERA. (Text in English, French, German, Portuguese, Spanish) 1990. s-a. (plus irreg. supplements). $40 (foreign $40) (effective 1996). Association for Tropical Lepidoptera, Box 141210, Gainesville, FL 32614-1210. TEL 352-372-3505. FAX 352-373-3249. Ed. J.B. Heppner. adv.; bibl.; illus.; tr.lit.; index, cum.index. circ. 1,250. (back issues avail.) **Document type:** academic/scholarly publication.
    —BLDSC (9056.320000).
    Description: General taxonomy and conservation of tropical and subtropical moths and butterflies.
    Refereed Serial

595.7   JA
TSUISO/WEEKLY BUTTERFLY'S TSUISO. (Text in Japanese) 1975. 3/m. 300 Yen per no. Mokuyosha, 53-15-402 Eifuku 3-chome, Suginami-ku, Tokyo 168, Japan. TEL 81-3-3324-1153. Ed. Yasusuke Nishiyama.

BIOLOGY — GENETICS

595.7   US   ISSN 0068-6417
QL461   CODEN: UCPEAH
UNIVERSITY OF CALIFORNIA PUBLICATIONS IN ENTOMOLOGY. 1906. irreg., vol.115, 1995. price varies. University of California Press, 2120 Berkeley Way, Berkeley, CA 94720. TEL 510-642-4247. FAX 510-643-7127. (Orders to: California-Princeton Fulfillment Services, 1445 Lower Ferry Rd., Ewing, NJ 08618. TEL 800-777-4726. FAX 800-999-1958) Ed.Bd. (back issues avail.) **Indexed:** Abstr.Hyg., Biol.Abstr., Curr.Adv.Ecol.Sci., Rev.Appl.Entomol., Trop.Dis.Bull. **Document type:** monographic series.
—CISTI; Linda Hall.
  Description: Researches the biology of various insect species from all parts of the world.
  Refereed Serial

595.7   PL   ISSN 0867-1966
QL461   CODEN: AUSEEA
UPPER SILESIAN MUSEUM IN BYTOM. ANNALS. ENTOMOLOGY. (Text in English; summaries in Polish) 1990. a. $25. Muzeum Gornoslaskie, Pl. Sobieskiego 2, 41-902 Bytom, Poland. **Document type:** proceedings.
—BLDSC (1035.004000).

UTTAR PRADESH JOURNAL OF ZOOLOGY. see *BIOLOGY — Zoology*

WEED RESEARCH. see *BIOLOGY — Botany*

595.7   NZ   ISSN 0111-7696
THE WETA; news bulletin. 1977. 2/yr. NZ.$5 (foreign $4.50) per issue (effective 1997). Entomological Society of New Zealand, Mt. Albert Research Centre, Private Bag 92169, Auckland, New Zealand. FAX 64-9-8497093. E-mail: mplmjb@dslak.co.nz. **Document type:** bulletin.

WORLD CROP PESTS. see *AGRICULTURE — Crop Production And Soil*

595.7   US   ISSN 0884-6677
                                CODEN: YESQES
Y E S QUARTERLY. 1984. q. $45. Young Entomologists' Society, Inc., International Headquarters, 1915 Peggy Place, Lansing, MI 48910. TEL 517-887-0499. URL: YESbug@aol.com. Ed. Gary A. Dunn. bk.rev.; index. circ. 750. **Indexed:** Entomol.Abstr. **Document type:** academic/scholarly publication.
—BLDSC (9418.335700).

595.7   JA   ISSN 0513-417X
QL541
YADORIGA/LEPIDOPTEROLOGICAL SOCIETY OF JAPAN. JOURNAL. (Text in Japanese) 1955. q. Nihon Rinshi Gakkai - Lepidopterological Society of Japan, c/o Ogata Bldg., 2-17 Imabashi 3-chome, Chuo-ku, Osaka 541, Japan. Ed. Toshio Inomata. adv.; bk.rev. circ. 1,500. (back issues avail.) **Document type:** academic/scholarly publication.
—CISTI.

595.7   JA   ISSN 0917-5695
YOSEGAKI/SAITAMA ENTOMOLOGIST'S ASSOCIATION. JOURNAL. (Text in Japanese) 1963. q. 3000 Yen. Saitama Konchu Danwakai - Saitama Entomologist's Association, c/o Mr. Makibayashi, 2-864 Amanumacho, Omiya-shi, Saitama-ken 330, Japan. TEL 81-48-642-4023. Ed. T. Usui. circ. 400. **Document type:** proceedings.

595.7   JA   ISSN 0387-5695
YUGATO/JOURNAL OF RESEARCH ON MOTHS. (Text in Japanese; summaries in English) 1959. q. 5000 Yen membership. Yugakai - Yugato Society, c/o Dr. Rikio Sato, 2-27-29, Shindori-nishi, Niigata-shi, Niigata-ken 950-21, Japan. TEL 81-25-262-5176. FAX 81-25-261-2936. Ed. Rikio Sato. bk.rev. circ. 300. **Document type:** bulletin.

ZEITSCHRIFT FUER PFLANZENKRANKHEITEN UND PFLANZENSCHUTZ. see *BIOLOGY — Botany*

595.7   GW   ISSN 0044-5223
QL461   CODEN: EMZMAJ
ZOOLOGISCHES MUSEUM HAMBURG. ENTOMOLOGISCHE MITTEILUNGEN. (Text in English, French, German; summaries in English) 1952. s-a. exchange basis. Zoologisches Museum Hamburg, Martin-Luther-King-Platz 3, 20146 Hamburg, Germany. FAX 49-40-4123-3937. (Co-sponsor: Universitaet Hamburg, Zoologisches Institut) Ed. H. Struempel. bk.rev.; cum.index. circ. 400. (looseleaf format; back issues avail.) **Indexed:** Biodet.Abstr., Biol.Abstr., Entomol.Abstr., IBR, Rev.Appl.Entomol., Zoo.Rec. **Document type:** academic/scholarly publication.
—BLDSC (3781.900000).

BIOLOGY — Genetics

573   II   ISSN 0258-0357
GN289.   CODEN: ACANDO
ACTA ANTHROPOGENETICA; international journal of research in human genetics. (Text and summaries in English) 1977. q. $100. Saraswati Press, 2-43 Ansari Rd., New Delhi 110002, India. Ed. Dr. P.K. Shrivastava. adv.; bk.rev.; index. circ. 1,000. (back issues avail.) **Indexed:** Anthropol.Lit., Biol.Abstr., Dent.Ind., Excerp.Med., Ind.Med.
—CASDDS; CISTI; Linda Hall.

575.1   YU   ISSN 0534-0012
QH431.A1   CODEN: GNTKDF
ACTA BIOLOGICA IUGOSLAVICA. SERIJA F: GENETIKA. 1969. 3/yr. $78. Unija Bioloskih Naucnih Drustava Jugoslavije - Yugoslav Union of Biological Sciences, Nemanjina 6, fah 127, 11080 Belgrade Zemun, Yugoslavia. (Co-sponsor: Drustvo Geneticara Jugoslavije) Ed. Janko Dumanovic. **Indexed:** Chem.Abstr., Curr.Adv.Ecol.Sci., Curr.Cont.
—BLDSC (4115.250000); CASDDS; Linda Hall.

575.1   UY   ISSN 0797-6852
ACTA GENETICA ET TERATOLOGICA. (Text in Spanish; summaries in English) 1991. a. $20. Fernando Mane-Garzon, Ed. & Pub., Casilla de Correo 157, Montevideo, Uruguay. illus.; index. circ. 500. (back issues avail.) **Document type:** academic/scholarly publication.

ACTA GENETICAE MEDICAE ET GEMELLOLOGIAE: TWIN RESEARCH. see *MEDICAL SCIENCES*

ACTA MICROBIOLOGICA POLONICA. see *BIOLOGY — Microbiology*

575.1 591.15
581.15   XR   ISSN 0085-0748
                                 CODEN: FMDLAJ
ACTA MUSEI MORAVIAE. SUPPLEMENTUM: FOLIA MENDELIANA. (Supplement to: Moravske Zemske Muzeum. Casopis. Vedy Prirodni (ISSN 0521-2359)) (Text in English, French, German; summaries in English) 1966. a. $18. Moravske Zemske Muzeum, Zelny trh 6, 659 37 Brno, Czech Republic. TEL 420-5-42321205. FAX 420-5-42212792. E-mail: mzm@mzm.anet.cz. Ed. Anna Matalova. **Indexed:** A.I.C.P., Biol.Abstr. **Document type:** academic/scholarly publication.
—KNAW; Linda Hall.

575.1   US   ISSN 1067-568X
QP624.7   CODEN: ADNAEO
ADVANCES IN DNA SEQUENCE SPECIFIC AGENTS. 1992. irreg., vol.3, 1997. $109.50. J A I Press Inc., 55 Old Post Rd., No. 2, Box 1678, Greenwich, CT 06830-1678. TEL 203-661-7602. FAX 203-661-0792. E-mail: jai@jaipress.com. (Subscr. in UK and Europe to: JAI Press Ltd., 38 Tavistock St., Covent Garden, London WC2E 7PB, England. TEL 44-171-379-8834. FAX 44-171-379-8835) Ed. Laurence Hurley. **Document type:** academic/scholarly publication.
—BLDSC (0704.249000); CASDDS.

575.082   US   ISSN 0065-2660
QH431.A1   CODEN: ADGEAV
ADVANCES IN GENETICS. (Supplement avail. (ISSN 0065-2679)) 1947. irreg., vol.36, 1997. Academic Press, Inc., 525 B St., Ste. 1900, San Diego, CA 92101-4495. TEL 619-231-0926. FAX 619-699-6715. (Subscr. to: Order Dept., 6277 Sea Harbor Dr., 4th Fl., Orlando, FL 32887. TEL 800-321-5068) Ed. M. Demerec. (reprint service avail. from ISI) **Indexed:** Abstr.Hyg., Anim.Breed.Abstr., ASCA, Biol.Abstr., Biol.& Agr.Ind., Cott.& Trop.Fibr.Abstr., Curr.Adv.Ecol.Sci., Ind.Med., Ind.Sci.Rev., INIS Atomind., Plant Breed.Abstr., Poult.Abstr., Sci.Cit.Ind., Telegen, Trop.Dis.Bull. **Document type:** monographic series.
—BLDSC (0708.000000); CASDDS; CISTI; KR SourceOne; Linda Hall; SWETS; UnCover. **CCC.**
  Incorporates (1991-1995): Molecular Genetic Medicine (ISSN 1057-2805)
  Refereed Serial

575.1   US   ISSN 0065-2679
ADVANCES IN GENETICS. SUPPLEMENT. 1966. irreg. price varies. Academic Press, Inc., 525 B. St., Ste. 1900, San Diego, CA 92101-4495. TEL 619-230-1840. FAX 619-699-6800. (Subscr. to: Order Dept., 6277 Sea Harbor Dr., 4th Fl., Orlando, FL 32887. TEL 800-321-5068) **Document type:** monographic series.
—CISTI; Linda Hall.

575.1   US   ISSN 1067-5701
QH447   CODEN: AGBIE9
ADVANCES IN GENOME BIOLOGY. 1992. irreg. $97.50. J A I Press Inc., 55 Old Post Rd., No. 2, Box 1678, Greenwich, CT 06836-1678. TEL 203-661-7602. FAX 203-661-0792. Ed. Ram Verma. **Document type:** academic/scholarly publication.
—BLDSC (0708.030000); CASDDS; CISTI. **CCC.**

573.21   US   ISSN 0065-275X
QH431.A1   CODEN: ADHGA8
ADVANCES IN HUMAN GENETICS. 1970. irreg., vol.23, 1997. price varies. Plenum Publishing Corp., 233 Spring St., New York, NY 10013-1578. TEL 212-620-8000. FAX 212-463-0742. TELEX 23-421139. E-mail: books@plenum.com. Eds. K. Hirschhorn, H. Harris. **Indexed:** ASCA, Biol.Abstr., Biol.& Agr.Ind., Chem.Abstr., Curr.Adv.Ecol.Sci., Excerp.Med., Ind.Med., Ind.Sci.Rev., INIS Atomind., Sci.Cit.Ind. **Document type:** monographic series.
—BLDSC (0709.070000); CASDDS; CISTI; EMDOCS; Genuine Article; KNAW; KR SourceOne; Linda Hall; SWETS; UnCover. **CCC.**
  Refereed Serial

575.1   SZ
ADVANCES IN LIFE SCIENCES. (Text in English) irreg. 88 SFr. Birkhaeuser Verlag, P.O. Box 133, CH-4010 Basel, Switzerland. TEL 41-61-2050730. FAX 41-61-2050791. E-mail: subscriptions@birkhauser.ch. **Document type:** academic/scholarly publication, monographic series.

575.1   NR   ISSN 0795-6762
AFRICAN JOURNAL OF GENETICS. French edition: Journal Africain de Genetique. (Text in English) q. $15. University of Benin, P.M.B. 1154, Ugbowo Campus, Benin City, Nigeria. TEL 234-52-200250. TELEX 41365. Ed. O.S.A. Aromose. **Document type:** academic/scholarly publication.

BIOLOGY — GENETICS

573.21 US ISSN 0002-9297
QH431.A1 CODEN: AJHGAG
AMERICAN JOURNAL OF HUMAN GENETICS; a record of research, review and bibliographic material relating to heredity in man. 1948. m. $495 to non-member individuals & institutions (Canada $529.65; elsewhere $495) (effective 1998). (American Society of Human Genetics) University of Chicago Press, Journals Division, Box 37005, Chicago, IL 60637. TEL 773-753-3347. FAX 773-753-0811. TELEX 25-4603. E-mail: subscriptions@journals.uchicago.edu; URL: http://www.journals.uchicago.edu/AJHG/. Ed. Dr. Peter H. Byers. adv.: page $355; trim 8 1/4 x 10 7/8. bk.rev.; charts; illus.; stat.; index. circ. 4,800. (also avail. in microform from MIM,UMI; reprint service avail.) **Indexed:** A.I.C.P., Abstr.Anthropol., Abstr.Hyg., Anim.Breed.Abstr., ASCA, Bibl.Dev.Med.& Child Neur., Biol.Abstr., Biol.& Agr.Ind., Biostat., Chem.Abstr., Curr.Adv.Cancer Res., Curr.Adv.Ecol.Sci., Curr.Adv.Genetics & Molec.Biol., Curr.Cont., Dairy Sci.Abstr., DSH Abstr., Excerp.Med., Helminthol.Abstr., Ind.Med., Ind.Sci.Rev., INIS Atomind., Med.& Surg.Dermat., Neurosci.Cit.Ind., Sci.Cit.Ind., So.Pac.Per.Ind., Sociol.Abstr., Telegen, THA. **Document type:** academic/scholarly publication.
—BLDSC (0825.000000); CASDDS; CISTI; EMDOCS; Genuine Article; KNAW; KR SourceOne; Linda Hall; SWETS; UMI; UnCover. **CCC.**
Description: Examines research into and the application of genetic principles in medicine, psychology, anthropology, and social services, as well as in related areas of molecular and cell biology.
Refereed Serial

612 US ISSN 0148-7299
RB155 CODEN: AJMGDA
AMERICAN JOURNAL OF MEDICAL GENETICS. (Supplement avail. (ISSN 1040-3787)) 1977. 36/yr. $5395 (foreign $6025) (effective 1998). John Wiley & Sons, Inc., Journals, 605 Third Ave., New York, NY 10158. TEL 212-850-6645. FAX 212-850-6021. TELEX 12-7063. E-mail: SUBINFO@JWILEY.COM; URL: http://www.wiley.co.uk. (Subscr. outside the Americas to: John Wiley & Sons Ltd., Baffins Ln., Chichester, W. Sussex PO19 1UD, England. TEL 44-1243-779777. FAX 44-1243-776128) Ed. John M. Opitz. adv.: B&W page £640, color page £1515; trim 279 x 210. bk.rev.; charts; illus.; index. circ. 150. (also avail. in microform from UMI; back issues avail.; reprint service avail. from ISI) **Indexed:** ASCA, Bibl.Dev.Med.& Child Neur., Biol.Abstr., Curr.Adv.Ecol.Sci., Curr.Adv.Genetics & Molec.Biol., Curr.Cont., Dent.Ind., Excerp.Med., Fam.Ind., Helminthol.Abstr., Ind.Med., Ind.Sci.Rev., INIS Atomind., Kidney, Med.& Surg.Dermat., Neurosci.Cit.Ind., Nutr.Abstr., Risk Abstr., Sci.Cit.Ind, SSCI, THA. **Document type:** academic/scholarly publication.
●Also available online.
—BLDSC (0827.900000); CISTI; EMDOCS; Genuine Article; KNAW; SWETS; UnCover. **CCC.**
Description: Covers all the biological and medical aspects of genetic disorders.
Refereed Serial

612 US ISSN 1040-3787
CODEN: AJMSED
AMERICAN JOURNAL OF MEDICAL GENETICS. SUPPLEMENT. 1986. irreg. John Wiley & Sons, Inc., Journals, 605 Third Ave., New York, NY 10158. TEL 212-850-6000. FAX 212-850-6088. TELEX 12-7063. E-mail: SUBINFO@JWILEY.COM. (Subscr. outside the Americas to: John Wiley & Sons Ltd., Baffins Ln., Chichester, W. Sussex PO19 1UD, England. TEL 44-1243-779777. FAX 44-1243-776128) **Document type:** monographic series.
—CISTI.

575.1 591.15 UK ISSN 0268-9146
CODEN: ANGEE3
ANIMAL GENETICS. 1970. bi-m. £223($406.50) (foreign £245) (effective 1998). (International Society for Animal Genetics) Blackwell Science Ltd., Osney Mead, Oxford OX2 0EL, England. TEL 44-1865-206206. FAX 44-1865-721205. E-mail: journals.cs@blacksci.co.uk; URL: http://www.black.co.uk. Ed. Dr. A. Archibald; Pub. Allen Stevens. R&P contact: Sarah Pollard. adv. contact: Martine Cariou-Keen. bk.rev.; illus.; index. circ. 485. (also avail. in microform from UMI; back issues avail.) **Indexed:** Anim.Breed.Abstr., ASCA, Biol.Abstr., Chem.Abstr., Curr.Adv.Ecol.Sci., Curr.Cont., Dairy Sci.Abstr., Excerp.Med., Ind.Med., Ind.Sci.Rev., Ind.Vet., Pig News & Info., Sci.Cit.Ind., Sport Fish.Abstr., Vet.Bull., Wild.Rev., Zoo.Rec. **Document type:** academic/scholarly publication.
—BLDSC (0903.572000); CASDDS; CISTI; EMDOCS; Genuine Article; KNAW; Linda Hall; SWETS; UMI; UnCover. **CCC.**
Formerly (until 1986): Animal Blood Groups and Biochemical Genetics (ISSN 0003-3480)
Refereed Serial

575.1 FR ISSN 0003-3995
CODEN: AGTQAH
ANNALES DE GENETIQUE. (Text and summaries in English, French) 1958. 4/yr. 1600 F. to individuals (foreign 1780 F.); students 800 F. (foreign 890 F.) (effective 1997). (Semaine des Hopitaux) Expansion Scientifique Francaise, 31 bd. de la Tour Maubourg, 75343 Paris Cedex 07, France. TEL 33-1-40626400. FAX 33-1-45556920. (Subscr. to: 15 rue St-Benoit, 75278 Paris Cedex 06, France. TEL 33-1-45484260. FAX 33-1-45448155) Ed. C. Stoll. bk.rev.; charts; illus. circ. 1,000. **Indexed:** Abstr.Anthropol., Anim.Breed.Abstr., ASCA, Bibl.Dev.Med.& Child Neur., Biol.Abstr., Chem.Abstr., Curr.Adv.Cancer Res., Curr.Adv.Ecol.Sci., Curr.Adv.Genetics & Molec.Biol., Curr.Cont., Dairy Sci.Abstr., Dent.Ind., Excerp.Med., Helminthol.Abstr., Ind.Med., Ind.Sci.Rev., Sci.Cit.Ind., Sport Fish.Abstr., SSCI, Wild.Rev., Zoo.Rec. **Document type:** academic/scholarly publication.
—BLDSC (0975.300000); CASDDS; CISTI; EMDOCS; Genuine Article; KNAW; SWETS; UnCover. **CCC.**

573.21 UK ISSN 0003-4800
HQ750.A1 CODEN: ANHGAA
ANNALS OF HUMAN GENETICS. 1925. bi-m. £144($248) (effective 1998). Cambridge University Press, Edinburgh Bldg., Shaftesbury Rd., Cambridge CB2 2RU, England. TEL 44-1223-312393. FAX 44-1223-315052. TELEX 851817256. E-mail: information@cup.cam.ac.uk; URL: http://www.cup.org/journals/CUPJNLS.html. (N. American addr.: Cambridge University Press, 40 W. 20th St., New York, NY 10011. TEL 212-924-3900. FAX 212-691-3239) Eds. C.A.B. Smith, D.A. Hopkinson. R&P contact: Linda Nicol. adv. contact: Rebecca Symons. bk.rev.; charts; illus.; index. (also avail. in microform from UMI; back issues avail.; reprint service avail. from SWZ) **Indexed:** A.I.C.P., Abstr.Anthropol., Abstr.Hyg., Anim.Breed.Abstr., Anthropol.Lit., ASCA, Bibl.Dev.Med.& Child Neur., Biol.Abstr., Chem.Abstr., Curr.Adv.Ecol.Sci., Curr.Cont., Dairy Sci.Abstr., Excerp.Med., Helminthol.Abstr., Ind.Med., Ind.Sci.Rev., Math.R., Nutr.Abstr., Psychol.Abstr., Sci.Cit.Ind., SSCI, Stat.Theor.Meth.Abstr., THA, Trop.Dis.Bull. **Document type:** academic/scholarly publication.
—BLDSC (1041.000000); CASDDS; CISTI; EMDOCS; Genuine Article; KNAW; KR SourceOne; Linda Hall; SWETS; UMI; UnCover. **CCC.**
Formerly: Annals of Eugenics.
Description: Concerned with the application of scientific techniques to the study of human inheritance, such as gene mapping, cytogenetics, clinical genetics or mathematical models.

591.15 575.1 US ISSN 0066-4197
QH431.A1 CODEN: ARVGB7
ANNUAL REVIEW OF GENETICS. 1967. a. $60 to individuals (foreign $65); institutions $120 (foreign $130) (effective 1998). Annual Reviews Inc., 4139 El Camino Way, Box 10139, Palo Alto, CA 94303-0139. TEL 650-493-4400; 800-523-8635. FAX 650-424-0910. E-mail: service@annurev.org; URL: http://www.annurev.org. Ed. Allan Campbell. R&P contact: Jeanne Kunz. bibl.; index, cum.index. (also avail. in microfilm from UMI; back issues avail.; reprint service avail.) **Indexed:** Abstr.Hyg., Anim.Breed.Abstr., ASCA, Bibl.Agri., Biol.Abstr., Biol.& Agr.Ind., Biotech.Abstr., Chem.Abstr., Curr.Adv.Biochem., Curr.Adv.Cell & Devel.Biol., Curr.Adv.Ecol.Sci., Curr.Adv.Genetics & Molec.Biol., Curr.Cont., Diar.Dis.Res., Excerp.Med., Forest.Abstr., Forest Prod.Abstr., Gen.Sci.Ind., Helminthol.Abstr., Ind.Med., Ind.Sci.Rev., INIS Atomind., M.M.R.I., Plant Breed.Abstr., Rev.Plant Path, Sci.Cit.Ind., THA, Trop.Dis.Bull. **Document type:** academic/scholarly publication.
●Also available online. Vendor(s): Information Access Co.
—BLDSC (1522.565000); ADONIS; CASDDS; CISTI; EMDOCS; Genuine Article; KNAW; KR SourceOne; Linda Hall; SWETS; UMI; UnCover. **CCC.**
Description: Original critical reviews of the significant literature and current developments in genetics.

575.1 US ISSN 1087-2906
QP623.5.A58 CODEN: AREDEI
ANTISENSE AND NUCLEIC ACID DRUG DEVELOPMENT. 1991. bi-m. $111 to individuals (foreign $165); institutions $185 (foreign $223) (effective through 1998). Mary Ann Liebert, Inc. Publishers, 2 Madison Ave., Larchmont, NY 10538. TEL 914-834-3100. FAX 914-834-3688. E-mail: liebert@pipeline.com. Eds. Arthur M. Krieg, C.A. Stein. **Indexed:** ASCA, Curr.Cont., Excerp.Med. (1993-), Ind.Med. (1992-), Ind.Sci.Rev., Sci.Cit.Ind. **Document type:** academic/scholarly publication.
—CASDDS; CISTI; EMDOCS; Genuine Article; UnCover.
Formerly (until 1997): Antisense Research and Development (ISSN 1050-5261)
Description: Deals with man-made substances and their effects on gene expression at the RNA and DNA levels both in vitro and in vivo.

575.1 618 US ISSN 1056-5191
RB155.6
APPLIED CYTOGENETICS. 1975. bi-m. $105. Association of Cytogenetic Technologists, c/o A C T Association Manager, Box 15945-288, Lenexa, KS 66285. TEL 913-541-9077. FAX 931-541-0156. Ed. Barbara J. Kaplan. adv. contact: Leslee Urhahn. bk.rev. circ. 1,700. (back issues avail.) **Document type:** trade publication.
—KNAW.
Formerly (until 1990): Karyogram (ISSN 0732-8745)
Description: Covers clinical cytogenetics and molecular cytogenetics for laboratory and medical personnel.

575.1 US ISSN 0271-7107
CODEN: AGNEEN
APPLIED GENETICS NEWS. 1980. m. $395. Business Communications Co., Inc. (Norwalk), 25 Van Zant St., Ste. 13, Norwalk, CT 06855. TEL 203-853-4266. FAX 203-853-0348. TELEX 6502934929 WUI. Ed. Jack T. Miskell. **Indexed:** BPIA, Curr.Biotech.Abstr.
●Also available online. Vendor(s): Data-Star, Information Access Co., Knight-Ridder Information, Inc., NewsNet (BT03).
—CISTI. **CCC.**
Description: Covers the biotechnology industry from technical and economic perspectives

575.1 IT ISSN 0066-9830
CODEN: AAGNA3
ASSOCIAZIONE GENETICA ITALIANA. ATTI. (Text and summaries in English or Italian) 1955. a. L.20000($7) Associazione Genetica Italiana, c/o Istituto di Biologia Animale, Via Loredan 10, 35100 Padova, Italy. Ed. G.A. Danieli. circ. 300. **Indexed:** Anim.Breed.Abstr., Biol.Abstr., Curr.Adv.Ecol.Sci., Curr.Cont., INIS Atomind.
—BLDSC (1778.050000); CISTI; Linda Hall.

BIOLOGY — GENETICS

575.1 614.4   AT
AUSTRALIAN AND NEW ZEALAND DIRECTORY OF GENETICS SUPPORT GROUPS, SERVICES AND INFORMATION. 1992. biennial. Aus.$20. New South Wales Genetics Education Program, P.O. Box 317, St. Leonards, N.S.W. 2065, Australia. TEL 61-2-99267324. FAX 61-2-99067529. Ed. Kristine Barlow-Stewart. R&P contact: Kristine Barlow-Stewart. circ. 2,000. (looseleaf format) **Document type:** directory.
  Description: Provides information about genetic support groups and services for the health professionals, students, teachers, and general community.

573.21   NE   ISSN 0167-4781
B B A - GENE STRUCTURE AND EXPRESSION. (Section of: Biochimica et Biophysica Acta (ISSN 0006-3002)) 1962. 18/yr. fl.3418($1964) (effective 1998). Elsevier Science B.V., P.O. Box 211, 1000 AE Amsterdam, Netherlands. TEL 31-20-4853911. FAX 31-20-4853598. TELEX 18582 ESPA NL. E-mail: nlinfo-f@elsevier.nl; usinfo-f@elsevier.com; forinfo-kyf04035@niftyserve.or.jp; URL: http://www.elsevier.nl/. (Subscr. in the Americas to: Elsevier Science, Regional Sales Office, Box 945, New York, NY 10159-0945. TEL 212-633-3730. FAX 212-633-3680; Subscr. in Australasia and the Far East to: Elsevier Science (Singapore) Pte Ltd, No.1 Temasek Ave., No.17-01 Millenia Tower, Singapore 039192, Singapore. TEL 65-434-3727. FAX 65-337-2230; Subscr. in Japan to: Elsevier Science Japan, 9-15 Higashi-Azabu 1-chome, Minato-ku, Tokyo 106, Japan. TEL 81-3-5561-5033. FAX 81-3-5561-5047) Ed.Bd. (also avail. in microform from UMI; back issues avail.) **Indexed:** ASCA, Biodet.Abstr., Biol.Abstr., Chem.Abstr., Curr.Cont., Excerp.Med., Ind.Chem., Ind.Med. **Document type:** academic/scholarly publication.
  —ADONIS; CISTI; EMDOCS; Genuine Article; SWETS. **CCC.**
  Description: Examines DNA and RNA structures. Includes sequence data, nucleic acid and protein interaction, DNA modifying enzymes and replication. Explores transcription mechanisms and factors as well as control of gene expression.
  Refereed Serial

B B A - MOLECULAR BASIS OF DISEASE. see *MEDICAL SCIENCES*

B T I A; la revue francaise de la genetique et de la reproduction. (Bulletin Technique de l'Insemination Artificielle) see *AGRICULTURE — Poultry And Livestock*

BABRAHAM INSTITUTE. REPORT. see *BIOLOGY — Physiology*

575.1 610   US   ISSN 0001-8244
CODEN: BHGNAT
BEHAVIOR GENETICS; an international journal devoted to research in the inheritance of behavior in animals and man. 1970. bi-m. $495 (foreign $580) (effective 1998). Plenum Publishing Corp., 233 Spring St., New York, NY 10013-1578. TEL 212-620-8000. FAX 212-463-0742. TELEX 23-421139. (Editorial addr.: c/o Institute for Behavioral Genetics, Campus Box 447, University of Colorado, Boulder, CO 80309) Ed. Dr. David W. Fulker. adv.; bk.rev.; bibl.; charts; illus.; stat.; index. (also avail. in microfilm from UMI; back issues avail.) **Indexed:** Abstr.Anthropol., Anim.Breed.Abstr., Apic.Abstr., ASCA, Biol.Abstr., Child Devel.Abstr., Curr.Adv.Ecol.Sci., Curr.Cont., Dairy Sci.Abstr., Excerp.Med., Fam.Ind., Ind.Med., Ind.Sci.Rev., INIS Atomind., Neurosci.Cit.Ind., Psychol.Abstr. (1970-), Sci.Cit.Ind., Sport Fish.Abstr., SSCI, Wild.Rev., Zoo.Rec., 013345422. **Document type:** academic/scholarly publication.
  —BLDSC (1876.691000); CISTI; EMDOCS; Genuine Article; KNAW; SWETS; UMI; UnCover. **CCC.**
  Refereed Serial

BILTEN ZA HMELJ, SIRAK I LEKOVITO BILJE. see *AGRICULTURE — Agricultural Economics*

BIOCHEMICAL GENETICS. see *BIOLOGY — Biological Chemistry*

BIOETHICS. see *PHILOSOPHY*

576.5   US   ISSN 0006-3363
QP251.A1   CODEN: BIREBV
BIOLOGY OF REPRODUCTION. (Supplement avail. (ISSN 0523-6754)) 1969. m. (in 2 vols.) $190 includes supplement (foreign $225) (effective 1997). Society for the Study of Reproduction, 1603 Monroe St., Madison, WI 53711-2021. TEL 608-256-2777. FAX 608-256-4610. E-mail: ssr@ssr.org; URL: http://www.ssr.org/ssr. Ed. Gordon D. Niswender. R&P contact: Judith Jansen. adv. contact: Judith Jansen. abstr.; bibl.; charts; illus.; s-a. index; circ. 3,700 (paid). (also avail. in microform from UMI; back issues avail.) **Indexed:** Abstr.Anthropol., Abstr.Anthropol., Anim.Breed.Abstr., ASCA, Bibl.Agri., Biol.Abstr., Chem.Abstr., Curr.Adv.Ecol.Sci., Curr.Cont., Dairy Sci.Abstr., Excerp.Med., Helminthol.Abstr., Ind.Med., Ind.Sci.Rev., Ind.Vet., INIS Atomind., Neurosci.Cit.Ind., Pig News & Info., Poult.Abstr., Rev.Med.& Vet.Mycol., Sci.Cit.Ind., Small Anim.Abstr., Sport Fish.Abstr., Vet.Bull., Wild.Rev., Zoo.Rec. **Document type:** academic/scholarly publication.
  —BLDSC (2087.220000); CASDDS; CISTI; EMDOCS; Genuine Article; KNAW; Linda Hall; SWETS; UMI; UnCover. **CCC.**
  Description: Publishes original research on a variety of topics in the field of reproductive biology, as well as review articles on topics of importance or controversy.
  Refereed Serial

575.1 332.1   US   ISSN 0899-5702
BIOTECH BUSINESS. 1988. m. $150 (outside N. America $165). Worldwide Videotex, Box 3273, Boynton Beach, FL 33424-3273. TEL 407-738-2276. Ed. Mark Wright; Pub. Mark Wright. pat. **Document type:** newsletter.
  ●Also available online. Vendor(s): Data-Star, Information Access Co., Knight-Ridder Information, Inc., NewsNet (BT06).
  —**CCC.**
  Description: Focuses on the latest fast-breaking developments in the technology and business of biotechnology. Provides news on patents, international business deals, licensing agreements, and developments in human, animal, and plant genetic engineering.

591.15   AG   ISSN 0067-9720
QH442
BOLETIN GENETICO. (Text and summaries in English and Spanish) 1965. irreg., no.15, 1989. $15 or exchange. Instituto Nacional de Tecnologia Agropecuaria, Centro de Investigaciones en Ciencias Agronomicas, Departamento de Genetica, Casilla de Correo No. 25, 1712 Castelar, Argentina. **Indexed:** Biol.Abstr.

575.1 574.8   BL   ISSN 0100-8455
CODEN: RBGED3
BRAZILIAN JOURNAL OF GENETICS/REVISTA BRASILEIRA DE GENETICA. (Text in English; summaries in English and Portuguese) 1978. q. Cr.$60($90) (effective 1997). Sociedade Brasileira de Genetica, R. Cap. Adelmio Norberto da Silva 736, 14025-670 Ribeirao Preto SP, Brazil. TEL 55-16-6218540. FAX 55-16-6201251. E-mail: rbg@genbov.fmrp.usp.br. Ed. Francisco A. Moura Duarte. R&P contact: Francisco A. Moura Duarte. adv.; bk.rev.; abstr.; index. circ. 2,000. (back issues avail.) **Indexed:** Anim.Breed.Abstr., Biol.Abstr., Chem.Abstr., Curr.Adv.Ecol.Sci., Curr.Cont., Excerp.Med., Genet.Abstr., Maize Abstr., Plant Breed.Abstr., Plant Grow.Reg.Abstr., Ref.Zh., Sci.Cit.Ind., Seed Abstr., Sorghum & Millets Abstr., Soyabean Abstr., Triticale Abstr. **Document type:** academic/scholarly publication.
  —BLDSC (2277.410000); CASDDS; CISTI; EMDOCS; Genuine Article; KNAW; Linda Hall.
  Refereed Serial

575.1   JA   CODEN: IKZAAD
BREEDING SCIENCE. (Text and summaries in English and Japanese) 1951. q. 6500 Yen (effective 1995). Japanese Society of Breeding, c/o Faculty of Agriculture, University of Tokyo, Bunkyo-ku, Tokyo 113, Japan. TEL 03-3812-2111. FAX 03-3815-5851. Ed. Fumio Kikuchi; Pub. Genkichi Takeda. adv. contact: Yutaka Hirai. circ. 2,000. (back issues avail.) **Indexed:** ASCA, Biol.Abstr., Chem.Abstr., Curr.Cont., Field Crop Abstr., Hort.Abstr., Maize Abstr., Ornam.Hort., Plant Grow.Reg.Abstr., Potato Abstr., Rice Abstr., Seed Abstr., Sorghum & Millets Abstr., Soyabean Abstr., SSCI, Triticale Abstr., Trop.Oil Seeds Abstr. **Document type:** academic/scholarly publication.
  —CASDDS; EMDOCS; Genuine Article; SWETS; UnCover.
  Formerly: Japanese Journal of Breeding (ISSN 0536-3683)
  Refereed Serial

575.1   PO   ISSN 0870-7235
CODEN: BRGED7
BROTERIA GENETICA. (Text in English, French, German, Italian, Portuguese and Spanish) 1902. q. $19. (Sociedade Portuguesa de Genetica) Edicoes Broteria, Rua Maestro Antonio Taborda 14, 1293 Lisbon Codex, Portugal. TEL 351-1-3961660. Ed. Luis J. Archer. bk.rev.; bibl.; charts; illus.; index, cum.index: 1902-1917; 1918-1959. circ. 1,000. (also avail. in microfiche from IDC) **Indexed:** Biol.Abstr., Chem.Abstr., M.L.A., Pig News & Info., Sport Fish.Abstr., Wild.Rev., Zoo.Rec. **Document type:** academic/scholarly publication.
  —Linda Hall.
  Supersedes (in 1980): Broteria: Ciencias Naturais (ISSN 0007-2427)

C A S BIOTECH UPDATES. GENETIC ENGINEERING. see *BIOLOGY — Abstracting, Bibliographies, Statistics*

CANCER GENE THERAPY. see *MEDICAL SCIENCES — Oncology*

CANCER GENETICS & CYTOGENETICS. see *MEDICAL SCIENCES — Oncology*

CELL DIFFERENTIATION. see *BIOLOGY — Cytology And Histology*

575.1   US   ISSN 0898-5138
QH426
CHINESE JOURNAL OF GENETICS. Selective English translation of: Yichuan Xuebao (CC ISSN 0379-4172) 1988. q. $590 (effective 1998). (Zhongguo Kexueyuan, Yichuan Yanjiusuo, CC - Chinese Academy of Sciences, Institute of Genetics) Allerton Press, Inc., 150 Fifth Ave., New York, NY 10011. TEL 212-924-3950. FAX 212-463-9684. Ed. Sheng Zu-jia. (back issues avail.) **Document type:** academic/scholarly publication.
  —CISTI. **CCC.**
  Description: Covers genetic research in mainland China, including molecular genetics and genetic engineering.

575.1   GW   ISSN 0009-5915
QH301   CODEN: CHROAU
CHROMOSOMA. Online edition (GW ISSN 1432-0886) (Text in English) 1939. 8/yr. DM.1648.20 (foreign DM.1658.60) (effective 1998). Springer-Verlag, Heidelberger Platz 3, 14197 Berlin, Germany. TEL 49-30-82787-0. FAX 49-30-82787448. E-mail: subscriptions@springer.de; URL: http://link.springer.de. (Subscr. in N. America to: Springer-Verlag New York, Inc., 333 Meadowlands Pkwy., Secaucus, NJ 07094. TEL 212-460-1500. FAX 212-473-6272) Eds. W. Hennig, P.B. Moens. adv.; bibl.; charts; illus.; index. (also avail. in microform from UMI; back issues avail.; reprint service avail. from ISI) **Indexed:** Abstr.Anthropol., Anim.Breed.Abstr., ASCA, Bibl.Agri., Bio-Contr.News & Info., Biol.Abstr., Chem.Abstr., Curr.Adv.Cell & Devel.Biol., Curr.Adv.Ecol.Sci., Curr.Adv.Genetics & Molec.Biol., Curr.Cont., Dent.Ind., Excerp.Med., Helminthol.Abstr., Ind.Med., Ind.Sci.Rev., Ornam.Hort., Plant Breed.Abstr., Rev.Appl.Entomol., Sport Fish.Abstr., Wild.Rev., Zoo.Rec. **Document type:** academic/scholarly publication.
  ●Also available online.
  —BLDSC (3184.000000); CASDDS; CISTI; EMDOCS; Genuine Article; KNAW; Linda Hall; SWETS; UMI; UnCover. **CCC.**
  Description: Links classic cytology and cytogenetics with research in molecular biology.

BIOLOGY — GENETICS

575.1 UK ISSN 0967-3849
CODEN: CRRSEE
CHROMOSOME RESEARCH. 1993. 8/yr. £105($175) to individuals; institutions £328($555) (effective 1996). Rapid Science Publishers, The Old Malthouse, Paradise St., Oxford OX1 1LD, England. TEL 44-1865-790447. FAX 44-1865-244012. E-mail: marketing@rapidcom.co.uk. (Subscr. in US to: 115 Fifth Ave., 4th Fl., New York, NY 10003. TEL 212-780-6234. FAX 212-260-1363) Ed. Herbert Macgregor. adv. contact: Julie Gribben. **Indexed:** ASCA, Curr.Cont., Excerp.Med. (1994-), Ind.Med. (1994-), Ind.Sci.Rev. **Document type:** academic/scholarly publication.
● Also available on CD-ROM.
—BLDSC (3184.250000); ADONIS; CASDDS; CISTI; EMDOCS; Genuine Article; KNAW; UnCover. **CCC.**
   Description: Provides a forum covering the wide area of chromosomology, including its supramolecular, molecular and evolutionary aspects.
Refereed Serial

575.1 JA
CODEN: SNSHBT
CHROMOSOME SCIENCE/KROMOSOME. (Text in English, Japanese) 1946. q. 12000 Yen (effective 1998). Senshokutai - Society of Chromosome Research, Laboratory of Plant Chromosome and Gene Stock, Faculty of Science, Hiroshima University, 1-4-3 Kagamiyama, Higashi-Hiroshima City 739, Japan. TEL 81-824-24-7490. FAX 81-824-24-0738. E-mail: kkondo@ue.ipc.hiroshima-u.ac.jp. Ed. Ryuso Tanaka. R&P contact: Katsuhiko Kondo. adv. contact: Katsuhiko Kondo. **Document type:** academic/scholarly publication.
—CASDDS; Linda Hall; UnCover.
   Former titles: Sensyokutai - Kromosomo (ISSN 0385-4655); (until 1976): Senshokutai (ISSN 0371-1641)

575.1 574.87 UK ISSN 0260-5872
CLINICAL CYTOGENETICS. 1981. s-m. (diskette m.) £125 (diskette £120; both £180) (effective 1997). S U B I S, Mansion House, 19 Kingfield Rd., Sheffield S11 9AS, England. TEL 44-114-2554433. FAX 44-114-2554626. E-mail: subis@sheffac. demon.co.uk; URL: http://www.shef.ac.uk/uni/companies/shap. (also avail. in diskette format) **Document type:** abstracting/indexing.
—CCC.
   Description: Current awareness service for researchers. Covers chromosomal birth defects, banding techniques, DNA cytometry, DNA probes and gene mapping, leukemias and lymphomas, solid tumors, genetic amniocentesis.

613.94 DK ISSN 0009-9163
RB155 CODEN: CLGNAY
CLINICAL GENETICS; an international journal of genetics and molecular biology in medicine. (Text in English) 1970. m. DKK 3410 in Europe (US, Canada and Japan DKK 3480) (effective 1997). Munksgaard International Publishers Ltd., 35 Noerre Soegade, P.O. Box 2148, DK-1016 Copenhagen K, Denmark. TEL 45-33-127030. FAX 45-33-129387. E-mail: fsub@mail.munksgaard.dk. (In N. America: Commerce Place, 350 Main St., Malden, MA 02148-5018. TEL 617-388-8273. FAX 617-388-8274) Ed. Kaare Berg. adv.; bibl.; charts; illus. circ. 1,100. (reprint service avail. from ISI,SWZ) **Indexed:** Abstr.Anthropol., ASCA, Bibl.Dev.Med.& Child Neur., Biol.Abstr., Chem.Abstr., Curr.Adv.Ecol.Sci., Curr.Adv.Genetics & Molec.Biol., Curr.Cont., Curr.Tit.Dent., Dairy Sci.Abstr., Dent.Ind., Dok.Arbeitsmed., Excerp.Med., Ind.Med., Ind.Sci.Rev., INIS Atomind., Med.& Surg.Dermat., Neurosci.Cit.Ind., Nutr.Abstr., Risk Abstr., Sci.Cit.Ind, SSCI. **Document type:** academic/scholarly publication.
—BLDSC (3286.287000); CASDDS; CISTI; EMDOCS; Genuine Article; KNAW; SWETS; UnCover. **CCC.**
Refereed Serial

573.21 SZ ISSN 1422-2795
▼**COMMUNITY GENETICS.** (Text in English) Announced for publication in 1998. q. 76 SFr.($59) to individuals; institutions 443 SFr.($338) (effective 1998). S. Karger AG, Allschwilerstr. 10, P.O. Box, CH-4009 Basel, Switzerland. TEL 41-61-3061111. E-mail: karger@karger.ch; URL: http://www.karger.ch/journals/cmg/cmgdes.ht. Ed. L.P. ten Kate. **Document type:** academic/scholarly publication.
   Description: International forum for research in the expanding field of community genetics, an area of medical care responding to the explosion of developments in human genetics which impact both the individual and society.

575.1 NE ISSN 0929-712X
CONTEMPORARY ISSUES IN GENETICS AND EVOLUTION. (Text in English) 1993. irreg., vol.4, 1995. price varies. Kluwer Academic Publishers, Postbus 17, 3300 AA Dordrecht, Netherlands. TEL 31-78-6392392. FAX 31-78-6392254. TELEX 29245 KAPG NL. E-mail: services@wkap.nl; URL: http://www.wkap.nl. (Dist. by: Kluwer Academic Publishers Group, P.O. Box 322, 3300 AH Dordrecht, Netherlands. TEL 31-78-6392392. FAX 31-78-6546474; N. America dist. addr.: Box 358, Accord Sta., Hingham, MA 02018-0358. TEL 617-871-6600. FAX 617-871-6528) **Document type:** monographic series.
—BLDSC (3425.184215); KNAW.
Refereed Serial

575.1 US ISSN 1045-4403
QH450 CODEN: CRGEEJ
CRITICAL REVIEWS IN EUKARYOTIC GENE EXPRESSION. 1990. q. $89 to individuals; institutions $391 (effective 1997). Begell House Inc., 79 Madison Ave., Ste. 1205, New York, NY 10016-7892. TEL 212-213-8368. FAX 212-725-1999. E-mail: begellhouse@worldnet.att.net. Ed.Bd.; Pub. William Begell. R&P contact: Jung K. Ra. adv. contact: Jung K. Ra. **Indexed:** ASCA, Ind.Med. (1992-). **Document type:** academic/scholarly publication.
—BLDSC (3487.475300); CASDDS; CISTI; EMDOCS; Genuine Article; KNAW; Linda Hall; SWETS; UnCover. **CCC.**
   Description: Assimilates and presents timely concepts and experimental approaches that contribute to the advances in understanding gene regulation, organization and structure.

CURRENT DIRECTIONS IN AUTOIMMUNITY. see *MEDICAL SCIENCES — Allergology And Immunology*

575.1 GW ISSN 0172-8083
QH426 CODEN: CUGED5
CURRENT GENETICS; eukaryotes with emphasis on yeasts, fungi, protists, cell organelles. Online edition (GW ISSN 1432-0983) (Text in English) 1980. m. DM.2270.80 (foreign DM.2286.40) (effective 1998). Springer-Verlag, Heidelberger Platz 3, 14197 Berlin, Germany. TEL 49-30-82787-0. FAX 49-30-82787448. E-mail: subscriptions@springer.de; URL: http://link.springer.de. (Subscr. in N. America to: Springer-Verlag New York, Inc., 333 Meadowlands Pkwy., Secaucus, NJ 07094. TEL 212-460-1500. FAX 212-473-6272) Ed. Les Grivell. adv. (also avail. in microform from UMI; reprint service avail. from ISI) **Indexed:** ASCA, Biotech.Abstr., Chem.Abstr., Crop Physiol.Abstr., Curr.Adv.Ecol.Sci., Curr.Biotech.Abstr., Curr.Cont., Excerp.Med., Fababean Abstr., Ind.Sci.Rev., INIS Atomind., Maize Abstr., Plant Breed.Abstr., Rice Abstr., Sci.Cit.Ind., Sorghum & Millets Abstr., Soyabean Abstr., Triticale Abstr. **Document type:** academic/scholarly publication.
● Also available online.
—BLDSC (3496.960000); CASDDS; CISTI; EMDOCS; Genuine Article; KNAW; Linda Hall; SWETS; UMI; UnCover. **CCC.**
   Description: Covers the genetics of eukaryotes, with an emphasis on yeasts, other fungi, protists, and cell organelles.

CURRENT OPINION IN GENETICS & DEVELOPMENT. see *BIOLOGY — Abstracting, Bibliographies, Statistics*

573.21 US
CURRENT PROTOCOLS IN HUMAN GENETICS. 2 base vols. (plus q. updates). $385 (CD-ROM $486) (effective 1996). John Wiley & Sons, Inc., Journals, 605 Third Ave., New York, NY 10158. TEL 212-850-6645. FAX 212-850-6021. E-mail: subinfo@jwiley.com. (looseleaf format) **Document type:** academic/scholarly publication.
● Also available on CD-ROM.

575.1 610 SZ ISSN 0301-0171
QH431 CODEN: CGCGBR
CYTOGENETICS AND CELL GENETICS. (Text in English, French and German) 1962. 16/yr. (in 4 vols.) 1198 SFr.($936) to individuals; institutions 2384 SFr.($1872) (effective 1998). S. Karger AG, Allschwilerstr. 10, P.O. Box, CH-4009 Basel, Switzerland. TEL 41-61-3061111. FAX 41-61-3061234. E-mail: karger@karger.ch; URL: http://www.karger.ch. Ed. H.P. Klinger. adv.; charts; illus.; index. circ. 1,800. (also avail. in microform; reprint service avail. from KTO) **Indexed:** Abstr.Anthropol., Abstr.Hyg., Anim.Breed.Abstr., ASCA, Biol.Abstr., Chem.Abstr., Curr.Adv.Ecol.Sci., Curr.Cont., Excerp.Med., Ind.Med., Ind.Sci.Rev., Ind.Vet., Neurosci.Cit.Ind., Pig News & Info., Poult.Abstr., Sci.Cit.Ind., Trop.Dis.Bull., Vet.Bull. **Document type:** academic/scholarly publication.
—BLDSC (3506.770000); CASDDS; CISTI; EMDOCS; Genuine Article; KNAW; Linda Hall; SWETS. **CCC.**
   Formerly: Cytogenetics (ISSN 0011-4537)
Refereed Serial

575.1 616.97 UK ISSN 1043-4666
QR185.8.C95 CODEN: CYTIE9
CYTOKINE. 1989. m. £172($287) to individuals; institutions £370 (effective 1998). Academic Press Ltd. (Subsidiary of: Harcourt Brace & Company Ltd.), 24-28 Oval Rd., London NW1 7DX, England. TEL 44-171-267-4466. FAX 44-171-482-2293. TELEX 25775 ACPRES G. E-mail: apsubs@acad. com; URL: http://www.hbuk.co.uk/ap/cytokine; http://www.europe.idealibrary.com/. (Subscr. to: Harcourt Brace & Company Ltd., Foots Cray High St., Sidcup, Kent DA14 5HP, England. TEL 44-181-300-3322. FAX 44-181-309-0807) Eds. Gordon W. Duff, Scott K. Durum. R&P contact: Catherine John. adv. contact: Nik Screen. (reprint service avail. from SWZ) **Indexed:** ASCA, Biol.Abstr., Chem.Abstr., Curr.Cont., Excerp.Med. (1993-), Ind.Med., Ind.Sci.Rev., Sci.Cit.Ind. **Document type:** academic/scholarly publication.
● Also available online.
—BLDSC (3506.778000); ADONIS; CASDDS; CISTI; EMDOCS; Genuine Article; KNAW; SWETS; UnCover. **CCC.**
   Description: Publishes original work on all cytokines including interleukins, cytotoxins, hematopoietic factors, transforming growth factors, interferons, and other known or new cytokines.

575.21 US ISSN 0095-4527
QH426 CODEN: CYGEDX
CYTOLOGY AND GENETICS. English translation of Tsitologiya i Genetika (KR ISSN 0564-3783) 1974. bi-m. $1060 (effective 1997). (Ukrainian Academy of Sciences, KR) Allerton Press, Inc., 150 Fifth Ave., New York, NY 10011. TEL 212-924-3950. FAX 212-463-9684. Ed. A.A. Sozinov. bibl.; charts; illus.; index. **Indexed:** Biol.Abstr., Excerp.Med., Sport Fish.Abstr., Wild.Rev., Zoo.Rec. **Document type:** academic/scholarly publication.
—BLDSC (0411.088000); CISTI; SWETS; UnCover. **CCC.**
   Description: Covers genetic structure of populations, genotoxic effects in plants, animals and humans, breeding, genetic diagnostics, etc.

575.1 UK ISSN 0142-8640
D N A. (Deoxyribonucleic Acid) m. £85 (effective 1997). S U B I S, Mansion House, 19 Kingfield Rd., Sheffield S11 9AS, England. TEL 44-114-2554433. FAX 44-114-2554626. E-mail: subis@sheffac. demon.co.uk; URL: http://www.shef.ac.uk/uni/companies/shap. (looseleaf format; back issues avail.) **Indexed:** Curr.Adv.Biochem. **Document type:** abstracting/indexing.
—CCC.
   Description: Current awareness service for researchers in clinical and life sciences.

575.1 616 UK ISSN 0266-6308
D N A PROBES. 1985. s-m. (diskette m.) £115 (diskette £120; both £180) (effective 1997). S U B I S, Mansion House, 19 Kingfield Rd., Sheffield S11 9AS, England. TEL 44-114-2554433. FAX 44-114-2554626. E-mail: subis@sheffac. demon.co.uk; URL: http://www.shef.ac.uk/uni/companies/shap. (also avail. in diskette format) **Document type:** abstracting/indexing.
—CCC.
   Description: Covers probes for all organisms: RFLP's, DNA fingerprinting, polymerase chain reaction.

BIOLOGY — GENETICS

575.1 NE ISSN 1042-5179
QP624 CODEN: DNSEES
D N A SEQUENCE; the journal of DNA sequencing and mapping. 1990. 6/yr. (in 1 vol., 6 nos./vol.). $138 (effective 1998). Gordon and Breach - Harwood Academic, Amsteldisk 166, 1st Fl., 1079 LH Amsterdam, Netherlands. URL: http://www.gbhap.com/DNA__Sequence/. (Subscr. to: International Publishers Distributor, Box 32160, Newark, NJ 07102. TEL 800-545-8398. FAX 215-750-6343) Ed. Bart Barrell. (also avail. in microform) **Indexed:** ASCA, Curr.Cont., Food Sci.& Tech.Abstr.
●Also available online.
Also available on CD-ROM.
—BLDSC (3605.723500); CASDDS; CISTI; EMDOCS; KNAW; SWETS. **CCC.**
Description: Covers mapping data, full DNA sequences and their analyses, new sequencing procedures, computer methods to analyze sequences, and compilations of DNA and protein motifs.
Refereed Serial

575.1 US ISSN 0192-253X
QH453 CODEN: DGNTDW
DEVELOPMENTAL GENETICS. 1979. 8/yr. $955 (foreign $1095) (effective 1998). John Wiley & Sons, Inc., Journals, 605 Third Ave., New York, NY 10158. TEL 212-850-6645. FAX 212-850-6021. TELEX 12-7063. E-mail: SUBINFO@JWILEY.COM; URL: http://www.wiley.co.uk. (Subscr. outside the Americas to: John Wiley & Sons Ltd., Baffins Ln., Chichester, W. Sussex PO19 1UD, England. TEL 44-1243-779777. FAX 44-1243-776128) Ed. Gerald M. Kidder. adv.: B&W page £640, color page £1515; trim 279 x 210. bk.rev.; bibl.; illus. circ. 550. (also avail. in microform from UMI; back issues avail.) **Indexed:** Anim.Breed.Abstr., ASCA, Bibl.Agri., Biol.Abstr., Chem.Abstr., Curr.Adv.Biochem., Curr.Adv.Cell & Devel.Biol., Curr.Adv.Ecol.Sci., Curr.Adv.Genetics & Molec.Biol., Curr.Cont., Excerp.Med., Ind.Sci.Rev., Maize Abstr., Pig News & Info., Plant Grow.Reg.Abstr., Poult.Abstr., Sci.Cit.Ind. **Document type:** academic/scholarly publication.
—BLDSC (3579.054500); CASDDS; CISTI; EMDOCS; Genuine Article; KNAW; SWETS; UnCover. **CCC.**
Description: Covers molecular and developmental genetics and provides a forum for research on all organisms, including prokaryotes, plants, insects, worms, and mammals.
Refereed Serial

576.5 NE ISSN 0168-7972
CODEN: DPGBD6
DEVELOPMENTS IN PLANT GENETICS AND BREEDING. (Text in English) 1983. irreg., vol.3, 1991. price varies. Elsevier Science B.V., Books Division, P.O. Box 211, 1000 AE Amsterdam, Netherlands. TEL 31-20-4853911. FAX 31-20-4853705. TELEX 18582 ESPA NL. E-mail: nlinfo@elsevier.nl; usinfo-f@elsevier.com; forinfo-kyf04035@niftyserve.or.jp; URL: http://www.elsevier.nl/. (Subscr. in the Americas to: Elsevier Science, Regional Sales Office, Box 945, New York, NY 10159-0945. TEL 212-633-3730. FAX 212-633-3680; Subscr. in Australasia and the Far East to: Elsevier Science (Singapore) Pte Ltd, No.1 Temasek Ave., No.17-01 Millenia Tower, Singapore 039192, Singapore. TEL 65-434-3727. FAX 65-337-2230; Subscr. in Japan to: Elsevier Science Japan, 9-15 Higashi-Azabu 1-chome, Minato-ku, Tokyo 106, Japan. TEL 81-3-5561-5033. FAX 81-3-5561-5047) (back issues avail.) **Document type:** monographic series.
—BLDSC (3579.086130); CASDDS; CISTI.
Refereed Serial

575.1 581 US ISSN 0744-8163
QK981 CODEN: DIVEE8
DIVERSITY; a news journal for the international genetic resources community. 1984. q. $35 to government and non-profit agencies and individuals in N. America (elsewhere $50); others in N. America $55 (elsewhere $70). Genetic Resources Communications Systems, Inc., 4905 Del Ray Ave., Ste. 401, Bethesda, MD 20814-2527. TEL 301-907-9350. FAX 301-907-9328. E-mail: diversitymag@igc.apc.org; URL: http://www.amseed.com/div. Ed. Deborah G. Strauss. adv. contact: Carol Jaka. bk.rev.; illus. circ. 2,688. **Indexed:** ASCA, Environ.Per.Bibl., SSCI.
—BLDSC (3604.271070); CISTI; Genuine Article; SWETS. **CCC.**
Description: Serves as a forum for the presentation and discussion of issues pertinent to the plant genetic resources community. Includes news on biodiversity, genetic resources, international affairs and regional and governmental developments.

575.1 US ISSN 0070-7333
QL537.M6
DROSOPHILA INFORMATION SERVICE. 1934. irreg. (approx. a.). $15 (foreign $18). Zoology Department, University of Oklahoma, Norman, OK 73019. TEL 405-325-4821. FAX 405-325-7560. Ed. James Thompson. circ. 1,200. **Indexed:** Curr.Adv.Ecol.Sci. **Document type:** academic/scholarly publication.

575.1 574.8 UA ISSN 0046-161X
QH426 CODEN: EJGCA9
EGYPTIAN JOURNAL OF GENETICS AND CYTOLOGY. 1972. s-a. $54. Egyptian Society of Genetics and Cytology, University of Cairo, Faculty of Agriculture, Department of Genetics, Giza, Egypt. Ed. A.R. Selim. adv. circ. 500. (reprint service avail. from UMI) **Indexed:** Anim.Breed.Abstr., Biol.Abstr., Cott.& Trop.Fibr.Abstr., Curr.Adv.Ecol.Sci., Curr.Cont., Dairy Sci.Abstr., Excerp.Med. (until 19??), Fababean Abstr., Genet.Abstr., Maize Abstr., Seed Abstr., Soyabean Abstr., Triticale Abstr., Weed Abstr., Zoo.Rec. **Document type:** academic/scholarly publication.
—BLDSC (3664.380000); CISTI.

575.1 GW ISSN 0256-1514
ENDOCYTOBIOSIS AND CELL RESEARCH. (Text in English) 1984. 3/yr. DM.135. (International Society on Endocytobiology) Tuebingen University Press, Wilhelmstr. 5, 72074 Tuebingen, Germany. TEL 07071-292502. FAX 07071-293287. Ed.Bd. adv.; bk.rev.; index. (back issues avail.) **Indexed:** ASCA, Curr.Cont., Ind.Sci.Rev., Sci.Cit.Ind. **Document type:** academic/scholarly publication.
—BLDSC (3743.095000); CISTI; Genuine Article.

ENTREZ DOCUMENT RETRIEVAL SYSTEM. see MEDICAL SCIENCES — Abstracting, Bibliographies, Statistics

575 US ISSN 0893-6692
QH465.C5 CODEN: EMMUEG
ENVIRONMENTAL AND MOLECULAR MUTAGENESIS. (Supplement avail. (ISSN 0898-3003) 1979. 9/yr. $472 (foreign $629.5) (effective 1998). (Environmental Mutagen Society) John Wiley & Sons, Inc., Journals, 605 Third Ave., New York, NY 10158. TEL 212-850-6645. FAX 212-850-6021. TELEX 12-7063. URL: http://www.wiley.co.uk. (Subscr. outside the Americas to: John Wiley & Sons Ltd., Baffins Ln., Chichester, W. Sussex PO19 1UD, England. TEL 44-1243-779777. FAX 44-1243-776128) Ed. Errol Zeiger. adv.: B&W page £640, color page £1515; trim 254 x 174. bk.rev.; bibl.; illus. circ. 1,500. **Indexed:** ASCA, Biol.Abstr., Chem.Abstr., Curr.Adv.Cancer Res., Curr.Adv.Ecol.Sci., Curr.Adv.Genetics & Molec.Biol., Curr.Cont., Dok.Arbeitsmed., Excerp.Med., Food Sci.& Tech.Abstr., Ind.Med., Ind.Sci.Rev., Lab.Haz.Bull., NRN, Sci.Cit.Ind., Sel.Water Res.Abstr., Sport Fish.Abstr., Wild.Rev. **Document type:** academic/scholarly publication.
●Also available online.
—BLDSC (3791.383100); ADONIS; CASDDS; CISTI; EMDOCS; Genuine Article; Linda Hall; SWETS; UnCover. **CCC.**
Formerly: Environmental Mutagenesis (ISSN 0192-2521)
Description: Provides an international forum for research on basic mechanisms of mutation, the detection of mutagens, and the implications of environmental mutagens for human health.
Refereed Serial

575 US ISSN 0898-3003
ENVIRONMENTAL AND MOLECULAR MUTAGENESIS. SUPPLEMENT. 1987. irreg. (Environmental Mutagen Society) John Wiley & Sons, Inc., Journals, 605 Third Ave., New York, NY 10158-0012. TEL 212-850-6645. (Subscr. outside the Americas to: John Wiley & Sons Ltd., Baffins Ln., Chichester, W. Sussex PO19 1UD, England. TEL 44-1243-779777. FAX 44-1243-776128) (back issues avail.) **Indexed:** Biol.Abstr., Excerp.Med., Ind.Med. **Document type:** academic/scholarly publication.
—BLDSC (3791.383110); CISTI.

613.94 US
EUGENICS SPECIAL INTEREST GROUP BULLETIN. 1970. irreg. $6. Eugenics Special Interest Group, Box 138, East Schodack, NY 12163. TEL 518-732-2390. Ed. Willard Hoyt. **Document type:** bulletin.

575.1 FR ISSN 1148-5493
CODEN: ECYNEJ
EUROPEAN CYTOKINE NETWORK. (Text in English) 1990. 4/yr. 1150 F. to individuals (outside EU 1220 F.); institutions 1750 F. (outside EU 1820 F.) (effective 1997). John Libbey Eurotext, 127 av. de la Republique, 92120 Montrouge, France. TEL 1-46730660. FAX 1-40840999. E-mail: marketing@jle.com. (Subscr. to: A T E I, 3 av. Pierre Kerautret, 93230 Romainville, France. TEL 33-1-48408686. FAX 33-1-48400731) Eds. Jacques Bertoglio, Didier Fradelizi. **Indexed:** ASCA, Curr.Cont., Excerp.Med. (1993-), Ind.Sci.Rev. **Document type:** academic/scholarly publication.
—BLDSC (3829.688820); CASDDS; EMDOCS; Genuine Article; KNAW.
Description: Serves as a link between immunological, biological, molecular, hematological and oncological researchers and clinicians.

EUROPEAN JOURNAL OF GENETICS IN SOCIETY; an ethical approach to genetics. see PHILOSOPHY

575.1 UK ISSN 1018-4813
CODEN: EJHGEU
EUROPEAN JOURNAL OF HUMAN GENETICS. (Text in English) 1993. bi-m. 688 SFr.($573) to institutions (effective 1997). (European Society of Human Genetics) Stockton Press (Subsidiary of: Macmillan Press Ltd.), Houndmills, Basingstoke, Hants RG21 6XS, England. TEL 44-1256-351898. FAX 44-1256-328339. (US subscr. to: Stockton Press, 345 Park Ave. S., 10th Fl., New York, NY 10010-1707. TEL 800-221-2123. FAX 212-689-9711) Ed. G.-J. Buan Ommen. (also avail. in microform from UMI) **Indexed:** ASCA, Curr.Cont., Excerp.Med. (1994-), Ind.Med. (1994-). **Document type:** academic/scholarly publication.
—BLDSC (3829.730020); CASDDS; CISTI; EMDOCS; Genuine Article; KNAW; SWETS. **CCC.**
Description: Contains information on the development of research, education and medical application in the field of human genetics.
Refereed Serial

575.1 UK ISSN 0960-7420
QR184 CODEN: EJOIE3
EUROPEAN JOURNAL OF IMMUNOGENETICS. 1974. bi-m. £292($533) (foreign £321) (effective 1998). Blackwell Science Ltd., Osney Mead, Oxford OX2 0EL, England. TEL 44-1865-206206. FAX 44-1865-721205. E-mail: journals.cs@blacksci.co.uk; URL: http://www.black.co.uk. Ed. E.D. Alben; Pub. Allen Stevens. R&P contact: Sarah Pollard. adv. contact: Martine Cariou-Keen. bk.rev.; abstr.; bibl.; illus.; index. circ. 450. (also avail. in microform from UMI; back issues avail.; reprint service avail. from ISI) **Indexed:** Abstr.Hyg., Anim.Breed.Abstr., Biol.Abstr., Chem.Abstr., Curr.Adv.Ecol.Sci., Curr.Biotech.Abstr., Curr.Cont., Dairy Sci.Abstr., Excerp.Med., Helminthol.Abstr., Ind.Med., Ind.Sci.Rev., Ind.Vet., Sci.Cit.Ind., Trop.Dis.Bull., Vet.Bull. **Document type:** academic/scholarly publication.
—BLDSC (3829.730050); ADONIS; CASDDS; CISTI; EMDOCS; Genuine Article; KNAW; SWETS; UMI; UnCover. **CCC.**
Formerly: Journal of Immunogenetics (ISSN 0305-1811)
Refereed Serial

BIOLOGY — GENETICS

575 US ISSN 0014-3820
QH301 CODEN: EVOLAO
EVOLUTION; international journal of organic evolution. 1947. bi-m. $170 (foreign $180) (effective 1997). (Society for the Study of Evolution) Allen Press, Inc., 1041 New Hampshire Ave., Box 1897, Lawrence, KS 66044-8897. TEL 800-627-0629. FAX 913-843-1274. Ed. Geerat Vermeij. adv.; bk.rev.; bibl.; charts; illus.; stat.; index. circ. 4,500. (also avail. in microform from UMI) **Indexed:** Agroforest.Abstr., Anim.Breed.Abstr., Apic.Abstr., ASCA, Bibl.Agri., Bio-Contr.News & Info., Biol.Abstr., Biol.& Agr.Ind., Chem.Abstr., Curr.Adv.Ecol.Sci., Curr.Cont., Deep Sea Res.& Oceanogr.Abstr., Ecol.Abstr., Excerp.Med., Field Crop Abstr., Forest.Abstr., Forest Prod.Abstr., Gen.Sci.Ind., Geo.Abstr., Geol.Abstr., GeoRef., Helminthol.Abstr., Ind.Sci.Rev., Ind.Sci.Rev., Ind.Vet., Int.Aerosp.Abstr., Key Word Ind.Wildl.Res., Maize Abstr., Ornam.Hort., Plant Breed.Abstr., Protozool.Abstr., Sci.Cit.Ind., Seed Abstr., Sh.& Vib.Dig., So.Pac.Per.Ind., Sport Fish.Abstr., SSCI, Vet.Bull., Weed Abstr., Wild.Rev., Zoo.Rec. **Document type:** academic/scholarly publication.
●Also available online. Vendor(s): Information Access Co.
—BLDSC (3834.000000); CASDDS; CISTI; EMDOCS; KR SourceOne; Linda Hall; SWETS; UMI.
Refereed Serial

575.005 US ISSN 0071-3260
QH366.A1 CODEN: EVBIAI
EVOLUTIONARY BIOLOGY. 1967. irreg. vol.29, 1996. price varies. Plenum Publishing Corp., 233 Spring St., New York, NY 10013-1578. TEL 212-620-8000. FAX 212-463-0742. TELEX 23-421139. E-mail: books@plenum.com. Eds. Max Hecht, Bruce Wallace. **Indexed:** ASCA, Biol.Abstr., Curr.Adv.Ecol.Sci., Deep Sea Res.& Oceanogr.Abstr., GeoRef., Ind.Sci.Rev., Sci.Cit.Ind, Sport Fish.Abstr., SSCI, Wild.Rev., Zoo.Rec. **Document type:** monographic series.
—BLDSC (3834.400000); CASDDS; CISTI; Genuine Article; KNAW; Linda Hall; UnCover. **CCC**.
Refereed Serial

EVOLUTIONARY COMPUTATION. see *BIOLOGY — Computer Applications*

575.1 SZ ISSN 0254-9670
CODEN: ECIME4
EXPERIMENTAL AND CLINICAL IMMUNOGENETICS. 1984. q. 193 SFr.($147.50) to individuals; institutions 386 SFr.($295) (effective 1998). S. Karger AG, Allschwilerstr. 10, P.O. Box, CH-4009 Basel, Switzerland. TEL 41-61-3061111. FAX 41-61-3061234. E-mail: karger@karger.ch; URL: http://www.karger.ch. Ed. E. K. Bauer. adv.; illus.; index. circ. 800. (also avail. in microform from UMI) **Indexed:** Anim.Breed.Abstr., ASCA, Curr.Cont., Excerp.Med., Ind.Sci.Rev., Sci.Cit.Ind. **Document type:** academic/scholarly publication.
—BLDSC (3838.640000); CASDDS; CISTI; EMDOCS; Genuine Article; KNAW; SWETS; UnCover. **CCC**.
Refereed Serial

575.1 US ISSN 0533-1242
FOCUS (GAITHERSBURG). 1969. q. free. Life Technologies, Inc., Box 6482, Rockville, MD 20849-6482. TEL 301-840-8000. URL: http://www.lifetech.com. Ed. Doreen Cupo. R&P contact: Doreen Cupo. index, cum.index: vols.1-18. circ. 45,000. (back issues avail.) **Document type:** newsletter.
  Description: Describes novel techniques, improvements of common techniques, simplified protocols, and trouble shooting of life science techniques.
Refereed Serial

GAMMA FIELD SYMPOSIA. see *AGRICULTURE*

GENBANK. see *BIOLOGY — Computer Applications*

575.1 NE ISSN 0378-1119
QH442 CODEN: GENED6
GENE; an international journal focusing on gene cloning and gene structure and function. Online edition: Gene - COMBIS. 1977. 3/m. fl.11193($6433) (effective 1998). Elsevier Science B.V., P.O. Box 211, 1000 AE Amsterdam, Netherlands. TEL 31-20-4853911. FAX 31-20-4853598. TELEX 18582 ESPA NL. E-mail: nlinfo-f@elsevier.nl; usinfo-f@elsevier.com; forinfo-kyf04035@niftyserve.or.jp; URL: http://www.elsevier.nl/. (Subscr. in the Americas to: Elsevier Science, Regional Sales Office, Box 945, New York, NY 10159-0945. TEL 212-633-3730. FAX 212-633-3680; Subscr. in Australasia and the Far East to: Elsevier Science (Singapore) Pte Ltd, No.1 Temasek Ave., Elsevier Science (Singapore) Singapore 039192, Singapore. TEL 65-434-3727. FAX 65-337-2230; Subscr. in Japan to: Elsevier Science Japan, 9-15 Higashi-Azabu 1-chome, Minato-ku, Tokyo 106, Japan. TEL 81-3-5561-5033. FAX 81-3-5561-5047) Ed. W. Szybalski. adv. (also avail. in microform from UMI; back issues avail.; reprint service avail. from SWZ) **Indexed:** Abstr.Anthropol., Anim.Breed.Abstr., ASCA, Bibl.Agri., Bio-Contr.News & Info., Biol.Abstr., Biol.& Agr.Ind., Biotech.Abstr., Chem.Abstr., Curr.Adv.Biochem., Curr.Adv.Cancer Res., Curr.Adv.Cell & Devel.Biol., Curr.Adv.Ecol.Sci., Curr.Adv.Genetics & Molec.Biol., Curr.Biotech.Abstr., Curr.Cont., Excerp.Med., Food Sci.& Tech.Abstr., Helminthol.Abstr., Ind.Med., Ind.Sci.Rev., Ind.Vet., Maize Abstr., Neurosci.Cit.Ind., Pig News & Info., Potato Abstr., Poult.Abstr., Protozool.Abstr., Rev.Med.& Vet.Mycol., Rice Abstr., Risk Abstr., Sci.Cit.Ind., Small Anim.Abstr., Soils & Fert., Sorghum & Millets Abstr., Sport Fish.Abstr., Telegen, Triticale Abstr., Vet.Bull., Wild.Rev. **Document type:** academic/scholarly publication.
●Also available online.
—BLDSC (4096.402000); ADONIS; CASDDS; CISTI; EMDOCS; Genuine Article; KR SourceOne; Linda Hall; SWETS; UnCover. **CCC**.
  Description: Publishes original scientific papers on the analysis of gene structure, function and regulation, recombinant DNA techniques, mapping, sequencing and study of plant, animal, human and microbial genomes, as well as basic and practical applications of genetic engineering and recombinant nucleic acid technology.
Refereed Serial

575.1 NE ISSN 0275-2778
CODEN: GAAND8
GENE AMPLIFICATION AND ANALYSIS SERIES. 1981. irreg., vol.5, 1987. price varies. Elsevier Science B.V., Books Division, P.O. Box 211, 1000 AE Amsterdam, Netherlands. TEL 31-20-4853911. FAX 31-20-4853705. TELEX 18582 ESPA NL. E-mail: nlinfo-f@elsevier.nl; usinfo-f@elsevier.com; forinfo-kyf04035@niftyserve.or.jp; URL: http://www.elsevier.nl/. (Subscr. in the Americas to: Elsevier Science, Regional Sales Office, Box 945, New York, NY 10159-0945. TEL 212-633-3730. FAX 212-633-3680; Subscr. in Australasia and the Far East to: Elsevier Science (Singapore) Pte Ltd, No.1 Temasek Ave., No.17-01 Millenia Tower, Singapore 039192, Singapore. TEL 65-434-3727. FAX 65-337-2230; Subscr. in Japan to: Elsevier Science Japan, 9-15 Higashi-Azabu 1-chome, Minato-ku, Tokyo 106, Japan. TEL 81-3-5561-5033. FAX 81-3-5561-5047) **Indexed:** Chem.Abstr. **Document type:** monographic series.
—CASDDS; CISTI.
Refereed Serial

575.1 US
THE GENE EXCHANGE. 1990. q. free. Union of Concerned Scientists (Washington), 1616 P St., N.W., Ste. 310, Washington, DC 20036. TEL 202-332-0900. FAX 202-332-0905. Eds. Margaret Mellon, Jane Rissler. bk.rev.; illus. circ. 3,500. **Indexed:** Per.Islam. (1995-). **Document type:** newsletter.
●Also available online.
  Description: Covers biotechnology and sustainable agriculture. Includes news and legislation notes on the fields.

GENE EXPRESSION. see *BIOLOGY — Abstracting, Bibliographies, Statistics*

575.1 US ISSN 1052-2166
QH450 CODEN: GEEXEJ
GENE EXPRESSION. 1991. bi-m. $435 (foreign $460) (effective 1998). Cognizant Communication Corporation, 3 Hartsdale Rd., Elmsford, NY 10523-3701. TEL 914-592-7720. FAX 914-592-8981. Ed. Samson Jacob; Pub. Robert N. Miranda. R&P contact: Robert N. Miranda. adv. contact: Lori Miranda. **Indexed:** Ind.Med. **Document type:** academic/scholarly publication.
—BLDSC (4096.402395); CASDDS; CISTI; Genuine Article; KNAW. **CCC**.
  Description: Publishes papers on all aspects of gene including its structure, function and regulation in prokaryotes, eukaryotes and viruses. Topics on DNA replication, DNA repair, gene transcription, transcriptional control, RNA processing, posttranscriptional control, oncogenes, molecular mechanisms of action of hormones, molecular mechanisms of cellular differentiation, growth and development, protein syntheses, and posttranslational control.

573.21 US
▼**THE GENE LETTER**. 1996. bi-m. E-mail: webmaster@shriver.org; URL: http://www.geneletter.org. **Document type:** newsletter.
●Available online only.
  Description: Covers the scientific, ethical, legal and social aspects of genetics.

GENE THERAPY (SHEFFIELD). see *MEDICAL SCIENCES — Abstracting, Bibliographies, Statistics*

575.1 US ISSN 0890-9369
QH426 CODEN: GEDEEP
GENES & DEVELOPMENT. 1987. s-m. $125 to individuals (foreign $220); institutions $640 (foreign $735); students $95 (foreign $190) (effective 1998). Cold Spring Harbor Laboratory Press, Publications Department, Box 100, Cold Spring Harbor, NY 11724. TEL 800-843-4388. FAX 516-349-1946. E-mail: cshpress@cshl.org; URL: http://www.cshl.org. (And: Genetical Society of Britain, MRC Human Genetics Unit, Western General Hospital, Crewe Rd., Edinburgh EH4 2XU, Scotland) Eds. T. Grodzicker, N. Hastie. adv. contact: Marcie Ebenstein. (reprint service avail.) **Indexed:** Anim.Breed.Abstr., ASCA, Biol.& Agr.Ind., Curr.Adv.Cell & Devel.Biol., Curr.Adv.Genetics & Molec.Biol., Curr.Cont., Ind.Sci.Rev., Ornam.Hort., Poult.Abstr., Sci.Cit.Ind., SSCI, Telegen. **Document type:** academic/scholarly publication.
—BLDSC (4111.759700); CASDDS; CISTI; EMDOCS; Genuine Article; KNAW; KR SourceOne; Linda Hall; SWETS; UMI; UnCover. **CCC**.
  Description: Publishes research papers of general interest and biological significance in molecular biology, molecular genetics, and related areas.
Refereed Serial

575 UK ISSN 1360-7413
▼**GENES AND FUNCTION**. Announced for publication in 1997. bi-m. £195($357) (foreign £215) (effective 1998). Blackwell Science Ltd., Osney Mead, Oxford OX2 0EL, England. TEL 44-1865-206206. FAX 44-1865-721205. E-mail: journals.cs@blacksci.co.uk; URL: http://www.black.co.uk. Ed. F. Grosveld; Pub. Allen Stevens. R&P contact: Sarah Pollard. adv. contact: Martine Cariou-Keen. **Document type:** academic/scholarly publication.
—BLDSC (4111.759800). **CCC**.

BIOLOGY — GENETICS

575.1   **JA**   ISSN 1341-7568
QH426   CODEN: GGSYF5
GENES & GENETIC SYSTEMS. (Text in English) 1921. bi-m. $130. Genetics Society of Japan - Nihon Iden Gakkai, c/o National Institute of Genetics, 1111 Yata, Mishima-shi, Shizuoka-ken 411, Japan. TEL 81-849-36-2111. FAX 81-849-36-2024. E-mail: nakata@fupharm.fukuyama-u.ac.jp. (Dist. by: Business Center for Academic Societies Japan, 5-16-9 Honkomagome, Bunkyo-ku, Tokyo 113, Japan. TEL 03-5814-5811) Ed. Atsuo Nakata. adv.; bk.rev. circ. 2,000. (back issues avail.) **Indexed:** Agrindex, Anim.Breed.Abstr., ASCA, Biol.Abstr., Chem.Abstr., Curr.Cont., Excerp.Med., Fababean Abstr., Field Crop Abstr., Ind.Med., Ind.Sci.Rev., INIS Atomind., Jap.Per.Ind., JTA, Plant Breed.Abstr., Rice Abstr., Sci.Cit.Ind., Seed Abstr., Soyabean Abstr., Sport Fish.Abstr., Triticale Abstr., Wild.Rev., Zoo.Rec. **Document type:** academic/scholarly publication.
—BLDSC (4111.762100); CASDDS; CISTI; EMDOCS; Genuine Article; KNAW; Linda Hall; SWETS; UnCover.
Formerly (until vol.70, no.6, 1996): Japanese Journal of Genetics - Idengaku Zasshi (ISSN 0021-504X)
Description: Covers a wide range in the field of genetics: general genetics, molecular genetics, cytogenetics, population genetics and evolution, and genome research.
Refereed Serial

575.1 616.99   **US**   ISSN 1045-2257
RC268.4   CODEN: GCCAES
GENES, CHROMOSOMES & CANCER. 1989. m. $795 (foreign $1005) (effective 1998). John Wiley & Sons, Inc., Journals, 605 Third Ave., New York, NY 10158. TEL 212-850-6645. FAX 212-850-6021. TELEX 12-7063. E-mail: SUBINFO@JWILEY.COM; URL: http://www.wiley.co.uk. (Subscr. outside the Americas to: John Wiley & Sons Ltd., Baffins Ln., Chichester, W. Sussex PO19 1UD, England. TEL 44-1243-779777. FAX 44-1243-776128) Eds. Felix Mitelman, Janet D. Rowley. adv.: B&W page £640, color page £1515; trim 279 x 210. circ. 800. (also avail. in microform from UMI; back issues avail.) **Indexed:** ASCA, Curr.Cont., Ind.Sci.Rev., Sci.Cit.Ind. **Document type:** academic/scholarly publication.
—BLDSC (4111.763000); CASDDS; CISTI; EMDOCS; Genuine Article; KNAW; SWETS; UnCover. **CCC.**
Description: Covers all aspects of genomic abnormalities related to neoplasia. Particular emphasis is placed on work combining molecular and cytogenetic analysis of the acquired genetic alterations of cancer cells.
Refereed Serial

GENETIC ANALYSIS, BIOMOLECULAR ENGINEERING. see BIOLOGY — Biotechnology

573.21   **SZ**   ISSN 1015-8146
RB155.7   CODEN: GECOEG
GENETIC COUNSELING. (Supplement avail.) (Summaries in English, French and German) 1952. 4/yr. 205 SFr. to individuals; institutions 270 SFr. (effective 1997). Editions Medecine et Hygiene, Case Postale 456, CH-1211 Geneva 4, Switzerland. TEL 41-22-7029311. FAX 41-22-7029355. E-mail: abonnements@medecinehygiene.ch. Ed.Bd. adv.; bk.rev.; abstr.; charts; illus.; stat.; index, cum.index. circ. 800. (reprint service avail. from IRC) **Indexed:** Anthropol.Lit., ASCA, Bibl.Dev.Med.& Child Neur., Biol.Abstr., Chem.Abstr., Dent.Ind., Excerp.Med., Ind.Med., Ind.Sci.Rev., Int.Nurs.Ind., Sci.Cit.Ind., SSCI. **Document type:** academic/scholarly publication.
—BLDSC (4111.845000); CISTI; EMDOCS; Genuine Article; KNAW; Linda Hall; SWETS; UMI; UnCover. **CCC.**
Formerly (until 1990): Journal de Genetique Humaine (ISSN 0021-7743)

575.1 576   **US**   ISSN 0196-3716
QH442   CODEN: GENGDC
GENETIC ENGINEERING; principles and methods. 1979. irreg., vol.19, 1997. price varies. Plenum Publishing Corp., 233 Spring St., New York, NY 10013-1578. TEL 212-620-8000. FAX 212-463-0742. TELEX 23-421139. E-mail: books@plenum.com. Eds. A. Hollaender, J.K. Setlow. **Indexed:** Biotech.Abstr., Chem.Abstr., Curr.Biotech.Abstr. **Document type:** monographic series.
—BLDSC (4111.847000); CASDDS; CISTI; KNAW; UnCover. **CCC.**
Refereed Serial

575.1 660   **JA**
GENETIC ENGINEERING. (Text in English) 1985. irreg. Associazione Biologica Italo-Giapponese - Nichii Seibutsugaku Kyokai, Nagoya Daigaku Rigakubu Rinkai Jikkenjo, Furocho, Chikusa-ku, Nagoya-shi, Aichi-ken 464, Japan.

575.1 660   **UN**   ISSN 1012-537X
GENETIC ENGINEERING AND BIOTECHNOLOGY: MONITOR. 1982. q. $40 (free in developing countries). United Nations Industrial Development Organization, Industrial Information Section, P.O. Box 300, A-1400 Vienna, Austria. TEL 43-1-21131-3736. E-mail: drhind@unido.org; URL: http://www.unido.org. Ed. V. Campbell. circ. 1,800.

575.1 660   **NE**   ISSN 0921-2604
TP248.2
GENETIC ENGINEERING AND BIOTECHNOLOGY YEARBOOK. 1986. irreg., latest 1989. price varies. Elsevier Science B.V., Books Division, P.O. Box 211, 1000 AE Amsterdam, Netherlands. TEL 31-20-4853911. FAX 31-20-4853705. TELEX 18582 ESPA NL. E-mail: nlinfo-f@elsevier.nl; usinfo-f@elsevier.com; forinfo-kyf04035@niftyserve.or.jp; URL: http://www.elsevier.nl/. (Subscr. in the Americas to: Elsevier Science, Regional Sales Office, Box 945, New York, NY 10159-0945. TEL 212-633-3730. FAX 212-633-3680; Subscr. in Australasia and the Far East to: Elsevier Science (Singapore) Pte Ltd, No.1 Temasek Ave., No.17-01 Millenia Tower, Singapore 039192, Singapore. TEL 65-434-3727. FAX 65-337-2230; Subscr. in Japan to: Elsevier Science Japan, 9-15 Higashi-Azabu 1-chome, Minato-ku, Tokyo 106, Japan. TEL 81-3-5561-5033. FAX 81-3-5561-5047) **Document type:** monographic series.
—CISTI.
Refereed Serial

575.1 660   **US**   ISSN 0270-6377
TP248.6   CODEN: GENNDX
GENETIC ENGINEERING NEWS; the information source of the biotechnology industry. 1981. bi-w. $276 to institutions (foreign $317) (effective through 1998). Mary Ann Liebert, Inc. Publishers, 2 Madison Ave., Larchmont, NY 10538. TEL 914-834-3100. FAX 914-834-3688. E-mail: liebert@pipeline.com. adv.; bk.rev.; pat.; stat.; tr.lit. circ. 10,000. **Indexed:** ASCA, Bibl.Agri., Chem.Abstr., SSCI, Telegen. **Document type:** trade publication.
—CASDDS; CISTI; Genuine Article; SWETS.
Description: Covers the biotechnology-bioprocess industry. Examines significant issues, regulatory and scale-up guidelines, R&D, financial news (including public offerings, mergers, and venture capital), corporate profiles, reports, and news.

575.1   **US**   ISSN 0741-0395
GENETIC EPIDEMIOLOGY. bi-m. $1095 (foreign $1200) (effective 1998). John Wiley & Sons, Inc., Journals, 605 Third Ave., New York, NY 10158. TEL 212-850-6645. FAX 212-850-6021. TELEX 12-7063. E-mail: SUBINFO@JWILEY.COM; URL: http://www.wiley.co.uk. (Subscr. outside the Americas to: John Wiley & Sons Ltd., Baffins Ln., Chichester, W. Sussex PO19 1UD, England. TEL 44-1243-779777. FAX 44-1243-776128) Eds. J.M. Mulvihill, A. Chakravarti. adv.: B&W page £640, color page £1515; trim 254 x 174. bk.rev. circ. 850. (also avail. in microform from UMI; back issues avail.) **Indexed:** Anim.Breed.Abstr., ASCA, Biol.Abstr., Chem.Abstr., Curr.Adv.Ecol.Sci., Curr.Adv.Genetics & Molec.Biol., Curr.Cont., Excerp.Med., Ind.Sci.Rev., Sci.Cit.Ind., SSCI, THA. **Document type:** academic/scholarly publication.
●Also available online.
—BLDSC (4111.848000); CISTI; EMDOCS; Genuine Article; KNAW; SWETS; UMI; UnCover. **CCC.**
Description: Provides a forum for research concerned with the etiology, distribution, and control of disease in groups of relatives and with the inherited predisposition to, or causes of, diseases in populations.
Refereed Serial

GENETIC EPISTEMOLOGIST. see PSYCHOLOGY

575.1 614   **US**
GENETIC RESOURCE. 1983. 2/yr. $15. New England Regional Genetics Group, Box 670, Mount Desert, ME 04660-0670. TEL 207-839-5324. FAX 207-839-8637. Ed. Robin J.R. Blatt. R&P contact: Joseph Robinson. TEL 207-288-2704. bk.rev. circ. 7,000. **Document type:** newsletter.
Description: Covers clinical genetics and related public health policy issues for lay and professional readers.

GENETIC RESOURCES AND CROP EVOLUTION; an international journal. see BIOLOGY — Botany

575.1   **US**   ISSN 0272-9032
   CODEN: GTNEEA
GENETIC TECHNOLOGY NEWS. (Includes 3 supplements: Patent Update; Strategic Partners Report; Market Forecast) 1981. m. $650 (foreign $710). Technical Insights (Subsidiary of: John Wiley & Sons, Inc.), 32 N. Dean St., Englewood, NJ 07631-2807. TEL 201-568-4744. FAX 201-568-8247. E-mail: gtninfo@insights.com; URL: http://www.insights.com. Ed. Albert S. Hester; Pub. Peter Katz. abstr.; bibl.; charts; pat.; stat.; tr.lit. (back issues avail.) **Indexed:** Curr.Biotech.Abstr. **Document type:** newsletter.
—BLDSC (4111.923000); CASDDS; CISTI. **CCC.**
Description: Explores genetic engineering and its uses in the chemical, pharmaceutical, food processing and energy industries, as well as in agriculture, animal breeding and medicine.

575.1   **US**   ISSN 1090-6576
▼**GENETIC TESTING.** 1997. q. $101 to individuals (foreign $146); institutions $201 (foreign $236) (effective through 1998). Mary Ann Liebert, Inc. Publishers, 2 Madison Ave., Larchmont, NY 10538. TEL 914-834-3100. FAX 914-834-3688. E-mail: liebert@pipeline.com. Ed. Dr. Fred Gilbert. **Document type:** academic/scholarly publication.
Description: Focuses on all aspects of genetic testing, including prenatal diagnosis, risk assessment, methodologies, ethical and legal uses.

575.1   **NE**   ISSN 0016-6707
QH301   CODEN: GENEA3
GENETICA; an international journal of genetics. (Text in English) 1919. 9/yr. fl.2298 to institutions; $1179 to institutions in U.S. (effective 1998). Kluwer Academic Publishers, Postbus 17, 3300 AA Dordrecht, Netherlands. TEL 31-78-6392392. FAX 31-78-6392254. TELEX 29245 KAPG NL. E-mail: services@wkap.nl; URL: http://www.wkap.nl. (Dist. by: Kluwer Academic Publishers Group, P.O. Box 322, 3300 AH Dordrecht, Netherlands. TEL 31-78-6392392. FAX 31-78-6546474; N. America dist. addr.: Box 358, Accord Sta., Hingham, MA 02018-0358. TEL 617-871-6600. FAX 617-871-6528) Ed. J. MacDonald. adv.; illus. (also avail. in microform from UMI; back issues avail.; reprint service avail. from SWZ) **Indexed:** Anim.Breed.Abstr., ASCA, Bio-Contr.News & Info., Biol.Abstr., Chem.Abstr., Curr.Adv.Ecol.Sci., Curr.Cont., Excerp.Med., Field Crop Abstr., Helminthol.Abstr., Herb.Abstr., Ind.Med., Ind.Sci.Rev., Plant Breed.Abstr., Rev.Appl.Entomol., Sci.Cit.Ind., Small Anim.Abstr., Sport Fish.Abstr., SSCI, Weed Abstr., Wild.Rev., Zoo.Rec. **Document type:** academic/scholarly publication.
—BLDSC (4112.000000); CASDDS; CISTI; EMDOCS; Genuine Article; Linda Hall; SWETS; UMI; UnCover. **CCC.**
Refereed Serial

BIOLOGY — GENETICS

575.1   UK   ISSN 0016-6723
QH431.A1   CODEN: GENRA8
GENETICAL RESEARCH. 1960. bi-m. £206($358) (effective 1998). Cambridge University Press, Edinburgh Bldg., Shaftesbury Rd., Cambridge CB2 2RU, England. TEL 44-1223-312393. FAX 44-1223-315052. TELEX 851817256. E-mail: information@cup.cam.ac.uk; URL: http://www.cup.cam.ac.uk. (N. American addr.: Cambridge University Press, Journals Dept., 40 W. 20th St., New York, NY 10011. TEL 212-924-3900. FAX 212-691-3239) Ed.Bd. R&P contact: Linda Nicol. adv. contact: Rebecca Symons. bk.rev.; charts; illus.; index. (also avail. in microform from UMI; back issues avail.; reprint service avail. from SWZ,UMI) **Indexed:** Abstr.Anthropol., Abstr.Hyg., Anim.Breed.Abstr., ASCA, Biol.Abstr., Biol.& Agr.Ind., Biostat., Biotech.Abstr., Chem.Abstr., Curr.Adv.Biochem., Curr.Adv.Ecol.Sci., Curr.Adv.Genetics & Molec.Biol., Curr.Biotech.Abstr., Curr.Cont., Dent.Ind., Excerp.Med., Helminthol.Abstr., Ind.Med., Ind.Sci.Rev., Maize Abstr., Math.R., Plant Breed.Abstr., Rev.Appl.Entomol., Sci.Cit.Ind., Soils & Fert., Sport Fish.Abstr., Telegen, Triticale Abstr., Trop.Dis.Bull., Weed Abstr., Wild.Rev., Zoo.Rec. **Document type:** academic/scholarly publication.
—BLDSC (4114.250000); CASDDS; CISTI; Genuine Article; KNAW; KR SourceOne; SWETS; UMI; UnCover. **CCC.**
Description: Covers current research in all branches of genetics: for geneticists, molecular and developmental biologists, and plant and animal breeders.

575.1   US   ISSN 0016-6731
QH431   CODEN: GENTAE
GENETICS; a periodical record of investigations bearing on heredity and variation. 1916. m. $430 to institutions (foreign $450) (effective 1997). Genetics Society of America, 9650 Rockville Pike, Bethesda, MD 20814. TEL 301-571-1825. FAX 301-530-7001. (Subscr. to: FASEB, Subscriptions, Rm. L2310, 9650 Rockville Pike, Bethesda, MD 20814. TEL 301-530-7026) abstr.; bibl.; charts; illus.; index. circ. 5,000. (also avail. in microform from MIM,UMI,PMC; reprint service avail. from UMI) **Indexed:** Abstr.Anthropol., Abstr.Hyg., Anim.Breed.Abstr., Anim.Breed.Abstr., Apic.Abstr., ASCA, Biol.Abstr., Biol.& Agr.Ind., Biotech.Abstr., Chem.Abstr., Compumath, Cott.& Trop.Fibr.Abstr., Curr.Adv.Biochem., Curr.Adv.Cell & Devel.Biol., Curr.Adv.Ecol.Sci., Curr.Adv.Genetics & Molec.Biol., Curr.Cont., Curr.Ref.Fish Res., Dairy Sci.Abstr., Excerp.Med., Fababean Abstr., Food Sci.& Tech.Abstr., Forest.Abstr., Gen.Sci.Ind., Geo.Abstr., Ind.Med., Ind.Sci.Rev., INIS Atomind., Maize Abstr., Ornam.Hort., Plant Breed.Abstr., Potato Abstr., Sci.Cit.Ind., Seed Abstr., Soils & Fert., Sorghum & Millets Abstr., Sport Fish.Abstr., Triticale Abstr., Trop.Dis.Bull., Weed Abstr., Wild.Rev., Zoo.Rec.
—BLDSC (4115.000000); CASDDS; CISTI; Genuine Article; KNAW; KR SourceOne; Linda Hall; SWETS; UMI; UnCover. **CCC.**
Refereed Serial

575.1   SA   ISSN 0259-0301
GENETICS NEWSLETTER/GENETIKA NUUSBRIEF. (Text in Afrikaans and English) 1968. q. membership. South African Genetic Society, c/o Department of Genetics, University of Stellenbosch, Stellenbosch, South Africa. Ed. Dr. A. E. Retief. bk.rev.; circ. controlled. (processed)

591.15 636.081   FR   ISSN 0999-193X
SF105   CODEN: GSEVE9
GENETICS, SELECTION, EVOLUTION. (Text mainly in English; summaries in English, French) 1969. bi-m. 1381 F. to institutions (US $264; elsewhere 1730 F.) (effective 1998). (Institut National de la Recherche Agronomique) Editions Scientifiques et Medicales Elsevier, 141 rue de Javel, 75747 Paris, France. TEL 33-1-45589022. FAX 33-1-45589421. URL: http://www.elsevier.nl/. (Subscr. in U.S. and Canada to: Elsevier Science Inc., Box 945, Madison Sq. Sta., New York, NY 10159-0945. TEL 212-633-3730. FAX 212-633-3680) Eds. B. Bibe, JR David. bk.rev.; charts; illus.; index. circ. 2,000. (also avail. in microform from UMI; reprint service avail. from ISI) **Indexed:** Anim.Breed.Abstr., ASCA, Biol.Abstr., Chem.Abstr., Curr.Adv.Ecol.Sci., Curr.Cont., Dairy Sci.Abstr., Ecol.Abstr., Food Sci.& Tech.Abstr., Forest.Abstr., Genet.Abstr., Ind.Vet., Pig News & Info., Poult.Abstr., Protozool.Abstr., Sci.Cit.Ind., Sport Fish.Abstr., Triticale Abstr., Vet.Bull., Wild.Rev., Zoo.Rec. **Document type:** academic/scholarly publication.
—BLDSC (4115.158000); CASDDS; CISTI; EMDOCS; Genuine Article; Linda Hall; SWETS; UnCover. **CCC.**
Former titles: Genetique, Selection, Evolution (ISSN 0754-0264); Annales de Genetique et de Selection Animale (ISSN 0003-4002)
Description: International journal open to original research papers in the field of animal genetics and evolution. Areas of interest include all aspects related to cytogenetics: cellular, biotechnical, factorial, mathematical, quantitative and population genetics.
Refereed Serial

575.1 011   CN   ISSN 0316-4357
QH426
GENETICS SOCIETY OF CANADA BULLETIN. 1959. q. Can.$25 (foreign Can.$30) (effective 1997). Genetics Society of Canada, 141 Laurier Av. W., Ste. 1112, Ottawa, ON K1P 5J3, Canada. TEL 613-232-9459. FAX 613-594-5190. Ed. Michael Bentley; Pub. Michael Bentley. R&P contact: Michael Bentley. adv. contact: Michael Bentley. bk.rev. circ. 450. **Document type:** bulletin.
—Linda Hall.

575.1   RU   ISSN 0016-6758
CODEN: GNKAA5
GENETIKA. English translation: Russian Journal of Genetics (US ISSN 1022-7954) (Text in English and Russian) 1965. m. $322 (effective 1998). (Rossiiskaya Akademiya Nauk) Izdatel'stvo Nauka, 90 Profsoyuznaya ul., 117864 Moscow, Russia. (Dist. in U.S. by: Victor Kamkin Inc., 4956 Boiling Brook Pkwy, Rockville, MD 20852. TEL 301-881-5973) bk.rev.; index. **Indexed:** Anim.Breed.Abstr., Bibl.Dev.Med.& Child Neur., Biol.Abstr., Biotech.Abstr., Chem.Abstr., Cott.& Trop.Fibr.Abstr., Curr.Adv.Ecol.Sci., Curr.Cont., Dent.Ind., Excerp.Med., Helminthol.Abstr., Hort.Abstr., Ind.Med., Ind.Sci.Rev., INIS Atomind., Maize Abstr., Pig News & Info., Plant Grow.Reg.Abstr., Potato Abstr., Poult.Abstr., Risk Abstr., Sci.Cit.Ind., Seed Abstr., Sport Fish.Abstr., SSCI, Triticale Abstr., Wild.Rev., Zoo.Rec. **Document type:** academic/scholarly publication.
—BLDSC (0047.080000); CASDDS; CISTI; Genuine Article; KNAW; Linda Hall; SWETS. **CCC.**

575.1   XR   ISSN 0862-8629
CODEN: SUSLDO
GENETIKA A SLECHTENI/GENETICS AND PLANT BREEDING; vedecky casopis. (Text and summaries in Czech or Slovak, English) 1965. q. $51 in Europe; elsewhere $53 (effective 1997). Ustav Zemedelskych a Potravinarskych Informaci, Slezska 7, 120 56 Prague 2, Czech Republic. TEL 420-2-24257939. FAX 420-2-24253938. E-mail: izlk@uzpi.cz. Eds. M. Braunova, H. Malikova. bk.rev. circ. 300. (back issues avail.) **Indexed:** Bibl.Agri., Biol.Abstr., Chem.Abstr., Crop Physiol.Abstr., Field Crop Abstr., Helminthol.Abstr., Herb.Abstr., Hort.Abstr., INIS Atomind., Landwirt.Zentralbl., Maize Abstr., Plant Breed.Abstr., Plant Grow.Reg.Abstr., Potato Abstr., Ref.Zh., Seed Abstr., Soyabean Abstr., Triticale Abstr.
—BLDSC (4115.300000); CASDDS.
Formerly (until 1989): U V T I Z Sbornik - Genetika a Slechteni (ISSN 0036-5378)
Description: Publishes original scientific studies concerning genetics, plant selection, seed growing, biology of plants, and phytopathology.

575.1   BU   ISSN 0016-6766
CODEN: GESKAC
GENETIKA I SELEKTSIIA/GENETICS AND PLANT BREEDING. (Text in Bulgarian; summaries in English and Russian) 1968. bi-m. 1.40 lv. per no. (Akademiia na Selskostopanskite Nauki) Publishing House of the Bulgarian Academy of Sciences, Acad. G. Bonchev St., Bldg. 6, 1113 Sofia, Bulgaria. (Dist. by: Hemus, 6, Rouski Blvd., 1000 Sofia, Bulgaria.) Ed. Khristo Daskalov. bk.rev.; bibl.; charts; illus. circ. 1,010. (back issues avail.; reprint service avail. from IRC) **Indexed:** Anim.Breed.Abstr., Biol.Abstr., BSL Biol., Chem.Abstr., Curr.Adv.Ecol.Sci., Dairy Sci.Abstr., Hort.Abstr., Ind.Vet., INIS Atomind., Maize Abstr., Pig News & Info., Plant Grow.Reg.Abstr., Poult.Abstr., Seed Abstr., Weed Abstr.
—BLDSC (0047.090000); CASDDS; CISTI; Linda Hall.

575   US   ISSN 0740-9737
CODEN: GEWAE6
GENEWATCH. 1984. bi-m. $24 to individuals (Canada & Mexico $29; elsewhere $32); institutions $30 (Canada & Mexico $35; elsewhere $38); students $15 (Canada & Mexico $20; elsewhere $28) (effective 1998). Council for Responsible Genetics (CRG), 5 Upland Rd., Ste. 3, Cambridge, MA 02140-2717. TEL 617-868-0870. FAX 617-491-5344. E-mail: crg@essential.org; URL: http://www.essential.org/crg. Ed. Wendy McGoodwin. R&P contact: Ben McKelway. adv. contact: Rebecca Lange. bk.rev.; bibl.; illus.; circ. 2,000 (paid). (back issues avail.) **Indexed:** Alt.Press Ind., Telegen. **Document type:** newsletter.
—CISTI; Genuine Article; UMI.
Description: Articles, commentary, international news, and legislative updates on social issues pertaining to genetic engineering and biotechnology.
Refereed Serial

575.1 574.8   CN   ISSN 0831-2796
QH431.A1   CODEN: GENOE3
GENOME. (Text mainly in English, occasionally in French) 1959. bi-m. Can.$120 to individuals (foreign $130); institutions Can.$300 (foreign $300) (effective 1996). (Genetics Society of Canada) National Research Council of Canada, Research Journals, Ottawa, ON K1A 0R6, Canada. TEL 613-993-9084. FAX 613-952-7656. URL: http://www.cisti.nrc.ca/cisti/journals/. Ed. Dr. Peter Moens. adv.: B&W page Can.$600; trim 8 1/2 x 11; adv. contact: Hoda Jabbour. charts; illus.; stat.; index. circ. 1,400. (also avail. in microfilm from PMC; back issues avail.) **Indexed:** Anim.Breed.Abstr., ASCA, Bio-Contr.News & Info., Biol.Abstr., Biol.& Agr.Ind., Chem.Abstr., Cott.& Trop.Fibr.Abstr., Curr.Adv.Cell & Devel.Biol., Curr.Adv.Ecol.Sci., Curr.Adv.Genetics & Molec.Biol., Curr.Biotech.Abstr., Curr.Cont., Excerp.Med., Helminthol.Abstr., Hort.Abstr., Ind.Med., Ind.Sci.Rev., Ind.Vet., INIS Atomind., Maize Abstr., Ocean.Abstr., Ornam.Hort., Plant Breed.Abstr., Plant Grow.Reg.Abstr., Pollut.Abstr., Potato Abstr., Rev.Appl.Entomol., Rev.Plant Path., Rice Abstr., Sci.Cit.Ind., Seed Abstr., Sorghum & Millets Abstr., Soyabean Abstr., Sport Fish.Abstr., Triticale Abstr., Vet.Bull., Weed Abstr., Wild.Rev., Zoo.Rec. **Document type:** academic/scholarly publication.
—BLDSC (4116.312000); ADONIS; CASDDS; CISTI; EMDOCS; Genuine Article; KNAW; KR SourceOne; Linda Hall; SWETS; UMI; UnCover. **CCC.**
Formerly: Canadian Journal of Genetics and Cytology - Journal Canadien de Genetique et de Cytologie (ISSN 0008-4093)
Description: Publishes papers in applied and basic genetics and cytology.
Refereed Serial

BIOLOGY — GENETICS

575.1 US ISSN 0888-7543
QH445.2 CODEN: GNMCEP
GENOMICS; international journal for analysis of the human and other genomes. 1987. 24/yr. $1100 (foreign $1300) (effective 1997). Academic Press, Inc., Journal Division, 525 B St., Ste. 1900, San Diego, CA 92101-4495. TEL 619-230-1840. FAX 619-699-6800. E-mail: apsubs@acad.com; URL: http://www.apnet.com/www/journal/ge.htm; http://www.idealibrary.com/. (Subscr. to: Box 861213, Orlando, FL 32886-1213. TEL 407-347-4040. FAX 407-363-9661) Ed.Bd. (back issues avail.). **Indexed**: ASCA, Bibl.Agri., Curr.Adv.Cell & Devel.Biol., Curr.Adv.Genetics & Molec.Biol., Curr.Cont., Ind.Sci.Rev., Neurosci.Cit.Ind., Sci.Cit.Ind., SSCI, Telegen. **Document type**: academic/scholarly publication.
●Also available online.
—BLDSC (4116.314000); CASDDS; CISTI; EMDOCS; Genuine Article; KNAW; Linda Hall; SWETS; UnCover. **CCC**.
 Description: Emphasizes the integration of basic and applied research in human and comparative gene mapping, molecular cloning, large-scale restriction mapping, and DNA sequencing and computational analysis.
 Refereed Serial

575.1 340 GW ISSN 0939-2211
GENTECHNIKGESETZ. 1991. irreg. DM.86. Erich Schmidt Verlag GmbH & Co. (Berlin), Genthiner Str. 30G, 10785 Berlin, Germany. TEL 49-30-250085-0. FAX 49-30-25008521. (looseleaf format) **Document type**: bulletin.

575.1 616.9 US ISSN 1063-0627
CODEN: HAIRE4
HARVARD AIDS INSTITUTE SERIES ON GENE REGULATION OF HUMAN RETROVIRUSES. 1991. irreg. price varies. Lippincott - Raven Publishers (Subsidiary of: Wolters Kluwer N.V.), 227 E. Washington Sq., Philadelphia, PA 19106. TEL 215-238-4200. FAX 215-238-4227. URL: http://www.lrpub.com. (Subscr. to: Box 1600. Hagerstown, MD 21741-1600. TEL 800-777-2295. FAX 301-824-7390) R&P contact: Alice McElhinney. (reprint service avail. from UMI) **Document type**: proceedings, monographic series.
—BLDSC (4265.545000); CASDDS; CISTI.
 Refereed Serial

HEMOCHROMATOSIS AWARENESS; a quarterly update on hereditary and acquired iron-overload. see
MEDICAL SCIENCES

575.1 574.8 SW ISSN 0018-0661
QH431.A1 CODEN: HEREAY
HEREDITAS; a periodical devoted to the publication of original research in all aspects of genetics and cytology. (Text in English) 1920. bi-m. SEK 1570 in Scandinavian countries; elsewhere SEK 1585. (Scandinavian Association of Geneticists) Mendelian Society of Lund, Department of Genetics, S-223 62 Lund, Sweden. TEL 46-46-12-02-36. FAX 46-46-14-78-74. (Subscr. to: Hereditas-Distribution, P.O. Box 1601, S-221 01 Lund, Sweden) Ed. Karl Fredga. abstr.; bibl.; illus.; index, cum.index: vols.1-40. circ. 1,000. (also avail. in microfilm from UMI; back issues avail.) **Indexed**: Abstr.Anthropol., Anim.Breed.Abstr., Biol.Abstr., Chem.Abstr., Crop Physiol.Abstr., Curr.Adv.Ecol.Sci., Curr.Cont., Dent.Ind., Excerp.Med., Fababean Abstr., Field Crop Abstr., Helminthol.Abstr., Herb.Abstr., Ind.Med., Ind.Sci.Rev., Ind.Vet., Plant Breed Abstr., Plant Grow.Reg.Abstr., Rev.Plant Path., Sci.Cit.Ind., Seed Abstr., Soils & Fert., Sport Fish.Abstr., Telegen, Triticale Abstr., Vet.Bull., Wild.Rev., Zoo.Rec. **Document type**: academic/scholarly publication.
—BLDSC (4299.000000); CASDDS; CISTI; KNAW; Linda Hall; SWETS; UMI; UnCover.
 Formerly: Hereditas-Genetiskt Arkiv.

575.1 UK ISSN 0018-067X
QH431 CODEN: HDTYAT
HEREDITY; an international journal of genetics. 1947. m. £252($465) (foreign £277) (effective 1998). (Genetical Society of Great Britain) Blackwell Science Ltd., Osney Mead, Oxford OX2 0EL, England. TEL 44-1865-206206. FAX 44-1865-721205. E-mail: journals.cs@blacksci.co.uk; URL: http://www.black.co.uk. Ed. T.J. Crawford; Pub. Allen Stevens. R&P contact: Sarah Pollard. adv. contact: Martine Cariou-Keen. bk.rev.; bibl.; charts; illus.; index. circ. 1,120. (also avail. in microform from UMI; back issues avail.) **Indexed**: Abstr.Anthropol., Abstr.Hyg., Anim.Breed.Abstr., Apic.Abstr., ASCA, Bio-Contr.News & Info., Biol.Abstr., Biol.& Agr.Ind., Chem.Abstr., Curr.Adv.Cell & Devel.Biol., Curr.Adv.Ecol.Sci., Curr.Adv.Genetics & Molec.Biol., Curr.Cont., Curr.Ref.Fish Res., Ecol.Abstr., Excerp.Med., Field Crop Abstr., Food Sci.& Tech.Abstr., Forest.Abstr., Helminthol.Abstr., Herb.Abstr., Hort.Abstr., Ind.Med., Ind.Sci.Rev., Ind.Vet., Ornam.Hort., Plant Breed Abstr., Potato Abstr., Poult.Abstr., Rev.Appl.Entomol., Rev.Plant Path., Rice Abstr., Sci.Cit.Ind., Seed Abstr., Soils & Fert., Sport Fish.Abstr., THA, Triticale Abstr., Trop.Dis.Bull., Vet.Bull., Weed Abstr., Wild.Rev., Zoo.Rec. **Document type**: academic/scholarly publication.
—BLDSC (4300.000000); CASDDS; CISTI; EMDOCS; Genuine Article; KR SourceOne; Linda Hall; SWETS; UMI; UnCover. **CCC**.
 Refereed Serial

575.1 599 JA ISSN 0918-5976
CODEN: MMGCEK
HONYU DOBUTSU SHIKEN BUNKAKAI KAIHO/MAMMALIAN MUTAGENICITY STUDY GROUP COMMUNICATIONS. (Text in English, Japanese) 1988. a. 2000 Yen. Nihon Kankyo Hen'igen Gakkai, Honyu Dobutsu Shiken Bunkakai - Environmental Mutagen Society of Japan, Mammalian Mutagenicity Study Group, Shokuhin Yakuhin Anzen Senta Hadano Kenkyujo, 729-5 Ochiai, Hadano-shi, Kanagawa-ken 257, Japan. Ed. Makoto Hayashi. adv.; bk.rev. **Document type**: academic/scholarly publication.
—BLDSC (5357.550000); CASDDS.
 Description: Contains papers reporting results (including negative data) of original research concerning mutagenesis, chromosome breakage, and related subjects in mammalian cells and mammals.
 Refereed Serial

575.1 150 US ISSN 1063-2158
HUMAN EVOLUTION, BEHAVIOR, AND INTELLIGENCE. 1992. irreg. price varies. Praeger Publishers (Subsidiary of: Greenwood Publishing Group Inc.), 88 Post Rd. W., Box 5007, Westport, CT 06881-5007. TEL 203-226-3571. FAX 203-222-1502. **Document type**: monographic series.

575.1 US ISSN 1043-0342
RB155.8 CODEN: HGTHE3
HUMAN GENE THERAPY. 1990. 18/yr. $181 to individuals (foreign $450); institutions $862 (foreign $937) (effective through 1998). Mary Ann Liebert, Inc. Publishers, 2 Madison Ave., Larchmont, NY 10538. TEL 914-834-3100. FAX 914-834-3688. E-mail: liebert@pipeline.com. Ed. Dr. W. French Anderson. **Indexed**: ASCA, Curr.Cont., Excerp.Med. (1993-), Ind.Sci.Rev., Sci.Cit.Ind. **Document type**: academic/scholarly publication.
—BLDSC (4336.092000); CASDDS; CISTI; EMDOCS; Genuine Article; KNAW; SWETS; UnCover.
 Description: Containss papers on the transfer of genes in mammals, including humans. Covers improvements in vector development, delivery systems and animal models, as well as ethical, legal, and regulatory issues.

573.21 GW ISSN 0340-6717
CODEN: HUGEDQ
HUMAN GENETICS. Online edition (GW ISSN 1432-1203) (Text in English) 1964. m. DM.4643 (foreign DM.4672.40) (effective 1998). Springer-Verlag, Heidelberger Platz 3, 14197 Berlin, Germany. TEL 49-30-82787-0. FAX 49-30-82787448. E-mail: subscriptions@springer.de; URL: http://link.springer.de. (Subscr. in N. America to: Springer-Verlag New York, Inc., 333 Meadowlands Pkwy., Secaucus, NJ 07094. TEL 212-460-1500. FAX 212-473-6272) Ed.Bd. adv.; charts; illus. (also avail. in microform from UMI; back issues avail.; reprint service avail. from ISI) **Indexed**: Anim.Breed.Abstr., ASCA, Bibl.Dev.Med.& Child Neur., Biol.Abstr., Chem.Abstr., Curr.Adv.Cancer Res., Curr.Adv.Ecol.Sci., Curr.Cont., Excerp.Med., Ind.Med., Ind.Sci.Rev., INIS Atomind., Med.& Surg.Dermat., Rev.Appl.Entomol., Sci.Cit.Ind., SSCI. **Document type**: academic/scholarly publication.
●Also available online.
—BLDSC (4336.095000); CASDDS; CISTI; EMDOCS; Genuine Article; KNAW; Linda Hall; SWETS; UMI; UnCover. **CCC**.
 Continues: Humangenetik (ISSN 0018-7348)
 Description: Covers human genetics, cytogenetics, biochemical genetics, population genetics, immunogenetics, pharmacogenetics, genetic diagnosis and counseling.

573.21 US ISSN 0172-7699
HUMAN GENETICS. SUPPLEMENT. 1978. irreg. price varies. Springer-Verlag, 175 Fifth Ave., New York, NY 10010. TEL 212-460-1500. FAX 212-473-6272. (Also: Berlin, Heidelberg, Tokyo and Vienna) (also avail. in microform from UMI; reprint service avail. from ISI) **Indexed**: Ind.Med. **Document type**: academic/scholarly publication.
—CISTI.

573.21 US ISSN 1050-6101
QH447 CODEN: HGNEFX
HUMAN GENOME NEWS. 1989. q. free. Human Genome Management Information System, Oak Ridge National Laboratory, 1060 Commerce Park, Oak Ridge, TN 37830. TEL 423-576-6669. FAX 423-574-9888. E-mail: mansfieldbk@ornl.gov; URL: http://www.ornl.gov/hqmis. (Subscr. to: Oak Ridge National Laboratory, 1060 Commerce Park, Oak Ridge, TN 37830) (U.S. Department of Energy) Ed. Betty K. Mansfield. bk.rev.; charts; illus.; circ. 14,300 (controlled). **Indexed**: ASCA, SSCI. **Document type**: government publication, newsletter.
●Also available online.
—Genuine Article.
 Description: Facilitates communication among genome researchers and informs persons interested in genetic research.

573.21 US
HUMAN GENOME PROGRAM REPORT. 1990. biennial. free. U.S. Department of Energy, Human Genome Program, Office of Health and Environmental Research, ER-72 GTN, Washington, DC 20585. TEL 301-903-6488. FAX 301-903-5051. E-mail: adamsonae@ornl.gov; URL: http://www.ornl.gov/hgmis. (Orders to: National Technical Information Service, 5285 Port Royal Rd., Springfield, VA 22161. TEL 703-487-4650. FAX 703-321-8547; Or: Human Genome Management Information System, Oak Ridge National Laboratory, 1060 Commerce Park, Oak Ridge, TN 37830. FAX 423-576-6669) (Co-sponsor: Oak Ridge National Laboratory. Human Genome Management Information System) Eds. Daniel W. Drell, Anne E. Adamson. R&P contact: Betty Mansfield. circ. 12,300. circ. 12,300 (controlled). **Document type**: government publication.
●Also available online.

BIOLOGY — GENETICS

573.21 SZ ISSN 0001-5652
RB155 CODEN: HUHEAS
HUMAN HEREDITY; international journal of human and medical genetics. (Text in English) 1950. bi-m. 256.50 SFr.($207.50) to individuals; institutions 533 SFr.($415) (effective 1998). S. Karger AG, Allschwilerstr. 10, P.O. Box, CH-4009 Basel, Switzerland. TEL 41-61-3061111. FAX 41-61-3061234. E-mail: karger@karger.ch; URL: http://www.karger.ch. Ed. J. Ott. adv.; bibl.; charts; illus.; stat.; index. circ. 1,000. (also avail. in microform) Indexed: A.I.C.P., Abstr.Anthropol., Abstr.Hyg., Anim.Breed.Abstr., Anthropol.Lit., ASCA, Bibl.Dev.Med.& Child Neur., Biol.Abstr., Chem.Abstr., Curr.Adv.Ecol.Sci., Curr.Cont., Dok.Arbeitsmed., Excerp.Med., Ind.Med., Ind.Sci.Rev., Nutr.Abstr., Rural Recreat.Tour.Abstr., Sci.Cit.Ind., THA, World Agri.Econ.& Rural Sociol.Abstr. **Document type:** academic/scholarly publication.
—BLDSC (4336.150000); CASDDS; CISTI; Genuine Article; KNAW; Linda Hall; SWETS; UnCover. **CCC.**
Formerly: Acta Genetica et Statistica Medica.
Refereed Serial

575.1 UK ISSN 0964-6906
RB155.5 CODEN: HMGEE5
HUMAN MOLECULAR GENETICS. 1992. 13/yr. £425 (foreign $725) (effective 1998). Oxford University Press, Academic Division, Great Clarendon St., Oxford OX2 6DP, England. TEL 44-1865-267907. FAX 44-1865-267485. TELEX 837330-OXPRES-G. E-mail: jnl.info@oup.co.uk; URL: http://www.oup.co.uk/journals. (Subscr. in U.S. to: Oxford University Press Inc., 2001 Evans Rd., Cary, NC 27513. TEL 800-852-7323. FAX 919-677-1714) Eds. H.F. Willard, K.E. Davies; Pub. Martin Richardson. R&P contact: Joolz Longley. adv. circ. 2,200. (reprint service avail. from SWZ) Indexed: ASCA, Curr.Cont., Excerp.Med. (1993-), Genet.Abstr., Ind.Med. (1993-), Ind.Sci.Rev., Neurosci.Cit.Ind., Sci.Cit.Ind. **Document type:** academic/scholarly publication.
●Also available online.
—BLDSC (4336.198000); CASDDS; CISTI; EMDOCS; Genuine Article; KNAW; Linda Hall; SWETS; UnCover. **CCC.**

575.1 US ISSN 1059-7794
RB155.5 CODEN: HUMUE3
HUMAN MUTATION. 1992. 13/yr. $545 (foreign $772.5) (effective 1998). John Wiley & Sons, Inc., Journals, 605 Third Ave., New York, NY 10158-0012. TEL 212-850-6645. FAX 212-850-6021. TELEX 12-7063. E-mail: SUBINFO@JWILEY.COM; URL: http://www.wiley.co.uk. (Subscr. outside the Americas to: John Wiley & Sons Ltd., Baffins Ln, Chichester, W. Sussex PO19 1UD, England. TEL 44-1243-779777. FAX 44-1243-776128) Eds. R.G.H. Cotton, Haig. H. Kazazian, Jr. adv.: B&W page £640, color page £1515; trim 279 x 210. bk.rev. circ. 750. (also avail. in microform from UMI; back issues avail.) Indexed: ASCA, Curr.Cont., Excerp.Med. (1993-), Ind.Med. (1993-). **Document type:** academic/scholarly publication.
—BLDSC (4336.217000); CASDDS; CISTI; EMDOCS; Genuine Article; KNAW; SWETS. **CCC.**
Description: Publishes original research articles, mutation updates, briefs on new mutations and reviews on broad aspects of mutation research as related to understanding the human genome and medical aspects of genetic disorders. For molecular, human and medical geneticists in academic, industrial and clinical research settings.
Refereed Serial

575.1 JA ISSN 0387-0022
CODEN: IDENBZ
IDEN/HEREDITY. (Irregular supplements avail.) (Text in Japanese) 1947. m. 900 Yen per no. (Idengaku Fukyukai - Association for Propagation of the Knowledge of Genetics) Shokabo Publisher Co., Ltd., 8-1, Yonbancho, Chiyoda-ku, Tokyo 102, Japan.
—BLDSC (4300.020000); CASDDS; CISTI.

IMMUNOGENETICS. see *MEDICAL SCIENCES — Allergology And Immunology*

IN VITRO CELLULAR & DEVELOPMENTAL BIOLOGY - ANIMAL. see *BIOLOGY — Microbiology*

IN VITRO CELLULAR & DEVELOPMENTAL BIOLOGY - PLANT. see *BIOLOGY — Microbiology*

575.1 II ISSN 0019-5200
SB123 CODEN: IJGBAG
INDIAN JOURNAL OF GENETICS AND PLANT BREEDING. 1960. q. plus a. supplement. Rs.450($70) (effective 1996). Indian Society of Genetics and Plant Breeding, Division of Genetics, 7A, Satyen Dutta Rd., Calcutta 700 029, India. TEL 91-33-466-1431. FAX 91-33-248-9200. Ed. Mihir Sen. adv.: B&W page $422, color page $845. bk.rev.; charts; illus.; index, cum.index: vols.1-20, vols.21-30. circ. 9,000. Indexed: Biol.Abstr., Chem.Abstr., Cott.& Trop.Fibr.Abstr., Curr.Cont., Fababean Abstr., Field Crop Abstr., Helminthol.Abstr., Herb.Abstr., Hort.Abstr., Maize Abstr., Plant Breed.Abstr., Plant Grow.Reg.Abstr., Rev.Plant Path., Rice Abstr., Seed Abstr., Soils & Fert., Soyabean Abstr., Triticale Abstr., Trop.Oil Seeds Abstr., Weed Abstr. **Document type:** academic/scholarly publication.
—CASDDS; Linda Hall; SWETS; UnCover.
Description: Covers electrical and electronics, metallurgy, mechanical, chemical, software engineering and computer science, mining, steel, environmental technology, power and energy.

630 II ISSN 0374-826X
CODEN: INJHA9
INDIAN JOURNAL OF HEREDITY. (Text in English) 1969. q. $38. Genetic Association of India, Izatnagar 243 122, India. Ed. N.S. Sidhu. adv.; bk.rev. circ. 500. (back issues avail.) Indexed: Anim.Breed.Abstr., Biol.Abstr., Chem.Abstr., Curr.Adv.Ecol.Sci., Excerp.Med., Plant Breed.Abstr.
—CASDDS; CISTI; Linda Hall.

INDIAN JOURNAL OF PHYSICAL ANTHROPOLOGY AND HUMAN GENETICS. see *ANTHROPOLOGY*

INDIAN JOURNAL OF PLANT GENETIC RESOURCES. see *BIOLOGY — Botany*

INDUSTRIAL CROPS AND PRODUCTS. see *AGRICULTURE — Crop Production And Soil*

INFORMATIONS ANNUELLES DE CARYOSYSTEMATIQUE ET CYTOGENETIQUE. see *BIOLOGY — Botany*

575.1 US
INSIDE THE JACKSON LABORATORY. 1952. q. free. Jackson Laboratory, 600 Main St., Bar Harbor, ME 04609. TEL 207-288-3371. Ed. Jeffre Witherly. charts; illus. circ. 14,000.
Former titles: Jax (ISSN 0021-5570); Jackson Laboratory News.

INSTITUT PASTEUR. ANNALES. ACTUALITES. see *BIOLOGY — Microbiology*

591.15 KE
INSTITUTE OF PRIMATE RESEARCH. ANNUAL REPORT. 1981. a. Institute of Primate Research, P.O. Box 24481, Karen, Nairobi, Kenya. FAX 254-2-882546. TELEX 254-2-22892.

575.1 SI ISSN 0218-1932
QH447 CODEN: IJGREY
INTERNATIONAL JOURNAL OF GENOME RESEARCH. 1992. bi-m. $240 to institutions; individuals & institutions of developing countries $120. World Scientific Publishing Co. Pte. Ltd., Farrer Rd., P.O. Box 128, Singapore 9128, Singapore. TEL 65-3825663. FAX 65-3825919. TELEX RS-28561-WSPC. (UK addr.: 73 Lynton Mead, Totteridge, London N20 8DH, England. TEL 44-181-446-2461; US addr.: 1060 Main St., Ste. 1B, River Edge, NJ 07661. TEL 800-227-7562) Indexed: Food Sci.& Tech.Abstr., SSCI. **Document type:** academic/scholarly publication.
—CASDDS; Genuine Article. **CCC.**
Description: Publishes research on human genomes, as well as other organisms and simple genomes such as those of Drosophila melanogaster and bacteria.

575 RU ISSN 0301-391X
ITOGI NAUKI I TEKHNIKI: GENETIKA CHELOVEKA. irreg., latest vol.6, 1982. price varies. Vsesoyuznyi Institut Nauchno-Tekhnicheskoi Informatsii (VINITI), Ul. Baltiiskaya, 14, Moscow A-219, Russia. (Subscr. to: Mezhdunarodnaya Kniga, Dimitrova ul. 39, 113095 Moscow, Russia)

J E M S NEWS. (Japan - Environmental Mutagen Society) see *ENVIRONMENTAL STUDIES*

616.8 US ISSN 0447-3353
CODEN: JALEBX
JAMES ARTHUR LECTURE ON THE EVOLUTION OF THE HUMAN BRAIN. 1956. irreg., no.57, 1987. price varies. American Museum of Natural History, Central Park W. at 79th St., New York, NY 10024-5192. TEL 212-769-5545. FAX 212-769-5009. E-mail: scipubs.@amnh.org. Ed. Brenda Jones. circ. 1,000. Indexed: Biol.Abstr. **Document type:** monographic series.
—BLDSC (4645.500000); CISTI.

573.21 JA ISSN 0021-5074
CODEN: JJHGEH
JAPANESE JOURNAL OF HUMAN GENETICS/JINRUI IDENGAKU ZASSHI. 1956. q. DM.278 (effective 1998). (Japan Society of Human Genetics - Nihon Jinrui Iden Gakkai) Springer-Verlag Tokyo, 3-113, Hongo 3-chome, Bunkyo-ku, Tokyo 113, Japan. TEL 81-3-38120331. FAX 81-3-38120719. E-mail: svt-ebs@ppp.bekkoame.or.jp. (Subscr. to: Springer-Verlag, Heidelberger Platz 3, 14197 Berlin, Germany. TEL 49-30-82787-0. FAX 49-30-82787448) adv.; bk.rev. circ. 1,200. Indexed: ASCA, Biol.Abstr., Chem.Abstr., Curr.Adv.Cancer Res., Curr.Cont., Excerp.Med., Helminthol.Abstr., Ind.Med., Ind.Sci.Rev., INIS Atomind., INSPEC, Jap.Per.Ind., Sci.Cit.Ind., THA. **Document type:** academic/scholarly publication.
—CASDDS; CISTI; Linda Hall; SWETS; UnCover.

JEAN PIAGET SYMPOSIA. see *PSYCHOLOGY*

JOURNAL OF ANIMAL SCIENCE. see *AGRICULTURE — Poultry And Livestock*

JOURNAL OF ANIMAL SCIENCE. SUPPLEMENT. BIENNIAL SYMPOSIUM ON ANIMAL REPRODUCTION. see *AGRICULTURE — Poultry And Livestock*

575.1 PL ISSN 1234-1983
SB123 CODEN: JAGEFC
JOURNAL OF APPLIED GENETICS; an international journal of genetics. (Text in English) 1960. q. $112 (effective 1998); $120 (effective 1998). Polska Akademia Nauk, Instytut Genetyki Roslin - Polish Academy of Sciences, Institute of Plant Genetics, Strzeszynska 34, 60-479 Poznan, Poland. TEL 48-61-233511. FAX 48-61-233671. E-mail: edyb@igr.poznan.pl; URL: http://saturn.ci.uw.edu.pl/psjc/; http://ciuw.warman.net.pl/. (Subscr. to: Ars Polona, Krakowskie Przedmiescie 7. 00-068 Warsaw, Poland) Ed. Zygmunt Kaczmarek. R&P contact: Eleonora Dybizbanska. TEL 48-61-233687. adv. contact: Bogumila Szymanska. bk.rev.; abstr.; bibl.; charts; illus.; index. circ. 350. Indexed: AgroAgen, AgroLibrex, Anim.Breed.Abstr., Biol.Abstr., Chem.Abstr., Curr.Adv.Biochem., Curr.Adv.Cell & Devel.Biol., Curr.Adv.Ecol.Sci., Curr.Adv.Genetics & Molec.Biol., Curr.Cont., Excerp.Med., Field Crop Abstr., Helminthol.Abstr., Herb.Abstr., Hort.Abstr., Ind.Sci.Rev., Ind.Vet., INIS Atomind., Maize Abstr., Plant Breed.Abstr., Plant Grow.Reg.Abstr., Sci.Cit.Ind., Seed Abstr., Soils & Fert., Triticale Abstr., Vet.Bull. **Document type:** academic/scholarly publication.
—BLDSC (4942.612000); CASDDS; CISTI. **CCC.**
Formerly (until 1995): Genetica Polonica (ISSN 0016-6715)
Description: Publishes original scientific papers on plant and animal genetics and breeding, on microorganisms and human genetics.
Refereed Serial

575.1 US ISSN 1087-0571
RS189 CODEN: JBISF3
▼**JOURNAL OF BIOMOLECULAR SCREENING.** 1996. q. $139 to individuals (foreign $146); institutions $201 (foreign $236) (effective through 1998). (Society for Biomolecular Screening) Mary Ann Liebert, Inc. Publishers, 2 Madison Ave., Larchmont, NY 10538. TEL 914-834-3100. FAX 914-834-3688. E-mail: liebert@pipeline.com. Ed. Dr. Michael Kozlowski. **Document type:** academic/scholarly publication.
—BLDSC (4953.845000); CASDDS.
Description: Covers chemistry, biology, automation and information management, including all aspects of the discovery process, from basic research through the early stages of product development.

575.1 312 301 UK ISSN 0021-9320
HQ750.A1 CODEN: JBSLAR
JOURNAL OF BIOSOCIAL SCIENCE. 1969. q. £80($140) (effective 1998). Cambridge University Press, Edinburgh Bldg., Shaftesbury Rd., Cambridge CB2 2RU, England. TEL 44-1223-312393. FAX 44-1223-315052. E-mail: information@cup.cam.ac.uk; URL: http://www.cup.cam.ac.uk. (N. American addr.: Cambridge University Press, Journals Dept., 40 W. 20th St., New York, NY 10011. TEL 212-924-3900. FAX 212-691-3239) Ed. C.G.N. Mascie-Taylor. R&P contact: Linda Nicol. adv. contact: Rebecca Symons. bk.rev.; index, cum.index: 1969-1978. circ. 600. (back issues avail.) **Indexed:** A.I.C.P., Abstr.Anthropol., Abstr.Hyg., Adol.Ment.Hlth.Abstr., Anthropol.Lit., Arts & Hum.Cit.Ind., ASCA, Biol.Abstr., Curr.Cont., Curr.Lit.Fam.Plan., Dent.Ind., Diar.Dis.Res., Excerp.Med., Fam.Ind., Geo.Abstr., IDA, Ind.Med., Ind.Sci.Rev., Lang.& Lang.Behav.Abstr., Mid.East: Abstr.& Ind., Mult.Ed.Abstr., Nutr.Abstr., Popul.Ind., Psychol.Abstr. (1976-), Rural Recreat.Tour.Abstr., Sci.Cit.Ind., Sociol.Abstr., SSCI, Stud.Wom.Abstr., THA, Trop.Dis.Bull., World Agri.Econ.& Rural Sociol.Abstr. **Document type:** academic/scholarly publication.
—BLDSC (4954.100000); KNAW; SWETS; UnCover. **CCC**.
Description: Contains original papers and lectures dealing with biosocial science, the common ground between biology and sociology.
Refereed Serial

575.1 DK ISSN 0270-4145
QL991 CODEN: JCGBDF
JOURNAL OF CRANIOFACIAL GENETICS AND DEVELOPMENTAL BIOLOGY. (Text in English) 1981. q. DKK 1650 in Europe (US, Canada and Japan DKK 1620) (effective 1997). (Society of Craniofacial Genetics) Munksgaard International Publishers Ltd., P.O. Box 2148, DK-1016 Copenhagen K, Denmark. TEL 45-33-127030. FAX 45-33-129387. E-mail: fsub@mail.munksgaard.dk. (In N. America: Commerce Place, 350 Main St., Malden, MA 02148-50018. TEL 617-388-8273. FAX 617-388-8274) Eds. Michael Melnick, Harold C. Slavkin. adv.; bibl.; charts; illus.; index. circ. 400. (reprint service avail.) **Indexed:** Abstr.Anthropol., ASCA, Biol.Abstr., Chem.Abstr., Curr.Cont., Curr.Tit.Dent., Dent.Ind., Excerp.Med., Ind.Med., Ind.Sci.Rev., Sci.Cit.Ind. **Document type:** academic/scholarly publication.
—BLDSC (4965.475000); ADONIS; CASDDS; CISTI; EMDOCS; Genuine Article; KNAW; SWETS; UnCover. **CCC**.
Refereed Serial

575.1 II ISSN 0253-7605
CODEN: JCGEDO
JOURNAL OF CYTOLOGY AND GENETICS. (Text in English) 1966. s-a. Rs.100($30) to individuals; institutions Rs.250($45) (effective Jan. 1997). Society of Cytologists and Geneticists, Department of Botany, Bangalore University, Bangalore 560 056, India. TEL 91-81-3355036. Ed. Dr. B.H.M. Nijalingappa. bk.rev.; circ. 350 (controlled). **Indexed:** Chem.Abstr., Curr.Cont., Helminthol.Abstr., Plant Breed.Abstr. **Document type:** academic/scholarly publication.
—CASDDS; CISTI; Linda Hall; UnCover.
Refereed Serial

575 SZ ISSN 1010-061X
QH359 CODEN: JEBIEQ
JOURNAL OF EVOLUTIONARY BIOLOGY. (Text in English) 1988. 6/yr. 727 SFr. (foreign 745.50 SFr.) (effective 1997). (European Society for Evolutionary Biology) Birkhaeuser Verlag, P.O. Box 133, CH-4010 Basel, Switzerland. TEL 41-61-2050730. FAX 41-61-2050791. E-mail: subscriptions@birkhauser.ch. (Dist. in N. America by: Springer-Verlag, Mercedes Distribution Center, 160 Imlay St., Brooklyn, NY 11231, USA) Ed. R.F. Hoekstra. index. circ. 900. (back issues avail.) **Indexed:** Anim.Breed.Abstr., ASCA, Biol.Abstr., Curr.Adv.Biochem., Curr.Adv.Cell & Devel.Biol., Curr.Adv.Genetics & Molec.Biol., Curr.Cont., Ecol.Abstr., Ind.Sci.Rev. **Document type:** academic/scholarly publication.
•Also available online.
—BLDSC (4979.642100); CASDDS; CISTI; EMDOCS; Genuine Article; SWETS; UMI; UnCover. **CCC**.
Description: Original research on any aspect of evolutionary biology from botany, zoology and theory.

THE JOURNAL OF GENETIC PSYCHOLOGY; developmental and clinical psychology. see *PSYCHOLOGY*

575.1 II ISSN 0022-1333
QH301 CODEN: JOGNAU
JOURNAL OF GENETICS. (Text in English) 1910. 3/yr. Rs.150($100) (effective 1997). Indian Academy of Sciences, C.V. Raman Avenue, P.B. 8005, Bangalore 560 080, India. TEL 91-80-3342546. FAX 91-80-3346094. TELEX 845-2178-ACAD-IN. E-mail: jgenet@ias.ernet.in. Ed. H. Sharat Chandra. bk.rev.; charts; illus.; stat. circ. 1,000. (processed; reprint service avail. from IRC) **Indexed:** Anim.Breed.Abstr., Apic.Abstr., ASCA, Biol.Abstr., Biol.& Agr.Ind., Chem.Abstr., Compumath, Curr.Cont., Excerp.Med., Hort.Abstr., Ind.Sci.Rev., Ind.Vet., Plant Breed.Abstr., Rev.Plant Path., Risk Abstr., Sci.Cit.Ind., Vet.Bull. **Document type:** academic/scholarly publication.
—BLDSC (4990.000000); CASDDS; CISTI; Genuine Article; Linda Hall; SWETS; UnCover.

JOURNAL OF GENETICS & BREEDING. see *AGRICULTURE*

573.21 US ISSN 0022-1503
S494.A2 CODEN: JOHEA8
JOURNAL OF HEREDITY. 1910. bi-m. £40($48) to individuals; institutions £115($170); students £18($24) (effective 1998). (American Genetic Association) Oxford University Press, Journals, 2001 Evans Rd., Cary, NC 27513. TEL 919-677-0977; 800-852-7323. FAX 919-677-1714. E-mail: jnlorders@oup-usa.org; URL: http://www.oup-usa.org/. (Subscr. outside N. America to: Oxford University Press, Journals, Great Clarendon St., Oxford OX2 6DP, England. TEL 44-1865-267907. FAX 44-1865-267485) Ed. Dr. Stephen O'Brien. adv.; bk.rev.; bibl.; charts; illus. circ. 1,860. (also avail. in microform from UMI,PMC; microfiche from IDC; back issues avail.; reprint service avail. from UMI) **Indexed:** Apic.Abstr., ASCA, Bibl.Agri., Bio-Contr.News & Info., Biol.Abstr., Biol.& Agr.Ind., Biotech.Abstr., Chem.Abstr., Cott.& Trop.Fibr.Abstr., Curr.Adv.Ecol.Sci., Curr.Cont., Curr.Ref.Fish Res., Excerp.Med., Field Crop Abstr., Forest.Abstr., Forest Prod.Abstr., Gen.Sci.Ind., GeoRef., Helminthol.Abstr., Hort.Abstr., Ind.Med., Ind.Sci.Rev., Ind.Vet., INIS Atomind., Maize Abstr., Ornam.Hort., Plant Breed.Abstr., Poult.Abstr., Psychol.Abstr., Rev.Appl.Entomol., Sci.Cit.Ind., Seed Abstr., Small Anim.Abstr., Sorghum & Millets Abstr., Soyabean Abstr., Sport Fish.Abstr., Telegen, THA, Triticale Abstr., Vet.Bull., Weed Abstr., Wild.Rev., Zoo.Rec. **Document type:** academic/scholarly publication.
—BLDSC (4998.000000); CASDDS; CISTI; Genuine Article; KNAW; KR SourceOne; Linda Hall; SWETS; UMI; UnCover. **CCC**.
Description: Publishes original research, review and historical articles in organismic genetics.
Refereed Serial

JOURNAL OF HUMAN ECOLOGY; international, interdisciplinary journal of man-environment relationship. see *ENVIRONMENTAL STUDIES*

573.2 UK ISSN 0047-2484
GN281 CODEN: JHEVAT
JOURNAL OF HUMAN EVOLUTION. 1972. m. £172($304) to individuals; institutions £454 (effective 1998). Academic Press Ltd. (Subsidiary of: Harcourt Brace & Company Ltd.), 24-28 Oval Rd., London NW1 7DX, England. TEL 44-171-267-4466. FAX 44-171-482-2293. TELEX 25775 ACPRES G. E-mail: apsubs@acad.com; URL: http://www.hbuk.co.uk/ap/journals/hu. (Subscr. to: Harcourt Brace & Company Ltd., Foots Cray High St., Sidcup, Kent DA14 5HP, England. TEL 44-181-300-3322. FAX 44-181-309-0807) Eds. L. Aiello, T. Harrison. R&P contact: Catherine John. adv. contact: Nik Screen. bk.rev.; charts; illus.; index. (reprint service avail. from SWZ) **Indexed:** A.I.C.P., Abstr.Anthropol., Anthropol.Lit., Arts & Hum.Cit.Ind., ASCA, Biol.Abstr., Biostat., Br.Archaeol.Abstr., Curr.Adv.Ecol.Sci., Curr.Cont., Ecol.Abstr., Excerp.Med., Geo.Abstr.H.G., Geo.Abstr.P.G., Geol.Abstr., Ind.Sci.Rev., Mid.East: Abstr.& Ind., NAA, Sci.Cit.Ind., SSCI. **Document type:** academic/scholarly publication.
•Also available online.
—BLDSC (5003.415000); Genuine Article; KNAW; Linda Hall; SWETS; UnCover. **CCC**.
Description: Concentrates on papers covering all aspects of human evolution.

613.94 UK ISSN 0022-2593
QH431 CODEN: JMDGAE
JOURNAL OF MEDICAL GENETICS. 1964. m. £220($330) B M J Publishing Group, B.M.A. House, Tavistock Sq., London WC1H 9JR, England. TEL 44-171-383-6270. FAX 44-171-383-6402. (N. American subscr. to: Box 590A, Kennebunkport, ME 04046. TEL 800-2-FON-BMJ. FAX 800-2-FAX-BMJ) Ed. Martin Bobrow. adv. contact: Steve McAuley. bk.rev.; charts; illus.; index. (also avail. in microform from UMI; reprint service avail. from UMI) **Indexed:** Abstr.Anthropol., Abstr.Hyg., Anim.Breed.Abstr., Arts & Hum.Cit.Ind., ASCA, Bibl.Dev.Med.& Child Neur., Biol.Abstr., Chem.Abstr., Curr.Adv.Cell & Devel.Biol., Curr.Adv.Ecol.Sci., Curr.Adv.Genetics & Molec.Biol., Curr.Cont., Dent.Ind., Excerp.Med., Helminthol.Abstr., Ind.Med., Ind.Sci.Rev., Ind.Vet., INIS Atomind., Med.& Surg.Dermat., Neurosci.Cit.Ind., Nutr.Abstr., Risk Abstr., Sci.Cit.Ind., So.Pac.Per.Ind., SSCI, Trop.Dis.Bull., Vet.Bull. **Document type:** academic/scholarly publication.
—BLDSC (5017.070000); CASDDS; CISTI; Genuine Article; KNAW; SWETS; UMI; UnCover. **CCC**.
Description: Devoted to all areas of medical genetics, including clinical applications of molecular genetics, dysmorphology (the delineation and genetic basis of new syndromes), ethical and social aspects of medical genetics, and the development of medical genetic services.
Refereed Serial

575.1 US ISSN 0022-2844
QH366.A1 CODEN: JMEVAU
JOURNAL OF MOLECULAR EVOLUTION. Online edition (US ISSN 1432-1432) (Text mainly in English) 1971. m. $1063 (effective 1998). (International Society of Molecular Evolution) Springer-Verlag, Life Science Journals, 175 Fifth Ave., New York, NY 10010. TEL 212-460-1500. FAX 212-473-6272. E-mail: orders@springer-ny.com; URL: http://www.springer-ny.com. (N. American subscr. to: Journal Fulfillment Services, Box 2485, Secaucus, NJ 07096-2485. TEL 800-777-4643. FAX 201-348-4505; Elsewhere: Heidelberger Platz 3, 14197 Berlin, Germany. TEL 49-30-8207-0. FAX 49-30-8207448) Ed. Emile Zuckerkandl. R&P contact: Ian Gross. adv. contact: Robert Vrooman. (also avail. in microform from UMI; reprint service avail. from ISI) **Indexed:** Anim.Breed.Abstr., ASCA, Bibl.Agri., Biol.& Agr.Ind., Chem.Abstr., Chem.Cit.Ind., Curr.Adv.Ecol.Sci., Curr.Cont., Dairy Sci.Abstr., Excerp.Med., Food Sci.& Tech.Abstr., Helminthol.Abstr., Ind.Med., Ind.Sci.Rev., Int.Aerosp.Abstr., Plant Breed.Abstr., Poult.Abstr., Sci.Cit.Ind., Sport Fish.Abstr., Wild.Rev., Zoo.Rec. **Document type:** academic/scholarly publication.
•Also available online.
—BLDSC (5020.710000); ADONIS; CASDDS; CISTI; Ei; Genuine Article; KNAW; KR SourceOne; Linda Hall; SWETS; UMI. **CCC**.
Description: Covers molecular evolution and molecular biology. Includes a new focus on the evolutionary aspects of molecular population genetics.
Refereed Serial

KANKYO HEN'IGEN KENKYU/ENVIRONMENTAL MUTAGEN RESEARCH. see *ENVIRONMENTAL STUDIES*

575.1 JA ISSN 0080-8539
CODEN: SEZIA3
KIHARA SEIBUTSUGAKU KENKYUJO. SEIKEN JIHO/KIHARA INSTITUTE FOR BIOLOGICAL RESEARCH. REPORT. (Text in Japanese) 1941. a. 1000 Yen($8) membership. Yokohama City University, Kihara Institute for Biological Research - Yokohama Shiritsu Daigaku Kihara Seibutsugaku Kenkyujo, 122-20 Mutsukawa 3-chome, Minami-ku, Yokohama-shi, Kanagawa-ken 232, Japan. **Indexed:** Agrindex, Biol.Abstr., INIS Atomind., Jap.Per.Ind., VITIS. **Document type:** bulletin.
—CISTI.

575 JA
KIKAN KEISEI KENKYUKAI KAISHI/JAPANESE SOCIETY FOR BASIC AND APPLIED ORGAN RESEARCH. BULLETIN. (Text in Japanese) a. Kikan Keisei Kenkyukai, Nagoya Daigaku Igakubu, Koku Gekagaku Kyoshitsu, 65 Tsurumaicho, Showa-ku, Nagoya-shi, Aichi-ken 466, Japan.

KIKAN KEISEI KENKYUKAI KOEN YOSHISHU/JAPANESE SOCIETY FOR BASIC AND APPLIED ORGAN RESEARCH ABSTRACTS OF THE MEETING. see *BIOLOGY — Abstracting, Bibliographies, Statistics*

BIOLOGY — GENETICS

575 JA
KIKAN KEISEI NYUSU/JAPANESE SOCIETY FOR BASIC AND APPLIED ORGAN RESEARCH NEWS. (Text in Japanese) 1989. irreg. Kikan Keisei Kenkyukai - Japanese Society for Basic and Applied Organ Research, Nagoya Daigaku Igakubu, Koku Gekagaku Kyoshitsu, 65 Tsurumaicho, Showa-ku, Nagoya-shi, Aichi-ken 466, Japan.

KOEN BISEIBUTSU KENKYUKAI KOEN YOSHISHU/CONFERENCE ON THE BIOLOGY OF HALOPHILIC MICROORGANISMS. PROCEEDINGS. see BIOLOGY — Microbiology

575.1 616.99 KO ISSN 0254-5934
QH426 CODEN: KJGEDG
KOREAN JOURNAL OF GENETICS. (Text in English or Korean) 1979. 4/yr. 64000 Won (foreign $100). Genetics Society of Korea, c/o Department of Molecular Biology, College of Natural Science, Chungam National University, Daejon 305-764, S. Korea. TEL 82-42-821-5496. FAX 82-42-822-9690. E-mail: sgpaik@hanbat.chungnam.ac.kr. Ed. Tae In Ahn. adv.; bk.rev. circ. 500. Indexed: ASCA, Biol.Abstr., Chem.Abstr., Curr.Adv.Genetics & Molec.Biol., Genet.Abstr. Document type: academic/scholarly publication, proceedings.
—BLDSC (5113.551000); CASDDS; CISTI.
Description: Publishes original reports on any field of genetics.

573.21 US
LINKAGE NEWSLETTER. 1987. irreg. (2-3/yr.). free. Rockefeller University, Laboratory of Statistical Genetics, Box 192, 1230 York Ave., New York, NY 10021-6399. TEL 212-960-2507. FAX 212-327-7996. E-mail: ott@rockvax.rockefeller.edu; URL: http://www.rockefeller.edu. Ed. Jurg Ott. adv.
Description: Focuses on human linkage analysis with particular emphasis on statistical problems and computer programs.

LYSOSOMES AND ENDOCYTOSIS. see BIOLOGY — Biological Chemistry

572.86 611.01816 US ISSN 0938-8990
QL738.5 CODEN: MAMGEC
MAMMALIAN GENOME. Online edition (US ISSN 1432-1777) 1991. m. $590 (effective 1998). (International Mammalian Genome Society) Springer-Verlag, Life Science Journals, 175 Fifth Ave., New York, NY 10010. TEL 212-460-1500. FAX 212-473-6272. E-mail: orders@springer-ny.com; URL: http://www.springer-ny.com. (N. American subscr. to: Journal Fulfillment Services, Box 2485, Secaucus, NJ 07094-2485. TEL 800-777-4643. FAX 201-348-4505; Elsewhere: Heidelberger Platz 3, 14197 Berlin, Germany. TEL 49-30-8207-0. FAX 49-30-8207448) Ed.Bd. R&P contact: Ian Gross. adv. contact: Robert Vrooman. (also avail. in microform from UMI; back issues avail.; reprint service avail. from ISI) Indexed: ASCA, Curr.Cont., Ind.Med. (1992-), Sci.Cit.Ind. Document type: academic/scholarly publication.
●Also available online.
—BLDSC (5357.450000); ADONIS; CASDDS; CISTI; Genuine Article; KNAW; SWETS; UnCover. CCC.
Incorporates (1949-1997): Mouse Genome (ISSN 0959-0587)
Description: Presents articles on experimental, theoretical, and technical aspects of genome organization, the evolution of mice, humans, and other mammalian species.
Refereed Serial

MANKIND QUARTERLY; an international quarterly journal dealing with both physical and cultural anthropology including related subjects such as psychology, demography, genetics, linguistics and mythology. see ANTHROPOLOGY

575.1 GW ISSN 0936-5931
CODEN: MGENEZ
MEDIZINISCHE GENETIK. 1989. 4/yr. DM.120 (effective 1996). Berufsverband Medizinische Genetik e.V., Goethestr. 29, 80336 Munich, Germany. TEL 49-89-532516. FAX 49-89-5438382. E-mail: medgen@pedgen.med.uni-muenchen.de. (Co-sponsor: Gesellschaft fuer Humangenetik e.V.) Ed. Christine Scholz. adv.: B&W page DM.2100, color page DM.3580; trim 260 x 176; adv. contact: Wolfgang Kroner. circ. 2,000. Indexed: Excerp.Med. (1994-). Document type: academic/scholarly publication.
—BLDSC (5535.076700); EMDOCS.

575.1 II ISSN 0970-9649
MENDEL; multidisciplinary international journal of science. (Text in English) 1984. q. Rs.100($50) to individuals; institutions Rs.250($150). Mendelian Society of India, 194-B, S.K. Puri, Patna 800001, India. TEL 91-612-233741. Eds. R.N. Trivedi, S.N. Chaturvedi. adv.; bk.rev.; circ. 750 (controlled). (reprint service avail.) Document type: academic/scholarly publication.
—BLDSC (5678.439700).
Description: Publishes papers and general articles of common interest in all fields of science and medicine.

575.1 AG ISSN 0325-223X
MENDELIANA. (Text in Spanish; summaries in English) 1976. s-a. Arg.$10($15) (effective 1997-98). Sociedad Argentina de Genetica, CC 25, 1712 Castelar, Argentina. FAX 54-111-1917. Ed. Sol L. Rabasa. bk.rev. circ. 650. (back issues avail.) Indexed: Biol.Abstr., Excerp.Med., Genet.Abstr., Ref.Zh.
—KNAW.
Description: Covers all areas of genetics.

METHODS IN CELL SCIENCE. see BIOLOGY — Microbiology

575.1 US ISSN 1067-2389
CODEN: MEMGE6
METHODS IN MOLECULAR GENETICS. 1993. irreg., latest vol.8. Academic Press, Inc., 525 B St., Ste. 1900, San Diego, CA 92101-4495. TEL 619-230-1840. FAX 619-699-6800. URL: http://www.apnet.com. Document type: monographic series.
—BLDSC (5748.202200); CASDDS; CISTI. CCC.

575.1 574.87 660 US
CODEN: GSTEFY
MICROBIAL & COMPARATIVE GENOMICS. 1994. q. $876 to individuals (foreign $290); institutions $431 (foreign $466) (effective through 1998). Mary Ann Liebert, Inc. Publishers, 2 Madison Ave., Larchmont, NY 10538. TEL 914-834-3100. FAX 914-834-3688. E-mail: liebert@pipeline.com. Ed. J. Craig Venter. Document type: academic/scholarly publication.
●Also available on CD-ROM.
—CASDDS; CISTI.
Formerly: Genome Science and Technology (ISSN 1070-2830)
Description: Offers a unique repository for genome and DNA sequencing; mapping, informatics, biological interpretations, human disease, ethical, legal, and social issues, new technology, and computational approaches.
Refereed Serial

575.1 GW ISSN 0026-8925
QH431 CODEN: MGGEAE
MOLECULAR AND GENERAL GENETICS; an international journal. Short title: M G G. Online edition (GW ISSN 1432-1874) (Text in English) 1908. 24/yr. DM.4980 (foreign DM.5038.80) (effective 1998). Springer-Verlag, Heidelberger Platz 3, 14197 Berlin, Germany. TEL 49-30-82787-0. FAX 49-30-82787448. E-mail: subscriptions@springer.de; URL: http://link.springer.de/link/service/journals/00438/index.htm. (Subscr. in N. America to: Springer-Verlag New York, Inc., 333 Meadowlands Pkwy., Secaucus, NJ 07094. TEL 212-460-1500. FAX 212-473-6272) Ed. J. Campos-Ortega. adv.; charts; illus. (also avail. in microform from UMI; back issues avail.; reprint service avail. from ISI) Indexed: ASCA, Bibl.Agri., Biol.Abstr., Biol.& Agr.Ind., Biotech.Abstr., Chem.Abstr., Cott.& Trop.Fibr.Abstr., Crop Physiol.Abstr., Curr.Adv.Biochem., Curr.Adv.Ecol.Sci., Curr.Adv.Genetics & Molec.Biol., Curr.Biotech.Abstr., Curr.Cont., Dairy Sci.Abstr., Excerp.Med., Field Crop Abstr., Food Sci.& Tech.Abstr., Helminthol.Abstr., Ind.Med., Ind.Sci.Rev., Maize Abstr., Ornam.Hort., Plant Breed.Abstr., Potato Abstr., Rice Abstr., Sci.Cit.Ind., Seed Abstr., Soils & Fert., Soyabean Abstr., Triticale Abstr., Weed Abstr. Document type: academic/scholarly publication.
●Also available online.
—BLDSC (5900.764000); ADONIS; CASDDS; CISTI; Genuine Article; KR SourceOne; Linda Hall; SWETS; UMI; UnCover. CCC.
Formerly: Zeitschrift fuer Vererbungslehre.
Description: For biotechnicians, microbiologists, virologists, and biochemists. Covers the genetics of prokaryotes, including plastids, mitochondria, plasmids, "jumping genes", and transposable elements. Provides background research on the molecular genetics of eukaryotes, and its practical applications in genetic engineering.

575.1 US ISSN 0891-4168
QH506
MOLECULAR GENETICS, MICROBIOLOGY AND VIROLOGY. English translation of: Molekulyarnaya Genetika, Mikrobiologiya i Virusologiya (UR ISSN 0208-0613) 1986. bi-m. $790 (effective 1998). (Biotechnologicheskaya Akademiya, RU - Biotechnology Academy) Allerton Press, Inc., 150 Fifth Ave., New York, NY 10011. TEL 212-924-3950. FAX 212-463-9684. Ed. E.D. Sverdlov. Document type: academic/scholarly publication.
—BLDSC (0416.235500); CISTI. CCC.
Description: Covers microbiology, virology, genetic engineering, immunology, DNA, methodology of molecular genetics.
Refereed Serial

MOLECULAR NEUROBIOLOGY; a review journal. see MEDICAL SCIENCES — Psychiatry And Neurology

575.1 US ISSN 1055-7903
QH367.5 CODEN: MPEVEK
MOLECULAR PHYLOGENETICS AND EVOLUTION. 1992. bi-m. $235 (foreign $285) (effective 1997). Academic Press, Inc., Journal Division, 525 B St., Ste. 1900, San Diego, CA 92101-4495. TEL 619-230-1840. FAX 619-699-6800. E-mail: apsubs@acad.com; URL: http://www.apnet.com/www/journal/fy.htm; http://www.idealibrary.com/. (Subscr. to: Box 861213, Orlando, FL 32886-1213. TEL 407-347-4040. FAX 407-363-9661) Ed. Morris Goodman. adv. (back issues avail.) Indexed: ASCA, Chem.Abstr., Ind.Med. (1993-). Document type: academic/scholarly publication.
●Also available online.
—BLDSC (5900.819800); CASDDS; CISTI; Genuine Article; SWETS; UnCover. CCC.
Description: Provides a forum for molecular studies that advance our understanding of phylogeny and evolution. Encourages collaboration of molecular biologists and computer scientists, with systematic and evolutionary biologists.
Refereed Serial

MOLECULAR PLANT - MICROBE INTERACTIONS. see BIOLOGY — Botany

BIOLOGY — GENETICS

577.1 576.64   **RU**   ISSN 0208-0613
QR74   CODEN: MGMVDU
MOLEKULYARNAYA GENETIKA, MIKROBIOLOGIYA I VIRUSOLOGIYA. English translation: Molecular Genetics, Microbiology and Virology (US ISSN 0891-4168) (Text in Russian; summaries in English) 1983. q. $144 (effective 1998). (Biotechnologicheskya Akademiya) Izdatel'stvo Meditsina, Petroverigskii pereulok 6-8, 101000 Moscow, Russia. TEL 7-095-9248785. FAX 7-095-9286003. TELEX 412282 MEDIZ SU. (Dist. by: Mezhdunarodnaya Kniga, B. Yakimanka 39, 117049 Moscow, Russia. TEL 7-095-2384967. FAX 7-095-2384634) Ed. Ye.D. Sverdlov. adv. contact: O.A. Fadeeva. circ. 500. **Indexed:** Biol.Abstr., Chem.Abstr., Curr.Cont., Ind.Med.
—CASDDS; CISTI; KNAW; Linda Hall.
    Description: Deals with fundamental and applied problems of molecular genetics, molecular microbiology and molecular virology.

613.9   **SZ**   ISSN 0077-0876
QH431   CODEN: MOHGAD
MONOGRAPHS IN HUMAN GENETICS. (Text in English) 1966. irreg. (approx. 1/yr.). price varies. S. Karger AG, Allschwilerstr. 10, P.O. Box, CH-4009 Basel, Switzerland. TEL 41-61-3061111. FAX 41-61-3061234. E-mail: karger@karger.ch; URL: http://www.karger.ch. (reprint service avail. from ISI) **Indexed:** Biol.Abstr., Chem.Abstr., Curr.Cont., Ind.Med. **Document type:** monographic series.
—BLDSC (5915.450000); CASDDS; CISTI; KNAW. **CCC.**
    Description: Sophisticated genetic studies transformed into clear interpretations of their medical importance.
Refereed Serial

575   **US**   ISSN 0341-5376
MONOGRAPHS ON THEORETICAL AND APPLIED GENETICS. 1975. irreg., vol.21, 1994. price varies. Springer-Verlag, 175 Fifth Ave., New York, NY 10010. TEL 212-460-1500. FAX 212-473-6272. Ed.Bd. (reprint service avail. from ISI) **Indexed:** Biol.Abstr. **Document type:** monographic series.
—BLDSC (5917.773000); CISTI.

575.1   **UK**   ISSN 0267-8357
QH465.A1   CODEN: MUTAEX
MUTAGENESIS. 1986. bi-m. £255 (foreign $405) (effective 1998). (U.K. Environmental Mutagen Society) Oxford University Press, Academic Division, Great Clarendon St., Oxford OX2 6DP, England. TEL 44-1865-267907. FAX 44-1865-267485. TELEX 837330-OXPRES-G. E-mail: jnl.info@oup.co.uk; URL: http://www.oup.co.uk/journals. (Subscr. in U.S. to: Oxford University Press Inc., 2001 Evans Rd., Cary, NC 27513. TEL 800-852-7323. FAX 919-677-1714) Ed.Bd.; Pub. Steven Johnson. R&P contact: Joolz Longley. adv.; bk.rev.; illus.; index. circ. 600. (back issues avail.; reprint service avail. from SWZ) **Indexed:** ASCA, Biol.Abstr., Chem.Abstr., Curr.Adv.Ecol.Sci., Curr.Cont., Excerp.Med., Ind.Sci.Rev., Sci.Cit.Ind. **Document type:** academic/scholarly publication.
—BLDSC (5991.895500); CASDDS; CISTI; EMDOCS; Genuine Article; KNAW; SWETS; UMI; UnCover. **CCC.**
    Description: International, multi-disciplinary journal for genetic toxicology research. Includes genetic mutation studies, mutagenicity testing guidelines, test program results, letters, and reviews.

575.29   **NE**   ISSN 0921-8262
MUTATION RESEARCH; international journal on mutagenesis, chromosome breakage and related subjects. (Consists of: Fundamental and Molecular Mechanisms of Mutagenesis (ISSN 0027-5107); D N A Repair (ISSN 0921-8777); Genetic Toxicology and Environmental Mutagenesis; Mutation Research Genomics (ISSN 1383-5726); Mutation Research Letters (ISSN 0165-7992); Reviews in Genetic Toxicology (ISSN 0165-1110); Reviews in Mutation Research (ISSN 1383-5742)) (Text in English, French and German) 1964. 63/yr. fl.11952($7378) (effective 1997). Elsevier Science B.V., P.O. Box 211, 1000 AE Amsterdam, Netherlands. TEL 31-20-4853911. FAX 31-20-4853598. TELEX 18582 ESPA NL. E-mail: nlinfo-f@elsevier.nl; usinfo-f@elsevier.com; forinfo-kyf04035@niftyserve.or.jp; URL: http://www.elsevier.nl/. (Subscr. in the Americas to: Elsevier Science, Regional Sales Office, Box 945, New York, NY 10159-0945. TEL 212-633-3730. FAX 212-633-3680; Subscr. in Australasia and the Far East to: Elsevier Science (Singapore) Pte Ltd, No.1 Temasek Ave., No.17-01 Millenia Tower, Singapore 039192, Singapore. TEL 65-434-3727. FAX 65-337-2230; Subscr. in Japan to: Elsevier Science Japan, 9-15 Higashi-Azabu 1-chome, Minato-ku, Tokyo 106, Japan. TEL 81-3-5561-5033. FAX 81-3-5561-5047) Ed.Bd. adv.; charts; illus. (also avail. in microform from UMI) **Indexed:** Anim.Breed.Abstr., Biol.Abstr., C.I.S. Abstr., Chem.Abstr., Chem.Cit.Ind., Crop Physiol.Abstr., Curr.Adv.Cell & Devel.Biol., Curr.Adv.Ecol.Sci., Curr.Adv.Genetics & Molec.Biol., Curr.Cont., Dairy Sci.Abstr., Dent.Ind., Dok.Arbeitsmed., Excerp.Med., Fababean Abstr., Field Crop Abstr., Food Sci.& Tech.Abstr., Helminthol.Abstr., Ind.Med., Ind.Sci.Rev., Ind.Vet., Lab.Haz.Bull., Maize Abstr., Plant Breed.Abstr., Plant Grow.Reg.Abstr., Poult.Abstr., Protozool.Abstr., Rev.Appl.Entomol., Rev.Med.& Vet.Mycol., Rev.Plant Path., Risk Abstr., Sci.Cit.Ind., Seed Abstr., Sel.Water Res.Abstr., Soils & ils & Fert., Sport Fish.Abstr., SSCI, Triticale Abstr., Trop.Dis.Bull., W.R.C.Inf., Weed Abstr., Wild.Rev., Zoo.Rec. **Document type:** academic/scholarly publication.
—CISTI; Genuine Article; Linda Hall. **CCC.**
Incorporates: Environmental Mutagen Society Newsletter (ISSN 0013-9319)
Refereed Serial

575.29   **NE**   ISSN 0921-8777
       CODEN: MDRRE
MUTATION RESEARCH - D N A REPAIR. (Section of: Mutation Research (ISSN 0921-8262)) 1983. 9/yr. fl.1706($980) (effective 1998). Elsevier Science B.V., P.O. Box 211, 1000 AE Amsterdam, Netherlands. TEL 31-20-4853911. FAX 31-20-4853598. TELEX 18582 ESPA NL. E-mail: nlinfo-f@elsevier.nl; usinfo-f@elsevier.com; forinfo-kyf04035@niftyserve.or.jp; URL: http://www.elsevier.nl/. (Subscr. in the Americas to: Elsevier Science, Regional Sales Office, Box 945, New York, NY 10159-0945. TEL 212-633-3730. FAX 212-633-3680; Subscr. in Australasia and the Far East to: Elsevier Science (Singapore) Pte Ltd, No.1 Temasek Ave., No.17-01 Millenia Tower, Singapore 039192, Singapore. TEL 65-434-3727. FAX 65-337-2230; Subscr. in Japan to: Elsevier Science Japan, 9-15 Higashi-Azabu 1-chome, Minato-ku, Tokyo 106, Japan. TEL 81-3-5561-5033. FAX 81-3-5561-5047) Ed. F.H. Sobels. (also avail. in microform from UMI; back issues avail.) **Indexed:** ASCA, Biol.Abstr., Bull.Signal., Chem.Abstr., Curr.Cont., Curr.Cont., Excerp.Med., Ind.Med., Ind.Sci.Rev. **Document type:** academic/scholarly publication.
—ADONIS; EMDOCS; Genuine Article; KNAW; SWETS. **CCC.**
Formerly (until 1988): Mutation Research - D N A Repair - Reports (ISSN 0167-8817)
    Description: Topics include: comparisons of cell-to-tissues systems; cloned DNA repair genes; trasformation and mutagen testing.
Refereed Serial

575.29   **NE**   ISSN 0027-5107
QH431   CODEN: MUREAV
MUTATION RESEARCH - FUNDAMENTAL AND MOLECULAR MECHANISMS OF MUTAGENESIS. (Section of: Mutation Research (ISSN 0921-8262)) (Text in English, French, German) 1964. 16/yr. (in 8 vols.). fl.9499($4999) includes 6 sub-sections (effective 1995). Elsevier Science B.V., P.O. Box 211, 1000 AE Amsterdam, Netherlands. TEL 31-20-4853911. FAX 31-20-4853598. TELEX 18582 ESPA NL. E-mail: nlinfo-f@elsevier.nl; usinfo-f@elsevier.com; forinfo-kyf04035@niftyserve.or.jp; URL: http://www.elsevier.nl/. (Subscr. in the Americas to: Elsevier Science, Regional Sales Office, Box 945, New York, NY 10159-0945. TEL 212-633-3730. FAX 212-633-3680; Subscr. in Australasia and the Far East to: Elsevier Science (Singapore) Pte Ltd, No.1 Temasek Ave., No.17-01 Millenia Tower, Singapore 039192, Singapore. TEL 65-434-3727. FAX 65-337-2230; Subscr. in Japan to: Elsevier Science Japan, 9-15 Higashi-Azabu 1-chome, Minato-ku, Tokyo 106, Japan. TEL 81-3-5561-5033. FAX 81-3-5561-5047) Ed.Bd. adv.; charts; illus.; index. (also avail. in microform from UMI; back issues avail.) **Indexed:** ASCA, Biol.Abstr., Chem.Abstr., Curr.Cont., Excerp.Med., Food Sci.& Tech.Abstr., Ind.Med., Ind.Sci.Rev. **Document type:** academic/scholarly publication.
—BLDSC (5991.900000); ADONIS; CASDDS; CISTI; Genuine Article; SWETS; UnCover. **CCC.**
Refereed Serial

575.29   **NE**
       CODEN: MRGTE
MUTATION RESEARCH - GENETIC TOXICOLOGY AND ENVIRONMENTAL MUTAGENESIS. (Section of: Mutation Research (ISSN 0921-8262)) 1988. 27/yr. fl.5117($2941) (effective 1998). Elsevier Science B.V., P.O. Box 211, 1000 AE Amsterdam, Netherlands. TEL 31-20-4853911. FAX 31-20-4853598. TELEX 18582 ESPA NL. E-mail: nlinfo-f@elsevier.nl; usinfo-f@elsevier.com; forinfo-kyf04035@niftyserve.or.jp; URL: http://www.elsevier.nl/. (Subscr. in the Americas to: Elsevier Science, Regional Sales Office, Box 945, New York, NY 10159-0945. TEL 212-633-3730. FAX 212-633-3680; Subscr. in Australasia and the Far East to: Elsevier Science (Singapore) Pte Ltd, No.1 Temasek Ave., No.17-01 Millenia Tower, Singapore 039192, Singapore. TEL 65-434-3727. FAX 65-337-2230; Subscr. in Japan to: Elsevier Science Japan, 9-15 Higashi-Azabu 1-chome, Minato-ku, Tokyo 106, Japan. TEL 81-3-5561-5033. FAX 81-3-5561-5047) Ed. F.H. Sobels. (also avail. in microform from UMI; back issues avail.) **Indexed:** ASCA, Curr.Cont., Excerp.Med., Food Sci.& Tech.Abstr., Ind.Med., Ind.Sci.Rev. **Document type:** academic/scholarly publication.
—ADONIS; Genuine Article; SWETS. **CCC.**
Former titles (until 1997): Mutation Research - Genetic Toxicology; (until 1994): Mutation Research - Genetic Toxicology Testing (ISSN 0165-1218); **Incorporates** (in 1996): Mutation Research - Environmental Mutagenesis and Related Subjects; Which had former titles (until 1994): Mutation Research - Section on Environmental Mutagenesis and Related Subjects including Methodology; Mutation Research - Section on Environmental Mutagenesis and Related Subjects (ISSN 0165-1161)
    Description: Covers all aspects of genetic toxicology and biomonitoring of environmental and occupational exposure to mutagens.
Refereed Serial

BIOLOGY — GENETICS

575.29 NE ISSN 0165-7992
CODEN: MRLED
MUTATION RESEARCH LETTERS. (Section of: Mutation Research (ISSN 0921-8262)) 1988. 12/yr. (in 3 vols.; 4 nos./vol.) fl.1326($698) (effective 1995). Elsevier Science B.V., P.O. Box 211, 1000 AE Amsterdam, Netherlands. TEL 31-20-4853911. FAX 31-20-4853598. TELEX 18582 ESPA NL. E-mail: nlinfo-f@elsevier.nl; usinfo-f@elsevier.com; forinfo-kyf04035@niftyserve.or.jp; URL: http://www.elsevier.nl/. (Subscr. in the Americas to: Elsevier Science, Regional Sales Office, Box 945, New York, NY 10159-0945. TEL 212-633-3730. FAX 212-633-3680; Subscr. in Australasia and the Far East to: Elsevier Science (Singapore) Pte Ltd, No.1 Temasek Ave., No.17-01 Millenia Tower, Singapore 039192, Singapore. TEL 65-434-3727. FAX 65-337-2230; Subscr. in Japan to: Elsevier Science Japan, 9-15 Higashi-Azabu 1-chome, Minato-ku, Tokyo 106, Japan. TEL 81-3-5561-5033. FAX 81-3-5561-5047) Eds. S. Galloway, J.M. Gentile. (also avail. in microform from UMI; back issues avail.) **Indexed:** ASCA, Curr.Cont., Excerp.Med., Food Sci.& Tech.Abstr., Ind.Med. **Document type:** academic/scholarly publication.
—Genuine Article. **CCC.**
Description: Specializes in the rapid publication of short communications on progressive work in the field of mutation research.
Refereed Serial

575.1 NE ISSN 1383-5726
▼**MUTATION RESEARCH - MUTATION RESEARCH GENOMICS.** (Section of: Mutation Research (ISSN 0921-8262)) (Text in English) 1997. q. fl.569($327) (effective 1998). Elsevier Science B.V., P.O. Box 211, 1000 AE Amsterdam, Netherlands. TEL 31-20-4853757. FAX 31-20-4853432. E-mail: nlinfo-f@elsevier.nl; usinfo-f@elsevier.nl; URL: http://www.elsevier.nl/. (Subscr. in the Americas to: Elsevier Science, Regional Sales Office, Box 945, New York, NY 10159-0945. TEL 212-633-3730. FAX 212-633-3680; Subscr. in Australasia and the Far East to: Elsevier Science (Singapore) Pte Ltd, No.1 Temasek Ave., No.17-01 Millenia Tower, Singapore 039192, Singapore. TEL 35-434-3727. FAX 35-337-2230; Subscr. in Japan to: Elsevier Science Japan, 9-15 Higashi-Azabu 1-chome, Minato-ku, Tokyo 106, Japan) **Document type:** academic/scholarly publication.
Refereed Serial

575.29 NE ISSN 0165-1110
MUTATION RESEARCH - REVIEWS IN GENETIC TOXICOLOGY. (Section of: Mutation Research (ISSN 0921-8262)) 1988. bi-m. fl.938($572) (effective 1996). Elsevier Science B.V., P.O. Box 211, 1000 AE Amsterdam, Netherlands. TEL 31-20-4853911. FAX 31-20-4853598. TELEX 18582 ESPA NL. E-mail: nlinfo-f@elsevier.nl; usinfo-f@elsevier.com; forinfo-kyf04035@niftyserve.or.jp; URL: http://www.elsevier.nl/. (Subscr. in the Americas to: Elsevier Science, Regional Sales Office, Box 945, New York, NY 10159-0945. TEL 212-633-3730. FAX 212-633-3680; Subscr. in Australasia and the Far East to: Elsevier Science (Singapore) Pte Ltd, No.1 Temasek Ave., No.17-01 Millenia Tower, Singapore 039192, Singapore. TEL 65-434-3727. FAX 65-337-2230; Subscr. in Japan to: Elsevier Science Japan, 9-15 Higashi-Azabu 1-chome, Minato-ku, Tokyo 106, Japan. TEL 81-3-5561-5033. FAX 81-3-5561-5047) Eds. F.H. Sobels, Frederick J. de Serres. (also avail. in microform from UMI; back issues avail.) **Indexed:** ASCA, Biol.Abstr., Bull.Signal., Chem.Abstr., Curr.Cont., Excerp.Med., Ind.Med., Ind.Sci.Rev. **Document type:** academic/scholarly publication.
—ADONIS; CISTI; Genuine Article. **CCC.**
Description: Provides a medium for the dissemination of advanced reviews in the field of genetic toxicology.
Refereed Serial

575.29 NE ISSN 1383-5742
MUTATION RESEARCH - REVIEWS IN MUTATION RESEARCH. (Text in English) bi-m. fl.1137($653) (effective 1998). Elsevier Science B.V., P.O. Box 211, 1000 AE Amsterdam, Netherlands. TEL 31-20-4853757. FAX 31-20-4853432. E-mail: nlinfo-f@elsevier.nl; usinfo-f@elsevier.com; kyf04035@niftyserve.or.jp; URL: http://www.elsevier.nl/. (Subscr. in the Americas to: Elsevier Science, Regional Sales Office, Box 945, New York, NY 10159-0945. TEL 212-633-3730. FAX 212-633-3680; Subscr. in Australasia and the Far East to: Elsevier Science (Singapore) Pte Ltd, No.1 Temasek Ave., No.17-01 Millenia Tower, Singapore 039192, Singapore. TEL 65-434-3727. FAX 65-337-2230; Subscr. in Japan to: Elsevier Science Japan, 9-15 Higashi-Azabu 1-chome, Minato-ku, Tokyo 106, Japan. TEL 81-3-5561-5033. FAX 81-3-5561-5047) **Document type:** academic/scholarly publication.
—SWETS. **CCC.**

575 JA ISSN 0077-4995
QH431.A1
NATIONAL INSTITUTE OF GENETICS. ANNUAL REPORT (ENGLISH EDITION). Japanese edition: Kokuritsu Idengaku Kenkyujo Nenpo. (Text in English) 1949. a. free. Ministry of Education, National Institute of Genetics - Monbusho Kokuritsu Idengaku Kenkyujo, 1111 Yata, Mishima-shi, Shizuoka-ken 411, Japan. circ. 600.
—BLDSC (1364.700000); KNAW; Linda Hall.

575.1 US ISSN 1061-4036
QH431 CODEN: NGENEC
NATURE GENETICS. (Supplement to: Nature (ISSN 0028-0836)) 1992. m. $530 (Canada $567; Central & Sourh America $675) (effective 1998). Macmillan Magazines Ltd. (Subsidiary of: Macmillan Publishers Ltd.), 1234 National Press Bldg., Washington, DC 20045. TEL 202-626-2513; 202-628-1609. (Subscr. to: Nature, 345 Park Ave. S., New York, NY 10160-1743. TEL 800-524-0384; Subscr. in UK and Europe to: Macmillan Magazines Ltd., Brunel Rd., Basingstoke, Hants RG21 2XS, England. TEL 44-256-29242) Ed. Kevin Davies. adv. contact: Marion Delancy. circ. 3,000. **Indexed:** Arts & Hum.Cit.Ind., ASCA, Bibl.Agri., Biol.& Agr.Ind., Curr.Cont., Diab.Cont., Excerp.Med. (1993-), Ind.Sci.Rev., Sci.Cit.Ind., SSCI. **Document type:** academic/scholarly publication.
—BLDSC (6046.625000); CASDDS; CISTI; EMDOCS; Genuine Article; KNAW; KR SourceOne; SWETS; UnCover. **CCC.**
Description: Comprehensive coverage of new developments and issues in all branches of genetics, with particular emphasis on the human genome project and genetic aspects of disease.

575.1 616.8 US
NEURO-FIBROMA-TOSIS. q. National Neurofibromatosis Foundation, Inc., 95 Pine St., Fl. 16, New York, NY 10005-1611. TEL 212-344-6633. FAX 212-747-0004. E-mail: nnff@aol.com; URL: http://www.nf.org.

575.1 616.8 US
NEURO-FIBROMA-TOSIS RESEARCH NEWSLETTER. s-a. free. National Neurofibromatosis Foundation, Inc., 95 Pine St., Fl. 16, New York, NY 10005-1611. TEL 212-344-6633. FAX 212-747-0004. E-mail: nnff@aol.com; URL: http://www.nf.org. Ed. Bruce Korff. **Document type:** newsletter.

NEUROGENETICS. see *MEDICAL SCIENCES — Psychiatry And Neurology*

NIHON IDEN GAKKAI TAIKAI PUROGURAMU YOKOSHU/GENETICS SOCIETY OF JAPAN. ABSTRACTS OF THE ANNUAL MEETING. see *BIOLOGY — Abstracting, Bibliographies, Statistics*

NIHON JINRUI IDEN GAKKAI TAIKAI SHOROKUSHU/JAPAN SOCIETY OF HUMAN GENETICS. ABSTRACTS OF THE ANNUAL MEETING. see *BIOLOGY — Abstracting, Bibliographies, Statistics*

NIHON SENSHOKUTAI KENSA GAKKAI SHOROKUSHU/JAPANESE ASSOCIATION FOR CHROMOSOME ANALYSIS. ABSTRACT OF ANNUAL MEETING. see *BIOLOGY — Abstracting, Bibliographies, Statistics*

581 JA ISSN 0917-8155
NIHON SENSHOKUTAI KENSA GAKKAI ZASSHI/JAPANESE ASSOCIATION FOR CHROMOSOME ANALYSIS. OFFICIAL JOURNAL. (Text in English, Japanese; summaries in English) 1983. q. Nihon Senshokutai Kensa Gakkai, c/o Kurasuta Koa Kenkyujo Idenshi Kenkyubu, 11-18, Tsubamesawa Higashi 3-chome, Miyagino-ku, Sendai-shi, Miyagi-ken 983, Japan.

575.1 UK
NORWICH RESEARCH PARK NEWSLETTER. 1987. s-a. $10. University of East Anglia, School of Biological Sciences, Norwich, Norfolk NR4 7TJ, England. TEL 0603-592197. FAX 0603-259492. Ed. Richard James. circ. 600. (tabloid format; back issues avail.) **Document type:** newsletter.
Formerly: Biological Research in Norwich.

NUCLEUS; international journal of cytology and allied topics. see *BIOLOGY — Cytology And Histology*

ON THE BEAM. see *HANDICAPPED — Visually Impaired*

ONCOGENE. see *MEDICAL SCIENCES — Oncology*

ONCOGENES. see *MEDICAL SCIENCES — Abstracting, Bibliographies, Statistics*

OXFORD MONOGRAPHS ON MEDICAL GENETICS. see *MEDICAL SCIENCES*

575.1 UK ISSN 0265-072X
QH359 CODEN: OSEBE3
OXFORD SURVEYS IN EVOLUTIONARY BIOLOGY. 1984. a. price varies. Oxford University Press, Oxford Journals, Walton St., Oxford OX2 6DP, England. TEL 01865-267907. FAX 01865-267773. TELEX 837330-OXPRES-G. E-mail: jnlorders@oup.co.uk. (U.S. subscr. to: Oxford University Press Inc., 2001 Evans Rd., Cary, NC 27513. TEL 919-677-0977. FAX 919-677-1714) bk.rev. **Indexed:** Anim.Breed.Abstr., Curr.Adv.Genetics & Molec.Biol., Sport Fish.Abstr., Wild.Rev., Zoo.Rec. **Document type:** academic/scholarly publication.
—CISTI; UnCover.

375.1 UK ISSN 0265-0738
QH426 CODEN: OSEGEI
OXFORD SURVEYS ON EUKARYOTIC GENES. 1984. a. price varies. Oxford University Press, Oxford Journals, Walton St., Oxford OX2 6DP, England. TEL 44-1865-267907. FAX 44-1865-267773. TELEX 837330-OXPRES-G. E-mail: jnlorders@oup.co.uk. (U.S. subscr. to: Oxford University Press Inc., 2001 Evans Rd., Cary, NC 27513. TEL 919-677-0977. FAX 919-677-0977) Ed. Norman Maclean. **Indexed:** Anim.Breed.Abstr., Ind.Med., Pig News & Info. **Document type:** academic/scholarly publication.
—CASDDS; CISTI; KNAW; Linda Hall.
Description: Forum for authoritative reviews of particular genes or gene families whose structure or function is better understood as a result of recent research.

575.1 615.7 UK ISSN 0960-314X
CODEN: PHMCEE
PHARMACOGENETICS. 1991. bi-m. $110 to individuals; institutions $325 (effective 1996). Chapman & Hall, Journals Department (Subsidiary of: International Thomson Publishing Group), 2-6 Boundary Row, London SE1 8HN, England. TEL 44-171-8650066. FAX 44-171-5229623. TELEX 290164 CHAPMA G. E-mail: jhelp@chall.co.uk; URL: http://www.chaphall.com/chaphall/journals.html. (Dist. by: International Thomson Publishing Services Ltd., Cheriton House, North Way, Andover, Hants. SP10 5BE, England. TEL 44-1264-342713. FAX 44-1264-342807; Subscr. in US & Canada to: 400 Market St., Philadelphia, PA 19106. TEL 800-552-5866) Ed.Bd. (reprint service avail.) **Indexed:** ASCA, Chem.Abstr., Curr.Cont., Excerp.Med. (1993-), Ind.Med. (1993-), SSCI. **Document type:** academic/scholarly publication.
●Also available online.
—BLDSC (6446.249000); ADONIS; CASDDS; CISTI; EMDOCS; Genuine Article; KNAW; SWETS. **CCC.**
Description: Devoted to the rapid publication of research papers, brief review articles, and short communications on genetic variation in response to drugs in humans and animals.
Refereed Serial

BIOLOGY — GENETICS

575.1 SZ ISSN 0301-0139
CODEN: PGTCA4
PIGMENT CELL. (Text in English) 1973. irreg. (approx. 1/yr.). price varies. S. Karger AG, Allschwilerstr. 10, P.O. Box, CH-4009 Basel, Switzerland. TEL 41-61-3061111. FAX 41-61-3061234. E-mail: karger@karger.ch; URL: http://www.karger.ch. (reprint service avail. from ISI) **Indexed:** Biol.Abstr., Chem.Abstr. **Document type:** academic/scholarly publication.
—CASDDS; CISTI; KNAW. **CCC**.
Refereed Serial

PLANT MOLECULAR BIOLOGY REPORTER. see *BIOLOGY — Botany*

575.1 US ISSN 1057-2600
PROBE (BELTSVILLE). 1991. q. free. U.S. National Agricultural Library, U.S. Department of Agriculture, 10301 Baltimore Ave., 4th Fl., Beltsville, MD 20705-2351. TEL 301-504-6613. FAX 301-504-7098. E-mail: pgenome@nal.usda.gov; URL: http://www.nalusda.gov:80/answers/info_center/pgdic/probe/v4n3_4.html. Ed. Susan McCarthy. R&P contact: Susan McCarthy. **Document type:** government publication.
●Also available online.
Description: Designed to facilitate interaction throughout the plant genome-mapping community and beyond.

575 US ISSN 0733-9003
CODEN: PTCYDB
PROGRESS AND TOPICS IN CYTOGENETICS. 1981. irreg., vol.8, 1989. price varies. John Wiley & Sons, Inc., Journals, 605 Third Ave., New York, NY 10158. TEL 212-475-7700. **Indexed:** Biol.Abstr., Chem.Abstr.
—CASDDS; CISTI; KNAW. **CCC**.
Refereed Serial

575.1 NE ISSN 0731-2849
CODEN: PMRSDJ
PROGRESS IN MUTATION RESEARCH. 1981. irreg., vol.5, 1985. price varies. Elsevier Science B.V., Books Division, P.O. Box 211, 1000 AE Amsterdam, Netherlands. TEL 31-20-4853911. FAX 31-20-4853705. TELEX 18582 ESPA NL. E-mail: nlinfo-f@elsevier.nl; usinfo-f@elsevier.com; forinfo-kyf04035@niftyserve.or.jp; URL: http://www.elsevier.nl/. (Subscr. in the Americas to: Elsevier Science, Regional Sales Office, Box 945, New York, NY 10159-0945. TEL 212-633-3730. FAX 212-633-3680; Subscr. in Australasia and the Far East to: Elsevier Science (Singapore) Pte Ltd, No.1 Temasek Ave., No.17-01 Millenia Tower, Singapore 039192, Singapore. TEL 65-434-3727. FAX 65-337-2230; Subscr. in Japan to: Elsevier Science Japan, 9-15 Higashi-Azabu 1-chome, Minato-ku, Tokyo 106, Japan. TEL 81-3-5561-5033. FAX 81-3-5561-5047) **Document type:** monographic series.
—CASDDS. **CCC**.
Refereed Serial

575.1 UK ISSN 0955-8829
CODEN: PSGEEX
PSYCHIATRIC GENETICS. 1990. q. £69($115) to individuals; institutions £165($280) (effective 1996). Rapid Science Publishers, The Old Malthouse, Paradise St., Oxford OX1 1LD, England. TEL 44-1865-790447. FAX 44-1865-244012. E-mail: marketing@rapidcom.co.uk. (Subscr. in US to: 115 Fifth Ave., 4th Fl., New York, NY 10003. TEL 212-780-6234. FAX 212-260-1363) Ed. John Nurnberger. adv. contact: Julie Gribben. bk.rev. **Indexed:** ASCA, Excerp.Med. (1993-), Ind.Med. (1994-), Neurosci.Cit.Ind., Psychol.Abstr. (1990-), Psychol.Abstr., SSCI. **Document type:** academic/scholarly publication.
●Also available on CD-ROM.
—BLDSC (6946.214050); ADONIS; CISTI; EMDOCS; Genuine Article; KNAW. **CCC**.
Description: Forum for novel approaches using new technologies to better understand the normal and abnormal brain.
Refereed Serial

R N A. (Ribonucleic Acid) see *BIOLOGY — Biological Chemistry*

RINBOKU NO IKUSHU/FOREST TREE BREEDING. see *FORESTS AND FORESTRY*

ROCZNIKI NAUKOWE ZOOTECHNIKI/ANNALS OF ANIMAL SCIENCE. see *AGRICULTURE — Poultry And Livestock*

575.1 RU ISSN 1062-3604
QL951 CODEN: RJDBE2
RUSSIAN JOURNAL OF DEVELOPMENTAL BIOLOGY. English translation of: Ontogenez (RU ISSN 0475-1450) 1970. bi-m. $1235 in US; elsewhere $1445 (effective 1998). (Russian Academy of Sciences) Maik Nauka - Interperiodica, Mezhdunarodnyi Otdel, Ul. Profsoyuznaya, 90, 117864 Moscow, Russia. TEL 7-095-3360066. FAX 7-095-3360666. (Dist. by: Plenum Publishing Corp., 233 Spring St., New York, NY 10013-1578, U.S.A. TEL 212-620-8468. FAX 212-463-0742) Ed. Sergei G. Vassetsky. (also avail. in microfilm from UMI; back issues avail.) **Indexed:** Biol.Abstr., Curr.Adv.Ecol.Sci., Ind.Med., Psychol.Abstr. **Document type:** academic/scholarly publication.
—CASDDS; CISTI; SWETS; UMI; UnCover. **CCC**.
Formerly (until 1993): Soviet Journal of Developmental Biology (ISSN 0049-173X)
Refereed Serial

575.1 574.8 RU ISSN 1022-7954
QH431 CODEN: RJGEEQ
RUSSIAN JOURNAL OF GENETICS. English translation of: Genetika (RU ISSN 0016-6758) 1966. m. $1595 in US; elsewhere $1865 (effective 1998). (Russian Academy of Sciences) Maik Nauka - Interperiodica, Mezhdunarodnyi Otdel, Ul. Profsoyuznaya, 90, 117864 Moscow, Russia. TEL 7-095-3360066. FAX 7-095-3360666. (Dist. by: Plenum Publishing Corp., 233 Spring St., New York, NY 10013-1578. TEL 212-620-8468. FAX 212-463-0742) Ed. G.P. Georgiev. (also avail. in microfilm from UMI; back issues avail.) **Indexed:** Biol.Abstr., Curr.Adv.Ecol.Sci., Excerp.Med., Ind.Med., Int.Abstr.Biol.Sci., Sport Fish.Abstr., Wild.Rev. **Document type:** academic/scholarly publication.
—BLDSC (0420.760960); CASDDS; CISTI; SWETS; UMI; UnCover. **CCC**.
Formerly (until 1994): Soviet Genetics (ISSN 0038-5409)
Refereed Serial

SEQUENCES OF PROTEINS OF IMMUNOLOGICAL INTEREST. see *MEDICAL SCIENCES — Abstracting, Bibliographies, Statistics*

575.1 JA ISSN 0911-0445
SHINKA SEIBUTSUGAKU KENKYUJO KENKYU HOKOKU/RESEARCH INSTITUTE OF EVOLUTIONARY BIOLOGY. SCIENCE REPORT. (Text in English, Japanese) 1982. irreg. Shinka Seibutsugaku Kenkyujo, 4-28 Kamiyoga 2-chome, Setagaya-ku, Tokyo 158, Japan.

575.1 634.9 GW ISSN 0037-5349
CODEN: SIGEAQ
SILVAE GENETICA; Zeitschrift fuer Forstgenetik und Forstpflanzenzuechtung. (Text in English, French and German) 1951. 6/yr. DM.500.40 (foreign DM.507) (effective 1997). J.D. Sauerlaender's Verlag, Finkenhofstr. 21, 60322 Frankfurt a.M., Germany. TEL 49-69-555217. FAX 49-69-5964344. Ed. H.J. Muhs. adv.; bk.rev.; abstr.; charts; illus.; index. **Indexed:** Abstr.Bull.Inst.Pap.Chem., ASCA, Biol.Abstr., Chem.Abstr., Curr.Adv.Ecol.Sci., Curr.Cont., Forest.Abstr., Forest Prod.Abstr., Plant Grow.Reg.Abstr., Sci.Cit.Ind., Seed Abstr., Soils & Fert., VITIS. **Document type:** academic/scholarly publication.
—BLDSC (8281.500000); CASDDS; EMDOCS; Genuine Article; SWETS; UnCover. **CCC**.
Description: Includes announcements and reports on meetings and congresses on forest tree breeding and genetics as well as other related fields.

613.94 US ISSN 0037-766X
HQ750.A1 CODEN: SOBIAL
SOCIAL BIOLOGY. 1954. q. $75 (effective 1998). Society for the Study of Social Biology, Box 2349, Port Angeles, WA 98362. TEL 608-233-1487. E-mail: rb-osb@olympus.net. Ed. Richard H. Osborne. adv.; bk.rev.; abstr.; charts; illus.; index. circ. 1,650. (also avail. in microform from UMI; back issues avail.; reprint service avail. from UMI) **Indexed:** Abstr.Anthropol., Abstr.Hyg., Anthropol.Lit., Arts & Hum.Cit.Ind., ASCA, ASSIA, Biol.Abstr., Biol.& Agr.Ind., Biol.Dig., Chem.Abstr., Curr.Adv.Ecol.Sci., Curr.Cont., Curr.Lit.Fam.Plan., Dairy Sci.Abstr., Diar.Dis.Res., Excerp.Med., Fam.Ind., IBR, Ind.Med., Indian Psychol.Abstr., Lang.& Lang.Behav.Abstr., Nutr.Abstr., P.A.I.S., Popul.Ind., Psychol.Abstr. (1969-), Risk Abstr., Soc.Sci.Ind. (until 1994), Sociol.Abstr., SSCI, Trop.Dis.Bull., World Agri.Econ.& Rural Sociol.Abstr. **Document type:** academic/scholarly publication.
—BLDSC (8318.055000); CISTI; Genuine Article; KNAW; KR SourceOne; SWETS; UMI; UnCover.
Formerly: Eugenics Quarterly (ISSN 0097-2762)
Description: Furthers knowledge of the biological and cultural forces affecting human evolution and their evolution.
Refereed Serial

SOCIETY FOR IN VITRO BIOLOGY. MONOGRAPH SERIES. see *BIOLOGY — Microbiology*

575.1 574.8 US ISSN 0740-7750
QH426 CODEN: SCMGDN
SOMATIC CELL AND MOLECULAR GENETICS. 1975. bi-m. $575 (foreign $670) (effective 1998). Plenum Publishing Corp., 233 Spring St., New York, NY 10013-1578. TEL 212-620-8000. FAX 212-463-0742. TELEX 23-421139. Ed. Richard L. Davidson. adv. (also avail. in microfilm from UMI) **Indexed:** Anim.Breed.Abstr., ASCA, Biol.Abstr., Biotech.Abstr., Chem.Abstr, Curr.Adv.Biochem., Curr.Adv.Cell & Devel.Biol., Curr.Adv.Ecol.Sci., Curr.Adv.Genetics & Molec.Biol., Curr.Cont., Excerp.Med., Ind.Med., Ind.Sci.Rev., Sci.Cit.Ind., Telegen. **Document type:** academic/scholarly publication.
—BLDSC (8327.808800); CASDDS; CISTI; EMDOCS; Genuine Article; KNAW; Linda Hall; SWETS; UMI; UnCover. **CCC**.
Formerly (until 1984): Somatic Cell Genetics (ISSN 0098-0366)
Refereed Serial

575.1 US ISSN 0081-4148
QH431.A1 CODEN: SGSYBV
STADLER GENETICS SYMPOSIUM. PROCEEDINGS. 1971. irreg., latest 1993. price varies. Plenum Publishing Corp., 233 Spring St., New York, NY 10013-1578. TEL 212-620-8000. FAX 212-463-0742. TELEX 23-421139. E-mail: books@plenum.com. Ed. J.P. Gustafson. **Indexed:** Anim.Breed.Abstr., Biol.Abstr., Chem.Abstr., Ref.Zh. **Document type:** proceedings.
—CASDDS; KNAW; Linda Hall.
Refereed Serial

BIOLOGY — GENETICS

575.1 GW ISSN 0040-5752
SB123 CODEN: THAGA6
THEORETICAL AND APPLIED GENETICS; international journal of breeding research and cell genetics. Short title: T A G. Online edition (GW ISSN 1432-2242) (Text in English) 1929. 16/yr. DM.5028 (foreign DM.5067.20) (effective 1998). Springer-Verlag, Heidelberger Platz 3, 14197 Berlin, Germany. TEL 49-30-82787-0. FAX 49-30-82787448. E-mail: subscriptions@springer.de; URL: http://link.springer.de. (Subscr. in N. America to: Springer-Verlag New York, Inc., 333 Meadowlands Pkwy., Secaucus, NJ 07094. TEL 212-460-1500. FAX 212-473-6272) Ed. G. Wenzel. (also avail. in microform from UMI; back issues avail.; reprint service avail. from ISI) **Indexed:** Abstr.Bull.Inst.Pap.Chem., Anim.Breed.Abstr., Apic.Abstr., ASCA, Bibl.Agri., Biol.Abstr., Biotech.Abstr., Chem.Abstr., Cott.& Trop.Fibr.Abstr., Crop Physiol.Abstr., Curr.Adv.Ecol.Sci., Curr.Adv.Genetics & Molec.Biol., Curr.Biotech.Abstr., Curr.Cont., Dairy Sci.Abstr., Excerp.Med., Fababean Abstr., Field Crop Abstr., Food Sci.& Tech.Abstr., Forest.Abstr., Forest Prod.Abstr., Helminthol.Abstr., Herb.Abstr., Hort.Abstr., Ind.Sci.Rev., Irr.& Drain.Abstr., Nutr.Abstr., Ornam.Hort., Plant Breed.Abstr., Plant Grow.Reg.Abstr., Potato Abstr., Poult.Abstr., Rev.Plant Path., Sci.Cit.Ind., Seed Abstr., Soils & Fert., Sorghum & Millets Abstr., Soyabean Abstr., Sport Fish.Abstr., Triticale Abstr., Trop.Oil Seeds Abstr., VITIS, Weed Abstr., Wild.Rev., World Agri.Econ.& Rural Sociol.Abstr., Zoo.Rec. **Document type:** academic/scholarly publication.
•Also available online.
—BLDSC (8814.552000); CASDDS; CISTI; EMDOCS; Genuine Article; Linda Hall; SWETS; UMI; UnCover. **CCC**.
Supersedes: Zuechter.
Description: Reflects the continuing progress of plant and animal breeding genetics, including fundamental and applied aspects.

TOMATO GENETICS COOPERATIVE REPORT. see BIOLOGY — Botany

591.15 660 UK ISSN 0962-8819
QH442.6 CODEN: TRSEES
TRANSGENIC RESEARCH. 1991. bi-m. $105 to individuals; institutions $335 (effective 1996). Chapman & Hall, Journals Department (Subsidiary of: International Thomson Publishing Group), 2-6 Boundary Row, London SE1 8HN, England. TEL 44-171-8650066. FAX 44-171-5229623. TELEX 290164 CHAPMA G. E-mail: jhelp@chall.co.uk; URL: http://www.chaphall.com/chaphall/journals.html. (Dist. by: International Thomson Publishing Services Ltd., Cheriton House, North Way, Andover, Hants. SP10 5BE, England. TEL 44-1264-342713. FAX 44-1264-342807; Subscr. in US & Canada to: 400 Market St., Philadelphia, PA 19106. TEL 800-552-5866) Ed.Bd. adv. (reprint service avail.) **Indexed:** ASCA, Biotech.Abstr., Chem.Abstr., Curr.Cont., Ind.Med. (1993-), Ind.Sci.Rev. **Document type:** academic/scholarly publication.
•Also available online.
—BLDSC (9020.713000); ADONIS; CASDDS; CISTI; EMDOCS; Genuine Article; KNAW; SWETS. **CCC**.
Description: Dedicated to the rapid publication of research in transgenic higher organisms, including their production and properties resulting from the transgenic state, use as experimental tools, exploitation and application, and environmental impact.
Refereed Serial

576.5 NE ISSN 1023-6171
CODEN: TADTEF
TRANSGENICS. Key Title: Transgenics (Basel). 1993. 6/yr. $118 (effective 1998). Gordon and Breach - Harwood Academic, Amsteldisk 166, 1st Fl., 1079 LH Amsterdam, Netherlnads. URL: http://www.gbhap.com/Transgenics/. (Subscr. to: International Publishers Distributor, Box 32160, Newark, NJ 07102. TEL 800-545-8398. FAX 215-750-6343) Ed. Julius Cruse. (back issues avail.) **Indexed:** Excerp.Med. (1995-). **Document type:** academic/scholarly publication.
•Also available online.
Also available on CD-ROM.
—BLDSC (9020.713500); CASDDS; CISTI; KNAW.
Formerly (until 1994): Transgene (ISSN 1068-3283)
Description: Presents original reports of biological analysis through DNA transfer in vivo and in vitro.

TRENDS IN CELL BIOLOGY (REFERENCE EDITION). see BIOLOGY — Cytology And Histology

576.8 577 UK ISSN 0968-0012
TRENDS IN ECOLOGY AND EVOLUTION (REFERENCE EDITION). 1986. a. £345($514) includes m. Trends in Ecology and Evolution (effective 1995). Elsevier Science Ltd., P.O. Box 800, Kidlington, Oxford OX5 1DX, England. TEL 44-1865-843000. FAX 44-1865-843010. E-mail: nlinfo-f@elsevier.nl; usinfo-f@elsevier.com; forinfo-kyf04035@niftyserve.or.jp; URL: http://www.elsevier.nl/. (Subscr. to: Elsevier Science, Regional Sales Office, P.O. Box 211, 1000 AE Amsterdam, Netherlands. TEL 31-20-4853757. FAX 31-20-4853432; Subscr. in the Americas to: Elsevier Science, Regional Sales Office, Box 945, New York, NY 10159-0945. TEL 212-633-3730. FAX 212-633-3680; Subscr. in Australasia and the Far East to: Elsevier Science (Singapore) Pte Ltd, No.1 Temasek Ave., No.17-01 Millenia Tower, Singapore 039192, Singapore. TEL 65-434-3727. FAX 65-337-2230) Ed. Andrew Sugden. (back issues avail.) **Document type:** academic/scholarly publication.
—CISTI. **CCC**.
Description: Compendium of archival material from Trends in Ecology and Evolution.
Refereed Serial

610 575.1 UK ISSN 0168-9525
QH426 CODEN: TRGEE2
TRENDS IN GENETICS; DNA, differentiation and development. Library compendium: Trends in Genetics (Reference Edition) (ISSN 0168-9479) 1985. m. fl.1349($775) to institutions (effective 1998). Elsevier Science Ltd., P.O. Box 800, Kidlington, Oxford OX5 1DX, England. TEL 44-1865-843000. FAX 44-1865-843010. E-mail: nlinfo-f@elsevier.nl; usinfo-f@elsevier.com; forinfo-kyf04035@niftyserve.or.jp; URL: http://www.elsevier.nl/. (Subscr. to: Elsevier Science, Regional Sales Office, P.O. Box 211, 1000 AE Amsterdam, Netherlands. TEL 31-20-4853757. FAX 31-20-4853432; Subscr. in the Americas to: Elsevier Science, Regional Sales Office, Box 945, New York, NY 10159-0945. TEL 212-633-3730. FAX 212-633-3680; Subscr. in Australasia and the Far East to: Elsevier Science (Singapore) Pte Ltd, No.1 Temasek Ave., No.17-01 Millenia Tower, Singapore 039192, Singapore. TEL 65-434-3727. FAX 65-337-2230) Ed. A. Stewart. adv.; bk.rev.; index. (back issues avail.; reprint service avail. from SWZ) **Indexed:** Anim.Breed.Abstr., ASCA, Bibl.Agri., Biol.Abstr., Chem.Abstr., Curr.Adv.Biochem., Curr.Adv.Cell & Devel.Biol., Curr.Adv.Genetics & Molec.Biol., Curr.Cont., Excerp.Med., Food Sci.& Tech.Abstr., Ind.Sci.Rev., Maize Abstr., Plant Grow.Reg.Abstr., Potato Abstr., Poult.Abstr., Sci.Cit.Ind. **Document type:** academic/scholarly publication.
—BLDSC (9049.598000); ADONIS; CASDDS; CISTI; Genuine Article; SWETS. **CCC**.
Description: Covers all aspects of genetics - molecular genetics, differentiation, development, clinical genetics, recombinant DNA.
Refereed Serial

575.1 610 UK ISSN 0168-9479
QH426
TRENDS IN GENETICS (REFERENCE EDITION). 1985. a. Elsevier Science Ltd., P.O. Box 800, Kidlington, Oxford OX5 1DX, England. TEL 44-1865-843000. FAX 44-1865-843010. E-mail: nlinfo-f@elsevier.nl; usinfo-f@elsevier.com; forinfo-kyf04035@niftyserve.or.jp; URL: http://www.elsevier.nl/. (Subscr. to: Elsevier Science, Regional Sales Office, P.O. Box 211, 1000 AE Amsterdam, Netherlands. TEL 31-20-4853757. FAX 31-20-4853432; Subscr. in the Americas to: Elsevier Science, Regional Sales Office, Box 945, New York, NY 10159-0945. TEL 212-633-3730. FAX 212-633-3680; Subscr. in Australasia and the Far East to: Elsevier Science (Singapore) Pte Ltd, No.1 Temasek Ave., No.17-01 Millenia Tower, Singapore 039192, Singapore. TEL 65-434-3727. FAX 65-337-2230) Ed. Alison Stewart. (back issues avail.) **Document type:** academic/scholarly publication.
—CISTI; UnCover. **CCC**.
Description: Compendium of archival material from Trends in Genetics.
Refereed Serial

TRISOMY 21; an international, multidisciplinary journal of Downs Syndrome. see MEDICAL SCIENCES — Pediatrics

575.1 KR ISSN 0564-3783
CODEN: TGANAK
TSITOLOGIYA I GENETIKA; nauchnyi zhurnal. English translation: Cytology and Genetics (US ISSN 0095-4527) 1965. bi-m. $209 (effective 1998). Akademiya Nauk Ukrainy, Institut Klitynnoi Biologii ta Genetychnoi Inzhenerii, Vul. Akad. Zabolotnogo, 152, 252143 Kiev 143, Ukraine. TEL 38-44-2669266. Ed. I.A. Shevtov. **Indexed:** Anim.Breed.Abstr., Bio-Contr.News & Info., Biol.Abstr., Chem.Abstr., Cott.&Trop.Fibr.Abstr., Curr.Adv.Ecol.Sci., Dent.Ind., Excerp.Med., Ind.Med., Int.Aerosp.Abstr., Pig News & Info., Plant Breed.Abstr., Plant Grow.Reg.Abstr., Potato Abstr., Poult.Abstr., Seed Abstr., Sorghum & Millets Abstr., Soyabean Abstr., Triticale Abstr.
—BLDSC (0397.030000); CASDDS; CISTI; EMDOCS; KNAW; Linda Hall. **CCC**.

575.1 XO
UNIVERZITA KOMENSKEHO. PEDAGOGICKA FAKULTA V TRNAVE. PRIRODNE VEDY: BIOLOGIA-GENETIKA. irreg., (approx. a.). price varies. c/o Study and Information Center, Safarikova nam. 6, 818 06 Bratislava, Slovakia.

VIRUS GENES. see BIOLOGY — Microbiology

575.1 CC ISSN 0253-9772
QH426 CODEN: ICHUDW
YICHUAN/HEREDITAS. (Text in Chinese) 1972. bi-m. $47.40. Science Press, Marketing and Sales Department, 16 Donghuangchenggen North St., Beijing 100717, People's Republic of China. TEL 4010642. FAX 4019810. adv.; bk.rev. circ. 31,000. **Indexed:** Anim.Breed.Abstr., Seed Abstr., Zoo.Rec. **Document type:** academic/scholarly publication.
—CASDDS; Linda Hall.
Description: Contains research reports, breeding work based on genetic theories, information on study results in stages, exchange of teaching instructions, and stories and news tidbits on personalities.

575.1 CC ISSN 0379-4172
QH431 CODEN: ICHPCG
YICHUAN XUEBAO/ACTA GENETICA SINICA. English translation: Chinese Journal of Genetics (US ISSN 0898-5138) (Text in Chinese; summaries in English) 1973. bi-m. $92.50. (Chinese Academy of Sciences, Institute of Genetics) Science Press, Marketing and Sales Department, 16 Donghuangchenggen North St., Beijing 100717, People's Republic of China. TEL 4010642. FAX 4019810. adv. circ. 16,000. **Indexed:** Anim.Breed.Abstr., Biol.Abstr., Chem.Abstr., Cott.& Trop.Fibr.Abstr., Curr.Adv.Biochem., Curr.Adv.Genetics & Molec.Biol., Excerp.Med., Fababean Abstr., Field Crop Abstr., Helminthol.Abstr., Maize Abstr., Ornam.Hort., Pig News & Info., Plant Breed.Abstr., Plant Grow.Reg.Abstr., Poult.Abstr., Rice Abstr., Seed Abstr., Sorghum & Millets Abstr., Soyabean Abstr., Triticale Abstr. **Document type:** academic/scholarly publication.
—CASDDS; CISTI.
Description: Covers genetics research in mainland China, including molecular genetics, genetic engineering, medical genetics, and genetics of plants, animals and microorganisms.
Refereed Serial

571.8 UK ISSN 0967-1994
QH491 CODEN: ZYGOEB
ZYGOTE; the biology of gametes and early embryos. 1993. q. £112($190) (effective 1998). Cambridge University Press, Edinburgh Bldg., Shaftesbury Rd., Cambri-ge CB2 2RU, England. TEL 44-1223-312393. FAX 44-1223-315052. TELEX 851817256. E-mail: information@cup.cam.ac.uk; URL: http://www.cup.cam.ac.uk. (N. American addr.: Cambridge University Press, Journals Dept., 40 W. 20th St., New York, NY 10011. TEL 212-924-3900. FAX 212-691-3239) Ed.Bd. R&P contact: Linda Nicol. adv. contact: Rebecca Symons. bk.rev. (back issues avail.) **Indexed:** ASCA, Curr.Cont., Ind.Med. (1994-). **Document type:** academic/scholarly publication.
—BLDSC (9538.885000); CASDDS; CISTI; Genuine Article; KNAW; UMI; UnCover. **CCC**.
Description: Provides a multidisciplinary forum for reports on all aspects of early developmental biology. Concentrates on the programming of developmental information during gametogenesis, through its modification at fertilization to the integration of the maternal and embryonic genomes.
Refereed Serial

BIOLOGY — Microbiology

576   US   ISSN 0044-7897
CODEN: ASMNBO
A S M NEWS (WASHINGTON). 1935. m. $37 to non-members; members free (effective 1997). American Society for Microbiology, 1325 Massachusetts Ave., N.W., Washington, DC 20005. TEL 202-737-3600. E-mail: executivedirector@asmusa.org; URL: http://www.asmusa.org/jnlsrc/asmnew1.htm. Ed. Michael I. Goldberg. adv.; bk.rev.; stat.; index. circ. 42,000. (also avail. in microform from UMI; back issues avail.; reprint service avail. from UMI) **Indexed**: Biodet.Abstr., Biol.Abstr., CAD CAM Abstr., Environ.Abstr., Ind.Med., Ind.Vet., Poult.Abstr., Rev.Med.& Vet.Mycol., SSCI, Telegen. **Document type**: trade publication.
●Also available online.
—BLDSC (1745.171000); CISTI; Genuine Article; SWETS; UMI. **CCC**.
Description: Provides information on a broad range of scientific and policy issues to microbiologists; letters; opinion pieces; meetings calendar; reports of legislative activity; and classified employment listings.

576
QR383   US
A T C C ANIMAL VIRUSES AND ANTISERA, CHLAMYDIAE, AND RICKETTSIAE. 1975. irreg., 7th ed., 1996. $36 in N. America; elsewhere $48. American Type Culture Collection, 12301 Parklawn Dr., Rockville, MD 20852. TEL 800-638-6597. FAX 301-816-4361. E-mail: sales@atcc.org. Eds. C. Buck, G. Paulino. **Document type**: catalog.
—CISTI. **CCC**.
Formerly: A T C C Catalogue of Animal Viruses and Antisera, Chlamydiae, and Rickettsiae (ISSN 1057-6495); Which supersedes in part (in 1990): American Type Culture Collection. Catalogue of Animal and Plant Viruses, Chlamydiae, Rickettsiae and Virus Antisera (ISSN 0898-4182); Which supersedes in part (in 1986): American Type Culture Collection. Catalogue of Strains 2: Animal Cell Lines, Animal Viruses, Bacterial Viruses, Mycoviruses, Plant Viruses, Rickettsiae, Chlamydiae (ISSN 0363-2989)

589.9   US
A T C C BACTERIA & BACTERIOPHAGES. 1985. irreg., 19th ed., 1996. $45 in N. America; elsewhere $55. American Type Culture Collection, 12301 Parklawn Dr., Rockville, MD 20852. TEL 800-638-6597. FAX 301-816-4361. E-mail: sales@atcc.org. Ed.Bd. **Document type**: catalog.
—CISTI.
Formerly: A T C C Catalogue of Bacteria and Bacteriophages (ISSN 1050-8120); Which supersedes in part: American Type Culture Collection. Catalogue of Strains 1.

576   US
A T C C CATALOGUE OF PLANT VIRUSES AND ANTISERA. 1975. irreg., 7th, 1993. $5. American Type Culture Collection, 12301 Parklawn Dr., Rockville, MD 20852. TEL 800-638-6597. FAX 301-816-4361. E-mail: Sales@ATCC.org. Ed.Bd. **Document type**: catalog.
—CISTI. **CCC**.
Supersedes in part (in 1990): American Type Culture Collection. Catalogue of Animal and Plant Viruses, Chlamydiae, Rickettsiae and Virus Antisera (ISSN 0898-4182); Which supersedes in part (in 1986): American Type Culture Collection. Catalogue of Strains 2: Animal Cell Lines, Animal Viruses, Bacterial Viruses, Mycoviruses, Plant Viruses, Rickettsiae, Chlamydiae (ISSN 0363-2989)

576.64   US
A T C C CATALOGUE OF PROTISTS. ALGAE - PROTOZOA. 1985. irreg., 18th, 1993. $5. American Type Culture Collection, 12301 Parklawn Dr., Rockville, MD 20852. TEL 800-638-6597. FAX 301-816-4361. E-mail: Sales@ATCC.org. Ed. T.A. Nerad. **Document type**: catalog.

576.64 589.9   US
A T C C CATALOGUE OF RECOMBINANT D N A MATERIALS. irreg., 3rd, 1993. $5. American Type Culture Collection, 12301 Parklawn Dr., Rockville, MD 20852. TEL 800-638-6597. FAX 301-816-4361. E-mail: sales@atcc.org. Eds. D.R. Maglott, W.C. Nierman. **Document type**: catalog.
—**CCC**.
Formerly: American Type Culture Collection. Catalogue of Recombinant D N A Collections; Supersedes in part: American Type Culture Collection. Catalogue of Bacteria, Phages, and D N A Vectors; American Type Culture Collection. Catalogue of Strains 1: Algae, Bacteria, Bacteriophages, Plasmids, Fungi, Plant Viruses and Antisera and Protozoa; Former titles: American Type Culture Collection. Catalogue of Strains 1: Algae, Bacteria, Bacteriophages, Fungi, Plant Viruses and Antisera and Protozoa; American Type Culture Collection. Catalogue of Strains: Algae, Bacteria, Bacteriophages, Fungi and Protozoa (ISSN 0363-2970)

576.64 589.9   US
A T C C CELL LINES AND HYBRIDOMAS. irreg., 8th, 1994. $22 in N. America; elsewhere $32. American Type Culture Collection, 12301 Parklawn Dr., Rockville, MD 20852. TEL 800-638-6597. FAX 301-816-4361. E-mail: sales@ATCC.org. Ed. R. Hay. **Document type**: catalog.
Former titles: A T C C Catalogue of Cell Lines and Hybridomas; Supersedes in part: American Type Culture Collection. Catalogue of Strains 2: Animal Cell Lines, Animal Viruses, Bacterial Viruses, Mycoviruses, Plant Viruses, Rickettsiae, Chlamydiae; Which was formerly titled: American Type Culture Collection. Catalogue of Strains 2: Animal Cell Lines, Animal Viruses, Bacterial Viruses, Mycoviruses, Rickettsiae, Chlamydiae; American Type Culture Collection. Catalogue of Strains: 2. Animal Viruses, Rickettsiae, Chlamydiae; American Type Culture Collection. Catalogue of Viruses, Rickettsiae, Chlamydiae.

576.64   US
A T C C CONNECTION. 1981. q. free. American Type Culture Collection, 12301 Parklawn Dr., Rockville, MD 20852. TEL 800-638-6597. FAX 301-816-4361. E-mail: news@atcc.org. Ed. E.M. Brown. circ. 18,500. **Indexed**: Telegen. **Document type**: newsletter.
—CISTI. **CCC**.
Former titles: A T C C Quarterly Newsletter (ISSN 0894-9026); (until 1985): American Type Culture Collection. Quarterly Newsletter (ISSN 0743-4758)
Description: Characterization, preservation, and use of biological cultures.

576.64
QK600.73.U62   US
A T C C FILAMENTOUS FUNGI. 1986. irreg., 19th, 1996. $34 in N. America; elsewhere $44. American Type Culture Collection, 12301 Parklawn Dr., Rockville, MD 20852. TEL 800-638-6597. FAX 301-816-4361. E-mail: sales@ATCC.org. Ed.Bd. **Document type**: catalog.
—CISTI.
Formerly: A T C C Catalogue of Filamentous Fungi (ISSN 1065-0598); Supersedes in part (in 1991): American Type Culture Collection. Catalogue of Fungi - Yeasts (ISSN 1053-3370); Which supersedes in part: American Type Culture Collection. Catalogue of Strains 1: Algae, Bacteria, Bacteriophages, Plasmids, Fungi, Plant Viruses and Antisera and Protozoa.

576.64   US
A T C C PRESERVATION METHODS: FREEZING & FREEZE-DRYING. 1991. irreg. $45 (foreign $50). American Type Culture Collection, 12301 Parklawn Dr., Rockville, MD 20852. TEL 800-638-6597. FAX 301-816-4361. Eds. F.P. Simione, E.M. Brown.

576.64   US
A T C C QUALITY CONTROL METHODS FOR CELL LINES. 1992. irreg. $40 (foreign $45). American Type Culture Collection, 12301 Parklawn Dr., Rockville, MD 20852. TEL 800-638-6597. FAX 301-816-4361. E-mail: Sales@ATCC.org.

576.64   US
A T C C YEASTS. 1986. irreg., 19th, 1995. $35 in N. America; elsewhere $47. American Type Culture Collection, 12301 Parklawn Dr., Rockville, MD 20852. TEL 800-638-6597. FAX 301-816-4361. Eds. S.C. Jong, M.J. Edwards. **Document type**: catalog.
—CISTI.
Formerly (until 1995): A T C C Catalogue of Yeasts; Supersedes in part (in 1991): American Type Culture Collection. Catalogue of Fungi - Yeasts (ISSN 1053-3370); Which supersedes in part: American Type Culture Collection. Catalogue of Strains 1.

576
QR1   YU   ISSN 0581-1538
CODEN: MIKJAT
ACTA BIOLOGICA IUGOSLAVICA. SERIJA B: MIKROBIOLOGIJA. 1964. s-a. $72. Unija Bioloskih Naucnih Drustava Jugoslavije - Yugoslav Union Biological Sciences, Nemanjina 6, fah 127, 11080 Belgrade Zemun, Yugoslavia. Ed. Zivojin Tesic. (back issues avail.) **Indexed**: Abstr.Hyg., Biol.Abstr., Biotech.Abstr., Chem.Abstr., Dairy Sci.Abstr., Excerp.Med., Geo.Abstr., Hort.Abstr., Ind.Med., Ind.Vet., Nutr.Abstr., Rev.Appl.Entomol., Soils & Fert., Trop.Dis.Bull., Vet.Bull.
—BLDSC (5761.630000); CASDDS; CISTI; Linda Hall.

ACTA BOTANICA CROATICA. see *BIOLOGY — Botany*

576   BU   ISSN 0204-8809
CODEN: AMBUDI
ACTA MICROBIOLOGICA BULGARICA. (Text in Bulgarian, Russian; summaries in English, Russian) 1973. s-a. price varies. (Bulgarska Akademiia na Naukite, Institut po Mikrobiologiia) Publishing House of the Bulgarian Academy of Sciences, Acad. G. Bonchev St., Bldg. 6, 1113 Sofia, Bulgaria. circ. 500. (reprint service avail. from IRC) **Indexed**: Abstr.Bulg.Sci.Med.Lit., Abstr.Hyg., Biodet.Abstr., Biol.Abstr., Biotech.Abstr., Chem.Abstr., Curr.Adv.Ecol.Sci., Dairy Sci.Abstr., Excerp.Med., Ind.Med., Ind.Vet., Sugar Ind.Abstr., Trop.Dis.Bull., Vet.Bull.
—BLDSC (0637.976000); CASDDS; CISTI; KNAW; Linda Hall. **CCC**.
Formed by the merger of: Acta Microbiologica, Virologica et Immunologica; Prilozhna Mikrobiologiia.

616.01
QR1   HU   ISSN 1217-8950
CODEN: AMIHEF
ACTA MICROBIOLOGICA ET IMMUNOLOGICA HUNGARICA. (Text in English) 1954. q. $144 (effective 1998). (Magyar Tudomanyos Akademia) Akademiai Kiado Rt, P.O. Box 245, H-1519 Budapest, Hungary. TEL 36-1-2043976. FAX 36-1-2043973. Ed. Istvan Nasz. adv.; bibl.; charts; illus.; index. **Indexed**: Abstr.Hyg., ASCA, Biol.Abstr., Chem.Abstr., Curr.Adv.Ecol.Sci., Curr.Biotech.Abstr., Curr.Cont., Dent.Ind., Excerp.Med., Helminthol.Abstr., Ind.Med., Ind.Sci.Rev., Ind.Vet., INIS Atomind., Sci.Cit.Ind., Trop.Dis.Bull., Vet.Bull. **Document type**: academic/scholarly publication.
—BLDSC (0637.978000); CASDDS; CISTI; Genuine Article; KNAW; Linda Hall; SWETS; UnCover. **CCC**.
Former titles (until 1994): Acta Microbiologica Hungarica (ISSN 0231-4622); (until 1982): Academiae Scientiarum Hungaricae. Acta Microbiologica (ISSN 0001-6187)
Description: Publishes research on medical and veterinary bacteriology, bacterial genetics, virology, mycology, parasitology. Includes immunology and epidemiology, agricultural and industrial microbiology.

BIOLOGY — MICROBIOLOGY

576   PL   ISSN 0137-1320
CODEN: AMPOAX
ACTA MICROBIOLOGICA POLONICA. (Text and summaries in English) 1952. q. 24 Zl. (foreign $100) (effective 1998). Polskie Towarzystwo Mikrobiologow, Ul. Chocimska 24, 00-791 Warsaw, Poland. TEL 48-22-497781. FAX 48-22-497484. E-mail: pzh@medstat.waw.pl. (Dist. by: Ars Polona, Krakowskie Przedmiescie 7, 00-950 Warsaw, Poland. TEL 48-22-8261201. FAX 48-22-8268673) Ed. Krystyna I. Wolska. R&P contact: Jolanta Szych. bk.rev.; charts; illus.; index. circ. 800. **Indexed:** AgroAgen, ASCA, Biodet.Abstr., Biol.Abstr., Biotech.Abstr., Bull.Signal., Chem.Abstr., Curr.Adv.Ecol.Sci., Curr.Biotech.Abstr., Curr.Cont., Excerp.Med., Field Crop Abstr., Food Sci.& Tech.Abstr., Geo.Abstr., Helminthol.Abstr., Herb.Abstr., Ind.Med., Ind.Sci.Rev., Ind.Vet., INIS Atomind., Microbiol.Abstr., Pig News & Info., Plant Breed.Abstr., Poult.Abstr., Rev.Plant Path., Rural Recreat.Tour.Abstr., Sci.Cit.Ind., Sel.Water Res.Abstr., Soils & Fert., Vet.Bull., World Agri.Econ.& Rural Sociol.Abstr. **Document type:** academic/scholarly publication.
—BLDSC (0638.000000); CASDDS; CISTI; Genuine Article; KNAW; Linda Hall; UnCover.
Formed by the 1976 merger of: Acta Microbiologica Polonica. Series A: Microbiologica Generalis (ISSN 0567-7815); Acta Microbiologica Polonica. Series B: Microbiologica Applicata (ISSN 0567-7823); Which supersedes (in 1969): Acta Microbiologica Polonica (ISSN 0001-6195)

571.999   PL   ISSN 1230-2821
QL757   CODEN: ACTPEO
ACTA PARASITOLOGICA. (Text in English; abstracts in Polish) 1953. q. $140 (effective 1996). Polska Akademia Nauk, Instytut Parazytologii Witolda Stefanskiego - Polish Academy of Sciences, Witold Stefanski Institute of Parasitology, Ul. Pasteura 3, 00-937 Warsaw, Poland. TEL 48-22-222562. (Dist. by: Ars Polona, Krakowskie Przedmiescie 7, 00-068 Warsaw, Poland) Ed. Katarzyna Niewiadomska. bk.rev.; bibl.; illus.; index. **Indexed:** Abstr.Hyg., AgroAgen, Biol.Abstr., Chem.Abstr., Curr.Adv.Ecol.Sci., Excerp.Med., Helminthol.Abstr., Ind.Vet., Key Word Ind.Wild.Res., Poult.Abstr., Protozool.Abstr., Rev.Appl.Entomol., Trop.Dis.Bull., Vet.Bull. **Document type:** academic/scholarly publication.
—BLDSC (0643.300000); CASDDS; CISTI; Genuine Article; KNAW; UnCover.
Formerly (until vol.37, 1992): Acta Parasitologica Polonica (ISSN 0065-1478)
Description: Original papers and research reports on theoretical and practical questions on parasitologic research.
Refereed Serial

576 616.9   XO   ISSN 0001-723X
CODEN: AVIRA2
ACTA VIROLOGICA; international journal. (Text and summaries in English) 1957. bi-m. £140($56) (effective 1998). (Slovak Academy of Sciences, Institute of Virology) Vydavatel'stvo S A P, s.r.a. - Slovak Academic Press Ltd., P.O. Box 57, Nam. Slobody 6, 810 05 Bratislava, Slovakia. TEL 42-7-211728. URL: http://www.europe.idealibrary.com/. (Dist. by: Mezhdunarodnaya Kniga, B. Yakimanka 39, 117049 Moscow, Russia. TEL 7-095-2384967. FAX 7-095-2384634) J. Zemla. bk.rev.; charts; illus.; index. circ. 1,200. **Indexed:** Abstr.Hyg., ASCA, Biol.Abstr., Biotech.Abstr., Chem.Abstr., Curr.Adv.Ecol.Sci., Curr.Cont., Dairy Sci.Abstr., Dent.Ind., Excerp.Med., Ind.Med., Ind.Sci.Rev., Ind.Vet., INIS Atomind., Poult.Abstr., Rev.Appl.Entomol., Sci.Cit.Ind., Sport Fish.Abstr., Telegen, Trop.Dis.Bull., Vet.Bull., Virol.Abstr., Wild.Rev., Zoo.Rec. **Document type:** academic/scholarly publication.
●Also available online.
—BLDSC (0671.500000); CASDDS; CISTI; EMDOCS; Genuine Article; KNAW; SWETS; UnCover. **CCC.**
Description: Devoted to original experimental papers in all fields of general virology and molecular biology of viruses, as well as of human and veterinary virology and rickettsiology.

576   IT   ISSN 0732-0574
QR82.A35   CODEN: ACTID2
ACTINOMYCETES. 1965. 3/yr. $85 (effective 1997). Centro per l'Ecologia Teorica e Applicata, Via Vittorio Veneto 19, 34170 Gorizia, Italy. TEL 39-481-536466. FAX 39-432-536470. (Subscr. to: Prof. R. Locci, Chair of Mycology, University of Udine, Aera Rizzi, Via Delle Scienze 208, 33100 Udine, Italy) (Co-sponsor: Dipartimento Biologia Applicata alla Difesa delle Pianti) Ed. Romano Locci. adv. contact: Fulvio Bisani. bk.rev.; illus. circ. 250. **Indexed:** Biol.Abstr., Chem.Abstr. **Document type:** newspaper.
—CASDDS; CISTI.
Former titles: Biology of the Actinomycetes and Related Organisms; Nocardial Biology.

576   US   ISSN 0065-2164
QR1   CODEN: ADAMAP
ADVANCES IN APPLIED MICROBIOLOGY. 1959. irreg., vol.43, 1997. Academic Press, Inc., 525 B St., Ste. 1900, San Diego, CA 92101-4495. TEL 619-231-0926. FAX 619-699-6715. (Subscr. to: Order Dept., 6277 Sea Harbor Dr., 4th Fl., Orlando, FL 32887. TEL 800-321-5068) Ed. Wayne W. Umbreit. index. (reprint service avail. from ISI) **Indexed:** ASCA, Biol.Abstr., Biol.& Agr.Ind., Curr.Adv.Ecol.Sci., Curr.Biotech.Abstr., Dairy Sci.Abstr., Deep Sea Res.& Oceanogr.Abstr., Excerp.Med., Food Sci.& Tech.Abstr., Ind.Med., Ind.Sci.Rev., Ind.Vet., Plant Breed.Abstr., Rev.Appl.Entomol., Sci.Cit.Ind., Telegen, Vet.Bull., Weed Abstr., World Agri.Econ.& Rural Sociol.Abstr.
—BLDSC (0699.100000); CASDDS; CISTI; Ei; EMDOCS; KR SourceOne; Linda Hall; SWETS; UnCover. **CCC.**
Refereed Serial

579   US   ISSN 0147-4863
QR100   CODEN: AMIED5
ADVANCES IN MICROBIAL ECOLOGY. 1977. irreg., vol.15, 1997. price varies. Plenum Publishing Corp., 233 Spring St., New York, NY 10013-1578. TEL 212-620-8000. FAX 212-463-0742. TELEX 23-421139. E-mail: books@plenum.com. Eds. M. Alaxander, K.C. Marshall. **Indexed:** ASCA, Chem.Abstr., Curr.Adv.Ecol.Sci., Deep Sea Res.& Oceanogr.Abstr., Ind.Sci.Rev., Ind.Vet., Nutr.Abstr., Rev.Plant Path., Sci.Cit.Ind., Soils & Fert., Vet.Bull. **Document type:** monographic series.
—BLDSC (0709.415000); CASDDS; CISTI; Genuine Article; KNAW; Linda Hall; UnCover. **CCC.**
Refereed Serial

576   US   ISSN 0065-2911
QR84   CODEN: AMIPB2
ADVANCES IN MICROBIAL PHYSIOLOGY. 1967. irreg., vol.39, 1997. Academic Press, Inc., 525 B St., Ste. 1900, San Diego, CA 92101-4495. TEL 619-231-0926. FAX 619-699-6715. (Subscr. to: Order Dept., 6277 Sea Harbor Dr., 4th Fl., Orlando, FL 32887. TEL 800-321-5068) Eds. A.H. Rose, J.F. Wilkinson. (reprint service avail. from ISI) **Indexed:** Abstr.Hyg., ASCA, Biol.Abstr., Biol.& Agr.Ind., Chem.Abstr., Curr.Adv.Ecol.Sci., Deep Sea Res.& Oceanogr.Abstr., Excerp.Med., Ind.Med., Ind.Sci.Rev., Rev.Med.& Vet.Mycol., Sci.Cit.Ind., Trop.Dis.Bull. **Document type:** monographic series.
—BLDSC (0709.420000); CASDDS; CISTI; KNAW; KR SourceOne; Linda Hall; SWETS; UnCover. **CCC.**
Refereed Serial

576 616   US   ISSN 0065-3527
QR360   CODEN: AVREA8
ADVANCES IN VIRUS RESEARCH. 1953. irreg., vol.42, 1992. Academic Press, Inc., 525 B St., Ste. 1900, San Diego, CA 92101-4495. TEL 619-231-0926. FAX 619-699-6715. (Subscr. to: Order Dept., 6277 Sea Harbor Dr., 4th Fl., Orlando, FL 32887. TEL 800-321-5068) Ed.Bd. index. (reprint service avail. from ISI) **Indexed:** Abstr.Hyg., ASCA, Biol.Abstr., Chem.Abstr., Curr.Adv.Ecol.Sci., Excerp.Med., Forest.Abstr., Hort.Abstr., Ind.Med., Ind.Sci.Rev., Ind.Vet., Rev.Appl.Entomol., Rev.Plant Path., Sci.Cit.Ind., Trop.Dis.Bull., Vet.Bull.
—BLDSC (0712.000000); CASDDS; CISTI; Linda Hall; SWETS; UnCover. **CCC.**
Refereed Serial

576   IT   ISSN 1121-9750
CODEN: AAMJEP
ALPE ADRIA MICROBIOLOGY JOURNAL. Abbreviated title: A A M J. 1992. q. DM.60 to individuals; institutions DM.150 (effective Jan. 1998). (Associazione Microbiologici Clinici Italiani) Biomedia s.r.l., Via C. Farini 70, 21059 Milan, Italy. TEL 39-2-69001316. FAX 39-2-69001311. E-mail: giuseppe.botta@drmm.uniud.it; URL: http://www.mf.uni.lj.si/~gubina/aamj.html. Ed. Bela Lanyi. adv. circ. 2,500. **Indexed:** Excerp.Med. (1994-). **Document type:** academic/scholarly publication.
—BLDSC (0801.953000); CASDDS; EMDOCS.
Description: Publishes review articles, original papers, correspondence, and congress proceedings in the field of pathogenesis of infections, diagnostic microbiology, epidemiology of infectious diseases, and mechanisms of action of antimicrobial agents.
Refereed Serial

576 589.9   US   ISSN 1060-2011
QR1.A47   CODEN: AGMME8
AMERICAN SOCIETY FOR MICROBIOLOGY. ABSTRACTS OF THE GENERAL MEETING. 1948. a. $25. American Society for Microbiology, 1325 Massachusetts Ave., N.W., Washington, DC 20005-4171. TEL 202-737-3600. index. circ. 10,000. (reprint service avail. from UMI) **Indexed:** Biol.Abstr., Dairy Sci.Abstr., Food Sci.& Tech.Abstr., Ind.Vet., INIS Atomind., Nutr.Abstr., Soils & Fert., Vet.Bull., Weed Abstr. **Document type:** proceedings.
—BLDSC (0564.255000); Linda Hall. **CCC.**
Former titles: American Society for Microbiology. Abstracts of the Annual Meeting (ISSN 0094-8519); Bacteriological Proceedings (ISSN 0067-2777)

616.01   UK   ISSN 1075-9964
CODEN: ANAEF8
▼**ANAEROBE.** 1995. bi-m. £90($178) to individuals; institutions £180 (effective 1998). Academic Press Ltd. (Subsidiary of: Harcourt Brace & Company Ltd.), 24-28 Oval Rd., London NW1 7DX, England. TEL 44-171-482-2893. FAX 44-171-267-0362. TELEX 25775 ACPRES G. E-mail: apsubs@acad.com; URL: http://www.hbuk.co.uk/ap/anaerobe; http://www.europe.idealibrary.com/. (Subscr. to: Harcourt Brace & Company Ltd., Foots Cray High St., Sidcup, Kent DA14 5HP, England. TEL 44-181-300-3322. FAX 44-181-309-0807) Ed. Larry Barton. **Indexed:** ASCA, Curr.Cont., Excerp.Med. (1996-). **Document type:** academic/scholarly publication.
●Also available online.
—BLDSC (0859.882000); CASDDS; CISTI; EMDOCS; Genuine Article.
Description: Focuses on studies pertaining to obligate and facultative anaerobes. Seeks to foster communication among a variety of disciplines.
Refereed Serial

576   IT   ISSN 1120-9135
CODEN: NAIMAH
ANNALI DI IGIENE, MEDICINA PREVENTIVA E DI COMUNITA. (Text in Italian; summaries in English) 1895. bi-m. L.60000 (foreign L.120000). (Istituto di Igiene Giuseppe Sanarelli) Societa Editrice Universo, Via G.B. Morgagni 1, 00161 Rome, Italy. Ed. G.M. Fara. adv.; bk.rev.; illus.; index. circ. 3,000. **Indexed:** Abstr.Hyg., Biol.Abstr., C.I.S. Abstr., Chem.Abstr., Dairy Sci.Abstr., Dent.Ind., Ind.Med., Ind.Vet., Trop.Dis.Bull., Vet.Bull.
—BLDSC (1014.180000); CASDDS; CISTI.
Former titles (until 1989): Nuovi Annali di Igiene e Microbiologia (ISSN 0029-6287); (until 1950): Annali d'Igiene (ISSN 0365-4842); (until 1916): Annali d'Igiene Sperimentale (ISSN 0365-3161)

BIOLOGY — MICROBIOLOGY

576 574.192   IT   ISSN 0003-4649
CODEN: AMEZAB
ANNALI DI MICROBIOLOGIA ED ENZIMOLOGIA. (Text in English, French, Italian; abstracts in English) 1940. s-a. L.100000 to individuals; institutions L.200000 (effective 1995). Universita degli Studi di Milano, Dipartimento di Scienze e Tecnologie Alimentari e Microbiologiche, Via G. Celoria 2, 20133 Milan, Italy. TEL 39-2-23673444. FAX 39-2-70630829. Ed. G. Ottogalli. adv. contact: Giorgio Ottogalli. bk.rev.; bibl.; charts; illus.; index, cum.index. circ. 500. **Indexed:** ASCA, Biodet.Abstr., Biol.Abstr., Chem.Abstr., Curr.Adv.Ecol.Sci., Dairy Sci.Abstr., Excerp.Med., Food Sci.& Tech.Abstr., Helminthol.Abstr., Int.Abstr.Biol.Sci., Soils & Fert., VITIS.
—BLDSC (1016.025000); CASDDS; CISTI; Genuine Article; KNAW; Linda Hall.
Description: Covers non-medical microbiology: general, industrial, soil, food, enzymology, fermentation and microbial chemistry.
Refereed Serial

576   JA
ANNUAL REVIEW MEN'EKI/ANNUAL REVIEW. IMMUNITY. (Text in Japanese) 1988. a. 6180 Yen. Chugai Igakusha, 62, Yaraicho, Shinjuku-ku, Tokyo 162, Japan.

576   US   ISSN 0066-4227
QR1   CODEN: ARMIAZ
ANNUAL REVIEW OF MICROBIOLOGY. 1947. a. $60 to individuals (foreign $65); institutions $120 (foreign $130) (effective 1998). Annual Reviews Inc., 4139 El Camino Way, Box 10139, Palo Alto, CA 94303-0139. TEL 650-493-4400; 800-523-8635. FAX 650-424-0910. E-mail: service@annurev.org; URL: http://www.annurev.org. Ed. L. Nicholas Ornston. R&P contact: Jeanne Kunz. bibl.; index, cum.index. (also avail. in microfilm from UMI; back issues avail.; reprint service avail.)
Indexed: Abstr.Bull.Inst.Pap.Chem., Abstr.Hyg., ASCA, Biodet.Abstr., Biol.Abstr., Biol.& Agr.Ind., Biotech.Abstr., Chem.Abstr., Curr.Adv.Ecol.Sci., Curr.Biotech.Abstr., Curr.Cont., Dairy Sci.Abstr., Deep Sea Res.& Oceanogr.Abstr., Diar.Dis.Res., Excerp.Med., Food Sci.& Tech.Abstr., Forest.Abstr., Forest Prod.Abstr., Gen.Sci.Ind., Helminthol.Abstr., Hort.Abstr., Ind.Med., Ind.Sci.Rev., Ind.Vet., INIS Atomind., M.M.R.I., Nutr.Abstr., Plant Breed.Abstr., Protozool.Abstr., Rev.Med.& Vet.Mycol., Sci.Cit.Ind., Soils & Fert., THA, Trop.Dis.Bull., Vet.Bull., VITIS.
Document type: academic/scholarly publication.
●Also available online. Vendor(s): Information Access Co.
—BLDSC (1523.000000); ADONIS; CASDDS; CISTI; EMDOCS; Genuine Article; KNAW; KR SourceOne; Linda Hall; SWETS; UMI; UnCover. **CCC.**
Description: Original critical reviews of the significant primary literature and current developments in microbiology.

576   US   ISSN 0066-4804
RM265   CODEN: AACHAX
ANTIMICROBIAL AGENTS AND CHEMOTHERAPY. 1972. m. $311 to non-members; members $55) (effective 1996). American Society for Microbiology, 1325 Massachusetts Ave., N.W., Washington, DC 20005. TEL 202-737-3600. Ed. George A. Jacoby, Jr. adv.; index. circ. 7,885. (also avail. in microform from UMI; back issues avail.; reprint service avail. from UMI) **Indexed:** Abstr.Hyg., Abstr.Inter.Med., AIDS Abstr., ASCA, Biol.Abstr., Biotech.Abstr., Chem.Abstr., Chem.Cit.Ind., Curr.Adv.Cancer Res., Curr.Adv.Ecol.Sci., Curr.Adv.Genetics & Molec.Biol., Curr.Cont., Dairy Sci.Abstr., Dent.Ind., Diar.Dis.Res., Excerp.Med., Helminthol.Abstr., I.P.A., Ind.Med., Ind.Sci.Rev., Ind.Vet., Kidney, Med.& Surg.Dermat., Neurosci.Cit.Ind., Pig News & Info., Protozool.Abstr., Rev.Med.& Vet.Mycol., Rev.Plant Path., Sci.Cit.Ind., Small Anim.Abstr., Telegen, Trop.Dis.Bull., Vet.Bull.
Document type: academic/scholarly publication.
●Also available on CD-ROM.
—BLDSC (1549.151000); CASDDS; CISTI; EMDOCS; Genuine Article; KNAW; Linda Hall; SWETS; UMI; UnCover. **CCC.**
Description: Forum for new work relating to antimicrobial, antiviral, antiparasitic, and anticancer agents and chemotherapy.
Refereed Serial

576   NE   ISSN 0168-938X
RM265   CODEN: AAANEB
ANTIMICROBIAL AGENTS ANNUAL. 1986. irreg. price varies. Elsevier Science B.V., Books Division, P.O. Box 211, 1000 AE Amsterdam, Netherlands. TEL 31-20-4853911. FAX 31-20-4853705. TELEX 18582 ESPA NL. E-mail: nlinfo-f@elsevier.nl; usinfo-f@elsevier.com; forinfo-kyf04035@niftyserve.or.jp; URL: http://www.elsevier.nl/. (Subscr. in the Americas to: Elsevier Science, Regional Sales Office, Box 945, New York, NY 10159-0945. TEL 212-633-3730. FAX 212-633-3680; Subscr. in Australasia and the Far East to: Elsevier Science (Singapore) Pte Ltd, No.1 Temasek Ave., No.17-01 Millenia Tower, Singapore 039192, Singapore. TEL 65-434-3727. FAX 65-337-2230; Subscr. in Japan to: Elsevier Science Japan, 9-15 Higashi-Azabu 1-chome, Minato-ku, Tokyo 106, Japan. TEL 81-3-5561-5033. FAX 81-3-5561-5047) Eds. P.K. Peterson, J. Verhoef. **Indexed:** Protozool.Abstr.
Document type: monographic series.
—CISTI. **CCC.**
Refereed Serial

576.64 616.9   NE   ISSN 0166-3542
CODEN: ARSRDR
ANTIVIRAL RESEARCH; a multidisciplinary journal of antiviral agents, natural host defence mechanisms, interferons and antiviral vaccines. (Text in English) 1981. m. fl.2607($1498) (effective 1998). (International Society for Antiviral Research) Elsevier Science B.V., P.O. Box 211, 1000 AE Amsterdam, Netherlands. TEL 31-20-4853911. FAX 31-20-4853598. TELEX 18582 ESPA NL. E-mail: nlinfo-f@elsevier.nl; usinfo-f@elsevier.com; forinfo-kyf04035@niftyserve.or.jp; URL: http://www.elsevier.nl/. (Subscr. in the Americas to: Elsevier Science, Regional Sales Office, Box 945, New York, NY 10159-0945. TEL 212-633-3730. FAX 212-633-3680; Subscr. in Australasia and the Far East to: Elsevier Science (Singapore) Pte Ltd, No.1 Temasek Ave., No.17-01 Millenia Tower, Singapore 039192, Singapore. TEL 65-434-3727. FAX 65-337-2230; Subscr. in Japan to: Elsevier Science Japan, 9-15 Higashi-Azabu 1-chome, Minato-ku, Tokyo 106, Japan. TEL 81-3-5561-5033. FAX 81-3-5561-5047) Eds. R.J. Whitley, E. de Clerq. adv.; bk.rev.; illus.; index. (also avail. in microform from UMI; back issues avail.; reprint service avail. from SWZ) **Indexed:** Abstr.Hyg., AIDS Abstr., ASCA, Biol.Abstr., Chem.Abstr., Curr.Adv.Ecol.Sci., Curr.Adv.Genetics & Molec.Biol., Curr.Cont., Dairy Sci.Abstr., Excerp.Med., Ind.Med., Ind.Sci.Rev., Ind.Vet., Pig News & Info., Potato Abstr., Rev.Plant Path., Sci.Cit.Ind., Small Anim.Abstr., Vet.Bull.
Document type: academic/scholarly publication.
—BLDSC (1552.830000); ADONIS; CASDDS; CISTI; EMDOCS; Genuine Article; KNAW; Linda Hall; SWETS; UnCover. **CCC.**
Formerly: Journal of Antiviral Research.
Description: Publishes full-length original articles, short definitive papers and review articles, pertaining to the effective control of virus infections in animals and hunans, as well as in plants or lower organisms.
Refereed Serial

576   NE   ISSN 0003-6072
CODEN: ALJMAO
ANTONIE VAN LEEUWENHOEK; international journal of general and molecular microbiology. (Text in English) 1935. 8/yr. fl.1817 to institutions; $933 to institutions in U.S. (effective 1998). (Stichting Antonie van Leeuwenhoek) Kluwer Academic Publishers, Postbus 17, 3300 AA Dordrecht, Netherlands. TEL 31-78-6392392. FAX 31-78-6392254. TELEX 29245 KAPG NL. E-mail: services@wkap.nl; URL: http://www.wkap.nl. (Dist. by: Kluwer Academic Publishers Group, P.O. Box 322, 3300 AH Dordrecht, Netherlands. TEL 31-78-6392392. FAX 31-78-6546474; N. America dist. addr.: Box 358, Accord Sta., Hingham, MA 02018-0358. TEL 617-871-6600. FAX 617-871-6528) Ed. A.H. Stouthamer. charts; stat.; index. (also avail. in microform from UMI; reprint service avail. from SWZ) **Indexed:** Abstr.Hyg., ASCA, Biodet.Abstr., Biol.Abstr., Biotech.Abstr., Bull.Signal., Chem.Abstr., Curr.Adv.Ecol.Sci., Curr.Biotech.Abstr., Curr.Cont., Dairy Sci.Abstr., Deep Sea Res.& Oceanogr.Abstr., Excerp.Med., Food Sci.& Tech.Abstr., Helminthol.Abstr., Ind.Med., Ind.Sci.Rev., Ind.Vet., Pig News & Info., Rev.Med.& Vet.Mycol., Rev.Plant Path., Sci.Cit.Ind., Small Anim.Abstr., Soils & Fert., Sugar Ind.Abstr., Vet.Bull., W.R.C.Inf.
Document type: academic/scholarly publication.
—BLDSC (1553.000000); CASDDS; CISTI; EMDOCS; Genuine Article; KNAW; Linda Hall; SWETS; UMI; UnCover. **CCC.**
Supersedes (in 1934): Nederlandsch Tijdschrift voor Hygiene, Microbiologie en Serologie (ISSN 0369-3821)
Description: Publishes fundamental and applied research connected with microbiology, including food microbiology, medical microbiology and applications of microbiology in biotechnology.
Refereed Serial

576   US   ISSN 0099-2240
QR1   CODEN: AEMIDF
APPLIED AND ENVIRONMENTAL MICROBIOLOGY. 1953. m. $322 to non-members; members $58 (effective 1997). American Society for Microbiology, 1325 Massachusetts Ave., N.W., Washington, DC 20005. TEL 202-737-3600. Ed. Lars G. Ljungdahl. adv.; bibl.; charts; index. circ. 9,000. (also avail. in microform from UMI; back issues avail.; reprint service avail. from UMI) **Indexed:** Abstr.Bull.Inst.Pap.Chem., Agri.Eng.Abstr., Agroforest.Abstr., ASCA, Bibl.Agri., Bio-Contr.News & Info., Biodet.Abstr., Biol.Abstr., Biol.& Agr.Ind., C.I.S.Abstr., Chem.Abstr., Chem.Cit.Ind., Chem.Cit.Ind., Comput.Dtbs., Crop Physiol.Abstr., Curr.Adv.Biochem., Curr.Adv.Ecol.Sci., Curr.Adv.Genetics & Molec.Biol., Curr.Biotech.Abstr., Curr.Cont., Curr.Pack.Abstr., Dairy Sci.Abstr., Dent.Ind., Diar.Dis.Res., E&P Hlth. (1993-), Ecol.Abstr., Energy Info.Abstr., Environ.Abstr., Environ.Per.Bibl. (1975-), Excerp.Med., Field Crop.Abstr., Food Sci.& Tech.Abstr., Forest Abstr., Forest.Prod.Abstr., Gas Process.& Ppl. (1993-), Gen.Sci.Ind., Geo.Abstr.P.G., Geol.Abstr., Helminthol.Abstr., Herb.Abstr., I.P.A., IBR, Ind.Med., Ind.Sci.Rev., Ind.Vet., INIS Atomind., Irr.& Drain.Abstr., Maize Abstr., Mat.Sci.Cit.Ind., Nutr.Abstr., Ocean.Abstr., Off.Tech. (1993-), Paper & Bd.Abstr., Petrol.Abstr. (1977-), Pig News & Info., Plant Grow.Reg.Abstr., Pollut.Abstr., Potato Abstr., Poult.Abstr., Protozool.Abstr., Repindex, Rev.Med.& Vet.Mycol., Rev.Plant Path., Risk Abstr., Sci.Cit.Ind., Sel.Water Res.Abstr., Soils & Fert., Soyabean Abstr., Sport Fish.Abstr., Sugar Ind.Abstr., Telegen, Triticale Abstr., Trop.Dis.Bull., Vet.Bull., W.R.C.Inf., Weed Abstr., Wild.Rev., Zoo.Rec. **Document type:** academic/scholarly publication.
●Also available on CD-ROM.
—BLDSC (1571.440000); CASDDS; CISTI; Ei; EMDOCS; Genuine Article; KNAW; KR SourceOne; Linda Hall; SWETS; UMI; UnCover. **CCC.**
Formerly (until 1976): Applied Microbiology (ISSN 0003-6919)
Description: Addresses all aspects of applied and environmental microbiology, including biotechnology, food microbiology, industrial microbiology, and microbial ecology.
Refereed Serial

APPLIED BIOCHEMISTRY AND MICROBIOLOGY. see *BIOLOGY — Biological Chemistry*

APPLIED MICROBIOLOGY AND BIOTECHNOLOGY. see *BIOLOGY — Biotechnology*

BIOLOGY — MICROBIOLOGY

576   US   ISSN 0070-217X
QR1   CODEN: CTMIA3
CURRENT TOPICS IN MICROBIOLOGY AND IMMUNOLOGY. irreg., vol.208, 1996. price varies. Springer-Verlag, 175 Fifth Ave., New York, NY 10010. TEL 212-460-1500. FAX 212-473-6272. E-mail: orders@springer-ny.com; URL: http://www.springer-ny.com. (Also: Berlin, Heidelberg, Tokyo and Vienna) (reprint service avail. from ISI) **Indexed:** Abstr.Hyg., AIDS Abstr., ASCA, Biol.Abstr., Chem.Abstr., Curr.Adv.Ecol.Sci., Excerp.Med., Ind.Med., Ind.Sci.Rev., Ind.Vet., Sci.Cit.Ind., Trop.Dis.Bull., Vet.Bull. **Document type:** monographic series.
—BLDSC (3504.890000); CASDDS; CISTI; EMDOCS; Genuine Article; KNAW; Linda Hall; SWETS; UnCover. **CCC.**
Formerly: Ergebnisse der Mikrobiologie und Immunitaetsforschung.
Description: Publishes research and studies in microbiology and immunology.

CURRENTS IN HEMATOIMMUNOLOGY. see *MEDICAL SCIENCES — Hematology*

576 616.7   SZ   ISSN 1013-9982
CODEN: CYTKEF
CYTOKINES. (Text in English) 1989. irreg. price varies. S. Karger AG, Allschwilerstr. 10, P.O. Box, CH-4009 Basel, Switzerland. TEL 41-61-3061111. FAX 41-61-3061234. E-mail: karger@karger.ch; URL: http://www.karger.ch. **Indexed:** Ind.Med. (1992-). **Document type:** monographic series.
—BLDSC (3506.780000); CASDDS; CISTI; KNAW.
Description: Covers cellular and molecular biological aspects of clinical perspectives in biomedical research. Discusses information on cell regulation in physiological and pathological processes, from which direct therapeutic consequences for the treatment of a variety of diseases are expected to emerge.
Refereed Serial

DENMARK. STATENS HUSDYRBRUGSFORSOEG. BERETNING/DENMARK. DANISH INSTITUTE OF ANIMAL SCIENCE. REPORT. see *AGRICULTURE — Poultry And Livestock*

DEVELOPMENTAL AND COMPARATIVE IMMUNOLOGY; ontogeny - phylogeny - aging. see *MEDICAL SCIENCES — Allergology And Immunology*

576   NE   ISSN 0070-4563
QR53   CODEN: DIMCAL
DEVELOPMENTS IN INDUSTRIAL MICROBIOLOGY SERIES. Represents: Society for Industrial Microbiology. Proceedings of the Annual Meeting. (Supplement to: Journal of Industrial Microbiology (ISSN 0169-4146)) 1960. irreg., vol.33, 1993. price varies. (Society for Industrial Microbiology, US) Elsevier Science B.V., Books Division, P.O. Box 211, 1000 AE Amsterdam, Netherlands. TEL 31-20-4853911. FAX 31-20-4853705. TELEX 18582 ESPA NL. E-mail: nlinfo@elsevier.nl; usinfo-f@elsevier.com; forinfo-kyf04035@niftyserve.or.jp; URL: http://www.elsevier.nl/. (Subscr. in the Americas to: Elsevier Science, Regional Sales Office, Box 945, New York, NY 10159-0945. TEL 212-633-3730. FAX 81-3-5561-5033; Subscr. in Australasia and the Far East to: Elsevier Science (Singapore) Pte Ltd, No.1 Temasek Ave., No.17-01 Millenia Tower, Singapore 039192, Singapore. TEL 65-434-3727. FAX 65-337-2230; Subscr. in Japan to: Elsevier Science Japan, 9-15 Higashi-Azabu 1-chome, Minato-ku, Tokyo 106, Japan. TEL 81-3-5561-5033. FAX 81-3-5561-5047) circ. 2,000. (back issues avail.) **Indexed:** Biodet.Abstr., Biol.Abstr., Biotech.Abstr., Chem.Abstr., Curr.Biotech.Abstr., Dairy Sci.Abstr., Excerp.Med., Food Sci.& Tech.Abstr., Ind.Sci.Rev., INIS Atomind., Rev.Plant Path., Sci.Cit.Ind. **Document type:** monographic series, proceedings.
—BLDSC (3579.082050); CASDDS; CISTI; Linda Hall. **CCC.**
Refereed Serial

576.64 616.0194   NE   ISSN 0167-8256
CODEN: DMVIDD
DEVELOPMENTS IN MOLECULAR VIROLOGY. (Text in English) 1981. irreg. price varies. Kluwer Academic Publishers, Postbus 17, 3300 AA Dordrecht, Netherlands. TEL 31-78-6392392. FAX 31-78-6392254. TELEX 29245 KAPG NL. E-mail: services@wkap.nl; URL: http://www.wkap.nl. (Dist. by: Kluwer Academic Publishers Group, P.O. Box 322, 3300 AH Dordrecht, Netherlands. TEL 31-78-6392392. FAX 31-78-6546474; N. America dist. addr.: Box 358, Accord Sta., Hingham, MA 02018-0358. TEL 617-871-6600. FAX 617-871-6528) **Document type:** monographic series.
—CASDDS; CISTI; KNAW.
Refereed Serial

576 616.9   US   ISSN 0732-8893
RB37.A1   CODEN: DMIDDZ
DIAGNOSTIC MICROBIOLOGY AND INFECTIOUS DISEASE. 1983. m. fl.1372($789) (effective 1998). Elsevier Science Inc., Box 945, New York, NY 10159-0945. TEL 212-633-3730. FAX 212-633-3680. TELEX 420643 AEP UI. E-mail: usinfo-f@elsevier.com; URL: http://www.elsevier.nl/. (Subscr. outside the Americas to: Elsevier Science, Regional Sales Office, P.O. Box 211, 1000 AE Amsterdam, Netherlands. TEL 31-20-4853757. FAX 31-20-4853432; Subscr. in Australasia and the Far East to: Elsevier Science (Singapore) Pte Ltd, No.1 Temasek Ave., No.17-01 Millenia Tower, Singapore 039192, Singapore. TEL 65-434-3727. FAX 65-337-2230; Subscr. in Japan to: Elsevier Science Japan, 9-15 Higashi-Azabu 1-chome, Minato-ku, Tokyo 106, Japan. TEL 81-3-5561-5033. FAX 81-3-5561-5047) Ed. Dr. Ronald N. Jones. adv.; bk.rev.; index. (also avail. in microform from UMI; back issues avail.) **Indexed:** Biol.Abstr., Chem.Abstr., Curr.Adv.Ecol.Sci., Curr.Cont., Diar.Dis.Res., Excerp.Med., Ind.Med., Ind.Sci.Rev., INSPEC, Med.& Surg.Dermat., Protozool.Abstr., Sci.Cit.Ind. **Document type:** academic/scholarly publication.
—BLDSC (3579.662000); ADONIS; CASDDS; CISTI; EMDOCS; Genuine Article; KNAW; SWETS; UnCover. **CCC.**
Description: Provides information on latest developments in clinical microbiology and the diagnosis and treatment of infectious diseases.
Refereed Serial

DISEASES OF AQUATIC ORGANISMS. see *BIOLOGY — Zoology*

DOJO BISEIBUTSU KENKYUKAI KOEN YOSHISHU/SOIL MICROBIOLOGICAL SOCIETY OF JAPAN. ABSTRACTS OF THE MEETING. see *BIOLOGY — Abstracting, Bibliographies, Statistics*

576   US
ECONOMIC MICROBIOLOGY. 1977. irreg., vol.8, 1983. Academic Press, Inc., 525 B St., Ste. 1900, San Diego, CA 92101-4495. TEL 619-231-0926. FAX 619-699-6715. (Subscr. to: Order Dept., 6277 Sea Harbor Dr., 4th Fl., Orlando, FL 32887. TEL 800-321-5068) Ed. A.H. Rose. (reprint service from ISI) **Indexed:** Chem.Abstr., Food Sci.& Tech.Abstr.
Refereed Serial

576   UA   ISSN 0301-8172
QR1   CODEN: EJMBA2
EGYPTIAN JOURNAL OF MICROBIOLOGY. (Text in English; summaries in Arabic and English) 1966. q. $107 (effective 1997). (Society of Applied Microbiology, Research Department) National Information and Documentation Centre (NIDOC), Tahrir St., Dokki, Awqaf P.O., Cairo, Egypt. TEL 20-2-3371696. Ed. S.A.Z. Mahmoud. charts; illus. circ. 1,000. (reprint service avail. from IRC) **Indexed:** Biol.Abstr., Chem.Abstr., Curr.Adv.Ecol.Sci., Curr.Biotech.Abstr., Dairy Sci.Abstr., Diar.Dis.Res., Field Crop Abstr., Food Sci.& Tech.Abstr., Herb.Abstr. **Document type:** academic/scholarly publication.
—BLDSC (3664.405000); CASDDS; CISTI; Linda Hall.
Formerly: Journal of Microbiology of the United Arab Republic (ISSN 0022-2704)

ENFERMEDADES INFECCIOSAS Y MICROBIOLOGIA. see *MEDICAL SCIENCES — Communicable Diseases*

ENZYME AND MICROBIAL TECHNOLOGY; biotechnology research and reviews. see *BIOLOGY — Biotechnology*

614.4 576 616.07   XR   ISSN 1210-7913
QR1   CODEN: EMIME6
EPIDEMIOLOGIE, MIKROBIOLOGIE, IMUNOLOGIE. (Text in Czech or Slovak; summaries in Czech and English) 1952. 4/yr. $112 (effective 1997 & 1998). (Ceska Lekarska Spolecnost J.E. Purkyne - Czech Medical Association) Nakladatelske Stredisko C L S J.E. Purkyne, Sokolska 31, 120 26 Prague 2, Czech Republic. TEL 420-2-24911420. FAX 420-2-24911420. (Dist. by: Abont s.r.o., Chlumova 17, 130 00 Prague 3, Czech Republic) Ed. Dr. B. Tichacek. adv.; bk.rev.; abstr.; bibl.; charts; illus.; stat.; index. circ. 800. **Indexed:** Abstr.Hyg., Biol.Abstr., C.I.S. Abstr., Chem.Abstr., Curr.Adv.Ecol.Sci., Dairy Sci.Abstr., Dok.Arbeitsmed., Excerp.Med., Ind.Med., Ind.Vet., Protozool.Abstr., Rev.Appl.Entomol., Rev.Med.& Vet.Mycol., Rev.Plant Path., Trop.Dis.Bull., Vet.Bull.
—BLDSC (3793.573000); CASDDS; CISTI. **CCC.**
Formerly: (until 1994): Ceskoslovenska Epidemiologie, Mikrobiologie, Imunologie (ISSN 0009-0522)
Refereed Serial

EPIDEMIOLOGY AND INFECTION. see *MEDICAL SCIENCES — Communicable Diseases*

576   GW   ISSN 0934-9723
CODEN: EJCDEU
EUROPEAN JOURNAL OF CLINICAL MICROBIOLOGY & INFECTIOUS DISEASES. 1982. 12/yr. DM.498($322) (effective 1997). M M V Medizin Verlag, Neumarkter Str. 18, 81673 Munich, Germany. TEL 49-89-43189-0. FAX 49-89-43189633. Ed. I. Braveny. adv. circ. 3,000. **Indexed:** Abstr.Hyg., Abstr.Inter.Med., ASCA, Biol.Abstr., Chem.Abstr., Curr.Adv.Ecol.Sci., Curr.Cont., Dairy Sci.Abstr., Dent.Ind., Diar.Dis.Res., Excerp.Med., Ind.Med., Ind.Sci.Rev., Med.& Surg.Dermat., Protozool.Abstr., Rev.Med.& Vet.Mycol., Sci.Cit.Ind. **Document type:** academic/scholarly publication.
—BLDSC (3829.727700); ADONIS; CASDDS; CISTI; EMDOCS; Genuine Article; KNAW; SWETS; UnCover. **CCC.**
Formerly: European Journal of Clinical Microbiology.
Description: Presents information and opinions in the fields of clinical microbiology and infectious diseases.
Refereed Serial

576   US
EXPERIMENTAL VIROLOGY. 1978. irreg., vol.4, 1983. Academic Press, Inc., 525 B St., Ste. 1900, San Diego, CA 92101-4495. TEL 619-231-0926. FAX 619-699-6715. (Subscr. to: Order Dept., 6277 Sea Harbor Dr., 4th Fl., Orlando, FL 32887. TEL 800-321-5068) Eds. T.W. Tinsley, F. Brown. (reprint service avail. from ISI)
Refereed Serial

EXTREMOPHILES; life under extreme conditions. see *BIOLOGY — Biotechnology*

BIOLOGY — MICROBIOLOGY

576 NE ISSN 0928-8244
QR46 CODEN: FIMIEV
F E M S. IMMUNOLOGY AND MEDICAL MICROBIOLOGY. (Section of: F E M S Microbiology (ISSN 0921-8254)) (Text in English) m. fl.1596($917) (effective 1998). (Federation of European Microbiological Societies) Elsevier Science B.V., P.O. Box 211, 1000 AE Amsterdam, Netherlands. TEL 31-20-4853911. FAX 31-20-4853598. TELEX 18582 ESPA NL. E-mail: nlinfo-f@elsevier.nl; usinfo-f@elsevier.com; forinfo-kyf04035@niftyserve.or.jp; URL: http://www.elsevier.nl/. (Subscr. in the Americas to: Elsevier Science, Regional Sales Office, Box 945, New York, NY 10159-0945. TEL 212-633-3730. FAX 212-633-3680; Subscr. in Australasia and the Far East to: Elsevier Science (Singapore) Pte Ltd, No.1 Temasek Ave., No.17-01 Millenia Tower, Singapore 039192. TEL 65-434-3727. FAX 65-337-2230; Subscr. in Japan to: Elsevier Science Japan, 9-15 Higashi-Azabu 1-chome, Minato-ku, Tokyo 106, Japan. TEL 81-3-5561-5033. FAX 81-3-5561-5047) Ed. Duncan E.S. Stewart-Tull. (also avail. in microform from UMI) **Indexed:** ASCA, Bibl.Agri., Curr.Cont., Excerp.Med. (1988-), Ind.Sci.Rev., Sci.Cit.Ind., Telegen. **Document type:** academic/scholarly publication.
—BLDSC (3905.291000); ADONIS; CASDDS; CISTI; EMDOCS; Genuine Article; KNAW; Linda Hall; SWETS; UnCover. **CCC.**
Formerly (until 1993): F E M S. Microbiology Immunology (ISSN 0920-8534)
Description: Focuses on works describing the mechanisms of immunity and how these can be exploited in the diagnosis and treatment of disease.
Refereed Serial

576 NE ISSN 0168-6496
CODEN: FMECEZ
F E M S. MICROBIOLOGY ECOLOGY. (Section of: F E M S Microbiology (ISSN 0921-8254)) (Text in English) m. fl.1596($917) (effective 1998). (Federation of European Microbiological Societies) Elsevier Science B.V., P.O. Box 211, 1000 AE Amsterdam, Netherlands. TEL 31-20-4853911. FAX 31-20-4853598. TELEX 18582 ESPA NL. E-mail: nlinfo-f@elsevier.nl; usinfo-f@elsevier.com; forinfo-kyf04035@niftyserve.or.jp; URL: http://www.elsevier.nl/. (Subscr. in the Americas to: Elsevier Science, Regional Sales Office, Box 945, New York, NY 10159-0945. TEL 212-633-3730. FAX 212-633-3680; Subscr. in Australasia and the Far East to: Elsevier Science (Singapore) Pte Ltd, No.1 Temasek Ave., No.17-01 Millenia Tower, Singapore 039192. TEL 65-434-3727. FAX 65-337-2230; Subscr. in Japan to: Elsevier Science Japan, 9-15 Higashi-Azabu 1-chome, Minato-ku, Tokyo 106, Japan. TEL 81-3-5561-5033. FAX 81-3-5561-5047) Ed. T.H. Blackburn. (also avail. in microform from UMI; back issues avail.) **Indexed:** ASCA, Bibl.Agri., Biodet.Abstr., Curr.Cont., Ecol.Abstr., Environ.Abstr., Excerp.Med., Geo.Abstr.P.G., Geol.Abstr., Ind.Sci.Rev., Protozool.Abstr., Sel.Water Res.Abstr., Telegen, Zoo.Rec. **Document type:** academic/scholarly publication.
—BLDSC (3905.296000); ADONIS; CASDDS; CISTI; Genuine Article; SWETS; UnCover. **CCC.**
Description: Details fundamental aspects of the ecology of micro-organisms in a variety of environments and situations.
Refereed Serial

576 NE ISSN 0168-6445
QR1 CODEN: FMREE4
F E M S. MICROBIOLOGY REVIEWS. (Section of: F E M S Microbiology (ISSN 0921-8254)) (Text in English) 1977. q. fl.544($313) (effective 1998). (Federation of European Microbiological Societies) Elsevier Science B.V., P.O. Box 211, 1000 AE Amsterdam, Netherlands. TEL 31-20-4853911. FAX 31-20-4853598. TELEX 18582 ESPA NL. E-mail: nlinfo-f@elsevier.nl; usinfo-f@elsevier.com; forinfo-kyf04035@niftyserve.or.jp; URL: http://www.elsevier.nl/. (Subscr. in the Americas to: Elsevier Science, Regional Sales Office, Box 945, New York, NY 10159-0945. TEL 212-633-3730. FAX 212-633-3680; Subscr. in Australasia and the Far East to: Elsevier Science (Singapore) Pte Ltd, No.1 Temasek Ave., No.17-01 Millenia Tower, Singapore 039192, Singapore. TEL 65-434-3727. FAX 65-337-2230; Subscr. in Japan to: Elsevier Science Japan, 9-15 Higashi-Azabu 1-chome, Minato-ku, Tokyo 106, Japan. TEL 81-3-5561-5033. FAX 81-3-5561-5047) Ed. G. Gottschalk. (also avail. in microform from UMI) **Indexed:** ASCA, Biodet.Abstr., Biol.Abstr., Chem.Abstr., Chem.Cit.Ind., Curr.Cont., Excerp.Med., Food Sci.& Tech.Abstr., Ind.Sci.Rev., Mat.Sci.Cit.Ind., Protozool.Abstr., Sci.Cit.Ind., Zoo.Rec. **Document type:** academic/scholarly publication.
—BLDSC (3905.305000); ADONIS; CASDDS; CISTI; Genuine Article; Linda Hall; SWETS; UnCover. **CCC.**
Description: Covers the entire field of microbiology with an emphasis on topicality and readability.
Refereed Serial

576 US ISSN 0163-9188
CODEN: FEMSDW
F E M S SYMPOSIUM. irreg., vol.75, 1995. price varies. (Federation of European Microbiological Societies) Plenum Publishing Corp., 233 Spring St., New York, NY 10013-1578. TEL 212-620-8000. FAX 212-463-0742. TELEX 23-421139. E-mail: books@plenum.com. (back issues avail.) **Document type:** proceedings.
—BLDSC (3905.320000); CASDDS; CISTI; KNAW. **CCC.**
Refereed Serial

FITOPATOLOGIA BRASILEIRA. see *AGRICULTURE — Crop Production And Soil*

576 NE ISSN 0921-8254
F E M S. MICROBIOLOGY; international journal providing for the rapid publication of reports on microbiological research. (In 4 sections: Ecology, Immunology and Medical Microbiology, Letters, Reviews) (Text in English) 1977. 66/yr. (in 19 vols.). fl.8835($5078) (effective 1998). (Federation of European Microbiological Societies) Elsevier Science B.V., P.O. Box 211, 1000 AE Amsterdam, Netherlands. TEL 31-20-4853911. FAX 31-20-4853598. TELEX 18582 ESPA NL. E-mail: nlinfo-f@elsevier.nl; usinfo-f@elsevier.com; forinfo-kyf04035@niftyserve.or.jp; URL: http://www.elsevier.nl/. (Subscr. in the Americas to: Elsevier Science, Regional Sales Office, Box 945, New York, NY 10159-0945. TEL 212-633-3730. FAX 212-633-3680; Subscr. in Australasia and the Far East to: Elsevier Science (Singapore) Pte Ltd, No.1 Temasek Ave., No.17-01 Millenia Tower, Singapore 039192, Singapore. TEL 65-434-3727. FAX 65-337-2230; Subscr. in U.S. and Canada to: Elsevier Science Inc., Box 882, Madison Sq. Sta., New York, NY 10159-0882. TEL 81-3-5561-5033. FAX 81-3-5561-5047) Ed.Bd. cum.index. (also avail. in microform from UMI; back issues avail.) **Indexed:** Apic.Abstr., Biol.Abstr., Chem.Abstr., Curr.Cont., Excerp.Med. **Document type:** academic/scholarly publication.
Refereed Serial

576 NE ISSN 0378-1097
QR1 CODEN: FMLED7
F E M S. MICROBIOLOGY LETTERS; an international journal providing for the rapid publication of short reports on microbiological research. (Section of: F E M S Microbiology (ISSN 0921-8254)) 1977. 24/yr. fl.5904($3393) (effective 1998). (Federation of European Microbiological Societies) Elsevier Science B.V., P.O. Box 211, 1000 AE Amsterdam, Netherlands. TEL 31-20-4853911. FAX 31-20-4853598. TELEX 18582 ESPA NL. E-mail: nlinfo-f@elsevier.nl; usinfo-f@elsevier.com; forinfo-kyf04035@niftyserve.or.jp; URL: http://www.elsevier.nl/. (Subscr. in the Americas to: Elsevier Science, Regional Sales Office, Box 945, New York, NY 10159-0945. TEL 212-633-3730. FAX 212-633-3680; Subscr. in Australasia and the Far East to: Elsevier Science (Singapore) Pte Ltd, No.1 Temasek Ave., No.17-01 Millenia Tower, Singapore 039192, Singapore. TEL 65-434-3727. FAX 65-337-2230; Subscr. in Japan to: Elsevier Science Japan, 9-15 Higashi-Azabu 1-chome, Minato-ku, Tokyo 106, Japan. TEL 81-3-5561-5033. FAX 81-3-5561-5047) Ed. C.A. Fewson. adv. (also avail. in microform from UMI; reprint service avail. from ISI) **Indexed:** ASCA, Bibl.Agri., Biodet.Abstr., Biol.Abstr., Biotech.Abstr., Chem.Abstr., Curr.Adv.Biochem., Curr.Adv.Ecol.Sci., Curr.Adv.Genetics & Molec.Biol., Curr.Biotech.Abstr., Curr.Cont., Dairy Sci.Abstr., Deep Sea Res.& Oceanogr.Abstr., Excerp.Med., Food Sci.& Tech.Abstr., Helminthol.Abstr., Ind.Sci.Rev., Ind.Vet., INIS Atomind., Nutr.Abstr., Pig News & Info., Protozool.Abstr., Rev.Med.& Vet.Mycol., Sci.Cit.Ind., Soils & Fert., Sport Fish.Abstr., Telegen, Vet.Bull., Weed Abstr., Wild.Rev., Zoo.Rec. **Document type:** academic/scholarly publication.
—BLDSC (3905.300000); ADONIS; CASDDS; CISTI; EMDOCS; Genuine Article; SWETS; UnCover. **CCC.**
Description: Covers all aspects of microbiology and microbial chemistry.
Refereed Serial

576 UK ISSN 0015-5632
CODEN: FOMIAZ
FOLIA MICROBIOLOGICA. (Text and summaries in English) 1956. bi-m. £154 (effective 1997). (Czech Academy of Sciences, Institute of Microbiology, XR) W.B. Saunders Co. Ltd. (Subsidiary of: Harcourt Brace & Company Ltd.), 24-28 Oval Rd., London NW1 7DX, England. TEL 44-171-267-4466. FAX 44-171-482-2293. (Subscr. to: Harcourt Brace & Company Ltd., Foots Cray High St., Sidcup, Kent DA14 5HP, England. TEL 44-181-300-3322. FAX 44-181-309-0807; Editorial addr.: Videnska 1083, 142 20 Prague 4, Czech Republic) (Co-sponsor: Ceskoslovenska Spolecnost Mikrobiologicka) Eds. V. Krumphanzl, J. Cudlin. adv.; bk.rev.; abstr.; charts; illus.; mkt.; index. circ. 1,200. **Indexed:** Abstr.Hyg., ASCA, Biol.Abstr., Biotech.Abstr., Chem.Abstr., Curr.Adv.Ecol.Sci., Curr.Biotech.Abstr., Curr.Cont., Dairy Sci.Abstr., Deep Sea Res.& Oceanogr.Abstr., Excerp.Med., Food Sci.& Tech.Abstr., Helminthol.Abstr., Ind.Med., Ind.Sci.Rev., Ind.Vet., Microbiol.Abstr., Nutr.Abstr., Plant Grow.Reg.Abstr., Rev.Med.& Vet.Mycol., Rev.Plant Path., Sci.Cit.Ind., Soils & Fert., Triticale Abstr., Trop.Dis.Bull., Vet.Bull., W.R.C.Inf., Weed Abstr. **Document type:** academic/scholarly publication.
—BLDSC (3971.500000); CASDDS; CISTI; Genuine Article; KNAW; Linda Hall; SWETS; UnCover. **CCC.**
Formerly (until 1958): Ceskoslovenska Mikrobiologie.
Description: Publishes original papers on anatomy, embryology, histology, electron microscopy, cyto- and histochemistry, somatic anthropology, and contributions of a technical nature.

FOLIA PARASITOLOGICA. see *MEDICAL SCIENCES — Communicable Diseases*

BIOLOGY — MICROBIOLOGY

576 664   UK   ISSN 0740-0020
QR115   CODEN: FOMIE5
FOOD MICROBIOLOGY. 1984. bi-m. £108($185) to individuals; institutions £250 (effective 1998). Academic Press Ltd. (Subsidiary of: Harcourt Brace & Company Ltd.), 24-28 Oval Rd., London NW1 7DX, England. TEL 44-171-267-4466. FAX 44-171-482-2293. TELEX 25775 ACPRES G. E-mail: apsubs@acad.com; URL: http://www.hbuk.co.uk/ap/foodmicro; http://www.europe.idealibrary.com/. (Subscr. to: Harcourt Brace & Company Ltd., Foots Cray High St., Sidcup, Kent DA14 5HP, England. TEL 44-181-300-3322. FAX 44-181-309-0807) Ed. C.A. Batt. R&P contact: Catherine John. adv. contact: Nik Screen. bk.rev. (reprint service avail. from SWZ) **Indexed:** ASCA, Bibl.Agri., Biodet.Abstr., Curr.Adv.Ecol.Sci., Curr.Cont., Dairy Sci.Abstr., Excerp.Med., Food Sci.& Tech.Abstr., Ind.Vet., Rev.Med.& Vet.Mycol., Sci.Cit.Ind., Vet.Bull. **Document type:** academic/scholarly publication.
●Also available online.
—BLDSC (3981.300000); CASDDS; CISTI; EMDOCS; Genuine Article; Linda Hall; SWETS; UnCover. **CCC**.
 Description: Publishes primary research papers, short research communications, reviews, reports of meetings, and news items dealing with all aspects of the microbiology of foods.

576   GW   ISSN 0724-441X
              CODEN: FMMIEP
FORTSCHRITTE DER MEDIZINISCHEN MIKROBIOLOGIE/PROGRESS IN MEDICAL MICROBIOLOGY. (Text in English or German; summaries in English) 1983. irreg. price varies. Gustav Fischer Verlag, Wollgrasweg 49, 70599 Stuttgart, Germany. TEL 49-711-458030. FAX 49-711-4580334. (Subscr. to: Postfach 720143, 70577 Stuttgart, Germany; Subscr. in N. America to: Lubrecht & Cramer Ltd., 38 Rte. 48, Forestburgh, NY 12777-6400, USA) Ed. Dr. Ullmann. circ. 5,000. (back issues avail.) **Document type:** academic/scholarly publication.
—CASDDS; CISTI; KNAW. **CCC**.

576   GW
FRONTIERS OF VIROLOGY. (Text in English) irreg., latest no.2. Springer-Verlag, Heidelberger Platz 3, 14197 Berlin, Germany. TEL 49-30-82787-0. FAX 49-30-82787448. E-mail: subscriptions@springer.de. Eds. Yechiel Becker, Gholamreza Darai. **Document type:** academic/scholarly publication.

575 660   UK   ISSN 1356-9597
QH441.5   CODEN: GECEFL
▼**GENES TO CELLS.** 1996. m. £360($657) (foreign £396) (effective 1998). (Molecular Biology Society of Japan) Blackwell Science Ltd., Osney Mead, Oxford OX2 OEL, England. TEL 44-1865-206206. FAX 44-1865-721205. E-mail: journals.cs@blacksci.co.uk; URL: http://www.black.co.uk. Ed. Dr. Jun-ichi Tomizawa; Pub. Allen Stevens. R&P contact: Sarah Pollard. adv. contact: Martine Cariou-Keen. circ. 1,000. **Document type:** academic/scholarly publication.
—BLDSC (4111.762500); CASDDS; Genuine Article; SWETS. **CCC**.
 Description: Provides an international forum for papers relating to physiological, biophysical, and evolutionary ecology.
 Refereed Serial

ENETIC ENGINEERING; principles and methods. see BIOLOGY — Genetics

575.1 660   US   ISSN 1088-9051
QP606.D46   CODEN: GEREFS
GENOME RESEARCH. 1991. m. $105 to individuals (foreign $157); institutions $595 (foreign $647) students $79 (foreign $131) (effective 1998). Cold Spring Harbor Laboratory Press, Publications Department, Box 100, Cold Spring Harbor, NY 11724. TEL 516-367-8492; 800-843-4388. FAX 516-367-8334. E-mail: cshpress@cshl.org; URL: http://www.cshl.org. Ed. J. Cuddihy. adv. contact: Marcie Ebenstein. **Indexed:** ASCA, Excerp.Med. (1993-), Food Sci.& Tech.Abstr., Ind.Med. (1992-). **Document type:** academic/scholarly publication.
●Also available online.
—BLDSC (4116.313800); CASDDS; CISTI; EMDOCS; Genuine Article; KNAW; Linda Hall; SWETS. **CCC**.
 Formerly (until Aug. 1995): P C R Methods and Applications (Polymerase Chain Reaction) (ISSN 1054-9803)
 Description: Focuses on genome studies in all species, including genetic and physical mapping, DNA sequencing, gene discovery, informatics, statistical and mathematical methods and genome structure as well as technological innovations and applications.
 Refereed Serial

576   US   ISSN 0149-0451
QR103   CODEN: GEJODG
GEOMICROBIOLOGY JOURNAL; an international journal of geomicrobiology and microbial biogeochemistry. 1978. q. £121($199) to institutions (effective 1998). Taylor & Francis Inc., 1900 Frost Rd., Ste. 101, Bristol, PA 19007-1598. TEL 215-785-5800; 800-821-8312. FAX 215-785-5515. E-mail: info@tandf.co.uk; URL: http://www.tandf.co.uk/. (Subscr. in Europe to: Taylor & Francis Ltd., Rankine Rd., Basingstoke, Hants. RG24 8PR, England. TEL 44-1256-840366. FAX 44-1256-479438) Eds. Henry L. Ehrlich, William C. Ghiorse. adv.; bk.rev.; abstr.; index. **Indexed:** ASCA, Biol.Abstr., Chem.Abstr., Curr.Adv.Ecol.Sci., Curr.Biotech.Abstr., Curr.Cont., Deep Sea Res.& Oceanogr.Abstr., E&P Hlth. (1993-), Ecol.Abstr., Gas Process.& Ppl. (1993-), Geol.Abstr., Ind.Sci.Rev., Microbiol.Abstr., Off.Tech. (1993-), Petrol.Abstr. (1989-), Sci.Cit.Ind., Sel.Water Res.Abstr., Soils & Fert., SSCI, W.R.C.Inf. **Document type:** academic/scholarly publication.
—BLDSC (4147.590000); CASDDS; CISTI; EMDOCS; Genuine Article; KR SourceOne; Linda Hall; PADDS; SWETS; UnCover. **CCC**.
 Description: Explores the geologic impact of microbial transformations of materials that make up the Earth's crust, oceans, sea lakes, bottom sediments, soils, mineral deposits, and rocks.
 Refereed Serial

576   CN   ISSN 1201-4907
GERMS AND IDEAS/GERMES D'I D. q. Can.$30($28) to individuals (foreign Can.$45($35)); institutions Can.$38 (foreign Can.$60($50)) (effective 1997). (Canadian Association of Clinical Microbiology and Infectious Diseases) Pulsus Group Inc., 2902 S. Sheridan Way, Oakville, ON L6J 7L6, Canada. TEL 905-829-4770. FAX 905-829-4799. E-mail: pulsus@pulsus.com; mkrajden@torhosp.toronto.on.ca; URL: http://www.pulsus.com. Ed. Mel Krajden. circ. 3,200. (back issues avail.)
—BLDSC (4162.178920).
 Formerly: C A C M I D Newsletter.

576   IT   ISSN 0390-5462
              CODEN: GBVID3
GIORNALE DI BATTERIOLOGIA, VIROLOGIA ED IMMUNOLOGIA. 1926. s-a. Ospedale Maria Vittoria, Via Cibrario 72, 10144 Turin, Italy. TEL 74 92 345. abstr. **Indexed:** Biol.Abstr., Chem.Abstr., Ind.Med., Ind.Vet., Rev.Med.& Vet.Mycol., Trop.Dis.Bull., Vet.Bull.
—CASDDS; CISTI.
 Supersedes: Giornale di Batteriologia, Virologia ed Immunologia ed Annali dell'Ospedale Maria Vittoria di Torino. Parte 1. Microbiologia (ISSN 0301-1453); Which superseded in part: Giornale di Batteriologia, Virologia ed Immunologia ed Annali dell'Ospedale Maria Vittoria di Torino (ISSN 0017-0267)

576   IT   ISSN 0017-0380
GIORNALE DI MICROBIOLOGIA. (Text in English, French, German, Italian and Spanish) 1955. q. Istituto Microbiologia, Via L. Mangiagalli 31, 20133 Milan, Italy. Ed. Romolo Deotto. index. circ. 650. **Indexed:** Biol.Abstr., Chem.Abstr., Excerp.Med., INIS Atomind.
—CISTI; Linda Hall.

GLYCOCONJUGATE JOURNAL. see BIOLOGY — Biological Chemistry

576   CC   ISSN 1001-6678
QR53   CODEN: GOWEEK
GONGYE WEISHENGWU/INDUSTRIAL MICROBIOLOGY. (Text in Chinese) 1986. q. $100 (effective 1997 & 1998). Shanghai Gongye Weishengwu Yanjiusuo - Shanghai Institute of Industrial Microbiology, 353 Guiping Rd., Shanghai 200233, People's Republic of China. TEL 64822988. (Co-sponsor: National Information Center of Industrial Microbiology) Ed. Lei Zhaozu. adv.; bk.rev. circ. 5,000. **Indexed:** Sugar Ind.Abstr. **Document type:** academic/scholarly publication.
—BLDSC (4457.895000); CASDDS.
 Description: Covers the industrial application of biotechnology.

571.999   CC   ISSN 1001-1072
GUOWAI YIXUE (JISHENGBING FENCE)/FOREIGN MEDICAL SCIENCES (PARASITOSIS). (Text in Chinese) bi-m. Zhongguo Yufang Yixue Kexueyuan, Jishengchongbing Yanjiusuo - Chinese Academy of Preventive Medicine, Institute of Parasitic Diseases, 207 Ruijin 2 Lu, Shanghai 200025, People's Republic of China. TEL 86-21-6437-7008. Ed. Xiao Shuhua. **Document type:** academic/scholarly publication.

579   US   ISSN 1083-4389
▼**HELICOBACTER.** 1996. q. $150 (foreign $175) (effective 1996). Blackwell Science Inc., 350 Main St., Malden, MA 02418. TEL 617-876-7000; 800-759-6102. FAX 617-388-8255. **Document type:** academic/scholarly publication.
—BLDSC (4285.102500); CISTI. **CCC**.

IMMUNOHISTOCHEMISTRY. see BIOLOGY — Cytology And Histology

576   US   ISSN 1071-2690
QH585   CODEN: IVCAED
IN VITRO CELLULAR & DEVELOPMENTAL BIOLOGY - ANIMAL. (Second March issue consists of abstracts for June annual meeting) 1965. m. (11/yr.) $335 (foreign $380) (effective 1997). Society for In Vitro Biology, 9315 Largo Dr. W. Ste. 255, Largo, MD 20774. TEL 301-324-5054. FAX 301-324-5057. (Subscr. to: Box 73230, Baltimore, MD 21273) Ed. Dr. Wallace L. McKeehan; Pub. Marietta Ellis. adv. contact: Marietta Ellis. bk.rev.; abstr.; circ. 2,300 (paid). (also avail. in microform from UMI; back issues avail.) **Indexed:** Abstr.Bull.Inst.Pap.Chem., Anim.Breed.Abstr., ASCA, Biol.Abstr., Chem.Abstr., Curr.Adv.Biochem., Curr.Adv.Cancer Res., Curr.Adv.Cell & Devel.Biol., Curr.Biotech.Abstr., Curr.Cont., Dairy Sci.Abstr., Dent.Ind., Excerp.Med., Helminthol.Abstr., Hort.Abstr., Ind.Med., Ind.Sci.Rev., Ind.Vet., INIS Atomind., Neurosci.Cit.Ind., Plant Grow.Reg.Abstr., Sci.Cit.Ind., Small Anim.Abstr., Sorghum & Millets Abstr., Soyabean Abstr., Vet.Bull. **Document type:** academic/scholarly publication.
—BLDSC (4372.500520); CASDDS; CISTI; EMDOCS; Genuine Article; KNAW; Linda Hall; SWETS; UMI; UnCover. **CCC**.
 Supersedes in part (in 1991): In Vitro Cellular and Developmental Biology (ISSN 0883-8364); Which was formerly: In Vitro (ISSN 0073-5655)
 Description: Publishes papers dealing with in vitro cultivation of cells, tissues, organs or tumors from multicellular animals.
 Refereed Serial

BIOLOGY — MICROBIOLOGY

576 US ISSN 1054-5476
QK725 CODEN: IVCPEO
IN VITRO CELLULAR & DEVELOPMENTAL BIOLOGY - PLANT. 1965. q. $115 in N. America (overseas $145); with Animal section $335 in N. America (overseas $380) (effective 1997). Society for In Vitro Biology, 9315 Largo Dr. W. Ste. 255, Largo, MD 20774. TEL 301-324-5054. FAX 301-324-5057. Ed. Trevor A. Thrope. adv. contact: Marietta Ellis. bk.rev.; index. circ. 1,400. (also avail. in microform from UMI; back issues avail.) **Indexed:** ASCA, Biol.Abstr., Chem.Abstr., Curr.Cont., Ind.Med., Sci.Cit.Ind. **Document type:** academic/scholarly publication.
—BLDSC (4372.500800); CASDDS; CISTI; EMDOCS; Genuine Article; KNAW; Linda Hall; SWETS; UMI; UnCover. **CCC.**
Supersedes in part (in 1991): In Vitro Cellular and Developmental Biology (ISSN 0883-8364); Which was formerly: In Vitro (ISSN 0073-5655)
Description: Publishes original papers in plant cellular and developmental biology with emphasis on the developmental, molecular and cellular biology of cells, tissues, and organs.
Refereed Serial

579 US ISSN 1077-3975
IN VITRO REPORT. 1950. bi-m. $40 (foreign $55) (effective 1997). Society for In Vitro Biology, 9315 Largo Dr. W., Ste. 255, Largo, MD 20774. TEL 301-324-5054. FAX 301-324-5057. (Subscr. to: Box 73230, Baltimore, MD 21273) Ed. Sandra Schneider; Pub. Marietta Ellis. circ. 2,100. **Document type:** academic/scholarly publication, monographic series, proceedings.
—CISTI.
Formerly (until 1994): T C A Report (ISSN 0163-772X)
Description: Contains news and notes about branches, sections, committees, and members of the society, placement service, notice of events of interest, and short articles.
Refereed Serial

576 II ISSN 0046-8991
QR1 CODEN: IJMBAC
INDIAN JOURNAL OF MICROBIOLOGY. (Text in English) 1961. q. $80. (Association of Microbiologists of India) Hindustan Publishing Corp., 4805-24, 1st Fl., Bharat Ram Rd., Darya Ganj, New Delhi 110 002, India. E-mail: hpcpd@giasdl01.vsnl.net.in. Ed. Dr. K.S. Gopalkrishnan. adv.; bk.rev. circ. 2,000. **Indexed:** Biol.Abstr., Biotech.Abstr., Chem.Abstr., Dairy Sci.Abstr., Diar.Dis.Res., Excerp.Med., Food Sci.& Tech.Abstr., Ind.Med., Ind.Vet., Nutr.Abstr., Rev.Plant Path., Rice Abstr., Soils & Fert., Vet.Bull.
—BLDSC (4417.300000); CASDDS; CISTI; Linda Hall; UnCover.

576 II ISSN 0303-4097
CODEN: IJMPAK
INDIAN JOURNAL OF MYCOLOGY AND PLANT PATHOLOGY. (Text in English) 1971. 3/yr. $100. Society of Mycology and Plant Pathology, Rajasthan College of Agriculture, Udaipur, Rajasthan 313 001, India. TELEX 28612 PP. (Dist. overseas by: HPC Publishers' Distributors Pvt. Ltd., 4805-24, 1st Fl., Bharat Ram Rd., Darya Ganj, New Delhi 110 002, India. TEL 91-11-3954401. FAX 91-11-6863511) Ed.Bd. adv.; bk.rev.; bibl.; charts; illus. circ. 500. **Indexed:** Agri.Eng.Abstr., Bibl.Agri., Biol.Abstr., Chem.Abstr., Cott.& Trop.Fibr.Abstr., Crop Physiol.Abstr., Fababean Abstr., Field Crop Abstr., Forest.Abstr., Herb.Abstr., Hort.Abstr., Indian Sci.Abstr., Maize Abstr., Ornam.Hort., Plant Grow.Reg.Abstr., Potato Abstr., Rev.Med.& Vet.Mycol., Rev.Plant Path., Rice Abstr., Seed Abstr., Soils & Fert., Sorghum & Millets Abstr., Triticale Abstr., Trop.Oil Seeds Abstr.
—CASDDS; Linda Hall; UnCover.

INDIAN JOURNAL OF NEMATOLOGY. see *AGRICULTURE*

INDIAN JOURNAL OF PATHOLOGY & MICROBIOLOGY. see *MEDICAL SCIENCES*

INDIAN POTATO ASSOCIATION. JOURNAL. see *AGRICULTURE — Crop Production And Soil*

INFECTION AND IMMUNITY. see *MEDICAL SCIENCES — Allergology And Immunology*

INFECTOLOGIA Y MICROBIOLOGIA CLINICA. see *MEDICAL SCIENCES — Communicable Diseases*

INFEKTIONS KLINIK - MIKROBIOLOGIE UND KRANKENHAUSHYGIENE. see *MEDICAL SCIENCES — Communicable Diseases*

576 UK ISSN 0952-1127
INNOVATION IN MICROBIOLOGY SERIES. 1983. irreg., vol.5, 1993. £55. Research Studies Press Ltd., 24 Belvedere Rd., Taunton, Somerset TA1 1HD, England. TEL 44-1823-336197. FAX 44-1823-253252. E-mail: vaw@rspltd.demon.co.uk. (Dist. by: John Wiley & Sons Ltd., Baffins Ln., Chichester, W. Sussex PO19 1UD, England. TEL 44-1243-779777. FAX 44-1243-775878) Ed. A.N. Sharpe. **Document type:** monographic series.
—CISTI.

576 575.1 FR ISSN 0924-4204
QR1 CODEN: AIPAEZ
INSTITUT PASTEUR. ANNALES. ACTUALITES. 1990. q. 529 F. (institutions in the Americas $101; elsewhere 620F.) (effective 1998). Editions Scientifiques et Medicales Elsevier, 141 rue de Javel, 75747 Paris, France. TEL 33-1-45589022. FAX 33-1-45589421. URL: http://www.elsevier.nl/. (Subscr. in U.S. and Canada to: Elsevier Science Inc., Box 945, Madison Sq. Sta., New York, NY 10159-0945. TEL 212-633-3730. FAX 212-633-3680) Ed. G.N. Cohen. bk.rev. (also avail. in microform from UMI; back issues avail.) **Indexed:** Excerp.Med. (1993-). **Document type:** academic/scholarly publication.
—BLDSC (0926.500000); CISTI; EMDOCS; KNAW. **CCC.**
Description: Presents the scientific activities of the institute which is involved in many fields from medical bacteriology to sophisticated genetics through embryogenesis and neurobiology.
Refereed Serial

INSTITUT PASTEUR. BULLETIN. see *MEDICAL SCIENCES — Communicable Diseases*

INSTITUT PASTEUR D'ALGERIE. ARCHIVES. see *MEDICAL SCIENCES — Communicable Diseases*

576 595.7 SG ISSN 0377-3418
QR64.S382
INSTITUT PASTEUR DE DAKAR. RAPPORT SUR LE FONCTIONNEMENT TECHNIQUE. (Text in French) 1938. a. free. Institut Pasteur Dakar, P.O. Box 220, 36 av. Pasteur, Dakar, Senegal. FAX 221-23-87-72. E-mail: moreaujp@pasteur.sn. Ed. Jean-Paul Moreau. circ. 600. **Indexed:** Biol.Abstr. **Document type:** corporate report.
Description: Reports on medical research activities in virology, immunology and vaccinology, edidemiology and entomology, bacteriology.

INSTITUT PASTEUR HELLENIQUE. ARCHIVES. see *MEDICAL SCIENCES — Communicable Diseases*

576 JA ISSN 0073-8751
QR1
INSTITUTE FOR FERMENTATION, OSAKA. RESEARCH COMMUNICATIONS/HAKKO KENKYUJO HOKOKU. (Text and summaries in English) 1963. biennial; no.18, 1997. 1300 Yen per no. Institute for Fermentation, Osaka - Hakko Kenkyujo, 17-85 Juso-honmachi 2-chome, Yodogawa-ku, Osaka 532, Japan. FAX 81-6-300-6814. Ed. Masao Takeuchi. cum.index. circ. 1,300. (back issues avail.) **Indexed:** Biol.Abstr., Curr.Biotech.Abstr., Rev.Plant Path. **Document type:** bulletin.
—CISTI.
Formerly (until no.4, 1969): Institute for Fermentation, Osaka. Annual Report.
Description: Provides information on the institute's taxonomical research studies of microorganisms, basic studies on animal cells, and on the culture collection of the institute.

579 BL ISSN 0073-9855
R25 CODEN: RIALA6
INSTITUTO ADOLFO LUTZ. REVISTA. (Text in English or Portuguese; summaries in English and Portuguese) 1941. s-a. exchange basis; free to qualified personnel. Instituto Adolfo Lutz, Diretoria Geral, Av. Dr. Arnaldo 355, C.P. 7027, 01246-902 Sao Paulo SP, Brazil. TEL 55-11-8510111. FAX 55-11-8533505. Ed. Luiz Carlos Meneguetti. bibl.; charts; illus.; index. circ. 1,200. **Indexed:** Abstr.Hyg., Agrindex, Anal.Abstr., Biol.Abstr., Chem.Abstr., Dairy Sci.Abstr., Excerp.Med., Food Sci.& Tech.Abstr., Ind.Med., Ind.Vet., Microbiol.Abstr., Rev.Med.& Vet.Mycol., Tox.Abstr., Trop.Dis.Bull., Vet.Bull., Virol.Abstr. **Document type:** government publication.
—BLDSC (7816.000000); CASDDS.
Description: Original papers in experimental and laboratory medicine or public health laboratory with emphasis on microbiology, epidemiology, chemistry and food chemistry.
Refereed Serial

INSTITUTO DE SALUD PUBLICA DE CHILE. BOLETIN. see *PUBLIC HEALTH AND SAFETY*

INSTITUTUL DE CERCETARI PENTRU PROTECTIA PLANTELOR. ANALELE/RESEARCH INSTITUTE FOR PLANT PROTECTION. ANNALS. see *AGRICULTURE*

576.64 US ISSN 0276-1076
QR187.5 CODEN: INRFDC
INTERFERON. 1979. irreg., vol.9, 1987. Academic Press, Inc., 525 B St., Ste. 1900, San Diego, CA 92101-4495. TEL 619-231-0926. FAX 619-699-6715. (Subscr. to: Order Dept., 6277 Sea Harbor Dr., 4th Fl., Orlando, FL 32887. TEL 800-321-5068) Ed. I. Gresser. (reprint service avail. from ISI) **Indexed:** Curr.Adv.Ecol.Sci.
—CASDDS; CISTI.

INTERNATIONAL JOURNAL FOR PARASITOLOGY. see *MEDICAL SCIENCES — Communicable Diseases*

576 NE ISSN 0924-8579
CODEN: IAAGEA
INTERNATIONAL JOURNAL OF ANTIMICROBIAL AGENTS. (Text in English) 1991. 8/yr. fl.1372($788) (effective 1998). Elsevier Science B.V., P.O. Box 211, 1000 AE Amsterdam, Netherlands. TEL 31-20-4853911. FAX 31-20-4853598. TELEX 18582 ESPA NL. E-mail: nlinfo-f@elsevier.nl; usinfo-f@elsevier.com; forinfo-kyf04035@niftyserve.or.jp; URL: http://www.elsevier.nl/. (Subscr. in the Americas to: Elsevier Science, Regional Sales Office, Box 945, New York, NY 10159-0945. TEL 212-633-3730. FAX 212-633-3680; Subscr. in Australasia and the Far East to: Elsevier Science (Singapore) Pte Ltd, No.1 Temasek Ave., No.17-01 Millenia Tower, Singapore 039192, Singapore. TEL 65-434-3727. FAX 65-337-2230; Subscr. in Japan to: Elsevier Science Japan, 9-15 Higashi-Azabu 1-chome, Minato-ku, Tokyo 106, Japan. TEL 81-3-5561-5033. FAX 81-3-5561-5047) Ed. Jan Verhoef. adv. (also avail. in microform from UMI; back issues avail.) **Indexed:** ASCA, Curr.Cont., Excerp.Med., Ind.Sci.Rev. **Document type:** academic/scholarly publication.
—BLDSC (4542.084000); CASDDS; CISTI; EMDOCS; Genuine Article; KNAW; SWETS. **CCC.**
Description: Provides information on the physical, chemical, pharmacological, in vitro and clinical properties of individual antimicrobial agents, and immunotherapy.
Refereed Serial

BIOLOGY — MICROBIOLOGY

576   NE   ISSN 0168-1605
CODEN: IJFMDD
INTERNATIONAL JOURNAL OF FOOD MICROBIOLOGY. (Text and summaries in English) 1984. 21/yr. fl.3760($2161) (effective 1998). (International Union of Microbiological Societies) Elsevier Science B.V., P.O. Box 211, 1000 AE Amsterdam, Netherlands. TEL 31-20-4853911. FAX 31-20-4853598. TELEX 18582 ESP NL. E-mail: nlinfo-f@elsevier.nl; usinfo-f@elsevier.com; forinfo-kyf04035@niftyserve.or.jp; URL: http://www.elsevier.nl/. (Subscr. in the Americas to: Elsevier Science, Regional Sales Office, Box 945, New York, NY 10159-0945. TEL 212-633-3730. FAX 212-633-3680; Subscr. in Australasia and the Far East to: Elsevier Science (Singapore) Pte Ltd, No.1 Temasek Ave., No.17-01 Millenia Tower, Singapore 039192, Singapore. TEL 65-434-3727. FAX 65-337-2230; Subscr. in Japan to: Elsevier Science Japan, 9-15 Higashi-Azabu 1-chome, Minato-ku, Tokyo 106, Japan. TEL 81-3-5561-5033. FAX 212-633-3990) (Co-sponsor: International Committee on Food Microbiology and Hygiene) Ed. M. Jakobsen. adv.; bk.rev.; abstr.; bibl.; charts; illus. circ. 700. (also avail. in microform from UMI; back issues avail.) **Indexed:** Abstr.Hyg., Apic.Abstr., ASCA, Bibl.Agri., Curr.Adv.Ecol.Sci., Curr.Cont., Dairy Sci.Abstr., Excerp.Med., Food Sci.& Tech.Abstr., Ind.Sci.Rev., Ind.Vet., Maize Abstr., Pig News & Info., Poult.Abstr., Protozool.Abstr., Rev.Med.& Vet.Mycol., Sci.Cit.Ind., SSCI. **Document type:** academic/scholarly publication.
—BLDSC (4542.253000); CASDDS; CISTI; Ei; Genuine Article; KNAW; Linda Hall; SWETS; UnCover. **CCC.**
Description: Covers all aspects of microbiological safety, quality and acceptability of foods.
Refereed Serial

589.9   US   ISSN 0020-7713
QR1   CODEN: IJSBA8
INTERNATIONAL JOURNAL OF SYSTEMATIC BACTERIOLOGY. 1951. q. $172 to non-members; members $$51 (effective 1997). (International Union of Microbiological Societies, International Committee on Systematic Bacteriology) American Society for Microbiology, 1325 Massachusetts Ave., N.W., Washington, DC 20005. TEL 202-737-3600. Ed. E. Stackebrandt. adv.; bk.rev.; bibl.; charts; illus.; index. circ. 1,930. (also avail. in microform from UMI; back issues avail.; reprint service avail. from UMI) **Indexed:** Abstr.Bull.Inst.Pap.Chem., Abstr.Hyg., ASCA, Biol.Abstr., Chem.Abstr., Curr.Cont., Dairy Sci.Abstr., Deep Sea Res.& Oceanogr.Abstr., Excerp.Med., Food Sci.& Tech.Abstr., Helminthol.Abstr., Ind.Med., Ind.Sci.Rev., Ind.Vet., Potato Abstr., Poult.Abstr., Rev.Med.& Vet.Mycol., Rev.Plant Path., Sci.Cit.Ind., Small Anim.Abstr., Soils & Fert., Trop.Dis.Bull., Vet.Bull., W.R.C.Inf. **Document type:** academic/scholarly publication.
●Also available on CD-ROM.
—BLDSC (4542.690000); CASDDS; CISTI; Genuine Article; KNAW; Linda Hall; SWETS; UMI; UnCover. **CCC.**
Formerly: International Bulletin of Bacteriological Nomenclature and Taxonomy.
Description: Publishes papers concerned with the systematics of bacteria, yeasts, and yeastlike organisms, including taxonomy, nomenclature, identification, characterization, and culture preservation.
Refereed Serial

576   TU   ISSN 0259-8426
INTERNATIONAL QUARTERLY OF VIROLOGY. (Text in English) 1987. q. $125. Tahsin Yazicioglu, P. Kutusu 1318, Sirkeci, Istanbul 34438, Turkey. Ed.Bd. adv.; bk.rev. **Indexed:** Biol.Abstr., Curr.Cont., Excerp.Med., Ref.Zh., Sci.Cit.Ind.

576 615   US   ISSN 0733-6373
CODEN: POCHES
INTERSCIENCE CONFERENCE ON ANTIMICROBIAL AGENTS AND CHEMOTHERAPY. PROGRAM AND ABSTRACTS. Former attached title: I C A A C Program and Abstracts. 1961. a. $25. American Society for Microbiology, 1325 Massachusetts Ave., N.W., Washington, DC 20005-4171. TEL 202-737-3600. (back issues avail.) **Document type:** proceedings.
—Linda Hall.
Refereed Serial

576.64   SZ   ISSN 0300-5526
QR355   CODEN: IVRYAK
INTERVIROLOGY; international journal of basic and medical virology. (Text in English) 1973. bi-m. 278.60 SFr.($219.10) to individuals; institutions 796 SFr.($626) (effective 1998). S. Karger AG, Allschwilerstr. 10, P.O. Box, CH-4009 Basel, Switzerland. TEL 41-61-3061111. FAX 41-61-3061234. E-mail: karger@karger.ch; URL: http://www.karger.ch. Ed. R.W. Braun. adv.; bibl.; charts; illus. circ. 1,200. (also avail. in microform) **Indexed:** Abstr.Hyg., AIDS Abstr., Biol.Abstr., Chem.Abstr., Curr.Cont., Dairy Sci.Abstr., Excerp.Med., Forest.Abstr., Ind.Med., Ind.Vet., Int.Sci.Rev., Pig News & Info., Poult.Abstr., Rev.Plant Path., Sci.Cit.Ind., Trop.Dis.Bull., Vet.Bull. **Document type:** academic/scholarly publication.
—BLDSC (4557.472000); CASDDS; CISTI; EMDOCS; Genuine Article; KNAW; Linda Hall; SWETS; UnCover. **CCC.**
Description: Features various aspects of virology.
Refereed Serial

INVERTEBRATE NEUROSCIENCE. see *BIOLOGY — Entomology*

576 616.97   JA   ISSN 0916-4804
CODEN: NIGZE4
JAPANESE JOURNAL OF MEDICAL MYCOLOGY/NIHON ISHINKIN GAKKAI ZASSHI. (Text in English) 1960. q. 10300 Yen. (Japanese Society for Medical Mycology) Business Center for Academic Societies Japan, 5-16-9 Honkomagome, Bunkyo-ku, Tokyo 113, Japan. TEL 03-5814-5811. FAX 03-5814-5822. TELEX 2722268 BCJSP J. adv.; bk.rev.; index. circ. 1,000. (back issues avail.) **Indexed:** Ind.Vet., Rev.Med.& Vet.Mycol., Small Anim.Abstr., Soils & Fert., Vet.Bull. **Document type:** academic/scholarly publication.
—CASDDS; CISTI; EMDOCS.
Formerly (until 1990): Shinkin to Shinkinsho (ISSN 0583-0516)

576   US   ISSN 1054-2744
QR46
JAWETZ, MELNICK & ADELBERG'S MEDICAL MICROBIOLOGY. 1954. biennial, 20th ed., 1995. $37.95. Appleton & Lange (Subsidiary of: Simon & Schuster Company), Box 120041, Stamford, CT 06912-0041. TEL 203-406-4500.
—BLDSC (4663.424250); CISTI. **CCC.**
Former titles (until 1991): Medical Microbiology; (until 1989): Review of Medical Microbiology (ISSN 0486-6118)
Description: Descriptions of basic microbiology and virology; covers developments in the fields of biochemistry, genetics, pharmacology and immunology.
Refereed Serial

589.9   UK   ISSN 1364-5072
QR1   CODEN: JAMIFK
JOURNAL OF APPLIED MICROBIOLOGY. 1938. m. £565($1029) (foreign £620) (effective 1998). (Society for Applied Bacteriology) Blackwell Science Ltd., Osney Mead, Oxford OX2 0EL, England. TEL 44-1865-206206. FAX 44-1865-721205. E-mail: journals.cs@blacksci.co.uk; URL: http://www.black.co.uk. Ed. Duncan E.S. Stewart-Tull; Pub. Allen Stevens. R&P contact: Sarah Pollard. adv. contact: Martine Cariou-Keen. bk.rev.; abstr.; bibl.; index. circ. 2,765. (also avail. in microform from UMI; back issues avail.) **Indexed:** Abstr.Hyg., ASCA, Biol.Abstr., Biol.& Agr.Ind., Biotech.Abstr., Chem.Abstr., Curr.Biotech.Abstr., Curr.Cont., Curr.Leather Lit., Dairy Sci.Abstr., Deep Sea Res.& Oceanogr.Abstr., Dent.Ind., Ecol.Abstr., Excerp.Med., Field Crop Abstr., Food Sci.& Tech.Abstr., Geo.Abstr.P.G., Helminthol.Abstr, Herb.Abstr., IDA, Ind.Med., Ind.Sci.Rev., Ind.Vet., INIS Atomind., Maize Abstr., Nutr.Abstr., Ornam.Hort., Packag.Sci.Tech., Pig News & Info., Plant Grow.Reg.Abstr., Potato Abstr., Poult.Abstr., Rev.Med.& Vet.Mycol., Rev.Plant Path., Risk Abstr., Sci.Cit.Ind., Sel.Water Res.Abstr., Soils & Fert., Soyabean Abstr., Telegen, Triticale Abstr., Trop.Dis.Bull., Vet.Bull., W.R.C.Inf. **Document type:** academic/scholarly publication.
—BLDSC (4943.070000); ADONIS; CASDDS; CISTI; Ei; EMDOCS; Genuine Article; KR SourceOne; Linda Hall; SWETS; UMI; UnCover. **CCC.**
Former titles(until 1997): Journal of Applied Bacteriology (ISSN 0021-8847); Society for Applied Bacteriology. Proceedings.
Refereed Serial

589.9   UK
JOURNAL OF APPLIED MICROBIOLOGY. SUPPLEMENT. a. Blackwell Science Ltd., Osney Mead, Oxford OX2 0EL, England. TEL 44-1865-206206. FAX 44-1865-721205. E-mail: journals.cs@blacksci.co.uk; URL: http://www.black.co.uk. Pub. Allen Stevens. R&P contact: Sarah Pollard. adv. contact: Martine Cariou-Keen. **Indexed:** Food Sci.& Tech.Abstr. **Document type:** academic/scholarly publication.
—ADONIS; EMDOCS. **CCC.**
Formerly: Journal of Applied Bacteriology. Symposium Supplement (ISSN 0267-4440)

JOURNAL OF APPLIED PHYCOLOGY. see *BIOLOGY — Botany*

589.9   US   ISSN 0021-9193
QR1   CODEN: JOBAAY
JOURNAL OF BACTERIOLOGY. 1916. s-m. $448 to non-members; members $82 (effective 1997). American Society for Microbiology, 1325 Massachusetts Ave., N.W., Washington, DC 20005. TEL 202-737-3600. Ed. Graham C. Walker. adv.; abstr.; bibl.; illus.; index. circ. 6,970. (also avail. in microform from UMI; back issues avail.; reprint service avail. from UMI) **Indexed:** Abstr.Bull.Inst.Pap.Chem., Abstr.Hyg., ASCA, Bibl.Agri., Bio-Contr.News & Info., Biol.Abstr., Biol.& Agr.Ind., Biotech.Abstr., Chem.Abstr., Curr.Cont., Curr.Adv.Biochem., Curr.Adv.Genetics & Molec.Biol., Curr.Biotech.Abstr., Curr.Cont., Dairy Sci.Abstr., Deep Sea Res.& Oceanogr.Abstr., Dent.Ind., Diar.Dis.Res., Field Crop Abstr., Food Sci.& Tech.Abstr., Gen.Sci.Ind., Helminthol.Abstr., Herb.Abstr., Hort.Abstr., Ind.Med., Ind.Sci.Rev., Ind.Vet., INIS Atomind., Int.Aerosp.Abstr., Maize Abstr., Med.& Surg.Dermat., Nutr.Abstr., Plant Grow.Reg.Abstr., Rev.Appl.Entomol., Rev.Med.& Vet.Mycol., Rev.Plant Path., Sci.Cit.Ind., Seed Abstr., Soils & Fert., Soyabean Abstr., Telegen, Triticale Abstr., Trop.Dis.Bull., Vet.Bull., W.R.C.Inf. **Document type:** academic/scholarly publication.
●Also available on CD-ROM.
—BLDSC (4951.000000); CASDDS; CISTI; Genuine Article; KNAW; KR SourceOne; Linda Hall; SWETS; UMI; UnCover. **CCC.**
Description: Devoted to the advancement of fundamental knowledge concerning bacteria and other microorganisms, including fungi and other unicellular, eucaryotic organisms.
Refereed Serial

576   GW   ISSN 0233-111X
QR1   CODEN: JBMIEQ
JOURNAL OF BASIC MICROBIOLOGY; an international journal on biochemistry, physiology, genetics, morphology and ecology of microorganisms. (Text in English) 1960. 6/yr. DM.195 (foreign DM.207) to individuals; institutions DM.595 (foreign DM.625) (effective 1997). Akademie Verlag GmbH, Muehlenstr. 33-34, 13187 Berlin, Germany. TEL 49-30-47889348. FAX 49-30-47889357. E-mail: info@akademie-verlag.de. (Subscr. in the Americas to: John Wiley & Sons, Inc., 605 Third Ave., New York, NY 10158. TEL 212-850-6645. FAX 212-850-6021) Eds. H. Malke, D. Groeger. adv.; bk.rev.; charts; illus.; index. **Indexed:** Abstr.Hyg., ASCA, Biol.Abstr., Chem.Abstr., Curr.Adv.Biochem., Curr.Biotech.Abstr., Curr.Cont., Dairy Sci.Abstr., Deep Sea Res.& Oceanogr.Abstr., Excerp.Med., Helminthol.Abstr., Ind.Med., Ind.Vet., INIS Atomind., Rev.Plant Path., Rice Abstr., Sci.Cit.Ind., Soils & Fert., SSCI, Trop.Dis.Bull., Vet.Bull., W.R.C.Inf. **Document type:** academic/scholarly publication.
—BLDSC (4951.125000); CASDDS; CISTI; EMDOCS; Genuine Article; Linda Hall; SWETS; UnCover. **CCC.**
Formerly: Zeitschrift fuer Allgemeine Mikrobiologie (ISSN 0044-2208)
Description: Publishes results of fundamental research on procariotic and eucariotic microorganisms.

JOURNAL OF BIOMOLECULAR SCREENING. see *BIOLOGY — Genetics*

BIOLOGY — MICROBIOLOGY

576 US ISSN 0095-1137
QR46 CODEN: JCMIDW
JOURNAL OF CLINICAL MICROBIOLOGY. 1975. m. $312 to non-members; members $55 (effective 1997). American Society for Microbiology, 1325 Massachusetts Ave., N.W., Washington, DC 20005. TEL 202-737-3600. Ed. Richard C. Tilton. adv.; s-a. index. circ. 13,470. (also avail. in microform from UMI; back issues avail.; reprint service avail. from UMI) **Indexed:** Abstr.Hyg., AIDS Abstr., ASCA, Biol.Abstr., Chem.Abstr., Curr.Adv.Genetics & Molec.Biol., Curr.Cont., Dairy Sci.Abstr., Deep Sea Res.& Oceanogr.Abstr., Dent.Ind., Diar.Dis.Res., Excerp.Med., Food Sci.& Tech.Abstr., Helminthol.Abstr., Ind.Med., Ind.Sci.Rev., Ind.Vet., INIS Atomind., Kidney, Med.& Surg.Dermat, Pig News & Info., Poult.Abstr., Protozool.Abstr., Rev.Med.& Vet.Mycol., Rev.Plant Path., Sci.Cit.Ind., Small Anim.Abstr., Sport Fish.Abstr., Telegen, Trop.Dis.Bull., Vet.Bull., Wild.Rev., Zoo.Rec. **Document type:** academic/scholarly publication.
●Also available on CD-ROM.
—BLDSC (4958.570000); CASDDS; CISTI; Genuine Article; KNAW; SWETS; UMI; UnCover. **CCC.**
   Description: Concerns the microbiological aspects of human and animal infections and infestations, with emphasis given to their etiological agents, diagnosis, and epidemiology.
   Refereed Serial

JOURNAL OF ELECTRON MICROSCOPY. see *BIOLOGY — Microscopy*

576 JA ISSN 0022-1260
QR1 CODEN: JGAMA9
JOURNAL OF GENERAL AND APPLIED MICROBIOLOGY. (Text in English) 1955. bi-m. $145. Microbiology Research Foundation - Oyo Biseibutsugaku Kenkyu Shoreikai, Japan Academic Societies Center Bldg., 16-9 Honkomagome 5-chome, Bunkyo-ku, Tokyo 113, Japan. (Dist. by: Intercontinental Marketing Corp., I.P.O. Box 5056, Tokyo 100-30, Japan. TEL 81-3-3661-7458. FAX 81-3-3667-9646) Ed. Shozo Koga. charts; illus. (also avail. in microform from UMI; reprint service avail. from UMI) **Indexed:** ASCA, Biol.Abstr., Biotech.Abstr., Chem.Abstr., Curr.Adv.Ecol.Sci., Curr.Biotech.Abstr., Curr.Cont., Dairy Sci.Abstr., Excerp.Med., Field Crop Abstr., Food Sci.& Tech.Abstr., Forest.Abstr., Helminthol.Abstr., Herb.Abstr., Hort.Abstr., Ind.Sci.Rev., Ind.Vet., INIS Atomind., JTA, Rev.Med.& Vet.Mycol., Rev.Plant Path., Sci.Cit.Ind., Sel.Water Res.Abstr., Soils & Fert., W.R.C.Inf. **Document type:** academic/scholarly publication.
—BLDSC (4987.700000); CASDDS; CISTI; Ei; Genuine Article; Linda Hall; SWETS; UnCover.

576 UK ISSN 0022-1317
QR360 CODEN: JGVIAY
JOURNAL OF GENERAL VIROLOGY. 1967. m. $480 (foreign $840) (effective 1997). Society for General Microbiology, Marlborough House, Basingstoke Rd., Spencers Wood, Reading RG7 1AE, England. TEL 44-1734-885577. FAX 44-1734-885656. Ed. G. Darby. adv. contact: John Brimelow. bibl.; charts; illus.; index. circ. 2,300. **Indexed:** AIDS Abstr., Anim.Breed.Abstr., ASCA, Bibl.Agri., Bio-Contr.News & Info., Biol.Abstr., Biotech.Abstr., Chem.Abstr., Curr.Adv.Cancer Res., Curr.Adv.Ecol.Sci., Curr.Adv.Genetics & Molec.Biol., Curr.Biotech.Abstr., Curr.Cont., Dairy Sci.Abstr., Dent.Ind., Diar.Dis.Res., Excerp.Med., Food Sci.& Tech.Abstr., Ind.Med., Ind.Sci.Rev., Ind.Vet., Neurosci.Cit.Ind., Nutr.Abstr., Pig News & Info., Poult.Abstr., Rev.Plant Path., Rice Abstr., Sci.Cit.Ind., Small Anim.Abstr., Soils & Fert., Sport Fish.Abstr., Triticale Abstr., Trop.Dis.Bull., Trop.Oil Seeds Abstr., Vet.Bull., W.R.C.Inf., Wild.Rev., Zoo.Rec. **Document type:** academic/scholarly publication.
—BLDSC (4989.300000); CASDDS; CISTI; Genuine Article; KNAW; Linda Hall; SWETS; UnCover. **CCC.**

JOURNAL OF HUMAN VIROLOGY. see *MEDICAL SCIENCES — Communicable Diseases*

JOURNAL OF INDUSTRIAL MICROBIOLOGY AND BIOTECHNOLOGY. see *BIOLOGY — Biotechnology*

576 US ISSN 1053-6388
  CODEN: JMAMEL
JOURNAL OF MEDICAL AND APPLIED MALACOLOGY. (Text in English, Spanish) 1989. a. $50 to non-members. International Society for Medical and Applied Malacology, Box 2715, Ann Arbor, MI 48106. TEL 313-764-0470. Ed. John B. Burch. abstr.; bibl.; charts; illus.; stat. circ. 200. (back issues avail.)
—BLDSC (5017.047500); CISTI; KNAW.
   Description: Contains original research on mollusks that are of medical, veterinary, agricultural and economic importance.

576 NE ISSN 0167-7012
QR65 CODEN: JMIMDQ
JOURNAL OF MICROBIOLOGICAL METHODS. (Text in English) 1983. m. fl.2550($1466) (effective 1998). Elsevier Science B.V., P.O. Box 211, 1000 AE Amsterdam, Netherlands. TEL 31-20-4853911. FAX 31-20-4853598. TELEX 18582 ESPA NL. E-mail: nlinfo-f@elsevier.nl; usinfo-f@elsevier.com; forinfo-kyf04035@niftyserve.or.jp; URL: http://www.elsevier.nl/. (Subscr. in the Americas to: Elsevier Science, Regional Sales Office, Box 945, New York, NY 10159-0945. TEL 212-633-3730. FAX 212-633-3680; Subscr. in Australasia and the Far East to: Elsevier Science (Singapore) Pte Ltd, No.1 Temasek Ave., No.17-01 Millenia Tower, Singapore 039192, Singapore. TEL 65-434-3727. FAX 65-337-2230; Subscr. in Japan to: Elsevier Science Japan, 9-15 Higashi-Azabu 1-chome, Minato-ku, Tokyo 106, Japan. TEL 81-3-5561-5033. FAX 81-3-5561-5047) Eds. D. White, C. Knowles. (also avail. in microform from UMI; back issues avail.) **Indexed:** Abstr.Bull.Inst.Pap.Chem., Abstr.Hyg., ASCA, Biodet.Abstr., Biol.Abstr., Chem.Abstr., Curr.Adv.Biochem., Curr.Adv.Ecol.Sci., Curr.Biotech.Abstr., Curr.Cont., Dairy Sci.Abstr., Excerp.Med., Food Sci.& Tech.Abstr., Ind.Sci.Rev., Ind.Vet., Protozool.Abstr., Sci.Cit.Ind., Sel.Water Res.Abstr., Soils & Fert., Vet.Bull., W.R.C.Inf. **Document type:** academic/scholarly publication.
—BLDSC (5019.260000); ADONIS; CASDDS; CISTI; Genuine Article; Linda Hall; SWETS; UnCover. **CCC.**
   Description: Publishes original papers and short reviews covering methods on all aspects of microbiology, excluding virology.
   Refereed Serial

JOURNAL OF MOLECULAR GRAPHICS. see *COMPUTERS — Computer Graphics*

JOURNAL OF MOLECULAR NEUROSCIENCE. see *MEDICAL SCIENCES — Psychiatry And Neurology*

JOURNAL OF PARASITOLOGY. see *MEDICAL SCIENCES — Communicable Diseases*

576 US ISSN 1060-3999
QR69.A88 CODEN: JRMMEE
JOURNAL OF RAPID METHODS AND AUTOMATION IN MICROBIOLOGY. 1992. q. $70 to individuals (foreign $89); institutions $90 (foreign $109). Food and Nutrition Press, Inc., 2 Corporate Dr., Box 374, Trumbull, CT 06611. TEL 203-261-8587. FAX 203-261-9724. Ed. Daniel Y.C. Fung. **Indexed:** Food Sci.& Tech.Abstr. **Document type:** academic/scholarly publication.
—BLDSC (5046.200000); CASDDS; CISTI.
   Description: Publishes information on methods developed by scientists for the rapid isolation, detection, enumeration, and identification of microorganisms.

576.64 NE ISSN 0166-0934
  CODEN: JVMEDH
JOURNAL OF VIROLOGICAL METHODS. (Text in English) 1980. m. fl.4064($2336) (effective 1998). Elsevier Science B.V., P.O. Box 211, 1000 AE Amsterdam, Netherlands. TEL 31-20-4853911. FAX 31-20-4853598. TELEX 18582 ESPA NL. E-mail: nlinfo-f@elsevier.nl; usinfo-f@elsevier.com; forinfo-kyf04035@niftyserve.or.jp; URL: http://www.elsevier.nl/. (Subscr. in the Americas to: Elsevier Science, Regional Sales Office, Box 945, New York, NY 10159-0945. TEL 212-633-3730. FAX 212-633-3680; Subscr. in Australasia and the Far East to: Elsevier Science (Singapore) Pte Ltd, No.1 Temasek Ave., No.17-01 Millenia Tower, Singapore 039192, Singapore. TEL 65-434-3727. FAX 65-337-2230; Subscr. in Japan to: Elsevier Science Japan, 9-15 Higashi-Azabu 1-chome, Minato-ku, Tokyo 106, Japan. TEL 81-3-5561-5033. FAX 81-3-5561-5047) Ed. A.J. Zuckerman. adv. (tabloid format; also avail. in microform from UMI,PMC; back issues avail.; reprint service avail. from ISI) **Indexed:** Abstr.Hyg., AIDS Abstr., ASCA, Biol.Abstr., Chem.Abstr., Curr.Adv.Ecol.Sci., Curr.Adv.Genetics & Molec.Biol., Curr.Cont., Excerp.Med., Ind.Med., Ind.Sci.Rev., Ind.Vet., INIS Atomind., Sci.Cit.Ind., Small Anim.Abstr., Triticale Abstr., Trop.Dis.Bull., Vet.Bull. **Document type:** academic/scholarly publication.
—BLDSC (5072.486000); ADONIS; CASDDS; CISTI; EMDOCS; Genuine Article; SWETS; UnCover. **CCC.**
   Description: Publishes original papers covering techniques on all aspects of virology.
   Refereed Serial

576 US ISSN 0022-538X
QR360 CODEN: JOVIAM
JOURNAL OF VIROLOGY. 1967. m. $462 to non-members; members $89 (effective 1997). American Society for Microbiology, 1325 Massachusetts Ave., N.W., Washington, DC 20005. TEL 202-737-3600. Ed. Thomas E. Shenk. adv.; charts; illus.; s-a. index. circ. 5,330. (also avail. in microform from UMI; back issues avail.; reprint service avail. from UMI) **Indexed:** AIDS Abstr., ASCA, Bibl.Agri., Bio-Contr.News & Info., Biol.Abstr., Biol.& Agr.Ind., Biotech.Abstr., Chem.Abstr., Curr.Adv.Biochem., Curr.Adv.Cancer Res., Curr.Adv.Ecol.Sci., Curr.Adv.Genetics & Molec.Biol., Curr.Biotech.Abstr., Curr.Cont., Dairy Sci.Abstr., Dent.Ind., Diar.Dis.Res., Excerp.Med., Food Sci.& Tech.Abstr., Helminthol.Abstr., Hort.Abstr., Ind.Med., Ind.Sci.Rev., Ind.Vet., INIS Atomind., Neurosci.Cit.Ind., Pig News & Info., Poult.Abstr., Rev.Appl.Entomol., Sci.Cit.Ind., Small Anim.Abstr., Sport Fish.Abstr., Telegen, Trop.Dis.Bull., Vet.Bull., Wild.Rev. **Document type:** academic/scholarly publication.
●Also available on CD-ROM.
—BLDSC (5072.490000); CASDDS; CISTI; Genuine Article; KNAW; KR SourceOne; Linda Hall; SWETS; UMI; UnCover. **CCC.**
   Description: Devoted to the dissemination of fundamental knowledge concerning viruses of bacteria, plants, and animals.

KISEICHU BUNRUI KEITAI DANWAKAI KAIHO/JAPANESE SOCIETY FOR SYSTEMATIC PARASITOLOGY. CIRCULAR. see *MEDICAL SCIENCES — Communicable Diseases*

576 JA
KOEN BISEIBUTSU KENKYUKAI KOEN YOSHISHU/CONFERENCE ON THE BIOLOGY OF HALOPHILIC MICROORGANISMS. PROCEEDINGS. (Text in Japanese) a. Koen Biseibutsu Kenkyukai, Osaka Shiritsu Kankyo Kagaku Kenkyujo, 8-34 Tojocho, Tennoji-ku, Osaka 543, Japan.

576 574.192 JA ISSN 0368-5365
TP500 CODEN: KGBKBK
KOGYO GIJUTSUIN. BISEIBUTSU KOGYO GIJUTSU KENKYUJO. KENKYU HOKOKU/FERMENTATION RESEARCH INSTITUTE. REPORT. (Text and summaries in English or Japanese) 1943. 2/yr. exchange basis. Fermentation Research Institute, Technology Information Center - Kogyo Gijutsuin Biseibutsu Kogyo Gijutsu Kenkyujo, 1-1-3 Yatabe-machi, Tsukuba-gun, Ibaraki 305, Japan. Ed. Muneo Yamaguchi. circ. 850. **Indexed:** Abstr.Bull.Inst.Pap.Chem., Biol.Abstr., Chem.Abstr., Food Sci.& Tech.Abstr., JTA.
—BLDSC (7470.500000); CASDDS.
   Description: Presents research conducted in microbiology.

576.64 574   JA   ISSN 0075-7357
QR360   CODEN: ARIVAK
KYOTO UNIVERSITY. INSTITUTE FOR VIRUS RESEARCH. ANNUAL REPORT/KYOTO DAIGAKU UIRUSU KENKYUJO NENKAN KIYO.* (Text in English) 1958. a. (Kyoto University, Institute for Virus Research - Kyoto Daigaku Uirusu Kenkyujo) Kyoto University Press, Yoshida-Hon-cho, Sakyo-ku, Kyoto 606, Japan. Ed. Seiich Matsumoto. circ. controlled. **Indexed:** Biol.Abstr., Chem.Abstr., INIS Atomind.
—BLDSC (1306.800000); CASDDS.

576 637   UK
LACTIC ACID BACTERIA. 1992. irreg. price varies. Elsevier Science Ltd., Books Division, P.O. Box 800, Kidlington, Oxford OX5 1DX, England. TEL 44-1865-843000. FAX 44-1865-843010. E-mail: nlinfo-f@elsevier.nl; usinfo-f@elsevier.com; forinfo-kyf04035@niftyserve.or.jp; URL: http://www.elsevier.nl/. (Subscr. to: Elsevier Science, Regional Sales Office, P.O. Box 211, 1000 AE Amsterdam, Netherlands. TEL 31-20-4853757. FAX 31-20-4853432; Subscr. in the Americas to: Elsevier Science, Regional Sales Office, Box 945, New York, NY 10159-0945. TEL 212-633-3730. FAX 212-633-3680; Subscr. in Australasia and the Far East to: Elsevier Science (Singapore) Pte Ltd, No.1 Temasek Ave., No.17-01 Millenia Tower, Singapore 039192, Singapore. TEL 65-434-3727. FAX 65-337-2230) Ed.Bd. bibl. **Document type:** monographic series.
Description: Scholarly monographs pertaining to the bacteriology and microbiology of lactic acid bacteria in dairy products and related substances, incorporating relevant aspects of toxicological studies.
Refereed Serial

LE LAIT. see AGRICULTURE — Dairying And Dairy Products

589.9   UK   ISSN 0266-8254
QR1   CODEN: LAMIE7
LETTERS IN APPLIED MICROBIOLOGY. 1985. m. £408($863) (outside Europe £546) (includes Journal of Applied Microbiology & Annual Symposium) (effective 1997). (Society for Applied Bacteriology) Blackwell Science Ltd., Osney Mead, Oxford OX2 0EL, England. TEL 44-1865-206206. FAX 44-1865-721205. E-mail: journals.cs@blacksci.co.uk; URL: http://www.black.co.uk. Ed. D.M. Gibson; Pub. Allen Stevens. R&P contact: Sarah Pollard. adv. contact: Martine Cariou-Keen. **Indexed:** ASCA, Bibl.Agri., Curr.Cont., Ecol.Abstr., Food Sci.& Tech.Abstr., Sci.Cit.Ind., Sel.Water Res.Abstr., W.R.C.Inf. **Document type:** academic/scholarly publication.
—BLDSC (5185.126700); ADONIS; CASDDS; CISTI; EMDOCS; Genuine Article; Linda Hall; SWETS; UnCover. **CCC.**
Refereed Serial

576   FR
LA LETTRE DE L'INFECTIOLOGUE. (Monthly supplement avail.: Les Nouvelles) 1985. m. 65 F. per no. Edimark S A, 62-64 rue Jean-Jaures, 92800 Puteaux, France. TEL 33-1-41458000. FAX 33-1-41458025. Eds. Y. Mouton, A. Thabaut; Pub. C. Damour-Terrasson.
Formerly (until Dec. 1996): La Lettre de l'Infectiologue de la Microbiologie a la Clinique (ISSN 0296-9009)

576   GW   ISSN 0171-8630
QH541.5.S3   CODEN: MESEDT
MARINE ECOLOGY - PROGRESS SERIES. (Text in English) 1979. irreg. (16 vols.) DM.4750 (foreign DM.4880) (effective 1998). Inter-Research, Nordbuente 23, 21385 Oldendorf, Germany. TEL 49-4132-7127. FAX 49-4132-8883. E-mail: marita@int-res.com; URL: http://www.int-res.com. Ed. O. Kinne. adv. contact: H. Witt. circ. 900. (back issues avail.) **Indexed:** Aqua.Sci.& Fish.Abstr., ASCA, Biol.Abstr., Cadscan, Curr.Adv.Ecol.Sci., Curr.Cont., Ecol.Abstr., Geo.Abstr.H.G., Geo.Abstr.P.G., Geol.Abstr., IBR, Ind.Sci.Rev., INIS Atomind., Lead Abstr., Pollut.Abstr., Sel.Water Res.Abstr., Soils & Fert., Sport Fish.Abstr., Wild.Rev., Zincscan, Zoo.Rec. **Document type:** academic/scholarly publication.
—BLDSC (5373.904000); CASDDS; CISTI; EMDOCS; KNAW; Linda Hall; SWETS; UnCover.
Description: Presents original papers, short notes and reviews in environmental factors, physiological mechanisms, cultivation, dynamics and ocean management.

576 610   UK
▼**MEDICAL MICROBIOLOGIST.** Abbreviated title: Med Micro. 1996. 3/yr. Hayward Medical Communications Ltd., 44 Earlham St., Covent Garden, London WC2H 9LA, England. TEL 44-171-240-4493. FAX 44-171-240-4479. E-mail: hayward.medical@etgate.co.uk; URL: http://www.hayward.co.uk. (Subscr. to: Rosemary Huse, Lanades Park, Kentford, Near Newmarket, Suffolk CB8 7PW, England. TEL 44-1638-751515. FAX 44-4638-751517) Ed. Dr. Paul Wright. bk.rev. circ. 850. **Document type:** academic/scholarly publication.

576 616   PL   ISSN 0025-8601
R91   CODEN: MDMIAZ
MEDYCYNA DOSWIADCZALNA I MIKROBIOLOGIA. 1949. q. 29 Zl. (foreign $100) (effective 1998). Panstwowy Zaklad Higieny, Ul. Chocimska 24, 00-791 Warsaw, Poland. TEL 48-22-497781. FAX 48-22-497484. TELEX 816712. E-mail: pzh@medstat.waw.pl. (Dist. by: Ars Polona, Krakowskie Przedmiescie 7, 00-950 Warsaw, Poland. TEL 48-22-8261201. FAX 48-22-8268673) (Co-sponsor: Polskie Towarzystwo Mikrobiologow) Ed. Stanislaw Kaluzewski. R&P contact: Jolanta Szych. **Indexed:** Abstr.Hyg., Biol.Abstr., Chem.Abstr., Dent.Ind., Excerp.Med., I.P.A, Ind.Med., Ind.Vet., INIS Atomind., Rev.Med.& Vet.Mycol., Rev.Plant Path., Vet.Bull. **Document type:** academic/scholarly publication.
—BLDSC (5536.000000); CISTI; KNAW.

576   NE   ISSN 1381-5741
QH585   CODEN: MCSCFB
METHODS IN CELL SCIENCE. 1975. q. fl.343 to institutions; $176 to institutions in U.S. (effective 1998). (Society of In Vitro Biology) Kluwer Academic Publishers, Postbus 17, 3300 AA Dordrecht, Netherlands. TEL 31-78-6392392. FAX 31-78-6392254. E-mail: services@wkap.nl; URL: http://www.wkap.nl. (Dist. by: Kluwer Academic Publishers Group, P.O. Box 322, 3300 AH Dordrecht, Netherlands. TEL 31-78-6392392. FAX 31-78-6546474; N. America dist. addr.: Box 358, Accord Sta., Hingham, MA 02018-0358. TEL 617-871-6600. FAX 617-871-6528) Ed. Robert J. Hay. adv. (back issues avail.) **Indexed:** Biol.Abstr. (until 1979), Chem.Abstr., Curr.Cont., Excerp.Med. **Document type:** academic/scholarly publication.
—BLDSC (5747.305000); CASDDS; CISTI; SWETS; UMI; UnCover. **CCC.**
Former titles (until 1995): Journal of Tissue Culture Methods (ISSN 0271-8057); (until 1978): T C A Manual (Tissue Culture Association) (ISSN 0361-0268)
Description: Publishes papers describing techniques developed during cell, tissue and organ culture from multicellular animals and plants. Emphasis on detailed presentation of laboratory protocols for cell tissue and organ culture.
Refereed Serial

576   US   ISSN 0580-9517
                    CODEN: MMICEU
METHODS IN MICROBIOLOGY. 1969. irreg., latest vol.24. Academic Press, Inc., 525 B St., Ste. 1900, San Diego, CA 92101-4495. TEL 619-230-1840. FAX 619-699-6800. URL: http://www.apnet.com. **Document type:** monographic series.
—BLDSC (5748.201000); CASDDS; CISTI.

579.5   MX   ISSN 0187-8921
MICOLOGIA NEOTROPICAL APPLICADA. 1988. a. Mex.$50($30) Colegio de Posgraduados, Apdo. Postal 701, Puebla 72001, Mexico. (Co-sponsors: Consejo Nacional de Ciencia y Tecnologia; Institut Francais de Recherche Scientifique pour le Developpement en Cooperation; International Foundation for Science)
—BLDSC (5756.720000).

576   UK   ISSN 0966-6796
MICROBIAL CLEAN-UP. 1992. 10/yr. £250($295) 2-3 Cornwall Terr., Regent's Park, London NW1 4QP, England. TEL 0171-935-2382. FAX 0171-486-7083. (N. American subscr. to: Box 1897, Lawrence, KS 66044-8897. TEL 913-843-1221) (back issues avail.)
Description: Covers developments in the use of microbes to eliminate pollutants, effluents, and waste.

576.64 614.49   US   ISSN 1076-6294
QR177   CODEN: MDREFJ
▼**MICROBIAL DRUG RESISTANCE: MECHANISM, EPIDEMIOLOGY, AND DISEASE.** 1995. q. $1101 to individuals (foreign $164); institutions $240 (foreign $280) (effective through 1998). (European Society of Clinical Microbial and Infectious Diseases, FR) Mary Ann Liebert, Inc. Publishers, 2 Madison Ave., Larchmont, NY 10538. TEL 914-834-3100. FAX 914-834-3688. E-mail: liebert@pipeline.com. Ed. Alexander Tomasz. adv. **Indexed:** ASCA. **Document type:** academic/scholarly publication.
—BLDSC (5756.914900); CASDDS; CISTI; Genuine Article; KNAW; SWETS.
Description: Focuses on the emergence and spread of antibiotic-resistant microbial pathogens and resistance genes, along with the challenges they present to a wide variety of disciplines.
Refereed Serial

576   US   ISSN 0095-3628
QR100   CODEN: MCBEBU
MICROBIAL ECOLOGY; an international journal. Online edition (US ISSN 1432-184X) 8/yr. $481 (effective 1998). Springer-Verlag, Life Science Journals, 175 Fifth Ave., New York, NY 10010. TEL 212-460-1500. FAX 212-473-6272. E-mail: orders@springer-ny.com; URL: http://link.springer.de/link/service/journals/00248/index.htm. (N. American subscr. to: Journal Fulfillment Services, Box 2485, Secaucus, NJ 07096-2485. TEL 800-777-4643. FAX 201-348-4505; Elsewhere: Heidelberger Platz 3, 14197 Berlin, Germany. TEL 49-30-8207-0. FAX 49-30-8207448) Ed. James K. Fredrickson. R&P contact: Ian Gross. adv. contact: Robert Vrooman. (also avail. in microform from UMI; reprint service avail. from ISI) **Indexed:** ASCA, Bio-Contr.News & Info., Biol.Abstr., Biol.& Agr.Ind., Chem.Abstr., Curr.Adv.Ecol.Sci., Curr.Cont., Dairy Sci.Abstr., Deep Sea Res.& Oceanogr.Abstr., Ecol.Abstr., Excerp.Med., Field Crop Abstr., Forest.Abstr., Geo.Abstr.H.G., Helminthol.Abstr., IBR, Ind.Sci.Rev., Ind.Vet., Rev.Plant Path., Sci.Cit.Ind., Seed Abstr., Soils & Fert., Soyabean Abstr., Triticale Abstr., Vet.Bull., W.R.C.Inf., Weed Abstr. **Document type:** academic/scholarly publication.
●Also available online.
—BLDSC (5756.920000); CASDDS; CISTI; EMDOCS; Genuine Article; KR SourceOne; Linda Hall; SWETS; UMI; UnCover. **CCC.**
Description: Publishes original articles in all areas of ecology involving microorganisms.
Refereed Serial

576   UK   ISSN 0882-4010
QR175   CODEN: MIPAEV
MICROBIAL PATHOGENESIS; molecular and cellular biology of infectious disease. 1986. m. £94($151) to individuals; institutions £294 (effective 1998). Academic Press Ltd. (Subsidiary of: Harcourt Brace & Company Ltd.), 24-28 Oval Rd., London NW1 7DX, England. TEL 44-171-267-4466. FAX 44-171-482-2293. TELEX 25775 ACPRES G. E-mail: apsubs@acad.com; URL: http://www.hbuk.co.uk/ap/micpath; http://www.europe.idealibrary.com/. (Subscr. to: Harcourt Brace & Company Ltd., Foots Cray High St., Sidcup, Kent DA14 5HP, England. TEL 44-181-300-3322. FAX 44-181-309-0807) Ed.Bd. R&P contact: Catherine John. adv. contact: Nik Screen. index. (back issues avail.; reprint service avail. from SWZ) **Indexed:** ASCA, Curr.Adv.Ecol.Sci., Curr.Adv.Genetics & Molec.Biol., Curr.Cont., Diar.Dis.Res., Excerp.Med. (1993-), Food Sci.& Tech.Abstr-), Ind.Sci.Rev., Ind.Vet., Protozool.Abstr., Rev.Med.& Vet.Mycol., Sci.Cit.Ind., Vet.Bull. **Document type:** academic/scholarly publication.
●Also available online.
—BLDSC (5756.955000); ADONIS; CASDDS; CISTI; EMDOCS; Genuine Article; KNAW; Linda Hall; SWETS; UnCover. **CCC.**
Description: Publishes original contributions, mini-reviews, and notes on molecular and cellular mechanisms in infectious disease.

576   SP   ISSN 0213-4101
                    CODEN: MICBE3
MICROBIOLOGIA. 1985. q. 12800 ptas.($128) (effective 1996). (Sociedad Espanola de Microbiologia) Editorial Garsi, S.A., Grupo Masson, Av. Principe de Asturias 20, 08012 Barcelona, Spain. TEL 34-3-4154544. FAX 34-3-4161220. (SEM addr.: Hotaleza 104, 28004 Madrid, Spain) Ed. Ricardo Guerrero. circ. 2,500. **Indexed:** ASCA, Food Sci.& Tech.Abstr., Ind.SST.
—BLDSC (5756.985000); CASDDS; CISTI. **CCC.**

BIOLOGY — MICROBIOLOGY

616.01   IT   ISSN 1120-0146
MICROBIOLOGIA MEDICA. 1979. q. Associazione Microbiologici Clinici Italiani, Via C. Farini 70, 20159 Milano, Italy. TEL 2-66801190. **Indexed:** Excerp.Med. (1995-). **Document type:** academic/scholarly publication.

576   614.7   GW   ISSN 0944-5013
QR51   CODEN: MCRSEJ
MICROBIOLOGICAL RESEARCH. (Text in English, French and German; summaries in English and German) 1895. 4/yr. DM.406 (foreign DM.414) (effective 1996). Gustav Fischer Verlag Jena, Villengang 2, 07745 Jena, Germany. TEL 49-3641-626444. FAX 49-3641-626500. (Subscr. to: Postfach 100537, 07705 Jena, Germany) Ed. J. Woestemeyer. adv.: page DM.750; trim 210 x 280. bk.rev.; bibl.; charts; illus.; index. circ. 350. (reprint service avail. from ISI) **Indexed:** ASCA, Curr.Adv.Biochem., Curr.Adv.Genetics & Molec.Biol., Curr.Cont., Field Crop Abstr., Food Sci.& Tech.Abstr., Hort.Abstr., Plant Grow.Reg.Abstr., Potato Abstr., Rev.Med.& Vet.Mycol., Soils & Fert., Soyabean Abstr., Triticale Abstr., Trop.Oil Seeds Abstr., Weed Abstr. **Document type:** academic/scholarly publication.
—BLDSC (5757.590000); CASDDS; CISTI; EMDOCS; Genuine Article; Linda Hall; SWETS; UnCover. **CCC.**
Former titles (until 1993): Zentralblatt fuer Mikrobiologie (ISSN 0232-4393); Zentralblatt fuer Bakteriologie, Parasitenkunde, Infektionskrankheiten und Hygiene: Zweite Abteilung - Naturwissenschaft.

576   US   ISSN 0889-3381
MICROBIOLOGICAL UPDATE. 1983. m. $180 (foreign $195) (effective 1997). Microbiological Applications, Inc., 132 San Remo Dr., Islamorada, FL 33036. TEL 305-664-8513. FAX 305-664-8597. Ed. Murray S. Cooper. R&P contact: Claire Sandberg. bk.rev. **Document type:** newsletter.
—BLDSC (5757.630000).

576   UK   ISSN 1350-0872
QR1   CODEN: MROBEO
MICROBIOLOGY. 1947. m. £480($840) (effective 1997). Society for General Microbiology, Marlborough House, Basingstoke Rd., Spencers Wood, Reading RG7 1AE, England. TEL 44-1734-885577. FAX 44-1734-885656. Ed. J.R. Saunders. adv. contact: C. Sinclair. bibl.; charts; illus.; index. circ. 3,500. (also avail. in microfilm from PMC) **Indexed:** Abstr.Hyg., ASCA, Biol.Abstr., Biol.& Agr.Ind., Biotech.Abstr., Chem.Abstr., Chem.Cit.Ind., Curr.Adv.Biochem., Curr.Adv.Ecol.Sci., Curr.Adv.Genetics & Molec.Biol., Curr.Biotech.Abstr., Curr.Cont., Dairy Sci.Abstr., Deep Sea Res.& Oceanogr.Abstr., Dent.Ind., Excerp.Med., Field Crop Abstr., Food Sci.& Tech.Abstr., Gen.Sci.Ind., GeoRef., Helminthol.Abstr., Herb.Abstr., Hort.Abstr., Ind.Med., Ind.Sci.Rev., Ind.Vet., INIS Atomind., Mass Spectr.Bull., Med.& Surg.Dermat., Nutr.Abstr., Pig News & Info., Plant Breed.Abstr., Poult.Abstr., Rev.Appl.Entomol., Rev.Med.& Vet.Mycol., Rev.Plant Path., Rice Abstr., Sci.Cit.Ind., Small Anim.Abstr., Soils & Fert., Triticale Abstr., Trop.Dis.Bull., Vet.Bull., W.R.C.Inf., Weed Abstr. **Document type:** academic/scholarly publication.
—BLDSC (5757.750500); CASDDS; CISTI; EMDOCS; Genuine Article; KNAW; KR SourceOne; Linda Hall; SWETS; UnCover. **CCC.**
Formerly (until 1993): Journal of General Microbiology (ISSN 0022-1287).
Description: Original work on microorganisms in the laboratory and in the field; emphasis on fundamental studies.

576   RU   ISSN 0026-2617
QR1   CODEN: MIBLAO
MICROBIOLOGY. English translation of: Mikrobiologiya (RU ISSN 0026-3656) 1957. bi-m. $1645 in US; elsewhere $1925) (effective 1998). (Russian Academy of Sciences) Maik Nauka - Interperiodica, Mezhdunarodnyi Otdel, Ul. Profsoyuznaya, 90, 117864 Moscow, Russia. TEL 7-095-3360066. FAX 7-095-3360066. (Dist. by: Plenum Publishing Corp., 233 Spring St., New York, NY 10013-1578, U.S.A. TEL 212-620-8468. FAX 212-463-0742) Ed. M.V. Ivanov. charts; illus.; index. (also avail. in microfilm from UMI; back issues avail.) **Indexed:** ASCA, Biol.Abstr., Chem.Titles, Curr.Adv.Ecol.Sci., Curr.Biotech.Abstr., Curr.Cont., Deep Sea Res.& Oceanogr.Abstr., Food Sci.& Tech.Abstr., Ind.Med., Ind.Sci.Rev., Int.Abstr.Biol.Sci., Weed Abstr. **Document type:** academic/scholarly publication.
—BLDSC (0416.200000); CASDDS; CISTI; Genuine Article; Linda Hall; SWETS; UMI; UnCover. **CCC.**
Refereed Serial

576   JA   ISSN 0385-5600
QR1   CODEN: MIIMDV
MICROBIOLOGY AND IMMUNOLOGY. (Text in English) 1957. m. $255. (Japanese Society for Bacteriology) Center for Academic Publications Japan, 2-4-16 Yayoi, Bunkyo-ku, Tokyo 113, Japan. TEL 81-3-3817-5821. FAX 81-3-3817-5820. E-mail: capj@crisscross.com. (Dist. by: Business Center for Academic Societies Japan, 5-16-9 Honkomagome, Bunkyo-ku, Tokyo 113, Japan. TEL 81-3-5814-5811. FAX 81-3-5814-5822) (Co-sponsors: Japanese Society for Immunology; Society of Japanese Virologists) adv.; charts; illus. circ. 1,500. (also avail. in microform from PMC) **Indexed:** Abstr.Hyg., ASCA, Biol.Abstr., Biotech.Abstr., Chem.Abstr., Curr.Adv.Cancer Res., Curr.Adv.Ecol.Sci., Curr.Adv.Genetics & Molec.Biol., Curr.Biotech.Abstr., Curr.Cont., Dairy Sci.Abstr., Dent.Ind., Diar.Dis.Res., Excerp.Med., Helminthol.Abstr., Ind.Med., Ind.Sci.Rev., Ind.Vet., Nutr.Abstr., Poult.Abstr., Protozool.Abstr., Rev.Med.& Vet.Mycol., Rev.Plant Path., Sci.Cit.Ind., Telegen, Trop.Dis.Bull., Vet.Bull., W.R.C.Inf. **Document type:** academic/scholarly publication.
—BLDSC (5757.791000); CASDDS; CISTI; EMDOCS; Genuine Article; KNAW; Linda Hall; SWETS.
Formerly (until vol. 21, 1977): Japanese Journal of Microbiology (ISSN 0021-5139)
Refereed Serial

576   US   ISSN 1092-2172
QR1   CODEN: MMBRF7
MICROBIOLOGY AND MOLECULAR BIOLOGY REVIEWS. 1937. q. $151 to non-members; members $45 (effective 1997). American Society for Microbiology, 1325 Massachusetts Ave., N.W., Washington, DC 20005. TEL 202-737-3600. Ed. W.K. Joklik. adv.; bibl.; illus.; index. circ. 11,860. (also avail. in microform from UMI; back issues avail.; reprint service avail. from UMI) **Indexed:** Abstr.Bull.Inst.Pap.Chem., Abstr.Hyg., ASCA, Bio-Contr.News & Info., Biol.Abstr., Biol.& Agr.Ind., Biotech.Abstr., Chem.Abstr., Curr.Adv.Ecol.Sci., Curr.Biotech.Abstr., Curr.Cont., Dairy Sci.Abstr., Deep Sea Res.& Oceanogr.Abstr., Diar.Dis.Res., Excerp.Med., Food Sci.& Tech.Abstr., Gen.Sci.Ind., Helminthol.Abstr., Hort.Abstr., Ind.Med., Ind.Sci.Rev., Ind.Vet., Nutr.Abstr., Protozool.Abstr., Rev.Med.& Vet.Mycol., Rev.Plant Path., Sci.Cit.Ind., Soils & Fert., Telegen, Trop.Dis.Bull., Vet.Bull. **Document type:** academic/scholarly publication.
●Also available on CD-ROM.
—BLDSC (5757.791300); CASDDS; CISTI; Genuine Article; KNAW; KR SourceOne; Linda Hall; SWETS; UMI; UnCover. **CCC.**
Former titles (until 1997): Microbiological Reviews (ISSN 0146-0749); (until 1978): Bacteriological Reviews (ISSN 0005-3678)
Description: Presents current reviews to serve the interests of all microbiologists on microbiolgy, immunology, and molecular and cellular biology.
Refereed Serial

576   AT
▼**MICROBIOLOGY AUSTRALIA.** 1995. 5/yr. (Australian Society for Microbiology) Reed Business Publishing Pty. Ltd. (Subsidiary of: Reed International PLC), P.O. Box 5487, W. Chatswood, N.S.W. 2057, Australia. TEL 61-2-699-2411. FAX 61-2-698-3920. circ. 330. **Document type:** trade publication.
Description: For working scientists within microbiological research, food, clinical and industrial laboratories involved in vital hospital testing through to ground-breaking research investigation.

576   GW   ISSN 0945-8182
MICROBIOLOGY EUROPE. 1993. 6/yr. DM.170 (effective 1997). V C H Verlagsgesellschaft mbH, Postfach 101161, 69451 Weinheim, Germany. TEL 49-6201-606147. FAX 49-6201-606117. (US addr.: V C H Publishers Inc., 220 E. 23rd St., New York, NY 10010-4606. TEL 212-683-8333) Ed. Andrea Sharpe. adv. contact: Klaus Graef. circ. 22,000. (back issues avail.) **Indexed:** Food Sci.& Tech.Abstr. **Document type:** academic/scholarly publication.
—KNAW. **CCC.**
Formerly (until 1993): European Microbiology (ISSN 1064-4725)
Description: Provides a communication platform for microbiologists throughout Europe. Focuses on the latest developments, methods, and techniques in all areas of microbiology as they pertain to food, agriculture, biochemicals and pharmaceuticals, petroleum, water, hygiene, hospitals and medical centers, veterinary and academic institutions.
Refereed Serial

MICROBIOLOGY NEWSLETTER. see *FOOD AND FOOD INDUSTRIES*

576   US   ISSN 0092-6027
                       CODEN: MSERDS
MICROBIOLOGY SERIES. irreg., vol.18, 1987. price varies. Marcel Dekker, Inc., 270 Madison Ave., New York, NY 10016. TEL 212-889-9595. FAX 212-658-4540. TELEX 421419. Ed. Allan I. Laskin. Pub. Graham Garratt. R&P contact: Julia Mulligan. **Indexed:** Diar.Dis.Res., GeoRef. **Document type:** monographic series.
—CASDDS; CISTI.
Refereed Serial

576   610.28   UK   ISSN 0026-2633
QR46   CODEN: MCBIA7
MICROBIOS; a prestige international biomedical research journal of chemical and general microbiology. (Text in English) 1969. m. £350 (includes supplements). Faculty Press, 88 Regent St., Cambridge CB2 1DP, England. FAX 44-1553-840695. Ed.Bd. adv.; bk.rev.; abstr.; bibl.; charts; illus.; index. **Indexed:** ASCA, Biol.Abstr., Biol.Dig., Biotech.Abstr., Chem.Abstr., Curr.Adv.Biochem., Curr.Adv.Ecol.Sci., Curr.Adv.Genetics & Molec.Biol., Curr.Biotech.Abstr., Curr.Cont., Dairy Sci.Abstr., Deep Sea Res.& Oceanogr.Abstr., Excerp.Med., Helminthol.Abstr., Ind.Med., Ind.Sci.Rev., Ind.Vet., Protozool.Abstr., Ref.Zh., Rev.Med.& Vet.Mycol., Rev.Plant Path., Sci.Cit.Ind., Soils & Fert., Sugar Ind.Abstr., Vet.Bull.
—BLDSC (5757.800000); CASDDS; CISTI; KNAW; SWETS; UnCover. **CCC.**
Description: Devoted to fundamental studies of viruses, bacteria, micro-fungi, microscopic algae, and protozoa.

MICROCIRCULATION. see *MEDICAL SCIENCES*

576   KR   ISSN 0201-8462
QR1   CODEN: MZHUDX
MIKROBIOLOGICHNYI ZHURNAL; nauchnyi zhurnal. (Text and summaries in English, Russian, Ukrainian) 1934. bi-m. $209 (effective 1998). Akademiya Nauk Ukrainy, Institut Mikrobiologii i Virusologii im. D.K. Zabolotnogo, Vul. Akad. Zabolotnogo, 154, 252143 Kiev, Ukraine. TEL 38-44-2663487. Ed. V.V. Smirnov. bk.rev.; index. **Indexed:** Biol.Abstr., Biotech.Abstr., Chem.Abstr., Dairy Sci.Abstr., Djerelo, Excerp.Med., GeoRef., Ind.Med., Maize Abstr., Potato Abstr., Rev.Med.& Vet.Mycol. **Document type:** academic/scholarly publication.
—BLDSC (0114.900000); CASDDS; CISTI; KNAW; Linda Hall. **CCC.**

576   TU   ISSN 0374-9096
                       CODEN: MIBUBI
MIKROBIYOLOJI BULTENI. (Text in Turkish; summaries in English) 1965. 4/yr. TL.1000000 (foreign $50) (effective 1996). Ankara Microbiology Society, Hacettepe University Faculty of Medicine, Dept. of Microbiology, 06100 Ankara, Turkey. TEL 90-312-3114752. FAX 90-312-3115250. E-mail: hutfm-e@servis2.net.tr. Ed. Dr. Ayfer Gunalp; Pub. Dr. Ayfer Gunalp. R&P contact: Durdal Us. adv. contact: Gulsen Hascelik. abstr. **Indexed:** Apic.Abstr., Excerp.Med., Ind.Med. (until 1994). **Document type:** academic/scholarly publication.
—BLDSC (5761.665000); CASDDS; CISTI; EMDOCS.
Description: Covers microbiology, medical microbiology, infectious diseases and chemotherapy. Includes case reports and discussions of practical medical microbiology.
Refereed Serial

MIKROKOSMOS; Zeitschrift fuer angewandte Mikroskopie, Mikrobiologie, Mikrochemie und mikroskopische Technik. see *BIOLOGY — Microscopy*

576   JA   ISSN 0026-8054
MODERN MEDIA/MODAN MEDIA. (Text in Japanese) 1955. m. Eiken Chemical Co. Ltd. - Eiken Kagaku K K., 5-26-20 Oji, Kita-ku, Tokyo 114, Japan. TEL 81-3-3913-6231. FAX 81-3-3914-7027. Ed. Hiromitsu Enomoto. bk.rev.; charts; illus.; circ. controlled.
—BLDSC (5889.700000).

MOLECULAR AND BIOCHEMICAL PARASITOLOGY. see *BIOLOGY — Biological Chemistry*

MOLECULAR AND CELL BIOLOGY OF HUMAN DISEASES. see *BIOLOGY — Cytology And Histology*

BIOLOGY — MICROBIOLOGY

616.97 — US — ISSN 0270-7306
QH506 — CODEN: MCEBD4
MOLECULAR AND CELLULAR BIOLOGY. 1981. m. $450 to non-members; members $84 (effective 1997). American Society for Microbiology, 1325 Massachusetts Ave., N.W., Washington, DC 20005. TEL 202-737-3600. Ed. Alan M. Weiner. adv. circ. 5,965. (also avail. in microform from UMI; back issues avail.; reprint service avail. from UMI) Indexed: Anim.Breed.Abstr., ASCA, Biol.Abstr., Biol.& Agr.Ind., Biotech.Abstr., Chem.Abstr., Curr.Adv.Biochem., Curr.Adv.Cancer Res., Curr.Adv.Cell & Devel.Biol., Curr.Adv.Ecol.Sci., Curr.Adv.Genetics & Molec.Biol., Curr.Cont., Curr.Cont., Dairy Sci.Abstr., Dent.Ind., Excerp.Med., Helminthol.Abstr., Ind.Med., Ind.Sci.Rev., Neurosci.Cit.Ind., Poult.Abstr., Protozool.Abstr., Rev.Med.& Vet.Mycol., Sci.Cit.Ind., Telegen. Document type: academic/scholarly publication.
●Also available on CD-ROM.
—BLDSC (5900.757000); CASDDS; CISTI; EMDOCS; Genuine Article; KNAW; KR SourceOne; Linda Hall; SWETS; UMI; UnCover. **CCC.**
   Description: Covers the molecular biology of eucaryotic cells, of both microbial and higher organisms.
   Refereed Serial

576 574.8 — US — ISSN 1065-3074
QH607 — CODEN: MCDIEL
MOLECULAR & CELLULAR DIFFERENTIATION. 1992. q. $80 to individuals; institutions $285. C R C Press, Inc., 2000 Corporate Blvd., N.W., Boca Raton, FL 33431. TEL 561-994-0555; 800-272-7737. FAX 561-998-9784. TELEX 568689-CRC PRESS. Document type: academic/scholarly publication.
—BLDSC (5900.758000); CASDDS; CISTI; EMDOCS; Genuine Article; KNAW; SWETS. **CCC.**

MOLECULAR CARCINOGENESIS. see *MEDICAL SCIENCES — Oncology*

576 — UK — ISSN 0962-1083
QH541.15.M63 — CODEN: MOECEO
MOLECULAR ECOLOGY. 1992. m. £675($1231.50) (foreign £742) (effective 1998). Blackwell Science Ltd., Osney Mead, Oxford OX2 0EL. TEL 44-1865-206206. FAX 44-1865-721205. E-mail: journals.cs@blacksci.co.uk; URL: http://www.black.co.uk. Eds. Terry Burke, Harry Smith; Pub. Allen Stevens. R&P contact: Sarah Pollard. adv. contact: Martine Cariou-Keen. bk.rev.; bibl.; illus.; index. circ. 540. (also avail. in microform from UMI; back issues avail.) Indexed: ASCA, Bibl.Agri., Curr.Cont., Environ.Per.Bibl. (1993-), Ind.Med. (1993-), Ind.Sci.Rev., Sci.Cit.Ind. Document type: academic/scholarly publication.
—BLDSC (5900.817360); CASDDS; CISTI; EMDOCS; Genuine Article; SWETS; UMI. **CCC.**
   Refereed Serial

MOLECULAR GENETICS, MICROBIOLOGY AND VIROLOGY. see *BIOLOGY — Genetics*

576 660 — US — ISSN 1053-6426
QH90.A1 — CODEN: MMBBEQ
MOLECULAR MARINE BIOLOGY AND BIOTECHNOLOGY. 1992. bi-m. $195 (foreign $215) (effective 1996). (American Society of Molecular Marine Biology & Biotechnology) Blackwell Science Inc., 350 Main St., Malden, MA 02148. TEL 617-876-7000. FAX 617-388-8255. Ed. Dennis Powers. Indexed: ASCA, Ind.Med. (1993-). Document type: academic/scholarly publication.
—BLDSC (5900.817850); CASDDS; CISTI; EMDOCS; Genuine Article; KNAW; Linda Hall; SWETS; UMI; UnCover. **CCC.**
   Description: Addresses biotechnology applications of marine life, including the study of the biological processes of oceans and organisms.

576 — UK — ISSN 0950-382X
QR74 — CODEN: MOMIEE
MOLECULAR MICROBIOLOGY. 23/yr. £968($1768) (foreign £1065) (effective 1998). Blackwell Science Ltd., Osney Mead, Oxford OX2 0EL, England. TEL 44-1865-206206. FAX 44-1865-721205. E-mail: journals.cs@blacksci.co.uk; URL: http://www.black.co.uk. Ed. C. Higgins; Pub. Allen Stevens. R&P contact: Sarah Pollard. adv. contact: Martine Cariou-Keen. bibl.; illus.; index. circ. 1,450. (also avail. in microform from UMI; back issues avail.) Indexed: ASCA, Bibl.Agri., Curr.Adv.Biochem., Curr.Adv.Genetics & Molec.Biol., Curr.Cont., Dairy Sci.Abstr., Food Sci.& Tech.Abstr., Hort.Abstr., Ind.Sci.Rev., Ind.Vet., Plant Grow.Reg.Abstr., Protozool.Abstr., Sci.Cit.Ind., Telegen, Vet.Bull., Weed Abstr. Document type: academic/scholarly publication.
—BLDSC (5900.817960); ADONIS; CASDDS; CISTI; EMDOCS; Genuine Article; Linda Hall; SWETS; UMI; UnCover. **CCC.**
   Incorporates: Microbiological Sciences (ISSN 0265-1351)
   Refereed Serial

MOLECULAR PLANT - MICROBE INTERACTIONS. see *BIOLOGY — Botany*

576 — US — ISSN 1040-452X
QP251 — CODEN: MREDEE
MOLECULAR REPRODUCTION AND DEVELOPMENT. 1988. m. $2295 (foreign $2505) (effective 1998). John Wiley & Sons, Inc., Journals, 605 Third Ave., New York, NY 10158. TEL 212-850-6645. FAX 212-850-6021. TELEX 12-7063. E-mail: subinfo@jwiley.com; URL: http://www.wiley.co.uk. (Subscr. outside the Americas to: John Wiley & Sons Ltd., Baffins Ln., Chichester, W. Sussex PO19 1UD, England. TEL 44-1243-779777. FAX 44-1243-776128) Ed. Ralph B. Gwatkin. adv.: B&W page £640, color page £1515; trim 279 x 210. bk.rev. circ. 800. (also avail. in microform from UMI; back issues avail.) Indexed: ASCA, Curr.Cont., Ind.Sci.Rev., Sci.Cit.Ind. Document type: academic/scholarly publication.
—BLDSC (5900.828000); CASDDS; CISTI; EMDOCS; Genuine Article; KNAW; Linda Hall; SWETS. **CCC.**
   Incorporates: Gamete Research.
   Description: Covers molecular biology of spermatogenesis, oogenesis, and embryonic and fetal development.
   Refereed Serial

MOLEKULYARNAYA GENETIKA, MIKROBIOLOGIYA I VIRUSOLOGIYA. see *BIOLOGY — Genetics*

MONOGRAFIE PARAZYTOLOGICZNE. see *VETERINARY SCIENCE*

576 — SZ — ISSN 0077-0965
— CODEN: MONVAK
MONOGRAPHS IN VIROLOGY. (Text in English) 1967. irreg. (approx. 1/yr.). price varies. S. Karger AG, Allschwilerstr. 10, P.O. Box, CH-4009 Basel, Switzerland. TEL 41-61-3061111. FAX 41-61-3061234. E-mail: karger@karger.ch; URL: http://www.karger.ch. Ed. H.W. Doerr. (reprint service avail. from ISI) Indexed: Biol.Abstr., Chem.Abstr., Curr.Cont., Ind.Med. Document type: monographic series.
—BLDSC (5917.780000); CISTI; KNAW. **CCC.**
   Description: Reference tools for virologists and non-virologists alike.
   Refereed Serial

MYCOBACTERIA. see *BIOLOGY — Abstracting, Bibliographies, Statistics*

589.2 — NE — ISSN 0301-486X
QK600 — CODEN: MYCPAH
MYCOPATHOLOGIA. (Text in English) 1938. m. fl.2200 to institutions; $1130 to institutions in U.S. (effective 1998). (C A B International Mycological Institute, UK) Kluwer Academic Publishers, Postbus 17, 3300 AA Dordrecht, Netherlands. TEL 31-78-6392392. FAX 31-78-6392254. TELEX 29245 KAPG NL. E-mail: services@wkap.nl; URL: http://www.wkap.nl. (Dist. by: Kluwer Academic Publishers Group, P.O. Box 322, 3300 AH Dordrecht, Netherlands. TEL 31-78-6392392. FAX 31-78-6546474; N. America dist. addr.: Box 358, Accord Sta., Hingham, MA 02018-0358. TEL 617-871-6600. FAX 617-871-6528) Ed.Bd. adv.; bk.rev.; illus. (also avail. in microform from UMI; reprint service avail. from SWZ) Indexed: Abstr.Hyg., Apic.Abstr., ASCA, ASCA, Bio-Contr.News & Info., Biol.Abstr., Biotech.Abstr., Chem.Abstr., Crop Physiol.Abstr., Curr.Adv.Ecol.Sci., Curr.Cont., Dairy Sci.Abstr., Excerp.Med., Food Sci.& Tech.Abstr., Forest.Abstr., Forest Prod.Abstr., Hort.Abstr., Ind.Med., Ind.Sci.Rev., Ind.Vet., Pig News & Info., Poult.Abstr., Rev.Med.& Vet.Mycol., Rev.Plant Path., Rice Abstr., Sci.Cit.Ind., Seed Abstr., Small Anim.Abstr., Soils & Fert., Soyabean Abstr., Triticale Abstr., Trop.Dis.Bull., Vet.Bull. Document type: academic/scholarly publication.
—BLDSC (5995.740000); CASDDS; CISTI; EMDOCS; Genuine Article; KNAW; Linda Hall; SWETS; UMI; UnCover. **CCC.**
   Formerly: Mycopathologia et Mycologia - Applicata (ISSN 0027-5530)
   Description: Studies the role of fungi in disease and biodeterioration.
   Refereed Serial

576 — GW — ISSN 0178-7888
— CODEN: MYREET
MYCOTOXIN RESEARCH. (Text in English) 1985. s-a. DM.73.50. Postfach 3628, 55026 Mainz, Germany. TEL 06131-320071. FAX 06131-381314. Ed. Dr. Rainer Schmidt. adv.; bk.rev. circ. 1,000. Indexed: Food Sci.& Tech.Abstr., Rev.Med.& Vet.Mycol., Triticale Abstr.
—BLDSC (5995.762000); CASDDS; CISTI; UnCover. **CCC.**

576 — NE — ISSN 0958-3165
QH506 — CODEN: NNOBE7
NANOBIOLOGY; journal of research on nanoscale living systems. 1992. q. $95 (effective 1998). Gordon and Breach - Harwood Academic, Amsteldisk 166, 1st Fl., 1079 LH Amsterdam, Netherlands. (Subscr. to: International Publishers Distributor, Box 32160, Newark, NJ 07102. TEL 800-545-8398. FAX 215-750-6343) Eds. Martyn C. Davies, Saul J.B. Tendler. Indexed: ASCA. Document type: academic/scholarly publication.
—BLDSC (6015.335520); CASDDS; CISTI; Genuine Article; UMI; UnCover. **CCC.**
   Description: Devoted to fundamental and applied research in biomolecular structure at the nanoscale and the impact of nanotechnology on these systems.
   Refereed Serial

576 — SZ — ISSN 1018-8916
— CODEN: NAIMEL
NATURAL IMMUNITY. (Text in English) 1981. 6/yr. 212 SFr.($162) to individuals; institutions 424 SFr.($324) (effective 1998). S. Karger AG, Allschwilerstr. 10, P.O. Box, CH-4009 Basel, Switzerland. TEL 41-61-3061111. FAX 41-61-3061234. E-mail: karger@karger.ch; URL: http://www.karger.ch. Ed. R.B. Herberman. adv.; bk.rev.; charts; illus.; index. circ. 800. (also avail. in microform from UMI; back issues avail.) Indexed: ASCA, Biol.Abstr., Chem.Abstr., Curr.Adv.Cancer Res., Curr.Adv.Ecol.Sci., Curr.Cont., Excerp.Med., Ind.Med. Document type: academic/scholarly publication.
—BLDSC (6040.723000); CASDDS; CISTI; EMDOCS; Genuine Article; KNAW; SWETS; UnCover. **CCC.**
   Former titles: Natural Immunity and Cell Growth Regulation (ISSN 0254-7600); (until 1984): Stem Cells (ISSN 0250-6793)
   Refereed Serial

BIOLOGY — MICROBIOLOGY

616.01   NE   ISSN 0929-0176
CODEN: NMMIE
NEDERLANDS TIJDSCHRIFT VOOR MEDISCHE MICROBIOLOGIE. 1993. q. (Nederlandse Vereniging voor Medische Microbiologie - Dutch Association of Medical Microbiology) Misset (Subsidiary of: Reed Elsevier plc), P.O. Box 1110, 3600 BC Maarssen, Netherlands. TEL 31-346-558222. FAX 31-546-554287. Ed. Dr. J. Kaan. adv. contact: G. van den Brink. circ. 750. **Indexed:** Excerp.Med. (1995-). **Document type:** academic/scholarly publication.
—KNAW.
Refereed Serial

576 610   UK   ISSN 0143-4179
CODEN: NRPPDD
NEUROPEPTIDES (EDINBURGH). 1979. bi-m. £105($150) to individuals; institutions £555 ($825) (effective 1998). Churchill Livingstone (Subsidiary of: Pearson Professional), Robert Stevenson House, 1-3 Baxter's Pl., Leith Walk, Edinburgh EH1 3AF, Scotland. TEL 44-131-556-2424. FAX 44-131-535-1704. URL: http://www.churchillmed.com. (Subscr. to : Pearson Professional Ltd., P.O. Box 77 Fourth Ave., Harlow, Essex CM19 5BQ, England. TEL 44-1279-623924. FAX 44-1279-639609; U.S. subscr. to: Churchill Livingstone, Box 3217, Secaucus, NJ 07096-3217. TEL 800-553-5426. FAX 201-319-9659) Eds. Drs. M.J. Brownstein, J. Hughes. adv. contact: David Dunnachie. bk.rev.; bibl. circ. 390. (back issues avail.) **Indexed:** Curr.Adv.Ecol.Sci., Curr.Cont., Ind.Med., Ind.Sci.Rev. **Document type:** academic/scholarly publication.
—BLDSC (6081.516000); ADONIS; CASDDS; CISTI; Genuine Article; KNAW; SWETS; UnCover. **CCC.**

576   IT   ISSN 1121-7138
CODEN: MIBLDR
THE NEW MICROBIOLOGICA; quarterly journal of microbiological sciences. (Text and summaries in English) 1978. q. L.190000 (effective Jan. 1992). (University of Bologna, Institute of Microbiology) Luigi Penzie e Figlio Publishers, Via D. da Catalogna 1-3, 27100 Pavia, Italy. TEL 0382-35000. TELEX 0382-304435. Ed. Michele La Placa. adv.; bk.rev. circ. 500. **Indexed:** Biol.Abstr., Curr.Adv.Ecol.Sci., Curr.Cont., Excerp.Med., Food Sci.& Tech.Abstr., Ind.Vet., Microbiol.Abstr., Pig News & Info., Protozool.Abstr., Rev.Med.& Vet.Mycol., Sci.Cit.Ind., Telegen, Vet.Bull. **Document type:** academic/scholarly publication.
—BLDSC (5757.400000); CASDDS; CISTI; Genuine Article; KNAW; SWETS; UnCover.
Formerly (until 1992): Microbiologica (ISSN 0391-5352)

NIHON ARCHAEBACTERIA KENKYUKAI KOENKAI YOSHISHU/JAPAN SOCIETY FOR ARCHAEBACTERIOLOGY. ABSTRACTS OF ANNUAL MEETING. see *BIOLOGY — Abstracting, Bibliographies, Statistics*

576   JA   ISSN 0911-7830
NIHON BISEIBUTSU SEITAI GAKKAIHO/JAPANESE SOCIETY OF MICROBIAL ECOLOGY. BULLETIN. (Text in English, Japanese; summaries in English) 1986. s-a. Nihon Biseibutsu Seitai Gakkai - Japanese Society of Microbial Ecology, c/o Mr. Yoshichika Takamura, Ibaraki Daigaku Nogakubu Nogei Kagakka, Amimachi, Inashiki-gun, Ibaraki-ken 300-03, Japan.

NIHON BOKIN BOBAI GAKKAI. NENJI TAIKAI YOSHISHU/SOCIETY FOR ANTIBACTERIAL AND ANTIFUNGAL AGENTS, JAPAN. ABSTRACTS OF THE MEETING. see *BIOLOGY — Abstracting, Bibliographies, Statistics*

576   JA   ISSN 0914-5818
CODEN: ACTIF4
NIHON HOSENKIN GAKKAISHI/ACTINOMYCETOLOGICA. (Text in English, Japanese; summaries in English) 1962. s-a. 7000 Yen. Nihon Hosenkin Gakkai - Society for Actinomycetes, Japan, Biseibutsu Kagaku Kenkyujo, 14-23 Kamiosaki 3-chome, Shinagawa-ku, Tokyo 141, Japan.
—BLDSC (0675.405500); CASDDS.

576.64   JA
NIHON UIRUSU GAKKAI HOKKAIDO SHIBU KAIHO/SOCIETY OF JAPANESE VIROLOGISTS. HOKKAIDO BRANCH. NEWS. (Text in Japanese) a. Nihon Uirusu Gakkai, Hokkaido Shibu - Society of Japanese Virologists, Hokkaido Branch, Hokkaido Daigaku Juigakubu Jui Koshu Eiseigaku Koza, Nishi 9-chome, Kita 18-jo, Kita-ku, Sapporo-shi, Hokkaido 060, Japan.

576.64   JA
NIHON UIRUSU GAKKAI KAIHO/SOCIETY OF JAPANESE VIROLOGISTS. BULLETIN. (Text in Japanese) s-a. Nihon Uirusu Gakkai, Nihon Gakkai Jimu Senta, 16-9, Honkomagome 5-chome, Bunkyo-ku, Tokyo 113, Japan.

576.64   JA
NIHON UIRUSU GAKKAI SOKAI ENZETSU SHOROKU/SOCIETY OF JAPANESE VIROLOGISTS. PROCEEDINGS OF THE ANNUAL MEETING. (Text in Japanese) 1953. a. Nihon Uirusu Gakkai, Nihon Gakkai Jimu Senta, 16-9 Honkomagome 5-chome, Bunkyo-ku, Tokyo 113, Japan. **Document type:** proceedings.

NORWICH RESEARCH PARK NEWSLETTER. see *BIOLOGY — Genetics*

O I E BULLETIN. (Office International des Epizooties) see *VETERINARY SCIENCE*

O I E REVUE SCIENTIFIQUE ET TECHNIQUE/O I E SCIENTIFIC AND TECHNICAL REVIEW. (Office International des Epizooties) see *VETERINARY SCIENCE*

576 574.12   GW
OLD HERBORN UNIVERSITY SEMINAR MONOGRAPHS. (Text in English) irreg., no.5, 1994. Institute for Microbiology and Biochemistry, Kornmarkt 34, 35745 Herborn-Dill, Germany. TEL 02772-41033. FAX 02772-41039. Ed.Bd. **Document type:** monographic series.

576 610   UK   ISSN 1362-6809
▼**OPINION: SPECIALIST REVIEWS OF KEY PAPERS IN MICROBIOLOGY.** Abbreviated title: Opinion: Micro. 1996. 3/yr. Hayward Medical Communications Ltd., 44 Earlham St., Covent Garden, London WC2H 9LA, England. TEL 44-171-240-4493. FAX 44-171-240-4479. E-mail: hayward.medical@etgate.co.uk; URL: http://www.hayward.co.uk. (Subscr. to: Rosemary House, Lanwades Park, Kentford, Near Newmarket, Suffolk CB8 7PW, England. TEL 44-1638-751515. FAX 44-1638-751517) circ. 1,800. **Document type:** academic/scholarly publication.

576 616.77   DK   ISSN 0902-0055
CODEN: OMIMEE
ORAL MICROBIOLOGY AND IMMUNOLOGY. (Text in English) 1987. bi-m. DKK 1630 in Europe (US, Canada and Japan DKK 1650) (effective 1997). Munksgaard International Publishers Ltd., 35 Noerre Soegade, P.O. Box 2148, DK-1016 Copenhagen K, Denmark. TEL 45-33-127030. FAX 45-33-129387. E-mail: fsub@mail.munksgaard.dk. (In N. America: Commerce Place, 350 Main St., Malden, MA 02148-5018. TEL 617-388-8273. FAX 617-388-8274) Ed. Joergen Slots. illus. circ. 625. **Indexed:** ASCA, Biol.Abstr., Chem.Abstr., Curr.Cont., Curr.Tit.Dent., Ind.Sci.Rev., Int.Abstr.Biol.Sci., Sci.Cit.Ind. **Document type:** academic/scholarly publication.
—BLDSC (6277.590000); CASDDS; CISTI; EMDOCS; Genuine Article; KNAW; SWETS; UnCover. **CCC.**
Refereed Serial

576   IT   ISSN 0390-5454
OSPEDALE MARIA VITTORIA DI TORINO. ANNALI. s-a. Ospedale Maria Vittoria, Via Cibrario 72, 10144 Turin, Italy. TEL 74 92 345. **Indexed:** Biol.Abstr., Dent.Ind., Trop.Dis.Bull.
—CISTI.
Supersedes: Giornale di Batteriologia, Virologia ed Immunologia ed Annali dell'Ospedale Maria Vittoria di Torino. Parte 2. Sezione Clinica (ISSN 0301-1445); Which superseded in part: Giornale di Batteriologia, Virologia ed Immunologia ed Annali dell'Ospedale Maria Vittoria di Torino (ISSN 0017-0267)

P H L S DIRECTORY. (Public Health Laboratory Service) see *MEDICAL SCIENCES — Communicable Diseases*

P H L S FOOD AND ENVIRONMENT BULLETIN. (Public Health Laboratory Service) see *MEDICAL SCIENCES — Communicable Diseases*

P H L S LIBRARY BULLETIN. (Public Health Laboratory Service) see *MEDICAL SCIENCES — Communicable Diseases*

P H L S MICROBIOLOGY DIGEST. (Public Health Laboratory Service) see *MEDICAL SCIENCES — Communicable Diseases*

PARASITE. see *MEDICAL SCIENCES — Communicable Diseases*

571.999   CL   ISSN 0716-0720
RC119
PARASITOLOGIA AL DIA. (Text in Spanish; summaries in English) 1977. q. $55 (effective 1996 & 1997). Sociedad Chilena de Parasitologia, Casilla 50470, Santiago 9, Chile. FAX 56-2-5416840. TELEX JUMAR. (Co-sponsor: Federacion Latinoamericano de Parasitologos) Ed. Hector Alcaino A. adv.; bk.rev.; charts; illus. circ. 3,000. **Indexed:** Abstr.Hyg., Ind.Med. **Document type:** academic/scholarly publication.
Refereed Serial

571.999   HU   ISSN 0303-688X
PARASITOLOGIA HUNGARICA. (Text in English) 1968. a. $20 (effective 1997). Magyar Termeszettudomanyi Muzeum - Hungarian Natural History Muzeum, Baross u. 13, 1088 Budapest, Hungary. TEL 36-1-31300035. (Co-sponsor: Hungarian Society of Parasitologists) Eds. Eva Murai, A. Gubanyi. circ. 500.
—BLDSC (6405.400000); CISTI.

PARASITOLOGY RESEARCH. see *MEDICAL SCIENCES — Communicable Diseases*

PARASITOLOGY TODAY; international review journal in the field of medical and veterinary parasites. see *MEDICAL SCIENCES — Communicable Diseases*

PARASITOLOGY TODAY (REFERENCE EDITION). see *MEDICAL SCIENCES — Communicable Diseases*

PARAZITOLOGIYA/PARASITOLOGY. see *MEDICAL SCIENCES — Communicable Diseases*

PATHOBIOLOGY; journal of immunopathology, molecular and cellular biology. see *MEDICAL SCIENCES*

578   NE   ISSN 0168-7069
CODEN: PMVIEA
PERSPECTIVES IN MEDICAL VIROLOGY. (Text in English) 1985. irreg., vol.4, 1992. price varies. Elsevier Science B.V., Books Division, P.O. Box 211, 1000 AE Amsterdam, Netherlands. TEL 31-20-4853911. FAX 31-20-4853705. TELEX 18582 ESPA NL. E-mail: nlinfo-f@elsevier.nl; usinfo-f@elsevier.com; forinfo-kyf04035@niftyserve.or.jp; URL: http://www.elsevier.nl/. (Subscr. in the Americas to: Elsevier Science, Regional Sales Office, Box 945, New York, NY 10159-0945. TEL 212-633-3730. FAX 212-633-3680; Subscr. in Australasia and the Far East to: Elsevier Science (Singapore) Pte Ltd, No.1 Temasek Ave., No.17-01 Millenia Tower, Singapore 039192, Singapore. TEL 65-434-3727. FAX 65-337-2230; Subscr. in Japan to: Elsevier Science Japan, 9-15 Higashi-Azabu 1-chome, Minato-ku, Tokyo 106, Japan. TEL 81-3-5561-5033. FAX 81-3-5561-5047) **Document type:** monographic series.
—CISTI; KNAW.
Refereed Serial

576   PL   ISSN 0079-4252
QR1   CODEN: PMKMAV
POSTEPY MIKROBIOLOGII. (Text in Polish; summaries in English, Polish) 1962. q. 24 Zl. (foreign $55) (effective 1998). Polskie Towarzystwo Mikrobiologow, Ul. Chocimska 24, 00-791 Warsaw, Poland. TEL 48-22-497781. FAX 48-22-497484. E-mail: pzh@medstat.waw.pl. (Dist. by: Ars Polona, Krakowskie Przedmiescei 7, 00-950 Warsaw, Poland. TEL 48-22-8261201. FAX 48-22-8268673) Ed. Jerzy Hrebenda. R&P contact: Jolanta Szych. adv. circ. 1,000. **Indexed:** AgroLibrex Chem.Abstr., Curr.Adv.Ecol.Sci., Excerp.Med. **Document type:** monographic series.
—CASDDS; CISTI.

PRIKLADNAYA BIOKHIMIYA I MIKROBIOLOGIYA. see *BIOLOGY — Biological Chemistry*

BIOLOGY — MICROBIOLOGY

576 NE ISSN 0079-6352
QR53 CODEN: PIMRAS
PROGRESS IN INDUSTRIAL MICROBIOLOGY. 1959. irreg., latest 1992. price varies. Elsevier Science B.V., Books Division, P.O. Box 211, 1000 AE Amsterdam, Netherlands. TEL 31-20-4853911. FAX 31-20-4853705. TELEX 18582 ESPA NL. E-mail: nlinfo-f@elsevier.nl; usinfo-f@elsevier.com; forinfo-kyf04035@niftyserve.or.jp; URL: http://www.elsevier.nl/. (Subscr. in the Americas to: Elsevier Science, Regional Sales Office, Box 945, New York, NY 10159-0945. TEL 212-633-3730. FAX 212-633-3680; Subscr. in Australasia and the Far East to: Elsevier Science (Singapore) Pte Ltd, No.1 Temasek Ave., No.17-01 Millenia Tower, Singapore 039192, Singapore. TEL 65-434-3727. FAX 65-337-2230; Subscr. in Japan to: Elsevier Science Japan, 9-15 Higashi-Azabu 1-chome, Minato-ku, Tokyo 106, Japan. TEL 81-3-5561-5033. FAX 81-3-5561-5047) Ed. M.E. Bushell. **Indexed:** Biol.Abstr., Chem.Abstr., Curr.Biotech.Abstr., Food Sci.& Tech.Abstr. **Document type:** monographic series.
—BLDSC (6868.500000); CASDDS; CISTI; Linda Hall; SWETS; UnCover. **CCC.**
Refereed Serial

PROGRESS IN MEDICAL VIROLOGY. see *MEDICAL SCIENCES — Communicable Diseases*

576 FR ISSN 0923-2508
QR1 CODEN: ANMBCM
RESEARCH IN MICROBIOLOGY. (Text in English) 1886. 9/yr. 2282 F. (institutions in the Americas $436; elsewhere 2820 F.) (effective 1998). (Institut Pasteur) Editions Scientifiques et Medicales Elsevier, 141 rue de Javel, 75747 Paris, France. TEL 33-1-45589022. FAX 33-1-45589421. URL: http://www.elsevier.nl/. (Subscr. in U.S. and Canada to: Elsevier Science Inc., Box 945, Madison Sq. Sta., New York, NY 10159. TEL 212-633-3730. FAX 212-633-3680) Ed. M. Hofnung. adv.; bk.rev.; abstr.; illus.; index. circ. 2,100. (also avail. in microform from RPI,PMC; reprint service avail. from ISI) **Indexed:** Abstr.Hyg., ASCA, Biol.Abstr., Biotech.Abstr., Bull.Signal., Chem.Abstr., Curr.Adv.Biochem., Curr.Adv.Ecol.Sci., Curr.Adv.Genetics & Molec.Biol., Curr.Cont., Dairy Sci.Abstr., Excerp.Med., Food Sci.& Tech.Abstr., Ind.Med., Ind.Sci.Rev., Ind.Vet., INIS Atomind., Pig News & Info., Poult.Abstr., Rev.Med.& Vet.Mycol., Sci.Cit.Ind., Soils & Fert., Trop.Dis.Bull., Vet.Bull. **Document type:** academic/scholarly publication.
—BLDSC (7742.720000); ADONIS; CASDDS; CISTI; EMDOCS; Genuine Article; Linda Hall; SWETS; UnCover. **CCC.**
Former titles: Institut Pasteur. Annales. Microbiologie (ISSN 0769-2609); (until 1985): Annales de Microbiologie (ISSN 0300-5410); Which supersedes in part: Institut Pasteur. Annales (ISSN 0020-2444)
Description: Publishes original reports, brief notes and position papers on general and molecular microbiology, physiology and microbial genetics, environmental and applied microbiology, industrial microbiology, mycology and medical microbiology.
Refereed Serial

576 UK ISSN 0954-139X
QR46 CODEN: RMEMER
REVIEWS IN MEDICAL MICROBIOLOGY. 1990. q. £245 (foreign $405) (effective 1998). (Pathological Society of Great Britain and Ireland) Thomson Science (Subsidiary of: International Thomson Publishing Group), 2-6 Boundary Row, London SE1 8HN, England. TEL 44-171-865-0198. FAX 44-171-928-7876. TELEX 290164 CHAPMA G. E-mail: journal@rapidcom.co.uk; URL: http://www.thomsonscience.com. (Subscr. to: International Thomson Publishing Services Ltd., Cheriton House, North Way, Andover, Hants. SP10 5BE, England. TEL 44-1264-342713. FAX 44-1264-342807; Subscr. in US & Canada to: 400 Market St., Philadelphia, PA 19106. TEL 800-552-5866) Ed. Ian Poxton. adv. contact: Gemma Heiser. (reprint service avail.) **Indexed:** Diar.Dis.Res., Excerp.Med. **Document type:** academic/scholarly publication.
●Also available online.
—BLDSC (7792.210000); EMDOCS; Genuine Article; KNAW. **CCC.**
Description: Provides balanced coverage of the entire field of medical microbiology, along with state-of-the-art reviews of the latest techniques and developments in medical microbiology, virology, mycology, parasitology, clinical microbiology, and nosocomial infection.
Refereed Serial

576.64 UK ISSN 1052-9276
QR1 CODEN: RMVIEW
REVIEWS IN MEDICAL VIROLOGY. 1991. q. $445 (foreign $445) (effective 1998). John Wiley & Sons Ltd., Journals, Baffins Ln., Chichester, W. Sussex PO19 1UD, England. TEL 44-1243-779777. FAX 44-1243-775878. E-mail: info-assets@wiley.co.uk; URL: http://www.wiley.co.uk. (Subscr. in the Americas to: John Wiley & Sons, Inc., 605 Third Ave., New York, NY 10158. TEL 212-850-6645. FAX 212-850-6021) Ed. Paul Griffiths. adv.: B&W page £595, color page £1495; trim 297 x 210; adv. contact: Bob Kern. circ. 200. (also avail. in microform from UMI; back issues avail.; reprint service avail. from SWZ) **Indexed:** ASCA, Curr.Cont., Excerp.Med. (1994-), Ind.Sci.Rev., Sci.Cit.Ind. **Document type:** academic/scholarly publication.
—BLDSC (7792.500000); CASDDS; Genuine Article; KNAW; SWETS; UMI. **CCC.**
Description: Reviews current research and new information on all viruses of medical importance.
Refereed Serial

576 616.97 AG ISSN 0325-7541
QR1 CODEN: RAMID4
REVISTA ARGENTINA DE MICROBIOLOGIA. (Text in English and Spanish) 1968. q. $40 (foreign $50) (effective 1997). Asociacion Argentina de Microbiologia, Bulnes 44, P.B. B, 1176 Buenos Aires, Argentina. TEL 54-1-9584888. FAX 54-1-9824888. E-mail: aam@aam.org.ar. Ed. Dr. Elsa Damonte. adv. circ. 1,500. **Indexed:** Abstr.Hyg., Biol.Abstr., Chem.Abstr., Dairy Sci.Abstr., Excerp.Med., Food Sci.& Tech.Abstr., Ind.Med., Ind.Vet., Protozool.Abstr., Trop.Dis.Bull., Vet.Bull. **Document type:** academic/scholarly publication.
—BLDSC (7841.400000); CASDDS; CISTI.
Refereed Serial

576 BL ISSN 0001-3714
QR6 CODEN: RMBGBP
REVISTA DE MICROBIOLOGIA. (Text in English) 1970. q. $50 (effective 1996). Sociedade Brasileira de Microbiologia, c/o Luiz Rachid Trabulsi, Ed., Depto. de Microbiologia, Instituto de Ciencias Biomedicas USP, Av. Prof. Lineu Prestes, 1374, 05508-900 Sao Paulo, SP, Brazil. TEL 55-11-8139647. FAX 55-11-81396747. R&P contact: Luiz Rachid Trabulsi. adv. contact: Nancy Yuri Kawakosi de Amo. bk.rev.; index. circ. 1,500. (back issues avail.; reprint service avail. from ISI) **Indexed:** Abstr.Hyg., ASCA, Biol.Abstr., Chem.Abstr., Curr.Adv.Ecol.Sci., Curr.Cont., Dairy Sci.Abstr., Excerp.Med., Food Sci.& Tech.Abstr., Helminthol.Abstr., Ind.Med., Ind.Vet., Poult.Abstr., Rev.Med.& Vet.Mycol., Rev.Med.& Vet.Mycol., Rev.Plant Path., Sugar Ind.Abstr., Trop.Dis.Bull., Vet.Bull. **Document type:** academic/scholarly publication.
●Also available online.
—BLDSC (7866.425000); CASDDS; CISTI; Genuine Article; KNAW; UMI.
Refereed Serial

576 SP ISSN 0213-4829
REVISTA ESPANOLA DE MICROBIOLOGIA CLINICA. 11/yr. 5800 ptas. Saned, S.A., Paseo de la Habana 202-bis, 28036 Madrid, Spain. TEL 1-3594092. Ed. Dr. Diego Damasco. circ. 10,000.
—**CCC.**

REVISTA IBEROAMERICANA DE MICOLOGIA. see *MEDICAL SCIENCES*

576 MX ISSN 0187-4640
QR1 CODEN: RLMIAA
REVISTA LATINOAMERICANA DE MICROBIOLOGIA. 1958. q. $40. (Asociacion Mexicana de Microbiologia) Asociacion Latinoamericana de Microbiologia, Apdo. Postal 4-862, 06400 Mexico D.F., Mexico. TEL 525-3414795. FAX 525-3963503. Ed. Dr. Jorge Ortigoza-Ferado. bk.rev. circ. 2,500. **Indexed:** Abstr.Hyg., Biol.Abstr., Chem.Abstr., Dairy Sci.Abstr., Deep Sea Res.& Oceanogr.Abstr., Excerp.Med., Food Sci.& Tech.Abstr., Helminthol.Abstr., Ind.Med., Ind.Vet., Rev.Med.& Vet.Mycol., Rev.Plant Path., Soils & Fert., Sugar Ind.Abstr., Trop.Dis.Bull., Vet.Bull. **Document type:** academic/scholarly publication.
—BLDSC (7863.500000); CASDDS; CISTI; KNAW; SWETS.
Former titles (until 1970): Revista Latinoamericana de Microbiologia y Parasitologia (ISSN 0370-5986); (until 1966): Revista Latinoamericana de Microbiologia (ISSN 0034-9771)
Description: Original papers in medical bacteriology, virology, immunology, genetics and molecular biology, parasitology, and industrial and agricultural microbiology.

REVISTA MEXICANA DE MICOLOGIA. see *BIOLOGY — Botany*

576 PY ISSN 0556-6908
QR22.P37
REVISTA PARAGUAYA DE MICROBIOLOGIA. (Text in Spanish; summaries in English) 1966. a. $10. Universidad Nacional de Asuncion, Facultad de Ciencias Medicas, Catedra de Bacteriologia y Parasitologia, Casilla de Correo 1102, Asuncion, Paraguay. Ed. Dr. Arquimedes Canese. illus. **Indexed:** Excerp.Med., Ind.Vet., Rev.Appl.Entomol., Trop.Dis.Bull., Vet.Bull.

REVUE ROUMAINE DE VIROLOGIE/RUMANIAN JOURNAL OF VIROLOGY. see *MEDICAL SCIENCES — Communicable Diseases*

RIVISTA DI PARASSITOLOGIA. see *MEDICAL SCIENCES — Communicable Diseases*

ROMANIAN ARCHIVES OF MICROBIOLOGY AND IMMUNOLOGY. see *MEDICAL SCIENCES — Allergology And Immunology*

576.64 US ISSN 1068-3747
QR355
RUSSIAN PROGRESS IN VIROLOGY. English translation of: Voprosy Virusologii (UR ISSN 0507-4088) 1980. bi-m. $1040 (effective 1998). (Rossiiskaya Akademiya Meditsinskikh Nauk, RU - Russian Academy of Medicine) Allerton Press, Inc., 150 Fifth Ave., New York, NY 10011. TEL 212-924-3950. FAX 212-463-9684. Ed. O.G. Andzhaparidze. **Document type:** academic/scholarly publication.
—BLDSC (0420.784000); CISTI. **CCC.**
Formerly: Soviet Progress in Virology (ISSN 0734-0311)
Description: Covers viral diagnostics, AIDS, epidemiology of viral diseases, antiviral drugs, virus reproduction, viral infection, etc.

589.9 JA
SAIKINGAKU GIJUTSU SOSHO/TECHNICAL JOURNAL OF BACTERIOLOGY. (Text in Japanese) a. 4000 Yen. Nihon Saikin Gakkai, Kyoiku linkai - Japanese Society for Bacteriology, Board of Education, Nihon Gakkai Jimu Senta, 16-9 Honkomagome 5-chome, Bunyo-ku, Tokyo 113, Japan.

SCHWEIZERISCHE ZEITSCHRIFT FUER PILZKUNDE/BULLETIN SUISSE DE MYCOLOGIE/BOLLETTINO SVIZZERO DI MICOLOGIA. see *BIOLOGY — Botany*

BIOLOGY — MICROBIOLOGY

576   JA   ISSN 0919-3758
TP500   CODEN: SEKAEA
SEIBUTSU KOGAKU KAISHI. (Text in Japanese; summaries in English) 1977. bi-m. 10000 Yen (effective 1997). Society for Fermentation and Bioengineering, Japan - Seibutsu Kogakkai, c/o Osaka University, Faculty of Engineering, 2-1 Yamadaoka, Suita-shi, Osaka 565, Japan. TEL 81-6-876-2731. FAX 81-6-829-2074. E-mail: sfbj@iijnet.or.jp. Ed. Itaru Urabe; Pub. Tohru Kodama. adv. contact: Takekuma Kuroki. abstr. **Indexed:** ASCA, Biol.Abstr., Chem.Abstr., Curr.Cont., Excerp.Med. **Document type:** academic/scholarly publication.
—BLDSC (8219.044000); CASDDS; CISTI; Genuine Article; Linda Hall. **CCC.**
Formerly (until 1993): Hakkokogaku (ISSN 0385-6151)

576.64   US   ISSN 1044-5773
QR355   CODEN: SEVIEL
SEMINARS IN VIROLOGY. 1990. bi-m. $180 (foreign $216) (effective 1997). Academic Press, Inc., Journal Division, 525 B ST., Ste. 1900, San Diego, CA 92101-4495. TEL 619-230-1840. FAX 619-699-6800. E-mail: apsubs@acad.com; URL: http://www.hbuk.co.uk/ap/journals/vi.htm; http://www.idealibrary.com/. (Subscr. to: Box 861213, Orlando, FL 32886-1213. TEL 407-347-4040. FAX 407-363-9661) Ed.Bd. (reprint service avail. from SWZ) **Indexed:** ASCA, Curr.Cont., Ind.Sci.Rev. **Document type:** academic/scholarly publication.
● Also available online.
—BLDSC (8239.487500); CASDDS; CISTI; Genuine Article; KNAW; SWETS; UnCover. **CCC.**
Description: Contains material of interest to scientists in the life sciences.

576   FR   ISSN 0081-1068
SOCIETE FRANCAISE DE MICROBIOLOGIE. ANNUAIRE. 1961. triennial. membership. Institut Pasteur, 28 rue du Docteur-Roux, Paris 75015, France.

576   US
SOCIETY FOR APPLIED BACTERIOLOGY. SYMPOSIUM SERIES. 1971. irreg., vol.12, 1984. Academic Press, Inc., 525 B St., Ste. 1900, San Diego, CA 92101-4495. TEL 619-231-0926. FAX 619-699-6719. (Subscr. to: Order Dept., 6277 Sea Harbor Dr., 4th Fl., Orlando, FL 32887. TEL 800-321-5068) (reprint service avail. from ISI) **Indexed:** Biol.Abstr., Chem.Abstr., Curr.Adv.Ecol.Sci., Food Sci.& Tech.Abstr., Ind.Med., Soils & Fert.
Refereed Serial

576   US
SOCIETY FOR APPLIED BACTERIOLOGY. TECHNICAL SERIES. irreg., vol.21, 1985. Academic Press, Inc., 525 B St., Ste. 1900, San Diego, CA 92101-4495. TEL 619-231-0926. FAX 619-699-6715. (Subscr. to: Order Dept., 6277 Sea Harbor Dr., 4th Fl., Orlando, FL 32887. TEL 800-321-5068) (reprint service avail. from ISI) **Indexed:** Biol.Abstr., Chem.Abstr., Food Sci.& Tech.Abstr.
Refereed Serial

576   UK   ISSN 0142-7547
SOCIETY FOR GENERAL MICROBIOLOGY. QUARTERLY. 1974. q. £34($65) Society for General Microbiology, Marlborough House, Basingstoke Rd., Spencers Wood, Reading RG7 1AE, England. TEL 44-1734-885577. FAX 44-1734-885656. Ed. D. Roberts. adv. contact: Janice Meekings. bk.rev. **Indexed:** Abstr.Hyg., Curr.Adv.Ecol.Sci., Dairy Sci.Abstr., Ind.Vet., Res.High.Educ.Abstr., Vet.Bull. **Document type:** academic/scholarly publication.
—BLDSC (8254.560215); CISTI; KNAW; Linda Hall; UnCover.
Formerly: Society for General Microbiology Proceedings (ISSN 0306-2708)

576   UK   ISSN 0081-1394
QR1   CODEN: SSGMAI
SOCIETY FOR GENERAL MICROBIOLOGY. SYMPOSIUM. 1961. irreg., no.41, 1987. price varies. Cambridge University Press, Edinburgh Bldg., Shaftesbury Rd., Cambridge CB2 2RU, England. TEL 44-1223-312393. FAX 44-1223-315052. TELEX 851817256. E-mail: information@cup.cam. ac.uk; URL: http://www.cup.cam.ac.uk. (N. American addr.: Cambridge University Press, Journals Dept., 40 W. 20th St., New York, NY 10011. TEL 212-924-3900. FAX 212-691-3239) R&P contact: Linda Nicol. index. **Indexed:** Biol.Abstr., Chem.Abstr., Curr.Biotech.Abstr., Rev.Plant Path. **Document type:** proceedings.
—BLDSC (8585.010000); CASDDS; KNAW. **CCC.**

579   US
SOCIETY FOR IN VITRO BIOLOGY. MONOGRAPH SERIES. irreg. price varies. Society for In Vitro Biology, 9315 Largo Dr. W., Ste. 255, Largo, MD 20774. TEL 301-324-5054. FAX 301-324-5057. (Subscr. to: Box 73230, Baltimore, MD 21273) **Document type:** monographic series.
Formerly: Tissue Culture Association. Monograph Series.
Description: Covers specific topics of interest to tissue culture researchers.
Refereed Serial

579   US
QH585
SOCIETY FOR IN VITRO BIOLOGY. PROCEEDINGS. irreg. price varies. Society for In Vitro Biology, 9315 Largo Dr. W., Ste. 255, Largo, MD 20774. TEL 301-324-5054. FAX 301-324-5057. (Subscr. to: Box 73230, Baltimore, MD 21273) **Document type:** proceedings.
Formerly: Tissue Culture Association. Proceedings of the Annual Meeting (ISSN 0272-6564)
Description: Publishes the proceedings of various meetings and specific topics of interest to tissue culture researchers.
Refereed Serial

STATION BIOLOGIQUE DE BESSE EN CHANDESSE. ANNALES. see *BIOLOGY — Abstracting, Bibliographies, Statistics*

576   GW   ISSN 0723-2020
QR1   CODEN: SAMIDF
SYSTEMATIC AND APPLIED MICROBIOLOGY. (Text in English, French and German) 1980. irreg. (4 nos./vol.) DM.768 (foreign £337) (effective 1997). Gustav Fischer Verlag, Villengang 2, 07745 Jena, Germany. TEL 49-3641-626430. FAX 49-3641-626421. E-mail: office.j@gfischer.de. (Subscr. to: Stockton Press, Subscription Dept., Houndmills, Basingstoke, Hants RG21 6XS, England) Eds. K.H. Schleifer, M. Teufer. **Indexed:** Abstr.Hyg., ASCA, Biol.Abstr., Chem.Abstr., Curr.Adv.Ecol.Sci., Curr.Cont., Dairy Sci.Abstr., Deep Sea Res.& Oceanogr.Abstr., Excerp.Med., Food Sci.& Tech.Abstr., Helminthol.Abstr., Ind.Med., Ind.Sci.Rev., Ind.Vet., Rev.Appl.Entomol., Rev.Med.& Vet.Mycol., Rev.Plant Path., Sci.Cit.Ind., Trop.Dis.Bull., Vet.Bull. **Document type:** academic/scholarly publication.
—BLDSC (8589.176000); CASDDS; CISTI; EMDOCS; Genuine Article; KNAW; Linda Hall; SWETS; UMI; UnCover. **CCC.**
Formerly: Zentralblatt fuer Bakteriologie, Mikrobiologie und Hygiene (ISSN 0172-5564)

576   KO   ISSN 0253-3162
QR1   CODEN: TMHCDX
TAEHAN MISAENGMUL HAKHOE CHI/KOREAN SOCIETY FOR MICROBIOLOGY. JOURNAL.* (Text in Korean; summaries and table of contents in English) 1957. bi-m. $70. Korean Society for Microbiology - Taehan Misaengmul Hakhoe, c/o Dept. of Microbiology, Yonsei University College of Medicine, 134 Shinchon-dong, Seodaemun-gu, Seoul 120-749, S. Korea. TEL 82-2-293-2111. FAX 82-2-293-1629. Ed. Pyung-Woo Lee. adv.; bibl.; charts. circ. 400. **Indexed:** Chem.Abstr., Excerp.Med. (until 1993). **Document type:** academic/scholarly publication.
—BLDSC (4812.346200); CASDDS; KNAW.
Description: Devoted to the dissemination of new knowledge concerning the microbiological aspects of human and animal infections, particularly regarding their etiologic agents, diagnosis, pathogenesis, epidemiology, and antimicrobial agents and chemotherapy.

TREE PHYSIOLOGY; an international botanical journal. see *BIOLOGY — Botany*

576   UK   ISSN 0966-842X
QR1   CODEN: TRMIEA
TRENDS IN MICROBIOLOGY. Library compendium: Trends in Microbiology (Reference Edition) (ISSN 0968-0055) 1993. m. fl.1349($775) to institutions (effective 1998). Elsevier Science Ltd., P.O. Box 800, Kidlington, Oxford OX5 1DX, England. TEL 44-1865-843000. FAX 44-1865-843010. E-mail: nlinfo-f@elsevier.nl; usinfo-f@elsevier.com; forinfo-kyf04035@niftyserve.or.jp; URL: http://www.elsevier.nl/. (Subscr. to: Elsevier Science, Regional Sales Office, P.O. Box 211, 1000 AE Amsterdam, Netherlands. TEL 31-20-4853757. FAX 31-20-4853432; Subscr. in the Americas to: Elsevier Science, Regional Sales Office, Box 945, New York, NY 10159-0945. TEL 212-633-3730. FAX 212-633-3680; Subscr. in Australasia and the Far East to: Elsevier Science (Singapore) Pte Ltd, No.1 Temasek Ave., No.17-01 Millenia Tower, Singapore 039192, Singapore. TEL 65-434-3727. FAX 65-337-2230) Ed. C.P.J. Ash. adv.; bk.rev.; bibl.; index. (also avail. in microform from UMI; back issues avail.) **Indexed:** ASCA, Excerp.Med. (1993-), Food Sci.& Tech.Abstr., Ind.Med. (1994-). **Document type:** academic/scholarly publication.
—BLDSC (9049.664000); ADONIS; CISTI; EMDOCS; Genuine Article; KNAW; SWETS; UnCover. **CCC.**
Description: Provides a forum for the discussion of all aspects of infection, covering dynamics, cell biology, immunology, genetics and evolution of infectious organisms, including fungi, bacteria and viruses, as well as their plant and animal hosts.
Refereed Serial

576   UK   ISSN 0968-0055
QR1
TRENDS IN MICROBIOLOGY (REFERENCE EDITION). 1993. a. Elsevier Science Ltd., P.O. Box 800, Kidlington, Oxford OX5 1DX, England. TEL 44-1865-843000. FAX 44-1865-843010. E-mail: nlinfo-f@elsevier.nl; usinfo-f@elsevier.com; forinfo-kyf04035@niftyserve.or.jp; URL: http://www.elsevier.nl/. (Subscr. to: Elsevier Science, Regional Sales Office, P.O. Box 211, 1000 AE Amsterdam, Netherlands. TEL 31-20-4853757. FAX 31-20-4853432; Subscr. in the Americas to: Elsevier Science, Regional Sales Office, Box 945, New York, NY 10159-0945. TEL 212-633-3730. FAX 212-633-3680; Subscr. in Australasia and the Far East to: Elsevier Science (Singapore) Pte Ltd, No.1 Temasek Ave., No.17-01 Millenia Tower, Singapore 039192, Singapore. TEL 65-434-3727. FAX 65-337-2230) Ed. Caroline Ash. **Document type:** academic/scholarly publication.
—CISTI. **CCC.**
Description: Compendium of archival material from Trends in Microbiology.
Refereed Serial

576   JA   ISSN 0912-2184
TSUCHI TO BISEIBUTSU/SOIL MICROORGANISMS. (Text in English, Japanese) 1954. 2/yr. 3500 Yen (foreign 4500 Yen) (effective 1997). Dojo Biseibutsu Kenkyukai - Soil Microbiological Society of Japan, Nogyo Kankyo Gijutsu Kenkyujo, 1-1 Kannondai 3-chome, Tsukuba-shi, Ibaraki-ken 305, Japan. TEL 81-298-38-8300. FAX 81-298-38-8199. E-mail: nowmat@niaes.affrc. go.jp. Ed. Masanori Saito. **Document type:** academic/scholarly publication.
—CCC.

576 616.97   TU   ISSN 0258-2171
TURK MIKROBIYOLOGI CEMIYETI DERGISI.* (Text in Turkish; summaries in English) 1971. q. $40. Turk Mikrobiyoloji Cemiyeti - Turkish Microbiological Society, Marmara Universitesi Tip Fakultesi, Mikrobiyoloji Anabilim Dali, 81326 Haydarpasa, Istanbul, Turkey. adv.; bk.rev. circ. 1,000. (back issues avail.) **Indexed:** Biol.Abstr., Helminthol.Abstr. **Document type:** academic/scholarly publication.

UNIVERSITY OF TOKYO. INSTITUTE OF APPLIED MICROBIOLOGY. REPORTS. see *BIOLOGY — Abstracting, Bibliographies, Statistics*

UNIVERSITY OF WAIKATO. ANTARCTIC RESEARCH UNIT. REPORT. see *EARTH SCIENCES — Geology*

VETERINARY MICROBIOLOGY; an international journal. see *VETERINARY SCIENCE*

BIOLOGY — MICROBIOLOGY

576.64 616.92   US   ISSN 0042-6822
QR360   CODEN: VIRLAX
VIROLOGY. CD-ROM edition (US ISSN 1089-862X) 1955. 26/yr. $1995 (foreign $2400) (effective 1997). Academic Press, Inc., Journal Division, 525 B St., Ste. 1900, San Diego, CA 92101-4495. TEL 619-230-1840. FAX 619-688-6800. E-mail: apsubs@acad.com; URL: http://www.apnet.com/ www/journal/vy.htm; http://www.idealibrary.com/. (Subscr. to: Box 861213, Orlando, FL 32886-1213. TEL 407-347-4040. FAX 407-363-9661) Ed. Robert Lamb. adv.; bibl.; charts; illus.; index. (back issues avail.) **Indexed:** Abstr.Hyg., AIDS Abstr., Anim.Breed.Abstr., ASCA, Bibl.Agri., Bio-Contr.News & Info., Biol.Abstr., Biol.& Agr.Ind., Biotech.Abstr., Chem.Abstr., Curr.Adv.Cancer Res., Curr.Adv.Ecol.Sci., Curr.Adv.Genetics & Molec.Biol., Curr.Cont., Dairy Sci.Abstr., Dent.Ind., Excerp.Med., Food Sci.& Tech.Abstr., Helminthol.Abstr., Hort.Abstr., Ind.Med., Ind.Sci.Rev., Ind.Vet., Neurosci.Cit.Ind., Nutr.Abstr., Pig News & Info., Poult.Abstr., Rev.Appl.Entomol., Rev.Plant Path., Sci.Cit.Ind., Small Anim.Abstr., So.Pac.Per.Ind., Sport Fish.Abstr., Triticale Abstr., Vet.Bull., W.R.C.Inf., Wild.Rev. **Document type:** academic/scholarly publication.
●Also available online.
Also available on CD-ROM.
—BLDSC (9240.500000); ADONIS; CASDDS; CISTI; Genuine Article; KNAW; KR SourceOne; Linda Hall; SWETS; UnCover. **CCC.**
Description: Publishes the results of basic research in all branches of virology, including the viruses of vertebrates and invertebrates, plants, bacteria, and yeast and fungi.
Refereed Serial

576 616   US   ISSN 0083-6591
QR360   CODEN: VIRMB3
VIROLOGY MONOGRAPHS/VIRUSFORSCHUNG IN EINZELDARSTELLUNGEN. 1968. irreg., vol.18, 1981. price varies. Springer-Verlag, 175 Fifth Ave., New York, NY 10010. TEL 212-460-1500. FAX 212-473-6272. (Also: Berlin, Heidelberg, Tokyo and Vienna) (reprint service avail. from ISI) **Indexed:** Biol.Abstr., Ind.Med. **Document type:** monographic series.
—CISTI.
Formerly: Handbuch der Virusforschung.

576 616   JA   ISSN 0042-6857
     CODEN: UIRUAF
VIRUS/UIRUSU. (Text in Japanese; summaries in English) 1951. s-a. Society of Japanese Virologists - Nihon Uirusu Gakkai, Nihon Gakkai Jimu Senta, 16-9 Honkomagome 5-chome, Bunkyo-ku, Tokyo 113, Japan. (Overseas Distributor: Japan Publications Trading Co., Ltd., Box 5030, Tokyo International, Tokyo 100-31, Japan; or 1255 Howard St., San Francisco, CA 94103) Ed. Dr. Isao Yoshioka. adv.; bk.rev.; abstr.; charts; illus.; index. circ. 1,200. **Indexed:** Biol.Abstr., Chem.Abstr., Excerp.Med., Ind.Med., Ind.Vet., Jap.Per.Ind., Rev.Plant Path., Vet.Bull.
—BLDSC (9240.850000); CASDDS; CISTI.

576.64 575.1   US   ISSN 0920-8569
     CODEN: VIGEET
VIRUS GENES. 1987. bi-m. fl.840 to institutions; $431 to institutions in U.S. (effective 1998). Kluwer Academic Publishers Boston, Box 358, Accord Sta., Hingham, MA 02018-0358. TEL 617-871-6600. FAX 617-871-6528. TELEX 200190. E-mail: services@wkap.nl; URL: http://www.wkap.nl. (Dist. outside N. America by: Kluwer Academic Publishers Group, P.O. Box 322, 3300 AH Dordrecht, Netherlands. TEL 31-78-6392392. FAX 31-78-6546474) Ed. Yechiel Becker. adv.; bk.rev. (also avail. in microform from UMI; back issues avail.; reprint service avail. from SWZ,UMI) **Indexed:** ASCA, Biol.Abstr., Chem.Abstr., Curr.Cont., Excerp.Med., Ind.Med., Ind.Sci.Rev., Sci.Cit.Ind. **Document type:** academic/scholarly publication.
—BLDSC (9240.850500); ADONIS; CASDDS; CISTI; EMDOCS; Genuine Article; KNAW; SWETS; UMI; UnCover. **CCC.**
Description: Publishes the results of studies on the structure and function of virus genes (animal, insect, plant and bacterial).
Refereed Serial

576   NE   ISSN 0168-1702
     CODEN: VIREDF
VIRUS RESEARCH; an international journal of molecular and cellular virology. (Text in English) 1984. m. fl.3826($2199) to institutions (effective 1998). Elsevier Science B.V., P.O. Box 211, 1000 AE Amsterdam, Netherlands. TEL 31-20-4853911. FAX 31-20-4853598. TELEX 18582 ESPA NL. E-mail: nlinfo-f@elsevier.nl; usinfo-f@elsevier.com; forinfo-kyf04035@niftyserve.or.jp; URL: http://www.elsevier.nl/. (Subscr. in the Americas to: Elsevier Science, Regional Sales Office, Box 945, New York, NY 10159-0945. TEL 212-633-3730. FAX 212-633-3680; Subscr. in Australasia and the Far East to: Elsevier Science (Singapore) Pte Ltd, No.1 Temasek Ave., No.17-01 Millenia Tower, Singapore 039192, Singapore. TEL 65-434-3727. FAX 65-337-2230; Subscr. in Japan to: Elsevier Science Japan, 9-15 Higashi-Azabu 1-chome, Minato-ku, Tokyo 106, Japan. TEL 81-3-5561-5033. FAX 81-3-5561-5047) Ed.Bd. adv.; bk.rev.; bibl.; charts; illus.; index. circ. 1,000. (also avail. in microform from UMI; back issues avail.; reprint service avail. from ISI) **Indexed:** AIDS Abstr., ASCA, Biol.Abstr., Chem.Abstr., Curr.Adv.Ecol.Sci., Curr.Adv.Genetics & Molec.Biol., Curr.Cont., Excerp.Med., Ind.Sci.Rev., Ind.Vet., Poult.Abstr., Vet.Bull. **Document type:** academic/scholarly publication.
—BLDSC (9240.852000); ADONIS; CASDDS; CISTI; Genuine Article; Linda Hall; SWETS; UnCover. **CCC.**
Description: Publishes original papers on fundamental research concerning virus structure, replication, and pathogenesis.
Refereed Serial

576.64   RU   ISSN 0507-4088
     CODEN: VVIRAT
VOPROSY VIRUSOLOGII/PROBLEMS OF VIROLOGY. English translation: Russian Progress in Virology (US ISSN 1068-3747) (Text in Russian; summaries in English) 1956. bi-m. $245 (effective 1998). (Rossiiskaya Akademiya Meditsinskikh Nauk) Izdatel'stvo Meditsina, Petroverigskii pereulok 6-8, 101000 Moscow, Russia. TEL 7-095-9248785. FAX 7-095-9286003. TELEX 412282 MEDIZ SU. (Dist. by: Mezhdunarodnaya Kniga, B. Yakimanka 39, 117049 Moscow, Russia. TEL 7-095-2384967. FAX 7-095-2384634) Ed. O.G. Andzhaparidze. adv. contact: O.A. Fadeeva. circ. 850. **Indexed:** Abstr.Hyg., ASCA, Biol.Abstr., Biotech.Abstr., Chem.Abstr., Curr.Adv.Ecol.Sci., Curr.Cont., Dent.Ind., Excerp.Med., Ind.Med., Ind.Vet., Sci.Cit.Ind., Small Anim.Abstr., Trop.Dis.Bull., Vet.Bull.
—BLDSC (0041.900000); CASDDS; CISTI; EMDOCS; Genuine Article; KNAW; SWETS. **CCC.**
Description: Deals with advances achieved in virology in Russia and abroad. Publishes papers about viral diseases of man, animals and plants.

576 591.192   FI   ISSN 0358-6758
WALTER AND ANDREE DE NOTTBECK FOUNDATION SCIENTIFIC REPORTS. (Text and summaries in English) 1976. irreg. free. Walter and Andree de Nottbeck Foundation, c/o Department of Ecology and Systematics, P.O. Box 7, Unioninkatan 44, FIN-00014 University of Helsinki, Finland. TEL 358-9-191-86-01. FAX 358-0-191-86-56. E-mail: carl-adam.haeggstrom@helsinki.fi. (Dist. by: Tvarminne Zoological Station, FIN-10900 Hangoe, Finland) Ed. Carl-Adam Haeggstrom. circ. 500. (back issues avail.) **Document type:** academic/scholarly publication.

576   CC   ISSN 1002-056X
WEISHENGWU XUE ZAZHI/JOURNAL OF MICROBIOLOGY. (Text in Chinese) 1979. q. $20. Liaoning Weishengwu Yanjiusuo - Liaoning Institute of Microbiology, No.22, Wenhua Lu 2 Duan, Chaoyang, Liaoning 122000, People's Republic of China. TEL 0421-2814613. Ed. Ding Jian.
—BLDSC (5019.285600).

576   CC   ISSN 0001-6209
QR1   CODEN: WSHPA8
WEISHENGWU XUEBAO/ACTA MICROBIOLOGICA SINICA. (Text in Chinese; summaries in English) 1953. bi-m. $100.80. (Chinese Academy of Sciences, Institute of Microbiology) Science Press, Marketing and Sales Department, 16 Donghuangchenggen North St., Beijing 100717, People's Republic of China. TEL 4010642. FAX 4019810. adv.; charts; illus. circ. 11,000. **Indexed:** Bio-Contr.News & Info., Biodet.Abstr., Biol.Abstr., Curr.Adv.Biochem., Curr.Adv.Ecol.Sci., Curr.Adv.Genetics & Molec.Biol., Dairy Sci.Abstr., Helminthol.Abstr., Hort.Abstr., Ind.Vet., Pig News & Info., Rev.Appl.Entomol., Rev.Med.& Vet.Mycol. **Document type:** academic/scholarly publication.
—BLDSC (0638.500000); CASDDS; CISTI; KNAW; Linda Hall.
Description: Contains theses on the theory and application of microbiology in industrial, agricultural, medical, and veterinary sciences, as well as virology (including taxomorphology, physio-biochemistry, genetics, and serology.)
Refereed Serial

576   CC   ISSN 0253-2654
QR1   CODEN: WSWPDI
WEISHENGWUXUE TONGBAO/BULLETIN OF MICROBIOLOGY. (Text in Chinese) 1973. bi-m. Y53.40. (Chinese Academy of Sciences, Institute of Microbiology) Science Press, Marketing and Sales Department, 16 Donghuangchenggen North St., Beijing 100717, People's Republic of China. TEL 4010642. FAX 4019810. adv. circ. 16,000. **Indexed:** Cott.& Trop.Fibr.Abstr. **Document type:** academic/scholarly publication.
—BLDSC (5757.730000); CASDDS.
Description: Aims to expand the reader's knowledge of microbiology. Carries information on new results, techniques, and methods from the spheres of industry, agriculture, medicine, and veterinary medicine.

576   CC   ISSN 1000-0674
QE719   CODEN: WEXUE9
WEITI GUSHENGWU XUEBAO/ACTA MICROPALAEONTOLOGICA SINICA. (Text in Chinese; summaries in English) 1984. q. $130.80. (Zhongguo Kexueyuan, Nanjing Dizhi Gushengwu-suo) Science Press, Marketing and Sales Department, 16 Donghuangchenggen North St., Beijing 100717, People's Republic of China. TEL 4010642. FAX 4019810. adv.; bk.rev. circ. 6,000. **Document type:** academic/scholarly publication.
—CISTI.
Description: Publishes the latest results of studies in morphology, taxonomy, systematics, evolution, stratigraphy, paleobiogeography, and paleoecology. Covers various groups of microfossils, and provides news about academic activities, both in China and abroad.
Refereed Serial

576   JA
WORLD DIRECTORY OF COLLECTIONS OF CULTURES OF MICROORGANISMS. (Text in English) 1989. irreg., 4th ed., 1993. 15450 Yen. W F C C World Data Centre on Microorganisms - Baiyo Seibutsu Sekai Deta Senta, Center for Information Biology, National Institute of Genetics, 1111 Yata, Mishima, Shizuoka 411, Japan. (Subscr. to: Japan Publications Trading Co., Ltd., P.O. Box 5030 Tokyo International 100-31, Japan. FAX 81-3-3292-0410) Ed. Hideaki Sugawara.
Formerly: Guide to World Data Center on Microorganism (ISSN 0915-6682)
Description: Lists of scientific names of 334,312 strains of bacteria and 351,263 strains of fungi and yeasts.

BIOLOGY — MICROSCOPY

576 660   UK   ISSN 0959-3993
QR53   CODEN: WJMBEY
WORLD JOURNAL OF MICROBIOLOGY AND BIOTECHNOLOGY. 1985. bi-m. £135($230) to individuals; institutions £270($460); developing countries £175 (effective 1996). (International Union of Microbiological Societies) Rapid Science Publishers, The Old Malthouse, Paradise St., Oxford OX1 1LD, England. TEL 44-1865-790447. FAX 44-1865-244012. E-mail: marketing@rapidcom.co.uk. (Subscr. in US to: 115 Fifth Ave., 4th Fl., New York, NY 10003. TEL 212-780-6234. FAX 212-260-1363) Ed. Colin Ratledge. adv. contact: Julie Gribben. bk.rev. **Indexed:** ASCA, Biol.Abstr., Crop Physiol.Abstr., Curr.Adv.Biochem., Curr.Biotech.Abstr., Curr.Cont., Dairy Sci.Abstr., Diar.Dis.Res., Field Crop Abstr., Food Sci.& Tech.Abstr., Forest.Abstr., Herb.Abstr., Hort.Abstr., Maize Abstr., Rev.Med.& Vet.Mycol., Soils & Fert., Triticale Abstr., Trop.Oil Seeds Abstr.
●Also available on CD-ROM.
—BLDSC (9356.073500); ADONIS; CASDDS; CISTI; EMDOCS; Genuine Article; SWETS; UMI. **CCC.**
Formerly (until 1990): Mircen - Journal of Applied Microbiology and Biotechnology (ISSN 0265-0762)
Description: Presents papers describing the results of original work in applied microbiology and biotechnology, on topics relevant to the needs of the developing world.

576   US   ISSN 1054-772X
QR46
YEAR BOOK OF CLINICAL MICROBIOLOGY. 1991. a. C R C Press, Inc., 2000 Corporate Blvd. N.W., Boca Raton, FL 33431. TEL 561-994-0555; 800-272-7737. FAX 561-998-9784. TELEX 568689-CRC PRESS.

YEAST; a forum for yeast researchers. see *BIOLOGY — Biotechnology*

ZENTRALBLATT FUER BAKTERIOLOGIE. see *MEDICAL SCIENCES — Communicable Diseases*

ZHENJUN XUEBAO/ACTA MYCOLOGICA SINICA. see *BIOLOGY — Botany*

571.999   CC   ISSN 1000-7423
                                  CODEN: ZJYZET
ZHONGGUO JISHENGCHONGXUE YU JISHENGCHONGBING ZAZHI/CHINESE JOURNAL OF PARASITOLOGY AND PARASITIC DISEASES. (Text in Chinese) bi-m. Zhongguo Yufang Yixue Kexueyuan, Jishengchongbing Yanjiusuo - Chinese Academy of Preventive Medicine, Institute of Parasitic Diseases, 207 Ruijin 2 Lu, Shanghai 200025, People's Republic of China. TEL 86-21-6437-7008. Ed. Feng Zheng. R&P contact: Feng Zheng. adv. contact: Minyi Yao. **Document type:** academic/scholarly publication.
—BLDSC (3180.465000).

576 636.089   CC   ISSN 1002-2694
ZHONGGUO RENSHOU GONGHUANBING ZAZHI/CHINESE JOURNAL OF ZOONOSES. (Text in Chinese) 1985. bi-m. Y27 (foreign $12). Health and Anti-epidemic Center, Fuzhou Zhongjunhou No. 5, Fuzhou, Fujian 350001, People's Republic of China. TEL 86-591-7552018. (Dist. overseas by: China International Book Trading Corp., P.O. Box 399, P.R. China) (Co-sponsor: Zhongguo Weishengwu Xuehui - Chinese Microbiology Society) Ed. Yu Enshu. **Document type:** academic/scholarly publication.
Description: Discusses and examines bacteria and diseases common both to human beings and animals.

BIOLOGY — Microscopy

A A F M PROCEEDINGS OF ANNUAL MEETING. (American Association of Feed Microscopists) see *MEETINGS AND CONGRESSES*

578   US
▼**ADVANCES IN ACOUSTIC MICROSCOPY.** 1995. irreg., vol. 2, 1996. price varies. Plenum Publishing Corp., 233 Spring St., New York, NY 10013-1578. TEL 212-620-8035. FAX 212-463-0742. TELEX 23-421139. E-mail: books@plenum.com. Ed. G. Andrew D. Briggs. **Document type:** monographic series.

ANTIMICROBIAL AGENTS ANNUAL. see *BIOLOGY — Microbiology*

578 574   AG   ISSN 0327-9545
                                CODEN: BOCEEZ
BIOCELL. (Text in English) 1972. 3/yr. (in 1 vol., 3 nos./vol.). $80 to individuals; institutions $100 (effective 1995). (Universidad Nacional de Cuyo, Facultad de Ciencias Medicas, Instituto de Histologia y Embriologia) Centro Regional de Investigaciones Cientificas y Tecnologicas, Casilla de Correo 131, 5500 Mendoza, Argentina. TEL 54-61-205020 ext. 2670. FAX 54-61-380232. E-mail: biocell@fmed2.uncu.edu.ar. (Co-sponsors: Latin American Electron Microscopy Society; Sociedad Iberoamericana de Biologia Celular) Eds. Mario H. Burgos, Ramon S. Piezzi. adv.: B&W page $200, color page $300; adv. contact: Gabriel Puebla. charts; illus.; index; circ. 300 (controlled). (reprint service avail. from ISI) **Indexed:** ASCA, Biol.Abstr., Curr.Cont., Curr.Cont., Excerp.Med. (until 1988), Ind.Med., Ind.Sci.Rev. **Document type:** academic/scholarly publication.
—BLDSC (2066.809400); CASDDS; CISTI; Genuine Article.
Former titles (until 1993): Microscopia Electronica y Biologia Celular - Electronic Microscopy and Cellular Biology (ISSN 0326-3142); (until 1983): Revista de Microscopia Electronica.
Description: Covers all aspects of biological electron microscopy and cell biology, from the molecular level to cell and tissue organization.
Refereed Serial

BIOLOGY OF THE CELL. see *BIOLOGY — Cytology And Histology*

570.282   US   ISSN 1052-0295
QH613   CODEN: BIHIEU
BIOTECHNIC AND HISTOCHEMISTRY; a journal for microtechnic and histochemistry. 1926. bi-m. $83 to individuals (foreign $123); institutions $142 (foreign $182) (effective 1998). (Biological Stain Commission) Williams & Wilkins (Subsidiary of: Waverly International), 351 W. Camden St., Baltimore, MD 21201. TEL 410-528-4068; 800-222-3790. FAX 410-528-4452-2436. E-mail: djones@wwilkins.com; URL: http://www.wwilkins.com. Ed. G.S. Nettleton. adv. contact: David Jones. bk.rev.; bibl.; charts; illus.; stat.; index. circ. 1,700. (also avail. in microfilm from WWS) **Indexed:** Abstr.Bull.Inst.Pap.Chem., Abstr.Hyg., Anim.Breed.Abstr., ASCA, Biol.Abstr., Chem.Abstr., Curr.Adv.Ecol.Sci., Curr.Cont., Dent.Ind., Excerp.Med., Field Crop Abstr., Helminthol.Abstr., Hort.Abstr., Ind.Med., Ind.Sci.Rev., Ind.Vet., Int.Aerosp.Abstr., Nutr.Abstr., Potato Abstr., Rev.Med.& Vet.Mycol., Rev.Plant Path., Sci.Cit.Ind., Seed Abstr., SSCI, Trop.Dis.Bull., Vet.Bull. **Document type:** academic/scholarly publication.
—BLDSC (2089.777000); CASDDS; CISTI; EMDOCS; Genuine Article; KNAW; Linda Hall; SWETS; UnCover. **CCC.**
Formerly: Stain Technology (ISSN 0038-9153)
Description: Covers new materials, apparatus, and methods involved in the preparation of biological specimens.
Refereed Serial

578 616   NE   ISSN 0923-0475
                                CODEN: EMBME5
ELECTRON MICROSCOPY IN BIOLOGY AND MEDICINE. (Text in English) 1984. irreg., vol.9, 1991. price varies. Kluwer Academic Publishers, Postbus 17, 3300 AA Dordrecht, Netherlands. TEL 31-78-6392392. FAX 31-78-6392254. TELEX 29245 KAPG NL. E-mail: services@wkap.nl; URL: http://www.wkap.nl. (Dist. by: Kluwer Academic Publishers Group, P.O. Box 322, 3300 AH Dordrecht, Netherlands. TEL 31-78-6392392. FAX 31-78-6546474; N. America dist. addr.: Box 358, Accord Sta., Hingham, MA 02018-0358. TEL 617-871-6600. FAX 617-871-6528) **Document type:** monographic series.
—BLDSC (3699.760400); CISTI.
Refereed Serial

578 535.84   SA
                                CODEN: VESADE
ELECTRON MICROSCOPY SOCIETY OF SOUTHERN AFRICA. PROCEEDINGS/MIKROSKOPIEVERENIGING VAN SUIDELIKE AFRIKA. VERRIGTINGS. (Text mainly in English; occasionally in Afrikaans) 1971. a. R.57. Microscopy Society of Southern Africa, Unit for Electron Microscopy, Faculty of Biological & Agricultural Sciences, University of Pretoria, Pretoria 0002, South Africa. TEL 27-12-4203297. FAX 27-12-4203266. circ. 200. (back issues avail.) **Indexed:** Biol.Abstr., Chem.Abstr., Curr.Adv.Ecol.Sci., Excerp.Med, INSPEC. **Document type:** proceedings, abstracting/indexing.
—CASDDS; KNAW.
Formerly: Electron Microscopy Society of Southern Africa. Proceedings (ISSN 0250-0418)
Description: Publishes abstracts accepted for presentation at the annual conference.

578   GW   ISSN 0936-6911
ELEKTRONENMIKROSKOPIE. 1989. irreg. (2-3/yr.). DM.40 (effective 1997). (Deutsche Gesellschaft fuer Elektronenmikroskopie e.V.) Wissenschaftliche Verlagsgesellschaft mbH, Postfach 101061, 70009 Stuttgart, Germany. TEL 49-711-2582-0. FAX 49-711-2582290. **Document type:** academic/scholarly publication.

578   IS   ISSN 0071-2647
EUROPEAN CONGRESS ON ELECTRON MICROSCOPY. quadrennial; 6th, Jerusalem, 1976. (Israel Society of Electron Microscopy) Tal International, Inquire: Prof. D. Danon, Weizmann Institute of Science, Rehovot, Israel.

578   XN   ISSN 0015-9298
                                CODEN: FRBAAB
FRAGMENTA BALCANICA MUSEI MACEDONICI SCIENTIARUM NATURALIUM.* 1954. irreg., (5-9/yr.). Prirodnauen Muzej na Makedonija, Bulevar Ilinden 66, 91000 Skopje, Macedonia. **Indexed:** Biol.Abstr., Curr.Adv.Ecol.Sci., Deep Sea Res.& Oceanogr.Abstr., Rev.Appl.Entomol.

JOURNAL OF COMPUTER-ASSISTED MICROSCOPY. see *COMPUTERS — Computer Simulation*

578 610   UK   ISSN 0022-0744
QC373.E4   CODEN: JELJA7
JOURNAL OF ELECTRON MICROSCOPY. 1953. 6/yr. £170 (foreign $275) (effective 1998). (Japanese Society of Electron Microscopy) Oxford University Press, Academic Division, Great Clarendon St., Oxford OX2 6DP, England. TEL 44-1865-267907. FAX 44-1865-267485. E-mail: jnl.info@oup.co.uk; URL: http://www.oup.co.uk/journals. (Subscr. in U.S. to: Oxford University Press Inc., 2001 Evans Rd., Cary, NC 27513. TEL 800-852-7323. FAX 919-677-1714) adv.; bk.rev.; abstr.; charts; illus.; stat. circ. 3,900. (also avail. in microform from UMI) **Indexed:** Abstr.Bull.Inst.Pap.Chem., Alloys Ind., ASCA, Biol.Abstr., Chem.Abstr., Chem.Cit.Ind., Curr.Cont., Dairy Sci.Abstr., Deep Sea Res.& Oceanogr.Abstr., Dent.Ind., Eng.Mat.Abstr., Excerp.Med., Helminthol.Abstr., Ind.Med., Ind.Sci.Rev., Ind.Vet., INIS Atomind., INSPEC, JTA, Mat.Sci.Cit.Ind., Met.Abstr., Met.Abstr.Ind., Nonfer.Met.Alert, PCC Alert, Sci.Cit.Ind., Steels Alert, Vet.Bull., W.R.C.Inf., World Alum.Abstr. **Document type:** academic/scholarly publication.
—BLDSC (4974.880000); AskIEEE; CASDDS; CISTI; Ei; Genuine Article; KR SourceOne; Linda Hall; SWETS; UMI; UnCover. **CCC.**

BIOLOGY — MICROSCOPY

578   UK   ISSN 0022-2720
CODEN: JMICAR
JOURNAL OF MICROSCOPY. 1878. m. £490($895) (foreign £539) (effective 1998). (Royal Microscopical Society) Blackwell Science Ltd., Osney Mead, Oxford OX2 0EL, England. TEL 44-1865-206206. FAX 44-1865-721205. E-mail: journals.cs@blackscl.co.uk; URL: http://www.black.co.uk. Ed. P. Echlin; Pub. Allen Stevens. R&P contact: Sarah Pollard. adv. contact: Martine Cariou-Keen. bk.rev.; abstr.; bibl.; charts; illus.; index. circ. 1,355. (also avail. in microform from UMI; back issues avail.; reprint service avail. from ISI) **Indexed:** Abstr.Bull.Inst.Pap.Chem., Alloys Ind., ASCA, Biol.Abstr., C.I.S.Abstr., Chem.Abstr., Chem.Cit.Ind., Compumath, Curr.Adv.Cancer Res., Curr.Adv.Ecol.Sci., Curr.Cont., Deep Sea Res.& Oceanogr.Abstr., Dent.Ind., Eng.Mat.Abstr., Excerp.Med., Field Crop Abstr., GeoRef., Helminthol.Abstr., Herb.Abstr., Hort.Abstr., Ind.Med., Ind.Sci.Rev., Ind.Vet., INIS Atomind., INSPEC, Int.Aerosp.Abstr., Mat.Sci.Cit.Ind., Met.Abstr., Met.Abstr.Ind., Nonfer.Met.Alert, Ornam.Hort., PCC Alert, Photo.Abstr., Phys.Ber., Plant Breed.Abstr., Sci.Cit.Ind., Seed Abstr., Soils & Fert., Soyabean Abstr., Steels Alert, World Alum.Abstr. **Document type:** academic/scholarly publication.
—BLDSC (5019.695000); ADONIS; AskIEEE; CASDDS; CISTI; Genuine Article; KR SourceOne; Linda Hall; SWETS; UMI; UnCover. **CCC.**
Formerly (until 1969): Royal Microscopical Society. Journal (ISSN 0368-3974)
Refereed Serial

578   US   ISSN 1059-910X
QH212.E4   CODEN: MRTEEO
JOURNAL OF MICROSCOPY RESEARCH AND TECHNIQUE. 1984. 24/yr. $3195 (foreign $3615) (effective 1998). John Wiley & Sons, Inc., Journals, 605 Third Ave., New York, NY 10158. TEL 212-850-6645. FAX 212-850-6021. TELEX 12-7063. E-mail: SUBINFO@JWILEY.COM; URL: http://www.wiley.co.uk. (Subscr. outside the Americas to: John Wiley & Sons Ltd., Baffins Ln., Chichester, W. Sussex PO19 1UD, England. TEL 44-1243-779777. FAX 44-1243-776128) Ed. Arthur M. Jonson, Jr. adv.: B&W page £640, color page £1515; trim 279 x 210. bk.rev.; bibl.; illus. circ. 700. (also avail. in microform from UMI; back issues avail.) **Indexed:** Abstr.Bull.Inst.Pap.Chem., Chem.Abstr., Curr.Adv.Cell & Devel.Biol., Curr.Cont., Excerp.Med., Ind.Vet., Protozool.Abstr., Rev.Med.& Vet.Mycol. **Document type:** academic/scholarly publication.
—BLDSC (5760.600850); CASDDS; CISTI; EMDOCS; Genuine Article; KNAW; Linda Hall; SWETS; UnCover. **CCC.**
Formerly: Journal of Electron Microscopy Technique (ISSN 0741-0581)
Description: Encompasses all aspects of advanced microscopy, focusing on equipment, methodology, and applications in the biological, materials, and medical sciences.
Refereed Serial

KLINICHNA LABORATORIIA. see *BIOLOGY — Biological Chemistry*

578   JA   ISSN 0918-4287
RB43.5   CODEN: MELMEJ
MEDICAL ELECTRON MICROSCOPY. (Text in English) 1993. q. DM.260 (effective 1998). (Clinical Electron Microscopy Society of Japan - Nihon Rinsho Denshi Kenbikyo Gakkai) Springer-Verlag Tokyo, 3-13, Hongo 3-chome, Bunkyo-ku, Tokyo 113, Japan. TEL 81-3-3812-4644. FAX 81-3-3812-0719. E-mail: svt-ebs@ppp.bekkoame.or.jp; URL: http://www.springer-ny.com. (Dist. outside Japan by: Springer-Verlag, Heidelberger Platz 3, 14197 Berlin, Germany. TEL 49-30-82787-0. FAX 49-30-82787448; In N. America: Springer-Verlag New York, Inc., 333 Meadowlands Pkwy., Secaucus, NJ 07094. TEL 212-460-1500. FAX 212-473-6272) Ed. M. Mori. **Document type:** academic/scholarly publication.
—BLDSC (5527.192500); CASDDS; CISTI; EMDOCS. **CCC.**
Supersedes the English part of: Nihon Rinsho Denshi Kenbikyo Gakkaishi (ISSN 0021-4981)
Description: Investigates the electron microscopic examination of structures, molecules, organelles, cells, tissues, and organs.

578   GW   ISSN 0076-6771
METHODENSAMMLUNG DER ELEKTRONENMIKROSKOPIE. 1970. irreg., no.11, 1984. DM.817 to non-members; members DM.653.60. (Deutsche Gesellschaft fuer Elektronenmikroskopie e.V) Wissenschaftliche Verlagsgesellschaft mbH, Postfach 101061, 70009 Stuttgart, Germany. TEL 49-711-2582-0. FAX 49-711-2582-290. Eds. G. Schimmel, W. Vogell. **Document type:** monographic series.

573   NE   ISSN 0275-9586
METHODS IN MICROANALYSIS. irreg., latest vol.6. price varies. Gordon and Breach - Harwood Academic, Amsteldisk 166, 1st Fl., 1079 LH Amsterdam, Netherlands. (Subscr. to: International Publishers Distributor, Box 32160, Newark, NJ 07102. TEL 800-545-8398. FAX 215-750-6343) Ed. J. Kuck. **Document type:** monographic series.
Refereed Serial

578   US   ISSN 0026-265X
CODEN: MICJAN
MICROCHEMICAL JOURNAL; devoted to the application of microtechniques in all branches of chemistry. 1957. 9/yr. $520 (foreign $583) (effective 1997). Academic Press, Inc., Journal Division, 525 B St., Ste. 1900, San Diego, CA 92101-4495. TEL 619-230-1840. FAX 619-699-6800. E-mail: apsubs@acad.com; URL: http://www.apnet.com/www/journal/mj.htm; URL: http://www.idealibrary.com/. (Subscr. to: Box 861213, Orlando, FL 32886-1213. TEL 407-347-4040. FAX 407-363-9661) Ed. Joseph Sneddon. adv.; bk.rev.; abstr.; bibl.; illus.; index. (back issues avail.) **Indexed:** Abstr.Bull.Inst.Pap.Chem., Anal.Abstr., Art & Archaeol.Tech.Abstr., ASCA, Biol.Abstr., Cadscan, Chem.Abstr., Chem.Cit.Ind., Curr.Adv.Ecol.Sci., Curr.Cont., Dairy Sci.Abstr., Deep Sea Res.& Oceanogr.Abstr., Excerp.Med., Food Sci.& Tech.Abstr., Ind.Sci.Rev., Ind.Vet., Lead Abstr., Nutr.Abstr., Sci.Cit.Ind., Vet.Bull., Zincscan. **Document type:** academic/scholarly publication.
●Also available online.
—BLDSC (5758.400000); ADONIS; CASDDS; CISTI; Ei; Genuine Article; Linda Hall; SWETS; UnCover. **CCC.**
Description: Focuses on microscale chemical analysis including clinical methods and procedures.
Refereed Serial

578   UK   ISSN 0968-4328
QH201   CODEN: MCONEN
MICRON; the international research and review journal for microscopy. 1969. bi-m. fl.1585($911) (effective 1998). Elsevier Science Ltd., Pergamon, P.O. Box 800, Kidlington, Oxford OX5 1DX, England. TEL 44-1865-843000. FAX 44-1865-843010. E-mail: nlinfo-f@elsevier.nl; usinfo-f@elsevier.com; forinfo-kyf04035@niftyserve.or.jp; URL: http://www.elsevier.nl/. (Subscr. to: Elsevier Science, Regional Sales Office, P.O. Box 211, 1000 AE Amsterdam, Netherlands. TEL 31-20-4853757. FAX 31-20-4853432; Subscr. in the Americas to: Elsevier Science, Regional Sales Office, Box 945, New York, NY 10159-0945. TEL 212-633-3730. FAX 212-633-3680; Subscr. in Australasia and the Far East to: Elsevier Science (Singapore) Pte Ltd, No.1 Temasek Ave., No.17-01 Millenia Tower, Singapore 039192, Singapore. TEL 65-434-3727. FAX 65-337-2230) Eds. R.W. Horne, D.J. Cockayne. (also avail. in microfilm from UMI; back issues avail.) **Indexed:** Abstr.Bull.Inst.Pap.Chem., ASCA, Br.Ceram.Abstr., Curr.Adv.Ecol.Sci., Curr.Cont., Deep Sea Res.& Oceanogr.Abstr., Ind.Med. (1994-), Ind.Sci.Rev., Met.Abstr., Sci.Cit.Ind., W.R.C.Inf., World Alum.Abstr. **Document type:** academic/scholarly publication.
—BLDSC (5759.300000); CASDDS; CISTI; EMDOCS; Genuine Article; Linda Hall; SWETS; UMI; UnCover. **CCC.**
Incorporates (1987-1992): Electron Microscopy Reviews (ISSN 0892-0354); **Formerly** (until 1993): Micron and Microscopica Acta (ISSN 0739-6260); **Supersedes:** Micron (ISSN 0047-7206)
Description: Publishes original research and reviews covering the design, application, practice or theory of microscopy and microanalysis; also covers optical and electron beam systems linked to computer image processing and other image analytical methods.
Refereed Serial

502.82 578   US   ISSN 0026-282X
QH201   CODEN: MICRAD
MICROSCOPE. 1937. q. $65 (effective 1997). McCrone Research Institute, 2820 S. Michigan Ave., Chicago, IL 60616-3292. TEL 312-842-7100. FAX 312-842-1078. E-mail: dstoney@mcri.org; URL: http://www.mcri.org. Ed. David Stoney. adv. contact: Debra Gilliand. bk.rev.; bibl.; charts; illus.; pat.; stat.; tr.lit.; index, cum.index. circ. 1,200. (also avail. in microfiche; back issues avail.) **Indexed:** Abstr.Bull.Inst.Pap.Chem., Alloys Ind., Art & Archaeol.Tech.Abstr., Chem.Abstr., Curr.Cont., Deep Sea Res.& Oceanogr.Abstr., Excerp.Med., GeoRef., INSPEC, Met.Abstr.Ind., Met.Abstr., Nonfer.Met.Alert, PCC Alert, Sci.Cit.Ind., Steels Alert, World Alum.Abstr.
—BLDSC (5760.000000); AskIEEE; CASDDS; CISTI; Genuine Article; KR SourceOne; Linda Hall; SWETS; UMI; UnCover. **CCC.**
Description: Dedicated to the advancement of all forms of microscopy for the biologist, mineralogist, metallographer or chemist.
Refereed Serial

758   US   ISSN 1051-404X
MICROSCOPE BOOK.* 1990. s-a. Cambrex Group, 79 Milk St., Ste. 81101, Boston, MA 02109-3903. TEL 617-742-8290. FAX 617-742-4942. **Document type:** catalog.
Description: For users of microscopes for analytical procedures.

758   US   ISSN 1041-0716
MICROSCOPE TECHNOLOGY & NEWS.* 1990. m. $197. Cambrex Group, 79 Milk St., Ste. 811, Boston, MA 02109-3903. TEL 617-742-8290. FAX 617-742-4942. **Document type:** newsletter.
—**CCC.**

578   CN   ISSN 0383-1825
CODEN: BMSCDG
MICROSCOPICAL SOCIETY OF CANADA. BULLETIN. (Text in English, French) 1973. q. Can.$38. Microscopical Society of Canada - Societe de Microscopie du Canada, c/o F. Leggett, 2918 13th Ave. S., Lethbridge, AB T1K 0T2, Canada. TEL 403-327-4342. FAX 403-382-3156. E-mail: leggett@em.agr.ca. Ed. Carolyn Emerson. R&P contact: Pierre Charest. adv.: page Can.$399; trim 6 x 9; adv. contact: Dianne Moyles. bk.rev.; circ. 650 (paid). (back issues avail.) **Document type:** proceedings.
—CISTI.
Description: Presents new developments in microscopy-instrumentation, applications, and biological and materials sciences.
Refereed Serial

578   CN   ISSN 0381-1751
CODEN: PMSCDA
MICROSCOPICAL SOCIETY OF CANADA. PROCEEDINGS. (Text mainly in English; occasionally in French) 1974. a. Can.$25 (foreign $25). Microscopical Society of Canada - Societe de Microscopie du Canada, Dept. of Pathology, Rm. 2V17, McMaster Univ., 1200 Main St., Hamilton, ON L8N 3Z5, Canada. TEL 905-525-9140. FAX 905-577-0198. adv. circ. 650. **Indexed:** Biol.Abstr., GeoRef. **Document type:** proceedings.
—CASDDS; Linda Hall.

578   UK   ISSN 0958-1952
MICROSCOPY AND ANALYSIS. 1987. bi-m. £40.50 (Europe £75; rest of world £106). Rolston Gordon Communications, 1 Gable Cottages, Post House Lane, Bookham, Surrey KT23 3EA, England. TEL 44-1372-454891. FAX 44-1372-459957. Ed. Larry Stoter. R&P contact: Agnes Murphy. adv.: B&W page £1390, color page £2070; trim 210 x 297; adv. contact: Jean Gordon. bk.rev. circ. 39,000. **Indexed:** Alloys Ind., Eng.Mat.Abstr., Met.Abstr.Ind., Met.Abstr., Nonfer.Met.Alert, PCC Alert, Steels Alert, World Alum.Abstr., World Surf.Coat. **Document type:** academic/scholarly publication.
—BLDSC (5760.600100); SWETS.
Description: For users of all types of microscopes in all areas of work.

MICROSCOPY AND MICROANALYSIS. see *INSTRUMENTS*

MICROSCOPY MICROANALYSIS MICROSTRUCTURES. see *PHYSICS — Optics*

BIOLOGY — MICROSCOPY

578   YU   ISSN 0351-6768
MIKROGRAFIJA U INFORMACIONIM SISTEMIMA/MICROGRAPHY IN INFORMATION SYSTEMS. (Text in Serbo-Croatian, Slovenian; summaries in English, Serbo-Croatian) 1976. bi-m. $228. Jugoslovenski Centar za Tehnicku i Naucnu Dokumentaciju - Yugoslav Center for Technical and Scientific Documentation (YCTSD), Sl. Penezica-Krcuna 29-31, Box 724, 11000 Belgrade, Yugoslavia. Ed. Ljiljana Kojic-Bogdanovic.

578   GW   ISSN 0026-3680
QH201   CODEN: MKKSA2
MIKROKOSMOS; Zeitschrift fuer angewandte Mikroskopie, Mikrobiologie, Mikrochemie und mikroskopische Technik. 1907. bi-m. DM.121 (foreign DM.134) (effective 1997). Gustav Fischer Verlag, Villengang 2, 07745 Jena, Germany. TEL 49-3641-626430. FAX 49-3641-626421. E-mail: office.j@gfischer.de. (Subscr. to: Stockton Press, Subscription Dept., Houndmills, Basingstoke, Hants RG21 6XS, England) Ed. Dr. O. Schlecht. adv.: bk.rev.; bibl.; charts; illus.; index. circ. 1,900. **Indexed:** Biol.Abstr., Chem.Abstr., Excerp.Med., GeoRef. **Document type:** academic/scholarly publication.
—CASDDS; CISTI; Linda Hall; SWETS. **CCC.**
Description: Covers applied microscopy, microbiology, microchemistry, and microscopal technology.

MYU. see PHYSICS — Optics

NAGOYA DAIGAKU DENSHI KOGAKU KENKYU NO AYUMI/PROGRESS IN ELECTRON OPTICS RESEARCH. see PHYSICS — Optics

578   JA   ISSN 0021-4981
     CODEN: NRDGBQ
NIHON RINSHO DENSHI KENBIKYO GAKKAISHI/JOURNAL OF CLINICAL ELECTRON MICROSCOPY. (Text in Japanese) 1969. q. Clinical Electron Microscopy Society of Japan - Nippon Rinsho Denshi Kenbikyo Gakkai, Shiga Ika Daigaku, Seta Tsukinowacho, Otsu-shi, Siga-ken 520-21, Japan. Ed. Dr. Kazumasa Kurosumi. bk.rev. circ. 2,000. **Indexed:** Biol.Abstr., Excerp.Med., INIS Atomind.
—BLDSC (4651.373500); CISTI.

578   NE   ISSN 0165-201X
     CODEN: PMEMD4
PRACTICAL METHODS IN ELECTRON MICROSCOPY. 1973. irreg., vol. 14, 1992. price varies. Elsevier Science B.V., Books Division, P.O. Box 211, 1000 AE Amsterdam, Netherlands. TEL 31-20-4853911. FAX 31-20-4853705. TELEX 18582 ESPA NL. E-mail: nlinfo-f@elsevier.nl; usinfo-f@elsevier.com; forinfo-kyf04035@niftyserve.or.jp; URL: http://www.elsevier.nl/. (Subscr. in the Americas to: Elsevier Science, Regional Sales Office, Box 945, New York, NY 10159-0945. TEL 212-633-3730. FAX 212-633-3680; Subscr. in Australasia and the Far East to: Elsevier Science (Singapore) Pte Ltd, No.1 Temasek Ave., No.17-01 Millenia Tower, Singapore 039192, Singapore. TEL 65-434-3727. FAX 65-337-2230; Subscr. in Japan to: Elsevier Science Japan, 9-15 Higashi-Azabu 1-chome, Minato-ku, Tokyo 106, Japan. TEL 81-3-5561-5033. FAX 81-3-5561-5047) Ed. A.M. Glauert. (back issues avail.) **Document type:** monographic series.
—CASDDS.
Refereed Serial

578   NE   ISSN 1355-185X
▼**PROBE MICROSCOPY.** 1996. q. $90 (effective 1998). Gordon and Breach - Harwood Academic, Amsteldijk 166, 1st Fl., 1079 LH Amsterdam, Netherlands. (Subscr. to: International Publishers Distributor, Box 32160, Newark, NJ 07102. TEL 800-545-8398. FAX 215-750-6343) Ed.Bd. **Document type:** academic/scholarly publication.
—CCC.
Description: Publishes papers relating to science and technology using local probe methods, covering physics, chemistry, materials science, biology and engineering applications.

502.8 576 616.9   UK
PROCEDURES IN ELECTRON MICROSCOPY. 1993. base vol. (plus s-a. updates). £495($770) for new orders; update service £95 ($145) (effective 1997). John Wiley & Sons Ltd., Journals, Baffins Ln., Chichester, W. Sussex PO19 1UD, England. TEL 44-1243-779777. FAX 44-1243-843232. E-mail: cs-journals@wiley.co.uk; URL: http://www.wiley.co.uk. (Subscr. in the Americas to: John Wiley & Sons, Inc., 605 Third Ave., New York, NY 10158-0012. TEL 212-850-6347) (looseleaf format) **Document type:** academic/scholarly publication.

578 616   UK   ISSN 0969-3823
QH201   CODEN: QJMIEN
QUEKETT JOURNAL OF MICROSCOPY. 1868. s-a. £30 (foreign £40) to non-members. Quekett Microscopical Club, 31 High St., Stanford in the Vale, Faringdon, Oxon SN7 8LH, England. TEL 44-1367-710223. FAX 44-1367-718963. Ed. D. Edwards. adv.; bk.rev.; illus. circ. 650. **Indexed:** Bibl.Agri., Biol.Abstr., Chem.Abstr., Deep Sea Res.& Oceanogr.Abstr., Excerp.Med., GeoRef., Hort.Abstr., W.R.C.Inf. **Document type:** academic/scholarly publication.
—BLDSC (7216.089500); CISTI; Linda Hall; UnCover.
Formerly (until 1993): Microscopy (ISSN 0026-2838)
Description: Covers light and electron microscopy, aquatic biology, cytology and cytochemistry, histology and histochemistry, microbiology, photography and photomicrography.

578   UK
ROYAL MICROSCOPICAL SOCIETY. ANNUAL IMMUNOCYTOCHEMISTRY MEETING. a. Royal Microscopical Society, 37-38 St. Clements, Oxford OX4 1AJ, England. TEL 44-1865-248768. FAX 44-1865-791237. **Document type:** proceedings.

578   UK   ISSN 0035-9017
QH201
ROYAL MICROSCOPICAL SOCIETY. PROCEEDINGS. 1966. q. £143($260.50) (foreign £157) (effective 1998). Blackwell Science Ltd., Osney Mead, Oxford OX2 OEL, England. TEL 44-1865-206206. FAX 44-1865-721205. E-mail: journals@blacksci.co.uk; URL: http://www.black.co.uk. Ed. P.J. Evenett; Pub. Allen Stevens. R&P contact: Sarah Pollard. adv. contact: Martine Cariou-Keen. abstr.; illus.; index. circ. 2,000. (back issues avail.; reprint service avail. from ISI) **Indexed:** Curr.Adv.Cell & Devel.Biol., Deep Sea Res.& Oceanogr.Abstr., Excerp.Med., Fuel & Energy Abstr. **Document type:** academic/scholarly publication, proceedings.
—BLDSC (6799.500000); CISTI; Linda Hall; SWETS; UMI. **CCC.**

578   UK
ROYAL MICROSCOPICAL SOCIETY. U K ANNUAL SCANNED PROBE MICROSCOPY MEETING. a. Royal Microscopical Society, 37-38 St. Clements, Oxford OX4 1AJ, England. TEL 44-1865-248768. FAX 44-1865-791237. **Document type:** proceedings.

578   US   ISSN 0161-0457
QH212.S3   CODEN: SCNNDF
SCANNING; journal of scanning microscopy. 1978. 8/yr. $175 to individuals (foreign $185); institutions $325 (foreign $370) (effective Jan. 1996). (Foundation for Advances in Medicine & Science, Inc.) F A M S, Inc., Box 832, Mahwah, NJ 07430-0832. TEL 201-818-1010. FAX 201-818-0086. TELEX 2-208-83 TAUR. Ed. Alan Boyde; Pub. Tony Bourgholtzer. R&P contact: Jean Johnson. adv. contact: Carole Taseal. bk.rev.; index. circ. 6,984. **Indexed:** ASCA, Curr.Adv.Ecol.Sci., Curr.Cont., Food Sci.& Tech.Abstr., Ind.Med. (1993-), Ind.Sci.Rev., INSPEC (1984-), Mat.Sci.Cit.Ind., Photo.Abstr., Sci.Cit.Ind. **Document type:** trade publication.
—BLDSC (8087.704000); AskIEEE; CASDDS; CISTI; Ei; Genuine Article; KR SourceOne; Linda Hall; SWETS; UnCover. **CCC.**

502.82   US   ISSN 0891-7035
QH212.S3   CODEN: SCMIEU
SCANNING MICROSCOPY; an international journal of scanning electron microscopy, related techniques, and applications. (Supplements avail.) 1968. q. $164 (foreign $189). Scanning Microscopy International, Inc., Box 66507, AMF O'Hare, Chicago, IL 60666-0507. TEL 708-529-6677. FAX 708-980-6698. Ed. Om Johari. cum.index. circ. 1,500. (back issues avail.) **Indexed:** Abstr.Bull.Inst.Pap.Chem., Alloys Ind., Anal.Abstr., ASCA, Biol.Abstr., Bull.Signal., Chem.Abstr., Curr.Cont., Dairy Sci.Abstr., Deep Sea Res.& Oceanogr.Abstr., Dent.Ind., Eng.Mat.Abstr., Excerp.Med., Food Sci.& Tech.Abstr., Geo.Abstr., GeoRef., Ind.Med., Ind.Sci.Rev., INSPEC, Mass Spectr.Bull., Mat.Sci.Cit.Ind., Met.Abstr., Met.Abstr.Ind., Nonfer.Met.Alert, PCC Alert, Rev.Plant Path., Sci.Cit.Ind., SSCI, Steels Alert, World Alum.Abstr. **Document type:** academic/scholarly publication.
—BLDSC (8087.705300); AskIEEE; CASDDS; CISTI; Ei; EMDOCS; Genuine Article; KNAW; KR SourceOne; Linda Hall; SWETS; UnCover. **CCC.**
Supersedes (in 1986): Scanning Electron Microscopy (ISSN 0586-5581); Which incorporated: Scanning Electron Microscope Symposium. Proceedings.
Description: Theory, instruments, advancements and physical and biological applications related to scanning microscopes and related techniques.
Refereed Serial

578   US   ISSN 0892-953X
     CODEN: SMSUEU
SCANNING MICROSCOPY SUPPLEMENT; proceedings of the Pfefferkorn Conference. 1987. a. price varies. Scanning Microscopy International, Inc., Box 66507, AMF O'Hare, Chicago, IL 60646. TEL 708-529-6677. FAX 708-980-6677. Ed. Om Johari. circ. 1,000. (back issues avail.) **Indexed:** INSPEC (1990-). **Document type:** proceedings.
—BLDSC (8087.705330); AskIEEE; CASDDS; CISTI; KNAW; KR SourceOne. **CCC.**
Supersedes (1982-1985): Pfefferkorn Conference. Proceedings.
Description: Covers fundamental problems of interest to electron microscopists and users of related techniques.

SCHWEIZERISCHE ZEITSCHRIFT FUER PILZKUNDE/BULLETIN SUISSE DE MYCOLOGIE/BOLLETTINO SVIZZERO DI MICOLOGIA. see BIOLOGY — Botany

SEMINARS IN OPHTHALMOLOGY. see MEDICAL SCIENCES — Ophthalmology And Optometry

578   NE   ISSN 0304-3991
QH212.E4   CODEN: ULTRD6
ULTRAMICROSCOPY; journal devoted to the technical and theoretical advancement of structural research. 1975. 20/yr. fl.2817($1619) to institutions (effective 1998). North-Holland (Subsidiary of: Elsevier Science B.V.), P.O. Box 211, 1000 AE Amsterdam, Netherlands. TEL 31-20-4853911. FAX 31-20-4853598. TELEX 18582 ESPA NL. (Subscr. in the Americas to: Elsevier Science, Regional Sales Office, Box 945, New York, NY 10159-0945. TEL 212-633-3730. FAX 212-633-3680; Subscr. in Australasia and the Far East to: Elsevier Science (Singapore) Pte Ltd, No.1 Temasek Ave., No.17-01 Millenia Tower, Singapore 039192, Singapore. TEL 65-434-3727. FAX 65-337-2230; Subscr. in Japan to: Elsevier Science Japan, 9-15 Higashi-Azabu 1-chome, Minato-ku, Tokyo 106, Japan. TEL 81-3-5561-5033. FAX 81-3-5561-5047) Ed. E. Zeitler. (also avail. in microform from UMI; back issues avail.; reprint service avail. from SWZ) **Indexed:** Alloys Ind., ASCA, Biol.Abstr., Chem.Cit.Ind., Compumath, Curr.Adv.Biochem., Curr.Adv.Cell & Devel.Biol., Curr.Adv.Ecol.Sci., Curr.Cont., Dairy Sci.Abstr., Eng.Mat.Abstr., Excerp.Med., Helminthol.Abstr., Ind.Med., Ind.Sci.Rev., INSPEC (1975-), Mat.Sci.Cit.Ind., Met.Abstr., Met.Abstr.Ind., Nonfer.Met.Alert, PCC Alert, Photo.Abstr., Phys.Ber., Sci.Cit.Ind., Steels Alert, World Alum.Abstr. **Document type:** academic/scholarly publication.
—BLDSC (9082.783000); AskIEEE; CASDDS; CISTI; Ei; EMDOCS; Genuine Article; KNAW; KR SourceOne; Linda Hall; SWETS; UnCover. **CCC.**
Description: Covers all fundamental and technical aspects pertaining to ultramicroscopic elucidation of structure, ranging from particle optics to radiation interaction.
Refereed Serial

BIOLOGY — Ornithology

see also Agriculture–Poultry and Livestock; Pets

598.2 US ISSN 0199-543X
CODEN: AFAWE5
A F A WATCHBIRD. 1974. bi-m. $30 membership. American Federation of Aviculture, 3118 W. Thomas Rd., No. 713, Phoenix, AZ 85017-5308. TEL 602-484-0931. FAX 602-484-0109. URL: http://www.afa.birds.org/afa. Ed. Dale Thompson. R&P contact: Robert Berry. TEL 713-434-8076. adv. contact: Sharon Rosenblat. bk.rev.; illus. circ. 5,000. **Indexed:** Sport Fish.Abstr., Wild.Rev. **Document type:** academic/scholarly publication.
 Description: Contains articles by aviculturists and avian veterinarians on husbandry, care and management of exotic bird species and on nutrition, diseases and disease control.

598.2 GW ISSN 0343-7647
A Z - NACHRICHTEN. 1954. m. DM.50. Vereinigung fuer Artenschutz, Vogelhaltung und Vogelzucht (AZ) e.V., Postfach 1168, 71522 Backnang, Germany. TEL 49-7191-82439. FAX 49-7191-85957. Ed. Theo Pagel. adv. contact: Helmut Uebele. bk.rev.; illus.; tr.lit.; index. circ. 27,000. (back issues avail.) **Document type:** newsletter.

598.2 PL ISSN 0001-6454
QL671 CODEN: AORNAK
ACTA ORNITHOLOGICA. (Text English; summaries in Polish) 1933. irreg., latest vol.31, no.2. price varies. Polska Akademia Nauk, Muzeum i Instytut Zoologii, Ul. Wilcza 64, 00-679 Warsaw, Poland. TEL 48-2-6293221. FAX 48-2-6296302. Ed. M. Luniak. abstr. circ. 1,200. **Indexed:** AgroLibrex, Biol.Abstr., Curr.Adv.Ecol.Sci., Ecol.Abstr., IBR, Key Word Ind.Wildl.Res., Ref.Zh., Sport Fish.Abstr., Wild.Rev., Zoo.Rec. **Document type:** academic/scholarly publication.
 —BLDSC (0642.010000); CISTI; UnCover.

598.2 LI ISSN 0135-3861
QL690.L5 CODEN: AOLIED
ACTA ORNITHOLOGICA LITUANICA. 1989. irreg. Institute of Ecology, Laboratory of Ornithology, Akademijos st. 2, 2600 Vilnius, Lithuania. **Indexed:** Sport Fish.Abstr., Wild.Rev., Zoo.Rec. **Document type:** academic/scholarly publication.
 —Linda Hall.

598.2 SA
AFRICA BIRDS & BIRDING; a magazine for birdwatchers. (Text in English) 1949. bi-m. $62 to individuals; institutions $72 (includes subscr. to Ostrich). Birdlife South Africa, P.O. Box 84394, Greenside, Johannesburg 2034, South Africa. TEL 27-11-8884147. adv.; bk.rev.; charts; illus. circ. 5,500. (back issues avail.) **Indexed:** Biol.Abstr., Ind.S.A.Per., Key Word Ind.Wildl.Res., Sport Fish.Abstr., Wild.Rev., Zoo.Rec.
 —Linda Hall; UnCover.
 Former titles (until 1996): Birding in Southern Africa (ISSN 1017-1533); (until Sept. 1989): Bokmakierie (ISSN 0006-5838)

598.2 PL ISSN 0137-1746
AKADEMIA ROLNICZA, POZNAN. ROCZNIKI. ORNITOLOGIA STOSOWANA. (Text in Polish; summaries in English) 1966. irreg. price varies. Wydawnictwo Akademii Rolniczej w Poznaniu, Ul. Witosa 45, 60-667 Poznan, Poland. TEL 48-61-487809. FAX 48-61-487802. E-mail: wgolob@owl.poznan.pl; URL: http://swan.au.poznan.pl/bib/bghome.html. R&P contact: Elzbieta Zagorska. TEL 48-61-487806. **Indexed:** Bibl.Agri. **Document type:** academic/scholarly publication.
 Description: Covers ornithology, ecology, populating, biology, survival, and rate descriptions of food breeding birds; investigation of the phenomenon of breeding territorialism, biological control of forest, field and pests.

598.2 FR ISSN 0002-4619
CODEN: ALUDAI
ALAUDA; revue internationale d'ornithologie. (Supplemented by records (30cm)) (Text in French; summaries in English) 1929. q. 280 F. (foreign 320 F.) (effective 1997). Museum National d'Histoire Naturelle, Laboratoire d'Ecologie Generale, 4 av. du Petit-Chateau, 91800 Brunoy, France. FAX 33-1-60465719. adv.; bk.rev.; bibl.; illus.; stat.; cum.index: 1929-1972, 1973-1989. circ. 1,150. (back issues avail.) **Indexed:** Biol.Abstr., Bull.Signal., Curr.Adv.Ecol.Sci., Ecol.Abstr., Geo.Abstr., IBR, Key Word Ind.Wildl.Res., Sport Fish.Abstr., Wild.Rev., Zoo.Rec. **Document type:** academic/scholarly publication.

598.2 GI ISSN 1352-8734
CODEN: ALCTEE
ALECTORIS. 1978. a. Gibraltar Ornithological & Natural History Society, Gibraltar Natural History Field Centre, Jew's Gate, Upper Rock Nature Reserve, P.O. Box 843, Gibraltar. Ed. John E. Cortes. **Indexed:** Sport Fish.Abstr., Wild.Rev., Zoo.Rec. **Document type:** academic/scholarly publication, monographic series.

598.2 333.7 US ISSN 0748-8319
QL696.F3
AMERICAN HAWKWATCHER. 1982. a. $25 membership. Wildlife Information Center, Inc., Box 198, Slatington, PA 18080-0198. TEL 610-760-8889. Ed. Donald S. Heintzelman. (back issues avail.) **Indexed:** Wild Life Rev. **Document type:** academic/scholarly publication.
 Description: Reports original raptor research results, especially regarding hawk migrations in North America.
 Refereed Serial

598.2 US ISSN 0892-6387
AMERICAN PHEASANT AND WATERFOWL SOCIETY MAGAZINE. 1975. 10/yr. $25 (foreign $35) (effective 1998). American Pheasant and Waterfowl Society, W. 2270 US Hwy. 10, Granton, WI 54436. TEL 715-238-7291. Ed. Lloyd Ure. adv.; bk.rev.; circ. 1,800 (paid). **Document type:** newsletter.

598.2 GW ISSN 0003-3154
ANGEWANDTE ORNITHOLOGIE/APPLIED ORNITHOLOGY. (Text mainly in German, occasionally in English, French, Italian) 1961. irreg. DM.15. Biologie-Verlag, Schlossallee 10a, 65388 Schlangenbad, Germany. Ed. Herbert Bruns. **Indexed:** Biol.Abstr. **Document type:** academic/scholarly publication.

598.2 GW ISSN 0232-5519
ANNALEN FUER ORNITHOLOGIE. (Supplement to: Mitteilungen aus dem Zoologischen Museum zu Berlin) 1977. a. Akademie Verlag GmbH, Muehlenstr. 33-34, 13187 Berlin, Germany. TEL 49-30-47889348. FAX 49-30-47889357. E-mail: info@akademie-verlag.de. (U.S. subscr. to: VCH Publishers Inc., 303 N.W. 12th Ave., Deerfield Beach, FL 33442-1788) **Document type:** academic/scholarly publication.
 —CISTI; Linda Hall.

598.2 SW ISSN 0347-9595
CODEN: ANSEET
ANSER. (Supplement avail. (ISSN 0347-9609)) 1974. q. Skaanes Ornitologiska Foerening, Ekologihuset, S-22362 Lund, Sweden. **Indexed:** Sport Fish.Abstr., Wild.Rev., Zoo.Rec.

598.2 SW ISSN 0347-9609
CODEN: ANSUE9
ANSER. SUPPLEMENT. 1976. irreg. Skaanes Ornitologiska Foerening, Ekologihuset, S-22362 Lund, Sweden. **Indexed:** Zoo.Rec.

AQUILO. SERIE ZOOLOGICA. see BIOLOGY — Zoology

598.2 NE ISSN 0373-2266
QL671 CODEN: ADEAA9
ARDEA. (Text in English) 1912. s-a. fl.65 to individuals; institutions fl.100. Nederlandse Ornithologische Unie - Netherlands Ornithological Union, c/o Akelei 42, 4102 JM Culemborg, Netherlands. TEL 31-345-519849. (Subscr. to: c/o P. Starmans, Oude Arnhemseweg 261, 3705 BD Zeist, Netherlands) Ed. C.J. Camphuysen. R&P contact: Theo Boudewyn. adv. contact: C.J. Camphuysen. bk.rev.; illus.; index. circ. 1,450. (back issues avail.) **Indexed:** ASCA, Biol.Abstr., Curr.Adv.Ecol.Sci., Curr.Cont., Ecol.Abstr., Geo.Abstr., Helminthol.Abstr., Ind.Sci.Rev., Key Word Ind.Wildl.Res., Sci.Cit.Ind., So.Pac.Per.Ind., Sport Fish.Abstr., Vet.Bull., Wild.Rev., Zoo.Rec. **Document type:** academic/scholarly publication.
 —BLDSC (1663.390000); CISTI; EMDOCS; Genuine Article; Linda Hall; SWETS; UnCover.
 Description: Publishes papers reporting significant new findings in ornithology, with emphasis on ecology, ethology, taxonomy and zoogeography.

598.2 SP ISSN 0570-7358
CODEN: ARDEDF
ARDEOLA; revista iberica de ornitologia. 1954. a. 2000 ptas. Sociedad Espanola de Ornitologia, c/o Fac. de Biologia, Univ. Complutense de Madrid, Ciudad Universitaria, 28040 Madrid, Spain. Ed. Eulalia Moreno. **Indexed:** Ind.SST, Key Word Ind.Wildl.Res., Sport Fish.Abstr., Wild.Rev., Zoo.Rec. **Document type:** bulletin.

598.2 US ISSN 0004-8038
QL671 CODEN: AUKJAF
AUK; a journal of ornithology. 1884. q. $70 (foreign $85) (effective 1997). American Ornithologists' Union, c/o Frederick Sheldon, Museum of Natural History, 119 Foster Hall, Louisiana State University, Baton Rouge, LA 70803. TEL 504-388-2855. E-mail: auk@selway.umt.edu; URL: http://www.nmh.si.edu. Ed. Gary D. Schnell. adv.; bk.rev.; bibl.; charts; illus.; index, cum.index every 10 yrs. circ. 4,500. (also avail. in microform from UMI; microfiche from IDC; reprint service avail. from KTO) **Indexed:** ASCA, Biol.Abstr., Biol.& Agr.Ind., Biol.& Agr.Ind., Chem.Abstr., Curr.Adv.Ecol.Sci., Curr.Cont., Deep Sea Res.& Oceanogr.Abstr., Environ.Per.Bibl. (1974-), Geo.Abstr., GeoRef., IBR, Ind.Sci.Rev., Key Word Ind.Wildl.Res., Key Word Ind.Wildl.Res., Ornithol.Abstr. (1955-), Psychol.Abstr. (1952-), Ref.Sour., Sci.Cit.Ind., Sport Fish.Abstr., Vet.Bull., Wild.Rev., Zoo.Rec. **Document type:** academic/scholarly publication.
 —BLDSC (1792.000000); CISTI; EMDOCS; Genuine Article; KR SourceOne; Linda Hall; SWETS; UMI; UnCover.
 Supersedes (1876-1883): Nuttall Ornithological Club. Bulletin.
 Refereed Serial

598.2 AT ISSN 0311-8150
AUSTRALIAN BIRDS. 1966. q. Aus.$25($23) New South Wales Field Ornithologists Club Inc., P.O. Box C436, Clarence St., Sydney, N.S.W. 2000, Australia. Ed. Peter Roberts. bk.rev. circ. 700. **Indexed:** Sport Fish.Abstr., Wild.Rev. **Document type:** academic/scholarly publication.
 —UnCover.
 Formerly (until Sep. 1974): Birds.
 Description: Covers biology, distribution and status of birds in New South Wales.

598.2994 AT ISSN 0045-0316
AUSTRALIAN BIRDWATCHER. 1959. q. Aus.$22 (foreign Aus.$34). Bird Observers Club of Australia, P.O. Box 185, Nunawading, Vic. 3131, Australia. TEL 61-3-98775342. FAX 61-3-98944048. Ed. Stephen Debus. R&P contact: Zoe Wilson. bk.rev.; cum.index every 2 yrs.; circ. 1,500 (paid). **Indexed:** Aus.Sci.Ind., Biol.Abstr., Sport Fish.Abstr., Wild.Rev., Zoo.Rec. **Document type:** academic/scholarly publication.
 —Linda Hall; UnCover.
 Refereed Serial

BIOLOGY — ORNITHOLOGY

598.2 — BE — ISSN 0005-1993 — CODEN: AVESAJ
AVES. (Text in French; summaries in Dutch, English, German) 1964. q. 800 BEF (effective 1996 & 1997). (Societe d'Etudes Ornithologiques Aves) Aves a.s.b.l., Maison de l'Environnement, 36 Rue de la Regence, B-4000 Liege, Belgium. TEL 32-4-2222025. FAX 32-4-2221689. URL: http://www.biol.ucl.ac.be/ecol/html/organis/fbdb/aves/. Ed. Emile Clotuche; Pub. Emile Clotuche. R&P contact: Emile Clotuche. adv. contact: Emile Clotuche. bk.rev.; abstr.; charts; illus.; index; circ. 2,600 (paid). **Indexed:** Biol.Abstr., Key Word Ind.Wildl.Res., Sport Fish.Abstr., Wild.Rev., Zoo.Rec. **Document type:** bulletin.

AVIAN DISEASES. see *VETERINARY SCIENCE*

598 — AT
AVIARY-BIRD AND WILDLIFE. 1968. m. Aus.$20. Avicultural and Wildlife Association, c/o Mrs. Sandra Davis, 12 Birch St., Maddington, W.A. 6109, Australia. TEL 61-9-4599530. Ed. David Coombes.

598.2 636 — CN — ISSN 0317-5650
AVICULTURAL JOURNAL. 1977. bi-m. Can.$25($25) (foreign Can.$32) (effective 1996 & 1997). Avicultural Advancement Council of Canada, P.O. Box 5126, Sta. B, Victoria, B.C. V8R 6N4, Canada. TEL 604-477-9982. FAX 604-477-9935. E-mail: aacc@islandnet.com; URL: http://www.islandnet.com/~aacc. Ed. Mark Curtis. R&P contact: Mark Curtis. adv.: page Can.$55; adv. contact: Mark Curtis. bk.rev. circ. 300. (back issues avail.) **Document type:** newsletter.
Description: Aticles dealing with the keeping, breeding and showing of non-indigenous birds in Canada and the conservation and protection of all endangered birds.
Refereed Serial

636.5 — UK — ISSN 0005-2256
QL671
AVICULTURAL MAGAZINE. 1894. q. £18 (foreign £21) (effective 1996). Avicultural Society, c/o Bristol Zoological Gardens, Clifton, Bristol, Avon B58 3HA, England. TEL 44-117-970-6176. FAX 44-117-973-6814. Ed. Malcolm Ellis. R&P contact: Malcolm Ellis. adv. contact: Malcolm Ellis. bk.rev.; illus.; index; circ. 500 (paid). (also avail. in microform from UMI; reprint service avail. from UMI) **Indexed:** Biol.Abstr., Sport Fish.Abstr., Wild.Rev., Zoo.Rec. **Document type:** academic/scholarly publication.
—BLDSC (1839.000000); UMI; UnCover.
Description: Contains articles on a wide range of the world's birds, both common and rare.

598.2 — GW — ISSN 1430-8819
AVIFAUNISTISCHER INFORMATIONSDIENST BAYERN. 1994. 4/yr. DM.65; newsstand price: DM.8. Ornithologische Gesellschaft in Bayern e.V., c/o Institut fuer Vogelkunde, Am Kreuzweiher 3, 91746 Weidenbach, Germany. TEL 49-9826-9730. FAX 49-9826-1610. (Subscr. to: Andreas Bernt, Asternstr. 45, 90765 Fuerth, Germany) Ed. Helmut Ranftl. circ. 1,150. **Document type:** newsletter.

598.05 — UK — ISSN 0962-0877
CODEN: BCLIE8
B O U CHECKLIST. 1976. a. British Ornithologists' Union, Akeman St., Tring, Herts. HP23 6AP, Tring, Herts. HT23 6AP, England. TEL 44-1442-890080. FAX 44-1442-890693. Ed. L.G. Grimes. **Indexed:** Biol.Abstr. (1983-). **Document type:** monographic series.

598.207 — UK — ISSN 0005-3392
QL690.G7 — CODEN: BTNWA5
B T O NEWS. a bulletin for bird watchers. 1964. bi-m. £19. British Trust for Ornithology, The Nunnery, Nunnery Pl., Thetford, Norfolk IP24 2PU, England. TEL 01842-750050. FAX 01842-750030. Ed. Paul Green. adv.; illus. circ. 11,000. **Indexed:** Curr.Adv.Ecol.Sci., Geo.Abstr., Zoo.Rec. **Document type:** bulletin.
—Linda Hall.

598.2 — UK — ISSN 1363-0601
▼**B W P JOURNAL.** (Birds of the Western Palearctic) 1997. 3/yr. £82 (foreign $140) (effective 1998). Oxford University Press, Academic Division, Great Clarendon St., Oxford OX2 6DP, England. TEL 44-1865-267907. FAX 44-1865-267485. E-mail: jnl.info@oup.co.uk; URL: http://www.oup.co.uk/journals. (Subscr. in U.S. to: Oxford University Press Inc., 2001 Evans Rd., Cary, NC 27513. TEL 800-852-7323. FAX 919-677-1714) Pub. Steven Johnson. R&P contact: Joolz Longley. **Document type:** academic/scholarly publication.
Refereed Serial

BARDSEY OBSERVATORY REPORT. see *BIOLOGY*

598 — JA
BATTARIGISU/JAPANESE SOCIETY OF ORTHOPTERA. BULLETIN. (Text in Japanese) 1978. irreg. 600 Yen per no. Nihon Chokushirui Kenkyukai - Japanese Society of Orthoptera, c/o Mr. Yasutsugu Kano, 1-31 Kikyogaoka 5-chome, Nabari-shi, Mie-ken 518-04, Japan.

598.29 — GW — ISSN 0174-1039
BEITRAEGE ZUR AVIFAUNA DES RHEINLANDES. 1972. a. Gesellschaft Rheinischer Ornithologen e.V., Im Rauland 37, 50127 Bergheim, Germany. TEL 49-2271-92121. Ed. Hans-Eckart Joachim. circ. 1,000. **Document type:** monographic series.

598.2 152 — US — ISSN 0156-1383
QL698.3 — CODEN: BBEHDU
BIRD BEHAVIOR; an international and interdisciplinary multimedia journal. 1977. q. $120 (foreign $145) (effective 1998); newsstand price: $2. Cognizant Communication Corporation, 3 Hartsdale Rd., Elmsford, NY 10523-3701. TEL 914-592-7720. FAX 914-592-8981. Ed. Dr. David B. Miller; Pub. Robert N. Miranda. R&P contact: Robert N. Miranda. adv. contact: Lori Miranda. bk.rev.; illus.; stat.; index. circ. 300. (also avail. in microform; reprint service avail. from UMI) **Indexed:** Anim.Behav.Abstr., Aus.Sci.Ind., Biol.Abstr., Curr.Adv.Ecol.Sci., Curr.Cont., Ecol.Abstr., Environ.Per.Bibl. (1991-), Ind.Sci.Rev., Psychol.Abstr., Sci.Cit.Ind., Sport Fish.Abstr., Vet.Bull., Wild.Rev., Zoo.Rec. **Document type:** academic/scholarly publication.
—Linda Hall. **CCC.**
Formerly: Babbler (ISSN 0314-5921)
Description: Research on descriptive and quantitative analyses of behavior, behavior ecology, experimental psychology and behavioral physiology of birds.

598.2 636 — US — ISSN 1073-5186
SF461.A1
BIRD BREEDER. 1928. bi-m. $29.97 (Canada $35.22; elsewhere $37.97) (effective 1997). Fancy Publications, Inc., 3 Burroughs, Irvine, CA 92618-2804. TEL 714-855-8822. FAX 714-855-3045. URL: http://www.petchannel.com. (Subscr. to: Neodata, Box 58025, Boulder, CO 80322. TEL 800-365-4221. FAX 393-604-7455) Ed. Kathleen Samuelson. adv.: B&W page $610, color page 1200; 5 1/2 x 8 1/2. bk.rev.; illus. circ. 25,000. **Indexed:** Sport Fish.Abstr., Wild.Rev. **Document type:** consumer publication.
—UnCover.
Incorporates (1978-1999?): Bird World (ISSN 0199-5979); Former titles (until 1994): American Cage-Bird Magazine (ISSN 0002-7782); (until 1950): American Canary Magazine.

598.2 — UK — ISSN 0959-2709
QL676.5 — CODEN: BCOIEN
BIRD CONSERVATION INTERNATIONAL. 1991. q. £87($142) (effective 1998). (BirdLife International) Cambridge University Press, The Edinburgh Bldg., Shaftesbury Rd., Cambridge CB2 2RU, England. TEL 44-1223-312393. FAX 44-1223-315052. TELEX 851817256. E-mail: information@cup.cam.ac.uk; URL: http://www.cup.org/journals/CUPJNLS.html. (N. American addr.: Cambridge University Press, Journals Dept., 40 W. 20th St., New York, NY 10011-4211. TEL 212-924-3900. FAX 212-691-3239) Ed. Dr. C.F. Mason. R&P contact: Linda Nicol. adv. contact: Rebecca Symons. bk.rev. (back issues avail.) **Indexed:** Ecol.Abstr., Environ.Abstr., Environ.Per.Bibl. (1990-), IDA, Key Word Ind.Wildl.Res., Zoo.Rec. **Document type:** academic/scholarly publication.
—BLDSC (2090.625000); UMI; UnCover. **CCC.**
Description: Focuses on conservation issues affecting birds, especially globally threatened species, and their habitats.

636.5 — AT — ISSN 0045-2076
BIRD KEEPING IN AUSTRALIA. 1958. m. Aus.$35. Avicultural Society of South Australia, P.O. Box 3234, Rundle Mall, Adelaide, S.A. 5000, Australia. TEL 61-8-82643295. Ed. Neroli Price. R&P contact: Neroli Price. adv. contact: Neroli Price. bk.rev. circ. 1,500. (also avail. in microform from UMI; back issues avail.; reprint service avail. from UMI) **Indexed:** Pinpointer. **Document type:** academic/scholarly publication.

598.2 — UK — ISSN 0006-3649
BIRD LIFE. 1965. bi-m. £8 membership. Young Ornithologist's Club, Royal Society for the Protection of Birds, The Lodge, Sandy, Bedfordshire SG19 2DL, England. TEL 44-1767-680551. FAX 44-1767-692365. Ed. Mark Boyd. adv.; bk.rev.; illus. circ. 140,000. **Document type:** bulletin.

598.2 — SA
BIRD NUMBERS. (Text in English) 1993. s-a. R.10 to non-members (members free). Avian Demography Unit, c/o Dept. of Statistical Sciences, University of Cape Town, Rondebosch 7700, South Africa. Ed. James A. Harrison. illus.
Supersedes (in 1993): S A B A P News.

598.2994 — AT — ISSN 0313-5888
CODEN: BOBSE4
BIRD OBSERVER. m. foreign Aus.$60. Bird Observers' Club of Australia, B.O.C.A. Centre, 183 Springvale Rd., Nunawading, Vic. 3131, Australia. TEL 61-3-98775342. FAX 61-3-98944048. Ed. Zoe Wilson. R&P contact: Zoe Wilson. adv. contact: Zoe Wilson. **Indexed:** Sport Fish.Abstr., Wild.Rev., Zoo.Rec. **Document type:** newsletter.

598.2 — UK
BIRD RESEARCH.* 1937. irreg. World Bird Research Station, Glanton, Northumberland NE66 4AH, England.

598.2 — UK — ISSN 0006-3657
QL671 — CODEN: BISTAC
BIRD STUDY. 1954. 3/yr. British Trust for Ornithology, The Nunnery, Nunnery Pl., Thetford, Norwich IP24 2PU, England. Ed. A. Gosler. adv.; bk.rev.; abstr.; bibl.; charts; illus.; maps; stat.; index. circ. 2,400. (also avail. in microform from UMI; back issues avail.) **Indexed:** ASCA, Biol.Abstr., Curr.Adv.Ecol.Sci., Curr.Cont., Ecol.Abstr., Environ.Abstr., Environ.Per.Bibl. (1990-), Forest.Abstr., Forest Prod.Abstr., Geo.Abstr., Ind.Sci.Rev., Key Word Ind.Wildl.Res., Poult.Abstr., Sci.Cit.Ind., Sport Fish.Abstr., Wild.Rev., Zoo.Rec. **Document type:** academic/scholarly publication.
—BLDSC (2092.000000); EMDOCS; Genuine Article; Linda Hall; SWETS; UMI; UnCover.
Refereed Serial

BIRD TALK. see *PETS*

598.2 — US — ISSN 0164-3037
QL677.5
BIRD WATCHER'S DIGEST. 1978. bi-m. $18.95 (Canada & Mexico 23.95; elsewhere $28.95) (effective 1997). Pardson, Inc., Box 110, Marietta, OH 45750. TEL 614-373-5285. FAX 614-373-8443. E-mail: readbwd@aol.com; URL: http://www.petersononline.com/birds/bird/about/bird.html. Ed. W.H. Thompson, III; Pubs. Elsa & W.H. Thompson. adv.: B&W page $1173, color page $1850; 5 1/4 x 7 7/8; adv. contact: Andrew Thompson. bk.rev.; illus.; cum.index. circ. 90,000. (also avail. in microform from UMI; back issues avail.) **Indexed:** Biol.Dig., Wild Life Rev. **Document type:** consumer publication.
●Also available online.
—UnCover.
Description: Discusses birds in the backyard and beyond, and the people who watch them.

598.2 333.7 — UK — ISSN 0269-1434
BIRD WATCHING. 1986. m. £27 (foreign £30) (effective 1997). E M A P - Pursuit Publishing, Bretton Ct., Bretton, Peterborough, Cambs. PE3 8DZ, England. TEL 44-1733-264666. FAX 44-1733-465939. (Subscr. to: Tower Publishing Services Ltd., Tower House, Sovereign Park, Lathkill St., Market Harborough, Leics. LE16 9EF, England. TEL 44-1858-468811. FAX 44-1858-432164) Ed. David Cromack; Pub. Karen Borsberry-Woods. adv.; bk.rev.; video rev.; circ. 21,020 (paid). (back issues avail.) **Document type:** consumer publication.

BIOLOGY — ORNITHOLOGY

598.2   US   ISSN 0895-495X
QL671
BIRDER'S WORLD. 1987. bi-m. $25 (foreign $29.88). Kalmbach Publishing Co., 210272 Crossroads Cir., Waukesha, WI 53187. TEL 414-796-8776. FAX 414-796-1142. Ed. Eldon D. Greij. adv. contact: David S. Yoder. bk.rev. circ. 75,000. **Indexed:** Sport Fish.Abstr., Wild.Rev. **Document type:** consumer publication.
—Linda Hall; UnCover.

598.2   US   ISSN 0161-1836
QL677.5   CODEN: BIRDEV
BIRDING. 1969. bi-m. $36 to individuals (foreign $45); libraries $41 (foreign $50); students $18 (foreign $27) (includes Winging It, A Bird's Eye View) (effective 1997). American Birding Association, Box 6599, Colorado Springs, CO 80934. TEL 719-578-1614; 800-850-2473. FAX 719-578-1480. E-mail: member@aba.org. Ed. Paul Lehman; Pub. George G. Daniels. adv. contact: Langdon R. Stevenson. bk.rev.; illus.; cum.index every 2 yrs. circ. 18,900. **Indexed:** Sport Fish.Abstr., Wild.Rev. **Document type:** academic/scholarly publication.
—UnCover.
Description: Presents articles of relevance to the birder (birdwatcher). Includes primarily bird-finding, bird indentification, bird-conservation information.

598.2   UK
BIRDLIFE CONSERVATION SERIES. (Former name of issuing body: International Council for Bird Preservation) 1980. irreg. price varies. BirdLife International, Wellbrook Ct., Girton Rd., Cambridge CB3 0NA, England. TEL 44-1223-277318. FAX 44-1223-277200. TELEX 818794 ICBP G. E-mail: birdlife@gn.apc.org. (U.S. addr.: Smithsonian Institution Press, Box 960, Herndon, VA 22070-0960. TEL 703-435-7064. FAX 703-689-0660) Ed. Duncan Brooks. (back issues avail.) **Indexed:** Sport Fish.Abstr., Wild.Rev., Zoo.Rec. **Document type:** monographic series.
—CISTI.
Former titles (until 1994): I C B P Technical Publications; I C B P Parrot Working Group Meeting. Proceedings (ISSN 0277-1330)
Description: Covers a wide range of bird conservation issues on a global scale aimed at the international scientific community.

333.95   UK
BIRDLIFE INTERNATIONAL. STUDY REPORT. irreg., no.55, 1995. BirdLife International, Wellbrook Ct., Girton Rd., Cambridge CB3 0NA, England. TEL 44-1223-277318. FAX 44-1223-277200. (Dist. in Americas by: Smithsonian Institution Press, Box 960, Herndon, VA 22070-0960. TEL 703-435-7064. FAX 703-689-0660) **Document type:** monographic series.
Formerly: International Council for Bird Preservation. Study Report.

598.2   UK   ISSN 1357-6860
CODEN: BIRDAR
BIRDS. 1903. q. membership only. Royal Society for the Protection of Birds, The Lodge, Sandy, Bedfordshire SG19 2DL, England. TEL 44-1767-680551. FAX 44-1767-692365. TELEX 82469 RSPB G. Ed. Rob Hume. adv.; bk.rev.; illus. circ. 544,653. **Indexed:** Biol.Abstr., Child.Lit.Abstr., Geo.Abstr., Key Word Ind.Wildl.Res., Sport Fish.Abstr., Wild.Rev., Zoo.Rec. **Document type:** consumer publication.
—UnCover.
Former titles (until 1994): Birds Magazine; (until 1987): Birds (ISSN 0006-3665); (until 1966): Bird Notes; Incorporates: R S P B Annual Report and Accounts (ISSN 0080-4509)

598.2   US
A BIRD'S-EYE VIEW. q. $5 (effective 1997). American Birding Association, Box 6599, Colorado Springs, CO 80934. TEL 719-578-1614; 800-850-2473. FAX 719-578-1480. E-mail: member@aba.rog. Ed. Matthew L. Pelikan. **Document type:** newsletter.
Description: Contains articles written by teenage students for students and others interested in the study of birds.

598   US   ISSN 1061-5466
QL681   CODEN: BNOAE8
BIRDS OF NORTH AMERICA. 1992. 2 vols./yr. (40 nos./vol.). $215 per vol.; (18 vols. set $3295). Academy of Natural Sciences of Philadelphia, 1900 Benjamin Franklin Pkwy., Philadelphia, PA 19103-1195. TEL 215-299-1178; 800-627-0629. FAX 215-299-1028. E-mail: rwalker@allenpress.com; URL: http://www.acnatsci.org/bna. (Co-sponsor: American Ornithologists' Union) illus. **Document type:** monographic series.
—CCC.
Description: Provides comprehensive descriptive information on all species of birds in North America.

598.22   GW   ISSN 0177-4034
CODEN: BITUEO
BIRDS OF TURKEY/TURKIYE KUSLARI. 1983. irreg. DM.10. Max Kasparek Verlag, Bleichstr. 1, 69120 Heidelberg, Germany. TEL 49-6221-475069. FAX 49-6221-471858. **Indexed:** Zoo.Rec. **Document type:** monographic series.

598.2   US   ISSN 1041-6676
BIRDSCOPE. 1987. 4/yr. membership. Cornell University, Laboratory of Ornithology, 159 Sapsucker Woods Rd., Ithaca, NY 14850. TEL 607-254-2473. FAX 607-254-2415. Ed. Tim Gallagher. circ. 40,000. **Indexed:** Zoo.Rec. **Document type:** newsletter.
—BLDSC (2092.507000).
Formerly: Cornell University. Cooperative Research Newsletter.
Description: Explains research programs of the laboratory in lay terms.

598.2   UK
BIRDWATCH. 1992. m. £27 (Europe £38) (effective 1996); newsstand price: £2.25. Solo Publishing Ltd., Bow House, 153-159 Bow Rd., London E3 2SE, England. TEL 44-181-983-1855. FAX 44-181-983-0246. (Subscr. to: Fulham House, Goldsmith Rd., Woking, Surrey GU21 1LY, England. TEL 44-1483-733886. FAX 44-1483-756792) Ed. Dominic Mitchell. adv.: B&W page £730, color page £1250; trim 210 x 297; adv. contact: Steve Swaby. bk.rev.; circ. 16,000 (paid). (back issues avail.) **Document type:** bulletin.
Former titles: Birdwatch Monthly; (until 1992): Birdwatch Magazine (ISSN 0967-1870)

598.2   639.9   UK
BIRDWATCHER'S YEARBOOK AND DIARY. 1981. a. £12.50($30) (1996 edition). Buckingham Press, 25 Manor Park, Maids Moreton, Buckingham, Bucks. MK18 1QX, England. TEL 44-1280-813931. Ed. John E. Pemberton. bk.rev.; bibl.; charts; illus. circ. 3,000. **Document type:** directory.
—BLDSC (2092.510500).
Formerly: Birdwatcher's Yearbook (ISSN 0144-364X)
Description: Lists bird recorders, bird reports, bird clubs, bird hospitals, and national and international organizations. Also contains feature articles.

598.294   DK   ISSN 0906-0146
BLAAVAND FUGLESTATION. 1985. a. DKK 20. (Blaavand Fuglestation) Dansk Ornitologisk Forening, Tempovej 7-11, DK-2750 Ballerup, Denmark.
Formerly (until 1988): Blaavand (ISSN 0901-0637).

598.2   DK   ISSN 0109-257X
BLADSMUTTEN. 1983. q. DKK 40. Danske Ornithologisk Forening i Vestsjaellands Amt, Drosselvej 12, 4100 Ringsted, Denmark. Ed. Arne H. Larsen. adv.; bk.rev.
Former titles: Buteo (ISSN 0109-0755); Vaagen.

598.2   IC   ISSN 0256-4181
CODEN: BLIKES
BLIKI; timarit um fugla. (Text in Icelandic; summaries in English) 1983. irreg. (1-2/yr.). ISK 1150 price varies. Natturufraedistofnun Islands - Icelandic Institute of Natural History, Department of Zoology, Hlemmur 3, P.O. Box 5320, 125 Reykjavik, Iceland. TEL 354-562-9822. FAX 354-562-0815. E-mail: ni@nattfs.is. (Co-sponsor: Icelandic Society for the Protection of Birds) Ed.Bd. bk.rev.; bibl.; charts; illus.; stat. circ. 1,200. (back issues avail.) **Indexed:** Sport Fish.Abstr., Wild Life Rev., Wild.Rev., Zoo.Rec. **Document type:** academic/scholarly publication.
Refereed Serial

598.2   CN   ISSN 0382-5655
BLUE BILL. 1954. q. membership. Kingston Field Naturalists, Box 831, Kingston, ON K7L 4X6, Canada. TEL 613-545-6139. FAX 613-545-6617. Ed. A.A. Crowder. bk.rev. circ. 350. **Document type:** bulletin.

598.207   IT   ISSN 1121-3701
BOLLETTINO DELL'ATTIVITA DI INANELLAMENTO/BULLETIN OF BIRD RINGING ACTIVITY. (Supplement avail.: Bollettino dell'Attivita di Inanellamento. Supplemento (ISSN 1121-3779)) (Text in Italian) 1981. irreg. exchange basis. Istituto Nazionale per la Fauna Selvatica, Via Ca Fornacetta 9, 40064 Ozzano Emilia (Bo), Italy. FAX 39-51-796628. Ed. Mario Spagnesi. stat. circ. 400. (back issues avail.) **Document type:** bulletin.

598.2   UK   ISSN 0007-0335
CODEN: BRBIAP
BRITISH BIRDS. 1907. m. £57($108) (effective July 1996). British Birds Ltd., Fountains, Park Ln., Blunham, Bedford MK44 3NJ, England. TEL 01767-640467. FAX 01767-640025. URL: http://birdcare.com/birdon/birdaction/british__birds.html. Ed. J.T.R. Sharrock. adv. contact: Erika Sharrock. bk.rev.; illus.; index. circ. 10,000. (also avail. in microform from UMI; microfiche from IDC; reprint service avail. from UMI) **Indexed:** Biol.Abstr., Curr.Adv.Ecol.Sci., Curr.Cont., Helminthol.Abstr., IBR, Ind.Sci.Rev., Key Word Ind.Wildl.Res., Sci.Cit.Ind., Sport Fish.Abstr., Wild.Rev., Zoo.Rec. **Document type:** academic/scholarly publication.
—BLDSC (2291.000000); Linda Hall; SWETS; UMI; UnCover. **CCC**.
Description: Independent magazine run by and for the benefit of birdwatchers; covers bird identification, behavior, distribution, ecology, and conservation.
Refereed Serial

BRITISH HOMING WORLD'S PIGEON RACING GAZETTE.
see *SPORTS AND GAMES*

598.2   UK   ISSN 0007-1595
CODEN: BBOCAS
BRITISH ORNITHOLOGISTS' CLUB. BULLETIN. 1892. q. £22($45) to non-members. British Ornithologists' Club, Dene Cottage, West Harting, Petersfield, Hants. GU31 5PA, England. TEL 44-1730-825280. (Subscr. to: Hon. Treasurer, B.O.C., c/o B.O.U. British Museum, Tring, Herts. HP23 6AP, England) Ed. Dr. David W. Snow. bk.rev.; bibl.; charts; illus.; index, cum.index: 1950-59; circ. 800 (paid). (also avail. in microfiche from IDC) **Indexed:** Biol.Abstr., Key Word Ind.Wildl.Res., So.Pac.Per.Ind., Sport Fish.Abstr., Wild.Rev., Zoo.Rec. **Document type:** academic/scholarly publication.
—BLDSC (2423.000000); Linda Hall; UnCover.
Description: Emphasizes taxonomy, descriptions on new forms, distribution information, and field studies.

598.2   UK   ISSN 0068-2675
BRITISH TRUST FOR ORNITHOLOGY. ANNUAL REPORT. 1935. a. membership. British Trust for Ornithology, The Nunnery, Nunnery Pl., Thetford, Norfolk IP24 2PU, England. TEL 01842-750050. FAX 01842-750030. Ed. Paul Green. circ. 10,000. **Document type:** corporate report.

598.71   UK   ISSN 0045-3323
BUDGERIGAR BULLETIN. 1925. q. membership. Budgerigar Society, 12 Abel Close, Hemel Hempstead, Herts, England. Ed. J.E. Watmough. adv.; illus. circ. 6,000. **Document type:** bulletin.

598.2   CN   ISSN 0007-5256
BULLETIN ORNITHOLOGIQUE. 1956. q. Can.$20 to individuals; families Can.$28. Club des Ornithologues de Quebec, Inc., 2000 bd. Montmorency, Quebec, PQ G1J 5E7, Canada. TEL 418-667-6373. bk.rev.; charts. circ. 500. (processed) **Document type:** bulletin.

BIOLOGY — ORNITHOLOGY

598.2 US ISSN 0362-9902
QL684.C6 CODEN: CFOJDN
C F O JOURNAL. 1965. q. $16 to individuals; institutions $25 (membership only). Colorado Field Ornithologists, c/o Mona Hill, Sec., 3910 Heidelberg Dr., Boulder, CO 80303. TEL 719-275-8208. Ed. Cynthia Meliher; Pub. Mona Hill. R&P contact: Mona Hill. bk.rev.; bibl.; charts; illus. circ. 300. (also avail. in microform from UMI) **Indexed:** Biol.Abstr., Sport Fish.Abstr., Wild Life Rev, Wild.Rev., Zoo.Rec. **Document type:** academic/scholarly publication.
—UMI; UnCover.
 Formerly: Colorado Field Ornithologist.
 Description: Covers identification, distribution, behavior and ecology of Colorado's avifauna.

598.2 636 UK ISSN 0007-9561
CAGE & AVIARY BIRDS. 1902. w. £46.80 (foreign £52) (effective 1996). I P C Magazines, Specialist Magazine Group (Subsidiary of: Reed Elsevier group), King's Reach Tower, Stamford St., London SE1 9LS, England. TEL 44-171-261-5000. FAX 44-1444-445599. Ed. Brian Byles. adv.: B&W page £1200. bk.rev.; charts; illus.; tr.lit. circ. 41,305.
 Description: Covers all aspects of keeping and breeding birds for the serious enthusiasts.

598.2 SW ISSN 0346-9395
CALIDRIS. 1972. q. SEK 100 (effective 1990). Oelands Ornitologiska Foerening, P.O. Box 15, S-386 00 Faerjestaden, Sweden. **Indexed:** Key Word Ind.Wildl.Res.

598.2 US ISSN 0162-8186
CARDINAL. 1970. bi-m. membership. Indiana Audubon Society, Inc., 2505 E. Maynard Dr., Indianapolis, IN 46227. TEL 765-529-5225. Ed. Mary R. Gough. circ. 600 (paid). **Document type:** newspaper.
 Description: Features activities of the society, state and federal environmental and conservation issues, and more.

598.2 GW ISSN 0174-1004
CHARADRIUS; Zeitschrift fuer Vogelkunde, Vogelschutz und Naturschutz im Rheinland und in Westfalen. (Text in German; summaries in English and German) 1965. q. DM.50. Gesellschaft Rheinischer Ornithologen e.V., Im Rauland 37, 50127 Bergheim, Germany. TEL 49-2271-92121. (Co-sponsor: Westfaelische Ornithologen Gesellschaft e.V.) bk.rev.; index. circ. 1,450. **Indexed:** Key Word Ind.Wildl.Res., Sport Fish.Abstr., Wild.Rev. **Document type:** bulletin.

598.2 US ISSN 0009-1987
QL671
CHAT. 1937. q. $15 to individuals; institutions $15; students $10. Carolina Bird Club, Inc., Box 29555, Raleigh, NC 27626-0555. TEL 919-334-5391. Ed. Robert Wood. bk.rev.; illus.; index. circ. 1,100. **Indexed:** Biol.Abstr., Sport Fish.Abstr., Wild.Rev., Zoo.Rec. **Document type:** academic/scholarly publication.
 Description: The ornithological journal of the Carolinas.

598.2 UK ISSN 0959-9096
CHESHIRE AND WIRRAL BIRD REPORT. 1968. a. £4.95 (effective 1997). Cheshire - Wirral Ornithological Society, 113 Nantwich Rd., Middlewich, Ches. CW10 9 HD, England. (Ed. addr.: S. Barber, 14 Thornfield Grove, Cheadle Hulme, Ches. SK8 6AZ, England) R&P contact: D. Cogger. adv.; illus.; charts. circ. 600. **Document type:** corporate report.
—BLDSC (3172.457000).
 Former titles (until 1989): Cheshire Ornithological Association. Bird Report (ISSN 0262-7655); (until 1978): Cheshire Bird Report.
 Refereed Serial

598 JA
CHORUI HYOSHIKI CHOSA HOKOKUSHO/BIRD MIGRATION RESEARCH CENTER. REPORT. (Text in Japanese) a. (Yamashina Chorui Kenkyujo - Yamashina Institute for Ornithology) Kankyocho - Environment Agency, 2-2 Kasumigaseki 1-chome, Chiyoda-ku, Tokyo 100, Japan.

598.2 US ISSN 0738-6028
QL671 CODEN: COWAEW
COLONIAL WATERBIRDS. 1981. s-a. $25. Colonial Waterbird Society, Oakland University, Rochester, MI 48309. TEL 810-370-3222. E-mail: mccrimmon@oakland.edu. Ed. Donald A. McCrimmon. R&P contact: Donald A. McCrimmon. adv. contact: Donald A. McCrimmon. bk.rev. circ. 550. **Indexed:** ASCA, Curr.Cont., Key Word Ind.Wildl.Res., Sport Fish.Abstr., Wild.Rev., Zoo.Rec. **Document type:** academic/scholarly publication.
—BLDSC (3320.375000); Genuine Article; Linda Hall; UnCover.
 Refereed Serial

598.2 US ISSN 0010-5422
QL671 CODEN: CNDRAB
CONDOR (TEMPE). 1899. q. $90 (effective 1997). Cooper Ornithological Society, Inc., c/o Glenn E. Walsberg, Ed., Zoology Department, Arizona State University, Tempe, AZ 85287-1501. FAX 602-965-3209. E-mail: rhole@interaktv.com. (Subscr. to: Ornithological Societies of North America, Box 1897, Lawrence, KS 66044-8897) adv.; bk.rev.; charts; illus.; maps; index, cum.index: 1899-1958. circ. 3,300. (also avail. in microfiche from UMI) **Indexed:** Biol.Abstr., Biol.& Agr.Ind., Chem.Abstr., Curr.Cont., Environ.Per.Bibl., GeoRef., Ind.Sci.Rev., Ind.Vet., Ornithol.Abstr. (1955-), Sport Fish.Abstr., Vet.Bull., Wild.Rev., Zoo.Rec. **Document type:** academic/scholarly publication.
—BLDSC (3406.000000); EMDOCS; Genuine Article; KR SourceOne; Linda Hall; SWETS; UMI; UnCover.
 Description: Devoted to the biology of wild species of birds.

598.2 BL
CONGRESSO BRASILEIRO DE ORNITOLOGIA. RESUMOS. 1991. a. Conselho Nacional da Desenvolvimento Cientifico e Tecnologico, Museu Paraense Emilio Goeldi, Caixa Postal 399, 66000 Belem, Para, Brazil. FAX 091-299-1412. (Co-sponsor: Sociedade Brasileira de Ornitologia)

598.2 US ISSN 1077-0283
CODEN: CWARET
CONNECTICUT WARBLER; a journal of Connecticut ornithology. 1981. q. $12 membership (effective 1995 & 1996). Connecticut Ornithological Association, Inc., 314 Unquowa Rd., Fairfield, CT 06430-5018. TEL 203-259-2623. Ed. Betty Kleiner. R&P contact: Carl Trichka. bk.rev.; circ. 550 (paid). (back issues avail.) **Indexed:** Sport Fish.Abstr., Wild.Rev., Zoo.Rec. **Document type:** academic/scholarly publication.
 Refereed Serial

598.2 UK
CONNOISSEURS BIRD JOURNAL. 1981. bi-m. £6. Flight Publishing Ltd., 41 Sugden Rd., Thames Ditton, Surrey, England. Ed. M. Desnaux. circ. 20,000.

CONSERVE WILDLIFE. see *CONSERVATION*

598.2 GW ISSN 0589-686X
CORAX; Veroeffentlichungen der ornithologischen Arbeitsgemeinschaft fuer Schleswig-Holstein und Hamburg e.V. (Text in German; summaries in English) 1965. irreg. (2-4 yr.). DM.60. Zum Brook 16, 24238 Bauersdorf, Germany. TEL 49-4384-1537. (Subscr. to: Karl-Heinz Reiser, Ruhwinkel 8, 24994 Medelby, Germany) Ed. Dr. Fridtjof Ziesemer; Pub. Dr. Fridtjof Ziesemer. bk.rev. circ. 850. (back issues avail.) **Indexed:** Biol.Abstr., IBR, Key Word Ind.Wildl.Res., Sport Fish.Abstr., Wild.Rev., Zoo.Rec. **Document type:** academic/scholarly publication.
 Refereed Serial

598.207 AT ISSN 0155-0438
CODEN: CRRLDQ
CORELLA. 1962. 4/yr. Aus.$35 (foreign Aus.$45) (effective 1997). Australian Bird Study Association, P.O. Box A313, S. Sydney, N.S.W. 1235, Australia. TEL 61-2-92318166. FAX 61-2-92517231. Ed. A.E. Cam. R&P contact: Alan Leishman. bk.rev.; abstr.; charts; illus.; index; circ. 600 (paid). **Indexed:** Biol.Abstr., Sport Fish.Abstr., Wild.Rev., Zoo.Rec. **Document type:** monographic series, newsletter.
—BLDSC (3470.803000); UnCover.
 Formerly (until Jan. 1977): Australian Bird Bander (ISSN 0004-8747)
 Description: Contains original articles on ornithology.
 Refereed Serial

598.2 FR ISSN 0751-7963
CODEN: CRMNE8
LE CORMORAN. 1969. a. 80 F. (effective 1996). Groupe Ornithologique Normand, Universite de Caen, 14032 Caen Cedex, France. TEL 31-43-52-56. FAX 31-93-27-07. Ed. Bruno Lang. **Indexed:** Sport Fish.Abstr., Wild.Rev., Zoo.Rec. **Document type:** academic/scholarly publication.
 Refereed Serial

598.2 FR ISSN 0011-0477
LE COURRIER DE LA NATURE; revue nationale de protection de la nature. 1967. bi-m. 195 F. (foreign 225 F.) (effective 1997). Societe Nationale de Protection de la Nature, 57 rue Cuvier, 75221 Paris Cedex 05, France. TEL 33-1-47073195. Ed. M. Gallois. adv.; bk.rev.; bibl.; illus.; index. circ. 20,000. (back issues avail.) **Indexed:** Biol.Abstr.
—BLDSC (3482.969000).
 Formerly: Courrier de la Nature, l'Homme et l'Oiseau (ISSN 1162-4671)

639.9782 CN ISSN 0011-3093
CURLEW. 1954. 8/yr. Can.$18 to individuals; families Can.$20 (effective 1996). Willow Beach Field Naturalists, P.O. Box 421, Port Hope, ON L1A 3W4, Canada. (Subscr. to: c/o Editor, 64 Young St., Port Hope, ON L1A 1M6, Canada) Ed. Norma Wallace. bk.rev. circ. 136. **Document type:** newsletter.

598.2 US ISSN 0742-390X
QL671 CODEN: CUROEN
CURRENT ORNITHOLOGY. 1983. irreg., vol.13, 1996. price varies. Plenum Publishing Corp., 233 Spring St., New York, NY 10013-1578. TEL 212-620-8000. FAX 212-463-0742. TELEX 23-421139. E-mail: books@plenum.com. Ed. D.M. Power. charts; illus.; stat. (back issues avail.) **Indexed:** Sport Fish.Abstr., Wild.Rev., Zoo.Rec. **Document type:** monographic series.
—BLDSC (3500.790000); CISTI; Linda Hall; UnCover.
 Description: Publishes contributions from international ornithologists on a broad spectrum of topics relating to the ecology, biology, and behavior of birds.
 Refereed Serial

598.29489 DK
QL671
D O F NYT. (Text in Danish and English) 1906. irreg. (2-4/yr.). DKK 235 membership (under 18 and over 67 DKK 130) (effective 1997). Dansk Ornitologisk Forening - Danish Ornithological Society, Vesterbrogade 140, DK-1620 Copenhagen V, Denmark. (Co-sponsor: BirdLife International) Ed. Kaj Kampp. adv.; bk.rev.; bibl.; illus.; index. circ. 8,500. **Indexed:** Biol.Abstr., Key Word Ind.Wildl.Res., Sport Fish.Abstr., Wild.Rev., Wildlife Rev., Zoo.Rec. **Document type:** consumer publication.
—BLDSC (3526.800000).
 Formerly (until Aug. 1995): Dansk Ornitologisk Forenings Tidsskrift (ISSN 0011-6394)

598.2 NE ISSN 0167-2878
CODEN: DUBID3
DUTCH BIRDING. 1979. bi-m. fl.70 (Europe fl.67.50; elsewhere fl.72.50) (effective 1997). Stichting Dutch Birding Association, Postbus 75611, 1070 AP Amsterdam, Netherlands. TEL 31-23-5378024. FAX 31-23-5376749. URL: http://www.mebweb.nl/dutchbirding. Ed. Arnoud B. van den Berg. adv.; bk.rev. circ. 2,300. **Indexed:** Biol.Abstr., Ecol.Abstr., Sport Fish.Abstr., Wild.Rev., Zoo.Rec., Zoo.Rec. **Document type:** academic/scholarly publication, consumer publication.
—UnCover.
 Description: Covers birds in the western Palearctic region.
 Refereed Serial

598.2 AU ISSN 0013-2373
EGRETTA; vogelkundliche Nachrichten aus Oesterreich. 1958. s-a. S.300 (foreign S.440) (effective 1997 & 1998). BirdLife Austria, Museumsplatz 1-10-8, A-1070 Vienna, Austria. TEL 43-1-5234651. FAX 43-1-5247040. Ed. Gerhard Loupal. bk.rev.; bibl.; charts; illus.; cum.index every 4 yrs. circ. 2,000. **Indexed:** Biol.Abstr., IBR, Key Word Ind.Wildl.Res., Sport Fish.Abstr., Wild.Rev., Zoo.Rec. **Document type:** academic/scholarly publication.
—BLDSC (3664.215700).
 Description: Publishes articles on ornithological topics with special regard to Austria.

BIOLOGY — ORNITHOLOGY

598.2 614.7   US   ISSN 0013-6069
CODEN: ELPABT
ELEPAIO. 1939. 9/yr. $10 (effective 1998). Hawaii Audubon Society, 850 Richards St., Ste. 505, Honolulu, HI 96813-4709. TEL 808-528-1432. Ed. Ron Welton. R&P contact: Ron Welton. bk.rev.; charts. circ. 2,600. (processed) **Indexed:** Biol.Abstr., Sport Fish.Abstr., Wild.Rev., Zoo.Rec. **Document type:** newsletter.

598.2   AT   ISSN 0158-4197
QL671   CODEN: EMUUAI
EMU. 1901. q. Aus.$75 to individuals; institutions Aus.$120 (foreign Aus.$140). Royal Australasian Ornithologists Union, 415 Riversdale Rd., E. Hawthorn, Vic. 3123, Australia. TEL 61-3-98822622. FAX 61-3-98822677. URL: http://www.ducks.org/. Ed. I.C. Rowley. R&P contact: Bill Fenton. adv. contact: Bill Fenton. bk.rev. circ. 1,500. (also avail. in microfilm from UMI; microfiche from IDC; reprint service avail. from UMI) **Indexed:** ASCA, Aus.Sci.Ind., Biol.Abstr., Curr.Adv.Ecol.Sci., Curr.Cont., Ecol.Abstr., Geol.Abstr., GeoRef., Helminthol.Abstr., IBR, Ind.Sci.Rev., Key Word Ind.Wildl.Res., Nutr.Abstr., So.Pac.Per.Ind., Sport Fish.Abstr., Wild.Rev., Zoo.Rec. **Document type:** academic/scholarly publication.
—BLDSC (3738.000000); EMDOCS; Genuine Article; Linda Hall; SWETS; UMI; UnCover. **CCC.**

598.2   CN   ISSN 0707-7165
ENVOL/FLIGHT. (Text in English and French) 1978. irreg. membership. Club d'Amateurs d'Oiseaux de Montreal, 228 de la Salle, Mont St. Hilaire, PQ J3H 3C2, Canada.

ESSENTIAL ORNITHOLOGICAL ABSTRACTS. see BIOLOGY — Abstracting, Bibliographies, Statistics

598.2   SW   ISSN 0281-790X
FAAGLAR I BLEKINGE. Variant title: Nya Faaglar i Blekinge. 1984. q. SEK 100 membership (effective 1997). Blekinge Ornitologiska Foerening, Stenhagsvaegen 14, S-374 33 Karlshamn, Sweden. Ed. Thomas Nilsson. adv.; bk.rev. circ. 450.
Formed by merger of: Faaglar i Blekinge. Aktuellt; Faaglar i Blekinge. Aarsskrift; Meddelanden fraan Torhamns Faagelstation.

598.2   SW   ISSN 0281-4374
FAAGLAR I DALARNA. 1968. q. SEK 75 membership (effective 1991). Dalarnas Ornitologiska Foerening (DOF), c/o Thorhild Jonsson, Traedgaardsgatan 2, S-771 50 Ludvika, Sweden. Ed. Bertil Rahm. **Document type:** newsletter.
Formerly (until 1980): Dalarnas Ornitologiska Foerening. Meddelanden.

598.2   SW   ISSN 0282-4760
FAAGLAR I JAEMTLAND - HAERJEDALEN. (Text in Swedish; some summaries in English) 1981. q. SEK 90 membership (effective 1990). Jaemtlands Laens Ornitologiska Foerening (JORF), c/o Thomas Holmberg, Ed., Roedoen 1824, S-835 91 Krokom, Sweden. TEL 46-63-34240. FAX 46–63-34240. circ. 400.
Description: Focuses on ornithology of the Jaemtland region of Sweden. Includes an annual report from the Aansjoen Bird Observatory with English summaries.

598.2   SW   ISSN 0282-5554
FAAGLAR I MEDELPAD. 1978. s-a. SEK 50 (effective 1991). Medelpads Ornitologiska Foerening, c/o N. Lundmark, Skarpskyttev. 6, S-852 43 Sundsvall, Sweden.

598.2   SW   ISSN 0349-3970
FAAGLAR I NAERKE. 1978. q. SEK 50 membership (effective 1991). Naerkes Ornitologiska Foerening (NOF), c/o E. Toernvall, Storg. 48, S-703 63 Oerebro, Sweden.

598.2   SW   ISSN 0281-4153
FAAGLAR I NORDVAESTSKAANE. (Supplement avail.: Faaglar i Nordvaestskaane. Supplement (ISSN 1100-7540)) 1981. a. SEK 50 membership (effective 1988). Kullabygdens Ornitologiska Foerening (KOF), c/o C. Strid, Nils Kaggs gata 15 A, S-252 54 Helsingborg, Sweden.

598.2   SW   ISSN 0281-6903
FAAGLAR I NORRBOTTEN. (Supplements avail.) 1982. q. SEK 100 in Sweden; elsewhere SEK 150. Norrbottens Ornitologiska Foerening, P.O. Box 193, S-971 06 Luleaa, Sweden. Ed. Tord Gustafsson. adv.; bk.rev. circ. 500. **Document type:** bulletin.
Description: Contains articles on birdlife in Norrbotten, the northernmost province of Sweden, and news of events held by Norbottens Ornitologiska Foerening.

598.2   SW   ISSN 1100-0813
FAAGLAR I NORRKOEPINGSTRAKTEN. 1980. q. SEK 100 (effective 1994). Faagelfoereningen i Norrkoeping (FiNk), c/o Juhani Vuorinen, ed., Bergslagsgatan 37, SE-602 18 Norrkoeping, Sweden. TEL 45-11-121-682. FAX 46-11-121-682. E-mail: juhani.vuorinen@facere.se.lars.g.Johansson@asdo.se; URL: http://www.torget.se/users/c/cinclus/finkinfo.htm. Ed. Juhani Vuorinen. adv.; circ. 350 (controlled). **Document type:** newsletter.
Description: Focuses on the study of bird life within the community boundaries of Norrkoeping and the neighbouring communities of Soederkoeping and Valdemarsvik.

598.2   SW   ISSN 1100-9748
FAAGLAR I OESTRA SMAALAND. 1989. q. SEK 80 (effective 1990). Oestra Smaalands Ornitologiska Foerening, c/o T. Larsson, Granholmsg. 8, S-572 40 Oskarshamn, Sweden.

598.2   SW   ISSN 0345-3820
FAAGLAR I SOERMLAND. (Supplement avail.: Faaglar i Soermland. Supplement (ISSN 0281-1413)) 1968. s-a. SEK 70 (effective 1990). Foereningen Soedermanlands Ornitologer (FSO), c/o Swenzen, Skaaneg. 5, S-641 36 Ktrineholm, Sweden.

598.2   SW   ISSN 0280-2430
FAAGLAR I VAESTMANLAND. 1970. q. SEK 85 membership (effective 1997). Vaestmanlands Ornitologiska Foerening, c/o Daniel Green, Knutsgatan 5 b, S-722 14 Vaesteraas, Sweden. E-mail: daniel.gren@vlt.se. Daniel Green. bk.rev. circ. 500.
Formerly (until 1980): Meddelanden fraan Vaestmanlands Ornitologiska Foerening.

598.2   SW   ISSN 0346-9662
FAAGLAR I X-LAEN. 1970. q. SEK 50 (effective 1990). Gaevleborgs Laens Ornitologiska Foerening (GLOF), c/o P.-O. Lock, Svang. 4 D, S-803 46 Gaevle, Sweden.
Former titles (until 1975): Faaglar i Gstr och Hls; (until 1972): Fraan V F's Rapportkommittee Foer Gaestrikland och Haelsingland.

598.2   SW   ISSN 0348-1530
FAAGLAR PAA VAESTKUSTEN. (Supplement avail.) 1965. a. SEK 75 membership (effective 1991). Goeteborgs Ornitologiska Foerening (GOF), P.O. Box 166, S-421 22 Vaestra Froelunda, Sweden.
Formed by the 1972 merger of: Faaglar paa Vaestkusten; Meddelanden fraan Goeteborgs Ornitologiska Foerening.

598.2 636   SW   ISSN 0345-3812
FAAGLEHOBBY; medlemsblad foer Sveriges samarbetand burfaagelfoereningar. 1971. 10/yr. SEK 140 (effective 1990). Faagelhobby, c/o U. Magnusson, Fylkingag. 49, S-212 29 Malmoe, Sweden.

598.2411   UK   ISSN 0427-9190
CODEN: RFBOD2
FAIR ISLE BIRD OBSERVATORY. REPORT. 1949. a. £4.50 per report. Fair Isle Bird Observatory Trust, The Lodge, Fair Isle, Shetland ZE2 9JU, Scotland. TEL 44-1595-760-258. FAX 44-1595-760-258. E-mail: fairisle.birdobs@zetnet.co.uk. R&P contact: Wendy Christie. adv. contact: Wendy Christie. circ. 650. **Indexed:** Sport Fish.Abstr., Wild.Rev., Zoo.Rec.
—BLDSC (7467.300000).

THE FALCONERS AND RAPTOR CONSERVATION MAGAZINE. see CONSERVATION

598.2   GW   ISSN 0323-357X
CODEN: FALKA6
DER FALKE; Journal fuer Vogelbeobachter. m. DM.78 (student DM.60) (effective 1996). Aula Verlag GmbH, Postfach 1366, 65003 Wiesbaden, Germany. TEL 49-611-379599. FAX 49-611-373060. adv.: B&W page DM.980. illus. **Indexed:** Biol.Abstr., IBR, Key Word Ind.Wildl.Res., Sport Fish.Abstr., Wild.Rev., Zoo.Rec. **Document type:** academic/scholarly publication.
Description: Information and news about ornithology and bird protection.

FAUNA D'ITALIA; repertorio generale delle specie animali esistenti in Italia. see BIOLOGY — Zoology

598.2   NO   ISSN 0332-7701
QL690.N8   CODEN: FNSCD9
FAUNA NORVEGICA SERIES C. NORWEGIAN JOURNAL OF ORNITHOLOGY. (Text in English) 1978. s-a. NOK 120 to Norwegian non-members; members NOK 90; non-members outside Norway NOK 160; members NOK 130 (effective 1997). (Norsk Ornitologisk Forening) Norsk Institutt for Naturforskning (NINA), c/o Kjetil Bevanger, Tungasletta 2, N-7005 Trondheim, Norway. TEL 47-73-58-05-00. FAX 47-73-91-54-33. E-mail: kjetil.bevanger@nina.nina.no. Ed. Svein Haftorn. R&P contact: Kjetil Bevanger. adv. contact: Kjetil Bevanger. bk.rev.; cum.index. circ. 700. (back issues avail.) **Indexed:** Ecol.Abstr., IBR, Sport Fish.Abstr., Wild.Rev., Zoo.Rec. **Document type:** academic/scholarly publication.
—BLDSC (3899.260000); CISTI. **CCC.**
Description: Publishes original research dealing with the Norwegian fauna.

598.2   US
FIELD NOTES OF RHODE ISLAND BIRDS. m. $10. Audubon Society of Rhode Island, 12 Sanderson Rd., Smithfield, RI 02917-2606. TEL 401-949-5454. FAX 401-949-5788. (Co-sponsor: Rhode Island Ornithological Club) Ed. David Emerson. circ. 300. (back issues avail.) **Document type:** newsletter.
Description: Birds seen in Rhode Island during the previous month.

598.2   US   ISSN 0738-999X
QL684.F6   CODEN: FFNADO
FLORIDA FIELD NATURALIST. 1972. q. $15. Florida Ornithological Society, Florida State Museum, University of Florida, Gainesville, FL 32611. TEL 352-376-6481. E-mail: engstrom@bio.fsu.edu. Ed. R. Todd Engstrom. adv.; bk.rev.; cum.index every 5 yrs. circ. 575. **Indexed:** Biol.Abstr., Key Word Ind.Wildl.Res., Sport Fish.Abstr., Wild Life Rev., Wild.Rev., Zoo.Rec. **Document type:** academic/scholarly publication.
—UnCover.
Refereed Serial

FOREST AND BIRD. see CONSERVATION

598.2948   DK   ISSN 0903-1731
FUGLE OG DYR I NORDJYLLAND. no. 18, 1981. a. DKK 110. Foreningen Fugle og Dyr i Nordjylland, Liljevej 3, DK-7800 Skive, Denmark. Ed. Gorm Waehrens. illus.
Former titles: Fugle i Nordjylland (ISSN 0108-7282); Nordjysk Ornitologisk Kartotek. Rapport.

598.2   SA
CODEN: GGBREY
G A B A R. (Growth and Biology of African Raptors) s-a. Raptor Conservation Group, P.O. Box 72155, Parkview 2122, South Africa. **Indexed:** Sport Fish.Abstr., Wild.Rev., Zoo.Rec.

GAME CONSERVANCY MAGAZINE. see CONSERVATION

GAME CONSERVANCY REVIEW. see CONSERVATION

598.2   SP   ISSN 0212-923X
CODEN: GARCER
LA GARCILLA; boletin - circular de la sociedad. 1984. 3/yr. 3000 ptas. Sociedad Espanola de Ornitologia, c/o Fac. de Biologia, Univ. Complutense de Madrid, Ciudad Universitaria, 28040 Madrid, Spain. Ed. Juan Varela. **Indexed:** Ind.SST, Sport Fish.Abstr., Wild.Rev., Zoo.Rec.

BIOLOGY — ORNITHOLOGY

598.2 GW ISSN 0016-5816
CODEN: GEWEBF
GEFIEDERTE WELT; Fachzeitschrift fuer Vogelpfleger und Vogelzuechter. 1874. m. DM.124.20. Verlag Eugen Ulmer GmbH, Wollgrasweg 41, 70599 Stuttgart, Germany. TEL 49-711-4507-0. FAX 49-711-4507120. (Subscr. to: Postfach 700561, 70574 Stuttgart, Germany) Ed. Dr. J. Steinbacher. R&P contact: G. Friedrich. adv. contact: A. Purwing. bk.rev.; abstr.; bibl.; illus.; index, cum.index. circ. 7,400. **Indexed:** Biol.Abstr., RILM, Sport Fish.Abstr., Wild.Rev., Zoo.Rec. **Document type:** consumer publication.
—Linda Hall. **CCC.**
Incorporates: Vogel-Kosmos.

508 GI ISSN 1352-8726
CODEN: NGOSE9
GIBRALTAR NATURE NEWS. Key Title: Gibraltar Ornithological & Natural History Society. Newsletter. $1979 3/yr. Gibraltar Ornithological & Natural History Society, Gibraltar Natural History Field Centre, Jew's Gate, P.O. Box 843, Upper Rock Nature Reserve, Gibraltar. Ed. John E. Cortes. **Indexed:** Zoo.Rec.

598.2 JM ISSN 1017-348X
GOSSE BIRD CLUB BROADSHEET. 1963. s-a. $10 to individuals; institutions $20. Gosse Bird Club, 93 Old Hope Rd., Kingston 6, Jamaica, W.I. TEL 809-978-5881. FAX 809-978-5881. URL: http://www.jatoday.com.jm/goosebird.html. Ed. Catherine Levy. adv.; bk.rev.; cum.index every 10 nos. circ. 250. (looseleaf format; back issues avail.) **Indexed:** Sport Fish.Abstr., Wild.Rev.
Description: Devoted to the study and conservation of Jamaican birds.

598.2 US ISSN 0164-971X
GULL. 1917. 11/yr. $10 (effective 1995). Golden Gate Audubon Society, 2530 San Pablo Ave., Ste. G, Berkeley, CA 94702. TEL 510-843-2222. FAX 510-843-5351. Ed. John Gibbons. R&P contact: Arthur Feinstein. TEL 510-843-2222. adv. contact: Arthur Feinstein. bk.rev.; circ. 6,000 (paid). **Document type:** newsletter.

598.2 US
CODEN: HMSTE8
HAWK MIGRATION STUDIES. 1977. s-a. membership. Hawk Migration Association of North America (HMANA), c/o Jeffery Dodge, Ed., 432 Manitou Beach Rd., Hilton, NY 14468. TEL 716-392-5685. bk.rev. (back issues avail.) **Indexed:** Sport Fish.Abstr., Wild.Rev., Zoo.Rec.
Formerly: Hawk Migration Association of North America. Newsletter.

598.207 639.9 US
HAWK MOUNTAIN NEWS. 1939. biennial. $25 membership. Hawk Mountain Sanctuary Association, Rt. 2, Kempton, PA 19529. TEL 610-756-6961. FAX 610-756-4468. URL: http://www.hawknountain.org. Ed. Nancy J. Keeler. R&P contact: Nancy Keeler. bk.rev.; charts. circ. 10,000. **Indexed:** Sport Fish.Abstr., Wild.Rev.
Description: Reports on events at the Sanctuary, including studies on and conservation of the birds of prey.

HERON CONSERVATION NEWSLETTER. see *ANIMAL WELFARE*

598.2 RH ISSN 0018-456X
HONEYGUIDE. 1954. q. Z.$110 to individuals; foreign institutions Z.$200 (effective 1997). Ornithological Association of Zimbabwe, P.O. Box CY 161, Causeway, Harare, Zimbabwe. E-mail: birds@harare.iafrica.com. Ed. M.P.S. Irwin. adv.; bk.rev.; abstr.; charts; illus.; cum.index. circ. 1,000. **Indexed:** Wild Life Rev., Zoo.Rec. **Document type:** academic/scholarly publication.
Description: Covers all aspects of ornithology in Zimbabwe.

598.2 CC ISSN 1017-1118
CODEN: HKBRE5
HONG KONG BIRD REPORT. 1959. a. HK.$240. Hong Kong Bird Watching Society, G.P.O. Box 12460, Hong Kong, People's Republic of China. Ed. G.J. Carey. circ. 1,000. **Indexed:** Sport Fish.Abstr., Wild.Rev., Zoo.Rec.

598.2 AG ISSN 0073-3407
CODEN: HRNOAX
HORNERO. (Text in Spanish; occasionally in English, Portuguese) 1917. a. $25. Asociacion Ornitologica del Plata, 25 de Mayo 749, 2o 6, 1002 Buenos Aires, Argentina. TEL 541-312-8958. FAX 541-312-8958. E-mail: hornero@aorpla.org.ar. Eds. Rosendo Fraga, Juan Carlos Reboreda; Pub. Juan Carlos Reboreda. adv. contact: Andres Bosso. bk.rev.; index. circ. 1,000. **Indexed:** Biol.Abstr., Sport Fish.Abstr., Wild.Rev., Zoo.Rec. **Document type:** academic/scholarly publication.

598.2 UK ISSN 1012-6201
CODEN: ICMOE6
I C B P MONOGRAPHS. (International Council for Bird Preservation) (Former name of issuing body: International Council for Bird Preservation) 1988. irreg., latest 1989. BirdLife International, Wellbrook Ct., Girton Rd., Cambridge CB3 0NA, England. TEL 44-1223-277318. FAX 44-1223-277200. TELEX 818794 ICBP G. (back issues avail.) **Indexed:** Zoo.Rec. **Document type:** monographic series.
—BLDSC (4360.295400).
Description: Provides information on biological diversity and conservation issues on a regional basis with particular relevance to birds.

598.2 US
I C F BUGLE. 1974. q. $25 (foreign $30). International Crane Foundation, P.O. Box 447, Baraboo, WI 53913-0447. TEL 608-356-9462. FAX 608-356-9465. TELEX 297778 ICF UR. Ed. Marshal Case. R&P contact: Marshal Case. bk.rev. circ. 7,500. (tabloid format; back issues avail.) **Document type:** newsletter, academic/scholarly publication.
Formerly: Brogla Bugle.
Description: Promotes the study and preservation of cranes through news of the foundation and current research and conservation programs.

598.2 US ISSN 0019-1019
QL671 CODEN: IBISAL
IBIS. 1859. q. $200 (effective 1997). (British Ornithologists' Union) Allen Press, Inc., 1041 New Hampshire Ave., Box 1897, Lawrence, KS 66044. TEL 913-843-1221; 800-627-0629. FAX 913-843-1274. adv.; bk.rev.; rec.rev.; abstr.; bibl.; charts; illus.; index. circ. 2,650. **Indexed:** Anim.Breed.Abstr., Biol.Abstr., Curr.Adv.Ecol.Sci., Curr.Cont., Ecol.Abstr., Environ.Abstr., Environ.Per.Bibl. (1989-1993), Geol.Abstr., Helminthol.Abstr., Ind.Sci.Rev., Ind.Vet., Key Word Ind.Wildl.Res., Sport Fish.Abstr., Vet.Bull., Wild.Rev., Zoo.Rec. **Document type:** academic/scholarly publication.
—BLDSC (4360.000000); CISTI; EMDOCS; Genuine Article; KR SourceOne; Linda Hall; SWETS; UMI.

598 JA
IGURETTA/EGRETTA. (Text in Japanese) 1986. s-a. free. Shirasagi Kinen Hakubutsukan - Shirasagi Memorial Museum, 172, Daiyama, Urawa-shi, Saitama-ken 337, Japan. TEL 81-48-878-0500. FAX 81-48-878-3335. Ed. T. Sunose. circ. 800. **Document type:** newsletter.
Description: Covers natural conservation for insects and others.

598.2 US ISSN 0019-6525
INDIANA AUDUBON QUARTERLY. 1950. q. membership (libraries $17). Indiana Audubon Society, Inc., 2505 E. Maynard Dr., Indianapolis, IN 46227. TEL 317-529-5225. (Subscr. to: Shirley Keller, 2505 E. Maynard Dr., Indianapolis, IN 46227. TEL 317-786-5822) Ed Charles E. Keller. bk.rev.; charts; illus.; index. circ. 632. **Indexed:** Biol.Abstr., Sport Fish.Abstr., Wild.Rev., Zoo.Rec. **Document type:** academic/scholarly publication, bulletin.
—UnCover.
Description: Features state Christmas count data, state May Day count data, winter feeder count data, official list of Indiana birds, seasonal field data for birds in the state, essays, travel essays (for birds), illustrations, book reviews, software reviews, index in last yearly issue.

598.2 AU ISSN 0074-7211
INTERNATIONAL ORNITHOLOGICAL CONGRESS. PROCEEDINGS. quadrennial, 1994, 21st, Vienna. International Ornithological Congress - Congres Ornithologique International, c/o Prof. John Dittami, Institute of Zoology, A-1090 Vienna, Austria. TEL 43-1-31-33-61-307. **Indexed:** Biol.Abstr., Chem.Abstr., Key Word Ind.Wildl.Res., Sport Fish.Abstr., Wild.Rev. **Document type:** proceedings.

598.2 US ISSN 0021-0455
QL671 CODEN: IOBLAM
IOWA BIRD LIFE. 1931. q. $15 (effective 1997). Iowa Ornithologists' Union, 4024 Arkansas Dr., Ames, IA 50014. TEL 515-292-3152. E-mail: oldcoot@iastate.edu. Ed. James J. Dinsmore. bk.rev.; charts; illus.; cum.index every 5 yrs.; circ. 575 (paid). **Indexed:** Biol.Abstr., Sport Fish.Abstr., Wild Life Rev., Wild.Rev., Zoo.Rec. **Document type:** academic/scholarly publication.
—UnCover.

598 JA
IPPITSU KEIJO/WILD BIRD SOCIETY OF JAPAN. WAKAYAMA PREFECTURE BRANCH. SURVEY REPORT. (Text in Japanese) 1980. q. Nihon Yacho no Kai, Wakayamaken Shibu - Wild Bird Society of Japan, Wakayama Prefecture Branch, Kenritsu Hidaka Koko, 45 Shima, Gobo-shi, Wakayama-ken 644, Japan.

598.2 IE ISSN 0332-0111
QL690.I7 CODEN: IBIRDL
IRISH BIRDS. 1977. a. I£10. Irish Wildbird Conservancy, Ruttledge House, 8 Longford Pl., Monkstown, Co. Dublin, Ireland. TEL 353-1-2804322. FAX 353-1-2844407. Ed. Brennan Kavanagh. adv. contact: Oran O'Sullivan. bk.rev.; illus. circ. 1,500. **Indexed:** Biol.Abstr., Zoo.Rec. **Document type:** academic/scholarly publication.
—BLDSC (4570.610000).
Incorporates: Irish Bird Report.
Description: All aspects of birds in Ireland.
Refereed Serial

598.2 US ISSN 0021-3845
QL671 CODEN: JPWBAD
JACK-PINE WARBLER. 1922. bi-m. $15 (foreign $20) (effective 1997). Michigan Audubon Society, 6011 W. St. Joseph, Ste. 403, Box 80527, Lansing, MI 48908-0527. TEL 517-886-9144. FAX 517-886-9466. Ed. John Elder. adv.; bk.rev.; charts; illus. circ. 8,500. (also avail. in microfilm from UMI; reprint service avail. from UMI) **Indexed:** Biol.Abstr., Mich.Mag.Ind., Sport Fish.Abstr., Wild.Rev., Zoo.Rec. **Document type:** newsletter.
—Linda Hall; UMI.
Incorporates: Michigan Audubon (ISSN 0731-9126); Which was formerly: Michigan Audubon Newsletter.
Description: Covers the ornithology and natural history of the Great Lakes region. Includes society news and activities and scientific bird surveys and articles.

598.2 JA ISSN 0913-400X
CODEN: JJOREH
JAPANESE JOURNAL OF ORNITHOLOGY. (Text in English, Japanese) 1915. q. 5500 Yen to non-members. Ornithological Society of Japan - Nihon Cho Gakkai, c/o National Science Museum, Department of Zoology, 3-23-1 Hyakunin-cho, Shinjuku-ku, Tokyo 169, Japan. TEL 03-3364-2311. Ed. Dr. Hiroyuki Morioka. adv.; bk.rev.; charts; illus. circ. 900. **Indexed:** Biol.Abstr., Jap.Per.Ind., Sport Fish.Abstr., Wild.Rev., Zoo.Rec.
Formerly: Tori.

598.2 GW ISSN 0021-8375
QL671 CODEN: JORNAH
JOURNAL FUER ORNITHOLOGIE. 1853. q. DM.421 in Europe; rest of world DM.418 (effective 1998). (Deutsche Ornithologen-Gesellschaft e.V.) Blackwell Wissenschaft, Kurfuerstendamm 57, 10707 Berlin, Germany. TEL 49-30-327906-0. FAX 49-30-32790610. E-mail: aboverwalt@blackwis.de; URL: http://www.blackwis.com. Ed. Einhard Bezzel. adv. contact: Wolfgang Stauber. bk.rev.; charts; illus.; index. circ. 3,000. (also avail. in microfiche from IDC) **Indexed:** ASCA, Biol.Abstr., Chem.Abstr., Curr.Cont., Ecol.Abstr., IBR, Ind.Sci.Rev., Sport Fish.Abstr., Wild.Rev., Zoo.Rec. **Document type:** academic/scholarly publication.
—BLDSC (5027.500000); CISTI; Linda Hall; SWETS UMI; UnCover.
Refereed Serial

BIOLOGY — ORNITHOLOGY

598.2   DK   ISSN 0908-8857
QL671   CODEN: JAVBE9
JOURNAL OF AVIAN BIOLOGY. (Text in English) 1970. q. DKK 740 in Europe (US, Canada and Japan DKK 770) (effective 1997). (Scandinavian Ornithologists' Union) Munksgaard International Publishers Ltd., 35 Noerre Soegade, P.O. Box 2148, DK-1016 Copenhagen K, Denmark. TEL 45-33-127030. FAX 45-33-129387. (In N. America: Commerce Place, 350 Main St., Malden, MA 82148-5018. TEL 617-388-8273. FAX 617-388-8274) Ed.Bd. bk.rev.; bibl.; charts; index. circ. 750. (back issues avail.; reprint service avail. from ISI) **Indexed:** ASCA, Biol.Abstr., Curr.Adv.Ecol.Sci., Curr.Cont., Ecol.Abstr., Geo.Abstr., IBR, Ind.Sci.Rev., Int.Abstr.Biol.Sci., Key Word Ind.Wldl.Res., Sci.Cit.Ind., Sport Fish.Abstr., Wlld.Rev., Zoo.Rec. **Document type:** academic/scholarly publication.
—BLDSC (4949.950000); EMDOCS; Genuine Article; Linda Hall; SWETS; UnCover. **CCC**.
   Formerly (until 1994): Ornis Scandinavica (ISSN 0030-5693)
   Refereed Serial

598.207   US   ISSN 0273-8570
CODEN: JFORDM
JOURNAL OF FIELD ORNITHOLOGY. 1930. q. $45 (foreign $51) (effective 1997). Association of Field Ornithologists, Inc., Dept. of Biology, Georgia Southern University, Statesboro, GA 30460. TEL 608-363-2314. FAX 608-363-2052. URL: http://www.nmnh.sci.edu/BIRNET/AFO/journal.html. (Subscr. to: c/o Ornithological Societies of North America, Box 1897, Lawrence, KS 66044-8897. TEL 913-843-1221) Ed. C. Ray Chandler. R&P contact: Elissa Landre. adv.; bk.rev.; bibl.; illus.; cum.index: 1951-1960. circ. 2,200. (also avail. in microform from UMI; reprint service avail. from UMI) **Indexed:** ASCA, Biol.Abstr., Curr.Cont., Deep Sea Res.& Oceanogr.Abstr., Helminthol.Abstr., Ind.Sci.Rev., Key Word Ind.Wldl.Res., Ornithol.Abstr. (1955-), Sci.Cit.Ind., Sport Fish.Abstr., Wild.Rev., Zoo.Rec. **Document type:** academic/scholarly publication.
—BLDSC (4984.110000); Genuine Article; Linda Hall; SWETS; UMI; UnCover.
   Formerly: Bird-Banding (ISSN 0006-3630)
   Description: Publishes original and methodological papers dealing with the ecology, behavior, taxonomy, life history, and zoogeography of birds in their natural habitats.

598.9   US   ISSN 0892-1016
CODEN: JRREEF
JOURNAL OF RAPTOR RESEARCH. 1967. q. $30 to individuals ($35 outside U.S.); institutions $50 ($55 outside U.S.) (effective 1997). Raptor Research Foundation, Inc., c/o O S N A, Box 1897, 810 E. 10th St., Lawrence, KS 66044-8897. TEL 612-437-4359. FAX 612-438-2908. URL: http://www.nmnh.si.edu/BIRDNET/RRF/index.html#RRFJournal. Ed. Dr. Mark Bechard. bk.rev.; circ. 1,200 (paid). (back issues avail.) **Indexed:** ASCA, Biol.Abstr., Curr.Cont., Ecol.Sci.Rev., Key Word Ind.Wldl.Res., Sci.Cit.Ind., Sport Fish.Abstr., Wild.Rev., Zoo.Rec. **Document type:** academic/scholarly publication.
—BLDSC (5046.500000); Genuine Article; UnCover.
   Formerly (until vol.20, 1987): Raptor Research (ISSN 0099-9059)
   Refereed Serial

598.2   GW
KANARIENFREUND. 1947. s-a. DM.100. Hanke Verlag GmbH, Lindenstr. 50, Postfach 1040, 75175 Pforzheim, Germany. TEL 49-7231-17700. FAX 49-7231-352148. Ed. Ruediger Henecka. adv.; bk.rev. **Document type:** newsletter.

598.2   US   ISSN 0022-8729
CODEN: KOSBBW
KANSAS ORNITHOLOGICAL SOCIETY. BULLETIN. 1950. q. $15 (effective 1997). Kansas Ornithological Society, c/o Max C. Thompson, Ed., Department of Biology, Southwestern College, 100 College St., Winfield, KS 67156-2499. TEL 316-221-8304. FAX 316-221-8382. E-mail: maxt@jinx.sckans.edu. Ed. Max Thompson. bk.rev.; rec.rev.; charts; illus.; stat. circ. 450. **Indexed:** Biol.Abstr., Sport Fish.Abstr., Wild Life Rev., Wild.Rev., Zoo.Rec. **Document type:** academic/scholarly publication.
—Linda Hall.

598.2   US   ISSN 0160-5070
CODEN: KEWAA
KENTUCKY WARBLER. 1925. q. Kentucky Ornithological Society, c/o Donna Coates, Treas., Rte. 1, Box 124, Cox's Creek, KY 40013. **Indexed:** Sport Fish.Abstr., Wild.Rev., Zoo.Rec.
—BLDSC (5089.665000).

598.2   US   ISSN 0023-1606
QL671   CODEN: KNGBAW
KINGBIRD. 1950. q. $18 (foreign $25) (effective 1996). Federation of New York State Bird Clubs, Inc., c/o Berna Lincoln, Box 296, Somers, NY 10589. TEL 914-277-8264. Ed. Donald A. Windsor. charts; illus.; circ. 900 (paid). (back issues avail.) **Indexed:** Biol.Abstr., Sport Fish.Abstr., Wild.Rev., Zoo.Rec. **Document type:** academic/scholarly publication.
—UnCover.
   Description: Covers ornithology of New York State.

598.2   SX
CODEN: LANIEC
LANIOTURDUS ORNITHOLOGISCHE ARBEITSGRUPPE MITTEILUNGEN. (Text and summaries in English, German) 1965. m. membership. Namibia Scientific Society, P.O. Box 67, Windhoek, Namibia. TEL 061-225372. **Indexed:** Sport Fish.Abstr., Wild.Rev., Zoo.Rec. **Document type:** academic/scholarly publication.
—BLDSC (5862.900000).
   Formerly: Ornithologische Arbeitsgruppe Mitteilungen (ISSN 0030-5731)

598.2   CI   ISSN 0350-5189
QL671   CODEN: LARSAO
LARUS. 1947. a. Hrvatska Akademija Znanosti i Umjetnosti, Institut za Ornitologiju - Croatian Academy of Arts and Sciences, Institute of Ornithology, Ilirski trg 9-2, 41000 Zagreb, Croatia. **Indexed:** Sport Fish.Abstr., Wild.Rev., Zoo.Rec. **Document type:** academic/scholarly publication.
—BLDSC (5156.000000).

598.2   GW   ISSN 0932-9153
CODEN: LIMIET
LIMICOLA; Zeitschrift fuer Feldornithologie. (Text in German; summaries in English) 1987. bi-m. DM.75. Limicola Verlag, Ueber-dem-Salzgraben 11, 37574 Einbeck-Drueber, Germany. TEL 05561-82224. FAX 05561-82289. Ed. Peter Barthel. adv. contact: Christine Barthel. bk.rev.; illus.; index. circ. 3,000. (back issues avail.) **Indexed:** Key Word Ind.Wldl.Res., Sport Fish.Abstr., Wild.Rev., Zoo.Rec. **Document type:** academic/scholarly publication.
—Linda Hall.

598.2   NE   ISSN 0024-3620
CODEN: LIMOA9
LIMOSA. (Summaries in English) 1929. q. fl.43 to individuals; institutions fl.76. Nederlandse Ornithologische Unie - Netherlands Ornithological Union, c/o Akelei 42, 4102 JM Culemborg, Netherlands. TEL 31-345-519849. (Subscr. to: L. Hellenberghof 32, 2202 XT Noordwijk, Netherlands) Ed. F. de Roder. R&P contact: Theo Boudweyn. adv. contact: R. Noordhuis. bk.rev.; charts; illus.; index. circ. 2,200. (back issues avail.) **Indexed:** Biol.Abstr., Ecol.Abstr., Sport Fish.Abstr., Wild.Rev., Zoo.Rec.
—BLDSC (5220.000000); Linda Hall; SWETS.
   Description: Publishes papers on field ornithology in the Netherlands.

598.2   US   ISSN 1059-521X
QL671   CODEN: LIBIE8
LIVING BIRD. 1962. q. $35 membership. Cornell University, Laboratory of Ornithology, 159 Sapsucker Woods Rd., Ithaca, NY 14850. TEL 607-254-2473. FAX 607-254-2415. URL: http://www.omith.cornell.edu/PUBS/LB/main.html. Ed. Tim Gallagher. adv.: B&W page $750, color page $1000; 8 1/2 x 11; adv. contact: Barbara Guttridge. bk.rev.; illus. circ. 22,000. (also avail. in microform from UMI) **Indexed:** Biol.Abstr., Ecol.Abstr., Sport Fish.Abstr., Wild.Rev., Zoo.Rec. **Document type:** academic/scholarly publication.
—BLDSC (5282.470000); Linda Hall; UMI; UnCover.
   Former titles (until 1991): Living Bird Quarterly (ISSN 0732-9210); (until 1982): Living Bird (ISSN 0459-6137)
   Description: Covers bird biology, behavior, conservation, art, travel, and reviews of bird equipment.

598.2   UK   ISSN 0141-4348
CODEN: LOBIBD
LONDON BIRD REPORT. 1936. a. £5. London Natural History Society, 5 Temple Close, Cassiobury, Watford, Herts WD1 3DR, England. TEL 44-1923-233706. FAX 44-1923-226095. Ed. M. Hardwick. R&P contact: M. Hardwick. circ. 1,200. (back issues avail.) **Indexed:** Sport Fish.Abstr., Wild.Rev., Zoo.Rec. **Document type:** bulletin.
—BLDSC (5293.000000).

598.207   CN   ISSN 0317-9575
LONG POINT BIRD OBSERVATORY NEWSLETTER. 1969. 3/yr. Can.$30 membership. Long Point Bird Observatory, P.O. Box 160, Port Rowan, ON N0E 1M0, Canada. TEL 519-586-3531. FAX 519-586-3532. E-mail: bsc@nornet.on.ca. Eds. Michael S.W. Bradstreet, J.D. McCracken. bk.rev. circ. 1,500. **Indexed:** Sport Fish.Abstr., Wild.Rev. **Document type:** newsletter.
   Description: Focuses on bird-banding and monitoring techniques.

598.2   US   ISSN 0024-645X
CODEN: LOONAO
LOON. 1929. q. $20 to individuals; families $30; supporting $50; youth $15 (foreign $25) membership (effective 1997). Minnesota Ornithologists' Union, James Ford Bell Museum of Natural History, University of Minnesota, 10 Church St., S.E., Minneapolis, MN 55455-0104. TEL 612-459-4150. FAX 612-459-6621. E-mail: etbell@aol.com; URL: http://biosci.cbs.umn.edu/~mou/mou.html. Ed. Anthony Hertzel. R&P contact: R.B. Janssen. bk.rev.; charts; illus.; stat.; index. circ. 1,200. (back issues avail.; reprint service avail. from ISI,UMI) **Indexed:** Biol.Abstr., Sport Fish.Abstr., Wild.Rev., Zoo.Rec.
—BLDSC (5294.519000); UnCover.
   Formerly (until 1964): Flicker (ISSN 0199-9672)
   Description: Information on birds, with emphasis on birds in Minnesota.

598.2   GW   ISSN 0024-7391
CODEN: LUSCAJ
LUSCINIA; vogelkundliche Zeitschrift fuer Hessen. 1927. a. DM.18. Vogelkundliche Beobachtungsstation Untermain e.V., Postfach 640163, 60355 Frankfurt a.M., Germany. TEL 49-69-724637. E-mail: eidam@t-online.de; URL: http://www.t-online.de/home/eidw/. Ed. Ulrich Eidam. adv.; bk.rev.; charts; illus.; maps; stat.; cum.index. circ. 1,000. **Indexed:** Apic.Abstr., Biol.Abstr., Key Word Ind.Wldl.Res., Sport Fish.Abstr., Wild.Rev., Zoo.Rec. **Document type:** academic/scholarly publication.

598.2   US
MAIL BAG. 1943. q. membership. Brooks Bird Club, Inc., 423 Warwood Ave., Wheeling, WV 26003. TEL 614-635-9246. Ed. William Murray. bk.rev. circ. 600.
   Formerly: B B C Mail Bag.
   Description: News of club events, environmental matters, news of club members, correspondence, poetry, and news and items of general interest to members.

MANITOBA NATURALISTS SOCIETY BULLETIN. see *CONSERVATION*

598.2   SA   ISSN 1018-3337
QL671   CODEN: MAOREL
MARINE ORNITHOLOGY. (Text in English) 1976. s-a. $50 (effective 1996). African Seabird Group, P.O. Box 34113, Rhodes Gift 7707, South Africa. TEL 27-21-6503294. FAX 27-21-6503295. TELEX 521439. E-mail: jcooper@botzoo.uct.ac.za. Ed. John Cooper. adv.; bk.rev.; bibl.; illus.; circ. 400 (paid). (back issues avail.) **Indexed:** Ecol.Abstr., Ind.S.A.Per., Sport Fish.Abstr., Wild Life Rev., Wild.Rev., Zoo.Rec. **Document type:** academic/scholarly publication.
—Linda Hall; UnCover.
   Formerly (until 1990): Cormorant (ISSN 0250-0213)
   Refereed Serial

BIOLOGY — ORNITHOLOGY

598.2 US ISSN 0147-9725
CODEN: MBIREW
MARYLAND BIRDLIFE. 1945. q. $10 (effective 1997). Maryland Ornithological Society, Inc., Patuxent Wildlife Research, Laurel, MD 20708-4015. TEL 301-497-5641. FAX 301-497-5624. Ed. Chandler S. Robbins. adv.; bk.rev.; charts; illus.; cum.index every 5 yrs.; circ. 2,200 (controlled). **Indexed:** Sport Fish.Abstr., Wild.Rev., Zoo.Rec. **Document type:** academic/scholarly publication.
Refereed Serial

598.2 US ISSN 1065-2043
QL684.I3
MEADOWLARK; a journal of Illinois birds. 1992. q. Can.$25($20) (foreign Can.$30) (effective 1998). Illinois Ornithological Society, Box 1971, Evanston, IL 60204-1971. Ed. Sheryl DeVore. R&P contact: Eric Walters. adv. contact: Michael Hogg. circ. 700 (paid). **Document type:** academic/scholarly publication.
Description: Serves professional and amateur ornithologists interested in the avian fauna of Illinois.
Refereed Serial

598.2 MM ISSN 1013-3933
CODEN: ILMEE5
IL-MERILL. (Text in English) 1970. irreg. Malta Ornithological Society, P.O. Box 498, Valetta, Malta. Ed. Joe Sultana. R&P contact: Norman Chetchoti. **Indexed:** Sport Fish.Abstr., Wild.Rev., Zoo.Rec. **Document type:** academic/scholarly publication.

598.2 US ISSN 0026-3575
CODEN: MGNTAQ
MIGRANT. 1930. q. $4. Tennessee Ornithological Society, c/o Dr. Gary O. Wallace, Ed., Route 7, Sunrise Dr., Box 338, Elizabethton, TN 37643. TEL 615-542-8612. bk.rev.; bibl.; cum.index every 3 yrs. circ. 1,000. **Indexed:** Biol.Abstr., GeoRef., Sport Fish.Abstr., Wild.Rev., Zoo.Rec.
—BLDSC (5761.527000).

598.2 591 IT ISSN 1121-9181
MIGRATORI ALATI; rivista di gestione dell'ambiente e della fauna. 1978. bi-m. L.32000 (effective 1997). R G F di Realini Gianfranco e C. s.a.s., Via Cascine, 4, 21027 Ispra (VA), Italy. TEL 0332-781057. (Subscr. to: Via Valmaggia 6, 20139 Milan, Italy. TEL 39-2-5696090) Ed. Gianfranco Realini. adv.; bk.rev. circ. 5,000.
Formerly (until 1986): Migratori Acquatici (ISSN 1121-9173)
Refereed Serial

598.2 IT
MIGRAZIONE E CACCIA. 1959. bi-m. membership. Associazione Nazionale Uccellatori e Uccellinai (ANUU), Associazione dei Migratoristi Italiani per la Conservazione dell'Ambiente Naturale, Via Baschenis 11C, 24100 Bergamo, Italy. TEL 39-35-243825. FAX 39-35-236925. Ed. Pier Luigi Chierici. adv.; B&W page L.2500000, color page L.3800000. bk.rev.; bibl. circ. 65,000.
Former titles (until 1979): Uccellagione e Piccola Caccia; (until 1963): Bollettino dell'Ucellatore.

598.2 US ISSN 0737-0393
MISSISSIPPI KITE. 1965. s-a. $10. Mississippi Ornithological Society, Box Z, Mississippi State, MS 39762. E-mail: picus@ra.msstate.edu. (Subscr. to: Jan Dubuisson, 22410 Glad Acres, Pass Christian, MS 39571) Ed. Jerome A. Jackson. bk.rev. circ. 200. **Indexed:** Sport Fish.Abstr., Wild.Rev. **Document type:** academic/scholarly publication.
Refereed Serial

598.2 AU ISSN 1018-6190
CODEN: MONTEI
MONTICOLA. 1966. 2/yr. S.200. Internationale Arbeitsgemeinschaft fuer Alpenornithologie, c/o Dr. Franz Niederwolfsgruber, Pontlatzer Str. 49, A-6020 Innsbruck, Austria. **Indexed:** Sport Fish.Abstr., Wild.Rev., Zoo.Rec. **Document type:** academic/scholarly publication.

500.9 598.2 333.7 US ISSN 0886-6619
N J AUDUBON. (Supplement avail.: Records of New Jersey Birds) 1940. q. $25. New Jersey Audubon Society, 790 Ewing Ave., Box 125, Franklin Lakes, NJ 07417. TEL 201-891-1211. Ed. Peter Dunne. adv.; bk.rev.; charts; illus. circ. 8,000. (also avail. in microform from UMI; reprint service avail. from ISI) **Indexed:** Sport Fish.Abstr., Wild.Rev.
Formerly (until 1978): New Jersey Nature News (ISSN 0028-5862)
Description: Covers New Jersey's environment and the life, both wild and human, that it sustains. Emphasis is on conservation, education and research.

598.2 US ISSN 1078-5477
QL671
NATIONAL AUDUBON SOCIETY FIELD NOTES. 1947. q. $30 to individuals; institutions $35. National Audubon Society, 700 Broadway, New York, NY 10003. TEL 212-979-3000. URL: http://www.audubon.org/. Ed. Susan Roney Orennan. adv.; bk.rev.; illus.; maps; index. circ. 6,000. (also avail. in microform from UMI) **Indexed:** Biol.Abstr., Biol.& Agr.Ind., Biol.Dig., Deep Sea Res.& Oceanogr.Abstr., Key Word Ind.Wildl.Res., Sport Flsh.Abstr., Wild.Rev., Zoo.Rec. **Document type:** consumer publication.
—KR SourceOne; Linda Hall; UMI; UnCover.
Former titles (until 1994): American Birds (ISSN 0004-7686); (until 1971): Audubon Field Notes (ISSN 0097-7144)
Description: Devoted to bird life of North America.

NATURE SOCIETY NEWS; North America's backyard journal. see CONSERVATION

598.2 US ISSN 0028-1816
CODEN: NBBRA4
THE NEBRASKA BIRD REVIEW; a magazine of the ornithology of the Nebraska region. 1932. q. $12.50 (Canada & Mexico $15; elsewhere $17.50) (effective 1997). Nebraska Ornithologists' Union, Inc., 3018 O St., Lincoln, NE 68510-1529. TEL 402-435-3382. Ed. Rosalind Morris. R&P contact: Rosalind Morris. bk.rev.; charts; illus.; stat.; circ. 303 (paid). **Indexed:** Biol.Abstr., Sport Fish.Abstr., Wild.Rev., Zoo.Rec. **Document type:** academic/scholarly publication.
—BLDSC (6068.000000); Linda Hall; UnCover.

NEERLANDS POSTDUIVEN ORGAAN. see SPORTS AND GAMES

NEMOURIA. see BIOLOGY — Zoology

NEW HAMPSHIRE AUDUBON. see CONSERVATION

598.2 US
NEW HAMPSHIRE BIRD RECORDS. 1982. q. $15 to non-members; members $10. Audubon Society of New Hampshire, 3 Silk Farm Rd., Concord, NH 03301-8200. TEL 603-224-9909. FAX 603-226-0902. E-mail: nhaudubon@igc.apc.org. Ed. Becky Suomala. circ. 300. **Document type:** bulletin.
Description: Describes bird sightings in New Hampshire.

598.2 II ISSN 0028-9426
NEWSLETTER FOR BIRDWATCHERS. (Text in English) 1960. bi-m. Rs.40($20) (Birdwatchers Field Club of India) Navbharath Enterprises, No.10, Sirur Park "B" St., Sheshadripuram, Bangalore 560 020, India. TEL 91-80-364142. Ed. Zafar Futehally; Pub. S. Sridhar. adv.; bk.rev.; index. circ. 800. (processed) **Document type:** newsletter.

598 JA ISSN 0914-4307
NIHON CHORUI HYOSHIKI KYOKAISHI/JAPANESE BIRD BANDING ASSOCIATION. BULLETIN. (Text in Japanese; summaries in English) 1986. 3/yr. Nihon Chorui Hyoshiki Kyokai - Japanese Bird Banding Association, Yamashina Chorui Kenkyujo, Konoyama, Abiko-shi, Chiba-ken 270-11, Japan.

598.2 JA ISSN 1341-5360
NIHON KIJI MIZUTORI KYOKAISHI/REVIEW OF PHEASANT AND WATERFOWL OF THE WORLD BULLETIN. (Text in English, Japanese) 1968. 4/yr. 3600 Yen. Nihon Kiji Mizutori Kyokai - Pheasant and Waterfowl Society of Japan, 17-11 Kuwazu 3-chome, Higashisumiyoshi-ku, Osaka 546, Japan. FAX 81-06-719-2616. Ed. Yukio Nakata. bk.rev. **Document type:** bulletin.
Description: Covers ornithology through studies of the avian biology, and the biochemical and physiological mechanism of birds.
Refereed Serial

598.207 US ISSN 0363-8979
QL677.5 CODEN: NABBDK
NORTH AMERICAN BIRD BANDER. 1923. q. $15 membership. 35 Logan Hill Rd., Candor, NY 13743. E-mail: rjpl@cornell.edu. (Co-publishers: Inland Bird Banding Association; Eastern Bird Banding Association; Western Bird Banding Association) Ed. Robert Pantle. R&P contact: Robert Pantle. adv. contact: Roy Slack. bk.rev.; charts; illus. circ. 2,000. (also avail. in microform from UMI; back issues avail.) **Indexed:** Biol.Abstr., Sport Fish.Abstr., Wild.Rev., Zoo.Rec. **Document type:** academic/scholarly publication.
—Linda Hall; UMI; UnCover.
Incorporates (as of 1986): Inland Bird Banding Newsletter; Formed by the 1976 merger of: Western Bird Bander; (until vol.39): E B B A News (ISSN 0012-7485)
Description: Presents research results which involve banding as a tool.
Refereed Serial

598.2 333.7 US
NORTH AMERICAN SWANS. 1969. q. membership. Trumpeter Swan Society, 3800 County Rd. 24, Maple Plain, MN 55359. TEL 612-476-4663. FAX 612-1514. Ed. David K. Weaver. circ. 500. (back issues avail.) **Indexed:** Sport Fish.Abstr., Wild.Rev. **Document type:** newsletter.
Formerly (until June 1997): Trumpeter Swan Society Newsletter (ISSN 0742-2792)

598.2 SZ ISSN 0029-3725
CODEN: NOOIAV
NOS OISEAUX. (Text in French) 1913. q. 35 SFr. (foreign 40 SFr.). Societe Romande pour l'Etude et la Protection des Oiseaux, c/o Musee d'histoire naturelle, CH-2300 La Chaux-de-Fonds, Switzerland. TEL 41-22-7359982. FAX 41-22-7359982. (Subscr. to: C.C.P. 20-117-8, Neuchatel, Switzerland) Ed. Claude Guex. adv.; bk.rev.; abstr.; charts; illus.; cum.index every 2 yrs. circ. 2,700. **Indexed:** Biol.Abstr., Key Word Ind.Wildl.Res., Sport Fish.Abstr., Wild.Rev., Zoo.Rec. **Document type:** academic/scholarly publication.
Refereed Serial

598.2 PL ISSN 0550-0842
CODEN: NOORAO
NOTATKI ORNITOLOGICZNE/ORNITHOLOGICAL PAPERS. (Text in Polish; summaries in English) 1960. q. 25 Zl. (foreign $15). Polskie Towarzystwo Zoologiczne - Polish Zoological Society, Ul. Sienkiewicza 21, 50-335 Wroclaw, Poland. TEL 48-71-225041. FAX 48-71-222817. E-mail: keller@delta.sggw.waw.pl. Ed. Marek Keller. adv. contact: Tadeusz Stawarczyk. bk.rev. circ. 15,000. **Indexed:** AgroLibrex, Biol.Abstr., Ref.Zh., Sport Fish.Abstr., Wild.Rev., Zoo.Rec. **Document type:** academic/scholarly publication.
—BLDSC (6155.300000).
Description: Publishes scientific papers, original research reports from all fields of ornithology.
Refereed Serial

598.2 NZ ISSN 0029-4470
QL671 CODEN: NTNSAN
NOTORNIS. 1939. q. NZ.$40 to members (foreign NZ.$50); institutions NZ.$80 (effective 1992). Ornithological Society of New Zealand Inc., P.O. Box 12-397, Wellington, New Zealand. TEL 64-6-3546540. FAX 64-6-3546731. E-mail: glovei@hort.cri.nz. Ed. G.L. Lovei. bk.rev.; index. circ. 1,300. **Indexed:** Biol.Abstr., Geo.Abstr., So.Pac.Per.Ind., Sport Fish.Abstr., Wild.Rev., Zoo.Rec. **Document type:** academic/scholarly publication.
—BLDSC (6174.900000); UnCover. CCC.
Description: Publishes scientific articles and short notes on birds, with emphasis on New Zealand, the Pacific and the subantarctic areas.
Refereed Serial

BIOLOGY — ORNITHOLOGY

598.2 — CN
NOVA SCOTIA BIRDS. 1959. 3/yr. Can.$15 to individuals; institutions Can.$25 (effective 1997). Nova Scotia Bird Society, c/o Nova Scotia Museum, 1747 Summer St., Halifax, NS B3H 3A6, Canada. TEL 902-429-4610. FAX 902-477-6036. Ed. J. Shirley Cohrs. bk.rev.; illus. circ. 750. **Indexed:** Sport Fish.Abstr., Wild.Rev. **Document type:** academic/scholarly publication.
Formerly: Nova Scotia Bird Society. Newsletter (ISSN 0383-9567)

598.2 — US
NUTTALL ORNITHOLOGICAL CLUB. MEMOIRS. 1886. irreg., vol.12, 1995. price varies. Nuttall Ornithological Club, c/o Museum of Comparative Zoology, Harvard University, Cambridge, MA 02138. TEL 617-495-2471. Ed. Raymond A. Paynter, Jr. R&P contact: Raymond A. Paynter, Jr. **Document type:** monographic series.

598.2 — US — ISSN 0550-4082
CODEN: NUOPAQ
NUTTALL ORNITHOLOGICAL CLUB. PUBLICATIONS. 1957. irreg., no.25, 1995. price varies. Nuttall Ornithological Club, c/o Museum of Comparative Zoology, Harvard University, Cambridge, MA 02138. TEL 617-495-2471. Ed. R.A. Paynter, Jr. bibl.; charts; illus.; stat. circ. 1,000. (back issues avail.) **Indexed:** Zoo.Rec. **Document type:** academic/scholarly publication, monographic series.
—BLDSC (7099.400000).
Description: Scholarly monographs on ornithological topics from all areas of the world.
Refereed Serial

598.2 — NZ — ISSN 0111-2686
O S N Z NEWS. 1977. q. NZ.$40 to individual members (foreign $40); institutional members NZ.$80 (foreign $80). Ornithological Society of New Zealand Inc., P.O. Box 12-397, Wellington, New Zealand. TEL 64-6-3546540. FAX 65-6-3546731. E-mail: glovei@hort.cri.nz. Ed. Tony Crocker. adv.: page NZ.$150; adv. contact: Tony Crocker. bk.rev.; rec.rev.; software rev. **Indexed:** Sport Fish.Abstr., Wild.Rev. **Document type:** newsletter.
—BLDSC (6301.435000).

598.2 — GW — ISSN 0937-2695
OEKOLOGIE DER VOEGEL. BEIHEFTE. irreg. Kuratorium fuer Avifaunistische Forschung in Baden-Wuerttemberg e.V., Auf der Schanz 23-2, 71640 Ludwigsburg, Germany. **Indexed:** IBR, Key Word Ind.Wildl.Res.

598.2 — US — ISSN 0474-0750
CODEN: OOSBA7
OKLAHOMA ORNITHOLOGICAL SOCIETY. BULLETIN. 1968. q. $15. Oklahoma Ornithological Society, Box 65, Ada, OK 74821. E-mail: mduggan@mailclrek.ecok.edu. Ed. Charles R. Brown. illus. circ. 500. **Indexed:** Biol.Abstr., Sport Fish.Abstr., Wild Life Rev., Wild.Rev., Zoo.Rec. **Document type:** bulletin.

598.07234713 — CN — ISSN 0822-3890
CODEN: ONBIE8
ONTARIO BIRDS. 1983. 3/yr. Ontario Field Ornithologists, P.O. Box 62014 Postal Outlet, Burlington, ON L7R 4K2, Canada. E-mail: crinsb2@epo.gov.on.ca; ofo@interlog.com; URL: http://www.interlog.com/~ofo. Ed. William Crins; Pub. Jean Iron. bk.rev. circ. 800. **Indexed:** Zoo.Rec.
Description: Includes notes and articles about the status, distribution, identification and behavior of Ontario's birds, as well as site guides, letters and the annual report of the Ontario Bird Records Committee.
Refereed Serial

598.2 — NE — ISSN 0030-3224
SF461.A1
ONZE VOGELS. 1939. m. fl.60. Nederlandse Bond van Vogelliefhebbers, Postbox 74, 4600 AB Bergen Op Zoom, Netherlands. TEL 31-1640-35007. FAX 31-1640-39020. Ed.Bd. adv.: B&W page fl.1980, color page fl.2480; adv. contact: Piet Deley. bk.rev.; charts; illus.; index; circ. 43,000 (controlled). **Document type:** bulletin.

598.2 — US — ISSN 0030-5553
QL671 **CODEN: OROLA4**
ORIOLE. 1936. q. $10 to libraries. Georgia Ornithological Society, c/o Dr. Carolina H. Lane, 869 Clifton Rd., N.E., Atlanta, GA 30307. Ed. Terry Moore. adv.; bk.rev.; charts; illus.; cum.index every 5 yrs. circ. 450. **Indexed:** Biol.Abstr., Sport Fish.Abstr., Wild.Rev., Zoo.Rec.

598.2 — FI — ISSN 0030-5685
QL671 **CODEN: ORFEA6**
ORNIS FENNICA. (Text in English; summaries in Finnish or Swedish) 1924. q. FIM 140 in the Nordic countries; elsewhere $40 (effective 1997). Finnish Ornithological Society, University of Helsinki, Department of Ecology and Systematics, Division of Population Biology, P.O. Box 17, SF-00014 Helsinki, Finland. TEL 358-81-5531214. FAX 358-81-5531227. E-mail: mmonkkon@cc.oulu.fi. Ed. Mikko Monkkonen. R&P contact: Mikko Monkkonen. adv. contact: Esa Lammi. bk.rev.; abstr.; bibl.; charts; illus.; index; circ. 1,100 (controlled). (back issues avail.) **Indexed:** ASCA, Biol.Abstr., Chem.Abstr., Curr.Adv.Ecol.Sci., Curr.Cont., Ecol.Abstr., IBR, Key Word Ind.Wildl.Res., Sport Fish.Abstr., Wild Life Rev., Wild.Rev., Zoo.Rec. —BLDSC (6292.000000); Genuine Article; UnCover.
Description: Publishes descriptive, analytical and experimental papers on the ecology, behavior, and biogeography of birds, with particular geographical emphasis on Fennoscandia.
Refereed Serial

598.2 — HU — ISSN 1215-1610
ORNIS HUNGARICA. 1991. s-a. 500 Ft. to non-members; members 300 Ft; foreign $25. Hungarian Ornithological and Nature Conservation Society, Kolto u. 21, 1121 Budapest, Hungary. E-mail: 397MOS@huella.bitnet. (Ed. addr.: Ecological Research Group, Hungarian Natural History Museum, Baross u. 13, 1088 Budapest, Hungary. TEL 36-1-3130035. FAX 36-1-1171669) Ed. Csaba Moskat. adv.; bk.rev. **Document type:** academic/scholarly publication.
—BLDSC (6292.100000).
Description: Publishes research reports and short articles on the ecology, behaviour and biogeography of birds.
Refereed Serial

598.2 — US — ISSN 0078-6594
QL671 **CODEN: ORMNBZ**
ORNITHOLOGICAL MONOGRAPHS. 1964. irreg. American Ornithologists' Union, c/o Frederick Sheldon, Museum of Natural History, 119 Foster Hall, Louisiana State University, Baton Rouge, LA 70803. TEL 504-388-2855. (Alt. addr.: National Museum of Natural History, Smithsonian Institution, Washington, DC 20560) Ed. John Hagen. circ. 500. **Indexed:** Deep Sea Res.& Oceanogr.Abstr., Ornithol.Abstr. (1964-), Sport Fish.Abstr., Wild.Rev., Zoo.Rec. **Document type:** monographic series.
—BLDSC (6292.900000).

598.2 — US — ISSN 0274-564X
ORNITHOLOGICAL NEWSLETTER. 1976. bi-m. Ornithological Societies of North America, Business Office, Box 1897, Lawrence, KS 66044. TEL 913-843-1221. FAX 913-843-1274. Ed. Kevin McGowan. bk.rev. circ. 4,600. **Document type:** newsletter.
Description: Publishes society news and activities, reports of governmental actions concerning birds, announcements and other items of interest to members.

598.2 — UK — ISSN 0959-6739
CODEN: BOSEED
ORNITHOLOGICAL SOCIETY OF THE MIDDLE EAST BULLETIN. 1978. s-a. Ornithological Society of the Middle East, c/o The Lodge, Sandy, Beds. SG19 2DL, England. FAX 0767-692365. Ed. Mark Boyd. bk.rev. circ. 900. **Indexed:** Sport Fish.Abstr., Wild.Rev., Zoo.Rec. **Document type:** bulletin.
Formerly: Ornithological Society of Turkey Bulletin.
Description: General and topical aspects of birdwatching and ornithology in Turkey and the Middle East.

598.2 — SZ — ISSN 0030-5707
CODEN: ORBEAK
DER ORNITHOLOGISCHE BEOBACHTER. (Text in German; summaries in English) 1902. 4/yr. 55 SFr. (foreign 65 SFr.) (effective 1996). Ala - Schweizerische Gesellschaft fuer Vogelkunde und Vogelschutz, Ruettenenweg 63, CH-4313 Moehlin, Switzerland. Ed. Dr. Christian Marti. adv.; bk.rev.; bibl.; charts; illus.; index. circ. 1,500. **Indexed:** Biol.Abstr., Ecol.Abstr., IBR, Key Word Ind.Wildl.Res., Sport Fish.Abstr., Wild.Rev., Zoo.Rec. **Document type:** academic/scholarly publication.
—BLDSC (6293.170000).

598.2 — GW — ISSN 0030-5723
QL671 **CODEN: ORMIAJ**
ORNITHOLOGISCHE MITTEILUNGEN. (Text mainly in German; occasionally in English) 1948. m. DM.62 (foreign DM.67). Biologie-Verlag, Schlossallee 10a, 65388 Schlangenbad, Germany. Ed. Herbert Bruns. adv.; bk.rev.; bibl.; charts; illus.; index. **Document type:** academic/scholarly publication.
—Linda Hall.

598.2 — GW — ISSN 0940-3256
QL671 **CODEN: ORANEC**
ORNITHOLOGISCHER ANZEIGER. (Summaries in English) 1919. 3/yr. DM.65. Ornithologische Gesellschaft in Bayern e.V., c/o the Secretary General, Werdenfelserstr. 19, 82490 Frachant, Germany. TEL 49-8821-68305. E-mail: ksc@pbs.esri.isar.de. Ed. Tino Mischler. bk.rev.; abstr.; illus.; stat.; index. circ. 1,200. **Indexed:** Biol.Abstr., IBR, Key Word Ind.Wildl.Res., Sport Fish.Abstr., Wild.Rev., Zoo.Rec. **Document type:** academic/scholarly publication.
Incorporates (in 1996): Ornithologische Verhandlungen (ISSN 0940-3248); Which was formerly (until 1991): Ornithologischen Gesellschaft in Bayern. Verhandlungen (ISSN 0177-1671); Formerly: Ornithologischen Gesellschaft in Bayern. Anzeiger (ISSN 0030-5715)

598.2 581 550
333.7 — GW — ISSN 0179-5813
ORNITHOLOGISCHER VEREIN ZU HILDESHEIM. MITTEILUNGEN. 1977. s-a. DM.15($7.50) Ornithologischer Verein zu Hildesheim e.V., c/o Josef Aberle, Kurzer Anger 8, 31139 Hildesheim, Germany. FAX 05067-25212. Ed. Peter Becker. bk.rev. circ. 400.

598.2 — SA — ISSN 0030-6525
QL671 **CODEN: OSTHAO**
OSTRICH. (Text in English; summaries occasionally in Afrikaans) 1930. q. $55 to individuals; institutions $60 (includes subscr. to Africa Birds & Birding). Birdlife South Africa, P.O. Box 84394, Greenside, Johannesburg 2034, South Africa. TEL 27-11-8884147. bk.rev.; abstr.; index. circ. 1,500. (back issues avail.) **Indexed:** Biol.Abstr., Curr.Adv.Ecol.Sci., Curr.Cont., Geo.Abstr., Ind.S.A.Per., Key Word Ind.Wildl.Res., Sport Fish.Abstr., Wild Life Rev., Wild.Rev., Zoo.Rec.
—Genuine Article; Linda Hall; UMI; UnCover.

OSTRICH NEWS. see *AGRICULTURE — Poultry And Livestock*

OSTRICH NEWS RATITE DIRECTORY. see *AGRICULTURE — Poultry And Livestock*

598.2 — US
PACIFIC SEABIRDS. 1974. 2/yr. $25 to institutions (foreign $30) (effective 1996 & 1997). Pacific Seabird Group, 4505 University Way, N.E., Box 179, Seattle, WA 98105. E-mail: sspeich@azstarnet.com; URL: http://www-nmnh.sci.edu/BIRDNET/PacBirds/index.htm#pubs. (Subscr. to: P S G, c/o Jan Hodder, Treas., Oregon Institute of Marine Biology, Charleston, OR 94970. TEL 541-888-2581. FAX 541-888-3250) Ed. Steven Speich. R&P contact: Steven Speich. adv.; bk.rev. circ. 400. **Indexed:** Sport Fish.Abstr., Wild.Rev., Zoo.Rec. **Document type:** bulletin.
Formerly: Pacific Seabird Group Bulletin (ISSN 0740-3771)
Description: Covers issues pertaining to seabird management.
Refereed Serial

598.2 — US — ISSN 0031-2703
QL671 **CODEN: PPGNAZ**
PASSENGER PIGEON; a magazine of Wisconsin bird study. 1939. q. $18. Wisconsin Society for Ornithology, W330 N8275 W. Shore Dr., Hartland, WI 53029. TEL 414-966-1072. FAX 414-966-1072. Ed. Rebecca Isenring. R&P contact: Alex Kailing. adv. contact: Alex Kailing. bk.rev.; rec.rev.; charts; illus.; cum.index. circ. 1,300. **Indexed:** Biol.Abstr., Key Word Ind.Wildl.Res., Sport Fish.Abstr., Wild.Rev., Zoo.Rec. **Document type:** academic/scholarly publication.
—UnCover.

BIOLOGY — ORNITHOLOGY

598.2 II ISSN 0031-3297
QL671 CODEN: PAVOA8
PAVO; the Indian journal of ornithology. (Text in English) 1963. s-a. Rs.95 (foreign $25). Society of Animal Morphologists & Physiologists, c/o Maharaja Sayajirao University of Baroda, Dept. of Zoology, Faculty of Science, Baroda 390002, India. Ed. Bonny Pilo. R&P contact: Bonny Pilo. adv.; bk.rev.; charts; illus.; index. circ. 200. **Indexed:** Biol.Abstr., Chem.Abstr., Curr.Adv.Ecol.Sci., IBR, Nutr.Abstr. **Document type:** academic/scholarly publication.
—CASDDS; UnCover.

598.4 US
CODEN: SPNWEW
PENGUIN CONSERVATION. 1988. 3/yr. $15. Cynthia Cheney, Ed. & Pub., 8060 Upper Applegate Rd., Jacksonville, OR 97530-9314. TEL 541-899-1114. FAX 541-899-1131. E-mail: hgpf@teleport.com. bk.rev.; software rev. circ. 450. **Indexed:** Sport Fish.Abstr., Wild.Rev., Zoo.Rec. (1992-). **Document type:** academic/scholarly publication.
—UnCover.
Formerly: Spheniscus Penguin Newsletter (ISSN 1045-0076)
Description: Publishes material dealing with the management, conservation, behavior and biology of penguins in captivity and in the wild.

PEREGRINE FUND NEWSLETTER. see *CONSERVATION*

598.2 AT ISSN 0812-8014
R A O U REPORT. irreg. Royal Australasian Ornithologists Union, 415 Riversdale Rd., E. Hawthorn, Vic. 3123, Australia. TEL 61-3-98822622. FAX 61-3-98822677. R&P contact: Bill Fenton. **Document type:** bulletin.
—UnCover. **CCC.**

RACING PIGEON PICTORIAL. see *PETS*

598 JA
RAICHO CHOSA HOKOKUSHO/RESEARCH REPORT ON PTARMIGAN. (Text in Japanese) a. Toyama Raicho Kenkyukai - Toyama Ptarmigan Association, Toyama Prefectural Government, 1-7 Shinsogawa, Toyama-shi, Toyama-ken 930, Japan.

598.2 333.7 US ISSN 1048-8030
THE RAPTOR REPORT. 1973-1983; resumed 1993. a. $15 (overseas $25) (for 2 yrs.). Society for the Preservation of Birds of Prey, c/o J. Richard Hilton, Ed., Mar Vista Sta., Box 66070, Los Angeles, CA 90066. TEL 310-285-3091. bk.rev.; illus.; stat. circ. 800. **Document type:** newsletter.
Supersedes: California Condor.

598.2 US ISSN 0034-0146
CODEN: RAVNAR
RAVEN (LYNCHBURG). 1930. s-a. $15. Virginia Society of Ornithology, c/o Thelma Dalmas, 520 Rainbow Forest Dr., Lynchburg, VA 24502. FAX 804-239-2730. Ed. Teta Kain. bk.rev.; bibl.; charts; stat.; index. circ. 700. **Indexed:** Zoo.Rec. **Document type:** academic/scholarly publication.
Description: Features articles about Virginia birdlife.

509 598.2 US
RECORDS OF NEW JERSEY BIRDS. (Supplement to: N J Audubon) q. New Jersey Audubon Society, Box 693, Bernardsville, NJ 07924. TEL 908-766-5787. (Subscr. to: Box 125, Franklin Lakes, NJ 07417) **Indexed:** Sport Fish.Abstr., Wild.Rev.
Formerly: (until 1994): N J Audubon. Supplement.
Description: Listings of bird sightings in New Jersey, plus reports on wildlife research.

598.207 US ISSN 0034-2165
CODEN: RDSTAH
REDSTART. 1933. q. $14 to non-members. Brooks Bird Club, Inc., 423 Warwood Ave., Wheeling, WV 26003. TEL 614-635-9246. Ed. Albert R. Buckelew, Jr. bk.rev.; charts; illus.; stat.; index. circ. 650. (back issues avail.) **Indexed:** Biol.Abstr., Sport Fish.Abstr., Wild.Rev.
—UnCover.
Description: Original papers in the field of natural history. Contains field and banding notes and reports of the Foray, Sortie, Christmas Count and other events.

RICERCHE DI BIOLOGIA DELLA SELVAGGINA. SUPPLEMENTO. see *BIOLOGY — Zoology*

598.2 PL ISSN 0035-5429
QL671 CODEN: RINGBN
THE RING; ringing - migration - monitoring. (Text in English) 1954. s-a. $30 (effective 1997). Polish Zoological Society, Przebendowo, 84-210 Choczewo, Poland. TEL 4858-72-33-15-220. Ed. Dr. Przemyslaw Busse. bk.rev.; charts; illus.; cum.index every 3 yrs. circ. 600. **Indexed:** Key Word Ind.Wildl.Res., Sport Fish.Abstr., Wild.Rev., Zoo.Rec. **Document type:** academic/scholarly publication.
—BLDSC (7971.490000); Linda Hall.

598.2 UK ISSN 0307-8698
QL671 CODEN: RIMIDQ
RINGING AND MIGRATION. 1975. 3/yr. £12.50 to non-members; members £8. British Trust for Ornithology, The Nunnery, Nunnery Pl., Thetford, Norfolk IP24 2PU, England. TEL 01842-750050. FAX 01842-750030. **Indexed:** Biol.Abstr., Curr.Adv.Ecol.Sci., Ecol.Abstr., Geo.Abstr., Sport Fish.Abstr., Wild.Rev., Zoo.Rec.
—BLDSC (7971.492000); Linda Hall; UnCover.

598.2 IT ISSN 0035-6875
QL690.I8 CODEN: RIORAQ
RIVISTA ITALIANA DI ORNITOLOGIA. 1909. s-a. L.50000 (effective 1996). Societa Italiana di Scienze Naturali, Corso Venezia 55, 20121 Milan, Italy. TEL 39-2-62085405. Ed. Cesare Conci. bk.rev.; illus.; index. circ. 850. (back issues avail.) **Indexed:** Biol.Abstr., IBR, Sport Fish.Abstr., Wild.Rev., Zoo.Rec. **Document type:** academic/scholarly publication.
—BLDSC (7987.450000).

598.65 BE ISSN 0778-2152
ROYALE FEDERATION COLOMBOPHILE BELGE. BULLETIN NATIONAL. Dutch edition: Koninklijke Belgische Duivenliefhebbersbond. Bondsblad (ISSN 0778-2144) (Text in French) 1956. bi-m. 250 BEF. Royale Federation Colombophile Belge - Koninklijke Belgische Duivenliefhebbersbond, 39 rue de Livourne, 1050 Brussels, Belgium. FAX 32-2-538-5721. Ed. Marcel Van Den Driessche. adv. **Document type:** bulletin.
Formerly: Royale Federation Colombophile Belge. Bulletin Federal (ISSN 0035-9319)

598.2 DK ISSN 0108-9315
SANDEVIFTEN. 1983. q. membership. Dansk Ornithologisk Forening i Ringkoebing Amt, Vesterbrogade 140, 1620 Copenhagen V, Denmark. Ed.Bd. adv.; bk.rev.; illus. circ. 300.
Formerly: Fugleiagttagelser i Ringkoebing Amt.

598.2 UK ISSN 0260-4736
CODEN: SANDE6
SANDGROUSE. 1980. s-a. £7 includes Bulletin. Ornithological Society of the Middle East, c/o The Lodge, Sandy, Beds. SG19 2DL, England. FAX 0767-692365. Ed. Duncan Brooks. circ. 900. **Indexed:** Ref.Zh., Sport Fish.Abstr., Wild Life Rev., Wild.Rev., Zoo.Rec.
—BLDSC (8072.955500).
Formerly: Turkish Bird Report.
Description: All aspects of ornithology in Turkey and Middle East.

598.2 US
SANDPIPER. 1968. m. Redwood Region Audubon Society, Box 1054, Eureka, CA 95501. Ed. Chad Roberts. circ. 1,500. (also avail. in microfilm from LIB)
Description: Describes current programs and conservation issues of relevance to the society.

598.2 CN ISSN 0080-6552
SASKATCHEWAN NATURAL HISTORY SOCIETY. SPECIAL PUBLICATIONS. 1958. irreg. price varies. Nature Saskatchewan, 1860 Lorne St., Rm. 206, Regina, SK S4P 2L7, Canada. TEL 306-780-9273. FAX 306-780-9263. Ed. Mary Gilliland. **Indexed:** Wild Life Rev. **Document type:** academic/scholarly publication.

598.2 US ISSN 0582-2637
CODEN: SCSSEM
SCISSORTAIL. 1951. q. $15. Oklahoma Ornithological Society, Box 65, Ada, OK 74821. E-mail: mduggan@mailclerk.ecok.edu. Ed. Richard A. Stuart. circ. 500. **Indexed:** Sport Fish.Abstr., Wild.Rev., Zoo.Rec. **Document type:** newsletter.

598.2 KE ISSN 0250-4162
QL692.E16
SCOPUS. (Text in English) 1977. 3/yr. £10($16) dM.30. East Africa Natural History Society, Ornithological Sub-Committee, P.O. Box 15194, Nairobi, Kenya. TEL 254-2-891419. Ed. Graeme Backhurst. R&P contact: D.A. Turner. adv. contact: D.A. Turner. bk.rev.; circ. 265 (paid). **Indexed:** P.L.E.S.A. **Document type:** academic/scholarly publication.
—BLDSC (8205.941000).
Description: Publishes original contributions on all aspects of the ornithology of eastern Africa, from the Sudan to Mozambique.
Refereed Serial

598.2 UK ISSN 0268-3199
SCOTTISH BIRD NEWS. 1986. q. Scottish Ornithologists Club, 21 Regent Terrace, Edinburgh EH7 5BT, Scotland. TEL 44-131-556-6042. Ed. Stan da Prato. adv. contact: Sylvia Laing. **Document type:** newsletter.
—BLDSC (8206.340000).

598.2 UK ISSN 0036-9144
QL690.S4 CODEN: SCTBB7
SCOTTISH BIRDS. 1958. s-a. £30. Scottish Ornithologists Club, 21 Regent Terrace, Edinburgh EH7 5BT, Scotland. TEL 44-131-556-6042. Ed. Stan Da Prato. adv. contact: Sylvia Lang. bk.rev.; charts; illus.; cum.index every 2 yrs. circ. 3,000. **Indexed:** Biol.Abstr., Geo.Abstr., Key Word Ind.Wildl.Res., Sport Fish.Abstr., Wild Life Rev., Wild.Rev., Zoo.Rec. **Document type:** academic/scholarly publication.
—BLDSC (8206.400000).
Refereed Serial

598.2 UK ISSN 0267-9310
CODEN: SEABEV
SEABIRD. 1969. a. £10 to individuals; libraries £15. Seabird Group, c/o R.S.P.B., The Lodge, Sandy, Beds. SG19 2DL, England. Ed. S. Wanless. bk.rev. circ. 500. **Indexed:** Sport Fish.Abstr., Wild.Rev., Zoo.Rec. **Document type:** academic/scholarly publication.
—BLDSC (8213.703000).
Former titles (until 1984): Seabird Report (ISSN 0080-8415); Seabird Bulletin.
Description: Papers on all aspects of seabird ecology, behavior, taxonomy and conservation.
Refereed Serial

598.2 GW ISSN 0722-2947
QL671
SEEVOEGEL. (Text in English, German) 1980. q. DM.48 membership. Verein Jorsand zum Schutze der Seevoegel und der Natur e.V., c/o Uwe Schneider, Haus der Natur Wulfsdorf, 22926 Ahrensburg, Germany. TEL 49-4102-32656. FAX 49-4102-31983. Ed. Eike Hartwig. adv. contact: Uwe Schneider. bk.rev. circ. 6,000. **Indexed:** Key Word Ind.Wildl.Res. **Document type:** academic/scholarly publication.

598.2 SP
SOCIEDAD ESPANOLA DE ORNITOLOGIA. MONOGRAFIAS. 1988. irreg. price varies. Sociedad Espanola de Ornitologia, c/o Fac. de Biologia, Univ. Complutense de Madrid, Ciudad Universitaria, 28040 Madrid, Spain. Ed. Juan Varela. **Indexed:** Sport Fish.Abstr., Wild.Rev. **Document type:** monographic series.

SOCIETA SARDA DI SCIENZE NATURALI. BOLLETTINO. see *BIOLOGY*

598.2 UK ISSN 0081-2048
SOMERSET BIRDS. 1924. a. £3. Somerset Ornithological Society, Barnfield, Tower Hill Rd., Crewkerne, Somerset, England. Ed. D.K. Ballance. circ. 500.

598.8 JA
SONGU POSUTO/SONG POST. (Text in Japanese) 1983 bi-m. 3500 Yen. Nihon Yacho no Kai, Kyoto Shibu - Wild Bird Society of Japan, Kyoto Branch, Hashimoto Bunka Bldg., 2-1, Saga-Yanagida-cho, Ukyo-ku, Kyoto 616, Japan. TEL 81-771-25-7103. FAX 81-771-25-7103. Ed. Tetsuo Sawashima. **Document type:** newsletter.
Description: Contains bird walk schedules, bird watching spot guide, research reports and other bird related information.

BIOLOGY — ORNITHOLOGY

598.2   US   ISSN 0038-3252
CODEN: SDBNAR
SOUTH DAKOTA BIRD NOTES. 1949. q. $9 to non-members. South Dakota Ornithologists' Union, Northern State University, Mathematics and Sciences, 1200 S. Jay St., Aberdeen, SD 57401-7198. TEL 605-626-2456. FAX 605-626-3022. E-mail: tallmand@wolf.northern.edu. Ed. Dan Tallman. adv.; bk.rev.; charts; illus.; cum.index every 5 yrs. circ. 400. **Indexed:** Biol.Abstr., Sport Fish.Abstr., Wild Life Rev., Wild.Rev., Zoo.Rec. **Document type:** academic/scholarly publication.

598.2 639.9   SA   ISSN 1018-7634
CODEN: SOBIDO
SOUTHERN BIRDS. (Text in English) 1975. irregg. price varies. Witwatersrand Bird Club, P.O. Box 72091, Parkview 2122, South Africa. Ed. Carl J. Vernon. adv.; bk.rev.; abstr.; bibl. circ. 600. (back issues avail.) **Indexed:** Biol.Abstr., Ind.S.A.Per., Sport Fish.Abstr., Wild.Rev., Zoo.Rec.

598.2   DK   ISSN 0109-274X
STIGSNAES; rapport. 1981. a. DKK 30. Dansk Ornithologisk Forening i Vestsjaellands, Stigsnaes Fuglestation - Stignaes Bird Observatory, Lille Valmosevej 1, DK-4160 Herlufmagle, Denmark. Ed. Bent Moeller Soerensen. illus.

598   JA   ISSN 0910-6901
STRIX/NIHON YACHO NO KAI KENKYU HOKOKU; a journal of field ornithology. (Text in Japanese; summaries in English, Japanese) 1982. a. Nihon Yacho no Kai - Wild Bird Society of Japan, 15-8 Nanpeidai, Shibuya-ku, Tokyo 150, Japan. TEL 81-3-3463-8862. FAX 81-3-3463-8844. E-mail: KGB00707@niftyserve.or.jp.
—BLDSC (8474.167000).

598.2   US   ISSN 0197-9922
CODEN: SABIET
STUDIES IN AVIAN BIOLOGY. 1978. irregg. price varies. Cooper Ornithological Society, Inc. (Riverside), Department of Biology, University of California at Riverside, Riverside, CA 92521. FAX 909-787-4286. Ed. John T. Rotenberry. R&P contact: John T. Rotenberry. circ. 1,000 (controlled). **Indexed:** Ornithol.Abstr. (1955-), Sport Fish.Abstr., Wild.Rev., Zoo.Rec. **Document type:** monographic series, academic/scholarly publication.
—BLDSC (8489.580000); Linda Hall.
    Supersedes (1900-1974): Pacific Coast Avifauna.
    Description: Monographic studies in various aspects of avian biology.
    Refereed Serial

598.2   AT   ISSN 1037-258X
CODEN: SUNBE4
THE SUNBIRD. 1970. q. Aus.$25. Queensland Ornithological Society, P.O. Box 97, St. Lucia, Qld. 4067, Australia. Ed. Peter Britton. adv.; bk.rev.; charts; illus.; index. circ. 500. **Indexed:** Sport Fish.Abstr., Wild.Rev., Zoo.Rec. **Document type:** academic/scholarly publication.
—BLDSC (8533.530000).

598.2   CN   ISSN 0834-7050
TCHEBEC. 1970-1985; resumed 1992. a. Can.$25 membership. Quebec Society for the Protection of Birds, Box 43, Station B, Montreal, PQ H3B 3J5, Canada. TEL 514-247-2185. Ed. David Smith. illus.; stat. circ. 750. (back issues avail.) **Document type:** newsletter.
    Description: Reports on bird sightings in the Montreal area and activities of the PQSPB.

598.2   US
TENNESSEE WARBLER. 1979. s-a. Tennessee Ornithological Society, Box 402, Norris, TN 37828.

598.2   US   ISSN 0040-4543
CODEN: TOSBAS
TEXAS ORNITHOLOGICAL SOCIETY. BULLETIN. 1967. a. $10 membership. Texas Ornithological Society, c/o Angelo State University, Department of Biology, San Angelo, TX 76909. Ed. Terry C. Maxwell. bk.rev.; abstr.; illus. circ. 800. **Indexed:** Biol.Abstr., Zoo.Rec. (until 19??).

598.2 333.95   UK
THREATENED BIRDS OF AFRICA AND RELATED ISLANDS; the ICBP-IUCN Red Data Book. (Former name of issuing body: International Council for Bird Preservation) 1985. irregg. £27.30($52.25) BirdLife International, Wellbrook Ct., Girton Rd., Cambridge CB3 0NA, England. TEL 44-1223-277318. FAX 44-1223-277200. TELEX 818794 ICBP G. (Subscr. to: University Press Marketing, The Old Mill, Mill St., Wantage, Oxon. OX12 9AB, England. TEL 44-1235-766662. FAX 44-1235-766545; Subscr. in the Americas to: Smithsonian Institution Press, Box 960, Herndon, VA 22070-0960. TEL 703-435-7064. FAX 703-689-0660) (Co-sponsor: United Nations. International Union for Conservation of Nature and Natural Resources) illus.
    Description: Describes threatened species of African birds with diagnoses of local threats and specific conservation recommendations.

598.2 333.95   UK
THREATENED BIRDS OF THE AMERICAS; the ICBP-IUCN Red Data Book. (Former name of issuing body: International Council for Bird Preservation) 1992. irregg. £32.30($77.25) BirdLife International, Wellbrook Ct., Girton Rd., Cambridge CB3 0NA, England. TEL 44-1223-277318. FAX 44-1223-227200. TELEX 818794 ICBP G. (Subscr. to: University Press Marketing, The Old Mill, Mill St., Wantage, Oxon. OX12 9AB, England. TEL 44-1235-766662. FAX 44-1235-766545; Subscr. in the Americas to: Smithsonian Institution Press, Box 960, Herndon, VA 22070-0960. TEL 703-435-7064. FAX 703-689-0660) (Co-sponsor: United Nations. International Union for Conservation of Nature and Natural Resources) illus. **Document type:** academic/scholarly publication.
    Description: Describes threatened species of North, South, and Central American birds, with diagnoses of local threats and specific conservation recommendations.

598.2 636.596   SZ
TIERWELT. w. 69 SFr. (foreign 118 SFr.). (Schweizerische Gesellschaft fuer Ornithologie, Gefluegel-, Kaninchen-, und Taubenzucht) Tierwelt Verlag, CH-4800 Zofingen, Switzerland. TEL 063-509494. FAX 063-511059.

598   JA
TOKUSHU CHORUI CHOSA. (Text in Japanese) a. (Nihon Yacho no Kai - Wild Bird Society of Japan) Kankyocho - Environment Agency, 2-2 Kasumigaseki 1-chome, Chiyoda-ku, Tokyo 100, Japan.

598.2   IS   ISSN 0333-7383
QL696.F3   CODEN: TORGE8
TORGOS. (Text in Hebrew; summaries in English) s-a. IS.26. Society for the Protection of Nature in Israel, 4 Hashfela St., Tel Aviv 66183, Israel. TEL 972-3-375063. Ed.Bd. **Indexed:** Sport Fish.Abstr., Wild.Rev., Zoo.Rec.
    Incorporates: Tzufit (ISSN 0334-1240)
    Description: Features articles about birds found in Israel.

598   JA
TOSHICHO KENKYUKAI KAISHI/URBAN BIRDS. (Text in Japanese) 4/yr. Toshicho Kenkyukai - Urban Bird Society of Japan, 31-16-901 Honcho, Wako-shi, Saitama-ken 351-01, Japan.

598.2 639.9   US   ISSN 1064-6094
SK325.T8
TURKEY CALL. 1973. bi-m. $25. National Wild Turkey Federation, Inc., Box 530, 770 Augusta Rd., Edgefield, SC 29824-0530. TEL 803-637-3106. FAX 803-637-0034. Ed. Jay Langston. R&P contact: Jay Langston. adv. contact: Danny Young. illus.; stat. circ. 120,000. **Document type:** consumer publication. —UnCover.
    Description: Dedicated to the education, enlightenment, and entertainment of wild turkey enthusiasts everywhere - people who hunt, study, and actively support the restoration and conservation of the American wild turkey.

598.2   IT   ISSN 0393-1218
UCCELLI D'ITALIA; e pagine del museo. (Text in Italian; summaries in English) 1976. a. L.40000 (foreign L.50000). Societa Ornitologica Italiana, c/o Museo Ornitologico e di Scienze Naturali, Loggettta Lombardesca, 48100 Ravenna, Italy. TEL 39-544-482874. FAX 39-544-213641. adv.; bk.rev.; bibl.; charts; illus.; stat.; index. (back issues avail.) **Indexed:** Key Word Ind.Wildl.Res.

598.2   US
UNIVERSITY OF CALIFORNIA AT DAVIS. GAME BIRD WORKSHOP. PROCEEDINGS. 1971. biennial. price varies. University of California at Davis, Department of Avian Sciences, Davis, CA 95616. TEL 916-752-3513. FAX 916-752-8960. E-mail: raernst@ucdavis.edu. Ed. Dr. R.A. Ernst. circ. 100.

598.2   SW   ISSN 0042-2649
QL671   CODEN: VARFAR
VAAR FAAGELVAERLD. (Supplement avail. (ISSN 0504-9520)) (Text in Swedish; summaries in English) 1942. 8/yr. SEK 390 (foreign SEK 470). Sveriges Ornitologiska Foerening, Ekhagsvaegen 3, S-104 05 Stockholm, Sweden. TEL 46-8-612-25-30. FAX 46-8-612-25-36. Ed. Anders Wirdheim. adv. contact: Anders Wirdheim. bk.rev.; abstr.; bibl.; charts; illus.; maps; stat.; index. circ. 10,000. (back issues avail.) **Indexed:** Biol.Abstr., Sport Fish.Abstr., Wild.Rev., Zoo.Rec.

598.2   SW   ISSN 0348-1360
VAERMLANDSORNITOLOGEN. 1973. s-a. SEK 50 membership (effective 1994). Wermlands Ornitologiska Foerening, c/o J.-E. Hermansson, Goestav. 35, S-663 02 Hammaroe, Sweden.

598.2   CN   ISSN 0316-8239
VANCOUVER ISLAND CAGE BIRD SOCIETY BULLETIN. 1954. m. Can.$16. Vancouver Island Cage Bird Society, 1064 Marigold Rd., Victoria, BC V8Z 4S2, Canada. TEL 604-479-1338. Ed. Wayne Green. adv.; bk.rev.; charts; illus. circ. 2,200. (back issues avail.)
    Description: Promotes captive breeding.

598.2   FR   ISSN 1248-2056
VIVRE AVEC LES OISEAUX.* 1947. bi-m. 168 F. (foreign 192 F.). Societe Europeenne de Magazines, 59 rue du Faubourg Poissonniere, 75009 Paris, France. TEL 1-47-70-94-62. FAX 1-45-23-36-81. Ed. Francoise De Korte; Pub. Gilles Barissat. adv.: B&W page 10000 F., color page 16000 F.; trim 235 x 171; adv. contact: Dominique Balen. illus.
    Former titles (until 1993): Journal des Oiseaux (ISSN 0181-8910); Journal des Oiseaux du Monde; Journal des Oiseaux (ISSN 0075-4080)

639.978   GW   ISSN 0173-0266
VOGEL UND UMWELT; Zeitschrift fuer Vogelkunde und Naturschutz in Hessen. 1980. 3/yr. DM.25. Hessisches Ministerium fuer Landesentwicklung, Wohnen, Landwirtschaft, Forsten und Naturschutz, Hoelderlinstr. 1-3, 65187 Wiesbaden, Germany. TEL 0611-817-0. FAX 0611-841649. bk.rev. circ. 2,000. (back issues avail.) **Indexed:** Key Word Ind.Wildl.Res. **Document type:** government publication.

598.2   NE   ISSN 0042-7985
CODEN: VOGLEO
VOGELJAAR. (Text in Dutch; some summaries in English or German) 1953. bi-m. fl.25 (foreign fl.35). Stichting Het Vogeljaar, Bilderdijklaan 25, 3743 HR Baarn, Netherlands. TEL 31-355-420303. Ed. Jaap Taapken. adv.; bk.rev.; abstr.; bibl.; charts; illus.; cum.index. circ. 16,000. **Indexed:** Excerp.Med., Sport Fish.Abstr., Wild.Rev., Zoo.Rec.

598.2 591   GW   ISSN 0340-403X
VOGELKUNDLICHE BERICHTE AUS NIEDERSACHSEN. (Text in German; summaries in English) 1969. 2/yr. DM.40. Niedersaechsische Ornithologische Vereinigung, Muehlenstr. 9, 21755 Hechthausen, Germany. TEL 49-4753-708. FAX 49-4753-8185. Ed. Juergen Ludwig. bk.rev.; bibl.; charts; illus.; index. circ. 1,000. (back issues avail.) **Indexed:** Biol.Abstr. **Document type:** academic/scholarly publication.
—BLDSC (9251.370000).

598.2   GW   ISSN 0178-0239
VOGELKUNDLICHE HEFTE EDERTAL.* 1975. a. DM.8. Hessische Gesellschaft fuer Ornithologie und Naturschutz, Arbeitskreis Edertal, c/o W. Luebcke, Rathausweg 1, 34549 Edertal, Germany. Ed.Bd. bk.rev. circ. 750. **Indexed:** IBR.

598.2   NE   ISSN 0167-8280
VOGELS. 1968. 6/yr. fl.45 membership. Vogelbeschirming Nederlands, Driebergseweg 16C, 3708 JB Zeist, Netherlands. TEL 31-30-6937700. FAX 31-30-6918844. Ed. Frans Buissink. R&P contact: H. Peeters. adv. contact: Th. Hesen. **Document type:** bulletin.
—SWETS.
    Formerly (until 1981): Lepelaar (ISSN 0166-8056)

BIOLOGY — ORNITHOLOGY

598.2   GW   ISSN 0049-6650
CODEN: VOGLAK
VOGELWARTE. 1930. 2/yr. DM.65.30 per no. (Vogelwarte Helgoland and Vogelwarte Radolfzell) Verlagsdruckerei Schmidt GmbH, Nuernbergerstr. 27-31, 91413 Neustadt, Germany. TEL 49-9161-8860-0. FAX 49-9161-1378. Eds. G. Thielcke, W. Winkel. bk.rev. circ. 3,000. **Indexed:** Biol.Abstr., Curr.Adv.Ecol.Sci., Ecol.Abstr., IBR, Key Word Ind.Wildl.Res., Sport Fish.Abstr., Wild.Rev., Zoo.Rec. **Document type:** academic/scholarly publication.
—BLDSC (9251.380000).

598.2   GW   ISSN 0042-7993
CODEN: VGLWAM
DIE VOGELWELT; Beitraege zur Vogelkunde. 1880. bi-m. DM.68 (effective 1997). (Dachverband Deutscher Avifaunisten) Aula Verlag GmbH, Postfach 1366, 65003 Wiesbaden, Germany. TEL 49-611-379599. FAX 49-611-373060. E-mail: aula-verlag@t-online.de. Eds. A.J. Helbig, M. Flade. R&P contact: Irmgard Meissl. adv. contact: Petra Muen. bk.rev.; abstr.; charts; illus.; index. **Indexed:** Biol.Abstr., IBR, Key Word Ind.Wildl.Res., Sport Fish.Abstr., Wild.Rev., Zoo.Rec. **Document type:** academic/scholarly publication.
—BLDSC (9251.400000); Linda Hall; UnCover. **CCC.**
Incorporates (1949-1993): Beitraege zur Vogelkunde (ISSN 0005-8211).
Description: Publishes original papers, review articles and short notes on all aspects of ornithology.

615   GW   ISSN 0344-9270
DIE VOLIERE. (Text in German; summaries in Dutch and English) 1978. 12/yr. DM.107.50 (foreign DM.131.90) (effective 1997). Verlag M. und H. Schaper GmbH, Kalandstr. 4, 31061 Alfeld, Germany. TEL 49-5181-8009-0. FAX 49-5181-800933. (Subscr. to: Postfach 1642, 31046 Alfeld, Germany) Ed. B. Hachfeld. adv.; bk.rev.; illus. circ. 5,900. **Indexed:** Vet.Bull. **Document type:** academic/scholarly publication.
—**CCC.**

598.2 639.9   SA
VULTURE NEWS. (Text in English) 1979. s-a. R.30($30) membership. Vulture Study Group, P.O. Box 72334, Parkview 2122, South Africa. TEL 27-11-6468617. FAX 27-11-4861506. Ed. Steven Piper. adv.; bk.rev.; abstr.; bibl.; charts; illus.; stat. circ. 1,000. **Indexed:** Key Word Ind.Wildl.Res.

598.296822   SA   ISSN 0250-1481
CODEN: WBCNEW
W B C NEWS. 1952. q. Witwatersrand Bird Club, P.O. Box 72091, Parkside 2122, South Africa. **Indexed:** Sport Fish.Abstr., Wild.Rev., Zoo.Rec.

598.2   UK   ISSN 0963-326X
CODEN: WPAJE6
W P A JOURNAL. a. $50. World Pheasant Association, P.O. Box 5, Lower Basildon, Reading RG8 9PF, England. TEL 44-1734-845140. FAX 44-1734-843369. (U.S. subscr. to: World Pheasant Association, 1800 S. Canyon Park Circle, Ste. 402, Edmond, OK 73013-6631) Ed. Ed Jenkins. R&P contact: Ron Sumner. adv. contact: Ron Sumner. **Indexed:** Sport Fish.Abstr., Wild.Rev., Zoo.Rec. **Document type:** bulletin.

598.2   UK   ISSN 0963-3278
CODEN: WPANEI
W P A NEWS. 1975. q. $50. World Pheasant Association, P.O. Box 5, Lower Basildon, Reading RG8 9PF, England. TEL 44-1734-845140. FAX 44-1734-843369. E-mail: rsumner@icnet.net. (U.S. subscr. to: World Pheasant Association, 1800 S. Canyon Park Circle, Ste. 402, Edmond, OK 73013-6631. TEL 405-348-9700. FAX 405-348-9772) R&P contact: Ron Sumner. **Indexed:** Poult.Abstr., Sport Fish.Abstr., Wild.Rev., Zoo.Rec. **Document type:** bulletin.
Description: Contains news, reports and articles concerning conservation and aviculture of the Galliformes (game birds).

598.2 333.78   UK
WATERFOWL. 1971. s-a. £20 membership (rest of Europe £28; elsewhere £35). British Waterfowl Association, Gill Cottage, New Gill, Bishopdale, Leyburn, N. Yorks. DL8 3TQ, England. TEL 44-1969-663693. Ed. M. Thompson. adv.; bk.rev.; bibl. circ. 1,600. (processed) **Document type:** newsletter.

598.2   GW   ISSN 0178-7373
WELLENSITTICH MAGAZIN; internationale Fachzeitschrift fuer Zuechter, Halter und Aussteller. 1986. 12/yr. DM.102.50 (foreign DM.121.40) (effective 1997). Verlag M. und H. Schaper GmbH, Kalandstr. 4, 31061 Alfeld, Germany. TEL 49-5181-8009-0. FAX 49-5181-800933. (Subscr. to: Postfach 1642, 31046 Alfeld, Germany) **Document type:** trade publication.
—**CCC.**

598.2   US   ISSN 0160-1121
CODEN: WSBDAA
WESTERN BIRDS. 1973. q. $18 (foreign $23). Western Field Ornithologists, c/o Dorothy Myers, 6011 Saddletree Ln., Yorba Linda, CA 92686. TEL 714-779-2201. Ed. Philip Unitt. adv. contact: Dori Myers. bk.rev.; illus.; index; circ. 1,000 (paid). **Indexed:** Sport Fish.Abstr., Wild.Rev., ZooRec. **Document type:** academic/scholarly publication.
—Linda Hall; UMI; UnCover.
Formerly (until 1973): California Birds (ISSN 0045-3897)
Description: Dedicated to the promotion and scientific values of ornithology in the western U.S., Canada, and Baja California, Mexico. Sponsors field trips in California.
Refereed Serial

598.2   UK   ISSN 1353-7792
WETLAND BIRD SURVEY (YEAR): WILDFOWL AND WADER COUNTS. a. £15 to non-members. Wildfowl and Wetlands Trust, Slimbridge, Gloucester GL2 7BT, England. TEL 44-1453-890333. FAX 44-1453-890827. E-mail: wwt@va.wsl.ac.uk. (Co-sponsors: British Trust for Ornithology; Royal Society for the Protection of Birds; Joint Nature Conservation Committee) Ed.Bd. circ. 4,000. **Document type:** bulletin.
—BLDSC (9317.245500).
Formerly: Wildfowl and Wader Counts (ISSN 0965-3708)
Description: Summary results of comprehensive waterfowl monitoring scheme in the UK.

598.2   BE   ISSN 0043-5260
DE WIELEWAAL. 1933. m. 900 BEF. (Vereniging voor Vogel en Natuurstudie de Wielewaal) De Wielewaal V.Z.W., Graatakker 11, B-2300 Turnhout, Belgium. TEL 014-41-22-52. Ed. G. Luyts. adv.; bk.rev.; illus. circ. 6,200.

598.207   US   ISSN 0892-5534
QL677.5
WILDBIRD. 1987. m. $23.97 (Canada $34.47; elsewhere $39.97) (effective 1997). Fancy Publications, Inc., 3 Burroughs, Irvine, CA 92618-2804. TEL 714-855-8822. FAX 714-855-3045. URL: http://www.petchannel.com. (Subscr. to: Neodata, Box 58025, Boulder, CO 80322. TEL 800-365-4221. FAX 303-604-7455) Ed. Paul Konrad. adv. circ. 150,000. **Indexed:** Sport Fish.Abstr., Wild.Rev. **Document type:** consumer publication.
—Linda Hall; UnCover.
Description: Contains a variety of birding and ornithology features, including tips on bird-watching, species profiles, birding "hotspots," product directories, field testing of the latest equipment, attracting, bird feeding, and bird identification advice.

598.2   UK   ISSN 0954-6324
SK351   CODEN: WLDFAB
WILDFOWL. 1948. a. £11 to members; libraries and non-members £21 (effective 1997). Wildfowl and Wetlands Trust, Slimbridge, Gloucester GL2 7BT, England. TEL 44-1453-890333. FAX 44-1453-890827. E-mail: wwt@dial.pipex.com; URL: http://www.washington.co.uk/wwt.wwtinfo.html. Ed. Janet Kear. bk.rev. circ. 2,500. **Indexed:** Biol.Abstr., Curr.Adv.Ecol.Sci., Ecol.Abstr., IBR, Ind.Vet., Key Word Ind.Wildl.Res., Sport Fish.Abstr., Vet.Bull., Wild Life Rev., Wild.Rev., Zoo.Rec. **Document type:** bulletin.
—BLDSC (9317.245000); Linda Hall; UnCover.

598.2   UK   ISSN 0960-4421
WILDFOWL AND WETLANDS. 1950. q. £2. Wildfowl and Wetlands Trust, Slimbridge, Gloucester GL2 7BT, England. TEL 44-1453-890333. FAX 44-1453-890827. E-mail: wwt@va.wsl.ac.uk. Ed. Nikki Straughan. adv.; bk.rev. circ. 37,000. (back issues avail.) **Document type:** bulletin.
—BLDSC (9317.245800).

598.2   US   ISSN 0043-5643
CODEN: WILBAI
WILSON BULLETIN; a quarterly magazine of ornithology. 1889. q. $40 (foreign $45) (effective 1997). Wilson Ornithological Society, c/o Charles R. Blem, Ed., Department of Biology, Virginia Commonwealth University, Richmond, VA 23289-2012. TEL 804-367-1562. FAX 804-367-0503. E-mail: cblem@felix.vcu.edu; URL: http://www.ummx.lsa.umich.edu/birds/bulletin.html. (Subscr. to: Ornithological Societies of North America, Box 1897, Lawrence, KS 66044-8897. TEL 913-843-1221. FAX 913-843-1274) R&P contact: Charles R. Blem. bk.rev.; bibl.; charts; illus.; index; circ. 3,500 (paid). (also avail. in microform from UMI) **Indexed:** ASCA, Biol.Abstr., Curr.Adv.Ecol.Sci., Curr.Cont., Gen.Sci.Ind., Helminthol.Abstr., Ind.Sci.Rev., Ind.Sci.Rev., Ind.Vet., Ornithol.Abstr. (1955-), Sci.Cit.Ind., Sport Fish.Abstr., Vet.Bull., Wild.Rev., Zoo.Rec. **Document type:** academic/scholarly publication.
●Also available online. Vendor(s): Information Access Co.
—BLDSC (9319.079000); CISTI; EMDOCS; Genuine Article; KNAW; KR SourceOne; Linda Hall; SWETS; UMI; UnCover.
Description: Publishes original studies of birds and short communications describing observations of particular interest.

598.2   US   ISSN 1042-511X
WINGING IT. 1989. m. $36 to individuals (foreign $45); libraries $41 (foreign $50); students $18 (foreign $27 (includes Birding & A Bird's Eye View) (effective 1997). American Birding Association, Box 6599, Colorado Springs, CO 80934. TEL 719-578-1614; 800-850-2473. FAX 719-578-1480. E-mail: member@aba.org. Ed. Virginia Maynard. illus. **Document type:** newsletter.

598.2   AT   ISSN 1036-7810
QL671   CODEN: WINSEF
WINGSPAN. 1969. q. Aus.$44. Royal Australasian Ornithologists Union, 415 Riversdale Rd., W. Hawthorn, Vic. 3123, Australia. TEL 61-3-98822622. FAX 61-3-98822677. Ed. Merrilyn Julian. R&P contact: David Baker-Gabb. adv. contact: Bill Fenton. circ. 5,000. (back issues avail.) **Indexed:** Curr.Adv.Ecol.Sci., Sport Fish.Abstr., Wild.Rev., Zoo.Rec. **Document type:** consumer publication.
—BLDSC (9319.417647); SWETS. **CCC.**
Formerly (until 1990): R A O U Newsletter (ISSN 0817-5748)

598.2 333.95   UK
WORLD BIRDWATCH. (Former name of issuing body: International Council for Bird Preservation) 1979. q. £25($35) to members. BirdLife International, Wellbrook Ct., Girton Rd., Cambridge CB3 0NA, England. TEL 44-1223-277318. FAX 44-1223-277200. TELEX 818794 ICBP G. (Dist. in Americas by: Smithsonian Institution Press, Box 960, Herndon, VA 22070-0960. TEL 703-435-7064. FAX 703-689-0660) bk.rev. circ. 4,000. (tabloid format) **Indexed:** Key Word Ind.Wildl.Res. **Document type:** newsletter.
Formerly: I C B P Newsletter (ISSN 0144-4476)
Description: Reports on world bird conservation.

598   JA   ISSN 0910-4488
YACHO/WILD BIRDS. (Text in Japanese) 1934. m. 600 Yen per no. Nihon Yacho no Kai - Wild Bird Society of Japan, 15-8 Nanpeidai, Shibuya-ku, Tokyo 150, Japan. TEL 81-3-3463-8919. FAX 81-3-3463-8844. E-mail: KGB00707@niftyserve.or.jp. Ed. Kyogoku Toru; Pub. Kuroda Nagahisa. **Document type:** bulletin.

598   JA
YACHOEN DAYORI/YATOMI WILD BIRD SANCTUARY NEWS. (Text in Japanese) 1976. 2/yr. Aichiken Yatomi Yachoen Jimusho - Aichi Prefecture, Yatomi Wild Bird Sanctuary Office, 2-10 Ueno, Yatomimachi, Kaifu-gun, Aichi-ken 498, Japan.

598   JA   ISSN 0910-2388
YAMAGUCHI YACHO/JOURNAL OF THE WILD BIRDS OF YAMAGUCHI. (Text in Japanese) a. membership. Nihon Yacho no Kai, Yamaguchiken Shibu - Wild Bird Society of Japan, Yamaguchi Prefecture Branch, c/o Mr. Ogawa, Iwanaga Shimogo, Shuhocho, Mine-gun, Yamaguchi 754-05, Japan.

598.2　　　　　　　JA
YAMASHINA INSTITUTE FOR ORNITHOLOGY. JOURNAL/YAMASHINA CHORUI KENKYUJO KENKYU HOKOKU. (Text in English and Japanese) 1952. s-a. 10000 Yen (effective 1997 & 1998). Yamashina Institute for Ornithology - Yamashina Chorui Kenkyujo, 115 Aza-Tsutsumine Konoyama, Abiko-shi, Chiba-ken 270-11, Japan. TEL 81-471-82-1101. FAX 81-471-82-1106. Ed. Nariko Oka. charts; illus. circ. 700. (back issues avail.) **Indexed:** Biol.Abstr., Jap.Per.Ind. **Document type:** academic/scholarly publication.
—BLDSC (4917.503000).
　Former titles: Yamashina Institute for Ornithology. Miscellaneous Reports (ISSN 0044-0183); Yamashina Institute for Ornithology and Zoology. Miscellaneous Reports.
　Description: Covers original reports on scientific study of birds, including bird protection.

598.2　　　　　　　UK
YORKSHIRE NATURALISTS' UNION. BIRD REPORT. a. £8 membership. Yorkshire Naturalists' Union, University of Bradford, Bradford, W. Yorks BD7 1DP, England. TEL 44-1274-384212. FAX 44-1274-384231. E-mail: m.r.d.seaward@bradford.ac.uk. Ed. M.R.D. Seaward. **Document type:** academic/scholarly publication.

598.2　　　ZA　ISSN 0378-4533
ZAMBIAN ORNITHOLOGICAL SOCIETY. NEWSLETTER. 1971. m. £20($30) Zambian Ornithological Society, P.O. Box 33944, Lusaka 10101, Zambia. Ed. C. Beel. bibl.; index. circ. 200. (back issues avail.) **Indexed:** Sport Fish.Abstr., Wild.Rev. **Document type:** newsletter.
　Description: Bird records, announcements, occasional reviews.

598.2　　　　　　　ZA
ZAMBIAN ORNITHOLOGICAL SOCIETY OCCASIONAL PAPERS. 1979. irreg., latest no.3, 1991. price varies. Zambian Ornithological Society, P.O. Box 33944, Lusaka 10101, Zambia. circ. 500. **Document type:** monographic series.

BIOLOGY — Physiology

see also Medical Sciences

ACTA BOTANICA CROATICA. see *BIOLOGY — Botany*

571　　　BU　ISSN 0323-9950
　　　　　　　　　CODEN: APPBDI
ACTA PHYSIOLOGICA ET PHARMACOLOGICA BULGARICA. (Text in English; summaries in Russian) 1974. q. 1.70 lv.($6) per no. (Bulgarska Akademiia na Naukite) Publishing House of the Bulgarian Academy of Sciences, Acad. G. Bonchev St., Bldg. 6, 1113 Sofia, Bulgaria. (Dist. by: Hemus, 6, Rouski Blvd., 1000 Sofia, Bulgaria) circ. 456. (reprint service avail. form IRC) **Indexed:** Abstr.Bulg.Sci.Med.Lit., Biol.Abstr., BSL Biol., Chem.Abstr., Curr.Adv.Ecol.Sci., Dairy Sci.Abstr., Excerp.Med., GeoRef., Ind.Med.
—BLDSC (0650.900000); CASDDS; CISTI; EMDOCS; KNAW; Linda Hall; UnCover.
　Supersedes: Bulgarska Akademiia na Naukite, Sofia, Institut po Fiziologiia. Izvestiia.

571　　　HU　ISSN 0231-424X
QP1　　　　　　　CODEN: APHHDU
ACTA PHYSIOLOGICA HUNGARICA. (Text in English) 1950. q. $148 (effective 1998). (Magyar Tudomanyos Akademia) Akademiai Kiado Rt., P.O. Box 245, H-1519 Budapest, Hungary. TEL 36-1-2043976. FAX 36-1-2043973. Eds. Peter Balint, Jeno Bartha. adv.; bk.rev.; bibl.; charts; illus.; index. (also avail. in microform from PMC) **Indexed:** ASCA, Biol.Abstr., Biotech.Abstr., Chem.Abstr., Curr.Adv.Ecol.Sci., Curr.Cont., Excerp.Med., Ind.Med., Ind.Sci.Rev., INIS Atomind., Neurosci.Cit.Ind., Nutr.Abstr., Sci.Cit.Ind, Vet.Bull. **Document type:** academic/scholarly publication.
—BLDSC (0652.500000); CASDDS; CISTI; EMDOCS; Genuine Article; KNAW; Linda Hall; SWETS; UnCover. **CCC.**
　Formerly (until 1982): Academiae Scientiarum Hungaricae. Acta Physiologica (ISSN 0001-6756)
　Description: Publishes new research papers in experimental medical sciences, covering physiology, pathophysiology and pharmacology.

571　　　AG　ISSN 0327-6309
　　　　　　　　　CODEN: APTLEZ
ACTA PHYSIOLOGICA PHARMACOLOGICA ET THERAPEUTICA LATINOAMERICANA; fisiologia, farmacologia, bioquimica y ciencias afines. (Text in English, French, Portuguese, Spanish; abstracts in English, Spanish) 1950. q. foreign $140 (effective 1997). Asociacion Latinoamericana de Ciencias Fisiologicas, Obligado 2490, 1428 Buenos Aires, Argentina. TEL 541-855-7204. FAX 541-8562751. (Co-sponsor: Asociacion Latinoamericana de Farmacologia) Ed. Dr. Enri S. Borda. adv. contact: Dr. Enri S. Borda. charts; illus.; index. circ. 1,000. (also avail. in microfilm) **Indexed:** Biol.Abstr., Chem.Abstr., Curr.Adv.Ecol.Sci., Curr.Cont., Dairy Sci.Abstr., Excerp.Med., Ind.Med., Ind.Sci.Rev., Nutr.Abstr., Sci.Cit.Ind. **Document type:** academic/scholarly publication.
—BLDSC (0653.500000); CASDDS; CISTI; EMDOCS; KNAW; Linda Hall; SWETS; UMI.
　Former titles (until 1990): Acta Physiologica et Pharmacologica Latino Americana (ISSN 0326-6656); (until 1984): Acta Physiologica Latinoamericana (ISSN 0001-6764)

571　　　UK　ISSN 0001-6772
QP1　　　　　　　CODEN: APSCAX
ACTA PHYSIOLOGICA SCANDINAVICA. 1940. m. £228($416.50) (foreign £251) (effective 1998). (Scandinavian Physiological Society) Blackwell Science Ltd., Osney Mead, Oxford OX2 OEL, England. TEL 44-1865-206206. FAX 44-1865-721205. E-mail: journals.cs@blacsci.co.uk; URL: http://www.black.co.uk. Ed. B. Uvnas; Pub. Allen Stevens. R&P contact: Sarah Pollard. adv. contact: Martine Cariou-Keen. abstr.; bibl.; charts; illus. circ. 1,300. (also avail. in microform from UMI; back issues avail.; reprint service from SWZ) **Indexed:** Anim.Breed.Abstr., ASCA, Biol.Abstr., Biotech.Abstr., C.I.S.Abstr., Chem.Abstr., Curr.Adv.Ecol.Sci., Curr.Cont., Dairy Sci.Abstr., Dent.Ind., Excerp.Med., Helminthol.Abstr., Ind.Med., Ind.Sci.Rev., Ind.Vet., Neurosci.Cit.Ind., Nutr.Abstr., Pig News & Info., Poult.Abstr., Sci.Cit.Ind., Sport Fish.Abstr., Sugar Ind.Abstr., THA, Vet.Bull., Wild.Rev., Zoo.Rec. **Document type:** academic/scholarly publication.
—BLDSC (0654.800000); ADONIS; CASDDS; CISTI; EMDOCS; Genuine Article; KNAW; Linda Hall; SWETS; UMI; UnCover. **CCC.**
　Formerly: Skandinavisches Archiv fur Physiologie.
　Refereed Serial

571　　　UK　ISSN 0302-2994
QP1　　　　　　　CODEN: APSSAD
ACTA PHYSIOLOGICA SCANDINAVICA. SUPPLEMENTUM. 1940. irreg. (Scandinavian Physiological Society) Blackwell Science Ltd., Osney Mead, Oxford OX2 OEL, England. TEL 44-1865-206206. FAX 44-1865-721205. E-mail: journals.cs@blacksci.co.uk; URL: http://www.black.co.uk. Pub. Allen Stevens. R&P contact: Sarah Pollard. adv. contact: Martine Cariou-Keen. **Indexed:** Excerp.Med., Ind.Med., Sport Fish.Abstr., Wild.Rev., Zoo.Rec. **Document type:** academic/scholarly publication.
—BLDSC (0655.000000); ADONIS; CASDDS; CISTI; EMDOCS; KNAW; Linda Hall; SWETS; UnCover.
　Formerly: Skandinavisches Archiv fur Physiologie. Supplementum.

ADVANCES IN ANIMAL PHYSIOLOGY AND ANIMAL NUTRITION/FORTSCHRITTE IN DER TIERPHYSIOLOGIE UND TIERERNAEHRUNG. see *BIOLOGY — Zoology*

ADVANCES IN ELECTROMAGNETIC FIELDS IN LIVING SYSTEMS. see *BIOLOGY — Bioengineering*

ADVANCES IN ENZYME REGULATION. see *MEDICAL SCIENCES*

612 370　　US　ISSN 1043-4046
ADVANCES IN PHYSIOLOGY EDUCATION. 1989. s-a. $16 to individual non-members (foreign $18.50); institutions $23 (foreign $26); free to members (effective 1997). American Physiological Society, 9650 Rockville Pike, Bethesda, MD 20814. TEL 301-530-7071. FAX 301-571-8313. E-mail: info@aps.faseb.org; URL: http://www.faseb.org/aps. Ed. P.A. Hansen. adv.: B&W page $1050, color page $1400. bibl.; charts; illus. circ. 9,250. **Indexed:** ASCA, C.I.J.E. **Document type:** academic/scholarly publication.
—CISTI; Genuine Article; UMI. **CCC.**
　Description: Concerned with issues of education in physiology at all educational levels, covering scholarly essays on the direction and scope of physiology training as well as practical aids to teaching.

AGING. see *GERONTOLOGY AND GERIATRICS*

ALFRED BENZON SYMPOSIUM. PROCEEDINGS. see *MEDICAL SCIENCES*

571　　　US　ISSN 0002-9513
QP1　　　　　　　CODEN: AJPHAP
AMERICAN JOURNAL OF PHYSIOLOGY. (Consolidates papers published in all 8 American Journal of Physiology individual journals) 1897. m. $1064 to individual non-members (Canada and Mexico $1184; elsewhere $1364); institutions $1595 (Canada and Mexico $1715; elsewhere $1895); members $532 (effective 1997). American Physiological Society, 9650 Rockville Pike, Bethesda, MD 20814. TEL 301-530-7164. FAX 301-571-3813. E-mail: info@aps.faseb.org; URL: http://www.faseb.org/aps. Ed. Brenda Rauner. adv.: B&W page $775, color page $1125. bibl.; charts; illus.; index, cum.index. circ. 2,500. (also avail. in microform from UMI,PMC; reprint service avail. from ISI,UMI) **Indexed:** Abstr.Hyg., Anim.Breed.Abstr., Bibl.Agri., Biol.Abstr., Biol.& Agr.Ind., Biotech.Abstr., Chem.Abstr., Curr.Adv.Biochem., Curr.Adv.Cell. & Devel.Biol., Curr.Adv.Ecol.Sci., Curr.Adv.Genetics & Molec.Biol., Curr.Cont., Curr.Ref.Fish Res., Dairy Sci.Abstr., Dent.Ind., Gen.Sci.Ind., Helminthol.Abstr., Ind.Med., Ind.Sci.Rev., Ind.Vet., INIS Atomind., Int.Abstr.Biol.Sci., Key Word Ind.Wildl.Res., Kidney, Neurosci.Cit.Ind., Nutr.Abstr., Pig News & Info., Poult.Abstr., Ref.Zh., Sci.Cit.Ind., Small Anim.Abstr., Sport Fish.Abstr., SSCI, Trop.Dis.Bull., Vet.Bull., Wild.Rev., Zoo.Rec. **Document type:** academic/scholarly publication.
—BLDSC (0834.000000); CASDDS; CISTI; Genuine Article; KNAW; KR SourceOne; Linda Hall; UMI; UnCover. **CCC.**
　Refereed Serial

AMERICAN JOURNAL OF PHYSIOLOGY: CELL PHYSIOLOGY. see *BIOLOGY — Cytology And Histology*

573.4　　　US　ISSN 0193-1849
QP187.A1
AMERICAN JOURNAL OF PHYSIOLOGY: ENDOCRINOLOGY AND METABOLISM. 1977. m. $150 to individual non-members (Canada and Mexico $190; elsewhere $210); institutions $225 (Canada and Mexico $265; elsewhere $285); members $75 (effective 1997). American Physiological Society, 9650 Rockville Pike, Bethesda, MD 20814. TEL 301-530-7071. FAX 301-571-8313. E-mail: info@aps.faseb.org; URL: http://www.faseb.org/aps. Ed. J.E. Pessin. circ. 700. (also avail. in microform from UMI; reprint service avail. from UMI) **Indexed:** Abstr.Hyg., Anim.Breed.Abstr., ASCA, Biol.Abstr., Biol.& Agr.Ind., Biotech.Abstr., Chem.Abstr., Curr.Cont., Dairy Sci.Abstr., Dent.Ind., Excerp.Med., Ind.Med., Ind.Sci.Rev., Ind.Vet., Key Word Ind.Wildl.Res., Nutr.Abstr., Ref.Zh., Sci.Cit.Ind., Trop.Dis.Bull., Vet.Bull. **Document type:** academic/scholarly publication.
—CISTI; EMDOCS; Genuine Article; SWETS; UMI. **CCC.**
　Supersedes in part (in 1980): American Journal of Physiology: Endocrinology, Metabolism and Gastrointestinal Physiology (ISSN 0363-6100)
　Description: Examines organisms at all levels of endocrine and metabolic systems development, from the subcellular and molecular to the level of whole animal.
　Refereed Serial

BIOLOGY — PHYSIOLOGY

573.3 US ISSN 0193-1857
QP145
AMERICAN JOURNAL OF PHYSIOLOGY: GASTROINTESTINAL AND LIVER PHYSIOLOGY. 1977. m. $150 to individuals (Canada and Mexico $190; elsewhere $205); institutions $210 (Canada and Mexico $242; elsewhere $264); members $75. American Physiological Society, 9650 Rockville Pike, Bethesda, MD 20814. TEL 301-530-7164. FAX 301-571-8313. E-mail: info@aps.faseb.org; URL: http://www.faseb.org/aps. Ed. D.H. Alpers. circ. 550. **Indexed:** Abstr.Hyg., ASCA, Biol.Abstr., Biol.& Agr.Ind., Biotech.Abstr., Chem.Abstr., Curr.Cont., Dairy Sci.Abstr., Dent.Ind., Excerp.Med., Helminthol.Abstr., Ind.Med., Ind.Sci.Rev., Ind.Vet., Int.Abstr.Biol.Sci., Key Word Ind.Wildl.Res., Nutr.Abstr., Ref.Zh., Sci.Cit.Ind., Trop.Dis.Bull., Vet.Bull. **Document type:** academic/scholarly publication.
—CISTI; EMDOCS; Genuine Article; SWETS; UMI. **CCC.**
Supersedes in part (in 1980): American Journal of Physiology: Endocrinology, Metabolism and Gastrointestinal Physiology (ISSN 0363-6100)
Description: Presents original papers dealing with normal or abnormal function of the alimentary canal and its accessory organs including the salivary glands, pancreas, gallbladder, and liver.
Refereed Serial

573.1 US ISSN 0363-6135
QP101.2
AMERICAN JOURNAL OF PHYSIOLOGY: HEART AND CIRCULATORY PHYSIOLOGY. 1977. m. $316 to individual non-members (Canada and Mexico $356; elsewhere $406); institutions $475 (Canada and Mexico $515; elsewhere $565); members $158 (effective 1997). American Physiological Society, 9650 Rockville Pike, Bethesda, MD 20814. TEL 301-530-7164. FAX 301-571-8313. E-mail: info@aps.faseb.org; URL: http://www.faseb.org/aps. Ed. H.J. Granger. circ. 950. (also avail. in microform from UMI; reprint service avail. from UMI) **Indexed:** Abstr.Hyg., ASCA, Biol.Abstr., Biol.& Agr.Ind., Biotech.Abstr., Chem.Abstr., Curr.Cont., Dent.Ind., Excerp.Med., Helminthol.Abstr., Ind.Med., Ind.Sci.Rev., Ind.Vet., Int.Abstr.Biol.Sci., Key Word Ind.Wildl.Res., Nutr.Abstr., Ref.Zh., Sci.Cit.Ind., Trop.Dis.Bull., Vet.Bull. **Document type:** academic/scholarly publication.
—CISTI; EMDOCS; Genuine Article; SWETS; UMI. **CCC.**
Description: Presents experimental and theoretical studies of cardiovascular function at all levels of organization ranging from the intact animal to the cellular, subcellular, and molecular levels.
Refereed Serial

612 US ISSN 1040-0605
QP121.A1 CODEN: APLPE7
AMERICAN JOURNAL OF PHYSIOLOGY: LUNG CELLULAR AND MOLECULAR PHYSIOLOGY. 1989. m. $138 to individual non-members (Canada and Mexico $178; elsewhere $198); institutions $206 (Canada and Mexico $246; elsewhere $266); members $69 (effective 1997). American Physiological Society, 9650 Rockville Pike, Bethesda, MD 20814. TEL 301-530-7164. FAX 301-571-8313. E-mail: info@aps.faseb.org; URL: http://www.faseb.org/aps. Ed. D.E. Rannels. circ. 1,150. **Indexed:** ASCA, Curr.Cont., Ind.Sci.Rev. **Document type:** academic/scholarly publication.
—CISTI; EMDOCS; Genuine Article; SWETS; UMI. **CCC.**
Description: Presents original investigative and theoretical papers dealing with molecular, cellular, and morphological aspects of normal and abnormal function and response of respiratory cell components of the respiratory system.
Refereed Serial

571 US ISSN 0363-6119
QP33
AMERICAN JOURNAL OF PHYSIOLOGY: REGULATORY, INTEGRATIVE AND COMPARATIVE PHYSIOLOGY. 1977. m. $200 to individual non-members (Canada and Mexico $240; elsewhere $275); institutions $300 (Canada and Mexico $340; elsewhere $375); members $100 (effective 1997). American Physiological Society, 9650 Rockville Pike, Bethesda, MD 20814. TEL 301-530-7164. FAX 301-571-3813. E-mail: info@aps.faseb.org; URL: http://www.faseb.org/aps. Ed. J.E. Hall. circ. 500. (also avail. in microform from UMI; reprint service avail. from UMI) **Indexed:** Abstr.Hyg., ASCA, Biol.Abstr., Biol.& Agr.Ind., Biotech.Abstr., Chem.Abstr., Curr.Cont., Dent.Ind., Excerp.Med., Helminthol.Abstr., Ind.Med., Ind.Sci.Rev., Ind.Vet., Int.Abstr.Biol.Sci., Key Word Ind.Wildl.Res., Nutr.Abstr., Ref.Zh., Sci.Cit.Ind., Trop.Dis.Bull., Vet.Bull. **Document type:** academic/scholarly publication.
—CISTI; EMDOCS; Genuine Article; SWETS; UMI. **CCC.**
Description: Presents original articles that emphasize relationships between organ systems and control of physiological processes in the whole organism, and articles on comparative physiology.
Refereed Serial

571.1 US ISSN 0363-6127
QP249
AMERICAN JOURNAL OF PHYSIOLOGY: RENAL, FLUID AND ELECTROLYTE PHYSIOLOGY. 1977. m. $190 to individual non-members (Canada and Mexico $225; elsewhere $247); institutions $236 (Canada and Mexico $280; elsewhere $303); members $95 (effective 1997). American Physiological Society, 9650 Rockville Pike, Bethesda, MD 20814. TEL 301-530-7164. FAX 301-571-3813. E-mail: info@aps.faseb.org; URL: http://www.faseb.org/aps. Ed. S.C. Hebert. circ. 950. (also avail. in microform from UMI; reprint service avail. from UMI) **Indexed:** Abstr.Hyg., ASCA, Biol.Abstr., Biol.& Agr.Ind., Biotech.Abstr., Chem.Abstr., Curr.Cont., Dent.Ind., Excerp.Med., Helminthol.Abstr., Ind.Med., Ind.Sci.Rev., Ind.Vet., Int.Abstr.Biol.Sci., Key Word Ind.Wildl.Res., Nutr.Abstr., Ref.Zh., Sci.Cit.Ind., Trop.Dis.Bull., Vet.Bull. **Document type:** academic/scholarly publication.
—CISTI; EMDOCS; Genuine Article; SWETS; UMI. **CCC.**
Description: Covers subject matter relating to the kidney, urinary tract, and epithelial cell layers. Also covers body fluid volume control and composition.
Refereed Serial

ANALOGUES IN CANCER AND HUMAN REPRODUCTION.
see *MEDICAL SCIENCES* — Oncology

611 SA
ANATOMIESE VERENIGING VAN SUIDER-AFRIKA. KONGRESVERRIGTINGE/ANATOMICAL SOCIETY OF SOUTHERN AFRICA. PROCEEDINGS OF ANNUAL CONGRESS. (Text in Afrikaans, English) 1971? a., 24th, 1994, Pretoria. price varies. Anatomiese Vereniging van Suider-Afrika - Anatomical Society of Southern Africa, c/o Dr. H.B. Groenwald, Dept. Anatomie, Fakulteit Veerartsenykunde, Privaatsak X04, Onderstepoort 0110, South Africa. **Document type:** proceedings.

571 GW ISSN 0340-2061
QL951 CODEN: ANEMDG
ANATOMY AND EMBRYOLOGY. Online edition (GW ISSN 1432-0568) (Text in English) 1892. m. DM.4105 (foreign DM.4134.40) (effective 1998). Springer-Verlag, Heidelberger Platz 3, 14197 Berlin, Germany. TEL 49-30-82787-0. FAX 49-30-82787448. E-mail: subscriptions@springer.de; URL: http://link.springer.de. (Subscr. in N. America to: Springer-Verlag New York, Inc., 333 Meadowlands Pkwy., Secaucus, NJ 07094. TEL 212-460-1500. FAX 212-473-6272) Ed.Bd. adv.; bibl.; charts; illus. (also avail. in microform from UMI; back issues avail.; reprint service avail. from ISI) **Indexed:** Anim.Breed.Abstr., ASCA, Biol.Abstr., Chem.Abstr., Curr.Adv.Cell & Devel.Biol., Curr.Adv.Ecol.Sci., Curr.Cont., Dairy Sci.Abstr., Dent.Ind., Excerp.Med., Ind.Med., Ind.Sci.Rev., Ind.Vet., INIS Atomind., Neurosci.Cit.Ind., Pig News & Info., Poult.Abstr., Sci.Cit.Ind., Vet.Bull. **Document type:** academic/scholarly publication.
●Also available online.
—BLDSC (0900.030000); ADONIS; CASDDS; CISTI; EMDOCS; Genuine Article; KNAW; Linda Hall; SWETS; UMI; UnCover. **CCC.**
Former titles: Journal of Anatomy and Embryology; Zeitschrift fuer Anatomie und Entwicklungsgeschichte (ISSN 0044-2232)

612.6 US ISSN 0090-5348
HQ768
ANNUAL EDITIONS: HUMAN DEVELOPMENT. 1972. a. $12.95. Dushkin Publishing Group, Sluice Dock, Guilford, CT 06437-9989. TEL 203-453-4351. FAX 203-453-6000. Eds. Larry Fenson, Judi Fenson; Pub. Ian Nielsen. illus. **Document type:** academic/scholarly publication.
Refereed Serial

571 US ISSN 0066-4278
QP1 CODEN: ARPHAD
ANNUAL REVIEW OF PHYSIOLOGY. 1939. a. $62 to individuals (foreign $67); institutions $124 (foreign $134) (effective 1998). Annual Reviews Inc., 4139 El Camino Way, Box 10139, Palo Alto, CA 94303-0139. TEL 650-493-4400; 800-523-8635. FAX 650-424-0910. E-mail: service@annurev.org; URL: http://www.annurev.org. Ed. Joseph F. Hoffman. R&P contact: Jeanne Kunz. bibl.; index, cum.index. (also avail. in microfilm from UMI; back issues avail.; reprint service avail.) **Indexed:** Abstr.Hyg., Anim.Breed.Abstr., ASCA, Biol.Abstr., Biol.& Agr.Ind., Chem.Abstr., Curr.Adv.Ecol.Sci., Curr.Cont., Dairy Sci.Abstr., Deep Sea.Res.& Oceanogr.Abstr., Dent.Ind., Diar.Dis.Res., Excerp.Med., Helminthol.Abstr., Ind.Med., Ind.Sci.Rev., Ind.Vet., INIS Atomind., M.M.R.I., Nutr.Abstr., Psychol.Abstr. (1939-), Sci.Cit.Ind., SSCI, THA. **Document type:** academic/scholarly publication.
—BLDSC (1527.000000); ADONIS; CASDDS; CISTI; EMDOCS; Genuine Article; KNAW; KR SourceOne; Linda Hall; SWETS; UMI; UnCover. **CCC.**
Description: Original critical reviews of the significant primary literature and current developments in physiology.

612 NE ISSN 0920-5268
CODEN: AAPAED
APPLIED CARDIOPULMONARY PATHOPHYSIOLOGY; the interface between laboratory and clinical practice. Abbreviated title: A C P. (Text in English) 1988. q. fl.385 to institutions; $197.50 to institutions in U.S. (effective 1998). Kluwer Academic Publishers, Postbus 17, 3300 AA Dordrecht, Netherlands. TEL 31-78-6392392. FAX 31-78-6392254. TELEX 29245 KAPG NL. E-mail: services@wkap.nl; URL: http://www.wkap.nl. (Dist. by: Kluwer Academic Publishers Group, P.O. Box 322, 3300 AH Dordrecht, Netherlands. TEL 31-78-6392392. FAX 31-78-6546474; N. America dist. addr.: Box 358, Accord Sta., Hingham, MA 02018-0358. TEL 617-871-6600. FAX 617-871-6528) Ed. Omar Prakash. (also avail. in microform from UMI) **Indexed:** ASCA, Bull.Signal., Curr.Cont., Excerp.Med. (1992-), Ind.Sci.Rev., Sci.Cit.Ind., Sci.Cit.Ind. **Document type:** academic/scholarly publication.
—BLDSC (1571.921330); CASDDS; CISTI; Ei; EMDOCS; Genuine Article; KNAW; UMI. **CCC.**
Refereed Serial

BIOLOGY — PHYSIOLOGY

612 301 JA ISSN 1341-3473
APPLIED HUMAN SCIENCE; journal of physiological anthropology. (Text in English) 1982. m. 3500 Yen. Japan Society of Physiological Anthropology - Seiri Jinrui Gakkai, c/o Business Center for Academic Societies Japan, 5-16-9 Honkomagome, Bunkyou-ku, Tokyo 113, Japan. TEL 81-3-5814-5801. FAX 81-3-5814-5820. E-mail: iwanaga@dergo2.tech.chiba-u.ac.jp. (Alt. addr.: Dept. of Ergonomics, Faculty of Engineering, Chiba University, 1-33 Yayoi-cho, Inage-ku, Chiba 263, Japan) Eds. N. Nagai, L. Harada. **Indexed:** Biol.Abstr., Excerp.Med., Ind.Med.
—BLDSC (1572.995000); KNAW.
  Formerly: Annals of Physiological Anthropology (ISSN 0287-8429)
  Description: Contains original articles, reviews, reports, technical reports and brief communications.

AQUILO. SERIE BOTANICA. see *BIOLOGY — Botany*

ARCHIVES ITALIENNES DE BIOLOGIE; an Italian journal of neuroscience. see *MEDICAL SCIENCES — Psychiatry And Neurology*

571 NE ISSN 1381-3455
QP1 CODEN: APBIF5
ARCHIVES OF PHYSIOLOGY AND BIOCHEMISTRY. (Text in English and French) 1904. 7/yr. fl.719($435) (effective 1997). Swets & Zeitlinger bv, P.O. Box 825, 2160 SZ Lisse, Netherlands. TEL 31-252-435111. FAX 31-252-415888. E-mail: orders@swets.nl; URL: http://www.swets.nl. (Dist. in N. America by: Swets & Zeitlinger, Box 613, Royersford, PA 19468. TEL 800-447-9387. FAX 610-524-5366) Eds. Dr. J. Lecomte, Dr. D. Lagneaux. R&P contact: J.v.d. Valk. adv. contact: Patrick Kleian. charts; illus.; index, cum.index. (also avail. in microfilm from PMC) **Indexed:** Biol.Abstr., Chem.Abstr., Curr.Adv.Ecol.Sci., Curr.Cont., Excerp.Med., Helminthol.Abstr., Ind.Med., Ind.Sci.Rev., Nutr.Abstr., Sci.Cit.Ind., Vet.Bull. **Document type:** academic/scholarly publication.
●Also available online.
—BLDSC (1639.570000); CASDDS; CISTI; EMDOCS; Genuine Article; KNAW; Linda Hall; SWETS; UnCover. **CCC.**
  Former titles (until vol.104): Archives Internationales de Physiologie, de Biochimie et de Biophysique (ISSN 0778-3124); Archives Internationales de Physiologie et de Biochimie (ISSN 0003-9799)
  Description: Publishes original research papers relating to the different parts of the physiological and biochemical sciences.
  Refereed Serial

571 IT ISSN 0004-0096
QP1 CODEN: ARFIAY
ARCHIVIO DI FISIOLOGIA. 1904. q. L.10000. Societa Italiana di Fisiologia, Viale Margagni 65, Florence, Italy. bk.rev. (also avail. in microfiche from BHP) **Indexed:** Biol.Abstr., Chem.Abstr., Excerp.Med., Ind.Med., Nutr.Abstr.
—CISTI.

571.1 AT ISSN 0310-7841
QK710 CODEN: AJPPCH
AUSTRALIAN JOURNAL OF PLANT PHYSIOLOGY. 1974. 8/yr. Aus.$475($475) for print ed.; online Aus.$450($450); both Aus.$500($500) (effective 1998). C.S.I.R.O. (Australia) C.S.I.R.O. Publishing, 150 Oxford St., Collingwood, Vic. 3066, Australia. TEL 61-3-96627620. FAX 61-3-96627611. E-mail: laurie.martinelli@publish.csiro.au; URL: http://www.publish.csiro.au/journals/ajpp. Ed. L.W. Martinelli. adv.; index. circ. 800. (also avail. in microform from UMI; back issues avail.) **Indexed:** Abstr.Bull.Inst.Pap.Chem., ASCA, Biol.Abstr., Biotech.Abstr., Chem.Abstr., Cott.& Trop.Fibr.Abstr., Crop Physiol.Abstr., Curr.Adv.Biochem., Curr.Adv.Ecol.Sci., Curr.Cont., Ecol.Abstr., Excerp.Med., Field Crop Abstr., Food Sci.& Tech.Abstr., Forest Abstr., Forest Prod.Abstr., Geo.Abstr.P.G., Herb.Abstr., Hort.Abstr., IDA, Ind.Sci.Rev., INIS Atomind., Irr.& Drain.Abstr., Maize Abstr., Ornam.Hort., Plant Breed.Abstr., Plant Grow.Reg.Abstr., Rev.Plant Path., Rice Abstr., Sci.Cit.Ind., Seed Abstr., Sel.Water Res.Abstr., Soils & Fert., Sorghum & Millets Abstr., Soyabean Abstr., Triticale Abstr., Trop.Oil Seeds Abstr., VITIS, Weed Abstr. **Document type:** academic/scholarly publication.
●Also available online.
—BLDSC (1811.120000); CASDDS; CISTI; EMDOCS; Genuine Article; Linda Hall; SWETS; UMI; UnCover. **CCC.**
  Description: Covers all aspects of plant physiology including biochemistry and biophysics, cell biology, geetics, plant-environment interactions, plant-microbe interactions and molecular biology.

612 AT ISSN 0067-2084
  CODEN: PAPPCH
AUSTRALIAN PHYSIOLOGICAL AND PHARMACOLOGICAL SOCIETY. PROCEEDINGS. 1970. 2/yr. Aus.$55. Australian Physiological and Pharmacological Society (APPS), c/o C.E. Hill, Division of Neuroscience, John Curtin School of Medical Research, G.P.O. Box 334, Canberra, A.C.T. 2601, Australia. FAX 61-6-2492687. E-mail: caryl@eccles.anu.edu.au. Ed. I. McCance. adv.: page Aus.$330; adv. contact: C.E. Hill. bk.rev. circ. 550. **Indexed:** Biol.Abstr., Chem.Abstr. **Document type:** proceedings.
—BLDSC (6655.500000); CASDDS; CISTI; KNAW; UnCover.
  Formerly: Australian Physiological Society. Proceedings.

612.89 NE ISSN 1047-5125
  CODEN: ANSYEL
AUTONOMIC NERVOUS SYSTEM. irreg., latest vol.10. price varies. Gordon and Breach - Harwood Academic, Amsteldisk 166, 1st Fl., 1079 LH Amsterdam, Netherlands. (Subscr. to: International Publishers Distributor, Box 32160, Newark, NJ 07102. TEL 800-545-8398. FAX 215-750-6343) Ed. Geoffrey Burnstock. (also avail. in microform) **Document type:** monographic series.
—BLDSC (1835.053000); CASDDS. **CCC.**
  Refereed Serial

591 UK ISSN 1354-8425
BABRAHAM INSTITUTE. REPORT. 1960. a. price varies. Babraham Institute, Babraham, Cambs. CB2 4AT, England. TEL 44-1223-832312. FAX 44-1223-836122. Ed. Caroline Edmonds. illus. circ. 1,500. **Indexed:** Anim.Breed.Abstr. **Document type:** corporate report.
—BLDSC (1854.610700).
  Former titles (until 1994): Institute of Animal Physiology and Genetics Research. Report (ISSN 0959-5783); Institute of Animal Physiology. Report (ISSN 0065-4507)

612 UK ISSN 0308-5384
BIOLOGICAL STRUCTURE AND FUNCTION. irreg., no.9, 1983. price varies. Cambridge University Press, Edinburgh Bldg., Shaftesbury Rd., Cambridge CB2 2RU, England. TEL 44-1223-312393. FAX 44-1223-315052. TELEX 851817256. E-mail: information@cup.cam.ac.uk; URL: http://www.cup.cam.ac.uk. (N. American addr.: Cambridge University Press, Journals Dept., 40 W. 20th St., New York, NY 10011. TEL 212-924-3900. FAX 212-691-3239) Eds. R.J. Harrison, R.M.H. McMinn. R&P contact: Linda Nicol. **Document type:** academic/scholarly publication.
—CISTI; KNAW.

BIOLOGY OF REPRODUCTION. SUPPLEMENT. see *BIOLOGY*

612.015 NE ISSN 0167-8450
QP801.U24 CODEN: BCAQDA
BIOMEDICAL AND CLINICAL ASPECTS OF COENZYME Q. (Text in English) 1977. irreg., vol.6, 1990. price varies. Elsevier Science B.V., Books Division, P.O. Box 211, 1000 AE Amsterdam, Netherlands. TEL 31-20-4853911. FAX 31-20-4853705. E-mail: nlinfo-f@elsevier.nl; usinfo-f@elsevier.com; forinfo-kyf04035@niftyserve.or.jp; URL: http://www.elsevier.nl/. (Subscr. in the Americas to: Elsevier Science, Regional Sales Office, Box 945, New York, NY 10159-0945. TEL 212-633-3730; Subscr. in Australasia and the Far East to: Elsevier Science (Singapore) Pte Ltd, No.1 Temasek Ave., No.17-01 Millenia Tower, Singapore 039192, Singapore. TEL 65-434-3727. FAX 65-337-2230; Subscr. in Japan to: Elsevier Science Japan, 9-15 Higashi-Azabu 1-chome, Minato-ku, Tokyo 106, Japan. TEL 81-3-5561-5033. FAX 81-3-5561-5047) **Document type:** proceedings.
—BLDSC (2087.753000); CASDDS.
  Refereed Serial

THE BREAST JOURNAL. see *MEDICAL SCIENCES — Obstetrics And Gynecology*

BUREIN SAIENSU/BRAIN SCIENCE. see *MEDICAL SCIENCES — Psychiatry And Neurology*

BUREIN SAIENSU SAIZENSEN/FRONTIERS OF BRAIN SCIENCE. see *MEDICAL SCIENCES — Psychiatry And Neurology*

612 JA ISSN 0387-9666
BYOTAI SEIRI (TOKYO)/JOURNAL OF PATHOLOGICAL PHYSIOLOGY. (Text in Japanese) 1964. irreg. Tokyo Hokenkai, Byotai Seiri Kenkyujo - Tokyo Hokenkai Foundation, Pathological Physiology Laboratory, 47-11, Kumanocho, Itabashi-ku, Tokyo 173, Japan.

612.1 JA ISSN 0917-6225
BYOTAI SEIRI TO SHINDAN CHIRYO/SANWA KAGAKU CO. MEDICAL REPORT. (Text in Japanese) 1980. s-a. Sanwa Kagaku Kenkyujo - Sanwa Kagaku Co., Ltd., 35, Higashisotoboricho, Higashi-ku, Nagoya-shi, Aichi-ken 461, Japan.

CACTACEAS Y SUCULENTAS MEXICANAS. see *BIOLOGY — Botany*

571 UK ISSN 0951-077X
  CODEN: CESSDT
CAMBRIDGE TEXTS IN THE PHYSIOLOGICAL SCIENCES. 1979. irreg., no.4, 1984. price varies. Cambridge University Press, Edinburgh Bldg., Shaftesbury Rd., Cambridge CB2 2RU, England. TEL 44-1223-312393. FAX 44-1223-315052. TELEX 851817256. E-mail: information@cup.cam.ac.uk; URL: http://www.cup.cam.ac.uk. (N. American addr.,: Cambridge University Press, Journals Dept., 40 W. 20th St., New York, NY 10011. TEL 212-924-3900. FAX 212-691-3239) Ed.Bd. R&P contact: Linda Nicol. **Indexed:** Biol.Abstr. **Document type:** monographic series.

BIOLOGY — PHYSIOLOGY

571   CN   ISSN 0008-4212
CODEN: CJPPA3
CANADIAN JOURNAL OF PHYSIOLOGY AND PHARMACOLOGY/JOURNAL CANADIEN DE PHYSIOLOGIE ET PHARMACOLOGIE. (Text mainly in English, occasionally in French) 1944. m. Can.$142 to individuals (foreign $152); institutions Can.$390 (foreign $390) (effective 1996). National Research Council of Canada, Research Journals, Ottawa, ON K1A 0R6, Canada. TEL 613-993-9084. FAX 613-952-7656. E-mail: research.journals@nrc.ca; URL: http://www.cisti.nrc.ca/cisti/journals/cjpp.html. Eds. Drs. J.S. Davison, J.F. Brien. adv.: B&W page Can.$600; trim 8 1/2 x 11; adv. contact: Hoda Jabbour. bibl.; illus.; index. circ. 1,100. (also avail. in microform from UMI,PMC; back issues avail.; reprint service avail. from UMI) **Indexed:** Anal.Abstr., Anim.Breed.Abstr., Apic.Abstr., ASCA, Biodet.Abstr., Biol.Abstr., Biotech.Abstr., Chem.Abstr., Curr.Adv.Cell & Devel.Biol., Curr.Adv.Ecol.Sci., Curr.Cont., Dairy Sci.Abstr., Dent.Ind., Dok.Arbeitsmed., Excerp.Med., Helminthol.Abstr., Hort.Abstr., Ind.Med., Ind.Sci.Rev., Ind.Vet., INIS Atomind., Med.& Surg.Dermat., Neurosci.Cit.Ind., Nutr.Abstr., Pig News & Info., Sci.Cit.Ind., THA, Vet.Bull. **Document type:** academic/scholarly publication.
●Also available online.
—BLDSC (3034.300000); ADONIS; CASDDS; CISTI; EMDOCS; Genuine Article; KNAW; Linda Hall; SWETS; UMI; UnCover. **CCC.**
Formerly (until 1964): Canadian Journal of Biochemistry and Physiology (ISSN 0576-5544); Which supersedes in part (in 1954): Canadian Journal of Medical Sciences (ISSN 0316-4403); Which was formerly (until 1951): Canadian Journal of Research. Section E: Medical Sciences (ISSN 0366-743X)
Refereed Serial

CANADIAN SOCIETY OF PLANT PHYSIOLOGISTS. BULLETIN/SOCIETE CANADIENNE DE PHYSIOLOGIE VEGETALE. BULLETIN. see *BIOLOGY — Botany*

CANCER BIOLOGY AND MEDICINE. see *MEDICAL SCIENCES — Oncology*

CARBOHYDRATE LETTERS. see *BIOLOGY — Biological Chemistry*

612 616.1   UK   ISSN 0142-8012
CARDIOVASCULAR PHYSIOLOGY. m. £80 (effective 1997). S U B I S, Mansion House, 19 Kingfield Rd., Sheffield S11 9AS, England. TEL 44-114-2554433. FAX 44-114-2554626. E-mail: subis@sheffac.demon.co.uk; URL: http://www.shef.ac.uk/uni/companies/shap. (looseleaf format; back issues avail.) **Document type:** abstracting/indexing.
—CCC.
Description: Current awareness service for researchers in clinical and life sciences.

CELLULAR PHYSIOLOGY AND BIOCHEMISTRY. see *BIOLOGY — Biological Chemistry*

571.1   XR   ISSN 1210-6313
QP1   CODEN: CEFYAD
CESKOSLOVENSKA FYZIOLOGIE/CZECHOSLOVAK PHYSIOLOGY. 1952. 4/yr. $112 (effective 1997 & 1998). (Ceska Lekarska Spolecnost J.E. Purkyne) Nakladatelske Stredisko C L S J.E. Purkyne, Sokolska 31, 120 26 Prague 2, Czech Republic. TEL 420-2-24911420. FAX 420-2-24911420. (Dist. by: Abont s.r.o., Chlumova 17, 130 00 Prague 3, Czech Republic) Ed. Jan Mares. bk.rev.; charts; illus.; index, cum.index every 11 yrs. circ. 500. **Indexed:** Biol.Abstr., C.I.S. Abstr., Chem.Abstr., Ind.Med., INIS Atomind., Nutr.Abstr.
—BLDSC (3122.050000); CASDDS; CISTI; Linda Hall.
Formerly (until 1993): Ceskoslovenska Fysiologie (ISSN 0009-0557)
Description: Review articles on topics of current interest in human and animal physiology, pathological physiology, biochemistry, pharmacology and perspectives in biology and medicine; reports of new methods.
Refereed Serial

571   UK   ISSN 0379-864X
QP455   CODEN: CHSED8
CHEMICAL SENSES. 1974. bi-m. £220 (foreign $355) (effective 1998). (European Chemoreception Organization) Oxford University Press, Academic Division, Great Clarendon St., Oxford OX2 6DP, England. TEL 44-1865-267907. FAX 44-1865-267485. TELEX 837330-OXPRES-G. E-mail: jnl.info@oup.co.uk; URL: http://www.oup.co.uk/chemse. (U.S. subscr. to: Oxford University Press Inc., 2001 Evans Rd., Cary, NC 27513. TEL 800-852-7323. FAX 919-677-1714) (Co-sponsor: Association for Chemoreception Sciences) Ed.Bd.; Pub. Steven Johnson. R&P contact: Joolz Longley. adv.; index. circ. 1,050. (back issues avail.; reprint service avail. from SWZ) **Indexed:** Anim.Breed.Abstr., ASCA, Chem.Abstr., Curr.Adv.Ecol.Sci., Curr.Cont., Curr.Ref.Fish Res., Excerp.Med., Food Sci.& Tech.Abstr., Ind.Med. (1994-), Ind.Sci.Rev., Neurosci.Cit.Ind., Potato Abstr., Psychol.Abstr. (1974-), Sci.Cit.Ind., SSCI, Sugar Ind.Abstr. **Document type:** academic/scholarly publication.
—BLDSC (3151.510000); CASDDS; CISTI; EMDOCS; Genuine Article; Linda Hall; SWETS; UMI; UnCover. **CCC.**
Formerly: Chemical Senses and Flavour (ISSN 0302-2471)
Description: International forum for chemoreception research at morphological, biochemical, physiological and psychophysical levels. Covers development and specific application of new methods.

571   CC   ISSN 0258-6428
CHINESE JOURNAL OF PHYSIOLOGICAL SCIENCES. Chinese edition: Shengli Xuebao (ISSN 0371-0874) (Text in English) 1985. q. $145 to individuals (foreign $165); institutions $245 (foreign $265) (effective 1996). (Shanghai Institute of Physiology - Shanghai Shenglixue Yanjiusuo) Science Press, Marketing and Sales Department, 16 Donghuangchenggen North St., Beijing 100717, People's Republic of China. TEL 4010642. FAX 4019810. (Overseas dist. by: Science Press New York, Ltd., 84-04 58th Ave., Elmhurst, NY 11373. TEL 718-476-0238) adv. circ. 6,000. pp./issue: 96. **Document type:** academic/scholarly publication.
—BLDSC (3180.530000); CISTI; EMDOCS; KNAW.
Refereed Serial

571   CH   ISSN 0304-4920
QP1   CODEN: CJPHDG
CHINESE JOURNAL OF PHYSIOLOGY/CHUNG-KUO SHENG LI HSUEH TSA CHIH. (Text in English) 1927. q. NT.$1600($80) Chinese Physiological Society - Chung-kuo Sheng Li Hsueh Hui, Department of Physiology, National Yan-Ming Medical College, Shih-pai, Taipei, Taiwan 11221, Republic of China. FAX 02-826-4049. Ed. Paulus S. Wang. adv.; abstr.; bibl.; charts; illus. circ. 1,000. **Indexed:** Chem.Abstr., Excerp.Med., Ind.Med. **Document type:** academic/scholarly publication.
—BLDSC (3180.550000); CASDDS; EMDOCS; KNAW.
Description: Contains original papers concerned with all fields of physiology, pharmacology, anatomy, and biochemistry.

612 617.8   JA   ISSN 0300-0338
CHOKAKU GENGO SHOGAI/COMMUNICATION DISORDER RESEARCH. (Text in Japanese; summaries in English) 1972. q. 4000 Yen. Chokaku Gengo Shogai Kenkyukai - Research Association of Communication Disorder, Tokyo Gakugei Daigaku Tokushu Kyoiku Shisetsu, 1-1, Nukui Kitamachi 4-chome, Koganei-shi, Tokyo 184, Japan.

612 617.8   JA
CHONO GENGOGAKU KENKYU/JAPANESE JOURNAL OF COMMUNICATION DISORDERS. (Text in Japanese; summaries in English, Japanese) 1983. 3/yr. 2000 Yen. Nihon Chono Gengo Gakkai - Japanese Speech - Language - Hearing Association, 2-15-6-202 Minamicho, Kokubunji-shi, Tokyo 185, Japan. TEL 81-423-24-7397. FAX 81-423-28-7071. Ed. Bensaku Nishimura. **Document type:** academic/scholarly publication.

612   IT   ISSN 0392-3436
CINESIOLOGIA. Variant title: Quaderni di Cinesiologia. 1971. q. L.8000. Edizioni Quattroventi, Via Dini 16, 61029 Urbino, Italy. TEL 39-722-2588. FAX 39-722-320998. Ed. Osvaldo Cappellini.

615.7   AT   ISSN 0305-1870
CODEN: CEXPB9
CLINICAL AND EXPERIMENTAL PHARMACOLOGY AND PHYSIOLOGY. (Supplement avail. (ISSN 0143-9294)) 1974. m. Aus.$720 (foreign Aus.$995) (effective 1997). (Australasian Society of Clinical and Experimental Pharmacologists) Blackwell Science Pty Ltd, P.O. Box 378, Carlton South, Vic. 3053, Australia. TEL 61-3-93470300. FAX 61-3-93493016. adv.: B&W page $790, color page $1650. circ. 780. (back issues avail.; reprint service avail. from UMI) **Indexed:** ASCA, Biotech.Abstr., Chem.Abstr., Curr.Adv.Ecol.Sci., Curr.Cont., Dent.Ind., Excerp.Med., Ind.Med., Ind.Sci.Rev., Neurosci.Cit.Ind., Nutr.Abstr., Sci.Cit.Ind., THA. **Document type:** academic/scholarly publication.
—BLDSC (3286.252000); ADONIS; CASDDS; CISTI; EMDOCS; Genuine Article; KNAW; Linda Hall; SWETS; UMI; UnCover. **CCC.**
Incorporates: Australian Society for Medical Research Proceedings (ISSN 0067-2130)
Description: Covers original contributions relating to the broad fields of pharmacology and physiology.

612   UK   ISSN 0962-8827
CODEN: CDYSEJ
CLINICAL DYSMORPHOLOGY. 1992. q. $95 to individuals; institutions $278 (effective 1996). Chapman & Hall, Journals Department (Subsidiary of: International Thomson Publishing Group), 2-6 Boundary Row, London SE1 8HN, England. TEL 44-171-8650066. FAX 44-171-5229623. TELEX 290164 CHAPMA G. E-mail: jhelp@chall.co.uk; URL: http://www.chaphall.com/chaphall/journals.html. (Dist. by: International Thomson Publishing Services Ltd., Cheriton House, North Way, Andover, Hants. SP10 5BE, England. TEL 01264-342713. FAX 01264-342807; Subscr. in US & Canada to: 400 Market St., Philadelphia, PA 19106. TEL 212-564-1060. FAX 212-564-1505) Ed.Bd. adv.; bk.rev.; illus. (reprint service avail.) **Indexed:** ASCA, Excerp.Med. (1994-), Ind.Med. (1993-), Neurosci.Cit.Ind. **Document type:** academic/scholarly publication.
●Also available online.
—BLDSC (3286.273700); ADONIS; CISTI; EMDOCS; Genuine Article; KNAW; SWETS. **CCC.**
Description: Devoted to publishing reports of multiple congenital anomaly syndromes, original studies and review articles on etiology, clinical delineation, genetic mapping, and molecular embryology of birth defects.
Refereed Serial

CLINICAL PHYSIOLOGY. see *MEDICAL SCIENCES*

612   US
CLINICAL PHYSIOLOGY SERIES. 1977-1991. irreg. price varies. American Physiological Society, 9650 Rockville Pike, Bethesda, MD 20814. TEL 301-530-7164. FAX 301-571-8313. E-mail: info@aps.faseb.org; URL: http://www.faseb.org/aps. Ed.Bd. **Document type:** academic/scholarly publication.
Description: Series is designed as a bridge between basic science and clinical medicine.

591.1   AT
COMMONWEALTH SCIENTIFIC AND INDUSTRIAL RESEARCH ORGANISATION. DIVISION OF ANIMAL PRODUCTION. DIVISIONAL INFORMATION SHEETS. 1969. irreg. free. C.S.I.R.O., Division of Animal Production, Public Affairs & Communication, Locked Bag No. 1, Delivery Centre, Blacktown N.S.W. 2148, Australia. TEL 61-2-98402700. FAX 61-2-98402940. E-mail: p.wilson@prospect.anprod.csiro.au; URL: http://www.anprod.csir.au. Ed. Pat Wilson. R&P contact: Pat Wilson. TEL 61-2-98402741. **Document type:** government publication.
Former titles (until 1993): C.S.I.R.O. Division of Animal Production. Technical Report; (until 1975): C.S.I.R.O. Division of Animal Physiology. Technical Report (ISSN 0084-9014)

BIOLOGY — PHYSIOLOGY

591.1   AT
COMMONWEALTH SCIENTIFIC AND INDUSTRIAL RESEARCH ORGANIZATION. DIVISION OF ANIMAL PRODUCTION. DIVISIONAL INFORMATION. irreg. C.S.I.R.O., Division of Animal Production, Public Affairs & Communication, Locked Bag No. 1, Delivery Centre, Blacktown, N.S.W. 2148, Australia. TEL 61-2-98402700. FAX 61-2-98402940. E-mail: p.wilson@prospect.anprod.csiro.au; URL: http://www.anprod.csiro.au. Ed. Pat Wilson. R&P contact: Pat Wilson. TEL 61-2-98402741. **Indexed:** Biol.Abstr. **Document type:** corporate report.
—CISTI.
    Former titles (until 1993): C.S.I.R.O. Division of Animal Production. Research Report (ISSN 0155-7742); (until 1976): C.S.I.R.O. Division of Animal Physiology. Report (ISSN 0069-7281)

COMPARATIVE BIOCHEMISTRY AND PHYSIOLOGY. PART A: COMPARATIVE PHYSIOLOGY. see *BIOLOGY — Biological Chemistry*

COMPARATIVE BIOCHEMISTRY AND PHYSIOLOGY. PART B: COMPARATIVE BIOCHEMISTRY. see *BIOLOGY — Biological Chemistry*

COMPARATIVE PHYSIOLOGY AND ECOLOGY. see *BIOLOGY*

571   UK   ISSN 0143-2044
                            CODEN: CRLED9
CRYO - LETTERS. 1979. bi-m. £42($84) to individuals; libraries £88 ($180) (effective 1997). 7 Wootton Way, Cambridge CB3 9LX, England. TEL 44-1223-504309. FAX 44-1223-504309. E-mail: cryoletters@dial.pipex.com. Ed. Dr. Felix Franks. adv.; bk.rev.; circ. 250 (paid). **Indexed:** Anim.Breed.Abstr., ASCA, Bibl.Agri., Biol.Abstr., Chem.Abstr., Curr.Adv.Biochem., Curr.Adv.Cell & Devel.Biol., Curr.Adv.Ecol.Sci., Curr.Cont., Ind.Sci.Rev., Sci.Cit.Ind. **Document type:** academic/scholarly publication, newsletter, proceedings.
—BLDSC (3490.133000); CASDDS; CISTI; EMDOCS; Genuine Article; SWETS; UnCover. **CCC**.
    Refereed Serial

CURRENT ADVANCES IN ENDOCRINOLOGY & METABOLISM. see *MEDICAL SCIENCES — Abstracting, Bibliographies, Statistics*

CURRENT MEDICAL LITERATURE. GROWTH HORMONE AND GROWTH FACTORS. see *MEDICAL SCIENCES — Abstracting, Bibliographies, Statistics*

DENMARK. STATENS HUSDYRBRUGSFORSOEG. BERETNING/DENMARK. DANISH INSTITUTE OF ANIMAL SCIENCE. REPORT. see *AGRICULTURE — Poultry And Livestock*

DEVELOPMENT (CAMBRIDGE). see *BIOLOGY*

591.1852   NE   ISSN 0924-5278
DEVELOPMENTS IN BIOMECHANICS. (Text in English) 1982. irreg. price varies. Kluwer Academic Publishers, Postbus 17, 3300 AA Dordrecht, Netherlands. TEL 31-78-6392392. FAX 31-78-6392254. TELEX 29245 KAPG NL. E-mail: services@wkap.nl; URL: http://www.wkap.nl. (Dist. by: Kluwer Academic Publishers Group, P.O. Box 322, 3300 AH Dordrecht, Netherlands. TEL 31-78-6392392. FAX 31-78-6546474; N. America dist. addr.: Box 358, Accord Sta., Hingham, MA 02018-0358. TEL 617-871-6600. FAX 617-871-6528) **Document type:** monographic series.
—KNAW.
    Refereed Serial

612.821   US   ISSN 1053-0797
BF1074   CODEN: DRMGEW
DREAMING. 1991. q. $195 (foreign $230) (effective 1998). (Association for the Study of Dreams) Human Sciences Press, Inc. (Subsidiary of: Plenum Publishing Corp.), 233 Spring St., New York, NY 10013. TEL 212-620-8000. FAX 212-463-0742. TELEX 23-421139. Ed. Ernest Hartmann. adv. **Indexed:** Arts & Hum.Cit.Ind., ASCA, Curr.Cont., Fam.Ind., Psychol.Abstr. (1991-). **Document type:** academic/scholarly publication.
—BLDSC (3623.341400); Genuine Article; UnCover. **CCC**.
    Description: Provides a forum for biological and physiological studies involving sleep and dream research, psychological studies, psychoanalytic investigations, and papers on the link between dreams and art, literature, and other human activities.
    Refereed Serial

571   UA   ISSN 0301-8660
QH301   CODEN: EJPLAD
EGYPTIAN JOURNAL OF PHYSIOLOGICAL SCIENCE. (Text in English; summaries in Arabic and English) 1974. s-a. $57 (effective 1997). (Egyptian Physiological Society, Research Department) National Information and Documentation Centre (NIDOC), Tahrir St., Dokki, Awqaf P.O., Cairo, Egypt. TEL 20-2-3371696. Ed. H. Hamdi. abstr.; charts; illus. circ. 1,000. (back issues avail.; reprint service avail. from IRC) **Indexed:** Biol.Abstr., Chem.Abstr., Hort.Abstr., Nutr.Abstr. **Document type:** academic/scholarly publication.
—BLDSC (3664.417000); CASDDS; CISTI; Linda Hall; SWETS.
    Formerly: Egyptian Journal of Physiology.

ELECTROMYOGRAPHY AND CLINICAL NEUROPHYSIOLOGY. see *MEDICAL SCIENCES*

ENDOCRINE. see *MEDICAL SCIENCES — Endocrinology*

ENDOTHELIUM. see *BIOLOGY — Abstracting, Bibliographies, Statistics*

ETHEL BROWNING'S TOXICITY AND METABOLISM OF INDUSTRIAL SOLVENTS. see *ENVIRONMENTAL STUDIES — Toxicology And Environmental Safety*

EUROPEAN JOURNAL OF ANATOMY. see *MEDICAL SCIENCES*

571   GW   ISSN 0301-5548
QP1   CODEN: EJAPCK
EUROPEAN JOURNAL OF APPLIED PHYSIOLOGY AND OCCUPATIONAL PHYSIOLOGY. Online edition (GW ISSN 1432-1025) (Text in English) m. DM.3794.80 (foreign DM.3810.40) (effective 1998). Springer-Verlag, Heidelberger Platz 3, 14197 Berlin, Germany. TEL 49-30-82787-0. FAX 49-30-82787448. E-mail: subscriptions@springer.de; URL: http://link.springer.de. (Subscr. in N. America to: Springer-Verlag New York, Inc., 333 Meadowlands Pkwy., Secaucus, NJ 07094. TEL 212-460-1500. FAX 212-473-6272) Eds. R. Goldsmith, W. Isselhard. (also avail. in microform from UMI; reprint service avail. from ISI) **Indexed:** ASCA, Biol.Abstr., C.I.S. Abstr., Chem.Abstr., Curr.Adv.Biochem., Curr.Adv.Ecol.Sci., Curr.Cont., Ergon.Abstr., Excerp.Med., HRIS, Ind.Med., Ind.Sci.Rev., INIS Atomind., Neurosci.Cit.Ind., Nutr.Abstr., Phys.Ed.Ind., Risk Abstr., Sci.Cit.Ind., Sportsearch (1975-), SSCI, THA, Trop.Dis.Bull. **Document type:** academic/scholarly publication.
●Also available online.
—BLDSC (3829.722500); CASDDS; CISTI; EMDOCS; Genuine Article; KNAW; SWETS; UMI; UnCover. **CCC**.
    Formerly: Internationale Zeitschrift fuer Angewandte Physiologie Einschliesslich Arbeitsphysiologie (ISSN 0020-9376)

611 571.3   NE   ISSN 0924-3860
QL799   CODEN: EJMOEB
EUROPEAN JOURNAL OF MORPHOLOGY. (Text in English) 1956. 5/yr. fl.363($220) to individuals; institutions fl.696($422) (effective 1997). Swets & Zeitlinger bv, P.O. Box 825, 2160 SZ Lisse, Netherlands. TEL 31-252-435111. FAX 31-252-415888. TELEX 41325. E-mail: orders@swets.nl; URL: http://www.swets.nl. (Dist. in N. America by: Swets & Zeitlinger, Box 613, Royersford, PA 19468. TEL 800-447-9387. FAX 610-524-5366) Eds. J. Drukker, A. Huson. R&P contact: J.v.d. Valk. adv. contact: Patrick Kliean. bk.rev.; bibl.; charts; index. circ. 600. (reprint service avail. from SWZ) **Indexed:** Anim.Breed.Abstr., ASCA, Biol.Abstr., Chem.Abstr., Curr.Adv.Ecol.Sci., Curr.Cont., Dent.Ind., Excerp.Med., Helminthol.Abstr., Ind.Med., Ind.Sci.Rev., Sci.Cit.Ind, Sport Fish.Abstr., Vet.Bull., Wild.Rev., Zoo.Rec. **Document type:** academic/scholarly publication.
●Also available online.
—BLDSC (3829.731660); CASDDS; CISTI; EMDOCS; Genuine Article; KNAW; Linda Hall; SWETS; UnCover. **CCC**.
    Incorporates (in 1995): European Archives of Biology (ISSN 0777-0553); Which was formerly titled (1886-1989): Archives de Biologie (ISSN 0003-9624); **Formerly:** Acta Morphologica Neerlando-Scandinavica (ISSN 0001-6225)
    Description: Covers the entire filed of vertebrate morphology, with emphasis on human embryology and anatomy.

612   UK   ISSN 0958-0670
QP1   CODEN: EXPHEZ
EXPERIMENTAL PHYSIOLOGY. 1908. bi-m. £197($336) (effective 1998). (Physiological Society) Cambridge University Press, Edinburgh Bldg., Shaftesbury Rd., Cambridge CB2 2RU, England. TEL 44-1223-312393. FAX 44-1223-315052. TELEX 851817256. E-mail: information@cup.cam.ac.uk; URL: http://www.cup.cam.ac.uk. (N. American addr.: Cambridge University Press, Journals Dept., 40 W. 20th St., New York, NY 10011. TEL 212-924-3900. FAX 212-691-3239) Ed. J. Gillespie. R&P contact: Linda Nicol. adv. contact: Rebecca Symons. bk.rev. (also avail. in microform from UMI,PMC; back issues avail.) **Indexed:** ASCA, Biol.Abstr., Curr.Adv.Biochem., Curr.Adv.Ecol.Sci., Curr.Cont., Dairy Sci.Abstr., Excerp.Med., Ind.Med., Ind.Sci.Rev., Ind.Vet., Neurosci.Cit.Ind., Nutr.Abstr., Poult.Abstr., Rice Abstr., Sci.Cit.Ind., Small Anim.Abstr., THA, Vet.Bull. **Document type:** academic/scholarly publication.
—BLDSC (3840.040000); CASDDS; CISTI; EMDOCS; Genuine Article; KNAW; Linda Hall; SWETS; UMI; UnCover.
    Former titles: Quarterly Journal of Experimental Physiology; Quarterly Journal of Experimental Physiology and Cognate Medical Sciences (ISSN 0144-8757)
    Description: Contains research papers on all aspects of experimental physiology from molecular to animal studies.

571   KR   ISSN 0533-1153
                            CODEN: FAVUAI
FIZIOLOGICHESKI AKTIVNYE VESHCHESTVA; respublikanskii mezhvedomstvennyi sbornik nauchnykh trudov. (Text in Russian) 1966. a. (Akademiya Nauk Ukrainy, Institut Organicheskoi Khimii) Vidavnitstvo Naukova Dumka, Vul. Tereshchenivska 3, 252601 Kiev, Ukraine. TEL 044-224-4068. FAX 044-224-7060. (Dist. by: Mezhdunarodnaya Kniga, B. Yakimanka 39, 117049 Moscow, Russia) Ed. M.O. Lozinskii. **Indexed:** Chem.Abstr.
—CASDDS; Linda Hall. **CCC**.

571   KR   ISSN 0201-8489
QP1   CODEN: FIZHDO
FIZIOLOGICHESKII ZHURNAL (KIEV)/FIZIOLOGICHNYI ZHURNAL; nauchno-teoreticheskii zhurnal. (Text in Russian and Ukrainian; summaries in English) 1955. bi-m. $42 (effective 1998). Akademiya Nauk Ukrainy, Institut Fiziologii im. Bogomol'tsya, Vul. Bogomol'tsya, 4, 252601 Kiev 1, Ukraine. TEL 38-44-2930745. (Dist. by: Mezhdunarodnaya Kniga, B. Yakimanka 39, 117049 Moscow, Russia. TEL 7-095-2384967. FAX 7-095-2384634) Ed. Ph.N. Serkov. bk.rev.; illus.; index. **Indexed:** Biol.Abstr., Chem.Abstr., Djerelo, Excerp.Med., Ind.Med., Ind.Sci.Rev., INIS Atomind., Neurosci.Cit.Ind., Poult.Abstr., Vet.Bull.
—BLDSC (0390.050000); CASDDS; CISTI; Genuine Article; KNAW; Linda Hall. **CCC**.
    Formerly (until 1978): Fiziologichnyi Zhurnal (ISSN 0015-3311)

571   RU
QP1   CODEN: FZLZAM
FIZIOLOGICHESKII ZHURNAL IM. SECHENOVA/SECHENOV PHYSIOLOGICAL JOURNAL. (Text in Russian; summaries in English) 1917. m. $256 (effective 1996 & 1997). (Rossiiskaya Akademiya Nauk, S.-Peterburgskoe Otdelenie) Izdatel'stvo Nauka, S.-Peterburgskoe Otdelenie, Mendeleevskaya Linija, 1, 199034 St. Petersburg B-34, Russia. TEL 812-218-37-12. (Dist. by: Mezhdunarodnaya Kniga, B. Yakimanka 39, 117049 Moscow, Russia. TEL 7-095-2384967. FAX 7-095-2384634; Dist. in U.S. by Victor Kamkin Inc., 4956 Boiling Brook Pkwy., Rockville, MD 20852. TEL 301-881-5973) Ed. Y.V. Natochin. bk.rev.; bibl.; charts; illus.; index. circ. 2,000. **Indexed:** Biol.Abstr., Chem.Abstr., Curr.Adv.Ecol.Sci., Dent.Ind., Excerp.Med., Helminthol.Abstr., Ind.Med., Ind.Vet., Int.Aerosp.Abstr., Nutr.Abstr., Poult.Abstr., Psychol.Abstr. (1932-), Sci.Cit.Ind., SSCI, Vet.Bull.
—CASDDS; CISTI; Linda Hall. **CCC**.
    Formerly: Fiziologicheskii Zhurnal S.S.S.R. im. Sechenova (ISSN 0015-329X)

BIOLOGY — PHYSIOLOGY

571　　　　　　　　RU　ISSN 0131-1646
QP34.5　　　　　　　　　CODEN: FICHDB
FIZIOLOGIYA CHELOVEKA. English translation: Human Physiology (US ISSN 0362-1197) 1975. bi-m. $236 (effective 1998). (Rossiiskaya Akademiya Nauk) Izdatel'stvo Nauka, 90 Profsoyuznaya ul., 117864 Moscow, Russia. TEL 234-05-84. (Dist. by: Mezhdunarodnaya Kniga, ul. Dimitrova D.39, 113095 Moscow, Russia) Ed. N.P. Bekhtereva. illus. **Indexed:** Biol.Abstr., Chem.Abstr., Ind.Med., INIS Atomind., Int.Aerosp.Abstr.
—BLDSC (0390.590000); CASDDS; CISTI; KNAW; Linda Hall.

571　　　　　　　　KR　ISSN 0256-1425
QK710　　　　　　　　　CODEN: FBKRAT
FIZIOLOGIYA I BIOKHIMIYA KUL'TURNYKH RASTENII/PHYSIOLOGY AND BIOCHEMISTRY OF CULTIVATED PLANTS; nauchno-teoreticheskii zhurnal. (Text in Russian; summaries in English and Russian) 1969. bi-m. $124. Akademiya Nauk Ukrainy, Institut Fiziologii Roslin ta Genetiki, Vul. Vasil'kivs'ka, 31-17, 252022 Kiev 22, Ukraine. TEL 38-44-2649921. (Dist. by: Mezhdunarodnaya Kniga, B. Yakimanka 39, 117049 Moscow, Russia; Dist. in U.S. by: Victor Kamkin Inc., 4956 Boiling Brook Pkwy., Rockville, MD 20852. TEL 301-881-5973) Ed. L.K. Ostrovskaya. abstr. **Indexed:** Biol.Abstr., Chem.Abstr., Cott.& Trop.Fibr.Abstr., Crop Physiol.Abstr., Curr.Adv.Ecol.Sci., Djerelo, Field Crop Abstr., Herb.Abstr., Hort.Abstr., Ind.Sci.Rev., INIS Atomind., Maize Abstr., Plant Breed.Abstr., Plant Grow.Reg.Abstr., Potato Abstr., Rev.Plant Path., Rice Abstr., Sci.Cit.Ind., Seed Abstr., Soils & Fert., Soyabean Abstr., Weed Abstr.
—CISTI.

573.8　　　　UK　ISSN 1353-6508
　　　　　　　　　CODEN: FNEUES
FRONTIERS IN NEUROBIOLOGY. 1994. irreg. £65($110.50) (effective 1997). Portland Press Ltd., 59 Portland Pl., London W1N 3AJ, England. TEL 44-171-580-5530. FAX 44-171-323-1136. E-mail: sales@portlandpress.co.uk; URL: http://www.portlandpress.co.uk. (Subscr. to: Commerce Way, P.O. Box 32, Colchester, Essex CO2 8HP, England. TEL 44-1206-796351. FAX 44-1206-799331) Ed. A.J. Turner. R&P contact: Adam Marshall. **Document type:** monographic series.
—BLDSC (4042.039500); CASDDS; CISTI.
Refereed Serial

612 616.3　　　UK　ISSN 0142-8098
GASTRIC SECRETION. 1987. s-m. (diskette m.) £120 (diskette £120; both £180) (effective 1997). S U B I S, Mansion House, 19 Kingfield Rd., Sheffield S11 9AS, England. TEL 44-114-2554433. FAX 44-114-2554626. E-mail: subis@sheffac.demon.co.uk; URL: http://www.shef.ac.uk/uni/companies/shap. (also avail. in diskette format) **Document type:** abstracting/indexing.
—CCC.
Description: Current awareness service for researchers in clinical and life sciences.

571　　　　　　　　XO　ISSN 0231-5882
QP1　　　　　　　　　CODEN: GPBIE2
GENERAL PHYSIOLOGY AND BIOPHYSICS. (Text in English) 1982. bi-m. 162 Kcs. Slovak Academy of Sciences, Institute of Molecular Physiology and Genetics, Vlarska 5, 933 34 Bratislava, Slovakia. (Dist. by: Slovart, Nam. Slobody 6, 817 64 Bratislava, Slovakia) Ed. Jozef Zachar. **Indexed:** ASCA, Curr.Adv.Ecol.Sci., Curr.Cont., Dairy Sci.Abstr., Ind.Med., Ind.Sci.Rev., Sci.Cit.Ind. **Document type:** academic/scholarly publication.
—BLDSC (4106.725000); CASDDS; CISTI; EMDOCS; Genuine Article; KNAW; SWETS; UnCover.
Description: Publishes original scientific studies within the sphere of general physiology, biophysics and biochemistry at the cellular and molecular levels, along with papers relating the progress and development of the respective research techniques and methods.

612　　　　　　　　JA
GIFU DAIGAKU IGAKUBU HANSHA KENKYU SHISETSU GYOSEKISHU/GIFU UNIVERSITY. SCHOOL OF MEDICINE. INSTITUTE OF EQUILIBRIUM RESEARCH. BULLETIN. (Text in English, Japanese) 1974. biennial. Gifu Daigaku, Igakubu, Hansha Kenkyu Shisetsu Hansha Seirigaku Bumon, 40, Tsukasamachi, Gifu-shi, Gifu-ken 500, Japan.

612　　　　　　　　NE　ISSN 0897-7194
QP552.G76　　　　　　　CODEN: GRFAEC
GROWTH FACTORS. 1989. 8/yr. (in 2 vols., 4 nos./vol.). $129 (effective 1998). Gordon and Breach - Harwood Academic, Amsteldisk 166, 1st Fl., 1079 LH Amsterdam, Netherlands. URL: http://www.gbhap.com/Growth_Factors/. (Subscr. to: International Publishers Distributor, Box 32160, Newark, NJ 07102. TEL 800-545-8398. FAX 215-750-6343) Ed. A.W. Burgess. (also avail. in microform) **Indexed:** ASCA, Curr.Cont., Food Sci.& Tech.Abstr., Ind.Sci.Rev., Sci.Cit.Ind.
●Also available online.
Also available on CD-ROM.
—BLDSC (4223.032950); CISTI; EMDOCS; KNAW; SWETS; UnCover. **CCC.**
Refereed Serial

571　　　　　　　　US　ISSN 0072-9876
HANDBOOK OF PHYSIOLOGY. 1959. irreg. price varies. American Physiological Society, 9650 Rockville Pike, Bethesda, MD 20814. TEL 301-530-7164. FAX 301-571-8313. E-mail: info@aps.faseb.org; URL: http://www.faseb.org/aps. **Indexed:** Biol.Abstr. **Document type:** monographic series.
Description: Provides a comprehensive but critical presentation of the state of knowledge in the various fields of functional biology.
Refereed Serial

612　　　　　　　　JA　ISSN 0385-5716
HEIKO SHINKEI KAGAKU/EQUILIBRIUM RESEARCH. (Text in Japanese; summaries in English) 1971. q. Nihon Heiko Shinkeika Gakkai - Japan Society for Equilibrium Research, c/o Kyoto Daigaku Igakubu Jibi Inko Kagaku Kyoshitsu, Shogoin Kawaracho, Sakyo-ku, Kyoto 606, Japan. **Indexed:** Excerp.Med.
—BLDSC (3794.509700); EMDOCS; KNAW.

612　　　　　　　　JA　ISSN 0916-0337
HEIKO SHINKEI KAGAKU. SUPPLEMENT/EQUILIBRIUM RESEARCH. SUPPLEMENT. (Text in Japanese; summaries in English) 1987. irreg. Nihon Heiko Shinkeika Gakkai - Japan Society for Equibrium Research, c/o Kyoto Daigaku Igakubu Jibi Inko Kagaku Kyoshitsu, Shogoin Kawaracho, Sakyo-ku, Kyoto 606, Japan.
—BLDSC (3794.509710).

571　　　　　　　　JA　ISSN 0916-3786
　　　　　　　　　CODEN: COPBEY
HIKAKU SEIRI SEIKAGAKU/COMPARATIVE PHYSIOLOGY AND BIOCHEMISTRY. (Text in English, Japanese) 1979. q. 2400 Yen per no. Nihon Hikaku Seiri Seikagakkai - Japanese Society for Comparative Physiology and Biochemistry, Tokyo Daigaku Rigakubu Dobutsugaku Kyoshitsu, 3-1 Hongo 7-chome, Bunkyo-ku, Tokyo 113, Japan. **Indexed:** Chem.Abstr.
—CASDDS.

612　　　　　　　　JA　ISSN 0913-0241
HIRO TO KYUYO NO KAGAKU/SCIENCE OF FATIGUE AND REST. (Text in Japanese; summaries in English) 1986. a. Hiro Kenkyukai - Society for the Study of Fatigue, Tokyo Jikeikai Ika Daigaku, Dai 2 Seirigaku Kyoshitsu, 25-8, Nishishinbashi 3-chome, Minato-ku, Tokyo 105, Japan.

HUMAN BRAIN MAPPING. see *MEDICAL SCIENCES — Psychiatry And Neurology*

612　　　　　　　　SZ　ISSN 0018-716X
　　　　　　　　　CODEN: HUDEA8
HUMAN DEVELOPMENT. (Text in English) 1958. bi-m. 83.80 SFr.($64) to individuals; institutions 335 SFr.($256) (effective 1998). S. Karger AG, Allschwilerstr. 10, P.O. Box, CH-4009 Basel, Switzerland. TEL 41-61-3061234. FAX 41-61-3061234. E-mail: karger@karger.ch; URL: http://www.karger.ch. Ed. B. Rogoff. adv.; bk.rev.; bibl.; charts; illus.; index. circ. 2,200. (also avail. in microform; reprint service avail. from SWZ) **Indexed:** Adol.Ment.Hlth.Abstr., Arts & Hum.Cit.Ind., Biol.Abstr., C.I.J.E., CLOA, Curr.Adv.Ecol.Sci., Curr.Cont., Educ.Ind., Excerp.Med., IBR, Ind.Med., M.L.A., Mid.East; Abstr.& Ind., Psychol.Abstr. (1958-), Psycscan D.P., Rehabil.Lit., SSCI, SSCI. **Document type:** academic/scholarly publication.
—BLDSC (4336.050000); Genuine Article; KNAW; KR SourceOne; SWETS; UnCover. **CCC.**
Formerly: Vita Humana.
Description: Scholarly articles on psychological development over an entire lifespan, from infancy through aging.
Refereed Serial

612　　　　　　　　RU　ISSN 0362-1197
QP34.5　　　　　　　　CODEN: HUPHDC
HUMAN PHYSIOLOGY. English translation of: Fiziologiya Cheloveka (RU ISSN 0131-1646) 1975. bi-m. $1165 in US; elsewhere $1365 (effective 1998). (Russian Academy of Sciences) Maik Nauka - Interperiodica, Mezhdunarodnyi Otdel, Ul. Profsoyuznaya, 90, 117864 Moscow, Russia. TEL 7-095-3360066. FAX 7-095-3360066. (Dist. by: Plenum Publishing Corp, 233 Spring St., New York, NY 10013-1578, U.S.A. TEL 212-620-8000. FAX 212-463-0742) Ed. V.I. Medvedev. (also avail. in microfilm from UMI; back issues avail.) **Indexed:** Biol.Abstr., Curr.Adv.Ecol.Sci., Ergon.Abstr., Excerp.Med., Ind.Med., Int.Abstr.Biol.Sci., Psychol.Abstr. (1979-). **Document type:** academic/scholarly publication.
—BLDSC (0412.087700); CASDDS; CISTI; SWETS; UMI; UnCover. **CCC.**
Refereed Serial

612 616.858　　　UK　ISSN 0142-811X
HUMAN SEXUALITY. s-m. (diskette m.) £90 (diskette £120; both £180) (effective 1997). S U B I S, Mansion House, 19 Kingfield Rd., Sheffield S11 9AS, England. TEL 44-114-2554433. FAX 44-114-2554626. E-mail: subis@sheffac.demon.co.uk; URL: http://www.shef.ac.uk/uni/companies/shap. (also avail. in diskette format; looseleaf format; back issues avail.) **Document type:** abstracting/indexing.
—CCC.
Description: Current awareness service for researchers in clinical and life sciences.

INDIAN JOURNAL OF COMPARATIVE ANIMAL PHYSIOLOGY. see *BIOLOGY — Zoology*

571　　　　　　　　II　ISSN 0019-5499
QP1　　　　　　　　　CODEN: IJPPAZ
INDIAN JOURNAL OF PHYSIOLOGY AND PHARMACOLOGY. (Text in English) 1957. q. Rs.1000($50) Association of Physiologists and Pharmacologists of India, Department of Physiology, All India Institute of Medical Sciences, Ansari Nagar, New Delhi 110 029, India. (Dist. by: HPC Publisher's Distributors (Pvt.) Ltd., 4805-24, 1st Fl., Bharat Ram Rd., Darya Ganj, New Delhi 110 002, India. TEL 91-11-3254402. FAX 91-11-6863511) Ed. Dr. R.L. Bijlani. adv.; bk.rev.; bibl.; charts; illus.; index. circ. 1,000. **Indexed:** Appl.Mech.Rev., Biol.Abstr., Chem.Abstr., Curr.Adv.Ecol.Sci., Excerp.Med., ExtraMED, Ind.Med., Rev.Med.& Vet.Mycol., Vet.Bull. **Document type:** academic/scholarly publication.
●Also available on CD-ROM.
—BLDSC (4420.130000); CASDDS; CISTI; KNAW; Linda Hall; UnCover.
Refereed Serial

571　　　　　　　　FR　ISSN 0073-8565
　　　　　　　　　CODEN: AIMPCT
INSTITUT MICHEL PACHA. ANNALES. 1968. biennial. price varies. Institut Michel Pacha, Laboratoire Maritime de Physiologie, Tamaris-sur-Mer, France. Ed. G. Peres. bk.rev. **Indexed:** Biol.Abstr., Bull.Signal., Chem.Abstr.
—CASDDS; CISTI.

612 661.8　　　　US
INSTITUTE FOR ORGONOMIC SCIENCE. ANNALS. 1984. a. $15. Institute for Orgonomic Science, Box 304, Gwynedd Valley, PA 19437. bk.rev. circ. 600.

INTEGRATIVE PHYSIOLOGICAL AND BEHAVIORAL SCIENCE. see *PSYCHOLOGY*

612 591　　　　UK　ISSN 0261-4952
INVERTEBRATE NEUROBIOLOGY. 1982. s-m. (diskette m.) £110 (diskette £120; both £180) (effective 1997). S U B I S, Mansion House, 19 Kingfield Rd., Sheffield S11 9AS, England. TEL 44-114-2554433. FAX 44-114-2554626. E-mail: subis@sheffac.demon.co.uk; URL: http://www.shef.ac.uk/uni/companies/shap. (also avail. in diskette format) **Document type:** abstracting/indexing.
—CCC.
Description: Current awareness service for researchers. Examines invertebrate neuroscience: development, structure, physiology, biochemistry, peptides and transmitters.

ITALIAN JOURNAL OF MINERAL & ELECTROLYTE METABOLISM. see *MEDICAL SCIENCES*

BIOLOGY — PHYSIOLOGY

571   RU   ISSN 0134-2673
QP1   CODEN: INTFCL
ITOGI NAUKI I TEKHNIKI: FIZIOLOGIYA CHELOVEKA I ZHIVOTNYKH. irreg., latest vol.35-38, 1989. 6.60 Rub. Vsesoyuznyi Institut Nauchno-Tekhnicheskoi Informatsii (VINITI), Baltiiskaya ul. 14, Moscow A-219, Russia. (Subscr. to: Mezhdunarodnaya Kniga, Dimitrova ul. 39, 113095 Moscow, Russia)

571   JA   ISSN 0021-521X
QP1   CODEN: JJPHAM
JAPANESE JOURNAL OF PHYSIOLOGY. (Text in English) 1951. bi-m. $160. (Physiological Society of Japan) Center for Academic Publications Japan, 2-4-16 Yayoi, Bunkyo-ku, Tokyo 113, Japan. TEL 03-3817-5821. FAX 03-3817-5830. E-mail: capj@crisscross.com. (Dist. by: Business Center for Academic Societies Japan, 5-16-9 Konkomagome, Bunkyo-ku, Tokyo 113, Japan. TEL 03-5814-5811. FAX 03-5814-5822) Ed. Hiroyuki Suga. circ. 1,600. **Indexed:** ASCA, Biol.Abstr., Chem.Abstr., Curr.Cont., Dairy Sci.Abstr., Dent.Ind., Excerp.Med., Ind.Med., Ind.Sci.Rev., INIS Atomind., Neurosci.Cit.Ind., SSCI, THA. **Document type:** academic/scholarly publication. —BLDSC (4658.000000); CASDDS; CISTI; Genuine Article; KNAW; Linda Hall; SWETS; UnCover.
Refereed Serial

JOURNAL OF ANIMAL MORPHOLOGY AND PHYSIOLOGY. see *BIOLOGY — Zoology*

JOURNAL OF ANIMAL SCIENCE. see *AGRICULTURE — Poultry And Livestock*

JOURNAL OF ANIMAL SCIENCE. SUPPLEMENT. BIENNIAL SYMPOSIUM ON ANIMAL REPRODUCTION. see *AGRICULTURE — Poultry And Livestock*

JOURNAL OF APPLIED BIOMECHANICS. see *MEDICAL SCIENCES — Sports Medicine*

571   US   ISSN 8750-7587
QP1   CODEN: JAPHEV
JOURNAL OF APPLIED PHYSIOLOGY. 1948. m. $410 to individual non-members (Canada and Mexico $450; elsewhere $500); institutions $615 (Canada and Mexico $655; elsewhere $705); members $205 (effective 1997). American Physiological Society, 9650 Rockville Pike, Bethesda, MD 20814. TEL 301-530-7164. FAX 301-571-8313. E-mail: info@aps.faseb.org; URL: http://www.faseb.org/aps. Ed. J.E. Remmers. adv.: B&W page $775, color page $1125. bibl.; charts; illus.; index. cum.index: vols.1-39 (1948-1975). circ. 4,475. (also avail. in microform from UMI; reprint service avail. from UMI) **Indexed:** Abstr.Anthropol., ASCA, Biol.Abstr., Biol.& Agr.Ind., Biotech.Abstr., C.I.S. Abstr., Chem.Abstr., Curr.Cont., Dairy Sci.Abstr., Dent.Ind., Ergon.Abstr., Excerp.Med., Ind.Sci.Rev., INSPEC, Int.Abstr.Biol.Sci., Neurosci.Cit.Ind., Nutr.Abstr., Phys.Ed.Ind., Ref.Zh., Sci.Cit.Ind., Sport Fish.Abstr., Sportsearch (1974-), SSCI, Trop.Dis.Bull., Vet.Bull., Wild.Rev., Zoo.Rec. **Document type:** academic/scholarly publication.
●Also available online. Vendor(s): OCLC. —BLDSC (4946.000000); CASDDS; CISTI; EMDOCS; Genuine Article; KNAW; KR SourceOne; Linda Hall; SWETS; UMI; UnCover. **CCC.**
Former titles: Journal of Applied Physiology: Respiratory, Environmental and Exercise Physiology (ISSN 0161-7567); (until 1977): Journal of Applied Physiology (ISSN 0021-8987)
Description: Presents original papers that deal with normal or abnormal function in four areas: respiratory physiology, environmental physiology, exercise physiology, and temperature regulation.
Refereed Serial

571   US   ISSN 0021-9541
QP1   CODEN: JCLLAX
JOURNAL OF CELLULAR PHYSIOLOGY. (Supplement avail.) 1932. m. $3355 (foreign $3355) (effective 1998). John Wiley & Sons, Inc., Journals, 605 Third Ave., New York, NY 10158. TEL 212-850-6645. FAX 212-850-6021. TELEX 12-7063. E-mail: subinfo@jwiley.com; URL: http://www.wiley.co.uk. (Subscr. outside the Americas to: John Wiley & Sons Ltd., Baffins Ln., Chichester, W. Sussex PO19 1UD, England. TEL 44-1243-779777. FAX 44-1243-776128) Ed. Claudio Basilico. adv.: B&W page £640, color page £1515; trim 279 x 210. abstr.; bibl.; charts. circ. 1,400. (also avail. in microform from UMI; back issues avail.; reprint service avail. from SWZ) **Indexed:** Anim.Breed.Abstr., ASCA, Biol.Abstr., Biol.& Agr.Ind., Chem.Abstr., Curr.Adv.Biochem., Curr.Adv.Cancer Res., Curr.Adv.Cell & Devel.Biol., Curr.Adv.Genetics & Molec.Biol., Curr.Cont., Dairy Sci.Abstr., Dent.Ind., Excerp.Med., Helminthol.Abstr., Ind.Med., Ind.Sci.Rev., INIS Atomind., Neurosci.Cit.Ind., Sci.Cit.Ind., SSCI. **Document type:** academic/scholarly publication.
●Also available online. —BLDSC (4955.020000); ADONIS; CASDDS; CISTI; Genuine Article; KNAW; KR SourceOne; Linda Hall; SWETS; UnCover. **CCC.**
Formerly: Journal of Cellular and Comparative Physiology.
Description: Presents research papers concerned with physiology and pathology at the cellular level, including the biochemical and biophysical mechanisms concerned in the regulation of cellular growth, differentiation, and function.
Refereed Serial

571.1   GW   ISSN 0340-7594
QP1   CODEN: JCPADN
JOURNAL OF COMPARATIVE PHYSIOLOGY. A: SENSORY, NEURAL, AND BEHAVIORAL PHYSIOLOGY. Online edition (GW ISSN 1432-1351) (Text in English) 1924. m. DM.4195 (foreign DM.4224.40) (effective 1998). Springer-Verlag, Heidelberger Platz 3, 14197 Berlin, Germany. TEL 49-30-82787-0. FAX 49-30-82787448. E-mail: subscriptions@springer.de; URL: http://link.springer.de. (Subscr. in N. America to: Springer-Verlag New York, Inc., 333 Meadowlands Pkwy., Secaucus, NJ 07094. TEL 212-460-1500. FAX 212-473-6272) Ed.Bd. adv.; charts; illus.; cum.index. (also avail. in microform from UMI,PMC; reprint service avail. from ISI) **Indexed:** Apic.Abstr., ASCA, Bibl.Agri., Bio-Contr.News & Info., Biol.Abstr., Chem.Abstr., Curr.Adv.Biochem., Curr.Adv.Cell & Devel.Biol., Curr.Cont., Curr.Ref.Fish Res., Deep Sea Res.& Oceanogr.Abstr., Dent.Ind., Excerp.Med., Helminthol.Abstr., Ind.Sci.Rev., Neurosci.Cit.Ind., Nutr.Abstr., Rev.Appl.Entomol., Sci.Cit.Ind., Sport Fish.Abstr., SSCI, Wild.Rev., Zoo.Rec. **Document type:** academic/scholarly publication.
●Also available online. —BLDSC (4963.210000); CASDDS; CISTI; EMDOCS; Genuine Article; Linda Hall; SWETS; UMI; UnCover. **CCC.**
Supersedes in part (in 1984): Zeitschrift fuer Vergleichende Physiologie (ISSN 0044-362X)
Description: Concerned with invertebrates, vertebrates, and non-human mammals, particularly with the sense organs, neural processes as well as with the experimental analysis of behavior.

571   GW   ISSN 0174-1578
QP33   CODEN: JPBPDL
JOURNAL OF COMPARATIVE PHYSIOLOGY. B: BIOCHEMICAL, SYSTEMATIC, AND ENVIRONMENTAL PHYSIOLOGY. Online edition (GW ISSN 1432-136X) (Text in English) 1924. 8/yr. DM.2013.20 (foreign DM.2020.40) (effective 1998). Springer-Verlag, Heidelberger Platz 3, 14197 Berlin, Germany. TEL 49-30-82787-0. FAX 49-30-82787448. E-mail: subscriptions@springer.de; URL: http://link.springer.de. (Subscr. in N. America to: Springer-Verlag New York, Inc., 333 Meadowlands Pkwy., Secaucus, NJ 07094. TEL 212-460-1500. FAX 212-473-6272) Ed.Bd. adv.; charts; illus.; cum.index. (also avail. in microform from UMI,PMC; reprint service avail. from ISI) **Indexed:** Apic.Abstr., ASCA, Biol.Abstr., Curr.Cont., Deep Sea Res.& Oceanogr.Abstr., Excerp.Med., Helminthol.Abstr., Ind.Sci.Rev., Ind.Vet., Nutr.Abstr., Poult.Abstr., Rev.Appl.Entomol., Sci.Cit.Ind., Sport Fish.Abstr., Wild.Rev., Zoo.Rec. **Document type:** academic/scholarly publication.
●Also available online. —BLDSC (4963.211000); CASDDS; CISTI; Genuine Article; Linda Hall; SWETS; UMI; UnCover. **CCC.**
Formerly: Journal of Comparative Physiology. B. Systematic and Environmental Physiology (ISSN 0340-7616); Supersedes in part (in 1984): Zeitschrift fuer Vergleichende Physiologie (ISSN 0044-362X)
Description: Provides information from the molecular level up to the organismic levels of animals, including comparative aspects of metabolism and enzymology, physiology of body fluids, and muscular physiology.

612.8   UK   ISSN 0307-5095
JOURNAL OF ELECTROPHYSIOLOGICAL TECHNOLOGY. 1949. q. £10 (foreign £20) (effective 1997). Electrophysiological Technologists' Association, c/o E.E.G. Department, St. Bartholomew's Hospital, W. Smithfield, London EC1A 7BE, England. TEL 44-171-601-8859. FAX 44-171-601-7875. Eds. C.R. Green, R. Pottinger. R&P contact: Christopher Green. adv. contact: L. O'Neill. bk.rev.; abstr.; bibl.; charts; illus.; index. circ. 700. **Indexed:** Excerp.Med., Ind.Med. **Document type:** academic/scholarly publication, abstracting/indexing. —BLDSC (4976.150000); CISTI; UnCover.
Formerly: Electrophysiological Technologists' Association. Proceedings and Journal (ISSN 0013-4597)
Description: Publishes original articles and reviews on all technical and clinical aspects of human neurophysiology, particularly EEG, EPs and EMG.
Refereed Serial

JOURNAL OF EVOLUTIONARY BIOCHEMISTRY AND PHYSIOLOGY. see *BIOLOGY — Biological Chemistry*

571   US   ISSN 0022-1295
QP1   CODEN: JGPLAD
JOURNAL OF GENERAL PHYSIOLOGY. 1918. m. (in 2 vols., 6 nos./vol.). $365 to institutions; includes Woods Hole Symposium (effective 1997). (Society of General Physiologists) Rockefeller University Press, 1114 First Ave., New York, NY 10021. TEL 212-327-8572. FAX 212-327-7944. URL: http://www.jgp.org; http://www.rockefeller.edu/rupress. (Subscr. to: Box 5108, GPO, New York, NY 10087-5108) Ed. Dr. Olaf S. Andersen. adv. contact: Charles E. Lych. bibl.; illus.; index. circ. 1,527. (also avail. in microform from UMI; reprint service avail. from ISI,UMI) **Indexed:** Abstr.Hyg., ASCA, Biol.Abstr., Biol.& Agr.Ind., Chem.Abstr., Curr.Adv.Ecol.Sci., Curr.Cont., Excerp.Med., Gen.Sci.Ind., Ind.Med., Ind.Sci.Rev., Ind.Vet., INIS Atomind., INSPEC, Neurosci.Cit.Ind., Nutr.Abstr., Sci.Cit.Ind., Sport Fish.Abstr., Trop.Dis.Bull., Vet.Bull., Wild.Rev., Zoo.Rec. **Document type:** academic/scholarly publication. —BLDSC (4989.000000); CASDDS; CISTI; Genuine Article; KNAW; KR SourceOne; Linda Hall; SWETS; UMI; UnCover. **CCC.**
Description: Articles concerned with the mechanisms of broad physiological significance covering research of prime importance for cellular and molecular physiology.
Refereed Serial

JOURNAL OF LONG-TERM EFFECTS OF MEDICAL IMPLANTS. see *MEDICAL SCIENCES*

JOURNAL OF MAMMARY GLAND BIOLOGY AND NEOPLASIA. see *MEDICAL SCIENCES — Obstetrics And Gynecology*

BIOLOGY — PHYSIOLOGY

JOURNAL OF MUSCLE RESEARCH AND CELL MOTILITY. see *MEDICAL SCIENCES*

573.8   **US**   **ISSN 0022-3034**
QP351   **CODEN: JNEUBZ**
JOURNAL OF NEUROBIOLOGY; an international journal. 1969. 16/yr. $1895 (foreign $2175) (effective 1998). John Wiley & Sons, Inc., Journals, 605 Third Ave., New York, NY 10158. TEL 212-850-6645. FAX 212-850-6021. TELEX 12-7063. E-mail: subinfo@jwiley.com. (Subscr. outside the Americas to: John Wiley & Sons Ltd., Baffins Ln., Chichester, W. Sussex PO19 1UD, England. TEL 44-1234-779777. FAX 44-1234-776128) Eds. Darcy B. Kelley, Eduardo Macagno. adv.: B&W page £640, color page £1515; trim 279 x 210. bk.rev. circ. 750. (also avail. in microform from UMI; back issues avail.; reprint service avail. from UMI) **Indexed:** Apic.Abstr., ASCA, Biol.Abstr., Chem.Abstr., Curr.Adv.Ecol.Sci., Curr.Cont., Dent.Ind., Excerp.Med., Helminthol.Abstr., Ind.Med., Ind.Sci.Rev., INIS Atomind., Neurosci.Cit.Ind., Sci.Cit.Ind., Sport Fish.Abstr., THA, Wild.Rev., Zoo.Rec. **Document type:** academic/scholarly publication.
—BLDSC (5021.450000); CASDDS; CISTI; Genuine Article; KNAW; Linda Hall; SWETS; UMI; UnCover. **CCC.**
Description: Covers neuroscience from molecular, genetic and cellular approaches. Vertebrate and invertebrate nervous systems are examined at the levels of the individual cell, the ensemble, and overall behavior.
Refereed Serial

573.8   **US**   **ISSN 0022-3077**
QP351   **CODEN: JONEA4**
JOURNAL OF NEUROPHYSIOLOGY. 1938. m. $375 to individual non-members (Canada and Mexico $415; elsewhere $445); institutions $563 (Canada and Mexico $603; elsewhere $633); members $187 (effective 1997). American Physiological Society, 9650 Rockville Pike, Bethesda, MD 20814. TEL 301-530-7164. FAX 301-571-3813. E-mail: info@aps.faseb.org; URL: http://www.faseb.org/aps. Ed. P.L. Strick. adv.: B&W page $525, color page $878. abstr.; charts; illus.; index. circ. 2,100. (also avail. in microform from UMI,PMC; reprint service avail. from UMI) **Indexed:** ASCA, Biol.Abstr., Biotech.Abstr., Chem.Abstr., Compumath, Curr.Adv.Cell & Devel.Biol., Curr.Adv.Ecol.Sci., Curr.Cont., Dent.Ind., Excerp.Med., Ind.Med., Ind.Sci.Rev., INIS Atomind., Int.Abstr.Biol.Sci., Neurosci.Cit.Ind., Nutr.Abstr., Psychol.Abstr. (1938-), Sci.Cit.Ind., SSCI. **Document type:** academic/scholarly publication.
—BLDSC (5022.000000); CASDDS; CISTI; Genuine Article; KNAW; Linda Hall; SWETS; UMI; UnCover. **CCC.**
Description: Presents original articles on the function of the nervous system.
Refereed Serial

JOURNAL OF PAIN AND SYMPTOM MANAGEMENT. see *MEDICAL SCIENCES — Anaesthesiology*

571   **UK**   **ISSN 0022-3751**
QP1   **CODEN: JPHYA7**
JOURNAL OF PHYSIOLOGY. 1878. 24/yr. £1156($1976) (effective 1998). (Physiological Society, London) Cambridge University Press, Edinburgh Bldg., Shaftesbury Rd., Cambridge CB2 2RU, England. TEL 44-1223-312393. FAX 44-1223-315052. TELEX 851817256. E-mail: information@cup.cam.ac.uk; URL: http://www.cup.cam.ac.uk. (N. American addr.: Cambridge University Press, Journals Dept., 40 W. 20th St., New York, NY 10011. TEL 212-924-3900. FAX 212-691-3239) Eds. R.E.J. Dyball. R&P contact: Linda Nicol. adv. contact: Rebecca Symons. bibl.; charts; illus.; index, cum.index. (also avail. in microform from UMI,PMC; back issues avail.) **Indexed:** Anim.Breed.Abstr., Apic.Abstr., ASCA, Biol.Abstr., Biol.& Agr.Ind., Biotech.Abstr., Chem.Abstr., Curr.Adv.Biochem., Curr.Adv.Ecol.Sci., Curr.Cont., Curr.Ref.Fish Res., Dairy Sci.Abstr., Deep Sea Res.& Oceanogr.Abstr., Dent.Ind., Ergon.Abstr., Excerp.Med., Helminthol.Abstr., Ind.Med., Ind.Sci.Rev., Ind.Vet., INIS Atomind., INSPEC, Int.Abstr.Biol.Sci., Mass Spectr.Bull., Neurosci.Cit.Ind., Nutr.Abstr., Pig News & Info., Poult.Abstr., Sci.Cit.Ind., Small Anim.Abstr., Sport Fish.Abstr., SSCI, Vet.Bull., Wild.Rev., Zoo.Rec. **Document type:** academic/scholarly publication.
—BLDSC (5039.000000); CASDDS; CISTI; Genuine Article; KNAW; KR SourceOne; Linda Hall; SWETS; UMI; UnCover.
Description: Covers physiological research in vertebrates: respiration, circulation, excretion, reproduction, digestion and homeostasis. Emphasis is on neurophysiology and muscle contraction.
Refereed Serial

573.8   **FR**   **ISSN 0928-4257**
QP1   **CODEN: JHYSEM**
JOURNAL OF PHYSIOLOGY (PARIS); an integrative neuroscience journal. 1899. bi-m. 2480 F.($371) 2480F. to institutions in Europe (effective 1998). Editions Scientifiques et Medicales Elsevier, 141 rue de Javel, 75747 Paris, France. TEL 33-1-45589022. FAX 33-1-45589421. URL: http://www.elsevier.nl/. (Subscr. in U.S. and Canada to: Elsevier Science Inc., Box 945, Madison Sq. Sta., New York, NY 10159-0945. TEL 212-633-3730. FAX 212-633-3680) Ed. M. Imbert. bk.rev.; illus.; index. circ. 850. (also avail. in microform from UMI; reprint service avail. from ISI) **Indexed:** Anim.Breed.Abstr., Apic.Abstr., ASCA, Biol.Abstr., Chem.Abstr., Curr.Cont., Curr.Ref.Fish Res., Dairy Sci.Abstr., Dent.Ind., Ergon.Abstr., Excerp.Med., Ind.Med., Ind.Sci.Rev., INIS Atomind., Neurosci.Cit.Ind., Nutr.Abstr., Psychol.Abstr., Sci.Cit.Ind., Sport Fish.Abstr., SSCI, Wild.Rev., Zoo.Rec. **Document type:** academic/scholarly publication.
—BLDSC (5039.020000); CASDDS; CISTI; EMDOCS; Genuine Article; KNAW; Linda Hall; SWETS; UnCover. **CCC.**
Formerly (until 1992): Journal de Physiologie (ISSN 0021-7948)
Description: Covers all aspects of neurobiology relevant to a better understanding of behavior and cognition and the integrative functions of the brain, with a focus on functional imaging, development and plasticity, cellular neurobiology, systems, behavioral and neuromuscular physiology, endocrinology, and cognition.
Refereed Serial

612 615.1   **PL**   **ISSN 0867-5910**
QP1   **CODEN: JPHPEI**
JOURNAL OF PHYSIOLOGY AND PHARMACOLOGY. (Text in English) 1950. q. $115 (effective 1997). Polskie Towarzystwo Fizjologiczne - Polish Physiological Society, Ul. Grzegorzecka 16, 31-531 Krakow, Poland. TEL 48-12-211006. FAX 48-12-211578. Ed.Bd. bk.rev.; illus. circ. 600. **Indexed:** AgroAgen, Apic.Abstr., ASCA, Biol.Abstr., Chem.Abstr., Curr.Cont., Excerp.Med., Ind.Ind., Ind.Med, INIS Atomind., INSPEC (1973-1983), Nutr.Abstr., Vet.Bull. **Document type:** academic/scholarly publication.
—BLDSC (5039.500000); CASDDS; CISTI; EMDOCS; KNAW; Linda Hall; SWETS; UnCover.
Formerly (until 1991): Acta Physiologica Polonica (ISSN 0044-6033)
Refereed Serial

612   **JA**   **ISSN 0916-8818**
CODEN: JREDEF
JOURNAL OF REPRODUCTION AND DEVELOPMENT. (Includes 2 additional issues in Japanese) (Text in English) 1955. q. 6000 Yen to members; non-members 9000 Yen. Japanese Society of Animal Reproduction, c/o Dept. of Veterinary Physiology, University of Tokyo, 1-1-1 Yayoi, Bunkyo-ku, Tokyo 113, Japan. TEL 81-3-3812-2111. FAX 81-3-3815-4266. Ed. Dr. Michio Takahashi. adv.; bk.rev. (back issues avail.) **Indexed:** Anim.Breed.Abstr., Dairy Sci.Abstr., Ind.Vet., INIS Atomind., Pig News & Info., Sugar Ind.Abstr., Vet.Bull. **Document type:** academic/scholarly publication.
—BLDSC (5049.570000); CASDDS.
Formerly (until Feb. 1992): Japanese Journal of Animal Reproduction (ISSN 0385-9932)
Description: Publishes new findings and concepts in reproductive biology, reproductive endocrinology, reproductive immunology, and developmental biology.
Refereed Serial

JOURNAL OF REPRODUCTION AND FERTILITY. see *BIOLOGY — Biological Chemistry*

JOURNAL OF REPRODUCTION AND FERTILITY. ABSTRACT SERIES. see *BIOLOGY — Abstracting, Bibliographies, Statistics*

JOURNAL OF REPRODUCTION AND FERTILITY. SUPPLEMENT. see *BIOLOGY*

JOURNAL OF SEROTONIN RESEARCH. see *BIOLOGY — Biological Chemistry*

JOURNAL OF VASCULAR RESEARCH. see *BIOLOGY — Biological Chemistry*

612   **US**   **ISSN 0957-4271**
QP471   **CODEN: JVEREH**
JOURNAL OF VESTIBULAR RESEARCH: EQUILIBRIUM AND ORIENTATION. 1991. bi-m. fl.734($422) (effective 1998). Elsevier Science Inc., Box 945, New York, NY 10159-0945. TEL 212-633-3730. FAX 212-633-3680. E-mail: nlinfo-f@elsevier.nl; usinfo-f@elsevier.com; forinfo-kyf04035@niftyserve.or.jp; URL: http://www.elsevier.nl/. (Subscr. outside the Americas to: Elsevier Science, Regional Sales Office, P.O. Box 211, 1000 AE Amsterdam, Netherlands. TEL 31-20-4853757. FAX 31-20-4853432; Subscr. in Australasia and the Far East to: Elsevier Science (Singapore) Pte Ltd, No.1 Temasek Ave., No.17-01 Millenia Tower, Singapore 039192, Singapore. TEL 65-434-3727. FAX 65-337-2230; Subscr. in Japan to: Elsevier Science Japan, 9-15 Higashi-Azabu 1-chome, Minato-ku, Tokyo 106, Japan. TEL 81-3-5561-5033. FAX 81-3-5561-5047) Eds. Ralph M. Jell, Desmond J. Ireland. (also avail. in microfilm from UMI; back issues avail.) **Indexed:** ASCA, Excerp.Med. (1994-), Ind.Med. (1993-), INSPEC (1990-), Neurosci.Cit.Ind., Psychol.Abstr. (1990-), SSCI. **Document type:** academic/scholarly publication.
—BLDSC (5072.340000); AskIEEE; CISTI; EMDOCS; Genuine Article; KNAW; KR SourceOne; SWETS; UMI. **CCC.**
Description: Includes experimental and observational studies and theoretical papers based upon the current facts of vestibular science.
Refereed Serial

612   **YU**   **ISSN 0352-1311**
CODEN: JMBIEE
JUGOSLAVENSKA MEDICINSKA BIOKEMIJA. (Text in English and Serbo-Croatian; summaries in English) 1982. 4/yr. Drustvo Medicinksih Biokemicara Jugoslavije - Yugoslav Society of Medical Biochemists, P.O. Box 146, Vojvode Stepe 450, 11000 Belgrade, Yugoslavia. adv.; bk.rev. circ. 1,000. (back issues avail.) **Indexed:** ASCA, Chem.Abstr., Excerp.Med. (until 1993; 1994-). **Document type:** academic/scholarly publication.
—CASDDS; EMDOCS.
Description: Publishes scientific papers on clinical chemistry.

612.98 617.582   NE   ISSN 0968-0160
RD561   CODEN: KNEEF2
THE KNEE. (Text in English) 1994. q. fl.435($250) (effective 1998). Elsevier Science B.V., P.O. Box 211, 1000 AE Amsterdam, Netherlands. TEL 31-20-4853757. FAX 31-20-4853432. E-mail: nlinfo-f@elsevier.nl; usinfo-f@elsevier.nl; URL: http://www.elsevier.nl/. (Subscr. in the Americas to: Elsevier Science, Regional Sales Office, Box 945, New York, NY 10159-0945. TEL 212-633-3730. FAX 212-633-3680; Subscr. in Australasia and the Far East to: Elsevier Science (Singapore) Pte Ltd, No.1 Temasek Ave., No.17-01 Millenia Tower, Singapore 039192, Singapore. TEL 65-434-3727. FAX 65-337-2230; Subscr. in Japan to: Elsevier Science Japan, 9-15 Higashi-Azabu 1-chome, Minato-ku, Tokyo 106, Japan. TEL 81-3-5561-5033. FAX 81-3-5561-5047) adv. (also avail. in microfilm from UMI; back issues avail.) **Document type:** academic/scholarly publication.
—BLDSC (5099.863500); CISTI; KNAW; UMI.
Refereed Serial

571   KO   ISSN 0300-4015
KOREAN JOURNAL OF PHYSIOLOGY. Key Title: Taehan Saengli Hakhoe Chi. (Text in English) 1967. s-a. $30 (effective 1991). Korean Physiological Society, Department of Physiology, College of Medicine, Seoul National University, 28 Yunkeun-dong, Chongno-gu, Seoul 110-799, S. Korea. TEL 02-765-2210. FAX 02-763-9667. Ed. Jong Sik Hah. abstr.illus. circ. 500. (also avail. in microfilm from UMI) **Indexed:** Excerp.Med. **Document type:** academic/scholarly publication.
—EMDOCS.

LEFTHANDER. *see CLUBS*

571   US
LIPPINCOTT-RAVEN PRESS SERIES IN PHYSIOLOGY. irreg. Lippincott - Raven Publishers (Subsidiary of: Wolters Kluwer N.V.), 227 E. Washington Sq., Philadelphia, PA 19106. TEL 215-238-4200. FAX 215-238-4227. URL: http://www.lrpub.com. (Subscr. to: Box 1600, Hagerstown, MD 21741-1600. TEL 800-777-2295. FAX 301-824-7390) R&P contact: Alice McElhinney. (reprint service avail. from UMI) **Document type:** monographic series.
Former titles: Raven Press Series in Physiology; Raven Press Series in Experimental Physiology.
Refereed Serial

LUNG BIOLOGY IN HEALTH AND DISEASE. *see MEDICAL SCIENCES — Respiratory Diseases*

571.79   UK   ISSN 0964-7600
MAMMARY GLAND. 1992. s-m. (diskette m.). £90 (diskette £120; both £180) (effective 1997). S U B I S, Mansion House, 19 Kingfield Rd., Sheffield S11 9AS, England. TEL 44-114-2554433. FAX 44-114-2554626. E-mail: subis@sheffac.demon.co.uk; URL: http://www.shef.ac.uk/uni/companies/shap. (also avail. in diskette format) **Document type:** abstracting/indexing.

612   NE
MANUAL OF BIOLOGICAL MARKERS OF DISEASE. (Text in English) 1994. base vol. (plus irreg. supplement). $69.50. Kluwer Academic Publishers, Postbus 17, 3300 AA Dordrecht, Netherlands. TEL 31-78-6392392. FAX 31-78-6392254. TELEX 29245 KAPG NL. E-mail: services@wkap.nl; URL: http://www.wkap.nl. (Dist. by: Kluwer Academic Publishers Group, P.O. Box 322, 3300 AH Dordrecht, Netherlands. TEL 31-78-6392392. FAX 31-78-6546474; N. America dist. addr.: Box 358, Accord Sta., Hingham, MA 02018-0358. TEL 617-871-6600. FAX 617-871-6528) Eds. W.J. van Venrooij, R.N. Maini. (looseleaf format) **Document type:** academic/scholarly publication.
Description: Presents information on recent advances in the study of autoantibodies of interest to immunologists, molecular biologists, and clinicians treating autoimmune disorders.

571   US
METHODS IN PHYSIOLOGY SERIES. 1994. irreg., vol.2, 1994. price varies. American Physiological Society, 9650 Rockville Pike, Bethesda. TEL 301-530-7164. FAX 301-571-8313. E-mail: info@aps.faseb.org; URL: http://www.faseb.org/aps. Ed.Bd. (back issues avail.) **Document type:** monographic series.
Refereed Serial

612   NE   ISSN 0168-1745
MICROCIRCULATION REVIEWS. (Text in English) 1982. irreg. price varies. Kluwer Academic Publishers, Postbus 17, 3300 AA Dordrecht, Netherlands. TEL 31-78-6392392. FAX 31-78-6392254. TELEX 29245 KAPG NL. E-mail: services@wkap.nl; URL: http://www.wkap.nl. (Dist. by: Kluwer Academic Publishers Group, P.O. Box 322, 3300 AH Dordrecht, Netherlands. TEL 31-78-6392392. FAX 31-78-6546474; N. America dist. addr.: Box 358, Accord Sta., Hingham, MA 02018-0358. TEL 617-871-6600. FAX 617-871-6528) **Document type:** monographic series.
—CISTI.
Refereed Serial

MINERAL AND ELECTROLYTE METABOLISM. *see MEDICAL SCIENCES*

571   KR   ISSN 0028-2561
QP361   CODEN: NEFZB2
NEIROFIZIOLOGIYA/NEUROPHYSIOLOGY; nauchno-teoreticheskii zhurnal. (Text in Russian; summaries in English) 1969. bi-m. 10.20 Rub.($18.60) Akademiya Nauk Ukrainy, Institut Fiziologii im. A.A. Bogomol'tsya, Vul. Bogomol'tsya, 4, 252601 Kiev 1, Ukraine. TEL 38-44-2930745. Ed. Prof. P.G. Kostyuk. bk.rev.; illus. circ. 900. **Indexed:** Biol.Abstr., Chem.Abstr., Dent.Ind., Djerelo, Excerp.Med., Ind.Med. (until 1992), Neurosci.Cit.Ind.
—CASDDS; CISTI; KNAW; Linda Hall.

612   US   ISSN 0197-4580
QP376   CODEN: NEAGDO
NEUROBIOLOGY OF AGING; experimental and clinical research. 1980. bi-m. fl.1887($1085) (effective 1998). Elsevier Science Inc., Box 945, New York, NY 10159-0945. TEL 212-633-3730. FAX 212-633-3680. E-mail: nlinfo-f@elsevier.nl; usinfo-f@elsevier.com; forinfo-kyf04035@niftyserve.or.jp; URL: http://www.elsevier.nl/. (Subscr. outside the Americas to: Elsevier Science, Regional Sales Office, P.O. Box 211, 1000 AE Amsterdam, Netherlands. TEL 31-20-4853757. FAX 31-20-4853432; Subscr. in Australasia and the Far East to: Elsevier Science (Singapore) Pte Ltd, No.1 Temasek Ave., No.17-01 Millenia Tower, Singapore 039192, Singapore. TEL 65-434-3727. FAX 65-337-2230; Subscr. in Japan to: Elsevier Science Japan, 9-15 Higashi-Azabu 1-chome, Minato-ku, Tokyo 106, Japan. TEL 81-3-5561-5033. FAX 81-3-5561-5047) Ed. Paul D. Coleman. abstr.; illus.; index. (also avail. in microfilm from UMI; reprint service avail. from ISI,UMI) **Indexed:** ASCA, Biol.Abstr., Chem.Abstr., Curr.Adv.Ecol.Sci., Curr.Cont., Excerp.Med., Ind.Med., Ind.Sci.Rev., Neurosci.Cit.Ind., Psychol.Abstr. (1980-), Sci.Cit.Ind., SSCI, THA. **Document type:** academic/scholarly publication.
—BLDSC (6081.311000); ADONIS; CASDDS; CISTI; Genuine Article; KNAW; SWETS; UMI; UnCover. CCC.
Description: Fosters better understanding and treatment of functional changes associated with aging.
Refereed Serial

612   UK   ISSN 0142-8241
NEUROPHYSIOLOGY. 1972. s-m. (diskette m.). £120 (diskette £120; both £180) (effective 1997). S U B I S, Mansion House, 19 Kingfield Rd., Sheffield S11 9AS, England. TEL 44-114-2554433. FAX 44-114-2554626. E-mail: subis@sheffac.demon.co.uk; URL: http://www.shef.ac.uk/uni/companies/shap. (also avail. in diskette format) **Indexed:** Biol.Abstr., Chem.Abstr., Curr.Adv.Ecol.Sci., Excerp.Med., Ind.Sci.Rev., Psychol.Abstr., Sci.Cit.Ind. **Document type:** abstracting/indexing.
—CCC.
Description: Current awareness service for researchers. Covers the electrophysiology and pharmacology of the vertebrate central, autonomic and peripheral nervous systems.

NEUROPSYCHOBIOLOGY; international journal of experimental and clinical research in biological psychiatry, pharmacopsychiatry, biological psychology, pharmacopsychology and pharmacoelectroencephalography. *see MEDICAL SCIENCES — Psychiatry And Neurology*

612   US   ISSN 0886-1714
QP1   CODEN: NEPSEY
NEWS IN PHYSIOLOGICAL SCIENCES; an international journal of physiology. Abbreviated title: N I P S. 1986. bi-m. $75 to individual non-members in N. America (elsewhere $85); institutions $110 in N. America (elsewhere $120); members free (effective 1997). American Physiological Society, 9650 Rockville Pike, Bethesda, MD 20814. TEL 301-530-7164. FAX 301-571-3813. E-mail: info@aps.faseb.org; URL: http://www.faseb.org/aps. (Subscr. to: Subscription Department, 9650 Rockville Pike, Bethesda, MD 20814. TEL 301-530-7180. FAX 301-571-8313) (Co-publisher: International Union of Physiological Sciences) Ed. S.G. Schultz. adv.: B&W page $950, color page $1300. charts; illus.; index. circ. 11,600. (also avail. in microform from UMI; microfiche; back issues avail.; reprint service avail. from UMI) **Indexed:** ASCA, Curr.Cont., Neurosci.Cit.Ind., Sci.Cit.Ind., SSCI. **Document type:** academic/scholarly publication.
—BLDSC (6105.385000); CASDDS; CISTI; Genuine Article; KNAW; Linda Hall; SWETS; UMI; UnCover. CCC.
Description: Designed to keep physiologists informed about current developments in their field.
Refereed Serial

612   JA
NEWSLETTER: FRONTIER RESEARCH PROGRAM. 1987. 4/yr. Rikagaku Kenkyujo, Kokusai Furontia Kenkyu Shuishinbu - Institute of Physical and Chemical Research, Division of Frontier Research Program, 2-1 Hirosawa, Wako-shi, Saitama-ken 351-01, Japan. TEL 0484-621111. FAX 0484-658048. **Document type:** newsletter.
Description: Monitors program which conducts basic research in bio-homeostasis, frontier materials research, brain mechanisms of mind and behavior.

612   JA   ISSN 0917-5946
NEWSLETTER, RESEARCH ON H F S P IN JAPAN. (Human Frontier Science Program) Japanese edition (ISSN 0917-5954) (Text in English) 1990. a. (Nihon Kagaku Gijutsu Shinko Zaidan - Japan Science Foundation) Rikagaku Kenkyujo - Institute of Physical and Chemical Research, 2-1 Hirosawa, Wako-shi, Saitama-ken 351-01, Japan.

612   JA   ISSN 0916-1104
NIHON DAEKISEN GAKKAISHI/JAPAN SALIVARY GLAND SOCIETY. JOURNAL. (Text in Japanese) 1959. a. Nihon Daekisen Gakkai, 1604, Shimosakunobe, Takatsu-ku, Kawasaki-shi, Kanagawa-ken 213, Japan.

NIHON SEIRI JINRUI GAKKAI TAIKAI SHOROKUSHU/JAPAN SOCIETY OF PHYSIOLOGICAL ANTHROPOLOGY. ABSTRACTS OF THE MEETING. *see BIOLOGY — Abstracting, Bibliographies, Statistics*

571 612   JA   ISSN 0031-9341
                        CODEN: NISEAV
NIHON SEIRIGAKU ZASSHI/PHYSIOLOGICAL SOCIETY OF JAPAN. JOURNAL. (Text in Japanese; summaries in English) 1937. m. 1000 Yen per no. Nihon Seiri Gakkai, 30-10, Hongo 3-chome, Bunkyo-ku, Tokyo 113, Japan. TEL 81-3-3815-1624. FAX 81-3-5684-2539. Ed. Akimichi Kaneko. adv.; bk.rev.; stat.; cum.index; circ. 3,500 (paid). (also avail. in microform) **Indexed:** ASCA, Biol.Abstr., Chem.Abstr., Curr.Adv.Ecol.Sci., Dent.Ind., Excerp.Med., Ind.Med.
—CASDDS; CISTI.

571   JA   ISSN 0911-2057
NIHON SHIKKAN MODERU DOBUTSU KENKYUKAI KIROKU/JAPANESE ASSOCIATION OF ANIMAL MODELS FOR HUMAN DISEASES. PROCEEDINGS. (Text in Japanese; summaries in English) 1985. a. Nihon Shikkan Moderu Dobutsu Kenkyukai, Wakayama Kenritsu Ika Daigaku, Dai 2 Seirigaku Kyoshitsu, 9, 9 Bancho, Wakayama-shi, Wakayama-ken 640, Japan. **Document type:** proceedings.

571   JA   ISSN 0446-6578
CODEN: NTAZAD
NIHON TAISHITSUGAKU ZASSHI/JAPANESE JOURNAL OF CONSTITUTIONAL MEDICINE. (Text in Japanese; summaries in English) 1932. a. Nihon Taishitsu Gakkai - Japanese Society of Constitutional Medicine, c/o Kumamoto Daigaku Igakubu, Fuzoku Iden Igaku Kenkyu Shisetsu, 24-1, Kuhonji 4-chome, Kumamoto-shi, Kumamoto-ken 862, Japan. Ed. Hiromichi Okuda. adv. contact: Norio Fujiki. **Document type:** academic/scholarly publication.
—CASDDS.

NO NO IGAKU SEIBUTSUGAKU KONWAKAI SHOROKU/ABSTRACTS OF CONFERENCE ON MEDICINE AND BIOLOGY OF THE BRAIN. see *BIOLOGY — Abstracting, Bibliographies, Statistics*

571   JA   ISSN 0387-494X
OSAKA SHIKA DAIGAKU SEIRIGAKU KYOSHITSU RONBUNSHU/OSAKA DENTAL UNIVERSITY. DEPARTMENT OF PHYSIOLOGY. COLLECTION OF PAPERS. (Text in English, Japanese) irreg. Osaka Shika Daigaku, Seirigaku Kyoshitsu, 1-47, Kyobashi, Higashi-ku, Osaka 540, Japan.

P A S C A L. F 53: ANATOMIE ET PHYSIOLOGIE DES VERTEBRES. see *BIOLOGY — Abstracting, Bibliographies, Statistics*

PAKISTAN JOURNAL OF PATHOLOGY. see *MEDICAL SCIENCES*

016.574   UK   ISSN 0142-825X
PANCREATIC AND SALIVARY SECRETION. s-m. (diskette m.). £115 (diskette £120; both £180) (effective 1997). S U B I S, Mansion House, 19 Kingfield Rd., Sheffield S11 9AS, England. TEL 44-114-255-4433. FAX 44-114-255-4626. E-mail: subis@sheffac.demon.co.uk; URL: http://www.shef.ac.uk/uni/companies/shap. (also avail. in diskette format) **Document type:** abstracting/indexing.
—CCC.
Description: Provides a current-awareness service for researchers. Covers the pharmacology, structure and function of the pancreatic and salivary glands.

612   NE   ISSN 0928-4680
CODEN: PTHOE7
PATHOPHYSIOLOGY. (Text in English) 1994. q. fl.571($328) (effective 1998). (International Society for Pathophysiology) Elsevier Science B.V., P.O. Box 211, 1000 AE Amsterdam, Netherlands. TEL 31-20-4853911. FAX 31-20-4853598. TELEX 18582 ESPA NL. E-mail: nlinfo-f@elsevier.nl; usinfo-f@elsevier.com; forinfo-kyf04035@niftyserve.or.jp; URL: http://www.elsevier.nl/. (Subscr. in the Americas to: Elsevier Science, Regional Sales Office, Box 945, New York, NY 10159-0945. TEL 212-633-3730. FAX 212-633-3680; Subscr. in Australasia and the Far East to: Elsevier Science (Singapore) Pte Ltd, No.1 Temasek Ave., No.17-01 Millenia Tower, Singapore 039192, Singapore. TEL 65-434-3727. FAX 65-337-2230; Subscr. in Japan to: Elsevier Science Japan, 9-15 Higashi-Azabu 1-chome, Minato-ku, Tokyo 106, Japan. TEL 81-3-5561-5033. FAX 81-3-5561-5047) Ed. T. Yoshikawa. (also avail. in microform from UMI; back issues avail.) **Indexed:** Excerp.Med. (1995-). **Document type:** academic/scholarly publication.
—BLDSC (6412.834000); CASDDS; CISTI; EMDOCS; KNAW. **CCC.**
Description: Publishes original interdisciplinary papers on the etiology, development and elimination of pathological processes.
Refereed Serial

PERSPECTIVES ON DEVELOPMENTAL NEUROBIOLOGY. see *MEDICAL SCIENCES — Psychiatry And Neurology*

PFLUEGERS ARCHIV/EUROPEAN JOURNAL OF PHYSIOLOGY. see *MEDICAL SCIENCES*

571.1   UK   ISSN 0862-8408
QP1   CODEN: PHRSEJ
PHYSIOLOGICAL RESEARCH. 1952. bi-m. £122 (effective 1996). (Czech Academy of Sciences, Institute of Physiology, CS) Academic Press Ltd. (Subsidiary of: Harcourt Brace & Company Ltd.), 24-28 Oval Rd., London NW1 7DX, England. TEL 44-171-267-4466. FAX 44-171-482-2293. TELEX 25775 ACPRES G. (Subscr. to: Harcourt Brace & Company Ltd., Foots Cray High St., Sidcup, Kent DA14 5HP, England. TEL 44-181-300-3322. FAX 44-181-309-0807) Ed. P. Hwik. charts; illus.; index. circ. 850. **Indexed:** ASCA, Biol.Abstr., C.I.S. Abstr., Chem.Abstr., Curr.Adv.Ecol.Sci., Curr.Cont., Dairy Sci.Abstr., Dent.Ind., Excerp.Med., Helminthol.Abstr., Ind.Med., Ind.Sci.Rev., Ind.Vet., Int.Abstr.Biol.Sci., Neurosci.Cit.Ind., Nutr.Abstr., Pig News & Info., Psychol.Abstr., Sci.Cit.Ind., Vet.Bull. **Document type:** academic/scholarly publication.
—BLDSC (6484.950000); CASDDS; CISTI; EMDOCS; Genuine Article; KNAW; SWETS. **CCC.**
Former titles: Physiologia Bohemoslovaca (ISSN 0369-9463); Physiologia Bohemoslovencia (ISSN 0031-9309)
Description: Publishes articles dealing with normal and pathological physiology, biochemistry, biophysics, and pharmacology. Preference is given to papers concerned with evolutionary physiology and neurophysiology.

571   US   ISSN 0031-9333
QP1   CODEN: PHREA7
PHYSIOLOGICAL REVIEWS. 1921. q. $169 to individual non-members (Canada and Mexico $209; elsewhere $219); institutions $225 (Canada and Mexico $237; elsewhere $247); members $84.50 (effective 1997). American Physiological Society, 9650 Rockville Pike, Bethesda, MD 20814. TEL 301-530-7164. FAX 301-571-8313. E-mail: info@aps.faseb.org/aps. Ed. W.F. Boron. bibl.; charts; illus.; cum.index: 1936-1951, 1952-1966, 1967-1981. circ. 3,200. (also avail. in microfilm from UMI,PMC; reprint service avail. from UMI) **Indexed:** Anim.Breed.Abstr., ASCA, Biol.Abstr., Biol.& Agr.Ind., Biotech.Abstr., Chem.Abstr., Curr.Adv.Ecol.Sci., Curr.Cont., Dairy Sci.Abstr., Dent.Ind., Excerp.Med., Gen.Sci.Ind., Ind.Med., Ind.Sci.Rev., Nutr.Abstr., Sci.Cit.Ind., Sport Fish.Abstr., SSCI, Trop.Dis.Bull., Weed Abstr., Wild.Rev., Zoo.Rec. **Document type:** academic/scholarly publication.
●Also available online. Vendor(s): Information Access Co.
—BLDSC (6485.000000); CASDDS; CISTI; Genuine Article; KNAW; KR SourceOne; Linda Hall; SWETS; UMI; UnCover. **CCC.**
Description: Contains invited critical reviews of physiological topics, as well as reviews in biochemistry, nutrition, general physiology, biophysics, and neuroscience.
Refereed Serial

571   US   ISSN 0079-2020
CODEN: PHSMA2
PHYSIOLOGICAL SOCIETY, LONDON. MONOGRAPHS. 1953. irreg., no.6, 1985. Academic Press, Inc., 525 B St., Ste. 1900, San Diego, CA 92101-4495. TEL 619-231-0926. FAX 619-699-6715. (Subscr. to: Order Dept., 6277 Sea Harbor Dr., 4th Fl., Orlando, FL 32887. TEL 800-321-5068) Ed.Bd. (reprint service avail. from ISI) **Indexed:** Biol.Abstr., Ind.Med. (until 1992), Nutr.Abstr. **Document type:** monographic series.
—BLDSC (5914.717300); CISTI.

571   US   ISSN 0031-9376
QP1   CODEN: PYSOAP
PHYSIOLOGIST. 1958. bi-m. $36.50 to individual non-members (foreign $46.50); institutions $53 (foreign $67); free to members (effective 1997). American Physiological Society, 9650 Rockville Pike, Bethesda, MD 20814. TEL 301-530-7164. FAX 301-571-8313. E-mail: info@aps.faseb.org; URL: http://www.faseb.org/aps. Ed. M. Frank. adv.: B&W page $950, color page $1300. charts; illus. circ. 9,900. (also avail. in microform from UMI; reprint service avail. from UMI) **Indexed:** Biol.Abstr., C.I.J.E., Chem.Abstr., Dent.Ind., Excerp.Med., Ind.Med., Int.Aerosp.Abstr. **Document type:** academic/scholarly publication.
●Also available online.
—BLDSC (6487.200000); CISTI; KNAW; Linda Hall; SWETS; UMI; UnCover. **CCC.**
Description: Contains articles on the society's affairs and announcements, as well as articles of importance to physiologists that are not suitable for other society publications
Refereed Serial

534 130   US   ISSN 0031-9384
QP351   CODEN: PHBHA4
PHYSIOLOGY AND BEHAVIOR; an international journal. 1966. 15/yr. fl.4541($2610) (effective 1998). Elsevier Science Inc., Box 945, New York, NY 10159-0945. TEL 212-633-3730. FAX 212-633-3680. E-mail: usinfo-f@elsevier.com; URL: http://www.elsevier.nl/. (Subscr. outside the Americas to: Elsevier Science, Regional Sales Office, P.O. Box 211, 1000 AE Amsterdam, Netherlands. TEL 31-20-4853757. FAX 31-20-4853432; Subscr. in Australasia and the Far East to: Elsevier Science (Singapore) Pte Ltd, No.1 Temasek Ave., No.17-01 Millenia Tower, Singapore 039192, Singapore. TEL 65-434-3727. FAX 65-337-2230; Subscr. in Japan to: Elsevier Science Japan, 9-15 Higashi-Azabu 1-chome, Minato-ku, Tokyo 106, Japan. TEL 81-3-5561-5033. FAX 81-3-5561-5047) Ed. Matthew J. Wayner. adv.: B&W page $550, color page $1350. bk.rev.; charts; illus.; stat.; index. circ. 1,800. (also avail. in microfiche from MIM; microfilm from UMI; reprint service avail. from UMI) **Indexed:** Anim.Breed.Abstr., Apic.Abstr., ASCA, Biol.Abstr., Chem.Abstr., Curr.Adv.Ecol.Sci., Curr.Cont., Dairy Sci.Abstr., Dent.Ind., Excerp.Med., Food Sci.& Tech.Abstr., IBR, Ind.Med., Ind.Sci.Rev., Ind.Vet., Lang.& Lang.Behav.Abstr., Maize Abstr., Neurosci.Cit.Ind., Nutr.Abstr., Pig News & Info., Potato Abstr., Poult.Abstr., Psychol.Abstr. (1966-), Sci.Cit.Ind., Soyabean Abstr., Sport Fish.Abstr., SSCI, Sugar Ind.Abstr., THA, Vet.Bull., Wild.Rev., Zoo.Rec. **Document type:** academic/scholarly publication.
—BLDSC (6488.100000); ADONIS; CASDDS; CISTI; Genuine Article; KNAW; SWETS; UMI; UnCover. **CCC.**
Description: Publishes original research contributions in the areas of neural control of eating, drinking, body composition and body fluids; hormonal control of behavior; sleep activity; rhythms; taste and olfaction; and learning and memory.
Refereed Serial

PHYSIOLOGY AND ECOLOGY JAPAN. see *ENVIRONMENTAL STUDIES*

PHYSIOLOGY CANADA. see *MEDICAL SCIENCES*

612   SA   ISSN 1022-1220
PHYSIOLOGY SOCIETY OF SOUTHERN AFRICA. PROCEEDINGS. (Text in English) 1993. a. Physiology Society of Southern Africa, c/o University of Pretoria Faculty of Medicine, Dept. of Physiology, Pretoria 0002, South Africa. **Document type:** proceedings.

591.332 618.34   UK   ISSN 0143-4004
QP281   CODEN: PLACDF
PLACENTA. 1980. 8/yr. £123 in Europe (rest of world $209) to individuals; institutions £214 (effective 1997). W.B. Saunders Co. Ltd. (Subsidiary of: Harcourt Brace & Company Ltd.), 24-28 Oval Rd., London NW1 7DX, England. TEL 44-171-267-4466. FAX 44-171-482-2293. URL: http://www.hbuk.co.uk/wbs/pla/. (Subscr. to: Harcourt Brace & Company Ltd., Foots Cray High St., Sidcup, Kent DA14 5HP, England. TEL 44-181-300-3322. FAX 44-181-309-0807) Eds. C.P. Sibley, L. Myatt. adv.; bk.rev.; bibl.; charts; illus.; stat.; index. (back issues avail.; reprint service avail. from SWZ) **Indexed:** ASCA, Biol.Abstr., Chem.Abstr., Curr.Adv.Cell & Devel.Biol., Curr.Adv.Ecol.Sci., Curr.Cont., Excerp.Med., Ind.Med., Ind.Sci.Rev., Sci.Cit.Ind., THA. **Document type:** academic/scholarly publication.
—BLDSC (6506.800000); CASDDS; CISTI; Genuine Article; KNAW; SWETS; UnCover. **CCC.**
  Description: Examines relevant areas of placental morphology, physiology, endocrinology, immunology, pharmacology, cell biology, placental microbiology, pathology, and toxicology.

PLANT TISSUE CULTURE MANUAL; fundamentals and applications. see *BIOLOGY — Biotechnology*

573.159 610   UK   ISSN 0142-8265
PLATELETS (SHEFFIELD). 1976. s-m. (diskette m.). £115 (diskette £120; both £180) (effective 1997). S U B I S, Mansion House, 19 Kingfield Rd., Sheffield S11 9AS, England. TEL 44-114-2554433. FAX 44-114-2554626. E-mail: subis@sheffac.demon.co.uk; URL: http://www.shef.ac.uk/uni/companies/shap. (also avail. in diskette format) **Indexed:** Sci.Cit.Ind. **Document type:** abstracting/indexing.
—**CCC.**
  Description: Current awareness service for researchers. Covers thrombocytopoiesis, pharmacology, aggregation, structure, biochemistry and functions of platelets.

PRIMARY SENSORY NEURON; the international interdisciplinary journal reporting basic and clinical research on sensory receptors and primary afferent neurons. see *MEDICAL SCIENCES — Psychiatry And Neurology*

573.8   UK   ISSN 0301-0082
QP356   CODEN: PGNBA5
PROGRESS IN NEUROBIOLOGY; an international review journal. 1973. 18/yr. fl.3530($2029) (effective 1998). Elsevier Science Ltd., Pergamon, P.O. Box 800, Kidlington, Oxford OX5 1DX, England. TEL 44-1865-843000. FAX 44-1865-843010. E-mail: info@elsevier.nl; usinfo-f@elsevier.com; forinfo-kyf04035@niftyserve.or.jp; URL: http://www.elsevier.nl/. (Subscr. to: Elsevier Science, Regional Sales Office, P.O. Box 211, 1000 AE Amsterdam, Netherlands. TEL 31-20-4853757. FAX 31-20-4853432; Subscr. in the Americas to: Elsevier Science, Regional Sales Office, Box 945, New York, NY 10159-0945. TEL 212-633-3730. FAX 212-633-3680; Subscr. in Australasia and the Far East to: Elsevier Science (Singapore) Pte Ltd, No.1 Temasek Ave., No.17-01 Millenia Tower, Singapore 039192, Singapore. TEL 65-434-3727. FAX 65-337-2230) Eds. G.A. Kerkut, J.W. Phillis. (also avail. in microfilm from UMI) **Indexed:** ASCA, Biol.Abstr., Chem.Abstr., Curr.Adv.Cell & Devel.Biol., Curr.Adv.Ecol.Sci., Curr.Cont., Excerp.Med., Ind.Med., Ind.Sci.Rev., Neurosci.Cit.Ind., Nutr.Abstr., Psychol.Abstr. (1994-), Sci.Cit.Ind., Sport Fish.Abstr., THA, Wild.Rev., Zoo.Rec. **Document type:** academic/scholarly publication.
—BLDSC (6870.300000); ADONIS; CASDDS; CISTI; EMDOCS; Genuine Article; KNAW; Linda Hall; SWETS; UMI; UnCover. **CCC.**
  Description: Reviews advances in the field of neurobiology with coverage of all relevant disciplines. *Refereed Serial*

PROGRESS IN REPRODUCTIVE BIOLOGY AND MEDICINE. see *MEDICAL SCIENCES — Nurses And Nursing*

PSYCHOPHYSIOLOGY; an international journal. see *MEDICAL SCIENCES*

571   UK   ISSN 0265-1742
RECENT ADVANCES IN PHYSIOLOGY. 1925. irreg., vol.10. Churchill Livingstone (Subsidiary of: Pearson Professional), Robert Stevenson House, 1-3 Baxter's Pl., Leith Walk, Edinburgh EH1 3AF, Scotland. TEL 44-131-556-2424. FAX 44-131-459-1177. URL: http://www.churchillmed.com. (US subscr. to: Churchill Livingstone, 650 Ave. of the Americas, New York, NY 10011. TEL 212-206-5000) **Document type:** academic/scholarly publication, monographic series.

RECEPTORS AND SIGNAL TRANSDUCTION. see *BIOLOGY — Biological Chemistry*

REDOX REPORT; communications in free radical research. see *BIOLOGY — Biological Chemistry*

REFERATIVNYI ZHURNAL. FIZIOLOGIYA I MORFOLOGIYA CHELOVEKA I ZHIVOTNYKH. see *BIOLOGY — Abstracting, Bibliographies, Statistics*

RENAL PHYSIOLOGY. see *MEDICAL SCIENCES — Urology And Nephrology*

612 616.4   UK   ISSN 0143-4284
RENIN, ANGIOTENSIN & KININS. 1980. s-m. (diskette m.). £110 (diskette £120; both £180) (effective 1997). S U B I S, Mansion House, 19 Kingfield Rd., Sheffield S11 9AS, England. TEL 44-114-2554433. FAX 44-114-2554626. E-mail: subis@sheffac.demon.co.uk; URL: http://www.shef.ac.uk/uni/companies/shap. (also avail. in diskette format) **Document type:** abstracting/indexing.
—**CCC.**
  Description: Current awareness service for researchers.

REPRODUCTIVE TOXICOLOGY. see *ENVIRONMENTAL STUDIES — Toxicology And Environmental Safety*

612   NE   ISSN 0034-5687
QP121.A1   CODEN: RSPYAK
RESPIRATION PHYSIOLOGY. 1965. m. fl.2336($1343) (effective 1998). Elsevier Science B.V., P.O. Box 211, 1000 AE Amsterdam, Netherlands. TEL 31-20-4853911. FAX 31-20-4853598. TELEX 18582 ESPA NL. E-mail: nlinfo-f@elsevier.nl; usinfo-f@elsevier.com; forinfo-kyf04035@niftyserve.or.jp; URL: http://www.elsevier.nl/. (Subscr. in the Americas to: Elsevier Science, Regional Sales Office, Box 945, New York, NY 10159-0945. TEL 212-633-3730. FAX 212-633-3680; Subscr. in Australasia and the Far East to: Elsevier Science (Singapore) Pte Ltd, No.1 Temasek Ave., No.17-01 Millenia Tower, Singapore 039192, Singapore. TEL 65-434-3727. FAX 65-337-2230; Subscr. in Japan to: Elsevier Science Japan, 9-15 Higashi-Azabu 1-chome, Minato-ku, Tokyo 106, Japan. TEL 81-3-5561-5033. FAX 81-3-5561-5047) Ed. P. Scheid. illus. (also avail. in microform from UMI) **Indexed:** ASCA, Biol.Abstr., C.I.S.Abstr., Chem.Abstr., Curr.Adv.Biochem., Curr.Adv.Ecol.Sci., Curr.Cont., Dent.Ind., Excerp.Med., Ind.Med., Ind.Sci.Rev., Ind.Vet., Neurosci.Cit.Ind., Pig News & Info., Poult.Abstr., Risk Abstr., Sport Fish.Abstr., THA, Vet.Bull., Wild.Rev., Zoo.Rec. **Document type:** academic/scholarly publication.
—BLDSC (7777.650000); CASDDS; CISTI; Genuine Article; KNAW; SWETS; UnCover. **CCC.**
  Description: For researchers in respiratory, pulmonary and circulatory physiology. *Refereed Serial*

612.015   UK   ISSN 0142-8780
RESPIRATORY SYSTEM. m. £80 (effective 1997). S U B I S, Mansion House, 19 Kingfield Rd., Sheffield S11 9AS, England. TEL 44-114-2554433. FAX 44-114-2554626. E-mail: subis@sheffac.demon.co.uk; URL: http://www.shef.ac.uk/uni/companies/shap. (looseleaf format; back issues avail.) **Document type:** abstracting/indexing.
—**CCC.**
  Description: Current awareness service for researchers in clinical and life sciences.

612 610   US   ISSN 0892-1253
REVIEW OF MEDICAL PHYSIOLOGY. 1963. biennial. Appleton & Lange (Subsidiary of: Simon & Schuster Company), Box 120041, Stamford, CT 06912-0041. TEL 203-406-4500. **Document type:** academic/scholarly publication, monographic series.
—BLDSC (7792.400000); CISTI.

571   US   ISSN 0303-4240
QP1   CODEN: RPBEA5
REVIEWS OF PHYSIOLOGY, BIOCHEMISTRY AND PHARMACOLOGY. irreg. price varies. Springer-Verlag, 175 Fifth Ave., New York, NY 10010. TEL 212-460-1500. FAX 212-473-6272. (Also: Berlin, Heidelberg, Tokyo and Vienna) (reprint service avail. from ISI) **Indexed:** ASCA, Biol.Abstr., Chem.Abstr., Curr.Adv.Ecol.Sci., Ind.Med., Ind.Sci.Rev., Sci.Cit.Ind. **Document type:** monographic series.
—BLDSC (7794.020000); CASDDS; CISTI; Genuine Article; KNAW; Linda Hall; SWETS. **CCC.**
  Formerly: Ergebnisse der Physiologie, Biologischen Chemie und Experimentellen Pharmakologie (ISSN 0080-2042)
  Refereed Serial

REVIEWS OF REPRODUCTION. see *BIOLOGY*

REVISTA ESPANOLA DE FISIOLOGIA/JOURNAL OF PHYSIOLOGY AND BIOCHEMISTRY. see *MEDICAL SCIENCES*

571   RM   ISSN 1220-840X
                          CODEN: RMEPDZ
REVUE ROUMAINE DE PHYSIOLOGIE/ROMANIAN JOURNAL OF PHYSIOLOGY. (Text in English, French, German, Russian and Spanish) q. (Academia de Stiinte Medicale) Editura Academiei Romane, Calea 13 Septembrie 13, 76117 Bucharest, Rumania. (Dist. by: Rodipet SA, Piata Presei Libere 1, Sec.1, P.O. Box 33-57, Bucharest, Rumania. TEL 401-6185103. FAX 401-2226407) Ed. Prof. P. Groza. bk.rev.; charts; illus.; index. circ. 600. **Indexed:** Biol.Abstr., Chem.Abstr., Curr.Adv.Ecol.Sci., Excerp.Med. (until 1993), Ind.Med. **Document type:** academic/scholarly publication.
—CASDDS; CISTI; KNAW; Linda Hall.
  Formerly (until 1990): Physiologie (ISSN 1011-6206); Which supersedes in part (in 1975): Revue Roumaine de Morphologie et de Physiologie (ISSN 0377-4953); Which was formed by the 1974 merger of: Revue Roumaine de Physiologie (ISSN 0035-399X); Revue Roumaine de Morphologie et d'Embryologie (ISSN 0377-4945); Which was formed by the 1973 merger of: Morfologia Normala si Patologia (ISSN 0027-1063); Revue Roumaine d'Embryologie et de Cytologie. Serie de Cytologie (ISSN 0556-8056); Revue Roumaine d'Embryologie (0300-063X); Which was (1964-1972): Revue Roumaine d'Embryologie et de Cytologie. Serie d'Embryologie (ISSN 0035-4007).

RINSHO KOKYU SEIRI/JOURNAL OF CLINICAL RESPIRATORY PHYSIOLOGY. see *MEDICAL SCIENCES — Respiratory Diseases*

612   JA   ISSN 0285-3299
                          CODEN: SGKHEB
SEIRIGAKU GIJUTSU KENKYUKAI HOKOKU/REPORT OF PHYSIOLOGICAL TECHNOLOGY. (Text in Japanese) 1979. a. Okazaki Kokuritsu Kyodo Kenkyu Kiko, Seirigaku Kenkyujo - Okazaki National Research Institutes, National Institute for Physiological Sciences, 38, Saigo Naka, Myodaiji, Okazaki-shi, Aichi-ken 444, Japan. **Indexed:** Chem.Abstr.
—CASDDS.

612   JA   ISSN 0913-0322
                          CODEN: SGHOEH
SEIRIGAKU KENKYUJO GIJUTSUKA HOKOKU/NATIONAL INSTITUTE FOR PHYSIOLOGICAL SCIENCES. TECHNICAL DIVISION. ANNUAL REPORT. (Text in Japanese) 1986. a. Okazaki Kokuritsu Kyodo Kenkyu Kiko, Seirigaku Kenkyujo - Okazaki National Research Institutes, National Institute for Physiological Sciences, 38, Saigo Naka, Myodaiji, Okazaki-shi, Aichi-ken 444, Japan. **Indexed:** Chem.Abstr.
—BLDSC (1465.955000); CASDDS.

612   JA
SEIRIGAKU KENKYUJO NENPO/NATIONAL INSTITUTE FOR PHYSIOLOGICAL SCIENCES. ANNUAL REPORT. (Text in English, Japanese) 1980. a. Okazaki Kokuritsu Kyodo Kenkyu Kiko, Seirigaku Kenkyujo - Okazaki National Research Institutes, National Institute for Physiological Sciences, 38, Saigo Naka, Myodaiji, Okazaki-shi, Aichi-ken 444, Japan.

BIOLOGY — PHYSIOLOGY

612 JA
SEIRIKEN SAKYURA/OKAZAKI NATIONAL RESEARCH INSTITUTES. NATIONAL INSTITUTE FOR PHYSIOLOGICAL SCIENCES. CIRCULAR. (Text in Japanese) 1978. a. Okazaki Kokuritsu Kyodo Kenkyu Kiko, Seirigaku Kenkyujo, 38, Saigo Naka, Myodaiji, Okazaki-shi, Aichi-ken 444, Japan.

SEMINARS IN NEPHROLOGY. see *MEDICAL SCIENCES — Urology And Nephrology*

SEMINARS IN NUCLEAR MEDICINE. see *MEDICAL SCIENCES — Radiology And Nuclear Medicine*

571 CC ISSN 0559-7765
QP1 CODEN: SLKHA8
SHENGLI KEXUE JINZHAN/PROGRESS IN PHYSIOLOGICAL SCIENCES. (Text in Chinese) 1957. q. $20 (effective 1994). Zhongguo Shengli Xuehui - Chinese Association for Physiological Sciences, 38 Xueyuan Rd., Beijing Medical University, Beijing 100083, People's Republic of China. TEL 861-209-1150. FAX 861-202-9252. Ed. Han Jisheng. adv.; bk.rev.; circ. 3,000 (paid). **Indexed:** Chem.Abstr., ExtraMED. **Document type:** academic/scholarly publication.
●Also available on CD-ROM.
—BLDSC (6873.490000); CASDDS; Linda Hall.
Description: Covers physiology, biochemistry, molecular biology, pharmacology, biophysics, pathophysiology and nutrition.
Refereed Serial

571 CC ISSN 0371-0874
QP1 CODEN: SLHPAH
SHENGLI XUEBAO/ACTA PHYSIOLOGICA SINICA. English edition: Chinese Journal of Physiological Sciences (ISSN 0258-6428) (Text in Chinese; summaries in English) 1927. bi-m. $59.60. (Shanghai Institute of Physiology - Shanghai Shenglixue Yanjiusuo) Science Press, Marketing and Sales Department, 16 Donghuangchenggen North St., Beijing 100717, People's Republic of China. TEL 4010642. FAX 4019810. adv. circ. 7,000. **Indexed:** Biol.Abstr., Excerp.Med., Psychol.Abstr. (1965-). **Document type:** academic/scholarly publication.
—BLDSC (0655.500000); CASDDS; CISTI; EMDOCS; Linda Hall.
Description: Contains mostly original research papers on physiology. Also includes short communications and reviews.
Refereed Serial

612 616.3 UK ISSN 0261-4928
SMOOTH MUSCLE. m. £80 (effective 1997). S U B I S, Mansion House, 19 Kingfield Rd., Sheffield S11 9AS, England. TEL 44-114-2554433. FAX 44-114-2554626. E-mail: subis@sheffac.demon.co.uk; URL: http://www.shef.ac.uk/uni/companies/shap. (looseleaf format; back issues avail.) **Document type:** abstracting/indexing.
—CCC.
Description: Current awareness service for researchers in clinical and life sciences.

612 UK ISSN 0954-7800
CODEN: SHUBAC
SOCIETY FOR THE STUDY OF HUMAN BIOLOGY. SYMPOSIUM SERIES. 1960. irreg., latest vol.36, 1995. price varies. (Society for the Study of Human Biology) Cambridge University Press, Edinburgh Bldg., Shaftesbury Rd., Cambridge CB2 2RU, England. TEL 44-1223-312393. FAX 44-1223-315052. TELEX 851817256. E-mail: information@cup.cam.ac.uk; URL: http://www.cup.cam.ac.uk. (N. American addr.: Cambridge University Press, Journals Dept., 40 W. 20th St., New York, NY 10011. TEL 212-924-3900. FAX 212-691-3239) Ed.Bd. R&P contact: Linda Nicol. circ. 200. **Indexed:** Biol.Abstr., Curr.Adv.Ecol.Sci.
—BLDSC (8585.040000); CASDDS.
Formerly (until 1986): Society for the Study of Human Biology. Symposia (ISSN 0081-153X)
Refereed Serial

571 UK ISSN 0899-0220
QP450 CODEN: SMOREZ
SOMATOSENSORY AND MOTOR RESEARCH. 1983. q. £72($96) to individuals; institutions £156 ($236) (effective 1997). Carfax Publishing Co., P.O. Box 25, Abingdon, Oxon OX14 3UE. TEL 44-1235-401000. FAX 44-1235-401550. E-mail: enquiries@carfax.co.uk. (N. American subscr. to: Carfax Publishing Co., 875-81 Massachusetts Ave., Cambridge, MA 02139. FAX 617-354-6875) Ed. Thomas Woolsey. adv.; charts; illus.; index. circ. 500. (back issues avail.; reprint service avail. from UMI) **Indexed:** ASCA, Biol.Abstr., Chem.Abstr., Curr.Adv.Cell & Devel.Biol., Curr.Adv.Ecol.Sci., Curr.Cont., Excerp.Med., Ind.Med., Ind.Sci.Rev., Neurosci.Abstr., Neurosci.Cit.Ind., Psychol.Abstr. (1983-), Sci.Cit.Ind., SSCI. **Document type:** academic/scholarly publication.
—BLDSC (8327.809150); CASDDS; CISTI; EMDOCS; Genuine Article; KNAW; SWETS; UMI; UnCover. **CCC.**
Formerly: Somatosensory Research (ISSN 0736-7244)
Description: Original research on somatic sensation and its neural mechanisms. Experimental and descriptive studies.
Refereed Serial

612 NE ISSN 0888-4803
QH301 CODEN: SRFREP
SOVIET SCIENTIFIC REVIEWS. SECTION F: PHYSIOLOGY AND GENERAL BIOLOGY REVIEWS. a. 164 ECU (effective 1997). Gordon and Breach - Harwood Academic, Amsteldisk 166, 1st Fl., 1079 LH Amsterdam, Netherlands. (Subscr. to: International Publishers Distributor, Box 32160, Newark, NJ 07102. TEL 800-545-8398. FAX 215-750-6343) Ed. T.M. Turpaev. (also avail. in microform) **Document type:** academic/scholarly publication.
—CISTI. **CCC.**
Refereed Serial

571.74 US ISSN 0039-128X
QP752.S7 CODEN: STEDAM
STEROIDS. 1963. m. fl.1382($794) (effective 1998). Elsevier Science Inc., Box 945, New York, NY 10159-0945. TEL 212-633-3730. FAX 212-633-3680. E-mail: usinfo-f@elsevier.com; URL: http://www.elsevier.nl/. (Subscr. outside the Americas to: Elsevier Science, Regional Sales Office, P.O. Box 211, 1000 AE Amsterdam, Netherlands. TEL 31-20-4853757. FAX 31-20-4853432; Subscr. in Australasia and the Far East to: Elsevier Science (Singapore) Pte Ltd, No.1 Temasek Ave., No.17-01 Millenia Tower, Singapore 039192, Singapore. TEL 65-434-3727. FAX 65-337-2230; Subscr. in Japan to: Elsevier Science Japan, 9-15 Higashi-Azabu 1-chome, Minato-ku, Tokyo 106, Japan. TEL 81-3-5561-5033. FAX 81-3-5561-5047) Eds. Richard Hochberg, William Rosner. adv.; bk.rev.; abstr.; bibl.; charts; index. (also avail. in microform from UMI; back issues avail.) **Indexed:** Anal.Abstr., Anim.Breed.Abstr., ASCA, Biol.Abstr., Biotech.Abstr., Chem.Abstr., Chem.Cit.Ind., Curr.Adv.Ecol.Sci., Curr.Chem.React, Curr.Cont., Dairy Sci.Abstr., Dent.Ind., Excerp.Med., Ind.Chem., Ind.Med., Ind.Sci.Rev., Ind.Vet., Mass Spectr.Bull., Nutr.Abstr., Ocean.Abstr., Ornam.Hort., Sci.Cit.Ind., Vet.Bull. **Document type:** academic/scholarly publication.
—BLDSC (8464.600000); CASDDS; CISTI; Genuine Article; KNAW; Linda Hall; SWETS; UMI; UnCover. **CCC.**
Description: Forum for the communication of articles dealing with all aspects of steroid hormones.
Refereed Serial

STUDIES IN FERTILITY AND STERILITY. see *BIOLOGY*

612 NE ISSN 0926-9738
STUDIES IN HUMAN BIOLOGY. (Text in English) 1990. irreg. price varies. Kluwer Academic Publishers, Postbus 17, 3300 AA Dordrecht, Netherlands. TEL 31-78-6392392. FAX 31-78-6392254. TELEX 29245 KAPG NL. E-mail: services@wkap.nl; URL: http://www.wkap.nl. (Dist. by: Kluwer Academic Publishers Group, P.O. Box 322, 3300 AH Dordrecht, Netherlands. TEL 31-78-6392392. FAX 31-78-6546474; N. America dist. addr.: Box 358, Accord Sta., Hingham, MA 02018-0358. TEL 617-871-6600. FAX 617-871-6528) **Document type:** monographic series.
—KNAW.

571 UK ISSN 0969-8116
STUDIES IN PHYSIOLOGY. 1993. irreg., vol.4, 1996. Portland Press Ltd., 59 Portland Pl., London W1N 3AJ, England. TEL 44-171-580-5530. FAX 44-171-323-1136. E-mail: sales@portlandpress.co.uk; URL: http://www.portlandpress.co.uk. (Subscr. to: Commerce Way, P.O. Box 32, Colchester, Essex CO2 8HP, England. TEL 44-1206-796351. FAX 44-1206-796351) R&P contact: Adam Marshall. **Document type:** academic/scholarly publication, monographic series.
—BLDSC (8491.223200); CISTI.
Refereed Serial

571 SI
STUDIES OF NONLINEAR PHENOMENA IN LIFE SCIENCE. (Text in English) 1990. irreg., vol.5, 1996. price varies. World Scientific Publishing Co. Pte. Ltd., Farrer Rd., P.O. Box 128, Singapore 9128, Singapore. TEL 65-3825663. FAX 65-3825919. TELEX RS 28561 WSPC. E-mail: wspcl@signet.com.sg; sales@wspc2.demon.co.uk; wspc@wspc.com.sg; URL: http://www.singnet.com.sg/~wspclib/. (UK addr.: 57 Shelton St., Covent Garden, London WC2H 9HE, England. TEL 44-171-836-0888. FAX 44-171-836-2020; US addr.: 1060 Main St., River Edge, NJ 07661. TEL 800-227-7562. FAX 201-487-9656) Ed. B.J. West. **Document type:** monographic series.

TOKYO SHIKA DAIGAKU SEIRIGAKU KYOSHITSU GYOSEKISHU/TOKYO DENTAL COLLEGE. DEPARTMENT OF PHYSIOLOGY. BIBLIOGRAPHY. see *BIOLOGY — Abstracting, Bibliographies, Statistics*

UTTAR PRADESH JOURNAL OF ZOOLOGY. see *BIOLOGY — Zoology*

571 PL ISSN 0860-9063
WYZSZA SZKOLA PEDAGOGICZNA IM. KOMISJI EDUKACJI NARODOWEJ W KRAKOWIE. ROCZNIK NAUKOWO-DYDAKTYCZNY. PRACE FIZJOLOGICZNE. 1988. irreg., no.2, 1991. price varies. Wydawnictwo Naukowe W S P, Ul. Karmelicka 41, 31-128 Krakow, Poland. TEL 33-78-20. (Co-sponsor: Ministerstwo Edukacji Narodowej)

ZHIWU SHENGLI XUEBAO/ACTA PHYTOPHYSIOLOGICA SINICA. see *BIOLOGY — Botany*

ZHIWU SHENGLIXUE TONGXUN/PLANT PHYSIOLOGY COMMUNICATIONS. see *BIOLOGY — Botany*

571 CC ISSN 1000-6834
CODEN: ZYSZE2
ZHONGGUO YINGYONG SHENGLIXUE ZAZHI/CHINESE JOURNAL OF APPLIED PHYSIOLOGY. (Text in Chinese; abstracts and table of contents in English) 1985. q. Y24 (foreign $17.12) (effective 1997 & 1998). (Zhongguo Shengli Xuehui - Chinese Association for Physiological Sciences) Zhongguo Yingyong Shenglixue Zazhi Bianjibu, One Da Li Dao, Tianjin 300050, People's Republic of China. TEL 86-22-841-3063. FAX 86-22-331-4818. (Dist. outside China by: Guoji Shudian - China International Book Trading Corp., P.O. Box 399, Beijing 100044, P.R.C.) Ed. Lu Yongda. adv.; page $500; adv. contact: Xiuying Zhu. circ. 4,000 (paid). **Document type:** academic/scholarly publication.
Description: Covers environmental physiology, pathophysiology, clinical physiology, cellular physiology, molecular physiology, ergonomics, medical engineering and veterinary physiology.
Refereed Serial

ZHURNAL EVOLYUTSIONNOI BIOKHIMII I FIZIOLOGII. see *BIOLOGY — Biological Chemistry*

616.8 RU ISSN 0044-4677
CODEN: ZVNDAM
ZHURNAL VYSSHEI NERVNOI DEYATEL'NOSTI. (Text in Russian; summaries in English) 1951. bi-m. $202 (effective 1998). (Rossiiskaya Akademiya Nauk, Otdelenie Fiziologii im. I.P. Pavlova) Izdatel'stvo Nauka, 90 Profsoyuznaya ul., 117864 Moscow, Russia. TEL 095-336-0266. FAX 095-420-2220. (Dist. in U.S. by: Victor Kamkin Inc., 4956 Boiling Brook Pkwy., Rockville, MD 20852. TEL 301-881-5973. FAX 301-881-1637) Ed. Prof. P.V. Simonov. bk.rev.; index. **Indexed:** ASCA, Biol.Abstr., Chem.Abstr., Curr.Adv.Ecol.Sci., Curr.Cont., Dent.Ind., Excerp.Med., Ind.Med., Ind.Sci.Rev., Neurosci.Cit.Ind., Psychol.Abstr. (1991-), Sci.Cit.Ind., SSCI.
—BLDSC (0060.650000); CASDDS; CISTI; Genuine Article; KNAW; Linda Hall. **CCC.**

ZOOLOGY - ANALYSIS OF COMPLEX SYSTEMS. see BIOLOGY — Zoology

612 JA ISSN 0917-5792
CODEN: CIGAEC
13C IGAKU/SOCIETY FOR THE MEDICAL APPLICATION OF CARBON THIRTEEN. BULLETIN. (Text in English, Japanese) 1991. a. 13C Igaku Oyo Kenkyukai, c/o Toho Daigaku Igakubu Dai 2 Seirigaku Kyoshitsu, 21-16, Omori Nishi 5-chome, Ota-ku, Tokyo 143, Japan.
—CASDDS.

BIOLOGY — Zoology

see also Pets; Veterinary Science

591 560 069 US ISSN 1041-5300
A M U NEWS. 1960. s-a. $25 membership. American Malacological Union, Inc., c/o Dr. Raymond W. Neck, Houston Museum of Natural Science, One Hermann Circle Dr., Houston, TX 77030. TEL 713-639-4678. FAX 713-523-4125. (Subscr. to: c/o David Hargreave, Department of Science Studies, Western Michigan University, Kalamazoo, MI 49008. TEL 616-387-2723) bk.rev. circ. 800. (back issues avail.) **Document type:** newsletter.
Description: Focuses on the study of mollusks.

A S C NEWSLETTER (WASHINGTON). (Association of Systematics Collections) see MUSEUMS AND ART GALLERIES

598.1 UK ISSN 0142-5145
A S R A JOURNAL. 1979. a. membership. Association for the Study of Reptilia and Amphibia, c/o Cotswold Wild Life Park, Burford, Oxon, England. Ed. Jenny Swainston. circ. 500.

591 US
A Z A COMMUNIQUE. 1959. m. membership. American Zoo and Aquarium Association, Oglebay Park, Wheeling, WV 26003. TEL 304-242-2160. FAX 304-242-2283. E-mail: azaoms@aol.com; URL: http://www.aza.org. Ed. Barbara Ray. adv.; stat. circ. 6,500. (processed) **Document type:** newsletter.
Former titles: A A Z P A Communique; A A Z P A Newsletter (ISSN 0001-0308)

591 SA ISSN 1021-9102
CODEN: AARDEW
AARDVARK. (Text mostly in English, occasionally in Afrikaans) 1970. 2/yr. $40 membership (effective 1993). Zoological Society of Southern Africa, Kaffrarian Museum, P.O. Box 1434, 5600 King Williams Town, South Africa. TEL 27-433-24506. FAX 27-431-21569. Ed. Pierre Swaneroel. bk.rev. circ. 800. **Indexed:** Zoo.Rec. **Document type:** newsletter.
Formerly (until July, 1990): Zoological Society of South Africa Newsletter.

590 HU ISSN 1217-8837
QL1
ACADEMIA SCIENTIARUM HUNGARICA. ACTA ZOOLOGICA. (Text in English) 1954. a. $60 (effective 1998). Magyar Termeszettudomanyi Muzeum, Baross u. 13, 1088 Budapest, Hungary. TEL 36-1-3130035. FAX 36-1-11171669. E-mail: perego@zoo.zoo.nhmus.hu; URL: http://www.nhmus.hu/hgannal.html. Ed. I. Matskasi. adv.; illus.; index. circ. 250. (back issues avail.) **Indexed:** ASCA, Biol.Abstr., Chem.Abstr., Curr.Adv.Ecol.Sci., Curr.Cont., Helminthol.Abstr., Ind.Sci.Rev., Key Word Ind.Wildl.Res., So.Pac.Per.Ind. **Document type:** academic/scholarly publication.
—BLDSC (0672.700500); CISTI; Genuine Article; Linda Hall. CCC.
Former titles: Acta Zoologica Hungarica (ISSN 0236-7130); (until 1983): Academiae Scientiarum Hungaricae. Acta Zoologica (ISSN 0001-7264)
Description: Publishes original papers in zoological taxonomy and systematics, zoogeography, animal ecology, community ecology, population genetics, population biology, biodiversity studies and nature conservation.
Refereed Serial

594.42 FR ISSN 0044-586X
QL458.A2 CODEN: ACRLAW
ACAROLOGIA. (Supplements accompany some vols.) (Text in English, French, German, Italian, Spanish) 1959. a. (in 4 vols.) 520 F. to individuals; institutions 800 F. (effective 1997). 61 rue de Buffon, 75231 Paris Cedex 05, France. FAX 33-1-40-79-35-76. E-mail: crustace@mnhn.fr. Ed. Yves Coineau. adv.; bk.rev.; illus.; index. circ. 300. (back issues avail.) **Indexed:** Abstr.Hyg., Apic.Abstr., ASCA, Bio-Contr.News & Info., Biodet.Abstr., Biol.Abstr., Biotech.Abstr., Curr.Adv.Ecol.Sci., Curr.Cont., Helminthol.Abstr., Ind.Med., Ind.Sci.Rev., Ind.Vet., Rev.Appl.Entomol., Sci.Cit.Ind., So.Pac.Per.Ind., Soils & Fert., Sport Fish.Abstr., Trop.Dis.Bull., Vet.Bull., Wild.Rev., Zoo.Rec. **Document type:** academic/scholarly publication.
—BLDSC (0570.600000); CASDDS; Genuine Article; Linda Hall; SWETS; UnCover.
Description: International review of fundamental and applied zoology diffusing publications concerning Acari.
Refereed Serial

595.4 JA ISSN 0001-5202
CODEN: AACHBY
ACTA ARACHNOLOGICA. (Text in English, French, German, Japanese; abstracts in English) 1936. s-a. 7000 Yen (students 5000 Yen) membership. Arachnological Society of Japan - Nihon Kumo Gakkai, Biological Laboratory, Otemon-Gakuin University, 2-1-15 Nishiai, Ibaraki, Osaka 567, Japan. FAX 81-726-43-5427. Ed. Tadashi Miyashita. adv.; bk.rev.; charts; illus. circ. 600. **Indexed:** Biol.Abstr., Jap.Per.Ind. **Document type:** academic/scholarly publication.
—BLDSC (0596.000000); CASDDS; CISTI; UnCover.
Refereed Serial

591 PL ISSN 0001-530X
QL1 CODEN: ABCZAQ
ACTA BIOLOGICA CRACOVIENSIA. ZOOLOGIA. (Text in English) 1958. a. price varies. (Polska Akademia Nauk, Oddzial w Krakowie, Komisja Biologiczna) Ossolineum, Publishing House of the Polish Academy of Sciences, Pl. Solny 14a, 50-062 Wroclaw, Poland. TEL 48-71-343-6961. FAX 48-71-448-103. TELEX 0712771 OSS PL. Ed. Cz. Jura. charts; illus.; index. circ. 780. **Indexed:** AgroAgen, Anim.Breed.Abstr., ASCA, Biol.Abstr., Bull.Signal, Chem.Abstr., Curr.Adv.Ecol.Sci., Curr.Cont., Helminthol.Abstr., IBR, Ind.Vet., Key Word Ind.Wildl.Res., Sci.Cit.Ind., Vet.Bull. **Document type:** academic/scholarly publication.
—BLDSC (0602.420000); CASDDS; CISTI; KNAW; Linda Hall; UnCover.
Description: Original research papers. Forum for zoologists involved in investigating function and structure of animals from cell level.

597 YU ISSN 0579-7152
ACTA BIOLOGICA IUGOSLAVICA. SERIJA E: ICHTHYOLOGIA. 1969. a. $6. Unija Bioloskih Naucnih Drustava Jugoslavije - Yugoslav Union of Biological Sciences, Nemanjina 6, fah 127, 11080 Belgrade Zemun, Yugoslavia. Ed. Dobrila Habekovic. **Indexed:** Biol.Abstr., Helminthol.Abstr.
—Linda Hall.

591 YU ISSN 0354-9410
QL462 CODEN: AEJGAP
ACTA ENTOMOLOGICA SERBICA. (Text in English; summaries in Serbian) 1971. s-a. $30 to individuals; institutions $50. Entomological Society of Serbia, Faculty of Forestry, Kneza Viseslava 1, 11030 Belgrade, Yugoslavia. E-mail: actaent@bf.bio.bg.ac.yu. (Subscr. to: Jugoslovenska Knjiga Import-Export Booksellers, P.O. Box 36, 11001 Belgrade, Yugoslavia. TEL 381-11-625970) Ed. Dr. Zivko R. Adamovic. bk.rev. **Indexed:** Bio-Contr.News & Info., Biol.Abstr., Rev.Appl.Entomol.
—BLDSC (0615.400000); Linda Hall.
Formerly: Acta Entomologica Jugoslavica (ISSN 0350-5510)

ACTA ICHTHYOLOGICA ET PISCATORIA. see FISH AND FISHERIES

ACTA PROTOZOOLOGICA. see BIOLOGY

591 SW ISSN 0072-4807
QL1 CODEN: ARSZAE
ACTA REGIAE SOCIETATIS SCIENTIARUM ET LITTERARUM GOTHOBURGENSIS. ZOOLOGICA. (Text in various languages) 1967. irreg., no.15, 1994. price varies; also exchange basis. Kungliga Vetenskaps- och Vitterhets-Samhaelle, c/o Goeteborgs Universitetsbibliotek, P.O. Box 5096, S-402 22 Goeteborg, Sweden. circ. 700. **Indexed:** Biol.Abstr. **Document type:** monographic series.
—CISTI; Linda Hall.
Supersedes in part: Goeteborgs Kungliga Vetenskaps- och Vitterhets-Samhaelle. Handlingar.

591 PL ISSN 0001-7051
QL700 CODEN: ATRLAF
ACTA THERIOLOGICA. (Text and summaries in English) 1954. q. $59 to individuals; institutions $89 (effective 1998). Polska Akademia Nauk, Zaklad Badania Ssakow - Polish Academy of Sciences, Mammal Research Institute, Ul. Gen. Waszkiewicza 1, 17-230 Bialowieza, Poland. TEL 48-835-12289. FAX 48-835-12289. E-mail: acta@bison.zbs.bialowieza.pl. Ed. Zdzislaw Pucek. R&P contact: Agata Jaroszewicz. adv. contact: Malgorzata Rychlik. bk.rev.; bibl.; illus.; index. circ. 700. (back issues avail.) **Indexed:** AgroAgen, Anim.Breed.Abstr., ASCA, Biol.Abstr., Biotech.Abstr., Bull.Signal, Chem.Abstr., Curr.Adv.Ecol.Sci., Curr.Cont., Dairy Sci.Abstr., Ecol.Abstr., Field Crop Abstr., Helminthol.Abstr., Herb.Abstr., Ind.Sci.Rev., Key Word Ind.Wildl.Res., Ref.Zh., Sci.Cit.Ind., So.Pac.Per.Ind., Soils & Fert., Sport Fish.Abstr., Wild Life Rev., Wild.Rev., Zoo.Rec. **Document type:** academic/scholarly publication.
—BLDSC (0665.000000); CASDDS; CISTI; EMDOCS; Genuine Article; KNAW; Linda Hall; SWETS; UnCover.
Description: Covers all aspects of mammalian biology. Publishes original research reports and short communications.
Refereed Serial

591 572 PL ISSN 1230-0527
QL1
ACTA UNIVERSITATIS LODZIENSIS: FOLIA ZOOLOGICA. (Text in Polish; summaries in various languages) 1955-1974; N.S. 1981. irreg. Wydawnictwo Uniwersytetu Lodzkiego, Ul. Jaracza 34, Lodz, Poland. TEL 331671. (Dist. by: Ars Polona-Ruch, Krakowskie Przedmiescie 7, Warsaw, Poland) **Document type:** academic/scholarly publication.
—BLDSC (0585.208777); CISTI; KNAW; Linda Hall.
Formerly (until 1992): Acta Universitatis Lodziensis: Folia Zoologica et Anthropologica (ISSN 0208-6166); **Supersedes in part:** Uniwersytet Lodzki. Zeszyty Naukowe. Seria 2: Nauki Matematyczno-Przyrodnicze (ISSN 0076-0366)

591 PL ISSN 0554-9051
QL1
ACTA UNIVERSITATIS WRATISLAVIENSIS. PRACE ZOOLOGICZNE. (Text in Polish; summaries in English) 1962. irreg. price varies. (Uniwersytet Wroclawski) Wydawnictwo Uniwersytetu Wroclawskiego, Spolka z o.o., Pl. Uniwersytecki 9-13, 50-137 Wroclaw, Poland. TEL 48-71-441006. FAX 48-71-402735. Ed. Andrzej Witkowski. circ. 250. **Indexed:** AgroLibrex. **Document type:** academic/scholarly publication.
—KNAW; Linda Hall.

BIOLOGY — ZOOLOGY

591 QL1 — UK — ISSN 0001-7272 — CODEN: AZOSAT
ACTA ZOOLOGICA; international journal for zoology. (Text in English, French and German) 1920. q. fl.824($473) (effective 1998). Elsevier Science Ltd., Pergamon, P.O. Box 800, Kidlington, Oxford OX5 1DX, England. TEL 44-1865-843000. FAX 44-1865-843010. E-mail: nlinfo-f@elsevier.nl; usinfo-f@elsevier.com; forinfo-ky04035@niftyserve.or.jp; URL: http://www.elsevier.nl/. (Subscr. to: Elsevier Science, Regional Sales Office, P.O. Box 211, 1000 AE Amsterdam, Netherlands. TEL 31-20-4853757. FAX 31-20-4853432; Subscr. in the Americas to: Elsevier Science, Regional Sales Office, Box 945, New York, NY 10159-0945. TEL 212-633-3730. FAX 212-633-3680; Subscr. in Australasia and the Far East to: Elsevier Science (Singapore) Pte Ltd, No.1 Temasek Ave., No.17-01 Millenia Tower, Singapore 039192, Singapore. TEL 65-434-3727. FAX 65-337-2230) (Co-sponsors: Royal Swedish Academy of Sciences; Royal Danish Academy of Sciences and Letters) Ed. Claus Nielsen. bibl.; charts; illus. circ. 1,200. (also avail. in microform from UMI; back issues avail.) **Indexed:** ASCA, Biol.Abstr., Bull.Signal., Chem.Abstr., Curr.Adv.Ecol.Sci., Curr.Cont., Excerp.Med., Helminthol.Abstr., Ind.Sci.Rev., Sci.Cit.Ind., Sport Fish.Abstr., Vet.Bull., Wild.Rev., Zoo.Rec. **Document type:** academic/scholarly publication.
—BLDSC (0672.650000); CISTI; EMDOCS; Genuine Article; SWETS; UnCover. **CCC.**
Description: Publishes original contributions in the fields of animal organization, structure and function.
Refereed Serial

591 B6 — BU — ISSN 0324-0770 — CODEN: AZBUD7
ACTA ZOOLOGICA BULGARICA. (Text in various languages) 1975. irreg. 1.60 lv. per no. (Bulgarska Akademiia na Naukite, Zoologicheski Institut) Publishing House of the Bulgarian Academy of Sciences, Acad. G. Bonchev St., Bldg. 6, 1113 Sofia, Bulgaria. (Dist. by: Hemus, 6, Rouski Blvd., 1000 Sofia, Bŭlgaria) illus. circ. 520. (reprint service avail. from IRC) **Indexed:** Bio-Contr.News & Info., Biol.Abstr., BSL Biol., Curr.Adv.Ecol.Sci., Forest.Abstr., Helminthol.Abstr., Protozool.Abstr., Soils & Fert.
—BLDSC (0672.750000); CASDDS; CISTI; KNAW; Linda Hall.
Supersedes: Bulgarska Akademiia na Naukite, Sofia. Zoologicheski Institut S Muzei. Izvestiia (ISSN 0068-3981)

590 QL1 — PL — ISSN 0065-1710 — CODEN: AZCRAY
ACTA ZOOLOGICA CRACOVIENSIA. (Text in English, French, German, Polish, Russian) 1956. a. price varies. Polska Akademia Nauk, Instytut Systematyki i Ewolucji Zwierzat, Ul. Slawkowska 17, 31-016 Krakow, Poland. TEL 48-12-221891. FAX 48-12-224294. (Co-sponsor: Polish Academy of Sciences, Institute of Systematics and Evolution of Animals) Ed. Zygmunt Bochenski. bibl.; charts; illus. circ. 750. **Indexed:** AgroAgen, Biol.Abstr., Ecol.Abstr., Geo.Abstr., GeoRef. **Document type:** academic/scholarly publication.
—BLDSC (0672.800000); CISTI; UnCover.
Description: Covers biology, systematics, palaeontology of terrestrial animals.
Refereed Serial

591 QH7 — FI — ISSN 0001-7299 — CODEN: AZFEAA
ACTA ZOOLOGICA FENNICA. (Text in English) 1926. irreg., (1-4/yr.). price varies. (Academy of Finland) Finnish Zoological and Botanical Publishing Board, P.O. Box 17, P. Rautatiekatu 13, FIN-00014 University of Helsinki, Finland. TEL 358-9-191-7405. FAX 358-9-191-7443. E-mail: elmor__kr@cc.helsinki.fi; URL: sekj.oc.helsinki.fi/journals. (Distr. by: Tiedekirja OY, Kirkokatu 14, FIN-00170, Finland. TEL 358-9-635177) Ed. Krzysztof Raciborski. illus.; cum.index: nos.1-50, 51-100, 101-150. circ. 850. (also avail. in microfiche from IDC) **Indexed:** Biol.Abstr., Curr.Adv.Ecol.Sci., Deep Sea Res.& Oceanogr.Abstr., Ecol.Abstr., GeoRef., IBR, Key Word Ind.Wildl.Res., Ref.Zh., Rev.Appl.Entomol., Sport Fish.Abstr., Wild.Rev., Zoo.Rec. **Document type:** academic/scholarly publication.
—BLDSC (0673.000000); CISTI; KNAW; Linda Hall; UnCover.
Description: Contains monographs and collections of papers from symposia and conference proceedings connected with Finnish and other North European research.

590 QL1 — AG — ISSN 0065-1729 — CODEN: AZOLA8
ACTA ZOOLOGICA LILLOANA. (Text in Spanish; summaries in English, French, German, Italian) 1943. irreg., vol.41, 1992. (Secretaria de Ciencia y Tecnologia) Fundacion Miguel Lillo, Miguel Lillo 251, 4000 Tucuman, Argentina. Ed. Jose A. Haedo Rossi. charts; bibl.; illus. (back issues avail.) **Indexed:** Anim.Behav.Abstr., Aqua.Sci.& Fish.Abstr., Biol.Abstr., Bull.Signal., Chem.Abstr., Ecol.Abstr., Entomol.Abstr., Ref.Zh., Zoo.Rec.
—CASDDS; CISTI; Linda Hall; UnCover.

590 — MX — ISSN 0065-1737 — CODEN: AZMEEF
ACTA ZOOLOGICA MEXICANA; nueva serie. (Text in English, German and Spanish) 1965-1971 (vol.10, no.4); resumed N.S. irreg. (approx. 4/yr.). $15. Instituto de Ecologia, Apdo. Postal 63, 91000 Xalapa, Veracruz, Mexico. FAX 52-28-187809. index. (back issues avail.) **Indexed:** Biol.Abstr., Sport Fish.Abstr., Wild.Rev., Zoo.Rec. **Document type:** academic/scholarly publication.
—BLDSC (0674.000000).

591 QL307.2 — CH — ISSN 1019-5858
ACTA ZOOLOGICA TAIWANICA/DONGWU XUEKAN. (Text in Chinese, English) 1988. s-a. National Taiwan University, College of Science, Department of Zoology - Guoli Taiwan Daxue Lixueyuan Dongwu Xuexi, Taipei, Taiwan 10764, Republic of China. Ed. Yao-Sung Lin. **Document type:** academic/scholarly publication.
—BLDSC (0675.010000); CISTI.

591 574.1 — GW — ISSN 0301-2743 — CODEN: FTPTAG
ADVANCES IN ANIMAL PHYSIOLOGY AND ANIMAL NUTRITION/FORTSCHRITTE IN DER TIERPHYSIOLOGIE UND TIERERNAEHRUNG. (Supplement to: Journal of Animal Physiology and Animal Nutrition) (Text and summaries in English, French, German) 1972. irreg., no.23, 1996. price varies. Blackwell Wissenschaft, Kurfuerstendamm 57, 10707 Berlin, Germany. TEL 49-30-32790627. FAX 49-30-32790610. E-mail: aboverwalt@blackwis.de; URL: http://www.blackwis.com. Eds. K.D. Guenther, M. Kirchgessner. bibl.; illus.; index. (reprint service avail. from ISI) **Indexed:** Biol.Abstr., Biotech.Abstr., Chem.Abstr., Dairy Sci.Abstr., Food Sci.& Tech.Abstr., Ind.Med., Ind.Vet., Nutr.Abstr. **Document type:** monographic series.
—CASDDS.

591 BF1 — GW — ISSN 0931-4202 — CODEN: AEHYAZ
ADVANCES IN ETHOLOGY. (Supplement to: Ethology) (Text and summaries in English, French, German) 1953. irreg. price varies. Verlag Paul Parey (Berlin), Seelbuschring 9-17, 12105 Berlin, Germany. TEL 030-70784-0. FAX 030-70784199. **Indexed:** Biol.Abstr., Curr.Cont., Psychol.Abstr., Zoo.Rec. **Document type:** academic/scholarly publication.
—BLDSC (0706.030000).
Formerly: Fortschritte der Verhaltensforschung (ISSN 0301-2808)

578 616.9 QH547 — US — ISSN 0065-308X — CODEN: ADPRAD
ADVANCES IN PARASITOLOGY. 1963. irreg., vol.39, 1997. Academic Press, Inc., 525 B St., Ste. 1900, San Diego, CA 92101-4495. TEL 619-231-0926. FAX 619-699-6715. (Subscr. to: Order Dept., 6277 Sea Harbor Dr., 4th Fl., Orlando, FL 32887. TEL 800-321-5068) Ed. Ben Dawes. index. (reprint service avail. from ISI) **Indexed:** Abstr.Hyg., ASCA, Biol.Abstr., Biol.& Agr.Ind., Curr.Adv.Ecol.Sci., Diar.Dis.Res., Excerp.Med., Helminthol.Abstr., Ind.Med., Ind.Sci.Rev., Ind.Vet., Nutr.Abstr., Rev.Appl.Entomol., Sci.Cit.Ind., Trop.Dis.Bull., Vet.Bull. **Document type:** monographic series.
—BLDSC (0709.580000); CASDDS; CISTI; EMDOCS; KNAW; KR SourceOne; Linda Hall; SWETS. **CCC.**
Refereed Serial

591 — US — ISSN 0587-4416 — CODEN: ADPYA
ADVANCES IN PRIMATOLOGY. irreg., latest 1993. Plenum Publishing Corp., 233 Spring St., New York, NY 10013-1578. TEL 212-620-8000. FAX 212-463-0742. TELEX 23-421139. E-mail: books@plenum.com. Eds. John G. Fleagle, Ross D.E. MacPhee. (back issues avail.) **Document type:** monographic series.
—KNAW.
Refereed Serial

591 — UK
ADVOCATES FOR ANIMALS. ANNUAL REPORT. (Former name of issuing body: Scottish Society for Prevention of Vivisection) 1912. a. free. Advocates for Animals, 10 Queensferry St., Edinburgh EH2 4PG, Scotland. TEL 44-131-225-6039. FAX 44-131-220-6377. Dir. Les Ward; Pub. Les Ward. R&P contact: Les Ward. adv. contact: Les Ward. bk.rev. circ. 10,000.
Formerly (until 1990): Scottish Society for Prevention of Vivisection. Annual Report.

AFRICAN JOURNAL OF ECOLOGY. see CONSERVATION

599 — SA — CODEN: AFSNEY
AFRICAN SMALL MAMMAL NEWSLETTER. a. c/o G.N. Bronner, Ed., Dept. of Mammals, Transvaal Museum, P.O. Box 413, Pretoria 0001, South Africa. **Indexed:** Sport Fish.Abstr., Wild.Rev., Zoo.Rec. **Document type:** newsletter.

AFRICAN WILDLIFE. see CONSERVATION

591.1 — II
AFRO-ASIAN NEMATOLOGY NETWORK. (Text in English) 1992. s-a. Rs.75($10) membership. Afro-Asian Society of Nematologists, c/o Narendra Deva University of Agriculture & Technology, Narendra Nagar (Kumarganj), Faizabad 224 229, India. Eds. M. Mashkoor Alam, B.A. Oteifa.

AKADEMIA ROLNICZA IM. HUGONA KOLLATAJA W KRAKOWIE. ZESZYTY NAUKOWE. SERIA: ZOOTECHNIKA. see AGRICULTURE — Poultry And Livestock

636 — PL — ISSN 0137-1770
AKADEMIA ROLNICZA, POZNAN. ROCZNIKI. ZOOTECHNIKA. (Text in Polish; summaries in English) 1967. irreg. price varies. Wydawnictwo Akademii Rolniczej w Poznaniu, Ul. Witosa 45, 60-667 Poznan, Poland. TEL 48-61-487809. FAX 48-61-487802. E-mail: wgolab@owl.au.poznan.pl; URL: http://sawn.au.poznan.pl/bib/bghome.html. **Indexed:** AgroLibrex, Bibl.Agri., Soyabean Abstr. **Document type:** academic/scholarly publication.
Description: Features works on animal breeding, such as: cattle, pigs, horses, sheep; also articles on animal feeding and fodder; also on fishing.

591 — JA
AKAMATA/OKINAWA HERPETOLOGICAL SOCIETY. RESEARCH REPORT. (Text in Japanese) a. Okinawa Ryosei Hachurui Kenkyukai - Okinawa Herpetological Society, Okinawa Kenritsu Hakubutsukan, Shurionakacho, Naha-shi, Okinawa-ken 903, Japan.

599.8 179.3 — CN — ISSN 0835-5851
ALCES; a journal devoted to the biology and management of moose. 1963. q. Can.$38($30) (effective 1997). Lakehead University Bookstore, 855 Oliver Rd., Thunder Bay, ON P7B 5E1, Canada. TEL 807-343-8528. FAX 807-346-7796. E-mail: MLANKEST@GALE.LAKEHEADU.CA. Eds. W. Ballard, A. Rodgers. charts; illus. circ. 300. (also avail. in microfiche; back issues avail.) **Indexed:** Environ.Abstr., Key Word Ind.Wildl.Res., Sport Fish.Abstr., Wild.Rev., Zoo.Rec. **Document type:** academic/scholarly publication.
—BLDSC (0786.716000); CISTI; UnCover.
Formerly (until 1981): North American Moose Conference. Proceedings (ISSN 0836-8716)
Description: Original research relating in the broadest sense to the biology and management of moose.
Refereed Serial

BIOLOGY — ZOOLOGY

591　　　　　　　HU　ISSN 0002-5658
　　　　　　　　　　CODEN: ALLKAS
ALLATTANI KOZLEMENYEK/ZOOLOGICAL PROCEEDINGS.
(Text in Hungarian; summaries in English, German or Russian) 1902. q. $30. Magyar Biologiai Tarsasag, Fo u. 68, 1027 Budapest, Hungary. Ed. I. Andrassy. bk.rev.; bibl.; charts; illus. **Indexed:** Biol.Abstr., Curr.Cont., Helminthol.Abstr.
　—CISTI; KNAW.

597 598　　　　　FR　ISSN 0753-4973
　　　　　　　　　　CODEN: ALTSES
ALYTES; international journal of batrachology. (Text in English, French, Spanish) 1982. q. 250 F.($50) to individuals; institutions 500 F. ($100). International Society for the Study and Conservation of Amphibians, c/o Laboratoire des Reptiles et Amphibians, Museum National d'Histoire Naturelle, 25 rue Cuvier, 75005 Paris, France. Ed. Alain Dubois. **Indexed:** Ref.Zh., Zoo.Rec. **Document type:** academic/scholarly publication.
　—BLDSC (0806.254400); Linda Hall.
　Refereed Serial

594 745.55 508　US　ISSN 1072-2440
AMERICAN CONCHOLOGIST. 1973. q. $20 (effective 1997). (Conchologists of America, Inc.) Lipps-National Press, 1222 Holsworth Lane, Louisville, KY 40222-6616. TEL 502-423-0469. FAX 502-426-4336. E-mail: amconch@ix.netcom.com; URL: http://www.coa.acnatsci.org/conchnet/. Ed. Lynn Scheu. adv. contact: Glen A. Deuel. bk.rev. circ. 1,400. (back issues avail.) **Document type:** academic/scholarly publication, bulletin.
　Formerly (until 1987): Conchologists of America Bulletin (ISSN 0747-105X)

597　　　　　　　US　ISSN 1070-7352
E839.5
AMERICAN CURRENTS. 1972. q. $11 membership (foreign $14). North American Native Fishes Association, 123 W. Mt. Airy Ave., Philadelphia, PA 19119. TEL 215-247-0384. (Subscr. to: Robert E. Schmidt, Simon's Rock, Alford Rd., Great Barrington, MA 01230) Ed. Bruce Gebhardt. adv.; bk.rev.; bibl.; charts; illus.; index, cum.index: 1982-1987. circ. 400. (back issues avail.) **Indexed:** Sport Fish.Abstr., Wild.Rev. **Document type:** academic/scholarly publication.
　—UnCover.
　Description: Covers news, features articles on ecology, ichthyology and live maintenance and study of North American fishes.

599.8　　　　　　US　ISSN 0275-2565
QL737.P9　　　　　　CODEN: AJPTDU
AMERICAN JOURNAL OF PRIMATOLOGY. 1981. m. $1596 (foreign $1806) (effective 1998). John Wiley & Sons, Inc., Journals, 605 Third Ave., New York, NY 10108. TEL 212-850-6645. FAX 212-850-6021. TELEX 12-7063. E-mail: SUBINFO@JWILEY.COM; URL: http://wiley.co.uk. (Subscr. outside the Americas to: John Wiley & Sons Ltd., Baffins Ln., Chichester, W. Sussex PO19 1UD, England. TEL 44-1243-779777. FAX 44-1243-776128) Ed. M.J. Raleigh. adv.: B&W page £640, color page £1515; trim 254 x 174. bk.rev.; bibl.; charts; illus.; index. circ. 650. (also avail. in microfilm from UMI; back issues avail.) **Indexed:** Abstr.Anthropol., Anthropol.Lit., ASCA, Biol.Abstr., Chem.Abstr., Curr.Adv.Biochem., Curr.Adv.Ecol.Sci., Curr.Cont., Excerp.Med., Ind.Sci.Rev., Ind.Vet., Psychol.Abstr. (1981-), Sci.Cit.Ind., Sport Fish.Abstr., SSCI, Vet.Bull., Wild.Rev., Zoo.Rec. **Document type:** academic/scholarly publication.
●Also available online.
　—BLDSC (0834.400000); CASDDS; EMDOCS; Genuine Article; KNAW; Linda Hall; SWETS; UnCover. **CCC.**
　Description: Examines topics relevant to the study of primates, including all aspects of their anatomy, behavior, development, ecology, evolution, genetics, nutrition, physiology, reproduction, systematics, conservation, husbandry, and use in biomedical research.
　Refereed Serial

594　　　　　　　　US　ISSN 0740-2783
QL401
AMERICAN MALACOLOGICAL BULLETIN. 1931; N.S. 1982. 2/yr. $32 to non-members (foreign $37). American Malacological Union, Inc., c/o Dr. Ronald Toll, Biology Department, Wesleyan College, Macon, GA 31297. TEL 912-474-7057. FAX 912-477-7572. (Subscr. to: c/o David Hargreave, Department of Science Studies, Western Michigan University, Kalamazoo, MI 49008. TEL 616-387-2723) index. circ. 800. **Indexed:** ASCA, Curr.Adv.Ecol.Sci., Curr.Cont., Deep Sea Res.& Oceanogr.Abstr., GeoRef, So.Pac.Per.Ind. **Document type:** bulletin.
　—BLDSC (0841.300000); Genuine Article; Linda Hall; UnCover.
　Former titles (until 1982): American Malacological Union. Bulletin (ISSN 0096-5537); (until 1970): American Malacological Union. Annual Reports (ISSN 0096-9486)
　Refereed Serial

500.9　　　　　　　US　ISSN 0003-0082
QL1　　　　　　　　　CODEN: AMUNAL
AMERICAN MUSEUM NOVITATES. 1921. irreg. price varies. American Museum of Natural History, Central Park W. at 79th St., New York, NY 10024-5192. TEL 212-769-5545. FAX 212-769-5009. E-mail: scipubs@amnh.org. Ed. Brenda Jones. circ. 1,000. **Indexed:** AESIS, Apic.Abstr., Biol.Abstr., Bull.Signal., Deep Sea Res.& Oceanogr.Abstr., GeoRef., Key Word Ind.Wildl.Res., Zoo.Rec. **Document type:** monographic series.
　—CISTI; Linda Hall; UMI.
　Description: Brief professional research papers in zoology, primarily systematics and evolutionary biology.
　Refereed Serial

591 069　　　　　　US　ISSN 0003-0090
QH1　　　　　　　　　CODEN: BUMNAE
AMERICAN MUSEUM OF NATURAL HISTORY. BULLETIN. 1881. irreg. price varies. American Museum of Natural History, Central Park W. at 79th St., New York, NY 10024-5192. TEL 212-769-5545. FAX 212-769-5009. E-mail: scipubs@amnh.org. Ed. Brenda Jones. circ. 1,200. (also avail. in microform from UMI,PMC; reprint service avail. from UMI) **Indexed:** ASCA, Biol.Abstr., Bull.Signal., Curr.Adv.Ecol.Sci., Curr.Cont., Deep Sea Res.& Oceanogr.Abstr., Geo.Abstr., GeoRef., Ind.Sci.Rev., Sci.Cit.Ind., Sport Fish.Abstr., Wild.Rev., Zoo.Rec. **Document type:** monographic series.
　—BLDSC (2390.000000); CASDDS; CISTI; UMI; UnCover.
　Description: Professional basic research papers in zoology, primarily on systematics and evolutionary biology.

591　　　　　　　　US　ISSN 0569-8219
　　　　　　　　　　　CODEN: AMAMBL
AMERICAN SOCIETY OF MAMMALOGISTS. SPECIAL PUBLICATIONS. 1967. irreg, no.10, 1993. price varies. American Society of Mammalogists, c/o Dr. H. Duane Smith, Sec.-Treas., Monte L. Bean Life Science Museum, Brigham Young University, Provo, UT 84602. TEL 801-378-2492. **Indexed:** Biol.Abstr.
　—BLDSC (8372.348000); CISTI.
　Refereed Serial

590.744　　　　　　US
QL77.5
AMERICAN ZOO AND AQUARIUM ASSOCIATION. PROCEEDINGS. a. $80 to non-members; members $45; libraries $50. American Zoo and Aquarium Association, Oglebay Park, Wheeling, WV 26003. TEL 304-242-2160. FAX 304-242-2283. E-mail: azaoms@aol.com; URL: www.aza.org. illus. **Indexed:** Biol.Abstr., Key Word Ind.Wildl.Res., Sport Fish.Abstr., Wild.Rev. **Document type:** proceedings.
　Formerly: American Association of Zoological Parks and Aquariums. Annual Conference. Proceedings (ISSN 0090-4473)

591　　　　　　　　US　ISSN 0003-1569
QL1　　　　　　　　　CODEN: AMZOAF
AMERICAN ZOOLOGIST. 1961. bi-m. $240 to individuals (Canada & Mexico $255; elsewhere $270); institutions $485 (Canada & Mexico $500; elsewhere $530) (effective 1998). Society for Integrative and Comparative Biology, 401 N. Michigan Ave., Box 809278, Chicago, IL 60611-9278. TEL 312-527-6697; 800-955-1236. FAX 312-245-1085. E-mail: sicb@sba.com; URL: http://sicb.org. Ed. James Hanken. R&P contact: Laura Jungen. adv. contact: Liz Klinger. bk.rev.; charts; illus.; index. circ. 6,300. (also avail. in microfilm from UMI; back issues avail.; reprint service avail. from UMI) **Indexed:** Anim.Breed.Abstr., ASCA, Biol.Abstr., Biol.& Agr.Ind., Biol.Dig., Chem.Abstr., Curr.Adv.Ecol.Sci., Curr.Cont., Curr.Ref.Fish Res., Dairy Sci.Abstr., Deep Sea Res.& Oceanogr.Abstr., Ecol.Abstr., Environ.Per.Bibl. (1991-1993), Gen.Sci.Ind., Geo.Abstr., Geol.Abstr., Helminthol.Abstr., Ind.Sci.Rev., Ind.Vet., Key Word Ind.Wildl.Res., Key Word Ind.Wildl.Res., Neurosci.Cit.Ind., Nutr.Abstr., Sport Fish.Abstr., Vet.Bull., Wild.Rev., Zoo.Rec. **Document type:** academic/scholarly publication.
　—BLDSC (0858.400000); CASDDS; CISTI; Genuine Article; KNAW; KR SourceOne; Linda Hall; SWETS; UMI; UnCover. **CCC.**
　Description: Contains papers from symposia dealing with a wide variety of zoological disciplines.
　Refereed Serial

598.1　　　　　　　NE　ISSN 0173-5373
QL640　　　　　　　　CODEN: AMREEH
AMPHIBIA REPTILIA. (Text in English, French, German and Spanish) 1980. 4/yr. fl.247($145) eo non-members; members DM.90 (effective 1998). (Societas Europaea Herpetologica) E.J. Brill, P.O. Box 9000, 2300 PA Leiden, Netherlands. TEL 31-71-5353500. FAX 31-71-5317532. TELEX 39296 BRILL NL. E-mail: cs@brill.nl. (In N. America: E.J. Brill, 24 Hudson St., Kinderhook, NY 12106. TEL 800-962-4406. FAX 518-758-1959) Eds. G. Gollmann, V. Perez-Mellado. R&P contact: Elizabeth Vennekamp. adv.; bk.rev.; illus. (back issues avail.) **Indexed:** Biol.Abstr., Curr.Adv.Ecol.Sci., Curr.Adv.Genetics & Molec.Biol., Ecol.Abstr., Geo.Abstr., Zoo.Rec. **Document type:** academic/scholarly publication.
　—BLDSC (0859.452500); CISTI; Linda Hall; UnCover. **CCC.**
　Refereed Serial

591　　　　　　　　AG　ISSN 0326-8489
　　　　　　　　　　　CODEN: ARPTEJ
AMPHIBIA & REPTILIA. Variant title: Amphibia & Reptilia (Conservacion). 1986. q. Fundacion Vida Silvestre Argentina, Av. L.N. Alem 968, 1001 Buenos Aires, C.F., Argentina. **Indexed:** Sport Fish.Abstr., Wild.Rev., Zoo.Rec.

BIOLOGY — ZOOLOGY

591.5 UK ISSN 0003-3472
QL750 CODEN: ANBEA8
ANIMAL BEHAVIOUR. 1952. m. £390 (effective 1998). (Association for the Study of Animal Behaviour) Academic Press Ltd. (Subsidiary of: Harcourt Brace & Company Ltd.), 24-28 Oval Rd., London NW1 7DX, England. TEL 44-171-267-4466. FAX 44-171-482-2293. TELEX 25775 ACPRES G. E-mail: apsubs@acad.com; URL: http://www.hbuk.co.uk/ap/abehav; http://www.europe.idealibrary.com/. (Subscr. to: Harcourt Brace & Company Ltd., Foots Cray High St., Sidcup, Kent DA14 5HP, England. TEL 44-181-300-3322. FAX 44-181-309-0807) (Co-sponsor: Animal Behaviour Society) Eds. Michael Beecher, C.J. Barnard. R&P contact: Catherine John. adv. contact: Nik Screen. index. (also avail. in microform from UMI,PMC; reprint service avail. from SWZ) **Indexed:** Acad.Ind., Anim.Breed.Abstr., Apic.Abstr., ASCA, Bibl.Agri., Biol.Abstr., Biol.& Agr.Ind., Biotech.Abstr., Chem.Abstr., Child Devel.Abstr., Curr.Adv.Ecol.Sci., Curr.Cont., Curr.Ref.Fish Res., Dairy Sci.Abstr., Deep Sea Res.& Oceanogr.Abstr., Ecol.Abstr., Excerp.Med., Gen.Sci.Ind., Geo.Abstr., Helminthol.Abstr., Ind.Med., Ind.Sci.Rev., Ind.Vet., Key Word Ind.Wildl.Res., Nutr.Abstr., Ocean.Abstr., Pollut.Abstr., Poult.Abstr., Psychol.Abstr. (1953-), Rev.Appl.Entomol., Risk Abstr., Sci.Cit.Ind., Small Anim.Abstr., Sport Fish.Abstr., SSCI, Wild.Rev., Zoo.Rec. **Document type:** academic/scholarly publication.
●Also available online.
—BLDSC (0902.950000); CASDDS; CISTI; EMDOCS; Genuine Article; KR SourceOne; Linda Hall; SWETS; UMI; UnCover. **CCC.**
Description: Contains critical reviews, original papers, and research articles about all aspects of animal behavior for biologists and veterinarians.

ANIMAL GENETICS. see *BIOLOGY — Genetics*

591 333.7 US ISSN 0164-9531
ANIMAL KEEPERS' FORUM. 1974. m. membership. American Association of Zoo Keepers, Inc., 635 S.W. Gage Blvd., Topeka, KS 66606-2066. TEL 913-273-1980; 800-242-4519. FAX 913-273-1980. Ed. Susan D. Chan. R&P contact: Susan D. Chan. adv. contact: Susan D. Chan. bk.rev.; index. circ. 2,700. (back issues avail.) **Indexed:** Sport Fish.Abstr., Wild Life Rev., Wild.Rev.
Description: Contains articles on exotic animal husbandry, research, and exhibit design.
Refereed Serial

ANIMAL NATURAL HISTORY SERIES. see *SCIENCES: COMPREHENSIVE WORKS*

591 SP ISSN 0214-3151
ANIMALIA; revista especializada en animales de compania. 11/yr. 11500 ptas.($115) (effective 1996). Elsevier Prensa S.A., Avda Paral.lel, 180, Apdo. No. 350 F.D., 08015 Barcelona, Spain. TEL 34-3-3255350. FAX 34-3-4252880. Ed. Antoni Prats i Esteve; Pub. Manuel Masip. adv. contact: Manuel Fernandez de Liencres. circ. 7,000. **Document type:** trade publication.
Description: Dedicated to pets, including health care, medicines, diet, show activities and more.

591 CN ISSN 1198-5445
ANIMALWATCH. 1994. 5/yr. Can.$8.49($7.49) (foreign $7.99) (effective 1997). Animal Knowledge & Information Network, P.O. Box 402, Stn. M, Calgary, AB T2P 2J1, Canada. TEL 403-241-2344. E-mail: animal@cuug.ab.ca; URL: http://www.cuug.ab.ca:8001/~animal/. Ed. Allex Michael. R&P contact: Allex Michael. bk.rev.; illus.; index. **Document type:** academic/scholarly publication.
Description: Nonpartisan global report providing the latest information about all animal species and their habitats.

591 636 FR ISSN 0003-424X
CODEN: AZOOAH
ANNALES DE ZOOTECHNIE. (Text and summaries in English, French) 1952. 6/yr. 1450 F. to institutions (US $277; outside the Americas 1790F. (effective 1998). (Institut National de la Recherche Agronomique) Editions Scientifiques et Medicales Elsevier, 141 rue de Javel, 75747 Paris, France. TEL 33-1-45589022. FAX 33-1-45589421. URL: http://www.elsevier.nl/. (Subscr. in U.S. and Canada to: Elsevier Science Inc., Box 945, Madison Sq. Sta., New York, NY 10159-0945. TEL 212-63337300. FAX 212-633-3680) Ed. C. Demarquilly. adv.; bk.rev.; charts; illus.; index. circ. 2,000. (also avail. in microform; reprint service avail. from ISI) **Indexed:** Anim.Breed.Abstr., ASCA, Bibl.Agri., Biol.Abstr., Chem.Abstr., Curr.Adv.Ecol.Sci., Curr.Cont., Dairy Sci.Abstr., Field Crop Abstr., Food Sci.& Tech.Abstr., Helminthol.Abstr., Herb.Abstr., Ind.Sci.Rev., Ind.Vet., Maize Abstr., Nutr.Abstr., Pig News & Info., Poult.Abstr., Sci.Cit.Ind., Sport Fish.Abstr., Sugar Ind.Abstr., Triticale Abstr., Vet.Bull., Wild.Rev., Zoo.Rec. **Document type:** academic/scholarly publication.
—BLDSC (1004.300000); CASDDS; Genuine Article; Linda Hall; SWETS; UnCover. **CCC.**
Description: Publishes original articles, reviews, short notes and national and international symposia proceedings on general or comparative zootechny.
Refereed Serial

591 FR ISSN 0003-4339
QH3 CODEN: ASNBAQ
ANNALES DES SCIENCES NATURELLES. ZOOLOGIE ET BIOLOGIE ANIMALE. (Summaries in English, French) 1824. 4/yr. 1477 F. (foreign 1744 F.) (effective 1997). Masson - Periodiques, 120 bd. St. Germain, 75006 Paris, France. TEL 33-1-40466200. FAX 33-1-40466201. (Subscr. to: Societe de Periodiques Specialises, B.P. 22-F, 41354 Vineuil Cedex, France. TEL 33-2-54504612. FAX 33-2-54504611) Eds. A. de Ricques, P. de Puytorac. bibl.; charts; illus. circ. 450. (also avail. in microform from UMI; microfiche from IDC; reprint service avail. from ISI) **Indexed:** ASCA, Biol.Abstr., Chem.Abstr., Curr.Adv.Ecol.Sci., Curr.Cont., Helminthol.Abstr., Ind.Sci.Rev., Key Word Ind.Wildl.Res., Sci.Cit.Ind., Sport Fish.Abstr., Wild.Rev., Zoo.Rec. **Document type:** academic/scholarly publication.
—BLDSC (0997.000000); CASDDS; CISTI; Genuine Article; Linda Hall; SWETS; UMI; UnCover. **CCC.**
Description: Contains original works on problems in biology, cytology, protistology, endocrinology, ethology, animal sociology, and compared anatomy.

591 PL ISSN 0003-4541
QL1 CODEN: AZOGAR
ANNALES ZOOLOGICI. (Text in various languages) 1922. irreg., latest vol.46, no.1-2. price varies. Polska Akademia Nauk, Muzeum i Instytut Zoologii, Ul. Wilcza 64, 00-679 Warsaw, Poland. TEL 48-2-6293221. FAX 48-2-6296302. Ed. S.A. Slipinski. charts; index. circ. 770. **Indexed:** AgroAgen, Biol.Abstr., Rev.Appl.Entomol., Soils & Fert. **Document type:** academic/scholarly publication.
—CISTI; Linda Hall; UnCover.

591 FI ISSN 0003-455X
CODEN: AZOFAO
ANNALES ZOOLOGICI FENNICI. (Text in English) 1934. q. FIM 500($96) (Academy of Finland) Finnish Zoological and Botanical Publishing Board, P.O. Box 17, P. Rautatiekatu 13, FIN-00014 University of Helsinki, Finland. TEL 358-9-191-7405. FAX 358-9-191-7443. E-mail: elmor__kr@cc.helsinki.fi; URL: http://sekj.pc.helsinki.fi/journals. (Dist. by: Tiedekirja OY, Kirkokatu 14, FIN-00170 Helsinki, Finland. TEL 358-9-635-177) (Co-sponsors: Finnish Academy of Sciences; Societas Scientarum Fennica; Societas pro Fauna et Flora Fennica) Ed. Krzysztof Raciborski. charts; illus.; stat.; index. circ. 750. **Indexed:** Acid Rain Abstr., Acid Rain Ind., ASCA, Biol.Abstr., Chem.Abstr., Curr.Adv.Ecol.Sci., Curr.Cont., Curr.Ref.Fish Res., Ecol.Abstr., Excerp.Med., Forest.Abstr., Forest Prod.Abstr., Geo.Abstr., Helminthol.Abstr., Hort.Abstr., Ind.Sci.Rev., Key Word Ind.Wildl.Res., Ocean.Abstr., Sci.Cit.Ind., Sel.Water Res.Abstr., Soils & Fert., Sport Fish.Abstr., W.R.C.Inf., Wild.Rev., Zoo.Rec. **Document type:** academic/scholarly publication.
—BLDSC (1004.250000); CASDDS; CISTI; EMDOCS; Genuine Article; Linda Hall; SWETS; UnCover.
Description: Contains research reports and reviews on ecology, conservation biology, game and fisheries research of general interests, ecological physiology, faunistics and systematics.

591 II ISSN 0003-5009
QL1 CODEN: AZLGAC
ANNALS OF ZOOLOGY. (Text in English) 1955. q. $32. Academy of Zoology, Khandari Rd., Agra 282 002, Uttar Pradesh, India. Ed. Prof. Beni Charan Mahendra. bk.rev. circ. 1,800. **Indexed:** Biol.Abstr., Chem.Abstr., Deep Sea Res.& Oceanogr.Abstr.
—CASDDS; CISTI.

ANNUAIRE DES ARACHNOLOGISTES MONDIAUX; acarologistes exceptes. see *BIOLOGY — Entomology*

597 UK ISSN 0959-8030
SH171 CODEN: ARFDEN
ANNUAL REVIEW OF FISH DISEASES. 1990. 1 issue/yr. fl.455($281) (effective 1997). Elsevier Science Ltd., Pergamon, P.O. Box 800, Kidlington, Oxford OX5 1DX, England. TEL 44-1865-843000. FAX 44-1865-843010. E-mail: nlinfo-f@elsevier.nl; usinfo-f@elsevier.com; forinfo-kyf04035@niftyserve.or.jp; URL: http://www.elsevier.nl/. (Subscr. to: Elsevier Science, Regional Sales Office, P.O. Box 211, 1000 AE Amsterdam, Netherlands. TEL 31-20-4853757. FAX 31-20-4853432; Subscr. in the Americas to: Elsevier Science, Regional Sales Office, Box 945, New York, NY 10159-0945. TEL 212-633-3730. FAX 212-633-3680; Subscr. in Australasia and the Far East to: Elsevier Science (Singapore) Pte Ltd, No.1 Temasek Ave., No.17-01 Millenia Tower, Singapore 039192, Singapore. TEL 65-434-3727. FAX 65-337-2230) Eds. M. Faisal, F.M. Hetrick. index. (also avail. in microfilm from UMI; back issues avail.) **Indexed:** Environ.Per.Bibl. (1991-1993), Sport Fish.Abstr., Wild.Rev., Zoo.Rec. **Document type:** academic/scholarly publication.
—BLDSC (1522.530000); CISTI; SWETS; UMI; UnCover. **CCC.**
Description: Publishes current reviews and theoretical papers in aquatic animal health. Topics covered include infections of fish caused by viruses, bacteria, fungi or parasites; valence factors of fish pathogens; epidemiology of fish diseases, and other related issues.
Refereed Serial

591 572 FR ISSN 0758-5683
ANTHROPOLOGIE - MARITIME. (Text in English or French) 1984. biennial. 80 F.($15) Centre d'Ethno-Technologie en Milieux Aquatiques (CETMA), Laboratoire d'Ichtyologie, 43, rue Cuvier, 75005 Paris, France. TEL 1-40797732. FAX 1-40793771. bk.rev. (also avail. in microfiche from BHP) **Indexed:** Anthropol.Lit.
Description: Publishes works and research results which contribute to the development of the knowledge of fish.

BIOLOGY — ZOOLOGY

591 156   FR   ISSN 0761-3032
GN476.76
ANTHROPOZOOLOGICA. (Supplement avail. (ISSN 0994-7213)) 1984. s-a. 275 F. to non-members (foreign 300 F.); members 220 F. (foreign 265 F.) (effective 1997). (L'Homme et l'Animal, Societe de Recherche Interdisciplinaire) H.A.S.R.I., c/o Laboratoire d'Anatomie Comparee, Museum National d'Histoire Naturelle, 55 rue Buffon, 75005 Paris, France. TEL 33-1-40793310. FAX 33-1-40793314. Ed. Jean-Denis Vigne.
Indexed: InterActions Bibl. (1990-).

591   FR   ISSN 0994-7213
ANTHROPOZOOLOGICA NUMERO SPECIAL. 1987. irreg. (L'Homme et l'Animal, Societe de Recherche Interdisciplinaire) H.A.S.R.I., c/o Laboratoire d'Anatomie Comparee, Museum National d'Histoire Naturelle, 55 rue Buffon, 75005 Paris, France. TEL 33-1-40793310. FAX 33-1-40793314.

ANTHROZOOS; a multidisciplinary journal on the interactions of people and animals. see *ANTHROPOLOGY*

591   IT   ISSN 0391-5522
APITALIA; notiziario quindicinale d'informazioni. 1974. s-m. L.30000 (foreign L.55000). Federazione Apicoltori Italiani, Corso Vittorio Emanuele 101, 00186 Rome, Italy. TEL 39-6-6877175. FAX 39-6-6852287. TELEX 612533. Ed. Raffaele Cirone. adv.; bk.rev.; index. circ. 20,000. (back issues avail.) **Document type:** bulletin.

591   NE   ISSN 0168-1591
               CODEN: AABSEV
APPLIED ANIMAL BEHAVIOUR SCIENCE; an international scientific journal reporting on the application of ethology to animals used by man. (Text in English) 1975. 20/yr. fl.2425($1394) (effective 1998). Elsevier Science B.V., P.O. Box 211, 1000 AE Amsterdam, Netherlands. TEL 31-20-4853911. FAX 31-20-4853598. TELEX 18582 ESPA NL. E-mail: nlinfo-f@elsevier.nl; usinfo-f@elsevier.com; forinfo-kyf04035@niftyserve.or.jp; URL: http://www.elsevier.nl/. (Subscr. in the Americas to: Elsevier Science, Regional Sales Office, Box 945, New York, NY 10159-0945. TEL 212-633-3730. FAX 212-633-3680; Subscr. in Australasia and the Far East to: Elsevier Science (Singapore) Pte Ltd, No.1 Temasek Ave., No.17-01 Millenia Tower, Singapore 039192, Singapore. TEL 65-434-3727. FAX 65-337-2230; Subscr. in Japan to: Elsevier Science Japan, 9-15 Higashi-Azabu 1-chome, Minato-ku, Tokyo 106, Japan. TEL 81-3-5561-5033. FAX 81-3-5561-5047) Ed. A.F. Fraser. adv.; bk.rev.; bibl.; illus.; index. (also avail. in microform from UMI) **Indexed:** Agri.Eng.Abstr., Anim.Behav.Abstr., Anim.Breed.Abstr., ASCA, Bibl.Agri., Biol.Abstr., Curr.Adv.Ecol.Sci., Curr.Cont., Dairy Sci.Abstr., Ecol.Abstr., Field Crop Abstr., Herb.Abstr., Ind.Sci.Rev., Ind.Vet., InterActions Bibl. (1989-), Key Word Ind.Wildl.Res., Pig News & Info., Poult.Abstr., Psychol.Abstr., Small Anim.Abstr., Sport Fish.Abstr., SSCI, Triticale Abstr., Vet.Bull., Wild.Rev., Zoo.Rec. **Document type:** academic/scholarly publication.
—BLDSC (1571.446000); EMDOCS; Genuine Article; SWETS; UnCover. CCC.
   Formerly (until 1985): Applied Animal Ethology (ISSN 0304-3762)
   Description: Deals with the behaviour of domesticated and utilized animals.
   Refereed Serial

APPLIED ENTOMOLOGY AND ZOOLOGY. see *BIOLOGY — Entomology*

AQUACULTURE INTERNATIONAL. see *FISH AND FISHERIES*

639.34 597   NE   ISSN 0003-729X
               CODEN: AQUUA2
HET AQUARIUM. 1930. 11/yr. fl.70. Nederlandse Bond "Aqua-Terra", Havenstraat 83, 1211 K H Hilversum, Netherlands. TEL 31-35-6216597. Ed. L.G. van den Berkmortel. adv.; bk.rev.; charts; illus.; index. circ. 15,000. **Indexed:** Biol.Abstr., Zoo.Rec. **Document type:** bulletin.
   Description: Articles cover: aquariums, aquatic plants and animals, terraria, reptiles, amphibia, ponds, bog plants, insects, and more.

591   US   ISSN 0167-5427
AQUATIC MAMMALS. 1972. 3/yr. $95 (effective 1997); $100 (effective 1998). European Association for Aquatic Mammals, Hawaii Institute of Marine Biology, Box 1106, Kailua, HI 96734. TEL 808-236-4001. FAX 808-247-5831. E-mail: nachtig@nosc.mil. Ed. Paul E. Nachtigall. R&P contact: Paul E. Nachtigall. bk.rev. circ. 300. (back issues avail.) **Indexed:** Anim.Behav.Abstr., Aqua.Sci.& Fish.Abstr., Biol.Abstr., Deep Sea Res.& Oceanogr.Abstr., Ind.Vet., Key Word Ind.Wildl.Res., Sport Fish.Abstr., Vet.Bull, Wild.Rev., Zoo.Rec. **Document type:** academic/scholarly publication.
—BLDSC (1582.390000); CISTI; UnCover.
   Description: Contains scientific papers dealing with all aspects of the science, conservation, care, and medicine of marine and aquatic mammals.
   Refereed Serial

591 598.2   FI   ISSN 0570-5177
               CODEN: AQZOA9
AQUILO. SERIE ZOOLOGICA. (Text in English) 1950. s-a. price varies. Societas Amicorum Naturae Ouluensis, Department of Zoology, University of Oulu, Linnanmaa, FIN-90570 Oulu, Finland. Ed. Eino Erkinaro. circ. 350. (back issues avail.) **Indexed:** Biol.Abstr., Chem.Abstr., Curr.Adv.Ecol.Sci., Deep Sea Res.& Oceanogr.Abstr., Ecol.Abstr., Geo.Abstr. **Document type:** proceedings.
—BLDSC (1583.120000).

ARASTIRMA ESERLERI SERISI. see *BIOLOGY — Entomology*

ARCHAEOZOOLOGIA; revue international d'archeozoologie. see *ARCHAEOLOGY*

ARCHIV FUER FISCHEREI UND MEERESFORSCHUNG. see *FISH AND FISHERIES*

594   GW   ISSN 0003-9284
               CODEN: AMKUAQ
ARCHIV FUER MOLLUSKENKUNDE. 1869. 2/yr. DM.85. Senckenbergische Naturforschende Gesellschaft, Senckenberganlage 25, 60325 Frankfurt a.M., Germany. TEL 49-69-7542-1. FAX 49-69-746238. E-mail: sjessel@sng.uni-frankfurt.de. Ed. Ronald Janssen. **Indexed:** Biol.Abstr., Chem.Abstr., Curr.Adv.Ecol.Sci., GeoRef., IBR. **Document type:** academic/scholarly publication.
—BLDSC (1621.000000); CISTI; Linda Hall; UMI; UnCover.

ARCHIVES OF ORAL BIOLOGY; a multidisciplinary journal in oral research. see *MEDICAL SCIENCES — Dentistry*

594   IT   ISSN 0394-3399
ARGONAUTA; international journal of malacology. (Text in English) 1985. q. L.50000 (foreign $50; institutions $60) (effective 1996) or exchange basis. Associazione Malacologica Internazionale, Casella Postale 322, 00126 Acilia (Rome), Italy. TEL 39-6-5259331. Ed. Gabriella Raybaudi Massilia. bk.rev.; illus. **Document type:** academic/scholarly publication.
—BLDSC (1664.345800).
   Description: Devoted to molluscan biology and taxonomy.
   Refereed Serial

ARNOLDIA ZIMBABWE. see *BIOLOGY*

591   BL   ISSN 0066-7870
               CODEN: ARQZA4
ARQUIVOS DE ZOOLOGIA. (Text in English, Portuguese and other languages) 1940. irreg. $25 (effective 1997). Universidade de Sao Paulo, Museu de Zoologia, Caixa Postal 42699, 04299-970 Sao Paulo SP, Brazil. Ed. Carlos Roberto Ferreira Brandao. circ. 600. (back issues avail.) **Indexed:** Biol.Abstr., Curr.Adv.Ecol.Sci., Rev.Appl.Entomol., Zoo.Rec. **Document type:** monographic series.
—BLDSC (1696.000000); Linda Hall.

591   NE   ISSN 1384-5950
ARTIS. 1955. bi-m. fl.55. (Zoological Society Amsterdam) Stichting tot Instandhouding van de Diergaarde van het Koninklijk Zoologisch Genootschap Natura Artis Magistra, Plantage Kerklaan 40, 1018 CZ Amsterdam, Netherlands. E-mail: tsartis@xs4all.nl. Ed. G. van der Sijde. bk.rev.; illus.; index. circ. 30,000. **Indexed:** RILA. **Document type:** consumer publication.
—CISTI.
   Former titles (until 1996): Dieren (ISSN 0168-6631); (until 1984): Artis (ISSN 0004-3834)

591   JA
ASA DOBUTSU KOEN SHIIKU KIROKUSHU/ASA ZOOLOGICAL PARK OF HIROSHIMA. RECORD OF BREEDING. (Text in Japanese) 1974. biennial. Hiroshimashi Dobutsuen Kyokai - Hiroshima City Zoological Park Society, Hiroshimashi Asa Dobutsu Koen, Dobutsuen, Asacho, Asa Kita-ku, Hiroshima-shi, Hiroshima-ken 731-33, Japan. Ed. Hiroshi Morimoto. **Document type:** bulletin.

591   US   ISSN 0066-8222
ASCIDIAN NEWS. 1966. 2/yr. $5. California State University, Fullerton, Department of Biology, Fullerton, CA 92634. TEL 714-773-3481. FAX 714-773-3426. E-mail: clambert@fulleton.edu. Eds. Charles Lambert, Gretchen Lambert. bk.rev. circ. 200. **Document type:** newsletter.

591 639.2   PH   ISSN 0116-6514
ASIAN FISHERIES SCIENCE. (Text in English) 1987. 4/yr. $15 to individual members $38 (non-members $27); institutional members $38 (non-members $60). International Center for Living Aquatic Resources Management, Asian Fisheries Society, M.C.P.O. Box 2631, 0718 Makati City, Philippines. TEL 63-2-812-86-41. FAX 63-2-816-31-83. Ed. Sena S. De Silva. adv.: page $200. **Indexed:** Food Sci.& Tech.Abstr.
—BLDSC (1742.417600).
   Description: Covers all aspects of Asian fisheries and aquaculture research.

594   IT
ASSOCIAZIONE MALACOLOGICA INTERNAZIONALE. NOTIZIARIO. 3/yr. included with Argonauta. Associazione Malacologica Internazionale, Casella Postale 322, 0126 Acilia (RO), Italy. TEL 39-6-5259331. adv. contact: Roberto Ubaldi. **Document type:** newsletter.

AUSTASIA AQUACULTURE. see *FISH AND FISHERIES*

594   AT
AUSTRALASIAN SHELL NEWS. 1953. q. included in subscription to Molluscan Research. Malacological Society of Australasia, Division of Invertebrate Zoology, Australian Museum, 6 College St., Sydney, N.S.W. 2000, Australia. TEL 61-2-3206275. FAX 61-2-3206050. E-mail: alisonm@amsg. Austmus.gov.au. Ed. J. Stanisic. adv.; bk.rev. circ. 500. **Document type:** newsletter.
   Former titles: Australian Shell News (ISSN 0310-1304); (until 197?): Australian Newsletter.
   Description: Discusses malacology.

BIOLOGY — ZOOLOGY

591   **AT**   ISSN 0004-959X
QL1   CODEN: AJZOAS
AUSTRALIAN JOURNAL OF ZOOLOGY. 1953. bi-m. Aus.$320($320) (effective 1998). (C.S.I.R.O. Australia) C.S.I.R.O. Publishing, 150 Oxford St., Collingwood, Vic. 3066, Australia. TEL 61-3-96627622. FAX 61-3-96627611. E-mail: dwm@publish.csiro.au; URL: http://www.publish.csiro.au/journals/ajz. Eds. D.W. Morton, S.L. Farrer. adv.; index. circ. 700. (also avail. in microform from UMI; back issues avail.) **Indexed:** Abstr.Hyg., Anim.Breed.Abstr., ASCA, Bio-Contr.News & Info., Biol.Abstr., Chem.Abstr., Curr.Adv.Cell & Devel.Biol., Curr.Adv.Ecol.Sci., Curr.Cont., Curr.Ref.Fish Res., Dairy Sci.Abstr., Deep Sea Res.& Oceanogr.Abstr., Ecol.Abstr., Environ.Abstr., Excerp.Med., Forest.Abstr., Forest Prod.Abstr., GeoRef., Helminthol.Abstr., Ind.Sci.Rev., Ind.Vet., Key Word Ind.Wildl.Res., Nutr.Abstr., Ocean.Abstr., Pollut.Abstr., Protozool.Abstr., Rev.Appl.Entomol., Sci.Cit.Ind., So.Pac.Per.Ind., Sport Fish.Abstr., Triticale Abstr., Trop.Dis.Bull., Vet.Bull., Wild.Rev., Zoo.Rec. **Document type:** academic/scholarly publication. **●Also available online.**
—BLDSC (1813.000000); CASDDS; CIS; CISTI; EMDOCS; Genuine Article; Linda Hall; SWETS; UMI; UnCover. **CCC.**
Description: Covers all branches of zoology including anatomy, physiology, genetics, behavior, ecology, and zoogeography.

599   **AT**   ISSN 0310-0049
CODEN: AUMACY
AUSTRALIAN MAMMALOGY. 1972. a. Aus.$48. Australian Mammal Society Inc., c/o Dr. Graham Ross, Ed., Australian Biological Resources Study (Fauna), G.P.O. Box 636, Canberra, A.C.T. 2601, Australia. TEL 06-250-9435. FAX 06-250-9448. (Subscr. to: c/o ACTS, G.P.O. Box 2200, Canberra, A.C.T. 2601, Australia) Ed. Graham Ross. bk.rev. circ. 680. **Indexed:** Apic.Abstr., Aus.Sci.Ind., Biol.Abstr., GeoRef, Sport Fish.Abstr., Wild.Rev., Zoo.Rec. **Document type:** academic/scholarly publication.
—BLDSC (1814.060000); Linda Hall; UnCover.
Refereed Serial

AUSTRALIAN MUSEUM, SYDNEY. RECORDS. see *SCIENCES: COMPREHENSIVE WORKS*

AUSTRALIAN MUSEUM, SYDNEY. RECORDS SUPPLEMENTS. see *SCIENCES: COMPREHENSIVE WORKS*

599.8 333.9   **AT**   ISSN 0817-9573
CODEN: AUMACY
AUSTRALIAN PRIMATOLOGY. 1986. q. Aus.$25 to members; institutions Aus.$35; students Aus.$15 (effective 1997). Australasian Primate Society, P.O. Box 500, One Tree Hill, S.A. 5114, Australia. TEL 61-8-82807670. E-mail: gc00274@dany.snetad.cpg.com.au. Ed. Greaeme Crook. adv.; bk.rev. circ. 150. **Document type:** bulletin.
—BLDSC (1818.310000).
Description: Presents papers and short communications in all areas of primatology.
Refereed Serial

591.0994   **AT**   ISSN 1033-4874
CODEN: AZOREU
AUSTRALIAN ZOOLOGICAL REVIEWS. 1989. irreg. included with Australian Zoologist. Royal Zoological Society of New South Wales, P.O. Box 20, Mosman, N.S.W. 2088, Australia. TEL 61-2-99697336. **Indexed:** Sport Fish.Abstr., Wild.Rev., Zoo.Rec. **Document type:** monographic series.

591   **AT**   ISSN 0067-2238
QL1   CODEN: AUZOA3
AUSTRALIAN ZOOLOGIST. 1914. irreg. Aus.$50 includes Australian Zoological Reviews. Royal Zoological Society of New South Wales, P.O. Box 20, Mosman, N.S.W. 2088, Australia. TEL 61-2-99697336. Ed. Dan Lunney. adv.; bk.rev. circ. 1,450. **Indexed:** Biol.Abstr., Curr.Adv.Ecol.Sci., Deep Sea Res.& Oceanogr.Abstr., Ecol.Abstr., Environ.Per.Bibl. (1990-1991), Geo.Abstr.H.G., Sport Fish.Abstr., Wild.Rev., Zoo.Rec.
—BLDSC (1825.000000); CISTI; Linda Hall; UnCover.

598.2   **IT**   ISSN 0404-4266
CODEN: AVOCEP
AVOCETTA. (Text in English, French, Italian) 1955. s-a. L.50000 (effective 1997). Centro Italiano Studi Ornitologici, c/o Dipartimento di Biologia Animale, Via Accademia Albertina 17, 10123 Turin, Italy. TEL 39-11-8122374. FAX 39-11-8124561. E-mail: bedini@discau.unipi.it. (Subscr. to: CISO, Dipartimento di Scienze del Comportamento Animale, Via. A. Volta 6, 56126 Pisa, Italy) Ed.Bd. adv. contact: N.E. Baldaccini. bk.rev.; abstr.; charts; illus. **Indexed:** Anim.Behav.Abstr., Ecol.Abstr., Sport Fish.Abstr., Wild.Rev., Zoo.Rec. **Document type:** academic/scholarly publication.
—UnCover.
Description: Stimulates and organizes ornithological research in Italy.
Refereed Serial

AZABU DAIGAKU JUIGAKUBU KENKYU HOKOKU/AZABU UNIVERSITY. VETERINARY MEDICINE. BULLETIN. see *VETERINARY SCIENCE*

591 639.9   **UK**   ISSN 0265-3656
B B C WILDLIFE. 1963. m. £30 (Europe & Ireland £34.95; rest of world £37.50) (effective 1996). B B C Worldwide Publishing, Broadcasting House, Whiteladies Rd., Bristol GS8 2LR, England. TEL 44-181-576-2000. FAX 44-181-576-2931. (Subscr. to.: B B C Wildlife Subscriptions, P.O. Box 425, Woking, Surrey GU21 1GP, England. TEL 44-1483-733716. FAX 44-1483-756792) Ed. Rosamund Kidman Cox; Pub. Heather Aylott. adv. contact: Jonathan Gifford. bk.rev.; charts; illus.; index. circ. 117,859. (also avail. in microfilm from UMI; back issues avail.) **Indexed:** Biol.Abstr., Biol.Dig., Curr.Adv.Ecol.Sci., Ecol.Abstr., Energy Ind., Energy Info.Abstr., Environ.Abstr., Environ.Per.Bibl. (1973-), Geo.Abstr., GeoRef., IDA, Key Word Ind.Wildl.Res. **Document type:** academic/scholarly publication.
—BLDSC (1871.360700); UnCover.
Formerly (until Nov. 1983): Wildlife (ISSN 0003-3618)
Description: Features articles covering animals, plants, conservation and environment issues, in a general-interest format.

591   **PL**   ISSN 0137-6683
BADANIA FIZJOGRAFICZNE NAD POLSKA ZACHODNIA. SERIA C. ZOOLOGIA. (Text in Polish; summaries in English) 1948. irreg., vol.41, 1994. price varies. Poznanskie Towarzystwo Przyjaciol Nauk, Ul. Sew. Mielzynskiego 27-29, 61-725 Poznan, Poland. TEL 48-61-527-441. Ed. Zofia Michalska. bibl. circ. 300. **Indexed:** AgroLibrex.
—BLDSC (1856.208000).
Supersedes in part (in 1974): Badania Fizjograficzne nad Polska Zachodnia. Seria B. Biologia (ISSN 0373-7497)

591.05   **BG**   ISSN 0304-9027
QL334.B34   CODEN: BJZOA5
BANGLADESH JOURNAL OF ZOOLOGY. (Text in English) 1973. s-a. Tk.800 (foreign $40) (effective 1997). Zoological Society of Bangladesh, c/o Dept. of Zoology, University of Dhaka, Dhaka 1000, Bangladesh. TEL 880-2-868333. FAX 880-2-865583. E-mail: zool.du@citechco.net. Ed. S.M.H. Kabir. adv.; bk.rev.; illus. circ. 600. **Indexed:** Biol.Abstr., Entomol.Abstr., Hort.Abstr., Rice Abstr., Zoo.Rec. **Document type:** academic/scholarly publication.
—BLDSC (1861.710000); CISTI; Linda Hall; UnCover.
Description: Publishes research papers on all branches of zoology, both pure and applied.
Refereed Serial

594   **NE**   ISSN 0005-6219
QL401   CODEN: BSTRAD
BASTERIA. (Text in Dutch, English, French or German) 1936. s-a. fl.62.50. Nederlandse Malacologische Vereniging - Dutch Malacological Society, c/o R.G. Moolenbeek, Zoologisch Museum, Mauritskade 57, P.O. Box 94766, 1090 GT Amsterdam, Netherlands. bk.rev.; charts; illus.; index, cum.index every 5 yrs. circ. 600. (also avail. in microfiche from IDC) **Indexed:** Biol.Abstr. **Document type:** proceedings.
—BLDSC (1866.000000); Linda Hall; UnCover.

599.4   **US**   ISSN 0005-6227
BAT RESEARCH NEWS. 1960. q. $15. c/o Dr. G. Roy Horst, Ed., Dept. of Biology, State University of New York at Potsdam, Potsdam, NY 13676. TEL 315-267-2259. adv.; bk.rev.; abstr.; bibl.; charts; cum.index every 5 yrs. circ. 800. (processed) **Indexed:** Biol.Abstr., Sport Fish.Abstr., Wild Life Rev., Wild.Rev., Zoo.Rec. **Document type:** newsletter.

591   **US**   ISSN 1049-0043
QL737.C5   CODEN: BATSEU
BATS. 1983. q. $30 includes membership. Bat Conservation International, Box 162603, Austin, TX 78716. TEL 512-327-9721. FAX 512-327-9724. Ed. Sara McCabe. R&P contact: Andrew Puntch. bk.rev. circ. 14,000. pp./issue: 20. **Indexed:** Sport Fish.Abstr., Wild.Rev., Zoo.Rec. **Document type:** newsletter.
—UnCover.

591   **NE**   ISSN 0067-4745
CODEN: BUFOAG
BEAUFORTIA; series of miscellaneous publications. (Text in English, French or German) 1951. irreg., vol.46, 1996. DM.130 per no. Universiteit van Amsterdam, Instituut voor Systematisch en Populatie Biologie (Zoologisch Museum), P.O. Box 94766, 1090 GT Amsterdam, Netherlands. TEL 31-20-5256901. FAX 31-20-5255402. E-mail: soest@bio.uva.nl. Ed. R.W.M. van Soest. circ. 900. **Indexed:** Biol.Abstr., Deep Sea Res.& Oceanogr.Abstr., GeoRef., Zoo.Rec. **Document type:** monographic series.
—BLDSC (1871.800000); CISTI; Linda Hall.
Description: Publishes research in taxonomy and systematics.
Refereed Serial

591.5   **NE**   ISSN 0005-7959
BF671   CODEN: BEHAA8
BEHAVIOUR; an international journal of behavioural biology. (Text in English and German) 1947. 10/yr. fl.705($414) (effective 1998). E.J. Brill, P.O. Box 9000, 2300 PA Leiden, Netherlands. TEL 31-71-5353500. FAX 31-71-5317532. TELEX 39296 BRILL NL. E-mail: cs@brill.nl. (In N. America: E.J. Brill, 24 Hudson St., Kinderhook, NY 12106. TEL 800-962-4406. FAX 518-758-1959) Ed. J.G. van Rhijn, M. Daly. R&P contact: Elizabeth Vennekamp. bibl.; charts; illus.; cum.index: vols.1-132. (also avail. in microform from SWZ,PMC) **Indexed:** Anim.Breed.Abstr., ASCA, Biol.Abstr., Chem.Abstr., Curr.Adv.Ecol.Sci., Curr.Cont., Dairy Sci.Abstr., Deep Sea Res.& Oceanogr.Abstr., Ecol.Abstr., Ind.Sci.Rev., Key Word Ind.Wildl.Res., M.L.A., Nutr.Abstr., Poult.Abstr., Psychol.Abstr. (1950-), Sci.Cit.Ind., Sport Fish.Abstr., SSCI, Wild.Rev., Zoo.Rec. **Document type:** academic/scholarly publication.
—BLDSC (1876.650000); CISTI; Genuine Article; Linda Hall; SWETS; UnCover. **CCC.**
Description: Covers the scientific study of animal behavior.
Refereed Serial

591   **GW**   ISSN 0067-6098
BERLINER TIERPARK-BUCH. 1957. irreg., no. 26, 1974. price varies. Tierpark Berlin, Am Tierpark 41, 10319 Berlin, Germany. **Document type:** monographic series.

BHARTIYA KRISHI ANUSANDHAN PATRIKA; quarterly research journal of plant and animal sciences. see *AGRICULTURE*

591 028.5   **GW**   ISSN 0342-8095
BIMBO; der kleine Tierfreund. 1977. m. DM.39.60. Johann Michael Sailer Verlag GmbH, Aeusserer-Laufer-Platz 22, 90403 Nuernberg, Germany. TEL 49-911-53961. Ed. Andrea Hoesel. bk.rev.; illus. circ. 140,000. (back issues avail.) **Document type:** consumer publication.
Description: Information about nature, animals and environmental protection for children aged 6-8.

BIOACOUSTICS; the international journal of animal sound and its recording. see *PHYSICS — Sound*

597 639.2 NE
BIOCHEMISTRY & MOLECULAR BIOLOGY OF FISHES. (Text in English) 1991. irreg., vol.5, 1995. price varies. Elsevier Science B.V., Books Division, P.O. Box 211, 1000 AE Amsterdam, Netherlands. TEL 31-20-4853911. FAX 31-20-4853705. TELEX 18582 ESPA NL. E-mail: nlinfo@elsevier.nl; usinfo-f@elsevier.com; forinfo-kyf04035@niftyserve.or.jp; URL: http://www.elsevier.nl/. (Subscr. in the Americas to: Elsevier Science, Regional Sales Office, Box 945, New York, NY 10159-0945. TEL 212-633-3730. FAX 212-633-3680; Subscr. in Australasia and the Far East to: Elsevier Science (Singapore) Pte Ltd, No.1 Temasek Ave., No.17-01 Millenia Tower, Singapore 039192, Singapore. TEL 65-434-3727. FAX 65-337-2230; Subscr. in Japan to: Elsevier Science Japan, 9-15 Higashi-Azabu 1-chome, Minato-ku, Tokyo 106, Japan. TEL 81-3-5561-5033. FAX 81-3-5561-5047) Eds. P.W. Hochachka, T.P. Mommsen. (back issues avail.) **Document type:** monographic series.
Refereed Serial

BIOLOGIA. see *BIOLOGY*

591 XO
CODEN: BLOAAO
BIOLOGIA. SECTION ZOOLOGY. (Two other sections avail: Botany; Cellular and Molecular Biology) (Text in English) 1946. s-a. $50 ($138 for 3 sections). Slovak Academy of Sciences, Institute of Zoology, Dubravska cesta 9, 842 06 Bratislava, Slovakia. TEL 421-7-3789756. FAX 421-7-3789757. E-mail: uzaelabu@savba.sk. (Dist. by: Slovak Academic Press, Ltd., P.O. Box 57, Nam. Slobody 6, 810 05 Bratislava, Slovakia) Eds. Milan Labuda, Maria Kazimirova. adv.; bk.rev.; charts; illus.; index. **Indexed:** Biodet.Abstr., Biol.Abstr., Chem.Abstr., Crop Physiol.Abstr., Helminthol.Abstr., Ind.Med., INIS Atomind., Sel.Water Res.Abstr., Small Anim.Abstr., Sport Fish.Abstr., Triticale Abstr., Vet.Bull., Wild.Rev., Zoo.Rec. **Document type:** academic/scholarly publication.
—BLDSC (2072.700000); CASDDS; CISTI; Genuine Article; KNAW; Linda Hall.
Formerly (until 1994): Biologia. B: Zoologia (ISSN 0862-1136); **Supersedes in part** (in 1969): Biologia (ISSN 0006-3088)
Description: Presents original experimental and descriptive works in basic biological research in zoology (taxonomy, study of vertebrates and invertebrates, physiology).

BIOLOGICAL SOCIETY OF WASHINGTON. PROCEEDINGS. see *BIOLOGY*

BIOLOGISCHE ZEITSCHRIFT. see *BIOLOGY — Entomology*

591 US ISSN 0893-312X
CODEN: BMBZEB
BISHOP MUSEUM BULLETINS IN ZOOLOGY. 1922. irreg., no.2, 199? price varies. (Bernice Pauahi Bishop Museum) Bishop Museum Press, 1525 Bernice St., Box 19000-A, Honolulu, HI 96817. TEL 808-847-3511. FAX 808-841-8968. circ. 300. (reprint service avail. from UMI)
—CISTI; Linda Hall.
Supersedes in part (in 1987): Bernice P. Bishop Museum Bulletin (ISSN 0005-9439)
Description: Covers zoology of Hawaii and the Pacific Basin.

580 590 PO ISSN 0523-7904
CODEN: BCGNAS
BOCAGIANA. 1959. irreg., no.153, 1992. exchange basis. (Camara Municipal do Funchal) Museu Municipal do Funchal, Rua da Mouraria, 31, 9000 Funchal, Madeira, Portugal. FAX 351-91-25180. TELEX 72529 MMFP. Eds. Manuel J. Biscoito, G.E. Maul. R&P contact: Antonio Domingos Abreu. circ. 750. **Indexed:** Biol.Abstr., Curr.Adv.Ecol.Sci., Deep Sea Res.& Oceanogr.Abstr., Zoo.Rec. **Document type:** bulletin, academic/scholarly publication.
—BLDSC (2116.750000).

591 BL ISSN 0101-3580
QL242 CODEN: BOZOD9
BOLETIM DE ZOOLOGIA. (Text in English, French and Portuguese) 1937. a. exchange basis. Universidade de Sao Paulo, Departamento de Zoologia, Caixa Postal 8191, 05508-900 Sao Paulo, SP, Brazil. (Co-sponsor: Instituto de Biologia Marinha) Ed. Walter Narchi. circ. 500. **Indexed:** Biol.Abstr., Zoo.Rec.
—Linda Hall.
Supersedes in part (since 1976): Boletim de Zoologia e Biologia Marinha. Nova Serie (ISSN 0067-9623)

591 IT ISSN 0394-7149
QL401
BOLLETTINO MALACOLOGICO. (Text in English, French, Italian, Spanish; summaries in English) 1965. 3/yr. L.60000 to individuals (foreign L.85000); institutions L.81000 (foreign L.105000) (effective 1995). Societa Italiana di Malacologia, c/o Acquario Civico, Viale Gadio 2, 20121 Milan, Italy. FAX 39-2-468563. E-mail: propal@mbox.vol.it. Ed. Mauro Mariani. adv. contact: Riccardo Giannuzzi-Savelli. bk.rev.; index. circ. 1,000. (back issues avail.) **Indexed:** Biol.Abstr., Zoo.Rec. **Document type:** academic/scholarly publication.
—BLDSC (2239.090000).
Refereed Serial

BOMBUS; faunistische Mitteilungen aus Nordwestdeutschland. see *BIOLOGY — Entomology*

591 GW ISSN 0006-7172
QL1 CODEN: BZOBAN
BONNER ZOOLOGISCHE BEITRAEGE. (Text in English, French, German) 1950. 4/yr. DM.90. Zoologisches Forschungsinstitut und Museum Alexander Koenig, Adenauerallee 160, 53113 Bonn, Germany. TEL 49-228-9122-216. FAX 49-228-216979. Ed. Dr. Rainer Hutterer. bk.rev.; charts; illus.; maps. circ. 350. **Indexed:** Biol.Abstr., Deep Sea Res.& Oceanogr.Abstr., Entomol.Abstr., Key Word Ind.Wildl.Res., Sport Fish.Abstr., Wild.Rev., Zoo.Rec., Zoo.Rec. **Document type:** academic/scholarly publication.
—BLDSC (2247.700000); CISTI.

590 GW ISSN 0302-671X
CODEN: BZMNAF
BONNER ZOOLOGISCHE MONOGRAPHIEN. (Text in English, French or German) 1971. irreg. (1-3/yr.). Zoologisches Forschungsinstitut und Museum Alexander Koenig, Adenauerallee 160, 53113 Bonn, Germany. TEL 49-228-9122-216. FAX 49-228-216979. Ed. Dr. Goetz Rheinwald. circ. 150. **Indexed:** Biol.Abstr., Sport Fish.Abstr., Wild.Rev., Zoo.Rec. **Document type:** monographic series.
—BLDSC (2247.720000); CISTI; Linda Hall.

591 GW ISSN 0174-3384
QH5
BRAUNSCHWEIGER NATURKUNDLICHE SCHRIFTEN. 1980. a. exchange basis. Staatliches Naturhistorisches Museum, Pockelsstr. 10, 38106 Braunschweig, Germany. TEL 49-531-3914351. FAX 49-531-3914370. **Indexed:** Ecol.Abstr., Geo.Abstr., IBR. **Document type:** proceedings.
—BLDSC (2277.013000).

591 US ISSN 0006-9698
QL1 CODEN: BRVRAG
BREVIORA. 1952. irreg. (3-6/yr.), no.506, 1996. price varies. Harvard University, Museum of Comparative Zoology, Cambridge, MA 02138. TEL 617-495-2468. Ed. Kenneth J. Boss. bibl.; charts; illus. circ. 700. (back issues avail.) **Indexed:** Biol.Abstr., Deep Sea Res.& Oceanogr.Abstr., GeoRef. **Document type:** academic/scholarly publication.
—CISTI; Linda Hall; UnCover.

913 500.907 US ISSN 0193-4406
QL155 CODEN: BRIMD7
BRIMLEYANA; the zoological journal of the southeastern United States. 1979. 2/yr. $15 to individuals; institutions $20. North Carolina State Museum of Natural Sciences, 102 N. Salisbury St., Box 29555, Raleigh, NC 27626-0555. TEL 919-733-7450. Ed. Richard A. Lancia. bk.rev. circ. 300. (back issues avail.) **Indexed:** ASCA, Biol.Abstr., Biol.Dig., Curr.Adv.Ecol.Sci., Curr.Cont., Geo.Abstr., Key Word Ind.Wildl.Res., Sport Fish.Abstr., Wild Life Rev., Wild.Rev., Zoo.Rec. **Document type:** academic/scholarly publication.
—BLDSC (2284.170000); Genuine Article; Linda Hall; UnCover.
Description: Publishes original research in systematics, evolution, zoogeography, ecology, behavior and palaeozoology on the fauna of the southeastern U.S.
Refereed Serial

595.4 UK ISSN 0524-4994
QL451 CODEN: BACBBR
BRITISH ARACHNOLOGICAL SOCIETY. BULLETIN. 1969. 3/yr. £24 to non-members; members £18 (effective 1996-1997). British Arachnological Society, c/o Dr. P. Merrett, Ed., 6 Hillcrest, Swanage, Dorset BH19 2HS, England. bk.rev.; charts; illus.; stat.; index; circ. 700 (controlled). **Indexed:** Biol.Abstr., Geo.Abstr., Sport Fish.Abstr., Wild.Rev., Zoo.Rec. **Document type:** academic/scholarly publication.
—BLDSC (2412.550000); Linda Hall; UnCover.
Supersedes: British Spider Study Group. Bulletin.
Refereed Serial

595.4 UK ISSN 0959-2261
CODEN: NBASE6
BRITISH ARACHNOLOGICAL SOCIETY. NEWSLETTER. 1985. 3/yr. British Arachnological Society, c/o J.E. Dalingwater, 50 Westgate, Hale, Altrincham, Cheshire WA15 9AZ, England. **Indexed:** Zoo.Rec. **Document type:** newsletter.
—BLDSC (6106.396700).

597.6 UK ISSN 0260-5805
CODEN: BBHSEB
BRITISH HERPETOLOGICAL SOCIETY. BULLETIN. 1980. q. (subscr. includes Herpetological Journal). British Herpetological Society, c/o Zoological Society of London, Regents Park, London NW1 4RY, England. adv.; bk.rev.; illus. circ. 900. **Indexed:** Sport Fish.Abstr., Wild.Rev., Zoo.Rec. **Document type:** academic/scholarly publication, bulletin.
—BLDSC (2414.900000); UnCover.
Formerly: British Herpetological Society. Newsletter.

591 US ISSN 0068-2780
BROOKFIELD BANDARLOG. 1949. irreg. membership. Chicago Zoological Society, Zoological Park, Brookfield, IL 60513. TEL 312-485-0263. Ed. George B. Rabb.
—Linda Hall.

591 US ISSN 8756-3479
BROOKFIELD ZOO BISON. 1966. 2/yr. $10 for 4 issues. Chicago Zoological Society, Zoological Park, Brookfield, IL 60513. TEL 312-485-0263. circ. 30,000.
—Linda Hall; UnCover.
Formerly: Brookfield Bison.

591 US ISSN 0108-0326
BRYOZOA (YEAR). (Text in English) 1980. a. $40 to individuals for 3/yrs.; libraries $10. International Bryozoology Association, c/o Department of Geology, University of Illinois, Urbana, IL 61801. TEL 217-333-3833. FAX 217-244-4996. Ed. Daniel B. Blake. circ. 250.
Description: Includes membership list, recent publications, and news items.

BUDGERIGAR WORLD. see *PETS*

BULLETIN DE LA MURITHIENNE. see *EARTH SCIENCES*

591 II ISSN 0970-0765
QL1 CODEN: BPAAS:A
BULLETIN OF PURE & APPLIED SCIENCES. SECTION A: ZOOLOGY. 1982. 2/yr. Rs.300($50) Dr. A.K. Sharma, Ed. & Pub., 140 (RPS) D.D.A. Flat, Mansarovar Park, Shahdara, New Delhi 110 032, India. TEL 91-11-2117408. adv.; bk.rev. circ. 600. **Document type:** academic/scholarly publication.
—CISTI; Linda Hall. CCC.

BIOLOGY — ZOOLOGY

590.744   AT   ISSN 0084-8182
BULLETIN OF ZOO MANAGEMENT. 1969. a. free. Royal Zoological Society of South Australia, Inc., Zoological Gardens, Frome Road, Adelaide, S.A. 5000, Australia. Ed. David Langdon. bk.rev.; circ. 250 (controlled).

591   UK   ISSN 0007-5167
                   CODEN: BZONAP
BULLETIN OF ZOOLOGICAL NOMENCLATURE. 1943. q. £95($175) (effective 1997). International Commission on Zoological Nomenclature, c/o Natural History Museum, Cromwell Rd., London. TEL 44-171-938-9387. E-mail: iczn@nhm.ac.uk. (Co-sponsor: International Trust for Zoological Nomenclature) Ed. P.K. Tubbs. circ. 300 (paid). **Indexed:** Biol.Abstr., GeoRef., Helminthol.Abstr., Sport Fish.Abstr., Wild.Rev., Zoo.Rec. **Document type:** academic/scholarly publication.
—BLDSC (2926.000000); CISTI; Linda Hall; SWETS; UnCover.
Refereed Serial

591   UK   ISSN 0305-0351
C I P DESCRIPTIONS OF PLANT-PARASITIC NEMATODES. 1972. irreg. price varies. CAB International, Institute of Parasitology, Wallingford, Oxon. OX10 8DE, England. TEL 44-491-832111. FAX 44-491-833508. TELEX 847964 COMAGG G. (U.S. subscr. to: CAB International, North American Office, 845 N. Park Ave., Tucson, AZ 85179. TEL 800-528-4841) Ed.Bd. (looseleaf format; back issues avail.) **Indexed:** Helminthol.Abstr. **Document type:** academic/scholarly publication.

CALIFORNIA COOPERATIVE OCEANIC FISHERIES INVESTIGATIONS REPORTS. see *FISH AND FISHERIES*

CALIFORNIA FISH AND GAME. see *CONSERVATION*

591   CN   ISSN 0008-4301
QL1   CODEN: CJZOAG
CANADIAN JOURNAL OF ZOOLOGY/JOURNAL CANADIEN DE ZOOLOGIE. (Text mainly in English, occasionally in French) 1929. m. Can.$188 to individuals (foreign $198); institutions Can.$515 (foreign $515) (effective 1996). National Research Council of Canada, Research Journals, Ottawa, ON K1A 0R6, Canada. TEL 613-993-9084. FAX 613-952-7656. URL: http://www.cisti.nrc.ca/cisti/journals/. Ed. Drs. K.G. Davey, A.S.M. Saleuddin. adv.; B&W page Can.$600; trim 8 1/2 x 11; adv. contact: Hoda Jabbour. bibl.; charts; illus.; index. circ. 1,300. (also avail. in microform from UMI,PMC; back issues avail.; reprint service avail. from UMI) **Indexed:** Abstr.Bull.Inst.Pap.Chem., Abstr.Hyg., Acid Rain Abstr., Acid Rain Ind., Anim.Breed.Abstr., Apic.Abstr., ASCA, Bibl.Agri., Bio-Contr.News & Info., Biodet.Abstr., Biol.Abstr., Biol.& Agr.Ind., Chem.Abstr., Curr.Adv.Ecol.Sci., Curr.Cont., Curr.Ref.Fish Res., Dairy Sci.Abstr., Deep Sea Res.& Oceanogr.Abstr., Ecol.Abstr., Ecol.Zoo.& Plant Sci.Abstr. (1945-), Environ.Abstr., Environ.Per.Bibl. (1975-1994), Excerpt.Med., Field Crop Abstr., Forest.Abstr., Forest Prod.Abstr., Geo.Abstr., Geol.Abstr., GeoRef., Helminthol.Abstr., Hort.Abstr., Ind.Sci.Rev., Ind.Vet., INIS Atomind., Key Word Ind.Wildl.Res., Maize Abstr., Neurosci.Cit.Ind., Nucl.Sci.Abstr., Nutr.Abstr., Ocean.Abstr., Plant Breed.Abstr., Pollut.Abstr., Poult.Abstr., Protozool.Abstr., Rev.Appl.Entomol., Risk Abstr., Sci.Cit.Ind., Sel.Water Res.Abstr., So.Pac.Per.Ind., Soils & Fert., Sport Fish.Abstr., Trop.Dis.Bull., Vet.Bull., Weed Abstr., Wild.Rev., World Text.Abstr., Zoo.Rec. **Document type:** academic/scholarly publication.
—BLDSC (3037.000000); CASDDS; CIS; CISTI; EMDOCS; Genuine Article; KNAW; KR SourceOne; Linda Hall; SWETS; UMI; UnCover. **CCC.**
Formerly (until 1950): Canadian Journal of Research. Section D: Zoological Sciences (ISSN 0366-7413); Which superseded in part (in 1935): Canadian Journal of Research (ISSN 0366-6581)
Refereed Serial

599.742   SW   ISSN 0283-9474
CANIS LUPUS; Varggruppens medlemstidning. 1984. q. SEK 125 membership (effective 1993). Foereningen Varggruppen - Wolf Group, P.O. Box 15061, S-104 65 Stockholm, Sweden. Susie Gustawson. adv.; bk.rev. circ. 1,800. **Document type:** newsletter.
Description: Directed to members of the organization Varggruppen, dedicated to the preservation of a free-ranging wolf population in Scandinavia.

597.6   US
CAPTIVE BREEDING. q. $20. Snake Bite, Box 87100, Canton, MI 48187. Ed. Richard Aquiline.

CARCINOLOGICAL SOCIETY OF JAPAN. CANCER. see *MEDICAL SCIENCES — Oncology*

CAROLINEA; Beitraege zur Naturkundlichen Forschung in Suedwestdeutschland. see *EARTH SCIENCES*

594   US   ISSN 0084-862X
CATALOG OF DEALERS' PRICES FOR MARINE SHELLS. (Text in English and Latin) 1965. a. $19.50. Of Sea & Shore Publications, Box 219, Port Gamble, WA 98364. TEL 360-297-2426. FAX 360-297-2426. E-mail: ofseashr@pacific.telebyte.com. Ed. Thomas C. Rice. circ. 2,000. (reprint service avail. from UMI)
Description: Provides information on the value of shells.

591   US
                   CODEN: CAPBAY
CATALOGUE OF AMERICAN AMPHIBIANS AND REPTILES. 1963. irreg., approx. 20/yr. $20 to member individuals (overseas $24); institutions $25. Society for the Study of Amphibians and Reptiles, c/o Robert Aldridge, St. Louis Univ., Dept. of Biology, 3507 Laclede Ave., St. Louis, MO 63103-2010. Ed. Robet Powell. R&P contact: Robert Aldridge. TEL 314-977-3916. circ. 900. (back issues avail.) **Indexed:** Biol.Abstr., Sport Fish.Abstr., Wild.Rev., Zoo.Rec. **Document type:** academic/scholarly publication, catalog.

591   AU   ISSN 1018-6093
CATALOGUS FAUNAE AUSTRIAE. irreg. price varies. Verlag der Oesterreichischen Akademie der Wissenschaften, Dr. Ignaz-Seipel-Platz 2, A-1010 Vienna, Austria. TEL 43-1-51581401. FAX 43-1-51581400. E-mail: verlag@oeaw.ac.at; URL: http://www.ac.at/einheiten/verlag. **Indexed:** Biol.Abstr. **Document type:** monographic series.
—BLDSC (5086.950000).
Description: Catalogs all animal life in Austria.

591 551 560   UK   ISSN 0260-681X
CEPHALOPOD NEWSLETTER. 1977. s-a. £7. c/o Dr. J.R. Senior, Dept. of Adult Education, 32 Old Elvet, Durham DH1 3JB, England. Ed. Dr. Marion Nixon. bk.rev.; abstr.; bibl. circ. 400. (back issues avail.)

591 133   US   ISSN 0747-9840
CHAMP CHANNELS. 1983. 4/yr. $9 (foreign $10). Lake Champlain Phenomena Investigation, Box 2134, Wilton, NY 12866. TEL 518-587-7638. Ed. Joseph W. Zarzynski. bk.rev.; illus. circ. 200. (back issues avail.)
Description: Examines the subject of the Lake Champlain and Loch Ness monsters.

591   UK
CHESTER ZOO NEWS. 1962. q. membership. North of England Zoological Society, Zoological Gardens, Upton by Chester, Cheshire CH2 1LH, England. TEL 0244-380280. FAX 0244-371273. Ed.Bd. bk.rev. circ. 5,000.
Former titles (until 1986): Chez Nous (ISSN 0300-4988); Our Zoo News.
Description: News items and informational articles on exhibits and events at the Chester Zoo, with announcements of members' meetings, activities, and lists of new arrivals and births.

598.1   US   ISSN 0009-3564
QL640   CODEN: CHSBAU
CHICAGO HERPETOLOGICAL SOCIETY. BULLETIN. 1966. m. $22 to individuals (foreign $34); institutions $38 (foreign $25) (effective 1997). Chicago Herpetological Society, Publications Secretary, Chicago Academy of Sciences, 2060 N. Clark St., Chicago, IL 60614. FAX 312-549-5199. Ed. Michael Dloogatch. adv. contact: Ralph Shepstone. bk.rev.; charts; illus.; circ. 1,300 (paid). **Indexed:** Biol.Abstr., Sport Fish.Abstr., Wild.Rev., Zoo.Rec. **Document type:** bulletin.
Formerly: Reptile Review.

591   GW   ISSN 0341-5414
CHINCHILLA-POST.* 1956. bi-m. DM.60. Europaeischen Chinchilla-Zucht, c/o W. Schmettkamp, Weidenbachweg 6a, 5303 Bornheim 3, Germany. adv. circ. 3,500.
Description: Reports on keeping and breeding chinchillas.

591 639.3   JA   ISSN 0577-9316
CHIRIBOTAN/MALACOLOGICAL SOCIETY OF JAPAN. NEWSLETTER. 1960. q. 7500 Yen (includes Venus). Malacological Society of Japan - Nihon Kairui Gakkai, c/o National Science Museum - Kokuritsu Kagaku Hakubutsukan, 3-23-1 Hyakunin-cho, Shinjuku-ku, Tokyo 169, Japan. Eds. Eiji Tsuchida, Masatoyo Okamoto. circ. 900.

CHOJU KANKEI TOKEI/ANNUAL STATISTICS OF BIRDS AND ANIMALS. see *BIOLOGY — Abstracting, Bibliographies, Statistics*

591   PO   ISSN 0378-875X
QH540   CODEN: CBMBEU
CIENCIA BIOLOGICA: BIOLOGIA MOLECULAR E CELULAR. (Text in English, French, German, Portuguese; summaries in two languages) 1934. q. $10. Universidade de Coimbra, Departamento de Zoologia, Coimbra, Portugal. TEL 351-39-34729. FAX 351-39-26798. Dir. Arselio Pato de Carvalho. bk.rev.; charts; illus.; index, cum.index; circ. 600 (controlled). **Indexed:** Biol.Abstr., Chem.Abstr., Dairy Sci.Abstr., Deep Sea Res.& Oceanogr.Abstr., Field Crop Abstr., Helminthol.Abstr., Rev.Appl.Entomol., Seed Abstr., Sport Fish.Abstr., Wild.Rev., Zoo.Rec. **Document type:** academic/scholarly publication.
—BLDSC (3194.995000); CASDDS; CISTI; KNAW.
Former titles (until 1972): Universidade de Coimbra. Museum Zoologico. Memorias e Estudos (ISSN 0041-8765); Universidade de Coimbra. Departamento de Zoologia. Ciencia Biologica.

CLADISTICS: THE INTERNATIONAL JOURNAL OF THE WILLI HENNIG SOCIETY. see *BIOLOGY — Botany*

COMMONWEALTH SCIENTIFIC AND INDUSTRIAL RESEARCH ORGANIZATION. DIVISION OF ANIMAL PRODUCTION. DIVISIONAL INFORMATION. see *BIOLOGY — Physiology*

599.8   JA   ISSN 0915-9681
COMPARATIVE PRIMATOLOGY MONOGRAPHS. (Text in English) biennial. Distributor of Comparative Primatology Monographs - Hikaku Reichoruigaku Senmonshi Hanpukai, 16 Shimogamo Minamichanokicho, Sakyo-ku, Kyoto 606, Japan. **Document type:** monographic series.

594   IT   ISSN 0394-0152
QL401
LA CONCHIGLIA/SHELL; international shell magazine. (Monographic supplement avail.) (Editions in English, Italian) 1969. q. L.60000 (foreign $50) (effective 1996). Conchiglia, Via C. Federici 1, 00147 Rome, Italy. TEL 39-6-5110192. FAX 39-6-5110192. Ed. Maria Antonietta Fontana Angioy; Pub. Catherine Nicolaidou. R&P contact: Paolo Angioy. adv.; bk.rev.; index. circ. 2,500. (back issues avail.)
Description: Presents papers on taxonomy, ethology, and environmental issues related to malacology. Lists events, shows and symposia.
Refereed Serial

594   UK   ISSN 0144-9826
CONCHOLOGICAL SOCIETY SPECIAL PUBLICATION. 1980. irreg. Conchological Society of Great Britain and Ireland, c/o Mr. M.D. Weideli, 35 Bartlemy Rd., Newbury, Berks. RG14 6LD, England. Ed. P.G. Oliver. **Document type:** monographic series.

594   UK   ISSN 0573-2336
CONCHOLOGISTS' NEWSLETTER. 1961. q. £23 to individuals; institutions £32 (foreign £35) (membership); £5 for non-member subscribers to the Journal of Conchology. Conchological Society of Great Britain and Ireland, c/o Mr. M.D. Weideli, 35 Bartlemy Rd., Newbury, Berks. RG14 6LD, England. Ed. R. Hill. circ. 650. **Document type:** newsletter.

CONGRESSO BRAILEIRO DE ZOOLOGIA E CONGRESSO LATINO-AMERICANO DE ZOOLOGIA. RESUMOS. see *BIOLOGY — Abstracting, Bibliographies, Statistics*

CONSERVE WILDLIFE. see *CONSERVATION*

591 NE
QL1
CONTRIBUTIONS TO ZOOLOGY/BIJDRAGEN TOT DE TIERKUNDE. (Text in English, French and German; summaries in English) 1848. q. $150 (effective 1996). Universiteit van Amsterdam, Commissie voor de Artis Bibliotheek, Plantage Middenlaan 45A, 1018 DC Amsterdam, Netherlands. (Subscr. to: S P B Academic Publishing b.v., P.O. Box 11188, 1001 GD Amsterdam, Netherlands. TEL 31-20-6278070. FAX 31-20-6380524) (Co-sponsor: Koninklijk Zoologisch Genootschap Natura Artis Magistra) Ed.Bd. index. circ. 1,000. **Indexed:** Anim.Behav.Abstr., Aqua.Sci.& Fish.Abstr., ASCA, Biol.Abstr., Bull.Signal., Curr.Adv.Ecol.Sci., Curr.Cont., Deep Sea Res.& Oceanogr.Abstr., Ecol.Abstr., Geo.Abstr., GeoRef., Helminthol.Abstr., Ind.Sci.Rev., Key Word Ind.Wildl.Res., Ocean.Abstr., Pollut.Abstr., Ref.Zh., Sci.Cit.Ind., Sport Fish.Abstr., SSCI, Wild Life Rev., Wild.Rev., Zoo.Rec. **Document type:** academic/scholarly publication.
—BLDSC (3461.490000); CISTI; Genuine Article; Linda Hall; SWETS; UnCover.
Formerly (until vol.65, 1995): Bijdragen tot de Dierkunde (ISSN 0067-8546)
Refereed Serial

591 US ISSN 0045-8511
QL1 CODEN: COPAAR
COPEIA. 1913. q. $50 membership. American Society of Ichthyologists and Herpetologists, c/o Dean A. Hendrickson, Sec., A S I H - Texas Natural History Collection, University of Texas - R4000, Austin, TX 78712-1100. TEL 512-471-0998. FAX 512-471-8775. E-mail: ASIH@mail.utexas.edu; URL: http://www.utexas.edu.depts/asih/. Ed. Dr. Michael E. Douglas. R&P contact: Dean Hendrickson. bk.rev.; index. circ. 3,600 (controlled). (also avail. in microform from UMI; back issues avail.) **Indexed:** Anim.Breed.Abstr., ASCA, Biol.Abstr., Biol.& Agr.Ind., Br.Geol.Lit., Chem.Abstr., Curr.Adv.Ecol.Sci., Curr.Cont., Curr.Ref.Fish Res., Deep Sea Res.& Oceanogr.Abstr., Geo.Abstr., Helminthol.Abstr., Ind.Sci.Rev., Nutr.Abstr., Ocean.Abstr., Pollut.Abstr., Sci.Cit.Ind., Sel.Water Res.Abstr., So.Pac.Per.Ind., Sport Fish.Abstr., Wild.Rev., Zoo.Rec. **Document type:** academic/scholarly publication.
—BLDSC (3466.000000); EMDOCS; Genuine Article; KR SourceOne; Linda Hall; SWETS; UMI; UnCover.
Description: Serves as a publication outlet for scientific publications in ichthyology and herpetology. Includes news of members and their activities, and a summary of the annual meetings.
Refereed Serial

594.32 US ISSN 1079-4182
THE COWRY NEW SERIES. 1960-1968; N.S. 1994. s-a. $20 to individuals (foreign $25); institutions $40 (foreign $45). Jiri Zidek, Ed. & Pub., Box 95, Socorro, NM 87801.
Supersedes (in 1994): Cowry (ISSN 0574-3737)
Description: Publishes both neontological and paleontological contributions on all aspects of the taxonomy, biology, and phylogeny of Cypraecea and Velutinacea.
Refereed Serial

595.3 NE ISSN 0168-6356
CODEN: CRISD2
CRUSTACEAN ISSUES. (Text in English) 1983. irreg., vol.10, 1995. price varies. A.A. Balkema, P.O. Box 1675, 3000 BR Rotterdam, Netherlands. TEL 31-10-4145822. FAX 31-10-4135947. E-mail: sales@balkema.nl; URL: http://www.jcn.nl/ima/balkema/. (Dist. in U.S. by: Ashgate Publishing Co., Old Post Rd., Brookfield, VT 05036. TEL 800-535-9544. FAX 802-276-3837) **Indexed:** Zoo.Rec. **Document type:** monographic series.
—BLDSC (3490.110000); CISTI. **CCC.**

595.3 NE ISSN 0011-216X
QL435.A1 CODEN: CRUSAP
CRUSTACEANA; international journal of crustacean research. (Supplement avail. (ISSN 0167-6563)) (Text and summaries in English, French, German) 1960. 9/yr. fl.617($362) (effective 1998). (Universiteit van Amsterdam, Zoologisch Museum) E.J. Brill, P.O. Box 9000, 2300 PA Leiden, Netherlands. TEL 31-71-5353500. FAX 31-71-5317532. TELEX 39296 BRILL NL. E-mail: cs@brill.nl. (In N. America: E.J. Brill, 24 Hudson St., Kinderhook, NY 12106. TEL 800-962-4406. FAX 518-758-1959) Ed.Bd. R&P contact: Elizabeth Vennekamp. abstr.; charts; illus.; cum.index: vols.1-68. (also avail. in microform from SWZ) **Indexed:** ASCA, Biol.Abstr., Curr.Adv.Ecol.Sci., Curr.Cont., Deep Sea Res.& Oceanogr.Abstr., Ecol.Abstr., Forest.Abstr., Forest Prod.Abstr., Geo.Abstr.H.G., Helminthol.Abstr., Ind.Sci.Rev., Ocean.Abstr., Pollut.Abstr., Sci.Cit.Ind., Sel.Water Res.Abstr., So.Pac.Per.Ind., Sport Fish.Abstr., Wild.Rev., Zoo.Rec. **Document type:** academic/scholarly publication.
—BLDSC (3490.120000); EMDOCS; Genuine Article; Linda Hall; SWETS; UnCover. **CCC.**
Description: Papers on taxonomy, ecology, physiology, anatomy, genetics and biometry in crustacean research.
Refereed Serial

595.3 NE ISSN 0167-6563
QL435.A1 CODEN: CRUSBQ
CRUSTACEANA. SUPPLEMENTS; international journal of Crustacean research. (Supplement to: Crustaceana (ISSN 0011-216X)) 1968. irreg., vol.16, 1990. price varies. E.J. Brill, P.O. Box 9000, 2300 PA Leiden, Netherlands. TEL 31-71-5353500. FAX 31-71-5317532. TELEX 39296 BRILL NL. E-mail: ejbrill@brill.nl. (In N. America: E.J. Brill, 24 Hudson St., Kinderhook, NY 12106. TEL 800-962-4406. FAX 518-758-1959) R&P contact: Elizabeth Vennekamp. (back issues avail.) **Indexed:** Biol.Abstr., Ind.Sci.Rev., Zoo.Rec. **Document type:** monographic series.
Refereed Serial

591 US ISSN 0736-7023
QL89
CRYPTOZOOLOGY. 1982. a. $42 to individuals; institutions $65 (includes receipt of The ISC Newsletter quarterly) (effective 1997). International Society of Cryptozoology, Box 43070, Tucson, AZ 85733. TEL 602-884-8369. FAX 602-884-8369. Ed. J. Richard Greenwell. adv.; bk.rev. circ. 800. (back issues avail.) **Document type:** academic/scholarly publication.
—Linda Hall.
Description: Zoological, historical, philosophical and psychological aspects of crytozoology.

591 MX ISSN 0188-9508
CUADERNOS MEXICANOS DE ZOOLOGIA. irreg. Mex.$100. Sociedad Mexicana de Zoologia, Apdo. 101-13, 04530 Mexico D.F., Mexico. Eds. Ma Eugenia Moncayo Lopez, Hector Espinosa Perez.

575.1 CU
CUBA. CENTRO DE INFORMACION Y DOCUMENTACION AGROPECUARIO. BOLETIN DE RESENAS. SERIE: MEJORAMIENTO ANIMAL. (Abstracts in English) 1974. irreg. exchange basis. Centro de Informacion y Documentacion Agropecuario, Gaveta Postal 4149, Havana 4, Cuba. **Indexed:** Agrindex.
Formerly: Cuba. Centro de Informacion y Divulgacion Agropecuario. Boletin de Resenas. Serie: Genetica y Reproduccion.

591 US ISSN 0899-577X
QL700
CURRENT MAMMALOGY. 1987. irreg., vol.2, 1990. price varies. Plenum Publishing Corp., 233 Spring St., New York, NY 10013-1578. TEL 212-620-8000. FAX 212-463-0742. TELEX 23-421139. E-mail: books@plenum.com. Ed. Hugh H. Genoways. (back issues avail.) **Document type:** monographic series.
—CISTI; KNAW.
Refereed Serial

BIOLOGY — ZOOLOGY 831

591 II ISSN 0971-0116
CURRENT NEMATOLOGY. (Text in English) 1990. s-a. Rs.100 to individuals (foreign $50); institutions Rs.500 (foreign $125). Bioved Research Society, c/o Brijesh K. Dwivedi, General Secretary, 252A-4A Om Gayatri Nagar, Teliarganj, Allahabad 211 004, U.P., India. TEL 91-532-640429. Ed. B.K. Dwivedi. **Document type:** academic/scholarly publication.
—BLDSC (3500.550000). **CCC.**

CURRENT PRIMATE REFERENCES. see *BIOLOGY — Abstracting, Bibliographies, Statistics*

CURRENT TOPICS IN MEMBRANES AND TRANSPORT. see *BIOLOGY — Cytology And Histology*

CYPRIS; international ostracoda newsletter. see *PALEONTOLOGY*

597 GW ISSN 0724-7435
D C G INFORMATIONEN.* 1970. m. DM.60. Deutsche Cichliden-Gesellschaft e.V., Rudolf-Diesel-Str. 3, 68780 St. Leon Rot, Germany. Ed. Rainer Stawikowski. adv.; bk.rev.; bibl.; index. circ. 3,000. (back issues avail.)

591.9489 DK ISSN 0109-7164
DANMARKS DYRELIV/ANIMAL LIFE OF DENMARK. (Text in Danish, summaries in English) 1984. irreg., vol.7, 1996. price varies. Apollo Books Aps, Kirkeby Sand 19, DK-5771 Stenstrup, Denmark. TEL 45-62-26-37-37. FAX 45-62-26-37-80. (back issues avail.) **Document type:** monographic series.
Description: Covers the insect fauna of Denmark and Fennoscandia or the whole of Northern Europe.

591.9489 DK ISSN 0108-1551
DANSK FAUNISTIK BIBLIOTEK. (Text in Danish, summaries in English) 1981. irreg., latest vol.4. price varies. Apollo Books Aps, Kirkeby Sand 19, DK-5771 Stenstrup, Denmark. TEL 45-62-26-37-37. FAX 45-62-26-37-80. (back issues avail.) **Document type:** monographic series.
Description: Provides identification and distribution of Danish insect families.

597 US
DARTER. 1989. 6/yr. $11 membership (foreign $14). North American Native Fishes Association, 123 W. Mt. Airy Ave., Philadelphia, PA 19119. TEL 215-247-0384. (Subscr. to: Robert E. Schmidt, Simon's Rock, Alford Rd., Great Barrington, MA 01230) **Document type:** newsletter.
Description: Covers news about fishes native to North America, including conservation, study and research topics.

DEFENDERS. see *CONSERVATION*

591 069 NE ISSN 0923-9308
DEINSEA. (Text in Dutch, English, German) 1994. a. fl.79. (Natuurmuseum Rotterdam - Natural History Museum of Rotterdam) Backhuys Publishers, P.O. Box 321, 2300 AH Leiden, Netherlands. TEL 31-71-5170208. FAX 31-71-5171856. E-mail: backhuys@euronet.nl; URL: http://www.euronet.nl/users/backhuys/. **Document type:** academic/scholarly publication.
Description: Publishes original research papers on topics in zoology, with particular emphasis on Europe.

DESERT TORTOISE COUNCIL. PROCEEDINGS OF SYMPOSIUM. see *EARTH SCIENCES*

594 GW ISSN 0418-8861
DEUTSCHE MALAKOZOOLOGISCHE GESELLSCHAFT. MITTEILUNGEN. 1962. irreg. Senckenbergische Naturforschende Gesellschaft, Senckenberganlage 25, 60325 Frankfurt a.M., Germany. TEL 49-69-7542-1. FAX 49-69-746238. E-mail: sjessel@sng.uni-frankfurt.de. (Co-sponsor: Deutsche Malakozoologische Gesellschaft) **Document type:** academic/scholarly publication.
—BLDSC (5839.490000).

BIOLOGY — ZOOLOGY

590   GW   ISSN 0070-4342
CODEN: VDZGAN
DEUTSCHE ZOOLOGISCHE GESELLSCHAFT. VERHANDLUNGEN. a. price varies. Gustav Fischer Verlag, Wollgrasweg 49, 70599 Stuttgart, Germany. TEL 49-711-458030. FAX 49-711-4580334. (Subscr. to: Postfach 720143, 70577 Stuttgart, Germany; U.S. address: Lubrecht & Cramer Ltd., 38 Rte. 48, Forestburgh, NY 12777-6400) **Indexed**: Anim.Breed.Abstr., Biol.Abstr., Chem.Abstr., Deep Sea Res.& Oceanogr.Abstr., Helminthol.Abstr., Rev.Appl.Entomol. **Document type**: proceedings.
—BLDSC (9163.500000); CASDDS; KNAW; Linda Hall; UMI. **CCC**.

591   NE   ISSN 0167-9309
CODEN: DAFSDF
DEVELOPMENTS IN AQUACULTURE AND FISHERIES SCIENCE. 1976. irreg., vol.25, 1992. price varies. Elsevier Science B.V., Books Division, P.O. Box 211, 1000 AE Amsterdam, Netherlands. TEL 31-20-4853911. FAX 31-20-4853705. TELEX 18582 ESPA NL. E-mail: nlinfo-f@elsevier.nl; usinfo-f@elsevier.com; forinfo-kyf04035@niftyserve.or.jp; URL: http://www.elsevier.nl/. (Subscr. in the Americas to: Elsevier Science, Regional Sales Office, Box 945, New York, NY 10159-0945. TEL 212-633-3730. FAX 212-633-3680; Subscr. in Australasia and the Far East to: Elsevier Science (Singapore) Pte Ltd, No.1 Temasek Ave., No.17-01 Millenia Tower, Singapore 039192, Singapore. TEL 65-434-3727. FAX 65-337-2230; Subscr. in Japan to: Elsevier Science Japan, 9-15 Higashi-Azabu 1-chome, Minato-ku, Tokyo 106, Japan. TEL 81-3-5561-5033. FAX 81-3-5561-5047) (back issues avail.) **Indexed**: Agri.Eng.Abstr. **Document type**: monographic series.
—BLDSC (3579.064000); CASDDS; CISTI.
Refereed Serial

597   NE   ISSN 0924-5316
DEVELOPMENTS IN ENVIRONMENTAL BIOLOGY OF FISHES. (Text in English) 1981. irreg., vol.14, 1993. price varies. Kluwer Academic Publishers, Postbus 17, 3300 AA Dordrecht, Netherlands. TEL 31-78-6392392. FAX 31-78-6392254. TELEX 29245 KAPG NL. E-mail: services@wkap.nl; URL: http://www.wkap.nl. (Dist. by: Kluwer Academic Publishers Group, P.O. Box 322, 3300 AH Dordrecht, Netherlands. TEL 31-78-6392392. FAX 31-78-6546474; N. America dist. addr.: Box 358, Accord Sta., Hingham, MA 02018-0358. TEL 617-871-6600. FAX 617-871-6528) **Document type**: monographic series.
—BLDSC (3579.071420).
Refereed Serial

591   GW   ISSN 0177-5103
CODEN: DAOREO
DISEASES OF AQUATIC ORGANISMS. (Text in English) 1985. 12/yr. (4 vols., 3 nos./vol.). DM.1232 (foreign DM.1252) (effective 1998). Inter-Research, Nordbuente 23, 21385 Oldendorf, Germany. TEL 49-4132-7127. FAX 49-4132-8883. E-mail: marita@int-res.com; URL: http://www.int-res.com. **Indexed**: ASCA, Curr.Cont., Curr.Ref.Fish Res., Ecol.Abstr., Ind.Sci.Rev., Ind.Vet., Protozool.Abstr., Sci.Cit.Ind., Sport Fish.Abstr., Vet.Bull., Wild.Rev., Zoo.Rec. **Document type**: academic/scholarly publication.
—BLDSC (3598.125000); CASDDS; CISTI; EMDOCS; Linda Hall; SWETS; UnCover.
Description: Presents original papers, short notes and reviews on disease phenomena in aquatic organisms.

DIVREI HA-AKADEMIA HA-LEUMIT HA-YISRAELIT LEMADAIM-HA-HATIVA LE-MADAEI HA-TEVA. see *SCIENCES: COMPREHENSIVE WORKS*

591   JA   ISSN 0287-0223
QL352
DOBUTSU BUNRUI GAKKAISHI/JAPANESE SOCIETY OF SYSTEMATIC ZOOLOGY. PROCEEDINGS. (Text in English, Japanese) 1965. 2/yr. 50 Yen to members. Dobutsu Bunrui Gakkai - Japanese Society of Systematic Zoology, National Science Museum, Tokyo, Dept. of Zoology, 23-1, Hyakunincho 3-chome, Shinjuku-ku, Tokyo 160, Japan. Ed. S. Mawatari. **Indexed**: Jap.Per.Ind.

591   JA   ISSN 0916-8419
CODEN: DSKEEN
DOBUTSU SHINRIGAKU KENKYU/JAPANESE JOURNAL OF ANIMAL PSYCHOLOGY. (Text in English or Japanese; summaries in English) 1947. s-a. 1700 Yen per no. Nihon Dobutsu Shinri Gakkai - Japanese Society for Animal Psychology, c/o University of Tsukuba, Institute of Psychology, 1-1-1 Ten'noudai, Tsukuba-shi 305, Japan. TEL 81-298-53-4720. E-mail: makinoju@human.tsukuba.ac.jp. (Subscr. to: Japan Publishing Trading Co. Ltd., P.O. Box 5030, Tokyo International, Tokyo, Japan) Ed. Junshiro Makino. adv.; index. circ. 500. (back issues avail.) **Indexed**: Biol.Abstr., Jap.Per.Ind., Psychol.Abstr. (1956-). **Document type**: academic/scholarly publication.
Formerly (until 1990): Dobutsu Shinrigaku Nenpo - Annual of Animal Psychology (ISSN 0003-5130)

591   JA   ISSN 0288-4887
CODEN: DOBUBT
DOBUTSU TO DOBUTSUEN/ANIMALS AND ZOOS. (Text in Japanese) 1949. m. 3600 Yen($64) Tokyo Dobutsuen Kyokai - Tokyo Zoological Park Society, Ueno Dobutsuen, 9-83, Ueno Koen, Taito-ku, Tokyo 110, Japan. Ed. Kazuharu Tashiro. **Indexed**: Sport Fish.Abstr., Wild.Rev., Zoo.Rec. **Document type**: academic/scholarly publication.

591   JA   ISSN 0386-7498
DOBUTSUEN SUIZOKUKAN ZASSHI/JAPANESE ASSOCIATION OF ZOOLOGICAL GARDENS AND AQUARIUMS. JOURNAL. (Text in Japanese; summaries in English, Japanese) 1959. q. Nihon Dobutsuen Suizokukan Kyokai - Japanese Association of Zoological Gardens and Aquariums, 13-2, Ueno 2-chome, Taito-ku, Tokyo 110, Japan.

591   SP   ISSN 0210-5985
QL606.55.S7   CODEN: DAVEEK
DONANA (ACTA VERTEBRATA). 1974. s-a. 2300 ptas. (foreign 3300 ptas.) (effective 1997-98). Estacion Biologica de Donana, Avda. Maria Luisa, s-n, Pabellon Peru, 41013 Seville, Spain. TEL 34-54-232340. FAX 34-54-621125. Eds. Carmen Diaz Paniagua, Francisco Palomares. **Indexed**: Ind.SST, Key Word Ind.Wildl.Res., Sport Fish.Abstr., Wild.Rev., Zoo.Rec. **Document type**: academic/scholarly publication.
Description: Covers animal behavior, vertebrate ecology, population biology, and nature conservation.
Refereed Serial

591   CC   ISSN 1000-0739
QL35I   CODEN: DFXUEB
DONGWU FENLEI XUEBAO/ACTA ZOOTAXONOMICA SINICA. (Text in Chinese; summaries in English) 1964. q. $52.80. (Chinese Academy of Sciences, Institute of Zoology) Science Press, Marketing and Sales Department, 16 Donghuangchenggen North St., Beijing 100717, People's Republic of China. TEL 4010642. FAX 4019810. adv. circ. 6,000. **Indexed**: Apic.Abstr., Protozool.Abstr., Rev.Appl.Entomol.
—Linda Hall.
Description: Contains theses on zootaxonomy, its theory and practice, scientific notes and academic discussions.
Refereed Serial

591   CC   ISSN 0001-7302
QL1   CODEN: TWHPA3
DONGWU XUEBAO/ACTA ZOOLOGICA SINICA. (Text in Chinese; summaries in English) 1935. q. $49.20. (Chinese Academy of Sciences, Institute of Zoology) Science Press, Marketing and Sales Department, 16 Donghuangchenggen North St., Beijing 100717, People's Republic of China. TEL 4010642. FAX 4019810. adv.; charts; illus.; maps. circ. 11,000. **Indexed**: Bio-Contr.News & Info., Biol.Abstr., Chem.Abstr., Curr.Adv.Ecol.Sci., Curr.Cont., Ecol.Abstr., Geol.Abstr., Helminthol.Abstr., Ind.Sci.Rev., Ind.Vet., Key Word Ind.Wildl.Res., Pig News & Info., Poult.Abstr., Protozool.Abstr., Sci.Cit.Ind., Sport Fish.Abstr., Vet.Bull., Wild.Rev., Zoo.Rec. **Document type**: academic/scholarly publication.
—BLDSC (0675.000000); CASDDS; CISTI; KNAW; Linda Hall.
Description: Contains original theses on zoology, including taxonomy, faunistics, morphology, ecology, and experimental zoology. Also includes information about research progress and discussions among various schools of research and academic viewpoints.
Refereed Serial

591   CC   ISSN 0254-5853
QL1   CODEN: DOYADI
DONGWUXUE YANJIU/ZOOLOGICAL RESEARCH. (Text in Chinese) 1980. q. $2.50 per no. Guoji Shudian, Qikan Bu - China International Book Trading Corp., Chegongzhuang Xilu 21, P.O. Box 2820, Beijing, People's Republic of China. **Indexed**: Biol.Abstr., Chem.Abstr., Rev.Appl.Entomol., Sport Fish.Abstr., Wild.Rev., Zoo.Rec. **Document type**: academic/scholarly publication.
—BLDSC (9520.060000); CASDDS; Linda Hall.

591   CC   ISSN 0250-3263
QL1   CODEN: TWHCDZ
DONGWUXUE ZAZHI/CHINESE JOURNAL OF ZOOLOGY. (Text in Chinese) 1957. bi-m. $49.80. (Chinese Academy of Sciences, Institute of Zoology) Science Press, Marketing and Sales Department, 16 Donghuangchenggen Beijie, Beijing 100707, People's Republic of China. TEL 4010642. FAX 4012180. TELEX 210247-SPBJ-CN. adv.; bk.rev. **Indexed**: Chem.Abstr. **Document type**: academic/scholarly publication.
—BLDSC (3180.700000); CASDDS; CISTI; Linda Hall.
Description: Aims to exchange information, experience, knowledge, and research results in zoology. Contains articles on research development, academic activities, experimental techniques, and news briefs.
Refereed Serial

DOSEI KYOKAI KAIHO/JAPANESE ASSOCIATION OF VETERINARY BIOLOGISTS. BULLETIN. see *VETERINARY SCIENCE*

591   US
DREISSENA!. 1990. bi-m. $60. Zebra Mussel Information Clearinghouse, Morgan III, SUNY College at Brockport, Brockport, NY 14420-2928. TEL 716-395-2516. FAX 716-395-2729. Ed. Charles R. O'Neill, Jr. **Document type**: newsletter.
Formerly: Dreissena Polymorpha Information Review (ISSN 1065-8408)
Description: Presents summaries of research, meetings, legislation, and sightings of the zebra mussel (Dreissena polymorpha) to encourage and facilitate communication among stakeholders.

DROSERA; Naturkundliche Mitteilungen aus Nordwestdeutschland. see *BIOLOGY*

591   FR   ISSN 1256-7779
DUMERILIA. (Text in English, French) 1994. irreg. 130 F. to individuals ($26); institutions 260 F. ($52). (Association des Amis du Laboratoire des Reptiles et Amphibiens du Museum National d'Histoire Naturelle) A A L R A M, c/o Alain Dubois, 25 rue Cuvier, 75005 Paris, France. TEL 33-1-40793487. E-mail: ohler@cimrs1.mnhn.fr. (Subscr. in US to: AALRAM, c/o Patricia B. Zug, Division of Amphibians and Reptiles, NHB Mail Stop 162, National Museum of Natural History, Smithsonian Institution, Washington, DC 20560) Ed. Roger Bour.
Refereed Serial

591   SA   ISSN 0012-723X
CODEN: DMNOAM
DURBAN MUSEUM NOVITATES. (Text in English) 1952. a. R.40($20) or exchange basis. Durban Natural Science Museum, P.O. Box 4085, Durban 4000, South Africa. TEL 27-31-3006211. FAX 27-31-3006302. Ed. Aldo Berruti. circ. 280 (controlled). **Indexed**: Biol.Abstr., Deep Sea Res.& Oceanogr.Abstr., IBR, Ind.S.A.Per., Rev.Appl.Entomol. **Document type**: academic/scholarly publication.
—BLDSC (3632.000000); CISTI; Linda Hall; UnCover.
Description: Original and review articles on taxonomy, systematics, and biogeography, particularly relating to the zoology of Southeastern Africa.
Refereed Serial

591   DK   ISSN 0109-1190
DYR I NATUR OG MUSEUM. 1984. 2/yr. DKK 50 (effective 1997). Zoologisk Museum, Universitetsparken 15, DK-2100 Copenhagen Oe, Denmark. TEL 45-32-10-00. FAX 45-35-10-10-55. Ed. Torben Wolff. illus. (back issues avail.)

BIOLOGY — ZOOLOGY

591 US
EASTERN PUMA NETWORK NEWS. 1981. 3/yr. $15. Eastern Puma Network, P.O. Box 3562, Baltimore, MD 21214. TEL 410-254-2517. FAX 410-254-2517. Ed. John Lutz. R&P contact: R. Pennington Smith. bk.rev.; stat.; circ. 400. circ. 253 (paid). (back issues avail.) **Document type:** newsletter.
  Description: For research network of volunteers interested in proving the existence of the eastern sub-species of felis concolor couguar and felis concolor niger. Publishes news of puma, panther and mountain lion sightings.

591 US
ECDYSIAST. 1981. s-a. membership. Crustacean Society, c/o Karen Hickey, Box 1897, Lawrence, KS 66044-8897. TEL 913-843-1221. circ. 800. (processed) **Document type:** newsletter.

593.91 NE ISSN 0168-6100
CODEN: ECSTD6
ECHINODERM STUDIES. (Text in English) 1983. biennial. price varies. A.A. Balkema, P.O. Box 1675, 3000 BR Rotterdam, Netherlands. TEL 31-10-4145822. FAX 31-10-4135947. E-mail: sales@balkema.nl; URL: http://www.jcn.nl/balkema/. (Dist. in U.S. by: Ashgate Publishing Co., Old Post Rd., Brookfield, VT 05036. TEL 800-535-9544. FAX 802-276-3837) **Indexed:** Zoo.Rec. **Document type:** academic/scholarly publication.
—BLDSC (3647.364500); CASDDS. **CCC.**

597.092 639.2 DK ISSN 0906-6691
QL624 CODEN: EFFIEW
ECOLOGY OF FRESHWATER FISH. (Text in English; summaries in Spanish) 1992. q. DKK 1295 in Europe (US, Canada and Japan DKK 1310) (effective 1997). Munksgaard International Publishers Ltd., 35 Noerre Soegade, P.O. Box 2148, DK-1016 Copenhagen K, Denmark. TEL 45-33-127030. FAX 45-33-129387. E-mail: fsub@mail.munksgaard.dk. (In N. America: Commerce Place, 350 Main St., Malden, MA 02148-5018. TEL 617-388-8273. FAX 617-388-8274) Eds. Javier Lobon-Cervia, Erik Mortensen. adv.; bk.rev.; illus. **Indexed:** Biol.Abstr., Ecol.Abstr. **Document type:** academic/scholarly publication.
—BLDSC (3650.043100); CISTI; UnCover. **CCC.**
  Description: Publishes original articles on all aspects of fish ecology and fishery sciences in lakes, rivers and estuaries.
  Refereed Serial

591 JA ISSN 0389-1445
EDAPHOLOGIA. (Text in English, French, German, Japanese; abstracts in English) 1967. 2/yr. 6000 Yen to individuals; institutions 9000 Yen; students 4000 Yen. Nihon Dojo Dobutsu Gakkai - Japanese Society of Soil Zoology, Natural History Museum & Institute, Chiba, 955-2 Aoba-cho, Chiba 260, Japan. TEL 81-43-265-3274. FAX 81-43-266-2481. E-mail: j90053@simail.ne.jp; URL: http://wwwsoc.nacsis.ac.jp/jssz/index.html. Ed. Shoichi Yoshida. R&P contact: Yasunori Hagino. circ. 300. **Indexed:** Agrindex. **Document type:** academic/scholarly publication.

LAINMAAILMA. see *PETS*

MPORIA STATE RESEARCH STUDIES. see *HISTORY — History Of North And South America*

597 NE ISSN 0378-1909
QL614 CODEN: EBFID3
ENVIRONMENTAL BIOLOGY OF FISHES. (Text in English) 1976. m. fl.2247 to institutions; $1153.50 to institutions in U.S. (effective 1998). Kluwer Academic Publishers, Postbus 17, 3300 AA Dordrecht, Netherlands. TEL 31-78-6392392. FAX 31-78-6392254. TELEX 29245 KAPG NL. E-mail: services@wkap.nl; URL: http://www.wkap.nl. (Dist. by: Kluwer Academic Publishers Group, P.O. Box 322, 3300 AH Dordrecht, Netherlands. TEL 31-78-6392392. FAX 31-78-6546474; N. America dist. addr.: Box 358, Accord Sta., Hingham, MA 02018-0358. TEL 617-871-6600. FAX 617-871-6528) Ed. Eugene K. Balon. adv.; bk.rev. (also avail. in microform from UMI) **Indexed:** Arts & Hum.Cit.Ind., ASCA, Bio-Contr.News & Info., Biol.Abstr., Chem.Abstr., Curr.Adv.Ecol.Sci., Curr.Cont., Curr.Ref.Fish Res., Deep Sea Res.& Oceanogr.Abstr., Ecol.Abstr., Environ.Abstr., Environ.Per.Bibl. (1992-), Excerpt.Med., Geo.Abstr.H.G., Helminthol.Abstr., Ind.Sci.Rev., Int.Abstr.Biol.Sci., Ocean.Abstr., Sci.Cit.Ind., Sel.Water Res.Abstr., So.Pac.Per.Ind., Sport Fish.Abstr., W.R.C.Inf., Wild.Rev., Zoo.Rec. **Document type:** academic/scholarly publication.
—BLDSC (3791.405000); CASDDS; CISTI; EMDOCS; Genuine Article; Linda Hall; SWETS; UMI; UnCover. **CCC.**
  Description: Publishes original studies of the ecology, life history, epigenetics, behavior, physiology, morphology, systematics and evolution of marine and freshwater fishes.
  Refereed Serial

EQUUS. see *SPORTS AND GAMES — Horses And Horsemanship*

ETHNOZOOTECHNIE. see *ANTHROPOLOGY*

591 GW ISSN 0179-1613
QL750 CODEN: ETHOEM
ETHOLOGY. (Text in English; summaries in English, German) 1937. 12/yr. DM.1478 in Europe; rest of world DM.1468 (effective 1998). Blackwell Wissenschaft, Kurfuerstendamm 57, 10707 Berlin, Germany. TEL 49-30-32790679. FAX 49-30-32790610. E-mail: aboverwalt@blackwis.de; URL: http://www.blackwis.com. Ed.Bd. adv.: B&W page DM.560; trim 190 x 122. bk.rev.; illus.; stat.; index. circ. 650. (back issues avail.) **Indexed:** Anim.Breed.Abstr., Apic.Abstr., ASCA, Biol.Abstr., Curr.Adv.Ecol.Sci., Curr.Cont., Dairy Sci.Abstr., Deep Sea Res.& Oceanogr.Abstr., Ind.Med., Ind.Vet., M.L.A., MLA Intl.Bibl., Nutr.Abstr., Psychol.Abstr. (1937-), Sci.Cit.Ind., So.Pac.Per.Ind., Sport Fish.Abstr., SSCI, Vet.Bull., Wild.Rev., Zoo.Rec. **Document type:** academic/scholarly publication.
—BLDSC (3815.240000); CISTI; EMDOCS; Genuine Article; SWETS; UnCover. **CCC.**
  Formerly: Zeitschrift fuer Tierpsychologie (ISSN 0044-3573).
  Description: Contains contributions from all branches of behavior research on all species of animals, both in the field and in the laboratory.

591 IT ISSN 0394-9370
QL750 CODEN: EEEVEP
ETHOLOGY ECOLOGY & EVOLUTION. (Text and summaries in English) 1890; N.S. 1967. q. L.55000($40) to individuals; institutions L.225000 ($150). Universita degli Studi di Firenze, Dipartimento di Biologia Animale e Genetica, Via Romana 17, 50125 Florence, Italy. TEL 39-55-222448. FAX 39-55-222565. E-mail: csfet@ifiidg.fi.cnr.it. (Dist. by: Sedicesimo, Via Mannelli, 29r, 50136 Florence, Italy. TEL 39-55-2476781) Ed. Francesco Dessi-Fulgheri. bk.rev.; illus.; index, cum.index. circ. 400. (reprint service avail. from ISI, back issues avail.) **Indexed:** Apic.Abstr., ASCA, Biol.Abstr., Chem.Abstr., Curr.Adv.Ecol.Sci., Curr.Cont., Deep Sea Res.& Oceanogr.Abstr., Helminthol.Abstr., Ind.Sci.Rev., Sport Fish.Abstr., SSCI, Wild.Rev., Zoo.Rec. **Document type:** academic/scholarly publication.
—BLDSC (3815.270000); CASDDS; CISTI; EMDOCS; Genuine Article; Linda Hall; SWETS; UnCover. **CCC.**
  Formerly (until 1989): Monitore Zoologico Italiano - Italian Journal of Zoology (ISSN 0026-9786).
  Description: Publishes research and review articles on all aspects of animal behavior. Emphasizes the gain in understanding of the function, ecology, or evolution of behavior.

591 150 SP ISSN 1130-3204
QL750 CODEN: ETOLEE
ETOLOGIA. (Text in English and Spanish) 1989. a. 5500 ptas. to individuals (foreign 7000 ptas.); institutions 12500 ptas. (foreign 13000 ptas.) (effective 1997). Sociedad Espanola de Etologia, c/o Museu de Zoologia, Apdo. 593, 08080 Barcelona, Spain. TEL 34-3-3196912. FAX 34-3-3104999. E-mail: mzoolbcn@lix.intercom.es. Eds. J.C. Senar, L. Arias de Reyna. adv. contact: Luisa Arroyo. bibl.; charts; illus. **Indexed:** Ind.SST. **Document type:** bulletin, academic/scholarly publication.
—BLDSC (3816.344089).
  Description: Covers the field of animal behavior research, both theoretical and applied.
  Refereed Serial

EUROPEAN AQUACULTURE SOCIETY. SPECIAL PUBLICATIONS. see *EARTH SCIENCES — Oceanography*

EVOLUTION & HUMAN BEHAVIOR. see *SOCIAL SCIENCES: COMPREHENSIVE WORKS*

590 NO ISSN 0014-8881
QL289 CODEN: FUNAAO
FAUNA. (Text in Norwegian; summaries in English) 1948. q. NOK 250 in Nordic countries; elsewhere NOK 300 (effective through 1998). Norsk Zoologisk Forening - Norwegian Zoological Society, P.O. Box 102 Blindern, N-0314 Oslo, Norway. Ed. Roar Solheim. adv.; bk.rev.; charts; illus.; cum.index. circ. 1,700. **Indexed:** Aqua.Sci.& Fish.Abstr., Biol.Abstr., INIS Atomind., Key Word Ind.Wildl.Res., Ref.Zh., Sel.Water Res.Abstr., Zoo.Rec. **Document type:** academic/scholarly publication.
—BLDSC (3897.820000); CISTI; Linda Hall. **CCC.**

591 IT ISSN 0430-1226
CODEN: FIITA
FAUNA D'ITALIA; repertorio generale delle specie animali esistenti in Italia. 1956. s-a. price varies. (Unione Zoologica Italiana) Edizioni Calderini, Via Emilia Levante 31, 40139 Bologna, Italy. TEL 39-51-492211. FAX 39-51-490200. (Co-sponsor: Accademia Nazionale Italiana Entomologica) Ed. Alessandro Minelli. circ. 2,000. (back issues avail.) **Indexed:** Biol.Abstr.

591 SP
FAUNA IBERICA. 1990. irreg. price varies. Museo Nacional de Ciencias Naturales, Jose Gutierrez Abascal 2, 28006 Madrid, Spain. TEL 34-1-4111328. FAX 34-1-5645078. Ed. M. Angeles Ramos. **Document type:** catalog.

590 NO ISSN 0332-768X
QL289 CODEN: FNSAD3
FAUNA NORVEGICA SERIES A. NORWEGIAN FAUNA EXCEPT ENTOMOLOGY AND ORNITHOLOGY. (Text in English; summaries in Norwegian) 1980. a. NOK 70 to non-members in Norway; members NOK 50; non-members outside Norway NOK 90; members NOK 70 (effective 1997). Norsk Instituit for Naturforskning (NINA), c/o Kjetil Bevanger, Tungasletta 2, N-7005 Trondheim, Norway. TEL 47-73-58-05-00. FAX 47-73-91-54-33. E-mail: kjetil.bevanger@nina.nina.no. Ed. Thrine Moen Heggberget. R&P contact: Kjetil Bevanger. adv. contact: Kjetil Bevanger. bk.rev.; cum.index every 3 yrs. circ. 700. (back issues avail.) **Indexed:** Ecol.Abstr., IBR, Key Word Ind.Wildl.Res. **Document type:** academic/scholarly publication.
—BLDSC (3899.258000); CISTI; Linda Hall. **CCC.**
  Refereed Serial

590.993 NZ ISSN 0111-5383
QL340
FAUNA OF NEW ZEALAND. 1982. irreg. latest no.36. price varies. Manaaki Whenua Press, P.O. Box 40, Lincoln 8152, New Zealand. TEL 64-3-3256700. FAX 64-3-3252127. E-mail: comfortg@landcare.cri.nz; URL: http://www.landcare.cri.nz/mwpress/. Ed. C. Tymone Duval. R&P contact: Greg Comfort. bibl.; illus. circ. 400. (back issues avail.) **Indexed:** Bio-Contr.News & Info., Biol.Abstr., Curr.Adv.Ecol.Sci., Entomol.Abstr., Zoo.Rec. **Document type:** monographic series.
—BLDSC (3899.254000); Linda Hall.
  Description: Describes systematic taxonomy of New Zealand invertebrates.

591 IS
FAUNA OF RUSSIA AND ADJACENT COUNTRIES. (Text in English) irreg. Israel Program for Scientific Translations, P.O. Box 7145, Jerusalem, Israel.

BIOLOGY — ZOOLOGY

591   **IS**
FAUNA OF THE U.S.S.R.. (Text in English) irreg. Israel Program for Scientific Translations, P.O. Box 7145, Jerusalem, Israel.

591   **IS**
FAUNA PALAESTINA. (Text in English) 1975. irreg., latest 1992. price varies. Israel Academy of Sciences and Humanities, 43 Jabotinsky St., P.O. Box 4040, 91040 Jerusalem, Israel. TEL 972-2-636211. FAX 972-2-666059. Ed. Zofia Lasman. adv. contact: Tami Korman. circ. 700. **Document type:** monographic series. **Description:** Scholarly monographs on specific orders of insects, arachnids, molluscs and fish. *Refereed Serial*

591   **PL**   ISSN 0303-4909
FAUNA POLSKI. 1973. irreg., no.18, 1995. price varies. Polska Akademia Nauk, Muzeum i Instytut Zoologii, Ul. Wilcza 64, 00-069 Warsaw, Poland. TEL 48-2-6293221. FAX 48-2-6296302. Ed. A. Riedel. **Document type:** catalog.
—BLDSC (3899.350000); CISTI.

591   **PL**   ISSN 0071-4089
FAUNA SLODKOWODNA POLSKI. (Text in Polish) 1935. irreg., no.10A, 1990. price varies. (Polska Akademia Nauk, Polskie Towarzystwo Hydrobiologiczne) Wydawnictwo Naukowe P W N, Ul. Miodowa 10, 00-251 Warsaw, Poland. TEL 48-22-260207. FAX 48-22-6954288. TELEX 813763. (Dist. by: Ars Polona, Krakowskie Przedmiescie 7, 00-068 Warsaw, Poland. TEL 48-22-261201) Ed. Andrzej Piechocki. circ. 550 (paid). **Document type:** monographic series.
—BLDSC (3899.370000).
Description: Presents a group of animals of Polish freshwater fauna and provides information about their biology and ecology. *Refereed Serial*

591   **JA**   ISSN 0917-9046
FAUNAUKITAMU/FAUNA IN OIITAMA DISTRICT. (Text in Japanese) 1990. m. Yonezawa Shiritsu Uesugi Hakubutsukan - Yonezawa Municipal Uesugi Museum, 1-4 Marunouchi, Yonezawa-shi, Yamagata-ken 992, Japan. TEL 81-238-23-7302. FAX 81-238-22-7302. Ed. Koichi Kusakari. **Document type:** academic/scholarly publication. **Description:** Lists of insects in Yamagata Prefecture.

591   **GW**   ISSN 0430-1285
QH540   CODEN: FOEMA7
FAUNISTISCH-OEKOLOGISCHE MITTEILUNGEN. 1952. irreg. DM.8. (Faunistisch-Oekologische Arbeitsgemeinschaft) Wachholtz Verlag GmbH, Rungestr. 4, 24537 Neumuenster, Germany. TEL 49-4321-906276. FAX 49-4321-906275. Ed.Bd. **Indexed:** IBR. **Document type:** academic/scholarly publication.
Formerly (until 1966): Faunistische Mitteilungen aus Norddeutschland (ISSN 0933-6559).

591   **US**   ISSN 0015-0754
QL1   CODEN: FLDZAK
FIELDIANA: ZOOLOGY. 1895. irreg. (Field Museum of Natural History, Library - Publications Division) Field Museum Press, Roosevelt Rd. at Lake Shore Dr., Chicago, IL 60605-2498. TEL 312-922-9410. FAX 312-427-7269. bibl.; charts; illus.; stat. circ. 600. (also avail. in microform from BHP; back issues avail.; reprint service avail. from UMI) **Indexed:** Biol.Abstr., Chem.Abstr., Curr.Adv.Ecol.Sci., Deep Sea Res.& Oceanogr.Abstr., Sport Fish.Abstr., Wild.Rev., Zoo.Rec.
—BLDSC (3925.100000); CISTI; Linda Hall; UnCover.
Description: Covers taxonomic, morphologic, evolutionary and zoogeographic studies involving Field Museum collections and research in the field. *Refereed Serial*

FISH & FISHERIES WORLDWIDE. see *FISH AND FISHERIES — Abstracting, Bibliographies, Statistics*

591   **NE**   ISSN 0920-1742
CODEN: FPBIEP
FISH PHYSIOLOGY & BIOCHEMISTRY. (Text in English) 1986. 8/yr. fl.904 to institutions; $464 to institutions in U.S. (effective 1998). Kugler Publications B.V., P.O. Box 11188, 1001 GD Amsterdam, Netherlands. TEL 31-20-6278070. FAX 31-20-6380524. Ed. J. Leatherland. (back issues avail.) **Indexed:** ASCA, Curr.Adv.Biochem., Curr.Adv.Cell & Devel.Biol., Curr.Cont., Curr.Ref.Fish Res., Ind.Sci.Rev., Ind.Vet., Neurosci.Cit.Ind., Sel.Water Res.Abstr., Sport Fish.Abstr., Wild.Rev., Zoo.Rec. **Document type:** academic/scholarly publication.
—BLDSC (3935.126000); CASDDS; CISTI; Genuine Article; SWETS; UMI; UnCover. **CCC**.
Description: Publishes original research papers in all aspects of the physiology and biochemistry of fishes.

FISHERIES BULLETIN. see *FISH AND FISHERIES*

FISHERIES OCEANOGRAPHY. see *FISH AND FISHERIES*

597   **US**
FISHES OF THE WESTERN NORTH ATLANTIC. 1948. irreg., part 9, 1989. price varies. Sears Foundation for Marine Research, Peabody Museum of Natural History, 170 Whitney Ave., Box 208118, New Haven, CT 06520-8118. TEL 203-432-3762. FAX 203-432-9816. (back issues avail.) **Document type:** monographic series.

595.1   **US**   ISSN 0360-7550
CODEN: FPNCAT
FLORIDA. DEPARTMENT OF AGRICULTURE AND CONSUMER SERVICES. NEMATOLOGY CIRCULAR. 1962. bi-m. free. Department of Agriculture and Consumer Services, Division of Plant Industry, 1911 S.W. 34th St., Box 147100, Gainesville, FL 32614-7100. TEL 904-372-3505. FAX 904-955-2301. Ed. Maeve McConnell. R&P contact: Maeve McConnell. (looseleaf format) **Indexed:** Bio-Contr.News & Info., Biol.Abstr., Ornam.Hort., Weed Abstr. **Document type:** government publication.

FLORIDA NATURALIST. see *CONSERVATION*

591   **XR**   ISSN 0139-9713
CODEN: FMRZEX
FOLIA MUSEI RERUM NATURALIUM BOHEMIAE OCCIDENTALIS. ZOOLOGICA. 1971. s-a. Zapadoceske Muzeum, Kopeckeho Sady 2, 301 35 Plzen, Czech Republic. **Indexed:** Sport Fish.Abstr., Wild.Rev., Zoo.Rec. **Document type:** academic/scholarly publication.

599.8   **SZ**   ISSN 0015-5713
QL737.P9   CODEN: FPRMAB
FOLIA PRIMATOLOGICA; international journal of primatology. (Text in English, French, German) 1963. bi-m. 230 SFr.($176) to individuals; institutions 460 SFr.($352) (effective 1998). S. Karger AG, Allschwilerstr. 10, P.O. Box, CH-4009 Basel, Switzerland. TEL 41-61-3061111. FAX 41-61-3061234. E-mail: karger@karger.ch; URL: http://www.karger.ch. Ed. R.H. Crompton. adv.; bk.rev.; bibl.; charts; illus.; index. circ. 850. (also avail. in microform) **Indexed:** A.I.C.P., Anthropol.Lit., ASCA, Biol.Abstr., Chem.Abstr., Curr.Adv.Ecol.Sci., Curr.Cont., Dairy Sci.Abstr., Dent.Ind., GeoRef., Ind.Med., Ind.Sci.Rev., Ind.Vet., Nutr.Abstr., Psychol.Abstr. (1963-), Sci.Cit.Ind., Sport Fish.Abstr., SSCI, Vet.Bull., Wild.Rev., Zoo.Rec. **Document type:** academic/scholarly publication.
—BLDSC (3973.580000); CASDDS; CISTI; Genuine Article; KNAW; Linda Hall; SWETS; UnCover. **CCC**.
Description: Discusses various aspects of the study of primates. *Refereed Serial*

591   **XR**   ISSN 0139-7893
QL1   CODEN: FOZODJ
FOLIA ZOOLOGICA. (Text in English or German; summaries in English) 1938. q. fl.318($170) (effective 1995). Academy of Sciences of the Czech Republic, Institute of Landscape Ecology, Kvetna 8, 60365 Brno, Czech Republic. TEL 42-5-43321306. FAX 42-5-43211346. E-mail: penaz@dior.ics.muni.cz. Ed. Milan Penaz. bk.rev.; charts; illus.; tr.lit.; index. circ. 1,100. **Indexed:** ASCA, Biol.Abstr., Bull.Signal., Curr.Adv.Cell & Devel.Biol., Curr.Adv.Ecol.Sci., Curr.Cont., Ecol.Abstr., Forest.Abstr., Forest Prod.Abstr., Helminthol.Abstr., Ind.Sci.Rev., INIS Atomind., Key Word Ind.Wildl.Res., Ref.Zh., Sci.Cit.Ind., Sport Fish.Abstr., Wild.Rev., Zoo.Rec. **Document type:** academic/scholarly publication.
—BLDSC (3974.320000); CISTI; EMDOCS; Genuine Article; Linda Hall; UnCover. **CCC**.
Former titles (until 1955): Zoologicke a Entomologicke Listy (Folia Zoologica et Entomologica) (ISSN 0044-5142); (until 1951): Entomologicke Listy (Folia Entomologica).
Description: Comprehensive articles on the results of original research on vertebrates, e.g. mammalogy, ornithology, ichthyology and morphology. *Refereed Serial*

591   **GW**   ISSN 0071-7991
QL1   CODEN: FOZOAG
FORTSCHRITTE DER ZOOLOGIE/PROGRESS IN ZOOLOGY. (Text in English, French, German) 1935. irreg. price varies. (Deutsche Zoologische Gesellschaft) Gustav Fischer Verlag, Wollgrasweg 49, 70599 Stuttgart, Germany. TEL 49-711-458030. FAX 49-711-4580334. (Subscr. to: Postfach 720143, 70577 Stuttgart, Germany; U.S. addr.: Lubrecht & Cramer Ltd., 38 Rte. 48, Forestburgh, NY 12777-6400) Ed. M. Lindauer. **Indexed:** Biol.Abstr., Chem.Abstr., Deep Sea Res.& Oceanogr.Abstr., Ind.Sci.Rev., Sci.Cit.Ind., VITIS. **Document type:** monographic series.
—BLDSC (4024.000000); CASDDS; CISTI; KNAW; Linda Hall; UMI. **CCC**.
Supersedes: Ergebnisse und Fortschritte der Zoologie.

FOTOGRAFIE DRAUSSEN; Erleben aus erster Hand. see *PHOTOGRAPHY*

591   **PL**   ISSN 0015-9301
QL1   CODEN: FRGFAH
FRAGMENTA FAUNISTICA. (Text in English, Polish) 1930. irreg., latest vol.39, no.16. price varies. Polska Akademia Nauk, Muzeum i Instytut Zoologii, Ul. Wilcza 64, 00-679 Warsaw, Poland. TEL 48-2-6293221. FAX 48-2-6296302. Ed. R. Pisarska. bibl.; charts; illus.; index. circ. 550. **Indexed:** AgroLibrex, Biol.Abstr., Deep Sea Res.& Oceanogr.Abstr., Rev.Appl.Entomol., Rev.Plant Path. **Document type:** academic/scholarly publication.
—CISTI; Linda Hall; UnCover.

591   **US**
FRESHWATER CRAYFISH; a journal of astacology. 1972. irreg., no.10, 1996. International Association of Astacology, c/o IAA Secretariat, Box 44650, University of Southwestern Louisiana, Lafayette, LA 70504. TEL 318-482-5239. FAX 318-482-5395.

FRONTIERS OF ORAL BIOLOGY. see *MEDICAL SCIENCES — Dentistry*

FUNCTIONAL ECOLOGY. see *CONSERVATION*

BIOLOGY — ZOOLOGY

591   FR   ISSN 1164-5571
QL391.N4   CODEN: FAPNE5
FUNDAMENTAL AND APPLIED NEMATOLOGY. (Text in English) 1978. 6/yr. 1100 F. (foreign 1450 F.) (effective 1997). (O R S T O M) Gauthier-Villars, 5 rue Laromiguiere, 75005 Paris, France. TEL 33-1-40466201. FAX 33-1-40466201. TELEX 634 916 F. E-mail: gauthier.villars.publisher@mail.sgip.fr; URL: http://www.gauthier-villars.fr. (Subscr. to: Societe de Periodiques Specialises, B.P. 22-F, 41354 Vineuil Cedex, France. TEL 33-2-54504612. FAX 33-2-54504611) Ed. Pierre Baujard. (back issues avail.) Indexed: ASCA, Bio-Contr.News & Info., Chem.Abstr., Curr.Adv.Ecol.Sci., Curr.Cont., Excerp.Med., Forest.Abstr., Helminthol.Abstr., Hort.Abstr., Ind.Sci.Rev., Irr.& Drain.Abstr., Maize Abstr., Plant Grow.Reg.Abstr., Potato Abstr., Rice Abstr., Soils & Fert., Weed Abstr.
—BLDSC (4056.030300); CASDDS; CISTI; EMDOCS; Genuine Article; Linda Hall; SWETS; UnCover. **CCC.**
Formerly: Revue de Nematologie (ISSN 0183-9187)
Description: Publishes papers concerning plant-parasitic, insect-parasitic, and soil free-living nematodes.

GAN NO SHINPOJUMU/SYMPOSIUM ON WILD GEESE. see *CONSERVATION*

GAN NO TAYORI/GOOSE LETTER. see *CONSERVATION*

GANKAMOKA NO CHORUI NO CHOSA HOKOKUSHO/ANNUAL CENSUS ON WILD GEESE, DUCKS AND SWANS IN JAPAN ADVOCATED BY THE ENVIRONMENTAL AGENCY. see *CONSERVATION*

591   PO   ISSN 0870-0001
GARCIA DE ORTA: SERIE DE ZOOLOGIA. 1972. 2/yr. price varies. Instituto de Investigacao Cientifica Tropical, Rua da Junqueira 30, 1300 Lisbon, Portugal. TEL 351-1-3622621. FAX 351-1-3631460. E-mail: cdi@iict.pt; URL: http://www.iict.pt. (Subscr. to: Centro de Documentacao e Informacao, Rau Jau 47, 1300 Lisbon, Portugal) circ. 1,000. **Document type:** academic/scholarly publication.

591   CL   ISSN 0016-531X
QL1   CODEN: GBCZAO
GAYANA: ZOOLOGIA. (Text in English or Spanish) 1961. a. Universidad de Concepcion, Facultad de Ciencias Naturales y Oceanograficas, Casilla 2407, Concepcion, Chile. FAX 56-41-240280. (Subscr. to: Editorial Universidad de Concepcion, Depto. Ventas, Cas.1557, Concepcion, Chile) Ed. Andres O. Angulo. adv. contact: Alejandro Wittker. circ. 1,000. Indexed: Apic.Abstr., Biol.Abstr., Deep Sea Res.& Oceanogr.Abstr., GeoRef. **Document type:** abstracting/indexing, directory.
—BLDSC (4089.590000); Linda Hall.

591   XR
GAZELLA. ANNUAL REPORT AND SCIENTIFIC ARTICLES. (Text and summaries in Czech and English) 1969. a. exchange basis. Zoologicka Zahrada v Praze - Zoological Garden of Prague, U Trojskeho Zamku 3-120, 171 00 Prague 7, Czech Republic. TEL 420-2-6880480. FAX 420-2-6890369. Ed. Evzen Kus. Indexed: Key Word Ind.Wildl.Res., Sport Fish.Abstr., Wild.Rev. **Document type:** academic/scholarly publication, bulletin.
Formerly: Zoologicka Zahrada v Praze. Vyrocni Zprava.
Refereed Serial

594   UY   ISSN 0037-8607
                     CODEN: CSMLA5
GAZETA DE BAIXADA.* 1961. s-a. P.300($2) Sociedad Malacologica del Uruguay, Casilla 1401, Montevideo, Uruguay. bk.rev.; bibl.; charts; illus.; index, cum.index. circ. 300. (looseleaf format)

599.5   JA   ISSN 1340-9409
GEIKEN TSUSHIN/WHALES RESEARCH INSTITUTE NEWS. (Text in Japanese) 1984. 4/yr. exchange basis. Nihon Geirui Kenkyusho - Institute of Cetacean Research, 4-18 Toyomicho, Chuo-ku, Tokyo 104, Japan. Ed. Seiji Ohsumi. **Document type:** newsletter.

593   JA   ISSN 0388-3752
GENSEI DOBUTSUGAKU ZASSHI/JAPANESE JOURNAL OF PROTOZOOLOGY. (Text in English, Japanese) 1968. a. Nihon Gensei Dobutsu Gakkai - Japan Society of Protozoology, Gifu Daigaku Igakubu Seikagaku Kyoshitsu, 40 Tsukasamachi, Gifu-shi, Gifu-ken 500, Japan.

591   FR   ISSN 0761-9243
QL1   CODEN: GFSAER
GIBIER FAUNE SAUVAGE/GAME AND WILDLIFE. (Text in French, English; occasionally German, Spanish. Abstracts in French, English, German) 1974. q. 286 F. (foreign 331 F.); students 197 F. (foreign 232 F.) (effective 1997). Office National de la Chasse, 85 bis ave. de Wagram, 75017 Paris, France. TEL 33-1-44151717. FAX 33-1-44151704. Ed. Yves Tachker; Pub. Jean-Marie Ballu. R&P contact: Marcel Birkan. TEL 33-1-34652421. bk.rev.; abstr.; circ. 229 (paid). Indexed: Sport Fish.Abstr., Wild.Rev., Zoo.Rec. **Document type:** academic/scholarly publication, proceedings.
—BLDSC (4172.366500).
Formerly (until 1984): France. Office National de la Chasse. Bulletin Special Scientifique (ISSN 1148-6538)
Description: Publishes original papers on game and wildlife. Concerned with all scientific disciplines and geographical regions dealing with these animals, but focuses on papers that contribute to species conservation and management.

591.5   JA   ISSN 0911-0461
GIFU FURUSATO TO DOBUTSU TSUSHIN/MAMMALS' NEWSLETTER IN HOMELAND GIFU. (Text in Japanese) 1984. bi-m. Gifuken Honyu Dobutsu Chosa Kenkyukai - Gifu Prefecture Mammalian Research Society, Takano, Mugegawacho, Mugi-gun, Gifu-ken 501-26, Japan. **Document type:** newsletter.

591   BL   ISSN 0103-6076
QL242   CODEN: GOZOEV
GOELDIANA ZOOLOGIA. 1990. irreg., no.13, 1992. Cr.$10000($2) Conselho Nacional de Desenvolvimento Cientifico e Tecnologico, Museu Paraense Emilio Goeldi, Caixa Postal 399, 66017-970 Belem, Para, Brazil. TEL 091-228-2341. FAX 091-299-1412. TELEX 091-1419.

GOOSE STUDY. see *CONSERVATION*

GORILLA. see *PSYCHOLOGY*

591   SP   ISSN 0367-5041
QL461   CODEN: GRAEAT
GRAELLSIA. (Monographic supplements avail.) (Text in English, Spanish; summaries in English) 1944. a. 4000 ptas. (foreign 5000 ptas.) to individuals; institutions 7000 ptas. (foreign 10000 ptas.) (effective 1996). Museo Nacional de Ciencias Naturales, Jose Gutierrez Abascal 2, 28006 Madrid, Spain. TEL 34-1-4111328. FAX 34-1-5645078. E-mail: MCNAC22@cc.csic.es. Eds. M. Angeles Ramos, Ana I. Camacho. bk.rev. circ. 500. Indexed: Ind.SST. **Document type:** newspaper, monographic series.
Description: Covers contributions to the advancement of knowledge in zoological biodiversity, including taxonomy, fauna, biogeography and evolution and conservation studies.
Refereed Serial

GRASDUINEN. see *BIOLOGY — Botany*

GREAT BASIN NATURALIST. see *BIOLOGY — Botany*

GREAT BASIN NATURALIST MEMOIRS. see *BIOLOGY — Botany*

GUJIZHUI DONGWU XUEBAO/VERTEBRATA PALASIATICA. see *PALEONTOLOGY*

597   JA   ISSN 0388-788X
                     CODEN: GYKEDT
GYOBYO KENKYU/FISH PATHOLOGY. (Text in English and Japanese) 1966. q. 6000 Yen (foreign 8000 Yen). Japanese Society of Fish Pathology - Nihon Gyobyo Gakkai, c/o Dept. of Fisheries, Faculty of Agriculture, University of Tokyo, Yayoi 1-1-1, Bunkyo-ku, Tokyo 113, Japan. TEL 81-3-3812-2111. FAX 81-3-3813-2776. (Subscr. to: Business Center for Academic Societies Japan, Hon-Komagome 5-16-9, Bunkyo-ku, Tokyo 113, Japan. TEL 81-3-5814-5811; Editorial abr.: National Research Institute of Aquaculture, Nansei, Mie 516-01, Japan. TEL 81-5996-6-1830. FAX 81-5886-6-1962) Ed. Y. Inui. R&P contact: Mitsuru Ototake. adv. contact: Hiroshi Yokoyama. bk.rev. circ. 1,000. (back issues avail.) Indexed: ASCA, Curr.Cont., Curr.Ref.Fish Res., Ind.Vet., Protozool.Abstr., Sci.Cit.Ind., Sport Fish.Abstr., Vet.Bull., Wild.Rev., Zoo.Rec. **Document type:** academic/scholarly publication.
—BLDSC (3935.120000); CASDDS; Genuine Article; SWETS; UnCover.
Description: Publishes research articles, short communications and reviews on disease phenomena of fishes and shellfishes.
Refereed Serial

598.1   JA   ISSN 0285-3191
                     CODEN: HRYZAJ
HACHU RYOSEIRUIGAKU ZASSHI/JAPANESE JOURNAL OF HERPETOLOGY. (Text in English, Japanese) 1964. s-a. Nihon Hachu Ryoseirui Gakkai - Herpetological Society of Japan, Kyoto Daigaku Rigakubu Dobutsugaku Kyoshitsu, Kitashirakawa Oiwakecho, Sakyo-ku, Kyoto 606, Japan.

597   II
                     CODEN: HAMAE7
HAMADRYAD. a. Madras Crocodile Bank, Vadanemmeli Village, Perur P.O., Mahabalipuram Rd., Madras 603 104, India. Indexed: Sport Fish.Abstr., Wild.Rev., Zoo.Rec.

595   GW   ISSN 0072-9612
                     CODEN: MHZMA4
HAMBURGISCHES ZOOLOGISCHES MUSEUM UND INSTITUT. MITTEILUNGEN. 1883. a. price varies. Universitaet Hamburg, Zoologisches Institut, Martin-Luther-King-Platz 3, 20146 Hamburg, Germany. TEL 49-4123-3960. FAX 49-4123-3937. (Co-sponsor: Zoologisches Museum der Universitaet Hamburg) Ed. Heinrich Hoerschelmann, Hans Georg Andres. circ. 600. Indexed: Biol.Abstr., Deep Sea Res.& Oceanogr.Abstr., Entomol.Abstr., Rev.Appl.Entomol., Sport Fish.Abstr., Wild.Rev., Zoo.Rec. **Document type:** newsletter.
—Linda Hall.
Refereed Serial

594   US   ISSN 0017-8624
QL401   CODEN: HWSNAM
HAWAIIAN SHELL NEWS. (Print version ceased in Jan. 1997) 1952. m. $30 (Canada & Mexico $31; elsewhere $33). Hawaiian Malacological Society, Box 22130, Honolulu, HI 96823-2130. E-mail: g-b.cook@juno.com; URL: http://www.hits.net/~hsn. Ed. Dwayne Minton. adv. contact: Olive Schoenberg-Dole. bk.rev.; charts; illus.; maps; stat. Indexed: Biol.Abstr., Curr.Tit.Ocean, Zoo.Rec.
●Available only online.
—Linda Hall; UMI.
Description: Nonscientific educational journal of events, opinions and problems in the shell world.

597.9   JA
HEBIKEN NYUSU/JAPAN SNAKE INSTITUTE NEWS. (Text in Japanese) irreg. Nihon Hebizoku Gakujutsu Kenkyujo - Japan Snake Institute, 3318 Yunoiri, Yabutsuka Honmachi, Nitta-gun, Gunma-ken 379-23, Japan.

HELICTITE; journal of Australasian cave research. see *EARTH SCIENCES — Geology*

BIOLOGY — ZOOLOGY

591 XO ISSN 0440-6605
QL392 CODEN: HMTGA4
HELMINTHOLOGIA. (Text in English) 1959. 4/yr. $174 (effective 1998). Slovak Academy of Sciences, Parasitological Institute, Hlinkova 3, 04001 Kosice, Slovakia. TEL 42-95-6331411. FAX 42-95-3631414. E-mail: helminth@linux.saske.sk. (Dist. by: Slovart, Nam. Slobody 6, 817 64 Bratislava, Slovakia; Subscr. to: Slovak Academi Press, Ltd., P.O. Box 57, Nam. Slobody 6, 810 05 Bratislava, Slovakia; Dist. also by: Mezhdunarodnaya Kniga, B. Yakimanka 39, 117049 Moscow, Russia. TEL 7-095-2384967. FAX 7-095-2384634) Ed. P. Dubinski. adv.; bk.rev.; illus.; index. circ. 700.
Indexed: Abstr.Bulg.Sci.Med.Lit., Abstr.Hyg., ASCA, Biol.Abstr., Chem.Abstr., Curr.Cont., Excerp.Med. (until 19??), Ind.Vet., Poult.Abstr., Sport Fish.Abstr., Trop.Dis.Bull., Vet.Bull., Wild.Rev., Zoo.Rec. **Document type:** academic/scholarly publication.
—BLDSC (4285.900000); CASDDS; CISTI; Genuine Article; UnCover.
Description: For physicians, students of medicine, and other scientific and specialized workers engaged in parasitology.
Refereed Serial

595.1 US ISSN 1049-233X
QL386 CODEN: JHSWE4
HELMINTHOLOGICAL SOCIETY OF WASHINGTON. JOURNAL. 1934. s-a. $40 (Canada & Mexico $42; elsewhere $45) (effective 1997). Allen Press, Inc., 1041 New Hampshire St., Lawrence, KS 66044. TEL 913-843-1221. FAX 913-843-1274. Ed. Sherman Hendrix. bk.rev. circ. 1,100. (back issues avail.) **Indexed:** Abstr.Hyg., ASCA, Bibl.Agri., Biol.Abstr., Biotech.Abstr., Curr.Adv.Ecol.Sci., Curr.Cont., Excerp.Med., Helminthol.Abstr., Ind.Vet., Pig News & Info., Poult.Abstr., Protozool.Abstr., Rev.Appl.Entomol., So.Pac.Per.Ind., Sport Fish.Abstr., Trop.Dis.Bull., Vet.Bull., Wild.Rev., Zoo.Rec. **Document type:** academic/scholarly publication.
—BLDSC (4758.001000); CISTI; EMDOCS; Genuine Article; Linda Hall; SWETS; UnCover.
Formerly: Helminthological Society of Washington. Proceedings (ISSN 0018-0130)

598 AT ISSN 0725-1424
CODEN: HRPFEK
HERPETOFAUNA. 1967. s-a. Aus.$40 for 3 years. Australasian Affiliation of Herpetological Societies, P.O. Box R307, Royal Exchange, Sydney, N.S.W. 2000, Australia. Ed. G. Swan. bk.rev. circ. 1,200. **Indexed:** Ecol.Abstr., Sport Fish.Abstr., Wild.Rev., Zoo.Rec.
—BLDSC (4300.280000); CISTI; UnCover.

597.6 GW ISSN 0172-7761
CODEN: HERFE7
HERPETOFAUNA. 1979. irreg. Herpetofauna-Verlags GmbH, Roemerstr. 21, 71384 Weinstadt, Germany. **Indexed:** Zoo.Rec. **Document type:** academic/scholarly publication.

598.1 US ISSN 0018-0831
QL640 CODEN: HPTGAP
HERPETOLOGICA. (Annual supplement avail.: Herpetological Monograph (ISSN 0733-1347)) 1936. q. $95 (effective 1997). Herpetologists League, c/o East Tennessee State University, Dept. of Biology, Box 70726, Johnson City, TN 37614. TEL 423-929-6929. FAX 423-929-5958. Ed. Robert G. Jaeger. R&P contact: Rebecca Pyles. bk.rev.; index; circ. 2,000 (paid). (also avail. in microfilm from UMI; back issues avail; reprint service avail. from UMI) **Indexed:** ASCA, Biol.Abstr., Chem.Abstr., Curr.Cont., Deep Sea Res.& Oceanogr.Abstr., Ecol.Abstr., Helminthol.Abstr., Sci.Cit.Ind., So.Pac.Per.Ind., Sport Fish.Abstr., SSCI, Wild.Rev., Zoo.Rec. **Document type:** academic/scholarly publication.
—BLDSC (4300.300000); CISTI; EMDOCS; Linda Hall; SWETS; UMI; UnCover.
Description: Publishes original research papers and essays dealing with the biology of amphibians and reptiles.

591 SA ISSN 0441-6651
CODEN: HAAJA4
HERPETOLOGICAL ASSOCIATION OF AFRICA. JOURNAL. (Text in English) 1965. irreg. R.30($20) Herpetological Association of Africa, c/o National Museum, P.O. Box 266, 9300 Bloemfontein, South Africa. Ed. W.R. Branch. adv.; bk.rev. circ. 500. **Indexed:** Sport Fish.Abstr., Wild.Rev., Zoo.Rec. **Document type:** academic/scholarly publication.
—UnCover.

598.1 UK ISSN 0268-0130
CODEN: HEJOES
HERPETOLOGICAL JOURNAL. 1948. q. £40($80) British Herpetological Society, c/o Zoological Society of London, Regents Park, London NW1 4RY, England. Ed. R. Griffits. adv.; bk.rev. circ. 800. **Indexed:** ASCA, Curr.Adv.Ecol.Sci., Curr.Cont., Deep Sea Res.& Oceanogr.Abstr., Geo.Abstr., Sport Fish.Abstr., Wild.Rev., Zoo.Rec. **Document type:** academic/scholarly publication.
—BLDSC (4300.328000); CASDDS; CISTI; EMDOCS; Genuine Article; Linda Hall; UnCover.
Formerly (until 1985): British Journal of Herpetology (ISSN 0007-1056)

597.6 US ISSN 0733-1347
QL640 CODEN: HEMOE9
HERPETOLOGICAL MONOGRAPH. (Supplement to: Herpetologica (ISSN 0018-0831)) 1982. a. price varies. Herpetologists League, c/o East Tennessee State University, Dept. of Biology, Box 37614, Lafayette, LA 70504. TEL 423-929-6929. FAX 423-929-5958. Ed. Darrel Frost. R&P contact: Darrel Frost. **Indexed:** Ecol.Abstr., Sport Fish.Abstr., Wild.Rev., Zoo.Rec. **Document type:** monographic series.
—BLDSC (4300.329000); CISTI; SWETS; UnCover.

598.1 US ISSN 0018-084X
QL640 CODEN: HEPRBU
HERPETOLOGICAL REVIEW. 1967. q. $24 to non-members. Society for the Study of Amphibians and Reptiles, c/o Robert Aldridge, St Louis Univ., Dept. of Biology, 3507 Laclede Ave., St. Louis, MO 63103-2010. Ed. Robert Hansen. R&P contact: Robert Aldridge. TEL 314-977-3916. adv.; bk.rev.; abstr.; bibl.; charts; illus.; stat.; circ. 2,500 (paid). **Indexed:** Biol.Abstr., Curr.Adv.Ecol.Sci., Sport Fish.Abstr., Wild.Rev., Zoo.Rec. **Document type:** newsletter.
—BLDSC (4300.330000); CISTI; Linda Hall; SWETS; UnCover.
Formerly: Ohio Herpetological Society Newsletter.
Refereed Serial

591 GW ISSN 0721-6874
HESSISCHE FAUNISTISCHE BRIEFE. 1981. a. DM.30. Naturwissenschaftlicher Verein Darmstadt, Havelstr. 7, 64295 Darmstadt, Germany. TEL 49-6151-133288. Ed. Michael Hoellwarth. adv.; bk.rev. circ. 500. **Document type:** academic/scholarly publication.
—BLDSC (4300.890000).

599.74 JA ISSN 0389-8148
HIGUMA/HOKKAIDO BROWN BEAR. (Text in Japanese) 1976. a. 500 Yen. Noboribetsu Kuma Bokujo - Norboribetsu Bear Park, 224 Noboribetsu Onsencho, Noboribetsu-shi, Hokkaido 059-05, Japan.

HIMALAYAN JOURNAL OF ENVIRONMENT AND ZOOLOGY. see ENVIRONMENTAL STUDIES

590 570 JA ISSN 0386-3166
QH301 CODEN: SRLUDT
HIROSHIMA UNIVERSITY. LABORATORY FOR AMPHIBIAN BIOLOGY. SCIENTIFIC REPORT. (Text in English) 1972. a. exchange basis. Hiroshima University, Laboratory for Amphibian Biology - Hiroshima Daigaku Rigakubu Fuzoku Ryoseirui Kenkyu Shisetsu, 1-3, Kagamiyama, Higashihiroshima-shi, Hiroshima-ken 724, Japan. **Indexed:** Biol.Abstr.
—BLDSC (8198.550000); CISTI.

591 JA
HIROSHIMASHI ASA DOBUTSU KOEN NENPO/ASA ZOOLOGICAL PARK OF HIROSHIMA. ANNUAL REPORT. (Text in Japanese) 1971. a. Hiroshimashi Asa Dobutsuen Kyokai - Asa Zoological Park of Hiroshima, Dobutsuen, Asacho, Asakita-ku, Hiroshima-shi, Hiroshima-ken 731-33, Japan. Dir. Hiroshi Morimoto. **Document type:** corporate report.

594 JA ISSN 0912-1900
HITACHIOBI. (Text in Japanese) 1974. irreg. Tokyo Kairui Dokokai - Tokyo Malacological Society, 4-40-9, Yamato-cho, Nakano-ku, Tokyo 165, Japan. Ed. S. Kato.

591 IT
HOBBY ZOO. 1983. m. Editoriale Olimpia S.p.A., Viale Milton 7, 50129 Florence, Italy. TEL 39-055-50161. FAX 39-055-5016280. Dir. Attilio Vallecchi. adv.; B&W page L.1550000, color page L.2800000; adv. contact: Roololfo Somigliane. circ. 14,000. **Document type:** trade publication.

591 JA ISSN 0285-3760
HOKURIKU JOURNAL OF ZOOTECHNICAL SCIENCE. (Text in Japanese) 1951. s-a. 600 Yen. Japan Zootechnical Society, Hokuriku Branch, c/o Department of Animal Husbandry, Faculty of Agriculture, Niigata University, Niigata 950-21, Japan. TEL 025-262-6662. FAX 025-263-1659. Ed. K. Yamamoto. circ. 800. (back issues avail.)

599 JA ISSN 0916-7625
HONYU DOBUTSU RANSHI GAKKAISHI/JOURNAL OF MAMMALIAN OVA RESEARCH. (Text in English, Japanese) 1984. s.a. membership. Honyu Dobutsu Ranshi Gakkai - Japanese Society of Mammalian Ova Research, Nihon Daigaku Nojuigakubu Jui Serigaku Kyoshitsu, 1866 Kameino, Fujisawa-shi, Kanagawa-ken 252, Japan.

HONYU DOBUTSU SHIKEN BUNKAKAI KAIHO/MAMMALIAN MUTAGENICITY STUDY GROUP COMMUNICATIONS. see BIOLOGY — Genetics

599 JA ISSN 0385-437X
QL700 CODEN: HONKE4
HONYURUI KAGAKU/MAMMALIAN SCIENCE. (Text in English, Japanese) s-a. membership. Nihon Honyurui Gakkai - Mammalogical Society of Japan, Nihon Gakkai Jimu Senta, 16-9, Honkomagome 5-chome, Bunkyo-ku, Tokyo 113, Japan. **Indexed:** Biol.Abstr.
—BLDSC (5357.600000).

599.323 IT ISSN 0394-1914
CODEN: HYSTEO
HYSTRIX. 1986. irreg. Associazione Teriologica Romana, Secretaria di Redazione, Casella Postale 7249, 00100 Rome, Italy. **Indexed:** Sport Fish.Abstr., Wild.Rev., Zoo.Rec. **Document type:** academic/scholarly publication.

591 US ISSN 1023-8174
I A A NEWSLETTER. 1972. q. $35 for 2 yrs. International Association of Astacology, c/o IAA Secretariat, Box 44650, University of Southwestern Louisiana, Lafayette, LA 70504. TEL 318-482-5239. FAX 318-482-5395. E-mail: jhnner@usd.edu. Ed. Glen Whisson. R&P contact: Jay Hune. bk.rev. **Document type:** newsletter.

597 594 595.3 DK ISSN 0109-2510
SH171
I C E S IDENTIFICATION LEAFLETS FOR DISEASES AND PARASITES OF FISH AND SHELLFISH/FICHES D'IDENTIFICATION DES MALADIES ET PARASITES DES POISSONS, CRUSTACES ET MOLLUSQUES. (Text in English, French) 1984. irreg. latest no.50, 1991. DKK 15 per no. International Council for the Exploration of the Sea, Palaegade 2-4, DK-1261 Copenhagen K, Denmark. FAX 33-934215. E-mail: postmaster@server.ices.inst.dk; URL: http://www.ices.inst.dk. (Subscr. to: C.A. Reitzels Boghandel, Noerregade 20, DK-1165 Copenhagen K, Denmark) Ed. G. Olivier. circ. 500. (back issues avail.) **Document type:** monographic series.
—BLDSC (4362.440000).

I C L A R M CONFERENCE PROCEEDINGS. (International Center for Living Aquatic Resources Management) see FISH AND FISHERIES

I L A R JOURNAL. (Institute of Laboratory Animal Resources) see MEDICAL SCIENCES — Experimental Medicine, Laboratory Technique

591 US ISSN 0741-5362
CODEN: ISNWEB
THE I S C NEWSLETTER. q. $42 to individuals; institutions $65 (includes receipt of Cryptozoology annually) (effective 1997). International Society of Cryptozoology, Box 43070, Tucson, AZ 85733. TEL 602-884-8369. FAX 602-884-8369. Ed. J. Richard Greenwell. circ. 800. **Document type:** newsletter.
Description: News on cryptozoology, including field reports, references, new books and interviews.

594 SP ISSN 0212-3010
CODEN: IBERDZ
IBERUS. 1981. a. 6000 ptas. Sociedad Espanola de Malacologia, c/o Museo Nac. de Ciencias Naturales Jose Gutierrez Abascal 2, 28006 Madrid, Spain. Ed. Angel A. Luove del Villar. **Document type:** academic/scholarly publication.

BIOLOGY — ZOOLOGY

591   GW   ISSN 0936-9902
CODEN: IEFRES
ICHTHYOLOGICAL EXPLORATION OF FRESHWATERS; international journal for field-orientated ichthyology. 1990. q. DM.150 to individuals; institutions DM.280 (effective 1996 & 1997). Verlag Dr. Friedrich Pfeil, Postfach 650086, 81214 Munich, Germany. TEL 49-89-7428270. FAX 49-89-7242772. Ed. Maurice Kottelat. index. circ. 500. (back issues avail.) **Indexed**: Environ.Per.Bibl. (1991-1993). **Document type**: academic/scholarly publication.
—BLDSC (4361.950950).

591   BL   ISSN 0073-4721
QL1   CODEN: IHZOAY
IHERINGIA. SERIE ZOOLOGIA. (Text in English, French, German, Italian, Portuguese, Spanish; abstracts in English) 1957. s-a. price varies. Fundacao Zoobotanica do Rio Grande do Sul, Museu de Ciencias Naturais, Caixa Postal 1188, 90690-000 Porto Alegre, RS, Brazil. TEL 55-51-336151. FAX 55-51-361778. E-mail: ebib@pampa.tche.br. Ed. Maria Helena M. Galileo. bibl.; illus.; charts; stat. circ. 600. **Indexed**: Apic.Abstr., Biol.Abstr., Entomol.Abstr., Sport Fish.Abstr., Wild.Rev., Zoo.Rec. **Document type**: bulletin, proceedings.
—BLDSC (4363.540000); CISTI. **CCC**.
Description: Original research articles on all aspects of zoology in South America, with a focus on Brazil.
Refereed Serial

591   II   ISSN 0537-0744
INDIA. ZOOLOGICAL SURVEY. ANNUAL REPORT. a. Zoological Survey of India, 34 Chittaranjan Ave., Calcutta 12, India.

591   II
INDIA. ZOOLOGICAL SURVEY. NEWSLETTER. (Text in English) 197? irreg. Zoological Survey of India, 34 Chittaranjan Ave., Calcutta 12, India.

591   II
INDIA. ZOOLOGICAL SURVEY. RECORDS. q. Rs.81($9) Zoological Survey of India, 34 Chittaranjan Ave., Calcutta 12, India.

591   II   ISSN 0255-7150
CODEN: ICAPDG
INDIAN JOURNAL OF COMPARATIVE ANIMAL PHYSIOLOGY. (Text in English) 1983. s-a. Rs.45($20) to individuals; institutions Rs.100($50). Indian Society for Comparative Animal Physiologists, Dept. of Zoology, Sri Venkateswara University, Tirupati 517502, India. TEL 91-8574-24166. FAX 91-8574-24111. Ed. P. Venkateswara Rao. circ. 300. **Indexed**: Chem.Abstr., Sport Fish.Abstr., Wild.Rev., Zoo.Rec. **Document type**: academic/scholarly publication.
—CASDDS; CISTI.
Refereed Serial

INDIAN JOURNAL OF FISHERIES. see *FISH AND FISHERIES*

591   II   ISSN 0971-104X
QL1   CODEN: IJZLA5
INDIAN JOURNAL OF ZOOLOGICAL SPECTRUM. (Text in English) 1974. 6/yr. Rs.60($20) to individuals; institutions Rs.100($75). Saifia College of Science & Technology, Department of Zoology, Bhopal, India. Ed. Masroor Ali Khan. adv.: page Rs.500. bk.rev.; bibl.; illus. circ. 500. (back issues avail.) **Indexed**: Biol.Abstr., Chem.Abstr., Curr.Cont., Helminthol.Abstr.
—BLDSC (4422.070000); CASDDS; CISTI; Linda Hall.
Formerly (until 1990): Indian Journal of Zoology (ISSN 0302-7562)

597   US   ISSN 0736-0460
INDO-PACIFIC FISHES. 1982. irreg. price varies. (Bishop Museum, Division of Ichthyology) Bishop Museum Press, 1525 Bernice St., Box 19000-A, Honolulu, HI 96817. TEL 808-848-4135. Eds. Dr. John Randall, Helen Randall. (reprint service avail. from UMI)
Description: Revisions of general or higher categories of fish in the Indo-West Pacific region.
Refereed Serial

591   CU   ISSN 0138-6832
INFORMACION EXPRESS. SERIE: GENETICA Y REPRODUCCION. 1977. 3/yr. $6 in N. America; S. America $9; Europe $10; others $14; or exchange basis. Centro de Informacion y Documentacion Agropecuario, Gaveta Postal 4149, Havana 4, Cuba. (Dist. by: Ediciones Cubanas, Obispo No. 527, Apdo. 605, Havana, Cuba) **Indexed**: Agrindex.

591   SP   ISSN 0210-6191
INSTITUCIO CATALANA D'HISTORIA NATURAL. BUTLLETI. SECCIO DE ZOOLOGIA. 1975. irreg. 1400 ptas. Institucion Catalana de Historia Natural, Carme 47, 08001 Barcelona, Spain. **Document type**: monographic series.

594   JA   ISSN 0288-1527
INSTITUTE OF MALACOLOGY OF TOKYO. BULLETIN. (Text in English) 1979. s-a. 1500 Yen membership (effective 1997 & 1998). Institute of Malacology of Tokyo - Tokyo Nantai Dobutsugaku Kenkyujo, 6-36, Midoricho 3-chome, Tanashi-shi, Tokyo 188, Japan. TEL 81-424-63-0851. FAX 81-424-61-1752. Ed. Sadao Kosuge. R&P contact: Sadao Kosuge. **Document type**: academic/scholarly publication.
—BLDSC (2866.750000).

INSTITUTE OF PRIMATE RESEARCH. ANNUAL REPORT. see *BIOLOGY — Genetics*

614.07205   BL   ISSN 0073-9901
CODEN: MIBUAH
INSTITUTO BUTANTAN. MEMORIAS. (Text and summaries in English, Portuguese) 1918. biennial. $20 (effective 1997). Instituto Butantan, Av. Vital Brasil 1500, 05503-900 Sao Paulo, Brazil. TEL 55-11-8137222. FAX 55-11-8151505. TELEX BUTA BR 011-83325. Ed. Eva Maria A. Kelen. index, cum.index: 1918-1989; circ. 800 (controlled). **Indexed**: Abstr.Hyg., Biol.Abstr., Chem.Abstr., Ind.Med., Ind.Vet., Trop.Dis.Bull., Vet.Bull., Zoo.Rec. **Document type**: corporate report, academic/scholarly publication.
—BLDSC (5659.000000); CASDDS; CISTI.
Description: Reports on the institute's activities.

591   PO   ISSN 0020-4021
INSTITUTO DE ZOOLOGIA "DR. AUGUSTO NOBRE". PUBLICACOES. (Text in English, French, German, Portuguese; summaries occasionally in English, French) 1940. irreg. (3-5/yr.) exchange basis. Instituto de Zoologia "Dr. Augusto Nobre", Universidade do Porto, Praca Gomes Teixeira, 4000 Porto, Portugal. bibl.; charts; illus.; stat. circ. 1,000. **Indexed**: Biol.Abstr., Deep Sea Res.& Oceanogr.Abstr., Key Word Ind.Wildl.Res., Zoo.Rec. **Document type**: academic/scholarly publication.

INSTITUTUL DE CERCETARI PENTRU PROTECTIA PLANTELOR. ANALELE/RESEARCH INSTITUTE FOR PLANT PROTECTION. ANNALS. see *AGRICULTURE*

599.8 340   US   ISSN 1064-1564
INTERNATIONAL BEAR NEWS. 1968. q. $20 (effective 1997). International Association for Bear Research and Management, c/o Kate Kendall, U.S.G.S. - B.R.D., Science Center, Glacier National Park, West Glacier, MT 59936-0128. TEL 406-888-7994. FAX 406-888-7990. E-mail: ibaibn@aol.com; katherine__kendall@nbs.gov.us; URL: http://weber.u.washington.edu/~hammill/iba/iba.html. bk.rev. circ. 600. (looseleaf format) **Document type**: newsletter.
Description: Studies of bear biology and management.

597.58 333.7   SP   ISSN 0377-368X
SH351.T8   CODEN: RICTEA
INTERNATIONAL COMMISSION FOR THE CONSERVATION OF ATLANTIC TUNAS. REPORT. (Published in 2 parts for even and odd numbered years) (Editions in English, French, Spanish) biennial. 3500 ptas.($26) to non-qualified personnel or on exchange basis. International Commission for the Conservation of Atlantic Tunas, Estebanez Calderon 3, 8I, 28020 Madrid, Spain. TEL 34-1-5793352. FAX 34-1-5715299. Ed. P.M. Miyake. (also avail. in microfiche from CIS) **Indexed**: IIS.
—BLDSC (7523.946000).

576   IT   ISSN 0074-3860
INTERNATIONAL CONGRESS OF PARASITOLOGY. PROCEEDINGS. 1964. quadrennial; 5th, Toronto, 1982. price varies. World Federation of Parasitologists, c/o A. Mantovani, Sec., Facolta di Medicina Veterinaria, Via S. Giacomo 9/2, 40126 Bologna, Italy.

INTERNATIONAL CONGRESS OF PRIMATOLOGY. PROCEEDINGS. see *ANTHROPOLOGY*

591   US   ISSN 1064-3826
INTERNATIONAL DIRECTORY OF PRIMATOLOGY. 1992. biennial. price varies. University of Wisconsin Press, 114 N. Murray St., Madison, WI 53715-1299. TEL 608-262-8782. FAX 608-262-7560. E-mail: jacobsen@primate.wisc.edu. (Dist. by: Wisconsin Regional Primate Research Center, 1220 Capitol Ct., Madison, WI 53715-1299. TEL 608-263-3512. FAX 608-263-4031) Ed. Larry Jacobsen. adv. contact: Larry Jacobsen. bk.rev.; stat. **Document type**: directory.
Refereed Serial

599.8   US   ISSN 0164-0291
QL737.P9   CODEN: IJPRDA
INTERNATIONAL JOURNAL OF PRIMATOLOGY. 1980. bi-m. $425 (foreign $495) (effective 1998). Plenum Publishing Corp., 233 Spring St., New York, NY 10013-1578. TEL 212-620-8000. FAX 212-463-0742. TELEX 23-421139. (Editorial adr.: c/o Dept. of Anthropology, University of Chicago, 1126 E. 59th St., Chicago, IL 60637) Ed. Russell H. Tuttle. adv.; bk.rev. (also avail. in microfilm from UMI; back issues avail.) **Indexed**: Anthropol.Lit., ASCA, Biol.Abstr., Chem.Abstr., Curr.Cont., Ecol.Abstr., Ind.Sci.Rev., Psychol.Abstr. (1981-), Ref.Zh., Sci.Cit.Ind., Sport Fish.Abstr., SSCI, Wild.Rev., Zoo.Rec. **Document type**: academic/scholarly publication.
—BLDSC (4542.484000); CASDDS; CISTI; EMDOCS; Genuine Article; KNAW; Linda Hall; SWETS; UMI; UnCover. **CCC**.
Refereed Serial

599.2 636.1   XR
INTERNATIONAL STUDBOOK EQUUS PRZEWALSKI. (Supplement every 5 yrs. avail.: General Studbook) (Text in Czech and English) 1960. a. free to qualified personnel. Zoologicka Zahrada v Praze, U Trojskeho Zamku 3-120, 171 00 Prague 1, Czech Republic. TEL 420-2-6880624. FAX 420-2-6890369. Ed. Evzen Kus. (reprint service avail.)

INTERNATIONAL WHALING COMMISSION. ANNUAL REPORT. see *FISH AND FISHERIES*

INTERNATIONAL WOLF. see *CONSERVATION*

591   UK   ISSN 0020-9155
INTERNATIONAL ZOO NEWS. 1951. 8/yr. £35($75) 80 Cleveland Rd., Chichester, W. Sussex PO19 2HF, England. TEL 44-1243-782803. FAX 44-1243-782803. Ed. Nicholas Gould. R&P contact: Nicholas Gould. adv.; bk.rev.; bibl.; illus.; stat. circ. 500. **Indexed**: Sport Fish.Abstr., Wild.Rev. **Document type**: newsletter.
—BLDSC (4552.550000); UnCover.
Description: Exchange of news, information and ideas between zoos worldwide.

591   UK   ISSN 0074-9664
QL76   CODEN: IZYBAE
INTERNATIONAL ZOO YEARBOOK. 1960. a. price varies. Zoological Society of London, Regent's Park, London NW1 4RY, England. FAX 071-483-4436. Ed. Peter Olney. index, cum.index. (reprint service avail. from UMI) **Indexed**: Anim.Breed.Abstr., Biol.Abstr., Dairy Sci.Abstr., Ind.Vet., Key Word Ind.Wildl.Res., Sport Fish.Abstr., Vet.Bull., Wild.Rev.
—BLDSC (4552.600000); Linda Hall; SWETS; UnCover.

BIOLOGY — ZOOLOGY

592 US ISSN 1077-8306
QH201 CODEN: TAMSAJ
INVERTEBRATE BIOLOGY. 1880. q. $75 (Canada & Mexico $75; elsewhere $100) (effective 1997). (American Microscopical Society) Allen Press, Inc., 1041 New Hampshire Ave., Box 1897, Lawrence, KS 66044. TEL 913-843-1234. (Co-sponsor: American Society of Zoologists. Division of Invertebrate Zoology) Ed. Dr. Vicki Pearse. adv.; bk.rev.; bibl.; illus.; index, cum.index: vols.1-80 (1880-1961). circ. 1,200. (also avail. in microfilm from PMC; back issues avail.) **Indexed:** Abstr.Bull.Inst.Pap.Chem., ASCA, Biol.Abstr., Biol.& Agr.Ind., Chem.Abstr., Curr.Adv.Ecol.Sci., Curr.Cont., Dairy Sci.Abstr., Deep Sea Res.& Oceanogr.Abstr., Helminthol.Abstr., Ind.Med., Ind.Sci.Rev., Ocean.Abstr., Pollut.Abstr., Sport Fish.Abstr., Wild.Rev., Zoo.Rec. **Document type:** academic/scholarly publication.
—BLDSC (4557.703195); CASDDS; CISTI; Genuine Article; KNAW; KR SourceOne; Linda Hall; SWETS; UnCover. **CCC.**
Formerly: American Microscopical Society. Transactions (ISSN 0003-0023)
Refereed Serial

INVERTEBRATE NEUROBIOLOGY. see *BIOLOGY — Physiology*

597 CL ISSN 0716-1328
SH237
INVESTIGACION PESQUERA. (Text in Spanish; summaries in English) 1965. a. $10. Instituto de Fomento Pesquero, Casilla 8-V, Valparaiso, Chile. Ed. Zaida Young U. abstr.; bibl.; charts; stat. circ. 600. (processed) **Indexed:** Biol.Abstr. **Document type:** academic/scholarly publication.
—CISTI.
Formed by the 1984 merger of: Instituto de Fomento Pesquero. Serie Investigacion Pesquera (ISSN 0716-4920); Instituto de Fomento Pesquero. Serie Informes Pesqueros (ISSN 0716-4939); Both of which were formed by the 1974 merger of: Instituto de Fomento Pesquero. Publicacion (ISSN 0080-6153); Instituto de Fomento Pesquero. Circular (ISSN 0716-4912); Instituto de Fomento Pesquero. Boletin Cientifico (ISSN 0374-8200)

591 IS ISSN 0021-2210
CODEN: IJZOAE
ISRAEL JOURNAL OF ZOOLOGY. (Text in English) 1951. 4/yr. $190 (effective 1996). Laser Pages Publishing (1992) Ltd., P.O. Box 50257, Jerusalem 91502, Israel. TEL 972-2-370699. FAX 972-2-370625. Ed. Y. Heller. charts; illus.; index. circ. 425. **Indexed:** Anim.Breed.Abstr., ASCA, Biol.Abstr., Chem.Abstr., Curr.Cont., Deep Sea Res.& Oceanogr.Abstr., Ecol.Abstr., Field Crop Abstr., Geol.Abstr., GeoRef, Helminthol.Abstr., Herb.Abstr., Ind.Sci.Rev., Ind.Vet., Key Word Ind.Wildl.Res., Rev.Appl.Entomol., Sci.Cit.Ind, Sport Fish.Abstr., Vet.Bull., VITIS, Wild.Rev., Zoo.Rec. **Document type:** academic/scholarly publication.
—BLDSC (4583.818000); CISTI; Genuine Article; KNAW; Linda Hall; SWETS; UnCover. **CCC.**
Description: Publishes research and review articles in all fields of zoology, with special emphasis on the fauna of terrestrial and marine environments in Israel, the Near East, the Red Sea and Eastern Mediterranean region.
Refereed Serial

590 IT ISSN 1121-4120
ISTITUTO NAZIONALE PER LA FAUNA SELVATICA. DOCUMENTI TECNICI. 1986. irreg. exchange basis. Istituto Nazionale per la Fauna Selvatica, Via Ca Fornacetta 9, 40064 Ozzano Emilia (BO), Italy. FAX 39-51-796628. E-mail: infsammi@iperbole. bologna.it. Ed. Mario Spagnesi. circ. 2,000. **Document type:** monographic series.

591 IT ISSN 0373-4137
QL1 CODEN: BZOOAS
ITALIAN JOURNAL OF ZOOLOGY. (Text and summaries in English) 1930. q. Lit.160000 (foreign Lit.190000) (effective 1997). (Unione Zoologica Italiana - Italian Society of Zoology) Mucchi Editore s.r.l., Via Emilia Est. 1527, 41100 Modena, Italy. TEL 39-59-374094. FAX 39-59-282628. (Edit. addr.: Dipartimento di Biologia Animale, Universita di Modena, Via Universita 4, 41100 Modena, Italy. TEL 39-59-225067) Ed. Pierangelo Luporini. adv.; bk.rev.; circ. 500 (controlled). **Indexed:** ASCA, Biol.Abstr., Curr.Adv.Ecol.Sci., Curr.Cont., Deep Sea Res.& Oceanogr.Abstr., GeoRef., INIS Atomind., Rev.Appl.Entomol., Zoo.Rec.
—BLDSC (4588.341620); CISTI; Genuine Article.
Formerly: Bollettino di Zoologia (ISSN 0373-4137)

591 RU ISSN 0202-702X
QL673
ITOGI NAUKI I TEKHNIKI: ZOOLOGIYA POZVONOCHNYKH. (Text in Russia) irreg., latest vol.16, 1989. 6.60 Rub. Vsesoyuznyi Institut Nauchno-Tekhnicheskoi Informatsii (VINITI), Baltiiskaya ul. 14, Moscow A-219, Russia. (Subscr. to: Mezhdunarodnaya Kniga, Dimitrova ul. 39, 113095 Moscow, Russia)

591 SA ISSN 0251-1258
QL614 CODEN: ICHBB7
J L B SMITH INSTITUTE OF ICHTHYOLOGY. ICHTHYOLOGICAL BULLETIN. (Text in English) 1956. irreg., no.66, 1997. $30 includes Special Publications (effective 1996 & 1997). J L B Smith Institute of Ichthyology, Private Bag 1015, Grahamstown 6140, South Africa. TEL 27-461-311002. FAX 27-461-22403. TELEX 244219 SA. E-mail: ihph@giraffe.ru.ac.za; URL: http://www.ru.ac.za/affiliates/JLB/. (Co-sponsors: South African Foundation for Research Development; South Africa Ministry of Arts, Culture, Science and Technology) Ed. Phillip C. Heemstra. abstr.; bibl.; cum.index; circ. 1,000 (controlled). (back issues avail.) **Indexed:** Biol.Abstr., Sport Fish.Abstr., Wild.Rev., Zoo.Rec. **Document type:** academic/scholarly publication, bulletin.
—BLDSC (4361.950900).
Formerly (until 1972): Ichthyological Bulletin (ISSN 0073-4381)
Description: Discusses latest research conducted on a wide variety of topics pertaining to fish.
Refereed Serial

591 SA ISSN 0075-2088
QL614 CODEN: SPSIEF
J L B SMITH INSTITUTE OF ICHTHYOLOGY. SPECIAL PUBLICATION. (Continues numbering of publication issued under former name of body, Dept. of Ichthyology, Rhodes University) (Text in English) 1967. irreg., no.56, 1993. $30 includes Ichthyological Bulletin (effective 1996 & 1997). J L B Smith Institute of Ichthyology, Private Bag 1015, Grahamstown 6140, South Africa. TEL 27-461-27124. FAX 27-461-22403. TELEX 244219 SA. (Co-sponsors: South African Foundation for Research Development; South Africa Ministry of Arts, Culture, Science, and Technology) Ed. Phillip C. Heemstra. abstr.; bibl.; charts; illus.; stat.; index; circ. 1,000 (controlled). (back issues avail.) **Indexed:** Biol.Abstr., Ocean.Abstr., Sport Fish.Abstr., Wild.Rev., Zoo.Rec. **Document type:** academic/scholarly publication.
Description: Publishes short original research papers on fish systematics, zoogeography, ecology and biology.
Refereed Serial

591 JA
JAPAN ETHOLOGICAL SOCIETY. NEWSLETTER. (Text in Japanese) 1983. s-a. Nippon Dobutsu Kodo Gakkai - Japan Ethological Society, Kyoto Daigaku Rigakubu Dobutsugaku Kyoshitsu, Kitashirakawa Oiwakecho, Sakyo-ku, Kyoto 606-01, Japan. **Document type:** newsletter.

JAPANESE JOURNAL OF APPLIED ENTOMOLOGY AND ZOOLOGY/NIHON OYO DOBUTSU KONCHU GAKKAISHI. see *BIOLOGY — Entomology*

597 JA ISSN 0021-5090
CODEN: GYOZA7
JAPANESE JOURNAL OF ICHTHYOLOGY/GYORUIGAKU ZASSHI. (Text in English, French, Japanese; summaries in English) 1950. q. $95. (Ichthyological Society of Japan - Nihon Gyorui Gakkai) Business Center for Academic Societies Japan, 5-16-9 Honkomagome, Bunkyo-ku, Tokyo 113, Japan. TEL 03-5814-5811. FAX 03-5814-5822. TELEX 2722268 BCJSP J. adv.; bk.rev.; abstr.; bibl.; charts; illus.; stat.; index. circ. 700. **Indexed:** Agrindex, Aqua.Sci.& Fish.Abstr., ASCA, Biol.Abstr., Chem.Abstr., Curr.Adv.Genetics & Molec.Biol., Curr.Cont., Curr.Ref.Fish Res., Helminthol.Abstr., Ind.Sci.Rev., Ind.Vet., Jap.Per.Ind., Sci.Cit.Ind., So.Pac.Per.Ind., Vet.Bull., Zoo.Rec. **Document type:** academic/scholarly publication.
—BLDSC (4655.350000); CISTI; Genuine Article; Linda Hall; UnCover.

591 636.089 JA ISSN 0424-7086
QL99 CODEN: ESDBAK
JAPANESE JOURNAL OF SANITARY ZOOLOGY/EISEI DOBUTSU. (Text in English, Japanese) 1950. q. 10300 Yen. (Japan Society of Sanitary Zoology) Business Center for Academic Societies Japan, 5-16-9 Honkomagome, Bunkyo-ku, Tokyo 113, Japan. TEL 03-5814-5811. FAX 03-5814-5822. TELEX 2722268 BCJSP J. circ. 1,000. (back issues avail.) **Indexed:** Abstr.Hyg., Bio-Contr.News & Info., Biol.Abstr., Chem.Abstr., Helminthol.Abstr., Ind.Vet., Protozool.Abstr., Rev.Appl.Entomol., So.Pac.Per.Ind., Trop.Dis.Bull., Vet.Bull. **Document type:** academic/scholarly publication.
—CASDDS; CISTI; UnCover.

599.74 570 JA
JAPANESE PELAGIC INVESTIGATION ON FUR SEALS. 1958. a. free to qualified personnel. National Research Institute of Far Seas Fisheries, 7-1, Orido 5-chome, Shimizu, Shizuoka 424, Japan. TEL 0543-340-715. FAX 0543-359-642. Ed.Bd. circ. 100.

594 AT ISSN 0021-7719
CODEN: JCNYAE
JOURNAL DE CONCHYLIOLOGIE. (Text and summaries in English, French and other languages) 1850. q. price varies. Ed. Dr. P.H. Fischer, 18/55 Prince Albert St., Mosman, N.S.W. 2088, Australia. bk.rev.; abstr.; bibl.; charts; illus.; index, cum.index. **Indexed:** GeoRef.
—Linda Hall.

591 BE ISSN 0776-7943
QL336
JOURNAL OF AFRICAN ZOOLOGY. (Text in English, French) 1911. bi-m. 5000 BEF (Europe 5200 BEF; N. America $149; elsewhere 5600 BEF) (effective 1994). (Musee Royal de l'Afrique Centrale - Koninklijk Museum voor Midden-Afrika) Editions AGAR a.s.b.l., 39 Venelle du Bois de Saras, B-1300 Wavre, Belgium. Ed. H.M. Andre. charts; illus.; index. **Indexed:** Bio-Contr.News & Info., Biol.Abstr., Ecol.Abstr., Helminthol.Abstr., IDA, Poult.Abstr., Protozool.Abstr., Rev.Appl.Entomol., Zoo.Rec. **Document type:** academic/scholarly publication.
—BLDSC (4919.997250); CISTI; Linda Hall; SWETS UnCover.
Former titles (until vol.108, 1994): Revue de Zoologie Africaine (ISSN 0251-074X); (until 1974): Revue de Zoologie et de Botanique Africaines (ISSN 0035-1814)

JOURNAL OF ANIMAL ECOLOGY. see *BIOLOGY*

591 II ISSN 0021-8804
QL801 CODEN: JAMPA2
JOURNAL OF ANIMAL MORPHOLOGY AND PHYSIOLOGY. (Text in English) 1954. s-a. Rs.125 (foreign $35). Society of Animal Morphologists & Physiologists, c/ Maharaja Sayajirao University of Baroda, Dept. of Zoology, Faculty of Science, Baroda 390002, India. TEL 91-265-336492. Ed. Bonny Pilo. adv. contact: Bonny Pilo. bk.rev.; charts; illus.; index. circ. 300. **Indexed:** Anim.Breed.Abstr., Biol.Abstr., Chem.Abstr., Excerp.Med., Ind.Vet., Vet.Bull. **Document type:** academic/scholarly publication.
—CASDDS; CISTI; Linda Hall; SWETS.

BIOLOGY — ZOOLOGY

591 GW ISSN 0931-2439
SF95 CODEN: ZTTFAA
JOURNAL OF ANIMAL PHYSIOLOGY AND ANIMAL NUTRITION/ZEITSCHRIFT FUER TIERPHYSIOLOGIE UND TIERERNAEHRUNG. (Text in English, French or German; summaries in English, German) 1938. 10/yr. DM.1135 in Europe; rest of world DM.1138 (effective 1998). Blackwell Wissenschaft, Kurfuerstendamm 57, 10707 Berlin, Germany. TEL 49-30-32790679. FAX 49-30-32790610. E-mail: aboverwalt@blackwis.de; URL: http://www.blackwis.com. Eds. K.D. Guenther, M. Kirchgessner. adv.: B&W page DM.560; trim 190 x 122. bk.rev.; abstr.; bibl.; charts; illus.; index. circ. 400. (reprint service avail. from ISI; back issues avail.) **Indexed:** ASCA, Biol.Abstr., Biotech.Abstr., Chem.Abstr., Curr.Cont., Dairy Sci.Abstr., Excerp.Med., Fababean Abstr., Field Crop Abstr., Food Sci.& Tech.Abstr., Geo.Abstr., Helminthol.Abstr., Herb.Abstr., Ind.Sci.Rev., Ind.Vet., Key Word Ind.Wildl.Res., Maize Abstr., Nutr.Abstr., Pig News & Info., Potato Abstr., Poult.Abstr., Psychol.Abstr., Seed Abstr., Sport Fish.Abstr., Triticale Abstr., Vet.Bull., Wild.Rev., Zoo.Rec. **Document type:** academic/scholarly publication.
—BLDSC (4936.600000); CASDDS; Genuine Article; SWETS; UnCover. **CCC.**
Formerly (until 1986): Zeitschrift fuer Tierphysiologie, Tierernaehrung und Futtermittelkunde (ISSN 0044-3565)
Description: Publishes research in the fields of animal physiology, physiology and biochemistry of nutrition, animal feeding, feed technology, and food preservation.

591 II ISSN 0971-2119
CODEN: JANREH
JOURNAL OF APPLIED ANIMAL RESEARCH. (Text in English; summaries in Hindi) 1992. q. $100 (effective 1992). Garuda Scientific Publications, 151 Janakpuri, P.O. Box 6, Izatnagar 243 122, India. TEL 91-581-479723. FAX 91-581-450147. Ed. D.K. Agrawal. R&P contact: Shashi Agrawal. adv. contact: Shashi Agrawal. bk.rev.; illus. (reprint service avail.) **Indexed:** ASCA, Curr.Cont., Food Sci.& Tech.Abstr. **Document type:** academic/scholarly publication.
—BLDSC (4939.920000); CASDDS; Genuine Article. **CCC.**
Description: Publishes original research work on all aspects of biological sciences applied to domestic and wild animals.
Refereed Serial

JOURNAL OF APPLIED ENTOMOLOGY/ZEITSCHRIFT FUER ANGEWANDTE ENTOMOLOGIE. see *BIOLOGY — Entomology*

597 GW ISSN 0175-8659
QL614 CODEN: ZAICEL
JOURNAL OF APPLIED ICHTHYOLOGY/ZEITSCHRIFT FUER ANGEWANDTE ICHTHYOLOGIE. (Text and summaries in English, French, German) 1984. q. DM.483 in Europe; rest of world DM.489 (effective 1998). Blackwell Wissenschaft, Kurfuerstendamm 57, 10707 Berlin, Germany. TEL 49-30-32790679. FAX 49-30-32790610. E-mail: aboverwalt@blackwis.de; URL: http://www.blackwis.com. Ed. Dr. H. Rosenthal. adv.: B&W page DM.560; trim 190 x 122. circ. 340. **Indexed:** ASCA, Curr.Adv.Ecol.Sci., Curr.Cont., Curr.Ref.Fish Res., Ind.Vet., Sport Fish.Abstr., Vet.Bull., Wild.Rev., Zoo.Rec. **Document type:** academic/scholarly publication.
—BLDSC (4942.620000); CASDDS; CISTI; Genuine Article; Linda Hall; SWETS; UnCover. **CCC.**
Description: Publishes articles by scientists of international repute on ichthyology, aquaculture, marine fisheries, environmental toxicology using fishes as test organisms, and basic research on fish management.

599.636 II ISSN 0971-6777
JOURNAL OF CAMEL PRACTICE AND RESEARCH. (Text in English) 1994. s-a. Rs.125($30) to individuals; institutions Rs.250($25) (effective 1997). Camel Publishing House, Gahlot Kutir, Nagani Rd., Bikaner 334 001, India. TEL 91-151-25232. (Subscr. to: Dr. T.K. Gahlot, Dept. of Surgery and Radiology, College of Veterinary & Animal Science, Bikaner 334 001, India. TEL 91-151-527029. FAX 91-151-527673) Ed. T.K. Gahlot. adv.: B&W page $750, color page $1200; adv. contact: T.K. Gahlot. bk.rev. circ. 750. **Document type:** academic/scholarly publication.
—BLDSC (4954.742400).
Description: Publishes manuscripts, postgraduate theses abstracts, news and other information related to the new and old world camelids.

JOURNAL OF COMPARATIVE PATHOLOGY. see *VETERINARY SCIENCE*

594 UK ISSN 0022-0019
JOURNAL OF CONCHOLOGY. 1874. s-a. £37 to non-members (foreign £40); with newsletter £42 (foreign £45) (free with membership) (effective 1997 & 1998). Conchological Society of Great Britain and Ireland, c/o Mr. M.D. Weideli, 35 Bartelmy Rd., Newbury, Berks. RG14 6LD, England. Ed. P.G. Oliver. bk.rev.; charts; illus.; cum.index every 3 yrs. circ. 800. (also avail. in microform from UMI) **Indexed:** ASCA, Biol.Abstr., Curr.Cont., Geo.Abstr.P.G., Ind.Sci.Rev., Sci.Cit.Ind., Zoo.Rec. **Document type:** academic/scholarly publication.
—BLDSC (4965.000000); CISTI; SWETS; UnCover.

595.3 US ISSN 0278-0372
QL435.A1 CODEN: JCBIDB
JOURNAL OF CRUSTACEAN BIOLOGY. 1981. q. $98 (foreign $125) (effective 1996). Crustacean Society, 810 E. 10th St., Box 1897, Lawrence, KS 66044. TEL 913-843-1221. FAX 913-843-1274. Ed. Arthur G. Humes. bk.rev. circ. 1,100. (back issues avail.) **Indexed:** Aqua.Sci.& Fish.Abstr., ASCA, Biol.Abstr., Chem.Abstr., Curr.Cont., Deep Sea Res.& Oceanogr.Abstr., Ecol.Abstr., Ind.Sci.Rev., Mar.Sci.Cont.Tab., Ocean.Abstr., Sci.Cit.Ind. **Document type:** academic/scholarly publication.
—BLDSC (4965.680000); CASDDS; EMDOCS; Genuine Article; Linda Hall; SWETS; UnCover.
Description: Provides international exchange of information among persons interested in any aspect of crustacean studies.
Refereed Serial

591 JA ISSN 0289-0771
QL750 CODEN: JOETE8
JOURNAL OF ETHOLOGY. (Text in English) 1983. s-a. Nippon Dobutsu Kodo Gakkai - Japan Ethological Society, Kyoto Daigaku Rigakubu Dobutsugaku Kyoshitsu, Kitashirakawa Oiwakecho, Sakyo-ku, Kyoto 606-01, Japan. FAX 81-3-5814-5822. (Dist. by: Business Center for Academic Societies Japan, 16-9, Honkagome 5-chome, Bunkyo-ku, Tokyo 113, Japan. TEL 81-3-5814-5811) **Indexed:** ASCA, Biol.Abstr., Curr.Cont., Sport Fish.Abstr., Wild.Rev., Zoo.Rec. **Document type:** academic/scholarly publication.
—BLDSC (4979.602500); EMDOCS; Genuine Article; UnCover.
Description: Contains scientific papers of ethology and related research areas.

593 US ISSN 1066-5234
QL366 CODEN: JEMIED
THE JOURNAL OF EUKARYOTIC MICROBIOLOGY. 1954. 6/yr. $152 (foreign $165) (effective 1997). (Society of Protozoologists) Allen Press, Inc., 1041 New Hampshire Ave., Box 1897, Lawrence, KS 66044. TEL 913-843-1221. FAX 913-843-1274. Ed. E. Kaneshiro. adv.; bk.rev.; bibl.; charts; illus. circ. 1,800. **Indexed:** Abstr.Hyg., ASCA, Bibl.Agri., Bio-Contr.News & Info., Biol.Abstr., Biol.& Agr.Ind., Biol.Dig., Biotech.Abstr., Chem.Abstr., Curr.Adv.Ecol.Sci., Curr.Cont., Curr.Ref.Fish Res., Dairy Sci.Abstr., Deep Sea Res.& Oceanogr.Abstr., Dent.Ind., Ecol.Abstr., Excerp.Med., Geol.Abstr., Helminthol.Abstr., Ind.Med., Ind.Sci.Rev., Ind.Vet., INIS Atomind., Ocean.Abstr., Pollut.Abstr., Poult.Abstr., Protozool.Abstr., Rev.Appl.Entomol., Sci.Cit.Ind., Soils & Fert., Sport Fish.Abstr., Trop.Dis.Bull., Vet.Bull., W.R.C.Inf., Wild.Rev., Zoo.Rec. **Document type:** academic/scholarly publication.
—BLDSC (4979.602740); CASDDS; CISTI; EMDOCS; Genuine Article; KNAW; KR SourceOne; Linda Hall; SWETS; UMI; UnCover.
Formerly: Journal of Protozoology (ISSN 0022-3921)
Refereed Serial

591 US ISSN 0022-104X
QL1 CODEN: JEZOAO
JOURNAL OF EXPERIMENTAL ZOOLOGY. (Supplement avail. (ISSN 1059-8324)) 1904. 18/yr. $3295 (foreign $3610) (effective 1998). John Wiley & Sons, Inc., Journals, 605 Third Ave., New York, NY 10158. TEL 212-850-6645. FAX 212-850-6021. TELEX 12-7063. E-mail: SUBINFO@JWILEY.COM; URL: http://www.wiley.co.uk. (Subscr. outside the Americas to: John Wiley & Sons Ltd., Baffins Ln., Chichester, W. Sussex PO19 1UD, England. TEL 44-1243-779777. FAX 44-1243-776128) Ed. Francis Ruddle. adv.: B&W page £640, color page £1515; trim 279 x 210. abstr.; bibl.; charts; illus.; index. circ. 1,200. (also avail. in microform from SWZ,PMC,UMI; back issues avail.; reprint service avail. from SWZ) **Indexed:** Anim.Breed.Abstr., ASCA, Bio-Contr.News & Info., Biol.Abstr., Biol.& Agr.Ind., Chem.Abstr., Curr.Adv.Biochem., Curr.Adv.Cell & Devel.Biol., Curr.Adv.Genetics & Molec.Biol., Curr.Cont., Curr.Ref.Fish Res., Dairy Sci.Abstr., Deep Sea Res.& Oceanogr.Abstr., Excerp.Med. (until 1992), Helminthol.Abstr., Ind.Med., Ind.Sci.Rev., Ind.Vet., INIS Atomind., Key Word Ind.Wildl.Res., Neurosci.Cit.Ind., Nutr.Abstr., Poult.Abstr., Rev.Appl.Entomol., Sci.Cit.Ind, Sport Fish.Abstr., Vet.Bull., Wild.Rev., Zoo.Rec. **Document type:** academic/scholarly publication.
● Also available online.
—BLDSC (4983.000000); CASDDS; CISTI; EMDOCS; Genuine Article; KNAW; KR SourceOne; Linda Hall; SWETS; UnCover. **CCC.**
Description: Reports research results; includes investigations of all levels of biological organization, from the molecular to the organismal.
Refereed Serial

591 US ISSN 1059-8324
CODEN: JEZSE6
JOURNAL OF EXPERIMENTAL ZOOLOGY. SUPPLEMENT. 1987. irreg. approx a. John Wiley & Sons, Inc., Journals, 605 Third Ave., New York, NY 10158-0012. TEL 212-850-6645. FAX 212-850-6021. (Subscr. outside the Americas to: John Wiley & Sons Ltd., Baffins Ln., Chichester, W. Sussex PO19 1UD, England. TEL 44-1243-779777. FAX 44-1243-776128) (back issues avail.) **Indexed:** Ind.Med., Sport Fish.Abstr., Wild.Rev., Zoo.Rec. **Document type:** academic/scholarly publication.
—CISTI
Refereed Serial

BIOLOGY — ZOOLOGY

597 UK ISSN 0022-1112
QL614 CODEN: JFIBA9
JOURNAL OF FISH BIOLOGY. 1969. m. £674 (effective 1998). (Fisheries Society of the British Isles) Academic Press Ltd. (Subsidiary of: Harcourt Brace & Company Ltd.), 24-28 Oval Rd., London NW1 7DX, England. TEL 44-171-267-4466. FAX 44-171-482-2293. TELEX 25775 ACPRES G. E-mail: apsubs@acad.com; URL: http://hbukco.uk/ap/jfb; http://www.europe.idealibrary.com/. (Subscr. to: Harcourt Brace & Company Ltd., Foots Cray High St., Sidcup, Kent DA14 5HP, England. TEL 44-181-300-3322. FAX 44-181-309-0807) Ed. J.E. Thorpe. R&P contact: Catherine John. adv. contact: Nik Screen. (reprint service avail. from SWZ) **Indexed:** Acid Rain Abstr., Acid Rain Ind., Anim.Breed.Abstr., ASCA, Biol.Abstr., Chem.Abstr., Curr.Adv.Genetics & Molec.Biol., Curr.Cont., Curr.Ref.Fish Res., Deep Sea Res.& Oceanogr.Abstr., Energy Info.Abstr., Environ.Abstr., Excerp.Med., Food Sci.& Tech.Abstr., GeoRef, Helminthol.Abstr., Ind.Sci.Rev., Ind.Vet., Nutr.Abstr., Oceanic.Abstr., Pollut.Abstr., Rev.Med.& Vet.Mycol., Sci.Cit.Ind, Sel.Water Res.Abstr., Sport Fish.Abstr., Vet.Bull., W.R.C.Inf., Wild.Rev., Zoo.Rec. **Document type:** academic/scholarly publication.
● Also available online.
—BLDSC (4984.280000); CASDDS; CISTI; EMDOCS; Genuine Article; Linda Hall; SWETS; UnCover. **CCC.**
Description: Covers all aspects of fish and fisheries biological research, both freshwater and marine.

598.1 US ISSN 0022-1511
QL640 CODEN: JHERAH
JOURNAL OF HERPETOLOGY. 1967. q. $40 to individuals; institutions $70; students $30 (includes Herpetological Review). Society for the Study of Amphibians and Reptiles, c/o Robert Aldridge, St. Louis Univ., Dept. of Biology, 3507 Laclede Ave., St. Louis, KS 67601-0626. Ed. Rich Siegel. R&P contact: Robert Aldridge. TEL 314-977-3916. charts; illus.; index; circ. 2,500 (paid). (back issues avail.) **Indexed:** ASCA, Biol.Abstr., Biol.& Agr.Ind., Chem.Abstr., Curr.Adv.Ecol.Sci., Curr.Cont., Ecol.Abstr., Geol.Abstr., GeoRef, Helminthol.Abstr., Ind.Sci.Rev., Sci.Cit.Ind, So.Pac.Per.Ind., Sport Fish.Abstr., Wild.Rev., Zoo.Rec. **Document type:** academic/scholarly publication.
—BLDSC (4998.100000); CASDDS; CISTI; Genuine Article; KR SourceOne; Linda Hall; SWETS; UnCover.
Formerly: Ohio Herpetological Society. Journal.
Refereed Serial

597 RU ISSN 0032-9452
SH1 CODEN: JITHAZ
JOURNAL OF ICHTHYOLOGY. English translation of: Voprosy Ikhtiologii (US ISSN 0042-8752) 1968. 9/yr. $1198 (Canada and Mexico $1288; elsewhere $1321.75) (effective 1996). (Russian Academy of Sciences, RU) Maika Nauka - Interperiodica, Mezhdunarodnyi Otdel, Ul. Profsoyuznaya, 90, 117864 Moscow, Russia. (Dist. by: Maik Nauka - Interperiodica, Subscription Office, Box 1831, Birmingham, AL 35201-1831, U.S.A.. TEL 205-9995-1567. FAX 205-995-1588) Ed. Robert J. Behnke. adv.; bk.rev.; bibl.; charts; illus.; index. (also avail. in microform from UMI) **Indexed:** Anim.Breed.Abstr., Aqua.Sci.& Fish.Abstr., Biol.Abstr., Curr.Adv.Ecol.Sci., Deep Sea Res.& Oceanogr.Abstr., Ecol.Abstr., Sel.Water Res.Abstr., Sport Fish.Abstr., Wild.Rev., Zoo.Rec. **Document type:** academic/scholarly publication.
—BLDSC (0415.120000); CISTI; SWETS; UMI; UnCover.
Formerly (until 1970): Problems of Ichthyology (ISSN 0193-5119)
Description: Covers fisheries management, fish culture, aquaculture, physiology and biochemistry of both marine and freshwater fish.

591 US ISSN 1064-7554
QL708.5 CODEN: JMEVEY
JOURNAL OF MAMMALIAN EVOLUTION. 1993. q. $165 (foreign $195) (effective 1998). Plenum Publishing Corp., 233 Spring St., New York, NY 10013-1578. TEL 212-620-8000. FAX 212-807-1047. TELEX 23-421139. Eds. W. Patrick Luckett, Jean-Louis Hartenberger. bk.rev. (also avail. in microfilm from UMI) **Indexed:** Ecol.Abstr. **Document type:** academic/scholarly publication.
—BLDSC (5010.880000); CISTI; UnCover.
Description: Investigates all aspects of the comparative and evolutionary biology of mammals, with contributions from specialists in the fields of paleontology, molecular biology, comparative anatomy, developmental biology and cytogenics.
Refereed Serial

599 US ISSN 0022-2372
QL700 CODEN: JOMAAL
JOURNAL OF MAMMALOGY. 1919. q. $45 (effective 1996 & 1997). American Society of Mammalogists, c/o Dr. H. Duane Smith, Sec.-Treas., Monte L. Bean Life Science Museum, Brigham Young University, Provo, UT 84602. TEL 801-378-2492. adv.; bk.rev.; bibl.; charts; illus.; index. (also avail. in microform from UMI,PMC; back issues avail.; reprint service avail. from UMI) **Indexed:** Abstr.Anthropol., Anim.Breed.Abstr., ASCA, Bibl.Agri., Biol.Abstr., Biol.& Agr.Ind., Curr.Adv.Ecol.Sci., Curr.Cont., Dairy Sci.Abstr., Deep Sea Res.& Oceanogr.Abstr., Ecol.Abstr., Forest.Abstr., Forest Prod.Abstr., Gen.Sci.Ind., Geo.Abstr.H.G., Geol.Abstr., GeoRef, Ind.Med., Ind.Sci.Rev., Ind.Vet., INIS Atomind., Key Word Ind.Wildl.Res., Nucl.Sci.Abstr., Nutr.Abstr., Ocean.Abstr., Pollut.Abstr., Sci.Cit.Ind., Sel.Water Res.Abstr., So.Pac.Per.Ind., Sport Fish.Abstr., SSCI, Vet.Bull., Wild Life Rev., Wild.Rev., Zoo.Rec. **Document type:** academic/scholarly publication.
—BLDSC (5011.000000); CISTI; EMDOCS; KNAW; KR SourceOne; Linda Hall; SWETS; UMI; UnCover.
Refereed Serial

599.8 DK ISSN 0047-2565
QL737.P9 CODEN: JMPMAO
JOURNAL OF MEDICAL PRIMATOLOGY. (Text in English) 1972. bi-m. DKK 2430 in Europe (US, Canada and Japan DKK 2400) (effective 1997). Munksgaard International Publishers Ltd., P.O. Box 2148, DK-1016 Copenhagen K, Denmark. TEL 45-33-127030. FAX 45-33-129387. E-mail: fsub@mail.munksgaard.dk. (In N. America: Commerce Place, 350 Main St., Malden, MA 02148-5018. TEL 617-388-8233. FAX 617-388-8274) Ed. J. Eichberg. adv.; bk.rev.; abstr.; charts; illus.; stat. circ. 500. (reprint service avail. from ISI) **Indexed:** ASCA, Biol.Abstr., Chem.Abstr., Curr.Adv.Ecol.Sci., Curr.Cont., Dairy Sci.Abstr., Excerp.Med., Helminthol.Abstr., Ind.Med., Ind.Sci.Rev., Ind.Sci.Rev., Ind.Vet., Nutr.Abstr., Protozool.Abstr., Sci.Cit.Ind, Vet.Bull. **Document type:** academic/scholarly publication.
—BLDSC (5017.082000); CASDDS; CISTI; Genuine Article; KNAW; SWETS; UnCover. **CCC.**
Refereed Serial

594 UK ISSN 0260-1230
QL401 CODEN: JMSTDT
JOURNAL OF MOLLUSCAN STUDIES. 1893. q. £125 (foreign $220) (effective 1998). (Malacological Society of London) Oxford University Press, Academic Division, Great Clarendon St., Oxford OX2 6DP, England. TEL 44-1865-267907. FAX 44-1865-267485. TELEX 837330-OXPRESS-G. E-mail: jnl.info@oup.co.uk; URL: http://www.oup.co.uk/journals. (U.S. subscr. to: Oxford University Press Inc., 2001 Evans Rd., Cary, NC 27513. TEL 800-852-7323. FAX 919-677-1714) Ed. J.D. Taylor; Pub. Steven Johnson. R&P contact: Joolz Longley. adv.; bk.rev.; index. circ. 750. **Indexed:** Arts & Hum.Cit.Ind., ASCA, Biol.Abstr., Curr.Adv.Ecol.Sci., Curr.Cont., Deep Sea Res.& Oceanogr.Abstr., Ecol.Abstr., Geol.Abstr., Helminthol.Abstr., Ind.Sci.Rev., Potato Abstr., Sci.Cit.Ind. **Document type:** academic/scholarly publication.
—BLDSC (5020.820000); EMDOCS; Genuine Article; Linda Hall; SWETS; UMI; UnCover. **CCC.**
Formerly: Malacological Society of London. Proceedings.
Description: Presents neurophysiological and behavioral research using molluscs as experimental material and natural populations.

595.1 US ISSN 0022-300X
QL386.A1 CODEN: JONEB5
JOURNAL OF NEMATOLOGY. 1969. q. $100 (effective 1997). Society of Nematologists, c/o Dr. M. McClure, 3012 Skyview Dr., Lakeland, FL 33801-7072. TEL 815-665-4481. FAX 815-665-1297. Ed. Don W. Dickson. bk.rev.; abstr.; bibl.; charts; illus.; index; circ. 1,145 (paid). (back issues avail.) **Indexed:** Agroforest.Abstr., Apic.Abstr., ASCA, Bibl.Agri., Bio-Contr.News & Info., Biol.Abstr., Biol.& Agr.Ind., Chem.Abstr., Cott.& Trop.Fibr.Abstr., Curr.Adv.Ecol.Sci., Curr.Cont., Excerp.Med., Helminthol.Abstr., Hort.Abstr., Ind.Sci.Rev., Potato Abstr., Poult.Abstr., Sci.Cit.Ind., Seed Abstr., Soils & Fert., Soyabean Abstr., Sport Fish.Abstr., Triticale Abstr., Trop.Oil Seeds Abstr., Weed Abstr., Wild.Rev., Zoo.Rec. **Document type:** academic/scholarly publication.
—BLDSC (5021.399000); CASDDS; EMDOCS; Genuine Article; KR SourceOne; Linda Hall; SWETS; UMI; UnCover.
Description: Presents original scientific papers on research of animal-parasitic, free-living, and plant-parasitic nematodes.
Refereed Serial

591 II ISSN 0253-7230
CODEN: JSREDL
JOURNAL OF SCIENTIFIC RESEARCH. (Text in English) 1978. q. Rs.25($25) Saifia College, Department of Zoology, Bhopal, India. Ed. M.A. Qayyum. adv.; bibl.; illus. circ. 750.
—BLDSC (5059.900000); CASDDS; CISTI. **CCC.**

594 US ISSN 0730-8000
SH370.A1 CODEN: JSHRDA
JOURNAL OF SHELLFISH RESEARCH. 1981. s-a. $125 (foreign $130) (effective 1997). National Shellfisheries Association, Inc., Natural Science Division, Southampton College, Southampton, NY 11968. TEL 516-287-8407. FAX 516-287-8419. Ed. Sandra E. Shumway. R&P contact: Sandra E. Shumway. bk.rev.; index, cum.index: 1930-1972. circ. 950. **Indexed:** ASCA, Biol.Abstr., Chem.Abstr., Curr.Adv.Ecol.Sci., Curr.Cont., Deep Sea Res.& Oceanogr.Abstr., Environ.Per.Bibl., Ind.Sci.Rev., Nutr.Abstr., Rice Abstr., Sci.Cit.Ind. **Document type:** academic/scholarly publication.
—BLDSC (5064.100000); CASDDS; CISTI; EMDOCS; Genuine Article; Linda Hall; SWETS; UnCover.
Formerly: National Shellfisheries Association. Proceedings (ISSN 0077-5711)
Description: Contains original papers dealing with all aspects of shellfish research.
Refereed Serial

JOURNAL OF SOIL BIOLOGY AND ECOLOGY. see *BIOLOGY*

JOURNAL OF VENOMOUS ANIMALS AND TOXINS. see *PHARMACY AND PHARMACOLOGY*

JOURNAL OF WILDLIFE REHABILITATION. see *BIOLOGY*

591 II ISSN 0253-7273
QL1 CODEN: JZRED2
JOURNAL OF ZOOLOGICAL RESEARCH. (Text in English) 1977. s-a. Rs.30($15) to individuals; institutions Rs.60($40). Sardar Mahmood Khan, Ed. & Pub., 1 Talat Lodge Amir Nishan, Aligarh-20200, India. adv. bk.rev. circ. 200. (back issues avail.) **Indexed:** Biol.Abstr., Chem.Abstr. **Document type:** newspaper.
—CASDDS; CISTI.

BIOLOGY — ZOOLOGY

591   **GW**   ISSN 0947-5745
QL351   CODEN: ZZSEAA
JOURNAL OF ZOOLOGICAL SYSTEMATICS AND EVOLUTIONARY RESEARCH. (Supplement avail.: Fortschritte in der zoologischen Systematik und Evolutionsforschung) (Text in English, French, or German; summaries in French, German, Spanish) 1963. 4/yr. DM.614 in Europe; rest of world DM.619 (effective 1998). Blackwell Wissenschaft, Kurfuerstendamm 57, 10707 Berlin, Germany. TEL 49-30-32790679. FAX 49-30-32790610. E-mail: aboverwalt@blackwis.de; URL: http://www.blackwis.com. Ed.Bd. adv.; B&W page DM.560; trim 195 x 122. bk.rev.; illus.; index. circ. 400. (reprint service avail. from ISI; back issues avail.). **Indexed:** Apic.Abstr., ASCA, Biol.Abstr., Curr.Adv.Ecol.Sci., Curr.Cont., Helminthol.Abstr., Sci.Cit.Ind., Sport Fish.Abstr., Wild.Rev., Zoo.Rec. **Document type:** academic/scholarly publication.
—BLDSC (5072.780700); CASDDS; Genuine Article; SWETS; UnCover. **CCC.**
   Formerly (until 1994): Zeitschrift fuer Zoologische Systematik und Evolutionsforschung (ISSN 0044-3808)
   Description: Provides an international forum for papers on zoological systematics and evolutionary research.

594   **JA**   ISSN 0912-2192
KAI NAKAMA/HANSHIN SHELL CLUB. REPORT. (Text in Japanese) 1967. irreg. Hanshin Kairui Danwakai - Hanshin Shell Club, Kikuchi Kairui Kenkyujo, 1-41 Ohamacho, Nishinomiya-shi, Hyogo-ken 662, Japan.

KANDOKON/JAPANESE JOURNAL OF ENVIRONMENT ENTOMOLOGY AND ZOOLOGY. see *BIOLOGY — Entomology*

591   **PL**   ISSN 0075-5230
KATALOG FAUNY PASOZYTNICZEJ POLSKI. 1970. irreg. $20 (effective 1996). Polskie Towarzystwo Parazytologiczne (Warsaw), Ul. Pasteura 3, 00-973 Warsaw, Poland. TEL 48-2-222562. Ed. Bozena Grabda-Kazubska. **Document type:** catalog.

591   **PL**   ISSN 0453-3623
KATALOG FAUNY POLSKI. (Text in Polish) 1960. irreg., no.55, 1996. price varies. Polska Akademia Nauk, Muzeum i Instytut Zoologii, Ul. Wilcza 64, 00-679 Warsaw, Poland. TEL 48-2-6293221. FAX 48-2-6296302. Ed. M. Mroczkowski. bibl. circ. 550. **Indexed:** Biol.Abstr., Rev.Appl.Entomol. **Document type:** catalog.

KEY WORD INDEX OF WILDLIFE RESEARCH. see *SCIENCES: COMPREHENSIVE WORKS — Abstracting, Bibliographies, Statistics*

591   **NE**
KEYS TO THE FAUNA OF THE U S S R. (Text in English) irreg., vol.158, 1994. price varies. E.J. Brill, P.O. Box 9000, 2300 PA Leiden, Netherlands. TEL 31-71-5353500. FAX 31-71-5317532. TELEX 39296 BRILL NL. E-mail: ejbrill@brill.nl. (In N. America: E.J. Brill, 24 Hudson St., Kinderhook, NY 12106. TEL 800-962-4406. FAX 518-758-1959) R&P contact: Elizabeth Vennekamp. **Document type:** monographic series.
   Refereed Serial

591   **GW**   ISSN 0375-5290
KOELNER ZOO. ZEITSCHRIFT. (Summaries in English) 1958. q. DM.20. Aktiengesellschaft Zoologischer Garten, Riehlerstr. 173, 50735 Cologne, Germany. TEL 0221-7785-0. FAX 0221-7785111. Ed. U. Ruempler. adv. **Indexed:** Biol.Abstr., IBR, Key Word Ind.Wildl.Res.
—BLDSC (9442.800000).

595.3   **JA**   ISSN 0287-3478
KOKAKURUI NO KENKYU/CRUSTACEAN RESEARCH. (Text in English, Japanese) 1963. a. Nihon Kokakurui Gakkai - Carcinological Society of Japan, Tokyo University of Fisheries, Dept. of Aquatic Bioscience, 4-5-7 Konan, Minato-ku, Tokyo 108, Japan. TEL 81-3-5463-0535. FAX 81-3-5463-0684. **Document type:** academic/scholarly publication.

KONINKLIJK BELGISCH INSTITUUT VOOR NATUURWETENSCHAPPEN. STUDIEDOCUMENTEN/INSTITUT ROYAL DES SCIENCES NATURELLES DE BELGIQUE. DOCUMENTS DE TRAVAIL. see *BIOLOGY*

591   **KO**   ISSN 1018-192X
THE KOREAN JOURNAL OF SYSTEMATIC ZOOLOGY. (Text in English or Korean; summaries in English) 1985. s-a. $20 to non-members; institutions $23. (Ministry of Education, Korean Federation of Science and Technology Societies) Korean Society of Systematic Zoology, c/o Byung-Hoon Lee, Pub., Dept. of Biology Education, Jeonbuk National University, Jeonju 560-756, S. Korea. TEL 0654-702783. (Subscr. to: c/o Byung Lae Choe, Ed., Dept. of Biology, Sung Kyun Kwan University, Suwon 440-746, S. Korea. TEL 0331-290-5316. FAX 0331-290-5362) **Document type:** academic/scholarly publication.
—BLDSC (5113.574750).
   Description: Publishes original papers on theory and practice of systematic biologies, including classification, phylogeny and evolution in all animal kingdom.

591   **KO**   ISSN 0440-2510
QL1   CODEN: TOHJAV
KOREAN JOURNAL OF ZOOLOGY. Key Title: Tongmul Hakhoe Chi. (Text in English, Korean) 1959. q. 30000 Won($40) Zoological Society of Korea, c/o Department of Zoology, Seoul National University, Seoul 151, Korea. Ed.Bd. circ. 500. (back issues avail.). **Indexed:** Biol.Abstr.
—BLDSC (5113.580000); CASDDS; CISTI.

599.5   **JA**   ISSN 0913-2244
KUJIRA/WEST JAPAN WHALES SOCIETY. NEWS. (Text in Japanese) 1986. a. Nishinihon Kujira Kenkyukai - West Japan Whales Society, Suisan Daigakko, 1944 Nagatahonmachi, Shimonoseki-shi, Yamaguchi-ken 759-65, Japan.

KUWAIT BULLETIN OF MARINE SCIENCE. see *FISH AND FISHERIES*

594   **JA**   ISSN 0911-985X
KYUSHU NO KAI/SHELLS OF KYUSHU. (Text in Japanese) s-a. Kyushu Kairui Danwakai, c/o Mr. Kinzo Matsubayashi, 720 Hinamigo, Togitsucho, Nishisonogi-gun, Nagasaki-ken 851-21, Japan.

LABORATORY ANIMAL SCIENCE. see *MEDICAL SCIENCES — Experimental Medicine, Laboratory Technique*

LABORATORY ANIMALS. see *MEDICAL SCIENCES — Experimental Medicine, Laboratory Technique*

598.1   **NE**   ISSN 0023-7051
LACERTA. 1942. bi-m. $50 (effective Oct. 1996). Nederlandse Vereniging voor Herpetologie en Terrariumkunde - Dutch Society for Herpetology, c/o P.D. Gorseman, Prins Hendrikstraat 95, 3331 XR Zwijndrecht, Netherlands. TEL 31-78-6123908. FAX 31-78-6121550. Ed. H.A.J. in den Bosch. adv.; bk.rev.; charts; illus.; maps; index; circ. 1,900 (paid). **Indexed:** Biol.Abstr., Zoo.Rec. **Document type:** bulletin.
—BLDSC (5142.900000); CISTI; UMI.
   Refereed Serial

591   **AU**
LANDESMUSEUM JOANNEUM. ZOOLOGIE. MITTEILUNGEN. (Text and summaries in German, English) 1972. irreg. (2-4/yr.) price varies. Landesmuseum Joanneum, Zoologie, Raubergasse 10, A-8010 Graz, Austria. TEL 43-316-8017-4760. FAX 43-316-80174800. TELEX 311838-LRGGR-A. Ed. Karl Adlbauer. R&P contact: Karl Adlbauer. bk.rev.; illus.; tr.lit.; charts; illus. circ. 600. **Document type:** academic/scholarly publication.
   Formerly: Landesmuseum Joanneum. Abteilung fuer Zoologie. Mitteilungen.

LIBRARY NEWS FOR ZOOS AND AQUARIUMS. see *LIBRARY AND INFORMATION SCIENCES*

591   **UK**   ISSN 0024-4082
QH1   CODEN: ZJLSA7
LINNEAN SOCIETY. ZOOLOGICAL JOURNAL; an international journal. m. £552 (effective 1998). Academic Press Ltd. (Subsidiary of: Harcourt Brace & Company Ltd.), 24-28 Oval Rd., London NW1 7DX, England. TEL 44-171-267-4466. FAX 44-171-482-2293. TELEX 25775 ACPRES G. E-mail: apsubs@acad.com; URL: http://www.hbuk.co.uk/ap/zjls; http://www.europe.idealibrary.com/. (Subscr. to: Harcourt Brace & Company Ltd., Foots Cray High St., Sidcup, Kent DA14 5HP, England. TEL 44-181-300-3322. FAX 44-181-309-0807) Ed. J.P. Thorpe. R&P contact: Catherine John. adv. contact: Nik Screen. illus.; index. (also avail. in microfiche from BHP; reprint service avail. from SWZ) **Indexed:** ASCA, Bio-Contr.News & Info., Biol.Abstr., Chem.Abstr., Curr.Adv.Ecol.Sci., Curr.Cont., Deep Sea Res.& Oceanogr.Abstr., Helminthol.Abstr., Ind.Sci.Rev., Nutr.Abstr., Rev.Appl.Entomol., Sci.Cit.Ind., So.Pac.Per.Ind., Sport Fish.Abstr., Wild.Rev., Zoo.Rec. **Document type:** academic/scholarly publication.
●Also available online.
—BLDSC (9519.700000); CISTI; Genuine Article; SWETS; UnCover. **CCC.**
   Formerly: Linnean Society of London. Journal.
   Description: Examines zoology with an emphasis on the diversity, systematics, interrelationships, and habits of animals both living and extinct.

591.4 551 576   **AT**   ISSN 0047-4746
LINNEAN SOCIETY OF NEW SOUTH WALES. PROCEEDINGS. 1875. a. (4 parts per no.). Aus.$70 (effective 1997). Southwood Press Pty. Ltd., P.O. Box 457, Milsons Point, N.S.W. 2061, Australia. TEL 61-2-99290253. Ed.Bd. index; circ. 600 (paid). **Indexed:** AESIS, Biol.Abstr., Chem.Abstr., Curr.Adv.Ecol.Sci., Field Crop Abstr., Forest.Abstr., Forest Prod.Abstr., GeoRef., Herb.Abstr., Rev.Appl.Entomol., Rev.Plant Path., So.Pac.Per.Ind., Soils & Fert. **Document type:** academic/scholarly publication, proceedings.
—UnCover.
   Refereed Serial

597.9   **NE**   ISSN 0926-3527
             CODEN: LSEEED
LITTERATURA SERPENTIUM (ENGLISH EDITION). Dutch edition (ISSN 0926-3586) 1980. bi-m. fl.30 (foreign fl.40). European Snake Society, Dahliastraat 13, 3911 WB Rhenen, Netherlands. TEL 31-317-613804. E-mail: r.a.a.vandervlugt@ipo.dlo.nl; URL: http://pcm0053.let.ruu.nl/ess.htm. (Subscr. to: c/o G. Gomes, Pauwenweld 18, 2727 DE Zoetermeer, Netherlands. TEL 31-79-3416592) Eds. Cecile & Rene van der Vlugt. adv. contact: G. Gomes. bk.rev.; cum.index: vols.1-10. circ. 1,000. **Indexed:** Zoo.Rec. **Document type:** consumer publication.
   Supersedes in part (in 1983): Litteratura Serpentium (ISSN 0926-3594)
   Description: Articles and information by and for amateur herpetologists.

636.089   **US**   ISSN 0887-9923
LLAMAS MAGAZINE; information for Camelid lovers everywhere. 1979. 7/yr. $25 (Canada $30; elsewhere $35). Clay Press, Inc., 46 Main St., Jackson, CA 95642-2322. TEL 209-223-0469. FAX 209-223-0466. E-mail: claypress@aol.com. Ed. Cheryl Dal Porto. adv. contact: Tina Stone. bk.rev.; cum.index: 1979-1995; circ. 6,000 (paid). (back issues avail.) **Document type:** trade publication.
—UnCover.
   Formerly: 3 L Llama Magazine (ISSN 0739-1064)

599   **NE**   ISSN 0024-7634
             CODEN: LUTAAI
LUTRA. (Text in Dutch, English, French, German; summaries in English) 1960. s-a. fl.65 (foreign fl.80) (effective 1996 & 1997). (Vereniging voor Zoogdierkunde en Zoogdierbescherming - Society for the Study and Protection of Mammals) Bureau V Z Z, Emmalaan 41, 3581 HP Utrecht, Netherlands. TEL 31-30-2544642. Ed. C. Smeenk. R&P contact: C. Smeenk. bk.rev.; charts; illus. circ. 800. **Indexed:** Biol.Abstr., Key Word Ind.Wildl.Res., Sport Fish.Abstr., Wild.Rev., Zoo.Rec. **Document type:** academic/scholarly publication.
—BLDSC (5308.130000).
   Description: Presents papers on mammalogy as relating to Europe, with an emphasis on the Netherlands and Belgium.
   Refereed Serial

BIOLOGY — ZOOLOGY

599   XR   ISSN 0024-7774
LYNX; novitates mammaliologicae. (Text in Czech, English, German, Russian, Slovak) 1962. irreg. price varies. Narodni Muzeum, Prirodovedecke Muzeum, Vaclavske nam. 68, 115 79 Prague 1, Czech Republic. FAX 42-2-24226488. Ed. Ivan Heran. bk.rev.; bibl.; cum.index. **Indexed:** Biol.Abstr., Key Word Ind.Wildl.Res. **Document type:** academic/scholarly publication.

599.8 333.95   SZ
MADAGASCAR PRIMATES. Variant title: Lemur News. a. $15. International Union for Conservation of Nature and Natural Resources, Species Survival Commission - Primate Specialist Group, Rue Mauverney 28, CH-1196 Gland, Switzerland. TEL 41-22-9990001. FAX 41-22-9990002. TELEX 419624-IUCN-CH. (Subscr. to: Conservation International, 1015 18th St., N.W., Ste. 1000, Washington, DC 20036) **Document type:** newsletter.

591   HU   ISSN 0076-2474
QL262
MAGYARORSZAG ALLATVILAGA/FAUNA HUNGARIAE. (Text in Hungarian) 1960. irreg., vol.172, 1996. price varies. (Magyar Tudomanyos Akademia) Akademiai Kiado Rt., P.O. Box 245, H-1519 Budapest, Hungary. TEL 36-1-2043976. FAX 36-1-2043973. **Indexed:** Biol.Abstr. **Document type:** academic/scholarly publication.

591 594   US   ISSN 0076-2997
QL401   CODEN: MALAAJ
MALACOLOGIA. (Text in English, French, German, Russian, Spanish) 1962. irreg., vol.36, 1995. $36 to individuals; institutions $55. Institute of Malacology, c/o Department of Malacology, Academy of Natural Sciences of Philadelphia, 1900 Benjamin Franklin Pkwy., Philadelphia, PA 19103. TEL 215-299-1130. FAX 215-299-1170. Ed. G.M. Davis. index. circ. 700. **Indexed:** ASCA, Biol.Abstr., Chem.Abstr., Curr.Adv.Ecol.Sci., Curr.Cont., Deep Sea Res.& Oceanogr.Abstr., GeoRef, Helminthol.Abstr., Ind.Sci.Rev., INIS Atomind., Sci.Cit.Ind., So.Pac.Per.Ind., SSCI. **Document type:** academic/scholarly publication.
—BLDSC (5354.100000); CASDDS; Linda Hall; SWETS; UnCover.
Description: Covers the morphology, ecology, evolution, fossil record, classification, distribution, physiology, biochemistry, cytology, genetics and parasitism of mollusks.

591   US   ISSN 0076-3004
QL401   CODEN: MLGRBL
MALACOLOGICAL REVIEW; international journal for biology of mollusks. (Text in English; occasionally in French, Spanish or German) 1968. a. $17 to individuals (foreign $20); institutions $30 (foreign $33). Society for Experimental and Descriptive Malacology, Box 3037, Ann Arbor, MI 48106. TEL 313-764-0470. Ed. J.B. Burch. bk.rev.; abstr.; index. circ. 600. **Indexed:** Biol.Abstr., Curr.Adv.Ecol.Sci., GeoRef., Helminthol.Abstr., Zoo.Rec. **Document type:** academic/scholarly publication.
—BLDSC (5354.150000); CISTI; Linda Hall; SWETS; UMI; UnCover.
Description: Publishes original research and articles on all aspects of the biology and paleontology of mollusks.

591   UK   ISSN 0305-1838
QL700   CODEN: MMLRAI
MAMMAL REVIEW. 1970. q. £118($216) (foreign £130) (effective 1998). (Mammal Society) Blackwell Science Ltd., Osney Mead, Oxford OX2 0EL, England. TEL 44-1865-206206. FAX 44-1865-721205. E-mail: journals.cs@blacksci.co.uk; URL: http://www.black.co.uk. Eds. D.W. Yalden, G.R. Hosey; Pub. Allen Stevens. R&P contact: Sarah Pollard. adv. contact: Martine Cariou-Keen. circ. 1,270. (also avail. in microform from UMI; back issues avail.; reprint service avail. from ISI) **Indexed:** ASCA, Biol.Abstr., Curr.Adv.Ecol.Sci., Curr.Cont., Ecol.Abstr., Geo.Abstr., Helminthol.Abstr., Ind.Sci.Rev., Ind.Vet., Key Word Ind.Wildl.Res., Nutr.Abstr., Sci.Cit.Ind., Sport Fish.Abstr., Vet.Bull., Wild.Rev., Zoo.Rec. **Document type:** academic/scholarly publication.
—BLDSC (5356.800000); CISTI; Genuine Article; Linda Hall; SWETS; UMI; UnCover. CCC.
Refereed Serial

591   UK   ISSN 0141-3392
MAMMAL SOCIETY. OCCASIONAL PUBLICATION. 1977. irreg., no.16. Mammal Society, 15 Cloisters Business Centre, 8 Battersea Park Rd., London SW8 4BG, England. TEL 44-171-498-4358. **Document type:** monographic series.
—BLDSC (6225.792400).

599   FR   ISSN 0025-1461
QL700   CODEN: MAMLAN
MAMMALIA; journal de morphologie, biologie, systematique des mammiferes. (Text in English, French) 1936. q. 900 F. (effective 1997). Museum National d'Histoire Naturelle, Mammiferes et Oiseaux, 55 rue Buffon, 75005 Paris, France. TEL 33-1-40793069. FAX 33-1-40793063. Ed. Jean Dorst; Ed. P. Dorst. adv. contact: P. Petter. bk.rev.; charts; illus.; circ. 670 (controlled). **Indexed:** Anim.Breed.Abstr., ASCA, Biol.Abstr., Curr.Adv.Ecol.Sci., Curr.Cont., Dairy Sci.Abstr., Ecol.Abstr., Geo.Abstr., GeoRef., Ind.Sci.Rev., Key Word Ind.Wildl.Res., Sci.Cit.Ind., Sport Fish.Abstr., Wild.Rev., Zoo.Rec. **Document type:** academic/scholarly publication, bibliography, proceedings.
—BLDSC (5357.000000); CISTI; EMDOCS; Genuine Article; Linda Hall; SWETS; UnCover.
Refereed Serial

591.4   US   ISSN 0076-3519
    CODEN: MLNSBP
MAMMALIAN SPECIES. 1969. irreg. $15. American Society of Mammalogists, c/o Dr. H. Duane Smith, Sec.-Treas., Monte L. Bean Life Science Museum, Brigham Young University, Provo, UT 84602. TEL 801-378-2492. Ed. Joseph Merritt. circ. 1,400. (processed) **Indexed:** Biol.Abstr., GeoRef., Key Word Ind.Wildl.Res., Sport Fish.Abstr., Wild.Rev., Zoo.Rec.
—Linda Hall.
Refereed Serial

599   JA   ISSN 0914-1855
QL700
MAMMALOGICAL SOCIETY OF JAPAN. JOURNAL. (Text in English) 1952. 2/yr. Nihon Honyu Dobutsu Gakkai - Mammalogical Society of Japan, Nihon Gakkai Jimu Senta, 16-9 Honkomagome 5-chome, Bunkyo-ku, Tokyo 113, Japan. **Indexed:** Biol.Abstr.

639.32   US   ISSN 1045-3555
MARINE FISH MONTHLY. m. $22 (Canada $28; elsewhere $38) (effective 1997). Publishing Concepts Corp., 3243 Hwy. 61 E., Luttrell, TN 37779. TEL 423-992-3892. FAX 423-992-5259. adv.; bk.rev. circ. 32,420.
Description: For hobbyists and collectors of marine fish.

MARINE INVERTEBRATES OF SCANDINAVIA. see *BIOLOGY*

591   US
MARINE MAMMAL NEWS. 1975. m. $67.50 (foreign $79.50) (effective 1998). Nautilus Press, Inc., 1201 National Press Bldg., Washington, DC 20045. TEL 202-347-6643. Ed. John R. Botzum, Jr. (looseleaf format; back issues avail.) **Document type:** newsletter.
Description: Covers government actions with an impact on whales, dolphins, and seals.

MARINE MAMMAL SCIENCE. see *EARTH SCIENCES — Oceanography*

598.1   US   ISSN 0025-4231
QL653.M3   CODEN: MHSBB5
MARYLAND HERPETOLOGICAL SOCIETY. BULLETIN. 1965. q. $25 (foreign $30) (effective 1997). (Natural History Society of Maryland, Inc.) Maryland Herpetological Society, 2643 N. Charles St., Baltimore, MD 21218. TEL 410-969-1431. Ed. Herbert S. Harris Jr. adv. contact: Herbert S. Harris, Jr. bk.rev.; bibl.; charts; illus.; stat.; circ. 300 (paid) (also avail. in microfilm) **Indexed:** Biol.Abstr., Sport Fish.Abstr., Wild Life Rev., Wild.Rev., Zoo.Rec. **Document type:** academic/scholarly publication.
—CISTI; Linda Hall; UnCover.
Description: Research with amphibians and reptiles.

MASSEY UNIVERSITY. FACULTY OF AGRICULTURAL AND HORTICULTURAL SCIENCES. RESEARCH AND EXTENSION REPORT (YEARS). see *AGRICULTURE*

591 581   SP   ISSN 0210-5004
    CODEN: MDTRDW
MEDITERRANEA. SERIE DE ESTUDIOS BIOLOGICOS. (Text in Spanish; summaries in English) 1976. a. 2000 ptas. Universidad de Alicante, Facultad de Ciencias, Departamento de Ecologia, Apdo. 99, 03080 Alicante, Spain. TEL 96-590-3400. FAX 96-590-3464. TELEX 66616. Ed.Bd. circ. 600 (controlled). **Indexed:** Biol.Abstr., Ind.SST, Sport Fish.Abstr., Wild.Rev., Zoo.Rec. **Document type:** monographic series.
Description: Publishes scientific works on land ecology of the Mediterranean climate.

595.146   CN   ISSN 0380-9633
    CODEN: MGDLAK
MEGADRILOGICA. (Text in English, French; summaries in English, French, and other languages) 1968. irreg. Can.$5 per no. Oligochaetology Laboratory, Sir Sandford Fleming College, P.O. Box 8000, Lindsay, ON K9V 5E6, Canada. TEL 705-324-9144. FAX 705-878-9312. E-mail: jreynold@flemingc.on.ca. Ed. Dr. J.W. Reynolds. bibl. circ. 1,000. (back issues avail.) **Indexed:** Bibl.Agri., Biol.Abstr., Curr.Adv.Ecol.Sci., Forest Abstr., Zoo.Rec. **Document type:** academic/scholarly publication.
—Linda Hall.
Refereed Serial

591   PL   ISSN 0076-6372
    CODEN: MEZOAN
MEMORABILIA ZOOLOGICA. (Text in English; summaries in Polish, Russian) 1958. irreg., no.50, 1996. price varies. Polska Akademia Nauk, Muzeum i Instytut Zoologii, Ul. Wilcza 64, 00-679 Warsaw, Poland. TEL 48-2-6296302. FAX 48-2-6296302. circ. 1,000. **Indexed:** AgroAgen, AgroLibrex, Biol.Abstr., Rev.Appl.Entomol. **Document type:** monographic series.
—BLDSC (5642.550000); CISTI; Linda Hall.
Description: Research results on flora and fauna in various environments.

591   GW   ISSN 0934-6643
MERTENSIELLA. (Supplement to: Salamandra (ISSN 0036-3375)) (Text in English, German) 1988. irreg. price varies. Deutsche Gesellschaft fuer Herpetologie und Terrarienkunde e.V., Postfach 1421, 53351 Rheinbach, Germany. Eds. Hartmut Greven, Burkhard Thiesmeier. illus. circ. 2,000. **Document type:** academic/scholarly publication.
—BLDSC (5682.281963).

597   JA   ISSN 0287-6108
MIE UNIVERSITY. FISHERIES RESEARCH LABORATORY. REPORT/MIE DAIGAKU SUISAN KENKYUJO HOKOKU. (Editions in English, Japanese) 1978. irreg. Mie Daigaku, Suisan Kenkyujo - Mie University, Fisheries Research Laboratory, 4190-172 Wagu, Shima-cho, Shima-gun, Mie-ken 517-07, Japan. Ed. Washiro Kida. circ. 500. **Indexed:** Curr.Adv.Ecol.Sci.

MIGRATORI ALATI; rivista di gestione dell'ambiente e della fauna. see *BIOLOGY — Ornithology*

591   GW   ISSN 0076-8839
MILU: WISSENSCHAFTLICHE UND KULTURELLE MITTEILUNGEN AUS DEM TIERPARK BERLIN. 1960. irreg., vol.3, 1973. DM.15. Tierpark Berlin, Am Tierpark 41, 10319 Berlin, Germany. Ed. H. Dathe. index. **Indexed:** Key Word Ind.Wildl.Res.

591   SP   ISSN 0211-6529
QL1   CODEN: MZOODG
MISCEL.LANIA ZOOLOGICA. (Text in English, Spanish; abstracts in English) 1958. s-a. (in 1 vol.). 3000 ptas. to individuals (Europe 3400 ptas.; elsewhere 3500 ptas.); institutions 10000 ptas. (Europe 10400 ptas.; elsewhere 10500 ptas.) (effective 1997). Museu de Zoologia, Attn: Dr. Anna Omedes, Ed., Apdo. de Correus 593, 08080 Barcelona, Spain. TEL 34-3-3196912. FAX 34-3-3104999. E-mail: mzoolbcn@lix.intercom.es. R&P contact: Dr. Anna Omedes. adv. contact: Anna Omedes. bibl.; charts; illus.; stat. circ. 1,500. **Indexed:** Acoust.Abstr., Agrindex, Anim.Behav.Abstr., Aqua.Sci.& Fish.Abstr., Behav.Abstr., Biol.Abstr., Biol.& Agr.Ind., Ecol.Abstr., Entomol.Abstr., Environ.Ind., Genet.Abstr., Helminthol.Abstr., Ind.SST, Ocean.Abstr., Ref.Zh., Zoo.Rec. **Document type:** academic/scholarly publication.
—BLDSC (5828.405000).
Formerly (until 1979): Miscelanea Zoologica (ISSN 0540-3278)
Description: Disseminates zoological research.
Refereed Serial

591 CU ISSN 0255-7843
MISCELANEA ZOOLOGICA. 1975. irreg. exchange basis. Academia de Ciencias de Cuba, Instituto de Ecologia y Sistematica, Industria 452, Havana 2, Cuba. **Indexed:** Zoo.Rec. **Document type:** academic/scholarly publication.

591 HU ISSN 0230-9017
MISCELLANEA ZOOLOGICA HUNGARICA. (Text in English) 1982. a. $24 (effective 1998). Magyar Termeszettudomanyi Muzeum - Hungarian Natural History Museum, Baross u. 13, 1088 Budapest, Hungary. TEL 36-1-3130035. FAX 36-1-11171669. Ed. L. Forro. illus.; circ. 300 (paid). (back issues avail.) **Document type:** academic/scholarly publication.
—BLDSC (5812.530000).
Description: Contains papers written by museum staff members or based on materials deposited there. Does not cover entomology.

594 JA ISSN 0912-1390
MITAMAKI/SAGAMI SHELL CLUB. NEWS. (Text in Japanese) 1967. irreg. Sagami Kairui Dokokai - Sagami Shell Club, Yokosukashi Shizen Hakubutsukan, 95 Fukadadai, Yokosuka-shi, Kanagawa-ken 238, Japan.

591 GW ISSN 0373-8493
QL1 CODEN: MTZMAK
MITTEILUNGEN AUS DEM ZOOLOGISCHEN MUSEUM IN BERLIN. (Text and summaries in English, French, German) 1898. 3/yr. DM.295 (foreign DM.310) (effective 1997). Akademie Verlag GmbH, Muehlenstr. 33-34, 13187 Berlin, Germany. TEL 49-30-47889348. FAX 49-30-47889357. E-mail: info@akademie-verlag.de. (Subscr. in the Americas to: John Wiley & Sons, Inc., 605 Third Ave., New York, NY 10058. TEL 212-850-6645. FAX 212-850-6021) Ed. R. Guenther. charts; illus.; index. **Indexed:** Biol.Abstr., IBR. **Document type:** academic/scholarly publication.
—BLDSC (5876.350000); CISTI.

594 AT
QL401
MOLLUSCAN RESEARCH. 1957. a. Aus.$45 includes Australian Shell News (effective 1997). Malacological Society of Australasia, Division of Invertebrate Zoology, Australian Museum, 6 College St., Sydney, N.S.W. 2000, Australia, Australia. TEL 61-2-3206275. FAX 61-2-3206050. E-mail: alisonm@amsg.Austmus.gov.au. Ed. Dr. F.E. Wells. bk.rev. circ. 650. **Indexed:** Biol.Abstr., Curr.Adv.Ecol.Sci., GeoRef. **Document type:** academic/scholarly publication.
Formerly (until vol.15, 1994): Malacological Society of Australia. Journal (ISSN 0085-2988)
Refereed Serial

MOLOCHNO-M'YASNE SKOTARSTVO; mizhvidomchyi temetichnyi naukovyi zbirnik. see *AGRICULTURE — Dairying And Dairy Products*

594 IT ISSN 1122-6358
MONDO DI CONCHIGLIE/WORLD SHELLS. (Text in English, Italian) 1992. q. L.50000($40) (effective 1996). P.O. Box 561, 00187 Rome, Italy. TEL 39-6-5943797. FAX 39-6-5430104. Ed. Alessandro Prati Muestti; Pub. Luigi Raybausi Massilia.

599.8 JA ISSN 0026-9794
MONKEY/MONKI. (Text in Japanese) 1957. bi-m. 3000 Yen (effective 1997). Japan Monkey Centre - Nihon Monki Senta, Kanrin Inuyama 26, Aichi 484, Japan. TEL 81-568-61-2327. FAX 81-568-62-6823. Ed. Shigetaka Kotera. R&P contact: Shigetaka Kotera. bk.rev.; film rev.; bibl.; charts; illus.; circ. 2,000 (controlled). **Document type:** academic/scholarly publication.

591 PL ISSN 0137-2173
CODEN: MGFPA8
MONOGRAFIE FAUNY POLSKI. (Text in Polish, English, French, German) 1973. irreg., vol.13, 1983. price varies. Polska Akademia Nauk, Zaklad Zoologii Systematycznej i Doswiadczalnej, Ul. Slawkowska 17, 31-016 Krakow, Poland. TEL 48-12-221901. FAX 48-12-224294. TELEX 0322414 PAN PL. Ed. Jozef Razowski. bibl. circ. 900. **Indexed:** Biol.Abstr., Ecol.Abstr. **Document type:** monographic series.
—CISTI; KNAW.

594 NE
MONOGRAPH OF LIVING CHITONS (MOLLUSCA: POLYPLACOPHORA). 1985. irreg., no.5, 1994. price varies. E.J. Brill, P.O. Box 9000, 2300 PA Leiden, Netherlands. TEL 31-71-5353500. FAX 31-71-5317532. TELEX 39296 BRILL NL. E-mail: ejbrill@brill.nl. (In N. America: E.J. Brill, 24 Hudson St., Kinderhook, NY 12106. TEL 800-962-4406. FAX 518-758-1959) Eds. P. Kaas, R.A. Van Belle. R&P contact: Elizabeth Vennekamp. illus.; maps. (back issues avail.) **Document type:** monographic series.
Refereed Serial

599.8 US ISSN 0740-9729
CODEN: MONPD5
MONOGRAPHS IN PRIMATOLOGY. 1983. irreg., vol.13, 1990. price varies. John Wiley & Sons, Inc., Journals, 605 Third Ave., New York, NY 10158. **Indexed:** Biol.Abstr. **Document type:** monographic series.
—CISTI. CCC.
Refereed Serial

594 US ISSN 0162-8321
CODEN: MMMOEI
MONOGRAPHS OF MARINE MOLLUSCA. 1978. irreg. $35 per no. Box 7279, Silver Springs, MD 20907. Ed. Ruediger Bieler. circ. 700. **Indexed:** Biol.Abstr., GeoRef., Zoo.Rec. **Document type:** academic/scholarly publication, monographic series.
—Linda Hall.

591 BE ISSN 0379-1785
QL337.C6 CODEN: MRAZBN
MUSEE ROYAL DE L'AFRIQUE CENTRALE. ANNALES - SCIENCES ZOOLOGIQUES. SERIE IN 8/KONINKLIJK MUSEUM VOOR MIDDEN-AFRIKA. ANNALEN - ZOOLOGISCHE WETENSCHAPPEN. REEKS IN 8. 1948. irreg., no.278, 1996. price varies. Musee Royal de l'Afrique Centrale - Koninklijk Museum voor Midden-Afrika, 13 Steenweg op Leuven, B-3080 Tervuren, Belgium. TEL 32-2-7695299. FAX 32-2-7670242. charts; illus. **Indexed:** Biol.Abstr., Forest.Abstr., Rev.Appl.Entomol. **Document type:** monographic series.

591 BE ISSN 0778-466X
MUSEE ROYAL DE L'AFRIQUE CENTRALE. DOCUMENTATION ZOOLOGIQUE/KONINKLIJK MUSEUM VOOR MIDDEN-AFRIKA. ZOOLOGISCHE DOCUMENTATIE. 1961. irreg., no.23, 1993. Musee Royal de l'Afrique Centrale - Koninklijk Museum voor Midden-Afrika, 13 Steenweg op Leuven, B-3080 Tervuren, Belgium. TEL 32-2-7695299. FAX 32-2-7670242. **Indexed:** Biol.Abstr. **Document type:** monographic series.
Description: Scholarly publications relating to the fauna of Africa and neighboring areas.

591 AG ISSN 0373-9066
QL1 CODEN: RMAZDB
MUSEO ARGENTINO DE CIENCIAS NATURALES "BERNARDINO RIVADAVIA." INSTITUTO NACIONAL DE INVESTIGACION DE LAS CIENCIAS NATURALES. REVISTA. ZOOLOGIA. 1948. irreg., vol.15, no.8, 1991. Museo Argentino de Ciencias Naturales "Bernardino Rivadavia", Instituto Nacional de Investigacion de las Ciencias Naturales, Avda. Angel Gallardo 470, Casilla de Correo 220-Sucursal 5, Buenos Aires, Argentina. **Indexed:** Sport Fish.Abstr., Wild.Rev., Zoo.Rec. **Document type:** academic/scholarly publication.
—CISTI.
Continues its: Revista, Ciencias Zoologicas.

591 UY ISSN 0027-0113
QL71.M7 CODEN: CZMMAN
MUSEO NACIONAL DE HISTORIA NATURAL. COMUNICACIONES ZOOLOGICAS. (Text in English, French,Spanish) 1943. irreg. (6-8/yr.). exchange basis only. Museo Nacional de Historia Natural, Casilla de Correos 399, 11000 Montevideo, Uruguay. illus. circ. 1,200. **Indexed:** Biol.Abstr., Sport Fish.Abstr., Wild.Rev., Zoo.Rec.
—BLDSC (3396.400000).

MUSEU BOCAGE. ARQUIVOS. see *ANTHROPOLOGY*

591 SP
MUSEU DE ZOOLOGIA. COL.LECCIONS. (Text in Catalan, Spanish) irreg. (1-2/yr.). exchange basis. Museu de Zoologia, Attn: Dr. Anna Omedes, Ed., Apdo. 593, 08080 Barcelona, Spain. TEL 34-3-3196912. FAX 34-3-3104999. E-mail: mzoolbcn@lix.intercom.es. adv. contact: Anna Omedes. **Document type:** academic/scholarly publication.
Description: Details the collections of the Zoology Museum of Barcelona, including journals.

591 SP ISSN 0211-0687
CODEN: TMZODN
MUSEU DE ZOOLOGIA. TREBALLS. (Text in English, Spanish; summaries in Catalan, English, Spanish) 1917-1957; N.S. 1979. irreg. Museu de Zoologia, Attn: Dr. Anna Omedes, Ed., Apdo. 593, 08080 Barcelona, Spain. TEL 34-3-3196912. FAX 34-3-3104999. E-mail: mzoolbcn@lix.intercom.es. **Indexed:** Acoust.Abstr., Agrindex., Anim.Behav.Abstr., Aqua.Sci.& Fish.Abstr., Behav.Abstr., Biol.& Agr.Ind., Ecol.Abstr., Entomol.Abstr., Environ.Ind., Genet.Abstr., Helminthol.Abstr., IBR, Ind.SST, Mar.Sci.Cont.Tab., Ocean.Abstr., Ref.Zh., Zoo.Rec. **Document type:** monographic series.
Supersedes (in 1979): Museo de Zoologia. Trabajos. Nueva Serie Zoologica (ISSN 0211-0695); Which was formerly (until 1956): Museo de Ciencias Naturales de Barcelona. Trabajos. Nueva Serie Zoologica (ISSN 0211-0709); (until 1937): Museu de Ciencies Naturals de Barcelona. Treballs (ISSN 0211-0717); (until 1918): Musei Barcinonensis Scientiarum Naturalium Opera.
Refereed Serial

946.9 PO ISSN 0870-3876
DP702.M11 CODEN: BMMFA2
MUSEU MUNICIPAL DO FUNCHAL. BOLETIM. 1945. a. exchange basis. (Camara Municipal do Funchal) Museu Municipal do Funchal, Rua da Mouraria, 31, 9000 Funchal, Madeira, Portugal. FAX 351-91-225180. TELEX 72529 MMFP. Ed.Bd. R&P contact: Antonio Domingos Abreu. circ. 750. **Indexed:** Biol.Abstr., Curr.Adv.Ecol.Sci., Deep Sea Res.& Oceanogr.Abstr., Zoo.Rec. **Document type:** bulletin.
—BLDSC (2139.000000).

591 BL ISSN 0080-312X
QL1 CODEN: BMJZAD
MUSEU NACIONAL, RIO DE JANEIRO. BOLETIM. NOVA SERIE. ZOOLOGIA. (Text in Portuguese; summaries mainly in English, occasionally in French and German) 1942. irreg., no.355, 1992. exchange only. Museu Nacional, Quinta da Boa Vista, 20941-360 Rio de Janeiro RJ, Brazil. TEL 55-21-5678676. E-mail: mmbib@acd.ujrj.br. bibl.; charts. **Indexed:** Biol.Abstr.
—CISTI; Linda Hall.

591 BL
MUSEU PARAENSE EMILIO GOELDI. BOLETIM. SERIE ZOOLOGIA. (Text mainly in Portuguese; occasionally in English, French) 1957. s-a. $10 per no. Conselho Nacional de Desenvolvimento Cientifico e Tecnologico, Museu Paraense Emilio Goeldi, Caixa Postal 399, 66017-970 Belem, Para, Brazil. TEL 091-228-2341. FAX 091-229-1412. TELEX 091-1419. abstr.; bibl.; illus. circ. 1,000. **Indexed:** Biol.Abstr., Curr.Adv.Ecol.Sci., GeoRef, Zoo.Rec.
—BLDSC (2143.500000).
Formerly (until 1983, no.124): Museu Paraense Emilio Goeldi. Boletim. Nova Serie: Zoologia (ISSN 0077-2232)
Description: Original papers in zoological research.

MUSEUM D'HISTOIRE NATURELLE "GRIGORE ANTIPA". TRAVAUX. see *BIOLOGY*

BIOLOGY — ZOOLOGY

591　　　　　　　　FR
QL1　　　　　CODEN: BMNADT
MUSEUM NATIONAL D'HISTOIRE NATURELLE. ZOOSYSTEMA. q. 800 F. (effective 1997). Museum National d'Histoire Naturelle, 57 rue Cuvier, 75005 Paris, France. TEL 33-1-40793000. FAX 33-1-40793484. TELEX MUSNAHN 202641F. E-mail: dhenry@mnhn.fr. (Dist. outside of France by: Universal Book Services, Dr. W. Backhuys, Warmonderweg 80, NL-2341 KZ Oegstgeest, Netherlands. TEL 31-71-5170208. FAX 31-71-5171856) Eds. Christian Erard, Daniele Defaye. **Indexed:** Sport Fish.Abstr., Wild.Rev., Zoo.Rec. **Document type:** academic/scholarly publication.
—BLDSC (2626.141000); CISTI; Linda Hall.
　Formerly: Museum National d'Histoire Naturelle. Bulletin - Section A (Zoologie et Ecologie Animales) (ISSN 0181-0626)

MUSEUM NATIONAL D'HISTOIRE NATURELLE, PARIS. MEMOIRES. see *SCIENCES: COMPREHENSIVE WORKS*

591　　　　　　　　US　　ISSN 0027-4100
QL1　　　　　CODEN: MCZBA4
MUSEUM OF COMPARATIVE ZOOLOGY. BULLETIN. 1863. irreg. (3-4/yr.), vol.154, no.4, 1996. price varies. Harvard University, Museum of Comparative Zoology, 26 Oxford St., Cambridge, MA 02138. TEL 617-495-2468. Ed. Kenneth J. Boss. bibl.; illus. circ. 1,000. (also avail. in microfilm from BHP; back issues avail.; reprint service avail. from KTO) **Indexed:** Biol.Abstr., Deep Sea Res.& Oceanogr.Abstr., GeoRef., Sport Fish.Abstr., Wild.Rev., Zoo.Rec. **Document type:** academic/scholarly publication.
—BLDSC (2624.000000); CISTI; Linda Hall.
　Formerly: Harvard University. Museum of Comparative Zoology. Bulletin.
　Description: Publishes natural sciences research papers.

591 500.907　　AT　　ISSN 0814-1827
GN665　　　　　CODEN: MMVMAJ
MUSEUM OF VICTORIA. MEMOIRS. 1906. irreg. (1-2/yr). Aus.$30 per issue. Museum of Victoria Council, 328 Swanston St., Melbourne, Vic. 3000, Australia. FAX 61-3-416-0475. Ed. Gary Poore. R&P contact: Gary Poore. circ. 600. **Indexed:** A.I.C.P., AESIS, Bull.Signal., Deep Sea Res.& Oceanogr.Abstr., Geo.Abstr., GeoRef., IBR, Sport Fish.Abstr., Wild.Rev., Zoo.Rec. **Document type:** monographic series.
—KNAW; Linda Hall; UnCover.
　Formerly: National Museum of Victoria. Memoirs (ISSN 0083-5986)

591 500.907　　AT　　ISSN 0814-1819
QH197　　　　　CODEN: OPMVEE
MUSEUM OF VICTORIA. OCCASIONAL PAPERS. 1984. irreg. Museum of Victoria Council, 285-328 Swanston St., Melbourne, Vic. 3000, Australia. Ed. Gary Poore. R&P contact: Gary Poore. **Indexed:** IBR, Sport Fish.Abstr., Wild.Rev., Zoo.Rec. **Document type:** monographic series.

591　　　　　　　　GW　　ISSN 0580-3896
QL737.C5
MYOTIS; Mitteilungsblatt fuer Fledermauskundler. (Text in English, German) 1963. a. price varies. Zoologisches Forschungsinstitut und Museum Alexander Koenig, Adenauerallee 160, 53113 Bonn, Germany. TEL 49-228-9122-216. FAX 49-228-216979. Ed. Dr. H. Roer. adv.; bk.rev. circ. 300. **Indexed:** Biol.Abstr. **Document type:** academic/scholarly publication.
—CISTI.
　Description: Publication devoted to scientific research on bats. Covers biology, behavior, reproduction, and conservation of all types in different areas. Includes list and reports of events.

NAGA: I C L A R M QUARTERLY. (International Center for Living Aquatic Resources Management) see *FISH AND FISHERIES*

NASIONALE MUSEUM, BLOEMFONTEIN. NAVORSINGE/NATIONAL MUSEUM, BLOEMFONTEIN. RESEARCHES. see *SCIENCES: COMPREHENSIVE WORKS*

591　　　　　　　　SA　　ISSN 0304-0798
Q85　　　　　CODEN: ANMUA9
NATAL MUSEUM. ANNALS/NATALSE MUSEUM. ANNALE. (Text in English, French, German; summaries in English) 1906. a. price varies. Natal Museum, Private Bag 9070, Pietermaritzburg 3200, South Africa. TEL 27-331-451404. FAX 27-331-450561. Ed. D. Barraclough. R&P contact: D. Barraclough. cum.index. circ. 320. (back issues avail.) **Indexed:** Anthropol.Lit., Biol.Abstr., Deep Sea Res.& Oceanogr.Abstr., GeoRef., IBR, Ind.S.A.Per., Zoo.Rec. **Document type:** academic/scholarly publication.
—BLDSC (1030.000000); UnCover.
　Description: Research articles on systematic zoology, mainly entomology, arachnology, malacology, and lower invertebrates.
Refereed Serial

591　　　　　　　　NE　　ISSN 0459-1801
　　　　　　　　　CODEN: ZOBJAX
NATIONAAL NATUURHISTORISCH MUSEUM. ZOOLOGISCHE BIJDRAGEN. Key Title: Zoologische Bijdragen. (Text in Dutch, English, German; summaries in English) 1955. irreg., no.40, 1994. price varies. Nationaal Natuurhistorisch Museum, Postbus 9517, 2300 RA Leiden, Netherlands. E-mail: inform@nnm.nl. (Subscr. to: Backhuys Publishers - Universal Book Services, P.O. Box 321, 2300 AH Leiden, Netherlands. TEL 31-71-5170208. FAX 31-71-5171856) Pub. Haan Moll. R&P contact: Haan Moll. circ. 800. (back issues avail.) **Indexed:** Curr.Adv.Ecol.Sci., Sport Fish.Abstr., Wild.Rev., Zoo.Rec. **Document type:** monographic series.
—BLDSC (9522.000000); KNAW.
　Formerly: Rijksmuseum van Natuurlijke Historie. Zoologische Bijdragen.

591　　　　　　　　NE　　ISSN 0024-0672
QL1　　　　　CODEN: ZMRHAP
NATIONAAL NATUURHISTORISCH MUSEUM. ZOOLOGISCHE MEDEDELINGEN. Key Title: Zoologische Mededelingen. (Text mainly in English, occasionally in French or German) 1915. s-a. price varies. Nationaal Natuurhistorisch Museum, Postbus 9517, 2300 RA Leiden, Netherlands. (Subscr. to: Backhuys Publishers - Universal Book Services, P.O. Box 321, 2300 AH Leiden, Netherlands. TEL 31-71-5171208. FAX 31-71-5171856) R&P contact: C. van Achterberg. charts; illus. circ. 800. (back issues avail.) **Indexed:** Biol.Abstr., Curr.Adv.Ecol.Sci., Sport Fish.Abstr., Wild.Rev., Zoo.Rec. **Document type:** academic/scholarly publication.
—BLDSC (9526.000000); KNAW.
　Formerly: Rijksmuseum van Natuurlijke Historie. Zoologische Mededelingen.

591　　　　　　　　NE　　ISSN 0024-1652
QL1　　　　　CODEN: ZVRHAK
NATIONAAL NATUURLHISTORISCH MUSEUM. ZOOLOGISCHE VERHANDELINGEN. Key Title: Zoologische Verhandelingen. (Text in English, occasionally in French, German; summaries in English) 1948. irreg., vol.309, 1996. price varies. Nationaal Natuurhistorisch Museum, Postbus 9517, 2300 RA Leiden, Netherlands. (Subscr. to: Backhuys Publishers - Universal Book Services, P.O. Box 321, 2300 AH Leiden, Netherlands. TEL 31-71-5170208. FAX 31-71-5171856) R&P contact: C. van Achterberg. circ. 800. (back issues avail.) **Indexed:** Biol.Abstr., Curr.Adv.Ecol.Sci., Sport Fish.Abstr., Wild.Rev., Zoo.Rec. **Document type:** academic/scholarly publication.
—BLDSC (9527.000000); CISTI; KNAW.
　Formerly: Rijksmuseum van Natuurlijke Historie. Zoologische Verhandelingen.

NATIONAL RESEARCH INSTITUTE OF FAR SEAS FISHERIES. BULLETIN. see *FISH AND FISHERIES*

NATIONAL RESEARCH INSTITUTE OF FAR SEAS FISHERIES. S SERIES. see *FISH AND FISHERIES*

591.9　　　　　　　JA　　ISSN 0385-2423
QL325　　　　　CODEN: BMAZD5
NATIONAL SCIENCE MUSEUM. BULLETIN. SERIES A: ZOOLOGY/KOKURITSU KAGAKU HAKUBUTSUKAN KENKYU HOKOKU. A RUI: DOBUTSUGAKU. (Text in English) 1939. q. Monbusho, Kokuritsu Kagaku Hakubutsukan - Ministry of Education, Science and Culture, National Science Museum, 7-20 Ueno Park, Taito-ku, Tokyo 110, Japan. illus. **Indexed:** Biol.Abstr., Deep Sea Res.& Oceanogr.Abstr., INIS Atomind.
—BLDSC (2644.020000); CISTI; UnCover.
　Supersedes in part (in 1975): National Science Museum. Bulletin (ISSN 0028-0119)

NATUR UND TIERSCHUTZ KALENDER DES DEUTSCHEN TIERSCHUTZBUNDES. see *CHILDREN AND YOUTH — For*

591　　　　　　　　UK　　ISSN 0968-0470
QL1
NATURAL HISTORY MUSEUM. BULLETIN. ZOOLOGY. 1949. s-a. £78.75. Intercept Ltd., P.O. Box 716, Andover, Hants. SP10 1YG, England. TEL 01264-334748. FAX 01264-334058. illus.; stat. circ. 750. **Indexed:** Biol.Abstr., GeoRef., Helminthol.Abstr., Sport Fish.Abstr., Wild.Rev., Zoo.Rec. **Document type:** bulletin.
—BLDSC (2644.275000); CISTI; Linda Hall; UnCover.
　Formerly (until 1992): British Museum (Natural History). Bulletin. Zoology (ISSN 0007-1498)

NATURHISTORISCHES MUSEUM IN WIEN. ANNALEN. SERIE B: BOTANIK UND ZOOLOGIE. see *SCIENCES: COMPREHENSIVE WORKS*

591　　　　　　　　GW　　ISSN 0173-7481
　　　　　　　　　CODEN: AVNHAV
NATURWISSENSCHAFTLICHER VEREIN IN HAMBURG. ABHANDLUNGEN. 1937. irreg. price varies. Gustav Fischer Verlag, Wollgrasweg 49, 70599 Stuttgart, Germany. TEL 49-711-458030. FAX 49-711-4580334. Ed. Otto Kraus. bk.rev.; bibl.; illus.; index. (reprint service avail. from ISI) **Indexed:** Biol.Abstr., Chem.Abstr., GeoRef. **Document type:** monographic series.
—CISTI; Linda Hall.
　Supersedes in part: Naturwissenschaftlicher Verein in Hamburg. Abhandlungen und Verhandlungen (ISSN 0301-2697)

591　　　　　　　　GW　　ISSN 0173-749X
Q49
NATURWISSENSCHAFTLICHER VEREIN IN HAMBURG. VERHANDLUNGEN. irreg. (Naturwissenschaftlicher Verein in Hamburg) Gustav Fischer Verlag, Wollgrasweg 49, 70599 Stuttgart, Germany. TEL 49-711-458030. FAX 49-711-4580334. adv.; bk.rev.; bibl.; illus.; index. **Document type:** proceedings.
—CISTI; Linda Hall.
　Supersedes in part: Naturwissenschaftlicher Verein in Hamburg. Abhandlungen und Verhandlungen (ISSN 0301-2697)

NATURWISSENSCHAFTLICHER VEREIN WUPPERTAL. JAHRESBERICHTE. see *PALEONTOLOGY*

594　　　　　　　　US　　ISSN 0028-1344
QL401　　　　　CODEN: NUTLA5
NAUTILUS (SANIBEL ISLAND); a quarterly devoted to the interests of malacologists. 1886. q. $45 (overseas $50) (effective 1997). Bailey-Matthews Shell Museum, Box 1580, Sanibel Island, FL 33957. TEL 941-395-2233. FAX 941-395-6706. E-mail: Jhleal@aol.com. Ed. M.G. Harasewych. R&P contact: Jose P. Leal. adv.; bk.rev.; bibl.; charts; illus.; index. circ. 800. (back issues avail.; reprint service avail. from KTO) **Indexed:** Biol.Abstr., Curr.Adv.Ecol.Sci., Deep Sea Res.& Oceanogr.Abstr., Geo.Abstr., GeoRef., Helminthol.Abstr., Ind.Sci.Rev., Ocean.Abstr. Sel.Water Res.Abstr., So.Pac.Per.Ind., Soils & Fert., Zoo.Rec. **Document type:** academic/scholarly publication.
—BLDSC (6063.100000); CISTI; Genuine Article; Linda Hall; SWETS; UnCover.
　Formerly: Conchologists' Exchange.
Refereed Serial

591　　　　　　NE　　ISSN 0923-5701
NEDERLANDSE MALACOLOGISCHE VERENIGING. CORRESPONDENTIEBLAD. (Text in Dutch or language of contributor) 1934. 6/yr. fl.42.50. Nederlandse Malacologische Vereniging - Dutch Malacological Society, c/o R.G. Moolenbeek, Zoologisch Museum, Mauritskade 57, P.O. Box 94766, 1090 GT Amsterdam, Netherlands. FAX 31-20-5255402. bk.rev.; cum.index. circ. 600. **Document type:** newsletter.
—CISTI.

595.1　　　　　　BL　　ISSN 0102-2997
QL391.N4　　　　　　　CODEN: NEBRET
NEMATOLOGIA BRASILEIRA. 1974. a. $20 membership (effective 1996). Sociedade Brasileira de Nematologia, Secao de Nematologia, Caixa Postal 28, 13020-902 Campinas SP, Brazil. TEL 55-192-415188. FAX 55-192-314943. Ed. Rubens R.A. Lordello. bk.rev. **Indexed:** Helminthol.Abstr., Zoo.Rec. **Document type:** academic/scholarly publication.
—BLDSC (6075.493000); CASDDS.
Formerly (until 1983): Sociedade Brasileira de Nematologia. Publicacao (ISSN 0101-7020)
Refereed Serial

595.1　　　　　　NE　　ISSN 0028-2596
QL391.N4　　　　　　　CODEN: NEMAAT
NEMATOLOGICA; international journal of nematological research. (Text in English, French, German) 1956. 6/yr. fl.558($328) (effective 1998). E.J. Brill, P.O. Box 9000, 2300 PA Leiden, Netherlands. TEL 31-71-5353500. FAX 31-71-5317532. TELEX 39296 BRILL NL. E-mail: cs@brill.nl. (In N. America: E.J. Brill, 24 Hudson St., Kinderhook, NY 12106. TEL 800-962-4406. FAX 518-758-1959) Ed R. Cook. R&P contact: Elizabeth Vennekamp. bk.rev.; charts; illus.; index. (also avail. in microform from SWZ; back issues avail; reprint service avail. from SWZ) **Indexed:** ASCA, Bio-Contr.News & Info., Biol.Abstr., Biotech.Abstr., Chem.Abstr., Curr.Adv.Ecol.Sci., Curr.Cont., Ecol.Abstr., Excerp.Med., Helminthol.Abstr., Hort.Abstr., Ind.Sci.Rev., Maize Abstr., Plant Breed.Abstr., Plant Grow.Reg.Abstr., Potato Abstr., Sci.Cit.Ind., Soils & Fert., Triticale Abstr., VITIS, Weed Abstr., Zoo.Rec. **Document type:** academic/scholarly publication.
—BLDSC (6075.500000); CASDDS; CISTI; EMDOCS; Genuine Article; Linda Hall; SWETS; UnCover. **CCC.**
Description: Covers methodology, morphological, biochemical and molecular taxonomy and systematics of soil, plant, insect and marine nematodes.
Refereed Serial

590 598　　　　　US　　ISSN 0085-3887
QL1　　　　　　　CODEN: NOPHD2
NEMOURIA. Variant titles: Delaware Museum of Natural History. Occasional Papers. 1970. irreg., no.40, 1995. price varies. Delaware Museum of Natural History, Box 3937, Wilmington, DE 19807-0937. TEL 302-658-9111. FAX 302-658-2610. E-mail: tpearce@wittnet.com. Ed. Timothy A. Pearce. R&P contact: Paula M. Mikkelsen. circ. 100 (paid). (back issues avail.) **Indexed:** Biol.Abstr., M.L.A. **Document type:** academic/scholarly publication.
—Linda Hall.
Description: Publishes research papers on natural history, especially in the fields of malacology and ornithology.
Refereed Serial

599.8 333.95　　　SZ
NEOTROPICAL PRIMATES. a. $15. International Union for Conservation of Nature and Natural Resources, Species Survival Commission - Primate Specialist Group, Rue Mauverney 28, CH-1196 Gland, Switzerland. TEL 41-22-9990001. FAX 41-22-9990002. TELEX 419624-IUCN-CH. (Subscr. to: Conservation International, 1015 18th St., N.W., Ste. 1000, Washington, DC 20036 USA) **Document type:** newsletter.

591　　　　　　　　ISSN 0028-2960
QL1　　　　　　　CODEN: NEJZAL
NETHERLANDS JOURNAL OF ZOOLOGY. (Text in English) 1947. q. fl.247($145) to non-members; members fl.92 (effective 1998). (Nederlands Diekundige Vereniging - Netherlands Zoological Society) E.J. Brill, P.O. Box 9000, 2300 PA Leiden, Netherlands. TEL 31-71-5353500. FAX 31-71-5317532. E-mail: cs@brill.nl. (In N. America: E.J. Brill, 24 Hudson St., Kinderhook, NY 12106. TEL 800-962-4406. FAX 518-758-1959) Ed. R.G. Bout. charts; illus.; stat. (also avail. in microform from SWZ) **Indexed:** Apic.Abstr., ASCA, Bio-Contr.News & Info., Biol.Abstr., Chem.Abstr., Curr.Cont., Curr.Ref.Fish Res., Deep Sea Res.& Oceanogr.Abstr., Ecol.Abstr., Geo.Abstr., Helminthol.Abstr., IDA, Ind.Sci.Rev., Ind.Vet., Sci.Cit.Ind., Sport Fish.Abstr., Wild.Rev., Zoo.Rec. **Document type:** academic/scholarly publication.
—BLDSC (6077.025000); CISTI; Genuine Article; Linda Hall; SWETS; UnCover.
Formerly (until 1968): Archives Neerlandaise de Zoologie (ISSN 0365-5164)
Description: Publishes studies with an experimental or functional approach to topics in behavioral and physiological ecology, ecological and functional morphology, environmental physiology and biosystematics.
Refereed Serial

NETTAI DOSHOKUBUTSU TOMO NO KAI KAIHO/NEWS OF THE TROPICAL PLANTS AND ANIMALS. see *BIOLOGY — Botany*

NEUE DENKSCHRIFTEN DES NATURHISTORISCHEN MUSEUMS IN WIEN. see *EARTH SCIENCES*

NEW YORK STATE CONSERVATIONIST. see *CONSERVATION*

591　　　　　　NZ　　ISSN 0301-4223
QL340　　　　　　　CODEN: NZJZAW
NEW ZEALAND JOURNAL OF ZOOLOGY. 1974. q. NZ.$140($90) to individuals; institutions NZ.$300 ($200) (effective 1997). (Royal Society of New Zealand) S I R Publishing, P.O. Box 399, Wellington, New Zealand. TEL 64-4-472-7421. FAX 64-4-473-1841. E-mail: nzjz@rsnz.govt.nz; URL: http://www.rsnz.govt.nz (US subscr. to: SIR Publishing, 810 East 10th St., Box 1897, Lawrence, KS 66044-8897, USA. TEL 913-843-1221) Ed. C.M. King. circ. 300. (back issues avail.) **Indexed:** ASCA, Bio-Contr.News & Info., Biol.Abstr., Curr.Adv.Ecol.Sci., Curr.Cont., Curr.Ref.Fish Res., Dairy Sci.Abstr., Deep Sea Res.& Oceanogr.Abstr., Ecol.Abstr., Environ.Abstr., Field Crop Abstr., Forest.Abstr., Geo.Abstr., Helminthol.Abstr., Herb.Abstr., Hort.Abstr., Ind.Sci.Rev., Ind.Vet., Key Word Ind.Wildl.Res., Rev.Appl.Entomol., So.Pac.Per.Ind., Soils & Fert., Triticale Abstr., Vet.Bull. **Document type:** academic/scholarly publication.
—BLDSC (6095.300000); CASDDS; CISTI; Genuine Article; KNAW; Linda Hall; UnCover. **CCC.**
Description: Publishes papers on all aspects of Zoology in the Pacific and Antarctic regions.
Refereed Serial

595.7　　　　　　NR　　ISSN 0331-0094
QL461　　　　　　　CODEN: NJENDW
NIGERIAN JOURNAL OF ENTOMOLOGY. 1974. s-a. £N20. Entomological Society of Nigeria, c/o Anthony Youdeowei, Department of Agricultural Biology, University of Ibadan, Ibadan, Oyo State, Nigeria. Ed. Olupomi Ajayi. illus. circ. 500. **Indexed:** Biol.Abstr., Chem.Abstr., Field Crop Abstr., Herb.Abstr., Rev.Appl.Entomol. **Document type:** academic/scholarly publication.
—CASDDS.
Supersedes: Entomological Society of Nigeria. Bulletin (ISSN 0425-1067)

591　　　　　　JA　　ISSN 0285-385X
NIHON DOBUTSU GAKKAI CHUGOKU SHIKOKU SHIBU KAIHO/ZOOLOGICAL SOCIETY OF JAPAN. CHUGOKU - SHIKOKU BRANCH. PROCEEDINGS. (Text in English, Japanese) 1947. a. membership. Nihon Dobutsu Gakkai, Chugoku Shikoku Shibu - Zoological Society of Japan, Chugoku - Shikoku Branch, Hiroshima Daigaku Rigakubu Dobutsugaku Kyoshitsu, 1-89 Higashisendamachi 1-chome, Naka-ku, Hiroshima-shi, Hiroshima-ken 730, Japan. **Document type:** proceedings.

591　　　　　　JA
NIHON DOBUTSUEN SUIZOKUKAN NENPO/JAPANESE ASSOCIATION OF ZOOLOGICAL GARDENS AND AQUARIUMS. ANNUAL REPORT. (Text in Japanese) 1951. a. Nihon Dobutsuen Suizokukan Kyokai - Japanese Association of Zoological Gardens and Aquariums, 13-2 Ueno 2-chome, Taito-ku, Tokyo 110, Japan.

NIHON GYORUI GAKKAI NENKAI KOEN YOSHI/ICHTHYOLOGY SOCIETY OF JAPAN. ADVANCE ABSTRACTS FOR THE ANNUAL MEETING. see *BIOLOGY — Abstracting, Bibliographies, Statistics*

NIHON JIKKEN DOBUTSU GAKKAI SOKAI KOEN YOSHISHU/JAPANESE ASSOCIATION FOR LABORATORY ANIMAL SCIENCE. ABSTRACTS OF GENERAL MEETING. see *MEDICAL SCIENCES — Abstracting, Bibliographies, Statistics*

NIHON JIKKEN DOBUTSU GIJUTSUSHA KYOKAI HOKKAIDO SHIBU KAISHI/JAPANESE ASSOCIATION FOR EXPERIMENTAL ANIMAL TECHNOLOGISTS. HOKKAIDO BRANCH. JOURNAL. see *MEDICAL SCIENCES — Experimental Medicine, Laboratory Technique*

594　　　　　　JA
NIHON KABUTOGANI O MAMORU KAI KAIHO/HORSESHOE CRAB. (Text in Japanese) 1979. a. membership. Nihon Kabutogani o Mamoru Kai - Japanese Horseshoe Crab Observation Association, Kabutogani Hogo Senta, 1950-3, Yokoshima, Kasaoka-shi, Okayama-ken 714, Japan.

599.8　　　　　　JA
NIHON MONKI SENTA NENPO/JAPAN MONKEY CENTER. ANNUAL REPORT. (Text in Japanese) 1988. a. Nihon Monki Senta - Japan Monkey Center, 26, Inuyama Kanrin, Inuyama-shi, Aichi-ken 484, Japan. TEL 81-568-61-2327. FAX 81-568-62-6823. Dir. Mitsuo Iwamoto. circ. 500. **Document type:** corporate report.

NIHON OYO DOBUTSU KONCHU GAKKAI CHUGOKU SHIBU KAIHO/JAPANESE SOCIETY OF APPLIED ENTOMOLOGY AND ZOOLOGY. CHUGOKU BRANCH. JOURNAL. see *BIOLOGY — Entomology*

591 595.7　　　　　JA
NIHON OYO DOBUTSU KONCHU GAKKAI KYUSHU SHIBU KAIHO/DELPHAX. (Text in Japanese) a. Nihon Oyo Dobutsu Konchu Gakkai, Kyushu Shibu - Japanese Society of Applied Entomology and Zoology, Kyushu Branch, Kyushu Nogyo Shikenjo Chiiki Kiban Kenkyubu, 2421 Suya, Nishigoshimachi, Kikuchi-gun, Kumamoto-ken 861-11, Japan.

599.8　　　　　　JA
NIHON REICHORUI GAKKAI TAIKAI YOKOSHU/PRIMATE SOCIETY OF JAPAN. PREPRINTS OF THE ANNUAL MEETING. (Text in English, Japanese) 1985. a. Nihon Reichorui Gakkai - Primate Society of Japan, Kyoto Daigaku Reichorui Kenkyujo, Inuyama Kanrin, Inuyama-shi, Aichi-ken 484, Japan. Ed. Osamu Takenaka. **Document type:** academic/scholarly publication.

595.1　　　　　　JA　　ISSN 0919-343X
NIHON SENCHU GAKKAI NYUSU/JAPAN NEMATOLOGY NEWS. (Text in Japanese) 1972. s-a. Nihon Senchu Gakkai - Japanese Nematological Society, National Agriculture Research Center, Kannondai, Tsukuba, Ibaraki-ken 305, Japan. TEL 81-298-38-8839. FAX 81-298-38-8837. E-mail: kshimz@narc.affrc.go.jp. Ed. N. Minagawa.
Formerly (until 1993): Nihon Senchu Kenkyukai Nyusu (ISSN 0911-7350)

595.1　　　　　　JA　　ISSN 0919-6765
NIHON SENCHU GAKKAISHI/JAPANESE JOURNAL OF NEMATOLOGY. (Text in English, Japanese) 1972. s-a. $35. Nihon Senchu Gakkai - Japanese Nematological Society, National Agriculture Research Center, Kannondai, Tsukuba, Ibaraki-ken 305, Japan. Ed. N. Minagawa. R&P contact: N. Minagawa. **Indexed:** Agrindex. **Document type:** academic/scholarly publication.
—BLDSC (4656.637000).
Formerly: Nihon Senchu Kenkyukaishi (ISSN 0388-2357)

NIPPON DOBUTSU KODO GAKKAI TAIKAI HAPPYO YOSHISHU/JAPAN ETHOLOGICAL SOCIETY. ABSTRACTS OF MEETING. see *BIOLOGY — Abstracting, Bibliographies, Statistics*

BIOLOGY — ZOOLOGY

591   JA
NOGEYAMA DOBUTSUEN NENPO/NOGEYAMA ZOOLOGICAL GARDENS. ANNUAL REPORT. (Text in Japanese) a. Yokohamashi Nogeyama Dobutsuen - Nogeyama Zoological Gardens of Yokohama, 63-10 Oimatsucho, Nishi-ku, Yokohama-shi, Kanagawa-ken 220, Japan.

590   UK   ISSN 0078-0952
NOMENCLATOR ZOOLOGICUS. 1939. irreg., vol.7, 1975. £30. Zoological Society of London, Regent's Park, London NW1 4RY, England.
FAX 071-483-4436. Eds. Marcia A. Edwards, H. Gwynne Vevers.
Description: Records of bibliographic origins of published generic and subgeneric names in zoology.

592.092905   CN
NORTH AMERICAN BENTHOLOGICAL SOCIETY. BULLETIN. 1984. 3/yr. $25. North American Benthological Society, c/o Lynda Corkum, Sec., Dept. of Biological Sciences, University of Windsor, Windsor, ON N9B 3PA, Canada.
TEL 519-253-4232. FAX 519-971-3609. (Subscr. to: NABS, Box 1897, Lawrence, KS 66044-8897. TEL 800-627-0629; Editorial addr.: c/o Chadwick & Associates, 5575 S. Sycamore St., Ste. 101, Littleton, CO 80120. TEL 303-794-5530. FAX 303-794-5041) Ed. Steven P. Canton. adv.; bk.rev.; abstr.; bibl.; index. **Document type:** bulletin, bibliography.
Description: Promotes better understanding of the benthic biological community and its role in aquatics ecosystems. Communicates information about society functions and activities, including abstracts of meetings.

592.092905   CN   ISSN 0887-3593
QL141   CODEN: JNASEC
NORTH AMERICAN BENTHOLOGICAL SOCIETY. JOURNAL. 1982. q. $60 to institutions (effective 1995). North American Benthological Society, c/o Lynda Corkum, Sec., Dept. of Biological Sciences, University of Windsor, Windsor, ON N9B 3PA, Canada.
TEL 519-253-4232. FAX 519-971-3609. (Subscr. to: NABS, Box 1897, Lawrence, KS 66044-8897. TEL 800-627-0629) Ed. Rosemary Mackay. (back issues avail.) **Indexed:** ASCA, Curr.Cont., Sport Fish.Abstr., Wild.Rev., Zoo.Rec. **Document type:** academic/scholarly publication.
—BLDSC (4833.740000); EMDOCS; Linda Hall; SWETS; UnCover.
Formerly (until 1986): Freshwater Invertebrate Biology (ISSN 0738-2189)
Description: Promotes better understanding of the biotic communities of lake and stream bottoms and their role in aquatic ecosystems.
Refereed Serial

591   US   ISSN 0078-1304
QL155   CODEN: XIWFAS
NORTH AMERICAN FAUNA. (Subseries of: Biological Science Reports (ISSN 1081-292X)). 1889. irreg. U.S. National Biological Service, Information Transfer Center, c/o Managing Editor, 1201 Oak Ridge Dr., Ste. 200, CO 80525-5589. TEL 970-226-9401. FAX 970-226-9455. (Orders to: U.S. Fish and Wildlife Service, Publications Unit, MS-130, Webb Bldg., 4401 N. Fairfax Dr., Arlington, VA 22203) (also avail. in microform from NTI; microfiche from BHP) **Indexed:** Biol.Abstr., Ecol.Abstr., Sport Fish.Abstr., Wild.Rev., Zoo.Rec. **Document type:** academic/scholarly publication, monographic series, government publication.
●Also available online.
—BLDSC (6148.000000); CISTI; Linda Hall.
Description: Publishes high-quality original scientific and review articles and reports.
Refereed Serial

591   US   ISSN 1051-1733
QL1   CODEN: NNATEP
NORTHWESTERN NATURALIST; a journal of vertebrate biology. 1920. 3/yr. $20 to individuals (foreign $25); institutions $50; students $12 (effective 1997). (Society for Northwestern Vertebrate Biology) Allen Press, 1041 New Hampshire Ave., Box 1897, Lawrence, KS 66044.
TEL 913-843-0629. FAX 913-843-1274. Ed. Paul Steven Corn. adv.; bk.rev.; charts; illus.; stat.; cum.index every 10 yrs. circ. 600. (also avail. in microform from UMI; back issues avail.; reprint service avail. from UMI) **Indexed:** Biol.Abstr., Ecol.Abstr., Ref.Zh., Sport Fish.Abstr., Wild Life Rev., Wild.Rev., Zoo.Rec. **Document type:** academic/scholarly publication.
—CISTI; UnCover.
Formerly: Murrelet (ISSN 0027-3716)
Description: Publishes original contributions dealing with the biology of terrestrial vertebrates of northwestern North America.
Refereed Serial

914.5   IT   ISSN 1121-161X
NOTIZIARIO S I M. 1983. 3/yr. membership. Societa Italiana di Malacologia, Viale Gadio 2, 20121 Milan. FAX 39-2-468563. E-mail: socitmal@mbox.vol.it. Ed. Riccardo Giannuzzi-Savelli. adv.; bk.rev. **Document type:** newsletter.

NYALA. see *CONSERVATION*

551.46   SA   ISSN 0078-320X
GC1   CODEN: ORIIAX
OCEANOGRAPHIC RESEARCH INSTITUTE. INVESTIGATIONAL REPORT. 1961. irreg., no.69, 1996. exchange basis. Oceanographic Research Institute, P.O. Box 10712, Marine Parade, Durban 4056, South Africa. TEL 27-31-373536. FAX 27-31-372132. (Co-sponsor: South African Association for Marine Biological Research) Ed. R.P. Van der Elst. R&P contact: R.P. Van der Elst. circ. 400 (controlled). (back issues avail.) **Indexed:** Aqua.Sci.& Fish.Abstr., Biol.Abstr., Deep Sea Res.& Oceanogr.Abstr., Ecol.Abstr., Ocean.Abstr., Zoo.Rec. **Document type:** academic/scholarly publication.
—BLDSC (4560.120000).
Description: Presents detailed results of current marine biological research.
Refereed Serial

OCEANOGRAPHIC RESEARCH INSTITUTE. POSTER SERIES. see *EARTH SCIENCES — Oceanography*

OCEANOGRAPHIC RESEARCH INSTITUTE. SPECIAL PUBLICATION. see *EARTH SCIENCES — Oceanography*

594   US   ISSN 0030-0055
   CODEN: OSSHDM
OF SEA AND SHORE. 1970. q. $15. Of Sea & Shore Publications, Box 219, Port Gamble, WA 98364. TEL 360-297-2426. FAX 360-297-2426. E-mail: ofseashr@pacific.telebyte.com. Ed. Thomas C. Rice. adv.; bk.rev.; illus.; index. (also avail. in microfilm from UMI; reprint service avail. from UMI)
—CISTI; Linda Hall; UMI.
Description: Covers all aspects of shell collection.

591 333.7   US
OF THE WORLD SERIES. 1986. a. $27.95. Facts on File, Inc., 11 Penn Plaza, 15th Fl., New York, NY 10001. TEL 212-967-8800. bibl.; index.
Description: Book series on all kinds of wild animals and insects.

OHIO FISH AND WILDLIFE REPORT. see *CONSERVATION*

OPERA LILLOANA. see *BIOLOGY — Botany*

590   HU   ISSN 0473-1034
QL1   CODEN: OPUZAS
OPUSCULA ZOOLOGICA. (Text in English, German) 1956. s-a. $12. Universitas Budapestinensis, Institutum Zoosystematicum et Oecologicum, Puskin u. 3, 1088 Budapest 8, Hungary. Eds. I. Andrassy, A. Berczik. charts; illus.; stat. circ. 800. **Indexed:** Biol.Abstr., Helminthol.Abstr.
—BLDSC (6277.200000); CISTI; Linda Hall.

591   SZ   ISSN 1010-5220
QL461   CODEN: OZFLEJ
OPUSCULA ZOOLOGICA FLUMINENSIA. 1984. irreg. (approx. 14/yr.). price varies. Flumserberg Scientific Publishers, Casa d'Uors, Postfach 34, CH-8896 Flumserberg, Switzerland. TEL 081-332214. Ed. Dr. B. Kiauta. adv.; bk.rev. circ. 600. **Indexed:** Chem.Abstr., Entomol.Abstr. **Document type:** academic/scholarly publication.
—BLDSC (6277.212000).
Description: Original research papers in the field of invertebrate zoology and entomology, with emphasis on taxonomic revisions and descriptions of new taxa, mostly insects.
Refereed Serial

ORYX. see *CONSERVATION*

591.16   UK   ISSN 0260-0854
QP251   CODEN: ORRBDQ
OXFORD REVIEWS OF REPRODUCTIVE BIOLOGY. 1979. a. $120. Oxford University Press, Oxford Journals, Walton St., Oxford OX2 6DP, England.
TEL 44-1865-56767. FAX 44-1865-56646. (Subscr. in US to: Oxford University Press Inc., 2001 Evans Rd., Cary, NC 27513. TEL 919-677-0977. FAX 919-677-1714) Ed. C.A. Finn. illus. (also avail. in microform from UMI) **Indexed:** ASCA, Chem.Abstr., Curr.Adv.Biochem., Curr.Adv.Cell & Devel.Biol., Curr.Adv.Genetics & Molec.Biol., Ind.Sci.Rev., Ind.Vet., Poult.Abstr., Vet.Bull. **Document type:** academic/scholarly publication.
—CASDDS; CISTI; Linda Hall; UMI; UnCover. **CCC**.
Refereed Serial

P A S C A L. T 260: ZOOLOGIE FONDAMENTALE ET APPLIQUEE DES INVERTEBRES. see *BIOLOGY — Abstracting, Bibliographies, Statistics*

PACHYDERM. see *CONSERVATION*

591   PK   ISSN 1013-3461
QL1   CODEN: PKCZEK
PAKISTAN CONGRESS OF ZOOLOGY. PROCEEDINGS. (Text in English) a., no.15, 1995. $100. Zoological Society of Pakistan - Pakistan Anjuman Hayawaniyyat, c/o Department of Zoology, University of the Punjab, New Campus, Lahore, Pakistan. TEL 92-42-5868376. Eds. Dr. Muzaffer Ahmad, Dr. A.R. Shakoori. R&P contact: A.R. Shakoori. circ. 300. **Document type:** proceedings, academic/scholarly publication.
—BLDSC (6848.575000); CASDDS.
Refereed Serial

595.182 581.5   PK   ISSN 0255-7576
   CODEN: PJNEE5
PAKISTAN JOURNAL OF NEMATOLOGY. (Text in English) 1983. s-a. Rps.100($43) (effective 1996). Pakistan Society of Nematologists, National Nematological Research Centre, University of Karachi, Karachi 75270, Pakistan.
FAX 92-21-4963373. E-mail: mag@nema.khi.crum.com.pk. Ed. Abdul Ghaffar. R&P contact: M.A. Maqbool. adv. contact: M.A. Maqbool. circ. 600 (controlled). (back issues avail.; reprint service avail. from ISI, UMI) **Indexed:** Zoo.Rec. **Document type:** academic/scholarly publication.
—BLDSC (6341.600000).
Refereed Serial

591   PK   ISSN 0030-9923
QL1   CODEN: PJZOAN
PAKISTAN JOURNAL OF ZOOLOGY. (Text in English) 1969. q. $100. Zoological Society of Pakistan, c/o Department of Zoology, University of the Punjab, New Campus, Lahore, Pakistan.
TEL 92-42-5868376. Eds. Muzaffer Ahmad, A.R. Shakoori. R&P contact: A.R. Shakoori. adv.; bk.rev.; charts; illus.; stat.; index. circ. 500. (also avail. in microfilm; back issues avail.) **Indexed:** Apic.Abstr., Biol.Abstr., Chem.Abstr., Curr.Cont., Deep Sea Res.& Oceanogr.Abstr., Food Sci.& Tech.Abstr., Helminthol.Abstr., Ind.Med., Ind.Vet., Maize Abstr., Ocean.Abstr., Pollut.Abstr., Protozool.Abstr., Rev.Appl.Entomol., Soils & Fert., Triticale Abstr., Trop.Oil Seeds Abstr., Vet.Bull., Zoo.Rec. **Document type:** academic/scholarly publication.
—BLDSC (6343.015000); CASDDS; CISTI; Linda Hall; UnCover. **CCC**.
Refereed Serial

PALAEO ICHTHYOLOGICA. see *PALEONTOLOGY*

BIOLOGY — ZOOLOGY

591   **BL**   ISSN 0031-1049
QL1   CODEN: PAZOAS
PAPEIS AVULSOS DE ZOOLOGIA. (Text in various languages) 1941. irreg. $15 (effective 1997). Universidade de Sao Paulo, Museu de Zoologia, Caixa Postal 42699, 04299-970 Sao Paulo SP, Brazil. Ed. Carlos Roberto Ferreira Brandao. illus.; index. circ. 800. (back issues avail.) **Indexed:** Abstr.Bull.Inst.Pap.Chem., Biol.Abstr., Curr.Adv.Ecol.Sci., Rev.Appl.Entomol., Zoo.Rec. **Document type:** monographic series.
—BLDSC (6358.100000); CISTI; Linda Hall.

591   **US**   ISSN 0738-4394
QL750
PERSPECTIVES IN ETHOLOGY. 1973. irreg., vol.11, 1995. price varies. Plenum Publishing Corp., 233 Spring St., New York, NY 10013-1578. TEL 212-620-8000. FAX 212-463-0742. TELEX 23-421139. E-mail: books@plenum.com. Eds. P.P.G. Bateson, P.H. Klopfer. (back issues avail.) **Document type:** monographic series.
—KNAW.
Refereed Serial

596   **NE**   ISSN 0169-7277
                        CODEN: PVSCD5
PERSPECTIVES IN VERTEBRATE SCIENCE. (Text in English) 1980. irreg. price varies. Kluwer Academic Publishers, Postbus 17, 3300 AA Dordrecht, Netherlands. TEL 31-78-6392392. FAX 31-78-6392392. TELEX 29245 KAPG NL. E-mail: services@wkap.nl; URL: http://www.wkap.nl. (Dist. by: Kluwer Academic Publishers Group, P.O. Box 322, 3300 AH Dordrecht, Netherlands. TEL 31-78-6392392. FAX 31-78-6546474; N. America dist. addr.: Box 358, Accord Sta., Hingham, MA 02018-0358. TEL 617-871-6600. FAX 617-871-6528) **Document type:** monographic series.
—BLDSC (6428.179000); CASDDS; CISTI.
Refereed Serial

591   **BL**   ISSN 0373-8418
QL1   CODEN: PQZOA4
PESQUISAS: PUBLICACOES DE ZOOLOGIA. Key Title: Pesquisas. Zoologia. (Numbering continues those of articles published in Pesquisas) 1957. irreg. price varies or exchange basis. (Universidade do Vale do Rio dos Sinos, Instituto Anchietano de Pesquisas) Unisinos, Av. Unisinos, 950, 93022-000 Sao Leopoldo RS, Brazil. TEL 55-51-5903333 ext. 1951. FAX 55-51-5921035. **Document type:** academic/scholarly publication.
—CISTI.
Supersedes in part (in 1960): Instituto Anchietano de Pesquisas. Pesquisas (ISSN 0480-1873)

591   **US**   ISSN 0031-935X
QL1   CODEN: PHZOA9
PHYSIOLOGICAL ZOOLOGY; a bi-monthly journal of zoological research. 1928. bi-m. $67 to non-member individuals (Canada $82.69; elsewhere $78); institutions $298 (Canada $329.86; elsewhere $309); students $40 (Canada $53.80; elsewhere $51); members $53 (Canada $67.71; elsewhere $64) (effective 1998). (American Society of Zoologists, Division of Comparative Physiology and Biochemistry) University of Chicago Press, Journals Division, Box 37005, Chicago, IL 60637. TEL 773-753-3347. FAX 773-753-0811. TELEX 25-4603. E-mail: subscriptions@journals.uchicago.edu; URL: http://www.journals.uchicago.edu/PZ/. Ed. Charlotte Magnumen. adv.: page $355; trim 8 1/2 x 11. bk.rev.; bibl.; charts; illus.; index. circ. 1,400. (also avail. in microform from UMI,PMC; reprint service avail. from UMI,ISI) **Indexed:** Anim.Breed.Abstr., Apic.Abstr., ASCA, Bio-Contr.News & Info., Biol.Abstr., Biol.& Agr.Ind., Chem.Abstr., Curr.Adv.Ecol.Sci., Curr.Cont., Curr.Ref.Fish Res., Dairy Sci.Abstr., Deep Sea Res.& Oceanogr.Abstr., Ecol.Abstr., Excerp.Med., Ind.Sci.Rev., Ind.Vet., Int.Abstr.Biol.Sci., Nutr.Abstr., Poult.Abstr., Protozool.Abstr., Rev.Appl.Entomol., Sci.Cit.Ind., Sci.Cit.Ind., Soils & Fert., Sport Fish.Abstr., SSCI, Vet.Bull., Wild.Rev., Zoo.Rec. **Document type:** academic/scholarly publication.
—BLDSC (6487.000000); CASDDS; CISTI; EMDOCS; Genuine Article; KNAW; KR SourceOne; Linda Hall; SWETS; UMI; UnCover. **CCC.**
Description: Provides an outlet for research in environmental and adaptational physiology and biochemistry. Explores comparative physiology, as well as physiological ecology.
Refereed Serial

591 581   **AG**   ISSN 0326-1441
                        CODEN: PHSAC2
PHYSIS. (In 3 sections: Section A (ISSN 0325-0342), Section B (ISSN 0325-0350), Section C (ISSN 0325-0369)) (Text mainly in Spanish, occasionally in English, French; summaries in English, Spanish) 1912. s-a. $100 (effective 1996). Asociacion Argentina de Ciencias Naturales, Museo Argentino de Ciencias Naturales "Bernardino Rivadavia", Avenida Angel Gallardo 470, 1405 Buenos Aires, Argentina. TEL 54-1-9828370. FAX 54-1-9824494. E-mail: physis@muanbe.gov.ar. Ed. Juan Carlos Giacchi. bk.rev.; charts; illus.; cum.index: 1912-1982. circ. 500. (back issues avail.) **Indexed:** Biol.Abstr., Curr.Adv.Ecol.Sci., Curr.Cont., Deep Sea Res.& Oceanogr.Abstr., Geo.Abstr., GeoRef, Helminthol.Abstr., Math.R. **Document type:** academic/scholarly publication.
—CISTI.
Description: Devoted to zoology and botany (systematics, physiology, distribution, ecology, histology, embryology and anatomy) mainly of South America.
Refereed Serial

PISCIUM CATALOGUS. see *PALEONTOLOGY*

590   **CU**   ISSN 0257-6902
QH109.C9   CODEN: PZCCAI
POEYANA. (Text in Spanish; abstracts in English) 1964. irreg., no.454, 1995. Academia de Ciencias de Cuba, Instituto de Ecologia y Sistematica, Apdo. Postal 8010, 10800 Havana 8, Cuba. bibl.; charts; illus. circ. 2,000. **Indexed:** Biol.Abstr., Deep Sea Res.& Oceanogr.Abstr., Rev.Appl.Entomol., Sport Fish.Abstr., Wild.Rev., Zoo.Rec.
Formerly (until Mar. 1974): Serie Poeyana (ISSN 0032-2229); Formed by the 1970 merger of: Poeyana. Serie A (ISSN 0554-4068); Poeyana. Serie B (ISSN 0554-4076)

594   **NZ**   ISSN 0032-2377
POIRIERIA. 1962. 2/yr. membership. Auckland Museum and Institute, Conchology Section, Private Bag 92018, Auckland, New Zealand. Ed. Glenys Stace. adv. contact: Glenys Stace. bk.rev. circ. 200. **Document type:** academic/scholarly publication.
—BLDSC (6541.873000). **CCC.**
Description: Provides information relevant to mollosc shell and related aspects of marine biology.

636   **PL**   ISSN 0137-1649
                        CODEN: PMZTAP
POLSKA AKADEMIA NAUK. INSTYTUT GENETYKI I HODOWLI ZWIERZAT. PRACE I MATERIALY ZOOTECHNICZNE. 1963. irreg. Polska Akademia Nauk, Instytut Genetyki i Hodowli Zwierzat, 05-551 Mrokow, Jastrzebiec, Poland. **Indexed:** AgroLibrex. **Document type:** academic/scholarly publication.
—BLDSC (6588.935000); CASDDS.
Former titles (until 1973): Polska Akademia Nauk. Instytut Genetyki i Hodowli Zwierzat. Biuletyn (ISSN 0137-2157); (until 1970): Polska Akademia Nauk. Zaklad Hodowli Doswiadczalnej Zwierzat. Biuletyn (ISSN 0554-5943)

636   **PL**   ISSN 1231-8388
POLSKA AKADEMIA NAUK. INSTYTUT GENETYKI I HODOWLI ZWIERZAT. PRACE I MATERIALY ZOOTECHNICZNE. ZESZYT SPECJALNY. 1992. irreg. Polska Akademia Nauk, Instytut Genetyki i Hodowli Zwierzat, 05-551 Mrokow, Jastrzebiec, Poland. **Document type:** academic/scholarly publication.

597 639.3   **PO**
PORTUGAL. INSTITUTO PORTUGUES DE INVESTIGACAO MARITIMA. BOLETIM. (Text in English, French, Portuguese; summaries in English, Portuguese) 1952. irreg., no.17, 1992. $20 or exchange basis. Instituto Portugues de Investigacao Maritima, Av. de Brasilia, 1400 Lisbon, Portugal. TEL 351-1-3010814. FAX 351-1-3015948. TELEX 15857 IPIMAR. Ed. Maria de Lourdes Paes da Franca. circ. 500. **Indexed:** Aqua.Sci.& Fish.Abstr., Sel.Water Res.Abstr. **Document type:** academic/scholarly publication, government publication.
Formerly: Portugal. Instituto Nacional de Investigacao das Pescas. Boletim (ISSN 0870-1245); Supersedes (in 1979): Notas e Estudos, Serie Recursos e Ambiente Aquaticos (ISSN 0251-091X); Lisbon. Instituto de Biologia Maritima. Notas e Estudos (ISSN 0020-3777)

597 639.3   **PO**   ISSN 0872-914X
SH281
PORTUGAL. INSTITUTO PORTUGUES DE INVESTIGACAO MARITIMA. PUBLICACOES AVULSAS. 1982. irreg., no.24, 1993. $20 or exchange basis. Instituto Portugues de Investigacao Maritima, Av. de Brasilia, 1400 Lisbon, Portugal. TEL 351-1-3010814. FAX 351-1-3015948. TELEX 15857 IPIMAR. Ed. Maria de Lourdes Paes da Franca. **Indexed:** Aqua.Sci.& Fish.Abstr. **Document type:** academic/scholarly publication, government publication.
Formerly: Portugal. Instituto Nacional de Investigacao das Pescas. Publicacoes Avulsas (ISSN 0870-0435)

POULTRY AND AVIAN BIOLOGY REVIEWS. see *AGRICULTURE — Poultry And Livestock*

593.6   **JA**   ISSN 0918-726X
PRECIOUS CORALS & OCTOCORAL RESEARCH. (Text in English) 1993. s-a. 6000 Yen. Nihon Nantai Dobutsu Gakkai - Laboratory for Biological, Economic and Technological Research of Organic Jewelry, 6-36, Midoricho 3-chome, Tanashi-shi, Tokyo 188, Japan. TEL 81-424-63-0851. FAX 81-424-61-1752. Ed. Sadao Kosuge. R&P contact: Sadao Kosuge. adv. contact: Sadao Kosuge.

PRIMATE REPORT. see *ANTHROPOLOGY*

599.8   **JA**   ISSN 0032-8332
QL737.P9   CODEN: PRMTBU
PRIMATES; journal of primatology. (Text in English) 1957. q. 15000 Yen to foreign individuals; institutions 22000 Yen (effective 1997). Japan Monkey Centre - Nihon Monki Senta, Kanrin Inuyama 26, Aichi 484, Japan. TEL 81-568-61-2327. FAX 81-568-62-6823. Ed. Yukimaru Sugiyama. R&P contact: Mitsuo Iwamoto. adv.; bk.rev.; abstr.; charts; illus.; stat. circ. 800. **Indexed:** Abstr.Anthropol., Anthropol.Lit., Curr.Cont., Ind.Sci.Rev., Ind.Vet., Psychol.Abstr. (1966-), Sci.Cit.Ind., Sport Fish.Abstr., SSCI, Vet.Bull., Wild.Rev., Zoo.Rec. **Document type:** academic/scholarly publication.
—BLDSC (6612.925000); CASDDS; CISTI; Genuine Article; KNAW; Linda Hall; SWETS; UnCover.

591   **JA**
PROBLEMS IN MODERN ZOOLOGY. (Text in Japanese) irreg.? Zoological Society of Japan, Toshin Bldg., 2-27-2 Hongo, Bunkyo-ku, Tokyo 113, Japan. TEL 81-3-5814-5811. FAX 81-3-3814-5352. Ed. Seiichiro Kawashima. **Document type:** monographic series.

593   **US**
PROGRESS IN PROTOZOOLOGY. (Published in host country) 1961. quadrennial, 9th, 1993, Berlin, Germany. International Congress on Protozoology, c/o Lea Bleyman, Baruch College - CUNY, Dept. of Natural Sciences, 17 Lexington Ave., Box A0505, New York, NY 10010. TEL 212-387-1240. FAX 212-387-1258. **Document type:** proceedings, academic/scholarly publication.
Formerly: International Conference on Protozoology. Proceedings (ISSN 0074-3267)

PROGRESSIVE FISH-CULTURIST. see *FISH AND FISHERIES*

591   **US**
PROTOCOLS IN PROTOZOOLOGY. irreg. $50 hardbound; looseleaf $40 (members $35; students $30). (Society of Protozoologists) Allen Press, Inc., Box 1897, Lawrence, KS 66044-8897. TEL 913-843-1221. FAX 913-843-1274. Eds. J.J. Lee, A.T. Soldo. (looseleaf format) **Document type:** academic/scholarly publication.
Description: Aims to advance the science by training students and educating others in the understanding and use of protozoa.

BIOLOGY — ZOOLOGY

591   PL   ISSN 0033-247X
QL1   CODEN: PZOOAC
PRZEGLAD ZOOLOGICZNY. (Text in Polish; contents and summaries in English) 1957. q. 16 Zl. Polskie Towarzystwo Zoologiczne, Ul. Sienkiewicza 21, 50-335 Wroclaw, Poland. TEL 48-71-225041. FAX 48-71-222817. (Dist. by: ORPAN, Palac Kultury i Nauki, 00-901 Warsaw, Poland) Ed. S. Bednarz. adv. contact: R.J. Pomorski. bk.rev.; bibl.; illus.; index. circ. 1,420. **Indexed:** AgroLibrex, Biol.Abstr., Bull.Signal., Chem.Abstr., Deep Sea Res.& Oceanogr.Abstr., GeoRef., Ind.Vet., Ref.Zh., Vet.Bull. **Document type:** academic/scholarly publication.
—BLDSC (6944.960000); CASDDS; CISTI; Linda Hall.

591   PK   ISSN 1016-1597
                  CODEN: PUJJZEN
PUNJAB UNIVERSITY JOURNAL OF ZOOLOGY. 1931-47; N.S. 1967; N.S. 1983. a. $40 per vol. (effective 1996 & 1997). University of the Punjab, Department of Zoology, Quaid-e-Azam Campus, Lahore 54590, Pakistan. TEL 92-42-5864028. Ed. Dr. Firdausia Azam Ali. circ. 300. **Indexed:** Biol.Abstr., Sport Fish.Abstr., Wild.Rev., Zoo.Rec. **Document type:** academic/scholarly publication.
—BLDSC (7160.330500); CISTI. **CCC.**
    Formerly (until 1983): University of the Punjab. Department of Zoology. Bulletin. New Series (ISSN 0079-8045)
    Refereed Serial

591   SI   ISSN 0217-2445
                  CODEN: RBUZEZ
RAFFLES BULLETIN OF ZOOLOGY. vol.36, 1988. s-a. fl.60 (effective 1996). National University of Singapore, Department of Zoology, Lower Kent Ridge Rd., Singapore 119260, Singapore. TEL 65-772-2969. FAX 65-779-2486. E-mail: zoolab6@nus.sg; URL: http://www.science.nus.sg:80/~zoology/raffles/. (Dist. by: Backhuys Publishers - Universal Book Services, P.O. Box 321, 2300 AH Leiden, Netherlands. TEL 31-71-5170208. FAX 31-71-5171856) Ed. Peter Ng. R&P contact: Peter Ng. bk.rev. circ. 100. (back issues avail.) **Indexed:** ASCA, Curr.Cont., Zoo.Rec. **Document type:** academic/scholarly publication.
—BLDSC (7242.652000); Genuine Article.
    Description: Publishes articles on systematics, faunistics, ecology and other aspects of zoology in tropical Southeast Asia.

599.73   NO   ISSN 0333-256X
RANGIFER; research, management and husbandry of reindeer and other northern ungulates. (Supplement avail.: Rangifer. Special Issue (ISSN 0801-6399)) (Text in English) 1981. irreg. (2-4/yr.) NOK 160 in Nordic countries (students NOK 75); Europe NOK 175 ; elsewhere NOK 200 (non-Nordic students NOK 100) (effective 1997). Nordisk Organ for Reinforskning (NOR) - Nordic Council for Reindeer Research, c/o NVH. Institute of Arctic Veterinary Medicine, N-9005 Tromsoe, Norway. TEL 47-77-68-43-10. FAX 47-77-68-44-11. Ed. Rolf Egil Haugerud. bk.rev. **Indexed:** Key Word Ind.Wildl.Res., Sport Fish.Abstr., Wild.Rev., Zoo.Rec. **Document type:** academic/scholarly publication, proceedings.
—BLDSC (7254.425300); UnCover.
    Description: Publishes articles on any arctic species of ungulates but primarily on reindeer, caribouu and muskox, reindeer management and husbandry.
    Refereed Serial

599.73   NO   ISSN 0801-6399
RANGIFER. SPECIAL ISSUE. (Supplement to: Rangifer (ISSN 0333-256X)) 1982. irreg. price varies. Nordisk Organ for Reinforskning (NOR) - Nordic Council for Reindeer Research, c/o NVH. Institute of Arctic Veterinary Medicine, N-9005 Tromsoe, Norway. TEL 47-77-68-43-10. FAX 47-77-68-44-11. Ed.Bd. **Document type:** academic/scholarly publication, proceedings.
—BLDSC (7254.425400).

591   IS   ISSN 0334-1461
RE'EM. (Text in Hebrew) a. (Israel Mammal Information Center) Society for the Protection of Nature in Israel, 4 Hashfela St., Tel Aviv 66183, Israel. TEL 972-3-375063. Eds. B. Shalmon, D. Simon.
    Description: Articles on mammals found in Israel.

599.8   JA   ISSN 0912-4047
REICHORUI KENKYU/PRIMATE RESEARCH. (Text in English, Japanese) 1985. s-a. 3000 Yen per no. Nihon Reichorui Gakkai - Primate Society of Japan, Primate Research Institute, Kyoto University, Inuyama-shi, Aichi-ken 484, Japan.
—BLDSC (6612.923500). **CCC.**

REPTILE & AMPHIBIAN MAGAZINE. see *PETS*

591   US   ISSN 1068-1965
REPTILES. 1993. m. $27.97 (Canada $38.47; elsewhere $43.97) (effective 1996); newsstand price: $3.50. Fancy Publications, Inc., 3 Burroughs, Irvine, CA 92618-2804. TEL 714-855-8822. FAX 714-855-3045. URL: http://www.petchannel.com. (Subscr. to: Neodata, Box 58025, Boulder, CO 80322. TEL 800-365-4221. FAX 303-604-7455) **Document type:** consumer publication.

597.6   US   ISSN 0966-7911
REPTILIAN. 1992. m. $60. c/o Zoo Med Laboratories, Inc., 3100 McMillan Rd., San Luis Obispo, CA 93401. URL: http://reptilian.co.uk. Ed. Tom Burgess; Pub. Tom Burgess. adv. contact: Chris Newman.

594   SP
RESENAS MALACOLOGICAS. 1981. irreg. 6000 ptas. Sociedad Espanola de Malacologia, c/o Museo Nac. de Ciencias Naturales, Jose Gutierrez Abascal, 2, 28006 Madrid, Spain. Ed. Angel A. Luove del Villar. **Document type:** academic/scholarly publication.

597 639.3   UK   ISSN 0960-3166
QL614   CODEN: RFBFEA
REVIEWS IN FISH BIOLOGY AND FISHERIES. q. £65 (foreign £110) to individuals; institutions £215 (foreign £360) (effective 1998). Thomson Science (Subsidiary of: International Thomson Publishing Group), 2-6 Boundary Row, London SE1 8HN, England. TEL 44-171-8650066. FAX 44-171-5229623. TELEX 290164 CHAPMA G. E-mail: jhelp@chall.co.uk; URL: http://www.thomsonscience.com. (Dist. by: International Thomson Publishing Services Ltd., Cheriton House, North Way, Andover, Hants. SP10 5BE, England. TEL 44-1264-342713. FAX 44-1264-342807; N. American subscr. to: Chapman & Hall, Journals Promotion Department, One Penn Plaza, 41st Fl., New York, NY 10119. TEL 800-552-5866) Eds. T. Pitcher, P. Hart. adv.; bk.rev. (reprint service avail.; back issues avail.) **Indexed:** ASCA, Curr.Cont., Ecol.Abstr., Environ.Per.Bibl. (1993-), Geo.Abstr.P.G., Ind.Sci.Rev., Sci.Cit.Ind., Sport Fish.Abstr., Wild.Rev., Zoo.Rec. **Document type:** academic/scholarly publication.
●Also available online.
—BLDSC (7790.568000); CISTI; Genuine Article; SWETS; UnCover.
    Description: Directed to people with an interest in fish biology and fisheries; includes information about physiology, evolutionary biology, taxonomy, and related subjects.
    Refereed Serial

REVISTA CUBANA DE CIENCIA AGRICOLA. see *AGRICULTURE*

REVISTA DE INVESTIGACION Y DESARROLLO PESQUERO. see *FISH AND FISHERIES*

590   MX   ISSN 0188-1884
REVISTA DE ZOOLOGIA. (Text and summaries in English and Spanish) no.2, 1996. s-a. Mex.$55($12) (effective 1997). Universidad Nacional Autonoma de Mexico, Escuela Nacional de Estudios Profesionales Iztacala, c/o Museo de las Ciencias Biologicas, Ave. de los Barrios s-n, Tlanepantla, Los Reyes Iztacala, 54090 Estado de Mexico, Mexico. TEL 52-5-6231386. FAX 52-5-6231212. Ed. Tizoc Adrian Altamirano Alvarez.
    Description: Covers paleontology, ecology, taxonomy, physiology, ornithology and other fields related to zoology.

597.9   SP   ISSN 0213-6686
REVISTA ESPANOLA DE HERPETOLOGIA. 1986. a. 3500 ptas. Asociacion Herpetologica Espanola, c/o Museo Nac. de Ciencias Naturales, Jose Gutierrez Abascal 2, 28006 Madrid, Spain. **Indexed:** Ind.SST.

REVISTA INVESTIGACIONES MARINAS. see *EARTH SCIENCES* — *Oceanography*

REVISTA PARAGUAYA DE MICROBIOLOGIA. see *BIOLOGY* — *Microbiology*

REVISTA VETERINARIA Y ZOOTECNICA DE CALDAS. see *VETERINARY SCIENCE*

595.4   FR   ISSN 0398-4346
REVUE ARACHNOLOGIQUE. (Text in English, French; summaries in French) 1977. irreg., vol.10, no.11, 1996. 180 F. J.C. Ledoux, Ed. & Pub., 43 rue Paul Bert, 30390 Aramon, France. (back issues avail.) **Indexed:** Biol.Abstr., Zoo.Rec.
    Refereed Serial

591   FR
REVUE FRANCAISE D'AQUARIOLOGIE, HERPETOLOGIE. (Text in English, French; summaries in English, French, German, Italian, Spanish, Portuguese) q. 160 F. (foreign 180 F.). Musee de Zoologie, 34 rue Sainte-Catherine, 54000 Nancy, France. Eds. B. Conde, D. Terver. bk.rev. (back issues avail.) **Indexed:** Zoo.Rec. **Document type:** bulletin.
    Refereed Serial

591   RM   ISSN 0377-8142
                  CODEN: RRBADA
REVUE ROUMAINE DE BIOLOGIE. SERIE BIOLOGIE ANIMALE. (Text in English, French, German, Russian, Spanish) 1956. s-a. (Academia Romana, Institutul de Stiinte Biologice) Editura Academiei Romane, Calea 13 Septembrie 13, 75117 Bucharest, Rumania. (Dist. by: Rodipet SA, Piata Presei Libere 1, Sec. 1, P.O. Box 33-57, Bucharest, Rumania. TEL 401-6185103. FAX 401-226407) Ed. Mihai Bacescu. bk.rev.; abstr.; charts; illus.; index. **Indexed:** Biol.Abstr., Chem.Abstr., Curr.Adv.Ecol.Sci., Excerp.Med., Helminthol.Abstr., Ocean.Abstr., Pollut.Abstr., Soils & Fert. **Document type:** academic/scholarly publication.
—BLDSC (7946.090000); CASDDS; CISTI; KNAW; Linda Hall.
    Supersedes in part (in 1976): Revue Roumaine de Biologie (ISSN 0250-6572); Which was formed by the 1975 merger of: Revue Roumaine de Biologie. Serie Zoologie (ISSN 0035-3922); Revue Roumaine de Biologie. Serie Botanique (ISSN 0035-3914); Both of which supersede (in 1964): Revue de Biologie (ISSN 0484-8462)

591   SZ   ISSN 0035-418X
QL1   CODEN: RSZOA6
REVUE SUISSE DE ZOOLOGIE. (Text in English, French, German, Italian; abstracts in English) 1893. q. 225 SFr. (foreign 230 SFr.) (effective 1996). Museum d'Histoire Naturelle de Geneve, B.P. 6434, CH-1211 Geneva 6, Switzerland. TEL 41-22-4186333. FAX 41-22-4186300. E-mail: mahnert@musinfo.ville-ge.ch. Ed. Volker Mahnert. R&P contact: Volker Mahnert. adv. contact: Denise Maier. bibl.; charts; illus.; index. circ. 280. (also avail. in microfiche from IDC) **Indexed:** ASCA, Biol.Abstr., Chem.Abstr., Curr.Adv.Ecol.Sci., Curr.Cont., Curr.Ref.Fish Res., Deep Sea Res.& Oceanogr.Abstr., Entomol.Abstr., Helminthol.Abstr., Ind.Sci.Rev., Key Word Ind.Wildl.Res., Ocean.Abstr., Pollut.Abstr., Sci.Cit.Ind., So.Pac.Per.Ind., Sport Fish.Abstr., Wild.Rev., Zoo.Rec. **Document type:** academic/scholarly publication.
—BLDSC (7953.400000); CASDDS; Genuine Article; KNAW; Linda Hall; SWETS; UnCover.

591   IT   ISSN 0375-0736
QL1   CODEN: RBSVA9
RICERCHE DI BIOLOGIA DELLA SELVAGGINA. (Supplement avail. (ISSN 1121-3973)) (Text in Italian; summaries in English, Italian) 1930. irreg. exchange basis. Istituto Nazionale per la Fauna Selvatica, Via Ca Fornacetta 9, 40064 Ozzano Emilia (BO), Italy. FAX 39-51-796628. E-mail: infsammi@iperbole.bologna.it. Ed. Mario Spagnesi. circ. 2,000. **Indexed:** Biol.Abstr., Key Word Ind.Wildl.Res., Sport Fish.Abstr., Wild.Rev., Zoo.Rec. —CISTI.
    Formerly: Ricerche di Zoologia Applicata alla Caccia (ISSN 0044-5061)

BIOLOGY — ZOOLOGY

591   **IT**   ISSN 1121-3973
CODEN: SRBSB5
RICERCHE DI BIOLOGIA DELLA SELVAGGINA. SUPPLEMENTO. (Supplement to: Ricerche di Biologia della Selvaggina (ISSN 0375-0736)) (Text and summaries in English, Italian) 1939. irreg. Istituto Nazionale per la Fauna Selvatica, Via Ca Fornacetta 9, 40064 Ozzano Emilia (BO), Italy. FAX 39-51-796628. E-mail: infsammi@iperbole.bologna.it. Eds. Mario Spagnesi, Silvano Toso. circ. 2,000. **Indexed:** Sport Fish.Abstr., Wild.Rev., Zoo.Rec. **Document type:** proceedings.
—BLDSC (7965.071000).
    Formerly (until 1976): Ricerche di Zoologia Applicata alla Caccia. Supplemento (ISSN 0375-149X)

ROYAL ONTARIO MUSEUM. LIFE SCIENCES. CONTRIBUTIONS. see BIOLOGY

591   **UK**
ROYAL ZOOLOGICAL SOCIETY OF SCOTLAND. ANNUAL REPORT. a. Royal Zoological Society of Scotland, Scottish National Zoological Park, 134 Corstorphine Rd., Edinburgh EH12 6TS, Scotland. TEL 44-131-334-9171. FAX 44-131-316-4050. Ed. Roger Wheater. **Document type:** proceedings.

591   **UK**
ROYAL ZOOLOGICAL SOCIETY OF SCOTLAND. ZOO GUIDE. 1958. irreg. £2.75. Royal Zoological Society of Scotland, Scottish National Zoological Park, 134 Corstorphine Rd., Edinburgh EH12 6TS, Scotland. TEL 44-131-334-9171. FAX 44-131-316-4050. adv. circ. 100,000. **Document type:** directory.

598.1   **JA**   ISSN 0285-287X
RYOSEI HACHURUI KENKYUKAISHI/NIPPON HERPETOLOGICAL JOURNAL. (Text in Japanese; summaries in English) 1975. irreg. 1000 Yen per no. Nippon Ryosei Hachurui Kenkyukai - Nippon Herpetological Society, c/o Mr. Kinebuchi, 2140 Katabata, Uchino, Niigata-shi, Niigata-ken 950-21, Japan.

591   **GW**   ISSN 0036-2344
CODEN: STKMBC
SAEUGETIERKUNDLICHE MITTEILUNGEN. (Text in English, French, German) 1953. q. DM.320. Postfach 1153, 31069 Delligsen, Germany. Ed. G. Kirk. bk.rev.; bibl.; illus.; index. circ. 400. **Indexed:** Anim.Breed.Abstr., Biol.Abstr., Helminthol.Abstr., Ind.Vet., Key Word Ind.Wildl.Res., Vet.Bull.
—CISTI; Linda Hall.

598.1   **GW**   ISSN 0036-3375
QL640   CODEN: SALAAH
SALAMANDRA; Zeitschrift fuer Herpetologie und Terrarienkunde. (Supplement avail.: Mertensiella) (Text in German; abstracts in English) 1965. 4/yr. DM.80. Deutsche Gesellschaft fuer Herpetologie und Terrarienkunde e.V., Postfach 1421, 53351 Rheinbach, Germany. Ed. Dr. Klaus Henle. bk.rev.; abstr.; bibl.; charts; illus.; index. circ. 4,500. **Indexed:** Biol.Abstr., Bull.Signal., Ref.Zh. **Document type:** academic/scholarly publication.
—BLDSC (8070.560000); CISTI; Linda Hall.

597 574.5   **FR**   ISSN 0220-1429
SAUMONS. q. 25 F. Association Nationale de Defense des Rivieres a Saumons, 1 Place Edouard Renard, 75012 Paris, France. Ed. Rene Richard.

598.1   **GW**   ISSN 0176-9391
CODEN: SAUREF
SAURIA; Herpetologie und Terraristik. (Text in German; summaries in English) 1979. q. DM.45. Terrariengemeinschaft Berlin e.V., Planetenstr. 45, 12057 Berlin, Germany. TEL 49-30-6847140. Ed. Wolfgang Grossmann. adv. contact: Manfred Buhle. bk.rev.; bibl.; charts; illus.; index. circ. 1,700. (back issues avail.) **Indexed:** Sport Fish.Abstr., Wild.Rev., Zoo.Rec. **Document type:** newsletter.
Refereed Serial

599   **JA**   ISSN 0917-0537
QL737.C4   CODEN: SRCTEG
SCIENTIFIC REPORTS OF CETACEAN RESEARCH/NIHON GEIRUI KENKYUSHO KENKYU HOKOKU. (Text in English) 1990. a. 5000 Yen. Institute of Cetacean Research - Nihon Geirui Kenkyusho, Tokyo Suisan Bldg., 4-18 Toyomi-cho, Chuo-ku, Tokyo 104, Japan. TEL 81-3-3536-6521. FAX 81-3-3536-6522. Ed. Seiji Ohsumi. R&P contact: Seiji Ohsumi. circ. 750. **Indexed:** Biol.Abstr., Curr.Adv.Ecol.Sci., Deep Sea Res.& Oceanogr.Abstr., Ocean.Abstr., Pollut.Abstr. **Document type:** academic/scholarly publication, bulletin.
    Supersedes (in Sep. 1990): Whales Research Institute, Tokyo, Japan. Scientific Reports (ISSN 0083-9086)
Refereed Serial

597   **US**
SEINE. bi-m. Society on North American Fishes, 123 W. Mt. Airy Ave., Philadelphia, PA 19119. TEL 215-247-0384. Ed. Bruce Gebhardt. adv.
    Description: Includes news and feature articles on ecology, icthyology, and live maintenance and study of North American fishes.

SEMINARS IN VETERINARY MEDICINE AND SURGERY: SMALL ANIMAL. see VETERINARY SCIENCE

591   **GW**   ISSN 0037-2102
QH5   CODEN: SBBOAG
SENCKENBERGIANA BIOLOGICA. 1919. 2/yr. DM.98 (effective 1997). Senckenbergische Naturforschende Gesellschaft, Senckenberganlage 25, 60325 Frankfurt a.M., Germany. TEL 49-69-7542-1. FAX 49-69-746238. TELEX 413129. E-mail: sjessel@sng.uni-frankfurt.de. Ed. Willi Ziegler. **Indexed:** Bio-Contr.News & Info., Biol.Abstr., Chem.Abstr., Curr.Adv.Ecol.Sci., Deep Sea Res.& Oceanogr.Abstr., Ecol.Abstr., Forest.Abstr., Geo.Abstr., GeoRef., IBR, Ocean.Abstr., Pollut.Abstr., Rev.Appl.Entomol., Sport Fish.Abstr., VITIS, Wild.Rev., Zoo.Rec. **Document type:** academic/scholarly publication.
—BLDSC (8240.000000); CISTI; Linda Hall; UMI; UnCover.

597.31   **US**
SHARK FEAR, SHARK AWARENESS. 1994. 2/yr. $3 per issue. Society of Shark Fear, 1420 N.W. Gilman Blvd., Ste. 2400, Issaquah, WA 98027-7001. Ed. Darin Johnson. bk.rev.; circ. 5,000 (paid). (back issues avail.) **Document type:** newsletter.
    Description: Studies the shark's predatory nature, and the sociological impact of their nature on human society.

597.31   **UK**   ISSN 1361-7397
SHARK NEWS. 1994. 3/yr. £5 per no. (I U C N, Shark Specialist Group) Nature Conservation Bureau Ltd., 36 Kingfisher Ct., Hambridge Rd., Newbury, Berks. RG14 5SJ, England. TEL 44-1635-550380. FAX 44-1635-550230. E-mail: post@naturebureau.co.uk. Eds. Sarah Fowler, Merry Camhi. adv.; circ. 1,500. **Document type:** newsletter.
●Also available online.
    Description: Provides a forum for the exchange of information on all aspects of chondrichthyan conservation matters.

594   **US**   ISSN 0085-607X
SHELLER'S DIRECTORY OF CLUBS, BOOKS, PERIODICALS AND DEALERS. 1968. a. $4.95. Of Sea & Shore Publications, Box 219, Port Gamble, WA 98364. TEL 360-297-2426. FAX 360-297-2426. E-mail: ofseashr@pacific.telebyte.com. Ed. Thomas C. Rice. adv. circ. 1,000. (reprint service avail. from UMI) **Document type:** directory.

594   **JA**   ISSN 0917-7159
SHIBUKITSUBO/NIIGATA SHELL CLUB. REPORT. (Text in Japanese) irreg. Niigata Kaiyukai - Niigata Shell Club, c/o Mr. Murayama, 301-2 Nakazawa 4-chome, Nagaoka-shi, Niigata-ken 940, Japan.

SHIMA MARINELAND. SCIENCE REPORT. see BIOLOGY

SHINRIN YASEI DOBUTSU KENKYUKAISHI/JAPANESE WILDLIFE RESEARCH SOCIETY. JOURNAL. see CONSERVATION

591   **CC**   ISSN 1000-1050
SHOULEI XUEBAO/ACTA THERIOLOGICA SINICA. (Text in Chinese; summaries in English) 1981. q. $61.60. (Xibei Gaoyuan Shengwu Yanjiusuo) Science Press, Marketing and Sales Department, 16 Donghuangchenggen North St., Beijing 100717, People's Republic of China. TEL 4010642. FAX 4019810. Ed. Wang Zuwang. adv.; bk.rev. circ. 5,500. **Indexed:** Ecol.Abstr., Geo.Abstr., Geol.Abstr. **Document type:** academic/scholarly publication.
    Description: Contains original theses on basic theories and applications of mammalian zoology. Includes taxonomy, morphology, ecology, physiology, biochemistry, paleontology and evolution, raising, domestication, natural protection, hunting, and prevention of cruelty.
Refereed Serial

691   **JA**
SHUKAN ASAHI HYAKKA/WEEKLY ASAHI ENCYCLOPEDIA. (Text in Japanese) 1975. w. Asahi Shimbun Publishing Co., 3-2, Tsukuji 5-chome, Chuo-ku, Tokyo 104-11, Japan. (Order to: Oversea Courier Service Co., Ltd., 9, Shibaura 2-chome, Minato-ku, Tokyo 108, Japan) Ed. Tsuyosi Nogami.

SIMIAN. see PETS

SKYHOPPER. see CONSERVATION

590   **US**   ISSN 0081-0282
QL1   CODEN: SMCZBU
SMITHSONIAN CONTRIBUTIONS TO ZOOLOGY. 1969. irreg., no.565, 1994. free. Smithsonian Institution Press, 470 L'Enfant Plaza, Ste. 7100, Washington, DC 20560. TEL 202-287-3738. FAX 202-287-3637. Ed. Don Fisher. circ. 2,000. (reprint service avail. from UMI) **Indexed:** Abstr.Hyg., Bio-Contr.News & Info., Biol.Abstr., Deep Sea Res.& Oceanogr.Abstr., GeoRef, Ocean.Abstr., Pollut.Abstr., Rev.Appl.Entomol., Sport Fish.Abstr., Wild.Rev., Zoo.Rec. **Document type:** monographic series.
—BLDSC (8311.620000); CISTI; Linda Hall.

597.6   **JA**   ISSN 0386-3425
QL640   CODEN: NJGKBV
SNAKE. (Text in English, Japanese) 1969. s-a. 2000 Yen($15) Japan Snake Institute - Nihon Hebizoku Gakujutsu Kenkyujo, 3318, Yunoiri, Yabutsuka Honmachi, Nitta-gun, Gunma-ken 379-23, Japan. TEL 81-277-78-5193. FAX 81-277-78-5520. Ed. Y. Sawai. adv.; bk.rev. circ. 1,000. **Indexed:** Biol.Abstr., Chem.Abstr., Sport Fish.Abstr., Wild.Rev., Zoo.Rec. **Document type:** academic/scholarly publication.
—BLDSC (8313.800000); CASDDS; CISTI; Linda Hall. CCC.
    Description: Publishes papers on the biology of snakes as well as medical aspects of snake venom and snakebites.

SOCIETA SARDA DI SCIENZE NATURALI. BOLLETTINO. see BIOLOGY

SOCIETE LINNEENNE DE BORDEAUX. BULLETIN. see BIOLOGY — Entomology

SOCIETE LINNEENNE DE PROVENCE. BULLETIN. see BIOLOGY — Botany

591   **FR**   ISSN 0037-962X
QL1   CODEN: BZOFAZ
SOCIETE ZOOLOGIQUE DE FRANCE. BULLETIN; evolution et zoologie. (Supplement avail.: (ISSN 0151-1173)) (Text mainly in French; occasionally English or German) 1876. q. 500 F. to non-members (effective 1997). Societe Zoologique de France, 195 rue Saint-Jacques, 75005 Paris, France. TEL 33-1-40793110. Ed. Jean-Loup d'Hondt. bk.rev.; illus.; index. circ. 1,300. (also avail. in microform from BHP; microfiche from IDC,BHP). **Indexed:** Anim.Breed.Abstr., ASCA, Bio-Contr.News & Info., Biol.Abstr., Chem.Abstr., Curr.Adv.Ecol.Sci., Curr.Cont., Dairy Sci.Abstr., Deep Sea Res.& Oceanogr.Abstr., Excerp.Med., Helminthol.Abstr., Ind.Sci.Rev., Maize Abstr., Sci.Cit.Ind., Sport Fish.Abstr., Wild.Rev. **Document type:** academic/scholarly publication.
—BLDSC (2758.000000); CASDDS; CISTI; KNAW; Linda Hall; SWETS.
Refereed Serial

BIOLOGY — ZOOLOGY

591   FR   ISSN 0750-747X
SOCIETE ZOOLOGIQUE DE FRANCE. MEMOIRES. (Text in French, occasionally in English; summaries in English, French) 1888. irreg. price varies. Societe Zoologique de France, 195 rue Saint Jacques, 75005 Paris, France. TEL 33-1-40793110. Ed. Jean-Loup d'Hondt. index. (back issues avail.) **Document type:** academic/scholarly publication.
   Refereed Serial

SOUTH AFRICAN JOURNAL OF WILDLIFE RESEARCH/SUID-AFRIKAANSE TYDSKRIF VIR NATUURNAVORSING. see *CONSERVATION*

591   SA   ISSN 0254-1858
QL337.S65   CODEN: SAJZDH
SOUTH AFRICAN JOURNAL OF ZOOLOGY/SUID-AFRIKAANSE TYDSKRIF VIR DIERKUNDE. (Text and summaries in English) 1965. q. R.118 to individuals; institutions R.138 (foreign $45) (effective 1997). (Zoological Society of Southern Africa) Foundation for Education, Science & Technology, P.O. Box 1758, Pretoria 0001, South Africa. TEL 27-12-3226404. FAX 27-12-3207803. E-mail: buro@shuttle.up.ac.za. Ed. S.W. Nicolson. adv. contact: S.W. Nicholson. charts; illus. circ. 850. **Indexed:** Anim.Breed.Abstr, Apic.Abstr., ASCA, Bio-Contr.News & Info., Biol.Abstr., Chem.Abstr., Curr.Adv.Ecol.Sci., Curr.Cont., Curr.Ref.Fish Res., Dairy Sci.Abstr., Deep Sea Res.& Oceanogr.Abstr., Ecol.Abstr., Geo.Abstr, Helminthol.Abstr, Herb.Abstr., Ind.S.A.Per., Ind.Vet., Key Word Ind.Wildl.Res., Sci.Cit.Ind., Soils & Fert., Sport Fish.Abstr., Vet.Bull., Wild Life Rev., Wild.Rev., Zoo.Rec. **Document type:** academic/scholarly publication.
  —BLDSC (8340.360000); CISTI; Genuine Article; KNAW; Linda Hall; UnCover. **CCC.**
   Formerly (until vol.13, 1978): Zoologica Africana (ISSN 0044-5096).
   Description: Publishes original research articles and brief discussions on research in the field of zoology in Africa, especially ecology, ethology, physiology and taxonomy.
   Refereed Serial

590   GW   ISSN 0341-8391
QL1   CODEN: SPIXD9
SPIXIANA; journal of zoology. (Supplement avail.: Spixiana Supplemente (ISSN 0177-7424)) (Text in English, French, German) 1950. 3/yr. DM.120. Zoologische Staatssammlung Muenchen, Muenchhausenstr. 21, 81247 Munich, Germany. TEL 49-89-81070. FAX 49-89-8107300. Ed. M. Baehr. bk.rev. circ. 450. **Indexed:** Biol.Abstr., Deep Sea Res.& Oceanogr.Abstr., IBR, Key Word Ind.Wildl.Res., Sport Fish.Abstr., Wild.Rev., Zoo.Rec. **Document type:** bulletin.
  —BLDSC (8417.350000); CISTI; UnCover.
   Formerly (until 1976): Zoologischen Staatssammlung Muenchen. Veroeffentlichungen.

590   GW   ISSN 0177-7424
QL1   CODEN: SPSUDG
SPIXIANA SUPPLEMENTE. (Supplement to: Spixiana (ISSN 0341-8391)) (Text in English, French, German) irreg., no.23, 1997. DM.125. Zoologische Staatssammlung Muenchen, Muenchhausenstr. 21, 81247 Munich, Germany. TEL 49-89-81070. FAX 49-89-8107300. Ed. M. Baehr. **Indexed:** Zoo.Rec. **Document type:** monographic series.
  —BLDSC (8417.351000); CISTI.

591   GW   ISSN 0375-2135
    CODEN: SMTFBL
STAATLICHES MUSEUM FUER TIERKUNDE DRESDEN. FAUNISTISCHE ABHANDLUNGEN. (Text in English, French, German) 1963. a. price varies. Staatliches Museum fuer Tierkunde Dresden, Augustusstr. 2, 01067 Dresden, Germany. TEL 49-351-4952503. FAX 49-351-4952525. Ed. Rainer Emmrich. bk.rev. circ. 400. (back issues avail.) **Indexed:** Biol.Abstr., IBR, Key Word Ind.Wildl.Res., Sport Fish.Abstr., Wild.Rev., Zoo.Rec. **Document type:** academic/scholarly publication.
  —CISTI; Linda Hall.
   Description: Focuses on the faunistics of Arachnida, Insecta and Vertebrata.

594   GW   ISSN 0070-7260
QL401   CODEN: SMTMB8
STAATLICHES MUSEUM FUER TIERKUNDE DRESDEN. MALAKOLOGISCHE ABHANDLUNGEN. (Text in English, French, German) 1964. a. price varies. Staatliches Museum fuer Tierkunde Dresden, Augustusstr. 2, 01067 Dresden, Germany. TEL 49-351-4952503. FAX 49-351-4952525. Ed. Rainer Emmrich. bk.rev. circ. 300. (back issues avail.) **Indexed:** Biol.Abstr., Ref.Zh., Zoo.Rec. **Document type:** academic/scholarly publication.
  —CISTI; Linda Hall.
   Description: Explores taxonomy, systematics, morphology, bionomics, ecology, zoogeography and faunistics of Mollusca.

591   GW   ISSN 0375-5231
    CODEN: ZASMAT
STAATLICHES MUSEUM FUER TIERKUNDE DRESDEN. ZOOLOGISCHE ABHANDLUNGEN. (Text in English, French, German) 1961. a. price varies. Staatliches Museum fuer Tierkunde Dresden, Augustusstr. 2, 01067 Dresden, Germany. TEL 49-351-4952503. FAX 49-351-4952525. Ed. Rainer Emmrich. bk.rev. circ. 700. (back issues avail.) **Indexed:** Biol.Abstr., IBR, Key Word Ind.Wildl.Res., Sport Fish.Abstr., Wild.Rev., Zoo.Rec. **Document type:** academic/scholarly publication.
  —BLDSC (9520.800000); CISTI.
   Description: Explores taxonomy, systematics, morphology, bionomics, ecology and zoogeography of Vertebrata.

STATE BIOLOGICAL SURVEY OF KANSAS. TECHNICAL BULLETIN. see *BIOLOGY — Botany*

591   DK   ISSN 0375-2909
QL1   CODEN: STRUB3
STEENTRUPIA; journal on systematic zoology and zoogeography. (Text and summaries in English) 1970. a. DKK 250 (effective 1997). Zoologisk Museum, Universitetsparken 15, DK-2100 Copenhagen Oe, Denmark. TEL 45-35-32-10-00. FAX 45-35-32-10-10. E-mail: <nlbruce@zmuc.ku.dk>; URL: <http://www.aki.ku.dk/zmuc/ento/stenstr.htm> Ed. Henrik Enghoff. index. (back issues avail.) **Indexed:** Biol.Abstr., Curr.Adv.Ecol.Sci., Deep Sea Res.& Oceanogr.Abstr., IBR, Zoo.Rec.
  —BLDSC (8464.109500); CISTI; Linda Hall.

STRANGE MAGAZINE. see *PARAPSYCHOLOGY AND OCCULTISM*

591   PL   ISSN 0082-5565
STUDIA SOCIETATIS SCIENTIARUM TORUNENSIS. SECTIO E. ZOOLOGIA. (Text in Polish; summaries in English, French, German) 1948. irreg., vol.10, no.5, 1987. price varies. Towarzystwo Naukowe w Toruniu, Ul. Wysoka 16, 87-100 Torun, Poland. TEL 48-56-23941. TELEX 552388 FSBH PL. Ed. Melityna Gromadska. **Indexed:** AgroLibrex, Biol.Abstr. **Document type:** monographic series.
  —BLDSC (8482.008000); CISTI.

591   NE   ISSN 0165-0521
QL235   CODEN: SNFEDP
STUDIES ON NEOTROPICAL FAUNA AND ENVIRONMENT. (Text in English) 1956. q. fl.601($364) (effective 1996). Swets & Zeitlinger bv, P.O. Box 825, 2160 SZ Lisse, Netherlands. TEL 31-252-435111. FAX 31-252-415888. TELEX 41325. E-mail: orders@swets.nl; URL: http://www.swets.nl. (Dist. in N. America by: Swets & Zeitlinger, Box 613, Royersford, PA 19468. TEL 800-447-9387. FAX 610-524-5366) Ed.Bd. R&P contact: J.v.d. Valk. adv. contact: Patrick Kleian. charts; illus. (also avail. in microform from SWZ; reprint service avail. from SWZ) **Indexed:** ASCA, Biol.Abstr., Curr.Cont., Ecol.Abstr., Helminthol.Abstr, Sport Fish.Abstr., Wild.Rev., Zoo.Rec. **Document type:** academic/scholarly publication.
  •Also available online.
  —BLDSC (8491.155200); Genuine Article; Linda Hall; SWETS; UnCover. **CCC.**
   Formerly: Studies on the Neotropical Fauna.

591 570   NE   ISSN 1381-2467
QH109.A1
STUDIES ON THE NATURAL HISTORY OF THE CARIBBEAN REGION. (Text in English) 1953. irreg., vol.72, 1995. Foundation for Scientific Research in the Caribbean Region - Natuurwetenschappelijke Studekring voor het Caraibische Gebied, Instituut voor Taxonomische Zoologie, Plantage Middenlaan 45, 1018 DC Amsterdam, Netherlands. TEL 31-20-5255926. FAX 31-20-5256612. Ed. Louise J. van der Steen. R&P contact: Louise J. Westerman. (back issues avail.) **Document type:** monographic series.
   Formerly (until vol.71, 1992): Studies on the Fauna of Curacao and Other Caribbean Islands (ISSN 0166-5189)

570   RM   ISSN 1220-5273
QH301   CODEN: SCBADI
STUDII SI CERCETARI DE BIOLOGIE. SERIA BIOLOGIE ANIMALA. 1948. s-a. (Academia Romana) Editura Academiei Romane, Calea 13 Septembrie 13, 76117 Bucharest, Rumania. (Dist. by: Rodipet SA, Piata Presei Libere 1, Sec.1, P.O. Box 33-57, Bucharest, Rumania. TEL 401-6185103. FAX 401-226407) Ed. Mihai Bacescu. **Indexed:** Biol.Abstr., Chem.Abstr., Ind.Vet., Sport Fish.Abstr., Vet.Bull., Wild.Rev., Zoo.Rec. **Document type:** academic/scholarly publication.
  —CISTI; Linda Hall.
   Formerly (until 1989): Studii si Cercetari de Biologie. Seria Zoologia (ISSN 1220-1634); Supersedes in part (in 1975): Studii si Cercetari de Biologie (ISSN 1015-2237); Which was formed by the merger of (1958-1973): Studii si Cercetari de Biologie. Seria Botanica (ISSN 0370-8934); Which was formerly (until 1963): Studii si Cercetari de Biologie. Seria Biologie Vegetala (ISSN 0365-5997); And (1958-1973): Studii si Cercetari de Biologie. Seria Zoologie (ISSN 0370-8950): Which was formerly (until 1963): Studii si Cercetari de Biologie. Seria Biologia Animala (ISSN 0365-5962).

591   JA   ISSN 0389-6838
SUZUKURI/ASA ZOOLOGICAL PARK NEWS. (Text in Japanese) 1972. q. 200 Yen per no. Hiroshimashi Dobutsuen Kyokai - Hiroshima City Zoological Park Society, Hiroshimashi Asa Dobutsu Koen, Dobutsuen, Asacho, Asa Kita-ku, Hiroshima-shi, Hiroshima-ken 731-33, Japan. Ed. Hiroshi Morimoto. **Document type:** newsletter.

333.95   US
SYDNEY'S KOALA CLUB NEWS. 1974. bi-m. $15. Zoological Society of San Diego, Box 551, San Diego, CA 92112. TEL 619-231-1515. (Subscr. to: Membership Department, Box 271, San Diego, CA 92112) Ed. Karen E. Worley. R&P contact: Karen E. Worley. circ. 135,000. **Document type:** newsletter.
   Formerly: Koala Club News.
   Description: Animal stories and information about the San Diego Zoo and San Diego Wild Animal Park for children.

591   NE   ISSN 0082-1101
    CODEN: SBFSDH
SYNOPSES OF THE BRITISH FAUNA. 1970-1981; N.S 1984. irreg., vol.53, 1997. price varies. (Linnean Society of London, UK) Backhuys Publishers, P.O. Box 321, 2300 AH Leiden, Netherlands. TEL 31-71-5170208. FAX 31-71-5171856. E-mail backhuys@euronet.nl; URL: http://www.euronet.nl/users/backhuys/. (back issues avail.) **Indexed:** Biol.Abstr., GeoRef., Zoo.Rec. **Document type:** monographic series.
  —BLDSC (8586.225000); CISTI; Linda Hall.
   Refereed Serial

BIOLOGY — ZOOLOGY

591   RH   ISSN 1011-7881
SYNTARSUS. (Text and summaries in English) 1956; N.S. 1983. irreg., latest 1991. price varies. (Natural History Museum of Zimbabwe) National Museums and Monuments of Zimbabwe, P.O. Box 240, Bulawayo, Zimbabwe. TEL 60045. Ed. A. Kumarai. illus.; index. circ. 400. (back issues avail.) Indexed: Biol.Abstr., GeoRef., Ind.S.A.Per., Rev.Appl.Entomol., Sport Fish.Abstr., Wild.Rev., Zoo.Rec. Document type: academic/scholarly publication.
    Former titles: Smithersia (ISSN 0250-300X); National Museums and Monuments Administration. Occasional Papers. Series B: Natural Sciences; National Museums and Monuments of Rhodesia. Occasional Papers. Series B: Natural Sciences (ISSN 0304-5315); Which superseded in part: National Museums and Monuments of Rhodesia. Occasional Papers (ISSN 0027-9730)
    Description: Theses and surveys discussing research in natural history in southern Africa.

591   US   ISSN 1063-5157
QH83   CODEN: SYBIER
SYSTEMATIC BIOLOGY. 1952. q. £55($90) to institutions (effective 1998). (Society of Systematic Biologists) Taylor & Francis Inc., 1900 Frost Rd., Ste. 101, Bristol, PA 19007-1598. TEL 800-821-8312. FAX 215-785-5515. E-mail: info@tandf.co.uk; URL: http://www.tandf.co.uk/. Ed. M.M. Miyamoto. bk.rev.; charts; illus.; index. circ. 2,800. (also avail. in microform from UMI; reprint service avail. from UMI) Indexed: ASCA, Biol.Abstr., Biol.& Agr.Ind., Chem.Abstr., Compumath, Curr.Adv.Ecol.Sci., Curr.Cont., Curr.Ref.Fish Res., Deep Sea Res.& Oceanogr.Abstr., Helminthol.Abstr., Ind.Sci.Rev., Sci.Cit.Ind., Sport Fish.Abstr., SSCI, Wild.Rev., Zoo.Rec. Document type: academic/scholarly publication.
    —BLDSC (8589.180700); CISTI; Genuine Article; KR SourceOne; Linda Hall; SWETS; UMI; UnCover.
    Formerly (until 1991): Systematic Zoology (ISSN 0039-7989)
    Refereed Serial

591   US   ISSN 0199-2988
QL63
TAXIDERMY REVIEW.* 1976. bi-m. $10. 15011 Hollyvale Dr., Houston, TX 77062-2908. TEL 303-623-3965. Ed. Joseph Kish. adv.; bk.rev.; illus.; tr.lit. circ. 2,700. (back issues avail.)
    Formerly: Wide World of Taxidermy.

639   US   ISSN 0886-1269
SK449
TENNESSEE WILDLIFE. 1977. bi-m. $5. Wildlife Resources Agency, Box 40747, Nashville, TN 37204. TEL 615-781-6504. FAX 615-741-4606. Ed. Dave Woodward. R&P contact: Cheri Irwin. circ. 62,000. Indexed: Sport Fish.Abstr., Wild.Rev.
    —UnCover.
    Description: Reports about Tennessee wildlife and related articles and information.
    Refereed Serial

THALASSIA SALENTINA. see *BIOLOGY — Botany*

591   SZ   ISSN 1017-1576
DAS TIER; internationale Tier-Zeitschrift. 1960. m. 66 SFr. (foreign 72 SFr.). Hallwag AG, Nordring 4, CH-3001 Bern, Switzerland. TEL 41-31-3323131. FAX 41-31-3314133. TELEX 912661-CH. Ed. Peter Viktor Kulig. adv.; bk.rev.; illus.; index. circ. 87,712. (back issues avail.) Document type: academic/scholarly publication.
    Formerly (until 1982): Grzimeks Tier, Sielmanns Tierwelt (ISSN 0721-2569); Which was formed by the merger of (1960-1981): Tier (ISSN 0040-7291); (1977-1981): Sielmanns Tierwelt (ISSN 0344-8614); Which was formerly: Tier-Park (ISSN 0170-4648)
    Description: Discusses new findings in zoology.

TIERFREUND; die Jugendzeitschrift fuer Tier-, Natur- und Umweltschutz. see *CHILDREN AND YOUTH — For*

591   GW   ISSN 0040-7305
CODEN: TRRHAS
DAS TIERREICH; eine Zusammenstellung und Kennzeichnung der rezenten Tierformen. (Text in English, French, German) 1897. irreg., no.112, 1997. price varies. Walter de Gruyter und Co., Genthiner Str. 13, 10785 Berlin, Germany. TEL 49-30-260050. FAX 49-30-26005251. TELEX 184027. E-mail: wdg-info@degruyter.de. (In US and Canada: Walter de Gruyter, Inc., 200 Saw Mill Rd., Hawthorne, N.Y. 10532) Eds. H. Wermuth, Maximilian Fischer. bibl.; illus. circ. 250. (back issues avail.) Indexed: Zoo.Rec. Document type: monographic series.
    —Linda Hall.

590   GW   ISSN 0082-4305
TIERWELT DEUTSCHLANDS. irreg., vol. 67, 1989. price varies. Gustav Fischer Verlag Jena, Villengang 2, 07745 Jena, Germany. TEL 49-3641-626444. FAX 49-3641-626500. (Subscr. to: Postfach 100537, 07705 Jena, Germany) Eds. K. Senglaub, H.-J. Hannemann, H. Schumann. (reprint service avail. from ISI) Document type: monographic series.

591   JA
TOKYOTO TAMA DOBUTSU KOEN JIGYO GAIYO/TAMA ZOOLOGICAL PARK. ANNUAL REPORT. (Text in Japanese) 1973. a. Tokyoto Tama Dobutsu Koen - Tama Zoological Park, 1-1 Hodokubo 7-chome, Hino-shi, Tokyo 191, Japan.

591 069   SA   ISSN 0496-1102
CODEN: TRMBAJ
TRANSVAAL MUSEUM. BULLETIN. 1955. irreg., no.22, 1987. price varies. Transvaal Museum, P.O. Box 413, Pretoria 0001, South Africa. TEL 27-12-3227632. FAX 27-12-3327939. R&P contact: Anita Dreyer. Indexed: Art & Archaeol.Tech.Abstr., Biol.Abstr., Zoo.Rec. Document type: bulletin.
    Description: Comprises articles in zoology, and newsworthy contributions on the activities of the Transvaal Museum.

TRANSVAAL MUSEUM. MONOGRAPHS. see *MUSEUMS AND ART GALLERIES*

597   SP   ISSN 1130-6130
TREBALLS D'ICTIOLOGIA I HERPETOLOGIA. 1984. irreg. 2500 ptas. Sociedad Catalana de Ictiologia y Herpetologia, Museo de Zoologia, Apdo. 593, 08080 Barcelona, Spain.
    Formerly (until 1989): Societat Catalana d'Ictiologia i Herpetologia. Treballs (ISSN 0213-0165)

570   IO   ISSN 0082-6340
TREUBIA; a journal of zoology of the Indo-Australian archipelago. (Text in English) 1915. irreg. price varies. Indonesian Institute of Sciences, R & D Centre for Biology, Jalan Juanda 18, Bogor, Indonesia. TEL 62-251-321038. FAX 62-251-325854. Ed.Bd. index. circ. 500. Indexed: Biol.Abstr., Zoo.Rec.
    —BLDSC (9050.000000); Linda Hall.

591   IT   ISSN 0394-6975
QL109   CODEN: TRZOEP
TROPICAL ZOOLOGY. 1966. 2/yr. L.100000. Universita degli Studi di Firenze, Dipartimento di Biologia Animala e Genetica, Via Romana 17, Florence 50125, Italy. TEL 39-55-222448. FAX 39-55-222565. E-mail: csfet@ifiidg.fi.cnr.it. (Dist. by: Sedicesimo, Via Mannelli 29r, 50136 Florence, Italy. TEL 39-55-2476781) (Co-sponsor: Consiglio Nazionale delle Ricerche, Centro di Studio per la Faunistica ed Ecologia Tropicali) Ed. Franco Ferrara. index. (back issues avail.; reprint service avail. from ISI) Indexed: ASCA, Biol.Abstr., Chem.Abstr., Curr.Adv.Ecol.Sci., Curr.Cont., Sport Fish.Abstr., Wild.Rev., Zoo.Rec. Document type: academic/scholarly publication.
    —BLDSC (9057.010000); CISTI; Genuine Article; UnCover. CCC.
    Formerly (until 1988): Monitore Zoologico Italiano. Supplemento (ISSN 0374-9444)
    Description: Publishes original papers in the field of experimental and descriptive zoology and zoogeography concerning tropical areas with particular attention to Africa.

591 581   US   ISSN 0082-6782
QL1   CODEN: TSZBAN
TULANE STUDIES IN ZOOLOGY AND BOTANY. 1953. irreg. $8. Tulane University, Museum of Natural History, Belle Chasse, LA 70037. TEL 504-394-1711. FAX 504-394-5045. E-mail: hank@museum.tulane.edu; URL: http://www.museum.tulane.edu/museum/museum.html. Ed. Henry L. Bart, Jr. R&P contact: Henry L. Bart. circ. 800. (back issues avail.) Indexed: Biol.Abstr., Curr.Adv.Ecol.Sci., Sport Fish.Abstr., Wild.Rev., Zoo.Rec., Zoo.Rec. Document type: monographic series.
    —Linda Hall.
    Formerly: Tulane Studies in Zoology.
    Refereed Serial

591   TU   ISSN 1300-0179
CODEN: DTZDEY
TURKISH JOURNAL OF ZOOLOGY/TURK ZOOLOJI DERGISI. (Text in English, Turkish) 1976. 4/yr. $100 (effective 1996 & 1997). Scientific and Technical Research Council of Turkey - TUBITAK - Turkiye Bilimsel ve Teknik Arastirma Kurumu, Ataturk Bulvari, No. 221, Kavaklidere, 06100 Ankara, Turkey. TEL 90-312-4685300. FAX 90-312-4271336. TELEX 43186 BTAK TR. E-mail: bdym@tubitak.gov.tr. Ed. Aykut Kence. Indexed: Ecol.Abstr., Food Sci.& Tech.Abstr., Geo.Abstr.P.G., Zoo.Rec. Document type: academic/scholarly publication.
    —BLDSC (9072.498000); CASDDS; CISTI.
    Formerly (until 1994): Doga Turkish Journal of Zoology - Doga Turk Zooloji Dergisi (ISSN 1011-0895)
    Refereed Serial

591   SP   ISSN 0213-3997
QL1   CODEN: ABBAEI
UNIVERSIDAD DE MURCIA. ANALES DE BIOLOGIA. SECCION BIOLOGIA ANIMAL. (Subseries of: Anales de Biologia) (Text mainly in English and Spanish; occasionally in other European languages) 1984. a. 2000 ptas. (effective 1997). Universidad de Murcia, Servicio de Publicaciones, Santo Cristo 1, 30080 Murcia, Spain. TEL 34-68-249200. FAX 34-68-835418. E-mail: vgm@pas.um.es; URL: http://www.um.es/~spumweb. Ed. Diego Rivera Nunez. bk.rev. circ. 500. (back issues avail.) Indexed: Bio-Contr.News & Info., Ind.SST. Document type: academic/scholarly publication.
    —CISTI.

591   SP   ISSN 0213-313X
UNIVERSIDAD DE NAVARRA. PUBLICACIONES DE BIOLOGIA. SERIE ZOOLOGIA. 1980. irreg. price varies. Servicio de Publicaciones de la Universidad de Navarra, S.A., Apdo. 177, 31080 Pamplona, Spain. TEL 94-25-2700. Indexed: Ind.SST.

591   MX   ISSN 0368-8720
UNIVERSIDAD NACIONAL AUTONOMA DE MEXICO. INSTITUTO DE BIOLOGIA. ANALES: SERIE ZOOLOGIA. (Text in English, French, Spanish; summaries in English, French, Spanish) 1967. s-a. Mex.$100($30) per no. (effective 1998). Universidad Nacional Autonoma de Mexico, Instituto de Biologia, Apdo. Postal 70-233, Ciudad Universitaria, 04510 Mexico DF, Mexico. TEL 52-5-6225690. FAX 52-5-6225687. E-mail: javier@mail.ibiologia.unam.mx; URL: http://www.ibiologia.unam.mx. Ed. Algondo N. Garcia Aldrete. adv. contact: Javier Domingues Galicia. abstr.; charts; illus.; stat. circ. 1,500. (back issues avail.) Indexed: Ecol.Abstr., Rev.Appl.Entomol. Document type: monographic series.
    —Linda Hall.
    Supersedes in part: Universidad Nacional Autonoma de Mexico. Instituto de Biologia. Anales (ISSN 0076-7174)
    Description: Publishes articles in the area of Zoology.

UNIVERSITE D'ANKARA. FACULTE DES SCIENCES. COMMUNICATIONS. SERIE C. BIOLOGIE. see *BIOLOGY*

591   FR   ISSN 1144-5955
UNIVERSITE DE CLERMONT-FERRAND II. ANNALES SCIENTIFIQUES. SERIE BIOLOGIE ANIMALE. 1963. irreg. price varies. Universite de Clermont-Ferrand II, Faculte des Sciences, 63177 Aubiere, France. circ. 250. (back issues avail.)
    Formerly (until 1985): Universite de Clermont-Ferrand II. Faculte des Sciences. Annales. Biologie Animale (ISSN 0069-4681)

BIOLOGY — ZOOLOGY

591 NE ISSN 0165-9464
QL1 CODEN: BZMAAA
UNIVERSITEIT VAN AMSTERDAM. ZOOLOGISCH MUSEUM. BULLETIN. Key Title: Bulletin - Zoologisch Museum, Universiteit van Amsterdam. (Text in English, French, German) 1966. irreg. price varies. Universiteit van Amsterdam, Zoologisch Museum, P.O. Box 94766, 1090 AT Amsterdam, Netherlands. TEL 31-20-5257234. FAX 31-20-5255402. E-mail: spoel@bio.uva.nl. Ed. S. van der Spoel. **Indexed:** Biol.Abstr., Deep Sea Res.& Oceanogr.Abstr., GeoRef., Zoo.Rec. **Document type:** academic/scholarly publication, bulletin.
—CISTI.

590 US ISSN 0068-6506
CODEN: UCPZAC
UNIVERSITY OF CALIFORNIA PUBLICATIONS IN ZOOLOGY. 1902. irreg., vol.128, 1996. price varies. University of California Press, 2120 Berkeley Way, Berkeley, CA 94720. TEL 510-642-4247. FAX 510-643-7127. (Orders to: California-Princeton Fulfillment Services, 1445 Lower Ferry Rd., Ewing, NJ 08618. TEL 800-777-4726. FAX 800-999-1958) Ed.Bd. (also avail. in microfiche from BHP; back issues avail.; reprint service avail. from UMI) **Indexed:** Abstr.Hyg., Biol.Abstr., Curr.Adv.Ecol.Sci., Deep Sea Res.& Oceanogr.Abstr., Rev.Appl.Entomol., Sport Fish.Abstr., Trop.Dis.Bull., Wild.Rev., Zoo.Rec. **Document type:** monographic series.
—BLDSC (9106.150000); CISTI; Linda Hall.
Description: Explores the biology of vertebrate animals in detail.
Refereed Serial

590 US ISSN 0076-8405
QL1 CODEN: MUZPA2
UNIVERSITY OF MICHIGAN. MUSEUM OF ZOOLOGY. MISCELLANEOUS PUBLICATIONS. 1916. irreg., approx. a. price varies. University of Michigan, Museum of Zoology, Ann Arbor, MI 48109-1079. TEL 313-764-0476. FAX 313-763-4080. Ed. Gerald Smith. R&P contact: Fritz Paper. TEL 313-764-0470. circ. 400. (back issues avail.) **Indexed:** Biol.Abstr., Rev.Appl.Entomol. **Document type:** monographic series, academic/scholarly publication.
—BLDSC (5820.000000); CISTI; Linda Hall; UnCover.
Description: Contains in-depth monographic, systematic, anatomical, behavioral, and faunal studies, as well as U.M.M.Z.-type specimen catalogues.
Refereed Serial

590 US ISSN 0076-8413
QL1 CODEN: MUZOAX
UNIVERSITY OF MICHIGAN. MUSEUM OF ZOOLOGY. OCCASIONAL PAPERS. Key Title: Occasional Papers of the Museum of Zoology, University of Michigan. 1913. irreg. price varies. University of Michigan, Museum of Zoology, Ann Arbor, MI 48109-1079. TEL 313-764-0476. FAX 313-763-4080. Ed. Gerald Smith. R&P contact: Fritz Paper. TEL 313-764-0470. cum.index. circ. 400. (also avail. in microfiche from BHP; back issues avail.) **Indexed:** Biol.Abstr., Rev.Appl.Entomol. **Document type:** monographic series, academic/scholarly publication.
—CISTI.
Description: Original studies based on museum collection of material.
Refereed Serial

591 US ISSN 1053-6477
CODEN: SPUZE8
UNIVERSITY OF MICHIGAN. MUSEUM OF ZOOLOGY. SPECIAL PUBLICATIONS. 1990. irreg. price varies. University of Michigan, Museum of Zoology, Ann Arbor, MI 48109-1079. TEL 313-764-0476. FAX 313-764-4080. Ed. Gerald Smith. R&P contact: Fritz Paper. TEL 313-764-0470. (back issues avail.) **Document type:** monographic series, academic/scholarly publication.
—CISTI.
Description: Contains subjects beyond the scope of the regular series.

591 PL ISSN 0554-8136
UNIWERSYTET IM. ADAMA MICKIEWICZA. ZOOLOGIA. (Text in Polish; summaries in English) 1962. irreg., vol.38, 1993. price varies. Adam Mickiewicz University Press, Nowowiejskiego 55, 61-734 Poznan, Poland. TEL 48-61-527380. FAX 48-61-527701. TELEX 413260 UAMPL. Pub. Maria Jankowska. R&P contact: Malgorzata Bis. circ. 380. **Indexed:** AgroLibrex. **Document type:** academic/scholarly publication, monographic series.
—BLDSC (9120.480900); CISTI.
Formerly: Uniwersytet im. Adama Mickiewicza w Poznaniu. Wydzial Biologii i Nauk o Ziemi. Prace. Seria Zoologia (ISSN 0208-6484)
Description: Every volume contains current research results of one author in the field of zoology, including Ph.D. works and monographs.

591 PL ISSN 0083-4416
UNIWERSYTET JAGIELLONSKI. ZESZYTY NAUKOWE. PRACE ZOOLOGICZNE. (Text in English, Polish; summaries in English, Russian) 1957. a. price varies. Uniwersytet Jagiellonski, Ul. Golebia 24, 31-007 Warsaw, Poland. (Dist. by: Ars Polona, Krakowskie Przedmiescie 7, 00-068 Warsaw, Poland) Ed. Czeslaw Jura. bibl.; illus. **Indexed:** AgroLibrex.
—CISTI.

597 JA ISSN 0388-5461
UO/FISHES. (Text in English, Japanese; summaries in English) 1948. irreg. membership. Uo no Kai - Japanese Society of Ichthyologists, Ito Gyogaku Kenkyu Shinko Zaidan, 26-11 Kamimeguro 1-chome, Meguro-ku, Tokyo 153, Japan.

591 333.7 614.7 US ISSN 0882-5858
URBAN WILDLIFE NEWS.* (Supplement avail.: Urban Wildlife Manager's Notebook) 1977. q. $25. National Institute for Urban Wildlife, 5130 West Running Brook Rd., Columbia, MD 21044-1523. Ed. Louise E. Dove. bk.rev. circ. 1,000. (back issues avail.)
Description: Serves as clearinghouse for current urban wildlife resource activities. Coordinates recent information on non-game and urban wildlife management and lists publications and meetings of interest to conservationists.

595.7 574.1 591 II ISSN 0256-971X
QL1
UTTAR PRADESH JOURNAL OF ZOOLOGY. (Text and summaries in English) 1981. 3/yr. Rs.100($20) to individuals; institutions Rs.200($30). Uttar Pradesh Zoological Society, c/o PG-Dept. of Zoology, Muzaffarnagar 251001, India. TEL 91-131-409053. FAX 91-131-402510. Sanatan Dharm College. adv.; bk.rev. circ. 225. (back issues avail.) **Indexed:** Biol.Abstr., Rice Abstr., Triticale Abstr. **Document type:** academic/scholarly publication.
—BLDSC (9135.619000).
Refereed Serial

594 US ISSN 0042-3211
QL401 CODEN: VLGHAL
VELIGER. 1958. q. $40 to individuals (foreign $50); institutions $72 (foreign $82) (effective 1995), California Malacozoological Society, Inc., Department of Invertebrate Zoology, Santa Barbara Museum of Natural History, 2559 Puesta del Sol Rd., Santa Barbara, CA 93105. TEL 802-682-4711. FAX 805-963-9679. E-mail: inverts@sbmnh.rain.org. Ed. Barry Roth. bk.rev.; circ. 650 (paid). (reprint service avail. from ISI) **Indexed:** ASCA, Biol.Abstr., Curr.Adv.Ecol.Sci., Curr.Cont., Deep Sea Res.& Oceanogr.Abstr., Helminthol.Abstr., Ind.Sci.Rev., Ocean.Abstr., Sci.Cit.Ind., Sel.Water Res.Abstr., So.Pac.Per.Ind., SSCI.
—BLDSC (9154.300000); CISTI; Genuine Article; Linda Hall; UnCover.
Description: International journal devoted to disseminating information about mollusks and promoting the science of malacology.
Refereed Serial

594 JA ISSN 0042-3580
VENUS: JAPANESE JOURNAL OF MALACOLOGY/KAIRUIGAKU ZASSHI. (Text in English, Japanese) 1928. q. 7500 Yen (includes Chiribotan). Malacological Society of Japan - Nihon Kairui Gakkai, c/o National Science Museum, 3-23-1 Hyakunin-cho, Shinjuku-ku, Tokyo 169, Japan. Ed. Akihiko Inaba. bk.rev.; illus.; index. circ. 900.
Indexed: Biol.Abstr., Ocean.Abstr., Pollut.Abstr.
—CISTI; UnCover.

VERSUCHSTIERKUNDE. see *MEDICAL SCIENCES — Experimental Medicine, Laboratory Technique*

591 KR ISSN 0084-5604
CODEN: VEZOAK
VESTNIK ZOOLOGII/ZOOLOGICAL RECORD/VISNYK ZOOLOGII. (Text in Russian; summaries in English) 1967. bi-m. $72 (effective 1998). Akademiya Nauk Ukrainy, Institut Zoologii im. I.I. Shmal'gauzena, Vul. Khmiel'nits'kogo, 15, 252601 Kiev 22, Ukraine. TEL 38-44-2255365. E-mail: narolsky%izoology.keiv.ua@relay.ussr.eu.net. (Dist. by: Mezhdunarodnaya Kniga, B. Yakimanka 39, 117049 Moscow, Russia; Dist. in U.S. by: Victor Kamkin Inc., 4956 Boiling Brook Pkwy., Rockville, MD 20852. TEL 301-881-5973. FAX 301-881-1637) Ed. V.A. Topachevskii. abstr. **Indexed:** Bio-Contr.News & Info., Biol.Abstr., Chem.Abstr., Deep Sea Res.& Oceanogr.Abstr., Djerelo, Forest.Abstr., Geo.Abstr, Helminthol.Abstr., Ind.Vet., Poult.Abstr., Rev.Appl.Entomol., Vet.Bull.
—BLDSC (0033.150000); CASDDS; KNAW; Linda Hall; UMI.

VETERINARSKI ARHIV. see *VETERINARY SCIENCE*

591 NZ ISSN 0375-5363
VICTORIA UNIVERSITY OF WELLINGTON ZOOLOGY PUBLICATIONS. 1949. irreg. no.75, 1981. exchange basis. (Victoria University of Wellington, Zoology Department) Victoria University Press, P.O. Box 600, Wellington, New Zealand. Ed. Prof. J.B.J. Wells. cum.index. circ. 400. **Indexed:** Biol.Abstr., Deep Sea Res.& Oceanogr.Abstr., Zoo.Rec. **Document type:** academic/scholarly publication.
—CISTI.

591 US ISSN 1047-2665
SF515 CODEN: VVRMET
VIVARIUM (ESCONDIDO). 1988. bi-m. $26 to individuals (foreign $34); institutions $46. American Federation of Herpetoculturists, Box 300067, Escondido, CA 92030-0067. TEL 619-747-4948. FAX 619-747-5224. adv.; bk.rev. **Document type:** consumer publication.
Description: Covers amphibians and reptiles.

591 GW ISSN 0179-1281
VIVARIUM, DARMSTADTS TIERGARTEN; the Darmstadt animal park Vivarium informs. 1973. irreg. DM.10. Vivarium, Darmstadts Tiergarten, Schnampelweg 4, 64287 Darmstadt, Germany. FAX 49-6151-132932. Ed. Hartmut Wilke. adv. circ. 3,500. (back issues avail.) **Document type:** newsletter.

VOGELKUNDLICHE BERICHTE AUS NIEDERSACHSEN. see *BIOLOGY — Ornithology*

597 RU ISSN 0042-8752
QL614 CODEN: VOIKAR
VOPROSY IKHTIOLOGII. English translation: Journal of Ichthyology (US ISSN 0032-9452) 1961. bi-m. $208 (effective 1998). (Rossiiskaya Akademiya Nauk, Otdelenie Obshchei Biologii) Izdatel'stvo Nauka, 90 Profsoyuznaya ul., 117864 Moscow, Russia. TEL 234-05-85. Ed. G.V. Nikolskii. bk.rev.; index. (tabloid format) **Indexed:** Biol.Abstr., Chem.Abstr., Deep Sea Res.& Oceanogr.Abstr., GeoRef., Sel.Water Res.Abstr. **Document type:** academic/scholarly publication.
—BLDSC (0042.830000); CASDDS; CISTI; Linda Hall. **CCC.**

591 UK
W I PUBLICATION. (Former name of issuing body: International Waterfowl and Wetlands Research Bureau) no.12, 1990. irreg. price varies. Wetlands International, Slimbridge, Gloucester GL2 7BX, England. TEL 44-1453-890624. FAX 44-1453-890697. E-mail: nhbs@nhbs.co.uk; URL: www.nhbs.co.uk. (Orders to: National History Book Service Ltd., 2-3 Wills Rd., Totnes, Devon TQ9 5XN, England. TEL 44-1803-865913) (back issues avail.) **Document type:** monographic series, academic/scholarly publication, proceedings.
Formerly (until 1996): I W R B Publication.
Description: Covers research on waterfowl and wetland ecosystems.

BIOLOGY — ZOOLOGY

594   US   ISSN 1053-637X
QL401
WALKERANA; transactions of the P O E T S society. (Text in English, Spanish) 1980. irreg. price varies. Society for Experimental and Descriptive Malacology, Box 3037, Ann Arbor, MI 48106. TEL 313-747-2189. Ed. John B. Burch. bibl.; charts; illus. circ. 200. (back issues avail.) **Document type:** academic/scholarly publication.
   Description: Publishes original research and review articles and monographs on mollusks.

591   US   ISSN 0511-7542
QL1
WESTERN FOUNDATION OF VERTEBRATE ZOOLOGY. OCCASIONAL PAPERS. 1968. irreg. price varies. Western Foundation of Vertebrate Zoology, 439 Calle San Pablo, Camarillo, CA 93012-8506. TEL 805-388-9944. (back issues avail.) **Indexed:** Biol.Abstr., Zoo.Rec. **Document type:** monographic series.
   Description: Consists of short papers reporting original research in vertebrate zoology.

591   US   ISSN 0511-7550
QL605   CODEN: PWFVA2
WESTERN FOUNDATION OF VERTEBRATE ZOOLOGY. PROCEEDINGS. 1963. irreg. price varies. Western Foundation of Vertebrate Zoology, 439 Calle San Pablo, Camarillo, CA 93012-8506. TEL 805-388-9944. (back issues avail.) **Document type:** proceedings.
—BLDSC (6834.090000).
   Description: Contains articles on the biological and systematic phases of vertebrate zoology.

594   US   ISSN 0361-1175
QL401   CODEN: ARWMDW
WESTERN SOCIETY OF MALACOLOGISTS. ANNUAL REPORT. Key Title: Annual Report - Western Society of Malacologists. 1968. a. $15. Western Society of Malacologists, c/o Dr. Henry Chaney, 1633 Posilipo Ln., Santa Barbara, CA 93108. Ed. Dr. Hans Bertsch. illus. circ. 250. **Indexed:** Biol.Abstr., Zoo.Rec.
   Formerly: Western Society of Malacologists. Echo; Abstracts and Proceedings of the Annual Meeting.

591   UK
WETLANDS INTERNATIONAL. (Former name of issuing body: International Waterfowl and Wetlands Research Bureau) 1989. s-a. £12($24) International Waterfowl and Wetlands Research, Slimbridge, Gloucester GL2 7BX, England. TEL 44-1453-890624. FAX 44-1453-890697. TELEX 437145 WWF G. E-mail: nhbs@nhbs.co.uk; URL: www.nhbs.co.uk. (Dist. by: Natural History Book Service Ltd. (NHBS), 2-3 Willis Rd., Totnes, Devon TQ9 5XN, England. TEL 44-1803-865913. FAX 44-1803-865280) Ed. Simon Nash. bk.rev.; maps; circ. 300 (paid); 1,700 (controlled). **Document type:** newsletter.
   Formerly (until 1996): I W R B News (ISSN 1016-1317)
   Description: Reports on Wetlands International activities and global wetlands news. Also alerts members of important conferences and symposia.

WHALING ACCOUNT. see *EARTH SCIENCES — Oceanography*

591   333.7   SZ   ISSN 0250-3832
WILDBIOLOGIE. 1978. q. 43 SFr. (foreign 50 SFr.). Infodienst Wildbiologie & Oekologie, Strickhofstr. 39, CH-8057 Zurich, Switzerland. TEL 41-1-6356131. FAX 41-1-6356819. E-mail: wild@wild.unizh.ch; URL: http://www.unizh.ch/wild/. Ed. Barbara Falk. circ. 2,200. **Indexed:** Key Word Ind.Wildl.Res. **Document type:** academic/scholarly publication.
   Formerly (until 1992): Wildtiere - Wildbiologie.
   Description: Provides information on wild animals in Europe, including biology, behaviour, ecology and protection of the environment.

WILDLIFE AUSTRALIA. see *CONSERVATION*

598.294   333.95   DK   ISSN 0909-6396
QL1   CODEN: DRGBAH
WILDLIFE BIOLOGY. (Text in English; summaries in Danish and Russian) 1995. q. DKK 320 in EU countries; elsewhere DKK 400. Nordic Council for Wildlife Research, c/o Jan Bertelsen, Techn. Ed., Grenaavej 14, Kaloe, DK-8410 Roende, Denmark. TEL 45-89-20-15-08. FAX 45-89-20-15-15. E-mail: ffjb@dmu.dk. Ed. Harto Linden. circ. 2,200. **Indexed:** Biol.Abstr., Curr.Adv.Ecol.Sci., Geo.Abstr., Key Word Ind.Wildl.Res., Nutr.Abstr., Poult.Abstr., Sport Fish.Abstr., Wild.Rev., Wildlife Rev., Zoo.Rec. **Document type:** academic/scholarly publication.
—BLDSC (9317.273000); EMDOCS; Linda Hall; UnCover.
   Formed by the merger of (1945-1995): Danish Review of Game Biology (ISSN 0374-7344) & Finnish Game Research (ISSN 0783-4365); Which was formerly (1948-1988): Riistatieteelisiaa Jukaisuja (ISSN 0015-2447); Swedish Wildlife Research (ISSN 0349-5116); Which was formerly (1955-1979): Viltrevy (ISSN 0505-611X)
   Description: Publishes high-quality practical and theoretical research from all areas of wildlife science, with the primary task of creating the scientific basis for the enhancement of conservation and management practices for wildlife species and their environments. Promotes the discussion of important issues.
Refereed Serial

WILDLIFE DISEASE REVIEW. see *MEDICAL SCIENCES*

WILDLIFE MONOGRAPHS. see *CONSERVATION*

WILDLIFE RESEARCH. see *CONSERVATION*

WILDLIFE RESEARCH REPORT. see *CONSERVATION*

WILDLIFE SOCIETY BULLETIN. see *CONSERVATION*

591   US
WOLF! MAGAZINE. 1982. q. $22.50 (Canada & Mexico $29; elsewhere $37.50). North American Wildlife Park Foundation, 4004 E. 800 N., Battle Ground, IN 47920. TEL 765-567-2265. FAX 765-567-4299. E-mail: wolf!@dcwi.com; URL: http://www.tigerden.com/wolf-park. Ed. Holly Jaycox Di Maio; Pub. Erich Klinghammer. R&P contact: Holly Jaycox Di Maio. adv. contact: Holly Jaycox Di Maio.

591   US
WOLF PARK NEWS. vol.6, 1979. q. $20. North American Wildlife Park Foundation Inc., Wolf Park, Battle Ground, IN 47920. TEL 317-567-2265. FAX 317-567-2084. Ed. Erich Klinghammer. bk.rev.; film rev.; abstr.; illus.; stat. circ. 3,000. (tabloid format) **Indexed:** Biol.Dig. **Document type:** newsletter.
   Formerly (until 1985): Predator.

591   636   NE
WORLD ANIMAL SCIENCE. (Consists of: Series A, Basic Information; Series B, Disciplinary Approach; Series C, Production System Approach) (Text in English) 1981. irreg., latest vol.B9, 1993. price varies. Elsevier Science B.V., Books Division, P.O. Box 211, 1000 AE Amsterdam, Netherlands. TEL 31-20-4853911. FAX 31-20-4853705. TELEX 18582 ESPA NL. E-mail: nlinfo-f@elsevier.nl; usinfo-f@elsevier.com; forinfo-kyf04035@niftyserve.or.jp; URL: http://www.elsevier.nl/. (Subscr. in the Americas to: Elsevier Science, Regional Sales Office, Box 945, New York, NY 10159-0945. TEL 212-633-3730. FAX 212-633-3680; Subscr. in Australasia and the Far East to: Elsevier Science (Singapore) Pte Ltd, No.1 Temasek Ave., No.17-01 Millenia Tower, Singapore 039192, Singapore. TEL 65-434-3727. FAX 65-337-2230; Subscr. in Japan to: Elsevier Science Japan, 9-15 Higashi-Azabu 1-chome, Minato-ku, Tokyo 106, Japan. TEL 81-3-5561-5033. FAX 81-3-5561-5047) (back issues avail.) **Document type:** monographic series.
Refereed Serial

WORLD BIODIVERSITY DATABASE SERIES. see *EARTH SCIENCES*

591   FR   ISSN 1257-5011
WORLD RABBIT SCIENCE. q. 498 F. (foreign 625 F.) (effective 1997). Association Francaise de Cuniculture, B.P. 50, 63370 Lempdes, France. TEL 33-4-73920152. FAX 33-4-73928680. Ed. F. Lebas. adv.; bibl.; illus. circ. 1,500. **Indexed:** Anim.Breed.Abstr., Food Sci.& Tech.Abstr., Ind.Vet., Nutr.Abstr., Soyabean Abstr., Trop.Oil Seeds Abstr., Vet.Bull.
—BLDSC (9358.560000).
   Formed by the merger of (1980-1992): Journal of Applied Rabbit Research (ISSN 0738-9760); (1983-1992): Cuni - Sciences (ISSN 0984-7847)

595.1   628.4   US
WORM DIGEST; worms deepening our connection to food and soil. 1993. q. $12; newsstand price: $3.50. Edible City Resource Center, Box 544, Eugene, OR 97440-0544. TEL 541-896-9058. FAX 541-896-9058. E-mail: wormdigest@aol.com. Eds. S. Zorba Frankel, Stephen White. adv.: page $22; adv. contact: S. Zorba Frankel. bk.rev. circ. 8,500. (back issues avail.) **Document type:** newspaper.
   Description: Reports on worms, worm composting and worm technologies for organic waste utilization.

WYOMING WILDLIFE. see *CONSERVATION*

591   PL   ISSN 0239-7994
WYZSZA SZKOLA PEDAGOGICZNA IM. KOMISJI EDUKACJI NARODOWEJ W KRAKOWIE. ROCZNIK NAUKOWO-DYDAKTYCZNY. PRACE ZOOLOGICZNE. (Text in Polish; summaries in English, Russian) 1967. irreg. Wydawnictwo Naukowe W S P, Ul. Karmelicka 41, 31-128 Krakow, Poland. TEL 33-79-20. bibl.; illus.

639.34   597   NE   ISSN 0166-8706
HET ZEE-AQUARIUM. 1949. m. fl.56.50. Nederlandse en Belgische Bond van Zee-Aquarium-Verenĩgingen (NBBZ), Postbus 45, 7680 AA Vroomshoop, Netherlands. TEL 31-546-641925. FAX 31-546-645500. Ed. A.M.H. Wisselaar. R&P contact: A.M.H. Wisselaar. adv.; bk.rev.; charts; illus. circ. 4,000. **Document type:** academic/scholarly publication, consumer publication.
   Formerly (until 1979): Kor (ISSN 1382-2306)

591   GW   ISSN 0044-2291
                         CODEN: ZANZA9
ZEITSCHRIFT FUER ANGEWANDTE ZOOLOGIE; german journal for applied zoology. 1914. q. price varies. Duncker and Humblot GmbH, Postfach 410329, 12113 Berlin, Germany. TEL 49-30-7900060. FAX 49-30-79000631. E-mail: duh-werbung@t-online.de. Ed. P.-D. Hensen. bk.rev.; charts; illus.; index. **Indexed:** Apic.Abstr., Biol.Abstr., Biotech.Abstr., Chem.Abstr., Excerp.Med., Forest.Abstr., Key Word Ind.Wildl.Res., Prod.Abstr., Ind.Vet., Rev.Appl.Entomol., Soils & Fert., Vet.Bull. **Document type:** academic/scholarly publication.
—BLDSC (9451.000000); CASDDS; Linda Hall; SWETS. CCC.

597   GW   ISSN 0939-6330
ZEITSCHRIFT FUER FISCHKUNDE. 1991. biennial. DM.34. Verlag Natur und Wissenschaft, Postfach 170209, 42624 Solingen, Germany. TEL 49-212-819878. FAX 49-212-816216. Ed. Harro Hieronimus. adv.: B&W page DM.200. bk.rev. **Indexed:** IBR. **Document type:** academic/scholarly publication.
   Description: Contains information about all areas of ichthyology.

ZEITSCHRIFT FUER JAGDWISSENSCHAFT. see *SPORTS AND GAMES*

BIOLOGY — ZOOLOGY

594 GW ISSN 0044-3468
QL700 CODEN: ZSAEA7
ZEITSCHRIFT FUER SAEUGETIERKUNDE; international journal of mammalian biology. (Text in English, French, German) 1926. 6/yr. DM.410 (foreign DM.422) (effective 1996). (Deutsche Gesellschaft fuer Saeugetierkunde) Gustav Fischer Verlag Jena, Villengang 2, 07745 Jena, Germany. TEL 49-3641-626444. FAX 49-3641-626500. Eds. Dr. Dieter Kruska, Dr. Peter Langer. adv.: page DM.750; trim 170 x 240. bk.rev.; illus.; index. circ. 900. (reprint service avail. from ISI; back issues avail.) **Indexed:** Anim.Breed.Abstr., ASCA, Biol.Abstr., Curr.Adv.Ecol.Sci., Curr.Cont., Dairy Sci.Abstr., Helminthol.Abstr., Ind.Sci.Rev., Ind.Vet., Key Word Ind.Wildl.Res., Sci.Cit.Ind., So.Pac.Per.Ind., Sport Fish.Abstr., Vet.Bull., Wild.Rev., Zoo.Rec. **Document type:** academic/scholarly publication.
—BLDSC (9485.500000); CISTI; EMDOCS; Genuine Article; KNAW; KR SourceOne; Linda Hall; SWETS; UnCover. **CCC.**

ZIVA; casopis pro biologickou praci. see BIOLOGY

591 BE ISSN 0044-5029
QL77.A6 CODEN: ZOOAB4
ZOO ANVERS. Dutch edition: Zoo Antwerpen. 1935. q. 420 BEF. Societe Royale de Zoologie d'Anvers - Koninklijke Maatschappij voor Dierkunde van Antwerpen, Koningin Astridplein 26, 2018 Antwerp, Belgium. TEL 32-3-2024540. FAX 32-3-2310018. Ed. F.J. Daman. R&P contact: I. Segers. adv. contact: I. Segers. bk.rev.; charts; illus.; index. circ. 37,000. **Indexed:** Biol.Abstr., Ind.Vet., Sport Fish.Abstr., Wild.Rev., Zoo.Rec.
—CISTI.
Description: News of recent arrivals at the zoo, scientific activities undertaken by zoo staff, as well as educational and cultural activities and other items of interest to a general audience, and especially our members.
Refereed Serial

591 US ISSN 0733-3188
QL77.5 CODEN: ZOBIDX
ZOO BIOLOGY. bi-m. $795 (foreign $900) (effective 1998). John Wiley & Sons, Inc., Journals, 605 Third Ave., New York, NY 10158. TEL 212-850-6645. FAX 212-850-6021. TELEX 12-7063. E-mail: SUBINFO@JWILEY.COM; URL: http://www.wiley.co.uk. (Subscr. outside the Americas to: John Wiley & Sons Ltd., Baffins Ln., Chichester, W. Sussex PO19 1UD, England. TEL 44-1243-779777. FAX 44-1243-776128) Ed. Donald G. Lindburg. adv.: B&W page £640, color page £1515; trim 229 x 152. bk.rev. circ. 600. (also avail. in microform from UMI; back issues avail.) **Indexed:** ASCA, Biol.Abstr., Chem.Abstr., Curr.Adv.Ecol.Sci., Curr.Adv.Genetics & Molec.Biol., Curr.Cont., Ind.Vet., Psychol.Abstr. (1982-), Sport Fish.Abstr., Vet.Bull., Wild.Rev., Zoo.Rec. **Document type:** academic/scholarly publication.
●Also available online.
—BLDSC (9516.100000); CASDDS; CISTI; Genuine Article; Linda Hall; SWETS; UnCover. **CCC.**
Description: Concerned with reproduction, demographics behavior, medicine, husbandry, management, conservation, and all empirical aspects of the exhibition and maintenance of wild animals in wildlife parks, zoos, and aquariums.
Refereed Serial

591 GW
ZOO - NACHRICHTEN; Allwetterzoo - Nachrichten. 1980. 3/yr. DM.20. Westfaelischer Zoologischer Garten Muenster GmbH, Sentruperstr. 315, 48161 Muenster, Germany. TEL 49-251-89040. FAX 49-251-890490. Ed. Ilona Zuehlke. adv.; bk.rev. circ. 5,000. (back issues avail.) **Document type:** consumer publication.
Description: Reports and news about animals and events at the Allwetterzoo.

591 JA
ZOO YOKOHAMA/ZOOLOGICAL SOCIETY OF YOKOHAMA. REPORT. (Text in Japanese) irreg. Yohohamashi Dobutsuen Tomo no Kai - Zoological Society of Yokohama, Nogeyama Dobutsuen, 63-10, Oimatsucho, Nishi-ku, Yokohama-shi, Kanagawa-ken 220, Japan.

591 028.5 US ISSN 0737-9005
ZOOBOOKS. 1980. m. $20.95 (Canada $25.95; elsewhere $31.95). Wildlife Education Ltd., 9820 Willow Creek Rd., Ste. 300, San Diego, CA 92131-1112. TEL 619-578-2440. FAX 619-578-9658. Ed. Ed Shadek; Pub. Ed Shadek. R&P contact: Sally Mercer. circ. 425,000 (paid). **Document type:** consumer publication.
—KR SourceOne; UnCover.
Description: Examines wildlife and their habitats for children 5-12.

591 VE ISSN 0798-7811
▼**ZOOCRIADEROS.** (Text in English, Spanish, Portuguese; summaries in English) 1996. 3/yr. $800 (effective 1997). Centro de Investigacion y Reproduccion de Especies Silvestres, Apdo. Postal 397, Merida 5101, Venezuela. TEL 58-74-712939. E-mail: cires@ciens.ula.ve; URL: http://www.ciens.ula.ve/~cires. Ed. Hector Fernando Aguilar. adv. contact: Lieselotte Hoeger de Aguilar. bk.rev.; bibl.; illus. circ. 2,500. **Indexed:** Biol.Abstr.
●Also available online.
Refereed Serial

590 IT
ZOOESPRESSO. 1969. m. L.3800. B.S.C., Via G. Servais 126, 10146 Turin, Italy. Ed. Bosco Pier Carlo. adv. circ. 17,000.

591 GW
DER ZOOFREUND. 1971. q. Zoofreunde Hannover e.V., Adenaueralle 3, 30175 Hannover, Germany. TEL 49-511-280740. FAX 49-511-28074-56. Ed. Frank-Dieter Busch. bk.rev. **Document type:** newsletter.

591 US ISSN 0163-416X
ZOOGOER. 1963. bi-m. $25 membership. Friends of the National Zoo, National Zoological Park, Washington, DC 20008. TEL 202-673-4711. FAX 202-673-4738. E-mail: susan@fonz.org; URL: http://www.fonz.org. Ed. Susan Lumpkin; Pub. Clinton A. Fields. R&P contact: Howard Youth. adv.: color page $1800; adv. contact: Susan Lumpkin. bk.rev.; illus. circ. 25,000. **Document type:** consumer publication.
Formerly: Spots and Stripes (ISSN 0038-8424)
Description: Articles, news, and photography pertaining to wildlife conservation, natural history and animal behavior.

591 GW ISSN 0044-5088
CODEN: ZLGAAA
ZOOLOGICA; Originalabhandlungen aus dem Gebiet der Zoologie. (Text in English, German) 1888. 2/yr. price varies. E. Schweizerbart'sche Verlagsbuchhandlung, Johannesstr. 3A, 70176 Stuttgart, Germany. TEL 49-711-625001. FAX 49-711-625005. Eds. F. Schaller, W. Funke. **Indexed:** Biol.Abstr., Deep Sea Res.& Oceanogr.Abstr., GeoRef. **Document type:** academic/scholarly publication.
—CISTI. **CCC.**

591 SP ISSN 1130-4251
QL293
ZOOLOGICA BAETICA. 1989. a. Universidad de Granada, Departamento de Biologia Animal, Ecologia y Genetica, Servicio de Publicaciones, Antiguo Colegio Maximo, Campus de Cartuja, 18071 Granada, Spain. TEL 34-58-243930. FAX 34-58-242827. **Indexed:** Ind.SST. **Document type:** academic/scholarly publication.

591 PL ISSN 0044-510X
QL1 CODEN: ZOPOAG
ZOOLOGICA POLONIAE; Archivum Societatis Zoologorum Poloniae. (Text in English; summaries in Polish) 1935. q. 15 Zl. (foreign $20). Polskie Towarzystwo Zoologiczne, Ul. Sienkiewicza 21, 50-335 Wroclaw, Poland. TEL 48-71-225041. FAX 48-71-222817. Ed. Antoni Ogorzalek. R&P contact: Ewa Swidnicka. charts; illus.; index. circ. 700. (also avail. in microfilm) **Indexed:** AgroLibrex, Biol.Abstr., Chem.Abstr., Deep Sea Res.& Oceanogr.Abstr., Ind.Vet., Ref.Zh., Sport Fish.Abstr., Vet.Bull., Wild.Rev., Zoo.Rec. **Document type:** academic/scholarly publication.
—BLDSC (9519.000000); CASDDS; CISTI; KNAW; Linda Hall.
Refereed Serial

591 UK ISSN 0300-3256
QL1 CODEN: ZLSCA8
ZOOLOGICA SCRIPTA; an international journal of evolutionary zoology. (Text in English) 1971. q. fl.980($563) to institutions (effective 1998). (Kungliga Svenska Vetenskapsakademien, SW - Royal Swedish Academy of Sciences) Elsevier Science Ltd., Pergamon, P.O. Box 800, Kidlington, Oxford OX5 1DX, England. (Subscr. to: Elsevier Science, Regional Sales Office, P.O. Box 211, 1000 AE Amsterdam, Netherlands; Subscr. in the Americas to: Elsevier Science, Regional Sales Office, Box 945, New York, NY 10159-0945) (Co-sponsor: Norwegian Academy of Science and Letters) Eds. Fredrik Pleijel, Per Sundberg. charts; illus.; index. circ. 800. (also avail. in microfilm from UMI; back issues avail.) **Indexed:** ASCA, Curr.Cont., Ind.Sci.Rev. **Document type:** academic/scholarly publication.
—BLDSC (9519.300000); CISTI; EMDOCS; Genuine Article; Linda Hall; SWETS; UMI; UnCover. **CCC.**
Supersedes: Arkiv for Zoologi (ISSN 0004-2110)
Description: Publishes original research in the areas of taxonomy, phylogeny, and biogeography.
Refereed Serial

591 914.106 UK
ZOOLOGICAL CORNWALL AND THE ISLES OF SCILLY. 1991. biennial. price varies. (Institute of Cornish Studies) University of Exeter Pess, Trevithick Centre, Trevenson Rd., Pool Redruth, Redruth, Corn. TR15 3PL, England. TEL 01209-712203. Eds. Colin French, Stella Turk. (back issues avail.) **Document type:** academic/scholarly publication.
Description: Studies the zoology of Cornwall and the Isles of Scilly.

591 US
ZOOLOGICAL PARKS & AQUARIUMS IN THE AMERICAS. 1930. a. $85 to non-members; members $40; libraries $60. American Zoo and Aquarium Association, Oglebay Park, Wheeling, WV 26003. TEL 304-242-2160. FAX 304-242-2283. E-mail: azaoms.aol.org; URL: www.aza.org. Ed. Linda Boyd. adv.; stat.; index. circ. 3,700. **Document type:** directory.
—CISTI.
Formerly: Zoos and Aquariums in the Americas (ISSN 0740-7610)

ZOOLOGICAL RECORD. see BIOLOGY — Abstracting, Bibliographies, Statistics

ZOOLOGICAL RECORD SEARCH GUIDE. see BIOLOGY — Abstracting, Bibliographies, Statistics

ZOOLOGICAL RECORD SERIAL SOURCES. see BIOLOGY — Abstracting, Bibliographies, Statistics

591 JA ISSN 0289-0003
QL1 CODEN: ZOSCEX
ZOOLOGICAL SCIENCE; an international journal. (Text in English) 1984. bi-m. DM.560 (effective 1997). Zoological Society of Japan, Toshin Bldg., 2-27-2 Hongo, Bunkyo-ku, Tokyo 113, Japan. TEL 81-3-3812-2111. FAX 81-3-3816-1965. (Dist. by: Business Center for Academic Societies Japan, 5-16-9 Honkomagome, Bunkyo-ku, Tokyo 113, Japan. TEL 81-3-5814-5811; Dist. overseas by: V S P, P.O. Box 346, 3700 AH Zeist, Netherlands. TEL 31-30-6925790. FAX 31-30-6932081) Ed. Noriyuki Satoh. adv.; bk.rev. circ. 3,400. (also avail. in microform from UMI; back issues avail.; reprint service avail. from UMI) **Indexed:** Anim.Breed.Abstr., Apic.Abstr., ASCA, Biol.Abstr., Chem.Abstr., Curr.Adv.Ecol.Sci., Curr.Cont., Deep Sea Res.& Oceanogr.Abstr., Helminthol.Abstr., Ind.Sci.Rev., Ind.Vet., Neurosci.Cit.Ind., Protozool.Abstr., Sci.Cit.Ind., Zoo.Rec. **Document type:** academic/scholarly publication.
—BLDSC (9520.150000); CASDDS; CISTI; EMDOCS; Genuine Article; KNAW; Linda Hall; SWETS; UMI; UnCover. **CCC.**
Formerly: Annotationes Zoologicae Japonenses (ISSN 0003-5092)
Description: Original and review articles on all aspects of zoology.
Refereed Serial

591 II ISSN 0373-5893
CODEN: PZSIAE
ZOOLOGICAL SOCIETY, CALCUTTA. PROCEEDINGS. (Text in English) 1948. s-a. Rs.200($25) Zoological Society, Calcutta, 35 Ballygunge Circular Rd., Calcutta 700 019, India. TEL 75-3681. Ed. A.S. Mukherjee. adv. circ. 450. **Indexed:** Biol.Abstr., Curr.Cont.
—CISTI.

591 QL1	II	ISSN 0049-8769 CODEN: JZSIAG

ZOOLOGICAL SOCIETY OF INDIA. JOURNAL. (Text in English) 1948. s-a. Rs.60($15) Zoological Society of India, Department of Zoology, Utkal University, Bhubaneswar, 751004 Orissa, India. (Dist. by: HPC Publisher's Distributors (Pvt.) Ltd., 4805-24, 1st Fl., Bharat Ram Rd., Darya Ganj, New Delhi 110 002, India. TEL 91-11-3254402. FAX 91-11-6863511) adv.; bk.rev.; charts; illus. circ. 400. (tabloid format) **Indexed:** Biol.Abstr., GeoRef., Zoo.Rec. **Document type:** academic/scholarly publication.
—CISTI; Linda Hall.

591 QL1	UK	ISSN 0084-5612 CODEN: SZSLAM

ZOOLOGICAL SOCIETY OF LONDON. SYMPOSIA. 1966. irreg., vol.67, 1995. price varies. Oxford University Press, Walton St., Oxford OX2 6DP, England. TEL 44-1865-56767. FAX 44-1865-56646. (Subscr. in U.S. to: Oxford University Press Inc., 2001 Evans Rd., Cary, NC 27513. TEL 919-677-0977. FAX 919-677-1714) (reprint service avail. from ISI) **Indexed:** Anim.Breed.Abstr., Biol.Abstr., Chem.Abstr., Curr.Adv.Ecol.Sci., Deep Sea Res.& Oceanogr.Abstr., GeoRef., Ind.Vet., Sport Fish.Abstr., Vet.Bull., Wild.Rev., Zoo.Rec. **Document type:** proceedings.
—BLDSC (8585.080000); CASDDS; CISTI; Linda Hall; SWETS. **CCC.**
Refereed Serial

591 QL307.2	CH	ISSN 1021-5506

ZOOLOGICAL STUDIES. (Summaries in Chinese) 1962. q. $60 to individuals; institutions $100. Academia Sinica, Institute of Zoology - Chung Yang Yen Chiu Yuan Tung Wu Hsueh Yen Chiu So, Nankang, Taipei, Taiwan 11529, Republic of China. TEL 886-2-7899507. FAX 886-2-7858059. Ed. Lucia Liu. circ. 700. (reprint service avail. from ISI) **Indexed:** Anim.Breed.Abstr., Biol.Abstr., Chem.Abstr., Curr.Adv.Ecol.Sci., Curr.Cont., Helminthol.Abstr., Ind.Vet., Math.R., Protozool.Abstr., Sci.Cit.Ind., Sport Fish.Abstr., Vet.Bull., Wild.Rev., Zoo.Rec. **Document type:** academic/scholarly publication.
—BLDSC (9520.250000); CASDDS; CISTI; Genuine Article; Linda Hall; UnCover.
Formerly (until 1994): Academia Sinica. Institute of Zoology. Bulletin (ISSN 0001-3943)
Refereed Serial

591 574 QL309	II	ISSN 0255-9587

ZOOLOGICAL SURVEY OF INDIA. BULLETIN. (Text in English) 1978. q. price varies. Zoological Survey of India, 34, Chittaranjan Ave., Calcutta 700012, India. circ. 400. (back issues avail.) **Indexed:** Abstr.Hyg., Rev.Appl.Entomol.
—CISTI; Linda Hall.

591 574	II	ISSN 0379-3540

ZOOLOGICAL SURVEY OF INDIA. MEMOIRS. (Text in English) 1907. irreg. price varies. Zoological Survey of India, 34, Chittaranjan Ave., Calcutta 700012, India. circ. 450. (back issues avail.) **Indexed:** Biol.Abstr., Rev.Appl.Entomol.

591	II	

ZOOLOGICAL SURVEY OF INDIA. NEWS. (Text in English) 1978. 2/yr. Zoological Survey of India, 34, Chittaranjan Ave., Calcutta 700012, India. circ. 600. (back issues avail.) **Indexed:** Rev.Appl.Entomol.

591	RU	ISSN 0044-5134 CODEN: ZOLZAT

ZOOLOGICHESKII ZHURNAL. (Text in Russian; summaries in English) 1916. m. $267 (effective 1998). (Rossiiskaya Akademiya Nauk, Otdelenie Obshchei Biologii) Izdatel'stvo Nauka, 90 Profsoyuznaya ul., 117864 Moscow, Russia. TEL 095-336-0266. FAX 095-420-2220. (Dist. in U.S. by: Victor Kamkin Inc., 4956 Boiling Brook Pkwy., Rockville, MD 20852. TEL 301-881-5973. FAX 301-881-1637) bk.rev.; index. (tabloid format) **Indexed:** Anim.Breed.Abstr., ASCA, Bio-Contr.News & Info., Biol.Abstr., Chem.Abstr., Curr.Adv.Ecol.Sci., Curr.Cont., Deep Sea Res.& Oceanogr.Abstr., Forest.Abstr., Forest Prod.Abstr., Geo.Abstr., Helminthol.Abstr., Ind.Sci.Rev., Nutr.Abstr., Ocean.Abstr., Pollut.Abstr., Protozool.Abstr., Rev.Appl.Entomol., Sci.Cit.Ind., Sel.Water Res.Abstr., Soils & Fert., Sport Fish.Abstr., Wild.Rev., Zoo.Rec. **Document type:** academic/scholarly publication.
—BLDSC (0072.240000); CASDDS; CISTI; Genuine Article; KNAW. **CCC.**

ZOOLOGISCH-BOTANISCHE GESELLSCHAFT IN OESTERREICH. VERHANDLUNGEN. see *BIOLOGY — Botany*

ZOOLOGISCH - BOTANISCHE GESELLSCHAFT, VIENNA. ABHANDLUNGEN. see *BIOLOGY — Botany*

591 QL1	GW	ISSN 0044-5150 CODEN: ZOBEAI

ZOOLOGISCHE BEITRAEGE; Neue Folge. (Text and summaries in English, German) 1883. s-a. price varies. Duncker und Humblot GmbH, Postfach 410329, 12113 Berlin, Germany. TEL 49-30-7900060. FAX 49-30-79000631. E-mail: duh-werbung@t-online.de. Ed.Bd. charts; illus.; index per vol. **Indexed:** Biol.Abstr., Rev.Appl.Entomol., Zoo.Rec. **Document type:** academic/scholarly publication.
—BLDSC (9521.000000); CASDDS; CISTI; KNAW. **CCC.**

591	GW	ISSN 0044-5169 CODEN: ZOGAAV

DER ZOOLOGISCHE GARTEN; Zeitschrift fuer die gesamte Tiergaertnerei. (Text and summaries in English and German) 1929. 6/yr. DM.234 (foreign DM.249) (effective 1996). (Verband Deutscher Zoodirektoren) Gustav Fischer Verlag Jena, Villengang 2, 07745 Jena, Germany. TEL 49-3641-626444. FAX 49-3641-626500. (Subscr. to: Postfach 100537, 07705 Jena, Germany) (Co-sponsor: International Union of Directors of Zoological Gardens) Ed. W. Grummt. adv.: page DM.900; trim 170 x 240. bk.rev.; abstr.; bibl.; charts; illus.; index. circ. 900. (reprint service avail. from ISI) **Indexed:** Biol.Abstr., Ind.Vet., Key Word Ind.Wildl.Res., Protozool.Abstr., Ref.Zh., Sport Fish.Abstr., Vet.Bull., Wild.Rev., Zoo.Rec. **Document type:** academic/scholarly publication.
—BLDSC (9522.500000). **CCC.**

591	GW	ISSN 0044-5231 CODEN: ZOANA6

ZOOLOGISCHER ANZEIGER. (Text in English and German; summaries in English) 1878. 4/yr. DM.466 (foreign DM.474) (effective 1996). Gustav Fischer Verlag Jena, Villengang 2, 07745 Jena, Germany. TEL 49-3641-626444. FAX 49-3641-626500. (Subscr. to: Postfach 100537, 07705 Jena, Germany) Ed. H.-E. Gruner. adv.: page DM.750; trim 210 x 280. bibl.; charts; illus.; index. circ. 350. (also avail. in microform from SWZ; reprint service avail. from ISI) **Indexed:** Anim.Breed.Abstr., ASCA, Bio-Contr.News & Info., Biol.Abstr., Chem.Abstr., Curr.Adv.Ecol.Sci., Curr.Cont., Deep Sea Res.& Oceanogr.Abstr., Ecol.Abstr., Helminthol.Abstr., Ind.Vet., Ref.Zh., Sci.Cit.Ind., Sport Fish.Abstr., Vet.Bull., Wild.Rev., Zoo.Rec. **Document type:** academic/scholarly publication.
—BLDSC (9528.000000); CASDDS; CISTI; Genuine Article; KNAW; Linda Hall; SWETS; UnCover. **CCC.**
Incorporates (1886-1995): Zoologische Jahrbuecher. Abteilung fuer Systematik, Oekologie und Geographie der Tiere (ISSN 0044-5193)

591 QL1	GW	ISSN 0944-2006 CODEN: ZOLGEA

ZOOLOGY - ANALYSIS OF COMPLEX SYSTEMS. (Text in English) 1886. 4/yr. DM.456 (foreign DM.464) (effective 1996). Gustav Fischer Verlag Jena, Villengang 2, 07745 Jena, Germany. TEL 49-3641-626444. FAX 49-3641-626500. (Subscr. to: Postfach 100537, 07705 Jena, Germany) Ed.Bd. adv.: page DM.825; trim 210 x 280. bk.rev.; bibl.; charts; illus.; index. circ. 350. (reprint service avail. from ISI) **Indexed:** Apic.Abstr., ASCA, Biol.Abstr., Chem.Abstr., Curr.Cont., Deep Sea Res.& Oceanogr.Abstr., Ecol.Abstr., Ind.Sci.Rev., Neurosci.Cit.Ind., Ref.Zh., Sci.Cit.Ind., SSCI, VITIS. **Document type:** academic/scholarly publication.
—BLDSC (9529.330000); CASDDS; CISTI; Genuine Article; Linda Hall. **CCC.**
Supersedes (in 1993): Zoologische Jahrbuecher. Abteilung fuer Allgemeine Zoologie und Physiologie der Tiere (ISSN 0044-5185) & Zoologische Jahrbuecher. Abteilung fuer Anatomie und Ontogenie der Tiere (ISSN 0044-5177)

591	GW	ISSN 0939-7140

ZOOLOGY IN THE MIDDLE EAST. (Text in English, German) 1986. irreg. (1-2/yr.). DM.27. Max Kasparek Verlag, Bleichstr. 1, 69120 Heidelberg, Germany. TEL 49-6221-475069. FAX 49-6221-471858. adv. **Indexed:** Biol.Abstr., Wild Life Rev., Zoo.Rec. **Document type:** academic/scholarly publication.
Description: Covers the whole scope of zoology in the Middle East.
Refereed Serial

ZOOMORPHOLOGY; an international journal of comparative and functional morphology. see *BIOLOGY*

ZOONOOZ. see *CONSERVATION*

591	US	

ZOOSLETTER. 1961. bi-m. membership. Indianapolis Zoological Society, Inc., 1200 W. Washington St., Indianapolis, IN 46222. TEL 317-638-8072. Ed. Vaughn Bidwell. adv. contact: Meg Beasley. bk.rev.; illus. circ. 40,000. **Document type:** newsletter.
Formerly: Zoo's Letter (ISSN 0044-5304)

591	FR	ISSN 0984-4708

30 MILLIONS D'AMIS - LA VIE DES BETES. 1978. m. 250 F. 30 Millions d'Amis, 78 rue Jules Guesde, 92300 Levallois-Perret, France. TEL 40-87-40-00. FAX 40-87-40-7. Ed. Loic Michel. illus. **Indexed:** Pt.de Rep. (1987-). **Document type:** newspaper.
Formerly (until 1987): Vie des Betes.

BIOPHYSICS

see *Biology–Biophysics*

BIOTECHNOLOGY

see *Biology–Biotechnology*

BIRTH CONTROL

see also *Population Studies*

613.9	GW	ISSN 0931-3613

A L F A - RUNDBRIEF. 1985. q. DM.20. Aktion Lebensrecht fuer Alle, Bornheimerstr. 90, 5311 Bonn, Germany. TEL 0228-656481. FAX 0228-696216. Ed. Jochen Beuckers. bk.rev. circ. 5,000. (back issues avail.)
Description: Information about new fertility techniques, abortions, debate about bioethics and the ethical questions of abortion.

613.9 340.5	UK	

A L R A NEWSLETTER. q. £12 to members. Abortion Law Reform Association, 11-13 Charlotte St., London WlP IHD, England. TEL 0171-637-7264. Ed. Jane Roe. adv.; bk.rev. circ. 2,000.
Former titles (until 1995): Breaking Chains (ISSN 0309-7978); (until 1977): A L R A Newsletter.
Description: Presents a pro-choice forum for the association.

613.942	US	

A V S C NEWS. 1963. 4/yr. membership. (Association for Voluntary Surgical Contraception) A V S C International, 79 Madison Ave., 7th fl., New York, NY 10016-7802. TEL 212-561-8000. FAX 212-779-9439. E-mail: info@avsc.org. Ed. Joanne Tzanis. R&P contact: Pamela Beyer Harper. TEL 212-561-8043. illus.; stat. circ. 8,000. **Indexed:** Curr.Lit.Fam.Plan. **Document type:** newsletter.
Formerly: A V S News (ISSN 0001-2904)
Description: Reports news and information related to family planning and reproductive health worldwide.

ABORTION REVIEW. see *WOMEN'S HEALTH*

BIRTH CONTROL

613.9405 NE ISSN 0267-4874
CODEN: ADCOEB
ADVANCES IN CONTRACEPTION. (Text in English; summaries in French, Spanish) 1985. q. fl.460 to institutions; $236 to institutions in U.S. (effective 1998). (Society for the Advancement of Contraception, US) Kluwer Academic Publishers, Postbus 17, 3300 AA Dordrecht, Netherlands. TEL 31-78-6392392. FAX 31-78-6392254. TELEX 29245 KAPG NL. E-mail: services@wkap.nl; URL: http://www.wkap.nl. (Dist. by: Kluwer Academic Publishers Group, P.O. Box 322, 3300 AH Dordrecht, Netherlands. TEL 31-78-6392392. FAX 31-78-6546474; N. America dist. addr.: Box 358, Accord Sta., Hingham, MA 02018-0358. TEL 617-871-6600. FAX 617-871-6528) Ed. G.I. Zatuchni. adv.; bibl.; charts; illus.; stat.; index. (also avail. in microform from UMI; back issues avail.; reprint service avail. from SWZ) **Indexed:** ASCA, Curr.Cont., Excerp.Med., Ind.Med., Popul.Ind., Rev.Med.& Vet.Mycol. **Document type:** academic/scholarly publication.
—BLDSC (0704.145000); CASDDS; CISTI; EMDOCS; Genuine Article; KNAW; SWETS; UMI; UnCover. **CCC.**
Description: Publishes papers concerned with research in reproduction and clinical aspects of contraception. Aims to stimulate knowledge of fertility regulation and family planning.
Refereed Serial

613.94 US ISSN 1012-8689
CODEN: ACDSEL
ADVANCES IN CONTRACEPTIVE DELIVERY SYSTEMS. 1980. q. $180 to individuals (foreign $190); institutions $200 (foreign $210) (effective 1996). (World Federation of Contraception - Health) Reproductive Health Center, 78 Surfsong Rd., Kiawah Island, SC 29455. TEL 803-768-5556. FAX 803-769-6494. Ed. E. Hafez. adv.; bk.rev.; charts; illus.; index. circ. 500. (also avail. in microform) **Indexed:** Biol.Abstr., Chem.Abstr., Curr.Cont., Excerp.Med., Ind.Sci.Rev., Sci.Cit.Ind. **Document type:** academic/scholarly publication.
—BLDSC (0704.146000); CASDDS; CISTI; EMDOCS; KNAW; SWETS; UnCover.
Formerly (until 1984): Contraceptive Delivery Systems (ISSN 0143-6112)
Refereed Serial

338.96 KE ISSN 0250-698X
AFRICA LINK. French ed.: Africa Link (Edition Francaise) (ISSN 1012-5019) (Text in English, French) 1971. s-a. free. Africa Regional Secretariat, Planned Parenthood Federation, Madison Insurance House, Upper Hill, P.O. Box 30234, Nairobi, Kenya. TEL 254-2-720280. FAX 254-2-726596. E-mail: ippfaro@ken.healthnet.org. Ed. Dorothy Nyong'o. R&P contact: Marc Okunnu. adv.; bk.rev.; circ. 3,000 (Eng.ed.); 2,000 (Fr.ed.) (controlled). (processed) **Document type:** trade publication.
—BLDSC (0732.160800).
Description: Covers the activities of the family planning associations in Sub-Saharan Africa. Addresses sexual and reproductive health issues.

ASIAN AND PACIFIC WOMEN'S RESOURCE AND ACTION SERIES. see *WOMEN'S INTERESTS*

613.7 BG
BANGLADESH ASSOCIATION FOR VOLUNTARY STERILIZATION. ANNUAL REPORT. (Text in English) a. Tk.25. Bangladesh Association for Voluntary Sterilization, 526 Dhanmondi Residential Area, Rd. No. 8, Dhaka, Bangladesh.

613.9 323.4 US ISSN 1065-3902
THE BODY POLITIC; monthly pro-choice news report. 1991. m. (exept Nov.-Dec.). $18. Body Politic, Inc., Box 2363, Binghamton, NY 13902. TEL 607-648-2760. Ed. Anne Bower.

613.9 UK ISSN 0144-8625
CODEN: BJFPDD
BRITISH JOURNAL OF FAMILY PLANNING. 1977. q. £32 (foreign £45). Faculty of Family Planning and Reproductive Health Care, 27 Sussex Pl., Regent's Park, London NW1 4RG, England. TEL 0171-724-2441. FAX 0171-723-0575. Ed. Dr. Jeanette Cayley. adv.; bk.rev.; illus. circ. 9,000. **Indexed:** ASCA, ASSIA, Biol.Abstr., Curr.Cont., Curr.Lit.Fam.Plan., Excerp.Med., Fam.Ind. **Document type:** academic/scholarly publication.
—BLDSC (2308.300000); Genuine Article; KNAW; SWETS. **CCC.**
Description: Presents original papers and review articles by leading authorities on all aspects of reproductive health care.

613.9 AQ
CARIBBEAN FAMILY PLANNING AFFILIATION. ANNUAL REPORT. 1981. a. free to qualified personnel. (International Planned Parenthood Federation, Western Hemisphere Region) Caribbean Family Planning Affiliation Limited, Airport and Factory Rds., P.O. Box 419, St. John's, Antigua, W.I. FAX 809-462-1187. Ed.Bd. circ. 2,000.
Description: Report on the year's activities in family life education and family planning.

613.9 312 US
CELEBRATE LIFE (STAFFORD). 1978. bi-m. $12.95. American Life League, Inc., 1179 Courthouse Rd., Box 1350, Stafford, VA 22555. TEL 504-659-4171. FAX 504-659-2586. Ed. Steve Dunham; Pub. Judie Brown. adv.; bk.rev.; index. circ. 130,000. **Document type:** consumer publication.
Formerly (until 1994): All About Issues (ISSN 0733-1231)
Description: Covers abortion, euthanasia, life and family issues from a pro-life perspective.

301.426 II
CENTRE CALLING. (Text in English) 1966. m. free. Department of Family Welfare, Ministry of Health and Family Welfare, Kotla Rd., Box 5410, New Delhi 110002, India. (Subscr. to: Editor, Post Box 5410, New Delhi 110002, India) Ed. Uma Shankar Mishra. bk.rev. circ. 40,000.

CHOICES; sexual health and family planning in Europe. see *POPULATION STUDIES*

301.426 PN
CONCIENCIA. 1967. m. free. Asociacion Panamena para el Planeamiento de la Familia, Apartado Postal 4637, Panama 5, Panama. TEL 507-2607005. FAX 507-2362979. Ed. Julio A. Lavergne; Pub. Alfonso Lavergne. illus. circ. 5,000. **Document type:** bulletin.

613.943 US ISSN 0010-7824
RG136.A1 CODEN: CCPTAY
CONTRACEPTION. 1970. m. fl.948($545) to institutions (effective 1998). Elsevier Science Inc., Box 945, New York, NY 10159-0945. TEL 712-633-3730. FAX 212-633-3680. E-mail: usinfo-f@elsevier.com; URL: http://www.elsevier.nl/. (Subscr. outside the Americas to: Elsevier Science, Regional Sales Office, P.O. Box 211, 1000 AE Amsterdam, Netherlands. TEL 31-20-4853757. FAX 31-20-4853432; Subscr. in Australasia and the Far East to: Elsevier Science (Singapore) Pte Ltd, No.1 Temasek Ave., No.17-01 Millenia Tower, Singapore 039192, Singapore. TEL 65-434-3727. FAX 65-337-2230; Subscr. in Japan to: Elsevier Science Japan, 9-15 Higashi-Azabu 1-chome, Minato-ku, Tokyo 106, Japan. TEL 81-3-5561-5033. FAX 81-3-5561-5047) Ed. Dr. Daniel R. Mishell Jr. adv.; bibl.; charts; illus.; s-a. index. (also avail. in microfilm from UMI; back issues avail.; reprint service avail. from UMI) **Indexed:** Anim.Breed.Abstr., ASCA, Bibl.Repro., Biol.Abstr., Biotech.Abstr., Chem.Abstr., Cott.& Trop.Fibr.Abstr., Curr.Adv.Cancer Res., Curr.Adv.Ecol.Sci., Curr.Cont., Curr.Lit.Fam.Plan., Dairy Sci.Abstr., Excerp.Med., Fam.Ind., Field Crop Abstr., Hort.Abstr., I.P.A., Ind.Med., Ind.Sci.Rev., Intl.Polym.Sci.& Tech., Nutr.Abstr., Popul.Ind., RAPRA, Risk Abstr., Seed Abstr., SSCI. **Document type:** academic/scholarly publication.
—BLDSC (3425.750000); ADONIS; CASDDS; CISTI; EMDOCS; Genuine Article; KNAW; SWETS; UMI; UnCover. **CCC.**
Description: Research reports in clinical and experimental contraception.
Refereed Serial

613.9 301.426 FR ISSN 1165-1083
CONTRACEPTION - FERTILITE - SEXUALITE. 1973. m. 880 F. (foreign 1430 F.); students 520 F. (effective 1997). S.A.R.L. Contraception - Fertilite - Sterilite, 55 rue des Petits-Champs, 75001 Paris, France. TEL 33-1-42969725. FAX 33-1-42860426. Ed. Jean Cohen. adv.; bk.rev. circ. 5,000. **Indexed:** ASCA, Biol.Abstr., Bull.Signal., Curr.Adv.Cancer Res., Curr.Adv.Cell & Devel.Biol., Curr.Cont., Excerp.Med., SSCI.
—BLDSC (3425.760000); CISTI; EMDOCS; Genuine Article; KNAW; SWETS. **CCC.**
Former titles (until 1992): Fertilite, Contraception, Sexualite (ISSN 1164-7418); (until 1992): Contraception Fertilite Sexualite (ISSN 1157-8181); (until 1991): Fertilite Contraception Sexualite (ISSN 0980-3904); (until 1986): Contraception Fertilite Sexualite (ISSN 0301-861X)
Description: Explores various planned parenthood issues.

301.426 613.9 UK
CONTRACEPTIVE EDUCATION BULLETIN. 1976. q. £12 (foreign £18) (effective 1997). Family Planning Association, 2-12 Pentonville Rd., London N1 9FP, England. TEL 44-171-837-5432. FAX 44-171-837-3042. Ed. Jane Hobden. R&P contact: Jane Hobden. adv.; bk.rev.; bibl. circ. 5,000. **Indexed:** Biol.Abstr., Curr.Lit.Fam.Plan. **Document type:** bulletin.
Supersedes (in 1996): Family Planning Today (ISSN 0309-1112); Which supersedes: Family Planning (ISSN 0014-7338)
Description: Contains news, information, and commentary about contraception, reproductive health and sexual health issues.

613.9 US ISSN 0091-9721
RG136.A1
CONTRACEPTIVE TECHNOLOGY. biennial. Irvington Publishers, Inc., 522 E. 82nd St., Ste. 1, New York, NY 10028.
—BLDSC (3425.770000).

613.9 US ISSN 0274-726X
CONTRACEPTIVE TECHNOLOGY UPDATE. 1980. m. $219. American Health Consultants, Inc., 3525 Piedmont Rd., N.E., Bldg. 6, Ste. 400, Atlanta, GA 30305. TEL 404-262-7436; 800-688-2421. FAX 800-284-3291. Ed. Virginia Mason. bk.rev. circ. 1,710. (also avail. in microfilm from UMI; back issues avail.; reprint service avail.) **Indexed:** Curr.Lit.Fam.Plan. **Document type:** newsletter.
●Also available online. Vendor(s): Lexis-Nexis.
—BLDSC (3425.773000); UMI.
Incorporates (1989-1991): Reproductive Technology Update.
Description: Addresses the needs of family planning professionals and is oriented toward clinical information.
Refereed Serial

301.4 UA
E P F P R. (Egyptian Population and Family Planning Review) (Text in Arabic, English) 1968. 2/yr. £E5($15) Cairo University, Institute of Statistical Studies and Research, Tharwat St., Orman, Cairo, Egypt. FAX 20-2-3482533. TELEX 94372. Ed. Ibrahim Farag Eissa. bk.rev.; bibl.; stat. circ. 400. **Indexed:** Popul.Ind. **Document type:** academic/scholarly publication.

301.426 CK
ESTUDIOS DE PLANIFICACION FAMILIAR. vol.9, 1975. 2/yr. Asociacion Colombiana para el Estudio Cientifico de la Poblacion, Carrera 18 No. 33-95, Canal Ramirez-Antares, Bogota, Colombia. Ed. Dr. Guillermo Lopez Escobar.

613.943 UK ISSN 1362-5187
▼**EUROPEAN JOURNAL OF CONTRACEPTION AND REPRODUCTIVE HEALTH CARE.** 1996. q. £70($120) to individuals; institutions £125($210) (effective 1998). (European Society of Contraception) Parthenon Publishing Group, Casterton Hall, Carnforth, Lancs LA6 2LA, England. TEL 44-15242-72084. FAX 44-15242-71587. URL: http://www.parthpub.com/contra/home.html. (In US: Box 1564, Pearl River, NY 10965. TEL 914-735-9363. FAX 914-735-1385) adv. contact: Julia Tissington. **Document type:** academic/scholarly publication.
—BLDSC (3829.728227); ADONIS.
Refereed Serial

BIRTH CONTROL

613.9   BG
F P A B HIGHLIGHTS. (Text in English) 1978. q. Family Planning Association of Bangladesh, 2 Naya Paltan, Dhaka 2, Bangladesh. TEL 88-02-316134. FAX 88-02-833008. TELEX 632379 IFIC BJ. Eds. Ahmad Neaz, M. Emamul Haque. circ. 1,000. **Document type:** newsletter.

301.426   CH
F P A C MONTHLY REPORT.* (Text in Chinese and English) 1961. m. free. Family Planning Association of China, No.1, Lane 160, Fuhsing S. Rd. Sec. 2, Taipei, Taiwan 106, Republic of China.

301.4   PK
F P A P ANNUAL REPORT. (Text in English) 1964. a. Family Planning Association of Pakistan, 3-A Temple Rd., Lahore, Pakistan. Ed.Bd. circ. 1,000 (controlled). **Document type:** corporate report.
    Former titles: F P A P Biennial Report (ISSN 0071-3759)

613.9   PH
THE F P O P BULLETIN. 1969. q. free. Family Planning Organization of the Philippines, 50 Dona Magdalina Hemady Ave., New Manila, Quezon City, Philippines. TEL 721-71-01. FAX 721-40-67. Ed. Javier Gil C. Montemayor. circ. 2,000. **Document type:** bulletin.

613.9   DK   ISSN 0108-8793
FAMILIEPLANLAEGNING; information og debat. 1982. a. free. Foreningen Sex og Samfund, c/o Nell Rasmussen, Skindergade 28, 1, DK-1159 Copenhagen K, Denmark. TEL 45-33-93-10-10. FAX 45-33-93-10-09. E-mail: Danish-FPA@dk-online.dk. Ed. Benta Klarskov. bk.rev. circ. 6,000. **Document type:** newsletter.
    Description: Details fundamental issues within the scope of contraception and family planning.

613.9   FJ
FAMILY PLANNING ASSOCIATION OF FIJI. NEWS. (Text in English) no.37, 1976. bi-m. Family Planning Association of Fiji, Box 619, Suva, Fiji. charts; illus.

301.42   II   ISSN 0377-7774
FAMILY PLANNING ASSOCIATION OF INDIA. REPORT. (Text in English) 1950. a. free. Family Planning Association of India, Bajaj Bhavan, Nariman Point, Mumbai 400 021, India. illus. circ. 2,000. **Document type:** newsletter.

301.42   KE
FAMILY PLANNING ASSOCIATION OF KENYA. ANNUAL REPORT. Key Title: Annual Report - Family Planning Association of Kenya. 1971. a. free. Family Planning Association of Kenya, Harabee P, Haile Selassie Ave., P.O. Box 30581, Nairobi, Kenya. Ed. Inzoberi John. illus. circ. 2,000. **Document type:** corporate report.

362.8   NP   ISSN 0303-4755
HQ766.5.N37
FAMILY PLANNING ASSOCIATION OF NEPAL. ANNUAL REPORT. (Text in English) 1960. a. free. Family Planning Association of Nepal, P.O. Box 486, Katmandu, Nepal. TEL 977-1-524440. FAX 977-1-524211. TELEX 2307 FPAN NP. stat. circ. 75.
    Description: Provides information on the programs and activities of the FPAN throughout the year.

362.8   NP
FAMILY PLANNING ASSOCIATION OF NEPAL. NEWSLETTER. (Text in English) 1973. bi-m. free. Family Planning Association of Nepal, P.O. Box 486, Katmandu, Nepal. TEL 977-1-524440. FAX 977-1-524211. TELEX 2307 FPAN NP. **Document type:** newsletter.
    Description: Provides news and information of the association.

613.94   GM   ISSN 0796-0174
FAMILY PLANNING ASSOCIATION OF THE GAMBIA. NEWSLETTER. (Text in English) 1972. q. free. Family Planning Association of the Gambia, P.O. Box 325, Banjul, Gambia. Ed. J.T. Taylor-Thomas. adv. circ. 150. **Document type:** newsletter.
    Formerly (until 1987): What's On.
    Description: Reports on workshops, training programs, resource development and association activities.

613.9   PH
FAMILY PLANNING NEWSLETTER. 1973. bi-m. exchange basis. National Family Planning Office, Ministry of Health, San Lazaro Hospital Compound, Rizal Ave., Manila, Philippines. Ed. Florentina G. Moran. circ. 3,000. (tabloid format)

FAMILY PLANNING PERSPECTIVES. see *MEDICAL SCIENCES — Obstetrics And Gynecology*

362.8   US   ISSN 0095-3121
HQ766.5.U5
FAMILY PLANNING PROGRAMS IN OKLAHOMA; annual statistical report. 1971. a. Department of Health, Maternal and Infant Health Service, 1000 N.E. 10th St., Oklahoma City, OK 73117-1299. TEL 405-271-4470. illus. circ. 450. **Document type:** government publication.

FERTILITAET, STERILITAET, IN-VITRO-FERTILISATION, SEXUALITAET, KONTRAZEPTION. see *MEDICAL SCIENCES — Obstetrics And Gynecology*

613.9   GD
GRENADA PLANNED PARENTHOOD ASSOCIATION. ANNUAL REPORT. a. Grenada Planned Parenthood Association, Scott St., St. George's, Grenada, W.I. FAX 809-440-8057. circ. 300. **Document type:** corporate report.

613.9   CC   ISSN 1001-3490
GUOWAI YIXUE (JIHUA SHENGYU FENCE)/FOREIGN MEDICAL SCIENCES (BIRTH CONTROL). (Text in Chinese) q. Tianjin Yixue Keji Qingbao Yanjiusuo - Tianjin Institute of Medical Science Information, 131 Chengdu Dao, Heping-qu, Tianjin 300050, People's Republic of China. TEL 302570. Ed. Yu Aifeng.

301.426   II   ISSN 0253-6803
RA529
HEALTH AND POPULATION: PERSPECTIVES AND ISSUES. 1972. q. $15. National Institute of Health and Family Welfare, New Mehrauli Rd., Munirka, New Delhi 110 067, India. (Dist. by: HPC Publishers' Distributors Pvt. Ltd., 4805-24, 1st Fl., Bharat Ram Rd., Darya Ganj, New Delhi 110 002, India. TEL 91-11-3254401. FAX 91-11-6863511) Ed. Somnath Roy. adv.; bk.rev. circ. 1,000. **Indexed:** Abstr.Hyg., Diar.Dis.Res., Excerp.Med., ExtraMED, Popul.Ind., Trop.Dis.Bull.
    ●Also available on CD-ROM.
    —BLDSC (4274.833000).
    Formed by the merger of: N I H A E Bulletin (ISSN 0378-6196); Journal of Population Research (ISSN 0377-0478); Which was formerly: National Institute of Family Planning. Newsletter.
    Description: Focuses on planned parenthood.

613.9   US   ISSN 0194-8032
HQ767
HEARTBEAT (ORLANDO). 1978. q. $25 (includes Pulse). Institute for Women and Children, 4680 Lake Underhill Rd., Orlando, FL 32807. TEL 407-277-1942. FAX 407-381-0907. Ed.Bd. adv.; bk.rev.; charts; illus. circ. 4,000.

613.9   IO
I P P A NEWSLETTER. (Text in English) 1977. q. Rps.8000($5) Indonesian Planned Parenthood Association - Perkumpulan Keluarga Berencana Indonesia, Jalan Hang Jebat 111-F3, P.O. Box 18, Kebayaran Baru, Jakarta 12120, Indonesia. TEL 62-21-715905. FAX 62-21-7394088. Ed. Kustiniyati Muchtar. stat. circ. 2,000. **Indexed:** Curr.Lit.Fam.Plan. **Document type:** newsletter.
    Description: Discusses methods used to curtail population growth.

I P P F ANNUAL REPORT. (International Planned Parenthood Federation) see *POPULATION STUDIES*

I P P F MEDICAL BULLETIN. (International Planned Parenthood Federation) see *POPULATION STUDIES*

I P P F OPEN FILE. (International Planned Parenthood Federation) see *POPULATION STUDIES*

I P P F PLANNED PARENTHOOD CHALLENGES. (International Planned Parenthood Federation) see *POPULATION STUDIES*

I U S S P NEWSLETTER/U I E S P BULLETIN DE LIAISON. (International Union for the Scientific Study of Population) see *POPULATION STUDIES*

I U S S P PAPERS/U I E S P DOCUMENTS DE L'UNION. (International Union for the Scientific Study of Population) see *POPULATION STUDIES*

613.94   EC
INFORME ANUAL DE LAS ACTIVIDADES DE LAS UNIDADES OPERATIVAS DE SALUD EN EL PROGRAMA DE PLANIFICACION FAMILIAR DEL MINISTERIO DE SALUD. a. Ministerio de Salud Publica, Departamento Nacional de Poblacion, Quito, Ecuador.

301.426   II
INSTITUTE OF ECONOMIC RESEARCH. PUBLICATIONS ON FAMILY PLANNING. (Text in English) irreg. price varies. Institute of Economic Research, Director, Vidyagiri, Dharwar 580004, Karnataka, India. FAX 836-41001.

INTERNATIONAL FAMILY PLANNING PERSPECTIVES. see *MEDICAL SCIENCES — Obstetrics And Gynecology*

INTERNATIONAL POPULATION CONFERENCE. PROCEEDINGS. see *POPULATION STUDIES*

301.426   JA   ISSN 0911-0755
J O I C F P NEWS. (Text in English) 1974. m. free. Japanese Organization for International Cooperation in Family Planning, Inc., Hoken Kaikan Bekkan, 6th Fl., 1-1 Sadohara-cho, Ichigaya, Shinjuku-ku, Tokyo 162, Japan. TEL 03-3268-5875. FAX 03-3235-7090. TELEX 2324584-JOICFP-J. Ed. Chojiro Kunii. bk.rev. circ. 5,000. **Document type:** newsletter.
    Description: Reports on population and family planning activities in Japan and the world, especially on Integrated Project, promoted worldwide by JOICFP.

JOHNS HOPKINS UNIVERSITY. POPULATION INFORMATION PROGRAM. POPULATION REPORTS. ENGLISH EDITION.. see *POPULATION STUDIES*

JOHNS HOPKINS UNIVERSITY. POPULATION INFORMATION PROGRAM. POPULATION REPORTS. FRENCH EDITION. see *POPULATION STUDIES*

JOHNS HOPKINS UNIVERSITY. POPULATION INFORMATION PROGRAM. POPULATION REPORTS. PORTUGUESE EDITION. see *POPULATION STUDIES*

JOHNS HOPKINS UNIVERSITY. POPULATION INFORMATION PROGRAM. POPULATION REPORTS. SPANISH EDITION. see *POPULATION STUDIES*

613.9   II   ISSN 0022-1074
HQ750.A2
JOURNAL OF FAMILY WELFARE. (Text in English) 1954. q. Rs.40 (foreign $10). Family Planning Association of India, Bajaj Bhavan, Nariman Point, Mumbai 400021, India. TEL 91-22-202-9080. FAX 91-22-202-9038. (Dist. by: HPC Publishers' Distributors Pvt. Ltd., 4805-24, 1st Fl., Darya Ganj, New Delhi 110 002, India. TEL 91-11-3254401. FAX 91-11-6863511) Ed. Smt. Avabai B. Wadia. bk.rev.; abstr.; charts. circ. 3,000. (reprint service avail. from ISI) **Indexed:** ASCA, Curr.Cont., Curr.Lit.Fam.Plan., ExtraMED, Fam.Ind., IMFL, Mult.Ed.Abstr., Popul.Ind., SSCI, Stud.Wom.Abstr. **Document type:** academic/scholarly publication.
    ●Also available on CD-ROM.
    —BLDSC (4983.750000); Genuine Article; UnCover.

301.42   KO   ISSN 0259-9112
JOURNAL OF POPULATION AND HEALTH STUDIES. (Text in English, Korean) 1974. s-a. free. Korea Institute for Population and Health, SAN 42-14 Bulgwang-Dong, Eunpyung-Ku, Seoul 122, S. Korea. Ed. Joung Joo Lee. stat.; circ. controlled. **Indexed:** IDA, Popul.Ind., Rural Recreat.Tour.Abstr., World Agri.Econ.& Rural Sociol.Abstr.
    Former titles: Journal of Population and Health; Family Planning Quarterly & Journal of Family Planning Studies.
    Description: Covers planned parenthood issues.

613.9   IO   ISSN 0216-0269
KABAR. 1980. q. Rps.9600($6) Indonesian Planned Parenthood Association, Jalan Hang Jebat 111-F3, P.O. Box 18, Kebayaran Baru, Jakarta 12120, Indonesia. TEL 62-21-715905. FAX 62-21-7394088. circ. 5,000. **Indexed:** So.Pac.Per.Ind.

BIRTH CONTROL

613.9   UK
KEY NOTE MARKET REPORT: CONTRACEPTIVES. Variant title: Contraceptives. 1993. irreg. £205. Key Note Ltd., Field House, 72 Oldfield Rd., Hampton, Middlesex TW12 2HQ, England. TEL 44-181-783-0755. FAX 44-181-783-0049. **Document type:** trade publication.
● Also available online.
Also available on CD-ROM.
Formerly: Key Note Report: Contraceptives (ISSN 1352-6561)

179 306.874   US   ISSN 0882-116X
L F L REPORTS. 1981. irreg. donations. Libertarians for Life, 13424 Hathaway Dr., Wheaton, MD 20906. TEL 301-460-4141. E-mail: DORIS.GORDON@IAD.BLKCAT.COM; URL: http://www.cris.com/~bwjass/lfl. Ed. John Walker. bk.rev. circ. 1,000. (back issues avail.) **Document type:** newsletter.
Description: Focuses on the issue of abortion from a non-religious, libertarian pro-life perspective, and the philosophical foundation of parental obligation.

MALAYSIAN JOURNAL OF REPRODUCTIVE HEALTH. see MEDICAL SCIENCES — Obstetrics And Gynecology

618   IO   ISSN 0216-4027
MANTAP: MAJALAH ILMAIH P K M I/INDONESIAN ASSOCIATION FOR SECURE CONTRACEPTION. JOURNAL. (Text mainly in Indonesian; occasionally in English) 1981. q. $200. Perkumpulan Kontrasepsi Mantap Indonesia (PKMI) - Indonesian Association for Secure Contraception, Jalan Kramat Sentiong 49A, Jakarta 10450, Indonesia. TEL 62-21-3155122. FAX 62-21-3155125. Ed. Azrul Azwar. circ. 1,000. (reprint service avail. from IRC) **Document type:** academic/scholarly publication.

301.42   II   ISSN 0077-4944
N I F P GENERAL SERIES. 1965. irreg., no.22, 1977. free (or on exchange basis). National Institute of Health and Family Welfare, New Mehrauli Rd., Munirka, New Delhi 110067, India. Ed. S. Pramanik. circ. 3,000.

301.42   II   ISSN 0077-4952
N I F P MANUAL SERIES. 1966. irreg. free (or on exchange basis). National Institute of Health and Family Welfare, New Mehrauli Rd., Munirka, New Delhi 110067, India. Ed. S. Pramanik. circ. 3,000.

301.42   II   ISSN 0077-4960
N I F P MONOGRAPH SERIES. 1966. irreg., no.19, 1973. free. National Institute of Health and Family Welfare, New Mehrauli Rd., Munirka, New Delhi 110067, India. Ed. S. Pramanik. circ. 3,000.

301.42   II   ISSN 0077-4979
N I F P REPORT SERIES. 1966. irreg., no.12, 1973. on exchange basis. National Institute of Health and Family Welfare, New Mehrauli Rd., Munirka, New Delhi 110067, India. Ed. S. Pramanik. circ. 3,000.

301.42   II   ISSN 0077-4987
N I F P TECHNICAL PAPER SERIES. 1966. irreg., no.17, 1973. on exchange basis. National Institute of Health and Family Welfare, New Mehrauli Rd., Munirka, New Delhi 110067, India. Ed. S. Pramanik. circ. 3,000.

613.9 618 616.95   US   ISSN 0270-3637
NETWORK (DURHAM). (Editions in English, French, Spanish) 1979. q. free to qualified personnel. Family Health International, Research Triangle Park Branch, Box 13950, Durham, NC 27709. FAX 919-544-7040. TELEX 579442. URL: http://www.fhi.org. Ed. Nash Herndon. R&P contact: Debbie Crumpler. circ. 65,000 (controlled). (back issues avail.) **Document type:** academic/scholarly publication, newsletter.
● Also available online.
—CISTI.
Description: Covers contraceptive methods, concern for maternal and child mortality; AIDS; sexually transmitted diseases.

NEW PARENT. see MEDICAL SCIENCES — Obstetrics And Gynecology

ON THE ISSUES; the progressive woman's quarterly. see WOMEN'S INTERESTS

301.426   II
ORISSA FAMILY PLANNING BULLETIN. (Text in English) 1971. m. free. State Family Welfare Bureau, Directorate of Family Welfare, Orissa, Bhubaneswar, India. Ed. Dr. N.N. Parida. charts. circ. 1,200.

OUTLOOK (SEATTLE); drug regulation and reproductive health. see PUBLIC HEALTH AND SAFETY

613.9   AT   ISSN 1323-675X
OVULATION METHOD RESEARCH AND REFERENCE CENTRE OF AUSTRALIA. BULLETIN. 1974. q. Aus.$15. Ovulation Method Research and Reference Centre of Australia, Billings Family Life Centre, 27 Alexandra Parade, N. Fitzroy, Melbourne, Vic. 3068, Australia. TEL 61-3-94811722. FAX 61-3-94824208. Ed. John J. Billings. R&P contact: J.J. Billings. bk.rev.; cum.index every 2 yrs. circ. 3,500. (tabloid format; back issues avail.) **Document type:** bulletin.
Formerly (until vol.22, no.1, 1995): Natural Family Planning Council of Victoria. Bulletin (ISSN 0312-7567)
Description: Covers philosophy and theology of marriage, scientific research into reproductive biology pertaining to natural family planning, and the teaching of natural family planning.
Refereed Serial

613.9   US
OVULATION METHOD TEACHERS ASSOCIATION (PUBLICATION). 1975. q. $10. Ovulation Method Teachers Association, Box 10-1780, Anchorage, AK 99510-1780. TEL 907-343-4623. FAX 907-344-8606. Ed.Bd. adv.; bk.rev. circ. 500. (looseleaf format; back issues avail.)
Description: Covers ovulation method of natural family planning and related health issues.

301.426   GH
P P A G NEWSLETTER. 1971. q. free. Planned Parenthood Association of Ghana, P.O. Box 13580, Accra, Ghana. circ. 300. **Document type:** newsletter.

PASSAGES. see CHILDREN AND YOUTH — About

301.426   UK   ISSN 0301-5645
HQ763
PEOPLE. French edition: Peuples (ISSN 0306-8331) 1973. q. £33($56) (International Planned Parenthood Federation) Longman Group UK Ltd., Longman House, Burnt Mill, Harlow, Essex CM20 2JE, England. TEL 44-1279-426721. FAX 44-1279-431-431059. E-mail: longhe@cityscape.co.uk. (Subscr. to: Pearson Professional, P.O. Box 77, Fourth Ave., Harlow, Essex CM19 5BQ, England. TEL 44-1279-623924. FAX 44-1279-639609) Ed. J. Rowley. adv.; bk.rev.; film rev.; abstr.; charts; illus.; stat. circ. 22,000. **Indexed:** Abstr.Hyg., Can.B.P.I., Geo.Abstr., Helminthol.Abstr., Rural Recreat.Tour.Abstr., Trop.Dis.Bull., World Agri.Econ.& Rural Sociol.Abstr.
—UMI. **CCC.**

PEOPLE & THE PLANET. see POPULATION STUDIES

PERSPECTIVAS INTERNACIONALES EN PLANIFICACION FAMILIAR. see MEDICAL SCIENCES — Obstetrics And Gynecology

PERSPECTIVES INTERNATIONALES SUR LE PLANNING FAMILIAL. see MEDICAL SCIENCES — Obstetrics And Gynecology

613.94   II
PLANNED PARENTHOOD. 1953. m. free. Family Planning Association of India, Bajaj Bhavan, Nariman Point, Mumbai 400 021, India. Ed. Jaishree Kochavara. circ. 7,000. (also avail. in microfilm from UMI) **Document type:** academic/scholarly publication.

PRE- AND PERI-NATAL PSYCHOLOGY JOURNAL. see MEDICAL SCIENCES — Obstetrics And Gynecology

363.460971   CN   ISSN 0836-7221
PRO-CHOICE NEWS. 1975. 3/yr. Can.$10($13) Canadian Abortion Rights Action League - Association Canadienne pour le Droit a l'Avortement, 344 Bloor St. W., Ste. 306, Toronto, ON M5S 3A7, Canada. TEL 416-961-1507. FAX 416-961-5771. E-mail: caral@interlog.com; URL: http://www.interlog.com/~caral. bk.rev. circ. 12,000. (tabloid format) **Document type:** newsletter.
Description: Provides a national forum for news and opinion on abortion rights.

613.9   US
PRO-LIFE ACTION NEWS. 1981. q. $10 donation. Pro-Life Action League, 6160 N. Cicero Ave., Ste. 600, Chicago, IL 60646. TEL 312-777-2900. FAX 312-777-3061. Ed. Ann Scheilder. adv.; bk.rev. circ. 7,500. (tabloid format) **Document type:** newspaper.
Description: Includes material relating to pro-life activism such as protests and sidewalk counseling.

PROLIFE NEWS. see PUBLIC HEALTH AND SAFETY

613.9   US
PULSE (ORLANDO). q. $29 includes Heartbeat. Institute for Women and Children, 4680 Lake Underhill Rd., Orlando, FL 32807. TEL 407-277-1942. FAX 407-381-0907.

613.9   CC
REN SHENG. English edition: Life. (Editions in Chinese, English) bi-m. (Zhongguo Jihua Shengyu Xiehui - China Family Planning Association) Ren Sheng Zazhishe, 7, Xicheng Jiaochang Hutong, Beijing 100034, People's Republic of China. TEL 664397. Ed. Tao Shaozeng.

RENKOUXUE YU JIHUA SHENGYU/POPULATION STUDIES AND BIRTH CONTROL. see POPULATION STUDIES

REPORTER ON HUMAN REPRODUCTION & THE LAW; cases, statutes and materials on law and life sciences. see LAW

RESUMENES SOBRE POBLACION DOMINICANA. see POPULATION STUDIES

S I E C C A N NEWSLETTER. (Sex Information and Education Council of Canada) see PHYSICAL FITNESS AND HYGIENE

613.9   DK   ISSN 1395-3036
SEX OG SAMFUND/SEX AND SOCIETY; om almet sexologiske emner, praevention og seksuelt overfortbare sygdomme. 1986. 4/yr. DKK 60. Danish Family Planning Association, Aurehoejvej 2, DK-2900 Hellerup, Denmark. TEL 45-39-62-56-88. FAX 45-39-62-02-82. E-mail: danish__fpa@dk-online.dk. Ed. Gitte Just. R&P contact: Gitte Just. illus. circ. 1,000. **Document type:** bulletin.
Former titles: Sex og Sundhed (ISSN 0901-9685); Mer om Sex og Sikkerhed (ISSN 0108-7851); Mer om Koenssygdomme (ISSN 0108-7843)

613.9   CC   ISSN 0253-357X
           CODEN: SCYYDZ
SHENGZHI YU BIYUN/REPRODUCTION & CONTRACEPTION. (Editions in Chinese, English) 1980. bi-m. Y31 (English ed. $12) (effective 1996 & 1997). (Shanghai Jihua Shengyu Kexue Yanjiusuo - Shanghai Institute of Planned Parenthood Research) Shengzhi yu Biyun Bianjibu, 2140 Xietu Lu, Shanghai 200032, People's Republic of China. TEL 86-21-4049215. FAX 85-21-4046128. (Dist. overseas by: China International Book Trading Corp., P.O. Box 399, Beijing 100044, P.R. China) Ed. Yueting Gong. R&P contact: Jianhua Lu. adv. contact: Jianhua Lu. circ. 4,000. pp./issue: 84. **Document type:** academic/scholarly publication.
—BLDSC (7713.598300); CASDDS.
Description: Covers birth control related issues in China.

SINGAPORE JOURNAL OF OBSTETRICS & GYNAECOLOGY. see MEDICAL SCIENCES — Obstetrics And Gynecology

618 614   US
U.S. CENTERS FOR DISEASE CONTROL. ABORTION SURVEILLANCE. ANNUAL SUMMARY. a. free. U.S. Centers for Disease Control, 1600 Clifton Rd., N.E., Atlanta, GA 30333. TEL 404-639-3311. **Indexed:** Curr.Lit.Fam.Plan. **Document type:** academic/scholarly publication.
Formerly: Abortion Surveillance.

362.8   US   ISSN 0094-4424
HQ763
U.S. CENTERS FOR DISEASE CONTROL. FAMILY PLANNING SERVICES: ANNUAL SUMMARY. Key Title: Family Planning Services; Annual Survey. a. U.S. Centers for Disease Control, Atlanta, GA 30333. TEL 404-639-3311. stat. **Document type:** government publication.

WOMEN'S GLOBAL NETWORK FOR REPRODUCTIVE RIGHTS. NEWSLETTER. see WOMEN'S HEALTH

613.9 US
WORLD FEDERATION OF HEALTH AGENCIES FOR THE ADVANCEMENT OF VOLUNTARY SURGICAL CONTRACEPTION. COMMUNIQUE.* (Text in Arabic, English, French, Spanish) a. 2/yr. free. World Federation of Health Agencies for the Advancement of Voluntary Surgical Contraception, 79 Madison Ave., 7th Fl., New York, NY 10016-7802. TEL 212-351-2525. FAX 212-599-0959. TELEX 425604 AVS Ul. Ed. Lynn Bakamjian. illus. circ. 5,500.

BIRTH CONTROL — Abstracting, Bibliographies, Statistics

ALTERNATIVE ALTERNATIVE. see SOCIOLOGY — Abstracting, Bibliographies, Statistics

613.9 UK ISSN 0140-5314
HQ767.5.G7
GREAT BRITAIN. GOVERNMENT STATISTICAL SERVICE. ABORTION STATISTICS. 1974. irreg. (Department of Health, Statistics Division) Government Statistical Service, SD2, Rm. 804, Hannibal House, Elephant and Castle, London SE1 6TE, England. TEL 0171-972-2193. (Orders to: Department of Health Leaflets, P.O. Box 21, Stanmore, Mddx. HA7 1AY, England) **Document type:** government publication.

301 US ISSN 0095-3105
HQ767.5.U5
NEBRASKA STATISTICAL REPORT OF ABORTIONS. a. free. Division of Health Data Systems, Lincoln, NE 68500. TEL 402-471-2871. **Document type:** government publication.

301.426 016 II ISSN 0028-4327
NEW BOOKS ON FAMILY PLANNING. (Text in English) 1968. bi-m. exchange basis. National Institute of Health and Family Welfare, New Mehrauli Rd., Munirka, New Delhi 110067, India. bibl.; circ. 1,250 (controlled). (processed)

613.94 618.88 DK ISSN 0106-7729
STATISTIK OM PRAEVENTION OG ABORTER. (Included in the series: Vitalstatistik) (Text in Danish; summaries in English) 1978. biennial. DKK 60. Sundhedsstyrelsen, Amaliegade 13, 1012 Copenhagen K, Denmark. (Subscr. to: Statens Informationt, P.O. Box 1003, 1009 Copenhagen K, Denmark)
Formerly: Statistik om Legale Aborter.

618 US ISSN 0300-6972
U.S. CENTERS FOR DISEASE CONTROL. ABORTION SURVEILLANCE REPORT. 1969. q. free. U.S. Centers for Disease Control, 1600 Clifton Rd., Atlanta, GA 30333. TEL 404-639-3311. stat.; circ. controlled. **Document type:** government publication.

BOATS AND BOATING

see Sports and Games–Boats and Boating

BOTANY

see Biology–Botany

BUDDHISM

see Religions and Theology–Buddhist

BUILDING AND CONSTRUCTION

see also Building and Construction–Carpentry and Woodwork; Building and Construction–Hardware; Architecture; Engineering–Civil Engineering; Heating, Plumbing and Refrigeration; Housing and Urban Planning

690 US
A A M A QUARTERLY REVIEW. 1985. q. American Architectural Manufacturers Association, 1827 Walden Office Sq., Ste. 104, Schaumburg, IL 60173-4268. TEL 847-303-5664. FAX 847-303-5774. E-mail: webmaster@AAMANET.org; URL: http://www.AAMANET.org. Ed. A.S. Coorlim. R&P contact: A.S. Coorlim. circ. 15,000. (tabloid format; back issues avail.) **Document type:** trade publication.

690 US
A A M A UPDATE. 1975. m. American Architectural Manufacturers Association, 1827 Walden Office Sq., Ste. 104, Schaumburg, IL 60173-4268. TEL 847-333-5664. FAX 847-303-5774. E-mail: webmaster@AAMANET.org; URL: http://www.AAMANET.org. R&P contact: A.S. Coorlim. **Document type:** newsletter.

692.8 US ISSN 1062-3698
A B C TODAY. 1953. s-w. $60 to non-members; members $42. Associated Builders & Contractors, Inc., 1300 N. 17th St., 8th Fl., Rosslyn, VA 22209. TEL 703-812-2000. FAX 703-812-8203. Eds. Pam Hunter, Lisa Nardone; Pub. Dan Bennet. adv.: B&W page $1975; trim 10 3/4 x 16; adv. contact: Robert H. Kruhm. bk.rev.; software rev. circ. 20,000. (tabloid format) **Document type:** newsletter, trade publication.
Former titles: A B C Newsline (ISSN 0888-014X); (until 1985): Merit Shop Scoop (ISSN 0279-9464)

690 368 UK
A B I - B C I S HOUSE REBUILDING COST INDEX. (Association for British Insurers) Issued with: B C I S Guide to House Rebuilding Costs (ISSN 1350-9500) 1993. m. £65.80 (effective Apr. 1997). Building Cost Information Service Ltd., Royal Institution of Chartered Surveyors, 85-87 Clarence St., Kingston-upon-Thames, Surrey KT1 1RB, England. TEL 44-181-546-7554. FAX 44-181-547-1238. (Co-sponsor: Association for British Insurers) **Document type:** bulletin.
Description: Updates B.C.I.S. house rebuilding cost figures published annually in the Guide to House Rebuilding Costs for Insurance Valuation.

691.3 US ISSN 0065-7875
TA439
A C I MANUAL OF CONCRETE PRACTICE. (In 5 Vols.) 1967. a. $423 per set to non-members. American Concrete Institute, Box 19150, Redford Sta., Detroit, MI 48219. TEL 313-532-2600. FAX 313-538-0655.
—BLDSC (0576.650000); CISTI. **CCC.**

690 US ISSN 0889-325X
TA439.A36 CODEN: AMAJEF
A C I MATERIALS JOURNAL. 1929. bi-m. $109 (foreign $117) (effective 1996). American Concrete Institute, Box 19150, Redford Sta., Detroit, MI 48219. TEL 513-532-2600. FAX 313-538-0655. URL: http://www.aci-int.org/. Ed. Helayne H. Beavers. index. circ. 11,700. (also avail. in microfilm; microfiche; reprint service avail. from UMI) **Indexed:** A.S.& T.Ind., ASCA, C.R.I.Abstr., C.R.I.Curr.Cont., Curr.Cont., Geotech.Abstr., HRIS, Mat.Sci.Cit.Ind., Sci.Cit.Ind. **Document type:** academic/scholarly publication.
—BLDSC (0576.655000); CASDDS; CISTI; Ei; Genuine Article; KR SourceOne; Linda Hall; SWETS; UMI; UnCover. **CCC.**
Supersedes in part: American Concrete Institute. Journal (ISSN 0002-8061)
Description: Focuses on properties, uses, research, and handling of materials used in concrete.

691 US ISSN 0889-3241
TA680 CODEN: ASTJEG
A C I STRUCTURAL JOURNAL. 1929. proceedings, 1905. bi-m. $109 (foreign $117) (effective 1996). American Concrete Institute, Box 19150, Redford Sta., Detroit, MI 48219. TEL 513-532-2600. FAX 313-538-0655. URL: http://www.aci-int.org/. Ed. Helayne H. Beavers. charts; illus.; index, cum.index: 1905-1959, 1960-1989 (publications); vols. 1-78 (proceedings). circ. 17,400. (also avail. in microform from UMI; back issues avail.; reprint service avail. from UMI) **Indexed:** A.S.& T.Ind., Abstr.J.Earthq.Eng., Appl.Mech.Rev., ASCA, C.R.I.Abstr., C.R.I.Curr.Cont., Chem.Abstr., Concr.Abstr., Curr.Cont., Eng.Ind., Excerp.Med., GeoRef., Geotech.Abstr., HRIS, Intl.Civil Eng.Abstr., J.of Ferroc., Mat.Sci.Cit.Ind., Sci.Cit.Ind., Soft.Abstr.Eng., W.R.C.Inf. **Document type:** academic/scholarly publication.
—BLDSC (0576.821000); CASDDS; CISTI; Ei; Genuine Article; KR SourceOne; Linda Hall; SWETS; UMI; UnCover. **CCC.**
Supersedes in part: American Concrete Institute. Journal (ISSN 0002-8061)
Description: Focuses on the structural design and analysis of concrete elements and structures.

A D S C MEMBERSHIP DIRECTORY. (Association of Drilled Shaft Contractors) see BUSINESS AND ECONOMICS — Trade And Industrial Directories

690 US
A D S C PRODUCTS AND SERVICES GUIDE. a. $25 (foreign $35). Association of Drilled Shaft Contractors, Box 280379, Dallas, TX 75228. TEL 214-343-2091; 214-343-2384. Ed. Scot Litke. adv.; bk.rev. circ. 1,800. **Document type:** catalog.

690 US
A D S C TECHNICAL LIBRARY CATALOG. s-a. free. Association of Drilled Shaft Contractors, Box 280379, Dallas, TX 75228. TEL 214-343-2091. FAX 214-343-2384. **Document type:** catalog.

A F E NEWSLINE. (Association for Facilities Engineering) see ENGINEERING

692.8 US
A G C - OHIO. 1991. bi-m. $20 (effective 1995). Associated General Contractors of Ohio, 1755 Northwest Blvd., Columbus, OH 43212. TEL 614-486-6446. FAX 614-486-6498. Ed. Rich Hobbs. adv.: page $745; trim 8 3/8 x 10 7/8; adv. contact: Mindy Meyer. circ. 3,000. (back issues avail.) **Document type:** trade publication.
Description: Contains up-to-date information on industry trends, safety, and legislative issues. Written for the general contractor and owners-buyers of construction services.

A J FOCUS; products in practice. see ARCHITECTURE

690 UK
A M E C TIMES. 6/yr. 1 Golden Lane, London EC1Y ORR, England. TEL 44-171-574-8999. FAX 44-171-574-3601. TELEX 296618. Ed. S. Hankin. circ. 20,000. **Document type:** newspaper.

690 FR
A PROPOS (AURILLAC).* q. Chambre Syndicale des Entrepreneurs du Batiment et des Travaux Publics du Central, Ave. Georges-Pompidou, 15000 Aurillac, France. adv.

BUILDING AND CONSTRUCTION

A R T B A TRANSPORTATION OFFICIALS AND ENGINEERS DIRECTORY, STATE AND FEDERAL TRANSPORTATION AGENCY PERSONNEL. (American Road and Transportation Builders Association) see *TRANSPORTATION — Roads And Traffic*

A S C. (Architects Standard Catalogue) see *ARCHITECTURE*

690 720   IT   ISSN 0394-5952
A U BIS SUPPLEMENTO TECNICO. (Arredo Urbano) 1980. q. L.18000. Istituto Nazionale dell'Arredo Urbano delle Strutture Ambientali, Via dell'Acqua Traversa,255, 00135 Rome, Italy. TEL (06)3273990. Ed. Renato Cecilia.
   Description: Deals with urban design and architecture, including diagrams and blue prints of future construction and projects.

690   VE
A - Z DE LA CONSTRUCCION Y LA DECORACION. 1975. a. Publicaciones Araguaney, Calle 8, Edificio Lec, piso 3, La Urbina, Caracas 107, Venezuela.

690   DK   ISSN 1395-7953
AALBORG UNIVERSITY. DEPARTMENT OF BUILDING TECHNOLOGY AND STRUCTURAL ENGINEERING. R. 1977. irreg. price varies. Aalborg University, Department of Building Technology and Structural Engineering, Sohngaardsholmvej 57, DK-9000 Aalborg, Denmark. FAX 45-98-148243. illus. **Document type:** government publication, academic/scholarly publication.
   Former titles: Aalborg Universitetscenter. Instituttet for Bygningsteknik. R (ISSN 0902-7513); (until 1984): Aalborg Universitetscenter. Instituttet for Bygningsteknik. Report (ISSN 0105-7421)

690   DK   ISSN 1395-8232
AALBORG UNIVERSITY. DEPARTMENT OF BUILDING TECHNOLOGY AND STRUCTURAL ENGINEERING. U. 1976. irreg. price varies. Aalborg Universitetscenter, Instituttet for Bygningsteknik - Department of Building Technology and Structural Engineering, Sohngaardsholmvej 57, DK-9000 Aalborg, Denmark. FAX 45-98-148243. illus. **Document type:** government publication, academic/scholarly publication.
   Former titles: Aalborg Universitetscenter. Instituttet for Bygningsteknik. U (ISSN 0902-8005); (until 1984): Aalborg Universitetscenter. Instituttet for Bygningsteknik. Note (ISSN 0105-8185)

690   NE   ISSN 0926-9894
AANNEMER. (Supplement avail.: BouwSpecialist) 1990. 10/yr. fl.125. Misset (Subsidiary of: Reed Elsevier plc), Postbus 4, 7000 BA Doetinchem, Netherlands. TEL 31-314-349371. FAX 31-314-363638. adv.: B&W page fl.3616, color page fl.5815; trim 218 x 298; adv. contact: Cor van Nek. illus. circ. 7,560. **Document type:** trade publication.
   —SWETS.
   Formerly (until 1991): BouwWereld - Aannemer (ISSN 0926-9886)
   Description: Covers business and technical aspects of the contracting profession.

691.3   US   ISSN 1051-5526
TA680   CODEN: ABCCET
ABERDEEN'S CONCRETE CONSTRUCTION. 1956. m. $27 (Canada & Mexico $36; elsewhere $93). Aberdeen Group, 426 S. Westgate St., Addison, IL 60101. TEL 630-543-0870. FAX 630-543-3112. URL: http://www.wocnet.com/mags/cc.htm. Ed. Ward Malisch; Pub. Michael J. Porcaro. R&P contact: Anne Balogh. adv. contact: Jan Gurath. bk.rev.; charts; illus.; tr.lit.; cum.index; circ. 75,000 (paid). (also avail. in microfilm; back issues avail.; reprint service avail. from UMI) **Indexed:** A.S.& T.Ind., C.R.I.Abstr., C.R.I.Curr.Cont., Concr.Abstr., Eng.Ind., HRIS, Ind.Sci.Rev., Intl.Civil Eng.Abstr., J.of Ferroc., Soft.Abstr.Eng. **Document type:** trade publication.
   —BLDSC (0538.057400); CASDDS; CISTI; Ei; KR SourceOne; Linda Hall; SWETS; UMI; UnCover. **CCC.**
   Formerly (until 1990): Concrete Construction (ISSN 0010-5333)
   Description: Contains information on the design, placement, specification and utilization of concrete.

691   US   ISSN 1051-4821
    CODEN: ACDIFQ
ABERDEEN'S CONCRETE REPAIR DIGEST. 1990. 6/yr. $21 (Canada & Mexico $28; elsewhere $78). Aberdeen Group, 426 S. Westgate St., Addison, IL 60101. TEL 630-543-0870. FAX 630-543-3112. Ed. Martin McGovern; Pub. Michael J. Porcaro. R&P contact: Martin McGovern. adv. contact: Jan Gurath. charts; illus.; tr.lit. circ. 17,000. (back issues avail.) **Document type:** trade publication.
   —BLDSC (0538.057500); CISTI. **CCC.**
   Description: Contains how-to information about the repair, rehabilitation and restoration of concrete. Covers solving concrete problems, state-of-the-art technology, materials, equipment, accessories, and related products.

690   US   ISSN 1050-9860
TH915
ABERDEEN'S CONCRETE SOURCEBOOK. a. (CD-ROM s-a). $30. Aberdeen Group, 426 S. Westgate St., Addison, IL 60101. TEL 630-543-0870. FAX 630-543-3112. URL: http://www.supernetwork.com. Ed. Bradley Stott; Michael J./Porcaro. adv. contact: Jan Gurath. **Document type:** directory.
   •Also available online.
   Also available on CD-ROM.
   Description: Provides information for the concrete and masonry construction marketplace.

690   US   ISSN 1051-483X
ABERDEEN'S CONSTRUCTION MARKETING TODAY. 1990. 10/yr. $39. Aberdeen Group, 426 S. Westgate St., Addison, IL 60101. TEL 630-543-0870. FAX 630-543-3112. URL: http://www.supernetwork.com. Ed. Diana Granitto; Pub. Diana Granitto. R&P contact: Diana Granitto. adv. contact: Joan Hager. cum.index: 1990-1993. (tabloid format; back issues avail.) **Document type:** trade publication.
   •Also available online.
   —**CCC.**
   Description: For those who sell construction products, CMT publishes news and features about the construction market, marketing moves of construction manufacturers, sales and distribution, and marketing methods.

691   US   ISSN 1055-4408
TH1199   CODEN: AMMCEK
ABERDEEN'S MAGAZINE OF MASONRY CONSTRUCTION. 1988. m. $27 (Canada & Mexico $36; elsewhere $93). Aberdeen Group, 426 S. Westgate St., Addison, IL 60101. TEL 630-543-0870. FAX 630-543-3112. E-mail: cschierhorn@wocnet.com; URL: http://www.supernetwork.com; http://www.wocnet.com/mags/mc.htm. Ed. Carolyn Schierhorn; Pub. Michael J. Porcaro. R&P contact: Carolyn Schierhorn. adv. contact: Jan Gurath. bk.rev.; charts; illus.; stat.; tr.lit.; index; circ. 40,000 (paid). **Indexed:** C.R.I.Abstr., C.R.I.Curr.Cont., Eng.Ind. **Document type:** trade publication.
   •Also available online.
   —BLDSC (0538.059000); CISTI; UMI. **CCC.**
   Formerly (until 1990): Magazine of Masonry Construction (ISSN 0898-6088)
   Description: Provides how-to information for contractors who build with masonry materials.

ACCESS CONTROL & SECURITY INTEGRATION; perimeter access to internal control. see *CRIMINOLOGY AND LAW ENFORCEMENT — Security*

ACCESS CONTROL & SECURITY INTEGRATION BUYERS' GUIDE. see *BUSINESS AND ECONOMICS — Trade And Industrial Directories*

690   UK   ISSN 1352-7517
ACCESS INTERNATIONAL. 1994. q. £45($69) K H L International Ltd., Southfields, Southview Rd., Wadhurst, E. Sussex TN5 6TP, England. TEL 44-1892-784088. FAX 44-1892-784086. E-mail: cranes@khl.com; URL: http://ourworld.compuserve.com/homepages/cranes. Ed. Murray Pollok; Pub. James King. R&P contact: Peter Watlinson. adv. contact: Trevor Pease. **Document type:** trade publication.

620.1 690   UK
ACCESS YEARBOOK (YEAR). a. £39.95($60) K H L International Ltd., Southfields, Southview Rd., Wadhurst, E. Sussex TN5 6TP, England. TEL 44-1892-784088. FAX 44-1892-784086. E-mail: cranes@khl.com; URL: http://ourworld.compuserve.com/homepages/cranes. Pub. James King. R&P contact: Peter Watkinson. **Document type:** directory.

669.1   FR   ISSN 0001-4931
ACIER DANS LE MONDE. 1966. bi-m. free. Office Technique pour l'Utilisation de l'Acier (O T U A), 19, Le Parvis, Elysees la Defense, 92072 Paris cedex 35, France. FAX 47-67-85-77. TELEX 611672. Dir. Bernard Trancher. bk.rev.; illus. circ. 30,000.
   Description: Covers steel usage.

330 340   US   ISSN 1052-1674
KF842
ACQUISITION ISSUES. 1991. m. $299. Holbrook & Kellogg, Inc., 1960 Gallows Rd., Ste. 120, Vienna, VA 22182. TEL 703-506-0600. FAX 703-506-1948. Ed. Peter G. Wacht. **Document type:** newspaper.
   Description: Contains information on federal contracting.

ACTA ACADEMIAE AGRICULTURAE AC TECHNICAE OLSTENENSIS. AEDIFICATIO ET MECHANICA/AGRICULTURAL AND TECHNICAL ACADEMY IN OLSZTYN. MECHANICS AND BUILDING ENGINEERING. see *ENGINEERING — Mechanical Engineering*

ACTA POLYTECHNICA SCANDINAVICA. CIVIL ENGINEERING AND BUILDING CONSTRUCTION SERIES. see *ENGINEERING — Civil Engineering*

ACTA STRUCTILIA; wetenskaplijke tydskrif. see *ARCHITECTURE*

ADOBE JOURNAL. see *ARCHITECTURE*

691   UK   ISSN 0951-7197
    CODEN: ACEREN
ADVANCES IN CEMENT RESEARCH. 1987. q. £75 (foreign £111) (effective 1997). Thomas Telford Services Ltd., Thomas Telford House, 1 Heron Quay, London E14 4JD, England. TEL 44-171-987-6999. FAX 44-171-538-9620. TELEX 298105-CIVILS-G. E-mail: ttjournals@ice.org.uk. Ed. F.P. Glasser. R&P contact: Joanna Brown. adv. contact: Joanna Brown. bk.rev. circ. 300. **Indexed:** C.R.I.Abstr., C.R.I.Curr.Cont. **Document type:** academic/scholarly publication.
   —BLDSC (0703.320000); CASDDS; CISTI; Ei; Linda Hall; SWETS; UnCover. **CCC.**
   Description: Deals with the fundamentals of cement science and includes original papers on current research on cements from all parts of the world.
   Refereed Serial

692.8   FR   ISSN 0001-9666
AFFICHES D'ALSACE ET DE LORRAINE - MONITEUR DES SOUMISSIONS ET DES VENTES DE BOIS DE L'EST. 1919. s-w. 300 F. Affiches Moniteur, 1 b, rue de Bouxurller, B.P. 238-R6, 67006 Strasbourg Cedex, France. TEL 88-21-59-79. FAX 88-23-56-24. Ed. Gilbert Bretillon. adv. contact: Gilbert Bretillon. bk.rev.; bibl.; index. circ. 11,000. **Document type:** newspaper.

691   SA
AFRICAN BUILDING CONTRACTOR. Short title: A B C. (Text in English) bi-m. R.18 (foreign R.70). Emden Publishing Co., P.O. Box 1123, Pinegowrie 2123, South Africa. TEL 27-11-8860208. FAX 27-11-7895223. Ed. Dennis Bird. adv.; illus. circ. 12,000. **Document type:** trade publication.
   Description: For informal building contractors. Aims to encourage black building entrepreneurs, and improve the skills of the black builder.

690   FR   ISSN 0762-3399
AFRIQUE EXPANSION. (Supplements avail.: Les Marches Afrique Expansion (ISSN 0762-3402); La Lettre des Marches Afrique Expansion (ISSN 1153-5954); La Lettre Afrique Expansion (ISSN 0996-9888)) (Text in English and French) 1979. w. 3500 F. (foreign 3600 F.). Groupe Moniteur, 17 rue d'Uzes, 75002 Paris, France. FAX 33-1-42333819. TELEX 220 528F. Ed. Michel Levron. circ. 850. **Document type:** trade publication.
   Formerly (until 1984): Construction Afrique.

BUILDING AND CONSTRUCTION 861

690 US ISSN 1046-7947
TH4911
AGRICULTURAL BUILDING COST GUIDE (YEAR). a. E.H. Boeckh (Subsidiary of: Thomson Publishing Corp.), 2885 S. Calhoun Rd., Box 510291, New Berlin, WI 53151-0291. TEL 414-780-2800. FAX 414-780-0306.
Description: Aims to assist insurance, appraisal, and assessment industries to estimate the replacement cost of agricultural buildings in the U.S.

AIRPORT FORUM; airport construction and operation, air transport, air traffic control. see TRANSPORTATION — Air Transport

690 620.1 MG
AKORA SOA; revue technique sur la qualite des materiaux et du batiment. q. 12 F.($2) Centre d'Information et de Documentation Scientifique et Technique, B.P. 6224, Antananarivo 101, Madagascar. TEL 33288. Ed. Juliette Ratsimandrava. **Document type:** proceedings.

AKTIV. see FORESTS AND FORESTRY — Lumber And Wood

690 US ISSN 0002-4155
ALABAMA BUILDER.* 1958. m. membership. Home Builders Association of Alabama, Inc., Box 1431, Montgomery, AL 36102-1431. Ed. Teresa Owens. adv.; tr.lit. circ. 3,000.

ALL OF HOUSING/KATEI-BAN HYAKKA SERIES. see HOUSING AND URBAN PLANNING

690 AU ISSN 0002-5798
ALLGEMEINE BAUZEITUNG. q. S.120. Johann L. Bondi und Sohn, Industriestr. 2, A-2380 Perchtoldsdorf, Austria. TEL 01-864921. FAX 01-86492144. Ed. Franz Bondi. circ. 1,800. **Document type:** trade publication.

690 GW ISSN 0002-5801
ALLGEMEINE BAUZEITUNG. 1930. w. DM.187.20 (effective 1998). Patzer Verlag GmbH und Co. KG, Koenigsallee 65, 14193 Berlin, Germany. TEL 49-30-8959030. FAX 49-30-89590317. Ed.Bd. adv.; bk.rev.; abstr.; charts; illus.; pat.; stat.; tr.lit. circ. 30,000. (back issues avail.) **Document type:** newspaper.

643.7 GW ISSN 0342-8494
ALTES HAUS MODERN; Magazin fuer Modernisierung, Instandsetzung und Neubau von Haus und Wohnung. 1964. q. DM.24. Verlag Deutsche Wohnungswirtschaft GmbH, Cecilienallee 45, 40474 Duesseldorf, Germany. TEL 0211-47817-0. FAX 0211-4781723. bibl. circ. 60,000. **Document type:** trade publication.
Description: Information about reconstruction, renovation and modernization of houses and buildings.

643.7 GW ISSN 0943-061X
ALTHAUS MODERNISIEREN. 1973. bi-m. DM.30 (foreign DM.42) (effective 1997). Fachschriften Verlag GmbH, Hoehenstr. 17, 70736 Fellbach, Germany. TEL 49-711-5206-256. FAX 49-711-5281424. TELEX 7254709-FSVF-D. Ed. Kurt Jeni; Pub. Ottmar Strebel. adv.: B&W page DM.8640, color page DM.15552; trim 187 x 247; adv. contact: Wolfgang Kriwan. bk.rev. circ. 52,000. **Document type:** trade publication.
Formerly (until 1992): Althaus Modernisierung (ISSN 0343-1762)

690 GW ISSN 0175-6273
ALUMINIUM-KURIER; die Zeitschrift der Aluminium-Zentrale fuer Verarbeiter und Anwender. 1984. 6/yr. DM.124.80. Callwey Verlag, Postfach 800409, 81604 Munich, Germany. TEL 49-89-436005-36. FAX 49-89-43600513. Ed.Bd. circ. 13,000. **Indexed:** Alloys Ind., Eng.Mat.Abstr., Met.Abstr.Ind., Met.Abstr., Nonfer.Met.Alert, PCC Alert, World Alum.Abstr. **Document type:** consumer publication.
—CCC.

690 US
AMERICAN BUILDER MAGAZINE. (Published in several regional editions) m. Transcontinental Publishing Inc., Box 45454, Phoenix, AZ 85064-5454. TEL 602-331-8900. FAX 602-331-8448. E-mail: transpub@aol.com. Pub. Phillip T. Zeni, Sr. adv.; circ. (controlled). (reprint service avail.) **Document type:** trade publication.
Description: Contains material of interest to regional residential building professionals, including architects, builders, designers, developers, remodelers, subcontractors, and suppliers.

691.3 US ISSN 0065-7646
AMERICAN CEMENT DIRECTORY; directory of cement companies and personnel, United States, Canada, Mexico, Central and South America. 1910. a. $67 (effective 1997). Bradley Pulverizer Co., Box 1318, 123 S. Third St., Allentown, PA 18105-1318. TEL 610-434-5191. FAX 610-770-9400. Ed. David J. Fronheiser. R&P contact: David J. Fronheiser. adv.; index. circ. 800. **Document type:** directory.

625.84 691 US ISSN 0517-0745
AMERICAN CONCRETE INSTITUTE. COMPILATION. 1962. irreg. price varies. American Concrete Institute, Box 19150, Redford Sta., Detroit, MI 48219. TEL 313-532-2600. FAX 313-538-0655.
—CISTI.

691 US ISSN 0065-7891
AMERICAN CONCRETE INSTITUTE. SPECIAL PUBLICATION. 1962. irreg., latest 1991. price varies. American Concrete Institute, Box 19150, Redford Sta., Detroit, MI 48219. TEL 513-532-2600. FAX 313-538-0655. **Indexed:** Chem.Abstr.
—BLDSC (0576.800000). **CCC**.

690 UK
▼**AMERICAN CONSTRUCTION CATALOG**. 1995. a. $55. Data Distribution Publications, Apex House, London Rd., Northfleet, Gravesend, Kent DA11 9JA, England. TEL 01322-277788. FAX 01322-569627. **Document type:** catalog.

720 690 US
AMERICAN CONTRACTOR. (Published in several local editions) m. Transcontinental Publishing Inc., Box 45454, Phoenix, AZ 85064-5454. TEL 602-331-8900. FAX 602-331-8448. E-mail: transpub@aol.com. Pub. Phillip T. Zeni, Sr. adv.; circ. controlled. (reprint service avail.) **Document type:** trade publication.
Formerly: America's Architects and Engineers.
Description: Contains articles and features of interest to regional commercial construction professionals, including architects, contractors, designers, developers, engineers, government officials, subcontractors, and suppliers.

690 US
AMERICAN HOMESTYLE'S BUILD IT!. 1993. a. $6.95. Family Circle, Inc. (Subsidiary of: New York Times Company Inc.), 110 Fifth Ave., New York, NY 10011. TEL 212-463-1574. FAX 212-463-1662. Pub. Jesse Iverson. adv.; circ. 200,000 (paid). **Document type:** consumer publication.

690 US
AMERICAN HOMESTYLE'S BUILD IT! ULTRA. 1993. a. $10. Family Circle, Inc. (Subsidiary of: New York Times Company Inc.), 110 Fifth Ave., New York, NY 10011. TEL 212-463-1574. FAX 212-463-1662. Pub. Jesse Iverson. circ. 50,000 (paid). **Document type:** consumer publication.

AMERICAN INSTITUTE OF BUILDING DESIGN NEWSLETTER. see ARCHITECTURE

690 US ISSN 0146-7557
TA1
AMERICAN PROFESSIONAL CONSTRUCTOR. 1973. q. $100 in U.S. & Canada; elsewhere $150 (effective 1995 & 1996). American Institute of Constructors, 466 94th Ave., N., St. Petersburg, FL 33702-2522. TEL 813-578-0317. FAX 813-578-9982. URL: http://www.aicnet.org. Ed. Francis Eubanks. charts; illus.; stat. circ. 1,500. **Document type:** academic/scholarly publication.
—BLDSC (0853.270000); CISTI.
Description: Publishes articles on technical and management issues for the professional constructor. Refereed Serial

690 US ISSN 0065-9940
AMERICAN RAILWAY BRIDGE AND BUILDING ASSOCIATION. PROCEEDINGS. vol. 74, 1969. a. $30 per issue. American Railway Bridge and Building Association, Cary Bldg., 18154 Harwood Ave., Homewood, IL 60430. TEL 708-799-4650. FAX 708-799-4703. adv. circ. 800. **Document type:** proceedings.

AMERICAN SOCIETY FOR TESTING AND MATERIALS. COMPILATION OF A S T M STANDARDS IN BUILDING CODES. see ENGINEERING — Engineering Mechanics And Materials

ANCIENT MONUMENTS SOCIETY TRANSACTIONS. see ARCHITECTURE

690 UK
ANGLIA BUILDER. 1988. q. £17 outside East Anglia; others free (overseas £25). B C Publications, 16C Market Pl., Diss, Norfolk IP22 3AB, England. TEL 44-1379-644200. FAX 44-1379-650480. Ed. Brian Chester. adv. contact: Brian Chester. stat. (back issues avail.) **Document type:** trade publication.

ANLAEG BRUTTO. see BUSINESS AND ECONOMICS — Marketing And Purchasing

ANLAEG NETTO. see BUSINESS AND ECONOMICS — Marketing And Purchasing

ANNUAL BOOK OF A S T M STANDARDS. VOLUME 04.01. CEMENT; LIME; GYPSUM. see ENGINEERING — Engineering Mechanics And Materials

ANNUAL BOOK OF A S T M STANDARDS. VOLUME 04.02. CONCRETE AND AGGREGATES (INCLUDING MANUAL OF AGGREGATE AND CONCRETE TESTING). see ENGINEERING — Engineering Mechanics And Materials

ANNUAL BOOK OF A S T M STANDARDS. VOLUME 04.05. CHEMICAL-RESISTANT MATERIALS; VITRIFIED CLAY, CONCRETE; FIBER-CEMENT PRODUCTS; MASONRY; MORTARS. see ENGINEERING — Engineering Mechanics And Materials

ANNUAL BOOK OF A S T M STANDARDS. VOLUME 04.06. THERMAL INSULATION; ENVIRONMENTAL ACOUSTICS. see ENGINEERING — Engineering Mechanics And Materials

ANNUAL BOOK OF A S T M STANDARDS. VOLUME 04.08. SOIL AND ROCK; DIMENSION STONE; GEOSYNTHETICS. see ENGINEERING — Engineering Mechanics And Materials

ANNUAL BOOK OF A S T M STANDARDS. VOLUME 08.04. PLASTIC PIPE AND BUILDING PRODUCTS. see ENGINEERING — Engineering Mechanics And Materials

338.3 US
APARTMENT AND CONDOMINIUM PERSONAL PROPERTY COST GUIDE. a. $28. (American Appraisal Associates) E.H. Boeckh (Subsidiary of: Thomson Publishing Corp.), 2885 S. Calhoun Rd., Box 510291, New Berlin, WI 53151-0291. TEL 414-780-2800; 800-285-1288. FAX 414-780-0306.

690 US
APPLICATOR. 1977. 3/yr. $20. Sealant, Waterproofing and Restoration Institute, 2841 Main St., Kansas City, MO 64108. TEL 816-472-7974. FAX 816-472-7765. Ed. Sheila Navis; Pub. Ken Bouman. adv.; circ. 800 (controlled). **Document type:** trade publication.
Description: Contains articles on application, techniques and problems in the sealant, waterproofing and restoration industry.

AQUA: THE BUSINESS MAGAZINE FOR THE SPA AND POOL INDUSTRY. see BUSINESS AND ECONOMICS — Marketing And Purchasing

BUILDING AND CONSTRUCTION

690   LE   ISSN 0255-8572
ARAB CONSTRUCTION WORLD. (Text in Arabic, English) 1983. 6/yr. $60. Chatila Publishing House, P.O. Box 135121, Chouran, Beirut, Lebanon. TEL 961-1-352413. FAX 961-1-352419. E-mail: chatila@cyberia.net.lb. Ed. Riyadh Chihab; Pub. Fathi Chatila. adv. contact: Mona Chatila. bk.rev. circ. 9,949. **Document type:** trade publication.
    Description: Covers articles of interest to importers, wholesalers, contractors, and distributors serving the building and construction industry of the Middle East, Anglophone Africa and other countries.

690   GW   ISSN 0863-4424
ARBEIT UND TECHNIK IN DER SCHULE. 1959. 11/yr. DM.89.10 (effective 1997); newsstand price: DM.10.20. Paedagogischer Zeitschriftenverlag, Postfach 269, 10107 Berlin, Germany. TEL 49-30-20183592. FAX 49-30-20183593. (Subscr. to: CVK Cornelsen Verlagskontor, Postfach 100271, 33502 Bielefeld, Germany) Ed. Juergen Loeffler. adv.; bk.rev.; charts; illus.; index. circ. 2,500. **Indexed:** IBR. **Document type:** academic/scholarly publication.
—SWETS.
    Formerly: Polytechnische Bildung und Erziehung (ISSN 0032-4116)

ARBOUW JOURNAAL. see *OCCUPATIONAL HEALTH AND SAFETY*

690 720   GW   ISSN 0587-3452
ARCH PLUS; Zeitschrift fuer Architektur, Staedtebau und Design. 1968. 4/yr. DM.79 (foreign DM.89) (effective 1997). Arch Plus Verlag GmbH, Charlottenstr. 14, 52070 Aachen, Germany. TEL 49-241-508329. FAX 49-241-54831. Ed.Bd. adv.: B&W page DM.2480, color page DM.4820; trim 188 x 269; adv. contact: Andreas Bittis. bk.rev.; bibl.; illus. circ. 10,000. **Indexed:** Avery Ind.Archit.Per. **Document type:** trade publication.

ARCHITECT & BUILDER. see *ARCHITECTURE*

693.7722 693.96   SA   ISSN 1027-6785
ARCHITECT & SPECIFIERN BUILDING. 1994. q. A A A M S A, P.O. Box 15852, Verwoerdburg 0140, South Africa. Ed. Hans A. Schefferlie. adv.: color page R.5000. illus.; circ. 7,000 (controlled). **Document type:** trade publication.
    Formerly (until 1997): Aluminium and Glass in Building (ISSN 1024-3453)

691 728   UK
ARCHITECT, BUILDER, CONTRACTOR & DEVELOPER. Abbreviated title: A B C & D. 1988. m. £19. Ascent Publishing Ltd., 91-93 High St., Bromsgrove, Worcs. B61 8AQ, England. TEL 44-1527-836600. FAX 44-1527-574388. Ed. Emma Home. adv. contact: Mark Hargreaves. bk.rev.; software rev.; charts; illus.; pat.; circ. 24,344 (controlled). (back issues avail.) **Document type:** trade publication.
    Description: Covers developments in the British building materials and construction industries for architects and other building professionals.

ARCHITECTS CATALOG. see *BUSINESS AND ECONOMICS — Trade And Industrial Directories*

692   US   ISSN 0066-6157
TH435
ARCHITECTS, CONTRACTORS & ENGINEERS GUIDE TO CONSTRUCTION COSTS. 1968. a. $36 (effective 1997). A C & E Publishing Co., 6129 Beard Ave. S., Minneapolis, MN 55410. TEL 612-920-9699. Ed. Donald S. Roth; Pub. Donald S./Roth. R&P contact: Donald S. Roth. adv. contact: Donald S. Roth. **Document type:** trade publication.
—CISTI.

ARCHITECTS' JOURNAL. see *ARCHITECTURE*

ARCHITECTURAL REVIEW. see *ARCHITECTURE*

690 720   UK   ISSN 1361-326X
NA968
ARCHITECTURAL TECHNOLOGY. 1989. bi-m. British Institute of Architectural Technologists, 397 City Rd., London EC1V 1NE, England. TEL 44-171-278-2206. FAX 44-171-837-3194. Ed. Tanya Keelty. bk.rev. circ. 25,000. (back issues avail.) **Document type:** trade publication.
    Formerly (until Sep. 1995): B I A T Bulletin.
    Description: Official publication of BIAT. Provides articles on architectural technology, updates on technical and practical news, and news of the institute. For architectural and technical professionals within the construction industry.

ARCHITECTURE. see *ARCHITECTURE*

ARCHITECTURE AND BUILDING INDUSTRY. see *ARCHITECTURE*

DER ARCHITEKT UND DER BAUINGENIEUR. see *ARCHITECTURE*

ARCHITEKTUR UND BAU FORUM NEWSLETTER. see *ARCHITECTURE*

690   GW   ISSN 0949-7153
ARCONIS; Wissen zum Planen und Bauen und zum Baumarkt. (Supplement avail.: Bulldok Bauschaden (ISSN 0177-8285)) 1983. q. DM.60 (effective 1997). (Fraunhofer Informationszentrum Raum und Bau) Fraunhofer I R B Verlag, Nobelstr. 12, 70569 Stuttgart, Germany. TEL 49-711-9702500. FAX 49-711-9702507. E-mail: irb@irb.fhg.de; URL: http://www.irb.fhg.de. **Document type:** trade publication.
    Formerly (until 1996): I R B Aktuell (ISSN 0724-3065)

AREA DEVELOPMENT - CANADIAN ISSUE. see *HOUSING AND URBAN PLANNING*

AREA DEVELOPMENT SITES & FACILITY PLANNING. see *HOUSING AND URBAN PLANNING*

ARKHITEKTURA I STROITEL'STVO BELARUSI. see *ARCHITECTURE*

ARKHITEKTURA I STROITEL'STVO ROSSII. see *ARCHITECTURE*

ARQUITETURA Y CONSTRUCAO; a revista para construir ou reformar sua casa. see *ARCHITECTURE*

690 720   IT   ISSN 0394-5944
ARREDO URBANO. Key Title: A U. Arredo Urbano. (Text in Italian; summaries in English) 1980. bi-m. L.95000($95) Istituto Nazionale dell'Arredo Urbano delle Strutture Ambientali, Via Acqua, Traversa 255, 00135 Rome, Italy. TEL 39-6-3310490. FAX 39-6-3313055. Ed. Renato Cecilia. adv.: B&W page L.4600000, color page L.5400000. bk.rev. circ. 5,000. (back issues avail.)
—SWETS.
    Description: Deals with urban design and architecture. Includes diagrams and blue prints of future construction and projects.

690   SP   ISSN 0212-8578
ARTE Y CEMENTO. 1950. fortn. 22000 ptas. (effective 1995) 25000 ptas. (effective 1996). Arte y Cemento S.A., C. Zancoeta 9, 48013 Bilbao, Spain. TEL 344-4410750. FAX 344-4425116. Ed. Isaac Rodrigo Keller. adv.: B&W page 180000 ptas., color page 275000 ptas.; 180 x 270. bk.rev.; bibl.; pat.; stat.; tr.lit.; index. circ. 30,000. **Document type:** trade publication.
—CISTI.
    Formerly (until 1959): Radar (ISSN 0212-856X)

690   FR   ISSN 0995-0206
ARTISANS INFO B.T.P.. 1945. 4/yr. C A P E B des Bouches-du-Rhone, 7 bd. Pebre, 13295 Marseille Cedex 08, France. TEL 33-4-91774017. FAX 33-4-91765541. Ed. Roger Cecchini. adv. contact: Cecile Cigolini. circ. 3,500. **Document type:** bulletin, corporate report.

ASBESTOS INFORMATION ASSOCIATION - NORTH AMERICA. NEWS AND NOTES. see *MINES AND MINING INDUSTRY*

666.95   CN   ISSN 0478-4049
ASBESTOS PRODUCER/PRODUCTEUR D'AMIANTE. (Text in English, French) 1954. irreg. Quebec Asbestos Mining Association, 2000 rue Peel, Ste. 750, Montreal, PQ H3H 2W5, Canada. TEL 514-844-4751. illus.

ASBESTOS WORKER. see *LABOR UNIONS*

ASIAN ARCHITECT & CONTRACTOR. see *ARCHITECTURE*

690   SI
ASIAN BUILDING & CONSTRUCTION. (Text in English) bi-m. Trend Publishing & Promotion Centre, 35 Tannery Rd., 06-01 Tannery Block, Ruby Industrial Complex, Singapore 347740, Singapore. TEL 7423313. FAX 7424366. adv.: B&W page S.$1700, color page S.$2200; 190 x 271. circ. 18,000.

690   SP   ISSN 0571-3226
ASINTO. 1954. q. 2000 ptas. Asociacion de Ingenieros de Construccion y Electricidad del Arma de Ingenieros, Victoria 2, 28012 Madrid, Spain. **Indexed:** Ind.SST.

625   US   ISSN 1055-9205
ASPHALT CONTRACTOR; paving America. 1986. m. $48 (effective Jan. 1997). Group III Communications, 204 W. Kansas Ave., No. 103, Independence, MO 64050-3714. TEL 816-254-8735. FAX 816-254-2128. (Subscr. to: 112 E. Davis, Fayette, MO 65248. TEL 816-248-1860. FAX 816-248-1843) Ed. Lucy Avera; Pub. William Neeley. adv.: B&W page $1597; trim 7 x 10; adv. contact: Chris Harrison. circ. 10,000 (controlled). **Document type:** trade publication.
●Also available online.
    Description: Serves asphalt producers, contractors, pavement maintenance contractors, dealers, manufacturers and public works specifiers. Includes information on asphalt issues, equipment, techniques and products.

690   PO   ISSN 0870-0214
ASSOCIACAO DE EMPRESAS DE CONSTRUCAO E OBRAS PUBLICAS DO SUL. INDUSTRIA DA CONSTRUCAO; revista tecnica de construcao civil e obras publicas. 1978. m. Esc.8500 (effective 1993). Associacao de Empresas de Construcao e Obras Publicas do Sul (AECOPS), Rua Duque de Palmela 20, 1250 Lisbon, Portugal. TEL 351-1-3110200. FAX 351-1-3554810. E-mail: aecops@mail.telepac.pt. adv.; bk.rev. circ. 7,500. **Document type:** trade publication.
    Description: Covers building, public works, and construction economics, technology, materials, and equipment.

621.9   US   ISSN 0164-0593
HD9715.U5
ASSOCIATED EQUIPMENT DISTRIBUTORS. RENTAL RATES COMPILATION; nationally averaged rental rates for construction equipment including complete model specifications. Key Title: Rental Rates Compilation. 1944. a. $32.50. Associated Equipment Distributors, 615 W. 22nd St., Oak Brook, IL 60521. TEL 708-574-0650. Ed. David Loftus. illus. circ. 20,000.
    Formerly: Associated Equipment Distributors. Rental Compilation (ISSN 0364-8893)

690   CN   ISSN 0833-8388
ASSOCIATION DE LA CONSTRUCTION DE MONTREAL ET DU QUEBEC. BULLETIN. English edition: Construction Association of Montreal and the Province of Quebec. Bulletin (ISSN 0833-8396) vol.12, 1975. m. free. Association de la Construction de Montreal et du Quebec, 4970 Place de la Savane, Montreal, Que. H4P 1Z6, Canada. TEL 514-739-2381. Ed. Jaques Theoret. circ. 5,000. **Document type:** bulletin.
    Formerly (until 1986): Association de la Construction de Montreal et du Quebec. Nouvelles.

ASU E NO J C C A/JAPAN CONSTRUCTION CONSULTANTS ASSOCIATION. NEWS. see *ENGINEERING — Civil Engineering*

ATARASHII ZAIRYO KOHO KIKAI KOSHUKAI KOEN GAIYO/LECTURES ON NEW MATERIALS, METHODS AND MACHINERY IN CONSTRUCTION. SUMMARIES. see *ENGINEERING — Civil Engineering*

BUILDING AND CONSTRUCTION

690   AT   ISSN 1032-240X
AUSTRALIAN BUILDING CONSTRUCTION AND HOUSING. 1907-1973; N.S. 1974. m. Aus.$42 (overseas Aus.$60). Master Builders Association of New South Wales, Private Bag 9, Broadway, N.S.W. 2007, Australia. TEL 02-660-7188. FAX 02-660-4437. Pub. Jerry Grover. adv./ bk.rev.; charts; illus.; mkt.; stat.; tr.lit. circ. 10,000. (back issues avail.)
    Document type: trade publication.
    Incorporates (in July, 1988): Builder N.S.W; Which was formerly (until 1973): Construction (ISSN 0010-6674)

690   AT   ISSN 1030-1925
AUSTRALIAN BUILDING NEWS. 1959-1982; resumed 1985. bi-m. $40. Sydney Building Information Centre Ltd., 525 Elizabeth St., Surry Hills, N.S.W. 2010, Australia. TEL 02-318-2988. FAX 02-319-1890. TELEX AA 75555. Ed. Richard Pakalnis. adv./ B&W page Aus.$2200, color page Aus.$3500; adv. contact: Simon Lawson. bk.rev./ circ. 17,656 (controlled). (back issues avail.)
    Document type: trade publication.
    Formerly: Building News (ISSN 0045-3420)
    Description: Covers industry standards and regulations, new products, seminars and exhibitions, building business, law and more.

AUSTRALIAN BUILDING REGULATION REPORTER. see *LAW*

691   AT   ISSN 1035-4611
AUSTRALIAN CLAY JOURNAL & CERAMIC NEWS. 1933. bi-m. Aus.$30 (foreign Aus.$42) (effective 1997). Hamilton Press Pty. Ltd., P.O. Box 386, Manly, N.S.W. 2095, Australia. TEL 61-2-99776046. FAX 61-2-99763190. Ed. Barry McCrea; Pub. Barry/McCrea. adv./ B&W page Aus.$1836, color page Aus.$2456; trim 245 x 355; adv. contact: Barry McCrea. circ. 350. (back issues avail.) **Indexed:** Br.Ceram.Abstr. **Document type:** trade publication.
    Incorporates: Australian National Clay; Formerly (until 1959): Australian Clay Products Association. Journal.
    Description: For Australian and overseas manufacturers of clay and concrete products, and of plant and equipment.

691   AT   ISSN 1034-7860
AUSTRALIAN CONCRETE CONSTRUCTION. 1988. bi-m. Aus.$42. (Steel Reinforcement Institute of Australia) Intermedia Group Pty. Ltd., P.O. Box 606, Rozell, N.S.W. 2039, Australia. TEL 61-2-818-4111. FAX 61-2-818-4738. Ed. Juliet Pratley. adv./ B&W page Aus.$1470, color page Aus.$ 2650; trim 297 x 210. circ. 10,321. (back issues avail.)
    Document type: trade publication.
    Description: Promotes the use of concrete in all construction areas.

690   AT   ISSN 0818-0571
AUSTRALIAN INSTITUTE OF BUILDING PAPERS. a. Aus.$40 (foreign Aus.$50). Australian Institute of Building, 217 Northbourne Ave., Turner, A.C.T. 2601, Australia. TEL 61-2-477433. FAX 61-2-489030. Ed. Peter Williams. R&P contact: Peter Williams. TEL 61-3-93446440. **Document type:** academic/scholarly publication.
    —BLDSC (1801.673100); CISTI.

690   US   ISSN 0899-5540
TH4819.P7
AUTOMATED BUILDER. (Annual buyers' guide avail. in Jan.) 1963. 11/yr. $50 in US and Canada; elsewhere $100; free to qualified personnel. C M N Publications (Subsidiary of: C M N Associates, Inc.), 4371 Carpinteria Ave., Box 120, Carpinteria, CA 93014. TEL 805-684-7659. FAX 805-684-1765. E-mail: abmag@autbldmag.com; URL: http://www.autbldrmag.com. Ed. Don O. Carlson; Pub. Don O. Carlson. adv. contact: Lance Carlson. charts; illus. circ. 26,000. (also avail. in microfilm; back issues avail.; reprint service avail. from UMI) **Indexed:** Avery Ind.Archit.Per., PROMT. **Document type:** trade publication.
    —CISTI; Linda Hall; UMI; UnCover.
    Former titles (until 1988): Automation in Housing and Manufactured Home Dealer (ISSN 0740-3534); Automation in Housing-Systems Building News (ISSN 0362-0395); Formed by the merger of: Automation in Housing (ISSN 0005-1217); Systems Building News.
    Description: For production builders and manufacturers of mobile homes, panelized homes, modular homes, special commercial units and independent component manufacturers. Presents profile stories and articles on all aspects of manufacturing in industrialized housing, with emphasis on automated machine tools for home building in factories.

AUTOMATION IN CONSTRUCTION; an international journal for the building industry. see *COMPUTERS — Automation*

690 720   CN
AWARD MAGAZINE. 1986. 6/yr. $19.95. Canada Wide Magazines & Communications Ltd., 4180 Lougheed Hwy., Ste. 401, Burnaby, BC V5C 6A7, Canada. TEL 604-299-7311. FAX 604-299-9188. Eds. Marisa Paterson, Janet Collins. adv. contact: Dan Chapman. bk.rev. circ. 7,500. **Document type:** trade publication.
    Formerly (until 1990): Award: Construction in Profile (ISSN 0841-8802)
    Description: Covers architectural and design trends, company and project profiles for architects, interior designers, landscape architects, general contractors, developers and engineers.

AZULEJO; ceramica noble. see *CERAMICS, GLASS AND POTTERY*

690   UK
B A C M I IN (YEAR). a. free. British Aggregate Construction Materials Industries, 156 Buckingham Palace Rd., London SW1W 9TR, England. TEL 0171-730-8194. FAX 0171-730-4355. **Document type:** corporate report.

690   GW
B B A BAU - BERATUNG - ARCHITEKTUR; kennziffer-Zeitschrift Architekten, Planer, Bauingenieure. X. 10/yr. DM.140 (foreign DM.142) (effective 1997). Konradin Verlag Robert Kohlhammer GmbH, Ernst-Mey-Str. 8, 70771 Leinfelden-Echterdingen, Germany. TEL 49-711-7594-0. FAX 49-711-7594-398. Ed. Juergen Ostrowski. adv./ B&W page DM.7600, color page DM.9750; trim 190 x 270; adv. contact: Klaus Paletta. circ. 20,046. **Indexed:** Excerp.Med. **Document type:** trade publication.
    —CCC.
    Former titles: B B A Planen und Bauen (ISSN 0171-1555); Planen und Bauen.
    Description: Provides practical information and solutions in the fields of architecture, building and surveying.

690   AU
B B B - BAUMASCHINE - BAUGERAET - BAUSTELLE; Fachzeitschrift fuer Bau- und Baunebengewerbe. 1965. 10/yr. S.560. Technopress Fachzeitschriften Verlagsgesellschaft mbH, Iglaseegasse 21-23, Postfach 176, A-1191 Vienna, Austria. TEL 43-1-3207427. FAX 43-1-327427. Ed. Friedrich Kovacs. adv./ bk.rev.; abstr.; illus.; circ. 15,000 (controlled). (tabloid format) **Document type:** trade publication.
    Formerly: Baumaschine Baugeraet Baustoff (ISSN 0005-6685)

690 368   UK   ISSN 1350-9500
B C I S GUIDE TO HOUSE REBUILDING COSTS. 1978. a. £35 (effective Apr. 1997). Building Cost Information Service Ltd., The Royal Institution of Chartered Surveyors, 85-87 Clarence St., Kingston-upon-Thames, Surrey KT1 1RB, England. TEL 0181-546-7554. FAX 0181-547-1238. **Document type:** trade publication.
    —BLDSC (1871.384150).
    Formerly: Guide to House Rebuilding Costs for Insurance Valuation (ISSN 0261-2054)

690 368   UK   ISSN 0260-6216
B C I S QUARTERLY REVIEW OF BUILDING PRICES. 1981. q. £210 (effective Apr. 1997). Building Cost Information Service Ltd., Royal Institution of Chartered Surveyors, 85-87 Clarence St., Kingston-upon-Thames, Surrey KT1 1RB, England. TEL 0181-546-7554. FAX 0181-547-1238. Ed. J.L.N. Martin. circ. 1,600. **Document type:** trade publication.
    —BLDSC (1871.384200).

691   GW   ISSN 0005-6723
B D BAUMASCHINENDIENST. 1964. m. DM.51.60. Krafthand Verlag Walter Schulz, Gottlieb-Daimler-Str. 10, 86824 Bad Woerishofen, Germany. adv.; index.
    —CCC.

690.028 691   SA
B E M SPECIFIER. (Text in English) 1969. m. Communications Group, P.O. Box 7870, Johannesburg 2000, South Africa. Ed. H. Snow. adv. circ. 7,147. (tabloid format)
    Former titles (until 1992): Building Equipment and Materials; Building Equipment and Materials for South Africa (ISSN 0007-344X)

692.8   US   ISSN 0194-6587
B I D SERVICE WEEKLY. 1954. w. $109.37 per q. Trade Publishing Co. Ltd., 287 Mokauea St., Honolulu, Hawaii, HI 96819. TEL 808-848-0711. FAX 808-841-3053. Ed. Alfonso Rivera. adv.; charts; illus.; mkt.; stat.; tr.lit.; index. circ. 1,380.
    Former titles: Building Industry Digest; Builders Report Pacific (ISSN 0007-3296)
    Description: Contains information about construction and bidding (city, state & federal) for the Pacific area, including awarded bid results, supplies, and services.

690   UK
B M I BUILDING MAINTENANCE PRICE BOOK. 1980. a. £42. Building Maintenance Information, 85-87 Clarence St., Kingston-upon-Thames, Surrey KT1 1RB, England. FAX 0181-547-1238. Ed. Michael Matthews. adv.; bk.rev.; circ. 3,000 (paid). **Document type:** trade publication.
    Formerly: B M C I S Building Maintenance Price Book (ISSN 0261-2933)

690   UK   ISSN 0144-9060
B M P FORECASTS. (Building Material Producers) 1979. 3/yr. £375 to non-members; free to members. National Council of Building Material Producers, 26 Store St., London WC1E 7BT, England. TEL 44-171-323-3770. FAX 44-171-323-0307. E-mail: 101326.2660@compuserve.com. Ed. M. Christensen. **Document type:** trade publication.

690   UK   ISSN 0144-9052
B M P INFORMATION. (Building Material Producers) 1947. m. £80 to non-members; free to members. National Council of Building Material Producers, 26 Store St., London WC1E 7BT, England. TEL 44-171-323-3770. FAX 44-171-323-0307. E-mail: 101326.2660@compuserve.com. Ed. P. Blake. circ. 650. **Document type:** trade publication.
    Description: Monthly digest of news and facts about the building material production trade.

690   UK   ISSN 0144-9036
B M P MONTHLY STATISTICAL BULLETIN. (Building Material Producers) 1974. m. £200 to non-members; free to members. National Council of Building Material Producers, 26 Store St., London WC1E 7BT, England. TEL 44-171-323-3770. FAX 44-171-323-0307. E-mail: 101326.2660@compuserve.com. Ed. M. Christensen. circ. 250. **Document type:** bulletin.
    Description: Monthly statistics of the building material production trade, housing starts, completions and renovations.

BUILDING AND CONSTRUCTION

690   UK
B M P STATE OF TRADE. (Building Material Producers) 1989. s-a. £150 to non-members; free to members. National Council of Building Material Producers, 26 Store St., London WC1E 7BT, England. TEL 44-171-323-3770. FAX 44-171-323-0307. E-mail: 101326.2660@compuserve.com. **Document type:** trade publication.

690   US
B O C A BULLETIN. 1950. bi-m. membership. Building Officials and Code Administrators International, 4051 W. Flossmoor Rd., Country Club Hills, IL 60478-5795. TEL 708-799-2300. Ed. Paul K. Heilstedt; Pub. Bill J. Even. R&P contact: Bill J. Even. adv. contact: Bill J. Even. circ. 14,000. **Document type:** newsletter.

690 340   US   ISSN 0897-0068
KF5701.A73
B O C A NATIONAL BUILDING CODE. 1950. triennial, 13th ed., 1996. $42 to members; non-members $65. Building Officials and Code Administrators International, 4051 W. Flossmoor Rd., Country Club Hills, IL 60478-5795. TEL 708-799-2300. FAX 708-799-4981. E-mail: boca@bocai.org. Ed. Paul K. Heilstedt; Pub. Bill J. Even. R&P contact: Bill J. Even. adv. contact: Bill J. Even.
—CISTI.
Formerly: B O C A Basic National Building Code.
Description: Covers administration, use or occupancy, general building limitations, types of construction, fireresistant materials and construction, interior finishes, energy conservation, foundations and retaining walls, building materials, plumbing systems and much more.

343   US   ISSN 1055-6192
KF5701.Z95
B O C A NATIONAL PROPERTY MAINTENANCE CODE. 1978. triennial, 5th ed., 1996. $20 to members; non-members $30. Building Officials and Code Administrators International, 4051 W. Flossmoor Rd., Country Club Hills, IL 60478-5795. TEL 708-799-2300. FAX 708-799-4981. E-mail: boca@bocai.org. Ed. Paul K. Heilstedt; Pub. Bill J. Even. R&P contact: Bill J. Even. adv. contact: Bill J. Even. index.
—CISTI.
Former titles: B O C A National Existing Structure Code (ISSN 0897-0076); B O C A Basic Housing - Property Maintenance Code (ISSN 0525-0110)
Description: Covers general administration, light, ventilation and occupancy limitations, plumbing facilities, rubbish and garbage, and exterior property areas.

690   UK
CODEN: BREDAP
B R E PROFESSIONAL DEVELOPMENT. (Consists of 12 Digests, 8 Good Building Guides, 12 Good Repair Guides, 18 Information Papers, 5 B R E News of Construction Research) 1931. m. £80. (Building Research Establishment) Construction Research Communications, 151 Rosebery Ave., London EC1R 4QX, England. TEL 44-171-505-6622. FAX 44-171-505-6606. TELEX 923 220. (Ed. addr.: Building Research Establishment, Garston, Watford, Herts. WD2 7JR. TEL 44-923-894040. FAX 44-923-664010) Ed. Paul Graver; Pub. Rowan Crowley. R&P contact: Beryl Cook. index. circ. 5,000. (back issues avail.) **Indexed:** Biodet.Abstr., J.of Ferroc., World Surf.Coat. **Document type:** government publication.
—BLDSC (2363.668000); CISTI; UMI.
Incorporates: Great Britain. Building Research Establishment. B R E Digests (ISSN 0144-8536)
Description: Contains a combination of papers dealing with current practice, latest results, defect diagnosis, practical solutions, and advice.

690   JA   ISSN 1341-2930
▼**B R I PROCEEDINGS.** (Text in English) 1995. irreg. Ministry of Construction, Building Research Institute, 1 Tatehara, Tsukuba-sh, Ibaraki-ken 305, Japan. **Document type:** proceedings.
—BLDSC (2283.630000); CISTI.

690   JA   ISSN 0453-4972
B R I RESEARCH PAPERS. (Text in English) 1960. irreg. exchange basis. Ministry of Construction, Building Research Institute, Research Planning and Information Department - Kensetsusho Kenchiku Kenkyujo, 1 Tatehara, Tsukuba-shi, Ibaraki-ken 305, Japan. circ. 400. **Document type:** academic/scholarly publication.
—CISTI.

690 333.3   UK   ISSN 0953-9905
B S A ANNUAL REPORT. 1942. a. £5 (effective 1997). Building Societies Association, 3 Savile Row, London W1X 1AF, England. TEL 44-171-437-0655. FAX 44-171-287-0109. **Document type:** corporate report.
Former titles: Building Societies Association. Annual Report; Building Societies Association. Report of the Council (ISSN 0262-8155)
Description: Provides review of the activities of the association, its council and committees, in relationship to domestic matters and in the context of wider developments in the fields of housing, legislation, taxation and international developments.

690   CN   ISSN 0829-559X
B S D A NEWS. 1969. q. free. Building Supply Dealers Association of British Columbia, 630 Columbia St., No. 101, New Westminster, BC V3M 1B2, Canada. TEL 604-524-8658. FAX 604-524-6070. Ed. G.R. Tracy. adv. contact: Cindi Mueller. circ. 1,400. **Document type:** trade publication.
Formerly: Building Supply Dealers Association. Survey (ISSN 0383-2430)

690 624   UK
B S HANDBOOK 3. SUMMARIES OF BRITISH STANDARDS FOR BUILDING. 1979. a. £420. British Standards Institution, Linford Wood, Milton Keynes, Bucks. MK14 6LE, England. TEL 44-1908-220022. FAX 44-1908-320856. TELEX 825777. **Document type:** trade publication.

690 628   XK   ISSN 1010-5700
B T - L M & S. (Building Technology - Land Management & Safety) 1985. q. $10. A L K I M Communication Production Company, Box MA 020, Marchand Post Office, Castries, St. Lucia, W.I. Ed. Albert Deterville. adv. contact: Albert Deterville. circ. 5,000. **Document type:** academic/scholarly publication, consumer publication.
—CCC.

690   FR   ISSN 1161-6032
B T P INFOS PLUS. 8/yr. Editions Faure et Associes, 2 bis, rue Georges Lardennois, 75019 Paris, France. TEL 44-52-56-20. FAX 48-03-13-62. Ed. Alain Faure. circ. 15,000.

690   FR   ISSN 0299-1705
B T P MAGAZINE. 1986. 10/yr. 415 F. (effective 1997). 33 rue du Mont Valerien, 92210 Saint-Cloud, France. TEL 33-1-47711442. FAX 33-1-49110005. Ed. Jean Cayola. adv. circ. 18,000.

690   GW   ISSN 0723-6131
B Z BAUZENTRALBLATT. die Fachzeitschrift fuer Bauunternehmer im Hoch-, Tief- und Strassenbau. 1961. m. DM.45.50. Giesel Verlag fuer Publizitaet GmbH, Rehkamp 3, 30916 Isernhagen, Germany. TEL 49-511-7304-0. FAX 49-511-7304157. Ed. Volker Mueller. adv.; bk.rev. circ. 30,600. **Document type:** trade publication.
—CCC.
Formerly (until 1982): Bau-Zentralblatt (ISSN 0341-4000)

690   US
BADGER BUILDER. bi-m. $25 for non-members. Wisconsin Builders Association, 6400 Gisholt Dr., No. 203, Box 6096, Madison, WI 53713-6096. TEL 608-222-7630. FAX 608-222-0262. Ed. Pam Moen; Pub. Barbara Slack. adv. contact: Beth Vander Grinten. circ. 6,500. **Document type:** trade publication.
Description: Provides economic and industrial trend information for the home building industry. Includes input and feedback by members, advertisers, and affiliated businesses.

690   IT   ISSN 0392-2723
BAGNO E ACCESSORI. Cover title: Bagno e Accessori International. (Supplement avail.: Album) (Text in English, Italian) 1974. 6/yr. Lit.98000 in Europe; Oceania Lit.198000; elsewhere Lit.152000 (effective 1997). Gruppo Editoriale Faenza Editrice s.p.a., Via Pier. de Crescenzi, 44, 48018 Faenza, Italy. TEL 39-546-663488. FAX 39-546-660440. E-mail: gefe.vendita@uno.dinamica.it; gefe.info@uno.dinamica.it. Ed. Grazia Gamberoni. R&P contact: Luisa Teston. adv.: B&W page Lit.5610000, color page Lit.7650000; adv. contact: Elvio Neri. illus. circ. 24,000. **Indexed:** Br.Ceram.Abstr. **Document type:** trade publication.
Description: Promotes design, production, market and distribution of bathrooms.

BARBOUR INDEX BUILDING PRODUCT COMPENDIUM.
see INTERIOR DESIGN AND DECORATION

690 330.9   UK
BARCLAYS BANK. CONSTRUCTION SURVEY. (Part of the Industry Reports series) q. £120 (academic institutions and students £60). Barclays Bank plc., Economics Department, P.O. Box 12, Barclays House, 1 Wimborne Rd., Poole, Dorset BH15 2BB, England. TEL 01202-344023. FAX 01202-402303.
Description: Provides an analysis and outlook for the construction industry.

691   FR   ISSN 0765-040X
BAREME DES COEFFICIENTS; cours des materiaux du batiment. 1947. m. 1250 F. Editions Charles Massin et Cie, 16-18, rue de l'Amiral Mouchez, 75686 Paris Cedex 14, France. TEL 45-65-48-48. FAX 45-65-47-00. TELEX 264 918 TRACE. adv.

690   FR   ISSN 0223-0011
BATIMENT ARTISANAL. 1953. m. Confederation de l'Artisanat et des Petites Entreprises du Batiment, 46, av. d'Ivry, B.P. 353, 75625 Paris Cedex 13, France. TEL 1-45-82-40-00. FAX 1-45-82-49-10. TELEX 201 057. adv.

690   FR   ISSN 1266-8176
BATIMENT INFORMATION; la revue du materiel compact. 10/yr. 190 F. (Europe 250 F.; elsewhere 350 F.) (effective 1997). (Societe d'Editions pour la Location) Groupe Chantiers de France, Bord de Seine, 202 quai de Clichy, 92110 Clichy, France. TEL 33-1-47561723. FAX 33-1-47561432. Eds. Arlette Surchamp, Marc Montagnon; Pub. Arlette Surchamp. adv. contact: Helene Tellier. circ. 7,000. **Document type:** newspaper, trade publication.
Formerly (until 1995): Location Actualite (ISSN 0997-380X)
Description: For those interested in the hiring of public work, handling, roadwork, transport and quarry equipment.

690   FR   ISSN 0223-758X
BATIMENT PARISIEN. 1978. 4/yr. 58 rue Rochechouart, 75009 Paris, France. TEL 48-78-41-52. FAX 45-26-09-33. Ed. M. Simon. circ. 4,000.

691   FR   ISSN 0987-7282
BATIPRIX. 1983. a. Publication du Moniteur, 17 rue d'Uzes, 75002 Paris, France. TEL 1-40-13-34-32. FAX 1-40-26-33-87. TELEX UPRESSE 680876F. Ed. Gilbert Lemaire. circ. 10,000.

690 720   FR   ISSN 0988-5188
BATISSEUR EUROPEEN. 1988. 9/yr. Sedibat, 8 rue Neuve, 34510 Florensac, France. TEL 67-77-71-75. FAX 67-77-75-67. Ed. Patrice Genet. circ. 10,000.

690   GW   ISSN 0931-394X
BAU - AKTUELL. Key Title: Bau Aktuell Rheinhessen-Pfalz. 1979. m. Pfalzischer Baugewerbeverband, Richard-Wagner-Str 19, 76185 Kaiserslautern, Germany. TEL 0631-12085.
Formerly (until 1986): Bau Aktuell Rheinland-Pfalz (ISSN 0174-4518)

660   SZ
BAU & HOLZ. (Text in French, German and Italian) w. Schweizerische Bau und Holzarbeiter Verband, Strassburgstr. 5, P.O. Box 8021, CH-8004 Zurich, Switzerland. adv. circ. 37,000.

690   SZ
BAU FLASH. 10/yr. Kretz AG, Postfach, CH-8706 Feldmeilen, Switzerland. TEL 41-1-9237656. FAX 41-1-9237657. Ed. Thomas Aeschmann. adv.: B&W page 2750 SFr., color page 3805 SFr.; trim 185 x 265; adv. contact: Esther Kretz. circ. 7,500. **Document type:** trade publication.

690   AU
BAU IM SPIEGEL. q. Heinestr. 3, A-1020 Vienna, Austria. TEL 01-2143344. FAX 01-2167929. Ed. Walter Polacek. circ. 12,600.

669   GW
BAU INFORMATION. m. Landesverband Bauindustrie Rheinland-Pfalz, Sudallee 31-35, 56068 Koblenz, Germany. TEL 0261-3703334.

BUILDING AND CONSTRUCTION

690   GW   ISSN 0005-643X
BAU UND BAUSTOFF. 1964. q. DM.36. Gert Wohlfarth GmbH Verlag Fachtechnik und Mercator-Verlag, Stresemannstr. 20-22, 47051 Duisburg, Germany. TEL 49-203-30527-0. FAX 49-203-337765. E-mail: wohlfarth@t-online.de. Ed. Wolfgang Metzmacher. adv.; bk.rev. circ. 75,000. **Document type:** trade publication.

690   GW
BAU-Z; Fachmagazin fuer Bauen und Baurecht. (Supplement avail.: Renova (ISSN 0947-8914)) 1947. m. DM.140 (foreign DM.170) (effective 1997). (Verband der Bauingenieure) Verlag fuer Bauwesen GmbH, Am Friedrichshain 22, 10407 Berlin, Germany. TEL 49-30-42151388. FAX 49-30-42151232. Ed. Peter Fritsch. adv.; bk.rev.; charts; illus.; tr.lit.; index. (back issues avail.) **Indexed:** C.I.S. Abstr., Geotech.Abstr., IBR, Intl.Civil Eng.Abstr., Soft.Abstr.Eng. **Document type:** trade publication.
—BLDSC (1871.120000); Linda Hall.
Formerly: Bauzeitung (ISSN 0005-6871)

690   GW   ISSN 0933-3924
BAUAUFSICHTLICHE ZULASSUNGEN. 1967. irreg. DM.468. Erich Schmidt Verlag GmbH & Co. (Berlin), Genthiner Str. 30G, 10785 Berlin, Germany. TEL 49-30-250085-0. FAX 49-30-25008521. (looseleaf format) **Document type:** bulletin.

690   SZ   ISSN 1019-4258
BAUDOC BULLETIN. 1969. 10/yr. Schweizer Baudokumentation, CH-4223 Blauen, Switzerland. TEL 41-61-7614141. FAX 41-61-7612233. Ed. Urs Graf. circ. 8,000. **Document type:** bulletin.
Formerly (until 1991): Docu-Bulletin (ISSN 1019-424X)

690   GW
BAUELEMENTE BAU; Marketingmagazin fuer Bauausstatter - Fenster - Tueren - Fassaden. 1976. m. DM.115. Verlag fuer Fachpublizistik GmbH, Moerikestr. 15, 70178 Stuttgart, Germany. TEL 49-711-6491031. Ed. Rudolf Engert, Hans U. Rohwer. **Document type:** trade publication.

690   GW   ISSN 0170-0138
BAUEN. 1975. bi-m. DM.42 (foreign DM.48) (effective 1997). Fachschriften Verlag GmbH, Hoehenstr. 17, 70736 Fellbach, Germany. TEL 49-711-5206-256. FAX 49-711-5281424. Ed. Hans-Peter Bauer-Boeckler; Pub. Ottmar Strebel. adv. contact: Wolfgang Kriwan. illus.; tr.lit.; circ. 76,253. **Document type:** trade publication.
Formerly (until 1978): Bauen und Moderniseren (ISSN 0170-4095)

690   GW   ISSN 0171-7952
BAUEN FUER DIE LANDWIRTSCHAFT. 1964. 3/yr. DM.40. (Bundesverband der Deutschen Zementindustrie e.V.) Beton-Verlag GmbH, Postfach 110134, 40501 Duesseldorf, Germany. TEL 0211-550090. FAX 0211-5500955. Ed. Joerg Brandt. adv.; bk.rev. circ. 6,500. **Document type:** trade publication.
—CCC.
Formerly: Beton-Landbau (ISSN 0005-9897)

BAUEN IN STAHL/CONSTRUIRE EN ACIER/COSTRUIRE IN ACCIAIO. see *ARCHITECTURE*

690   GW   ISSN 0934-1773
BAUEN MIT KUNSTSTOFFEN. 1958. bi-m. DM.90. Institut fuer das Bauen mit Kunstoffen e.V., Osannstr. 37, 64285 Darmstadt, Germany. FAX 06151-421101. Eds. Dieter Arlt, Wolfgang Hasemann. adv.; bk.rev. circ. 2,500. **Indexed:** Nonwov.Abstr.

BAUFORUM; Fachzeitschrift fuer Architektur-Bautechnik-Bauwirtschaft-Industrial Design. see *ARCHITECTURE*

690   GW   ISSN 0005-6626
BAUGESCHAEFT UND BAUUNTERNEHMER. 1966. q. DM.48($20) Zeitungs- und Zeitschriftenverlag Heinrichs, Brueggekamp 1, 30890 Barsinghausen, Germany. TEL 49-5155-2289. Ed. G. Heinrichs; Pub. G. Heinrichs. adv.; bk.rev.; stat.; tr.lit. circ. 5,400. (tabloid format) **Document type:** trade publication.

690   GW   ISSN 0343-0375
BAUGEWERBE - MITTEILUNGEN WESTFALEN. 1976. m. Fachverband Zimmerei und Holzbau, Westfalendamm 229, 44141 Dortmund, Germany. TEL 433918.

690   GW   ISSN 0173-5365
BAUHANDWERK; Ausbau und Modernisierung. 1979. m. DM.115. Bertelsmann Fachzeitschriften GmbH, Postfach 120, 33111 Guetersloh, Germany. TEL 05241-802332. FAX 05241-73055. Ed. Burkhard Froehlich. adv.: B&W page DM.5480, color page DM.8430; trim 270 x 186. bk.rev. circ. 11,900. **Document type:** trade publication.
Description: Trade publication for the building industry, featuring restoration, renovation and modernization of existing buildings and houses as well as extensions and additions. Lists new products, materials and appliances.

690   GW   ISSN 0937-1826
BAUIDEE. 1988. q. newsstand price: DM.12. Heinrich Bauer Verlag, Burchardstr. 11, 20095 Hamburg, Germany. TEL 49-40-30193040. FAX 49-40-335923. (Dist. in US by: GLP International, 153 S. Dean St., Englewood, NJ 07631-3513. TEL 201-871-1010; Dist. in UK by: Powers International, 517-523 Fulham Rd., London SW6 1HD, England. TEL 44-171-385-8855. FAX 44-171-381-5555) Ed. Ute Stahmann. adv.: B&W page DM.12120, color page DM.19404; adv. contact: Karl Keller. circ. 88,000 (paid). **Document type:** consumer publication.
Description: Ideas and tips for building and construction.

690   AU
BAUIMPULS. s-a. Dietrichgasse 39, A-1030 Vienna, Austria. TEL 01-7130598. circ. 12,800.

690   GW   ISSN 0940-7367
BAUINDUSTRIE AKTUELL. m. Hauptverband der Deutschen Bauindustrie, Abraham-Lincoln-Str. 30, 65189 Wiesbaden, Germany. TEL 49-611-7720. **Document type:** trade publication.
Incorporated (in 1986): Baukonjunkturspiegel (ISSN 0343-141X); **Formerly** (until 1986): Bauindustriebrief (ISSN 0343-7795)

690   GW   ISSN 0938-7536
NA2728
BAUINFORMATIK. 1990. bi-m. DM.148. Verlagsgesellschaft Rudolf Mueller GmbH & Co. KG, Stolberger Str. 84, 50933 Cologne, Germany. TEL 49-221-5497-0. FAX 49-221-5497326. adv.: B&W page DM.5840, color page DM.9440; trim 188 x 267. circ. 15,000. **Document type:** trade publication.

690   GW   ISSN 0005-6650
TA3   CODEN: BANGAS
BAUINGENIEUR; Zeitschrift fuer das gesamte Bauwesen. 1920. 11/yr. DM.548 (effective 1997). Springer V D I Verlag, Heinrichstr. 24, 40239 Duesseldorf, Germany. TEL 49-211-6103-0. FAX 49-221-6103414. Ed. Thomas Burska-Erler. adv.: B&W page DM.3440, color page DM.5600; trim 250 x 175; adv. contact: Renate Birkenstock. bk.rev.; bibl.; charts; illus.; index. (also avail. in microform from UMI; back issues avail.; reprint service avail. from ISI) **Indexed:** Alloys Ind., Appl.Mech.Rev., Chem.Abstr., Concr.Abstr., Dok.Str., Eng.Ind., Eng.Mat.Abstr., Excerp.Med., Geotech.Abstr., INIS Atomind., Intl.Civil Eng.Abstr., Met.Abstr., Met.Abstr.Ind., Nonfer.Met.Alert, PCC Alert, Soft.Abstr.Eng., Steels Alert, World Alum.Abstr. **Document type:** trade publication.
—BLDSC (1867.000000); CISTI; Linda Hall; SWETS; UMI. **CCC.**

690   AU
BAUJOURNAL. 1989. 9/yr. S.300. Baujournal Fachzeitschriften GmbH, Rahlgasse 1, A-1060 Vienna, Austria. TEL 01-5870860. FAX 01-587509611. Ed. Herbert Zach. adv. contact: Katharina Hallal. bk.rev. **Document type:** trade publication.

660   SZ
NA9000
BAUKADER - AKTUELLES BAUEN. 1963. 12/yr. 83 SFr. (foreign 103 SFr.). Schueck Soehne AG, Bahnhofstr. 24, CH-8803 Rueschlikon, Switzerland. TEL 01-7241044. FAX 01-7242258. Ed. Karl-Josef Verding. adv.: B&W page 2250 SFr., color page 3350 SFr.; trim 185 x 260; adv. contact: Werner Staehli. bk.rev. circ. 10,800. **Indexed:** Archit.Per.Ind., Avery Ind.Archit.Per., Br.Tech.Ind. **Document type:** trade publication.
Former titles: Aktuelles Bauen; Schweizer Baumarkt (ISSN 0255-6898); Aktuelles Bauen.

690   GW   ISSN 0341-2717
BAUMARKT. m. DM.163.20. Bertelsmann Fachzeitschriften GmbH, Postfach 120, 33111 Guetersloh, Germany. TEL 05241-802332. FAX 05241-73055. Eds. A. Langer, Volker Horschig. adv.: B&W page DM.5960, color page DM.8810; trim 270 x 186. circ. 15,899. (back issues avail.) **Indexed:** Excerp.Med., Key to Econ.Sci. **Document type:** trade publication.
Incorporates (in Apr. 1978): Bauanalysis.
Description: Covers business and technical questions in connection with underground and surface engineering and road building.

690   GW   ISSN 0723-5062
BAUMARKT TIP; der aktuelle Chef-Brief. 1977. w. DM.312. Bertelsmann Fachzeitschriften GmbH, Postfach 120, 33111 Guetersloh, Germany. TEL 05241-802332. FAX 05241-73055. Ed. Fritz O. Bornemann. circ. 1,000. **Document type:** trade publication.
Description: For executives in the building sector.

690   GW   ISSN 0005-6715
BAUMASCHINEN- UND BAUGERAETE-HANDEL. 1966. q. DM.48($20) Zeitungs- und Zeitschriftenverlag Heinrichs, Brueggekamp 1, 30890 Barsinghausen, Germany. TEL 49-5105-2289. Ed. G. Heinrichs; Pub. G. Heinrichs. adv.; bk.rev.; stat.; tr.lit. circ. 3,500. (tabloid format) **Document type:** trade publication.

BAUMEISTER; Zeitschrift fuer Architektur. see *ARCHITECTURE*

690   GW   ISSN 0179-2563
BAUMETALL; Klempnertechnik im Hochbau. 1985. bi-m. DM.92.40 (foreign DM.114) (effective 1996). Technischer Fachverlag GmbH, Forststr. 131, 70193 Stuttgart, Germany. TEL 49-711-63672-0. FAX 49-711-6367211. Ed. Manfred Haselbach. adv. contact: Annette Haselbach. circ. 5,200. **Document type:** trade publication.

690 531   GW   ISSN 0171-5445
TH6014   CODEN: BAUPDP
BAUPHYSIK. 1979. bi-m. DM.295 (foreign DM.325) (students DM.95 (foreign DM.107)) (effective 1997). Ernst und Sohn, Muehlenstr. 33-34, 13187 Berlin, Germany. TEL 49-30-47889200. FAX 49-30-47889284. (Subscr. to: Wiley - V C H, Postfach 101161, 69451 Weinheim, Germany. TEL 49-6201-606147. FAX 49-6201-606117; Subscr. in the Americas to: John Wiley & Sons, Inc., 605 Third Ave., New York, NY 10158. TEL 212-850-6645. FAX 212-850-6021) Ed. H.P. Luehr. adv. circ. 1,835. **Indexed:** Acoust.Abstr., Excerp.Med., INIS Atomind. **Document type:** trade publication.
—BLDSC (1867.800000); CASDDS; CISTI; Linda Hall; SWETS. **CCC.**
Description: Covers topics such as the problems of thermal insulation, humidity control, acoustics, fire design, lighting and micro-climate control relating to buildings.

690 720   GW   ISSN 0938-1694
BAUPLAN - BAUORGA; internationale technisch-wirtschaftliche Zeitschrift. 1980. 6/yr. DM.51.36 (foreign DM.60). Verlag Heinrich Graefen GmbH, Im Dreispitz 30, 47249 Duisburg, Germany. TEL 49-203-702672. FAX 49-203-702672. adv.; bk.rev. circ. 8,000. **Document type:** trade publication.

BUILDING AND CONSTRUCTION

690   GW   ISSN 0724-7931
BAUPRAXIS-ZEITUNG. Abbreviated title: B P Z. 11/yr. DM.114.60 (foreign DM.123) (effective 1997). Konradin Verlag Robert Kohlhammer GmbH, Ernst-Mey-Str. 8, 70771 Leinfelden-Echterdingen, Germany. TEL 49-711-7594-0. FAX 49-711-7594-390. Ed. Peter Schaeuble. adv.: B&W page DM.6820, color page DM.8800; trim 190 x 270; adv. contact: Klaus Paletta. circ. 21,440. (back issues avail.) **Document type:** trade publication.
  Description: Presents data on the building industry, construction technology, processes, machinery, materials and components.

690   GW   ISSN 0340-7489
BAURECHT; Zeitschrift fuer das gesamte oeffentliche und zivile Baurecht. Short title: BauR. 1970. bi-m. DM.303.40 (effective 1996). Werner-Verlag GmbH, Karl-Rudolf-Str. 172, 40215 Duesseldorf, Germany. TEL 49-211-38798-0. FAX 49-211-383104. Eds. Konrad Gelzer, Hermann Korbion. Indexed: Dok.Str., IBR, INIS Atomind. **Document type:** trade publication.
—SWETS. **CCC.**

690 340   GW   ISSN 0941-2182
BAURECHT FUER DAS LAND BRANDENBURG. 1992. irreg. DM.196. Erich Schmidt Verlag GmbH & Co. (Berlin), Genthiner Str. 30G, 10785 Berlin, Germany. TEL 49-30-250085-0. FAX 49-30-25008521. (looseleaf format) **Document type:** bulletin.

690 340   GW
BAURECHT FUER DAS LAND MECKLENBURG-VORPOMMERN. 1992. irreg. DM.196. Erich Schmidt Verlag GmbH & Co. (Berlin), Genthiner Str. 30G, 10785 Berlin, Germany. TEL 49-30-250085-0. FAX 49-30-25008521. (looseleaf format) **Document type:** bulletin.

690 340   GW   ISSN 0941-2190
BAURECHT FUER DAS LAND SACHSEN-ANHALT. 1992. irreg. DM.196. Erich Schmidt Verlag GmbH & Co. (Berlin), Genthiner Str. 30G, 10785 Berlin, Germany. TEL 49-30-250085-0. FAX 49-30-25008521. (looseleaf format) **Document type:** bulletin.

690 340   GW   ISSN 0941-2204
BAURECHT FUER DAS LAND THUERINGEN. 1992. irreg. DM.196. Erich Schmidt Verlag GmbH & Co. (Berlin), Genthiner Str. 30G, 10785 Berlin, Germany. TEL 49-30-250085-0. FAX 49-30-25008521. (looseleaf format) **Document type:** bulletin.

690 340   GW   ISSN 0941-2212
BAURECHT FUER DEN FREISTAAT SACHSEN. 1992. irreg. DM.196. Erich Schmidt Verlag GmbH & Co. (Berlin), Genthiner Str. 30G, 10785 Berlin, Germany. TEL 49-30-250085-0. FAX 49-30-25008521. (looseleaf format) **Document type:** bulletin.

690 340   AU
▼**BAURECHTLICHE BLAETTER.** Announced for publication in 1998. q. DM.70 (effective 1998). Springer-Verlag, Sachsenplatz 4-6, P.O. Box 89, A-1201 Vienna, Austria. TEL 43-1-3302415. FAX 43-1-3302426. E-mail: springer@springer.co.at. (Subscr. in N. America to: Springer-Verlag New York, Inc., 175 Fifth Ave., New York, NY 10010. TEL 212-460-1500. FAX 212-473-6272) **Document type:** academic/scholarly publication.

690   GW   ISSN 0939-4680
BAUSANIERUNG. bi-m. Bertelsmann Fachzeitschriften GmbH, Postfach 120, 33111 Guetersloh, Germany. TEL 05241-802332. FAX 05241-73055. adv.: B&W page DM.5440, color page DM.8140; trim 279 x 189. circ. 9,923. **Document type:** trade publication.

690   GW   ISSN 0174-3058
BAUSPAR-JOURNAL. 1979. q. membership. Deutsche Bausparkasse AG, Heinrichstr. 2, 64283 Darmstadt, Germany. Ed. E. Nierich. adv.: bk.rev.; charts; illus. circ. 120,000.
  Formerly (1927-1968): Heim und Herd (ISSN 0017-968X)

690   GW   ISSN 0721-7854
BAUSTOFF-TECHNIK; Fachzeitschrift fuer Baustoffe und Baustoff-Anwendung. 1982. m. DM.60. Gert Wohlfarth GmbH Verlag Fachtechnik und Mercator-Verlag, Stresemannstr. 20-22, 47051 Duisburg, Germany. TEL 49-203-30527-0. FAX 49-203-337765. E-mail: wohlfarth@t-online.de. Ed. Wilfried Behr; Pub. Gert Wohlfarth. circ. 6,210. **Document type:** trade publication.

660   GW   ISSN 0343-5903
HD9715.G3
BAUSTOFF UMSCHAU. 1977. 9/yr. Baader Verlag, Postfach 1220, 72522 Muensingen, Germany. adv. circ. 7,400.

690   GW   ISSN 0005-6804
BAUSTOFF- UND BAUBEDARFS-GROSSHANDEL. 1966. q. DM.48($20) Zeitungs- und Zeitschriftenverlag Heinrichs, Brueggekamp 1, 30890 Barsinghausen, Germany. TEL 49-5105-2289. Ed. G. Heinrichs; Pub. G. Heinrichs. adv.: bk.rev.; stat.; tr.lit. circ. 3,500. (tabloid format) **Document type:** trade publication.

691   GW   ISSN 0005-6448
BAUSTOFFMARKT; Fachzeitschrift fuer den Baustoff-, Heimwerker- und Keramik-markt. 1969. m. DM.144. (Bundesverband Deutscher Baustoffhaendler e.V.) Gert Wohlfarth GmbH Verlag Fachtechnik und Mercator-Verlag, Stresemannstr. 20-22, 47051 Duisburg, Germany. TEL 49-203-30527-0. FAX 49-203-337765. E-mail: wohlfarth@t-online.de. Ed. Wilfried Behr; Pub. Gert Wohlfarth. circ. 6,980. **Document type:** trade publication.

690   GW   ISSN 0179-2857
BAUSUBSTANZ; Fachmagazin fuer Bauwerkserhaltung. 10/yr. DM.152.40 (foreign DM.176.40) (effective 1997). Meininger Verlag GmbH, Maximilianstr. 7-17, 67433 Neustadt, Germany. TEL 49-6321-8908-0. FAX 49-6321-890873. Ed. Thomas Wieckhorst. circ. 14,103. **Document type:** trade publication.

690   GW   ISSN 0932-8351
BAUTECHNIK. 1924. m. DM.495 (foreign DM.555) (students DM.165 (foreign DM.189)) (effective 1997). Ernst und Sohn, Muehlenstr. 33-34, 13187 Berlin, Germany. TEL 49-30-47889200. FAX 49-30-47889284. (Subscr. to: Wiley - V C H, Postfach 101161, 69451 Weinheim, Germany. TEL 49-6201-606147. FAX 49-6201-606117; Subscr. in the Americas to: John Wiley & Sons, Inc., 605 Third Ave., New York, NY 10158. TEL 212-850-6645. FAX 212-850-6021) Ed. Doris Greiner-Mai. circ. 3,780. Indexed: Alloys Ind., Eng.Mat.Abstr., Geotech.Abstr., I.M.M.Abstr., Met.Abstr.Ind., Met.Abstr., Nonfer.Met.Alert, PCC Alert, Steels Alert, World Alum.Abstr. **Document type:** trade publication.
—CISTI; Ei; SWETS; UMI. **CCC.**
  Formed by 1983 merger of: Bautechnik. Ausgabe A (ISSN 0341-1052); Bautechnik. Ausgabe B (ISSN 0340-5044)
  Description: Theory and practice in civil engineering, building technology and related fields, developments in building machinery and construction methods, reviews, and technical reports.

690   GW   ISSN 0170-9267
                CODEN: BABADL
BAUTENSCHUTZ UND BAUSANIERUNG; Zeitschrift fuer Bauinstandhaltung und Denkmalpflege. Short title: B und B. (Text in German; summaries in English and German) 1977. 8/yr. DM.172 (foreign DM.178). Verlagsgesellschaft Rudolf Mueller GmbH & Co. KG, Stolberger Str. 84, 50933 Cologne, Germany. TEL 49-221-5497-202. FAX 49-221-5497326. TELEX 8881256. (Subscr. to: Postfach 410949, 50869 Cologne, Germany) Ed. Franz Lubinski. adv.: B&W page DM.4450, color page DM.7740; trim 188 x 267. bk.rev.; index. circ. 7,000. (reprint service avail.) **Document type:** trade publication.
—BLDSC (1870.320000); CASDDS; CISTI. **CCC.**

690   GW   ISSN 0005-6847
DIE BAUVERWALTUNG. 1938. m. DM.276 (foreign DM.311) (effective 1997). (Bundesministerium fuer Raumordnung, Bauwesen und Staedtebau) Vincentz Verlag, Schiffgraben 43, 30175 Hannover, Germany. TEL 49-511-9910310. FAX 49-511-9910399. E-mail: zeitschriftendienst@vincentz.de. (Subscr. to: Postfach 6247, 30062 Hannover, Germany) Ed. Jola Horschig. adv.: B&W page DM.3340, color page DM.5740. bk.rev.; illus.; stat.; tr.lit.; index. circ. 4,825. Indexed: Dok.Str. **Document type:** government publication.
—CCC.
  Incorporates: Baurechtliche Mitteilungen; Bauamt und Gemeindebau (ISSN 0005-6472)

690   GW   ISSN 1433-0148
BAUWIRTSCHAFT; das Monatsmagazin fuer Fuehrungskraefte im Bauwesen. 1947. m. DM.320 (foreign DM.356) (effective 1998). (Hauptverband der Deutschen Bauindustrie) Bauverlag GmbH, Postfach 1460, 65004 Wiesbaden, Germany. TEL 49-6123-700-0. FAX 49-6123-700122. E-mail: bauverlag.zeitschr.-journals@t-online.de. (Co-sponsor: Bundesverband Steine und Erden e.V.) Eds. U. Morchutt, D. Lemser. adv. contact: A. Mayer. bk.rev.; charts; illus.; pat.; stat. circ. 12,500. Indexed: Dok.Str. **Document type:** trade publication.
  Formerly: Bauwirtschaft. Ausgabe A (ISSN 0341-3810)
  Description: Trade publication for the building industry featuring planning, completion, materials, and trade. Articles on prefabrication, road building, and the building market. Lists events and industry news.

690 330   GW   ISSN 0170-9097
BAUWIRTSCHAFT IM ZAHLENBILD. s-a. Hauptverband der Deutschen Bauindustrie, Abraham-Lincoln-Str. 30, 65189 Wiesbaden, Germany. TEL 49-611-7720. **Document type:** bulletin.

BEIKOKU TOKKYO SHOROKU. YU'YU KIKAI, KENSETSU, DOBOKU HEN/U.S. PATENT ABSTRACTS. TRANSPORTING MACHINE, CONSTRUCTION, CIVIL ENGINEERING. see PATENTS, TRADEMARKS AND COPYRIGHTS — Abstracting, Bibliographies, Statistics

960   US
BERGER BUILDING & DESIGN COST FILE. UNIT PRICES. VOL. 1: GENERAL CONSTRUCTION TRADES. a. Building Cost File, Inc., 2906 Anthony St., Wantagh, NY 11793-2330.
  Formed by the 1981 merger of: Berger Design Cost File; Berger Building Cost File; Which was formerly: Building Cost File (ISSN 0091-3499)

690   US
BERGER BUILDING & DESIGN COST FILE. UNIT PRICES. VOL. 2: MECHANICAL AND ELECTRICAL TRADES. a. Building Cost File, Inc., 2906 Anthony St., Wantagh, NY 11793-2330.
  Formed by the 1981 merger of: Berger Design Cost File; Berger Building Cost File; which was formerly: Building Cost File (ISSN 0091-3499)

690   GW   ISSN 0940-3825
BERLIN - BRANDENBURGISCHE BAUWIRTSCHAFT. 1949. s-m. DM.185 (foreign DM.234) (effective 1998). Bauverlag GmbH (Berlin), Nikolsburgerstr. 11, 10717 Berlin, Germany. TEL 49-30-8835888. FAX 49-30-8833109. E-mail: bauverlag.zeitschr.-journals@t-online.de. Ed. Gabriela Schulz. adv.: bk.rev.; bibl.; illus.; stat.; index. circ. 7,000. **Document type:** trade publication.
  Formerly: Berliner Bauwirtschaft (ISSN 0045-1762)

690   GW   ISSN 0723-5895
BERTELSMANN BAUKATALOG. 1929. a. DM.44.80. Bertelsmann Fachzeitschriften GmbH, Postfach 120, 33111 Guetersloh, Germany. TEL 05241-802332. FAX 05241-73055. adv. circ. 34,961. **Document type:** catalog.
  Formerly (until 1980): Bauwelt Katalog (ISSN 0067-4664)
  Description: Entries provide product information for the architect, planner, master craftsman, specialist engineer and building contractor.

BESKRIVELSESTEKSTER. see BUSINESS AND ECONOMICS — Marketing And Purchasing

BUILDING AND CONSTRUCTION

690   333.33   US
BEST SELLERS COLLECTIONS. 4/yr. $10 (effective 1996 & 1997). Drawing Board Atlanta, Inc., Box 15556, Atlanta, GA 30333-0556. TEL 404-624-3999. Ed. Phillip Andrew Jessup. circ. 5,000. **Document type:** trade publication.
    Description: Contains house design sketches and data of most popular homes.

BEST-SELLING HOME PLANS. see *ARCHITECTURE*

691.3   GW   ISSN 0005-9846
                             CODEN: BTONAH
BETON. (Text in German; summaries in English and French) 1951. m. DM.330. (Bundesverband der Deutschen Zementindustrie e.V.) Beton-Verlag GmbH, Postfach 110134, 40501 Duesseldorf, Germany. TEL 0211-550090. FAX 0211-5500955. Ed. Rainer Buechel. adv.; bk.rev.; illus.; index. circ. 6,500. **Indexed:** Concr.Abstr., Dok.Str., INIS Atomind., Intl.Civil Eng.Abstr., Key to Econ.Sci., Soft.Abstr.Eng. **Document type:** trade publication.
    —BLDSC (1942.680000); CISTI; Linda Hall; SWETS. **CCC.**

691.3   BE
BETON. (Text in Dutch, French) 1969. 5/yr. 1200 BEF. FeBe - Federation de l'Industrie du Beton, Bd. Aug. Reyers 207-209, 1030 Brussels, Belgium. TEL 32-2-7358015. FAX 32-2-7347794. Ed. W. Simons. adv.: B&W page 20500 BEF, color page 49000 BEF; trim 210 x 297. bk.rev.; index; circ. 8,500. (controlled). (back issues avail.) **Document type:** trade publication.
    Description: For the precast concrete industry.

691.3   RU   ISSN 0005-9889
TA680   CODEN: BTZBA2
BETON I ZHELEZOBETON. English translation: Russian Journal of Concrete and Reinforced Concrete. (Contents page in English, French and German) 1955. bi-m. $122 (effective 1998). Gosstroi, Moscow, Russia. Ed. K.V. Mikhailov. bk.rev.; bibl.; charts; illus.; index. circ. 14,700. **Indexed:** Alloys Ind., Appl.Mech.Rev., C.R.I.Abstr., C.R.I.Curr.Cont., Chem.Abstr., Concr.Abstr., Eng.Ind., Eng.Mat.Abstr., INIS Atomind., Intl.Civil Eng.Abstr., Met.Abstr.Ind., Met.Abstr., Nonfer.Met.Alert, PCC Alert, Soft.Abstr.Eng., Steels Alert, World Alum.Abstr.
    —BLDSC (0015.700000); CASDDS; CISTI; Linda Hall.

620.135   GW   ISSN 0342-7617
BETON-KALENDER. 1906. a. DM.196. Ernst und Sohn, Muehlenstr. 33-34, 13187 Berlin, Germany. TEL 49-30-47889200. FAX 49-30-47889240. Ed. J. Eibl. circ. 18,000. **Document type:** trade publication.

691.3   GW   ISSN 0005-9900
TA680   CODEN: BESTAI
BETON- UND STAHLBETONBAU. 1901. m. DM.435 (foreign DM.495) (students DM.165 (foreign DM.189)) (effective 1997). Ernst und Sohn, Muehlenstr. 33-34, 13187 Berlin, Germany. TEL 49-30-47889200. FAX 49-30-47889284. (Subcr. to: Wiley - V C H, Postfach 101161, 69451 Weinheim, Germany. TEL 49-6201-606147. FAX 49-6201-606117; Subscr. in the Americas to: John Wiley & Sons, Inc., 605 Third Ave., New York, NY 10158. TEL 212-850-6645. FAX 212-850-6021) Ed.Bd. adv.; bk.rev.; charts; illus.; index. circ. 4,864. (back issues avail.) **Indexed:** Appl.Mech.Rev., Chem.Abstr., Concr.Abstr., Eng.Ind., Excerp.Med., Geotech.Abstr., HRIS, INIS Atomind., Intl.Civil Eng.Abstr., Soft.Abstr.Eng. **Document type:** trade publication.
    —CISTI; Ei; Linda Hall; SWETS; UMI. **CCC.**
    Description: Deals specifically with problems related to concrete and reinforced concrete construction methods.

691.3   NO   ISSN 0332-8384
BETONGPRODUKTER. 1970. q. NOK 500. Betongindustriens Landsforening, Forskningsveien 3B, Postboks 53 Blindern, 0313 Oslo, Norway. TEL 02-96 58 60. FAX 02-56-42-38. Ed. Arne Skjelle. adv.; bk.rev. circ. 4,500.

691.3   FI   ISSN 1235-2136
BETONI. 1930. 4/yr. FIM 140 includes a. Finnish Concrete (effective 1997). Suomen Betonitieto Oy, Mikonkatu 18 B 12, FIN-00100 Helsinki, Finland. TEL 358-0-651-411. FAX 358-0-651-145. Ed. Maritta Koivisto. adv. contact: Erkki Monkavaara. bk.rev.; charts; illus. circ. 8,500. **Indexed:** C.R.I.Abstr., Chem.Abstr., Concr.Abstr., Intl.Civil Eng.Abstr., Soft.Abstr.Eng. **Document type:** bulletin.
    —BLDSC (1944.100000).
    Formed by the 1992 merger of: Betoni ja Laatu (ISSN 0785-8396); Betonituote (ISSN 0005-9919); Tiedotuslehti - Suomen Betoniyhdistys-Finska Betongfoereningen (ISSN 0356-3332)
    Description: Provides information about concrete architecture, concrete technologies, research, industry conditions, and new developments.

690   FI
BETONI. 1930. q. FIM 140 (effective 1997). Betonitieto Oy, Mikonkatu 18 B 12, SF-00100 Helsinki, Finland. TEL 358-9-651411. FAX 358-9-651145. Ed. Maritta Koivisto. adv. **Document type:** bulletin.
    Formerly: Suomen Betoniteollisuuden Keskusjarjesto. Julkaisuja (ISSN 0358-0407)
    Description: Professional reference publication series.

691   NE   ISSN 0166-137X
BETONIEK. 1970. 10/yr. fl.28.50. Stichting Beton Prisma, Sint Teunislaan 1, Postbus 3532, 5203 DM 's-Hertogenbosch, Netherlands. **Document type:** trade publication.

691.3   GW   ISSN 0409-2740
BETONTECHNISCHE BERICHTE. (Text in German; summaries English and French) 1960. irreg. DM.49.80. (Verein Deutscher Zementwerke e.V.) Beton-Verlag GmbH, Postfach 110134, 40501 Duesseldorf, Germany. TEL 0211-550090. FAX 0211-5500955. Ed. Gert Wischers. index, cum.index. circ. 1,500. **Indexed:** Dok.Str., Ref.Zh. **Document type:** monographic series.
    —CISTI; Linda Hall.

691   GW   ISSN 0373-4331
TH1491   CODEN: BWFTAB
BETONWERK UND FERTIGTEIL-TECHNIK; concrete precasting plant and technology. (Text in English and German; summaries in French) 1934. m. DM.337 (foreign DM.367) (effective 1998). Bauverlag GmbH, Postfach 1460, 65004 Wiesbaden, Germany. TEL 49-6123-700-0. FAX 49-6123-700122. E-mail: bauverlag.zeitschr.-journals@t-online.de. Ed. R. Kroemer. adv. contact: E. Gross. bk.rev.; charts; illus.; stat.; index. circ. 5,400. **Indexed:** C.R.I.Abstr., Chem.Abstr., Concr.Abstr., Dok.Str., Eng.Ind., Excerp.Med., IBR, Intl.Civil Eng.Abstr., Soft.Abstr.Eng., W.R.C.Inf. **Document type:** trade publication.
    —BLDSC (1946.100000); CASDDS; CISTI; Ei; Linda Hall; SWETS. **CCC.**
    Formerly: Betonstein-Zeitung (ISSN 0005-9927)
    Description: Trade publication for the concrete building and manufacturing industry. Covers construction, quality control, production, prefabrication, pipes and shafts, industry news, events, announcements, and positions available.

BETTER HOMES AND GARDENS GARDEN, DECK AND LANDSCAPE PLANNER. see *GARDENING AND HORTICULTURE*

643.7   US   ISSN 1051-0427
TH4816
BETTER HOMES AND GARDENS HOME PRODUCTS GUIDE. Key Title: Home Products Guide. 1989. s-a. (effective 1997); newsstand price: $3.99 (Canada $4.99). Meredith Corporation, Special Interest Publications, 1716 Locust St., Des Moines, IA 50336. TEL 515-284-3000. Pub. Steve Levinson. adv.: B&W page $20250; adv. contact: Peggy Leib. circ. 450,000 (paid). **Document type:** consumer publication.
    Description: Covers materials needed when building or remodeling a home. Directed to consumers.

BETTER HOMES & GARDENS REMODELING IDEAS. see *ARCHITECTURE*

690   IS
BETUMAN. bi-m. free. Paz Co., Ltd., P.O. Box 434, Haifa 31 003, Israel. TEL 04-567111. Ed. Zvi Dvorsky.

BIRU SHINBUN/BUILDING NEWSPAPER. see *ENGINEERING — Civil Engineering*

BLUEPRINTS. see *ARCHITECTURE*

BODEN, WAND, DECKE. see *INTERIOR DESIGN AND DECORATION*

690   US
BOECKH BUILDING CODE MODIFIER. 6/yr. $115. E.H. Boeckh (Subsidiary of: Thomson Publishing Corp.), 2885 S. Calhoun Rd., Box 510291, New Berlin, WI 53151-0291. TEL 414-780-2800; 800-285-1288. FAX 414-780-0306.

690   SW   ISSN 0281-5060
BOFAST. 1983. 18/yr. SEK 290. SABO Foerlags AB, P.O. Box 1206, S-171 23 Solna, Sweden. TEL 46-8-82-06-20. FAX 46-8-83-14-95. Ed. Boo Ehlin; Pub. Bengt Owe Birgersson. adv.: B&W page SEK 15200, color page SEK 21800; trim 187 x 259; adv. contact: Svem-Erik Bjarnesson. circ. 13,500. cols./p.: 5; pp./issue: 48. **Document type:** newspaper.

690   UK
BOOK OF BRITISH EXCELLENCE. a. free to qualified personnel. Custom Publishing Company Ltd., 45 Station Rd., Redhill, Surrey RH1 1QH, England. TEL 44-1737-767213. FAX 44-1737-771662. adv.: page £2,500; adv. contact: John Bailey. circ. 150,000 (controlled). **Document type:** directory.
    Description: Lists British construction products and contains company profiles. Distributed by embassies, architects, and building consultants throughout the European Community.

690   720   NE   ISSN 0366-2330
BOUW. 1946. bi-w. fl.179. Misset (Subsidiary of: Reed Elsevier plc), Postbus 4, 7000 BA Doetinchem, Netherlands. TEL 31-314-349371. FAX 31-314-363638. adv.: B&W page fl.3269, color page fl.5769; trim 225 x 297; adv. contact: Cor van Nek. bk.rev.; illus. circ. 5,170. **Indexed:** Avery Ind.Archit.Per., Br.Tech.Ind., C.I.S. Abstr., ELLIS, Int.Build.Serv.Abstr., Key to Econ.Sci. **Document type:** trade publication.
    —BLDSC (2264.300000); CISTI; SWETS.
    Description: For the house building, industrial and commercial building industries, and persons in related fields, including planning, architecture and building technology.

690   NE   ISSN 0923-5108
BOUW EN BEHEER. 1889. 10/yr. fl.60. Bureau van Vliet B.V., Postbus 20, 2040 AA Zandvoort, Netherlands. TEL 02507-14745. FAX 02507-17680. Ed. J.L. Gerritsen. adv.; bk.rev.; illus.; stat. circ. 3,550. **Document type:** trade publication.
    Formerly (until 1988): Patrimonium (ISSN 0031-3149)

690   NE   ISSN 0165-3520
DE BOUWADVISEUR. Key Title: B A. De Bouwadviseur. 1958. 10/yr. fl.167.50. Samsom Bedrijfsinformatie B.V. (Subsidiary of: Wolters Kluwer N.V.), Postbus 4, 2400 MA Alphen aan den Rijn, Netherlands. TEL 31-172-466775. FAX 31-172-440681. Ed. M.J.M. van Duijn. adv.; bk.rev.; charts; illus.; circ. 4,660 (controlled). **Indexed:** Excerp.Med., Key to Econ.Sci. **Document type:** trade publication.
    —SWETS.
    Formerly (until 1977): Raadgevend Ingenieur (ISSN 0033-7226)

691   624   NE   ISSN 0166-6363
BOUWEN MET STAAL. 1967. bi-m. fl.89 (foreign fl.134). Staalbouw Instituut, Postbus 29075, 3001 GB Rotterdam, Netherlands. TEL 31-10-4110435. FAX 31-10-4121221. Ed. C.H. van Eldik. adv.; bk.rev.; bibl.; index. circ. 5,000. (back issues avail.) **Document type:** trade publication.
    —SWETS.
    Description: Technical and scientific information for the design and construction in steel of structural, architectural, and civil engineering projects.

BUILDING AND CONSTRUCTION

690 NE ISSN 0165-2648
BOUWKOSTEN. 1972. m. Misset (Subsidiary of: Reed Elsevier plc), Postbus 4, 7000 BA Doetinchem, Netherlands. TEL 31-8340-49911. FAX 31-8340-43839. TELEX 45481. Ed. W. Pasman. (looseleaf format) **Document type:** trade publication, monographic series.
Description: Cost information for total cost information during all stages of construction of housing and utility building.

690 BE
BOUWKRONIEK; moniteur du batiment et des travaux publics. 1921. w. 9730 BEF($295) N.V. Drukkerij de Bouwkroniek, Zennestraat 37, B-1000 Brussels, Belgium. TEL 32-2-5138295. FAX 32-2-5117015. Ed. M. Depraekere. adv. contact: Leo van Hoorick. charts; illus. circ. 12,000. **Indexed:** Key to Econ.Sci. **Document type:** trade publication.

621.9 NE ISSN 0006-8373
BOUWMACHINES. 1965. m. fl.189. Misset (Subsidiary of: Reed Elsevier plc), Postbus 4, 7000 BA Doetinchem, Netherlands. TEL 31-314-349371. FAX 31-314-363638. TELEX 45481. Ed. Th. de Rijk. adv.: B&W page fl.3479, color page fl.5270; trim 215 x 285; adv. contact: Cor van Nek. charts; illus.; stat. circ. 5,080. **Indexed:** Excerp.Med. **Document type:** trade publication.
—SWETS.
Description: Aimed at building contractors in housing and public buildings, earth-moving projects, highways and waterways, dredging works.

690 NE ISSN 0925-6466
BOUWMANAGEMENT EN TECHNISCH BEHEER. 1990. irreg., vol.14, 1995. price varies. (Onderzoeksinstituut OTB) Delft University Press, Mekelweg 4, 2628 CD Delft, Netherlands. TEL 31-15-2783254. FAX 31-15-2781661. E-mail: dup@dup.tudelft.nl. (back issues avail.) **Document type:** monographic series.

691 NE ISSN 0520-6804
BOUWMARKT; actuele bouwkosten informatie. 1961. 10/yr. fl.415. Delwel Uitgeverij B.V., Postbus 19110, 2500 CC The Hague, Netherlands. TEL 31-70-3624800. FAX 31-70-3605606. Ed. Bd. illus. **Indexed:** Key to Econ.Sci. **Document type:** trade publication.
—SWETS.
Description: Provides current information on building and construction costs.

690 340 NE ISSN 0165-1528
BOUWRECHT. 1964. m. fl.350 (effective 1996). (Stichting Instituut voor Bouwrecht) Uitgeverij Kluwer B.V., Postbus 23, 7400 GA Deventer, Netherlands. TEL 31-570-647111. FAX 31-570-631419. (Editorial addr.: Instituut voor Bouwrecht, Wassenaarseweg 23, 2596 CE The Hague, Netherlands. TEL 31-70-3245544) adv. **Document type:** trade publication.
—SWETS.

690 NE ISSN 0923-229X
BOUWREVUE. (Includes s-a. supplement: Documentatie Revue) 1979. 10/yr. free to qualified personnel. Misset (Subsidiary of: Reed Elsevier plc), Postbus 4, 7000 BA Doetinchem, Netherlands. TEL 31-314-349371. FAX 31-314-363638. TELEX 45481. Ed. J.F.F. van Bruggen. adv.: B&W page fl.14103; trim 280 x 380; adv. contact: Cor van Nek. bk.rev.; illus.; circ. 14,000 (controlled). **Document type:** trade publication.
—SWETS.
Description: Presents information on new products and applications in the building industry.

690 NE
BOUWSPECIALIST. (Supplement to: Aannemer (ISSN 0926-9894)) 10/yr. Misset (Subsidiary of: Reed Elsevier plc), Postbus 4, 7000 BA Doetinchem, Netherlands. TEL 31-314-349371. FAX 31-314-363638. Ed. A. Grevers. adv.: B&W page fl.2348, color page fl.4098; trim 240 x 320; adv. contact: Cor van Nek. **Document type:** trade publication.
Description: For building contractors, subcontractors, and building specialists.

690 NE ISSN 0165-6457
BOUWTIPS EDITIE A: GRONINGEN, FRIESLAND, DRENTHE. 1958. w. fl.1650 (effective 1996). Bouwtips B.V., Postbus 64, 7800 AB Emmen, Netherlands. TEL 31-591-648030. FAX 31-591-648093. circ. 2,000 (paid). (back issues avail.) **Document type:** trade publication.
Description: Publishes information on current and scheduled construction projects (commercial, industrial, offices and public works) in the Netherlands.

690 NE ISSN 0165-6503
BOUWTIPS EDITIE B: OVERIJSSEL, GELDERLAND, UTRECHT, FLEVOLAND. 1958. w. fl.1650 (effective 1996). Bouwtips B.V., Postbus 64, 7800 AB Emmen, Netherlands. TEL 31-591-648030. FAX 31-591-648093. circ. 2,000 (paid). (back issues avail.) **Document type:** trade publication.
Description: Publishes information on current and scheduled construction projects (commercial, industrial, offices and public works) in the Netherlands.

690 NE ISSN 0165-6554
BOUWTIPS EDITIE C: NOORD-HOLLAND EN ZUID-HOLLAND. 1958. w. fl.1650 (effective 1996). Bouwtips B.V., Postbus 64, 7800 AB Emmen, Netherlands. TEL 31-591-648030. FAX 31-591-648093. (back issues avail.) **Document type:** trade publication.
Description: Publishes information on current and scheduled construction projects (commercial, industrial, offices and public works) in the Netherlands.

690 NE ISSN 0165-6600
BOUWTIPS EDITIE D: ZEELAND, NOORD-BRABANT, LIMBURG. 1958. w. fl.1650 (effective 1996). Bouwtips B.V., Postbus 64, 7800 AB Emmen, Netherlands. TEL 31-591-648030. FAX 31-591-648093. (back issues avail.) **Document type:** trade publication.
Description: Publishes news of current and scheduled construction projects (commercial, industrial, offices and public works) in the Netherlands.

690 NE ISSN 0026-5942
BOUWWERELD. 1905. bi-w. fl.219. Misset (Subsidiary of: Reed Elsevier plc), Postbus 4, 7000 BA Doetinchem, Netherlands. TEL 31-314-349371. FAX 31-314-363638. TELEX 45481. Ed. H. Mulder. adv.: B&W page fl.4267, color page fl.6562; trim 215 x 285; adv. contact: Cor van Nek. bk.rev.; charts; illus.; mkt.; index. circ. 13,120. **Indexed:** Excerp.Med., Int.Build.Serv.Abstr., Key to Econ.Sci. **Document type:** trade publication.
—SWETS.
Formerly: Misset's Bouwwereld.
Description: Technical and practical information for designers, architects and building contractors.

BRITAIN'S TOP 1000 CONSTRUCTION COMPANIES. see BUSINESS AND ECONOMICS — Trade And Industrial Directories

BRONX REALTOR NEWS. see REAL ESTATE

690 SZ
BRUCKENBAUER. w. Limmatplatz 6, CH-8023 Zurich, Switzerland. TEL 01-2720300. FAX 01-2773582. circ. 1,096,028.

690 IS ISSN 0334-0430
B'SDEH HABNIYA. (Text in Hebrew) 1955. a. IS.120($40) Technion - Israel Institute of Technology, National Building Research Institute, Technion City, Haifa 32000, Israel. TEL 972-4-8292242. FAX 972-4-8324534. TELEX 46406-TECON-IL. Ed. Joab H. Rektor.

690 721 KR
BUDIVNITSTVO UKRAINY; virobnicho-tekhnichnii zagal'nogaluzevnii zhurnal. (Text in Ukrainian) 1959. bi-m. $7.20. (Akademiya Budivnystva i Arkhitektury Ukrainy) Vydavnytstvo Ukrarkhbudinform, Prorizna, 15, 252601 Kiev 3, Ukraine. TEL 7-44-2280787. bk.rev.; illus.; index. (tabloid format) **Indexed:** Chem.Abstr. Geotech.Abstr.
—CISTI.
Formerly (until 1993): Promyshlennoe Stroitel'stvo i Inzhenernye Sooruzheniya (ISSN 0033-1198)

690 PL ISSN 0867-4485
TH4
BUDOWNICTWO I GOSPODARKA MIEJSKA. 1960. m. 6 Zl. (effective 1996). Centralny Osrodek Informacji Budownictwa, Ul. Bartycka 26, 00-716 Warsaw, Poland. TEL 48-22-6511454. FAX 48-22-404228. TELEX 817123. Ed. Janina Stachurko-Zakrzewska. adv.; bk.rev.; charts; illus.; pat.; stat.; tr.lit. circ. 5,000. (also avail. in microform; reprint service avail.) **Indexed:** INIS Atomind. **Document type:** bulletin.
Former titles (until 1991): Biuletyn Informacyjny. Budownictwo. Gospodarka Mieszkaniowa (ISSN 0860-407X); (until 1987): Biuletyn Informacyjny o Budownictwie (ISSN 0137-2696); Centralny Osrodek Informacji Budownictwa. Biuletyn-Informacja (ISSN 0008-9591)

692.8 721 IE ISSN 0790-8830
BUILD. 1953. 11/yr. £14.74. 28 Lower Baggot St., Dublin 2, Ireland. TEL 766192. FAX 619781. Ed. John Low. adv.; bk.rev.; abstr.; bibl.; charts; illus.; stat.; tr.lit.; circ. 4,400 (controlled). **Indexed:** Build.Manage.Abstr., C.R.I.Abstr., C.R.I Curr.Cont.
Incorporates: Transport Management; Equipment Review.

690 AT ISSN 0313-2560
BUILD. 1973. q. Aus.$12. Finecraft Publishing Co., Box 260, Neutral Bay Junction, N.S.W. 2089, Australia. Ed. John Walters. **Indexed:** World Surf.Coat.
Formerly: B.N.I.A. (ISSN 0310-9534)

690 UK ISSN 0958-7438
BUILD & DESIGN PROFESSIONAL. q. Bergius House, Clifton St., Glasgow G3 7LA, Scotland. TEL 041-331-1022. FAX 041-331-1395. Ed. M. Travers. circ. 10,500.

690 US
BUILD IT!. 1992. s-a. New York Times Magazine Group, 5520 Park Ave., Box 395, Trumbull, CT 06611. TEL 203-373-7155. FAX 203-371-2199.

690 UK ISSN 0958-2681
BUILD - IT. m. £30. Build It Publications Ltd., 9 White Lion St., London N1 9XJ, England. TEL 44-171-837-8727. FAX 44-171-837-7124. Ed. Rosalind Renshaw; Pub. Kath Agres. R&P contact: Rosalind Renshaw. adv. contact: Kieran Killeen. circ. 70,000 (paid). **Document type:** consumer publication.

BUILD IT! HOME PLANS. see ARCHITECTURE

691 683 CN
TH13.2.C2
BUILDCORE PRODUCT SOURCE; construction materials, equipment & furniture available in Canada. 1974. a. Can.$162.49. Buildcore Product Source, 280 Yorkland Blvd., North York, ON M2J 4Z6, Canada. TEL 416-494-4990. FAX 416-756-2767. E-mail: info@buildcore.com; URL: http://www.buildcore.com. Ed. Nigel Heseltine; Pub. Susan Steele. adv. contact: Richard Wheller. tr.lit. circ. 8,500. **Document type:** catalog, directory, trade publication.
Formed by the merger of: Buildcore Index (ISSN 0227-0595) & Buildcore Product Review (ISSN 1182-3798)

690 US ISSN 0744-1193
HD9715.U5
BUILDER (WASHINGTON). 1942. m. $29.95. (National Association of Home Builders of the United States) Hanley-Wood Inc., One Thomas Circle, N.W., Ste. 600, Washington, DC 20005. TEL 202-452-0800. FAX 202-785-1974. E-mail: johnbutter@builderonline.com; URL: http://www.builderonline.com. Ed. Boyce Thompson; Pub. Michael Tucker. adv.; bk.rev.; illus.; tr.lit. circ. 194,000. (also avail. in microform from UMI) **Indexed:** Archit.Per.Ind., B.P.I., PROMT, Search (1988-), SRI. **Document type:** trade publication.
●Also available online.
—CISTI; KR SourceOne; SWETS; UMI; UnCover.
Former titles: N A H B Builder; Builder (Washington) (ISSN 0162-0533); N A H B Journal-Scope (ISSN 0098-2865); Which was formed by the merger of: N A H B Journal (ISSN 0027-5832); N A H B Washington Scope (ISSN 0027-5840)
Description: For builders, architects, dealers and subcontractors.

BUILDING AND CONSTRUCTION

690 US
BUILDER & REMODELER. 1982. m. $12. Sheahan Publications, Inc., Box 826, Westhamption Beach, NY 11978. TEL 516-288-5400. Ed. Denis Sheahan. adv.; bk.rev.; charts; illus.; stat. circ. 8,500. (tabloid format) **Indexed:** Avery Ind.Archit.Per., Build.Manage.Abstr., Tr.& Indus.Ind. **Document type:** trade publication.
    Formerly (until Sep. 1990): Builder; **Supersedes:** Long Island Builder (ISSN 0024-6247)

692.8 US   ISSN 0891-0332
BUILDER ARCHITECT.* 1938. m. $18. Sunshine Media, Inc., Box 37707, Phoenix, AZ 85069-7707. Ed. Linda Kilbourne. adv.; illus. circ. 3,300.
    Formerly: Builder Architect-Contractor Engineer (ISSN 0193-7472); Which was formed by the merger of: Builder-Architect (ISSN 0007-327X); Arizona-New Mexico Contractor and Engineer (ISSN 0004-1580)

BUILDER INSIDER. see *ARCHITECTURE*

690 US
BUILDER PROFILE; magazine of the Chicagoland residential & light commercial building industry. 1988. bi-m. $30. Progressive Publishing, Inc., Box 354, Bloomingdale, IL 60108. TEL 630-582-8888. FAX 630-582-8895. E-mail: Almanac123@aol.com; profiles@mindspring.com; URL: http://www.villageprofile.com. Ed. Juli Bridgers; Pub. Dan Nugara. adv. contact: Joseph Nugara. bk.rev.; circ. 7,500 (controlled). **Document type:** trade publication.
    Description: Contains news, industry forecasts, new product information, technology trends and features on residential and light commercial builders.

690 US
BUILDERS ASSOCIATION NEWS. 1954. m. $3. Builders Association of Fort Worth & Tarrant County, 6464 Brentwood Stair Rd., Ste. 100, Fort Worth, TX 76112-3242. TEL 817-457-2864. FAX 817-457-2870. Ed. Patricia A. Pembroke. adv.; stat.; tr.lit. circ. 1,500.

690 747 US   ISSN 1055-3460
NA7205
BUILDER'S BEST HOME DESIGNS. 1991. q. $4.95 per no. Hanley-Wood Inc., One Thomas Circle, N.W., Ste. 600, Washington, DC 20005. TEL 202-452-0800. FAX 202-785-1974. Ed. Bob Hoffman. circ. 85,000. **Document type:** trade publication.
    Description: Features new home plans.

690 330 US
BUILDERS' COMPUTER NEWSLETTER. 1982. 12/yr. Charles Mann & Associates, Microcomputer Division, 113 Wattenbarger Rd., Sweetwater, TN 37874-6135. TEL 800-484-4074. FAX 423-337-0222. Ed. Ray Burr. bk.rev. circ. 92,171.

690 UK
BUILDERS' MERCHANT NEWS. 1977. m. £44 (foreign £56) (effective Sept. 1995). B & M Publications (London) Ltd., P.O. Box 13, Hereford House, Bridle Path, Croydon, Surrey CR9 4NL, England. TEL 44-181-680-4200. FAX 44-181-681-5049. Ed. Tony Jackson. circ. 7,591 (controlled). **Document type:** trade publication.
    Description: Covers building materials, their distribution, and their sale.

690 UK   ISSN 0268-1323
HD9715.G7
BUILDERS MERCHANTS JOURNAL; the business journal for building supplies distributions. 1920. m. £63 (foreign £75) (effective 1996). Miller Freeman plc, Miller Freeman House, Calderwood St., London SE18 6QH, England. TEL 44-181-855-7777. FAX 44-181-854-8058. Ed. Christopher Pateman; Pub. Graham Beardwell. adv. contact: Mike Knoth. bk.rev.; charts; illus.; mkt.; index. circ. 7,533. **Document type:** trade publication.
    —BLDSC (2358.970000).
    Former titles (until 1985): Builders and Timber Merchant (ISSN 0262-6063); (until 1982): Builders and Home Improvement Merchants Journal (ISSN 0262-6055); (until 1978): Builders Merchants Journal (ISSN 0007-3288); (until 1964): Builders Merchants Journal and Builders Ironmonger.

690 UK
BUILDERS MERCHANTS REVIEW. 1983. 3/yr. £2. B & M Publications (London) Ltd., P.O. Box 13, Hereford House, Bridle Path, Croydon, Surrey CR9 4NL, England. TEL 44-181-680-4200. FAX 44-181-381-5049. **Document type:** trade publication.

690 CN   ISSN 1185-3654
TH1
BUILDING; the newsmagazine for Canada's development industry. 1952. 6/yr. Can.$34 (US $55; elsewhere $60) (effective 1998). Crailer Communications, 360 Dupont St., Toronto, ON M5R 1V9, Canada. TEL 416-966-9944. FAX 416-966-9946. E-mail: crailer@interlog.com. Ed. Al Warson; Pub. Sheri Craig. R&P contact: Sheri Craig. adv.: B&W page Can.$2595, color page Can.$3700; trim 8 x 10 1/2; adv. contact: John Bauslaugh. bk.rev.; charts; illus.; mkt.; tr.lit.; index. circ. 14,503. (also avail. in microform from UMI; reprint service avail. from UMI) **Indexed:** Can.B.P.I., RICS. **Document type:** trade publication.
    —BLDSC (2359.290000); CISTI.
    Formerly (until 1991): Canadian Building (ISSN 0008-3070); **Incorporates:** Real Estate Development Annual.
    Description: For developers, contractors, architects, engineers and facility managers. Covers residential, commercial-industrial, retail, and institutional development.

BUILDING; for the design and construction team. see *ARCHITECTURE*

BUILDING. see *ARCHITECTURE*

694 340 AT
BUILDING AND CONSTRUCTION CONTRACTS IN AUSTRALIA. 1990. 4/yr. Aus.$380 with updates. L B C, 50 Waterloo Rd., N. Ryde, N.S.W. 2113, Australia. TEL 61-2-9936444. FAX 61-2-8889706. TELEX ASBOOK 27995. Eds. John Dorter, John Sharkey. (looseleaf format)
    Description: Thorough analysis of general principles of contract law, with analysis of the four main Australian building and engineering contracts.

690 UK
HD9715.G7
BUILDING & CONSTRUCTION INDEX. 1923. a. £66.50 (Europe £79; rest of world £87) (effective 1997). Miller Freeman Information Services (Subsidiary of: United News & Media), Riverbank House, Angel Ln., Tonbridge, Kent TN9 1SE, England. TEL 44-1732-362666. FAX 44-1732-767301. URL: http://www.mfplc.com. Ed. Gwen Young. adv. contact: Elaine Soni. bk.rev. circ. 5,000. **Document type:** directory.
    Former titles: Sell's Building and Construction Index (ISSN 0966-0399); Sell's Building Index (ISSN 0080-8717)
    Description: A buyers' guide for builders, architects, engineers, surveyors, contractors, merchants, and government departments.

690 340 AT   ISSN 0815-6050
BUILDING AND CONSTRUCTION LAW JOURNAL. 1985. bi-m. Aus.$295. L B C Information Services, 50 Waterloo Rd., N. Ryde, N.S.W. 2113, Australia. TEL 61-2-99366444. FAX 61-2-98889706. TELEX ASBOOK 27995. Ed. John Dorter. (back issues avail.) **Indexed:** Leg.Per.
    —BLDSC (2359.332300); KR SourceOne; UnCover.
    Description: Changes and direction of law in the building industry.

332.6 US
BUILDING & CONSTRUCTION MARKET FORECAST. 1983. m. $299 (foreign $319). Cahners Publishing Company (Newton), Division of Reed Elsevier Inc., 275 Washington St., Newton, MA 02158-1630. TEL 617-630-2131. FAX 617-630-2100. URL: http://members.aol.com/cahners/. (Subscr. to: Cahners Publishing Co., Box 7610, Highlands Ranch, CO 80126. TEL 800-662-7776) Ed. Kim Kennedy. circ. 8,000. pp./issue: 6. **Document type:** newsletter.
    Description: Includes analyses and two-year forecasts for construction activity in: residential - new and remodeling; non-residential - new commercial, industrial, institutional and non-building construction

690 720 BA   ISSN 0217-5541
BUILDING & CONSTRUCTION NEWS; Asia's weekly construction newspaper. (Text in English) 1983. w. $495. Al Hilal Publishing & Marketing Group, P.O. Box 224, Manama, Bahrain. TEL 973-293131. FAX 973-293400. TELEX 8981 HILAL BN. (In Singapore: Al Hilal Publishing (Far East) Pte. Ltd., 50 Jalan Sultan, 20-06 Jalan Sultan Centre, Singapore 0719, Singapore. TEL 63-2939233. FAX 63-2970862; In the U.K.: Al Hilal Publishing International (UK) Ltd., Crescent Ct., 102 Victor Rd., Teddington, Mddx. TW11 8SS, England. TEL 44-181-9433630. FAX 44-181-9433701) Ed. Gurdip Singh; Pub. Gurdip Singh. adv.: B&W page $2800, color page $3920; trim 400 x 275. circ. 7,175 (controlled). (tabloid format; back issues avail.) **Document type:** trade publication, newspaper.
    Description: Covers the building and construction industry and the supporting industries of the building trade.

690 CN   ISSN 1186-1398
BUILDING & CONSTRUCTION TRADES TODAY; the independent seasonal newspaper linking with builders, contractors,suppliers and the design community. 1990. q. Can.$15.99 (foreign $15.99). Heisey Publishing, c/o 29s Bernard Ave., Toronto, ON M5R 1R3, Canada. TEL 416-944-1217. FAX 416-944-0133. E-mail: hize@compuserve.com. Ed. Alan Heisey; Pub. Alan Heisey. adv.: B&W page Can.$1680; trim 10 3/8 x 14 3/4; adv. contact: Alexandra Irving. circ. 4,000. (tabloid format) **Document type:** trade publication.
    Description: Covers news and current developments in the building and construction trades in the Greater Toronto area.

690 UK   ISSN 0360-1323
TH1   CODEN: BUSCBC
BUILDING AND ENVIRONMENT. (Text in English, French and German) 1965. bi-m. fl.1406($808) (effective 1998). Elsevier Science Ltd., Pergamon, P.O. Box 800, Kidlington, Oxford OX5 1DX, England. TEL 44-1865-843000. FAX 44-1865-843010. E-mail: nlinfo-f@elsevier.nl; usinfo-f@elsevier.com; forinfo-kyf04035@niftyserve.or.jp; URL: http://www.elsevier.nl/. (Subscr. to: Elsevier Science, Regional Sales Office, P.O. Box 211, 1000 AE Amsterdam, Netherlands. TEL 31-20-4853757. FAX 31-20-4853432; Subscr. in the Americas to: Elsevier Science, Regional Sales Office, Box 945, New York, NY 10159-0945. TEL 212-633-3730. FAX 212-633-3680; Subscr. in Australasia and the Far East to: Elsevier Science (Singapore) Pte Ltd, No.1 Temasek Ave., No.17-01 Millenia Tower, Singapore 039192, Singapore. TEL 65-434-3727. FAX 65-337-2230) Ed. C.B. Wilson. adv.; bk.rev.; charts; illus. circ. 1,000. (also avail. in microfilm from UMI) **Indexed:** Abstr.J.Earthq.Eng., Agri.Eng.Abstr., ASCA, Avery Ind.Archit.Per., Br.Ceram.Abstr., Br.Tech.Ind., Cadscan, Chem.Abstr., Curr.Adv.Ecol.Sci., Curr.Cont., Energy Info.Abstr., Energy Rev., Eng.Ind., Environ.Abstr., Environ.Per.Bibl. (1979-1994), IDA, J.of Ferroc., Lead Abstr., Zincscan. **Document type:** academic/scholarly publication.
    —BLDSC (2359.355000); CISTI; Ei; EMDOCS; Genuine Article; KR SourceOne; Linda Hall; SWETS; UMI; UnCover. **CCC.**
    Formerly (until 1976): Building Science (ISSN 0007-3628)
    Description: Publishes building and architectural research, applications in building design and construction, environmental behavior of buildings, components and materials.
    Refereed Serial

690 MY
BUILDING & INVESTMENT. (Text in English) q. B & I Publishing, 32-2A Jl Pandan, 3-2 Pandan Jaya, 55100 Kuala Lumpur, Malaysia. TEL 3-9858223. FAX 3-9857409. Ed. Joane Hou. adv. contact: Eric Tan.

BUILDING AND CONSTRUCTION

643.7 US ISSN 1077-2030
BUILDING & REMODELING NEWS. (Issued in 7 regional editions) 1987. m. $24.95 (foreign $34.95). S R Sound Inc., 600C Lake St., Ramsey, NJ 07446-1245. TEL 201-327-1600. FAX 201-327-3185. E-mail: renee@opcenter.net. Ed. Renee Rewiski. adv. contact: Don Smith. bk.rev.; circ. 75,000 (controlled). **Document type:** trade publication.
  Supersedes (in 1994): Remodeling News (Northern - Central New Jersey edition) (ISSN 1053-1505); Remodeling News (Baltimore - Washington, DC, edition; Remodeling News (Greater Boston - New England Edition) (ISSN 1053-1491); Remodeling News (Greater Philadelphia - Delaware edition) (ISSN 1053-1483); Remodeling News (Long Island - Metro New York edition) (ISSN 1052-4177); Remodeling News (Westchester, Rockland, Putnam, Orange, Fairfield & New Haven edition) (ISSN 1053-1475); Which superseded: Remodeling News (ISSN 1043-2183).
  Description: Provides professional builders and remodeling contractors with business information, product knowledge and how-to techniques. Geared to residential remodeling, custom building and light construction industries.

BUILDING AND WOOD. see LABOR UNIONS

690 CC
BUILDING ANNUAL. (Text in Chinese) a. Wealth Trade Press Ltd., Flat D, 15-F, Sun Kai Mansion, 38 Hennessy Rd., Wanchai, Hong Kong, People's Republic of China. TEL 852-2527-1282. FAX 852-2865-6529. adv.: B&W page HK.$7000, color page HK.$9800; trim 210 x 280. circ. 30,000.

690 001.6 IT
BUILDING AUTOMATION. q. L.50000 (foreign L.70000). Tecnomedia s.r.l., Via Sansovino 28, 20133 Milan, Italy. TEL 02-70602276. FAX 02-23680468. adv.: B&W page L.1340000, color page L.1940000; trim 175 x 266. circ. 8,529.

690 US
BUILDING BUSINESS AND APARTMENT MANAGEMENT. 1938. m. $36. Building Industry Association of Southeastern Michigan, 30375 Northwestern Hwy., Ste. 100, Farmington Hills, MI 48334-3233. Ed. Susan Adler. R&P contact: Susan Adler. adv.; charts; illus.; stat. circ. 7,300. **Document type:** trade publication.
  Formerly: Bildor (ISSN 0006-2448)

690 IS
BUILDING CENTRE OF ISRAEL BULLETIN/BABINIYA. (Text in Hebrew) 1970. bi-m. $12. Building Centre of Israel, P.O. Box 39027, Tel-Aviv 61390, Israel. TEL 03-425222. FAX 03-6425221. Ed. Lerner Miriam. adv.; bk.rev.; charts; illus.; stat. circ. 3,000.
  Former titles: Building Centre of Israel Journal; (until 1983): Babniyah Building Centre of Israel Quarterly (ISSN 0334-3863)

690 354.71 AT
BUILDING CODE OF AUSTRALIA - LOOSELEAF UPDATING SERVICE. irreg., no.8, 1995. price varies. Law Press (Victoria), 52-58 Chetwynd St., W. Melbourne, Vic. 3003, Australia. TEL 61-3-93208686. FAX 61-3-93208699. (Subscr. addr.: P.O. Box 334, N. Melbourne, Vic. 3051, Australia. TEL 61-3-93208623) (looseleaf format) **Document type:** government publication.

692.8 917.306 US
BUILDING CONCERNS. 1980. q. $45. National Association of Minority Contractors, 666 11th St., N.W., Ste. 520, Washington, DC 20001. TEL 202-347-8259. FAX 202-628-1876. Ed. Samuel Carradine. adv.; bk.rev. circ. 4,000. (back issues avail.)
  Description: Details national news of relevance. Presents major corporation and chapters' reports as well as members in the news.

692 US ISSN 0068-3531
TH435
BUILDING CONSTRUCTION COST DATA (YEAR). 1942. a. $76.95. R.S. Means Company, Inc., 100 Construction Plaza, Box 800, Kingston, MA 02364-0800. TEL 800-334-3509. FAX 617-585-7466. Ed. Philip R. Waier. index.
  —CISTI.
  Description: Provides over 20,000 cost entries for estimating.

690.028 691 AT ISSN 1031-3745
BUILDING CONSTRUCTION MATERIALS & EQUIPMENT. 1959. m. free. Federal Publishing Company, 180 Bourke Rd., Alexandria, N.S.W. 2015, Australia. TEL 61-2-93530926. Ed. Barry Tranter; Pub. Michael Hannan. R&P contact: Mark Marshall. adv. contact: Stephen Donaldson. circ. 17,059. **Indexed:** C.I.S. Abstr. **Document type:** trade publication.
  —CISTI.
  Former titles (until 1984): Australia - New Zealand Building Construction Materials and Equipment (ISSN 0811-0670); (until 1983): Australia - New Zealand Building Materials and Equipment (ISSN 0811-0662); (until 1980): Building Materials and Equipment (ISSN 0007-3512)

690 US ISSN 0192-7590
BUILDING CONSTRUCTION NEWS; a publication of the building construction industry in Northern Ohio. vol.4, 1979. m. $12 (free to qualified personnel). Builders Exchange, Inc., 981 Keynote Circle, Cleveland, OH 44131-1842. Ed. Gregg Mazurek. adv.; bk.rev.; circ. controlled.

690 368 UK
BUILDING COST INFORMATION SERVICE. DIGESTS. q. £45 (effective Apr. 1997). Building Cost Information Service Ltd., Royal Institution of Chartered Surveyors, 85-87 Clarence St., Kingston-upon-Thames, Surrey KT1 1RB, England. TEL 0181-546-7554. FAX 0181-547-1238.

690 368 UK
BUILDING COST INFORMATION SERVICE. ELEMENTAL ANALYSIS. a. £210 (effective Apr. 1997). Building Cost Information Service Ltd., Royal Institution of Chartered Surveyors, 85-87 Clarence St., Kingston-upon-Thames, Surrey KT1 1RB, England. TEL 0181-546-7554. FAX 0181-547-1238.

690 368 UK
BUILDING COST INFORMATION SERVICE. INDICES & FORECASTS. q. £210 (effective Apr. 1997). Building Cost Information Service Ltd., Royal Institution of Chartered Surveyors, 85-87 Clarence St., Kingston-upon-Thames, Surrey KT1 1RB, England. TEL 0181-546-7554. FAX 0181-547-1238.

690 UK
BUILDING COST INFORMATION SERVICE. LABOUR, HOURS & WAGES. a. £150 (effective Apr. 1997). Building Cost Information Service Ltd., Royal Institution of Chartered Surveyors, 85-87 Clarence St., Kingston-upon-Thames, Surrey KT1 1RB, England. TEL 0181-546-7554. FAX 0181-547-1238.

690 368 UK
BUILDING COST INFORMATION SERVICE. SURVEYS OF TENDER PRICES. q. £210 (effective Apr. 1997). Building Cost Information Service Ltd., Royal Institution of Chartered Surveyors, 85-87 Clarence St., Kingston-upon-Thames, Surrey KT1 1RB, England. TEL 0181-546-7554. FAX 0181-547-1238.

BUILDING DESIGN. see ARCHITECTURE

690 US ISSN 0007-3407
TH1
BUILDING DESIGN & CONSTRUCTION. 1950. m. $99.90 (Canada $144.90; Mexico $139.90; elsewhere $169.90). Cahners Publishing Company (Des Plaines), Division of Reed Elsevier Inc., 1350 E. Touhy Ave., Box 5080, Des Plaines, IL 60018-5080. TEL 847-390-2650. FAX 847-390-2769. E-mail: marketaccess@cahners.com; URL: http://www.bdcmag.com. (Subscr. to: 8773 Ridgeline Blvd., Highlands Ranch, CO 80126-2329. TEL 800-662-7776) Ed. Christopher Olson; Pub. Robert A. Lindsey. adv.: B&W page $8780. charts; illus.; tr.lit.; index. circ. 79,000. (microfiche from CIS; reprint service avail. from UMI) **Indexed:** Avery Ind.Archit.Per., Bus.Ind., C.R.I.Abstr., Concr.Abstr., Intl.Civil Eng.Abstr., Search (1988-), Soft.Abstr.Eng., SRI, Tr.& Indus.Ind. **Document type:** trade publication.
  —BLDSC (2359.715000); CISTI; Linda Hall; SWETS; UMI; UnCover. **CCC.**
  Formerly (until 1958): Building Construction.
  Description: For nonresidential building owners, contractors, engineers and architects. Includes design innovations, industry news, law, emerging technology, and financing.

338.4 690 AT ISSN 0007-3431
BUILDING ECONOMIST. 1962. q. Aus.$65. Australian Institute of Quantity Surveyors, National Surveyors' House, 27-29 Napier Close, Deakin, A.C.T. 2600, Australia. TEL 61-6-282-2222. FAX 61-6-285-2427. Ed. Ian Blyth. adv.; bk.rev.; charts; illus. circ. 3,300. (back issues avail.) **Indexed:** Archit.Per.Ind., Build.Manage.Abstr.
  —BLDSC (2359.750000); CISTI; UnCover.
  Incorporates: Quantity Surveyor (ISSN 0048-6108)

693 658.8 UK
BUILDING ECONOMIST. 1983. m. £180 in the UK. Builder Group plc., Builder House, 1 Millharbour, London E14 9RA, England. TEL 44-171-560-4000. FAX 44-171-560-4004. (Subscr. to: Building, Freepost (LE6522), Leicester LE87 4DH, England. TEL 44-1858-468811) Ed. Alistair Stewart; Pub. Pam Barker. adv. contact: Ben Greenish. charts; illus.; stat. circ. 552. (back issues avail.) **Indexed:** Archit.Per.Ind. **Document type:** trade publication.
  Formerly (until Jan. 1995): Building Market Report (ISSN 0267-2561)

690 UK
BUILDING FOR LEISURE. 1990. bi-m. Stable Publishing, 19-21 High St., Sutton, Surrey SM1 1DJ, England. TEL 081-770-1080. FAX 081-643-9846. adv.; circ. 12,000 (controlled). (back issues avail.) **Document type:** trade publication.

690 SA ISSN 1018-838X
BUILDING, HARDWARE AND HOUSEWARES (YEAR). (Text in English) a. Reed Business Information South Africa (Pty.) Ltd., P.O. Box 653207, Benmore 2010, South Africa. TEL 27-11-784-1110. FAX 27-11-883-4729. **Document type:** directory.
  Formerly: Hardware and Building (Year).

690 AT
BUILDING IN AUSTRALIA (YEAR). a. Aus.$1750 (effective 1997). B I S Shrapnel Pty. Ltd., 8th Fl., 181 Miller St., N. Sydney, N.S.W. 2060, Australia. TEL 61-2-99595924. FAX 61-2-99595795. Ed. Robert Mellor. circ. 300.
  Description: Reports on the medium to long term prospects for building activity.

690 SA ISSN 0378-9020
BUILDING INDUSTRIES FEDERATION. ANNUAL REPORT. 1904. a. free. Building Industries Federation, Attn.: Information Services Manager, 14 Alexandra Ave., Halfway House 1685, South Africa. TEL 27-11-8051985. FAX 27-11-3151644. circ. 6,000 (controlled). **Document type:** corporate report.
  Description: Annual overview of the Executive Director - financial year June to May.

690 US
BUILDING INDUSTRY. 1954. m. Trade Publishing Co. Ltd., 287 Mokauea St., Honolulu, HI 96819-3143. TEL 808-848-0711. Ed. Jim Crabtree. circ. 4,750. **Document type:** trade publication.
  Formerly: Building History.

690 AT
BUILDING INDUSTRY PROSPECTS. m. Aus.$1270 (effective 1997). B I S Shrapnel Pty. Ltd., 8th Fl., 181 Miller St., N. Sydney, N.S.W. 2060, Australia. TEL 61-2-995959246. FAX 61-2-99595795. Ed. Robert Mellor. circ. 450.
  Description: Regular monitoring of developments affecting the building industry with detailed numerical forecasts of dwelling and non-dwelling.

634.9 AT
BUILDING INNOVATION. 6/yr. Aus.$42 (effective 1998). C.S.I.R.O., Division of Building, Construction and Engineering, P.O. Box 606, Rozell, N.S.W. 2039, Australia. TEL 61-2-98184111. FAX 61-2-98184738. TELEX AA 33766. Ed. June Cummings; Pub. J. Grover. R&P contact: V. York. adv. contact: John Andrews. bibl.; charts. circ. 10,000. **Indexed:** AESIS, Br.Ceram.Abstr., C.R.I.Abstr., C.R.I.Curr.Cont., Forest.Abstr., Forest Prod.Abstr. **Document type:** trade publication.
  —CISTI; Linda Hall.
  Formerly (until 1995): Focus (ISSN 1032-9315); Which supersedes (in 1989): Rebuild (ISSN 0312-620X)

BUILDING AND CONSTRUCTION

690   CN
BUILDING INSPECTORS' ASSOCIATION OF NOVA SCOTIA. REPORTER. 1989. q. free. Building Inspectors' Association of Nova Scotia, 2543 Barrington St., Halifax, NS B3K 2X2, Canada. adv.; circ. 250 (controlled). **Document type:** newsletter.

690   CC   ISSN 1022-5560
BUILDING JOURNAL HONG KONG CHINA. (Text in English) 1973. m. HK.$480($180) Trend Publishing (H.K.) Ltd., Sup Tower, Rm. 603, 75-83 King's Rd., North Point, Hong Kong, People's Republic of China. TEL 2802-6299. FAX 2802-6458. Ed. Jimmy Yuen; Pub. Felix Leung. adv. contact: Bobo Chan. tr.lit. circ. 20,000. (reprint service avail.) **Indexed:** HongKongiana. **Document type:** trade publication.
—BLDSC (2360.725000).
   Formerly: Building Journal China.
   Description: News about architectural design and building projects.

BUILDING LAW MONTHLY. see *LAW*

BUILDING LAW REPORTS. see *LAW*

690   US
BUILDING MATERIAL RETAILER. Short title: B M R. 1984. m. National Lumber and Building Material Dealers Association, 40 Ivy St., S.E., Washington, DC 20003. TEL 202-547-2230. adv. circ. 23,000.
—Linda Hall.
   Supersedes: Retail Lumberman (ISSN 0034-608X); Northwestern Lumberman (ISSN 0092-0681); Which was formerly: Northwestern and Mississippi Valley Lumberman (ISSN 0091-6390); Which was formed by the merger of: Northwestern Lumber Dealer (ISSN 0029-3504); Mississippi Valley Lumberman (ISSN 0026-6426)

690   US
BUILDING MATERIALS DIRECTORY. a. Underwriters Laboratories Inc., Publications, 33 Pfingsten Rd., Northbrook, IL 60062-2096. TEL 708-272-8800. FAX 708-272-8129. **Document type:** directory.
   Description: Lists all manufacturers of building materials complying with UL standards.

BUILDING OFFICIAL AND CODE ADMINISTRATOR. see *PUBLIC ADMINISTRATION — Municipal Government*

690   US   ISSN 1071-2879
BUILDING OKLAHOMA. 1989. m. $12. Oklahoma Retailer Publishing Co., Inc., 4500 N. Sewell, Ste. 12, Oklahoma City, OK 73118. TEL 405-528-0903. Ed. Fred Singleton; Pub. Fred Singleton. R&P contact: Fred Singleton. adv.: B&W page $824; adv. contact: Fred Singleton. circ. 3,000 (controlled). (tabloid format) **Document type:** trade publication.
   Description: Covers commercial and residential building, remodeling, and construction industries in Oklahoma.

690   US   ISSN 0007-3490
TH3301   CODEN: BUOMAL
BUILDING OPERATING MANAGEMENT; the national magazine for commercial, industrial and institutional buildings-remodeling, expansion, retrofit, replacement and operations. 1954. m. $55. Trade Press Publishing Corp., Box 694, 2100 W. Florist Ave., Milwaukee, WI 53209. TEL 414-228-7701. FAX 414-228-1134. Ed. Ed Sullivan; Pub. Robert Wisniewski. adv.; bk.rev.; illus.; tr.lit. circ. 65,000. (also avail. in microform from UMI; reprint service avail. from UMI) **Indexed:** Intl.Mgmt.Info. **Document type:** trade publication.
—CASDDS; CISTI; UMI.
   Formerly: Building Maintenance and Modernization.

690 534   CN   ISSN 0843-6487
BUILDING PERFORMANCE NEWS. (Included in: Construction Innovation) (Editions in English, French) q. free. National Research Council of Canada, Institute for Research in Construction, Ottawa, ON K1A 0R6, Canada. TEL 613-993-2463; 800-672-7990. FAX 613-952-7673. URL: http://www.cisti.nrc.ca/cisti/journals/.
—CISTI. **CCC.**
   Description: Contains information on building performance, indoor environment and acoustics.

690   US   ISSN 0007-3555
BUILDING PERMIT ACTIVITY IN FLORIDA. 1959. m. $45 (diskette version $90). University of Florida, College of Business Administration, Bureau of Economic and Business Research, Box 117145, 221 Matherly Hall, Gainesville, FL 32611-7145. TEL 352-392-0171. FAX 352-392-4739. Ed. Carol McLarty. stat. circ. 200. (also avail. in microfiche from CIS; diskette format) **Indexed:** SRI. **Document type:** bulletin.

BUILDING PERMITS LAW BULLETIN. see *HOUSING AND URBAN PLANNING*

690   US
BUILDING PLANNED LIST.* 1967. m. $100 per no. Live Leads Corp., 35 W. 76th St., 4, New York, NY 10023-1521. Ed. Thomas Szabo. charts; stat. circ. 150.

690   US   ISSN 1055-0216
BUILDING PRODUCTS. 1990. q. $36. Hanley-Wood Inc., One Thomas Circle, Ste. 600, Washington, DC 20006. TEL 202-736-3301. FAX 202-785-1974. E-mail: jdimeohwi@aol.com. Ed. Jean Dimeo; Pub. Michael J. Tucker. adv. contact: Warren Nesbitt. circ. 80,000 (controlled). (tabloid format; back issues avail.) **Document type:** trade publication.
   Description: Includes product reviews, as well as articles on product trends and information on how builders and remodelers can use specific products to promote their businesses.

674 691   US   ISSN 0742-5694
BUILDING PRODUCTS DIGEST. 1982. m. $25. Cutler Publishing, Inc., 4500 Campus Dr., Ste. 480, Newport Beach, CA 92660. TEL 714-852-1990. FAX 714-852-0231. URL: http://www.building-products.com. Ed. David Koenig; Pub. David Cutler. R&P contact: David Cutler. adv. contact: Chuck Casey. bk.rev. circ. 12,750. **Document type:** trade publication.
   Description: Covers industry news, how-to, new products, new literature, association news, business trends for home centers, lumber and building material retailers and wholesalers and wood treaters in 13 southern states.

BUILDING PRODUCTS FILE. see *BUSINESS AND ECONOMICS — Trade And Industrial Directories*

691   AT
BUILDING PRODUCTS NEWS. Abbreviated title: B P N. 1960-199?; resumed 1995. m. Aus.$88($88) (effective 1996). Reed Business Publishing Pty. Ltd. (Subsidiary of: Reed International PLC), P.O. Box 5487, W. Chatswood, N.S.W. 2057, Australia. TEL 61-2-699-2411. FAX 61-2-698-3920. Ed. Gill Marsden. adv.; bk.rev. circ. 15,938. **Document type:** trade publication.
   Former titles: S.A. Building Products News (ISSN 0007-3369); S.A. Building and Decorating Materials (ISSN 0038-2035)
   Description: Covers building products and materials; focusing on in-depth application stories, project overviews, news and articles by respected industry figures.

691   AT   ISSN 0007-358X
BUILDING PRODUCTS NEWS (CHIPPENDALE). 1967. m. Aus.$69. Thomson Business Publishing, 47 Chippen St., Chippendale, N.S.W. 2008, Australia. TEL 02-699-2411. FAX 02-698-3920. Ed. Ron Krueger. adv.; bk.rev.; illus. circ. 16,004.

690   AT
BUILDING REGULATION AUSTRALIA. 2 base vol. (plus updates 6/yr). Aus.$388 (effective 1997). Butterworths, Division of Reed International Books Australia Pty. Ltd. (Subsidiary of: Reed Elsevier Australia Pty. Ltd.), 271-273 Lane Cove Rd., North Ryde, N.S.W. 2113, Australia. TEL 61-2-93354444. FAX 61-2-93354655. R&P contact: Deanne Castellino. adv. contact: Rebecca Browning. (looseleaf format)
   Supersedes (in 1992): Regulation of Building Standards N S W.

690   UK   ISSN 0961-3218
TH1   CODEN: BREIEA
BUILDING RESEARCH AND INFORMATION; the international journal of research, development and demonstration. (Text in English; occasionally in French) 1970. bi-m. £235 (foreign $390) (effective 1998). (International Council for Building Research, Studies and Documentation (CIB)) Thomson Professional (Subsidiary of: International Thomson Publishing Group), 2-6 Boundary Row, London SE1 8HN, England. TEL 44-171-8650066. FAX 44-171-5229623. TELEX 290164 CHAPMA G. E-mail: journal@rapidcom.co.uk; URL: http://jpr.thomsonprofessional.com. (Subscr. to: Chapman & Hall, International Thomson Publishing Services Ltd., North Way, Andover, Hants. SP10 5BE, England. TEL 44-1264-342713. FAX 44-1264-342807; Subscr. in US & Canada to: 400 Market St., Philadelphia, PA 19106. TEL 800-552-5866) Ed. Anthony Kirk. adv.; bk.rev.; illus. circ. 4,000. (reprint service avail.) **Indexed:** ASCA, Avery Ind.Archit.Per., Br.Ceram.Abstr., Br.Tech.Ind., Build.Manage.Abstr., C.R.I.Abstr., C.R.I.Curr.Cont., Eng.Ind., Geo.Abstr.H.G., IDA, J.of Ferroc., RICS. **Document type:** academic/scholarly publication.
●Also available online.
—BLDSC (2363.527000); CISTI; Ei; EMDOCS; Genuine Article; KR SourceOne; Linda Hall; SWETS; UMI; UnCover. **CCC.**
   Formerly: Batiment International, Building Research and Practice (ISSN 0182-3329); Which was formed by the 1970 merger of: Building Research and Practice (ISSN 0306-9931); Batiment International (ISSN 0373-4277)
   Description: Covers all aspects of building research and technology.
   Refereed Serial

BUILDING RESEARCH ESTABLISHMENT. REPORTS. see *FIRE PREVENTION*

690   CC
BUILDING REVIEW. (Text in Chinese, English) 1976. m. HK.$420. Building Review Publishing Co., Block D, 15F, Sun Kai Mansion, 38 Hennessy Rd., Wanchai, Hong Kong, People's Republic of China. TEL 852-2527-1282. FAX 852-2865-6529. E-mail: wtg@hkstar.com. Ed. Daisy Wong; Pub. Peter Lee C.S. adv.: B&W page HK.$8000, color page HK.$10800; trim 210 x 280; adv. contact: A. Read. circ. 30,000. **Document type:** trade publication.
   Description: Covers architectural project, interior features, products and technology, company profiles, trade reports and more.

690   US
BUILDING SCIENCES. 1974. bi-m. $35 to non-members. National Institute of Building Sciences, 1201 L St., N.W., Ste. 400, Washington, DC 20005. TEL 202-289-7800. Ed. Nell/Sandler. R&P contact: Nell Sandler. **Document type:** newsletter.
   Description: Covers building industry issues. Includes Institute's activities, calendar of events and industry briefs.

BUILDING SERVICE N.S.W. (BCA). see *LAW*

690 600   UK   ISSN 0143-6244
TH1.B8473   CODEN: BSETDF
BUILDING SERVICES ENGINEERING RESEARCH & TECHNOLOGY. 1980. q. £40 to non-members. Chartered Institution of Building Services Engineers, Delta House, 222 Balham High Rd., London SW12 9BS, England. Ed. Barry Copping. bk.rev.; charts; illus.; index. circ. 800. (also avail. in microfilm from UMI) **Indexed:** Build.Manage.Abstr., Ergon.Abstr., Gas Abstr., INSPEC (1980-), Int.Build.Serv.Abstr.
—BLDSC (2365.670000); AskIEEE; CISTI; Ei; KR SourceOne; Linda Hall; UMI.

BUILDING SERVICES JOURNAL. see *HEATING, PLUMBING AND REFRIGERATION*

BUILDING SOCIETIES ACT OF 1986 PRACTICE MANUAL. see *LAW*

690   JM
BUILDING SOCIETIES ASSOCIATION OF JAMAICA FACTBOOK. 1974. a. free. Building Societies Association of Jamaica, Ltd., 17 Belmont Rd., P.O. Box 141, Kingston 10, Jamaica, W.I. TEL 809-96-83855. Ed. Gayon Clarke. circ. 500. **Document type:** trade publication.
   Description: Statistical presentation of annual financial performances in the building society movement.

BUILDING AND CONSTRUCTION

333.33   UK
BUILDING SOCIETY ANNUAL ACCOUNTS MANUAL. base vol. (plus irreg. updates). £115 to non-members; members £85 (effective 1996-97). Building Societies Association, 3 Savile Row, London W1X 1AF, England. TEL 44-171-437-0655. FAX 44-171-287-0109. (Co-sponsor: Council of Mortgage Lenders) (looseleaf format) **Document type:** trade publication.
    Description: Provides updated commentary and analysis on the Building Societies Regulations of 1992, the Building Societies Act of 1986, the Companies Act of 1985, and other material on accounting standards of interest to building societies.

BUILDING SOCIETY LEAGUE TABLES (FINANCIAL). see *REAL ESTATE*

BUILDING SOCIETY LEAGUE TABLES (OPERATIONAL). see *REAL ESTATE*

BUILDING SOCIETY PEER GROUPS (FINANCIAL). see *REAL ESTATE*

BUILDING SOCIETY PEER GROUPS (OPERATIONAL). see *REAL ESTATE*

BUILDING SOCIETY TAXATION MANUAL. see *LAW — Estate Planning*

690   US   ISSN 0270-1197
TH1
BUILDING STANDARDS; the national magazine for building officials. 1933. bi-m. $25 (effective 1997). International Conference of Building Officials, 5360 Workman Mill Rd., Whittier, CA 90601-2298. TEL 310-699-0541. FAX 310-699-8031. Ed. Mark Edelstein. adv. contact: Greg West. cum.index. circ. 16,000. (back issues avail.) **Document type:** trade publication.
—CISTI; Ei.
    Description: Articles on earthquake damage, fires, architecture and building officials and inspectors. Education section offers seminars to individuals interested in being certified with ICBO as building inspectors, plumbing inspectors.

690   US   ISSN 1048-2555
TH1
BUILDING STANDARDS NEWSLETTER. 1933. bi-m. included in subscr. to Building Standards. International Conference of Building Officials, 5360 Workman Mill Rd., Whittier, CA 90601-2298. TEL 562-699-0541. FAX 562-699-9721. circ. 16,000. **Document type:** newsletter, trade publication.
—Linda Hall.

691   US   ISSN 0749-6133
TA676
BUILDING STONE MAGAZINE.* 1960. bi-m. $50 (foreign $100). Building Stone Institute, Box 507, Purdys, NY 10578-0507. TEL 914-232-5723. FAX 914-232-5259. Ed. Dorothy Kender. adv.; bk.rev. circ. 15,386.
    Formerly: Building Stone News (ISSN 0007-3679)

691   US
TH1
BUILDING SUPPLY BUSINESS. 1917. m. $70 (Canada $102; Mexico $109.90; elsewhere $149.90). Cahners Publishing Company (Des Plaines), Division of Reed Elsevier Inc., 1350 E. Touhy Ave., Box 5080, Des Plaines, IL 60018-5080. TEL 847-635-8800. FAX 847-635-9950. (Subscr. to: 44 Cook St., Denver, CO 80206. TEL 800-662-7776) Ed. Eric Benderoff; Pub. Jack Hollfelder. adv.; charts; illus.; mkt.; tr.lit. circ. 42,179. **Indexed:** PROMT, Tr.& Indus.Ind. **Document type:** trade publication.
●Also available online. Vendor(s): Dow Jones News Retrieval, Information Access Co., Knight-Ridder Information, Inc.
—UMI. **CCC.**
    Former titles (until July 1995): Building Supply Home Centers (ISSN 0890-9008); Building Supply News (ISSN 0007-3695)
    Description: For retailers of lumber and building materials. Features new products, marketing, management and merchandising ideas for selling to the do-it-yourself consumer, professional builder and remodeling contractor customer.

690 380.1   CN
BUILDING SUPPLY DEALERS ASSOCIATION OF BRITISH COLUMBIA. BUYER'S GUIDE AND PRODUCT SOURCE DIRECTORY. a. Building Supply Dealers Association of British Columbia, 630 Columbia St., No. 101, New Westminster, BC V3M 1B2, Canada. TEL 604-850-1040. Eds. George Tracy, Cindi Mueller. adv. contact: Cindi Mueller. **Document type:** directory.

690   US
BUILDING SYSTEMS MAGAZINE. (Includes a. Building Product Suppliers Directory & Housing Manufacturers Directory) 1980. m. $39 (foreign $85). Home Buyer Publications, Inc., Box 22039, 4200-T Lafayette Center Dr., Chantilly, VA 22021-2970. TEL 703-222-9411. FAX 703-222-3209. Ed. Rick Morgan; Pub. Rick Peterson. adv. contact: Tim Lee. bk.rev.; tr.lit. circ. 18,000. **Document type:** trade publication.
    Former titles: Building Systems Builder & Builder - Dealer (ISSN 0279-6368); Log Home and Alternative Housing Builder.

694   UK   ISSN 0954-0652
BUILDING TODAY. 1877. w. £77.50($126.33) Construction Publication, Elm House, 10-16 Elm St., London WCl, England. Ed. J. Belk. adv.; bk.rev.; charts; film rev.; illus.; mkt.; pat.; tr.lit.; index. circ. 17,564. (reprint service avail. from UMI) **Indexed:** Archit.Per.Ind., Br.Ceram.Abstr., Build.Manage.Abstr., Cadscan, Copper Abstr., Lead Abstr., RICS, Stud.Wom.Abstr., World Surf.Coat., Zincscan. **Document type:** trade publication.
—CISTI.
    Former titles: Building Trades Journal (ISSN 0306-3216); Illustrated Carpenter and Builder (ISSN 0019-2406)

690   UK
BUILDING, TRADE & INDUSTRY. 1985. m. £15 (foreign £25) (effective 1996). 1st Fl., 131-133 Duckmoor Rd., Ashton Gate, Bristol, Avon BS3 2BH, England. TEL 0272-660441. FAX 0272-664239. Ed. J. Heal, Jr. adv. contact: Nikki Cook. circ. 27,000. (tabloid format) **Document type:** trade publication.

690   US
BUILDING TRADES EMPLOYERS' ASSOCIATION OF THE CITY OF NEW YORK. UPDATE;* matters of interest to the building industry. 1974? 10/yr. membership. Building Trades Employers Association of the City of New York, 44 W. 28th St., 12 Fl., New York, NY 10001-4212. TEL 212-697-2860. Ed.Bd. charts; illus. circ. 1,800.
    Supersedes (1933-1974): Building Trades Employers' Association of the City of New York. News and Opinion.

BUILDING TRADESMAN. see *LABOR UNIONS*

690 658   US   ISSN 0007-3725
                                          CODEN: BUILEQ
BUILDINGS; the facilities construction and management magazine. 1906. m. $70 (Canada $85; elsewhere $100) (effective 1997). Stamats Communications, Inc., Box 1888, Cedar Rapids, IA 52406-1888. TEL 319-364-6167; 800-553-8878. FAX 319-364-4278. URL: http://www.buildings.com. Ed. Linda K. Monroe; Pub. Wayne Bayliss. R&P contact: Linda Monroe. adv. contact: Gail Utt. illus.; index; circ. 56,600 (controlled). (also avail. in microform from UMI; back issues avail.; reprint service avail.) **Indexed:** Avery Ind.Archit.Per., B.P.I., Tr.& Indus.Ind. **Document type:** trade publication.
●Also available online. Vendor(s): Information Access Co., Knight-Ridder Information, Inc., UMI.
—BLDSC (2366.035000); CASDDS; CISTI; KR SourceOne; Linda Hall; UMI; UnCover. **CCC.**
    Description: Covers the facilities construction and management of commercial and institutional buildings. Forecasts trends of the year to come.

690 621.042   US   ISSN 0891-3730
BUILDINGS ENERGY TECHNOLOGY; a current awareness bulletin. m. $145. (U.S. Department of Energy, Office of Scientific and Technical Information) U.S. National Technical Information Service, 5825 Port Royal Rd., Springfield, VA 22161. TEL 703-487-4630. Ed. D. Lamar Cason.
    Formerly (until 1987): Buildings Energy Conservation (ISSN 8755-0237)
    Description: Presents worldwide information on the technology required for economic energy conservation in buildings and communities.

690   SZ
BULLETIN C R B. (Text in German) 1964. 5/yr. 60 SFr. Schweizerische Zentralstelle fuer Baurationalisierung, Zentralstr. 153, CH-8040 Zurich, Switzerland. TEL 41-1-4564545. FAX 41-1-4564566. Ed. Felix Trefzer. bk.rev. circ. 7,000. **Document type:** bulletin.

690   FR   ISSN 1148-5531
BULLETIN EUROPEEN DU MONITEUR. 1990. w. 4100 F. (foreign 4340 F.). Groupe Moniteur, 17 rue d'Uzes, 75002 Paris, France. FAX 33-1-42333819. TELEX 220 528F. Ed. Michel Levron. circ. 650. **Document type:** bulletin.

690 330   TH
BUSINESS & CONSTRUCTION MAGAZINE. m. Business & Construction Magazine Co. Ltd., 198-31 Soi Anamai, Srinakarin, Bangkok 10250, Thailand. FAX 2-3229324. Ed. Supreeya Sukkasang. adv. contact: Weerapol Rakthorn. circ. 40,000.

BUSINESS RATIO PLUS: BUILDING & CIVIL ENGINEERING - INTERMEDIATE. see *ENGINEERING — Civil Engineering*

BUSINESS RATIO PLUS: BUILDING & CIVIL ENGINEERING - MAJOR. see *ENGINEERING — Civil Engineering*

690 330.9   UK   ISSN 1355-8641
BUSINESS RATIO PLUS: CONSTRUCTIONAL STEELWORK MANUFACTURERS. 1978. a. £249. I C C Business Publications Ltd., Field House, 72 Oldfield Rd., Hampton, Mddx. TW12 2HQ, England. TEL 44-181-783-0922. FAX 44-181-783-1940. charts; stat. **Document type:** trade publication.
    Formerly: Business Ratio Report: Constructional Steelwork Manufacturers (ISSN 0261-7730)
    Description: Analyses and compares the financial performance of leading companies. Provides industry performance summaries, trends, and forecasts.

BUSINESS RATIO PLUS: HEATING & VENTILATING CONTRACTORS. see *HEATING, PLUMBING AND REFRIGERATION*

695   UK   ISSN 1359-4486
BUSINESS RATIO PLUS: ROOFING CONTRACTORS. 1986. a. I C C Business Publications, Field House, 72 Oldfield Rd., Hampton, Mddx. TW12 2HQ, England. TEL 44-181-783-0922. FAX 44-181-783-1940.
    Formerly (until 1994): Business Ratio Report: Roofing Contractors (ISSN 0269-2074)

690 658.8   UK   ISSN 0261-7307
BUSINESS RATIO REPORT: ARCHITECTURAL IRONMONGERS; an industry sector analysis. 1980. a. I C C Business Ratios Ltd., Freepost, Field House, Hampton, Mddx. TW12 1BR, England. TEL 081-783-0977. FAX 081-783-1940. charts; stat. **Document type:** trade publication.

690 658.8   UK   ISSN 0261-7501
BUSINESS RATIO REPORT: BUILDERS MERCHANTS; an industry sector analysis. 1974. a. I C C Business Ratios Ltd., Freepost, Field House, Hampton, Mddx. TW12 1BR, England. TEL 081-783-0977. FAX 081-783-1940. charts; stat. **Document type:** trade publication.

690 658.8   UK   ISSN 0951-8894
BUSINESS RATIO REPORT: BUILDING INSULATION CONTRACTORS; an industry sector analysis. 1987. a. I C C Business Ratios Ltd., Freepost, Field House, Hampton, Mddx. TW12 1BR, England. TEL 081-783-0977. FAX 081-783-1940. charts; stat. **Document type:** trade publication.

690 658.8   UK   ISSN 0261-7684
BUSINESS RATIO REPORT: CONSTRUCTION EQUIPMENT; an industry sector analysis. 1978. a. I C C Business Ratios Ltd., Freepost, Field House, Hampton, Mddx. TW12 1BR, England. TEL 081-783-0977. FAX 081-783-1940. charts; stat. **Document type:** trade publication.

690 658.8   UK   ISSN 0261-8435
BUSINESS RATIO REPORT: HOUSEBUILDERS; an industry sector analysis. 1978. a. I C C Business Ratios Ltd., Freepost, Field House, Hampton, Mddx. TW12 1BR, England. TEL 081-783-0977. FAX 081-783-1940. charts; stat. **Document type:** trade publication.

BUILDING AND CONSTRUCTION

690 658.8   UK   ISSN 0261-9377
BUSINESS RATIO REPORT: PLANT HIRE; an industry sector analysis. 1973. a. I C C Business Ratios Ltd., Freepost, Field House, Hampton, Mddx. TW12 1BR, England. TEL 081-783-0977. FAX 081-783-1940. charts; stat. **Document type:** trade publication.

693 658.8   UK   ISSN 0261-9415
BUSINESS RATIO REPORT: PRE-CAST CONCRETE MANUFACTURERS; an industry sector analysis. 1979. a. I C C Business Ratios Ltd., Freepost, Field House, Hampton, Mddx. TW12 1BR, England. TEL 081-783-0977. FAX 081-783-1940. charts; stat. **Document type:** trade publication.

691 658.8   UK   ISSN 0261-9466
BUSINESS RATIO REPORT: READY MIXED CONCRETE & AGGREGATES; an industry sector analysis. 1973. a. I C C Business Ratios Ltd., Freepost, Field House, Hampton, Mddx. TW12 1BR, England. TEL 081-783-0977. FAX 071-783-1940. charts; stat. **Document type:** trade publication.

693.1   IT
BUSINESS STONE; mensile di informazioni per il settore lapideo. (Supplement avail.: Work Stone) 1992? m. Ever s.n.c. di Emilia Gallini & C., Galleria Ghandi 15, 20017 Rho - Milan, Italy. TEL 39-2-93900750. FAX 39-2-93900727. adv.: B&W page L.1239000, color page L.1764000; 210 x 297. circ. 4,500.
Description: Italian news for the stone and technology field.

690   US   ISSN 1054-1136
TH4818.W6
BUYER'S GUIDE TIMBER FRAME HOMES. 1991. q. $15.95 (Canada $21.95) (effective 1991); newsstand price: $3.95. Home Buyer Publications, Inc., Box 220039, 4200-T Lafayette Center Dr., Chantilly, VA 22021. TEL 703-222-9411. FAX 703-222-3209. Ed. Janice Brewster; Pub. John P. Kupferer. adv.: page $4890; trim 8 1/4 x 10 7/8; adv. contact: Laorie V. Sloan. circ. 45,000 (paid). (back issues avail.) **Document type:** consumer publication.
Description: A consumer guide to buying and building timber frame homes.

338.4   DK
BYG-TEK & BYGGERI; building magazine for the building industry. 1968. m. DKK 380. Odsgard ApS, Hovedvejen 182, DK-2600 Glostrup, Denmark. TEL 45-43-45-34-91. FAX 45-43-43-13-28. Ed. Peter Odsgard. adv.: B&W page DKK 31720, color page DKK 35700; trim 261 x 370. circ. 26,000 (controlled). **Document type:** trade publication.
Formed by the 1990 merger of: Byg-Teknik; Byggeri (ISSN 0107-1866); **Formerly:** Anlaegsteknik; Moderne Jordflytning (ISSN 0026-8623).

690   SW   ISSN 0281-658X
TH4
BYGG & TEKNIK. 1909. 8/yr. SEK 490. Foerlags AB Bygg & Teknik, P.O. Box 19099, S-104 32 Stockholm, Sweden. TEL 46-8-612-17-50. FAX 46-8-612-54-81. Ed. Stig Dahlin. adv.: B&W page SEK 10700, color page SEK 15800; trim 185 x 270; adv. contact: Roland Dahlin. illus.; circ. 6,595 (controlled). **Indexed:** Chem.Abstr.
Former titles (until 1984): Byggnadskonst (ISSN 0007-7593); (until 1966): Tidning for Byggnadskonst.
Description: Devoted to Swedish building technology, architecture and engineering.

690   DK   ISSN 0107-9514
BYGGEFORUM; oekonomisk-teknisk tidsskrift for bygge- og boligforhold. 8/yr. DKK 400 (effective 1994). (Byggesocietetet) Odsgard ApS, Hovedvejen 182, DK-2600 Glostrup, Denmark. TEL 45-43-45-34-91. FAX 45-43-43-13-28. Ed. Peter Odsgard. adv.: B&W page DKK 10945, color page DKK 15265; trim 176 x 262. illus. circ. 7,000. **Document type:** trade publication.

690   DK   ISSN 0007-750X
BYGGEINDUSTRIEN/DANISH BUILDING INDUSTRY. 1950. 8/yr. DKK 405. Teknisk Forlag A-S, Skelbaekgade 4, DK-1780 Copenhagen V, Denmark. TEL 45-31-21-68-01, FAX 45-31-21004-01. Ed. Poul W. Udengaard. adv.: B&W page DKK 7990, color page DKK 12190; trim 265 x 185. illus.; circ. 2,793 (controlled).
—BLDSC (2939.500000); CISTI.
Description: Provides comprehensive reports and authoritative comment on the industrial and advanced building trades.

690   NO   ISSN 0332-7086
BYGGEINDUSTRIEN. 1968. m. NOK 595. B A Media A-S, P.O. Box 128 Blindern, N-0314 Oslo, Norway. TEL 47-22-96-59-22. FAX 47-22-46-00-25. Ed. Per Helge Pedersen. adv. circ. 10,000. **Document type:** trade publication.

690   NO   ISSN 0333-3477
BYGGENYTT. 1955. s-m. (20/yr.). NOK 360. Hausmannsgate 21 4, Oslo 1, Norway. FAX 02-364771. Ed. Arvid Aastad. adv.; bk.rev. circ. 13,000.
Formerly (until 1962): Ukens Byggenytt (ISSN 0801-311X)

690   DK   ISSN 0906-1037
BYGGERIET. 1991. Byggeriets Arbejdsgivere, Kejsergade 2, DK-1195 Copenhagen K, Denmark. Dir. Kurt Jensen. adv. circ. 2,000.
Formed by the merger of (1958-1990): Murermesteren (ISSN 0027-3651); (1958-1990): Byggehaandvaerket (ISSN 0007-7496)

691.029   DK   ISSN 0900-9337
BYGGEVAREFORTEGNELSE. 1986. a. Teknisk Forlag AS, Skelbaekgade 4, DK-1780 Copenhagen, Denmark. TEL 45-31-21-68-01. FAX 45-31-21-09-83. adv.: B&W page DKK 16500, color page DKK 19500. circ. 3,000.
Description: Building materials.

690   SW   ISSN 1101-8437
BYGGFAKTA PROJEKTNYTT. 1989. 6/yr. SEK 118. Byggfakta AB, S-827 81 Ljusdal, Sweden. TEL 46-651-194-00. E-mail: jbn@byggfakta.se. Ed. Jan Nilsson. adv.: B&W page SEK 18900, color page SEK 22900; trim 185 x 270; adv. contact: Kjell Hoeok. circ. 22,400 (controlled). cols./p.: 4; pp./issue: 60. **Document type:** trade publication.

690   SW   ISSN 1102-3686
BYGGFORSKNING. 1980. 6/yr. SEK 300 (effective 1997). Byggforskningsraadet - Swedish Council for Building Research, P.O. Box 866, S-112 98 Stockholm, Sweden. TEL 46-8-617-73. FAX 46-8-617-73-80. Ed. Birgitta Bruzelius. **Document type:** academic/scholarly publication.
Former titles (until vol.5, 1991): Tidskriften Byggforskning; (until vol.4, 1991): Byggforskningen.

690   NO   ISSN 0332-6152
BYGGHERREN.* 1974. 10/yr. NOK 220. (Byggherreforeningen) Teknisk Presse A.S, Box 6754, Rodeloekka, N-0503 Oslo, Norway. TEL 47-2-52-10-40. FAX 47-2-50-66-48. Ed. Anders Thomassen. adv. circ. 8,725.
—CCC.

690   SW   ISSN 1104-5981
TH4
BYGGINDUSTRIN; organ foer byggentreprenoererna. (Includes: Arets Byoggen) 1931. 38/yr. SEK 800 (effective 1997). Byggfoerlaget, P.O. Box 5456, S-114 81 Stockholm, Sweden. TEL 46-8-665-36-51. FAX 46-8-667-72-78. E-mail: morgan@byggforlaget.se; URL: http://www.byggindustrin.com. Ed. Morgan Andersson. R&P contact: H.-P. Moeller. adv. contact: Gun Arvidsson. bk.rev.; charts; illus.; stat.; circ. 16,200. **Indexed:** C.I.S.Abstr., Geotech.Abstr., Int.Build.Serv.Abstr. **Document type:** trade publication.
Former titles (until 1994): Tidningen Byggindustrin (ISSN 0349-3733); (until vol.6, 1980): Byggindustrin; (until 1980): Byggnadsindustrin; (until 1971): Byggnadsindustrin med Nyhetsextra; (until 1936): Stockholms Byggmaestareforening. Meddelande.

690   NO   ISSN 0332-7221
BYGGMESTEREN. 1926. 11/yr. NOK 370. Byggforlaget A S, Box 5475 Majorstua, 0305 Oslo pl., Norway. TEL 22-961150. FAX 22-697364. Ed. Per B. Lotherington. adv. circ. 10,000. **Indexed:** Archit.Per.Ind.
Formerly (until 1952): Bygg- og Tomrermesteren (ISSN 0802-5274)

338.4369   DK   ISSN 0108-0229
BYGNINGSDELE. Variant title: V & S Priser, Bygningsdele. 1982. a. DKK 1310 (effective 1997). V & S Byggedata A-S, Frederikssundvej 194, DK-2700 Broenshoej, Denmark. TEL 45-38-60-77-11. FAX 45-38-60-77-44.

338.4 690   DK   ISSN 0106-3715
TA645   CODEN: BYMEAF
BYGNINGSSTATISKE MEDDELELSER. (Text in Danish and English) 1929. irreg., approx. 4/yr. DKK 230. Dansk Selskab for Bygningsstatik, Bygning 118, Lundtoftevej 100, 2800 Lyngby, Denmark. Ed. L. Pilegaard Hansen. bibl.; charts; illus. circ. 950. **Indexed:** Appl.Mech.Rev., Concr.Abstr.
—BLDSC (2941.200000); CISTI; Linda Hall.

690   RU   ISSN 0007-7690
TH9   CODEN: BYSTAM
BYULLETEN' STROITEL'NOI TEKHNIKI. 1944. m. $198 (effective 1998). Gosstroi, Moscow, Russia. Ed. V.I. Sichov. charts; illus.; index. circ. 26,400. (tabloid format) **Indexed:** Chem.Abstr.
—BLDSC (0024.800000); CISTI; Linda Hall.

690   CK
C A M A C O L. ASAMBLEA NACIONAL. DOCUMENTO. 1957. a. $20. Camara Colombiana de la Construccion (CAMACOL), Presidencia Nacional, Carrera 10 No. 19-65, piso 10, Apdo. 28588, Bogota D.E., Colombia. TEL 2345186. adv. circ. 10,000.

690   US   ISSN 0883-7880
C A M MAGAZINE. 1978. m. $36 (effective 1997). Construction Association of Michigan, 1625 S. Woodward Ave., Box 3204, Bloomfield Hill, MI 48302-3204. TEL 810-972-1000. FAX 810-972-1001. Ed. Phyllis L. Brooks; Pub. Curt Hacias. adv.: page $945; 7 3/4 x 10; adv. contact: Amanda Tackett. circ. 4,200 (controlled). **Document type:** trade publication.
Description: Provides a forum on new construction industry technology and practices, current information on new construction projects, products and services, and information on industry personnel changes and advancements.

691   SW   ISSN 0282-6283
C B I INFORMERAR. (Text in Swedish) 1985. irreg. SEK 50 per no. Cement- och Betonginstitutet - Swedish Cement and Concrete Research Institute, S-100 44 Stockholm, Sweden. TEL 46-696-11-00. FAX 46-8-24-31-37. Ed. Lise Langseth. **Document type:** academic/scholarly publication.
Formerly: C B I Rekommendationer-Recommendations (ISSN 0348-2790)
Description: Covers research on cement and concrete.

690   US   ISSN 1059-406X
HD9715.A1
C B R CONSTRUCTION BUSINESS REVIEW. 1991. bi-m. $39.95 (foreign $54.95). H L K Global Communications, Inc., 8133 Leesburg Pike, Ste. 750, Vienna, VA 22182. TEL 703-734-0017; 800-922-7123. FAX 703-734-2908. Ed. Fred Maavnezadeh; Pub. Robin L. Olsen. adv. contact: Levi K. Gain.
—CISTI.

630   CN   ISSN 1188-0783
C C M C NEWS. French edition (ISSN 1188-0821) (Included in: Construction Innovation) q. free. National Research Council of Canada, Institute for Research in Construction, Ottawa, ON K1A OR6, Canada. TEL 613-993-2463; 800-672-7990. FAX 613-952-7673. URL: http://www.cisti.nrc.ca/cisti/.
—CISTI. **CCC.**
Description: Contains information on evaluations of innovative building products and services.

C E E NEWS. see *ENGINEERING — Electrical Engineering*

BUILDING AND CONSTRUCTION

690 332 US
C F M A BUILDING PROFITS. 1988. bi-m. Construction Financial Management Association, 707 State Rd., Ste. 223, Princeton, NJ 08540-1413. TEL 609-683-5000. FAX 609-683-4821. Ed. Paula A. Patt-Pronek. adv.: B&W page $1315; adv. contact: Sarah G. Patt. circ. 6,500. **Document type:** trade publication.
  Description: Features industry news and technical articles in the field of construction financial management.

690 SP ISSN 0211-9919
C I C INFORMACION. 1963. 22/yr. 13000 ptas. (Europe 16000 ptas.; elsewhere 18000 ptas.). Centro Informativo de la Construccion, Roger de Lluria, 117, 08037 Barcelona, Spain. TEL 34-3-4870455. FAX 34-3-2158415. Ed. Ferran Cabellos Romero. adv.: B&W page 134000 ptas., color page 220000 ptas.; trim 210 x 297. bk.rev. circ. 17,500. **Indexed:** Ind.SST. **Document type:** trade publication.

690 SP
C I C PRODUCTOS. 3/yr. free to qualified personnel. Centro Informativo de la Construccion, Roger de Lluris 117, 08037 Barcelona, Spain. TEL 34-3-4870455. FAX 34-3-2158415. adv.: B&W page 445000 ptas.; 297 x 420. circ. 20,000 (paid).

690 SI
C I D B CATALOGUE (YEAR). (Text in English) a. (in 2 vols.). $60. (Construction Industry Development Board) Times Trade Directories Pte. Ltd., Times Centre, One New Industrial Rd., Singapore 536196, Singapore. TEL 65-2848844. FAX 65-2850161. TELEX RS 25713 TIMES. (Co-sponsor: Singapore Institute of Architects Building Centre) Pub. Leslie Lim. R&P contact: Leslie Lim. adv. contact: Joseph Liang. **Document type:** catalog.
  Description: Reference source for the building and construction industries. Provides information on a building materials, and decorative products, as well as construction plant and equipment.

C I R I A ANNUAL REPORT. (Construction Industry Research and Information Association) see ENGINEERING — Civil Engineering

C I R I A NEWS. (Construction Industry Research and Information Association) see ENGINEERING — Civil Engineering

C I R I A REPORT. (Construction Industry Research and Information Association) see ENGINEERING — Civil Engineering

C I R I A TECHNICAL NOTE. (Construction Industry Research and Information Association) see ENGINEERING — Civil Engineering

690 US
C M ADVISOR. 1983. bi-m. membership. Construction Management Association of America, 7918 Jones Branch Dr., Ste. 540, McLean, VA 22102. TEL 703-356-2622. FAX 703-356-6388. E-mail: cmaa@access.digex/net; URL: http://www.access.digex.ney/~cmaa/. Ed. Carl F. Borgstrom. adv. contact: Karen Hermann. bk.rev. (back issues avail.) **Document type:** trade publication, newsletter.
  Description: Focuses on current issues affecting construction managers and association events.

691.3 US
C M NEWS. 1962. m. free to qualified personnel. National Concrete Masonry Association, 2302 Horse Pen Rd., Herndon, VA 22071-3406. TEL 703-713-1900. FAX 703-713-1910. E-mail: ncma@ncma.org; URL: http://ncma.org. Ed. Randi Hertzberg. adv.: B&W page $1425, color page $2175; adv. contact: Randi Hertzberg. bk.rev.; abstr.; charts; illus.; stat.; tr.lit. circ. 5,000. **Document type:** newsletter, trade publication.
  Former titles: Concrete Masonry News; C - M News; C - M Newsletter; C - M News (ISSN 0007-8662)
  Description: Covers subjects related to manufacture and marketing of concrete masonry products.

690 US ISSN 0163-5018
C S I NEWSDIGEST. m. membership. Construction Specifications Institute, 601 Madison St., Alexandria, VA 22314-1791. TEL 703-684-0300. FAX 703-684-0465. Ed. Sharon Hammel. adv. circ. 19,000.
  Description: Targeted towards CSI members, covers member news - technical and educational, calendar of events, and employment.

690 US
C W A NEWS. 1953. q. membership. Construction Writers Association, Box 5586, Buffalo Grove, IL 60089-5586. TEL 847-398-7756. Ed. Shelia Wertz. R&P contact: Sheila Wertz. adv. contact: Shelia Wertz. circ. 650. **Document type:** newsletter.
  Formerly: Construction Writers Association. Newsletter (ISSN 0069-9217)
  Description: Covers news of interest to and activities of the association.

690 FR ISSN 0241-6794
CAHIERS TECHNIQUES DU BATIMENT. 1970. 9/yr. 460 F. (foreign 520 F.). Groupe Moniteur, 17 rue d'Uzes, 75002 Paris, France. FAX 33-1-42333819. TELEX 220 528F. Ed. Frederic Lenne. illus. circ. 12,500.
  —BLDSC (2952.330000); CISTI.
  Former titles (until 1975): Cahiers Techniques du Moniteur; Urbat (ISSN 0049-5697)

690 US ISSN 0045-3900
TA1
CALIFORNIA BUILDER AND ENGINEER.* 1893. s-m. $65. California Builder and Engineer, Inc., Box 2370, Riverside, CA 92516-2370. TEL 415-494-8822. FAX 415-494-1023. Ed. Alan D. Stafford; Pub. Fred Johnston. R&P contact: Leah Gayheart. adv. contact: Bob Story. bk.rev.; illus.; stat.; tr.lit. circ. 9,951. **Document type:** trade publication.
  Description: Regional trade publication serving heavy construction industries of California, Nevada and Hawaii.

690 US ISSN 1085-7729
CALIFORNIA CONSTRUCTION NEWS COVERING EAST BAY. 1992. w. McGraw-Hill Companies, Princeton Rd. S-2, Box 689, Hightstown, NJ 08520-0689. TEL 800-325-2030. adv. **Document type:** newsletter, trade publication.
  ●Also available online.
  Description: Provides information on what jobs are coming up for bid or negotiation.

690 US ISSN 1085-780X
CALIFORNIA CONSTRUCTION NEWS COVERING GOLD COAST. 1988. w. McGraw-Hill Companies, Princeton Rd. S-2, Box 689, Hightstown, NJ 08520-0689. TEL 800-325-2030. adv. **Document type:** newsletter, trade publication.
  ●Also available online.
  Description: Provides information on what jobs are coming up for bid or negotiation.

690 US ISSN 1085-777X
CALIFORNIA CONSTRUCTION NEWS COVERING INLAND EMPIRE. 1988. w. McGraw-Hill Companies, Princeton Rd. S-2, Box 689, Hightstown, NJ 08520-0689. TEL 800-325-2030. adv. **Document type:** newsletter, trade publication.
  ●Also available online.
  Description: Provides information on what jobs are coming up for bid or negotiation.

690 US ISSN 1085-7761
CALIFORNIA CONSTRUCTION NEWS COVERING LOS ANGELES. 1988. w. McGraw-Hill Companies, Princeton Rd. S-2, Box 689, Hightstown, NJ 08520-0689. TEL 800-325-2030. adv. **Document type:** newsletter, trade publication.
  ●Also available online.
  Description: Provides information on what jobs are coming up for bid or negotiation.

690 US ISSN 1085-7753
CALIFORNIA CONSTRUCTION NEWS COVERING NORTH COAST. 1993. w. McGraw-Hill Companies, Princeton Rd. S-2, Box 689, Hightstown, NJ 08520-0689. TEL 800-325-2030. adv. **Document type:** newsletter, trade publication.
  ●Also available online.
  Description: Provides information on what jobs are coming up for bid or negotiation.

690 US ISSN 1085-7788
CALIFORNIA CONSTRUCTION NEWS COVERING ORANGE COUNTY. 1988. w. McGraw-Hill Companies, Princeton Rd. S-2, Box 689, Hightstown, NJ 08520-0689. TEL 800-325-2030. adv. **Document type:** newsletter, trade publication.
  ●Also available online.
  Description: Provides information on what jobs are coming up for bid or negotiation.

690 US ISSN 1085-7796
CALIFORNIA CONSTRUCTION NEWS COVERING SAN DIEGO. 1988. w. McGraw-Hill Companies, Princeton Rd. S-2, Box 689, Hightstown, NJ 08520-0689. TEL 800-325-2030. adv. **Document type:** newsletter, trade publication.
  ●Also available online.
  Description: Provides information on what jobs are coming up for bid or negotiation.

690 US ISSN 1085-7745
CALIFORNIA CONSTRUCTION NEWS COVERING SAN FRANCISCO. 1993. w. McGraw-Hill Companies, Princeton Rd. S-2, Box 689, Hightstown, NJ 08520-0689. TEL 800-325-2030. adv. **Document type:** newsletter, trade publication.
  ●Also available online.
  Description: Provides information on what jobs are coming up for bid or negotiation.

690 US ISSN 1085-7737
CALIFORNIA CONSTRUCTION NEWS COVERING SOUTH BAY. 1992. w. McGraw-Hill Companies, Princeton Rd. S-2, Box 689, Hightstown, NJ 08520-0689. TEL 800-325-2030. adv. **Document type:** newsletter, trade publication.
  ●Also available online.
  Description: Provides information on what jobs are coming up for bid or negotiation.

CALIFORNIA STATE CONTRACTS REGISTER. see BUSINESS AND ECONOMICS

690 CK ISSN 0120-5102
CAMACOL REVISTA. 1978. q. Col.$25500($30) (effective 1994). Camara Colombiana de la Construccion (CAMACOL), Presidencia Nacional, Carrera 10 No. 19-65, Piso 10, Apdo. 28588, Bogota D.E., Colombia. TEL 2177166. FAX 2119559. Dir. Alberto Vasquez Restrepo. adv.; charts; illus.; stat.; cum.index: no.1-49. circ. 25,000.
  Description: Analysis of construction and public works, legislation, finance and marketing, and macroeconomics.

690 CK
CAMARA COLOMBIANA DE LA CONSTRUCCION. BOLETIN MENSUAL DE ESTADISTICA.* 1973. m. Camara Colombiana de la Construccion (CAMACOL), Presidencia Nacional, Carrera 10 No. 19-65, Piso 10, Apdo. 28588, Bogota D.E., Colombia. charts; stat. **Document type:** bulletin.

690 CK
CAMARA COLOMBIANA DE LA CONSTRUCCION. BOLETIN TRIMESTRIAL.* 1973. q. Camara Colombiana de la Construccion (CAMACOL), Presidencia Nacional, Carrera 10 No. 19-65, Piso 10, Apdo. 28588, Bogota D.E., Colombia. charts; stat. **Document type:** bulletin.

690 946 SP
CAMARA OFICIAL DE LA PROPIEDAD URBANA DE LA PROVINCIA DE AVILA. BOLETIN INFORMATIVO. 1965. q. Camara Oficial de la Propiedad Provincia, Martin Carramolino 10, Spain. circ. 4,000. **Document type:** government publication.

691 PN
CAMARA PANAMENA DE LA CONSTRUCCION. LISTA DE PRECIOS DE MATERIALES DE CONSTRUCCION. 1961. s-a. $30. Camara Panamena de la Construccion, Apdo. 6793, Panama 5, Panama. TEL 507-265-2500. FAX 507-265-2571. circ. 500.
  Description: Lists local prices of construction materials and equipment rentals.

690 331.2 PN
CAMARA PANAMENA DE LA CONSTRUCCION. PRESTACIONES LABORALES EN LA CONSTRUCCION. 1984. irreg., latest 1987. $30. Camara Panamena de la Construccion, Apdo. 6793, Panama 5, Panama. TEL 507-265-2500. FAX 507-265-2571. Ed. Eduardo Rodriguez, Jr. circ. 400.
  Description: Contains analysis of labor benefits and basic salary rates as set by Panamanian labor code.

BUILDING AND CONSTRUCTION

690   **CN**
CANADIAN AGGREGATES AND ROAD BUILDING CONTRACTOR. 1987. 8/yr. Can.$35($35) Franmore Communications Inc., 4999 St. Catherines St. W., Ste. 215, Westmount, PQ H3Z 1T3, Canada. TEL 514-487-9868. FAX 514-487-9276. Ed. Robert L. Consediwe; Pub. Robert L. Consediwe. adv.: B&W page $2729; trim 8 1/8 x 10 7/8; adv. contact: Clifford Allum. circ. 7,847. **Document type:** trade publication.
Formerly (until 1993): Canadian Aggregates (ISSN 0836-799X)

690.028   **CN**   **ISSN 0832-6533**
CANADIAN HEAVY EQUIPMENT GUIDE. 1986. 9/yr. Can.$37.45 (US Can.$45). Baum Publications Ltd., 1625 Ingleton Ave., Burnaby, BC V5C 4L8, Canada. TEL 604-291-9900. FAX 604-291-1906. Ed. Len Webster. adv.: B&W page $5366, color page $6551; adv. contact: John F. Bleuler. circ. 31,093. (tabloid format)
Description: Describes new products and industry developments. Industry experts explain the best way to use and maintain heavy equipments.

690   **CN**   **ISSN 0837-015X**
CANADIAN MASONRY CONTRACTOR. 1987. 4/yr. $16 (foreign $24). Perks Publications Inc., 1735 Bayly St., Ste. 7A, Pickering, ON L1W 3G7, Canada. TEL 416-831-4711. FAX 416-831-4725. Ed. Tanja Nowotny. adv.: B&W page $930; trim 8 1/2 X 11; adv. contact: Mike Nosko. circ. 4,194.
—CISTI.

695   **CN**   **ISSN 0829-3511**
CANADIAN ROOFING CONTRACTOR. 4/yr. $16. Perks Publications Inc., 1735 Bayly St., Ste. 7A, Pickering, ON L1W 3G7, Canada. TEL 416-831-4711. FAX 416-831-4725. Ed. E.B. Perks. adv.: B&W page $930; trim 8 1/2 X 11; adv. contact: Mary Beattie. circ. 4,066.
—CISTI.

690   **CN**   **ISSN 0068-984X**
CANADIAN TECHNICAL ASPHALT ASSOCIATION. PROCEEDINGS OF THE ANNUAL CONFERENCE. 1956. a. Can.$50 per no. to non-members. Polyscience Publications Inc., 44 Seize Arpents, P.O. Box 148, Morin Heights, PQ J0R 1H0, Canada. TEL 514-226-5870; 800-840-5870. FAX 514-226-5866. E-mail: polysci@ietc.com. (Dist. in US by: Polyscience Publications Inc., 100 Walnut St., Champlain, NY 12919) Ed. E. Thompson. circ. 1,000. **Document type:** proceedings.
—BLDSC (6840.267000).

690   **SZ**   **ISSN 0376-6926**
CANTIERI. (Text in Italian) m. Swiss Society of Builders, Muehlerain 31, CH-4614 Haegendorf, Switzerland. TEL 062-462215. Ed. Ruedi Moser. circ. 7,052.

690   **IT**   **ISSN 0393-8220**
CANTIERI STRADE COSTRUZIONI. Key Title: Costruzioni Strade Cantieri. 1984. m. Lit.168000 (effective 1997). Gesto s.r.l., Via Cesare Battisti 21, 20122 Milan, Italy. TEL 39-2-55187581. FAX 39-2-5465310. Ed. Ferdinando Tagliabue. adv.: color page Lit.5250000.
Description: Technical and economic news for the building industry.

690   **AT**
CARPENTER AND JOINER. 1960. irreg. (Building Workers' Industrial Union of Australia, Victorian Branch) Industrial Printing and Publicity Co. Ltd., 122 Dover St., Richmond, Vic. 3121, Australia. Ed. A. Zeeno.

691   **IT**
CATALOGO EDILE. (In 4 vols.) 1990. a. L.190000 (effective Oct. 1996). BE-MA Editrice s.r.l., Via Teocrito 50, 20128 Milan, Italy. TEL 39-2-2552451. FAX 39-2-27000692. Ed. Gaetano Bertini Malgarini. adv.: B&W page L.2800000, color page L.4500000. circ. 5,000. **Document type:** catalog.
●Also available on CD-ROM.

691   **NE**   **ISSN 0008-8811**
CEMENT; vakblad voor de betonwereld. 1949. 11/yr. fl.130 to individuals; students fl.45. Stichting Beton Prisma, Sint Teunislaan 1, Postbus 3532, 5203 DM s-Hertogenbosch, Netherlands. Ed.Bd. adv.; bk.rev.; abstr.; charts; illus.; index, cum.index every 5 yrs. circ. 4,200. **Indexed:** C.R.I.Abstr., Concr.Abstr., Excerp.Med., HRIS. **Document type:** trade publication.
—CISTI; SWETS.

691.5   **CI**   **ISSN 0008-882X**
            CODEN: CEZAA7
CEMENT; casopis industrije cementa jugoslavije. (Text in Croatian; summaries in English, French) 1957. irreg. $20. J U C E M A - Association of the Yugoslav Cement and Asbestos-Cement Producers, Prilaz JNA 30, 41000 Zagreb, Croatia. FAX 41-278-101. TELEX 21406 YU CEMA. Ed. S. Zuliani. adv.; bk.rev.; charts; illus.; index. circ. 650. **Indexed:** C.R.I.Abstr., C.R.I.Curr.Cont., Chem.Abstr., Concr.Abstr.
—BLDSC (3098.760000); CASDDS.

691   **UK**   **ISSN 0958-9465**
TA418.9.C6   **CODEN: CCOCEG**
CEMENT AND CONCRETE COMPOSITES. 1979. bi-m. fl.1065($612) (effective 1998). Elsevier Science Ltd., P.O. Box 800, Kidlington, Oxford OX5 1DX, England. TEL 44-1865-843000. FAX 44-1865-843010. E-mail: nlinfo-f@elsevier.nl; usinfo-f@elsevier.com; forinfo-kyf04035@niftyserve.or.jp; URL: http://www.elsevier.nl/. (Subscr. to: Elsevier Science, Regional Sales Office, P.O. Box 211, 1000 AE Amsterdam, Netherlands. TEL 31-20-4853757. FAX 31-20-4853432; Subscr. in the Americas to: Elsevier Science, Regional Sales Office, Box 945, New York, NY 10159-0945. TEL 212-633-3730. FAX 212-633-3680; Subscr. in Australasia and the Far East to: Elsevier Science (Singapore) Pte Ltd, No.1 Temasek Ave., No.17-01 Millenia Tower, Singapore 039192, Singapore. TEL 65-434-3727. FAX 65-337-2230) Ed. R.N. Swamy. adv.; bk.rev. circ. 550. (also avail. in microform from UMI; reprint service avail. from UMI) **Indexed:** Alloys Ind., Appl.Mech.Rev., ASCA, C.R.I.Abstr., C.R.I.Curr.Cont., Chem.Abstr., Concr.Abstr., Eng.Ind., Eng.Mat.Abstr., HRIS, Intl.Polym.Sci.& Tech., J.of Ferroc., Met.Abstr.Ind., Met.Abstr., Nonfer.Met.Alert, PCC Alert, RAPRA, RICS, Steels Alert, World Alum.Abstr. **Document type:** academic/scholarly publication.
—BLDSC (3098.986000); CASDDS; CISTI; Ei; Genuine Article; Linda Hall; SWETS; UMI; UnCover. CCC.
Formerly (until 1990): International Journal of Cement Composites and Lightweight Concrete (ISSN 0262-5075); Formed by the 1981 merger of: International Journal of Cement Composites (ISSN 0142-095X); International Journal of Lightweight Concrete (ISSN 0142-0968)
Refereed Serial

691   **UK**   **ISSN 0008-8846**
TA434   **CODEN: CCNRAI**
CEMENT AND CONCRETE RESEARCH. (Text in English, French, German and Russian) 1971. m. fl.2227($1280) (effective 1998). Elsevier Science Ltd., Pergamon, P.O. Box 800, Kidlington, Oxford OX5 1DX, England. TEL 44-1865-843000. FAX 44-1865-843010. E-mail: nlinfo-f@elsevier.nl; usinfo-f@elsevier.com; forinfo-kyf04035@niftyserve.or.jp; URL: http://www.elsevier.nl/. (Subscr. to: Elsevier Science, Regional Sales Office, P.O. Box 211, 1000 AE Amsterdam, Netherlands. TEL 31-20-4853757. FAX 31-20-4853432; Subscr. in the Americas to: Elsevier Science, Regional Sales Office, Box 945, New York, NY 10159-0945. TEL 212-633-3730. FAX 212-633-3680; Subscr. in Australasia and the Far East to: Elsevier Science (Singapore) Pte Ltd, No.1 Temasek Ave., No.17-01 Millenia Tower, Singapore 039192, Singapore. TEL 65-434-3727. FAX 65-337-2230) Ed. Della M. Roy. adv.; bk.rev. circ. 1,500. (also avail. in microform from UMI; back issues avail.) **Indexed:** Alloys Ind., Appl.Mech.Rev., ASCA, Br.Ceram.Abstr., C.R.I.Abstr., C.R.I.Curr.Cont., Chem.Abstr., Chem.Cit.Ind., Concr.Abstr., Curr.Cont., Eng.Ind., Eng.Mat.Abstr., Excerp.Med., Intl.Civil Eng.Abstr., J.of Ferroc., Mat.Sci.Cit.Ind., Met.Abstr., Met.Abstr.Ind., Nonfer.Met.Alert, PCC Alert, Petrol.Abstr., Risk Abstr., Sci.Cit.Ind., Soft.Abstr.Eng., Steels Alert, W.R.C.Inf., World Alum.Abstr. **Document type:** academic/scholarly publication.
—BLDSC (3098.990000); CASDDS; CISTI; Ei; Genuine Article; Linda Hall; SWETS; UMI; UnCover. CCC.
Description: Covers research in cement, cement composites, concrete and other allied materials.
Refereed Serial

693   **JA**
CEMENT ASSOCIATION OF JAPAN. REVIEW OF THE GENERAL MEETING. (Text in English) 1947. a. 3,000 Yen. Cement Association of Japan, c/o Hattori Bldg., 1-1 Kyobashi, Chuo-ku, Tokyo 104, Japan. abstr.

620.1   **JA**
CEMENT ASSOCIATION OF JAPAN. REVIEW OF THE GENERAL MEETING. TECHNICAL SESSION. (Text in English) 1973. a. 3,500 Yen. Cement Association of Japan, c/o Hattori Bldg., 1-1 Kyobashi, Chuo-ku, Tokyo 104, Japan. abstr.

691   **II**   **ISSN 0970-2148**
CEMENT INDUSTRY ANNUAL REVIEW. (Text in English) 1982. a. Amakgamated Press, Narang House, 41 Ambalal Doshi Marg, Fort, Mumbai 400 001, India. TEL 91-22-265-4184. FAX 91-22-264-1275. adv.: B&W page £600; 230 x 175.

690   **US**
CEMENT: LATIN AMERICAN INDUSTRIAL REPORT. (Avail. for each of 22 Latin American countries) 1985. a. $435 per country report. Aquino Productions, Box 125, Rochester, VT 05767. Ed. Andres C. Aquino.

690   **UK**
▼**CEMENT PLANT ENVIRONMENTAL YEAR BOOK.** 1997. a. Tradeship Publications Ltd., Old Kings Head Ct., 15 High St., Dorking, Surrey RH4 1AR, England. TEL 44-1306-740363. Ed. David Hargreaves. **Document type:** trade publication.

691.5   **UK**   **ISSN 0008-8889**
CEMENT SPECIAL. 1961. q. free. Lafarge Aluminous Cement Co., Box 13, Fondu Works, 730 London Rd., Grays, Essex RM16 1NJ, England. charts; illus.; stat. circ. 10,000.

693   **BE**   **ISSN 1018-5852**
CEMENT STANDARDS OF THE WORLD. 1948. irreg., latest 1991. 6000 BEF (effective 1993). Cembureau, Rue d'Arlon 55, B-1040 Brussels, Belgium. TEL 32-2-2341011. FAX 32-2-2304720. **Description:** Details of cement standards in 112 countries and imported standards used in those countries which do not have their own.

691.5   **PL**   **ISSN 0008-8897**
            CODEN: CMWGAW
CEMENT, WAPNO, GIPS. 1929. m. $61. (Zrzeszenie Producentow Cementu - Association of Cement Producers, Sosnowiec) Wydawnictwo Czasopism i Ksiazek Technicznych SIGMA - NOT, Ul. Ratuszowa 11, P.O. Box 1004, 00-950 Warsaw, Poland. TEL 48-22-180918. FAX 48-22-192187. TELEX 814550 SIGMA PL. (Dist. by: SIGMA NOT Ltd., Ul. Bartycka 20, 00-716 Warsaw, Poland) Ed. Wieslaw Kurdowski. adv.; bk.rev.; charts; illus.; mkt.; tr.lit.; index. circ. 700. **Indexed:** C.R.I.Abstr., Ceram.Abstr., Chem.Abstr., Concr.Abstr., INIS Atomind., Ref.Zh.
—CASDDS; CISTI.

691   **AG**
CEMENTO. 1967. bi-m. free. Instituto del Cemento Portland Argentino, San Martin 1137, Buenos Aires, Argentina. TEL 54-1-3123040. FAX 54-1-3121700. E-mail: icpa@spi-cis.com. Ed. Julio Cesar Caballero; Pub. Raul N. Cippitelli. R&P contact: Julio Cesar Caballero. adv.: B&W page $1600, color page $2300; trim 200 x 280; adv. contact: Raul N. Cippiteelli. bk.rev.; bibl.; charts; illus. circ. 8,000. **Indexed:** C.R.I.Abstr., C.R.I.Curr.Cont. **Document type:** proceedings.
—CISTI.
Formerly (until 1994): Boletin del Cemento Portland (ISSN 0523-9095)
Description: Promotes and disseminates information about Portland cement and its applications.
Refereed Serial

691   **SP**   **ISSN 0008-8919**
TA680   **CODEN: CMHOAF**
CEMENTO - HORMIGON; revista tecnica. 1929. m. $175 in Latin America; elsewhere $195 (effective 1997). Ediciones Cemento, S.L., Calle Maignon 26, 08024 Barcelona, Spain. TEL 34-93-2844318. FAX 34-93-2108082. Ed. Patricio Palomar. adv. contact: Carlos Palomar. bk.rev.; abstr.; bibl.; charts; illus.; stat.; index. circ. 4,000. **Indexed:** Chem.Abstr., Ind.SST. **Document type:** trade publication.
—CASDDS; CISTI; SWETS.

BUILDING AND CONSTRUCTION

690   US   ISSN 0082-934X
CENSUS OF CONSTRUCTION INDUSTRIES: FINAL REPORTS. (Issued in 3 series: Geographic Area Series, Industry Series, and Special Report Series.) 1930. quinquennial, latest 1992. $60 for Geographic Area Series (foreign $75); Industry Series $85 (foreign $106.25). U.S. Bureau of the Census, Customer Services, Washington, DC 20233. TEL 301-457-4100. FAX 301-457-4714. URL: http://www.census.gov/. (Subscr. to: Superintendent of Documents, U.S. Government Printing Office, Box 371954, Pittsburgh, PA 15250-7954. TEL 202-512-1800. FAX 202-512-2250; Or: Bernan, 4611-F Assembly Dr., Lanham, MD 20706. TEL 301-459-7666. FAX 301-459-0056) **Document type:** government publication.
●Also available online.
Also available on CD-ROM.

690   II
CENTRAL BUILDING RESEARCH INSTITUTE. BUILDING RESEARCH NOTE. (Text in English) 1963; N.S. 1982. irreg. Rs.5 for 5 nos. Central Building Research Institute, Roorkee, Uttar Pradesh, India. TEL 91-1332-72243. FAX 91-1332-72272. Ed. R.C. Satiya. **Document type:** academic/scholarly publication.
—CISTI.
    Formerly (until 1982): Central Building Research Institute. Building Digest (ISSN 0557-319X)
    Description: Each issue covers a specific topic of research at the CBRI.

690   US
CENTRAL OKLAHOMA HOME BUILDER. bi-m. Central Oklahoma Home Builders Association, 623 W. Interstate 44 Service Rd., Oklahoma City, OK 73118-6032. TEL 405-843-1508. FAX 405-843-6714. Ed. Terri Akers. circ. 600.

690   FR   ISSN 0008-9850
CENTRE SCIENTIFIQUE ET TECHNIQUE DU BATIMENT. CAHIERS. Short title: Cahiers. (Includes cum.index: Repertoire de Cahiers et des Avis Techniques Publics) 1948. 10/yr. 1090 F. (effective 1997). Centre Scientifique et Technique du Batiment, 4 av. du Recteur Poincare, 75782 Paris Cedex 16, France. Ed. Alain Maugard. R&P contact: M. Rubinstein. TEL 33-1-40502828. adv.; bk.rev.; abstr.; charts; illus.; tr.mk.; index, cum.index. every 3 yrs. circ. 6,000. **Indexed:** Archit.Per.Ind., Br.Ceram.Abstr., Int.Build.Serv.Abstr. **Document type:** academic/scholarly publication.
—CISTI.

691   IT   ISSN 0392-4890
CERAMICA PER L'EDILIZIA - INTERNATIONAL. (Supplement avail.: Fashion Ceramic Tiles) (Text in English and Italian) 1967. bi-m. Lit.122000 in Europe; Oceania Lit.210000; elsewhere Lit.172000 (includes supplement) (effective 1997). Gruppo Editoriale Faenza Editrice s.p.a., Via Pier. de Crescenzi, 44, 48018 Faenza, Italy. TEL 39-546-663488. FAX 39-546-660440. E-mail: gefe.vendita@uno.dinamica.it; gefe.info@uno.dinamica.it. Ed. Alda Hauner. R&P contact: Luisa Teston. adv.: color page Lit.5080000; adv. contact: Elvio Neri. illus. circ. 16,000. **Indexed:** Br.Ceram.Abstr. **Document type:** trade publication.
    Formerly (until vol.13, no.59, 1979): Ceramica Italiana nell'Edilizia (ISSN 0009-028X)
    Description: Provides information on manufacturing companies, distributors, products, technologies, events, and initiatives in the ceramic building materials sector.

690   BE
CHAMBRE SYNDICALE DE LA CONSTRUCTION. BULLETIN. (Text in French) 22/yr. 5 Gallerie de la Sauvenier, B-4000 Liege, Belgium. adv. circ. 2,400. **Document type:** bulletin.

690   FR   ISSN 0009-1596
CHANTIERS COOPERATIFS. 1948. m. 35 F. Federation Nationale des Cooperatives Ouvrieres de Production du Batiment, des Travaux Publics et des Activites Annexes, 88 rue de Courcelles, Paris (8e), France. TEL 46-22-40-48. FAX 46-22-47-83. Ed. Claude Leturcq. adv.; bibl.; illus.

690   FR   ISSN 0397-4650
CHANTIERS DE FRANCE; l'officiel des materiels de travaux publics et de batiment. 1962. 10/yr. 300 F. (Europe 500 F., elsewhere 800 F.) (effective 1997). Groupe Chantiers de France, Bord de Seine, 202 quai de Clichy, 92110 Clichy, France. TEL 33-1-47561723. FAX 33-1-47561432. Eds. Arlette Surchamp, Marc Montagnon; Pub. Arlette Surchamp. adv. contact: Sophie Yon. charts; illus.; tr.lit. circ. 15,000. **Document type:** newspaper, trade publication.
—CISTI.
    Incorporates: Levage Actualite (ISSN 1158-0038)
    Description: Provides up to date news on public works as well as the latest earth-moving equipment and civil engineering projects.

690 200   FR   ISSN 0009-160X
LES CHANTIERS DU CARDINAL. 1963. q. 15 F. 106 rue du Bac, 75341 Paris Cedex 07, France. TEL 33-1-42224686. Ed. M. Thizon. adv.; illus. circ. 70,000. **Document type:** bulletin.
    Description: Presents construction and maintenance of churches in Ile-de-France.

690   FR   ISSN 1149-1051
CHARPENTE - MENUISERIE - SERRURERIE. Short title: C M S. Variant title: Charpente, Menuiserie, Serrurerie, Fermeture, Tolerie. 1972. 9/yr. 345 F. Editions Bernard Begassat, 17 rue du Louvre, 75001 Paris, France. TEL 42-36-05-13. FAX 40-13-98-51. Ed. Bernard Begassat. circ. 6,000.
    Formerly (until 1989): Nouveau Journal de Charpente, Menuiserie, Metallique, Serrurerie (ISSN 0291-8366)
    Description: Technical review of metalwork and PVC in the building trade.

690   AT   ISSN 1324-0900
CHARTERED BUILDING PROFESSIONAL. 1972. q. Aus.$20 (foreign Aus.$30) (effective 1997). Australian Institute of Building, 217 Northbourne Ave., Turner, A.C.T. 2601, Australia. TEL 61-62-477433. FAX 61-62-489030. Ed. David Green. R&P contact: Don Debus. TEL 61-6-2477433. adv. contact: David Green. circ. 3,000 (controlled). **Indexed:** Build.Manage.Abstr. **Document type:** newsletter.
—BLDSC (3129.991700).
    Formerly (until May 1995): Chartered Builder (ISSN 0311-1903); Which incorporated (1988-1990): A I B Newsletter (ISSN 1032-8467)
    Description: Provides new about the institute and matters relevant to the building profession in Australia.

690   UK
CHARTERED INSTITUTE OF BUILDING. HANDBOOK. 1968. a. £60. Chartered Institute of Building, c/o Peter Harlow, Englemere, Kings Ride, Ascot, Berks. SL5 8BJ, England. TEL 01334-23355. FAX 01334-23467. adv. circ. 10,000. (reprint service avail. from UMI) **Document type:** trade publication.
    Former titles (until 1987): Chartered Institute of Building. Year Book (ISSN 0260-7727); Chartered Institute of Building. Year Book and Directory of Members (ISSN 0073-9014)

CHECKLIST SUPPLEMENT AND ILLUSTRATIVE FINANCIAL STATEMENTS FOR CONSTRUCTION CONTRACTORS. see BUSINESS AND ECONOMICS — Accounting

690   CC
CHINA BUILDING DEVELOPMENT. (Text in English) 6/yr. HK.$480 (foreign $180). Trend Publishing (H.K.) Ltd., Sup Tower, Rm. 603, 75-83 King's Rd., North Point, Hong Kong, People's Republic of China. TEL 2802-6299. FAX 2802-6458. **Document type:** trade publication.

690   BE
CHRONIQUE. (Text in French) 1945. w. S.A. Orena, 140 bld. Lambermont, B-1030 Brussels, Belgium. adv. circ. 21,900.

690   FR
CHRONIQUE DES TRAVAUX PUBLICS ET PARTICULIERS. w. 268 bd. Clemenceau, 59707 Marcq-en-Baroeul, France. TEL 20-72-87-14. FAX 20-45-93-28. TELEX 810 946. Ed. Gerard Ferlin. circ. 3,750.

CHURCH BUSINESS. PRODUCTS & TECHNOLOGY. see RELIGIONS AND THEOLOGY

690   UK
CI-NET EUROPEAN CONSTRUCTION FORECAST. a. £195. National Council of Building Material Producers, 26 Store St., London WC1E 7BT, England. TEL 44-171-323-3770. FAX 44-171-323-0307. E-mail: 101326.2660@compuserve.com. Ed. A. Wilen. **Document type:** trade publication.

691   FR   ISSN 0397-006X
TA2   CODEN: CBPCDD
CIMENTS, BETONS, PLATRES, CHAUX. (Text in English, French) 1905. 6/yr. 738.18 F. (foreign 953 F.) (effective 1997). Septima, 14 rue Falguiere, 75015 Paris, France. TEL 33-1-44384800. FAX 33-1-44384809. Ed. D. Lecat. adv.; bk.rev.; abstr.; bibl.; charts; illus.; index. circ. 1,650. **Indexed:** Art & Archaeol.Tech.Abstr., Br.Ceram.Abstr., C.R.I.Abstr., C.R.I.Curr.Cont., Ceram.Abstr., Chem.Abstr., Concr.Abstr., Excerp.Med., GeoRef. **Document type:** trade publication.
—BLDSC (3198.405000); CASDDS; CISTI; Linda Hall; SWETS. CCC.
    Formerly: Revue des Materiaux de Construction et de Travaux Publics (ISSN 0035-2144)
    Description: Covers cement, gypsum and lime.

CITY COMMERCIAL - RESIDENTIAL CODES. see HOUSING AND URBAN PLANNING

690 621.3   US
CITY OF CHICAGO BUILDING CODE. 1951. a. $102.44. Index Publishing Corporation, 415 N. State St., Chicago, IL 60610. TEL 312-644-7800. FAX 312-644-4255. Ed. Joanne Reed; Pub. Sylvia Youpel. adv. contact: Thomas Youpel. circ. 2,037. **Document type:** government publication.
    Description: Compilation of Chicago regulations governing structural and mechanical requirements for new construction and existing buildings.

CIVIC TRUST AWARDS. see ARCHITECTURE

690   CN   ISSN 1181-7925
CLASSIC HOMESTYLES. 1990. a. Can.$4.95. Giroux Publishing, 102 Ellis St., Penticton, BC V2A 4L5, Canada. TEL 604-493-0942. FAX 604-493-7526. E-mail: cgiroux@vip.net. Ed. Michael A. Giroux. adv. contact: Dennis Thatchuk. circ. 13,500. **Document type:** consumer publication, catalog.
    Description: Features designs from Canadian home designers and the latest housing innovations. Contains house plans for a range of styles and budgets.

690.24   UK
CLEANING MAINTENANCE AND SUPPORT SERVICES. 1953. 11/yr. £62 (foreign £81) (effective 1997). Turret Group Plc., Turret House, 171 High St., Rickmansworth, Herts WD3 1SN, England. TEL 44-1923-777000. FAX 44-1923-771297. Ed. Neil Nixon. adv.; illus. circ. 13,000. **Indexed:** Br.Tech.Ind., PROMT, RICS, World Text.Abstr. **Document type:** trade publication.
    Former titles: Cleaning Maintenance; Cleaning Maintenance and Big Buildings Management (ISSN 0143-0963); Which incorporated: Buildings Maintenance and Services (ISSN 0308-5651)

647.9   US
CLEANING MANAGEMENT. 1927. m. $45. National Trade Publications, Inc., 13 Century Hill, Latham, NY 12110-2197. TEL 518-783-1281. FAX 518-783-1386. E-mail: cleannet@cleannet.com; URL: http://cleanet.com. Ed. Steve Kane; Pub. Alice Savino. adv.: B&W page $3090, color page $4935; trim 8 1/8 x 10 7/8; adv. contact: Greg Torrito. charts; illus.; index; circ. 42,000 (controlled). **Indexed:** RILM. **Document type:** trade publication.
—UnCover. CCC.
    Former titles: Cleaning Management (ISSN 1051-5720); National Custodian (ISSN 0027-9099)
    Description: For directors, managers, administrators, supervisors and executives in charge of institutional, industrial and commercial building cleaning services.

690   UK   ISSN 0020-2789
TH57
CLERK OF WORKS. 1893. m. £12. Institute of Clerks of Works of Great Britain Inc., 41 The Mall, Ealing, London W5 3TJ, England. TEL 01-579-2917. FAX 081-570-0554. Ed. Arthur L. Watts. adv.; bk.rev.; tr.lit. circ. 4,500.
—BLDSC (3278.637000).
    Description: About control of building quality performance and standards.

BUILDING AND CONSTRUCTION

690   331.8   US   ISSN 0009-8779
CLEVELAND CITIZEN. 1891. m. $6.50 (effective 1995). (Cleveland Building and Construction Trades Council) Citizen Publishing, 2012 W. 25th St., Ste. 900, Cleveland, OH 44113. TEL 216-861-4283. Ed. William G. Obbagy. adv.: page $713.60; adv. contact: Henry Q. Speeth. circ. 10,600. (tabloid format; also avail. in microfilm; back issues avail.) **Document type:** newspaper.
   Description: Contains news of interest to union members in the building & construction trades.

690   NE   ISSN 0010-0064
COBOUW; vakdagblad voor de bouwwereld. 1856. d. (Mon.-Fri.). fl.780 (foreign fl.1245) (effective 1996). Ten Hagen & Stam b.v. (Subsidiary of: Wolters Kluwer N.V.), Postbus 34, 2501 AG The Hague, Netherlands. TEL 31-70-3045700. FAX 31-70-3045812. Ed. W. Egels. adv. contact: Herman Voois. illus.; circ. 19,433 (paid). (broadsheet format) **Indexed:** Key to Econ.Sci. **Document type:** trade publication, newspaper.
—SWETS.
   Description: News on the Dutch building and construction fields: civil and utility building, earth and soil removal, road and waterway works.

COCKSHAW'S CONSTRUCTION LABOR NEWS & OPINION. see *BUSINESS AND ECONOMICS — Labor And Industrial Relations*

690   340   US   ISSN 0735-9330
KF0459.A1
CODE NEWS. 1981. bi-m. $175. Banks - Baldwin Law Publishing Co., Box 318063, Cleveland, OH 44131-8063. TEL 216-520-5600. FAX 216-520-5655. Ed. David S. Collins. (looseleaf format) **Document type:** newsletter.
   Description: Covers construction law and building code enforcement in Ohio.

690   FR   ISSN 0758-7317
CODE PERMANENT: CONSTRUCTION ET URBANISME. 3 base vols. plus m. updates. 1060 F. for base vols. (updates 330 F.) (effective 1995). Editions Legislatives et Administratives, 80 ave. de la Marne, 92546 Montrouge Cedex, France. TEL 40-92-68-68. FAX 46-56-00-15. TELEX 632 855 F. (looseleaf format)
   Description: For architects, lawyers, decorators, entrepreneurs, appraisers, construction companies and building supervisors whose work involves urbanization.

CODES & STANDARDS. see *HOUSING AND URBAN PLANNING*

690   US   ISSN 1071-0264
COLORADO CONSTRUCTION WEEKLY. w. McGraw-Hill Companies, Princeton Rd. S-2, Box 689, Hightstown, NJ 08520-0689. TEL 800-325-2030. adv. **Document type:** newsletter, trade publication.
●Also available online.
   Former titles: Colorado Construction News (ISSN 1041-1976); Construction Bulletin and Trades Report. Colorado (ISSN 0889-5287)

690   622   US
COMIMEX.* 1991. m. Construccion Mexicana, Inc., 9500 S. Dadeland Blvd., Ste. 550, Miami, FL 33156-2819. TEL 305-670-4818. FAX 305-670-4820. Ed. Martha Oliveros. adv. circ. 8,384.

614.8   FR   ISSN 0010-244X
TA192
COMITES DE PREVENTION DU BATIMENT ET DES TRAVAUX PUBLICS. CAHIERS. 1946. bi-m. 130 F. (foreign 240 F.). Organisme Professionnel de Prevention du Batiment et des Travaux Publics, Tour Amboise B 3, 204 Rond Point du Pont de Sevres, 92516 Boulogne Billancourt Cedex, France. TEL 46-09-26-81. FAX 46-09-27-40. Dir. Michel Deroide. bk.rev.; bibl.; charts; illus.; stat.; index. circ. 20,000. **Document type:** trade publication.
—CISTI.

690   US
COMMERCIAL, INSTITUTIONAL, LIGHT INDUSTRIAL BUILDING COST GUIDE. $95. E.H. Boeckh (Subsidiary of: Thomson Publishing Corp.), 2885 S. Calhoun Rd., Box 510291, New Berlin, WI 53151-0291. TEL 414-780-2800. FAX 414-780-0306.
   Description: Aims to assist insurance, appraisal, and assessment industries to estimate the replacement cost of commercial, institutional, and light industrial buildings in the U.S.

690   US
COMMERCIAL SQUARE FOOT. 1991. a. $49.95. Saylor Publications, Inc., 9420 Topanga Canyon Blvd., Ste. 203, Chatsworth, CA 91311. TEL 818-718-5966. FAX 818-718-8024. E-mail: saylor@pacificnet.net. Ed. Stanley J. Strychaz. R&P contact: Stanley J. Strychaz. **Document type:** trade publication.

690   660   GW
CONCHEM JOURNAL. 1993. q. DM.118 (effective 1997). H. Ziolkowsky GmbH, Beethovenstr. 16, 86150 Augsburg, Germany. TEL 49-821-519345. FAX 49-821-517953. Ed. Dr. Bernd Ziolkowsky. adv. contact: Robert Fischer. **Document type:** trade publication.
   Description: Covers chemical and technical developments within the building material industry.

691   UK   ISSN 0010-5317
                                CODEN: CCRTAA
CONCRETE. 1966. bi-m. £50($75) The Concrete Society, No. 3 Eatongate, Windsor Rd., Slough, Berks. SL1 2JA, England. TEL 44-1753-693313. FAX 44-1753-692333. Ed. M. Walker. R&P contact: T.W. Kirkbride. adv. contact: J. Pengeley. bk.rev.; charts; illus. circ. 6,500. (tabloid format; also avail. in microform from UMI; reprint service avail. from UMI) **Indexed:** Appl.Mech.Rev., Archit.Per.Ind., Avery Ind.Archit.Per., Br.Tech.Ind., C.R.I.Abstr., C.R.I.Curr.Cont., Chem.Abstr., Concr.Abstr., Eng.Ind., Excerp.Med., Geotech.Abstr., HRIS, INIS Atomind., Intl.Civil Eng.Abstr., PROMT, Soft.Abstr.Eng., W.R.C.Inf. **Document type:** trade publication.
—BLDSC (3399.600000); CASDDS; CISTI; Ei; Linda Hall; SWETS; UMI; UnCover.
   Incorporates: Concrete Works International.

691.3   II   ISSN 0010-5341
CONCRETE CONSTRUCTION AND ARCHITECTURE. (Text in English) 1968. m. Rs.40. Pandeya Publications, Block F, 105-C, New Alipore, Calcutta 700053, India. Ed. L.K. Pandeya. adv.: B&W page Rs.500, color page Rs.1100; trim 220 x 280; adv. contact: O.N. Pandeya.

691.3   AT
CONCRETE IN AUSTRALIA. q. (Concrete Institute of Australia) Engineers Australia Pty. Ltd., 2 Ernest St., P.O. Box 588, Crows Nest, N.S.W. 2065, Australia. TEL 61-2-94381533. FAX 61-2-9438-5934. E-mail: ea.editorial@eol.ieaust.org.au; URL: http://members.australis.net.au/~engineer. Ed. Bob Jackson. adv. contact: Maria Mamone. circ. 2,000.
   Description: Contains news items and articles of interest to persons in the building and construction industry.
   Refereed Serial

691.3   US
TA680   CODEN: CIDCD2
CONCRETE INTERNATIONAL. 1979. m. $109 (foreign $117) (effective 1996). American Concrete Institute, Box 19150, Redford Sta., 22400 Seven Mile Rd., Detroit, MI 48219. TEL 313-532-2600. FAX 313-538-0655. Ed. William J. Semioli. adv. circ. 20,000. **Indexed:** A.S.& T.Ind., Abstr.J.Earthq.Eng., C.R.I.Abstr., C.R.I.Curr.Cont., Chem.Abstr., Concr.Abstr., J.of Ferroc.
—BLDSC (3402.050000); CASDDS; CISTI; Ei; KR SourceOne; Linda Hall; SWETS; UnCover. **CCC.**
   Formerly: Concrete International - Design and Construction (ISSN 0162-4075)
   Description: Publishes current reports on concrete, products, and materials related to concrete.

639.5   US   ISSN 0045-8015
CONCRETE PIPE NEWS. 1952. q. $15. American Concrete Pipe Association, 222 Las Colinas Blvd. W., Ste. 641, Irving, TX 75039-5423. TEL 703-821-1990. FAX 703-821-3054. URL: http://www.concrete-pipe.org. Ed. Mike Saubert. R&P contact: Mike Saubert. charts; illus. circ. 12,000. **Indexed:** Concr.Abstr. **Document type:** trade publication.
—Linda Hall.
   Description: Contains articles about the installation of concrete pipe throughout the world & stories about both innovative & standard installations.

691.3   UK   ISSN 0264-0236
CONCRETE PLANT AND PRODUCTION. 1982. m. £24($50) Hayden Jeffery, Ed. & Pub., 12 Grimsdells Lane, Amersham, Bucks HP6 6HF, England. TEL 0494-726273. FAX 0494-726273. adv.; bk.rev. circ. 1,800. **Indexed:** C.R.I.Abstr., C.R.I.Curr.Cont., Concr.Abstr.
—CISTI; Linda Hall.
   Description: For people who batch, mix, pump, transport, pour and compact concrete.

691   US
THE CONCRETE PRODUCER. 1983. m. Aberdeen Group, 426 S. Westgate St., Addison, IL 60101. TEL 630-543-0870. FAX 630-543-3112. URL: http://www.supernetwork.com. Ed. Ward Malisch; Pub. Michael J. Porcaro. R&P contact: Allan Benson. adv. contact: Jan Gurath. charts; illus.; tr.lit.; index; circ. 15,500 (controlled). (back issues avail.) **Indexed:** Eng.Ind. **Document type:** trade publication.
●Also available online.
   Formerly (until 1997): Aberdeen's Concrete Journal (ISSN 1055-0356)
   Description: For producers of concrete products in the major concrete producing market segments: ready mixed concrete, precast and prestressed concrete and concrete block, tile and pipe, pavers and architectural precast.

691.3   US   ISSN 0010-5368
CONCRETE PRODUCTS. 1947. m. $36. Intertec Publishing Corp., 29 N. Wacker Dr., Chicago, IL 60606. TEL 312-726-2802. FAX 312-726-2574. TELEX 270258 EXP. Ed. A. Don Marsh; Pub. Robert Dimond. R&P contact: Don Marsh. adv. contact: Ker Hughes. charts; illus.; stat.; tr.lit. circ. 20,000. (also avail. in microfilm from UMI) **Indexed:** C.R.I.Abstr., C.R.I.Curr.Cont., Concr.Abstr., PROMT. **Document type:** trade publication.
●Also available online. Vendor(s): Information Access Co.
—BLDSC (3402.800000); CISTI; Linda Hall; UMI. **CCC.**
   Description: For manufacturers and users of concrete products.

691   620   US   ISSN 1055-2936
TA680
CONCRETE REPAIR BULLETIN. 1988. bi-m. membership. International Concrete Repair Institute, 1323 Shepard Dr., Ste. D, Sterling, VA 20164. TEL 703-450-0116. FAX 703-450-0119. E-mail: concrepair@aol.com. Ed. Karen Morey; Pub. Milt Collins. adv. contact: Sally Collins. charts; illus.; stat.; tr.lit.; index. circ. 11,000. (back issues avail.) **Indexed:** Corros.Abstr. **Document type:** trade publication.
—BLDSC (3404.040000).
   Description: For contractors, engineers, manufacturers and anyone concerned with the repair of concrete.

691.3   UK   ISSN 0305-1986
                          CODEN: CSTRDR
CONCRETE SOCIETY. TECHNICAL REPORTS. no. 2, 1970. irreg., no. 42, 1993. The Concrete Society, No. 3 Eatongate, Windsor Rd., Slough, Berks. SL1 2JA, England. TEL 44-1753-693313. FAX 44-1753-692333. Ed. M. Walker. R&P contact: T.W. Kirkbride. **Indexed:** Concr.Abstr., HRIS, I.M.M.Abstr. **Document type:** trade publication.
—BLDSC (3404.400000); CISTI.

BUILDING AND CONSTRUCTION

690   US
CONCRETE TECHNOLOGY TODAY. 1980. 3/yr. Portland Cement Association, 5420 Old Orchard Rd., Skokie, IL 60077-1083. TEL 847-966-6200. FAX 847-966-8389. E-mail: steve_kosmatka@portcement.org; URL: http://www.portcement.org. Ed. Steve Kosmatkah. R&P contact: Patricia Dyer. TEL 847-966-6200 ext.367. bk.rev.; cum.index: 1980-1996. circ. 18,000. (back issues avail.) **Document type:** newsletter.
   Description: How to use concrete to advantage and avoid problems. For decision makers in design, management, or construction of building projects.

691.3   UK   ISSN 0069-8288
THE CONCRETE YEARBOOK. 1924. a. £62.50 (foreign £79) (effective 1996). Thomas Telford Ltd., 1 Heron Quay, London E14 4JD, England. TEL 44-171-987-6999. FAX 44-171-538-4101. TELEX 298105-CIVILS-G. Ed. David Sanders. adv. circ. 1,200. (reprint service avail. from UMI)
—BLDSC (3405.000000); CISTI.
   Description: Directory of information on every aspect of the UK concrete and construction industries, their associated materials, products and services.

690   US
CONNECTICUT CONSTRUCTION HIGHLIGHTS OF THE WEEK. 1984. w. Connecticut Construction Industries Association, Inc., 912 Silas Deane Hwy., Wethersfield, CT 06109. TEL 860-529-6855. FAX 860-563-0616. Ed. Brian Holmes. circ. 650 (controlled). (back issues avail.) **Document type:** newsletter.
   Description: Covers state and national construction news for construction industry readers.

331.83 690
CONNECTICUT HOUSING PRODUCTION AND PERMIT AUTHORIZED CONSTRUCTION.* 1982. a. $5. Department of Housing, Research Unit, 505 Hudson St., Hartford, CT 06106-2502. TEL 203-566-4682. FAX 203-566-8600. Ed. Sandy Bergin. circ. 4,000. (also avail. in microfiche from CIS) **Indexed:** SRI.
   Formed by the merger of: Housing Units in Connecticut. Annual Summary & Connecticut. Department of Community Affairs Division of Research and Program Evaluation. Construction Activity Authorized by Building Permits. Summary (ISSN 0069-9020)

669.142   US   ISSN 1076-5522
CONNECTION (ARLINGTON). 1971. q. membership. National Institute of Steel Detailing, Inc., c/o Don Pope, Box 121484, Arlington, TX 76012. TEL 817-860-9890. FAX 817-860-9891. Ed. Ronald R. Montes. adv.: B&W page $250. **Document type:** newsletter.

690   US   ISSN 0893-5629
CONNSTRUCTION MAGAZINE. 1961. 4/yr. $28. McHugh Design, 62 LaSalle Rd., Ste. 211, W. Hartford, CT 06107. TEL 203-523-7518. FAX 203-231-8808. Ed. Thomas S. Jakups. adv. contact: Janet Hutson. bk.rev.; circ. 7,000 (controlled). (back issues avail.) **Document type:** trade publication.
   Former titles: Connecticut Construction; Connecticut Construction and Road Builder; Connecticut Road Builder.

690   SP   ISSN 0210-4601
CONSTRUC; revista tecnica de la construccion. 1952. q. 6800 ptas. (effective 1997). Ediciones Construc s.l., Ronda General Mitre 107, 08022 Barcelona, Spain. TEL 34-3-4175419. FAX 34-3-2115741. Dir. Juan Farre Sierra. adv.: B&W page 95000 ptas., color page 120000 ptas.; trim 190 x 270; adv. contact: Alex Farre Sierra. bk.rev. circ. 40,000.

690   BL   ISSN 0102-0501
CONSTRUCAO MINAS CENTRO OESTE. 1977. m. $177 (effective 1997). Editora Pini Ltda., Rua Anhaia 964, Bom Retiro, 01130-900 Sao Paulo, Brazil. TEL 55-11-2248811. Ed. Mario Sergio Pini. adv. contact: Luiz Carlos F. Oliveira. charts; illus.; stat. **Document type:** directory.

690   BL   ISSN 0102-051X
CONSTRUCAO NORTE NORDESTE. 1973. m. $177 (effective 1997). Editora Pini Ltda., Rua Anhaia 964, Bom Retiro, 01130-900 Sao Paulo, Brazil. TEL 55-11-2248811. Ed. Mario Sergio Pini. adv. contact: Luiz Carlos F. Oliveira. bk.rev.; illus. **Document type:** directory.

690 624   BL   ISSN 0102-0528
CONSTRUCAO REGIAO SUL. 1968. m. $177 (effective 1997). Editora Pini Ltda., Rua Anhaia 964, Bom Retiro, 01130-900 Sao Paulo, Brazil. TEL 55-11-2248811. Ed. Mario Sergio Pini. adv. contact: Luiz Carlos F. Oliveira. bk.rev.; charts; illus.; tr.lit. **Document type:** directory.

690 624   BL   ISSN 0100-1671
CONSTRUCAO RIO DE JANEIRO. 1970. m. $177. Editora Pini Ltda., Rua Anhaia 964, Bom Retiro, 01130-900 Sao Paulo, Brazil. TEL 55-11-2248811. Ed. Mario Sergio Pini. adv. contact: Luiz Carlos F. Oliveira. bk.rev.; charts; illus.; stat.; tr.lit. **Document type:** directory.

690   BL   ISSN 0010-6631
CONSTRUCAO SAO PAULO. 1948. w. $627 (effective 1997). Editora Pini Ltda., Rua Anhaia 964, Bom Retiro, 01130-900 Sao Paulo, Brazil. TEL 55-11-2248811. Ed. Mario Sergio Pini. adv. contact: Luiz Carlos F. Oliveira. bk.rev.; illus.; mkt.; stat. **Document type:** directory.

690   US
CONSTRUCCION DEL NORTE. (Text in Spanish) 1993. q. $22. McGraw-Hill Companies (Phoenix), 2050 E. University Ave., Ste. 1, Phoenix, AZ 85034. TEL 602-258-1641. FAX 602-495-9407. adv.: B&W page $1670; trim 8 x 10 3/4. circ. 9,241. **Document type:** trade publication.
   Description: Covers construction in Northern Mexico.

690   US   ISSN 0192-4230
CONSTRUCCION PAN-AMERICANA.* (Text in Spanish) 1972. m. $30. International Construction Publishing Inc., 9500 S. Dadeland Blvd., Ste. 550, Miami, FL 33156-2819. TEL 305-670-4818. Ed. Juan Escalante. circ. 12,203. (back issues avail.)

CONSTRUCCION PAN-AMERICANA INTERNATIONAL BUYER'S GUIDE. see *BUSINESS AND ECONOMICS — Trade And Industrial Directories*

690   US   ISSN 1084-3884
CONSTRUCCION Y OBRAS PUBLICAS LATINOAMERICA. (Text in Spanish) 1994. bi-m. $125 (effective 1997). MacDonald Communications, Inc., 3300 S. Gessner, Ste. 118, Houston, TX 77063. TEL 713-266-0610. FAX 713-266-6657. Pub. Peter Bryant. R&P contact: Peter Bryant. adv.: B&W page $2500, color page $4000; trim 8 1/4 x 11. circ. 14,101. **Document type:** trade publication.

691   MX   ISSN 0187-7895
   CODEN: CNTTEX
CONSTRUCCION Y TECNOLOGIA. 1963. m. $40 (effective 1997). Instituto Mexicano del Cemento y del Concreto, A.C., Insurgentes sur No. 1846, 01030 Mexico D.F., Mexico. FAX 5348806. Heraclio Esqueda Huidobro. adv.; bk.rev.; index. circ. 10,000. **Indexed:** Appl.Mech.Rev., C.R.I.Abstr., C.R.I.Curr.Cont., Intl.Civil Eng.Abstr., Soft.Abstr.Eng.
—BLDSC (3420.690500); CISTI; Linda Hall.
   Formerly: Revista I M C Y C (ISSN 0034-9607)
   Description: Contains practical and quality technological reports on cement and concrete useful for application to work done in Mexico.

669.142   AT   ISSN 1030-2581
TS350
CONSTRUCT IN STEEL. 1972. q. Aus.$70 (foreign Aus.$110) including Steel Construction. Australian Institute of Steel Construction, P.O. Box 6366, North Sydney, N.S.W. 2059, Australia. TEL 61-2-99296666. FAX 61-2-99555406. Ed. Karen Hayward. R&P contact: Karen Hayward. adv. contact: Karen Hayward. bk.rev.; charts; illus.; tr.lit.; cum.index. circ. 4,500. (back issues avail.) **Indexed:** Appl.Mech.Rev., Aus.Rd.Ind. **Document type:** consumer publication.
—BLDSC (3420.730000); Linda Hall.
   Formerly (until Aug. 1987): Steel Fabrication Journal (ISSN 0311-015X)
   Description: Aimed at engineers; covers use of fabricated steel in construction.

690   IE
CONSTRUCTION. m. (10/yr.) I£35. (Construction Industry Federation of Ireland) Tara Publishing Co. Ltd., Poolbeg House, 1-2 Poolbeg St., Dublin 2, Ireland. TEL 01-6719244. FAX 01-6719263. Ed. Fergus Farrell. adv.: B&W page I£1255, color page I£1800. bk.rev. circ. 3,504. **Document type:** trade publication.

690   BE
CONSTRUCTION. Dutch edition: Bouwbedrijf. (Supplement avail.) (Text in French) 1944. w. 6500 BEF. National Confederation of Building Contractors - Confederation Nationale de la Construction, 34-42 rue du Lombard, B-1000 Brussels, Belgium. TEL 32-2-5455719. FAX 32-2-5455908. Ed.Bd.; Pub. Robert de Meulenaere. adv. contact: Christian Nekkebroeck. circ. 21,200 (8,950 French ed.; 12,250 Dutch ed.). **Document type:** trade publication.
   Description: Provides relevant technical, social, economic and fiscal information for the construction industry.

690   UK
CONSTRUCTION. q. £22 (overseas £28). B & M Publications (London) Ltd., Hereford House., Bridle Path, Croydon, Surrey CR9 4NL, England. TEL 44-181-680-4200. FAX 44-181-681-5049. adv.; bk.rev. circ. 10,000. **Document type:** trade publication.
   Description: Contains technical information for building scientists, architects, and engineers in government departments.

690   US   ISSN 0010-6704
CONSTRUCTION (GUILFORD). 1933. fortn. $55. H E S, Inc., 26 Long Hill Rd., Box 362, Guilford, CT 06437-0362. TEL 203-453-3717. FAX 203-453-3717. E-mail: cn@hes.com. Ed. Sally E. Bahner; Pub. Herb Swartz. R&P contact: Herb Swartz. adv. contact: Harold Cook. illus.; circ. 6,900 (controlled). **Indexed:** Chem.Abstr., Eng.Ind.
—UnCover.

690   UK
CONSTRUCTION AFRICA. (Supplement to: African Review of Business & Technology) m. free. Alain Charles Publishing Ltd., Alain Charles House, 27 Wilfred St., London SW1E 6PR, England. TEL 44-171-834-7676. FAX 44-171-973-0076. TELEX 297165 ACPLTD G. **Document type:** trade publication.
   Description: Covers all aspects of building construction.

690 620   CN   ISSN 0700-9178
CONSTRUCTION ALBERTA NEWS. 1974. 2/w. Can.$235. Construction Alberta News Ltd., 10536 106th St., Edmonton, AB T5H 2X8, Canada. TEL 403-424-1146. FAX 403-425-5886. Ed. Don Coates; Pub. Don Coates. adv. contact: Jack Turner. circ. 4,125 (controlled). **Document type:** trade publication.

690.028 621.9   US
CONSTRUCTION AND AGGREGATES MACHINERY EN ESPANOL. (Text in Spanish) 1987. q. $60 (free to qualified personnel). Construction & Aggregates Machinery Group, 5600 S.W. 135th Ave., Ste. 107, Miami, FL 33283-3447. TEL 305-388-4890. FAX 305-388-4991. Ed. Jose A. Climent; Pub. Jerry Estevez. adv.: B&W page $2143, color page $3152; trim 8 x 10 7/8; adv. contact: Pablo Aguila. illus.; tr.lit. circ. 17,016. **Document type:** trade publication.
   Supersedes in part: Construction and Mining Machinery en Espanol.
   Description: Contains technical news, new product reviews, job stories and machinery applications stories for readers in 22 Spanish-speaking countries.

BUILDING AND CONSTRUCTION 879

690 624 UK ISSN 0950-0618
TA401 CODEN: CBUMEZ
CONSTRUCTION AND BUILDING MATERIALS. 1987. 8/yr. fl.923($530) (effective 1998). Elsevier Science Ltd., P.O. Box 800, Kidlington, Oxford OX5 1DX, England. TEL 44-1865-310366. FAX 44-1865-310898. TELEX 83111 BHPOXF G. E-mail: nlinfo-f@elsevier.nl; usinfo-f@elsevier.com; foringo-kyf04035@niftyserve.or.jp; URL: http://www.elsevier.nl/. (Subscr. to: Elsevier Science, Regional Sales Office, P.O. Box 211, 1000 AE Amsterdam, Netherlands. TEL 31-20-4853757. FAX 31-20-4853432; Subscr. in the Americas to: Elsevier Science, Regional Sales Office, Box 945, New York, NY 10159-0945. TEL 212-633-3730. FAX 212-633-3680; Subscr. in Australasia and the Far East to: Elsevier Science (Singapore) Pte Ltd, No.1 Temasek Ave., No.17-01 Millenia Tower, Singapore 039192, Singapore. TEL 65-434-3727. FAX 65-337-2230) Ed. B. Donovan. bk.rev. (also avail. in microform from UMI; back issues avail.) Indexed: Alloys Ind., ASCA, Biodet.Abstr., C.R.I.Abstr., C.R.I.Curr.Cont., Eng.Mat.Abstr., HRIS, Intl.Polym.Sci.& Tech., Mat.Sci.Cit.Ind., Met.Abstr., Met.Abstr.Ind., Nonfer.Met.Alert, PCC Alert, RAPRA, Steels Alert, World Alum.Abstr., World Surf.Coat. **Document type:** academic/scholarly publication.
—BLDSC (3420.950900); CISTI; Ei; Genuine Article; SWETS; UMI. **CCC**.
Description: Covers the development, application and performance of materials in all aspects of major project architecture and civil engineering.
Refereed Serial

690 624 CC ISSN 1022-5579
CONSTRUCTION AND CONTRACT NEWS. (Text in Chinese and English) 1981. bi-m. HK.$480($180) Trend Publishing (H.K.) Ltd., Sup Tower, Rm. 603, 75-83 King's Rd., North Point, Hong Kong, People's Republic of China. TEL 2802-6299. FAX 2802-6458. Ed. Jimmy Yuen; Pub. Felix Leung. R&P contact: Felix Leung. adv.: B&W page HK.$4500, color page HK.$7600; trim 213 x 289; adv. contact: Bobo Chan. tr.lit. circ. 10,000. **Document type:** trade publication.
Description: News about civil engineering in Hong Kong and China.

340 690 US ISSN 8755-7568
KF901.A75
CONSTRUCTION AND DESIGN LAW DIGEST. 1984. m. $550 (effective 1997). (National Institute of Construction Law, Inc.) Michie Company, Box 7587, Charlottesville, VA 22906-7587. TEL 804-972-7600. (looseleaf format; back issues avail.) **Document type:** newsletter.

690 PH ISSN 0115-1312
CONSTRUCTION & ENGINEERING. 1968. m. P.115($60) Asiaworld Publishing House Inc., 7514 Bagtikan, Cnr. Pasang Tamo, Makati, Metro Manilla 3117, Philippines. Ed. Rod F. Concepcion. adv. contact: Isabelo R. Mojica. circ. 11,484.

690 624 RH
CONSTRUCTION AND ENGINEERING ZIMBABWE. 1989. m. Z.$36 (effective 1995). Argosy Press, P.O. Box 2677, Harare, Zimbabwe. TEL 263-4-755084. FAX 263-4-752162. TELEX 26334 ZW. Ed. Desmond Kumbuka. adv. contact: Ruth P. Mahleka. circ. 5,000. (back issues avail.) **Document type:** trade publication.
Description: For the construction industry and all engineering disciplines.

CONSTRUCTION AND INTERIOR DIRECTORY. see BUSINESS AND ECONOMICS — Trade And Industrial Directories

690 IE ISSN 0376-7213
CONSTRUCTION AND PROPERTY NEWS. 1973. fortn. 15p. Construction and Property News Ltd., 175 N. Strand Rd., Dublin 1, Ireland. TEL 742265. FAX 741242. Ed. Andrew Murphy. adv.; bk.rev. circ. 5,202.

CONSTRUCTION & SURETY LAW NEWSLETTER. see LAW

690 340 US ISSN 0162-3176
CONSTRUCTION BRIEFINGS. 1978. m. $584 (effective 1998). Federal Publications Inc., 1120 20th St., N.W., Ste. 500 S., Washington, DC 20036-3484. TEL 202-337-7000; 800-922-4330. FAX 202-223-0755. E-mail: bbolger@fedpub.com; URL: http://www.fedpub.com. Ed. Diane Davis. (looseleaf format; back issues avail.) **Document type:** newsletter.
Description: Contains practical analysis of construction contract law topics.

690 US ISSN 0891-6535
CONSTRUCTION BULLETIN (ATLANTA). 1984. s-w. $1079. Construction Market Data, Inc., 4126 Pleasantdale Rd., Ste. A8, Atlanta, GA 30340. TEL 800-949-0276. FAX 770-613-5978. Ed. David Fullem. adv. circ. 4,500. (back issues avail.) **Document type:** bulletin.
●Also available online.

690 US
CONSTRUCTION BULLETIN (NEW HOPE). 1893. w. $125. Chapin Publishing Co., 9443 Science Center Dr., New Hope, MN 55428. TEL 612-537-7730. FAX 612-537-1363. Ed. George R. Rekela; Pub. Chris Casey. R&P contact: Chris Casey. adv. contact: John Saunders. bk.rev. circ. 5,800. **Document type:** trade publication, bulletin.
Description: Serves heavy, highway and non-residential construction industry in MN, ND and SD.

692.8 CN ISSN 0228-8788
CONSTRUCTION CANADA. (Text in English, French) 1959. bi-m. Can.$30 (effective 1997). (Construction Specifications Canada) N I B Publishing, 316 Adelaide St., W., Toronto, ON M5V 1R1, Canada. TEL 416-977-8104. FAX 416-598-0658. Ed. Jim Tobros; Pub. Jim Tobros. adv.: B&W page Can.$2135, color page Can.$3225; trim 8 1/4 x 10 3/4; adv. contact: Jim Tobros. illus.; tr.lit. circ. 8,016.
—BLDSC (3421.025000); CISTI.
Formerly (until 1980): Specification Associate (ISSN 0038-691X)
Description: Covers construction products, technology, building science for architects, engineers, specifiers and project managers.

690 340 US ISSN 0742-0889
KF901.A53
CONSTRUCTION CLAIMS CITATOR. 1982. m. $365. Select Press, Construction Industry Press, Box 9838, San Rafael, CA 94912. TEL 415-924-1612. Ed. Bruce M. Jervis. index. (looseleaf format) **Document type:** trade publication.
●Also available online. Vendor(s): NewsNet (BC12).
Description: Compiles cases involving contract claims and bid disputes.

690 340 US ISSN 0272-4561
KF901.A15
CONSTRUCTION CLAIMS MONTHLY; devoted exclusively to the problems of construction contracting. (Includes Focus on Construction Claims) 1979. m. $198 (effective Sep. 1992). Business Publishers, Inc., 951 Pershing Dr., Silver Spring, MD 20910-4464. TEL 301-587-6300. FAX 301-585-9075. Ed. Bruce M. Jervis. index. (looseleaf format) **Document type:** newsletter.
●Also available online. Vendor(s): NewsNet.
—CCC.
Description: Designed to help one avoid construction claims, settle claims quickly when they arise, and win disputes that require legislation.

690 340 US ISSN 0899-5982
CONSTRUCTION CLAIMS TRAINING GUIDE. 1988. m. $216 (effective Sep. 1992). Business Publishers, Inc., 951 Pershing Dr., Silver Spring, MD 20910-4464. TEL 301-587-6300. FAX 301-585-9075. Ed. Bruce M. Jervis. (looseleaf format) **Document type:** newsletter.
●Also available online. Vendor(s): NewsNet.
Description: Explanation of actual construction law statutes.

CONSTRUCTION CLIENT NEWSLETTER. see BUSINESS AND ECONOMICS — Accounting

CONSTRUCTION COMPANY STRATEGIST. see BUSINESS AND ECONOMICS — Management

690 US ISSN 0162-3168
CONSTRUCTION CONTRACTOR. bi-w. $680 (effective 1998). Federal Publications Inc., 1120 20th St., N.W., Ste. 500 S., Washington, DC 20036-3484. TEL 202-377-7000; 800-922-4330. FAX 202-659-2233. E-mail: bbolger@fedpub.com; URL: http://www.fedpub.com. Ed. Richard L. Shea. (looseleaf format) **Document type:** newsletter.
—CCC.
Description: Contains news and analysis of construction contract law developments and cases.

690 AT
CONSTRUCTION CONTRACTOR. m. Aus.$88($125) (effective 1996). Reed Business Publishing Pty. Ltd. (Subsidiary of: Reed International PLC), P.O. Box 5487, W. Chatswood, N.S.W. 2057, Australia. TEL 61-2-699-2411. FAX 61-2-698-3920. circ. 10,401. **Document type:** trade publication.
Description: A news magazine for the construction industry with articles relating to civil engineering, earthmoving, public works and commercial and industrial building.

690 AT
CONSTRUCTION CONTRACTOR SPECIFICATION GUIDE. a. Aus.$75 (effective 1996). Reed Business Publishing Pty. Ltd. (Subsidiary of: Reed International PLC), P.O. Box 5487, W. Chatswood, N.S.W. 2057, Australia. TEL 61-2-699-2411. FAX 61-2-698-3920. **Document type:** trade publication.
Description: Details the operating specifications of all construction plant and equipment including cranes, excavators, loaders, pumps and work platforms.

690 US ISSN 1087-9412
CONSTRUCTION DATA & NEWS COVERING OREGON. 1993. w. McGraw-Hill Companies, Princeton Rd. S-2, Box 689, Hightstown, NJ 08520-0689. TEL 800-325-2030. adv. **Document type:** newsletter, trade publication.
●Also available online.

690 US ISSN 1084-9696
CONSTRUCTION DATA & NEWS COVERING SACRAMENTO. w. McGraw-Hill Companies, Princeton Rd. S-2, Box 689, Hightstown, NJ 08520-0689. TEL 800-325-2030. adv. **Document type:** newsletter, trade publication.
●Also available online.

690 US
CONSTRUCTION DATA & NEWS COVERING WASHINGTON & ALASKA. w. McGraw-Hill Companies, Princeton Rd. S-2, Box 689, Hightstown, NJ 08520-0689. TEL 800-325-2030. adv. **Document type:** newsletter, trade publication.
●Also available online.

690 US ISSN 0010-6739
CONSTRUCTION DIGEST. 1926. s-m. $65. Construction Magazine Group Inc., Box 6132, Indianapolis, IN 46206-6132. TEL 317-329-3100. FAX 317-329-3110. URL: http://www.cmgnews.com. Ed. Bill Orth; Fred G. Johnston, Jr. R&P contact: Leah Gayheart. adv. contact: Pat Wagner. bk.rev.; circ. 11,276 (controlled). **Document type:** trade publication.
Description: For those involved in the purchase, sale, or related services of new construction equipment.

690 US ISSN 0194-8903
CONSTRUCTION DIMENSIONS MAGAZINE.* 1974. m. $30. Association of the Wall and Ceiling Industries International, 307 Annandale Rd., Ste. 200, Falls Church, VA 22042-2454. TEL 703-684-2924. FAX 703-684-2935. Ed. Kathy B. Sedgwick. adv.; bk.rev.; abstr.; stat.; tr.lit.; index. circ. 18,000. —CISTI.
Incorporating: G D C I Drywall; Which was formerly titled: Drywall Newsmagazine (ISSN 0300-7197)

690 SI ISSN 0218-1258
CONSTRUCTION ECONOMICS REPORT. (Text in English) 1988. q. $500; newsstand price: $140. Construction Industry Development Board, 9 Maxwell Rd., No. 03-00, Annexe A, MND Complex, Singapore 069112, Singapore. TEL 65-2256711. FAX 65-2257301. E-mail: cidb_enquiry@cidb.gov.sg. Ed. Teng Yew Geok. circ. 1,000.

BUILDING AND CONSTRUCTION

690   UK
CONSTRUCTION EMPLOYERS FEDERATION. BULLETIN. m. Construction Employers Federation Ltd., 143 Malone Rd., Belfast BT9 6SU, N. Ireland. TEL 44-1232-661711. FAX 44-1232-666323. E-mail: federation@cef.eunet.co.uk. Ed. Tony Doran. **Document type:** bulletin.
   Formerly: Federation of Building and Civil Engineering Contractors. Federation Bulletin.

690   US   ISSN 0192-3978
TA1
CONSTRUCTION EQUIPMENT. 1949. m. (plus a. Buyers' Guide). $95.90 (Canada $139.90; Mexico $129.90; elsewhere $179.90). Cahners Publishing Company (Des Plaines), Division of Reed Elsevier Inc., 1350 E. Touhy Ave., Box 5080, Des Plaines, IL 60018-5080. TEL 847-390-2176. FAX 847-390-2690. E-mail: marketaccess@cahners.com; URL: http://www.coneq.com; http://www.packdigest.com/mainmag/ce.htm. (Subscr. to: 8773 S. Ridgeline Blvd., Highland Ranch, CO 80126. TEL 303-470-4544) Ed. Kirk Landers; Pub. Daniel Pels. R&P contact: Kirk Landers. adv.: B&W page $8185, color page $10485; adv. contact: Maureen Phyferon. charts; illus.; stat.; tr.lit.; index. circ. 80,500. (reprint service avail. from UMI) **Indexed:** Bus.Ind., Concr.Abstr., Intl.Civil Eng.Abstr., Soft.Abstr.Eng., Tr.& Indus.Ind. **Document type:** trade publication.
   ●Also available online.
   —CISTI; SWETS; UMI. **CCC.**
   Former titles: Construction Equipment Magazine (ISSN 0010-6763); Construction Equipment and Materials Magazine.
   Description: Detailed coverage of heavy equipment and trucks. Concerned with management, purchasing, maintenance, used and new product evaluation, as well as with trends in industry, government and the economy.

690 634.9 622   US
CONSTRUCTION EQUIPMENT BUYERS' GUIDE. (Published as an issue of: Construction Equipment (ISSN 0192-3978)) vol.72, 1985. a. $44.95 per no. (included in subscr. to: Construction Equipment). Cahners Publishing Company (Des Plaines), Division of Reed Elsevier Inc., 1350 E. Touhy Ave., Box 5080, Des Plaines, IL 60018-5080. TEL 847-635-8800. FAX 847-390-2690. (Subscr. to: 8773 S. Ridgeline Blvd., Highlands Ranch, CO 80126-2329. TEL 303-470-4445) Ed. Kirk Landers; Pub. Daniel Pels. R&P contact: Kirk Landers. adv. contact: Maureen Pyferon. circ. 80,000. (reprint service avail.) **Document type:** directory.

690   US   ISSN 0010-6755
HD9715.U5
CONSTRUCTION EQUIPMENT DISTRIBUTION. 1936. m. $40 to non-members; members $20. Associated Equipment Distributors, 615 W. 22nd St., Oak Brook, IL 60521. TEL 708-574-6050. Ed. Edward Salek. adv.; illus. circ. 4,600.

690   US   ISSN 1058-787X
CONSTRUCTION EQUIPMENT GUIDE (MIDATLANTIC EDITION). 1957. fortn. $60. Edwin M. McKeon, Ed. & Pub., 2627 Mt. Carmel Ave., Glenside, PA 19038. TEL 215-885-2900. FAX 215-885-2910. Ed. Beth Baker. adv.; tr.lit. circ. 27,256. (tabloid format) **Document type:** newspaper, trade publication.
   Description: Provides current construction news, new and used equipment, auctions and projects.

690   US   ISSN 1081-7034
CONSTRUCTION EQUIPMENT GUIDE (MIDWEST EDITION). bi-w. $60. Edwin M. McKeon, Ed. & Pub., 2627 Mt. Carmel Ave., Glenside, PA 19038. TEL 215-885-2900. FAX 215-885-2910. circ. 29,106. **Document type:** newspaper, trade publication.

690   US
CONSTRUCTION EQUIPMENT GUIDE (NORTHEAST EDITION). fortn. Edwin M. McKeon, Ed. & Pub., 2627 Mt. Carmel Ave., Glenside, PA 19038. TEL 215-885-2900. FAX 215-885-2910. **Document type:** newspaper, trade publication.
   Description: Provides current construction news, new and used equipment, auctions and projects.

690   US   ISSN 1058-6474
CONSTRUCTION EQUIPMENT GUIDE (SOUTHEAST EDITION). bi-m. $60. Edwin M. McKeon, Ed. & Pub., 2627 Mt. Carmel Ave., Glenside, PA 19038. TEL 215-885-2900. FAX 215-885-2910. circ. 26,641. **Document type:** newspaper, trade publication.

690.028   US   ISSN 0010-6771
CONSTRUCTION EQUIPMENT OPERATION AND MAINTENANCE. 1948. bi-m. $12. Construction Publications, Inc., Box 1689, Cedar Rapids, IA 52406. TEL 319-366-1597. FAX 319-362-8808. Ed. Barry Butters; Pub. Clark K. Parks. R&P contact: Barry Butters. adv. contact: Gavin McComas. bk.rev.; tr.lit.; circ. 64,200. (tabloid format) **Document type:** trade publication.
   Description: Includes "how-to-do-it" type information for users of construction equipment as well as industry news and features.

690   UK   ISSN 0964-0665
CONSTRUCTION EUROPE. 1990. m. $140. K H L International Ltd., Southfields, Southview Rd., Wadhurst, E. Sussex TN5 6TP, England. TEL 44-1892-784088. FAX 44-1892-784086. E-mail: cranes@khl.com; URL: http://ourworld.compuserve.com/homepages/cranes. Ed. Paul Marsden; Pub. James King. R&P contact: Peter Watkinson. adv.: B&W page £3335, color page £4575; trim 297 x 210; adv. contact: Peter Gilmore. bk.rev. circ. 15,454. **Document type:** trade publication.
   Description: Reports on the effects of the single European market on Europe's construction industry and general construction related information.

690 720   UK   ISSN 0267-7768
TH15
CONSTRUCTION HISTORY. 1985. a. £55 (foreign £70). Chartered Institute of Building, Englemere, Kings Ride, Ascot, Berks. SL5 8BJ, England. TEL 01334-23355. FAX 01344-23467. Eds. Robert Thorne, Christopher Powell. abstr. (back issues avail.) **Indexed:** Amer.Hist.& Life (1985-), Hist.Abstr. (1985-).
   —BLDSC (3421.294000).
   Formerly: Construction Science.

338.4   US   ISSN 0069-9187
CONSTRUCTION IN HAWAII. 1967. a. free. Bank of Hawaii, Economics Department, Box 2900, Honolulu, HI 96846. TEL 808-537-8307. FAX 808-536-9433. URL: http://www.boh.com/econ/. Ed. Paul H. Brewbaker. circ. 8,000. (back issues avail.)
   Formerly: Housing Activity in Hawaii.
   Description: Reports all facets of construction activities in Hawaii in the previous year, and includes industry forecast.

690   II
CONSTRUCTION INDUSTRIES AND TRADE ANNUAL. 1968. a. Ad International, Sayajiganj, Baroda 390005, India. TEL 64158. (Alt. addr.: c/o Public Relations and Mass Communications, Palejwala Bldg., Sayajiganj, Baroda 5, India) Parshuram Bldg. adv. contact: C.M. Pandit. circ. 4,200.
   Formerly: Construction Industries and Trade Journal (ISSN 0010-6828)

CONSTRUCTION INDUSTRIES OF MASSACHUSETTS DIRECTORY; a directory and catalog of highway and heavy construction in New England. see *BUSINESS AND ECONOMICS — Trade And Industrial Directories*

690 332   US
CONSTRUCTION INDUSTRY ANNUAL FINANCIAL SURVEY. 1989. a. $149. Construction Financial Management Association, 707 State Rd., Ste. 223, Princeton, NJ 08540-1413. TEL 609-683-5000. FAX 609-683-4821. Ed. Paula A. Wristen. adv.: B&W page $1550; adv. contact: Sarah G. Patt. circ. 2,000. (back issues avail.) **Document type:** trade publication.
   Description: Construction industry's only financial performance report. Includes financial data, accounting methods, insurance issues, and corporate policies and procedures.

690   AT
CONSTRUCTION INDUSTRY IN TOOWOOMBA. 1987. irreg. Toowoomba Regional Development Corporation Ltd., Town Hall, 541 Ruthven St., Toowoomba, Qld. 4350, Australia. TEL 076-385977.
   Description: Details of businesses related to construction within the city of Toowoomba, Queensland.

CONSTRUCTION INDUSTRY LAW LETTER. see *LAW*

CONSTRUCTION INJURY LIABILITY MONTHLY. see *LAW*

690   CN
CONSTRUCTION INNOVATION/INNOVATION EN CONSTRUCTION. (Consists of: Building Performance News (ISSN 0843-6487); C C M C News (ISSN 1188-0783); Materials News (ISSN 1188-4096); N B C - N F C News (ISSN 0848-600X); Structures News (ISSN 1188-407X); Alberta Fire News (ISSN 0848-4259)) q. free. National Research Council of Canada, Institute for Research in Construction, Ottawa, ON K1A 0R6, Canada. TEL 613-993-2463; 800-672-7990. FAX 613-952-7673. Ed.Bd.

CONSTRUCTION LABOR NEWS. see *BUSINESS AND ECONOMICS — Labor And Industrial Relations*

CONSTRUCTION LABOR REPORT. see *BUSINESS AND ECONOMICS — Labor And Industrial Relations*

690   US
CONSTRUCTION: LATIN AMERICAN INDUSTRIAL REPORT. (Avail. for each of 22 Latin American countries) 1985. a. $435 per country report. Aquino Productions, Box 125, Rochester, VT 05767. Ed. Andres C. Aquino.

690 340   UK
CONSTRUCTION LAW. 10/yr. £149 (foreign £195) (effective Oct. 1996). Eclipse Group Ltd., School of Business and Industrial Management, 18-20 Highbury Pl., London N5 1QP, England. TEL 44-171-384-5858. FAX 44-171-226-8106. stat. **Document type:** trade publication.
   Description: Focuses on the legal issues that arise in management in the construction industry.

690 340   US   ISSN 1071-7668
KF1950.A15
CONSTRUCTION LAW ADVISER; monthly practical advice for lawyers and construction professionals. 1983. m. $295. Clark - Boardman - Callaghan Company, Inc., 155 Pfingsten Rd., Deerfield, IL 60015. TEL 800-323-1336. FAX 708-948-9340. Ed. Bob Bouchard. index. (looseleaf format) **Document type:** newsletter.

690 340   UK   ISSN 0267-2359
K3
CONSTRUCTION LAW JOURNAL. 1984. q. £146. Sweet & Maxwell, South Quay Plaza, 7th Fl., 183 Marsh Wall, London E14 9FT, England. TEL 071-538-8686. FAX 071-538-9508. Ed. Harry Ulaeto. adv. contact: Jackie Wood. (reprint service avail. from RRI,WSH) **Indexed:** Euro.LJI, L.R.I., LJI. **Document type:** trade publication.
   —BLDSC (3421.328000).

692.8   CN   ISSN 0827-3480
CONSTRUCTION LAW LETTER. 1984. bi-m. Can.$120 (foreign $120). Build - Law Publications Inc., 253 College St., Ste. 286, Toronto, Ont. M5T 1R5, Canada. TEL 416-978-4799. FAX 416-395-0459. Ed. Paul Sandori. bk.rev.; index. circ. 1,500. (back issues avail.)
   Description: Summaries of construction-related court decisions across Canada.

CONSTRUCTION LAW REPORTS. see *LAW*

690 340   US   ISSN 0272-0116
KF1950.A15
CONSTRUCTION LAWYER. 4/yr. $40 (effective 1997). (American Bar Association, Forum Committee on the Construction Industry) A B A Press, 750 N. Lake Shore Dr., Chicago, IL 60611. TEL 312-988-6063. FAX 312-988-6281. URL: http://www.abanet.org. Ed. Charles A. Meeker. R&P contact: Richard Vittenson. circ. 3,455. **Indexed:** C.L.I., L.R.I. **Document type:** newsletter.
   —UnCover.
   Description: Legal developments in the construction industry.

BUILDING AND CONSTRUCTION

690 340   US   ISSN 0279-1102
KF901.A75
CONSTRUCTION LITIGATION REPORTER; recent decisions of national significance. 1979. m. $340. Clark - Boardman - Callaghan Company, Inc., 155 Pfingsten Rd., Deerfield, IL 60015. TEL 800-422-2101. Ed. Mark Schneier. bibl.; index. (looseleaf format; back issues avail.) **Document type**: newsletter.
—CCC.
Description: Legal developments and summaries of cases affecting construction law.

690 658   UK   ISSN 0268-2478
CONSTRUCTION MANAGEMENT.* 1983. bi-m. R.J. Dodd Publishing Ltd., c/o Millbank Publications Ltd., 25 Catherine St., London WC23 5JW, England. Ed. Richard Kruger. adv. circ. 9,600. **Indexed**: Build.Manage.Abstr.

690   UK
CONSTRUCTION MANAGEMENT AND ECONOMICS. 1983. bi-m. £395 (foreign $660) (effective 1998). Thomson Professional (Subsidiary of: International Thomson Publishing Group), 2-6 Boundary Row, London SE1 8HN, England. TEL 44-171-8650066. FAX 44-171-5229623. TELEX 290164 CHAPMA G. E-mail: journal@rapidcom.co.uk; URL: http://jpr.thomsonprofessional.com. (Dist. by: International Thomson Publishing Services Ltd., Cheriton House, North Way, Andover, Hants. SP10 5BE, England. TEL 44-1264-342713. FAX 44-1264-342807; Subscr. in US & Canada to: 400 Market St., Philadelphia, PA 19106. TEL 800-552-5866) Eds. Ranko Bon, Will Hughes. adv.; bk.rev. (reprint service avail.) **Indexed**: ABI Inform., Build.Manage.Abstr. **Document type**: academic/scholarly publication.
●Also available online.
—BLDSC (3421.358100); CISTI; SWETS; UMI; UnCover. **CCC**.
Incorporates (1986-198?): International Journal of Construction Management and Technology; **Formerly**: Journal of Construction Industry Economics and Management (ISSN 0144-6193)
Description: Focuses on research, case studies and innovative practice in the building industry; subjects include architecture, building, civil engineering, economics, management, planning and surveying.
Refereed Serial

690   UK
TH1
CONSTRUCTION MANAGER. 1963. m. £40 (foreign £50). (Chartered Institute of Building) Englemere Services Ltd., Englemere, Kings Ride, Ascot, Berks. SL5 7TB, England. TEL 44-1344-23355. FAX 44-1344-23467. Ed. Connal Vickers. adv. contact: Pauline Sargent. bk.rev. circ. 25,000. (also avail. in microform from UMI; reprint service avail. from UMI) **Indexed**: Archit.Per.Ind., Br.Tech.Ind., C.I.S. Abstr., Int.Build.Serv.Abstr., Intl.Civil Eng.Abstr., RICS, Soft.Abstr.Eng., World Surf.Coat. **Document type**: trade publication.
—CISTI; Linda Hall; UMI.
Former titles (until 1995): Chartered Builder (ISSN 0957-8773); Building Technology and Management (ISSN 0007-3709)
Description: Contains articles on technical and management aspects of building, together with reports on conferences and seminars.

690   CN   ISSN 0832-5804
CONSTRUCTION MANITOBA. 1987. q. Can.$12. (Winnipeg Construction Association) Sanford Evans Communications Ltd., 1077 Church Ave., Box 6900, Winnipeg, MB R3C 3B1, Canada. TEL 204-775-0201. FAX 204-783-7488. Ed. G. Greasley. adv. circ. 1,064.
Description: Covers the construction industry in the province of Manitoba.

690   KO
CONSTRUCTION MATERIAL PRICES/WOLGAN KONSOL MULKA. (Text in Korean) 1970. m. 9000 Won($12) Construction Association of Korea, 71-2 Nonhyun-dong, Kangnam-ku, Seoul 135-701, S. Korea. Ed. Suh Joo-Whan. adv. circ. 2,000.

690   UK
CONSTRUCTION MIDLANDS. 10/yr. Sta. Bldgs., Maclure Rd., Rochdale, Lancs OL11 1DN, England. TEL 0706-58880. FAX 071-0706-59403. Ed. J. McClelland. circ. 11,600.

690   UK
CONSTRUCTION MONITOR. Issued with: Building (ISSN 0007-3318) 10/yr. free. Department of Environment, Rm. C1-01a, 2 Marsham St., London SW1P 3EB, England. TEL 44-171-276-6600. FAX 44-171-276-3826. Ed. David Broyd. circ. 35,000. **Document type**: newsletter, government publication.
Formerly (until 1994): Euronews Construction.
Description: Provides information about the construction industry in the U.K., including health, legal, financial and governmental aspects. Includes calendar of events.

690   UK   ISSN 0010-6860
CONSTRUCTION NEWS. (Supplement avail.) 1871. w. £72.50 (rest of Europe £95; elsewhere £125). Construction Publications Ltd., 2-6 Boundary Row, London SE1 8HN, England. TEL 44-171-410-6611. FAX 44-171-522-9648. Ed. John Pullin; Pub. Geoff Hall. adv. contact: Simon Elgar. bk.rev.; illus. **Indexed**: Archit.Per.Ind., Build.Manage.Abstr., C.I.S. Abstr., Fluidex, RICS, W.R.C.Inf. **Document type**: trade publication.
—BLDSC (3421.750000); CISTI.

690   US   ISSN 0160-5607
TH1
CONSTRUCTION NEWS.* 1934. s-m. $65. Construction News Publishing Company, 10825 Financial Centre Pkwy., Ste. 133, Little Rock, AR 72211-3555. TEL 501-376-1931. FAX 501-375-5831. Ed. Robert J. Alvey. adv.; bk.rev. circ. 7,500. **Indexed**: Fluidex, RICS, W.R.C.Inf. **Document type**: trade publication.
Description: Covers Arkansas, Oklahoma, western Tennessee, Mississippi, Louisiana.

690   UK   ISSN 0267-5137
CONSTRUCTION NEWS PRODUCTS.* 1983. bi-m. E M A P - Construct, 151 Rosebery Ave., London EC1 4QR, England. TEL 071-935-6611. FAX 071-722-0257. TELEX 299973-ITP-LM-G. Ed. D. Taylor. circ. 41,000.
—BLDSC (3421.752200).

690   US   ISSN 1088-3711
▼**CONSTRUCTION NEWS WEEKLY COVERING LONG ISLAND**. 1995. w. McGraw-Hill Companies, Princeton Rd. S-2, Box 689, Hightstown, NJ 08520-0689. TEL 800-325-2030. adv. **Document type**: newsletter, trade publication.
●Also available online.
Description: Provides information on what jobs are coming up for bid or negotiation.

690   US   ISSN 0892-3337
CONSTRUCTION NEWS WEST. w. McGraw-Hill Companies, Princeton Rd. S-2, Box 689, Hightstown, NJ 08520-0689. TEL 800-325-2030. adv.
Document type: newsletter, trade publication.
●Also available online.
Formerly: Construction Week (ISSN 0744-1568)

CONSTRUCTION NEWSLETTER. see *OCCUPATIONAL HEALTH AND SAFETY*

CONSTRUCTION NICHE BUILDER. see *BUSINESS AND ECONOMICS — Public Finance, Taxation*

690   UK
CONSTRUCTION NORTH. 10/yr. Sta. Bldgs., Maclure Rd., Rochdale OL11 1DN, England. TEL 0706-58880. FAX 0706-59403. Ed. J. McCleland. circ. 10,600.

690   UK
THE CONSTRUCTION PLANT - HIRE ASSOCIATION BULLETIN. 10/yr. membership. 28 Eccleston St., London SW1W 9PY, England. TEL 44-171-730-7117. FAX 0171-730-7110. Ed. Linda Malcolm. R&P contact: Linda Malcolm. **Document type**: trade publication.
Description: Contains information relating to plant hire companies in the U.K.

CONSTRUCTION RECORD. see *ENGINEERING — Civil Engineering*

691   UK   ISSN 0967-0726
CODEN: CEPAET
CONSTRUCTION REPAIR. 1985. bi-m. £54($110) Palladian Publications Ltd., The Old Forge, Elstead, Surrey GU8 6DD, England. TEL 01252-703900. FAX 01252-703901. Ed. Paul Maxwell-Cook. adv. contact: Rod Hardy. circ. 2,000. (back issues avail.) **Indexed**: Biodet.Abstr., W.R.C.Inf., World Surf.Coat. **Document type**: trade publication.
—BLDSC (3421.765500); CISTI; Ei; Linda Hall; SWETS; UMI.
Former titles: International Journal of Construction Maintenance and Repair (ISSN 0959-5090); (until 1990): Construction Repair (ISSN 0951-0346); Construction Repair and Maintenance.

690   US
CONSTRUCTION RISK MANAGEMENT. 1984. q. $226 (renewal $133). International Risk Management Institute, Inc., 12222 Merit Dr., Ste. 1660, Dallas, TX 75251-2217. TEL 214-960-7693. FAX 214-960-6037. Ed. Ann Rudd. (looseleaf format)
Description: Covers insurance and risk management considerations for contracting organizations of any type.

690   US   ISSN 0010-6925
TH425   CODEN: COSPAJ
CONSTRUCTION SPECIFIER; for commercial and industrial construction. 1950. m. $36 to non-members; universities $30. Construction Specifications Institute, 601 Madison St., Alexandria, VA 22314. TEL 703-684-0300. FAX 708-684-0465. URL: http://www.csinet.org. Ed. Jack Reeder; Pub. Jack Reeder. R&P contact: Jack Reeder. adv.; bk.rev.; index. circ. 19,000. **Indexed**: Avery Ind.Archit.Per., Concr.Abstr., Eng.Ind., Search (1990-).
—BLDSC (3421.865000); CISTI; Ei; Linda Hall; UnCover. **CCC**.
Description: Covers technology, materials and law, in non-residential commercial construction.

690   AT
CONSTRUCTION SUPERVISOR. 1967. bi-m. Aus.$0.30 per no. (Australian Institute of Construction Supervisors) Percival Publishing Co. Pty. Ltd., 862-870 Elizabeth St., Waterloo, N. S. W. 2017, Australia. **Indexed**: Build.Manage.Abstr.

690 330   US
CONSTRUCTION SURVEY. m. $30. Dun & Bradstreet, Economic Analysis Department, 220 E. 42nd St., 9th Fl., New York, NY 10017-4717. FAX 212-883-3400. (Subscr. to: Box 1861, New York, NY 10163-1861)
Description: Nationwide survey of 200 construction firms regarding their current conditions and expectations for the upcoming months.

690   US   ISSN 0744-2149
CONSTRUCTION TIMES. 1977. m. $12. Webco Publishing, Inc., Box 268, Stillwater, MN 55082. TEL 612-430-1113. Ed. Bill Baker. adv. circ. 15,365.

691   AT   ISSN 0010-695X
CONSTRUCTIONAL REVIEW. 1927. q. Aus.$40 (Asia & Oceania Aus.$50; elsewhere Aus.$60). Cement and Concrete Association of Australia, 25 Berry St., N. Sydney, N.S.W. 2060, Australia. TEL 61-2-99233213. FAX 61-2-99231925. Ed. Diane Kell. adv. contact: Diane Kell. bk.rev.; abstr.; charts; illus.; circ. 2,000 (paid). **Indexed**: Aus.Rd.Ind., Br.Tech.Ind., C.R.I.Abstr., C.R.I.Curr.Cont., Geotech.Abstr., Intl.Civil Eng.Abstr., Soft.Abstr.Eng. **Document type**: trade publication.
—CISTI; Linda Hall; UnCover. **CCC**.
Description: Reviews buildings constructed of concrete.

690   FR   ISSN 0010-6976
CONSTRUCTIONS EQUIPEMENTS POUR LES LOISIRS. (Annual Number) (Text in French; summaries in English, German) 1961. bi-m. 75 F.($15) Techno-Loisirs, 3 rue Sivel, Paris -14e, France. Ed. Georges E. Caille. adv.; bk.rev.; bibl.; charts; illus.; cum.index. circ. 7,000. **Document type**: trade publication.

BUILDING AND CONSTRUCTION

690   AG   ISSN 0010-7018
CONSTRUCTOR. 1901. w. Arg.$96($96) for 6 mos. Constructor s.r.l., Hipolito Yrigoyen 615, Piso 7, 1086 Buenos Aires, Argentina. TEL 54-1-343-0716. FAX 54-1-331-9368. Ed. Marcelo Daniel Donadio. adv.; bk.rev. circ. 15,000. (tabloid format)

690   US   ISSN 0162-6191
TH1
CONSTRUCTOR; the management magazine of the construction industry. 1919. m. $100 to non-members; members $15. (Associated General Contractors of America) A G C Information Inc., 1957 E St., N.W., Washington, DC 20006. TEL 202-393-2040. FAX 202-628-7369. URL: http://agc.org. Ed. Ben Herring; Pub. Donald Scott. R&P contact: Ben Herring. TEL 202-383-2768. adv.; B&W page $3450, color page $3850; adv. contact: Jeff Smith. bk.rev.; tr.lit.; index. circ. 44,000. Indexed: Build.Manage.Abstr., Concr.Abstr., HRIS, Intl.Civil Eng.Abstr., Soft.Abstr.Eng. **Document type:** trade publication.
—BLDSC (3423.000000); CISTI; Linda Hall; UnCover.
    Description: Contains feature material on markets, equipment, manpower and money.

690   SP   ISSN 1135-402X
CONSTRUCTORS. 1977. 11/yr. 3500 ptas. Editorial Interpress' S.L., C. Benedicto Mateo 8-10, Bjs., 08034 Barcelona, Spain. TEL 3-280-05-22. FAX 3-205-46-20. Ed. J. Fernandez Martorell. adv. circ. 5,000.
    Formerly (until 1994): Gremi de Constructors d'Obres de Barcelona i Comarques. Revista.

690   SZ   ISSN 0010-7034
CONSTRUIRE. m. 30 Fr. Federation Romande de Metiers du Batiment, 10 rue de Beaumont, Case 339, 1211 Geneva 25, Switzerland. (Co-sponsor: Groupement Romand des Maitres Ferblantiers et Appareilleurs) Ed. P. Schuetz. adv.; illus.; stat. circ. 2,565.

690   MR   ISSN 0851-0210
CONSTRUIRE; hebdomadaire du batiment et des travaux publics du Maroc. 1940. w. DH.340 (foreign DH.440) (effective 1994). Societe Nouvelle Construire, 25 rue d'Azilal, B.P. 10902 Casa Bandoeng, Casablanca, Morocco. Ed. Bouchaib Talal. adv. **Document type:** trade publication.
    Description: Covers the construction and public works sector in Morocco

690   CN   ISSN 0833-0239
CONSTRUIRE. (Text in French) 1986. bi-m. Can.$28.43($60) Association de la Construction du Quebec, 4970 Place de la Savane, Montreal, PQ H4P 1Z6, Canada. TEL 514-739-2381. FAX 514-739-8933. E-mail: acqprov@total.net. (Dist. addr.: 7875 Trans-Canada Rd., St. Laurent, PQ H4S 1L3, Canada. TEL 514-333-7480. FAX 514-332-6915; Subscr. to: 4970 Place de la Savane, Montreal, PQ H4P 1Z6, Canada. TEL 514-739-2381. FAX 514-739-8933) Ed. Christiane Rioux. adv.; B&W page Can.$2075, color page Can.$2675, trim 8 1/8 x 10 7/8; adv. contact: Pierre Leduc. circ. 18,683 (controlled). (back issues avail.) **Document type:** trade publication.
—CISTI.
    Incorporated (1988-1990): Contact C S S T (ISSN 1182-1558)
    Description: Focuses on major construction projects within the renovation, building materials, research and development projects, professional continuing education, and health and security sectors on project sites.

CONSUMER HOME AND GARDEN. see *GARDENING AND HORTICULTURE*

692.8   UK
HD9715.G72
CONTRACT JOURNAL. 1879. w. £102. Reed Business Information (Subsidiary of: Reed Elsevier group), Quadrant House, The Quadrant, Sutton, Surrey SM2 5AS, England. TEL 44-181-652-4805. FAX 44-181-652-4804. (Subscr. to: Quadrant Subscription Services, Oakfield House, Perrymount Rd., Haywards Heath, W. Sussex RH16 3DH, England. TEL 44-1444-445566) Ed. L. Clifford. adv.; bk.rev.; charts; illus.; mkt.; pat.; tr.lit. circ. 45,000. (also avail. in microfilm) Indexed: Archit.Per.Ind., Br.Tech.Ind., Build.Manage.Abstr., C.I.S.Abstr., Fuel & Energy Abstr., Geo.Abstr.P.G., HRIS, Intl.Civil Eng.Abstr., Key to Econ.Sci., RICS, Soft.Abstr.Eng., W.R.C.Inf. **Document type:** trade publication.
—BLDSC (3425.800000); CISTI; Ei; EMDOCS; KR SourceOne; UMI. **CCC**.
    Former titles (until 1979): U K Plant Hire Guide (ISSN 0307-2630); Contract Journal (ISSN 0010-7859)

690   US   ISSN 0897-7135
HD9715.U5
CONTRACTOR; the newsmagazine of mechanical contracting. 1954. m. $79.90 (Canada $104.90; Mexico $99.90; elsewhere $149.90). Cahners Publishing Company (Des Plaines), Division of Reed Elsevier Inc., 1350 E. Touhy Ave., Box 5080, Des Plaines, IL 60018-5080. TEL 847-390-2110. FAX 847-390-2690. E-mail: b.mader@cahners.com; URL: http://www.contractormag.com. (Subscr. to: Box 7500, Highlands Ranch, CO 80126-7500. TEL 303-470-4000) Ed. Robert Miodonski; Pub. Bill Everham. R&P contact: Robert Miodonski. adv. contact: Pam Raca. charts; illus.; stat.; tr.lit. circ. 52,200. (tabloid format; also avail. in microfilm; back issues avail.; reprint service avail. from UMI) Indexed: Tr.& Indus.Ind. **Document type:** trade publication.
—CISTI; UMI. **CCC**.
    Description: For air conditioning, heating, fire protection, piping, refrigeration, plumbing, contractors.

692.8   US
CONTRACTORS EQUIPMENT GUIDE. 1960. bi-w. $70. 50 Central Ave., Box 324, Needham Heights, MA 02194. TEL 617-449-1250; 800-225-8448. FAX 617-449-7768. adv.; B&W page $950. circ. 29,969. (tabloid format) **Document type:** catalog.
    Description: Covers new and used construction equipment.

690 720   US   ISSN 0273-5954
CONTRACTORS GUIDE; the guide to the roofing, insulation, siding, solar, and window industries. 1978. 12/yr. $26. Century Communications Corp., 6201 W. Howard St., Niles, IL 60714-3435. TEL 847-647-1200. FAX 847-647-7055. Ed. Greg Ettling. adv.; bk.rev.; circ. 32,000 (controlled). (also avail. in microform from UMI) **Document type:** trade publication.
—UMI.
    Formerly: Insulator's Guide (ISSN 0192-8457)

658   US   ISSN 0192-6330
CONTRACTORS HOT LINE. w. $99 in US; Canada $109; Mexico $119. Heartland Communications Group, Inc., 1003 Central Ave., Fort Dodge, IA 50501. TEL 515-955-1600; 800-247-2000. FAX 515-955-6636. URL: http:www.contractorshotline.com. circ. 50,000. (tabloid format)
    Description: Brings together buyers and sellers of new and used construction equipment nationwide.

CONTRACTORS HOT LINE EQUIPMENT GUIDE ANNUAL AND MONTHLY UPDATES. see *PUBLISHING AND BOOK TRADE*

690   TH
CONTRACTORS MAGAZINE. m. Nirapai Turakij, 1909-376 Soi Ruampattana, Charansanidwong, Bangkoknoi, Bangkok 10700, Thailand. TEL 02-4355888. FAX 02-4357958. Ed. Rattapol Khanchit. adv. contact: Jiraphorn Nirapai.

CO-OPSERVATIONS. see *HOUSING AND URBAN PLANNING*

690   AT
CORDELL CONSTRUCTION REPORTS. (In 7 Sections: Commercial; Community; Civil Engineering; Industrial; Flats & Units; Housing; Mining) 1972. w. price varies. Cordell Building Information Services (Subsidiary of: Thomson Publications (Australia) Pty. Ltd.), P.O. Box 124, St. Leonards, N.S.W. 2065, Australia. TEL 61-2-934-5555. circ. 6,500.
    ●Also available online.

690   AT   ISSN 1320-4319
CORDELL'S BUILDING COST GUIDE. COMMERCIAL AND INDUSTRIAL. 1971. q. Aus.$330($434) Cordell Building Information Services (Subsidiary of: Thomson Publications (Australia) Pty. Ltd.), P.O. Box 124, St. Leonards, N.S.W. 2065, Australia. adv. circ. 6,000.
    Former titles: Cordell's Building Cost Guide. New Construction; Cordell's Building Cost Book and Estimating Guide. New South Wales (ISSN 0311-2497); Cordell's Building Price Book and Estimating Guide. New South Wales.

690   AT   ISSN 1320-4653
CORDELL'S BUILDING COST GUIDE. HOUSING. q. Aus.$330($434) Cordell Building Information Services (Subsidiary of: Thomson Publications (Australia) Pty. Ltd.), P.O. Box 124, St. Leonards, N.S.W. 2065, Australia.
    Formerly: Cordell's Cost Guide. Housing Alterations and Additions.

690   AT   ISSN 0311-7472
CORDELL'S PRICE INDEX OF BUILDING MATERIALS. fortn. Aus.$330. Cordell Building Information Services (Subsidiary of: Thomson Publications (Australia) Pty. Ltd.), P.O. Box 124, St. Leonards, N.S.W. 2065, Australia.

690   AT
CORDELL'S WHO'S WHO IN BUILDING: ARCHITECTS. a. Cordell Building Information Services (Subsidiary of: Thomson Publications (Australia) Pty. Ltd.), P.O. Box 124, St. Leonards, N.S.W. 2065, Australia. TEL 61-2-934-5555. FAX 61-2-934-5501. **Document type:** directory.
    Formerly: Cordell's Who's Who in Building: Non-Housing.

690   AT
CORDELL'S WHO'S WHO IN BUILDING: BUILDERS. a. Cordell Building Information Services (Subsidiary of: Thomson Publications (Australia) Pty. Ltd.), P.O. Box 124, St. Leonards, N.S.W. 2065, Australia. TEL 61-2-934-5555. FAX 61-2-934-5501. **Document type:** directory.
    Formerly: Cordell's Who's Who in Building: Housing.

690 721   AT
CORDELL'S WHO'S WHO IN BUILDING: DEVELOPERS. a. Cordell Building Information Services (Subsidiary of: Thomson Publications (Australia) Pty. Ltd.), P.O. Box 124, St. Leonards, N.S.W. 2065, Australia. TEL 61-2-934-5555. FAX 61-2-934-5501. **Document type:** directory.
    Formerly: Cordell's Who's Who in Design Specifying.

690   SP
CORREO DE LA CONSTRUCCION. fortn. Ediciones Roda, S.L., Corcega 204 bajos, Barcelona, Spain. TEL 93-3223951. FAX 93-419-24-63. adv.; B&W page 173000 ptas., color page 231000 ptas. circ. 23,000. **Document type:** newspaper.

690   IT   ISSN 0391-6286
CORRIERE DEI COSTRUTTORI. Variant title: Nuovo Corriere dei Costruttori. 1921. m. L.95000 (foreign L.180000) (effective 1996). (Associazione Nazionale Costruttori Edili) Edilstampa s.r.l., Via Guattani 24, 00161 Rome, Italy. TEL 39-6-84881. FAX 39-6-44232981. Ed. Alfredo Martini. adv.; bk.rev.; bibl.; illus. circ. 25,000. **Document type:** trade publication.

690   IT   ISSN 1121-6336
COSTRUIRE. 1982. 12/yr. L.93000 (foreign L.131000). Editrice Abitare Segesta S.p.A., Corso Monforte 15, 20122 Milan, Italy. TEL 39-2-760901. FAX 39-2-76021904. Ed. Prof. Leonardo Fiori. adv. contact: Pierluigi Bollini. circ. 39,647. **Document type:** consumer publication.
    Formerly (until 1987): Costruire per Abitare (ISSN 1121-6328)

BUILDING AND CONSTRUCTION

690   IT   ISSN 0589-8765
COSTRUTTORI ITALIANI NEL MONDO. 1955. 4/yr. L.90000 (foreign L.150000) (effective 1996). (Associazione Nazionale Costruttori Edili, Settore Lavori all'Estero) Edilstampa s.r.l., Via Guattani 24, 00161 Rome, Italy. TEL 39-6-84881. FAX 39-6-44232981. Ed. Luciano Melini. circ. 3,000.

690   IT   ISSN 0010-9657
COSTRUTTORI ROMANI. 1965; N.S. vol.4 no.9, 1990. m. free. Associazione dei Costruttori Edili di Roma e Provincia, Via di Villa Patrizi, 11, 00161 Rome, Italy. TEL 06-440-3886. FAX 06-440-3885. Ed. Piero Sacchetti. adv. contact: Fabio Cauli. bk.rev.; charts; illus. circ. 5,000. (tabloid format) **Document type:** bulletin.

COSTRUZIONI; tecnica ed organizzazione dei cantieri. see *ENGINEERING — Civil Engineering*

COSTRUZIONI METALLICHE; rivista dei tecnici dell'acciaio. see *ENGINEERING — Civil Engineering*

690   US
COUNCIL OF AMERICAN BUILDING OFFICIALS. ONE AND TWO FAMILY DWELLING CODE. (Includes supplements) 1971. a. $40 to non-members; members $30. (Council of American Building Officials) International Conference of Building Officials, 5360 Workman Mill Rd., Whittier, CA 90601-2298. TEL 310-699-0541. **Document type:** trade publication.
   Formerly (until 1983): International Conference of Building Officials. One and Two Family Dwelling Code.

COUNCIL ON TALL BUILDINGS AND URBAN HABITAT. COLLECTED PAPERS. see *HOUSING AND URBAN PLANNING*

COUNCIL ON TALL BUILDINGS AND URBAN HABITAT. PROCEEDINGS. see *HOUSING AND URBAN PLANNING*

690 747   US
COUNTRY LIVING DREAM HOMES. 1988-1989; resumed 1994. a. newsstand price: $2.95. Hearst Corporation, Country Living, 224 W. 57th St., New York, NY 10019. TEL 212-649-3500. URL: http://www.hearstcorp.com. Ed. Pam Abrahams; Pub. Brian Doyle. adv.; illus. circ. 250,000. **Document type:** consumer publication.

690 720   US
COUNTRYPOLITAN HOMES & PLANS. q. newsstand price: $4.95. HomeStyles, E. 4th St., 4th Fl., St. Paul, MN 55101. TEL 612-602-5000. FAX 612-602-5001. Ed. Eric Erglund. R&P contact: Kris Donnelly. adv. contact: Kevin Miller. **Document type:** consumer publication.

690.028   US   ISSN 1070-0188
CRANE WORKS. 1992. bi-m. $28 (effective 1997 & 1998). Group II Communications, 204 W. Kansas, Ste.103, Independence, MO 64050. TEL 816-254-8735. FAX 816-254-2128. (Subscr. to: 112 E. Davis, Fayette, MO 65248. TEL 816-248-1860. FAX 816-248-1843) Ed. Suzanne Harbison; Pub. Terry Ford. adv. contact: Bev O'Dell. circ. 8,000. **Document type:** trade publication.
   Description: Covers the how-to of crane and rigging operations. Focuses on safety standards, procedures of crane operations, and information on the latest equipment and technology.

690.028   UK   ISSN 0260-745X
CRANES TODAY HANDBOOK. 1974. a. £55($99) (effective 1997). Wilmington Business Publishing, Apex House, London Rd., Northfleet, Kent DA11 9JA, England. TEL 44-1322-277788. FAX 44-1474-569418. E-mail: wbp@wilmington.co.uk. (Subscr. to: WDIS, P.O. Box 200, Ruislip, Middlesex HA4 0SY, England) Ed. Mark Aldwinckle. adv. circ. 5,000. **Document type:** trade publication.

690   UK   ISSN 1359-2742
CRANES U K. q. $69. K H L International Ltd., Southfields, Southview Rd., Wadhurst, E. Sussex TN5 6TP, England. TEL 44-1892-784088. FAX 44-1892-784086. E-mail: cranes@khl.com; URL: http://ourworld.compuserve.com/homepages/cranes. Ed. Tim Whiteman. R&P contact: Peter Watkinson. **Document type:** trade publication.

690   UK
CROWN JOURNAL. 1916. q. free. Higgs and Hill plc., Crown House, Kingston Rd., New Malden, Surrey KT3 3ST, England. TEL 44-181-942-8921. FAX 44-181-949-9280. Ed. David Helsen. circ. 10,000 (controlled). **Indexed:** Build.Manage.Abstr. **Document type:** trade publication.

CUNZHEN JIANSHE/TOWN OR VILLAGE DEVELOPMENT. see *ARCHITECTURE*

692.8   US   ISSN 0161-7257
TH435
CURRENT CONSTRUCTION COSTS. 1963. a. $54.95. Saylor Publications, Inc., 9420 Topanga Canyon Blvd., Ste. 203, Chatsworth, CA 91311. TEL 818-718-5966. FAX 818-718-8024. Ed. Stanley J. Strychaz. R&P contact: Stanley J. Strychaz. circ. 8,000. **Document type:** trade publication.

CURRENT CONSTRUCTION REPORTS: EXPENDITURES FOR RESIDENTIAL IMPROVEMENTS AND REPAIRS. see *HOUSING AND URBAN PLANNING*

CURRENT CONSTRUCTION REPORTS: HOUSING COMPLETIONS. see *HOUSING AND URBAN PLANNING*

CURRENT CONSTRUCTION REPORTS: HOUSING STARTS. see *HOUSING AND URBAN PLANNING*

CURRENT CONSTRUCTION REPORTS: HOUSING UNITS AUTHORIZED BY BUILDING PERMITS; states and selected metropolitan areas. see *HOUSING AND URBAN PLANNING*

CURRENT CONSTRUCTION REPORTS: NEW ONE-FAMILY HOUSES SOLD. see *HOUSING AND URBAN PLANNING*

CURRENT CONSTRUCTION REPORTS: NEW RESIDENTIAL CONSTRUCTION IN SELECTED METROPOLITAN AREAS. see *HOUSING AND URBAN PLANNING*

CURRENT CONSTRUCTION REPORTS: VALUE OF NEW CONSTRUCTION PUT IN PLACE. see *HOUSING AND URBAN PLANNING*

621.475   US   ISSN 0895-2493
TJ810
CUSTOM BUILDER; the business magazine for custom home builders. 1976. bi-m. $23 (foreign $35). Gruner & Jahr U.S.A. Publishing, 110 Fifth Ave., New York, NY 10011-5601. TEL 207-828-4470. FAX 207-828-4478. E-mail: custmbld96@aol.com. Ed. Laurence Oberwager; Pub. Paul Gillenger. R&P contact: Shannon Meserve. adv. contact: Cathy Smith. illus.; circ. 30,000 (controlled). **Indexed:** A.S.& T.Ind., AESIS, ASCA, Bus.Ind., Energy Ind., Energy Info.Abstr., Energy Rev., Environ.Per.Bibl., INSPEC, Key to Econ.Sci., PROMT, Search (1988-1989, 1992-), Tr.& Indus.Ind. **Document type:** trade publication.
   ●Also available online. Vendor(s): Information Access Co.
   —BLDSC (3506.114000); CISTI; KR SourceOne; Linda Hall; UMI; UnCover. **CCC.**
   Former titles (until 1987): Progressive Builder (ISSN 0888-9171); (until 1986): Solar Age (ISSN 0160-8401)
   Description: Covers innovations in building techniques, practices and products directly to the builder of custom homes.

338.769 690.83   US
▼**CUSTOM BUILDERS AND THEIR COMMUNITIES.** 1995. a. $4.95. Living Partners Ltd., 5501 LBJ Freeway, Ste. 300, Dallas, TX 75240. TEL 214-239-2399. FAX 214-239-7850. Ed. Nancy Meza. adv.: Color page $2995; trim 8 x 10 7/8; adv. contact: Ray L. Baker. circ. 40,000 (controlled). **Document type:** directory, consumer publication.
   Description: Lists custom home builders in the over $250,000 price range in the Dallas/Ft. Worth area.

690   US   ISSN 1055-3479
NA7208
CUSTOM HOME. 6/yr. $24. Hanley-Wood Inc., One Thomas Circle, Ste. 600, Washington, DC 20005. TEL 202-452-0800. FAX 202-785-1974. Ed. Leslie Ensor. circ. 40,000. **Document type:** trade publication.

690   PL   CODEN: CZTEAY
CZASOPISMO TECHNICZNE. SERIA B: BUDOWNICTWO. (Contents page in 4 languages) 1877. irreg. 20 Zl. (effective 1997). Politechnika Krakowska, Ul. Warszawska 24, 31-155 Krakow, Poland. TEL 48-12-37-42-89. FAX 48-12-335773. TELEX 322468 PK PL. E-mail: Marcinek@biblos.pk.edu.pl. bk.rev.; charts; illus.; index. circ. 12,000. **Indexed:** Chem.Abstr. **Document type:** academic/scholarly publication.
   —CASDDS.
   Supersedes in part: Czasopismo Techniczne (ISSN 0011-4561); Which was formerly (until 1883): Dzwignia (ISSN 1230-2791).

D B - DEUTSCHE BAUZEITUNG; Fachzeitschrift fuer Architekten und Bauingenieure. see *ARCHITECTURE*

D C A NEWS. (Distribution Contractors Association) see *PETROLEUM AND GAS*

690 607.4   US
D E C. (Demolition & Environmental Contractor) 1967. m. $35 (foreign $72). Duane Publishing, Inc., Box 850769, Braintree, MA 02184. TEL 617-848-6150. FAX 617-848-6160. Ed. H. Tobias Duan III. adv. contact: Susan Cellucci. illus.; mkt. circ. 16,000. **Document type:** trade publication.
   Supersedes (in Jan. 1997): Wrecking and Salvage Journal (ISSN 0043-9460)
   Description: Provides a publication that recognizes the prevalence of environmental issues such as asbestos, lead, PCB's and contaminated soil in today's demolition and renovation projects. Contains news of current and upcoming jobs, and features on techniques and problems particular to the demolition, excavation, and remediation industries. Covers new equipment and current legal requirements.

D E M M. (Digest of Equipment, Materials and Management) see *ENGINEERING*

691.2   GW   ISSN 0178-3343
D N I. (Die Naturstein Industrie) 1965. 9/yr. DM.171 (foreign DM.189) (effective 1997); newsstand price: DM.22. Stein-Verlag GmbH, Josef-Herrmann-Str. 1-3, 76473 Iffezheim, Germany. TEL 49-7229-606-0. FAX 49-7229-60610. Ed. Thorsten Block; Pub. Wilhelm Joesch. R&P contact: Jutta Senn. adv. contact: Alfons John. circ. 7,800. **Indexed:** Dok.Str. **Document type:** trade publication.
   —BLDSC (6048.830000).
   Formerly (until 1979): Naturstein-Industrie (ISSN 0028-1034)
   Description: Magazine of the German stone industry and its associations.

690   GW   ISSN 0174-5336
D S B. (Die Schweizer Baustoff-Industrie) (Text in French, German) 1969. 9/yr. DM.166 (foreign DM.184) (effective 1997); newsstand price: DM.22. Stein-Verlag GmbH, Josef-Herrmann-Str. 1-3, 76473 Iffezheim, Germany. TEL 49-7229-606-0. FAX 49-7229-60610. Ed. Thorsten Block; Pub. Wilhelm Joesch. R&P contact: Jutta Senn. adv. contact: Alfons John. circ. 2,600. **Document type:** trade publication.

695   SZ
DACH UND WAND; Schweizerischer Dachdeckmeister-Zeitung. (Text in French, German) 1907. m. 55 SFr. (Schweizerischer Dachdeckermeister Verband) Verlag Dach und Wand, Lindenstr. 4, CH-9240 Uzwil, Switzerland. TEL 073-517244. Ed.Bd. **Document type:** trade publication.
   Description: Covers all aspects of roofing.

691   AU
DACH UND WAND ABDICHTUNG. m. S.580. (Bundes- und Landesinnungen der Dachdecker) Oesterreichischer Wirtschaftsverlag, Nikolsdorfergasse 7-11, A-1051 Vienna, Austria. TEL 0222-555585. TELEX 1-11669. Ed. Dr. Wolfgang Biedermann. adv.; bk.rev.; illus. circ. 1,000.
   Formerly: Oesterreichische Dachdecker- und Pflasterer-Zeitung (ISSN 0029-8999)

BUILDING AND CONSTRUCTION

690 GW
DAS DACHDECKER-HANDWERK; Zeitschrift fuer Wand-, Dach- und Abdichtungs-Technik. Short title: D D H. 1879. s-m. DM.245 (foreign DM.267). (Zentralverband des Dachdeckerhandwerks e.V) Verlagsgesellschaft Rudolf Mueller GmbH & Co. KG, Stolberger Str. 84, 50933 Cologne, Germany. TEL 49-221-5497-200. FAX 49-221-5497326. (Subscr. to: Postfach 410949, 50869 Cologne, Germany) Ed. Volker Rutkowski. adv.: B&W page DM.5750, color page DM.9200; trim 188 x 267. circ. 12,000. (back issues avail.) **Document type:** trade publication.
Formerly: Deutsches Dachdecker-Handwerk (ISSN 0012-124X)

695 GW ISSN 0343-382X
DER DACHDECKERMEISTER. m. DM.105.60. Verlag F.H. Kleffmann GmbH, Hernerstr. 299, 44809 Bochum, Germany. TEL 49-234-95391-0. FAX 49-234-9539130. E-mail: kleffmann@mediacom.de; URL: http://www.mediacom.de/kleffmann. circ. 9,500. (back issues avail.) **Document type:** trade publication.
—BLDSC (3509.500000).

690
DAEMM JOURNAL; Informationszeitung ueber den Nutzen des Daemmens fuer Mensch und Umwelt. 1988. irreg. Gesamtverband Daemmstoffindustrie, Ferdinand-Porsche-Str. 16, 60486 Frankfurt a.M., Germany. TEL 069-423896. circ. 800,000.

690 CN ISSN 0317-3178
DAILY COMMERCIAL NEWS AND CONSTRUCTION RECORD. 1929. d. (5/w.). Can.$662.33 (foreign Can.$846). Daily Commercial News (Subsidiary of: Southam Inc.), 280 Yorkland Blvd., North York, ON M2J 4Z6, Canada. TEL 416-494-4990. FAX 416-756-2767. Ed. Scott Button; Pub. Ian Hardy. adv. contact: Dave Watson. circ. 4,600.
Indexed: Can.B.P.I.
—CISTI.
Formerly: Daily Commercial News and Building Record (ISSN 0317-316X)

690 KO
THE DAILY CONSTRUCTION NEWS. d. Construction Association of Korea, 71-2 Nonhyun-dong, Kangnam-ku, Seoul 135-701, S. Korea. **Document type:** newspaper.
Formerly: Construction Association of Korea. Construction News Service.

692.8 US ISSN 0011-5401
DAILY CONSTRUCTION SERVICE. (Local ed. in El Segundo also avail.) 1919. d. $979 (effective Jan. 1995). Construction Market Data, Inc., 4126 Pleasantdale Rd., Ste. A8, Atlanta, CA 30340. TEL 800-949-0276. FAX 770-613-5978. Ed. William B. Wallace. adv.: page $750; trim 8 1/2 x 11; adv. contact: William B. Wallace. bk.rev.; m. index; circ. 2,500 (paid). **Document type:** trade publication.
Description: Detailed descriptions of construction projects out for bid.

DAILY MAIL BOOK OF HOME PLANS. see ARCHITECTURE

690 US
DAILY PACIFIC BUILDER. 1895. d. (5/w.). $1536. McGraw-Hill Companies, 1221 Ave. of the Americas, New York, NY 10020. TEL 212-512-2000. Ed. Doug Hebbard. adv.; charts; illus.; stat. circ. 2,000. (tabloid format) **Document type:** newspaper, trade publication.
Description: Provides sales leads.

690 JA ISSN 0914-3890
DAINIPPON KOBOKU K.K. GIJUTSU SHIRYO/DAI NIPPON CONSTRUCTION CO., LTD. TECHNICAL MATERIALS. (Text in Japanese) 1963. a. Dainippon Koboku K.K. Komu Honbu, 6-8, Usa Minami 1-chome, Gifu-shi, Gifu-ken 162, Japan.

693.5 DK ISSN 0109-758X
DANSK BETON/DANISH CONCRETE. 1972. q. DKK 210. (Dansk Beton Industriforening) Parita Grafik, Gribskovvej 2, DK-2100 Copenhagen, Denmark. TEL 45-75-92-10-00. FAX 45-75-93-49-48. (Co-sponsors: Dansk Betonforening; Dansk Betonelementforening; Dansk Fabriksbetonforening) Ed. S.E. Kaarsholm. adv.: B&W page DKK 7200, color page DKK 13600; trim 247 x 171; adv. contact: Bente Stricker. illus. circ. 6,800. **Document type:** trade publication.
Formerly (until 1984): Dansk Beton Industri (ISSN 0901-3091)

690 IT
DEDALO. 1985. 10/yr. L.25000 (foreign L.40000). (Assimpredil) A I E Servizi s.r.l., Via S. Maurilio 21, 20123 Milan, Italy. TEL 39-2-809081. FAX 39-2-8056802. TELEX 326345 EDILMI I. Ed. Mario Rotondi. adv.: B&W page L.1050000, color page L.1650000; 210 x 297. circ. 10,000.
Description: For the construction industry in Milan. Informs on projects, works in progress, and industry trends.

690 NE ISSN 1386-1077
▼**DELFT MARITIEM.** 1995. irreg., vol.3, 1995. price varies. Delft University Press, Mekelweg 4, 2628 CD Delft, Netherlands. TEL 31-15-2783254. FAX 31-15-2781661. E-mail: dup@dup.tudelft.nl. **Document type:** monographic series.

690 US
TH153
DEMOLITION; the voice of the demolition industry. 1973. m. $40. (National Association of Demolition Contractors) Construction Safety Associates, Inc., 16 N. Franklin St., Ste. 200-B, Doylestown, PA 18901. TEL 215-348-8282. FAX 215-348-8422. Ed. Michael R. Taylor; Pub. Michael R. Taylor. R&P contact: Michael R. Taylor. adv. contact: Michael R. Taylor. circ. 4,400. **Document type:** trade publication.
—CISTI.
Formerly: Demolition Age (ISSN 0362-7772)

690 UK
DEMOLITION & DISMANTLING. q. Computer House, 65 Mortimer Rd., Mitcham CR4 3HS, England. TEL 081-648-9286. FAX 081-685-9473. Ed. John Bergen. circ. 4,000.
Description: Received by demolition companies, construction organizations, manufacturers and distributors of machinery, plants and vehicles.

343.489078 DK ISSN 0108-9803
DENMARK. BOLIGMINISTERIET. BUILDING REGULATIONS. 1977. irreg. Boligministeriet - Ministry of Housing, Slotsholmsgade 1, 3, 1216 Copenhagen K, Denmark.

690 US
DENVER DAILY JOURNAL. 1897. d. $1208 (effective Jan. 1993). (Information Systems Co.) McGraw-Hill Companies, 1221 Ave. of the Americas, New York, NY 10020. TEL 212-512-2000. Ed. Jack Phinney. adv.; charts; illus.; stat. circ. 10,000. (also avail. in microfiche) **Document type:** newspaper, trade publication.
Description: Provides sales leads for Denver construction industry.

690 721 US
TH1
DESIGN - BUILD BUSINESS. 1935. m. $24 (effective 1997). McKellar Publications, Inc., 333 E. Glenoaks Blvd., Ste. 204, Glendale, CA 91207-2074. TEL 818-241-0250. FAX 818-241-4406. Ed. Doyle Peck. adv. contact: Jean Koehler. bk.rev.; circ. 60,000 (controlled). (back issues avail.) **Document type:** trade publication.
—UnCover.
Former titles (until 1996): Sun - Coast Architect - Builder (ISSN 0744-8872); Formed by the merger of: Western Building Design (ISSN 0192-1568) & Pacific Coast Builder (ISSN 0192-1703)
Description: Features, news, project examples, departments, etc.; of interest to builders, architects, designers and remodelers.

DESIGN COST & DATA; the cost estimating magazine for architects, builders and specifiers. see ARCHITECTURE

DESIGN LINE. see ARCHITECTURE

691 US
DESIGN MANUAL. s-a. $25 per no. Steel Deck Institute, Box 25, Fox River Grove, IL 60021-0025. TEL 847-462-1930. FAX 847-462-1940. R&P contact: Steven A. Roehrig.

DESIGNER'S BEST HOME PLANS. see ARCHITECTURE

670 US ISSN 0897-6228
DESIGNERS' COLLECTION HOME PLANS. 1988. q. $15. HomeStyles, 213 E. 4th St., 4th Fl., St. Paul, MN 55101. TEL 612-602-5000; 888-626-2026. FAX 612-602-5002. Ed. Eric Erglund. R&P contact: Kris Donnelly. adv. contact: Kevin Miller. circ. 70,000.
Description: Contains executive and luxury home designs by American designers.

DETAIL; Zeitschrift fuer Architektur & Baudetail. see ARCHITECTURE

690 GW
DEUTSCHE BAUINDUSTRIE - JAHRESBERICHT. a. Hauptverband der Deutschen Bauindustrie, Abraham-Lincoln-Str. 30, 65189 Wiesbaden, Germany. TEL 49-611-7720. **Document type:** bulletin.

DEUTSCHER BAUKATALOG. see ARCHITECTURE

690 GW ISSN 0939-8791
DEUTSCHES BAUBLATT. m. Im Bondorf 30, 53545 Linz, Germany. TEL 08387-399-0. FAX 038387-299-33. TELEX 541121. (Dist. by: Buchdruckerei Holzer, Fridolin-Holzer-Str. 22, Postfach 159, D-8999 Weiler, Germany) Ed. Martin A. Schmitt. circ. 28,500.
Supersedes (1974-1988): Baugeraetemarkt.

690 333.333 US ISSN 0888-6067
DEVELOPMENT (HERNDON). 1969. 4/yr. $39 to non-members; members $24. National Association of Industrial and Office Parks, 2201 Cooperative Way, 3rd Fl., Herndon, VA 22071-3024. TEL 703-904-7100. Eds. Ron Derven, Ellen Rand. adv.: B&W page $1875. bk.rev.: tr.lit.; circ. 7,500 (paid). **Indexed:** Avery Ind.Archit.Per. **Document type:** trade publication.
Formerly: N A I O P News.
Description: Covers the full range of commercial real estate.

349 FR ISSN 0012-2467
DICTIONNAIRE PERMANENT: CONSTRUCTION. 1962. 3 base vols. plus m. updates. 1660 F. for base vols. (updates 520 F.) (effective 1995). Editions Legislatives et Administratives, 80, ave. de la Marne, 92456 Montrouge Cedex, France. TEL 40-92-68-68. FAX 46-56-00-15. TELEX 632 855 F. bibl.; index, cum.index. circ. 9,000. (looseleaf format)
Description: Examines judicial problems encountered in construction and urbanization.

690 US
DIGEST OF BUILDING CONTRACT AWARDS; the hard facts - comparables on actual project listings. a. $49.95. Marshall & Swift, 1617 Beverly Blvd., Box 26307, Los Angeles, CA 90026-0307. TEL 800-544-2678. FAX 213-250-9811. Ed. James Gudnecht. illus.
Formerly (until 1988): Dodge Digest of Building Cost Data.
Description: Details actual bid prices on nearly 1,000 structures furnished by architects and engineers, for numerous types of commercial and residential occupancies.

690 US ISSN 0883-0258
DIMENSIONAL STONE MAGAZINE. 1985. 12/yr. $50 (Canada & Mexico $55; elsewhere $60). Dimensional Stone Institute, Inc., 6300 Variel Ave., Ste. I, Woodland Hills, CA 91367-2513. TEL 818-704-5555. FAX 818-704-6500. TELEX 181545. Ed. William Campbell; Pub. Jerry Fisher. R&P contact: William Campbell. adv.: B&W page $1935, color page $2665; 7 x 10; adv. contact: Gary Gelt. bk.rev.; circ. 15,000(controlled). (back issues avail.) **Document type:** trade publication.
—CCC.
Description: Contains dimensional stone industry trends and events. Features articles on quarrying, installation, fabrication and cutting techniques, sales and marketing, finance, equipment and new products.

BUILDING AND CONSTRUCTION

DIRECTIVOS CONSTRUCCION. see REAL ESTATE

690 II
DIRECTORY OF BUILDERS AND CONTRACTORS. (Text in English) 1987. irreg. $20. Architects Publishing Corp. of India, 51 Sujata, Ground Fl., Rani Sati Marg, Malad East, Mumbai 400 097, India. TEL 91-22-883-4442. Ed. A.K. Gupta. adv.; charts; illus. circ. 5,000. **Document type:** directory.
  Description: Regional listing of names, addresses and telephone numbers of builders and property developers, civil, electrical, sanitary and painting contractors.

DIRECTORY OF BUILDING CODES & REGULATIONS. see HOUSING AND URBAN PLANNING

DIRECTORY OF CONSULTANTS AND CONTRACTORS ACTIVE IN EASTERN EUROPE. see BUSINESS AND ECONOMICS — Trade And Industrial Directories

DIRECTORY OF CONSULTANTS AND CONTRACTORS ACTIVE IN LATIN AMERICA AND THE CARIBBEAN. see BUSINESS AND ECONOMICS — Trade And Industrial Directories

DIRECTORY OF CONSULTANTS AND CONTRACTORS ACTIVE IN THE FAR EAST. see BUSINESS AND ECONOMICS — Trade And Industrial Directories

DIRECTORY OF CONSULTANTS AND CONTRACTORS ACTIVE IN THE MIDDLE EAST AND AFRICA. see BUSINESS AND ECONOMICS — Trade And Industrial Directories

DIRECTORY OF CONSULTANTS AND CONTRACTORS ACTIVE IN THE UNITED STATES AND CANADA. see BUSINESS AND ECONOMICS — Trade And Industrial Directories

DIRECTORY OF CONSULTANTS AND CONTRACTORS ACTIVE IN WESTERN EUROPE. see BUSINESS AND ECONOMICS — Trade And Industrial Directories

690 US
DIRECTORY OF LICENSED PRODUCTS. 1961. a. free. Air Movement and Control Association, 30 W. University Dr., Arlington Heights, IL 60004. TEL 708-394-0150. FAX 708-253-0088. Ed. Mark Stevens. circ. 12,000. **Document type:** directory.

DIRECTORY OF MANUFACTURERS & DEALERS OF BUILDING INDUSTRY. see BUSINESS AND ECONOMICS — Trade And Industrial Directories

691 670 US
DIRECTORY OF MEMBERSHIP & PRECAST CONCRETE PRODUCTS.* a. $150 to non-members. National Precast Concrete Association, 10333 N. Meridian St., Ste. 272, Indianapolis, IN 46290-1081. TEL 317-253-0486. FAX 317-259-7230.
  Description: Lists over 800 producers and associate members of the Association; over 250 precast concrete products.

690 BL ISSN 0012-3358
DIRIGENTE CONSTRUTOR. 1964. m. $70. Editora Visao Ltda., Rua Alvaro de Carvalho, 350, 2o andar, C.P. 3082, 01050 Sao Paulo, Brazil. TEL 256-5011. FAX 258-1919. TELEX 1121436. Ed. Hamilton Lucas de Oliviera. adv.; bk.rev.; charts; illus.; stat.; index, cum.index. circ. 23,889.

690 US ISSN 0897-6236
NA7205
DISTINGUISHED HOME PLANS. 1981. q. $20. HomeStyles, 213 E. 4th St., 4th Fl., St. Paul, MN 55101. TEL 612-602-5000; 888-626-2026. FAX 612-602-5002. Ed. Eric Erglund. R&P contact: Kris Donnelly. adv. contact: Kevin Miller. circ. 73,000.
  Description: Contains home plans for classic and traditional homes with emphasis on construction and affordable family living.

728 US
DISTINGUISHED HOME PLANS & PRODUCTS - CUSTOM HOME PLANS GUIDE. 1950. q. $1.75. Master Plan Service, Inc., c/o National Home Plan, 37 Mountain Ave., Springfield, NJ 07087. Ed. Kenneth Miller. adv. circ. 70,000.
  Formerly: Distinguished Home Plans and Products.

690 US ISSN 0012-4281
TA1
DIXIE CONTRACTOR. 1926. s-m. $15. Dixie Contractor, Inc., 209-A Swanton Way, Box 280, Decatur, GA 30031. TEL 404-377-2683. FAX 404-371-1509. Ed. Steve Hudson. adv.; illus.; tr.lit. circ. 10,000. (back issues avail.)

690 US ISSN 1085-1925
DODGE BUILDING REVIEW COVERING CENTRAL INDIANA. 1992. w. McGraw-Hill Companies, Princeton Rd. S-2, Box 689, Hightstown, NJ 08520-0689. TEL 800-325-2030. adv. **Document type:** newsletter, trade publication.
  ●Also available online.
  Description: Provides information on what jobs are coming up for bid or negotiation.

690 US ISSN 1085-1933
DODGE BUILDING REVIEW COVERING NORTHERN INDIANA. 1992. w. McGraw-Hill Companies, Princeton Rd. S-2, Box 689, Hightstown, NJ 08520-0689. TEL 800-325-2030. adv. **Document type:** newsletter, trade publication.
  ●Also available online.
  Description: Provides information on what jobs are coming up for bid or negotiation.

690 US ISSN 1085-1917
DODGE BUILDING REVIEW COVERING SOUTHERN INDIANA. 1992. w. McGraw-Hill Companies, Princeton Rd. S-2, Box 689, Hightstown, NJ 08520-0689. TEL 800-325-2030. adv. **Document type:** newsletter, trade publication.
  ●Also available online.
  Description: Provides information on what jobs are coming up for bid or negotiation.

690 US ISSN 0012-480X
DODGE CONSTRUCTION NEWS. CHICAGO EDITION. 1946. d. $1245. McGraw-Hill Companies, 1221 Ave. of the Americas, New York, NY 10020. TEL 212-512-2000. adv.; charts; illus.; mkt.; stat.; tr.mk. **Document type:** trade publication, newspaper.
  Formerly: Chicago Construction News.
  Description: Classified, legal and display ads for Chicago construction projects.

690 US
DODGE CONSTRUCTION NEWS. LOS ANGELES EDITION. 1865. d. $1392. McGraw-Hill Companies, 1221 Ave. of the Americas, New York, NY 10020. TEL 212-512-2000. adv.; charts; illus.; stat. circ. 4,250. **Document type:** trade publication.
  Description: Classified, legal and display ads for Los Angeles construction projects.

690 US ISSN 1085-2204
DODGE CONSTRUCTION NEWS WEEKLY COVERING ALABAMA. w. McGraw-Hill Companies, Princeton Rd. S-2, Box 689, Hightstown, NJ 08520-0689. TEL 800-325-2030. adv. **Document type:** newsletter, trade publication.
  ●Also available online.
  Description: Provides information on what jobs are coming up for bid or negotiation.

690 US ISSN 1085-8148
DODGE CONSTRUCTION NEWS WEEKLY COVERING ALBANY. 1993. w. McGraw-Hill Companies, Princeton Rd. S-2, Box 689, Hightstown, NJ 08520-0689. TEL 800-325-2030. adv. **Document type:** newsletter, trade publication.
  ●Also available online.
  Description: Provides information on what jobs are coming up for bid or negotiation.

690 US ISSN 1086-6256
DODGE CONSTRUCTION NEWS WEEKLY COVERING ARKANSAS. 1992. w. McGraw-Hill Companies, Princeton Rd. S-2, Box 689, Hightstown, NJ 08520-0689. TEL 800-325-2030. adv. **Document type:** newsletter, trade publication.
  ●Also available online.
  Description: Provides information on what jobs are coming up for bid or negotiation.

690 US ISSN 1085-2190
DODGE CONSTRUCTION NEWS WEEKLY COVERING ASHEVILLE - CHARLOTTE. w. McGraw-Hill Companies, Princeton Rd. S-2, Box 689, Hightstown, NJ 08520-0689. TEL 800-325-2030. adv. **Document type:** newsletter, trade publication.
  ●Also available online.
  Description: Provides information on what jobs are coming up for bid or negotiation.

690 US ISSN 1086-6167
▼**DODGE CONSTRUCTION NEWS WEEKLY COVERING AUSTIN.** 1995. w. McGraw-Hill Companies, Princeton Rd. S-2, Box 689, Hightstown, NJ 08520-0689. TEL 800-325-2030. adv. **Document type:** newsletter, trade publication.
  ●Also available online.
  Description: Provides information on what jobs are coming up for bid or negotiation.

690 US ISSN 1086-5330
DODGE CONSTRUCTION NEWS WEEKLY COVERING BALTIMORE. w. McGraw-Hill Companies, Princeton Rd. S-2, Box 689, Hightstown, NJ 08520-0689. TEL 800-325-2030. adv. **Document type:** newsletter, trade publication.
  ●Also available online.
  Description: Provides information on what jobs are coming up for bid or negotiation.

690 US ISSN 1086-6213
▼**DODGE CONSTRUCTION NEWS WEEKLY COVERING BATON ROUGE.** 1995. w. McGraw-Hill Companies, Princeton Rd. S-2, Box 689, Hightstown, NJ 08520-0689. TEL 800-325-2030. adv. **Document type:** newsletter, trade publication.
  ●Also available online.
  Description: Provides information on what jobs are coming up for bid or negotiation.

690 US
DODGE CONSTRUCTION NEWS WEEKLY COVERING BEAUMONT - LAKE CHARLES. w. McGraw-Hill Companies, Princeton Rd. S-2, Box 689, Hightstown, NJ 08520-0689. TEL 800-325-2030. adv. **Document type:** newsletter, trade publication.
  ●Also available online.
  Description: Provides information on what jobs are coming up for bid or negotiation.

690 US ISSN 1085-8202
▼**DODGE CONSTRUCTION NEWS WEEKLY COVERING BROOKLYN - QUEENS.** 1995. w. McGraw-Hill Companies, Princeton Rd. S-2, Box 689, Hightstown, NJ 08520-0689. TEL 800-325-2030. adv. **Document type:** newsletter, trade publication.
  ●Also available online.
  Description: Provides information on what jobs are coming up for bid or negotiation.

690 US ISSN 1085-8156
DODGE CONSTRUCTION NEWS WEEKLY COVERING BUFFALO. 1994. w. McGraw-Hill Companies, Princeton Rd. S-2, Box 689, Hightstown, NJ 08520-0689. TEL 800-325-2030. adv. **Document type:** newsletter, trade publication.
  ●Also available online.
  Description: Provides information on what jobs are coming up for bid or negotiation.

690 US ISSN 1085-195X
DODGE CONSTRUCTION NEWS WEEKLY COVERING CENTRAL AND SOUTHERN ILLINOIS. w. McGraw-Hill Companies, Princeton Rd. S-2, Box 689, Hightstown, NJ 08520-0689. TEL 800-325-2030. adv. **Document type:** newsletter, trade publication.
  ●Also available online.
  Description: Provides information on what jobs are coming up for bid or negotiation.

690 US ISSN 1085-8237
DODGE CONSTRUCTION NEWS WEEKLY COVERING CENTRAL NEW JERSEY. w. McGraw-Hill Companies, Princeton Rd. S-2, Box 689, Hightstown, NJ 08520-0689. TEL 800-325-2030. adv. **Document type:** newsletter, trade publication.
  ●Also available online.
  Description: Provides information on what jobs are coming up for bid or negotiation.

690 US ISSN 1085-8253
DODGE CONSTRUCTION NEWS WEEKLY COVERING CENTRAL PENNSYLVANIA. w. McGraw-Hill Companies, Princeton Rd. S-2, Box 689, Hightstown, NJ 08520-0689. TEL 800-325-2030. adv. **Document type:** newsletter, trade publication.
  ●Also available online.
  Description: Provides information on what jobs are coming up for bid or negotiation.

BUILDING AND CONSTRUCTION

690 US ISSN 1085-1879
▼DODGE CONSTRUCTION NEWS WEEKLY COVERING CHICAGO ENGINEERING. 1995. w. McGraw-Hill Companies, Princeton Rd. S-2, Box 689, Hightstown, NJ 08520-0689. TEL 800-325-2030. adv. **Document type:** newsletter, trade publication.
●Also available online.
  Description: Provides information on what jobs are coming up for bid or negotiation.

690 US ISSN 1085-1887
▼DODGE CONSTRUCTION NEWS WEEKLY COVERING CHICAGO GENERAL BUILDING. 1995. w. McGraw-Hill Companies, Princeton Rd. S-2, Box 689, Hightstown, NJ 08520-0689. TEL 800-325-2030. adv. **Document type:** newsletter, trade publication.
●Also available online.
  Description: Provides information on what jobs are coming up for bid or negotiation.

690 US ISSN 1087-0997
▼DODGE CONSTRUCTION NEWS WEEKLY COVERING CINCINNATI AND VICINITY. 1995. w. McGraw-Hill Companies, Princeton Rd. S-2, Box 689, Hightstown, NJ 08520-0689. TEL 800-325-2030. adv. **Document type:** newsletter, trade publication.
●Also available online.
  Description: Provides information on what jobs are coming up for bid or negotiation.

690 US ISSN 1088-1425
DODGE CONSTRUCTION NEWS WEEKLY COVERING CLEVELAND - AKRON - CANTON. w. McGraw-Hill Companies, Princeton Rd. S-2, Box 689, Hightstown, NJ 08520-0689. TEL 800-325-2030. adv. **Document type:** newsletter, trade publication.
●Also available online.
  Description: Provides information on what jobs are coming up for bid or negotiation.

690 US ISSN 1085-2271
DODGE CONSTRUCTION NEWS WEEKLY COVERING COLUMBIA - CHARLESTON. w. McGraw-Hill Companies, Princeton Rd. S-2, Box 689, Hightstown, NJ 08520-0689. TEL 800-325-2030. adv. **Document type:** newsletter, trade publication.
●Also available online.
  Description: Provides information on what jobs are coming up for bid or negotiation.

690 US ISSN 1087-0970
▼DODGE CONSTRUCTION NEWS WEEKLY COVERING COLUMBUS AND VICINITY. 1995. w. McGraw-Hill Companies, Princeton Rd. S-2, Box 689, Hightstown, NJ 08520-0689. TEL 800-325-2030. adv. **Document type:** newsletter, trade publication.
●Also available online.
  Description: Provides information on what jobs are coming up for bid or negotiation.

690 US ISSN 1085-8121
DODGE CONSTRUCTION NEWS WEEKLY COVERING CONNECTICUT. 1992. w. McGraw-Hill Companies, Princeton Rd. S-2, Box 689, Hightstown, NJ 08520-0689. TEL 800-325-2030. adv. **Document type:** newsletter, trade publication.
●Also available online.
  Description: Provides information on what jobs are coming up for bid or negotiation.

690 US ISSN 1086-6183
▼DODGE CONSTRUCTION NEWS WEEKLY COVERING DALLAS. 1995. w. McGraw-Hill Companies, Princeton Rd. S-2, Box 689, Hightstown, NJ 08520-0689. TEL 800-325-2030. adv. **Document type:** newsletter, trade publication.
●Also available online.
  Description: Provides information on what jobs are coming up for bid or negotiation.

690 US ISSN 1087-0989
▼DODGE CONSTRUCTION NEWS WEEKLY COVERING DAYTON AND VICINITY. 1995. w. McGraw-Hill Companies, Princeton Rd. S-2, Box 689, Hightstown, NJ 08520-0689. TEL 800-325-2030. adv. **Document type:** newsletter, trade publication.
●Also available online.
  Description: Provides information on what jobs are coming up for bid or negotiation.

690 US ISSN 1085-1895
▼DODGE CONSTRUCTION NEWS WEEKLY COVERING DETROIT METRO. 1995. w. McGraw-Hill Companies, Princeton Rd. S-2, Box 689, Hightstown, NJ 08520-0689. TEL 800-325-2030. adv. **Document type:** newsletter, trade publication.
●Also available online.
  Description: Provides information on what jobs are coming up for bid or negotiation.

690 US ISSN 1087-1012
DODGE CONSTRUCTION NEWS WEEKLY COVERING EASTERN KENTUCKY. w. McGraw-Hill Companies, Princeton Rd. S-2, Box 689, Hightstown, NJ 08520-0689. TEL 800-325-2030. adv. **Document type:** newsletter, trade publication.
●Also available online.
  Description: Provides information on what jobs are coming up for bid or negotiation.

690 US
DODGE CONSTRUCTION NEWS WEEKLY COVERING EASTERN MASSACHUSETTS. w. McGraw-Hill Companies, Princeton Rd. S-2, Box 689, Hightstown, NJ 08520-0689. TEL 800-325-2030. adv. **Document type:** newsletter, trade publication.
●Also available online.
  Description: Provides information on what jobs are coming up for bid or negotiation.

690 US ISSN 1085-1844
DODGE CONSTRUCTION NEWS WEEKLY COVERING EASTERN MISSOURI. 1993. w. McGraw-Hill Companies, Princeton Rd. S-2, Box 689, Hightstown, NJ 08520-0689. TEL 800-325-2030. adv. **Document type:** newsletter, trade publication.
●Also available online.
  Description: Provides information on what jobs are coming up for bid or negotiation.

690 US ISSN 1085-8261
▼DODGE CONSTRUCTION NEWS WEEKLY COVERING EASTERN NORTH CAROLINA. 1995. w. McGraw-Hill Companies, Princeton Rd. S-2, Box 689, Hightstown, NJ 08520-0689. TEL 800-325-2030. adv. **Document type:** newsletter, trade publication.
●Also available online.
  Description: Provides information on what jobs are coming up for bid or negotiation.

690 US
DODGE CONSTRUCTION NEWS WEEKLY COVERING EASTERN OKLAHOMA. w. McGraw-Hill Companies, Princeton Rd. S-2, Box 689, Hightstown, NJ 08520-0689. TEL 800-325-2030. adv. **Document type:** newsletter, trade publication.
●Also available online.
  Description: Provides information on what jobs are coming up for bid or negotiation.

690 US ISSN 1086-6205
▼DODGE CONSTRUCTION NEWS WEEKLY COVERING FORT WORTH. 1995. w. McGraw-Hill Companies, Princeton Rd. S-2, Box 689, Hightstown, NJ 08520-0689. TEL 800-325-2030. adv. **Document type:** newsletter, trade publication.
●Also available online.
  Description: Provides information on what jobs are coming up for bid or negotiation.

690 US ISSN 1085-2220
DODGE CONSTRUCTION NEWS WEEKLY COVERING GEORGIA. w. McGraw-Hill Companies, Princeton Rd. S-2, Box 689, Hightstown, NJ 08520-0689. TEL 800-325-2030. adv. **Document type:** newsletter, trade publication.
●Also available online.
  Description: Provides information on what jobs are coming up for bid or negotiation.

690 US ISSN 1086-6159
▼DODGE CONSTRUCTION NEWS WEEKLY COVERING HOUSTON. 1995. w. McGraw-Hill Companies, Princeton Rd. S-2, Box 689, Hightstown, NJ 08520-0689. TEL 800-325-2030. adv. **Document type:** newsletter, trade publication.
●Also available online.
  Description: Provides information on what jobs are coming up for bid or negotiation.

690 US ISSN 1069-1820
DODGE CONSTRUCTION NEWS WEEKLY COVERING IOWA. w. McGraw-Hill Companies, Princeton Rd. S-2, Box 689, Hightstown, NJ 08520-0689. TEL 800-325-2030. adv. **Document type:** newsletter, trade publication.
●Also available online.
  Description: Provides information on what jobs are coming up for bid or negotiation.

690 US ISSN 1085-2247
DODGE CONSTRUCTION NEWS WEEKLY COVERING JACKSONVILLE AND VICINITY. w. McGraw-Hill Companies, Princeton Rd. S-2, Box 689, Hightstown, NJ 08520-0689. TEL 800-325-2030. adv. **Document type:** newsletter, trade publication.
●Also available online.
  Description: Provides information on what jobs are coming up for bid or negotiation.

690 US ISSN 1087-4070
DODGE CONSTRUCTION NEWS WEEKLY COVERING KANSAS. w. McGraw-Hill Companies, Princeton Rd. S-2, Box 689, Hightstown, NJ 08520-0689. TEL 800-325-2030. adv. **Document type:** newsletter, trade publication.
●Also available online.
  Description: Provides information on what jobs are coming up for bid or negotiation.

690 US ISSN 1086-623X
DODGE CONSTRUCTION NEWS WEEKLY COVERING KANSAS CITY. 1992. w. McGraw-Hill Companies, Princeton Rd. S-2, Box 689, Hightstown, NJ 08520-0689. TEL 800-325-2030. adv. **Document type:** newsletter, trade publication.
●Also available online.
  Description: Provides information on what jobs are coming up for bid or negotiation.

690 US ISSN 1084-9580
▼DODGE CONSTRUCTION NEWS WEEKLY COVERING KNOXVILLE AND VICINITY. 1995. w. McGraw-Hill Companies, Princeton Rd. S-2, Box 689, Hightstown, NJ 08520-0689. TEL 800-325-2030. adv. **Document type:** newsletter, trade publication.
●Also available online.
  Description: Provides information on what jobs are coming up for bid or negotiation.

690 US ISSN 1087-1020
▼DODGE CONSTRUCTION NEWS WEEKLY COVERING LEXINGTON AND VICINITY. 1995. w. McGraw-Hill Companies, Princeton Rd. S-2, Box 689, Hightstown, NJ 08520-0689. TEL 800-325-2030. adv. **Document type:** newsletter, trade publication.
●Also available online.
  Description: Provides information on what jobs are coming up for bid or negotiation.

690 US ISSN 1086-5292
DODGE CONSTRUCTION NEWS WEEKLY COVERING MAINE. w. McGraw-Hill Companies, Princeton Rd. S-2, Box 689, Hightstown, NJ 08520-0689. TEL 800-325-2030. adv. **Document type:** newsletter, trade publication.
●Also available online.
  Description: Provides information on what jobs are coming up for bid or negotiation.

690 US ISSN 1084-9572
▼DODGE CONSTRUCTION NEWS WEEKLY COVERING MEMPHIS AND VICINITY. 1995. w. McGraw-Hill Companies, Princeton Rd. S-2, Box 689, Hightstown, NJ 08520-0689. TEL 800-325-2030. adv. **Document type:** newsletter, trade publication.
●Also available online.
  Description: Provides information on what jobs are coming up for bid or negotiation.

690 US ISSN 1086-5357
DODGE CONSTRUCTION NEWS WEEKLY COVERING METRO PHILADELPHIA. w. McGraw-Hill Companies, Princeton Rd. S-2, Box 689, Hightstown, NJ 08520-0689. TEL 800-325-2030. adv. **Document type:** newsletter, trade publication.
●Also available online.
  Description: Provides information on what jobs are coming up for bid or negotiation.

BUILDING AND CONSTRUCTION

690　　　　US　　ISSN 1084-9548
▼**DODGE CONSTRUCTION NEWS WEEKLY COVERING MIAMI AND VICINITY.** 1995. w. McGraw-Hill Companies, Princeton Rd. S-2, Box 689, Hightstown, NJ 08520-0689. TEL 800-325-2030. adv. **Document type:** newsletter, trade publication.
●Also available online.
　Description: Provides information on what jobs are coming up for bid or negotiation.

690　　　　US　　ISSN 1085-5785
DODGE CONSTRUCTION NEWS WEEKLY COVERING MINNESOTA - NORTHWEST WISCONSIN. 1991. w. McGraw-Hill Companies, Princeton Rd. S-2, Box 689, Hightstown, NJ 08520-0689. TEL 800-325-2030. adv. **Document type:** newsletter, trade publication.
●Also available online.
　Description: Provides information on what jobs are coming up for bid or negotiation.

690　　　　US　　ISSN 1084-9556
▼**DODGE CONSTRUCTION NEWS WEEKLY COVERING NASHVILLE AND VICINITY.** 1995. w. McGraw-Hill Companies, Princeton Rd. S-2, Box 689, Hightstown, NJ 08520-0689. TEL 800-325-2030. adv. **Document type:** newsletter, trade publication.
●Also available online.
　Description: Provides information on what jobs are coming up for bid or negotiation.

690　　　　US　　ISSN 1085-5777
DODGE CONSTRUCTION NEWS WEEKLY COVERING NEBRASKA. w. McGraw-Hill Companies, Princeton Rd. S-2, Box 689, Hightstown, NJ 08520-0689. TEL 800-325-2030. adv. **Document type:** newsletter, trade publication.
●Also available online.
　Description: Provides information on what jobs are coming up for bid or negotiation.

690　　　　US　　ISSN 1086-5284
DODGE CONSTRUCTION NEWS WEEKLY COVERING NEW HAMPSHIRE. w. McGraw-Hill Companies, Princeton Rd. S-2, Box 689, Hightstown, NJ 08520-0689. TEL 800-325-2030. adv. **Document type:** newsletter, trade publication.
●Also available online.
　Description: Provides information on what jobs are coming up for bid or negotiation.

690　　　　US　　ISSN 1086-6191
▼**DODGE CONSTRUCTION NEWS WEEKLY COVERING NEW ORLEANS.** 1995. w. McGraw-Hill Companies, Princeton Rd. S-2, Box 689, Hightstown, NJ 08520-0689. TEL 800-325-2030. adv. **Document type:** newsletter, trade publication.
●Also available online.
　Description: Provides information on what jobs are coming up for bid or negotiation.

690　　　　US　　ISSN 1086-5233
DODGE CONSTRUCTION NEWS WEEKLY COVERING NORFOLK. w. McGraw-Hill Companies, Princeton Rd. S-2, Box 689, Hightstown, NJ 08520-0689. TEL 800-325-2030. adv. **Document type:** newsletter, trade publication.
●Also available online.
　Description: Provides information on what jobs are coming up for bid or negotiation.

690　　　　US　　ISSN 1088-3533
DODGE CONSTRUCTION NEWS WEEKLY COVERING NORTH AND SOUTH DAKOTA. w. McGraw-Hill Companies, Princeton Rd. S-2, Box 689, Hightstown, NJ 08520-0689. TEL 800-325-2030. adv. **Document type:** newsletter, trade publication.
●Also available online.
　Description: Provides information on what jobs are coming up for bid or negotiation.

690　　　　US　　ISSN 1085-1860
DODGE CONSTRUCTION NEWS WEEKLY COVERING NORTHEAST WISCONSIN - UPPER PENINSULA. w. McGraw-Hill Companies, Princeton Rd. S-2, Box 689, Hightstown, NJ 08520-0689. TEL 800-325-2030. adv. **Document type:** newsletter, trade publication.
●Also available online.
　Description: Provides information on what jobs are coming up for bid or negotiation.

690　　　　US　　ISSN 1086-6132
▼**DODGE CONSTRUCTION NEWS WEEKLY COVERING NORTHERN MISSISSIPPI.** 1995. w. McGraw-Hill Companies, Princeton Rd. S-2, Box 689, Hightstown, NJ 08520-0689. TEL 800-325-2030. adv. **Document type:** newsletter, trade publication.
●Also available online.
　Description: Provides information on what jobs are coming up for bid or negotiation.

690　　　　US　　ISSN 1085-8229
DODGE CONSTRUCTION NEWS WEEKLY COVERING NORTHERN NEW JERSEY. w. McGraw-Hill Companies, Princeton Rd. S-2, Box 689, Hightstown, NJ 08520-0689. TEL 800-325-2030. adv. **Document type:** newsletter, trade publication.
●Also available online.
　Description: Provides information on what jobs are coming up for bid or negotiation.

690　　　　US　　ISSN 1085-2255
DODGE CONSTRUCTION NEWS WEEKLY COVERING NORTHWEST FLORIDA. w. McGraw-Hill Companies, Princeton Rd. S-2, Box 689, Hightstown, NJ 08520-0689. TEL 800-325-2030. adv. **Document type:** newsletter, trade publication.
●Also available online.
　Description: Provides information on what jobs are coming up for bid or negotiation.

690　　　　US　　ISSN 1085-1941
DODGE CONSTRUCTION NEWS WEEKLY COVERING NORTHWEST ILLINOIS. 1992. w. McGraw-Hill Companies, Princeton Rd. S-2, Box 689, Hightstown, NJ 08520-0689. TEL 800-325-2030. adv. **Document type:** newsletter, trade publication.
●Also available online.
　Description: Provides information on what jobs are coming up for bid or negotiation.

690　　　　US　　ISSN 1085-2239
DODGE CONSTRUCTION NEWS WEEKLY COVERING ORLANDO AND VICINITY. w. McGraw-Hill Companies, Princeton Rd. S-2, Box 689, Hightstown, NJ 08520-0689. TEL 800-325-2030. adv. **Document type:** newsletter, trade publication.
●Also available online.
　Description: Provides information on what jobs are coming up for bid or negotiation.

690　　　　US　　ISSN 1087-0938
DODGE CONSTRUCTION NEWS WEEKLY COVERING PITTSBURGH AND VICINITY. w. McGraw-Hill Companies, Princeton Rd. S-2, Box 689, Hightstown, NJ 08520-0689. TEL 800-325-2030. adv. **Document type:** newsletter, trade publication.
●Also available online.
　Description: Provides information on what jobs are coming up for bid or negotiation.

690　　　　US　　ISSN 1077-3568
DODGE CONSTRUCTION NEWS WEEKLY COVERING RALEIGH - DURHAM. w. McGraw-Hill Companies, Princeton Rd. S-2, Box 689, Hightstown, NJ 08520-0689. TEL 800-325-2030. adv. **Document type:** newsletter, trade publication.
●Also available online.
　Description: Provides information on what jobs are coming up for bid or negotiation.

690　　　　US　　ISSN 1086-5241
DODGE CONSTRUCTION NEWS WEEKLY COVERING REGIONAL ALLIANCE. w. McGraw-Hill Companies, Princeton Rd. S-2, Box 689, Hightstown, NJ 08520-0689. TEL 800-325-2030. adv. **Document type:** newsletter, trade publication.
●Also available online.
　Description: Provides information on what jobs are coming up for bid or negotiation.

690　　　　US　　ISSN 1086-5268
DODGE CONSTRUCTION NEWS WEEKLY COVERING RHODE ISLAND. w. McGraw-Hill Companies, Princeton Rd. S-2, Box 689, Hightstown, NJ 08520-0689. TEL 800-325-2030. adv. **Document type:** newsletter, trade publication.
●Also available online.
　Description: Provides information on what jobs are coming up for bid or negotiation.

690　　　　US　　ISSN 1085-8180
DODGE CONSTRUCTION NEWS WEEKLY COVERING RICHMOND. w. McGraw-Hill Companies, Princeton Rd. S-2, Box 689, Hightstown, NJ 08520-0689. TEL 800-325-2030. adv. **Document type:** newsletter, trade publication.
●Also available online.
　Description: Provides information on what jobs are coming up for bid or negotiation.

690　　　　US　　ISSN 1086-6221
▼**DODGE CONSTRUCTION NEWS WEEKLY COVERING RIO GRANDE.** 1995. w. McGraw-Hill Companies, Princeton Rd. S-2, Box 689, Hightstown, NJ 08520-0689. TEL 800-325-2030. adv. **Document type:** newsletter, trade publication.
●Also available online.
　Description: Provides information on what jobs are coming up for bid or negotiation.

690　　　　US　　ISSN 1086-5349
DODGE CONSTRUCTION NEWS WEEKLY COVERING ROANOKE. w. McGraw-Hill Companies, Princeton Rd. S-2, Box 689, Hightstown, NJ 08520-0689. TEL 800-325-2030. adv. **Document type:** newsletter, trade publication.
●Also available online.
　Description: Provides information on what jobs are coming up for bid or negotiation.

690　　　　US　　ISSN 1085-8164
DODGE CONSTRUCTION NEWS WEEKLY COVERING ROCHESTER. 1994. w. McGraw-Hill Companies, Princeton Rd. S-2, Box 689, Hightstown, NJ 08520-0689. TEL 800-325-2030. adv. **Document type:** newsletter, trade publication.
●Also available online.
　Description: Provides information on what jobs are coming up for bid or negotiation

690　　　　US　　ISSN 1085-1828
DODGE CONSTRUCTION NEWS WEEKLY COVERING ST. LOUIS. w. McGraw-Hill Companies, Princeton Rd. S-2, Box 689, Hightstown, NJ 08520-0689. TEL 800-325-2030. adv. **Document type:** newsletter, trade publication.
●Also available online.
　Description: Provides information on what jobs are coming up for bid or negotiation.

690　　　　US　　ISSN 1086-6175
▼**DODGE CONSTRUCTION NEWS WEEKLY COVERING SHREVEPORT.** 1995. w. McGraw-Hill Companies, Princeton Rd. S-2, Box 689, Hightstown, NJ 08520-0689. TEL 800-325-2030. adv. **Document type:** newsletter, trade publication.
●Also available online.
　Description: Provides information on what jobs are coming up for bid or negotiation.

690　　　　US　　ISSN 1085-2212
DODGE CONSTRUCTION NEWS WEEKLY COVERING SOUTH CAROLINA. w. McGraw-Hill Companies, Princeton Rd. S-2, Box 689, Hightstown, NJ 08520-0689. TEL 800-325-2030. adv. **Document type:** newsletter, trade publication.
●Also available online.
　Description: Provides information on what jobs are coming up for bid or negotiation.

690　　　　US
DODGE CONSTRUCTION NEWS WEEKLY COVERING SOUTHERN CALIFORNIA INCLUDING NEVADA. w. McGraw-Hill Companies, Princeton Rd. S-2, Box 689, Hightstown, NJ 08520-0689. TEL 800-325-2030. adv. **Document type:** newsletter, trade publication.
●Also available online.
　Description: Provides information on what jobs are coming up for bid or negotiation.

690　　　　US　　ISSN 1086-6124
▼**DODGE CONSTRUCTION NEWS WEEKLY COVERING SOUTHERN MISSISSIPPI.** 1995. w. McGraw-Hill Companies, Princeton Rd. S-2, Box 689, Hightstown, NJ 08520-0689. TEL 800-325-2030. adv. **Document type:** newsletter, trade publication.
●Also available online.
　Description: Provides information on what jobs are coming up for bid or negotiation.

888 BUILDING AND CONSTRUCTION

690   US   ISSN 1085-8245
DODGE CONSTRUCTION NEWS WEEKLY COVERING SOUTHERN NEW JERSEY. w. McGraw-Hill Companies, Princeton Rd. S-2, Box 689, Hightstown, NJ 08520-0689. TEL 800-325-2030. adv. **Document type:** newsletter, trade publication.
●Also available online.
Description: Provides information on what jobs are coming up for bid or negotiation.

690   US   ISSN 1087-092X
▼DODGE CONSTRUCTION NEWS WEEKLY COVERING SOUTHERN PENINSULA. 1995. w. McGraw-Hill Companies, Princeton Rd. S-2, Box 689, Hightstown, NJ 08520-0689. TEL 800-325-2030. adv. **Document type:** newsletter, trade publication.
●Also available online.
Description: Provides information on what jobs are coming up for bid or negotiation.

690   US   ISSN 1085-1852
▼DODGE CONSTRUCTION NEWS WEEKLY COVERING SOUTHERN WISCONSIN. 1995. w. McGraw-Hill Companies, Princeton Rd. S-2, Box 689, Hightstown, NJ 08520-0689. TEL 800-325-2030. adv. **Document type:** newsletter, trade publication.
●Also available online.
Description: Provides information on what jobs are coming up for bid or negotiation.

690   US   ISSN 1086-6140
▼DODGE CONSTRUCTION NEWS WEEKLY COVERING STATE OF MISSISSIPPI. 1995. w. McGraw-Hill Companies, Princeton Rd. S-2, Box 689, Hightstown, NJ 08520-0689. TEL 800-325-2030. adv. **Document type:** newsletter, trade publication.
●Also available online.
Description: Provides information on what jobs are coming up for bid or negotiation.

690   US   ISSN 1085-8172
DODGE CONSTRUCTION NEWS WEEKLY COVERING SYRACUSE. 1994. w. McGraw-Hill Companies, Princeton Rd. S-2, Box 689, Hightstown, NJ 08520-0689. TEL 800-325-2030. adv. **Document type:** newsletter, trade publication.
●Also available online.
Description: Provides information on what jobs are coming up for bid or negotiation.

690   US   ISSN 1085-8210
▼DODGE CONSTRUCTION NEWS WEEKLY COVERING THE BRONX - MANHATTAN - STATEN ISLAND. 1995. w. McGraw-Hill Companies, Princeton Rd. S-2, Box 689, Hightstown, NJ 08520-0689. TEL 800-325-2030. adv. **Document type:** newsletter, trade publication.
●Also available online.
Description: Provides information on what jobs are coming up for bid or negotiation.

690   US   ISSN 1086-525X
DODGE CONSTRUCTION NEWS WEEKLY COVERING THE HUDSON VALLEY. 1993. w. McGraw-Hill Companies, Princeton Rd. S-2, Box 689, Hightstown, NJ 08520-0689. TEL 800-325-2030. adv. **Document type:** newsletter, trade publication.
●Also available online.
Description: Provides information on what jobs are coming up for bid or negotiation.

690   US   ISSN 1085-813X
DODGE CONSTRUCTION NEWS WEEKLY COVERING THE LEHIGH VALLEY. w. McGraw-Hill Companies, Princeton Rd. S-2, Box 689, Hightstown, NJ 08520-0689. TEL 800-325-2030. adv. **Document type:** newsletter, trade publication.
●Also available online.
Description: Provides information on what jobs are coming up for bid or negotiation.

690   US   ISSN 1086-5276
DODGE CONSTRUCTION NEWS WEEKLY COVERING THE NORTH SHORE. w. McGraw-Hill Companies, Princeton Rd. S-2, Box 689, Hightstown, NJ 08520-0689. TEL 800-325-2030. adv. **Document type:** newsletter, trade publication.
●Also available online.
Description: Provides information on what jobs are coming up for bid or negotiation.

690   US
DODGE CONSTRUCTION NEWS WEEKLY COVERING THE SOUTH SHORE. w. McGraw-Hill Companies, Princeton Rd. S-2, Box 689, Hightstown, NJ 08520-0689. TEL 800-325-2030. adv. **Document type:** newsletter, trade publication.
●Also available online.
Description: Provides information on what jobs are coming up for bid or negotiation.

690   US   ISSN 1087-0954
▼DODGE CONSTRUCTION NEWS WEEKLY COVERING TOLEDO AND VICINITY. 1995. w. McGraw-Hill Companies, Princeton Rd. S-2, Box 689, Hightstown, NJ 08520-0689. TEL 800-325-2030. adv. **Document type:** newsletter, trade publication.
●Also available online.
Description: Provides information on what jobs are coming up for bid or negotiation.

690   US   ISSN 1085-8199
DODGE CONSTRUCTION NEWS WEEKLY COVERING VERMONT. w. McGraw-Hill Companies, Princeton Rd. S-2, Box 689, Hightstown, NJ 08520-0689. TEL 800-325-2030. adv. **Document type:** newsletter, trade publication.
●Also available online.
Description: Provides information on what jobs are coming up for bid or negotiation.

690   US   ISSN 1088-3541
DODGE CONSTRUCTION NEWS WEEKLY COVERING WAL-MART. w. McGraw-Hill Companies, Princeton Rd. S-2, Box 689, Hightstown, NJ 08520-0689. TEL 800-325-2030. adv. **Document type:** newsletter, trade publication.
●Also available online.
Description: Provides information on what jobs are coming up for bid or negotiation.

690   US   ISSN 1086-5322
DODGE CONSTRUCTION NEWS WEEKLY COVERING WASHINGTON GENERAL BUILDING. w. McGraw-Hill Companies, Princeton Rd. S-2, Box 689, Hightstown, NJ 08520-0689. TEL 800-325-2030. adv. **Document type:** newsletter, trade publication.
●Also available online.
Description: Provides information on what jobs are coming up for bid or negotiation.

690   US   ISSN 1085-2263
DODGE CONSTRUCTION NEWS WEEKLY COVERING WEST CENTRAL FLORIDA. w. McGraw-Hill Companies, Princeton Rd. S-2, Box 689, Hightstown, NJ 08520-0689. TEL 800-325-2030. adv. **Document type:** newsletter, trade publication.
●Also available online.
Description: Provides information on what jobs are coming up for bid or negotiation.

690   US   ISSN 1084-9564
▼DODGE CONSTRUCTION NEWS WEEKLY COVERING WEST PALM BEACH AND VICINITY. 1995. w. McGraw-Hill Companies, Princeton Rd. S-2, Box 689, Hightstown, NJ 08520-0689. TEL 800-325-2030. adv. **Document type:** newsletter, trade publication.
●Also available online.
Description: Provides information on what jobs are coming up for bid or negotiation.

690   US   ISSN 1087-0962
▼DODGE CONSTRUCTION NEWS WEEKLY COVERING WEST VIRGINIA. 1995. w. McGraw-Hill Companies, Princeton Rd. S-2, Box 689, Hightstown, NJ 08520-0689. TEL 800-325-2030. adv. **Document type:** newsletter, trade publication.
●Also available online.
Description: Provides information on what jobs are coming up for bid or negotiation.

690   US   ISSN 1087-1004
▼DODGE CONSTRUCTION NEWS WEEKLY COVERING WESTERN KENTUCKY. 1995. w. McGraw-Hill Companies, Princeton Rd. S-2, Box 689, Hightstown, NJ 08520-0689. TEL 800-325-2030. adv. **Document type:** newsletter, trade publication.
●Also available online.
Description: Provides information on what jobs are coming up for bid or negotiation.

690   US   ISSN 1086-5306
DODGE CONSTRUCTION NEWS WEEKLY COVERING WESTERN MASSACHUSETTS. w. McGraw-Hill Companies, Princeton Rd. S-2, Box 689, Hightstown, NJ 08520-0689. TEL 800-325-2030. adv. **Document type:** newsletter, trade publication.
●Also available online.
Description: Provides information on what jobs are coming up for bid or negotiation.

690   US   ISSN 1086-6248
DODGE CONSTRUCTION NEWS WEEKLY COVERING WESTERN MISSOURI. 1992. w. McGraw-Hill Companies, Princeton Rd. S-2, Box 689, Hightstown, NJ 08520-0689. TEL 800-325-2030. adv. **Document type:** newsletter, trade publication.
●Also available online.
Description: Provides information on what jobs are coming up for bid or negotiation.

690   US   ISSN 1085-827X
DODGE CONSTRUCTION NEWS WEEKLY COVERING WESTERN NORTH CAROLINA. w. McGraw-Hill Companies, Princeton Rd. S-2, Box 689, Hightstown, NJ 08520-0689. TEL 800-325-2030. adv. **Document type:** newsletter, trade publication.
●Also available online.
Description: Provides information on what jobs are coming up for bid or negotiation.

690   US   ISSN 1086-6108
▼DODGE CONSTRUCTION NEWS WEEKLY COVERING WESTERN OKLAHOMA. 1995. w. McGraw-Hill Companies, Princeton Rd. S-2, Box 689, Hightstown, NJ 08520-0689. TEL 800-325-2030. adv. **Document type:** newsletter, trade publication.
●Also available online.
Description: Provides information on what jobs are coming up for bid or negotiation.

690   US   ISSN 1085-1909
▼DODGE CONSTRUCTION NEWS WEEKLY COVERING WESTERN PENNSYLVANIA. 1995. w. McGraw-Hill Companies, Princeton Rd. S-2, Box 689, Hightstown, NJ 08520-0689. TEL 800-325-2030. adv. **Document type:** newsletter, trade publication.
●Also available online.
Description: Provides information on what jobs are coming up for bid or negotiation.

690   US   ISSN 1085-2182
DODGE CONSTRUCTION NEWS WEEKLY COVERING WINSTON - SALEM. w. McGraw-Hill Companies, Princeton Rd. S-2, Box 689, Hightstown, NJ 08520-0689. TEL 800-325-2030. adv. **Document type:** newsletter, trade publication.
●Also available online.
Formerly: Dodge Construction News Weekly Covering Winston - Salem - Greensboro (ISSN 1077-3576)
Description: Provides information on what jobs are coming up for bid or negotiation.

690   US   ISSN 1087-0946
DODGE CONSTRUCTION NEWS WEEKLY COVERING YOUNGSTOWN AND VICINITY. w. McGraw-Hill Companies, Princeton Rd. S-2, Box 689, Hightstown, NJ 08520-0689. TEL 800-325-2030. adv. **Document type:** newsletter, trade publication.
●Also available online.
Description: Provides information on what jobs are coming up for bid or negotiation.

690   US   ISSN 1085-6552
DODGE DAILY BULLETIN. AKRON - YOUNGSTOWN. d. McGraw-Hill Companies, Princeton Rd. S-2, Box 689, Hightstown, NJ 08520-0689. TEL 800-325-2030. adv. **Document type:** bulletin, trade publication.
●Also available online.
Description: Provides information on what jobs are coming up for bid or negotiation.

690   US   ISSN 1085-5998
DODGE DAILY BULLETIN. ALABAMA. 1971. d. McGraw-Hill Companies, Princeton Rd. S-2, Box 689, Hightstown, NJ 08520-0689. TEL 800-325-2030. adv. **Document type:** bulletin, trade publication.
●Also available online.
Description: Provides information on what jobs are coming up for bid or negotiation.

BUILDING AND CONSTRUCTION

690   US   ISSN 1085-7826
DODGE DAILY BULLETIN. ARIZONA. 1965. d.
McGraw-Hill Companies, Princeton Rd. S-2, Box 689, Hightstown, NJ 08520-0689. TEL 800-325-2030. adv. **Document type:** newsletter, trade publication.
●Also available online.
   Description: Provides information on what jobs are coming up for bid or negotiation.

690   US
DODGE DAILY BULLETIN. ATLANTA AND VICINITY ENGINEERING. d. McGraw-Hill Companies, Princeton Rd. S-2, Box 689, Hightstown, NJ 08520-0689. TEL 800-325-2030. adv. **Document type:** bulletin, trade publication.
●Also available online.
   Description: Provides information on what jobs are coming up for bid or negotiation.

690   US   ISSN 1085-5947
DODGE DAILY BULLETIN. AUSTIN - SAN ANTONIO. d. McGraw-Hill Companies, Princeton Rd. S-2, Box 689, Hightstown, NJ 08520-0689. TEL 800-325-2030. adv. **Document type:** bulletin, trade publication.
●Also available online.
   Description: Provides information on what jobs are coming up for bid or negotiation.

690   US   ISSN 1088-369X
DODGE DAILY BULLETIN. BALTIMORE. 1988. d. McGraw-Hill Companies, Princeton Rd. S-2, Box 689, Hightstown, NJ 08520-0689. TEL 800-325-2030. adv. **Document type:** bulletin, trade publication.
●Also available online.
   Description: Provides information on what jobs are coming up for bid or negotiation.

690   US   ISSN 1088-3940
DODGE DAILY BULLETIN. BALTIMORE - DELAWARE. 1991. d. McGraw-Hill Companies, Princeton Rd. S-2, Box 689, Hightstown, NJ 08520-0689. TEL 800-325-2030. adv. **Document type:** bulletin, trade publication.
●Also available online.
   Description: Provides information on what jobs are coming up for bid or negotiation.

690   US   ISSN 1085-6420
DODGE DAILY BULLETIN. BIRMINGHAM ENGINEERING. 1971. d. McGraw-Hill Companies, Princeton Rd. S-2, Box 689, Hightstown, NJ 08520-0689. TEL 800-325-2030. adv. **Document type:** bulletin, trade publication.
●Also available online.
   Description: Provides information on what jobs are coming up for bid or negotiation.

690   US   ISSN 1085-6390
DODGE DAILY BULLETIN. BROWARD COUNTY. 1968. d. McGraw-Hill Companies, Princeton Rd. S-2, Box 689, Hightstown, NJ 08520-0689. TEL 800-325-2030. adv. **Document type:** bulletin, trade publication.
●Also available online.
   Description: Provides information on what jobs are coming up for bid or negotiation.

690   US   ISSN 1085-6471
DODGE DAILY BULLETIN. BUFFALO AND VICINITY. 1972. d. McGraw-Hill Companies, Princeton Rd. S-2, Box 689, Hightstown, NJ 08520-0689. TEL 800-325-2030. adv. **Document type:** bulletin, trade publication.
●Also available online.
   Description: Provides information on what jobs are coming up for bid or negotiation.

690   US   ISSN 1085-651X
DODGE DAILY BULLETIN. BUFFALO METRO. 1972. d. McGraw-Hill Companies, Princeton Rd. S-2, Box 689, Hightstown, NJ 08520-0689. TEL 800-325-2030. adv. **Document type:** bulletin, trade publication.
●Also available online.
   Description: Provides information on what jobs are coming up for bid or negotiation.

690   US   ISSN 1088-3673
DODGE DAILY BULLETIN. CENTRAL PENNSYLVANIA. 1967. d. McGraw-Hill Companies, Princeton Rd. S-2, Box 689, Hightstown, NJ 08520-0689. TEL 800-325-2030. adv. **Document type:** bulletin, trade publication.
●Also available online.
   Description: Provides information on what jobs are coming up for bid or negotiation.

690   US   ISSN 1085-6463
DODGE DAILY BULLETIN. CINCINNATI. 1972. d. McGraw-Hill Companies, Princeton Rd. S-2, Box 689, Hightstown, NJ 08520-0689. TEL 800-325-2030. adv. **Document type:** bulletin, trade publication.
●Also available online.
   Description: Provides information on what jobs are coming up for bid or negotiation.

690   US   ISSN 1085-6498
DODGE DAILY BULLETIN. CLEVELAND AND VICINITY. 1968. d. McGraw-Hill Companies, Princeton Rd. S-2, Box 689, Hightstown, NJ 08520-0689. TEL 800-325-2030. adv. **Document type:** bulletin, trade publication.
●Also available online.
   Description: Provides information on what jobs are coming up for bid or negotiation.

690   US   ISSN 1085-6560
DODGE DAILY BULLETIN. COLUMBUS. 1968. d. McGraw-Hill Companies, Princeton Rd. S-2, Box 689, Hightstown, NJ 08520-0689. TEL 800-325-2030. adv. **Document type:** bulletin, trade publication.
●Also available online.
   Description: Provides information on what jobs are coming up for bid or negotiation.

690   US   ISSN 1088-3959
DODGE DAILY BULLETIN. CONNECTICUT. 1967. d. McGraw-Hill Companies, Princeton Rd. S-2, Box 689, Hightstown, NJ 08520-0689. TEL 800-325-2030. adv. **Document type:** bulletin, trade publication.
●Also available online.
   Description: Provides information on what jobs are coming up for bid or negotiation.

690   US   ISSN 1085-5831
DODGE DAILY BULLETIN. DALLAS. 1967. d. McGraw-Hill Companies, Princeton Rd. S-2, Box 689, Hightstown, NJ 08520-0689. TEL 800-325-2030. adv. **Document type:** bulletin, trade publication.
●Also available online.
   Description: Provides information on what jobs are coming up for bid or negotiation.

690   US   ISSN 1085-6455
DODGE DAILY BULLETIN. DETROIT. 1972. d. McGraw-Hill Companies, Princeton Rd. S-2, Box 689, Hightstown, NJ 08520-0689. TEL 800-325-2030. adv. **Document type:** bulletin, trade publication.
●Also available online.
   Description: Provides information on what jobs are coming up for bid or negotiation.

690   US   ISSN 1085-6528
DODGE DAILY BULLETIN. DETROIT CENTRAL. 1991. d. McGraw-Hill Companies, Princeton Rd. S-2, Box 689, Hightstown, NJ 08520-0689. TEL 800-325-2030. adv. **Document type:** bulletin, trade publication.
●Also available online.
   Description: Provides information on what jobs are coming up for bid or negotiation.

690   US   ISSN 1085-6439
DODGE DAILY BULLETIN. EASTERN & CENTRAL TENNESSEE. 1971. d. McGraw-Hill Companies, Princeton Rd. S-2, Box 689, Hightstown, NJ 08520-0689. TEL 800-325-2030. adv. **Document type:** bulletin, trade publication.
●Also available online.
   Description: Provides information on what jobs are coming up for bid or negotiation.

690   US
DODGE DAILY BULLETIN. EASTERN AND CENTRAL TENNESSEE ENGINEERING. d. McGraw-Hill Companies, Princeton Rd. S-2, Box 689, Hightstown, NJ 08520-0689. TEL 800-325-2030. adv. **Document type:** bulletin, trade publication.
●Also available online.
   Description: Provides information on what jobs are coming up for bid or negotiation.

690   US   ISSN 1088-3967
DODGE DAILY BULLETIN. EASTERN MASSACHUSETTS. 1967. d. McGraw-Hill Companies, Princeton Rd. S-2, Box 689, Hightstown, NJ 08520-0689. TEL 800-325-2030. adv. **Document type:** bulletin, trade publication.
●Also available online.
   Description: Provides information on what jobs are coming up for bid or negotiation.

690   US   ISSN 1085-5874
DODGE DAILY BULLETIN. EASTERN OKLAHOMA. 1967. d. McGraw-Hill Companies, Princeton Rd. S-2, Box 689, Hightstown, NJ 08520-0689. TEL 800-325-2030. adv. **Document type:** bulletin, trade publication.
●Also available online.
   Description: Provides information on what jobs are coming up for bid or negotiation.

690   US   ISSN 1088-3932
DODGE DAILY BULLETIN. FIVE BOROS. 1966. d. McGraw-Hill Companies, Princeton Rd. S-2, Box 689, Hightstown, NJ 08520-0689. TEL 800-325-2030. adv. **Document type:** bulletin, trade publication.
●Also available online.
   Description: Provides information on what jobs are coming up for bid or negotiation.

690   US   ISSN 1085-5971
DODGE DAILY BULLETIN. FORT WORTH. 1967. d. McGraw-Hill Companies, Princeton Rd. S-2, Box 689, Hightstown, NJ 08520-0689. TEL 800-325-2030. adv. **Document type:** bulletin, trade publication.
●Also available online.
   Description: Provides information on what jobs are coming up for bid or negotiation.

690   US   ISSN 1088-4068
DODGE DAILY BULLETIN. FOUR BOROS. 1966. d. McGraw-Hill Companies, Princeton Rd. S-2, Box 689, Hightstown, NJ 08520-0689. TEL 800-325-2030. adv. **Document type:** bulletin, trade publication.
●Also available online.
   Description: Provides information on what jobs are coming up for bid or negotiation.

690   US   ISSN 1085-6013
DODGE DAILY BULLETIN. GEORGIA. 1968. d. McGraw-Hill Companies, Princeton Rd. S-2, Box 689, Hightstown, NJ 08520-0689. TEL 800-325-2030. adv. **Document type:** bulletin, trade publication.
●Also available online.
   Description: Provides information on what jobs are coming up for bid or negotiation.

690   US
DODGE DAILY BULLETIN. GEORGIA ENGINEERING. d. McGraw-Hill Companies, Princeton Rd. S-2, Box 689, Hightstown, NJ 08520-0689. TEL 800-325-2030. adv. **Document type:** bulletin, trade publication.
●Also available online.
   Description: Provides information on what jobs are coming up for bid or negotiation.

690   US   ISSN 1085-6544
DODGE DAILY BULLETIN. GREATER LEXINGTON AND VICINITY. 1989. d. McGraw-Hill Companies, Princeton Rd. S-2, Box 689, Hightstown, NJ 08520-0689. TEL 800-325-2030. adv. **Document type:** bulletin, trade publication.
●Also available online.
   Description: Provides information on what jobs are coming up for bid or negotiation.

690   US   ISSN 1085-6536
DODGE DAILY BULLETIN. GREATER LOUISVILLE. 1989. d. McGraw-Hill Companies, Princeton Rd. S-2, Box 689, Hightstown, NJ 08520-0689. TEL 800-325-2030. adv. **Document type:** bulletin, trade publication.
●Also available online.
   Description: Provides information on what jobs are coming up for bid or negotiation.

690   US   ISSN 1085-5955
DODGE DAILY BULLETIN. HOUSTON. 1967. d. McGraw-Hill Companies, Princeton Rd. S-2, Box 689, Hightstown, NJ 08520-0689. TEL 800-325-2030. adv. **Document type:** bulletin, trade publication.
●Also available online.
   Description: Provides information on what jobs are coming up for bid or negotiation.

690   US   ISSN 1085-6501
DODGE DAILY BULLETIN. INDIANA. 1989. d. McGraw-Hill Companies, Princeton Rd. S-2, Box 689, Hightstown, NJ 08520-0689. TEL 800-325-2030. adv. **Document type:** bulletin, trade publication.
●Also available online.
   Description: Provides information on what jobs are coming up for bid or negotiation.

BUILDING AND CONSTRUCTION

690　　　　　　US　　ISSN 1085-603X
DODGE DAILY BULLETIN. JACKSONVILLE AND VICINITY. 1989. d. McGraw-Hill Companies, Princeton Rd. S-2, Box 689, Hightstown, NJ 08520-0689. TEL 800-325-2030. adv. **Document type:** bulletin, trade publication.
●Also available online.
　Description: Provides information on what jobs are coming up for bid or negotiation.

690　　　　　　US　　ISSN 1085-598X
DODGE DAILY BULLETIN. KANSAS. 1967. d. McGraw-Hill Companies, Princeton Rd. S-2, Box 689, Hightstown, NJ 08520-0689. TEL 800-325-2030. adv. **Document type:** bulletin, trade publication.
●Also available online.
　Description: Provides information on what jobs are coming up for bid or negotiation.

690　　　　　　US　　ISSN 1085-5823
DODGE DAILY BULLETIN. KANSAS CITY. 1988. d. McGraw-Hill Companies, Princeton Rd. S-2, Box 689, Hightstown, NJ 08520-0689. TEL 800-325-2030. adv. **Document type:** bulletin, trade publication.
●Also available online.
　Description: Provides information on what jobs are coming up for bid or negotiation.

690　　　　　　US　　ISSN 1088-3975
DODGE DAILY BULLETIN. LONG ISLAND. 1966. d. McGraw-Hill Companies, Princeton Rd. S-2, Box 689, Hightstown, NJ 08520-0689. TEL 800-325-2030. adv. **Document type:** bulletin, trade publication.
●Also available online.
　Description: Provides information on what jobs are coming up for bid or negotiation.

690　　　　　　US　　ISSN 1085-5912
DODGE DAILY BULLETIN. LOUISIANA. 1972. d. McGraw-Hill Companies, Princeton Rd. S-2, Box 689, Hightstown, NJ 08520-0689. TEL 800-325-2030. adv. **Document type:** bulletin, trade publication.
●Also available online.
　Description: Provides information on what jobs are coming up for bid or negotiation.

690　　　　　　US　　ISSN 1088-3983
DODGE DAILY BULLETIN. MAINE - NEW HAMPSHIRE - VERMONT. 1967. d. McGraw-Hill Companies, Princeton Rd. S-2, Box 689, Hightstown, NJ 08520-0689. TEL 800-325-2030. adv. **Document type:** bulletin, trade publication.
●Also available online.
　Description: Provides information on what jobs are coming up for bid or negotiation.

690　　　　　　US　　ISSN 1088-4041
DODGE DAILY BULLETIN. MANHATTAN. 1966. d. McGraw-Hill Companies, Princeton Rd. S-2, Box 689, Hightstown, NJ 08520-0689. TEL 800-325-2030. adv. **Document type:** bulletin, trade publication.
●Also available online.
　Description: Provides information on what jobs are coming up for bid or negotiation.

690　　　　　　US　　ISSN 1085-6005
DODGE DAILY BULLETIN. MIAMI. 1968. d. McGraw-Hill Companies, Princeton Rd. S-2, Box 689, Hightstown, NJ 08520-0689. TEL 800-325-2030. adv. **Document type:** bulletin, trade publication.
●Also available online.
　Description: Provides information on what jobs are coming up for bid or negotiation.

690　　　　　　US　　ISSN 1085-6072
DODGE DAILY BULLETIN. MIAMI ENGINEERING. 1968. d. McGraw-Hill Companies, Princeton Rd. S-2, Box 689, Hightstown, NJ 08520-0689. TEL 800-325-2030. adv. **Document type:** bulletin, trade publication.
●Also available online.
　Description: Provides information on what jobs are coming up for bid or negotiation.

690　　　　　　US　　ISSN 1085-5793
DODGE DAILY BULLETIN. MINNEAPOLIS - ST. PAUL. 1972. d. McGraw-Hill Companies, Princeton Rd. S-2, Box 689, Hightstown, NJ 08520-0689. TEL 800-325-2030. adv. **Document type:** bulletin, trade publication.
●Also available online.
　Description: Provides information on what jobs are coming up for bid or negotiation.

690　　　　　　US　　ISSN 1085-5858
DODGE DAILY BULLETIN. MINNESOTA - NORTHWEST WISCONSIN. d. McGraw-Hill Companies, Princeton Rd. S-2, Box 689, Hightstown, NJ 08520-0689. TEL 800-325-2030. adv. **Document type:** bulletin, trade publication.
●Also available online.
　Description: Provides information on what jobs are coming up for bid or negotiation.

690　　　　　　US　　ISSN 1085-5904
DODGE DAILY BULLETIN. MISSISSIPPI. 1972. d. McGraw-Hill Companies, Princeton Rd. S-2, Box 689, Hightstown, NJ 08520-0689. TEL 800-325-2030. adv. **Document type:** bulletin, trade publication.
●Also available online.
　Description: Provides information on what jobs are coming up for bid or negotiation.

690　　　　　　US　　ISSN 1088-405X
DODGE DAILY BULLETIN. NASSAU - SUFFOLK. 1992. d. McGraw-Hill Companies, Princeton Rd. S-2, Box 689, Hightstown, NJ 08520-0689. TEL 800-325-2030. adv. **Document type:** bulletin, trade publication.
●Also available online.
　Description: Provides information on what jobs are coming up for bid or negotiation.

690　　　　　　US　　ISSN 1085-5890
DODGE DAILY BULLETIN. NEBRASKA & SOUTHWEST IOWA. d. McGraw-Hill Companies, Princeton Rd. S-2, Box 689, Hightstown, NJ 08520-0689. TEL 800-325-2030. adv. **Document type:** bulletin, trade publication.
●Also available online.
　Description: Provides information on what jobs are coming up for bid or negotiation.

690　　　　　　US　　ISSN 1085-5963
DODGE DAILY BULLETIN. NEW MEXICO. 1967. d. McGraw-Hill Companies, Princeton Rd. S-2, Box 689, Hightstown, NJ 08520-0689. TEL 800-325-2030. adv. **Document type:** bulletin, trade publication.
●Also available online.
　Description: Provides information on what jobs are coming up for bid or negotiation.

690　　　　　　US
DODGE DAILY BULLETIN. NEW MEXICO - WEST TEXAS. d. McGraw-Hill Companies, Princeton Rd. S-2, Box 689, Hightstown, NJ 08520-0689. TEL 800-325-2030. adv. **Document type:** bulletin, trade publication.
●Also available online.
　Description: Provides information on what jobs are coming up for bid or negotiation.

690　　　　　　US　　ISSN 1085-584X
DODGE DAILY BULLETIN. NEW ORLEANS. 1972. d. McGraw-Hill Companies, Princeton Rd. S-2, Box 689, Hightstown, NJ 08520-0689. TEL 800-325-2030. adv. **Document type:** bulletin, trade publication.
●Also available online.
　Description: Provides information on what jobs are coming up for bid or negotiation.

690　　　　　　US　　ISSN 1085-5920
DODGE DAILY BULLETIN. NEW ORLEANS ENGINEERING. 1972. d. McGraw-Hill Companies, Princeton Rd. S-2, Box 689, Hightstown, NJ 08520-0689. TEL 800-325-2030. adv. **Document type:** bulletin, trade publication.
●Also available online.
　Description: Provides information on what jobs are coming up for bid or negotiation.

690　　　　　　US　　ISSN 1085-5866
DODGE DAILY BULLETIN. NORTH & SOUTH DAKOTA. d. McGraw-Hill Companies, Princeton Rd. S-2, Box 689, Hightstown, NJ 08520-0689. TEL 800-325-2030. adv. **Document type:** bulletin, trade publication.
●Also available online.
　Description: Provides information on what jobs are coming up for bid or negotiation.

690　　　　　　US　　ISSN 1085-6064
DODGE DAILY BULLETIN. NORTH CAROLINA. 1968. d. McGraw-Hill Companies, Princeton Rd. S-2, Box 689, Hightstown, NJ 08520-0689. TEL 800-325-2030. adv. **Document type:** bulletin, trade publication.
●Also available online.
　Description: Provides information on what jobs are coming up for bid or negotiation.

690　　　　　　US
DODGE DAILY BULLETIN. NORTH CAROLINA ENGINEERING. d. McGraw-Hill Companies, Princeton Rd. S-2, Box 689, Hightstown, NJ 08520-0689. TEL 800-325-2030. adv. **Document type:** bulletin, trade publication.
●Also available online.
　Description: Provides information on what jobs are coming up for bid or negotiation.

690　　　　　　US
DODGE DAILY BULLETIN. NORTHERN FLORIDA ENGINEERING. d. McGraw-Hill Companies, Princeton Rd. S-2, Box 689, Hightstown, NJ 08520-0689. TEL 800-325-2030. adv. **Document type:** bulletin, trade publication.
●Also available online.
　Description: Provides information on what jobs are coming up for bid or negotiation.

690　　　　　　US　　ISSN 1088-4009
DODGE DAILY BULLETIN. NORTHERN NEW JERSEY. 1966. d. McGraw-Hill Companies, Princeton Rd. S-2, Box 689, Hightstown, NJ 08520-0689. TEL 800-325-2030. adv. **Document type:** bulletin, trade publication.
●Also available online.
　Description: Provides information on what jobs are coming up for bid or negotiation.

690　　　　　　US　　ISSN 1088-355X
DODGE DAILY BULLETIN. NORTHWEST AND WEST TEXAS. d. McGraw-Hill Companies, Princeton Rd. S-2, Box 689, Hightstown, NJ 08520-0689. TEL 800-325-2030. adv. **Document type:** bulletin, trade publication.
●Also available online.
　Description: Provides information on what jobs are coming up for bid or negotiation.

690　　　　　　US　　ISSN 1085-6021
DODGE DAILY BULLETIN. NORTHWEST FLORIDA. 1990. d. McGraw-Hill Companies, Princeton Rd. S-2, Box 689, Hightstown, NJ 08520-0689. TEL 800-325-2030. adv. **Document type:** bulletin, trade publication.
●Also available online.
　Description: Provides information on what jobs are coming up for bid or negotiation.

690　　　　　　US　　ISSN 1085-6404
DODGE DAILY BULLETIN. ORLANDO AND VICINITY. 1968. d. McGraw-Hill Companies, Princeton Rd. S-2, Box 689, Hightstown, NJ 08520-0689. TEL 800-325-2030. adv. **Document type:** bulletin, trade publication.
●Also available online.
　Description: Provides information on what jobs are coming up for bid or negotiation.

690　　　　　　US　　ISSN 1085-6412
DODGE DAILY BULLETIN. PALM BEACH. 1968. d. McGraw-Hill Companies, Princeton Rd. S-2, Box 689, Hightstown, NJ 08520-0689. TEL 800-325-2030. adv. **Document type:** bulletin, trade publication.
●Also available online.
　Description: Provides information on what jobs are coming up for bid or negotiation.

690　　　　　　US　　ISSN 1088-4076
DODGE DAILY BULLETIN. PHILADELPHIA HOUSING. 1967. d. McGraw-Hill Companies, Princeton Rd. S-2, Box 689, Hightstown, NJ 08520-0689. TEL 800-325-2030. adv. **Document type:** bulletin, trade publication.
●Also available online.
　Description: Provides information on what jobs are coming up for bid or negotiation.

690　　　　　　US　　ISSN 1085-648X
DODGE DAILY BULLETIN. PITTSBURGH. 1972. d. McGraw-Hill Companies, Princeton Rd. S-2, Box 689, Hightstown, NJ 08520-0689. TEL 800-325-2030. adv. **Document type:** bulletin, trade publication.
●Also available online.
　Description: Provides information on what jobs are coming up for bid or negotiation.

690　　　　　　US　　ISSN 1088-4017
DODGE DAILY BULLETIN. RHODE ISLAND. 1967. d. McGraw-Hill Companies, Princeton Rd. S-2, Box 689, Hightstown, NJ 08520-0689. TEL 800-325-2030. adv. **Document type:** bulletin, trade publication.
●Also available online.
　Description: Provides information on what jobs are coming up for bid or negotiation.

BUILDING AND CONSTRUCTION

690 US ISSN 1085-6056
DODGE DAILY BULLETIN. SOUTH CAROLINA. 1968. d. McGraw-Hill Companies, Princeton Rd. S-2, Box 689, Hightstown, NJ 08520-0689. TEL 800-325-2030. adv. **Document type:** bulletin, trade publication.
●Also available online.
Description: Provides information on what jobs are coming up for bid or negotiation.

690 US
DODGE DAILY BULLETIN. SOUTH CAROLINA ENGINEERING. d. McGraw-Hill Companies, Princeton Rd. S-2, Box 689, Hightstown, NJ 08520-0689. TEL 800-325-2030. adv. **Document type:** bulletin, trade publication.
●Also available online.
Description: Provides information on what jobs are coming up for bid or negotiation.

690 US ISSN 1085-6587
DODGE DAILY BULLETIN. SOUTHERN MICHIGAN PENINSULA. 1972. d. McGraw-Hill Companies, Princeton Rd. S-2, Box 689, Hightstown, NJ 08520-0689. TEL 800-325-2030. adv. **Document type:** bulletin, trade publication.
●Also available online.
Description: Provides information on what jobs are coming up for bid or negotiation.

690 US ISSN 1088-4033
DODGE DAILY BULLETIN. SOUTHERN NEW JERSEY AND PHILADELPHIA HOUSING. 1988. d. McGraw-Hill Companies, Princeton Rd. S-2, Box 689, Hightstown, NJ 08520-0689. TEL 800-325-2030. adv. **Document type:** bulletin, trade publication.
●Also available online.
Description: Provides information on what jobs are coming up for bid or negotiation.

690 US ISSN 1085-5939
DODGE DAILY BULLETIN. TEXAS ENGINEERING. d. McGraw-Hill Companies, Princeton Rd. S-2, Box 689, Hightstown, NJ 08520-0689. TEL 800-325-2030. adv. **Document type:** bulletin, trade publication.
●Also available online.
Description: Provides information on what jobs are coming up for bid or negotiation.

690 US ISSN 1085-6579
DODGE DAILY BULLETIN. TOLEDO. 1968. d. McGraw-Hill Companies, Princeton Rd. S-2, Box 689, Hightstown, NJ 08520-0689. TEL 800-325-2030. adv. **Document type:** bulletin, trade publication.
●Also available online.
Description: Provides information on what jobs are coming up for bid or negotiation.

690 US ISSN 1085-7834
DODGE DAILY BULLETIN. UTAH. 1972. d. McGraw-Hill Companies, Princeton Rd. S-2, Box 689, Hightstown, NJ 08520-0689. TEL 800-325-2030. adv. **Document type:** bulletin, trade publication.
●Also available online.
Description: Provides information on what jobs are coming up for bid or negotiation.

690 US ISSN 1088-4084
DODGE DAILY BULLETIN. WASHINGTON AND VICINITY. 1983. d. McGraw-Hill Companies, Princeton Rd. S-2, Box 689, Hightstown, NJ 08520-0689. TEL 800-325-2030. adv. **Document type:** bulletin, trade publication.
●Also available online.
Description: Provides information on what jobs are coming up for bid or negotiation.

690 US ISSN 1085-6048
DODGE DAILY BULLETIN. WEST CENTRAL FLORIDA. 1987. d. McGraw-Hill Companies, Princeton Rd. S-2, Box 689, Hightstown, NJ 08520-0689. TEL 800-325-2030. adv. **Document type:** bulletin, trade publication.
●Also available online.
Description: Provides information on what jobs are coming up for bid or negotiation.

690 US ISSN 1088-3991
DODGE DAILY BULLETIN. WESTCHESTER. 1966. d. McGraw-Hill Companies, Princeton Rd. S-2, Box 689, Hightstown, NJ 08520-0689. TEL 800-325-2030. adv. **Document type:** bulletin, trade publication.
●Also available online.
Description: Provides information on what jobs are coming up for bid or negotiation.

690 US ISSN 1088-4025
DODGE DAILY BULLETIN. WESTERN MASSACHUSETTS. 1967. d. McGraw-Hill Companies, Princeton Rd. S-2, Box 689, Hightstown, NJ 08520-0689. TEL 800-325-2030. adv. **Document type:** bulletin, trade publication.
●Also available online.
Description: Provides information on what jobs are coming up for bid or negotiation.

690 US ISSN 1085-5807
DODGE DAILY BULLETIN. WESTERN MISSOURI. 1967. d. McGraw-Hill Companies, Princeton Rd. S-2, Box 689, Hightstown, NJ 08520-0689. TEL 800-325-2030. adv. **Document type:** bulletin, trade publication.
●Also available online.
Description: Provides information on what jobs are coming up for bid or negotiation.

690 US ISSN 1085-5882
DODGE DAILY BULLETIN. WESTERN OKLAHOMA. 1967. d. McGraw-Hill Companies, Princeton Rd. S-2, Box 689, Hightstown, NJ 08520-0689. TEL 800-325-2030. adv. **Document type:** bulletin, trade publication.
●Also available online.
Description: Provides information on what jobs are coming up for bid or negotiation.

690 US ISSN 1085-5815
DODGE DAILY BULLETIN. WICHITA. 1988. d. McGraw-Hill Companies, Princeton Rd. S-2, Box 689, Hightstown, NJ 08520-0689. TEL 800-325-2030. adv. **Document type:** bulletin, trade publication.
●Also available online.
Description: Provides information on what jobs are coming up for bid or negotiation.

690 US
DODGE REPAIR & REMODEL COST BOOK; the sourcebook - labor and material costs for residential and light commercial construction. 1986. a. $74.95. Marshall & Swift, 1617 Beverly Blvd., Box 26307, Los Angeles, CA 90026-0307. TEL 800-544-2678. FAX 213-250-9811. Ed. Fred Atkinson. circ. 3,000.
Former titles (until 1992): Repair and Remodelling Quarterly; (until 1988): Dodge Remodelling and Retrofit Cost Data.
Description: Contains over 10,000 component costs categorized by C.S.I. 16-division format. Labor and material costs as well as productivity rates are constantly researched.

690 RU
DOMOSTROI. (Text in Russian) 1991. 26/yr. 0.40 Rub. Moskovskii Stroitel'nyi Komitet, Pr. Kalinina 19, k.1, 121019 Moscow, Russia. TEL 291-09-34. Ed. L.G. Kalinina. **Document type:** newspaper.

690 US
DOOR & OPERATOR INDUSTRY. bi-m. free. Door & Operator Dealers Association, Box 117, W. Milton, OH 45383. TEL 513-698-4188. Ed. Christopher S. Long. adv.; index.
Description: Provides news and information about the door and operator industry with a particular emphasis on the door and operator dealer.

338.4769 658 US
DOOR & WINDOW RETAILING.* 1989. bi-m. $15. Jervis & Associates, 11300 US Highway 1, Ste. 400, North Palm Beach, FL 33408-3208, West Palm Beach, FL 33401-4322. TEL 908-850-8100. Ed. John H. Jervis. adv. contact: Linda Callindritto. circ. 16,000. **Document type:** trade publication.
Former titles (until 1993): Door and Window Business; (until 1991): Door and Window Retailing.
Description: Provides news, technical reports, product descriptions, marketing concepts, trends, opinion and interviews about door and window marketing.

DOORS AND HARDWARE. see BUILDING AND CONSTRUCTION — Hardware

690 691 JA ISSN 0285-6018
DORO TO KONKURITO/ROAD AND CONCRETE. 1968. q. Cement Association of Japan, 4th Floor, Hattori Bldg., 1-10-3, Kyobashi, Chuo-Ku, Tokyo 104, Japan. circ. 2,500.

DROGOWNICTWO. see ENGINEERING — Civil Engineering

THE DROP CLOTH. see PAINTS AND PROTECTIVE COATINGS

690 US ISSN 1055-4505
DWELLING CONSTRUCTION UNDER THE UNIFORM MECHANICAL CODE. 1991. triennial. $25.75 to non-members; members $19.35 (effective 1997). International Conference of Building Officials, 5360 Workman Mill Rd., Whittier, CA 90601-2298. TEL 310-699-0541. FAX 310-699-8031. **Document type:** trade publication.

690 AT ISSN 0311-4783
E B S NOTES ON THE SCIENCE OF BUILDING. 1949. irreg. price varies. (Experimental Building Station) Australian Government Publishing Service, G.P.O. Box 84, Canberra, A.C.T. 2061, Australia. TEL 61-6-295-4612. FAX 61-6-295-4500. illus.; cum.index. circ. 6,000. **Indexed:** Aus.Rd.Ind. —CISTI. **CCC.**
Former titles (until 1973): C E B S Notes on the Science of Building (ISSN 0311-0427); Notes on the Science of Building (ISSN 0300-371X)

692.8 US ISSN 0896-3169
E C A MAGAZINE. 1957. m. $10. Engineering Contractors' Association, 8310 Florence Ave., Downey, CA 90240. TEL 213-861-0929. FAX 213-923-6179. Ed. John Simpson. adv.; bk.rev. circ. 2,034.
Formerly (until 1963): E G C A Magazine (Engineering and Grading Contractors Association).

692.8 US ISSN 1077-2154
E M R DIRECTORY OF CONSTRUCTION INFORMATION RESOURCES. 1978. biennial. $87 (effective 1995). McGraw-Hill Companies, 1221 Ave. of the Americas, New York, NY 10020. TEL 212-512-2000. (Dist. by: Utility Data Institute, 1200 G St., N.W., Ste. 250, Washington, DC 20005. TEL 800-486-3660. FAX 202-942-8789) Ed. Paul Herrmannsfeldt. **Document type:** directory.
—CISTI.
Supersedes (until 1993): Directory of Construction Associations (ISSN 0193-2764)
Description: Catalogs technical and business information resources and organizations.

E N R. (Engineering News Record) see ENGINEERING — Civil Engineering

692.8 US ISSN 1065-2205
TA12
E N R DIRECTORY OF CONTRACTORS - MIDWEST. 1974. biennial. $95 for set of 4 regional editions. McGraw-Hill Companies, 1221 Ave. of the Americas, New York, NY 10020. TEL 212-512-2000. (Dist. by: Utility Data Institute, 1200 G St., N.W., Ste. 250, Washington, DC 20005. TEL 800-486-3660. FAX 202-942-8789) Ed. Paul Herrmannsfeldt. illus. circ. 22,000. **Indexed:** PROMT. **Document type:** directory.
Supersedes in part (in 1992): E N R Directory of Contractors (ISSN 0098-6453)
Description: Lists high-volume contractors in the Midwest.

692.8 US ISSN 1065-2191
E N R DIRECTORY OF CONTRACTORS - NORTHEAST. 1974. biennial. for set of 4 regional editions. McGraw-Hill Companies, 1221 Ave. of the Americas, New York, NY 10020. TEL 212-512-2000. (Dist. by: Utility Data Institute, 1200 G St., N.W., Ste. 250, Washington, DC 20005. TEL 800-486-3660. FAX 202-942-8789) Ed. Paul Herrmannsfeldt. illus. circ. 22,000. **Indexed:** PROMT. **Document type:** directory.
Supersedes in part (in 1992): E N R Directory of Contractors (ISSN 0098-6453)
Description: Lists high-volume contractors in the Northeast.

692.8 US ISSN 1065-2213
E N R DIRECTORY OF CONTRACTORS - SOUTH. 1974. biennial. $95 for set of 4 regional editions. McGraw-Hill Companies, 1221 Ave. of the Americas, New York, NY 10020. TEL 212-512-2000. (Dist. by: Utility Data Institute, 1200 G St., N.W., Ste. 250, Washington, DC 20005. TEL 800-486-3660. FAX 202-942-8789) Ed. Paul Hermannsfeldt. illus. circ. 22,000. **Indexed:** PROMT. **Document type:** directory.
Supersedes in part (in 1992): E N R Directory of Contractors (ISSN 0098-6453)
Description: Lists high-volume directors in the US South.

BUILDING AND CONSTRUCTION

692.8   US   ISSN 1065-2183
E N R DIRECTORY OF CONTRACTORS - WEST. 1974. biennial. $95 for set of 4 regional editions. McGraw-Hill Companies, 1221 Ave. of the Americas, New York, NY 10020. TEL 212-512-2000. (Dist. by: Utility Data Institute, 1200 G St., N.W., Ste. 250, Washington, DC 20005. TEL 800-486-3660. FAX 202-942-8789) Ed. Paul Herrmannsfeldt. illus. circ. 22,000. **Indexed:** PROMT. **Document type:** directory.
   Supersedes in part (in 1992): E N R Directory of Contractors (ISSN 0098-6453)
   Description: Lists high-volume contractors in the U.S. West.

E N R DIRECTORY OF DESIGN FIRMS. see ENGINEERING

690   US
EARTH (LOS ANGELES). 1955. q. $20. Shepherd Media Group, Box 6789, Los Angeles, CA 90022. TEL 310-463-4043. FAX 310-699-0491. Ed. David J. Byrnes. R&P contact: Frank Weir. adv.; charts; illus.; circ. 5,200 (controlled). (also avail. in microform from UMI; reprint service avail. from UMI) **Document type:** trade publication.
   Description: Earthmoving and heavy construction in Southern California.

EARTHMOVER AND CIVIL CONTRACTOR. see ENGINEERING — Civil Engineering

690.24   FR
ECHO DES CONCIERGES; bulletin des loges. m. (10/yr.; double nos. for Jul.-Aug., Sep.-Oct.). 17 rue du Dragon, 75006 Paris, France. adv. circ. 15,000.

690   US   ISSN 1055-8284
ECONOMIC HOME OWNER.* (Supplement avail.) 1991. q. $29.99. Publishing & Business Consultants, 101 W. 64th St., Unit 3-2, Inglewood, CA 90302-1255. TEL 213-732-3477. FAX 213-732-9123. (Subscr. to: Box 75392, Los Angeles, CA 90075) Ed. Andeson Napoleon Atia. adv. circ. 120,000.
   Document type: consumer publication.
   Description: Provides helpful information on a variety of topics relating to home repair, with information on industry trends.

690   IT
EDILIZIA (MILAN). 10/yr. Eredi de Lettera Editore, Via A. Bazzini 17, 20131 Milan, Italy. TEL 2-26-66-345. FAX 2-26-64-781. Ed. Fiorino Ivan de Lettera. circ. 8,000.

690 720
EDILIZIA (TURIN). 22/yr. Via S. Francesco da Paola 37, 10123 Turin, Italy. TEL 11-540-796. Ed. Ezio Gianotti. circ. 4,000.

690   SP   ISSN 0213-6287
EDITECO. 1986. 11/yr. Plaza Republica del Ecuador 6, 28016 Madrid, Spain. TEL 1-250-99-43. FAX 1-458-26-06. Ed. Angel Bengoechea. circ. 8,500.

690   UN   ISSN 0251-463X
EDUCATIONAL BUILDING DIGEST. 1973. irreg. (5-6/yr.). free on exchange basis. UNESCO (Thailand), Principal Regional Office for Asia and the Pacific, P.O. Box 967, Prakanong Post Office, Bangkok 10110, Thailand. TEL 662-391-0577. FAX 662-391-0866. TELEX 20591 TH. charts; illus. circ. 3,000. **Indexed:** Archit.Per.Ind.
—CISTI.
   Formerly: School Building Digest.

696 333.79   US
Z5943.E5
THE EFFICIENT HOUSE SOURCEBOOK; an annotated bibliography and directory of helpful organizations. 1987. irreg., latest 1992. $15 (effective 1992). Rocky Mountain Institute, 1739 Snowmass Creek Rd., Snowmass, CO 81654-9199. TEL 970-927-3851. FAX 970-927-4178. Ed. Robert Sardinsky. bk.rev. **Document type:** bibliography, directory.
   Formerly (until 1992): Resource-Efficient Housing (ISSN 1063-0112)
   Description: Comprehensive annotated survey of literature on home energy conservation, including design, renovation and retrofitting. Also lists government, non-profit and other organizations providing educational materials on energy efficiency.

EHIMEKEN KENSETSU KENKYUJO KENKYUJOHO/EHIMEKEN CONSTRUCTION LABORATORY. REPORT. see ENGINEERING — Civil Engineering

690   AU
DAS EINFAMILIENHAUS. bi-m. C P Z Verlagsgesellschaft mbH, Wilhelminerstr. 80, A-1160 Vienna, Austria. TEL 01-454001. FAX 01-460287. Eds. Klaus Vetterle, Amei Cramer. adv. contact: Peter Ross. circ. 73,451. **Document type:** consumer publication.

690   RU   ISSN 0013-3116
EKONOMIKA STROITEL'STVA. 1959. m. $88. Troitskii 2-i per., 6a, stroen. 9, 129090 Moscow, Russia. TEL 7-095-2843295. (Dist. by: Mezhdunarodnaya Kniga, B. Yakimanka 39, 117049 Moscow, Russia; Dist. in U.S. by: Victor Kamkin Inc., 4956 Boiling Brook Pkwy., Rockville, MD 20852. TEL 301-881-5973. FAX 301-881-1637) index.

ELECTRICAL CONSTRUCTION MATERIALS DIRECTORY. see ENGINEERING — Electrical Engineering

690   GW   ISSN 0934-5914
ELEMENT UND BAU. 1982. bi-m. DM.82 (foreign DM.94) (effective 1998). Dr. Harnisch Verlagsgesellschaft mhH, Blumenstr. 15, 90402 Nuernberg, Germany. TEL 49-911-2018-0. FAX 49-911-2018100. E-mail: uepost@aol.com. Ed. Benno Keller. adv.: B&W page DM.3140, color page DM.5390; trim 171 x 255. circ. 6,600. **Document type:** trade publication.
—BLDSC (3726.850000).
   Formerly (until 1988): Element und Fertigbau.

690   US   ISSN 0013-614X
ELEVATOR CONSTRUCTOR. 1906. m. membership. International Union of Elevator Constructor Companies, Clark Bldg., Ste. 310, Columbia, MD 21044. TEL 410-997-9000. FAX 410-997-0243. Ed. Warner Baxter. circ. 17,500 (controlled). **Document type:** newspaper.

690   US   ISSN 0013-6158
TJ1370
ELEVATOR WORLD. 1953. m. $67 (foreign $110). Elevator World, Inc., Box 6507, Mobile, AL 36660. TEL 334-479-4514; 800-730-5093. FAX 334-479-7043. E-mail: sales@elevator-world.com; URL: http://www.elevator-world.com. Ed. Robert S. Caporale; Pub. Ricia S. Hendrick. R&P contact: Ricia S. Hendrick. adv. contact: Patricia Cartee. bk.rev.; charts; illus.; pat.; tr.lit.; index; circ. 6,100 (paid). **Indexed:** C.I.S.Abstr., HRIS. **Document type:** trade publication.
—BLDSC (3730.500000); Ei; Linda Hall; SWETS; UnCover. **CCC**.

EMDEN'S CONSTRUCTION LAW. see LAW

620.005   BL   ISSN 0103-7358
EMPREITEIRO.* (Text in Portuguese and Spanish) 1968. m. $60. E M E P Editorial Ltda., Rua Diogo Moriera 124, CEP 05423 Sao Paulo, Brazil. TEL 814-5022. FAX 813-0545. TELEX 1180007 EMEB BR. Ed. Joseph Young. adv.; bk.rev.; illus. circ. 25,000.

ENERGY AND BUILDINGS; an international journal of research applied to energy efficiency in the built environment. see ENERGY

690 720   US   ISSN 0741-3629
CODEN: EDUDEA
ENERGY DESIGN UPDATE; the monthly newsletter on energy-efficient housing. 1982. m. $337 (foreign $397). Cutter Information Corp., 37 Broadway, Arlington, MA 02174. TEL 617-648-8700. FAX 617-648-1950. URL: http://www.cutter.com. Ed. J.D. Ned Nisson; Pub. Karen Fine Coburn. R&P contact: Carolyn Licata. charts; illus.; pat.; stat. (back issues avail.) **Document type:** newsletter.
   ●Also available online. Vendor(s): NewsNet (BC08).
—CISTI. **CCC**.
   Description: Covers new products, research, and techniques for building energy-efficient, high-quality, and healthful houses. Includes discussion of mechanical systems, major appliances, and an objective look at products' promotional claims.

690   UK   ISSN 0969-9988
ENGINEERING CONSTRUCTION AND ARCHITECTURAL MANAGEMENT. 1994. q. £306($559.50) (foreign £337) (effective 1998). Blackwell Science Ltd., Osney Mead, Oxford OX2 OEL, England. TEL 44-1865-206206. FAX 44-1865-721205. E-mail: journals.cs@blacksci.co.uk; URL: http://www.black.co.uk. (Editorial addr.: Department of Civil and Building Engineering, Loughborough University of Technology, Loughborough, Leicestershire LE11 3TU, England) Ed. Ronald McCaffer; Pub. Allen Stevens. R&P contact: Sarah Pollard. adv. contact: Martine Cariou-Keen. bk.rev.; bibl.; illus.; index. (also avail. in microform from UMI) **Document type:** academic/scholarly publication.
—BLDSC (3758.609000); CISTI. **CCC**.
   Refereed Serial

690 624   SP
ENTORNO. 6/yr. Avda. Baron de Carcer 37, 46005 Valencia, Spain. TEL 6-352-53-69. FAX 3-42-52-880.

624   DK   ISSN 0109-4890
ENTREPRENOEREN. 1971. 10/yr. DKK 250. Entreprenoerforeningen - Danish Contractors Association, Noerre Voldgade 106, DK-1015 Copenhagen K, Denmark. TEL 45-33-138801. FAX 45-33-132450. TELEX 27049. Ed. Joern Damgaard. adv. circ. 5,935.

692.8   FR   ISSN 0014-9373
ENTREPRISE EUROPEENNE. (Text in English, French and German) 1954. irreg. 50 F. (Federation Europeenne de la Construction) Societe d'Editions et de Publications Internationales du Batiment et des Travaux Publics, 33 Av. Kleber, 75116 Paris, France. adv.; bk.rev.; charts; illus. circ. 3,000. **Indexed:** Avery Ind.Archit.Per.
—CISTI.
   Former titles: International Federation of European Contractors of Building and Public Works Review (ISSN 0020-6687); International Federation of Building and Public Works Review.

720   US   ISSN 1062-3957
TA401
ENVIRONMENTAL BUILDING NEWS; a bimonthly newsletter on environmentally sustainable design and construction. 1992. bi-m. $67 to individuals; institutions $127. West River Communications, R.R. 1, Box 161, Brattleboro, VT 05301-0161. TEL 802-257-7300. FAX 802-257-7304. E-mail: ebn@sover.net. Ed. Alex Wilson; Pub. Alex Wilson. R&P contact: Marianne Buettner. bk.rev.; circ. 1,800 (paid). **Indexed:** Environ.Per.Bibl. (1994-). **Document type:** newsletter.
—BLDSC (3791.405800); CISTI.
   Description: Offers building contractors and architects practical, in-depth insight into environmentally sustainable building materials, technologies, and construction methods. Also reviews new products and reports on news in the field.

690 721   HU   ISSN 0013-9661
EPITES- EPITESZETTUDOMANY/BUILDING AND ARCHITECTURAL SCIENCE. 1957. q. $48 (effective 1997). (Magyar Tudomanyos Akademia) Akademia Kiado, Publishing House of the Hungarian Academy of Sciences, P.O. Box 245, H-1519 Budapest, Hungary. TEL 36-1-2043976. FAX 36-1-2045600. Ed. J. Szabo. adv.; bk.rev.; illus. **Indexed:** Hung.Build.Bull. **Document type:** academic/scholarly publication.
—Linda Hall.
   Formerly (until 1968): Epites- es Kozlekedestudomanyi Kozlemenyek (ISSN 0423-278X)

BUILDING AND CONSTRUCTION

691 HU ISSN 0013-970X
TP785 CODEN: EPITAA
EPITOANYAG. (Text in Hungarian; summaries in English, German, Hungarian and Russian) 1949. q. 2000 Ft ($20) Szilikatipari Tudomanyos Egyesulet, Fo utca 68, 1027 Budapest, Hungary. TEL 36-1-2019360. (Dist. by: Kultura, Box 149, H-1389 Budapest, Hungary) Ed. Ilona Wojnarovits. R&P contact: Jozsef Talaber. adv.: B&W page $180, color page $450. bk.rev.; abstr.; charts; illus.; index. circ. 2,700. **Indexed:** Br.Ceram.Abstr., C.R.I.Abstr., Ceram.Abstr., Chem.Abstr., Concr.Abstr., Hist.Abstr. (1955-), Hung.Build.Bull., INIS Atomind. —BLDSC (3794.300000); CASDDS; CISTI; Linda Hall.
  Description: Serves the cement and lime, structural ceramics, ceramic houseware, high-tech ceramics, inorganic heat and sound insulation, glass, natural stone and gravel, and concrete industries.
  Refereed Serial

690.028 BE ISSN 0775-2075
EQUIPMENT CONSTRUCTION. (Text in Dutch, French) 1987. 11/yr. 1750 BEF. Benefalux S.A., Rue Jorez 21-23, 1070 Brussels, Belgium. TEL 32-2-5560356. FAX 32-2-5230355. **Document type:** trade publication.

977 622 US ISSN 0897-5159
EQUIPMENT ECHOES. 1986. q. $18 (foreign $21) (effective 1997). Historical Construction Equipment Association, Box 328, Grand Rapids, OH 43522. TEL 419-832-4232. FAX 419-832-4034. Ed. Donald W. Frantz. R&P contact: Donald W. Frantz. adv.; bk.rev.; illus.; pat.; tr.lit. circ. 2,900. (back issues avail.) **Document type:** academic/scholarly publication.

690 CN ISSN 0710-2720
EQUIPMENT JOURNAL. 1966. 17/yr. Can.$21($28) Pace Publishing Limited, 5160 Explorer Dr., Unit 6, Mississauga, ON L4W 4T7, Canada. TEL 905-629-7500; 800-667-8541. FAX 905-629-7988. E-mail: equipmentjournal@globalserve.net. Ed. Michael Anderson; Pub. E.E. Abel. R&P contact: John Baker. adv.: B&W page Can.$1415; color page Can.$1965; adv. contact: John Baker. circ. 20,000. (tabloid format) **Document type:** trade publication.

690.028 US ISSN 0891-141X
EQUIPMENT TODAY. 1966. m. $60 (foreign $120) (effective 1997). Johnson Hill Press, Inc. (Subsidiary of: Cygnus Publishing), 1233 Janesville Ave., Ft. Atkinson, WI 53538. TEL 920-563-6388. FAX 920-563-1699. Ed. Kate Miller; Pub. Bruce Rabe. adv. contact: Patti Brown. circ. 81,000 (controlled). (tabloid format)
  Formerly: Equipment Guide News (ISSN 0149-5240); Which incorporated: Reporter of Construction Equipment (ISSN 0034-480X)
  Description: Provides contractors with information on equipment selection, application, maintenance, safety and new products.

643.7 GW
ERFOLGREICH HEIMWERKEN. 1988. w. DM.4.20 per no. c/o Marshall Cavendish, Paulstr. 3, 20095 Hamburg, Germany. TEL 040-322175. FAX 040-338769.

STATE & PROPERTY NEWS. see REAL ESTATE

691 GW ISSN 0949-6459
▼**EUROPEAN AGGREGATES.** 1995. q. DM.88 (foreign DM.98) (effective 1997). (European Aggregates Association) Stein-Verlag GmbH, Josef-Herrmann-Str. 1-3, 76473 Iffezheim, Germany. TEL 49-7229-606-0. FAX 49-7229-60610. Ed. Anthony Fell; Pub. Wilhelm Joesch. adv. contact: Gisela Bellemann. **Document type:** trade publication. —BLDSC (3829.482974).

UROPEAN CEMENT ASSOCIATION. EUROPEAN ANNUAL REVIEW. see BUILDING AND CONSTRUCTION — Abstracting, Bibliographies, Statistics

690 UK
EUROPEAN DIRECTORY OF CONTRACTORS. 1889. a. £175($335) Biggar & Co. (Publishers) Ltd., 4 Trafalgar St., Cheltenham, Glos. GL50 1UH, England. FAX 0242-226381. adv.; bk.rev. circ. 25,000. **Document type:** directory.
  Former titles: Directory of Contractors and Public Works Annual and Construction Industries Buyers Guide; Directory of Contractors and Construction Industries Buyers Guide.
  Description: Lists contractors and clients for the construction industry in Europe.

690 UK
EUROPEAN EQUIPMENT INDEX. a. $60. K H L International Ltd., Southfields, Southview Rd., Wadhurst, E. Sussex TN5 6TP, England. TEL 44-1892-784088. FAX 44-1892-784086. E-mail: cranes@khl.com; URL: http://ourworld.compuserve.com/homepages/cranes. **Document type:** directory.

EVALUATING YOUR FIRM'S INJURY & ILLNESS RECORD. CONSTRUCTION INDUSTRIES. see OCCUPATIONAL HEALTH AND SAFETY

692.8 US ISSN 0014-3995
TA730.A3
EXCAVATING CONTRACTOR.* 1905. m. free to qualified personnel. Cummins Publishing Co., 6557 Forest Park Dr., Troy, MI 48098-1954. TEL 313-358-4900. Ed. R.J. Stevens. adv.; bk.rev.; abstr.; charts; illus.; stat.; index. circ. 35,000. (also avail. in microform from UMI; reprint service avail. from UMI)
  —Linda Hall; UMI.
  Formerly: Excavating Engineer.

691 FR ISSN 1251-7321
F D C - FONDATIONS - DEMOLITIONS - CARRIERES. 5/yr. (effective 1995). Editions Faure et Associes, 2 bis, rue George Lardennois, 75019 Paris, France. TEL 44-52-56-20. FAX 48-03-13-62. Ed. Alain Faure. circ. 4,000.

690 AU
F G W VORSCHAU. s-a. S.550. Forschungsgesellschaft fuer Wohnen, Bauen und Planen, Loewengasse 47, A-1030 Vienna, Austria. TEL 43-1-71262510. Ed. Hermann Lebeda. **Document type:** bulletin.

F M DATA MONTHLY. see ARCHITECTURE

F UND I-BAU; Bauen mit Systemen. see ARCHITECTURE

692.8 UK ISSN 0263-2772
TS177 CODEN: FCILEC
FACILITIES; monthly digest for the building administration manager. 1983. 14/yr. £1229($1899) (foreign Aus.$2389) (effective 1998). M C B University Press Ltd., 60-62 Toller Ln., Bradford, W. Yorks BD8 9BY, England. TEL 44-1274-777700. FAX 44-1274-785200. TELEX 51317-MCBUNI-G. URL: http://www.mcb.co.uk. Ed. Fari Akhlaghi. bk.rev.; charts; illus.; cum.index. (back issues avail.) **Indexed:** Anbar. **Document type:** academic/scholarly publication. —BLDSC (3863.430000); AskIEEE; Ei; KR SourceOne; UMI. CCC.

FACILITIES PLANNING HANDBOOK. see ARCHITECTURE

690 SW ISSN 1100-4894
FACKLIGT AKTUELLT; information foer medlemar i Byggnads. 1971. q. Svenska Byggnadsarbetarefoerbundet, S-106 32 Stockholm, Sweden. **Document type:** trade publication.
  Formerly (until vol.5, 1988): Byggnads Fackligt Aktuellt (ISSN 0345-1933)

FAMILY CIRCLE'S GREAT IDEAS. see HOME ECONOMICS

690 SW ISSN 0345-3251
FASADEN. q. AB Svenska Bostaeder, Box 95, 162 12 Vaellingby 1, Sweden. Ed. Katy Strandberg. adv.

690 GW ISSN 0941-7796
FASSADE. 8/yr. DM.84. Verlag F.H. Kleffmann GmbH, Hernerstr. 299, 44809 Bochum, Germany. TEL 49-234-95391-0. FAX 49-234-9539130. E-mail: kleffmann@mediacom.de; URL: http://www.mediacom.de/kleffmann. circ. 11,000. (back issues avail.) **Document type:** trade publication.
  Formerly (until 1992): Maler- und Lackiererhandwerk (ISSN 0343-4079)

690 GW ISSN 0948-1214
▼**FASSADENTECHNIK;** Know-How fuer Konstruktion und Montage. 1995. bi-m. DM.90 (foreign DM.105). Verlagsgesellschaft Rudolf Mueller GmbH & Co. KG, Stolberger Str. 84, 50933 Cologne, Germany. TEL 49-221-5497-0. FAX 49-221-5497326. Ed. Franz Lubinski. adv.: B&W page DM.4500, color page DM.7800; trim 188 x 267. circ. 12,000. **Document type:** trade publication.

690 333.33 US
FAVORITE HOMES. 4/yr. $10 (effective 1996 & 1997). Drawing Board Atlanta, Inc., Box 15556, Atlanta, GA 30333-0556. TEL 404-624-3999. Ed. Phillip Andrew Jessup. circ. 5,000. **Document type:** trade publication.
  Description: Contains house design sketches and data of architect-selected homes.

690 SP
FEDERACION DE ENTIDADES EMPRESARIALES DE LA CONSTRUCCION DE BARCELONA, BOLETIN. 12/yr. Federacion de Entidades Empresariales de la Construccion de Barcelona, Via Layetana 28, 08003 Barcelona, Spain. TEL 3-310-67-12.

690 UK
FENCING NEWS. 1981. bi-m. £9 (effective 1996). Grendon Publications Ltd., P.O. Box 1, Atherstone, Warks. CV9 1BE, England. TEL 44-1827-711722. FAX 44-1827-718081. E-mail: fn@zipmail.co.uk; URL: http://www.zipmail.co.uk/bg.htm. Ed. Bob Jennings. adv.: B&W page £570, color page £850; trim 180 x 265; adv. contact: Paul Carter. circ. 3,500. **Document type:** trade publication.

690 US ISSN 0895-450X
FENESTRATION; a magazine for manufacturers & distributors of windows, doors, & other fenestration products. 1987. 8/yr. free (foreign $21). Ashlee Publishing Co., Inc., 18 E. 41st St., Phse., New York, NY 10017-6222. TEL 212-376-7722. FAX 212-376-7723. Ed. John Swanson. circ. 14,000 (controlled). **Document type:** trade publication.
  —CCC.

LE FIERE; rassegna periodica tecnica di documentazione e informazione. see MEETINGS AND CONGRESSES

FINANCIAL MANAGEMENT AND ACCOUNTING FOR THE CONSTRUCTION INDUSTRY. see BUSINESS AND ECONOMICS — Accounting

FINANCIAL SURVEY. BRICK & TILE MANUFACTURERS AND DISTRIBUTORS. see BUSINESS AND ECONOMICS — Trade And Industrial Directories

FINANCIAL SURVEY. BUILDERS MERCHANTS. see BUSINESS AND ECONOMICS — Trade And Industrial Directories

FINANCIAL SURVEY. BUILDING CONTRACTORS; company data for success. see BUSINESS AND ECONOMICS — Trade And Industrial Directories

FINANCIAL SURVEY. CONSTRUCTION EQUIPMENT MANUFACTURERS & DISTRIBUTORS; company data for success. see BUSINESS AND ECONOMICS — Trade And Industrial Directories

643.7 635.9 UK
FINANCIAL SURVEY. THE D I Y AND GARDEN INDUSTRY. (Do-It-Yourself); company data for success. a. I C C Business Publications Ltd., Field House, 72 Oldfield Rd., Hampton, Mddx. TW12 2HQ, England. TEL 44-181-783-0922. FAX 44-181-783-1940. (also avail. in diskette format) **Document type:** trade publication.
  Description: Contains financial information and contact data for companies in the industry.

FINANCIAL SURVEY. PLANT HIRE; company data for success. see BUSINESS AND ECONOMICS — Trade And Industrial Directories

BUILDING AND CONSTRUCTION

690 US ISSN 0273-1398
TH4805
FINE HOMEBUILDING. 1980. 7/yr. $29. Taunton Press, Inc., 63 S. Main St., Box 5506, Newtown, CT 06470-5506. TEL 203-426-8171. FAX 203-426-3434. URL: http://www.taunton.com/fh/index.html. Ed. Kevin Ireton. adv. contact: Sam Vincent. circ. 243,000. **Indexed:** Access (1994-), Avery Ind.Archit.Per., Br.Tech.Ind., Ind.How To Do It (1981-), Search (1988-). **Document type:** trade publication.
—BLDSC (3927.752000); CISTI; UnCover.
Description: Provides professional-level information on residential building and remodeling with in-depth technique articles.

690 US ISSN 0015-3923
FLORIDA BUILDER MAGAZINE;* the magazine of Florida residential and commercial construction. 1946. bi-m. $18. 3650 N Federal Hwy., Ste. 202, Lighthouse Point, FL 33064-6649. TEL 813-835-4689. Ed. Joan B. Antoine. adv. contact: Duane Williams. bk.rev. circ. 10,125. **Document type:** trade publication.

690 US ISSN 0191-4618
FLORIDA FORUM. 1961. m. free. (Florida Roofing, Sheet Metal & Air Conditioning Contractors Association, Inc.) F R S A, Drawer 4850, Winter Park, FL 32793. TEL 407-671-3772. FAX 407-679-0010. Ed. Bonnie B. Pierce. adv.; bk.rev.; charts; illus.; stat.; index; circ. 9,200 (controlled). **Document type:** trade publication.
Description: For roofing, sheet metal and air conditioning contractors, builders, general contractors, manufacturers and distributors. Includes F.W. Dodge Construction reports, legislative updates, Association news, industry meetings and events and people and products.

690 US
FOCUS ON N A R I. 1982. m. membership only. National Association of the Remodeling Industry, 4900 Seminary Rd., Ste. 320, Alexandria, VA 22311-1811. TEL 703-575-1121. E-mail: narieditor@aol.com; URL: http://www.nari.org. Ed. Susan Maney; Pub. Susan Maney. R&P contact: Brigitte Junior. adv. contact: Brigitte Junior. circ. 7,500 (controlled). (tabloid format) **Document type:** newsletter, trade publication.
Formerly (until 1997): N A R I Focus.
Description: Features and technical articles on the remodeling industry, and association news.
Refereed Serial

FORM & FUNCTION. see *ARCHITECTURE*

690 747 720 GW ISSN 0429-1050
FORM & ZWECK; Fachzeitschrift fuer industrielle Formgestaltung. (Text in German; summaries in English, French, Russian) 1969. bi-m. DM.70.20. Amt fuer Industrielle Formgestaltung beim Ministerrat, Breite Str. 11, DDR-1020 Berlin, Germany. Ed.Bd. bk.rev. **Indexed:** Ergon.Abstr.
—BLDSC (4008.313000).

690 SP ISSN 1134-8232
FORMACIO. 1992. q. (Institut Gaudi de la Construccio) Editorial Interpress S.L., Benedicto Mateo 8-10 bajos, 08034 Barcelona, Spain. TEL 34-3-2800522. FAX 34-3-2054620. Ed. J. Fernandez Martorell. circ. 20,000 (controlled).

690 658.3 DK ISSN 0902-9303
FORMANDSBLADET.* 11/yr. Dansk Formands Forening, Vermslandsgade 71, 2, DK-2300 Copenhagen, Denmark. adv. circ. 3,677.

690 FR ISSN 0995-6220
FORUM B T P. Variant title: Forum T P. 1988. 9/yr. (effective 1995). Editions Faure et Associes, 2 bis, rue Georges Lardennois, 75019 Paris, France. TEL 44-52-56-20. FAX 48-03-13-62. Ed. Alain Faure. circ. 15,000.

690 US ISSN 0274-5186
FOUNDATION DRILLING; serving contractors, deep foundation design engineers, and manufacturers and suppliers of drilled foundation and anchored earth retention systems equipment and services throughout the world. 1980. 8/yr. $60 (foreign $75). Association of Drilled Shaft Contractors, Box 280379, Dallas, TX 75228. TEL 214-343-2091. FAX 214-343-2384. Ed. Scot Litke. adv. contact: Ted Ledgard. bk.rev. circ. 2,300. **Document type:** trade publication.
—UnCover.
Description: For the foundation drilling and anchored earth retention industries worldwide. Includes feature articles, news departments, insurance, personnel and management reports, and a calendar of monthly events.

690 NE ISSN 1385-514X
▼**FRAGBLAST;** the international for blasting and fragmentation. 1997. q. fl.150($5) to members; non-members fl.295($175). A.A. Balkema, P.O. Box 1675, 3000 BR Rotterdam, Netherlands. TEL 31-10-4145822. FAX 31-10-4135947. E-mail: sales@balkema.nl. Ed. H.P. Rossmanith.
Description: Serves as a means of communication for engineers, scientists, and practitioners developing and utilizing explosives in construction and resource removal.

690 747 IT
FRAMES ARCHITETTURA DEI SERRAMENTI; rivista internazionale degli infissi e dei sistemi di chiusura nell'edilizia. (Text in English, Italian) 1983. 6/yr. Lit.94000 in Europe; Oceania Lit.196000; elsewhere Lit.144000 (effective 1997). Gruppo Editoriale Faenza Editrice S.p.A., Via Pier. de Crescenzi, 44, 48018 Faenza RA, Italy. TEL 39-546-663488. FAX 39-546-660440. E-mail: gefe.vendita@uno.dinamica.it; gefe.info@uno.dinamica.it. Ed. Fabrizio Bianchetti. R&P contact: Luisa Teston. adv.: B&W page Lit.4790000, color page Lit.5210000; adv. contact: Elvio Neri. bk.rev. circ. 20,000. **Document type:** trade publication.
Formerly: Frames Porte e Finestre.
Description: For those interested in the role of window frames in architectural design. Contains technical research, news of innovations in the sector, and news on new products and designs.
Refereed Serial

690 FR
FRANCHE COMTE BATIMENT ET TRAVAUX PUBLICS. 4/yr. B.P. 1239, 25004 Besancon, France. TEL 81-83-25-11. FAX 81-83-17-70.

690 JA
FUDO GIJUTSU KENKYU HOKOKUSHU/FUDO TECHNICAL RESEARCH REPORTS. (Text in Japanese) 1981. a. Fudo Kensetsu K.K. Chuo Kenkyujo - Fudo Construction Co., Ltd., Central Research Institute, 2-1, Taito 1-chome, Taito-ku, Tokyo 110, Japan. **Document type:** academic/scholarly publication.

690 CC
FUJIAN JIANCAI/FUJIAN CONSTRUCTIONAL MATERIAL. (Text in Chinese) q. Y6. Fujian Sheng Jiancai Kexue Yanjiusuo, No.61, Liuqiao Yangqiao Lu, Fuzhou, Fujian 350002, People's Republic of China. TEL 713994. (Dist. overseas by: Jiangyu Publications Import & Export Corp., 56 Gao Yun Ling, Nanjing, Jiangsu, P.R.C.) Ed. Hu Yucai.

FUKUSHIMAKEN KENSETSU GIJUTSU. FUKUKEN/FUKUSHIMA ASSOCIATION OF CONSTRUCTION. NEWS. see *ENGINEERING — Civil Engineering*

690 333.33 US
FULL COLLECTION. 1989. a. $35 (effective 1996 & 1997). Drawing Board Atlanta, Inc., Box 15556, Atlanta, GA 30333-0556. TEL 404-624-3999. (Dist. by: 479 Waldo St., S.E., Atlanta, GA 030312) Ed. Phillip Andrew Jessup. R&P contact: Philip Andrew Jessup. adv. contact: Phillip Andrew Jessup. circ. 1,000. **Document type:** trade publication.
Description: Contains house design sketches and data.

690 AU
G D W INFORMATIONEN. 1965. bi-m. membership. Gemeinschaft der Wohnungseigentuemer, Wiedner Guertel 1D, A-1100 Vienna, Austria. Ed. Dr. Josef Mentschl. bk.rev. circ. 4,500. **Document type:** consumer publication.
Formerly: Gemeinschaft der Wohnungseigentuemer-Informationen (ISSN 0016-6219)

G I - GESUNDHEITS INGENIEUR. see *PUBLIC HEALTH AND SAFETY*

690 UK ISSN 1362-7295
▼**G L P.** (Gypsum, Lime and Building Products) 1996. q. £80($150) (effective 1997). Tradeship Publications Ltd., Old Kings Head Ct., 15 High St., Dorking, Surrey RH4 1AR, England. TEL 44-1306-740363. FAX 44-1306-740660. Ed. David Hargreaves. **Document type:** trade publication.

690 US
GARAGE DOOR BUSINESS. 1990. q. Door & Access Systems Manufacturers Association, 1300 Summer Ave., Cleveland, OH 44115-2851. TEL 216-241-7333. FAX 216-241-0105. Ed. William Wending. circ. 12,000. **Document type:** trade publication.
Formerly (until Jan. 1996): Door and Access Systems.
Description: Covers garage door systems, rolling doors, grilles, and electronics.

GEBOUWBEHEER. see *BUSINESS AND ECONOMICS — Management*

690 CN ISSN 0841-1948
GENERALS.* 1984. q. (Ontario General Contractors' Association) Kenilworth Publishing Inc., 27 W. Beaver Creek, Richmond Hill, ON L4B 1M8, Canada. TEL 905-771-7333. FAX 905-771-7336. adv.: B&W page Can.$1550, color page Can.$2150; trim 8 1/8 x 10 3/4. circ. 3,500.
Description: For the architectural, engineering and construction segments of the building industry.

690 IT
GEOMETRI INFORMAZIONE. 1979. m. L.30000($23) Chiandetti Editore s.r.l., Via Vittorio Veneto n.106, 33010 Reana del Roiale, Udine, Italy.

690 US
GEORGIA BUILDER.* bi-m. Thompson-Cook, Inc., 2781 W. Hannon Hill Dr., Tallahassee, FL 32308-8916. Ed. Pat Watkins. circ. 5,000.

690 IT
GEOTEC. 1988. 9/yr. L.60000 (effective 1994). Professional Press s.r.l., Piazzale Baracca 10, 20123 Milan, Italy. TEL 02-48-19-43-20. FAX 02-48-01-11-00. Ed. Andrea Bonalanza; Pub. Enrico Bassi. adv.: B&W page L.3160000, color page L.4750000; trim 190 x 277. circ. 18,000. **Document type:** trade publication.
Formerly: Georama.

GIJUTSU KENKYUJO SHOHO/INSTITUTE OF TECHNOLOGY AND DEVELOPMENT. TECHNICAL REPORTS. see *ENGINEERING — Civil Engineering*

GIJUTSU KENKYUJOHO/TECHNICAL RESEARCH INSTITUTE. TECHNICAL REPORTS. see *ENGINEERING — Civil Engineering*

691 IT
GIORNALE DEL MARMO/INTERNATIONAL STONE MAGAZINE. 1965. bi-m. Lit.64000 in Europe; Oceania Lit.134000; elsewhere Lit.94000 (effective 1997). Gruppo Editoriale Faenza Editrice S.p.A., Via Pier. de Crescenzi 44, 48018 Faenza RA, Italy. TEL 39-546-663488. FAX 39-546-660440. E-mail: gefe.vendita@uno.dinamica.it; gefe.info@uno.dinamica.it. Ed. Stefania/Battaglia. adv.: B&W page Lit.1850000, color page Lit.2060000; adv. contact: Elvio Neri. circ. 6,000.

690 IT
GIORNALE DEL RIVENDITORE EDILE. 12/yr. National Federation of Building Materials Traders, Via Trezzo d'Adda 16, 20144 Milan, Italy. TEL 2-42-39-446. FAX 2-48-95-28-89. Ed. Giorgio Panciroli. circ. 11,000.

690   IT
GIORNALE DEL SERRAMENTO; tecnologia del serramento e degli accessori. Short title: G D S. 1988. 7/yr. Lit.69000 in Europe; Oceania Lit.102000; elsewhere Lit.88000 (effective 1997). Gruppo Editoriale Faenza Editrice S.p.A., Via Pier. de Crescenzi, 44, 48018 Faenza RA, Italy. TEL 39-546-663488. FAX 39-546-660440. Ed. Stefania Battaglia. R&P contact: Luisa Teston. adv.: B&W page Lit.3025000, color page Lit.4950000; adv. contact: Elvio Neri. illus. circ. 16,000.

690   IT
GIORNALE DELL'EDILIZIA ITALIANA. 11/yr. Via Trezzo d'Adda 16, 20144 Milan, Italy. TEL 2-42-39-446. FAX 2-48-95-28-89. Ed. Giorgio Panciroli. circ. 35,000.

GLASS & GLAZING PRODUCTS. see CERAMICS, GLASS AND POTTERY

691   JA
GLASS BLOCK AND BRICK.* (Text in Japanese) 1961. s-a. exchange basis. Nippon Electric Glass Co. Ltd. - Nippon Denki Garasu K.K., 7-1, Seoran 2-chome, Otsu-shi, Shiga-ken 520, Japan.

GLASS DIGEST; management magazine serving the flat glass, architectural metal and allied products industry. see CERAMICS, GLASS AND POTTERY

690   UK
GLOBAL CEMENT REPORT. 1994. a. £210($400) (effective 1997). Tradeship Publications Ltd., Old Kings Head Ct., 15 High St., Dorking, Surrey RH4 1AR, England. TEL 44-1306-740363. FAX 44-1306-740660. Ed. David Hargreaves. adv. contact: David Hargreaves. **Document type**: trade publication.

643   DK   ISSN 0281-3041
GOER SAA HAER. Variant title: Goer Saa Haer i Hemmet. 1981. m. SEK 450; newsstand price: SEK 37.50. Bonniers Specialmagasiner A-S, Strandboulevarden 130, 2100 Copenhagen Oe, Denmark. TEL 45-39-295500. FAX 45-39-290199. Ed. Aksel Brinck Jensen. adv.: color page SEK19200. circ. 54,800 (paid). cols./p.: 4; pp./issue: 68. **Document type**: consumer publication.

690 796.352 380   US
GOLF COURSE BUILDERS ASSOCIATION OF AMERICA. DIRECTORY. a. $15. Golf Course Builders Association of America, 920 Airport Rd., Ste. 210, Chapel Hill, NC 27514-2619. TEL 919-942-8922. FAX 919-942-6955. Ed. Phil Arnold. adv. contact: Susan Monk. circ. 3,500. **Document type**: directory.
  Formerly: Golf Course Builders of America Directory.

690 621.9   CC   ISSN 1000-1212
GONGCHENG JIXIE/CONSTRUCTION MACHINERY & EQUIPMENT. (Text in Chinese) 1964. m. 3 King Si, Gu Rd., Tianjin 300131, People's Republic of China. TEL 86-22-571751. FAX 86-22-317045. TELEX CN 23206 TFIMP. Ed. Quingman Yan. adv.: B&W page $500, color page $1000; trim 185 x 258; adv. contact: Quingman Yan.

690   CC   ISSN 1000-8993
GONGYE JIANZHU/INDUSTRIAL CONSTRUCTION. (Text in Chinese) 1964. m. Y60 (foreign Y48). Yejin-bu, Jianzhu Yanjiu Zongyuan - Ministry of Metallurgical Industry, Central Research Institute of Construction, 33 Xitucheng Lu, Haidian-qu, Beijing 100088, People's Republic of China. TEL 86-10-6222-5599. FAX 86-10-6222-5938. (Dist. overseas by: Guoji Shudian - China International Book Trading Corp., P.O. Box 399, Beijing, P.R.C.) Ed. Fan Xisheng. adv.: color page $1,500; trim 260 x 187; adv. contact: Wang Shuting. bk.rev./ circ. 8,000 (controlled). (also avail. in microfiche) **Document type**: academic/scholarly publication.
  Refereed Serial

690   XV   ISSN 0017-2774
GRADBENI VESTNIK. (Text in Slovenian; summaries in English) 1951. m. $50. Zveza Drustev Gradbenih Inzenirjev in Tehnikov Slovenije, Erjavceva 15, Ljubljana, Slovenia. Ed. Sergej Bubnov. adv.; bk.rev.; abstr.; bibl.; charts; illus.; index. circ. 3,000. **Indexed**: Concr.Abstr., Intl.Civil Eng.Abstr., Soft.Abstr.Eng. —Linda Hall.

690   UK   ISSN 0957-9400
GREAT BRITAIN. BUILDING RESEARCH ESTABLISHMENT. ANNUAL REVIEW. a. free. Building Research Establishment, Garston, Watford, Herts. WD2 7JR, England. TEL 0923-894040. FAX 0923-664010. TELEX 923 220. circ. 8,000. (also avail. in microform from UMI; reprint service avail. from UMI) **Indexed**: Fluidex, Met.Abstr. **Document type**: corporate report.
—BLDSC (1519.982000). **CCC**.
  Former titles (until 1989): Great Britain. Building Research Establishment. Annual Report (ISSN 0141-1829); (until 1973): Great Britain. Building Research Station. Annual Report (ISSN 0068-354X); Incorporates: Forest Products Research (ISSN 0071-7517); Fire Research Annual Reports (ISSN 0071-5433)

GROENLAND, see BUSINESS AND ECONOMICS — Marketing And Purchasing

690   NE   ISSN 0920-8380
GRONDVERZET & BOUWTRANSPORT; grootse bouwmaterieelvakblad van Nederland. 1966. 11/yr. fl.290 (foreign fl.350). Ten Hagen & Stam b.v. (Subsidiary of: Wolters Kluwer N.V.), Postbus 34, 2501 AG The Hague, Netherlands. TEL 31-70-3045700. FAX 31-70-3045812. Ed. W. Mol. adv. contact: Herman Voois. bk.rev./ illus. circ. 6,970. (tabloid format) **Indexed**: Excerp.Med. **Document type**: trade publication.
  Formerly (until 1980): Machinepark (ISSN 0165-4012)
  Description: Information on building, construction and transportation machinery and tools.

GROUND ENGINEERING YEARBOOK. see BUSINESS AND ECONOMICS — Trade And Industrial Directories

669   FR
GROUPE DES CHAMBRES SYNDICALES DU BATIMENT ET DES TRAVAUX PUBLICS DU DEPARTEMENT DE L'OISE. MONTHLY REVIEW. m. Groupe des Chambres Syndicales du Batiment et des Travaux Publics du Departement de l'Oise, 19 Pl. Georges Clemenceau, 60000 Beauvais, France. TEL 774128. TELEX 430306.

690   FR
GUIDE ANNUAIRE ETANCHEITE. a. 213 F. (foreign 207 F.). Societe de Diffusion des Techniques et Specialites du Batiment, 6-14 rue la Perouse, 75784 Paris Cedex 16, France. TEL 33-.-40-70-94-57. FAX 33-1-40-70-04-58.

690   FR
GUIDE ANNUAIRE JOINTS ET FACADES. a. 118.60 F. (foreign 100 F.). Societe de Diffusion des Techniques et Specialites du Batiment, 6-14 rue la Perouse, 75784 Paris Cedex 16, France. TEL 33-1-40-70-94-57. FAX 33-1-40-70-04-58.

690   FR
GUIDE DE L'ENTREPRENEUR DU BATIMENT ET DES TRAVAUX PUBLICS. 6/yr. Editions S E R I P, 40 rue Guy-Moquet, 94501 Champigny Cedex, France. TEL 48-81-91-91. Ed. Yves de Kerautem. circ. 57,250.
  Description: Practical advice and prices of materials for the building trade.

690   FR
GUIDE PRATIQUE DE L'ENTREPRENEUR - BOIS - ALU - P V C. 6/yr. Editions S E R I P, 40 rue Guy Moquet, 94501 Champigny Cedex, France. TEL 48-81-91-91. FAX 48-81-81-77. Ed. Regine Heurteur. circ. 13,000.

690   FR   ISSN 1254-4019
GUIDE PRATIQUE DE L'ENTREPRENEUR - MACONNERIE. 6/yr. Editions S E R I P, 40 rue Guy Moquet, 94501 Champigny sur Marne Cedex, France. TEL 48-81-91-91. FAX 48-81-81-77. Ed. Reni Giacomo. circ. 15,000.

690 368   UK   ISSN 0950-3250
GUIDE TO DAYWORK RATES & UPDATING SERVICE. 1986. irreg. £135 (effective Apr. 1997). Building Cost Information Service Ltd., Royal Institution of Chartered Surveyors, 85-87 Clarence St., Kingston-upon-Thames, Surrey KT1 1RB, England. TEL 0181-546-7554. FAX 0181-547-1238. **Document type**: trade publication.

690   BA
GULF CONSTRUCTION & SAUDI ARABIA REVIEW. (Text in English) 1980. m. $95. Al Hilal Publishing & Marketing Group, P.O. Box 224, Manama, Bahrain. TEL 973-293131. FAX 973-293400. TELEX 8981 HILAL BN. (In the U.K.: Al Hilal International (UK) Ltd., Crescent Ct., 102 Victor Rd., Teddington, Middx. TW11 8SS, England. TEL 44-181-9433630. FAX 44-181-9433701) Ed. Bina Prabhu Goveas; Pub. A.M. Abdul Rahman. adv.: B&W page $2015, color page $2890; bleed 285 x 213. bk.rev.; circ. 10,200 (controlled). (back issues avail.) **Document type**: trade publication.
  Formerly: Gulf Construction.
  Description: Provides news, features, contracts and tenders, product and technical developments, scientific papers covering construction from architecture to landscaping, maintenance, finishings, interiors, and civil and structural work.

690.029   DK   ISSN 0107-5454
HAANDBOG FOR BYGNINGSINDUSTRIEN. 1931. biennial. DKK 422 (effective 1997). Nyt Nordisk Forlag Arnold Busck A-S, Koebmagergade 49, DK-1150 Copenhagen K, Denmark. TEL 45-33-11-11-03. FAX 45-33-93-44-90. adv. circ. 8,200. **Document type**: catalog.

AL-HANDASAH; a monthly construction, industrial & technological magazine for the Arab world. see ENGINEERING

690 666   US
HANDBOOK FOR CERAMIC TILE INSTALLATION. 1963. a. $3 (CD-ROM $9.95). Tile Council of America, Inc., Box 1787, Clemson, SC 29633-1787. TEL 864-646-8453. FAX 864-646-2821. E-mail: tcalink@carol.net; URL: http://www.tileUSA.com. Ed. Ken Erikson. R&P contact: Robert Daniele. TEL 864-646-8453. illus.; circ. 60,000. circ. 55,000 (paid). **Document type**: trade publication.
  Description: Presents architects and builders with ceramic tile installation standards.

695   US
HANDBOOK OF COMMERCIAL ROOFING SYSTEMS. a. 15. Advanstar Communications, Inc., 7500 Old Oak Blvd., Cleveland, OH 44130. TEL 216-826-2839. FAX 216-891-2726. (Subscr. to: 131 W. First St., Duluth, MN 55802. TEL 800-346-0085) Ed. Teresa O'Dea. adv. circ. 26,877. **Document type**: directory, trade publication.

690   GW   ISSN 0017-7202
HANDBUCH DES BAUHERRN; Neubau - Umbau - Modernisierung. 1964. a. membership. Heinze Verlag, Bremer Weg 184, 29219 Celle, Germany. TEL 49-5141-500. FAX 49-5141-50104. E-mail: heinzks@aol.com.de. adv. circ. 600,000. **Document type**: trade publication.

338.4   US   ISSN 0279-1242
HARD HAT NEWS. 1979. fortn. free to qualified personnel. Lee Publications, Inc., W. Grand St., Box 121, Palatine Bridge, NY 13428. TEL 518-673-3237. FAX 518-673-2699. Ed. M. Hilton. adv.: B&W page $700, color page $995. circ. 23,355. (tabloid format)
  Description: Covers heavy construction and roadbuilding industries.

690.028   US
HARDHAT (INDIANAPOLIS). 1991. m. Construction Magazine Group Inc., Box 6132, Indianapolis, IN 46206-6132. TEL 317-329-3100. Pub. Fred G. Johnston, Jr. adv. contact: Pat Wagner. circ. 29,869. **Document type**: trade publication.
  Description: For those involved in the purchase, sale or related services of used construction eqipment.

690   GW   ISSN 0017-8403
HAUS UND GRUND. 1915. m. DM.12. Verlag Haus und Grund GmbH, Luetticher Str. 1-3, 5000 Cologne 1, Germany. Ed. Henning Dreis. adv.; bk.rev.; illus.; stat.; index. circ. 135,000.

690 340   GW   ISSN 0171-8533
HAUS- UND GRUNDBESITZ IN RECHT UND PRAXIS. 1978. irreg. DM.300. Rudolf Haufe Verlag GmbH & Co. KG, Hindenburgstr. 64, 79102 Freiburg, Germany. TEL 49-761-3683-0. FAX 49-761-3683236. Eds. Julius Schoenhofer, Guenther Reinisch. (looseleaf format) **Document type**: proceedings.

BUILDING AND CONSTRUCTION

690　　　　　　　GW　ISSN 0934-8026
DAS HAUSBAU MAGAZIN. 1963. bi-m. DM.48 (foreign DM.54) (effective 1997). Fachschriften Verlag GmbH, Hoehenstr. 17, 70736 Fellbach, Germany. TEL 49-711-5206-256. FAX 49-711-5281424. Ed. Paul Daluden; Pub. Ottmar Strebel. adv. contact: Wolfgang Kriwan. bk.rev.; illus.; mkt.; tr.lit.; circ. 74,062. **Document type:** trade publication.
　　Former titles (until 1986): Bauen und Fertighaus (ISSN 0005-6510); Fertig Bauen (ISSN 0430-3253).
　　Description: News about house building and renovation.

HAUSTECHNISCHE RUNDSCHAU. see *HEATING, PLUMBING AND REFRIGERATION*

690　　　　　　　US
HAWAII BUILDING GUIDE (DIRECTORY). 1954. a. $20 free to qualified personnel. Trade Publishing Co. Ltd., 287 Mokauea St., Honolulu, HI 96819. TEL 808-848-0711. Ed. John Black. adv. circ. 4,500. **Document type:** directory.
　　Formerly: Building Industry Digest of Hawaii.

692.8　　　　　CN　ISSN 0017-9426
HEAVY CONSTRUCTION NEWS. 1957. fortn. Can.$36. Maclean Hunter Ltd., Business Publication Division, Maclean Hunter Bldg., 777 Bay St., Toronto, ON M5W 1A7, Canada. TEL 416-596-5844. FAX 416-593-3193. Ed. Russ Noble; Pub. David J. Fidler. adv. contact: Steven Feld. bibl.; charts; index. circ. 23,000. **Indexed:** Can.B.P.I.
　　—CISTI; UnCover. **CCC**.
　　Description: Focuses on business prospects, site stories, maintenance and new products.

HERON. see *ENGINEERING — Civil Engineering*

338.3　　　　　US
HIGH - VALUED DWELLING COST GUIDE. a. $49. (American Appraisal Associates) E.H. Boeckh (Subsidiary of: Thomson Publishing Corp.), 2885 S. Calhoun Rd., Box 510291, New Berlin, WI 53151-0291. TEL 414-780-2800; 800-285-1288. FAX 414-780-0306.

HIGHWAY BUILDER. see *ENGINEERING — Civil Engineering*

690　　　　　　　GW　ISSN 0342-5169
HOCH- UND TIEFBAU. 1948. 10/yr. DM.80 (foreign DM.100). Verlag Neuer Merkur GmbH, Ingolstaedter Str. 63a, 80939 Munich, Germany. TEL 089-318905-0. FAX 089-31890553. **Document type:** trade publication.

HOME; creative ideas for home design. see *ARCHITECTURE*

690　　　　　　　CN　ISSN 0840-4348
HOME BUILDER MAGAZINE. (Text in English) 1987. 6/yr. Can.$30. Work-4 Projects Ltd., 4819 St. Charles Blvd., Pierrefonds, PQ H9H 3C7, Canada. TEL 514-620-2200. FAX 514-620-6300. E-mail: work4@total.net. Ed. Frank O'Brien. R&P contact: Ady Artzy. adv.: B&W page Can.$3875, color page Can.$4975; adv. contact: Cheryl Carvery. circ. 25,138 (controlled). (back issues avail.) **Document type:** trade publication.
　　—CISTI.
　　Description: Covers new home construction and renovation markets in Canada.

690　　　　　　　US
HOME BUILDER NETWORK.* m. $38. (Association Publications Network, Inc.) A P L, Inc., Box 32500, Louisville, KY 40232-2500. Ed. Pam Moore.

THE HOME HANDYMAN. see *HOW-TO AND DO-IT-YOURSELF*

643.7　　　　　US
HOME MAGAZINE'S BEST KITCHEN & BATH. q. Hachette Filipacchi Magazines, Inc., 1633 Broadway, New York, NY 10019. TEL 212-767-5800. FAX 212-789-4216. Ed. Timothy A. Drew. circ. 123,420. **Document type:** consumer publication.

690　　　　　　　US　ISSN 1040-547X
NA7205
HOME PLANNER. 1989. 8/yr. $21.95. Home Planners, Inc., 3275 W. Ina Rd., Ste. 110, Tucson, AZ 85741. TEL 602-297-8200. FAX 602-297-6219. Ed. Paulette Mulvin; Pub. Rickard Bailey. adv. contact: Tom Low. circ. 100,000. **Document type:** consumer publication.
　　Description: Contains home plans, showing detailed exterior illustrations, floor plans, and planning pointers. Also contains in-depth how-to advice.

690　　　　　　　US
HOMEBUILDER.* 1980. m. $21. Thompson Publications, Inc., 2781 W. Hannon Hill Dr., Talahassee, FL 32308-8916. TEL 904-681-3583. FAX 904-224-1359. Ed. Paul M. Thompson. adv. circ. 22,000.

690　　　　　　　CN　ISSN 1187-0974
HOMES AND COTTAGES. 1989. 8/yr. Can.$14.98 (foreign Can.$35). In-Home Show Ltd., 6557 Mississauga Rd., No. D, Mississauga, ON L5N 1A6, Canada. TEL 905-567-1440. FAX 905-567-1442. E-mail: janhvc@pathcom.com; jimhc@pathcom.com; URL: http://homesandcottages.com. Ed. Janice E. Naisby; Pub. Steven Griffin. R&P contact: Jim Adair. adv. contact: Laurie Watson. bk.rev. circ. 64,000. (back issues avail.) **Document type:** trade publication, consumer publication.
　　Formerly (until 1990): In-Home Show News (ISSN 1186-6160)
　　Refereed Serial

690　　747　　　AT　ISSN 0817-4296
HOMES & LIVING. 1981. q. (plus 2 annuals: Renovations & Yearbook). Aus.$38 (effective May 1993). H B M Publishing, 33 Brisbane St., E. Perth, W.A. 6000, Australia. TEL 09-228-9334. FAX 09-227-8337. Ed. Diane Edge. adv. contact: Tania Ruttledge. bk.rev.; index. circ. 50,000. (back issues avail.) **Document type:** consumer publication.
　　Formerly (until 1984): W.A. Homes and Living (ISSN 0817-430X)
　　Description: Features homes, gardens for builders, decorators, renovators.
　　Refereed Serial

690　　　　　　　US　ISSN 0897-621X
NA7205
HOMESTYLES HOME PLANS. 1986. q. $15. HomeStyles, 213 E. 4th St., 4th Fl., St. Paul, MN 55101. TEL 612-602-5000; 888-626-2026. FAX 612-602-5002. Ed. Eric Erglund. R&P contact: Kris Donnelly. adv. contact: Kevin Miller. circ. 73,000.
　　Description: Contains home designs for which blueprints are available. For those who plan to build a new home.

HONG KONG. BUILDING DEVELOPMENT DEPARTMENT. BUILDING STATISTICS. see *PUBLIC ADMINISTRATION*

HONG KONG ARCHITECTS & DESIGNERS CATALOGUE (YEAR). see *ARCHITECTURE*

338.4　　　　　CC
HONG KONG BUILDER DIRECTORY (YEAR). (Text in Chinese, English) a. HK.$595 (foreign $100). Far East Trade Press Ltd., Kai Tak Commercial Bldg., 2nd Fl., 317 Des Voeux Rd., Central, Hong Kong, People's Republic of China. TEL 5453028. FAX 5446979. (Subscr. to: Times Publishing Group, Block C, 10th Fl. Seaview Estate, 2-8 Watson Rd., North Point, Hong Kong. TEL 852-566-8381. FAX 852-508-0255; People's Republic of China) Ed. Kenneth Ho; Pub. Kenneth Ho. adv.: B&W page HK.$8150, color page HK.$10900; trim 210 x 280. illus. circ. 8,000. **Document type:** directory.
　　Description: Covers construction products and services, building professionals, and relevant government departments.

691.3　　　　　SP　ISSN 1133-1380
HORMIGON PREPARADO. 1987. q. 4000 ptas. (foreign 5000 ptas.) (effective 1996). (Asociacion Nacional Espanola de Fabricas de Hormigon Preparado) Metalurgia y Electricidad, S.L., Antonio Gonzalez Porras 35, 2o, 28019 Madrid, Spain. TEL 34-1-4690420. FAX 34-1-4690304. adv.: B&W page 100000 ptas., color page 135000 ptas.; trim 260 x 185; adv. contact: Francisco Carmona. circ. 5,000 (paid). **Indexed:** Ind.SST. **Document type:** newspaper.
　　Description: For public works engineers, architects, technical schools, and concrete companies.

691　　　　　　　SP　ISSN 0439-5689
　　　　　　　　　　　　CODEN: HOACBE
HORMIGON Y ACERO. 1964. 4/yr. 8500 ptas. individual membership; institutional 21000 ptas. (effective 1995). Asociacion Tecnica Espanola del Pretensado, Apdo. 19002, 28080 Madrid, Spain. TEL 34-1-7660703. Ed. Rafael Pineiro. bk.rev. **Indexed:** Ind.SST.

690　　747　　　US
HOUSE BEAUTIFUL HOME BUILDING. 2/yr. newsstand price: $2.95. Hearst Corporation, 224 W. 57th St., New York, NY 10019-5970. TEL 212-649-3808. Ed. Jim Kemp; Pub. Connie Livsey. adv. contact: Mart T. Kennedy. circ. 250,000. **Document type:** consumer publication.

690　　　　　　　US　ISSN 0018-6430
HOUSE BEAUTIFUL'S BUILDING MANUAL. 1935. 3/yr. $2.95 per no. Hearst Corporation, 1700 Broadway, Ste. 2801, New York, NY 10019. TEL 212-903-5182. FAX 212-262-9401. Ed. Jim Kemp. adv.; illus. circ. 250,000.

690　　　　　　　UK　ISSN 0951-1334
HOUSE BUILDER; management journal of a 3 billion pound industry. 1941. m. £66 (foreign £99) (effective 1997). (House-Builders' Federation) Housebuilder Publications Ltd., 82 New Cavendish St., London W1M 8AD, England. TEL 44-171-580-5588. FAX 44-171-323-0890. (Co-sponsor: National House Building Council) Ed. Ben Roskrow; Pub. Alan Dawson. R&P contact: Alan Dawson. adv. contact: Alan Levett. tr.lit.; circ. 18,134. **Indexed:** Archit.Per.Ind. **Document type:** trade publication.
　　—BLDSC (4334.620000).

690　　　　　　　US
HOUSE MAGAZINE; the northeast builder's trade journal. 1993. bi-m. $18. Patrick Gass & Co., Inc., Box 235, Jericho, VT 05465. TEL 802-899-4838. FAX 802-899-1709. Ed. Richard A. Mindell. adv. contact: Richard Mindell. charts; illus.; stat.; tr.lit. circ. 25,000. (back issues avail.) **Document type:** trade publication.
　　Formerly: VT Builder Magazine.
　　Description: Covers the residential construction industry in the northeastern U.S. Includes new products and innovative building systems.

352.75　　　　　AT
HOUSING. 1948. bi-m. Aus.$50 to non-members; members Aus.$45 (effective 1997). (Housing Industry Association) H.I.A. Publishing Pty. Ltd., 70 Jolimont St., Jolimont, Vic. 3002, Australia. TEL 61-3-92808200. FAX 61-3-92808205. Ed. Kevin Randall. R&P contact: Penny Brown. adv. contact: Keith Park. bk.rev. circ. 30,000. **Document type:** trade publication.
　　Former titles: Housing Victoria - Tasmania (ISSN 1035-9265); Housing Victoria; Housing Products and Costing Guide; Housing Australia (ISSN 0046-8096)
　　Description: Covers housing industry nationally; new products, new developments, economic research, management and marketing coverage.

690　　333.33　　　UK
HOUSING FINANCE REVIEW. 1952. m. free. Nationwide Building Society, Planning Department, Nationwide House, Pipers Way, Swindon SN38 1XX, England. FAX 44-1793-455903. Ed. P.J. Sanderson. charts; stat.; cum.index: 1973-1994. circ. 50,000. (tabloid format) **Indexed:** Build.Manage.Abstr. **Document type:** bulletin.
　　Former titles: Nationwide Building Society. House Prices; Nationwide Anglia Building Society. House Prices (ISSN 0263-3639); Nationwide Anglia Building Society. Occasional Bulletin; Cooperative Permanent Building Society. Occasional Bulletin.

BUILDING AND CONSTRUCTION

HUSBYGNING BRUTTO. see *BUSINESS AND ECONOMICS — Marketing And Purchasing*

HUSBYGNING NETTO. see *BUSINESS AND ECONOMICS — Marketing And Purchasing*

HUTTLINGER'S PIPELINE REPORT. see *PETROLEUM AND GAS*

690   US   ISSN 1079-9931
TP882
I E E E CEMENT INDUSTRY TECHNICAL CONFERENCE. RECORD. a. price varies. (I E E E, Industry Applications Society) Institute of Electrical and Electronics Engineers, Inc., 345 E. 47th St., New York, NY 10017-2394. TEL 732-981-0060; 800-678-4333. FAX 732-981-9667. E-mail: customer.service@ieee.org; URL: http://www.ieee. org. (Subscr. to: 445 Hoes Ln., Box 1331, Piscataway, NJ 08855-1331) Indexed: INSPEC.
   Former titles: I E E E Cement Industry Technical Conference. Record of Conference Papers (ISSN 1050-3854); Cement Industry Technical Conference. Record (ISSN 0069-1402)
   Description: Development and application of electrical systems specifically related to the manufacture of cement.

690 620   PH
I F A W P C A NEWSLETTER. q. International Federation of Asian and Western Pacific Contractors' Associations, Padilla Building, 3rd Fl., Ortigas Commercial Center, Emerald Ave., Pasig, Metro Manila, Philippines. FAX 632-631-2789. TELEX 29083 IFAWPCA PH. Ed. Rodante D. Marcoleta.

330   GW   ISSN 0170-5687
I F O STUDIEN ZUR BAUWIRTSCHAFT. 1974. irreg., vol.19, 1995. price varies. I F O Institut fuer Wirtschaftsforschung, Poschingerstr. 5, 81679 Munich, Germany. TEL 49-89-9224-0. FAX 49-89-985369. circ. 400. **Document type:** monographic series.
   Description: Research results of the Department of Construction and Housing in Germany.

I S T C TODAY. (Iron and Steel Trades Confederation) see *LABOR UNIONS*

690   US   ISSN 0019-1914
ILLINOIS BUILDING NEWS.* 1932. m. $3.50. Illinois Lumber and Material Dealers Association, Inc., 932 S. Spring, Springfield, IL 62704. TEL 217-544-5405. Ed. Edwin F. Sembell. adv. circ. 1,356.

691   US
ILLINOIS DEALER DIRECTORY AND BUYER'S GUIDE.* 1932. a. $20. Illinois Lumber and Material Dealers Association, Inc., 932 S. Spring, Springfield, IL 62704. TEL 217-544-5405. adv. circ. 750.
   Formerly: Illinois Directory and Suppliers Listing (ISSN 0073-4799)

690   US   ISSN 1081-6569
IMAGE (FORT WORTH). 1969. m. $35 (foreign $45). National Association of Women in Construction, 327 S. Adams St., Fort Worth, TX 76104. TEL 817-877-5551. FAX 817-877-0324. E-mail: nawic@onamp.net; URL: http://www.nawic.org. Ed. Leona Priya Dalavai. R&P contact: Leona Priya Dalavai. adv.; circ. 6,500 (paid). **Document type:** trade publication.
   Description: Covers financial, legal, educational and career issues relating to women in construction.

690 333.33   GW   ISSN 0940-7987
IMMOBILIEN MANAGER. 1992. 10/yr. DM.145 (foreign DM.155). Verlagsgesellschaft Rudolf Mueller GmbH & Co. KG, Stolberger Str. 84, 50933 Cologne, Germany. TEL 49-221-5497-0. FAX 49-221-5497326. adv.: B&W page DM.7840, color page DM.10690; trim 164 x 250. circ. 20,000. **Document type:** trade publication.

690   IT
IMPRESE. 10/yr. L.12000. B.F.B. Editrice s.r.l., Via Medardo Rosso 18, 20159 Milan, Italy. TEL 39-2-6880206. FAX 39-2-6883529. Ed. Roberto Amghimomi. circ. 83,500.

IMPROVE YOUR CONSTRUCTION BUSINESS SERIES. see *BUSINESS AND ECONOMICS — Labor And Industrial Relations*

643.7   US
IN STEP WITH N S D A. 1934. w. membership. National Supply Distributors Association Inc., 5134 Bower Ave., Dayton, OH 45431. TEL 513-258-2424. FAX 513-258-3327. adv.; bk.rev. circ. 1,000. (processed)
   Former titles: National Supply Distributors Association Bulletin; Home Improvement Trends.

INCOME - EXPENSE ANALYSIS: CONVENTIONAL APARTMENTS. see *REAL ESTATE*

INCOME - EXPENSE ANALYSIS: FEDERALLY ASSISTED APARTMENTS. see *REAL ESTATE*

INCOME - EXPENSE ANALYSIS: SHOPPING CENTERS, OPEN AND ENCLOSED. see *REAL ESTATE*

690   II
INDIAN ARCHITECT & BUILDER. (Text in English) 1987. m. $70. Business Press, Transmission House, Compartment No. 82, Plot No. 6-19, Marol Co-op Industrial Estate, M.V. Rd., Andheri East, Mumbai 400 059, India. TEL 91-22-850-9100. FAX 91-22-850-2070. TELEX 011-78455 BPPL IN. Ed. Sarayu Ahuja; Pub. R.V. Pandit. adv.: B&W page Rs.7000, color page Rs.12500; trim 280 x 205. circ. 35,000.
   Formerly: Building and Construction.
   Description: Contains construction activities, international news briefs and interviews with leading architects and engineers.

691   II
INDIAN CEMENT INDUSTRY DESKBOOK. (Text in English) 1978. biennial. Rs.175($55) Technical Press Publications, 5-1 Convent St., Colaba, Mumbai 400 039, India. TEL 91-22-2021446. FAX 91-22-2871499. TELEX 011-83479 CHEM IN. Ed. J.P. de Sousa. adv.; bk.rev.; abstr.; charts; illus. circ. 6,400. (also avail. in microform from UMI) **Document type:** trade publication.

INDIAN CONCRETE JOURNAL. see *ENGINEERING — Civil Engineering*

690   II   ISSN 0971-1244
INDIAN CONSTRUCTION; journal of the builders' association of India. 1968. m. Rs.50($20) Builders' Association of India, Commerce Centre, J. Dadajee (Tardeo) Road, Bombay 400 034, India. Ed. N.A. Samant. adv.; bk.rev.; abstr. circ. 1,350. **Indexed:** C.R.I.Abstr., C.R.I.Curr.Cont.
—CISTI.
   Formerly (until 1979): Builders' Association of India. Bulletin (ISSN 0304-9507)

690   II
INDIAN TENDER JOURNAL. (Text in English) 1968. w. newsstand price: Rs.0.50. South Delhi Printers & Publishers, D-30, N.D.S.E. Part I, New Delhi 110 049, India. Pub. Tej Singh. adv.: page Rs.7600; 405 x 275. **Indexed:** Text.Tech.Dig.

690   US
INDIANA BUILDER MAGAZINE. 1990. m. $28. ProTec Publishing, Box 1494, Bloomington, IN 47402. TEL 812-332-1693. FAX 812-332-0117. Ed. C. Dale Risch. adv.: B&W page $900, color page $1250; trim 8 1/2 x 11; adv. contact: Mike Burns. circ. 12,444. **Document type:** trade publication.

690 720   US
INDIANA CONSTRUCTOR. 1990. bi-m. free to qualified personnel. (Associated General Contractors of Indiana) I B J Corp., 431 N. Pennsylvania St., Indianapolis, IN 46204. TEL 317-634-6200. FAX 317-263-5060. Ed. Jo Ann Welker. adv.; illus.; circ. 3,500 (controlled). **Document type:** trade publication.
   Description: Covers topics and issues of interest to the commercial, industrial and institutional construction industries in Indiana.

690 747   UK
INDIVIDUAL HOMES; designing, building & renovating your own home. m. £20 (U.A.E., Canada, Hong Kong £62; elsewhere £68) (effective 1997 & 1998). 91-93 High St., Bromsgrove, Worcs. B61 8AQ, England. TEL 44-1527-836600. FAX 44-1527-574388. E-mail: indhomes@cityscape.co.uk. Ed. Michael Holmes; Pub. Peter Harris. adv. contact: Joy Stanley. **Document type:** consumer publication.
   Description: Directed to those who want to build or develop their own home. Provides information during the decision-making process for designing, building materials, financing, and planning procedures.

690   IT
L'INDUSTRIA DEI LATERIZI. (Text in Italian; summaries in English) 1950. bi-m. Lit.64000 in Europe; Oceania Lit.139000; elsewhere Lit.101000 (effective 1997). (Associazione Nazionale degli Industriali dei Laterizi) Gruppo Editoriale Faenza Editrice S.p.A., Via Pier. de Crescenzi, 44, 48018 Faenza, Italy. TEL 39-546-663488. FAX 39-546-660440. E-mail: gefe.vendita@uno.dinamica.it; gefe.info@vendita.dinamica.it. Ed. Giovanni Biffi. adv.: B&W page Lit.1750000, color page Lit.1930000; adv. contact: Elvio Neri. bk.rev.; charts; mkt.; stat. circ. 3,300. **Indexed:** Br.Ceram.Abstr., Chem.Abstr. **Document type:** trade publication.
   Formed by the 1990 merger of: Refrattari e Laterizi (ISSN 0391-3848); Industria Italiana dei Laterizi (ISSN 0019-7610)
   Description: Presents an up-to-date on technological issues.

690   IT   ISSN 0579-4900
L'INDUSTRIA DELLE COSTRUZIONI. (Text in English and Italian) 1967. m. (10/yr.) L.125000 (Europe L.180000; elsewhere L.250000). (Associazione Nazionale Costruttori Edili) CopEditrice s.r.l., Via di Portonaccio 23-B, 00159 Rome, Italy. TEL 39-6-43530138. FAX 39-6-43530186. Ed. Giuseppe Nannerini. adv.; bk.rev. circ. 9,000. **Indexed:** Br.Tech.Ind. **Document type:** trade publication.
—BLDSC (4438.530000).

690   IT   ISSN 0019-7637
    CODEN: IICEAW
INDUSTRIA ITALIANA DEL CEMENTO. (Text in English and Italian) 1930. m. L.160000. (Associazione Italiana Tecnica Economica del Cemento) Pubblicemento s.r.l., Via di S. Teresa 23, 00198 Rome, Italy. Ed. Domenico Burattini. adv.; bk.rev.; charts; illus.; stat.; index. circ. 10,000. **Indexed:** Concr.Abstr.
—BLDSC (4439.000000); CISTI; Ei; Linda Hall.

691   BE   ISSN 0775-8413
INDUSTRIE CIMENTIERE BELGE/BELGISCHE CEMENTNIJVERHEID. (Text and summaries in Dutch, French) 1976. a. free. Federation de l'Industrie Cimentiere Belge - Federatie van de Belgische Cementnijverheid, 46 rue Cesar Franck, 1050 Brussels, Belgium. TEL 32-2-6455211. FAX 32-2-6400670. Ed. J.P. Latteur. stat. circ. 1,500. (also avail. in microform from DIN) **Document type:** corporate report.
   Description: Annual report of activity.

690   GW   ISSN 0935-2023
INDUSTRIEBAU. 1955. bi-m. DM.160 (foreign DM.185) (effective 1997). (Arbeitsgemeinschaft Industriebau e.V.) Vincentz Verlag, Schiffgraben 43, 30175 Hannover, Germany. TEL 49-511-9910310. FAX 49-511-9910399. E-mail: zeitschriftendienst@vincentz.de. (Subscr. to: Postfach 6247, 30062 Hannover, Germany) Ed. Yola Horschig. adv.: B&W page DM.3240, color page DM.5640; trim 250 x 175. bk.rev.; bibl.; charts; illus.; pat.; tr.lit. circ. 4,097. **Indexed:** C.I.S. Abstr., Excerp.Med. **Document type:** trade publication.
—SWETS. CCC.
   Formerly: Zentralblatt fuer Industriebau (ISSN 0044-4227)

690   CU
INFORMACION CONSTRUCCION.* 1975. bi-m. exchange basis. Comite Estatal de la Construccion, Centro Tecnico Superior de la Construccion, Ministry of Construction, Avda. Carlos M. de Cespedes y Calle 35, Havana, Cuba. Ed. Regino Gayoso. illus.

BUILDING AND CONSTRUCTION

690   VE
INFORMADOR DE LA CONSTRUCCION Y DE LA INDUSTRIA. 1957. a. $150. Publicaciones Sangar, C.A., Apdo. 2323 (1010A), Caracas, Venezuela. TEL 626853. Ed. Coral Garcia de Hernandez. adv. circ. 10,000.

690   SZ
INFORMATOR. (Text in French, German) 1976. 6/yr. 6 SFr. per no. Informator Verlags AG, Buhlmatt 9, CH-6277 Kleinwangen, Switzerland. TEL 041-883823. FAX 041-885956. Ed. Yolanda Allenspach. circ. 40,000. **Document type:** trade publication.

690   SP   ISSN 0020-0883
                       CODEN: ICOMA6
INFORMES DE LA CONSTRUCCION; revista de informacion tecnica. (Text in Spanish; summaries in English) 1948. bi-m. 9000 ptas. (foreign 13500 ptas.) (effective 1996). Instituto de Ciencias de la Construccion Eduardo Torroja, Instituto de Ciencias de la Construccion Eduardo Torroja, Vitruvio 8, 28006 Madrid, Spain. TEL 34-1-5612833. FAX 34-1-5629634. adv.; bk.rev.; bibl.; charts; illus.; cum.index: nos.1-100. circ. 2,500. (microform) **Indexed:** Appl.Mech.Rev., B.P.I., Br.Tech.Ind., Chem.Abstr., Concr.Abstr., Geotech.Abstr., IBR, Ind.SST.
—Linda Hall; SWETS.
     Description: Technical and scientific articles explaining the complete process of the construction field

INGEGNERI ARCHITETTI COSTRUTTORI. see ENGINEERING — Civil Engineering

690   IT
INGEGNERI E COSTRUTTORI.* vol.21, 1973. m. L.6000. Associazione Industriali, Mure Porta Castello, 9, 36100 Vicenza, Italy. Ed. Bruno Scaroni. adv.; charts; illus.

DER INGENIEUR. see ENGINEERING

INGENIOEREN/DANISH ENGINEER'S WEEKLY. see ENGINEERING

690 624   TU
INSAAT DUNYASI; uluslararasi muteahhitlik ve ticaret mecmuasi. (Text in Turkish; summaries in English, German, Turkish) 1982. m. TL.500000. Halic Uluslararasi Yayincilik Ltd. Sti., Cumhuriyet Cad., Babil Sok. 9-10, Harbiye 80230 Istanbul, Turkey. TEL 90-212-2325406. FAX 90-212-2325408. Ed. M. Vasi Pakman. adv. contact: Yasemin Boskurt. circ. 10,000. **Document type:** trade publication.
     Description: Covers new equipment, events, issues and developments affecting the civil engineering and construction sector.

690   SP   ISSN 0212-8519
INSTALACIONES DEPORTIVAS XXI; revista de la construccion deportiva materiales y accesorios. 1974. 7/yr. 17000 ptas.($148) (effective 1996). Elsevier Prensa S.A., Avda Paral.lel, 180, Apdo. No. 350 F.D., 08015 Barcelona, Spain. TEL 34-3-3255350. FAX 34-3-4252880. Ed. Marcel Lleal. adv. contact: Manuel Fernandez de Liencres. bk.rev.; charts; illus. circ. 4,000. **Document type:** trade publication.
     Description: Covers the building industry, equipment, maintenance, materials and accessories for sport installations.

690   GW   ISSN 0172-3006
INSTITUT FUER BAUTECHNIK. MITTEILUNGEN. 1970. bi-m. DM.160 (foreign DM.190) (effective 1997). (Institut fuer Bautechnik) Ernst und Sohn, Muehlenstr. 33-34, 13187 Berlin, Germany. TEL 49-30-47889200. FAX 49-30-47889240. circ. 3,000. **Document type:** trade publication.
—CISTI; SWETS. CCC.

690   FR   ISSN 0020-2568
TH2   CODEN: AITBAK
INSTITUT TECHNIQUE DU BATIMENT ET DES TRAVAUX PUBLICS. ANNALES. (Text in French; summaries in English, French, German and Spanish) 1936. 10/yr. 1110 F. (foreign 1400 F.). Societe d'Editions du Batiment et des Travaux Publics, 7, rue de la Perouse, 75784 Paris Cedex 16, France. (Subscr. to: 6-14, rue le Perouse, 75784 Paris Cedex 16, France) Ed. Jacques Rene Kramer. adv.; bk.rev.; abstr.; charts; illus.; index, cum.index every 5 yrs. circ. 5,500. **Indexed:** Appl.Mech.Rev., Br.Ceram.Abstr., C.I.S. Abstr., Chem.Abstr., Concr.Abstr., Eng.Ind., INIS Atomind.
—CISTI; Linda Hall.

690 720   RM   ISSN 1223-8120
INSTITUTUL POLITEHNIC DIN IASI. BULETINUL. SECTIA 6: CONSTRUCTII, ARHITECTURA. (Text in English, French, German, Italian, Russian, Spanish) 1946. q. exchange basis. Institutul Politehnic din Iasi, Bd. Copou 11, 6600 Jassy, Rumania. TEL 40-81-46577. FAX 40-81-47923. Eds. Alfred Braier, Hugo Rosman. adv.; bk.rev.; bibl. circ. 450. **Indexed:** Appl.Mech.Rev., Chem.Abstr., Math.R., Ref.Zh.
     Formerly: Institutul Politehnic din Iasi. Buletinul. Sectia 5: Constructii, Imbunatatiri Funciare; Which was formed by the merger of: Institutul Politehnic Iasi. Buletinul. Sectia 5: Constructii, Arhitectura; And: Institutul Politehnic din Iasi. Buletinul. Sectia VI: Imbunatatiri Funciare.

INSTYTUT TECHNIKI BUDOWLANEJ. PRACE. see ENGINEERING — Civil Engineering

690 696   US
INSULATION CONTRACTORS MONTHLY.* 1980. m. membership. Insulation Contractors Association of America, Box 26237, Alexandria, VA 22313-6237, adv.; bk.rev. circ. 1,000.
     Formerly: I C A A News.

690   UK
INSULATION HANDBOOK. a. £41 (foreign £44) (effective 1997). Turret Group Plc., Turret House, 171 High St., Rickmansworth, Herts WD3 1SN, England. TEL 44-1923-777000. FAX 44-1923-771297. **Document type:** directory.

690   UK   ISSN 0950-1940
TH1715.A1   CODEN: INJOEY
INSULATION JOURNAL. 1957. bi-m. £60. Turret Group Plc., Turret House, 171 High St., Rickmansworth, Herts. WC3 1SN, England. TEL 44-1923-777000. FAX 44-1923-771297. **Indexed:** Br.Tech.Ind., Hort.Abstr., Intl.Polym.Sci.& Tech., PROMT, RAPRA. **Document type:** trade publication.
—SWETS.

693.83   US
TH1715.A1
INSULATION OUTLOOK. 1956. m. $45. National Insulation Association, 99 Canal Center Plaza, Ste. 222, Alexandria, VA 22314. TEL 703-683-6480. FAX 703-549-4838. Ed. Kathleen H. Bova; Pub. William W. Pittkin. R&P contact: Stuart Hales. TEL 703-683-6422. adv.: B&W page $1421, color page $2472; trim 8 1/4 x 10 7/8; adv. contact: Dena Verdescape. bk.rev.; charts; illus.; stat.; tr.lit. circ. 4,000. **Document type:** trade publication.
     Former titles: Outlook (Alexandria) (ISSN 0898-5766); Insulation Outlook (ISSN 0270-3963); N I C A Outlook (ISSN 0047-8881)
     Description: Concerns commercial and industrial insulation industries.

690   US   ISSN 0888-0387
INTERIOR CONSTRUCTION. 1956. 6/yr. $35 (foreign $45). Ceilings & Interior Systems Construction Association, 1500 Lincoln Hwy., No. 202, St. Charles, IL 60174-3569. TEL 630-584-1919. FAX 630-584-2003. E-mail: cisca@juno.com; URL: http://www.cisca.org. Ed. Karen A. Newman; Pub. Jan Foxen. adv. contact: John Sanger. circ. 7,300. (back issues avail.) **Document type:** trade publication.
     Former titles: (until vol.29, 1985): Inside Contracting (ISSN 0193-2586); (until 1979): Sound Ideas (ISSN 0038-1837)

692.8   US   ISSN 0020-5656
INTERMOUNTAIN CONTRACTOR; building and engineering construction news. 1950. w. $357. McGraw-Hill Companies, 1221 Avenue of the Americas, New York, NY 10020. FAX 801-972-8975. Ed. Albert Van Dyk. adv.; bk.rev.; charts; illus.; stat. circ. 31,500. **Document type:** trade publication.

690   UK
INTERNATIONAL ASIAN BUILDING PRODUCTS CATALOGUE. 1985. a. $55. Data Distribution Publications, Apex House, London Rd., Northfield, Gravesend, Kent DA11 9JA, England. TEL 01322-277788. FAX 01322-569627. **Document type:** catalog.

INTERNATIONAL CAR PARK DESIGN AND CONSTRUCTION TRENDS. see TRANSPORTATION — Automobiles

690   UK   ISSN 0959-6038
INTERNATIONAL CEMENT REVIEW. m. £135($240) Tradeship Publications Ltd., Old Kings Head Ct., 15 High St., Dorking, Surrey RH4 1AR, England. TEL 44-1306-740363. FAX 44-1306-740660. Ed. David Hargreaves. circ. 4,000. **Indexed:** C.R.I.Abstr., C.R.I.Curr.Cont. **Document type:** trade publication.
—BLDSC (4538.416500); SWETS.
     Description: Concerned with features and forecasts, plus monthly round-ups of the world's tanker industry news; includes trading and technical developments from around the world.

690   US   ISSN 0896-9752
TH223
INTERNATIONAL CONFERENCE OF BUILDING OFFICIALS. ANALYSIS OF REVISIONS TO THE (YEAR) UNIFORM CODES. triennial. $16.30 to non-members; members $12.25 (effective 1997). International Conference of Building Officials, 5360 Workman Mill Rd., Whittier, CA 90601-2298. TEL 310-699-0541. FAX 310-699-8031. **Document type:** trade publication.
     Formerly: International Conference of Building Officials. Analysis of Revisions to the Uniform Building Code.

690   US
INTERNATIONAL CONFERENCE OF BUILDING OFFICIALS. BUILDING DEPARTMENT ADMINISTRATION. 1973. irreg. $49 (effective 1997). International Conference of Building Officials, 5360 Workman Mill Rd., Whittier, CA 90601-2298. TEL 310-699-0541. FAX 310-699-8031. **Document type:** trade publication.

690   US   ISSN 0579-3769
INTERNATIONAL CONFERENCE OF BUILDING OFFICIALS. CODE CHANGES COMMITTEE. ANNUAL REPORT. bi-m. International Conference of Building Officials, 5360 Workman Mill Rd., Whittier, CA 90601-2298. TEL 310-699-0541. FAX 310-699-8031. **Document type:** corporate report.

690   US   ISSN 0896-9728
KF5701.Z95
INTERNATIONAL CONFERENCE OF BUILDING OFFICIALS. DWELLING CONSTRUCTION UNDER THE UNIFORM BUILDING CODE. triennial. $15.60 to non-members; members $11.65 (effective 1997). International Conference of Building Officials, 5360 Workman Mill Rd., Whittier, CA 90601-2298. TEL 310-699-0541 FAX 310-699-8031. **Document type:** trade publication.
—CISTI.

690 352.7   US
INTERNATIONAL CONFERENCE OF BUILDING OFFICIALS. EVALUATION REPORTS. a. (with m. supplements). $170 to non-members; members $150 (effective 1997). International Conference of Building Officials, 5360 Workman Mill Rd., Whittier, CA 90601-2298. TEL 310-699-0541. FAX 310-699-8031. **Document type:** trade publication.

690   US
INTERNATIONAL CONFERENCE OF BUILDING OFFICIALS. PLAN REVIEW MANUAL. triennial. $32.60 to non-members; members $24.50 (effective 1997). International Conference of Building Officials, 5360 Workman Mill Rd., Whittier, CA 90601-2298. TEL 310-699-0541. FAX 310-699-8031. **Document type:** trade publication.

BUILDING AND CONSTRUCTION   899

690   US   ISSN 0896-9655
KF5701.A39
INTERNATIONAL CONFERENCE OF BUILDING OFFICIALS. UNIFORM BUILDING CODE. (3 vol. set) 1927. triennial. $173.90 to non-members; members $139.10 (effective 1997). International Conference of Building Officials, 5360 Workman Mill Rd., Whittier, CA 90601-2298. TEL 310-699-0541. FAX 310-699-8031. **Document type:** trade publication.
—BLDSC (9090.666000); CISTI.

690   US   ISSN 0896-971X
KF5701.Z95
INTERNATIONAL CONFERENCE OF BUILDING OFFICIALS. UNIFORM CODE FOR THE ABATEMENT OF DANGEROUS BUILDINGS. triennial. $12.65 to non-members; members $9.55 (effective 1997). International Conference of Building Officials, 5360 Workman Mill Rd., Whittier, CA 90601-2298. TEL 310-699-0541. FAX 310-699-8031. **Document type:** trade publication.
—CISTI.

690   US   ISSN 0896-9736
KF3975.Z95
INTERNATIONAL CONFERENCE OF BUILDING OFFICIALS. UNIFORM FIRE CODE. triennial (in 2 vols.). $139.50 to non-members; members $107.15 (effective 1997). International Conference of Building Officials, 5360 Workman Mill Rd., Whittier, CA 90601-2298. TEL 310-699-0541. FAX 310-699-8031. **Document type:** trade publication.
—CISTI.

690 692   US   ISSN 0501-1213
KF5701.Z95
INTERNATIONAL CONFERENCE OF BUILDING OFFICIALS. UNIFORM HOUSING CODE. 1955. triennial. $12.65 to non-members; members $9.55 (effective 1997). International Conference of Building Officials, 5360 Workman Mill Rd., Whittier, CA 90601-2298. TEL 310-699-0541. FAX 310-699-8031. **Document type:** trade publication.
—CISTI.

690   US   ISSN 0896-9671
KF5708.Z95
INTERNATIONAL CONFERENCE OF BUILDING OFFICIALS. UNIFORM MECHANICAL CODE. triennial. $44.65 to non-members; members $33.60 (effective 1997). International Conference of Building Officials, 5360 Workman Mill Rd., Whittier, CA 90601-2298. TEL 310-699-0541. FAX 310-699-8031. **Document type:** trade publication.
—CISTI.

INTERNATIONAL CONSTRUCTION LAW REVIEW. see LAW — International Law

INTERNATIONAL CONSTRUCTION MANAGEMENT SERIES. see BUSINESS AND ECONOMICS — Labor And Industrial Relations

690   UK   ISSN 0968-0365
INTERNATIONAL JOURNAL OF CONSTRUCTION INFORMATION TECHNOLOGY. 1992. 2/yr. £70 (effective 1996). University of Salford, Department of Surveying, Salford M5 4WT, England. TEL 44-161-745-5128. FAX 44-161-745-5130. E-mail: m.alshawi@surveying.salford.ac.uk. Eds. Mustafa Alshawi, Martin Skitmore. **Document type:** trade publication.
—BLDSC (4542.175750); CISTI.

690   UK   ISSN 0956-0599
INTERNATIONAL JOURNAL OF SPACE STRUCTURES. 1985. 4/yr. £117 in U.K.; Europe £127; rest of world £146 (effective 1997). Multi-Science Publishing Co. Ltd., 107 High St., Brentwood, Essex CM14 4RX, England. TEL 44-1277-224632. FAX 44-1277-223453. (U.S. subscr. to: Box 176, Avenel, NJ 07001) Ed. H. Nooshin. adv.; bk.rev.; charts; illus.; index. **Document type:** academic/scholarly publication.
—BLDSC (4542.660000); CISTI; Ei; SWETS; UnCover.
Formerly (until 1988): Space Structures (ISSN 0266-3511)
  Refereed Serial

690 621.393 747   NE   ISSN 0020-7853
TK1
INTERNATIONAL LIGHTING REVIEW. French edition: Revue Internationale de l'Eclairage (ISSN 0035-3388); German edition: Internationale Licht Rundschau (ISSN 0165-9863); Spanish edition: Revista Internacional de Luminotecnia (ISSN 0167-7608) (Text in English) 1950. q. fl.98. (Philips Lighting B.V.) Foundation Prometheus, Box 721, 5600 AS Eindhoven, Netherlands. FAX 31-40-756406. TELEX 35000-PHTC-NL. Ed. J.F. Caminada. bk.rev.; charts; illus.; index, cum.index. circ. 16,000. **Indexed:** Br.Tech.Ind., C.I.S. Abstr., Ergon.Abstr., HRIS, Int.Build.Serv.Abstr. **Document type:** trade publication.
—BLDSC (4543.000000); CISTI; SWETS.
  Description: Reports on lighting applications worldwide.

690   UK
INTERNATIONAL MIDDLE EAST BUILDING PRODUCTS CATALOGUE. 1976. a. $55. Data Distribution Publications, Apex House, London Rd., Northfleet, Gravesend, Kent DA11 9JA, England. TEL 01322-277788. FAX 01322-569627. circ. 7,000. **Document type:** catalog.
  Formerly: Middle East Construction Catalogue - Building Products Edition.

INTERNATIONAL PLUMBING CODE. see HEATING, PLUMBING AND REFRIGERATION

343   US   ISSN 1085-1151
▼**INTERNATIONAL PRIVATE SEWAGE DISPOSAL CODE.** 1995. biennial. $15 to members; non-members $22. Building Officials and Code Administrators International, 4051 W. Flossmoor Rd., Country Club Hills, IL 60478-5795. TEL 708-799-2300. FAX 708-799-4981. E-mail: boca@bocai.org. (Co-sponsor: International Code Council) Ed. Paul K. Heilstedt; Pub. Bill J. Even. R&P contact: Bill J. Even. adv. contact: Bill J. Even. index. **Document type:** trade publication.
  Description: Covers administration, definitions, general regulations, site evaluation and requirements, materials, soil absorption systems, pressure distribution systems, tanks, mound systems, cesspools, and inspections.

691   FI
INTERNATIONAL TRADE CONFERENCE OF WORKERS OF THE BUILDING, WOOD AND BUILDING MATERIALS INDUSTRIES. (BROCHURE). irreg, 7th, 1975. Trade Unions International of Workers of the Building, Wood and Building Materials Industries, P.O. Box 281, FIN-00101 Helsinki, Finland.

INTERNATIONAL UNION OF BRICKLAYERS AND ALLIED CRAFTSMEN. JOURNAL. see LABOR UNIONS

INTERNATIONAL WELDING ENGINEERING. see METALLURGY — Welding

690   GW   ISSN 0947-4498
▼**INTERNATIONALE ZEITSCHRIFT FUER BAUINSTANDSETZEN/INTERNATIONAL JOURNAL FOR RESTORATION OF BUILDINGS AND MONUMENTS.** (Text in English, German) 1995. 6/yr. DM.180. (Fraunhofer-Informationszentrum Raum und Bau) Fraunhofer I R B Verlag, Nobelstr. 12, 70569 Stuttgart, Germany. TEL 49-711-9702500. FAX 49-711-9702507. TELEX 7255168-IZS-D. E-mail: irb@irb.fhg.de; URL: http://www.irb.fhg.de. (Co-publisher: Aedificatio Verlag) Ed. Folker Wittmann. **Document type:** trade publication.
—BLDSC (4542.537000); CISTI.

690   IE   ISSN 0791-0878
IRISH BUILDING SERVICES NEWS. 1964. 10/yr. £20. Pressline Ltd., Walnut Lodge, Carysfort Ave., Blackrock, Co. Dublin, Ireland. TEL 831596. FAX 832980. Ed. Patrick Lehane. circ. 2,500. (back issues avail.)

690   IE   ISSN 0791-9786
IRISH CONSTRUCTION INDUSTRY. 1990. 12/yr. National & International Publications Ltd., 40 Fitzwilliam Sq., Dublin 2, Ireland. TEL 767018. FAX 767189. circ. 4,000.

690   IT   ISSN 0393-8069
ITALIAN BUILDING AND CONSTRUCTION. (Text in English) 1978. q. L.50000($50) (effective 1997). Casa Editrice la Fiaccola, Via Ravizza 62, 20149 Milan, Italy. FAX 39-2-4814834. Ed. Giuseppe Saronni. adv. contact: Mauro Nartelli. index. circ. 35,000. (back issues avail.)
  Description: Promotes the Italian building and construction industry.

IZGRADNJA/CONSTRUCTION. see ENGINEERING — Civil Engineering

690   JA   ISSN 0914-4528
J A C I C REPORT/J A C I C JOHO. (Text in Japanese) 1986. q. 1000 Yen per no. Japan Construction Information Center - Nihon Kensetsu Joho Sogo Senta, 10-20, Akasaka 7-chome, Minata-ku, Tokyo 107, Japan.

691.3   JA
J C I TRANSACTIONS. (Text in English) 1978. a. 16500 Yen($123) Japan Concrete Institute, No. 708 TBR Bldg., 5-7, Kohjimachi, Chiyoda-ku, Tokyo 102, Japan. TEL 81-3-3263-1571. FAX 81-3-3263-2115. Ed. Itsuo Honda. circ. 1,800. **Indexed:** C.R.I.Abstr., C.R.I.Curr.Cont.

690   JA
J S S C REPORT/J S S C REPOTO. (Text in Japanese) 1986. irreg. Society of Steel Construction of Japan - Nihon Kokozo Kyokai, Shintokyo Biru 848, 3-1, Marunouchi 3-chome, Chiyoda-ku, Tokyo, Japan.

690 352.7   JM
JAMAICA. MINISTRY OF CONSTRUCTION (WORKS). JAMAICA BUDGET (YEAR). a. Ministry of Construction (Works), Kingston, Jamaica, W.I. **Document type:** government publication.

690   JA
JAPAN'S CONSTRUCTION TODAY. (Text in English) a. exchange basis. Overseas Construction Association of Japan - Kaigai Kensetsu Kyokai, 24-2, Hatchobori 2-chome, Chuo-ku, Tokyo 104, Japan. TEL 81-3-3553-1631. FAX 81-3-3551-0148. Ed. Yoshio Yokoyama. R&P contact: Yoshio Yokoyama. **Document type:** bulletin.

690   JA
JARI JIHO/GRAVEL TIMES. (Text in Japanese) 1954. m. 300 Yen per no. Nihon Jari Kyokai - Japan Sand and Gravel Association, 9-12, Kudan Kita 1-chome, Chiyoda-ku, Tokyo 102, Japan.

JIANZHU ANQUAN. see OCCUPATIONAL HEALTH AND SAFETY

690   CC   ISSN 0412-0787
JIANZHU GONGREN/CONSTRUCTION WORKERS. (Text in Chinese; abstracts in Chinese, English) 1970. m. $20 (effective 1998). Beijing Shi Jianzhu Gongcheng Zonggongsi - Beijing Construction Engineering Company, No. 19, Nanlishi Lu, Fuxingmenwai, Beijing 100045, People's Republic of China. TEL 86-10-6853-2554. FAX 86-10-6853-3576. Ed. Peng Shenghao. adv.: B&W page $500, color page $1400; adv. contact: Xu Qingxiang. circ. 12,000 (paid).

690   CC   ISSN 1001-019X
JIANZHU GUANLI XIANDAIHUA/CONSTRUCTION MANAGEMENT MODERNIZATION. (Text in Chinese) 1985. q. Y1.50 per no. Harbin Jianzhu Daxue - Harbin University of Architecture and Engineering, 66 Xi Dazhi St., Harbin, Heilongjiang 150006, People's Republic of China. TEL 3643512. FAX 3635700. Ed. Guan Ke. **Document type:** academic/scholarly publication.

690   CC   ISSN 1000-6869
JIANZHU JIEGOU XUEBAO/JOURNAL OF BUILDING STRUCTURES. (Text in Chinese) bi-m. $2.30 per no. Guoji Shudian, Qikan Bu - China International Book Trading Corp., P.O. Box 399, Beijing 100044, People's Republic of China.

690 720   CC   ISSN 1000-4726
JIANZHU JISHU/ARCHITECTURAL TECHNOLOGY. (Text in Chinese; abstracts in Chinese, English) m. $50 (effective 1998). Beijing Jianzhu Gongcheng Zonggongsi - Beijing Architectural Engineering Corporation, 19 Nanlishi Lu, Fuxingmenwai, Beijing 100045, People's Republic of China. TEL 86-10-6853-2554. FAX 86-10-6853-3576. Ed. Peng Shenghao. adv.: color page $1000; adv. contact: Xu Qingxiang. circ. 70,000 (paid).

900 BUILDING AND CONSTRUCTION

690   CN   ISSN 0047-2115
JOURNAL CONSTRUCTO. (Text in French) 1963. s-w. Can.$299. Groupe Constructo, 1500 boul. Jules-Poitras, Ste. 200, St-Laurent, PQ H4N 1X7, Canada. TEL 514-745-5720. FAX 514-339-2267. Ed. Johanne Rouleau; Pub. Guy Choiniere. adv. contact: Johanne Rouleau. (also avail. in microfilm from BNQ) **Document type:** trade publication, newspaper.
—CISTI.

690   SZ   ISSN 0021-776X
JOURNAL DE LA CONSTRUCTION DE LA SUISSE ROMANDE. 1926. s-m. 68 SFr. Budron A, 1052 Le Mont-sur-Lausanne, Switzerland. TEL 021-329944. Ed. Gerard Geiger. adv.; bk.rev. circ. 6,000. **Indexed:** C.I.S. Abstr. **Document type:** trade publication.
Description: Trade publication for the construction industry, covering buildings, roads, association news, exhibitions, new products, etc.

JOURNAL DU BATIMENT ET DES TRAVAUX PUBLICS. see *ENGINEERING — Civil Engineering*

690   FR   ISSN 1148-554X
JOURNAL DU CHAUFFAGE ET DU SANITAIRE. 1989. 8/yr. 240 F. (foreign 340 F.). Groupe Moniteur, 17 rue d'Uzes, 75002 Paris, France. FAX 33-1-42333819. TELEX 220 528F. Ed. Michele Fourret. circ. 25,000.

691   CN   ISSN 0831-0122
JOURNAL INDUSTRIEL DU QUEBEC. 1985. 10/yr. Can.$25 (effective Jan. 1991). Info-Industriel Inc., 2370 E. Boul. Henri-Bourassa, Montreal, Que. H2B 1T6, Canada. TEL 514-388-8801. FAX 514-388-7871. Ed. Yvan Gauthier. adv.; circ. 25,000 (controlled).
Description: Provides information on various products needed in the industry. For executive management and purchasers.

693   TH   ISSN 0125-1759
TA444
JOURNAL OF FERROCEMENT. (Text in English) 1976. q. $35 to individuals in Asia (elsewhere $55); institutions in Asia $85 (elsewhere $99). International Ferrocement Information Center, Asian Institute of Technology, P.O. Box 2754, Bangkok 10501, Thailand. TEL 66-2-5245864. FAX 66-2-5162126. TELEX 84276 TH. E-mail: itic@ait.ac.th. Ed. Lilia Robles-Austriaco. adv.; bk.rev.; abstr.; illus.; index. circ. 700. (also avail. in microfilm from UMI; reprint service avail. from UMI) **Indexed:** AIT Reports, Alloys Ind., Appl.Mech.Rev., BMT, C.R.I.Abstr., C.R.I.Curr.Cont., Concr.Abstr., Eng.Mat.Abstr., Eng.Mat.Abstr., INSPEC, Met.Abstr., Met.Abstr.Ind., Nonfer.Met.Alert, PCC Alert, Ref.Zh., Steels Alert, World Alum.Abstr.
—BLDSC (4984.030000); CISTI; Ei; Linda Hall; SWETS; UMI; UnCover.
Former titles: N Z F C M A Bulletin; N Z F C M A Newsletter.
Description: Covers concrete, cement, low-cost composite materials and related topics.

JOURNAL OF FINANCIAL MANAGEMENT OF PROPERTY AND CONSTRUCTION. see *REAL ESTATE*

690   US   ISSN 1040-5224
JOURNAL OF LIGHT CONSTRUCTION. 1982. m. $32.50. Buildenberg Group Inc., RR 2, Box 146, Richmond, VT 05477. TEL 802-434-4747. Ed. Steven Bliss; Pub. Terri Shanahan. adv.; bk.rev.; circ. 45,000 (paid). **Indexed:** B.R.I., Search (1992-).
—CISTI.
Formerly: New England Builder.
Description: Provides practical information on building technology and business management for residential and light-commercial building contractors.

JOURNAL OF MEDIA ECONOMICS. see *COMMUNICATIONS*

690 352.7   UN   ISSN 1012-9812
TA401
JOURNAL OF THE NETWORK OF AFRICAN COUNTRIES ON LOCAL BUILDING MATERIALS AND TECHNOLOGIES. 1989. biennial. free. United Nations Centre for Human Settlements (Habitat), Box 30030, Nairobi, Kenya. TEL 254-2-621234. FAX 254-2-624266. TELEX 22996 UNHAB KE. Ed. Baris Der-Petrossian.
Description: Compiles and disseminates information, case studies and data on low-cost innovations in local building materials and construction technology. It is a medium for information exchange and facilitator for acquisition of suitable technologies and know-how by needy countries.

690   IS
KABLAN VEBONEH/CONTRACTOR AND BUILDER. 1952. q. IS.36.80. Contractors and Builders Center in Israel, 43 Hatarese Blvd., Tel Aviv 62 492, Israel. TEL 03-440560. Ed. Elnakam Artzieli. illus. circ. 3,500.

690   US   ISSN 1069-3297
KELLER'S CONSTRUCTION REGULATORY UPDATE. 1993. m. $90. J.J. Keller & Associates, Inc., 3003 W. Breezewood Lane, Neenah, WI 54957-0368. TEL 414-722-2848; 800-327-6868. FAX 414-727-7526. Ed. Jerry Woodson. (also avail. in looseleaf format)
Description: Provides news related to construction specific DOT, EPA and OSHA regulatory activities.

690   JA   ISSN 0451-6486
KENCHIKU KENKYU HOKOKU/BUILDING RESEARCH INSTITUTE. REPORT. (Text in Japanese; summaries in English, Japanese) 1949. irreg. Kensetsusho Kenchiku Kenkyujo, 1, Tachihara, Tsukuba-shi, Ibaraki-ken 305, Japan. TEL 81-298-64-2151. FAX 81-298-64-2909. Ed. Shin Okamoto. adv. contact: Hiroshi Matsumoto. **Indexed:** INIS Atomind. **Document type:** academic/scholarly publication, government publication.
Description: Reports the results of researches conducted by the Building Research Institute.

KENKI GIHO/CONSTRUCTION MACHINERY TECHNICAL REVIEW. see *MACHINERY*

690   JA
KENSETSU HAKUSHO/WHITE PAPER OF CONSTRUCTION WORKS. (Text in Japanese) 1949. a. 2600 Yen. (Kensetsusho - Ministry of Construction) Okurasho Insatsukyoku - Ministry of Finance, Printing Bureau, 2-4, Toranomon 2-chome, Minato-ku, Tokyo 105, Japan. **Document type:** government publication.

690 621.9   JA
KENSETSU KIKAI DOKO CHOSA HOKOKU/ANNUAL REPORT OF CONSTRUCTION MACHINERY AND EQUIPMENT. 1978. a. Tsusho Sangyosho, Kikai Joho Sangyokyoku - Ministry of International Trade and Industry, Machinery and Information Industries Bureau, 3-1, Kasumigaseki 1-chome, Chiyoda-ku, Tokyo 100, Japan. **Document type:** government publication.

690 621.9   JA   ISSN 0388-4066
KENSETSU KIKAIKA KENKYUJO NENPO/CONSTRUCTION METHOD AND MACHINERY RESEARCH INSTITUTE. ANNUAL REPORT. (Text in Japanese) 1965. a. Nihon Kensetsu Kikaika Kyokai, Kensetsu Kikaika Kenkyujo - Japan Construction Mechanization Association, Construction Method and Machinery Research Institute, 3154, Ohbuchi, Fuji-shi, Shizuoka-ken 417, Japan. FAX 0545-35-3719.

690 621.9   JA
KENSETSU KIKAIKAI KENKYUJO SEINO SHIKEN HOKOKU/JAPANESE CONSTRUCTION METHOD AND MACHINERY RESEARCH INSTITUTE. REPORT OF PERFORMANCE TESTS. (Text in Japanese) 1964. irreg. 500 Yen. Nihon Kensetsu Kikaika Kyokai, Kensetsu Kikaika Kenkyujo - Japan Construction Mechanization Association, Construction Method and Machinery Research Institute, 3154, Ohbuchi, Fuji-shi, Shizuoka-ken 417, Japan. TEL 0545-35-0212. FAX 0545-35-3719.

KENSETSU KOGAKU KENKYU SHINKOKAI NENPO/SOCIETY FOR THE PROMOTION OF CONSTRUCTION ENGINEERING. ANNUAL REPORT. see *ENGINEERING — Civil Engineering*

KENSETSU KOJI SAIGAI BOSHI TEIANSHU/PROPOSALS FOR INDUSTRIAL SAFETY OF CONSTRUCTION. see *OCCUPATIONAL HEALTH AND SAFETY*

690   JA
KENSETSU NIHON/CONSTRUCTION JAPAN. (Text in Japanese) 1967. 36/yr. 8000 Yen. Kensetsu Nihon Shinbunsha, 9-11, Edobori 1-chome, Nishi-ku, Osaka-shi, Osaka 550, Japan.

KENSETSU NO KIKAIKA/CONSTRUCTION MECHANIZATION. see *MACHINERY*

KENSETSU ROBOTTO SHINPOJUMU RONBUNSHU/SYMPOSIUM ON CONSTRUCTION ROBOTICS IN JAPAN. PROCEEDINGS. see *COMPUTERS — Robotics*

690   JA
KENSETSUSHO KINKI CHIHO KENSETSUKYOKU. JIGYO GAIYO/MINISTRY OF CONSTRUCTION. KINKI REGIONAL CONSTRUCTION BUREAU. ANNUAL REPORT.* (Text in Japanese) a. 2000 Yen. Kinki Kensetsu Kyokai - Kinki Association of Construction, c/o Ministry of Construction, 2-1 Kasumigascki, Chiyoda-ku, Tokyo, Japan.

690   UK
KEY NOTE MARKET REPORT: BRICKS & TILES. Variant title: Bricks & Tiles. irreg., no.10, 1994. £205. Key Note Ltd., Field House, 72 Oldfield Rd., Hampton, Middlesex TW12 2HQ, England. TEL 44-181-783-0755. FAX 44-181-783-0049. **Document type:** trade publication.
●Also available online.
Also available on CD-ROM.
Formerly: Key Note Report: Bricks and Tiles (ISSN 0951-9114)

690   UK
KEY NOTE MARKET REPORT: BUILDERS' MERCHANTS. Variant title: Builders' Merchants. irreg., vol.9, 1995. £205. Key Note Ltd., Field House, 72 Oldfield Rd., Hampton, Middlesex TW12 2HQ, England. TEL 44-181-783-0755. FAX 44-181-783-0049. Ed. Phillippa Smith. **Document type:** trade publication.
Formerly (until 1995): Key Note Report: Builders' Merchants (ISSN 0952-5351)

690   UK
KEY NOTE MARKET REPORT: BUILDING CONTRACTING. Variant title: Building Contracting. irreg., no.4, 1994. £205. Key Note Ltd., Field House, 72 Oldfield Rd., Hampton, Middlesex TW12 2HQ, England. TEL 44-181-783-0755. FAX 44-181-783-0049. **Document type:** trade publication.
●Also available online.
Also available on CD-ROM.
Formerly: Key Note Report: Building Contracting (ISSN 0269-901X)

690   UK
KEY NOTE MARKET REPORT: BUILDING MATERIALS. Variant title: Building Materials. irreg., no.7, 1992. £185. Key Note Ltd., Field House, 72 Oldfield Rd., Hampton, Middlesex TW12 2HQ, England. TEL 44-181-783-0755. FAX 44-181-783-1940. **Document type:** trade publication.
●Also available online.
Also available on CD-ROM.
Formerly: Key Note Report: Building Materials.

690   UK
KEY NOTE MARKET REPORT: BUILDING SOCIETIES. Variant title: Building Societies. irreg., no.9, 1994. £205. Key Note Ltd., Field House, 72 Oldfield Rd., Hampton, Middlesex TW12 2HQ, England. TEL 44-181-783-0755. FAX 44-181-783-0049. **Document type:** trade publication.
●Also available online.
Also available on CD-ROM.
Formerly: Key Note Report: Building Societies.

690 352.7   UK
KEY NOTE MARKET REPORT: HOUSEBUILDING. Variant title: Housebuilding. irreg., no.11, 1994. £205. Key Note Ltd., Field House, 72 Oldfield Rd., Hampton, Middlesex TW12 2HQ, England. TEL 44-181-783-0755. FAX 44-181-783-0049. **Document type:** trade publication.
●Also available online.
Also available on CD-ROM.
Formerly: Key Note Report: Housebuilding.

BUILDING AND CONSTRUCTION

690   UK
KEY NOTE MARKET REPORT: INSULATION PRODUCTS. Variant title: Insulation Products. irreg., no.7, 1993. £205. Key Note Ltd., Field House, 72 Oldfield Rd., Hampton, Middlesex TW12 2HQ, England. TEL 44-181-783-0755. FAX 44-181-783-0049. **Document type:** trade publication.
●Also available online.
Also available on CD-ROM.
    Formerly: Key Note Report: Insulation Products (ISSN 0951-3566)

690   UK
KEY NOTE MARKET REVIEW: U K CONSTRUCTION INDUSTRY. Variant title: U K Construction Industry. irreg., no.5, 1995. £410. Key Note Ltd., Field House, 72 Oldfield Rd., Hampton, Middlesex TW12 2HQ, England. TEL 44-181-783-0755. FAX 44-181-783-0049. **Document type:** trade publication.
●Also available online.
Also available on CD-ROM.

KIRSH'S CONSTRUCTION LIEN CASE FINDER. see *LAW*

643.3   US   ISSN 0730-2487
TT197
KITCHEN & BATH BUSINESS. Cover title: K B B. 1955. m. $70 (Canada & Mexico $75; elsewhere $90) (effective 1996). Miller Freeman Inc. (New York) (Subsidiary of: United News & Media), One Penn Plaza, New York, NY 10119. TEL 212-714-1300. FAX 212-279-3960. (Subscr. to: Box 1124, Skokie, IL 60076-8124. TEL 800-250-2430. FAX 708-647-5972) Ed. Leslie Hart. adv.; charts; illus.; index. circ. 50,000. **Document type:** trade publication.
—CCC.
    Formerly: Kitchen Business (ISSN 0023-1932)
    Description: Covers the residential kitchen and bathroom market.

643.7   US
KITCHEN BATH SPECIALIST. m. Kasmar Publications, Inc., Box 12638, Palm Desert, CA 92255. TEL 800-253-9992. FAX 619-773-2876. Ed. Greg Rohl.

690   JA
KOKUDO KENSETSU NO GENKYO/PRESENT STATE OF LAND CONSTRUCTION. (Text in Japanese) 1949. a. Kensetsusho - Ministry of Construction, 1-3, Kasumigaseki 2-chome, Chiyoda-ku, Tokyo 100, Japan. **Document type:** government publication.

KOKYO. see *ENGINEERING — Civil Engineering*

690   SZ
KOMMUNAL KATALOG; Nachschlagewerk fuer Behoerden und Einkaeufer. (Text in German) 1976. a. 25 SFr. Vogt-Schild AG, Zuchwilerstr. 21, CH-4501 Solothurn, Switzerland. TEL 065-247247. FAX 065-247235. Ed. Marianne Flury. adv.: B&W page 2600 SFr., color page 3700 SFr.; trim 185 x 260; adv. contact: Hansruedi Spiri. bk.rev. circ. 5,000. (tabloid format) **Document type:** catalog.

KOMPASS PROFESSIONNEL. BATIMENT ET GENIE CIVIL, MANUTENTION - LEVAGE, BOIS - MEUBLES. see *BUSINESS AND ECONOMICS — Trade And Industrial Directories*

KOMPASS PROFESSIONNEL. CHAUDRONNERIE, CONSTRUCTIONS METALLIQUES, TOLERIES, TUBES, CHAUFFAGE. see *BUSINESS AND ECONOMICS — Trade And Industrial Directories*

620.002548   DK   ISSN 0106-1135
KOMPASS SELECT EXPORT. BUILDING CONSTRUCTION, CONTRACTORS. Cover title: Euro Kompass Denmark. Construction. (Text in Danish, English, French, German and Spanish) 1966. a. DKK 300 (listed companies DKK 100). Forlaget Kompass-Danmark, Oeveroedvej 5, DK-Holte, Denmark. TEL 45-45-41-21-00. FAX 45-45-41-06-65. illus. **Document type:** directory.
●Also available on CD-ROM.
    Formerly: Kompass Select Denmark. Construction.

691.3   JA   ISSN 0387-1061
CODEN: KOKODX
KONKURITO KOGAKU/CONCRETE JOURNAL. (Text in Japanese; summaries in English) 1963. m. 15450 Yen($87) Japan Concrete Institute - Nihon Konkurito Kogaku Kyokai, No. 708 TBR Bldg., 5-7, Kohjimachi, Chiyoda-ku, Tokyo 102, Japan. TEL 81-3-3263-1571. FAX 81-3-3263-2115. Ed. Itsuo Honda. adv.; bk.rev.; abstr.; bibl.; charts; illus.; index. circ. 9,000. **Indexed:** Chem.Abstr., Corros.Abstr., INIS Atomind.
—CASDDS; CISTI; Linda Hall.
    Formerly: Konkurito Jaanaru (ISSN 0023-3544)

KONKURITO KOGAKU RONBUNSHU/CONCRETE RESEARCH AND TECHNOLOGY. see *ENGINEERING — Civil Engineering*

690   JA
KONOIKEGUMI GIJUTSU KENKYU HAPPYOKAI RONBUNSHU/KONOIKE CONSTRUCTION CO. PROCEEDINGS OF ANNUAL MEETING. (Text in Japanese) 1975. a. Konoikegumi Gijutsu Kenkyujo - Konoike Construction Co., Ltd., Technical Research Institute, 6-1, Kitakyuhoji-machi 3-chome, Chuo-ku, Osaka-shi, Osaka 541, Japan. **Document type:** academic/scholarly publication.

690   JA   ISSN 0914-6229
KONOIKEGUMI GIJUTSU KENKYU HOKOKU/KONOIKE CONSTRUCTION CO. TECHNICAL RESEARCH REPORTS. (Text and summaries in English, Japanese) 1988. a. Konoikegumi Gijutsu Kenkyujo - Konoike Construction Co. Ltd., Technical Research Institute, 6-1, Kitakyuhoji-machi 3-chome, Chuo-ku, Osaka-shi, Osaka 541, Japan.

960   GW   ISSN 0344-4570
DER KONSTRUKTEUR. 1970. 11/yr. DM.114 (foreign DM.130) (effective 1996). Verlag fuer Technik und Wirtschaft GmbH & Co., Lise-Meitner-Str. 2, 55129 Mainz, Germany. TEL 49-6131-992-0. FAX 49-6131-992100. (Subscr. to: Postfach 4029, 55030 Mainz, Germany) Ed. Michael Doeppert. adv.: B&W page DM.7900, color page DM.10300; trim 265 x 185; adv. contact: Michael Spahn. charts; illus. circ. 25,000. **Document type:** trade publication.
—BLDSC (5111.950000).

690   GW
KONSTRUKTION UND ENGINEERING. 1977. m. DM.112 (Europe DM.148; overseas DM.208). Verlag Moderne Industrie, Justus-von-Liebig-Str. 1, 86899 Landsberg, Germany. TEL 49-8191-125-0. FAX 49-8191-125-483. Ed. Franz Graf. adv.: B&W page DM.7980; trim 257 x 178; adv. contact: Walter Rojan. circ. 29,308. **Document type:** trade publication.
    Former titles: Konstruktion und Elektronik (ISSN 0177-7459); Konstruktion, Entwicklung und Design; Konstruktion und Design (ISSN 0344-6034)

690   US   ISSN 0075-6768
KONSTRUKTIONSBUECHER. (Text in German) 1955. irreg., latest no.27. price varies. Springer-Verlag, 175 Fifth Ave., New York, NY 10010. TEL 212-460-1500. FAX 212-473-6272. (Also: Berlin, Heidelberg, Tokyo and Vienna) (reprint service avail. from ISI) **Document type:** monographic series.

KUNST UND STADT. see *ARCHITECTURE*

KYORYO NENKAN/STEEL BRIDGE YEARBOOK. see *ENGINEERING — Civil Engineering*

691   UK   ISSN 0960-6823
LAXTON'S BUILDING PRICE BOOK. a. £89.50. Reed Information Services (Subsidiary of: Reed Elsevier group), Windsor Court, E. Grinstead House, E. Grinstead, W. Sussex RH19 1XA, England. TEL 01342-335832. FAX 01342-335948. TELEX 95127-INFSER-G. adv.; stat. circ. 6,000.
—BLDSC (5161.900000).
    Former titles: Laxton's National Building Price Book (ISSN 0960-6815); Laxton's Building Price Book (ISSN 0305-6589)

690 340   IT   ISSN 0392-503X
LEGISLAZIONE E NORMATIVA DELLE COSTRUZIONI. 1961. m. (11/yr.). L.42000. Editrice la Pace S.r.l., Via La Pace 1, 60004 Sassoferrata (Ancona) Italy. TEL 6-62-36-216. adv. circ. 8,200.

338.47624   SW   ISSN 0345-7133
LEVERANSTIDNINGEN ENTREPRENAD. 1960. 22/yr. SEK 499 (effective 1997). Svensk Leveranstidning AB, S-162 83 Vellingby, Sweden. TEL 46-8-620-24-04. FAX 46-8-89-70-05. URL: http://www.entreprenad.com. Ed. Torbjoern Albert. adv.: B&W page SEK 21700, color page SEK 33650; trim 250 x350; adv. contact: Aake Trygg. illus. circ. 16,000. **Document type:** newspaper.
    Formed by the merger of: Svensk Leveranstidning, (until vol.26, 1970): Entreprenad; (until vol.36, 1968): Entreprenadmeddelanden.

392.8   DK   ISSN 0024-287X
LICITATIONEN; dagbladet for bygge- og anlaegsvirksomhed. 1908. d. DKK 1360. Visholm Media AS, Sydvestvej 49, DK-2600 Glostrup, Denmark. Ed. Klaus Toltrop. adv. **Document type:** newspaper.
    Formerly: Haandvaerkets Dagblad.

690   LH
LIECHTENSTEINER BAU- UND HAUSZEITUNG. m. Postfach 983, FL-9490 Vaduz, Liechtenstein. TEL 41-75-2321414. FAX 41-75-2326510. Ed. Norman Kaufmann. circ. 2,000. **Document type:** trade publication.

LIFTING & TRANSPORTATION INTERNATIONAL. see *TRANSPORTATION — Trucks And Trucking*

690 621.3   US   ISSN 1069-0050
LIGHTING ANSWERS. 1993. irreg., approx. 4-6/yr. $8 per no. Rensselaer Polytechnic Institute, Lighting Research Center, Troy, NY 12180-3590. TEL 518-276-8716. FAX 518-276-2999. E-mail: lrs@rpi.edu; URL: http://www.lrc.rpi.edu. Ed. Robert Davis. R&P contact: Judith Block. bibl.; charts; illus. (back issues avail.) **Document type:** newsletter.
    Description: Presents educational information about specific lighting technology issues and topics, such as fluorescent lamps or light polarizers, in a question-and-answer format.

691.3   US   ISSN 0075-9457
LIGHTWEIGHT CONCRETE INFORMATION SHEETS. 1952. irreg. free. Expanded Shale, Clay and Slate Institute, 2225 E. Murray Holladay Rd., Ste. 102, Salt Lake City, UT 84117. TEL 801-272-7070. FAX 801-272-3377. Ed. John P. Ries. cum.index: 1952-1988. circ. 20,000. (back issues avail.) **Document type:** trade publication.
    Description: Information on ceramic lightweight aggregate which is used in concrete, concrete masonry, asphalt, horticulture, roof tile and insulation.

690   FR   ISSN 0990-1159
LOCAGUIDE; du BTP et de la manutention. a. 150 F. (Europe 200 F., elsewhere 270 F.) (effective 1997). (Societe d'Editions pour la Location) Groupe Chantiers de France, Bord de Seine, 202 quai de Clichy, 92110 Clichy, France. TEL 33-1-47561723. FAX 33-1-47561732. Eds. Arlette Surchamp, Marc Montagnon; Pub. Arlette Surchamp. adv. contact: Helene Tellier. circ. 10,000. **Document type:** newspaper, trade publication.
    Description: Lists addresses for drilling, pumping, sawing, cutting, air compression, concrete and other construction-related businesses.

LOCAL AUTHORITY BUILDING & MAINTENANCE. see *PUBLIC ADMINISTRATION — Municipal Government*

690   US
LODGING: AN INDUSTRY OVERVIEW. a. $395. Dun & Bradstreet Information Services (Murray Hill) (Subsidiary of: Dun & Bradstreet, Inc.), One Diamond Hill Rd., Murray Hill, NJ 07974. TEL 908-665-5224. FAX 908-771-7599. Ed. Robert Porreca.
    Description: Examines the transition of the lodging industry and its impact on related industries such as construction, banking, insurance, transportation services, tourism and furniture. Also analyzes the major trends of globalization, segmentation and consolidation.

BUILDING AND CONSTRUCTION

690   US   ISSN 1061-5857
LOG CABIN NEWS. 1989. q. $20 to individuals (Canada $23); historical societies $30 (Canada $35); libraries $10 (Canada $12); (effective 1997). Log Cabin Society of Michigan, 3503 Edwards Rd., Sodus, MI 49126. TEL 616-944-5719. FAX 616-944-5719. Ed. Virginia Handy. adv. contact: Virginia Handy. bk.rev. (back issues avail.) **Document type:** newsletter.
    Description: Promotes awareness of log cabins in Michigan and elsewhere for their historical value, encourages restoration of existing log cabins and construction of new ones, and presents news of related activities and festivals.

690   US   ISSN 1041-830X
TH4840
LOG HOME LIVING. (Supplement avail. a.: Log Home Plans) 1989. 10/yr. $28.95. Home Buyer Publications, Inc., Box 22039, 4200-T Lafayette Center Dr., Chantilly, VA 22021. TEL 703-222-9411. FAX 703-222-3209. Ed. Janice Brewster; Pub. John R. Kupferer. adv. contact: Laurie V. Sloan. circ. 200,000. (back issues avail.) **Document type:** consumer publication.
    Incorporates: Log Home Plans.
    Description: For people who own or want to own contemporary log homes.

692.8   US   ISSN 0195-7074
LOUISIANA CONTRACTOR. 1953. m. (plus a. Directory). $19.50. McGraw-Hill Companies, Louisiana Contractor, 2900 Westfork Dr., Ste. 345, Baton Rouge, LA 70827. TEL 504-292-8980. FAX 504-292-5089. Ed. Sam Barnes. adv. contact: Melane Rhodes. tr.lit. circ. 5,700.
    Formerly: Contractors Magazine.

690   US
LOUISVILLE BUILDER. 1987. m. $15 (effective 1997). Home Builders Association of Louisville, Inc., 100 N. Hurstbourne Pkwy., Louisville, KY 40223-6036. TEL 502-429-6036. FAX 502-429-6036. E-mail: newhomes@hbal.com; URL: http://www.hbal.com. Ed. Randy Gordon. adv.: B&W page $770; trim 8 1/8 x 10 7/8. illus. circ. 3,000. (back issues avail.) **Document type:** trade publication.

LOW BIDDER. see TRANSPORTATION — Roads And Traffic

LUXEMBOURG. SERVICE CENTRAL DE LA STATISTIQUE ET DES ETUDES ECONOMIQUES. INDICATEURS RAPIDES. SERIE B2: INDICES DE L'ACTIVITE DANS LA CONSTRUCTION. see BUILDING AND CONSTRUCTION — Abstracting, Bibliographies, Statistics

693.7   GW   ISSN 0934-3199
CODEN: MLVBAD
M & T - METALLHANDWERK & TECHNIK. 1899. m. DM.165. (Bundesverband Metall) Charles Coleman Verlag GmbH & Co. KG, Wahmstr. 56, 23552 Luebeck, Germany. TEL 49-451-79933-0. FAX 49-451-7993399. Ed. Dietrich Muhs; Pub. Guenter Sandscheper. adv. contact: Ulrich Claussen. bk.rev.; pat.; circ. controlled. **Document type:** trade publication.
—CASDDS; CISTI; Linda Hall. **CCC.**
    Incorporates (in 1995): Metallverarbeitung (ISSN 0026-0908); Former titles: Metallhandwerk and Metalltechnik (ISSN 0026-0789); Metallhandwerk.

691   US
M C A A INFO. m. Mason Contractors Association of America, 1910 S. Highland Ave, Ste. 101, Lombard, IL 60148. TEL 630-705-4200. FAX 630-705-4209. Pub. Michael Adelizzi. **Document type:** trade publication.

393   SW
M E - TIDNINGEN. 1957. m. (10/yr.). SEK 240. Maskinentreprenoernas Foerlags AB - Swedish Earth Moving Machine Owners Association, P.O. Box 1609, S-111 86 Stockholm, Sweden. TEL 46-8-762-70-65. FAX 46-8-611-85-41. Ed. Dag af Ekenstam. adv. contact: Christer Holmquist. bk.rev.; abstr.; charts; illus.; stat.; tr.lit. circ. 7,200. **Document type:** trade publication.
    Former titles: Maskinentreprenoeren (ISSN 0284-7140); (until 1986): S E R - Tidningen (ISSN 0037-2080)

690   US   ISSN 0274-9637
M H - R V BUILDERS NEWS; the magazine for builders of manufactured-mobile-modular-marine homes and recreational vehicles. 1965. bi-m. $20. Dan Kamrow & Associates, Inc., Box 72367, Roselle, IL 60172. TEL 747-891-8872. Ed. Patrick Finn. adv.; tr.lit.; index; circ. 9,000. (controlled). **Document type:** trade publication.
    Former titles: M H Builders News; M H-R V Builders News; M H Builders News (ISSN 0047-5254)

690   SZ
M O P. 5/yr. Weka Verlag AG, Hermetschloostr. 77, CH-8010 Zurich, Switzerland. TEL 41-1-4348888. FAX 41-1-4328201. Ed. Gaby Oehler. circ. 3,000. **Document type:** trade publication.

MAANSIIRTO/EARTHMOVING; maa- ja vesirakennusteknillinen aikakauslehti. see ENGINEERING — Civil Engineering

MADERA Y SU USO EN LA CONSTRUCCION. see FORESTS AND FORESTRY — Lumber And Wood

690   GW   ISSN 0024-9769
MAGAZIN FUER HAUS UND WOHNUNG. 1962. m. DM.42 (foreign DM.78) (effective 1997). Verlag fuer Bauwesen GmbH, Am Friedrichshain 22, 10407 Berlin, Germany. TEL 49-30-42151-0. FAX 49-30-42151232. Ed. Christiane Strehlau; Pub. Wolfgang Huss. adv. contact: Peter Schambier. bk.rev.; charts; illus.; index. circ. 60,116. **Document type:** consumer publication.

690   FR   ISSN 0987-7444
MAGAZINE DE LA CONSTRUCTION. 1980. 10/yr. Editions S E R I P, 40 rue Guy Moquet, 94501 Champigny Cedex, France. TEL 48-81-91-91. Ed. Alain Morvan. circ. 36,000. **Document type:** trade publication.
    Former titles (until 1987): Entrepreneur Magazine (ISSN 0767-4791); (until 1986): Guide Pratique de l'Entrepreneur du Batiment et de Travaux Publics. Magazine (ISSN 0755-4915)

666.89 620.136   UK   ISSN 0024-9831
TA680   CODEN: MCORAV
MAGAZINE OF CONCRETE RESEARCH. 1949. q. £106 (foreign £159) (effective 1997). Thomas Telford Services Ltd., Thomas Telford House, 1 Heron Quay, London E14 4JD, England. TEL 44-171-987-6999. FAX 44-171-538-9620. E-mail: ttjournals@ice.org.uk. Ed. P.C. Hewlett; Pub. Leon Heward-Mills. R&P contact: Joanna Brown. adv. contact: Joanna Brown. bk.rev.; abstr.; bibl.; illus. circ. 3,000. (reprint service avail. from UMI) **Indexed:** Abstr.J.Earthq.Eng., Alloys Ind., ASCA, Br.Ceram.Abstr., Br.Tech.Ind., Build.Manage.Abstr., C.R.I.Abstr., C.R.I.Curr.Cont., Chem.Abstr., Concr.Abstr., Curr.Cont., Eng.Ind., Eng.Mat.Abstr., Geotech.Abstr., HRIS, Ind.Sci.Rev., INSPEC, Intl.Civil Eng.Abstr., Intl.Polym.Sci.& Tech., J.of Ferroc., Mat.Sci.Cit.Ind., Met.Abstr.Ind., Met.Abstr., Nonfer.Met.Alert, PCC Alert, RAPRA, Sci.Cit.Ind., Soft.Abstr.Eng., Steels Alert, World Alum.Abstr. **Document type:** academic/scholarly publication.
—BLDSC (5333.000000); CASDDS; CISTI; Ei; Genuine Article; Linda Hall; SWETS; UMI; UnCover. **CCC.**
    Description: Publishes original research on the behavior of concrete and its constituent materials, both in the laboratory and in structures.
    Refereed Serial

690   IT
MAGAZZINO EDILE. 6/yr. Viale Don Minzoni 51, 20091 Bresso, Italy. TEL 2-61-08-119. Ed. Paolo Benna. circ. 8,250.

690.24   US   ISSN 1072-3560
MAINTENANCE SOLUTIONS. 1993. m. Trade Press Publishing Corp., 2100 W. Florist Ave., Milwaukee, WI 43209. TEL 414-228-7701. FAX 414-228-1134. Ed. Dan Hounsell. adv.: B&W page $3750; trim 10 7/8 x 14 7/8. circ. 35,000. **Document type:** trade publication.
    Description: Aimed at maintenance management, i.e., directors, managers, supervisors and other professionals responsible for the physical maintenance, engineering systems support and housekeeping functions in commercial and institutional buildings.

658.2   US   ISSN 0025-0929
MAINTENANCE SUPPLIES. 1956. m. $50. P T N Publishing Corp., 445 Broadhollow Rd., Melville, NY 11747-3601. Ed. Susan Brady; Pub. Mike Rossi. adv.; bk.rev.; charts; illus.; index. circ. 18,050. **Document type:** trade publication.

690   FR   ISSN 0244-1136
MAISON ET TRAVAUX. 1978. 6/yr. 140 F. Presse Pratique Parisienne, 16-18 rue de l'Amiral Mouchez, 75686 Paris Cedex 14, France. TEL 45-65-48-48. FAX 45-65-47-00. TELEX 240-918 TRACE. Ed. Jacqueline Louvet.
    Supersedes (in 1981): Batiguide (ISSN 0151-573X)

MALEREN. see PAINTS AND PROTECTIVE COATINGS

691   SP   ISSN 0210-1513
MANIPULACION DE MATERIALES EN LA INDUSTRIA. Short title: M A N I P. 1972. m. 4240 ptas. Publicaciones Internacionales S.A., P. Castellana, 210, 28046 Madrid, Spain. Ed. Tomas Blas Abascal. adv.; circ. 2,000 (controlled).

690   CN   ISSN 0714-3222
MANITOBA - WINNIPEG BUILDING & CONSTRUCTION TRADES COUNCIL YEARBOOK. 1971. a. Naylor Communications Ltd. (Winnipeg), 100 Sutherland Ave., Winnipeg, Man. R2W 3C7, Canada. TEL 204-947-0222. Ed. Janis Connolly. circ. 2,250.

690   US   ISSN 1086-4962
MANUFACTURED STRUCTURES NEWSLETTER. 1969. m. $115 (foreign $135). Hal Carlson, Ed. & Pub., 11 N. Ridge Ct., Box 6300, Battlement Mesa, CO 81636. TEL 970-285-7540. E-mail: scorehal@aol.com. R&P contact: Hal Carlson. (looseleaf format) **Document type:** newsletter, trade publication.
    Formerly: Manufactured Housing Newsletter (ISSN 0197-1816)
    Description: Covers conferences, industry news releases, regulatory and marketing news for all types of industrialized-modular, plus HUD-code manufactured homes and buildings in the US, Canada and internationally.

MANUTENZIONE E RESTAURO. see REAL ESTATE

MAQUINARIA Y EQUIPO. see MACHINERY

MARIN RODO/MARINE ROAD. see ENGINEERING — Civil Engineering

690   GW   ISSN 0949-0833
▼**MARKT- UND PLANUNGSDATEN FUER DIE BAUWIRTSCHAFT.** 1995. q. DM.90 (effective 1997). (Fraunhofer Informationszentrum Raum und Bau) Fraunhofer I R B Verlag, Nobelstr. 12, 70569 Stuttgart, Germany. TEL 49-711-9702500. FAX 49-711-9702507. E-mail: irb@irb.fhg.de; URL: http://www.irb.fhg.de. **Document type:** trade publication.

MARMI GRANITI PIETRE; rivista specializzata del settore marmifero. see MINES AND MINING INDUSTRY

693.1 720   IT
MARMO IN. (Text in English, Italian) 1990. s-a. free. (Italian Consortium for Marble) Ever s.n.c. di Emilia Gallini & C., Galleria Gandhi 15, 20017 Rho (MI), Italy. TEL 39-2-93900750. FAX 39-2-93900727.

MARYLAND BUILDER. see HOUSING AND URBAN PLANNING

MASCHINEN UND STAHLBAU. see MACHINERY

690 721   UZ
TH4
MASKAN; arkhitektura i stroitel'stvo Uzbekistana, Kazakhstana, Azerbaidzana, Kyrgyzstana, Tadzjikistana, Turkmenistana. 1966. m. 16.20 Rub. Ul. Gazety "Pravda", 41, 700000 Tashkent, Uzbekistan. charts; illus.; index. **Indexed:** Chem.Abstr. —Linda Hall.
    Formerly (until no.9, 1991): Stroitel'stvo i Arkhitektura Uzbekistana (ISSN 0039-243X)

BUILDING AND CONSTRUCTION

691 US ISSN 0025-4681
TH1199
MASONRY. 1961. 6/yr. $20 (effective 1997). Mason Contractors Association of America, 1910 S. Highland Ave., Ste. 101, Lombard, IL 60148. TEL 630-705-4200. FAX 630-705-4209. Ed. Richard Olson; Pub. Michael Adelizzi. adv.; bk.rev.; illus. circ. 8,200. **Document type:** trade publication.
—CISTI.

690 US
MASONRY DESIGN WEST. bi-m. Pleasanton Publishing Company, 6284 Wade Ct., Pleasanton, CA 95688. TEL 415-846-5623. FAX 415-846-1753. Ed. Alan Knapp. circ. 12,508.

690 624 US ISSN 0741-1294
CODEN: MSJUET
MASONRY SOCIETY JOURNAL. 1981. s-a. $55 in U.S. and Canada; elsewhere $60 (effective 1997). Masonry Society, 3970 Broadway St., Ste. 201-D, Boulder, CO 80304-1135. TEL 303-939-9700. FAX 303-541-9215. Ed. Rochelle C. Jaffe. bk.rev. circ. 2,500. (back issues avail.)
—BLDSC (5387.537000); CISTI; UnCover.
Description: Technical masonry research.
Refereed Serial

690 AT ISSN 1039-4532
MASTER BUILDER. 1949. 6/yr. Aus.$48 (foreign Aus.$60). Master Builders Association of Victoria, 332-334 Albert St., E. Melbourne, Vic. 3002, Australia. TEL 03-419-4555. FAX 03-417-7006. Ed. Giselle Grynbaum. adv.; bk.rev. circ. 5,246.
Formerly (until 1992): Australian Builder (ISSN 0004-878X).

690 UK ISSN 0025-4991
MASTER BUILDERS' JOURNAL. 1955. m. £19.70. (Federation of Master Builders) Construction Industry Services Ltd., 14-15 Great James St., Holborn, London WC1N 3DP, England. TEL 071-242-7583. FAX 071-404-0296. Ed. Ray Briggs. adv.; bk.rev.; illus.; tr.lit. circ. 21,000. **Indexed:** Br.Tech.Ind. **Document type:** trade publication.

690 US
▼**MASTER PLAN FOR PROFESSIONAL HOME REMODELING.** 1997. a. free to homeowners. National Association of the Remodeling Industry, 4900 Seminary Rd., Ste. 320, Alexandria, VA 22311-1811. TEL 703-575-1100; 800-440-6274. FAX 703-575-1121. E-mail: narieditor@aol.com; URL: http://www.nari.org. Ed. Susan Maney. R&P contact: Susan Maney. adv. **Document type:** consumer publication.
Description: Includes features about the remodeling industry to help homeowners successfully complete a remodeling project.

691 SP ISSN 0465-2746
TP875 CODEN: MCUAAA
MATERIALES DE CONSTRUCCION. (Text in English, Spanish) 1949. q. 6000 ptas. (foreign 7000 ptas.) (effective 1996). Instituto de Ciencias de la Construccion Eduardo Torroja, Apdo. 19002, 28080 Madrid, Spain. TEL 34-1-3020440. FAX 34-1-3020700. adv.; bk.rev. circ. 1,000. **Indexed:** Art & Archaeol.Tech.Abstr., Chem.Abstr., Concr.Abstr., Ind.SST, Intl.Civil Eng.Abstr., Soft.Abstr.Eng., W.R.C.Inf.
—BLDSC (5393.700000); CASDDS; Ei; Genuine Article; SWETS. **CCC.**

690 IT
MATERIALI DA COSTRUZIONE ED OPERE EDILI PREZZI INFORMATIVI. 1967. q. L.35000. Camera di Commercio, Industria, Artigianato e Agricoltura, Piazza della Vittoria, 42100 Reggio Emilia, Italy. TEL 0522-7961. FAX 0522-433750. Ed. Sergio Cecchieri. circ. 1,000.
Formerly: Materiali da Costruzione ed Opere Edili Prezzi Indicativi.

692.8 FR ISSN 0025-5432
CODEN: MCMSBP
MATERIALS AND STRUCTURES/MATERIAUX ET CONSTRUCTIONS; research and testing. 1968. 10/yr. £210 to institutions in the E.U. (N. America $360; elsewhere £225) (effective 1995). International Union of Testing and Research Laboratories for Materials and Structures (RILEM), Pavillon des Jardins 61, Av. du President Wilson, 94235 Cachan Cedex, France. Ed. M. Brusin. adv. (reprint service avail.) **Indexed:** Alloys Ind., ASCA, C.R.I.Abstr., C.R.I.Curr.Cont., Eng.Mat.Abstr., J.of Ferroc., Mat.Sci.Cit.Ind., Met.Abstr., Met.Abstr.Ind., Nonfer.Met.Alert, PCC Alert, Steels Alert, World Alum.Abstr. **Document type:** academic/scholarly publication.
—BLDSC (5394.103000); CASDDS; CISTI; Ei; Linda Hall; SWETS; UMI; UnCover. **CCC.**
Description: Presents technical papers on the properties and performance of building materials and structures in laboratory and service conditions; the standardization of test methods between countries; and the application of such results to the structural use of materials in building and civil engineering applications.
Refereed Serial

690 CN ISSN 1188-4096
MATERIALS NEWS. (Included in: Construction Innovation) (Editions in English, French) q. free. National Research Council of Canada, Institute for Research in Construction, Ottawa, ON K1A 0R6, Canada. TEL 613-993-2463; 800-672-7990. FAX 613-952-7673. URL: http://www.cisti.nrc.ca/. **Indexed:** Alloys Ind., Eng.Mat.Abstr., Met.Abstr., Met.Abstr.Ind., Nonfer.Met.Alert, PCC Alert, Steels Alert, World Alum.Abstr. **Document type:** academic/scholarly publication.
—CISTI. **CCC.**
Description: Contains information on materials: concrete, sealants, roofing materials, paints, masonry.

690 PL ISSN 0137-2971
MATERIALY BUDOWLANE. 1974. m. $30.50. Wydawnictwo Czasopism i Ksiazek Technicznych SIGMA - NOT, Ul. Ratuszowa 11, P.O. Box 1004, 00-950 Warsaw, Poland. TEL 48-22-180918. FAX 48-22-192187. TELEX 814550 SIGMA PL. (Dist. by: SIGMA NOT Ltd., Ul. Bartycka 20, 00-716 Warsaw, Poland) Ed. Tadeusz Bienias. adv.: B&W page $1260. circ. 2,000. **Indexed:** INIS Atomind.

691 FR
MATERIAUX DE CONSTRUCTION ET PRODUITS DE CARRIERES. 4/yr. 3 rue Alfred Roll, 75017 Paris, France. TEL 44-01-47-01. FAX 40-54-03-28. TELEX 641 394 F. Ed. Olivier Guinet. circ. 2,800.

691 721 GW ISSN 1432-3427
▼**DAS MAUERWERK.** 1997. q. DM.188 (foreign DM.208) (effective 1997). Ernst und Sohn, Muehlenstr. 33-34, 13187 Berlin, Germany. TEL 49-30-47889200. (Subscr. to: Wiley - V C H, Postfach 101161, 69451 Weinheim, Germany. TEL 49-6201-606147. FAX 49-6201-606117; Subscr. in the Americas to: John Wiley & Sons, Inc., 605 Third Ave., New York, NY 10158. TEL 212-850-6645. FAX 212-850-6021) Ed. P. Schubert. **Document type:** academic/scholarly publication.
Description: Forum for the exchange of knowledge and experience pertaining to buildings from all over Europe.

MAUSOLEE; arts et techniques des roches de qualite. see *ART*

691 US ISSN 0894-4342
TH435
MEANS ASSEMBLIES COST DATA (YEAR). 1976. a. $128.95. R.S. Means Company, Inc., 100 Construction Plaza, Box 800, Kingston, MA 02364-0800. TEL 800-334-3509. FAX 617-585-7466. Ed. Philip R. Waier.
—CISTI.
Former titles: Means Assemblies Costs; Means Systems Costs.

691 US ISSN 1075-0274
TA682.26
MEANS CONCRETE AND MASONRY COST DATA. 1982. a. $74.95. R.S. Means Company, Inc., 100 Construction Plaza, Box 800, Kingston, MA 02364-0800. TEL 617-585-7880; 800-334-3509. FAX 617-585-7466. Ed. Philip R. Waier. bk.rev.; charts; stat. circ. 3,000. (back issues avail.) **Document type:** trade publication.
Former titles (until 1994): Means Concrete Cost Data (Year) (ISSN 1075-0533); (until 1987): Concrete and Masonry Cost Data (ISSN 0739-8298)
Description: Includes cost facts for every concrete estimating problem, from complicated formwork to lavish brickwork.

692 US ISSN 1075-0789
MEANS FACILITIES CONSTRUCTION COST DATA. 1986. a. R.S. Means Company, Inc., 100 Construction Plaza, Box 800, Kingston, MA 02364-0800. TEL 617-585-7880; 800-448-8182. FAX 617-585-7466. Ed. Philip R. Waier. **Document type:** trade publication.
Formerly (until 1994): Means Facilities Cost Data (ISSN 0888-6709)

690 US ISSN 0893-5602
TH435
MEANS HEAVY CONSTRUCTION COST DATA. a. $82.95. R.S. Means Company, Inc., 100 Construction Plaza, Box 800, Kingston, MA 02364-0800. TEL 800-334-3509. FAX 617-585-7466.
Description: Provides current unit and systems prices for thousands of heavy construction installations.

690 US
MEANS INTERIOR COST DATA (YEAR). 1984. a. $79.95. R.S. Means Company, Inc., 100 Construction Plaza, Box 800, Kingston, MA 02364-0800. TEL 800-334-3509. FAX 617-585-7466. Ed. Roger Grant.
Formerly: Interior Cost Data (Year) (ISSN 8755-7541)

692 331 US
MEANS LABOR RATES FOR THE CONSTRUCTION INDUSTRY. 1973. a. $174.95. R.S. Means Company, Inc., 100 Construction Plaza, Box 800, Kingston, MA 02364-0800. TEL 800-334-3509. FAX 617-585-7466. Ed. Philip R. Waier.
Formerly: Labor Rates for the Construction Industry (ISSN 0098-3608)

690 US ISSN 0896-7601
TH4315
MEANS LIGHT COMMERCIAL COST DATA (YEAR). a. $72.95. R.S. Means Company, Inc., 100 Construction Plaza, Kingston, MA 02364. TEL 800-334-3509. charts; illus.

690 US
TH435
MEANS MECHANICAL COST DATA (YEAR). 1978. a. $79.95. R.S. Means Company, Inc., 100 Construction Plaza, Box 800, Kingston, MA 02364-0800. TEL 800-334-3509. FAX 617-585-7466. Ed. Melville J. Mossman.
—CISTI.
Former titles: Mechanical Cost Data (ISSN 0748-2698); Mechanical and Electrical Cost Data (ISSN 0193-1954)

690 US
MEANS OPEN SHOP BUILDING CONSTRUCTION COST DATA (YEAR). 1985. a. $76.95. R.S. Means Company, Inc., 100 Construction Plaza, Box 800, Kingston, MA 02364-0800. TEL 800-334-3509. FAX 617-585-7466. Ed. Philip R. Waier.
Formerly: Open Shop Building Construction Cost Data (Year) (ISSN 0883-8127)

691 US ISSN 0898-5006
TH3411
MEANS REPAIR AND REMODELING COST DATA (YEAR). 1980. a. $79.95. R.S. Means Company, Inc., 100 Construction Plaza, Box 800, Kingston, MA 02364-0800. TEL 617-585-7880. FAX 617-585-7466. Ed. Philip R. Waier.
—CISTI.
Formerly: Repair and Remodeling Cost Data (ISSN 0271-5945)

BUILDING AND CONSTRUCTION

691 US ISSN 0738-1239
TH435
MEANS RESIDENTIAL COST DATA. 1982. a. $72.95. R.S. Means Company, Inc., 100 Construction Plaza, Box 800, Kingston, MA 02364-0800. TEL 617-585-7880. FAX 617-585-7466. Ed. Philip R. Waier.
Formerly: Residential - Light Commercial Cost Data (ISSN 0733-6403)

691 US ISSN 1064-5128
TH435
MEANS SITE WORK AND LANDSCAPE COST DATA (YEAR). 1982. a. $82.95. R.S. Means Company, Inc., 100 Construction Plaza, Box 800, Kingston, MA 02364-0800. TEL 800-334-3509. FAX 617-585-7466.
Formerly (until 1992): Means Site Work Cost Data (ISSN 0734-8479)
Description: Covers every aspect of modern site work estimating: exploration, pollution control, soil retention, hidden utilities, security, and site enhancement.

MEANS SQUARE FOOT COSTS (YEAR); residential, commercial, industrial, institutional. see REAL ESTATE

621 600 US
MECHANICAL CONTRACTOR LITERATURE SHOWCASE. 2/yr. Cahners Publishing Company (Des Plaines), Division of Reed Elsevier Inc., 1350 E. Touhy Ave., Box 5080, Des Plaines, IL 60018-5080. TEL 847-635-8800. FAX 847-390-2329. (Subscr. to: 8773 S. Ridgeline Blvd., Highlands Ranch, CO 80126. TEL 303-470-4000) Ed. Robert Miodonski. adv. circ. 52,572. **Document type:** trade publication.

692.8 US
MECHANICAL CONTRACTORS ASSOCIATION OF AMERICA. STATISTICAL SURVEY REPORT.* s-a. $40 to non-members; members $20. Mechanical Contractors Association of America, 1385 Piccard Dr., Rockville, MD 20850. TEL 301-869-5800.

690 US
MECHANICS' AND CONSTRUCTION LIENS IN ALASKA, OREGON AND WASHINGTON. 1987. base vol. (plus supplement). $70. Butterworth Legal Publishers (Salem) (Subsidiary of: Reed Elsevier plc), 8 Industrial Way, Bldg. C, Salem, NH 03079. TEL 800-548-4001. FAX 603-898-9858. Ed. Brian A. Blum. (looseleaf format)

690 FI ISSN 1237-1130
MEIDAN TALO JA KOTI. 1960. 10/yr. FIM 397 (effective 1997). A-Lehdet Oy, Hitsaajankatu 7, FIN-00081 A-Lehdet, Finland. FAX 358-0-759-1268. Ed. Anja Tuomi. circ. 40,715. **Document type:** consumer publication.
Former titles (until 1992): Meidan Talo (ISSN 0356-6110); (until 1978): Rakennusviesti (ISSN 0355-5062)
Description: Useful information magazine for people who build, improve or maintain their own homes.

MEKHANIZATSIYA STROITEL'STVA. see ENGINEERING — Civil Engineering

MERCHANT MAGAZINE. see FORESTS AND FORESTRY — Lumber And Wood

690 658 SA
MERKELS' BUILDERS' PRICING AND MANAGEMENT MANUAL. 1948. a. R.307.80. Thomson Publications (Subsidiary of: Times Media Ltd.), P.O. Box 56182, Pinegowrie 2123, South Africa. TEL 27-11-789-2144. FAX 27-11-789-3196. adv. circ. 2,000. **Document type:** directory.

690 352.7 RU ISSN 0202-6317
MESTNYI PROIZVODSTVENNYI OPYT V STROITEL'STVE/LOCAL LEVEL EXPERIENCE IN THE CONSTRUCTION INDUSTRY; nauchno-tekhnicheskii referativnyi sbornik. 1975. m. 4.80 Rub. Moskovskii Gorodskoi Territorial'nyi Tsentr Nauchno-Tekhnicheskoi Informatsii i Propagandy, Pr. Serova 5, 101958 Moscow, Russia. TEL 921-67-05. (Co-sponsor: State Planning Committee of the R.S.F.S.R.) Ed. Arnold P. Kudryashov. circ. 2,060. (back issues avail.)

693.7 US ISSN 0026-0525
TH1611
METAL BUILDING REVIEW.* 1965. m. $16. Mill Hollow Publications, 100 Avenue of the Americas, 6th Fl., New York, NY 10013-1689. TEL 212-741-2095. Ed. Richard Merli. adv.; bk.rev.; illus. circ. 22,000.

690 669 US ISSN 0274-8843
METAL CONSTRUCTION NEWS. m. $45 (effective 1997). Modern Trade Communications, 7450 Skokie Blvd., Skokie, IL 60077. TEL 847-674-2200. FAX 847-674-3676. Ed. Shawn Zuver. R&P contact: Shawn Zuver. adv. contact: John Riester. circ. 32,800. **Document type:** trade publication.
Formerly: Metal Building News.

MICHERON BINIYA, ENERGIA VESHERUTIM NIVCHARIM. see ENERGY

692.8 US
MICHIGAN CONTRACTOR & BUILDER; engineering and construction. 1907. w. $125. Contractor Publishing Co., 1629 W. Lafayette, Detroit, MI 48216. TEL 313-962-3337. FAX 313-962-4560. Ed. Guy Snyder. adv.; bk.rev. circ. 3,693. **Indexed:** Mich.Mag.Ind.

MICHIGAN MASTER PLUMBER & MECHANICAL CONTRACTOR; a monthly magazine for Michigan's plumbing, heating, cooling industry. see HEATING, PLUMBING AND REFRIGERATION

692.8 US ISSN 0026-3044
MIDWEST CONTRACTOR MAGAZINE.* (In 2 editions: North & South) 1901. s-m. $38 per ed.; for both eds. $76. Midwest Contractor, 3101 Broadway St., Ste. 750, Kansas City, MO 64111-2416. Ed. Scott Judy. adv.; bk.rev.; illus. circ. 8,125. **Document type:** trade publication.
Description: Articles and information on bids-awards, planned work, business methods, new products and literature, legislation, association meetings, and manufacturer-distributor news pertaining to the engineered construction and public works industries in Iowa, Kansas, Nebraska, and western and northeastern Missouri.

MILJOE. see BUSINESS AND ECONOMICS — Marketing And Purchasing

MILLION DOLLAR PROJECT PLANNED LIST. see ARCHITECTURE

690 US ISSN 0895-7304
MILLWORK MANUFACTURING. 1985. bi-m. $15 per no. Associations Publications, Inc., Box 640, Collierville, TN 38027-9986. TEL 901-853-7470. Ed. Joyce Powell. adv. circ. 6,620.

690 US
MILLWORK PRODUCTS GUIDE. a. National Sash and Door Jobbers Association, 10225 Robert Trent Jones Pkwy, New Port Richey, FL 34655-4649.

MINNESOTA P - H - C CONTRACTOR MAGAZINE. see HEATING, PLUMBING AND REFRIGERATION

MITGLIEDERINFORMATION. see ARCHITECTURE

690 IS ISSN 0333-7502
MIVNIM. (Text in Hebrew) m. IS.11($5.50) Merav Publishing Industries Ltd., 12 Yad Harutzim, Tel Aviv 67778, Israel. TEL 972-2-6382942. FAX 972-3-6382939. Ed. Eilat El Gur. adv. circ. 6,000. **Document type:** trade publication.
Description: For the construction industry in Israel.

388.3 US ISSN 0733-6497
TL297
MOBILE - MANUFACTURED HOME BLUE BOOK. 2/yr. $100. National Market Reports, Inc., 29 N. Wacker Dr., Chicago, IL 60606-3297. TEL 312-855-0137. FAX 312-855-0137. Ed. Gary Dillow; Pub. George Stanton. R&P contact: George Stanton. (back issues avail.) **Document type:** directory.
Formerly (until 1982): Mobile Home Blue Book (ISSN 0733-6489)

333.33 US ISSN 1081-7808
MOBILE - MANUFACTURED HOUSING COST GUIDE. 198? a. $35. (American Appraisal Associates) E.H. Boeckh (Subsidiary of: Thomson Publishing Corp.), 2885 S. Calhoun Rd., Box 510291, New Berlin, WI 53151-0291. TEL 414-780-2800; 800-285-1288. FAX 414-780-0306.

MODERN BUILDING ARCHITECTURE AND ENGINEERING IN AUSTRALIA. see ARCHITECTURE

693.71 US ISSN 0026-8445
TA472
MODERN STEEL CONSTRUCTION. 1944. m. $30 (foreign $36) free to qualified personnel. American Institute of Steel Construction, Inc., One E. Wacker Dr., Ste. 3100, Chicago, IL 60601-2001. TEL 312-670-5407. FAX 312-670-5403. TELEX 910-350-6816. Ed. Scott Melnick. illus. circ. 35,000. **Indexed:** Alloys Ind., Appl.Mech.Rev., Avery Ind.Archit.Per., Eng.Mat.Abstr., HRIS, Met.Abstr., Met.Abstr.Ind., Nonfer.Met.Alert, PCC Alert, Sh.& Vib.Dig., Steels Alert, World Alum.Abstr.
—BLDSC (5897.500000); CISTI; Ei; SWETS; UnCover.
Supersedes (in 1961): Steel Construction Digest.

690 624 IT ISSN 0390-1025
MODULO. (Supplements avail.) 1975. m. (10/yr.). L.120000 (effective 1997). BE-MA Editrice s.r.l., Via Teocrito, 50, 20128 Milan, Italy. TEL 39-2-2552451. FAX 39-2-57000692. Ed. Giuseppe Biondo. adv.: B&W page L.4700000, color page L.6200000; trim 210 x 297. circ. 14,656.
Description: Covers technology and design for quality in building.

690 IT ISSN 0394-7874
MONDOCUCINA.* m. L.55000 (foreign L.80000). Armand Curcio Periodici S.p.A., Via IV Novembre 149, 00187 Rome, Italy. TEL 06-856041. Ed. Tarquino Maiorino.

MONITEUR DES TRAVAUX PUBLICS ET DU BATIMENT. see ENGINEERING — Civil Engineering

624 621.9 FR ISSN 0998-4577
LE MONITEUR - MATERIELS ET CHANTIERS. 1921. 9/yr. 260 F. (foreign 340 F.). Groupe Moniteur, 17 rue d'Uzes, 75002 Paris, France. FAX 33-1-42333819. TELEX 220 528F. Ed. Michel Roche. adv.; bk.rev. circ. 15,000.
Incorporates: Equipement Mecanique, Carrieres et Materiaux; Which was formerly: Equipment Mecanique des Chantiers (ISSN 0013-9882)

691 SP ISSN 0212-7091
MONITOR. 1888. 12/yr. Agrupacion Nacional de Constructores de Obras Publicas, Principe Vergara 74, 6o p., 28006 Madrid, Spain. TEL 1-563-05-04. FAX 1-262-58-444. TELEX 27646 SEOP. Ed. Paloma Tello Lucini. circ. 8,000.
Formerly (until 1983): Monitor de Obras Publicas (ISSN 0540-651X)

690 US
MONITOR (SKOKIE). m. Portland Cement Co., 5240 Old Orchard Rd., Skokie, IL 60077-1083. TEL 708-966-6200. Ed. Bill Toal.

690 RU ISSN 0027-0040
CODEN: MSRYA9
MONTAZHNYE I SPETSIAL'NYE RABOTY V STROITEL'STVE. 1941. m. $151 (effective 1998). Ministerstvo Stroitel'nogo, Dorozhnogo i Kommunal'nogo Mashinostroeniya, Moscow G-200, Russia. bk.rev.; bibl.; charts; illus. (tabloid format) **Indexed:** Chem.Abstr.
—BLDSC (0117.510000).

690 333.7 US
MOUNTAIN CONSTRUCTOR & RECLAMATIONIST.* 1990 bi-m. $25. Phoenix Publishing Corporation, Box 6048, Denver, CO 80206-0048. TEL 303-988-2784. Ed. James I. Clayton. circ. 11,201 (controlled).
Description: Covers heavy construction, reclamation, non-residential building, landscaping, soil conservation, mining and logging in the Western U.S.

BUILDING AND CONSTRUCTION

690 380   US   ISSN 0844-3459
TH4818.W6
MUIR'S ORIGINAL LOG HOME GUIDE FOR BUILDERS & BUYERS. (Supplements avail.) 1978. q. Can.$12($12) (foreign $25). Muir Publishing Co., Inc., 164 Middle Creek Rd., Cosby, TN 37722. TEL 800-345-5647. FAX 615-487-3249. Ed. Allan T. Muir. adv.: B&W page $6325, color page $7900. bk.rev.; charts; illus.; tr.lit. circ. 175,000. (back issues avail.)
   Formerly: Log Home Guide for Builders and Buyers (ISSN 0707-5006); Incorporates: Log Home Decor for Builders and Buyers.
   Description: Covers developments in the log home industry. Contains how-to articles on buying as well as (or in place of) building a log house in North America.

690 333.33   US   ISSN 0146-0919
MULTI-HOUSING NEWS. Cover title: M H N. 1966-1991; resumed 1992. 6/yr. $30 canada & Mexico $46; elsewhere $90 (effective 1996). Miller Freeman Inc. (New York) (Subsidiary of: United News & Media), One Penn Plaza, New York, NY 10119. TEL 212-869-1300. FAX 212-944-7164. (Subscr. to: Box 1055, Skokie, IL 60076-8055. TEL 800-682-8297) Ed. Laura Rowley. adv.; illus.; circ. 28,300 (controlled). **Document type:** trade publication.
—CCC.
   Formerly: Apartment Construction News (ISSN 0003-6358)
   Description: Covers finance, marketing, sales and other developments affecting the multi-unit building and management industry.

690   NO   ISSN 0332-5733
MUR; arkitektur og byggeteknikk. 1976. q. NOK 200($14) (effective 1997). Mur Sentret, Forskningsveien 3 b, NO-0371 Oslo, Norway. TEL 47-4-22--96-58-88. FAX 47-4-22-60-11-92. Ed. Mari Flaata. adv. circ. 4,000. **Document type:** trade publication.

690   IT
MURATURE OGGI.* 4/yr. Edizioni Lambda s.n.c., Via Gobetti 9, 37138 Verona, Italy. TEL 39-45-572697. FAX 39-45-572430. Ed. B. Martelli. circ. 37,490.

691   DK   ISSN 0108-8602
MURERHAANDBOG. 1963. a. DKK 5. Kalk- og Teglinformation, Teglbaekvej 20, 8361 Hassselager, Denmark. illus.

381.45   US   ISSN 1078-8824
HD9715.7.U62
N A D A MANUFACTURED HOUSING APPRAISAL GUIDE. 3/yr. $95. (National Automobile Dealers Association) N.A.D.A. Appraisal Guides, Box 7800, Costa Mesa, CA 92628-7800. TEL 800-966-6232. FAX 714-556-8715.
   Former titles (until 1993): N.A.D.A. Mobile - Manufactured Housing Appraisal Guide (ISSN 0742-9274); N.A.D.A. Mobile Home Appraisal Guide (ISSN 0095-6538)

690   US
N A H B REMODELOR. 1988. bi-m. National Association of Home Builders, Remodelors Council, 1201 15th St., N.W., Washington, DC 20005. TEL 202-822-0200. FAX 202-861-2170. Ed. Christopher P. Nicholson. circ. 5,000. **Document type:** newsletter.
   Description: Covers remodelling issues, technical advice and council news.

N A: NUEVA ARCHITECTURA CON ARCILLA COCIDA. see ARCHITECTURE

690   US
▼**N A R I REMODELER'S JOURNAL.** 1997. q. membership. National Association of the Remodeling Industry, 4900 Deminary Rd., Ste. 320, Alexandria, VA 22311-1811. TEL 703-575-1100. FAX 703-575-1121. E-mail: narieditor@aol.com; URL: http://www.nari.org. Ed. Susan Maney. R&P contact: Birgitte Junior. adv.; bk.rev.; circ. 7,500 (controlled).
   Description: Includes features and technical articles on the remodeling industry, association news, and business management issues.
   Refereed Serial

690   CN   ISSN 0848-600X
N B C - N F C NEWS. (National Building Code - National Fire Code) (Included in: Construction Innovation) (Editions in English, French) 1957. q. free. National Research Council of Canada, Institute for Research in Construction, Ottawa, ON K1A 0R6, Canada. TEL 613-993-2463; 800-672-7990. FAX 613-952-7673. URL: http://www.cisti.nrc.ca/cisti/. circ. 27,000.
—CISTI; Linda Hall. **CCC.**
   Formerly: N B C News (ISSN 0027-612X)
   Description: Monitors any changes in building and fire codes, evaluates standards in the construction industry, outlines schedule of code committee meetings, among other activities.

690 331   US
N C A NEWSLETTER. 1960. q. free to qualified personnel. National Constructors Association, 1730 M. St., N.W., Ste. 503, Washington, DC 20036-4571. TEL 202-466-8880. FAX 202-466-7512. Ed. David Mapledsen. R&P contact: Nick Fiore. circ. 600. **Document type:** newspaper.
   Description: Covers industrial construction matters relating to labor relations, union agreements, safety and health government regulations, tax and human resources issues, association meetings and events.

N C S B C S NEWS. (National Conference of States on Building Codes and Standards, Inc.) see HOUSING AND URBAN PLANNING

695   UK
N F R C ROOFING INDUSTRY DIRECTORY. 1979. a. (National Federation of Roofing Contractors) B P G Ltd., 2 West St., Bourne, Lincs PE10 9NE, England. TEL 0778-393747. FAX 0778-425453. Ed. S. McLoughlin. adv. contact: Rod Plowe. **Document type:** directory, trade publication.
   Formerly: N F R C Yearbook.

690   US   ISSN 1049-7579
TA435   CODEN: NBSSES
N I S T BUILDING SCIENCE SERIES. irreg. price varies. U.S. National Institute of Standards and Technology, Gaithersburg, MD 20899. TEL 301-975-3058. (Orders to: National Technical Information Service, 5285 Port Royal Rd., Springfield, VA 22161. TEL 703-487-4650. FAX 703-321-8547; Or: Bernan, 4611-F Assembly Dr., Lanham, MD 20706. TEL 800-274-4447. FAX 301-459-0056) **Indexed:** Alloys Ind., Eng.Mat.Abstr., INSPEC, Met.Abstr., Met.Abstr.Ind., Nonfer.Met.Alert, PCC Alert, Steels Alert, World Alum.Abstr., World Surf.Coat. **Document type:** government publication, monographic series.
—CISTI; Ei.
   Formerly: U.S. National Bureau of Standards. Building Science Series (ISSN 0083-1794)
   Description: Presents research results on test methods and performance criteria related to structural and environmental functions, durability and safety.
   Refereed Serial

N R C A MEMBERSHIP DIRECTORY. (National Roofing Contractors Association) see BUSINESS AND ECONOMICS — Trade And Industrial Directories

691.3   US   ISSN 0077-5355
                      CODEN: NRMCAO
N R M C A PUBLICATION. 1931. irreg., no.144, 1973. price varies. National Ready Mixed Concrete Association, 900 Spring St., Silver Spring, MD 20910. TEL 301-587-1400. Ed. R.D. Gaynor. circ. 2,000. **Indexed:** Concr.Abstr.

690   YU   ISSN 0350-2619
NASE GRADEVINARSTVO. (Supplement to: Tehnika) (Text in Serbo-Croatian; summaries in English, Russian) vol.30, 1976. m. $50. Savez Inzenjera i Tehnicara Jugoslavije, Kneza Milosa 9, Box 187, 11000 Belgrade, Yugoslavia. Ed. Mihailo Muravljov. **Indexed:** Concr.Abstr., Geotech.Abstr.

691   UK
NATIONAL ASSOCIATION OF SCAFFOLDING CONTRACTORS YEAR BOOK. 1979. a. Comprint Ltd., Penn House, Penn Ln., Rickmansworth, Herts. WD3 1SN, England. **Document type:** trade publication.

690   II
NATIONAL BUILDING. (Text in English) s-a. Rs.66($23.76) Government of India, Department of Publications, Civil Lines, Delhi 110 054, India. **Document type:** government publication.

690   II   ISSN 0255-8165
NATIONAL BUILDINGS CONSTRUCTION CORPORATION. BULLETIN. (Text and summaries in English) 1973. q. free. National Buildings Construction Corporation Limited, NBCC House, Lodi Road, New Delhi 110 003, India. TEL 690314. TELEX 31-66665 NBCC IN. Ed. V. Grover. circ. 2,000. **Document type:** bulletin.

690   II   ISSN 0027-8815
NATIONAL BUILDINGS ORGANISATION. JOURNAL. (Text in English) 1955. s-a. Rs.10($3.60) National Buildings Organisation, G Wing, Nirman Bhavan, Maulana Azad Rd., New Delhi 11, India. Ed. S. Pratap. adv.; bk.rev.; charts; illus.; stat. circ. 750. **Indexed:** Archit.Per.Ind., C.R.I.Abstr., C.R.I.Curr.Cont.
—CISTI.

NATIONAL CONFERENCE OF STATES ON BUILDING CODES AND STANDARDS. ANNUAL CONFERENCE PROCEEDINGS. see HOUSING AND URBAN PLANNING

666.8   II
NATIONAL COUNCIL FOR CEMENT AND BUILDING MATERIALS. ANNUAL REPORT. (Text in English) a. National Council for Cement and Building Materials, 34th Kilometer Stone, Delhi-Mathura Rd. (NA-2), Ballabgarh 121 004, India. TEL 91-129-242051. FAX 91-129-242100. illus. **Indexed:** Concr.Abstr. **Document type:** corporate report.
   Formerly: Cement Research Institute of India. Annual Report.

690   US
(YEAR) NATIONAL ELECTRICAL ESTIMATOR. 1985. a. $47.75. Craftsman Book Company, 6058 Corte del Cedro, Box 6500, Carlsbad, CA 92018. TEL 619-438-7828; 800-829-8123. FAX 619-438-0398. URL: http://www.craftsman-book.com. Ed. Laurence Jacobs; Pub. Gary Moselle. R&P contact: Laurence Jacobs. adv. contact: Bill Grote. circ. 5,000. (also avail. in diskette format) **Document type:** trade publication.
   Formerly: Electrical Construction Estimator (ISSN 1041-729X)
   Description: Labor and material costs for installing electrical in residential, commercial, and industrial construction.

690   JA
NATIONAL FEDERATION OF CONSTRUCTION WORKERS' UNIONS. ZENKENSOREN. bi-w. National Federation of Construction Workers' Unions, 7-15 Takadanobaba 2-chome, Shinjuku-ku, Tokyo, Japan.

691   UK   ISSN 0077-4480
NATIONAL FEDERATION OF PLASTERING CONTRACTORS. YEAR BOOK. 1958. a. free. Comprint Ltd., Penn House, Penn Ln., Rickmansworth, Herts WD3 1SN, England. Ed. K. Williams. adv. circ. 2,500. **Document type:** trade publication.

692.8   US   ISSN 0192-6772
NATIONAL HOME CENTER NEWS; the newspaper for retailers serving homeowners and contractors. 1975. bi-w. $79 (effective 1997). Lebhar-Friedman, Inc., 425 Park Ave., New York, NY 10022. TEL 212-756-5000. Ed. Donald Longo. adv. circ. 38,000. (also avail. in microfiche from CIS) **Indexed:** SRI. **Document type:** newspaper.
   ●Also available online. Vendor(s): Information Access Co.
—UMI. **CCC.**

690   US
NATIONAL INSTITUTE OF BUILDING SCIENCES. ANNUAL REPORT TO THE PRESIDENT. 1974. a. National Institute of Building Sciences, 1201 L St., N.W., Ste. 400, Washington, DC 20005. TEL 212-289-7800. R&P contact: Nell Sandler. circ. 2,000. **Document type:** corporate report.

690   US
NATIONAL SASH AND DOOR JOBBERS ASSOCIATION. BULLETIN. irreg. National Sash and Door Jobbers Association, 10225 Robert Trent Jones Pkwy, New Port Richey, FL 34655-4649. **Document type:** bulletin.

690   US
NATIONAL SASH AND DOOR JOBBERS ASSOCIATION. NEWSLETTER. m. National Sash and Door Jobbers Association, 10225 Robert Trent Jones Pkwy, New Port Richey, FL 34655-4649. **Document type:** newsletter.

BUILDING AND CONSTRUCTION

691 US
NATIONAL TERRAZZO AND MOSAIC ASSOCIATION. DIRECTORY.* a. National Terrazzo and Mosaic Association, 110 E. Market St., Ste. 200A, Leesburg, VA 20176-3122. TEL 312-635-7744. **Document type:** directory.

690 US ISSN 8750-6580
NATION'S BUILDING NEWS. s-m. National Association of Home Builders, 1201 15th St., N.W., Washington, DC 20005. TEL 202-822-0427. FAX 202-861-2131. Ed. Tim Ahern. circ. 160,000. **Document type:** newspaper.

691.2 UK ISSN 1356-5443
NATURAL STONE SPECIALIST. 1965. m. £35 (overseas £55). Herald House Ltd., 96 Dominion Rd., Worthing, W. Sussex BN14 8JP, England. TEL 01903-821082. FAX 01903-215904. Ed. E. Bignell. adv.; bk.rev.; abstr.; illus.; tr.lit.; circ. 2,500 (paid). **Indexed:** AESIS, Art & Archaeol.Tech.Abstr. **Document type:** trade publication.
—CISTI; Ei.
Formerly: Stone Industries (ISSN 0039-1778)
Description: Covers all aspects of dimensional stone industry from extraction to finished products in construction, memorial masonry, restoration, and sculpture.

690 GW ISSN 0028-1026
NATURSTEIN; Fachzeitschrift fuer Steinmetzen, Steinindustrie, Architekten, Baubehoerden. (Text in German; summaries in English) 1946. m. DM.159.80 (foreign DM.185). (Bundesinnungsverband des Deutschen Steinmetz-Stein- und Holzbildhauerhandwerks) Ebner Verlag GmbH, Postfach 3060, 89020 Ulm, Germany. TEL 49-731-152002. FAX 49-731-152088. Ed. Barbara Hollaender. adv.; bk.rev.; charts; illus.; stat.; index. circ. 6,158. **Document type:** trade publication.
—CCC.
Description: Devoted to stone-masonry. Covers stone and wood sculpture, stone-industry, technology, restoration, architecture, building authorities, and cemeteries. Includes association news, international news, and positions available.

690 NE ISSN 0165-6368
NATUURSTEEN. 1949. m. fl.95 (Europe fl.115). Wijlhuizen Vaktijdschriften, Wilhelminasingel 4, 6524 AK Nijmegen, Netherlands. TEL 31-80-605253. FAX 31-80-605210. Ed. Y. Wijlhuizen. adv. circ. 5,700. **Document type:** trade publication.
Description: Independent trade publication for the natural stone industrie in the Netherlands and Belgium.

690 AA ISSN 1010-4003
T4
NDERTUESI/CONSTRUCTEUR. q. $6.15. Ministria e Ndertimit - Ministere de la Construction, Tirana, Albania. TELEX 4208.

690 AU ISSN 0253-0198
NEUES VOM BAU. 1955. 6/yr. S.120. Hasnerstr. 36-1, A-4020 Linz, Austria. TEL 0732-656062. FAX 0732-666683. Ed. Rudolf Steininger. adv.; B&W page S.17400. circ. 14,200. **Document type:** trade publication.
—BLDSC (6077.948000).

NEW MEXICO CONSTRUCTION LAW. see LAW — Civil Law

690 330 US
NEW PLANT REPORT. 1981. m. $1200. Conway Data, Inc., 35 Technology Pkwy., Ste. 150, Norcross, GA 30092-9990. TEL 770-446-6996. FAX 770-263-8825. TELEX 80-4468ATL. Ed. Tim Venable; Pub. McKinley Conway. adv.; stat. (looseleaf format; also avail. in diskette format; back issues avail.)
Description: Covers current announcements of U.S. and foreign corporate expansion plans, acquisitions, facility construction and facility closings; focus is on manufacturing industries.

690 JA ISSN 0917-0782
NEW SETSUBI SHIZAI JOHO/INFORMATION ON NEW EQUIPMENTS. (Text in Japanese) 1990. m. Nikkan Kogyo Shinbunsha, 8-10, Kudan Kita 1-chome, Chiyoda-ku, Tokyo 102, Japan.

721 692.8 UK ISSN 0968-0098
TA684
NEW STEEL CONSTRUCTION. bi-m. £70 (foreign £90) (effective 1997). (Steel Construction Institute) Kingslea Press Ltd., 137 Newhall St., Birmingham B3 1SF, England. TEL 44-121-236-8112. FAX 44-121-200-1480. (Co-sponsor: British Constructional Steelwork Association Ltd.) Ed. John Rawson. adv.: page £858; trim 254 x 178; adv. contact: Sam Ichbia. bk.rev.; bibl.; illus.; pat.; tr.lit.; index. circ. 10,000. (back issues avail.) **Indexed:** Alloys Ind., Eng.Mat.Abstr., Met.Abstr.Ind., Met.Abstr., Nonfer.Met.Alert, PCC Alert, Steels Alert, World Alum.Abstr. **Document type:** trade publication.
—BLDSC (6088.766200); SWETS.
Formed by the 1993 merger of: Steel Construction Today (ISSN 0950-9216); Steel Construction (ISSN 0950-6039); Which was formerly (1985-1986): B S C A News (ISSN 0950-6020)
Description: Information for the constructional steelwork industry.

NEW YORK APARTMENT LAW INSIDER. see REAL ESTATE

690 340 US
NEW YORK BUILDING LAWS MANUAL.* 1911. irreg., latest 1990, amended 1993. $65. New York Society of Architects, 10 Columbus Circle, Ste. 1030, New York, NY 10019-1202. TEL 212-675-6646. adv. circ. 1,000. (looseleaf format)

NEW YORK CITY BUILDING CODE. see LAW

690 US ISSN 0028-7164
NEW YORK CONSTRUCTION NEWS; serving the entire construction industry in Metropolitan New York, Northern New Jersey, and Southern Connecticut. 1953. w. $39. New York Construction News, Inc. - McGraw-Hill, 1221 Ave. of the Americas, 41st Fl., New York, NY 10020. TEL 212-512-4770. FAX 212-512-2335. Ed. David Chartock. R&P contact: Heather Hatfield. adv.: B&W page $1020; trim 8 1/2 x 10 7/8; adv. contact: Paul Haynes. charts; illus.; mkt. circ. 6,200. (tabloid format) **Document type:** trade publication.

690 NZ ISSN 0549-0219
NEW ZEALAND CONCRETE CONSTRUCTION. 1957. bi-m. NZ.$72. (Cement and Concrete Research Association of New Zealand) A G M Publishing Ltd., Private Bag 99-915, Newmarket, Auckland, New Zealand. TEL 64-9-379-5393. FAX 64-9-308-9523. Ed. Barbara Glenie; Pub. Robin Beckett. R&P contact: Robin Beckett. adv. contact: Stephaniie Watson. bk.rev.; illus.; stat.; tr.lit.; index. circ. 1,300. (back issues avail.) **Indexed:** C.R.I.Abstr., C.R.I.Curr.Cont., Chem.Abstr., Eng.Ind., HRIS, J.of Ferroc. **Document type:** trade publication.
—BLDSC (6089.908000); CISTI. CCC.
Description: Covers research, development and marketing of concrete, concrete products, allied services, and company news and contains profiles on prominent industry personalities.

690 JA ISSN 0286-021X
NIHON KOKUDO KAIHATSU K.K. GIJUTSU KENKYU HOKOKU/JAPAN DEVELOPMENT AND CONSTRUCTION CORP. TECHNICAL REPORT. (Includes irregular special issues) (Text in Japanese) 1981. a. Nihon Kokudo Kaihatsu K.K., Gijutsu Kenkyujo - Japan Development and Construction Corp., Technical Research Institute, 4036-1, Nakatsu, Aikawa-machi, Aikogun, Kanagawa-ken 243-03, Japan. **Document type:** academic/scholarly publication.

690 NE
NIJGH CATALOGUS BOUWWERELD. a. fl.194.50. Nijgh Periodieken B.V., Postbus 122, 3100 AC Schiedam, Netherlands. TEL 31-10-4274100. FAX 31-10-4739911. E-mail: ncb@nijgh.nl. Pub. A.J.A. van der Post. adv.: B&W page fl.1990, color page fl.3780; 175 x 260. circ. 5,000. **Document type:** directory.

NIKKEI HOME DESIGN. see INTERIOR DESIGN AND DECORATION

690 JA ISSN 0285-3450
NISHIMATSU KENSETSU GIHO/NISHIMATSU TECHNICAL RESEARCH REPORT. (Text in Japanese) 1978. a. Nishimatsu Kensetsu K.K., Gijutsu Kenkyujo - Nishimatsu Construction Co., Ltd., Technical Research Institute, 2570-4, Shimotsuruma, Yamato-shi, Kanagawa-ken 242, Japan.

NISSAN KENSETSU. GIJUTSU HONBU. GIJUTSU REPOTO/NISSAN CONSTRUCTION. TECHNICAL DEPARTMENT. TECHNICAL REPORT. see ENGINEERING — Civil Engineering

690 JA
NISSAN KENSETSU. GIJUTSU HONBU. TEKUNIKARU REPOTO/NISSAN CONSTRUCTION. TECHNOLOGICAL REPORT. (Text in Japanese) 1980. q. Nissan Kensetsu K.K., Gijutsu Honbu, 2-6, Minamiaoyama 1-chome, Minato-ku, Tokyo 107, Japan. **Document type:** trade publication.

690 UK ISSN 0960-4405
CODEN: NOINEK
NO - DIG INTERNATIONAL. 1990. m. £42($75) (International Society for Trenchless Technology) Mining Journal Ltd., 60 Worship St., London EC2A 2HD, England. TEL 44-171-216-6060. FAX 44-171-216-6050. Ed. Ian Clarke. adv. contact: Mike Bellenger. circ. 4,552. **Indexed:** HRIS. **Document type:** trade publication.
—Ei.
Description: For the international trenchless construction sector.

NORGES LANDBRUKSHOEGSKOLE. INSTITUTT FOR TEKNISKE FAG. MELDINGER/AGRICULTURAL UNIVERSITY OF NORWAY. DEPARTMENT OF AGRICULTURAL ENGINEERING. REPORTS. see AGRICULTURE

NORGES LANDBRUKSHOEGSKOLE. INSTITUTT FOR TEKNISKE FAG. RAPPORTER/AGRICULTURAL UNIVERSITY OF NORWAY. DEPARTMENT OF AGRICULTURAL ENGINEERING. RESEARCH REPORTS. see AGRICULTURE

690 346 IT
NORMATIVA TECNICA AGGIORNAMENTI. bi-m. Schedario Tecnico Editore S.p.A., Via Cavour 100, 12011 Borgo San Dalmazzo (CN), Italy. TEL 0171-262296. FAX 0171-262357. Ed. Borgogno Giancarlo. adv.: B&W page L.2300000, color page L.3900000; trim 122 x 250. circ. 14,260.

690 US
NORTH AMERICAN BUILDING MATERIAL DISTRIBUTION ASSOCIATION. JOURNAL. m. membership only. North American Building Material Distribution Association, 401 N. Michigan Ave., Ste. 1150, Chicago, IL 60611-4274. TEL 312-321-6845. FAX 312-644-0310. Ed. Colleen Hynes. **Document type:** newsletter.
Formerly: National Building Materials Distributors. Journal.

691.3 US ISSN 1046-7270
TP880.N7
NORTH AMERICAN CEMENT DIRECTORY INCLUDING MEXICO AND THE CARIBBEAN. 1987. a. Intertec Publishing Corp., 29 N. Wacker Dr., Chicago, IL 60606. TEL 312-726-2802. FAX 312-726-2574. **Document type:** directory.
Formerly (until 1989): North American Cement Directory (ISSN 1048-3853)

NORTH CAROLINA BUILDER.* m. A P L, Inc., Box 32500, Louisville, KY 40232-2500. Ed. John Sheley. circ. 10,000.

690 UK
NORTHERN BUILDER. 1989. m. £1.50 per no. Northern Builder Ltd., Lisburn Enterprise Centre, Unit 22, Ballinderry Rd., Lisburn BT28 2SA, N. Ireland. TEL 0846-663390. FAX 0846-666242. Ed. Alan Bailie. adv.: B&W page £600, color page £850; adv. contact: John Hunter. circ. 5,000. (tabloid format) **Document type:** trade publication.

690 GW
NR 1. 1973. a. Aktienbaugesellschaft fuer Kleine Wohnungen, Elbestr. 48, 60329 Frankfurt a.M., Germany. TEL 49-69-2608-0. FAX 49-69-2608333. Eds. Petra Stoelting, Katie Hoeser. circ. 29,000. **Document type:** bulletin.

690 IT
IL NUOVO BAGNO. 1980. s-a. Di Baio Editore s.r.l., Via Settembrini, 11, 20124 Milan, Italy. TEL 02-669254. FAX 02-6709257. Ed. Giuseppe Maria Jonghi Lavarini. adv.: B&W page L.9500000.

BUILDING AND CONSTRUCTION

690　　　　　　　IT　　ISSN 0029-6325
IL NUOVO CANTIERE. 1966. 11/yr. L.110000 (Europe L.165000; elsewhere L.230000) (effective 1997). Tecniche Nuove s.p.a., Via C. Menotti 14, 20129 Milan, Italy. TEL 39-2-75701. FAX 39-2-7610351. E-mail: abbonamenti@tecnet.it; URL: http://www.tecnet.it. Ed. Toni Ligouri. adv.: B&W page L.3290000, color page L.5264000; trim 245 x 340. circ. 17,000. (back issues avail.)
　　Formerly: Cantiere (ISSN 0008-5715)
　　Description: Presents current events, technology trends and market data on the building sector.

O T B WERKDOCUMENTEN. (Onderzoeksinstituut OTB) see *PUBLIC ADMINISTRATION*

OBRAS. see *HOUSING AND URBAN PLANNING*

OEKO-HAUS; bauen, wohnen, renovieren. see *CONSUMER EDUCATION AND PROTECTION*

690　　　　　　　AU　　ISSN 0048-1416
OESTERREICHISCHE BAU-WIRTSCHAFT. 1961. q. S.400. Media Emap Verlag GmbH, Loquaiplatz 12, A-1061 Vienna, Austria. TEL 01-59960-0. FAX 01-5996021. adv. contact: Karl Englert. charts; illus. **Document type:** trade publication.

690　　　　　　　AU
OESTERREICHISCHE BAUCHRONIK; Querschnitt durch das Bauschaffen. q. S.60. Oswald Moebius Verlag, Amerlingstr. 19, A-1060 Vienna, Austria. Ed. Erwin H. Aglas.

690　　　　　　　AU　　ISSN 0029-8891
TH3
OESTERREICHISCHE BAUZEITUNG. 1962. w. S.1508. Oesterreichischer Wirtschaftsverlag, Nikolsdorfergasse 7-11, A-1051 Vienna, Austria. TEL 0222-555585. TELEX 1-11669. Ed. Peter Hauer. adv.; bk.rev.; illus. circ. 12,800. **Indexed:** C.I.S. Abstr.
　—BLDSC (6304.600000).

690　　　　　　　AU　　ISSN 0029-9499
DER OESTERREICHISCHE SPENGLER UND KUPFERSCHMIED; offizielles Fachorgan der Bundesinnung. 1947. m. S.350. Landesinnung Wien der Spengler und Kupferschmiede, Gruengasse 27, A-1050 Vienna, Austria. TEL 43-1-5873769. FAX 43-1-5870539. Ed. Irmtraud Strohmayer. adv.; bk.rev.; abstr.; illus.; stat.; tr.lit.; index. circ. 2,000. **Document type:** trade publication.

690　　　　　　　FR　　ISSN 0294-0752
OFFICE DES PRIX DU BATIMENT - EDITION MACONNERIE PEINTURE. 1975. 4/yr. 468 rue de la Croix-Verte, B.P. 1061, 34007 Montpellier Cedex, France. TEL 67-41-01-52. FAX 67-52-49-27. Ed. Guy Dumons. circ. 19,364.

690　　　　　　　FR　　ISSN 0245-9450
OFFICIEL DU BATIMENT ET DES TRAVAUX PUBLICS DE TOULOUSE ET DE MIDI-PYRENEES. 1964. 2/yr. 50 F. Societe d'Exploitation de l'Officiel du Batiment et des Travaux Publics de Toulouse et de Midi-Pyrenees (SODOFI), 11 bd des Recollets, 31078 Toulouse Cedex, France. TEL 61-53-03-13. adv.; bk.rev. circ. 7,000.

690　　　　　　　FR　　ISSN 1268-1393
L'OFFICIEL HEBDO; le journal des cuisinistes, bainistes et electromenagistes. (Supplements avail.: L'Officiel Magazine (ISSN 1270-1602); L'Officiel Compact) 1953. w. 1113.91 F. (foreign 1480 F.) (effective 1997). Officiel S.A., B.P. 9037, 34041 Montpellier Cedex, France. TEL 33-4-67588228. FAX 33-4-67923886. adv. circ. 4,500. (back issues avail.)
　　Supersedes: Lettre des Cuisinistes, des Bainistes et des Electromenagistes (ISSN 0988-4343) & Officiel des Cuisinistes (ISSN 0399-8290) & Officiel des Bainistes (ISSN 0299-3856) & Officiel des Electromenagistes (ISSN 0994-2785); Which was formerly: Officiel de l'Equipement Menager (ISSN 0183-7516)

690　　　　　　　US
OHIO BUILDER.* 1981. bi-m. (Ohio Home Builders Association) A P L, Inc., Box 32500, Louisville, KY 40232-2500. Ed. Pat Ellen. adv.: B&W page $869, color page $1189; trim 8 1/2 X 11. circ. 4,700.

690 331.8　　　　US　　ISSN 1063-9853
OHIO LABOR CITIZEN. 1988. m. $6.50. (Cleveland Building and Construction Trades Council) Citizen Publishing, 2012 W. 25th St., Ste. 900, Cleveland, OH 44113. TEL 216-861-4283. Ed. William G. Obbagy. adv.: page $612; adv. contact: Henry Speeth. circ. 14,100. (tabloid format; back issues avail.) **Document type:** newspaper.
　　Description: Contains news of interest to union members in the building and construction trades.

690　　　　　　　JA
OKINAWAKEN KENSETSU GIJUTSU SENTA SHIKEN NENPO/OKINAWA CONSTRUCTION TECHNOLOGICAL CENTER. ANNUAL REPORT. (Text in Japanese) a. Okinawaken Kensetsu Gijutsu Senta - Okinawa Construction Technological Center, 7-13, Yorimiya 1-chome, Naha-shi, Okinawa-ken 902, Japan.

729　　　　　　　US　　ISSN 0094-0178
TH3401
OLD-HOUSE JOURNAL. 1973. 6/yr. $27 (Canada $35; elsewhere $41). Dovetale Publishers, 2 Main St., Gloucester, MA 01930-5726. TEL 508-283-3200. FAX 508-283-4629. (Subscr. to: Box 58017, Boulder, CO 80322-8017. TEL 800-234-3797) Ed. Patricia Poore; Pub. William O'Donnell. R&P contact: Nicole Gaspar. adv. contact: Rebecca Bernie. bk.rev.; illus.; index. (back issues avail.) **Indexed:** Art & Archaeol.Tech.Abstr., Br.Tech.Ind., Gard.Lit. (1992-), Ind.How To Do It (1973-). **Document type:** consumer publication.
　—UnCover.
　　Description: How-to and technical data on restoration, plus period house styles, decorating and products for the pre-1939 home.

729 691　　　　　US
TH455
OLD-HOUSE JOURNAL RESTORATION DIRECTORY. 1976. a. $14.95 ($12.95 for subscribers to Old-House Journal). Dovetale Publishers, 2 Main St., Gloucester, MA 01930-5726. TEL 508-281-8803. FAX 508-283-4629. Ed. Patricia Poore; Pub. Patricia Poore. R&P contact: Nicole Gaspar. adv. contact: Rebecca Bernie. illus. circ. 20,000. **Document type:** directory.
　—CISTI.
　　Former titles: Old-House Journal Directory; Old-House Journal Catalog (ISSN 0271-7220); Old-House Journal Buyers' Guide.
　　Description: Extensively indexed listing of over 1,500 companies that provide restoration and renovation products and special services.

691　　　　　　　CN
ON THE LEVEL. a. Canadian Masonry Contractors' Association, 360 Superior Blvd., Mississauga, Ont. L5T 2N7, Canada. TEL 416-564-6622. FAX 416-564-5744.

690　　　　　　　NE
ONDERNEMINGSANALYSES BOUW. a. fl.89.50. Delwel Uitgeverij B.V., Postbus 19110, 2500 CC The Hague, Netherlands. TEL 31-70-3624800. FAX 31-70-3605606. Ed. H. Stevens.
　　Formerly (until 1992): Fact and Figures Bouw (Year) (ISSN 0927-1260)
　　Description: Financial and economic information on the construction industry in the Netherlands.

OPUS DESIGN FILE. see *BUSINESS AND ECONOMICS — Trade And Industrial Directories*

ORANGE COUNTY APARTMENT NEWS. see *REAL ESTATE*

690 720　　　　IT
ORDINE DEGLI INGEGNERI DELLA PROVINCIA DI PALERMO. BOLLETTINO. 6/yr. Ordine degli Ingegneri della Provincia di Palermo, Via Franceso Gristi 120, 90139 Milan, Italy. TEL 91-58-14-21. Ed. Roberta Messina. **Document type:** bulletin.

690　　　　　　　SZ
ORGANE DU SYNDICAT DU BATIMENT ET DU BOIS. (Text in French) 6/yr. 28 Avenue de Sevelin, CH-1000 Lausanne 20, Switzerland. TEL 021-6262627. FAX 021-6262628. Ed. Serge Baehler. circ. 26,000.

690　　　　　　　AT　　ISSN 0728-7275
OWNER BUILDER MAGAZINE. 1981. bi-m. Aus.$24 (New Zealand and Papua New Guinea Aus.$33). Russell Andrews & Association Pty. Ltd., 66 Broadway, Dunolly, Vic. 3472, Australia. TEL 61-3-546899. FAX 61-3-54681899. Eds. Valerie and Russell Andrews. adv.; bk.rev. circ. 15,100. (back issues avail.) **Indexed:** Pinpointer. **Document type:** consumer publication.
　　Description: "How to" build your own home or extensions; includes encouragement and inspirational stories of owner-builders in Australia.

P A S C A L. T 295: BATIMENT. TRAVAUX PUBLICS. see *ENGINEERING — Abstracting, Bibliographies, Statistics*

691.3　　　　　　US　　ISSN 0887-9672
TA680　　　　　　　　　CODEN: PCIJEE
P C I JOURNAL. 1956. bi-m. $35 (foreign $49). Precast - Prestressed Concrete Institute, 175 W. Jackson Blvd., Chicago, IL 60604. TEL 312-786-0300. FAX 312-786-0353. URL: http://www.pci.org. Eds. G.D. Nasser, Joe Hoyle. adv. contact: Joe hoyle. bk.rev.; abstr.; charts; illus.; tr.lit.; index, cum.index. 1956-1981; circ. 6,400 (paid). (also avail. in microfilm from UMI; back issues avail.) **Indexed:** ASCA, C.R.I.Abstr., C.R.I.Curr.Cont., Concr.Abstr., Curr.Cont., Eng.Ind., Geotech.Abstr., Intl.Civil Eng.Abstr., J.of Ferroc., Mat.Sci.Cit.Ind., Soft.Abstr.Eng. **Document type:** trade publication, academic/scholarly publication.
　—BLDSC (6413.612000); CISTI; Ei; Genuine Article; Linda Hall; SWETS; UMI; UnCover.
　　Formerly (until 1982): Prestressed Concrete Institute Journal (ISSN 0032-793X)
　　Description: Reports on current research, design, construction and innovations in the use of precast and prestressed concrete.

P E B EXCHANGE. (Programme on Educational Building) see *EDUCATION — School Organization And Administration*

690　　　　　　　SA　　ISSN 1023-2451
P W V HOME OWNER BUILDING & IMPROVEMENTS BUYERS GUIDE. (Pretoria - Witwatersrand - Vaal) (Text in English) 1994. a. R.72.50 (effective 1997). Avonwold Publishing Co. (Pty) Ltd., Avonwold House, 24 Baker St., Rosebank, Johannesburg 2196, South Africa. TEL 27-11-7881610. FAX 27-11-8802732. (Subscr. to: P.O. Box 52068, Saxonwold 2132, South Africa) adv.; illus. **Document type:** consumer publication.

690 620　　　　US　　ISSN 0030-8544
PACIFIC BUILDER AND ENGINEER. 1902. s-m. $29.75. Vernon Publications Inc., 3000 Northup Way, Ste. 200, Bellevue, WA 98004. TEL 206-827-9900. FAX 206-822-9372. Ed. Carl Molesworth. adv.; bk.rev.; illus.; mkt.; tr.lit.; index, cum.index. circ. 12,505. (also avail. in microform from UMI; reprint service avail.) **Document type:** trade publication.

PAINTING AND WALLCOVERING CONTRACTOR. see *PAINTS AND PROTECTIVE COATINGS*

690　　　　　　　UK　　ISSN 1361-1666
PANEL INDUSTRY MONITOR. 1988. 10/yr. £190 (Europe $225; elsewhere $340) (effective 1997). Data Transcripts, P.O. Box 14, Dorking, Surrey RG5 4YN, England. TEL 44-1306-884473. Ed. Ward Williams. (back issues avail.) **Document type:** newsletter.

690 790.1　　　UK　　ISSN 0969-482X
PANSTADIA INTERNATIONAL QUARTERLY REPORT; the definitive journal for the sports facility industry worldwide. 1993. q. £80 (effective 1997). Sports Development International Ltd., Stadium House, 12 Bonnersfield Ln., Harrow, Mddx. HA1 2JR, England. TEL 44-181-424-8554. FAX 44-181-424-0918. E-mail: piqr@globalnet.co.uk; URL: http://www.piqr.com. (Alt. addr.: Greater London House, 1 Hampstead Rd., London NW1 7QQ, England) Ed. Peter Fitzpatrick; Pub. Julian A. Reader. R&P contact: Matthew Brown. adv.: color page £4495($6742); adv. contact: Kevin Dukes. bk.rev. circ. 25,000. **Document type:** trade publication.
　—BLDSC (6357.476500).
　　Description: Publishes a mix of articles on the sports facility market, including new products, services and innovations, case studies of new staia-arenas or rebuild, and educational articles on all aspects of the planning, building, fitting-out, and management of stadia and arenas.

BUILDING AND CONSTRUCTION

690 FR ISSN 1153-026X
PARIS LE JOURNAL. 1977. m. 100 F. (foreign 150 F.). Association pour l'Information Municipale, Hotel de Ville, 75196 Paris R.P., France. TEL 33-1-42-77-11-20. (Subscr. to: Alter-Data - Paris le Journal, 49 rue de la Vanne, 92126 Montrouge Cedex, France. TEL 33-1-41-17-13-93) Ed. Patrice de Clinchamps. adv.; bk.rev. circ. 300,000.
 Formerly: Ville de Paris (ISSN 0220-8156)

PEOPLE & PROFITS; Bill Lee's tips, tactics and how-to's for the building supply, hardware and home center industry. see BUSINESS AND ECONOMICS — Marketing And Purchasing

690 US
PERMANENT BUILDINGS AND FOUNDATION CONTRACTOR. 1986. bi-m. $24 (effective 1995). R.W. Nielsen Co., 5245 N. Kensington, Box 11067, Kansas City, MO 64119. TEL 816-453-0590. FAX 816-453-0591. Ed. Roger W. Nielsen. adv. contact: David Nielsen. bk.rev. circ. 35,000.
 Formerly: Foundations.
 Description: Edited for residential, light commercial, and industrial contractors who use cast-in-place, pre-cast, or tilt-up concrete construction for footing, foundation, or total building construction. Case histories present management and construction methods.

PERSPECTIVE. see ARCHITECTURE

PERSPECTIVE (INDIANAPOLIS). see REAL ESTATE

PHILIPPINE ARCHITECTURE, ENGINEERING & CONSTRUCTION RECORD. see ARCHITECTURE

690 SP ISSN 0210-6868
PISCINAS XXI; revista de la construccion, mantenimiento, equipo y accesorios de la piscina. 1976. 8/yr. 13750 ptas.($125) (effective 1996). Elsevier Prensa S.A., Avda Paral.lel 180, Apdo. No. 350 F.D., 08015 Barcelona, Spain. TEL 34-3-3255350. FAX 34-3-4252880. Ed. Marcel Lleal; Pub. Manuel Masip. adv. contact: Manuel Fernandez de Liencres. circ. 6,000. **Document type:** trade publication.
 Description: Covers building, maintenance and equipment for swimming pools, spas and saunas.

690 FR ISSN 0295-5725
PISCINES - SPAS MAGAZINE; spas, equipment and maintenance of swimming pools and spas. 1967. 5/yr. 340 F.($32) Editions Christian Ledoux, S.A., 155 av. de Paris, 94807 Villejuif, France. TEL 46-77-70-70. FAX 46-77-32-55. TELEX 260 808 F TXFRA. (Subscr. to: Praxs s.a., 68 rue des Bruyeres, 93260 Les Lilas, France) Ed. Charlotte le Baron. adv.; charts; illus.; stat.; tr.lit. circ. 40,000.
 Formerly: Piscines (ISSN 0032-0285)
 Description: Review specializing in construction and equipping.

690 747 UK ISSN 0961-7442
PLANAHOME GUIDE. s-a. £1.95 per no. Custom Publishing Company Ltd. (Subsidiary of: Glendower Holdings Ltd.), 45 Station Rd., Redhill, Surrey RH1 1QH, England. TEL 44-1737-767213. FAX 44-1737-771662. Ed. David Hoppit. adv.: B&W page £1320; color page £1650; adv. contact: John Bailey. circ. 75,000 (paid). **Document type:** consumer publication.
 Former titles: Planahome Home Improvement Guide & Planahome Book of Home Plans.

PLANNING. see ARCHITECTURE

PLANNING AND DEVELOPMENT SERVICE (NEW SOUTH WALES). see LAW

PLANNING AND DEVELOPMENT VICTORIA. see LAW

PLANT MANAGERS JOURNAL. see BUSINESS AND ECONOMICS — Management

690 UK
PLANT WORLD. 1981. bi-w. £75. Sheen Publishing Ltd., 50 Queens Rd., Buckhurst Hill, Essex IG9 5DD, England. TEL 44-181-504-1661. FAX 44-181-505-4336. TELEX 296620-SHEEN-G. Ed. Carole Titmuss; Pub. Carole Titmuss. adv. contact: Sandie Hardworker. circ. 12,000. **Document type:** trade publication.
 Formerly: World Plant.

690 IE
PLANTMAN MAGAZINE. 1970. 12/yr. I£25 (effective 1997). 1 The Green, Kingswood Heights, Dublin 22, Ireland. TEL 353-1-4520898. FAX 353-1-4520898. Ed. Patrick Murphy. R&P contact: Patrick Murphy. circ. 4,700. **Document type:** trade publication.

PLASTERER AND CEMENT MASON. see LABOR UNIONS

690 668.4 US ISSN 0147-2429
PLASTICS IN BUILDING CONSTRUCTION. 1974. m. $225 (foreign $255) (effective 1997); $240 (foreign $270) (effective 1998). Technomic Publishing Co., Inc., 851 New Holland Ave., Box 3535, Lancaster, PA 17604. TEL 717-291-5609. FAX 717-295-45388. TELEX 230 753565 (TECHNOMIC UD). E-mail: marketing@techpub.com; URL: http://www.techpub.com. Ed. Joseph Eckenrode. bk.rev.; stat. circ. 130. (back issues avail.) **Indexed:** Alloys Ind., Eng.Ind., Eng.Mat.Abstr., Intl.Polym.Sci.& Tech., Met.Abstr., Met.Abstr.Ind., Nonfer.Met.Alert, PCC Alert, RAPRA, Steels Alert, World Alum.Abstr. **Document type:** academic/scholarly publication.
 —BLDSC (6531.910000); CISTI; Linda Hall; SWETS; UMI. **CCC.**
 Refereed Serial

690 PL ISSN 0860-7214
POLITECHNIKA CZESTOCHOWSKA. ZESZYTY NAUKOWE. BUDOWNICTWO. (Text in Polish; summaries in English and Russian) 1969; N.S. 1989. irreg. price varies. Politechnika Czestochowska, Ul. Deglera 31, 42-200 Czestochowa, Poland. TEL 50-954. (Dist. by: Ars Polona-Ruch, Krakowskie Przedmiescie 7, Warsaw, Poland) Ed. Stanislaw Lewowicki.
 Description: Covers general building and constructions, building on mining ares, building economics and organization, environmental engineering etc.

POLITECHNIKA GDANSKA. ZESZYTY NAUKOWE. BUDOWNICTWO LADOWE. see ENGINEERING — Civil Engineering

POLITECHNIKA LODZKA. ZESZYTY NAUKOWE. BUDOWNICTWO. see ENGINEERING — Civil Engineering

690 624 PL ISSN 0137-2297
POLITECHNIKA WARSZAWSKA. PRACE NAUKOWE. BUDOWNICTWO. 1953. irreg., no.130, 1996. Politechnika Warszawska, c/o Biblioteka Glowna, Pl. Politechniki 1, 00-661 Warsaw, Poland. E-mail: bgpw@bg.pw.edu.pl. **Document type:** academic/scholarly publication.
 —BLDSC (6590.781000); Linda Hall.
 Formerly (until 1968): Politechnika Warszawska. Zeszyty Naukowe. Budownictwo (ISSN 0509-7002)

690 PL ISSN 0324-9883
POLITECHNIKA WROCLAWSKA. INSTYTUT BUDOWNICTWA. PRACE NAUKOWE. KONFERENCJE. (Text in Polish and English; summaries in Russian) 1974. irreg., no.21, 1994. price varies. Oficyna Wydawnicza Politechniki Wroclawskiej, Wybrzeze Wyspianskiego 27, 50-370 Wroclaw, Poland. TEL 48-71-222940. FAX 48-71-223664. TELEX 172559 PWRPL. (Dist. by: Ars Polona, Krakowskie Przedmiescie 7, Warsaw, Poland) R&P contact: Halina Dudek. circ. 475. **Document type:** proceedings.
 —CISTI; Ei.

690 PL ISSN 0324-9875
TH4 CODEN: PIBWEQ
POLITECHNIKA WROCLAWSKA. INSTYTUT BUDOWNICTWA. PRACE NAUKOWE. MONOGRAFIE. (Text in Polish; summaries in English and Russian) 1985. irreg., no.30, 1996. price varies. Oficyna Wydawnicza Politechniki Wroclawskiej, Wybrzeze Wyspianskiego 27, 50-370 Wroclaw, Poland. TEL 48-71-222940. FAX 48-71-223664. TELEX 712559 PWRPL. (Dist. by: Ars Polona, Krakowskie Przedmiescie 7, Warsaw, Poland) R&P contact: Halina Dudek. **Indexed:** Chem.Abstr. **Document type:** monographic series.
 —BLDSC (6589.500000); CASDDS; CISTI; Linda Hall.

690 PL ISSN 0137-6241
POLITECHNIKA WROCLAWSKA. INSTYTUT BUDOWNICTWA. PRACE NAUKOWE. STUDIA I MATERIALY. (Text in Polish; summaries in English and Russian) 1971. irreg., no.16, 1991. price varies. Oficyna Wydawnicza Politechniki Wroclawskiej, Wybrzeze Wyspianskiego 27, 50-370 Wroclaw, Poland. TEL 48-27-222940. FAX 48-71-223664. TELEX 712254 PWRPL. (Dist. by: Ars Polona, Krakowskie Przedmiescie 7, Warsaw, Poland) Ed. Maria Lyko. R&P contact: Haline Dudek. **Document type:** academic/scholarly publication.

POLITECHNIKA WROCLAWSKA. INSTYTUT INZYNIERII CHEMICZNEJ I URZADZEN CIEPLNYCH. PRACE NAUKOWE. STUDIA I MATERIALY. see ENGINEERING — Chemical Engineering

690 IT ISSN 1120-2637
PORTE E CANCELLI. 9/yr. Edizioni di Protezione Civile s.r.l., Via Acqua Traversa 187, 00135 Rome, Italy. TEL 39-6-3313000. FAX 39-6-3313212. Ed. Daniela Matteucci; Pub. Pier Roberto Pais. adv. contact: Roberto Barberini. circ. 9,000. **Document type:** trade publication.

690 SP ISSN 0032-5600
POTENCIA; revista mensual para tecnicos y usuarios de maquinaria de construccion y obras publicas. 1964. m. 14950 ptas. in Europe; elsewhere 29900 ptas. (effective 1997). Miller Freeman, S.A., Maria Auxiliadora 5, 28040 Madrid, Spain. TEL 450-88-37. FAX 450-94-29. Ed. Jesus Elorz Muruzabal. adv.; bibl.; illus.; tr.lit. circ. 12,000. (cards) **Indexed:** Ind.SST. **Document type:** trade publication.
 —CCC.

PRACTICAL HOMEOWNER'S DO-IT-YOURSELF ANNUAL. see HOME ECONOMICS

690 CN ISSN 0226-9597
PRACTICAL HOMES. 1955. a., latest vol.30, 1996. (effective 1996); newsstand price: Can. $3.50. Giroux Publishing, 102 Ellis St., Penticton, BC V2A 4L5, Canada. TEL 604-493-0942. FAX 604-493-7526. E-mail: eqiroux@vip.net. Ed. Michael A. Giroux. adv.: page Can.$1858; trim 8 1/8 x 10 1/2; adv. contact: Michael Giroux. charts. circ. 10,000. (back issues avail.) **Document type:** consumer publication, catalog.
 Description: Features floor plans and architectural designs for houses by top Canadian designers.

747 UK ISSN 0079-4813
PRACTICAL HOUSEHOLDER. (Supplement avail.: Home Plus (ISSN 0266-3910)) 1955. m. $23.40 (rest of Europe £32.20; elsewhere £47.20) (effective 1996). Nexus Media Ltd., Boundary House, Hemel Hempstead, Herts HB2 7ST, England. TEL 44-1442-66551. FAX 44-1442-66998. Ed. John McGowan. R&P contact: Tony de Bell. adv.: B&W page £1095; adv. contact: Colin Back. circ. 76,778. **Indexed:** Pinpointer.
 Incorporates: New Homemaker (ISSN 0144-1620); Practical Home-Building and Decorating (ISSN 0032-6402)

690 IT
PRECAST. 5/yr. L.40000. BE-MA Editrice s.r.l., Via Teocrito 50, 20128 Milan, Italy. TEL 2-25-52-451. FAX 2-270-00-692. Ed. Dal Lago. adv.: B&W page L.2800000, color page L.3700000; trim 195 x 280. circ. 3,000. **Document type:** trade publication.
 Formerly: Produrre: La Qualita dei Manufatti in Calcestuzzo (ISSN 0390-6124)

693.97 IT ISSN 0032-7247
PREFABBRICARE. (Text in Italian; summaries in English) 1958. bi-m. L.32000. Associazione Italiana Prefabbricazione per l'Edilizia Industrializzata, Galleria Passarella 2, 20122 Milan, Italy. adv.; bk.rev.; charts; illus.; index. circ. 7,000.

PREVISIONS GLISSANTES DETAILLEES EN PERSPECTIVES SECTORIELLES (VOL.5): CONSTRUCTION DE MACHINES. see BUSINESS AND ECONOMICS — Economic Situation And Conditions

PREVISIONS GLISSANTES DETAILLEES EN PERSPECTIVES SECTORIELLES (VOL.28): BATIMENTS D'ACTIVITE. see BUSINESS AND ECONOMICS — Economic Situation And Conditions

PREVISIONS GLISSANTES DETAILLEES EN PERSPECTIVES SECTORIELLES (VOL.30): MATERIAUX DE CONSTRUCTION I. see *BUSINESS AND ECONOMICS — Economic Situation And Conditions*

PREVISIONS GLISSANTES DETAILLEES EN PERSPECTIVES SECTORIELLES (VOL.31): MATERIAUX ET COMPOSANTS DE CONSTRUCTION II. see *BUSINESS AND ECONOMICS — Economic Situation And Conditions*

690   IT
PREZZI INFORMATIVI PER OPERE EDILI DI MANUTENZIONE. 1985. 4/yr. L.180000. Maggioli Editore, Casella Postale 290, 47037 Rimini, Italy. TEL 0541-626777. FAX 0541-622020. (Co-publisher: Passoni Editore) Ed. Roberto Passoni. circ. 6,000.

690   GW   ISSN 0085-5154
PRIVATES BAUSPARWESEN. 1950. a. DM.30. Domus-Verlag GmbH, Servatiusstr. 8, 53129 Bonn, Germany. TEL 49-228-230041. FAX 49-228-230044. Ed. Andreas Zehnder.
 Document type: trade publication.

690   PL   ISSN 0555-2966
PROBLEMY ROZWOJU BUDOWNICTWA/PROBLEMS OF BUILDING GROWTH. (Text in Polish; contents page in English, French, German, Russian) 1963. bi-m. 15 Zl. (effective 1997); 18 Zl. (effective 1998). Instytut Gospodarki Mieszkaniowej, Ul. Filtrowa 1, 00-925 Warsaw 58, Poland. FAX 48-22-250683. Ed. Henryk Hajduk. bk.rev. circ. 2,000. (also avail. in microfiche) **Document type:** bulletin.
 Formerly (until 1969): Problemy Inwestowania i Rozwoju (ISSN 0032-9517)
 Refereed Serial

690   US   ISSN 1072-0561
TH1
PROFESSIONAL BUILDER. 1936. m. (14/yr.). $89.90 (Canada $159.90; Mexico $149.90; elsewhere $199.90). Cahners Publishing Company (Des Plaines), Division of Reed Elsevier Inc., 1350 E. Touhy Ave., Box 5080, Des Plaines, IL 60018-5080. TEL 847-390-2155. FAX 847-635-9950. URL: http://www.probuilder.com. (Subscr. to: 8773 S. Ridgeline Blvd., Highlands Ranch, CO 80126-2329. TEL 303-470-4445) Ed. Jim Carper; Pub. Jay McKenzie. R&P contact: Jim Carper. adv. contact: Marti Halik. bk.rev.; charts; illus.; mkt.; tr.lit. circ. 124,200. (also avail. in microfiche from CIS) **Indexed:** B.P.I., Bus.Ind., Energy Info.Abstr., Search (1991-), SRI, Tr.& Indus.Ind. **Document type:** trade publication.
 ●Also available online. Vendor(s): Information Access Co.
 —BLDSC (6857.300000); CIS; CISTI; KR SourceOne; UMI; UnCover. **CCC.**
 Former titles (until Aug. 1993): Professional Builder and Remodeler (ISSN 1053-6353); (until 1990): Professional Builder (ISSN 0885-8020); (until 1985): Professional Builder and Apartment Business (ISSN 0361-5316); (until 1972): Professional Builder (ISSN 0033-0043); (until 1967): Practical Builder.
 Description: Covers the residential and light commercial construction and remodeling industries, featuring legislation, news, market data, merchandising, technology, design, land development, financing and new products.

690   US
PROFESSIONAL BUILDER'S HOME PLAN DATABASE C D - R O M. a. Cahners Publishing Company (Des Plaines), Division of Reed Elsevier Inc., 1350 E. Touhy Ave., Box 5080, Des Plaines, IL 60017-5080. TEL 847-390-2101. FAX 847-635-9950. URL: http://www.cahners.com/mainmag/cd__rom/prbldcd.htm. Ed. Judy Brociek; Pub. Jay McKenzie.
 ●Available only on CD-ROM.
 Description: An extensive source to help new-home builders, architects, designers and consumers find and select the new-house plans that best fit their needs.

690   US
PROFESSIONAL REMODELER. 6/yr. Cahners Publishing Company (Des Plaines), Division of Reed Elsevier Inc., 1350 E. Touhy Ave., Box 5080, Des Plaines, IL 60017-5080. TEL 847-390-2170. FAX 847-299-9070. URL: http://www.cahners.com/mainmag/pr.htm. Ed. Rod Sutton; Pub. Dean Horowitz. circ. 50,000.
 Description: Source of industry information for remodelers, buyers and specifiers in top metro markets.

695   US   ISSN 0896-5552
TH2430
PROFESSIONAL ROOFING. m. $30 in U.S. and Canada (elsewhere $70). National Roofing Contractors Association, 10255 W. Higgins Rd., Ste. 600, Rosemont, IL 60018. TEL 847-299-9070. FAX 847-299-1183. Ed. Mari Paulson. adv. contact: Mary Carravallah. circ. 20,000. (back issues avail.) **Document type:** trade publication.
 —BLDSC (6864.214000); CISTI
 Formerly (until 1988): Roofing Spec (ISSN 0199-7742)
 Description: Examines commercial, industrial and residential roofing issues through features, columns, and technical articles.

690   SA
PROFESSIONS AND PROJECTS REGISTER. (Text in English) 1988. a. R.200 (effective 1997). Avonwold Publishing Co. (Pty) Ltd., Avonwold House, 24 Baker St., Rosebank, Johannesburg 2196, South Africa. TEL 27-11-788-1610. FAX 27-11-880-2732. (Subscr. to: P.O. Box 52068, Saxonwold 2132, South Africa) Ed E.T. Braby. circ. 6,250. **Document type:** trade publication.
 Description: Details for architects, quantity purveyors, engineers and land surveyors in the housing construction and engineering industries, including all major projects in Southern Africa.

690   IT
PROGETTARE & COSTRUIRE. 1981. a. L.55000. Antonio Ghiorzo Ed. & Pub., Via Casella 16, 20156 Milan, Italy. adv. circ. 8,000.

PROJECT PLANNING AND CONTROL FOR CONSTRUCTION. see *HOUSING AND URBAN PLANNING*

690   UK
PROJECT SCOTLAND. 1970. 24/yr. £50.30 (foreign £56.30) (effective 1996 & 1997). Peebles Publishing Group Ltd., Bergius House, Clifton St., Glasgow G3 7LA, Scotland. TEL 44-141-331-1022. FAX 44-141-331-1395. Ed. Mike Travers. adv.; bk.rev.; charts; illus.; stat. circ. 9,000. **Document type:** trade publication.
 Incorporates: Cope in Scotland.

690   MX
PROMACASA. 1971. m. Av. Cuauhtemoc, No. 1486-401-C, Mexico, D.F., Mexico. Ed. Rafael Cordova. adv. circ. 8,000.

PROMOZIONE SICUREZZA. see *LABOR UNIONS*

690   RU   ISSN 0033-118X
TH4   CODEN: PMSTAO
PROMYSHLENNOE STROITEL'STVO. (Contents page in English and German) 1923. m. 27 Rub. Gosstroi, Tretyakovskii pr. 1, komn. 2, Moscow K-12, Russia. Ed. P.I. Karalov. adv.; charts; illus.; stat.; index. circ. 12,000. **Indexed:** Chem.Abstr., Geotech.Abstr.
 —CASDDS; CISTI.

690   VE
PRONTUARIO TECNICO DE LA CONSTRUCCION. 1975. a. Prontuario Tecnico Comercial, Av. Miquel Angel, Prolonga-Lion el Casquillito, Resd. Hilton, P.O. Box, Ofc. No. 1 Colinas de Bella Monte, Caracas 105, Venezeula. adv.

PROPERTIES. see *REAL ESTATE*

691   US   ISSN 1055-3444
PROSALES. 1989. 9/yr. $36. Hanley-Wood Inc., One Thomas Circle, Ste. 600, Washington, DC 20005. TEL 202-452-0800. Ed. Boyce Thompson. circ. 38,000. **Document type:** trade publication.
 Description: Helps building product dealers, distributors, and wholesalers better understand the needs of their professional customers, home builders and remodeling contractors.

PROSPECT (EDINBURGH). see *ARCHITECTURE*

690   CN
PROVEN AND POPULAR HOME PLANS. 1994. a. Can.$5.95. Giroux Publishing, 102 Ellis St., Penticton, BC V2A 4L5, Canada. TEL 604-493-0942. FAX 604-493-7526. E-mail: cqiroux@vip.net. Ed. Michael A. Giroux; Pub. G.T. Giroux. adv. contact: Dennis Thatchuk. circ. 10,000. **Document type:** consumer publication, catalog.
 Description: Features designs from Canada's top home designers and editorial features on the latest housing innovations.

690   PL   ISSN 0033-2038
PRZEGLAD BUDOWLANY/BUILDING REVIEW. (Text in Polish; summaries in English, Polish and Russian) 1929. m. $36. (Polski Zwiazek Inzynierow i Technikow Budownictwa - Polish Association of Building Engineers and Technicians) Warszawskie Centrum Postepu Techniczno-Organizacyjnego Budownictwa, Ul. Swietokrzyska 14A, 00-950 Warsaw, Poland. (Dist. by: Zaklad Kolportazu SIGMA-NOT, Ul. Bartycka 20, P.O. Box 1004, 0-950 Warsaw, Poland) Ed. Jerzy Widera. adv.; bk.rev.; abstr.; bibl.; charts; illus.; index. circ. 5,000. (microform) **Indexed:** C.I.S. Abstr., Geotech.Abstr., Pol.Tech.Abstr.

PUBLIC WORKS RESEARCH INSTITUTE. JOURNAL OF RESEARCH. see *ENGINEERING — Civil Engineering*

690   CN   ISSN 0829-6359
PUBLIQUIP. 1983. m. Can.$29.95($50) Publiquip Inc., 10595 Louis Hlafomeline, Anjou, Que. H1J 2E8, Canada. TEL 514-351-1110. Ed. Gilles Chevigny; Pub. Gilles Chevigny. adv. contact: Michel Levasseur. circ. 31,000. (back issues avail.) **Document type:** trade publication.
 Formerly: Publiquip - Roucam.

674 690   DK   ISSN 0106-2018
PUFF; fagtidsskrift for traelast- og byggemarkeder. 1977. 11/yr. DKK 410. Odsgard Reklame - Marketing ApS, Hovedvejen 182, DK-2600 Glostrup, Denmark. TEL 45-43-45-34-91. FAX 45-43-43-13-28. Ed. Peter Odsgaard. adv.: B&W page DKK 7415, color page DKK 11995; trim 185 x 262. circ. 2,300. **Document type:** trade publication.
 Refereed Serial

690 624   JA   ISSN 0387-1983
PURESUTORESUTO KONKURITO/JOURNAL OF PRESTRESSED CONCRETE. (Text in Japanese) 1959. bi-m. Puresutoresuto Konkurito Gijyutsu Kyokai - Japan Prestressed Concrete Engineering Association, 4-6, Tsukudo-cho, Shinjuku-ku, Tokyo 162, Japan.
 —BLDSC (5042.225000).

690.2   US   ISSN 0098-9207
TH4816
QUALIFIED REMODELER. 1975. 12/yr. $36. Qualified Remodeler, Inc., 20 E. Jackson Blvd., 7th Fl., Chicago, IL 60604-2206. Ed. Kenneth W. Betz. adv.; illus. circ. 90,135.
 Incorporates (1985-1991): Kitchen and Bath Concepts (ISSN 8750-9504)

690   IT
QUARRY AND CONSTRUCTION.* 1962. m. L.80000. Edizioni P E I s.r.l., Strada Naviglio Alto 46, 43100 Parma, Italy. TEL 39-52-1771818. FAX 39-52-17735729. Ed. Carlo Cagozzi. adv.; illus. circ. 10,000. **Document type:** trade publication.
 Formerly: Frantoio.
 Description: Information on the Italian construction industry.

690   CN   ISSN 0709-0692
QUART DE ROND. (Text in French) 1959. 8/yr. Can.$36. Building Materials Retailer Association of Quebec, 474 Place Trans Canada, Longueuil, PQ J4G 1N8, Canada. TEL 514-646-5842. FAX 514-646-6171. E-mail: admacq@accent.net; URL: http://www.quart-de-rond.qc.ca. Ed. Gabriel Pollender. adv.: B&W page Can.$1970, color page Can.$2820; trim 8 1/8 x 10 7/8; adv. contact: Claude Dagenais. circ. 5,200. **Document type:** trade publication.
 —CISTI.

BUILDING AND CONSTRUCTION

690   **CN**
QUEBEC HABITATION. (Text in French) 1987. 6/yr. Can.$17.33. Association Provinciale des Constructeurs d'Habitations du Quebec, 5930 Blvd. Louis-H-Lafontaine, Anjou, PQ H1M 1S7, Canada. TEL 514-353-9960. FAX 514-353-4825. adv.: B&W page Can.$1445; adv. contact: Pierre Moreau. circ. 15,000.

R E D I REALTY REPORT. (Real Estate Data Inc.) see *REAL ESTATE*

693.83   **US**   **ISSN 0033-7129**
R S I. (Roofing, Siding, Insulation) 1945. m. $36 (effective 1996). Advanstar Communications, Inc., 7500 Old Oak Blvd., Cleveland, OH 44130. TEL 216-826-2839. FAX 216-891-2726. (Subscr. to: 131 W. First St., Duluth, MN 55802. TEL 800-346-0085) Ed. Michael Russo. adv.; charts; illus.; tr.lit. circ. 19,933. (also avail. in microform from UMI) **Indexed:** Alloys Ind., Cadscan, Eng.Mat.Abstr., Lead Abstr., Met.Abstr., Met.Abstr.Ind., Nonfer.Met.Alert, PCC Alert, PROMT, Steels Alert, World Alum.Abstr., Zincscan. **Document type:** trade publication.
—CISTI; UMI; UnCover. **CCC.**
Incorporates: Solar Contractor.
Description: Focuses on sales promotion, industry news, trends and new products.

624   **FI**   **ISSN 0033-9121**
RAKENNUSLEHTI. 1966. 39/yr. FIM 350 (foreign FIM 810) (effective 1997). Suomen Rakennuslehti Oy, Mannerheimintie 40, FIN-00100 Helsinki, Finland. TEL 358-9-584-44-00. FAX 358-9-584-44-600. Ed. Veikko Savolainen. adv.; bk.rev. circ. 30,323.
Incorporates: Rakennustuotanto (ISSN 0355-5526)

690 721   **FI**   **ISSN 0048-6663**
RAKENNUSTAITO. 1905. s-m. (10/yr.) FIM 320. Rakennustietosaatio Rakennusmestarien Keskusliitto, P.O. Box 1004, FIN-00101 Helsinki, Finland. TEL 358-9-549-5570. FAX 358-0-694-3252. Ed. Sirkka Saarinen. adv.; B&W page FIM 9888, color page FIM 16400; trim 210 x 297. bk.rev.; illus.; index. circ. 12,000.

690   **FI**   **ISSN 0355-8614**
RAKENTAJA; the paper of the construction workers. 1924. w. FIM 150. Rakennusliitto - Construction Union of Finland, Siltasaarenk 4, PL 307 00531 Helsinki, Finland. TEL 90-77021. FAX 7702239. Ed. Markku Salomaa. adv.; bk.rev. circ. 93,000. (also avail. in microfiche) **Document type:** trade publication.

690   **GW**   **ISSN 0173-9220**
RATIONELL REINIGEN. m. DM.108. (Bundesinnungsverband des Gebaeudereiniger-Handwerks) Lobrecht Verlag Max Rauscher GmbH & Co. KG, Postfach 1454, 86817 Bad Woerishofen, Germany. FAX 08247-5894. Ed. Heinz-Peter Senftleben; Pub. Max Rauchser. adv. contact: Petra Kollmannsberger. bk.rev. circ. 17,500.
—SWETS.
Formerly: Gebaeudigereiniger-Handwerk (ISSN 0016-5727)

690   **AT**   **ISSN 0810-8064**
RAWLINSONS AUSTRALIAN CONSTRUCTION HANDBOOK (YEAR). 1983. a. Aus.$190 (effective 1997); Aus.$195 (effective 1998). Rawlhouse Publishing Pty. Ltd., 1141 Hay St., W. Perth, W.A. 6005, Australia. TEL 61-9-93218951. FAX 61-9-94811914. Ed. Iain Baillie. R&P contact: Christine Morriss. adv. contact: Iain Baillie. circ. 3,750. (back issues avail.)
Description: Provides prices for all stages of the building construction process, for feasibility studies, estimating, budgeting, cost control and contract management.

RAWLINSONS NEW ZEALAND CONSTRUCTION HANDBOOK. see *BUSINESS AND ECONOMICS — Trade And Industrial Directories*

690   **US**   **ISSN 0744-530X**
REAL ESTATE NEW YORK. 1982. 10/yr. $35. 111 Eighth Ave., Fl. 1511, New York, NY 10011-5201. TEL 212-929-6900. FAX 212-929-7124. Ed. Michael Billig; Pub. Jonathan Schein. R&P contact: Jonathan Schein. adv.: B&W page $2150, color page $4545; adv. contact: Michelle Zere. circ. 15,003. (reprint service avail.) **Document type:** trade publication.
Formerly: Better Buildings.

REAL ESTATE NEWS AND BUYERS GUIDE. see *REAL ESTATE*

REALTY AND BUILDING. see *REAL ESTATE*

690   **GW**
RECHTSPRECHUNG ZUM PRIVATEN BAURECHT. 1954. base vol. (with m. updates). DM.400 (DM.225 for updates) (effective 1996). Werner-Verlag GmbH, Karl-Rudolf-Str. 172, 40215 Duesseldorf, Germany. TEL 49-211-38798-0. FAX 49-211-383104. Ed. Reiner Hochstein. cum.index: 1954-1977. (looseleaf format) **Document type:** bulletin.
Formerly: Rechtsprechung der Bau-Ausfuehrung (ISSN 0034-1371)

690   **UK**
REDLAND. ANNUAL REVIEW AND SUMMARY FINANCIAL STATEMENT (YEAR). a. Redland PLC, Redland House, Reigate, Surrey RH2 OSJ, England. TEL 44-1737-242488. FAX 44-1737-221938. **Document type:** corporate report.

690   **UK**
REDLAND. DIRECTORS' REPORT AND ACCOUNTS (YEAR). a. Redland PLC, Redland House, Reigate, Surrey RH2 OSJ, England. TEL 44-1737-242488. FAX 44-1737-221938. Ed. R.C. Monro. **Document type:** corporate report.

690   **FR**
REFLETS ET NUANCES. 5/yr. 240 F. U N P V F, 9 rue La Perouse, 75784 Paris Cedex 16, France. TEL 40-69-53-71. FAX 40-70-01-74. TELEX 611 975 F. Ed. Raphae'l Filpo. adv.; illus.

690   **UK**
REFURBISHMENT PROJECTS. 1986. bi-m. £24($48) Sheen Publishing Ltd., 50 Queens Rd., Buckhurst Hill, Essex IG9 5DD, England. TEL 44-181-504-1661. FAX 44-181-505-4336. TELEX 296620-SHEEN-G. Ed. Tony Prior; Pub. Carole Titmuss. adv. contact: Jane Andrews. circ. 11,400. **Document type:** trade publication.
Formerly: Refurbishment Products.

690   **US**   **ISSN 0885-8039**
TH4816
REMODELING. 1985. m. $44.95. Hanley-Wood Inc., One Thomas Circle, Ste. 600, Washington, DC 20005. TEL 202-452-0800. FAX 202-785-1974. E-mail: editor@builderonline.com; URL: http://www.remodeling.hw.net. Ed. Cheryl Weber. adv.; bk.rev.; charts; illus.; stat.; tr.lit. circ. 92,700. (also avail. in microform from UMI; reprint service avail. from UMI) **Document type:** trade publication.
Formerly: Remodeling World (ISSN 0745-2152); Incorporates (1948-1987): Remodeling Contractor (Washington); Which was formerly (until 1983): Home Improvement Contractor (ISSN 0146-5996); (until 1976): Home Improvements (ISSN 0018-4063); (until 1969): Building Specialties and Home Improvements.
Description: Provides current news and information for the residential remodeling market.

690   **US**
REMODELING - REPAIR CONSTRUCTION COSTS. 1991. a. $49.95. Saylor Publications, Inc., 9420 Topanga Canyon Blvd., Ste. 203, Chatsworth, CA 91311. TEL 818-718-5966. FAX 818-718-8024. Ed. Stanley J. Strychaz. R&P contact: Stanley J. Strychaz. **Document type:** trade publication.

RENEW; Canada's magazine of residential renovation and restoration. see *HOUSING AND URBAN PLANNING*

690   **GW**   **ISSN 0947-8914**
▼**RENOVA;** renovieren und modernisieren. (Supplement to: Bau Zeitung (ISSN 0005-6871)) 1995. q. DM.60. Verlag fuer Bauwesen GmbH, Am Friedrichshain 22, 10407 Berlin, Germany. TEL 49-30-42151388. FAX 49-30-42151232. adv.: B&W page DM.4950; 205 x 290. circ. 10,000. **Document type:** trade publication.

690   **NE**   **ISSN 0922-4114**
RENOVATIE & ONDERHOUD; maandblad voor stadsvernieuwing. 1976. 11/yr. fl.290 (foreign fl.350) (effective 1996). Ten Hagen & Stam b.v. (Subsidiary of: Wolters Kluwer N.V.), Postbus 34, 2501 AG The Hague, Netherlands. TEL 31-70-3045700. FAX 31-70-3045812. Ed. N. Meeder. adv.; B&W page fl.3165, color page fl.6415; trim 285 x 215; adv. contact: Herman Voois. illus. circ. 6,113. **Document type:** trade publication.
—SWETS.
Description: Covers all aspects of the architectural management of real estate, including economic, policy and planning issues and urban renovation.

690   **AU**
RENOVATION. q. Technopress Fachzeitschriften Verlagsgesellschaft mbH, Iglaseegasse 21-23, Postfach 176, A-1191 Vienna, Austria. TEL 43-1-322551. FAX 43-1-3207427. Ed. Wolfgang Kadrnoska. circ. 80,000. **Document type:** consumer publication.

643.7   **CN**
RENOVATION MAGAZINE. 1990. 2/yr. Homes Publishing Group, 178 Main St., Unionville, ON L3R 2G9, Canada. TEL 905-479-4663. FAX 905-479-4482. Ed. Diane McDougall. R&P contact: M. Rosset. adv. contact: Kathleen Kelly. circ. 50,000. **Document type:** consumer publication.
Formerly: Professional Renovation Magazine (ISSN 1182-0470)

690   **US**
▼**RENOVATION STYLE.** 1996. q. newsstand price: $4.95. Meredith Corporation, 125 Park Ave., 18th Fl., New York, NY 10017. TEL 212-551-7138. Ed. Karol DeWulf Nickell; Pub. Deborah Barrow. **Document type:** consumer publication.

RENOVERING OG DRIFT - NETTO. see *BUSINESS AND ECONOMICS — Marketing And Purchasing*

690 747   **FR**   **ISSN 1246-354X**
REPONSES BAIN. Abbreviated title: R B. 1993. 6/yr. 295 F. S 4 E Publications, B.P. 120, 40 rue Guy Mouquet, 94501 Champigny Cedex, France. TEL 1-48-84-91-91. FAX 1-48-81-81-77. Ed. Marianne Tournier. adv. contact: Christelle Granger. circ. 8,000.

REQUIREMENTS FOR ELECTRICAL INSTALLATIONS. see *ENGINEERING — Electrical Engineering*

690   **UK**   **ISSN 0034-5105**
RESALE WEEKLY. 1964. w. £8.50. Moffat Publishing Co. Ltd., 1-23 Queen's Rd. W., Plaistow, London E13 OAP, England. Ed. J.W. Branch. adv. circ. 9,500.

690   **FR**   **ISSN 1157-576X**
RESEAUX (SAINT CLOUD)/NETWORK. 1990. 8/yr. 250 F. Reseaux - Com, 33 rue du Mont-Valerien, 92210 Saint Cloud, France. TEL 47-71-12-03. FAX 49-11-00-05. adv. circ. 10,000. **Indexed:** Int.Ind.Film Per.
Description: Covers materials used in all forms of pipework and aerial wires: water, electricity, gas and phone.

RESIDENCES. see *INTERIOR DESIGN AND DECORATION*

690 368   **US**   **ISSN 1053-2986**
TH4815.8
RESIDENTIAL BUILDING COST GUIDE (YEAR). a. $49. E.H. Boeckh (Subsidiary of: Thomson Publishing Corp.), 2885 S. Calhoun Rd., Box 510291, New Berlin, WI 53151-0291. TEL 414-780-2800. FAX 414-780-0306.
Description: Aims to assist the insurance, appraisal, and assessment industries to estimate the replacement cost of homes in the U.S.

692.8   **US**
RESIDENTIAL CONSTRUCTION COSTS. 1982. a. $54.95. Saylor Publications, Inc., 9420 Topanga Canyon Blvd., Ste. 203, Chatsworth, CA 91311. TEL 818-718-5966. FAX 818-718-8024. Ed. Stanley J. Strychaz. R&P contact: Stanley J. Strychaz. circ. 4,000. **Document type:** trade publication.

BUILDING AND CONSTRUCTION

690 US
RESIDENTIAL SQUARE FOOT BUILDING COSTS (YEAR). 1993. a. $29.95. Saylor Publications, Inc., 9420 Topanga Canyon Blvd., Ste. 203, Chatsworth, CA 91311. TEL 818-718-5966. FAX 818-718-8024. Ed. Stanley J. Strychaz. R&P contact: Stanley J. Strychaz. **Document type:** trade publication.

690 SA
RESOURCE QUANTITIES AND PRICING GUIDE. Variant title: Build Aid Resource Quantities and Pricing Guide. 1993. a. B A & E Publishing, P.O. Box 979, Cramerview 2060, South Africa. **Document type:** trade publication.

690 US
RESTON SERIES IN CONSTRUCTION TECHNOLOGY. 1971. irreg. price varies. Reston Publishing Company, Inc., c/o Prentice Hall, Englewood Cliffs, NJ 07632-3501. Ed. Alice Barr. adv.; bk.rev.

691 AG
REVISTA A C O M A C. m. Asociacion de Comerciantes en Materiales para Construccion y Afines, Viamonte 2160, Buenos Aires, Argentina. Ed. Oscar M. Leguizamon. adv.; stat.

690 BL
REVISTA DE PRECOS PARA CONSTRUCAO DE PREDIOS. 1962. m. Editora Revista de Precos Ltda., Av. N. Sa de Copacabana, 749 gr. 801, 220550 Rio de Janeiro RJ, Brazil. TEL 55-21-2356397. FAX 55-21-2356923. Ed. Tatiana Salme Lowjagin; Pub. Sila Bardo do Couto. adv.: B&W page $1080, color page $1732; adv. contact: Luiz Antonio de Souza e Silva. circ. 16,000.

690 PN
REVISTA PANAMENA DE LA CONSTRUCCION. 1961. bi-m. $20. Camara Panamena de la Construccion, Apdo. 6793, Panama 5, Panama. TEL 507-265-2500. FAX 507-265-2571. Ed. Eduardo Rodriguez, Jr. adv. contact: Rebeca Y. de Burillo. circ. 1,250. **Document type:** trade publication.
Formerly (until 1984): Camara Panamena de la Construccion. Boletin Informativo.
Description: Covers many aspects of construction including permits, legal issues, and new technology.

690 624 FR
REVUE FRANCAISE DU BATIMENT ET DES TRAVAUX PUBLICS. 1981. q. 70 F. Societe Nouvelle Meridionale d'Imprimerie et d'Edition (S N M I E), Centre d'Affaires CAP SUD, Immeuble Orion, Route de Marseille, 84000 Avignon, France. TEL 90-86-03-33. FAX 90-27-05-67. Ed. Marie-Claire Forcina. adv.: B&W page 5500 F., color page 11000 F.; trim 252 x 189; adv. contact: Christian Hodapp.

690 FR   ISSN 0035-3132
REVUE GENERALE DE L'ETANCHEITE ET DE L'ISOLATION. 1949. q. 280 F. (foreign 400 F.). Societe de Diffusion des Techniques et Specialites du Batiment, 6-14, rue la Perouse, 75016 Paris, France. TEL 33-1-40-70-94-57. FAX 33-1-47-03-45-97. Ed. Yann Brett. adv. circ. 5,700.

690 FR   ISSN 0048-8186
REVUE TECHNIQUE DU BATIMENT ET DES CONSTRUCTIONS INDUSTRIELLES. 1953. bi-m. 580 F. (foreign 700 F.) (effective 1998). Diffusions et Relations Officielles, 50 rue Championnet, 75018 Paris, France. TEL 33-1-42541414. FAX 33-1-42522894. Ed. Jacqueline Mehr. adv.: B&W page 17000 F., color page 24800 F.; trim 180 x 260. bk.rev.; bibl.; illus. circ. 20,030. **Document type:** trade publication.

690 US
THE RHODE ISLAND BUILDER REPORT. 1951. 12/yr. membership. Rhode Island Builders Association, 450 Veterans Memorial Pkwy. No. 301, East Providence, RI 02914-5380. TEL 401-438-7400. FAX 401-438-7446. Ed. Paul F. Eno; Pub. Roger R. Warren. adv. contact: Janet Kortick. bk.rev.; circ. 3,400 (controlled). **Document type:** newsletter.
Formerly: Rhode Island Builder.
Description: For the residential construction industry.

690 IT   ISSN 0393-4411
RIABITA. 1985. m. L.70000 (foreign L.80000). Rima Editrice s.r.l., Viale Sarca 235-3, 20126 Milan, Italy. TEL 39-2-66103539. FAX 39-2-66103558. adv.: B&W page L.4200000, color page L.4900000; 240 x 310. circ. 19,000.
Description: Covers reconstruction, renovation and maintenance of private and public buildings.

690 340 IT   ISSN 0485-2435
RIVISTA GIURIDICA DELL'EDILIZIA. 1958. bi-m. Lit.200000 (foreign Lit.300000) (effective 1997). Casa Editrice Dott. A. Giuffre, Via Busto Arsizio 40, 20151 Milan, Italy. TEL 39-2-38089200. FAX 39-2-38009582. Ed.Bd. adv. circ. 6,200.
Indexed: IBR.

RIVISTA TRIMESTRALE DEGLI APPALTI; rivista di dottrina-legislazione-giurisprudenza, see LAW — Corporate Law

690 US
ROCK AND DIRT. 1949. 36/yr. $42. T A P Publishing Co., Crossville, TN 38555. TEL 615-484-5137. FAX 615-484-2532. Pub. Michael D. Stone. adv. contact: Barbara Patterson. illus. circ. 172,000. (tabloid format) **Document type:** trade publication.

690 US   ISSN 0192-3951
ROCKY MOUNTAIN CONSTRUCTION (SOUTH EDITION). North Edition (ISSN 0192-3943) (Annual Buyer's Guide & Directory avail.) 1925. fortn. $40. Rocky Mountain Construction Magazine, Inc., Associated Construction Publications, 2403 Champa, Denver, CO 80205-2694. TEL 303-295-0630. FAX 303-295-2159. Ed. F. Hol Wagner, Jr.; Pub. Lawrence Bell. adv. contact: Don Ludwig. charts; illus.; circ. 7,800 (controlled). **Document type:** trade publication.
—UnCover.

690 GW   ISSN 0344-8088
DER ROLLADEN - JALOUSIEBAUER. 1966. m. DM.122.40. Verlag F.H. Kleffmann GmbH, Hernerstr. 299, 44809 Bochum, Germany. TEL 49-234-95391-0. FAX 49-234-9539130. E-mail: kleffmann@mediacom.de; URL: http://www.mediacom.de/kleffmann. Ed. M. Scholz. circ. 8,000. **Document type:** trade publication.

695 720 US   ISSN 0279-4616
TH2391
ROOFER MAGAZINE. 1981. m. $36 (Canada $45; elsewhere $65) (effective 1996 & 1997). 12734 Kenwood Ln., Ste. 73, Ft. Myers, FL 33907-5638. TEL 813-489-2929. FAX 813-489-1747. URL: http://www.roofmag.com. Ed. Angela M. Williamson; Pub. Greg P. Abrell. adv.: B&W page $3490, color page $5645; trim 8 3/8 x 10 7/8; adv. contact: Greg P. Abrell. bk.rev.; charts; illus.; stat.; index. circ. 22,450. (also avail. in microfiche; back issues avail.) **Document type:** trade publication.
—BLDSC (8021.930000).
Description: Covers all aspects of the roofing industry.

695 UK
ROOFING. 1950. m. £35. (National Federation of Roofing Contractors) B P G Ltd., 2 West St., Bourne, Lincs PE10 9NE, England. TEL 0778-393747. FAX 0778-425453. Ed. S. McLoughlin. adv.; bk.rev.; illus.; tr.lit. circ. 13,250. **Indexed:** Br.Ceram.Abstr., RICS.
—CISTI.
Formerly: Roofing Contractor (ISSN 0035-8193)
Description: Covers roofing products, their manufacturers, distributors and suppliers.

695 NE   ISSN 0924-705X
ROOFING HOLLAND. (Text in Dutch) 1991. 11/yr. Mandate Publishers BV, Postbus 9198, 1800 GD Alkmaar, Netherlands. TEL 31-2513-20500. Ed. L.E.R. DuPuy. adv.; circ. 14,000 (controlled). (back issues avail.) **Document type:** trade publication.

695.025 US
ROOFING MATERIALS AND SYSTEMS DIRECTORY. a. Underwriters Laboratories Inc., Publications, 333 Pfingsten Rd., Northbrook, IL 60062-2096. TEL 708-272-8800. FAX 708-272-8129. **Document type:** directory.
Description: Lists all manufacturers of roofing materials and equipment complying with UL standards.

690 UK
ROYAL INSTITUTION OF CHARTERED SURVEYORS. CONTRACTS IN USE. a. Royal Institution of Chartered Surveyors, 12 Great George St., Parliament Sq., London SW1P 3AD, England. TEL 44-171-222-7000. FAX 44-171-222-9430. **Document type:** bulletin.

690 630 US   ISSN 0888-3025
RURAL BUILDER. 1966. 7/yr. $18.95 (free to qualified personnel) (effective 1997). Krause Publications, Inc., 700 E. State St., Iola, WI 54990. TEL 715-445-2214. FAX 715-445-4087. TELEX 556461 KRAUSE PUB UD. Ed. Erik Stottrup; Pub. Ulrich Groth. adv. contact: Claude Chmiel. bk.rev.; charts; illus. circ. 33,109.
—CCC.
Formerly (until 1986): Farm Building News (ISSN 0014-7869)
Description: For contractors, suppliers, and builders servicing non-urban America.

691.3 693.5 NE
RUSSIAN JOURNAL OF CONCRETE AND REINFORCED CONCRETE. English translation of: Beton i Zhelezobeton (RU ISSN 0005-9889) (Text in English) 1988. q. fl.475($250) (State Committee on Construction, RU) A.A. Balkema, P.O. Box 1675, 3000 BR Rotterdam, Netherlands. TEL 31-10-4145822. FAX 31-10-4135947. E-mail: sales@balkema.nl; URL: http://www.jcn.nl/ima/balkema/. **Indexed:** C.R.I.Abstr., C.R.I.Curr.Cont., J.of Ferroc. **Document type:** academic/scholarly publication.
—CISTI. CCC.
Formerly (until Dec. 1991): Soviet Journal of Concrete and Reinforced Concrete (ISSN 0970-244X)
Description: Includes papers of interest to the international construction industry. Excludes papers of only local interest and those dealing with management and economics of the Russian construction industry.

690 GW   ISSN 0036-102X
S B/SPORTS FACILITIES AND SWIMMING POOLS/EQUIPEMENT SPORTIF ET PISCINES/CONSTRUCCION DE INSTALLACIONES DEPORTIVAS Y PISCINAS. (Sportstaettenbau und Baederanlagen) (Text in English, French, German and Spanish) 1967. bi-m. DM.54 (foreign DM.84) (effective 1997 & 1998). (International Association for Sports and Leisure Facilities) S B 67 Verlagsgesellschaft mbH, Postfach 320340, 50797 Cologne, Germany. TEL 49-221-95644625. FAX 49-221-95644698. Ed. F. Roskam. adv.; bk.rev. circ. 7,500. **Indexed:** Sportsearch (1976-). **Document type:** trade publication.
Description: Contains information on sports facilities of all kinds and developments in sports equipment.

016.69 DK   ISSN 0107-900X
S B I - AARSBERETNING/S B I - ANNUAL REPORT. Variant title: Byggeforskningsinstitut - Aarsberetning. 1949. a. free. Statens Byggeforskningsinstitut - Danish Building Research Institute, Dr. Neergaards Vej 15, Postbox 119, 2970 Hoersholm, Denmark. TEL 45-42-86-55-33. FAX 45-42-86-75-35. E-mail: sbi@sbi.dk; URL: http://www.sbi.dk. illus.
Formerly: Denmark. Statens Byggeforskningsinstitut. Aarsberetning.

690 SZ
S E L EDILIZIA SVIZZERA. (Text in Italian) 24/yr. Gewerkschaft Bau und Holz, Postfach, CH-8021 Zurich, Switzerland. TEL 01-2951636. FAX 01-2951799. circ. 30,000.

690 FR
S N S O BULLETIN. 12/yr. 8 rue Catulle-Mendes, 75017 Paris, France. TEL 46-22-18-65. Ed. Sylvie Touchard-Cantie. circ. 5,000. **Document type:** bulletin.

720 RU
S.-PETERBURGSKAYA PANORAMA. 1936. m. 15.60 Rub. Nevskii pr., 53, 191025 St. Petersburg, Russia. TEL 7-812-113-1523. Ed.Bd. bibl.; charts; illus.; index. circ. 6,000. **Indexed:** Archit.Per.Ind., Br.Tech.Ind., Chem.Abstr.
Former titles (until Oct. 1991): Leningradskaya Panorama (ISSN 0233-7010); (until 1982): Stroitel'stvo i Arkhitektura Leningrada (ISSN 0039-2413)

BUILDING AND CONSTRUCTION

690   FR
SAGERET: ANNUAIRE NATIONAL DU BATIMENT ET DES TRAVAUX PUBLICS. (In 6 vols.) 1809. a. 3000 F. (effective 1996). Sageret, 7 rue Plumet, 75015 Paris, France. FAX 42-73-04-47. TELEX UJE 1111-699559. adv. circ. 60,000. **Document type:** directory.
   Formerly: Sageret: Annuaire General du Batiment et des Travaux Publics.

690 624   FR   ISSN 1157-1586
SAINT-LAMBERT, L'ANNUAIRE BATIMENT ET TRAVAUX PUBLICS. 1930. a. 495 F. (Mat. Presse-Saint Lambert Editeur) Guide Rosenwald, 10 rue Vineuse, 75116 Paris, France. TEL 33-1-44308100. FAX 33-1-44308111. E-mail: rosenwal@pratique.fr. Ed. Marie-Jeanne Fiant. adv. **Document type:** directory.
   Former titles: Officiel Batiment et Travaux Publics; Annuaire Batiment et Travaux Publics.

690   US   ISSN 1045-3792
ST. LOUIS CONSTRUCTION NEWS & REVIEW. 1969. m. $22. Finan Publishing Company, 8730 Big Bend Blvd., St. Louis, MO 63119-3730. TEL 314-961-6644. FAX 314-961-4809. Ed. Thomas J. Finan; Pub. Thomas J. Finan. R&P contact: Nancy Valentine. adv. contact: Nancy Valentine. charts; illus.; stat.; tr.lit. circ. 6,500. (back issues avail.) **Document type:** trade publication, newspaper.
   Description: Covers construction, architecture and engineering.

690   JA
SAISHIN NO SEKO GIJUTSU/LATEST CONSTRUCTION TECHNOLOGY. (Text in Japanese) 1985. a. Doboku Gakkai, Doboku Seko Kenkyu Iinkai - Japan Society of Civil Engineering, Committee on Construction Technology, Yotsuya 1-chome, Shinjuku-ku, Tokyo 160, Japan.

SAITAMA DAIGAKU KOGAKUBU KENSETSUKEI KENKYU HOKOKU/SAITAMA UNIVERSITY. FACULTY OF ENGINEERING. DEPARTMENT OF CONSTRUCTION. RESEARCH REPORT. see *ENGINEERING — Civil Engineering*

SALES PROSPECTOR. see *BUSINESS AND ECONOMICS — Production Of Goods And Services*

690   FR   ISSN 0036-505X
SAUVEGARDE DES CHANTIERS. 1951. bi-m. 65 F. (foreign 120 F.) Organisme Professionnel de Prevention du Batiment et des Travaux Publics, Tour Amboise B 3, 204 Rond Point du Pont de Sevres, 92516 Boulogne Billancourt Cedex, France. TEL 1-46-09-26-50. Dir. Pierre Verges. bibl.; charts; illus.; stat. circ. 18,150. **Indexed:** C.I.S. Abstr. **Document type:** trade publication.

690.24   US
SCAFFOLD INDUSTRY ASSOCIATION. NEWSLETTER. 1972. m. membership. Scaffold Industry Association, 14039 Sherman Way, Ste. 100, Van Nuys, CA 91405-2599. TEL 818-782-2012. FAX 818-786-3027. Ed. D. Victor Saleeby. R&P contact: D. Victor Saleeby. adv. contact: Gary Larson. **Document type:** newsletter, directory.

690   US
SCAFFOLD INDUSTRY ASSOCIATION. (YEAR) DIRECTORY AND HANDBOOK. 1980. a. $125. Scaffold Industry Association, 14039 Sherman Way, Ste. 100, Van Nuys, CA 91405-2599. TEL 818-782-2012. FAX 818-786-3027. Ed. D. Victor Saleeby. adv. contact: Gary Larson. illus. circ. 2,000. **Document type:** directory.
   Description: Lists S.I.A. members and the services they provide. Also compiles O.S.H.A. standards pertaining to scaffolding.

698.9 645.1   SA
SCHALK BURGER'S FLOORS IN AFRICA. Running title: Floors. 1985. bi-m. Schalk Burger Publications, P.O. Box 12532, Clubview, Verwoerdburg 0014, South Africa. adv.; illus. **Document type:** trade publication.
   Former titles: (until vol.13, 1995): Schalk Burger's Southern Africa Floorcovering Journal; (until vol.12, no.3, 1994): Schalk Burger's S.A. Floor Covering Journal; (until 1988): S.A. Floor Covering Journal (ISSN 0258-9958)

690.24   GW   ISSN 0943-4593
SCHORNSTEINFEGERHANDWERK. 1884. m. DM.90. Bundesverband des Schornsteinfegerhandwerks, Rubensstr. 1, 40237 Duesseldorf, Germany. TEL 0211-682464. FAX 0211-665626. Ed. B. Steinebach. adv.: B&W page DM.1905, color DM.3690; trim 253 x 184. bk.rev. circ. 12,000. **Document type:** trade publication.
   Description: Discusses the work of chimney sweeps.

690   AU
SCHULE- UND SPORTSTAETTE. 1965. bi-m. S.660 (effective 1996). (Oesterreichisches Institut fuer Schul- und Sportstaettenbau) Ostag Werbung und Verlag, Wickenburggasse 17, A-1082 Vienna, Austria. TEL 43-1-4027573. FAX 43-1-4088292. adv.: B&W page S.8310, color page S.17250; trim 245 x 180. abstr.; bibl.; charts; illus.; mkt.; pat.; stat.; tr.mk. circ. 2,650. (reprint service avail. from ISI) **Document type:** academic/scholarly publication.
   Formerly: Schul- und Sportstaettenbau (ISSN 0036-7095)

690   SZ   ISSN 0036-7303
SCHWEIZER BAUBLATT. 1889. s-w. 320 SFr. (foreign 108 SFr.) (effective 1996). Schueck Soehne AG, Bahnhofstr. 24, CH-8803 Rueschlikon, Switzerland. TEL 01-7247777. FAX 01-7247877. adv.; bk.rev.; illus.; pat.; stat.; tr.lit. **Document type:** trade publication.

690   SZ   ISSN 0376-6853
SCHWEIZER BAUWIRTSCHAFT/JOURNAL SUISSE DES ENTREPRENEURS/GIORNALE SVIZZERO DEGLI IMPRESARI COSTRUTTORI. (Text in French, German, Italian) 1911. w. 216 SFr. (Schweizerischer Baumeisterverband) AG Verlag Hoch- und Tiefbau, Postfach, CH-8023 Zurich, Switzerland. FAX 41-1-2610324. Ed. Rene Mueller. adv.; bibl.; charts; illus.; tr.lit. **Indexed:** C.I.S. Abstr., Geotech.Abstr. **Document type:** trade publication.
   Formerly: Hoch- und Tiefbau (ISSN 0046-7677)

SCHWEIZER JOURNAL. see *ARCHITECTURE*

690   GW   ISSN 0343-4958
SCHWIMMBAD UND SAUNA; Zeitschrift fuer Planung und Bau von Schwimmbaedern und Saunas. 1969. bi-m. DM.48 (foreign DM.54) (effective 1997). Fachschriften Verlag GmbH, Hoehenstr. 17, 70736 Fellbach, Germany. TEL 49-711-5206-256. FAX 49-711-5281424. Eds. Guenter Bayer, Karl-Heinz Linderich; Pub. Ottmar Strebel. adv. contact: Wolfgang Kriwan. tr.lit.; circ. 20,187. **Document type:** trade publication.

SCIENCE AND TECHNOLOGY OF BUILDING SEALS, SEALANTS, GLAZING, AND WATERPROOFING. see *ENGINEERING — Engineering Mechanics And Materials*

SCOPE (YEAR). see *BUSINESS AND ECONOMICS — Accounting*

690 624   UK   ISSN 0085-6002
TH61
SCOTTISH BUILDING & CIVIL ENGINEERING YEAR BOOK. 1960. a. $30. Edinburgh Pictorial Ltd., Smith's Place House, Edinburgh EH8 6NU, Scotland. FAX 44-131-555-2965. Ed. C.C. Cumming. R&P contact: C.C. Cumming. adv. contact: Ian Kirkhope. circ. 3,000. (processed) **Document type:** trade publication.

691   US
SCREENING INDUSTRY. 1974. q. (Screen Manufacturers Association) Fitzgerald Corporation, 2850 S. Ocean Blvd., Apt. 114, Palm Beach, FL 33480-5535. TEL 561-533-0991. FAX 561-533-7466. Ed. Frank S. Fitzgerald. circ. 1,000. **Document type:** newsletter.
   Formerly: Screening News.

690   JA   ISSN 0389-1879
SEKO/ARCHITECTURAL PRODUCT ENGINEERING. Variant title: Kenchiku no Gijutsu. (Text in Japanese) 1966. m. Shokokusha Publishing Co., Ltd., 25 Sakamachi, Shinjuku-ku, Tokyo 160, Japan. TEL 81-3-3359-3231. FAX 81-3-3357-3961. Ed. Kiyoshi Kamahara. adv.: B&W page 120000 Yen, color page 400000 Yen; adv. contact: Toshio Takahashi. circ. 50,000.

690 640   CN   ISSN 0833-1103
NA7241
SELECT HOME DESIGNS. 1983. a. Can.$9.95 (effective 1997). Planners Plus Enterprises Ltd., 611 Alexander St., Ste. 301, Vancouver, BC V6A 1E1, Canada. TEL 604-879-4144. FAX 604-251-3212. Ed. Brian Thorn. adv.: color page Can.$6980; adv. contact: Brian Thorn. bk.rev. circ. 85,000. **Document type:** consumer publication, trade publication.
   Description: New home designs and information on new home construction and products.

658.2 648   US   ISSN 0279-0548
TX955
SERVICES. 1981. m. $30 (foreign $60). Building Service Contractors Association International, 10201 Lee Hwy., Ste. 225, Fairfax, VA 22030. TEL 703-359-7090. FAX 703-352-0493. Ed. Donald E. Tepper. adv. contact: Jon Shonerd. circ. 17,000. (back issues avail.)
   Description: Articles on the janitorial industry, from cleaning to security services, both management and technical in every issue.

690   CC
SHANGHAI JIANSHE KEJI/SHANGHAI CONSTRUCTION SCIENCE AND TECHNOLOGY. (Text in Chinese) bi-m. Shanghai Jianshe Keji Qingbao Zhongxin Zhan, 75 Yuanping Lu, Shanghai 200032, People's Republic of China. TEL 4387445. Ed. Chen Zhengqian.

690   US   ISSN 0164-6559
SHELTER; magazine for distribution and marketing of products for building and home improvement. 1962. bi-m. $15. Associations Publications, Inc., Box 640, Collierville, TN 38027-9986. TEL 901-853-7470. Ed. Joyce Powell. adv.; illus.; stat.; tr.lit. circ. 23,517.
   Formerly: N S D J A Digest (National Sash and Door Jobbers Association).

SHIGONG JISHU/CONSTRUCTION TECHNOLOGY. see *ARCHITECTURE*

629   JA   ISSN 0289-8330
SHIMIZU KENSETSU KENKYU HOKOKU/SHIMIZU CONSTRUCTION TECHNICAL RESEARCH REPORT. (Text in Japanese; summaries in English, Japanese) 1962. s-a. exchange basis. Shimizu Kensetsu K.K., Gijutsu Kenkyujo - Shimizu Corporation, Institute of Technology, 4-17, Etchujima 3-chome, Koto-ku, Tokyo 135, Japan. TEL 03-3643-4311. FAX 03-3643-7260. Ed. Muneo Kawamura. circ. 600. **Indexed:** Eng.Mat.Abstr., INIS Atomind., Met.Abstr., Met.Abstr.Ind., Nonfer.Met.Alert, PCC Alert, Steels Alert, World Alum.Abstr. **Document type:** bulletin.
   Description: Contains selected original papers of Shimizu Corporation's research engineers.

690   JA   ISSN 0912-7518
SHIMIZU TECHNICAL RESEARCH BULLETIN. (Text in English) 1982. a. exchange basis. Shimizu Corporation, Institute of Technology, 4-17, Etchujima 3-chome, Koto-ku, Tokyo 135, Japan. TEL 03-3643-4311. FAX 03-3643-7260. Ed. Muneo Kawamura; Pub. Hiroshi Yamahara. circ. 300. **Indexed:** Alloys Ind., Eng.Mat.Abstr., Met.Abstr., Met.Abstr.Ind., Nonfer.Met.Alert, PCC Alert, Steels Alert, World Alum.Abstr. **Document type:** bulletin. —CISTI.
   Description: Contains original papers of the company's research engineers.

690   NE   ISSN 1383-7265
SHIP, PORT, AND OFFSHORE TECHNOLOGY. 1992. irreg., vol.2, 1997. price varies. Delft University Press, Mekelweg 4, 2628 CD Delft. TEL 31-15-2783254. FAX 31-15-2781661. E-mail: dup@dup.tudelft.nl. **Document type:** monographic series.

691   CC   ISSN 1001-6171
SHUINI JISHU/CEMENT TECHNOLOGY. (Text in Chinese) bi-m. Y300. Tianjin Shuini Gongye Sheji Yanjiuyuan - Tianjin Design Academy for Cement Industry, Yin He Qiao Li, Beijiao (North Star Suburb), Tianjin 300400, People's Republic of China. TEL 86-22-26391311. FAX 86-22-26390071. TELEX 23264 FRHTC CN. Ed. Zhu Zupei. adv. contact: Shen Ying. circ. 10,000.

SIL'S'KE BUDIVNYTSTVO. see *AGRICULTURE*

BUILDING AND CONSTRUCTION

690   GW   ISSN 0943-3880
SISTA AKTUELL. 1984. 4/yr. free. Wegra Verlag GmbH, Frankfurterstr. 10, 71732 Tamm, Germany. circ. 15,000. **Document type:** trade publication.
   Description: Information on sealing windows and concrete building elements with connecting sealant.

658.202   SW   ISSN 1103-5285
SKANDINAVISK UNDERHAALLSMARKNAD. 1991. 6/yr. SEK 392 in Nordic countries; elsewhere SEK 492 (effective 1998). Arbor Publishing AB, P.O. Box 26212, S-100 41 Stockholm, Sweden. TEL 46-8-611-60-30. FAX 46-8-679-54-40.

690 658   US   ISSN 0892-7847
HD1393.55
SKYLINES (WASHINGTON); news of the commercial real estate industry. 1916. 10/yr. $95 to non-members; members $75. Building Owners and Managers Association International, 1201 New York Ave., N.W., Ste. 300, Washington, DC 20005. TEL 202-408-2662. FAX 202-321-0181. Ed. Monique Silverio. adv.; bk.rev.; illus.; stat.; index. circ. 16,000. (also avail. in microform from UMI) **Indexed:** B.P.I. **Document type:** trade publication.
   —CISTI; UnCover.
   Formerly (until May 1981): Building Owner and Manager; Supersedes (in 1976): Skyscraper Management (ISSN 0037-6647)

SLOOP & RECYCLING. see ENVIRONMENTAL STUDIES — Waste Management

THE SOURCE (PRINCETON). see BUSINESS AND ECONOMICS — Trade And Industrial Directories

691   SA   ISSN 0038-2027
SOUTH AFRICAN BUILDER/SUID AFRIKAANSE BOUER. Short title: S.A. Builder - Bouer. (Text in Afrikaans, English) 1923. m. R.72 (foreign R.300). (Building Industries Federation South Africa - Bou-Industriee Federasie Suid-Afrika) Emden Publishing Co., P.O. Box 1123, Pinegowrie 2123, South Africa. TEL 27-11-8860208. FAX 27-11-7895223. Ed. Dennis Bird. adv.; bk.rev.; charts; illus.; index. circ. 8,300. **Indexed:** Ind.S.A.Per. **Document type:** trade publication.

690   SA
SOUTH AFRICAN CONSTRUCTION WORLD. 1982. m. R.60. Phase Four (Pty) Ltd., P.O. Box 784279, Sandton 2146, South Africa. TEL 011-444-4566. FAX 011-444-7888. Ed Arthur Tassell. circ. 5,100. (back issues avail.) **Indexed:** Ind.S.A.Per.
   Formerly: South African Construction News.

SOUTH AFRICAN HOME OWNER. see ARCHITECTURE

690   AT   ISSN 0157-938X
SOUTH AUSTRALIAN BUILDER. 1921. m. Aus.$40. Master Builders Association of South Australia, 47 South Terrace, Adelaide, S.A. 5000, Australia. Ed. Elke Langman. adv.; B&W page Aus.$700, color page Aus.$1000; trim 275 x 210. circ. 2,000 (controlled). **Indexed:** Aus.Rd.Ind. **Document type:** trade publication.

643.7 380   US
SOUTH CAROLINA BUILDER.* 6/yr. Home Builders Association of South Carolina, Box 5977, Columbia, SC 29250-5977. TEL 803-771-7408.

690   SI
SOUTHEAST ASIA BUILDING. (Text in English) 1974. m. $105. A P Trade Publications, 24 Peck Seah St., No. 03-00 Nehson's Building, Singapore 0207, Singapore. FAX 65-2225587. Ed. Margie T. Logarta. adv.; B&W page $1150, color page $1350; trim 205 x 275; adv. contact: Sherry Kang. bk.rev. circ. 6,500.
   Formerly (until 1988): Southeast Asian Building Annual.

690 624   SI
SOUTH EAST ASIA CONSTRUCTION. (Text in English) 1983. bi-m. A R Format Pte. Ltd., 1201 Wing on Life Bldg., 150 Cecil St., Singapore 0001, Singapore. TEL 2208777. TELEX RS 28179 FORMAT. Ed. Andrew Loh. adv. contact: Victor Rodrigues. circ. 10,000.

690   US   ISSN 0038-3864
SOUTHERN BUILDING. 1943. bi-m. $35. Southern Building Code Congress, International, 900 Montclair Rd., Birmingham, AL 35213. TEL 205-591-1853. FAX 205-592-7001. Ed. Karla Price Higgs. adv.; bk.rev.; illus. circ. 13,000.
   —CISTI.

690 624   US
SOUTHERN BUILDING CODE CONGRESS. STANDARD BUILDING CODE. triennial. Southern Building Code Congress, International, 900 Montclair Rd., Birmingham, AL 35213. TEL 205-591-1853. FAX 205-592-7001.

690 628.92   US
SOUTHERN BUILDING CODE CONGRESS. STANDARD FIRE PREVENTION CODE. triennial. Southern Building Code Congress, International, 900 Montclair Rd., Birmingham, AL 35213. TEL 205-591-1853. FAX 205-592-7001.

690   US
SOUTHERN BUILDING CODE CONGRESS. STANDARD GAS CODE. triennial. Southern Building Code Congress, International, 900 Montclair Rd., Birmingham, AL 35213. TEL 205-591-1853. FAX 205-592-7001.

690 621   US
SOUTHERN BUILDING CODE CONGRESS. STANDARD MECHANICAL CODE. triennial. Southern Building Code Congress, International, 900 Montclair Rd., Birmingham, AL 35213. TEL 205-591-1853. FAX 205-592-7001.

690 616.15   US
SOUTHERN BUILDING CODE CONGRESS. STANDARD PLUMBING CODE. triennial. Southern Building Code Congress, International, 900 Montclair Rd., Birmingham, AL 35213. TEL 205-591-1853. FAX 205-592-7001.

624 622   US   ISSN 1064-6914
SOUTHWEST CONTRACTOR. (In two editions: Arizona - New Mexico, Nevada) 1938. m. $36. McGraw-Hill Companies, Southwest Contractor, 2050 E. University, Phoenix, AZ 85034. TEL 602-258-1641. E-mail: sweditor@aol.com. Ed. Danielle Beaugureau. adv.; B&W page $920, color page $1415; trim 8 1/2 X 11. circ. 5,600 (controlled). **Document type:** trade publication.
   Incorporates: Southwest Builder.
   Description: Covers the commercial, residential, and industrial construction industry.

691   UK   ISSN 0950-6632
SPECIALIST BUILDING FINISHES. 1967. q. £12. (Federation of Plastering and Drywall Contractors) Phebruary Publications Ltd., 2 Bovingdon Close, Bovingdon, Hertfordshire HP3 0QU, England. TEL 44-1442-832908. Ed. Peter Hancocks. adv.; illus. circ. 5,000. **Document type:** newsletter.
   —BLDSC (8404.765400).
   Incorporates: Modern Plastering (ISSN 0026-8267)

690   IT
SPECIALIZZATA. 1990. m. (10/yr.). L.100000 (effective 1996). BE-MA Editrice s.r.l., Via Teocrito, 50, 20128 Milan, Italy. TEL 39-2-2552451. FAX 39-2-27000692. Ed. Dario Marabelli. adv.; B&W page L.3200000, color page L.4100000; trim 195 x 280. circ. 10,000. **Document type:** trade publication.
   Formerly: Impermeabilizzare.
   Description: Provides information on the latest technology in the sectors of civil engineering, residential and industrial building.

690   UK   ISSN 0081-3567
SPECIFICATION; building methods and products. 1898. a. £75. E M A P - Architecture, 33-39 Bowling Green Ln., London EC1R 0DA, England. TEL 44-171 837-1212. FAX 44-171-833-8072. Ed. Alan Williams. adv. circ. 20,000. **Document type:** directory.
   ●Also available on CD-ROM.
   Description: Provides a primer for students of architecture and persons involved in building procurement.

690 621.3   US   ISSN 1067-2451
SPECIFIER REPORTS. 1991. irreg., approx. 4/yr. $30 per no. Rensselaer Polytechnic Institute, Lighting Research Center, Troy, NY 12180-3590. TEL 518-276-8716. FAX 518-276-2999. E-mail: lrc@rpi.edu; URL: http://www.lrc.rpi.edu. Ed. Robert Davis. R&P contact: Judith Block. bibl.; charts; illus. (looseleaf format; back issues avail.) **Document type:** newsletter.
   Description: Publishes product-specific performance data and general technical information for lighting products marketed in the U.S., including electronic ballasts, compact fluorescent lamps, reflectors and power reducers.
   Refereed Serial

690   SA
SPECIFILE BUILDING COMPENDIUM. (Text in Afrikaans, English) 1976. a. R.95. Communications Group Specifile, Information Services Division, Handel Rd. & Northern Pkwy., Box 7870, Johannesburg 2000, South Africa. FAX 011-835-1943. TELEX 4-82735 SA. Ed. V. Shapiro. adv. circ. 5,500.
   Description: Lists addresses and phone numbers of manufacturers of building products, descriptions of their specific products.

690   SA
SPECIFILE NEWS AND PRODUCT UPDATE. (Text in English) 1980. bi-m. Communications Group, P.O. Box 7870, Johannesburg 2000, South Africa. circ. 2,500. (back issues avail.) **Document type:** trade publication.

690   UK
SPECIFY. 1980. m. £20. Jemma Publications (N.I.) Ltd., 151 University St., Belfast BT7 1HR, N. Ireland. FAX 0232-325736. Ed. Stanley Maxwell. adv.; bk.rev. circ. 4,500. (back issues avail.)

690   US
SPECTEXT; coordinated 16 division master guide specification in C S I format and style. 1979. q. price varies. Construction Sciences Research Foundation, 202 Wyndhurst Ave., Baltimore, MD 21210. TEL 410-323-8489. Ed.Bd. adv. circ. 2,200.

690   UK   ISSN 0306-3046
SPON'S ARCHITECTS' & BUILDERS' PRICE BOOK. 1873. a. £59.50. E. & F.N. Spon, 2-6 Boundary Row, London SE1 8HN, England. TEL 071-865-0066. FAX 071-522-9623. Ed.Bd. adv.; stat. circ. 13,000. **Document type:** directory.
   —BLDSC (8419.050000).
   Description: Essential work for those involved in the pricing of construction works, whether estimating or negotiating a new case.

690   UK   ISSN 0267-4181
SPON'S LANDSCAPE & EXTERNAL WORKS PRICEBOOK. 1972. a. £50. E. & F.N. Spon, 2-6 Boundary Row, London SE1 8HN, England. TEL 071-865-0066. FAX 071-522-9623. Ed.Bd. illus. circ. 3,000. **Document type:** directory.
   —BLDSC (8419.060500).
   Former titles: Spon's Landscape Pricebook (ISSN 0144-8404); Spon's Landscape Handbook (ISSN 0306-3054)

690 621.3   UK   ISSN 0305-4543
SPON'S MECHANICAL & ELECTRICAL SERVICES PRICE BOOK. 1968. a. £65. E. & F.N. Spon, 2-6 Boundary Row, London SE1 8HN, England. TEL 071-865-0066. FAX 071-522-9623. Ed.Bd. adv. **Document type:** directory.
   —BLDSC (8419.070000).

SPORT- BAEDER- FREIZEITBAUTEN; internationale Fachzeitschrift fuer Planung, Bau, Einrichtung, Betrieb und Forschung. see SPORTS AND GAMES

690 669   GW   ISSN 0176-3083
STAHLBAU - NACHRICHTEN. bi-m. Deutscher Stahlbau-Verband, Ebertplatz 1, 50668 Cologne, Germany. TEL 0221-77310. FAX 0221-7731121. **Document type:** trade publication.

690 669   AU
STAHLBAU - RUNDSCHAU - MITTEILUNGEN. 1954. bi-m. Oesterreichischer Stahlbauverband, Larochegasse 28, A-1130 Vienna, Austria. TEL 0222-826170. FAX 0222-8774836. **Document type:** newsletter.

STATE BAR OF WISCONSIN. CONSTRUCTION AND PUBLIC CONTRACT LAW SECTION. NEWSLETTER. see LAW

BUILDING AND CONSTRUCTION

STATE COMMERCIAL - RESIDENTIAL CODES. see *HOUSING AND URBAN PLANNING*

690   GW   ISSN 0949-2275
STAVEBNI MATERIALY. (Text in Czech) q. DM.88 (foreign DM.98) (effective 1997); newsstand price: DM.22. Stein-Verlag GmbH, Josef-Herrmann-Str. 1-3, 76473 Iffezheim, Germany. TEL 49-7229-606-0. FAX 49-7229-60610. Pub. Wilhelm Joesch. R&P contact: Jutta Senn. **Document type:** trade publication.

690 624 720   XO   ISSN 0039-078X
CODEN: STVCA2
STAVEBNICKY CASOPIS. (Text in Slovak; summaries in English and Russian) 1953. m. $44 in US (effective 1996). (Slovenska Akademia Vied, Ustav Stavebnictva a Architektury) Vydavatel'stvo S A P, s.r.o. - Slovak Academic Press Ltd., P.O. Box 57, Nam. Slobody 6, 810 05 Bratislava, Slovakia. TEL 42-78-211728. Ed. Jan Balas. bk.rev.; bibl.; charts; illus.; index, cum.index. circ. 1,250. **Indexed:** Appl.Mech.Rev., C.R.I.Abstr., C.R.I.Curr.Cont., Chem.Abstr., Eng.Ind., Geotech.Abstr., Ref.Zh.
—CISTI; Linda Hall.
Description: Deals with the problems of building mechanics, as well as various building materials, construction theories, elasticity and plasticity theories.

690 331.88   XR   ISSN 0039-0798
STAVEBNIK;* ctrnactideni pracujicich ve stavebnictvi. 1897. s-m. $22.30. Ustredni Rada Odboru, Stavba - Odborovy Svaz Ceske Republiky, Senovazne nam. 23, 112 82 Prague 1, Czech Republic. Ed. Ladislav Jencik. circ. 25,000.

693.71   AT   ISSN 0049-2205
STEEL CONSTRUCTION. 1967. q. Aus.$70 (foreign Aus.$110) including Construct in Steel. Australian Institute of Steel Construction, P.O. Box 6366, N. Sydney, N.S.W. 2059, Australia. TEL 61-2-99296666. FAX 61-2-99555406. Ed. Arun Syam. R&P contact: Arun Syam. circ. 4,500. **Indexed:** Appl.Mech.Rev., Aus.Rd.Ind.
—BLDSC (8462.550000).
Description: Provides technical literature on steel design mainly for the structural engineer.

690 669.142   SA
STEEL CONSTRUCTION. q. R.4. P.O. Box 1338, Johannesburg 2000, South Africa. adv. **Indexed:** Ind.S.A.Per. **Document type:** trade publication.
Description: Covers all aspects of the steel sector of the building industry.

STEEL DESIGN/CONSTRUCTION METALLIQUE. see *ARCHITECTURE*

691.2   GW   ISSN 0940-6905
STEIN. 1884. m. DM.196.80 (students DM.150) (effective 1997). Callwey Verlag, Postfach 800409, 81604 Munich, Germany. TEL 49-89-436005-0. FAX 49-89-43600513. Ed. Horst Wanetschek. adv.; bk.rev.; bibl.; illus.; stat.; index. circ. 7,800. **Indexed:** IBR. **Document type:** trade publication.
—CCC.
Former titles: Steinmetz und Bildhauer (ISSN 0039-1034); Steinmetz und Steinbildhauer.

690   GW   ISSN 0942-7538
TN950.A1
STEINTIME; bauen mit Naturstein. 1992. s-a. DM.35. Callwey Verlag, Postfach 800409, 81604 Munich, Germany. TEL 49-89-436005-0. FAX 49-89-43600513. circ. 23,000. **Indexed:** IBR. **Document type:** trade publication.

622.3   SW   ISSN 0346-1866
STEN; the Scandinavian stone industries magazine. 1939. q. SEK 280 (effective 1997). Sveriges Stenindustrifoerbund - Swedish Stone Industries Federation, P.O. Box 106, S-121 22 Johanneshov, Sweden. TEL 46-08-81-86-00. FAX 46-08-81-86-02. (Co-sponsor: Stenindustriens Landssammenslutning, Norge) Ed. Christer Kjellen. adv.: B&W page SEK 7700, color page SEK 11200; trim 190 x 260. circ. 8,800 (controlled). **Description:** Directed to architects and building contractors in the Scandinavian countries.

690 336.2   GW
STEUER-BRIEF FUER DAS BAU- UND BAUNEBENGEWERBE. m. DM.9.85 per no. (effective 1997). Verlag Peter Deubner GmbH, Wolfgang-Mueller-Str. 14, 50968 Cologne, Germany. TEL 49-221-9370180. FAX 49-221-93701890. **Document type:** bulletin.
Formerly: Steuer-Brief fuer das Baugewerbe (ISSN 0946-4603)

691 388   UK
STONE FEDERATION HANDBOOK. a. (Stone Federation of Great Britain) Ealing Publications Ltd., Herald House, 96 Dominion Rd., Worthing, W. Sussex BN14 8JP, England. TEL 44-1903-821082. FAX 44-1903-821081. (Alt. addr.: Stone Federation of Great Britain, 18 Mansfield St., London W1M 9FG, England) **Document type:** directory.
Description: Lists members of the Stone Federation of Great Britain and indicates their specific interests.

690 720   US   ISSN 0160-7243
NB1
STONE IN AMERICA. 1889. m. $30 (foreign $37). American Monument Association, 30 Eden Alley, Ste. 301, Columbus, OH 43215-2000. TEL 614-461-5852. FAX 614-461-1497. Ed. Pennie L. Sabel. R&P contact: Pennie L. Sabel. adv. contact: Pennie L. Sabel. bk.rev.; illus. circ. 2,200. **Document type:** trade publication.
Formerly (until 1977): Monumental News-Review (ISSN 0027-075X)

690   FR   ISSN 0183-455X
STORES ET FERMETURES. 7/yr. 320 F. (foreign 420 F.) (effective 1997); newsstand price: 55 F. Editions Ampere, Groupe C.E.P.P., 25 rue Dagorno, 75012 Paris, France. TEL 33-1-43473020. FAX 33-1-43465818.
Description: Treats windows, awnings, locks, shutters, blinds.

690   RU   ISSN 0039-2375
STROITEL'. 1955. m. 16.80 Rub. Tret'yakovskii pr., 1, 103012 Moscow, Russia. TEL 7-095-9283448. bk.rev.; bibl.; index. **Indexed:** Chem.Abstr.

STROITEL'NAYA MEKHANIKA I RASCHET SOORUZHENII. see *ENGINEERING — Engineering Mechanics And Materials*

691   BU
STROITELNI MATERIALI I SILIKATNA PROMISHLENOST. 1960. m. 4.10 lv.($18) Ministerstvo na Stroezhite i Arkhitekturata, Sofia, Bulgaria. (Dist. by: Hemus, 6, Rouski Blvd., 1000 Sofia, Bulgaria) circ. 2,500. **Indexed:** Art & Archaeol.Tech.Abstr., BSL Geo., Chem.Abstr.

690   KR
STROITEL'NYE MATERIALY I KONSTRUKTSII. (Text in Russian) 1959. q. $6. (Gosudarstvennyi Komitet Ukrainy po Delam Stroitel'stva i Arkhitektury) Izdatel'stvo Ukrarkhstroyinform, Menzhinskogo, 71, Kiev-135, Ukraine. (Co-sponsor: Ministerstvo Promyshlennosti Stroitel'nykh Materialov Ukrainskoi S.S.R.) Ed. G.A. Neporozhnaya. adv.; illus.; index. circ. 6,000. (tabloid format) **Indexed:** Chem.Abstr.
—BLDSC (0019.500000); Linda Hall.
Formerly (until 1975): Budivel'ni Materialy i Konstruktsii (ISSN 0007-2974)

690   BU   ISSN 0562-1852
CODEN: STRVA5
STROITELSTVO. (Text in Bulgarian; summaries in German and Russian) 1954. m. 6 lv.($12) Ministerstvo na Stroezhite i Arkhitekturata, Sofia, Bulgaria. (Dist. by: Hemus, 6, Rouski Blvd., 1000 Sofia, Bulgaria) (Co-sponsor: Nauchno- Tekhnicheski Suiuz po Stroitelstvo) circ. 3,997. **Indexed:** BSL Geo., BSL Indus., BSL Math., C.I.S. Abstr., Chem.Abstr., Geotech.Abstr.
—CASDDS.

690   KR   ISSN 0039-2405
STROITEL'STVO I ARKHITEKTURA. 1953. m. 24.60 Rub. Spilka Arkhitektiv Ukrayiny, Kiev, Ukraine. **Indexed:** Archit.Per.Ind., C.R.I.Abstr., C.R.I.Curr.Cont.
—Linda Hall.

STRUCTURAL MOVER. see *ENGINEERING — Civil Engineering*

692 620   UK   ISSN 0263-080X
TA630
STRUCTURAL SURVEY. 1982. 5/yr. £439($679) (foreign Aus.$849) (effective 1998). M C B University Press Ltd., 60-62 Toller Ln., Bradford, W. Yorks BD8 9BY, England. TEL 44-1274-777700. FAX 44-1274-785200. TELEX 51317-MCBUNI-G. URL: http://www.mcb.co.uk. Eds. Anthony Poole, Mike Hoxley. bk.rev.; cum.index. (reprint service avail. from SWZ) **Indexed:** Br.Ceram.Abstr., Br.Tech.Ind. **Document type:** bulletin.
●Also available on CD-ROM.
—BLDSC (8478.610000); CISTI. CCC.

693.6   GW   ISSN 0941-7583
STUCK - PUTZ - TROCKENBAU. 1947. 11/yr. DM.169 (foreign DM.180). (Stuckgewerbebund im Zentralverband des Deutschen Baugewerbes) C. Maurer Druck und Verlag, Schubartstr. 21, 73312 Geislingen, Germany. TEL 49-7331-930156. FAX 49-7331-930190. Ed. Paul Dolt. adv. contact: Sybille Lutz. circ. 5,800. **Document type:** trade publication.
Former titles (until 1992): Stukkateur (ISSN 0177-1477); (until 1984): Stuckgewerbe (ISSN 0344-8711)

690   GW
SUEDDEUTSCHE BAUWIRTSCHAFT. 1951. m. DM.42. Verlag Sueddeutsche Bauwirtschaft, Wilhelm-Hertz-Str. 14, 70192 Stuttgart, Germany. TEL 49-711-2573333. FAX 49-711-2573422. Ed. Horst Kimmich; Pub. Horst Kimmich. adv.: B&W page DM.2000; trim 250 x 180. bk.rev.; charts; illus.; stat.; tr.lit. circ. 5,000. **Document type:** consumer publication.

690   US   ISSN 0745-354X
SUN BELT BUILDING JOURNAL.* 1976. m. $11. Sun Belt Publishing Co., 5151 N. 16th St., Phoenix, AZ 85016-3908. Ed. Jerry Rockwell. adv.; bk.rev. circ. 8,263.

692.8   US
SUPERINTENDING FOR CONTRACTORS: HOW TO BRING JOBS IN ON TIME, ON BUDGET. 1987. irreg. $34.95. R.S. Means Company, Inc., 100 Construction Plaza, Kingston, MA 02364. TEL 617-585-7880. Ed. Bd. charts; illus.
Formerly (until 1991): Superintending for the General Contractor.

338.4   IR   ISSN 0301-7478
SURVEY OF CONSTRUCTION ACTIVITIES OF THE PRIVATE SECTOR IN URBAN AREAS OF IRAN. q. free. Bank Markazi Jomhouri Islami Iran, Economic Statistics Department - Central Bank of the Islamic Republic of Iran, P.O. Box 11365-8531, Tehran, Iran. FAX 98-21-390323. illus.; stat.

691   SW   ISSN 0284-432X
SVERIGES BYGG- OCH INSTALLATIONSVAROR; generalagenter - Tillverkare. 1987. a. SEK 655 (effective 1990). Svensk Byggtjaenst, S-171 88 Solna, Sweden.

SVERIGES LANTBRUKSUNIVERSITET. INSTITUTIONEN FOER JORDBRUKETS BIOSYSTEM OCH TEKNOLOGI. SPECIALMEDDELANDE/SWEDISH UNIVERSITY OF AGRICULTURAL SCIENCES. DEPARTMENT OF AGRICULTURAL BIOSYSTEMS AND TECHNOLOGY. SPECIAL REPORT. see *AGRICULTURE*

690   SW   ISSN 1401-1514
SWEDEN. BYGGFORSKNINGSRAADET. ANSLAGSRAPPORT. 1995. irreg. price varies. Byggforskningsraadet - Swedish Council for Building Research, Box 12866, S-112 98 Stockholm, Sweden. TEL 46-8-617-73-00. FAX 46-8-617-74-60. TELEX 10398. URL: http://www.bfr.se. (Subscr. to: Byggdok, St. Eriksg. 46, S-112 34 Stockholm, Sweden. TEL 46-8-617-74-00. FAX 46-8-617-74-60)
—BLDSC (7257.650000); CISTI.
Formed by the merger of (1975-1995): Sweden. Swedish Council for Building Research. Document (ISSN 0347-0962); Which was formerly (1969-1975): Sweden. National Swedish Building Research. Document (ISSN 0586-6766); (1992-1994): Sweden. Byggforskningsraadet - R (ISSN 1103-6346); Which was formerly (1980-1992): Sweden. Byggforskningsraadet - Rapport (ISSN 0349-3296); (1961-1979): Sweden. Byggforskningen - Rapport (ISSN 0346-5616)

BUILDING AND CONSTRUCTION

690   SW   ISSN 1400-6995
SWEDISH BUILDING RESEARCH. (Text in English) 1995. 4/yr. free. Byggforskningsraadet - Swedish Council for Building Research, Box 12866, S-112 98 Stockholm, Sweden. TEL 46-8-6177300. E-mail: kerstin.franklin@bfr.se; URL: http://www.bfr.se. Ed. Kerstin Franklin. **Document type:** academic/scholarly publication.
—BLDSC (8573.858600).
     Formed by the merger of (1987-1995): Sweden. Statens Raad foer Byggnadsforskning; (1990-1995): Newsletter of Swedish Building Research (ISSN 1102-3554); Which was formerly (1977-1990): Swedish Building Research News (ISSN 0349-0254)

690   CN   ISSN 1190-9072
SWEET'S CANADIAN CONSTRUCTION CATALOGUE. CD-ROM edition: Sweetsource. (Text in English, French) 1966. a. free. McGraw-Hill Information Systems Company of Canada, 270 Yorkland Blvd., North York, ON M2J 1R8, Canada. TEL 416-496-3100. FAX 416-496-3123. Ed. B.I. Fallis. circ. 7,000 (controlled). **Document type:** directory, catalog.
● Also available on CD-ROM.
—CISTI.
     Formerly (until 1988): Sweet's Canadian Construction Catalogue File (ISSN 0082-0431)

690   US
SWEET'S GENERAL BUILDING AND RENOVATION FILE. 1906. a. $350. Sweet's Catalog Files (Subsidiary of: McGraw-Hill, Inc.), 1221 Ave. of the Americas, New York, NY 10020. TEL 212-512-4450. FAX 212-512-2348. Pub. Robert Russell, Jr. circ. 25,000. **Document type:** catalog.
     Formerly: Sweet's General Building Catalog File.

690   US
SWEET'S HOMEBUILDING & REMODELING FILE. a. $60. Sweet's Catalog Files (Subsidiary of: McGraw-Hill, Inc.), 1221 Ave. of the Americas, New York, NY 10020. TEL 212-512-4450. FAX 212-512-2348. Pub. Robert Russell, Jr. circ. 29,000 (controlled). **Document type:** catalog.

690   US   ISSN 1056-5272
TA215
SWEET'S INDUSTRIAL CONSTRUCTION AND RENOVATION FILE. a. free to qualified personnel. Sweet's Catalog Files (Subsidiary of: McGraw-Hill, Inc.), 1221 Ave. of the Americas, New York, NY 10020. TEL 212-512-4450. FAX 212-512-2348. Pub. Robert Russell, Jr. circ. 25,000 (controlled). **Document type:** catalog.

690   US
SWEET'S INTERNATIONAL BUILDING PRODUCTS CATALOG FILE. a. free to qualified personnel. Sweet's Catalog Files (Subsidiary of: McGraw-Hill, Inc.), 1221 Ave. of the Americas, New York, NY 10020. TEL 212-512-4450. FAX 212-512-2348. Pub. Robert Russell, Jr. circ. controlled. **Document type:** catalog.
     Formerly: Sweet's International Construction File.

690   US
SWEET'S INTERNATIONAL PRODUCTLINE. 1993. q. Sweet's Catalog Files (Subsidiary of: McGraw-Hill, Inc.), 1221 Ave. of the Americas, New York, NY 10020. TEL 212-512-4750. FAX 212-512-4302. Ed. Brenda Griffin. adv.; circ. controlled. (tabloid format)
     Description: Provides the latest up-to-date information on building product materials for the international market.

749.63   US
SWEET'S LIGHT SOURCE. 1906. a. Sweet's Catalog Files, 1221 Ave. of the Americas, New York, NY 10020. TEL 212-512-4450. FAX 212-512-2348. Pub. Robert Russell, Jr. adv.; circ. 21,000 (controlled). **Document type:** catalog.

690   US
SWEET'S PRODUCTLINE. q. Sweet's Catalog Files (Subsidiary of: McGraw-Hill, Inc.), 1221 Ave. of the Americas, New York, NY 10020. TEL 212-512-4750. FAX 212-512-4302. Ed. Brenda Griffin; Pub. Gloria Glowacki. adv.; circ. 25,000 (controlled). (tabloid format); back issues avail.)
     Description: Provides up-to-date information, in a 4-color format, on building products.

797.21 690   US   ISSN 0899-1022
GV837.A1
SWIMMING POOL - SPA AGE. 1926. m. (plus a. Data & Reference directory). $48 (foreign $108). Intertec Publishing Corp. (Atlanta), 6151 Powers Ferry Rd., N.W., Atlanta, GA 30339-2941. TEL 770-955-2500. FAX 770-955-0400. Ed. Michael Pallerino. adv.; charts; illus.; tr.lit. circ. 17,149. (tabloid format; also avail. in microform from UMI; reprint service avail. from UMI) **Document type:** trade publication.
—UMI. CCC.
     Former titles (until 1988): Swimming Pool Age and Spa Merchandiser (ISSN 0279-134X); Swimming Pool Weekly and Swimming Pool Age (ISSN 0039-7393); **Supersedes:** Swimming Pool Age.
     Description: Covers news about the design, building, installation, operation and maintenance of swimming pools, spas and hot tubs, and the wholesale and retail distribution of their supplies and accessories.

690 797.2   US
SWIMMING POOL - SPA AGE PRODUCT DIRECTORY. 1933. a. $44.95. Intertec Publishing Corp. (Atlanta), 6151 Powers Ferry Rd., N.W., Atlanta, GA 30339-2941. TEL 770-955-2500. FAX 770-955-0400. Ed. Michael Pallerino. adv. circ. 17,149. **Document type:** directory.
     Former titles (until 1992): Swimming Pool - Spa Age Data and Reference Annual; Swimming Pool Age Data and Reference Annual; Swimming Pool Weekly - Age - Data and Reference Annual.

690   FR   ISSN 0989-2583
SYCODES INFORMATIONS. 1989. 6/yr. 350 F. Agency of Quality Construction, 9 bd. Malesherbes, 75008 Paris, France. TEL 44-51-03-51. FAX 47-42-81-71. Ed. Pierre Debomy. adv. circ. 5,000.

690   US   ISSN 1059-4450
SYSTEMS BUILDING REVIEW. 1990. q. free to qualified personnel. Systems Builders Association, Inc., 28 Lowry Dr., Box 117, W. Milton, OH 45383. TEL 513-698-4188. FAX 513-698-6153. Ed. Christopher Long. adv.; illus.; tr.lit.
     Description: Provides information on technical, legal, and general developments in the systems building industry, for the building, design, development, and financial communities.

690   NE
T N O BUILDING AND CONSTRUCTION RESEARCH. ANNUAL REPORT. (Text in Dutch, English) 1954. a. free. T N O Building and Construction Research, P.O. Box 49, 2600 AA Delft, Netherlands. TEL 31-15-2842000. FAX 31-15-2843990. TELEX 38270. E-mail: info@bouw.tno.nl; URL: http://www.bouw.tno.nl; http://www.tno.nl/instit/bouw/home.html. bibl.; charts; illus. circ. 2,500. **Document type:** corporate report.
     Formerly: Institute T N O for Building Materials and Building Structures. Annual Report.

690   JA   ISSN 0387-2254
CODEN: TKGJAW
TAISEI KENSETSU GIJUTSU KENKYUJOHO/TAISEI TECHNICAL RESEARCH REPORT. (Text in Japanese; summaries in English, Japanese) 1968. a. Taisei Kensetsu K.K., Gijutsu Kenkyujo - Taisei Corp., Technology Research Center, 344-1, Nase-cho, Tosuka-ku, Yokohama-shi, Kanagawa-ken 245, Japan. **Indexed:** Alloys Ind., Chem.Abstr., Eng.Mat.Abstr., INIS Atomind., Met.Abstr., Met.Abstr.Ind., Nonfer.Met.Alert, PCC Alert, Steels Alert, World Alum.Abstr.
—CASDDS.

690   JA   ISSN 0285-5445
TAISEI QUARTERLY. (Text in Japanese; summaries in English) 1961. q. Taisei Kensetsu K.K., 25-1 Nishishinjuku 1-chome, Shinjuku-ku, Tokyo 160, Japan.

690   JA   ISSN 0374-4663
TAKENAKA GIJUTSU KENKYU HOKOKU/TAKENAKA TECHNICAL RESEARCH REPORT. 1966. s-a. free. (Takenaka Komuten Gijutsu Kenkyujo - Takenaka Technical Research Laboratory) Takenaka Komuten Co., Ltd., 1-13, Hon-machi 4-chome, Chuo-ku, Osaka-shi, Osaka 541, Japan. (back issues avail.) **Indexed:** Eng.Ind., INIS Atomind., INSPEC (1971-), JTA.
—BLDSC (8601.077000); AskIEEE; KR SourceOne.

690 340.5   GW   ISSN 0935-7211
TASCHENLEXIKON BAU- UND ARCHITEKTENRECHTLICHER ENTSCHEIDUNGEN. 1978. irreg. DM.118. Erich Schmidt Verlag GmbH & Co. (Berlin), Genthiner Str. 30G, 10785 Berlin, Germany. TEL 49-30-250085-0. FAX 49-30-25008521. **Document type:** bulletin.

690   AT
TASMANIAN MASTER BUILDER. 1950. m. Aus.$55 (effective 1998). Master Builders' Association of Tasmania, G.P.O. 992 K, Hobart, Tas. 7001, Australia. TEL 61-03-6232377. FAX 61-03-6234194. Ed. Wesley Phillips. adv.: color page Aus.$1000; adv. contact: Wesley Phillips. bk.rev. circ. 900. **Document type:** newsletter, trade publication.
     Formerly: Tasmanian Building Journal.
     Refereed Serial

TEAM S P I NEWS. see *PHYSICAL FITNESS AND HYGIENE*

690   BL   ISSN 0104-1053
TECHNE. 1992. bi-m. $75 (effective 1997). Editora Pini Ltda., Rua Anhaia 964, Bom Retiro, 01130-900 Sao Paulo, SP, Brazil. TEL 55-11-2248811. Ed. Mario Sergio Pini. adv. contact: Luiz Carlos F. Oliveira. **Document type:** directory.

690   IS   ISSN 0792-0776
TECHNION - ISRAEL INSTITUTE OF TECHNOLOGY. RESEARCH REPORTS. (Text in English) biennial. free. Technion - Israel Institute of Technology, National Building Research Institute, Technion City, Haifa 32000, Israel. TEL 972-4-8292242. FAX 972-4-8324534. TELEX 46406-TECON-IL. Ed. Monica Paciuk.

690   GW   ISSN 0178-5796
TECHNISCHE UNIVERSITAET BRAUNSCHWEIG. INSTITUT FUER BAUSTOFFE, MASSIVBAU UND BRANDSCHUTZ. SCHRIFTENREIHE. 1963. irreg. (approx. 6/yr.). Technische Universitaet Braunschweig, Institut fuer Baustoffe, Massivbau und Brandschutz, Beethovenstr. 52, 38106 Braunschweig, Germany. TEL 49-531-3915454. FAX 49-531-3914573. E-mail: o.dienelt@tu-bs.de. **Document type:** monographic series, proceedings.
     Formerly (until 1978): Institut fuer Baustoffkunde und Stahlbetonbau. Schriftenreihe (ISSN 0178-580X)

690   AU
TECHNOPRESS BAU MAGAZIN; fuer Baustoffe, Elemente und Zubehoer. 1974. q. S.160($9.60) Technopress Fachzeitschriften Verlagsgesellschaft mbH, Iglaseegasse 21-23, Postfach 176, A-1191 Vienna, Austria. TEL 43-1-322551. FAX 43-1-3207427. adv.; bk.rev.; abstr.; illus. circ. 21,000 (controlled). **Document type:** trade publication.
     Formerly: Bau Magazin.

690   IT   ISSN 0040-1803
TECNICA E RICOSTRUZIONE. 1946. bi-m. L.3500. Ordine degli Ingegneri della Provincia di Catania, Via Giuffrida 202, 95125 Catania, Sicily, Italy. Ed. Sebastiano Quatarone. adv.; bk.rev.; illus.; mkt.

690   VE   ISSN 0798-9601
TECNOLOGIA Y CONSTRUCCION. 1985. s-a. Bs.1500($20) to individuals; institutions Bs.2000 ($25). Instituto de Desarrollo Experimental de la Construccion, Facultad de Arquitectura y Urbanismo, Apdo. Postal 47169, Caracas 1041-A, Venezuela. TEL 58-2-6931269. FAX 58-2-6931183. Dir. Maria Elena Hobaica. abstr.; bibl.; charts; maps; index.
     Refereed Serial

691   DK   ISSN 0040-2141
TEGL. 1897. q. DKK 110. Murerfagets Oplysningsraad - Information Council of the Masons Association, Peblinge Dossering 36, DK-2200 Copenhagen N, Denmark. TEL 31-37-25-00. FAX 31-39-70-37. Ed. Soeren Boegh. adv.; bk.rev.; charts; illus.; tr.lit. circ. 10,500. **Indexed:** Chem.Abstr.
—BLDSC (8763.537000).

690 669   JA
TEKKOTSU/STEEL FRAME. (Text in Japanese) 1983. s-a. Tekkotsu Kensetsugyo Kyokai - Japan Steel Constructors Association, 2-18, Ginza 2-chome, Chuo-ku, Tokyo 104, Japan.

BUILDING AND CONSTRUCTION

690   SI
TENDERS ESTIMATING DATA SERVICE. (Text in English) 1988. s-a. $200. Construction Industry Development Board, 9 Maxwell Rd., No. 03-00, Annexe A, MND Complex, Singapore 069112, Singapore. TEL 65-2256711. FAX 65-2257301. E-mail: cidb__enquiry@cidb.gov.sg. circ. 200.

729.7
TERRAZZO TOPICS.* vol.59, 1970. 10/yr. membership. National Terrazo and Mosaic Association, 110 E. Market St., Ste. 200A, Leesburg, VA 20176-3122. circ. 1,500. **Document type:** newsletter.
  Formerly: Terrazzo Trends.
  Description: Covers activities of the association.

690   US   ISSN 0164-8012
TEXAS BUILDER. 1989. bi-m. $12. Oliver Publications, Box 8619, Ft. Worth, TX 76124-0619. TEL 817-451-8951. Ed. Rene Adams; Pub. Becky Oliver. adv.; circ. 10,000 (paid). **Document type:** trade publication.

690   US   ISSN 1077-1867
TEXAS CONSTRUCTION. 1993. m. $23.50. McGraw-Hill Companies, Texas Construction, 2900 Westfork Dr., Ste. 345, Baton Rouge, LA 70827. TEL 713-529-4895. FAX 713-524-7639. Ed. Maretta Tubb. adv. contact: Maelane Rhodes. circ. 6,500. **Document type:** trade publication.
  Description: Focuses on Texas construction and industrial markets.

692.8
TEXAS CONTRACTOR. 1923. s-m. $40. Peters Publishing Co. of Texas, Box 551359, Dallas, TX 75355-1359. TEL 972-271-2693. FAX 972-278-4652. Ed. Trey Randal; Pub. Weldon K. McDonald. R&P contact: Trey Randal. adv. contact: Don Schmidt. circ. 7,050. **Document type:** trade publication.

THAI BUILDERS DIRECTORY. see *BUSINESS AND ECONOMICS — Trade And Industrial Directories*

643.7   US   ISSN 1086-2633
TH4805
▼**THIS OLD HOUSE.** 1995. bi-m. $21; newsstand price: $3.50 (Can.$4.50). Time Publishing Ventures, Inc., 20 W. 43rd Fl., 8th Fl., New York, NY 10036. TEL 212-522-9465; 800-898-7237. E-mail: letters@toh.timeinc.com. (Subscr. to: Box 58368, Boulder, CO 80323-8368) Ed. Stephen L. Petranek; Pub. Tom Ott. R&P contact: Brooke Deterling. adv. contact: Marie Isabelle. illus.; tr.lit. **Document type:** consumer publication.
  Description: Covers the renovation and decoration of old houses.

690.028   AT
THOMSON'S CONSTRUCTION AUSTRALIA. 1968. m. Aus.$69. Thomson Business Publishing, 47 Chippen St., Chippendale, N.S.W. 2008, Australia. TEL 02-699-2411. FAX 02-698-3920. Ed. June Cummings. adv.: B&W page Aus.$1650, color page Aus.$ 2780. illus.; tr.lit. circ. 10,420. (back issues avail.) **Document type:** trade publication.
  Formerly (until 1986): C E N (Construction Equipment News) (ISSN 0007-8247)
  Description: For private construction and civil engineering companies, subcontractors, suppliers and manufacturers.
  Refereed Serial

690   GW   ISSN 0944-8780
TIEFBAU. 1889. m. DM.60. Erich Schmidt Verlag GmbH & Co. (Bielefeld), Viktoriastr. 44A, 33602 Bielefeld, Germany. TEL 49-521-58308-0. (Subscr. to: Postfach 102451, 33524 Bielefeld, Germany) Ed.Bd. adv.; bk.rev. circ. 26,520. **Indexed:** C.I.S.Abstr., Dok.Str., Geotech.Abstr. **Document type:** trade publication.
  —SWETS. **CCC.**
  Formerly: Tiefbauberufsgenossenschaft (ISSN 0340-952X)

690 338.4 747   FI   ISSN 0356-3987
TIKKURILAN VIESTI. Swedish edition: Dickursby Meddelanden (ISSN 0356-3995) 1929. s-a. free. Tikkurila Oy, Kuninkaalantie 1, P.O. Box 53, FIN-01301 Vantaa. TEL 358-0-85-72-71. FAX 358-0-8577-6900. Ed. Visa pekkarinen. circ. 30,000. (back issues avail.) **Document type:** trade publication.

TILE AND DECORATIVE SURFACES. see *CERAMICS, GLASS AND POTTERY*

TILE NEWS. see *CERAMICS, GLASS AND POTTERY*

TILING NEWS. see *CERAMICS, GLASS AND POTTERY*

690   US   ISSN 1061-9860
TH1101
TIMBER FRAMING. 1985. q. $20 (effective 1997). Timber Framers Guild of North America, Box 1075, Bellingham, WA 98227. TEL 360-733-4001. FAX 360-733-4002. E-mail: tfguild@telcomplus.com; URL: http://www.tfguild.org. Ed. Kenneth Rower; Pub. Ken Rower. R&P contact: Ken Rower. adv. contact: Ken Rower. bk.rev.; index. (back issues avail.) **Document type:** trade publication.
  Formerly: Timber Framers News.
  Description: Reports on the guild's work and membership activities with articles about history, house design, engineering, mechanical systems, traditional building, timber framing abroad, and forest preservation for builders, owners, and designers.

TIMES (BETHLEHEM). see *HOUSING AND URBAN PLANNING*

690   JA   ISSN 0910-917X
TODA KENSETSU GIJUTSU KENKYU HOKOKU/TODA TECHNICAL RESEARCH REPORT. (Text in English, Japanese) 1974. a. Toda Kensetsu K.K., Gijutsu Kenkyujo - Toda Corp., Technical Research Laboratory, 315, Kaname, Tsukuba-shi, Ibaraki-ken 300-26, Japan.

690   JA
TOKEN GEPPO/TOKEN MONTHLY. (Text in Japanese; summaries in English, Japanese) 1951. m. 300 Yen per no. Tokyo Kensetsugyo Kyokai - Associated General Contractors of Tokyo, 5-1, Hatchobori 2-chome, Chuo-ku, Tokyo 104, Japan.

690   JA   ISSN 0285-4546
TOKYU KENSETSU GIJUTSU KENKYUJOHO/TOKYU CONSTRUCTION TECHNICAL REPORTS. (Text in Japanese; summaries in English, Japanese) 1973. a. Tokyu Kensetsu K.K., Gijutsu Kenkyujo - Tokyu Construction Co., Ltd., Technological Research Institute, 13-9, Miyazaki 2-chome, Miyamae-ku, Kawasaki-shi, Kanagawa-ken, Japan.

690   US
TOLERANCES VARIATIONS AND PRE-EXISTING SITE CONDITIONS FOR THE WALL AND CEILING INDUSTRIES. 1990. 2/yr. $45. Foundation of the Wall and Ceiling Industry, 307 E. Annandale Rd., Ste. 200, Falls Church, VA 22042-2433. TEL 703-538-1614. FAX 703-534-8307. **Document type:** directory.

690 669   JA
TOMOEGUMI TEKKOJO GIHO/TOMOEGUMI IRON WORKS TECHNICAL REPORT. (Text in Japanese; summaries in English, Japanese) 1988. a. Tomoegumi Tekkojo, 2-10, Ginza 6-chome, Chuo-ku, Tokyo 104, Japan.

TOP CONTACTS. see *BUSINESS AND ECONOMICS — Trade And Industrial Directories*

690 658   UK
TOP SOCIETY. 1978. q. free. National Merchant Buying Society, 3 Chancery Place, Millstone Ln., Leicester LE1 5JN, England. TEL 44-116-253-0531. FAX 44-116-251-7589. Ed. Denis Gray. adv. contact: Laura Gray. circ. 2,500. (back issues avail.) **Document type:** newsletter.

690   JA   ISSN 1340-3249
TOYO CONSTRUCTION TECHNICAL RESEARCH REPORTS. (Text in English, Japanese) 1976. a. Toyo Kensetsu K.K. Gijutsu Kenkyujo, Gijutsu Kenkyujo - Toyo Construction Co., Ltd., Technical Research Institute, 17-6, Naruohama 3-chome, Nishinomiya-shi, Hyogo-ken 663, Japan. TEL 0798-43-0661. FAX 0798-40-0694. **Document type:** academic/scholarly publication.
  Formerly: Gijutsu Kenkyujo Hokoku - Technical Research Institute. Report (ISSN 0911-338X)

690.028 388.324   US
TRACK AND TIRE. 1991. 17/yr. $19.95. 29829 Greenfield Rd., Ste. 101, Southfield, MI 48076-2201. TEL 800-872-2574. FAX 313-557-4156. Ed. John H. Osborne. adv.: B&W page $485; 6 1/4 x 9 3/4. circ. 30,100 (controlled). **Document type:** trade publication.
  Description: Contractors source for equipments, parts, trucks and related services.

690   US   ISSN 0898-0284
TRADITIONAL BUILDING. 1988. bi-m. $18. Historical Trends Corporation, 69A Seventh Ave., Brooklyn, NY 11217. TEL 718-636-0788. FAX 718-636-0750. URL: http://www.traditional-building.com. Ed. Clem Labine. R&P contact: Magnolia Shepherd. adv. contact: Susan Littman. bk.rev. circ. 16,800. **Document type:** trade publication.
  Description: Reviews products and materials for builders and restorers of historical buildings, and includes source lists for hard-to-find items.

690   GW   ISSN 0179-8006
TROCKENBAU AKUSTIK. 1984. 10/yr. DM.150 (foreign DM.155). Verlagsgesellschaft Rudolf Mueller GmbH & Co. KG, Stolberger Str. 84, 50933 Cologne, Germany. TEL 49-221-5497-0. FAX 49-221-5497326. adv.: B&W page DM.5820, color page DM.9840; trim 188 x 267. index. circ. 15,000. **Document type:** trade publication.

690   RU
TA680   CODEN: TSMTAC
TSEMENT I EGO PRIMENENIE. (Text in Russian) 1901. bi-m. $117 (effective 1998). Stroiizdat, S.-Peterburgskoe Otdeleniye, Volkhovsky per., 3, 199053 St. Petersburg, Russia. (Dist. by: Mezhdunarodnaya Kniga, ul. Dimitrova 39, Moscow G-200, Russia) Ed. Nataliya Tushenkova. adv. contact: N.A. Surovtseva. bk.rev., illus. circ. 2,300. **Indexed:** C.R.I.Abstr., C.R.I.Curr.Cont., Ceram.Abstr., Chem.Abstr.
  —CASDDS; CISTI. **CCC.**
  Formerly: Tsement (ISSN 0041-4867)

693.71   UK   ISSN 0041-3909
                           CODEN: TUSTAM
TUBULAR STRUCTURES. 1963. 3/yr. free to qualified personnel. British Steel Corp., Tubes Division, Corby Works, Corby, Northants, England. charts; illus.; stat. circ. 8,000. **Indexed:** Alloys Ind., Eng.Mat.Abstr., Met.Abstr., Met.Abstr.Ind., Nonfer.Met.Alert, PCC Alert, Steels Alert, World Alum.Abstr.
  —BLDSC (9068.300000); CISTI; Linda Hall.

TUNNELLING ACTIVITIES IN JAPAN. see *ENGINEERING — Civil Engineering*

TURKISH CONSTRUCTION CATALOG. see *ENGINEERING — Civil Engineering*

U I T B B BULLETIN. (Trade Unions International of Workers of the Building, Wood and Building Materials Industries) see *LABOR UNIONS*

691   FR
U N I C E M ANNUAIRE OFFICIEL. 1945. a. 370 F. (Union Nationale des Industries de Carrieres et Materiaux de Construction) Union Francaise d'Annuaires Professionnels, 130 av. des Bouleaux, 78192 Trappes Cedex, France. TEL 01-30-13-82-00. FAX 01-30-13-82-11. adv. circ. 5,000. **Document type:** directory.

690   US
U S COURT AND TRACK BUILDERS ASSOCIATION NEWSLINE. q. $25 (foreign $35) (effective 1997). U S Tennis Court & Track Builders Association, 3225 Ellicott Mills Dr., Apt. N, Ellicott City, MD 21043-4547. TEL 410-418-4800. FAX 410-418-4875. Ed. Carol T. Shaner. bk.rev.; circ. 750 (paid). **Document type:** newsletter.
  Description: Covers the design and building of tennis courts and tracks. Reviews new products and companies.

691   US   ISSN 0041-7661
U S GLASS, METAL & GLAZING. Variant title: U S Glass. Metal, Glazing, Auto Glass and Windows. 1966. m. $39 (effective 1997). Key Communications, Inc., Box 569, Garrissonville, VA 22463. TEL 540-720-5584. FAX 540-720-5687. E-mail: usglass@aol.com; URL: http://www.usglassmag.com. Ed. Helen Price; Pub. Debra Levy. adv. contact: Tina Czar. bk.rev.; charts; illus.; stat.; tr.lit.; circ. 20,000 (controlled). (back issues avail.) **Document type:** trade publication.
  —CISTI; Linda Hall.
  Description: Covers manufacturing and marketing segments and wholesale, retail trade relating to flat glass, auto glass, architectural metal and related products.

690   UK
ULSTER BUILDER AND ALLIED TRADES JOURNAL. 1946. m. £2.20. c/o William H. Guilfoyle, 27 Dunlambert Park, Belfast BT15 3NJ, N. Ireland.

BUILDING AND CONSTRUCTION

690 665 US
UNDERGROUND FOCUS; the magazine of below-ground damage prevention. 1986. bi-m. $20 (Canada $35; elsewhere $55). Canterbury Communications, Inc., Box 638, Spooner, WI 54801. TEL 715-635-7975. FAX 715-635-7977. E-mail: ufmagazine@underspace.com. Ed. R.N. Rosencrans; Pub. R.N. Rosencrans. R&P contact: R.N. Rosencrans. adv. contact: Scott Landers. tr.lit. circ. 25,000. **Indexed:** Corros.Abstr. **Document type:** trade publication.
Description: Covers placement and protection of below ground facilities. Includes new products, news briefs, accident file, trench cave-ins, and contractor's view.

UNDERNEATH IT ALL. see ENGINEERING

669 FR
UNION DEPARTEMENTALE DES SYNDICATS D'ENTREPRENEURS ET D'ARTISANS DU BATIMENT ET DES TRAVAUX PUBLICS DE LA HAUTE-GARONNE. OFFICIEL DU BATIMENT. m. Union Departementale des Syndicats d'Entrepreneurs et d'Artisans du Batiment et des Travaux Publics de la Haute-Garonne, 11 Blvd. des Recollets, 31078 Toulouse Cedex, France. TEL 727476.

691 FR
UNION NATIONALE DES ENTREPRENEURS PLATRIERS-PLAQUISTES, STAFFEURS ET STUCATEURS. BULLETIN. 1987. s-a. membership. Union Nationale des Entrepreneurs Platriers-Plaquistes, Staffeurs et Stucateurs, 33 Av. Kleber, 75784 Paris Cedex 16, France. adv. **Document type:** bulletin.

690 RM ISSN 1224-6026
UNIVERSITATEA POLITEHNICA DIN TIMISOARA. BULETINUL STIINTIFIC. SERIA CONSTRUCTII. (Text in English, French, German, Rumanian) 1920. a. $20 (effective 1997). Universitatea Politehnica din Timisoara, Piata Victoriei 2, 1900 Timisoara, Rumania. TEL 40-56-200333. FAX 40-56-190321. bk.rev. circ. 500. **Document type:** bulletin.
—CISTI.
Formerly: Institutul Politehnic Timisoara. Buletinul Stiintific si Tehnic. Seria Constructii (ISSN 0373-4374); Which superseded in part: Institutul Politehnic din Timisoara. Buletinul de Stiinta si Tehnica (ISSN 0563-5594).

690 US
UNIVERSITY OF ILLINOIS. SCHOOL OF ARCHITECTURE - BUILDING RESEARCH COUNCIL. COUNCIL NOTES. 1945. irreg. University of Illinois at Urbana-Champaign, School of Architecture, Building Research Council, One E. St. Mary's Rd., Champaign, IL 61820. TEL 217-333-1801; 800-336-0616. FAX 217-244-2204. circ. 3,900. (back issues avail.) **Document type:** trade publication.
—CISTI.
Formerly: University of Illinois. Small Homes Council. Building Research Council. Circulars (ISSN 0073-5396).
Description: Provides practical consumer-oriented advice on home planning, construction, and maintenance.

690 US ISSN 0073-5426
UNIVERSITY OF ILLINOIS. SCHOOL OF ARCHITECTURE - BUILDING RESEARCH COUNCIL. TECHNICAL NOTES. 1945. irreg., no.18, 1990. University of Illinois at Urbana-Champaign, School of Architecture, Building Research Council - Small Homes Council, One E. St. Mary's Rd., Champaign, IL 61820. TEL 217-333-1801. FAX 217-244-2204. **Document type:** academic/scholarly publication.
—CISTI; Linda Hall.
Description: Contains semitechnical reports on specific building problems.

690 SA ISSN 0258-9265
UNIVERSITY OF STELLENBOSCH. BUREAU FOR ECONOMIC RESEARCH. BUILDING AND CONSTRUCTION. Key Title: Building and Construction (Stellenbosch). (Text in English) 1969. q. R.650 (effective 1996 & 1997). University of Stellenbosch, Bureau for Economic Research, Private Bag 5050, University, Stellenbosch 7599, South Africa. TEL 27-21-8872810. FAX 27-21-8899225. TELEX 520-383 SA. E-mail: odjs@maties.sun.ac.za. Ed. C.H. Martin. stat.; cum.index. circ. 600. **Indexed:** Ind.S.A.Per.
Former titles (until 1986): Report on Business Conditions in the Building Industry (ISSN 0586-4941); Building Survey (ISSN 0045-3447)
Description: Discusses current conditions, problems and opportunities in the building and construction sectors.

690 PO
URBANISMO E CONSTRUCAO. 26/yr. Apdo. 9002, Repoliek, 2700 Amadora, Portugal. TEL 495-97-69. FAX 496-08-14. Ed. Mario Pedro.

690 US ISSN 0042-1383
UTAH CONSTRUCTION REPORT. 1958. q. free (foreign $20). University of Utah, Bureau of Economic and Business Research, 401 Kendall Dr., Garff Bldg., Salt Lake City, UT 84112. TEL 801-581-6333. FAX 801-581-3354. Dir. R. Thayne Robson. R&P contact: R. Thayne Robson. TEL 801-581-8274. charts; stat. circ. 2,000. **Document type:** trade publication.

690 US
UTILITY CONSTRUCTION AND MAINTENANCE. 1990. 4/yr. $12 (Canada $18; elsewhere $35) (effective 1997). Practical Communications, Inc., Box 183, Cary, IL 60013-0183. TEL 847-639-2200. FAX 847-639-9542. Ed. Alan Richter; Pub. Judith Chance. R&P contact: Alan Richter. circ. 25,500 (controlled). **Document type:** trade publication.
Description: Focuses on construction, maintenance, and equipment for managers in the utilities, public works, municipalities. Includes CATV operators and related contractors.

V & S GENERALBESKRIVELSE. see BUSINESS AND ECONOMICS — Marketing And Purchasing

V OG S GENERALBESKRIVELSE, SUPPLEMENT. see BUSINESS AND ECONOMICS — Marketing And Purchasing

V & S REGLER FOR OPMAALING AF BYGGERI. see BUSINESS AND ECONOMICS — Marketing And Purchasing

V W D - BAUWIRTSCHAFT. (Vereinigte Wirtschaftsdienste GmbH) see BUSINESS AND ECONOMICS — Investments

690 333 NE
VASTGOEDMARKT. m. fl.560 (foreign fl.760). Ten Hagen & Stam b.v. (Subsidiary of: Wolters Kluwer N.V.), Postbus 34, 2501 AG The Hague, Netherlands. TEL 31-70-3045700. FAX 31-70-3045812. adv. contact: Herman Voois. circ. 4,050 (paid); 7,955 (controlled). (tabloid format) **Document type:** trade publication.
Description: Covers the housing and office construction markets in the Netherlands.

690 GW ISSN 0507-6714
VEREIN DEUTSCHER ZEMENTWERKE. FORSCHUNGSINSTITUT DER ZEMENTINDUSTRIE. TAETIGKEITSBERICHT. (Editions in English, German) 1948. triennial. free. Verein Deutscher Zementwerke e.V., Tannenstr. 2, 40476 Duesseldorf, Germany. TEL 49-211-45781. FAX 49-211-4578296. circ. 2,000. **Document type:** trade publication.
—CISTI.

690 340 AT
VICTORIA BUILDING LEGISLATION SERVICE - UPDATES. irreg., latest Feb. 1995. price varies. Law Press (Victoria), 52-58 Chetwynd St., W. Melbourne, Vic. 3003, Australia. TEL 61-3-93208686. FAX 61-3-93208699. (Subscr. addr.: P.O. Box 334, N. Melbourne, Vic. 3051, Australia. TEL 61-3-93208623) (looseleaf format) **Document type:** government publication.

690 US
VIRGINIA BUILDER. 1988. 9/yr. $18 to non-members. Mid-Atlantic Trade Exposition Inc., 2117 Smith Ave., Chesapeake, VA 23320. TEL 757-420-2434. FAX 804-424-5954. Ed. Stacey E. Klemenc; Pubs. Joyce F. Hearn, Sandra Amidon. R&P contact: Joyce Hearn. adv.: B&W page $1300, color page $1850; trim 7 1/2 x 10; adv. contact: Michele Weatherly. circ. 5,000. **Document type:** trade publication.
Description: Features recent and upcoming HBAV events, lobbying efforts, educational programs, information on national building trends and products, and calendar listings.
Refereed Serial

VIRGINIA POLYTECHNIC INSTITUTE AND STATE UNIVERSITY. SARDO PALLET AND CONTAINER RESEARCH LABORATORY. LABORATORY REPORT. see FORESTS AND FORESTRY — Lumber And Wood

690 II ISSN 0042-7217
VISWASILPI.* (Text in Telugu) vol.3, 1970. m. Rs.3. Cherravuru Nagabhushanacharyulu, V.B. Bhavan, Narasaraopet, P.O. Guntur. Dist., Andhra Pradesh, India. adv.; bk.rev.; film rev.; play rev.; illus. circ. 1,000.

690 GW
VOITH ANNUAL REPORT. a. Voith Dienstleistungsgesellschaft mbH, Postfach 1940, 89509 Heidenheim, Germany. TEL 49-7321-37-0. FAX 49-7321-377000. **Document type:** corporate report.

690 US
THE VOLATILE WORLD OF THE CONSTRUCTION INDUSTRY. 1991. a. $395. Dun & Bradstreet Information Services (Murray Hill) (Subsidiary of: Dun & Bradstreet, Inc.), One Diamond Hill Rd., Murray Hill, NJ 07974. TEL 908-665-5224. FAX 908-771-7599. Ed. Mark Smith.
Description: Examines all facets of the construction industry and its impact on the overall economy. Also analyzes different types of construction companies and their financial condition by geographic region.

VOLKSHUISVESTINGSBELEID EN BOUWMARKT. see HOUSING AND URBAN PLANNING

690 AU
VORSCHAU. 1969. a. S.550. Forschungsgesellschaft fuer Wohnen, Bauen und Planen, Loewengasse 47, A-1030 Vienna, Austria. TEL 43-1-71262510. FAX 43-1-712625121. adv.; stat.; index; circ. controlled. **Document type:** bulletin.

690 VE
VOZ DE LA CONSTRUCCION.* 1962. m. Editor Ferga, C.A., Edif. Halven, Avda. Universidad esq. Monroy, Apdo. 16044, Caracas, Venezuela. TEL 562-28-96. TELEX 21381 CABIC VC. Ed. Eduardo Arcila Farias. circ. 5,000.

691 US ISSN 0043-0161
TH8120
WALLS & CEILINGS. 1938. m. $42 (Canada $54.94; elsewhere $78). Business News Publishing Co., 755 W. Big Beaver, Ste. 1000, Troy, MI 48084. TEL 810-362-3700. FAX 810-362-0317. URL: http://www.wco.org. (Subscr. to: Box 3212, Northbrook, IL 60065) Ed. Greg Campbell; Pub. Paula Graham. adv. contact: Mary Roberts. bk.rev.; charts; illus.; stat.; tr.lit. circ. 20,000. **Document type:** trade publication.
Formerly: Plastering Industries.
Description: For contractors, specifiers, manufacturers, architects and suppliers engaged in drywall, lath, plaster, metal framing, ceiling systems, exterior insulation, acoustics and fireproofing.

WEEKEND PROPERTY HOME FINDER. see REAL ESTATE

690 US
WEST VIRGINIA CONSTRUCTION NEWS. 1937. bi-m. $8 to non-members; members $7. Contractors Association of West Virginia, 2114 Kanawha Blvd., E., Charleston, WV 25311. TEL 304-342-1166. FAX 304-342-1074. Ed. Michael L. Clowser. adv. contact: Tom Gesner. bk.rev. circ. 1,500. **Document type:** trade publication.
Description: Articles, commentary, news items, and announcements on the legislative, economic, and regulatory issues affecting the building, highway, and heavy utility contracting industries in the state.

BUILDING AND CONSTRUCTION

690   US   ISSN 0043-3535
WESTERN BUILDER; building and engineering construction news of Wisconsin, upper Michigan, northern Illinois. 1911. w. $89. Western Builder Publishing Co., 6526 River Pkwy., Milwaukee, WI 53213. TEL 414-453-7700. FAX 414-453-8075. (Affiliate: Associated Construction Publications) Ed. John A. Keyes; Pub. John A. Keyes. adv. contact: James E. Keyes. bk.rev.; illus. circ. 4,450. **Document type:** trade publication.
—Linda Hall.

690   US   ISSN 0164-5803
WESTERN ROOFING - INSULATION - SIDING. 1978. bi-m. $12. (Western State Roofing Contractors Association) Dodson Publications Inc., 546 Court St., Reno, NV 89501-1711. TEL 702-333-1080. FAX 702-333-1081. Ed. Marc Dodson. R&P contact: Marc Dodson. adv. contact: Marc Dodson. bk.rev.; circ. 1,800 (paid); 20,000 (controlled). (also avail. in microform) **Document type:** trade publication.

690   UK   ISSN 0142-9094
WHAT'S NEW IN BUILDING. 1978. m. £48($90) Morgan-Grampian (Construction Press) Ltd. (Subsidiary of: Morgan-Grampian plc), Morgan-Grampian House, 30 Calderwood St., London SE18 6QH, England. TEL 0181-855-7777. FAX 0181-316-3169. Ed. Janice Purath. adv. contact: Ian Withum. circ. 30,000. **Document type:** trade publication.
—CCC.

698.9 643.7   US
WHO'S WHO IN THE WALL AND CEILING INDUSTRY.* a. Association of the Wall and Ceiling Industries International, 307 Annandale Rd., Ste. 200, Falls Church, VA 22042-2454. TEL 703-684-2924. FAX 703-684-2935. **Document type:** directory.

WILEY CONSTRUCTION LAW UPDATE. see *LAW*

338.476 690   US   ISSN 1087-2272
WINDOW & DOOR FABRICATOR.* 1993. bi-m. free to qualified personnel. (National Glass Association) Jervis and Associates, 11300 US Hwy. 1, Ste. 400, North Palm Beach, FL 33408-3208. E-mail: nga@glass.org; URL: http://ourworld.compuserve.com/homepages/nga. Ed. Jennifer Cetta; Pub. Nicole Harris. adv.: color page $2090; adv. contact: Mike Gribbin. circ. 8,000. **Document type:** trade publication.
Former titles: D W G Fabricator; (until 1995): D and W Fabricator.
Description: Serves fabricators and manufacturers of windows and doors. Reports the latest industry developments, technical information, management strategies, and new product information.

WINDOW INDUSTRIES. see *CERAMICS, GLASS AND POTTERY*

690 666   UK
WINDOW TRADE NEWS. 10/yr. 33-39 Bowling Green Ln., London EC1R 0DA, England. TEL 071-837-1212. FAX 071-278-4003. Ed. Peter Taylor. circ. 6,210.

690   SZ
WIR BAUEN. a. Postfach 261, CH-8840 Einsiedeln, Switzerland. TEL 055-531853. FAX 055-535915. circ. 18,000.

690   SZ
DAS WOHNEN. m. Schweizerischer Verband fuer Wohnungs Wesen, Bucheggstr. 107, CH-8057 Zurich, Switzerland. TEL 1-284240.

WOHNEN PLUS; Zeitschrift der gemeinnuetzigen Bauvereinigungen in Oesterreich. see *HOUSING AND URBAN PLANNING*

340 690   GW   ISSN 0344-8738
DER WOHNUNGSEIGENTUEMER. 1971. q. DM.16. Verlag Deutsche Wohnungswirtschaft GmbH, Cecilienallee 45, 40474 Dusseldorf, Germany. Ed. Theodor Paul. cum.index: 1971-1982, 1983-1984, 1985-1986, 1987-1988. (reprint service avail. from SCH)

690   GW   ISSN 0043-7166
WOHNUNGSEIGENTUM. 1949. m. DM.12. Verlag der Eigenwohner GmbH, Tangstedter Landstr. 83, 22415 Hamburg, Germany. adv.; bk.rev. circ. 6,910.
Formerly: Eigenwohner.

690   KO
WOLGAN KORE KAGIOK. (Text in Korean) m. Construction Association of Korea, Construction Bldg., 71-2 Nonhyun-dong, Kangnam-ku, Seoul 135-701, S. Korea. TEL 2-5476101. FAX 2-5276979.

WOOD/BOIS. see *FORESTS AND FORESTRY — Lumber And Wood*

WOOD DESIGN AND BUILDING. see *FORESTS AND FORESTRY — Lumber And Wood*

693.1   IT
WORK STONE. (Former sponsoring body: Associazione Costruttori Macchine Marmo ed Affini) (Text in English, Italian) 1983? bi-m. $60. Ever s.n.c. di Emilia Gallini & C., Galleria Ghandi 15, 20017 Milan, Italy. TEL 39-2-93900740. FAX 39-2-93900727. Ed. Giancarlo Lazzaroni. adv.: B&W page L.1239000, color page L.1764000; 210 x 297. illus. circ. 5,000.
Formerly: A C I M M per il Marmo.

691   UK   ISSN 0263-6050
TP875   CODEN: WOCEDR
WORLD CEMENT. 1928. m. £80($180) Palladian Publications Ltd., The Old Forge, Elstead, Surrey GU8 6DD, England. TEL 01252-703900. FAX 01252-703901. Ed. Paul Maxwell-Cook. adv. contact: Rod Hardy. bk.rev.; charts; illus.; pat. circ. 3,000. (also avail. in microform from UMI; back issues avail.; reprint service avail. from UMI) **Indexed:** Br.Ceram.Abstr., Br.Tech.Ind., C.R.I.Abstr., C.R.I.Curr.Cont., Ceram.Abstr., Chem.Abstr., Eng.Ind., Excerp.Med., PROMT. **Document type:** trade publication.
—BLDSC (9353.075000); CASDDS; CISTI; Ei; Linda Hall; SWETS; UMI; UnCover.
Former titles: World Cement Technology (ISSN 0308-8855); Cement Technology (ISSN 0008-8854); Cement and Lime Manufacture.

693   BE   ISSN 1013-9532
WORLD CEMENT DIRECTORY. 1958. quinquennial. $1200 (effective 1996). (European Cement Association) Cembureau, Rue d'Arlon 55, 1040 Brussels, Belgium. TEL 32-2-2341011. FAX 32-2-2304720. adv.; illus. circ. 1,500. **Document type:** directory.
Description: Information on the international cement industry; covers company management, locations of plants and their access to ports, number and types of kilns, fuel used, and production and capacity figures.

690   UK
WORLD CRANE GUIDE. a. $60. K H L International Ltd., Southfields, Southview Rd., Wadhurst, E. Sussex TN5 6TP, England. TEL 44-1892-784088. FAX 44-1892-784086. E-mail: cranes@khl.com; URL: http://ourworld.compuserve.com/homepages/cranes. R&P contact: Peter Watkinson. **Document type:** directory.

690   BE   ISSN 0777-5288
WORLD DIRECTORY OF CEMENT & CONCRETE ASSOCIATIONS. 1989. irreg., latest 1996. $40 (effective 1996). (European Cement Association) Cembureau, Rue d'Arlon 55, 1040 Brussels, Belgium. TEL 32-2-2341011. FAX 32-2-2304720. **Document type:** directory.
Description: Lists more than 200 national and international cement, precast and ready-mixed concrete associations and research institutes.

690   US   ISSN 1054-5115
WORLD FENCE NEWS. 1983. m. $24.95. World Fence News, 6101 W. Courtyard Dr., No. 3-115, Austin, TX 78730-5029. TEL 512-349-2536. Ed. Rick Henderson; Pub. Rodger D. Duke. R&P contact: Rick Henderson. adv.: B&W page $1910, color page $2635; trim 10 3/4 x 14 1/4. circ. 12,600. **Document type:** newspaper, trade publication.
Description: Contains current information on events, trends, products and services that affect the fence industry.

WORLDWIDE DIRECTORY OF CONSULTANTS AND CONTRACTORS. see *BUSINESS AND ECONOMICS — Trade And Industrial Directories*

690 334   GW
WUERTTEMBERGISCHE BAU-BERUFSGENOSSENSCHAFT. JAHRESBERICHT. a. Wuerttembergische Bau-Berufsgenossenschaft, Friedrich-Gerstlacher-Str. 15, 71032 Boeblingen, Germany. TEL 07031-6250. Ed. Petra Krisa. **Document type:** trade publication.

690 690   GW   ISSN 0172-2514
WUERTTEMBERGISCHE BAU-BERUFSGENOSSENSCHAFT. MITTEILUNGEN. 1960. 4/yr. Wuerttembergische Bau-Berufsgenossenschaft, Friedrich-Gerstlacher-Str. 15, 71032 Boeblingen, Germany. TEL 07031-625-0. FAX 07031-625-100. Ed. Horst Haun. adv.; bk.rev.; charts; illus. circ. 24,000. **Indexed:** C.I.S. Abstr. **Document type:** trade publication.
Formerly: Bau (ISSN 0005-6413)
Description: Covers safety and health protection in the building industry. Features accident prevention, safety rules, reports of events, lists of courses in safety, forthcoming events and exhibitions.

YAPI; aylik kultur, sanat ve mimarlik dergisi. see *ARCHITECTURE*

YOUR HOME. see *HOUSING AND URBAN PLANNING*

ZBORNIK ISTRAZIVACKIH RADOVA IZ OBLASTI MATERIJALA I KONSTRUKCIJA U GRADJEVINARSTVU. see *ENGINEERING — Civil Engineering*

ZEICHNEN FACHZEITSCHRIFT FUER KONSTRUIEREN UND GESTALTEN. see *ARCHITECTURE*

690   AU   ISSN 0514-2946
TA680   CODEN: ZMBEA4
ZEMENT UND BETON. 1953. q. S.240 (foreign S.320). Zement und Beton Handels- und Werbe-GmbH, Reisnerstr. 53, A-1030 Vienna, Austria. TEL 43-1-714668553. FAX 43-1-714668526. Eds. Brigitte Simma, Ernst Roubin. R&P contact: Ernst Roubin. bk.rev.; adv.; illus. circ. 4,700. **Indexed:** C.R.I.Abstr., C.R.I.Curr.Cont., Chem.Abstr. **Document type:** trade publication.
—CASDDS; Linda Hall.

692.8   JA   ISSN 0044-4006
ZENKEN JOURNAL/ZENKEN JANARU. (Text in Japanese) 1962. m. 1200 Yen. Associated General Contractors of Japan Inc. - Zenkoku Kensetsu Gyomukai, 2-5-1 Hatcho-bori, Chuo-ku, Tokyo 104, Japan. Eds. Yashio Murata, Yasuo Takata. stat.; index. circ. 10,000.

ZHILISHCHNOE I KOMMUNAL'NOE KHOZYAISTVO. see *BUSINESS AND ECONOMICS — Production Of Goods And Services*

690   RU   ISSN 0044-4472
ZHILISHCHNOE STROITEL'STVO. 1958. m. $149 (effective 1998). Gosstroi, Moscow, Russia. bk.rev.; bibl.; index. circ. 12,600. (tabloid format)
—BLDSC (0058.200000); CISTI; Linda Hall.

690 621   CC   ISSN 1001-7151
ZHONGGUO DIANTI/CHINA ELEVATOR. (Text in Chinese) 1985. bi-m. Y192 (foreign $144) (effective 1997 & 1998). China Elevator Association, 61 Jinguang Ave., Langfang, Hebei 065000, People's Republic of China. TEL 86-316-204-0577. FAX 86-316-201-0248. (Co-sponsor: China Academy of Building Research, Institute of Building Mechanization) Ed. Kerong Peng. R&P contact: Zengjian Li. adv.: color page $1680; adv. contact: Li Zengjian. circ. 5,500. **Document type:** trade publication.
Formerly: Elevator Bulletin.
Description: Comprehensive elevator, escalator, passenger converyor, parking system publication concerned with technology and market.

690   CC
ZHONGGUO JIANZHUYE NIANJIAN/CHINA BUILDING INDUSTRY ALMANAC. (Text in Chinese) 1985. a. Y60. Zhongguo Jianzhu Gongye Chubanshe, Xijiao, Baiwanzhuang, Beijing, People's Republic of China. TEL 86-10-6839-3529. FAX 86-10-6834-8830.

BUILDING AND CONSTRUCTION — ABSTRACTING, BIBLIOGRAPHIES, STATISTICS

690   GW
ZULIEFERER UND MASCHINENAUSRUESTER VON A - Z. 1985. a. Vogel Verlag und Druck GmbH & Co. KG, Max-Planck-Str. 7-9, 97082 Wuerzburg, Germany. TEL 49-931-4182145. FAX 49-931-4182905. (Subscr. to: Vogel Verlag, 97064 Wuerzburg, Germany; Dist. in US by: Vogel Europublishing, Inc., 632 Sunflower Ct., San Ramos, CA 94583. TEL 510-648-1170. FAX 510-648-1171) adv. contact: Kurt Kleindienst. circ. 30,000. **Document type:** trade publication.

BUILDING AND CONSTRUCTION —
Abstracting, Bibliographies, Statistics

690 310   US
A A M A INDUSTRY STATISTICAL REVIEW AND FORECAST. 1970. a. $100. American Architectural Manufacturers Association, 1827 Walden Office Sq., Ste. 104, Schaumburg, IL 60173-4268. TEL 847-303-5664. FAX 847-303-5774. E-mail: webmaster@AAMANET.org; URL: http://www.AAMANET.org. circ. 514. (back issues avail.) **Document type:** trade publication.

ABSTRACTS OF BULGARIAN SCIENTIFIC LITERATURE. INDUSTRY, BUILDING AND TRANSPORT. see *BUSINESS AND ECONOMICS — Abstracting, Bibliographies, Statistics*

AMERICAN IRON AND STEEL INSTITUTE. ANNUAL STATISTICAL REPORT. see *ENGINEERING — Abstracting, Bibliographies, Statistics*

690   UN   ISSN 0066-3840
HD9715.A1
ANNUAL BULLETIN OF HOUSING AND BUILDING STATISTICS FOR EUROPE. (Text in English, French, and Russian) 1957. a. price varies. Economic Commission for Europe (ECE), Palais des Nations, 1211 Geneva 10, Switzerland. TEL 022-917-2436. FAX 022-917-0036. TELEX 412962. (Orders in N. America to: United Nations Publications, Rd. DC2-853, New York, NY 10017. TEL 212-963-8302. FAX 212-963-3489; Or: Unipub, 4611-F Assembly Dr., Lanham, MD 20706. TEL 301-459-7666. FAX 301-459-0056) charts. (processed; also avail. in microfiche from CIS) **Indexed:** Geo.Abstr., IIS. **Document type:** government publication, bulletin.
—CISTI.
Formerly: U N Quarterly Housing Construction Summary for Europe (ISSN 0041-7424)
Description: Compiles statistical data on building and housing trends in Europe and North America.

695   CN   ISSN 0380-5786
ASPHALT ROOFING/PAPIER-TOITURE ASPHALTE. (Text in English and French) 1932. m. Can.$62 (foreign $62) (effective 1998). Statistics Canada, Operations and Integration Division, Circulation Management, Jean Talon Bldg., 2-C12, Tunney's Pasture, Ottawa, ON K1A 0T6, Canada. TEL 613-951-7277; 800-267-6677. FAX 613-951-1584. URL: http://www.statcan.ca. circ. 250. (also avail. in microform from MML; back issues avail.)
Description: Covers production and shipments, domestic and export of asphalt roofing shingles, sidings, tar and asphalt felts and sheathing.

690   AT   ISSN 0818-3511
AUSTRALIA. BUREAU OF STATISTICS. BUILDING ACTIVITY, AUSTRALIA: DWELLING UNIT COMMENCEMENTS, PRELIMINARY. 1953. q. Aus.$11 per no. Australian Bureau of Statistics, P.O. Box 10, Belconnen, A.C.T. 2616, Australia. **Document type:** government publication.
Description: Contains estimates of the number of dwelling units commenced for both private and public sectors, in originally and seasonally adjusted terms.

690   AT   ISSN 1031-0169
AUSTRALIA. BUREAU OF STATISTICS. BUILDING ACTIVITY, AUSTRALIAN CAPITAL TERRITORY. 1961. q. Aus.$12 per no. Australian Bureau of Statistics, P.O. Box 10, Belconnen, A.C.T. 2616, Australia. **Document type:** government publication.
Description: Contains number of dwelling units and value of residential buildings, value of alterations and additions to residential buildings, and value of non-residential building.

AUSTRALIA. BUREAU OF STATISTICS. BUILDING APPROVALS, AUSTRALIA. see *HOUSING AND URBAN PLANNING — Abstracting, Bibliographies, Statistics*

690 310   AT
AUSTRALIA. BUREAU OF STATISTICS. CONSTRUCTION INDUSTRY, AUSTRALIA: SUMMARY OF PRIVATE SECTOR OPERATIONS. 1978. irreg., latest 1989. Aus.$20. Australian Bureau of Statistics, P.O. Box 10, Belconnen, A.C.T. 2616, Australia. **Document type:** government publication.
Formerly: Construction Industry Survey: Private Sector Construction Establishments, Summary of Operations, Australia.
Description: Number of establishments operating during the year, employment, wages and salaries, components of turnover, stocks, purchases and selected expenses.

690 352.7   AT   ISSN 0729-2058
AUSTRALIA. BUREAU OF STATISTICS. NEW SOUTH WALES OFFICE. BUILDING ACTIVITY, NEW SOUTH WALES. 1948. q. Aus.$12 per no. Australian Bureau of Statistics, New South Wales Office, St. Andrews House, Sydney Square, George St., Sydney, N.S.W. 2000, Australia. **Document type:** government publication.
Description: Contains number of dwelling units and value of residential buildings, value of alterations and additions to residential buildings, and value of non-residential buildings.

690   AT   ISSN 1321-4861
AUSTRALIA. BUREAU OF STATISTICS. PRICE INDEX OF MATERIALS USED IN BUILDING OTHER THAN HOUSE BUILDING, SIX STATE CAPITAL CITIES AND CANBERRA. 1969. m. Aus.$13 per no. Australian Bureau of Statistics, P.O. Box 10, Belconnen, A.C.T. 2616, Australia. **Document type:** government publication.
Former titles: Price Index of Materials Used in Building Other Than House Building, Eight Capital Cities (ISSN 1030-9411); Price Index of Materials Used in Building Other Than House Building, Six State Capital Cities and Darwin.
Description: Measures price movements of materials delivered on site for use in constructing buildings other than houses.

690   AT   ISSN 1031-394X
AUSTRALIA. BUREAU OF STATISTICS. PRICE INDEX OF MATERIALS USED IN HOUSE BUILDING, SIX STATE CAPITAL CITIES AND CANBERRA. 1970. m. Aus.$10 per no. Australian Bureau of Statistics, P.O. Box 10, Belconnen, A.C.T. 2616, Australia. **Document type:** government publication.
Formerly: Price Index of Materials Used in House Building, Six State Capital Cities.
Description: Measures price movements of materials delivered on site for use in constructing houses.

690 352.7   AT   ISSN 0812-8332
AUSTRALIA. BUREAU OF STATISTICS. QUEENSLAND OFFICE. BUILDING ACTIVITY, QUEENSLAND. 1982. q. Aus.$12. Australian Bureau of Statistics, Queensland Office, 313 Adelaide St., Brisbane, Qld. 4000, Australia. TEL 07-222-6022. FAX 07-229-6171. TELEX AA 40271. **Document type:** government publication.
Description: Provides the number and value of dwelling units by type of new residential building. Includes statistics on buildings commenced, under construction and completed, as well as value of work done and yet to be completed by ownership and total state.

690   AT   ISSN 0726-1896
AUSTRALIA. BUREAU OF STATISTICS. SOUTH AUSTRALIAN OFFICE. BUILDING ACTIVITY, SOUTH AUSTRALIA. 1981. q. Aus.$14. Australian Bureau of Statistics, South Australian Office, G.P.O. Box 2272, Adelaide, S.A. 5001, Australia. FAX 61-8-82377566. charts. **Document type:** government publication.
Description: Contains information about the number and value of residential building commenced and completed.

AUSTRALIA. BUREAU OF STATISTICS. SOUTH AUSTRALIAN OFFICE. DWELLING UNIT COMMENCEMENTS REPORTED BY APPROVING AUTHORITIES, SOUTH AUSTRALIA. see *HOUSING AND URBAN PLANNING — Abstracting, Bibliographies, Statistics*

690 352.7   AT   ISSN 0725-5535
AUSTRALIA. BUREAU OF STATISTICS. TASMANIAN OFFICE. BUILDING ACTIVITY, TASMANIA. 1980. q. Aus.$13.50 per no. Australian Bureau of Statistics, Tasmanian Office, G.P.O. Box 66A, Hobart, Tas. 7001, Australia. **Document type:** government publication.
Description: Contains number of dwelling units and value of residential buildings for both private and public sectors.

690 352.7   AT   ISSN 0812-3071
AUSTRALIA. BUREAU OF STATISTICS. VICTORIAN OFFICE. BUILDING ACTIVITY, VICTORIA. 1950. q. Aus.$12. Australian Bureau of Statistics, Victorian Office, G.P.O. Box 2796Y, Melbourne, Vic. 3001, Australia. **Document type:** government publication.
Description: Contains number of dwelling units and value of residential buildings, value of alterations and additions to residential buildings, and value of non-residential buildings.

AUSTRALIA. BUREAU OF STATISTICS. VICTORIAN OFFICE. BUILDING APPROVALS BY STATISTICAL LOCAL AREAS, VICTORIA - SMALL AREA SUMMARY DATA REPORTS. see *HOUSING AND URBAN PLANNING — Abstracting, Bibliographies, Statistics*

AUSTRALIA. BUREAU OF STATISTICS. VICTORIAN OFFICE. BUILDING APPROVALS, VICTORIA. see *HOUSING AND URBAN PLANNING — Abstracting, Bibliographies, Statistics*

AUSTRALIA. BUREAU OF STATISTICS. WESTERN AUSTRALIAN OFFICE. DWELLING UNIT COMMENCEMENTS REPORTED BY APPROVING AUTHORITIES, WESTERN AUSTRALIA. see *HOUSING AND URBAN PLANNING — Abstracting, Bibliographies, Statistics*

690   AT   ISSN 1031-7120
HD7379.W47
AUSTRALIA. BUREAU OF STATISTICS. WESTERN AUSTRALIAN OFFICE. ESTIMATED STOCKS OF DWELLING, WESTERN AUSTRALIA. 1986. a. Aus.$18 per no. (effective 1996). Australian Bureau of Statistics, Western Australian Office, 30 Terrace Rd., E. Perth, W.A. 6004, Australia. **Document type:** government publication.
Formerly: Estimated Stocks of Dwellings in Census Collection Districts and Statistical Local Areas, Western Australia.
Description: Contains estimates of population and private dwellings.

690   AU
AUSTRIA. STATISTISCHES ZENTRALAMT. BAUSTATISTIK. (Subseries of: Beitraege zur Oesterreichischen Statistik) a. S.450 for part I, part II S.480. Oesterreichisches Statistisches Zentralamt, Hintere Zollamtsstr. 2b, A-1033 Vienna, Austria. TEL 43-1-71128-0. FAX 43-1-7156828. **Document type:** government publication.
Description: Data on classification in construction branches and customers.

331 314   AU   ISSN 1013-5626
AUSTRIA. STATISTISCHES ZENTRALAMT. WOHNUNGSDATEN. (Subseries of: Beitraege zur Oesterreichischen Statistik) 1956. a. S.350. Hintere Zollamtsstr. 2b, A-1033 Vienna, Austria. TEL 43-1-71128-0. FAX 43-1-7156828. circ. 400. **Document type:** government publication.
Formerly: Austria. Statistisches Zentralamt. Die Wohnbautaetigkeit (ISSN 0067-2300)
Description: Presents statistics on the reconstruction of homes and on the stock of occupied dwellings.

690   MX   ISSN 0187-4950
HD9715.C5
AVANCE DE INFORMACION ECONOMICA. INDUSTRIA DE LA CONSTRUCCION. 1986. q. Mex.$48($16) Instituto Nacional de Estadística, Geografía e Informatica, Secretaria de Programacion y Presupuesto, Prol. Heroe de Nacozari 2301 Sur, Puerta 11, Acceso, 20270 Aguascalientes Ags., Mexico. TEL 49-18-19-48. FAX 491-807-39. circ. 800.

690   UK
B A C M I STATISTICAL YEARBOOK. a. £20. British Aggregate Construction Materials Industries, 156 Buckingham Palace Rd., London SW1W 9TR, England. TEL 0171-730-8194. FAX 0171-730-4355. **Document type:** trade publication.

BUILDING AND CONSTRUCTION — ABSTRACTING, BIBLIOGRAPHIES, STATISTICS

B M P MONTHLY STATISTICAL BULLETIN. (Building Material Producers) see BUILDING AND CONSTRUCTION

690 333.33 UK ISSN 0261-6416
B S A MONTHLY STATISTICS DIGEST (PRESS RELEASE). 1978. m. £48 by post; by fax £125 (effective 1997). Building Societies Association, 3 Savile Row, London W1X 1AF, England. TEL 44-171-437-0655. FAX 44-171-287-0109. (also avail. by fax) **Document type:** trade publication.
Description: Provides all the information supplied in the B.S.A. monthly figures press release on mortgage lending and savings; includes a commentary.

690 314 GW ISSN 0084-7739
BAUSTATISTISCHES JAHRBUCH. 1960. a. DM.65. Hauptverband der Deutschen Bauindustrie, Abraham-Lincoln-Str. 30, 65189 Wiesbaden, Germany. TEL 49-611-7720. Ed.Bd. **Document type:** corporate report.

690 SZ
BAUTAETIGKEIT UND BAUVORHABEN IN DER SCHWEIZ/CONSTRUCTIONS EXECUTEES ET CONSTRUCTIONS PROJETEES. (Text in French and German) 1986. a. 20 SFr. Bundesamt fuer Statistik, Schwarztorstr. 96, CH-3003 Bern, Switzerland. TEL 41-31-3236060. FAX 41-31-3236061. URL: http://www.admin.ch/bfs. **Document type:** government publication.

690 331.83 BE ISSN 0772-7720
BELGIUM. INSTITUT NATIONAL DE STATISTIQUE. STATISTIQUES DE LA CONSTRUCTION ET DU LOGEMENT. Key Title: Statistiques de la Construction et du Logement - Institut National de Statistique. Dutch edition: Statistiek over Bouwnijverheid en Huisvesting (ISSN 0772-7712) (Text in French) a. 275 BEF (foreign 395 BEF) (effective 1997). Institut National de Statistique, 44 rue de Louvain, 1000 Brussels, Belgium. TEL 32-2-5486211. FAX 32-2-5486367. **Document type:** government publication.
Formerly (until 1971): Belgium. Institut National de Statistique. Batiments et Logements (ISSN 0067-544X)

690 US
BOECKH BUILDING COST INDEX. 6/yr. $115. E.H. Boeckh (Subsidiary of: Thomson Publishing Corp.), 2885 S. Calhoun Rd., Box 510291, New Berlin, WI 53151-0291. TEL 414-780-2800; 800-285-1288. FAX 414-780-0306. **Document type:** abstracting/indexing.

310 330.9 CC
BUILDING, CONSTRUCTION AND REAL ESTATE SECTORS. SURVEY. (Text in Chinese, English) 1984. a. HK.$31. Census and Statistics Department, Wanchai Tower, 12 Harbour Rd., Central, Hong Kong, People's Republic of China. TEL 852-2598-8179. FAX 852-2598-7482. (Subscr. to: Director of Information Services, Information Services Dept., 28-F Siu On Centre, 188 Lockhart Rd., Wanchai, Hong Kong; People's Republic of China) Ed. Wanda Yue. **Document type:** government publication.

690.2021 NO ISSN 0804-1334
BYGGINFO. 1992. m. NOK 370 (effective 1997); newsstand price: NOK 35. Statistisk Sentralbyraa, Box 8131 Dep., N-0033 Oslo, Norway. TEL 47-22-86-45-00. FAX 47-22-86-49-76. URL: http://www.ssb.no. circ. 4,200. **Document type:** government publication.

691 016 II ISSN 0576-9922
TA680
C R I ABSTRACTS. (Cement Research Institute of India); digest of developments & research in cement, concrete, building materials and allied industries. 1968. q. Rs.80($40) National Council for Cement and Building Materials, 34th Kilometer Stone, Delhi-Mathura Rd. (NA-2), Ballabgarh 121 004, India. TEL 91-129-242051. FAX 91-129-242100. Ed. C. Rajkumar. abstr. circ. 600. **Indexed:** C.R.I.Abstr., C.R.I.Curr.Cont. **Document type:** abstracting/indexing.

691 016 II ISSN 0970-7891
C R I CURRENT CONTENTS; a documentation list of current literature on cement, concrete, building materials and allied industries. 1969-70. bi-m. Rs.50($25) National Council for Cement and Building Materials, 34th Kilometer Stone, Delhi-Mathura Rd. (NA-2), Ballabarh 121004, India. TEL 91-129-242051. FAX 91-129-242100. Ed. G. Ramaseshan. circ. 450. **Indexed:** C.R.I.Abstr., C.R.I.Curr.Cont. **Document type:** abstracting/indexing.

690 016 SA
C S I R BUILDING TECHNOLOGY. COMPLETE LIST OF PUBLICATIONS. 1980. a. R.45. C S I R Building Technology - W N N R Boutegnologie, P.O. Box 395, Pretoria 0001, South Africa. (also avail. in diskette format) **Document type:** bibliography.
Supersedes: National Building Research Institute. Complete List of N B R I Publications (ISSN 0077-3581)
Description: Comprehensive listing of research publications in building and construction.

690 CN ISSN 0318-8809
TH26
CANADA. STATISTICS CANADA. BUILDING PERMITS/PERMIS DE BATIR. (Text in English and French) 1922. m. Can.$248 (foreign $248) (effective 1998). Statistics Canada, Operations and Integration Division, Circulation Management, Jean Talon Bldg., 2-C12, Tunney's Pasture, Ottawa, ON K1A 0T6, Canada. TEL 613-951-7277; 800-267-6677. FAX 613-951-1584. URL: http://www.statcan.ca. (also avail. in microform from MML) **Document type:** government publication.
Description: Statistics of building permits issued by municipalities; number of new dwelling units by type; value of residential, commercial, governmental and institutional building construction for individual municipalities, metropolitan areas, census divisions and provinces.

690 CN ISSN 0575-7975
HD9715.C3
CANADA. STATISTICS CANADA. BUILDING PERMITS, ANNUAL SUMMARY/PERMIS DE BATIR, SOMMAIRE ANNUEL. (Text in English and French) 1966. a. Can.$62 (foreign $62) (effective 1998). Statistics Canada, Operations and Integration Division, Circulation Management, Jean Talon Bldg., 2-C12, Tunney's Pasture, Ottawa, ON K1A 0T6, Canada. TEL 613-951-7277; 800-267-6677. FAX 613-951-1584. URL: http://www.statcan.ca. (also avail. in microform from MML) **Document type:** government publication.
—CISTI.
Description: Provides the number and value of building permits issued in more than 1600 Canadian municipalities. Includes data analysis and definitions.

690 CN ISSN 0229-6098
HD9623.C2
CANADA. STATISTICS CANADA. MINERAL WOOL INCLUDING FIBROUS GLASS INSULATION/LAINE MINERALE Y COMPRIS LES ISOLANTS EN FIBRE DE VERRE. (Text in English and French) 1950. m. Can.$62 (foreign $62) (effective 1998). Statistics Canada, Operations and Integration Division, Circulation Management, Jean Talon Bldg., 2-C12, Tunney's Pasture, Ottawa, ON K1A 0T6, Canada. TEL 613-951-7277; 800-267-6677. FAX 613-951-1584. URL: http://www.statcan.ca. (also avail. in microform from MML) **Document type:** government publication.
Description: Covers production and factory shipments of mineral wool including fibrous glass insulation used in construction.

690 BL ISSN 0103-6882
CENSO DA CONSTRUCAO. 1985. quinquennial. Fundacao Instituto Brasileiro de Geografia e Estatistica, Centro de Documentacao e Disseminacao de Informacoes, Rua General Canabarro 706, 2o andar, Maracana 20271-201 Rio de Janeiro, Brazil. TEL 55-21-2645424. FAX 55-21-2841959. **Document type:** government publication.
Description: Presents data on the number of construction establishments, employed persons, salaries and wages, withdrawals and other payments, construction costs, operational revenue, gross production value, and construction costs and expenditures.

690 US
CENSUS OF CONSTRUCTION INDUSTRIES: PRELIMINARY REPORTS. quinquennial, latest 1992. $48 for Industry Series (foreign $60); United States Summary Report $5; Subject Series $5 per no. U.S. Bureau of the Census, Customer Services, Washington, DC 20233. TEL 301-457-4100. FAX 301-457-4714. URL: http://www.census.gov/. (Subscr. to: Superintendent of Documents, U.S. Government Printing Office, Box 371954, Pittsburgh, PA 15250-7954. TEL 202-512-1800. FAX 202-512-2250; Or: Bernan, 4611-F Assembly Dr., Lanham, MD 20706. TEL 301-459-7666. FAX 301-459-0056) **Document type:** government publication.
●Also available on CD-ROM.

016 690 II
CENTRAL BUILDING RESEARCH INSTITUTE. PUBLICATIONS INDEX. (Text in English) irreg. free. Central Building Research Institute, Roorkee, Uttar Pradesh, India. TEL 91-1332-72243. FAX 91-1332-72272. (also avail. in diskette format) **Document type:** bibliography.
Formerly: Central Building Research Institute. List of Publications (ISSN 0557-322X)
Description: List of all available CBRI publications.

690 UK
CHARTERED INSTITUTE OF PUBLIC FINANCE AND ACCOUNTANCY. DIRECT SERVICE ORGANISATION STATISTICS. ACTUALS. 1982. a. £105. Chartered Institute of Public Finance and Accountancy, Statistical Information Service, 3 Robert St., London WC2N 6BH, England. TEL 44-171-543-5600. FAX 44-171-543-5700. (back issues avail.)
Former titles: Chartered Institute of Public Finance and Accountancy. Direct Labour Organisation Statistics. Actuals; Chartered Institute of Public Finance and Accountancy. Direct Labour Statistics. Actuals (ISSN 0263-2977)

690 CL
CHILE. INSTITUTO NACIONAL DE ESTADISTICAS. EDIFICACION. 1980. a. Ch.$2000 (US $13.50; elsewhere $15.90) (effective 1995). Instituto Nacional de Estadisticas, Av. Bulnes 418, Casilla 498, Correo 3 Santiago, Chile. TEL 56-2-6991441. FAX 56-2-6712169.

COMMON CARRIER MICROWAVE CONSTRUCTION PERMIT FILE. see COMMUNICATIONS — Abstracting, Bibliographies, Statistics

690.3 016 US ISSN 0045-8007
TP875 CODEN: CNASB
CONCRETE ABSTRACTS. 1972. bi-m. $194 to non-members (foreign $207); members $166 (foreign $177) (effective 1996). American Concrete Institute, Box 19150, Redford Sta., Detroit, MI 48219. TEL 313-532-2600. FAX 313-538-0655. Ed. Helayne H. Beavers. circ. 800. (back issues avail.) **Indexed:** C.R.I.Abstr., C.R.I.Curr.Cont., Corros.Abstr., J.of Ferroc. **Document type:** abstracting/indexing.
—CISTI. CCC.
Description: Summarizes and indexes US and international publications which report developments in concrete and concrete technology.

690 016 UK
CONSTRUCTION INFORMATION FILE - C I F. 1976. bi-m. £60 (overseas £75). Chartered Institute of Building, Englemere, Kings Ride, Asoct, Berks. SL5 8BJ, England. TEL 01344-23355. FAX 01344-23467. circ. 6,500. (reprint service avail. from UMI) **Indexed:** Br.Tech.Ind.
—CISTI.
Incorporates: Building Management Abstracts (ISSN 0308-9665); Formerly (until 1992): Technical Information Service - T I S (ISSN 0262-6632); Which was formed by the merger of (1971-1982): Chartered Institute of Building. Estimating Information Service (ISSN 0308-8073); (1971-1982): Chartered Institute of Building. Site Management Information Service (ISSN 0308-8081); (1977-1982): Chartered Institute of Building. Maintenance Information Service (ISSN 0140-9665); (1979-1982): Chartered Institute of Building. Surveying Information Service (ISSN 0143-649X).

BUILDING AND CONSTRUCTION — ABSTRACTING, BIBLIOGRAPHIES, STATISTICS

690 352 US ISSN 0010-6917
HD9715.U5
CONSTRUCTION REVIEW. 1955. q. $18 (foreign $22.50). U.S. International Trade Administration, Basic Industries Division, Department of Commerce, Herbert C. Hoover Bldg., ITA Rm. H4039, 14th St. and Constitution Ave., Washington, DC 20230. TEL 202-482-0132. FAX 202-482-0382. (Subscr. to: Superintendent of Documents, U.S. Government Printing Office, Box 371954, Pittsburgh, PA 15250-7954. TEL 202-512-1800. FAX 202-512-2250) Ed. Patrick H. MacAuley. charts; mkt.; stat.; cum.index; circ. 1,500 (paid). (also avail. in microform from MIM,UMI; microfiche from CIS; back issues avail.; reprint service avail. from CIS) Indexed: Amer.Stat.Ind. (1974-), B.P.I., Build.Manage.Abstr., Bus.Ind., Concr.Abstr., HongKongiana, Ind.U.S.Gov.Per., P.A.I.S., PROMT, Tr.& Indus.Ind. **Document type:** government publication.
●Also available online. Vendor(s): Information Access Co., Knight-Ridder Information, Inc., UMI.
—CISTI; KR SourceOne; Linda Hall; UMI.
Description: Compiles most federal government statistics on construction and building products.

690 CY
HD9715.C95
CYPRUS. DEPARTMENT OF STATISTICS AND RESEARCH. CONSTRUCTION AND HOUSING STATISTICS. (Text in English, Greek) a. £C5. Ministry of Finance, Department of Statistics and Research, 13 Lord Byron Ave., Nicosia, Cyprus. TEL 357-2-302349. FAX 357-2-456712. **Document type:** government publication.
Formerly: Cyprus. Department of Statistics and Research. Construction and Housing Report (ISSN 0253-8725)
Description: Presents statistical data on the construction industry and housing.

690 EC
ECUADOR. INSTITUTO NACIONAL DE ESTADISTICA Y CENSOS. ENCUESTA ANUAL DE EDIFICACIONES. a. Esc.57000($130) (effective 1993). Instituto Nacional de Estadistica y Censos, Av. 10 de Agosto 229, Quito, Ecuador. TEL 593-2-581900. FAX 593-2-580041. **Document type:** government publication.

690 MX ISSN 0186-9035
ENCUESTA TRIMESTRAL SOBRE LA INDUSTRIA DE LA CONSTRUCCION. q. Mex.$6.50($2) Instituto Nacional de Estadistica, Geografia e Informatica, Secretaria de Programacion y Presupuesto, Prol. Heroe de Nacazari 2301 Sur, Puerta 11, Acceso, 20270 Aguascalientes Ags., Mexico. TEL 49-18-19-48. FAX 491-807-39.

310 SP
ESTADISTICA DEL CEMENTO. a. 2000 ptas. Ministerio de Industria, Paseo de la Castellana, 160, Madrid 28046, Spain. FAX 259-84-80.

690 BE ISSN 1010-7185
EUROPEAN CEMENT ASSOCIATION. EUROPEAN ANNUAL REVIEW. (Text in English, French) 1951; N.S. 1979. a., no.18, 1997. $200 (effective 1996). Cembureau, Rue d'Arlon 55, 1000 Brussels, Belgium. TEL 32-2-2341011. FAX 32-2-2304720.
Formerly (until 1979): Cement Market and Outlook.
Description: Annual round-up of the European Cement Association.

338 690 BE ISSN 0777-611X
EUROPEAN CEMENT ASSOCIATION. WORLD STATISTICAL REVIEW. Key Title: World Statistical Review - Cembureau. 1959. a. $200 (effective 1996). Cembureau, Rue d'Arlon 55, 1040 Brussels, Belgium. TEL 32-2-2341011. FAX 32-2-2304720.
—BLDSC (9360.041630).
Formerly: European Cement Association. Statistical Review.
Description: Data on cement production, imports, exports and consumption.

FACHBUCHVERZEICHNIS BAUWESEN - ARCHITEKTUR (YEAR). see ARCHITECTURE — Abstracting, Bibliographies, Statistics

690 FJ ISSN 0259-6016
FIJI. BUREAU OF STATISTICS. CENSUS OF BUILDING AND CONSTRUCTION. a., latest 1993. $5 (effective 1997). Bureau of Statistics, P.O. Box 2221, Suva, Fiji. **Document type:** government publication.

690 310 FR
FRANCE. MINISTERE DE L'URBANISME ET DU LOGEMENT. STATISTIQUES DE LA CONSTRUCTION. 4/yr. 300 F. (Europe 315 F., elsewhere 330 F.) (effective 1997). Documentation Francaise, 29-31 quai Voltaire, 75344 Paris Cedex 07, France. TEL 33-1-40157000. FAX 33-1-40157230. TELEX 215 666 DOCFRAN. (Subscr. to: 124 rue Henri Barbusse, 93308 Aubervilliers Cedex, France. TEL 33-1-48395600. FAX 33-1-48395601) (also avail. in microfiche from DFR) **Document type:** government publication.
Formerly: France. Direction du Batiment, des Travaux Publics et de la Conjoncture. Statistiques de la Construction (ISSN 0338-4160)

690 314 GW ISSN 0072-1719
GERMANY. STATISTISCHES BUNDESAMT. AUSGEWAEHLTE ZAHLEN FUER DIE BAUWIRTSCHAFT. m. DM.286.60 (effective 1997). 65180 Wiesbaden, Germany. TEL 49-611-75-1. FAX 49-611-724000. TELEX 61186-STBA-D. URL: http://www.statistik-bund.de. **Document type:** government publication.

690 314 GW
GERMANY. STATISTISCHES BUNDESAMT. FACHSERIE 4, PRODUZIERENDES GEWERBE, REIHE 5: BAUGEWERBE. (Consists of three subseries: Reihe 5.1: Beschaeftigung, Umsatz und Geraetbestand der Betriebe im Baugewerbe; Reihe 5.2: Beschaeftigung, Umsatz und Investitionen der Unternehmen im Baugewerbe; Reihe 5.3: Kostenstruktur der Unternehmen im Baugewerbe) a. price varies. Statistisches Bundesamt, 65180 Wiesbaden, Germany. TEL 49-611-75-1. FAX 49-611-724000. TELEX 61186-STBA-D. URL: http://www.statistik-bund.de. **Document type:** government publication.
Formerly: Germany (Federal Republic, 1949-) Statistisches Bundesamt. Fachserie 4, Reihe 5: Beschaeftigung, Umsatz, Investitionen und Kosten Struktur im Baugewerbe (ISSN 0072-1727)

690 314 GW ISSN 0072-1735
HD9715 .G33
GERMANY. STATISTISCHES BUNDESAMT. FACHSERIE 5, BAUTAETIGKEIT UND WOHNUNGEN, REIHE 1: BAUTAETIGKEIT. a. DM.23 (effective 1997). 65180 Wiesbaden, Germany. TEL 49-611-75-1. FAX 49-611-724000. TELEX 61186-STBA-D. URL: http://www.statistik-bund.de. **Document type:** government publication.

690 314 GW ISSN 0072-1743
HD7339.A3
GERMANY. STATISTISCHES BUNDESAMT. FACHSERIE 5, BAUTAETIGKEIT UND WOHNUNGEN, REIHE 2: BEWILLIGUNGEN IM SOZIALEN WOHNUNGSBAU. a. DM.15.30 (effective 1997). 65180 Wiesbaden, Germany. TEL 49-611-75-1. FAX 49-611-724000. TELEX 61186-STBA-D. URL: http://www.statistik-bund.de. **Document type:** government publication.

690 314 GW ISSN 0072-1751
HD9715.G3
GERMANY. STATISTISCHES BUNDESAMT. FACHSERIE 5, BAUTAETIGKEIT UND WOHNUNGEN, REIHE 3: BESTAND AN WOHNUNGEN. a. DM.11. 65180 Wiesbaden, Germany. TEL 49-611-75-1. FAX 49-611-724000. TELEX 61186-STBA-D. URL: http://www.statistik-bund.de. **Document type:** government publication.

692 314 GW ISSN 0720-4124
GERMANY. STATISTISCHES BUNDESAMT. FACHSERIE 17, PREISE, REIHE 5: KAUFWERTE FUER BAULAND. q. DM.37.20. Statistisches Bundesamt, 65180 Wiesbaden, Germany. TEL 49-611-75-1. FAX 49-611-724000. TELEX 61186-STBA-D. URL: http://www.statistik-bund.de. **Document type:** government publication.
Supersedes: Germany (Federal Republic, 1949-) Statistisches Bundesamt. Preise, Loehne, Wirtschaftsrechnungen. Reihe 5: Preise und Preisindizes fuer Bauwerke und Bauland (ISSN 0072-3908)

690 310 UK ISSN 0308-9819
HD7333.A3
GREAT BRITAIN. DEPARTMENT OF THE ENVIRONMENT. HOUSING AND CONSTRUCTION STATISTICS. 1972. 8/yr. £50 (effective 1997). (Department of the Environment) Stationery Office, 51 Nine Elms Ln., London SW8 5DR, England. TEL 44-171-873-0011. FAX 44-171-873-8463. (Subscr. to: P.O. Box 276, London SW8 5DT, England. TEL 44-171-873-8222) (Co-sponsors: Scottish Development Department, Welsh Office) circ. 2,300. **Document type:** government publication.
—BLDSC (4335.090400). CCC.

690 UK ISSN 0964-4571
GREAT BRITAIN. DEPARTMENT OF THE ENVIRONMENT. PRICE ADJUSTMENT FORMULAE FOR CONSTRUCTION CONTRACTS: MONTHLY BULLETIN OF INDICES. £69. (Department of the Environment) Stationery Office, 51 Nine Elms Ln., London SW8 5DR, England. TEL 44-171-873-0011. FAX 44-171-873-8247. (Subscr. to: Stationery Office, Publications Centre, P.O. Box 276, London SW8 5DT, England. TEL 44-171-873-8499. FAX 44-171-873-8222) stat.; circ. 2,800 (paid). (back issues avail.) **Document type:** government publication.
Formed by the 1984 merger of: Monthly Bulletin Construction Indices for Use with National Economic Development Office Price Adjustment Formulae (ISSN 0262-0642); Price Adjustment Formulae for Building Contracts: Bulletin of Indices (ISSN 0262-0634)
Description: Enables tenderers to price building work.

690 GR ISSN 0256-7970
HD7357.5.A3
GREECE. NATIONAL STATISTICAL SERVICE. BUILDING ACTIVITY STATISTICS. 1977. a. $13. National Statistical Service of Greece, Statistical Information and Publications Division - Ethniki Statistiki Yperesia tes Ellados, 14-16 Lykourgou, 101 66 Athens, Greece. TEL 30-1-3289-307. FAX 30-1-3241-102. TELEX 216734 ESYE GR. (back issues avail.) **Document type:** government publication.

690 330 GR
GREECE. NATIONAL STATISTICAL SERVICE. REVISED PRICE INDICES OF NEW BUILDING DWELLINGS CONSTRUCTION (YEAR). (Text in English, Greek) 1983. decennial. $4. National Statistical Service of Greece, Statistical Information and Publications Division - Ethniki Statistiki Yperesia tes Ellados, 14-16 Lykourgou, 101 66 Athens, Greece. TEL 30-1-3244-748. FAX 30-1-3241-102. TELEX 216734 ESYE GR. (back issues avail.) **Document type:** government publication.

690 CN ISSN 0840-8106
TH4817
HOMEOWNER REPAIR AND RENOVATION EXPENDITURE IN CANADA/DEPENSES SUR LES REPARATIONS ET RENOVATIONS EFFECTUEES PAR LES PROPRIETAIRES DE LOGEMENT AU CANADA. (Catalogue 62-201) 1987. a. Can.$30 (foreign $42). Statistics Canada, Operations and Integration Division, Circulation Management, Jean Talon Bldg., 2-C12, Tunney's Pasture, Ottawa, ON K1A 0T6, Canada. TEL 613-951-7277; 800-267-6677. FAX 613-951-1584. URL: http://www.statcan.ca. adv. contact: Kathryn Bonner. **Document type:** government publication.

690 314 HU
HUNGARY. KOZPONTI STATISZTIKAI HIVATAL. BERUHAZASI, EPITOIPARI, LAKASEPITESI EVKONYV. a. 438 Ft. Statisztikai Kiado Vallalat, Kaszasdulo u. 2, P.O. Box 99, 1300 Budapest 3, Hungary. TEL 36-1-180-3311. FAX 36-1-168-8635. TELEX 22-6699. (Subscr. to: Kultura, Box 149, H-1389 Budapest, Hungary) stat. **Document type:** government publication.
—BLDSC (5143.923000).
Former titles: Hungary. Kozponti Statisztikai Hivatal. Lakasstatisztikai Evkonyv (ISSN 0236-9524); Hungary. Kozponti Statisztikai Hivatal. Lakasepites es Megszunes (ISSN 0209-5513)

BUILDING AND CONSTRUCTION — ABSTRACTING, BIBLIOGRAPHIES, STATISTICS

690   HU   ISSN 0139-3510
HUNGARY. KOZPONTI STATISZTIKAI HIVATAL. BERUHAZASI, EPITOIPARI, LAKASEPITESI ZSEBKONYV. (Supplement avail. a.: Idegen Nyelvu Melleklet - Pocket Book (ISSN 0230-9459)) 1979. a. 69 Ft. Statisztikai Kiado Vallalat, Kaszasdulo u. 2, P.O. Box 99, 1300 Budapest 3, Hungary. TEL 36-1-180-3311. FAX 36-1-168-8635. TELEX 22-6699. (Subscr. to: Kultura, Box 149, 1389 Budapest, Hungary) stat. circ. 1,000. **Document type:** government publication.

690   CR
INDICES DE PRECIOS DE LOS INSUMOS BASICOS DE LA INDUSTRIA DE LA CONSTRUCCION. m. Direccion General de Estadistica y Censos, Apdo. 10163, 1000 San Jose, Costa Rica.

330   IE   ISSN 0791-2951
IRELAND. CENTRAL STATISTICS OFFICE. BUILDING AND CONSTRUCTION: AVERAGE EARNINGS AND HOURS WORKED. q. I£8. Central Statistics Office, Skehard Rd., Cork, Ireland. TEL 353-21-359000. FAX 353-21-359090. E-mail: information@cso.ie; URL: http://www.cso.ie. (processed) **Document type:** government publication.
Description: Estimates of the average hours worked and average earnings per hour and per week of each of the main categories of employee in private sector construction firms employing ten or more persons.

330   IE   ISSN 0791-2943
IRELAND. CENTRAL STATISTICS OFFICE. BUILDING AND CONSTRUCTION. MONTHLY INDEX OF EMPLOYMENT IN PRIVATE FIRMS WITH FIVE OR MORE PERSONS ENGAGED. m. I£24. Central Statistics Office, Skehard Rd., Cork, Ireland. TEL 353-21-359000. FAX 353-21-359090. E-mail: information@cso.ie; URL: http://www.cso.ie. (processed) **Document type:** government publication.
Formerly: Ireland. Central Statistics Office. Building Employment Index.
Description: Measures changes in the employment levels of private construction firms employing five or more persons.

330   IE   ISSN 0791-2978
IRELAND. CENTRAL STATISTICS OFFICE. BUILDING AND CONSTRUCTION PLANNING PERMISSIONS. q. I£8. Central Statistics Office, Skehard Rd., Cork, Ireland. TEL 353-21-359000. FAX 353-21-359090. E-mail: information@cso.ie; URL: http://www.cso.ie. (processed) **Document type:** government publication.
Description: Details of the number and floor area of planning permissions granted in each county, county borough and planning region; classified by four types of development and eight functional categories.

330   IE   ISSN 0791-296X
IRELAND. CENTRAL STATISTICS OFFICE. CENSUS OF BUILDING AND CONSTRUCTION. RESULTS FOR PRIVATE FIRMS WITH 20 OR MORE PERSONS ENGAGED. a. I£2. Central Statistics Office, Skehard Rd., Cork, Ireland. TEL 353-21-359000. FAX 353-21-359090. E-mail: information@cso.ie; URL: http://www.cso.ie. **Document type:** government publication.
Formerly: Ireland. Central Statistics Office. Census of Building and Construction.
Description: Covers the activities of private sector firms in the building, civil engineering and allied trades.

690   IS   ISSN 0069-9195
ISRAEL. CENTRAL BUREAU OF STATISTICS. CONSTRUCTION IN ISRAEL/HA-BINUI BE-YISRAEL. (Text in Hebrew) 1960. irreg., latest 1994. price varies. Central Bureau of Statistics, P.O. Box 13015, Jerusalem 91130, Israel. TEL 972-2-6553400. FAX 972-2-6553325. (also avail. in diskette format) **Document type:** government publication.

690   IT
ITALY. ISTITUTO NAZIONALE DI STATISTICA. STATISTICHE DELL'ATTIVITA EDILIZIA. 1955. a. L.26000 (effective 1992). Istituto Nazionale di Statistica, Via Cesare Balbo 16, 00100 Rome, Italy. FAX 39-6-46735198.
Supersedes in part: Italy. Istituto Centrale di Statistica. Annuario Statistico dell'Attivita Edilizia e delle Opere Pubbliche (ISSN 0075-1804)

690   IT
ITALY. ISTITUTO NAZIONALE DI STATISTICA. STATISTICHE DELLE OPERE PUBBLICHE. 1955. a. L.15000 (effective 1992). Istituto Nazionale di Statistica, Via Cesare Balbo 16, 00100 Rome, Italy. FAX 39-6-46735198. **Document type:** government publication.
Supersedes in part: Italy. Istituto Centrale di Statistica. Annuario Statistico dell'Attivita Edilizia e delle Opere Pubbliche (ISSN 0075-1804)

690   JO
JORDAN. DEPARTMENT OF STATISTICS. CONSTRUCTION STATISTICS. (Text in Arabic, English) 1987. a. $15. Department of Statistics, P.O. Box 2015, Amman, Jordan. TEL 962-6-842171. FAX 962-6-833518. TELEX 24117 STATIS JO. **Document type:** government publication.

690   JA   ISSN 0916-653X
KENSETSU TOKEI GEPPO/MONTHLY OF CONSTRUCTION STATISTICS. (Text in Japanese) 1973. m. 980 Yen per no. Kensetsu Bukka Chosakai - Construction Prices Investigation Institute, 11-8, Nihonbashi Odenmacho, Chuo-ku, Tokyo 103, Japan.

690 338   KU
KUWAIT. CENTRAL STATISTICAL OFFICE. ANNUAL SURVEY OF ESTABLISHMENTS - CONSTRUCTION/KUWAIT. AL-IDARAH AL-MARKAZIYYAH LIL-IHSA'. AL-BAHTH AL-SANAWI LIL-MANSHAAT - AL-TASHYID WAL-BINA'. (Text in Arabic, English) 1983. a., latest 1994. Central Statistical Office - Al-Idarah al-Markaziyyah lil-Ihsa', P.O. Box 26188, Safat 13122, Kuwait. TEL 965-2428200. FAX 965-2430464. TELEX 22468 TAKHTET KT. **Document type:** government publication.

690   KU
KUWAIT. CENTRAL STATISTICAL OFFICE. CONSTRUCTION STATISTICS RESULTS/KUWAIT. AL-IDARAH AL-MARKAZIYYAH LIL-IHSA'. NATA'IJ IHSA'AT AL-TASHYID WAL-BINA'. (Text in Arabic, English) 1979. a., latest 1995. Central Statistical Office - Al-Idarah al-Markaziyyah lil-Ihsa', P.O. Box 26188, Safat 13122, Kuwait. TEL 965-2428200. FAX 965-2430464. TELEX 22468 TAKHTET KT. **Document type:** government publication.

690   SZ
LEERWOHNUNGSBESTAND IN DER SCHWEIZ 1. JUNI (YEAR)/LOGEMENTS VACANTS EN SUISSE DENOMBRES AU 1ER JUIN (YEAR). (Text in French and German) 1988. a. 7 SFr. Bundesamt fuer Statistik, Schwarztorstr. 96, CH-3003 Bern, Switzerland. TEL 41-31-3236060. FAX 41-31-3236061. URL: http://www.admin.ch/bfs. **Document type:** government publication.
Formerly: Leerwohnungszaehlung 1. Juni (Year).

690   LY   ISSN 0075-9279
LIBYA. CENSUS AND STATISTICS DEPARTMENT. REPORT OF THE SURVEY OF LICENSED CONSTRUCTION UNITS. (Text in Arabic and English) 1967. a. free. Secretariat of Planning, Census and Statistics Department, P.O. Box 600, Tripoli, Libya. **Document type:** government publication.

690 016   GW   ISSN 0722-060X
LITERATURINFORMATIONDIENST SCHRIFTTUM BAUWESEN: GESAMTAUSGABE. 1976. m. DM.828. (Fraunhofer Informationszentrum Raum und Bau) Fraunhofer I R B Verlag, Nobelstr. 12, 70569 Stuttgart, Germany. TEL 49-711-9702500. FAX 49-711-9702507. TELEX 7255168-IZS-D. E-mail: irb@irb.fhg.de; URL: http://www.irb.fhg.de. adv.; bk.rev.; abstr. circ. 900. **Document type:** trade publication.
Formerly (until 1981): Schrifttum Bauwesen: Gesamtausgabe (ISSN 0343-4494); Which superseded: Schrifttumkartei Bauwesen (ISSN 0036-6994); (1963-1975): Schrifttumkartei Beton (ISSN 0036-7001)

LOCAL GOVERNMENT INDEX (NEW SOUTH WALES). see LAW — Abstracting, Bibliographies, Statistics

690   LU   ISSN 1012-6597
LUXEMBOURG. SERVICE CENTRAL DE LA STATISTIQUE ET DES ETUDES ECONOMIQUES. INDICATEURS RAPIDES. SERIE A2: INDICES DES PRIX DE LA CONSTRUCTION. s-a. 1000 Fr. for complete series (effective 1997). Service Central de la Statistique et des Etudes Economiques, 6 bd. Royal, B.P. 304, 2013 Luxembourg, Luxembourg. TEL 352-478-4268. FAX 352-464289. E-mail: statec.post@statec.etat.lu; URL: http://statec.gouvernement.lu. (looseleaf format) **Document type:** government publication.

690   LU
LUXEMBOURG. SERVICE CENTRAL DE LA STATISTIQUE ET DES ETUDES ECONOMIQUES. INDICATEURS RAPIDES. SERIE B2: INDICES DE L'ACTIVITE DANS LA CONSTRUCTION. m. 1000 Fr. for complete series (effective 1997). Service Central de la Statistique et des Etudes Economiques, 6 bd. Royal, B.P. 304, 2013 Luxembourg, Luxembourg. TEL 352-478-4268. FAX 352-464289. E-mail: statec.post@statec.etat.lu; URL: http://statec.gouvernement.lu. (looseleaf format) **Document type:** government publication.

690   LU   ISSN 1012-666X
LUXEMBOURG. SERVICE CENTRAL DE LA STATISTIQUE ET DES ETUDES ECONOMIQUES. INDICATEURS RAPIDES. SERIE G: AUTORISATIONS DE BATIR - BATIMENTS, LOGEMENTS ET VOLUME BATI. m. 1000 F. for complete series (effective 1997). Service Central de la Statistique et des Etudes Economiques, 6 bd. Royal, B.P. 304, 2013 Luxembourg, Luxembourg. TEL 352-478-4268. FAX 352-464289. E-mail: statec.post@statec.etat.lu; URL: http://statec.gouvernement.lu. (looseleaf format) **Document type:** government publication.

690   MH
MACAO. DIRECCAO DOS SERVICOS DE ESTATISTICA E CENSOS. INDICES E PRECOS DOS MATERIAS DE CONSTRUCAO/MACAO. CENSUS AND STATISTICS DEPARTMENT. INDEXES AND PRICES OF CONSTRUCTION MATERIALS. (Text in Chinese, Portuguese) 1992. q. free. Direccao dos Servicos de Estatistica e Censos, Rua Inacio Baptista, No. 4-6, P.O. Box 3022, Macao. TEL 853-3995311. FAX 853-307825. **Document type:** government publication.

690   MH
MACAO. DIRECCAO DOS SERVICOS DE ESTATISTICA E CENSOS. RECENSEAMENTO A CONSTRUCAO/MACAO. CENSUS AND STATISTICS DEPARTMENT. CONSTRUCTION SURVEY. (Text in Chinese, Portuguese) 1991. a. free. Direccao dos Servicos de Estatistica e Censos, Rua Inacio Baptista, No. 4-6, P.O. Box 3022, Macao. TEL 853-3995311. FAX 853-307825. **Document type:** government publication.

690 310   US   ISSN 0361-9591
MEANS CONSTRUCTION COST INDEXES. q. $198. R.S. Means Company, Inc., 100 Construction Plaza, Box 800, Kingston, MA 02364-0800. TEL 800-334-3509. FAX 617-585-7466. Ed.Bd. charts; stat.

690 011   II   ISSN 0027-6138
N B O ABSTRACTS. 1956. m. exchange basis. National Buildings Organisation, G Wing, Nirman Bhavan, Maulana Azad Rd., New Delhi 11, India. Ed. S. Protar. bk.rev.; film rev.; stat.; cum.index. circ. 500. (processed)

690 016   US
N T I S ALERTS: BUILDING INDUSTRY TECHNOLOGY. w. $135 (foreign $195). U.S. National Technical Information Service, 5285 Port Royal Rd., Springfield, VA 22161. TEL 703-487-4630. FAX 703-321-8547. TELEX 64617. index. (also avail. in microform from NTI; back issues avail.) **Document type:** abstracting/indexing.
Former titles: Abstract Newsletter: Building Industry Technology (ISSN 0163-1500); Weekly Abstract Newsletter: Building Industry Technology; Weekly Government Abstracts. Building Industry Technology; Weekly Government Abstracts. Building Technology.

BUILDING AND CONSTRUCTION — CARPENTRY AND WOODWORK

690 310   NL   ISSN 0984-2594
NEW CALEDONIA. INSTITUT TERRITORIAL DE LA STATISTIQUE ET DES ETUDES ECONOMIQUES. INDICE ET INDEX DU B T P. 1983. m. CFPF1000 (foreign CFPF1700) (effective 1997). Institut Territorial de la Statistique et des Etudes Economiques, P.O. Box 823, Noumea, New Caledonia. TEL 687-275481. FAX 687-288148. E-mail: itsee@cipac.nc. Ed. Gerard Baudchon. **Document type:** government publication.
    Formerly: New Caledonia. Institut Territorial de la Statistique et des Etudes Economiques. Index Batiment, Indice des Couts des Materiaux de Construction (ISSN 0758-0347)

331   NR
NIGERIA. FEDERAL MINISTRY OF LABOUR AND PRODUCTIVITY. QUARTERLY BULLETIN OF LABOUR STATISTICS. 1981. q. free. Federal Ministry of Labour and Productivity, Planning, Research and Statistics Department, Federal Secrctariat, Phase I, Ikoyi, P.M.B. 12576, Lagos, Nigeria. circ. 500. (processed) **Document type:** government publication.

690 310   NR
NIGERIA. NATIONAL INTEGRATED SURVEY OF HOUSEHOLDS. BUILDING AND CONSTRUCTION SURVEY. a. Federal Office of Statistics, Dissemination Division, National Integrated Survey of Households, c/o Mrs. M.T. Osita, P.M.B. 12528, 36-38 Broad St., Lagos, Nigeria. TEL 234-1-2601710-4. **Document type:** government publication.
    Supersedes: Nigeria. Federal Office of Statistics. Building and Construction Survey.

690.021   NO   ISSN 0550-7162
HA1501 subser.
NORWAY. STATISTISK SENTRALBYRAA. BYGGEAREALSTATISTIKK. (Subseries of its Norges Offisielle Statistikk) 1967. q. NOK 250 (effective 1997). Statistisk Sentralbyraa - Statistics Norway, P.O. Box 8131 Dep, N-0033 Oslo, Norway. TEL 47-22-86-45-00. FAX 47-22-86-49-73. E-mail: ssb@ssb.no. Eds. Peder Naes, John Egil Bjoerke.

690 016   SW   ISSN 0281-7276
NYA BYGGREGLER. 1968. 6/yr. SEK 525. Institutet foer Byggdokumentation - Swedish Institute of Building Documentation, Sankt Eriksgatan 46, S-112 34 Stockholm, Sweden. TEL 08-6177450. FAX 08-6177460. E-mail: info@byggdok.se; URL: http://www.byggdok.se. Ed. Olle Malm. (reprint service avail.) **Document type:** abstracting/indexing.
    Formerly (until 1984): Nya Byggnormer (ISSN 0280-7815)
    Description: News about building regulations and standards in Sweden.

690   PP   ISSN 0479-4826
PAPUA NEW GUINEA. NATIONAL STATISTICAL OFFICE. BUILDING STATISTICS. 1963. q. K.7 (foreign K.12). National Statistical Office, P.O. Box 337, Waigani, N.C.D., Papua New Guinea. TEL 675-3011226. FAX 675-3251869. TELEX FINANCE NE 22312. Ed. Francis K. Kasau. circ. 250. **Document type:** government publication.
    Formerly: Building (ISSN 0033-5339)
    Description: Covers building construction activity in urban areas. Contains the number and values of dwellings and other types of buildings, by ownership, building type and provinces. Also includes tables on the value of repairs, additions and replacements, and employment in the building industry.

690   PO   ISSN 0871-9969
PORTUGAL. INSTITUTO NACIONAL DE ESTATISTICA. ESTATISTICAS DA CONSTRUCAO DE EDIFICIOS. LICENCIAMENTO - HABITACAO. 1970. a. Esc.4000 (effective 1997). Instituto Nacional de Estatistica, Av. Antonio Jose de Almeida, 1078 Lisbon, Portugal. TEL 351-1-8470050. FAX 351-1-8478578. TELEX 351-63738 PCDINE P. circ. 500. **Document type:** government publication.
    Formerly (until 1991): Estatisticas da Construcao e da Habitacao - Statistiques du Batiment et de l'Habitation (ISSN 0377-2225)

QUARTERLY REPORT OF EMPLOYMENT & VACANCIES AT CONSTRUCTION SITES. see *OCCUPATIONS AND CAREERS — Abstracting, Bibliographies, Statistics*

R I C S LIBRARY INFORMATION SERVICE ABSTRACTS AND REVIEWS. (Royal Institution of Chartered Surveyors) see *ENGINEERING — Abstracting, Bibliographies, Statistics*

690 016   CU
SERVICIO REFERATIVO DE LA CONSTRUCCION.* Cover title: S R Construccion. 1967. bi-m. exchange basis. Comite Estatal de la Construccion, Centro Tecnico Superior de la Construccion, Ministry of Construction, Avda. Carlos M. de Cespedes y Calle 35, Havana, Cuba. Ed. Angel Fernandez Chavez. circ. 3,000. **Document type:** abstracting/indexing.
    Formerly: Revista Referativa de la Construccion (ISSN 0035-0427)

690 316.8   SA
SOUTH AFRICA. CENTRAL STATISTICAL SERVICE. BUILDING PLANS PASSED AND BUILDINGS COMPLETED. (Report No. 50-11-01) a., latest 1991. R.25 (foreign R.27.50). Central Statistical Service - Sentrale Statistiekdiens, Private Bag X44, Pretoria 0001, South Africa. TEL 27-12-310-8911. FAX 27-12-310-8500. (Orders to: Government Printing Works, Private Bag X85, Pretoria 0001, South Africa) **Document type:** government publication.
    Formerly: South Africa. Department of Statistics. Building Plans and Buildings Completed.

690 316.8   SA
SOUTH AFRICA. CENTRAL STATISTICAL SERVICE. CENSUS OF CONSTRUCTION. (Report No. 50-01-01) triennial, latest 1988. R.8 (foreign R.8.80). Central Statistical Service - Sentrale Statistiekdiens, Private Bag X44, Pretoria 0001, South Africa. TEL 27-12-310-8911. FAX 27-12-310-8500. (Orders to: Government Printing Works, Private Bag X85, Pretoria 0001, South Africa) **Document type:** government publication.

690 316.8   SA
SOUTH AFRICA. CENTRAL STATISTICAL SERVICE. STATISTICAL RELEASE. BUILDING INDUSTRY ADVISORY COUNCIL CONTRACT PRICE ADJUSTMENT PROVISIONS - WORKGROUP INDICES (HAYLETT). (No. P0151) m. free. Central Statistical Service - Sentrale Statistiekdiens, Private Bag X44, Pretoria 0001, South Africa. TEL 27-12-310-8911. FAX 27-12-310-8500. **Document type:** government publication.

690 316.8   SA
SOUTH AFRICA. CENTRAL STATISTICAL SERVICE. STATISTICAL RELEASE. BUILDING PLANS PASSED AND BUILDINGS COMPLETED. (No. P5041.3) a. free. Central Statistical Service - Sentrale Statistiekdiens, Private Bag X44, Pretoria 0001, South Africa. TEL 27-12-310-8911. FAX 27-12-310-8500. **Document type:** government publication.

690 316.8   SA
SOUTH AFRICA. CENTRAL STATISTICAL SERVICE. STATISTICAL RELEASE. BUILDING STATISTICS - PRIVATE SECTOR. (No. P5041.1) m. free. Central Statistical Service - Sentrale Statistiekdiens, Private Bag X44, Pretoria 0001, South Africa. TEL 27-12-310-8911. FAX 27-12-310-8500. **Document type:** government publication.
    Supersedes: South Africa. Central Statistical Service. Statistical News Release. Building Statistics - Private Sector - Building Plans Passed and Buildings Completed - Summary Statistics - Preliminary.

690 316.8   SA
SOUTH AFRICA. CENTRAL STATISTICAL SERVICE. STATISTICAL RELEASE. CENSUS OF CONSTRUCTION. (No. P5001) irreg., latest 1988. free. Central Statistical Service - Sentrale Statistiekdiens, Private Bag X44, Pretoria 0001, South Africa. TEL 27-12-310-8911. FAX 27-12-310-8500. **Document type:** government publication.

690 316.8   SA
SOUTH AFRICA. CENTRAL STATISTICAL SERVICE. STATISTICAL RELEASE. CONSTRUCTION AND TOWNSHIP DEVELOPERS: WORK ON HAND AND WORK DONE. (No. P5042) q. free. Central Statistical Service - Sentrale Statistiekdiens, Private Bag X44, Pretoria 0001, South Africa. TEL 27-12-310-8911. FAX 27-12-310-8500. **Document type:** government publication.

690 316.8   SA
SOUTH AFRICA. CENTRAL STATISTICAL SERVICE. STATISTICAL RELEASE. CONTRACT PRICE INDEX FOR BUILDINGS. (No. P0153) q. free. Central Statistical Service - Sentrale Statistiekdiens, Private Bag X44, Pretoria 0001, South Africa. TEL 27-12-310-8911. FAX 27-12-310-8500. **Document type:** government publication.
    Description: Compiled from information received from bills of quantities for accepted tenders.

690 310   SP   ISSN 0561-4902
SPAIN. MINISTERIO DE LA VIVIENDA. ESTADISTICA DE LA INDUSTRIA DE LA CONSTRUCCION. (Subseries of Spain. Ministerio de la Vivienda. Documentos Informativos) a. Ministerio de la Vivienda, Secretaria General Tecnica, Madrid, Spain.

690   US
SPEC-DATA PROGRAM; concise manufacturer's product literature in C S I format and proprietary specification on specific products. 1966. q. $250 to non-members. Construction Specifications Institute, 601 Madison St., Alexandria, VA 22314. TEL 703-684-0300. FAX 703-684-0465. adv. circ. 12,600.
    Former titles: Spec-Data Manu-Spec System; Spec-Data System.
    Description: Technical data on products available in commercial, industrial and institutional markets.

690   US
SPEC-DATA PROGRAM INDEX. 1968. a. Construction Specifications Institute, 601 Madison St., Alexandria, VA 22314. TEL 703-684-0300. FAX 703-684-0465. Ed. Carol E. Duke. adv. contact: Carol E. Duke. circ. 22,000. (also avail. in microfiche) **Document type:** abstracting/indexing, directory.
    Former titles: Spec-Data Manu-Spec Program Index; Spec-Data Manu-Spec System Index; Spec-Data Manu-Spec Index.
    Description: Listing of building products and manufacturers in the SPEC-DATA Program.

690 314   SW   ISSN 0085-6991
HD9715.S85
SWEDEN. STATISTISKA CENTRALBYRAAN. STATISTISKA MEDDELANDEN. SERIE BO, BOSTAEDER OCH BYGGNADER. (Text in Swedish; tables heads and summaries in English) 1966. irreg. SEK 980. Statistiska Centralbyraan, Publishing Unit, S-701 89 Oerebro, Sweden. circ. 1,375.

315.61   TU   ISSN 1013-5529
HA1911
TURKEY. DEVLET ISTATISTIK ENSTITUSU. BINA INSAAT ISTATISTIKLERI/TURKEY. STATE INSTITUTE OF STATISTICS. BUILDING CONSTRUCTION STATISTICS. (Text in English, Turkish) 1969. a., latest 1992. $60 (effective 1996). Devlet Istatistik Enstitusu - State Institute of Statistics, Necatibey Caddesi No. 114, 06100 Ankara, Turkey. TEL 90-312-4185027. FAX 90-312-4170432. circ. 1,151. **Document type:** government publication.
    Description: Provides statistical information on building construction and occupancy, including regional data.

690   TU   ISSN 1300-6754
TURKEY. STATE INSTITUTE OF STATISTICS. QUARTERLY BUILDING CONSTRUCTION COST INDEX. (Text in English, Turkish) 1992. a. $45 (effective 1996). Devley Istatistik Enstitusu - State Institute of Statistics, Necatibey Caddesi No. 114, 06100 Ankara, Turkey. TEL 90-312-4185027. FAX 90-312-4170432. **Document type:** government publication.

690   UN   ISSN 0257-9073
UNITED NATIONS. DEPARTMENT OF INTERNATIONAL ECONOMIC AND SOCIAL AFFAIRS. STATISTICAL OFFICE. CONSTRUCTION STATISTIC YEARBOOK. 1982. a. United Nations Publications, Sales and Marketing Section, Room DC2-0853, New York, NY 10017. TEL 212-963-8302; 800-253-9646. FAX 212-963-3489. E-mail: publications@un.org; URL: http://www.un.org/publications.

690   SZ   ISSN 1018-2292
WOHNBAUTAETIGKEIT IN DER SCHWEIZ/CONSTRUCTION DE LOGEMENTS EN SUISSE. (Text in French and German) 1987. a. 7 SFr. Bundesamt fuer Statistik, Schwarztorstr. 96, CH-3003 Bern, Switzerland. TEL 41-31-3236060. FAX 41-31-3236061. URL: http://www.admin.ch/bfs. **Document type:** government publication.

BUILDING AND CONSTRUCTION — Carpentry And Woodwork

A I T I M BOLETIN DE INFORMACION TECNICA. (Asociacion de Investigacion Tecnica de las Industrias de la Madera) see *FORESTS AND FORESTRY — Lumber And Wood*

BUILDING AND CONSTRUCTION — CARPENTRY AND WOODWORK

A W I NEWSBRIEFS. (Architectural Woodwork Institute) see *ARCHITECTURE*

698.3   SP
ACOMAT. 6/yr. Isabel la Catolica 12, 2o D, 28013 Madrid, Spain. TEL 1-247-18-32. FAX 1-247-18-37. Ed. J.M. Fernandez Sanz.

AMBIENTE. see *INTERIOR DESIGN AND DECORATION*

694   US   ISSN 0895-9005
AMERICAN WOODTURNER. 1986. q. $25 (Canada $30; elsewhere $40). American Association of Woodturners, 3200 Lexington Ave., Shoreview, MN 55126. TEL 612-484-9094. FAX 612-484-1724. E-mail: 75037.2123@compuserve.com; URL: http://www.RTPnet.org/~twnc/. Ed. Rick Mastelli. adv.; bk.rev.; illus.; circ. 6,600 (paid). **Indexed:** Ind.How To Do It (1990-). **Document type:** trade publication.

694 674.2 618.1   AT
AUSTRALASIAN CABINETMAKER & TIMBER TRADE JOURNAL. q. Aus.$48 in Australia & New Zealand; elsewhere Aus.$68. (Cabinetmakers Association of Western Australia) Furnishing Publications Pty. Ltd., Courtyard, Monash Homemaker Centre, 1207 Prices Hwy., Clayton, Vic. 3168, Australia. TEL 61-3-95629177. FAX 61-3-95629477. (Co-sponsors: Victorian Cabinet Manufacturing Industry Association; Kitchen and Allied Trades Association of Newcastle) Ed. Keith Dunn; Pub. Keith Dunn. R&P contact: Keith Dunn. adv. contact: Grahame Waterson.
    Incorporates: Australian Shop and Office Fittings Today.
    Description: Contains editorials on timbers, wood machinery, veneers, laminates, MDF particle boards spray equipment, cabinet hardware and handtools.

694   AT   ISSN 0818-0261
AUSTRALIAN WOODWORKER. 1985. bi-m. Aus.$25 (foreign Aus.$41). Skills Book Publishing Pty. Ltd., 40-44 Red Lion St., Rozelle, N.S.W. 2039, Australia. TEL 61-2-98106222. FAX 61-2-98185675. Ed. Steven Burrows. R&P contact: Barbara Burrons. adv. contact: Peter Douglas. bk.rev. circ. 22,450. (back issues avail.) **Document type:** consumer publication.
    Description: Directed toward the professional and serious amateur woodworker.

694   GW   ISSN 0005-6545
BAUEN MIT HOLZ. 1899. m. DM.166.80 (foreign DM.205.20; students DM.112.20) (effective 1997). Bruderverlag Albert Bruder GmbH, Bismarckstr. 21, 76133 Karlsruhe, Germany. TEL 49-721-91388-0. FAX 49-721-9138898. Ed. Klaus Fritzen. R&P contact: Volker Rutkowski. adv. contact: Anton Hummel. bk.rev.; abstr.; bibl.; charts; illus.; pat.; stat.; tr.lit.; index. circ. 9,500. (tabloid format) **Document type:** trade publication.
—SWETS. **CCC.**

BERGISCHE HANDWERK. see *ART*

BETTER HOMES AND GARDENS DECORATIVE WOODCRAFTS. see *ARTS AND HANDICRAFTS*

BETTER HOMES AND GARDENS WOOD. see *HOW-TO AND DO-IT-YOURSELF*

694 338 658.8   UK   ISSN 0261-8591
BUSINESS RATIO REPORT: JOINERY MANUFACTURERS; an industry sector analysis. 1978. a. I C C Business Ratios Ltd., Freepost, Field House, Hampton, Mddx. TW12 1BR, England. TEL 081-783-0977. FAX 081-783-1940. charts;stat. **Document type:** trade publication.

BYGG & JAERNHANDELN/BUILDING MATERIAL AND HARDWARE TRADE JOURNAL. see *BUSINESS AND ECONOMICS — Marketing And Purchasing*

694   SW   ISSN 0007-7569
BYGGNADSARBETAREN. 1949. 22/yr. SEK 215. Svenska Byggnadsarbetarefoerbundet, S-106 32 Stockholm, Sweden. TEL 46-8-7284900. FAX 46-8-7284980. Ed. Haakan Olander. adv.; bk.rev.; play rev.; charts; illus.; mkt.; stat.; tr.lit.; index. circ. 168,000.

CANADIAN WORKSHOP; the do-it-yourself magazine. see *HOW-TO AND DO-IT-YOURSELF*

694 331.8   US   ISSN 0008-6843
HD6350.C2
THE CARPENTER. 1881. bi-m. $10. United Brotherhood of Carpenters and Joiners of America, 101 Constitution Ave., N.W., Washington, DC 20001. TEL 202-546-6206. FAX 202-547-8979. Ed. Dave Ransom; Pub. Andris J. Silins. R&P contact: Dave Ransom. adv. contact: David Patterson. illus.; circ. 500,000 (controlled). **Document type:** trade publication, consumer publication.
    Description: Directed to people who follow carpentry and its allied trades.

694   FR
CHARPENTE - MENUISERIE - PARQUETS; revue technique du travail du bois. 1910. m. 370 F. Editions Bernard Begassat, 17 rue du Louvre, 75001 Paris, France. TEL 42-36-05-13. FAX 40-13-98-51. adv.; bk.rev.; charts; illus.; index. circ. 5,950.
    Former titles: Nouveau Journal de Charpente - Menuiserie - Parquets (ISSN 0029-4675); (until 1959): Nouveau Journal de Charpente - Menuiserie (ISSN 1141-1945)

CHIP CHATS. see *ARTS AND HANDICRAFTS*

698.3   US
CLASSIFIED EXCHANGE.* m. Miller Publishing Company, Box 34908, Memphis, TN 38184-0908. TEL 901-372-8166. FAX 901-373-6180. Ed. Joanne Avanzi. circ. 18,200.

694   US   ISSN 0010-6968
CONSTRUCTIONEER; news-photo coverage of construction in New York, Pennsylvania, New Jersey, Delaware. 1945. fortn. $50. H E S, Inc., 26 Long Hill Rd., Box 362, Guilford, CT 06437. TEL 203-453-3717. FAX 203-453-4390. E-mail: cr@hes.com. Ed. Sally E. Bahner. adv.; charts; illus.; tr.lit.; circ. 15,000 (controlled). **Indexed:** Concr.Abstr. —Linda Hall.

CONTRACTOR'S BUSINESS MANAGEMENT REPORT. see *BUSINESS AND ECONOMICS — Accounting*

698.3   US   ISSN 1055-6729
CREATIVE WOODWORKS AND CRAFTS. 1988. bi-m. $29.70. All American Crafts Publishing, Inc., 243 Newton-Sparta Rd., Newton, NJ 07860. TEL 201-383-8080; 800-877-5527. FAX 201-383-8133. (Dist. by: Kable, 641 Lexington Ave., New York, NY 10022. TEL 212-705-4600) Ed. Robert Becker. adv. contact: Robert Becker. circ. 95,000. **Document type:** consumer publication.
    Description: Concentrates solely on woodworking - woodcrafting, mostly instructional with a few articles on other wood workers and their accomplishments, along with occasional articles on uses and techniques with materials and tools for woodworking.

694   US   ISSN 1058-403X
CUSTOM WOODWORKING BUSINESS. 1991. m. $25 (effective 1995). Vance Publishing Corporation (Lincolnshire), Box 1414, Lincolnshire, IL 60069-1414. TEL 708-634-2600; 800-621-2845. FAX 708-634-4379. Ed. Richard Christianson. adv.; circ. 60,000 (controlled). **Document type:** trade publication.
    Description: Covers the business, design and technical needs of custom woodworking operations.

D D S - DAS MAGAZIN FUER MOEBEL UND AUSBAU; Fachzeitschrift fuer die Holz- und Kunststoffverarbeitung. see *INTERIOR DESIGN AND DECORATION — Furniture And House Furnishings*

684.1   IT   ISSN 0393-330X
DATALIGNUM. (Text in English, German and Italian) 1982. m. L.90000($100) Milla International S.r.l., Via Stefano Ussi 4, 20125 Milan, Italy. TEL 39-2-66101160. FAX 39-2-66100433. Ed. Pietro Stroppa. R&P contact: Silvia Buchi. adv. contact: Silvia Buchi. bk.rev. circ. 9,000. **Document type:** monographic series.

694   RU   ISSN 0011-9008
TS800   CODEN: DVPYAN
DEREVOOBRABATYVAYUSHCHAYA PROMYSHLENNOST. 1952. bi-m. $82 (effective 1998). (Ministerstvo Derevoobrabatyvayushchei Promyshlennosti) Izdatel'stvo Lesnaya Promyshlennost, Ul. 25 Let Oktyabrya, 17, 103645 Moscow K-25, Russia. (Subscr. to: Mezhdunarodnaya Kniga, ul. Dimitrova 39, Moscow G-200, Russia) Ed. L.P. Myasnikov. adv.; bk.rev.; bibl.; charts; illus.; tr.lit.; index. circ. 15,300. **Indexed:** Abstr.Bull.Inst.Pap.Chem., Biodet.Abstr., Chem.Abstr., Forest.Abstr., Forest Prod.Abstr.
—BLDSC (0053.000000); CASDDS; CISTI; Linda Hall.

694   XO   ISSN 0012-6144
    CODEN: DRVOAT
DREVO/WOOD. (Text in Slovak or Czech; summaries in English, German and Russian) 1946. m. $36. Statny Drevarsky Vyskumny Ustav - State Forest Products Research Institute, Lamacska cesta 1, 833 30 Bratislava, Slovakia. TEL 42-7-371301. FAX 42-7-372063. Ed. Vaclav Sehnal. R&P contact: Stanislav Florek. adv.: B&W page $580; adv. contact: Vaclav Sehnal. bk.rev.; charts; illus.; pat.; index. circ. 3,000. **Indexed:** Abstr.Bull.Inst.Pap.Chem., Biodet.Abstr., C.I.S. Abstr., Chem.Abstr., Forest.Abstr., Forest Prod.Abstr. **Document type:** academic/scholarly publication.
—CASDDS; CISTI; Linda Hall.
    Description: Wood and wood products application

FINE TOOL JOURNAL. see *ANTIQUES*

694   US   ISSN 0361-3453
TT180
FINE WOODWORKING. 1975. bi-m. $32; newsstand price: $6.95 (Canada Can.$7.95; UK £4.25). Taunton Press, Inc., 63 S. Main St., Box 5506, Newtown, CT 06470-5506. TEL 203-426-8171. FAX 203-426-3434. Ed. Scott Gibson; Pub. Jim Chiavelli. R&P contact: Scott Gibson. adv.: B&W page $11075, color page $15180; trim 8 7/8 x 10 7/8; adv. contact: Dick West. bk.rev.; illus.; circ. 268,000 (paid). **Indexed:** Access (1994-), Art Ind., DAAI, Ind.How To Do It (1976-), MELSA. **Document type:** consumer publication.
—BLDSC (3927.775000); KR SourceOne; UnCover.
    Description: Contains articles on making beautiful, practical things out of wood, covering the gamut of furniture styles and projects.

694   US   ISSN 1079-087X
FRAME BUILDING NEWS. 1987. 5/yr. free to qualified personnel. Krause Publications, Inc., 700 E. State St., Iola, WI 54990-0001. TEL 715-445-2214. FAX 715-445-4087. Ed. Dave Natzke; Pub. Ulrich Groth. adv. contact: Claude Chmiel. circ. 23,159. **Document type:** trade publication.

694.26   GW   ISSN 0016-3236
FUSSBODEN-ZEITUNG.* 1952. m. Verlag Michael Steinert, An der Alster 21, 2000 Hamburg 1, Germany. TEL 040-240852. FAX 040-2803788. Ed. M. Steinert. adv.; bk.rev.; abstr.; charts; illus.; pat.; tr.mk.; index. circ. 8,100. **Indexed:** Art & Archaeol.Tech.Abstr., Intl.Polym.Sci.& Tech., Key to Econ.SCi., RAPRA, Text.Tech.Dig. **Document type:** trade publication.

GENAU. see *PLASTICS*

657.6 350.6   US
GOVERNMENT ACCOUNTING AND AUDITING DISCLOSURE MANUAL. base vol. (plus a. supplement). $145.95 (overseas $215.45) (effective 1995). Warren, Gorham & Lamont, One Penn Plaza, New York, NY 10119. TEL 212-971-5000. FAX 212-971-5113. (Subscr. to: The Park Square Bldg., 31 St. James Ave., Boston, MA 02116-4112. TEL 800-950-1207) Eds. Allan B. Afterman, Rowan H. Jones. (looseleaf format) **Document type:** trade publication.
    Description: Covers all aspects of disclosure and reporting requirements for the financial statements of state and local governments.

645   IT
GUIDA: ANNUARIO DEI FORNITORI DELL'INDUSTRIA DEL MOBILE. a. Lit.70000 (effective 1997). Industria del Mobile s.r.l., Via Giambologna 21, 20136 Milan, Italy. TEL 39-2-8394780. FAX 39-2-8372547.
    Description: Lists firms in the woodworking machinery field.

BUILDING AND CONSTRUCTION — CARPENTRY AND WOODWORK

694   **FR**
GUIDE PRATIQUE DE L'ENTREPRENEUR - MENUISERIE. 6/yr. Editions S E R I P, 40 rue Guy Moquet, 94501 Champigny Cedex, France. TEL 48-81-91-91. FAX 48-81-81-77. Ed. Regine Heurteur. circ. 13,000.
Description: Studies carpentry and joinery.

H O B - DIE HOLZBEARBEITUNG. see *FORESTS AND FORESTRY — Lumber And Wood*

694 674   **US**
H P V A EXECUTIVE BRIEF. q. $16. Hardwood Plywood & Veneer Association, 1825 Michael Faraday Dr., Box 2789, Reston, VA 20195. TEL 703-435-2900. FAX 703-435-2537. Ed. Sally Peck. adv. **Document type:** newsletter.
Formerly: H P M A Executive Brief.

694   **US**   **ISSN 0897-022X**
HARDWOOD FLOORS. 1988. bi-m. $36 (foreign $45). (National Wood Flooring Association) Athletic Business Publications, Inc., 1846 Hoffman St., Madison, WI 53704. TEL 608-249-0186. FAX 608-249-1153. E-mail: hfmag@aol.com. Ed. Rick Berg. R&P contact: Rick Berg. adv. contact: Kris Currie. circ. 24,153 (controlled). **Document type:** trade publication.
Description: Geared towards floor covering retailers, builders and interior designers. Includes association news and issues facing the industry.

694 674   **US**
HARDWOOD PLYWOOD & VENEER NEWS. bi-m. $30. Hardwood Plywood & Veneer Association, 1825 Michael Faraday Dr., Box 2789, Reston, VA 20195. TEL 703-435-2900. FAX 703-435-2537. Ed. Sally Peck. **Document type:** newsletter.

694   **GW**   **ISSN 0945-1994**
TS840
HOLZ; Zeitschrift fuer Moebelhersteller, Laden- und Innenausbau. (Supplement avail.: A K Holz) 1947. m. DM.166. Holz-Verlag GmbH und Co. KG, Postfach 1260, 86407 Mering, Germany. TEL 49-8233-32761. FAX 49-8233-32762. Ed. Manfred Kittel. adv.: B&W page DM.3000, color page DM.4500; trim 185 x 270. bk.rev.; illus.; tr.lit.; index. **Document type:** trade publication.
Former titles (until 1993): Holz-Kunststoff (ISSN 0933-4580); Holz-Kunststoff-Moebelfertigung (ISSN 0341-0331); Holz-Kunststoff (ISSN 0018-375X)

694   **GW**   **ISSN 0943-3864**
HOLZ PRAXIS; Informationen fuer das Holz- und Kunststoffverarbeitende Handwerk. 1978. 3/yr. free. Wegra Verlag GmbH, Frankfurterstr. 10, 71732 Tamm, Germany. circ. 50,000. **Document type:** trade publication.

HOLZARBEITER-ZEITUNG. see *LABOR UNIONS*

694   **GW**   **ISSN 0723-4856**
HOLZBAU - REPORT. 1976. m. membership. Landesinnungsverband des Bayerischen Zimmererhandwerks, Postfach 402064, Eisenacher Str. 17, 80804 Munich, Germany. TEL 089-367056. FAX 089-361-5854. (Subscr. to: Josef M. Greska GmbH, Morassistr. 26, 8000 Munich 5, Germany) (Co-Sponsor: Verbaende des Bayerischen Zimmerer- und Holzbaugewerbes) adv.; bk.rev. circ. 4,000. (looseleaf format; back issues avail.) **Document type:** trade publication.

694   **NE**   **ISSN 0923-5574**
HET HOUTBLAD; vaktijdschrift voor het houtvak en de bouwsector. 1989. 8/yr. free to qualified personnel. (Centrum Hout - Timber Information Center) Het Houtblad B.V., Postbus 1375, 1300 BJ Almere, Netherlands. TEL 31-36-5327331. FAX 31-36-5329708. Ed. J.J. de Groot. adv.: B&W page fl.3595, color page fl.5705; trim 210 x 297. circ. 18,500 (controlled). **Document type:** trade publication.
—SWETS.
Description: For architects, housing associations, building inspectors, construction firms, wood traders and the furniture industry.

684.1   **IT**   **ISSN 0019-753X**
INDUSTRIA DEL MOBILE. (Includes a. industry directory) 1959. m. Lit.140000 (foreign Lit.260000) (effective 1997). Industria del Mobile s.r.l., Via Giambologna, 21, 20136 Milan, Italy. TEL 39-2-8394780. FAX 39-2-8372547. adv.; illus. circ. 6,000.

694   **UK**
INDUSTRIAL WOODWORKER. 1991. m. £25 (foreign £60). Willowe Magazines Ltd., 47-49 Cinque Ports St., Rye, E. Sussex TN31 7AN, England. TEL 44-1797-227300. FAX 44-1797-222445. Ed. John Emslie. adv.: color page £995; trim 360 x 270; adv. contact: Bill Lowe. illus.; software rev.; tr.lit.; circ. 13,000. (back issues avail.) **Document type:** trade publication.
Description: Aimed at professional trade woodworkers, joiners, furniture manufacturers, door and window manufacturers, cabinet makers, etc.

694   **SZ**
INDUSTRIEL SUR BOIS. 1923. m. 60 SFr. Federation Romande des Entreprises de Menuiserie, Ebenisterie, Charpentes, des Fabriques de Meubles et des Parqueteurs, Case postale 193, CH-1052 Le Mont, Switzerland. TEL 41-21-6521553. FAX 41-21-6521565. adv.: B&W page 1255 SFr., color page 2800 SFr.; trim 185 x 262; adv. contact: Corinne Meylan. circ. 2,600. **Document type:** trade publication.

694   **SP**
INFORMACIONES. 24/yr. Association of Cabinetmakers, Diputacion 195 1o, 08011 Barcelona, Spain. TEL 3-323-32-00. FAX 3-75-12-440. Ed. M. Muntane Muixench. circ. 7,936.

694   **UK**
INSTITUTE OF CARPENTERS JOURNAL. 1900. q. membership. Institute of Carpenters, 12 Valley Gardens, Downend, Bristol BS16 6SF, England. TEL 44-177-94924188. FAX 4-115-9491664. Ed. W.K. Jefferies. bk.rev. circ. 2,800. (back issues avail.)

694   **PL**   **ISSN 0032-6240**
TA401   **CODEN: PITDAL**
INSTYTUT TECHNOLOGII DREWNA. PRACE. (Contents page and summaries in English and Russian) 1954. q. 24 Zl. per issue (effective 1998). Instytut Technologii Drewna, Ul. Winiarska 1, 60-654 Poznan, Poland. TEL 48-61-224081. FAX 48-61-224372. Ed. Edmund G. Urbanik. bibl.; illus. circ. 200. **Indexed:** AgroLibrex, Chem.Abstr., Forest Abstr., Forest Prod.Abstr., Ref.Zh. **Document type:** academic/scholarly publication.
—BLDSC (6582.450000); CASDDS; CISTI.
Description: Articles presenting the results of research works in the field of wood technology. *Refereed Serial*

694   **GW**
INTERN (TAUBERBISCHOFSHEIM). (Text in English, French, German, Italian and Spanish) s-a. Michael Weinig AG, Weinigstr. 2-4, 97941 Tauberbischofsheim, Germany. TEL 49-9341-860. Ed. Rudi Walz. adv. contact: Rudi Walz. circ. 3,000. **Document type:** consumer publication.

694   **AU**
HD9750.1
INTERNATIONALER HOLZMARKT UND HOLZ IM HANDWERK. 1909. m. S.1160. Zeitungsverlag Kuhn und Co. GmbH, Kutschkergasse 42, A-1180 Vienna, Austria. TEL 43-1-47686. FAX 43-1-4768621. Ed. Eveline Kozma. adv.: B&W page S.27000, color S.40200; trim 265 x 185; adv. contact: Monika Grassl. mkt. circ. 10,000. **Indexed:** Key to Econ.Sci. **Document type:** trade publication.
Formed by the merger of: Internationaler Holzmarkt (ISSN 0020-9422) & Holz im Handwerk (ISSN 0018-3776)

684   **US**   **ISSN 1049-9547**
JOINERS' QUARTERLY; the journal of timber framing. 1983. q. $18 (Canada $22; foreign $25) (effective Jan. 1997); newsstand price: $4.50. Fox Maple Press, Inc., Snowville Rd., Box 249, Brownfield, ME 04010. TEL 207-935-3720. FAX 207-935-4575. E-mail: foxmaple@dns.nxi.com. Ed. Laurie LaMountain. R&P contact: Steve Chappell. adv.: page $1280; trim 8 1/8 x 10 7/8; adv. contact: Janot Mendler. bk.rev.; software rev., charts, illus, tr.lit.; cum.index: 1994-1997, no. 3; circ. 6,500 (paid). (back issues avail.) **Document type:** trade publication.
Description: Deals with timber frame construction and design, log building, scribe-rule, architecture, sustainable building, historical building techniques and natural house building, and straw, clay, thatch, strawbale, and forestry practices.

JOURNAL OF AMERICAN ORGANBUILDING. see *MUSIC*

KEY NOTE MARKET REPORT: TIMBER & JOINERY. see *FORESTS AND FORESTRY — Lumber And Wood*

IL LEGNO (MILAN). see *FORESTS AND FORESTRY — Lumber And Wood*

NATIONAL ASSOCIATION OF HOME AND WORKSHOP WRITERS NEWSLETTER. see *JOURNALISM*

694   **AU**   **ISSN 0029-9677**
DER OESTERREICHISCHE ZIMMERMEISTER. 1962. m. S.580. Oesterreichischer Wirtschaftsverlag, Nikolsdorfergasse 7-11, A-1051 Vienna, Austria. TEL 0222-55585. TELEX 1-11669. Ed. Wolfgang Biedermann. adv.; illus. circ. 1,600.

694 684.1   **FR**
OFFICIEL DU BOIS (EDITION ROUGE). 1930. w. 240 F. Societe "le Bois National", 3 rue Claude Odde, 42007 St. Etienne Cedex, France. TEL 77-74-39-99. FAX 77-93-11-26. TELEX 300 818. adv.
Formerly: Bois National (Edition Rouge).

698.3   **US**
PALLET DIGEST. bi-m. Dixie Publications, 257 N. Main St., Box 489, Wadley, GA 30477. TEL 912-252-5237. FAX 912-252-1140. Ed. Jack D. Smith.

694 684.1   **NE**   **ISSN 1385-2019**
▼**PARKETBLAD.** 1995. 6/yr. fl.50.75 (Belgium fl.57.50; elsewhere fl.72.50). Uitgeverij Lakerveld B.V., Mangaanstraat 86, Postbus 43250, 2504 AG The Hague, Netherlands. TEL 31-70-3218218. FAX 31-70-3298744. E-mail: publish@lakerveld.nl. Ed. Jos Krijnen; Pub. Ad van Gaalen. adv. contact: Hans de Jong. illus. circ. 2,500. (back issues avail.) **Document type:** trade publication.
Description: Covers parquet business.

694   **US**   **ISSN 0884-8823**
TT180
POPULAR WOODWORKING. 1981. bi-m. $19.97. F & W Publications, Inc., 1507 Dana Ave., Cincinnati, OH 45207. TEL 513-531-2222. FAX 513-531-4082. Ed. Steve Shanesy. adv.; bk.rev.; illus. circ. 200,000. (back issues avail.) **Indexed:** Ind.How To Do It (1990-). **Document type:** consumer publication.
Formerly (until 1984): Popular Woodworker (ISSN 0277-576X)

694 697   **UK**
PROFESSIONAL BUILDER; small builders and contractors business magazine. 1972. m. (11/yr.). £30 (foreign £42.50). Hamerville Magazines Ltd., Regal House, Regal Way, Watford, Herts. WD2 4YJ, England. TEL 01923-237799. FAX 01923-246901. Ed. Dawn Leahey. adv.; bk.rev.; illus. circ. 105,050. **Indexed:** B.P.I. **Document type:** trade publication.
Former titles: Professional Builder and House Remodeller (ISSN 0263-7936); B J - Builder's Journal (ISSN 0260-5120); Builder and Decorator.

634.9 674   **FI**   **ISSN 0355-953X**
PUUMIES. 1955. m. FIM 270. Puumiesten Liitto ry - Association of Finnish Woodworking Technicians and Engineers, Kauppakatu 6 A 1, SF-40100 Jyvaaskylaa, Finland. TEL 941-215-636. FAX 941-215-652. Ed. Ritva Varis. adv.; bk.rev. circ. 3,050. **Document type:** trade publication.

REDWOOD NEWS. see *ARCHITECTURE*

RENOVATOR'S SUPPLY. see *INTERIOR DESIGN AND DECORATION*

RODALE'S AMERICAN WOODWORKER. see *HOW-TO AND DO-IT-YOURSELF*

698.3   **UK**   **ISSN 0968-266X**
ROUTING. 1993. q. Argus Specialist Publications Ltd. (Subsidiary of: Argus Press Group), Argus House, Boundary Way, Hemel Hempstead, Herts. HP2 7ST, England. TEL 01442-66551. FAX 01442-66998. (Subscr. to: Argus Subscription Services, Queensway House, 2 Queensway, Redhill, Surrey RH1 1QS, England. TEL 01737-768611) **Document type:** trade publication.
Description: Discusses woodworking techniques using a router.

SCHWEIZER HOLZ-BOERSE; Fachblatt fuer alle Gebiete der Holzwirtschaft. see *FORESTS AND FORESTRY*

BUILDING AND CONSTRUCTION — CARPENTRY AND WOODWORK

694 SZ
SCHWEIZER HOLZBAU. 1934. m. 85 SFr. Hoch- und Tiefbau Verlag AG, Postfach 7039, CH-8023 Zurich, Switzerland. TEL 0258-8333. FAX 0261-0324. Ed. Walter Bogusch. adv. contact: Alexander Eugster. illus. circ. 8,100. **Indexed:** C.I.S. Abstr. **Document type:** trade publication.
Formerly (until 1982): Holzbau (ISSN 0018-3814)

694 SZ ISSN 0036-7753
SCHWEIZERISCHE SCHREINERZEITUNG. 1889. w. 128 SFr. non-members. Verband Schweizerischer Schreinermeister und Moebelfabrikanten, Schmelzbergstr. 56, CH-8044 Zurich, Switzerland. TEL 01-2678100. FAX 01-2878152. Ed. Alois Bohnet. adv.; bk.rev.; abstr.; mkt.; illus.; stat.; tr.lit.; index. circ. 10,400. **Indexed:** C.I.S. Abstr. **Document type:** trade publication.

694 US ISSN 1062-9696
SHOPNOTES. 1992. bi-m. $19.95. August Home Publishing Co., 2200 Grand Ave., Des Moines, IA 50312-5306. TEL 515-282-7000. FAX 515-282-6741. E-mail: augusthome@aol.com; URL: http://www.augusthome.com. Ed. Tim Robertson; Pub. Donald B. Peschke. R&P contact: Julia Fish. illus. circ. 165,000. **Indexed:** Ind.How To Do It. **Document type:** consumer publication.
Description: For woodworking hobbyists.

SIA; skogsindustriarbetaren. see *FORESTS AND FORESTRY — Lumber And Wood*

SLOVENIJALES; glasilo mednarondega podjetja za trgovino, inzeniring, proizvodnjo, zastopanje in konsignacijo. see *BUSINESS AND ECONOMICS*

TIMBER FACTS. see *FORESTS AND FORESTRY — Lumber And Wood*

694 NE ISSN 0040-7933
TIMMERFABRIKANT. 1951. m. fl.96.50 (Europe fl.130). (Nederlandse Bond van Timmerfabrikanten) Wijlhuizen Vaktijdschriften, Wilhelminasingel 4, 6524 AK Nijmegen, Netherlands. TEL 31-24-3605253. FAX 31-24-3605210. adv.; illus.; stat.; circ. 1,400 (paid). **Document type:** trade publication.

694 AU ISSN 0040-8131
DER TISCHLER. 1962. s-m. S.812. (Bundesinnung und Landesinnung der Tischler Oesterreichs) Oesterreichischer Wirtschaftsverlag, Nikolsdorfergasse 7-11, A-1051 Vienna, Austria. TEL 0222-555585. TELEX 1-11669. Ed. Manfred Traber. adv.; bk.rev.; illus. circ. 6,400.

694 UK ISSN 0954-0156
TRADITIONAL WOODWORKING. 1988. m. £28.20 (foreign £45.70) (effective 1997); newsstand price: £2.35. Waterways World Ltd., The Well House, High St., Burton-on-Trent, Staffs DE14 2JQ, England. TEL 44-1283-564290. FAX 44-1283-531431. (Dist. by: Comag, Tavistock Rd., Middlesex UB7 7QE, England. TEL 44-1895-444055) Ed. Helen Adkins. adv. contact: Rod Straw. tr.lit.; index; circ. 35,000. (paid). (back issues avail.) **Document type:** consumer publication.

694 DK ISSN 0041-0624
TRAE NYT. 1966. 11/yr. free. Teknisk Forlag A - S, Skelbaekgade 4, DK-1717 Copenhagen V, Denmark. TEL 45-31-21-68-01. FAX 45-31-21-04-01. TELEX 16368 TEKFO DK. Ed. Peter Friis. adv.: B&W page DKK 10810, color page DKK 16510; trim 257 x 175. bk.rev.; charts; illus. circ. 15,452 (controlled). **Document type:** trade publication.
Description: Provides information to members of the wood-working industry through articles about new products in wood-working machines, workshop methods, storage and internal transport, semimanufactures and accessories for the furniture industry.

694 674 DK
TRAE NYTS LEVERANDOERREGISTER. a. Teknisk Forlag A - S, Skelbaekgade 4, DK-1780 Copenhagen V, Denmark. TEL 45-31-21-68-01. FAX 45-31-21-23-96. TELEX 16368 TEKFO DK. Ed. Erik Kuhlman. adv. circ. 15,521. **Document type:** trade publication.

694 SW ISSN 0346-2846
TRAEINDUSTRIN/WOODWORKING INDUSTRY. 1918. 18/yr. SEK 810 in Nordic countries; elsewhere SEK 740 (effective 1998). Arbor Publishing AB, P.O. Box 26212, S-100 41 Stockholm, Sweden. TEL 46-8-611-60-30. FAX 46-8-679-90-50. Ed. Camilla Myrsten. adv. contact: Alf Hitterdahl. circ. 4,400. **Document type:** trade publication.
Formed by the merger of: Trae; Svensk Snickeritidskrift (ISSN 0039-6729)

698.3 IT ISSN 0393-4373
VERNICIATURA DEL LEGNO. 1982. bi-m. L.40000 (foreign L.80000). Rivista del Colore s.r.l., Via degli Imbriani 10, 20158 Milan, Italy. Ed. Danilo O. Malavolti. adv.; bk.rev.; abstr.; tr.lit.; index. circ. 10,000. **Indexed:** World Surf.Coat.

694 305.818 US
VESTERHEIM WOODWORKING NEWSLETTER; newsletter for woodworkers in the Norwegian-American tradition. q. $35 (Canada & Mexico $39; elsewhere $40) (includes museum membership). Vesterheim Norwegian-American Museum, Box 379, 502 Water St., Decorah, IA 52101. TEL 319-382-9681. FAX 319-382-8828. Ed. John Boots. **Document type:** newsletter.
Description: Covers all aspects of the Norwegian folk art of woodcarving.

VICTORIAN HOMES. see *INTERIOR DESIGN AND DECORATION*

694 UK ISSN 0042-5842
VIEWPOINT (LONDON, 1970). 1970. q. free. Union of Construction, Allied Trades and Technicians, UCATT House, 177 Abbeville Rd., Clapham, London SW4 9RL, England. Ed. A. Vedeille. adv.; bk.rev. circ. 80,000. **Document type:** trade publication.
Incorporates: U C A T T Journal; Woodworkers and Painters Journal (ISSN 0049-7940)

694 US
THE VITAL LINK. 1977. m. $35. Woodworking Machinery Distributors Association, 251 W. DeKalb Pike, A-109, King of Prussia, PA 19406. TEL 610-265-6658. FAX 610-265-3419. Ed. R. Franklin Brown, Jr. circ. 125. **Document type:** newsletter.
Formerly: Bits 'n Chips.
Description: Covers industry, general management and government news of interest to machinery distributors. Includes news of the association.

694 US
W M D A MEMBERSHIP DIRECTORY AND BUYERS GUIDE; who's who in woodworking machinery distribution. 1960. $35 (foreign $45). Woodworking Machinery Distributors Association, 251 W. DeKalb Pike, Ste. A-109, King of Prussia, PA 19406. TEL 610-265-6658. FAX 610-265-3419. Ed. R. Franklin Brown, Jr. circ. 2,100. (back issues avail.) **Document type:** directory, newsletter.
Description: Information on companies distributing industrial woodworking machinery and sawmill equipment in the U.S. and Canada.

694 GW
WEINIG INFO. (Text in Chinese, English, French, German, Italian, Japanese and Spanish) 1960. s-a. Michael Weinig AG, Weinigstr. 2-4, 97941 Tauberbischofsheim, Germany. TEL 49-9341-86-0. FAX 49-9341-7080. Ed. Rudi Walz. circ. 70,000. **Document type:** consumer publication.

694 674 US
WHERE TO BUY HARDWOOD PLYWOOD AND VENEER. 1960. a. $5. Hardwood Plywood & Veneer Association, 1825 Michael Faraday Dr., Box 2789, Reston, VA 20195. TEL 703-435-2900. FAX 703-435-2537. adv. contact: Ketti Tyree. circ. 6,000. **Document type:** directory.
Description: Lists manufacturers of hardwood plywood and veneer, prefinishers of hardwood plywood, industry suppliers, and wholesale stocking distributors.

694 UK
WOOD & EQUIPMENT NEWS. 1968. bi-m. £41 (overseas £50) (effective 1997). Turret Group Plc., Turret House, 171 High St., Rickmansworth, Herts WD3 1SN, England. TEL 44-1923-777000. FAX 44-1923-771297. Ed. Mark Corliss. adv. circ. 7,500. (processed) **Document type:** trade publication. —CCC.
Formerly: Wood and Equipment News Plus Woodworking Materials (ISSN 0263-1180); Which superseded (in 1977): Wood and Equipment News (ISSN 0043-7646)

674 US
WOOD FINISHER. 1986. q. $10. Mitchell Kohanek, Ed. & Pub., Box 64, Rosemount, MN 55068. bk.rev. circ. 5,000.

698.3 US
WOOD FINISHING QUARTERLY. 1981. q. free. Dakota County Area Vocational Technical Institute, Wood Finishing Trade Program, Co. Rd. 42 and Akron Ave., Rosemount, MN 55068. TEL 612-423-8362. Ed. Dan McGraw. adv. circ. 10,000.

WOOD NEWS; products-processes machines. see *FORESTS AND FORESTRY — Lumber And Wood*

694.5 US
WOOD STROKES & WOODCRAFTS. 1992. bi-m. $24. E G W Publishing Co., 1041 Shary Circle, Concord, CA 94518. TEL 510-671-9852. FAX 510-671-0692. Ed. Sandra Wagner. circ. 120,000 (paid). (back issues avail.) **Document type:** consumer publication.
Formerly: Wood Strokes and Weekend Woodcrafts; Which was formed by the merger of: Wood Strokes (ISSN 1069-6962) & Weekend Woodcrafts (ISSN 1058-9821)

698.3 UK ISSN 0965-9463
WOODCARVING. 1992. 10/yr. £65. (Guild of Master Craftsmen) G M C Publications Ltd., 166 High St., Lewes, E. Sussex BN7 1 XU, England. TEL 01273-477374. FAX 44-1273-478606. Ed. Nick Hough; Pub. A.E. Phillips. adv.: B&W page £800, color page £1080; trim 210 x 298; adv. contact: Linda Grace. circ. 25,000. **Indexed:** Ind.How To Do It (1993-). **Document type:** consumer publication.
Description: Covers the craft of woodcarving in all aspects.

694 US ISSN 0894-5403
WOODSHOP NEWS. 1986. m. $15.97. Soundings Publications, Inc., Pratt St., Essex, CT 06426-1122. TEL 860-767-8227. FAX 860-767-1048. URL: http://www.woodshopnews.com. Ed. Ian C. Bowen; Pub. John Turner. adv. contact: Glenn Mallory. circ. 90,000. (tabloid format) **Document type:** newspaper, consumer publication.
Description: News for and about people who work with wood.

694 US ISSN 0164-4114
WOODSMITH. 1979. bi-m. $19.95. August Home Publishing Co., 2200 Grand Ave., Des Moines, IA 50312-5306. TEL 515-282-7000. FAX 515-282-6741. E-mail: augusthome@aol.com; URL: http://www.augusthome.com. Ed. Terry Strohman; Pub. Donald B. Peschke. R&P contact: Robin Hutchinson. illus. circ. 400,000. **Indexed:** Ind.How To Do It (1979-). **Document type:** consumer publication. —UnCover.
Description: For woodworking hobbyists.

698 UK ISSN 0958-9457
WOODTURNING. 1990. 10/yr. £65. (Guild of Master Craftsmen) G M C Publications Ltd., 166 High St., Lewes, E. Sussex BN7 1XU, England. TEL 01273-477374. FAX 01273-478606. Ed. Neil Bell; Pub. A.E. Phillips. adv. contact: Linda Grace. circ. 31,311. **Indexed:** Ind.How To Do It (1993-). **Document type:** consumer publication.
Description: Covers the craft of woodturning. Includes information on tools, materials, and equipment.

WOODWORK. see *HOW-TO AND DO-IT-YOURSELF*

694   UK   ISSN 0043-776X
WOODWORKER. 1901. m. £24. Argus Specialist Publications Ltd. (Subsidiary of: Argus Press Group), Argus House, Boundary Way, Hemel Hempstead, Herts. HP2 7ST, England. TEL 01442-66551. FAX 01442-66998. (Subscr. to: Argus Subscription Services, Queensway House, 2 Queensway, Redhill, Surrey RH1 1QS, England. TEL 01737-768611) Ed. Zac Taylor. adv.; bk.rev.; charts; illus.; index. **Indexed:** Gdlns., Ind.How To Do It, Pinpointer. **Document type:** consumer publication.
—BLDSC (9346.800000).
    Formerly: Woodworker Annual (ISSN 0084-1196)
    Description: Appeals to beginner and expert woodworkers alike with new projects, how-to advice, and product reviews.

WOODWORKER'S JOURNAL. see *HOW-TO AND DO-IT-YOURSELF*

684   US   ISSN 1080-0042
WOODWORKERS WEST. 1988. bi-m. $12 (foreign $18) (effective 1997). Goldman Communications, Box 66751, Los Angeles, CA 90066. TEL 310-398-5931. E-mail: editor@woodwest.com; URL: http://www.woodwest.com/wood/. Ed. Ronald Goldman; Pub. Ronald Goldman. adv. circ. 10,000. **Document type:** consumer publication.
●Also available online.
    Formerly: Southern California Woodworker (ISSN 0898-3550)
    Description: Covers the people and events within the woodworking community in the western US. Includes news, shows, exhibits, clubs, classes and profiles.

694   CN   ISSN 0838-4185
WOODWORKING; Canada's leading magazine serving the producers of wood and wood products. 1987. 6/yr. Can.$35($55) Action Communications Inc., 135 Spy Court, Markham, ON L3R 5H6, Canada. TEL 905-477-3222. FAX 905-477-4320. Ed. Maurice Holtham; Pub. Blair Tullis. adv.; charts; illus.; stat.; tr.lit.; circ. 11,000 (controlled). (tabloid format; back issues avail.)
—UMI.
    Description: Directed to makers of furniture, kitchen cabinets, millwork and for sawmill operators.

698.3   UK
WOODWORKS. q. Nexus Special Interests Ltd., Nexus House, Boundary Way, Hemel Hempstead, Herts HP2 7ST, England. TEL 44-1442-66551. FAX 44-1442-66998. (Subscr. to: Argus Subscription Services, Queensway House, 2 Queensway, Redhill, Surrey, England. TEL 44-1737-768611) **Document type:** consumer publication.
    Description: Offers step-by-step instructions and advice for the home woodworker.

694   GW   ISSN 0342-6521
DER ZIMMERMANN. m. DM.83.40 (foreign DM.112.20) (effective 1997). Bruderverlag Albert Bruder GmbH, Bismarckstr. 21, 76133 Karlsruhe, Germany. TEL 49-721-91388-0. FAX 49-721-9138898. Ed. Peter Kuebler. R&P contact: Volker Rutkowski. adv. contact: Anton Hummel. circ. 10,000. **Document type:** trade publication.
—CCC.

BUILDING AND CONSTRUCTION — Hardware

APPLIANCE. see *ENGINEERING — Electrical Engineering*

683   CC   ISSN 0254-1149
ASIAN SOURCES HARDWARES. 1976. m. $40. Asian Sources Media Group, 22-F Vita Tower, 29 Wong Chuk Hang Rd., Aberdeen, Hong Kong, People's Republic of China. TEL 852-2555-4777. FAX 852-2873-0488. E-mail: asmgroup@singnet.com.sg. (Subscr. to: Wordright Enterprises Inc., Box 3062, Evanston, IL 60204-3062. TEL 708-475-1900) Ed. Michael Hay. adv. circ. 21,200. **Indexed:** HongKongiana. **Document type:** trade publication.
    Description: Covers home center products, auto parts & accessories, machinery and industrial supplies.

683   FI   ISSN 0788-5822
ASU HYVIN. 1959. m. FIM 150. Kauppiaitten Kustannus Oy, Kanavakatu 3.B, FIN-00160 Helsinki, Finland. TEL 358-0-228821. Ed. Hannu Hotakainen. adv.; charts; illus.; circ. 29,414 (controlled).
    Former titles (until 1990): Asu Hyvin - Rautavieisti; (until 1988): Rautavieisti (ISSN 0355-3086); (until 1972): K-Rautaviesti (ISSN 0022-7404)

683   AT   ISSN 0004-9255
AUSTRALIAN HARDWARE JOURNAL. 1886. m. Aus.$60 (foreign $116). Glenvale Publications Pty. Ltd., 4 Palmer Court, Mount Waverley, Vic. 3149, Australia. TEL 61-3-544-2233. FAX 61-3-543-1150. Ed. Sarah Maybery. adv.: B&W page Aus.$2080, color page Aus.$2520. bk.rev.; illus.; mkt.; stat. circ. 6,066. **Document type:** trade publication.

B H F DIRECTORY. (British Hardware Federation) see *BUSINESS AND ECONOMICS — Trade And Industrial Directories*

683   GW   ISSN 0005-6480
BAUBESCHLAG MAGAZIN. 1953. m. DM.30. Gert Wohlfarth GmbH Verlag Fachtechnik und Mercator-Verlag, Stresemannstr. 20-22, 47051 Duisburg, Germany. TEL 49-203-30527-0. FAX 49-203-337765. E-mail: wohlfarth@t-online.de. Ed. Matthias Fischer. circ. 23,000. **Document type:** trade publication.
    Formerly: Baubeschlag Magazin mit Praktikus; Incorporates (in 1974): Praktikus (ISSN 0171-3361)

683   GW   ISSN 0067-4583
BAUBESCHLAG-TASCHENBUCH. 1952. a. DM.34. Gert Wohlfarth GmbH Verlag Fachtechnik und Mercator-Verlag, Stresemannstr. 20-22, 47051 Duisburg, Germany. TEL 49-203-30527-0. FAX 49-203-337765. E-mail: wohlfarth@t-online.de. Pub. Gert Wohlfarth. adv.; bk.rev. circ. 5,600. **Document type:** trade publication.

683   SP
BRICOLAGE DISTRIBUCION. 4/yr. Via Augusta 59, 8o Of. 812, 08006 Barcelona, Spain. TEL 3-237-88-65. FAX 3-415-86-88. Ed. Salvador Beltran Nunez. circ. 10,000.

BRUSH AND ALLIED TRADES INTERNATIONAL DIRECTORY. see *BUSINESS AND ECONOMICS — Trade And Industrial Directories*

683.8 679.6   US   ISSN 0007-2710
TS2301.B8
BRUSHWARE. 1898. bi-m. $35 (foreign $70). Centaur South, 5515 Dundee Rd., Huddleston, VA 24104. TEL 540-297-1517. FAX 540-297-1519. Ed. Leslie W. Neff; Pub. Carl H. Wurzer. adv. contact: Carl H. Wurzer. bk.rev.; illus.; stat.; circ. 1,800 (paid). **Document type:** trade publication.
—CISTI.

BUILDCORE PRODUCT SOURCE; construction materials, equipment & furniture available in Canada. see *BUILDING AND CONSTRUCTION*

BUILDING, HARDWARE AND HOUSEWARES (YEAR). see *BUILDING AND CONSTRUCTION*

BYGG & JAERNHANDELN/BUILDING MATERIAL AND HARDWARE TRADE JOURNAL. see *BUSINESS AND ECONOMICS — Marketing And Purchasing*

683.3   CN   ISSN 1203-1771
CANADIAN LOCKSMITH; the technical news magazine for the locksmith and security industry. 1982. 5/yr. Can.$42 (effective 1997). 137 Vaughan Rd., Toronto, ON M6C 2L9, Canada. TEL 416-653-2199. FAX 416-656-3048. E-mail: tclarsin@interlog.com. Ed. Arnold Sintnicolaas. adv. circ. 500. (back issues avail.) **Document type:** trade publication.

683   CN   ISSN 0847-9968
CENTRE MAGAZINE. Key Title: Hardware & Home Centre Magazine. 1977. 8/yr. Can.$20 (foreign Can.$42) (effective 1997). Southam Magazine Group, 1450 Don Mills Rd., Don Mills, ON M3B 2X7, Canada. TEL 416-445-6641. FAX 416-510-6875. Ed. Elena Opasini. adv. contact: Debra Chapman. circ. 17,358.
    (until 1988): Hardware, Home, Building Supply Centre (ISSN 0847-995X); (until 1986): Centre (ISSN 0703-4598)
    Description: Brings up-to-date news on the industry, latest products, merchandising, buying skills and ways of increasing profit.

683   US   ISSN 8755-254X
TS200
CHILTON'S HARDWARE AGE; serving the North American hardware - home center market. (Catalog and Directory number avail.; annual buyers' guide avail.) 1855. m. $75. Chilton Co., Chilton Way, Radnor, PA 19089. TEL 610-964-4282. URL: http://www.homemkt.com. Ed. Jim Cory. adv.; bk.rev.; illus.; tr.lit. circ. 68,644. (also avail. in microfilm from UMI; microfiche from UMI; reprint service avail. from UMI) **Indexed:** Bus.Ind., Chem.Abstr., Tr.& Indus.Ind. **Document type:** trade publication.
●Also available online. Vendor(s): Knight-Ridder Information, Inc.
—UMI; UnCover. **CCC.**
    Former titles (until 1983): Hardware Age; (until 1981): Chilton's Hardware Age (ISSN 0162-5896); Hardware Age (ISSN 0017-7660)

D I Y SUPERSTORE. (Do It Yourself) see *HOW-TO AND DO-IT-YOURSELF*

683   UK   ISSN 0967-2257
HD9745.G7
D I Y TRADE BUYERS' GUIDE; the year book for the D I Y, hardware trades, housewares and garden equipment industries. 1908. a. £73.50 (Europe £86; rest of world £94) (effective 1997). Miller Freeman Information Services (Subsidiary of: United News & Media), Riverbank House, Angel Ln., Tonbridge, Kent TN9 1SE, England. TEL 44-1732-362666. FAX 44-1732-757829. URL: http://www.mfplc.com. index. circ. 1,500. **Document type:** directory.
    Former titles: Benn's Guide (Year) (ISSN 0954-8548); Benn's Hardware Directory and D I Y Buyers Guide (ISSN 0261-1465); Benn's Hardware Directory (ISSN 0067-5725)
    Description: Contains classified lists covering D.I.Y. hardware, housewares, and garden trades detailing manufacturers, wholesalers, retailers, and trade names.

D I Y WEEK. (Do It Yourself) see *HOW-TO AND DO-IT-YOURSELF*

DIRECTORY OF AUTOMOTIVE AFTERMARKET SUPPLIERS (YEAR). see *BUSINESS AND ECONOMICS — Trade And Industrial Directories*

DO-IT-YOURSELF RETAILING; hardware, home centers, lumberyards. see *HOW-TO AND DO-IT-YOURSELF*

683 690   US   ISSN 0361-5294
TS200
DOORS AND HARDWARE. 1936. m. $49 (foreign $89). Door and Hardware Institute, 14170 Newbrook Dr., Chantilly, VA 20151. TEL 703-222-2010. FAX 703-222-2410. E-mail: publications@dhi.org; URL: http://www.dhi.org. Ed. Janice Cooper; Pub. Donna Munari. R&P contact: Donna Munari. adv. contact: Nina Dadgar. illus.; tr.lit.; index; circ. 11,000 (controlled). **Document type:** trade publication.
●Also available online. Vendor(s): Information Access Co.
—CISTI.
    Incorporating (as of 1975): American Society of Architectural Hardware Consultants. News and Views (ISSN 0044-7935); Formerly (until May 1975): Hardware Consultant (ISSN 0017-7687)
    Description: Designed primarily for the door and architectural hardware wholesale commercial markets.
Refereed Serial

683   FR
DROGUERIE FRANCAISE. 24/yr. 12 rue Martel, 75010 Paris, France. TEL 45-23-38-33. FAX 42-46-05-05. Ed. Georges Abbou. circ. 8,500.

BUILDING AND CONSTRUCTION — HARDWARE

683   **GW**
EISENWAREN ZEITUNG; Markt fuer Werkzeuge, Beschlaege, Heimwerken & Garten. 1948. 13/yr. DM.115.20. (Fachverband des Deutschen Eisenwaren- und Hausrathandels - Federation of German Hardware and Houseware Retailers) Eisenwaren-Zeitung GmbH, Rheinwallgraben 11, 41460 Neuss, Germany. TEL 49-2131-916521. FAX 49-2131-916515. Ed. Achim Mecklenbeck. adv.: B&W page DM.4080, color page DM.7220; trim 185 x 260. bk.rev.; illus. circ. 10,000. **Document type:** trade publication.
    Formerly: E Z Eisenwaren; Which supersedes in part (in 1992): E Z - Eisenwaren und Hausrat (ISSN 0938-2011); (until 1989): Eisenwaren- und Hausrat-Zeitung (ISSN 0931-5411); (until 1986): Eisenwaren-Zeitung (ISSN 0013-2861)

683   **GW**   **ISSN 0013-2853**
EISENWARENBOERSE. 1904. 6/yr. DM.72 (foreign DM.98). Verlag Kramer, Postfach 101726, 33517 Bielefeld, Germany. adv.; bk.rev.; bibl.; illus.; stat.; index. circ. 15,614. **Document type:** trade publication.
    —CCC.

683   **FR**
ESSOR DE LA QUINCAILLERIE. 1965. a. 500 F. Union Francaise d'Annuaires Professionnels, 130 av. de Bouleaux, B.P. 36, 78192 Trappes Cedex, France. TEL 01-30-13-82-00. FAX 01-30-13-82-11. **Document type:** directory.
    Formerly: Memento General Tequi Quincaillerie (ISSN 0025-9055); Which incorporates: Memento General de la Quincaillerie; Repertoire Tequi Quincaillerie.

683 621.042   **UK**
EUROPEAN DIRECTORY OF SUSTAINABLE AND ENERGY EFFICIENT BUILDING - COMPONENTS SERVICES MATERIALS. 1993. a. £39.50($65) James & James (Science Publishers) Ltd., Waterside House, 47 Kentish Town Rd., London NW1 8NZ, England. TEL 44-171-284-3833. FAX 44-171-284-3737. E-mail: jxj.com; URL: http://www.jxj.com/. (Dist. in N. America by: Books International, Box 605, Herndon, VA 20172. TEL 703-435-7064. FAX 703-689-0660) Eds. Owen Lewis, John Goulding; Pub. Edward Milford. adv.: B&W page £2795, color page £3495; adv. contact: Paul Diamond. **Document type:** directory.
    —CISTI.
    Formerly: European Directory of Energy Efficient Building - Components Services Materials (ISSN 1352-0172)
    Description: Contains a wide range of contributions providing an overview of current practices in energy efficient design and construction.

683   **US**   **ISSN 0746-2441**
TJ1320
FASTENER TECHNOLOGY INTERNATIONAL. 1977. bi-m. $35 (foreign $70) free to qualified personnel (effective 1997). Initial Publications Inc., 3869 Darrow Rd., Ste. 109, Stow, OH 44224. TEL 216-686-9544. FAX 216-686-9563. E-mail: 104251.426@compuserve.com. Ed. Michael J. McNulty; Pub. John L. Jones. adv.; pat.; circ. 13,000 (controlled). **Document type:** trade publication.
    —CISTI.
    Former titles: Fastener Technology (ISSN 0191-8508); F T Fastener Technology (ISSN 0272-7331)

683   **IT**
FERRAMENTA E CASALINGHI. 1959. m. L.80000 (foreign L.170000). Editrice Collins Gestione Editoriale, Piazza S. Carmillo De Lellis 1, 20141 Milan, Italy. TEL 39-2-66984880. FAX 39-2-66984771. Ed. Osvaldo Giardino. adv.: B&W page L.2650000, color page L.3500000; trim 180 x 297. circ. 14,463.

683   **SP**
FERRETERIA ACTUALIDAD. 6/yr. Via Augusta 59 8o, Of. 812, 08006 Barcelona, Spain. TEL 3-237-88-65. FAX 3-415-86-88. Ed. Salvador Beltran Nunez. circ. 10,000.

683   **SP**   **ISSN 0212-8276**
FERRETICA. 9/yr. $100. Mazustegui 21 4o planta, 48006 Bilbao, Spain. TEL 415-90-22. FAX 416-27-43. Ed. Teresa del hoyo. circ. 5,200.

683   **IT**
FINESTRA INTERNATIONAL. (Text in English, French, Spanish) s-a. Tecnomedia s.r.l., Via Sansovino 28, 20133 Milan, Italy. TEL 02-70602276. FAX 02-23680468. adv.: B&W page L.1930000, color page L.2720000; trim 195 x 270. circ. 7,430.

683   **NE**   **ISSN 0929-5674**
GEREEDSCHAP; vakblad voor de detailhandel in gereedschappen, ijzerwaren en doe het zelf proauicten. 1950. 6/yr. fl.64. Uitgeverij Scala bv, Postbus 28009, 3828 ZG Hoogland, Netherlands. TEL 31-33-4806896. FAX 31-33-4802281. Pub. M. Fetvacian. adv. circ. 6,000. **Indexed:** Key to Econ.Sci. **Document type:** trade publication.
    Former titles (until 1992): Vakhandel (ISSN 0927-6653); (until 1991): D H Z - Vakhandel (ISSN 0922-5293); (until 1988): Gereedschap (ISSN 0016-8602)

683   **CN**
GUIDE DES CENTRES ET DES QUINCAILLERIES DU QUEBEC. 1993. a. Publedition Inc., 620 Industriel Blvd., St-Jean-sur-Richelieu, PQ J3B 7X4, Canada. TEL 514-856-7821. FAX 514-359-0836. Ed. Martine Breton. adv.: B&W page Can.$1030, color page Can.$1330; trim 8 1/4 x 10 7/8. circ. 3,000.

HARDWARE AGE "WHO MAKES IT" BUYERS' GUIDE. see BUSINESS AND ECONOMICS — Trade And Industrial Directories

683   **UK**   **ISSN 0266-0539**
HARDWARE AND GARDEN REVIEW. 1968. m. £47 (foreign £63) ($100)) (effective 1997). Faversham House Group Ltd., Faversham House, 232a Addington Rd., South Croydon, Surrey CR2 8LE, England. TEL 44-181-651-7100. FAX 44-181-651-7117. Ed. Liam O'Brien; Pub. Martin Albert. adv. contact: Mark Skelton. bk.rev.; circ. 14,970. (tabloid format; back issues avail.) **Document type:** trade publication.
    Former titles: Hardware Review (ISSN 0017-7733); Hardware Trades Review.

683   **CN**   **ISSN 0017-7717**
HARDWARE MERCHANDISING. (Annual directory: Hardware Handbook) 1888. 10/yr. Can.$35 (Includes annual directory). Maclean Hunter Ltd., 777 Bay St., Toronto, ON M5W 1A7, Canada. TEL 416-596-5284. FAX 416-596-5553. Ed. Michael McLarney. adv.; illus.; mkt.; stat.; tr.lit. circ. 15,621.

683 658   **SA**
HARDWARE RETAILER. 1985. m. R.60. Complete Publishing (Pty.) Ltd., P.O. Box 87745, Houghton 2041, South Africa. TEL 27-11-7892112. FAX 27-11-7895347. adv.; illus. circ. 6,584. **Document type:** trade publication.

683   **UK**
HARDWARE TODAY. m. membership. British Hardware Federation, 225 Bristol Rd., Edgbaston, Birmingham B5 7UB, England. TEL 44-121-446-6688. FAX 44-121-446-5215. Ed. John Morgan; Pub. Michael I. Weedon. R&P contact: Michael I. Weedon. adv.: B&W page £695, color page £1130; trim 297 x 210; adv. contact: Roger Loweth. bk.rev.; illus.; stat. circ. 9,850. **Indexed:** Food Sci.& Tech.Abstr. **Document type:** trade publication.
    Formerly: N F I Bulletin (ISSN 0027-6502)

683   **US**
HARDWARE TRADE. 1891. bi-m. $24. Screened Porch Publishing Co., 10510 France Ave. S., No. 225, Bloomington, MN 55431-3538. TEL 612-944-3172. Ed. Patt Peterson; Pub. Sue Connelly. adv.: B&W page $1700, color $2300; trim 8 1/2 x 11; adv. contact: P. Connelly. illus.; tr.lit.; circ. 17,242. **Document type:** trade publication.
    Former titles: Northern Hardware; Northern Hardware Trade (ISSN 0191-6807)

683   **AU**
HARTWARENMARKT. m. Verlag Lorenz, Ebendorferstr. 10, A-1010 Vienna, Austria. TEL 43-1-4056695. FAX 43-1-4068693. Ed. Gabriele Kaiser. adv.: B&W page S.18700, color page S.33900. circ. 4,300. **Document type:** trade publication.
    Formerly: Eisenwarenhandel.

HONG KONG ENTERPRISE. see GIFTWARE AND TOYS

683.8   **CC**   **ISSN 1021-8882**
HONG KONG HOUSEHOLD. (Text in English) 1983. s-a. $54 for 2 yrs. in Asia; elsewhere $72. Hong Kong Trade Development Council, 36-39th Fl., Office Tower, Convention Plaza, 1 Harbour Rd., Wanchai, Hong Kong, People's Republic of China. TEL 2584-4333. FAX 2824-0249. Ed. Saul Lockhart. adv.; illus.; stat. circ. 30,000. **Indexed:** HongKongiana. **Document type:** trade publication.

683   **IE**   **ISSN 0047-1461**
IRISH HARDWARE AND ALLIED TRADER. 1938. m. £20. (Irish Hardware Association) Jemma Publications Ltd., Marino House, 53 Glasthule Rd., Sandycove, Co. Dublin, Ireland. TEL 2800000. FAX 2801818. (Subscr. to: P.O. Box 1973, Rathmines, Dublin 6, Ireland) Ed. Pat Nolan. adv.; bk.rev.; tr.lit. circ. 1,774.

ISENKRAMBRANCHEN. see INTERIOR DESIGN AND DECORATION — Furniture And House Furnishings

KETENS IN KAART. see HOW-TO AND DO-IT-YOURSELF

683.3   **UK**   **ISSN 0262-4478**
KEYWAYS. 1979. 6/yr. membership. Master Locksmiths Association, Units 4-5, The Business Park, Woodford Halse, Daventry, Northants NN11 3PZ, England. TEL 44-1327-262255. FAX 44-1327-262539. Ed. Mick Friend. R&P contact: Roman Russocki. adv. contact: Lorraine Stanley. illus. **Document type:** bulletin.

683.3   **US**   **ISSN 0193-3191**
LOCKSMITH GAZETTE; the magazine of professional locksmithing. 1977. q. $16. Box 14321, Columbus, OH 43214. Ed. Victor Fanberg. adv.; bk.rev. circ. 3,500. **Document type:** trade publication.

683.3   **US**   **ISSN 1050-2254**
TS519
LOCKSMITH LEDGER INTERNATIONAL. 1939. m. $38 (Canada $52; elsewhere $65; includes directory issue) (effective 1997). Locksmith Publishing Corp., 850 Busse Hwy., Park Ridge, IL 60068-5980. TEL 847-692-5940. FAX 847-692-4604. E-mail: lledger@simon-net.com. Ed. Gale Johnson; Pub. Steven Lasky. adv. contact: Nancy L. Campanale. charts; illus.; mkt.; pat.; tr.lit.; tr.mk.; index. circ. 19,500. (reprint service avail.) **Document type:** trade publication.
    Former titles (until 1988): Locksmith Ledger (ISSN 0273-625X); Locksmith Ledger and Security Register (ISSN 0024-5720)
    Description: Technical news magazine of the physical and electronic security industry.

LOCKSMITH LEDGER - INTERNATIONAL DIRECTORY. see CRIMINOLOGY AND LAW ENFORCEMENT — Security

MARKET; commerce de l'equipement du cadre de vie. see INTERIOR DESIGN AND DECORATION — Furniture And House Furnishings

683.3   **US**
MASTER LOCK NEWS TODAY. 1947. q. free to qualified personnel. Master Lock Co., 2600 N. 32nd St., Milwaukee, WI 53210. TEL 414-444-2800. FAX 414-449-3193. TELEX 26-9444. Ed. Richard P. Simons. circ. 1,900 (controlled). **Description:** Informs employees of company-related news and other topics of interest to them.

683 674   **US**
MEMBERS. 1991. m. (except Dec.). Cotter & Company, 8600 W. Bryn Mawr Ave., Chicago, IL 60631. TEL 312-695-5224. FAX 312-695-6785. Ed. Shelley Berryhill. R&P contact: Shelley Berryhill. adv.: color page $3495; trim 7 3/8 x 10; adv. contact: Tom Delph. circ. 10,000. **Document type:** trade publication.

683   **SP**
MENAJE TOTAL. 6/yr. Via Augusta 59, 8o, Of. 812, 08006 Barcelona, Spain. TEL 3-237-11-98. Ed. Salvador Beltran Nunez. circ. 25,000.

BUSINESS AND ECONOMICS

683 UK
NATURAL STONE DIRECTORY. 1968. biennial. £40. Herald House Ltd., 96 Dominion Rd., Worthing, W. Sussex BN14 8JP, England. TEL 01903-821082. FAX 01903-215904. **Document type:** directory.
Description: Lists all quarries and stone available in the U.K. and Ireland, as well as imported materials. Provides information on suppliers of related equipment and services for specifiers and users of stone.

683 NZ ISSN 0028-8160
NEW ZEALAND HARDWARE JOURNAL. vol.16, 1971. m. NZ.$8. (New Zealand Wholesale Hardware Guilds' Federation) Akron Consolidated Ltd., Box 51-182, Auckland 6, New Zealand. (Co-sponsor: N.Z. Retail Hardware Federation) Ed. L. Soffe. adv.; bk.rev.; illus. circ. 1,000. **Document type:** trade publication.
—CCC.

683 SP ISSN 0213-0823
NUEVA FERRETERIA; revista para los profesionales de la ferreteria y afines. 1985. m. 10900 ptas. (foreign 21300 ptas.) (effective 1997). Tecnipublicaciones S.A., C. Albacete 5, 28027 Madrid, Spain. TEL 34-1-3261440. FAX 34-1-3262341. adv. circ. 85,000.

683 IT ISSN 0394-3216
NUOVA FINESTRA; serramenti e componenti per l'edilizia. 1980. m. (11/yr.). L.95000 (foreign L.160000). Tecnomedia s.r.l., Via Sansovino 28, 20133 Milan, Italy. TEL 2-70602276. FAX 392-203264. TELEX 323047 TECMEA I. Ed. Renata Giusiana. adv.: B&W page L.1470000, color page L.2140000; trim 175 x 266. bk.rev. circ. 7,000.

683 AU
DER OESTERREICHISCHER BAUSTOFFMARKT. 8/yr. Verlag Lorenz, Ebendorferstr. 10, A-1010 Vienna, Austria. TEL 43-1-4056695. FAX 43-1-4068693. Ed. Raimund Ossinger. adv.: B&W page S.23400, color page S.38700. circ. 4,800. **Document type:** trade publication.

683 SZ ISSN 0031-5923
PERSPECTIVE. (Text in French and German) 1912. s-m. 85 SFr. (foreign 89 SFr.) (effective 1997 & 1998). Association of Swiss Ironmongers, Talstr. 66, CH-8001 Zurich, Switzerland. TEL 41-1-2242084. FAX 41-1-2242088. Ed. Christoph Rotermund. adv. contact: Ursula Merkle. bk.rev.; illus.; stat.; tr.lit. circ. 2,000. **Indexed:** Bus.Ind. **Document type:** trade publication.
Formerly: Eisenwarenhandel.
Description: Trade journal covering the hardware industry: tools, fittings, appliances, machinery, housewares, glass, camping equipment.

683 CN ISSN 0318-8531
QUINCAILLERIE MATERIAUX. 1887. 6/yr. Can.$20 (foreign Can.$49). Maclean Hunter Ltd., 777 Bay St., Toronto, ON M5W 1A7, Canada. TEL 416-596-5284. FAX 416-596-5553. Ed. Joanne Marchand. adv.; illus.; stat.; tr.lit. circ. 4,474.
Formerly (until 1976): Quincaillier (ISSN 0318-8515)

683 FR
QUINCAILLERIE MODERNE. m. 345 F. (foreign 440 F.) (effective 1997). S.E.P., 106 bd. Malesherbes, 75017 Paris, France. TEL 33-1-42128080. FAX 33-1-46229879. Pub. Joelle Letessier. adv. circ. 8,000. **Document type:** trade publication.

683 GW ISSN 0934-411X
ROLLADEN & SONNENSCHUTZ; Fachzeitschrift fuer das Rolladen- und Jalousiebauer-Handwerk. 1961. 10/yr. DM.95 (foreign DM.130) (effective 1996). Bundesverband Rolladen & Sonnenschutz e.V., Hopmannstr. 2, 53177 Bonn, Germany. TEL 49-228-952100. FAX 49-228-328099. Ed. Hans Stoffels. adv.: B&W page DM.895; trim 260 x 180. bk.rev.; pat. circ. 1,700. **Document type:** trade publication.
Description: Trade publication for the shutter and sunscreen industry. Covers marquees, shades, blinds, awnings, security shutters. Includes list of advertisers.

683 IT ISSN 1120-7876
S E C. (Serramenti e Componenti) m. (9/yr.). L.65000 (Europe L.130000; elsewhere L.175000) (effective 1997). Tecniche Nuove s.p.a., Via C. Menotti, 14, 20129 Milan, Italy. TEL 39-2-75701. FAX 39-2-7610351. adv.: B&W page L.1430000, color page L.2288000; trim 210 x 297. circ. 6,500.

683 GW ISSN 0179-1591
SCHLOSS & BESCHLAG & MARKT; Fachzeitschrift fuer den Ausstattungs- und Sicherheitsmarkt. 1986. m. DM.96. Gert Wohlfarth GmbH Verlag Fachtechnik und Mercator-Verlag, Stresemannstr. 20-22, 47051 Duisburg, Germany. TEL 49-203-30527-0. FAX 49-203-337765. E-mail: wohlfarth@t-online.de. Ed. Uwe Hennig; Pub. Gert Wohlfarth. circ. 4,592. **Document type:** trade publication.

683 SZ
SCHWEIZER BAUSTOFF INDUSTRIE. 8/yr. Buberbergplatz 9, CH-3001 Bern, Switzerland. TEL 031-3262626. FAX 031-3262629. circ. 2,700. **Document type:** trade publication.

683 365.64 US ISSN 1045-831X
TH9739
SECURITY SALES; technology for security installation and service. 1979. m. (plus Factbook in Dec.). $35 (Canada $42; elsewhere $53). (National Alarm Association of America) Bobit Publishing Company, 2512 Artesia Blvd., Redondo Beach, CA 90278-3210. TEL 310-376-8788. FAX 310-376-9043. E-mail: peggyn@bobit.com. (Co-sponsor: National Alarm Association of America) Ed. Jason Knott. adv.; bk.rev.; circ. 23,500 (controlled). **Document type:** trade publication.
Former titles (until 1988): A I D (Agoura Hills) (ISSN 0885-7784); (until 1987): Alarm Installer and Dealer (ISSN 0195-8178)
Description: Practical applications, features and new technology developments for the security alarm dealer.

683 AU ISSN 0561-7855
TA684
STAHLBAU - RUNDSCHAU; Fach- und Informationszeitschrift des oesterreichischen Stahlbauverbandes. 1955. s-a. S.374. (Oesterreichischer Stahlbau-Verband) Bohmann Druck und Verlag GmbH & Co. KG, Leberstr. 122, A-1110 Vienna, Austria. TEL 43-1-74095-0. FAX 43-1-74095-183. TELEX 132312. Ed. H. Massiczek. adv. circ. 6,100. **Indexed:** Eng.Ind. **Document type:** trade publication.
—Ei; Linda Hall.

683 FR
T N SERRURERIE - MIROITERIE. (Techniques Nouvelles) 1967. 10/yr. 520 F. (effective 1996). 28 rue Andre Bonnenfant, 78100 Saint-Germain en Laye, France. TEL 39-73-50-31. FAX 39-73-53-31. Ed. Olivier Millet. adv.; circ. 6,000. circ. 6,000. **Document type:** trade publication.

683 US
TOOLS & HARDWARE: LATIN AMERICAN INDUSTRIAL REPORT. (Avail. for each of 22 Latin American countries) 1985. a. $435 per country report. Aquino Productions, Box 125, Rochester, VT 05767.

683 US
TOP DRAWER.* 1963? q. free. Axia Incorporated, 100 W. 22nd St., Ste. 134, Lombard, IL 60148-4877. TEL 312-654-3350. Ed. Ethel C. Stahnke. circ. 2,000.

VAKBLAD MIX; voor de doe-het-zelf en ijzerwaren- en tuinhandel. see HOW-TO AND DO-IT-YOURSELF

BUSINESS AND ECONOMICS

see also Advertising and Public Relations; Business and Economics–Accounting; Business and Economics–Banking and Finance; Business and Economics–Banking and Finance–Computer Applications; Business and Economics–Chamber of Commerce Publications; Business and Economics–Computer Applications; Business and Economics–Cooperatives; Business and Economics–Domestic Commerce; Business and Economics–Economic Situation and Conditions; Business and Economics–Economic Systems and Theories, Economic History; Business and Economics–International Commerce; Business and Economics–International Development and Assistance; Business and Economics–Investments; Business and Economics–Labor and Industrial Relations; Business and Economics–Macroeconomics; Business and Economics–Management; Business and Economics–Marketing and Purchasing; Business and Economics–Office Equipment and Services; Business and Economics–Personnel Management; Business and Economics–Production of Goods and Services; Business and Economics–Public Finance, Taxation; Business and Economics–Small Business; Business and Economics–Trade and Industrial Directories; Consumer Education and Protection; Insurance; Labor Unions; Occupations and Careers; Real Estate; also specific industries

330 368 US ISSN 1054-5913
RA413.5.U5
A A P P O JOURNAL. 1991. bi-m. $50 (foreign $80). (American Association of Preferred Provider Organizations) Health Care Communications, Inc., 1 Bridge Plaza, Fort Lee, NJ 07024. TEL 201-947-5455. FAX 201-947-8406. Ed. Douglas L. Elden. adv. circ. 23,000. (back issues avail.) **Indexed:** I.P.A.
Description: Highlights research and trends within managed health care.
Refereed Serial

330 AT ISSN 1037-8286
A B A R E RESEARCH REPORTS. no.4, 1971. irreg. (8-15/yr.). Aus.$220 (effective 1997). Australian Bureau of Agricultural and Resource Economics, G.P.O. Box 1563, Canberra, A.C.T. 2601, Australia. TEL 61-6-2722211. FAX 61-6-2722330. E-mail: deniseflemia@abare.gov.au. Ed. Andrew Wright. **Indexed:** Food Sci.& Tech.Abstr., Ind.Vet., Nutr.Abstr., Rural Recreat.Tour.Abstr., Vet.Bull., World Agri.Econ.& Rural Sociol.Abstr. **Document type:** government publication.
—BLDSC (0537.724475). **CCC.**
Formerly (until Apr., 1989): Australian Bureau of Agricultural Economics. Occasional Papers (ISSN 0815-1458)
Description: Contains economic analyses and commodity analyses.

330 MW
A B A TODAY. 1982. m. African Businessmen's Association of Malawi, P.O. Box 5861, Limbe, Malawi. Ed. Rex Chalera.

A C C A DOCKET. (American Corporate Counsel Association) see LAW — Corporate Law

330 PH
A D B BUSINESS OPPORTUNITIES. (Text in English) m. $30. Asian Development Bank, P.O. Box 789, 1099 Manila, Philippines. TEL 632-711-3851. FAX 632-741-7961. TELEX 63587 ADB PN. (also avail. in microfiche from CIS) **Indexed:** Ind.Phil.Per.
Description: Covers proposed projects, advance action on procurement, consultant recruitment and retroactive financing, procurement notices, and contract awards.

BUSINESS AND ECONOMICS

330 SZ ISSN 0982-832X
A G E F I MAGAZINE. (Supplement to: Agence Economique et Financiere (ISSN 0755-1940)) m. Societe de l'Agence Economique et Financiere SA, 7 rue de Geneve, Case Postale 2113, CH-1002 Lausanne, Switzerland. TEL 021-200316. FAX 021-202464. TELEX 450211. Ed. Alain Fabarez. circ. 6,300.

330 AU
A K AKTUELL. 5/yr. Maximilianstr. 7, A-6020 Innsbruck, Austria. TEL 05222-5340. FAX 05222-5340208. Ed. Elmar Schiffkorn. circ. 200,000. **Document type:** bulletin.

330 FR
A LA BARRE DE L'ENTREPRISE. 1957. q. 24-26 rue Hamelin, 75116 Paris, France. adv. circ. 2,000.

330 US ISSN 0892-1067
A O I BUSINESS VIEWPOINT.* 1960. bi-m. Associated Oregon Industries, Inc., 1149 Court St., N.E., Salem, OR 97301-4030. TEL 503-588-2458. FAX 503-588-0052. Ed. Donna Lewis. adv.

A R W WHOLESALER NEWS. (Air-Conditioning & Refrigeration Wholesalers) see HEATING, PLUMBING AND REFRIGERATION

330 SI ISSN 0217-4472
HC441.A1
A S E A N ECONOMIC BULLETIN. 1984. 3/yr. $29 to individuals (Europe & N. America $35); institutions $36 (Europe & N. America $44). (Association of South East Asian Nations, Economic Research Unit) Institute of Southeast Asian Studies, Heng Mui Keng Terrace, Pasir Panjang, Singapore 119596, Singapore. TEL 65-7780955. FAX 65-7756259. E-mail: pubsunit@merlion.iseas.ac.sg; URL: http://www.iseas.ac.sg/pub.html; http://mertion.iseas.ac.sg/aeb.html. Ed. Joseph Tan. bk.rev.; abstr.; bibl.; charts; stat.; index. (also avail. in microform from UMI; back issues avail.) **Indexed:** Asian-Pac.Econ.Lit., P.A.I.S., Per.Islam. (1991-), World Agri.Econ.& Rural Sociol.Abstr. **Document type:** academic/scholarly publication.
—BLDSC (1739.952000); SWETS; UMI; UnCover.
  Description: Current economic issues pertaining to the countries of the Association of Southeast Asian Nations: Indonesia, Philippines, Thailand, Malaysia, Singapore, Brunei, and Vietnam. Also covers ASEAN's relations with its major trade partners: the USA, Japan, EEC, East Asia, and Australasia, and its relationships with the world political economy.

A W H P ACTION. (Association for Worksite Health Promotion) see PHYSICAL FITNESS AND HYGIENE

ABSTRACT OF AMERICAN INDUSTRIAL TREND ANALYSIS. see BUSINESS AND ECONOMICS — Labor And Industrial Relations

330 CH ISSN 1018-161X
ACADEMIA ECONOMIC PAPERS. (Text in Chinese and English) 1973. q. free. Academia Sinica, Institute of Economics - Chung Yang Yen Chiu Yuan Ching Chi Yen Chiu So, Nankang, Taipei, Taiwan 11529, Republic of China. TEL 02-782-2791. FAX 02-785-3946. Ed. Jia-Dong Shea. bk.rev. circ. 2,000. **Indexed:** Asian-Pac.Econ.Lit. **Document type:** academic/scholarly publication.
—BLDSC (0570.469200).
  Refereed Serial

330 UK ISSN 0958-5206
HF5341
ACCOUNTING, BUSINESS AND FINANCIAL HISTORY. 1990. 3/yr. £55 (foreign $90) to individuals; institutions £125 (foreign $210); print & online eds. combined £150 (foreign $250) (effective 1998). Thomson Professional (Subsidiary of: International Thomson Publishing Group), 2-6 Boundary Row, London SE1 8HN, England. TEL 44-171-865-0066. FAX 44-171-522-9621. E-mail: journal@rapidcom.co.uk; URL: http://abfh.thomsonprofessional.com. (Subscr. to: ITPS Ltd., Cheriton House, Andover, Hants. SP10 5BE, England. TEL 44-1264-342713. FAX 44-1264-342807) Eds. J.R. Edwards, R.H. Parker. circ. 600. (back issues avail.) **Document type:** academic/scholarly publication.
●Also available online.
—BLDSC (0573.592300); SWETS. **CCC.**
  Description: Analyzes past developments in business and finance history; explains present structure and practices; and aims to create a platform for solving current problems and predicting future developments.
  Refereed Serial

330 HU ISSN 0001-6373
HB9.M28 CODEN: AOECDR
ACTA OECONOMICA. (Text in English) 1966. q. $148 (effective 1998). (Magyar Tudomanyos Akademia) Akademiai Kiado Rt., P.O. Box 245, H-1519 Budapest, Hungary. TEL 36-1-2043976. FAX 36-1-2043973. Ed. Tamas Foldi. adv.; bk.rev.; charts. **Indexed:** ASCA, Curr.Cont., Geo.Abstr., IBR, J.of Econ.Lit., Key to Econ.Sci., P.A.I.S., Rural Recreat.Tour.Abstr., SSCI, World Agri.Econ.& Rural Sociol.Abstr. **Document type:** academic/scholarly publication.
—BLDSC (0641.690000); Genuine Article; SWETS; UnCover. **CCC.**
  Description: Publishes articles on Hungary's economic development, policy, management system and planning, and reforms. Includes issues of world economics and trade.

330 370 PL ISSN 0208-6018
HB3
ACTA UNIVERSITATIS LODZIENSIS: FOLIA OECONOMICA. (Text in Polish; summaries in various languages) 1975. irreg. Wydawnictwo Uniwersytetu Lodzkiego, Ul. Jaraczca 34, Lodz, Poland. TEL 331671. (Dist. by: Ars Polona-Ruch, Krakowskie Przedmiescie 7, Warsaw, Poland) **Document type:** academic/scholarly publication.
—BLDSC (0585.207600); KNAW.
  Supersedes in part (in 1980): Uniwersytet Lodzki. Zeszyty Naukowe. Seria 3: Nauki Ekonomiczne i Socjologiczne (ISSN 0076-0374)
  Description: Research on political economy, econometrics and statistics, accounting, informatics, planning and economic policy, marketing, foreign trade and more.

330 PL ISSN 0208-5305
HB9
ACTA UNIVERSITATIS NICOLAI COPERNICI. NAUKI HUMANISTYCZNO-SPOLECZNE. EKONOMIA. 1972. irreg. price varies. Uniwersytet Mikolaja Kopernika, Wydawnictwo, Ul. Gagarina 11, 87-100 Torun, Poland. TEL 48-56-14295. TELEX 212242. (Dist. by: Osrodek Rozpowszechniania Wydawnictw Naukowych PAN, Palac Kultury i Nauki, 00-901 Warsaw, Poland) **Document type:** academic/scholarly publication.
  Formerly (until 1973): Uniwersytet Mikolaja Kopernika w Toruniu. Nauki Humanistyczno-Spoleczne. Zeszyty Naukowe. Ekonomia (ISSN 0208-5380)

300 HU ISSN 0554-5374
ACTA UNIVERSITATIS SZEGEDIENSIS DE ATTILA JOZSEF NOMINATAE. SECTIO OECONOMICO-POLITICA. (Supplement to: Politikai Gazdasgtan (ISSN 0563-0622)) (Text in Hungarian; summaries in English and Russian) 1959. a. exchange basis. Attila Jozsef University, c/o E. Szabo, Exchange Librarian, Dugonics ter 13, P.O. Box 393, 6701 Szeged, Hungary. (Subscr. to: Kultura, Box 149, 1389 Budapest, Hungary) Ed. Lajos Nagy. circ. 200.
  Description: Disseminates the academic staff's economic research in Hungary and abroad.

330 PL
ACTA UNIVERSITATIS WRATISLAVIENSIS. EKONOMIA. (Text in Polish; summaries in English or German) 1993. irreg. price varies. (Uniwersytet Wroclawski) Wydawnictwo Uniwersytetu Wroclawskiego, Spolka z o.o., Pl. Uniwersytecki 9-13, 50-137 Wroclaw, Poland. TEL 48-71-441006. FAX 48-71-402735. Ed. Leon Olszewski. circ. 300. **Document type:** academic/scholarly publication.

ACTA UNIVERSITATIS WRATISLAVIENSIS. PRZEGLAD PRAWA I ADMINISTRACJI. see PUBLIC ADMINISTRATION

338 370 NE ISSN 0165-0246
ACTU ECO; werkkrant voor het economie-onderwijs. 1974. 5/yr. price varies. WoltersgroepGroningen b.v. (Subsidiary of: Wolters Kluwer N.V.), Postbus 58, 9700 MB Groningen, Netherlands. TEL 31-50-5226524. FAX 31-50-5264866. illus.

330 UK
▼**ACTUALIDAD ECONOMICA EN C D - R O M.** 1996. a. Chadwyck-Healey Ltd., The Quorum, Barnwell Rd., Cambridge CB5 8SW, England. TEL 44-1223-215512. FAX 44-1223-215514. E-mail: marketing@chadwyck.co.uk; URL: http://www.chadwyck.com. (In N. America: Chadwyck-Healey Inc., 1101 King St., Alexandria, VA 22314. TEL 800-752-0515. FAX 703-683-7589)
●Available only on CD-ROM. Producer(s): Chadwyck-Healey Inc.
  Description: Publishes the full text of the weekly Spanish business magazine Actualidad Economica.

330 CN ISSN 0001-771X
HB3
ACTUALITE ECONOMIQUE. 1925. q. Can.$60 (effective 1997). (Societe Canadienne de Science Economique) Ecole des Hautes Etudes Commerciales, 3000 chemin de la Cote-Sainte-Catherine, Montreal, PQ H3T 2A7, Canada. TEL 514-340-6437. Ed. Paul Lanoie. adv.; bk.rev.; bibl.; charts; index, cum.index: 1925-1950, 1950-1960, 1960-1970, 1980-1990. circ. 1,200. **Indexed:** Amer.Hist.& Life, Can.B.P.I., Can.Per.Ind., ELLIS, Geo.Abstr., Hist.Abstr., IBR, Int.Lab.Doc., J.of Econ.Lit., P.A.I.S.For.Lang.Ind., Pt.de Rep. (1979-), SSCI. **Document type:** academic/scholarly publication.
—BLDSC (0677.105000).

330 US ISSN 1088-016X
ADVANCE (SAN FRANCISCO). (Text in Spanish) 1989. bi-m. $10 (effective 1996). 3247 24th St., San Francisco, CA 94110-3927. TEL 415-647-8029. FAX 415-821-4127. E-mail: mtmeza@aol.com. Ed. Marco T. Meza; Pub. Marco T. Meza. adv.; page $2500; trim 8 1/2 x 11; adv. contact: Marco T. Meza. bk.rev.; film rev.; music rev.; play rev.; software rev.; tele.rev.; video rev.; charts; illus.; stat.; tr.lit. circ. 35,000. (back issues avail.)
  Formerly (until 1996): Avance Hispano (ISSN 1088-0151)
  Description: Covers different issues of today's business world, such as computers and technology, especially for business people and college students.

330 US
ADVANCE NEWS JOURNAL. 1978. w. $15 (out of state $22). Advance Publishing Company, 1101 N. Cage, Twin Palm Plaza, Ste. C1, Pharr, TX 78577. TEL 210-783-0036. Ed. Gregg Wendorf; Pub. Gregg Wendorf. adv.; tr. rev. 4,000,000 (paid); 3,500 (controlled). **Document type:** trade publication.

ADVANCES IN ARTIFICIAL INTELLIGENCE IN ECONOMICS, FINANCE, AND MANAGEMENT. see COMPUTERS — Artificial Intelligence

ADVANCES IN THE ECONOMICS OF SPORT. see SPORTS AND GAMES

330 MK
AL-ADWA'. s-m. Oman Publishing House, P.O. Box 580, Muscat, Sultanate of Oman. TEL 704353. TELEX 3376. Ed. Habib Muhammad Nasib. circ. 15,600. **Indexed:** Per.Islam. (1993-).

330 659.1 059 GW
AFRICAN INTERPRETER; journal on African and Arab affairs. (Text in English) 1975. m. DM.48($45) African Interpreter Publishing Co., Raderbergguertel 11, 50968 Cologne, Germany. Ed. David Ogunsade. adv.; bk.rev. circ. 23,000. (back issues avail.)

AFRICAN REVIEW OF BUSINESS AND TECHNOLOGY. see TECHNOLOGY: COMPREHENSIVE WORKS

BUSINESS AND ECONOMICS   931

330   GW
AFRIKA STUDIEN. 1964. irreg., vol.123, 1994. Weltforum Verlag, Marienburgerstr. 22, 50963 Cologne, Germany. TEL 49-221-93763-0. FAX 49-221-9376399. circ. 500. **Indexed:** Agroforest.Abstr., Geo.Abstr. Document type: monographic series.

AFRIQUE EXPANSION. see BUILDING AND CONSTRUCTION

AGENCY EXPERTISE. see ADVERTISING AND PUBLIC RELATIONS

330   IT   ISSN 0065-4264
AGENDA DEL DIRIGENTE DI AZIENDA. a. Editoriale Emme Elle s.r.l., Via Reno, 30, Rome, Italy.

330   IT
L'AGENTE. m. Vallardi & C. s.a.s., Via G. Galilei 6, 20124 Milan, Italy. TEL 392-6555545. FAX 392-6555640. adv.: B&W page L.4800000; trim 187 x 275. circ. 4,275. **Document type:** trade publication.
    Description: For salespeople, representatives and agents.

330   US
▼**AGILITY AND GLOBAL COMPETITION.** 1997. q. $150 (foreign $174) (effective 1998). John Wiley & Sons, Inc., Journals, 605 Third Ave., New York, NY 10158. TEL 212-850-6645. FAX 212-850-6021. E-mail: subinfo@jwiley.com; URL: http://www.wiley.co.uk. (Subscr. outside the Americas to: John Wiley & Sons Ltd., Baffins Ln., Chichester, W. Sussex PO19 1UD, England. TEL 44-1243-779777. FAX 44-1243-775878) Ed. Kenneth Preiss. **Document type:** trade publication.
    Description: Covers all areas of a new business paradigm called agility in which goods and services are provided in an information-rich environment by coordinated intercompany processes.

AIDS WEEKLY PLUS. see MEDICAL SCIENCES — Communicable Diseases

AIRLINE FINANCIAL NEWS. see TRANSPORTATION — Air Transport

330   PL   ISSN 0324-8445
HB9   CODEN: PNAWDL
AKADEMIA EKONOMICZNA IM. OSKARA LANGEGO WE WROCLAWIU. PRACE NAUKOWE. (Subseries avail.: Monografie i Opracowania (ISSN 0239-8532)) 1956. irreg., no.666, 1994. price varies. Akademia Ekonomiczna we Wroclawiu, Ul. Komandorska 118-120, 53-345 Wroclaw, Poland. TEL 48-71-681155. FAX 48-71-672778. TELEX 0712427 AE PL. adv.; bk.rev.; illus. (also avail. in microform) **Document type:** academic/scholarly publication.
    —BLDSC (6589.060000); CASDDS.
    Formerly (until 1974): Wyzsza Szkola Ekonomiczna we Wroclawiu. Prace Naukowe (ISSN 0524-4560)

330   PL   ISSN 0239-8532
AKADEMIA EKONOMICZNA IM. OSKARA LANGEGO WE WROCLAWIU. PRACE NAUKOWE. SERIA: MONOGRAFIE I OPRACOWANIA. 1981. irreg. price varies. Akademia Ekonomiczna im. Oskara Langego we Wroclawiu, Ul. Komandorska 118-120, 53-345 Wroclaw, Poland. TEL 48-71-681155. FAX 48-71-672778. TELEX 0712427 AE PL. Ed. Alicja Ziolkowska. **Document type:** academic/scholarly publication, monographic series.

330   PL   ISSN 1230-1477
AKADEMIA EKONOMICZNA, KRAKOW. RECTOR'S LECTURES. Key Title: Rector's Lectures. (Text in English, Polish) 1992. irreg. price varies. Akademia Ekonomiczna, Krakow, Ul. Rakowicka 27, 31-510 Krakow, Poland. FAX 48-12-210536. circ. 120.

330   PL   ISSN 0208-7944
HB9   CODEN: ZAEKDO
AKADEMIA EKONOMICZNA, KRAKOW. ZESZYTY NAUKOWE. (Text in Polish; summaries in English) 1955. irreg. price varies. Akademia Ekonomiczna, Krakow, Ul. Rakowicka 27, 31-510 Krakow, Poland. FAX 48-12-210536. TELEX 0325414. circ. 120. **Indexed:** AgroLibrex, Chem.Abstr.
    —CASDDS.
    Formerly: Wyzsza Szkola Ekonomiczna. Zeszyty Naukowe (ISSN 0075-5125)

330   PL   ISSN 0209-1674
AKADEMIA EKONOMICZNA, KRAKOW. ZESZYTY NAUKOWE. SERIA SPECJALNA: MONOGRAFIE. (Text in Polish; summaries in English) 1961. irreg. price varies. Akademia Ekonomiczna, Krakow, Ul. Rakowicka 27, 31-510 Krakow, Poland. FAX 48-12-210536. TELEX 0325414. circ. 170. **Document type:** monographic series.
    —BLDSC (9512.142000).
    Formerly: Wyzsza Szkola Ekonomiczna, Krakow. Zeszyty Naukowe. Seria Specjalna: Monografie.

330   PL   ISSN 0208-4902
HB54   CODEN: ZNASDH
AKADEMIA EKONOMICZNA, POZNAN. ZESZYTY NAUKOWE. SERIA 1. 1961. irreg. price varies. Akademia Ekonomiczna, Poznan, Al. Niepodleglosci 10, 60-967 Poznan, Poland. TEL 48-61-699261. FAX 48-61-668924. TELEX 0413390 AE PL. circ. 300. **Indexed:** Food Sci.& Tech.Abstr., Zent.Math. **Document type:** academic/scholarly publication.
    —BLDSC (9512.143000); CASDDS.
    Formerly (until 1974): Wyzsza Szkola Ekonomiczna, Poznan. Zeszyty Naukowe. Seria 1 (ISSN 0079-4546)

330   PL   ISSN 0079-4554
AKADEMIA EKONOMICZNA, POZNAN. ZESZYTY NAUKOWE. SERIA 2. PRACE HABILITACYJNE I DOKTORSKIE. (Former name of issuing body: Wyzsza Szkola Ekonomiczna) 1957. irreg. price varies. Akademia Ekonomiczna, Poznan, Al. Niepodleglosci 10, 60-967 Poznan, Poland. TEL 48-61-699261. FAX 48-61-668924. TELEX 0413390 AE PL. circ. 200. **Indexed:** Food Sci.& Tech.Abstr. **Document type:** academic/scholarly publication.

330   AJ
AKADEMIYA NAUK AZERBAIJANA. IZVESTIYA. SERIYA EKONOMICHESKIKH NAUK. (Text in Azerbaijani and Russian) 1967. q. 8.40 Rub. Izdatel'stvo Elm, Ul. Narimanova, 37, 370073 Baku, Azerbaijan. (Subscr. to: Mezhdunarodnaya Kniga, ul. Dimitrova 39, Moscow G-200, Russia) Ed. A. Sumbadzade. index. circ. 1,940.
    Formerly: Akademiya Nauk Azerbaidzhanskoi S.S.R. Izvestiya. Seriya Ekonomicheskikh Nauk (ISSN 0002-3094)

650   US   ISSN 1055-4645
HC107.A4
ALABAMA BUSINESS AND ECONOMIC INDICATORS. 1930. m. free. University of Alabama, Center for Business and Economic Research, Box 870221, Tuscaloosa, AL 35487-0221. TEL 205-348-6191. FAX 205-348-2951. URL: http://www.sba.ua.edu/-cber. Ed. Annette Watters. stat. circ. 3,750. (also avail. in microfiche from CIS) **Indexed:** P.A.I.S., SRI. **Document type:** newsletter.
    Former titles (until 1990): Alabama Business (ISSN 0002-4163); (until 1955): University of Alabama Business News (ISSN 0735-8725); Incorporating (1955-1973): Alabama Retail Trade (ISSN 0002-4333)

ALABAMA LIBERTY. see POLITICAL SCIENCE

330 338   US   ISSN 8756-4092
ALASKA BUSINESS MONTHLY. 1985. m. $21.95. Alaska Business Publishing Co., Box 241288, Anchorage, AK 99524-1288. TEL 907-276-4373. FAX 907-279-2900. Ed. Ron Dalby; Pub. Vern McCorkle. R&P contact: Ron Dalby. adv. contact: Jim Martin. stat.; index. circ. 10,000. (back issues avail.) **Document type:** trade publication.
    ●Also available online. Vendor(s): Information Access Co., Knight-Ridder Information, Inc., Lexis-Nexis. —UMI.
    Description: Promotes economic growth in Alaska through coverage of people, issues and trends affecting the state's business sector.

330   EC
ALFA-GAMMA. m. Box 5391, Guayaquil, Ecuador. Dir. Maria A. Game de Gomendirrutia. circ. 5,000.

600   IT
ALLESTIRE; politica-tecnica-economia per mostre fiere congressi vetrine negozi stand. 1984. 5/yr. L.40000 (foreign L.70000). Edintorni s.r.l., Via Montepulciano 7, 20124 Milan, Italy. TEL 39-2-66988188. FAX 39-2-66988190. Ed. Fabio Contini. adv.: B&W page L.2100000, color page L.3200000; trim 165 x 235. illus. **Document type:** trade publication.
    Description: Covers political, technical and economic matters relating to the holding of exhibitions and trade fairs.

330   FR   ISSN 0247-3739
ALTERNATIVES ECONOMIQUES. 1980. 11/yr. 180 F. (foreign 230 F.) (effective 1997). S C O P Alternatives Economiques, 12 rue du Cap Vert, 21800 Quetigny, France. TEL 33-1-44882890. FAX 33-1-40284358. E-mail: 10173223@ compuserve.com. Ed. Philippe Fremeaux; Pub. Denis Clerc. R&P contact: Delphine Guyet. TEL 33-3-80481025. adv. contact: Pierre Liret. bk.rev. circ. 100,000. **Indexed:** Per.Islam. (1993-). **Document type:** newspaper.
    —BLDSC (0803.683000).
    Description: Provides economic and social news.

334   NE   ISSN 0002-6999
AMBT EN PLICHT. vol.18, 1970. m. fl.40. (Gereformeerd Maatschappelijk Verbond) Bureau G.M.V., Postbus 547, 8000 AM Zwolle, Netherlands. FAX 038-218629. Ed. Ms. N. Westerbeek de Wit. R&P contact: J. Westert. bk.rev.; bibl. **Document type:** bulletin, consumer publication.

330   CL
AMERICA ECONOMIA. 1986. m. $50 in N. America; elsewhere $150. Nanbei Ltd., Marchant Pereira 160, Casilla 113, Correo 35, Santiago, Chile. TEL 56-2-2516139. FAX 56-2-223-1903. (Subscr. to: Dow Jones & Co., Inc., Box 7005, Chicopee, MA 01021-7005. TEL 413-592-7761. FAX 413-592-4782) Ed. Ricardo Zisis; Pub. David Taggart. R&P contact: Ricardo Zisis. circ. 48,000.
    Description: Covers business and finance in Latin America.

AMERICAN BUSINESS LAW JOURNAL. see LAW — Corporate Law

330   US   ISSN 0743-2348
AMERICAN BUSINESS REVIEW. 1983. s-a. $14. University of New Haven, School of Business, West Haven, CT 06516. Ed. Thomas Katsaros. illus. **Document type:** academic/scholarly publication.
    —UnCover.
    Refereed Serial

330   US
AMERICAN COUNCIL OF HIGHWAY ADVERTISERS. NEWSLETTER. m. American Council of Highway Advertisers, Box 388, Shady Side, MD 20764. TEL 301-261-9197. FAX 410-867-1764. E-mail: rico45acp@aol.com. Ed. Richard Roberts. R&P contact: R.R. Roberts. **Document type:** newsletter.
    Formerly: Roadside Business Association. Newsletter.

AMERICAN FIREWORKS NEWS. see ENGINEERING — Chemical Engineering

330   US   ISSN 0034-5407
HC101
AMERICAN INSTITUTE FOR ECONOMIC RESEARCH. RESEARCH REPORTS. 1934. s-m. $59. American Institute for Economic Research, Box 1000, Great Barrington, MA 01230. TEL 413-528-1216. FAX 413-528-0103. Ed. Lawrence Pratt. bk.rev.; charts; stat.; index. circ. 8,000.

BUSINESS AND ECONOMICS

330 301   US   ISSN 0002-9246
H1   CODEN: AJESA3
AMERICAN JOURNAL OF ECONOMICS AND SOCIOLOGY. 1941. q. $25 to individuals (foreign $30); institutions & libraries $50 (foreign $56); students $15 (foreign $20) (effective 1997). (Robert Schalkenbach Foundation) American Journal of Economics & Sociology, Inc., 41 E. 72nd St., New York, NY 10021-0310. TEL 212-988-1680. FAX 212-399-6465. (Co-sponsor: Francis Neilson Fund) Ed. Frank Genovese. bk.rev.; stat.; index. circ. 2,200. (also avail. in microfiche from UMI; microfilm from UMI; reprint service avail. from KTO,ISI,NTI,UMI) **Indexed:** A.B.C.Pol.Sci., ABI Inform., Abstr.Crim.& Pen., Acad.Ind., Amer.Hist.& Life (1963-), Amer.Hist.& Life, Arts & Hum.Cit.Ind., ASCA, Asian-Pac.Econ.Lit., Bk.Rev.Ind. (1965-1980), BPIA, Bull.Signal., C.I.J.E., C.R.E.J., Child.Bk.Rev.Ind. (1965-1980), Cont.Pg.Manage., Crim.Just.Abstr., Curr.Cont., Energy Ind., Fam.Ind., Hist.Abstr. (1963-), IBR, IMFL, Int.Polit.Sci.Abstr., J.of Econ.Lit., Key to Econ.Sci., Lang.& Lang.Behav.Abstr., Mid.East: Abstr.& Ind., Mult.Ed.Abstr., P.A.I.S., Popul.Ind., PSI, Rural Recreat.Tour.Abstr., Sage Pub.Admin.Abstr., Sage Urb.Stud.Abstr., Soc.Sci.Ind., Soc.Work Res.& Abstr., Sociol.Abstr. (1952-), Sociol.Educ.Abstr., Sp.Ed.Needs Abstr., SSCI, Stud.Wom.Abstr., Work Rel.Abstr., World Agri.Econ.& Rural Sociol.Abstr. **Document type:** academic/scholarly publication. ●Also available online. Vendor(s): Information Access Co., UMI.
—BLDSC (0824.350000); Genuine Article; KR SourceOne; SWETS; UMI; UnCover. **CCC.**
    Description: Presents an interdisciplinary synthesis in social sciences and philosophy, studying economic, social, and political problems of representative democratic societies. Articles based on empirical research.

AMERICA'S FUTURE. see *POLITICAL SCIENCE*

330   SP   ISSN 0213-7569
ANALES DE ESTUDIOS ECONOMICOS Y EMPRESARIALES. 1986. irreg., vol.8, 1993. 4000 ptas. Universidad de Valladolid, Secretariado de Publicaciones, Facultad de Ciencias Economicas y Empresariales, C. Juan Membrilla, 14, 47003 Valladolid, Spain. TEL 3 4-83-423000. FAX 34-83-290300. TELEX 26357. **Document type:** academic/scholarly publication, monographic series.
—CINDOC.

330   SP   ISSN 0214-4646
ANALISE EMPRESARIAL. 3/yr. Pi y Margall 72, bajo, Apdo. 1331, 36202 Vigo, Spain. TEL 86-29-94-48. FAX 86-20-56-04. Ed. Alfonso Rivas Fraga. circ. 3,000.

330   UY
ANALISIS; administracion contabilidad economia. 1992. Fundacion de Cultura Universitaria, 25 de Mayo 568, Casilla de Correo 1155, 11000 Montevideo, Uruguay. TEL 96-11-52.

330   SP   ISSN 1130-4413
ANDALUCIA ECONOMICA. 12/yr. Rep. Argentina 26, bis. 4, 41011 Seville, Spain. TEL 5-428-13-62. FAX 5-428-31-05. Ed. Rafael Camacho. circ. 2,000.
    Description: Covers international finance and economy, emphasizing Europe.

330   PL   ISSN 0459-9586
ANNALES UNIVERSITATIS MARIAE CURIE-SKLODOWSKA. SECTIO H. OECONOMIA. (Text and summaries in English, French, German, Polish) 1967. a. price varies. Uniwersytet Marii Curie-Sklodowskiej, Wydawnictwo, Pl. M. Curie-Sklodowskiej 5, 20-031 Lublin, Poland. TEL 48-81-375304. FAX 48-81-336699. TELEX 0643223. Ed. Ryszard Orlowski. circ. 350. **Indexed:** Hort.Abstr., Potato Abstr., Poult.Abstr. **Document type:** academic/scholarly publication.

338.9 910 352.7   GW   ISSN 0570-1864
HT390
ANNALS OF REGIONAL SCIENCE; international journal of urban, regional and environmental research and policy. (Text in English) 1967. q. DM.471.60 (foreign DM.475.20) (effective 1998). Springer-Verlag, Heidelberger Platz 3, 14197 Berlin, Germany. TEL 49-30-82787-0. FAX 49-30-82787448. E-mail: subscriptions@springer.de; URL: http://link.springer.de. (Subscr. in N. America to: Springer-Verlag New York, Inc., 333 Meadowlands Pkwy., Secaucus, NJ 07094. TEL 212-460-1500. FAX 212-473-6272) Ed.Bd. adv.; bk.rev.; cum.index every 5 yrs. circ. 1,100. (back issues avail.) **Indexed:** A.B.C.Pol.Sci., ASCA, Avery Ind.Archit.Per., C.R.E.J., Curr.Cont., E.I., Forest.Abstr., Geo.Abstr.H.G., GeoRef., IDA, J.of Econ.Lit., Popul.Ind., Risk Abstr., Rural Devel.Abstr., Sage Urb.Stud.Abstr., SSCI, World Agri.Econ.& Rural Sociol.Abstr. **Document type:** academic/scholarly publication.
—BLDSC (1043.650000); CISTI; Genuine Article; SWETS; UMI; UnCover. **CCC.**

330   FR
ANNUAIRE DES ADMINISTRATEURS ET DES SOCIETES. vol.62, 1978. a. 1876 F. D A F S A, 42 rue Emeriau, 75015 Paris, France. FAX 40-60-51-51. TELEX 206 065.
    Formerly: Annuaire Desfosses.

330   FR   ISSN 1169-4475
ANNUAIRE DES DOCTEURS EN SCIENCES ECONOMIQUES. Key Title: Annuaire - A N D E S E. 1954. a. (Association Nationale des Docteurs en Sciences Economiques) Editions de L'Andese, 120 rue d'Assas, 75006 Paris, France. TEL 1-42-93-69-55. FAX 1-45-22-64-55. Ed. Rene Le Moal. **Document type:** directory.
    Formerly (until 1991): Association Nationale des Docteurs en Sciences Economiques. Annuaire (ISSN 1152-7528)

ANNUAIRE TELEXPORT; les exportateurs et importateurs francais. see *BUSINESS AND ECONOMICS — Chamber Of Commerce Publications*

330 170 100   US
ANNUAL EDITIONS: BUSINESS ETHICS. 1989. a. $12.95. Dushkin Publishing Group, Sluice Dock, Guilford, CT 06437-9989. TEL 203-453-4351; 800-243-6532. FAX 203-543-6000. Ed. John E. Richardson; Pub. Ian Nielsen. illus. **Document type:** academic/scholarly publication.
Refereed Serial

330   US
ANNUAL EDITIONS: ECONOMICS. 1971. a. $12.95. Dushkin Publishing Group, Sluice Dock, Guilford, CT 06437-9989. TEL 203-453-4351. FAX 203-453-6000. Ed. Don Cole; Pub. Ian Nielsen. illus. **Document type:** academic/scholarly publication.
    Formerly: Annual Editions: Readings in Economics (ISSN 0090-4430)
Refereed Serial

330   UN   ISSN 1020-4407
HC59.69
ANNUAL WORLD BANK CONFERENCE ON DEVELOPMENT ECONOMICS. (Supplement to: World Bank Economic Review (ISSN 0258-6770); World Bank Research Observer (ISSN 0257-3032)) 1989. a. $24.95. World Bank, International Bank for Reconstruction and Development, Office of the Publisher, 1818 H St., N.W., Washington, DC 20433. TEL 202-473-1155. FAX 202-522-2627. E-mail: books@worldbank.org. (U.S. orders to: Box 7247-8619, Philadelphia, PA 19170-8619) Eds. Michael Bruno, Boris Pleskovic, (also avail. in microfiche from CIS) **Indexed:** ABI Inform., Asian-Pac.Econ.Lit., Human Resour.Abstr., IIS, Sage Pub.Admin.Abstr. **Document type:** proceedings.
●Also available online. Vendor(s): Knight-Ridder Information, Inc.
—BLDSC (1539.355200); UnCover.
    Formerly (until 1995): World Bank Annual Conference on Development Economics. Proceedings (ISSN 1014-7268)
    Description: Provides a forum to discuss and debate important policy issues affecting developing nations, with emphasis on how empirical and basic research can contribute to better understanding development processes and formulating sound development policies.

330   IT
ANNUARIO NAZIONALE DEI DOTTORI COMMERCIALISTI. 1980. a. Consiglio Nazionale dei Dottori Commercialisti, Via Poli 29, 00187 Rome, Italy. TEL 39-6-675861. FAX 39-6-67586348. Ed. Francesco Serao. adv.: B&W or color page L.6800000; adv. contact: Luciano Alcaro Menichini. circ. 40,000.

330   GP   ISSN 0987-4216
ANTIANE ECO; revue economique des Antilles et de la Guyane. 1986. q. 100 Fr. (foreign 125 Fr.). Institut National de la Statistique et des Etudes Economiques, Service Interregional Antilles - Guyane, Tour SECID, 7th & 8th Fls., B.P. 300, 97175 Pointe-a-Pitre, Guadeloupe. TELEX 919912. Dir. F. Vennat. circ. 1,500. (back issues avail.)

ANTITRUST & COMMERCE REPORT. see *LAW — Corporate Law*

ANTITRUST LAW AND ECONOMICS REVIEW. see *LAW — Corporate Law*

330   AG
ANUARIO DE LA ECONOMIA ARGENTINA/ARGENTINE ECONOMY ANNUAL. (Text in English, Spanish) 1961. a. $200. Consejo Tecnico de Inversiones, S.A., Tucuman 834,m 1o, 1049 Buenos Aires, Argentina. FAX 541-322-4887.

330 301   II   ISSN 0378-4568
ANVESAK. (Text in English) 1972. s-a. Rs.40($20) Sardar Patel Institute of Economics and Social Research, Spiesr, Thaltej Rd., Ahmedabad 380 084, India. TEL 91-79-441598. Ed. G.V.S.N. Murty. adv.; bk.rev. circ. 200. **Indexed:** Pub.Admin.Abstr., Rural Devel.Abstr., World Agri.Econ.& Rural Sociol.Abstr. **Document type:** academic/scholarly publication.

330   US   ISSN 0003-6595
APPALACHIA. 1967. q. U.S. Appalachian Regional Commission, 1666 Connecticut Ave. N.W., Washington, DC 20235. TEL 202-884-7770. FAX 202-884-7682. Ed. Jack Russell. bk.rev.; charts; illus.; stat.; cum.index. circ. 20,000. (also avail. in microfiche) **Indexed:** Amer.Hist.& Life (1986-1988), Biol.Abstr., C.I.J.E., Geo.Abstr., GeoRef., Hist.Abstr. (1986-1988), Ind.U.S.Gov.Per., P.A.I.S., Sportsearch, Telegen. **Document type:** government publication.
—BLDSC (1569.040000); UMI; UnCover.
    Formerly: Appalachian Digest.
    Description: Devoted to regional development.

330   US   ISSN 0503-5422
HC107.A133
APPALACHIAN REGIONAL COMMISSION. ANNUAL REPORT. 1965. a. free. U.S. Appalachian Regional Commission, 1666 Connecticut Ave. N.W., Washington, DC 20235. TEL 202-884-7770. FAX 202-884-7682. Ed. Jack Russell. circ. 3,000. (back issues avail.) **Indexed:** P.A.I.S. **Document type:** government publication, corporate report.

APPLAUSE; the international live music business monthly. see *MUSIC*

330   II   ISSN 0570-4839
APPLIED ECONOMIC PAPERS. (Text in English) 1961. s-a. Osmania University, Department of Commerce, Hyderabad 500007, Andhra Pradesh, India. bk.rev. charts.

BUSINESS AND ECONOMICS

330   UK   ISSN 0003-6846
HB1   CODEN: APPEBP
APPLIED ECONOMICS. (Suppl. avail.: Applied Economics Letters (ISSN 1350-5851); Applied Financial Economics (ISSN 0960-3107)) 1969. m. £685 to institutions in the EU (N. America $1140; elsewhere £705) (effective 1997) (includes Applied Financial Economics and Applied Economics Letters). Routledge, 11 New Fetter Ln., London EC4P 4EE, England. TEL 44-171-583-9855. FAX 44-171-842-2298. E-mail: info.journals@ routledge.com; URL: http://www.routledge.com/routledge/journal/journals.html. (Subscr. to: ITPS Ltd., Cheriton House, North Way, Andover, Hants SP10 5BE, England. TEL 44-1264-342919. FAX 44-1264-342807; Subscr. in US & Canada to: 29 W. 35th St., New York, NY 10001-2299. TEL 212-244-3336. FAX 212-564-7854) Ed. Maurice H. Preston. adv.; charts. (reprint service avail. from ISI,SCH,UMI) **Indexed:** ABI Inform., Abstr.Health Care Manage.Stud., ASCA, Asian-Pac.Econ.Lit., Asian-Pac.Econ.Lit., B.P.I., BPIA, C.R.E.J., Cont.Pg.Manage., Crim.Just.Abstr., Curr.Cont., Geo.Abstr.H.G., IDA, Int.Lab.Doc., J.Cont.Quant.Meth., Maize Abstr., Risk Abstr., Rural Recreat.Tour.Abstr., Soyabean Abstr., SSCI, Tr.& Indus.Ind., Triticale Abstr., World Agri.Econ.& Rural Sociol.Abstr. **Document type:** academic/scholarly publication.
●Also available online. Vendor(s): Information Access Co.
—BLDSC (1571.970000); Genuine Article; KR SourceOne; SWETS; UMI; UnCover. **CCC.**
   Description: Encourages economic analysis to economics problems in the private and public sectors.
   Refereed Serial

330   UK   ISSN 1350-4851
APPLIED ECONOMICS LETTERS. (Supplement to: Applied Economics (ISSN 0003-6846)) 1994. m. £150 in the E.U. (N. America $260; rest of world £168) (effective 1997). Routledge, 11 New Fetter Ln., London EC4P 4EE, England. TEL 44-171-583-9855. FAX 44-171-842-2298. E-mail: info.journals@routledge.com; URL: http://www.routledge.com/routledge/journal/journals.html. (Dist. by: International Thomson Publishing Services Ltd., Cheriton House, North Way, Andover, Hants. SP10 5BE, England. TEL 44-1264-342919. FAX 44-1264-342807; Subscr. in US & Canada to: 29 W. 35th St., New York, NY 10001-2299. TEL 212-244-3336. FAX 212-564-7854) Ed. Maurice H. Preston. adv. (reprint service avail.) **Indexed:** ASCA, Crim.Just.Abstr., Curr.Cont. **Document type:** academic/scholarly publication.
●Also available online.
—**CCC.**
   Description: Publishes short accounts of new and original research within two months of receipt.
   Refereed Serial

330   UK
ARAB - BRITISH BUSINESS. 50/yr. membership only. Arab - British Chamber of Commerce, 6 Belgrave Sq., London SW1X 8PH, England. TEL 44-171-235-4363. FAX 44-171-235-1748. Ed. Wendy Field.

330   UK
ARAB - BRITISH TRADE. 10/yr. free. Arab - British Chamber of Commerce, 6 Belgrave Sq., London SW1X 8PH, England. TEL 44-171-235-4363. FAX 44-171-253-1748. Ed. Atef Sultan. circ. 10,000.
   Formerly: Arab - British Commerce.

ARAB WORLD AGRIBUSINESS/AL-ZIRA'AH FI-L-ALAM AL-ARABI. see *AGRICULTURE*

330   CN   ISSN 0830-8888
ARABUSINESS INTERNATIONAL. (Text in Arabic, English) 1986. 24/yr. $72 (foreign $100). Allam Arabic Publishing & Advertising Co., 370 Queen St. E., Toronto, ON M5A 1T1, Canada. TEL 416-861-0238. FAX 416-861-0238. TELEX 416-861-0238. Ed. Salah Allam. adv.

330   GW   ISSN 0342-6270
ARCHIV UND WIRTSCHAFT. 1967. q. DM.50. Vereinigung Deutscher Wirtschaftsarchivare e.V., Am Bergbaumuseum 28, 44791 Bochum, Germany. Ed. Detlef Krause. adv.; bk.rev.; bibl.; film rev.; illus.; index. circ. 800. (back issues avail.) **Document type:** bulletin.

ARCHIVUM TREBONENSE. see *HISTORY — History Of Europe*

330   GW
ARGUMENTE ZU UNTERNEHMENSFRAGEN. m. (Institut der Deutschen Wirtschaft) Deutscher Instituts Verlag GmbH, Postfach 510670, 50942 Cologne, Germany. TEL 49-221-4981452. FAX 49-221-4981592. **Document type:** academic/scholarly publication.

330   LE
L'ARGUS DE L'ECONOMIE LIBANAISE. (Text in French) 1966. m. $300 (effective 1998). Bureau of Lebanese and Arab Documentation, P.O. Box 165403, Beirut, Lebanon. TEL 961-1-219113. (Subscr. to: Marcel Tawil, Bureau of Documentation, Postfach 2412, 79514 Loerrach, Germany. TEL 49-7621-2472. FAX 49-7621-2472) **Document type:** bulletin.
   Description: Survey of economic developments in Lebanon, including trade and industry, finance and taxation, public works and reconstruction, transports and communications, labor and social affairs.

330   FR   ISSN 0752-4471
ARGUS DU FONDS DE COMMERCE ET DE L'INDUSTRIE. * 1982. 6/yr. Groupe ICF, Tour Centre Affaire, Avenir Ouest, 92025 Nanterre Cedex. TEL 42-94-97-74. Ed. Marie-Jose Plumas. circ. 30,000.

330   US   ISSN 0273-6950
ARIZONA BUSINESS GAZETTE. 1880. w. $45. Phoenix Newspapers, Inc., Box 1950, Phoenix, AZ 85001. TEL 602-271-7373. FAX 602-271-7363. Ed. Jim Fickess. adv. contact: Colleen Brady. circ. 15,123. **Indexed:** Tr.& Indus.Ind. **Document type:** newspaper.
●Also available online. Vendor(s): Dow Jones News Retrieval, Knight-Ridder Information, Inc., Lexis-Nexis, MediaStream.

330   US
ARIZONA ECONOMIC INDICATORS (TUCSON). Issued with: Arizona's Economy. 1984. s-a. $16 (foreign $22). University of Arizona, College of Business and Public Administration, McClelland Hall 204K, Economic and Business Research Program, Tucson, AZ 85721. TEL 520-621-2155. FAX 520-621-2150. E-mail: pmontoya@bpa.arizona.edu. Ed. Diana Hunter. circ. 1,000.
   Description: Presents historical data for some 530 measures of economic activity for the state of Arizona and its counties. Provides useful information for both public and private sector professionals.

330   US
ARIZONA ECONOMIC TRENDS. q. free. Department of Economic Security, Research Administration, Box 6123, Site Code 733A, Phoenix, AZ 85005. TEL 602-542-3871. FAX 602-542-6474. Ed. Brent Fine. circ. 4,500. **Document type:** government publication.
   Description: Provides an update and analysis of state and county employment and economic data, as well as information on state and national programs and policies that affect the nation's and Arizona's labor markets.

330   650   US   ISSN 0004-1742
HC107.A8   CODEN: ABRVBM
ARKANSAS BUSINESS AND ECONOMIC REVIEW. 1933. q. free in N. America only. University of Arkansas, College of Business Administration, Bureau of Business and Economic Research, Fayetteville, AR 72701. TEL 501-575-4151. FAX 501-575-7687. E-mail: sbarger@comp.uark.edu. Ed. Donald R. Market. R&P contact: Sherryl Barger. charts; illus.; stat.; cum.index. circ. 3,900. (also avail. in microfiche from CIS) **Indexed:** ABI Inform., BPIA, Bus.Ind., INSPEC (1981-1984), Manage.Cont., P.A.I.S., Pers.Manage.Abstr., SRI, Tr.& Indus.Ind. **Document type:** academic/scholarly publication.
●Also available online. Vendor(s): Information Access Co., Knight-Ridder Information, Inc., UMI.
—UMI; UnCover.
   Formerly: Arkansas Business Bulletin.
   Refereed Serial

ART MATERIALS TODAY. see *ART*

330   II   ISSN 0004-3559
HC431
ARTHA VIJNANA. (Text in English) 1959. q. Rs.200 (foreign $50). Gokhale Institute of Politics and Economics, c/o D.C. Wadhwa, Ed., Pune 411 004, India. TEL 91-212-344287. (Subscr. in U.S. to: Asian Society. University of California Press, Berkeley, CA 94720) adv.; bk.rev.; charts; stat.; index. circ. 465. (back issues avail.) **Indexed:** C.R.E.J., Forest.Abstr., IDA, Int.Lab.Doc., Key to Econ.Sci., P.A.I.S., Pub.Admin.Abstr., Rice Abstr., Rural Recreat.Tour.Abstr., Sorghum & Millets Abstr., Trop.Oil Seeds Abstr., World Agri.Econ.& Rural Sociol.Abstr. **Document type:** academic/scholarly publication.
—BLDSC (1733.750000); UnCover.

330   II
ARTHA VIJNANA REPRINT SERIES. (Text in English) 1975. irreg., no. 15, 1991. price varies. Gokhale Institute of Politics and Economics, Pune 411 004, India. TEL 0212-344287.

330   II   ISSN 0004-3575
ARTHANITI. (Text in English) 1957. s-a. Rs.15($4) University of Calcutta, Department of Economics, 56-A Barrackapore Trunk Rd., Calcutta 700050, India. Ed. Amlan Datta. bk.rev.; charts; stat. circ. 400. **Indexed:** IBR.

330   II   ISSN 0970-7654
ARTHIK PRASANGA. English edition: Economic Studies (ISSN 0013-0362) 1952-1985; resumed 1988. q. Rs.25($7) Economic Studies and Journals Publishing Co., 2 Private Rd., Dum Dum, Calcutta 700 074, West Bengal, India. TEL 551-2288. (Subscr. to: P.O. Box 10868, Calcutta 700 009, West Bengal, India) Ed. Dwijendranath Mukherjea. adv.; bk.rev.; charts; illus.; pat.; stat.; tr.lit.; tr.mk. circ. 16,201. **Document type:** newspaper.

330   IT
ARTIGIANATO DI SICILIA. 1965. m. Associazione Artigiani Provincia di Palermo, Artigianato di Sicilia, Via Roma, 391, 90133 Palermo, Italy. circ. 20,000.

ARZNEIMITTEL ZEITUNG. see *PHARMACY AND PHARMACOLOGY*

ASIA ENVIRONMENTAL BUSINESS JOURNAL. see *ENVIRONMENTAL STUDIES*

ASIA LAW. see *LAW*

330   UK   ISSN 1360-2381
HC460.5.A1
ASIA - PACIFIC BUSINESS REVIEW. 1994. q. £35($48) to individuals; institutions £130 ($180) (effective 1998). Frank Cass, Newbury House, 890-900 Eastern Ave., Newbury Park, Ilford, Essex IG2 7HH, England. TEL 44-181-599-8866. FAX 44-181-599-0984. E-mail: jnlsubs@frankcass.com; URL: http://www.frankcass.com. (Dist. in US by: ISBS, 5804 N.E. Hassalo St., Portland, OR 97213-3644. TEL 800-944-6190. FAX 503-280-8832) Ed.Bd. adv.: B&W page £195 ($275); adv. contact: Anne Kidson. bk.rev.; index. **Indexed:** Asian-Pac.Econ.Lit, Geo.Abstr.H.G., Geo.Abstr.P.G., IDA, Intl.Bibl.S.S.Pol.Sci., Mgmt.& Market.Abstr. **Document type:** academic/scholarly publication.
—BLDSC (1742.257600); EMDOCS; KR SourceOne.
   Formerly (until 1995): Journal of Far Eastern Business (ISSN 1351-0363).
   Description: Concentrates on the way the economic transformation of the Pacific Rim has reshaped the global economy, explaining and investigating the rise of Far Eastern businesses and their international competitiveness.
   Refereed Serial

BUSINESS AND ECONOMICS

330   UK   ISSN 1358-6653
HC411
▼**ASIA - PACIFIC ECONOMIC REVIEW.** 1995. 3/yr. £75($120) (effective 1998). (Economic Modelling Bureau of Australia, AT) Cambridge University Press, Edinburgh Bldg., Shaftesbury Rd., Cambridge CB2 2RU, England. TEL 44-1223-312393. FAX 44-1223-315052. TELEX 851817256. E-mail: information@cup.cam.ac.uk; URL: http://www.cup.org/journals/CUPJNLS.html. (N. American addr.: Cambridge University Press, Journals Dept., 40 W. 20th St., New York, NY 10011. TEL 212-924-3900. FAX 212-691-3239) Eds. Colin Hargreaves, Peter C.B. Phillips. R&P contact: Linda Nicol. adv. contact: Rebecca Symons. bk.rev. **Indexed:** Asian-Pac.Econ.Lit. **Document type:** academic/scholarly publication.
—BLDSC (1742.260320); SWETS.
   Description: Covers the economic expansion of the Asia-Pacific region.

330   AT   ISSN 1036-3793
DS501
ASIA PACIFIC PROFILES. 1990. a. Aus.$500 (foreign $500). Australian National University, Research School of Pacific and Asian Studies, Asia Pacific Economics Group, Canberra, A.C.T. 0200, Australia. TEL 61-6-249-4705. FAX 61-6-257-2886. (Subscr. to: Bibliotech, Canberra, A.C.T. 0200, Australia) Ed. Maree Tait. stat.
   Description: A review of the economics of East Asia and the Pacific region with current statistics and projections.

330 332.6   AT   ISSN 0813-2844
ASIA TODAY; Australia's regional business magazine. 1983. m. Aus.$110 (Asia $110). East Asia News and Features (Australia) Pty. Ltd., Level 29 Chifley Tower, 2 Chifley Sq., Sydney, N.S.W. 2000, Australia. TEL 61-2-99706477. FAX 61-2-99132003. E-mail: 100356.3100@compuserve.com. Ed. Florence Chong; Pub. Barry Pearton. R&P contact: Barry Pearton. adv.: B&W page Aus.$2495, color page Aus.$3275; trim 260 x 179; adv. contact: Barry Pearton. circ. 8,217. **Document type:** trade publication.
   Description: Identifies business opportunities in Asia and changes in Asian government policies affecting foreign trade, investment, taxation, economic development.

330   CC
ASIA YEARBOOK. 1960. a. $42 for softcover; hardcover $55. Review Publishing Co. Ltd., G.P.O. Box 160, Hong Kong, People's Republic of China. TEL 852-2508-4300. FAX 852-2503-1549. TELEX 66452 REVCD HX. Ed. Michael Westlake. adv. **Indexed:** GdIns.
   Formerly: Far Eastern Economic Review. Yearbook (ISSN 0071-3821)
   Description: Observes and interprets economic, political and social trends of all Asian countries.

330   SI   ISSN 0218-9275
▼**ASIAN CASE RESEARCH JOURNAL.** (Text in English) 1997. s-a. $60 (foreign $60) (effective 1998). John Wiley & Sons (Asia) Pte. Ltd., 2 Clementi Loop 02-01, Jin Xing Distripark, Singapore 129809, Singapore. TEL 65-4632400. FAX 65-4634605. E-mail: csd___ord@wiley.com.sg. Ed. Wee Chow Hou. adv.: B&W page £640, color page £1515. **Document type:** academic/scholarly publication.
   Description: Aims to provide case instructors, whether academics, consultants, or company in-house trainers, with a selection of high-quality cases on Asian companies and MNCs operating in Asia-Pacific.

330   PH   ISSN 0117-0481
HC411
ASIAN DEVELOPMENT OUTLOOK. (Text in English) a. Asian Development Bank, P.O. Box 789, 1099 Manila, Philippines. TEL 632-711-3851. FAX 632-741-7961.
—BLDSC (1742.407740).
   Description: Provides a broad view of economic progress in developing Asia and the Pacific, and offers analysis and assessment of recent trends.

330   II   ISSN 0004-4555
HB9
ASIAN ECONOMIC REVIEW. (Text in English) 1958. 3/yr. Rs.210 (foreign $60) (effective 1994). Indian Institute of Economics, 11-6-841 Red Hills, Hyderabad 500 004, India. TEL 91-40-225083. TELEX 0425-6038 FAP IN. Ed. M. Venkata Rao. bk.rev.; bibl.; charts; stat. circ. 400. **Indexed:** Asian-Pac.Econ.Lit., BPIA, C.R.E.J., Cott.& Trop.Fibr.Abstr., Per.Islam. (1991-), Pub.Admin.Abstr. **Document type:** academic/scholarly publication.
   Description: Publishes articles and reviews on specific economic, social projects undertaken in various developing countries as well as discussions of policy implications.

338   JA   ISSN 0002-2942
HC411
ASIAN ECONOMIES/AJIA KEIZAI. (Text in Japanese) 1960. m. 12000 Yen. Institute of Developing Economies - Ajia Keizai Kenkyusho, 42 Ichigaya-Hommura-cho, Shinjuku-ku, Tokyo 162, Japan. TEL 3353-4231. FAX 3226-8475. Ed. Toshiaki Kayashi. bk.rev.; cum.index. circ. 2,000. **Indexed:** Amer.Hist.& Life (1969-1989), Asian-Pac.Econ.Lit., Hist.Abstr. (until 1922), SSCI.
—BLDSC (0785.480000); UnCover.

330 382   US
ASIAN INDUSTRIAL REPORTER. 1983. 6/yr. Keller International Publishing Corporation, 150 Great Neck Rd., Great Neck, NY 11021. TEL 516-829-9210. FAX 516-829-7265. Ed. Felicia M. Morales. adv. circ. 24,129. (tabloid format) **Document type:** trade publication.

ASIAN JOURNAL OF PUBLIC ADMINISTRATION. see PUBLIC ADMINISTRATION

ASIAN MEETINGS AND INCENTIVES. see MEETINGS AND CONGRESSES

ASIAN REVIEW OF BUSINESS AND TECHNOLOGY. see TECHNOLOGY: COMPREHENSIVE WORKS

330   AG
ASOCIACION DE ECONOMISTAS ARGENTINOS. COLECCION INSTITUTO SUPERIOR. irreg, no.3, 1976. Editorial el Coloquio, Junin 735, Buenos Aires, Argentina. charts, stat.

330   PO
ASSOCIACAO COMERCIAL DO PORTO. BOLETIM. m. Associacao Comercial do Porto, Camara de Comercio e Industria do Porto, Palacio da Bolsa, 4000 Porto, Portugal.

330   UK
ASSOCIATION. q. Society of Association Executives, Courtleigh, Westbury Leigh, Westbury, Wilts BA13 3TA, England. TEL 01380-830964. FAX 01380-830574. Ed. Leslie Rocker. circ. 1,000. **Document type:** newsletter.

330   JA   ISSN 0004-5683
ASSOCIATION OF ECONOMIC GEOGRAPHERS. ANNALS. (Text in English and Japanese) 1954. s-a. 1800 Yen($6) Association of Economic Geographers - Keizai Chiri Gakkai, c/o Graduate School, Meiji University, 1-1 Kanda Surugadai, Chiyoda-ku, Tokyo, Japan. Ed. Isamu Ota. bk.rev.; abstr.; bibl.; charts; illus.
—CCC.

330   US   ISSN 1066-8691
ASSOCIATION SOURCE. 1985. m. $15 (effective 1995). Florida Society of Association Executives, Box 11119, Tallahassee, FL 32302-3119. TEL 904-222-7994. FAX 904-222-6350. Ed. Tom Burchnell. adv. contact: Brian Pinsker. bk.rev. circ. 1,100. **Document type:** trade publication.
   Formerly: Source (Casselberry) (ISSN 0898-8811)
   Description: Designed for association executives and their staff members, with emphasis on feature articles relating to association management.

330   UK
ASTON UNIVERSITY. PUBLIC SECTOR MANAGEMENT RESEARCH CENTRE. WORKING PAPER. irreg., no.19, 1992. Aston University, Public Sector Management Research Centre, Birmingham B4 7ET, England. TEL 0121-359-3611. **Document type:** monographic series.
   Formerly: Aston University. Public Sector Management Research Unit. Working Paper (ISSN 0954-3554)

330   QA
ASWAQ AL-KHALIJ. 1980. w. Dar al-Nabaa Press, Printing and Publishing, P.O. Box 3344, Doha, Qatar. TEL 438326. FAX 439859. Ed. Mohamed Salim al-Kuwari; Pub. Mohamed Salim al-Kuwari. circ. 6,000.

330   GR   ISSN 1105-8536
ATHENS FINANCIAL GAZETTE. (Text in English) 1987. fortn. Dr.50000 (foreign $300). Enimeroseis - Dioscuri Ltd., 21 Sarandapichou St., 114 71 Athens, Greece. TEL 361-5497. FAX 363-8274. E-mail: eladop@enternet.gr; URL: http://www.enternet.gr/afg. Ed. Olga Palagia; Pub. Eugene Ladopoulos. R&P contact: Eugene Ladopoulos. (looseleaf format; back issues avail.) **Document type:** newsletter.
● Also available online.
   Description: Examines the political economy, outlook and prospects, and leading economic indicators of Greece.

330   CN   ISSN 0319-003X
ATLANTIC CANADA ECONOMICS ASSOCIATION. ANNUAL CONFERENCE: A C E A PAPERS. no.4, 1975. a. Can.$25 (effective 1998). Atlantic Canada Economics Association, c/o Christina Fader, Ed., Department of Economics, Acadia University, Wolfville, NS B0P 1X0, Canada. TEL 902-585-1491. FAX 902-585-1070. R&P contact: Christina Fader. charts; stat. circ. 150. **Document type:** academic/scholarly publication.
—BLDSC (0573.799000).

330   US   ISSN 0197-4254
HB1
ATLANTIC ECONOMIC JOURNAL. 1973. q. $159 (Canada $166; elsewhere $174) (effective 1998). Atlantic Economic Society, c/o John M. Virgo, Ed., Box 1101, Southern Illinois University, Edwardsville, IL 62026-1101. TEL 618-692-2291. FAX 618-692-3400. E-mail: iaes@iaes.org; URL: http://www.iaes.org. R&P contact: Mary Ellen Kissling. adv. contact: Mary Ellen Kissing. bk.rev.; abstr.; charts; illus.; stat. circ. 1,500. (also avail. in microform from UMI; back issues avail.) **Indexed:** ABI Inform., BPIA, C.R.E.J., Curr.Cont., J. of Econ.Lit., Manage.Cont., P.A.I.S., Soc.Sci.Ind., Tr.& Indus.Ind. **Document type:** academic/scholarly publication.
● Also available online. Vendor(s): Information Access Co., Knight-Ridder Information, Inc.
—BLDSC (1765.899500); SWETS; UMI; UnCover.

330   US   ISSN 1092-3012
▼**ATTAINMENT BUSINESS STARTUPS JOURNAL.** 1997. 8-10/yr. Abiogenesis Publications, Box 9, Bellingham, WA 98227-0009. E-mail: attainment@abiogenesis.com; URL: http://www.abiogenesis.com/attainment. Ed. Julie Petersen. **Document type:** newsletter.
● Available only online.
   Description: Practical, how-to resources for startup businesses which focus on early phase financing, production and marketing.

AUCTION PRICES OF AMERICAN ARTISTS. see ART

330   US   ISSN 1064-4555
HF3000
AUDACITY; the magazine of business experience. 1992. q. $15 (free to qualified personnel). (International Paper) Forbes, Inc., 60 Fifth Ave., New York, NY 10011. TEL 212-620-2200. (Subscr. to: Box 6606, Syracuse, NY 13217. TEL 800-825-0061) Ed. Catherine Calhoun. illus.; circ. 100,000 (controlled).
—CCC.
   Description: Historical perspective on current issues in business events and trends around the world.

| 330 | | 658 | AT | ISSN 0729-2384 |

AUDITOPICS. 1980. m. Aus.$20. Institute of Internal Auditors, Victorian Branch, P.O. Box 82, North Balwyn, Vic. 3104, Australia. FAX 61-3-857-4487. (Subscr. to: G.P.O. Box 817F, Melbourne, Vic. 3001, Australia) Ed. Jim Shaw. adv.; bk.rev. circ. 600. (back issues avail.)

| 330 | | | GW | ISSN 0944-9337 |

AUSBILDER HANDBUCH. irreg. (4-6/yr.). DM.148. Deutscher Wirtschaftsdienst, Marienburgerstr. 22, 50968 Cologne, Germany. TEL 49-221-93763-0. FAX 49-221-9376399. (looseleaf format) **Document type:** bulletin.

AUSBILDER IN DER CHEMISCHEN INDUSTRIE. see *CHEMISTRY*

AUSTIN BOOK OF LISTS. see *PUBLISHING AND BOOK TRADE*

| 330 | | | US | ISSN 0892-869X |

AUSTIN BUSINESS JOURNAL.* 1981. w. $54. American City Business Journals, Inc. (Austin), 505 Powcl St., Austin, TX 78703-5121. TEL 512-328-0180. FAX 512-328 7304. adv. circ. 7,100. (also avail. in microform from UMI) **Indexed:** Tr.& Indus.Ind. **Document type:** newspaper.
●Also available online. Vendor(s): UMI.
—UMI. **CCC.**

| 330 | | | US | |

AUSTIN MINORITY BUSINESS GUIDE.* 1990. a. $54. American City Business Journal, Inc. (Austin), 111 Congress Ave., Ste. 750, Austin, TX 78701-4043. TEL 512-328-0180. FAX 512-328-7304. Ed. Beth Zacharias; Pub. Lisa Bormaster. R&P contact: Beth Zacharias. adv. contact: Donna Sangwin. circ. 9,000. **Document type:** newspaper.

| 330 | | | AT | ISSN 1039-5083 |

AUSTRALIA - JAPAN ECONOMIC INSTITUTE. ECONOMIC BULLETIN. 12/yr. Aus.$48 (foreign Aus.$68) (effective 1997). Australia - Japan Economic Institute, Level 11, The Chifley Tower, Chifley Sq., Sydney, N.S.W. 2000, Australia. TEL 61-2-92338533. FAX 61-2-92338503. Ed. Manuel Panagiotopoulos. bk.rev.; circ. 210 (paid). **Document type:** bulletin.
Former titles: Australia - Japan Economic Institute. Newsletter (ISSN 1034-9081); (until 1989): A J E I Newsletter (ISSN 0725-0401)
Description: Features relevant articles dealing with the Japanese economy, investment and the Australia-Japan business relationship, as well as economic updates and monthly reviews.
Refereed Serial

AUSTRALIAN AGRICULTURAL AND RESOURCE ECONOMICS SOCIETY. PAPERS PRESENTED AT ANNUAL CONFERENCE (MICROFICHE). see *AGRICULTURE*

| 330 | | | AT | |

AUSTRALIAN BUSINESS ADVISERS GUIDE. (In 2 vols.) 1991. m. C C H Australia Ltd., P.O. Box 230, North Ryde, N.S.W. 2113, Australia. TEL 61-21-300300224. FAX 61-1-300306224. (looseleaf format)
Description: Designed to assist in giving advice on all aspects of starting, running or even leaving a business.

| 330 | 374.013 | | AT | ISSN 1036-2878 |

AUSTRALIAN BUSINESS EDUCATION DIRECTORY. s-m. Aus.$195. Mount Wise Press Pty. Ltd., P.O. Box 49, Burnley, Vic. 3121, Australia. FAX 03-824-2935.
Formerly: Australian Directory of Conferences, Seminars and Short Courses.

AUSTRALIAN CHICKEN FARMER. see *AGRICULTURE — Poultry And Livestock*

AUSTRALIAN CONSUMER SALES AND CREDIT LAW REPORTER. see *LAW*

| 330 | | | AT | |

AUSTRALIAN CORPORATE PRACTICE MANUAL. (In 2 vols.) 1978. 3/yr. C C H Australia Ltd., P.O. Box 230, North Ryde, N.S.W. 2113, Australia. TEL 61-1-300300224. FAX 61-1-300306224. (looseleaf format)
Formerly: Australian Company Secretary's Practice Manual.
Description: Provides a practical guide to the day-to-day running of a company.

| 330 | | | AT | ISSN 0004-900X |
HB1

AUSTRALIAN ECONOMIC PAPERS. 1962. s-a. Aus.$35 (foreign Aus.$40) (effective 1996 & 1997). University of Adelaide, Economics Department, Adelaide, Australia. TEL 61-8-83035908. FAX 61-8-2231460. TELEX UNIVAD AA89141. E-mail: mraimondo@economics.adelaide.edu.au. (Co-sponsor: Flinders University of South Australia) Ed.Bd. R&P contact: D. Damania. adv. contact: D. Hackett. bibl.; charts; illus.; stat.; index. circ. 1,250. **Indexed:** Asian-Pac.Econ.Lit., Aus.P.A.I.S., C.R.E.J., Curr.Cont., Geo.Abstr.H.G., IBR, IDA, Int.Lab.Doc., J.of Econ.Lit., P.A.I.S., Risk Abstr., Rural Recreat.Tour.Abstr., SSCI, World Agri.Econ.& Rural Sociol.Abstr. **Document type:** academic/scholarly publication.
—BLDSC (1798.670000); SWETS; UnCover.

| 330 | | | UK | ISSN 0004-9018 |
HC601

AUSTRALIAN ECONOMIC REVIEW. 1968. q. £112($177) (foreign.£112) (effective 1997). (University of Melbourne, Institute of Applied Economic and Social Research) Blackwell Publishers Ltd., 108 Cowley Rd., Oxford OX4 1JF, England. TEL 44-1865-791100. FAX 44-1865-791347. E-mail: jnlinfo@blackwellpublishers.co.uk; URL: http://www.blackwellpublishers.co.uk. Ed.Bd. charts; stat. circ. 900. (tabloid format; also avail. in microform from UMI) **Indexed:** Arts & Hum.Cit.Ind., Asian-Pac.Econ.Lit., Aus.P.A.I.S., C.R.E.J., Gdlns, Geo.Abstr.H.G., IDA, Int.Lab.Doc., J.of Econ.Lit., P.A.I.S., PROMT, World Agri.Econ.& Rural Sociol.Abstr., World Bank.Abstr. **Document type:** academic/scholarly publication.
●Also available online. Vendor(s): UMI.
—BLDSC (1798.680000); SWETS; UMI; UnCover. **CCC.**
Description: Contains articles on applied economic and social issues.
Refereed Serial

| 330 | | | AT | |

AUSTRALIAN INSOLVENCY MANAGEMENT PRACTICE. (In 2 vols.) 1984. bi-m. C C H Australia Ltd., P.O. Box 230, North Ryde, N.S.W. 2113, Australia. TEL 61-1-300300224. FAX 61-1-300306224. (looseleaf format)
Description: Provides practical assistance for implementing the procedures required for dealing with individual and corporate insolvency management. This step-by-step guide is organized in chronological sequence.

| 330 | | | AT | ISSN 0310-0057 |

AUSTRALIAN PROPERTY NEWS. m. Aus.$96. B R W Media, Level 2, 469 La Trobe St., Melbourne, Vic. 3000, Australia. TEL 61-3-96033888. FAX 61-3-96704328. Ed. Howard Brenchley. adv. contact: John Briggs.
Description: Covers all aspects of commercial property in Australia, New Zealand and Asia. Reports and comments on sales, deals and trends within the industry.

| 348 | 338 | | AT | |

AUSTRALIAN TRADE PRACTICES REPORTER. (In 3 vols.) 1972. every 3 wks. C C H Australia Ltd., P.O. Box 230, North Ryde, N.S.W. 2113, Australia. TEL 61-1-300300224. FAX 61-1-300306224. (looseleaf format)
Description: Contains commentary on restrictive trade practices and consumer production under the Trade Practices Act, legislation and reporting of court and Trade Practices Tribunal decisions and Trade Practices Commission determinations.

AUSTRIAN ECONOMIC QUARTERLY. see *BUSINESS AND ECONOMICS — Economic Situation And Conditions*

AUTOMOTIVE DEALERS DIGEST. see *TRANSPORTATION — Automobiles*

| 330 | | | IT | |

AVVISATORE. 1867. w. L.5000. Vittorio Pierallini, Ed. & Pub., Viale della Liberta 135, 90143 Palermo, Italy. TEL 91-305-273. FAX 91-302464. adv. circ. 18,000.

BUSINESS AND ECONOMICS 935

| 650 | | | US | ISSN 1079-4255 |
HC107.A6

AZ B - ARIZONA BUSINESS. 1954. m. $18 to residents; out-of-state $24; foreign $30. Arizona State University, Center for Business Research, College of Business, Box 874406, Tempe, AZ 85287-4406. TEL 602-965-3961. FAX 602-965-5458. Ed. Nan Beams. charts; stat.; index; circ. 1,097 (paid); 630. (also avail. in microfilm from UMI; microfiche from CIS; reprint service avail. from UMI) **Indexed:** ABI Inform., B.P.I., BPIA, Bus.Ind., Manage.Cont., P.A.I.S., Pers.Manage.Abstr., SRI, Tr.& Indus.Ind. **Document type:** newsletter.
●Also available online. Vendor(s): Information Access Co., UMI.
Also available on CD-ROM.
—BLDSC (1668.430800); UMI.
Former titles (until 1995): Arizona Business (ISSN 0093-0717); Arizona Business Bulletin (ISSN 0004-1440)
Description: Offers a broad perspective of information on the Arizona economy, including regular articles on Consumer Price Index, building permits, economic indicators, population and migration, and winter residents.

| 330 | | | IT | |

AZIENDA E FISCO. 1991. fortn. L.215000 (foreign L.430000). I P S O A s.r.l. (Subsidiary of: Wolters Kluwer N.V.), Strada 1, Palazzo F6, 20090 Assago Milanofiori (MI), Italy. TEL 39-2-824761. Ed. Massimiliano Galioni. adv.: B&W page L.3000000, color page L.5000000; adv. contact: Luciano Alcaro Menichini. **Document type:** consumer publication.

| 330 | | | GW | |

B & H. (Bausortiment & Holz und Ausbaubedarf); Fachzeitschrift fuer den Holzhandel und Baumaerkte. 1975. m. DM.79.20 (foreign DM.97.80) (effective 1997). D R W Verlag Weinbrenner GmbH & Co., Fasanenweg 18, 70771 Leinfelden-Echterdingen, Germany. TEL 49-711-7591-0. Ed. Karl Widermuth. adv.; bk.rev. circ. 26,000. (back issues avail.) **Document type:** trade publication.

| 650 | 350 | | US | ISSN 0361-7653 |
HF5001 | | | | CODEN: BPUAEI

B & P A. (Business & Public Affairs) 1975. s-a. free. Murray State University, College of Business and Public Affairs, Murray, KY 42071. TEL 502-762-4188. FAX 502-762-3482. Ed. James F. Thompson. circ. 1,000 (controlled). **Indexed:** P.A.I.S. **Document type:** academic/scholarly publication.
—BLDSC (2933.220500).
Supersedes: Business Dynamics (ISSN 0045-3625)
Description: Covers any issue concerning business or public administration.
Refereed Serial

| 650 | 700 | | US | ISSN 0005-2841 |

B C A NEWS. 1968. q. $55 (foreign $65; not-for-profit organizations $30). Business Committee for the Arts, Inc., 1775 Broadway, Ste. 510, New York, NY 10019. TEL 212-664-0600. FAX 212-956-5980. Ed. Jemma Fried. illus.; stat. circ. 1,000. **Document type:** newsletter.
Description: Focuses on the alliances between business and the arts. Features interviews with business leaders, information about new business arts alliances, issues and trends.

| 330 | | | CN | ISSN 0829-481X |

B C BUSINESS. Variant title: British Columbia Business. 1972. m. $22.95. Canada Wide Magazines & Communications Ltd., 4180 Lougheed Hwy., 4th Fl., Burnaby, BC V5C 6A7, Canada. TEL 604-299-7311. Ed. Bonnie Irving; Pub. Peter Legge. adv. contact: Bev Malcom. circ. 13,000 (paid); 13,000. (also avail. in microform) **Indexed:** Can.B.P.I., Can.Per.Ind., CMI, Tr.& Indus.Ind. **Document type:** trade publication.
●Also available online. Vendor(s): Information Access Co., Knight-Ridder Information, Inc.
Former titles (until 1983): B C Business Magazine; (until 1975): Business in B C (ISSN 0384-0573)
Description: Covers prominent business leaders and key developments in the local area. Provides data on business trends and opportunities.

BUSINESS AND ECONOMICS

330   **GW**   **ISSN 0937-2385**
B D I HANDBUCH DER FORSCHUNGS- UND INNOVATIONSFOERDERUNG. 1979. bi-m. DM.248. Deutscher Wirtschaftsdienst, Marienburgerstr. 22, 50968 Cologne, Germany. TEL 49-221-937630. FAX 49-221-9376399. Eds. J. von Freyend, C. Kreklau. (looseleaf format) **Document type:** bulletin.

330   **US**   **ISSN 1051-208X**
B N A C COMMUNICATOR; topics and resources for training. 1980. q. free to qualified personnel. B N A Communications, Inc. (Subsidiary of: The Bureau of National Affairs, Inc.), 9439 Key West Ave., Rockville, MD 20850-3396. TEL 301-948-0540. FAX 301-948-2085. URL: http://www.bna.com/bnac. Ed. Tony Cornish; Pub. Rohit Patel. R&P contact: Theresa McGrail. adv.; bk.rev.; circ. 230,000 (controlled). (back issues avail.) **Document type:** trade publication.
    Description: Covers topics and resources for training in the areas of human resource development, safety, labor relations, and equal employment opportunity.

330   **AT**
B P ACCELERATOR. (British Petroleum) 1932. m. free. B P Australia Ltd., 360 Elizabeth St., Melbourne, Vic. 3001, Australia. TEL 03-2684824. Ed. N.J. McMaster. circ. 3,500. **Document type:** newsletter.
    Description: Covers BP's involvement in community and oil industry issues relating to Australia and Papua New Guinea.

B V - EUROLETTER; E G-Binnenmarkt: Tips, Trends, Termine. (Bayerische Vereinsbank AG) see *BUSINESS AND ECONOMICS — Banking And Finance*

BALANCE SHEETS. see *BUSINESS AND ECONOMICS — Abstracting, Bibliographies, Statistics*

330   **US**   **ISSN 0747-1823**
BALTIMORE BUSINESS JOURNAL. 1983. w. $59.85 (effective 1996). American City Business Journals, Inc. (Baltimore), 117 Water St., 9th Fl., Baltimore, MD 21202. TEL 410-576-1161. FAX 410-752-3112. Ed. Marsie Freaney. adv. contact: Marianne Pfeffer. circ. 13,500. (also avail. in microform from UMI) **Indexed:** Tr.& Indus.Ind. **Document type:** trade publication.
    ●Also available online. Vendor(s): Information Access Co., Knight-Ridder Information, Inc.
    —UMI. **CCC.**
    Description: Covers local business news on a weekly basis with emphasis on local finance, health care and real estate.

330   **CL**   **ISSN 0716-2391**
BANCO CENTRAL DE CHILE. ESTUDIOS MONETARIOS. 1967. irreg., no.11, 1989. Ch.$5000($25) Banco Central de Chile, Casilla 967, Santiago, Chile. TEL 56-2-6702000. FAX 56-2-6984847. **Document type:** monographic series.

330   **CL**   **ISSN 0716-2502**
BANCO CENTRAL DE CHILE. SERIE DE ESTUDIOS ECONOMICOS. 1981. irreg., no.40, 1996. Ch.$4700($25) Banco Central de Chile, Casilla 967, Santiago, Chile. TEL 56-2-6702000. FAX 56-2-6984847. **Document type:** monographic series.

330   **BG**
BANGLADESH ARTHANAITIKA JARIP. (Editions in Bengali, English) 1971. a. free. Ministry of Finance, Economic Adviser's Wing, Bangladesh Secretariat, Bldg. No. 6, Dhaka 1000, Bangladesh. circ. 2,000.
    Formerly (until 1974): Bangladesh Economic Survey (ISSN 0070-8704)

330   **MM**   **ISSN 1017-7841**
BANK OF VALLETTA REVIEW. (Text in English) 1990. s-a. free. Bank of Valletta, Zachary St., Valletta VLT 04, Malta. TEL 356-313134. FAX 356-313139. E-mail: cpu@bov.com. (Subscr. to: Bank of Valletta, Strategic Planning Unit, BOV Centre, Gaiety Ln., Sliema SLM16, Malta) Ed. Lino Briguglio. circ. 900. **Document type:** academic/scholarly publication.
    Refereed Serial

330   **GW**   **ISSN 0170-6659**
BANKFACHKLASSE. m. DM.89 (foreign DM.98) (effective 1997). Betriebswirtschaftlicher Verlag Dr. Th. Gabler GmbH, Abraham-Lincoln-Str. 46, 65189 Wiesbaden, Germany. TEL 49-611-7878129. FAX 49-611-7878423. **Document type:** trade publication.
    —**CCC.**

BANKRUPTCY SERVICE CURRENT AWARENESS ALERT. see *LAW — Corporate Law*

BANKRUPTCY SERVICE LAWYERS EDITION. see *LAW — Corporate Law*

BANKS, INVESTMENT & STOCKMARKET. see *BUSINESS AND ECONOMICS — Banking And Finance*

BANQUES ET ENTREPRISES AU MAROC. see *BUSINESS AND ECONOMICS — Banking And Finance*

330   **UK**   **ISSN 0261-3786**
BARCLAYS BANK. INTERNATIONAL INDUSTRIAL SURVEY. (Part of the Industry Reports series) 1978-1985; resumed. q.? Barclays Bank plc., Economics Department, P.O. Box 12, Barclays House, 1 Wimborne Rd., Poole, Dorset BH15 2BB, England. TEL 01202-344023. FAX 01202-402303.
    Formerly (until 1981): Barclays Bank. U K Industrial Survey (ISSN 0260-5341)
    Description: Surveys and analyzes the current situation and the outlook of various industries worlwide and in the context of their U.K. counterparts.

330   **FR**
BAREME SOCIAL PERIODIQUE. q. 285 F. (effective Oct. 1995). Groupe Liaisons, 1 av. Edouard Belin, 92856 Rueil Malmaison, France. TEL 33-1-41299879. FAX 33-1-41299880.

330   **UA**
BARID ASH-SHARIKAT. 1952. d. P.O. Box 813, Alexandria, Egypt. Ed. S. Benaducci. circ. 15,000.
    Description: Covers domestic and international business news, including finance, insurance, import-export trade, and shipping.

BARRON'S GUIDE TO GRADUATE BUSINESS SCHOOLS. see *EDUCATION — Guides To Schools And Colleges*

BAUINDUSTRIE AKTUELL. see *BUILDING AND CONSTRUCTION*

BAUWIRTSCHAFT IM ZAHLENBILD. see *BUILDING AND CONSTRUCTION*

BAYERISCHER MONATSSPIEGEL. see *POLITICAL SCIENCE*

330.968   **SA**
BE IN. (Text in English) 1993. 3/yr. Black Enterprise Publishing and Marketing, P.O. Box 2185, Houghton 2041, South Africa. adv.; illus. **Document type:** trade publication.

330   **CC**
BEIJING CAIMAO XUEYUAN XUEBAO/BEIJING INSTITUTE OF FINANCE AND TRADE. JOURNAL. (Text in Chinese) bi-m. Beijing Caimao Xueyuan, 68 Nanxiange Jie, Guang'anmennei, Beijing 100053, People's Republic of China. TEL 365938. Ed. Shi Chunnian.

330   **GW**   **ISSN 0170-5784**
BEITRAEGE ZUR QUANTITATIVEN WIRTSCHAFTSFORSCHUNG. 1975. irreg., vol.5, 1996. price varies. I F O Institut fuer Wirtschaftsforschung, Poschingerstr. 5, 81679 Munich, Germany. TEL 49-89-9224-0. FAX 49-89-985369. **Document type:** monographic series.

330   **US**   **ISSN 1064-7716**
DK507.8
BELARUSIAN REVIEW. 1991. q. $20 (foreign $40). Byelorussian-American Association, Box 10353, Torrance, CA 90505. FAX 310-373-0793.

330   **CN**   **ISSN 0706-7852**
BENEFITS FOR SASKATCHEWAN INDUSTRY FROM RESOURCE DEVELOPMENT.* 1979. irreg. Government Printing Co., 2005 8th St., Regina, Sask. S4P 3V7, Canada. TEL 306-566-9393.

330.949   **DK**   **ISSN 0907-8274**
HC357.F3
BERETNING OM DEN OEKONOMISKE UDVIKLING PAA FAEROERNE. 1973. a. free. Raadgivende Udvalg Vedroerende Faeroerne, Statsministeriet, Copenhagen, Denmark. TEL 45-1-33-92-33-00. FAX 45-33-11-16-65. TELEX 27027. (Subscr. to: Rita Volsing, Prime Minister's Office, Christiansborg, DK-1218 Copenhagen K, Denmark) circ. 500. **Document type:** government publication.
    Formerly (until 1992): Oekonomiske Udvikling paa Faeroerne (ISSN 0108-6464)
    Description: Contains reports on economic development in the Faroe Islands.

330 301   **MY**
BERITA I D S DEVELOPMENT REVIEW. m.? M.$3.50 (foreign M$.5.50). Institute for Development Studies (Sabah), Ste. 7 CF01, 7th Fl., Block C, Kompleks Karamunsing, 88300 Kota Kinabalu, Sabah, Malaysia. TEL 088-246166. FAX 088-234707. TELEX IDS MA80067. **Document type:** newsletter.
    Description: Covers social, economic and current affairs with updates on research programmes and activities of the institute.

330   **GW**   **ISSN 0863-2952**
BERLINER MERKUR. 1990. m. DM.50. Merkur Verlag, Binzstr. 18, 13189 Berlin, Germany. TEL 49-30-4725393. FAX 49-30-4732251. Ed. Uwe Riemer. adv. contact: Liane Komoll. circ. 20,000. **Document type:** consumer publication.

330   **SZ**   **ISSN 0067-6128**
BERNER BEITRAEGE ZUR NATIONALOEKONOMIE. 1965. irreg., vol.80, 1997. price varies. Paul Haupt AG, Falkenplatz 14, CH-3001 Bern, Switzerland. TEL 41-31-3012345. FAX 41-31-3014669. Ed.Bd. **Document type:** monographic series.
    —**CCC.**

330   **BE**
BESTUUR EN BELEID V Z W. (Supplement avail.) (Text in Flemish) s-m. 4664 BEF. C E D Samsom (Subsidiary of: Wolters Samsom Belgie n.v.), Kouterveld 14, B-1831 Diegem, Belgium. TEL 32-2-7231111.
    Description: Covers regulations, subsidies, accounting, personnel and directional leadership.

330   **GW**   **ISSN 0341-1044**
BETRIEB UND PERSONAL. m. DM.179 (effective 1997). Stollfuss Verlag Bonn, Postfach 2428, 53014 Bonn, Germany. TEL 49-228-724-0. FAX 49-228-659223. **Document type:** bulletin.
    —SWETS. **CCC.**

330   **GW**
BETRIEBSERGEBNISSE BUCHFUEHRENDER BETRIEBE. 1970. a. DM.30. Landwirtschaftskammer Rheinland Endenicher Allee 60, 53115 Bonn, Germany. TEL 49-228-703-223. FAX 49-228-703498. Ed. Hans Peter Rehse. **Document type:** bulletin.

330   **GW**   **ISSN 0172-6196**
DER BETRIEBSWIRT. 1959. q. DM.75. Deutscher Betriebswirte Verlag GmbH, Postfach 1332, 76586 Gernsbach, Germany. TEL 49-7224-93970. FAX 49-7224-939780. Ed. Casimir Catz. adv.: B&W page DM.1250, color page DM.3050; trim 186 x 260; adv. contact: Horst Wannemacher. bk.rev. circ. 2,600. (back issues avail.) **Document type:** newsletter.

330   **GW**   **ISSN 0933-3614**
BETRIEBSWIRTSCHAFTLICHES ARBEITSBUCH. 1978. irreg. DM.128. Erich Schmidt Verlag GmbH & Co. (Berlin), Genthiner Str. 30G, 10785 Berlin, Germany. TEL 49-30-250085-0. FAX 49-30-25008521. (looseleaf format) **Document type:** bulletin.

330   **II**
BETTER BUSINESS. bi-m. Ad International, 212 Arun Chambers, Taredo Rd., Mumbai 34, India. Pub. R.C Pandit.

BIBLIOGRAPHIE DER WIRTSCHAFTSWISSENSCHAFTEN. see *BIBLIOGRAPHIES*

330   **RM**   **ISSN 0067-8082**
BIBLIOTHECA OECONOMICA. (Text in Rumanian; summaries in English, French and Russian) 1967; N.S. 1992. irreg. (Institutul de Cercetari Economice Editura Academiei Romane, Calea 13 Septembrie 13, 76117 Bucharest, Rumania. (Dist. by: Piata Presei Libere 1, Sec. 1 Bucharest, Rumania. TEL 401-6185103. FAX 401-2226407)

BUSINESS AND ECONOMICS

330 320   FR   ISSN 0755-2238
BILANS HEBDOMADAIRES. 1945. w. 3800 F. (foreign 4080 F.) (effective 1997). Societe Generale de Presse et d'Editions, 13 av. de l'Opera, 75001 Paris, France. TEL 40-15-17-89. FAX 40-15-17-15. TELEX SOGPRES 230023. Ed. Marianne Berard Quelin. (looseleaf format)
—CCC.
Description: Provides a summary of the political, economic and social news in France and the world.

BILL SHIPP'S GEORGIA. see *PUBLIC ADMINISTRATION*

BINGO MANAGER. see *SPORTS AND GAMES*

BIOTECH MARKET NEWS & LEGAL STRATEGIES. see *BIOLOGY — Biotechnology*

330   UK   ISSN 0956-8328
BIRKBECK COLLEGE DISCUSSION PAPERS IN ECONOMICS. 1972. irreg. free. University of London, Birkbeck College, Department of Economics, 7-15 Gresse St., London W1P 2LL, England. TEL 44-171-631-6401. FAX 44-171-631-6416. URL: http://www.econ.bbk.ac.uk/research/wpaper.htm/. circ. 200. **Indexed:** Rural Devel.Abstr. **Document type:** academic/scholarly publication, monographic series.
—BLDSC (3597.914800).
Formerly (until 1987): Birkbeck College Discussion Papers (ISSN 0956-831X)

330   CN
BIZ - HAMILTON-HALTON BUSINESS REPORT. 1986. q. Can.$9.95. Town Publishing Group Inc., 875 Main St. W., Hamilton, ON L8S 4R1, Canada. TEL 905-522-6117. FAX 905-529-2242. Ed. Wayne Narciso. adv. contact: Glenda MacDonald. bk.rev.; film rev.; play rev. circ. 21,000. (back issues avail.)
Formerly: Report Business Quarterly; Incorporates: Hamilton Report & Hamilton Business Report.

330   NE   ISSN 1380-8206
BIZZ - MISSETS ZAKENBLAD. Key Title: BiZZ. 1994. 9/yr. Misset (Subsidiary of: Reed Elsevier plc), Postbus 4, 7000 BA Doetinchem, Netherlands. TEL 31-314-349371. FAX 31-314-363638. adv.: B&W page fl.11062, color page fl.16417; trim 215 x 285; adv. contact: Cor van Nek. illus.; circ. 205,640 (controlled). **Document type:** trade publication.
Description: Provides topical information and practical ideas for the company manager, owner or entrepreneur.

650   US   ISSN 0006-4165
E185.8   CODEN: BLENDG
BLACK ENTERPRISE. 1970. m. $19.95 (foreign $29.95). Earl G. Graves Publishing Co., Inc., 130 Fifth Ave., New York, NY 10011. TEL 212-242-8000. FAX 212-886-9610. Ed. Alfred Edmond. adv.: page $13850; adv. contact: Dirk Caldwell. circ. 300,000. (also avail. in microfilm from UMI; microfiche from UMI; reprint service avail. from UMI) **Indexed:** ABI Inform., Acad.Ind., Account.Ind. (1987-), B.P.I., Bk.Rev.Ind. (1978-), BPIA, Bus.Ind., Child.Bk.Rev.Ind. (1978-), Ind.Per.Art.Relat.Law, Mag.Ind., P.A.I.S., PMR, PSI, R.G., R.G.Abstr., SRI, Tr.& Indus.Ind., Work Rel.Abstr. **Document type:** consumer publication, trade publication.
●Also available online. Vendor(s): Information Access Co., UMI.
—BLDSC (2105.925000); KR SourceOne; UMI; UnCover. CCC.
Description: Features business service information for black professionals and entrepreneurs.

330   GW   ISSN 0406-4224
BLICK DURCH DIE WIRTSCHAFT. 1958. 5/w. DM.32 per mo. (Europe DM.35.90; rest of world DM.47) (effective 1997). Frankfurter Allgemeine Zeitung GmbH, Hellerhofstr. 2-4, 60327 Frankfurt a.M., Germany. TEL 49-69-7591-0. FAX 49-69-75911743. Ed. Hans-Christoph Noack; Pub. Juergen Jeske. circ. 30,000. **Document type:** newspaper.

BLUEPRINT SERIES. see *ENVIRONMENTAL STUDIES*

330   FR   ISSN
BOARDROOM. 1978. m. £11.50. Ulster Magazines Ltd., 58 Rugby Rd., Belfast BT7 1NT, N. Ireland. TEL 44-1232-230425. FAX 44-1232-243595. Ed. Larry Nixon. adv.; bk.rev.; pat.; stat.; tr.lit. circ. 5,000. (tabloid format) **Document type:** trade publication.
Formerly: Trade and Industry in Ireland.

330   GW
BOERSEN ZEITUNG. 5/w. (Tue.-Sat.). DM.1648.80. Herausgebergemeinschaft Wertpapier-Mitteilungen Keppler, Lehmann GmbH & Co., Postfach 110932, 60044 Frankfurt a.M., Germany. TEL 49-69-2732-0. FAX 49-69-234473. TELEX 412066-BZFFM. Ed. Hans Herdt. **Document type:** newspaper.

330.9489   DK   ISSN 0900-1298
BOERSENS NYHEDSMAGASIN. 1966. m. (11/yr.). DKK 1175. Boersens Magasiner A-S, P.O. Box 2242, DK-1019 Copenhagen K, Denmark. TEL 45-33-32-44-00. FAX 45-33-11-59-06. (Dist. by: Forhandlerservice, Rosenkaeret 18, DK-2860 Soeborg, Denmark. TEL 45-39-69-00-22) Ed. Kristian Lund. adv.: B&W page DKK 4900; trim 420 x 280; adv. contact: Henrik Klitvad. circ. 16,000. (back issues avail.)
—Linda Hall.
Formed by the merger of (1982-1985): Politisk Ugebrev (ISSN 0109-0909); (1978-1985): Maaneds Boersen (ISSN 0105-8843); (1968-1985): Management (ISSN 0025-1631)
Description: Contains in-depth articles about the most important events in Danish trade and industry, a summary of current news, and portraits of influential corporate executives.

330   SP   ISSN 1130-1619
BOLETIN C.E.E. 1986. fortn. free. (Departamento de Economia y Hacienda) Gobierno de Navarra, Fondo de Publicaciones, Navas de Tolosa 21, 31002 Pamplona, Spain. TEL 34-48-107121. FAX 34-48-227673.

330   SP   ISSN 1131-5490
HC387.N3
BOLETIN DE ECONOMIA DE NAVARRA. 1985. s-a. 1800 ptas. (effective 1997). (Departamento de Economia y Hacienda) Gobierno de Navarra, Fondo de Publicaciones, Navas de Tolosa 21, 31002 Pamplona, Spain. TEL 34-48-427123. (back issues avail.) **Document type:** government publication.
—CINDOC.
Formerly (until 1991): Boletin de Economia (ISSN 1130-1635)

330   SP   ISSN 0006-6249
HB9
BOLETIN DE ESTUDIOS ECONOMICOS; revista de investigacion economica. 1942. 3/yr. 3500 ptas. (foreign 4000 ptas. effective 1993). (Universidad Comercial de Deusto) Asociacion de Licenciados en Ciencias Economicas, Apto. 20044, 48080 Bilbao, Spain. TEL 94-445-22-12. FAX 94-445-63-45. Eds. Susana Rodriguez Vidarte, Fernando Gomez-Bezares. adv.; bk.rev.; bibl.; index. circ. 5,000. **Indexed:** Amer.Hist.& Life (1958-1975), ELLIS, Excerp.Med., Hist.Abstr. (1958-1975), IBR, SCIMP (1982-).
—BLDSC (2203.840000); CINDOC; SWETS.
Formerly: Universidad de Deusto. Publicaciones. Economia.

330   MY   ISSN 0128-7397
HC448.B6
BORNEO REVIEW. (Text in English) 1990. s-a. M.$32. Institute for Development Studies (Sabah) - Institut Kajian Pembangunan (Sabah), Ste. 7 CF01, 7th Fl., Block C, Kompleks Karamunsing, 88300 Kota Kinabalu, Sabah, Malaysia. TEL 088-264166. FAX 088-234707. Ed. Pang Teck Wai. adv. **Indexed:** Asian-Pac.Econ.Lit.
Description: Publishes research pertaining to economic, social, political and public administrative developments.

330   US
BOSTON BUSINESS JOURNAL. 1981. w. $64. American City Business Journals, Inc., 505 Powell St., Austin, TX 78703-5121. (Subscr. to: 200 High St., Boston, MA 02110-3006) Ed. Charles Heschmeyer. adv.: B&W page $3975. circ. 20,000. (tabloid format) **Document type:** consumer publication.
●Also available online. Vendor(s): CompuServe, Inc., Data-Star, Dow Jones News Retrieval, Knight-Ridder Information, Inc., National Data Corp., UMI.

330   US   ISSN 0068-0354
BOSTWICK PAPER. 1968. irreg., no.6, 1988. $5. Bostwick Press, 5 Bostwick Ln., Richmond, VA 23226-3106. Ed. Thomas S. Berry. circ. 500. **Indexed:** Vert.File Ind. **Document type:** monographic series.

330   SA
BOTSWANA; review - commerce, industry and tourism. a. R.30 (effective 1996). Braby's (Subsidiary of: Kohler Packaging Ltd.), P.O. Box 1426, Pinetown 3600, South Africa. TEL 27-31-7017021. FAX 27-31-7017036.

330   BS
BOTSWANA BUSINESS MONTH MAGAZINE. 1988. bi-m. P.10.65 (foreign $15). News Company Botswana Pty. Ltd., P.O. Box 1605, Gaborone, Botswana. TEL 267-312833. FAX 267-312774. TELEX 2631 BD. Ed. Clara Olsen. adv.: B&W page P.1360, color page P.1950. circ. 500. **Document type:** trade publication.
Description: Encourages investment and economic development in Botswana.

330   BS
BOTSWANA BUSINESS NEWS. 1980. m. free. Ministry of Commerce and Industry, Department of Trade and Investment Promotion (T I P A), Private Bag 00367, Gaborone, Botswana. TEL 267-351790. FAX 267-305375. TELEX 2674 TRADE BD. Eds. Mukram Sheikh, Monty Letshwiti. circ. 3,000. **Document type:** newsletter, government publication.
Description: Covers a variety of subjects related to trade and investment promotion. Reviews commercial and industrial development.

657   CN   ISSN 0831-5477
BOTTOM LINE; the news and information publication for Canada's financial professionals. 1985. m. Can.$69. Butterworths Canada Ltd., 75 Clegg Rd., Markham, ON L6G 1A1, Canada. TEL 905-479-2665. FAX 905-479-3758. E-mail: tbl@butterworths.ca. Ed. Mike Lewis; Pub. Don Brillineer. R&P contact: Wendy King. adv.: B&W page Can.$3570; trim 10 1/4 x 15; adv. contact: Warren Beesley. bk.rev. circ. 30,000. (tabloid format; also avail. in microfiche) **Indexed:** Can.B.P.I., Can.Per.Ind., Tr.& Indus.Ind. **Document type:** trade publication.
Description: News about, for, or affecting accountants, consultants and financial managers.

330   BM
BOTTOM LINE. 1991. free. Bermuda Press (Holdings) Ltd., P.O. Box HM1025, Hamilton HMDX, Bermuda. TEL 441-295-5881. FAX 441-295-1513. Ed. David L. White; Pub. Keith R. Jensen. adv. contact: Gary L. Ritchie.

330   US
BRANDYWINE.NET BUSINESS REPORT. bi-w. $9 (effective 1997 & 1998). Ad Pro, Inc., Box 520, Oxford, PA 19363. TEL 610-932-2444. FAX 610-932-2246. E-mail: rolder@brandywine.net; URL: http://www.chestercounty.com/busrpt.htm. Ed. Joanne Silva; Pub. Robert Older. R&P contact: Randall Lieberman. adv. contact: Robert Older. circ. 6,000. **Document type:** newspaper.
●Also available online.
Former titles: Chester County Business Report; Chester County Biz.
Description: Contains business, technology information news and reports.

330   BL
BRASIL EM EXAME. 1970. a. Editora Abril, S.A., Av. Otaviano Alves de Lima 4400, 02909-900 Sao Paulo SP, Brazil. TEL 011-877-1322. FAX 011-877-1437. Ed. Jose Roberto Guzzo. adv.; bk.rev.; charts; illus.; stat. circ. 6,600. **Document type:** consumer publication.
Description: For professionals in administration, marketing, finance, human resources and industry.

330   UK
BRIEFCASE BUSINESS NEWS. 1987. 11/yr. £25 to non-members (effective 1997). (Redditch & Bromsgrove Chamber of Commerce) Lily Publishing Ltd., Crossgate House, Crossgate Rd., Park Farm, Redditch, Worcs B98 7SN, England. TEL 44-1527-502503. FAX 44-1527-502811. Ed. Claire Wolfe. R&P contact: Jeannette Laight. adv.: page £495; 186 x 270; adv. contact: Jeannette Laight. circ. 4,000. (back issues avail.) **Document type:** bulletin.

BUSINESS AND ECONOMICS

BRITISH COLUMBIA BUSINESS EDUCATION ASSOCIATION. JOURNAL. see *EDUCATION — Teaching Methods And Curriculum*

330 UK ISSN 0263-3523
BRITISH ECONOMY SURVEY. 1971. 3/yr. £6.99. Longman Group UK Ltd., Longman House, Burnt Mill, Harlow, Essex CM20 2JE, England. TEL 44-1279-426721. FAX 44-1279-431059. (Subscr. to: Pearson Professional, P.O. Box 77, Fourth Ave., Harlow, Essex CM19 5BQ, England. TEL 44-1279-623924. FAX 44-1279-639609) Ed. Brian Hodkinson. circ. 9,000. (back issues avail.; reprint service avail. from SCH) **Document type:** bulletin.
—BLDSC (2299.150000); SWETS.
Description: Contains current information on the British economy, written for high school students of economics.

330 UK
BRITISH-NORTH AMERICAN COMMITTEE PUBLICATIONS. 1970. irreg. price varies. British-North American Research Association, Grosvenor Gardens House, 35-37 Grosvenor Gardens, London SW1W 0BS, England. TEL 44-171-828-6644. FAX 44-171-828-5830. E-mail: 101564.1243@compuserve.com. Ed.Bd. bibl.; charts. **Document type:** bulletin.
Formerly: British-North American Research Association. Committee Publications.
Description: Discusses U.K., U.S. and Canadian relations.

330 UK
BRITISH-NORTH AMERICAN RESEARCH ASSOCIATION. OCCASIONAL PAPERS. 1972. irreg. price varies. British-North American Research Association, Grosvenor Gardens House, 35-37 Grosvenor Gardens, London SW1W 0BS, England. TEL 44-171-828-6644. FAX 44-171-828-5830. E-mail: 101564.1243@compuserve.com. bibl.; charts.
Description: Discusses policy issues relating to U.K. economic performance in world economy.

BRITISH PLASTICS FEDERATION. BUSINESS TRENDS SURVEY. see *PLASTICS*

330 350 US ISSN 1053-5365
BRONG'S BUSINESS SUCCESS NEWS; view from the trenches. 1990. bi-m. $95. G M B Partnership, 4530 Manastash Rd., Ellensburg, WA 98926-7826. TEL 509-962-8238. FAX 509-925-4566. Ed. Gerald Brong. R&P contact: Gerald Brong. adv.; bk.rev. circ. 2,000. **Document type:** newsletter.
Description: Provides news and opinion about business, government, politics, quality initiatives, and educational leadership for decision makers.

330 US ISSN 0745-1253
HI
BROOKINGS REVIEW. 1962. q. $17.95 (foreign $24.95). Brookings Institution, 1775 Massachusetts Ave., N.W., Washington, DC 20036-2188. TEL 202-797-6258. FAX 202-797-6195. (Subscr. to: Box 037, Washington, DC 20042-0037. TEL 202-797-6255) Ed. Brenda Szittya. R&P contact: Garry Sparks. TEL 202-797-2483. circ. 20,000. (also avail. in microform from UMI; reprint service avail. from UMI) **Indexed:** ABI Inform., Abstr.Mil.Bibl., Acad.Ind., BPIA, Int.Polit.Sci.Abstr., Mid.East: Abstr.& Ind., P.A.I.S., Polit.Sci.Abstr., PROMT, R.G.Abstr., Tr.& Indus.Ind., World Bank.Abstr. **Document type:** academic/scholarly publication.
●Also available online. Vendor(s): Information Access Co., UMI.
—BLDSC (2350.081000); KR SourceOne; SWETS; UMI; UnCover. **CCC.**
Formerly: Brookings Bulletin (ISSN 0007-229X)
Description: Offers articles on the economic, political, and foreign policy issues of the day.

330.9 US
BROOKLYN BUSINESS JOURNAL. m. Brooklyn Journal Publications, Inc., 129 Montague St., Brooklyn, NY 11201. TEL 718-624-6033. FAX 718-624-5302.

BRUCE BORTZ'S MARYLAND REPORT. see *PUBLIC ADMINISTRATION*

330 CN ISSN 0829-5239
BRUNSWICK BUSINESS JOURNAL. 1983. m. Can.$39.95. A B J Publishing Inc., 599 Main St., Ste. 203, Moncton, NB E1C 1C8, Canada. TEL 506-857-9696. FAX 506-859-7395. Ed. Suzanne McDonald Boyce; Pub. Dalten Jensen. adv. contact: Dalton Jenson. circ. 7,000. (tabloid format) **Document type:** newspaper.
●Also available online. Vendor(s): UMI.
—UMI.
Description: Focuses on trends and issues that affect business people in New Brunswick.

BUEROJOURNAL. see *HANDICAPPED — Visually Impaired*

330 US ISSN 0882-2859
BUFFALO BUSINESS JOURNAL. 1984. fortn. $25. 125 Broadway, Buffalo, NY 14203. TEL 716-855-3333. Ed. Norman Myer. adv. circ. 15,000.

BUILDING IN AUSTRALIA (YEAR). see *BUILDING AND CONSTRUCTION*

BUILDING INDUSTRY PROSPECTS. see *BUILDING AND CONSTRUCTION*

330 346 BU ISSN 0861-5640
BULGARIAN ECONOMIC REVIEW. Daily Bulgarian edition: Pari (ISSN 0861-5608) (Text in English) 1992. fortn. 2600 lv.($190) (effective 1995). Rubicon Ltd., Tsarigradsko Chaussee 47, Sofia 1504, Bulgaria. TEL 359-2-447317. FAX 359-2-445412. Ed. Stefan Pavlov. adv. contact: Veselin Iankov. circ. 6,000. (paid). (back issues avail.) **Document type:** newspaper.
Description: Provides business and finance coverage on Bulgaria: new economic laws, foreign trade and customs regulations, banking news and statistics.

BULLETIN ANALYTIQUE DE DOCUMENTATION POLITIQUE, ECONOMIQUE ET SOCIALE CONTEMPORAINE. see *POLITICAL SCIENCE*

BULLETIN L A R F. see *BUSINESS AND ECONOMICS — Banking And Finance*

330 UK ISSN 0307-3378
HB1
BULLETIN OF ECONOMIC RESEARCH. 1949. q. £107($226) (foreign £143) (effective 1997). Blackwell Publishers Ltd., 108 Cowley Rd., Oxford OX4 1JF, England. TEL 44-1865-791100. FAX 44-1865-791347. E-mail: jnlinfo@blackwellpublishers.co.uk; URL: http://www.blackwellpublishers.co.uk. Eds. John Treble, Ken Burdett. adv.; bk.rev.; charts; index. circ. 650. (also avail. in microform from UMI; reprint service avail. from SWZ) **Indexed:** ABI Inform, Amer.Hist.& Life (1955-1985), Asian-Pac.Econ.Lit., BPIA, Br.Hum.Ind., Bus.Ind., C.R.E.J., Cont.Pg.Manage., Geo.Abstr.H.G., Hist.Abstr. (1955-1985), IBR, IDA, Int.Lab.Doc., J.Cont.Quant.Meth., J.of Econ.Lit., Key to Econ.Sci., Mid.East: Abstr.& Ind., P.A.I.S., Tr.& Indus.Ind., World Bank.Abstr. **Document type:** academic/scholarly publication.
●Also available online. Vendor(s): Information Access Co.
—BLDSC (2849.620000); SWETS; UMI; UnCover. **CCC.**
Formerly: Yorkshire Bulletin of Economic and Social Research (ISSN 0044-0590)
Refereed Serial

330 XK ISSN 1010-5719
BUSINESS. 1985. q. $10. A L K I M Communication Production Company, Box MA 020, Marchand Post Office, Castries, St. Lucia, W.I. Ed. Albert Deterville. adv. circ. 5,000.
—CCC.

330 IT
BUSINESS (PARMA). 1985. m. L.60000 (foreign L.120000). Via dei Franese 17, 43100 Parma, Italy. TEL 39-521-233983. FAX 39-521-234774. Ed. Paolo Dalco. adv.: color page L.23500000. bk.rev.

BUSINESS ADVICE AND FINANCIAL PLANNING. see *BUSINESS AND ECONOMICS — Banking And Finance*

BUSINESS ADVISORY CLIENT NEWSLETTER. see *BUSINESS AND ECONOMICS — Accounting*

330 CN
THE BUSINESS ADVOCATE. 1987. m. free. London Chamber of Commerce, 244 Pall Mall St., Box 3295, London, ON N6A 5P6, Canada. TEL 519-432-7551. FAX 519-432-8063. Ed. John Redmond. circ. 10,000.

330 US ISSN 1050-091X
BUSINESS ALABAMA MONTHLY. 1986. m. $19.95. P M T Publishing Co., Inc., Box 66200, Mobile, AL 36660. TEL 205-473-6269. FAX 205-479-8822. Ed. Matthew Solon. adv. circ. 16,000.
Formerly (until 1987): Business Alabama (ISSN 0886-3024)
Description: For business owners, managers, and presidents of companies in Alabama.

330 US ISSN 1081-6216
BUSINESS ALERT. 1982. q. free. Long Island University, C.W. Post College, Center for Business Research, Brookville, NY 11548. TEL 516-299-2832. FAX 516-299-4170. E-mail: cbr@titan.liunet.edu. Ed. Nancy R. Marino. circ. 300. (back issues avail.) **Indexed:** Ind.S.A.Per. **Document type:** newsletter.

330 CC
BUSINESS ALERT; the latest developments in US trade policy. (Text in English) 1996. q. Hong Kong Trade Development Council, 38-F, Office Tower, Convention Plaza, 1 Harbour Rd., Wanchai, Hong Kong, People's Republic of China. TEL 852-2584-4333. FAX 852-2824-0249. URL: http://www.tdc.org.hk.

338.5 II ISSN 0007-6430
HB1
BUSINESS ANALYST. (Text in English) 1968. 2/yr. Rs.50($10) (£5). Shri Ram College of Commerce, Delhi 7, India. Ed. D.R. Miltal. adv.; bk.rev. circ. 1,000. (tabloid format; also avail. in record) **Document type:** academic/scholarly publication.

BUSINESS & CONSTRUCTION MAGAZINE. see *BUILDING AND CONSTRUCTION*

330 US ISSN 0894-6825
HF5343
BUSINESS AND ECONOMIC HISTORY. 1975. s-a. $20. College of William and Mary, Department of Economics, Williamsburg, VA 23187-8795. TEL 804-221-2381. Ed. William J. Hausman. R&P contact: William J. Hausman. circ. 500. **Indexed:** Amer.Hist.& Life (1987-), Hist.Abstr. (1987-). **Document type:** academic/scholarly publication.
—BLDSC (2933.192000); UMI.

650 330 US ISSN 0007-6465
HC107.S7 CODEN: BSERA6
BUSINESS & ECONOMIC REVIEW. 1954. q. free. University of South Carolina, College of Business Administration, Division of Research, The Francis M. Hipp Bldg., Columbia, SC 29208. TEL 803-777-2510. FAX 803-777-9344. E-mail: jstucker@darla.badm.sc.edu; URL: http://research.badm.sc.edu/research/bereview/contents.htm. Ed. Jan Collins Stucker. R&P contact: Jan Collins Stucker. charts; illus.; stat. circ. 5,419. (also avail. in microform from UMI; reprint service avail. from UMI) **Indexed:** ABI Inform., BPIA, P.A.I.S., Pers.Manage.Abstr., PSI. **Document type:** abstracting/indexing.
—UMI; UnCover.
Description: Covers business, economic, and environmental issues in South Carolina.

330 UK
▼**BUSINESS AND ECONOMICS RESEARCH DIRECTORY.** 1996. a. $225. Europa Publications Ltd., 18 Bedford Sq., London WC1B 3JN, England. TEL 44-171-580-8236. FAX 44-171-637-0922. Ed. Ian Preston. **Document type:** directory.

BUSINESS AND FINANCE CAREER DIRECTORY. see *OCCUPATIONS AND CAREERS*

BUSINESS AND ECONOMICS

650   US   ISSN 0007-6503
HF5001   CODEN: BUSOBE
BUSINESS AND SOCIETY; a journal of interdisciplinary exploration. 1960. q. $145 to institutions (effective Sep. 1996). (International Association for Business and Society, Research Committee) Sage Publications, Inc., 2455 Teller Rd., Thousand Oaks, CA 91320. TEL 805-499-0721. FAX 805-499-0871. E-mail: libraries@sagepub.com; URL: http://www.sagepub.co.uk/journals/usdetails/j0037.html. (Overseas subscr. to: Sage Publications Ltd., 6 Bonhill St., London EC2A 4PU, England; Sage Publications India Pvt. Ltd., P.O. Box 4215, New Delhi 110 048, India) Ed. Donna J. Wood. adv. contact: Margaret Travers. tr.lit. circ. 3,500. (also avail. in microform from UMI; back issues avail.; reprint service avail. from SCH,UMI) **Indexed:** BPIA, Bus.Ind., Comput.Rev., Intl.Mgmt.Info., Manage.Cont., Mid.East: Abstr.& Ind., Oper.Res.Manage.Sci., P.A.I.S., Pers.Manage.Abstr., Qual.Contr.Appl.Stat., Tr.& Indus.Ind., Work Rel.Abstr. **Document type:** academic/scholarly publication.
●Also available online. Vendor(s): Information Access Co.
—BLDSC (2933.225000); KR SourceOne; UMI; UnCover. CCC.
Description: Focuses on business and society, social issues in management, and business ethics.
Refereed Serial

650   US   ISSN 0045-3609
HD60.5.U5   CODEN: BUSRAM
BUSINESS AND SOCIETY REVIEW; a quarterly forum on the role of business in a free society. 1972. q. $56. Business and Society Review, c/o Hanover Publishers, 200 W. 57th St., New York, NY 10019. TEL 212-399-1088. FAX 212-245-1973. Ed. Theodore Cross. bk.rev.; circ. 2,000 (paid). (also avail. in microform from RRI,WSH) **Indexed:** ABI Inform., Account.Ind. (1974-), B.P.I., BPIA, Bus.Ind., Bus.Ind., C.L.I., Comput.Rev., Fut.Surv., Ind.Per.Art.Relat.Law, L.R.I., Leg.Per., Manage.Cont., Mgmt.& Market.Abstr., Mid.East: Abstr.& Ind., P.A.I.S., P.A.I.S., Pers.Lit., Pers.Manage.Abstr., PSI, SCIMP, Soc.Sci.Ind., Tr.& Indus.Ind., Work Rel.Abstr. **Document type:** academic/scholarly publication.
●Also available online. Vendor(s): Information Access Co.
—BLDSC (2933.226000); KR SourceOne; SWETS; UMI; UnCover.

330   CN
BUSINESS ANNUAL. (Supplement to: Business Times) 1992. a. Can.$5.95. Blackburn Group, 231 Dundas St., Ste. 203, London, ON N6A 1H1, Canada. TEL 519-679-4901. FAX 519-434-7842. Ed. Nadia Shousher. adv.: B&W page Can.$995; color page Can.$1400; trim 8 x 10 3/4. circ. 14,300.
Formerly: London Times Business Annual (ISSN 1194-4005)

330 020   UK
BUSINESS ARCHIVES COUNCIL. ANNUAL CONFERENCE PROCEEDINGS. a. £35 membership to institutions (foreign £40); corporate membership £80 (foreign £85) (includes Business Archives, quarterly newsletter). Business Archives Council, The Clove Bldg., 4 Maguire St., Butlers Wharf, London SE1 2NQ, England. Ed. Serena Kelly. R&P contact: W.S. Quinn. TEL 44-171-407-6110. **Document type:** proceedings.

330 020   UK
BUSINESS ARCHIVES COUNCIL. NEWSLETTER. q. £35 membership to institutions (overseas £40); corporate membership £80 (overseas £85) (includes Business Archives; conference proceedings). Business Archives Council, The Clove Bldg., 4 Maguire St., Butlers Wharf, London SE1 2NQ, England. Ed. Serena Kelly. R&P contact: W.S. Quinn. TEL 44-171-407-6110. **Document type:** newsletter.
—BLDSC (2933.270000).
Formerly (until 1969): Business Archives Council: Quarterly Newsletter (ISSN 0309-4200)

330 020   UK
BUSINESS ARCHIVES COUNCIL. PRINCIPLES AND PRACTICE. 1934. a. £35 membership to institutions (foreign £40); corporate members £80 (foreign £85) (includes: conference proceedings, quarterly newsletter). Business Archives Council, The Clove Bldg., 4 Maguire St., Butlers Wharf, London SE1 2NQ, England. Ed. Serena Kelly. R&P contact: W.S. Quinn. TEL 44-171-407-6110. adv. contact: W.S. Quinn. **Document type:** academic/scholarly publication.
—BLDSC (2933.240000); UnCover.
Supersedes in part: Business Archives (ISSN 0007-6538); Which was formerly (until 1962): Business Archives Council: Quarterly Bulletin.

330 020   UK
HF5736
BUSINESS ARCHIVES: SOURCES AND HISTORY. 1934. a. £35 membership to institutions (foreign £40); corporate membership £80 (overseas £85) (includes newsletter and conference proceedings). Business Archives Council, The Clove Bldg., 4 Maguire St., Butlers Wharf, London SE1 2NQ, England. Ed. Serena Kelly. R&P contact: W.S. Quinn. TEL 44-171-407-6110. adv. contact: W.S. Quinn. bk.rev.; cum.index. circ. 600. (back issues avail.) **Document type:** academic/scholarly publication, bulletin, newsletter, proceedings.
—BLDSC (2933.240000); UnCover.
Supersedes in part: Business Archives (ISSN 0007-6538); Which was formerly (until 1962): Business Archives Council: Quarterly Bulletin.

330   ISSN 0572-7545
BUSINESS ASIA. 1970. bi-w. £575($875) Economist Intelligence Unit, 111 W. 57th St., New York, NY 10019. TEL 212-554-0600; 800-938-4685. FAX 212-586-1182. TELEX 175567. URL: http://www.eiu.com. (UK addr.: Economist Intelligence Unit Ltd., Subscriptions Dept., P.O. Box 200, Harold Hill, Romford, Essex RM3 8UX, England. TEL 44-171-830-1007. FAX 44-1708-371850) (also avail. in microform from UMI) **Indexed:** Key to Econ.Sci. **Document type:** newsletter.
●Also available online. Vendor(s): Knight-Ridder Information, Inc.
—UMI.
Description: Provides up-to-the-minute coverage of what is happening throughout Asia and why, and what can be done about it for profit.

BUSINESS ASSOCIATE; partners in land conservation. see CONSERVATION

330 658   UK   ISSN 1352-5565
BUSINESS BASICS: GUIDE TO NATIONAL INSURANCE CONTRIBUTIONS. Key Title: Croner's Business Basics Bulletin. N I C. 1994. base vol. (plus m. updates). £80.40 (update service £56.40) (effective 1995). Croner Publications Ltd. (Subsidiary of: Wolters Kluwer N.V.), Croner House, 100 London Rd., Kingston-upon-Thames, Surrey TW2 6SR, England. TEL 44-181-547-3333. FAX 44-181-247-1300. TELEX 23778. (looseleaf format) **Document type:** trade publication.

330 020.1   US   ISSN 0741-8132
BUSINESS BOOK REVIEW.* 1984. bi-m. $45. Corporate Support Systems, 1802 S. Duncan, Champaign, IL 61821. Ed. Jagdish N. Sheth. bk.rev.; index. circ. 4,000. **Indexed:** Bk.Rev.Ind. (1984-), Child.Bk.Rev.Ind. (1984-).

330   UK
BUSINESS BULLETIN. 1981. bi-m. £25. Dart Publishing, Guildhall, Dartmouth, Devon, England. Ed. Philip K. Spann. adv.; bk.rev. circ. 14,000. **Indexed:** Build.Manage.Abstr. **Document type:** consumer publication.

330 320   UK   ISSN 1350-1240
HC244.A1   CODEN: BCEUE9
BUSINESS CENTRAL EUROPE. (Text in English) 1993. m. £35 (N. America $45) (effective 1997). Economist Newspapers, 25 St. James's St., London SW1A 1HG, England. TEL 44-171-839-7000. FAX 44-171-839-9386. (All subscr. to: International Subscription Services, P.O. Box 14, Harold Hill, Romford, Essex. RM3 3EQ, England. TEL 01708-381555. FAX 44-1708-381555; Editorial addr.: Schwarzenbergplatz 8-4, 1030 Vienna, Austria. TEL 0431-713-3363. FAX 0431-714-0113) Ed. Delia Math-Cohn; Pub. Simon Phillips. R&P contact: Caroline Bowen. TEL 44-171-830-7000. adv. contact: Stephen Howard. bk.rev. circ. 22,000. **Document type:** trade publication.
—BLDSC (2933.338680); SWETS.
Description: Covers politics, economics, business and finance in Central and Eastern Europe.

330   US   ISSN 1055-8217
BUSINESS CONCEPTS.* (Supplement avail.) 1991. q. $29.99. Publishing & Business Consultants, 101 W. 64th St. Unit 3-2, Inglewood, CA 90302-1255. TEL 213-732-3477. FAX 213-732-9123. (Subscr. to: Box 75392, Los Angeles, CA 90075) Ed. Andeson Napoleon Atia. adv. circ. 120,000. **Document type:** consumer publication.
Description: Presents money making ideas and new business opportunities.

330   AT   ISSN 0814-4273
BUSINESS COUNCIL OF AUSTRALIA BULLETIN. 1968. m. Aus.$125. Business Council of Australia, 15th Fl., 10 Queens Road, Melbourne, Vic. 3000, Australia. FAX 61-3-9274-7744. Ed. M. Soutter. adv. circ. 7,000. **Indexed:** Key to Econ.Sci.
—UnCover.
Formerly: A I D A Bulletin.

BUSINESS COUNSEL; a quarterly update of the litigation activities of the U.S. Chambers of Commerce. see LAW — Corporate Law

330 011   US
BUSINESS DATELINE. (Not avail. in printed format) 1985. w. U M I Company (Louisville), 620 S. Third St., Louisville, KY 40202-2475. TEL 800-626-2823. **Document type:** abstracting/indexing, bibliography.
●Also available online. Vendor(s): Dow Jones News Retrieval, Human Resources Information Network, Knight-Ridder Information, Inc., Lexis-Nexis. Also available on CD-ROM.
Description: Contains bibliographic information, indexing, and full-text articles from 375 city business journals, newspapers, and news services.

330   SA   ISSN 1015-0706
BUSINESS DAY. (Published in 2 editions: National; Final (Johannesburg)) (Text in English) 1985. 5/w. (Mon-Fri.). R.520 (R.2236 airmail to U.K.; R.3837 airmail to U.S.). B D F M Ltd., 4 Biermann Ave., Johannesburg 2000, South Africa. TEL 27-11-2803000. FAX 27-11-2805600. E-mail: busday@tml.co.za; URL: http://www.bday.co.za. Ed. Jim Jones; Pub. Alan Greenblo. R&P contact: Trevor Bisseker. TEL 27-11-2805504. adv. contact: Sarel Du Plessis. bk.rev.; film rev.; music rev.; play rev.; illus.; circ. 40,000 (paid). cols./p.: 10. (broadsheet format; back issues avail.) **Document type:** newspaper.
●Also available online.
Description: News and information of interest to the business and financial community.

330   UK
▼**BUSINESS DECISIONS;** inside the C I S. 1995. fortn. £550($880) (I.T.A.R. - T.A.S.S., RU) C I S Business Enterprises Ltd., Morley House, 314 Regent St., 2nd Fl., Ste. 38, London W1R 5AB, England. TEL 44-171-580-5507. FAX 44-171-580-4922. Eds. Alexander Sisnev, A.R. Hunter. **Document type:** trade publication.
Description: Updates business news and economic issues of the CIS.

330   II
BUSINESS DEEPIKA; economic & financial weekly. (Text in Malayalam) w. (Mon.). Rs.440 for 2 yrs.; newsstand price: Rs.5. Rashtra Deepika Ltd., Deepika Bldg., C.M.S. College Rd., P.B. No. 7, Kottayam 686 001, India. TEL 91-481-566706. FAX 91-481-567947. TELEX 0888-203-DPKA IN. adv.: page Rs.120000. circ. 50,000.

BUSINESS AND ECONOMICS

330 II
BUSINESS DEEPIKA INTERNATIONAL. (Text in Malayalam) w. (Mon.). Rashtra Deepika Ltd., Deepika Bldg., C.M.S. College Rd., P.B. No. 7, Kottayam 686 001, India. TEL 91-481-566706. FAX 91-481-567947. TELEX 0888-203 DPKA IN. adv.: page Rs.120000.

330 US ISSN 0895-3791
BUSINESS DIGEST OF CAPE COD & THE ISLANDS.
Variant title: Cape and Islands Business Digest. Variant title: Southeastern Massachusetts - Cape and Islands Business Digest. 1986. m. $28. Cape & Islands Business Digest, Inc., Box 64, Hyannis Port, MA 02647-0064. TEL 508-778-5042. FAX 508-778-5063. Ed. Anthony Alva. adv.: page $1075; bleed 8 1/2 x 11; adv. contact: Jeff Lyon. circ. 6,500. (back issues avail.) **Document type:** consumer publication.
   Former titles: Business Digest of Southeastern Massachusetts - Cape Cod; Business Digest of Southeastern Massachusetts.
   Description: Contains local business news and issues for Cape Cod, Massachusetts.

330 US ISSN 8750-2305
BUSINESS DIGEST OF GREATER BURLINGTON. 1984. m. $24. Mill Publishing, Inc., 1233 Shelburne Rd., E-5, S. Burlington, VT 05403. TEL 802-862-4109. FAX 802-862-9322. E-mail: busydigest@vermontguides.com; URL: http://www.vermontguides.com. Ed. Edna Tenney; Pub. Jack Tenney. adv. contact: Liz Swim. bk.rev.; circ. 5,800 (controlled). **Document type:** trade publication.

330 US ISSN 1046-168X
BUSINESS DIGEST OF GREATER WATERBURY. 1989. bi-m. $24. Four Stars Publishing Co., Inc., Box 9018, 197 Tranquility Rd., Middlebury, CT 06702-2230. TEL 203-754-9922. FAX 203-754-5192. Ed. Barbara J. Mitchell. adv.; circ. 6,300 (controlled).
   Formerly: Greater Waterbury Business Digest.
   Description: Tracks the movements of people within the 17 towns of the Greater Waterbury business community, new businesses, and new products and services. Includes interviews with business leaders and profiles of successful businesses.

330 US ISSN 0889-7549
BUSINESS DIGEST OF PIONEER VALLEY.* 1986. m. $17 (effective 1993). Apple Hill Communications, Inc., Box 195, Granville, MA 01034-0195. TEL 413-786-4000. FAX 413-786-1462. Ed. Maripat Jordan. adv. contact: Jay Jordan. circ. 9,000. **Document type:** consumer publication.
   Description: Includes news and issues of interest to the business community of the greater Springfield, Massachusetts area.

330 UK ISSN 0958-7918
BUSINESS EAST MIDLANDS. 1986. m. £19.50. Business Magazine Group, Briarwood House, St. John St., Mansfield, Notts NG18 1QH, England. TEL 0623-422522. FAX 0623-27479. Ed. Sue Allen. adv. circ. 11,207.
●Also available online.

330 US ISSN 0007-666X
HC101 CODEN: BECODS
BUSINESS ECONOMICS; designed to serve the needs of practicing business economists. 1965. q. $75 (foreign $100); students $30 (effective 1998). National Association of Business Economists, 1233 20th St., N.W., Ste. 505, Washington, DC 20036-2304. TEL 202-463-6223. FAX 202-463-6239. E-mail: busecon@cpcug.org; URL: http://www.nabe.com. Ed. Edmund A. Mennis. adv.; bk.rev.; bibl.; charts; illus.; stat. circ. 4,700. (also avail. in microform from UMI,IAC; back issues avail.; reprint service avail. from SCH,UMI) **Indexed:** ABI Inform., B.P.I., Bank.Lit.Ind., BPIA, Bus.Ind., C.R.E.J., J.of Econ.Lit., Mag.Ind., Manage.Cont., P.A.I.S., Tr.& Indus.Ind., Work Rel.Abstr. **Document type:** newsletter.
●Also available online. Vendor(s): Information Access Co., UMI.
Also available on CD-ROM.
—BLDSC (2933.455000); KR SourceOne; SWETS; UMI; UnCover. CCC.
   Description: Features articles on applied economics, including macro- and microeconomics, monetary and fiscal policy, short- and long-term business forecasting, interest rates, international economics, industry studies, and deregulation.

330 UK ISSN 0306-5049
BUSINESS ECONOMIST. 1969. 3/yr. £29 in U.K. & Europe; elsewhere £34 (effective 1997). Society of Business Economists, 11 Bay Tree Walk, Watford, Herts WD1 3RX, England. TEL 44-1923-37287. Ed. James Hirst. R&P contact: Marian Marshall. adv. contact: Kay Webb. bk.rev./; index. circ. 2,000. (back issues avail.) **Indexed:** Cont.Pg.Manage. **Document type:** academic/scholarly publication.
—BLDSC (2933.475000); SWETS.
   Description: Developments in the UK, overseas and world economics. Issues in applied economic theory and analysis of individual industries.

BUSINESS EDGE. see OCCUPATIONS AND CAREERS

330 370 US
BUSINESS EDUCATION FILMS CATALOG. 1950. biennial. free. Business Education Films, c/o Paul Weinberg, Ed., Box 449, Clarksville, NJ 08510. TEL 201-462-3522. FAX 908-294-0330. circ. 20,000.
   Description: Catalog of business education films available.

650.07 370 US ISSN 0007-6678
HF1101.U57
BUSINESS EDUCATION FORUM. 1947. 4/yr. $60 to libraries (includes Yearbook and Keying In newsletter). National Business Education Association, 1914 Association Dr., Reston, VA 22091. TEL 703-860-8300. FAX 703-620-4483. URL: http://www.nbea.com. Ed. Regina M. McDowell; Pub. Janet M. Treichel. R&P contact: Regina M. McDowell. adv. contact: Regina M. McDowell. illus. circ. 17,000. (also avail. in microform from UMI; reprint service avail. from UMI) **Indexed:** Bus.Educ.Ind., C.I.J.E., Cont.Pg.Educ., Educ.Ind., Tech.Educ.Abstr. **Document type:** academic/scholarly publication.
—BLDSC (2933.540000); KR SourceOne; UMI; UnCover.

330 US
BUSINESS EDUCATION GUIDE. 1986. q. $10. Box 2014, Neptune City, NJ 07754. TEL 908-280-2244. FAX 908-681-5482. Ed. Catherine Sims; Pub. Sky Sims. R&P contact: Jean Sims. adv. contact: Jim Ryan. circ. 75,000. **Document type:** catalog.
   Description: Includes articles and listings of seminars, courses, workshops and services.

330 FR ISSN 0982-0418
BUSINESS - ENTREPRISE. 1986. 6/yr. 23 rue des Apennins, 75017 Paris, France. TEL 42-28-59-00. FAX 42-28-24-58. Ed. John Martial. circ. 92,000.

332.6 SA
BUSINESS ENVIRONMENT FOCUS. 1994. irreg. Andrew Levy & Associates, P.O. Box 1431, Rivonia 2128, South Africa.

330 US ISSN 0894-6582
BUSINESS ETHICS; the magazine of socially responsible business. 1986. bi-m. $49 (foreign $59) (effective 1997). Business Ethics Magazine, 52 S. Tenth St., Ste. 110, Minneapolis, MN 55403-2001. TEL 612-962-4700; 800-601-9010. FAX 612-962-4706. E-mail: bizethics@aol.com; URL: http://condor.depaul.edu/ethics/bizethics.html. Ed. Marjorie Kelly; Pub. Marjorie Kelly. R&P contact: Karen McNichol. adv. contact: Jean Madson. bk.rev. circ. 20,000. **Indexed:** Alt.Press Ind. **Document type:** trade publication.
—BLDSC (2933.633500).
   Description: For socially responsible business; offers practical advice and views for enlightened businesspeople.

330 UK ISSN 0962-8770
HF5387 CODEN: BUETFV
BUSINESS ETHICS; a European review. 1992. q. £135($189) (foreign £135) (effective 1997). Blackwell Publishers Ltd., 108 Cowley Rd., Oxford OX4 1JF, England. TEL 44-1865-791100. FAX 44-1865-791347. E-mail: jnlinfo@blackwellpublishers.co.uk; URL: http://www.blackwellpublishers.co.uk. Ed. Jack Mahoney. **Document type:** academic/scholarly publication.
—BLDSC (2933.634000); SWETS; UMI. CCC.
   Description: Aims to enhance the quality of decision making at all levels of business throughout Europe.
Refereed Serial

330 US ISSN 1052-150X
HF5387
BUSINESS ETHICS QUARTERLY. 1991. q. $40 to individuals; institutions $98 (effective 1997). Society for Business Ethics, Rosemont College, Philosophy Dept., Rosemont, PA 19010. (Subscr. to: Philosophy Documentation Center, Bowling Green, OH 43403-0189. TEL 419-372-2419) Ed. Ron Duska; Pub. Ron Duska. R&P contact: Ron Duska. adv. contact: Ron Duska. (also avail. in microform from UMI) **Indexed:** B.P.I., Soc.Sci.Ind. (1994-). **Document type:** academic/scholarly publication.
—BLDSC (2933.637000); KR SourceOne; SWETS; UMI; UnCover.
   Description: Covers global business and economic concerns and issues of gender, race, ethnicity, and nationality.

330 UK ISSN 0966-3541
BUSINESS EUROPA; central Europe business magazine. 1992. 9/yr. £30 (N. America £45 ($90); elsewhere £48 ($95)). Central European Business Ltd. (Subsidiary of: Walden Publishing Ltd.), 2 Market St., Saffron Walden, Essex CB10 1H2, England. TEL 44-1799-521150. FAX 44-1799-524805. Ed. Anthony Axon; Pub. Anthony Axon. R&P contact: Donna Sharp. adv.: B&W page £1950, color page £2950; trim 270 x 210; adv. contact: Sue Hewitt. bk.rev. circ. 15,000. **Document type:** trade publication.
●Also available online. Vendor(s): Information Access Co.
   Description: Provides a country-by-country review of key business developments.

330 CN ISSN 0838-6048
BUSINESS EXAMINER (NORTH ISLAND EDITION). m. Business Examiner Ltd., 777 Poplar St., Nanaimo, BC V9S 2H7, Canada. TEL 250-754-8344. FAX 250-753-0788. Ed. Mark MacDonald. circ. 10,500.
   Supersedes in part (in 1987): Business Examiner (ISSN 0838-6056)

330 CN ISSN 0836-1142
BUSINESS EXAMINER (SOUTH ISLAND EDITION). 1984. 12/yr. Can.$32.05. Business Examiner Ltd., 1824 Store St., Victoria, BC V8T 4R4, Canada. TEL 604-381-3926. FAX 604-381-5606. Ed. Bjorn Stavrum. adv. circ. 14,000. **Document type:** newspaper.
   Supersedes in part (in 1987): Business Examiner (ISSN 0838-6056)

330 CN ISSN 0841-8675
BUSINESS EXAMINER PRESENTS. (Supplement to Business Examiner, South Island and North Island Editions) 1988. q. Can.$32.05. Business Examiner Ltd., 1824 Store St., Victoria, BC V8T 4R4, Canada. TEL 604-381-3926. FAX 604-381-5606. Ed. Mark MacDonald. adv. contact: John Palmer. circ. 24,500. **Document type:** newspaper.

330 MY
BUSINESS EXPECTATIONS SURVEY OF LIMITED COMPANIES MALAYSIA. (Text in English, Malay) a. M.$10. Department of Statistics - Jabatan Perangkaan, Wisma Statistik, Jalan Cenderasari, 50514 Kuala Lumpur, Malaysia. TEL 03-2922133. **Document type:** government publication.

330 UK ISSN 0262-7019
BUSINESS EXPRESS.* 1980. q. £6.50. Modern English Publications Ltd., Brunel Rd., Houndmills, Basingstoke, Hants. RG21 2XS, England. Ed. Hilary Rees-Parnall. circ. 2,000.

330 PH ISSN 0116-3590
BUSINESS EYE. 12/yr. Leader Promotions & Marketing, Fedman Suites, Salcedo St. Legaspi, Makati MM, Philippines. TEL 862561. Ed. Rodolfo Mazareno.

330 GD
BUSINESS EYE. bi-m. Business Eye International, Ltd., P.O. Box 360, Young St., St. George's, Grenada, W. TEL 809-440-3425.

BUSINESS AND ECONOMICS 941

330   US   ISSN 0749-9418
BUSINESS FIRST (BUFFALO); the business newspaper of Buffalo and Western New York. 1984. w. $59 (Canada $90). (American City Business Journals, Inc.) Business First of New York, Inc., 472 Delaware Ave., Buffalo, NY 14202. TEL 716-882-6200. FAX 716-882-3020. Ed. Donna Collins; Pub. Jack Connors. adv. contact: Shelley Rohaver. charts; illus.; stat.; circ. 15,000 (paid). (tabloid format; also avail. in microform from UMI; back issues avail.) **Document type:** newspaper.
●Also available online. Vendor(s): Information Access Co., Knight-Ridder Information, Inc., Lexis-Nexis.
—UMI. **CCC**.

330   US   ISSN 0748-6138
BUSINESS FIRST (LOUISVILLE); the business newspaper of Greater Louisville. 1984. w. $60 (effective 1997). A C B J Business Publications, Inc., 111 W. Washington St., Ste. 400, Louisville, KY 40202. TEL 502-583-1731. FAX 502-587-1703. E-mail: louisville@www.amc.ty.com. Ed. Carol Timmons; Pub. Tom Monahan. R&P contact: Carol Timmons. adv. contact: Maureen O'Meara. circ. 15,000. (tabloid format; back issues avail.) **Document type:** newspaper.
—UMI. **CCC**.
Description: Covers regional business news.

330   PL   ISSN 0867-7026
BUSINESS FORUM. 1991. 6/yr. Dom Wydawniczy Herold-Press, Ul. Sniadeckich 10, 00-656 Warsaw, Poland. TEL 48-22-256140. Ed. Bogdan Herbich. adv. circ. 10,000.

330   US   ISSN 0733-2408
HD28
BUSINESS FORUM (LOS ANGELES). 1975. q. $35 (foreign $45) (effective 1998). California State University, Los Angeles, School of Business & Economics, 5151 State University Dr., Los Angeles, CA 90032-8120. TEL 213-343-2806. FAX 213-343-5263. Ed. Tom H. Woods; Pub. Ronald S. Lemos. R&P contact: Tom H. Woods. adv. contact: Tom H. Woods. bk.rev.; illus.; circ. 3,000 (paid); 1,000 (controlled). (also avail. in microform from UMI; back issues avail.; reprint service avail. from UMI) **Indexed:** ABI Inform., Anbar, BPIA, Manage.Cont., P.A.I.S. **Document type:** academic/scholarly publication.
●Also available online. Vendor(s): Information Access Co., UMI.
—BLDSC (2933.667000); UMI; UnCover. **CCC**.
Formerly (until 1982): Los Angeles Business and Economics (ISSN 0278-3428)
Description: Research articles and interpretative commentary on contemporary issues of interest to all business and economics disciplines, for business executives, academicians, and public administrators.
Refereed Serial

650   UK   ISSN 0007-6791
HF11
BUSINESS HISTORY. 1959. q. £38($48) to individuals; institutions £150($225) (effective 1998). Frank Cass, Newbury House, 890-900 Eastern Ave., Newbury Park, Ilford, Essex IG2 7HH, England. TEL 44-181-599-8866. FAX 44-181-599-0984. E-mail: jnlsubs@frankcass.com; URL: http://www.frankcass.com/jnls/bh.htm. (Dist. in US by: ISBS, 5804 N.E. Hassalo St., Portland, OR 97213-3644. TEL 800-944-6190. FAX 503-280-8832) Eds. Charles Harvey, Geoffrey Jones. adv.: B&W page £195($275); adv. contact: Anne Kidson. bk.rev.; index. (also avail. in microform from UMI; back issues avail.; reprint service avail. from KTO) **Indexed:** Amer.Hist.& Life (1958-), Arts & Hum.Cit.Ind., ASCA, B.P.I., BPIA, Br.Hum.Ind., Curr.Cont., Geo.Abstr.H.G., Hist.Abstr. (1958-), IBR, IDA, Intl.Bibl.S.S.Soc.Cult.Anthro., Mid.East: Abstr.& Ind., P.A.I.S., SSCI, Tr.& Indus.Ind. **Document type:** academic/scholarly publication.
●Also available online. Vendor(s): Information Access Co.
Also available on CD-ROM.
—BLDSC (2933.710000); Genuine Article; KR SourceOne; SWETS; UMI; UnCover.
Description: Covers research articles in the field of business history, and is concerned with the long-term evolution and contemporary operation of business systems and enterprises.
Refereed Serial

650   US   ISSN 0007-6805
HF5001
BUSINESS HISTORY REVIEW. 1926. q. $35 to individuals; institutions $75; students $20 (effective 1997). Harvard Business School Publishing, 60 Harvard Way, Boston, MA 02163. TEL 617-495-6154. FAX 617-496-5985. E-mail: kdonahue@hbsp.harvard.edu. Ed. Thomas K. McCraw. R&P contact: Audrey Barrett. TEL 617-495-6849. adv. contact: Kristen Donahue. bk.rev.; charts; illus.; index, cum.index. circ. 2,000. (also avail. in microform from UMI; reprint service avail. from KTO) **Indexed:** Account.Ind. (1974-), Amer.Bibl.Slavic & E.Eur.Stud., Amer.Hist.& Life (1954-), Arts & Hum.Cit.Ind., ASCA, B.P.I., Bk.Rev.Dig., Bk.Rev.Ind. (1965-), Bus.Ind., Child.Bk.Rev.Ind. (1965-), Curr.Cont., Econ.Abstr., Hist.Abstr. (1954-), IBR, J.of Econ.Lit., Mar.Aff.Bibl., Mid.East: Abstr.& Ind., P.A.I.S., Soc.Sci.Ind., SSCI, Tr.& Indus.Ind., Work Rel.Abstr. **Document type:** academic/scholarly publication.
●Also available online. Vendor(s): Information Access Co., Knight-Ridder Information, Inc., UMI.
—BLDSC (2933.730000); KR SourceOne; SWETS; UMI; UnCover.
Formerly: Business Historical Society. Bulletin (ISSN 0017-856X)

330   II
BUSINESS HISTORY STUDIES. 1980. 4/yr. Rs.460($114) K.K. Roy (Private) Ltd., 55 Gariahat Rd., P.O. Box 10210, Calcutta 700 019, India. Ed. Dr. K.K. Roy. adv.; abstr.; bibl.; index. circ. 518.

650   US   ISSN 0007-6813
HF5001
BUSINESS HORIZONS. 1957. bi-m. $90 to individuals (foreign $110); institutions $195 (foreign $215) (effective 1998). (Indiana University School of Business) J A I Press Inc., 55 Old Post Rd., No. 2, Box 1678, Greenwich, CT 06830-1678. TEL 203-661-7602. FAX 203-661-0792. E-mail: jai@jaipress.com; URL: http://www.jaipress.com/jmlspub.htm. (Addr. in Europe: J A I Press Ltd., 38 Tavistock St., Covent Garden, London WC2E 7PB, England. TEL 44-171-379-8834. FAX 44-171-379-8835) Ed. Dennis Organ. adv.; bk.rev.; charts; index. circ. 3,000. (also avail. in microform from UMI) **Indexed:** AAR, Account.& Data Proc.Abstr., Account.Ind. (1974-), Anbar, ASEAN Manage.Abstr., B.P.I, Bank.Lit.Ind., Bk.Rev.Dig., Bk.Rev.Ind. (1977-1989), BPIA, Bus.Ind., C.R.E.J., Child.Bk.Rev.Ind. (1977-1989), Comput.Lit.Ind., Cont.Pg.Manage., Curr.Cont., Data Process.Dig., Educ.Admin.Abstr., Excerp.Med., Fut.Surv., IBR, INSPEC (1983-), Intl.Mgmt.Info., Key to Econ.Sci., Mag.Ind., Manage.Cont., Mgmt.& Market.Abstr., Mid.East: Abstr.& Ind., Oper.Res.Manage.Sci., Oper.Res.Manage.Sci., P.A.I.S., Pers.Lit., Pers.Manage.Abstr., PROMT, Q.Abstr., Qual.Contr.Appl.Stat., SCIMP (1978-), SSCI, Tr.& Dev.Alert, Tr.& Indus.Ind., Work Rel.Abstr. **Document type:** trade publication.
—BLDSC (2933.770000); AskIEEE; KR SourceOne; SWETS; UMI; UnCover. **CCC**.
Description: Covers approaches to management and marketing, studies of business situations, accounting, banking, business education, and corporation activities.

330   US   ISSN 0738-7024
BUSINESS IDEAS. 1954. m. (10/yr.). $50. Dan Newman Co., 1051 Bloomfield Ave., Clifton, NJ 07012. TEL 201-778-6677. Ed. J. Cangi. adv.; bk.rev. circ. 4,000. (back issues avail.) **Document type:** newsletter.
Description: Covers items of interest to businesspeople.

330   UK
BUSINESS IN BRIEF. 1990. m. £12 ((foreign £25). Community Publishers Ltd., 50 Prospect Pl., Swindon, Wiltshire SN1 3LG, England. TEL 44-1793-497799. FAX 44-1793-497744. Ed. D.L. Thomas. adv. contact: D.L. Thomas. circ. 14,500. (back issues avail.) **Document type:** bulletin.

330   CN   ISSN 1193-1698
BUSINESS IN CALGARY. 1992. m. Can.$30 (foreign Can.$49) (effective 1996); newsstand price: Can.$2.50. Ste. 600, Burns Bldg., 237 Eighth Ave. S.E., Calgary, AB T2G 5C3, Canada. TEL 403-299-0340. FAX 403-299-0349. Ed. Richard Bronstein; Pub. Pat Ottmann. adv. contact: Tim Ottmann. circ. 28,000. **Document type:** trade publication.
Description: Discusses all issues that affect business in the Calgary area.

330   FR   ISSN 1267-8023
HF3621
BUSINESS IN RUSSIA. (Text in English) 1990. 11/yr. $154 (effective 1998). S.C.I.I., 4 rue Brunel, 75017 Paris, France. FAX 33-1-42677548. (Dist. by: Mezhdunarodnaya Kniga, B. Yakimanka 39, 117040 Moscow, Russia. TEL 7-095-2384967. FAX 7-095-2384634; U.S. addr.: 1560 Broadway, Ste. 511, New York, NY 10036. TEL 212-227-6700) Ed. Vadim Biriukov. adv. contact: Jean-Charles Abeille.
Former titles (until 1995): Delovye Lyudi (International Edition) (ISSN 1167-2137); (until 1993): Business in the U.S.S.R. (International Edition) (ISSN 1150-4382)
Description: Includes news and analysis of the Soviet economic situation, with features on new business projects, international developments and joint ventures, portraits of business persons, forecasts, and more.

330   CN   ISSN 0849-5017
BUSINESS IN VANCOUVER. 1989. w. Can.$69 (foreign $106). B I V Publications Ltd., 1155 Pender St. W., Ste. 500, Vancouver, BC V6E 2P4, Canada. TEL 604-688-2398. FAX 604-688-1963. Ed. Peter Ladner; Pub. Peter Ladner. adv. contact: Sandi Gilmer. illus.; circ. 14,000 (paid) (tabloid format) **Document type:** newspaper.
Description: Covers business news in the Greater Vancouver area.

330   UK   ISSN 0263-1067
BUSINESS IN YORKSHIRE. 1982. m. £19.50. Business Magazine Group, Briarwood House, St. John St., Mansfield, Notts NG18 1QH, England. TEL 0532-443082. FAX 0532-443334. Ed. R. Harrison. adv.; bk.rev. circ. 11,251.
—BLDSC (2934.954000).

BUSINESS INFORMATION ALERT; what's new in business publications, databases and research techniques. see *LIBRARY AND INFORMATION SCIENCES*

330   LE   ISSN 0254-4342
BUSINESS INFORMATION DIGEST. (Text in English) m. free. Middle East Airlines, c/o Sr. Manager of Market Development, Middle East Airlines HQ, P.O. Box 206, Beirut, Lebanon.

BUSINESS INFORMATION FROM YOUR PUBLIC LIBRARY. see *LIBRARY AND INFORMATION SCIENCES*

THE BUSINESS INTERNET NEWSLETTER. see *COMMUNICATIONS*

330   IE   ISSN 0790-8636
BUSINESS IRELAND. 1986. 4/yr. free. Irish Industrial Development Agency, Wilton Park House, Wilton Pl., Dublin 2, Ireland. TEL 01-6686633. FAX 01-6603703. Ed. Gerry O'Shaughnessy. circ. 15,000. **Document type:** newsletter.
Description: Presents industrial and business information about Ireland for foreign readers.

330   KE
BUSINESS JOURNAL; Kenya's retail traders & financial newspaper. (Text in English and Swahili) 1978. m. KShs.50. Kenya National Chamber of Commerce and Industry, Nairobi, Kenya. TEL 254-2-220867. FAX 254-2-340664. Ed. Peter G. Muiruri. adv. contact: Peter G. Muiruri. illus. circ. 12,000. **Indexed:** Bank.Lit.Ind., Bus.Ind., Curr.Cont. **Document type:** trade publication.

BUSINESS AND ECONOMICS

330   US   ISSN 0895-1632
BUSINESS JOURNAL (PHOENIX); serving Phoenix & the Valley of the Sun. 1980. w. $48. Phoenix Business Journal, Inc., 2910 N. Central Ave., Phoenix, AZ 85012. TEL 602-230-8400. FAX 602-230-0955. Ed. Tom Jensen; Pub. Rob Fisher. adv. contact: Joelle Hadley. circ. 16,500. (tabloid format; back issues avail.) **Indexed:** Tr.& Indus.Ind. **Document type:** newspaper.
• Also available online. Vendor(s): Information Access Co., Knight-Ridder Information, Inc.
—UMI. **CCC**.
Formerly (until 1987): Greater Phoenix Business Journal (ISSN 0890-9644)
Description: Covers all facets of business news about the Phoenix metropolitan area.

330   US   ISSN 1048-8812
THE BUSINESS JOURNAL (SAN JOSE).* 1983. w. $59. American City Business Journals, Inc. (Austin), 505 Powell St., Austin, TX 78703-5121. TEL 408-295-3800. FAX 408-295-5028. Ed. Delbert Schafer. adv. contact: Matt Toledo. bk.rev.; circ. 14,812 (paid); 2,800 (controlled). **Indexed:** Tr.& Indus.Ind. **Document type:** newspaper.
—CCC.
Former titles (until 1988): San Jose Business Journal (ISSN 0886-5922); (until 1985): Business Journal (San Jose) (ISSN 0737-7274)

330   US
THE BUSINESS JOURNAL OF CHARLOTTE. w. American City Business Journals (Charlotte), 128 S. Tryon St., No.2250, Charlotte, NC 28202-5003. TEL 704-347-2340. FAX 704-347-2350. Ed. Joanne Skoog. circ. 14,500. **Document type:** newspaper.

330   US   ISSN 1040-6360
BUSINESS JOURNAL OF UPPER EAST TENNESSEE AND SOUTHWEST VIRGINIA. 1988. m. $22. Business Publishers Company, Box 643, Tri-Port Complex, 2333-D Hwy. 75, Blountville, TN 37617. TEL 615-323-7111. FAX 615-323-1479. Ed. Hank Hayes; Pub. Elizabeth W. Pardue. adv.: B&W page $1295, color page $1620; trim 11 x 14. bk.rev. circ. 10,000. (also avail. in microfiche) **Document type:** consumer publication.
• Also available online. Vendor(s): UMI.
—UMI.

330   US   ISSN 0740-2899
BUSINESS JOURNAL SERVING GREATER MILWAUKEE. 1983. w. $69.95. Business Journal of Milwaukee Inc., 600 W. Virginia St., Ste. 500, Milwaukee, WI 53204-1551. TEL 414-278-7788. FAX 414-278-7028. E-mail: bjmilw@execpc.com; URL: http://www.amcity.com/milwaukee. Ed. Gary Miller; Pub. Mark Sabljak. R&P contact: Gary Miller. adv. contact: James Denor. bk.rev.; circ. 13,015 (paid), **Indexed:** Tr.& Indus.Ind. **Document type:** newspaper.
• Also available online. Vendor(s): Information Access Co., UMI.
—UMI. **CCC**.
Description: Concentrates on business and business-related issues in Milwaukee and southeastern Wisconsin.

330   US   ISSN 1057-6061
BUSINESS JOURNAL SERVING SONOMA & MARIN COUNTIES. 1985. s-m. $17. Sloan Publications, 5510 Skylane Blvd., Ste. 201, Santa Rosa, CA 95403. TEL 707-579-2900. FAX 707-579-8475. Eds. Randy Sloan, Ken Clark; Pub. Ken Clark. R&P contact: Leda Wagner. adv. contact: Paul Pastorino. circ. 8,000 (paid). (tabloid format; back issues avail.) **Document type:** newspaper.
Formerly: Business Journal Serving Sonoma, Marin, and Mendocino Counties.

330   KO   ISSN 1016-5304
BUSINESS KOREA; economic & trade review. (Text in English) 1983. m. $90. Korea Trade Promotion Corp., Won Chang Bldg., 3rd. Fl., 26-3 Yoido-dong, Yongdung po-ku, Seoul 150-602, S. Korea. TEL 02-234-4010. FAX 02-253-4040. TELEX K 23695 KORTA. (Subscr. in US to: 460 Park Ave., Ste. 402, New York, NY 10022. TEL 212-826-0900. FAX 212-886-4930) Ed. Kim Kyong-Hae. adv.; illus. circ. 30,000. **Indexed:** P.A.I.S.
• Also available online. Vendor(s): UMI.

330   CE
BUSINESS LANKA. (Text in English) 1981. q. Rs.320. Sri Lanka Export Development Board, Trade Information Service, No. 115, Sir Chittampalam A Gardiner Mawatha, Colombo 3, Sri Lanka. TEL 438512-5. FAX 438404. TELEX 21457 EXDEV CE. E-mail: edb@Sri.Lanka.net. Ed. S. Samarasekera. adv. circ. 2,000.
Description: Provides information on Sri Lankan exports and products for business people.

330 340   AT
▼**BUSINESS LAW COMPLIANCE**. 1995. s-a. C C H Australia Ltd., P.O. Box 230, North Ryde, N.S.W. 2113, Australia. TEL 61-1-300300224. FAX 61-1-300306224. (looseleaf format)
Description: Provides information on all practical aspects of complying with current business regulations.

BUSINESS LAW MONOGRAPHS. see LAW — Corporate Law

BUSINESS LAW REPORTS (2ND SERIES). see LAW — Corporate Law

BUSINESS LAW REVIEW. see LAW — Corporate Law

BUSINESS LAW TODAY. see LAW — Corporate Law

BUSINESS LAWYER. see LAW — Corporate Law

330   US   ISSN 1060-8230
BUSINESS LEADER. 1989. m. $24. Business to Business Inc., 4109 Wake Forest Rd., Ste. 304, Raleigh, NC 27609. TEL 919-872-7077. FAX 919-872-1590. E-mail: editor@businessleader.com; URL: http://www.businessleader.com. Ed. Beverly Finnen; Pub. Dan Davies. R&P contact: Dan Davies. adv. contact: Vera Simms. circ. 11,000. (also avail. in microform from UMI).
—UMI.
Formerly (until 1991): Business Digest (ISSN 1058-6490)
Description: Covers business in the Triangle area (greater Raleigh-Durham). Profiles leaders, gives company success stories, and provides management ideas and advice.

330   US
THE BUSINESS LEDGER; the business newspaper for DuPage, Northwest Cook and the Fox Valley. 1993. m. $23 (effective 1997); newsstand price: $2. Ledger Publishing Co., 709 Enterprise Dr., Oak Brook, IL 60521-8814. TEL 708-571-8911. FAX 708-571-4053. Ed. Don Kopriva; Pub. James E. Elsner. adv. contact: Joe Castelluccio. bk.rev. circ. 17,000. (tabloid format; back issues avail.) **Document type:** newspaper.
Formerly: DuPage Business Ledger (ISSN 1082-8397)
Description: Covers trends, issues, industries, specific companies and business people in DuPage, N.W. Cook County and Fox Valley

330   US
BUSINESS MARKET NEWS. 1991. q. $24. Hemsing Advertising, 755 W. Big Beaver Rd., Ste. 416, Troy, MI 48084-4903. TEL 810-362-0448. FAX 810-362-3884. Ed. Jeffrey Bourque. bk.rev.; circ. controlled. **Document type:** newsletter.
Description: Provides economic and marketing management for business-to-business marketers.

330   US
BUSINESS MEDIA. 1986. q. $12. Business Media Publications, 9260 Baltimore St., N.E., Minneapolis, MN 55449. TEL 612-780-1018. FAX 612-780-8228. Ed. Valorie Arrowsmith. adv. contact: Gregg Kroll. bk.rev.; charts; illus.; stat. circ. 20,000.
Description: Covers business news, business people, and business management.

330   CN   ISSN 0834-020X
BUSINESS NEWS. 1986. m. Can.$35. St. John's Board of Trade, 10 Fort William Place, Box 5127, St. John's, NF A1C 5V5, Canada. TEL 709-726-2961. FAX 709-726-2003. Ed. Kyran Pittman Snair. adv.: B&W page Can.$615, color page Can.$1100; adv. contact: David Udle. circ. 1,400. **Document type:** newsletter.

330   XR
BUSINESS NEWS. (Supplement avail.) (Text in English) 1990. 5/w. $720. Ceska Tiskova Kancelar - Czech News Agency, Opletalova 5, 111 44 Prague 1, Czech Republic. TEL 42-4-2147. FAX 42-2-235-6804. TELEX 122841. Eds. Alexandr Kramer, Vera Maria Beedway. circ. 170.
Formerly: Ecoservice.
Description: Contains detailed information on economic developments in the Czech Republic and Slovakia.

330   IO
BUSINESS NEWS. (Editions in English, Indonesian) 1956. 3/w. (Indonesian ed.), 2/w. (English ed.). Rps.55000 per mo. P T Business News, Jalan H. Abdul Muis 70, Jakarta 10160, Indonesia. TEL 62-21-3848207. FAX 62-21-3454280. Ed. Sanjoto Sastromihardjo. adv.: B&W page Rps.2200000, color page Rps.7500000; trim 205 x 280; adv. contact: Heru Nuroso. circ. 15,000. **Document type:** bulletin.

330 341   US   ISSN 0882-5289
BUSINESS NEWS (WESTFORD). 1974. m. $100 to non-members. U.S. Business Council for Southeastern Europe, 7 Broadway, No. 1028, New York, NY 10004-1004. TEL 212-439-9025. FAX 908-439-9105. E-mail: usbc@aol.com; URL: http://www.usbizcouncil.com. Eds. Thorsten Knutsson, Ksenisa Saksic; Pubs. Thorsten Knutsson, Ksenisa Saksic. circ. 300 (controlled). (looseleaf format) **Document type:** newsletter.
Description: Reports on the economic conditions of Slovenia, Croatia, Macedonia, Bosnia and Herzegovina, and other areas which were formerly Yugoslavia.

330   PL   ISSN 1231-0573
BUSINESS NEWS FROM POLAND. (Text in English, Polish) 1990. fortn. Polska Agencja Prasowa (P.A.P.) - Polish Press Agency, P.O. Box 898, 00-950 Warsaw, Poland. TEL 48-2-6122489. FAX 48-2-6122495. TELEX 817720 PAPEX PL. E-mail: boss@ikp.atm.com.pl. Ed. Aneta Dylewska. adv.: page $200. circ. 600. **Document type:** bulletin, consumer publication.
Description: Covers Polish politics, economics, banking, finance, stock exchange, industry, legislation, transport, foreign trade.

338   US
BUSINESS NEWS NEW JERSEY. 1995. fortn. $39. Snowden Publications Inc., 391 George St., New Brunswick, NJ 08901. TEL 908-246-7677. FAX 908-249-8886. Ed. George M. Taber; Pub. Donald M. Wilson. adv. contact: Michelle McGowan. bk.rev. circ. 11,000. (tabloid format; also avail. in microform from UMI; back issues avail.) **Document type:** newspaper.
—UMI.
Formed by the merger of (1993-1995): Northern N J Business (ISSN 1071-281X); (1993-1995): Central N J Business; Which was formerly (1988-1993): Business for Central New Jersey (ISSN 1042-8704)
Description: Covers the major business-related events as they occur in the entire state of New Jersey. Also provides a focus on various industries of business in the state.

330   UK
BUSINESS NORTH EAST. 1987. m. £19.50. Business Magazine Group, Briarwood House, St. John St., Mansfield, Notts NG18 1QH, England. TEL 0642-232882. FAX 0623-232899. Ed. Ian Fammond. adv. circ. 11,213.
• Also available online.

THE BUSINESS OF FILM. see MOTION PICTURES

BUSINESS AND ECONOMICS

330 US
▼**BUSINESS OPERATIONS REPORTS**. (Includes: Egypt; Nigeria; Saudi Arabia; South Africa; Baltic States (Estonia, Latvia, & Lithuania); Belarus & Ukraine; Bulgaria & Romania; Central Asia Republics (Kazakhstan, Turkmenistan, & Uzbekistan); Croatia & Slovenia; Czech Republic & Slovakia; Hungary; Poland; Russia; China; India; Indonesia; Malaysia; Philippines; Thailand; Vietnam; Taiwan; Argentina; Brazil; Mexico; Myanmar, Laos & Cambodia; Turkey; Pakistan; South Korea) 1995. q. £295($495) in E. Europe; Middle East & Africa £425($625); elsewhere £365($595). Economist Intelligence Unit, 111 W. 57th St., New York, NY 10019. TEL 212-554-0600; 800-938-4685. FAX 212-586-1182. TELEX 175567. URL: http://www.eiu.com. (UK addr.: Economist Intelligence Unit Ltd., Subscriptions Dept., P.O. Box 200, Harold Hill, Romford, Essex RM3 8UX, England. TEL 44-171-830-1007. FAX 44-1708-371850)
Formerly (until 1997): Business Reports.
Description: Reports on business operational issues in 39 emerging markets. Coverage includes political climate, infrastructure, investment issues, land availability, labour and business services, finance, marketing and distribution.

330 BU
BUSINESS OPPORTUNITIES IN BULGARIA. (Text in English) 1980. 3/yr. $25. Bulgarian Chamber of Commerce and Industry, 42 Parchevich str., Sofia, Bulgaria. TEL 359-2-872631. FAX 359-2-873209. TELEX 22374. circ. 3,000.
Formerly (until 1997): Bulgaria - Economic Development (Year).
Description: Provides information on Bulgaria's economy and foreign economic relations.

BUSINESS ORGANIZATIONS: CORPORATE ACQUISITIONS AND MERGERS. see *LAW — Corporate Law*

330 340 US
BUSINESS ORGANIZATIONS: PROFESSIONAL CORPORATIONS AND ASSOCIATIONS. (Issued in 7 base vols. with supplements) 1970. irreg. $990. Matthew Bender & Co., Inc., 2 Park Ave., New York, NY 10016. TEL 212-448-2000. E-mail: international@bender.com; URL: http://www.bender.com. Ed. Berrien C. Eaton, Jr.
Description: Provides information on forming, operating, and changing ownership of a professional corporation or association.

330 HU ISSN 0237-3831
BUSINESS PARTNER HUNGARY. Hungarian edition: Kereskedelmi Partner Magyarország (ISSN 0237-546X) (Editions in English, German, Hungarian) 1986-1992. q. 22400 Ft.($160) (effective 1997). Kopint - Datorg Plc., Csokonai u. 3, 1081 Budapest, Hungary. TEL 36-1-2668200. FAX 36-1-2667165. TELEX 22-5646. E-mail: http://www.kopint-datorg.hu. Ed. Ilona Nemeth. R&P contact: Ilona Nemeth. adv. contact: Judith Boncz.
Description: Covers Hungarian trade acts and regulations, customs foreign exchange, investments. Includes foreign trade statistics, industry tests, commodity market reports, regional investment offers.

330 US ISSN 1051-094X
HF3163.F7
BUSINESS PEOPLE.* Variant title: Business People Magazine of Greater Fort Wayne. 1988. m. $15.75; newsstand price: $2.50. Michiana Business Publications, Inc., 205 Airport North Office Park, Fort Wayne, IN 46825-6702. TEL 219-484-1840. FAX 219-484-4234. Ed. Steve Harris; Pub. Daniel C. Copeland. adv.: B&W page $1125, color page $2020. circ. 8,400. **Document type:** trade publication.
—UMI.
Description: Deals with issues and information affecting business professionals in Allen County.

338 US ISSN 0896-3703
HC107.A13
BUSINESS PERSPECTIVES. 1963. q. free. University of Memphis, Bureau of Business & Economic Research, Memphis, TN 38152. TEL 901-678-2281. URL: http://www.peopl.memphis.edu/~bberlib. Ed. Dolores Bell. stat. circ. 2,500. (back issues avail.) **Indexed:** BPIA, Bus.Ind., Manage.Cont., P.A.I.S., Sage Pub.Admin.Abstr., Sage Urb.Stud.Abstr., SRI, Tr.& Indus.Ind. **Document type:** academic/scholarly publication.
● Also available online. Vendor(s): Information Access Co.
—BLDSC (2934.602000); UMI; UnCover.
Formerly: Mid-South Business Journal (ISSN 0279-8174); Which superseded in 1981: Mid-South Quarterly Business Review (ISSN 0885-4696); Which was formerly (until 1971): Memphis State Business Review (ISSN 0025-9209)

330 US
▼**BUSINESS POWER MAGAZINE.** 1996. m. Decision Media Group & Publishing Co., Transcend Visual Communications, Inc., Box 512, Appleton, WI 54912. E-mail: dmgedit@athenet.net; URL: http://www.athenet.net/~dmgedit/bpm.html. Ed. Diane Mathia Garrod.
● Available only online.
Description: Focuses on business issues of all types, including marketing, public relations, management, home-based to corporate, interviews, profiles, tips and more.

330 US ISSN 1045-8697
THE BUSINESS PRESS. 1988. w. $43. Carolyn Ashford, 314 Main St., Ste. 300, Ft. Worth, TX 76102-7407. TEL 817-336-8300. FAX 817-332-3038. Ed. Rachel Master; Pub. Gregg Moss. R&P contact: Greg Moss. adv. contact: Kathleen King. circ. 8,000. **Document type:** newspaper.

330 PL ISSN 0866-9287
BUSINESS PROMOTION. (Text in Polish) 1990. m. Business Publications Ltd., P.O. Box 1354, 40-096 Katowice, Poland. TEL 48-32-599647. Ed. Boguslaw Faciejew. circ. 2,000.

330 PR
BUSINESS PUERTO RICO. (Text in English) 4/yr. $29.70 for 6 nos. Puerto Rico Almanacs, Inc., Box 9582, Santurce, PR 00908-0582. TEL 787-725-3155. FAX 787-725-3196. Ed. Connie Garcia. adv.; illus.; stat. circ. 13,500. **Document type:** consumer publication.
Description: Covers economic events on the island.

330 AT
BUSINESS QUARTERLY. q. Monash University, E-mail: brenda.harkness@mcom.monash.edu.au; URL: http://www.monash.edu.au/pubs/busquart/index.html. Ed. Brenda Harkness.
● Available only online.
Description: Focuses on the effect that government, international relations, new products and new trends will have on Australian business in the future.

330 UK ISSN 0951-0532
BUSINESS RATIO REPORT: POLLUTION CONTROL; an industry sector analysis. 1980. a. I C C Business Ratios Ltd. (Subsidiary of: I C C Information Group Ltd.), Freepost, Field House, Hampton, Mddx. TW12 2HQ, England. TEL 081-783-0977. FAX 081-783-1940.
Former titles (until 1986): Business Ratio Report. Pollution Control Equipment Manufacturers (ISSN 0264-2743); (until 1980): Business Ratio Report. Pollution Control (ISSN 0261-9407)

330 US ISSN 0746-410X
BUSINESS RECORD (DES MOINES). 1983. w. $49. Business Publications Corporation, The Depot at Fourth, 100 Fourth St., Des Moines, IA 50309. TEL 515-288-3336. FAX 515-288-0309. Ed. Pete Katz; Pub. Connie Wimer. R&P contact: Connie Wimer. adv. contact: Lon Matejczyk. bk.rev. circ. 7,100. **Indexed:** Tr.& Indus.Ind. **Document type:** newspaper.
—UMI.

330 GW ISSN 0343-1975
BUSINESS REPORT (ABRIDGED VERSION). (Text in various languages) 1952. a. Bayer AG, Abteilung Publikationen, 51368 Leverkusen, Germany. TEL 49-214-3062875. FAX 49-214-3071985. circ. 750,000. **Document type:** corporate report.

330 GW
BUSINESS REPORT (UNABRIDGED VERSION). (Text in English, French, German) 1951. a. Bayer AG, Abteilung Publikationen, 51368 Leverkusen, Germany. TEL 49-214-3062875. FAX 49-214-3071985. circ. 37,000. **Document type:** corporate report.

331 JA
BUSINESS REVIEW/BIJINESU REBYU. (Text in Japanese) 1953. q. 800 Yen. Chikura Shobo, c/o Kyobashi Daiichi Seimei Bldg., 4-12 Kyobashi 2-chome, Chuo-ku, Tokyo 104, Japan. Ed. Ikujiro Nonaka. circ. 1,000. **Indexed:** JTA.

330 UK ISSN 1354-1110
BUSINESS REVIEW. 1994. 4/yr. (Sep.-Apr.) £14.95 (rest of Europe £23.50; elsewhere £29) (effective 1997 & 1998). Philip Allan Publishers Ltd., Market Pl., Deddington, Oxon. OX15 OSE, England. TEL 44-1869-338652. FAX 44-1869-338803. R&P contact: Ceri Jenkins. adv. contact: Ceri Jenkins. **Document type:** academic/scholarly publication, trade publication.

330 US
THE BUSINESS REVIEW OF NORTHEAST OHIO.* m. Board of Directors Club, Inc., Box 168, Wickliffe, OH 44092-0168. TEL 216-881-0550. FAX 216-881-2216. Ed. Patrick Christopher. circ. 20,000.

330 US ISSN 1357-0293
▼**BUSINESS RUSSIA (NEW YORK).** 1995. m. £495($775) Economist Intelligence Unit, 111 W. 57th St., New York, NY 10019. TEL 212-554-0600; 800-938-4685. FAX 212-586-1182. TELEX 175567. URL: http://www.eiu.com. (UK addr.: Economist Intelligence Unit Ltd., Subscriptions Dept., P.O. Box 200, Harold Hill, Romford, Essex RM3 8UX, England. TEL 44-171-830-1007. FAX 44-1708-371850)
Description: Provides information on all the issues that affect business across every part of the former Soviet Union.

330 UK ISSN 0958-7934
BUSINESS SOUTH WEST. 1980. m. £19.50. Business Magazine Group, 4 Armada Place, Stokes Croft, Bristol BS1 3SF, England. TEL 0272-249684. FAX 0272-441028. Ed. Sue Turner. adv.; bk.rev.; illus. circ. 11,594.
Formerly: Business West.

BUSINESS SPACE REGISTER. see *REAL ESTATE*

330 UK ISSN 0957-7939
BUSINESS SPAIN; the monthly report of business news & consumer market trends in Spain. (Supplement avail.: Business Spain Quarterly Index) 1988. m. £325 (outside Europe £335); with Quarterly Index £395 (outside Europe £405). 5 Newton Rd., Wimbledon, London SW19 3PJ, England. TEL 0181-540-8520. FAX 0181-542-9185. Ed. Graham Faiella; Pub. Graham Faiella. index.
Description: Provides the business community with comprehensive information about business trends in Spain.

650 II
BUSINESS STANDARD. (Text in English) 1975. m. newsstand price: Rs.4. Ananda Bazar Patrika Ltd., 6 Prafulla Sarkar St., Calcutta 700 001, India. TEL 033-274880. FAX 033-303240. Ed. T.N. Ninan. adv. contact: Gautam Gupta Bhaya. circ. 13,808. **Indexed:** Print.Abstr., WPM. **Document type:** newspaper.

330 US
BUSINESS STRATEGIES. 1983. s-m. $707. C C H Incorporated, 2700 Lake Cook Rd., Riverwoods, IL 60015. TEL 847-267-7000; 800-835-5224. FAX 800-224-8299.

330 US
BUSINESS STRATEGIES BULLETIN. 1983. m. $157. C C H Incorporated, 2700 Lake Cook Rd., Riverwoods, IL 60015. TEL 847-267-7000; 800-835-5224. FAX 800-224-8299. (looseleaf format) **Document type:** newsletter.

BUSINESS STRATEGY FOR THE BIO-ENVIRONMENT. see *ENVIRONMENTAL STUDIES*

BUSINESS AND ECONOMICS

330   UK   ISSN 0960-7730
BUSINESS STRATEGY INTERNATIONAL. biennial. £19.95. Cornhill Publications Ltd., Kings Ct., 2-16 Goodge St., London W1P IFF. Ed. Sylvie Aubry. adv. contact: Carol White. circ. 20,000. **Document type:** trade publication.

330   UK
BUSINESS STUDIES MAGAZINE. m. Stanley Thornes Publishers Ltd., Ellenborough House, Wellington St., Cheltenham, Glos GL50 1YD, England. TEL 01242-224234. **Document type:** trade publication.

330   IE
BUSINESS STUDIES SERIES. 1979. irreg. price varies. Irish Business and Employers Confederation, Confederation House, 84-86 Lower Baggot St., Dublin 2, Ireland. TEL 353-1-6601011. FAX 353-1-6601717. URL: http://www.iol.ie/ibec. Ed. Tony Donohoe. **Document type:** monographic series.

330 650   CH
BUSINESS TAIWAN; economic news weekly. (Text in English) 1975. w. NT.$1200($80) in Asia, Middle East, Oceania; elsewhere $100. China Economic News Service, 561 Chunghsiao E. Rd., Sec. 4, Taipei, Taiwan 10516, Republic of China. TEL 2-642-2629. FAX 2-642-7422. TELEX 27710-CENSPC. (Subscr. to: P.O. Box 43-60, Taipei, Taiwan, R.O.C.) Ed. Philip Liu. adv.; illus. circ. 10,000. (tabloid format)
Formerly: Economic News Overseas Weekly.

BUSINESS TAX PLANNING. see BUSINESS AND ECONOMICS — Public Finance, Taxation

BUSINESS TECH. see COMPUTERS — Computer Networks

330   NR   ISSN 0331-2585
BUSINESS TIMES; economic and business review. (Text in English) 1975. w. £N52. Daily Times of Nigeria Ltd., Publications Division, Latef Jakendi Rd., Ikeja, Lagos State, Nigeria. TEL 234-1-4977280. FAX 234-1-4977284. Ed. Godfrey Bamawo. circ. 270,800. **Document type:** trade publication.

330   MY
BUSINESS TIMES. (Text in English) 1976. d. (6/w.) M.232.50($2464.50) Financial Publications Sdn. Bhd., 31 Jalan Riong, 59100 Kuala Lumpur, Malaysia. TEL 2745444. Ed. Henry Chang. circ. 12,000. (back issues avail.)

330   SI
BUSINESS TIMES. (Text in English) 1976. d. (except Sun.). S.$265.20 (foreign S$2008). Singapore Press Holdings Ltd., Corporate Relations Department, 82 Genting Lane, News Centre, Singapore 349567, Singapore. TEL 743-8800. FAX 747-3835. TELEX RS 55050 SPHGC. E-mail: http://www.asia1.com.sg/biztimes. Ed. Cheong Yip Seng. adv. contact: Tham Khai Wor. bk.rev.; film rev.; music rev.; play rev.; illus.; circ. 35,908 (paid). cols./p.: 8; pp./issue: 48. (also avail. in microfiche) **Document type:** newspaper.
Description: Singapore's business newspaper.

330   TH   ISSN 0125-2313
BUSINESS TIMES. (Text in English) 1979. w. Thai Bldg., 1400 Rama IV Rd., Bangkok 10110, Thailand.

330   US
BUSINESS TIMES (NEW HAVEN EDITION). 1986. m. $26. Choice Media, 315 Peck St., Box 580, New Haven, CT 06513-0580. TEL 203-782-1420. FAX 203-782-3793. Ed. Joel MacClaren; Pub. Joel MacClaren. R&P contact: Joel MacClaren. adv. contact: Francesca Wood. circ. 10,000. **Document type:** trade publication.
Former titles: New Haven Business & Exclusively Connecticut; New Haven County Woman.
Description: Local business journal featuring small to medium size businesses.

330   CN   ISSN 1185-1600
BUSINESS TO BUSINESS. 1989. 7/yr. Can.$35($50) Bracebridge Examiner Ltd., 16 Manitoba St., Box 1049, Bracebridge, Ont. P0B 1C0, Canada. TEL 705-645-8771. FAX 705-645-1718. Ed. Mike Archer. adv.; circ. 6,034 (controlled).

THE BUSINESS - TO - BUSINESS MARKETER. see ADVERTISING AND PUBLIC RELATIONS

330   CN
BUSINESS TO BUSINESS NEWS. 1993. m. Can.$24 (US Can.$34, elsewhere Can.$40). Box 130, Durham, ON N0G 1R0, Canada. TEL 519-369-6950. FAX 519-369-6961. Pub. Geo Benninger. adv.: B&W page Can.$865; adv. contact: Roseanne Vermein. (tabloid format)

330   II
BUSINESS TODAY. (Text in English) 1992. fortn. Living Media India Pvt. Ltd., F-14-15, Connaught Place, New Delhi 11000, India. TEL 011-3315801. FAX 011-3315801. TELEX 31-61245 INTO IN. Ed. Aroon Purie. adv.: B&W page Rs.42000, color page Rs.60000; trim 19.1 x 27.3.

BUSINESS TORTS. see LAW — Corporate Law

330 340   US
▼**BUSINESS TRANSACTIONS IN EASTERN EUROPE.** 1996. 2 base vols. (plus a. update). $350 for base vols.; update $140. (Center for International Legal Studies) Matthew Bender & Co., Inc., 2 Park Ave., New York, NY 10016. TEL 212-448-2000. E-mail: international@bender.com; URL: http://www.bender.com. Ed. Stephen Breidenbach.
Description: Includes discussion of relevant business - legal information for 12 Eastern European jurisdictions.

BUSINESS TRAVELER INTERNATIONAL. see TRAVEL AND TOURISM

BUSINESS TRAVELLER. see TRAVEL AND TOURISM

330   US   ISSN 1060-2348
BUSINESS TRENDS REPORT; digest of America's leading investment, business, and travel newsletter. 1991. m. $35 (effective 1997). Business Research, 537 Newport Center Dr., Ste. 355, Newport Beach, CA 92660. TEL 714-644-8818. Ed. Thomas S. Thompson. bk.rev.; circ. 3,000 (paid). (back issues avail.) **Document type:** newsletter.

650   US   ISSN 0007-7135
HF5001   CODEN: BUWEA3
BUSINESS WEEK. (International ed. avail.) 1929. w. (last of volume is a double issue) $46.95 (effective 1997); newsstand price: $2.75. McGraw-Hill Companies, 1221 Ave. of the Americas, 39th Fl., New York, NY 10020. TEL 212-512-2000. E-mail: subtobw@aol.com; URL: http://www.businessweek.com/. (Subscr. to: Box 516, Hightstown, NJ 08520. TEL 800-635-1200) Ed. Stephen B. Shepard; Pub. David G. Ferm. adv.: B&W page $45100. bk.rev.; illus.; stat.; index. circ. 990,000. (also avail. in microform from UMI; back issues avail.; reprint service avail. from UMI) **Indexed:** ABI Inform., Abstr.Bull.Inst.Pap.Chem., Acad.Ind., Account.Ind. (1974-), ASCA, B.P.I., Bank.Lit.Ind., Bk.Rev.Ind. (1977-), BMT, BPIA, Bus.Ind., CAD CAM Abstr., Chem.Abstr., Child.Bk.Rev.Ind. (1977-), Comput.Bus., Comput.Indus.Up., Comput.Lit.Ind., Curr.Lit.Fam.Plan., Curr.Pack.Abstr., Energy Info.Abstr., Energy Rev., Environ.Abstr., Fut.Surv., High.Educ.Curr.Aware.Bull., Hlth.Ind., Ind.Bus.Rep., Ind.Per.Art.Relat.Law, Key to Econ.Sci., Mag.Ind., Manage.Cont., Mgmt.& Market.Abstr., Microcomp.Ind., Mid.East: Abstr.& Ind., Ocean.Abstr., Oper.Res.Manage.Sci., P.A.I.S., PCR2, Pers.Lit., PMR, Pollut.Abstr., Qual.Contr.Appl.Stat., R.G.Abstr., Resour.Ctr.Ind., Robomat., SRI, Tel.Abstr., Tel.Alert, Telegen, Text.Tech.Dig., Text.Tech.Dig., TOM, Tr.& Indus.Ind., Work Rel.Abstr. **Document type:** trade publication.
●Also available online. Vendor(s): Dow Jones News Retrieval, Knight-Ridder Information, Inc. (File no.624/McGRAW-HILL PUBLICATIONS ONLINE), Lexis-Nexis, NewsNet (GB555).
—BLDSC (2934.930000); CIS; CISTI; Genuine Article; KR SourceOne; SWETS; UnCover. **CCC.**
Description: Comprehensive coverage of news and developments affecting the business world. Includes information on computers, finance, labor, industry, marketing, science and technology.

382 330   US
BUSINESS WEEK - CHINA. (Selected Chinese translation of: Business Week (ISSN 0007-7135) & Business Week International) (Text in Chinese) 1986. bi-m. (Ministry of Foreign Economic Relations and Trade, Institute of International Trade, CC - Duiwai Jingji Maoyi Bu, Guoji Maoyi Yanjiuso) McGraw-Hill Companies, 1221 Ave. of the Americas, New York, NY 10020. TEL 212-512-3867. (Dist. by: MOFERT, 28 Donghouxiang, Andingmenwai, Beijing 100710, People's Republic of China. TEL 421-9332) Ed. Stephe Shepand. adv. circ. 60,000. (back issues avail.) **Document type:** trade publication.
Formerly: International Business and Management - Guoji Shangye yu Guanli (ISSN 1002-445X)
Description: Covers economics, management, and financial subjects.

330   UK
BUSINESS WEEK INTERNATIONAL. 1929. w. $150. McGraw-Hill, 34 Dover St., London W1X 4BR, England. TEL 071-491-8985. FAX 071-493-9896. (U.S. addr.: McGraw-Hill Inc., 1221 Ave. of the Americas, New York 10020) Ed. Paula Dwyer. adv.; bk.rev.; circ. 105,000. circ. 116,857 (paid). (also avail. in microform) **Indexed:** Mgmt.& Market.Abstr., WPM. **Document type:** trade publication.

330   CH   ISSN 1021-9536
BUSINESS WEEKLY/SHANG YEH CHOU K'AN. (Text in Chinese) 1987. w. (50/yr.). NT.$3800($180) (foreign NT.$4300). Business Weekly, Inc., 1F, no. 7, Lane 13, Yungkang St., Taipei, Taiwan, Republic of China. TEL 02-3121357. FAX 02-3936024. (Dist. in US by: World Journal Bookstore, 141-07 20th Ave., Whitestone, NY 11357) Ed. Li Meng-chou. adv.
Description: Reports on world business news.

330   NR
BUSINESS WEEKLY (LAGOS). (Text in English) w. P.M.B. 21340, Ikeja, Lagos State, Nigeria. **Document type:** trade publication.

330   UK   ISSN 0958-7942
BUSINESS WEST MIDLANDS. 1988. m. £19.50. Business Magazine Group, Briarwood House, St. John St., Mansfield, Notts NG18 1QH, England. TEL 021-308-0077. FAX 021-308-0385. Ed. Sue Allen. adv. circ. 11,825.
●Also available online.

330   II   ISSN 0970-8197
BUSINESS WORLD. (Text in English) 1980. fortn. newsstand price: Rs.12. 145 Atlanta, 209 Ceremonial Blvd., Nariman Point, Mumbai 400 021, India. TEL 91-22-240581. TELEX 112354. Ed. T.N. Ninan. adv.: B&W page Rs.30000, color page Rs.60000; trim 194 x 265; adv. contact: Bikash Banerjee. circ. 37,204. **Document type:** trade publication.

BUYERS GUIDE TO U.S. COTTON. see AGRICULTURE — Crop Production And Soil

330   US
BUYOUTS NEWSLETTER; the newsletter for management buyouts, leveraged acquisitions and special situations. 1985. bi-w. $1060. (Securities Data Company, Inc.) Securities Data Publishing, 40 W. 57th St., 11th Fl., New York, NY 10019. TEL 212-765-5311. FAX 212-765-6123. Ed. Kopin Tan. bk.rev.; charts. **Document type:** newsletter.
●Also available online. Vendor(s): Data-Star, Information Access Co., Knight-Ridder Information, Inc.
Formerly: Merger Management Report (ISSN 0885-8616)
Description: Contains interviews and articles about successful buyouts, restructurings and leveraged acquisitions.

330 659.1   US
B2B E-NEWSLETTER. s-m. $48. E-mail: B2B@Doyle.Marketing.com; URL: http://www.DoyleMarketing.com. **Document type:** newsletter.
●Available only online.
Description: Provides articles, studies and surveys about business to business advertising, direct marketing and internet communications.

C B D. (Corporate Business Design) see COMMUNICATIONS

BUSINESS AND ECONOMICS

330 350   US
C B D WEEKLY RELEASE. (Commerce Business Daily) w. $197. United Communications Group, 11300 Rockville Pike, Ste. 1100, Rockville, MD 20852-3030. TEL 301-816-8950. FAX 301-816-8945.
   Description: Lists all published procurements and awards by Federal Supply Code.

338   UK   ISSN 0268-2273
C B I ANNUAL REPORT. a. Confederation of British Industry, Centre Point, 103 New Oxford St., London WC1A 1DU, England. TEL 44-71-379-7400. FAX 44-71-240-1578. TELEX 21332. **Document type:** corporate report.
—BLDSC (1153.950000).

330   UK   ISSN 0961-6330
C B I - COOPERS & LYBRAND SURVEY OF FINANCIAL SERVICES. 1990. q. £225 to non-members. Confederation of British Industry, Centre Point, 103 New Oxford St., London WC1A 1DU, England. TEL 44-171-379-7400. FAX 44-171-240-1578. **Document type:** trade publication.
   Formerly: C B I - Coopers & Lybrand Deloitte Survey of Financial Services.

350   UK
C B I MONTHLY TRENDS SURVEY. m. included with C B I Quarterly Industrial Trends Survey. Confederation of British Industry, Centre Point, 103 New Oxford St., London WC1A 1DU, England. TEL 44-71-379-7400. FAX 44-71-240-1578.
   Former titles: C B I Monthly Trends Enquiry; C B I Monthly Trends Survey; C B I Monthly Trends Enquiry.

338   UK   ISSN 0261-6661
C B I NEWS. m. £25 to non-members (foreign £59). Confederation of British Industry, Centre Point, 103 New Oxford St., London WC1A 1DU, England. TEL 44-71-379-7400. FAX 44-71-240-1578. TELEX 21332. **Document type:** bulletin.
   Formerly: C B I Members Bulletin (ISSN 0140-2188)

338   UK
C B I QUARTERLY INDUSTRIAL TRENDS SURVEY. q. £430 with C B I Monthly Trends Survey; without £280. Confederation of British Industry, Centre Point, 103 New Oxford St., London WC1A 1DU, England. TEL 44-71-379-7400. FAX 44-71-240-1578. TELEX 21332.
—BLDSC (3095.480000).
   Formerly: C B I Industrial Trends Survey (ISSN 0142-6435)

330   US
C B M C CONTACT QUARTERLY; the magazine for business today. 1942. 4/yr. $12.95. Christian Business Men's Committee of USA, 1800 McCallie Ave., Box 3308, Chattanooga, TN 37404. TEL 423-698-4444. FAX 423-629-4434. Ed. Robert J. Tamasy; Pub. Phil Downer. R&P contact: Ginger West. adv. contact: Ginger West. bk.rev. circ. 25,000. (back issues avail.)
   Formerly: C B M C Contact (ISSN 0890-0442)
   Description: Devoted to helping Christian business and professional people apply Biblical principles more effectively in their personal, family, and business lives.

330   GW
C D H BAYERN. m. Wirtschaftsverband Bayerischer Handelsvertreter und Handelsmakler, Ismaninger Str. 63, 81675 Munich, Germany. TEL 471046.

330   CN   ISSN 0824-8001
HD9710.C2
C.D. HOWE INSTITUTE COMMENTARY. 1982. irreg. Can.$6 per issue. C.D. Howe Institute, 125 Adelaide St. E., Toronto, ON M5C 1L7, Canada. TEL 416-865-1904. FAX 416-865-1866. E-mail: cdhome@edhome.org; URL: http://www.cdhome.org. **Indexed:** G.Soc.Sci.& Rel.Per.Lit. **Document type:** monographic series.
   Description: Commentaries on Canadian economic and social policy issues.

C D - R O M AND ONLINE BUSINESS AND COMPANY DATABASES. see LIBRARY AND INFORMATION SCIENCES — Computer Applications

D SICHERHEITS-MANAGEMENT. (Criminal Digest) see CRIMINOLOGY AND LAW ENFORCEMENT — Security

380   SP
C E A M - REVISTA DE ECONOMIA INDUSTRIAL. 1952. q. 1000 ptas. Centro de Estudios y Asesoramiento Metalurgico, Jose Anselmo Clave 2, Barcelona 2, Spain. TEL 3-318-80-58. FAX 3-317-14-63. TELEX 59250 CEAM. Ed. Juan Ortega Galan. adv.; abstr.; bibl.; charts; illus.
   Description: Covers industrial economics.

330   FR   ISSN 0999-7598
C.E.C. MAGAZINE. 4/yr. E S E R, 3 Sente des Dorees, 75019 Paris, France. TEL 42-03-12-09. FAX 42-06-36-52. Ed. Gisele Mednick. circ. 30,000.

C E D E J EGYPTE - MONDE ARABE; droit, economie, societe. (Centre d'Etudes et de Documentation Economique, Juridique et Sociale) see POLITICAL SCIENCE

346.066   US
C E I UPDATE. 1988. m. $50 donation. Competitive Enterprise Institute, 1001 Connecticut Ave., N.W., Ste. 1250, Washington, DC 20036-5504. TEL 202-331-1010. FAX 202-331-0640. E-mail: info@cei.org; URL: http://www.cei.org. Ed. Jonathan H. Adler. Pub. Fred L. Smith. R&P contact: Jonathan H. Adler. bk.rev. circ. 7,500. (back issues avail.) **Document type:** newsletter.
   Description: Focuses on principles of limited government and free enterprise. Government regulations and current economic policies are critiqued according to whether they advance or hinder economic freedom.

330   US   ISSN 0887-9168
HD2771
C E O INTERVIEWS. 1986. w. Wall Street Transcript, 99 Wall St., New York, NY 10005-4301. TEL 212-747-9500. FAX 212-668-9824. Ed. Paul Smith.

330   US   ISSN 8756-7113
HG4026   CODEN: CFOMEX
C F O. (Chief Financial Officer); the magazine for senior financial executives. m. $50 (foreign $90); free to qualified subscribers. C F O Publishing Corporation (Subsidiary of: Economist Group), 253 Summer St., Boston, MA 02210. TEL 617-345-9700. FAX 617-951-4090. E-mail: jah@cfo.ccmail. compuserve.com; URL: http://www.cfonet.com. (Subscr. to: Box 530, Mt. Morris, IL 61054-0530) Ed. Julia Homer; Pub. David J. Laird. adv. contact: Alex Clemente. circ. 365,000 (controlled). (reprint service avail. from UMI. **Indexed:** ABI Inform., Account.Ind. (1986-). **Document type:** consumer publication.
●Also available online. Vendor(s): UMI.
—BLDSC (3128.516000); KR SourceOne; UMI. CCC.

330 300   IV   ISSN 1011-839X
HC501
C I R E S CAHIERS. (Text in French) 1970. q. 2400 Fr.CFA. Universite Nationale de Cote d'Ivoire, Centre Ivoirien de Recherches Economiques et Sociales, B.P. 1259, Abidjan 08, Ivory Coast. TEL 44-09-53. FAX 44-57-08. Ed. Paul T. Perrault. bk.rev.; bibl. circ. 250. **Indexed:** Documentatieblad.

330   GW   ISSN 0170-5679
C I R E T STUDIEN. 1963. irreg., vol.49, 1995. DM.50. Centre for International Research on Economic Tendency, Poschingerstr. 5, 81679 Munich, Germany. TEL 49-89-9224-0. FAX 49-89-985369. circ. 400. **Document type:** monographic series.

C K A G STUDIENFUEHRER EUROPA. WIRTSCHAFTSWISSENSCHAFTEN UND JURA. see EDUCATION — Guides To Schools And Colleges

C R S PERSPECTIVES. (Centre for Resource Studies) see MINES AND MINING INDUSTRY

330   RH
C Z I INDUSTRIAL REVIEW. m. Z.$106.80 (foreign Z.$128.40) (effective 1997). (Confederation of Zimbabwe Industries) Thomson Publications Zimbabwe (Pvt) Ltd., Thomson House, P.O. Box 1683, Harare, Zimbabwe. TEL 263-4-736835. FAX 263-4-752390. **Document type:** trade publication.
   Formerly: Industrial Review.

CAHIERS D'ECONOMIE APPLIQUEE AUX SCIENCES HUMAINES. see HUMANITIES: COMPREHENSIVE WORKS

330   SZ
CAHIERS ECONOMIQUES. (Text in French or German) 1974. a. price varies. Universitaetsverlag Freiburg, Perolles 42, CH-1705 Fribourg, Switzerland. TEL 41-26-4264311. FAX 41-26-4264300. **Document type:** bulletin.
   Formerly: Colloques Economiques.

330   CG   ISSN 0008-0209
HC501.A1
CAHIERS ECONOMIQUES ET SOCIAUX. (Editions in English and French) 1962. q. 1000 Fr.CFA($10.) Universite Nationale du Zaire, Kinshasa, Institut de Recherches Economiques et Sociales, B.P. 257, Kinshasa 11, Democratic Republic of the Congo. Ed. Sebisogo Muhima. adv.; bk.rev.; abstr.; charts; mkt.; stat.; index, cum.index. circ. 1,000. (also avail. in microfiche from IDC) **Indexed:** Curr.Cont.Africa, Documentatieblad, Int.Polit.Sci.Abstr., Key to Econ.Sci., P.A.I.S.For.Lang.Ind., P.A.I.S., Rural Ext.Educ.& Tr.Abstr. **Document type:** academic/scholarly publication.

CALIFORNIA REAL ESTATE REPORTER. see REAL ESTATE

330 692.8   US
CALIFORNIA STATE CONTRACTS REGISTER. 1981. s-m.; d. on the Internet. Department of General Services, Office of Small and Minority Business, 1531 I St., 2nd Fl., Sacramento, CA 95814-2016. TEL 916-323-5478. FAX 916-442-7855. URL: http://www.dgs.ca.gov/osmb. Ed.Bd. adv. circ. 6,200. **Document type:** government publication.
●Also available online.

330   US   ISSN 0888-8671
HG2037
CALLAHAN'S CREDIT UNION DIRECTORY. 1986. a. $135. Callahan & Associates, 1001 Connecticut Ave., N.W., Ste. 1022, Washington, DC 20036. TEL 202-223-3920. FAX 202-223-1311. Ed. Ray Springsteen; Pub. Chip Filson. R&P contact: Ray Springsteen. adv. contact: Ray Springsteen. circ. 3,500. (also avail. in diskette format) **Document type:** directory.

382   UY
CAMARA DE COMERCIO URUGUAYO - BRITANICA. BOLETIN INFORMATIVO. 1969. m. free. Camara de Comercio Uruguayo - Britanica, Av. Libertador Brig. Gral. Lavalleja, P. 2, Of. 201, 11000 Montevideo, Uruguay. TEL 5982-98-0349. FAX 5982-90-0936. stat.; circ. 150 (controlled).
   Formerly: Camara de Comercio Uruguayo - Britanica. Revista (ISSN 0008-1914)

330 338   VE
CAMARA DE INDUSTRIALES DE CARACAS. NOTI. m. Camara de Industriales de Caracas, Edificio Camara de Industriales, piso 2, Esq. de Puente Anauco, Caracas 1011-A, Venezuela. TEL 02-571-42-24. FAX 02-571-20-09. TELEX 24453 CAINC VC. circ. 20,000.
   Description: Directed to the industrial world.

330   UK
CAMBRIDGE ECONOMIC HANDBOOKS. NEW SERIES. irreg. price varies. Cambridge University Press, Edinburgh Bldg., Shaftesbury Rd., Cambridge CB2 2RU, England. TEL 44-1223-312393. FAX 44-1223-315052. TELEX 851817256. E-mail: information@cup.cam.ac.uk; URL: http://www.cup.cam.ac.uk. (N. American addr.: Cambridge University Press, Journals Dept., 40 W. 20th St., New York, NY 10011. TEL 212-924-3900. FAX 212-691-3239) Eds. P.S. Dasgupta, G.M. Heal. R&P contact: Linda Nicol. **Indexed:** I.M.M.Abstr. **Document type:** monographic series.

BUSINESS AND ECONOMICS

330　　　　　UK　ISSN 0309-166X
HB1.
CAMBRIDGE JOURNAL OF ECONOMICS. 1977. bi-m. £150 (foreign $255) (effective 1998). (Cambridge Political Economy Society) Oxford University Press, Academic Division, Great Clarendon St., Oxford OX2 6DP, England. TEL 44-1865-267907. FAX 44-1865-267485. E-mail: jnl.info@oup.co.uk; URL: http://www.oup.co.uk/journals. (Subscr. in U.S. to: Oxford University Press Inc., 2001 Evans Rd., Cary, NC 27513. TEL 800-852-7323. FAX 919-677-1714) Ed.Bd.; Pub. Martin Green. R&P contact: Joolz Longley. adv. contact: Jane Parker. circ. 1,950. (reprint service avail. from SWZ) **Indexed:** Arts & Hum.Cit.Ind., ASCA, Asian-Pac.Econ.Lit., C.R.E.J., Curr.Cont., Geo.Abstr.H.G., IDA, Int.Lab.Doc., J.of Econ.Lit., P.A.I.S., Pub.Admin.Abstr., Rural Devel.Abstr., Rural Recreat.Tour.Abstr., Soc.Sci.Ind., SSCI, World Agri.Econ.& Rural Sociol.Abstr., World Bank.Abstr. **Document type:** academic/scholarly publication.
—BLDSC (3015.956000); Genuine Article; KR SourceOne; SWETS; UnCover. **CCC.**
　Description: Provides a forum for the non-neoclassical approaches to economics.

CAMBRIDGE STUDIES IN POPULATION, ECONOMY AND SOCIETY IN PAST TIME. see *HISTORY*

330　　　　　UK　ISSN 0068-6832
CAMBRIDGE UNIVERSITY. DEPARTMENT OF APPLIED ECONOMICS. MONOGRAPHS. 1948. irreg., no.27, 1980. price varies. Cambridge University Press, Edinburgh Bldg., Shaftesbury Rd., Cambridge CB2 2RU, England. TEL 44-1223-312393. FAX 44-1223-315052. TELEX 851817256. E-mail: information@cup.cam.ac.uk; URL: http://www.cup.cam.ac.uk. (N. American addr.: Cambridge University Press, 40 W. 20th St., New York, NY 10011. TEL 212-924-3900. FAX 212-691-3239) R&P contact: Linda Nicol. **Document type:** monographic series.

330　　　　　UK　ISSN 0068-6840
CAMBRIDGE UNIVERSITY. DEPARTMENT OF APPLIED ECONOMICS. OCCASIONAL PAPERS. 1964. irreg., no.56, 1985. price varies. Cambridge University Press, Edinburgh Bldg., Shaftesbury Rd., Cambridge CB2 2RU, England. TEL 44-1223-312393. FAX 44-1223-315052. TELEX 851817256. E-mail: information@cup.cam.ac.uk; URL: http://www.cup.cam.ac.uk. (N. American addr.: Cambridge University Press, 40 W. 20th St., New York, NY 10011. TEL 212-924-3900. FAX 212-691-3239) **Document type:** monographic series.

CAMPAIGN FINANCE LAW. see *POLITICAL SCIENCE*

650　　　　　CN　ISSN 0008-3100
HF1　　　　　　　CODEN: CABUAL
CANADIAN BUSINESS. 1928. m. Can.$26.70 (foreign Can.$45) (effective 1997). Canadian Business Media, 777 Bay St., 5th Fl., Toronto, ON M5W 1A7, Canada. TEL 416-596-5100. FAX 416-596-5152. E-mail: letters@cbmedia.ca. Ed. Arthur Johnson; Pub. Paul Jones. adv.: B&W page Can.$9520, color page Can.$11900; trim 8 x 10 3/4; adv. contact: Deborah Rosser. bk.rev.; charts; illus.; tr.lit. circ. 83,000. **Indexed:** ABI Inform., B.P.I, BPIA, Bus.Ind., Can.B.P.I., Can.Per.Ind., CMI, INSPEC (1983-), Mag.Ind., Mgmt.& Market.Abstr., P.A.I.S., PROMT, Sportsearch (1984-), Tr.& Indus.Ind., Work Rel.Abstr. **Document type:** trade publication.
●Also available online. Vendor(s): Information Access Co.
—BLDSC (3018.250000); AskIEEE; CASDDS; CISTI; KR SourceOne; SWETS; UMI; UnCover. **CCC.**
　Description: Provides strategic management information and ideas for senior executives in top 500 companies.

330　　　　　CN　ISSN 0829-1349
CANADIAN BUSINESS LIFE. 1981. q. Can.$20. Better Business Bureau, Publication Division, 1 St. Johns Rd., 4th Fl., Toronto, ON M6P 4C7, Canada. TEL 416-766-5744. FAX 416-766-1970. Ed. Fiorella Grossi. adv. contact: Max Lieberman. circ. 48,000. **Indexed:** Can.B.P.I.

CANADIAN FRANCHISE GUIDE. see *LAW*

330　　　　　CN　ISSN 0825-0383
HD28　　　　　　　CODEN: CJASE9
CANADIAN JOURNAL OF ADMINISTRATIVE SCIENCES. (Text and summaries in English and French) 1984. q. Can.$60($60) (effective 1997). Administrative Sciences Association of Canada, Faculty of Commerce and Administration, Concordia University, 1455 de Maisonneuve Blvd. W., Montreal, QC H3G 1M8, Canada. TEL 514-848-2719. FAX 514-848-2839. Ed. A. Jalilvand. adv.; bk.rev.; circ. 900 (paid). (also avail. in microform from MML,UMI; back issues avail.) **Indexed:** ASCA, ASCA, Can.B.P.I., Can.Per.Ind., Curr.Cont., Soc.Sci.Ind., Sociol.Abstr., SSCI. **Document type:** academic/scholarly publication.
●Also available online. Vendor(s): UMI.
Also available on CD-ROM. Producer(s): UMI.
—BLDSC (3027.880000); Genuine Article; UMI.
　Description: Covers all fields of business administration, and publishes both theoretical and empirical papers.
Refereed Serial

330　　　　　CN　ISSN 0008-4085
HC111
CANADIAN JOURNAL OF ECONOMICS/REVUE CANADIENNE D'ECONOMIE. (Text in English, French) 1968. q. Can.$85($90) to institutions (effective 1998). (Canadian Economics Association) University of Toronto Press, Journals Department, 5201 Dufferin St., Downsview, ON M3H 5T8, Canada. TEL 416-667-7710. FAX 416-667-7881. E-mail: journals@gpu.utcc.utoronto.ca. (U.S. addr.: 340 Nagel Dr., Cheektowaga, NY 14225) Ed. B. Curtis Eaton. adv.; bk.rev.; index, cum.index: vols. 1-10. circ. 3,000. (also avail. in microform from UMI,PMC) **Indexed:** ABI Inform., Amer.Bibl.Slavic & E.Eur.Stud., ASCA, BPIA, C.L.I., C.R.E.J., Can.B.P.I., Can.Per.Ind., Curr.Cont., Geo.Abstr.H.G., Geo.Abstr., IBR, IDA, Int.Lab.Doc., J.of Econ.Lit., Key to Econ.Sci., Leg.Per., P.A.I.S., P.A.I.S.For.Lang.Ind., Rural Recreat.Tour.Abstr., Soc.Sci.Ind., SSCI, Tr.& Indus.Ind., Work Rel.Abstr., World Agri.Econ.& Rural Sociol.Abstr., World Bank.Abstr. **Document type:** academic/scholarly publication.
—BLDSC (3031.158000); Genuine Article; KR SourceOne; SWETS; UMI; UnCover. **CCC.**
　Supersedes in part: Canadian Journal of Economics and Political Science.

330　　　　　CN　ISSN 0318-0859
CANADIAN PROCESS EQUIPMENT & CONTROL NEWS. 1972. 6/yr. Can.$36($48) (foreign $48) (effective 1997). Canadian Process Equipment & Control News Ltd., 343 Eglinton Ave. E., Toronto, ON M4P 1L7, Canada. TEL 416-481-6483. FAX 416-481-6436. Ed. V. Sharp; Pub. J.P. Birchard. R&P contact: Rob Sommerville. adv. contact: Rob Sommerville. circ. 25,118 (controlled). **Document type:** trade publication.
　Description: Provides information on new and existing products and applications.

330　　　　　CN　ISSN 0383-7920
CANADIAN RENTAL SERVICE. (Text in English, French) 1976. 8/yr. Can.$39. A I S Communications Ltd., 145 Thames Rd. W., Exeter, ON N0M 1S3, Canada. TEL 519-235-2400. FAX 519-235-0798. Ed. Craig Power. adv. contact: Bill Branderhorst. tr.lit. circ. 3,690. (back issues avail.) **Document type:** trade publication.

330 320　　　　　CN　ISSN 1191-0860
F1001
CANADIAN SPEECHES: ISSUES OF THE DAY. 1987. 10/yr. Can.$85($85) (foreign Can.$100) (effective 1997). Canadian Speeches, Box 250, Woodville, ON K0M 2T0, Canada. TEL 705-439-2580. FAX 705-439-1208. Ed. Earle Gray. index. circ. 1,000. (also avail. in microfilm; back issues avail.) **Indexed:** Can.B.P.I.
●Also available online. Vendor(s): Knight-Ridder Information, Inc.
　Formerly: Canadian Speeches: Issues, Informed Thought (ISSN 0849-9918)
　Description: Presents full-text of speeches about issues which reflect broad national interest.

330　　　　　US
CAPE COD BUSINESS JOURNAL.* m. Tri-Coastal Publishing, Inc., Box 39, Orleans, MA 02653-0039. Ed. Anne B. Saint. circ. 11,000.

330　　　　　GW　ISSN 0008-5847
HB5
CAPITAL; das deutsche Wirtschaftsmagazin. 1962. m. DM.108 (Europe DM.151.20; elsewhere DM.282.60). Gruner und Jahr AG & Co., Am Baumwall 11, 20459 Hamburg, Germany. TEL 49-40-3703-0. FAX 49-40-37035617. Ed. Ulrike Fischer. adv. contact: Rolf-Ruediger Nausch. bk.rev.; charts; illus.; stat.; tr.lit. circ. 291,450. (also avail. in microfiche from NRP; microfilm from ALP) **Indexed:** Key to Econ.Sci. **Document type:** trade publication.
—SWETS.
　Description: Covers management strategies, analyses of selected industry and business sectors, political developments and current events for business executives.

330　　　　　II　ISSN 0008-5839
CAPITAL; India's oldest financial weekly dealing with economics, industry and public affairs. (Text in English) 1888. fortn. Rs.100. 1-2 Old Court House Center, P.O. Box 14, Calcutta 700001, India. TEL 33-200099. TELEX 217172. Ed. S. Banerjee. adv.; bk.rev.; mkt.; stat.; index. circ. 8,200. (tabloid format)

330　　　　　IT　ISSN 0392-3320
CAPITAL. 1980. m. L.67200. Rizzoli Editore-Corriere della Sera, Via A Rizzoli 2, 20132 Milan, Italy. TEL 39-2-2588. Ed. Myriam DeCesco. adv.: page L.36300000; adv. contact: Flavio Biondi. circ. 139,596.

330　　　　　FR　ISSN 1162-6704
HF5001
CAPITAL; l'essentiel de l'economie. 1991. m. Prisma Presse, 6 rue Daru, 75008 Paris, France. TEL 44-15-30-00. FAX 47-64-10-42. Ed. Remy Dessarts. adv. circ. 222,000. **Document type:** consumer publication.
　Description: Covers areas of interest to top executives, whether macro- or microeconomic.

330　　　　　II
CAPITALIST. (Text in English) 1978. m. Rs.40. Ikon Papyrus, D-4, Kalindi, New Delhi 110065, India. adv.

CAPITOL UPDATE. see *PUBLIC ADMINISTRATION*

CAREERS AND THE M B A. see *OCCUPATIONS AND CAREERS*

330　　　　　PE
CARETAS. m. Camana 615, Of. 308, Lima, Peru. TEL 287-520. Ed. Antonio Passano. circ. 90,000.

330　　　　　PR　ISSN 0194-8326
CARIBBEAN BUSINESS. (Text in English) 1973. w. $42 (foreign $52) (effective 1995). Casiano Communications Inc., 1700 Fernandez Juncos Ave., Stop 25, San Juan, PR 00909-2999. TEL 787-728-3000. FAX 787-728-7325. Ed. Alex Diaz. adv.; tr.lit. circ. 45,000. (tabloid format; reprint service avail.) **Indexed:** Tr.& Indus.Ind. **Document type:** newspaper.
　Description: Covers all topics of business in the Puerto Rico and Caribbean area.

330　　　　　AQ
CARIBBEAN HANDBOOK. 1983. a. $85. F T Caribbean, P.O. Box 1037, St. John's, Antigua, W.I. TEL 268-462-3392. FAX 268-462-3492. (Subscr. to: Subscription Department, Ste. 53, Omnibus Business Center, 39-41 North Rd., London N7 9DP, England. TEL 44-171-6073430. FAX 44-171-7000429) Ed. Lindsay Maxwell; Pub. Edna Fortescue. R&P contact: Edna Fortescue. adv.; bk.rev. circ. 10,000.

CARLTON COMMUNICATIONS PLC. ANNUAL REPORT AND ACCOUNTS. see *COMMUNICATIONS — Television And Cable*

BUSINESS AND ECONOMICS

330 NE ISSN 0167-2231
HD87
CARNEGIE-ROCHESTER CONFERENCE SERIES ON PUBLIC POLICY; bi-annual conference proceedings. 1978. s-a. fl.450($259) (effective 1998). North-Holland (Subsidiary of: Elsevier Science B.V.), P.O. Box 211, 1000 AE Amsterdam, Netherlands. TEL 31-20-4853911. FAX 31-20-4853598. TELEX 18582 ESPA NL. (Subscr. in the Americas to: Elsevier Science, Regional Sales Office, Box 945, New York, NY 10159-0945. TEL 212-633-3730. FAX 212-633-3680; Subscr. in Australasia and the Far East to: Elsevier Science (Singapore) Pte Ltd, No.1 Temasek Ave., No.17-01 Millenia Tower, Singapore 039192, Singapore. TEL 65-434-3727. FAX 65-337-2230; Subscr. in Japan to: Elsevier Science Japan, 9-15 Higashi-Azabu 1-chome, Minato-ku, Tokyo 106, Japan. TEL 81-3-5561-5033. FAX 81-3-5561-5047) Ed. Allan H. Meltzer. (also avail. in microform from UMI; back issues avail.; reprint service avail. from SWZ) **Indexed:** ABI Inform., C.R.E.J., J.of Econ.Lit. **Document type:** academic/scholarly publication, proceedings.
—BLDSC (3055.090000); SWETS; UMI; UnCover. CCC.
Description: Reviews selected policy problems and issues confronting policy makers.
Refereed Serial

330 US
CAROLINA BUSINESS. 1985. m. $27. Taylor Publications, Inc., Box 12006, New Bern, NC 28561. TEL 919-633-5106. FAX 919-633-2836. adv. circ. 20,403.
Description: Highlights regional business information with regular monthly listings of new corporations.

650 US ISSN 0008-6932
HC101
CARROLL BUSINESS BULLETIN. 1957. 2/yr. $2. John Carroll University, School of Business, University Heights, Cleveland, OH 44118. TEL 216-491-4391. Ed. Dr. Alfred Schneider. bk.rev.; charts; illus. circ. 5,500. **Indexed:** P.A.I.S.

330 DR
CARTA DOMINICANA. 1974. m. Avda. Tiradentes 56, Santo Domingo, Dominican Republic. TEL 566-0119. Dir. Juan Ramon Quinones M.

330 GW ISSN 0178-5125
CASH. bi-m. DM.62 (effective 1996). Cash Verlags GmbH, Brabandstr. 1, 22297 Hamburg, Germany. TEL 49-40-5144401. FAX 49-40-51444120. Ed. Josef Depenbrock; Pub. Dieter Jansen. adv. contact: Baerbel Landschoof. circ. 55,206. **Document type:** consumer publication.

330 PL ISSN 1230-5464
CASH. 1993. w. 11000 Zl. Ringier Polska S.A., Ul. Smolna 8, 00-375 Warsaw, Poland. TEL 84-22-260663. FAX 48-22-200653. Ed. Mariusz Ziomecki. adv. contact: Bozena Patek. circ. 50,000. (back issues avail.) **Document type:** consumer publication, newspaper.
Description: Covers investment analysis, information and advice, Polish stock market, privatization in Poland. For entrepreneurs and investors, everyday and business people.

330 AU
CASH FLOW. 11/yr. Stubenring 2, A-1010 Vienna, Austria. TEL 01-5138800. FAX 01-5138808. Ed. Ferenc Papp. circ. 50,000.

330 US
CASH FLOW MANAGEMENT STRATEGIES. m. $249 (effective 1997). Siefer Consultants, Inc., Box 1384, Storm Lake, IA 50588. TEL 712-732-7340. FAX 712-732-7906. Ed. Lynn Hardt. **Document type:** newsletter.
Description: Contains articles on what organizations are actually doing to increase cash flow, including accounts receivable and collections, accounts payable, procurement, banking services, tax planning, capital financing, new technology and more.

330 UK ISSN 0069-0937
CASS LIBRARY OF INDUSTRIAL CLASSICS. 1966. irreg., no.28, 1969. price varies. Frank Cass, Newbury House, 890-900 Eastern Ave., Newbury Park, Ilford, Essex IG2 7HH, England. TEL 44-181-530-4226. FAX 44-181-530-7795. E-mail: sales@frankcass.com; URL: http://www.frankcass.com. (Dist. in the U.S. by: I.S.B.S., 5804 N.E. Hassalo St., Portland, OR 97213-3644. TEL 800-944-6190. FAX 503-280-8832) **Document type:** academic/scholarly publication.

330 IT
CASSAMARCA; rivista trimestrale di politica economica finanziaria istituzionale e sociale. 1987. q. free. (Cassa di Risparmio della Marca Trivigiana) Cassamarca S.p.A., Piazza S. Leonardo 1, 31100 Treviso, Italy. TEL 39-422-6541. FAX 39-422-654316. Ed. Claudio Alessandri. circ. 6,000. (back issues avail.)

CATALOGO LEGALE. see *LAW*

CATTLE BUSINESS. see *AGRICULTURE — Poultry And Livestock*

330 CJ
CAYMAN EXECUTIVE. q. C.$33($40) in Caribbean, U.S. and Canada; elsewhere C.$42($50). Cayman Publishing Co. Ltd., Box 173GT, Grand Cayman, Cayman Islands, W.I. TEL 809-949-5111. Ed. Ryhaan Shah.

330 US
CECIL BUSINESS LEDGER. 1992. m. $12. Chesapeake Publishing Corp., 601 Bridge St., Elkton, MD 21922-0429. TEL 410-398-3311. FAX 410-398-4044. Pub. Jeffrey Mezzatesta. adv.: B&W page $650; trim 11 1/2 x 15; adv. contact: Gene Schwenk. circ. 2,895.
Description: Contains features and news articles on topics of interest to local business owners, managers, and professionals.

CENTRAL AMERICA REPORT. see *POLITICAL SCIENCE*

CENTRAL ASIA MONITOR. see *POLITICAL SCIENCE*

330 CE
CENTRAL BANK OF SRI LANKA. ECONOMIC BULLETIN. (Text in English) $6. Central Bank of Sri Lanka, Janadhipathi Mawatha, P.O. Box 590, Colombo 1, Sri Lanka. TEL 94-1-421191. FAX 94-1-445127. **Document type:** bulletin.

330 US ISSN 1058-3599
CENTRAL PENN BUSINESS JOURNAL. 1984. s-m. $44.95. Journal Publications, Inc., 409 S. Second St., Ste. 3D, Harrisburg, PA 17104-1612. TEL 717-236-4300. FAX 717-236-6803. Ed. Beth Mollard; Pub. David A. Schankweiler. adv. contact: Wes Bower. bk.rev.; illus.; circ. 16,000 (controlled). (also avail. in microform from UMI) **Document type:** trade publication.
●Also available online. Vendor(s): UMI.
—UMI.
Formerly: Strictly Business.
Description: Covers the latest local business news and offers analysis of trends.

330 RM ISSN 1221-3489
CENTRUL DE CERCETARI "GH. ZANE," IASI. ANUARUL. 1992. a. Editura Academiei Romane, Calea 13 Septembrie 13, 76117 Bucharest, Rumania. (Dist. by: Rodipet SA, Piata Presei Libere 1, Sec.1, PO Box 33-57, Bucharest, Rumania. TEL 401-6185103. FAX 401-2226407) Ed. Alexandru Puiu Tacu.

330 AU
CERCLE ECONOMIQUE. m. Elisabethstr. 13, A-1010 Vienna, Austria. TEL 01-5877707. FAX 01-5870752. Ed. Karl Hannes Schmidt. circ. 20,000.

330 301 PR
CETERIS PARIBUS; revista de investigaciones socio-economicas. 1991. s-a. $15 to individuals; institutions $20. Instituto de Estudios Socio-Economicos Regionales, Fac. de Artes y Ciencias, Recinto Univ. de Mayaguez, P.O. Box 5000, Mayaguez, PR 00681-5000. Ed. Jose A. Mari-Mutt. **Indexed:** P.A.I.S. **Document type:** academic/scholarly publication.
Description: Presents recent research in social sciences from the institute.

330 IS
CHADASHOT PENSIA. 1968. m. Kaliah Ltd., Rehov Ben-Yeduha 165, Tel Aviv 63471, Israel.

330 US ISSN 0577-5132
HC101 CODEN: CHLGBB
CHALLENGE (ARMONK); the magazine of economic affairs. 1952. bi-m. $45 to individuals (foreign $65); institutions $110 (foreign $170) (effective 1997). M.E. Sharpe, Inc., 80 Business Park Dr., Armonk, NY 10504. TEL 914-273-1800; 800-541-6563. FAX 914-273-2106. Ed. Jeffrey Madrick. R&P contact: Ginny Chandoha. adv.: page $750; 6 x 9; adv. contact: Barbara Ladd. bk.rev.; bibl.; charts; illus.; stat.; index. circ. 5,000. (also avail. in microform from UMI; back issues avail.) **Indexed:** Acad.Ind., Access, B.P.I., Curr.Cont., INIS Atomind., J.of Econ.Lit., Manage.Cont., P.A.I.S., Soc.Sci.Ind., Work Rel.Abstr. **Document type:** academic/scholarly publication.
—BLDSC (3129.100000); KR SourceOne; SWETS; UMI; UnCover. CCC.
Description: Provides information and analysis on economic issues.
Refereed Serial

330 CN ISSN 1192-4365
CHARITABLE BUSINESS. 1992. bi-m. Can.$18($30) Momentum Media Management, 4040 Creditview Rd., Unit 11, Box 1800, Mississauga, ON L5C 3Y8, Canada. TEL 905-813-7100. FAX 905-813-7117. E-mail: barwellj@momentummedia.com. Ed. Jay Barwell. R&P contact: Jay Barwell. adv.: B&W page Can.$1915, color page Can.$2750; trim 8 x 11; adv. contact: Hugh Parkinson. bk.rev.; circ. 11,100 (controlled). **Document type:** trade publication.
Description: Covers the administration and facility management needs of charities and nonprofit organizations for executive managers, administration and property managers.

330 IS
CHAROSHET; monthly review for the Israeli producer. (Text in Hebrew) m. IS.86. Kalia Press Ltd., Rehov Ben-Yehuda 165, Tel Aviv 63 471, Israel.

CHECK-IN; das Magazin fuer Geschaeftsreisende Business & Pleasure. see *TRAVEL AND TOURISM*

330 CC ISSN 1005-4332
CHENGSHI JINGJI, QUYUE JINGJI/CITY ECONOMICS, REGIONAL ECONOMICS. (Subseries of: Fuyin Baokan Ziliao) (Text in Chinese) bi-m. $42.56. Zhongguo Renmin Daxue, Shubao Ziliao Zhongxin - China People's University, Book & Newspaper Information Center, 3 Zhang Zizhong Rd., P.O. Box 1122, Beijing 100007, People's Republic of China. TEL 86-10-4015080. (Dist. in US by: China Publications Service, Box 49614, Chicago, IL 60649. TEL 312-288-3291. FAX 312-288-8570) pp./issue: 112.

330 US ISSN 1044-0844
CHICAGO ENTERPRISE. 1986. 6/yr. free. Commercial Club of Chicago, One First National Plaza, No. 2700, Chicago, IL 60603. TEL 312-853-1203. FAX 312-853-1209. Ed. David H. Roeder. adv.; bk.rev. circ. 9,100.
●Also available online. Vendor(s): Lexis-Nexis.
Description: Covers economic development and urban issues in Chicago area.

330 US
CHIEF EXECUTIVE OPINION. 1989. irreg. $15 to non-members; members $5. Conference Board, Inc., 845 Third Ave., New York, NY 10022. TEL 212-759-0900. FAX 212-980-7014. circ. 8,700. **Document type:** newsletter.
Description: Analysis of US CEO's views on major policy issues and business trends.

CHILDREN'S SOCIAL & ECONOMICS EDUCATION; an international journal. see *EDUCATION*

CHILE. INSTITUTO NACIONAL DE ESTADISTICAS. ESTADISTICA Y ECONOMIA. see *STATISTICS*

330 CC
CHINA & NORTH ASIA MONITOR. (Text in English) m. HK.$2700($350) Abraham Book Centre, 2802 Admiralty Centre, Tower One, 18 Harcourt Rd., Hong Kong, People's Republic of China. TEL 852-2529-0356. FAX 852-2565-8749.
Description: Provides country-by-country analysis of the most recent changes to the political and business environment in China, Hong Kong, Taiwan and N. & S. Koreas.

BUSINESS AND ECONOMICS

CHINA BUSINESS LAW GUIDE. see *LAW — Corporate Law*

330   US
CHINA HAND; investing, licensing and trading conditions today. 1981. m. £1245($1975) Economist Intelligence Unit, 111 W. 57th St., New York, NY 10019. TEL 212-554-0600; 800-938-4685. FAX 212-586-1182. TELEX 175567. URL: http://www.eiu.com. (UK addr.: Economist Intelligence Unit Ltd., Subscriptions Dept., P.O. Box 200, Harold Hill, Romford, Essex RM3 8UX, England. TEL 44-171-830-1007. FAX 44-1708-371-850) Ed. Lois Dougan Tretiak. circ. 1,000. (looseleaf format)
● Also available online.
Also available on CD-ROM.
Description: Covers laws and regulations full-text, including starting a new business, dealing with foreign trade corporations, plus negotiating and implementing joint ventures in the PRC.

CHINA LAW & PRACTICE; documenting & analysing the Chinese legal system. see *LAW*

CHINA LAW JOURNAL. see *LAW*

330   UK   ISSN 1353-6079
CHINA MONITOR/ZHONGGUO TOUSHI. (Text in Chinese, English) 1994. q.? Household World Ltd., 1 Ben Rhydding Rd., Ilkley LS29 8RJ, England. TEL 44-1943-602632. FAX 44-1943-6034973. Ed. Yingxian Soong; Pub. Sau Wan Chan. R&P contact: Sau Wan Chan. **Document type:** trade publication.
—BLDSC (3180.206000).

330   US
CHINA REPORT: ECONOMIC AFFAIRS. irreg. (approx. 130/yr.). $7 per no. (foreign $14 per no.). U.S. Joint Publications Research Service, Box 12507, Arlington, VA 22209. TEL 703-487-4630. (Orders to: NTIS, Springfield, VA 22161)

330   CC
CHINESE ECONOMIC MONTHLY. 12/yr. Manley Commercial Bldg., no.1206, 367-375 Queens Rd., Central, Hong Kong, People's Republic of China. TEL 5-443133. FAX 5-450774. Ed. Li Hung.

330   CH
CHINESE ECONOMIC REVIEW/CHUNG-KUO CHING CHI P'ING LUN. (Text in Chinese) 1969. q. NT$60 per no. in ROC; in Hong Kong $2.50; Asia $3.50; elsewhere $4.50. (Chinese Institute for Economic Development - Chung-kuo Ching Chi Chien She Yen Chiu Hui) Chinese Economic Review Publishers, 3F, No.7, Alley 2, Szewei Lane, Chung Cheng Rd., Hsintien, Taipei Hsien, Taiwan 23136, Republic of China. TEL 02-912-1811. Ed. Chou I-ping.

330   US   ISSN 0009-4552
HC426
CHINESE ECONOMIC STUDIES; a journal of translations. 1967. bi-m. $110 to individuals (foreign $176); institutions $630 (foreign $710) (effective 1997). M.E. Sharpe, Inc., 80 Business Park Dr., Armonk, NY 10504. TEL 914-273-1800; 800-541-6563. FAX 914-273-2106. Ed. Joseph Fewsmith. R&P contact: Ginny Chandoha. adv.: page $300; trim 5 x 8; adv. contact: Barbara Ladd. index. (back issues avail.) **Indexed:** Asian-Pac.Econ.Lit., C.R.E.J., Curr.Cont., Geo.Abstr.H.G., IDA, Int.Lab.Doc., J.of Econ.Lit., P.A.I.S., Rural Recreat.Tour.Abstr., SSCI, World Agri.Econ.& Rural Sociol.Abstr. **Document type:** academic/scholarly publication.
—BLDSC (3180.277000); Genuine Article; SWETS; UMI; UnCover. **CCC.**
Description: Presents ongoing developments in the Chinese economy. Articles by China's leading economists present analyses of the functioning of the economy, the problems of reform, and debates over economic policy. Special thematic issues concentrate on a specific area of focus.
Refereed Serial

CHINESE FILM MARKET. see *MOTION PICTURES*

330   US
CHRISTIAN BUSINESSMAN. Short title: C.B. 4/yr. $5 or membership. Christian Business Men's Committee of USA, 1800 McCallie Ave., Box 3308, Chattanooga, TN 37404. TEL 423-698-4444. FAX 423-629-4434. Ed. Robert J. Tamasy. R&P contact: Ginger West. adv.
Description: Contains news, information, and features about the ministry of Christian Business Men's Committee of USA.

CHRISTIANA ALBERTINA. see *EARTH SCIENCES*

330   CC
CHUANGYE ZHE/ENTREPRENEURS. (Text in Chinese) bi-m. Shanghai Fanyi Chuban Gongsi - Shanghai Translation Publishing Company, 597 Fuxing Zhonglu, Shanghai 200020, People's Republic of China. TEL 4332298. Ed. He Congying.

330   JA   ISSN 0910-8874
HD28
CHUBU UNIVERSITY. COLLEGE OF BUSINESS ADMINISTRATION AND INFORMATION SCIENCE. JOURNAL. Japanese edition: Keieijoho Gakubu Ronshu. 1985. s-a. exchange basis to libraries. Chubu University, College of Business Administration and Information Science, Kasugai, Aichi 487, Japan. TEL 81-568-51-1111. FAX 81-568-52-1505. Ed.Bd. bk.rev.
Description: Contains articles, research notes, reports of association attendance.

330   UK
CHURCHES PURCHASING SCHEME. 1989. s-a. Ecclesiastical Insurance Office, Desk Top Publishing Unit, Beaufort House, Brunswick Rd., Gloucester GL1 1JZ, England. TEL 0452-383080. FAX 0452-383621. adv. contact: Maggie Vinson. circ. 32,500 (controlled). (back issues avail.) **Document type:** academic/scholarly publication.
Description: Provides a means of supplying a wide range of goods and services at competitive prices by negotiating bulk discounts with suppliers, primarily for churches, charities, and educational organizations.

330 382   IT   ISSN 1120-4249
CINA NOTIZIE; rassegna informativa di attualita cinese. 1969. bi-m. L.150000. Camera di Commercio Italo Cinese, Via Carducci, 18, 20123 Milan, Italy. FAX 72000236. Ed. Carlo F. Butti. adv. circ. 1,500.
Document type: newsletter.
Description: Directed to Italian economic operators wishing to cooperate with Chinese partners, and supplies basic up-to-date information.

330   US   ISSN 0882-8861
CINCINNATI BUSINESS COURIER. 1984. w. $48. A C B J Business Publications Inc., 35 E. 7th St., Ste. 700, Cincinnati, OH 45202-2411. TEL 513-621-6665. FAX 513-621-2462. E-mail: louisville@www.amc.ty.com. Ed. Mark Gleason; Pub. Tom Manahan. R&P contact: Carol Timmons. adv. contact: Maureen O'Meara. bk.rev. circ. 12,800. (tabloid format; also avail. in microfiche; back issues avail.; reprint service avail. from UMI) **Document type:** trade publication, newspaper.
● Also available online. Vendor(s): Information Access Co.
—UMI. **CCC.**
Incorporates (1988-1996): Business Record (Cincinnati) (ISSN 1068-2899); Which was formerly (until 1993): Greater Cincinnati Business Record (ISSN 1044-9264)
Description: Serves the general business information needs of qualified recipients in the Cincinnati metropolitan area, including Northern Kentucky.

330   SP
CINCO DIAS. 1978. d. (except Sun.). 43600 ptas. (America 135000 ptas.). Estructura, S.A., Gran Via, 32, piso 2o, 28013 Madrid, Spain. TEL 538-61-00. FAX 523-06-82. adv. circ. 21,500. **Document type:** newspaper.

331.881   DK   ISSN 0108-0636
CIVILOEKONOMEN. 1953. m. (10/yr.). DKK 470 (effective 1997). F D C - Danske Civiloekonomer - Association of Danish Business Economists, Soetorvet 5, P.O. Box 2043, DK-1012 Copenhagen K, Denmark. TEL 45-33-14-11-49. FAX 45-33-14-11-49. Ed. Kim Haagen Andersen. adv.; bk.rev.; charts; illus.; stat.; index. circ. 14,078.

330   US   ISSN 1059-3055
CLEVELAND ENTERPRISE. 1991. q. $15.95. Enterprise Development, Inc., 11000 Cedar Ave., 4th Fl., Cleveland, OH 44106. TEL 216-229-9445. FAX 216-229-3236. Ed. Barbara Mooney; Pub. Sandra K. Siebenschuh. adv.: B&W page $3930, color page $4990; trim 8 3/8 x 10 7/8; adv. contact: George Allen. bk.rev. circ. 30,000. **Document type:** trade publication.
Description: For CEOs of growing businesses in Northeast Ohio. Features Northeast Ohio businesses only.

CLIENT DIRECTORY AND AGENCY LIST. see *ADVERTISING AND PUBLIC RELATIONS*

330   US   ISSN 1060-3417
COAST BUSINESS. 1989. bi-w. $22.50. Ship Island Holding Co., Box 1209, Gulfport, MS 39502-1209. TEL 601-868-1182. FAX 601-867-2986. E-mail: coastbusiness@nse.com. Ed. Lauren Thompson; Pub. Jeff Bell. R&P contact: Robert Freeman. adv. contact: Nell Schmidt. bk.rev.; circ. 8,000 (paid). (also avail. in microfilm from UMI) **Document type:** consumer publication.
● Also available online. Vendor(s): UMI.
—UMI.
Description: Covers the business news, people and opportunities in South Mississippi and surrounding counties.

CODE; das andere deutsche Nachrichtenmagazin. see *POLITICAL SCIENCE*

COLECCAO HORIZONTE UNIVERSITARIO. see *POLITICAL SCIENCE*

330   SP
COLECCION TABLERO. irreg. no. 8, 1982. Editorial Planeta, S.A., Corcega, 273-277, 08008 Barcelona, Spain.

330   SP
COLEGIO DE CORREDORES DE COMERCIO DE ZARAGOZA. BOLETIN DE COTIZACION OFICIAL. 52/yr. Colegio de Corredores de Comercio de Zaragoza - College of Business Agents of Zaragoza, San Clemete 21 3o, 50001 Zaragoza, Spain. Ed. Gonzalo Divar Loyola.

330   US
COLLEGE BOULEVARD NEWS. 1984. w. $42. Sun Publications, Inc., 7373 W. 107th St., Overland Park, KS 66212. TEL 913-381-1010. FAX 913-381-9889. Ed. Steve Hale. adv.; illus. circ. 30,000. (tabloid format; back issues avail.)

330 368   CK
COLOMBIA. SUPERINTENDENCIA BANCARIA. SEGUROS Y CAPITALIZACION. 1972. a. free. Superintendencia Bancaria, Apdo. Aereo 3460, Bogota DC, Colombia. TEL 57-1-2804060. FAX 57-1-2800864. circ. 500.

330   US   ISSN 1062-810X
COLORADO SPRINGS BUSINESS JOURNAL. 1989. w. $34.50. 31 E. Platte Ave., Ste. 300, Box 1541, Colorado Springs, CO 80901. TEL 719-634-5905. FAX 719-634-5157. E-mail: mail@scbj.com; editor@csbj.com. Ed. Becky Maxedon; Pub. Charles B. Sheldon. R&P contact: Charles B. Shelden. adv. contact: Roger C. Powell. circ. 9,500. (tabloid format; back issues avail.) **Document type:** trade publication.
● Also available online. Vendor(s): UMI.
Description: Provides local business news, and feature articles of interest to the business and professional community.

330   US   ISSN 0732-1015
HF5429.4.C6
COLORADO STATE AND COUNTY RETAIL SALES BY STANDARD INDUSTRIAL CLASSIFICATION. 1970. q. plus a $75 (subscr. includes Colorado City Retail Sales). University of Colorado, Business Research Division, Campus Box 420, Boulder, CO 80302-0420. TEL 303-492-8227. FAX 303-492-3620. circ. 60. (back issues avail.)
Supersedes in part: Colorado County and City Retail Sales by Standard Industrial Classification (ISSN 0091-4789)

COLUMBIA BUSINESS LAW REVIEW. see *LAW*

330   US   ISSN 0069-6331
COLUMBIA STUDIES IN ECONOMICS. 1968. irreg., no.10, 1979. Columbia University Press, 562 W. 113th St., New York, NY 10025. TEL 212-666-1000. Ed. Kate Witterberg. R&P contact: Lisa Simmars. **Document type:** monographic series.

650   US
COLUMBIA UNIVERSITY GRADUATE SCHOOL OF BUSINESS. DISSERTATIONS SERIES. irreg. price varies. (Columbia University, Graduate School of Business) Free Press, c/o Macmillan, 866 Third Ave., New York, NY 10022. TEL 212-935-2000. FAX 212-605-9364.

BUSINESS AND ECONOMICS 949

330   US
COLUMBUS BUSINESS JOURNAL.* m. $12. 110 N. High St., Gahanna, OH 43230-9069. Ed. Wynn Hollingshead. adv. circ. 18,500. (reprint service avail.)
●Also available online. Vendor(s): Knight-Ridder Information, Inc.
    Formerly: Buckeye Business Journal.

330   UY
LA COMARCA; negocios y empresas del Mercosur. m. Comarca Ltda., Colonia 881, piso 7, Esc. 21, 11100 Montevideo, Uruguay. TEL 911038. Ed. Jose A. Ripoll.

330   BO   ISSN 1017-8856
COMENTARIOS ECONOMICOS DE ACTUALIDAD. Abbreviated title: C E A. (Text in English, Spanish) 1983. s-m. foreign $120 (effective 1998). P.O Box 3-12097 S.M., La Paz, Bolivia. TEL 591-2-431550. FAX 591-2-432554. E-mail: veceba@utam.bolnet. bol. Ed. Guido Cespedes Argandona. **Document type:** newsletter.
    Description: Includes information, analysis and research about economic situations and conditions, investments, international commerce, macroeconomics, trade and industry, ecological development and small business.

330   FR   ISSN 1154-5305
COMMERCE ET FRANCHISE.* 1990. 11/yr. 64 rue du May 1945, 92025 Nanterre Cedex, France. TEL 46-95-10-10. FAX 47-24-76-76. Ed. Jean-Pierre Pamier. circ. 50,000.

330   FR
COMMERCE ET PERSPECTIVES. 1868. 4/yr. A E C C I P, 1 rue Armand-Moisant, 75015 Paris, France. TEL 43-20-98-70. Ed. Georges Guillot. adv. circ. 3,500.

330 004.678   US
COMMERCE EXTRA. m. free. E-mail: news@outreach.com; commerce-request@lists.outreach.com; URL: http://www.outreach.com/commercelink/issue1.html. **Document type:** newsletter.
●Available only online.

330   MK
THE COMMERCIAL. (Text in Arabic, English) m. P.O. Box 5002, Muscat, Sultanate of Oman. TEL 705972. TELEX 3189. adv.

COMMERCIAL AGENCY AND DISTRIBUTORSHIP IN THE ARAB MIDDLE EAST. see LAW

COMMERCIAL CRIME INTERNATIONAL. see CRIMINOLOGY AND LAW ENFORCEMENT

COMMERCIAL LAW REPORT. see LAW

381   IT
COMMERCIO VERONESE. 1971. m. free. Associazione Commercianti della Provincia di Verona, Corso Porta Nuova 4, 37122 Verona, Italy. TEL 045-591688. FAX 045-595846. circ. 10,000.

330   US
COMMITTEE ON THE STATUS OF WOMEN IN THE ECONOMICS PROFESSION. NEWSLETTER. 3/yr. $20 membership. American Economic Association, Committee on the Status of Women in the Economics Profession, Denison University, Granville, OH 43023. TEL 614-587-6574. FAX 614-587-6345. (Subscr. to: Joan Haworth, 4901 Tower Ct., Tallahasse, FL 32303) Ed. Robin Bartlett. **Document type:** newsletter.
    Description: Contains news of the organization and its members; lists career opportunities for women in the economics professions.

COMMON SENSE. see POLITICAL SCIENCE

330.9   US
COMMONWEALTH OF KENTUCKY. ANNUAL ECONOMIC REPORT (YEAR). 1972. a. single copy free. Center for Business & Economic Research, 301 Mathews Bldg., College of Business and Economics, University of Kentucky, Lexington, KY 40506-0047. TEL 606-257-7675. FAX 606-257-7671. Ed. Carol M. Straus. R&P contact: Marie Hart. circ. 1,800. (back issues avail.) **Document type:** academic/scholarly publication.
    Formerly: Kentucky. Council of Economic Advisors. Annual Report (ISSN 0270-238X)
    Description: Analysis of Kentucky's economy, including trends for personal income, employment and earnings by industry.

330   FR   ISSN 0988-3851
COMMUNICATION C B NEWS. 1986. 52/yr. 175-177 rue d'Aguesseau, 92100 Boulogne, France. TEL 46-04-12-12. FAX 46-04-38-52. Ed. Francoise Vidal. circ. 8,718.
    Formerly (until 1988): Communication and Business (ISSN 0299-0334)

330   US
COMMUNIQUE (WASHINGTON, 1971).* 1971. bi-m. membership. World President's Organization, Inc., 1 Canal Center Plz., Ste. 105, Alexandria, VA 22314-1595. TEL 202-508-0144. FAX 202-737-0654. TELEX 4972461 WORBUS. Ed. Ann Marie Ross. bk.rev. circ. 3,500.
    Description: Covers seminars, conferences, member news, and promotion of the organization.

330   UK   ISSN 1357-9428
COMPANY CAR POLICY U.K. a. Monks Partnership Ltd., The Mill House, Wendens Ambo, Saffron Walden, Essex CB11 4JX, England. TEL 44-1799-542222. FAX 44-1799-541805. Ed. Alison Smith. R&P contact: David Atkins. **Document type:** corporate report.

330   UK   ISSN 0966-5269
COMPANY DIGEST. 1982. m. £35($70) Piton Publishing House Ltd., 79-81 High St., Godalming, Surrey GU7 1AW, England. TEL 44-1483-425454. FAX 44-1483-414262. E-mail: digest@digest.co.uk; URL: http://www.companydigest.co.uk. Ed. Peter Tribe. adv.: page £1200; adv. contact: Suzanne Kimber. bk.rev.; charts; illus.; software rev.; circ. 11,200. (back issues avail.) **Document type:** bulletin.

330 320   NE   ISSN 1024-5294
▼**COMPETITION AND CHANGE**; the journal of global political economy. 1996. 4/yr. (in 1 vol., 4 nos./vol.). $46 (effective 1998). Gordon and Breach - Harwood Academic, Amsteldisk 166, 1st Fl., 1079 LH Amsterdam, Netherlands. (Subscr. to: International Publishers Distributor, Box 32160, Newark, NJ 07102. TEL 800-545-8398. FAX 215-750-6343) Eds. Richard Appelbaum, Jeffrey Henderson.
—CCC.
    Description: Examines the changing nature of business organization in a highly competitive global economy.

330   II
COMPETITION LEADER. (Text in English) 1977. m. 7 Old Court House St., Calcutta 700 001, India. Ed. S.C. Talukdar. circ. 97,000.

330   II
COMPETITION REFRESHER. (Text in English) 1984. m. (Bright Careers Institute) Competition Refresher Pvt. Ltd., 2767 Bright House, Darya Ganj, New Delhi 110 002, India. TEL 91-11-3282227. FAX 91-11-3269227. Ed. D.S. Phull; Pub. Pritam Singh Bright. adv.: B&W page Rs.25000, color page Rs.50000; trim 245 x 175. circ. 124,572. circ. 124,572 (paid).
    Refereed Serial

330   II
COMPETITION SUCCESS REVIEW. (Text in English) 1964. m. newsstand price: Rs.21. Competition Review Pvt. Ltd., 604 Prabhat Kiran, Rajendra Place, New Delhi 110 008, India. TEL 11-4712898. FAX 11-5754647. Ed. S.K. Sachdeva. adv.: B&W page Rs.50000, color page Rs.100000; trim 245 x 175. circ. 250,000.

COMPLETING THE INTERNAL MARKET OF THE EUROPEAN COMMUNITY: 1992 LEGISLATION - BUSINESS. see LAW — International Law

COMPUTER BUSINESS REVIEW. see COMPUTERS — Computer Industry

330   UK   ISSN 0965-0997
COMPUTER CONTRACTS AND TENDERS. 1991. w. £395. A L L M Systems and Marketing, 21 Beechcroft Rd., Bushey, Herts. WD2 2JU, England. TEL 44-1923-230150. FAX 44-1923-211148. E-mail: apritchard@cix.compulink.co.uk. Ed. Alan Pritchard; Pub. Alan Pritchard. circ. 200 (paid). (also avail. by e-mail). **Document type:** bulletin.
    Description: Provides information on public- and private-sector computer contracts, items for sale by bid or tender, and business opportunities.

330   US
COMSTOCK'S;* the business of California's capitol region. 1989. m. $30. Comstock Publishing Inc., 3054 Fite Cir., Ste. 108, Sacramento, CA 95827-1809. TEL 916-924-9815. FAX 916-924-9034. Ed. Janice Fillip. adv.; index. circ. 17,000. (back issues avail.) **Document type:** trade publication.
    Description: For top managers including CEOs, presidents, owners of companies, regional managers, government leaders, professionals and entrepreneurs. Profiles community leaders; discusses issues facing communities, and growth in the region.

330   US
CONCEPTS IN ACTION. q. Deloitte & Touche, 10 Westport Rd., C-2 N., Box 820, Wilton, CT 06897. TEL 203-761-3000.

330   US
CONCORD BUSINESS. 1989. a. $2.50. Box 2393, Concord, NH 03301. TEL 603-224-6566. Ed. Kathleen Sheaw; Pub. James C. Boyle. R&P contact: James C. Boyle. adv. contact: James C. Boyle. circ. 5,000. **Document type:** trade publication.
    Description: Covers economic and financial developments in the city of Concord. Written by area businessmen, stockbrokers and bankers.

330   SA   ISSN 0379-9840
THE CONDENSER. 1947. a. free to qualified personnel. Tongaat-Hulett Group Ltd., P.O. Box 3, Tongaat 4400, Natal, South Africa. TEL 27-322-21000. FAX 27-322-21094. TELEX 6-50171. Ed. G.Y. Balfour. circ. 14,000 (controlled). **Document type:** corporate report.
    Description: Expresses views on topics of current affairs that may affect the Tongaat-Hulett Group and its interests, and discusses Group policies. For shareholders, staff, major customers and suppliers.

CONFERENCE AND INCENTIVE TRAVEL. see TRAVEL AND TOURISM

338   US   ISSN 1043-5344
HG4028.C6
CONFERENCE BOARD. SURVEY OF CORPORATE CONTRIBUTIONS. (Subseries of: Conference Board. Report) a. $100 to non-members; members $25. Conference Board, Inc., 845 Third Ave., New York, NY 10022. TEL 212-759-0900. FAX 212-980-7014. (also avail. in microfiche from CIS) **Indexed:** B.P.I., P.A.I.S., SRI. **Document type:** monographic series.
    Former titles: Conference Board. Annual Survey of Corporate Contributions (ISSN 0146-0986); Conference Board. Report on Company Contributions (ISSN 0069-8369)

650 330   US   ISSN 0069-8350
CONFERENCE BOARD CUMULATIVE INDEX. 1963. a. free. Conference Board, Inc., 845 Third Ave., New York, NY 10022. TEL 212-759-0900. FAX 212-980-7014. Ed. Carol Estoppey. circ. 15,000. **Document type:** abstracting/indexing.
—CCC.

330 301   US   ISSN 0363-9460
CONFRONTATION - CHANGE REVIEW. Key Title: Confrontation - Change Literary Review. 1976. q. $16. Economic Research Center, Inc., 3955 Denlinger Rd., Dayton, OH 45426-2329. TEL 513-837-0498. FAX 513-837-5888. Ed. Frederick M. Finney. adv.; bk.rev.; film rev.; play rev.; bibl.; charts; illus.; stat.; index. circ. 1,000. **Indexed:** Psychol.Abstr.
    Incorporated: Journal of Applied Social and Economic Sciences.

CONJONCTURE ECONOMIQUE DES REGIONS DU QUEBEC EN (YEAR). see BUSINESS AND ECONOMICS — Production Of Goods And Services

BUSINESS AND ECONOMICS

330   AG
CONSEJO TECNICO DE INVERSIONES. INFORME ESPECIAL. (Text in English, Spanish) 1975. s-a. $100. Consejo Tecnico de Inversiones, S.A., Tucuman 834, 1o piso, 1049 Buenos Aires, Argentina. FAX 541-322-4887.
    Description: Current economic updates and 5-year projections.

CONSTRUCTION SURVEY. see *BUILDING AND CONSTRUCTION*

330   SG
CONSTRUIRE L'AFRIQUE. 1985. 6/yr. B.P. 3770, Dakar, Senegal. TEL 24-19-61. FAX 23-07-90. Ed. Cheikh-Ousmane Diallo.

330   IT
CONSULENZA; settimanale di informazione e commenti operativi per l'azienda. 1976. w. L.320000. Luigi Buffetti S.p.A., Via del Fosso di S. Maura snc, 00169 Rome, Italy. TEL 06-231951. FAX 06-2677347. TELEX 630096 BUFF. Ed. Sergio Milocco. adv. circ. 16,000.

330 346   IT
CONSULENZA AMBIENTE. 1993. m. L.230000 (foreign L.460000) (effective 1993). I P S O A s.r.l. (Subsidiary of: Wolters Kluwer N.V.), Strada 1, Palazzo F6, 20090 Milanofiori - Assago, Italy. TEL 02-82476328. FAX 02-82476645. Ed. Massimiliano Galioni.

330   US   ISSN 0887-0314
CONSULTING INTELLIGENCE. 1983. bi-m. $48. American Consultants League, 1290 Palm Ave., Sarasota, FL 34236. TEL 914-952-9290. FAX 914-379-6024. Ed. Hubert Bermont. adv. contact: Hubert Bermont. circ. 1,000. **Document type:** trade publication.

CONSULTING RATES AND BUSINESS PRACTICES. ANNUAL SURVEY. see *OCCUPATIONS AND CAREERS*

CONSULTING SUCCESS. see *ADVERTISING AND PUBLIC RELATIONS*

CONSUMER CREDIT CONTROL. see *LAW*

330   BG
CONSUMER - ECONOMIST. (Text in English) 1980. w. Tk.150($50) Newlook Publishers, 121 Jubilee Rd., Chittagong, Bangladesh. TEL 226288. FAX 880-31-227337. Ed. Moyeen Ul Alam. circ. 16,000. (reprint service avail.)
    Description: Covers development, economics, international relations and general interest.

CONSUMER PROTECTION, ANTITRUST & UNFAIR BUSINESS PRACTICES NEWSLETTER. see *CONSUMER EDUCATION AND PROTECTION*

330   US   ISSN 0273-2475
TX335
CONSUMERISM. (Subseries of: S I R S Social Issues (ISSN 0740-3127)) 1979. a. price varies; a. supplement $19. Social Issues Resources Series, Box 2348, Boca Raton, FL 33427-2348. TEL 561-994-0079; 800-232-SIRS. FAX 561-994-4704. E-mail: custserve@sirs.com; URL: http://www.sirs.com. Ed. Trudy Collins; Pub. Eleanor Goldstein. R&P contact: Bonnie Milnes. (looseleaf format; back issues avail.) **Document type:** academic/scholarly publication.
    Description: Reprints articles that cover consumer rights and marketing.

330   CU
CONTACTOS; la revista para hombres de negocios. 1993. m. $30. Camara de Comercio - Chamber of Commerce, Calle 21 No. 661, esq. A, Casilla 4237, Vedado, Havana, Cuba. TEL 30-3356. FAX 5-37-33-3042. TELEX 51-1752. Ed. Fernando Davalos. adv.: color page $1000; adv. contact: Sandra Gonzalez. **Document type:** trade publication.

330   FR   ISSN 1166-4231
CONTACTS A V A (Assurances Vieillesse des Artisans) 1963. 5/yr. free. Institution d'Assurances Vieillesse des Artisans, 28 bd. de Grenelle, 75737 Paris Cedex 15, France. TEL 33-1-44375232. FAX 33-1-44375205. Ed. Philippe Bollecker. R&P contact: Lucien Chauvier. bk.rev. circ. 1,180,000. **Document type:** trade publication.
    Description: Covers commercial, economic, and social security matters, as they affect artisans in France and the EU.

330   US   ISSN 1074-3529
HD72
CONTEMPORARY ECONOMIC POLICY. 1982. q. $110 (foreign $125) (effective 1997). Western Economic Association International, 7400 Center Ave., Ste. 109, Huntington Beach, CA 92647-3039. TEL 714-898-3222. (Dist. by: Allen Press, Inc., Box 1897, Lawrence, KS 66044) Ed. Darwin C. Hall. R&P contact: Eldon J. Dvorak. adv. circ. 3,000. (also avail. in microfilm from UMI) **Indexed:** ABI Inform., Amer.Hist.& Life (1982-), ASCA, Chic.Per.Ind., Crim.Just.Abstr., Curr.Cont., Energy Rev., Hist.Abstr. (1982-), Ind.Per.Art.Relat.Law, J.of Econ Lit., P.A.I.S., Polit.Sci.Abstr., Sage Pub.Admin.Abstr., Soc.Sci.Ind. (1994-), SSCI, SSCI, World Bank.Abstr., World Bibl.Soc.Sec. **Document type:** academic/scholarly publication.
    ●Also available online. Vendor(s): Information Access Co.
    —BLDSC (3425.179450); Genuine Article; KR SourceOne; SWETS; UMI; UnCover. **CCC.**
    Formerly (until 1994): Contemporary Policy Issues (ISSN 0735-0007)
    Refereed Serial

330 332   US
CONTEMPORARY STUDIES IN ECONOMIC AND FINANCIAL ANALYSIS; an international series of monographs. 1976. irreg., vol.79, 1996. $73.25. J A I Press Inc., 55 Old Post Rd., No. 2, Box 1678, Greenwich, CT 06830-1678. TEL 203-661-7602. FAX 203-661-0792. E-mail: jai@jaipress.com. (Subscr. in UK and Europe to: JAI Press Ltd., 38 Tavistock St., Covent Garden, London WC2E 7PB, England. TEL 44-171-379-8834. FAX 44-171-379-8835) charts; stat. **Document type:** monographic series.

330 658   US   ISSN 0045-8376
HF5429.3
CONTINENTAL FRANCHISE REVIEW. 1968. bi-w. $195 (foreign $225) (effective 1997). Sparks Publishing Co., Inc., 7009 S. Potomac, Ste 109, Englewood, CO 80112. TEL 303-799-1112; 800-938-1044. FAX 303-799-1115. Ed. Nancy Weingartner; Pub. Janet Sparks. R&P contact: Janet Sparks. bk.rev.; index. (looseleaf format; back issues avail.) **Document type:** newsletter.

330   GW   ISSN 0178-5737
CONTRASTE; Monatszeitung fuer Selbstverwaltung. 1984. m. DM.80. Contraste e.V., Postfach 104520, 69035 Heidelberg, Germany. TEL 49-6221-162467. FAX 49-6221-164489. **Document type:** newspaper.

330   IT
CONTRATTI. 1993. bi-m. L.140000 (foreign L.280000). I P S O A s.r.l. (Subsidiary of: Wolters Kluwer N.V.), Strada 1, Palazzo F6, 20090 Assago Milanofiori (MI), Italy. TEL 39-2-824761. Ed. Massimiliano Galioni. adv.: B&W page L.3000000, color page L.5000000; adv. contact: Luciano Alcaro Menichini. **Document type:** consumer publication.

330   BL
CONTRIBUICOES EM ECONOMIA. 1977. irreg. Editora Campus Ltda. (Subsidiary of: Elsevier Science B.V.), Rua Sete se Setembro 111-16 andar, 20159-900 Centro, Rio de Janeiro RJ, Brazil. TEL 021-221-5340. FAX 021-252-2904. Ed. Claudio M. Rothmuller. illus. **Document type:** monographic series.

330   US   ISSN 1081-9215
HG4001
CONTROLLER'S COST REPORT. 1979. m. $134.50 (foreign $191.35) (effective 1995). Warren, Gorham & Lamont, One Penn Plaza, New York, NY 10119. TEL 212-971-5000. FAX 212-971-5113. (Subscr. to: The Park Square Bldg., 31 St. James Ave., Boston, MA 02116-4112. TEL 800-950-1207) Ed. Paul J. Wendell. (also avail. in microform from UMI) **Document type:** newsletter.
    ●Also available online. Vendor(s): Information Access Co.
    —UMI.
    Former titles (until 1995): Wendell's Report for Controllers (ISSN 1067-7313); (until 1993): C F O Alert (Monthly) (ISSN 0894-4822); (until 1987): Corporate Controllers Report (ISSN 0745-3078); (until 1982): Corporate Controller's and Treasurer's Report (ISSN 0274-6107)
    Description: Focuses exclusively on all areas of crucial interest to chief financial officers, from taxes and legal developments to operations and compensation, giving quick access to the latest ideas and methods.

CONTUREN. see *LITERARY AND POLITICAL REVIEWS*

330   US
COOPERS & LYBRAND. MONOGRAPH SERIES. irreg., latest no.3, 1995. price varies. Coopers & Lybrand L.L.P., Publishing Division, 1530 Wilson Blvd., Arlington, VA 22209. TEL 703-908-1527; 800-247-6553. (back issues avail.) **Document type:** monographic series.

330   NQ
COORDINADORA REGIONAL DE INVESTIGACIONES ECONOMICAS Y SOCIALES. CUADERNOS. (In 5 series: Debates, Ensayos, Avances, Documentos, Bibliografias) 1982. irreg. Coordinadora Regional de Investigaciones Economicas y Sociales, Apdo. 3516, Managua, Nicaragua. Ed.Bd.

330   US
▼**COPYSOURCE QUARTERLY.** 1997. q. $199. Bureau of Business Practice, 24 Rope Ferry Rd., Waterford, CT 06386. TEL 860-442-4365. FAX 860-437-3555. URL: http://www.bbpnews.com. Ed. Kathy Cipriani; Pub. Peter Garabedian. R&P contact: Debra Ferraro. **Document type:** newsletter.
    Description: Resource for producing in-house newsletters. Includes topics such as: leadership and teamwork, financial planning, customer service, health and safety, personal and professional development, and sales.

330   CK
CORPORACION FINANCIERA COLOMBIANA. EJERCICIO. a. Corporacion Financiera Colombiana, Carrera nos. 26-45, Apdo Aereo 11843, Bogota, Colombia.

330   US
CORPORATE ALMANAC. a. Cognetics, Inc., 100 Cambridge Park Dr., Cambridge, MA 02140. Eds. David Birch, Anne Haggerty.

330 340   US   ISSN 1061-8775
KF1397
CORPORATE CONDUCT QUARTERLY; a practical guide for corporate ethics & compliance. 1991. q. $50. Rutgers University, Camden, 401 Cooper St., Camden, NJ 08102. TEL 609-225-6311. FAX 609-225-6559. E-mail: ccq@clam.rutgers.edu; URL: http://camden-www.rutgers.edu/~ccq. Eds. Jay A. Sigler, Joseph E. Murphy. R&P contact: Kevin Borrup. adv.; bk.rev.; video rev. circ. 1,400. **Document type:** newsletter.

330   US   ISSN 1062-368X
CORPORATE DETROIT MAGAZINE.* 1984. m. $29. Corporate Detroit, Inc., 19512 Livernois Ave., Detroit, MI 48221-1766. TEL 313-872-6000. FAX 313-872-6009. Ed. Claire Hinsberg; Pub. Dale Jaslove. adv.; circ. 27,000 (controlled). (also avail. in microform from UMI) **Indexed:** Tr.& Indus.Ind.
    ●Also available online. Vendor(s): Knight-Ridder Information, Inc., UMI.
    —UMI.
    Former titles (until 1991): Business Detroit (ISSN 1062-3671); (until 1990): Michigan Business (ISSN 0886-5639)

330   CN
CORPORATE ELITE. 1990. a. Financial Post Co., Ltd., 333 King St. E., Toronto, ON M5A 4N2, Canada. TEL 416-350-6176. FAX 416-599-6171. R&P contact: Theresa Butcher. adv.

330 338 US ISSN 0361-2309
HD60.5.U5
CORPORATE EXAMINER. 1972. 10/yr. $35 (Canada & Mexico $40; elsewhere $45) (effective 1998). Interfaith Center on Corporate Responsibility, Rm. 550, 475 Riverside Dr., New York, NY 10115-0500. TEL 212-870-2296. Ed. Diane Bratcher; Pub. Timothy Smith. bk.rev. circ. 1,500. **Indexed:** HR Rep. **Document type:** newsletter, trade publication.

330 US
KF1397.C65
CORPORATE EXECUTIVE. 1986. 6/yr. $350. Executive Press, Box 3895, San Francisco, CA 94119. TEL 510-685-5111. Ed. Jesse M. Brill. index. (back issues avail.) **Document type:** newsletter.

330 CN
CORPORATE EXECUTIVE; news atlantic. 1992. 9/yr. Can.$18. Nationwide Promotion Limited, 12 Dawn Dr., Dartmouth, NS B3B 1H9, Canada. TEL 902-468-5141. FAX 902-468-6219. Ed. Bill Harris. adv.: B&W page Can.$1525, color page Can.$2325; 9 1/4 x 11 7/8; adv. contact: Bill Harris. circ. 38,000. (tabloid format) **Document type:** newspaper.
Description: Current business articles directed at upper management covering all of the Atlantic Canada, New England, and Europe.

330 US ISSN 0163-3031
HG4057
CORPORATE FINANCE SOURCEBOOK; the guide to major capital investment sources and related financial services. 1980. a. $499.95. National Register Publishing, A Division of Reed Elsevier Inc., 121 Chanlon Rd., New Providence, NJ 07974. TEL 908-464-6800. FAX 908-665-6688. TELEX 138 755. E-mail: info@redref.com; URL: http://www.reedref.com. (Subscr. to: National Register Publishing, Box 31, New Providence, NJ 07974-9903. TEL 800-521-8110) adv.; tr.lit. circ. 10,122. **Document type:** directory.
—CCC.
Description: Includes 18 highly specialized chapters including: venture capital, major private lenders, commercial finance, leasing, commercial banks, US-based foreign banks, investment banks, foreign investment banks in the US, business intermediaries, pension managers, master trusts, cash managers, business insurance brokers, real estate services, securities analysts, and CPAs. Chapter 19 includes a listing of mergers and acquisitions, and a three-year financing retrospective.

330 UK ISSN 0964-8410
HD2741
CORPORATE GOVERNANCE; an international review. 1992. q. £170($238) (foreign £170) (effective 1997). Blackwell Publishers Ltd., 108 Cowley Rd., Oxford OX4 1JF, England. TEL 44-1865-791100. FAX 44-1865-791347. E-mail: jnlinfo@blackwellpublishers.co.uk; URL: http://www.blackwellpublishers.co.uk. Ed. Bob Tricker. **Indexed:** Cont.Pg.Manage. **Document type:** academic/scholarly publication.
—BLDSC (3472.066100); UMI. **CCC.**
Refereed Serial

332.6 US
CORPORATE GROWTH.* 1968. m. $198. Princeton Research Institute, Western Management Center, Box 2702, Scottsdale, AZ 85252-2072. TEL 609-396-0305. (Subscr. to: Box 2702, Scottsdale, AZ 85252) (also avail. in microform from UMI) **Indexed:** ABI Inform.
Description: Covers all aspects of mergers, acquisitions, divestitures, corporate growth and development world-wide.

330 384 UK
CORPORATE I T UPDATE. (Not avail. in print format) m. £100($170) (effective 1997). M2 Communications Ltd., P.O. Box 475, Coventry CV1 2ZW, England. TEL 44-1203-634700. FAX 44-1203-634144. E-mail: di@m2.com; URL: http://www.m2.com. Ed. Darren Ingram. **Document type:** trade publication.
●Available only online.
Description: Briefing for executives who need a jargon-free update on the issues, technologies and products relevant to the corporate organizations which emerge from the rapidly-changing IT and telecomms marketplace.

338.09 II
CORPORATE OBSERVER. 1982. q. $200. Pranava Industrial Services Pvt. Ltd., 18, Sagar Tarang, Bhulabhai Desai Road, Bombay 400 036, India. TEL 822-6236. Ed. P.J. Divatia.

330 US ISSN 0890-4278
HC107.W63
CORPORATE REPORT WISCONSIN. 1985. m. $18. The Brady Co., Inc., N80 W12878 Fond du Lac Ave., Box 878, Menomonee Falls, WI 53052-0878. TEL 414-255-9077. FAX 414-255-3388. Ed. Karl F. Ohm, Sr.; Pub. Karl F. Ohm, Sr. adv.: B&W page $2435, color page $2885. bk.rev. circ. 28,000 (controlled). (also avail. in microform from UMI)
●Also available online. Vendor(s): UMI.
—UMI.
Description: Monthly business magazine for executives in the state of Wisconsin.

338 US
CORPORATE RESPONSIBILITY.* 1972. bi-m. $85. 658 Counselors Way, Williamsburg, VA 23185-4059. Ed. Judith Mackey.

330 371.4 US ISSN 1050-2386
LB2342
CORPORATE SUPPORT OF EDUCATION. a. Council for Aid to Education, 342 Madison Ave., Ste. 1532, New York, NY 10173-0002. TEL 212-661-9766. FAX 212-661-5800. Ed. David Morgan. R&P contact: David Morgan. **Indexed:** SRI.
Formerly: Corporate Support of Higher Education (ISSN 0270-4501)

CORPORATE YELLOW BOOK; who's who at the leading U.S. companies. see BUSINESS AND ECONOMICS — Management

330 UK
CORPORATION OF LONDON. SUBJECT REPORT. irreg., vol.9, 1994. Corporation of London, Public Relations Office, Guildhall, London EC2P 2EJ, England. **Document type:** bulletin.

330 US
CORPUS CHRISTI BAY AREA BUSINESS. 1992. q. $8.95. (Corpus Christi Area Development Corporation) Woolford Publishing (Subsidiary of: Leah Woolford & Co., Inc.), 711 N. Carancahua St., Ste. 500, Corpus Christi, TX 78475-1301. TEL 512-883-8833. FAX 512-883-4329. (Co-sponsor: Corpus Christi Chamber of Commerce) Ed. Jeffrey R. Woolford. adv.: page $1000; adv. contact: Jeff Woolford. bk.rev.; stat.; circ. 6,500 (controlled). (back issues avail.) **Document type:** trade publication.
Description: Targets business and industry decision-makers with articles on business, small-business management, trade with Mexico, and sales and personnel management.

330 FR
CORRESPONDANCE ECONOMIQUE; quotidien d'informations économiques et sociales. 1945. d. 26700 F. (foreign 30680 F.) (effective 1997). Societe Generale de Presse et d'Editions, 13 av. de l'Opera, 75001 Paris, France. TEL 40-15-17-89. FAX 40-15-17-15. TELEX SOGPRESS 230023. Ed. Etienne Lacour; Pub. Marianne Berard Quelin. adv.
Description: Provides economic, social and financial information.

330 IT
CORRIERE TRIBUTARIO. 1978. w. L.380000 (foreign L.760000). I P S O A s.r.l. (Subsidiary of: Wolters Kluwer N.V.), Strada 1, Palazzo F6, 20090 Assago Milanofiori (MI), Italy. TEL 39-2-824761. Ed. Massimiliano Galioni. adv.: B&W page L.4500000; adv. contact: Luciano Alcaro Menichini. bk.rev.; index. circ. 39,500.

COSTA RICA ADVENTURE & BUSINESS. see GENERAL INTEREST PERIODICALS — Costa Rica

690 387.1 IT ISSN 1121-6352
COSTRUIRE CANTIERE. 1992. m. Editrice Abitare Segesta S.p.A., Corso Monforte 15, 20122 Milan, Italy. TEL 39-2-760901. FAX 39-2-76021904. Ed. Leonardo Fiori; Pub. Renato Mezzi. adv. contact: Pierluigi Bollini. **Document type:** trade publication.

330 BE
COTE LIBRE.* (Text in French) 5/w. Rue de Birmingham 131, 1070 Brussels, Belgium. TEL 2-5265666. FAX 2-5265526. adv. circ. 4,000. **Document type:** newspaper.

COTTON ECONOMIC REVIEW. see AGRICULTURE — Crop Production And Soil

332 382 US ISSN 1041-3553
HC10
COUNTRY FORECASTS (SYRACUSE). 1985. s-a. $495 (foreign $545) (effective 1997). The P R S Group, Box 248, East Syracuse, NY 13057-0248. TEL 315-431-0511. FAX 315-431-0200. URL: http://www.countrydata.com. Eds. William D. Coplin, Michael K. O'Leary. (also avail. in diskette format; back issues avail.)
●Also available online. Vendor(s): Data-Star (FSRI), Information Access Co., Knight-Ridder Information, Inc., NewsNet (IT933).
Incorporates (1981-1988): Political Climate for International Business (ISSN 0887-7637); (1986-1988): Political Risk Database (ISSN 0890-4928); (1986-1988): Country Database (ISSN 0890-4952); Former titles (until 1988): Country Facts (ISSN 0889-5007); Country Data Quarterly.
Description: Contains rankings and data for 100 countries on political, economic, and social variables; methods of data-gathering and forecasting; and assumptions underlying the forecasts.

330 US
COUP;* information for development executives. 1983. q. $100. Venture Capital Consultants America, 917 S. Park St., Owosso, MI 48867-4422. Eds. Ben Campbell, Jeff Campbell. adv.; bk.rev.; charts; illus.; pat.; stat.; tr.lit.; index. circ. 3,000. (looseleaf format; also avail. in microfilm; back issues avail.)
Formerly: Venture Capital.
Description: Reports on acquisitions, mergers, divestitures, venture capital, private placements, corporate financing, planning takeovers, writing investment proposals, and sources of secret business information for practitioners.

330 TI ISSN 0330-1516
COURRIER DE L'INDUSTRIE. 1977. bi-m. free. Agence de Promotion de l'Industrie - Industrial Promotion Agency, rue Isle de Syrie, 1002 Tunis Belvedere, Tunisia. TEL 792144. FAX 782482. TELEX 14166 TN. Ed.Bd. illus.; stat.; tr.lit. circ. 8,000. (back issues avail.)

330 333.33 FR
COURRIER DES EMPLOYES D'IMMEUBLES. 12/yr. 39 rue Vivienne, 75002 Paris, France. TEL 42-36-69-25. Ed. Jacques Simakis. circ. 22,000.

332 320 FR ISSN 0590-0239
COURRIER DES PAYS DE L'EST. 1964. m. (10/yr.). 640 F. (Europe 680 F., elsewhere 730 F.) (effective 1997). (Centre d'Etudes et de Documentation sur l'Ex-U R S S, la Chine et l'Europe de l'Est) Documentation Francaise, 29-31 quai Voltaire, 75344 Paris Cedex 07, France. TEL 33-1-40157000. FAX 33-1-40157230. (Subscr. to: 124 rue Henri Barbusse, 93308 Aubervilliers Cedex, France. TEL 33-1-48395600. FAX 33-1-48395601) (Co-sponsor: Centre d'Etudes Prospectives et d'Information Internationales) Ed. Martine Viallet. adv.; bk.rev.; index. circ. 1,300. (also avail. in microfiche from DFR) **Indexed:** Key to Econ.Sci., P.A.I.S.For.Lang.Ind., Pt.de Rep. (1989-). **Document type:** government publication.
—BLDSC (3483.080000); SWETS.

330 SZ
COURRIER UVACIM. m. Case Postale 1471, CH-1001 Lausanne, Switzerland. TEL 021-361871. FAX 021-364866. circ. 16,000.

330 US
COURT & COMMERCIAL RECORD. 1895. 3/w. $89. 431 N. Pennsylvania, Indianapolis, IN 46204. TEL 317-636-0200. FAX 317-263-5060. Ed. Chris Banquis; Pub. Glenda Russell. R&P contact: Glenda Russell. adv. contact: Judy Atwater. circ. 850 (paid). **Document type:** newspaper.
Formerly: Indianapolis Commercial (ISSN 1059-9649)

330 SP ISSN 1130-9784
COYUNTURA ECONOMICA DE NAVARRA. 1991. q. free. (Departamento de Economia y Hacienda) Gobierno de Navarra, Fondo de Publicaciones, Navas de Tolosa 21, 31002 Pamplona, Spain. TEL 34-48-107121. FAX 34-48-227673.

BUSINESS AND ECONOMICS

382 US ISSN 0149-6956
CRAIN'S CHICAGO BUSINESS. 1978. w. $81 (effective Jan. 1995). Crain Communications, Inc. (Chicago), 740 N. Rush St., Chicago, IL 60611-2525. TEL 312-649-5270. FAX 312-649-5228. (Subscr. to: 965 E. Jefferson Ave., Detroit, MI 48207-3185. TEL 800-678-9595) Ed. David Snyder. adv. contact: 50,000. (tabloid format; also avail. in microfiche from UMI; reprint service avail. from UMI.) Indexed: Tr.& Indus.Ind. **Document type:** consumer publication.
●Also available online. Vendor(s): Information Access Co., Knight-Ridder Information, Inc., Lexis-Nexis (CHIBUS).
—UMI. CCC.

330 US ISSN 0882-1992
CRAIN'S DETROIT BUSINESS. w. $40 (foreign $82). Crain Communications, Inc. (Detroit), 1400 Woodbridge Ave., Detroit, MI 48207-3187. TEL 313-446-0426. FAX 313-446-1650. (Subscr. to: 965 E. Jefferson Ave., Detroit, MI 48207-9966) Ed. Mary Kramer; Pub. Keith E. Crain. adv. contact: Judy Siner. circ. 35,042. Indexed: Tr.& Indus.Ind. **Document type:** newspaper.
●Also available online. Vendor(s): Information Access Co., Knight-Ridder Information, Inc., Lexis-Nexis.
—UMI. CCC.
Description: Covers metro Detroit business exclusively.

330 US ISSN 8756-789X
HC107.N7
CRAIN'S NEW YORK BUSINESS. 1985. w. $62; newsstand price: $2. Crain Communications, Inc. (New York), 220 E. 42nd St., Ste. 1306, New York, NY 10017. TEL 212-210-0277; 800-678-9595. FAX 212-210-0799. (Subscr. to: 965 E. Jefferson Ave., Detroit, MI 48207-9966. TEL 800-992-9970) Ed. Greg David. adv.; bk.rev. circ. 65,000. (tabloid format; also avail. in microform; back issues avail.) Indexed: Tr.& Indus.Ind. **Document type:** newspaper.
●Also available online. Vendor(s): Information Access Co., Knight-Ridder Information, Inc., Lexis-Nexis (NYBUS).
—UMI. CCC.
Description: Covers business and related issues in New York.

330 UK ISSN 0963-1690
HD35
CREATIVITY AND INNOVATION MANAGEMENT. 1992. q. £135($189) (foreign £135) (effective 1997). Blackwell Publishers Ltd., 108 Cowley Rd., Oxford OX4 1JF, England. TEL 44-1865-791100. FAX 44-1865-791347. E-mail: jnlinfo@ blackwellpublishers.co.uk; URL: http://www. blackwellpublishers.co.uk. Eds. Susan Moger, Tudor Rickards. Indexed: Cont.Pg.Manage. **Document type:** academic/scholarly publication.
—BLDSC (3487.250400); UMI. CCC.
Description: Promotes underderstanding and scholarship internationally in the fields of creativity and innovation.
Refereed Serial

330 US ISSN 1055-8225
CREDIT & FINANCE.* (Supplement avail.) 1991. q. $29.99. Publishing & Business Consultants, 101 W. 64th St. Unit 3-2, Inglewood, CA 90302-1255. TEL 213-732-3477. FAX 213-732-9123. (Subscr. to: Box 75392, Los Angeles, CA 90075) Ed. Andeson Napoleon Atia. adv. circ. 120,000. **Document type:** consumer publication.
Description: Covers consumer related credit issues.

330 CK
CRITERIO ECONOMICO. 1965. 3/yr. exchange basis. Sociedad Colombiana de Economistas, Apdo. Aereo 8429, Bogota, Colombia. adv.; bk.rev.; abstr.; illus.; stat. circ. 2,000.
Former titles (until no.27, 1976): Sociedad Colombiana de Economistas. Revista; Sociedad Colombiana de Economistas. Boletin Informativo.

330 340.5 UK
341.7582
CRONER'S MODEL BUSINESS CONTRACTS. Variant title: Model Business Contracts. 1988. base vol. (plus 3/yr. updates). £152 (updates £97) (effective 1995). Croner Publications Ltd. (Subsidiary of: Wolters Kluwer N.V.), Croner House, 100 London Rd., Kingston-upon-Thames, Surrey TW2 6SR, England. TEL 44-181-547-3333. FAX 44-181-547-2637. TELEX 267778. (looseleaf format) **Document type:** newsletter.
Description: Provides model forms of contracts for the purchase and sales of goods and services, in addition to building contracts, contracts of carriage, provision of financial services, and intellectual property rights protection.

330 UY
CRONICAS ECONOMICAS. 1981. w. Avda. del Libertador Brig. Gral. Lavalleja, Montevideo, Uruguay. Ed.Bd.

330 CL ISSN 0716-0046
CUADERNOS DE ECONOMIA. (Text in Spanish; summaries in English) 1963. 3/yr. Esc.10000 (Latin America $42; Europe & US $50) (effective 1997). Pontificia Universidad Catolica de Chile, Instituto de Economia, Casilla 76, Correo 17, Santiago, Chile. TEL 56-2-6864314. FAX 56-2-5521310. TELEX 240395-PUC-VA-CL. E-mail: cgarces@volcan.facea.puc.cl. Ed. Vittorio Corbo. R&P contact: Ana Maria Aguirre. adv.; bk.rev.; bibl.; charts; stat.; tr.lit.; circ. controlled. (looseleaf format; also avail. in record; back issues avail.) Indexed: Hisp.Amer.Per.Ind. (1970-), IBR, J.of Econ.Lit., P.A.I.S.For.Lang.Ind., P.A.I.S., Rural Recreat.Tour.Abstr., World Agri.Econ.& Rural Sociol.Abstr. **Document type:** academic/scholarly publication.
—BLDSC (3490.662800); SWETS.
Description: Emphasizes Latin American economic problems, includes theoretical issues related to Latin American countries. Focuses on applied work for use in the design and evaluation of economic policies.
Refereed Serial

330 SP ISSN 0210-0266
HC10
CUADERNOS DE ECONOMIA.* 1973. 3/yr. $20. Universidad de Barcelona, Departamento de Teoria Economica, Gran Via de les Cortes Catalanes 585, 08007 Barcelona, Spain. adv.; bk.rev.
—CINDOC.
Supersedes (1955-1969): Cuadernos de Informacion Economica (ISSN 0590-1979)

330 VE
HC10
CUADERNOS DE INFORMACION ECONOMICA. 1949. s-a. Corporacion Venezolana de Fomento, Unidad de Estudios, Edificio Norte, Centro Simon Bolivar, Caracas, Venezuela. charts; stat.

330 SP ISSN 1132-9386
CUADERNOS DE INFORMACION ECONOMICA. 1987. m. (10/yr.). 10000 ptas. (foreign 13000 ptas.) (effective 1997). Fundacion de las Cajas de Ahorros Confederadas para la Investigacion Economica y Social, Padre Damian, 48, 28036 Madrid, Spain. TEL 34-1-3596158. FAX 34-1-3504959. (Subscr. to: Juan Hurtado de Mendoza, 19, 28036 Madrid, Spain. TEL 34-1-3504400. FAX 34-1-3508040) Ed. Fernando Gonzalez Olivares; Pub. Victorio Valle Sanchez. circ. 2,500. (also avail. in microfiche) **Document type:** trade publication.
Description: Covers all economic and financial topics, both national and international.

330 CU ISSN 0864-4675
CUBA ECONOMICA. 1990. 4/yr. $20 in S. America; N. America $24; elsewhere $28. Ediciones Cubanas, Obispo No. 527, Apdo. 605, Havana, Cuba. circ. 8,000.

659 US
CUSTOMER SERVICE; a journal of theory, service and practices. 1990. s-a. $50. International Customer Service Association, 401 N. Michigan Ave., Chicago, IL 60611-4267. TEL 312-321-6800. FAX 312-321-6869. Ed. Mark Nelson. adv.: page $1600; adv. contact: Jennifer Maher. circ. 4,000. (back issues avail.) **Document type:** academic/scholarly publication.
Formerly: I C S A Journal (ISSN 1074-5467)
Description: Features in-depth articles on a variety of customer service issues.
Refereed Serial

330 003 BE
CYBERARIAN'S GUIDE TO CYBER - MARKETING. w.? I O Communications, 182 B Ch. de Charleroi, 1060 Brussels, Belgium. TEL 32-2-534-07-37. FAX 32-2-534-07-57. E-mail: mbauwens@iocom.be; URL: http://www.iocom.be/pilot/cybermarketing/. Ed. Michel Bauwens.
●Also available online.
Description: Summarizes resources in the field of interactive marketing, online advertising, electronic commerce, and their enabling technologies.

330 004.6 US
▼**CYBERHOUND'S GUIDE TO COMPANIES ON THE INTERNET.** 1996. irreg. $79. Gale Research, 835 Penobscot Bldg., 645 Griswold St., Detroit, MI 48226-4094. TEL 313-961-2242; 800-877-4253. FAX 800-414-5043. E-mail: daniel__snyder@gale.com. **Document type:** directory.
Description: Publishes information on more than 2000 corporate sites.

330 US ISSN 1081-6577
D B A HOUSTON. 1990. m. $22.95. Impax Enterprises Inc., 13111 Westheimer Rd., No. 315, Houston, TX 77077-5520. TEL 713-870-9933. FAX 713-870-9996. Ed. Cathy Schmerund; Pub. Bob Orkand. R&P contact: Bob Orkand. adv.: B&W page $3060, color page $3498; trim 8 3/8 x 10 7/8; adv. contact: Ellen Polansky. circ. 25,000.
Description: Covers business in the Houston area.

330 IE ISSN 1393-290X
▼**D C U B S RESEARCH PAPERS.** 1996. s-a. I£5 (overseas I£8). Dublin City University Business School, Glasnevin, Dublin 9, Ireland. TEL 353-1-7045452. E-mail: ohalpine@ccmail.dcu. ie. Ed. Eunan O'Halpin. **Document type:** academic/scholarly publication.
—BLDSC (7752.002000).

D J OE F - HAANDBOGEN; opslagsbog for tillidsrepraesentanter i D J OE F. (Danmarks Jurist- og Oekonomforbund) see *LAW*

330 PH ISSN 0116-7111
D L S U BUSINESS & ECONOMICS REVIEW. (Text in English) 1983. s-a. P.140($16) De La Salle University, College of Business and Economics, 2401 Taft Ave., Manila, Philippines. TEL 2-594832. FAX 632-521-9094. adv.; bk.rev. circ. 300. **Document type:** academic/scholarly publication.
Formerly: Journal of Business and Economics.
Description: Publishes scholarly articles reflecting significant quantitative or qualitative research. Includes speeches, research reports, and "state of the art" papers.

330 US
D R I - MCGRAW-HILL U S ECONOMIC OUTLOOK. m. D R I - McGraw-Hill, 24 Hartwell Ave., Lexington, MA 02173. TEL 617-863-5100. FAX 617-860-6332. TELEX 200 284. Ed. Cynthia Latta. **Document type:** trade publication.
Formerly: D R I - McGraw-Hill U S Executive Report.

330 SW ISSN 0346-640X
DAGENS INDUSTRI. Variant title: Di. (Supplement avail.: Svensk Handel) (Text in Swedish; summaries in English) 1976. 240/yr. SEK 1950 in Scandinavia; Europe SEK 4350; elsewhere SEK 5050. Dagens Industri AB, P.O. Box 3177, S-103 63 Stockholm, Sweden. TEL 46-8-736-50-00. FAX 46-8-789-88-67. Ed. Hasse Olsson. adv.: B&W page SEK 54000, color page SEK 86400; trim 280 x 385; adv. contact: Soeren Sunmo. circ. 83,500. cols./p.: 5. (tabloid format) Indexed: Paper & Bd.Abstr. **Document type:** newspaper.
Formed by the merger of (1961-1976): Elektroniknyhetarna (ISSN 0345-2824); (1946-1976): Ingenjoertidningen Teknisk Information (ISSN 0040-2311); (1965-1976): Modern Datateknik (ISSN 0026-7686); (1968-1976): Modern Kemi (ISSN 0047-7710); (1965-1976): Moderna Transporter (ISSN 0026-8585); Modern Ytbehandling (ISSN 0302-8321); (1962-1976): Pack-Distribution (ISSN 0030-9001); Plastvaerlden (ISSN 0032-132X).

BUSINESS AND ECONOMICS

330 340 US
DAILY BUSINESS REVIEW (BROWARD EDITION). 1962. d. (Mon.-Fri.) $239. Daily Business Review, Box 010589, Miami, FL 33101. TEL 305-377-3721. FAX 305-374-8474. Owner(s): American Lawyer Media, 600 Third Ave., New York, NY 10016. TEL 212-973-2800. Ed. Edward Wasserman; Pub. Donna T. Stotts. adv.; circ. 2,846 (paid). (also avail. in microfilm) **Document type:** newspaper.
   Formerly: Broward Review (ISSN 0887-4751)

330 US
DAILY BUSINESS REVIEW (MIAMI EDITION). 1926. d. (Mon.-Fri.). $239. Daily Business Review, Box 010589, Miami, FL 33101. TEL 305-377-3721. FAX 305-374-8474. Owner(s): American Lawyer Media, 600 Third Ave., New York, NY 10016. TEL 212-973-2800. Ed. Edward Wasserman; Pub. Donna T. Stotts. adv. contact: T. Alicia Coya. circ. 5,166 (paid). (also avail. in microfilm) **Document type:** newspaper.
   Formerly: Miami Review (ISSN 0888-0263)
   Description: Covers South Florida's daily business, real estate and legal issues.

330 US
DAILY BUSINESS REVIEW (PALM BEACH EDITION). 1976. 5/wk. (Mon.-Fri.) $239. Daily Business Review, Box 010589, Miami, FL 33101. TEL 305-347-3721. FAX 305-374-8474. Owner(s): American Lawyer Media, 600 Third Ave., New York, NY 10016. Tel 212-973-2800. Ed. Edward Wasserman; Pub. Donna T. Stotts. adv. contact: T. Alicia Coya. bk.rev./ circ. 2,090 (paid). **Document type:** newspaper.
   Former titles: Palm Beach Review (ISSN 0884-8785); Palm Beach Review and Business Record (ISSN 0199-0969); Law Review and Business Record of Palm Beach County (ISSN 0164-7652)
   Description: Serves the fields of business, real estate and law.

330 US ISSN 0889-2431
DAILY COMMERCIAL RECORD. 1888. d. (Mon.-Fri.). $168. 706 Main St., Dallas, TX 75202. TEL 214-741-6366. Ed. E.N. Cates. **Document type:** newspaper.

330 345.01 US
DAILY RECORD (KANSAS CITY). 1889. d. (Mon.- Fri.). $81. Record Newspaper Co., 3611 Troost Ave., Kansas City, MO 64109. TEL 816-931-2002. FAX 816-561-6675. Ed. Pam Weaver. R&P contact: Pam Weaver. adv. contact: Gary Smalley. circ. 670 (paid). **Document type:** newspaper.

330 340 US
THE DAILY RECORD (OMAHA).* 1886. d. $72. 3323 Leavenworth St., Omaha, NE 68105-1915. TEL 402-345-1303. FAX 402-345-2351. Ed. Ronald A. Henningsen. circ. 2,000. **Document type:** newspaper.
   Description: Business and law journal.

330 346.066 US ISSN 0743-8397
DAILY TERRITORIAL. 1930. d. (Mon.-Fri.). $100. Territorial Newspapers, P.O. Box 27087, Tucson, AZ 85726-7087. TEL 520-294-1200. FAX 520-294-4040. Ed. Stephen E. Jewett. adv. circ. 1,100. (tabloid format) **Document type:** newspaper.

330 US ISSN 0899-4129
DALLAS BUSINESS JOURNAL.* 1977. w. $55. Dallas Business Journal, Inc., 10670 N. Central Expwy., Ste. 710, Dallas, TX 75231-2111. TEL 214-520-1010. FAX 214-522-5606. E-mail: 73532.3142@compuserve.com. Ed. Huntley Payton; Pub. Gwin Grogan. adv. contact: Nickie Murchison. circ. 13,200 (paid). (also avail. in microfilm from UMI) **Indexed:** Tr.& Indus.Ind. **Document type:** newspaper.
   ●Also available online.
   —UMI. **CCC.**
   Supersedes in part in 1988: Dallas - Fort Worth Business Journal (ISSN 8750-6084)
   Description: Contains news and information essential to business executives, including features, data listing and how-to articles.

DANSK INDUSTRI EFTER 1870. see HISTORY — History Of Europe

330.9489 DK ISSN 0107-8224
DEN DANSKE BANK. ORIENTERING. 1976; N.S. 1990. m. free. Danske Bank, Oekonomisk Afdeling, c/o Library, Holmens Kanal 2-12, DK-1092 Copenhagen K, Denmark. TEL 45-33-44-00-00. Eds. Joergen Birger Christensen, Carsten Winkler. charts; stat. **Document type:** bulletin.
   Formerly: Danske Bank af 1871. Orientering.
   Description: Discusses economic issues and trends as they affect Denmark.

330 CN
DATELINE WINNIPEG. q. free. Better Business Bureau of Winnipeg & Manitoba, 301-365 Hargrave St., Winnipeg, MB R3B 2K3, Canada. TEL 204-942-7166. FAX 204-943-1489. Ed. T.S. Durham. adv. contact: T.S. Durham. circ. 2,000 (controlled). **Document type:** newsletter.

330 US ISSN 1063-3413
DAYTON BUSINESS REPORTER. (Monthly supplement avail.: Acquisition of Greater Dayton (ISSN 1063-3413)) 1991. bi-w. $28. Hannover Publishing Co., Inc., 6356 Far Hills Ave., Dayton, OH 45459-2782. TEL 937-291-1100. FAX 937-436-3426. E-mail: dbr_acq@CFANET.com; URL: http://www.daytonbusiness.com. Ed. Gene Fox; Pub. Thomas G. Thoms. R&P contact: Gene Fox. adv.: B&W page $2122, color page $2697; trim 11 3/8 x 15; adv. contact: Tina Rhodus. circ. 10,000. (also avail. in microform from UMI) **Document type:** newspaper.
   ●Also available online. Vendor(s): UMI.
   Also available on CD-ROM. Producer(s): UMI.
   —UMI. **CCC.**
   Description: Provides news and commentary about the area business community. Provides a forum for the exchange of opinions and ideas.

330 SP
DE ECONOMIA; revista de temas economicos. 1948. q. Consejo Economico Sindical Nacional, Paseo del Prado, 18, Madrid, Spain.

330 UK
DE MONTFORT UNIVERSITY. LEICESTER BUSINESS SCHOOL. OCCASIONAL PAPER. 1992. irreg., no.26. £3 per no. (effective 1996). De Montfort University, Leicester Business School, Department of Public Policy and Managerial Studies, Scraptcroft, Leicester LE7 9SU, England. TEL 0116-257-7780. FAX 0116-257-7795. E-mail: mdenscombe@dmu.ac.uk. Ed. Martyn Denscombe. **Document type:** monographic series.
   Refereed Serial

330 UK
DECISION. 1975. bi-m. free. Gildea & Co. Ltd., Suite 14D, Monkscoole House, Rathcoole, Co. Antrim BT37 9DA, N. Ireland. Ed. A.L. Gildea. adv.

330 UK
DEFENCE INDUSTRY DIGEST. 1984. m. £145($260) Longman Group UK Ltd., Law, Tax and Finance Division, 21-27 Lamb's Conduit St., London WC1N 3NJ, England. TEL 071-242-2548. FAX 071-831-8119. Ed. John Reed.
   Description: Digests news from the defense industry.

330 FR ISSN 0759-089X
DEFIS.* 1983. 11/yr. 230 F. c/o Free Lance S.A., 204 bd. Raspail, 75014 Paris, France. TEL 33-1-48017676. FAX 33-1-48009155. Ed. Nicolas Rousseaux. adv.; bk.rev. circ. 37,428. **Document type:** trade publication.

330 US ISSN 1061-4605
DELAWARE BUSINESS REVIEW.* 1978. w. $48. Independent Newspapers, Inc., Box 737, Dover, DE 19903. TEL 302-998-9580. FAX 302-998-1276. adv. circ. 9,661. **Document type:** newspaper.
   ●Also available online. Vendor(s): UMI.

330 US ISSN 1048-9827
HC107.L8
DELTA BUSINESS REVIEW. 1989. s-a. free. Northeast Louisiana University, Center for Business & Economic Research, Monroe, LA 71209-0101. TEL 318-342-1215. FAX 318-342-1209. E-mail: brwall@alpha.nlu.eduedu. Ed. Jerry L. Wall. bk.rev. circ. 750. **Document type:** academic/scholarly publication.
   —UMI.
   Formerly: Northeast Louisiana Business Review (ISSN 0736-9859)
   Description: Publishes articles examining issues facing the Lower Mississippi Delta region.
   Refereed Serial

DELTA PI EPSILON. SERVICE BULLETINS. see EDUCATION — Higher Education

DELTA PI EPSILON. (YEAR) RESEARCH CONFERENCE PROCEEDINGS. see EDUCATION — Higher Education

DELTA PI EPSILON JOURNAL. see EDUCATION — Higher Education

338.1060489 DK
HD2001
DENMARK. STATENS JORDBRUGS- OG FISKERIOEKONOMISKE INSTITUT. AARSBERETNING/DANISH INSTITUTE OF AGRICULTURAL AND FISHERIES ECONOMICS. ANNUAL REPORT. (Text in Danish; summaries in English) 1979. a. Statens Jordbrugs- og Fiskerioekonomiske Institut - Danish Institute of Agricultural and Fisheries Economics, Toftegaards Plads, Gammel Koege Landevej 1-3, DK-2500 Valby (Copenhagen), Denmark. TEL 45-36-44-20-80. FAX 45-36-44-11-10.
   Former titles: Denmark. Statens Jordbrugsoekonomiske Institut. Aarsberetning (ISSN 0108-7479); (until 1983): Denmark. Jordbrugsoekonomisk Institut. Aarsberetning (ISSN 0106-4967)

338.18489 DK ISSN 0106-1291
DENMARK. STATENS JORDBRUGS- OG FISKERIOEKONOMISKE INSTITUT. LANDBRUGETS OEKONOMI/DANISH AGRICULTURAL ECONOMY. Key Title: Landbrugets Oekonomi. 1979. a. price varies. Statens Jordbrugs- og Fiskerioekonomiske Institut - Danish Institute of Agricultural and Fisheries Economics, Toftegaards Plads, Gammel Koege Landevej 1-3, DK-2500 Valby (Copenhagen), Denmark. TEL 45-36-44-20-80. FAX 45-36-44-11-10. Ed. Arne Larsen.
   —BLDSC (5151.130000).

DENTAL ECONOMICS; revista de la gestion de la clinica dental. see MEDICAL SCIENCES — Dentistry

330 US ISSN 0893-7745
THE DENVER BUSINESS JOURNAL. w. $51 (effective 1995). American City Business Journals (Denver), 1700 Broadway, No. 515, Denver, CO 80290. TEL 303-837-3500. FAX 303-837-3535. Ed. Dougald Mc Donald. adv. circ. 15,000. **Document type:** newspaper.
   ●Also available online. Vendor(s): Information Access Co.
   —UMI. **CCC.**

330 332.1 CL ISSN 0716-2219
DEUDA EXTERNA DE CHILE. (Text in English, Spanish) 1977. a. Ch.$8200($25) Banco Central de Chile, Casilla 967, Santiago, Chile. TEL 56-2-6702000. FAX 56-2-6984847. TELEX 40569 CENBC CL. circ. 400. **Document type:** government publication.
   Description: Statement of Chilean external debt for each year with cumulative statistics.

330 GW ISSN 0340-1707
DEUTSCHES INSTITUT FUER WIRTSCHAFTSFORSCHUNG. VIERTELJAHRSHEFTE ZUR WIRTSCHAFTSFORSCHUNG. (Text in German; summaries in English) 1926. q. price varies. Duncker und Humblot GmbH, Postfach 410329, 12113 Berlin, Germany. TEL 49-30-7900060. FAX 49-30-79000631. E-mail: duh-werbung@t-online.de. Ed. Dr. Klaus Henkner. bk.rev.; bibl.; charts; stat.; index. **Indexed:** ELLIS, IBR, P.A.I.S.For.Lang.Ind. **Document type:** academic/scholarly publication.
   —BLDSC (9235.780000).

BUSINESS AND ECONOMICS

330 301   **II**
DHARAM NARAIN MEMORIAL LECTURE SERIES. (Text in English) 1981. irreg., no.7, 1988. Institute of Economic Growth, University Enclave, New Delhi 110007, India. TEL 2522201.

330   **PY**
DIA. 1981. d. 617100 g.($435) (effective 1997); newsstand price: 2000 g. Multimedia S.A., Mcal. Lopez 2948, Asuncion, Paraguay. TEL 595-21-6034000. FAX 595-21-606330. E-mail: eldia@infonet.com.pg. Ed. Manuel Godoy; Pub. Hugo Aranda. adv.: page $3300; trim 10 1/2 x 12; adv. contact: Guillermo Cortes. bk.rev.; film rev, software rev, tele.rev, video rev, tr.lit. Wire service(s): AFP, AP, REUTERS. cols./p.: 6; pp./issue: 32. (tabloid format; back issues avail.) **Document type:** newspaper.
    Formerly (until 1995): Hoy.
    Description: Articles of economy, business and related fields.

330   **BO**
DIAGRAMA ECONOMICO. m. Casilla 2762, La Paz, Bolivia. Ed. V. Rodriguez.

DIALOGO SOCIAL. see *SOCIOLOGY*

DIAMOND HARVARD BUSINESS. see *BUSINESS AND ECONOMICS — Management*

330   **PO**
DIARIO ECONOMICO. 260/yr. Rua de Santa Marta 47 r-c, 1100 Lisbon, Portugal. TEL 558071. FAX 690417. Ed. Silverio do Canto. circ. 24,000.

330 346.066   **FR**
DICTIONNAIRE JOLY CONCURRENCE. 2 base vols. plus s-a. updates. 1200 F. (effective 1997). Joly Editions, 1 av. Franklin D. Roosevelt, 75008 Paris, France. TEL 33-1-44951620. FAX 33-1-45638939. Ed.Bd. (looseleaf format) **Document type:** trade publication.

DICTIONNAIRE PERMANENT: DROIT DES AFFAIRES. see *LAW*

330   **LV**
DIENAS BIZNESS. (Text in Latvian; summaries in English, Russian) 1992. 3/w. $722 (effective 1998). Dienas Bizness, 1301 Balasta dombis 3, 1081 Riga, Latvia. TEL 371-2-464690. FAX 371-80-828287. (Dist. by: Mezhdunarodnaya Kniga, B. Yakimanka 39, 117049 Moscow, Russia. TEL 7-095-2384967. FAX 7-095-2384634) Ed. Juris Paiders. adv. contact: Andris Morkans. circ. 15,000. cols./p.: 5; pp./issue: 28. (tabloid format) **Document type:** newspaper.

330   **EC**   **ISSN 0012-2696**
HC121
DIFUSION ECONOMICA. vol.5, 1967. 3/yr. S/120($5) Universidad de Guayaquil, Instituto de Investigaciones Economicas y Politicas, Box 5725, Guayaquil, Ecuador. Ed. Enrique Salas Castilo. charts; stat.

330   **BO**   **ISSN 0012-2939**
DINAMICA ECONOMICA.* 1961. bi-m. Bs.20.($20) Universidad Mayor de San Andres, Facultad de Economia, Juridica y Ciencias Sociales, Casilla 4787, La Paz, Bolivia. Ed. Eduarde Nava Morales Eguia. adv.; bk.rev.; charts; illus. circ. 12,000.

330   **SP**
DINERO. w. Nuevo Projecto 50, Po. Odsteuala, 36, 28046 Madrid, Spain, Dir. Rafael Navas.

330   **IT**
DIPARTIMENTO DI ECONOMIA AZIENDALE. STUDI DI RAGIONERIA E DI ECONOMIA AZIENDALE. 1993. irreg., no.3, 1994. price varies. Liguori Editore s.r.l., Via Posillipo 394, 80123 Naples, Italy. TEL 39-81-7206111. FAX 39-81-7206244. Pub. Guido Liguori. adv. contact: Maria Liguori. **Document type:** monographic series.

330   **GW**
DIPLOMATISCHE VERTRETUNGEN DER BUNDESREPUBLIK DEUTSCHLAND IM AUSLAND. a. DM.98. Deutscher Wirtschaftsdienst, Marienburgerstr. 22, 50968 Cologne, Germany. TEL 49-221-93763-0. FAX 49-221-9376399. (reprint service avail. from SCH) **Document type:** bulletin.
    Formerly: Vertretungen der Bundesrepublik Deutschland im Ausland (ISSN 0431-509X)

330   **LY**
DIRASSAT;* Libyan economic and business review. (Text in Arabic, English) 1964. s-a. $15. University of Garyounis, Faculty of Economics and Commerce, Center of Economics and Business Research, Benghazi, Libya. charts; stat. circ. 3,000. **Indexed:** Chem.Abstr., Forest.Abstr., Soils & Fert.

330   **SP**   **ISSN 0210-0908**
DIRECCION Y PROGRESO. 1972. 6/yr. Association of Business Development, Montalban 3, 6o, 28014 Madrid, Spain. TEL 1-532-22-65. Ed. B. Herrero Nieto. circ. 4,736. **Indexed:** ELLIS.
—CINDOC.

DIRECTIVOS CONSTRUCCION. see *REAL ESTATE*

DIRECTORY OF FOREIGN INVESTMENT IN THE U S; real estate and business. see *BUSINESS AND ECONOMICS — Trade And Industrial Directories*

DIRECTORY OF M & A INTERMEDIARIES. see *BUSINESS AND ECONOMICS — Trade And Industrial Directories*

DIRITTO ED ECONOMIA; rivista-dibattito interdisciplinare quadrimestrale. see *LAW*

330   **UK**   **ISSN 1360-2438**
DISCUSSION PAPER IN ECONOMICS AND ECONOMETRICS. irreg. University of Nottingham, Department of Economics, University Park, Nottingham NG7 2RD, England. TEL 44-115-9515480. FAX 44-115-9514159. E-mail: lezst@lzn2.not.ac.uk. Ed. R. Falvey. circ. 120. **Document type:** academic/scholarly publication.
—BLDSC (3597.933850).
    Formerly: Discussion Paper in Economics and Econometrics.
    Refereed Serial

330   **UK**
DISCUSSION PAPERS IN ECONOMICS. irreg., no.95. University of York, Department of Economics and Related Studies, Heslington, York YO1 5DD, England. **Document type:** academic/scholarly publication, monographic series.
    Formerly: University of York. Institute for Research in the Social Sciences. Discussion Paper.

330   **UK**
DISCUSSION PAPERS IN PUBLIC SECTOR ECONOMICS. irreg. University of Leicester, Faculty of Social Sciences, Public Sector Economics Research Centre, Leicester LE1 7RH, England. TEL 01533-523952. FAX 01533-523949. **Document type:** monographic series.

330   **US**
DISTRIBUTOR'S LINK. q. $25. 4297 Corp. Sq. N., Naples, FL 33942. TEL 813-643-2713. FAX 813-643-5795. Ed. Leo J. Coar. adv. circ. 12,000. **Document type:** trade publication.

DOCUMENTS TARIFAIRES TRANSPORT. see *TRANSPORTATION*

330 340   **US**   **ISSN 1057-3836**
KU78.867
DOING BUSINESS IN AUSTRALIA. 1992. base vol. plus a. supplements. $165. Juris Publishing, Executive Park, One Odell Plaza, Yonkers, NY 10701. TEL 800-887-4064. FAX 914-375-6047. Ed. Edward J. Wright. (looseleaf format)
    Description: Provides practical information about the business, political, government, and economic climate in Australia. Provides analysis of the law, and relevant case law, regulations and statutes.

330 340   **US**
DOING BUSINESS IN BRAZIL. (Includes m. Legal Letter) 1979. base vol. plus s-a. supplements. $360. Juris Publishing, Executive Park, One Odell Plaza, Yonkers, NY 10701. TEL 800-887-4064. FAX 914-375-6047. (looseleaf format)
    Description: Provides analysis and description of the Brazilian government, legislature and judiciary, and detailed commentary of the principal commercial and financial laws that affect foreign investment.

330 340   **US**
DOING BUSINESS IN CHINA. 1990. base vol. plus a. supplements. $165. Juris Publishing, Executive Park, One Dell Plaza, Yonkers, NY 10701. TEL 800-887-4064. FAX 914-375-6047. Ed. William P. Streng. (looseleaf format)
    Description: Examines the variety of political, economic and governmental issues affecting business in today's China.

330 341.7   **US**
DOING BUSINESS IN FRANCE. 1983. 2 base vols. (plus a. update). $565 for base vols.; update $236. Matthew Bender & Co., Inc., 2 Park Ave., New York, NY 10016. TEL 212-448-2000. E-mail: international@bender.com; URL: http://www.bender.com.
    Description: Practice-oriented treatise covering taxation, banking and securities, foreign investment, auditing and accounting standards.

330 341.7   **US**
DOING BUSINESS IN IRELAND. 1987. base vol. (plus a. update). $165 for base vol.; update $130. Matthew Bender & Co., Inc., 2 Park Ave., New York, NY 10016. TEL 212-448-2000. E-mail: international@bender.com; URL: http://www.bender.com.
    Description: Focuses on Irish business and legal climate, particularly investment incentives, taxation, employment law, export-import restrictions, intellectual property and product liability.

330 340   **US**   **ISSN 1068-0683**
KGF333.B86
DOING BUSINESS IN MEXICO. (Includes bi-m. Legal Letter) (Text in English, Spanish) 1980. 4 base vols. plus s-a. supplements. $597.50. Transnational Publishers, Inc., 1 Bridge St., Irvington, NY 10533. TEL 914-591-4288; 800-914-8186. FAX 914-591-2688. E-mail: lawbooks@village.ios.com. Ed. Philip von Mehren. (looseleaf format) **Document type:** trade publication.
    Description: Source on legal, economic, and practical aspects affecting the conduct of business in Mexico.

330 341.7   **US**
DOING BUSINESS IN SPAIN. 1987. base vol. (plus a. update). $200 for base vol.; update $154. Matthew Bender & Co., Inc., 2 Park Ave., New York, NY 10016. TEL 212-448-2000. E-mail: international@bender.com; URL: http://www.bender.com. Ed. Fernando Pombo.
    Description: Guide to the business and legal environment in Spain, with coverage of foreign investment incentives, exchange controls, taxation, labor relations, business regulation and intellectual property.

330   **CC**
DONGFANG QIYEJIA/ORIENTAL ENTREPRENEURS. (Text in Chinese) m. Baihua Wenyi Chubanshe, 189 Zhangzizhong Lu, Heping Qu, Tianjin 300020, People's Republic of China. TEL 704723. Ed. Zheng Faqing.

330   **JA**   **ISSN 0387-3021**
DOSHISHA UNIVERSITY ECONOMIC REVIEW/DOSHISHA DAIGAKU KEIZAIGAKU RONSO. 1948. 6/yr. 3000 Yen. Doshisha University, Doshisha Economic Association - Doshisha Daigaku Keizaigaku-kai, Karasuma Imadegawa, Kamikyo-ku, Kyoto 602, Japan. Ed. Setsujiro Irie. circ. 2,500.
—BLDSC (3619.745000).

330   **DK**   **ISSN 0904-8022**
DRIFTSRESULTATER FOR SOMMERREGNSKABER.* 1982. a. free. Landbrugets Raadgivningscenter, Husmandsforeningernes Landskontor, Udkaervej 15, DK-8200 Aarhus N, Denmark. (Co-sponsors: Husmandsforeningerne. Landskontoret for Driftsoekonomi; Driftsoekonomiudvalget, Danske Husmandsforeninger) Ed. Per Koford Hansen. bk.rev circ. 11,000.
    Formerly (until 1985): Oekonomisk Analyse, Sommerregnskaber.

330 378   **SW**   **ISSN 0283-636X**
DROEMMEN OM ELIN. 1972. q. SEK 50 (effective 1990). (E L I N - Ekonomfoereningen vid Universitetet i Linkoeping) Linkoepings Universitet, Kaarallen, S-581 83 Linkoeping, Sweden.

DROIT ET ECONOMIE. see *LAW*

BUSINESS AND ECONOMICS

330   US
DUN'S 5,000 SURVEY. irreg. free. Dun & Bradstreet, Economic Analysis Department, 220 E. 42nd St., 9th Fl., New York, NY 10017-4717. FAX 212-883-3400. (Subscr. to: Box 1861, New York, NY 10163-1861)
    Description: Survey of 5,000 U.S. firms with results for companies in all size categories. Includes annual forecasts of employment and capital spending, as well as special topical surveys.

540 660   US   ISSN 0095-8808
DUPONT MAGAZINE. 1913. bi-m. E.I. du Pont de Nemours & Co., Montchanin Bldg., N - 9442, Wilmington, DE 19898. TEL 302-774-7988. FAX 302-774-2760. Ed. Jim Moore. charts; illus.; tr.lit. circ. 215,000. **Indexed:** Abstr.Bull.Inst.Pap.Chem., Br.Ceram.Abstr., CAD CAM Abstr., Fluidex, Graph.Arts Lit.Abstr., Int.Packag.Abstr., Print.Abstr., Text.Tech.Dig., World Text.Abstr.
—BLDSC (3630.760000); CISTI; EMDOCS; KR SourceOne; Linda Hall.

330   NE   ISSN 0922-9825
DUTCH COMPANY YEARBOOK. 1988. a. fl.99. Delwel Uitgeverij B.V., Postbus 19110, 2500 CC The Hague, Netherlands. TEL 31-70-3624800. FAX 31-70-3605606.
    Description: Provides financial data on the most successful businesses in the Netherlands.

330   NE
DYNAMIC ECONOMICS: THEORY AND APPLICATIONS (SERIES). 1976. irreg., vol.4, 1985. price varies. Elsevier Science B.V., Books Division, P.O. Box 211, 1000 AE Amsterdam, Netherlands. TEL 31-20-4853911. FAX 31-20-4853705. TELEX 18582 ESPA NL. E-mail: nlinfo-f@elsevier.nl; usinfo-f@elsevier.com; forinfo-kyf04035@niftyserve.or.jp; URL: http://www.elsevier.nl/. (Subscr. in the Americas to: Elsevier Science, Regional Sales Office, Box 945, New York, NY 10159-0945. TEL 212-633-3730. FAX 212-633-3680; Subscr. in Australasia and the Far East to: Elsevier Science (Singapore) Pte Ltd, No.1 Temasek Ave., No.17-01 Millenia Tower, Singapore 039192, Singapore. TEL 65-434-3727. FAX 65-337-2230; Subscr. in Japan to: Elsevier Science Japan, 9-15 Higashi-Azabu 1-chome, Minato-ku, Tokyo 106, Japan. TEL 81-3-5561-5033. FAX 81-3-5561-5047) Ed. Maurice Wilkinson. **Indexed:** Math.R. **Document type:** monographic series.
    Formerly: Dynamic Economics Series.
    Refereed Serial

338   NE   ISSN 0921-3619
DYNAMISCH OOST-NEDERLAND. 1981. bi-m. fl.47.50. Drukkerij Giethoorn B.V., Postbus 41, 7940 AA Meppel, Netherlands. adv.; bk.rev. circ. 10,000.
    Formerly: Dynamisch Overijssel.

330 658 338   GW   ISSN 0938-8702
E B; Handbuch fuer Selbstaendige und Unternehmer. 1982. m. DM.198. Verlag Norman Rentrop, Theodor-Heuss-Str. 4, 53177 Bonn, Germany. TEL 49-228-8205-0. FAX 49-228-364411. TELEX 17228309. Ed. Norman Rentrop. (looseleaf format; back issues avail.) **Document type:** bulletin.
    Formerly: Erfolgsberater.
    Description: A how-to publication on starting a new business in Germany.

330   UN
E D I DEVELOPMENT POLICY CASE SERIES. irreg., no.9, 1994. World Bank, Economic Development Institute, 1818 H St., N.W., Washington, DC 20433. TEL 202-473-1155. FAX 202-522-2627. E-mail: books@worldbank.org. (U.S. orders to: Box 7247-8619, Philadelphia, PA 19170-8619; Also avail. from: 66 av. D'lena, 75116 Paris, France. TEL 33-1-40-69-30-55. FAX 33-1-40-69-30-68)

330   US
E I U NEWSLETTERS. (Includes Business Asia, Business Africa, Business Latin America, Business Europe, Business Eastern Europe, Business China, and Crossborder Monitor) base vol. (plus m. updates). Economist Intelligence Unit, 111 W. 57th St., New York, NY 10019. TEL 212-554-0600; 800-938-4685. FAX 212-586-1182. TELEX 175567. (UK addr.: Economist Intelligence Unit Ltd., Subscriptions Dept., P.O. Box 200, Harold Hill, Romford, Essex RM3 8UX, England. TEL 44-1708-381-444. FAX 44-1708-371-850) **Document type:** newsletter.
    •Also available on CD-ROM.

330   DK   ISSN 0108-9773
E K - BLADET. 1983. q. membership. Erhverskvinders Klub, c/o Hanne Francia, Roerhoenevej 15, 2970 Hoersholm, Denmark. illus.

E N D S REPORT. see ENVIRONMENTAL STUDIES

330   US
▼**E S B N ONLINE.** (Entrepreneur - Small Business Newsletter) 1996. m. Portrait Press, 4652 Portrait Ln., Plano, TX 75024. TEL 214-491-2460. FAX 214-491-2460. E-mail: ppress@cyberhighway.net; URL: http://www.esbnonline.com/news/. **Document type:** trade publication.
    Description: Provides pertinent business information.

330 300   IE
E S R I ACCOUNTS AND BALANCE SHEET. a. Economic and Social Research Institute, 4 Burlington Rd., Dublin 4, Ireland. TEL 353-1-667-1525. FAX 353-1-668-6231. **Document type:** corporate report.

330 300   IE
E S R I ANNUAL REPORT. a. Economic and Social Research Institute, 4 Burlington Rd., Dublin 4, Ireland. TEL 353-1-6671525. FAX 353-1-6686231. **Document type:** corporate report.

330   BE
THE E U INSTITUTIONS' REGISTER - THE ORANGE BOOK. (European Union) a. 4100 BEF. Euroconfidentiel s.a., Rue de Rixensart 18, 1332 Genval, Belgium. TEL 32-2-6520284. FAX 32-2-6530180. **Document type:** directory.
    Formerly (until 1996): E U Institutions' Yellow Pages.
    Description: Lists key personnel of the major institutions of the European Union.

E U R O M A P ECONOMIC SURVEY. (European Plastics and Rubber Machinery Manufacturers Association) see PLASTICS

E UND W. (Elektro und Wirtschaft) see ENGINEERING — Electrical Engineering

330   US
EAST WEST EUROPEAN ECONOMIC INTERACTION. 1976. irreg. price varies. Springer-Verlag, 175 Fifth Ave., New York, NY 10010. TEL 212-460-1500. FAX 212-473-6272. (Also: Berlin, Heidelberg, Tokyo and Vienna) (reprint service avail. from ISI) **Document type:** monographic series.

330   AU
EAST - WEST REPORT; business information for the Central European investor. (Text in English) 1992. q. Bank Austria AG, Am Hof 2, A-1010 Vienna, Austria. TEL 01-71191-0. Eds. Alexander Vogel, Franz Himmer. **Document type:** trade publication.

330   KE   ISSN 1011-4750
HC501
EASTERN AFRICA ECONOMIC REVIEW. 1954-1977; N.S. 1985. s-a. $70. Kenya Literature Bureau, P.O. Box 30022, Nairobi, Kenya. Ed. J.K. Maitha. adv.; bk.rev.; bibl.; charts; stat. circ. 1,000. **Indexed:** Documentatieblad, J.of Econ.Lit., P.A.I.S., Rural Devel.Abstr., Rural Recreat.Tour.Abstr., SSCI, World Agri.Econ.& Rural Sociol.Abstr.
—BLDSC (3646.573000).
    Formerly (until 1969): East African Economic Review (ISSN 0424-0790)

330   US   ISSN 0094-5056
HB1
EASTERN ECONOMIC JOURNAL. 1974. q. $50 to individuals (foreign $55); libraries $75 (foreign $85). Eastern Economic Association, Iona College, New Rochelle, NY 10801. TEL 610-559-8050. FAX 610-250-8961. E-mail: hochmanh@lafayette.edu; URL: http://www.iona.edu/eea.thm. Ed. Harold Hochman. R&P contact: Hai Hochman. adv. contact: Jenifer C. Gamber. bk.rev.; bibl.; circ. 1,000 (paid). **Indexed:** BPIA, J.of Econ.Lit. **Document type:** academic/scholarly publication.
    •Also available online. Vendor(s): UMI.
—BLDSC (3646.587900); SWETS; UMI; UnCover.
    Description: Devoted to free and open intellectual inquiry from diverse philosophical perspectives in all areas of theoretical and applied research related to economics.
    Refereed Serial

330   US   ISSN 0012-8775
HC244.A1
EASTERN EUROPEAN ECONOMICS; a journal of translations from Bulgaria, Czechoslovakia, East Germany, Hungary, Poland, Rumania and Yugoslavia. 1962. bi-m. $110 to individuals (foreign $176); institutions $630 (foreign $710) (effective 1997). M.E. Sharpe, Inc., 80 Business Park Dr., Armonk, NY 10504. TEL 914-273-1800; 800-541-6563. FAX 914-273-2106. Ed. Josef Brada. adv.: page $300; 5 x 8; adv. contact: Barbara Ladd. index. **Indexed:** ASCA, C.R.E.J., Curr.Cont., IBR, J.of Econ.Lit., Key to Econ.Sci., P.A.I.S., SSCI. **Document type:** academic/scholarly publication.
—BLDSC (3646.595000); Genuine Article; SWETS; UMI; UnCover. **CCC.**
    Description: Covers economic thought and policy in "the new Europe." Discusses problems associated with the transition to mamrket economy, including inflation, unemployment, inadequate investment and savings, and other issues.
    Refereed Serial

330   US   ISSN 1074-9624
EASTERN PENNSYLVANIA BUSINESS JOURNAL. 1989. w. $36. Press - Enterprise, Inc. (Allentown), 5000 Tilghman St., Allentown, PA 18104. TEL 610-398-1026; 800-328-1026. FAX 610-398-6943. Ed. Larry Jalowiec. R&P contact: Debi Richards. adv.: B&W page $1472, color page $1602; 10 1/8 x 12 5/8; adv. contact: Ann Biernat-Rucker. circ. 12,000. **Document type:** newspaper.
    Description: Covers business and economic news including real estate transfers, new businesses, bankruptcies, and related subjects.

330   BE   ISSN 0776-409X
L'ECHO (BRUSSELS). (Text in French) 1881. 5/w. 7800 BEF (foreign 14920 BEF). Editeco S.A., 131 rue de Birmingham, 1070 Brussels, Belgium. TEL 02-526-5511. FAX 02-526-55-26. Ed. F. Melaet. adv.; bk.rev. circ. 54,000. **Document type:** newspaper.
    Formerly: Echo de la Bourse.

330   GW
ECHO-HANDELSJOURNAL. 1952. bi-m. DM.46.80. Rewe-Verlag GmbH, Domstr. 20, 50668 Cologne, Germany. TEL 49-221-149-0. FAX 49-221-1499552. Ed. Josef Rosen. circ. 55,000. **Document type:** trade publication.

330   NE   ISSN 1383-990X
ECLAIRE. 1979. 9/yr. (includes special issue). Economics Faculty Association Rotterdam (EFR), Burgmeester Oudlaan 50, Kamer C1-15, 3062 PA Rotterdam, Netherlands. TEL 31-10-4081146. FAX 31-10-4532928. E-mail: efr@few.eur.nl. Ed. E.A. Kerkuijk. bk.rev. circ. 3,000 (35,000 special issue).

330   SP
ECO. 12/yr. Via La Cierva 13, Polig. del Tambre, 15890 Santiago, Madrid, Spain. TEL 81-56-38-06. FAX 81-57-26-60. Ed. Jose M. Couselo. circ. 5,000.

333.7   US
ECO (MOUNT KISCO);* business & environment. 1993. q. $40. Eco, Inc., 420 Lexington Ave., New York, NY 10170-0002. TEL 914-242-0140. FAX 914-242-0046. Ed. Igor Gordevitch; Pub. Mary Anne Holley. adv. contact: Mary Anne Holley. bk.rev.; illus.; circ. 80,000 (controlled).
    Description: Business magazine focusing on environmental issues.

330 028.5 375   AT   ISSN 1320-968X
ECODATE. 1987. q. Aus.$45. Warringal Publications, 114 Argyle St., Fitzroy, Vic. 3065, Australia. TEL 61-3-94160200. FAX 61-3-94160402. Ed. Bronwyn Hession; Pub. Jane Arter. circ. 2,000. (back issues avail.)
    Description: Presents recent developments in Australian economics for 12th grade students.

BUSINESS AND ECONOMICS

330   FR   ISSN 0296-4449
ECOFLASH; mensuel d'informations economiques et sociales. 10/yr. 120 F. (foreign 136 F.) (effective 1997). Centre National de Documentation Pedagogique, 29 rue d'Ulm, 75230 Paris Cedex 05, France. TEL 33-1-46349000. FAX 33-1-46345544. (Subscr. to: CNDP - Abonnement, B750, 60732 Ste. Genevieve Cedex, France. FAX 33-3-44033013) Ed. Albert Cohen.
   Description: Each issue studies a sociological, economic, historical or geographical theme, with a methodological analysis and bibliography.

330   MR   ISSN 0851-5743
ECONOMAP; daily economic and financial news bulletin. (Text in French) 1976. d. DH.2985($370) Maghreb Arabe Presse, 122 Ave. Alial Ben Abdellah, B.P. 1049, Rabat, Morocco. TEL 76-40-83. FAX 670-97. TELEX 310-44. Ed. Abdeljalil Fenjiro. adv.; illus. circ. 800.

330   UK   ISSN 0012-9682
HB1   CODEN: ECMTA7
ECONOMETRICA. 1933. bi-m. £110($30) (foreign £174) (effective 1997). (Econometric Society) Blackwell Publishers Ltd., 108 Cowley Rd., Oxford OX4 1JF, England. TEL 44-1865-791100. FAX 44-1865-791347. E-mail: jnlinfo@blackwellpublishers.co.uk; URL: http://www.blackwellpublishers.co.uk Ed. A. Mas-Colell. adv.; charts; index, cum.index: vols.1-20 (1933-1952), vols.21-45 (1953-1977). circ. 6,000. (also avail. in microform from PMC,UMI; reprint service avail. from SWZ,UMI) **Indexed:** ASCA, Biostat., BPIA, C.R.E.J., Compumath, Compumath, Cont.Pg.Manage., Curr.Cont.(1958-), Fam.Ind., Geo.Abstr., Int.Polit.Sci.Abstr., J.Cont.Quant.Meth., J.of Econ.Lit., Key to Econ.Sci., Math.R., Mid.East: Abstr.& Ind., Oper.Res.Manage.Sci., Qual.Contr.Appl.Stat., Risk Abstr., Rural Recreat.Tour.Abstr., Sci.Cit.Ind., Soc.Sci.Ind., SSCI, Stat.Theor.Meth.Abstr. (1958-), Tr.& Indus.Ind., World Agri.Econ.& Rural Sociol.Abstr., Zent.Math. **Document type:** academic/scholarly publication.
   ●Also available online.
   —BLDSC (3650.100000); KR SourceOne; SWETS; UMI; UnCover.
   Refereed Serial

330   EC   ISSN 0012-9704
HC201
ECONOMIA. 1965. s-a. $10. Universidad Central del Ecuador, Instituto de Investigaciones Economicas, Ciudad Universitaria, Apdo. 17-03-0724, Quito, Ecuador. TEL 593-2-525018. FAX 593-2-229481. E-mail: secretar@iieuc.ecx.ec. Dir. Isaias Campana C. bk.rev.; stat.
   Description: Covers all aspects of the economy in Ecuador, past and present.

330   GT   ISSN 0046-113X
ECONOMIA. 3/yr. Q.5($5) Universidad de San Carlos de Guatemala, Instituto de Investigaciones Economicas y Sociales, Edificio S6 3er. Nivel, Ciudad Universitaria, zona 12, Guatemala, Guatemala. bk.rev.

330   JA   ISSN 0012-9712
ECONOMIA. 1950. q. exchange basis. Yokohama Kokuritsu Daigaku - Yokohama National University, Economic Society, 156 Tokiwadai, Hodogaya-ku, Yokohama 240, Japan. Ed. Hiroshi Matsumoto. bk.rev.; index; circ. 1,800 (controlled). **Document type:** academic/scholarly publication.

330   AG   ISSN 0325-0830
ECONOMIA. 1913. q. Viamonte 1582, Buenos Aires, Argentina.
   Formerly (until 1972): Revista de Ciencias Economicas. Temas de Economia (ISSN 0325-0822); Supersedes in part (in 1970): Revista de Ciencias Economicas (ISSN 0034-7779)

330   PE   ISSN 0254-4415
HC226
ECONOMIA. Variant title: Revista Economia. 1977. s-a. $28. Pontificia Universidad Catolica del Peru, Departamento de Economia, Fondo Editorial, Apdo. 1761, Lima 32, Peru. TEL 51-14-626390. FAX 5114-611785. E-mail: editorial@pucp.edu.pe; URL: http://www.pucp.edu.pe. Eds. Maximo Vega-Centeno, Jorge Rojas. bk.rev. circ. 500. **Indexed:** J.of Econ.Lit., P.A.I.S.For.Lang.Ind. **Document type:** academic/scholarly publication.
   Refereed Serial

330   IT
ECONOMIA. 1988. irreg. no.9, 1995. price varies. Liguori Editore s.r.l., Via Posillipo 394, 80123 Naples, Italy. TEL 39-81-7206111. FAX 39-81-7206244. Ed. Salvatore Vinci; Pub. Guido Liguori. adv. contact: Maria Liguori. **Document type:** monographic series.

330 650   PO   ISSN 0870-3531
HB1.A1
ECONOMIA (LISBON, 1977). (Text in English, French, Portuguese, Spanish) 1977. 3/yr. Esc.2000($40) to individuals; institutions Esc.2400($50); students Esc.1500($40). Universidade Catolica Portuguesa, Faculdade de Ciencias Economicas e Empresariais, Caminho da Palma de Cima, 1600 Lisbon, Portugal. TEL 351-1-7214000. FAX 351-1-7260546. TELEX 65094 UNICAP-P. Dir. Valentim Xavier Pintado. adv.; bk.rev.; bibl.; charts; stat. circ. 2,000. **Indexed:** IBR, J.of Econ.Lit., P.A.I.S.For.Lang.Ind. **Document type:** academic/scholarly publication.
   Description: Essays and research on economics and management science.

330 340   IT
ECONOMIA E DIRITTO DEL TERZIARIO. 1989. 3/yr. L.65000 (foreign L.85000) (effective 1993). Franco Angeli Editore, Viale Monza, 106, 20127 Milan, Italy. TEL 02-2895762. Ed.Bd.

330   IT   ISSN 0391-2078
HD28
ECONOMIA E POLITICA INDUSTRIALE. 1974. q. L.97000 (foreign L.130000) (effective 1993). Franco Angeli Editore, Viale Monza 106, 20127 Milan, Italy. TEL 02-28-27-651. Ed. Sergio Vacca.
   —BLDSC (3650.480000).

330   IT
ECONOMIA ED AMBIENTE. 1982. bi-m. L.85000. (Centro Italiano di Studi Economrici e Ambientali) C.I.S.P.E., Via Fotezza 1, 56100 Pisa, Italy. TEL 39-50-571181. FAX 39-50-571198. Ed. Romano Molesti. R&P contact: Silvio Truceo. adv. contact: A.C. Cappuccilli. bk.rev.; index. (back issues avail.) **Document type:** academic/scholarly publication.

330   BL   ISSN 1413-6090
ECONOMIA EM REVISTA. 1993. s-a. $8 (effective 1997 & 1998). Universidade Estadual de Maringa, Departamento de Economia, Av. Colombo 5790, 87020-900 Maringa PR, Brazil. TEL 55-442614305. FAX 55-442232676. E-mail: dco@uem.br; URL: http://www.uem.br/-dco. Ed. Maria de Fatima Garcia. R&P contact: Maria de Fatima Garcia. bk.rev.; bibl, charts; circ. 200 (paid). **Document type:** academic/scholarly publication.
   Description: Presents the results of research activities of the faculty members. Covers a wide range of topics in economics.
   Refereed Serial

330   MX   ISSN 0185-0849
ECONOMIA INFORMA. 1974. m. Universidad Nacional Autonoma de Mexico, Direccion General de Difusion Cultural, Villa Obregon, Ciudad Universitaria, Mexico 20, D.F., Mexico.

330   SP   ISSN 0012-9801
ECONOMIA INTERNACIONAL. 1956. m. 15500 ptas. (foreign 18500 ptas.). Balmes, 213, 08006 Barcelona, Spain. Ed. Jacinto Calm Domenech. adv.; bk.rev.; bibl.; charts; stat. circ. 20,000. **Document type:** academic/scholarly publication, consumer publication, trade publication.

330   IT   ISSN 0012-981X
HB7
ECONOMIA INTERNAZIONALE. (Text in English, French, Italian, Spanish) 1948. q. L.80000($85) (effective 1997). (Camera di Commercio, Industria, Artigianato e Agricoltura di Genova) Istituto di Economia Internazionale, Via Garibaldi 4, 16124 Genoa, Italy. TEL 39-10-2094201. FAX 39-10-2094300. TELEX 286325 COMGEN I. bk.rev.; bibl.; charts; index. circ. 1,000. (reprint service avail. from SWZ) **Indexed:** Asian-Pac.Econ.Lit., C.R.E.J., Curr.Cont.(1980-), IBR, J.of Econ.Lit., Key to Econ.Sci., P.A.I.S.For.Lang.Ind., Rural Recreat.Tour.Abstr., Stat.Theor.Meth.Abstr. (1980-), World Agri.Econ.& Rural Sociol.Abstr. **Document type:** academic/scholarly publication.
   —BLDSC (3650.860000); SWETS; UnCover.
   Description: International articles in several languages about international economic relations.

330   MX   ISSN 0185-0458
ECONOMIA MEXICANA. (Text in English, Spanish) 1979. s-a. Mex.$70 to individuals($40); institutions Mex.$100($95) (effective 1997). Centro de Investigacion y Docencia Economicas, Departamento de Economia, Apdo. Postal 116-114, 01130 Mexico DF, Mexico. TEL 52-5-7279885. FAX 52-5-7279885. Ed. Alejandro Villagomez. adv. circ. 1,000. **Indexed:** IBR. **Document type:** academic/scholarly publication.
   Description: Economic review for the analysis and discussion of the economic problems of Mexico and Latin America.

330 900   MX   ISSN 0531-8203
HC10
ECONOMIA POLITICA. 1965. q. $6. Instituto Politecnico Nacional, Escuela Superior de Economia, Unidad Profesional Zacatenco, Col. Lindavista, 07738 Mexico DF, Mexico. bk.rev.; illus. circ. 2,000.

330   HO   ISSN 0424-2483
HC145.A1
ECONOMIA POLITICA. 1962; N.S. 1972. irreg. $2. Universidad Nacional Autonoma de Honduras, Instituto de Investigaciones Economicas y Sociales, Ciudad Universitaria, Tegucigalpa DC, Honduras. Ed. Victor Meza. bk.rev. circ. 1,000. **Indexed:** Int.Lab.Doc.

330   IT   ISSN 1120-2890
ECONOMIA POLITICA; rivista di teoria e analisi. 1984. 3/yr. Lit.120000 (foreign Lit. 180000) (effective 1997). Societa Editrice Il Mulino, Strada Maggiore, 37, 40125 Bologna, Italy. TEL 39-51-256011. FAX 39-51-256034. E-mail: riviste@mulino.it. Ed. Alberto Quadrio Curzio. adv. contact: M. Luisa Vezzali. index. circ. 900. (back issues avail.) **Indexed:** J.of Econ.Lit.

ECONOMIA, SOCIETA E ISTITUZIONI. see *SOCIOLOGY*

330   CL   ISSN 0716-0100
ECONOMIA Y ADMINISTRACION. (Text and summaries in English, Spanish) 1964. 2/yr. Ch.$5000 (foreign $19) (effective 1997 & 1998). Universidad de Concepcion, Facultad de Ciencias Economicas y Administrativas, Casilla 1987, Concepcion, Chile. TEL 56-41-229946. FAX 56-41-231131. Dir. Rosa Aguilera V. adv.; bk.rev.; bibl.; charts; stat.; index, cum.index. circ. 500. **Document type:** academic/scholarly publication.
   —BLDSC (3651.148000).

330   VE   ISSN 0012-9895
H8.S7
ECONOMIA Y CIENCIAS SOCIALES.* vol.12, 1970. q. Universidad Central de Venezuela, Facultad de Ciencias Economicas y Sociales, Ciudad Universitaria, Los Chapuaramos, ZP 104, Caracas 1051, Venezuela. Dir. D.F. Maza Zavala. bibl.; charts. **Indexed:** Amer.Hist.& Life, Hisp.Amer.Per.Ind. (1970-1980), Hist.Abstr., Int.Polit.Sci.Abstr.

330   CU   ISSN 0252-8584
HB9   CODEN: ECDEEN
ECONOMIA Y DESARROLLO. (Summaries in English, French) 1970. bi-m. C.$300($13) in N. America; S. America $14; Europe $18; elsewhere $21. (Universidad de la Habana, Facultad de Economia) Ediciones Cubanas, Obispo No. 527, Apdo. 605, Havana, Cuba. Ed. Fernando Gonzalez. bibl.; charts; illus.; stat. circ. 11,000. **Indexed:** Hisp.Amer.Per.Ind. (1970-1990), IBR, P.A.I.S.For.Lang.Ind., Rural Recreat.Tour.Abstr., World Agri.Econ.& Rural Sociol.Abstr.

330   CL   ISSN 0717-0033
HD4811
ECONOMIA Y TRABAJO EN CHILE. Variant title: Revista de Economia y Trabajo. 1993. s-a. $20 to individuals; institutions $30; students $15. Programa de Economia del Trabajo, Santo Domingo 526, Santiago, Chile. TEL 6326128. FAX 56-6333671. Ed. Gonzalo Rivas. **Document type:** academic/scholarly publication.

330　　　　　　II　　ISSN 0424-2513
HC431
ECONOMIC AFFAIRS; a quarterly journal of economics. (Text in English) 1956. q. Rs.150($22.50) (effective 1998). Himansu Roy, Ed. & Pub., BC-144, Sector 1, Salt Lake City, Calcutta 700 064, India. TEL 91-33-373034. adv.; bk.rev.; index. circ. 2,000. (reprint service avail. from SCH) **Indexed:** Cont.Pg.Manage., IBR, Int.Lab.Doc., Irr.& Drain.Abstr., J.of Econ.Abstr., Rural Devel.Abstr., Rural Ext.Educ.& Tr.Abstr., Rural Recreat.Tour.Abstr., Soils & Fert., World Agri.Econ.& Rural Sociol.Abstr. **Document type:** academic/scholarly publication.
—BLDSC (3651.420000); UnCover.

330　320　　　UK　　ISSN 0265-0665
HB1
ECONOMIC AFFAIRS. 1980. q. £50($87) (foreign £55) (effective 1997). (Institute of Economic Affairs (London)) Blackwell Publishers Ltd., 108 Cowley Rd., Oxford OX4 1JF, England. TEL 44-1865-791100. FAX 44-1865-791347. E-mail: jnlinfo@blackwellpublishers.co.uk; URL: http://www.blackwellpublishers.co.uk. Ed. Colin Robinson; Pub. John Hayes. adv. contact: Griselda Anderson. bk.rev.; index. circ. 5,000. (reprint service avail. from SCH) **Indexed:** C.R.E.J., Rural Devel.Abstr. **Document type:** academic/scholarly publication.
—BLDSC (3651.422000); SWETS. **CCC.**
Formerly: Journal of Economic Affairs (ISSN 0260-8359)
Description: Each issue presents original research articles on an economic topic, such as market analysis, government policy, or inflation.
Refereed Serial

330　　　　　　AT　　ISSN 0313-5926
ECONOMIC ANALYSIS AND POLICY. 1970. 2/yr. Aus.$20 to individuals; institutions Aus.$25. Economic Society of Australia and New Zealand, Queensland Branch, c/o Queensland University of Technology, School of Economics & Finance, G.P.O. Box 2434, Brisbane, Qld. 4001, Australia. FAX 09-371-5896. TELEX UNIVQLD AA40315. Ed.Bd. adv.; bk.rev. circ. 550. **Indexed:** C.R.E.J., P.A.I.S.
—BLDSC (3651.441000); UnCover.

330　　　　　　YU　　ISSN 0351-286X
HD28
ECONOMIC ANALYSIS AND WORKERS MANAGEMENT. (Text in English, Serbo-Croatian) 1967. q. $30 to individuals; institutions $70. Udruzenje za Ekonomiju Samoupravljanja, Zmaj Jovina 12, P.O. Box 611, 11000 Belgrade, Yugoslavia. (Subscr. to: Prosveta, Terazije 16, Belgrade, Yugoslavia) Ed. Branko Horvat. adv.; bk.rev.; abstr.; bibl.; charts; stat. circ. 2,000. **Indexed:** C.R.E.J., J.of Econ.Lit., Mid.East: Abstr.& Ind., SSCI.
Formerly: Ekonomska Analiza - Economic Analysis (ISSN 0013-3213)

ECONOMIC ANALYSIS OF UNITED STATES SKI AREAS.
see SPORTS AND GAMES — Outdoor Life

338　　　　　　II　　ISSN 0012-995X
ECONOMIC & BUSINESS REVIEW. (Text in English) 1969. q. $10. S.S. Mohan, 31-13 East Patel Nagar, New Delhi 110 008, India. TEL 583926. adv.; bk.rev. circ. 2,100.

330　　　　　　UK　　ISSN 1351-3621
ECONOMIC & FINANCIAL REVIEW. 1994. q. £190 (outside Europe £205) (effective 1997). European Economics and Financial Centre, P.O. Box 2498, London W2 4LE, England. TEL 0171-229-0402. FAX 0171-221-5118. Ed. H.M. Scobie. **Document type:** academic/scholarly publication.
—BLDSC (3651.451500).
Description: Aims to provide a forum for communication among public sector, private sector and academic economists, removing the isolation that currently exists among these groups so that new theories will be more in tune with the real workings of the economy. Covers fiscal and economic policy-making on the government level as well as isssues facing market decision-makers who need to incorporate government actions into their forecasts.
Refereed Serial

ECONOMIC AND INDUSTRIAL DEMOCRACY; an international journal. see POLITICAL SCIENCE

330　320　　　II　　ISSN 0012-9976
HC431
ECONOMIC AND POLITICAL WEEKLY; a journal of current economic and political affairs. (Text in English) 1966. w. Rs.475 to individuals (foreign $100); institutions Rs.600 (foreign $150). Sameeksha Trust, Hitkari House, 284, Shahid Bhagatsingh Rd., Mumbai 400 038, India. TEL 91-22-2676072. FAX 91-22-269-6072. E-mail: epwl@shakti.ncst.ernet.in; URL: http://www.commercenetindia.com. Ed. Krishna Raj. adv.: page Rs.6000; trim 270 x 210. bk.rev.; charts; stat. circ. 12,000. (also avail. in microfiche from IDC) **Indexed:** Abstr.Rural Dev.Trop., Arts & Hum.Cit.Ind., ASCA, Asian-Pac.Econ.Lit., CLOSS, Cott.& Trop.Fibr.Abstr., Curr.Cont., Dairy Sci.Abstr., Geo.Abstr., IDA, Int.Lab.Doc., Int.Polit.Sci.Abstr., Irr.& Drain.Abstr., Mid.East: Abstr.& Ind., P.A.I.S., Popul.Ind., Pub.Admin.Abstr., Risk Abstr., Rural Devel.Abstr., Rural Recreat.Tour.Abstr., Soils & Fert., SSCI, Trop.Oil Seeds Abstr., World Agri.Econ.& Rural Sociol.Abstr. **Document type:** academic/scholarly publication.
—BLDSC (3651.480000); SWETS; UnCover.
Formerly: Economic Weekly.
Refereed Serial

330.1　　　　II　　ISSN 0070-8437
ECONOMIC AND SCIENTIFIC RESEARCH FOUNDATION. ANNUAL REPORT. 1967. a. free. Economic and Scientific Research Foundation, Federation House, New Delhi 110001, India. circ. 1,000.
Description: Features annual activities of the foundation.

330 300　　　　IE
ECONOMIC AND SOCIAL RESEARCH INSTITUTE. BROADSHEET SERIES. 1969. irreg., no.29, 1993. I£10. Economic and Social Research Institute, 4 Burlington Rd., Dublin 4, Ireland. TEL 353-1-6671525. FAX 353-1-6686231. Ed. B.J. Whelan. R&P contact: John Roughan. **Document type:** monographic series.

330　　　　　　IE
ECONOMIC AND SOCIAL RESEARCH INSTITUTE. GENERAL RESEARCH SERIES. 1961. irreg., no.170, 1996. I£12.95. (Economic and Social Research Institute) Oak Tree Press, Merrion Bldgs., Lower Merrion St., Dublin 2, Ireland. TEL 353-1-6761600. FAX 353-1-6761644. R&P contact: David Givens. **Indexed:** Geo.Abstr., Rural Recreat.Tour.Abstr., World Agri.Econ.& Rural Sociol.Abstr. **Document type:** academic/scholarly publication.
Former titles: Economic and Social Research Institute. Publications Series. Paper (ISSN 0070-8755); (until 1967, no.35): Economic Research Institute. Paper (ISSN 0332-3358)

330　　　　　　IE　　ISSN 0790-9470
HC10
ECONOMIC AND SOCIAL RESEARCH INSTITUTE. MEDIUM TERM REVIEW. a. I£35. Economic and Social Research Institute, 4 Burlington Rd., Dublin 4, Ireland. TEL 353-1-6671525. FAX 353-1-6686231. Ed. B.J. Whelan. R&P contact: John Roughan. **Document type:** corporate report.
Description: Assesses the effects of international developments and Irish economic policies on the domestic economy in recent years.

330 300　　　　IE
ECONOMIC AND SOCIAL RESEARCH INSTITUTE. MEMORANDUM SERIES. 1962. irreg., no.187, 1994. I£3 per no. Economic and Social Research Institute, 4 Burlington Rd., Dublin 4, Ireland. TEL 353-1-6671525. FAX 353-1-6686231. Ed. B.J. Whelan. R&P contact: John Roughan. **Document type:** monographic series.

330　　　　　　IE
ECONOMIC AND SOCIAL RESEARCH INSTITUTE. POLICY RESEARCH SERIES. irreg., no.29, 1996. I£12. Economic and Social Research Institute, 4 Burlington Rd., Dublin 4, Ireland. TEL 353-1-6671525. FAX 353-1-6686231. Ed. B.J. Whelan. R&P contact: John Roughan. **Indexed:** Rural Recreat.Tour.Abstr., World Agri.Econ.& Rural Sociol.Abstr. **Document type:** monographic series.

330 300　　　　IE
ECONOMIC AND SOCIAL RESEARCH INSTITUTE. TECHNICAL SERIES. 1986. irreg., no.11, 1995. Economic and Social Research Institute, 4 Burlington Rd., Dublin 4, Ireland. TEL 353-1-6671525. FAX 353-1-6686231. Ed. B.J. Whelan. R&P contact: John Roughan. **Document type:** monographic series.

330　300　　　IE　　ISSN 0012-9984
HC257.I6
ECONOMIC AND SOCIAL REVIEW. 1969. q. $35 to individuals; libraries $55. Economic and Social Studies, 4 Burlington Rd., Dublin 4, Ireland. TEL 353-1-6671525. FAX 353-1-6686231. Eds. G. Boyle, H. Tovey. R&P contact: C. O'Regan. adv.; bk.rev.; index. circ. 750. **Indexed:** Amer.Hist.& Life (1978-), ASCA, ASSIA, BPIA, Bus.Ind., C.R.E.J., Cont.Pg.Manage., Curr.Cont.(1983-), Fam.Ind., Geo.Abstr.H.G., Hist.Abstr. (1978-), IDA, IMFL, Int.Polit.Sci.Abstr., J.of Econ.Lit., Mid.East: Abstr.& Ind., P.A.I.S., Rural Recreat.Tour.Abstr., SSCI, Stat.Theor.Meth.Abstr., World Agri.Econ.& Rural Sociol.Abstr. **Document type:** academic/scholarly publication.
—BLDSC (3651.520000); Genuine Article; SWETS; UnCover.
Description: Publishes papers, both theoretical and applied, in all areas of social science.

330　　　　　　LY
ECONOMIC BULLETIN. m. Jamahiriya News Agency, Sharia al-Fateh, P.O. Box 2303, Tripoli, Libya. TEL 37106. TELEX 20841.

330　　　　　　UK　　ISSN 0343-754X
HC10
ECONOMIC BULLETIN (ALDERSHOT). 1963. m. £180 (outside Europe £207.50) (effective 1997). Ashgate Publishing Ltd. (Subsidiary of: Gower Publishing Co. Ltd.), Gower House, Croft Rd., Aldershot, Hants. GU11 3HR, England. TEL 44-1252-331551. FAX 44-1252-344405. TELEX 337210 BUREAU G. Ed.Bd. (back issues avail.) **Indexed:** Key to Econ.Sci. **Document type:** bulletin.

330　　　　　　GH　　ISSN 0013-0044
ECONOMIC BULLETIN OF GHANA.* 1957. q. $5.50. Economic Society of Ghana, P.O. Box 22, Legon, Accra, Ghana. Ed. J.C. Degraft-Johnson. **Document type:** bulletin.

330　　　　　　US　　ISSN 0428-1276
HC108.C7
ECONOMIC COMMENTARY. 1948. s-m. free. Federal Reserve Bank of Cleveland, Box 6387, Cleveland, OH 44101. TEL 216-579-3079. FAX 216-579-2477. Eds. Robin Ratliff, Tess Ferg. R&P contact: Kathy Popovich. cum.index: 1982-1990. circ. 12,000. (back issues avail.) **Indexed:** ABI Inform., Fed Print. **Document type:** newsletter.
●Also available online. Vendor(s): Information Access Co., UMI.
—UMI.
Supersedes: Business Trends.
Description: Presents scholarly papers on current issues pertaining to patterns and trends in foreign and domestic banking, trade, finance, and investment.

330　　　　　　UN　　ISSN 0251-0197
ECONOMIC COMMISSION FOR EUROPE. ANNUAL REPORT. French edition: Nations Unies. Commission Economique pour l'Europe. Rapport Annuel (ISSN 0251-0189); Russian edition: Organizatsiya Ob'edinennykh Natsii. Evropeiskaya Ekonomicheskaya Komissiya. God ovoi Doklad (ISSN 0251-0200) 1947. a. Economic Commission for Europe, Palais des Nations, 1211 Geneva 10, Switzerland. TEL 917-1234. FAX 917-0123. TELEX 412962.

330　　　　　　US　　ISSN 8755-8629
HT123
ECONOMIC DEVELOPMENT COMMENTARY. 1981. q. $30. National Council for Urban Economic Development, 1730 K. St., N.W., Washington, DC 20006. TEL 202-223-4735. FAX 202-223-4745. adv. circ. 2,000.
—UnCover.

330　　　　　　US　　ISSN 0424-2769
HG179
ECONOMIC EDUCATION BULLETIN. 1960. m. $25. American Institute for Economic Research, Box 1000, Great Barrington, MA 01230. TEL 413-528-1216. FAX 413-528-0103.

BUSINESS AND ECONOMICS

330   NZ   ISSN 0114-023X
HC661
ECONOMIC FORECASTS. 1988. 2/yr. NZ.$22.50 in New Zealand & Australia; elsewhere NZ.$25 (effective 1996-97). Reserve Bank of New Zealand, Corporate Services, 2 The Terrace, P.O. Box 2498, Wellington, New Zealand. TEL 64-4-472-2029. FAX 64-4-473-8554. TELEX NZ 3368. **Document type:** corporate report.

330   US   ISSN 0095-2583
HB1   CODEN: ECIND6
ECONOMIC INQUIRY. 1962. 4/yr. $150 (foreign $165) (effective 1997). Western Economic Association International, 7400 Center Ave., Ste. 109, Huntington Beach, CA 92647. TEL 714-898-3222. (Dist. by: Allen Press, Inc., Box 1897, Lawrence, KS 66044) Ed. William S. Neilson. R&P contact: Eldon J. Dvorak. adv.; charts; illus.; index. circ. 3,500. (also avail. in microform from UMI; back issues avail.; reprint service avail. from UMI) **Indexed:** ABI Inform., Amer.Hist.& Life (1978-), ASCA, Asian-Pac.Econ.Lit., BPIA, Bus.Ind., C.R.E.J., Cont.Pg.Manage., Curr.Cont., Fam.Ind., Hist.Abstr. (1978-), IBR, Ind.Per.Art.Relat.Law, Int.Bibl.Soc.Sci., J.of Econ.Lit., Mid.East: Abstr.& Ind., P.A.I.S., PHRA, Risk Abstr., Rural Recreat.Tour.Abstr., Sage Pub.Admin.Abstr., Sage Urb.Stud.Abstr., Soc.Sci.Ind., SSCI, Tr.& Indus.Ind., World Agri.Econ.& Rural Sociol.Abstr., World Bank.Abstr. **Document type:** academic/scholarly publication.
●Also available online. Vendor(s): Information Access Co., Knight-Ridder Information, Inc.
—BLDSC (3653.660000); Genuine Article; KR SourceOne; SWETS; UMI; UnCover. **CCC.**
Formerly: Western Economic Journal (ISSN 0043-3640)
Refereed Serial

330   UK   ISSN 0013-0133
HB1   CODEN: ECJOAB
ECONOMIC JOURNAL. 1891. bi-m. £115($196) (foreign £124) (effective 1997). (Royal Economic Society) Blackwell Publishers Ltd., 108 Cowley Rd., Oxford OX4 1JF, England. TEL 44-1865-791100. FAX 44-1865-791347. E-mail: jnlinfo@ blackwellpublishers.co.uk; URL: http://www. blackwellpublishers.co.uk. Ed. M. Wickens. adv.; bk.rev.; index. circ. 7,000. (also avail. in microfilm from UMI,PMC; reprint service avail. from UMI) **Indexed:** ABI Inform., Amer.Hist.& Life (1955-), ASCA, Asian-Pac.Econ.Lit., BPIA, Br.Hum.Ind., C.R.E.J., Cont.Pg.Manage., Curr.Cont., Excerp.Med., Geo.Abstr.H.G., Hist.Abstr. (1955-), HRIS, IBR, IDA, Int.Lab.Doc., J.of Econ.Abstr., J.of Econ.Lit., Key to Econ.Sci., Mid.East: Abstr.& Ind., P.A.I.S., PSI, Pub.Admin.Abstr., Ref.Sour., Risk Abstr., Rural Recreat.Tour.Abstr., SCIMP, Soc.Sci.Ind., SSCI, Tr.& Indus.Ind., Work Rel.Abstr., World Agri.Econ.& Rural Sociol.Abstr., World Bank.Abstr. **Document type:** academic/scholarly publication.
●Also available online. Vendor(s): Information Access Co.
—BLDSC (3653.800000); Genuine Article; KR SourceOne; SWETS; UMI; UnCover. **CCC.**
Refereed Serial

ECONOMIC JUSTICE REPORT; global issues of economic justice. see *POLITICAL SCIENCE — International Relations*

330   330.1   IT   ISSN 0391-5026
HB1
ECONOMIC NOTES. Italian edition: Note Economiche (ISSN 0391-8289) (Text and summaries in English) 1972. 3/yr. free. Monte dei Paschi di Siena, Piazza Salimbeni 3, 53100 Siena, Italy. TEL 0577-294401. FAX 0577-294084. TELEX 570080 M PASCHI. Ed. Lorenzo Maccari. bk.rev.; bibl.; charts; stat.; index, cum.index: 1972-1991. **Indexed:** Curr.Cont.(1973-), J.of Econ.Lit., Stat.Theor.Meth.Abstr. (1973-).
—BLDSC (3653.932000).
Description: Covers economic theory, methodology and international economics.

330   AT
ECONOMIC OUTLOOK. 1964. m. Aus.$900 (effective 1997). B I S Shrapnel Pty. Ltd., Level 8, 181 Miller St., N. Sydney, N.W.S. 2060, Australia. TEL 61-2-99595924. FAX 61-2-99595795. Ed. Frank Gelber. circ. 560.
Description: Analysis and forecasts of prospects for the Australian economy.

330   JO
ECONOMIC PERSPECTIVES. bi-w. $350. Media Services International, P.O. Box 9313, Amman, Jordan. TEL 648298. TELEX 21392. URL: http://www. arabia.com/ep/. Ed. Osama ash-Sharif. adv. contact: Mahmoud Fares. **Document type:** newspaper.
Formerly: Al-Ghad al-Iqtisadi.

330   UK   ISSN 0266-4658
HD87
ECONOMIC POLICY; a European forum. 1985. s-a. £69($109) (foreign £69) (effective 1997). (European Economic Association) Blackwell Publishers Ltd., 108 Cowley Rd., Oxford OX4 1JF, England. TEL 44-1865-791100. FAX 44-1865-791347. E-mail: jnlinfo@ blackwellpublishers.co.uk; URL: http://www. blackwellpublishers.co.uk. (Co-sponsors: Maison des Sciences de l'Homme, Centre for Economic Policy Research) Eds. Georges de Menil, Richard Portes. adv. (also avail. in microform from UMI; back issues avail.; reprint service avail. from SWZ) **Indexed:** Asian-Pac.Econ.Lit., ELLIS, Geo.Abstr.H.G., IDA, J.of Econ.Lit. **Document type:** academic/scholarly publication.
—BLDSC (3654.091300); SWETS; UMI; UnCover. **CCC.**
Refereed Serial

330   AT   ISSN 0013-0249
HC601
ECONOMIC RECORD. 1925. 4/yr. Aus.$55 to non-members (foreign Aus.$67) (effective 1997). Economic Society of Australia, c/o R.A. Williams, Ed., Dept. of Economics, Melbourne University, Melbourne, Vic. 3052, Australia. TEL 61-3-93447426. FAX 61-3-93446899. E-mail: g.isgro@acomfac.unimelb.edu.au. (Subscr. to: Brown Prior Anderson Pty. Ltd., 5 Evans St., Burwood, Vic. 3125, Australia) R&P contact: R.A. Williams. adv. contact: C. Orchard. bk.rev.; bibl.; index. circ. 3,800. (also avail. in microfilm from UMI; reprint service avail. from ISI,UMI) **Indexed:** ASCA, Asian-Pac.Econ.Lit., Aus.P.A.I.S., Aus.Rd.Ind., Bus.Ind., C.R.E.J., Curr.Cont., Geo.Abstr.H.G., IBR, IDA, J.of Econ.Lit., Key to Econ.Sci., Mid.East: Abstr.& Ind., P.A.I.S., Rural Recreat.Tour.Abstr., SSCI, Tr.& Indus.Ind., Work Rel.Abstr., World Agri.Econ.& Rural Sociol.Abstr., World Bank.Abstr. **Document type:** academic/scholarly publication.
●Also available online. Vendor(s): Information Access Co., UMI.
—BLDSC (3654.200000); Genuine Article; SWETS; UMI; UnCover. **CCC.**
Refereed Serial

330   US   ISSN 1058-661X
ECONOMIC REFORM TODAY. 1991. q. Center for International Private Enterprise, 1615 H St., N.W., Washington, DC 20062-2000. TEL 202-463-5901. FAX 202-887-3447. E-mail: cipe@cipe.org; URL: http://www.cipe.org. Ed.By.
—BLDSC (3654.220000).

330   PH   ISSN 0424-2904
ECONOMIC RESEARCH JOURNAL. 1953. q. University of the East, Faculty of the Graduate School, Sampaloc, Manila, Philippines.

338.9   PK   ISSN 0531-8955
HC440.5.A1
ECONOMIC REVIEW. (Text in English) 1970. m. Rs.500($75) Economic and Industrial Publications, Al-Masiha, 17 Abdullah Haroon Rd., P.O. Box 7843, Karachi 74400, Pakistan. Ed. Iqbal Haidari. adv.; bk.rev.; charts; stat. circ. 50,000. **Indexed:** BPIA, IBR, P.A.I.S., Tr.& Indus.Ind. **Document type:** trade publication.
●Also available online. Vendor(s): Information Access Co.

330   BG   ISSN 0070-8631
ECONOMIC REVIEW.* (Text in English) 1964. a. University of Dhaka, Economics Association, Ramna, Dhaka 1000, Bangladesh.

330   CE   ISSN 0259-9775
HC424.A1
ECONOMIC REVIEW. 1975. m. $35. People's Bank, Research Department, Sir Chittampalam A. Gardinar Mawatha, Colombo 2, Sri Lanka. TEL 01-327082. Ed. L. Siriwardene. **Indexed:** Rural Devel.Abstr. **Document type:** academic/scholarly publication.
—BLDSC (3654.575000).

330   IO   ISSN 0125-9571
ECONOMIC REVIEW. (Text in English) 1966. m. free. PT. Bank Negara Indonesia (Bank BNI), Jalan Jenderal Sudirman, Kav.1, P.O. Box 2955, Jakarta 10220, Indonesia. TEL 62-21-2511946. FAX 62-21-2511961. TELEX 65511 KBBNI IA. Ed. Muchlis Harun. circ. 2,000. (also avail. in microfiche from IDC)
Description: Serves as an informative communication media between Bank BNI and its clients.

330   UK   ISSN 0265-0290
ECONOMIC REVIEW. 1982. 4/yr. (Sept.-Apr.). £17.95 (Europe £23.50; rest of world £29) (effective 1997 & 1998). Philip Allan Publishers Ltd., Market Pl., Deddington, Oxon. OX15 0SE, England. TEL 44-1869-338652. FAX 44-1869-338803. R&P contact: Ceri Jenkins. adv. contact: Ceri Jenkins. **Document type:** academic/scholarly publication.
—BLDSC (3654.580000).

330   JA   ISSN 0013-0273
HB9
ECONOMIC REVIEW (KYOTO)/KEIZAI RONSO. (Text in Japanese; title and contents page in English) 1915. m. $50. Kyoto University, Economic Society - Kyoto Daigaku Keizai Gakkai, Sakyo-ku, Kyoto 606, Japan. index. circ. 1,600. **Indexed:** Amer.Hist.& Life (1955-1984), Hist.Abstr. (1955-1984).
—UnCover.

ECONOMIC REVIEW OF THE YEAR - THE GREEK ECONOMY. see *BUSINESS AND ECONOMICS — Economic Situation And Conditions*

330.9593   TH
ECONOMIC REVIEWS. (Text in English) s-a. Post Publishing Co., Ltd., Bangkok Post Bldg., 136 Nanong Rd., Off Sunthorn Kosa Rd., Klong Toey, Bangkok 10110, Thailand. TEL 662-240-3700. FAX 662-240-3790.
Description: Summarizes and analyzes Thailand's economy.

330   AT   ISSN 0812-0439
ECONOMIC SOCIETY OF AUSTRALIA. ECONOMIC PAPERS. 1941; N.S. 1982. 4/yr. Aus.$28 to non-members (foreign Aus.$40) (effective 1997). Economic Society of Australia Inc. (Ivanhoe), 23 Wallis Ave. E., Ivanhoe, Vic. 3079, Australia. TEL 61-2-2077709. FAX 61-2-3164960. Ed. Ivo Favotto. R&P contact: C. Orchard. adv. contact: C. Orchard. bk.rev.; bibl.; circ. 2,000. (paid). **Indexed:** Aus.P.A.I.S. **Document type:** academic/scholarly publication.
—BLDSC (3653.977000); UnCover.
Formerly: Economic Society of Australia and New Zealand. New South Wales and Victorian Branches. Economic Papers (ISSN 0013-0354)
Description: Contains papers dealing with issues in business, economics and economic policies.

330   II   ISSN 0013-0362
HC10
ECONOMIC STUDIES; a journal of economic outlook and trend. Bengali edition: Arthik Prasanga (ISSN 0970-7654) 1960-1985; resumed 1988. q. Rs.100 to individuals (foreign $40); institutions Rs.100 (foreign $40). Economic Studies & Journals Publishing Co., 2 Private Rd., Dum Dum, Calcutta 700 074, West Bengal, India. TEL 551-2288. (Subscr. to: P.O. Box 10868, Calcutta 700 009, West Bengal, India) Ed. Dwijendranath Mukherjea. adv.; bk.rev.; charts; illus.; pat.; stat.; tr.lit.; tr.mk. circ. 25,432. **Document type:** newspaper.
—UnCover.

330   BG   ISSN 1021-125X
ECONOMIC TIMES. (Text in English) 1989. w. $56. Munirul Huq, Ed. & Pub., 65-2 Laboratory Rd., South Dhanmondi, Dhaka 1205, Bangladesh. TEL 880-2-505376. FAX 880-2-834933. circ. 6,200. **Document type:** newspaper.

330   IE   ISSN 0332-3951
ECONOMIC TRENDS. 1970. m. Irish Business and Employers Confederation, Confederation House, 84-86 Lower Baggot St., Dublin 2, Ireland. TEL 353-1-6601011. FAX 353-1-6601717. URL: http://www.iol.ie/ibec. Ed. David Croughan. (reprint service avail. from SCH) **Document type:** bulletin.
Description: Provides commentary with graphical summary of the current economic situation.

BUSINESS AND ECONOMICS

330   US
ECONOMIC UPDATE. m. free. Ways & Means Committee, Economic Group, State Capitol, Rm. 412, Albany, NY 12248. TEL 518-455-4006. Ed. Edward Cupoli. **Document type:** government publication.
   Description: Covers the State's current economic conditions and financial plan.

330   UK   ISSN 0013-0427
HB1
ECONOMICA. 1921. q. £58($92) (foreign £58) (effective 1997). (London School of Economics & Political Science) Blackwell Publishers Ltd., 108 Cowley Rd., Oxford OX4 1JF, England. TEL 44-1865-791100. FAX 44-1865-791347. E-mail: jnlinfo@blackwellpublishers.co.uk; URL: http://www.blackwellpublishers.co.uk. Ed. Hugh Wills. adv.; bk.rev.; charts; stat.; index. circ. 3,800. (back issues avail.) **Indexed:** Amer.Hist.& Life (1954-1992), Arts & Hum.Cit.Ind., Asian-Pac.Econ.Lit., Br.Hum.Ind., C.R.E.J., Cont.Pg.Manage., Curr.Cont.(1981-), Excerp.Med., Geo.Abstr.H.G., Hist.Abstr. (1954-1992), IBR, IDA, Int.Polit.Sci.Abstr., J.of Econ.Lit., Mid.East: Abstr.& Ind., P.A.I.S., Rural Recreat.Tour.Abstr., SCIMP, Soc.Sci.Ind., Stat.Theor.Meth.Abstr. (1981-), World Agri.Econ.& Rural Sociol.Abstr., World Bank.Abstr.
—BLDSC (3656.900000); Genuine Article; KR SourceOne; SWETS; UMI; UnCover. **CCC.**
   Refereed Serial

330 375   AT
ECONOMICS. 1966. q. Aus.$20. Economics and Commercial Teachers' Association of New South Wales, Box 187, Rose Bay, N.S.W. 2029, Australia. Ed. A. Shellshear. bk.rev. circ. 1,000. **Indexed:** C.R.E.J., Per.Islam. (1994-).

330   US   ISSN 1058-1758
ECONOMICS. (Subseries of: S I R S Global Perspectives (ISSN 1058-1731)) 1991. a. $85. Social Issues Resources Series, Box 2348, Boca Raton, FL 33427-2348. TEL 561-994-0079; 800-232-SIRS. FAX 561-994-4704. E-mail: custserve@sirs.com; URL: http://www.sirs.com. Ed. Trudy Collins; Pub. Eleanor Goldstein. R&P contact: Bonnie Milnes. (looseleaf format; back issues avail.) **Document type:** academic/scholarly publication.
   Description: Reprints 70 articles exploring economic issues of global importance, as well as key U.S. economic issues.

ECONOMICS AND BUSINESS FOR THE FUTURE (YEAR); first degree courses in economics and business. see EDUCATION — Guides To Schools And Colleges

330   IO
ECONOMICS AND FINANCE IN INDONESIA. (Text in English) 1948. q. University of Indonesia, Institute for Economic and Social Research, Jalan Raya Salemba 4, Jakarta 10430, Indonesia. TEL 021-330225. FAX 021-334310. circ. 4,000.

ECONOMICS OF SCIENCE, TECHNOLOGY AND INNOVATION. see TECHNOLOGY: COMPREHENSIVE WORKS

330   FR   ISSN 0013-0494
HB3
ECONOMIE APPLIQUEE. 1948. q. 660 F. (foreign 690 F.). (Institut de Sciences Mathematiques et Economiques Appliquees, Paris) Presses Universitaires de Grenoble, B.P. 47, 38040 Grenoble Cedex 9, France. TEL 76-82-56-51. FAX 76-82-56-54. index. circ. 2,000. (reprint service avail. from KTO) **Indexed:** IBR, J.of Econ.Lit., Key to Econ.Sci., P.A.I.S.For.Lang.Ind., SSCI.
—BLDSC (3657.400000); SWETS.

330   CN   ISSN 1188-4304
ECONOMIE ET AFFAIRES AU QUEBEC. a. Can.$44.95 (effective 1997). Quebec dans le Monde, C.P. 8503, Sainte-Foy, PQ G1V 4N5, Canada. TEL 418-659-5540. FAX 418-659-4143. **Document type:** directory.
   Description: Contains listings of chambers of commerce, major firms, and banks in Quebec.

330.1   FR   ISSN 0070-8801
ECONOMIE ET SOCIETE. 1970. irreg. price varies. Editions du Seuil, 27 rue Jacob, 75261 Paris Cedex 06, France. Ed. Edmond Blanc. **Indexed:** Curr.Cont., Key to Econ.Sci.
—CCC.

330   FR
ECONOMIES ET SOCIETES. 1945. m. 1250 F. (foreign 1350 F.). Presses Universitaire de Grenoble, B.P. 47X, 38060 Grenoble Cedex, France. TEL 76-82-56-51. FAX 76-82-56-54. TELEX UNISOG 980810. **Indexed:** ELLIS, J.of Econ.Lit.
   Description: Concentrates on the different areas of economic research.

331   FR   ISSN 0068-4821
ECONOMIES ET SOCIETES. SERIE AB. ECONOMIE DU TRAVAIL. 1960. irreg., latest 1987. 350 F. Presses Universitaires de Grenoble, B.P. 47, 38040 Grenoble Cedex 9, France. Dir. H. Bartoli. circ. 1,600.
—SWETS.

330.1   FR   ISSN 0068-4872
ECONOMIES ET SOCIETES. SERIE T. INFORMATION - RECHERCHE INNOVATION. 1959. irreg. 350 F. Presses Universitaires de Grenoble, B.P. 47, 38040 Grenoble Cedex 9, France. Dir. F. Russo. circ. 1,600.

330 300   BE   ISSN 0013-0575
ECONOMISCH EN SOCIAAL TIJDSCHRIFT. (Text in Dutch, English, French, German) 1947. 4/yr. 850 BEF to individuals (Netherlands 1100 BEF; elsewhere 1650 BEF); institutions 1300 BEF (Netherlands 1550 BEF; elsewhere 1650 BEF) (effective 1998). Universitaire Faculteiten Sint-Ignatius te Antwerpen, Venusstraat 35, 2000 Antwerp, Belgium. TEL 32-3-2204523. FAX 32-3-2204524. E-mail: est.lerno.I@alpha.ufsia.ac.be. Ed. Paul Roosens. adv.; bk.rev.; charts; index. circ. 2,000. (also avail. in microform from UMI; reprint service avail. from UMI) **Indexed:** ELLIS, IBR, Key to Econ.Sci. **Document type:** academic/scholarly publication.
—SWETS; UMI.

330   NE   ISSN 0013-063X
HB9   CODEN: ENOME9
DE ECONOMIST. (Text in English) 1852. q. fl.400 to institutions; $202.50 to institutions in U.S. (effective 1998). (Royal Netherlands Economic Association) Kluwer Academic Publishers, Postbus 17, 3300 AA Dordrecht, Netherlands. TEL 31-78-6392392. FAX 31-78-6392254. TELEX 29245 KAPG NL. E-mail: services@wkap.nl; URL: http://www.wkap.nl. (Dist. by: Kluwer Academic Publishers Group, P.O. Box 322, 3300 AH Dordrecht, Netherlands. TEL 31-78-6392392. FAX 31-78-6546474; N. America dist. addr.: Box 358, Accord Sta., Hingham, MA 02018-0358. TEL 617-871-6600. FAX 617-871-6528) Ed. Theo. C.M.J. van de Klundert. adv.; bk.rev.; bibl.; index, cum.index every 10-20 yrs. circ. 3,000. (reprint service avail. from UMI) **Indexed:** ABI Inform., B.P.I., Bk.Rev.Dig., Bus.Ind., Deep Sea Res.& Oceanogr.Abstr., Excerp.Med., Geo.Abstr.H.G., IDA, J.of Econ.Lit., Key to Econ.Sci., Mid.East: Abstr.& Ind., P.A.I.S., PROMT, Risk Abstr., Soc.Sci.Ind., SSCI, Telegen, W.R.C.Inf. **Document type:** academic/scholarly publication.
—BLDSC (3659.310000); Genuine Article; SWETS; UMI; UnCover. **CCC.**
   Description: Publishes review articles and original studies dealing with theoretical issues in economics, as well as applied research, with a focus on Europe.
   Refereed Serial

330   PO   ISSN 0870-4236
ECONOMISTA. 1982. q? Cr.$2000 per no. Associacao Portuguesa de Economistas, R. Francisco Rodriguez lobo, 2 r-c., 1000 Lisbon, Portugal. TEL 65-99-50. FAX 65-14-30. Ed. Manuela Morgado.

330   MX
EL ECONOMISTA. 1989. 5/w. Mex.$450; newsstand price: Mex.$.45. Periodico Economista S.A. de C.V., Avda. Coyoacan 515, 03100 Mexico DF, Mexico. TEL 52-5-3265454. FAX 52-5-6829369. E-mail: econom@condor.dgsca.unam.mx; URL: http:serpiente.dgsca.unam.mx/el_economista/. Ed. Ricardo Medina; Pub. Luis E. Mercado. adv. contact: Jesus Hernandez. circ. 28,400 (paid). cols./p.: 4; pp./issue: 64. (tabloid format) **Document type:** newspaper.

330   SP   ISSN 0212-4386
ECONOMISTAS. 1983. q. Colegio de Economistas de Madrid, Flora 1, 28013 Madrid, Spain. TEL 34-1-5594602. Ed. Emilio Ontiveros Baeza.
—CINDOC.

ECONOMY AND SOCIETY. see SOCIAL SCIENCES: COMPREHENSIVE WORKS

ECONOMY AND THE FOREIGN POLICY. see BUSINESS AND ECONOMICS — Economic Systems And Theories, Economic History

330   CH
ECONOMY TODAY/CHIN JIH CHING CHI. (Text in Chinese) m. $22 in Hong Kong and Macao; Asia $25; elsewhere $28. 15 Foochow St., Taipei, Taiwan 10722, Republic of China. TEL 02-341-2338. adv.; illus.
   Description: Covers the economic situation for businesspeople, entrepreneurs, analysts. Also includes some general interest articles.

ECOS DE A L A D I. (Asociacion Latinoamericana de Integracion) see POLITICAL SCIENCE

330   GW
EDEKA HANDELS-RUNDSCHAU. 1907. s-m. DM.80.40. Edeka Verlag GmbH, New-York-Ring 6, 22297 Hamburg, Germany. TEL 040-6377-2200. FAX 040-6377-2478. Ed. Folker des Coudres. circ. 14,000. **Document type:** trade publication.

330   MP
EDIYN DZASGIYN BOLOVSROL/ECONOMIC EDUCATION. (Text in Mongolian) 18/yr. Mongolian People's Revolutionary Party, Ulan Bator, Mongolia. Ed. D. Surenjav. circ. 37,000.

330   FR   ISSN 0990-5413
EDUCATION ECONOMIE. 4/yr. 110 F. (foreign 135 F.). Centre National de Documentation Pedagogique, 29 rue d'Ulm, 75230 Paris Cedex 05, France. TEL 33-1-46349000. FAX 33-1-46345544. (Subscr. to: CNDP-Abonnement, B750, 60732 Ste. Genevieve Cedex, France. FAX 33-3-44033013)

330   US
EINHORN NEWSLETTER. q. Einhorn Associates, 2323 N. Mayfair Rd., Ste. 490, Milwaukee, WI 53226-1507. TEL 414-453-4488. FAX 414-453-4831. Ed. Stephen Einhorn. **Document type:** newsletter.

330   SP
EJECUTIVOS FINANCIEROS. 6/yr. Asociacion Espanola de Ejecutivos Financieros - Spanish Association of Financial Executives, Carranza, 25, 3o, 28004 Madrid, Spain. TEL 1-445-09-97. Ed. Luis G. Justicia. circ. 20,000.

330   IO
EKONOMI DAN PEMBANGUNAN. 1977. m. Lambung Mangkurat University, Faculty of Economics - Universitas Lambung Mangkurat, Fakultas Ekonomi, Jl. Lambung Mangkurat 20, Banjarmasin, Indonesia. **Indexed:** E.I.

330   IO   ISSN 0216-3659
EKONOMI INDONESIA. (Text in English) 1971. bi-m. Jalan Merdeka, Timur 11-12, Jakarta, Indonesia. TEL 021-494458. Ed. Z. Achmad. circ. 20,000. **Indexed:** Asian-Pac.Econ.Lit.

330   XO   ISSN 0013-3035
EKONOMICKY CASOPIS/ECONOMICAL JOURNAL. (Text in Slovak; contents page and summaries in English and Russian) 1953. m. $126 in US (effective 1996). (Slovenska Akademia Vied, Ekonomicky Ustav) Vydavatel'stvo S A P, s.r.o. - Slovak Academic Press Ltd., P.O. Box 57, Nam. Slobody 6, 810 05 Bratislava, Slovakia. TEL 42-7-211728. (Co-sponsor: Slovenska Akademie Vied, Prognosticky Ustav) Ed. Egon Hlavaty. bk.rev.; bibl.; stat.; index. **Indexed:** ASCA, Bus.Ind., Curr.Cont., Geo.Abstr.H.G., IDA, SCIMP, SSCI.
—Genuine Article.
   Description: Presents papers directed to economic problems and mathematical solutions. For economists in production and management centers, teachers and university and specialized secondary school students.

330 510   RU   ISSN 0424-7388
HB74.M3   CODEN: EMAMBV
EKONOMIKA I MATEMATICHESKIE METODY. 1965. q. $167 (effective 1998). Central Institute of Economics and Mathematics, Ul. Krasikova 32, 117418 Moscow, Russia. Ed. V.L. Makarov. circ. 3,500. **Document type:** academic/scholarly publication.
—BLDSC (0397.630000); KNAW.

BUSINESS AND ECONOMICS

335   RU
EKONOMIKA I ZHIZN. 1918. w. $260 (effective 1998). Bumazhny pr. 14, 101462 Moscow, Russia. TEL 7-095-2573456. FAX 7-095-2573965. (Dist. by: Mezhdunarodnaya Kniga, B. Yakimanka 39, 117049 Moscow, Russia. TEL 7-095-2384967. FAX 7-095-2384634; Dist. in U.S. by: Victor Kamkin Inc., 4956 Boiling Brook Pkwy., Rockville, MD 20852. TEL 301-881-5973) Ed. B.G. Vladimirov. adv.; illus. circ. 750,000. (tabloid format; also avail. in microform from UMI) **Indexed:** Curr.Dig.Sov.Press, PROMT.
   Formerly (until 1990): Ekonomicheskaya Gazeta (ISSN 0013-3132)

330   YU   ISSN 0353-443X
HD28
EKONOMIKA PREDUZECA. (Summaries in English) 1953. m. 1600 din.($150) Savez Ekonomista Srbije, Marsala Tita 16, Belgrade, Yugoslavia. Ed. Jovan Rankovic. adv.; abstr.; bibl.; charts. circ. 3,000.
   Former titles (until 1989): Ekonomika Udruzenog Rada (ISSN 0350-1434); (until 1984): Ekonomika Preduzeca (ISSN 0013-3078)

330   RU   ISSN 0235-2494
HD1491.R9
EKONOMIKA SEL'SKOKHOZYAISTVENNYKH I PERERABATYVAYUSHCHIKH PREDPRIYATII. 1926. m. $108 (effective 1996). Sadovaya-Spasskaya, 18, kom. 422, 107807 Moscow, Russia. TEL 7-095-2071580. FAX 7-095-2072870. (Dist. by: Mezhdunarodnaya Kniga, B. Yakimanka 39, 117049 Moscow, Russia. TEL 7-095-2384967. FAX 7-095-2384634) Ed. V.A. Orlov. circ. 18,600.
—BLDSC (0397.693000).

330   CY
EKONOMIKI KYPROS/CYPRUS ECONOMICS. 1987. m. 51 Dhigenis Akritas Ave., Nicosia, Cyprus. TEL 02-472510. Ed. Tassos Anastasiades. circ. 3,000.

330   SW   ISSN 0345-2646
EKONOMISK DEBATT/ECONOMIC DEBATE. 1973. 8/yr. SEK 415 (teachers and students SEK 300) (effective 1997). Nationalekonomiska Foereningen - Swedish Economic Society, c/o Nationalekonomiska Institutionen, Stockholms Universitet, S-106 91 Stockholm, Sweden. TEL 46-16-30-49. FAX 46-8-15-94-82. E-mail: http://www.ne.su.se/ed. (Subscr. to: STK-Distribution, Box 84, S-162 12 Vaellingby, Sweden. TEL 46-8-38-04-05) Eds. C-H Siven, M. Persson. adv.; index, cum.index: 1878-1926. circ. 4,000. **Indexed:** INIS Atomind.
   Supersedes: Nationalekonomiska Foereningens Foerhandlingar.

330   FI   ISSN 0013-3183
HC337.F5
EKONOMISKA SAMFUNDETS TIDSKRIFT/ECONOMIC SOCIETY OF FINLAND. JOURNAL. (Text in Swedish; summaries in English) 1913. 3/yr. FIM 150 (effective 1997). Economic Society of Finland, c/o Niklas Ahlgren, Swedish School of Economics, Dept. of Economics, P.O. Box 479, Arkadiagatan 22, FIN-00101 Helsinki, Finland. TEL 358-9-431-33-405. FAX 358-9-431-33-382. E-mail: ahlgren@shh.fi. Ed.Bd. adv.; bk.rev.; abstr.; illus.; stat.; index. circ. 1,400. **Indexed:** ASCA, Curr.Cont., IBR, Int.Lab.Doc., J.of Econ.Lit., Risk Abstr., SSCI. **Document type:** academic/scholarly publication.
—Genuine Article.

330   YU   ISSN 0013-3191
EKONOMIST. (Contents page and summaries in English, Russian) 1948. q. 11000 din. Savez Ekonomista Jugoslavije, Nusiceva 6-III, 11000 Belgrade, Yugoslavia. TEL 011-334-417. Ed. Oto Norcic.

330   TU
HC491.E374
EKONOMIST. 1991. w. Hurriyet Tesisleri, Kirecocagi Mevkii Evren Mah., Guneslikoy - Ankara, Turkey. TEL 90-212-5500050. FAX 90-212-5500082. adv.

330   PL   ISSN 0013-3205
EKONOMISTA. (Text in Polish; summaries in English, Russian) 1900. bi-m. 13 ZI. (foreign 26 ZI.) (effective 1997); 15 ZI. (foreign 30 ZI.) (effective 1998). Polskie Towarzystwo Ekonomiczne, Ul. Nowy Swiat 49, 00-242 Warsaw, Poland. TEL 48-22-275031. FAX 48-22-279904. (Dist. by: Ars Polona-Ruch, Krakowskie Przedmiescie 7, Warsaw, Poland) (Co-sponsor: Polska Akademia Nauk, Komitet Nauk Ekonomicznych) Ed. Zdzislaw Sadowski. R&P contact: W. Switalski. bk.rev.; bibl.; charts; index. circ. 1,300 (paid). **Indexed:** AgroLibrex, Amer.Hist.& Life (1955-), Hist.Abstr. (1955-). **Document type:** academic/scholarly publication.
—SWETS.
   Description: Key Text
   Refereed Serial

330   YU   ISSN 0013-323X
EKONOMSKA MISAO. (Text in Serbo-Croatian; summaries in English, Russian) 1968. q. 15000 din.($140) Savez Ekonomista Srbije, Marsala Tita 16, Belgrade, Yugoslavia. Ed. Ljubomir Madzar.

330   XV   ISSN 0013-3256
HB9
EKONOMSKA REVIJA. (Text in Slovenian; summaries in English) 1950. q. $17. Zveza Ekonomistov Slovenije, Titova 19-1, Ljubljana, Slovenia. Ed. Ivan Turk. adv.; bk.rev.; bibl.; charts; stat. circ. 3,100.

330   YU   ISSN 0013-3264
EKONOMSKI ANALI. (Text in Serbo-Croatian) 1951. q. 100 din. Ekonomski Fakultet u Beogradu, Kamenicka 6, 11000 Belgrade, Yugoslavia. Ed. Zarko Bulajic.

330   BN   ISSN 0013-3272
EKONOMSKI GLASNIK. (Text in Serbo-Croatian) 1968. q. 200 din. Savez Ekonomista Bosne i Herzegovine, Trg Oslobodenja 1, Sarajevo, Bosnia Hercegovina. Ed. Momir Cecez.

330   CI   ISSN 0424-7558
HB9
EKONOMSKI PREGLED. (Text in Serbo-Croatian; summaries in English, Russian) 1950. m. Savez Ekonomista Hrvatske, Berislaviceva 6, Croatia. Ed. Miljenko Rendulic. bibl.; charts; index. circ. 1,700. **Indexed:** Amer.Hist.& Life (1970-), Hist.Abstr. (1970-).

330   IO
EKSEKUTIF. (Text in Indonesian) 1979. m. P T Trend Media, P.O. Box 77 JKWK, Jakarta, Indonesia. TEL 7502513. FAX 7502627. adv.: color page Rps.3500000. circ. 22,000.
   Description: Covers business and economics.

330   US   ISSN 8750-6033
HF5001
EL PASO ECONOMIC REVIEW. 1964. bi-m. $15. University of Texas at El Paso, Texas Centers, Burges Hall, Rm. 410, El Paso, TX 79968-0541. TEL 915-747-5036. Ed. James E. Trumbly. charts; stat. circ. 1,000. (tabloid format; back issues avail.) **Indexed:** P.A.I.S. **Document type:** academic/scholarly publication.
   Former titles: El Paso Business Review (ISSN 0162-1041); El Paso Economic Review (ISSN 0013-4031)

338.9   ES
EL SALVADOR: COYUNTURA ECONOMICA; boletin informativo y analisis economico. 1985. bi-m. Col.36($16) (Instituto de Investigaciones Economicas) Universidad de El Salvador, Facultad de Ciencias Economicas, Aptdo. Postal 2830, San Salvador, El Salvador. TEL 257755. circ. 1,000.
   Supersedes (1950-19??): Revista de Economia de El Salvador.

330   FR
ELECTRICITE DE FRANCE. DIRECTION DES ETUDES ET RECHERCHES. COLLECTION DE NOTES INTERNES. ORGANISATION, INFORMATION, ENVIRONNEMENT SOCIAL ET ECONOMIQUE. 1992. irreg. free. Electricite de France (EDF), Directions des Etudes et Recherches, 1 av. du General de Gaulle, 92140 Clamart, France. TEL 1-47-65-43-21. FAX 1-47-65-31-24. TELEX 204 347 F. Ed. Jean-Marie Lecoeuvre.

330   GW   ISSN 0377-7332
HB1.A1
EMPIRICAL ECONOMICS. (Text in English) 1976. q. DM.751.60 (foreign DM.755.20) (effective 1998). (Institute for Advanced Studies, Vienna, AU) Physica-Verlag GmbH und Co. (Subsidiary of: Springer-Verlag), Postfach 105280, 69042 Heidelberg, Germany. TEL 49-6221-487492. FAX 49-6221-487177. E-mail: physica@springer.de; URL: http://www.springer.de. (Subscr. to: Springer Verlag GmbH, Postfach 311340, 10643 Berlin, Germany. TEL 49-30-82787-0. FAX 49-30-82787448; Dist. in N. America by: Springer-Verlag New York Inc., Box 2485, Secaucus, NJ 07096-2485, USA. TEL 212-460-1500. FAX 212-473-6272) Ed.Bd. (reprint service avail. from SWZ) **Indexed:** Geo.Abstr.H.G., IBR, IDA, Int.Abstr.Oper.Res., J.Cont.Quant.Meth., J.of Econ.Lit., Oper.Res.Manage.Sci., Qual.Contr.Appl.Stat., SCIMP (1991-), World Bibl.Soc.Sec. **Document type:** academic/scholarly publication.
—BLDSC (3737.010000); SWETS; UnCover. **CCC.**
   Description: Papers dealing with the confrontation of relevant economic theory with observed data through the use of adequate econometric methods.
   Refereed Serial

330   US   ISSN 0899-8833
HD5650.E46
EMPLOYEE OWNERSHIP REPORT. 1981. bi-m. $70 membership. National Center for Employee Ownership, Inc., 1201 Martin Luther King Jr. Way, Oakland, CA 94612. TEL 510-272-9461. FAX 510-272-9510. E-mail: nceo@nceo.org; URL: http://www.nceo.org. Ed. Corey Rosen. bk.rev. circ. 1,700. (back issues avail.)
   Formerly (until 1987): Employee Ownership.
   Description: Contains legal, regulatory, and financial news pertaining to employee ownership, tips on management and communication practices, research and case studies.

330   SP
EMPRESA Y SOCIEDAD. 4/yr. Aritjols 32, bajos, 08016 Barcelona, Spain. TEL 3-350-04-04. FAX 3-353-62-18. Ed. Antonio O. Ferreiro. circ. 30,000.

330   SP   ISSN 1131-6551
EMPRESARIO. 1978. 11/yr. 3900 ptas. (effective 1996). Confederacion Espanola de la Pequena y Mediana Empresa, Diego de Leon 50, 28006 Madrid, Spain. TEL 34-1-4116161. FAX 34-1-5645269. TELEX 45754 PYME E. Ed. Carlota Dominguez; Pub. Alfonso Picabia. adv. contact: Alfonso Picabia. circ. 15,000.
   Description: Contains economic and business information.

ENERGY BUSINESS REVIEW. see *ENERGY*

ENERGY ECONOMIC NEWS. see *ENERGY*

ENERGY ECONOMIST; an international analysis. see *ENERGY*

ENERGY USER NEWS. see *ENERGY*

ENGINEERING ECONOMIST. see *ENGINEERING*

330   US   ISSN 0099-0043
NE2720
ENGRAVERS JOURNAL. 1975. 12/yr. $49. Davis Farrell & Associates, Inc., Box 318, Brighton, MI 48116-0318. TEL 313-229-5725. FAX 313-229-8320. Ed. Michael J. Davis. adv.; illus. **Indexed:** Mag.Ind. **Document type:** trade publication.
—Linda Hall.

330   FR   ISSN 1167-2196
HC271
ENJEUX LES ECHOS. 12/yr. Echos Hera, 46 rue La Boetie, 75008 Paris, France. TEL 1-49-53-65-65. FAX 1-42-25-26-40. Ed. Olivier Jay. circ. 130,000.
   Formerly (until 1992): Dynasteurs (ISSN 0983-1517)
   Description: Provides financial and economic analysis and prospects.

ENROUTE; your complimentary in-flight magazine. see *TRAVEL AND TOURISM*

BUSINESS AND ECONOMICS

320 330   CK   ISSN 0120-4483
HC196
ENSAYOS SOBRE POLITICA ECONOMICA. 1982. s-a. Col.$3000($20) Banco de la Republica, Departamento Editorial, Calle 13 No. 35-51, Bogota, Colombia. circ. 2,300. **Indexed:** IBR, P.A.I.S.For.Lang.Ind.
Description: Deals with aiding those whose capacity is in economics research. Includes studies and analysis of economic problems.

330   US
ENTERPRISE (SALT LAKE CITY). 1971. w. $48. Digest Publishing of Utah Inc., Box 11778, Pioneer Sta., Salt Lake City, UT 84147. TEL 801-533-0556. Ed. George Gregersen. R&P contact: George Gregersen. adv. contact: Kirk Dyorich. illus./ stat. circ. 5,700. (also avail. in microform from UMI; back issues avail.) **Document type:** newspaper.

330   US
ENTERPRISES FINANCIAL AND ECONOMIC SURVIVAL LETTER. 1960. m. $300. Enterprises Unlimited, Box 31, F.D.R. Sta., New York, NY 10150. TEL 212-755-9363. E-mail: occult@juns.com. Ed. John Edwards. bk.rev. **Document type:** newsletter.

330   SZ
ENTREPRENDRE. s-a. 1000 SFr. to individuals; institutions 5000 SFr. (Jeune Chambre Economique de Geneve) Bercher SA, Rue de l'Athenee 34, CH-1206 Geneva, Switzerland. TEL 022-3473388. FAX 022-3462047. circ. 10,000. **Document type:** consumer publication.

330   FR
ENTREPRENDRE. 1984. 11/yr. 220 F. (foreign 360 F.) (effective 1997). 6 bis, rue Auguste Vitu, 75015 Paris, France. TEL 33-1-45774141. FAX 33-1-45792211. Ed. Robert Lafont. circ. 270,000.

330   CN   ISSN 1188-7427
ENTREPRENDRE; le magazine des gens qui ont l'esprit d'entreprise. 1987. bi-m. Can.$26.16; newsstand price: Can.$4.95. Editions Qualite Performante Inc., 1600 bd. St-Martin E., Tour B, Bureau 630, Ville de Laval, PQ H7G 4S7, Canada. TEL 514-669-8373; 800-479-1777. FAX 514-669-9078. E-mail: message@entreprendre.ca; URL: http://www.entreprendre.ca. Ed. Jean-Noel Tremblay; Pub. Edmond Bourque. adv.: B&W page Can.$4795, color page Can.$6495; trim 8 5/8 x 11 1/8; adv. contact: Edmond Bourque. circ. 20,000. circ. 30,000 (paid). **Document type:** trade publication.
Formerly (until 1992): Club Regional de l'Entrepreneurship (ISSN 0840-9145)
Description: Targets all decision-makers in the private or public sector, education, management or labour who are interested in promoting economic growth in Quebec and other parts of Canada.

330.9   CG
L'ENTREPRENEUR. (Text in French) 1978. 6/yr. $100 (effective 1996-1997). Association Nationale des Entreprises du Zaire, 10 av. des Aviateurs, B.P. 7247, Kinshasa, Democratic Republic of the Congo. TEL 22286. TELEX 21071 ANEZA ZR.
Description: Reprints articles from different authors on the enforcement of the laws and regulations of any business and trade. Provides paragraphs on business world events in Zaire and abroad; tenders, classified ads; economic aspects of Zaire.

330   UK   ISSN 0898-5626
HC79.I53
ENTREPRENEURSHIP & REGIONAL DEVELOPMENT. 1989. q. £99($163) to institutions (effective 1998). Taylor & Francis Ltd., Rankine Rd., Basingstoke, Hants. RG24 8PR, England. TEL 44-1256-840366. FAX 44-1256-479438. E-mail: info@tandf.co.uk; URL: http://www.tandf.co.uk/. (Subscr. in N. America to: Taylor & Francis Inc., 1900 Frost Rd., Ste. 101, Bristol, PA 19007-1598. TEL 800-821-8312. FAX 215-785-5515) Ed. Gerald Sweeney. **Indexed:** Geo.Abstr.H.G. **Document type:** bulletin.
—BLDSC (3790.547500); SWETS. **CCC.**
Description: Focuses on the roles entrepreneurial enterprises play in regional economic growth and prosperity.
Refereed Serial

ENTREPRESSE. see *JOURNALISM*

330 331   FR   ISSN 0995-4945
ENTREPRISE ET CARRIERES. 1989. w. 470 F. (effective 1995). Groupe Liaisons S.A., 1 av. Edouard Belin, 92856 Rueil Malmaison, France. TEL 33-1-41299879. FAX 33-1-41299880.

330   FR   ISSN 1161-2770
HF5001
ENTREPRISES ET HISTOIRE. s-a. 271 F. (foreign 380 F.) (effective 1995). Editions E S K A, 27 rue Dunois, 75013 Paris, France. TEL 44-06-80-42. FAX 44-24-06-94. Ed. Patrick Fridenson. **Document type:** trade publication.
Description: Covers all aspects of business in France and other industrial nations since the 18th century.

ENVIRONMENTAL AND RESOURCE ECONOMICS. see *ENVIRONMENTAL STUDIES*

ENVIRONMENTAL AND RESOURCE ECONOMICS. see *ENVIRONMENTAL STUDIES*

ENVIRONMENTAL BUSINESS JOURNAL; strategic information for a changing industry. see *ENVIRONMENTAL STUDIES*

ENVIRONMENTAL INDUSTRY YEARBOOK. see *ENVIRONMENTAL STUDIES*

ENVIRONMENTAL LAW IN REAL ESTATE AND BUSINESS TRANSACTIONS. see *ENVIRONMENTAL STUDIES*

EQUIPMENT LEASING TODAY. see *MACHINERY*

330   CN   ISSN 0823-6801
EQUITY. 1983. 10/yr. Can.$19.95. Pacific West Equities Ltd., 1178 West Pender St., Ste. 200, Vancouver, BC V6E 2R9, Canada. TEL 604-684-1414. FAX 604-684-6907. Ed. David A. Hanley; Pub. Ron Stern. adv. contact: Mark Hood. circ. 25,000. **Indexed:** Can.B.P.I.

330   DK   ISSN 0109-9310
ERHVERVS-ORIENTERING STAT AMT, KOMMUNE; kommunikationstidskrift for erhverv og institution. 1983. 8/yr. free. Mono-Marketing A-S, Gammel Kongevej 23, 1610 Copenhagen V, Denmark. adv.; illus. circ. 10,000.

330   DK   ISSN 0109-792X
ERHVERVSLEDEREN.* 1984. m. DKK 180. Dansk Erhvervsforlag, Worsaaesvej 24, 1972 Frederiksberg SC, Denmark. illus.

330   SZ
ESPRESSO. 10/yr. 49 SFr. (foreign 60 SFr.). Modapress AG, Koeschenruetistr. 109, Postfach, CH-8052 Zurich, Switzerland. TEL 41-1-3024044. FAX 41-1-3022022. circ. 56,000. **Document type:** bulletin.
Formerly: Professionnelle.

330   CK   ISSN 0121-4802
ESTRATEGIA ECONOMIA Y FINANCIERA. 1977. s-m. Col.$95100($180) (Europe $192) (effective 1997). Servicios de Informacion S.A., Calle 18 no. 3-82, Piso 3, Apdo. Aereo 53120, Bogota, Colombia. TEL 57-1-2437911. FAX 57-1-2837365. E-mail: estrateg@uniandes.edu.co. Ed. Marta Lasprilla. adv. contact: Elsa Pineda. bk.rev.; circ. 10,000 (paid).

330   VE   ISSN 0798-9733
ESTUDIOS DE COYUNTURA. 1989. s-a. Bs.300($20) or exchange basis. Universidad del Zulia, Facultad de Ciencias Economicas y Sociales, Apdo. 526, Maracaibo 4001A, Venezuela. TEL 061-428504. FAX 061-416025. Ed. Hernan Pardo. bk.rev.

330   CL   ISSN 0304-2758
ESTUDIOS DE ECONOMIA. (Editions in English, Spanish) 1973. s-a. $25 to individuals; institutions $35. Universidad de Chile, Facultad de Ciencias Economicas y Administrativas, Av. Ranacagua 257, Santiago, Chile. FAX 562-634-7342. Ed. Jorge Marshall. adv. circ. 400. **Document type:** academic/scholarly publication.
Refereed Serial

330   AG   ISSN 0425-368X
HB9
ESTUDIOS ECONOMICOS. 1962. a. exchange basis. Universidad Nacional del Sur, Departamento de Economia, 12 de Octubre y San Juan, 8000 Bahia Blanca, Argentina. TEL 54-91-25432. Ed. Elena Ortiz de Guevara. R&P contact: Ricardo Bara. bk.rev./ bibl. circ. 500. **Indexed:** Int.Lab.Doc., J.of Econ.Lit. **Document type:** academic/scholarly publication.

330.1   BL   ISSN 0101-4161
HB9
ESTUDOS ECONOMICOS. 1970. q. $60 (effective 1997). Fundacao Instituto de Pesquisas Economicas, Departamento de Publicacoes, Caixa Postal 11474, 05508-900 Sao Paulo, Brazil. TEL 55-11-212-5471. FAX 55-11-814-3379. Ed.Bd. adv. contact: Eny Elza Ceotto. bibl.; charts; stat.; index, cum.index. circ. 1,500. **Indexed:** Hisp.Amer.Per.Ind. (1980-), IBR. **Document type:** academic/scholarly publication.
Formerly (until 1971): Revista de Teoria e Pesquisa Economica (ISSN 0101-4110)
Description: Presents original papers in economic research.

330 381 382   GW   ISSN 0721-7072
ETAGE; Chef-Informationen. 1981. m. DM.198. Dr. Horst Kerlikowsky Verlag, Haimhauserstr. 5a, 80802 Munich, Germany. TEL 49-89-344012. FAX 49-89-390662. Ed. Horst Kerlikowsky. R&P contact: Horst Kerlikowsky. adv. contact: Fris Hilz. bk.rev.; index. circ. 2,000. (back issues avail.) **Document type:** bulletin.

330.9   FR   ISSN 0757-6714
ETAT DU MONDE; annuaire economique et geopolitique mondial. (Text and summaries in French) 1981. a. price varies. Editions La Decouverte, 9 bis, rue Abel-Hovelacque, 75013 Paris, France. TEL 44-08-84-00. FAX 44-08-84-19. Ed.Bd; Pub. Francois Geze. circ. 45,000. (back issues avail.)

ETHICS & POLICY. see *SOCIOLOGY*

ETHIKOS; examining ethical issues in business. see *PHILOSOPHY*

ETTELA'AT-E SIYASSI EQTESADI; mahnameh siyassi ve eqtesadi. see *POLITICAL SCIENCE*

330   GW   ISSN 0939-2734
EURO BRIEF. m. DM.330. Deutscher Wirtschaftsdienst, Marienburgerstr. 22, 50968 Cologne, Germany. TEL 49-221-93763-0. FAX 49-221-9376399. Ed. Hermann Bohle. (looseleaf format) **Document type:** bulletin.

EURO-CHALLENGE; international career guide for students and graduates. see *OCCUPATIONS AND CAREERS*

330 677   GW   ISSN 0942-9638
EURO DECOR. 1971. 10/yr. DM.168 (foreign DM.192) (effective 1997). Meininger Verlag GmbH, Maximilianstr. 7-17, 67433 Neustadt, Germany. TEL 49-6321-8908-0. FAX 49-6321-8908-73. Ed. Christoph Meininger. circ. 10,000. **Document type:** trade publication.
—**CCC.**
Former titles (until 1992): F T B-Handel (ISSN 0175-6575); (until 1984): Das Farbenfachgeschaeft (ISSN 0343-6047)

330   NE
EURONOMICS. 1993. m. $500 to non-members; members $250. International Business Consortium Alphen, P.O. Box 1154, 2400 BD Alphen aan den Rijn, Netherlands. TEL 31-1720-25529. FAX 31-1720-26099. E-mail: ibca@cistron.nl. Ed. Ruth Axtell. R&P contact: Ruth Axtell. circ. 450. **Document type:** newsletter.
●Also available online.
Description: Covers economic, social and political developments in Europe.

336 339.5   EI   ISSN 1145-0339
EURONOVA. 1989. m. I N F E D, 3 rue Blaise Pascal, 63960 Veyre-Monton, France. TEL 73-69-65-94. Ed. Brigitta Sirotteau.

BUSINESS AND ECONOMICS

947 UK ISSN 0966-8136
DK266.A2 CODEN: EASTER
EUROPE - ASIA STUDIES. 1949. 8/yr. £72($136) to individuals; institutions £248 ($418) (effective 1997). Carfax Publishing Co., P.O. Box 25, Abingdon, Oxon. OX14 3UE, England. TEL 44-1235-401000. FAX 44-1235-401550. E-mail: enquiries@carfax.co.uk. (Subscr. in the U.S. to: Carfax Publishing Co., 875-81 Massachusetts Ave., Cambridge, MA 02139) Ed. R.A. Clarke. adv.; bk.rev.; index. (also avail. in microfiche; back issues avail.) **Indexed:** A.B.C.Pol.Sci., Abstr.Mil.Bibl., Amer.Hist.& Life (1955-), Arts & Hum.Cit.Ind., ASCA, Br.Hum.Ind., Crim.Just.Abstr., Curr.Cont., Energy Ind., Energy Info.Abstr., Geo.Abstr.H.G., Hist.Abstr. (1955-), Hum.Ind., IDA, Int.Polit.Sci.Abstr., Key to Econ.Sci., Mid.East: Abstr.& Ind., P.A.I.S., Per.Islam. (1992-), Polit.Sci.Abstr., Rural Recreat.Tour.Abstr., Soc.Sci.Ind., SSCI, World Agri.Econ.& Rural Sociol.Abstr. **Document type:** academic/scholarly publication.
●Also available online. Vendor(s): Information Access Co.
—BLDSC (3829.461740); Genuine Article; KR SourceOne; SWETS; UMI; UnCover. **CCC.**
Formerly (until 1993): Soviet Studies (ISSN 0038-5859)
Refereed Serial

EUROPE FOR BUSINESS TRAVELERS. see *TRAVEL AND TOURISM*

330 UK ISSN 0264-7362
Z7165.E8
EUROPEAN ACCESS. 1989. bi-m. £130 (effective 1995). (European Commission, United Kingdom Offices, EI) Chadwyck-Healey Ltd., The Quorum, Barnwell Rd., Cambridge CB4 8SW, England. TEL 01223-215513. FAX 01223-66440. TELEX 9312102281 CH G. E-mail: mail@chadwyck.co.uk. (Subscr. in N. America to: Chadwyck-Healey, Inc. 1101 King St., Alexandria, VA 22314. TEL 703-683-4890; Ed. addr.: Ian Thompson, Ed., European Documentation Centre, U W C C, P.O. Box 430, Cardiff CF1 3XT, Wales. TEL 01222-215512) Ed. Ian Thomson. adv.: page £200; adv. contact: Emma Rintoul. bk.rev.; index. circ. 700. **Indexed:** LJI. **Document type:** bulletin.
—BLDSC (3829.482920); SWETS.
Description: A guide to the policies and activities of the European Communities that aids those in business, the professions, public authorities, pressure groups, and the academic community keep up with developments in Europe.

330 GW
EUROPEAN AND TRANSATLANTIC STUDIES. (Text in English) irreg. DM.98. Springer-Verlag, Heidelberger Platz 3, 14197 Berlin, Germany. TEL 49-30-8207-0. FAX 49-30-8214091. **Document type:** academic/scholarly publication, monographic series.

330 UK ISSN 1352-4518
HD70.E8
EUROPEAN BUSINESS & ECONOMIC DIGEST. 1990. bi-m. M C B University Press Ltd., 60-62 Toller Ln., Bradford, W. Yorks BD8 9BY, England. TEL 44-1274-777700. FAX 44-1274-785200. URL: http://www.mcb.co.uk. Ed. Martin Fojt. **Indexed:** Cont.Pg.Manage., Geo.Abstr. **Document type:** trade publication.
Former titles (until 1994): European Business and Economic Development (ISSN 0966-8004); (until 1992): European Research (ISSN 0958-9082)

330 UK
EUROPEAN BUSINESS INFORMATION CONFERENCE (YEAR) PROCEEDINGS. a. £75. T F P L Publishing, 17-18 Britton St., London EC1M 5NQ, England. TEL 44-171-251-5522. FAX 44-171-251-8318. E-mail: central@tfpl.com; URL: http://www.tfpl.com. **Document type:** proceedings.

330 UK ISSN 0957-0039
EUROPEAN BUSINESS INTELLIGENCE BRIEFING. 1989. m. (11/yr.). £235($335) (effective 1997). Headland Business Information (Subsidiary of: Bowker-Saur), Customer Services Department, Maypole House, Maypole Rd., E. Grinstead, W. Sussex RH19 1HU, England. TEL 44-1342-330-100. FAX 44-1342-330-191. E-mail: custserv@bowker-saur.co.uk. (Subscr. to: World Wide Subscription Services, Unit 4, Gibbs Reed Farm, Ticehurst, E. Sussex TN5 7HE, England) Ed. David Mort. **Document type:** newsletter.
—BLDSC (3829.551500).
Description: Evaluates European companies, markets and products in depth. Reviews the best business information available in newsletters, research reports, newspapers, business and consumer magazines, electronic databases, and publications of trade organizations and chambers of commerce.

330 UK ISSN 0955-808X
HF5152.A3
THE EUROPEAN BUSINESS JOURNAL. 1989. q. £99($190) (effective 1998). Whurr Publishers Ltd., 19b Compton Terrace, London N1 2UN, England. TEL 44-171-359-5979. FAX 44-171-226-5290. (Subscr. to: Turpin Distribution Services Ltd., Blackhorse Rd., Letchworth, Herts. SG6 1HN, England. TEL 44-1462-672555. FAX 44-1462-480947; Subscr. in N. America to: Whurr Publishers Ltd., Box 1897, Lawrence, KS 66044-8897. TEL 913-843-1221. FAX 913-843-1274) Ed. William Nicoll. adv.: page £200; adv. contact: Maggy Park. (also avail. in microform from UMI) **Indexed:** Cont.Pg.Manage., Intl.Polym.Sci.& Tech., Mgmt.& Market.Abstr., RAPRA. **Document type:** academic/scholarly publication.
●Also available online. Vendor(s): UMI.
—BLDSC (3829.552000); SWETS; UMI.
Description: Independent forum for the presentation and discussion of the major issues affecting business in the European Union.
Refereed Serial

330 UK ISSN 0955-534X
EUROPEAN BUSINESS REVIEW. bi-m. £1299($1999) (foreign Aus.$2499) (effective 1998). M C B University Press Ltd., 60-62 Toller Ln., Bradford, W. Yorks BD8 9BY, England. TEL 44-1274-777700. FAX 44-1274-785200. TELEX 51317-MCBUNI-G. (N. American subscr. to: MCB University Press Ltd., Box 1943, Birmingham, AL 35202) Ed. Richard Welford. (reprint service avail. from SWZ) **Indexed:** Anbar, Cont.Pg.Manage., Per.Islam. (1992-), SCIMP (1991-). **Document type:** academic/scholarly publication.
—BLDSC (3829.557200); SWETS; UMI. **CCC.**
Incorporates (1988-1996): New European (ISSN 0953-1432)
Description: Interdisciplinary focus on management issues in Europe.

338 EI ISSN 0010-2423
EUROPEAN COMMUNITIES. ECONOMIC AND SOCIAL COMMITTEE. BULLETIN.. (Text in Danish, Dutch, English, French, German, Greek, Italian, Portuguese, Spanish) 1961. 3/yr. free for Luxembourg. (European Communities, Economic and Social Committee, Division for Information, Publications and Relations with Socio-economic Groups) Office for Official Publications of the European Communities, B.P. 1003, L-2985 Luxembourg, Luxembourg. bibl. circ. 5,000. **Indexed:** EC Ind.

330 EI
EUROPEAN COMMUNITIES. ECONOMIC AND SOCIAL COMMITTEE. COMMISSION DOCUMENTS. irreg. $620. Office for Official Publications of the European Communities, L-2985 Luxembourg, Luxembourg. (Dist. in the U.S. by: Unipub, 4611-F Assembly Dr., Lanham, MD 20706-4391. TEL 800-274-4888. FAX 301-459-0056) (also avail. in microfiche)
—BLDSC (6272.030000).
Formerly: European Communities. Economic and Social Committee. Opinions and Reports (ISSN 0255-0717)

330 327 EI ISSN 1011-5269
EUROPEAN COMMUNITIES. ECONOMIC AND SOCIAL CONSULTATIVE ASSEMBLY. ANNUAL REPORT. (Text in Danish, Dutch, English, French, German, Greek, Italian, Portuguese, Spanish) a. $35. (European Communities, Economic and Social Committee, Division for Information, Publications and Relations with Socio-economic Groups) Office for Official Publications of the European Communities, L-2985 Luxembourg, Luxembourg. (Dist. in U.S. by: Unipub, 4611-F Assembly Dr., Lanham, MD 20706-4391. TEL 800-274-4888. FAX 301-459-0056)
Formerly (until 1986): European Communities. Economic and Social Committee. Annual Report (Year) (ISSN 0376-5458)
Description: Covers the Economic and Social Committee's work.

330 NE ISSN 0014-2921
HB1 CODEN: EERVAI
EUROPEAN ECONOMIC REVIEW. 1969. 9/yr. fl.2045($1175) (effective 1998). (European Economic Association) North-Holland (Subsidiary of: Elsevier Science B.V.), P.O. Box 211, 1000 AE Amsterdam, Netherlands. TEL 31-20-4853911. FAX 31-20-4853598. TELEX 18582 ESPA NL. (Subscr. in the Americas to: Elsevier Science, Regional Sales Office, Box 945, New York, NY 10159-0945. TEL 212-633-3730. FAX 212-633-3680; Subscr. in Australasia and the Far East to: Elsevier Science (Singapore) Pte Ltd, No.1 Temasek Ave., No.17-01 Millenia Tower, Singapore 039192, Singapore. TEL 65-434-3727. FAX 65-337-2230; Subscr. in Japan to: Elsevier Science Japan, 9-15 Higashi-Azabu 1-chome, Minato-ku, Tokyo 106, Japan. TEL 81-3-5561-5033. FAX 81-3-5561-5047) Ed. Francois Bourguignon. adv.; index, cum.index: vols.1-10. (also avail. in microfilm from UMI; reprint service avail. from SWZ) **Indexed:** ABI Inform., Arts & Hum.Cit.Ind., ASCA, BPIA, Bus.Ind., C.R.E.J., Cont.Pg.Manage., Curr.Cont., ELLIS, Geo.Abstr.H.G., IDA, J.of Econ.Lit., Key to Econ.Sci., Manage.Cont., Mid.East: Abstr.& Ind., P.A.I.S., Risk Abstr., Rural Recreat.Tour.Abstr., Soc.Sci.Ind., SSCI, Tr.& Indus.Ind., World Agri.Econ.& Rural Sociol.Abstr., World Bank.Abstr. **Document type:** academic/scholarly publication.
—BLDSC (3829.697000); Genuine Article; KR SourceOne; SWETS; UMI; UnCover. **CCC.**
Description: Publishes theoretical and empirical papers on topics in economics.
Refereed Serial

330 UK
EUROPEAN ENTREPRENEUR. q. Knightsbridge House, Headley, Berkshire RG15 8JY, England. TEL 0635-269055. Ed. Peter van der Sluijs.

340 330 US ISSN 0929-1261
K487.E3 CODEN: EJLEEA
EUROPEAN JOURNAL OF LAW AND ECONOMICS. 1993. bi-m. fl.750 to institutions; $385 to institutions in U.S. (effective 1998). Kluwer Academic Publishers Boston, Box 358, Accord St., Hingham, MA 02018-0358. TEL 617-871-6600. FAX 617-871-6528. E-mail: services@wkap.nl; URL: http://www.wkap.nl. (Dist. outside N. America by: Kluwer Academic Publishers Group, P.O. Box 322, 3300 AH Dordrecht, Netherlands. TEL 31-78-6392392. FAX 31-78-6546474) Eds. Jurgen G. Backhaus, Frank H. Stephen. adv.; bk.rev. (back issues avail.; reprint service avail. from SWZ,WSH) **Document type:** academic/scholarly publication.
—BLDSC (3829.730960); SWETS; UnCover. **CCC.**
Description: Publishes analytical studies of the impact of legal interventions into economic processes by legislators, courts and regulatory agencies, with an emphasis on the EC and EC law.
Refereed Serial

EUROPEAN PHARMACEUTICAL REVIEW. see *PHARMACY AND PHARMACOLOGY*

330 EI
EUROPEAN UNION. FINANCIAL REPORT. 1988. a. Office for Official Publications of the European Communities, B.P. 1003, 2 rue Mercier, L-2985 Luxembourg, Luxembourg. URL: http://europa.eu.int.
Formerly (until 1995): European Communities. Financial Report (ISSN 1016-023X)

BUSINESS AND ECONOMICS

330 UK
EUROPEAN WINDOW ON INDUSTRY. 1985. m. free to qualified personnel in the U.K. (overseas £32). Aydee Marketing Ltd., Nithsdale House, 159 Cambridge St., Aylesbury, Bucks. HP20 1BQ, England. TEL 44-1296-434381. FAX 44-1296-436936. Ed. Jenny Henderson; Pub. Richard Salmon. adv. contact: Neil Hampson. bk.rev.; tr.lit. circ. 15,000. (back issues avail.) **Document type:** trade publication.
Description: Discusses various aspects of the handling, packaging, and storage of products, as well as occupational health and safety in medium-sized firms.

330 BE ISSN 0778-4899
L'EVENEMENT IMMOBILIER. 1982. m. 980 BEF. Editions Dupuis, S.A., 52 rue Destree, B-6001 Marcinelle, Belgium. TEL 32-71-600500. FAX 32-71-600599. TELEX 64-168 DUPUIS B. Ed. Violaine Muuls; Pub. Jean-Pierre Dupuis. adv.; bk.rev.; illus.; circ. 30,000. (controlled). **Document type:** trade publication.
Formerly (until 1991): Magazine de l'Evenement Immobilier (ISSN 0773-6789)

330 BL ISSN 0102-2881
EXAME. (Supplement avail.: Exame Vip) 1971. fortn. $180. Editora Abril, S.A., R. Otaviano Alves de Lima, 4400, 02909-900 Sao Paulo, Brazil. TEL 011-877-1322. FAX 011-87-1437. (Subscr. to: Rua do Curtume, 769, 05065-900 Sao Paulo, Brazil. TEL 011-823-9100) Ed. Jose Roberto Guzzo. adv.; charts; illus.; stat. circ. 132,000. **Document type:** consumer publication.
Formerly: Negocios em Exame.
Description: For professionals in administration, marketing, finance, human resources and industry.

330 FR ISSN 1141-8141
EXCELLENCE. 4/yr. Societe d'Edition du Personnel Territorial, B.P. 215, 38506 Voiron Cedex, France. TEL 76-65-71-36. FAX 76-66-12-85. Ed. Maryse Deschambures. circ. 20,000.

330 CH ISSN 1011-2227
EXCELLENCE BUSINESS MONTHLY. (Text in Chinese) 1984. m. NT.$1980. Excellence Publications Co., 5-F No. 531-1, Chung Cheng Rd., Hsin-Tien City, Taipei 231, Taiwan, Republic of China. TEL 886-2-218-6988. FAX 886-2-218-6494. Ed. Angony Han; Pub. Chris J.F. Lin. adv.; B&W page $2900, color page $4500; trim 210 x 280; adv. contact: Saria Chou. bk.rev. circ. 66,000.
Description: Serves as a trends analyst of the business community. Covers companies and industries, investment and money market, government policies, economic forecast and economic viewpoints.

EXEC. see *MEN'S INTERESTS*

330 SA ISSN 1023-0572
EXECUBRIEF (ENGLISH EDITION); solutions for business. Afrikaans edition (ISSN 1019-2387) 1994. q. Coopers & Lybrand, P.O. Box 2536, Johannesburg 2000, South Africa. (looseleaf format)

330 RH
EXECUTIVE. vol.15, 1992. bi-m. Z.$15. (Institute of Management) Argosy Press, P.O. Box 2677, Harare, Zimbabwe. TEL 263-4-755084. FAX 263-4-752162. TELEX 26334 ZW. Ed. Michael Hamilton. adv.; illus. circ. 3,200.

330 PH
EXECUTIVE BRIEF: PHILIPPINE BUSINESS. 6/yr. $60. Leverage International (Consultants) Inc., PS Bank Bldg. 5F, C.P.O. Box 2296, Ayala Ave., Makati MM, Philippines. FAX 632-8101594.

330 US ISSN 0893-5467
EXECUTIVE BUSINESS MAGAZINE.* 10/yr. Executive Publications, 41 Cransford Rd., Cedar Grove, NJ 07009-1201. TEL 201-797-6666. FAX 201-794-9817. Ed. Renee Rewiski. circ. 47,061.

330 US ISSN 1080-5885
EXECUTIVE DENVER CORPORATE CONNECTION. 1986. bi-m. $14.95. 2601 Blake St., Ste. 203, Denver, CO 80205-2241. TEL 303-292-6424. FAX 303-296-8476. Ed. Jeff Rundles; Pub. Glenn Richardson. R&P contact: Jeff Rundles. adv.: B&W page $1850, color page $2300; trim 8 3/8 x 10 7/8; adv. contact: Glenn Richardson. circ. 10,125. **Document type:** consumer publication.
Formerly: Denver Corporate Connection (ISSN 1073-3078)

EXECUTIVE EDGE. see *PHYSICAL FITNESS AND HYGIENE*

330 BL
EXECUTIVE NEWS. (Text in English, Portuguese) bi-m. Cr.$36000. Icaro Editora Ltda., Rua Viera de Morais 1928, 04617 Sao Paulo SP, Brazil. TEL 011-887-4233. FAX 011-885-3717. TELEX 011-33608 ICED. Ed. Carlos Ivan Siqueira. circ. 80,000. **Document type:** consumer publication.

330 US
EXECUTIVE PLANNING SUMMARY. 1983. a. free. Missouri Department of Economic Development, Box 118, Jefferson City, MO 65102. TEL 314-751-4241. FAX 314-751-7385. URL: http://www.state.mo.us. Ed. Daniel Onunkwor. circ. 500. **Document type:** government publication.
Description: Overview of Missouri economy, demographics, and economic development opportunities.

330 US ISSN 0888-4110
EXECUTIVE SPEECHES. 1986. bi-m. $60 (Canada $70; Europe & South America $80; Far East $94). Executive Speaker Co., Box 292437, Dayton, OH 45429. TEL 937-294-8493. FAX 937-294-6044. Ed. Robert Skovard. (also avail. in microform from UMI) Indexed: ABI Inform., PSI. **Document type:** trade publication.
•Also available online. Vendor(s): UMI.
Also available on CD-ROM.
—BLDSC (3836.223850); UMI.
Description: Features the full text of 10-20 speeches by executives

650 US
EXECUTIVE SUITE.* 1991. m. $24. Eric Communications, 12138 Central Ave., Ste. 301, Mitchellville, MD 20721-1932. TEL 301-277-7080. FAX 301-439-7885. Ed. James Eric. adv.: B&W page $600, color page $750. circ. 10,000. **Document type:** trade publication.
Description: Targets African-American business owners in the Washington, DC-Baltimore corridor.

330 US
EXECUTIVE WOMEN INTERNATIONAL. PULSE. q. membership. Executive Women International, 515 S. 700 E., Ste. 2-E, Salt Lake City, UT 84102-2801. TEL 801-355-2800. FAX 801-355-2852. adv. contact: Janice Schrieber. **Document type:** corporate report.
Formerly: Executive Women International. Times.
Description: Publication for member firms and their key representatives.

330 US ISSN 0890-426X
EXIMBANK LETTER; trends in trade, project, and investment finance. 1986. s-m. $288. International Business Affairs Corporation, 4938 Hampden Ln., Bethesda, MD 20814-2914. TEL 301-907-8647. Ed. Richard Barovick. q. index. **Document type:** newsletter.

330 SP
EXPANSION. 1986. d. 47000 ptas. (effective 1997); newsstand price: 150 Ptas. Recoletos Compania Editorial, S.A, Recoletos 1, 5o, 28001 Madrid, Spain. TEL 34-1-3373220. FAX 34-1-3373266. E-mail: expansion@recoletos.es; URL: http://www.recoletos.es. Dir. Jesus Martinez Vazquez. adv.: page 725000 Ptas; trim 253 X 344; adv. contact: Angel Guardiola Moreno. cols./p.: 6; pp./issue: 43. (tabloid format; back issues avail.) **Document type:** newspaper.
•Also available online.
Also available on CD-ROM. Producer(s): Chadwyck-Healey Inc.
Description: Covers business and economics news

330 UK
▼**EXPANSION EN C D - R O M.** 1996. a. Chadwyck-Healey Ltd., The Quorum, Barnwell Rd., Cambridge CB5 8SW, England. TEL 44-1223-215512. FAX 44-1223-215514. URL: http://www.chadwyck.com. (In N. America: Chadwyck-Healey Inc., 110 King St., Alexandria, VA 22314. TEL 800-752-0515. FAX 703-683-7589)
•Available only on CD-ROM. Producer(s): Chadwyck-Healey Inc.
Description: Provides the complete text of the Spanish business newspaper Expansion.

330 FR ISSN 1254-3179
L'EXPANSION MANAGEMENT REVIEW; revue des responsables. 1976. q. 505 F. Groupe Expansion, 25 rue le Blanc, 75015 Paris, France. TEL 40-60-40-60. FAX 40-60-41-20. TELEX 205 581. Ed. Eric Meyer. circ. 8,000. Indexed: Pt.de Rep., SCIMP (1985-).
Formerly (until 1994): Harvard l'Expansion (ISSN 0397-5495)

330 RU
▼**EXPERT.** 1995. w. free. Kriyanovski ul., 24-35, b.2, 124036 Moscow, Russia. TEL 7-095-1246390. E-mail: ask@expert.ru; URL: http://www.expert.ru. Ed. Nikita V. Kirichenko. **Document type:** consumer publication.
•Also available online.
Description: Covers economy in Russia. Provides information about the top Russian companies for bankers and economists.

EXPRESS; magazine for account holders of D H L International. see *COMMUNICATIONS*

EXPRESSION D'ENTREPRISE; le magazine de la communication. see *COMMUNICATIONS*

330 PO ISSN 0870-1970
EXPRESSO. (Text in Portuguese) 1973. w. Esc.5200($40) Sociedade Jornalistica e Editorial, S.A., Rua Duque de Palmela, 37, 3o, 1296 Lisbon Codex, Portugal. TEL 1-526141. Ed. Maria Joao Avillez. adv. circ. 113,500. (also avail. in microfiche; back issues avail.)

330 301 UN ISSN 0259-2460
F A O ECONOMIC AND SOCIAL DEVELOPMENT PAPER. French edition: Etude F A O, Developpement Economique et Social (ISSN 0259-2215) (Text in English) 1978. irreg., latest no.123. price varies. Food and Agriculture Organization of the United Nations, Bernan Associates, 4611-F Assembly Dr., Lanham, MD 20706-4391. TEL 301-459-7666. FAX 301-459-0056. Indexed: Food Sci.& Tech.Abstr., IDA, Rice Abstr., World Agri.Econ.& Rural Sociol.Abstr. **Document type:** monographic series.
—BLDSC (3865.627500).

330 US
F & S REPORTS.* irreg. Frost & Sullivan, Inc., 90 West St., No. 1301, New York, NY 10005-1039. TEL 212-233-1080. Ed. Henry M. Berler.

330 US ISSN 0029-4012
F E E NOTES. 1952. m. included with The Freeman. Foundation for Economic Education, Inc., 30 S. Broadway, Irvington-on-Hudson, NY 10533. TEL 914-591-7230. circ. 19,000. (looseleaf format; also avail. in microform from UMI; reprint service avail. from UMI)
Description: Contains column by the president of the foundation and notices of offers and events.

330 GW ISSN 0934-6430
F I R UND I A W MITTEILUNGEN. 1968. q. Forschungs Institut fuer Rationalisierung und Institut fuer Arbeits Wissenschaft, Pontdriesch 14-16, 52062 Aachen, Germany. TEL 49-241-47705-0. FAX 49-241-402401. adv.; bk.rev. circ. 4,000. (back issues avail.) **Document type:** academic/scholarly publication.

330 GW ISSN 0071-769X
F I W - SCHRIFTENREIHE. 1962. irreg., vol.167, 1996. price varies. (Forschungsinstitut fuer Wirtschaftsverfassung und Wettbewerb e.V.) Carl Heymanns Verlag KG, Luxemburgerstr. 449, 50939 Cologne, Germany. TEL 49-221-46010-0. FAX 49-221-4601069. adv.; bk.rev. Indexed: ELLIS. **Document type:** monographic series.

FABIAN NEWSLETTER. see *POLITICAL SCIENCE*

BUSINESS AND ECONOMICS

330 NE ISSN 0924-8641
FACILITY MANAGEMENT MAGAZINE. 1988. bi-m. fl.110. (Nederlandse Facility Management Associatie) Arko Uitgeverij b.v., Essenkade 4, 3992 AA Houten, Netherlands. TEL 31-3403-76933. FAX 31-3403-80600. (Subscr. to: Postbus 616, 3430 AP Nieuwegein, Netherlands) Ed. F.W. van Waardhuizen. adv.; bk.rev.; charts; illus.; stat.; tr.lit. circ. 4,000. **Document type:** trade publication. —SWETS.
 Formerly: Gebouwmanagement (ISSN 0169-2305)
 Description: Features new product announcements, spatial organizing ideas, calendars of events and classes, as well as insights for upper management. Includes computer applications.

FACTOR D; kwartaalblad voor het economie-onderwijs en zijn didactiek. see EDUCATION

FACTS ON FILE. YEARBOOK. see HISTORY — History Of North And South America

FACTS ON FILE WORLD NEWS DIGEST WITH INDEX. see HISTORY

338 FI ISSN 1237-2196
FAILI. (Text in Finnish; summaries in English) 1963. 4/yr. FIM 250($50) Liikearkistoyhdistys r.y. - Finnish Business Archives Association, P.O. Box 271, FIN-00101 Helsinki, Finland. Ed. Carl-Magnus Roos. adv.; bk.rev. circ. 500. **Document type:** bulletin.
 Formerly (until 1994): Liikearkisto (ISSN 0356-7850)

330 FI ISSN 0358-626X
FAKTA. 1981. 11/yr. FIM 657 (effective 1997). A-Lehdet Oy, Hitsaajankatu 7, FIN-00081 A-Lehdet, Finland. TEL 358-9-75961. FAX 358-9-783526. TELEX 124698. Ed. Timo Holtari. adv. contact: Jyrki Rehumaki. bk.rev.; circ. 22,176 (controlled). **Document type:** consumer publication.
 Description: Focuses on management, development and entrepreneurship.

330 CC ISSN 1003-0670
FAZHAN YANJIU/DEVELOPMENT RESEARCH. (Text in Chinese) 1984. m. Y14.40. Fujian Sheng Jingji Yanjiu Zhongxin - Fujian Economics Studies Center, Sheng Zhengfu Dalou, 2nd Fl., Hualin Lu, Fuzhou, Fujian 350003, People's Republic of China. TEL 0591-7826106. FAX 0591-7826001. Ed. Wang Kaiming. **Document type:** academic/scholarly publication.
 Description: Covers social and economic development issues.

330 US ISSN 0889-9223
THE FED TRACKER; specializing in domestic and global money flow analysis. Key Title: Ken Coleman's The Fed Tracker. m. $96 (foreign $110). Seraphim Press, 4805 Courageous Ln., Carlsbad, CA 92008. TEL 619-720-0107. FAX 619-720-4208. Ed. S.R. Coleman; Pub. Kenneth Coleman. circ. 1,300. (back issues avail.) **Document type:** newsletter.
 Formed by the 1992 merger of: Fed Tracker Reality Theory Newsletter (ISSN 0739-3563); Fed Tracker Special Report (ISSN 0739-5256)

330 US ISSN 0195-2617
FEDERAL GRANTS MANAGEMENT HANDBOOK. 1978. 2 base vols. (plus m. updates). $269 ($35 per chapter for each federal granting agency) (subscr. includes newsletter). Thompson Publishing Group, Grants Management Advisory Service, 1725 K St., N.W., Ste. 700, Washington, DC 20006. TEL 202-872-4000. FAX 202-296-9657. E-mail: gran@thompson.com. Ed. Don Montuori; Pub. Daphne Musselwhite. R&P contact: Daphne Musselwhite. bk.rev. circ. 3,300. **Document type:** newsletter.
 —CCC.
 Description: Aimed at federal financial assistance recipients, it includes detailed guidance on obtaining grants, preparing to receive funds, preparing for audits, managing grant expenditures and handling grant disputes.

330 350 US
FEDERAL PROCUREMENT UPDATE. m. $167. United Communications Group, 11300 Rockville Pike, Ste. 1100, Rockville, MD 20852-3030. TEL 301-816-8950. FAX 301-816-8945. Ed. Joe Klem.
 Description: Describes the federal contracting process; includes news, how-to's, new regulations, and tips from other contractors on contract administrations, marketing and negotiations.

330 UK ISSN 1354-5701
▼**FEMINIST ECONOMICS.** 1995. 3/yr. £32 (U.S. and Canada $48; rest of world £34) to individuals; institutions £68 (U.S. and Canada $102; rest of world £72) (effective 1997). Routledge, 11 New Fetter Ln., London EC4P 4EE, England. TEL 44-171-583-9855. FAX 44-171-842-2298. E-mail: info.journals@routledge.com; URL: http://www.routledge.com/routledge/journal/journals.html. (Subscr. to: ITPS Ltd., Cheriton House, North Way, Andover, Hants SP10 5BE, England. TEL 44-1264-342919. FAX 44-1264-342807; Subscr. in US & Canada to: 29 W. 35th St., New York, NY 10001-2299. TEL 212-244-3336. FAX 212-564-7854) Ed. Diana Strassmann. adv.: page £150; trim 115 x 190. **Document type:** academic/scholarly publication.
 —BLDSC (3905.197230).
 Description: A review of cross-disciplinary perspectives and intellectual traditions in economics.

330 BN
FEROELEKTRO. (Text in Serbo-Croatian) 1978. m. free. Trg Oktobra bb, 71000 Sarajevo, Bosnia Hercegovina. TEL 071 35-607. Ed. Veljko Zugic. tr.lit. circ. 25,000. (looseleaf format)

FERRO ALLOYS MONTHLY. see METALLURGY

FESTIVAL MANAGEMENT & EVENT TOURISM. see TRAVEL AND TOURISM

330 HU ISSN 0015-086X
FIGYELO;* gazdasagpolitikai hetilap. 1957. w. $65. P.O. Box 18, 1355 Budapest, Hungary. (Subscr. to: Kultura, Box 149, H-1389 Budapest, Hungary) Ed. Gyorgy Varga. adv.; charts; illus.; stat. circ. 33,000. (also avail. in microfilm from NRP) **Indexed:** Hung.Build.Bull.

330 US
FINANCE AND COMMERCE DAILY NEWSPAPER.* 1887. d. (Tue.-Sat.). $119. Dolan Media (Minneapolis), 333 S. Seventh St., Ste. 2180, Minneapolis, MN 55402-2432. TEL 612-333-4244. FAX 612-333-3243. Ed. Pat Boulay. circ. 3,840. **Document type:** newspaper.

330 UG
FINANCIAL TIMES. d. Plot 17-19 Sta. Rd., POB 31399, Kampala, Uganda. TEL 245798. Ed. Dan Salasatta.

330 BE ISSN 0772-0890
DE FINANCIEEL ECONOMISCHE TIJD. (Text in Dutch) 1968. 5/w. 9150 BEF. Uitgeversbedrijf Tijd n.v., Franklin Building, Posthoflei 3, 2600 Berchem (Antwerp), Belgium. TEL 32-3-2860211. FAX 32-3-2860310. TELEX 32614 FETANT. Ed. Hans Maertens; Pub. Paul Huybrechts. adv. contact: Dirk Vandekerckhove. bk.rev.; circ. 31,000 (paid). **Indexed:** Key to Econ.Sci. **Document type:** newspaper.
 ●Also available online.
 Also available on CD-ROM.

330 NE
HET FINANCIEELE DAGBLAD. (Text in Dutch; summaries in English) 1796. d. (5/wk., Tue.-Sat.). fl.515 (Belgium fl.598) (effective 1997); newsstand price: fl.2.50(50BEF). Het Financieele Dagblad B.V., P.O. Box 216, 1000 AE Amsterdam, Netherlands. TEL 31-20-5928888. FAX 31-20-592800. URL: http://www.Nederlander.com.nl. Ed. Fred Bakker. R&P contact: L. Sieders. adv. contact: L. Sieders. abstr.; illus.; stat.; circ. 45,000 (paid). cols./p.: 10; pp./issue: 20. (broadsheet format; back issues avail.; reprint service avail.) **Document type:** newspaper.
 ●Also available online.
 Former titles: Dagelijksche Beurscourant; Amsterdamsch Effectenblad.
 Description: Publishes financial and business news from the Netherlands and Europe, and covers political issues relevant to the business community.

330 IT
FINANZA E FISCO. 1987. 12/yr. L.250000. Via Donna Olimpia 205, 00152 Rome, Italy. TEL 39-6-53-49-345. FAX 39-6-5346192. Ed. Eugenio Pompei. adv.: B&W page L.2500000, color page L.4250000. circ. 30,000.

330 SP ISSN 0210-4997
FINANZAS. 1960. 12/yr. Alcala 20, Apdo. 14776, 28014 Madrid, Spain. TEL 1-532-23-28. Ed. C. Munoz Hernandez.

330 GW ISSN 0863-2499
FINANZWIRTSCHAFT (BERLIN). 1990. m. DM.176.40 (foreign DM.212.40) (effective 1997). Verlag Die Wirtschaft GmbH, Am Friedrichshain 22, 10407 Berlin, Germany. TEL 49-30-42151421. FAX 49-30-4215123. Ed. Wolfgang Bergs. **Document type:** trade publication.

HJ1150.A2
330 US
FINER POINTS MAGAZINE. 1969. 4/yr. $10 (foreign $75). Industrial Diamond Association of America, Inc., Box 1070, Skyland, NC 28776. TEL 704-684-1986. FAX 704-684-7372. E-mail: 76113.1364@compuserve.com. Ed. Fred A. Gray. adv.: B&W page $1075, color page $1450. circ. 5,380. **Indexed:** Alloys Ind., Eng.Mat.Abstr., Met.Abstr., Met.Abstr.Ind., Nonfer.Met.Alert, PCC Alert, Steels Alert, World Alum.Abstr. **Document type:** trade publication.

FINLAND. TILASTOKESKUS. KUOLEMANSYYT/FINLAND. STATISTIKCENTRALEN. DOEDSORSAKER/FINLAND. STATISTICS FINLAND. CAUSES OF DEATH IN FINLAND. see BUSINESS AND ECONOMICS — Abstracting, Bibliographies, Statistics

FIRST CLASS EXECUTIVE TRAVEL. see TRAVEL AND TOURISM

330 NE
FISCAAL ADVIES. 4/yr. fl.35.50 (foreign fl.64.50) (effective 1998). B.V. Uitgeversmaatschappij Bonaventura (Subsidiary of: Elsevier N.V.), Postbus 2158, 1000 CD Amsterdam, Netherlands. TEL 31-20-6914111. FAX 31-20-5674398. adv.

FOCUS ON BRITISH BUSINESS AND MANAGEMENT SCIENCES RESEARCH. see BIBLIOGRAPHIES

338.7 SW
FOERETAGARNA I SKAANE. 1991. 9/yr. Foeretagarna i Skaane Service AB, Vallmogatan 7, S-263 33 Hoegnaas, Sweden. TEL 46-42-34-26-40. FAX 46-42-34-02-36. Ed. Bengt Kristoferson. adv.: B&W page SEK 8000, color page SEK 12200; trim 180 x 262. circ. 8,800. cols./p.: 3; pp./issue: 36.

330 PL ISSN 0071-674X
FOLIA OECONOMICA CRACOVIENSIA. (Text in Polish; summaries in English, Russian) 1960. a. price varies. Polska Akademia Nauk, Oddzial w Krakowie, Komisja Nauk Ekonomicznych, Ul. Slawkowska 17, 31-016 Krakow, Poland. TEL 48-12-224853. FAX 48-12-222791. Ed. Janusz Maciaszek. circ. 530. **Document type:** academic/scholarly publication. —KNAW.
 Description: Covers system-independent monetarized economy; investment rate changes; agricultural production; territorial and social differences of consumption.

330 US
FOLIO (OKLAHOMA CITY). bi-m. Department of Commerce, Box 26980, Oklahoma City, OK 73126-0980. FAX 405-815-5281. Ed. Tracy Allford. illus. circ. 7,000. (tabloid format) **Indexed:** B.P.I. **Document type:** government publication, newsletter.
 Former titles: Oklahoma Economic Development News; Oklahoma P.E.P; **Incorporates:** Oklahoma Now!

330 IT ISSN 1120-9445
FONDAZIONE ASSI. ANNALI DI STORIA DELL'IMPRESA. 1985. a. Societa Editrice Il Mulino, Strada Maggiore 37, 40125 Bologna, Italy. TEL 39-51-256011. FAX 39-51-256034. E-mail: riviste@mulino.it. Ed.Bd. adv. contact: M. Luisa Vezzali. circ. 1,000. (back issues avail.)

BUSINESS AND ECONOMICS

330   MX
FONDO DE CULTURA. SERIE DE LECTURAS. 1973. irreg. Mex.$25($35) per no. (effective 1997). Fondo de Cultura Economica, Carretera Picacho Ajusco 227, Col. Bosques del Pedregal, 14200 Mexico, D.F., Mexico. TEL 52-5-2274672. FAX 52-5-2274683. Ed. Carlos Bazdresch. adv.; bk.rev.; bibl. circ. 5,000.
Document type: academic/scholarly publication.

FORBES. see *BUSINESS AND ECONOMICS — Management*

FORBES F Y I. see *GENERAL INTEREST PERIODICALS — United States*

330   JA   ISSN 0916-9903
FORBES JAPAN. (Text in Japanese) 1992. m. 900 Yen. Gyosei Corporation Ltd., 19623 Ventura Blvd., Shinjuku-Ku, Tokyo 162. TEL 33269-4145. FAX 33268-2315. Ed. Kiyoshi Hashimoto. circ. 100,000.

330   CC
FORBES ZIBENJIA. (Text in Chinese) 1991. m. Capital Communications Corp. Ltd., 7-F Paramount Bldg., 12 Ka Yip St., Chaiwan, Hong Kong, People's Republic of China. TEL 2896-8688. FAX 2556-1627. Ed. Vincent Cheung. adv.: B&W page $7500, color page $9900; trim 206 x 273. circ. 50,000.
Description: For Chinese entrepreneurs and senior executives in South East Asia.

330   US   ISSN 0095-294X
FORECASTER. 1962. 40/yr. $150. Forecaster Publishing Co., Inc., 19623 Ventura Blvd., Tarzana, CA 91356. TEL 818-345-4421. Ed. John Kamin. R&P contact: John Kamin. bk.rev.; charts; illus.; stat.
Document type: newsletter.
Description: Publishes confidential economic reports about the future to benefit readers. Includes analysis of property, interest rates, speculation, gold, silver, coins, antiques, cars and travel.

FOREIGN REPORT (PRINT); the private intelligence behind the news. see *POLITICAL SCIENCE*

FOREIGN REPRESENTATIVES IN THE U.S. YELLOW BOOK; who's who in the U.S. offices of foreign corporations, foreign nations, the foreign press and intergovernmental organizations. see *POLITICAL SCIENCE — International Relations*

330 657   US   ISSN 8756-8888
HV8079.W47
FORENSIC ACCOUNTING REVIEW.* 1983. m. $125 (foreign $155). Computer Protection Systems, Inc., 12275 Appletree Dr., Plymouth, MI 48170-3739. TEL 313-459-8787. FAX 313-459-8787. Ed. Jack Bologna. (looseleaf format; back issues avail.)
Document type: newsletter.
Description: Digest of current incidents of corporate fraud, including insider trading, executive frauds, improper auditing, embezzlement, bank fraud and questionable accounting.

FORT HARE PAPERS. see *SCIENCES: COMPREHENSIVE WORKS*

330   DK   ISSN 0109-4955
FORTEGNELSE OVER DANSK UDVIKLINGSFORSKNING. 1984. a. DKK 30($5) Roskilde Universitetscenter, Foreningen af Aktive Udviklingsforskere - Association of Development Researchers in Denmark, c/o Roskilde Uiversitetscenter, Hus 05.2, Postbox 260, DK-4000 Roskilde, Denmark. bk.rev. circ. 400.

330   NE   ISSN 0738-5587
HF5001
FORTUNE INTERNATIONAL. bi-w. $95.90. Time Warner Publishing BV (Subsidiary of: Time Warner, Inc.), Ottho Heldring Straat 5, 1066 AZ Amsterdam, Netherlands. TEL 31-20-5104911. FAX 31-20-6175077. URL: http://fortune.com. Ed. John Huey; Pub. Stuart Arnold. R&P contact: Jo Mattern. adv. contact: Christopher Poleway. circ. 860,000. circ. 850,000 (paid). Indexed: Mgmt.& Market.Abstr. **Document type:** consumer publication.
●Also available online.
—SWETS.

330 332.6   US
FORUM (NEW YORK, 1986). q. membership. American Business Association, 292 Madison Ave., New York, NY 10017. TEL 212-949-5900. (Co-sponsors: National Association of the Professions; The Attorneys Group) Ed. William Driscoll. charts; illus. circ. 5,000. **Document type:** newsletter.
Formerly: A B A Business Briefs; Which was formerly (until 1978): A L A Brief; American Lawyers Association Brief.

330   FR   ISSN 0989-8778
FORUM ENSEIGNEMENTS. 1988. 3/yr. 16 Route Spontini, 75116 Paris, France. TEL 45-53-60-00. FAX 47-55-96-31. circ. 15,000.

FORUM LOCCUM. see *POLITICAL SCIENCE*

330   GW   ISSN 0340-7705
FORUM WARE. (Text in English, German) 1972. s-a. DM.100. Deutsche Gesellschaft fuer Warenkunde und Technologie, Carl-Peters-Str. 11, 36251 Bad Hersfeld, Germany. TEL 49-6621-3663. FAX 49-6221-41227. (Co-sponsors: Oesterreichische, und Internationale, Gesellschaft fuer Warenkunde und Technologie) Ed. Guenter Otto. bk.rev. **Document type:** academic/scholarly publication.
Description: Devoted to the commodity and its significance for man, economy and nature. Covers study and instruction, knowledge of commodities, ecological aspects, and consumer information.

650   UK
FOUNDATION FOR BUSINESS RESPONSIBILITIES. DIALOGUES. irreg., no.2, 1972. Foundation for Business Responsibilities, 40 Doughty St., London WC1N 2LF, England.
Formerly: Industrial Educational and Research Foundation. Dialogues.

650   UK   ISSN 0073-7410
FOUNDATION FOR BUSINESS RESPONSIBILITIES. DISCUSSION PAPER. 1965. irreg. price varies. Foundation for Business Responsibilities, 40 Doughty St., London WC1N 2LF, England. bk.rev.

650   UK   ISSN 0073-7429
FOUNDATION FOR BUSINESS RESPONSIBILITIES. OCCASIONAL PAPERS. 1965. irreg. price varies. Foundation for Business Responsibilities, 40 Doughty St., London WC1N 2LF, England. bk.rev.

658   UK   ISSN 0073-7437
FOUNDATION FOR BUSINESS RESPONSIBILITIES. RESEARCH PAPER. 1965. irreg. price varies. Foundation for Business Responsibilities, 40 Doughty St., London WC1N 2LF, England. bk.rev.

650   UK
FOUNDATION FOR BUSINESS RESPONSIBILITIES. SEMINAR PAPERS. 3/yr. $15. Foundation for Business Responsibilities, 40 Doughty St., London WC1N 2LF, England.

330   FR   ISSN 0995-3531
FRANCE. DIRECTION GENERALE DE LA CONCURRENCE, DE LA CONSOMMATION ET DE LA REPRESSION DES FRAUDS. ACTUALITES. m. (11/yr.). 150 F. Imprimerie Nationale, B.P. 514, 59505 Douai Cedex, France. TEL 27-93-70-70. FAX 27-93-70-96. TELEX 120 389 F.

330   FR
HC271
FRANCE. MINISTERE DE L'ECONOMIE, DES FINANCES ET DU BUDGET. ECONOMIE ET PREVISION. 1981. 5/yr. 310 F. (Europe 375 F., elsewhere 440 F.) (effective 1997). (Ministere de l'Economie, des Finances et du Budget) Documentation Francaise, 29-31 quai Voltaire, 75344 Paris Cedex 07, France. TEL 33-1-40157000. FAX 33-1-40157230. TELEX 215 666 DOCFRAN. (Subscr. to: 124 rue Henri Barbusse, 93308 Aubervilliers Cedex, France. TEL 33-1-48395600. FAX 33-1-48395601) charts. (also avail. in microfiche from DFR) **Document type:** government publication.
—BLDSC (3657.810000); SWETS.
Former titles: France. Ministere de l'Economie et des Finances. Economie et Prevision (ISSN 0249-4744); (until 1971) France. Ministere de l'Economie et des Finances. Statistiques et Etudes Financieres. Etudes Economiques. Serie Orange (ISSN 0338-4217)

310 658.5   FR
FRANCE. SERVICE D'ETUDE DES STRATEGIES ET DES STATISTIQUES INDUSTRIELLES. SOCIETES D'ETUDES ET DE CONSEILS, INGENIEURS-CONSEILS. Title varies slightly: France. Service d'Etude des Strategies et des Statistiques Industrielles. Ingenierie, Etudes et Conseils. 1968. a. 85 F. Service d'Etude des Strategies et des Statistiques Industrielles (SESSI), 85 bd. du Montparnasse, 75270 Paris Cedex 06, France. TEL 45-56-42-34. FAX 45-56-40-71.
Formerly: France. Service du Traitement de l'Information et des Statistiques Industrielles. Societe d'Etudes et de Conseils, Ingenieurs-Conseils.
Description: Statistics on engineering services in France.

FRANCHISE LAW JOURNAL. see *LAW*

330   US
FRANCHISE UPDATE.* bi-m. P.O. Box 20547, San Jose, CA 95160-0547. TEL 408-997-7795. Ed. Theresa Thilgen. circ. 10,000.

330 658   UK   ISSN 1359-852X
▼**FRANCHISING RESEARCH.** 1996. q. £99($149) (effective 1997). M C B University Press Ltd., 60-62 Toller Ln., Bradford, W. Yorks BD8 9BY, England. TEL 44-1274-777700. FAX 44-1274-785200. URL: http://www.mcb.co.uk. Ed. Sharon Parkinson. **Document type:** academic/scholarly publication.
—BLDSC (4032.782490). CCC.

330   SA
FREE STATE; review - commerce and industry. a. R.30 (effective 1996). Braby's (Subsidiary of: Kohler Packaging Ltd.), P.O. Box 1426, Pinetown 3600, South Africa. TEL 27-31-7017021. FAX 27-31-7017036. adv.
Formerly: Orange Free State.

FREEMAN; ideas on liberty. see *POLITICAL SCIENCE*

330   GW   ISSN 0067-5938
FREIE UNIVERSITAET BERLIN. OSTEUROPA-INSTITUT. WIRTSCHAFTSWISSENSCHAFTLICHE VEROEFFENTLICHUNGEN. 1954. irreg. price varies. Freie Universitaet Berlin, Osteuropa-Institut, Garystr. 55, 14195 Berlin, Germany. TEL 030-832081. FAX 030-8383788. Ed.Bd. circ. 500. **Document type:** monographic series.

330   SA
FREIGHT & TRADING WEEKLY. Short title: F & T Weekly. 1973. w. R.215 (effective 1995). Travel and Trade Publishing (Pty) Ltd., P.O. Box 662, Auckland Park 2006, South Africa. TEL 27-11-7263036. FAX 27-11-7263994. Ed. David Marsh. adv.: B&W page R.9745.86; trim 320 x 225; adv. contact: David Marsh. bk.rev.; circ. 3,493 (controlled). **Document type:** trade publication, newspaper.
Former titles: Freight and Container Weekly; (until 1983): F C Weekly; Which incorporates (in 1980): Southern Africa's Freighting News; Containering and Transport News.
Description: Covers all aspects of international trade from an importer's and exporter's point of view.

330   US
FRESNO BUSINESS JOURNAL.* 1986. w. $30. Fresno Business Journal, Inc., 1315 Van Ness Ave. 200, Fresno, CA 93721-1713. TEL 209-237-0114. FAX 209-237-3540. adv.: B&W page $500; trim 11 1/2 x 15. circ. 1,724. (also avail. in microfilm from LIB)
Description: Contains news about public and private companies, personality profiles, local business trends, advice and data.

052   UK   ISSN 0266-5883
FRONTIER. (Supplement avail.: Who's Who in Duty Free (ISSN 0953-6957)) 1984. 10/yr. $45. Reed Business Information (Subsidiary of: Reed Elsevier group), Quadrant House, The Quadrant, Sutton, Surrey SM2 5AS, England. TEL 44-181-652-4942. FAX 44-181-652-8991. (Subscr. to: Reed Business Information, Oakfield House, Perrymount Rd., Haywards Heath, W. Sussex RH16 3DH, England. TEL 44-1444-445566) Ed. Carolyn Lander. circ. 7,259. (back issues avail.) **Document type:** trade publication.
Description: Covers duty and tax free retailing on land, in air and sea.

FUNDACAO CENTRO DE PESQUISAS ECONOMICAS E SOCIAIS DO PIAUI. RELATORIO DE ATIVIDADES. see *SOCIOLOGY*

BUSINESS AND ECONOMICS

330 SP
FUNDACION DE LAS CAJAS DE AHORROS CONFEDERADAS PARA LA INVESTIGACION ECONOMICA Y SOCIAL. DOCUMENTOS DE TRABAJO. 1987. irreg., no.136, 1997. 1000 ptas. per no. Fundacion de las Cajas de Ahorros Confederadas para la Investigacion Economica y Social, Padre Damian, 48, 28036 Madrid, Spain. TEL 34-1-3596158. FAX 34-1-3504959. URL: http://www.funcas.ceca.es. (Subscr. to: Juan Hurtado de Mendoza, 19, 28036 Madrid, Spain. TEL 34-1-3504400. FAX 34-1-3508040) Ed. Fernando Gonzalez Olivares; Pub. Victorio Valle Sanchez. R&P contact: Fernando Gonzalez Olivares. circ. 500. **Document type:** monographic series.
  Formerly: Confedereacion Espanola de Cajas de Ahorros. Fundacion Fondo para la Investigacion Economica y Social. Documentos de Trabajo.
  Description: Publishes research conducted or promoted by the foundation.

330 SP
FUNDACION DE LAS CAJAS DE AHORROS CONFEDERADAS PARA LA INVESTIGACION ECONOMICA Y SOCIAL. ESTUDIOS. 1987. irreg., no.7, 1997. price varies. Fundacion de las Cajas de Ahorros Confederadas para la Investigacion Economica y Social, Padre Damian, 48, 28036 Madrid, Spain. TEL 34-1-3596158. FAX 34-1-3504959. (Subscr. to: Juan Hurtado de Mendoza, 19, 28036 Madrid, Spain. TEL 34-1-3504400. FAX 34-1-3508040) Ed. Fernando Gonzalez Olivares; Pub. Victorio Valle Sanchez. R&P contact: Fernando Gonzalez Olivares. circ. 2,000. **Document type:** monographic series.
  Formerly: Confederacion Espanola de Cajas de Ahorros. Fundacion Fondo para la Investigacion Economica y Social. Estudios.
  Description: Publishes research conducted or promoted by the foundation, whose results become manuals or reference works.

FUNK - SPOT; Radioservice des Instituts der deutschen Wirtschaft. see *COMMUNICATIONS — Radio*

FUTURIBLES; analyse et prospective. see *SOCIOLOGY*

330 US ISSN 0738-9264
FUTURIFIC. 1976. m. $70 to individuals (foreign $100); institutions $140 (foreign $170). (Foundation for Optimism) Futurific, Inc., 305 Madison Ave., Concourse 10B, New York, NY 10165. TEL 212-297-0502; 800-696-2836. Ed. Balint Szent-Miklosy; Pub. Balint Szent-Miklosy. adv.; bk.rev.; film rev.; software rev. circ. 10,000. **Document type:** academic/scholarly publication.
  Description: Newsmagazine of the future, focusing on solutions, not problems. Reviews current events and forecasts their eventual outcome high great accuracy.

665.7 FR ISSN 0072-0046
G; DOCUMENTATION TECHNIQUE ET COMMERCIALE DES VENDEURS DE GAZ. 1970. irreg. Gaz de France, Direction Commerciale, 23 rue Philibert-Delorme, 75017 Paris, France. circ. 3,000.
  Formerly: Gaz et L'Industrie.

330 378 US ISSN 1072-7612
G S B CHICAGO. 1979. q. University of Chicago, Graduate School of Business, 5801 Ellis Ave., Chicago, IL 60637. TEL 312-702-1234. (Subscr. to: 1101 E. 58th St., Chicago, IL 60637. TEL 312-702-7431. FAX 312-702-2973) Ed. William S. Bike. bk.rev.; circ. 35,000 (controlled).
  Description: Features business-related articles for the alumni.

330 SP
GACETA DE LOS NEGOCIOS. d. (312/yr.). O'Donnell 12, 1o planta, 28009 Madrid, Spain. TEL 586-33-00. FAX 577-62-33. Ed. Gregorio Gonzalez. circ. 50,000.

330 BO ISSN 0016-3767
GACETA ECONOMICA. 1967. m. $28.80. G. Mercado No. 996, Box 237, La Paz, Bolivia. Ed. Arturo Valdivieso. adv.; bk.rev.; bibl.; charts; illus.; stat.

GAIA; oekologische Perspektiven in Natur-, Geistes- und Wirtschaftswissenschaften. see *HUMANITIES: COMPREHENSIVE WORKS*

330 US
GAINESVILLE - OCALA BUSINESS. 1987. m. $18. Linda Young-Marks, Box 4649, Ocala, FL 32678. TEL 904-622-2995. FAX 904-622-9200. Ed. Vinod Chhabra. circ. 12,000. **Document type:** consumer publication.
  Formerly: Business in Gainesville.

330 CC ISSN 1000-064X
GANG AO JINGJI/ECONOMICS IN HONG KONG AND MACAO. (Text in Chinese) m. Guangdong Sheng Shehui Kexueyuan, Gang Ao Yanjiu Zhongxin - Guangdong Academy of Social Sciences, Hong Kong and Macao Research Center, No. 6, Xihepu, Dongshan, Guangzhou, Guangdong 510080, People's Republic of China. TEL 776123. Ed. Xu Long.

330 UA
AL-GARIDAH AT-TIGARIYYAH AL-MISRIYYAH. 1921. w. 25 Sharia Nubar Pasha, Cairo, Egypt. circ. 7,000.

330 US ISSN 1053-5527
HG4501
GARY NORTH'S REMNANT REVIEW. 1974. m. $97. American Bureau of Economic Research, c/o Agora, 1217 St. Paul St., Baltimore, MD 21202. TEL 410-234-0691; 800-433-1528. Ed. Gary North. adv. circ. 19,000. (back issues avail.)

330 IT
GAZZETTA DEI CONCORSI.* 1974. w. L.45000. Gruppo Editoriale Poker s.r.l., Via Gentile da Mogliano 16, 00176 Rome, Italy. TEL 06-7028090. FAX 06-2751173. Ed. Eraclite Corbi. adv. contact: Mirco Corbi.

330 300 IE
GEARY LECTURE SERIES. 1967. irreg., no.26, 1995. I£5. Economic and Social Research Institute, 4 Burlington Rd., Dublin 4, Ireland. TEL 353-1-6671525. FAX 353-1-6686231. Ed. B.J. Whelan. R&P contact: John Roughan. **Document type:** monographic series.

330 JA ISSN 0918-0591
HF5001
GEKKAN KEIDANREN. 1953. m. $5. Japan Federation of Economic Organizations - Keizai Dantai Rengokai (KEIDANREN), 9-4 Otemachi, 1-chome, Chiyoda-ku, Tokyo 100, Japan. TEL 81-3-3279-1411. FAX 81-3-5255-6255. TELEX 0222 3188 KDRTOKJ. adv.; charts; illus.; stat. circ. 15,000.
  Formerly (until 1992): Keidanren Geppo (ISSN 0453-4484)

GEORGE WASHINGTON JOURNAL OF INTERNATIONAL LAW AND ECONOMICS. see *LAW — International Law*

338 US ISSN 0279-3857
HC107.G4
GEORGIA BUSINESS AND ECONOMIC CONDITIONS. 1929. bi-m. free. University of Georgia, Terry College of Business, Selig Center for Economic Growth, Athens, GA 30602. TEL 706-542-4085. FAX 706-542-3835. Ed. Lorena Akioka. charts; stat.; cum.index. circ. 3,000. (also avail. in microfiche from CIS; back issues avail.) **Indexed:** P.A.I.S., SRI. **Document type:** academic/scholarly publication.
  Formerly: Georgia Business (ISSN 0016-8173)

330 US ISSN 0884-1179
HC107.G4
GEORGIA ECONOMIC OUTLOOK. a. $15. University of Georgia, Terry College of Business, Selig Center for Economic Growth, Georgia Economic Forecasting Project, Athens, GA 30602. TEL 706-542-4085. FAX 706-542-3835. **Document type:** academic/scholarly publication.

330 GW
GERMAN BRIEF. (Text in English) 1989. w. DM.895. Frankfurter Allgemeine Zeitung GmbH, Information Services, Hellerhofstr. 2-4, 60327 Frankfurt a.M., Germany. TEL 49-69-75912219. FAX 49-69-75912188. (U.S. and Canadian subscr. to: European Business Publications Inc., Box 891, Darien, CT 06820. TEL 203-656-2701. FAX 203-655-8332) Ed. David Hart. stat.; index. (back issues avail.) **Document type:** newsletter.
  ●Also available online.
  Description: Covers the economics and politics of Germany, covering important business trends, economic developments, ratings of key industrial situations, profiles of leading companies, and announcements of trade fairs and conferences.

330 US ISSN 0722-2416
HC14
GERMAN YEARBOOK ON BUSINESS HISTORY. 1981. a. price varies. Springer-Verlag, 175 Fifth Ave., New York, NY 10010. TEL 212-460-1500. FAX 212-473-6272. (Also: Berlin, Heidelberg, Tokyo and Vienna) Ed.Bd.

330 HU ISSN 0237-5478
GESCHAEFTSPARTNER UNGARN. 1986-1992; resumed 1996. q. 22400 Ft.($160) (effective 1997). Kopint - Datorg Plc., Csokonai u. 3, 1081 Budapest, Hungary. TEL 36-1-2668200. FAX 36-1-2667165. E-mail: mail@kopint-datorg.hu; URL: http://www.kopint-datorg.hu. Ed. Ilona Nemeth. R&P contact: Ilona Nemeth. adv. contact: Judit Boncz. circ. 1,000. **Document type:** newsletter.
  Description: Covers Hungarian trade acts and regulations, customs, foreign exchange, and investments. Includes foreign trade statistics, industry tests, market reports.

330 CN ISSN 0701-0028
GESTION; revue internationale de gestion. (Text in French) 1976. 4/yr. Can.$50 (effective 1997). Ecole des Hautes Etudes Commerciales, 3000 chemin de la Cote-Sainte-Catherine, Montreal, PQ H3T 2A7, Canada. TEL 514-340-6677. FAX 514-340-6382. E-mail: revue.gestion@hec.ca. Ed. Alain Gosselin. adv.; bk.rev. circ. 6,500. **Indexed:** Pt.de Rep. (1983-). **Document type:** trade publication.
  —BLDSC (4163.690000).

330 SZ
GEWERBE ZEITUNG. 11/yr. Oberergraben 12, CH-9001 St. Gallen, Switzerland. TEL 071-297777. FAX 071-297529. Ed. A. Muehlematter. circ. 9,000.

GEZONDHEIDSZORG, BELEID EN ORGANIZATIE. see *HOSPITALS*

330 IT ISSN 0017-0097
HB7 CODEN: GIAEAY
GIORNALE DEGLI ECONOMISTI E ANNALI DI ECONOMIA. (Text in English or Italian) 1875. m. L.110000 (foreign L.160000). Universita Commerciale Luigi Bocconi, Via Sarfatti 25, 20136 Milan, Italy. TEL 39-2-58365431. TELEX 316003 UNIBOC I. Ed. Mario Monti. adv.; bk.rev.; charts; index. circ. 1,450. (tabloid format; also avail. in microfiche from BHP) **Indexed:** Curr.Cont.(1991-), ELLIS, J.of Econ.Lit., P.A.I.S.For.Lang.Ind., SSCI, Stat.Theor.Meth.Abstr. (1991-).
  —BLDSC (4177.800000); SWETS.

330 IT
GIORNALE DEI COMMERCIANTI DELLE IMPRESE TURISTICHE DEI SERVIZI. 20/yr. Coop. Edizioni Commercio, Via Messina 19, 00198 Rome, Italy. TEL 06-86-83-96. Ed. Renzo Santelli. circ. 210,000.

330 IT
GIORNALE DEI DOTTORI COMMERCIALISTI. 1968. 12/yr. Consiglio Nazionale dei Dottori Commercialisti, Via Poli 29, 00187 Rome, Italy. TEL 39-6-675861. FAX 39-6-67586348. Ed. Giorgio Sganga. adv.; B&W page L.4300000, color page L.7000000. circ. 30,200.

GIORNALE DEL MEZZOGIORNO; economico-politico. see *POLITICAL SCIENCE*

330 SZ
GIORNALE SVIZZERO DEGLI IMPIEGATI DI COMMERCIO. m. Via Orico 9, CH-6500 Bellinzona, Switzerland. TEL 092-263909. Ed. Fulvio Ranzoni. circ. 2,000.

330 UK ISSN 0956-1056
GLOBAL BUSINESS. q. £15($35) Maxwell Communication Corp., Greater London House, Hampstead Rd., London NW1 7QQ, England. TEL 01-377-4633. FAX 01-383-7486. Ed. Sandra Harris.

330 SZ
HF1414
THE GLOBAL COMPETITIVENESS REPORT. a. 800 SFr. (effective 1996). World Economic Forum, 53 Ch. des Hauts-Crets, CH-1223 Geneva, Switzerland. TEL 41-4122-8691212. FAX 41-4122-7862744. TELEX 413280. E-mail: contact@weforum.org. Ed.Bd. **Document type:** trade publication.
  Formerly: World Competitiveness Report (ISSN 1015-5449)

330　　　　　　　US　　ISSN 1086-9123
▼GLOBAL MARKETPLACE. 1996. bi-m.; electronic edition w. & m. 7111 W. Indian School Rd., Ste. 101, Phoenix, AZ 85033. TEL 602-872-7900; 800-831-8899. FAX 603-530-4940. E-mail: subscribe@globalmarketnet.com; URL: http://www.globalmarketrit. Ed. Jerry Pedrotti; Pub. Ozzie Cortes.
●Also available online.

GOKHALE INSTITUTE MIMEOGRAPH SERIES. see POLITICAL SCIENCE

GOKHALE INSTITUTE OF POLITICS AND ECONOMICS. STUDIES. see POLITICAL SCIENCE

GOLF MARKET TODAY. see SPORTS AND GAMES — Ball Games

338　　　　　　　CC　　ISSN 1001-3024
GONGYE JINGJI/INDUSTRIAL ECONOMICS. (Subseries of: Fuyin Baokan Ziliao) (Text in Chinese) 1978. m. $121.13. Zhongguo Renmin Daxue, Shubao Ziliao Zhongxin - China People's University, Book & Newspaper Information Center, 3 Zhang Zizhong Rd., P.O. Box 1122, Beijing 100007, People's Republic of China. TEL 86-10-4015080. (Dist. in US by: China Publications Service, Box 49614, Chicago, IL 60649. TEL 312-288-3291. FAX 312-288-8570) pp./issue: 176.

330　　　　　　　UK
GOVERNMENT & INDUSTRY; a business guide to Westminster, Whitehall, and Brussels. 3/yr. Longman Group UK Ltd., Longman House, Burnt Mill, Harlow, Essex CM20 2JE, England. TEL 44-1279-426721. FAX 44-1279-431059. E-mail: longhe@cityscape.co.uk (Subscr. to: Pearson Professional, P.O. Box 77, Fourth Ave., Harlow, Essex CM19 5BQ, England. TEL 44-1279-623924. FAX 44-1279-639609) Ed. W. Rodgers. cum.index. (looseleaf format) Document type: trade publication.

330　　　　　　　PK　　ISSN 0424-2815
HC440.5.A1
GOVERNMENT COLLEGE. ECONOMIC JOURNAL. (Text in English) 1966. 2/yr. Rs.100($40) per no. (effective 1995). Government College, Department of Economics, Lahore, Pakistan. TEL 92-42-7228344. Eds. Shoaib Hashmi, Mohammed Aslam. R&P contact: Mohammad Aslam. bk.rev.; charts; stat. circ. 300. Document type: academic/scholarly publication.
—BLDSC (4203.925000).

330　　　　　　　UK　　ISSN 0268-8948
GOVERNMENT CONTRACTING REVIEW. 1986. q. £75($140) Longman Group UK Ltd., Law, Tax and Finance Division, 21-27 Lamb's Conduit St., London WC1N 3NJ, England. TEL 0171-242-2548. FAX 0171-831-8119. Ed. John Reed.
—CCC.
Description: Articles on procedures, practices and policies relating to government contracting.

330　　　　　　　IT　　ISSN 1121-9564
GRANDE DISTRIBUZIONE E DISTRIBUZIONE ORGANIZZATA. Key Title: G D O. Grande Distribuzione e Distribuzione Organizzata. 1970. fortn. L.80000. Agepe Gruppo Editoriale, Via D. Trentacoste 9, 20134 Milan, Italy. TEL 02-215621. FAX 02-2640330. TELEX 351491 AGEPE I. Ed. Livia Artuffo. adv.: color page L.17500000; trim 250 x 340; adv. contact: Angelo Borrello. circ. 41,500 (controlled). Document type: trade publication.
Former titles: Distribuzione Organizzata (ISSN 0394-8455); (until 1984): Droghiere. Distribuzione Organizzata (ISSN 0394-879X); (until 1983): Droghiere (ISSN 0394-8781); (until 1972): Rassegna de "Il Droghiere" (ISSN 0394-8773)

330　　　　　　　US
GREATER GREENWOOD BUSINESS JOURNAL.* 1992. m. $15. Kelly Publications, Inc., P.O. Box 7126, Greenwood, IN 46142-6422. TEL 317-882-8796. FAX 317-882-8830. Ed. Maggie Kelly; Publ. Brian Kelly. adv.: B&W page $495; color page $795; trim 10 1/4 x 13. bk.rev. circ. 14,000. (tabloid format; back issues avail.) Document type: newspaper.
Description: Presents extensive coverage of business events in greater Greenwood, Indiana. How-to tips for business owners featured regularly.

GREECE AND INTERNATIONAL TRANSPORT/ELLAS KAI DIEDNIS METAPHORES; monthly financial magazine. see TRANSPORTATION

GREEK ECONOMY IN FIGURES (YEAR). see BUSINESS AND ECONOMICS — Abstracting, Bibliographies, Statistics

333.7 620.85　　US　　ISSN 1056-490X
GREEN BUSINESS LETTER. m. $197 (online edition $95) (effective 1997 & 1998). Tilden Press Inc., 1519 Connecticut Ave., N.W, Washington, DC 20036. TEL 202-332-1700. FAX 202-332-3028. E-mail: jgamble@enn.com; URL: http://www.enn.com/gbl. Ed. Jennifer Gamble. Indexed: Environ.Abstr. Document type: newsletter.
●Also available online.
—CCC.
Description: Provides business advice for incorporating environmental concerns into all aspects of business operation. Includes product reviews and new-technology analysis.

330　　　　　　　GW
▼DIE GROSSHANDELSKAUFLEUTE. 1995. m. DM.66. Friedrich Kiehl Verlag GmbH, Pfaustr. 13, 67063 Ludwigshafen, Germany. TEL 49-621-63502-0. FAX 49-621-6350222. Ed. Lothar Kurz. adv. contact: Joern Mueller-Grote. circ. 2,800 (paid). Document type: academic/scholarly publication.

330　　　　　　　GU　　ISSN 1045-053X
HF4031.5
GUAM BUSINESS NEWS. m. Glimpses of Guam, Inc., P.O. Box 3191, Agana, Guam 96910. TEL 671-472-1829. FAX 671-472-2163. Ed. Jonathan Needham. Indexed: So.Pac.Per.Ind.

330　　　　　　　CC
GUANGDONG JIAGE YANJIU/GUANGDONG PRICE RESEARCH. (Text in Chinese) q. Guangdong Sheng Wujia Yanjiusuo - Guangdong Price Research Institute, Shengfu Dayuan, Dongfeng Zhonglu, Guangzhou, Guangdong 510031, People's Republic of China. TEL 330860. Ed. Liu Shijing.

330　　　　　　　VE
GUIA INDUSTRIAL DE VENEZUELA. 1955. a. Editorial Guia Industrial, Apdo. 60772, Chacao, Caracas 101, Venezuela.

THE GUIDE TO TRAINING IN SECRETARIAL AND OFFICE SKILLS. see OCCUPATIONS AND CAREERS

GULF STATES NEWSLETTER. see POLITICAL SCIENCE — International Relations

330　　　　　　　CC　　ISSN 1005-4316
GUOMIN JINGJI GUANLI YU JIHUA/NATIONAL ECONOMY MANAGEMENT AND PLANNING. (Subseries of: Fuyin Baokan Ziliao) (Text in Chinese) m. $128.93. Zhongguo Renmin Daxue, Shubao Ziliao Zhongxin - China People's University, Book & Newspaper Information Center, 3 Zhang Zizhong Rd., P.O. Box 1122, Beijing 100007, People's Republic of China. TEL 86-10-4015080. (Dist. in US by: China Publications Service, Box 49614, Chicago, IL 60649. TEL 312-288-3291. FAX 312-288-8570) pp./issue: 192.

330　　　　　　　HU　　ISSN 1217-9647
HC10
H V G; gazdasagi, politikai hirmagazin. 1978. w. 1922 Ft.($102) Heti Vilaggazdasag Rt., Szepvolgyi ut 35, 1037 Budapest, Hungary. TEL 361-1884329. FAX 361-1887101. E-mail: sztibor@hvg.hu; URL: http://www.hvg.hu/. (Edit. addr.: Nemetvolgyi ut 64, 1124 Budapest, Hungary. TEL 361-1555411) Ed. Ivan Lipovecz. adv.: B&W page 280000 Ft., color page 350000 Ft.; adv. contact: Henriette Kovacs. charts; illus.; stat.; tr.lit. circ. 114,000. Indexed: Hung.Build.Bull. Document type: consumer publication.
●Also available online.
Formerly (until 1992): Heti Vilaggazdasag (ISSN 0139-1682)
Description: Political, economic weekly paper. Read by educated middle-aged generation in the cities.

330　　　　　　　AU
H V MAGAZIN. (Handelsvertreter) m. S.270 (foreign S.462) (effective 1996). (Selbstaendigen Handelsvertreter und Vermittler Oesterreichs) Bastei Verlags- und Anzeigengesellschaft mbH, Nikolsdorfergasse 7-11, A-1051 Vienna, Austria. TEL 43-1-5452359. FAX 43-1-54664330. adv.: B&W page S.22700, color page S.36320; trim 176 x 242; adv. contact: Ingeborg Eisenkolb. circ. 12,000. Document type: trade publication.

330　　　　　　　GW　　ISSN 0179-2253
H W W A - REPORT. 1971. irreg. DM.20. H W W A - Institut fuer Wirtschaftsforschung Hamburg, Informationszentrum, Neuer Jungfernstieg 21, 20347 Hamburg, Germany. TEL 040-3562354. FAX 040-351900. Document type: monographic series.
—BLDSC (4340.290000).

330　　　　　　　GW　　ISSN 0344-2608
H Z DEUTSCHES WIRTSCHAFTSBLATT. 1948. bi-w. DM.36. Verlagsanstalt Handwerk, Postfach 8120, D-4000 Dusseldorf 1, Germany. TEL 0211-307073. FAX 0211-307070. TELEX 08587-140. Ed.Bd. adv.; bk.rev. circ. 178,833.

330　　　　　　　CC
HAINAN JISHU JINGJI XINXI. (Text in Chinese) m. Hainan Sheng Keji Qingbao Yanjiusuo - Hainan Institute of Science and Technology Information, No. 89, Haifu Dadao, Haikou, Hainan 570003, People's Republic of China. TEL 42232. Ed. Lin Fang'an.

330　　　　　　　GW　　ISSN 0938-2941
HANDBUCH DER DEUTSCHEN AKTIENGESELLSCHAFTEN. 1958. w. DM.2150. Verlag Hoppenstedt GmbH, Havelstr. 9, 64295 Darmstadt, Germany. TEL 49-6151-380-0. FAX 49-6151-380-360. Document type: directory.
Formerly: Aktiengesellschaften.

330　　　　　　　GW　　ISSN 0934-375X
HANDBUCH DER STEUERLICHEN BETRIEBSPRUEFUNG. 1977. irreg. DM.186. Erich Schmidt Verlag GmbH & Co. (Berlin), Genthiner Str. 30G, 10785 Berlin, Germany. TEL 49-30-250085-0. FAX 49-30-25008521. (looseleaf format) Document type: bulletin.

330　　　　　　　GW　　ISSN 0935-2279
HANDBUCH DER UNTERNEHMENSBERATUNG. irreg. DM.128. Erich Schmidt Verlag GmbH & Co. (Berlin), Genthiner Str. 30G, 10785 Berlin, Germany. TEL 49-30-250085-0. FAX 49-30-25008521. (looseleaf format) Document type: bulletin.

330　　　　　　　AU
HANDEL UND GEWERBE. m. Zeitungsverlag Kuhn und Co. GmbH, Kutschkergasse 42, A-1180 Vienna, Austria. TEL 43-1-47686. FAX 43-1-4768621. Ed. Gerd Volker Weege. circ. 4,900. Document type: trade publication.

330　　　　　　　SZ
HANDELS ZEITUNG. w. Seestr. 37, Postfach 539, CH-8027 Zurich, Switzerland. TEL 41-1-2883555. FAX 41-1-2883575. Ed. Kurt Speck. circ. 35,855. Document type: newspaper.
Formerly: Schweizer Handels Zeitung.

330　　　　　　　LU
HANDELSBLAT. (Text in French, German) 1950. bi-m. 500 Fr. Confederation du Commerce Luxembourgeois, 21-23 Allee Scheffer, L-2520 Luxembourg, Luxembourg. TEL 47-31-25. FAX 22-00-59. (Subscr. to: B.P. 482, L-2014 Luxembourg, Luxembourg) Ed. Romain Jeblick. adv. circ. 2,100. Document type: trade publication.

330 647.94 310　　GW　　ISSN 0323-3545
HANDELSHOCHSCHULE LEIPZIG. WISSENSCHAFTLICHE ZEITSCHRIFT. (Text in German; summaries in English, French, German, Russian) 1974. q. DM.21.60. Handelshochschule Leipzig, Markgrafenstr. 2, Postfach 640, 7010 Leipzig, Germany. Ed. E. Walther. bk.rev. circ. 1,200.

330　　　　　　　DK　　ISSN 0106-4363
HANDELSHOEJSKOLEN I AARHUS. INSTITUT FOR ERHVERVS- OG SAMFUNDSBESKRIVELSE. SKRIFTSERIE C. no.6, 1983. irreg. free. Handelshoejskolen i Aarhus, Institut for Erhvervs- og Samfundsbeskrivelse - Aarhus School of Business, Department of Applied Economics, Fuglesange Alle 20, DK-8210 Aarhus V, Denmark. circ. 200.

HANDELSPRAKTIJKEN EN MEDEDINGING/PRATIQUE DU COMMERCE ET CONCURRENCE. see LAW — Corporate Law

330 375　　　　　DK　　ISSN 0900-4505
HANDELSSKOLEN. 1968. 13/yr. Handelsskolernes Laererforening, Godthaabsvej 106, 2000 Copenhagen F, Denmark. adv. circ. 3,300.
Formed by the merger of (1911-1967): Danske Handelsskole (ISSN 0900-4483); (1941-1967): Handelsskolebladet (ISSN 0900-4491)

BUSINESS AND ECONOMICS

330 — DK — ISSN 0108-6987
HANDLEREN. 1980. 6/yr. free. Moderate Studenter ved Handelshoejskolen i Koebenhavn, Julius Thomsens Plads 10, Lokale 140, 1925 Frederiksberg C, Denmark. Ed. Anders Fauerskov. adv.; illus.

330 — GW
HANSEATISCHE WERTPAPIERBOERSE HAMBURG. AMTLICHE KURSBLATT. 1853. d. DM.45.50. Hanseatische Wertpapierboerse Hamburg, Postfach 11 15 09, 20415 Hamburg, Germany. TEL 040-361302-0. circ. 650. (tabloid format)

330 — US
HARFORD BUSINESS LEDGER. 1989. m. $15.75. Harford Business Ledger, Inc., Box 40, Aberdeen, MD 21001-0075. TEL 410-893-9191. FAX 410-272-4208. Ed. Don Dohler; Pub. Robert Carll. adv. contact: Philip Smith. bk.rev. circ. 8,100. **Document type:** newspaper.
●Also available online. Vendor(s): UMI.

650 — US — ISSN 0017-8012
HF5001 — CODEN: HABRAX
HARVARD BUSINESS REVIEW. 1922. bi-m. $85 (foreign $145). (Harvard University, Graduate School of Business Administration) Harvard Business School Publishing Corporation, 60 Harvard Way, Boston, MA 02163. TEL 617-495-6800. FAX 617-495-9933. TELEX 6817320. E-mail: custserv@cchbspub.harvard.edu; URL: http://www.hbsp.harvard.edu/groups/hbr/index.html. (Subscr. to: Box 52623, Boulder, CO 80322-2623. TEL 800-274-3214) Ed. Nan Stone. adv.: B&W page $16500, color page $19950; trim 8 3/16 x 10 3/4; adv contact: Catherine Donovan. bk.rev.; charts; cum.index. circ. 209,271. (also avail. in microform from UMI; reprint service avail. from KTO) **Indexed:** ABI Inform., Abstr.Bull.Inst.Pap.Chem., Abstr.Health Care Manage.Stud., Acad.Ind., Access (1980-), Account.& Data Proc.Abstr., Account.Ind. (1974-), Anbar, ASCA, ASEAN Manage.Abstr., Asian-Pac.Econ.Lit., B.P.I., Bank.Lit.Ind., Bk.Rev.Ind. (1978-), BMT, BPIA, Bus.Ind., C.I.J.E., CAD CAM Abstr., Child.Bk.Rev.Ind. (1978-), Comput.Bus., Comput.Lit.Ind., Comput.Rev., Cont.Pg.Manage., Curr.Cont., Curr.Cont., Curr.Cont., Environ.Abstr., Excerp.Med., Fut.Surv., High.Educ.Curr.Aware.Bull., IBR, INSPEC, Int.Lab.Doc., Intl.Mgmt.Info., Intl.Polym.Sci.& Tech., Key to Econ.Sci., L.I.I., Law Ofc.Info.Svc., Mag.Ind., Manage.Cont., Mark.Res.Abstr. (1963-), Mgmt.& Market.Abstr., Mid.East: Abstr.& Ind., Oper.Res.Manage.Sci., P.A.I.S., PCR2, Pers.Lit., Pers.Manage.Abstr., PROMT, Psychol.Abstr., Q.Abstr., R.G.Abstr., R.G., RAPRA, Ref.Pt.Food Indus.Abstr., Rehabil.Lit., Resour.Ctr.Ind., Risk Abstr., Robomat., SCIMP (1978-), SSCI, SSCI, Tel.Abstr., Telegen, Text.Tech.Dig., Tr.& Indus.Ind., Work Rel.Abstr., World Bank.Abstr. **Document type:** academic/scholarly publication.
●Also available online. Vendor(s): Data-Star (HBRO), Human Resources Information Network, Knight-Ridder Information, Inc. (File no.122), Lexis-Nexis, Ovid Technologies, Inc. (HBRO).
—BLDSC (4265.800000); CASDDS; CIS; Ei; Genuine Article; KR SourceOne; SWETS; UMI; UnCover.
Description: Publishes research and case studies on issues in corporate strategies, management, finance, regulatory policy, technology, international trends, and related subjects.

330 — US — ISSN 0749-5072
HARVARD BUSINESS SCHOOL. ANNUAL REPORT. a. $75. Harvard Business School, Annual Report Office, 2401 HBS Student Mail Ctr., Boston, MA 02163. TEL 617-495-5093. E-mail: annreport@hbs.edu. Ed. Oliver Ryan. adv. contact: Eric Chu. circ. 1,500 (paid). **Document type:** corporate report.

650 — US — ISSN 0017-8020
HF1134
HARVARD BUSINESS SCHOOL. BULLETIN. 1921. bi-m. $24 (foreign $40). Harvard University, Graduate School of Business Administration, Soldiers Field Rd., Boston, MA 02163. TEL 617-495-6554. Ed. Deborah Blagg. adv.; bk.rev.; charts; illus. circ. 55,000. (reprint service avail. from SCH) **Indexed:** P.A.I.S. **Document type:** bulletin.
—BLDSC (4265.850000); SWETS.

330 — SP
HARVARD - DEUSTO BUSINESS REVIEW. 6/yr. Ediciones Deusto S.A., Apdo. 4 FD, Alda Recalde, 27, 48009 Bilbao, Spain. TEL 425-1500.

330 — US — ISSN 0073-0505
HARVARD ECONOMIC STUDIES. irreg., vol.161, 1991. price varies. Harvard University Press, 79 Garden St., Cambridge, MA 02138. TEL 617-495-2600. FAX 617-495-5898. URL: http://www.hup.harvard.edu. R&P contact: Mindy Koyanis. TEL 617-495-2619. adv. contact: Denise Waddington. **Document type:** monographic series.
—BLDSC (4265.890000).
Refereed Serial

330 — IT
HARVARD - ESPANSIONE; trimestrale di management. 1978. q. L.60000 (foreign L.64200). Arnoldo Mondadori Editore S.p.A., Casella Postale 1833, 20101 Milan, Italy. TEL 3199345. Ed. Redento Mori. adv. circ. 7,312.

HARVEST BOOK SERIES. see *SOCIOLOGY*

330 — CN — ISSN 1183-6709
HEAD OFFICE AT HOME. bi-m. $35. Abaco Communications Ltd., 20 Crown Steel Dr., Unit 10, Markham, ON L3R 9X9, Canada. TEL 416-477-4349. Ed. Elizabeth Harris. circ. 50,000. **Document type:** trade publication.

HEALTHCARE TECHNOLOGY & BUSINESS OPPORTUNITIES. see *MEDICAL SCIENCES*

330 — GR
HELLENEWS. (Text in English) 1958. w. Dr.25000($125) (UK £80) (effective 1998). Hellenews Publications, Halandriou 39, Amaroussion 151 25, Athens, Greece. TEL 301-6899-400. FAX 301-6899-430. TELEX 219746. URL: http://www.kapatel.gr/express/hellen/news1.htm. Ed. John M. Germanos. R&P contact: John M. Germanos. TEL 301-6899407. circ. 6,200. (back issues avail.) **Document type:** newsletter.
Description: Contains the abridged or condensed version of the news reported in the "Express Financial Daily", and economic information from other sources as well.

330 — FI
HELSINGIN KAUPPAKORKEAKOULU. JULKAISUSARJA B. TUTKIMUKSIA. (Text in English, Finnish) irreg. Helsinki School of Economics, Runeberginkatu 22-24, FIN-00100 Helsinki, Finland.
—BLDSC (4286.394000).

330 — FI
HELSINGIN KAUPPAKORKEAKOULU. JULKAISUSARJA E. SELVITYKSIAE. (Text in English, Finnish) irreg. Helsinki School of Economics, Runeberginkatu 22-24, FIN-00100 Helsinki, Finland.

330 — FI — ISSN 1235-5674
HELSINGIN KAUPPAKORKEAKOULU. JULKAISUSARJA W. WORKING PAPERS. (Text in Finnish, English) 1980. irreg. exchange basis. Helsinki School of Economics, Runeberginkatu 22-24, FIN-00100 Helsinki, Finland. circ. 100.
Formerly (until 1993): Helsingin Kauppakorkeakoulu. Julkaisusarja F. Tyopapereita (ISSN 0358-2973)

330 — US
HERALD BUSINESS REVIEW. (Supplement avail.: Herald Extra) 1985. m. Box 2400, Allaire, NJ 07727. TEL 908-938-4400. Ed. Wendy Clayton. adv. circ. 14,000.

HERMES INTERNATIONAL; the English magazine for Cyprus. see *GENERAL INTEREST PERIODICALS — Cyprus*

330 — NP — ISSN 0259-1405
HIMALAYAN ECONOMIST. (Text in English) 1972. q. $5. Parthibeshar P. Timilsima, Ed.& Pub., 21-694-1 Dillibazar, Kathmandu, Nepal. adv. circ. 500.

330 — US — ISSN 0199-0349
HF3000
HISPANIC BUSINESS MAGAZINE. 1979. 10/yr. $18. Hispanic Business, Inc., 360 S. Hope Ave., Ste. 300C, Santa Barbara, CA 93105. TEL 805-682-5843. FAX 805-687-4546. E-mail: hbinfo@hninc.com; URL: http://www.hispanstar.com. Ed. Hector Cantu; Pub. Jesus Chavarria. adv. contact: Robert Filiatreaux. bk.rev. circ. 190,000. **Indexed:** B.P.I., Chic.Per.Ind., P.A.I.S., SRI. **Document type:** consumer publication.
—KR SourceOne; UnCover. **CCC.**
Description: Covers successful Hispanic-owned businesses, political, economic and social trends, and consumer products. Provides tips for aspiring entrepreneurs and for executives and professionals.

HISTORIJSKI ARHIV RIJEKA. VJESNIK. see *HISTORY — History Of Europe*

330 — JA — ISSN 0018-280X
HC461.A1
HITOTSUBASHI JOURNAL OF ECONOMICS. 1960. s-a. 5000 Yen (effective 1997). Hitotsubashi Daigaku, Hitotsubashi Gakkai - Hitotsubashi University, Hitotsubashi Academy, 2-1 Naka, Kunitachi-shi, Tokyo 186, Japan. (Subscr. to: Japan Publications Trading Co. Ltd., P.O. Box 5030, Tokyo International, Tokyo, Japan. TEL 81-3-3292-3751. FAX 81-3-3292-0410) Eds. H. Cjuma, T. Ito. bibl.; charts; illus.; stat.; index. circ. 1,100. **Indexed:** ASCA, C.R.E.J., Curr.Cont., J.of Econ.Lit., Key to Econ.Sci., P.A.I.S., SSCI, SSCI.
—BLDSC (4318.935000); UnCover.
Description: Presents papers that concern empirical, theoretical and-or historical aspects of the Japanese economy.

300 — JA — ISSN 0018-2818
H1
HITOTSUBASHI REVIEW/HITOTSUBASHI RONSO. (Text in Japanese) 1938. m. 8500 Yen. Hitotsubashi Daigaku, Hitotsubashi Gakkai - Hitotsubashi University, Hitotsubashi Academy, 2-1 Naka, Kunitachi-shi, Tokyo 186, Japan. (Subscr. to: Japan Publications Trading Co., Ltd., P.O. Box 5030 Tokyo International, Tokyo, Japan. TEL 81-3-3292-3751. FAX 81-3-3292-0410) Ed. A. Sakuma. bk.rev.; index. circ. 1,350. **Indexed:** Amer.Hist.& Life (1954-), Hist.Abstr. (1954-). **Document type:** academic/scholarly publication.
—UnCover.

330 — UK — ISSN 0073-2818
HC12
HOBART PAPERS. 1960. irreg. $85 (combined subscription for all series). Institute of Economic Affairs, 2 Lord North St., London SW1P 3LB, England. TEL 44-171-799-3745. FAX 44-171-799-2137. E-mail: iea@iea.org.uk; URL: http://www.iea.org.uk. Ed. Colin Robinson. (also avail. in microfiche) **Document type:** academic/scholarly publication.
—BLDSC (4319.750000).
Refereed Serial

HOBSONS FINANCE CASEBOOK. see *OCCUPATIONS AND CAREERS*

650 — US — ISSN 0073-2907
HOFSTRA UNIVERSITY YEARBOOK OF BUSINESS. (Each number has a distinctive title) 1964. irreg., ser.24, vol.1, 1989. prices varies. Hofstra University, Frank G. Zarb School of Business, Attn. Sr. Asst. Dean Rose Anne Manfredi, Weller Hall, Rm. 302, 134 Hofstra University, Hempstead, NY 11550-1090. TEL 516-463-5678. FAX 516-463-5268. E-mail: BIZRAM@VAXC.HOFSTRA.EDU.

330.08 — JA — ISSN 0916-4650
HB9
HOKKAIDO UNIVERSITY. ECONOMIC JOURNAL. (Text in English) 1969. a. free. Hokkaido University, Faculty of Economics - Hokkaido Daigaku Keizaigakubu, North 9, West 7, Kita-ku, Sapporo 060, Japan. TEL 81-11-706-4112. FAX 81-11-706-4947. Ed. Mieko Asakura. bk.rev.; circ. 560 (controlled). **Document type:** academic/scholarly publication.
—BLDSC (3653.830000).
Former titles (until vol.18, July 1989): Hokudai Economic Papers (ISSN 0441-7410); Hokkaido Economic Papers.
Description: Devoted to the coverage of economic developments.

330   IT
HOLDING; * rivista di economia pubblica e privata. 1981. bi-m. Gruppo I R I, Loc. Madonna delle Grazie 261, 06031 Bevagna, Italy. Ed. Demetrio De Stefano.
    Supersedes: I R I Notizie.

330   NE   ISSN 0927-4375
HOLLAND MANAGEMENT REVIEW. Cover title: H M R. 1984. 4/yr. fl.291.50. B.V. Uitgeversmaatschappij Bonaventura (Subsidiary of: Elsevier N.V.), Postbus 2158, 1000 CD Amsterdam, Netherlands. TEL 31-20-6914111. FAX 31-20-5674398. Ed. T.A.C. Otting. adv.; bk.rev.; cum.index. circ. 7,000. (back issues avail.)
    —BLDSC (4322.304747); SWETS.
    Formerly (until 1991): Harvard Holland Review (ISSN 0168-9444)

HOLLIS BUSINESS ENTERTAINMENT (YEAR). see HOTELS AND RESTAURANTS

HOLZBAU - REPORT. see BUILDING AND CONSTRUCTION — Carpentry And Woodwork

338   CN   ISSN 1198-5143
HOME BUSINESS REPORT. 1990. q. Can.$17.12($26) (effective 1997). H B Communications Group Inc., 2949 Ash St., Abbotsford, BC V2S 4G5, Canada. TEL 604-857-1788. FAX 604-854-3087. E-mail: hbr@cyberstore.ca. (Dist. by: Andrew Wood, International Publishing Consultants, Forest Green Square, 16715 - 12 Yonge St., Ste. 161, New Market, ON L3X 1X4. TEL 905-895-3208. FAX 905-895-3208) Ed. Alison Gardner; Pub. Barbara Scott. R&P contact: Barbara Mowat. adv.; B&W page Can.$3500, color page Can.$4485; trim 8 1/2 x 11; adv. contact: Brittany Mowat. bk.rev.; software rev, stat, tr.lit. circ. 50,000. (back issues avail.) Document type: trade publication.
    Formerly: B.C. Home Business Report.
    Description: Aimed at the wide variety of people taking on the challenge of operating a business from the home.

330   CN
HOME WORKPLACE; the Worksteaders Club. 1988. q. Can.$25($25) Worksteaders Club, 1126 Glengrove Ave., W., North York, ON M6B 2K4, Canada. Ed. Maurice Boychuk. adv. circ. 5,000. (looseleaf format) Document type: newsletter, directory.
    Description: Job and opportunity listings for home workers.

659.1   HO
HONDURAS. CONSEJO SUPERIOR DE PLANIFICACION ECONOMICA. PLAN OPERATIVO ANUAL. SECTOR INDUSTRIAL. a. Consejo Superior de Planificacion Economica, Secretaria Tecnica, Tegucigalpa D.C., Honduras.

HONDURAS. CONSEJO SUPERIOR DE PLANIFICACION ECONOMICA. PLAN OPERATIVO ANUAL. SECTOR TURISMO. see TRAVEL AND TOURISM

330   CC
HONG KONG BUSINESS. 1982. m. HK.$250; newsstand price: HK.$30. Communication Management Ltd., 1811 Hong Kong Plaza, 188 Connaught Rd. W., Hong Kong, People's Republic of China. TEL 852-2547-7117. FAX 852-2858-2671. Ed. Lina Ross; Pub. Lina Ross. adv. contact: Graham Abbott. circ. 15,000. Indexed: HongKongiana. Document type: consumer publication.
    Formerly: Hong Kong Business Today.
    Description: Covers Hong Kong, China and international business. Also contains news and features that affect business people in Hong Kong.

330   CC
HONG KONG ECONOMIC YEARBOOK. (Text in Chinese) a. Economic Information & Agency, 342 Hennessy Rd., 10th Fl., Wanchai, Hong Kong, People's Republic of China. TEL 852-573-8217. FAX 852-838-8304. TELEX 86990 EIA HX. adv. circ. 9,800.

330   UN
HOW TO DO BUSINESS WITH THE UNITED NATIONS; the complete guide to U.N. procurement. a. United Nations Association of the United States of America, Inc., 485 Fifth Ave., New York, NY 10016. Eds. Ralph L. Gwerman, Sandrine Tessonneyre. Document type: trade publication.

330 020   US   ISSN 1044-7784
JK404
HOW TO FIND BUSINESS INTELLIGENCE IN WASHINGTON. 1986. irreg., latest 12th ed, $295 (effective 1997). Washington Researchers, Ltd., Box 19005, 20th St. Sta., Washington, DC 20036-9005. TEL 202-333-3499. FAX 202-625-0656. E-mail: research@researchers.com; URL: http://www.researchers.com/pub/busintel/researchers.html. Ed. M. Newman. R&P contact: Ellen O'Kane. Document type: directory.
    Description: Informs executives on where to find industry reports, marketing data and analyses, market databases, and marketing publications issued by the U.S. government, many of which are free.

330 338   US   ISSN 0278-372X
HD2771
HOW TO FIND INFORMATION ABOUT COMPANIES; the corporate intelligence source book. (In 3 vols.; Includes supplement: Information Update) irreg. plus q. update. $395 for each part; all 3 parts $885 (effective 1997). Washington Researchers, Ltd., Box 19005, 20th St. Sta., Washington, DC 20036-9005. TEL 202-333-3499. FAX 202-333-0656. E-mail: research@researchers.com; URL: http://www.researchers.com/pub/busintel/researchers.html. Ed. M. Newman. R&P contact: Ellen O'Kane. Document type: directory.
    Description: Provides business managers worldwide with guidance on finding information about their competitors.

330 020   US   ISSN 1044-9737
HD38.7
HOW TO FIND INFORMATION ABOUT DIVISIONS, SUBSIDIARIES, & PRODUCTS. a. $145 (effective 1995). Washington Researchers, Ltd., Box 19005, 20th St. Sta., Washington, DC 20036-9005. TEL 202-333-3499. FAX 202-625-0656. E-mail: research@researchers.com; URL: http://www.researchers.com/pub/busintel/researchers.html. Ed. M. Newman. R&P contact: Ellen O'Kane. Document type: directory.
    Description: Tells where to look for obscure information about a segment of a company; how to determine which government agencies, trade associations, and industry experts can be of help; and how to tap the company's competitors for information.

330   CC   ISSN 1004-9754
HUAN BOHAI JINGJI LIAOWANG/ECONOMIC OUTLOOK ROUND THE BOHAI SEA. (Text in Chinese) 1987. bi-m. Y48($18) (effective 1997). Huan Bohai Diqu Jingji Xinxi Xiehui - Economic Information Association of the Bohai Sea Rim, 39 Youyi Lu, Hexi Qu, Tianjin 300201, People's Republic of China. TEL 86-22-813-1745. FAX 86-22-835-4270. Ed. Kaiming Lin; Pub. Yuelong Fan. R&P contact: Kaiming Lin. adv.: B&W page Y1800; adv. contact: Chenxiu Li. bk.rev.; circ. 20,000 (paid).
    Description: Regional economic magazine covering Bohai Sea Rim and Pacific Ocean Rim.
    Refereed Serial

330   CC   ISSN 1005-4901
HUANQIU SHICHANG XINXI DAOBAO/GLOBAL MARKET INFORMATION HERALD. (Text in Chinese) m. Zhongguo Shehui Kexueyuan, Wenxian Xinxi Zhongxin - Chinese Academy of Social Sciences, Centre for Documentation and Information, No. 5, Jianguomen-nei Dajie, Beijing 100732, People's Republic of China. TEL 86-10-6523-0096. FAX 86-10-5512-6393. (Dist. overseas by: China International Book Trading Corp., P.O. Box 399, Beijing 100044, P.R. China) Ed. Huiguo Li. R&P contact: Hongzhou Wang. adv. contact: Hongzhou Wang. Document type: academic/scholarly publication.
    Description: Analyzes Chinese and foreign market trends. Contains market studies, investment guides and interviews of prominent figures of various industries.

330   US   ISSN 1050-1096
HUDSON VALLEY BUSINESS JOURNAL. fortn. $20. County Business Journal Publications, Box 339, Pine Island, NY 10969-0339. TEL 914-258-4008. FAX 914-258-4111. Ed. Carol Betley.

330   II   ISSN 0419-0432
HUKERIKAR MEMORIAL LECTURE SERIES. (Text in English) 1964. irreg. price varies. Institute of Economic Research, Director, Vidyagiri, Dharwar 580004, Karnataka, India. FAX 836-41001.

330   HU   ISSN 0133-0365
HC300.2
HUNGARIAN ECONOMY/GAZDASAGI HETILAP FIGYELO; a quarterly economic and business review. (Text in English) 1972-199?; resumed. q. $19.50. (Ministry of Industry and Trade) Verzal Co. Ltd., Frangepan utca 66, 1135 Budapest XIII, Hungary. TEL 36-1-118-6064. FAX 36-1-118-0524. (Subscr. to: Kultura, Box 149, H-1389 Budapest, Hungary) Ed. Andras Hirschler. adv.; bk.rev. circ. 11,000. Indexed: Key to Econ.Sci., PROMT.

I C A LETTER. (International Carwash Association) see TRANSPORTATION — Automobiles

I C E BREAKER REPORT; covering the semiconductor industry. (Integrated Circuit Engineering Corporation) see ELECTRONICS

659   US
I C S A NEWS. 1981. q. $100. International Customer Service Association, 401 N. Michigan Ave., Chicago, IL 60611-4267. TEL 312-321-6800. FAX 312-321-6869. Ed. Kristin Stromberg. circ. 3,500. (back issues avail.) Document type: trade publication.
    Description: Communicates news, ideas and business trends in customer service for professionals. Includes association and industry news, chapter news, technology updates, management tips and new member listings.

330   JA
▼**I D E DEVELOPMENT AND THE ENVIRONMENT SERIES.** 1995. irreg. price varies. Institute of Developing Economies - Ajia Keizai Kenkyusho, 42 Ichigaya-Hommura-cho, Shinjuku-ku, Tokyo 162, Japan. (Dist. by: Maruzen Co. Ltd., Intl. Div. Information Group, P.O. Box 5050, Tokyo International 100-31, Japan. TEL 81-3-3273-3234. FAX 81-3-3271-6076)

338   JA   ISSN 0537-9202
I D E OCCASIONAL PAPERS SERIES. (Former issuing body: Institute of Asian Economic Affairs) (Text in English) irreg, no.33, 1997. price varies. Institute of Developing Economies - Ajia Keizai Kenkyusho, 42 Ichigaya-Hommura-cho, Shinjuku-ku, Tokyo 162, Japan. TEL 81-3-3353-4231. FAX 81-3-3226-8475. (Subscr. to: Maruzen Co. Ltd., Box 5050, Tokyo International 100-31, Tokyo, Japan) Indexed: IDA.
    Formerly (until 1969): I A E A Occasional Papers.

330   SP   ISSN 1133-4029
I E S E REVISTA. 4/yr. free to qualified personnel. (Universidad de Navarra, Instituto de Estudios Superiores de la Empresa) Estudios y Ediciones I E S E S.L., Juan de Alos 43, 08034 Barcelona, Spain. TEL 34-3-2044000. FAX 34-3-2801177. TELEX 50824 IESB E. Ed. Edurne Perez-Yarza. adv.: B&W page 210000 ptas., color page 275000 ptas.; trim 185 x 275; adv. contact: Antonio Morea. bk.rev.; circ. 15,834 (controlled).

332 368   TZ   ISSN 0856-4086
THE I F M JOURNAL OF FINANCE AND MANAGEMENT. 1992. s-a. Sh.4800 (foreign $28). Institute of Finance Management, Library, P.O. Box 3918, Dar es Salaam, Tanzania. TEL 255-51-112931. TELEX 41969 TZ. E-mail: ifm@costech.gn.apc.org. Ed. M.L. Arora. adv. circ. 1,000. Document type: academic/scholarly publication.
    Description: Contains in-depth articles and reports on topics in finance and management, accounting, insurance, social security, and related areas.

330   GW   ISSN 0170-7663
I F O DIGEST; a quarterly journal on economic trends in the Federal Republic of Germany. (Text in English) 1978. q. DM.100 (effective 1997). I F O Institut fuer Wirtschaftsforschung, Poschingerstr. 5, 81679 Munich, Germany. TEL 49-89-9224-0. FAX 49-89-985369. circ. 650. Indexed: C.R.E.J., Key to Econ.Sci.
    —BLDSC (4363.316500).

330   GW   ISSN 0945-1730
I F O DOKUMENTATION. 1993. irreg, vol.4, 1995. DM.25. I F O Institut fuer Wirtschaftsforschung, Poschingerstr. 5, 81679 Munich, Germany. TEL 49-89-9224-0. FAX 49-89-985369. Document type: monographic series.

BUSINESS AND ECONOMICS

330 GW
I F O DRESDEN BERICHTET; ueber Konjunktur, Struktur, Wirtschaftspolitik. bi-m. DM.50 (effective 1995). I F O Institut fuer Wirtschaftsforschung, Poschingerstr. 5, 81679 Munich, Germany. TEL 49-89-9224-0. FAX 49-89-985369. **Document type:** bulletin.

330 GW
I F O FORSCHUNGSBERICHTE DER ABTEILUNG ENTWICKLUNGSLAENDER. 1965. irreg., vol.85, 1995. DM.48. (I F O Institut fuer Wirtschaftsforschung) Weltforum Verlag, Marienburgerstr. 22, 50963 Cologne, Germany. TEL 49-221-93763-0. FAX 49-221-9376399. circ. 150. **Document type:** monographic series.
Description: Covers economic issues affecting developing nations.

330 GW ISSN 0947-3173
I F O IM (MONTH). m. DM.24 (effective 1995). I F O Institut fuer Wirtschaftsforschung, Poschingerstr. 5, 81679 Munich, Germany. TEL 49-89-9224-0. FAX 49-89-985369. **Document type:** bulletin.

330 GW ISSN 0445-0736
I F O INSTITUT FUER WIRTSCHAFTSFORSCHUNG. SCHRIFTENREIHE. 1949. irreg., vol.139, 1995. DM.86. Duncker und Humblot GmbH, Postfach 410329, 12113 Berlin, Germany. TEL 49-30-790006-0. FAX 49-30-79000631. E-mail: duh-werbung@t-online.de. **Document type:** monographic series.

330 GW
I F O KONJUNKTURPERSPEKTIVEN. 1974. m. DM.150 (effective 1995). I F O Institut fuer Wirtschaftsforschung, Poschingerstr. 5, 81679 Munich, Germany. TEL 49-89-9224-0. FAX 49-89-985369. (back issues avail.) **Document type:** bulletin.
Formerly (until 1991): Konjunkturperspektiven.

330 GW ISSN 0018-974X
I F O SCHNELLDIENST. 1948. 3/mo. DM.310. (I F O Institut fuer Wirtschaftsforschung) Duncker und Humblot GmbH, Postfach 410329, 12113 Berlin, Germany. TEL 49-30-7900060. FAX 49-30-79000631. E-mail: duh-werbung@t-online.de. bk.rev.; charts; stat. **Indexed:** ELLIS, INIS Atomind., Key to Econ.Sci., World Agri.Econ.& Rural Sociol.Abstr. **Document type:** academic/scholarly publication.
—BLDSC (4363.320000). **CCC.**

330 GW ISSN 0018-9731
HB5
I F O STUDIEN; Zeitschrift fuer empirische Wirtschaftsforschung. (Text in English, German; summaries in English) 1955. q. DM.198. (I F O Institut fuer Wirtschaftsforschung) Duncker und Humblot GmbH, Postfach 410329, 12113 Berlin, Germany. TEL 49-30-7900060. FAX 49-30-79000631. E-mail: duh-werbung@t-online.de. Ed. K.H. Oppenlaender. bk.rev.; index. **Indexed:** IBR, J.of Econ.Lit., P.A.I.S.For.Lang.Ind., SCIMP (1991-). **Document type:** academic/scholarly publication.
—SWETS. **CCC.**

330 GW ISSN 0170-5695
I F O STUDIEN ZU HANDELS- UND DIENSTLEISTUNGSFRAGEN. 1962. irreg., no.51, 1996. price varies. I F O Institut fuer Wirtschaftsforschung, Poschingerstr. 5, 81679 Munich, Germany. TEL 49-89-9224-0. FAX 49-89-985369. circ. 400. **Document type:** monographic series.
Formerly: I F O Institut fuer Wirtschaftsforschung. Studien zu Handelsfragen (ISSN 0073-4268)
Description: Research results concerning marketing and service sectors.

330 700 GW
I F O STUDIEN ZU KULTUR UND WIRTSCHAFT. 1990. irreg., vol.20, 1996. price varies. I F O Institut fuer Wirtschaftsforschung, Poschingerstr. 5, 81679 Munich, Germany. TEL 49-89-9224-0. FAX 49-89-985369. **Document type:** monographic series.

I F O STUDIEN ZUR BEVOELKERUNGSOEKONOMIE. see POPULATION STUDIES

330 GW ISSN 0944-0356
I F O STUDIEN ZUR INNOVATIONSFORSCHUNG. 1993. irreg., vol.3, 1995. price varies. I F O Institut fuer Wirtschaftsforschung, Poschingerstr. 5, 81679 Munich, Germany. TEL 49-89-9224-0. FAX 49-89-985369. **Document type:** monographic series.

330 GW ISSN 0176-0874
I F O STUDIEN ZUR STRUKTURFORSCHUNG. 1983. irreg., vol.24, 1996. price varies. I F O Institut fuer Wirtschaftsforschung, Poschingerstr. 5, 81679 Munich, Germany. TEL 49-89-9224-0. FAX 49-89-985369. **Document type:** monographic series.

330 613.1 GW ISSN 0175-8330
I F O STUDIEN ZUR UMWELTOEKONOMIE. 1984. irreg., vol.23, 1997. price varies. I F O Institut fuer Wirtschaftsforschung, Poschingerstr. 5, 81679 Munich, Germany. TEL 49-89-9224-0. FAX 49-89-985369. **Document type:** monographic series.

338 GW ISSN 0943-3007
HC281
I F O WIRTSCHAFTSKONJUNKTUR. 1949. m. DM.265. (I F O Institut fuer Wirtschaftsforschung) Duncker und Humblot GmbH, Postfach 410329, 12113 Berlin, Germany. TEL 49-30-7900060. FAX 49-30-79000631. E-mail: duh-werbung@t-online.de. adv.; bk.rev.; charts; stat. **Indexed:** Key to Econ.Sci., P.A.I.S.For.Lang.Ind. **Document type:** academic/scholarly publication.
—SWETS. **CCC.**
Formerly: Wirtschaftskonjunktur (ISSN 0043-6283)

330 BO ISSN 0034-9283
I I E REVISTA. Variant title: Revista Economica. 1945. s-a. $10. Universidad Boliviana Tecnica de Oruro, Instituto de Investigaciones Economicas, Casilla 441, Oruro, Bolivia.

330 GW
I K B DEUTSCHE INDUSTRIEBANK. GESCHAEFTSBEREICH VOLKSWIRTSCHAFT UND MARKETING. I K B - MITTEILUNGEN. 3/yr. I K B Deutsche Industriebank AG, Karl-Theodor-Str. 6, 40213 Duesseldorf, Germany. TEL 0211-8221-499. FAX 0211-8221-766. circ. 16,000. **Document type:** bulletin.
Former titles: Deutsche Industriebank. Geschaeftsbereich Volkswirtschaft. I K B - Mitteilungen (ISSN 0940-0001); Deutsche Industriebank. Volkswirtschaftliche Abteilung. V W - Mitteilungen.

I N A VJESNIK INDUSTRIJE NAFTE. see PETROLEUM AND GAS

330 AT ISSN 1030-4177
HB1
I P A REVIEW. 1947. q. $28. Institute of Public Affairs, 128-36 Jolimont Rd., Jolimont, Vic. 3002, Australia. TEL 61-3-96547499. FAX 61-3-96507627. Ed. Ken Baker. R&P contact: Ken Baker. adv. contact: Louise Cato. bk.rev. circ. 7,800. (back issues avail.) **Indexed:** Aus.P.A.I.S., Child.Lit.Abstr., P.A.I.S.
●Also available online. Vendor(s): UMI.
—UMI; UnCover.
Former titles (until 1986): Institute of Public Affairs. Review (ISSN 1030-4169); (until 1982): I P A Review (ISSN 0019-0268)
Description: Presents analysis and commnet on social, political and economic issues.

330.9 BL
I P E A SERIE P N P E. 1982. irreg., no.11, 1985. price varies. Instituto de Planejamento Economico e Social, Programa Nacional de Pesquisa Economica, Caixa Postal 2672, Rio de Janeiro, RJ, Brazil. TEL 021-220-5533. Ed. Hamilton N. Marques. circ. 1,000.

I R I SENTINEL. (Industrial Risk Insurers) see INSURANCE

330 SI ISSN 0218-2114
I S E A S CURRENT ECONOMIC AFFAIRS SERIES. (Text in English) 1991. irreg., no.13, 1996. price varies. Institute of Southeast Asian Studies, Heng Mui Keng Terrace, Pasir Panjang, Singapore 119596, Singapore. TEL 65-778-0955. FAX 65-775-6259. E-mail: pubsunit@merlion.iseas.ac.sg; URL: http://www.iseas.ac.sg/pub.html. Ed. Triena Ong. R&P contact: Triena Ong. **Document type:** academic/scholarly publication, monographic series.
Description: Covers current economic affairs in the Asia-Pacific region.

330 JA
I S E R REPRINT SERIES. a. Institute of Social and Economic Research, Osaka University, 10-1 Mihogaoka, Ibaraki-shi, Osaka 567. TEL 06-8775111.
Description: Reprints of articles published by ISER members or by others working in association with the institute.

330 GW ISSN 0344-919X
I W D. w. DM.154.85. (Institut der Deutschen Wirtschaft) Deutscher Instituts Verlag GmbH, Postfach 510670, 50942 Cologne, Germany. TEL 49-221-4981452. FAX 49-221-4981592. **Document type:** bulletin.

330 US ISSN 8750-4022
IDAHO BUSINESS REVIEW. 1984. w. $59. Box 8866, Boise, ID 83707. TEL 208-336-3768. Ed. Carl Miller. adv. contact: Kitty Fleishcman. bk.rev.; stat. circ. 2,550. (back issues avail.) **Document type:** newsletter.
Description: Provides current news, plus information about records and construction for business owners and managers.

330 SP
IDEAS EMPRESARIALES. 1982. 4/yr. free. Asociacion de Antiguos Alumnos del Instituto de Empresa, Maria de Molina 12 bajo izda., 28006 Madrid, Spain. TEL 39-1-4114511. FAX 39-1-4117923. Ed. Antonio Montes. adv. contact: Victoria Gimeno. circ. 9,000. **Document type:** academic/scholarly publication.

330 FR ISSN 0180-9709
IDEES LUCRATIVES. 10/yr. Maison des Chevaliers de Saint Jean, B.P. 266, 1 Place du Lycee, 68005 Colmar Cedex, France. TEL 89-24-04-64. FAX 89-23-58-27. Ed. Jean Luc Specht. circ. 15,000.

330 BU ISSN 0013-2993
HC407.B9
IKONOMICESKA MISAL. (Summaries in French, Russian) 1956. 12/yr. 0.75 lv. per no. (Bulgarska Akademiia na Naukite, Ikonomiceski Institut) Publishing House of the Bulgarian Academy of Sciences, Acad. G. Bonchev St., Bldg. 6, 1113 Sofia, Bulgaria. (Dist. by: Hemus, 6, Rouski Blvd., 1000 Sofia, Bulgaria) Ed. K. Kiriakov. bk.rev.; charts; index. circ. 6,220. (reprint service avail. from IRC) **Indexed:** BSL Econ., Geo.Abstr.
—BLDSC (0086.160000).

330 659.1 BU
IKONOMICHESKI ZHIVOT. (Text in Bulgarian) 1965. w. 260 lv.($120) Ikonomicheski Zhivot, Moskovska Str. 9, Sofia 1000, Bulgaria. TEL 35-92-879506. FAX 35-92-882140. Ed. Vasil Alexiev. adv. contact: Dimistar Ivanov. bk.rev.; charts; illus.; pat.; stat.; tr.lit. circ. 20,000. (tabloid format) **Document type:** newspaper.
Description: Publishes business news for businessmen, managers, accountants, insurance and advertising agents.

330 IT
IMPRENDITORIALITA; mensile di politica, economia e cultura. 1980. m. (11/yr.) L.50000 (foreign L.100000). Sviluppo Editoriale Pubblicitario s.r.l., Via del Pozzo delle Cornacchie 55, 00186 Rome, Italy. TEL 39-6-68-77-887. FAX 39-6-6896256. Ed. Maurizio Talamona. adv.: B&W page L.8000000, color page L.12000000. circ. 47,000.

330 IT
IMPRESA ARTIGIANA. 11/yr. Confederazione Generale Italiana dell'Artigianato, Via S. Giovanni Laterano 152, 00184 Rome, Italy. TEL 39-6-703741. Ed. Giovanni Vitelli. adv.: page L.15660000. circ. 420,000.

BUSINESS AND ECONOMICS   971

330   GW   ISSN 0720-9037
IMPULSE (HAMBURG). 1980. m. DM.105.60 (Europe DM.144.60; elsewhere DM.241.60). Gruner und Jahr AG & Co., Am Baumwall 11, 20459 Hamburg, Germany. TEL 49-40-3703-0. FAX 49-40-37035617. circ. 135,100. (also avail. in microfilm from ALP) **Document type:** consumer publication.
—SWETS.

330 600   US
IN TECHNOLOGY. * m. Pittsburgh High Technology Council, 2000 Technology Dr., Pittsburgh, PA 15219. TEL 412-687-2700. Ed. Lynne Glover.

IN VIVO; the business and medicine report. see *MEDICAL SCIENCES*

330   US   ISSN 1047-2347
HD62.7
INDEPENDENT BUSINESS. 1989. bi-m. Group IV Communications, Inc., 125 Auburn Ct., Ste. 100, Thousand Oaks, CA 91362-3617. TEL 805-496-6156. FAX 805-496-5469. Ed. Daniel Kehrer. adv.; bk.rev.; circ. 600,000 (controlled). **Document type:** trade publication.
Description: Information for the business owner and operator. Includes updates on legislation, employee benefits and relations, and public relations.

INDEX OF ECONOMIC FREEDOM. see *POLITICAL SCIENCE*

338   II
INDIA. MINISTRY OF HEAVY INDUSTRY. REPORT. (Text in English) 1973. irreg. Ministry of Heavy Industry, New Delhi, India. **Document type:** government publication.

330   US
INDIA BUSINESS INTELLIGENCE. (Supplements avail. 3/yr.) 1994. m. £445($745) Economist Intelligence Unit, 111 W. 57th St., New York, NY 10019. TEL 212-554-0600; 800-938-4685. FAX 212-586-1182. TELEX 175567. URL: http://www.eiu.com. (UK addr.: Economist Intelligence Unit Ltd., Subscriptions Dept., P.O. Box 200, Harold Hill, Romford, Essex RM3 8UX, England. TEL 44-171-830-1007. FAX 44-1708-371850) **Document type:** trade publication.
Formerly: Business South Asia.
Description: Provides analyses of foreign investment and market entry strategies in India. Covers issues such as market size, investment as well as corporate strategies of multinationals and Indian business groups.

INDIAN BUSINESS AND MANAGEMENT. see *ETHNIC INTERESTS*

330   II   ISSN 0019-4662
HC431
INDIAN ECONOMIC JOURNAL. (Text in English) 1953. q. Rs.200($30) Indian Economic Association, c/o Dynaram Electronics & Computers, No. 20, 1st Fl., South Cross Rd., Bosavanagadi, Bangalore 560004, India. TEL 91-80-602822. FAX 91-80-6600440. Ed. P.R. Bradhmananda; Pub. A.N. Mashruewala. adv.; bk.rev.; charts; index. circ. 2,500. (also avail. in microform from UMI; back issues avail.; reprint service avail. from UMI) **Indexed:** Int.Lab.Doc., J.of Econ.Lit., J.of Econ.Lit., Key to Econ.Sci., Mid.East: Abstr.& Ind., Pub.Admin.Abstr., Rural Recreat.Tour.Abstr., SSCI, World Agri.Econ.& Rural Sociol.Abstr. **Document type:** academic/scholarly publication.
—BLDSC (4396.330000); SWETS; UnCover.
Refereed Serial

330   II   ISSN 0019-4670
HB1.A1
INDIAN ECONOMIC REVIEW. 1952; N.S. 1966. s-a. Rs.300($50) (effective 1995). University of Delhi, Delhi School of Economics, Delhi 110 007, India. TEL 91-11-7257005. FAX 91-11-7257159. E-mail: ier@cdedse.ernet.in. Ed. V. Pandit. adv.; bk.rev.; charts; index. circ. 600. **Indexed:** C.R.E.J., J.of Econ.Lit., Rural Recreat.Tour.Abstr., World Agri.Econ.& Rural Sociol.Abstr. **Document type:** academic/scholarly publication.
—BLDSC (4396.340000); SWETS; UnCover.

330   II
HB9
INDIAN JOURNAL OF ECONOMICS. (Text in English) 1916. q. $125. University of Allahabad, Department of Economics and Commerce, Allahabad 211 002, Uttar Pradesh, India. FAX 91-532-609857. Ed. P.N. Mehrotra. adv.; bk.rev.; bibl.; charts; illus.; mkt.; pat.; tr.mk. circ. 500. (also avail. in microfiche from IDC) **Indexed:** C.R.E.J., Cott.& Trop.Fibr.Abstr., IBR, Int.Lab.Doc., P.A.I.S., Pub.Admin.Abstr., Rural Devel.Abstr., Sorghum & Millets Abstr., SSCI, Trop.Oil Seeds Abstr. **Document type:** academic/scholarly publication.
—BLDSC (4411.700000); SWETS; UnCover.
Refereed Serial

330 320   II   ISSN 0971-0396
INDIAN SCHOOL OF POLITICAL ECONOMY. JOURNAL. 1989. q. $80. New Age International Pvt. Ltd., Journals Division, 4835-24, Ansari Rd., Daryaganj, New Delhi 110 002, India. TEL 91-11-3261487. FAX 91-11-3267437. **Document type:** academic/scholarly publication.

650   US   ISSN 0019-6541
HC107.I6   CODEN: IBREAO
INDIANA BUSINESS REVIEW. 1926. q. free. Indiana University, School of Business, Bloomington, IN 47405. TEL 812-855-5507. Ed. Morton J. Marcus. charts; illus. circ. 4,000. (also avail. in microfiche from CIS) **Indexed:** ABI Inform, BPIA, Pers.Manage.Abstr., SRI.
●Also available online. Vendor(s): UMI.
—BLDSC (4431.500000); UMI; UnCover.

330   II
INDIANA JOURNAL OF COMMERCE AND INDUSTRY. 1988. m. $29.95. R & W Publishing, Inc., Box 3275, Evansville, IN 47731-3275. TEL 812-425-2210. FAX 812-422-4984. Ed. Barbara Stahura; Pub. Conrad L. Roe. R&P contact: Conrad L. Roe. adv. contact: Conrad L. Roe. circ. 12,000. **Document type:** newspaper.
●Also available online. Vendor(s): UMI.
Formerly: Evansville Business Journal.
Description: Provides domestic and international business news and analysis.

330   CL   ISSN 0716-2413
INDICADORES ECONOMICOS Y SOCIALES. (Text in English, Spanish) 1981. irreg., no.3, 1989. Ch.$23000($115) Banco Central de Chile, Casilla 967, Santiago, Chile. TEL 56-2-6702000. FAX 56-2-6984847. circ. 1,100.

330   IO
INDONESIA BUSINESS WEEKLY. (Text in English) w. Bisnis Indonesia Bldg., 5th Fl., Jl Let Jend S Parman Kav 12, Slipi, Jakarta 11410, Indonesia. TEL 5304016. FAX 5305868.

330   PN
INDUSTRIA. 1953. q. free. Sindicato de Industriales de Panama, Apdo. 6-4798, El Dorado, Panama 1, Panama. TEL 507-30-0169. Ed. Flor Ortega. adv. circ. 1,000. **Document type:** newsletter.

330   PO   ISSN 0872-6728
A INDUSTRIA DO NORTE - INFORMACAO. (Supplements avail.: Industria do Norte - Opiniao e Analise (semi-annual; A I P Ambiente (monthly)) 1846. m. Esc.3500 (free to qualified personnel) (effective 1997). Associacao Industrial Portuense - Porto Industrial Association, Exponor - Feira Internacional do Porto, 4450 Leca da Palmeira, Portugal. TEL 351-2-9981500. FAX 351-2-9957017. TELEX 25492 AIPORT P. Dir. Angelo Ludgero Marques; Pub. Angelo Ludgero Marques. adv. contact: Rene Brigido. circ. 5,000. **Document type:** trade publication.
Former titles (until 1994): Industria do Norte (ISSN 0019-7572); (until 1938): Trabalho Nacional (ISSN 0870-9505); (until 1915): Industrial Portuense.
Description: Deals with economical, technological, and juridical themes of industry.

330   VE
INDUSTRIA VENEZOLANA. 1971. 6/yr. Editorial Guia Industrial, Apdo. 60772, Chacao, Caracas 101, Venezuela. Ed. Jose Precedo.

INDUSTRIAL & TRADE DIRECTORY. see *BUSINESS AND ECONOMICS — Trade And Industrial Directories*

330   UK
INDUSTRIAL DEVELOPMENT ACT, 1982, ANNUAL REPORT. a. £25. H.M.S.O., 51 Nine Elms Ln., London SW8 5DR, England. TEL 44-171-873-0011. FAX 44-171-873-8247. (Dist. by: UNIPUB, 4611-F Assembly Dr., Lanham, MD 20706-4391. TEL 301-459-7666) **Document type:** government publication.
Description: Describes the powers under the Act including the powers under past legislation which the act consolidated.

330   US
INDUSTRIAL DEVELOPMENT AND THE SOCIAL FABRIC; an international series of historical monographs. 1979. irreg., vol.13, 1995. $73.25. J A I Press Inc., 55 Old Post Rd., No. 2, Box 1678, Greenwich, CT 06830-1678. TEL 203-661-7602. FAX 203-661-0792. E-mail: jai@jaipress.com. (Subscr. in UK and Europe to: JAI Press Ltd., 38 Tavistock St., Covent Garden, London WC2E 7PB, England. TEL 44-171-379-8834. FAX 44-171-379-8835) Ed. John P. McKay. **Document type:** monographic series.

330   US
INDUSTRIAL NEWS (IAEGER). 1926. w. $6. Box 180, Iaeger, WV 24844. TEL 304-938-2142. Ed. William A. Johnson. adv. circ. 2,510. **Document type:** newspaper.
●Also available on CD-ROM.

INDUSTRIAL REPORTS. see *LAW — Corporate Law*

338.09   II
INDUSTRIAL RESEARCHER. (Text in English) 1974. q. $200. Pranava Industrial Services Pvt. Ltd., 18, Sagar Tarang, Bhulabhai Desai Rd., Bombay 400 036, India. TEL 3633236. Ed. P.J. Divatia. adv. circ. 500.
●Also available online. Vendor(s): Knight-Ridder Information, Inc.

639 338   SP   ISSN 0212-7202
INDUSTRIAS PESQUERAS; revista maritima quincenal. (Text in Spanish; summaries in Spanish and English) 1927. fortn. 6000 ptas. (foreign 8000 ptas.). Servicios Industriales Pesqueros S.A., Policarpo Sanz 22-3, 36202 Vigo, Spain. TEL 34-86-438597. FAX 34-86-430625. TELEX 83058 IBISA E. Dir. Alfonso Paz-Andrade. adv.; B&W page 105000 ptas., color page 135000 ptas.; 185 x 260; adv. contact: Luis de Miguel. bk.rev.; abstr.; bibl.; charts; illus.; stat. circ. 5,000. **Indexed:** Ind.SST. **Document type:** consumer publication, trade publication.

330   SZ
INDUSTRIE FLASH. 10/yr. Kretz AG, Postfach, CH-8706 Feldmeilen, Switzerland. TEL 41-1-9237656. FAX 41-1-9237657. Ed. Rudolf Weber. adv.; B&W page 2870 SFr., color page 3930 SFr.; trim 185 x 265; adv. contact: Esther Kretz. circ. 6,900. **Document type:** trade publication.

330   UK
INDUSTRY AND EUROPEAN MARKET. 6/yr. 3 St. Faiths Ln., Norwich, Norfolk NR1 1NN, England. TEL 0603-765800. FAX 0603-760812. Ed. Peter Mercer.

330   CH   ISSN 0019-946X
INDUSTRY OF FREE CHINA. Key Title: Ziyou Zhongguo zhi Gongye. (Text in Chinese and English) 1954. m. (in 2 vols.). NT.$800 (Hong Kong $45; Asia & Pacific $60; elsewhere $75). (Council for Economic Planning and Development) Publishing Committee of Industry of Free China, 9th Fl., No. 87 Nanking E. Rd., Sec. 2, Taipei, Taiwan 10408, Republic of China. TEL 886-2-522-5404. FAX 886-2-562-2950. Ed. W.P. Chang. bibl.; stat.; index. circ. 2,500. **Indexed:** Asian-Pac.Econ.Lit., IBR, Key to Econ.Sci., P.A.I.S., Rural Devel.Abstr., Rural Recreat.Tour.Abstr., World Agri.Econ.& Rural Sociol.Abstr. **Document type:** government publication.
—BLDSC (4478.100000); UnCover.
Refereed Serial

BUSINESS AND ECONOMICS

330　　　　　　　　CN　ISSN 1194-8973
INFO - AFFAIRES. 1989. m. Gilles Belleau, Ed. & Pub., Box 399, Richibouctou, N.B. E0A 2M0, Canada. TEL 506-523-1123. FAX 506-523-1122. circ. 15,000.

330　　　　　　　　SZ
INFO-VENTE. 11/yr. Ligue Suisse de la Representation Commerciale, 20 rue Camille-Martin, CH-1203 Geneva, Switzerland. TEL 022-7960711. FAX 022-730530. Ed. Joseph Schafer. circ. 5,000.

330 338.4　　　　　SP
INFORMACION TECNICO ECONOMICA. 1977. q. (Asociacion de Investigacion de la Industria Papelera Espanola) Instituto Papelero Espanol, Carretera de la Coruna, Km. 7, 28040 Madrid, Spain. TEL 34-1-3070976. FAX 34-1-3572828. circ. 800.

332　　　　　　　　BL
INFORMACOES F I P E. m. $39 (effective 1997). Fundacao Instituto de Pesquisas Economicas, Departamento de Publicacoes, Caixa Postal 11474, 05508-900 Sao Paulo, Brazil. TEL 55-11-2125471. FAX 55-11-8186073. Ed. Helio Zylberstajn. adv. contact: Eny Elza Ceotto. charts; stat.

330　　　　　　　　PO
INFORMADOR FISCAL. 4/yr. Rua St. Idelfonso 42-1o, Porto, Portugal.

INFORMATION ECONOMICS AND POLICY. see *COMMUNICATIONS*

330　　　　　　US　ISSN 1070-4639
HF54.52.U5
THE (YEAR) INFORMATION PLEASE BUSINESS ALMANAC & DESK REFERENCE. Variant title: Information Please Business Almanac and Sourcebook. a. $21.95. Houghton Mifflin Co., 215 Park Ave. S., New York, NY 10003. TEL 212-420-5800. (Dist. by: Reference Press, Inc., 6448 Hwy. 290 E., Ste. E-104, Austin, TX 78723. TEL 512-454-7778. FAX 512-454-9401; Subscr to: Houghton Mifflin Co., Wayside Rd., Burlington, MA 01803. TEL 800-225-3362) Ed. Seth Godin. maps; stat.
Description: Provides a comprehensive reference of business addresses, media contacts, government agencies, area and zip codes, and other handy information for business professionals.

330　　　　　　　US
INFORMATION STRATEGY. Online edition (US ISSN 1365-6325) m. Economist Group, E-mail: isfeedback@info-strategy.com; URL: http://www.info-strategy.com/. Ed. Matthew May. **Document type**: trade publication.
●Also available online.

330　　　　　　FR　ISSN 0766-6241
INFORMATIONS M M M. 1964. 11/yr. 3200 F. Club M M M, 26 rue Cadet, 75009 Paris, France. TEL 45-23-01-07. FAX 45-23-02-88. Ed. Brigitte Guillot. circ. 2,000. **Document type**: bulletin.

330　　　　　　　　PN
INFORMATIVO INDUSTRIAL. m. Sindicato de Industriales de Panama, Apdo. 6-4798, El Dorado, Panama 1, Panama. TEL 507-2300169. Ed. Flor Ortega. **Document type**: newsletter.

330　　　　　　　　PE
INFORME NEGOCIACION COLECTIVA. 1990. m. Asesoramiento y Analisis Laborales S.A., Mariano Odicio 334, Miraflores, Lima 18, Peru. TEL 469477. Dir. Luis Aparicio Valdez. **Document type**: newsletter.

330　　　　　　　　PE
INFORME TRIBUTARIO. (Supplement to: Analisis Tributario) 1991? m. Asesoramiento y Analisis Laborales S.A., Mariano Odicio 334, Miraflores, Lima 18, Peru. TEL 469477.

INFORPRESS CENTROAMERICANA. see *POLITICAL SCIENCE*

INFOS DE L'EXPRESSION D'ENTREPRISE. see *COMMUNICATIONS*

330　　　　　　　　UK
INFRASTRUCTURE YEARBOOK. 1994. a. £95. Privatisation International Ltd., Butlers Wharf Business Centre, Ste. 404, 45 Curlew St., London SE1 2ND, England. TEL 44-171-378-1620. FAX 44-171-403-7876. E-mail: 100446.3646@compuserve.com. Ed. Rodney Lord. adv. contact: Diana Howarth. **Document type**: trade publication.
Description: Detailed review of developments in private financing of infrastructure projects all over the world.

380　　　　　　US　ISSN 1046-9958
HD2771
INGRAM'S MAGAZINE; for successful Kansas Citians. 1974. m. $36. Show-me Publishing, 306 E. 12th St., Ste. 1014, Kansas City, MO 64106. TEL 816-842-9994. FAX 816-474-1111. Ed. Russell Brown. adv. contact: Sue Barrelli. bk.rev. circ. 28,000. **Indexed**: Tr.& Indus.Ind.
—UMI.
Former titles (until 1989): Corporate Report; Corporate Report - Kansas City (ISSN 0273-9968); (until 1981): Outlook (ISSN 0191-6815)

330 600　　　　　　US
INNOVATION. 1994. w. $15. NewsScan Inc., 1290 Oxford Rd., Box 15010, Atlanta, GA 30306. E-mail: gehl@newsscan.com; URL: http://www.newsscan.com. Eds. John Gehl, Suzanne Douglas.
●Available only online.
Description: Covers trends, strategies and innovations in business and technology.

330　　　　　　GW　ISSN 0579-6415
INPUT - OUTPUT STUDIEN. 1969. irreg., vol.16, 1984. price varies. I F O Institut fuer Wirtschaftsforschung, Poschingerstr. 5, 81679 Munich, Germany. TEL 49-89-9224-0. FAX 49-89-985369. **Document type**: monographic series.

INSEGNARE DIRITTO ECONOMIA. see *LAW*

INSIDE MICHIGAN POLITICS. see *PUBLIC ADMINISTRATION*

330　　　　　　US　ISSN 1069-5184
INSIDE TUCSON BUSINESS. 1991. w. $39. Territorial Newspapers, P.O. Box 27087, Tucson, AZ 85726-7087. TEL 520-294-1200. FAX 520-294-4040. Ed. Rod Smith. adv. contact: David Stoler. circ. 8,000 (controlled). (tabloid format) **Document type**: newspaper.

330 332.6　　　　CN　ISSN 0821-0012
KE1485.A13
INSOLVENCY BULLETIN. (Text in English, French) 1980. q. free. Industry Canada, 365 Laurier Ave. W., 8th Fl., Ottawa, ON K1A 0G8, Canada. TEL 819-997-3825. Ed. Henri Massue-Monat. circ. 2,350. **Indexed**: Ind.Can.L.P.L.
Supersedes in part (in 1980): Canada Corporations. Bulletin. Bankruptcy and Insolvency (ISSN 0382-3288); Which was formerly (until 1976): Canada Corporations Act Bulletin (ISSN 0382-327X)
Description: Aimed at trustees, jurists, registrars, accountants, credit managers and those with an interest in bankruptcy and insolvency.

330 320.531　　　　FR
INSTITUT DES RECHERCHES MARXISTES. ISSUES. (Text in French) 1979. 4/yr. 200 F. (foreign 250 F.). Institut des Recherches Marxistes, 64 bd. Auguste Blanqui, 75013 Paris, France. adv.; bk.rev. circ. 2,000.
Former titles: S E P I R M Issues; Institut de Recherches Marxistes. Issues (ISSN 0222-7762)

330　　　　　　UK　ISSN 1367-5796
▼**INSTITUTE FOR FINANCIAL RESEARCH WORKING PAPERS**. 1995. irreg. free. University of London, Birbeck College, Department of Economics, 7-15 Gresse St., London W1P 2LL, England. TEL 44-171-631-6401. FAX 44-171-631-6316. URL: http://www.econ.bbk.ac.uk/research/fwpaper.htm/. **Document type**: monographic series.

330　　　　　　UK　ISSN 0073-909X
H11
INSTITUTE OF ECONOMIC AFFAIRS. OCCASIONAL PAPERS. 1963. irreg. $85 (combined subscription for all series). Institute of Economic Affairs, 2 Lord North St., London SW1P 3LB, England. TEL 44-171-799-3745. FAX 44-171-799-2137. E-mail: iea@iea.org.uk; URL: http://www.iea.org.uk. Ed. Colin Robinson. (also avail. in microfiche) **Document type**: academic/scholarly publication.
—BLDSC (6217.450000).
Refereed Serial

330　　　　　　UK　ISSN 0073-9103
INSTITUTE OF ECONOMIC AFFAIRS. RESEARCH MONOGRAPHS. 1966. irreg. $85 (combined subscription for all series). Institute of Economic Affairs, 2 Lord North St., London SW1P 3LB, England. TEL 44-171-799-3745. FAX 44-171-799-2137. E-mail: iea@iea.org.uk; URL: http://www.iea.org.uk. Ed. Colin Robinson. (also avail. in microfiche) **Document type**: academic/scholarly publication.
—BLDSC (7743.080000).
Refereed Serial

330　　　　　　　　II
INSTITUTE OF ECONOMIC GEOGRAPHY, INDIA. JOURNAL.* (Text in English) 1970. s-a. $4. Institute of Economic Geography, 4-1 Ashton Rd., Calcutta 20, India. illus.

330　　　　　　　　II
INSTITUTE OF ECONOMIC GROWTH. WORKING PAPERS. 1972. irreg., no.157, 1993. Institute of Economic Growth, University Enclave, New Delhi 110007, India. TEL 7257101.

330　　　　　　II　ISSN 0020-2851
INSTITUTE OF ECONOMIC RESEARCH. JOURNAL. (Text in English) 1966. s-a. Rs.50($20) Institute of Economic Research, Vidyagiri, Dharwad 580 004, Karnataka, India. FAX 836-41001. Ed. N. Vajra Kumar. adv.; bk.rev.; charts; illus.; stat.; index. circ. 200. (back issues avail.) **Indexed**: Rural Devel.Abstr., World Agri.Econ.& Rural Sociol.Abstr.
Description: Covers economic research in agriculture, housing and urban planning, population studies and social sciences.

330　　　　　　　　II
INSTITUTE OF ECONOMIC RESEARCH. PUBLICATIONS ON ECONOMICS. (Text in English) irreg. price varies. Institute of Economic Research, c/o Director, Vidyagiri, Dharwar 580004, Karnataka, India. FAX 836-41001.

INSTITUTE OF FINANCE MANAGEMENT. PROSPECTUS. see *EDUCATION — Adult Education*

330　　　　　　　　US
INSTITUTE OF SOCIAL AND ECONOMIC RESEARCH. REPORTS. 1963. irreg., no.58, 1985. price varies. University of Alaska, Institute of Social and Economic Research, 3211 Providence Dr., Anchorage, AK 99508. TEL 907-786-7710. FAX 907-786-7739. Ed. Linda Leask.
Formerly: Institute of Social, Economic and Government Research. Reports (ISSN 0065-5937)

330　　　　　　　　BL
INSTITUTO DE PESQUISA ECONOMICA APLICADA. BOLETIM CONJUNTURAL. (Supplement avail. 8/yr.: Carta de Conjuntura). q. $70 includes Carta de Conjuntura (effective Nov. 1994). Instituto de Pesquisa Economica Aplicada, Av. Pres. Antonio Carlos, 51 14o andar, 20020-010 Rio de Janeiro RJ, Brazil. TEL 55-21-220-5533. FAX 55-21-240-1920. circ. 700.

INSTRUCTIONAL STRATEGIES: AN APPLIED RESEARCH SERIES. see *EDUCATION — Teaching Methods And Curriculum*

INTELLIGENCE DIGEST - A REVIEW OF WORLD AFFAIRS; international political, economic and strategic intelligence. see *POLITICAL SCIENCE*

330 371.3　　　　CN　ISSN 0315-9892
INTERCOM (SASKATOON). 2/yr. Can.$20. (Saskatchewan Business Teachers' Association) Saskatchewan Teachers' Federation, 2317 Arlington Ave., Saskatoon, SK S7J 2H8, Canada. TEL 306-373-1660. adv. **Document type**: bulletin.

BUSINESS AND ECONOMICS

330   US   ISSN 1083-0898
▼INTERNATIONAL ADVANCES IN ECONOMIC RESEARCH. 1995. q. $90 (Canada $97; elsewhere $105) (effective 1997 & 1998). Atlantic Economic Society, c/o John M. Virgo, Ed., Campus Box 1101, Southern Illinois University, Edwardsville, IL 62026-1101. TEL 618-692-2291. FAX 618-692-3400. E-mail: iaes@iaes.org; URL: http://www.iaes.org. R&P contact: Mary Ellen Kissling. adv. contact: Mary Ellen Kissling. abstr.; charts; illus.; stat. circ. 1,000. **Document type:** academic/scholarly publication.

332.6   UK   ISSN 0969-5931
HD2755.5
INTERNATIONAL BUSINESS REVIEW. 1992. bi-m. fl.994($571) (effective 1998). Elsevier Science Ltd., Pergamon, P.O. Box 800, Kidlington, Oxford OX5 1DX, England. TEL 44-1865-843000. FAX 44-1865-843010. E-mail: nlinfo-f@elsevier.nl; usinfo-f@elsevier.com; forinfo-kyf04035@niftyserve.or.jp; URL: http://www.elsevier.nl/. (Subscr. to: Elsevier Science, Regional Sales Office, P.O. Box 211, 1000 AE Amsterdam, Netherlands. TEL 31-20-4853757. FAX 31-20-4853432; Subscr. in the Americas to: Elsevier Science, Regional Sales Office, Box 945, New York, NY 10159-0945. TEL 212-633-3730. FAX 212-633-3680; Subscr. in Australasia and the Far East to: Elsevier Science (Singapore) Pte Ltd, No.1 Temasek Ave., No.17-01 Millenia Tower, Singapore 039192, Singapore. TEL 65-434-3727. FAX 65-337-2230) Ed. Pervez N. Ghauri. (also avail. in microform from UMI; back issues avail.) **Indexed:** Mgmt.& Market.Abstr. **Document type:** academic/scholarly publication.
—BLDSC (4538.383500); SWETS; UMI. **CCC.**
Formerly (until 1993): Scandinavian International Business Review (ISSN 0962-9262)
Description: Publishes empirical studies with practical application, and discussions of theoretical and methodological issues in international business, especially marketing and management concerns.
Refereed Serial

330   CN   ISSN 0704-7584
INTERNATIONAL DEVELOPMENT RESEARCH CENTRE. ANNUAL REPORT/CENTRE DE RECHERCHES POUR LE DEVELOPPEMENT INTERNATIONAL. RAPPORT ANNUEL. (Text in English, French) 1971. a. International Development Research Centre, Box 8500, Ottawa, ON K1G 3H9, Canada. TEL 613-236-6163. FAX 613-563-2476. E-mail: kmorrow@idrc.ca; URL: http://www.idrc.ca. Ed. Robert Charbonneau. illus. **Indexed:** Potato Abstr., World Agri.Econ.& Rural Sociol.Abstr. **Document type:** corporate report.
●Available only online.
—CISTI.

330   UK   ISSN 0074-4646
INTERNATIONAL ECONOMIC ASSOCIATION. PROCEEDINGS OF THE CONFERENCES AND CONGRESSES. 1956. irreg. Macmillan Press Ltd., Houndmills, Basingstoke, Hants RG21 2XS, England. TEL 44-1256-329242. FAX 44-1256-330688. URL: http://www.macmillan-press.co.uk. **Document type:** proceedings.

330   US   ISSN 0020-6598
HB1   CODEN: INERAE
INTERNATIONAL ECONOMIC REVIEW. 1960. q. $50 to individuals; institutions $165; students $20 (effective 1998). University of Pennsylvania, Department of Economics, 3718 Locust Walk, University of Pennsylvania, Philadelphia, PA 19104-6297. TEL 215-898-5841. FAX 215-573-2072. E-mail: ier@econ.upenn.edu; URL: http://www.ssc.upenn.edu/econ/ierevi. (Co-sponsor: Osaka University Institute of Social and Economic Research Association) Eds. Andrew Postlewaite, Hajime Miyazaki. R&P contact: Navasha Barman-Roy. adv. contact: Navasha Barman-Roy. index, cum.index. circ. 2,000. (also avail. in microform from UMI; back issues avail., reprint service avail. from UMI) **Indexed:** ABI Inform., ASCA, Asian-Pac.Econ.Lit., B.P.I., BPIA, Bus.Ind., C.R.E.J., Curr.Cont., Geo.Abstr.H.G., IDA, J.of Econ.Lit., Mar.Aff.Bibl., Math.R., Mid.East: Abstr.& Ind., P.A.I.S., Soc.Sci.Ind., Soc.Sci.Ind., SSCI, Tr.& Indus.Ind., World Bank.Abstr., Zent.Math. **Document type:** academic/scholarly publication.
—BLDSC (4539.791000); Genuine Article; KR SourceOne; SWETS; UMI; UnCover. **CCC.**
Refereed Serial

INTERNATIONAL FEDERATION OF ADVERTISING AGENCIES. NEWSLETTER. see *ADVERTISING AND PUBLIC RELATIONS*

330 628   UK
INTERNATIONAL INSTITUTE FOR ENVIRONMENT AND DEVELOPMENT. ENVIRONMENTAL ECONOMICS PROGRAMME. DISCUSSION PAPER. Cover title: Environmental Economics Programme. Discussion Paper. irreg. International Institute for Environment and Development (IIED), Environmental Economics Programme, 3 Endsleigh St., London WC1H 0DD, England. TEL 44-171-388-2117. FAX 44-171-388-2826. **Document type:** monographic series.
Formerly (until 1994): London Environmental Economics Centre. Discussion Paper.
Description: Discusses environmental issues from an economics perspective.

330   US   ISSN 1083-4346
HF5001
INTERNATIONAL JOURNAL OF BUSINESS. 1992; N.S. 1996. s-a. $35 to individuals (foreign $45); institutions $120 (foreign $130). (California State University, Fresno, Craig School of Business) Premier Publishing, Inc., Box 27647, Fresno, CA 93729-7647. TEL 209-434-2886. FAX 209-434-2886. Ed. K.C. Chen. R&P contact: K.C. Chen. adv. contact: K.C. Chen. index. circ. 200. (also avail. in microform from UMI) **Document type:** academic/scholarly publication.
—BLDSC (4542.155850); SWETS.
Formerly (until 1996): Review of Business Studies (ISSN 1047-4595)
Refereed Serial

330   CN   ISSN 1206-7873
▼INTERNATIONAL JOURNAL OF BUSINESS, ECONOMY & INDUSTRY STUDIES. (Text in Arabic, English) 1997. q. Can.$400. P.O. Box 98029, S. Common Post, 2150 Burnhamthorpe Rd., Mississagua, ON L5L 3A0, Canada. FAX 416-277-2875. (And: P.O. Box 38552, Abdulla Al-Salem, Kuwait City 72256, Kuwait. FAX 965-489-1179) Ed. M.I. Ismail.
Description: Designed for concise, cooperative publication of simple and creative developmental ideas.
Refereed Serial

INTERNATIONAL JOURNAL OF FORECASTING. see *BUSINESS AND ECONOMICS — Economic Situation And Conditions*

330 301   UK   ISSN 0306-8293
HB1   CODEN: ISLEBC
INTERNATIONAL JOURNAL OF SOCIAL ECONOMICS. 1974. m. £3199($4959) (foreign Aus.$6229) (effective 1998). (International Institute of Social Economics) M C B University Press Ltd., 60-62 Toller Ln., Bradford, W. Yorks BD8 9BY, England. TEL 44-1274-777700. FAX 44-1274-785200. TELEX 51317-MCBUNI-G. URL: http://www.mcb.co.uk. Ed. John C. O'Brien. bk.rev.; charts; illus.; cum.index. (reprint service avail. from SWZ) **Indexed:** Anbar, Asian-Pac.Econ.Lit., ASSIA, BPIA, Bus.Ind., C.R.E.J., Curr.Cont., Geo.Abstr.H.G., IDA, Int.Lab.Doc., J.of Econ.Lit., Key to Econ.Sci., Manage.Cont., Mgmt.& Market.Abstr., Mult.Ed.Abstr., P.A.I.S., Per.Islam. (1992-), SCIMP (1978-), SSCI, Tech.Educ.Abstr., Tr.& Indus.Ind., World Bibl.Soc.Sec. **Document type:** academic/scholarly publication.
●Also available on CD-ROM.
—BLDSC (4542.555000); Genuine Article; SWETS; UMI; UnCover. **CCC.**
Incorporates: International Review of Economics and Ethics (ISSN 0268-392X)
Description: Contains articles that deal with socioeconomic problems. Covers socioeconomic systems, human resources policy, social indicators, environmental economics, income distribution and policy, social services, demographic trends, and ethical and religious influence.

330   UK   ISSN 1357-1516
INTERNATIONAL JOURNAL OF THE ECONOMICS OF BUSINESS. 1994. 3/yr. £48($70) to individuals; institutions £174 ($274) (effective 1997). Carfax Publishing Co., P.O. Box 25, Abingdon, Oxon. OX14 3UE, England. TEL 44-1235-401000. FAX 44-1235-401550. E-mail: enquiries@carfax.co.uk. (N. American subscr. to: Carfax Publishing Co., 875-81 Massachusetts Ave., Cambridge, MA 02139) Eds. Eleanor Morgan, Mick Silver. adv.: page £200; adv. contact: Steve Entwistle. bk.rev./; index. (also avail. in microfiche) **Document type:** academic/scholarly publication.
—BLDSC (4542.198000); UMI. **CCC.**
Formerly (until vol.1, no.2, 1994): Journal of the Economics of Business (ISSN 0962-1369)
Description: Presents original economics that are clearly applicable to business, both private and public sector, and related public policy problems or issues.
Refereed Serial

INTERNATIONAL MARINE BUSINESS JOURNAL; the voice of the marine industries worldwide. see *SPORTS AND GAMES — Boats And Boating*

330   II
INTERNATIONAL PRESS CUTTING SERVICE: LIST OF NEW INDUSTRIES APPROVED BY GOVERNMENT. (Text in English) w. Rs.615($75) International Press Cutting Service, P.O. Box 121, Allahabad 211001, India. **Document type:** newsletter.

338   US   ISSN 1053-9514
HC79.I52
INTERNATIONAL PRODUCTIVITY JOURNAL. 1990. 3/yr. $60 (foreign $80). International Productivity Service, 200 Constitution Ave., N.W., Rm. N-5119, Washington, DC 20210. TEL 202-219-7379. FAX 202-219-7308. **Document type:** academic/scholarly publication.
Description: Helps to facilitate a global flow of information on productivity, quality and competitiveness, labor-management relations and international comparisons.

650.07 373.246   DK   ISSN 0035-354X
INTERNATIONAL REVIEW FOR BUSINESS EDUCATION/REVUE INTERNATIONALE POUR L'ENSEIGNEMENT COMMERCIAL/INTERNATIONALE ZEITSCHRIFT FUER KAUFMAENNISCHES BILDUNGSWESEN/RIVISTA INTERNAZIONALE PER LA CULTURA COMMERCIALE/REVISTA INTERNACIONAL PARA LA ENSENANZA COMERCIAL. (Text in English, French, German, Italian, Spanish) 1901. s-a. 45 SFr. (effective 1997). International Society for Business Education, Hunderupvej 122 A, DK-5230 Odense M, Denmark. TEL 45-66-12-19-66. FAX 45-66-14-57-94. Ed. Erik Lange. adv.; bk.rev./; charts. circ. 2,900. **Indexed:** Bus.Educ.Ind. **Document type:** academic/scholarly publication.

330   UK   ISSN 0269-2171
HB1
INTERNATIONAL REVIEW OF APPLIED ECONOMICS. 1987. 2/yr. £48($84) to individuals; institutions £148 ($272) (effective 1997). Carfax Publishing Co., P.O. Box 25, Abingdon, Oxon. OX14 3UE, England. TEL 44-1235-401000. FAX 44-1235-401550. E-mail: enquiries@carfax.co.uk. (N. American subscr. to: Carfax Publishing Co., 875-81 Massachusetts Ave., Cambridge, MA 02139) adv.; bk.rev (back issues avail.) **Indexed:** J.of Econ.Lit. **Document type:** academic/scholarly publication.
—BLDSC (4546.160000); SWETS; UnCover. **CCC.**
Description: Examines the practical application of economic ideas.

330 332   UK   ISSN 1358-1937
INTERNATIONAL RISK MANAGEMENT. 1994. m. £85 (foreign £100) (effective 1996). E M A P - Finance & Freight Ltd., 33-39 Bowling Green Ln., London EC1R 0DA, England. TEL 44-171-505-8000. FAX 44-171-505-8185. Ed. Mike Handley. adv.; charts; stat.; tr.lit./; index. **Document type:** trade publication.

INTERNATIONAL STATUS REPORT ON PLASTICS INDUSTRY WORLDWIDE. see *PLASTICS*

BUSINESS AND ECONOMICS

330   NE   ISSN 0924-5170
INTERNATIONAL STUDIES IN ECONOMICS AND ECONOMETRICS. (Text in English) 1969. irreg., vol.30, 1994. price varies. Kluwer Academic Publishers, Postbus 17, 3300 AA Dordrecht, Netherlands. TEL 31-78-6392392. FAX 31-78-6392254. TELEX 29245 KAPG NL. E-mail: services@wkap.nl; URL: http://www.wkap.nl. (Dist. by: Kluwer Academic Publishers Group, P.O. Box 322, 3300 AH Dordrecht, Netherlands. TEL 31-78-6392392. FAX 31-78-6546474; N. America dist. addr.: Box 358, Accord Sta., Hingham, MA 02018-0358. TEL 617-871-6600. FAX 617-871-6528) (back issues avail.) **Document type:** monographic series.
—BLDSC (4549.771000). **CCC**.
Refereed Serial

330 341   US
INTERNATIONAL TRADE. q. $29.50 to non-members; free to members. International Trade Association, 8383 E. Evans, Scottsdale, AZ 85260. TEL 602-483-0001. FAX 602-998-8022. Eds. Robert G. Johnson, Samantha A. Graham; Pub. Samantha A. Graham. R&P contact: Samantha A. Graham. adv. contact: Samantha A. Graham. **Document type:** newspaper.
Formed by the merger of: World Trade News & World Trade Update.

INTERNATIONALE DIREKTINVESTIONEN. see *POLITICAL SCIENCE*

330   UK
INVEST IN BRITAIN ANNUAL REPORT. 1977. a. free. Invest in Britain Bureau, 1 Victoria St., London SW1H 0ET, England. TEL 44-171-215-2501. FAX 44-171-215-5651. Ed.Bd. charts; illus.; stat.; circ. 6,000 (controlled). (back issues avail.) **Document type:** government publication.
Description: Reviews activities and investments in the UK by foreign companies.

330   SP   ISSN 0210-1521
INVESTIGACIONES ECONOMICAS. REVISTA. (Text in Spanish; summaries in English) 1986. 3/yr. 2000 ptas.($27) to individuals; institutions 4000 ptas.($55). Fundacion Empresa Publica, Plaza Marques de Salamanca, 8, 28006 Madrid, Spain. TEL 575-88-12. FAX 575-56-41. bk.rev. **Indexed:** IBR, J.of Econ.Lit.
—CINDOC.
Description: Covers economic theory, history of economics and Spanish industrial and public economics.

INVESTMENT NEWS. see *BUSINESS AND ECONOMICS — Investments*

330   US   ISSN 1050-6551
HG1616.I5
INVESTMENT PERFORMANCE DIGEST. q. $389 (effective 1997). I D C Financial Publishing, Inc., Box 140, Hartland, WI 53029. TEL 414-367-7231. FAX 414-367-6497. Ed. John E. Rickmeier. R&P contact: John E. Rickmeier. (back issues avail.) **Document type:** trade publication.

330   IR
IRAN BUSINESS DIGEST. (Text in English) irreg. Sayar Communications Co., URL: http://gpg.com/ibd/news.html. **Document type:** bulletin.
●Available only online.
Description: Focuses on business and economic news in Iran.

330   IR
IRAN PRESS DIGEST (ECONOMIC). w. Iran Press Digest Establishment, Hafiz Ave., 4 Kucheh Hurtab, P.O. Box 11365-5551, Teheran, Iran. TEL 021-668114. TELEX 212300. Ed. J. Behrouz.

330   US   ISSN 1072-6136
HF5003
IRWIN BUSINESS AND INVESTMENT ALMANAC. 1977. a. $75 cloth. Irwin Professional Publishing, 1333 Burr Ridge Pkwy., Burr Ridge, IL 60521-6489. TEL 708-789-4000. Eds. Sumner N. Levine, Caroline Levine. circ. 7,600.
Former titles (until 1994): Business One Irwin Business and Investment Almanac (ISSN 1057-5014); (until 1991): Dow Jones-Irwin Business and Investment Almanac (ISSN 0733-2610); Dow Jones-Irwin Business Almanac (ISSN 0146-6534).

330   FJ
ISLANDS BUSINESS. (Text in English) 1980. m. $35 in N. America; Europe $55. 46 Gordon St., P.O. Box 12718, Suva, Fiji. TEL 6-79-303623. FAX 6-79-303943. E-mail: info@ibi.com.fj. Ed. Peter Lomas; Pub. Robert Keith-Reid. R&P contact: Godfrey Scoullar. adv. contact: Gordon Moore. bk.rev.; circ. 8,500 (paid). **Document type:** trade publication.
Former titles: Islands Business Politics; (until 1994): Islands Business Pacific; (until 1991): Islands Business.
Description: Covering Pacific Islands business, economics and politics.

ISSUES IN BUSINESS ETHICS. see *PHILOSOPHY*

330   IT   ISSN 0075-1529
ISTITUTO MOBILIARE ITALIANO. ANNUAL REPORT. (Editions in English, Italian) 1932. a. Istituto Mobiliare Italiano, 25 Viale dell'Arte, 00144 Rome, Italy. circ. 2,400.

320.945   US   ISSN 0952-3243
JN5201
ITALIAN POLITICS; a review. 1986. a. (Istituto Carlo Cattaneo, IT) St. Martin's Press, 175 Fifth Ave., New York, NY 10010. TEL 212-674-5151. Eds. Raffaella Nanetti, Raimondo Catanzaro. bibl.; charts; illus.; stat.; index. circ. 750. (back issues avail.) **Document type:** bulletin.
—BLDSC (4588.345500).
Description: Covers the major economic, social and political events of the year.

330   UK
THE J.S.G. WILSON LECTURE IN ECONOMICS. irreg., vol.3, 1996. University of Hull Press, Hull HU6 7RX, England. TEL 44-1482-46311. FAX 44-1482-465936. **Document type:** academic/scholarly publication, monographic series.

330   US
JACKSON BUSINESS JOURNAL. 1990. m. $18 (effective 1996 & 1997). Box 12727, Jackson, MS 39236-2727. TEL 601-956-0756. FAX 601-956-4047. Ed. Jack Criss; Pub. Jack Criss. R&P contact: Jack Criss. adv.: B&W page $750, color page $1420; adv. contact: Abby Askin-Bullard. bk.rev.; circ. 6,230 (paid); 4,007 (controlled). **Document type:** newspaper.
Formerly (until Jan. 1992): Metro Jackson Business News.

330   US   ISSN 0885-453X
JACKSONVILLE BUSINESS JOURNAL. 1985. w. American City Business Journals (Jacksonville), 1200 Gulf Life Dr., No. 501, Jacksonville, FL 32207-1808. TEL 904-396-3502. FAX 904-396-5706. Ed. Ben Eubanks. circ. 11,900.
—UMI. **CCC**.

330 320   GW
JAHRBUCH DER POLITIK UND WIRTSCHAFT IN NORDRHEIN-WESTFALEN. a. Bouvier Verlag Herbert Grundmann, Am Hof 28, 53113 Bonn, Germany. TEL 49-228-7290124. FAX 49-228-7290179. Ed. Monika Hallai-Hentschel.

330 340 336.2   GW   ISSN 0075-2886
JAHRESFACHKATALOG RECHT - WIRTSCHAFT - STEUERN. 1949. a. DM.48.50. Buchwerbung in Berlin GmbH, Luetzowstr. 105-106, 10785 Berlin, Germany. adv.; bk.rev. **Document type:** bibliography.
Description: Lists each year's new titles in law, economics and taxation.

330   JA
JAPAN BUSINESS LAW LETTER. 12/yr. Japan Legal Publisher Inc., P.O. Box 74, Kojimachi 102-91, Silky Heights no.701, 4-2-9 Kudan Minami, Chiyoda-ku, Tokyo 102, Japan. TEL 03-261-3147. FAX 03-261-3823. Ed. Masui Kazuhiro.

330   AT   ISSN 1038-2658
JAPAN MONITOR. 1992. q. Aus.$36. Japanese Economic and Management Centre, University of New South Wales, Sydney, N.S.W. 2052, Australia. TEL 61-2-3855802. FAX 61-2-3136775. E-mail: r.march@unsw.edu.au. Ed. Roger March. circ. 1,500. (back issues avail.) **Document type:** newsletter.
Description: Examines current issues in Japanese business and management and in Australia - Japan related business and trade.

330   UK   ISSN 1352-4739
HB9
JAPANESE ECONOMIC REVIEW. 1950. q. £59($93) (foreign £59) (effective 1997). Blackwell Publishers Ltd., 108 Cowley Rd., Oxford OX4 1JF, England. TEL 44-1865-791100. FAX 44-1865-791347. E-mail: jnlinfo@blackwellpublishers.co.uk; URL: http://www.blackwellpublishers.com. bk.rev. **Indexed:** C.R.E.J., J.of Econ.Lit. **Document type:** academic/scholarly publication.
—BLDSC (4650.762700); SWETS; UnCover. **CCC**.
Formerly (until 1995): Economic Studies Quarterly (ISSN 0557-109X)
Refereed Serial

330   US   ISSN 0021-4841
HC461
JAPANESE ECONOMIC STUDIES. 1972. bi-m. $138 to individuals (foreign $176); institutions $680 (foreign $770) (effective 1997). M.E. Sharpe, Inc., 80 Business Park Dr., Armonk, NY 10504. TEL 914-273-1800; 800-541-6563. FAX 914-273-2106. Ed. Kazuo Sato. adv.: page $300; trim 5 x 8; adv. contact: Barbara Ladd. (back issues avail.) **Indexed:** ASCA, C.R.E.J., Curr.Cont., IBR, Key to Econ.Sci., P.A.I.S., SSCI. **Document type:** academic/scholarly publication.
—BLDSC (4650.764000); Genuine Article; SWETS; UMI; UnCover. **CCC**.
Description: Contains translations of economic and management material from Japanese sources, primarily scholarly journals and books. Selections are intended to reflect developments in the Japanese economy and to be of interest to those professionally concerned with this field.
Refereed Serial

330   CC   ISSN 1002-851X
JIANZHU JINGJI. (Text in Chinese) 1985. m. Zhongguo Jianzhu Xuehui, Jianzhu Jingji Xueshu Weiyuanhui, No. 19, Chegongzhuang Dajie, Xizhimenwai, Beijing 100044, People's Republic of China. TEL 8992669. Ed. Yang Shen.

330   CC
JINGJI CANKAO/ECONOMIC INFORMATION. (Text in Chinese) d. $329.80. Xinhua Tongxun She - New China News Agency, 57 Xuanwumen Xidajie, Beijing 100803, People's Republic of China. TEL 601-3668. (Dist. in US by: China Books & Periodicals, Inc., 2929 24th St., San Francisco, CA 94110) **Document type:** newspaper.

JINGJI FAZHI. see *LAW — Corporate Law*

330   CC   ISSN 1003-3580
JINGJI LUNTAN/ECONOMIC TRIBUNE. (Text in Chinese) 1987. s-m. Hebei Sheng Shehui Kexueyuan - Hebei Academy of Social Sciences, 9 Shiyi Lu, Shijiazhuang, Hebei 050051, People's Republic of China. TEL 86-311-3035747. FAX 86-311-3036594. (Dist. overseas by: China International Book Trading Corp., P.O. Box 399, Beijing 100044, P.R. China) Ed. Liu Peng. pp./issue: 48. **Document type:** academic/scholarly publication.
Description: Provides timely information on Chinese economic development.

330   CC   ISSN 1005-3425
JINGJI PINGLUN/ECONOMIC REVIEW. (Text in Chinese) bi-m. Jingji Pinglun Zazhishe, Wuhan Daxue Jingji Xueyuan, Wuhan, Hubei 430072, People's Republic of China. TEL 86-27-7822712. (Dist. overseas by: China International Book Trading Corp., P.O. Box 399, Beijing 100044, P.R. China) Ed. Fu Yincai. adv. pp./issue: 96. **Document type:** academic/scholarly publication.
Description: Contains academic researches, reports and comments on economic theories and major practical issues.

330   CH
JINGJI RIBAO/ECONOMIC DAILY NEWS. (Text in Chinese) 1967. d. $240 for 3 mos. 555 Chung Hsaio E. Rd., Sec. 4, Taipei, Taiwan 105, Republic of China. TEL 886-2-763-8095. FAX 886-2-763-4124. Ed. Shyh Shyang Lui. adv.: B&W page NT.$250000; trim 395 x 545. circ. 275,000. **Document type:** newspaper.
Description: Contains economic, finance, trade, real estate, industry and commercial news.

330   CC
JINGJI SHIJIE - NANFANG/ECONOMIC WORLD - SOUTH. (Text in Chinese) m. Xinhua Tongxunshe, 57 Xuanwumen Xidajie, Beijing 100803, People's Republic of China. TEL 3073658. Ed. Ye Zhou.

BUSINESS AND ECONOMICS

330   **CC**
JINGJI WENTI/ECONOMIC ISSUES. (Text in Chinese) m. Shanxi Sheng Shehui Kexueyuan - Shanxi Academy of Social Sciences, 38 Bingzhou Nanlu, Taiyuan, Shanxi 030006, People's Republic of China. TEL 775841. Ed. Chen Dianmo.

330   **US**
JINGJI WENTI TANSUO. (Text in Chinese) bi-m. $30.50. China Books & Periodicals, Inc., 2929 24th St., San Francisco, CA 94110. TEL 415-282-2994. FAX 415-282-0994.

330   **CC**   ISSN 1000-8330
JINGJI YU SHEHUI FAZHAN/ECONOMICS AND SOCIAL DEVELOPMENT. (Text in Chinese) q. Taiyuan Jishu Jingji Yanjiu Zhongxin - Taiyuan Research Center of Technology and Economics, 21 Hanxiguan, Taiyuan, Shanxi 030002, People's Republic of China. TEL 345385. Ed. Yang Kaishan.

330   **CC**   ISSN 1002-9818
JINGJI YUCE YU XINXI/ECONOMIC FORECAST AND INFORMATION. (Text in Chinese) 1985. m. Guojia Jingji Xinxi Zhongxin, Jingji Xinxi-bu - National Economic Information Center, Bureau of Economic Information, No. 58, Sanlihe Lu, Beijing 100045, People's Republic of China. TEL 8091733. Ed. Wu Jiapei.

330   **CC**
JINGJI ZONGHENG. (Text in Chinese) 1985. m. Jilin Sheng Jingjixue Tuanti Lianhehui, 28, Xinfa Lu, Changchun, Jilin 130051, People's Republic of China. TEL 0431-829642. FAX 0431-826854. (Dist. outside China by: China International Book Trading Corp., P.O. Box 399, Beijing, P.R. China) Ed. Zhang Weida. adv.; bk.rev. circ. 7,000. **Document type:** academic/scholarly publication.
Description: Covers Chinese economic reforms and economic development strategies. Reviews Chinese and foreign economic theories and thoughts.

330   **CC**   ISSN 1004-4914
JINGJISHI/CHINA ECONOMIST. (Text in Chinese) 1986. bi-m. Shanxi Jingji Guanli Xueyuan - Shanxi Institute of Economics and Management, 46, Jiefang Lu, Taiyuan, Shanxi 030002, People's Republic of China. TEL 227266. Ed. Zhang Chengong. **Indexed:** Arts & Hum.Cit.Ind.

330.9   **CC**   ISSN 1001-3385
JINGJISHI/ECONOMICS HISTORY. (Subseries of: Fuyin Baokan Ziliao) (Text in Chinese) 1978. bi-m. $56,42. Zhongguo Renmin Daxue, Shubao Ziliao Zhongxin - China People's University, Book & Newspaper Information Service, 3 Zhang Zizhong Rd., P.O. Box 1122, Beijing 100007, People's Republic of China. TEL 86-10-4015080. (Dist. in US by: China Publications Service, Box 49614, Chicago, IL 60649. TEL 312-288-3291. FAX 312-288-8670) pp./issue: 160.

330   **CC**   ISSN 1002-8390
JINGJIXUE DONGTAI. (Text in Chinese) 1960. m. Zhongguo Shehui Kexueyuan, Jingji Yanjiusuo - Chinese Academy of Social Sciences, Institute of Economics, 2 Yuetan Beixiaojie, Beijing 100836, People's Republic of China. TEL 895023. Ed. Mao Tianqi.

330   **CC**   ISSN 1003-5656
HC427.92
JINGJIXUE JIA/ECONOMIST. (Text in Chinese) bi-m. Xinan Caijing Daxue - Southwest University of Finance and Economics, 55 Guanghua Cun, Chengdu Xijiao, Sichuan 610074, People's Republic of China. TEL 86-28-7784707. FAX 86-28-784689. (Dist. overseas by: China International Book Trading Corp., P.O. Box 399, Beijing 100044, P.R. China) Ed. Liu Shibai. adv. contact: Li Jianyong. pp./issue: 128. **Indexed:** Arts & Hum.Cit.Ind. **Document type:** academic/scholarly publication.
Description: Encourages academic discussions about economic theories.

330   **CC**
JINRONG YU JINGJI/FINANCE AND ECONOMICS. (Text in Chinese) m. Jiangxi Sheng Jinrong Xuehui - Jiangxi Finance Society, No. 302, Zhongshan Lu, Nanchang, Jiangxi 330009, People's Republic of China. TEL 52965. (Co-sponsor: Zhongguo Renmin Yinhang Jiangxi Sheng Fenhuang Jinrong Yanjiusuo) Ed. Peng Chunhua.

330   **CC**
JISHU JINGJI XINXI. (Text in Chinese) m. Guangxi Jingji Weiyuanhui - Guangxi Economics Commission, 1 Minle Lu, Nanning, Guangxi 530012, People's Republic of China. TEL 25294. Ed. Li Guanhua.

330   **JA**   ISSN 0446-8147
JITSUGYO NO NIHON/BUSINESS OF JAPAN. (Text in Japanese) 1897. m. 5760 Yen. Jitsugyo no Nihon Sha, Ltd., 3-9-Ginza, 1-chome, Chuo-ku, Tokyo 104, Japan. TEL 81-3-3562-1967. FAX 81-3-3562-3200. E-mail: lebo2234@niftyserve.or.jp. Ed. Toshio Kawajiri; Pub. Yoshikazu Masuda. adv.: B&W page 480000 Yen, color page 750000 Yen; trim 210 x; adv. contact: Maqaaki Ohara. bk.rev. circ. 48,000.
Description: Covers business in general, consumer affairs, as well as financial and investment trends.

JOB OPENINGS FOR ECONOMISTS. see OCCUPATIONS AND CAREERS

330   **RU**   ISSN 0869-5369
JOINT VENTURES/SOVMESTNYE PREDPRIYATIYA. (Text in Russian; summaries in English) 1990. bi-m. $60 (effective 1998). Assotsiatsiya Sovmestnykh Predpriyatii - Association of the Joint Ventures, Leningradsky Prospekt 55, 12513- Moscow, Russia. TEL 943-9481. FAX 148-71-14. Ed. Evgenii Minin. adv.: B&W page 30000 Rub.($1750), color page 83000 Rub.($6500). circ. 11,000.

330   **UK**   ISSN 0267-8152
JORDANS JOURNAL. 1985. q. free. Jordan Publishing Ltd., 21 St. Thomas St., Bristol BS1 6JS, England. TEL 0117-923-0600. FAX 0117-923-0063. Ed. Richard Hudson. circ. 7,200 (controlled). **Document type:** trade publication.

650   **US**   ISSN 1048-4701
JOSEPH I. LUBIN MEMORIAL LECTURES. 1961. a. price varies. (New York University, College of Business and Public Administration) New York University Press, 70 Washington Square S., New York, NY 10012. TEL 212-998-2575; 800-996-3833. FAX 212-995-3833. TELEX 235128 NYU UR. Ed. Dean Daniel E. Diamond. R&P contact: Kathe Sweeney. circ. 2,000. **Document type:** monographic series.
Formerly (until 1984): Charles C. Moskowitz Lectures (ISSN 0084-8727)

658   **US**   ISSN 0892-7626
JOURNAL OF APPLIED BUSINESS RESEARCH. 1985. q. $198.50 (effective 1997). Western Academic Press, Box 620760, Littleton, CO 80162. TEL 303-904-4750. FAX 303-978-0413. E-mail: cluter@wapress.com; URL: http://www.cluter@wapress.com. Ed. Ronald C. Clute. bk.rev. circ. 600. (back issues avail.) **Indexed:** Account.Ind. (1988-), B.P.I., Sociol.Abstr., World Bank.Abstr. **Document type:** academic/scholarly publication.
—BLDSC (4940.660000); KR SourceOne; UMI; UnCover. **CCC.**
Description: Provides a forum for research and debate for all areas of applied business and economics.
Refereed Serial

650   **US**   ISSN 0021-9398
BP163   CODEN: JOBUAQ
THE JOURNAL OF BUSINESS (CHICAGO). 1928. q. $27 to individuals (Canada $33.89; elsewhere $32); institutions $65 (Canada $74.55; elsewhere $70) (effective 1998). University of Chicago Press, Journals Division, Box 37005, Chicago, IL 60637. TEL 773-753-3347. FAX 773-753-0811. E-mail: subscriptions@journals.uchicago.edu; URL: http://www.nchicago.edu/JB/home.html. Ed. Douglas W. Diamond. adv.: page $355; trim 6 x 9. bk.rev.; bibl.; index, cum.index: vol.1-24 (1928-1951). circ. 4,200. (also avail. in microform from MIM,UMI,PMC; reprint service avail. from ISI,SCH,UMI) **Indexed:** ABI Inform., Acad.Ind., Account.Ind. (1974-), Amer.Hist.& Life (1967-1987), Asian-Pac.Econ.Lit., B.P.I., Bank.Lit.Ind., BPIA, Bus.Ind., Commun.Abstr., Comput.Lit.Ind., Curr.Cont., Hist.Abstr. (1967-1987), IBR, J.Cont.Quant.Meth., J.of Econ.Lit., Key to Econ.Sci., Manage.Cont., Med.Care Rev., Mgmt.& Market.Abstr., Mid.East: Abstr.& Ind., Oper.Res.Manage.Sci., P.A.I.S., PROMT, Qual.Contr.Appl.Stat., SSCI. **Document type:** academic/scholarly publication.
●Also available online. Vendor(s): Information Access Co.
—BLDSC (4954.650000); Genuine Article; KR SourceOne; SWETS; UMI; UnCover. **CCC.**
Formerly (until 1953): Journal of Business of the University of Chicago (ISSN 0740-9168)
Description: Publishes research, analysis, and inquiry into issues of theoretical and practical importance to the business community.
Refereed Serial

330   **US**
JOURNAL OF BUSINESS AND ECONOMIC PERSPECTIVES. 1975. s-a. $15 to individuals; libraries $26. University of Tennessee at Martin, School of Business Administration, 113 Business Administration Bldg., Martin, TN 38238-5015. TEL 901-587-7226. FAX 901-587-7241. Ed. Bob G. Fggins. adv. contact: Tammy McWherter. bk.rev. circ. 2,500. **Indexed:** P.A.I.S. **Document type:** academic/scholarly publication.
Formerly (until 1980): Business and Economics Perspectives.
Description: Publishes empirical research on business and economic issues.
Refereed Serial

650 330   **US**   ISSN 1063-343X
HF5001
JOURNAL OF BUSINESS AND ECONOMIC STUDIES. 1974. s-a. $30 to individuals; institutions $25. Salem State College, 352 Lafayette, Salem, MA 01970. TEL 508-741-6664. FAX 508-741-6027. E-mail: djacobson@shorenet. Ed. David Jacobson. R&P contact: Michael Tucker. adv. contact: David Jacobson. bk.rev.; charts; illus.; stat. circ. 1,700. **Indexed:** ABI Inform, P.A.I.S. **Document type:** academic/scholarly publication.
—BLDSC (4954.661020); UMI.
Former titles (until 1991): Northeast Journal of Business and Economics (ISSN 8755-5123); (until 1983): New England Journal of Business and Economics; **Supersedes:** Rhode Island Business Quarterly (ISSN 0035-4570)
Description: Scholarly research in all areas of business and economics, practical and theoretical.
Refereed Serial

JOURNAL OF BUSINESS & FINANCE LIBRARIANSHIP. see LIBRARY AND INFORMATION SCIENCES

JOURNAL OF BUSINESS & PSYCHOLOGY. see PSYCHOLOGY

650 301   **NR**   ISSN 0331-8583
JOURNAL OF BUSINESS & SOCIAL STUDIES. (Text in English) 1968; N.S. 1977. s-a. £N20($25) (University of Lagos, Faculty of Social Studies) Lagos University Press, Publishing Division, P.O. Box 132, Akoka, Yaba, Lagos State, Nigeria. (Co-sponsor: Faculty of Business Administration) Ed. Oladejo O. Okediji. adv.; bk.rev.; charts; illus.; maps. circ. 1,500. (also avail. in microform from UMI; reprint service avail. from UMI) **Indexed:** Curr.Cont.Africa, Geo.Abstr. **Document type:** academic/scholarly publication.
—BLDSC (4954.662000).
Description: Covers African economics, agriculture and general development issues.

BUSINESS AND ECONOMICS

330 US ISSN 1050-6519
HF5717 CODEN: JBTCE9
JOURNAL OF BUSINESS AND TECHNICAL COMMUNICATION. 1987. q. $158 to institutions (effective Sep. 1996). Sage Publications, Inc., 2455 Teller Rd., Thousand Oaks, CA 91320. TEL 805-499-0721. FAX 805-499-0871. E-mail: libraries@sagepub.com; URL: http://www.sagepub.com. (Overseas subscr. to: Sage Publications Ltd., 6 Bonhill St., London EC2A 4PU, England; Sage Publications India Pvt. Ltd., P.O. Box 4215, New Delhi 110 048, India) Ed. Charles Kostlenick. adv. contact: Margaret Travers. circ. 1,000. (back issues avail.; reprint service avail.) **Indexed:** Abstr.Anthropol., ASCA, C.I.J.E., Curr.Cont. **Document type:** academic/scholarly publication.
—BLDSC (4954.663000); Genuine Article; UnCover. **CCC.**
Formerly (until 1988): Iowa State Journal of Business and Technical Communication (ISSN 0892-5720)
Description: Provides information on the latest communication practices, problems, and trends in both industry and the academic world.

174 NE ISSN 0167-4544
JOURNAL OF BUSINESS ETHICS. (Text in English) 1982. 16/yr. fl.1275 to institutions; fl.654 to institutions in U.S. (effective 1998). Kluwer Academic Publishers, Postbus 17, 3300 AA Dordrecht, Netherlands. TEL 31-78-6392392. FAX 31-78-6392254. TELEX 29245 KAPG NL. E-mail: services@wkap.nl; URL: http://www.wkap.nl/kapis/CGI-BIN/WORLD/jounalhome.htm?01674544. (Dist. by: Kluwer Academic Publishers Group, P.O. Box 322, 3300 AH Dordrecht, Netherlands. TEL 31-78-6392392. FAX 31-78-6546474; N. America dist. addr.: Box 358, Accord Sta., Hingham, MA 02018-0358. TEL 617-871-6600. FAX 617-871-6528) Ed. Alex C. Michalos. adv.; bk.rev. (also avail. in microform from UMI; reprint service avail. from SWZ) **Indexed:** ABI Inform., Account.& Data Proc.Abstr., Account.Ind. (1986-), Arts & Hum.Cit.Ind., ASCA, B.P.I., BPIA, Commun.Abstr., Cont.Pg.Manage., Curr.Cont., IBR, IBZ, Manage.Cont., Mgmt.& Market.Abstr., P.A.I.S., Phil.Ind., Risk Abstr., Soc.Sci.Ind. (until 1994), SSCI, Tr.& Indus.Ind. **Document type:** academic/scholarly publication.
●Also available online. Vendor(s): Information Access Co., UMI.
—BLDSC (4954.686000); Genuine Article; KR SourceOne; SWETS; UMI; UnCover. **CCC.**
Description: Publishes original articles from a variety of methodological and disciplinary perspectives concerning ethical issues related to business.
Refereed Serial

JOURNAL OF BUSINESS FINANCE & ACCOUNTING. see BUSINESS AND ECONOMICS — Accounting

330 US ISSN 0278-6087
HB3730
JOURNAL OF BUSINESS FORECASTING METHODS AND SYSTEMS. 1981. q. $60 (foreign $90). Graceway Publishing Co., Box 670159, Flushing, NY 11367-0159. TEL 718-463-3914; 800-440-0499. FAX 718-544-9086. E-mail: ibf@ibf.org; URL: http://www.ibforecast.com/jbf.htm. Ed. Chaman L. Jain. R&P contact: Chaman L. Jain. adv. contact: Jean McCreary. bk.rev.; abstr.; bibl.; charts; illus.; index. circ. 3,500. (also avail. in microform from UMI; back issues avail.; reprint service avail.) **Indexed:** Account.Ind. (1982-), BPIA, Manage.Cont., Oper.Res.Manage.Sci. **Document type:** trade publication.
●Also available online. Vendor(s): UMI.
Also available on CD-ROM.
—BLDSC (4954.695000); SWETS; UMI; UnCover. **CCC.**
Description: Covers subjects such as how to prepare and use forecasts or set up a forecasting system, the problems that exist between forecasters and users and how they can be resolved, and experiences of different companies and individuals in the field. Gives forecasts of key economic variables in 47 countries.
Refereed Serial

JOURNAL OF BUSINESS LAW. see LAW — Corporate Law

330 US ISSN 0883-9026
CODEN: JBVEEP
JOURNAL OF BUSINESS VENTURING. 1985. bi-m. fl.757($435) (effective 1998). Elsevier Science Inc., Box 945, New York, NY 10159-0945. TEL 212-633-3730. FAX 212-633-3680. TELEX 420643 AEP UI. E-mail: usinfo-f@elsevier.com; URL: http://www.elsevier.nl:80/inca/publications/store/5/0/5/7/2/3/505723.pub.shtml. (Subscr. outside the Americas to: Elsevier Science, Regional Sales Office, P.O. Box 211, 1000 AE Amsterdam, Netherlands. TEL 31-20-4853757. FAX 31-20-4853432; Subscr. in Australasia and the Far East to: Elsevier Science (Singapore) Pte Ltd, No.1 Temasek Ave., No.17-01 Millenia Tower, Singapore 039192, Singapore. TEL 65-434-3727. FAX 65-337-2230; Subscr. in Japan to: Elsevier Science Japan, 9-15 Higashi-Azabu 1-chome, Minato-ku, Tokyo 106, Japan. TEL 81-3-5561-5033. FAX 81-3-5561-5047) Ed. Ian MacMillan. (also avail. in microform from UMI) **Indexed:** ABI Inform., ASCA, Cont.Pg.Manage., Curr.Cont., PIRA, SSCI. **Document type:** academic/scholarly publication.
—BLDSC (4954.718500); Genuine Article; SWETS; UMI; UnCover. **CCC.**
Description: Details research on entrepreneurship, either as independent start-ups or within existing corporations.
Refereed Serial

JOURNAL OF COMMON MARKET STUDIES. see POLITICAL SCIENCE

330 US ISSN 0147-5967
HB90
JOURNAL OF COMPARATIVE ECONOMICS. 1977. bi-m. $295 (foreign $332) (effective 1997). (Association for Comparative Economic Studies) Academic Press, Inc., Journal Division, 525 B St., Ste. 1900, San Diego, CA 92101-4495. TEL 619-230-1840. FAX 619-699-6800. E-mail: apsubs@acad.com; URL: http://www.apnet.com/www/journal/je.htm; http://www.idealibrary.com/. (Subscr. to: Box 861213, Orlando, FL 32886-1213. TEL 407-347-4040. FAX 407-363-9661) Ed. Josef C. Brada. adv.; bk.rev. (back issues avail.) **Indexed:** Amer.Bibl.Slavic & E.Eur.Stud., ASCA, Asian-Pac.Econ.Lit., BPIA, C.R.E.J., Curr.Cont., J.of Econ.Lit., P.A.I.S., Rural Recreat.Tour.Abstr., Soc.Sci.Ind., SSCI, Tr.& Indus.Ind., World Agri.Econ.& Rural Sociol.Abstr., Zent.Math. **Document type:** academic/scholarly publication.
●Also available online.
—BLDSC (4961.890000); Genuine Article; KR SourceOne; SWETS; UnCover. **CCC.**
Description: Devoted to the analysis and study of contemporary, historical, and hypothetical economic systems.

330 US
HF5686.M3 CODEN: JMINEU
JOURNAL OF COST MANAGEMENT. 1987. q. $123.98 (overseas $197.35) (effective 1995). Warren, Gorham & Lamont, One Penn Plaza, New York, NY 10119. TEL 212-871-5000. FAX 212-971-5113. (Subscr. to: The Park Square Bldg., 31 St. James Ave., Boston, MA 02116-4112. TEL 800-950-1207) Ed. Barry J. Brinker. circ. 2,649. (also avail. in microform from UMI) **Indexed:** Account.Ind. (1987-). **Document type:** trade publication.
—BLDSC (4965.431000); Ei; SWETS; UMI; UnCover. **CCC.**
Formerly: Journal of Cost Management for the Manufacturing Industry (ISSN 0899-5141)
Description: Provides information to help improve cost-management systems and techniques in order to pursue more vigorous marketing and pricing strategies.

658 US ISSN 1069-2533
HF5415.5 CODEN: JCMREQ
▼**JOURNAL OF CUSTOMER SERVICE IN MARKETING & MANAGEMENT;** innovations for service, quality & value. 1995. q. $40 to individuals (Canada $52; elsewhere $56); institutions $60 (Canada $78; elsewhere $84); libraries $150 (Canada $195; elsewhere $210) (effective 1996-1997). Haworth Press, Inc., 10 Alice St., Binghamton, NY 13904. TEL 607-722-5857; 800-342-9676. FAX 607-722-6362. E-mail: getinfo@haworth.com; URL: http://www.haworth.com. Ed. William J. Winston; Pub. Bill Cohen. R&P contact: Ruthann Heath. adv.: B&W page $300; trim 4 3/8 x 7 1/8; adv. contact: Jackie Blakeslee. (also avail. in microform from HAW,UMI; reprint service avail. from HAW) **Document type:** trade publication, academic/scholarly publication.
—BLDSC (4965.955400); Haworth; UnCover.
Description: Supplies practical, applied literary resources to professionals in a wide range of industries on customer-client service, quality enhancement, and value for services and products purchased or provided.
Refereed Serial

330 NE ISSN 0167-2681
HD28 CODEN: JEBOD9
JOURNAL OF ECONOMIC BEHAVIOR & ORGANIZATION. (Text in English) 1980. m. fl.2025($1164) (effective 1998). North-Holland (Subsidiary of: Elsevier Science B.V.), P.O. Box 211, 1000 AE Amsterdam, Netherlands. TEL 31-20-4853911. FAX 31-20-4853598. TELEX 18582 ESPA NL. (Subscr. in the Americas to: Elsevier Science, Regional Sales Office, Box 945, New York, NY 10159-0945. TEL 212-633-3730. FAX 212-633-3680; Subscr. in Australasia and the Far East to: Elsevier Science (Singapore) Pte Ltd, No.1 Temasek Ave., No.17-01 Millenia Tower, Singapore 039192, Singapore. TEL 65-434-3727. FAX 65-337-2230; Subscr. in Japan to: Elsevier Science Japan, 9-15 Higashi-Azabu 1-chome, Minato-ku, Tokyo 106, Japan. TEL 81-3-5561-5033. FAX 81-3-5561-5047) Ed. Richard H. Day. (also avail. in microform from UMI; reprint service avail. from SWZ) **Indexed:** ABI Inform., Arts & Hum.Cit.Ind., ASCA, BPIA, Bus.Ind., C.R.E.J., Curr.Cont., INSPEC (1990-), J.of Econ.Lit., Manage.Cont., Risk Abstr., SSCI, Tr.& Indus.Ind. **Document type:** academic/scholarly publication.
—BLDSC (4972.790000); AskIEEE; Genuine Article; KR SourceOne; SWETS; UMI; UnCover. **CCC.**
Description: Emphasizes theoretical and empirical research on economic decision, organization and behavior.
Refereed Serial

330 US ISSN 0022-0485
H62.5.U5
THE JOURNAL OF ECONOMIC EDUCATION. 1969. q. $37.50 to individuals; institutions $75. (Helen Dwight Reid Educational Foundation) Heldref Publications, 1319 18th St., N.W., Washington, DC 20036-1802. TEL 202-296-6267. FAX 202-296-5149. Ed. Rosalind Springsteen. adv. contact: Raymond Rallo. bk.rev.; abstr.; charts; stat. circ. 1,500. (also avail. in microform; back issues avail.; reprint service avail. from SCH) **Indexed:** ASCA, Bus.Educ.Ind., C.I.J.E., Cont.Pg.Educ., Curr.Cont., Educ.Ind., Educ.Tech.Abstr., IBR, J.of Econ.Lit., SSCI, Tech.Educ.Abstr. **Document type:** academic/scholarly publication.
●Also available on CD-ROM. Producer(s): UMI.
—BLDSC (4972.900000); Genuine Article; KR SourceOne; SWETS; UMI; UnCover. **CCC.**
Refereed Serial

330 KO ISSN 1225-651X
JOURNAL OF ECONOMIC INTEGRATION. (Text in English) 1986. q. $30 to individuals; institutions $60. Sejong University, Institute for International Economics, Seongdong-ku, Seoul 143-747, S. Korea. TEL 81-2-460-0338. FAX 82-2-460-0338. Ed. Myung-gun Choo. circ. 1,500. **Document type:** academic/scholarly publication.
—BLDSC (4973.051000).
Formerly (until 1992): Journal of International Economic Integration (ISSN 1015-356X)
Description: Publishes articles that investigate economic issues in international trade and finance.
Refereed Serial

330 UK ISSN 1350-178X
HB131
JOURNAL OF ECONOMIC METHODOLOGY. 1989. 2/yr. £32 (U.S. and Canada $50; rest of world £32) to individuals; institutions £74 (U.S. and Canada £118; rest of world £80) (effective 1997). Routledge, 11 New Fetter Ln., London EC4P 4EE, England. TEL 44-171-583-9855. FAX 44-171-842-2298. E-mail: sample.journals@routledge.com; URL: http://www.routledge.com/routledge/journal/journals.html. (Subscr. to: ITPS Ltd., Cheriton House, North Way, Andover, Hants SP10 5BE, England. TEL 44-1264-342919. FAX 44-1264-342807; Subscr. in US & Canada to: 29 W. 35th St., New York, NY 10001-2299. TEL 212-244-3336. FAX 212-564-7854) Ed.Bd. adv.: page £150; trim 115 x 190. circ. 850. **Document type:** academic/scholarly publication.
—BLDSC (4973.053500); SWETS; UnCover.
Formerly (until 1994): Methodus (ISSN 1018-5070)
Description: Explores current and historical developments in the field of economic practice and methodological work.
Refereed Serial

330 UK ISSN 0144-3585
HB1
JOURNAL OF ECONOMIC STUDIES. 1965; N.S. 1974. bi-m. £2879($4569) (foreign Aus.$5719) (effective 1998). M C B University Press Ltd., 60-62 Toller Ln., Bradford, W. Yorks BD8 9BY, England. TEL 44-1274-777700. FAX 44-1274-785200. TELEX 51317-MCBUNI-G. URL: http://www.mcb.co.uk. Ed. Frank M. Stephens. adv.; bk.rev.; charts; stat.; cum.index. (reprint service avail. from SWZ) **Indexed:** ABI Inform., Anbar, Bus.Ind., Curr.Cont., Geo.Abstr.P.G., IDA, J.of Econ.Lit., P.A.I.S., Rural Recreat.Tour.Abstr., SSCI, Tr.& Indus.Ind., World Agri.Econ.& Rural Sociol.Abstr. **Document type:** academic/scholarly publication.
●Also available on CD-ROM.
—BLDSC (4973.055000); SWETS; UMI; UnCover. **CCC.**
Formerly: Economic Studies.
Description: Maintains a sound balance between the theory and practice of economics. Covers new developments in the international monetary system, urban bias in developing countries, economic methodology, labor and regional economics, history of economic thought, finance, and dependency theory.

330 UK ISSN 0950-0804
HB1
JOURNAL OF ECONOMIC SURVEYS. 1987. q. £102($190) (foreign £120) (effective 1997). Blackwell Publishers Ltd., 108 Cowley Rd., Oxford OX4 1JF, England. TEL 44-1865-791100. FAX 44-1865-791347. E-mail: jnlinfo@blackwellpublishers.co.uk; URL: http://www.blackwellpublishers.co.uk. Ed.Bd. adv.; bk.rev. circ. 300. (back issues avail.; reprint service avail. from SWZ) **Indexed:** Asian-Pac.Econ.Lit., J.of Econ.Lit.
—BLDSC (4973.065000); SWETS; UMI; UnCover. **CCC.**
Description: Surveys of topics in economics: econometrics, economic history and business economics.
Refereed Serial

330 II
JOURNAL OF ECONOMICS. (Text in English) 1973. s-a. Rs.60($20) Meerut University Economics Association, 3-1 Professor's Lodge, Modinagar, India. Ed. O.P. Gupta. adv.; bk.rev. **Indexed:** Zent.Math.

330 US ISSN 0361-6576
HB1 CODEN: JOECFQ
JOURNAL OF ECONOMICS (VERMILLION). 1975. a. $16. Missouri Valley Economic Association, c/o Green A. Miller, 222 Combs, UPO 1280, MSU, Morehead, KY 40351. TEL 606-783-2721. FAX 606-783-2678. Ed. Mahmeood Yousefi. adv. contact: Robert S. Herren. bk.rev. circ. 350.

330 650 US ISSN 0148-6195
HC101 CODEN: JEBUDR
JOURNAL OF ECONOMICS AND BUSINESS. 1949. bi-m. fl.597($343) (effective 1998). (Temple University, School of Business Administration) Elsevier Science Inc., Box 945, New York, NY 10159-0945. TEL 212-633-3730. FAX 212-633-3680. TELEX 420643 AEP UI. E-mail: usinfo-f@elsevier.com; URL: http://www.elsevier.nl/. (Subscr. outside the Americas to: Elsevier Science, Regional Sales Office, P.O. Box 211, 1000 AE Amsterdam, Netherlands. TEL 31-20-4853757. FAX 31-20-4853432; Subscr. in Australasia and the Far East to: Elsevier Science (Singapore) Pte Ltd, No.1 Temasek Ave., No.17-01 Millenia Tower, Singapore 039192, Singapore. TEL 65-434-3727. FAX 65-337-2230; Subscr. in Japan to: Elsevier Science Japan, 9-15 Higashi-Azabu 1-chome, Minato-ku, Tokyo 106, Japan. TEL 81-3-5561-5033. FAX 81-3-5561-5047) Ed. David Meinster. adv.; bk.rev.; charts; mkt.; index, cum.index. (also avail. in microform from ISI,SWZ,UMI) **Indexed:** ABI Inform., B.P.I., Bank.Lit.Ind., BPIA, Bus.Ind., C.R.E.J., Curr.Cont., INIS Atomind., J.of Econ.Lit., Manage.Cont., Med. Care Rev., P.A.I.S., Pers.Manage.Abstr., Risk Abstr., SSCI, Tr.& Indus.Ind. **Document type:** academic/scholarly publication.
—BLDSC (4973.092000); Genuine Article; KR SourceOne; SWETS; UMI; UnCover. **CCC.**
Formerly: Economic and Business Bulletin (ISSN 0012-9933)
Description: Provides a forum for scholarly research in applied economics, finance and related disciplines that focus on the domestic and international aspects of business and society.
Refereed Serial

330 US ISSN 1055-0925
HB1
JOURNAL OF ECONOMICS AND FINANCE. 1989. 3/yr. $45 to non-members; members $25; students $20; libraries $35 (foreign $50). University of Southern Mississippi, Southern Sta., Box 5076, Hattiesburg, MS 39406-5076. TEL 601-266-4691. FAX 601-266-5992. (Alt. assoc. addr.: c/o Paul Merkle, Louisiana State University at Shreveport, One University Place, Shreveport, LA 71115. TEL 318-797-5240) (Co-sponsor: The Academy of Economics and Finance) circ. 375. **Document type:** academic/scholarly publication.
—UnCover.
Description: Examines economics and finance through theoretical and empirical research at higher academic levels.
Refereed Serial

339 AU ISSN 0931-8658
HB5 CODEN: ZENOA4
JOURNAL OF ECONOMICS - ZEITSCHRIFT FUER NATIONALOEKONOMIE. (Supplements avail.) (Text in English) 1929. bi-m. DM.844 (effective 1998). Springer-Verlag, Sachsenplatz 4-6, P.O. Box 89, A-1201 Vienna, Austria. TEL 43-1-3302415. FAX 43-1-3302426. E-mail: springer@springer.co.at. (Subscr. in N. America to: Springer-Verlag New York, Inc., 175 Fifth Ave., New York, NY 10010. TEL 212-460-1500. FAX 212-473-6272) Ed. D. Boes. adv.; bk.rev.; charts; illus.; index, cum.index: vol.1-15. (also avail. in microform from UMI; reprint service avail. from ISI,SWZ) **Indexed:** ASCA, Curr.Cont., IBR, J.of Econ.Lit., Key to Econ.Sci., Math.R., Risk Abstr., SSCI. **Document type:** academic/scholarly publication.
—BLDSC (4973.081000); Genuine Article; SWETS; UMI; UnCover. **CCC.**
Formerly: Journal of Economics (New York) (ISSN 0044-3158)
Description: Specializes in mathematical economic theory of medium- and high-level difficulty, with emphasis on microeconomic theory. Includes papers on macroeconomic topics.

650.07 370 US ISSN 0883-2323
HF1101
JOURNAL OF EDUCATION FOR BUSINESS. 1928. bi-m. $33 to individuals; institutions $56. (Helen Dwight Reid Educational Foundation) Heldref Publications, 1319 18th St., N.W., Washington, DC 20036-1802. TEL 202-296-6267. FAX 202-296-5149. Ed. Isabella Owen. adv. contact: Raymond Rallo. bk.rev.; bibl.; illus.; index. circ. 1,800. (also avail. in microform; reprint service avail.) **Indexed:** B.P.I., Bk.Rev.Ind. (1965-1977), Bus.Educ.Ind., C.I.J.E., Child.Bk.Rev.Ind. (1965-1977), Cont.Pg.Educ., Educ.Ind., IBR, Media Rev.Dig., Ref.Sour., Stud.Wom.Abstr., Tech.Educ.Abstr. **Document type:** academic/scholarly publication.
●Also available online. Vendor(s): UMI.
Also available on CD-ROM. Producer(s): UMI.
—BLDSC (4973.127500); KR SourceOne; SWETS; UMI; UnCover. **CCC.**
Formerly: Journal of Business Education (ISSN 0021-9444)
Refereed Serial

JOURNAL OF EMPLOYEE OWNERSHIP LAW AND FINANCE. see *LAW*

JOURNAL OF END USER COMPUTING; the international journal of information user management. see *COMPUTERS — Microcomputers*

330 SI ISSN 0218-4958
JOURNAL OF ENTERPRISING CULTURE. (Text in English) 4/yr. $110. World Scientific Publishing Co. Pte. Ltd., Farrer Rd., P.O. Box 128, Singapore 9128, Singapore. TEL 65-3825663. FAX 65-3825919. E-mail: wspcsl@singnet.com.sg; sales@wspc2.demon.co.uk; wspc@wspc.com; URL: http://www.singnet.com.sg/~wspclib/. (UK addr.: 57 Shelton St., Covent Garden, London WC3H 9HE, England. TEL 44-171-836-0888. FAX 44-171-836-2020; US addr.: 1060 Main St., Ste. 1B, River Edge, NJ 07661. TEL 800-227-7562. FAX 201-487-9656) Ed. Teck-Meng Tan.
Description: Publishes conceptual, research and case based works that can be of practical value to business persons, educators, students and advocates.

330 US ISSN 1044-002X
HC241.2 CODEN: JEBUES
JOURNAL OF EUROPEAN BUSINESS. 1989. bi-m. $99. Faulkner & Gray, Inc. (New York), 11 Penn Plaza, 17th Fl., New York, NY 10001. TEL 212-967-7000. FAX 212-967-7155. Ed. Heather Ogilne. adv.: B&W page $1775, color page $2700; trim 8 1/8 x 10 7/8. circ. 5,798 (paid); 6,202 (controlled). **Indexed:** Account.Ind. (1989-).
—UMI; UnCover.
Description: Focuses on how European business will change with the "new Europe" and what challenges and opportunities the single European market will present both within Europe and for other nations.

330 SZ ISSN 0304-405X
HG4501 CODEN: JFECDT
JOURNAL OF FINANCIAL ECONOMICS. (Text in English) 1974. m. fl.1944($1117) (effective 1998). Elsevier Science S.A., P.O. Box 564, CH-1001 Lausanne 1, Switzerland. TEL 41-21-3207381. FAX 41-21-3235444. TELEX 450620-ELSA-CH. (Subscr. to: Elsevier Science, Regional Sales Office, P.O. Box 211, 1000 AE Amsterdam, Netherlands. TEL 31-20-4853757. FAX 31-20-4853432; Subscr. in the Americas to: Elsevier Science, Regional Sales Office, Box 945, New York, NY 10159-0945. TEL 212-633-3730. FAX 212-633-3680; Subscr. in Australasia to: Elsevier Science (Singapore) Pte. Ltd., No. 1 Temasek Ave., No. 17 Millenia Tower, Singapore 039192, Singapore. TEL 65-434-3727. FAX 65-337-2230) Ed. Michael C. Jensen. adv.; bk.rev.; charts; illus. (also avail. in microform from UMI) **Indexed:** ABI Inform., ASCA, B.P.I., BPIA, Bus.Ind., C.R.E.J., Compumath, Cont.Pg.Manage., Curr.Cont., J.Cont.Quant.Meth., J.of Econ.Lit., Manage.Cont., Risk Abstr., SCIMP (1978-), SSCI, Tr.& Indus.Ind., World Bank.Abstr. **Document type:** academic/scholarly publication.
—BLDSC (4984.240000); Genuine Article; KR SourceOne; SWETS; UMI; UnCover. **CCC.**
Description: Provides a forum for the publication of research in the general area of financial economics.
Refereed Serial

BUSINESS AND ECONOMICS

330 332 US ISSN 0270-2592
HG1
JOURNAL OF FINANCIAL RESEARCH. 1978. q. $125 (foreign $131) (effective 1997 & 1998). (Southern Finance Association) Virginia Polytechnic Institute and State University, College of Business, Department of Finance, 1016 Pamplin Hall, Blacksburg, VA 24061-0221. TEL 540-231-7699. FAX 540-231-4706. E-mail: edjones@vt.edu; URL: http://www.vt.edu:10021/business/finance/jfr. (Co-sponsor: Southwestern Finance Association) Eds. Robert Hansen, Arthur Keown. adv. contact: C. Denise Jones. index. circ. 1,900. (also avail. in microform from UMI; back issues avail.; reprint service avail. from UMI) **Indexed:** ABI Inform, B.P.I., Cont.Pg.Manage., J.of Econ.Lit., Risk Abstr., SCIMP, SSCI. **Document type:** academic/scholarly publication.
●Also available online. Vendor(s): Information Access Co.
—BLDSC (4984.265000); Genuine Article; KR SourceOne; SWETS; UMI; UnCover. **CCC.**

330 US ISSN 1053-7287
HG3879
JOURNAL OF GLOBAL BUSINESS. 1990. s-a. $25 to individuals; institutions $35 (effective 1997 & 1998). Association for Global Business, Box 1381, Harrisonburg, VA 22801. TEL 540-433-7403. FAX 540-433-7403. Ed. Faramarz Damanpour. adv.: B&W page $250. bk.rev. circ. 1,000. (back issues avail.) **Document type:** academic/scholarly publication.
—BLDSC (4996.260000).
Description: Aims to provide a forum for the exchange of professional ideas, to enhance research in the field of international business and global concerns, and to create a general awareness of significant accomplishments in the area of global enterprises.
Refereed Serial

330 UK ISSN 0022-1821
HD1 CODEN: JIEOAF
JOURNAL OF INDUSTRIAL ECONOMICS. 1952. q. £79($151) (foreign £91) (effective 1997). Blackwell Publishers Ltd., 108 Cowley Rd., Oxford OX4 1JF, England. TEL 44-1865-791100. FAX 44-1865-791347. E-mail: jnlinfo@ blackwellpublishers.co.uk; URL: http://www. blackwellpublishers.co.uk. Ed. Michael Waterson. adv.; bibl.; charts; index. circ. 1,850. (also avail. in microform from MIM,UMI; reprint service avail. from UMI,KTO) **Indexed:** ABI Inform, ASCA, Asian-Pac.Econ.Lit., ASSIA, B.P.I., BPIA, Br.Hum.Ind., Bus.Ind., C.R.E.J., Cont.Pg.Manage., Curr.Cont., Energy Ind., Energy Info.Abstr., Geo.Abstr., IBR, IDA, J.of Econ.Lit., Key to Econ.Sci., Manage.Cont, Mark.Res.Abstr. (1965-), Mgmt.& Market.Abstr., Oper.Res.Manage.Sci., P.A.I.S., PROMT, Risk Abstr., SCIMP (1978-), SSCI, Tr.& Indus.Ind., Work Rel.Abstr., World Bank.Abstr. **Document type:** academic/scholarly publication.
●Also available online. Vendor(s): Information Access Co.
—BLDSC (5005.650000); Genuine Article; KR SourceOne; SWETS; UMI; UnCover. **CCC.**
Refereed Serial

330 UK ISSN 0260-1079
HB1
JOURNAL OF INTERDISCIPLINARY ECONOMICS. 1984. q. £89($179) A B Academic Publishers, P.O. Box 42, Bicester, Oxon. OX6 7NW, England. TEL 44-1869-320949. Ed. Ken Penney. adv.; bk.rev. (also avail. in microform) **Indexed:** Amer.Hist.& Life (1985-1987), Asian-Pac.Econ.Lit., ASSIA, C.R.E.J., Hist.Abstr. (1985-1987). **Document type:** academic/scholarly publication.
—BLDSC (5007.546000); UnCover. **CCC.**

650 CN ISSN 0047-2506
HF1
JOURNAL OF INTERNATIONAL BUSINESS STUDIES. 1970. q. $57 for individual membership; institutions $57 (outside N. America $63). University of Western Ontario, Western Business School, London, ON N6A 3K7, Canada. TEL 519-661-4031. FAX 519-661-3700. E-mail: pbeamish@novell. business.uwo.ca. (Co-sponsor: Academy of International Business) Ed. Paul Beamish. adv.: B&W page US$400. bk.rev.; charts. circ. 4,100. (processed; also avail. in microform from UMI; reprint service avail. from SCH,UMI) **Indexed:** ABI Inform, Account.& Data Proc.Abstr., Amer.Bibl.Slavic & E.Eur.Stud., ASCA, Asian-Pac.Econ.Lit., B.P.I., Bus.Ind., Cont.Pg.Manage., Curr.Cont., Manage.Cont., Mgmt.& Market.Abstr., Mid.East: Abstr.& Ind., P.A.I.S., PROMT, Risk Abstr., SCIMP (1978-), SSCI, Tr.& Indus.Ind. **Document type:** academic/scholarly publication.
●Also available online. Vendor(s): Information Access Co., UMI.
—BLDSC (5007.590000); Genuine Article; KR SourceOne; SWETS; UMI; UnCover. **CCC.**
Description: Publishes the results of basic or applied research in international or comparative business. Also publishes important conceptual or theoretical contributions that augment knowledge in the field or advance educational methodology.
Refereed Serial

330 NE ISSN 0022-1996
HF1 CODEN: JIECBE
JOURNAL OF INTERNATIONAL ECONOMICS. (Text in English) 1971. 8/yr. fl.1365($784) (effective 1998). North-Holland (Subsidiary of: Elsevier Science B.V.), P.O. Box 211, 1000 AE Amsterdam, Netherlands. TEL 31-20-4853911. FAX 31-20-4853598. TELEX 18582 ESPA NL. (Subscr. in the Americas to: Elsevier Science, Regional Sales Office, Box 945, New York, NY 10159-0945. TEL 212-633-3730. FAX 212-633-3680; Subscr. in Australasia and the Far East to: Elsevier Science (Singapore) Pte Ltd, No.1 Temasek Ave., No.17-01 Millenia Tower, Singapore 039192, Singapore. TEL 65-434-3727. FAX 65-337-2230; Subscr. in Japan to: Elsevier Science Japan, 9-15 Higashi-Azabu 1-chome, Minato-ku, Tokyo 106, Japan. TEL 81-3-5561-5033. FAX 81-3-5561-5047) Ed. Richard A. Brecher. adv.; bk.rev.; charts; illus.; index. (also avail. in microform from UMI; back issues avail.; reprint service avail. from SWZ) **Indexed:** ABI Inform, ASCA, Asian-Pac.Econ.Lit., BPIA, Bus.Ind., Curr.Cont., Geo.Abstr.P.G., IDA, J.of Econ.Lit., Key to Econ.Sci., Risk Abstr., Rural Recreat.Tour.Abstr., SCIMP, Soc.Sci.Ind., SSCI, Tr.& Indus.Ind., World Agri.Econ.& Rural Sociol.Abstr., World Bank.Abstr. **Document type:** academic/scholarly publication.
—BLDSC (5007.650000); Genuine Article; KR SourceOne; SWETS; UMI; UnCover. **CCC.**
Description: Publishes analytical work in the pure theory of international trade and payment analysis.
Refereed Serial

JOURNAL OF LAW AND ECONOMICS. see *LAW*

JOURNAL OF MODERN AFRICAN STUDIES. see *POLITICAL SCIENCE*

THE JOURNAL OF PEASANT STUDIES. see *SOCIOLOGY*

330 320 US ISSN 0022-3808
HB1 CODEN: JLPEAR
JOURNAL OF POLITICAL ECONOMY. 1892. bi-m. $46 to individuals (Canada $60.22; elsewhere $57); institutions $127 (Canada $146.89; elsewhere $138); students $30 (Canada $43.10; elsewhere $41) (effective 1998). University of Chicago Press, Journals Division, Box 37005, Chicago, IL 60637. TEL 773-753-3347. FAX 773-753-0811. TELEX 25-4603. E-mail: subscriptions@journals.uchicago. edu; jstor-info@umich.edu; URL: http://www.jstor. org/fcgi-bin/jstor/; http://www.journals.uchicago. edu/JPE/. Ed.Bd. adv.: page $410; trim 6 x 9. bk.rev.; abstr.; bibl.; charts; illus.; stat.; index. circ. 7,100. (also avail. in microform from MIM,UMI,PMC; reprint service avail. from UMI,ISI,WSH) **Indexed:** A.B.C.Pol.Sci., ABI Inform., Amer.Hist.& Life (until 1991), Arts & Hum.Cit.Ind., Asian-Pac.Econ.Lit., Bank.Lit.Ind., Bk.Rev.Dig., Bk.Rev.Ind. (1965-), Bus.Ind., C.R.E.J., Child.Bk.Rev.Ind. (1965-), Cont.Pg.Manage., Crim.Just.Abstr., Curr.Cont., Geo.Abstr.P.G., Hist.Abstr. (until 1991), IBR, IDA, J.of Econ.Lit., Key to Econ.Sci., Mid.East: Abstr.& Ind., Popul.Ind., Rural Recreat.Tour.Abstr., SCIMP, Soc.Sci.Ind., SSCI, Stud.Wom.Abstr., World Agri.Econ.& Rural Sociol.Abstr. **Document type:** academic/scholarly publication.
●Also available online.
—BLDSC (5040.850000); Genuine Article; KR SourceOne; SWETS; UMI; UnCover. **CCC.**
Description: Presents work in traditional areas of political economics: monetary theory, fiscal policy, labor economics, planning and developments, micro- and macroeconomic theory, and international trade and finance. Also publishes analyses in related fields such as economic thought and social economics.
Refereed Serial

330 US
HD1
JOURNAL OF REGIONAL ANALYSIS & POLICY. 1971. s-a. $35 to individuals; institutions $45. (Mid-Continent Regional Science Association) University of Nebraska at Lincoln, Bureau of Business Research, c/o Charles Lamphear, 114 C.B.A., Lincoln, NE 68588-0489. TEL 402-472-7928. bk.rev. circ. 500. **Indexed:** Geo.Abstr.P.G., J.of Econ.Lit. **Document type:** academic/scholarly publication.
—UnCover.
Formerly: Regional Science Perspectives (ISSN 0097-1197)

JOURNAL OF REPRINTS FOR ANTITRUST LAW & ECONOMICS. see *LAW*

330 US ISSN 0094-1190
HT321 CODEN: JUECDW
JOURNAL OF URBAN ECONOMICS. 1974. bi-m. $450 (foreign $555) (effective 1997). Academic Press, Inc., Journal Division, 525 B St., Ste. 1900, San Diego, CA 92101-4495. TEL 619-230-1840. FAX 619-699-6800. E-mail: apsubs@acad.com; URL: http://www.apnet.com/www/journal/ue.htm; http://www.idealibrary.com/. (Subscr. to: Box 861213, Orlando, FL 32886-1213. TEL 407-347-4040. FAX 407-363-9661) Ed. Jan K. Brueckner. (back issues avail.) **Indexed:** ASCA, Asian-Pac.Econ.Lit., B.P.I., BPIA, C.R.E.J., Crim.Just.Abstr., Curr.Cont., Excerpt.Med., Fam.Ind., J.of Econ.Lit., Manage.Cont., P.A.I.S., Pub.Admin.Abstr., SSCI, Tr.& Indus.Ind., Zent.Math. **Document type:** academic/scholarly publication.
●Also available online.
—BLDSC (5071.554000); Genuine Article; KR SourceOne; SWETS; UnCover. **CCC.**
Description: Illustrates empirical, theoretical, positive, or normative approaches to urban economics.

340 US ISSN 0737-5468
K10
JOURNAL RECORD. 1903. 5/w. $131 in Oklahoma; elsewhere $180. (Oklahoma Farmers Union) Dolan Media, Box 26370, Oklahoma City, OK 73126-0370. TEL 405-235-3100. FAX 405-278-6918. Ed. David Page. adv. contact: Bridgett Griffin. bk.rev.; circ. 3,500 (paid). (also avail. in microfiche) **Indexed:** Tr.& Indus.Ind. **Document type:** newspaper.
●Also available online.
Formerly: Daily Law Journal Record (ISSN 0011-5452)

BUSINESS AND ECONOMICS

330 US
JOURNEY (ANTIOCH). 1991. q. $39.95. Buker, Inc., 1425 Tri-State Pky., Ste. 120, Gurnee, IL 60031-4060. TEL 847-855-8554. FAX 847-855-0889. E-mail: nhorton@buker.com; URL: http://www.buker.com. Ed. James W. Bieal. adv. contact: Mike Stickler. bk.rev. **Document type:** corporate report, newsletter.
Description: Provides business managers with proven methods of improving their operating performance.

330 II
JUNIOR SCIENCE REFRESHER; science magazine. (Text in English) 1987. m. newsstand price: Rs.20. (Bright Careers Institute) Junior Science Refresher Pty. Ltd., 2769 Bright House, Darya Ganj, New Delhi 110 002, India. TEL 91-11-3276554. FAX 91-11-3269227. TELEX ND 31-76101. Ed. D.S. Phull; Pub. Pritam Singh Bright. R&P contact: P.S. Bright. adv.: B&W page Rs.18500, color page Rs.35000; 245 x 175. circ. 71,758.

JUTA'S BUSINESS LAW; the quarterly law review for people in business. see LAW — Corporate Law

330 332 339 KO
K D B REPORT. (Text and summaries in English) 1977. m. free. Korea Development Bank, 10-2 Kwanch'ol-dong, Chongno-gu, C.P.O. Box 28, Seoul, S. Korea. Ed. Bong Won Lee. circ. 2,800. (tabloid format)

KAERVEN; Foereningsbankens tidning. see BUSINESS AND ECONOMICS — Banking And Finance

330 CC
KAIFANG YUEKAN; Shanghai Xinchao Zazhi. (Text in Chinese) m. 62 Henshan Lu, Shanghai 200031, People's Republic of China. TEL 86-21-4313564. FAX 86-21-4315274. (Dist. overseas by: China International Book Trading Corp., P.O. Box 399, Beijing 100044, P.R. China)
Description: Covers the latest development in China's economic reform.

330
KANSAI UNIVERSITY ECONOMIC REVIEW/KANSAI DAIGAKU KEIZAI RONSHU. 1950. bi-m. Kansai University, Economic Society - Kansai Daigaku Keizai Gakkai, Senriyama, Suita, Osaka, Japan. bk.rev. **Indexed:** Account.& Data Proc.Abstr., Asian-Pac.Econ.Lit.
—BLDSC (3654.950000).

330 FI ISSN 0022-8427
HB9
KANSANTALOUDELLINEN AIKAKAUSKIRJA/FINNISH ECONOMIC JOURNAL. (Summaries in English) 1905. q. FIM 150 (students FIM 60). (Kansantaloudellinen Yhdistys) Finnish Economic Association - E T L A, Loennrotinkatu 4 B, SF-00120 Helsinki, Finland. TEL 358-0-609-900. FAX 358-0-601-753. E-mail: anna@etla.fi. Ed. Mika Widgen. adv.; bk.rev.; bibl. circ. 2,000. **Indexed:** World Bibl.Soc.Sec.

330 FI ISSN 0451-5560
KAUPPALEHTI. 1898. 5/w. FIM 982. Kustannus oy Kauppalehti, P.O. Box 189, SF-00101, Vetotie no.3, 01610 Vantaa, Finland. TEL 90 50781. Ed. Lauri Helve. circ. 84,068. **Indexed:** Paper & Bd.Abstr.
●Also available online. Vendor(s): Helsinki School of Economics.

330 JA ISSN 0022-9695
HC461
KEIDANREN REVIEW. (Text in English) 1964. bi-m. free. Japan Federation of Economic Organizations - Keizai Dantai Rengokai (KEIDANREN), 9-4 Otemachi, 1-chome, Chiyoda-ku, Tokyo 100, Japan. TEL 81-3-3279-1411. FAX 81-3-5255-6255. TELEX 0222 3188 KDRTOKJ. adv.; charts; illus.; stat. circ. 12,000.

330 JA ISSN 0386-9113
HD28
KEIEI SHIGAKU/JAPAN BUSINESS HISTORY REVIEW. (Text in Japanese) 1967. 4/yr. 4200 Yen. (Business History Society of Japan) University of Tokyo Press, 3-1 Hongo 7-chome, Bunkyo-ku, Tokyo 113, Japan.

650 JA ISSN 0453-4557
HF5001
KEIO BUSINESS REVIEW. (Text in English) vol.15, 1978. a. price varies. Keio University Society of Business and Commerce, c/o Faculty of Business and Commerce, Mita, Minato-ku, Tokyo 108, Japan. (Dist. by: Japan Publications Trading Co., Ltd., P.O. Box 5030, Tokyo International, Tokyo, Japan) Ed. Tadahiro Yamamasu. charts; stat. **Indexed:** Account.& Data Proc.Abstr., Cont.Pg.Manage., P.A.I.S.
—UnCover.

330 JA ISSN 0022-9709
HB9
KEIO ECONOMIC STUDIES. (Text in English) 1963. s-a. 3000 Yen. Keio Gijuku Daigaku, Keio Keizai Gakkai - Keio University, Keio Economic Society, 2-15-45 Mita, Minato-ku, Tokyo 108, Japan. TEL 81-3-3453-4511. FAX 81-3-3798-7480. Ed. Hiroaki Osana. R&P contact: Kunio Kawamata. adv. contact: Kunio Kawamata. circ. 800. **Indexed:** Asian-Pac.Econ.Lit., C.R.E.J., J.of Econ.Lit., SSCI. **Document type:** academic/scholarly publication.
—BLDSC (5088.870000).

650 JA ISSN 0075-5346
KEIO MONOGRAPHS OF BUSINESS AND COMMERCE. 1967. irreg. price varies. Keio University Society of Business and Commerce, c/o Faculty of Business and Commerce, Mita, Minato-ku, Tokyo 108, Japan. (Dist. by: Japan Publications Trading Co. Ltd., Box 5030, Tokyo International, Tokyo 100-31 Japan; Or: 1255 Howard St., San Francisco, CA 94103) **Document type:** monographic series.

330 JA ISSN 0022-9725
KEIZAI KAGAKU/ECONOMIC SCIENCE. (Text mainly in Japanese; occasionally in English) 1951. q. Nagoya Daigaku, Keizaigakubu - Nagoya University, School of Economics, Furo-cho, Chikusa-ku, Nagoya 464-01, Japan. TEL 81-52-789-2360. FAX 81-52-789-4924. E-mail: econsci@soec. nagoya-u.ac.jp; URL: http://www.soec.nagoya-u.ac.jp/index__e.html. Ed. Soshichi Kinoshita. bk.rev.; bibl.; charts; stat.; index, cum.index. circ. 400. **Document type:** academic/scholarly publication.
—BLDSC (3655.180000).
Refereed Serial

330 JA ISSN 0022-9733
HB9
KEIZAI KENKYU/ECONOMIC REVIEW (TOKYO, 1950). (Text and contents page in English and Japanese) 1950. q. 6300 Yen. (Hitotsubashi Daigaku, Keizai Kenkyujo - Hitotsubashi University, Institute of Economic Research) Iwanami Shoten Publishers, 5-5 Hitotsubashi 2-chome, Chiyoda-ku, Tokyo 101-02, Japan. FAX 03-239-9618. (Dist. overseas by: Japan Publications Trading Co., Ltd., Box 5030, Tokyo International, Tokyo 100-31, Japan; Or: 1255 Howard St., San Francisco, CA 94103) Ed. R. Minami. adv.; bk.rev.; bibl.; illus.; stat. circ. 1,500. **Indexed:** Amer.Hist.& Life (1958-1971), Hist.Abstr. (1958-1971), J.of Econ.Lit.
—UnCover.

330 JA
KEIZAI OHRAI/ECONOMIC REVIEW (TOKYO, 1926). (Text in Japanese) 1926. m. Keizaioraisha, 11 Yotsuya 4-chome, Shinjuku-ku, Tokyo 160, Japan. TEL 81-3-3357-0811. FAX 81-3-3357-0815. Ed. Yoshiya Sekine. adv. circ. 38,000.
Description: Covers business and economic affairs in Japan.

330 JA ISSN 0022-9741
KEIZAI SHIRIN/HOSEI UNIVERSITY ECONOMIC REVIEW. 1925. q. 3200 Yen. Hosei Daigaku, Keizai Gakkai - Hosei University, Economics Society, 4342 Aihara-machi, Machida-shi, Tokyo, Japan. TEL 81-427-83-2517. FAX 81-427-83-2611. Ed. Kazuko Ishige. bk.rev. **Indexed:** Amer.Hist.& Life (1958-1961), (1971-1971), Hist.Abstr. (1958-1961), (1971-). **Document type:** academic/scholarly publication.

330 JA ISSN 0022-975X
HB9
KEIZAIGAKU KENKYU/JOURNAL OF POLITICAL ECONOMY.* 1931. bi-m. exchange basis. Keizai Riron Gakkai - Society of Political Economy, c/o Rikkyo Daigaku Keizaigakubu, 3 Ikebukuro, Toshima-ku, Tokyo 171, Japan. Ed. Senzo Hidemura. bk.rev.; cum.index; circ. controlled. **Indexed:** Amer.Hist.& Life, Deep Sea Res.& Oceanogr.Abstr., Hist.Abstr.
—BLDSC (5040.880000).

330 JA ISSN 0453-4778
KEIZAIGAKU RONSAN/JOURNAL OF ECONOMICS. 1960. bi-m. Chuo Daigaku, Keizaigaku Kenkyukai - Chuo University, Economic Society, 742 Higashinakano, Hachioji-shi, Tokyo, Japan. Ed. Toshihiko Aono. **Indexed:** Amer.Hist.& Life (1959-1969), Hist.Abstr. (1959-1969). **Document type:** academic/scholarly publication.

330 JA ISSN 0022-9768
KEIZAIGAKU RONSHU/JOURNAL OF ECONOMICS. 1931. q. 5200 Yen. (University of Tokyo, School of Economics) University of Tokyo Press - Tokyo Daigaku Shuppankai, 3-1 Hongo 7-chome, Bunkyo-ku, Tokyo 113, Japan. (Dist. by: Business Center for Academic Societies Japan, 5-16-9 Honkomagome, Bunkyo-ku, Tokyo 113, Japan. TEL 03-5814-5811. FAX 03-5814-5822) bk.rev.; stat.; cum.index; circ. controlled. **Indexed:** Amer.Hist.& Life, C.R.E.J., Hist.Abstr. **Document type:** academic/scholarly publication.

330 JA ISSN 0910-8858
KEIZAIJIN. (Text in Japanese) 1947. m. Kansai Economic Federation, Nakanoshima Center Bldg., 6-2-27, Nakanoshima, Kita-ku, Osaka 530, Japan. TEL 81-6-441-0105. FAX 81-6-443-5347. Ed. A. Sakurauchi. circ. 2,600. **Document type:** bulletin.

330 JA
KEIZAIKAI. (Text in Japanese) 1972. s-m. 7900 Yen. Keizaikai Co., Ltd., 11 Mori Bldg., 2-6-4 Toranomon, Minato-ku, Tokyo, Japan. Ed. Yuzo Yasuda. adv.; bk.rev. circ. 156,000.
Formerly: Economic World.

330 US ISSN 0192-642X
KENTUCKY BUSINESS LEDGER.* 1975. m. $20. Kentucky Communications, Inc., Box 470867, Charlotte, NC 28247. Ed. Philip F. Van Pelt. adv. circ. 21,000. (reprint service avail.)
●Also available online. Vendor(s): Knight-Ridder Information, Inc.

330 338 US
THE KENTUCKY MANUFACTURER.* 1982. m. $20. Industrial Marketing, Inc., PO Box 4310, Lexington, KY 40544-4310. TEL 606-266-3303. FAX 606-266-3230. Ed. Jane E. Cummins. adv. circ. 11,000.
●Also available online. Vendor(s): UMI.

330 UK ISSN 0142-5048
HC252.2
KEY BRITISH ENTERPRISES. a. £438. Dun & Bradstreet Ltd., Holmers Farm Way, High Wycombe, Bucks. HP12 4UL, England. TEL 44-1494-422000. FAX 44-1494-422260. Ed. Laura Morel. **Document type:** directory.
●Also available online.
—CISTI.

330 UK
KEY BUSINESS RATIOS. 1987. a. £249. Dun & Bradstreet Ltd., Holmers Farm Way, High Wycombe, Bucks. HP12 4UL, England. TEL 44-1494-422000. FAX 44-1494-422260. Ed. Laura Morel. **Document type:** directory.

330 070 UK
KEY NOTE MARKET REPORT: BUSINESS PRESS. Variant title: Business Press. irreg., no.9, 1996. £205. Key Note Ltd., Field House, 72 Oldfield Rd., Hampton, Middlesex TW12 2HQ, England. TEL 44-181-783-0755. FAX 44-181-783-0049. **Document type:** trade publication.
●Also available online.
Also available on CD-ROM.
Formerly: Key Note Report: Business Press.

KEY NOTE MARKET REPORT: BUSINESS TRAVEL. see TRAVEL AND TOURISM

BUSINESS AND ECONOMICS

KEY NOTE MARKET REVIEW: BUSINESS INFORMATION IN THE U K. see *BUSINESS AND ECONOMICS — Trade And Industrial Directories*

650.07   US
KEYING IN. 1991. 4/yr. $60 to libraries (includes Business Education Forum and Yearbook). National Business Education Association, 1914 Association Dr., Reston, VA 22091. TEL 703-860-8300. FAX 703-620-4483. Ed. Susan Okula; Pub. Janet M. Treichel. R&P contact: Susan Okula. **Document type:** newsletter.

330   SU   ISSN 1018-3582
KING SAUD UNIVERSITY. JOURNAL. ADMINISTRATIVE SCIENCES. Key Title: Majallat Jami'at al-Malik Sa'ud, al-'Ulum al-Idariyyah. (Other sections avail.: Agricultural Sciences, Architecture and Planning, Arts, Computer and information Sciences, Educational Sciences and Islamic Studies, Engineering Sciences, Science) (Text in Arabic, English) 1989. s-a. $10. King Saud University, University Libraries, P.O. Box 22480, Riyadh 11495, Saudi Arabia. TEL 966-1-4676148. FAX 966-1-4676162. TELEX 401019 KSU SJ. Ed. Khalid A. Al-Hamoudi. R&P contact: Saad A. Al-Dobaian. charts; illus. circ. 3,000. **Document type:** academic/scholarly publication.
Refereed Serial

330   RW
KINYAMATEKA. 1933. fortn. 5 blvd. de l'OUA, B.P. 761, Kigali, Rwanda. TEL 6164. Ed. Andre Sibomana. circ. 11,000.

330   NA
KNOW HOW. (Text in English) m. Know How Group N.V., Schottegatweg Oost 56, P.O. Box 473, Curacao, Netherlands Antilles. TEL 367079. FAX 367080.

330   JA   ISSN 0075-6415
KOBE ECONOMIC AND BUSINESS RESEARCH SERIES. (Text in English) 1962. irreg. exchange basis. Kobe Daigaku, Research Institute for Economics and Business Administration - Kobe University, Rokko, Nada-ku, Kobe-shi, Hyogo-ken, Japan. Ed.Bd. circ. 400. **Document type:** monographic series.

330   JA   ISSN 0075-6407
HC461
KOBE ECONOMIC AND BUSINESS REVIEW. (Text in English) 1953. a. exchange basis. Kobe Daigaku, Research Institute for Economics and Business Administration - Kobe University, Rokko, Nada-ku, Kobe-shi, Hyogo-ken 657, Japan. TEL 81-78-881-1212. FAX 81-78-861-6434. Ed.Bd. circ. 550. **Indexed:** Account.Ind. (1979-), C.R.E.J. **Document type:** academic/scholarly publication.
—BLDSC (5100.575000); UnCover.
Description: Explores business and economic issues worldwide.

330   JA   ISSN 0454-1111
HB9
KOBE UNIVERSITY ECONOMIC REVIEW. (Text in English) 1955. a. exchange basis. Kobe Daigaku, Keizaigakubu - Kobe University, Faculty of Economics, Rokkodai-cho, Nada-ku, Kobe-shi, Hyogo-ken 657, Japan. FAX 81-78-803-0319. circ. 650. **Indexed:** Asian-Pac.Econ.Lit., C.R.E.J., IBR, J.of Econ.Lit., Key to Econ.Sci. **Document type:** academic/scholarly publication.
—BLDSC (5100.611000); UnCover.
Description: Analyzes business, labor, and economics industry throughout the world.

330   DK   ISSN 0906-0669
KOEBENHAVNS UNIVERSITET. OEKONOMISK INSTITUT. CYKELAFDELINGEN. MEMO. (Text in Danish, English) 1958. irreg. Koebenhavns Universitet, Oekonomisk Institut (Subsidiary of: Cykelafdelingen), Studiestraede 6, DK-1455 Copenhagen K, Denmark.
Former titles (until 1990): Koebenhavns Universitet. Oekonomisk Institut. Gult Memo (ISSN 0904-0943); (until 1987): Koebenhavns Universitet. Oekonomiske Institut. Cyckelafdelingen. Memo (ISSN 0902-0128); Supersedes in Part (in 1972): Koebenhavns Universitet. Oekonomisk Institut. Memorandum.

330   DK   ISSN 0107-3664
KOEBENHAVNS UNIVERSITET. OEKONOMISK INSTITUT. MEMO. Variant title: Koebrenhavns Universitet. Oekonomisk Institut. Blaat Memo. (Text in Danish, English) 1958. irreg. Koebenhavns Universitet, Oekonomisk Institut, Studiestraede 6, DK-1455 Copenhagen K, Denmark. illus.
Supersedes in part (in 1972): Koebenhavns Universitet. Oekonomiske Institut. Memorandum (ISSN 0574-0045).

330   DK   ISSN 0108-2221
KOEBENHAVNS UNIVERSITET. OEKONOMISK INSTITUT. ROED SERIE. (Text in Danish, English) 1981. irreg. Koebenhavns Universitet. Oekonomisk Institut, Studiestraede 6, DK-1455 Copenhagen K, Denmark.

330   JA   ISSN 0288-6340
HB9
KOKUGAKUIN UNIVERSITY ECONOMIC REVIEW/KOKUGAKUIN KEIZAIGAKU. (Text in Japanese) vol.15, 1966. q. 2000 Yen. Kokugakuin University, Faculty of Economics - Keizaibu, 4-10-28 Higashi, Shibuya-ku, Tokyo, Japan. TEL 03-5466-0342. FAX 03-5466-2340. Ed. Ichiro Nagai; Pub. Makoto Iki. bk.rev. circ. 2,000. **Indexed:** Amer.Hist.& Life (1962-1968), Hist.Abstr. (1954-1968). **Document type:** academic/scholarly publication.
—BLDSC (5101.776400).
Formerly: Seikei Ronso - Faculty of Politics, Law and Economics. Journal (ISSN 0582-4192)

330   RU
KOMMERSANT. 1989. w. $353 (effective 1998). Khoroshovskoe Shosse 41, Moscow, Russia. TEL (095) 941-09-00. (Dist. by: Mezhdunarodnaya Kniga, B. Yakimanka 39, 117049 Moscow, Russia. TEL 7-095-2384967. FAX 7-095-2384634) Ed. Vladimir Yakovlev. **Document type:** newspaper.

KOMPASS BUSINESS SERVICES AND TRANSPORT. see *BUSINESS AND ECONOMICS — Trade And Industrial Directories*

KOMPASS DIRECTORY. see *PLASTICS*

330   FR   ISSN 0295-7965
KOMPASS REGIONAL ECONOMIQUE ET INDUSTRIEL. ALSACE. 1979. a. Kompass France, 66 quai du Marechal Joffre, 92415 Courbevoie Cedex, France. Ed. Bertrand Macabeo; Pub. Bertrand Macabeo. R&P contact: Bertrand Macabeo. adv. contact: Mireille Girault. **Document type:** directory.
Formerly (until 1982): Inventaire Regional Economique et Industriel. Alsace (ISSN 0240-4753)

330   FR   ISSN 0295-7981
KOMPASS REGIONAL ECONOMIQUE ET INDUSTRIEL. AQUITAINE. 1979. a. Kompass France, 66 quai du Marechal Joffre, 92415 Courbevoie Cedex, France. Ed. Bertrand Macabeo; Pub. Bertrand Macabeo. R&P contact: Bertrand Macabeo. adv. contact: Mireille Girault. **Document type:** directory.
Formerly (until 1982): Inventaire Regional Economique et Industriel. Aquitaine (ISSN 0245-1158)

330   FR   ISSN 0295-7957
KOMPASS REGIONAL ECONOMIQUE ET INDUSTRIEL. AUVERGNE. 1977. a. Kompass France, 66 quai du Marechal Joffre, 92415 Courbevoie Cedex, France. Ed. Bertrand Macabeo; Pub. Bertrand Macabeo. R&P contact: Bertrand Macabeo. adv. contact: Mireille Girault. **Document type:** directory.
Formerly (until 1982): Inventaire Regional Economique et Industriel de l'Auvergne (ISSN 0183-8040)

330   FR   ISSN 0295-7922
KOMPASS REGIONAL ECONOMIQUE ET INDUSTRIEL. BOURGOGNE. a. Kompass France, 66 quai du Marechal Joffre, 92415 Courbevoie Cedex, France. Ed. Bertrand Macabeo; Pub. Bertrand Macabeo. R&P contact: Bertrand Macabeo. adv. contact: Mireille Girault. **Document type:** directory.
Formerly (until 1982): Inventaire Regional Economique et Industriel. Bourgogne (ISSN 0245-1166)

330   FR   ISSN 0759-3929
KOMPASS REGIONAL ECONOMIQUE ET INDUSTRIEL. BRETAGNE. 1981. a. Kompass France, 66 quai du Marechal Joffre, 92415 Courbevoie Cedex, France. Ed. Bertrand Macabeo; Pub. Bertrand Macabeo. R&P contact: Bertrand Macabeo. adv. contact: Mireille Girault. **Document type:** directory.

330   FR   ISSN 0759-3910
KOMPASS REGIONAL ECONOMIQUE ET INDUSTRIEL. CENTRE. 1981. a. Kompass France, 66 quai du Marechal Joffre, 92415 Courbevoie Cedex, France. Ed. Bertrand Macabeo; Pub. Bertrand Macabeo. R&P contact: Bertrand Macabeo. adv. contact: Mireille Girault. **Document type:** directory.

330   FR   ISSN 0295-7930
KOMPASS REGIONAL ECONOMIQUE ET INDUSTRIEL. CHAMPAGNE - ARDENNES. 1977. a. Kompass France, 66 quai du Marechal Joffre, 92415 Courbevoie Cedex, France. Ed. Bertrand Macabeo; Pub. Bertrand Macabeo. R&P contact: Bertrand Macabeo. adv. contact: Mireille Girault. **Document type:** directory.
Formerly (until 1982): Inventaire Regional Economique et Industriel. Champagne - Ardennes (ISSN 0183-8059)

330   FR   ISSN 0295-7949
KOMPASS REGIONAL ECONOMIQUE ET INDUSTRIEL. FRANCHE-COMTE. 1979. a. Kompass France, 66 quai du Marechal Joffre, 92415 Courbevoie Cedex, France. Ed. Bertrand Macabeo; Pub. Bertrand Macabeo. R&P contact: Bertrand Macabeo. adv. contact: Mireille Girault. **Document type:** directory.
Formerly (until 1982): Inventaire Regional Economique et Industriel. Franche-Comte (ISSN 0245-1174)

330   FR   ISSN 0759-3813
KOMPASS REGIONAL ECONOMIQUE ET INDUSTRIEL. ILE-DE-FRANCE. a. Kompass France, 66 quai du Marechal Joffre, 92415 Courbevoie Cedex, France. Ed. Bertrand Macabeo; Pub. Bertrand Macabeo. R&P contact: Bertrand Macabeo. adv. contact: Mireille Girault. **Document type:** directory.
Formerly (until 1982): Inventaire Regional Economique et Industriel. Ile-de-France (ISSN 0759-3805); Which was formed by the merger of: Inventaire Regional Economique et Industriel de l'Ile-de-France. Petite Couronne de Paris (ISSN 0152-9684); Inventaire Regional Economique et Industriel de l'Ile-de-France. Grande Couronne de Paris (ISSN 0152-9676)

330   FR   ISSN 0295-7795
KOMPASS REGIONAL ECONOMIQUE ET INDUSTRIEL. LANGUEDOC - ROUSSILLON. 1982. a. Kompass France, 66 quai du Marechal Joffre, 92415 Courbevoie Cedex, France. Ed. Bertrand Macabeo; Pub. Bertrand Macabeo. R&P contact: Bertrand Macabeo. adv. contact: Mireille Girault. **Document type:** directory.

330   FR   ISSN 0759-4755
KOMPASS REGIONAL ECONOMIQUE ET INDUSTRIEL. LIMOUSIN, POITOU - CHARENTES. 1972. a. Kompass France, 66 quai du Marechal Joffre, 92415 Courbevoie Cedex, France. Ed. Bertrand Macabeo; Pub. Bertrand Macabeo. R&P contact: Bertrand Macabeo. adv. contact: Mireille Girault. **Document type:** directory.
Former titles (until 1981): Qui Vend Quoi? Qui Achete Quoi? Limousin, Poitou, Charentes (ISSN 0184-4024); (until 1977): Annuaire des Entreprises Regionales. Limousin, Poitou - Charentes (ISSN 0184-4032)

330   FR   ISSN 0295-7914
KOMPASS REGIONAL ECONOMIQUE ET INDUSTRIEL. LORRAINE. 1980. a. Kompass France, 66 quai du Marechal Joffre, 92415 Courbevoie Cedex, France. Ed. Bertrand Macabeo; Pub. Bertrand Macabeo. R&P contact: Bertrand Macabeo. adv. contact: Mireille Girault. **Document type:** directory.
Formerly (until 1982): Inventaire Regional Economique et Industriel. Lorraine (ISSN 0752-7187)

330   FR   ISSN 0295-7787
KOMPASS REGIONAL ECONOMIQUE ET INDUSTRIEL. MIDI-PYRENEES. 1982. a. Kompass France, 66 quai du Marechal Joffre, 92415 Courbevoie Cedex, France. Ed. Bertrand Macabeo; Pub. Bertrand Macabeo. R&P contact: Bertrand Macabeo. adv. contact: Mireille Girault. **Document type:** directory.

BUSINESS AND ECONOMICS

330   FR   ISSN 0295-7973
KOMPASS REGIONAL ECONOMIQUE ET INDUSTRIEL. NORD, PAS-DE-CALAIS. 1982. a. Kompass France, 66 quai du Marechal Joffre, 92415 Courbevoie Cedex, France. Ed. Bertrand Macabeo; Pub. Bertrand Macabeo. R&P contact: Bertrand Macabeo. adv. contact: Mireille Girault. **Document type:** directory.
    Formerly (until 1982): Inventaire Regional Economique et Industriel du Nord et du Pas-de-Calais (ISSN 0152-9692)

330   FR   ISSN 0752-9309
KOMPASS REGIONAL ECONOMIQUE ET INDUSTRIEL. NORMANDIE. 1980. a. Kompass France, 66 quai du Marechal Joffre, 92415 Courbevoie Cedex, France. Ed. Bertrand Macabeo; Pub. Bertrand Macabeo. R&P contact: Bertrand Macabeo. adv. contact: Mireille Girault. **Document type:** directory.
    Formerly (until 1982): Inventaire Regional Economique et Industriel. Normandie (ISSN 0752-7179)

330   FR   ISSN 0295-7906
KOMPASS REGIONAL ECONOMIQUE ET INDUSTRIEL. PAYS DE LA LOIRE. 1980. a. Kompass France, 66 quai du Marechal Joffre, 92415 Courbevoie Cedex, France. Ed. Bertrand Macabeo; Pub. Bertrand Macabeo. R&P contact: Bertrand Macabeo. adv. contact: Mireille Girault. **Document type:** directory.
    Formerly (until 1982): Inventaire Regional Economique et Industriel. Pays-de-la-Loire (ISSN 0752-7195)

330   FR   ISSN 0759-5506
KOMPASS REGIONAL ECONOMIQUE ET INDUSTRIEL. PICARDIE. 1979. a. Kompass France, 66 quai du Marechal Joffre, 92415 Courbevoie Cedex, France. Ed. Bertrand Macabeo; Pub. Bertrand Macabeo. R&P contact: Bertrand Macabeo. adv. contact: Mireille Girault. **Document type:** directory.
    Formerly (until 1982): Inventaire Regional Economique et Industriel. Picardie (ISSN 0245-1182)

330   FR   ISSN 0759-3686
KOMPASS REGIONAL ECONOMIQUE ET INDUSTRIEL. PROVENCE, ALPES, COTE-D'AZUR, CORSE. 1982. a. Kompass France, 66 quai du Marechal Joffre, 92415 Courbevoie Cedex, France. Ed. Bertrand Macabeo; Pub. Bertrand Macabeo. R&P contact: Bertrand Macabeo. adv. contact: Mireille Girault. **Document type:** directory.

330   FR   ISSN 0752-921X
KOMPASS REGIONAL ECONOMIQUE ET INDUSTRIEL. RHONE - ALPES. 1979. a. Kompass France, 66 quai du Marechal Joffre, 92415 Courbevoie Cedex, France. Ed. Bertrand Macabeo; Pub. Bertrand Macabeo. R&P contact: Bertrand Macabeo. adv. contact: Mireille Girault. **Document type:** directory.
    Formerly (until 1982): Inventaire Regional Economique et Industriel. Rhone - Alpes (ISSN 0752-9201); Which was formed by the merger of: Inventaire Regional Economique et Industriel. Alpes (ISSN 0240-4745); Inventaire Regional Economique et Industriel. Rhone - Loire.

332 338   FR
KOMPASS REGIONAUX. (In 19 volumes: Alsace; Aquitaine; Auvergne; Bourgogne; Bretagne; Centre; Champagne-Ardennes; Franche-Comte; Ile-de-France; Languedoc-Roussillon; Limousin; Poitou-Charentes; Lorraine; Midi-Pyrennes; Nord, Pas-de-Calais; Normandie; Pays de la Loire; Picardie; Provence, Alpes, Cote-d'Azur, Corse; Rhones-Alpes) (Text in French) 1976. a. price varies. Kompass France, 66 quai du Marechal Joffre, 92415 Courbevoie Cedex, France. Ed. Bertrand Macabeo; Pub. Bertrand Macabeo. R&P contact: Bertrand Macabeo. charts; stat. **Document type:** directory.
    Formerly: Inventaires Economiques et Industriels Regionaux.

330   GW   ISSN 0722-0227
KONJUNKTURINDIKATOREN. 1976. m. DM.58 (effective 1995). I F O Institut fuer Wirtschaftsforschung, Poschingerstr. 5, 81679 Munich, Germany. TEL 49-89-9224-0. FAX 49-89-985369. Ed.Bd. **Document type:** bulletin.

330   DK   ISSN 0109-3533
KONSULENTORDNINGEN; byerhvervenes og arbejdsmarkedets konsulenter og deres arbejdsopgaver ultimo. 1983. a. free. (Teknologistyrelsen) Dansk Teknologisk Instituts Forlag, Teknologiparken, DK-8000 Aarhus C, Denmark.

330 600   RU   ISSN 0868-6378
KONVERSIYA. (Text in Russian; summaries in English) 1990. m. 320000 Rub. (effective 1997). Informatsionno-analiticheskaya i Izdatel'skaya Firma (IZANA), Izmailovski Ostrov, 105037 Moscow E-37, Russia. TEL 7-095-1654827. FAX 7-095-1660818. E-mail: izana@aha.ru. Ed. Dmitri V. Birukov. adv.: page $2000. index. circ. 5,000. (back issues avail.)
—BLDSC (0091.945000).

330   CN   ISSN 0842-0580
KOOTENAY BUSINESS JOURNAL. 1988. m. $18 (foreign $20). Catalyst Communications Inc., 2F-601 Front St., Nelson, BC V1L 5P5, Canada. TEL 604-352-6397. FAX 604-352-2588. Ed. Jeff Shecter. circ. 6,500 (controlled).

330   KO
KOREA BUSINESS WORLD. (Text in English) 1985. m. Korea Businessworld Ltd., 4-F, Suhgun Bldg., 107-6 Banpo-dong, Seocho-ku, Seoul 137-040, S. Korea. TEL 02-5321464. FAX 02-5947663. Pub. Lee Kie-Hong. adv.: B&W page $3402, color page $5230; trim 205 x 275; adv. contact: Willard Chang-Suk Lee. circ. 40,200.
    Description: Covers business and economics in South Korea.

KOREA TRADE & BUSINESS. see *BUSINESS AND ECONOMICS — International Commerce*

330   KO
KOREAN BUSINESS REVIEW. (Text in English) 1978. m. free. Federation of Korean Industries, 28-1, FKI Bldg., Yoido-dong, Yong-deungpo-ku, Seoul, S. Korea. TEL 02-780-1801. FAX 02-782-2271. TELEX K 25544 FEKOIS. Ed. Cho Kyu-Hah. adv.: color page $2000 trim 185 x 255; adv. contact: Kawk Sung-Young. bk.rev. circ. 20,000. **Indexed:** Key to Econ.Sci.

330   KO   ISSN 0023-3978
KOREAN ECONOMIC JOURNAL/KYONGJE NONJIP. (Text in Korean) 1962. q. exchange basis. Seoul National University, Institute of Economic Research - Seoul Daehakkyo Kyeongje Yeonguso, San 56-1, Sinlim-dong, Kwanak-ku, Seoul 151-742, S. Korea. TEL 02-877-1629. FAX 02-888-4454. Ed. Sung-Hwi Lee. bk.rev.; abstr.; bibl.; index. circ. 500. **Indexed:** Asian-Pac.Econ.Lit. **Document type:** academic/scholarly publication.

KOTTKE NATIONAL END OF SEASON SURVEY. see *SPORTS AND GAMES — Outdoor Life*

338   NO   ISSN 0452-7208
KRISTOFER LEHMKUHL FORELESNING. 1958. a. free to conferees. Norges Handelshoeyskole - Norwegian School of Economics and Business Administration, Helleveien 30, N-5035 Bergen-Sandviken, Norway. TEL 47-55-95-92-16. FAX 47-55-959100. TELEX 40642-NHH-N. circ. 800. **Document type:** academic/scholarly publication.
    Description: Presents lecture on economics and business administration.

332.632210   DK   ISSN 0905-4472
KURSLISTE FOR DANSKE AKTIESELSKABER OG ANPARTSSELSKABER SAMT GROENLANDSKE SELSKABER. 1979. a. DKK 475. Skatteministeriet, Told og Skattestyrelsen, Oestbanegade 123, DK-2100 Copenhagen Oe, Denmark. TEL 45-35297300.
    Formerly (until 1989): Kursliste og Selskabsfortegnelse for Danske Aktieselskaber og Anpartsselskaber samt Fortegnelse over Groenlandske Selskaber, Foreninger og Filialer af Udenlandske Selskaber (ISSN 0902-0233); Which was formed by the 1985 merger of: Fortegnelse over Danske Aktieselskaber, Anpartsselskaber, Filialer af Udenlandske Selskaber samt over Foreninger (ISSN 0106-2085); Kursliste Verdroerende Aktier i Danske Aktieselskaber samt Anparter i Anpartsselskaber (ISSN 0902-0225)

330   RU
KUZBASS-INFORM. 1991. m. 0.20 Rub. per issue. Institut Ekonomiki, Kemerovskii Otdel, Pr. Sovetskii 63, kabinet 59, 650000 Kemerovo, Russia. TEL 25-25-77. circ. 5,000.

330   SA   ISSN 1016-6645
KWAZULU; review - commerce and industry. 1989. a. R.30 (effective 1996). Braby's (Subsidiary of: Kohler Packaging Ltd.), P.O. Box 1426, Pinetown 3600, South Africa. TEL 27-31-7017021. FAX 27-31-7017036.

330   JA   ISSN 0023-6055
HB9
KYOTO UNIVERSITY ECONOMIC REVIEW/KYOTO DAIGAKU KEIZAI GAKUBU KIYO. Variant title: Kyoto University. Faculty of Economics. Memoirs. (Text in English) 1926. s-a. Kyoto University, Faculty of Economics, c/o Economic Research Office, 606 Sakyo-ku, Kyoto, Japan. (Co-sponsor: Imperial University of Kyoto. Department of Economics) circ. 500. **Indexed:** Asian-Pac.Econ.Lit.
—UnCover.

330.9 332   CK
L A R F REPORT. ANNUAL. (Former publisher: Andean Reserve Fund) (Editions in English, Spanish) 1979. a. free. Latin American Reserve Fund, Apdo. Aereo 241523, Bogota, Colombia. TEL 2858511. FAX 2881117. TELEX 45586. charts; illus.; stat. circ. 1,200 (300 English ed.; 900 Spanish ed.).
    Formerly: A R F Report. Annual.
    Description: Covers annual economic summary of the international economy and of the five member countries of the LARF: Bolivia, Colombia, Ecuador, Peru and Venezuela.

LABTRADER MAGAZINE. see *SCIENCES: COMPREHENSIVE WORKS*

LAMY DROIT COMMERCIAL. see *LAW — Corporate Law*

LAMY DROIT ECONOMIQUE; concurrence, distribution, consommation. see *LAW*

LAMY PROTECTION SOCIALE; regime general de securite sociale - salaries, regimes des non-salaries, retraites complementaires, regimes de retraite d'entreprise, prevoyance, aide sociale et action sociale. see *LAW — Corporate Law*

LAMY SOCIAL; droit du travail et de la securite sociale. see *LAW*

330   GW
LANDESVERBANDER SCHAUSTELLER UND DER MARKKAUFLEUTE NIEDERSACHSEN - NORD UND BREMEN. MARKTBERICHT. m. Landesverbander Schausteller und der Markkaufleute Niedersachsen - Nord und Bremen, Ausser der Schleifmuhle 33, 28203 Bremen, Germany. TEL 0421-323870.

330   US   ISSN 1063-925X
LANE REPORT. 1985. m. $29 (effective 1997). Lane Communications Group, 269 W. Main St., Lexington, KY 40507. TEL 606-244-3522. FAX 606-244-3544. Ed. Kevin Depew; Pub. Ed Lane. R&P contact: Ed Lane. adv.: B&W page $1725, color page $1995; trim 8 1/2 x 10 7/8; adv. contact: David Shropshire. circ. 7,500. **Document type:** consumer publication.
    ●Also available online. Vendor(s): UMI.
    Description: Contains business and economic news for executives, managers, professionals and entrepreneurs in Kentucky.

330 370   UK   ISSN 0968-2023
LANGUAGE MATTERS. s-a. Associated Examining Board, Stag Hill House, Guildford, Surrey GU2 5XJ, England. TEL 44-1483-506506. FAX 44-1483-300152. Ed. George Turnbull. circ. 13,000. **Document type:** newsletter.

330   US   ISSN 1071-2186
LAS VEGAS BUSINESS PRESS. 1993. w. $68. Wick Communications, 3535 Wynn Rd., Las Vegas, NV 89102. TEL 702-871-6780. FAX 702-871-3470. Ed. Len Butcher; Pub. Bruce Spotleson. R&P contact: Len Butcher. adv. contact: Ben Falk. circ. 11,256. (also avail. in microform from UMI; microfilm from LIB)
    ●Also available online. Vendor(s): Lexis-Nexis, UMI.
—UMI.

BUSINESS AND ECONOMICS

LATEINAMERIKA (HAMBURG); Analysen - Daten - Dokumentation. see *POLITICAL SCIENCE — International Relations*

LATIN AMERICAN LAW AND BUSINESS REPORT. see *LAW — Corporate Law*

330 320   IT
LAVORO E SOCIETA; economia-cultura-politica-sociologia. (Text in Italian, Sardinian) 1980. w. L.30000. Viale Mameli, 9, I-07100 Sassari, Sardinia, Italy. adv.; bk.rev.; bibl.; charts; illus.; stat. circ. 12,500. (back issues avail.)

LAW AND POLICY IN INTERNATIONAL BUSINESS. see *LAW — International Law*

LAW FOR BUSINESS. see *LAW — Corporate Law*

LECTURE NOTES IN ECONOMICS AND MATHEMATICAL SYSTEMS; operations research, computer science, social science. see *MATHEMATICS*

338   DK   ISSN 0902-3704
HB9
LEDELSE OG ERHVERVSOEKONOMI. (Text in Danish, Norwegian, Swedish) 1955. q. DKK 350 (effective 1997). F D C - Danske Civiloekonomer - Association of Danish Business Economists, Soetorvet 5, P.O. Box 2043, DK-1012 Copenhagen K, Denmark. TEL 45-33-14-11-49. FAX 45-33-14-11-49. Ed. Kim Haagen Andersen. adv.; bk.rev.; bibl.; illus.; stat.; index. circ. 7,000. **Document type:** academic/scholarly publication.
    Former titles (until 1987): Erhvervsoekonomisk Tidsskrift (ISSN 0014-0147)

330   US   ISSN 1042-0134
LEFT BUSINESS OBSERVER. 1986. m. $22 to individuals; institutions $55. Doug Henwood, Ed. & Pub., 250 W. 85th St., No. 7J, New York, NY 10024-3217. TEL 212-874-4020. FAX 212-874-3137. E-mail: dhenwood@panix.com; URL: http://www.panix.com/~dhenwood/lbo_home.html. Ed. Doug Henwood; Pub. Doug Henwood. R&P contact: Doug Henwood. bk.rev.; circ. 3,000 (paid). **Indexed:** Alt.Press Ind. **Document type:** newsletter.
    Description: Covers economics and politics worldwide, with emphasis on the US.

LEGAL BUSINESS. see *LAW*

LEGAL CONNECTION: CORPORATIONS AND LAW FIRMS; a directory of publicly-held corporations and their law firms. see *LAW*

330 352   UK   ISSN 0967-716X
LEICESTER ECONOMIC REVIEW. 1993. q. free to qualified persons. Leicester City Council, Economic Services, Environment and Development, New Walk Centre, Welford Pl., Leicester LE1 6ZG, England. Ed. Mathe Diseko. **Document type:** bulletin, government publication.
  —BLDSC (5181.916600).
    Description: Reports on the activities of the Leicester City Council, Economic Services, and how they affect the local economy.

330   GW   ISSN 0930-4460
LERNFELD BETRIEB. 1986. bi-m. DM.72. Dr. Josef Raabe Verlags GmbH, Postfach 103922, 70034 Stuttgart, Germany. **Document type:** trade publication.

330   SA   ISSN 1016-6653
HC920.A1
LESOTHO; review - commerce, industry and tourism. 1979. a. R.30 (effective 1996). Braby's (Subsidiary of: Kohler Packaging Ltd.), P.O. Box 1426, Pinetown 3600, South Africa. TEL 27-31-7017021. FAX 27-31-7017036. adv.

330   IS
LETAASIYAN. 1987. m. Manufacturers Association of Israel, 29 Hamered St., Tel Aviv 68125, Israel. TEL 972-3-5128800. FAX 972-3-5103060. TELEX 342651. Ed. Eli Laniado. adv. circ. 4,000.

330   FR
LETTRE M M M. 1991. w. 3395 F. Club M M M, 26 rue Cadet, 75009 Paris, France. TEL 45-23-01-07. FAX 45-23-02-88. Ed. Edmund Ballerand. (looseleaf format; back issues avail.)
    Description: Looks at the global economy.

330   CC
LIAONING JINGJI/LIAONING ECONOMICS. (Text in Chinese) m. Liaoning Fazhan Yanjiu Zhongxin - Liaoning Development Research Center, Beiling Dajie, Shenyang, Liaoning 110032, People's Republic of China. Ed. Liu Mingliang.

330 658   LB
LIBERIAN ECONOMIC AND MANAGEMENT REVIEW.* (Text in English) 1972. s-a. $6. University of Liberia, College of Business and Public Administration, Economic and Management Research Institute, Monrovia, Liberia. adv.; bk.rev.; charts; stat.

330   US
LIFE-LONG BUSINESS SUCCESS. m. free. E-mail: epth@cannet.com. Ed. Paul LaForge. **Document type:** newsletter.
  ●Available only online.
    Description: Contains valuable principles, tips, and strategies for succeeding in every area of business.

330   FI   ISSN 0024-3469
HD58.5
LIIKETALOUDELLINEN AIKAKAUSKIRJA/FINNISH JOURNAL OF BUSINESS ECONOMICS. (Text in English, Finnish; summaries in English) 1952. q. FIM 150 (foreign FIM 200). Liiketaloudellinen Yhdistys - Helsinki School of Economics, Helsingin Kauppakorkeakoulu, Runeberginkatu 14-16, FIN-00100 Helsinki, Finland. TEL 358-0-43131. FAX 358-0-4313678. Ed. Eero Kasanen. adv. contact: Mika Kaskimies. bk.rev.; bibl.; index. circ. 1,800. (reprint service avail. from UMI) **Indexed:** IBR, J.of Econ.Lit., P.A.I.S., SSCI. **Document type:** academic/scholarly publication.
  —BLDSC (5215.700000).
    Description: Publishes research reports on economics and business administration.

330   CC   ISSN 1005-4286
LILUN JINGJIXUE. (Subseries of: Fuyin Baokan Ziliao) (Text in Chinese) m. $85.13. Zhongguo Renmin Daxue, Shubao Ziliao Zhongxin - China People's University, Book & Newspaper Information Center, 3 Zhang Zizhong Rd., P.O. Box 1122, Beijing 100007, People's Republic of China. TEL 86-10-4015080. (Dist. in US by: China Publications Service, Box 49614, Chicago, IL 60649. TEL 312-288-3291. FAX 312-288-8570) pp./issue: 112.
    Description: Covers Chinese and Western economic theories.

330   IT
LINEA CAPITAL. 6/yr. Rizzoli Editore-Corriere della Sera, Via A. Rizzoli 2, 20132 Milan, Italy. Ed. Paolo Panerai. circ. 21,694.

330   GW   ISSN 0937-0862
LIST FORUM FUER WIRTSCHAFTS- UND FINANZPOLITIK. q. DM.70. (List Gesellschaft e.V.) Nomos Verlagsgesellschaft mbH und Co. KG, Waldseestr. 3-5, 76530 Baden-Baden, Germany. TEL 49-7221-21040. FAX 49-7221-210427. (Subscr. to: Postfach 610, 76484 Baden-Baden, Germany) Ed. Hans Besters. **Indexed:** IBR. **Document type:** bulletin.
  —BLDSC (5231.375000).

330   US
LITTLE FREE PRESS;* food for thought since 1969. 1969-1992 (Apr.); resumed 1993 (Oct.)-1994 (July); resumed. s-m. free. Little Free Press, 730 3rd St. NE, Little Falls, MN 56345-2412. TEL 612-632-2813. URL: http://www.smart.net/~banneker. Ed. Ernest Mann. bk.rev. circ. 200. (reprint service avail.; back issues avail.) **Document type:** newsletter.
    Description: To help create total freedom for each individual on planet Earth and free access to its abundance.

330   UK   ISSN 0968-6444
LLOYDS BANK - S B R T QUARTERLY SMALL BUSINESS MANAGEMENT REPORT. 1993. q. £55. Open University, Small Business Research Trust, Business School, Walton Hall, Milton Keynes, Bucks. MK7 6AA, England. TEL 44-1908-655831. FAX 44-1908-655898. E-mail: oubs-sbrt@open.ac.uk; URL: http://www-iet.open.ac.uk/iet/sbrt/sbrt.htm. **Document type:** trade publication.

LLOYD'S LIST INTERNATIONAL. see *TRANSPORTATION — Ships And Shipping*

330   UK   ISSN 0269-0942
LOCAL ECONOMY. 1986. 4/yr. £40 (foreign £50) to individuals; institutions £102 (foreign £112) (effective 1997). (South Bank Polytechnic, Local Economy Policy Unit) Pitman Publishing, 128 Long Acre, London WC2E 9AN, England. TEL 44-171-447-2000. FAX 44-171-240-5771. (Subscr. to: Galleon Ltd., Fulham House, Goldsworth Rd., Woking, Surrey GU21 1LY, England. TEL 44-1483-747008) Ed. S. Aaronovitch. adv.; bk.rev. circ. 700. (also avail. in microfilm; microfiche; back issues avail.; reprint service avail. from UMI) **Indexed:** Stud.Wom.Abstr. **Document type:** academic/scholarly publication.
  —BLDSC (5290.011420); UMI. CCC.
    Description: Covers economic situations and conditions, as well as cooperatives, and other related fields of business and economics.
  Refereed Serial

LOGISTICS EUROPE. see *TRANSPORTATION*

330   GW   ISSN 0172-9047
LOHN UND GEHALT; Zeitschrift fuer die Personalverguetung. bi-m. DM.148. Datakontext Fachverlag GmbH, Augustinusstr. 9d, 50226 Frechen-Koenigsdorf, Germany. TEL 49-2234-96610-0. FAX 49-2234-966109. adv.: B&W page DM.2700, color page DM.4800; trim 246 x 188; adv. contact: Gabriele Bender. circ. 6,500. **Document type:** trade publication.
  —SWETS. CCC.

330   II
LOKPRABHA. (Text in Marathi) 1974. w. Express Towers, Nariman Point, Mumbai 400 021, India. TEL 91-22-202-2627. FAX 91-22-285-2108. Ed. Pradeep Varma. adv.; bk.rev. circ. 34,401.

338   CN   ISSN 0820-5698
LONDON BUSINESS MONTHLY MAGAZINE. 1975. m. Can.$18.19. Bowes Publishers Ltd., P.O. Box 7400 Sta. E, London, ON N5Y 4X3, Canada. TEL 519-472-7601. FAX 519-473-2256. Ed. Janine Foster. adv. circ. 12,000. **Document type:** consumer publication.
  Formerly (until 1987): Western Ontario Business (ISSN 0383-6193)
    Description: Business news in London and St. Thomas.

330   UK   ISSN 0954-4763
LONDON GUILDHALL UNIVERSITY. DEPARTMENT OF ECONOMICS. WORKING PAPER. irreg., no.30, 1994. London Guildhall University, Department of Economics, 117-119 Houndsditch, London EC3A 7BU, England. TEL 0171-320-1000. FAX 0171-320-1337. Ed. David Wilson. **Document type:** monographic series.

330   US
LONG BEACH BUSINESS JOURNAL. 1987. bi-w. $17.50 (bulk rate $55). South Coast Publishing, 2599 E. 28th St., No. 212, Long Beach, CA 90806-2139. TEL 562-988-1222. FAX 562-988-1239. URL: http://www.lbcnet.com/journal. Pub. George Economides. R&P contact: George Economides. circ. 340,000. **Document type:** newspaper.

330   US   ISSN 0896-4688
LONG ISLAND. 1987. 11/yr. $30. Long Island Association, 80 Hauppauge Rd., Commack, NY 11725. TEL 516-499-4400. Ed. Valerie Z. Scibilia. adv. contact: Joseph Shea. circ. 10,000.
    Description: Focuses on issues of interest to the Long Island business community--taxes, environment, housing, economic data, government relations, transportation, labor supply, interviews and profiles, advice, small business news, viewpoints, association news and a calendar of events.

330   US   ISSN 0894-4806
LONG ISLAND BUSINESS NEWS. 1953. w. $59 (effective 1997). Long Island Commercial Review, Inc., 2150 Smithtown Ave., Ronkonkoma, NY 11779-7327. TEL 516-737-1700. FAX 516-737-1890. E-mail: editor@libiznews.com; URL: http://www.libiznews.com. Ed. Paul B. Townsend. adv.: Tom/Masterson. bk.rev. circ. 10,500. (tabloid format) **Indexed:** Tr.& Indus.Ind. **Document type:** newspaper.
  ●Also available online. Vendor(s): Information Access Co.
  —CCC.
    Former titles: Long Island - Business (ISSN 0893-5734); (until 1979): L I Business Review (ISSN 0274-9157)

BUSINESS AND ECONOMICS

330   AT
LONG TERM FORECASTS (YEAR). a. Aus.$1100 (effective 1997). B I S Shrapnel Pty. Ltd., 8th Fl., 181 Miller St., N. Sydney, N.S.W. 2060, Australia. TEL 61-2-99595924. FAX 61-2-99595795. Ed. Frank Gelber. circ. 200.
Description: Examines the medium- to long-term prospects of the Australian economy.

LOSINKA. see *PUBLIC ADMINISTRATION — Municipal Government*

330   UK
LOUGHBOROUGH ECONOMIC RESEARCH PAPERS. irreg. free. Loughborough University, Department of Economics, Loughborough, Leics. LE11 3TU, England. TEL 44-1509-222729. FAX 44-1509-223910. Ed. Leigh Drake. circ. 93. (back issues avail.) **Document type:** academic/scholarly publication.
Formerly: Loughborough Occasional Papers in Economics.

LUXEMBOURG. SERVICE CENTRAL DE LA STATISTIQUE ET DES ETUDES ECONOMIQUES. STATISTIQUES HISTORIQUES. see *BUSINESS AND ECONOMICS — Abstracting, Bibliographies, Statistics*

330   LU
LUXEMBOURG BUSINESS. (Text in English, French) 1987. 10/yr. 2200 F.($105) (effective 1997). International City Magazines, 25 rue Philippe II, L-2340 Luxembourg, Luxembourg. TEL 352-46-11-22. FAX 352-47-00-56. E-mail: e-mail@business.lu. Ed. Simon Gray; Pub. Pol Wirtz. adv.: B&W page 36800 Fr., color page 55700 Fr.; 286 x 186; adv. contact: Michele Gosselin. bk.rev.; illus. circ. 5,200. pp./issue: 56. **Document type:** newspaper.

LUYOU JINGJI. see *TRAVEL AND TOURISM*

DAS M B A STUDIUM. (Masters in Business Administration) see *OCCUPATIONS AND CAREERS*

650   TR
M D C BUSINESS JOURNAL. 1976. s-a. free. Management Development Centre, Library, Salvatori Bldg., P.O. Box 1301, Port-of-Spain, Trinidad & Tobago, W.I. TEL 809-623-1961. FAX 809-623-2111. Ed. Ingrid Jordan. circ. 1,200.

330   US
M O D A REPORT.* q. $15. M.O. Dickerson Associates, Inc., 2125 Reed St., Philadelphia, PA 19146-4533.

330   UK   ISSN 0269-0365
M O D CONTRACTS BULLETIN. 1986. 25/yr. £130($225) (Ministry of Defence) Longman Group UK Ltd., Law, Tax and Finance Division, 21-27 Lamb's Conduit St., London WC1N 3NJ, England. TEL 0171-242-2548. FAX 0171-831-8119. Indexed: Intl.Polym.Sci.& Tech., RAPRA. **Document type:** government publication, bulletin.
—UMI. CCC.
Description: Details of major Ministry of Defence tenders and contracts.

330   UK   ISSN 0951-8053
M O D NEWS. 1987. m. £69($130) (Ministry of Defence) Longman Group UK Ltd., Law, Tax and Finance Division, 21-27 Lamb's Conduit St., London WC1N 3NJ, England. TEL 071-242-2548. FAX 071-831-8119. Ed. Michael Bentley. **Document type:** government publication.
—CCC.
Description: News service of important information concerning the Ministry of Defence, including its press releases and government reports.

330   US
▼**S R B MANUAL.** (Municipal Security Rulemaking Board) 1977. bi-m. $297. C C H Incorporated, 2700 Lake Cook Rd., Riverwoods, IL 60015. TEL 847-267-7000; 800-835-5224. FAX 800-224-8299.

330   NE   ISSN 0024-8673
MAANDSCHRIFT ECONOMIE; tijdschrift voor algemeen economische en sociaaleconomische vraagstukken. 1932. m. fl.130 to individuals (foreign fl.140); institutions fl.270 (effective 1996). (Stichting Maandschrift Economie) WoltersgroepGroningen b.v. (Subsidiary of: Wolters Kluwer N.V.), Postbus 58, 9700 MB Groningen, Netherlands. TEL 31-50-5226524. FAX 31-50-5264866. Ed. Pieter J.F. Meulendijks. adv.; bk.rev.; charts. circ. 1,700. Indexed: ELLIS, Excerp.Med., Key to Econ.Sci., World Bibl.Soc.Sec.
—SWETS.

330   US   ISSN 1082-5479
MCALLEN NEWS JOURNAL. 1954. w. $18 (out of state $22). Advance Publishing Company, 1101 N. Cage, Twin Palm Plaza, Ste. C1, Pharr, TX 78577. TEL 210-783-0036. Ed. Gregg Wendorf; Pub. Gregg Wendorf. adv.; circ. 2,000 (paid); 1,000 (controlled). **Document type:** trade publication.
Formerly (until Nov. 1994): South Texas Business Journal (ISSN 0746-8482)
Description: Covers business and general interests.

MACAO. DIRECCAO DOS SERVICOS DE ESTATISTICA E CENSOS. ESTIMATIVAS DO PRODUTO INTERNO BRUTO/MACAO. CENSUS AND STATISTICS DEPARTMENT. GROSS DOMESTIC PRODUCT ESTIMATES. see *BUSINESS AND ECONOMICS — Abstracting, Bibliographies, Statistics*

MACAO. DIRECCAO DOS SERVICOS DE ESTATISTICA E CENSOS. INQUERITO INDUSTRIAL/MACAO. CENSUS AND STATISTICS DEPARTMENT. INDUSTRIAL SURVEY. see *BUSINESS AND ECONOMICS — Abstracting, Bibliographies, Statistics*

330 650   MH
MACAU INDUSTRY. 1977. a. Macau Business Centre, Edificio Ribeiro, P.O. Box 138, Macao. stat.

MACOMB COUNTY LEGAL NEWS. see *LAW*

333.33 917   US   ISSN 0889-0838
MADDUX REPORT. 1984. m. $75. Maddux Publishing, Inc., Box 202, St. Petersburg, FL 33731. TEL 813-823-4394. FAX 813-821-1645. Ed. Carlen Maddux. adv. circ. 16,500. (back issues avail.)

330   IT
MADE IN; mensile di economia. 1991. m. L.180000. Bergamo 15 s.r.l., Via Broseta 65, 24128 Bergamo, Italy. TEL 39-35-251176. FAX 39-35-250159. Ed. Mario Zambetti. adv.: B&W page L.1430000, color page L.2145000. circ. 4,000. (also avail. in diskette format) **Document type:** consumer publication.

330   IT
MADE IN BERGAMO. 1986. q. L.40000. Bergamo 15 s.r.l., Via Boseta 65, 24128 Bergamo, Italy. TEL 39-35-251176. FAX 39-35-250159. Ed. Mario Zambetti. adv.: B&W page L.1430000, color page L.2145000. circ. 6,500. **Document type:** consumer publication.

AL-MAGALLAH AL-QANUNIYYAH AL-IQTISADIYYAH. see *LAW*

330   CN
MAGAZINE QUEBEC ENTREPRISE. 1992. 6/yr. Can.$20. 483 Marie Claire Daveluy Rd., Boisbriand, PQ J7G 3G9, Canada. TEL 514-433-9971. FAX 514-433-0434. Ed. Daniel Boisvert. adv.: B&W page Can.$2100, color page Can.$3000; trim 8 1/8 x 10 7/8. circ. 25,000.

382 330   ISSN 0865-8986
MAGYAR KIADAS - BUSINESS WEEK. (Text in Hungarian) 1990. bi-m. $1080 (foreign Ft. 2160). McGraw-Hill Companies, 1220 Ave. of the Americas, New York, NY 10020. TEL 212-512-3867. (Dist. by: Hirlapkiado Vallalat, Blaha Lujza ter 3, 1959 Budapest 8, Hungary) Eds. Forgacs Katalin, Gomori Endre. adv. circ. 8,000. **Document type:** trade publication.
Description: Comprehensive coverage of news and developments affecting the business world.

330   GW
MAINFRAENKISCHE WIRTSCHAFT. 1946. m. DM.30. Industrie- und Handelskammer Wuerzburg, Mainaustr. 33, 97082 Wuerzburg, Germany. TEL 0931-4194-0. FAX 0931-4194-100. **Document type:** bulletin.

330   MW
MALAWI DEVELOPMENT CORPORATION. ANNUAL REPORT. (Text in English) 1965. a. free. Malawi Development Corporation, P.O Box 566, Blantyre, Malawi. TEL 265-620100. FAX 265-620584-33. TELEX 44146. circ. 1,000. **Document type:** corporate report.
Description: Presents information of the accounts of the Malawi Development Corporation for the year.

MALAYSIA. DEPARTMENT OF STATISTICS. BALANCE OF PAYMENTS REPORT MALAYSIA. see *STATISTICS*

MALAYSIA. DEPARTMENT OF STATISTICS. MONTHLY CONSUMER PRICE INDEX FOR MALAYSIA. see *STATISTICS*

330   MY   ISSN 0126-5504
HC445.5.A1
MALAYSIAN BUSINESS. (Text in English) 1972. bi-m. M.$67.20($24.80) Berita Publishing, 22 Jalan Liku, 59100 Kuala Lumpur, Malaysia. TEL 03-282-4322. FAX 03-282-1605. Ed. Rejal Arbee. adv.: B&W page M.$4100, color page M.$5200; trim 210 x 280; adv. contact: Peter Thumby Rajah. bk.rev.; charts; illus. circ. 35,000. **Document type:** trade publication.
Description: Covers business, investments, market analysis and technology updates, as well as political events that have an impact on business.

MANAGED CARE MEDICINE. see *MEDICAL SCIENCES*

MANCHETE. see *LITERARY AND POLITICAL REVIEWS*

330   NE   ISSN 1383-6803
▼**MANSHOLT STUDIES.** (Text in English) 1995. irreg. price varies. (Landbouwuniversiteit Wageningen) Backhuys Publishers, P.O. Box 321, 2300 AH Leiden, Netherlands. TEL 31-71-5170208. FAX 31-71-5171856. E-mail: backhuys@euronet.nl; URL: http://www.euronet.nl/users/backhuys/. **Document type:** monographic series.
—BLDSC (9261.196745).
Formed by the merger of (1989-1995): Wageningen Economic Papers (ISSN 0924-106X); (1988-1995): Wageningen Ruimtelijke Studies (ISSN 0923-4373); (1988-1995): Wageningen Sociologische Studies (ISSN 0923-4365); Which was formerly (1982-1988): Landbouwuniversiteit Wageningen. Vakgroepen voor Sociologie. Mededelingen (ISSN 0923-4381)

330   II   ISSN 0025-2921
HC431
MARGIN. (Text in English) 1968. q. $80. National Council of Applied Economic Research, Parisila Bhawan, 11 Indraprastha Estate, New Delhi 110 002, India. TEL 91-11-3317860. FAX 91-11-3327164. E-mail: slv@ncaev.ernet.in. Ed. Shashanka Bhide. bk.rev. circ. 1,000. (reprint service avail.) Indexed: J.of Econ.Lit., Pub.Admin.Abstr., Rural Ext.Educ.& Tr.Abstr. **Document type:** academic/scholarly publication.
—BLDSC (5373.510000).
Description: Articles on the Indian economy.

MARINEFACTS; topical directory of marine information. see *SPORTS AND GAMES — Boats And Boating*

330   IT
MARK UP; economia, produzione e politiche della distribuzione. 1994. m. L.200000 (foreign L.400000) (effective 1996). Quasar Editoriale s.r.l., Via Santa Lucia 2, 20122 Milan, Italy. TEL 39-2-58301946. FAX 39-2-58303803. Ed. Luigi Rubinelli; Pub. Giuseppe Dilettoso. adv.: color page L.30000000; adv. contact: Rosy Battaglia. circ. 60,000 (paid). **Document type:** newspaper.
Description: For entrepreneurs and managers of production, marketing, retailing and service sectors. Offers features and articles on European and international scenarios, analysis of operating profits, descriptions of market share and key factors in mass market.

MARKET INSIGHT. see *SPORTS AND GAMES — Ball Games*

BUSINESS AND ECONOMICS

330 JA
MARKET SHARE IN JAPAN (YEAR). 1990. a. 100000 Yen($750) Yano Research Institute Ltd., Pola Ebisu Bldg., 3-9-19 Higashi, Shibuya-ku, Tokyo 150, Japan. TEL 03-54854618. FAX 03-54854681.
  Description: Identifies rankings of over 5,000 major companies, charts yearly growth rates of over 900 products, finds emerging trends, determines production, tracks competitors, finds new suppliers and customers.

MARKETING JAHRBUCH WEIN. see *BEVERAGES*

330 US ISSN 1054-2264
MARKETPLACE MAGAZINE. 1989. 13/yr. $48 (free to qualified personnel). A D D Inc., 211 N. Lynndale Dr., Ste. 8, Appleton, WI 54913-1897. TEL 414-735-5969. FAX 414-735-5970. Ed. Steve Prestegard; Pub. Al Wells. R&P contact: Steve Prestegard. adv. contact: Brian Rasmussen. circ. 16,000 (controlled). (also avail. in microform from UMI)
  ●Also available online. Vendor(s): UMI.
  —UMI.
  Description: Provides in-depth analysis of business news and trends in Northeast Wisconsin, and company profiles.
  Refereed Serial

330 MR ISSN 0851-5115
MAROC BUSINESS. 1975. q. DH.3 per issue. 1 Rond Point St. Exupery, Casablanca, Morocco. Ed. Taieb Jamai. adv.; charts; illus.; stat.

330 US ISSN 0747-0320
MARYLAND BUSINESS & LIVING.* 1978. m. $6. (Mid-Atlantic Business Journal, Inc.) Philos Publications Inc., c/o D.N. Kuryk, 5 Light St., Ste. 950, Baltimore, MD 21202. Ed. Joni Lesage. adv.; bk.rev. circ. 25,000. **Indexed:** Tr.& Indus.Ind.
  ●Also available online. Vendor(s): Knight-Ridder Information, Inc.
  Former titles (until 1984): Maryland Business and Living Journal (ISSN 0746-5629); (until 1983): Maryland Business Journal (ISSN 0191-6203)

650 330 US
MASSACHUSETTS BUSINESS AND ECONOMIC REPORT. 1974. q. free. University of Massachusetts, School of Management, Management Research Center, Rm. 202, Amherst, MA 01003. TEL 413-545-0111. Ed. Louis Wigdor. charts; stat. circ. 2,500. (reprint service avail. from ISI)

MASSACHUSETTS COLLECTIONS MANUAL. see *LAW*

330 510 US ISSN 0025-1127
HB135
MATEKON; translations of Russian and East European mathematical economics. 1964. q. $110 to individuals (foreign $160); institutions $510 (foreign $570) (effective 1997). M.E. Sharpe, Inc., 80 Business Park Dr., Armonk, NY 10504. TEL 914-273-1800; 800-541-6563. FAX 914-273-2106. Ed. John Litwack. adv.: page $300; trim 5 x 8; adv. contact: Barbara Ladd. (back issues avail.) **Indexed:** C.R.E.J., Compumath, Curr.Cont, J.of Econ.lit., SSCI. **Document type:** academic/scholarly publication.
  —BLDSC (5390.810000); Genuine Article; SWETS; UMI; UnCover. **CCC.**
  Formerly: Mathematical Studies in Economics and Statistics in the U S S R and Eastern Europe.
  Description: For international specialists in the fields of mathematical economics, programming, and applied control theory.Makes available in English the applied mathematics tradition of the former Soviet Union and Eastern Europe. The journal draws, in particular on the publications of TsEMI - the Central Mathematical Economics Institute in Moscow.
  Refereed Serial

330 IS ISSN 0333-7839
MAURICE FALK INSTITUTE FOR ECONOMIC RESEARCH IN ISRAEL. REPORT AND DISCUSSION PAPER SERIES. (Editions in English and Hebrew) 1964. irreg. free. Maurice Falk Institute for Economic Research in Israel, P. Naphtali Bldg., The Hebrew University, Mt. Scopus, 91905 Jerusalem, Israel. TEL 972-2-883130. FAX 972-2-816071. circ. 500.
  —BLDSC (3597.495000).
  Formerly: Maurice Falk Center for Economic Research in Israel. Report. (ISSN 0076-5473)

330 JA
MAZAL U'BRACHA. (Text in English, Hebrew) m. $136 (effective 1997). Miller Freeman, Inc., Silver Bldg., 7 Abba Hillel St., Ramat Gan 52133, Israel. TEL 972-3-5750196. FAX 972-3-5754829. Ed. Chain Even-Zohar. R&P contact: Chaim Even-Zohar. adv. contact: Anat Rapaport. **Document type:** trade publication.

330 US
MECKLENBURG TIMES. 1924. 2/w. $51 (effective 1997). Legal and Business Publishers, Inc., Box 36306, Charlotte, NC 28236. TEL 704-377-6221. Ed. Jill T. Purdy. adv. contact: June D. Powell. bk.rev. circ. 926. (tabloid format; also avail. in microform; back issues avail.) **Document type:** newspaper.

MEETING & CONFERENCE EXECUTIVES. see *MEETINGS AND CONGRESSES*

338.7 II ISSN 0376-5423
HC438.M4
MEGHALAYA INDUSTRIAL DEVELOPMENT CORPORATION. ANNUAL REPORT. Key Title: Annual Report - Meghalaya Industrial Development Corporation. (Text in English) 1972. a. Meghalaya Industrial Development Corporation, Additional Civil Secretariat Bldg., Shillong 1, India.

330 CC ISSN 1002-9605
MEITAN JINGJI YANJIU/COAL ECONOMICS STUDY. (Text in Chinese) 1981. m. Y4.50 (foreign $6) (effective 1997). Zhongguo Meitan Kexue Yanjiu Zongyuan, Jingji Yanjiusuo, Hepingli, Beijing 100013, People's Republic of China. TEL 86-10-6423-4338. FAX 86-10-6422-1627. Ed. Zhang Yunzhang. circ. 10,000.
  ●Also available on CD-ROM.
  Description: Covers studies on the multifarious economic problems of the coal industry, as well as related government policies and statues.

330 CY ISSN 1016-9520
MEMO; a fortnightly newsletter of economic news from the Middle East. (Text in English) 1974. fortn. $400. Middle East Economic Consultants, P.O. Box 4351, Limassol, Cyprus. TEL 357-5-377095. FAX 357-5-375099. TELEX 5060 MEMORAB CY. Ed. Mounir Makhlouf. adv.; bk.rev.; charts; index. circ. 2,000. **Indexed:** Curr.Cont.M.E., Per.Islam. (1991-). **Document type:** newsletter.
  Formerly: An-Nahar Arab Report and Memo; Which was formed by the merger of: M E M O: Middle East Money; An-Nahar Arab Report (ISSN 0003-2379)

330 GW ISSN 0176-5833
MEMO-FORUM; Zirkular der Arbeitsgruppe Alternative Wirtschaftspolitik. 1983. irreg., no.17, 1991. DM.4. Arbeitsgruppe Alternative Wirtschaftspolitik, Postfach 330447, 28209 Bremen, Germany. TEL 0421-3498621. FAX 0421-498087. Ed. Axel Troost. circ. 3,500. (back issues avail.) **Document type:** bulletin.

330 US ISSN 0747-167X
MEMPHIS BUSINESS JOURNAL. 1979. w. $45. Mid-South Communications, Inc., 88 Union, Ste. 102, Memphis, TN 38103-5195. TEL 901-523-1000. FAX 901-526-5240. Ed. Barney DuBois. adv.; bk.rev. circ. 13,000. (also avail. in microform from UMI) **Indexed:** Tr.& Indus.Ind. **Document type:** trade publication.
  ●Also available online. Vendor(s): Information Access Co., Knight-Ridder Information, Inc., Lexis-Nexis, UMI.
  —UMI. **CCC.**
  Formerly (until Mar. 1984): Mid-South Business (ISSN 0274-8525)

330 AG
EL MENHIR. 1991. irreg., no.4, Oct. 1993. free. Universidad de Buenos Aires, Colegio de Economica, Olleros 2016, 6to piso, 1426 Buenos Aires C.F., Argentina. TEL 54-1-772-1666. FAX 54-1-821-4540. Ed. Maximiliano Montenegro. adv.; bk.rev. circ. 5,000.
  Description: Includes interviews, articles on Argentine and world economy written by people who work in either private or governmental institutions.

330 340 IT
MENSILE EUROPEO DI ECONOMIA, FINANZA, FISCO E NORME C E E. m. Repertorio Commerciale s.r.l., Via Monte Rosa 51, 20149 Milan, Italy. TEL 02-548001936. FAX 02-48003226. adv.: color page L.5000000; trim 185 x 240. circ. 16,413.

330 IT
MERCATI FINANZIARI.* d. Milano Finanza Editori S.p.A., Via Burigozzo 3, 20122 Milan, Italy. TEL 2-80-291. FAX 2-80-52-832. Ed. Lionello Cadorin. circ. 30,000.

330 US ISSN 0742-602X
HD2746.5
MERGER AND ACQUISITION SOURCEBOOK (YEAR). a. $325 (effective 1995). Quality Services Company, 5290 Overpass Rd., Ste. 126, Santa Barbara, CA 93111-9950. TEL 805-964-7841. Ed. Walter Jurek.
  Description: In depth review of 3000 plus mergers and acquisitions in the U.S. and world markets. Includes legal and financial data.

330 US
HD2746.5
MERGER YEARBOOK. 1980. a. $550. (Securities Data Company, Inc.) Securities Data Publishing, 40 W. 57th St., 11th Fl., New York, NY 10019. TEL 212-765-5311. FAX 212-765-6123. Ed. Daniel Bokser. adv.; charts; stat.; index. (back issues avail.) **Document type:** trade publication.
  Formed by the 1992 merger of: Merger Yearbook; International Edition (ISSN 1052-9942); (1978-1992): Merger Yearbook; Domestic Edition (ISSN 1052-9934); Which was formerly (until 1989): Yearbook on Corporate Mergers, Joint Ventures and Corporate Policy (ISSN 0732-5320)
  Description: Listing of acquisition announcements by industry, indexed by corporate and individual targets.

332.6 US ISSN 0026-0010
HG4028.M4 CODEN: AMACDR
MERGERS & ACQUISITIONS. Variant title: Mergers and Acquisitions Journal. 1965. bi-m. $425 (foreign $500) (effective 1997). Investment Dealers' Digest, 2 World Trade Center, 18th Fl., New York, NY 10048. TEL 212-432-0845. FAX 212-321-2336. E-mail: subscribe@iddis.com. Ed. Martin Sikora. adv.: B&W page $3185, color page $4185; trim 8 1/2 x 11; adv. contact: Todd Miller. charts; index; circ. 3,000 (paid). (also avail. in microform from UMI; microfiche from CIS; back issues avail.; reprint service avail. from UMI) **Indexed:** ABI Inform., Account.Ind. (1974-), B.P.I, BPIA, Bus.Ind., C.L.I., L.R.I., Manage.Cont, P.A.I.S., PROMT, SRI, Tr.& Indus.Ind. **Document type:** trade publication.
  ●Also available online. Vendor(s): Information Access Co., UMI.
  —BLDSC (5680.770000); KR SourceOne; SWETS; UMI; UnCover. **CCC.**
  Formed by the merger of: Mergers and Acquisitions Quarterly; Mergers and Acquisitions Monthly (ISSN 0543-5137)
  Description: Provides in-depth coverage of merger techniques and strategies, corporate development, and data on US merger and acquisition activity. For financial executives and legal, accounting, and banking professionals.

330 US
MERGERS & ACQUISITIONS REPORT. w. $1175 (foreign $1275) (effective 1997). Investment Dealers' Digest, 2 World Trade Center, 18th Fl., New York, NY 10048-0638. TEL 212-432-0045. FAX 212-321-2336. Ed. Mark Kollar. R&P contact: Denise Robbins. adv. contact: Todd Miller. **Document type:** newsletter.
  ●Also available online. Vendor(s): Information Access Co., UMI.

330 US
HD2746.5
MERGERS AND RESTRUCTURINGS. 1977. w. (50/yr.) $995 (by fax $1898). (Securities Data Company, Inc.) Securities Data Publishing, 40 W. 57th St., 11th Fl., New York, NY 10019. TEL 212-765-5311. FAX 212-765-6123. Ed. Jud Cohen. bk.rev.; charts; stat. (also avail. by fax) **Document type:** trade publication.
  ●Also available online. Vendor(s): Information Access Co., NewsNet.
  —CCC.
  Former titles (until May 1996): Mergers and Corporate Policy (ISSN 0273-6357); (until June 1980): Mergers and Federal Policy.
  Description: Lists merger announcements by industry in each issue.

BUSINESS AND ECONOMICS

330   UK   ISSN 0026-1386
METROECONOMICA; international review of economics. (Text in English, French, German or Italian) 1949. 3/yr. £81($128) (foreign £81) (effective 1997). Blackwell Publishers Ltd., 108 Cowley Rd., Oxford OX4 1JF, England. TEL 44-1865-791100. FAX 44-1865-791347. E-mail: jnlinfo@blackwellpublishers.co.uk; URL: http://www.blackwellpublishers.co.uk. Ed. S. Parrinello. adv.; bk.rev.; bibl.; charts; index, cum.index every 10 yrs. circ. 1,800. (reprint service avail. from SCH) **Indexed:** C.R.E.J., Geo.Abstr., IBR, J.of Econ.Lit., Math.R., Rural Recreat.Tour.Abstr., World Agri.Econ.& Rural Sociol.Abstr., Zent.Math. **Document type:** academic/scholarly publication.
—BLDSC (5748.750000); SWETS; UMI; UnCover. **CCC.**
Refereed Serial

330   CN   ISSN 0829-2558
HC118.T6
METROPOLITAN TORONTO BUSINESS AND MARKET GUIDE. 1985. a. Can.$60 to non-members; members Can.$45 (effective 1997). Board of Trade of Metropolitan Toronto, P.O. Box 60, 1 First Canadian Place, Toronto, ON M5X 1C1, Canada. TEL 416-366-6811. Ed. Mary de Reus. circ. 3,000. **Document type:** corporate report.
Description: Statistical, economic and demographic overview of the business community and marketplace in Toronto. Includes guide to establishing a business in Toronto.

330   IT
METROQUADRO. 1991. bi-m. L.20000 (foreign L.40000). Edizioni Living International, Via A.G. Bragaglia 33, 00123 Rome, Italy. TEL 39-6-30889282. FAX 39-6-30889944. Ed. Enrico Morelli. R&P contact: Giulia Trappani. adv.: B&W page L.8000000; adv. contact: Anna Maria Morelli.

330   MX
MEXICAN FORECAST; fortnightly forecast for management and investors on Mexican business and investment trends. (Text in English) 1992. s-m. $595 (effective 1997). Grupo Editorial Expansion, Salamanca No. 149, Col. Roma, 06700 Mexico D.F., Mexico. FAX 525-2072066. FAX 525-5116351. Ed. Lindajoy Fenley; Pub. David Estrello. R&P contact: David Estrello. adv. contact: Maria Elena Bayardo. **Document type:** newsletter.

MEZHDUNARODNI OTNOSHENIYA. see *HISTORY — History Of Europe*

330   US
MICHIGAN JOURNAL OF ECONOMICS. 1982. a. $3. University of Michigan, Economics Department, Lorch Hall, University of Michigan, Ann Arbor, MI 48109. TEL 810-763-8063. Ed. R. David Reading. bk.rev. circ. 150. (back issues avail.) **Document type:** academic/scholarly publication.

330   US   ISSN 0895-1772
HD28
MID-AMERICAN JOURNAL OF BUSINESS. 1986. s-a. $12 (foreign $17) (effective 1996 & 1997). Ball State University, Bureau of Business Research, Muncie, IN 47306. TEL 317-285-5926. FAX 317-285-8024. E-mail: jlane@wp.bsu.edu; URL: http://www.bbr.bsu.edu/majb. (Articles to: W. Rocky Newman, Ed., c/o Dept. of Management, Miami University, Oxford, OH 45056) Ed. Judy Lane. R&P contact: Judy Lane. adv. contact: Judy Lane. bk.rev.; charts; stat. circ. 3,000. (also avail. in microform from UMI; back issues avail.) **Indexed:** Bus.Educ.Ind., P.A.I.S. **Document type:** academic/scholarly publication.
●Also available online. Vendor(s): UMI.
—BLDSC (5761.313430).
Formed by the merger of (1971-1985): Ball State Business Review; (1929-1982): Ball State Journal for Business Educators; Which was formerly (until 1965): Ball State Commerce Journal.
Description: Publishes general business articles intended for business professionals - executives, consultants, and teachers.
Refereed Serial

650   US   ISSN 0732-9334
HF5001
MID-ATLANTIC JOURNAL OF BUSINESS. 1962. 3/yr. $40 to individuals (foreign $45); institutions $50 (foreign $75) (effective 1997). Seton Hall University, W. Paul Stillman School of Business, Division of Business Research, c/o Mary L. Williams, South Orange, NJ 07079-2692. TEL 201-761-9210. FAX 201-761-9217. URL: http://www.shu.edu/majb. Ed. A.D. Amar. bk.rev. circ. 1,000. (also avail. in microfilm from UMI; reprint service avail. from UMI) **Indexed:** ABI Inform, Account.Ind. (1974-), BPIA, Bus.Ind., Manage.Cont., PROMT, Tr.& Indus.Ind. **Document type:** academic/scholarly publication.
—BLDSC (5761.313940); UMI; UnCover. **CCC.**
Formerly (until vol.19, 1980): Journal of Business (South Orange) (ISSN 0021-9401)

THE MIDDLE EAST. see *LITERARY AND POLITICAL REVIEWS*

330 320   LE
MIDDLE EAST OBSERVER. (Text in Arabic) 1970. q. Dar Assayad S.A.L., P.O. Box 1038, Hazmieh, Beirut, Lebanon. FAX 961-1-456373. TELEX 44224 SAYAD LE. (U.K. addr.: c/o Contact PR & Mgt. (UK) Ltd., 3 Park Place, 12 Lawn Ln., London SW8, England. TEL 44-71-582-2220) adv. contact: Salim Zreik.

330   US
MIDDLESEX MAGAZINE. 1989. m. $20 (effective 1994). Chronicle Communications, 615 Main St., Cromwell, CT 06416. TEL 209-635-1819. FAX 203-632-7203. Ed. Ron Nolan; Pub. Ron Nolan. R&P contact: Ron Nolan. adv. contact: Ron Nolan. bk.rev. circ. 12,000. (also avail. in microform from UMI)
●Also available online. Vendor(s): UMI.
Formerly (until 1995): Middlesex Business Review.

330   US   ISSN 0194-4525
MIDLANDS BUSINESS JOURNAL;* published for the nation's industrial and agri-business heartland. 1975. w. $30. M B J Corporation, Box 24245, Omaha, NE 68124-0245. TEL 402-330-1760. Ed. Robert G. Haig.

MIDWEST LAW REVIEW. see *LAW*

MIND MATTERS REVIEW. see *PSYCHOLOGY*

330   US   ISSN 0883-3044
MINNEAPOLIS - ST. PAUL CITYBUSINESS; the business journal. 1983. w. $64. American City Business Journals, Inc. (Austin), 505 Powell St., Austin, TX 78703-5121. (Subscr. to: 527 Marquette Ave., Ste. 300, Minneapolis, MN 55402) Ed. Kevin Maler; Pub. Stuart Chamblin III. adv.: B&W page $3275; adv. contact: David Jost. bk.rev.; circ. 11,600 (paid); 6,000 (controlled). (tabloid format; also avail. in microfiche from UMI) **Document type:** consumer publication.
●Also available online. Vendor(s): CompuServe, Inc., Data-Star, Dow Jones News Retrieval, Knight-Ridder Information, Inc., Lexis-Nexis.
—UMI. **CCC.**
Formerly: CityBusiness - Twin Cities.
Description: Constains breaking business news for the Twin Cities area, smallbusiness information, and more.

330   US   ISSN 1050-3463
MINORITIES IN BUSINESS INSIDER. 1987. s-m. $322. (Community Development Services, Inc.) C D Publications, 8204 Fenton St., Silver Spring, MD 20910. TEL 301-588-6380. FAX 301-588-6385. Ed. Mark Brinker. R&P contact: Mike Gerecht. index. **Document type:** newsletter.
Description: Reports on affirmative action, minority employment, government contracts and education.

MINORITY M B A. see *OCCUPATIONS AND CAREERS*

330 327   RU   ISSN 0026-5829
HC10
MIROVAYA EKONOMIKA I MEZHDUNARODNYE OTNOSHENIYA. (Text in Russian; contents page in English) 1957. m. 6000 Rub. per issue (effective Apr. 1997). Rossiiskaya Akademiya Nauk, Institut Mirovoi Ekonomiki i Mezhdunarodnykh Otnoshenii, Profsoyuznaya ul., 23, 117418 Moscow, Russia. TEL 7-095-1280883. E-mail: imemoran@glas.apc.org. (Dist. by: Mezhdunarodnaya Kniga, ul. B. Yakimanka 39, 117049 Moscow, Russia; Dist. in U.S. by: Victor Kamkin Inc., 4956 Boiling Brook Pkwy, Rockville, MD 20852. TEL 301-881-5973) Ed. G.G. Deligenskii. bk.rev.; bibl.; charts; stat.; index. circ. 4,200. **Indexed:** Amer.Hist.& Life (1957-1961), (1973-), Curr.Dig.Sov.Press, Hist.Abstr. (1957-1961), (1973-), Int.Polit.Sci.Abstr., Rural Recreat.Tour.Abstr., World Agri.Econ.& Rural Sociol.Abstr. **Document type:** academic/scholarly publication.
—KNAW.

330   JA   ISSN 0026-6760
HB9
MITA GAKKAI ZASSHI/MITA JOURNAL OF ECONOMICS. (Text in Japanese) 1909. q. 8000 Yen($66.70) Keio Gijuku Daigaku, Keio Keizai Gakkai - Keio University, Keio Economic Society, 2-15-45 Mita, Minato-ku, Tokyo 108, Japan. TEL 81-3-3453-4511. FAX 81-3-3798-7480. (Dist. by: Japan Publications Trading Co., Box 5030, Tokyo International, Tokyo 100-31, Japan) Ed. Tamon Yamada. R&P contact: Kunio Kawamata. adv. contact: Kunio Kawamata. bk.rev.; abstr.; charts. **Indexed:** Amer.Hist.& Life (1966-1973), Hist.Abstr. (1966-1973). **Document type:** academic/scholarly publication.

MODERN TRUCKSTOP NEWS. see *TRANSPORTATION — Trucks And Trucking*

330   MX
MOMENTO ECONOMICO; informacion y analisis de la coyuntura mexicana. m. Mex.$2.70($15) Universidad Nacional Autonoma de Mexico, Instituto de Investigaciones Economicas, Torre 11 de Humanidades 1er Piso, Apdo. Postal 20-721, 04510 Mexico, D.F., Mexico. TEL 550-52-15. **Indexed:** Hisp.Amer.Per.Ind.
Description: Examines the economy and politics of Mexico, specifically, but not exclusively.

330   US
MONETARY AND ECONOMIC REVIEW. 1985. m. $150. F A M C Inc., 3500 J F K Pkwy., Fort Collins, CO 80525. TEL 970-223-4962. FAX 970-223-4996. Ed. Larry Bates. R&P contact: Sherry Shackleford. TEL 901-761-0115. adv. contact: Sherry Shackleford. bk.rev.; cum.index: 1985-1997; circ. 5,000 (paid). (back issues avail.) **Document type:** newsletter.
Description: Reviews the political, governmental and central bank actions as to how they affect the economy and certain investments.
Refereed Serial

330   US   ISSN 0272-9970
HC101
MONEY (BOCA RATON). (Subseries of: S I R S Social Issues (ISSN 0740-3127)) 1977. a. price varies; a. supplement $19. Social Issues Resources Series, Box 2348, Boca Raton, FL 33427-2348. TEL 561-994-0079; 800-232-SIRS. FAX 561-994-4704. E-mail: custserve@sirs.com; URL: http://www.sirs.com. Ed. Trudy Collins; Pub. Eleanor Goldstein. R&P contact: Bonnie Milnes. (looseleaf format; back issues avail.) **Indexed:** B.P.I., R.G.Abstr. **Document type:** academic/scholarly publication.
Description: Reprints articles that explore the sociological aspects of money.

330   AU   ISSN 1420-4576
MONEY TREND. (Text in German) 1968. 11/yr. S.550. Money Trend Verlag GmbH, Fuerstenberggasse 4, A-3002 Purkersdorf, Austria. TEL 43-1-9792385. FAX 43-1-9792894. Ed. Gerd-Volker Weege. R&P contact: Zuzanna Stauffer. adv.: B&W page $1000, color page $1700; trim 189 x 265; adv. contact: Zuzanna Stauffer. circ. 10,979. **Document type:** consumer publication.

330   FR   ISSN 0750-3598
MONITEUR DU COMMERCE ET DE L'INDUSTRIE. 1901. 24/yr. 13 rue d'Uzes, 75002 Paris, France. TEL 45-08-95-94. FAX 42-33-78-83. adv. circ. 20,000.

BUSINESS AND ECONOMICS

330　　　　　MY
MONOGRAPH SERIES ON MALAYSIAN ECONOMIC AFFAIRS. 1971. irreg., no.6, 1987. price varies. University of Malaya, Faculty of Economics & Administration, Lembah Pantai, 59100 Kuala Lumpur, Malaysia. TEL 755-4111. FAX 756-7252. bibl. circ. 1,000. **Document type:** monographic series.

650　　　　　US　　ISSN 0026-9921
HC107.M9　　　CODEN: MBQUA9
MONTANA BUSINESS QUARTERLY. Abbreviated title: M B Q. 1962. q. $25. University of Montana, Bureau of Business and Economic Research, Missoula, MT 59812. TEL 406-243-5113. FAX 406-243-2086. (Co-sponsor: University of Montana, School of Business Administration) Ed. Marlene Nesary. index. circ. 1,700. (also avail. in microfilm from UMI; back issues avail.) **Indexed:** ABI Inform, BPIA, Bus.Ind., P.A.I.S., Tr.& Indus.Ind. **Document type:** academic/scholarly publication.
●Also available online. Vendor(s): Information Access Co., UMI.
—BLDSC (5928.005400); UMI; UnCover.

330　　　　　CN　　ISSN 0835-7692
MONTREAL BUSINESS MAGAZINE. 1988. 6/yr. 275 St. Jacques St. W., Ste. 43, Montreal, PQ H2Y 1M9, Canada. TEL 514-286-8038. FAX 514-287-7346. Ed. Michael Carin. R&P contact: Mark Weller. adv.; bk.rev.; circ. 16,500. circ. 16,500 (controlled). **Document type:** trade publication.
Description: Includes commentaries on wealth management, industry sector reports, corporate profiles, professional advice in law, accounting, and management.

330 320　　　IT
MOSCA NEWS. 1989. m. Arnoldo Mondadori Editore S.p.A., Segrate (Milan), Italy. Ed. Stefano Troncini.

052 330　　　RU　　ISSN 0868-8400
MOSCOW MAGAZINE. (Editions in English, Russian) 1990. m. $54 (Europe $89; N. America $112). Dom Zhurnalista, Komn. 303, Suvorovsky Blvd. 8A, 121019 Moscow, Russia. TEL 203-3644. FAX 291-1787. (Subscr. outside U.S.S.R. to: P.O. Box 6805, 2001 JH Haarlem, Netherlands) adv./ bk.rev.; illus. circ. 60,000. (back issues avail.)
Description: Covers developments affecting the Soviet economy, including privatization, political and legislative changes; also provides information on business and cultural life in Moscow for foreign residents and visitors, with listings of restaurants and services.

330　　　　　RU　　ISSN 0130-0105
HB97.5
MOSKOVSKII UNIVERSITET. VESTNIK. SERIYA 7: EKONOMIKA. 1966. bi-m. $51 (effective 1998). Moskovskii Universitet, Ul. Gertsena 5-7, 103009 Moscow, Russia. (Dist. by: Mezhdunarodnaya Kniga, ul. Dimitrova 39, Moscow G-200, Russia) bk.rev.; bibl.; index. circ. 2,150.
Supersedes in part: Moskovskii Universitet. Vestnik. Seriya Ekonomika, Filosofiya (ISSN 0027-1365)

330　　　　　UK　　ISSN 0953-7929
MULTINATIONAL EMPLOYER. 1984. 11/yr. £175($290) (effective 1997). P.O. Box 149, Farnham, Surrey GU9 8YH, England. TEL 44-1252-726416. FAX 44-1252-713730. Ed. Beatrice Falzone; Pub. Sally Simone. R&P contact: Beatrice Falzone. bk.rev. **Document type:** bulletin.
Formerly (until 1988): Corporate Expatriate (ISSN 0267-2324)
Refereed Serial

330　　　　　CK　　ISSN 0121-6546
MUNDO Y MERCADO LATINO. 1993. bi-m. Latin Press Inc., Apdo. Postal 67252, Medellin, Colombia. TEL 57-4-284-5232. adv.; B&W page $2250, color page $3000. circ. 10,017.

330.1025　　　AT
MURRAY BRIDGE BUSINESS & COMMUNITY SERVICES GUIDE. 1990. a. free. Murray Bridge Information Centre, 3 South Tce, Murray Bridge, S.A. 5253, Australia. TEL 61-85-322900. FAX 61-85-322766. Ed. Beryl Price. R&P contact: Theresa Geister. TEL 61-85-323094. adv. **Document type:** consumer publication, directory.
Description: Provides community information and business listings.

330　　　　　BE
MUSEE ROYAL DE L'AFRIQUE CENTRALE. DOCUMENTATION ECONOMIQUE/KONINKLIJK MUSEUM VOOR MIDDEN-AFRIKA. ECONOMISCHE DOCUMENTATIE. (Text mainly in French, occasionally in Dutch) 1961. irreg., no.9, 1995. price varies. Musee Royal de l'Afrique Centrale - Koninklijk Museum voor Midden-Afrika, 13 Steenweg op Leuven, B-3080 Tervuren, Belgium. TEL 32-2-7695299. FAX 32-2-7670242. **Document type:** monographic series.

330　　　　　FR　　ISSN 0985-2433
MUTATIONS. 1987. a. free. Novespace, 15 rue des Halles, 75001 Paris, France. TEL 42-33-41-41. FAX 40-26-08-60. Ed. Jean-Pierre Fouquet. circ. 20,000. **Document type:** catalog.

330　　　　　PH
MYANMAR BUSINESS. (Text in English) m. $295. Options Publishing Services, 10 Garcia Villa St., San Lorenzo Village, Makati City, Metro Manila, Philippines. TEL 63-2-818-3289. FAX 63-2-819-3752. E-mail: opsi@mni.sequel.net. Pub. Melva C. Nath. **Document type:** newsletter.
Description: Focuses on how to trade and invest and make business connections in Myanmar.

330 320　　　SI　　ISSN 0218-8708
▼**MYANVIEW.** (Text in English) 1995. q. S.$180($130) Institute of Southeast Asian Studies, Heng Mui Keng Terrace, Pasir Panjang, Singapore 119596, Singapore. TEL 65-778-0955. FAX 65-775-6259. E-mail: khairani@merlion.iseas. ac.sg; URL: http://merlion.iseas.ac.sg/pub.html. Ed. Triena Ong. **Document type:** academic/scholarly publication.
Description: Reviews economic and political trends in Myanmar.

N A B T E REVIEW. (National Association for Business Teacher Education) see EDUCATION — Higher Education

N C STATE ECONOMIST. see AGRICULTURE — Agricultural Economics

330　　　　　UK
N E R A TOPICS. 1989. irreg. free. National Economic Research Associates, 15 Stratford Pl., London W1N 9AF, England. TEL 44-171-629-6787. FAX 44-171-495-3216. E-mail: annie_cleghorn@ nera.co.uk. Ed. Dermot Glynn. R&P contact: Annie Cleghorn. **Document type:** monographic series.

N I S E R OCCASIONAL PAPERS. (Nigerian Institute of Social and Economic Research) see SOCIAL SCIENCES: COMPREHENSIVE WORKS

330　　　　　US
N S A C I NEWS. m. North West Suburban Association of Commerce and Industry, 1450 E. American Ln., No. 140, Schaumberg, IL 60173. TEL 708-517-7110. FAX 708-517-7116. Ed. Janet Hart. circ. 1,600.

330　　　　　SI　　ISSN 0218-3269
N U S ECONOMIC JOURNAL. (Text in English) 1962. a. $5. National University of Singapore, Economics and Statistics Society, Kent Ridge Campus, Clementi Rd., Singapore 0511, Singapore. Ed. Chew Wei Min. adv. circ. 10,000.
—UnCover.
Formerly (until 1990): National University of Singapore. Economics and Statistics Society. Annual Journal - Suara Ekonomi (ISSN 0585-8127)
Description: Contains honor students' academic exercises, interviews with academicians & ministers, special speeches. Also discusses current economic and business issues.

330　　　　　SA
NAMIBIA; review - commerce, industry and tourism. 1987. a. R.30 (effective 1996). Braby's (Subsidiary of: Kohler Packaging Ltd.), P.O. Box 1426, Pinetown 3600, South Africa. TEL 27-31-7017021. FAX 27-31-7017036. adv.
Formerly: S W A - Namibia Review (ISSN 1016-3875)

330　　　　　CC　　ISSN 1001-4691
HB9
NANKAI JINGJI YANJIU/NANKAI ECONOMIC STUDIES. (Text in Chinese) 1985. bi-m. $30. Nankai Daxue, Jingji Xueyuan - Nankai University, College of Economics, 94 Weijin Road, Tianjin 300071, People's Republic of China. TEL 86-22-3342161. FAX 86-22-3344853. Ed. Yue Zhang. circ. 2,000. **Document type:** monographic series.

330　　　　　JA　　ISSN 0912-6139
NANZAN KEIZAI KENKYU/NANZAN JOURNAL OF ECONOMIC STUDIES. (Text in Japanese) 1961. 3/yr. free. Nanzan University, Society of Economics, 18 Yamazato-cho, Showa-ku, Nagoya 466, Japan. TEL 052-832-3111. FAX 052-835-1444. **Document type:** academic/scholarly publication.
—BLDSC (6015.343830).
Supersedes in part (in 1986): Akademia. Keizai Keieigaku Hen (ISSN 0389-844X); Which superseded in part (in 1975): Akademia (ISSN 0515-8680)

330　　　　　BU　　ISSN 0323-9004
NARODNOSTOPANSKI ARKHIV/ARCHIVES OF NATIONAL ECONOMY. (Text in Bulgarian; summaries in English, Russian) 1946. q. 4 lv.($7) Vissh Finansovo-Stopanski Institut, 5250 Svishtov, Bulgaria. (Dist. by: Hemus, 6, Rouski Blvd., 1000 Sofia, Bulgaria) Ed. Svetlozar Kaltchev. adv. contact: Svetlozar Kaltchev. bk.rev. circ. 1,700. **Indexed:** BSL Econ. **Document type:** academic/scholarly publication.

330　　　　　XV　　ISSN 0547-3101
NASE GOSPODARSTVO/OUR ECONOMY: REVIEW OF CURRENT PROBLEMS IN ECONOMICS. (Text in Slovenian; summaries in English) 1955. bi-m. $30. Ekonomsko-Poslovna Fakulteta, Razlagova 14, Maribor, Slovenia. (Co-sponsor: Ekonomski Center Maribor) Ed. Davor Savin. adv.; bk.rev.; charts; stat. circ. 8,000.

330　　　　　US　　ISSN 0889-2873
NASHVILLE BUSINESS JOURNAL. 1985. w. $45. Mid-South Communications, Box 23229, Nashville, TN 37202. TEL 615-248-2222. FAX 615-248-6246. E-mail: nbj@nc5.infi.net. Ed. Bill Lewis; Pub. Kevin Lorance. adv. contact: Steven Byars. circ. 10,000 (paid). (also avail. in microform from UMI) **Document type:** newspaper.
●Also available online. Vendor(s): Lexis-Nexis, UMI.
—UMI. CCC.
Description: Regional business magazine.

330 330.9　　　EI　　ISSN 0256-7601
NATIONAL ACCOUNTS E S A - AGGREGATES (YEARS). (Text in English) 1977. a. $20. Office for Official Publications of the European Communities, Rue Alcide de Gasperi, 2920 Luxembourg, Luxembourg. (Dist. in the U.S. by: Unipub, 4611-F Assembly Dr., Lanham, MD 20706-4391. TEL 800-274-4888. FAX 301-459-0056) Ed.Bd. circ. 4,100. (also avail. in microfiche from CIS) **Indexed:** IIS.
—BLDSC (6015.775000).
Formerly: Statistical Office of the European Communities. Comparison in Real Terms of E S A Aggregates.

330.72　　　US　　ISSN 0898-2937
HB1
NATIONAL BUREAU OF ECONOMIC RESEARCH. WORKING PAPER. irreg., approx. 450/yr. $870 to academic institutions (foreign $1260); corporations $1650 (foreign $2000). National Bureau of Economic Research, 1050 Massachusetts Ave., Cambridge, MA 02138. TEL 617-868-3900. R&P contact: Mar Fitz-Patrick. **Document type:** monographic series.
—BLDSC (6067.719500).
Description: Papers on economic issues ranging from corporate finance, industrial organization and taxation to monetary economics, international finance and macroeconomics.

330　　　　　AT　　ISSN 1036-4145
NATIONAL BUSINESS BULLETIN. 1991. m. Aus.$60. National Business Magazines, 361 Riley St., Surry Hills, N.S.W. 2010, Australia. TEL 61-2-2125588. FAX 61-2-2122709. E-mail: nbb@hutch.com.au. Ed. Doug Nettleship. adv.; B&W page Aus.$3650, color page Aus.$4950; trim 275 x 210; adv. contact: Stephen Cottier. circ. 41,989 (controlled). (back issues avail.)
Description: Written by chief executives for chief executives of top 500 companies in Australia.

NATIONAL DIRECTORY OF CORPORATE PUBLIC AFFAIRS. see BUSINESS AND ECONOMICS — Trade And Industrial Directories

330   UK   ISSN 0027-9501
HC10   CODEN: NIERAY
NATIONAL INSTITUTE ECONOMIC REVIEW. 1959. q. £90. National Institute of Economic and Social Research, 2 Dean Trench St., Smith Sq., London SW1P 3HE, England. TEL 44-171-222-7665. FAX 44-171-222-1435. charts; stat. circ. 2,000. (also avail. in microfiche) Indexed: ABI Inform., B.P.I., BPIA, Bus.Ind., C.R.E.J., Cont.Pg.Manage., ELLIS, Geo.Abstr., Int.Lab.Doc., J.of Econ.Lit., Mgmt.& Market.Abstr., P.A.I.S., PROMT, Rural Recreat.Tour.Abstr., Tr.& Indus.Ind., World Agri.Econ.& Rural Sociol.Abstr., World Bibl.Soc.Sec. **Document type:** academic/scholarly publication.
• Also available online. Vendor(s): Information Access Co., UMI.
— BLDSC (6025.580000); KR SourceOne; SWETS; UMI; UnCover. CCC.

330 300   UK
NATIONAL INSTITUTE OF ECONOMIC AND SOCIAL RESEARCH. REPORT SERIES. irreg., no.10, 1996. National Institute of Economic and Social Research, 2 Dean Trench St., Smith Sq., London SW1P 3HE, England. TEL 44-171-222-7665. FAX 44-171-222-1435. **Document type:** monographic series.

330 301   UK   ISSN 0070-8453
NATIONAL INSTITUTE OF ECONOMIC AND SOCIAL RESEARCH, LONDON. ECONOMIC AND SOCIAL STUDIES. 1946. irreg., no.34, 1985. price varies. Cambridge University Press, Edinburgh Bldg., Shaftesbury Rd., Cambridge CB2 2RU, England. TEL 44-1223-312393. FAX 44-1223-315052. TELEX 851817256. E-mail: information@cup.cam.ac.uk; URL: http://www.cup.cam.ac.uk. (N. American addr.: Cambridge University Press, Journals Dept., 40 W. 20th St., New York, NY 10011. TEL 212-924-3900. FAX 212-691-3239) R&P contact: Linda Nicol. index. **Document type:** academic/scholarly publication.

330   UK   ISSN 0077-4928
NATIONAL INSTITUTE OF ECONOMIC AND SOCIAL RESEARCH, LONDON. OCCASIONAL PAPERS. 1946. irreg., no.41, 1987. price varies. Cambridge University Press, Edinburgh Bldg., Shaftesbury Rd., Cambridge CB2 2RU, England. TEL 44-1223-312393. FAX 44-1223-315052. TELEX 851817256. E-mail: information@cup.cam.ac.uk; URL: http://www.cup.cam.ac.uk. (N. American addr.: Cambridge University Press, Journals Dept., 40 W. 20th St., New York, NY 10011. TEL 212-924-3900. FAX 212-691-3239) R&P contact: Linda Nicol. **Document type:** monographic series.

NATIONAL MARINE BUSINESS JOURNAL; the voice of the marine industries nationwide. see SPORTS AND GAMES — Boats And Boating

330   US
NATIONAL SUMMARY OF DOMESTIC TRADE RECEIVABLES. 1958. q. $200. Credit Research Foundation, Inc., 8815 Centre Park Dr., Ste. 200B, Columbia, MD 21045. TEL 410-740-5499. charts; illus.; stat. **Document type:** trade publication.

NATION'S BUSINESS. see BUSINESS AND ECONOMICS — Chamber Of Commerce Publications

330   PL   ISSN 0137-1428
NAUKI EKONOMICZNE. (Text in Polish; summaries in various languages) 1974. irreg., no.7, 1994. price varies. (Uniwersytet im. Adama Mickiewicza) Adam Mickiewicz University Press, Nowowiejskiego 55, 61-734 Poznan, Poland. TEL 48-61-527380. FAX 48-61-527701. TELEX 413260 UAMPL. Ed.Bd.; Pub. Maria Jankowska. R&P contact: Malgorzata Bis. **Document type:** academic/scholarly publication, monographic series.
Description: Each issue contains the Ph.D. thesis of one author.

NEBRASKA CHAMBER OF COMMERCE & INDUSTRY. LEGISLATIVE REPORT. see LAW

NEFTYANAYA I GAZOVAYA PROMYSHLENNOST'. NAUCHNO-TEKHNICHESKII INFORMATSIONNYI SBORNIK. SERIYA: EKONOMIKA I UPRAVLENIE NEFTEGAZOVOI PROMYSHLENNOSTI. see PETROLEUM AND GAS

330   CK
NEGOCIOS. 1983. m. Emiro Aristizabal, Pub., Av. 32, no. 14-46, Bogota, Colombia. TEL 245-4757. TELEX 45299 PANIB CO. Ed. Alberto Lopera. circ. 25,000.

330 004.678   BE
NET BUSINESS DAILY. d. I O Communications, 182 Ch. de Charleroi, 1060 Brussels, Belgium. TEL 32-2-534-07-37. FAX 32-5-534-07-57. E-mail: mbauwens@iocom.be; URL: http://www.iocom.be/nbd/. Ed. Miche Bauwens.
• Available only online.
Description: Webzine monitoring internet business developments in the fields of interactive marketing, online advertising and electronic commerce.

330   NE   ISSN 0927-5800
THE NETHERLANDER. (Text in English) 1992. w. (Fri.). fl.295 (Belgium fl.350; elsewhere fl.450) (effective 1996); newsstand price: fl.7. Het Financieele Dagblad B.V., P.O. Box 216, 1000 AE Amsterdam, Netherlands. TEL 31-20-5928888. FAX 31-20-5928600. E-mail: webmaster@netherlander.com; URL: http://www.netherlander.com. Ed. Fred Bakker. R&P contact: L. Sieders. adv. contact: L. Sieders. circ. 42,500. cols./p.: 5; pp./issue: 20. (tabloid format; back issues avail.; reprint service avail.) **Document type:** newspaper.
• Also available online.
Description: Publishes news articles covering the business and financial sectors in the Netherlands and Europe, as well as political and social and environmental issues relevant to the business community.

330   IS
NETO. bi-m. Raayonote Ltd., P.O. Box 26051, Tel Aviv 61 260, Israel. TEL 03-204029. Ed. Shlomo Smalsky. circ. 1,000.

NEUE MITTE; Stimme der Katholiken in Wirtschaft und Verwaltung. see RELIGIONS AND THEOLOGY — Roman Catholic

330   AU
DIE NEUE WIRTSCHAFT; Monatsmagazin fuer Unternehmer und Manager. 1945. m. S.700. Oesterreichischer Wirtschaftsverlag, Nikolsdorfergasse 7-11, A-1051 Vienna, Austria. TEL 0222-555585. TELEX 1-11669. Ed. Dr. Rudolf Weber. adv.; illus.; tr.lit. circ. 35,000.
Formerly: Wirtschaft (ISSN 0043-6100)

330   US
NEVADA BUSINESS JOURNAL. 1986. bi-m. $36. 2127 Paradise Rd., Las Vegas, NV 89104-2515. TEL 702-735-7003. FAX 702-733-5953. Ed. Connie Brennan; Pub. Lyle Brennan. adv.: B&W page $1940, color page $2840. circ. 10,000. **Document type:** trade publication.
Description: Covers Nevada business concerns and issues.

NEW AFRICAN YEARBOOK. see POLITICAL SCIENCE

330   UK
NEW ECONOMICS FOUNDATION. BRIEFINGS. 1993. irreg. free. New Economics Foundation, 88-94 Wentworth St., London E1 7SA, England. TEL 071-377-5696. **Document type:** monographic series.

330 374   US
NEW HAMPSHIRE BUSINESS EDUCATION ASSOCIATION. NEWSLETTER.* 1983. irreg. membership. New Hampshire Business Education Association (NHBEA), 16 Barnesdale Rd., Nashua, NH 03062-2157. TEL 603-882-7041. Ed. Maria Matarazzo. circ. 300. (back issues avail.) **Document type:** newsletter.
Formerly: New Hampshire Business Education Association. Journal.

330 346   US
NEW HAMPSHIRE CORPORATIONS, PARTNERSHIPS AND ASSOCIATIONS. a. $18. Butterworth Legal Publishers (Salem) (Subsidiary of: Reed Elsevier plc), 8 Industrial Way, Bldg. C, Salem, NH 03079. TEL 800-548-4001. FAX 603-898-9858. Ed.Bd.
Description: For corporate counsel, business executives and those involved in forming corporations, partnerships and associations.

330   US
NEW HAVEN BUSINESS DIGEST.* 1984. m. $17. Vought Communications, Inc., Box 846, Southport, CT 06490-0846. FAX 203-787-2027. Ed. Jean McAndrews. adv. circ. 10,000.

330   US
NEW JERSEY NOTES;* a bimonthly news summary of grants & funding. 1979. s-m. $35. Mitchell Guide, (Subsidiary of: Littman Associates, 23997 Cliff Dr., Worton, MD 21678-1322. TEL 800-831-4497. FAX 410-778-7949. Ed. Wendy P. Littman. circ. 350.
Description: News on private and public grants and funding in the state.

330   US   ISSN 0889-5937
HF3161.N6
NEW MEXICO BUSINESS, CURRENT ECONOMIC REPORT. 1948. m. (11/yr.). $22. University of New Mexico, Bureau of Business & Economic Research, 1920 Lomas N.E., Albuquerque, NM 87131-6021. TEL 505-277-2216. FAX 505-277-7066. Ed. Kevin Kargacin. charts; stat.; index, cum.index. circ. 500. (also avail. in microfilm from UMI; microfiche from CIS; reprint service avail. from UMI) Indexed: J.of Econ.Lit., Mkt.Inform.Guide, SRI. **Document type:** newsletter.
— UMI.
Formerly (until 1980): New Mexico Business (ISSN 0028-6168); Incorporating: Retail Food Price Bulletin (ISSN 0034-6055)

330   US   ISSN 0164-6796
NEW MEXICO BUSINESS JOURNAL. 1976. m. $24. Sierra Publishing Group, Inc., 420 Central SW, Ste.104, Albuquerque, NM 87102. TEL 505-243-3444. FAX 505-243-4118. E-mail: sierrapg@nmbiz.com. Ed. Robert J. Cochnar; Pub. Robert J. Cochnar. R&P contact: Kathryn Matousek. adv. contact: Claire Garner. bk.rev.; charts; illus.; stat. circ. 22,000. (also avail. in microform from UMI; back issues avail.; reprint service avail.) Indexed: Tr.& Indus.Ind. **Document type:** consumer publication.
• Also available online. Vendor(s): Information Access Co., Knight-Ridder Information, Inc., UMI.
— UMI.

330   US
NEW ORLEANS DAILY JOURNAL OF COMMERCE. 1922. d. (Mon.-Fri.). $426. Guide Publishing Co., 118 Terry Parkway, Gretna, LA 70056. TEL 504-368-8900. FAX 504-368-8999. Ed. Carlo Ragusa. adv. contact: Paul F. Serpas. circ. 11,300. **Document type:** newspaper, trade publication.

NEW PLANT REPORT. see BUILDING AND CONSTRUCTION

NEW WEST NOTES. see POLITICAL SCIENCE

NEW YORK STATE BAR ASSOCIATION. ANTITRUST LAW SECTION SYMPOSIUM. see LAW

NEW YORK UNIVERSITY BUSINESS MAGAZINE PUBLISHING SERIES. see PUBLISHING AND BOOK TRADE

330   NZ   ISSN 1172-7608
NEW ZEALAND. MINISTRY OF FOREIGN AFFAIRS AND TRADE. CORPORATE PLAN. 1987. a. NZ.$9.15. Ministry of Foreign Affairs and Trade, Private Bag 18-901, Wellington, New Zealand. TEL 64-4-4948500.
Former titles (until 1993): New Zealand. Ministry of External Relations and Trade. Corporate Plan (ISSN 0114-5533); (until 1989): New Zealand. Ministry of Foreign Affairs. Corporate Plan (ISSN 0113-3446)

330   NZ   ISSN 0113-4957
NEW ZEALAND BUSINESS. 1938. 11/yr. NZ.$54.45 (foreign NZ.$117.40) (effective 1994). Profile Publishing Ltd., P.O. Box 5544, Wellesley St., Auckland, New Zealand. TEL 64-9-6308940. FAX 64-9-6301046. E-mail: sprofile@iconz.co.nz. Ed. Ena Hutchinson. adv.; bk.rev. circ. 9,546. (back issues avail.) **Document type:** trade publication.
— BLDSC (6195.265000). CCC.
Formerly (until 1987): Better Business (ISSN 0110-7100)
Description: Information for business people on tax, economics, management, innovative companies and more.

BUSINESS AND ECONOMICS

330   NZ   ISSN 0077-9954
HB9
NEW ZEALAND ECONOMIC PAPERS. 1967. s-a. NZ.$70 to non-members; members NZ.$80 (effective 1997-98). New Zealand Association of Economists, P.O. Box 568, Wellington, New Zealand. TEL 64-3-4798655. FAX 64-3-4798174. E-mail: dowen@commerce.otago.ac.nz. Ed. Dorian Owen. bk.rev. circ. 800. **Indexed:** C.R.E.J., J.of Econ.Lit., Rural Recreat.Tour.Abstr., World Agri.Econ.& Rural Sociol.Abstr. **Document type:** academic/scholarly publication.
—BLDSC (6089.990000); UnCover.
   Refereed Serial

330   NZ   ISSN 0078-0057
NEW ZEALAND INSTITUTE OF ECONOMIC RESEARCH. ANNUAL REPORT. 1960. a. NZ.$13.50. New Zealand Institute of Economic Research, P.O. Box 3479, Wellington 1, New Zealand. TEL 64-4-4721880. FAX 64-4-4721211. E-mail: econ@nzier.org.nz. **Document type:** corporate report.

330   NZ   ISSN 0078-0049
NEW ZEALAND INSTITUTE OF ECONOMIC RESEARCH. DISCUSSION PAPER. 1961. a. price varies. New Zealand Institute of Economic Research, P.O. Box 3479, Wellington 1, New Zealand. TEL 64-4-4721880. FAX 64-4-4721211. E-mail: econ@nzier.org.nz. **Document type:** academic/scholarly publication.

330   NZ   ISSN 0110-4470
NEW ZEALAND INSTITUTE OF ECONOMIC RESEARCH. QUARTERLY SURVEY OF BUSINESS OPINION. 1961. q. NZ.$182.50. New Zealand Institute of Economic Research, P.O. Box 3479, Wellington 1, New Zealand. TEL 64-4-4721880. FAX 64-4-4721211. E-mail: econ@nzier.org.nz. **Document type:** academic/scholarly publication.
   Description: Reports surveys of business experiences and intentions.

330   NZ   ISSN 0113-1877
NEW ZEALAND INSTITUTE OF ECONOMIC RESEARCH. RESEARCH MONOGRAPHS. 1961. irreg. (approx. 6/yr.). price varies. New Zealand Institute of Economic Research, P.O. Box 3479, Wellington 1, New Zealand. TEL 64-4-4721880. FAX 64-4-4721211. E-mail: econ@nzier.org.nz. **Document type:** academic/scholarly publication.
—BLDSC (7743.124500).
   Formerly: New Zealand Institute of Economic Research. Research Paper (ISSN 0078-0065)

658   NZ   ISSN 1171-5375
NEW ZEALAND MANUFACTURER (WELLINGTON, 1992). 1949. 11/yr. NZ.$65 (Australia and Pacific Islands NZ.$95; elsewhere NZ.$140). New Zealand Manufacturers Federation, 3 Church St., P.O. Box 11-543, Wellington 1, New Zealand. TEL 64-4-4733000. FAX 64-4-4733004. E-mail: nzlmflgjp@manwlg.attmail.com. Ed. Gilbert Peterson. R&P contact: Gilbert Peterson. adv. contact: Jill Wood. bk.rev.; charts; illus.; mkt.; tr.lit.; circ. 3,000 (controlled). **Document type:** trade publication.
●Also available online. Vendor(s): UMI.
—UMI.
   Former titles (until 1992): Manufacturer (ISSN 0113-9320); (until Apr. 1988): New Zealand Manufacturer (Wellington, 1985) (ISSN 0113-0498); Which was formerly (until 1985): Manufacturer (Wellington, 1975) (ISSN 0110-6279); (until 1975): New Zealand Manufacturer (Wellington, 1949) (ISSN 0028-8411).

NEWSLINE (LAWRENCE). see *SPORTS AND GAMES — Ball Games*

330   US
NEWSWEEK BUSINESS PLUS. 1989. w. Newsweek, Inc., 251 W. 57th St., New York, NY 10019. TEL 212-445-4000. adv.: B&W page $45400, color page $74470, trim 8 x 10 3/4. circ. 1,000,000 (paid).

330   CN
NIAGARA BUSINESS REPORT. 1983. q. Rannie Printing and Publishing Ltd. (Subsidiary of: Burgoyne Community Newspapers Ltd.), 4309 Central Ave., Beamsville, ON L0R 1B0, Canada. TEL 905-563-1629. FAX 905-563-7977. Ed. Molly Harding. adv. contact: Jacquie Hoover. circ. 14,500.
   Formerly (until 1993): Let's Talk Business Niagara (ISSN 0831-9006)

330   NR   ISSN 0794-2877
HF3931
NIGERIA BUSINESS GUIDE ANNUAL; a practical guide for businessmen and foreign investors in Nigeria. (Text in English) 1986. a. $25. Comprehensive Guide Ltd., P.O. Box 29262, Ibadan, Oyo State, Nigeria. Ed. Joseph Ajiboye. adv.; bk.rev. circ. 250,000. **Document type:** trade publication.
—CCC.

338.1   NR   ISSN 0331-0361
HC517.N48
NIGERIAN ECONOMIC SOCIETY. PROCEEDINGS OF THE ANNUAL CONFERENCE. 1973. a. included with Nigerian Journal of Economic & Social Studies. Nigerian Economic Society, Department of Economics, University of Ibadan, Ibadan, Oyo State, Nigeria. Ed. E. Lambo. circ. 800. **Document type:** proceedings.

330   NR
NIGERIAN EXPORTER. (Text in English) 1985. m. Ohida & Sons Ltd., 41 Adewale Crescent, Oshodi, P.O. Box 742, Ikeja, Lagos State, Nigeria. Ed. Cyprian Agbor. **Document type:** trade publication.

NIGERIAN INSTITUTE OF SOCIAL AND ECONOMIC RESEARCH. ANNUAL REPORT. see *SOCIAL SCIENCES: COMPREHENSIVE WORKS*

330 300   NR   ISSN 0029-0092
HC517.N48
NIGERIAN JOURNAL OF ECONOMIC & SOCIAL STUDIES. (Text in English) 1959. 3/yr. $75 includes Proceedings of the Annual Conference. Nigerian Economic Society, Department of Economics, University of Ibadan, Ibadan, Oyo State, Nigeria. Ed. E. Lambo. cum.index. **Indexed:** C.R.E.J., Documentatieblad, Geo.Abstr., IDA, Int.Lab.Doc., Popul.Ind., Rural Ext.Educ.& Tr.Abstr., Rural Recreat.Tour.Abstr., World Agri.Econ.& Rural Sociol.Abstr. **Document type:** academic/scholarly publication.
—BLDSC (6112.120000). **CCC.**

330   JA
NIHON KEIZAI SHIMBUN. (International "Satellite Edition" avail.) (Text in Japanese) 1876. d. $90 for international ed. Nihon Keizai Shimbun, Inc., 1-9-5 Ote-machi, Chiyoda-ku, Tokyo 100-66, Japan. TEL 81-3-3270-0251. FAX 81-3-5255-2661. TELEX J22308 NIKKEI. (Intl. ed. dist. by: Nikkei America, Inc., 1325 Ave. of the Americas, Ste. 2500, New York, NY 10019. TEL 212-261-6200) Ed. Kenjiro Horikawa. adv. contact: Toshiharu Sakuma. bk.rev. circ. 3,000,000. (back issues avail.) **Document type:** newspaper.

330   JA
NIKKAN KOGYO SHINBUN/BUSINESS & TECHNOLOGY DAILY NEWS. (Text in Japanese) 1915. d. (5/w.). Nikkan Kogyo Shinbunsha, 8-10 Kudan Kita-1-chome, Chiyoda-ku, Tokyo 102, Japan. TEL 03-222-7240. Ed. Toshio Fujiyoshi. adv. circ. 550,110. **Document type:** newspaper.

330   JA
NIKKEI. ANNUAL FOREIGN CORPORATION REPORTS. a. Nihon Keizai Shimbun, Inc., 1-9-5 Ote-machi, Chiyoda-ku, Tokyo 100-66, Japan. TEL 81-3-3270-0251. FAX 81-3-5255-2661. TELEX J22308 NIKKEI. **Document type:** trade publication, corporate report.
   Description: Covers 3,700 companies from 40 countries.

330   JA
NIKKEI CORPORATE WHO'S WHO (YEAR). a. Nihon Keizai Shimbun, Inc., 1-9-5 Ote-machi, Chiyoda-ku, Tokyo 100-66, Japan. TEL 81-3-3270-0251. FAX 81-3-5255-2661. TELEX J22308 NIKKEI. **Document type:** directory.
   Description: Lists more than 20,000 directors and managers of 3,800 leading Japanese Corporations.

330   JA   ISSN 0912-3881
NIKKEI REGIONAL ECONOMIC REPORT. s-m. Nihon Keizai Shimbun, Inc., Nikkei Research Institute of Industry and Markets, 1-9-5 Ote-machi, Chiyoda-ku, Tokyo 100-66, Japan. TEL 81-3-3270-0251. FAX 81-3-5255-2661. TELEX J22308 NIKKEI. **Document type:** newsletter.
   Description: Contains regional economic and industrial information.

330   JA
NIKKEI VENTURE BUSINESS ALMANAC. a. Nihon Keizai Shimbun, Inc., 1-9-5 Ote-machi, Chiyoda-ku, Tokyo 100-66, Japan. TEL 81-3-3270-0251. FAX 81-3-5255-2661. TELEX J22308 NIKKEI. **Document type:** trade publication.
   Description: A reference work on 2,050 leading venture businesses in Japan.

330   JA   ISSN 0918-5348
HC461   CODEN: JECJAU
THE NIKKEI WEEKLY. (Text in English) 1962. w. $108. Nihon Keizai Shimbun, Inc., 1-9-5 Otemachi, Chiyoda-ku, Tokyo 100, Japan. TEL 81-3-3270-0251. FAX 81-3-5255-2661. TELEX J22308 NIKKEI. (US addr.: Nikkei America, Inc., 1325 Ave. of the Americas, Ste. 2500, New York, NY 10019. TEL 212-261-6200) Ed. Nobuo Ikeda. adv. contact: Kazuo Onotera. bk.rev.; illus.; mkt.; stat.; index. circ. 36,500. (also avail. in microfiche) **Indexed:** A.I.Abstr., BPIA, Br.Ceram.Abstr., CAD CAM Abstr., Chem.Abstr., Environ.Abstr., Key to Econ.Sci., Mgmt.& Market.Abstr., PROMT, Robomat., Tel.Abstr., Telegen, Text.Tech.Dig. **Document type:** newspaper.
●Also available online. Vendor(s): Lexis-Nexis.
—BLDSC (6113.178420); CASDDS; UMI.
   Formerly (until June 1991): Japan Economic Journal (ISSN 0021-4388)
   Description: Covers Japan's business, finance, industry, stocks and technology.

330.1   NO   ISSN 0078-1029
NORD-NORGE NAERINGSLIV OG OEKONOMI.* 1948. irreg. price varies. Icon A-S, Naeringri Nord, 8001 Bodoe, Norway. cum.index: vols.1-41 in vol.41.

330 374.013   GW
NORDBAYERN. LANDESARBEITSAMT. BUNDESANSTALT FUER ARBEIT. BERATUNGS- UND VERMITTLUNGSDIENSTE. INFORMATIONEN. 1950. w. DM.85. Landesarbeitsamt Nordbayern, Bundesanstalt fuer Arbeit, Regensburgerstr. 104, 90328 Nuernberg, Germany. FAX 0911-1792417. bk.rev. circ. 18,000. **Document type:** government publication.
   Description: Information for vocational and occupational guidance services of the Bundesanstalt.

330   SW   ISSN 1100-7559
HC341
NORDIC ECONOMIC OUTLOOK. Co-sponsor: Federation of Danish Industries. 1974. s-a. SEK 520 to non-members; members SEK 400 (effective 1997); newsstand price: SEK 200. Federation of Swedish Industries (FSI), Economic Policy Department, Box 5513, S-114 85 Stockholm, Sweden. TEL 46-8-783-80-49. FAX 46-8-662-35-95. TELEX 19990. Ed. Ola Virin. circ. 5,000. **Indexed:** Key to Econ.Sci.
—BLDSC (6117.913000).

NORFOLK ISLAND GOVERNMENT GAZETTE. see *PUBLIC ADMINISTRATION*

338.7   SW   ISSN 0283-0779
NORRA SVERIGES AFFAERER OCH FOERETAG. 1984. 10/yr. SEK 490. Media Foerlag Norra Sveriges Affaerer & Foeretag AB, P.O. Box 3737, S-903 13 Umeaa, Sweden. TEL 46-90-14-23-20. FAX 46-90-14-23-20. Ed. Anders Pauser. adv.: B&W page SEK 12500, color page SEK 14900; trim 185 x 266; adv. contact: Rolf Stenwall. cols./p.: 4; pp./issue: 52.
   Formerly (until 1986): Norra Sveriges Affaerer (ISSN 0282-2261)

330   SW   ISSN 0029-1838
NORRLAENDSK TIDSKRIFT. 1952. 8/yr. SEK 95($7) Norrlandsfoerbundet, Box 294, Kyrkogatan 26, 85 05 Sunsvall, Sweden. Ed. Hasse Bystroem. adv.; illus. circ. 10,000.

330   SU
NORTH SHORE BUSINESS. m. Computech Publishing, Inc., 42 Thomas Pattern Dr., Randolph, MA 02368-3902. TEL 617-961-2700. FAX 617-963-4616. Ed. Gary Pan.

BUSINESS AND ECONOMICS 989

330   US   ISSN 1078-5698
NORTHEAST PENNSYLVANIA BUSINESS JOURNAL. m. $29. Press - Enterprise, Inc., 3185 Lackawanna Ave., Bloomsburg, PA 17815-3329. TEL 717-784-2121. FAX 717-784-9226. E-mail: npbj@enterpe.com; URL: http://www.enterpe.com/npbj.html. Ed. Tom Sink. R&P contact: Tom Sink. adv. contact: Karen Nocerine. circ. 12,000. **Document type:** newspaper.
   Description: Provides business news and information for 10 counties in northeast Pennsylvania.

330   UK
NORTHERN BUSINESS AND FINANCE. 1991. bi-m. £15 (Europe £35; elsewhere £75). Northern Business Press Ltd., 46B Bradford Rd., Brighouse, W. Yorkshire HD6 1RY, England. TEL 44-1484-401484. FAX 44-1484-401114. E-mail: contact@n-b-p.co.uk. Ed. Keith J. Butterick; Pub. Keith J. Butterick. adv.: B&W page £1750; 210 x 297; adv. contact: Barry Denham. bk.rev.; circ. 17,000 (paid). (back issues avail.) **Document type:** trade publication.
   Formerly (until 1997): Finance North.

330   CN
NORTHERN ONTARIO BUSINESS. m. Can.$20. Laurentian Publishing Co., 158 Elgin St., Sudbury, ON P3E 3N5, Canada. TEL 705-673-5705. FAX 705-673-9542. Ed. Mark Sandford. adv.; circ. 10,000 (controlled). (also avail. in microform from UMI) **Document type:** newspaper.
   ●Also available online. Vendor(s): Lexis-Nexis, UMI.

330   US   ISSN 1041-7869
NORTHLAND BUSINESS LEDGER.* 1987. m. $12. Antioch Publications, 7007 N.E. Parvin Rd., Kansas City, MO 64117-1532. TEL 816-454-3222. FAX 816-454-4236. Ed. Pete Hall. adv.: B&W page $800; trim 11 1/2 x 13 1/2; adv. contact: Jack Watt. circ. 5,500. **Document type:** newspaper.

330   330.1   IT   ISSN 0391-8289
HB7
NOTE ECONOMICHE. English edition: Economic Notes (ISSN 0391-5026) (Text in Italian; summaries in Italian and English) 1971. 3/yr. free. Monte dei Paschi di Siena, Piazza Salimbeni 3, 53100 Siena, Italy. TEL 0577-294401. FAX 0577-294084. Ed. Lorenzo Maccari. bk.rev.; bibl.; charts; stat. **Indexed:** P.A.I.S.For.Lang.Ind.
   Description: Covers economic theory, the history of economic thought and methodology.

330   SP
NOTICIARIO ECONOMICO - M B. 1990. 46/yr. 34950($300) (foreign $265) (effective 1998). Canalejas 30, entlo. 2o, 08028 Barcelona, Spain. TEL 34-3-4226199. FAX 34-3-4211858. E-mail: revista.econo@redestb.es. Ed. Ricardo Rabella; Pub. Susana Torre. R&P contact: Ricardo Rabella. circ. 460,000. **Document type:** bulletin.
   Description: Includes investment, banking, commercial, personnel and international news. *Refereed Serial*

330   IT   ISSN 0391-0121
NOTIZIARIO ENASARCO. 1954. m. L.20000 (effective 1996). Ente Nazionale Agenti e Rappresentanti, Via A. Usodimare, 29, 00154 Rome, Italy. TEL 39-6-57931. FAX 39-6-5741019. Ed. Moreno Gori. adv.: B&W page L.5500000. circ. 270,000.

330   350
NOTTINGHAM TRENT UNIVERSITY. CENTRE FOR RESEARCH INTO REGULATION, ORGANIZATION AND LAW. OCCASIONAL PAPERS IN ECONOMICS. irreg., no.96-11. Nottingham Trent University, Centre for Research into Regulation, Organization and Law, Burton St., Nottingham NG1 4BU, England. TEL 44-115-941-8418. FAX 44-115-948-6808. **Document type:** monographic series.

330   SP   ISSN 0214-9389
▼**NUEVO CADUCEO MAGAZINE.** 1952. bi-m. P. de San Francisco de Sales 17, 3o, 28003 Madrid, Spain. TEL 1-549-86-09. FAX 1-549-56-52. Ed. E. Rinon Ramirez. circ. 150,000.
   Formerly (until 1981): Caduceo (ISSN 0409-7955)

330   SP   ISSN 1133-9535
NUEVO LUNES DE LA ECONOMIA Y LA SOCIEDAD. 1981. 48/yr. Plaza de Espana 18, Torre de Madrid, planta 7 ofc. 3, 28008 Madrid, Spain. TEL 1-24-73-101. FAX 1-248-04-06. TELEX 41777 LUNES E. Ed. Marivi Casanneva. circ. 25,000.

330   VE   ISSN 0798-2003
NUMERO. 1980. w. $300. Editora Triangulo C.A., Apdo. Postal 75570, El Marques, Caracas 1070, Venezuela. FAX 582-345885. Ed. Juan C. Malaguti. adv. contact: Nelly Cavo. bk.rev. circ. 20,000.

NUOVA ECONOMIA. see BUSINESS AND ECONOMICS — Chamber Of Commerce Publications

330   IT   ISSN 0029-6376
HC301.A1
NUOVO MEZZOGIORNO. 1958. m. L.100000. Edizioni Nuovo Mezzogiorno, Corso Vittorio Emanuele 154, 00186 Rome, Italy. TEL 39-6-68806288. FAX 39-6-68806288. Ed. Vittorio Ciampi. adv.: page L.2500000; adv. contact: Maria Novelli. bk.rev.; abstr.; bibl.; charts; illus.; index, cum.index. circ. 15,000.

330   CN   ISSN 0826-9947
OBSERVATION. 1974. irreg. price varies. C.D. Howe Institute, 125 Adelaide St. E., Toronto, ON M5C 1L7, Canada. TEL 416-865-1904. E-mail: cdhome@cdhome.org; URL: http://www.cdhome.org. (also avail. in microform from MML) **Indexed:** Can. B.P.I., PROMT. **Document type:** monographic series. —BLDSC (6198.290000).
   Formerly (until 1980): H R I Observations (ISSN 0381-5250)
   Description: Studies on Canadian and international economics policy issues.

330   NO
OBSERVATOR. 1947. m. NOK 100 to individuals; institutions NOK 200. Frederik, Studentgruppa i Norske Sosialoekonomers Forening, Postboks 1095, Blindern, 0317 Oslo 3, Norway. bk.rev. circ. 900.
   Formerly: Stimulator; et Fagblad for Socialoekonomer.

330   003   US   ISSN 0078-3390
OEKONOMETRIE UND UNTERNEHMENSFORSCHUNG/ECONOMETRICS AND OPERATIONS RESEARCH. (Text in German; occasionally in English) 1962. irreg. price varies. Springer-Verlag, 175 Fifth Ave., New York, NY 10010. TEL 212-460-1500. FAX 212-473-6272. (Also: Berlin, Heidelberg, Tokyo and Vienna) (reprint service avail. from ISI) **Indexed:** Biol.Abstr. **Document type:** academic/scholarly publication.

320   DK   ISSN 0030-1906
HC10
OEKONOMI OG POLITIK. 1927. q. DKK 360 (effective 1997). (Selskabet for Historie og Samfundsoekonomi) Jurist- og Oekonomforbundets Forlag, Gothersgade 133, DK-1123 Copenhagen K, Denmark. TEL 45-33-95-97-00. FAX 45-33-95-99-97. Ed. Peter Nedergaard. adv.; bk.rev.; stat.; index. circ. 1,500. (reprint service avail. from ISI) **Indexed:** Amer.Hist.& Life (until 1990), Hist.Abstr. (until 1990).

OESTERREICHISCHES INSTITUT FUER WIRTSCHAFTSFORSCHUNG. MONATSBERICHTE. see BUSINESS AND ECONOMICS — Economic Situation And Conditions

330   AU   ISSN 1013-9486
OESTERREICHISCHES RECHT DER WIRTSCHAFT. m. S.1594. Verlag Orac GesmbH & Co. KG, Graben 17, A-1010 Vienna, Austria. TEL 43-1-53452-0. FAX 43-1-53452141. adv.: B&W page S.17600; trim 167 x 249; adv. contact: Christian Braun. circ. 13,800. **Document type:** trade publication.

330   AU
OESTERREICHS WIRTSCHAFT. 9/yr. Eschenbachgasse 11, A-1072 Vienna, Austria. TEL 01-5873633. FAX 01-5870192. Ed. Evamaria Hawel. circ. 4,200.

330   341   RU
▼**OFFSHORE EXPRESS.** (Text in Russian) 1995. m. $60. B. Polianka ul., 15, 109108 Moscow, Russia. TEL 7-095-2307615. FAX 7-095-2307963. circ. 40,000. (back issues avail.)
   Description: Provides information for whose who are wishing to form a business or establish residence overseas.

OGGI E DOMANI. see PUBLIC ADMINISTRATION

OHIO & NORTHERN KENTUCKY GASOLINE DEALERS & GARAGE NEWS. see TRANSPORTATION — Automobiles

333   JA   ISSN 0287-0916
OITA DAIGAKU KEIZAI KENKYUJO KENKYUJOHO/OITA UNIVERSITY. RESEARCH INSTITUTE OF ECONOMICS. BULLETIN. (Text in Japanese) 1967. a. exchange basis. Oita Daigaku, Keizai Kenkyusho - Oita University, Research Institute of Economics, Oita, Japan. Ed. Fukuo Igarashi; Pub. Sunao Uchino. circ. 550. **Document type:** bulletin.

330   JA   ISSN 0474-0157
OITA DAIGAKU KEIZAI RONSHU/OITA UNIVERSITY ECONOMIC REVIEW. (Text in Japanese) 1949. 6/yr. 5000 Yen. Oita Daigaku, Keizai Gakkai - Oita University, Economic Society, Oita, Japan. Ed. Fukuo Igarashi; Pub. Katsuhiko Yoshime. circ. 1,300. **Document type:** bulletin.

330   CN   ISSN 1180-3975
OKANAGAN BUSINESS MAGAZINE. 1989. 10/yr. Can.$15. Byrne Publishing Group, Inc., Box 1479, Sta. A, Kelowna, BC V1Y 7V8, Canada. TEL 604-861-5399. FAX 604-7868-3040. Ed. Mike Haines; Pub. Paul Byrne. adv. contact: Gerry Lee. bk.rev. circ. 10,710. **Document type:** consumer publication.

330   US
OKLAHOMA COUNCIL ON ECONOMIC EDUCATION NEWSLETTER.* 1961. 3/yr. membership. Oklahoma Council on Economic Education, University of Central Oklahoma, Economics Department, Edmond, OK 73034-0182. TEL 405-341-2980. Dir. Jean Caldwell. circ. 3,600. **Document type:** newsletter.

330   650   US
OKLAHOMA STATE UNIVERSITY. COLLEGE OF BUSINESS ADMINISTRATION. WORKING PAPERS. 1966. irreg., latest no.91-5. free. Oklahoma State University, College of Business Administration, Office of Business and Economic Research, Stillwater, OK 74078-0555. TEL 405-744-5125.
   Supersedes: Oklahoma State University. College of Business Administration. Extension Service. Business Papers (ISSN 0078-4427)

330   340   BE
ONDERNEMER; praktisch jaarboek voor de Bedrijfsleider. French edition: Entreprise. (Text in Dutch) a. 2800 BEF includes data diskette. Kluwer Rechtswetenschappen Belgie (Subsidiary of: Wolters Kluwer N.V.), Santvoortbeeklaan 21-25, 2100 Antwerp, Belgium. FAX 32-3-3600467. Eds. Jack Misteli, Werner Van Minnebruggen.

ONLINE · C D - R O M BUSINESS SOURCEBOOK. see BUSINESS AND ECONOMICS — Trade And Industrial Directories

330   NZ   ISSN 0114-6602
OPERATIONAL RESEARCH SOCIETY OF NEW ZEALAND. PROCEEDINGS OF THE ANNUAL CONFERENCE. 1978. a. free to conference participants. Operational Research Society of New Zealand, P.O. Box 904, Wellington, New Zealand. circ. 120. **Document type:** proceedings.

330   658   US
OPERATIONS UPDATE (NEW YORK). irreg. $75 to non-members; members $50 (effective 1996). Securities Industry Association, 120 Broadway, 35th Fl., New York, NY 10271. TEL 212-608-1500. **Document type:** trade publication.
   Description: Presents developments of immediate interest to operations managers.

330   CK
OPINION ECONOMICA.* 1975. q. Sociedad Antioquena de Economistas, c/o Sociedad Colombiana de Economistas, Carrera 20, 36-41, Apdo. Aereo 8429, Bogota, Colombia.

BUSINESS AND ECONOMICS

330 US ISSN 0279-8190
HF5001
OREGON BUSINESS MAGAZINE. 1978. m. $19.95. Oregon Business Media, 610 S.W. Broadway, No. 200, Portland, OR 97205-3431.
TEL 503-223-0304. FAX 503-221-6544. URL: http://www.oregonbusiness.com. Ed. Kathy Dimond; Pub. David Rowe. R&P contact: Shirleen Holt. adv. contact: Roy Melani. bk.rev. circ. 20,487. (also avail. in microform from UMI) **Document type:** consumer publication.
● Also available online. Vendor(s): Information Access Co.
—UMI.
Description: Covers small and medium-sized businesses in Oregon.

330 US
OREGON BUSINESS NETWORK NEWS. 1981. bi-m. $36. Oregon Business Network, Box 5488, Portland, OR 97219. TEL 503-244-2689. FAX 503-618-8771. E-mail: royjay19@mail.idi.net. Ed. Roy Jay. adv. contact: Betty Davis. illus.; circ. 21,000 (controlled). **Document type:** newsletter.
Description: Covers business news, ideas and sales opportunities, marketing and related topics.

330 SZ
ORGANISATIONSENTWICKLUNG IN DER PRAXIS. 1981. irreg., vol.6, 1993. price varies. Paul Haupt AG, Falkenplatz 14, CH-3001 Bern, Switzerland.
TEL 41-31-3012345. FAX 41-31-3014669. **Document type:** monographic series.

ORGANIZING CORPORATE AND OTHER BUSINESS ENTERPRISES. see *LAW — Corporate Law*

330 US
ORLANDO BUSINESS JOURNAL.* w. American City Business Journals (Orlando), 315 E. Robinson St., Ste. 250, Orlando, FL 32801-1949.
TEL 407-649-8470. FAX 407-649-8469. Ed. Carolyn Cerbin. circ. 10,500.
● Also available online. Vendor(s): Information Access Co.

658 CN ISSN 1198-8215
T177.C3
ORTECH. ANNUAL REPORT. 1928. a. free. ORTECH, Dept. of Marketing, 2395 Speakman Dr., Mississauga, ON L5K 1B3, Canada.
TEL 905-822-4111. FAX 905-823-1446. Ed. John Convey. **Document type:** corporate report.
—CISTI.
Former titles: ORTECH International. Annual Report; Ontario Research Foundation. Annual Report (ISSN 0078-5083)

330 JA ISSN 0078-6640
OSAKA CITY UNIVERSITY ECONOMIC REVIEW. (Text in English, French, German and other languages) 1965. s-a. $15. Osaka City University, Faculty of Economics, 3-3-138 Sugimoto, Sumiyoshi-ku, Osaka 558, Japan. FAX 81-060605-2256. (Co-sponsor: Institute for Economic Research) Ed. Jun-ichi Hasegawa. adv. contact: Hitoshi Hoshno. bk.rev. circ. 500. **Document type:** academic/scholarly publication.
—BLDSC (6297.500000).

330 JA ISSN 0473-4548
OSAKA DAIGAKU KEIZAIGAKU/OSAKA ECONOMIC PAPERS. 1951. q. 6000 Yen. Osaka Daigaku, Keizaigakubu - Osaka University, Faculty of Economics, Toyonaka, Osaka 560, Japan. Ed. Hirofumi Shibata. bk.rev.; index, cum.index every 10 vols. circ. 1,500. **Indexed:** P.A.I.S. **Document type:** academic/scholarly publication.
Formerly: Osaka University. Economic Review (ISSN 0030-610X)

330 382 346 JA ISSN 1342-3274
OSAKA PREFECTURE UNIVERSITY. SERIES D: ECONOMICS, BUSINESS ADMINISTRATION AND LAW. (Text in European languages) 1957. a. exchange basis. Osaka Prefecture University - Osaka-furitsu Daigaku, 1-1 Gakuen-cho, Sakai-shi, Osaka 593, Japan. TEL 81-722-52-1161.
FAX 81-722-52-6798. **Document type:** academic/scholarly publication.
—BLDSC (2795.530000).
Former titles (until Apr. 1996): University of Osaka Prefecture. Bulletin. Series D: Economics, Business Administration and Law; University of Osaka Prefecture. Bulletin. Series D: Sciences of Economy, Commerce and Law (ISSN 0473-4637)

330 US ISSN 0197-3592
OSTARO'S MARKET NEWSLETTER;* charts gold, silver and DJIA for the next one month. 1980. 12/yr. $195. Box 20340, New York, NY 10001-0007.
TEL 212-686-4121. Ed. D. Ostaro. circ. 1,000.
Document type: newsletter.

330 GW ISSN 0030-6460
HC244
OSTEUROPA-WIRTSCHAFT. (Text in English and German) 1956. q. DM.89 (students DM.69) (effective 1997). (Deutsche Gesellschaft fuer Osteuropakunde) Deutsche Verlags-Anstalt GmbH, Postfach 106012, 70049 Stuttgart, Germany.
TEL 49-711-2631-0. FAX 49-711-2631110. Ed. F.-L. Altmann. bk.rev.#; stat.; index. circ. 650. (reprint service avail. from SWZ) **Indexed:** A.B.C.Pol.Sci., Amer.Hist.& Life (1979-), Hist.Abstr. (1979-), IBR, Key to Econ.Sci., P.A.I.S.For.Lang.Ind., P.A.I.S. **Document type:** trade publication.
—BLDSC (6312.250000); SWETS. **CCC.**

330 CN ISSN 0832-2546
OTTAWA BUSINESS NEWS. 1986. bi-w. Can.$22. Istari Corporation Publications, 77 Auriga Dr., Unit 3, Nepean, Ont. K2E 7Z7, Canada.
TEL 613-727-1400. FAX 613-727-1010. Ed. Mark Sutcliffe. adv. contact: Brian Warren. circ. 20,000. (back issues avail.)
Description: Business news and information from Canada's capital.

310 330 UK ISSN 0305-9049
HC10
OXFORD BULLETIN OF ECONOMICS AND STATISTICS. 1939. q. £99($205) (foreign £130) (effective 1997). Blackwell Publishers Ltd., 108 Cowley Rd., Oxford OX4 1JF, England. TEL 44-1865-791100. FAX 44-1865-791347. E-mail: jnlinfo@blackwellpublishers.co.uk; URL: http://www.blackwellpublishers.co.uk. Ed.Bd. adv.; index. circ. 1,500. **Indexed:** ABI Inform., ASCA, Asian-Pac.Econ.Lit., BPIA, Br.Hum.Ind., C.R.E.J., Compumath, Cont.Pg.Manage., Curr.Cont., Fam.Ind., Forest.Abstr., Forest Prod.Abstr., J.Cont.Quant.Meth., J.of Econ.Lit., Key to Econ.Sci., Mark.Res.Abstr. (1963-), Mid.East: Abstr.& Ind., P.A.I.S, Pub.Admin.Abstr., Rural Recreat.Tour.Abstr., SSCI, Tr.& Indus.Ind., World Agri.Econ.& Rural Sociol.Abstr., World Bank.Abstr. **Document type:** academic/scholarly publication.
● Also available online. Vendor(s): Information Access Co.
—BLDSC (6320.640000); Genuine Article; SWETS; UMI; UnCover. **CCC.**
Formerly: Oxford University. Institute of Statistics. Bulletin (ISSN 0030-767X)
Refereed Serial

330 UK ISSN 0030-7653
HB31
OXFORD ECONOMIC PAPERS. 1938. q. £96 (foreign $165) (effective 1998). Oxford University Press, Academic Division, Great Clarendon St., Oxford OX2 6DP, England. TEL 44-1865-267907.
FAX 44-1865-267485. TELEX 837330-OXPRES-G. E-mail: jnl.info@oup.co.uk; URL: http://www.oup.co.uk/journals. (U.S. subscr. to: Oxford University Press Inc., 2001 Evans Rd., Cary, NC 27513. TEL 800-852-7323. FAX 919-677-1714) Ed.Bd.; Pub. Martin Green. R&P contact: Joolz Longley. adv. contact: Jane Parker. index. circ. 2,300. (also avail. in microform from UMI; reprint service avail. from UMI) **Indexed:** ABI Inform., Amer.Hist.& Life (1955-1990), ASCA, Asian-Pac.Econ.Lit., Br.Hum.Ind., C.R.E.J., Cont.Pg.Manage., Curr.Cont., Excerpt.Med., Geo.Abstr.P.G., Hist.Abstr. (1955-1990), IDA, J.of Econ.Lit., Key to Econ.Sci., Mid.East: Abstr.& Ind., P.A.I.S., Pub.Admin.Abstr., Risk Abstr., Rural Devel.Abstr., Rural Recreat.Tour.Abstr., SCIMP (1978-), Soc.Sci.Ind., SSCI, World Agri.Econ.& Rural Sociol.Abstr., World Agri.Econ.& Rural Sociol.Abstr., World Bank.Abstr. **Document type:** academic/scholarly publication.
● Also available online. Vendor(s): Information Access Co.
—BLDSC (6320.700000); Genuine Article; KR SourceOne; SWETS; UMI; UnCover. **CCC.**
Description: Addresses theoretical and applied economics, economic history, public administration and scientific method.

338 UK ISSN 0266-903X
HC251
OXFORD REVIEW OF ECONOMIC POLICY. 1985. q. £130 (foreign $225) (effective 1998). Oxford University Press, Academic Division, Great Clarendon St., Oxford OX2 6DP, England. TEL 44-1865-267907.
FAX 44-1865-267485. TELEX 837330-OXPRES-G. E-mail: jnl.info@oup.co.uk; URL: http://www.oup.co.uk/journals. (U.S. subscr. to: Oxford University Press Inc., 2001 Evans Rd., Cary, NC 27513. TEL 800-852-7323. FAX 919-677-1714) Ed. T. Jenkinson; Pub. Martin Green. R&P contact: Joolz Longley. adv. contact: Jane Parker. charts; illus. circ. 1,600. (back issues avail.) **Indexed:** ASCA, C.R.E.J., Curr.Cont., IDA, J.of Econ.Lit., SSCI. **Document type:** academic/scholarly publication.
● Also available online.
—BLDSC (6321.610950); Genuine Article; SWETS; UMI; UnCover. **CCC.**
Description: Provides commentary, forecasts and articles on economic policy in the UK and the world.

330 UK ISSN 0963-8563
P E L OCCASIONAL PAPERS ON BUSINESS, ECONOMY AND SOCIETY. 1991. irreg., no.4, 1991. £10. Polytechnic of East London, Department of Business Studies, Longbridge Rd., Dagenham, Essex RM8 2AS, England. TEL 081-590-7722. Ed.Bd. **Document type:** monographic series.
—BLDSC (6224.337000).

330 PK
P I D E TIDINGS. 1981. 3/yr. free. Pakistan Institute of Development Economics, P.O. Box 1091, Islamabad 44000, Pakistan. TEL 92-51-9206610.
FAX 92-51-9210886. Ed. Sarafraz Khan Qureshi. circ. 1,000.

P M E AU QUEBEC. ETAT DE LA SITUATION. (Petite et Moyenne Entreprise) see *BUSINESS AND ECONOMICS — Production Of Goods And Services*

P O N S I REPORT; linking higher education with business, industry, and government. see *EDUCATION — Higher Education*

P S I DISCUSSION PAPERS. (Policy Studies Institute) see *SOCIAL SCIENCES: COMPREHENSIVE WORKS*

P S I: REPORT SERIES. (Policy Studies Institute) see *POLITICAL SCIENCE*

P T DISTRIBUTOR; helping power transmission distribution add value to products and services. (Power Transmission) see *ENGINEERING — Mechanical Engineering*

330 US ISSN 0030-8552
PACIFIC BUSINESS NEWS.* 1963. w. $54.95. American City Business Journals, Inc. (Austin), 505 Powell Ste., Austin, TX 78703-5121.
TEL 704-375-7404. Ed. Michelle Yamagichi; Pub. Mike Kallay. adv.; bk.rev. circ. 13,000. (tabloid format; also avail. in microfilm from UMI; back issues avail.) **Indexed:** Tr.& Indus.Ind.
● Also available online. Vendor(s): Knight-Ridder Information, Inc., Lexis-Nexis.
—UMI. **CCC.**
Description: News and public record information for business and professional readers in Hawaii.

PACIFIC DIALOGUE. see *ADVERTISING AND PUBLIC RELATIONS*

330 US
PAINEWEBBER WORKING PAPER SERIES. 1984. 4/yr. $240. Columbia University, Graduate School of Business, 6N Uris Hall, New York, NY 10027.
TEL 212-854-8344. FAX 212-316-9219. E-mail: jgla@admin.gsb.colombia.edu. Ed. Joy Glazener. **Document type:** academic/scholarly publication.
Formerly (until 1993): First Boston Working Paper Series (ISSN 1047-9546)
Description: Shares the faculty's research on money, economics and finance with academics, managers and government officials worldwide.

BUSINESS AND ECONOMICS

330.9   **PK**   ISSN 0253-1941
PAKISTAN AND GULF ECONOMIST. (Text in English) 1962. w. Rs.975 (foreign $160; US & Canada $190) (effective 1996 & 1997). Economist Publications (Pvt.) Limited, GSA House, 3rd Fl., 19 Timber Pond, Keamari Rd., P.O. Box No. 10449, Karachi 75620, Pakistan. TEL 92-21-2851190. FAX 92-21-2851815. URL: http://www.pak-economist.com/. Ed. Akhtar Adil Razvi. R&P contact: Suhail Abbas. adv.; bk.rev.; charts; illus.; stat.; index, cum.index. circ. 27,000. **Indexed:** Key to Econ.Sci., Mid.East: Abstr.& Ind., Rural Devel.Abstr., Rural Recreat.Tour.Abstr., World Agri.Econ.& Rural Sociol.Abstr. **Document type:** newspaper.
  Incorporating: Pakistan Economist (ISSN 0030-9745); Which was formerly: Finance and Industry.
  Description: Provides opinion, commentary and analysis on all key business, economic and financial developments in Pakistan.

338.9   **PK**   ISSN 0030-9729
HC440.5
PAKISTAN DEVELOPMENT REVIEW; international journal of development economics. (Text in English) 1961. q. $125. Pakistan Institute of Development Economics, P.O. Box 1091, Islamabad 44000, Pakistan. TEL 92-51-9206610. FAX 92-51-9210886. Ed. Sarfraz Khan Qureshi. bk.rev.; stat. circ. 1,500. (back issues avail.) **Indexed:** Abstr.Rural Dev.Trop., Agri.Eng.Abstr., Asian-Pac.Econ.Lit., Geo.Abstr.P.G., J.of Econ.Lit., Per.Islam. (1989-), Popul.Ind., Rice Abstr., Rural Ext.Educ.& Tr.Abstr., Triticale Abstr., Trop.Oil Seeds Abstr., World Agri.Econ.& Rural Sociol.Abstr. **Document type:** academic/scholarly publication.
—BLDSC (6340.680000); KR SourceOne; SWETS; UnCover.
  Description: Publishes empirical research on development economics with a focus on economic issues relating to Pakistan.

PAKISTAN ECONOMIC AND SOCIAL REVIEW. see BUSINESS AND ECONOMICS — International Development And Assistance

330   **PK**
PAKISTAN ECONOMIC JOURNAL. (Text in English) 1973. s-a. Rs.8($6) Pakistan Economic Association, University of the Punjab, Department of Economics, New Campus, Lahore, Pakistan. Ed. Moin Baqai. adv.; bibl.

338.9   **PK**   ISSN 0078-821X
PAKISTAN INSTITUTE OF DEVELOPMENT ECONOMICS. REPORT. (Text in English) 1962. irreg. Pakistan Institute of Development Economics, P.O. Box 1091, Islamabad 44000, Pakistan. TEL 92-51-9206610. FAX 92-51-9210886. Ed. Sarfraz Khan Qureshi. circ. 1,000. **Indexed:** World Agri.Econ.& Rural Sociol.Abstr. **Document type:** academic/scholarly publication.

338.9   **PK**   ISSN 0078-8228
PAKISTAN INSTITUTE OF DEVELOPMENT ECONOMICS. RESEARCH REPORTS. (Text in English) 1962. irreg., no.157, 1992. price varies. Pakistan Institute of Development Economics, P.O. Box 1091, Islamabad 44000, Pakistan. TEL 92-51-9206610. FAX 92-51-9210886. Ed. Sarfraz Khan Qureshi. circ. 500. (processed) **Indexed:** Rural Devel.Abstr. **Document type:** monographic series.
—BLDSC (7769.547300).

330 346   **BU**   ISSN 0861-5608
PARI. Fortnightly English edition: Bulgarian Economic Review (ISSN 0861-5640) (Text in Bulgarian) 1991. d. Rubicon Ltd., Tsarigradsko Chaussee 47, Sofia 1504, Bulgaria. TEL 359-2-447317. FAX 359-2-445412.

330   **FR**
PARTENAIRES. s-m. 250 F. (Ministere du Travail, de l'Emploi et de la Formation Professionnelle) Imprimerie Nationale, B.P. 514, 59505 Douai Cedex, France. **Document type:** government publication.
  Description: Offers a panorama of business activity in France and Europe.

PATHWAYS TO PROFITABILITY; a financial analysis of the decorating products centers in the U.S. see INTERIOR DESIGN AND DECORATION

330.948   **DK**   ISSN 0107-4873
PENGE OG PRIVATØKONOMI. 1977. m.(11/yr.). DKK 485. Boersen Magasiner A-S, Moentergade 19, P.O. Box 2242, DK-1019 Copenhagen K, Denmark. TEL 45-33-32-44-00. FAX 45-33-11-59-06. Ed. Ole Hoy Hansen. adv.: B&W page DKK 33500, color page DKK 41000; trim 420 x 297; adv. contact: Christian Samsoe. circ. 30,000. (back issues avail.)
  Formerly (until 1981): Penge og Investering (ISSN 0105-4376)
  Description: News about managing personal finances: investing in bonds, shares, real estate, tax regulations, deductions, cars, housing, savings.

330   **US**
PENNSYLVANIA CONFERENCE OF ECONOMISTS. PROCEEDINGS OF THE ANNUAL MEETING. 1951. a. $15. Pennsylvania Conference of Economists, c/o Alexander Garvin, Economics Dept., Indiana University of Pennsylvania, Indiana, PA 15701. TEL 412-357-2640. Ed. Joseph Horton. charts. circ. 500. (back issues avail.) **Document type:** proceedings.

330   **US**
PENNSYLVANIA ECONOMIC REVIEW. 1991. s-a. $25 to non-members. Pennsylvania Economic Association, Economics Dept., Millersville University, Box 1002, Millersville, PA 17551. TEL 717-872-3561. FAX 717-871-2326. E-mail: margolis@mu2.millersv.edu. Ed. Marvin S. Margolis. R&P contact: Marvis S. Margolis. adv. contact: Marvis S. Margolis. bk.rev.; circ. 200 (controlled). (back issues avail.) **Document type:** academic/scholarly publication.
Refereed Serial

330   **HO**
PENSAMIENTO ECONÓMICO. 19??-1975; resumed 1979. q. Colegio Hondureno de Economistas, Tegucigalpa, D.C., Honduras. Ed.Bd. adv.; bibl.; charts; stat. **Indexed:** P.A.I.S.

330   **IT**
PENSIERO ECONOMICO ITALIANO. 1993. s-a. L.40000 to individuals; institutions L.60000. (Universita degli Studi G. D'Annunzio di Chieti, Dipartimento di Storia e Critica della Politica) Gruppo Editoriale Internazionale, Via Ruggero Bonghi 11-B, 00187 Rome, Italy. TEL 39-6-70493456. FAX 39-6-70476605. (Subscr. to: G E I, Via Santa Bibbiana 30, 56127 Pisa, Italy. TEL 39-50-934242. FAX 39-50-934200)

330   **UK**   ISSN 0267-9035
PENSIONS INTELLIGENCE. 1985. m. £145($260) Longman Group UK Ltd., Law, Tax and Finance Division, 21-27 Lamb's Conduit St., London WC1N 3NJ, England. TEL 44-171-242-2548. FAX 44-171-831-8119. **Document type:** newsletter.
—CCC.
  Description: Covers all aspects of pension-fund management, investment and regulation.

PERFORMANCE CHEMICALS. see CHEMISTRY

330   **US**
PERSONAL SUCCESS T M - THE NEWSLETTER; real solutions for all your problems. 1972. m. $99. Du Vall Press Financial Publications, Box 14, Williamston, MI 48895-0014. FAX 517-655-5208. Ed. Dean F.V. Du Vall. adv.; tr.lit. circ. 25,000. **Document type:** newsletter.
  Former titles: Dax Money-Maker (ISSN 0147-1112); Dacs Money Maker Newsletter.

330   **BL**   ISSN 0100-039X
PERSPECTIVA ECONOMICA. 1966. 4/yr. $30 or exchange basis. (Universidade do Vale do Rio dos Sinos) Unisinos, Av. Unisinos, 950, 93022-000 Sao Leopoldo RS, Brazil. TEL 55-51-5920333 ext.1951. FAX 55-51-5921035. Ed. Nestor Saul. bk.rev. circ. 1,000. **Indexed:** IBR. **Document type:** academic/scholarly publication.
  Formerly: Vale do Rio dos Sinos (ISSN 0042-2274)

330   **FR**   ISSN 0304-3274
PERSPECTIVES ÉCONOMIQUES DE L'O E C D. English edition: O E C D Economic Outlook. s-a. Organization for Economic Cooperation and Development, 2 rue Andre-Pascal, 75775 Paris Cedex 16, France. (U.S. orders to: O.E.C.D. Publications and Information Center, 2001 L St., N.W., Ste. 650, Washington, DC 20036-4922. TEL 202-785-6323)

330   **US**
PERSPECTIVES ON ECONOMIC CHANGE. irreg. (approx. 2/yr.) Guilford Publications, Inc., 72 Spring St., New York, NY 10012. TEL 212-431-9800; 800-365-7006. FAX 212-966-6708. E-mail: info@guilford.com. Eds. Peter Dicken, Meric Gertler. **Document type:** monographic series.
  Description: Offers important developments in today's economy, particularly as they operate within, and impact on, space and place at all geographical scales.

330   **BL**   ISSN 0102-7603
HC186
PESQUISA E DEBATE. 1985. s-a. Cr.$1200. Pontificia Universidade Catolica de Sao Paulo, Programa de Estudos Pos-Graduados em Economia, Rua Monte Alegre, 984, 05014 Sao Paulo, SP, Brazil. TEL 62-0280. Ed. Marijane Vieira Lisboa.

PHARMACEUTICAL BUSINESS NEWS; the executive newsletter for the pharmaceutical industry. see PHARMACY AND PHARMACOLOGY

PHARMACEUTICAL COMPANY PROFILES. see PHARMACY AND PHARMACOLOGY

PHARMACOECONOMICS. see PHARMACY AND PHARMACOLOGY

PHARMACOECONOMICS AND OUTCOMES NEWS; rapid alerts to world pharmacoeconomic news, views and practical application. see PHARMACY AND PHARMACOLOGY

330   **PH**
PHILIPPINE BUSINESS REPORT. (Text in English) 1990. free. Department of Trade and Industry, Trade & Industry Information Center, 4th Fl., Industry & Investment Bldg., 385 Sen. Gil J. Puyat Ave., Makati, Metro Manila 3117, Philippines. TEL 02-895-3611. FAX 02-895-6487. Ed. Minerva R. Fajardo. R&P contact: Alfonso M. Valenzuela. **Document type:** government publication, newsletter.
  Description: Provides latest information on government policies, industry, investments, trade and business in the country.

330   **PH**   ISSN 0031-7500
HC451
PHILIPPINE ECONOMIC JOURNAL. 1962. q. P.120($20) Philippine Economic Society, P S S C Bldg., P.O. Box 205, U.P. Diliman, Quezon City, Philippines. Ed. Ruperto P. Alonzo. adv.; bk.rev.; bibl.; charts; stat.; index, cum.index. circ. 1,000. **Indexed:** Asian-Pac.Econ.Lit., C.R.E.J., Geo.Abstr., J.of Econ.Abstr., J.of Econ.Lit., P.A.I.S., Rural Recreat.Tour.Abstr., World Agri.Econ.& Rural Sociol.Abstr.

330   **PH**   ISSN 0031-7780
HC451
PHILIPPINE REVIEW OF ECONOMICS AND BUSINESS. 1964. s-a. $20. University of the Philippines, College of Business Administration, School of Economics, Diliman, Quezon City 1101, Philippines. TEL 632-928-45-71. FAX 632-928-45-74. E-mail: cba@nicole.upd.edu.ph. Eds. Raul Fabella, E.E. Patalinghug. adv.; bk.rev.; charts; index, cum.index. circ. 1,000. (also avail. in microfilm from UMI; reprint service avail. from UMI) **Indexed:** Asian-Pac.Econ.Lit., Ind.Phil.Per., J.of Econ.Lit., Rural Recreat.Tour.Abstr., World Agri.Econ.& Rural Sociol.Abstr.
  Description: Research work and articles about Philippine economic and business conditions.

330   **US**   ISSN 0746-746X
PINELLAS COUNTY REVIEW. 1952. w. $26. Warfield Media Co., Box 6130, Clearwater, FL 34618-6130. TEL 813-724-1112. Ed. Wayne Garcia; Pub. Dave Sutton. adv.; circ. 1,400 (paid); 10,000 (controlled). (tabloid format; back issues avail.) **Document type:** newspaper.
  Description: Covers news of interest to the Tampa Bay legal, financial, business and real estate communities.

BUSINESS AND ECONOMICS

330   US   ISSN 0883-7910
PITTSBURGH BUSINESS TIMES - JOURNAL. 1985. w. $68. Pittsburgh Business Times, 2313 E. Carson St., Ste. 200, Pittsburgh, PA 15203-2109. TEL 412-481-6397. FAX 412-481-9956. Ed. Paul Furiga; Pub. Alan Robertson. adv.: B&W page $4350; adv. contact: Rick Lindner. circ. 13,501 (paid). **Indexed:** Tr.& Indus.Ind. **Document type:** consumer publication.
 ● Also available online. Vendor(s): Information Access Co., UMI.
 —CCC.
 Formed by the merger of (1985-1985): Pittsburgh Business Times (ISSN 0279-330X) & Pittsburgh Business Journal (ISSN 0279-2915)

330   YU   ISSN 0554-2537
PLANIRANJE I ANALIZA POSLOVANJA. 1958. m. 1150 din. Zavod za Ekonomske Ekspertize, Palmira Toljatija 3, Belgrade, Yugoslavia. Ed. Sima Doncevic.
 —BLDSC (6508.553850).

PLANNING FOR SOCIAL CHANGE. see *SOCIOLOGY*

330   XV   ISSN 1318-1025
PODJETNIK. (Text in Slovenian) 1985. m. 14400 din.($32) T.O.Z.D. Delavska Enotnost, N.sol.o. Celovska 43, N.sub.o. CGP Delo, P.O. 313-VI, 61001 Ljubljana, Slovenia. Ed. Joze Vilfan.
 Formerly (until 1991): Revija za Razvoj (ISSN 0352-7832)

330   AT   ISSN 1032-6634
H97
POLICY. 1978. 4/yr. Aus.$40 (foreign Aus.$50). Centre for Independent Studies, Box 92, St. Leonards, N.S.W. 2065, Australia. TEL 61-2-94384377. FAX 61-2-94397310. E-mail: cis@cis.rog.au; URL: http://www.cis.org.au. Ed. Andrew Norton. bk.rev. circ. 2,000. **Indexed:** AESIS. **Document type:** academic/scholarly publication.
 —BLDSC (6543.320500); UnCover. CCC.
 Former titles: C I S Policy Report (ISSN 0814-9321) & C I S Newsletter (ISSN 0155-0144)
 Description: Provides regular, expert commentary on public affairs based on economic and social research.
 Refereed Serial

330   US
POLICY BITES. bi-m. free. Urban Institute, 2100 M St., N.W., Washington, DC 20037. TEL 202-833-7200. FAX 202-223-3043. Ed.Bd. **Document type:** academic/scholarly publication.
 Description: Comments on economic and social issues.

POLICY SCIENCES; an international journal devoted to the improvement of policy making. see *POLITICAL SCIENCE*

POLICY STUDIES. see *POLITICAL SCIENCE*

330   CN   ISSN 0832-7912
POLICY STUDY. 1986. irreg. price varies. C.D. Howe Institute, 125 Adelaide St. E., Toronto, ON M5C 1L7, Canada. TEL 416-865-1904. FAX 416-865-1866. E-mail: cdhome@cdhome.org; URL: http://www.cdhome.org. **Document type:** monographic series.
 —BLDSC (6543.329560).
 Description: Studies of Canadian and international economic and social policy issues.

330   PL   ISSN 0208-5666
POLITECHNIKA GDANSKA. ZESZYTY NAUKOWE. EKONOMIA. (Text in English, Polish; summaries in Russian and one West-European language) 1967. irreg. price varies. Politechnika Gdanska, Ul. G. Narutowicza 11-12, 80-952 Gdansk 6, Poland. (Dist. by: Osrodek Rozpowszechniania Wydawnictw Naukowych PAN, Palac Kultury i Nauki, 00-901 Warsaw, Poland) bibl.; charts; illus.; stat. **Document type:** academic/scholarly publication.
 Description: Deals with political economy and philosophy.

330   PL
POLITECHNIKA KRAKOWSKA. ZESZYTY NAUKOWE. NAUKI SPOLECZNE I EKONOMICZNE. (Text in Polish; summaries in English, French, German, Russian) 1967. irreg. price varies. Politechnika Krakowska, Ul. Warszawska 24, 31-155 Krakow, Poland. TEL 48-12-374289. FAX 48-12-335773. TELEX 322468 PK PL. E-mail: Marcinek@biblos.pk.edu.pl. bibl.; charts; illus. circ. 200. **Document type:** academic/scholarly publication, monographic series.
 Formerly: Politechnika Krakowska. Zeszyty Naukowe. Nauki Ekonomiczne (ISSN 0548-0442)

POLITECHNIKA LODZKA. ZESZYTY NAUKOWE. ORGANIZACJA I ZARZADZANIE. see *SOCIAL SCIENCES: COMPREHENSIVE WORKS*

330   PL
POLITECHNIKA WARSZAWSKA. OSRODEK NAUK SPOLECZNYCH. ZESZYTY NAUKOWE. 1972. irreg., no.8, 1996. Politechnika Warszawska, Osrodek Nauk Spolecznych, c/o Biblioteka Glowna, Pl. Politechniki 1, 00-661 Warsaw, Poland. E-mail: bgpw@bg.pw.edu.pl. **Document type:** academic/scholarly publication.
 Formerly: Politechnika Warszawska. Instytut Nauk Ekonomiczno-Spolecznych. Prace (ISSN 0137-2262)

POLITICA ED ECONOMIA/POLITICS AND ECONOMICS. see *POLITICAL SCIENCE*

POLITICAL AND ECONOMIC REVIEW. see *POLITICAL SCIENCE*

330   XR   ISSN 0032-3233
POLITICKA EKONOMIE/JOURNAL OF POLITICAL ECONOMY. (Text in Czech; summaries in English) 1953. bi-m. $110. Vysoka Skola Ekonomicka, Nam. W. Churchilla 4, 130 67 Prague 3, Czech Republic. TEL 42-2-24095819. FAX 42-2-24220675. E-mail: papers@vse.cz. Ed. Milan Zak. bk.rev.; bibl.; index. circ. 4,000. (reprint service avail. from SCH) **Indexed:** Acad.Ind., Amer.Hist.& Life (1955-1990), ASCA, Curr.Cont., Fam.Ind., Hist.Abstr. (1955-1990), IMFL, Int.Polit.Sci.Abstr., Risk Abstr., SSCI, Tr.& Indus.Ind., World Agri.Econ.& Rural Sociol.Abstr., World Bank.Abstr. **Document type:** academic/scholarly publication.
 —BLDSC (6543.932000).
 Description: A theoretical journal publishing results of scientific research into economics. Deals mainly with problems of intensive reproduction, planning, forecasting and improving the management system.
 Refereed Serial

POLITIK EKONOMIK BULTEN GAZETESI. see *POLITICAL SCIENCE*

POLITIKA. see *POLITICAL SCIENCE*

330   PL   ISSN 0079-3353
POLSKA AKADEMIA NAUK. ODDZIAL W KRAKOWIE. KOMISJA NAUK EKONOMICZNYCH. PRACE. (Text in Polish; summaries in English) 1960. irreg. price varies. Ossolineum, Publishing House of the Polish Academy of Sciences, Pl. Solny 14a, 50-062 Wroclaw, Poland. TEL 48-71-3436961. FAX 48-71-448103. TELEX 0712771 OSS PL. **Document type:** monographic series.

330   TH
POO JAD KARN MONTHLY. (Text in Thai) 1983. m. Manager Co., Ltd., 98-3 10 Phra-A-Thit Rd., Chanasongkhram, Phranakorn, Bangkok 10200, Thailand. TEL 02-2801300. FAX 02-2810033. Ed. Permpol Bhowperrmhem; Pub. Sondhi Limthongkul. adv.: B&W page B.40000, color page B.52000; trim 215 x 290; adv. contact: M. Hema.
 Description: Contains business, economical, political and social analysis for businessmen and executives.

330   IT
PORTAPORTESE. 1978. bi-w. L.360000 (foreign L.414000). S.E.G.E. s.r.l., Via di Porta Maggiore 95, 00185 Rome, Italy. TEL 06-70300005. FAX 06-70300007. Ed. Rosario Caccamo. adv. contact: Brunello Caccamo. circ. 105,000.

330.968   SA
PORTFOLIO OF BLACK BUSINESS IN SOUTHERN AFRICA. 1993. a. W R Publications, P.O. Box 7485, Johannesburg 2000, South Africa. illus.; maps.
 Formerly (until 1994): Portfolio of Black Business in South Africa.

PORTUGAL. INSTITUTO NACIONAL DE ESTATISTICA. INQUERITO AO EMPREGO. see *BUSINESS AND ECONOMICS — Small Business*

330   IT
IL POSTO. fortn. L.20000. Job Editore, Via in Arcione 111, Rome, Italy. TEL 06-6782828. Ed. Emilio Paolo Tria. adv.: B&W page L.9600000. circ. 77,000.

PRAEGER SERIES IN POLITICAL ECONOMY. see *POLITICAL SCIENCE*

330   XR   ISSN 1210-0455
HC267.B2
PRAGUE ECONOMIC PAPERS. (Text in English) 1959. q. $70. Vysoka Skola Ekonomicka, Nam. W. Churchilla 4, 130 67 Prague 3, Czech Republic. TEL 42-2-24095819. FAX 42-2-24220657. E-mail: papers@vse.cz. Ed. Milan Zak. bk.rev.; bibl. circ. 1,000. **Indexed:** C.R.E.J., J.of Econ.Lit. **Document type:** academic/scholarly publication.
 —BLDSC (6598.522000).
 Formerly (until 1992): Czechoslovak Economic Papers (ISSN 0590-5001)
 Description: Provides experts aborad with information concerning the evolution of economic theory as well as actual problems of the transformation, scientific life and new economic literature published in Czech Republic.
 Refereed Serial

330   NO   ISSN 0803-4680
PRAKTISK OEKONOMI & LEDELSE. 1985. 4/yr. NOK 810. (Norwegian Federation of Business Economists) Bedriftsoekomens Forlag, Lybekkergt.2, Postboks 9049, Vaterland, 0134 Oslo 1, Norway. FAX 02-17-06-00. adv.; bk.rev.; illus.; index. circ. 10,000. (back issues avail.) **Indexed:** Intl.Mgmt.Info.
 Former titles: Praktisk Oekonomi (ISSN 0800-8159)

330   GW   ISSN 0341-7948
PRAXIS DES RECHNUNGSWESENS; Buchfuehrung, Bilanzierung, Betriebsabrechnung, EDV Loesungen. 1973. bi-m. DM.250. Rudolf Haufe Verlag GmbH & Co. KG, Hindenburgstr. 64, 79102 Freiburg, Germany. TEL 49-761-3683-0. FAX 49-761-3683-195. bk.rev. **Document type:** trade publication.

330   GW   ISSN 0940-8428
PRAXIS HANDBUCH PERSONAL. 1991. bi-m. DM.198. Verlag Norman Rentrop, Theodor-Heuss-Str. 4, 53177 Bonn, Germany. TEL 49-228-8205-0. FAX 49-228-364411. TELEX 17228309-TTX-D. Ed. Peter Derschka. (looseleaf format; back issues avail.) **Document type:** bulletin.

330   GW   ISSN 0944-2499
PRAXISHANDBUCH BUCHFUEHRUNG UND STEUERN FUER FREIBERUFLER UND KLEINUNTERNEHMER. 1993. 6/yr. DM.199.80. Verlag Norman Rentrop, Theodor-Heuss-Str. 4, 53177 Bonn, Germany. TEL 49-228-82050. FAX 49-228-364411. TELEX 17228309. Ed. Dagmar Koempf. (looseleaf format) **Document type:** bulletin.
 Description: Information on taxation for small businesses.

330   US   ISSN 1060-5088
JC362   CODEN: PPMIEK
PRESIDENTS AND PRIME MINISTERS; international perspectives from world leaders. 1992. bi-m. $22.35 (foreign $41.35) (effective 1997). E Q E S Inc., 799 Roosevelt Rd., Bldg. 6, Ste. 208, Glen Ellyn, IL 60137-5925. TEL 708-858-6161. FAX 708-858-8787. Ed. Newal K. Agnihotri; Pub. Newal K. Agnihotri. R&P contact: Newal K. Agnihotri. adv.: B&W page $720, color page $1220; trim 8 1/4 x 10 7/8; adv. contact: Anu Agnihotri. circ. 1,200. (also avail. in microform from UMI) **Indexed:** P.A.I.S., Per.Islam. (1993-). **Document type:** consumer publication.
 —BLDSC (6609.910000); UMI. CCC.
 Description: Features articles and speeches by top government officials.

330　　　　　UK　　ISSN 1352-8157
PRICE WATERHOUSE CORPORATE REGISTER. 1989. a. £175 (rest of Europe £200; the Americas £219; Africa and Middle East £227; Asia and Australia £230) (effective 1997). Hemmington Scott Publishing Ltd., 26-31 Whiskin St., London EC1R OBP, England. TEL 44-171-278-7769. FAX 44-171-278-9808. Ed. Nicolee Stevens. stat. **Document type:** directory.
—BLDSC (6612.874000).
　Former titles (until 1995): Arthur Andersen Corporate Register; Hambro Corporate Register (ISSN 0956-2893)
　Description: Contains contact details and biographies for directors, officers and advisers of all U.K. stock market companies.

330　　　　　US　　ISSN 0079-5291
PRINCETON UNIVERSITY. ECONOMETRIC RESEARCH PROGRAM. RESEARCH MEMORANDUM. 1957. irreg., no.372, 1995. price varies. Princeton University, Econometric Research Program, c/o Program Secretary, Department of Economics, 203 Fisher Hall, Princeton, NJ 08544-1021. TEL 609-258-4030. FAX 609-258-5561. Ed. Gregory C. Chow. circ. 200. (also avail. in microform; back issues avail.) **Document type:** academic/scholarly publication.
—BLDSC (7742.550000).

PRIVATA AFFAERER. see *CONSUMER EDUCATION AND PROTECTION*

330　　　　　PH
PRIVATE DEVELOPMENT CORPORATION OF THE PHILIPPINES. ECONOMIC PERFORMANCE AND PROSPECTS; international-domestic economy. (Text in English) 1977. s-a. $30. Private Development Corporation of the Philippines - Pribadong Korporasyon sa Pagpapaunlad ng Pilipinas, P.O. Box 757 Makati, Metro Manila 3117, Philippines. TEL 02-8100231. FAX 02-8195376. TELEX RCA-22080. circ. 600.

330　　　　　UK　　ISSN 0961-4206
PRIVATISATION INTERNATIONAL; monthly intelligence report on privatisation and private financing of infrastructure. 1988. m. £450($695) (CD-ROM £850($1350)) (effective 1997). Privatisation International Ltd., Butlers Wharf Business Centre, Ste. 404, 45 Curlew St., London SE1 2ND, England. TEL 44-171-378-1620; 800-321-6388. FAX 44-171-403-7876. E-mail: 100446.3646@compuserve.com. Ed. Rodney Lord. adv.: B&W page £950, color page £1425; adv. contact: Diana Howarth. circ. 950. **Document type:** newsletter.
●Also available online. Vendor(s): Information Access Co.
Also available on CD-ROM.
　Description: Intelligence report on privatisation and private financing of infrastructure worldwide.

330　　　　　UK　　ISSN 1352-3139
PRIVATISATION YEARBOOK. 1992. a. £110. Privatisation International Ltd., Butlers Wharf Business Centre, Ste. 404, 45 Curlew St., London SE1 2ND, England. TEL 44-171-378-1620. FAX 44-171-403-7876. E-mail: 100446.3646@compuserve.com. Ed. Rodney Lord. adv. contact: Diana Howarth. **Document type:** trade publication.
—BLDSC (6617.069700).
　Description: Detailed review of privatization developments in approximately 75 different countries.

330　　　　　YU　　ISSN 0032-8979
PRIVREDNA IZGRADNJA. (Text mainly in Serbo-Croatian; occasionally in Hungarian, Rumanian, Ruthenian and Slovenian; summaries in English or Russian) 1951. q. $20. Savez Ekonomista Vojvodine - Association of Economists of Vojvodine, Zmaj Jovine 26, 21000 Novi Sad, Yugoslavia. TEL 021 24-971. Ed. Branko Bijelic. adv.; bk.rev.; abstr.; bibl.; charts; stat.; index. circ. 700.
●Also available online.
—BLDSC (6617.071800).
　Formerly: Privreda (Novi Sad).

330　　　　　CI　　ISSN 0032-8995
PRIVREDNI VJESNIK/ECONOMIC HERALD. (Text in Croatian) 1954. w. Privredni Vjesnik Holding, Kacićeva 9, 41000 Zagreb, Croatia. TEL 041-422-182. FAX 041-429-308. Ed. Franjo Zilic. index. circ. 11,200.

338　　　　　MX　　ISSN 0301-7036
HC121　　　　　CODEN: PRDEFC
PROBLEMAS DEL DESARROLLO; revista latinoamericana de economía. 1969. q. $40. Universidad Nacional Autonoma de Mexico, Instituto de Investigaciones Economicas, Torre 11 de Humanidades 1er Piso, Apdo. Postal 20-721, 04510 Mexico, D.F., Mexico. TEL 5505215 ext. 2904. Dir. Salvador Rodriguez y Rodriguez. adv.; bk.rev.; cum.index. circ. 2,000. (also avail. in microfiche; microfilm) **Indexed:** Curr.Cont., Hisp.Amer.Per.Ind. (1977-), IBR, Int.Lab.Doc.
—SWETS.
　Description: Examines economic issues and questions of political economy.

330　　　　　AA
PROBLEME EKONOMIKE. 1953. bi-m. $6.16. Academie des Sciences de la RPSA, Institut des Etudes Economiques, Tirana, Albania. TEL 042-26418. bk.rev. circ. 2,000. **Indexed:** Geo.Abstr.

330　　　　　FR　　ISSN 0032-9304
HC10
PROBLEMES ECONOMIQUES; selection de textes francais et etrangers. 1948. w. 440 F. (Europe 600 F., elsewhere 710 F.) (effective 1997). Documentation Francaise, 29-31 quai Voltaire, 75344 Paris Cedex 07, France. TEL 33-1-40157000. FAX 33-1-40157230. TELEX 215 666 DOCFRAN. (Subscr. to: 124 rue Henri Barbusse, 93308 Aubervilliers Cedex, France. TEL 33-1-48395600. FAX 33-1-48395601) index. circ. 22,000. (also avail. in microfiche from DFR) **Indexed:** Cott.& Trop.Fibr.Abstr., ELLIS, Int.Lab.Doc., Key to Econ.Sci., Pt.de Rep. (1989-), Triticale Abstr., Trop.Oil Seeds Abstr., World Bibl.Soc.Sec. **Document type:** government publication.
—BLDSC (6617.870300); SWETS.

330　　　　　US　　ISSN 1061-1991
HC10
PROBLEMS OF ECONOMIC TRANSITION; selected articles from Soviet economic journals in English translation. 1958. m. $138 to individuals (foreign $176); institutions $800 (foreign $900) (effective 1997). M.E. Sharpe, Inc., 80 Business Park Dr., Armonk, NY 10504. TEL 914-273-1800; 800-541-6563. FAX 914-273-2106. Ed. John Tedstrom. adv.: page $300; trim 5 x 8; adv. contact: Barbara Ladd. stat.; index. (back issues avail.) **Indexed:** C.R.E.J., Curr.Cont., Energy Ind., Energy Info.Abstr., Int.Lab.Doc., J.of Econ.Lit., Key to Econ.Sci., Mid.East Abstr.& Ind., P.A.I.S., Risk Abstr., SSCI. **Document type:** academic/scholarly publication.
—BLDSC (6617.883050); Genuine Article; SWETS; UMI; UnCover. **CCC.**
　Formerly: Problems in Economics (ISSN 0032-9436)
　Description: Scans Russian-language economic literature, from Voprosy ekonomiki to EDO, to allow readers to follow the principal theoretical and policy issues that constitute post-Soviet economic discourse in various regions of the former USSR. Topics covered include reform policy; foreign economic relations; industrial reorganization; labor economics and social policy; and regional economic development.
　Refereed Serial

PROCESO; informativo semanal. see *POLITICAL SCIENCE*

PRODUCTS LIABILITY REPORTS. see *LAW*

330 320　　　　　SP　　ISSN 0214-7130
PROFESIONALES Y CUADROS. 6/yr. Isla de Saipan 47, 28035 Madrid, Spain. TEL 1-373-47-50. FAX 1-316-91-77. Ed. J. Menendez Zapata. circ. 24,778.
　Formerly (until 1985): Cuadros (ISSN 0214-7637).

PROFESSIONAL LIABILITY TODAY. see *INSURANCE*

330　　　　　FR　　ISSN 0220-3480
PROFESSIONS DU SUD EST. 11/yr. 16 place General de Gaulle, 13231 Marseille Cedex 1, France. TEL 91-57-71-00. FAX 91-54-86-03. Ed. T. Debaille. circ. 20,000.

338.642　　　　　CN　　ISSN 1183-1324
PROFIT; the magazine for Canadian entrepreneurs. 1982. bi-m. Can.$16 (foreign Can.$30) (effective 1997). Canadian Business Media, 777 Bay St., 5th Fl., Toronto, ON M5W 1A7, Canada. TEL 416-596-9999. FAX 416-596-5152. E-mail: profit@cbmedia.ca. Ed. Rick Spence. adv. contact: Deborah Rosser. bk.rev. circ. 100,000. (also avail. in microfiche; microform from UMI; back issues avail.) **Indexed:** Can.B.P.I., Can.Per.Ind. **Document type:** consumer publication, trade publication.
—UMI.
　Former titles: Small Business (ISSN 0714-4210); Magazine That's All About Small Business.
　Description: Provides hands-on management information and ideas, covers entrepreneurial successes and failures, profiles Canada's fastest-growing companies and explores political and social issues as they affect business.

330　　　　　IT
PROGETTO MANAGER. 10/yr. Federazione Nazionale Dirigenti Aziende Industriali - National Federation of Industrial Company Directors, Via Palermo 12, 00184 Rome, Italy. TEL 06-47-40-351. Ed. Silvano Revelli. adv.: B&W page L.6000000, color page L.8000000. circ. 75,000.

330　　　　　AT
▼**PROPRIETARY COMPANIES GUIDE.** 1996. a. C C H Australia Ltd., P.O. Box 230, North Ryde, N.S.W. 2113, Australia. TEL 61-1-300300224. FAX 61-1-300306224. (looseleaf format)
　Description: Designed to help proprietary companies and advisers understand the statutory requirements through the course of a financial year.

330　　　　　US　　ISSN 0887-8226
PROVIDENCE BUSINESS NEWS. 1986. w. $69. Providence Business News, Inc., 300 Richmond St., Ste. 202, Providence, RI 02903-4288. TEL 401-273-2201. FAX 401-274-0670. Ed. Franklin S. Prosnitz; Pub. Roger Bergenheim. adv. contact: John S. Lamp. bk.rev. circ. 11,000. **Document type:** newspaper.
　Description: Covers local and regional business news.

PROVINCIAL LEGISLATIVE RECORD. see *PUBLIC ADMINISTRATION*

330　　　　　NE　　ISSN 0048-5829
JA1　　　　　CODEN: PUCHBX
PUBLIC CHOICE. 1966. 16/yr. fl.1560 to institutions; $800 to institutions in U.S. (effective 1998). (George Mason University, Center for the Study of Public Choice, US) Kluwer Academic Publishers, Postbus 17, 3300 AA Dordrecht, Netherlands. TEL 31-78-6392392. FAX 31-78-6392254. TELEX 29245 KAPG NL. E-mail: services@wkap.nl; URL: http://www.wkap.nl. (Dist. by: Kluwer Academic Publishers Group, P.O. Box 322, 3300 AH Dordrecht, Netherlands. TEL 31-78-6392392. FAX 31-78-6546474; N. America dist. addr.: Box 358, Accord Sta., Hingham, MA 02018-0358. FAX 617-871-6528) Eds. Charles K. Rowley, Robert D. Tollison. adv.; bk.rev.; bibl.; cum.index. (also avail. in microform from UMI; reprint service avail. from SWZ,UMI) **Indexed:** A.B.C.Pol.Sci., Arts & Hum.Cit.Ind., ASCA, Curr.Cont., Geo.Abstr., IBR, Int.Polit.Sci.Abstr., J.of Econ.Lit., Lang.& Lang.Behav.Abstr., Polit.Sci.Abstr., Sage Pub.Admin.Abstr., Sage Urb.Stud.Abstr., SSCI. **Document type:** academic/scholarly publication.
—BLDSC (6962.900000); Genuine Article; SWETS; UMI; UnCover. **CCC.**
　Description: Discusses issues at the intersection between economics and political science, and the application of economic methods to problems dealt with by political scientists.
　Refereed Serial

PUBLIC INTEREST. see *SOCIAL SCIENCES: COMPREHENSIVE WORKS*

330　　　　　FR　　ISSN 0297-7826
PUBLICATIONS COMMERCIALES. 100/yr. 63 rue Paradis, B.P. 228, 13253 Marseille Cedex 6, France. TEL 91-33-23-80. FAX 91-33-37-16. Ed. Y. Bertaudon. circ. 8,000.
　Description: Provides commercial, economic, legal information covering the Bouche-du-Rhone area.

BUSINESS AND ECONOMICS

330 US ISSN 8750-7757
PUGET SOUND BUSINESS JOURNAL. 1980. w. $26. Scripps Howard Business Publications (Seattle), 720 Third Ave., Ste. 800, Seattle, WA 98104. TEL 206-583-0701. Ed. Mike Flynn. adv. circ. 14,393. (tabloid format; also avail. in microform from UMI) **Indexed:** Tr.& Indus.Ind. **Document type:** trade publication.
●Also available online. Vendor(s): Information Access Co., Knight-Ridder Information, Inc.
—UMI. **CCC.**
Formerly: Seattle Business Journal (ISSN 0274-5453)

650 CN
PURPLE REPORT. 1986. w. McGill University, Graduate Business Students' Society, 1001 Sherbrooke St. W., Montreal, PQ H3C 3G1, Canada. TEL 514-348-4311. Ed. Wendy Tassiae Chan. illus. circ. 200.
Formerly: McGill Journal of Business (ISSN 0541-6159)

338 MY ISSN 0126-5466
PUSPANIAGA.* 1973. m. M.$6. Berita Publishing, 22 Jalan Liku, 59100 Kuala Lumpur, Malaysia. Ed. Zanial Abidin Safarnan. circ. 4,500.

Q J I. (Quarterly Journal of Ideology) see POLITICAL SCIENCE

QANOUN WAL IQTISAD/DROIT ET ECONOMIE POLITIQUE. see LAW

330 CC ISSN 1000-968X
QIYE JISHU JINBU. (Text in Chinese) bi-m. Qiye Jishu Jinbu Zazhishe, No. A-397, Guang'anmenwai Dajie, Beijing 100055, People's Republic of China. TEL 3261417. Ed. Li Hongdao.

330 FR ISSN 0767-9432
QUALITIQUE. (Text in French; summaries in English, German, Spanish) 1988. 10/yr. 695 F. (Europe 795 F.; elsewhere 895 F.) (effective 1998). Editions Labeau, 9 rue Albert Einstein, 77420 Champs-sur-Marne, France. TEL 33-1-64682193. FAX 33-1-64687904. TELEX 612 259. E-mail: 106334.3016@compuserve.com. (Subscr. to: ATEI, 3 av. Pierre Kerautret, 93230 Romainville, France. TEL 33-1-48408686. FAX 33-1-48400731) Ed. Jean-Luc Laffargue; Pub. Brigitte Monnier. R&P contact: Christelle Pasquier. adv. contact: Cecile Aivazis. illus.; tr.lit.; circ. 10,000 (paid). **Document type:** newspaper.
Description: Keeps track of evolution in all sectors of quality engineering, offers solutions to management and production problems, presents new products, technologies and strategic tools.
Refereed Serial

330 US ISSN 1057-9583
TS156.A1
QUALITY OBSERVER. 1991. m. $99 to individuals (foreign $139); institutions $168. Quality Observer, 3970 Chain Bridge Rd., Fairfax, VA 22030-3316. TEL 703-691-9496. Ed. Mike Matheny. adv. circ. 25,000. **Indexed:** Q.Abstr.
Description: Contains interviews, case studies, international news and columns covering a broad range of industries and organizations.

330 CC ISSN 1002-6584
QUANGUO QINGGONG XINXI/CHINA NATIONWIDE LIGHT INDUSTRIAL NEWS. (Text in Chinese) 1986. w. $100. Zhonguo Qinggongye Jingji Keji Xinxi Zhongxin - China Economic, Scientific and Technological Information Centre of Light Industry, 22B, Fuwai Dajie, Beijing 100833, People's Republic of China. TEL 86-10-6839-6607. FAX 86-10-6839-6607. Ed. Pang Zhenhua. **Document type:** government publication, bulletin.

330 AT
THE QUANTAS CLUB. 1987. m. membership only. (Australian Airlines Flight Deck Club) B R W Media, Level 2, La Trobe St., Melbourne, Vic. 3000, Australia. TEL 61-3-96428716. FAX 61-3-96420852. bk.rev. circ. 60,000. (back issues avail.)
Formerly (until Sep. 1994): Flight Deck (ISSN 0819-419X)

330 UK ISSN 0959-6798
QUARTERLY ACCOUNT. 1983. q. £15. Money Advice Association, Gresham House, 1st Fl., 24 Holborn Viaduct, London EC1A 2BN, England. TEL 44-171-236-3566. Ed. Steve Wilcox. R&P contact: Jane Guy. adv. contact: Jane Guy. bk.rev. circ. 500. **Indexed:** LJI. **Document type:** trade publication.
—BLDSC (7169.890000).
Description: Provides personal finance-related advice and information.
Refereed Serial

330 US ISSN 0888-787X
QUARTERLY DOMESTIC & GLOBAL FORECASTS OF KEY ECONOMIC INDICATORS. 1984. q. $105 for hard copy (foreign $150); with floppy disk $125 (foreign $170). (Institute of Business Forecasting) Graceway Publishing Co., Box 670159, Flushing, New York, NY 11367-0159. TEL 718-463-3914. FAX 718-544-9086. Ed. Dennis F. Ellis. R&P contact: Chaman L. Jain. adv. contact: Jean McCreary. circ. 450. (looseleaf format; back issues avail.) **Document type:** trade publication.
—**CCC.**
Description: Provides one-year-ahead forecasts of real economic growth rate, inflation, and balance of payments for 47 countries plus interest and foreign exchange rates forecasts for 7 major countries. Also provides consensus forecasts of 13 key variables of the US economy, and industry forecasts.

330 IE ISSN 0376-7191
HC257.I6
QUARTERLY ECONOMIC COMMENTARY. q. I£30 per no. Economic and Social Research Institute, 4 Burlington Rd., Dublin 4, Ireland. TEL 353-1-6671525. FAX 353-1-6686231. Ed. B.J. Whelan. R&P contact: John Roughan. **Document type:** bulletin.
—BLDSC (7181.242500).

330 338 US ISSN 0747-5535
HB1
QUARTERLY JOURNAL OF BUSINESS AND ECONOMICS. Short title: Q J B E. 1962. q. $16 to individuals (foreign $30); institutions $30 (foreign $40) (effective 1997). University of Nebraska at Lincoln, College of Business Administration, Bureau of Business Research, CBA Bldg., Lincoln, NE 68588-0407. TEL 402-472-3309. FAX 402-472-9777. E-mail: myoung@cbamail.unl.edu; URL: http://www.cba.unl.edu/mani2/pubs/qjbe/QJBE.html. Ed. George M. McCabe. R&P contact: Margo Young. TEL 402-472-7931. charts; illus.; circ. 400 (paid). (also avail. in microform from UMI; reprint service avail. from UMI) **Indexed:** ABI Inform., ASCA, Asian-Pac.Econ.Lit., BPIA, Bus.Ind., C.R.E.J., Human Resour.Abstr., J.of Econ.Lit., Manage.Cont., Mid.East: Abstr.& Ind., P.A.I.S., SSCI, Tr.& Indus.Ind., World Agri.Econ.& Rural Sociol.Abstr. **Document type:** academic/scholarly publication.
●Also available online. Vendor(s): Information Access Co.
—BLDSC (7187.930000); SWETS; UMI; UnCover. **CCC.**
Former titles (until 1983): N J E B: Nebraska Journal of Economics and Business (ISSN 0160-6557); Nebraska Journal of Economics and Business (ISSN 0028-1867)
Description: Features scholarly articles that empirically test theories in the fields of finance, accounting, economics, marketing and land management.
Refereed Serial

330 650 US ISSN 1062-9769
HC10 CODEN: QREBAE
THE QUARTERLY REVIEW OF ECONOMICS AND FINANCE. 1960. q. (plus a. supplement). $125 to individuals (foreign $150); institutions $255 (foreign $280) (effective 1998). (University of Illinois at Urbana-Champaign, Bureau of Economics and Business Research) J A I Press Inc., 55 Old Post Rd., No. 2, Box 1678, Greenwich, CT 06830-1678. TEL 203-661-7602. FAX 203-661-0792. E-mail: jai@jaipress.com. (Addr. in Europe: J A I Press Ltd., 38 Tavistock St., Covent Garden, London WC2E 7PB, England. TEL 44-171-379-8834. FAX 44-171-379-8835) Eds. Richard J. Arnould, Joseph E. Finnerty. adv.; bk.rev.; abstr. circ. 2,000. (also avail. in microform from MIM,UMI; back issues avail.; reprint service avail. from SCH,UMI) **Indexed:** ABI Inform., Amer.Hist.& Life (until 1992), ASCA, Asian-Pac.Econ.Lit., B.P.I., BPIA, Bus.Ind., Cont.Pg.Manage., Curr.Cont., Hist.Abstr. (1966-1992), J.of Econ.Abstr., J.of Econ.Lit., Manage.Cont., Oper.Res.Manage.Sci., P.A.I.S., Pers.Manage.Abstr., Risk Abstr., Rural Recreat.Tour.Abstr., SCIMP, SSCI, Tr.& Indus.Ind., Work Rel.Abstr., World Agri.Econ.& Rural Sociol.Abstr. **Document type:** academic/scholarly publication.
●Also available online. Vendor(s): Information Access Co.
—BLDSC (7206.501000); Genuine Article; KR SourceOne; SWETS; UMI; UnCover. **CCC.**
Former titles (until 1992): Quarterly Review of Economics and Business (ISSN 0033-5797); Current Economic Comment.

330 CM
QUE SAVOIR; industrie-commerce-tourisme. 1978. m. 10000 Fr.CFA. Consultants International, B.P. 1986, Douala, Cameroon. Ed.Bd. adv.; bk.rev. circ. 15,000.

QUEBEC (PROVINCE). MINISTERE DE L'ANALYSE DE LA CONJONCTURE INDUSTRIELLE. SECTEUR MANUFACTURIER ET LE COMMERCE. see BUSINESS AND ECONOMICS — Production Of Goods And Services

330 CN ISSN 0316-5078
HB31
QUEEN'S UNIVERSITY. INSTITUTE FOR ECONOMIC RESEARCH. DISCUSSION PAPER. 1969. irreg. Can.$180 (foreign Can.$210). Queen's University, Institute for Economic Research, Kingston. ON K7L 3N6, Canada. TEL 613-545-2260. FAX 613-545-6668. E-mail: pachecoe@qed.econ.queensu.ca. bibl. circ. 200. **Document type:** academic/scholarly publication.
—BLDSC (3597.590000).

QUESTE ISTITUZIONI; cronache del sistema politico. see POLITICAL SCIENCE

330 US
QUINCY BUSINESS NEWS. 1989. m. free. John R. Graham, Inc., 40 Oval Rd., Ste. 2, Quincy, MA 02170-3813. TEL 617-328-0069. FAX 617-471-1504. E-mail: info@grahamcomm.com. Ed. Cindy Cantrell. R&P contact: Cindy Cantrell. adv.; bk.rev.; circ. 2,850 (controlled). (back issues avail.) **Document type:** newsletter.
Description: For residents and businesses in Quincy.
Refereed Serial

330 NE ISSN 0920-8275
QUOTE. 1986. m. Quote B.V., P.O. Box 10209, 1001 EE Amsterdam, Netherlands. TEL 31-20-6244961. adv.
—SWETS.

660 JA
R & D ACTIVITIES OF MAJOR JAPANESE CHEMICAL COMPANIES. (Text in English) 1990. irreg. $550 per copy. Dodwell Marketing Consultants, Kowa No. 35 Bldg., 14-14, Akasaka 1-chome, Minato-ku, Tokyo 107, Japan. TEL 03-3589-0207. FAX 03-5570-7132. TELEX J22274 DODWELL.
Description: Covers business strategies of major chemical manufacturers in Japan with regard to current business operations and R & D activities.

BUSINESS AND ECONOMICS

330   **CN**
R & D OUTLOOK. 1985. a. Can.$250 to non-members. Conference Board of Canada, 255 Smyth Rd., Ste. 100, Ottawa, ON K1H 8M7, Canada. TEL 613-526-3280. FAX 613-526-4857.
Formerly (until 1989): Research and Development in the Canadian Corporate Sector (ISSN 0826-8983)

R B R R KALE MEMORIAL LECTURES. see *POLITICAL SCIENCE*

330   **US**
R I C O BUSINESS DISPUTES GUIDE. (Racketeer Influenced and Corrupt Organizations); business disputes and the "racketeering" laws--federal and state. 1985. m. $430. C C H Incorporated, 2700 Lake Cook Rd., Riverwoods, IL 60015. TEL 847-267-7000; 800-835-5224. FAX 800-224-8299.

R.U.E. REVUE; nyt fra Raadet for Uddannelses- og Erhvervsvejledning. see *EDUCATION*

330   **GW**   **ISSN 0933-0089**
R W I MITTEILUNGEN; Zeitschrift fuer Wirtschaftsforschung. (Text in German; summaries in English, French) 1950. q. price varies. (Rheinisch-Westfaelisches Institut fuer Wirtschaftsforschung, Essen) Duncker und Humblot GmbH, Postfach 410329, 12113 Berlin, Germany. TEL 49-30-7900060. FAX 49-30-79000631. E-mail: duh-werbung@t-online.de. abstr.; charts; stat.; index. circ. 600. Indexed: IBR. Document type: academic/scholarly publication.
—BLDSC (8053.489800). CCC.
Formerly: Rheinisch-Westfaelisches Institut fuer Wirtschaftsforschung. Mitteilungen (ISSN 0035-4465)

RAGAN REPORT; a weekly survey of ideas and methods for communication executives. see *COMMUNICATIONS*

330 658   **US**   **ISSN 0741-6261**
HD2763.A2   **CODEN: RJECEA**
RAND JOURNAL OF ECONOMICS. 1970. q. $152 (foreign $167) (effective 1996 & 1997). Rand Corporation, 1700 Main St., Box 2138, Santa Monica, CA 90407-2138. TEL 310-393-0411. FAX 310-393-4818. TELEX 9103436878. E-mail: rje@allenpress.com; URL: http://www.rje.org. Ed. James R. Hosek. R&P contact: Paula Larich. bk.rev. (also avail. in microform from UMI; back issues avail.) Indexed: ABI Inform., Account.Ind. (1974-), AESIS, ASCA, Asian-Pac.Econ.Lit., B.P.I., BPIA, Bus.Ind., C.R.E.J., Comput.Rev., Cont.Pg.Manage., Curr.Cont., Eng.Ind., HRIS, INSPEC, Int.Abstr.Oper.Res., J.of Econ.Lit., Key to Econ.Sci., Manage.Cont., Math.R., Mgmt.& Market.Abstr., Mid.East: Abstr.& Ind., Oper.Res.Manage.Sci., Rural Recreat.Tour.Abstr., Soc.Sci.Ind., SSCI, Tr.& Indus.Ind., Work Rel.Abstr., World Agri.Econ.& Rural Sociol.Abstr. Document type: academic/scholarly publication.
—BLDSC (7254.410300); AskIEEE; Genuine Article; KR SourceOne; SWETS; UMI; UnCover. CCC.
Former titles (until 1984): Bell Journal of Economics (ISSN 0361-915X); (until 1974): Bell Journal of Economics and Management Science (ISSN 0005-8556)
Description: Covers microeconomics with a focus on industrial organization, regulation, and law and economics. Includes both theoretical and quantitative papers that analyze market behavior and public policy.
Refereed Serial

RAND MCNALLY BUSINESS TRAVELER'S ROAD ATLAS; and trip planner. see *TRAVEL AND TOURISM*

RAPID READERS SERIES. see *EDUCATION — Higher Education*

330   **IT**
RAPPORTO I R S SUL MERCATO AZIONARIO. a. Societa Editoriale Media Economici Seme S.p.A., Via P. Lomazzo 52, 20154 Milan, Italy. TEL 02-331211. FAX 02-316905.

330   **IT**   **ISSN 1120-9518**
RAPPORTO SULL'ECONOMIA DEL MEZZOGIORNO. 1975. a. (Associazione per lo Sviluppo dell'Industria nel Mezzogiorno) Societa Editrice Il Mulino, Strada Maggiore 37, 40125 Bologna, Italy. TEL 39-51-256011. FAX 39-51-256034. E-mail: riviste@mulino.it. adv. contact: M. Luisa Vezzali. circ. 2,000. (back issues avail.)

330   **SP**
RATING. 11/yr. Plaza de Espana 18, Torre de Madrid, Planta 7, Ofc. 3, 28008 Madrid, Spain. TEL 1-247-30-11. FAX 1-248-04-06. Ed. Pedro Zamarro.

330   **UK**   **ISSN 0305-814X**
HC256.6
READING IN POLITICAL ECONOMY. 1967. irreg., no.39, 1993. $85 (combined subscription for all series). Institute of Economic Affairs, 2 Lord North St., London SW1P 3LB, England. TEL 44-171-799-3745. FAX 44-171-799-2137. E-mail: iea@iea.org.uk; URL: http://www.iea.org.uk. Ed. Colin Robinson. adv.; bk.rev. (also avail. in microfiche) Document type: academic/scholarly publication.
—BLDSC (4362.666000).
Formerly: Readings in Political Economy (ISSN 0079-9874)
Refereed Serial

330   **BE**   **ISSN 0770-4518**
HB3
RECHERCHES ECONOMIQUES DE LOUVAIN. Short title: R E L. (Text in English, French) 1929. q. 4560 BEF (Europe 4910 BEF; elsewhere 4960 BEF) (effective 1998). (Universite Catholique de Louvain, Institut des Sciences Economiques) De Boeck et Larcier S.A., Fond Jean-Paques 4, 1348 Louvain-la-Neuve, Belgium. TEL 32-10-482570. FAX 32-10-482519. Ed. Michel de Vroey. bk.rev.; charts. circ. 750. Indexed: Cont.Pg.Manage., IBR, J.of Econ.Lit., Numis.Lit., P.A.I.S., P.A.I.S.For.Lang.Ind. Document type: academic/scholarly publication.
—BLDSC (7308.400000); SWETS; UnCover.

DAS RECHT DER WIRTSCHAFT. see *LAW*

330   **UK**
RECOMMENDATION FOR SURVIVAL IN BUSINESS. 1981. irreg. £4.50. Marcus Tobias & Co., 65 Shakespeare Dr., Shirley, Solihull B90 2AN, England. TEL 0121-744-2912. FAX 0121-733-2902. Document type: monographic series.

330 340   **CN**
RECORDS RETENTION: LAW & PRACTICE. 1975. 2/yr. Can.$175. Carswell, One Corporate Plaza, 2075 Kennedy Rd., Scarborough, ON M1T 3V4, Canada. TEL 416-609-8000. FAX 416-298-5094. index. (looseleaf format) Document type: trade publication.

RED HERRING; technology strategy, finance and investment. see *TECHNOLOGY: COMPREHENSIVE WORKS*

THE REED MCCLURE LETTER. see *LAW*

330   **BE**   **ISSN 0034-2971**
HB3
REFLETS ET PERSPECTIVES DE LA VIE ECONOMIQUE. 1961. q. 2500 BEF (Europe 2850 BEF; elsewhere 2900 BEF) (effective 1998). (Recherche et Diffusion Economiques A.S.B.L.) De Boeck et Larcier S.A., Fond Jean Paques 4, 1348 Louvain-la-Neuve, Belgium. TEL 32-10-482570. FAX 32-10-482519. Ed. Monique Huybrechts-Deroubaix. adv.; bk.rev.; index. circ. 900. Indexed: ELLIS, Excerp.Med., P.A.I.S.For.Lang.Ind., World Bibl.Soc.Sec. Document type: academic/scholarly publication.
—BLDSC (7332.340000).

330   **SZ**
REGENSBURGER BEITRAEGE ZUR BETRIEBSWIRTSCHAFTLICHEN FORSCHUNG. 1983. irreg., vol.8, 1989. price varies. Paul Haupt AG, Falkenplatz 14, CH-3001 Bern, Switzerland. TEL 41-31-3012345. FAX 41-31-3014669. Document type: monographic series.

330   **UK**
REGIONAL AND INDUSTRIAL RESEARCH SERIES. 1989. a. price varies. University of Strathclyde, European Policies Research Centre, 141 St. James Rd., Glasgow G4 0LT, Scotland. TEL 0141-552-4400. Eds. John Bachtler, Keith Clement. (back issues avail.) Document type: academic/scholarly publication.
Description: Papers for academics and policy-makers on public policy in Europe.

330   **UK**
REGIONAL DEVELOPMENT INTERNATIONAL; the news magazine of industrial office & economic development. 1978. m. £45 (effective 1996 & 1997). Eurocom Ltd., Princess House, 74 Princess St., Luton, Beds. LU1 5AT, England. TEL 44-1582-452911. FAX 44-1582-483841. Ed. Sian Fretwell; Pub. Colin Robinson. adv. contact: Colin Robinson. bk.rev. circ. 28,000. (tabloid format; back issues avail.)
Former titles: Regional Development; Industrial Planning and Development (ISSN 0262-3161)
Description: Reports on regional development programs, promotes inward, cross-border and indigenous investment projects. Helps overseas, mainland European and U.K. corporate investors.

REGIONAL SCIENCE & URBAN ECONOMICS. see *HOUSING AND URBAN PLANNING*

330   **GW**   **ISSN 0721-4588**
RENO; Zeitschrift fuer Ausbildung und Praxis. m. DM.89 (foreign DM.98) (effective 1997). Betriebswirtschaftlicher Verlag Dr. Th. Gabler GmbH, Abraham-Lincoln-Str. 46, 65189 Wiesbaden, Germany. TEL 49-611-7878129. FAX 49-611-7878423. Document type: trade publication.
—CCC.

330   **IT**
REPERTORIO COMMERCIALE. 4/yr. L.139000. Repertorio Commerciale s.r.l., Via Monte Rosa 51, 20149 Milan, Italy. TEL 39-2-48001491. FAX 39-2-48003226. Ed. Edio Vallini. adv.: color page L.5000000. circ. 24,347.

330   **UK**
THE REPORT ON BUSINESS. m. £225 (fax service £445) (effective 1998). (Chartered Institute of Purchasing and Supply) N T C Publications Ltd., P.O. Box 69, Henley-on-Thames, Oxon RG9 1GB, England. TEL 44-1491-411000. FAX 44-1491-571188. (also avail. by fax) Document type: trade publication.

330   **CN**   **ISSN 0827-7680**
HD2807
REPORT ON BUSINESS MAGAZINE. 1984. m. free with subscr. to The Globe and Mail. Globe & Mail Publishing, 444 Front St. W., Toronto, ON M5V 2S9, Canada. TEL 416-585-5499. FAX 416-585-5641. Ed. Patricia Best; Pub. Stephen Petherbridge. adv. contact: Cheri Natale. circ. 270,000. Indexed: Can.B.P.I. Document type: consumer publication.
—CISTI. CCC.
Description: Provides informed journalism about business in Canada and the world.

REPORT ON CORPORATE EDUCATIONAL SUPPORT. see *EDUCATION — School Organization And Administration*

REPORTERO INDUSTRIAL; new equipment, machinery and techniques for industry. see *MACHINERY*

330   **CX**
REPUBLIQUE CENTRAFRICAINE. JOURNAL OFFICIEL. 1974. fortn. Republique Centrafricaine, B.P. 739, Bangui, Central African Republic. Ed. Gabriel Agba. Document type: government publication.
Description: Provides economic data.

BUSINESS AND ECONOMICS

330 US ISSN 0191-1937
HD28
RESEARCH IN CORPORATE SOCIAL PERFORMANCE AND POLICY; an annual compilation of research. 1978. irreg., vol.15, 1996. $73.25. J A I Press Inc., 55 Old Post Rd., No. 2, Box 1678, Greenwich, CT 06830-1678. TEL 203-661-7602. FAX 203-661-0792. E-mail: jai@jaipress.com. (Subscr. in the UK and Europe to: JAI Press Ltd., 38 Tavistock St., Covent Garden, London WC2E 7PB, England. TEL 44-171-379-8834. FAX 44-171-379-8835) Ed. James Post. **Document type**: monographic series.
—BLDSC (7737.200000). **CCC.**

330 UK ISSN 0035-5054
HC301
RESEARCH IN ECONOMICS/RICERCHE ECONOMICHE; an international review of economics. Online edition (UK ISSN 1090-9443) (Text in Italian and English) 1947. q. £61($103) to individuals; institutions £214 (effective 1998). (Universita degli Studi di Venezia, Dipartimento di Scienze Economiche, IT) Academic Press Ltd. (Subsidiary of: Harcourt Brace & Company Ltd.), 24-28 Oval Rd., London NW1 7DX, England. TEL 44-171-482-2293. TELEX 25775 ACPRES G. E-mail: apsubs@acad.com; URL: http://www.hbuk.co.uk/ap/re; http://www.europe.idealibrary.com/. (Subscr. to: Harcourt Brace & Company Ltd., Foots Cray High St., Sidcup, Kent DA14 5HP, England. TEL 44-181-300-3322. FAX 44-181-309-0807) Ed. Guglielmo Weber. R&P contact: Catherine John. adv. contact: Nik Screen. bk.rev.; charts; index, cum.index. circ. 1,200. (also avail. in microform from UMI; reprint service avail. from SCH,SWZ,UMI) **Indexed**: J.of Econ.Lit., P.A.I.S.For.Lang.Ind., Rural Recreat.Tour.Abstr., World Agri.Econ.& Rural Sociol.Abstr., Zent.Math. **Document type**: academic/scholarly publication.
●Also available online.
—UMI. **CCC.**
Description: Theoretical and empirical research in all fields of economic inquiry.

330.05 346.066 US ISSN 0193-5895
K18
RESEARCH IN LAW AND ECONOMICS. (Supplement avail.: Economics of Nonproprietary Organizations) 1979. irreg., vol.18, 1996. $73.25. J A I Press Inc., 55 Old Post Rd., No. 2, Box 1678, Greenwich, CT 06830-1678. TEL 203-661-7602. FAX 203-661-0792. E-mail: jai@jaipress.com. (Subscr. in the UK and Europe to: JAI Press Ltd., 38 Tavistock St., Covent Garden, London WC2E 7PB, England. TEL 44-171-379-8834. FAX 44-171-379-8835) Ed. Richard O. Zerbe, Jr. (reprint service avail. from WSH) **Indexed**: C.L.I., L.R.I., Leg.Per. **Document type**: monographic series.
—UnCover. **CCC.**

330 020 US ISSN 1067-0394
HF54.52.U5
RESEARCHING MARKETS, INDUSTRIES, AND BUSINESS OPPORTUNITIES. 1994. irreg., latest 3rd ed. $395 (effective 1997). Washington Researchers, Ltd., Box 19005, 20th St. Sta., Washington, DC 20036-9005. TEL 202-333-3499. FAX 202-625-0656. E-mail: research@researchers.com; URL: http://www.researchers.com/pub/busintel/researchers.html. R&P contact: Ellen O'Kane. **Document type**: directory, trade publication.
Description: Helps executives, analysts, and researchers assess the performance of companies and explore new business opportunities.

330 IT
▼**RESPONSABILITA E COMUNICAZIONE IMPRESA.** 1996. q. Lit.100000 (foreign Lit.150000) (effective 1997). Casa Editrece Dott. A. Giuffre, Via Busto Arsizio 40, 20151 Milan, Italy. TEL 39-2-38089200. FAX 39-2-38009582. Ed. U. Ruffolo.

330 305.896073 US ISSN 0034-6446
E185.5
REVIEW OF BLACK POLITICAL ECONOMY. 1970. q. $52 to individuals (foreign $84); institutions $108 (foreign $140) (effective 1997). (National Economic Association) Transaction Publishers, Transaction Periodicals Consortium, Department 3092, Rutgers University, New Brunswick, NJ 08903. TEL 908-445-2280. FAX 908-445-3138. (Co-sponsor: Southern Center for Studies in Public Policy of Clark College) Ed. Thomas D. Boston. adv.: page $250; 4 1/2 x 7. bk.rev. circ. 1,000. (also avail. in microform from UMI; reprint service avail. from UMI) **Indexed**: Amer.Hist.& Life (1983-), ASCA, Bus.Ind., Curr.Cont., Hist.Abstr. (1983-), J.of Econ.Lit., P.A.I.S., Sage Pub.Admin.Abstr., Sage Urb.Stud.Abstr., Soc.Sci.Ind., SSCI, Tr.& Indus.Ind., Work Rel.Abstr. **Document type**: academic/scholarly publication.
●Also available online. Vendor(s): Information Access Co., UMI.
—BLDSC (7788.700000); Genuine Article; KR SourceOne; SWETS; UMI; UnCover. **CCC.**
Description: Examines issues related to the economic status of black and Third World peoples. Identifies and analyzes policy prescriptions designed to reduce racial economic inequality.

650 US ISSN 0034-6454
REVIEW OF BUSINESS. 1964. q. free. St. John's University, College of Business Administration, Bent Hall, 8000 Utopia Pkwy., Jamaica, NY 11439. TEL 718-990-6768. FAX 718-990-1868. Ed. Charles Little. bk.rev.; charts; illus.; stat.; circ. 7,000 (controlled). (also avail. in microform from UMI) **Indexed**: ABI Inform., BPIA, Bus.Ind., P.A.I.S., Tr.& Indus.Ind. **Document type**: academic/scholarly publication.
●Also available online. Vendor(s): Information Access Co., UMI.
—BLDSC (7788.880000); UMI; UnCover.
Description: Provides information of current interest and relevance to a general business audience, especially material the business practitioner can use.
Refereed Serial

330
REVIEW OF COMMERCE STUDIES. 1972. a. Rs.10($2.50) University of Delhi, School of Economics, Department of Commerce, Delhi 110007, India. Ed. R.A. Sharma. (back issues avail.)

330 300 IE
REVIEW OF E S R I RESEARCH. a. Economic and Social Research Institute, 4 Burlington Rd., Dublin 4, Ireland. TEL 353-1-6671525. FAX 353-1-6686231. **Document type**: corporate report.

330 UK ISSN 0034-6527
HB1
REVIEW OF ECONOMIC STUDIES. 1933. q. £83($150) (foreign £83) (effective 1997). Blackwell Publishers Ltd., 108 Cowley Rd., Oxford OX4 1JF, England. TEL 44-1865-791100. FAX 44-1865-791347. E-mail: jnlinfo@blackwellpublishers.co.uk; URL: http://www.blackwellpublishers.co.uk. Eds. M. Dewatripont, J.H. Moore. adv.; cum.index: vol.1-25. (reprint service avail. from KTO) **Indexed**: ASCA, Br.Hum.Ind., C.R.E.J., Cont.Pg.Manage., Curr.Cont., Fam.Ind., IBR, J.Cont.Quant.Meth., J.of Econ.Abstr., J.of Econ.Lit., Key to Econ.Sci., Math.R., P.A.I.S., Rural Recreat.Tour.Abstr., SCIMP (1978-), Soc.Sci.Ind., SSCI, World Agri.Econ.& Rural Sociol.Abstr., World Bank.Abstr., Zent.Math. **Document type**: academic/scholarly publication.
—BLDSC (7790.200000); Genuine Article; KR SourceOne; SWETS; UMI; UnCover. **CCC.**

330 JA ISSN 0302-6574
REVIEW OF ECONOMICS AND BUSINESS. (Text in English) 1972. s-a. (Kansai University) Kansai University Press, 3-3-35 Yamate-cho, Suita-shi 564, Osaka, Japan. Ed. Shigeru Shoji. circ. 600. **Indexed**: Asian-Pac.Econ.Lit.
—BLDSC (7790.222000).

330 519.5 US ISSN 0034-6535
HA1 CODEN: RECSA9
THE REVIEW OF ECONOMICS AND STATISTICS. 1966. 4/yr. $45 to individuals (foreign $63); institutions $170 (foreign $188); students $25 (foreign 443) (effective 1997). (Harvard University, Economics Department) M I T Press, 5 Cambridge Center, Cambridge, MA 02142-1399. TEL 617-577-1545. FAX 617-577-1545. E-mail: jounrals-orders@mit.edu; URL: http://www-mitpress.mit.edu/. Ed.Bd. R&P contact: Paul Dzus. adv.; charts; index. circ. 3,500. (also avail. in microform from UMI; back issues avail.; reprint service avail. from KTO) **Indexed**: ABI Inform., Amer.Hist.& Life (1967-1974), ASCA, B.P.I., BPIA, Bus.Ind., C.R.E.J., Cont.Pg.Manage., Curr.Cont., Energy Ind., Energy Info.Abstr., Excerp.Med., Geo.Abstr.P.G., Hist.Abstr. (1967-1974), IBR, IDA, Int.Lab.Doc., Int.Polit.Sci.Abstr., J.Cont.Quant.Meth., J.of Econ.Lit., Key to Econ.Sci., Mag.Ind., Manage.Cont., Mar.Aff.Bibl., Med.Care Rev., Mid.East: Abstr.& Ind., P.A.I.S., Popul.Ind., Risk Abstr., Rural Recreat.Tour.Abstr., Sage Urb.Stud.Abstr., SCIMP (1978-), Soc.Sci.Ind., SSCI, Tr.& Indus.Ind., World Agri.Econ.& Rural Sociol.Abstr., World Bank.Abstr., World Bibl.Soc.Sec. **Document type**: academic/scholarly publication.
●Also available online.
—BLDSC (7790.250000); Genuine Article; KR SourceOne; SWETS; UMI; UnCover. **CCC.**
Description: Publishes theoretical, empirical and statistical analysis that characterizes modern economics.
Refereed Serial

338 330 US ISSN 1058-3300
HF5001
REVIEW OF FINANCIAL ECONOMICS. 1965. s-a. $75 to individuals (foreign $95); institutions $180 (foreign $200) (effective 1998). (University of New Orleans, Lake Front, College of Business Administration, Business and Economic Research Division) J A I Press Inc., 55 Old Post Rd., No. 2, Box 1678, Greenwich, CT 06830-1678. TEL 203-661-7602. FAX 203-661-0792. E-mail: jai@jaipress.com. (Addr. in Europe: J A I Press Ltd., 38 Tavistock St., Covent Garden, London WC2E 7PB, England. TEL 44-171-379-8834. FAX 44-171-379-8835) Ed. Gerald Whitney. circ. 1,000. (also avail. in microform from UMI; reprint service avail. from SCH,UMI) **Indexed**: ABI Inform., Account.Ind. (1981-), B.P.I., BPIA, Bus.Ind., C.R.E.J., Cont.Pg.Manage., Manage.Cont., P.A.I.S., SSCI, Tr.& Indus.Ind., World Bank.Abstr. **Document type**: academic/scholarly publication.
●Also available online. Vendor(s): Information Access Co.
—BLDSC (7790.564000); KR SourceOne; SWETS; UMI; UnCover. **CCC.**
Former titles (until 1991): Review of Business and Economics Research (ISSN 0362-7985); Mississippi Valley Journal of Business and Economics (ISSN 0026-6418).
Description: Academic journal for academicians and practitioners in the field of financial economics.
Refereed Serial

330 UK ISSN 0965-7576
HF1351
REVIEW OF INTERNATIONAL ECONOMICS. 1992. q. £145($198) (foreign £145) (effective 1997). Blackwell Publishers Ltd., 108 Cowley Rd., Oxford OX4 1JF, England. TEL 44-1865-791100. FAX 44-1865-791347. E-mail: jnlinfo@blackwellpublishers.co.uk; URL: http://www.blackwellpublishers.co.uk. Ed. Kwan Choi. (back issues avail.) **Document type**: academic/scholarly publication.
—BLDSC (7790.905000); SWETS; UMI; UnCover. **CCC.**
Refereed Serial

BUSINESS AND ECONOMICS

330   UK   ISSN 1355-6223
HG230.3
THE REVIEW OF POLICY ISSUES. 1994. q. (plus a. issue). £20 (foreign $35) to individuals; institutions £50 (foreign $90) (effective 1997 & 1998). Sheffield Hallam University, Unit 7, Sheffield Science Park, Howard St., Sheffield S1 2LX, England. TEL 44-114-2534462. FAX 44-114-2534467. E-mail: p.curwen@shu.ac.uk. Ed. Peter Curwen. R&P contact: Peter Curwen. bk.rev. circ. 150. **Document type:** academic/scholarly publication.
—BLDSC (7794.105000).
   Description: Exists to stimulate interest in policy-related issues both among the academic community and practitioners in business and management.
Refereed Serial

330 300   UK   ISSN 0034-6764
HB1
REVIEW OF SOCIAL ECONOMY. 1948. q. £36 (U.S. and Canada $54; rest of world £38) to individuals; institutions £65 (U.S. and Canada $98; rest of world £65) (effective 1997). (Association for Social Economics) Routledge, 11 New Fetter Ln., London EC4P 4EE, England. TEL 44-171-583-9855. FAX 44-171-842-2298. E-mail: sample.journal@ routledge.com; URL: http://www.routledge.com/ routledge/journal/journals.html. (Subscr. to: ITPS Ltd., Cheriton House, North Way, Andover, Hants. SP10 5BE, England. TEL 44-1264-342919. FAX 44-1264-342807) Ed. John B. Davis. adv.: page £175; trim 110 x 180. bk.rev.; bibl.; charts; index. circ. 2,000. (also avail. in microform from UMI; back issues avail.; reprint service avail. from SCH,UMI) **Indexed:** Amer.Bibl.Slavic & E.Eur.Stud., Amer.Hist.& Life (until 1995), Arts & Hum.Cit.Ind., ASCA, Asian-Pac.Econ.Lit., ASSIA, BPIA, Bus.Ind., C.R.E.J., Cath.Ind., Curr.Cont., Fam.Ind., Hist.Abstr., J.of Econ.Lit., P.A.I.S.For.Lang.Ind., Polit.Sci.Abstr., Rural Recreat.Tour.Abstr., SSCI, Tr.& Indus.Ind., World Agri.Econ.& Rural Sociol.Abstr. **Document type:** academic/scholarly publication.
●Also available online. Vendor(s): Information Access Co.
—BLDSC (7796.910000); Genuine Article; SWETS; UMI; UnCover. CCC.
   Description: Publishes papers on the many relationships between social values and economics.
Refereed Serial

330 300   AG   ISSN 0328-2058
REVISTA ARGENTINA DE ECONOMIA Y CIENCIAS SOCIALES. 1994. 3/yr. Universidad de Buenos Aires, Montaneses 2958, 5o A, 1429 Buenos Aires, Argentina. **Document type:** academic/scholarly publication.

330   BL   ISSN 0034-7140
HB9
REVISTA BRASILEIRA DE ECONOMIA. 1947. q. $90 (effective 1996). (Escola de Pos-Graduacao em Economia) Fundacao Getulio Vargas, C.P. 62591, 22257-970 Rio de Janeiro, R.J., Brazil. TEL 55-21-5369196. FAX 55-21-5369155. TELEX 21-36811. Ed. Clovis de Faro. adv. contact: Milton Gondim. bk.rev.; bibl.; stat. circ. 1,500. **Indexed:** Hisp.Amer.Per.Ind. (1970-), IBR, Int.Lab.Doc., P.A.I.S.For.Lang.Ind., Rural Recreat.Tour.Abstr., SSCI, World Agri.Econ.& Rural Sociol.Abstr. **Document type:** academic/scholarly publication.
—BLDSC (7844.200000); SWETS.
   Description: Reports on the national economic performance and the development of international economic thought.

338 332.6   BL   ISSN 0102-9797
HG4503
REVISTA BRASILEIRA DE MERCADO DE CAPITAIS. 1974. q. Cr.$210($21) Instituto Brasileiro de Mercado de Capitais, Av. Rio Branco, 108, 2o andar, 20040 Rio de Janeiro RJ, Brazil. TEL 242-6646. Ed. Joao Luiz Mascolo. adv.; bk.rev.; charts; illus.; stat.; index. circ. 2,500. **Indexed:** P.A.I.S.For.Lang.Ind.

330 658.5   BL   ISSN 0104-1029
HC186
REVISTA C N I. 1968. bi-m. free. Confederacao Nacional da Industria, Av. Nilo Pecanha, 50, Gr. 2608, 20044-900 Rio de Janeiro RJ, Brazil. TEL 532-0330. Ed. Fernando Luz. adv.; charts; illus.; pat.; stat. circ. 16,000.
—BLDSC (3287.311540).
   Former titles (until 1991): Industria e Produtividade (ISSN 0019-7718); Desenvolvimento e Conjuntura.
   Description: Covers Brazilian industry, economics and related themes.

330   PO
REVISTA DAS EMPRESAS. 12/yr. R. Francisco Rodriques Lobo 2 r-c Dto., 1000 Lisbon, Portugal. TEL 659950. FAX 65-14-30. Ed. Jose Nunes Pereira. circ. 18,000.

330   BL   ISSN 0556-5782
HB9
REVISTA DE ECONOMIA. 1960. irreg. Universidade Federal do Parana, Faculdade de Economia e Administracao, 80000 Curitiba, Parana, Brazil.

330 310   AG   ISSN 0034-8066
HB9
REVISTA DE ECONOMIA Y ESTADISTICA. 1939. q. exchange basis. Universidad Nacional de Cordoba, Facultad de Ciencias Economicas, Ciudad Universitaria, Estafeta 32, 5000 Cordoba, Argentina. bk.rev.; bibl.; charts. **Document type:** academic/scholarly publication.

330   PN
REVISTA DE INVESTIGACIONES ECONOMICAS. a.? Universidad de Panama, Centro de Investigacion Facultad de Economia, Estafeta Universitaria, Panama, Panama. TEL 23-0819.

REVISTA DEL DERECHO INDUSTRIAL. see *LAW*

330   VE   ISSN 1315-2467
REVISTA ECONOMIA; nueva etapa. 1961-1975; resumed 1987. a. $10. Universidad de Los Andes, Facultad de Economia, IIES, La Hechicera, Edf. B, 1r, Merida 5101, Venezuela. TEL 074-401081. FAX 074-401120. circ. 500. **Document type:** academic/scholarly publication.
●Also available online.
   Formerly: Economia (ISSN 0070-8399)
   Description: Covers scientific articles in the field of economics; includes statistics, administration, accounting and computer science.

330   AG
REVISTA ECONOMICA (BUENOS AIRES); industrial, comercial y financiera. 1985. m. Arg.$20 (N. America and Europe $100). Prensa Argentina S.R.L., Pinchincha 364, 1o B, Buenos Aires, Argentina. TEL 54-1-9527835. FAX 54-1-9542723. Ed. Luis A. Pineiro; Pub. Juan Luis Rechax. illus.
   Formerly: Revista Economica y Politica.

330   AG   ISSN 0013-0419
REVISTA ECONOMICA (LA PLATA). (Text in Spanish; summaries in English, Spanish) 1954. 2/yr. Arg.$30 (S. America $35; US & Europe $40). Universidad Nacional de la Plata, Instituto de Investigaciones Economicas, Calle 48 No. 555, Piso 5, Ofic. 523, 1900 La Plata, Argentina. TEL 54-21-229383. Ed. Mario L. Szychowski. adv.; bk.rev.; bibl.; charts; circ. 1,000 (controlled). **Indexed:** J. of Econ.Abstr., J.of Econ.Lit. **Document type:** academic/scholarly publication.

332   EC   ISSN 1016-7994
REVISTA ECUATORIANA DE HISTORIA ECONOMICA. 1987. s-a. $20. Banco Central del Ecuador, Casilla 29C, Sucursal no.15, Quito, Ecuador. TEL 561-521. Ed. Carlos Marchan Romero. circ. 2,000.
   Description: Contains studies of economic history related to Ecuador, the Andean region and South America, as well as methodological contributions to economic history from other areas.

330   SP   ISSN 0210-1025
REVISTA ESPANOLA DE ECONOMIA. 1971. s-a. 4000 ptas. Instituto de Estudios Fiscales, Avda de Cardenal Herrera Oria 378, 28035 Madrid, Spain. TEL 34-1-3398800. FAX 34-1-3398964. (Subscr. to: Ministerio de Economia y Hacienda, Centro de Publicaciones, Plaza del Campillo del Mundo Nuevo 3, 28005 Madrid, Spain. TEL 91-527-1437) bk.rev.; stat. circ. 2,000. **Indexed:** J.of Econ.Lit.
—CINDOC; SWETS.

330   PO
REVISTA NEGOCIOS. m. Rua do Norte 14-1o, 1200 Lisbon, Portugal. TEL 1-3469550. FAX 3475254. Ed. J. Gomes Motta. circ. 10,000.

REVUE ALGERIENNE DES SCIENCES JURIDIQUES. see *LAW*

330   FR   ISSN 0373-2630
HB3
REVUE D'ECONOMIE POLITIQUE. 1887. bi-m. 560 F. to individuals (foreign 700 F.); institutions 800 F. (foreign 900 F.) (effective 1996). Editions Sirey, 11 rue Soufflot, 75240 Paris Cedex 05, France. TEL 40-51-54-54. FAX 45-87-37-48. TELEX 206 446 F. (Subscr. to: 35 rue Tournefort, 75240 Paris Cedex 05, France. TEL 40-51-54-35) Ed. Henri Guitton. bk.rev.; charts. circ. 2,000. (reprint service avail. from SCH) **Indexed:** Amer.Hist.& Life (1954-1958), (1964-), Geo.Abstr., Hist.Abstr. (1954-1958), (1964-), IBR, Int.Lab.Doc., J.of Econ.Lit., Key to Econ.Sci., P.A.I.S.For.Lang.Ind. **Document type:** trade publication.
—BLDSC (7898.770000); KR SourceOne; SWETS. CCC.

330   MR   ISSN 0851-0431
K13
REVUE DE DROIT ET D'ECONOMIE. 1985. s-a. Universite Sidi Mohamed Ben Abdellah, B.P. 42, Dhar El Mahraz, Fes, Morocco.

330   FR   ISSN 0035-1350
HC277.F7
REVUE DE L'ECONOMIE DU CENTRE-EST. 1958. q. 120 F. (foreign 140 F.). Institut d'Economie Regionale Bourgogne-Franche-Comte, 4 bd. Gabriel, 21000 Dijon (Cote d'Or), France. Ed. Jack Perreur. bk.rev.; bibl.; charts; index, cum.index: 1958-1986. circ. 600.

330   FR   ISSN 0035-2764
HB3
REVUE ECONOMIQUE. (Text in French, summaries in English, French) 1950. bi-m. 430 F. to individuals (foreign 490 F.); institutions 680 F. (foreign 740 F.). Presses de la Fondation Nationale des Sciences Politiques, 27 rue Saint-Guillaume, 75341 Paris Cedex 07, France. FAX 1-45-48-04-41. Dir. Jeanne-Marie Parly. adv.; bk.rev.; bibl.; charts; index, cum.index every 10 yrs. circ. 1,850. (reprint service avail. from SCH) **Indexed:** Amer.Hist.& Life (1972-), C.I.S. Abstr., Hist.Abstr. (1972-), Int.Lab.Doc., Int.Polit.Sci.Abstr., J.of Econ.Lit., P.A.I.S.For.Lang.Ind., SSCI.
—BLDSC (7898.785000); Genuine Article; SWETS. CCC.

330 300   SZ   ISSN 0035-2772
HB3
REVUE ECONOMIQUE ET SOCIALE. 1943. 4/yr. 65 SFr. (foreign 80 SFr.) (effective 1998). Societe d'Etudes Economiques et Sociales, B F S H 1, CH-1015 Dorigny, Switzerland. TEL 41-21-6915347. FAX 41-21-6923385. E-mail: infosees@hec.unil.ch; URL: http://www.hec.unil.ch/assoc/sees. Ed. Kaj Noschis. R&P contact: Kaj Noschis. adv. contact: Marja Montserrat. bk.rev.; bibl.; charts; index, cum.index. circ. 1,200. (reprint service avail. from SCH) **Indexed:** ELLIS, Int.Lab.Doc., Int.Polit.Sci.Abstr., Key to Econ.Sci., P.A.I.S.For.Lang.Ind. **Document type:** academic/scholarly publication.
—BLDSC (7898.790000).

330   FR   ISSN 0035-2780
REVUE ECONOMIQUE FRANCAISE. 1878. q. 80 F. (foreign 100 F.). Societe de Geographie Humaineiale de Paris, 8 rue Roquepine, 75008 Paris, France. Ed. Pierre Gosselin. bk.rev.; bibl. circ. 1,100. **Indexed:** P.A.I.S.For.Lang.Ind.

REVUE EUROPEENNE DE DROIT DE LA CONSOMMATION. see *LAW*

REVUE INTERNATIONALE DE DROIT ECONOMIQUE. see *LAW*

BUSINESS AND ECONOMICS

330   CN   ISSN 1192-4551
REVUE OCCASIONS D'AFFAIRES. 1993. bi-m. Can.$14.95($13.95) Revue Occasions d'Affaires Ltee, 425 St.-Amable St., Ste. 145, Quebec, PQ G1R 5E4, Canada. TEL 418-640-1686; 800-361-1686. FAX 418-640-1687. URL: http://www.roa-mag.com. Ed. Pierre Bherer; Pub. Pierre Bherer. R&P contact: Regis Pelletier. adv.: color page Can.$4200; adv. contact: Christian Cloutier. circ. 30,000. circ. Roger/Robitaille. **Document type:** trade publication.

330
HC407.R8   RM   ISSN 1220-5397
REVUE ROUMAINE DE SCIENCES ECONOMIQUES. (Text in English, French and Russian) 1956. 2/yr. (Academia Romana) Editura Academiei Romane, Calea 13 Septembrie 13, 76117 Bucharest, Rumania. (Dist. by: Rodipet SA, Piata Presei Libere 1, Sec. 1, P.O. Box 33-57, Bucharest, Rumania. TEL 401-6185103. FAX 401-2226407) Ed. N.N. Constantinescu. bk.rev.; bibl.; charts; stat. **Indexed:** Amer.Hist.& Life, Hist.Abstr., P.A.I.S.For.Lang.Ind., P.A.I.S.
—BLDSC (7946.510000); KNAW.
    Formerly (until 1989): Revue Roumaine des Sciences Sociales. Serie de Sciences Economiques (ISSN 0035-404X); Which superseded in part (in 1964): Revue des Sciences Sociales (ISSN 0484-8640).

330   BE
RIJKSUNIVERSITEIT TE GENT. FACULTEIT VAN DE ECONOMISCHE WETENSCHAPPEN. WERKEN. irreg. Rijksuniversiteit te Gent, Faculteit van de Economische Wetenschappen, Hoveniersberg 4, B-9000 Ghent, Belgium. Eds. E. de Lembre, W. Georges.

330   JA   ISSN 0288-0180
RITSUMEIKAN KEIZAIGAKU/RITSUMEIKAN ECONOMIC REVIEW. (Text in Japanese) 1952. bi-m. Ritsumeikan Daigaku, Keizai Gakkai - Ritsumeikan University, Economic Society, 56-1, Toji-in Kitamachi, Kita-ku, Kyoto 603-77, Japan. TEL 81-75-465-8180. FAX 81-75-465-7856. **Document type:** academic/scholarly publication.
—BLDSC (7976.350000).

330 346   IT
RIVISTA DEI DOTTORI COMMERCIALISTI. 1949. bi-m. Lit.150000 (foreign Lit.225000) (effective 1997). (Ordine dei Dottori Commercialisti di Milano) Casa Editrice Dott. A. Giuffre, Via Busto Arsizio 40, 20151 Milan, Italy. TEL 39-2-38089200. FAX 39-2-38009582. Ed. Angelo Provasoli. circ. 6,700.

330   IT   ISSN 0035-6468
RIVISTA DI POLITICA ECONOMICA. (Supplement (1946-1988): Selected Papers (ISSN 0391-6170)) 1911. m. (plus 4 monographs in English). L.200000 (foreign L.250000($145)). Servizio Italiano Pubblicazioni Internazionali s.r.l., Viale L. Pasteur, 6, 00144 Rome, Italy. TEL 39-6-5918586. FAX 39-6-5924819. Ed. Mario Baldassarri. bk.rev.; charts; cum.index: 1911-1970, 1981-1990. circ. 1,000. (back issues avail.) **Indexed:** ELLIS, IBR, P.A.I.S.For.Lang.Ind., P.A.I.S., Rural Recreat.Tour.Abstr., World Agri.Econ.& Rural Sociol.Abstr. **Document type:** academic/scholarly publication.

330   IT   ISSN 1120-9534
RIVISTA ECONOMICA DEL MEZZOGIORNO. 1987. q. Lit.130000 (effective 1997). (Associazione per lo Sviluppo dell'Industria nel Mezzogiorno) Societa Editrice II Mulino, Strada Maggiore, 37, 40125 Bologna, Italy. TEL 39-51-256011. FAX 39-51-256034. E-mail: riviste@mulino.it. Ed. Salvatore Cafiero. adv. contact: M. Luisa Vezzali. index. circ. 1,300. (back issues avail.)

330 380   IT   ISSN 0035-6751
H7
RIVISTA INTERNAZIONALE DI SCIENZE ECONOMICHE E COMMERCIALI. (Text in English, French, German and Italian) 1954. q. L.200000 (foreign L.300000) (effective 1997). Casa Editrice Dott. Antonio Milani, Via Jappelli 5-6, 35121 Padua, Italy. TEL 39-49-656677. FAX 39-49-8752900. Ed. Aldo Montesano. adv.; bk.rev.; charts; illus.; index. circ. 1,200. **Indexed:** Cont.Pg.Manage., Curr.Cont., ELLIS, J.of Econ.Lit., P.A.I.S.For.Lang.Ind., P.A.I.S., SSCI.
—BLDSC (7987.150000); SWETS; UnCover.
    Description: Publishes original essays in doctrine, method, economic theory, finance, marketing, budgeting, politics and labor.

330   IT
RIVISTA ITALIANA DI RAGIONERIA E DI ECONOMIA AZIENDALE. m. L.310000 (effective 1996). R I R E A di Nobile Giovanna, Via delle Isole 30, 00198 Rome, Italy. TEL 39-6-8417690. FAX 39-6-8845732.

RIVISTA TRIMESTRALE DEGLI APPALTI; rivista di dottrina-legislazione-giurisprudenza. see *LAW — Corporate Law*

330   US
ROCHESTER BUSINESS.* 1984. m. $19.95. 131 Eastman Est., Rochester, NY 14622-1747. TEL 716-458-8280. FAX 716-458-9831. Ed. Kristina Hutch; Pub. Joseph Julian. adv.; bk.rev. circ. 11,000.

330   RM
ROMANIA: ECONOMIC HIGHLIGHTS. (Text in English) vol.27, 1976. w. $205 for 6 mos. Rompres, the National Press Agency, Piata Presei Libere 1, Bucharest, Rumania. TEL 2223233. FAX 2230089. Ed. Monica Mariana Grigorescu. **Document type:** bulletin.
    Formerly (until 1990): Romania: Articles - Features - Information (ISSN 1016-250X)

330   RM
ROMANIAN BUSINESS NEWS. (Supplement avail. m.: Romanian Financial and Banking News) 1993. m. (11/yr.). 100 lei (foreign $185) (effective 1996). Cosmos Development, P.O. Box 22-256, Bucharest, Rumania. TEL 401-6502504. (Foreign subscr. to: Cosmos, Inc., P.O. Box 30437, Bethesda, MD 20824. TEL 301-229-5875. FAX 301-229-5876) Ed. Andreas Tsantis. adv.; circ. 650 (paid). **Document type:** newsletter.
    Description: Provides an overview of the economy. Interprets current economic events, the stock exchange, general and regional news, and statistical information.

DER ROSENTHALER. see *CERAMICS, GLASS AND POTTERY*

330   DK   ISSN 0105-8827
ROSKILDE UNIVERSITETSCENTER. INSTITUT FOR SAMFUNDSOEKONOMI OG PLANLAEGNING. RESEARCH REPORT. 1981. irreg. free. Roskilde Universitetscenter, Institut for Samfundsoekonomi og Planlaegning, Roskilde, Denmark.

330   RU   ISSN 0869-5202
ROSSIISKII EKONOMICHESKII ZHURNAL. 1958. m. $108 (effective 1998). (Gosudarstvennyi Komitet po Narodnomu Ograzovaniyu) Izdatel'stvo Vysshaya Shkola, Neglinnaya ul. 29-14, Moscow, Russia. TEL 095-200-0456. FAX 095-973-2180. (Dist. in U.S. by: Victor Kamkin Inc., 4956 Boiling Brook Pkwy., Rockville, MD 20852. TEL 301-881-5973. FAX 301-881-1637) Ed. Yu. Melentev. adv.; bk.rev.; index. circ. 23,600. **Indexed:** Int.Lab.Doc., Rural Recreat.Tour.Abstr., World Agri.Econ.& Rural Sociol.Abstr., World Bibl.Soc.Sec.
    Formerly (until 1992): Ekonomicheskie Nauk (ISSN 0130-9757)

330   FI   ISSN 0780-4288
ROTARY NORDEN. (Text in Danish, Finnish, Icelandic, Norwegian, Swedish) 8/yr. Erikoislehdet Oy Business Publications, P.O. Box 16, SF-00381 Helsinki, Finland. circ. 65,000.

RUCH PRAWNICZY, EKONOMICZNY I SOCJOLOGICZNY. see *LAW*

RURAL DEVELOPMENT PERSPECTIVES. see *AGRICULTURE*

330 320   UK   ISSN 0967-2265
DK293
RUSSIA AND THE SUCCESSOR STATES BRIEFING SERVICE. bi-m. £145 (Europe £148; elsewhere £155). Longman Group UK Ltd., Longman House, Burnt Mill, Harlow, Essex CM20 2JE, England. TEL 44-1279-442601. FAX 44-1279-444501. E-mail: longhe@cityscape.co.uk. (Subscr. to: Pearson Professional, P.O. Box 77, Fourth Ave., Harlow, Essex CM19 5BQ, England. TEL 44-1279-623924. FAX 44-1279-639609) Ed. Martin McCauley. **Document type:** bulletin.

RUSSIA ONLINE AND WIRELESS. see *COMMUNICATIONS — Computer Applications*

330   US
RUSSIAN BUSINESS NEWS UPDATE. 1994. m. Josh Zander Financial and Management Consulting Services, 4286 Redwood Hwy., Ste. 376, San Rafael, CA 94903. TEL 415-492-3382. FAX 415-472-5709. Ed. Josh Zander. adv. circ. 500. (back issues avail.) **Document type:** newsletter.
    Description: Covers Russian business, economic and financial news.

349   US   ISSN 1051-9939
HG2150
S & L - SAVINGS BANK FINANCIAL QUARTERLY. (Savings and Loan) q. $389 (effective 1997). I D C Financial Publishing, Inc., Box 140, Hartland, WI 53029. TEL 800-525-5457. Ed. John E. Rickmeier. R&P contact: John E. Rickmeier. (back issues avail.) **Document type:** trade publication.
    Formerly (until 1986): S and L Financial Quarterly.

330   UK
S C I E S WORKING PAPER SERIES. irreg. membership. University of Surrey, Surrey Centre for International Economic Studies, Guildford, Surrey GU2 5XH, England. TEL 44-1483-259325. FAX 4401483-303775. **Document type:** monographic series.

340 011   US
S C M P NEWSLETTER.* q. membership. Society of Corporate Meeting Professionals, 2107 Del Monte Ave., Monterey, CA 93940-3711. TEL 408-649-6544. FAX 408-649-4124. **Document type:** newsletter.

330 333.79   UK
S E E C OCCASIONAL PAPER. 1993. irreg., no.2, 1995. £25 (foreign £30) (effective 1997). University of Surrey, Surrey Energy Economics Centre, Guildford GU2 5XH, England. TEL 44-1483-259379. FAX 44-1483-303775. E-mail: i.hildyard@surrey.ac.uk. Ed.Bd. circ. 150. **Document type:** monographic series.
    Description: Promotes research and teaching in the broad area of energy economics and policy.

330 333.79   UK   ISSN 0952-8490
S E E D S. (Surrey Energy Economics Discussion Paper Series) 1980. irreg. (approx. 5/yr.) £99 (foreign £105) to institutions; academic libraries £50 (foreign £60) (effective 1997). University of Surrey, Surrey Energy Economics Centre, Guildford GU2 5XH, England. TEL 44-1483-259379. FAX 44-1483-303775. E-mail: i.hildyard@surrey.ac.uk. **Document type:** monographic series.
—BLDSC (3597.970300).

330 333.79   UK
▼**S E E D S TECHNICAL PAPERS.** (Surrey Energy Economics Discussion Paper Series) 1996. irreg. £25 (foreign £30) (effective 1997). University of Surrey, Surrey Energy Economics Centre, Guildford GU2 5XH, England. TEL 44-1483-259379. FAX 44-1483-303775. E-mail: i.hildyard@surrey.ac.uk. **Document type:** monographic series.

S L U - E I S S I F NEWSLETTER. (Saint Louis University, Extension Institute for Small-Scale Industries Foundation) see *EDUCATION — Higher Education*

S N A BOLETIN ECONOMICO. (Sociedad Nacional de Agricultura) see *AGRICULTURE*

330   DR
SABADO ECONOMICO. w. $35. (Fundacion Economia y Desarrollo, Inc.) Editora Taller, Isabel la Catolica 260, Apdo. 2190, Santo Domingo, Dominican Republic. TEL 809-682-9369. FAX 809-689-7259. Ed. Andres Dauhajre, Jr.

BUSINESS AND ECONOMICS 999

330 US ISSN 8756-5897
SACRAMENTO BUSINESS JOURNAL; serving greater Sacramento. Key Title: Business Journal (Sacramento, Calif.). 1984. w. $65. American City Business Journals, Inc. (Austin), 505 Powell St., Austin, TX 78703-5121. (Subscr. to: Sacramento Business Journal, 1401 21st St., Ste. 200, Sacramento, CA 95814. TEL 916-447-7661. FAX 916-447-2243) Ed. Lee Wessman; Pub. Dan Kennedy. adv.: B&W page $4200. circ. 13,117 (paid). (tabloid format; also avail. in microfilm from LIB) **Document type:** newspaper.
● Also available online. Vendor(s): CompuServe, Inc., Data-Star, Dow Jones News Retrieval, Information Access Co., Knight-Ridder Information, Inc., Lexis-Nexis.
Also available on CD-ROM. Producer(s): UMI.
—UMI. **CCC.**

ST. GALLER STUDIEN ZUM PRIVAT-, HANDELS- UND WIRTSCHAFTSRECHT. see *LAW*

330 US
ST. LOUIS BUSINESS JOURNAL. 1980. w. $53. St. Louis Business Journal Corp. (Subsidiary of: American City Business Journals, Inc.), 1 Metropolitan Sq., Ste. 2170, St. Louis, MO 63102-2733. TEL 314-421-6200. Ed. Tom Wolf. adv.; bk.rev. circ. 18,490. (also avail. in microform from UMI) **Indexed:** Tr.& Indus.Ind. **Document type:** trade publication.
● Also available online. Vendor(s): Knight-Ridder Information, Inc.

ST. LOUIS COMPUTING. see *COMPUTERS — Personal Computers*

330 NA
ST. MAARTEN BUSINESS JOURNAL; the authoritative independent voice of the business community. 1985. m. $20. Box 372, Philipsburg, St. Maarten, Netherlands Antilles. Ed. Louis N. Peters. adv. circ. 500.
Formerly: St. Maarten Journal.

ST. PAUL LEGAL LEDGER. see *LAW — Corporate Law*

330 JA ISSN 0035-5356
ST. PAUL'S ECONOMIC REVIEW/RIKKYO KEIZAIGAKU KENKYU. 1938. q. 2000 Yen($20) (Rikkyo Daigaku, Rikkyo Keizaigaku Kenkyukai - Rikkyo University, St. Paul's Economic Society) Rikkyo Daigaku, Nishi-Ikebukuro, Toshima-ku, Tokyo 171, Japan. Ed.Bd. bk.rev. circ. 4,000. **Indexed:** Amer.Hist.& Life (1964-1968), Hist.Abstr. (1964-1968). **Document type:** academic/scholarly publication.
—BLDSC (7971.448100).

SALES COUNTER. see *PHOTOGRAPHY*

330 US ISSN 1077-9329
SALES MEMORY JOGGER. 1956. m. $22.80. Bureau of Business Practice, 24 Rope Ferry Rd., Waterford, CT 06386. TEL 860-442-4365. FAX 860-437-3555. URL: http://www.bbpnews.com. Ed. Sandy Fisher; Pub. Peter Garabedian. R&P contact: Debra Ferraro.

330 DK ISSN 0108-3937
SAMFUNDSOEKONOMEN. 1983. 8/yr. DKK 375 (effective 1997). Danmarks Jurist- og Oekonomforbund - Association of Danish Lawyers and Economists, 133 Gothersgade, P.O. Box 2126, DK-1015 Copenhagen, Denmark. TEL 45-33-95-97-00. FAX 45-33-95-99-99. Ed. Niels Ploug. adv.: B&W page DKK 5000; trim 200 x 145; adv. contact: Rosa Joergensen. **Document type:** academic/scholarly publication.

SAMSOM ARTSENPRAKTIJK. see *MEDICAL SCIENCES*

330 BE ISSN 0778-127X
SAMSOM BESLOTEN VENNOOTSCHAPPEN MET BEPERKTE AANSPRAKELIJKHEID. French edition: Samsom Societe Privee a Responsabilite Limitee (ISSN 0776-1562) (Supplement avail.) (Text in Flemish) 1986. s-m. 4558 BEF. C E D Samsom (Subsidiary of: Wolters Samsom Belgie n.v.), Kouterveld 14, B-1831 Diegem, Belgium. TEL 32-2-7231111.
Description: Helps professionals to sufficiently document business activities.

330 BE ISSN 0776-1511
SAMSOM COOPERATIEVE VENNOOTSCHAPPEN. French edition: Samsom Societe Cooperative (ISSN 0776-152X) (Supplement avail.) (Text in Flemish) 1988. s-m. 4552 BEF. C E D Samsom (Subsidiary of: Wolters Samsom Belgie n.v.), Kouterveld 14, B-1831 Diegem, Belgium. TEL 32-2-7231111.
Description: Disseminates information on subtle statutes and administration through fiscal questions, social problematics and economic dilemmas.

330 BE ISSN 0778-1261
SAMSOM NAAMLOZE VENNOOTSCHAPPEN. Variant title: N V Naamloze Vennootschappen. French edition: Samsom Societe Anonyme (ISSN 0778-0583) (Supplement avail.) (Text in Flemish) 1985. s-m. 4558 BEF. C E D Samsom (Subsidiary of: Wolters Samsom Belgie n.v.), Kouterveld 14, B-1831 Diegem, Belgium. TEL 2-7231111.
Description: Examines issues and concerns affecting limited liability companies.

382 BE ISSN 0776-4383
SAMSOM VRIJE BEROEPEN. French edition: Samsom Professions Liberales (ISSN 0777-2009) (Supplement avail.) (Text in Flemish) 1988. s-m. 4452 BEF. C E D Samsom (Subsidiary of: Wolters Samsom Belgie n.v.), Kouterveld 14, B-1831 Diegem, Belgium. TEL 32-2-7231111.

330 US ISSN 0895-1551
SAN ANTONIO BUSINESS JOURNAL. 1987. w. $48. American City Business Journals, Inc. (San Antonio), 8200 W. Interstate Hwy. 10, Ste. 300, San Antonio, TX 78230-3877. TEL 512-341-3202. FAX 512-341-3031. Ed. Bill Conroy; Pub. Kent Krauss. adv. contact: Mary Jonas. bk.rev.; circ. 12,000 (paid). **Document type:** newspaper.
● Also available online. Vendor(s): Information Access Co.
—UMI. **CCC.**
Description: Features news, statistics, and commentary about San Antonio's business community.

330 US
SAN DIEGO BUSINESS.* 1985. m. $18. Schmidt Communications, Box 33166, San Diego, CA 92163-3166. TEL 619-234-7997. Ed. Don Schmidt. adv.; bk.rev. circ. 12,500.

330 US ISSN 8750-6890
SAN DIEGO BUSINESS JOURNAL. 1980. w. $58. San Diego Business Journal, Inc., 4909 Murphy Canyon Rd., No. 200, San Diego, CA 92123. TEL 619-277-6359. FAX 619-571-3628. Ed. Martin Hill; Pub. Ted Owen. adv.: Kristi/Matula. circ. 21,500. (tabloid format; also avail. in microform from UMI) **Indexed:** Tr.& Indus.Ind. **Document type:** newspaper.
● Also available online. Vendor(s): Information Access Co., Knight-Ridder Information, Inc., UMI.
—UMI. **CCC.**

330 650 US ISSN 0068-5836
SAN DIEGO STATE UNIVERSITY. BUREAU OF BUSINESS AND ECONOMIC RESEARCH. MONOGRAPHS. Former title of issuing body--California. State College, San Diego. irreg. price varies. San Diego State University, Bureau of Business and Economic Research, School of Business Administration, San Diego, CA 92182. TEL 619-265-5200. **Document type:** monographic series.

330 650 US ISSN 0068-5844
SAN DIEGO STATE UNIVERSITY. BUREAU OF BUSINESS AND ECONOMIC RESEARCH. RESEARCH STUDIES AND POSITION PAPERS. Former title of issuing body--California. State College, San Diego. no.2, 1965. irreg., no.18, 1968. price varies. San Diego State University, Bureau of Business and Economic Research, School of Business Administration, San Diego, CA 92182. TEL 619-265-5200.

330 600 VN
SANG TAO/CREATIVITY. 1989. w. Central Council of Co-operatives, 80 Hang Gai, Hanoi, Socialist Republic of Vietnam. TEL 56122. Ed. Nguyen Huy Thong.

330 RU
SANKT-PETERBURGSKII UNIVERSITET. VESTNIK. SERIYA: EKONOMIKA. (Text in Russian; summaries in English) 1946. q. Sankt-Peterburgskii Universitet, Universitetskaya Nab. 7-9, St. Petersburg V-164, Russia.
—KNAW.
Formerly: Leningradskii Universitet. Vestnik. Seriya: Ekonomika (ISSN 0233-755X); Supersedes in part (in 1985): Leningradskii Universitet. Vestnik. Seriya: Ekonomika, Filosofiya, Pravo (ISSN 0024-0818).

658 KO ISSN 0036-4487
SANOP KWA KYONGYONG/YONSEI BUSINESS REVIEW. (Text in English and Korean) 1963. s-a. 8000 Won($12) Yonsei University, Industrial Management Research Centre, College of Business and Economics, 134 Sinchon-Dong, Sudaemoon-ku, Seoul, S. Korea. TEL 02-392-0192. FAX 02-313-5331. Ed. Hwi Suck Choo. adv.; bk.rev.; charts; stat. circ. 2,000.

330 320 JA
SAPIO. (Text in Japanese) 1989. bi-w. Shogakukan, Inc., 3-1 Hitotsubashi 2-chome, Chiyoda-ku, Tokyo 101-01, Japan. TEL 81-3-3230-5367. FAX 81-3-3264-8471. Ed. Kunimasa Endo; Pub. Mitsutoshi Igarashi. adv.: B&W page 800000 Yen, color page 1250000 Yen; trim 210 x 285; adv. contact: Hajime Yokoyama. circ. 150,000.
Description: Covers business, economics and politics.

330 300.9 CN
SASKATCHEWAN. DEPARTMENT OF INDUSTRY AND COMMERCE. INDUSTRIAL BENEFITS FROM RESOURCE DEVELOPMENT.* 1979. q. Government Printing Co., 2005 8th St., Regina, Sask. S4P 3V7, Canada. TEL 306-566-9393. circ. controlled.

330 CN ISSN 0709-0854
SASKATCHEWAN BUSINESS. 1979. bi-m. Can.$15.95. Sunrise Publishing Ltd., 2213-C Hanselman Ct., Saskatoon, SK S7L 6A8, Canada. TEL 306-244-5668. FAX 306-244-5679. Ed. Keith Moen; Pub. Twila Reddekopp. R&P contact: Twila Reddekopp. adv.: B&W page Can.$1898, color page Can.$2755; adv. contact: Twila Reddekopp. circ. 9,000. **Indexed:** Can.B.P.I. **Document type:** trade publication.
● Also available online. Vendor(s): Information Access Co.
Description: Profiles prominent business leaders and key developments in the Saskatchewan area. Provides data on business trends and opportunities.

330 SU
SAUDI ARABIA BUSINESS WEEK. (Text in English) w. P.O. Box 2894, Riyadh, Saudi Arabia.

330 SU ISSN 0252-967X
SAUDI ECONOMIC SURVEY; weekly review of Saudi Arabian economic and business activities. 1967. w. SRI.1550 ($475 outside the Arab world). Saudi Eco Survey, P.O. Box 1989, Jeddah 21441, Saudi Arabia. TEL 966-2-6428245. Ed. Abdelhakim Misbah Ghaith; Pub. S.A. Ashour. adv. circ. 3,000. (back issues avail.) **Document type:** bulletin, newsletter.
Description: Covers Saudi business transactions, trade and legal changes affecting business, contracts, tenders.

330 US ISSN 1073-1741
SAVANNAH BUSINESS JOURNAL; the business journal of Bryan, Chatham, Effingham, and Liberty counties. 1990. m. $15. Blum Publishing Co., 6203 Abercorn, Ste. 103E, Savannah, GA 31405. TEL 912-354-5553. FAX 912-232-0140. Ed. Donald R. Blum; Pub. Donald R. Blum. R&P contact: Donald R. Blum. TEL 912-233-5711. adv.: page $700; adv. contact: Donald R. Blum. bk.rev. circ. 5,000. (also avail. in microform from UMI) **Document type:** newspaper.
● Also available online. Vendor(s): UMI.
Description: Features selected area businesses, general business news, newly issued licenses and special topics.

BUSINESS AND ECONOMICS

338.948   SW
▼**SCANDINAVIA NOW ONLINE.** 1996. d. free. Elfwendahl & Co., Runebergsgatan 6, SE-114 29 Stockholm, Sweden. TEL 46-8-678-32-30. FAX 46-8-611-23-58. E-mail: eme.nova@intense.se; mailbox@elfco.se; URL: http://www.elfco.se/scandnow. Ed. Everett M. Ellestad. adv. contact: Tord Elfwendahl.
●Available only online.
Description: Focuses on Scandinavian trade, business and industry of interest to businesses and industries outside Scandinavia. Information on weather, economic and cultural aspects for each country is also included.
Refereed Serial

330   UK   ISSN 0347-0520
HB9
SCANDINAVIAN JOURNAL OF ECONOMICS. 1899. q. £118($204) (foreign £129) (effective 1997). Blackwell Publishers Ltd., 108 Cowley Rd., Oxford OX4 1JF, England. TEL 44-1865-791100. FAX 44-1165-791347. E-mail: jnlinfo@blackwellpublishers.co.uk; URL: http://www.blackwellpublishers.co.uk. Eds. Torben Andersen, Karl Moore. adv.; index. circ. 1,100. (reprint service avail. from SWZ) **Indexed:** ABI Inform., Amer.Hist.& Life (1954-1970), ASCA, BPIA, C.R.E.J., Curr.Cont., Fam.Ind., Hist.Abstr. (1954-1970), J.of Econ.Lit., Key to Econ.Sci., P.A.I.S., Risk Abstr., SSCI, Zent.Math. **Document type:** academic/scholarly publication.
—BLDSC (8087.505700); Genuine Article; KR SourceOne; SWETS; UMI; UnCover. **CCC.**
Former titles: Swedish Journal of Economics (ISSN 0039-7318); Ekonomisk Tidskrift.
Refereed Serial

330   UG
SCARCITY. (Text in English) vol.2, 1968. irreg. (approx. a.). Makerere Economics Society, Box 7062, Kampala, Uganda.

330   US
SCHOOL OF BUSINESS UPDATE. 1983. 3/yr. free to qualified personnel. University of Wisconsin at Madison, School of Business, 1155 Observatory Dr., Madison, WI 53706. TEL 608-262-2401. FAX 608-263-0477. Ed. Lari Fanlund. circ. 26,000. (back issues avail.)

330   UK
SCHOOL OF MANAGEMENT AND FINANCE. DISCUSSION PAPERS. irreg. £2.50. School of Management and Finance, Social Sciences Bldg., University of Nottingham, Nottingham NG7 2RD, England. TEL 0602-515251. **Document type:** academic/scholarly publication.

330   SZ
SCHWEIZERISCHE MARKT ZEITUNG. m. Binzmuehlestr. 223, CH-8056 Zurich, Switzerland. TEL 01-3715757. Ed. W.E. Fehr. circ. 4,000.

330 310   SZ   ISSN 0303-9692
SCHWEIZERISCHE ZEITSCHRIFT FUER VOLKSWIRTSCHAFT UND STATISTIK/REVUE SUISSE D'ECONOMIE POLITIQUE ET DE STATISTIQUE. (Text in English, French, German) 1863. 4/yr. 100 SFr. (effective 1996). (Schweizerische Gesellschaft fuer Statistik und Volkswirtschaft - Societe Suisse de Statistique et d'Economie Politique) Helbing und Lichtenhahn Verlag AG, Freie Str. 84, CH-4051 Basel, Switzerland. TEL 41-61-2721116. FAX 41-61-2721150. (Subscr. to: Sauerlaender AG, Laurenzenvorstadt 89, CH-5001 Aarau, Switzerland. TEL 41-64-268626. FAX 41-64-244580) Ed. Ernst Baltensperger. adv.; B&W page 525 SFr.; trim 125 x 190. bk.rev. circ. 1,850. (reprint service avail. from SCH) **Indexed:** Curr.Cont. (1979-), IBR, Int.Polit.Sci.Abstr., J.of Econ.Lit., Key to Econ.Sci., P.A.I.S.For.Lang.Ind., P.A.I.S., Stat.Theor.Meth.Abstr. (1979-). **Document type:** academic/scholarly publication.
●Also available online. Vendor(s): Knight-Ridder Information, Inc.
Also available on CD-ROM. Producer(s): SilverPlatter Information, Inc.
—BLDSC (7953.363000); SWETS.

330   FR   ISSN 0765-0027
SCIENCE ET VIE ECONOMIE. 1984. 11/yr. 220 F. (foreign 276 F.) (effective 1992). Excelsior Publications, 1 rue du Colonel Pierre Avia, 75503 Paris Cedex 15, France. TEL 46-48-48-48. FAX 46-48-48-09. TELEX 631 994 F. Ed. Marc Jezegabel. adv. contact: Gilles de Keranflech. circ. 115,273.
Description: Explores the economy from all angles.

330   US
SCORECARD. 1992. q. $99. 4751 Best Rd., Ste. 300, Atlanta, GA 30337-9894. TEL 404-763-5454. FAX 404-763-5473. E-mail: marcom@aeronomics.com; URL: http://www.aeronomics.com. Pub. Robert G. Cross. (back issues avail.)
Description: Includes information on revenue management.

330   UK   ISSN 0954-4976
SCOTTISH CHAMBERS BUSINESS SURVEY. 1984. q. £150. University of Strathclyde, Fraser of Allander Institute for Research on the Scottish Economy, Curran Bldg., 100 Cathedral St., Glasgow G4 0LN, Scotland. TEL 44-141-552-4400. FAX 44-141-552-5589. TELEX 77472-UNSLIB-G. Ed. Eleanor Malloy. adv. contact: Cliff Lockyer. **Document type:** bulletin.
Formerly: Scottish Business Survey (ISSN 0267-1212)

SCOTTISH ECONOMIC AND SOCIAL HISTORY. see *SOCIAL SCIENCES: COMPREHENSIVE WORKS*

330   UK   ISSN 0036-9292
HB1
SCOTTISH JOURNAL OF POLITICAL ECONOMY. 1954. 5/yr. £84($153) (foreign £97) (effective 1997). (Scottish Economic Society) Blackwell Publishers Ltd., 108 Cowley Rd., Oxford OX4 1JF, England. TEL 44-1865-791100. FAX 44-1865-791347. E-mail: jnlinfo@blackwellpublishers.co.uk; URL: http://www.blackwellpublishers.co.uk. Eds. L.C. Hunter, A. Muscatelli. adv.; bk.rev.; index. circ. 1,500. (reprint service avail. from KTO) **Indexed:** Amer.Hist.& Life (1955-1961), (1964-), ASCA, Asian-Pac.Econ.Lit., Br.Hum.Ind., Bus.Ind., C.R.E.J., Cont.Pg.Manage., Curr.Cont., Geo.Abstr.P.G., Hist.Abstr. (1955-1961), (1964-), IBR, IDA, Int.Lab.Doc., J.of Econ.Lit., Key to Econ.Sci., P.A.I.S., Rural Recreat.Tour.Abstr., SSCI, Work Rel.Abstr., World Agri.Econ.& Rural Sociol.Abstr., World Bank.Abstr. **Document type:** academic/scholarly publication.
—BLDSC (8210.600000); Genuine Article; SWETS; UMI; UnCover. **CCC.**
Refereed Serial

330   SP
SECTOR PUBLICO EMPRESARIAL DE LA COMUNIDAD AUTONOMA DE EUSKADI. (Text in Basque and Spanish) 1989. irreg., latest 1995. (Ogasun eta Finantza Saila - Departamento de Hacienda y Finanzas) Eusko Jaurlaritzaren Argitalpen-Zerbitzu Nagusia - Servicio Central de Publicaciones del Gobierno Vasco, C. Duque de Wellington 2, 01010 Vitoria-Gasteiz, Spain. circ. 1,500. **Document type:** government publication.

330   JA   ISSN 0387-4753
SEIJO UNIVERSITY ECONOMIC PAPERS/SEIJO DAIGAKU KEIZAI KENKYU. (Text in Japanese) 1953. q. 3000 Yen. Economic Institute of Seijo University - Seijo Daigaku Keizaigakkai, 1-20, Seijo 6, Setagaya-ku, Tokyo 157, Japan. Ed. Itaru Ueno. bk.rev. circ. 300. **Document type:** academic/scholarly publication.
—BLDSC (8219.655000).

330   JA
SEKISAN GIJUTSU/COST ESTIMATION ANALYSIS. (Text in Japanese) m. 850 Yen per no. Keizai Chosakai - Economic Research Association, 15-10, Ginza 3-chome, Chuo-ku, Tokyo 104, Japan.

330   UK   ISSN 1356-9627
SELF-ASSESSMENT; the magazine of continuous quality improvement. q. £120 (overseas £140($225)) (effective 1996). I F S International Ltd., Wolseley Business Park, Kempston, Bedford MK42 7PW, England. TEL 44-1234-853605. FAX 44-1234-854499. Ed. Dan M. Boland; Pub. Roy L. Chase. R&P contact: David Watts. adv. contact: David Watts. bk.rev.; illus. **Document type:** trade publication.
—BLDSC (8235.360000).
Description: Examines how the use of self-assessment leads to continuous improvement, superior competitive performance, and achievement of world-class status.

330   US   ISSN 1046-9036
THE SELLING ADVANTAGE. 1989. fortn. $94.56. Progressive Business Publications, 370 Technology Dr., Malvern, PA 19355-1315. TEL 610-695-8600. Ed. Philip Ahr; Pub. Edward Satell. **Document type:** newsletter.
Description: For sales professionals interested in improving performance.

330   PE   ISSN 0254-816X
SEMANA ECONOMICA. 1985. w. (48/yr.) $590 (effective 1997). Apoyo Comunicaciones, S.A., Juan de la Fuente 625, Lima 18, Peru. TEL 51-14-445555. FAX 51-14-445555. Ed. Augusto Alvarez Rodrich.

330   PO   ISSN 0872-1688
SEMANARIO ECONOMICO. 1987. w. Esc.10190. Rua de Santa Marta 47-2o, Dto., 1100 Lisbon, Portugal. TEL 01-352-85-25. FAX 01-315-18-41. Dir. Nicolau Santos. adv. contact: B/W. circ. 20,000. **Document type:** newspaper.

330   SP
SENAS. 1993. 46/yr. 37900 ptas. (foreign $320) (effective 1997). Canalejas 30, entlo. 2o, 08028 Barcelona, Spain. TEL 34-3-4226289. FAX 34-3-4211858. E-mail: revista.econo@redestb.es. Ed. Ricardo Rabella. circ. 460,000. **Document type:** bulletin.
Description: Contains business, investment, banking, and commercial news from Spain.
Refereed Serial

330   US
SENIOR POWER. 1983. m. Senior Power, Inc., 7802 E. Mission Crt., No. 1230, Spokane, WA 99212-2598. TEL 509-928-1677. FAX 509-924-3720. adv.; bk.rev.; illus. (tabloid format) **Document type:** newspaper.

330   KO   ISSN 1225-0279
SEOUL JOURNAL OF ECONOMICS. (Text in English) 1988. q. $20 to individuals; institutions $50. Seoul National University, Institute of Economic Research - Seoul Daehakkyo Kyeongje Yeonguso, Seoul 151-742, S. Korea. TEL 02-877-1629. FAX 02-888-4454. Ed. Cae-One Kim. circ. 500. **Document type:** academic/scholarly publication.
—BLDSC (8241.809700); SWETS.
Description: Deals with theoretical and empirical matters in all fields of economics, especially focusing on the economic development of East Asia.

338.4   UK   ISSN 0264-2069
HD9980.1
THE SERVICE INDUSTRIES JOURNAL. 1981. q. £48($60) to individuals; institutions £165($230) (effective 1998). Frank Cass, Newbury House, 890-900 Eastern Ave., Newbury Park, Ilford, Essex 1G2 7HH, England. TEL 44-181-599-8866. FAX 44-181-599-0984. E-mail: jnlsubs@frankcass.com; URL: http://www.frankcass.com. (Dist. in US by: ISBS, 5804 N.E. Hassalo St., Portland, OR 97213-3644. TEL 800-944-6190. FAX 503-280-8832) Ed.Bd. adv.: B&W page £195($275); adv. contact: Anne Kidson. bk.rev.; index. (also avail. in microfilm from UMI; back issues avail.) **Indexed:** ABI Inform., Anbar, Art.Hosp.& Tour., ASCA, Cont.Pg.Manage., Curr.Cont., Food Sci.& Tech.Abstr., Geo.Abstr.H.G., Geo.Abstr.P.G., IBR, IDA, Mgmt.& Market.Abstr., SSCI, World Bank.Abstr. **Document type:** academic/scholarly publication.
●Also available online. Vendor(s): UMI.
—BLDSC (8251.429000); Genuine Article; SWETS; UMI. **CCC.**
Description: Covers services, service industries, and management of services from an international, interdisciplinary, and academic perspective.
Refereed Serial

330   IT
SERVIZI; rivista di studi e ricerche. 1991. s-a. L.20000 (foreign L.30000) (effective 1991). (Confesercenti Provinciali de Pesaro e Urbino) Edizioni Quattroventi, Via Dini 16, Casella Postale 156, 61029 Urbino, Italy. TEL 0722-2588. FAX 0722-320998. Ed. Giancarlo Zuccarini.

330   CC   ISSN 1000-971X
SHANDONG JINGJI/SHANDONG ECONOMICS. (Text in Chinese) m. Shandong Jingji Xueyuan - Shandong Institute of Economics, Jing 10 Lu, Jinan, Shandong 250014, People's Republic of China. TEL 48920. Ed. Zhang Wenjie.

330   MY   ISSN 0126-9593
SHANG HAI. (Text in Chinese) 1979. m. Star Publications (M) Bhd., 13 Jalan 13-6, Petaling Jaya, Selangor, 46200 Kuala Lumpur, Malaysia. TEL 3-758-1188. FAX 3-755-4039. adv.: B&W page M.$1045, color page M.$1720; 187 x 265. circ. 9,312. **Document type:** trade publication.
Description: Covers business related economic, social, and political topics.

330   CC   ISSN 1000-4211
SHANGHAI JINGJI/SHANGHAI ECONOMICS. (Text in Chinese) 1981. bi-m. Y7.20 (effective 1993). Shanghai Shehui Kexueyuan, Bumen Jingji Yanjiusuo - Shanghai Academy of Social Sciences, Institute of Sector Economy, No.7, Alley 622, Huaihai Zhonglu, Shanghai 200020, People's Republic of China. TEL 3271170. FAX 86-21-270004. Ed. Xu Zhihe.

330   CC   ISSN 1005-1309
HC428.S47
SHANGHAI JINGJI YANJIU/SHANGHAI ECONOMIC RESEARCH. (Text in Chinese) m. Shanghai Shehui Kexueyuan, Jingji Yanjiusuo - Shanghai Academy of Social Sciences, Institute of Economics, No. 7, Alley 622, Huaihai Zhonglu, Shanghai 200020, People's Republic of China. TEL 86-21-6327-1170. Ed. Zhang Jiguang.

330 320.531   CC   ISSN 1005-4294
SHEHUIZHUYI JINGJI LILUN YU SHIJIAN/THEORY AND PRACTICE OF SOCIALIST ECONOMICS. (Subseries of: Fuyin Baokan Ziliao) (Text in Chinese) m. $162.01. Zhongguo Renmin Daxue, Shubao Ziliao Zhongxin - China People's University, Book & Newspaper Information Center, 3 Zhang Zizhong Rd., P.O. Box 1122, Beijing 100007, People's Republic of China. TEL 86-104015080. (Dist. in US by: China Publications Service, Box 49614, Chicago, IL 60649. TEL 312-288-3291. FAX 312-288-8570) pp./issue: 240.

330 628   CC
SHENGTAI JINGJI/ECOLOGICAL ECONOMICS. (Text in Chinese) bi-m. (Zhongguo Shengtai Jingji Xuehui) Shengtai Jingji Zashishe, Renmin Donglu, Kunming, Yunnan 650051, People's Republic of China. TEL 86-871-3317953. (Dist. overseas by: China International Book Trading Corp., P.O. Box 399, Beijing 100044, P.R. China) (Co-sponsor: Yunnan Sheng Shengtai Jingji Xuehui) pp./issue: 56.
Document type: academic/scholarly publication.
Description: Discusses theories of ecological economics. Advocates the balanced development of ecology and economics.

330   CC
SHIJIE JINGJI YICONG/WORLD ECONOMICS TRANSLATIONS. (Text in Chinese) m. Zhongguo Shehui Kexueyuan, Shijie Jingji yu Zhengzhi Yanjiusuo - Chinese Academy of Social Sciences, Institute of World Economics and Politics, 5 Jianguomennei Dajie, Beijing 100732, People's Republic of China. TEL 5137744. Ed. Gong Rongjin.

330   CC   ISSN 1007-0184
SHIJIE JINGJI YU ZHONGGUO/WORLD ECONOMY & CHINA. (Text in Chinese, English) q. $80. Zhongguo Shehui Kexueyuan, Shijie Jingji yu Zhengzhi Yanjiusuo - Chinese Academy of Social Sciences, Institute of World Economics and Politics, 5 Jianguomennei Dajie, Beijing 100732, People's Republic of China. TEL 86-10-5137744. (Co-sponsor: Chinese Society on World Economy) Ed. Yuanyang Gu.

330   JA
SHUKAN DAIYAMONDO/WEEKLY DIAMOND. (Text in Japanese) 1913. w. 16000 Yen. Diamond Inc., 4-2, 1-chome, Kasumigaseki, Chiyoda-ku, Tokyo 100, Japan. TEL 03-3504-6519. TELEX 24461. Ed. Teiji Kajima.

330   JA   ISSN 0918-5755
SHUKAN TOYO KEIZAI/WEEKLY TOYO KEIZAI. (Text in Japanese) 1895. w. Toyo Keizai Inc., 1-2-1 Nihombashi Hongoku-cho, Chuo-ku, Tokyo 103, Japan. TEL 81-3-3246-5601. FAX 81-3-3246-0679. (Subscr. in US to: 380 Lexington Ave., Ste. 4505, New York, NY 10168. TEL 212-949-6737. FAX 212-949-6648) Ed. Hiroshi Takahashi. adv.: B&W page 580000 Yen, color page 820000 Yen; trim 182 x 257; adv. contact: Shuji Kawase. circ. 61,024.

330   TS
SHU'UN AL-SINA'AH. 1985. q. Ministry of Finance and Industry, Information Department, P.O. Box 398, Abu Dhabi, United Arab Emirates. TEL 726000. FAX 823901. TELEX 22937 FEDFIN EM. Ed. Rafa'at al-Mugharbel. circ. 1,000.
Description: Provides news and information of interest to members of the business and industry communities, and serves as a forum for discussion of concerns.

SICHERHEITS-BESCHAFFUNGSDIENST; aktuelle Produkte und Dienstleistungen fuer Sicherheit in der Wirtschaft. see CRIMINOLOGY AND LAW ENFORCEMENT — Security

330   GW   ISSN 0943-3937
SIGNALE AUS DER WISSENSCHAFTLICHEN HOCHSCHULE FUER UNTERNEHMENSFUEHRUNG. (Text in English, French, German) 1986. 4/yr. DM.68 (effective 1997). Wissenschaftliche Hochschule fuer Unternehmensfuehrung, Otto-Beisheim-Hochschule, Burgplatz 2, 56179 Vallendar, Germany. TEL 49-261-6509128. FAX 49-261-6509111. Ed. Phoebe Schnurr. adv.: page DM.3500; adv. contact: Phoebe Schnurr. illus. (back issues avail.) **Document type:** academic/scholarly publication.

910.202   BE
SIGNATURE. (Editions in Dutch, Flemish, French) 1963. 5/yr. membership. (Diners Club Benelux) Continental Publishing, Lakborslei 114, B-2100 Antwerp, Belgium. TEL 32-3-3607800. FAX 32-3-3607801. Ed. Willy Van den Bossche; Pub. Jozef Govaerts. adv.: B&W page 260000 BEF, color page 315000 BEF. bk.rev. circ. 215,000 (85,000 Dutch ed.; 55,000 Flemish ed.; 70,000 French ed.). **Document type:** consumer publication.
Description: Business and lifestyle articles for Diners Club cardholders.

330 300   MR   ISSN 0851-4909
SIGNES DU PRESENT. (Editions in Arabic, English, French) 1936. irreg. DH.50 for 4 nos. Societe d'Etudes Economiques Sociales et Statistiques du Maroc, B.P. 535, Rabat-Chellah, Morocco. TEL 792-20. Ed. Abdelkhebir Khatibi. bk.rev.; cum.index. circ. 1,300. **Indexed:** P.A.I.S.For.Lang.Ind.
Formerly (until 1988): Bulletin Economique et Social du Maroc (ISSN 0007-4586)

330   TS
AL-SINA'AH/INDUSTRY. (Text in Arabic) 1988. m. Mu'assasat al-Aamah lil-Sina'ah, P.O. Box 4499, Abu Dhabi, United Arab Emirates. TEL 214900. FAX 325034. TELEX 22938 GICORP EM. Ed. Isa Abdul Rahman Atiq.
Description: Covers industrial concerns, with a focus on development and the future of industry in the U.A.E.

330   SI   ISSN 0217-5908
HB1
SINGAPORE ECONOMIC REVIEW. 1956. s-a. S.$40($20) Economic Society of Singapore, c/o Faculty of Business Administration, National University of Singapore, 10 Kent Ridge Crescent, Singapore 0511, Singapore. TEL 65-772-3075. Ed.Bd. adv.; bk.rev. circ. 800. (reprint service avail. from SCH) **Indexed:** ASCA, Asian-Pac.Econ.Lit., C.R.E.J., E.I., Geo.Abstr.P.G., IDA, Int.Lab.Doc., J.of Econ.Lit., Mid.East: Abstr.& Ind., P.A.I.S., Rice Abstr., SSCI. **Document type:** academic/scholarly publication. —BLDSC (8285.463050); SWETS; UnCover.
Formerly (until 1982): Malayan Economic Review (ISSN 0047-5599)

THE SINGAPORE LAW GAZETTE. see LAW

330   SI   ISSN 0217-7528
HF3800.67
SINGAPORE TRADE NEWS. (Text in English) 1984. bi-m. Singapore Trade Development Board, 1 Maritime Square No. 10-40, World Trade Centre, Telok Blangah Rd., Singapore 0409, Singapore. FAX 2740770. TELEX RS-28617-TRADEV. Ed. Jeanne Cheng. circ. 15,000. **Document type:** trade publication.
Description: Gives a general overview of Singapore and its business prospects.

330   CK   ISSN 0120-5463
SINTESIS ECONOMICA. 1975? w. Apdo. Postal Aereo 34284, Calle 70A, 10-52, Bogota, Colombia. TEL 212-7360. Dir. Daniel Mazuera Gomez. circ. 7,500.

330   CL   ISSN 0716-2456
HA992
SINTESIS ESTADISTICA DE CHILE. (Editions in English, Spanish) 1978. a. Ch.$5300($20) Banco Central de Chile, Casilla 967, Santiago, Chile. TEL 56-2-6702000. FAX 56-2-6984847. TELEX 405 69 CENBC CL. circ. 2,000. **Document type:** government publication.
Description: General and economic statistics of Chile.

650   UK
SIR FREDERIC HOOPER AWARD ESSAY. 1969. a. membership. Foundation for Business Responsibilities, 40 Doughty St., London WC1N 2LF, England.

338 320   UK   ISSN 0080-9780
SIR GEORGE EARLE MEMORIAL LECTURE ON INDUSTRY AND GOVERNMENT. 1966. a. price varies. Foundation for Business Responsibilities, 40 Doughty St., London WC1N 2LF, England. bk.rev.

330   IT
SISTEMA ITALIA. 1948. w. L.200000. Edizioni Sistema Italia S.p.A., Via Liszt 21, 00144 Rome, Italy. TEL 39-6-5992442. FAX 39-6-59926702. Ed. Lorenzo Guglielmi. adv.: B&W page L.8400000. circ. 35,000.

330   US   ISSN 1059-1958
SITUATIONS DIGEST.* 1991. q. $29.99. Publishing & Business Consultants, 101 W. 64th St., Unit 3-2, Inglewood, CA 90302-1255. TEL 213-732-3477. FAX 213-732-9123. (Subscr. to: Box 75392, Los Angeles, CA 90075) Ed. Andeson Napoleon Atia. **Document type:** consumer publication.

SKATTEN. ERHVERV. see BUSINESS AND ECONOMICS — Public Finance, Taxation

330   CN
SKEENA BUSINESS MAGAZINE. 1993. m. Can.$20 (US Can.$30). Sterling Newspapers Ltd., 413-3rd Ave., E., Prince Rupert, BC V8J 1K7, Canada. TEL 604-624-2613. FAX 604-624-2680. Ed. Mike Kelly; Pub. Les Yates. adv.: B&W page Can.$630; trim 8 x 10 5/8. circ. 4,500.

330 747 643.6   XV   ISSN 0353-1007
SLOVENIJALES; glasilo mednarondega podjetja za trgovino, inzeniring, proizvodnjo, zastopanje in konsignacijo. (Text in Slovenian) 1975. m. free. Mednarodno Podjetje Slovenijales, Titova 52, pp 94, 61001 Ljubljana, Slovenia. TEL 061-319-266. FAX 061-126-130. Ed. Janes Svajovic. illus. circ. 3,500. (tabloid format; back issues avail.)

330   XO
SLOVENSKY PROFIT; hospodarsky a podnikatel'sky tyzdennik. w. newsstand price: 12 Sk. Euroskop, Inc., Pribinova 25, 819 37 Bratislava, Slovakia. TEL 42-7-2103817. FAX 42-2-2104581. Ed. Iveta Seifertova. adv. contact: Includes supplement: Profit Invest. charts; illus.; stat. circ. 43,000. cols./p.: 5; pp./issue: 32. (tabloid format) **Document type:** newspaper.
Description: Reports business and financial news; provides information on investing.

330   NE
SOCIAAL-ECONOMISCHE RAAD. JAARVERSLAG/SOCIAAL-ECONOMISCHE RAAD. ANNUAL REPORT. a. free. Sociaal-Economische Raad, Postbus 90405, 2509 LK The Hague, Netherlands. TEL 31-70-3499499. FAX 31-70-3832535. bk.rev. **Document type:** corporate report.
Description: Discusses economic and social policy issues.

BUSINESS AND ECONOMICS

SOCIAL AND ECONOMIC STUDIES. see *SOCIAL SCIENCES: COMPREHENSIVE WORKS*

330   FR   ISSN 0769-055X
SOCIAL PRATIQUE. (Supplement avail. (ISSN 0997-1092)) bi-m. 618 F. (effective 1992). Groupe Liaisons S.A., 1 av. Edouard Belin, 92856 Rueil Malmaison, France. TEL 33-1-41299879. FAX 33-1-41299880.

340   BL
SOCIEDADES POR ACOES. 1977. irreg. Editora Resenha Universitaria, Rua Quatinga 12, 04140 Sao Paulo, Brazil.

330   BE
SOCIETE ROYALE D'ECONOMIE POLITIQUE DE BELGIQUE. SEANCES. 1855. 8/yr. 750 Fr. Societe Royale d'Economie Politique de Belgique, Avenue General Michel 1b, B-6000 Charleroi, Belgium. circ. 900. **Indexed:** P.A.I.S.For.Lang.Ind.
     Formerly (until 1964): Societe Royale d'Economie Politique de Belgique. Comptes Rendus des Travaux.

330 350   US
SOCIETY OF GOVERNMENT ECONOMISTS. BULLETIN. m. Society of Government Economists, c/o Thesia I. Garner, Bicentennial Bldg., Rm. 4103, Bureau of Labor Statistics, 600 E St., N.W., Washington, DC 20212. TEL 202-272-2610. FAX 202-272-2610. **Document type:** bulletin.
     Description: Aimed at economists employed by governments or those interested in economic policy issues.

330   DK   ISSN 0109-2863
SOENDERJYLLANDS ERHVERVSORIENTERING: PRODUKTION, HANDEL, KONTAKT. 1983. q. Langenberg Trykkeri, Falstersgade 2, 6400 Soenderborg, Denmark. illus.

330 614.7   US
SOFT DRINK RECYCLER. q. National Soft Drink Association, 1101 16th St., N.W., Washington, DC 20036. TEL 202-463-6700. Ed. Heather Beldon.

SOGO TOSHI KENKYU/COMPREHENSIVE URBAN STUDIES. see *SOCIOLOGY*

330   US   ISSN 0191-6327
SONOMA BUSINESS.* m. Mariposa Press, 50 Old Courthouse Sq., 105, Santa Rosa, CA 95404-4930. TEL 707-575-8282. Ed. James Dunn. circ. 7,500.

330 345.01   US
SONOMA COUNTY DAILY HERALD-RECORDER. 1899. 5/w. $188. Daily Journal Corporation (Los Angeles), 915 E. First St., Los Angeles, CA 90012. TEL 213-229-5300. Ed. Eric Cummins. adv.; bk.rev.; illus. circ. 500. (tabloid format) **Document type:** newspaper.
     Formerly: Sonoma County Herald-Recorder (ISSN 0038-142X)

330.1 339   CH   ISSN 0259-3769
SOOCHOW JOURNAL OF ECONOMICS AND BUSINESS. Key Title: Dongwu Jingji Shangxue Xuebao. (Text in Chinese and English) 1977. a. $15. Soochow University, Wai Shuang Hsi, Shih Lin, Taipei, Taiwan, Republic of China. FAX 886-02-8812317. Ed.Bd. circ. 500. (reprint service avail.) **Document type:** academic/scholarly publication.

330 320 306.3   NO   ISSN 0038-1624
SOSIALOEKONOMEN. (Text in Norwegian; articles occasionally in English) 1947. 10/yr. NOK 500 to individuals; students NOK 240 (effective 1997). Sosialoekonomenes Forening, P.O. Box 8872 Youngstorget, N-0028 Oslo, Norway. TEL 47-22-41-32-90. FAX 47-22-41-32-93. Ed. Torstein A. Bye. adv.; B&W page NOK 4300; trim 187 x 254. bk.rev.; charts; illus.; index. circ. 2,500.
     —BLDSC (8328.775000).
     Formerly (until 1958): Stimulator (ISSN 0332-9488)

330   CN   ISSN 0381-5471
SOUNDING BOARD. 1935. m. (11/yr.). Board of Trade, World Trade Centre, Ste. 400, 999 Canada Pl., Vancouver, BC V6C 3E1, Canada. TEL 604-641-1270. FAX 604-681-0437. Ed. Ron Stanaitis. adv. contact: Ron Stanaitis. circ. 12,000. (tabloid format) **Document type:** newspaper.

SOUNDINGS (NOTRE DAME); a series of books on ethics, economics and business. see *PHILOSOPHY*

330   CN
SOURCEBOOK (YEAR) BUSINESS PROGRAMS FOR NORTHERN ONTARIO. (Editions in English, French) 1988. irreg. free. Ministry of Northern Development and Mines, Communications Services, 159 Cedar St., 4th Fl., Sudbury, ON P3E 6A5, Canada. TEL 705-670-7107. FAX 705-670-7108. circ. 20,000. **Document type:** government publication.
     Formerly: Business Guide.
     Description: Information guide providing financial and advisory assistance for entrepreneurs operating or setting up in Northern Ontario.

330   SA   ISSN 0038-2280
HB9
SOUTH AFRICAN JOURNAL OF ECONOMICS/SUID-AFRIKAANSE TYDSKRIF VIR EKONOMIE. (Text in English; occasionally in Afrikaans; summaries in English) 1933. q. R.40 in South Africa; Namibia, southern & central Africa R.60; elsewhere $38 (effective 1993). Economic Society of South Africa, 4-44 EBW Bldg., University of Pretoria, Pretoria 0002, South Africa. TEL 012-420-3525. FAX 012-43-7589. Ed.Bd. adv.; bk.rev.; bibl.; stat.; index. circ. 1,700. (back issues avail.; reprint service avail. from SCH) **Indexed:** ASCA, C.R.E.J., Curr.Cont., Documentatieblad, Ind.S.A.Per., Int.Lab.Doc., J.of Econ.Lit., Key to Econ.Sci., P.A.I.S., Rural Devel.Abstr., Rural Recreat.Tour.Abstr., SSCI, Work Rel.Abstr., World Agri.Econ.& Rural Sociol.Abstr. **Document type:** academic/scholarly publication.
     —BLDSC (8338.860000); SWETS; UnCover.
     Description: Covers various aspects of the study of economics.

SOUTH AFRICAN MERCANTILE LAW JOURNAL/SUID-AFRIKAANSE TYDSKRIF VIR HANDELSREG. see *LAW*

330   US   ISSN 0745-4473
SOUTH CAROLINA BUSINESS JOURNAL. 1982. m. $15. South Carolina Chamber of Commerce, 1201 Main St., Columbia, SC 29201-3200. TEL 803-799-4601. FAX 803-779-6043. Ed. Preston McLaurin; Pub. Deborah K. Wooley. circ. 8,300. **Document type:** newspaper.

330   US
SOUTH CENTRAL INDIANA'S BUSINESS JOURNAL. Short title: S C I B J. 1991. m. $15; newsstand price: free. Times - Mail Special Products, 813 16th St., Box 849, Bedford, IN 47421. TEL 812-277-3470. FAX 812-277-3475. Ed. Jeff Routh; Pub. Debbie Morthland. R&P contact: Ellen Ware. TEL 812-275-3355. adv.: page $400; 11 x 14; adv. contact: Janelle Zack. bibl.; charts; illus.; stat.; tr.lit. circ. 3,200. (tabloid format; back issues avail.) **Document type:** newspaper.
     Description: Focuses on regional business. Direct mailed to Lawrence, Orange and contiguous counties' Chamber of Commerce members.

650   US   ISSN 0038-3260
HC107.S8   CODEN: SDBRA5
SOUTH DAKOTA BUSINESS REVIEW. 1942. q. free. University of South Dakota, School of Business, Business Research Bureau, 414 E. Clark St., Vermillion, SD 57069-2390. TEL 605-677-5287. FAX 605-677-5427. URL: http://www.brb.usd.edu. Ed. Steve Tracy. R&P contact: Nancy Nelson. charts; stat. circ. 1,350. (also avail. in microfiche from CIS) **Indexed:** ABI Inform., BPIA, Bus.Ind., P.A.I.S., SRI, Tr.& Indus.Ind. **Document type:** newsletter.
     ●Also available online. Vendor(s): Information Access Co., UMI.
     —UMI.

330   US   ISSN 0746-2271
SOUTH FLORIDA BUSINESS JOURNAL. 1980. w. $69 includes annual Book of Lists. American City Business Journals, Inc. (Miami), 1050 Lee Wagener Blvd., Ste. 302, Ft. Lauderdale, FL 33315-3500. FAX 305-594-1892. Ed. Ross Nethery; Pub. Gary Press. R&P contact: Ross Nethery. adv. contact: Joel Welker. circ. 14,000. (tabloid format; also avail. in microfiche from UMI) **Indexed:** Tr.& Indus.Ind.
     ●Also available online. Vendor(s): Information Access Co.
     —UMI. CCC.
     Formerly: Miami Business Journal.

330   AT   ISSN 0728-4764
THE SOUTH SEA DIGEST; the private newsletter of Pacific Islands affairs. 1981. 25/yr. Aus.$150 (foreign Aus.$175) (effective 1997 & 1998). G.P.O. Box 4245, Sydney, N.S.W. 2001, Australia. TEL 61-2-2881708. FAX 61-2-2883322. TELEX 20124. Ed. John Carter. R&P contact: John Carter. circ. 300. **Document type:** newsletter.
     Description: Covers important cultural, social and economic events in the Pacific Islands region.

330   CC   ISSN 0959-2601
HC441.A1
SOUTH EAST ASIA MONITOR. m. £220($350) Abraham Book Centre, 2802 Admiralty Centre, Tower One, 18 Harcourt Rd., Hong Kong, People's Republic of China. TEL 852-2529-0356. FAX 852-2565-8749. Ed. Anthony Beachey. **Indexed:** Per.Islam. (1991-).
     Description: Covers South East Asian markets. Provides country-by-country profiles. Each issue includes: political risk assessment; statistical summaries of key economic indicators; reliable forecasts; foreign trade debt and aid developments; investment and joint ventures; industrial performance; commodity reviews.

330   US   ISSN 1067-8751
SOUTHERN BUSINESS & DEVELOPMENT MAGAZINE. 1993. q. $17.95 (effective 1994). E H R Publishing Inc., Box 380545, Birmingham, AL 35238-0545. TEL 205-733-1970. FAX 205-733-1973. Ed. Michael C. Randle. circ. 25,000. **Document type:** trade publication.
     Description: Provides exclusive information on the southern states. Provides market reports, features, etc. on the South. Targeted to decision-making executives involved in corporate expansion and relocation.

330   US
HC101
SOUTHERN BUSINESS & ECONOMIC JOURNAL. 1977. q. $25 to individuals; libraries $30. Auburn University at Montgomery, School of Business, 7300 University Dr., Montgomery, AL 36117-3596. TEL 334-244-3523. FAX 334-244-3792. E-mail: hmoberly@monk.aum.edu. Ed. Dean Moberly. adv. contact: Dean Moberly. bk.rev. circ. 1,500. **Indexed:** P.A.I.S. **Document type:** academic/scholarly publication.
     —UnCover.
     Former titles (until 1987): Alabama Business and Economic Journal (ISSN 0743-779X); (until vol.5): Alabama Business and Economic Reports (ISSN 0735-2476)
     Description: Emphasizes applied academic studies with a preference for data-based research with practical application.
     Refereed Serial

330   US   ISSN 0038-4038
HC107.A13   CODEN: SECJAR
SOUTHERN ECONOMIC JOURNAL. 1933. s-m. $80 (foreign $90). University of North Carolina at Chapel Hill, Southern Economic Association, 300 Hanes Hall, CB 3540, Chapel Hill, NC 27514. TEL 919-966-5261. FAX 919-932-5469. Ed. Vincent J. Tarascio. R&P contact: Vincent J. Tarascio. adv. contact: Linda Tarascio. bk.rev.; bibl.; index, cum.index vols. 1-49; circ. 4,000 (paid). (also avail. in microform from MIM,UMI; reprint service avail. from UMI,SCH) **Indexed:** ABI Inform, Abstr.Health Care Manage.Stud., Amer.Bibl.Slavic & E.Eur.Stud., Amer.Hist.& Life (1954-), Arts & Hum.Cit.Ind., ASCA, B.P.I, BPIA, Bus.Ind., C.R.E.J., Compumath, Cont.Pg.Manage., Curr.Cont., Fam.Ind., Geo.Abstr.P.G., Hist.Abstr. (1954-), IDA, Int.Lab.Doc., J.of Econ.Lit., Key to Econ.Sci., Manage.Cont., P.A.I.S., Popul.Ind., Risk Abstr., Rural Recreat.Tour.Abstr., Sage Urb.Stud.Abstr., Soc.Sci.Ind., SSCI, Work Rel.Abstr., World Agri.Econ.& Rural Sociol.Abstr., World Bank.Abstr. **Document type:** academic/scholarly publication.
     ●Also available online. Vendor(s): Information Access Co.
     —BLDSC (8354.020000); KR SourceOne; SWETS; UMI; UnCover.
     Description: Presents theoretical and empirical research in economics addressed primarily to teachers, researchers, and other professionals in business, economics, and related fields.
     Refereed Serial

BUSINESS AND ECONOMICS

330   II
SOUTHERN ECONOMIC REVIEW. (Text in English) 1971. q. Rs.15($8) A. Ramaswami, 26 Clemens Rd., Vepery, Madras 600007, India. bk.rev.; charts; illus.; stat. circ. 1,000.

330   II   ISSN 0038-4046
HC431
SOUTHERN ECONOMIST. (Text in English) 1962. fortn. $80 (effective 1997). Southern Economist Private Ltd., Saleh Ahmed Bldg., 106-108 Infantry Rd., Bangalore 560 061, India. TEL 91-80-5592330. Ed. Susheela Subrahmanya; Pub. Susheela Subrahmanya. adv.: page Rs.2000; trim 270 x 215; adv. contact: K. Chithra. bk.rev. circ. 10,000.
Indexed: Int.Lab.Doc. **Document type:** newspaper.
     Description: For policy-makers, academics, and business professionals interested in various aspects of economics. Includes topics such as: banking, development finance, monetary policy and planning, and stock market trends as well as many others.

330   US   ISSN 8750-4294
HF5001
SOUTHWEST JOURNAL OF BUSINESS AND ECONOMICS. 1983. s-a. $20. University of Texas at El Paso, Texas Centers, El Paso, TX 79968. Ed. James E. Trumbly. **Indexed:** ABI Inform, Tr.& Indus.Ind. **Document type:** academic/scholarly publication.
●Also available online. Vendor(s): Information Access Co.
—UMI; UnCover.
     Formerly (until 1975): Southwest Business and Economic Review (ISSN 0195-198X)

SPACE FORUM; the international journal of space policy, science and technology for industrial applications. see *AERONAUTICS AND SPACE FLIGHT*

330   SP
SPAIN. INSTITUTO NACIONAL DE INDUSTRIA. INFORME ANUAL. (Text in English and Spanish) 1981. a. free. Instituto Nacional de Industria, Plaza de Salamanca 8, 28006 Madrid, Spain. TEL 341-401 40 04. charts, stat.
     Formerly: Spain. Instituto Nacional de Industria. Memoria I N I (Year).

330   SP   ISSN 0214-9958
SPAIN. REGISTRO MERCANTIL. BOLETIN OFICIAL. 1990. d. 14700 ptas. (foreign 27100 ptas.) for print ed.; microfiche ed. 22260 ptas. (foreign 24157 ptas.) (effective 1996). (Registro Mercantil) Boletin Oficial del Estado, Trafalgar, 27, 28071 Madrid, Spain. TEL 34-1-5382297. FAX 34-1-5382275. URL: http://www.boe.es. stat. (also avail. in microfiche)
●Also available online.

332.1   US   ISSN 0081-3559
SPECIAL PAPERS IN INTERNATIONAL ECONOMICS. 1955. irreg., no.19, 1996. $40 (includes Essays in International Finance; Reprints in International Finance; Studies in International Finance) (effective 1996 & 1997). Princeton University, International Finance Section, Dept. of Economics, Fisher Hall, Princeton, NJ 08544-1021. TEL 609-258-4048. FAX 609-258-6419. Ed. Margaret B. Riccardi. R&P contact: Margaret B. Riccardi. circ. 2,000. (back issues avail.; reprint service avail. from UMI)
Document type: monographic series.
—BLDSC (8370.100000).
     Description: Survey of the literature of international economics suitable for courses in colleges and universities.

SPORTS SPONSORSHIP MANUAL SERIES. see *SPORTS AND GAMES*

330   US   ISSN 1075-2803
SPRINGFIELD BUSINESS JOURNAL. 1980. w. $45.62. 313 Park Central, W., Springfield, MO 65806-1244. TEL 417-831-3230. FAX 417-831-5478. E-mail: news@sbj.net; URL: http://wwww.sbj.net. Ed. Paul Flemming; Pub. Dianne Elizabeth. R&P contact: Stanley E. Coffman. TEL 417-831-3238. adv.: B&W page $849, color page $1199; 10 1/8 x 13; adv. contact: Stanley E. Coffman. bk.rev. circ. 6,200. (also avail. in microform from UMI) **Document type:** newspaper.
●Also available online. Vendor(s): UMI.
—UMI.
     Former titles (until 1994): Greater Springfield Business Journal (ISSN 1058-1553); (until 1990): Springfield Business Journal (ISSN 0889-8634); (until 1983): Tops Executive Journal (ISSN 0745-0087)
     Description: Reports news concerning and of interest to locally owned businesses in the Springfield area.

079.881   GY
STABROEK NEWS. 1986. d. G.$37440($288) (effective 1997). Guyana Publications Limited, 46-47 Robb St., Lacytown, Georgetown, Guyana. TEL 592-278569. FAX 592-254637. E-mail: stabroeknewsguyana@solutions2000.net. Ed. Anand Persaud. adv.: page $220, Sun. page $390; trim 10 3/8 x 13; adv. contact: Cordelle Baird. bk.rev.; dance rev.; music rev.; play rev. Wire service(s): RN. circ. 17,500; Sun. 30,200 (paid). cols./p.: 6; pp./issue: 24. (tabloid format; back issues avail.)
Document type: newspaper.

330   UK
STAFFORDSHIRE UNIVERSITY. DIVISION OF ECONOMICS. WORKING PAPERS. 1980. irreg. (approx. 10/yr.). free. Staffordshire University, Division of Economics, Leek Rd., Stoke-on-Trent ST4 2DF, England. Ed. P. Reynolds. (also avail. in microform) **Indexed:** C.R.E.J. **Document type:** academic/scholarly publication.
     Former titles: Staffordshire Polytechnic. Department of Economics. Discussion Papers; North Staffordshire Polytechnic. Department of Economics. Discussion Papers.
     Description: Scholarly articles on economic theory and its application in a variety of areas.

330   UK   ISSN 0964-833X
STAFFORDSHIRE UNIVERSITY BUSINESS SCHOOL. WORKING PAPER. irreg., no.11, 1993. Staffordshire University, Business School, Brindley Bldg., Leek Rd., Stoke-on-Trent ST4 2DF, England. TEL 0782-412515. FAX 0782-747006. Eds. Colm Harmon, Ian Walker. **Document type:** monographic series.
—BLDSC (9349.957040).

330   US
STANDARD & POOR'S CORPORATION RECORDS. DAILY NEWS SECTION. Variant title: Standard and Poor's Daily News. Issued with: Standard & Poor's Corporation Records (ISSN 0196-4674) 1923. d. (5/wk.). 1465. Standard & Poor's (Subsidiary of: McGraw-Hill Companies, Inc.), 25 Broadway, New York, NY 10004. TEL 212-208-8000. Ed. John Daly. circ. 2,853. (back issues avail.) **Document type:** trade publication.
●Also available online. Vendor(s): Knight-Ridder Information, Inc. (File no.133).
Also available on CD-ROM.
     Description: Examines mergers and acquisitions, registrations, offerings, bankruptcies, litigation, management changes, new products, capital spending, redemptions, and trading data.

STAR TECH JOURNAL. see *BUSINESS AND ECONOMICS — Production Of Goods And Services*

330   US
STATE CHAMBER NEWS. 1981. 26/yr. membership only. Chamber of Commerce, One Commerce Center, Ste. 200, Wilmington, DE 19801. TEL 302-678-3616. Ed. Ruth L. Mankin. adv. circ. 18,000.

330   US
THE STATE JOURNAL. m. State Journal Corp., 904 Virginia St. E., Charleston, WV 25301-2815. TEL 304-344-1630. FAX 304-345-2721. Ed. Dan Page. circ. 10,000. (also avail. in microform from UMI)
●Also available online. Vendor(s): UMI.

330 338   US
HG4057
STATE SOURCES OF COMPANY INTELLIGENCE. 1976. irreg., latest 17th ed. $125 (effective 1997). Washington Researchers, Ltd., Box 19005, 20th St. Sta., Washington, DC 20036-9005. TEL 202-333-3499. FAX 202-625-0656. E-mail: research@researchers.com; URL: http://www.researchers.com/pub/businti/researchers.html. Ed. M. Newman. R&P contact: Ellen O'Kane. **Document type:** directory.
     Former titles (until 1995): How to Find Company Intelligence in State Documents (ISSN 1041-8024); Sources of State Information on Corporations.
     Description: Informs executives on company intelligence on plants, expansions, processes, finances, strategies, and executives, issued by each of the 50 states.

STATISTICS CANADA CATALOGUE. see *STATISTICS*

348.489026   DK   ISSN 0109-0798
STATUS. 1983. 20/yr. DKK 150($18) Statens Informationstjeneste, P.O. Box 1103, DK-1009 Copenhagen K, Denmark. TEL 01-929-200. (Subscr. to: Abonnement paa Status, Avispostkontoret, 1535 Copenhagen V, Denmark) Ed. Hanne Egebjerg. bk.rev.; s-a. index. circ. 20,000. (back issues avail.)

330 378   US
STERN BUSINESS REPORT. 1990. q. free. New York University, Leonard N. Stern School of Business, 25 W. Fourth St., New York, NY 10012. TEL 212-989-0962. FAX 212-995-4007. Ed. Colleen Troy. circ. 5,000.
     Description: News of the School of Business.

330   GW
STEUER - SPAR - BERATER. 1993. m. DM.298. Verlag Norman Rentrop, Theodor-Heuss-Str. 4, 53177 Bonn, Germany. TEL 49-228-82050. FAX 49-228-364411. TELEX 17228309. Ed. Hans Joachim Oberhettinger. (looseleaf format) **Document type:** bulletin.

DER STEUERENTSCHEID; Sammlung aktueller steuerrechtlicher Entscheidungen. see *LAW*

330   GW
STIFTUNG VOLKSWAGENWERK. SCHRIFTENREIHE. 1967. irreg., vol.25, 1994. DM.29.80. Vandenhoeck und Ruprecht, Robert-Bosch-Breite 6, 37079 Goettingen, Germany. TEL 49-551-6959-0. FAX 49-551-695917. (Subscr. to: 37070 Goettingen, Germany) Ed.Bd. **Document type:** monographic series.

330   XN   ISSN 0039-1816
HB9
STOPANSKI PREGLED/ECONOMIC REVIEW; spisanie na Sojuzot na drustvata na ekonomistite od SR Makedonija. (Text in Macedonian) 1950. bi-m. Sojuzot na Drustvata na Ekonomistite na SR Makedonija, Box 489, Skopje, Macedonia. Ed. Nikola Kljusek. circ. 1,600.

330   UK   ISSN 0258-0543
HD30.28
STRATEGIC DIRECTION. 1984. 10/yr. £769($1269) (foreign Aus.$1599) (effective 1998). M C B University Press Ltd., 60-62 Toller Ln., Bradford, W. Yorks BD8 9BY, England. TEL 44-1274-777700. FAX 44-1274-785200. TELEX 51317-MCBUNI-G. URL: http://www.mcb.co.uk. (N. American subscr. to: M C B University Press Limited, Box 1943, Birmingham, AL 35201) Ed. Eric Sandelands. (reprint service avail. from SWZ) **Document type:** academic/scholarly publication.
—BLDSC (8474.031440); SWETS. CCC.

330   US   ISSN 1083-706X
▼**STRATEGY & BUSINESS.** 1995. q. $38 (foreign $48) (effective 1997); newsstand price: 9.50. Booz, Allen & Hamilton, 101 Park Ave., New York, NY 10178. E-mail: Jkurtzman@aol.com; URL: http://www.bah.com. (Subscr. to: 49 Richmondville Ave., Westport, CT 06880-9555. TEL 888-557-5550; Editorial addr.: 67 Mount Vernon St., boston, MA 02108. TEL 617-523-7047. FAX 617-723-3989) Ed. Joel Kurtzman; Pub. Laurance Allen. (reprint service avail.) **Document type:** trade publication.
—BLDSC (8474.037500).

STRUCNI CASOPIS DURO DAKOVIC. see *ENGINEERING — Mechanical Engineering*

BUSINESS AND ECONOMICS

330   IT   ISSN 0039-2928
STUDI ECONOMICI. 1947. N.S. 3/yr. L.69000 (foreign L.90000) (effective 1993). Franco Angeli Editore, Viale Monza 106, 20127 Milan, Italy. TEL 02-28-27-651. Ed.Bd. bk.rev.; index. (reprint service avail. from SCH) Indexed: J.of Econ.Lit., P.A.I.S.For.Lang.Ind.
—BLDSC (8481.810000).

330   IT   ISSN 0391-8750
STUDI ECONOMICI E SOCIALI. 1966. q. L.48000 (foreign L.90000) (effective 1997). Centro Studi G. Toniolo, Piazza Giuseppe Toniolo 2, 56100 Pisa, Italy. TEL 39-50-571181. Ed. Romano Molesti. R&P contact: Silvio Truceo. adv. contact: A.C. Cappuccilli. bk.rev. **Document type:** academic/scholarly publication.

330   RM   ISSN 1224-8738
▼**STUDIA UNIVERSITATIS "BABES-BOLYAI". NEGOTIA.** (Text in English, Rumanian; summaries English, French, German) 1996. s-a. exchange basis. Universitatea "Babes-Bolyai", Biblioteca Centrala Universitara, Str. Clinicilor nr. 2, Cluj-Napoca 3400, Rumania. TEL 40-64-197092. FAX 40-64-197633. Ed. A. Marga. abstr. charts, illus.; index. **Document type:** academic/scholarly publication.

330   RM   ISSN 0578-5472
HB9
STUDIA UNIVERSITATIS "BABES-BOLYAI." OECONOMICA. (Text in English, Rumanian; summaries in English, French, German) 1960. s-a. exchange basis. Universitatea "Babes-Bolyai", Biblioteca Centrala Universitara, Str. Clinicilor nr. 2, Cluj-Napoca 3400, Rumania. TEL 40-64-197092. FAX 40-64-197633. Ed. A. Marga. abstr.; charts; illus.; index. **Document type:** academic/scholarly publication.

STUDIEREN FUER EUROPA. see OCCUPATIONS AND CAREERS

STUDIEREN NACH DEM STUDIUM. see OCCUPATIONS AND CAREERS

650   US   ISSN 0081-7635
STUDIES IN BUSINESS AND SOCIETY. 1965. irreg., latest 1986. price varies. (University of Chicago, Graduate School of Business) University of Chicago Press, 5801 S. Ellis Ave., Chicago, IL 60637. TEL 773-702-7899. E-mail: sales@press.uchicago.edu; URL: http://www.press.uchicago.edu. (Subscr. to: 11030 S. Langley, Chicago, IL 60628. TEL 800-621-2736. FAX 800-621-8471) (reprint service avail. from UMI,ISI)
—BLDSC (8489.770000).
Refereed Serial

STUDIES IN DEVELOPMENT AND PLANNING. see BUSINESS AND ECONOMICS — International Development And Assistance

330   II
STUDIES IN ECONOMIC DEVELOPMENT AND PLANNING. (Text in English) 1961. irreg., no.58, 1993. price varies. Institute of Economic Growth, University Enclave, New Delhi 110 007, India. TEL 2522201. **Formerly:** Studies in Economic Growth (ISSN 0081-7848)

STUDIES IN ECONOMIC ETHICS AND PHILOSOPHY. see PHILOSOPHY

330   JA
STUDIES IN ECONOMIC SCIENCE/KEIZAI SHUSHI. 1928. bi-m. Nihon University, Economic and Commercial Research Society - Nihon Daigaku Keizaigaku Shogaku Kenkyu-kai, 1-2 Kanda Misakicho, Chiyoda-ku, Tokyo, Japan. bk.rev.

STUDIES IN INDUSTRIAL ORGANIZATION. see BUSINESS AND ECONOMICS — Economic Systems And Theories, Economic History

330   NE
STUDIES IN INTERNATIONAL ECONOMICS. 1974. irreg., vol.8, 1984. price varies. Elsevier Science B.V., Books Division, P.O. Box 211, 1000 AE Amsterdam, Netherlands. TEL 31-20-4853911. FAX 31-20-4853705. TELEX 18582 ESPA NL. E-mail: nlinfo-f@elsevier.nl; usinfo-f@elsevier.com; forinfo-kyf04035@niftyserve.or.jp; URL: http://www.elsevier.nl/. (Subscr. in the Americas to: Elsevier Science, Regional Sales Office, Box 945, New York, NY 10159-0945. TEL 212-633-3730. FAX 212-633-3680; Subscr. in Australasia and the Far East to: Elsevier Science (Singapore) Pte Ltd, No.1 Temasek Ave., No.17-01 Millenia Tower, Singapore 039192, Singapore. TEL 65-434-3727. FAX 65-337-2230; Subscr. in Japan to: Elsevier Science Japan, 9-15 Higashi-Azabu 1-chome, Minato-ku, Tokyo 106, Japan. TEL 81-3-5561-5033. FAX 81-3-5561-5047) Eds. J.N. Bhagwati, J.S. Chipman. **Document type:** monographic series.
Refereed Serial

330   NE
STUDIES IN PRODUCTION AND ENGINEERING ECONOMICS. 1981. irreg., vol.10, 1991. price varies. Elsevier Science B.V., Books Division, P.O. Box 211, 1000 AE Amsterdam, Netherlands. TEL 31-20-4853911. FAX 31-20-4853705. TELEX 18582 ESPA NL. E-mail: nlinfo-f@elsevier.nl; usinfo-f@elsevier.com; forinfo-kyf04035@niftyserve.or.jp; URL: http://www.elsevier.nl/. (Subscr. in the Americas to: Elsevier Science, Regional Sales Office, Box 945, New York, NY 10159-0945. TEL 212-633-3730. FAX 212-633-3680; Subscr. in Japan to: Elsevier Science Japan, 9-15 Higashi-Azabu 1-chome, Minato-ku, Tokyo 106, Japan. TEL 65-434-3727. FAX 65-337-2230; Subscr. in U.S. and Canada to: Elsevier Science Inc., Box 882, Madison Sq. Sta., New York, NY 10159. TEL 81-3-5561-5033. FAX 81-3-5561-5047) Ed. R.W. Grubbstroem. **Document type:** monographic series.
Refereed Serial

330   SP   ISSN 0491-3949
SUBASTAS Y CONCURSOS. 10/yr. Orense 39, 28020 Madrid, Spain. TEL 1-556-42-14. Ed. Juan Jose Arnedo.

330   FR   ISSN 1143-9815
SUD AFFAIRES; le provencal et le meridional. 10/yr. Centre Mediterraneen de Presse, 248 av. Roger Salengro, 13501 Marseille, France. TEL 91-84-45-45. FAX 91-56-60-83. Ed. Christian Apothelol. circ. 229,707.

330 301   UK   ISSN 1362-3710
▼**SUDEBNIK.** (Text in English, Russian) 1996. q. (Moscow School of Social and Economic Sciences, Faculty of Law) Simmonds and Hill Publishing Ltd., 58 Carey St., London WC2A 2JB, England. TEL 44-171-405-5145. FAX 44-181-523-5926. Ed. W.E. Butler. **Document type:** academic/scholarly publication.
—BLDSC (8509.044000).

330   US
SUMMA. 1986. m. Col.$10200($45) Carvajal International, Inc., 901 Ponce de Leon Blvd., Ste. 901, Coral Gables, FL 33134-3073. TEL 305-448-6875; 800-622-6657. FAX 305-448-9942. Ed. Vicky Santana; Pub. David Ashe. adv. circ. 124,527. **Document type:** consumer publication.
Description: Selects and translates articles published by Forbes, The Economist, Time, the New York Times, Harvard Business Review, Sloan Management Review, and Management Review.

330 791.43 792   US
SUN BELT JOURNAL. 1980. bi-m. $75. Wiffden Company, 20640 N. 53rd. Ave., Glendale, AZ 85308-9309. Ed. Dennis Kienlen; Pub. Dennis Kienlen. adv. contact: Joseph Jacobs. bk.rev. circ. 171,000. (back issues avail.) **Document type:** consumer publication, newspaper, trade publication, corporate report.

330   AT
▼**SUNZINE - ABOUT QUEENSLAND AUSTRALIA.** 1995. d. P.O. Box 159, Peregian Beach, Qld. 4573, Australia. TEL 61-7-5448-1888. FAX 61-7-5448-1686. E-mail: webteam@sunzine.net; URL: http://www.sunzine.net/. Ed. Ian Wilks.
●Available only online.
Description: Covers travel, investment and real estate.

330   FI   ISSN 0355-6034
SUOMEN PANKKI. JULKAISUJA. SARJA A/BANK OF FINLAND. PUBLICATIONS. SERIES A/FINLANDS BANK. PUBLIKATIONER. SERIE A. (Vols. 1-35 in Finnish and Swedish) (Text in English, Finnish or Swedish) 1942. irreg. FIM 90 (effective 1997). Suomen Pankki - Bank of Finland, Publication and Language Services, P.O. Box 160, FIN-00101 Helsinki, Finland. TEL 358-9-1832566. FAX 358-9-174872. E-mail: publications@bof. circ. 1,600.
Formerly (until vol.35, 1972): Suomen Pankki. Taloustieteellinen Tutkimuslaitos. Julkaisuja. Series A: Taloudellisia Selvityksia (ISSN 0081-9476)

330   FI   ISSN 1238-1691
SUOMEN PANKKI. TUTKIMUKSIA. SARJA E/BANK OF FINLAND. STUDIES. SERIES E/FINLANDS BANK. UNDERSOEKNINGAR. SERIE E. (Text in English, Finnish or Swedish) 1995. irreg. FIM 90 (effective 1997). Suomen Pankki - Bank of Finland, Publication and Language Services, P.O. Box 160, FIN-00101 Helsinki, Finland. TEL 358-9-183-2566. FAX 358-9-174872. E-mail: publications@bof.fi. circ. 1,500.
Formed by the 1995 merger of: Suomen Pankki. Julkaisuja. Series B (ISSN 0357-4776); Which was formerly (1943-1969): Suomen Pankki. Taloustieteellinen Tutkimuslaitos. Julkaisuja. Series B (ISSN 0081-9484) & Suomen Pankki. Julkaisuja. Series C (ISSN 0781-4429); Which was formerly (1962-1970): Suomen Pankki. Taloustieteellisen Tutkimuslaitos. Julkaisuja. Series C (ISSN 0081-9492) & Suomen Pankki. Julkaisuja. Series D (ISSN 0355-6042); Which was formerly (1963-1972): Suomen Pankki. Taloustieteellinen Tutkimuslaitos. Julkaisuja. Series D. Mimeographed Series (ISSN 0081-9506).

330   UK
SURREY DIRECTOR. 1982. 10/yr. R S Publishing, 112 Churchill Rd., South Croydon, Surrey CR2 6HB, England. TEL 01-681-3773. Ed. Theo Spring. adv.; bk.rev.; play rev. circ. 3,800. (tabloid format)
Description: Business and branch information for Surrey Branch Institute of Directors.

330   CN   ISSN 0832-0772
SURVEY OF PREDECESSOR AND DEFUNCT COMPANIES. 1981. biennial. Can.$39.50. (Financial Post Co., Ltd.) Maclean-Hunter Ltd., Business Publication Division, Maclean-Hunter Bldg., 777 Bay St., Toronto, ON M5W 1A7, Canada. TEL 416-350-6186. Ed. John Byrne. adv. circ. 6,000.
—CISTI.
Formerly (until 1985): Financial Post Survey of Predecessor and Defunct Companies (ISSN 0712-3256)
Description: Aids in tracing mergers, amalgamations, name changes or charter cancellations of Canadian businesses.

339   US
SURVEYS OF APPLIED ECONOMICS. 1973. irreg. price varies. St. Martin's Press, 175 Fifth Avenue, New York, NY 10010.

330   UK   ISSN 0306-2201
SUSSEX BUSINESS TIMES. 1975. m. £12 (foreign £30). Sussex Business Times Ltd., 202 Church Rd., Hove, E. Sussex BN3 2DJ, England. TEL 44-1273-778168. FAX 44-1273-208278. Ed. John Nixon; Pub. Alan Havard. adv. contact: Brian Collins. bk.rev. circ. 5,300. **Document type:** trade publication.

330   IO   ISSN 0215-0050
SWA - SEMBRADA/BUSINESS MAGAZINE. (Text in Indonesian) 1985. m. Rps.59400($28.2) Yayasan Sembada Swakarya, Gedung Chandra, 2nd Fl., Jl. MH Thamrin 20, Jakarta Pusat, Indonesia. TEL 062-21-3103316. FAX 062-21-3103318. TELEX 62797-IA. (Singapore addr.: Media Link, 1 Sophia Rd., No. 04-26, Peace Centre, Singapore 0922. TEL 65-3361725; Japan addr.: Raira Enterprise Co., Ltd., 1-6-8-402, Shimoochiai, Shinjuku-ku, Tokyo 161, Japan. TEL 03-3360-9171) Ed. Geonawan Mohamad. adv.: B&W page $1898, color page $2609; trim 210 x 275; adv. contact: Dinny Harun. circ. 45,195. (reprint service avail.)
Description: Contains profiles of companies and successful business people.

330   SA   ISSN 1016-7064
SWAZILAND; review - commerce, industry and tourism. a. R.30 (effective 1996). Braby's (Subsidiary of: Kohler Packaging Ltd.), P.O. Box 1426, Pinetown 3600, South Africa. TEL 27-31-7017021. FAX 27-31-7017036. adv.

330   SW   ISSN 0082-0067
SWEDEN. KONJUNKTURINSTITUTET. OCCASIONAL PAPER. (Text in English) 1964. irreg., no.14, 1985. price varies. Konjunkturinstitutet - National Institute of Economic Research, P.O. Box 3116, S-103 62 Stockholm, Sweden.

330   SW   ISSN 0039-7296
HC371
THE SWEDISH ECONOMY. Swedish edition: Konjunkturlaeget (ISSN 0023-3463) (Text in English) 1961. q. (Konjunkturinstitutet (KI) - National Institute of Economic Research) Fritzes AB, S-106 47 Stockholm, Sweden. TEL 46-468-690-9090. FAX 46-468-205021. charts; stat.; index. circ. 900. **Indexed**: Key to Econ.Sci., P.A.I.S., PROMT.
• Also available online. Vendor(s): Information Access Co.

330   UK
SWINDON BUSINESS NEWS. 1982. every 6 wks £10. County Business Publishing Ltd., The Priory, Haselton, Near Cheltenham, Glos., England. TEL 0793-615393. (Subscr. to: 26 Wood St., Swindon, Wilts. SN1 4AB, England) Ed. L. Barling.

330   SZ   ISSN 0042-8590
SWITZERLAND. BUNDESAMT FUER INDUSTRIE, GEWERBE UND ARBEIT. VOLKSWIRTSCHAFT; das Magazin fuer Wirtschaftspolitik. French edition: Vie Economique (ISSN 0253-3987) 1928. m. 148 SFr. Bundesamt fuer Industrie, Gewerbe und Arbeit, Gurtengasse 3, CH-3003 Bern, Switzerland. TEL 41-31-3222786. FAX 41-31-3222740. Ed. Erwin Roos. adv.; bk.rev.; charts; stat.; tr.lit.; index. circ. 5,900 (1,900 French ed.; 4,000 German ed.). **Indexed**: P.A.I.S.For.Lang.Ind. **Document type**: government publication.

330   SZ
SWITZERLAND. KOMMISSION FUER KONJUNKTURFRAGEN. ALLFAELLIGE STUDIEN. French edition: Switzerland. Commission pour les Questions Conjoncturelles. Etudes Occasionnelles. (Supplement to: Switzerland. Eidgenoessisches Volkswirtschaftsdepartement. Volkswirtschaft und to Schweizerische Nationalbank. Monatsbericht) irreg., no.300, 1986. Bundesamt fuer Konjunkturfragen, Kommission fuer Konjunkturfragen, Effingerstr. 27, CH-3003 Bern, Switzerland. TEL 41-31-3222138. FAX 41-31-3249615. **Document type**: government publication.

330   TH   ISSN 0857-2968
HC445.A1
T D R I QUARTERLY REVIEW. (Text in English) 1985. q. B.300 (S.E. Asia $23; Asia & the Pacific $24; Europe & Australia $26; Africa $28; N. America $29; S. America $30). Thailand Development Research Institute, TDRI, 565 Ramkhamhaeng 39 (Thepleea 1), Ramkhamhaeng Rd., Wangthonglang, Bangkapi District, Bangkok 10310, Thailand. TEL 622-718-5460. FAX 622-718-5461-2. E-mail: publications@leela1.tdri.or.th; URL: http://www.info.tdri.or.th. Ed. Poonsin Wongkoltoot. adv. contact: Poonsin Wongkoltoot. **Indexed**: Asian-Pac.Econ.Lit. **Document type**: academic/scholarly publication.
—BLDSC (8612.589550).

T J F R BUSINESS NEWS REPORTER. see *JOURNALISM*

330 639.2   US
T S S A REPORT.* 1979. q. membership only. Tackle & Shooting Sports Agents Association, 1033 N. Fairfax St., Ste. 200, Alexandria, VA 22314-1540. TEL 708-381-3032. FAX 708-381-9518. Ed. Nancy Lerns. circ. 400 (controlled). (looseleaf format) **Document type**: newsletter.
   Formerly: T R A I Report.

T V V S; maandblad voor ondernemingsrecht en rechtspersonen. see *LAW*

TAKEOVERS AND RECONSTRUCTIONS IN AUSTRALIA. see *LAW — Corporate Law*

330   US
TAKING SIDES: CLASHING VIEWS ON CONTROVERSIAL ISSUES IN BUSINESS ETHICS AND SOCIETY. 1990. irreg., 2nd ed., 1992. $12.95. Dushkin Publishing Group, Sluice Dock, Guilford, CT 06437-9989. TEL 203-453-4351. FAX 203-453-6000. Eds. Maureen M. Ford, Lisa H. Newton; Pub. Lan Nielsen. illus. **Document type**: academic/scholarly publication.

330   CI
TALIJANSKA PRIVREDA DANAS; imprese e imprenditori italiani oggi. (Text in Serbo-Croatian; summaries in Italian) 1965. s-a. $5. Informator, Masarykova ul.1, 41001 Zagreb, Croatia. TEL 041 442-197. adv. circ. 10,000. (back issues avail.)
   Description: Describes cooperation between Italy and Yugoslavia.

330   US   ISSN 1067-067X
TALKING TO THE BOSS. 1986. 12/yr. $18. 4556 Oakton St., No.200, Skokie, IL 60076-3144. TEL 708-933-9659. FAX 708-933-9667. Ed. Myrna Petlicki; Pub. David Stein. R&P contact: David Stein. adv. contact: Michael Heimlich. bk.rev.; circ. 15,000 (controlled). **Document type**: newspaper.

330   FI   ISSN 0356-5106
HC337.F5
TALOUSELAMA. (Includes annual special issue: 500 Largest Companies in Finland) 1938. w. (42/yr.). FIM 920 (effective 1997). Oy Talentum Ab, P.O. Box 920, FIN-00101 Helsinki, Finland. TEL 358-9-148-801. FAX 358-9-685-6650. URL: http://www.talentum.fi. Ed. Pertti Monto. adv.: B&W page FIM 23700, color page FIM 40700; trim 200 x 273. bk.rev.; illus. circ. 60,525. **Indexed**: Paper & Bd.Abstr. **Document type**: trade publication.
   Description: Provides in-depth coverage of investment, management and marketing trends affecting Finnish business, with company profiles on major Finnish companies.

330   TZ   ISSN 0856-3373
HC885.A1
TANZANIA ECONOMIC TRENDS. 1988. q. University of Dar es Salaam, Economic Research Bureau, Economics Department, P.O. Box 35189, Dar es Salaam, Tanzania. **Indexed**: Documentatieblad.

330   TZ   ISSN 0856-2172
TANZANIA INDUSTRIAL STUDIES AND CONSULTING ORGANISATION. ANNUAL REPORT AND ACCOUNTS. 1978. a. free. Tanzania Industrial Studies and Consulting Organisation (TISCO), P.O. Box 2650, Dar es Salaam, Tanzania. Ed. E.M. Ntabaye. circ. 500. (back issues avail.) **Indexed**: Met.Abstr. **Document type**: corporate report.

330   TZ   ISSN 0856-4531
TANZANIA JOURNAL OF ECONOMICS. 1989. s-a. University of Dar es Salaam, Economics Research Bureau, Economics Department, P.O. Box 35189, Dar es Salaam, Tanzania. **Indexed**: P.L.E.S.A. **Document type**: academic/scholarly publication.

330   HU   ISSN 1218-9383
J335
TARSADALOM ES GAZDASAG KOZEP ES KELET-EUROPABAN. English edition: Society and Economy in Central and Eastern Europe (ISSN 1218-9391) 1979. a. (English ed. 3/yr.). exchange basis. Budapesti Kozgazdasagtudomanyi Egyetem, Fovam Ter 8, II-268, 1093 Budapest IX, Hungary. TEL 2176-524. FAX 2186-855. Ed. Barbara Csaki. bk.rev. circ. 400. **Document type**: academic/scholarly publication.
   Former titles (until 1994): Budapesti Kozgazdasagtudomanyi Egyetem Folyoirata. Aula. Tarsadalom es Gazdasag (ISSN 0866-6865); (until 1989): Marx Karoly Kozgazdasagtudomanyi Egyetem Folyoirata. Egyetemi Szemle (ISSN 0139-4045).
   Description: Articles by teachers and staff of the Budapest University of Economic Sciences.

330   AT
TASMANIA. DEVELOPMENT & RESOURCES. ANNUAL REPORT. 1985. a. free. Development & Resources, G.P.O. Box 646G, Hobart, Tas. 7001, Australia. TEL 61-3-62335888. FAX 61-3-62335800. E-mail: tdr@tdr.tas.gov.au; URL: http://www.tdr.tas.gov.au. Ed. Daryl Peebles. R&P contact: Daryl Peebles. TEL 61-3-62335875. circ. 3,000. **Document type**: government publication, directory.
   Formerly: Tasmanian Development Authority Annual Report (ISSN 0817-6418).

375 330   UK
HB1
TEACHING BUSINESS & ECONOMICS. 1947. q. £40 (overseas £54) (effective 1997). Economics and Business Education Association, 1A Keymer Rd., Hassocks, W. Sussex BN6 8AD, England. TEL 44-1273-846033. FAX 44-1273-844646. E-mail: ebeah@pavilion.co.uk. Ed. Barry Harrison. adv. contact: Richard Young. bk.rev. circ. 3,000. (also avail. in microform from UMI; reprint service avail. from UMI) **Indexed**: Br.Educ.Ind., C.I.J.E., Cont.Pg.Educ., Cont.Pg.Manage., P.A.I.S., PSI, Tech.Educ.Abstr. **Document type**: academic/scholarly publication.
—BLDSC (3656.930325); SWETS; UMI.
   Former titles: Economics and Business Education (ISSN 0969-2509); (until 1992): Economics (ISSN 0300-4287)

TEACHING BUSINESS ETHICS. see *PHILOSOPHY*

330   FR   ISSN 0184-4067
TECHNICA. bi-m. Association des Anciens Eleves de l'Ecole Centrale Lyonnaise, 7 rue Grolee, 69002 Lyon, France. TEL 78-37-48-05. Ed. Jean Soubiran. circ. 4,000.

TECHNICAL REVIEW MIDDLE EAST/AL-NASHRAH AL-TIQNIYYAH AL-SHARQ AL-AWSAT. see *TECHNOLOGY: COMPREHENSIVE WORKS*

330   PL   ISSN 0137-3730
TECHNIKA ZAGRANICZNA. 1971. m. Wydawnictwa Czasopism i Ksiazek Technicznych SIGMA - NOT, Ul. Ratuszowa 11, P.O. Box 1004, 00-950 Warsaw, Poland. Ed. Andrzej Kuszyk. circ. 60,000.

TECHNIQUES. see *EDUCATION — Teaching Methods And Curriculum*

330   US
TECHNOLOGY OPPORTUNITIES: RESEARCHING EMERGING & CRITICAL TECHNOLOGIES. irreg., latest 3rd ed. $295 (effective 1997). Washington Researchers, Ltd., Box 19005, 20th St. Sta., Washington, DC 20036-9005. TEL 202-333-3499. FAX 202-625-0656. E-mail: research@researchers.com; URL: http://www.researchers.com/pub/busintel/researchers.html. R&P contact: Ellen O'Kane. **Document type**: directory.
   Description: Provides managers with full contact information for organizations that monitor technology development, licensing, and commercial applications.

330   CK   ISSN 0120-0933
HD70.C55
TECNOLOGIA ADMINISTRATIVA. 1979. q. Col.$8000($15) Universidad de Antioquia, Facultad de Ciencias Economicas, Departamento de Administracion de Empresas y Consultorias Administrativas, Apdo. Aereo 1226, Medellin, Colombia. Ed. Alirio Ibarra. bk.rev. circ. 1,200.

330   IT
TECNORAMA. 2/yr. Pubblicita Edizioni Associati s.r.l., Via Simone d'Orsenigo 22, 20135 Milan, Italy. TEL 2-551-18-42. FAX 2-551-85-263. Ed. Ugo Carutti. circ. 6,600.

330   SA
TEGNIEK. (Text in Afrikaans) 1948. m. R.12. Tegniek, Ltd., Box 51, Stellenbosch 7600, South Africa. Ed. T.J.F. De Villiers.

TELE-SATELLIT; Europe's satellite magazine. see *COMMUNICATIONS — Television And Cable*

TELECONFERENCE MAGAZINE; the business communications magazine. see *COMMUNICATIONS*

330   VE   ISSN 0495-0615
TEMAS ECONOMICOS. 1951. m. Conde a Pinango 22, Apdo. 2570, Caracas, Venezuela. stat.

330   PO
TEMPO ECONOMICO. 26/yr. Rua Duque de Palmela 37, Lisbon, Portugal. **Indexed**: Mgmt.& Market.Abstr.

330   MX
TENDENCIAS. w. $233 in US & Canada; Latin America $250; Europe & Asia $269 (effective 1997). Grupo Editorial Expansion, Salamanca 35, Col. Roma, 06700 Mexico DF, Mexico. TEL 207-20-66. **Document type**: newsletter.
   Description: For bankers, investors and business managers in Mexico.

BUSINESS AND ECONOMICS

330 340   AG   ISSN 0325-5034
TENDENCIAS ECONOMICAS: LEGISLACION ECONOMICAS ARGENTINA/BUSINESS TRENDS: ARGENTINE ECONOMIC LEGISLATION. (Text in English and Spanish) 1964. w. $900. Consejo Tecnico de Inversiones, S.A., Tucuman 834, 1o piso, 1049 Buenos Aires, Argentina. FAX 541-322-4887. Ed. Jose Luis Blanco. adv. **Indexed:** Key to Econ.Sci. **Document type:** newsletter.
 Description: Report for business management.

330   CC   ISSN 1005-4308
TEQU YU KAIFAQU JINGJI. (Subseries of: Fuyin Baokan Ziliao) (Text in Chinese) m. $54.51. Zhongguo Renmin Daxue, Shubao Ziliao Zhongxin - China People's University, Book & Newspaper Information Center, 3 Zhang Zizhong Rd., P.O. Box 1122, Beijing 100007, People's Republic of China. TEL 86-10-4015080. (Dist. in US by: China Publications Service, Box 49614, Chicago, IL 60649. TEL 312-288-3291. FAX 312-288-8570) pp./issue: 80.
 Description: Covers the economic development of China's special economic zones.

650   US   ISSN 0040-4209
HC107.T4   CODEN: TXBRAK
TEXAS BUSINESS REVIEW. 1926. bi-m. free. University of Texas at Austin, Bureau of Business Research, Box 7459, Austin, TX 78713. TEL 512-471-1616. FAX 512-471-1063. E-mail: dhardy@mail.utexas.edu. Ed. Lois Shrout. R&P contact: Lois Shrout. bibl.; charts; illus.; stat.; index, cum.index: 1926-1961; 1975-1994. circ. 5,000. (also avail. in microform from UMI; reprint service avail. from UMI) **Indexed:** BPIA, P.A.I.S., Tr.& Indus.Ind. **Document type:** trade publication.
 ●Also available online. Vendor(s): Information Access Co.
 —BLDSC (8798.680000); UMI. **CCC.**
 Description: Focuses on current economic issues in Texas and competitiveness at the state's industries. Includes employment data.

330   TH   ISSN 0125-3905
THAI ECONOMIC REVIEW. (Text in English & Thai) 1972. 3/yr. Chulalongkorn University, Faculty of Economics, Phyathai Rd., Bangkok 10500, Thailand. Ed. Supachai Manuspaibool. adv.; charts; stat. **Document type:** academic/scholarly publication.

THAT WAS YUGOSLAVIA. see POLITICAL SCIENCE

330   MY   ISSN 0128-4134
HC59.69
THIRD WORLD ECONOMICS; trends & analysis. (Text in English) fortn. $55 for Third World countries; developed countries $75. Third World Network, 228 Macalister Rd., 10400 Penang, Malaysia. TEL 60-4-226-6728. FAX 60-4-226-4505. E-mail: twn@igc.apc.org; twnpen@twn.po.my; URL: http://www.twnside.org.sg. **Indexed:** Per.Islam. (1992-). **Document type:** academic/scholarly publication.
 —BLDSC (8820.145090).
 Description: Provides news and analyses that reflect the grassroots interests of people in the Third World.

330   CN   ISSN 0838-7087
THIS WEEK IN BUSINESS. 1987. 50/yr. 250 St. Antoine W., Montreal, PQ H2Y 3R7, Canada. TEL 514-987-2512. FAX 514-987-2638. Ed. James Ferrabee. adv. contact: Jean Sanche. circ. 192,949. **Indexed:** Can.B.P.I.

330   TU
TICARET. 1942. 6/w. (Mon.-Sat.). TL.150000000 (foreign $90). Ticaret Gazetesi, 1571 Sok No.: 16, Cinarli, 35110 Izmir, Turkey. TEL 90-232-4617196. FAX 90-232-4840799. Ed. Ahmet S. Tukel; Pub. Suha S. Tukel. adv. contact: Kamuran Oncel. circ. 4,700 (paid). (broadsheet format; back issues avail.) **Document type:** newspaper.
 Description: Publishes business news, current information on commodities and notices of tenders and bids.

330   SZ
TICINO MANAGEMENT; il mensile svizzera di finanza, economia e cultura. (Text in Italian) 1989. m. 90 SFr.($55) Ticino Management SA, Centro Galleria 2, CH-6928 Manno, Switzerland. TEL 41-91-508800. FAX 41-91-508820. Pub. Valerio De Giorgi. adv.: B&W page 3120 SFr., color page 4400 SFr.; trim 178 x 252; adv. contact: Claus Winterhalter. bk.rev.; film rev.; music rev.; tr.lit.; circ. 20,000 (paid). **Document type:** consumer publication.

330   BE   ISSN 0772-7674
HB9
TIJDSCHRIFT VOOR ECONOMIE EN MANAGEMENT. (Text in Dutch and English) 1956. q. 1500 BEF($40) (effective 1995). Katholieke Universiteit te Leuven, Faculteit der Economische en Toegepaste Economische Wetenschappen - Catholic University of Louvain, Faculty of Economic and Applied Economic Sciences, Naamsestraat 69, 3000 Leuven, Belgium. TEL 32-16-326688. FAX 32-16-326610. Ed. P. Sercu. adv.; charts. circ. 2,000. (back issues avail.) **Indexed:** C.R.E.J., J.of Econ.Lit., Key to Econ.Sci. **Document type:** academic/scholarly publication.
 —BLDSC (8839.550000).
 Formerly: Tijdschrift voor Economie (ISSN 0040-7461)

330   JA   ISSN 0911-7008
HC411
TOKYO BUSINESS TODAY. Japanese edition: Toyo Keizai. (Text in English) 1934. m. $54 in Asia; U.S. $99; Europe $105. Toyo Keizai Inc., 1-2-1, Nihonbashi Hongoku-cho, Chuo-ku, Tokyo 103, Japan. TEL 81-3-3246-5602. FAX 81-3-3246-0679. (Dist. by: Intercontinental Marketing Corp., I.P.O. Box 5056, Tokyo 100-30, Japan. TEL 81-3-3661-7458. FAX 81-3-3667-9646) Ed. Hiroshi Fukunaga. adv. contact: Kenji Murata. bk.rev.; stat.; index. circ. 60,000. **Indexed:** ABI Inform., Chem.Abstr., Cont.Pg.Manage., Key to Econ.Sci., Mid.East: Abstr.& Ind., P.A.I.S., PSI, Rural Recreat.Tour.Abstr., World Agri.Econ.& Rural Sociol.Abstr.
 —UMI; UnCover.
 Formerly: Oriental Economist (ISSN 0030-5294)
 Description: Provides insight into Japanese corporations, politics and society.

330   JA   ISSN 0493-4091
TOKYO KEIZAI UNIVERSITY. JOURNAL. (Text in mainly in Japanese, partly in English) 1949. 5/yr. Tokyo Keizai University - Tokyo Keizai Daigaku, 34-7 Minamicho 1-chome, Kokubunji, Tokyo 185, Japan. Ed.Bd. bk.rev. circ. 2,200.
 —BLDSC (4908.925000).
 Formerly: (until no.116, 1980): Tokyo College of Economics. Journal - Tokyo Keidai Gakkai-Shi.

330   US
TOLEDO BUSINESS JOURNAL. 1984. m. $15. Telex Communications, Inc., 27 Broadway St., Toledo, OH 43602-1701. TEL 419-244-8200. FAX 419-244-5773. Ed. Brian Taylor; Pub. Sanford Lubin. R&P contact: 419-244-8200. adv. contact: Jacqueline Bruecken. circ. 9,600. (also avail. in microform from UMI) **Document type:** newspaper.
 ●Also available online. Vendor(s): UMI.

TONGJIXUE, JINGJI SHUXUE FANGFA. see STATISTICS

330   IT
TOP NUOVA ECONOMIA.* m. Top Italia Editoriale Coop. a.r.l., Via Aurelia 641, 00165 Rome, Italy. TEL 39-6-3214040. adv.: page L.18000000. circ. 58,000. **Document type:** consumer publication.

TOP WOMAN. see WOMEN'S INTERESTS

TOPEKA METRO NEWS. see LAW

330 371.42   CN   ISSN 1199-6579
TORONTO REGION TOP EMPLOYERS GUIDE. 1992. a. Can.$60 to non-members; members Can.$45 (effective 1997). Board of Trade of Metropolitan Toronto, P.O. Box 60, 1 First Canadian Place, Toronto, ON M5X 1C1, Canada. TEL 416-366-6811. Ed. Mary de Reus. **Document type:** directory.
 Formerly: (until 1994): Guide to the Toronto Region's Top Employers (ISSN 1183-7373)

TOURISM ECONOMICS; the business and finance of tourism and recreation. see TRAVEL AND TOURISM

330   JA
TOYO KEIZAI. English edition: Tokyo Business Today. 1895. w. Toyo Keizai Inc., 1-2-1 Nihonbashi Hongokucho, Chuo-ku, Tokyo 103, Japan. TEL 81-3-3246-5602. FAX 81-3-3246-0679. Ed. Sasaburo Satoh. adv. circ. 52,669.

330   US
TRADE-MARK BUSINESS NETWORK NEWS. 1979. m. $5. Trade - Mark Corporation, 9045 S.W. Barbur Blvd., Ste. 3, Portland, OR 97219. TEL 503-244-2689. FAX 503-643-2876. Ed. Roy Jay. adv. contact: Roy Jay. **Document type:** newsletter.

TRAFIKOEKONOMISKE ENHEDSPRISER. see TRANSPORTATION — Roads And Traffic

330   UK
TRANSTERRA BUSINESS BRIEF. 1972. w. £225($445) Transterra Ltd., St. Julians, Kent TN15 0RX, England. TEL 44-1732-740850. FAX 44-1732-740849. Ed. R. McKeogh. R&P contact: S. Klenke. (back issues avail.) **Document type:** newsletter.

340   CY   ISSN 1015-6585
TRAPEZIKOS/BANK EMPLOYEE. (Text in Greek) 1960. m. P.O. Box 1235, Nicosia, Cyprus. TEL 357-2-366993. Ed. L. Hadjicostis. circ. 4,500. **Document type:** trade publication.

TRAVELER; business and travel magazine for international traders. see TRAVEL AND TOURISM

330   UK   ISSN 0961-5261
TREASURY TODAY. 1991. m. £160 (overseas £176). Accountancy Books, 399 Silbury Blvd., Central Milton Keynes, Bucks. MK9 2HL, England. TEL 44-1908-248000. FAX 44-1908-248001. **Document type:** trade publication, government publication.

650   AU   ISSN 0049-4623
TREND; das oesterreichische Wirtschaftsmagazin. 1970. m. S.495 (foreign S.716) (effective 1997). Wirtschafts-Trend Zeitschriftenverlagsgesellschaft mbH, Marc-Aurel-Str. 10-12, A-1010 Vienna, Austria. TEL 43-1-53470-0. FAX 43-1-53470349. E-mail: redaktion@trend.at. Eds. Thomas Martinek, Christian Rainer; Pubs. Helmut Gansterer, Christian Rainer. adv. contact: Hans Hudribusch. bk.rev.; charts; illus.; index. **Indexed:** Key to Econ.Sci. **Document type:** consumer publication.

330   GW   ISSN 0178-0727
TREND AKTUELL. 1977. bi-m. DM.720($480) Trend Aktuell Verlags GmbH, Leopoldstr. 32, 80802 Munich, Germany. TEL 49-89-347514. FAX 49-89-349282. Ed. Klaus Peinelt. circ. 100. **Document type:** trade publication.
 Description: Results of market and opinion research on economic, political and social titles.

330   GW   ISSN 0935-5596
TRENDLETTER MEGATRENDS AKTUELL. 1987. m. DM.357.60. Verlag Norman Rentrop, Theodor-Heuss-Str. 4, 53177 Bonn, Germany. TEL 49-228-8205-0. FAX 49-228-364411. TELEX 17228309-TTX-D. Ed. Armin Ziegler. **Document type:** bulletin.
 Formed by merger of: Trendletter; Megatrends Aktuell.

330   HU   ISSN 0133-7769
TRENDS IN WORLD ECONOMY. (Text in English) 1971. irreg. (4-6/yr.) price varies. Vilaggazdasagi Tudomanyos Tanacs, Kallo esperes u. 15, P.O.B. 36, 1531 Budapest, Hungary. FAX 162-0661. Ed. Gabor Foti. circ. 600. (processed)
 —BLDSC (9049.690000).

330   US   ISSN 1065-2094
THE TRENDS JOURNAL. 1991. q. $185 (foreign $192) (effective 1997). Trends Research Institute, Box 660, Rhinebeck, NY 12572-0660. TEL 914-876-6700. E-mail: 73441.3516@compuserve.com; URL: http://www.trendsresearch.com. Ed. Gerald Celente. **Document type:** newsletter.

330   CN
TRENDS MAGAZINE. 12/yr. Can.$22. Netmar Publications Inc., 1383 Confederation St., Sarnia, ON N7S 5P1, Canada. TEL 519-336-1100. FAX 519-336-1833. Ed. Dick With. adv. contact: Norma Sutton. circ. 5,000 (controlled).

330 US
TRIAD BUSINESS NEWS. 1986. w. $42. High Point Enterprise, Inc., Box 18249, Greensboro, NC 27419. TEL 910-854-3001. FAX 910-854-3013. Ed. Richard Barron. adv.; bk.rev.; charts; illus.; stat. circ. 10,500. (tabloid format) **Document type:** newspaper.
Formerly: Triad Business (ISSN 0897-0408)

330 US ISSN 0891-0022
TRIANGLE BUSINESS JOURNAL.* 1985. w. $36. American City Business Journals, Inc. (Austin), 505 Powell St., Austin, TX 78703-5121. TEL 919-878-0010. FAX 919-790-6885. Ed. Dale Gibson. adv.; bk.rev.; charts; illus.; stat. circ. 15,000. (tabloid format)
●Also available online. Vendor(s): Lexis-Nexis.
—UMI. **CCC.**
Description: Designed to inform decision-making executives about business growth and trends in Wake, Orange and Durham counties.

330 055.1 IT
TRIBUNA DELL'IRPINIA; settimanale di attualita. 1967. w. L.15000($22) (Societa per la Pubblicita in Italia (S.P.I.)) Editrice Periodici Settimanali, Via Touro 13, I-83100 Avellino, Italy. TEL (0825) 39.580. Ed. Scelza Maria Loreta. adv. circ. 1,000. (tabloid format; back issues avail.)
Description: Interest lies in the variety of subjects featured. Devoted to business and economics. Contains news items concerning Irpinia and subjects of culture in general.

330 US ISSN 1051-7367
TRIBUNE BUSINESS WEEKLY. 1990. w. $26. South Bend Tribune, 225 W. Colfax, South Bend, IN 46626. TEL 219-235-6474; 800-521-5045. FAX 219-239-2646. Ed. Phil A. Vitale; Pub. Pete Baker. adv. contact: Carol Smith. circ. 8,000 (controlled). (tabloid format; also avail. in microform from UMI) **Document type:** newspaper, trade publication.
—UMI.
Description: Contains business news, profiles of area business people and area businesses, feature stories, and information of interest to the local business community.

330 FR ISSN 1168-6944
TRIBUNE DESFOSSES. 1920. d. 42 rue Notre Dame des Victoires, 75002 Paris, France. TEL 1-42-33-21-30. FAX 1-42-33-12-36. TELEX 680 326. URL: http://www.edelweb.fr/Guests/LaTribune. Ed. Paul Francois Trioux. circ. 27,344. **Document type:** newspaper.
●Also available online.
Formed by the merger of (1920-1992): Cote Desfosses (ISSN 0750-0424); (1987-1992): Tribune de l'Expansion (ISSN 0989-1323)
Description: Covers the economy, stockmarket and finance.

330 IT
TRIESTE ECONOMICA. 1970. q. free. Camera di Commercio, Industria, Artigianato e Agricoltura di Trieste, Piazza della Borsa 14, Trieste, Italy. TEL 39-40-67011. FAX 39-40-6701321. Ed. Arcangelo Flaminio. adv. circ. 1,000. **Document type:** trade publication.

330 MX ISSN 0041-3011
HB9
TRIMESTRE ECONOMICO. 1934. q. $70 c. America; S. America and Spain $90; elsewhere $120 (effective 1997). Fondo de Cultura Economica, Carretera Picacho Ajusco 227, Col. Bosques del Pedregal, 14200 Mexico, D.F., Mexico. TEL 52-5-2274670. FAX 52-5-2274640. Ed. Rodolfo de la Torre. adv.; bk.rev.; bibl.; index, cum.index: 1934-1983. circ. 1,100. **Indexed:** ASCA, Hisp.Amer.Per.Ind. (1970-), IBR, Int.Lab.Doc., J.of Econ.Lit., P.A.I.S.For.Lang.Ind., Rural Recreat.Tour.Abstr., SSCI, World Agri.Econ.& Rural Sociol.Abstr. **Document type:** academic/scholarly publication.
—BLDSC (9050.650000); Genuine Article; SWETS.

330 US ISSN 0745-5747
TULSA BUSINESS CHRONICLE. 1982. w. $30 in Tulsa County; elsewhere in U.S. $60. World Publishing Co. (Tulsa), Box 1770, Tulsa, OK 24102. TEL 918-581-8560. (Subscr. to: P.O. Box 1770, Tulsa, OK 74102) Ed. Bill Sansing. adv.; charts; stat. circ. 2,000. (tabloid format; back issues avail.)
Description: Covers local business news, features, personal investing, real estate, and stocks for corporate individuals.

330 US
U A M R NEWSLETTER. 1975. m. $48. (United Association Manufacturers' Representatives) Keith Kittrell & Associates, Inc., P.O. Box 986, Dana Point, CA 92639. TEL 714-240-4966. Ed. H. Keith Kittrell. adv. circ. 1,650. (back issues avail.) **Document type:** newsletter.

THE U K BIOTECHNOLOGY HANDBOOK. see *BIOLOGY — Biotechnology*

320 US ISSN 0743-1694
U R P E NEWSLETTER. 1969. q. $15 to individuals; institutions and foreign $30 (effective 1997). Union for Radical Political Economics, One Summer St., Somerville, MA 02143. TEL 617-776-5888. FAX 617-628-2025. E-mail: urpe@igc.apc.org. Ed. Marc Schaberg. R&P contact: Bryan Snyder. adv. contact: Bryan Snyder. bk.rev. circ. 2,000. **Indexed:** Geo.Abstr. **Document type:** newsletter.

U S A FOR BUSINESS TRAVELERS. see *TRAVEL AND TOURISM*

U S REAL ESTATE REGISTER. see *REAL ESTATE*

UKRAINIAN REPORTER. see *POLITICAL SCIENCE*

330 UK
ULSTER BUSINESS JOURNAL. m. £1 per no. Ulster Journals Ltd., 39 Boucher Rd., Belfast BT12 6UT, N. Ireland. Ed. R. Johnston. adv. **Document type:** trade publication.

333.7 GW ISSN 0943-3481
UMWELTWIRTSCHAFTSFORUM. Short title: U W F. 1990. q. DM.183 (foreign DM.192.80) (effective 1998). (Institut fuer Umweltwirtschaftsanalysen Heidelberg e.V.) Springer-Verlag, Heidelberger Platz 3, 14197 Berlin, Germany. TEL 49-30-82787-0. FAX 49-30-82787448. (Subscr. in N. America to: Springer-Verlag New York, Inc., 333 Meadowlands Pkwy., Secaucus, NJ 07094. TEL 212-460-1500. FAX 212-473-6272) Ed. Dietfried Guenter Liesegang. adv. contact: Barbara Brecht. **Document type:** academic/scholarly publication, bulletin.
—BLDSC (9083.366000).
Formerly (until 1992): F O B - Forschungsinformationsdienst Oekologisch Orientierte Betriebswirtschaftslehre (ISSN 0937-5228)
Description: Provides a forum for ecological management in industry.

UNION. see *POLITICAL SCIENCE*

330 UK
UNIT TRUST ASSOCIATION. INDUSTRY REVIEW AND DIRECTORY (YEAR). 1988. a. Professional and Business Information plc, Munro House, 14 St. Cross St., London EC1N 8YY, England. TEL 071-430-2020. FAX 071-430-1773. Ed. Christine Stopp. adv. contact: Paul Wynter. **Document type:** directory.

330 300 UN
UNITED NATIONS. ECONOMIC AND SOCIAL COUNCIL. ANNEXES. (Text in English, French, Spanish) 1946. q. United Nations Publications, Sales and Marketing Section, Room DC2-0853, New York, NY 10017. TEL 212-963-8302; 800-253-9646. FAX 212-963-3489. E-mail: publications@un.org; URL: http://www.un.org/publications.

330 338.91 UN
UNITED NATIONS. ECONOMIC COMMISSION FOR AFRICA. PROPOSALS FOR PROGRAMME BUDGET. biennial. Economic Commission for Africa, Addis-Ababa, Ethiopia.

330 320 UN
UNITED NATIONS. GENERAL ASSEMBLY. ANNEXES. (Text in Arabic, Chinese, English, French, Russian, Spanish) 1946? a. United Nations Publications, Sales and Marketing Section, Room DC2-0853, New York, NY 10017. TEL 212-963-8302; 800-253-9646. FAX 212-963-3489. E-mail: publications@un.org; URL: http://www.un.org/publications.

330 320 UN
UNITED NATIONS. GENERAL ASSEMBLY. OFFICIAL RECORDS. (Supplement avail.) (Text in Arabic, Chinese, English, French, Russian, Spanish) a. United Nations Publications, Sales and Marketing Section, Room DC2-0853, New York, NY 10017. TEL 212-963-8302; 800-253-9646. FAX 212-963-3489. E-mail: publications@un.org; URL: http://www.un.org/publications.

330 320 UN
UNITED NATIONS. GENERAL ASSEMBLY. PROVISIONAL RECORDS. (Text in Arabic, Chinese, English, French, Russian, Spanish) 1946. a. United Nations Publications, Sales and Marketing Section, Room DC2-0853, New York, NY 10017. TEL 212-963-8302; 800-253-9646. FAX 212-963-3489. E-mail: publications@un.org; URL: http://www.un.org/publications.

UNITED NATIONS. TRUSTEESHIP COUNCIL. OFFICIAL RECORDS. ANNEXES - SESSIONAL FASCICLE. see *POLITICAL SCIENCE — International Relations*

UNITED NATIONS. TRUSTEESHIP COUNCIL. OFFICIAL RECORDS. RESOLUTIONS. see *POLITICAL SCIENCE — International Relations*

UNITED NATIONS. TRUSTEESHIP COUNCIL. OFFICIAL RECORDS. VERBATIM RECORDS OF PLENARY MEETINGS. see *POLITICAL SCIENCE — International Relations*

330 300 UN
UNITED NATIONS ECONOMIC AND SOCIAL COUNCIL. OFFICIAL RECORDS. SUPPLEMENTS AND SPECIAL SUPPLEMENTS. (Text in English, French, Spanish) 1946. q. United Nations Publications, Sales and Marketing Section, Room DC2-0853, New York, NY 10017. TEL 212-963-8302; 800-253-9646. FAX 212-963-3489. E-mail: publications@un.org; URL: http://www.un.org/publications.

330 300 UN ISSN 0251-9410
UNITED NATIONS ECONOMIC AND SOCIAL COUNCIL. RESOLUTIONS AND DECISIONS. Arabic edition (ISSN 0257-1145); Chinese edition (ISSN 0251-9380); French edition (ISSN 0251-9429); German edition (ISSN 0257-389X); Spanish edition (ISSN 0251-9399) (Text in English) 1946. q. United Nations Publications, Sales and Marketing Section, Room DC2-0853, New York, NY 10017. TEL 212-963-8302; 800-253-9646. FAX 212-963-3489. E-mail: publications@un.org; URL: http://www.un.org/publications.

330 300 UN
UNITED NATIONS ECONOMIC AND SOCIAL COUNCIL. SUMMARY RECORDS OF PLENARY MEETINGS. (Text in English, French, Spanish) 1946. q. United Nations Publications, Room DC2-0853, New York, NY 10017. TEL 212-963-8302; 800-253-9646. FAX 212-963-3489.

330 MX ISSN 0041-8498
UNIVERSIDAD AUTONOMA DE NUEVO LEON. CENTRO DE INVESTIGACIONES ECONOMICAS. BOLETIN BIMESTRAL. 1963. bi-m. Mex.$50($20) Universidad Autonoma de Nuevo Leon, Centro de Investigaciones Economicas, Loma Redonda 1515-A, Col. Loma Larga, Monterrey, Mexico. TEL 45-50-18. Ed. Jesus Ramones Saldana. stat. circ. 650. (processed)
Description: Presents research of the institute.

330 CL
UNIVERSIDAD DE CHILE. FACULTAD DE CIENCIAS ECONOMICAS Y ADMINISTRATIVAS. DESARROLLO. irreg. Universidad de Chile, Facultad de Ciencias Economicas y Administrativas, Av. Ranacagua 257, Santiago, Chile.

330 UY ISSN 0378-9918
UNIVERSIDAD DE LA REPUBLICA. FACULTAD DE CIENCIAS ECONOMICAS Y DE ADMINISTRACION. REVISTA. 1940; N.S. 1950. irreg. Universidad de la Republica, Facultad de Ciencias Economicas y de Administracion, Montevideo, Uruguay. bibl.; charts.

330 SP
UNIVERSIDAD DE SEVILLA. INSTITUTO GARCIA OVIEDO. CUADERNOS. irreg., latest no.2. price varies. Universidad de Sevilla, Instituto Garcia Oviedo, Servicio de Publicaciones, Calle Porvenir 27, 41013 Seville, Spain. TEL 34-5-4231958. FAX 34-5-4232245.

BUSINESS AND ECONOMICS

330 650   SP
UNIVERSIDAD DE SEVILLA. SERIE: CIENCIAS ECONOMICAS Y EMPRESARIALES. vol.2, 1976. irreg., latest no.27. Universidad de Sevilla, Servicio de Publicaciones, Calle Porvenir 27, 41013 Seville, Spain. TEL 34-5-4231958. FAX 34-5-4232245.
    Formerly (until 1967): Universidad Hispalense. Anales. Serie: Economicas y Empresariales.

330   AG   ISSN 0041-8668
UNIVERSIDAD NACIONAL DE CUYO. FACULTAD DE CIENCIAS ECONOMICAS. REVISTA. 1949. 3/yr. Universidad Nacional de Cuyo, Facultad de Ciencias Economicas, Casilla de Correo 594, Mendoza 5500, Argentina. Ed.Bd. bk.rev.; abstr.; charts; stat.; index, cum.index: 1949-1966. circ. 600.

330   AG
UNIVERSIDAD NACIONAL DEL LITORAL. FACULTAD DE CIENCIAS ECONOMICAS COMERCIALES Y POLITICAS. 1926. irreg. Universidad Nacional del Litoral, Facultad de Ciencias Economicas Comerciales y Politicas, Santa Fe, Argentina.

330   PE
UNIVERSIDAD NACIONAL MAYOR DE SAN MARCOS. FACULTAD DE CIENCIAS ECONOMICAS Y COMERCIALES. REVISTA. 1929. irreg. Universidad Nacional Mayor de San Marcos, Facultad de Ciencias Economicas y Comerciales, Casilla 2631, Lima, Peru. bibl.
    Formerly: Revista Economica y Financiera.

330   CK   ISSN 0120-3053
HC196
UNIVERSIDAD PEDAGOGICA Y TECNOLOGICA DE COLOMBIA. CENTRO DE ESTUDIOS ECONOMICOS. APUNTES DEL C E N E S. 1991. s-a. Col.$11000 (effective 1996). Universidad Pedagogica y Tecnologica de Colombia, Centro de Estudios Economicos, Apdo. Aereo 1094, Tunja, Boyaca, Colombia. TEL 425237. Ed. Manuel Caicedo. bk.rev. circ. 600. **Document type:** academic/scholarly publication, proceedings.
    Description: Publishes works and research by professors and students at the university. Includes proceedings on seminars, forums, and symposiums.

330   PO   ISSN 0870-4252
UNIVERSIDADE DE COIMBRA. FACULDADE DE DIREITO. BOLETIM DE CIENCIAS ECONOMICAS. (Text in Portuguese; summaries in English) 1952. a. $10.70. Coimbra Editora Lda., Rua do Arnado, Apdo. 101, 3002 Coimbra Codex, Portugal. TEL 039-25459. FAX 039-37531. bk.rev.; charts; stat. circ. 500.

330   IT
UNIVERSITA DEGLI STUDI DI PARMA. FACOLTA DI ECONOMIA E COMMERCIO. STUDI E RICERCHE. 1964. a. Universita degli Studi di Parma, Facolta di Economia e Commercio, P.le della Pace 7A, 43100 Parma, Italy.

330   IT
UNIVERSITA DI SASSARI. FACOLTA DI GIURISPRUDENZA. PUBBLICAZIONI. SERIE ECONOMICA. 1984. irreg. Casa Editrice Dott. A. Giuffre, Via Busto Arsizio 40, 20151 Milan, Italy. TEL 39-2-38089200. FAX 39-2-38009582.

330   GW
UNIVERSITAET HAMBURG. SEMINAR FUER ALLGEMEINE BETRIEBSWIRTSCHAFTLEHRE. SCHRIFTENREIHE. 1978. irreg., vol.34, 1990. DM.70. Vandenhoeck und Ruprecht, Robert-Bosch-Breite 6, 37079 Goettingen, Germany. TEL 49-551-6959-0. FAX 49-551-695917. (Subscr. to: 37070 Goettingen, Germany) **Document type:** monographic series.

330   GW
UNIVERSITAET HEIDELBERG. WIRTSCHAFTSWISSENSCHAFTLICHE FAKULTAET. DISKUSSIONSSCHRIFTEN. irreg., no.241. Universitaet Heidelberg, Wirtschaftswissenschaftliche Fakultaet, Grabengasse 14, 69117 Heidelberg, Germany. **Document type:** academic/scholarly publication, monographic series.

330   GW   ISSN 0531-0318
UNIVERSITAET ZU KOELN. INSTITUT FUER HANDELSFORSCHUNG. MITTEILUNGEN. SONDERHEFTE. 1954. irreg., no.41, 1992. price varies. Verlag Otto Schwartz und Co., Annastr. 7, 37075 Goettingen, Germany. TEL 49-551-31051. FAX 49-551-372812. Ed. Fritz Klein-Blenkers. **Document type:** monographic series.

330   CK   ISSN 0120-0941
UNIVERSITAS ECONOMICA. 1977. s-a. Col.$7000($8) (effective 1997). Pontificia Universidad Javeriana, Facultad de Ciencias Economicas y Administrativas, Calle 40 No. 6-23, Piso 7, Santafe de Bogota, Colombia. TEL 57-1-2870388. FAX 57-1-2857289. E-mail: jrey@javercol.javeriana.edu.co.

330   RM   ISSN 0379-7864
UNIVERSITATEA "AL. I. CUZA" DIN IASI. ANALELE STIINTIFICE. SECTIUNEA 3C: STIINTE ECONOMICE. (Text in English, French, Rumanian) a. 35 lei. Universitatea "Al. I. Cuza" din Iasi, Calea M. Eminescu 11, Jassy, Rumania. (Subscr. to: ILEXIM, Str. 13 Decembrie Nr. 3, P.O. Box 136-137, Bucharest, Rumania) Ed. M. Tarca. bk.rev.; abstr.; charts; illus. circ. 250.
    Description: New research in theoretical and applied economics.

338.9   CG
UNIVERSITE NATIONALE DU ZAIRE, KINSHASA. INSTITUT DE RECHERCHES ECONOMIQUES ET SOCIALES. LETTRE MENSUELLE. 1964. m. Universite Nationale du Zaire, Kinshasa, Institut de Recherches Economiques et Sociales, B.P. 257, Kinshasa 11, Democratic Republic of the Congo.

330   DK   ISSN 1396-2426
UNIVERSITY OF AARHUS, DENMARK. DEPARTMENT OF ECONOMICS. WORKING PAPER. 1974. irreg. University of Aarhus, Department of Economics, Building 350, DK-8000 Aarhus C, Denmark. TEL 45-89-42-11-33. FAX 45-86-13-63-34. Eds. Tom Engsted, Niels Haldrup.
    —BLDSC (9349.988643).
    Formerly (until 1996): Aarhus Universitet. Oekonomisk Institut. Memo (ISSN 0902-6223)

330   UK   ISSN 0143-4543
UNIVERSITY OF ABERDEEN. DEPARTMENT OF ECONOMICS. OCCASIONAL PAPER. 1993. irreg. £6. University of Aberdeen, Department of Economics, Edward Wright Bldg., Dunbar St., Aberdeen AB9 2TY, Scotland. **Document type:** academic/scholarly publication, monographic series.

UNIVERSITY OF ALASKA. INSTITUTE OF SOCIAL AND ECONOMIC RESEARCH. RESEARCH SUMMARY. see *SOCIOLOGY*

330 620   UK
UNIVERSITY OF BRIGHTON. BUSINESS SCHOOL. OCCASIONAL PAPERS SERIES. irreg., no.2, 1996. price varies. University of Brighton, Business School, Centre for Research in Innovation Management, Falmer, Brighton BN1 9PH, England. **Document type:** monographic series.

330   CN   ISSN 0317-0144
UNIVERSITY OF BRITISH COLUMBIA. DEPARTMENT OF ECONOMICS. DISCUSSION PAPER. 1968. irreg. exchange basis. University of British Columbia, Department of Economics, 1873 East Mall, Ste. 997, Vancouver, BC V6T 1Z1, Canada. TEL 604-822-2876. FAX 604-822-5915. circ. 300. **Document type:** academic/scholarly publication.

330   II   ISSN 0970-9657
UNIVERSITY OF CALCUTTA. BUSINESS STUDIES. 1975. s-a. Rs.20($4) University of Calcutta, University College of Business Studies, College Street, Calcutta-73, India. Ed. A.K. Dutta Gupta. bk.rev. circ. 250.

330 327   UK
UNIVERSITY OF CAMBRIDGE. FACULTY OF ECONOMICS AND POLITICS. RESEARCH PAPER. irreg., no.45. University of Cambridge, Faculty of Economics and Politics, Sidgwick Ave., Cambridge CB3 9DD, England. **Document type:** monographic series.

330   DK   ISSN 0902-6452
UNIVERSITY OF COPENHAGEN. INSTITUTE OF ECONOMICS. DISCUSSION PAPERS. (Text in English) 1987. irreg. Koebenhavns Universitet. Oekonomisk Institut, Studiestraede 6, DK-1455 Copenhagen K, Denmark.
    —BLDSC (3597.776000).

330   TZ
UNIVERSITY OF DAR ES SALAAM. ECONOMIC RESEARCH BUREAU. OCCASIONAL PAPER. Short title: E R B Occasional Paper Series. 1966. irreg. price varies. University of Dar es Salaam, Economic Research Bureau, Economics Department, P.O. Box 35096, Dar es Salaam, Tanzania. circ. 100. **Document type:** academic/scholarly publication, monographic series.

330   TZ   ISSN 0418-3746
UNIVERSITY OF DAR ES SALAAM. ECONOMIC RESEARCH BUREAU. PAPERS. Short title: E R B Papers. 1966. irreg. $3 per no. University of Dar es Salaam, Economic Research Bureau, Economics Department, P.O. Box 35096, Dar es Salaam, Tanzania. **Document type:** monographic series, academic/scholarly publication.

330   UK
UNIVERSITY OF EXETER. DISCUSSION PAPERS IN ECONOMICS. irreg. University of Exeter, Department of Economics, Amory Bldg., Rennes Dr., Exeter EX4 4RJ, England. TEL 44-1392-263219. FAX 44-1392-263240. TELEX 42894-EXUNIV-G. Ed. Ben Lockwood. **Document type:** academic/scholarly publication, monographic series.

UNIVERSITY OF GHANA. INSTITUTE OF STATISTICAL, SOCIAL AND ECONOMIC RESEARCH. DISCUSSION PAPERS. see *SOCIAL SCIENCES: COMPREHENSIVE WORKS*

330   UK
UNIVERSITY OF HERTFORDSHIRE. BUSINESS SCHOOL. WORKING PAPER SERIES. irreg. University of Hertfordshire, Business School, Mangrove Rd., Hertford, Herts SG13 8QF, England. TEL 44-1707-285468. FAX 44-1707-285489. Ed. Susan Barker. **Document type:** monographic series.

330   UK   ISSN 1352-8955
UNIVERSITY OF KEELE. DEPARTMENT OF ECONOMICS. WORKING PAPER. 1970. irreg. University of Keele, Department of Economics, Keele, Staffs ST5 5BG, England. TEL 44-1782-583091. FAX 44-1782-717577. E-mail: ecb01@keele.ac.uk; URL: http://www.keele.ac.uk/cwis.html. Ed. Michael Devereux. R&P contact: Michael Devereux. **Document type:** monographic series.
    —BLDSC (9350.845500).
    Formerly: University of Keele. Department of Economics and Management Science. Working Paper (ISSN 0952-1658)

330   UK   ISSN 0956-1110
UNIVERSITY OF LEEDS. SCHOOL OF BUSINESS AND ECONOMIC STUDIES. DISCUSSION PAPER SERIES. 1978. irreg. £5 to non-academics (foreign academics £10) (effective 1997). University of Leeds, School of Business and Economic Studies, ESS Bldg., Leeds LS2 9JT, England. TEL 44-113-233-4467. FAX 44-113-233-4465. E-mail: eleanor@lubs.leeds.ac.uk. Ed. John Bowers. R&P contact: Eleanor Lynn. **Document type:** monographic series.

330   UK   ISSN 1367-580X
▼**UNIVERSITY OF LONDON. PENSIONS INSTITUTE. DISCUSSION PAPERS.** 1996. irreg. £15 (foreign £20). University of London, Birbeck College, 7-15 Gresse St., London W1P 2LL, England. TEL 44-171-631-6401. FAX 44-171-631-6416. URL: http://www.econ.bbk.ac.uk/pi/wp.htm/. (Co-sponsor: University of London. Pensions Institute) **Document type:** monographic series.

330   US
UNIVERSITY OF MINNESOTA. ECONOMIC DEVELOPMENT CENTER. BULLETIN. irreg. University of Minnesota, Economic Development Center, Department of Economics, Minneapolis, MN 55455. **Document type:** bulletin, monographic series.

330 NR
UNIVERSITY OF NIGERIA. INAUGURAL LECTURE SERIES. irreg., latest no.8. University of Nigeria Press, Nsukka, Enugu State, Nigeria. (Dist. outside Africa by: African Books Collective Ltd., The Jam Factory, 27 Park End St., Oxford OX1 1HU, England. TEL 0865-726686. FAX 0865-793298) **Document type:** monographic series.

330 US ISSN 0081-8437
UNIVERSITY OF PENNSYLVANIA. WHARTON SCHOOL OF FINANCE AND COMMERCE. STUDIES IN QUANTITATIVE ECONOMICS. 1966. irreg. price varies. University of Pennsylvania, Wharton School of Finance and Commerce, Economics Research Unit, 3718 Locust Walk, Philadelphia, PA 19104. TEL 215-898-7601.

338.9
UNIVERSITY OF STELLENBOSCH. BUREAU FOR ECONOMIC RESEARCH. MANUFACTURING SURVEY. (Text in English) 1954. q. R.550 (effective 1996 & 1997). University of Stellenbosch, Bureau for Economic Research, Private Bag 5050, University, Stellenbosch 7599, South Africa. TEL 27-21-8872810. FAX 27-21-8839225. TELEX 520-383 SA. E-mail: odja@maties.sun.ac.za. Ed. P. Laubscher. circ. 360.
Formerly: University of Stellenbosch. Bureau for Economic Research. Opinion Survey (ISSN 0561-9998)
Description: Covers recent developments in South Africa's manufacturing sector, and looks at expected performance.

350 UK ISSN 0306-7866
HC257.S4
UNIVERSITY OF STRATHCLYDE. FRASER OF ALLANDER INSTITUTE FOR RESEARCH ON THE SCOTTISH ECONOMY. QUARTERLY ECONOMIC COMMENTARY. 1975. q. £50. University of Strathclyde, Fraser of Allander Institute for Research on the Scottish Economy, Curran Bldg., 100 Cathedral St., Glasgow G4 0LN, Scotland. TEL 44-141-552-4400. FAX 44-141-552-5589. TELEX 77472-UNSLIB-G. Ed. Eleanor Malloy. adv. contact: Brian Ashcroft. circ. 500. **Document type:** bulletin.
—BLDSC (7181.242800).
Description: A detailed analysis of the Scottish economy from a British-European context for the interested lay person and professional economist alike.

330 UK ISSN 0306-7408
UNIVERSITY OF STRATHCLYDE. FRASER OF ALLANDER INSTITUTE FOR RESEARCH ON THE SCOTTISH ECONOMY. RESEARCH MONOGRAPH. 1975. irreg. price varies. University of Strathclyde, Fraser of Allander Institute for Research on the Scottish Economy, Curran Bldg., 100 Cathedral St., Glasgow G4 0LN, Scotland. TEL 44-141-552-4400. FAX 44-141-552-5589. TELEX 77472-UNSLIB-G. bibl. **Indexed:** Rural Recreat.Tour.Abstr., World Agri.Econ.& Rural Sociol.Abstr. **Document type:** monographic series.

330 UK
UNIVERSITY OF SUSSEX. SCHOOL OF SOCIAL SCIENCES. ECONOMICS DISCUSSION PAPER. irreg. University of Sussex, School of Social Sciences, Falmer, Brighton BN1 9QN, England. Ed. Barry Reilly. **Document type:** monographic series.

330 AT
UNIVERSITY OF SYDNEY. DEPARTMENT OF ECONOMICS. WORKING PAPERS IN ECONOMICS. 1975. irreg., no.246, 1997. exchange basis. University of Sydney, Department of Economics, Room 324 Merewether Bldg., City Rd., Sydney, N.S.W. 2006, Australia. TEL 61-2-513074. FAX 61-2-5521118. E-mail: jackt@bullwinkle.econ.su.oz. Ed. W.E. Schworm. bibl.; circ. 200 (controlled). **Document type:** monographic series.
Former titles: University of Sydney. Department of Economics. Information and Research Monograph; University of Sydney. Faculty of Economics. Information and Research Monograph.
Refereed Serial

UNIVERSITY OF TECHNOLOGY, SYDNEY. RESEARCH REPORT. see *TECHNOLOGY: COMPREHENSIVE WORKS*

650 US ISSN 0495-2634
UNIVERSITY OF TEXAS AT AUSTIN. BUREAU OF BUSINESS RESEARCH. PUBLICATIONS. Key Title: Publications - Bureau of Business Research, the University of Texas at Austin. a. University of Texas at Austin, Bureau of Business Research, Box 7459, Austin, TX 78713. TEL 512-471-1616. FAX 512-671-1063. E-mail: dhardy@mail.utexas.edu. R&P contact: Lois Shrout. (reprint service avail. from UMI) **Document type:** monographic series.

650 US
UNIVERSITY OF TEXAS AT AUSTIN. BUREAU OF BUSINESS RESEARCH. RESEARCH IN USE SERIES. irreg. price varies. University of Texas at Austin, Bureau of Business Research, Box 7459, Austin, TX 78713. TEL 512-471-1616. FAX 512-471-1063. E-mail: dhardy@mail.utexas.edu. R&P contact: Lois Shrout. **Document type:** monographic series.
Description: Focuses on studies on business topics with immediate, practical applications.

650 US
UNIVERSITY OF TEXAS AT AUSTIN. BUREAU OF BUSINESS RESEARCH. RESEARCH MONOGRAPH SERIES. 1928. irreg., latest 1990. price varies. University of Texas at Austin, Bureau of Business Research, Box 7459, Austin, TX 78713. TEL 512-471-1616. FAX 512-471-1063. E-mail: dhardy@mail.utexas.edu. R&P contact: Lois Shrout. (reprint service avail. from UMI) **Document type:** monographic series.
Former titles: University of Texas, Austin. Bureau of Business Research. Research Report Series; University of Texas, Austin. Bureau of Business Research. Research Monograph (ISSN 0082-3279)

UNIVERSITY OF THE WEST INDIES. INSTITUTE OF SOCIAL AND ECONOMIC RESEARCH. WORKING PAPERS. see *SOCIOLOGY*

301 330 CN ISSN 0703-6949
H67.T65
UNIVERSITY OF TORONTO. INSTITUTE FOR POLICY ANALYSIS. ANNUAL REPORT. 1976. irreg. University of Toronto, Institute for Policy Analysis, 150 St. George St., Toronto, ON M5S 3G7, Canada. TEL 416-978-8623. FAX 416-978-6713. Dir. James Pesando. **Document type:** newsletter.
Supersedes: University of Toronto. Institute for the Quantitative Analysis of Social and Economic Policy. News Letter (ISSN 0082-5271)

301 330 CN ISSN 0829-4909
UNIVERSITY OF TORONTO. INSTITUTE FOR POLICY ANALYSIS. WORKING PAPER SERIES. (Print edition ceased in 1995) irreg. free. University of Toronto, Institute for Policy Analysis, 150 St. George St., Toronto, ON M5S 3G7, Canada. TEL 416-978-8623. FAX 416-978-6713. E-mail: ecolib@chass.utoronto.ca; URL: http://www.chass.utoronto.ca:8080/ecipa/wpa.html. (Co-sponsor: Department of Economics) Dir. James Pesando. **Document type:** academic/scholarly publication.
●Available only online.
Formerly: University of Toronto. Institute for the Quantitative Analysis of Social and Economic Policy. Working Paper Series (ISSN 0082-5301)

330 301 UK
UNIVERSITY OF WESTMINSTER. FACULTY OF BUSINESS, MANAGEMENT AND SOCIAL STUDIES. RESEARCH WORKING PAPER SERIES. irreg., no.2. £5. University of Westminster, Faculty of Business, Management and Social Studies, 32-38 Wells St., London W1P 3FG, England. TEL 0171-911-5000. FAX 0171-911-5175. Ed. Robin Theobald. **Document type:** monographic series.

330 XN
UNIVERZITET VO SKOPJE. EKONOMSKIOT FAKULTET. GODISNIK/UNIVERSITE DE SKOPJE. FACULTE DES SCIENCES ECONOMIQUE. ANNUAIRE. (Text in Macedonian; summaries in English, French, German and Russian) 1956. a. Univerzitet vo Skoplje, Ekonomskiot Fakultet, P.O. Box 576, Bulevar Krste Misirkov bb, 91000 Skopje, Macedonia. circ. 500.

330 335 PL ISSN 0208-4813
UNIWERSYTET GDANSKI. WYDZIAL EKONOMIKI TRANSPORTU. ZESZYTY NAUKOWE. INSTYTUT EKONOMII POLITYCZNEJ. PRACE I MATERIALY. (Text in Polish; summaries in English and Russian) 1971. irreg., latest no.16. price varies. Uniwersytet Gdanski, Wydzial Ekonomiki Transportu, c/o Biblioteka Glowna, Ul. Armii Krajowej 110, 81-824 Sopot, Poland. TEL 51-0061. TELEX 051-2247 BMOR PL. (Dist. by: Ars Polona-Ruch, Krakowskie Przedmiescie 7, 00-680 Warsaw, Poland) circ. 250. **Document type:** academic/scholarly publication.
Description: Covers economic growth, international trade and investment, history of economic thought, transnational corporations, economic efficiency of the centrally-planned economy, technological progress and policy, etc.

330 PL ISSN 0137-3056
UNIWERSYTET WARSZAWSKI. WYDZIAL NAUK EKONOMICZNYCH. EKONOMIA. (Text in Polish; summaries in English) 1959. irreg., no.56, 1993. price varies. Wydawnictwa Uniwersytetu Warszawskiego, Ul. Nowy Swiat 4, 00-497 Warsaw, Poland. TEL 48-22-6253044. FAX 48-22-6253044. (Dist. by: Ars Polona, Krakowskie Przedmiescie 7, 00-068 Warsaw, Poland) Ed. Wojciech Maciejewski. R&P contact: Jolanta Okonska. circ. 350. **Document type:** academic/scholarly publication.
Former titles (until no.33, 1975): Uniwersytet Warszawski. Instytut Nauk Ekonomicznych. Biuletyn Naukowy; (until no.24, 1970): Uniwersytet Warszawski. Wydzial Ekonomii Politycznej. Biuletyn Naukowy.

330 SZ
UNTERNEHMER. m. Fliederweg 9, CH-7203 Trimmis, Switzerland. TEL 081-225252. circ. 12,000.

330 GW ISSN 0938-3875
DIE UNTERNEHMERIN. 1960. q. DM.35 (foreign DM.60) (effective 1996). Verband Deutscher Unternehmerin e.V., Gustav-Heinemann-Ufer 94, Postfach 511030, 50968 Cologne, Germany. TEL 49-221-375074. FAX 49-221-343171. Ed. Irene Kuron. adv.; bk.rev. circ. 4,000. **Document type:** trade publication.

UN'YU TO KEIZAI/TRANSPORTATION AND ECONOMY. see *TRANSPORTATION*

330 IT
UOMINI & BUSINESS. 1989. m. L.61000 (foreign L.97900). Uomini & Business S.p.A., Corso Venezia 8, 20122 Milan, Italy. TEL 39-2-76009291. FAX 39-2-76009716. Ed. Giuseppe Turani. adv.: B&W page L.25000000. bk.rev. circ. 13,000. **Document type:** consumer publication.
Description: Covers economics, politics and culture.

UPTREND; Canadian penny market newsletter. see *BUSINESS AND ECONOMICS — Investments*

330 US ISSN 0092-7481
HT167
URBAN INSTITUTE. ANNUAL REPORT. Key Title: Urban Institute Report. 1970. a. Urban Institute, 2100 M Street, N.W., Washington, DC 20037. TEL 202-833-7200. FAX 202-223-3043. Ed. Felicity Skidmore. circ. 11,000. **Indexed:** Med.Care Rev. **Document type:** corporate report.
Description: Reports on the institute's activities concerning the social and economic problems confronting the nation and government policies and programs designed to alleviate them.

330 US ISSN 0741-8485
URBAN INSTITUTE. POLICY AND RESEARCH REPORT. 1971. 3/yr. free. Urban Institute, 2100 M St., N.W., Washington, DC 20037. TEL 202-223-3043. FAX 202-223-3043. Ed. Susan Brown. bk.rev.; charts; illus. circ. 11,000. (back issues avail.) **Document type:** academic/scholarly publication.
—BLDSC (6543.322650); UnCover.
Formerly (until 1979): Search (Washington, D.C.) (ISSN 0048-9921)
Description: Contains summaries of Urban Institute research that investigates the social and economic problems confronting the nation and government policies and programs designed to alleviate such problems.

BUSINESS AND ECONOMICS

330 650   US   ISSN 0042-1405
HC107.U8
UTAH ECONOMIC AND BUSINESS REVIEW. 1941. 9/yr. free (foreign $20). University of Utah, Bureau of Economic and Business Research, Salt Lake City, UT 84112. TEL 801-581-6333. FAX 801-531-3354. Dir. R. Thayne Robson. R&P contact: R. Thayne Robson. TEL 801-581-8284. charts; illus.; stat. circ. 4,000. (also avail. in microfiche from CIS.) **Indexed:** P.A.I.S., SRI. **Document type:** academic/scholarly publication.
—BLDSC (9135.160000).

330   US
UTAH FOUNDATION. RESEARCH REPORT AND RESEARCH BRIEFS. m. $80 to individuals; institutions $100. Utah Foundation, 10 W. 100 S., No. 323, Salt Lake City, UT 84101-1544. TEL 801-364-1837.
Description: Studies covering an agency, function, or problem of state and local government in Utah.

330 305.4   NE   ISSN 0929-5496
V B MAGAZINE; voor vrouwen in business. 1986. 10/yr. fl.105 (foreign fl.148) (effective 1998). Vrouw en Bedrijf BV (Subsidiary of: Reed Elsevier plc), Hoogoorddreef 60, 1101 BE Amsterdam, Netherlands. TEL 31-20-5674911. FAX 31-20-5674352. adv.; illus. **Document type:** consumer publication.
—SWETS.
Formerly (until 1993): Vrouw en Bedrijf (ISSN 0920-5764)

330   SZ
V H T L ZEITUNG.* 20/yr. V H T L, Postfach, CH-8036 Zurich, Switzerland. TEL 01-2423576. FAX 01-2429405. Ed. Urs Boller. circ. 18,000.

330   II
V.T. KRISHNAMACHARI MEMORIAL LECTURE SERIES. (Text in English) 1984. irreg., no.6, 1990. Institute of Economic Growth, University Enclave, New Delhi 110007, India. TEL 2522201.

VALVE MAGAZINE. see *MACHINERY*

330   US
VANCOUVER BUSINESS JOURNAL. 1994. fortn. $29. 2115 E. Fourth Plain Blvd., Vancouver, WA 98661-3959. TEL 360-695-2442. FAX 360-695-3056. URL: http://www.vbjusa.com. Ed. Jennifer Meacham; Pub. Allen Raines. R&P contact: Allen Raines. adv.: B&W page $1455, color page $1805; trim 10 x 13 1/2; adv. contact: Sandy Lowery. circ. 10,000. (tabloid format; back issues avail.) **Document type:** newspaper.
Description: Covers local Clark County business news.

330   DK   ISSN 0107-2013
HC241.2
VEDROERENDE UDVIKLINGEN I DE EUROPAEISKE FAELLESSKABER. BERETNING. 1973. a. free. (Nordgruppen) Underigsministeriet, Nordgruppen, Asiatisk Plads 2, DK-1448 Copenhagen, Denmark. FAX 33-92-03-46. TELEX 31292-ETR-DK. E-mail: um_n1@cyberrnet.dk. **Document type:** academic/scholarly publication.

VEHICLE LEASING TODAY. see *TRANSPORTATION — Automobiles*

330   VE   ISSN 0798-8656
VENEZUELA. OFICINA CENTRAL DE ESTADISTICA E INFORMATICA. MEMORIA Y CUENTA. 1978. a. free. Oficina Central de Estadistica e Informatica, Apdo. de Correos 4593, Carmelitas, Caracas 1010A, Venezuela. TEL 58-2-7811380. FAX 58-2-7811380. **Document type:** government publication.

VENEZUELA ANALITICA. see *POLITICAL SCIENCE*

330   US   ISSN 0897-7925
VERMONT BUSINESS MAGAZINE. (Supplements avail.: Book of Lists, Vermont Manufacturers Directory) 1972. m. $28 (effective 1997). Lake Iroquois Publishing, Inc., 2 Church St., Burlington, VT 05401. TEL 802-863-8038. FAX 802-863-8069. Ed. Lawrence Pyne. adv. contact: John P. Routin. circ. 16,000. (also avail. in microform from UMI.) **Indexed:** Tr.& Indus.Ind. **Document type:** consumer publication.
●Also available online. Vendor(s): Knight-Ridder Information, Inc., UMI.
—UMI.

330 384   US   ISSN 1071-2291
HE202.5
VERONIS, SUHLER & ASSOCIATES COMMUNICATIONS INDUSTRY FORECAST. (Vol. two of Veronis, Suhler, and Associates Communications Industry Research Library (3 vols.)) 1987. a. $995 (3 vol. Communications Industry Research Library $2,485) (effective 1997). Veronis, Suhler & Associates Inc., 350 Park Ave., New York, NY 10022. TEL 212-935-4990. FAX 212-935-0877. E-mail: madlangbay@vacomm.com; URL: http://www.vsacomm.com. Ed. John Suhler. **Document type:** trade publication.
Description: Provides an industry spending preview for 10 segments of the communications industry for the coming 5 years.

330 380   US   ISSN 1071-2283
P96.E252
VERONIS, SUHLER & ASSOCIATES COMMUNICATIONS INDUSTRY REPORT. (Volume three of: Veronis, Suhler & Associates Communications Industry Research Library (3 vols.)) 1983. a. $995 (3 vol. Communications Industry Research Library $2485) (effective 1997). Veronis, Suhler & Associates Inc., 350 Park Ave., New York, NY 10022. TEL 212-935-4990. FAX 212-935-0877. E-mail: madlangbay@vacomm.com; URL: http://www.vsacomm.com. Ed. John Suhler. **Document type:** trade publication.
Description: Analyzes the historical performance of every publicly reporting company in eleven segments of the communications industry over a five-year period.

330 384   UK
VERONIS, SUHLER & ASSOCIATES COMMUNICATIONS INDUSTRY REPORT. (Volume one of: Veronis, Suhler & Associates Communications Industry Research Library (3 vols.)) a. $995 (3 vol. Communications Industry Research Library $2485) (effective 1997). Veroniis, Suhler, & Associates Inc., 350 Park Ave., New York, NY 10022. TEL 212-935-4990. FAX 212-935-0877. E-mail: madlangbay@vsacomm.com; URL: http://www.vsacomm.com.
Description: Covers transactional data for more than 400 publicly traded media and communications companies. Includes listings of transactions by company, total transactions by segment, aggregate value of transactions, and average value on a year-by-year basis by category of transactions.

330   GW
VERTRAULICHE MITTEILUNGEN AUS POLITIK, WIRTSCHAFT UND GELDANLAGE. (Supplement avail.: Kontakt) 1951. w. DM.213. Verlag Arbeit und Wirtschaft GmbH, Junkerstr. 46, 78263 Buesingen, Germany. TEL 49-7734-6061. FAX 49-7734-7112. **Document type:** bulletin.

VIA FEDEX. see *COMMUNICATIONS*

330   PO   ISSN 0871-4320
VIDA ECONOMICA. 1983. w. Esc.13800 (effective 1995 & 1996). Rua Goncalo Cristerao, 111, 4000 Porto, Portugal. TEL 351-2-2003661. FAX 351-2-318098. Ed. Joao Luis de Sousa; Pub. Joao Peixoto de Sousa. adv. contact: Joao Pedro Freire. bk.rev.; circ. 30,000 (paid). **Document type:** newspaper.

330   FR   ISSN 0336-142X
VIE ET SCIENCES ECONOMIQUES. (Text in French and English) 1953. q. 800 F. per no. (Association Nationale des Docteurs es Sciences Economiques) Editions de L'Andese, 120 rue d'Assas, 75006 Paris, France. TEL 1-42-93-49-55. FAX 1-45-22-64-55. Ed. M. de l'Andese. adv.; bk.rev.; charts; stat. circ. 1,000. **Document type:** academic/scholarly publication.

330   FR   ISSN 0766-608X
VIE FORAINE. 11/yr. 69 bd. de Strasbourg, 75010 Paris, France. TEL 47-70-07-19. FAX 47-70-27-52. Ed. Jean Fotel. circ. 5,000.

330   SZ
DIE VIER IM SCHWEIZERISCHEN WIRTSCHAFTSLEBEN. q. Fritz Wagner's Erben, Katzenrutistr. 77, CH-8153 Ruemlang, Switzerland. adv. circ. 5,000.

330   US   ISSN 1076-0032
THE VIETNAM BUSINESS JOURNAL. 1993. bi-m. $30 (foreign $60); newsstand price: $4.95. Viam Communications Group Ltd., 114 E. 32nd St., Ste. 1010, New York, NY 10016. TEL 212-725-1717. E-mail: vbj@viam.com; URL: http://www.viam.com. Ed. Joshua Levine; Pub. Kenneth D. Felberbaum. R&P contact: Mitchell Klaif. adv. contact: Mitchell Klaif. bk.rev. circ. 18,200. **Document type:** trade publication.
●Also available online. Vendor(s): Dow Jones News Retrieval.
Description: Covers topics and business issues regarding Vietnam and Indochina.

330   VN
VIETNAM ECONOMIC TIMES. (Text in English) m. Ringiers - Association of Vietnamese Economists, 10 Duong Thanh, Honoi, Socialist Republic of Vietnam. TEL 252411. FAX 251888. Pub. Robert Ferguson. adv.: B&W page $1700, color page $2200; trim 210 x 295; adv. contact: Kurtis Law.
Description: For Vietnamese businessmen and foreign investors.

330   VN
VIETNAM RENOVATION. (Text in Chinese, English) 1991. q. D.10000($10) (Ministry of Trade) Vietnam Trade Review, 46 Ngo Quyen, Hanoi, Vietnam. TEL 84-4-8264606. FAX 84-4-8262311. Ed. Truong Duc Ngai. adv.: page $400. circ. 8,000.
Formerly (until Apr. 1994): Business.
Description: Covers business and socioeconomic situations in Vietnam.

330   US   ISSN 0888-1340
HC107.V8V437
VIRGINIA BUSINESS. 1986. m. $30 (effective 1997). Box C-32333, Richmond, VA 23261. TEL 804-649-6999. FAX 804-649-6311. Ed. Karl W. Rhodes; Pub. James Bacon. R&P contact: Karl W. Rhodes. adv. contact: Hunter Bendall. circ. 35,500.
Description: Focuses on business, economics, and public policy, as related to the business environment in Virginia.

330   GW   ISSN 0942-8615
VIS-A-VIS; Saar-Lor-Lux-Magazin. (Text in French, German) 1992. bi-m. DM.30. Verlag Haselbauer und Partner, Bergstr. 18, 53547 Dattenberg, Germany. TEL 49-2644-2011. FAX 49-2644-2014. Ed. W. Haselbauer. **Document type:** bulletin.

338   BE
DE VLAAMSE ONDERNEMER. (Text in Dutch) 1989. s-m. 1000 BEF. Pastoor Schoetersstraat 10, 2910 Essen, Belgium. TEL 32-3-6772456. FAX 32-3-6771092. Ed. L. Willemijns. adv.: color page 95000 BEF; adv. contact: G. Sparen. circ. 25,000. (tabloid format; back issues avail.) **Document type:** trade publication.
Formerly: Antwerpse Ondernemer (ISSN 0777-236X)
Description: Covers business and management issues of interest to companies in the province of Antwerp & Limburg.

650   US
VOICE OF WORKING WOMEN.* 1962. q. membership. New Jersey Federation of Business & Professional Women, Inc., 120 Finderne Ave., Bridgewater, NJ 08807-3670. TEL 908-233-0110. adv. circ. 2,000.
Formerly (until 1985): New Jersey Business Woman (ISSN 0028-5579)

330   SZ   ISSN 1011-386X
VOLKSWIRTSCHAFT. (Text in German) 1915. m. Bundesamt fuer Industrie, Gewerbe und Arbeit, Gurtengasse 3, CH-3003 Bern, Switzerland. TEL 41-31-3222786. FAX 41-31-3222740. Ed. Erwin Roos. circ. 6,000. **Document type:** government publication.
—BLDSC (9234.960000); SWETS.

BUSINESS AND ECONOMICS

330 RU ISSN 0042-8736
VOPROSY EKONOMIKI. 1929. m. $180 (effective 1998). (Rossiiskaya Akademiya Nauk, Institut Ekonomiki) Voprosy Ekonomii, Ul. Krasikova 27, 117218 Moscow, Russia. TEL 7-095-1245228. (Dist. by: Mezhdunarodnaya Kniga, ul. B. Yakimanka 39, 117049 Moscow, Russia; Dist. in U.S. by: Victor Kamkin Inc., 4956 Boiling Brook Pkwy, Rockville, MD 20852. TEL 301-881-5973) R&P contact: Sergei Popov. adv. contact: Sergei Popov. bk.rev./ stat. circ. 8,800. (also avail. in microform) **Indexed:** Amer.Hist.& Life (1954-1955), (1973-), Curr.Dig.Sov.Press, Dairy Sci.Abstr., Hist.Abstr. (1954-1955), (1973-), IBR, Int.Lab.Doc., Potato Abstr., Rural Recreat.Tour.Abstr., Seed Abstr., World Agri.Econ.& Rural Sociol.Abstr. **Document type:** academic/scholarly publication.

330 RU
VOPROSY RAZVITIYA PROIZVODITEL'NYKH SIL MURMANSKOI OBLASTI - APATITY. 1972. irreg. 0.48 Rub. Akademiya Nauk S.S.S.R., Kol'skii Nauchnyi Tsentr, Institut Ekonomicheskikh Problem, 184200 Apatity, Akademgorodok, Russia. TELEX 126118 PGI SU. Eds. Nikolai A. Peshev, Evgemii E. Lazarev. illus. circ. 228.
Formerly: Voprosy Ekonomiki Narodnogo Khozyaistva Murmanskoi Oblasti.

320 BE ISSN 1370-1290
VOULOIR. 1983. q. Victor Rousseau 28, Brussels, Belgium. Ed. Robert Steuckers.

332 II ISSN 0042-9325
VYAPAR (GUJARATI EDITION). (Editions in Gujarati, Hindi) 1949. s-w. Rs.330 (foreign Rs.2300); newsstand price: Rs.3. Saurashtra Trust, Janmabhoomi Bhavan, Janmabhoomi Marg, Fort, Bombay 400 001, India. TEL 022-2870831. FAX 022-2874097. TELEX 11-86859 BHOO IN. Ed. Shashikant Vasani; Pub. Dhirubhai J. Desai. adv. contact: N.G. Patel. bk.rev. circ. 31,549.
Description: Covers trade, business, industries, banking, labor, and more.

332 II
VYAPAR (HINDI EDITION). w. Rs.170 (foreign Rs.1150); newsstand price: Rs.3. Saurashtra Trust, Janmabhoomi Bhavan, Janmabhoomi Marg, Fort, Bombay 400001, India. TEL 022-2870831. FAX 022-2874097. Ed. Shashikant Vasani. circ. 19,274.
Description: Covers trade, business, industries, banking, labor, and more.

330 US
W D.* (Workforce Diversity) 1994. a. Equal Opportunity Publications, Inc., 1160 E. Jericho Tpke., Ste. 200, Huntington, NY 11743-5400. TEL 516-261-8899. FAX 516-261-8935. E-mail: info@eop.com; URL: http://www.eop.com. **Document type:** trade publication.

330 AU
W D F MAGAZIN. 11/yr. Lothringerstr. 12, A-1030 Vienna, Austria. TEL 01-7137968. FAX 01-71135. TELEX 131717. Ed. Gerald Schulze. circ. 3,500.

330 GW
W I R - WIRTSCHAFT IN ROSTOCK. m. DM.36 (foreign DM.52) (effective 1996). Schmidt-Roemhild Verlag, Mengstr. 16, 23552 Luebeck, Germany. TEL 49-451-703101. FAX 49-451-7031253. **Document type:** bulletin.

338 US
W N C BUSINESS JOURNAL. (Western North Carolina) 1987. m. $40 in NC; elsewhere in US $50 (foreign $75) (effective 1996). Nason & Associates, Box 8204, Asheville, NC 28814. TEL 704-298-1322. FAX 704-298-1312. Ed. Marilyn Nason; Pub. Marilyn Nason. R&P contact: Marilyn Nason. adv. contact: Michelle Ramsey. bk.rev./ circ. 19,000 (controlled). **Document type:** newsletter.
Former titles: W N C Business Beat (ISSN 1084-6352); (until 1995): Original W N C Business Journal (ISSN 1065-027X); W N C Business Journal.
Description: For business people throughout the 28 counties of western North Carolina.

W S I MITTEILUNGEN. (Wirtschafts- und Sozialwissenschaftliches Institut) see SOCIAL SCIENCES: COMPREHENSIVE WORKS

330 GW ISSN 0178-3521
W W T - WEITERBILDUNG IN WIRTSCHAFT UND TECHNIK;* Zeitschrift fuer die berufliche Weiterbildung. 1979. q. DM.48 (foreign DM.56). (Technische Akademie Esslingen) Expert Verlag GmbH, Wankelstr. 13, 71272 Renningen, Germany. Ed. W.J. Bartz. adv.; bk.rev. circ. 1,500.

WAGE-PRICE LAW & ECONOMICS REVIEW. see BUSINESS AND ECONOMICS — Macroeconomics

330 CC
WAIXIANG JINGJI. (Text in Chinese) m. Shandong Sheng Chuban Zongshe, Yantai Fenshe, No. 114, Dama Lu, Yantai, Shandong 364001, People's Republic of China. TEL 224311. Ed. Dong Ruiting.

330 GW ISSN 0083-7113
WALTER EUCKEN INSTITUT. WIRTSCHAFTSWISSENSCHAFTLICHE UND WIRTSCHAFTSRECHTLICHE UNTERSUCHUNGEN. 1962. irreg. price varies. (Walter Eucken Institut) Verlag Mohr Siebeck, Wilhelmstr. 18, 72074 Tuebingen, Germany. TEL 49-7071-923-0. FAX 49-7071-51104. E-mail: mohr-siebeck@t-online.de; URL: http://www.mohr.de. (Subscr. to: Postfach 2040, 72010 Tuebingen, Germany) R&P contact: Jill Sopper. **Document type:** monographic series.

330 US ISSN 1071-9555
HG4009
WARD'S PRIVATE COMPANY PROFILES. 1994. a. $139. Gale Research, 835 Penobscot Bldg., 645 Griswold St., Detroit, MI 48226-4094. TEL 313-961-2242; 800-877-4253. FAX 800-414-5043. E-mail: daniel__snyder@gale.com. bibl.; stat.; index. (back issues avail.) **Document type:** directory.
—CISTI.
Description: Profiles newsmaking, private companies in the US. Each volume includes 150 companies of various sizes from various industries. Entries include excerpted or full-text articles from recent publications.

650 UK
WARWICK BUSINESS SCHOOL RESEARCH PAPERS. 1982. irreg. £10 (foreign £15) (effective 1997). University of Warwick, Warwick Business School, Coventry CV4 7AL, England. TEL 44-1203-523523. FAX 44-1203-524965. Ed. Catherine Waddams. R&P contact: Sue Watts. circ. 100. **Document type:** academic/scholarly publication.
Former titles (until Dec. 1990): Warwick Papers in Management (ISSN 0955-4718); Warwick Papers in Industry, Business and Administration (ISSN 0263-5976); **Supersedes:** Warwick Industrial Economic and Business Research Papers; Warwick Research Industrial and Business Studies (ISSN 0083-7369).

330 JA ISSN 0388-1008
HF41
WASEDA BUSINESS AND ECONOMIC STUDIES. (Text in English) 1965. a. free. Waseda University, Graduate School of Commerce, 6-1 Nishi-Waseda 1-chome, Shinjuku-ku, Tokyo 169-50, Japan. charts; illus. circ. 500.

WASEDA SEIJI KEIZAIGAKU ZASSHI/WASEDA JOURNAL OF POLITICAL SCIENCE AND ECONOMICS. see POLITICAL SCIENCE

330 US ISSN 0149-7618
HF125.W2
WASHINGTON (STATE). DEPARTMENT OF REVENUE. QUARTERLY BUSINESS REVIEW. 1974. q. Department of Revenue, Research Division, Box 47459, Olympia, WA 98504-7459. TEL 360-753-2087. FAX 360-664-0972. circ. 1,100. **Document type:** government publication.

330 US ISSN 0737-3147
WASHINGTON BUSINESS JOURNAL. 1982. w. $49. American City Business Journals, Inc. (Arlington), 2000 14th St., N. Ste. 500, Arlington, VA 22201. TEL 703-875-2200. FAX 703-875-2231. Ed. Dave Yochum. adv. circ. 21,000. **Indexed:** Tr.& Indus.Ind.
●Also available online.
—UMI. **CCC.**
Description: Covers Washington metropolitan area business news and trends.

WASHINGTON STATE BAR ASSOCIATION. BUSINESS AND LAW SECTION. NEWSLETTER. see LAW

WEB INFORMANT (ELK GROVE); the complete monthly guide to web development. see COMPUTERS — Computer Networks

WEB INFORMANT (PORT WASHINGTON). see COMPUTERS — Computer Networks

330 370 011 540 GW
WELLA AKTIENGESELLSCHAFT. REPORT; Mitarbeitermagazin fuer Mitarbeiter und Pensionaere der weltweiten Wella-Unternehmen. (Text in German; summaries in English) 1979. m. free. Wella AG, Berliner Allee 65, 64274 Darmstadt, Germany. TEL 49-6151-342890. FAX 49-6151-343298. Ed. Peter Skopp. bk.rev. circ. 6,000. (back issues avail.) **Document type:** newsletter.
Formerly: Schnellreport.

330 GW ISSN 0043-2636
H5
WELTWIRTSCHAFTLICHES ARCHIV/REVIEW OF WORLD ECONOMICS. (Text and summaries in several languages) 1914. q. DM.168 (effective 1998). (Institut fuer Weltwirtschaft Kiel) Verlag Mohr Siebeck, Wilhelmstr. 18, 72074 Tuebingen, Germany. TEL 49-7071-923-0. FAX 49-7071-51104. E-mail: mohr-siebeck@t-online.de; URL: http://www.uni-kiel.de:8080/ifw/pub/wa/. (Subscr. to: Postfach 2040, 72010 Tuebingen, Germany) Ed. Horst Siebert. R&P contact: Jill Sopper. bk.rev.; bibl.; index. circ. 1,800. **Indexed:** ASCA, Asian-Pac.Econ.Lit., BPIA, Bus.Ind., C.R.E.J., Curr.Cont., IBR, Int.Lab.Doc., J.of Econ.Lit., Key to Econ.Sci., P.A.I.S.For.Lang.Ind., P.A.I.S., SCIMP (1980-), SSCI, Tr.& Indus.Ind. **Document type:** academic/scholarly publication.
—BLDSC (9295.050000); Genuine Article; SWETS; UnCover. **CCC.**
Description: Contains articles on international economics; emphasis on empirical research and study of national policies.

330 US
WENATCHEE BUSINESS JOURNAL. 1987. m. $18. Wenatchee Business Journal Inc., 304 S. Mission St., Wenatchee, WA 98801-3044. TEL 509-663-6730. E-mail: wbizjour@hcw.net. Ed. Mike Cassidy; Pubs. Jim Corcoran, Mike Cassidy. adv.: B&W page $940; trim 9 3/4 x 13 1/2; adv. contact: Jim Corcoran. circ. 3,400. **Document type:** trade publication.
●Also available online. Vendor(s): UMI.
Description: Contains profiles on business leaders and successful businesses, business news and advice, and management columns.

330 GW ISSN 0723-5275
WER LEITET; das Middle Management der deutschen Wirtschaft. 1982. a. DM.160 (effective 1997). Verlag Hoppenstedt GmbH, Havelstr. 9, 64295 Darmstadt, Germany. TEL 49-6151-380-0. FAX 49-6151-380-360. circ. 46,000. **Document type:** directory.

330 US
WEST CENTRAL BUSINESS JOURNAL; the business newspaper of west central Ohio. 1992. m. free. Ronald Freed, Ed. & Pub., Box 388, Lima, OH 45802-0388. TEL 419-991-6839. FAX 419-991-4762. R&P contact: Ronald Freed. adv.: B&W page $699; 10 x 12.25; adv. contact: Ronald Freed. circ. 10,000 (controlled). (tabloid format) **Document type:** newsletter.
Description: Covers all business matters in 10 west central Ohio counties.

330 US ISSN 0195-4644
HC107.W5
WEST VIRGINIA BUSINESS INDEX. 1938. m. $60. West Virginia Chamber of Commerce, Box 2789, Charleston, WV 25330. TEL 304-342-1115. **Document type:** trade publication.

WETBOEK ECONOMISCH EN FINANCIEEL RECHT - DEEL ECONOMISCH EN CONSUMENTENRECHT. see LAW — Corporate Law

WETTBEWERB IN RECHT UND PRAXIS. see LAW

WHAT IS TO BE READ. see LITERATURE

BUSINESS AND ECONOMICS

332   UK   ISSN 0263-8525
WHAT MORTGAGE. 1982. m. £2.50 per month. Charterhouse Communications, 4-8 Tabernacle St., 3rd Fl., London EC2A 4LU, England. TEL 44-171-638-1916. FAX 44-171-638-3128. Ed. Nia Williams; Pub. Ivan Elliot. R&P contact: Nia Williams. adv. contact: Mike Mortimore. circ. 35,000 (paid). **Document type:** consumer publication.

WHAT'S NEW IN BUSINESS INFORMATION. see *COMMUNICATIONS*

WHICH DEGREE. SOCIAL SCIENCES, BUSINESS, EDUCATION. see *SOCIAL SCIENCES: COMPREHENSIVE WORKS*

330   US
WHITFIELD'S UTILITY LETTER.* 1984. m. $49. J. Charles Whitfield, Ed. & Pub., 1512 Memorial Dr., Houston, TX 77007-7728. TEL 713-521-2536. circ. 500. **Document type:** newsletter.
     Description: Contains comments on the economy and governmental policies.

WHO'S WHO IN EUROPEAN BUSINESS. see *BIOGRAPHY*

WHO'S WHO IN FINANCE AND INDUSTRY. see *BIOGRAPHY*

330   US   ISSN 0894-4032
WICHITA BUSINESS JOURNAL. 1986. w. $53 (effective 1996). American City Business Journals, Inc. (Wichita), 110 S. Main St., Ste. 200, Wichita, KS 67202-3745. TEL 316-267-6406. FAX 316-267-8570. Ed. Kevin Bumgarner; Pub. Forrest Gossett. R&P contact: Kevin Bumgarner. adv. contact: Teresa Moore. circ. 5,800 (paid). (tabloid format) **Document type:** newspaper.
● Also available online. Vendor(s): Lexis-Nexis. —UMI. **CCC.**
     Description: Covers local business news.

330   US   ISSN 1048-3365
WICHITA JOURNAL. 1969. w. $31.75. Times Publishing of Kansas, Box 190, Derby, KS 67037. TEL 316-788-2835. FAX 316-788-0854. Ed. Sherry Blanchard; Pub. Jimmie R. Stephenson. R&P contact: 216-788-2835. adv. contact: Fay Osenbough. bk.rev.; tr.lit. rev. 750. (tabloid format) **Document type:** newspaper.
     Description: Covers news affecting the business community.

330   AU
WIENER WIRTSCHAFT. w. S.720. Oesterreichischer Wirtschaftsverlag, Nikolsdorfergasse 7-11, A-1051 Vienna, Austria. TEL 0222-555585. TELEX 1-11669. adv. circ. 60,500.

330   AU
WIENER WIRTSCHAFTSREPORT. 11/yr. Falkestr. 3-3, A-1010 Vienna, Austria. TEL 01-5127631. circ. 64,600.

330   US   ISSN 0084-0246
WILLIAM K. MCINALLY LECTURE. 1966. a. $5. University of Michigan, Graduate School of Business Administration, Division of Research, Tappan and Monroe Sts., Ann Arbor, MI 48109. TEL 313-764-1366. (reprint service avail. from UMI)

WINDS OF CHANGE; American Indian education & opportunity. see *ETHNIC INTERESTS*

WINE BUSINESS INSIDER. see *BEVERAGES*

WINE BUSINESS MONTHLY; & grower and cellar news. see *BEVERAGES*

330   GW   ISSN 0232-4768
DIE WIRTSCHAFT (BERLIN); Wochenzeitung fuer Wirtschaft, Handel und Finanzen. 1960. w. DM.260. Verlag Die Wirtschaft GmbH, Am Friedrichshain 22, 10407 Berlin, Germany. TEL 030-4287250. FAX 030-4261249. Ed. Harry Pollei. adv. contact: Claudia Brendel. bk.rev.; charts; illus.; tr.lit.; index. circ. 10,289. **Indexed:** C.I.S. Abstr. **Document type:** newspaper.
     Incorporates (in 1994): Innovation & Management (ISSN 0863-2790); **Formerly:** Wirtschaft: Ausgabe A (ISSN 0043-6119)

330   AU
WIRTSCHAFT AKTIV. q. Landgruppe Oe Oe, Bluetenstr.21, Postfach 3, A-4041 Linz, Austria. TEL 0732-23642622. Ed. K. Kurzthaler. circ. 42,000.

330   GW   ISSN 0936-5885
WIRTSCHAFT IM SUEDWESTEN. 1973. m. DM.36. Industrie- und Handelskammern im Regierungsbezirk Freiburg, Schnewlinstr. 11-13, 79098 Freiburg, Germany. TEL 49-761-32829. FAX 49-761-3858222. Ed. Ulrich Plankenhorn. adv.; bk.rev. **Document type:** trade publication.

330   GW
WIRTSCHAFT MARKT. m. DM.48. W und M Verlagsgesellschaft mbH, Neue Gruenstr. 18, 10179 Berlin, Germany. TEL 49-30-2793005. FAX 49-30-2793665. Ed. Klaus George. adv. contact: Margit Eschment. circ. 40,000. **Document type:** trade publication.
     Formerly: Wirtschaft und Markt (ISSN 0863-5323)

330   GW   ISSN 0944-6249
WIRTSCHAFT REGIONAL. m. Wirtschaft Regional Verlag GmbH, Villastr. 11, 70190 Stuttgart, Germany. TEL 0711-2686131. FAX 0711-2686139. Ed. Ulrich Pfaffenberger. adv. contact: Christian Schikora. circ. 103,000. **Document type:** trade publication.

330   AU   ISSN 0378-5130
HC261
WIRTSCHAFT UND GESELLSCHAFT. 1975. q. S.456. (Kammer fuer Arbeiter und Angestellte fuer Wien) Verlag Orac GesmbH & Co. KG, Graben 17, A-1010 Vienna, Austria. TEL 43-1-53452-0. FAX 43-1-53452141. Ed. G. Chaloupek. adv.; B&W page S.5000; adv. contact: Christian Braun. bk.rev. circ. 3,000. **Indexed:** IBR, Int.Polit.Sci.Abstr., P.A.I.S.For.Lang.Ind. **Document type:** trade publication.
—BLDSC (9325.415550).

WIRTSCHAFT UND GESELLSCHAFT IM BERUF. see *EDUCATION — Teaching Methods And Curriculum*

330 310   GW   ISSN 0043-6143
HC281
WIRTSCHAFT UND STATISTIK. 1949. m. DM.198. Statistisches Bundesamt, 65180 Wiesbaden, Germany. TEL 49-611-75-1. FAX 49-611-724000. TELEX 61186-STBA-D. URL: http://www.statistik-bund.de. (reprint service avail. from KTO) **Indexed:** Chem.Abstr., Key to Econ.Sci., P.A.I.S.For.Lang.Ind., Popul.Ind., Rural Recreat.Tour.Abstr., World Agri.Econ.& Rural Sociol.Abstr. **Document type:** government publication.
—SWETS. **CCC.**

330 370   GW
WIRTSCHAFT UND UNTERRICHT; Informationen fuer Paedagogen in Schule und Betrieb. 10/yr. Institut der Deutschen Wirtschaft, Gustav-Heinemann-Ufer 84-88, Postfach 510670, 50968 Cologne, Germany. TEL 0221-3708341. FAX 0221-3708192.

DIE WIRTSCHAFTLICHE ENTWICKLUNG IN DEN SOZIALISTISCHEN LAENDERN OSTEUROPAS ZUR JAHRESWENDE. see *POLITICAL SCIENCE*

330   GW   ISSN 0177-3518
DER WIRTSCHAFTSREDAKTEUR; Wirtschaft Wissenschaft und Medien Aktuell. 1965. s.a-m. DM.240. Presse- und Brancheninformationsdienst Bert Schnitzler GmbH, Binsberg 28, 85658 Egmating, Germany. TEL 49-8095-9090-0. FAX 49-8095-753. Ed. Bert Schnitzler. adv.; B&W page DM.2730, color page DM.4530; trim 180 x 260; adv. contact: Robert Grundl. bk.rev. circ. 1,600. **Document type:** newsletter.
—CCC.

330   GW   ISSN 0178-7209
WIRTSCHAFTS KOMPASS. 1983. a. Rudolf Haufe Verlag GmbH & Co. KG, Hindenburgstr. 64, 79102 Freiburg, Germany. TEL 49-761-3683-0. FAX 49-761-3683-195. TELEX 772442-HAUFE-D. Ed. Wolfgang Bohl.

330   GW   ISSN 0170-3390
WIRTSCHAFTS-KURIER. 11/yr. Wirtschafts-Kurier Verlagsgesellschaft mbH, Lindwurmstr. 201, 80337 Munich, Germany. TEL 089-774086. FAX 089-763938. Ed. Wilhelm Gaensler; Pub. Hans Englert. adv. contact: Anne-Marie Kwak. circ. 42,719. **Document type:** consumer publication.

330   GW   ISSN 0931-2552
WIRTSCHAFTS-NACHRICHTEN. 1955. m. DM.118 (effective 1996). Stuenings Verlag GmbH, Luisenstr. 100-104, 47799 Krefeld, Germany. TEL 49-2151-853-0. FAX 49-2151-853103. Ed. Lothar Neumann. adv.; B&W page DM.3596, color page DM.4760; trim 185 x 255. bk.rev.; stat. circ. 17,000. (back issues avail.) **Document type:** consumer publication.
     Formerly: Wirtschafts-Nachrichten fuer den Linken Niederrhein (ISSN 0344-0249)

330   GW   ISSN 0722-3358
WIRTSCHAFTS UND STEUER HEFTE. 1925. 24/yr. DM.222.64 (effective 1996). D I E Verlag H. Schaefer GmbH, Postfach 2243, 61292 Bad Homburg, Germany. TEL 49-6172-9583-0. FAX 49-6172-71288. Ed. Erika Bressel. adv. contact: Peter Vollrath. circ. 15,500. **Document type:** trade publication.
● Also available on CD-ROM.

330   GW   ISSN 0043-6275
WIRTSCHAFTSDIENST. 1917. m. DM.121 (foreign DM.142) (effective 1996). (H W W A - Institut fuer Wirtschaftsforschung, Hamburg) Nomos Verlagsgesellschaft mbH und Co. KG, Waldseestr. 3-5, 76530 Baden-Baden, Germany. TEL 49-7221-2104-0. FAX 49-7221-210427. Ed. Otto G. Mayer. adv.; bk.rev.; charts; index. (reprint service avail. from ISI) **Indexed:** ELLIS, Excerp.Med., IBR, Int.Lab.Doc., Irr.& Drain.Abstr., Key to Econ.Sci., P.A.I.S.For.Lang.Ind., P.A.I.S., Rural Recreat.Tour.Abstr., World Agri.Econ.& Rural Sociol.Abstr. **Document type:** trade publication.
—BLDSC (9325.550000); SWETS. **CCC.**

330   GW   ISSN 0722-9267
WIRTSCHAFTSECHO - HEIM UND WERK. m. DM.21.06. Heim und Werk GmbH, Benderstr. 168a, 40625 Duesseldorf, Germany. TEL 0211-283095. FAX 0211-283827. Ed. Rolf Scheer. adv. contact: Walter Rau. circ. 108,015. **Document type:** trade publication.

330   AU
WIRTSCHAFTSMAGAZIN. 8/yr. Meinhardtstr. 3, A-6020 Innsbruck, Austria. TEL 0512-52022-0. circ. 27,500.

330 340   GW   ISSN 0945-2346
WIRTSCHAFTSRECHTLICHE BERATUNG; Zeitschrift fuer Wirtschaftsanwaelte und Unternehmensjuristen. Abbreviated title: Wi B. 1994. s-m. DM.412 (effective 1997). Verlag C.H. Beck, 80791 Munich, Germany. TEL 49-89-38189-338. FAX 49-89-38189-398. Ed.Bd. adv.; B&W page DM.2600, color page DM.4550; trim 260 x 186. bk.rev. circ. 4,000. (back issues avail.) **Document type:** bulletin.

330   GW
WIRTSCHAFTSREPORT SIEGEN-OLPE-WITTGENSTEIN. m. Vorlaender und Rothmaler GmbH, Obergraben 39, 57072 Siegen, Germany. TEL 0271-5941. FAX 0271-594318. TELEX 872844-SGNZT-D. **Document type:** bulletin.

330   GW
WIRTSCHAFTSSPIEGEL; Kurier der Industrie- und Handelskammer zu Muenster. m. DM.36. Industrie- und Handelskammer zu Muenster, Sentmaringer Weg 61, 48151 Muenster, Germany. TEL 0251-707-232. FAX 0251-707-358. (back issues avail.) **Document type:** bulletin.

WIRTSCHAFTSTRENDS ZUM JAHRESWECHSEL. see *HISTORY — History Of Europe*

DIE WIRTSCHAFTSWISSENSCHAFTLICHEN FAKULTAETEN. see *OCCUPATIONS AND CAREERS*

BUSINESS AND ECONOMICS

330 GW ISSN 0340-1650
WIRTSCHAFTSWISSENSCHAFTLICHES STUDIUM; Zeitschrift fuer Ausbildung und Hochschulkontakt. Abbreviated title: Wi S T. 1972. m. DM.184 (students DM.136) (effective 1997). Verlag C.H. Beck, 80791 Munich, Germany. TEL 49-89-38189-338. FAX 49-89-38189-398. Ed.Bd. adv.: B&W page DM.2300, color page DM.4025; trim 260 x 186. bk.rev.; abstr.; bibl.; charts; stat.; index. circ. 3,200. (back issues avail.) **Indexed:** IBR, P.A.I.S.For.Lang.Ind. **Document type:** academic/scholarly publication.
—BLDSC (9325.636500); SWETS.

650 US ISSN 0084-0513
WISCONSIN BUSINESS MONOGRAPHS. 1968. irreg., no.14, 1987. price varies. University of Wisconsin at Madison, Bureau of Business Research, 110 Commerce Bldg., 1155 Observatory Dr., Madison, WI 53706. TEL 608-262-1550. **Document type:** monographic series.
Formerly: University of Wisconsin. Bureau of Business Research and Service. Monographs (ISSN 0512-0918)

330 US ISSN 0084-0599
WISCONSIN ECONOMY STUDIES. 1967. irreg., no.22, 1987. price varies. University of Wisconsin-Madison, Bureau of Business Research, 110 Commerce Building, 1155 Observatory Dr., Madison, WI 53706. TEL 608-262-1550.
Formerly: Wisconsin Commerce Studies.

WIWI-PRESS. see *COLLEGE AND ALUMNI*

WOLFE'S VERSION; a socio-political-economic analysis. see *POLITICAL SCIENCE*

650 US ISSN 0043-7441
HF5500.2
WOMEN IN BUSINESS. 1949. 6/yr. $16 (foreign $20). (American Business Women's Association) A B W A Company, Inc., 9100 Ward Parkway, Box 8728, Kansas City, MO 64114-0728. TEL 816-361-6621. FAX 816-361-4991. Ed. Wendy S. Myers; Pub. Carolyn B. Elman. R&P contact: Wendy Myers. adv. contact: Dawn Anderson. bk.rev.; software rev.; video rev.; tr.lit.; circ. 90,000 (paid). (also avail. in microform from UMI) **Indexed:** B.P.I., BPIA, PMR, Tr.& Indus.Ind. **Document type:** consumer publication, trade publication.
—KR SourceOne; UMI.
Description: Covers association news, business trends, women's work place issues, entrepreneurial and retirement issues.

330 US
WOMEN IN ECONOMICS; the C S W E P roster. 1973. biennial. $20. American Economic Association, Committee on the Status of Women in the Economics Profession, Denison University, Dept. of Economics, Granville, OH 43023. TEL 614-587-6574. FAX 614-587-6348. Ed. Robin Bartlett. circ. 6,000. **Document type:** directory.

WOMEN'S BUSINESS EXCLUSIVE. see *WOMEN'S INTERESTS*

330 UK ISSN 1351-4725
HC10
WORLD BUSINESS AND ECONOMIC REVIEW. a. £135. Kogan Page Ltd., 120 Pentonville Rd., London N1 9JN, England. TEL 44-171-278-0433. FAX 44-171-837-6348. TELEX 263088 KOGAN G. R&P contact: Linda Batman. stat. **Document type:** trade publication, directory.
Description: Contains political and economic analysis and statistics on 220 countries.

WORLD BUSINESS SOLUTION. see *PRINTING*

330 US
WORLD COMMODITY FORECASTS. (Consists of two parts: Food, Feedstuffs and Beverages (1363-2604); Industrial Raw Materials (ISSN 1363-2612)) 1989. q. £395($745) per part. Economist Intelligence Unit, 111 W. 57th St., New York, NY 10019. TEL 212-554-0600; 800-938-4685. FAX 212-586-1182. TELEX 175567. URL: http://www.eiu.com. (UK addr.: Economist Intelligence Unit Ltd., Subscriptions Dept., P.O. Box 154, Dartford, Kent DA1 1QB, England. TEL 322-289194) (also avail. in microform from UMI) **Indexed:** Food Sci.& Tech.Abstr. **Document type:** trade publication.
Description: For investors, planners, analysts and businessmen; uses monitored trends to generate forecasts of spot prices for the next 18 months of 27 commodities.

WORLD DIRECTORY OF BUSINESS INFORMATION LIBRARIES. see *LIBRARY AND INFORMATION SCIENCES*

330 382 UK ISSN 0378-5920
HF1410
THE WORLD ECONOMY. 1968. 7/yr. £232($446) (foreign £282) (effective 1997). Blackwell Publishers Ltd., 108 Cowley Rd., Oxford OX4 1JF, England. TEL 44-1865-791100. FAX 44-1865-791347. E-mail: jnlinfo@ blackwellpublishers.co.uk; URL: http://www. blackwellpublishers.co.uk. Eds. John Whalley, David Greenaway. adv.; bk.rev. circ. 1,800. (reprint service avail. from SWZ) **Indexed:** A.B.C.Pol.Sci., ABI Inform., B.P.I., BPIA, Bus.Ind., ELLIS, Geo.Abstr.P.G., IBR, IDA, Int.Lab.Doc., Int.Polit.Sci.Abstr., J.of Econ.Lit., Key to Econ.Sci., Manage.Cont., Mar.Aff.Bibl., P.A.I.S., SCIMP, Soyabean Abstr., SSCI, Tr.& Indus.Ind., World Bank.Abstr. **Document type:** academic/scholarly publication.
—BLDSC (9354.760000); Genuine Article; KR SourceOne; SWETS; UMI; UnCover. **CCC**.
Incorporates: Lectures in Commercial Diplomacy (ISSN 0309-1961)
Refereed Serial

WORLD ENVIRONMENTAL BUSINESS HANDBOOK. see *ENVIRONMENTAL STUDIES*

330 UK ISSN 0954-3074
WORLD IN (YEAR). a. Economist Newspaper Ltd., 25 St. James's St., London SW1A 1HG, England. TEL 44-71-839-7000. FAX 44-71-839-2968. TELEX 24344-ECON-G.

330 CH
WORLD INDUSTRY. 1964. m. 4-7L, 59 Chung Shan N. Rd., Sec. 1, Taipei, Taiwan, Republic of China. Ed. Evan Y.C. Fong. adv. circ. 71,000.

330 US ISSN 1046-4778
HD1393.25
WORLD M & A NETWORK. (Merger and Acquisition) 1988. 4/yr. $345 (foreign $375) (effective 1997). International Executive Reports, Ltd., 717 D St., N.W., Ste. 300, Washington, DC 20004-2807. TEL 202-628-7767. FAX 202-628-6618. E-mail: http://www.deadnet.com.manda. Ed. John Bailey. adv.; circ. 1,000 (paid); 15,000 (controlled). **Document type:** corporate report.
Description: Lists privately held companies for sale and companies looking to purchase other companies: more than 2,000 merger and acquisition leads annually. Included are manufacturing, distribution and service companies with annual revenues from $1 million to $100 million.

330 US
WORLD PRESS. 1982. w. World Press, 2547 Monroe St., Dearborn, MI 48123-2159. TEL 313-563-0360. FAX 313-563-1448. Ed. Stephen R. Castor. adv.; bk.rev. **Document type:** newspaper.

330 CN
▼**WORLDPROFIT ONLINE MAGAZINE.** (Text in English) 1996. m. free. Worldprofit, Inc., 9010 - 106 Ave., Ste. 208, Edmonton, AB T5H 4K3, Canada. TEL 403-425-2466. E-mail: webmaster@ worldprofit.com; URL: http://www.worldprofit.com. Ed. Sandra Hunter. R&P contact: George Kosch. adv. contact: George Kosch. **Document type:** consumer publication.
● Available only online.
Description: Publishes business articles, including such topics as home business, internet advertising, as well as technical and marketing related subjects.

808.066 US ISSN 1084-3620
▼**WRITER & CLIENT NEWSLETTER.** 1995. m. $24 donation. Box 5652, Glendale, AZ 85312-5652. E-mail: essncom@primenet.com; URL: http://www.primenet.com/~essncom/writer.html. Ed. John E. Patterson.
● Also available online.

330 PL ISSN 0084-2974
WROCLAWSKI ROCZNIK EKONOMICZNY. 1968. a. price varies. (Polskie Towarzystwo Ekonomiczne) Biuro Wydawnictw i Bibliotek PAN, P.O. Box 24, 00-901 Warsaw, Poland. (Dist. by: Ars Polona, Krakowskie Przedmiescie 7, 00-068 Warsaw, Poland) Ed.Bd. circ. 750.

330 PL ISSN 0239-7951
WYZSZA SZKOLA PEDAGOGICZNA IM. KOMISJI EDUKACJI NARODOWEJ W KRAKOWIE. ROCZNIK NAUKOWO-DYDAKTYCZNY. PRACE EKONOMICZNO-SPOLECZNE. 1974. irreg., no.6, 1991. price varies. Wydawnictwo Naukowe W S P, Ul. Karmelicka 41, 31-128 Krakow, Poland. TEL 33-78-20. (Co-sponsor: Ministerstwo Edukacji Narodowej)

330 CC ISSN 1001-6546
XIANDAI QIYEJIA/MODERN ENTREPRENEURS. (Text in Chinese) m. Liaoning Sheng Shehui Kexueyuan - Liaoning Academy of Social Sciences, 86 Taishan Lu, Huanggu Qu, Shenyang, Liaoning 110031, People's Republic of China. TEL 460511. Ed. Sun Chengci.

330 CC ISSN 1000-355X
HC462.9
XIANDAI RIBEN JINGJI/CONTEMPORARY JAPANESE ECONOMICS. (Text in Chinese) 1982. bi-m. Y12. Jilin Daxue, Xiandai Riben Jingji Bianjibu, 83 Jiefang Dalu, Changchun, Jilin 130023, People's Republic of China. TEL 86-431-823189. FAX 86-431-823907. (Co-sponsor: China Nationwide Japanese Economic Institute) Ed. Bingdiao Yu. adv.; bk.rev. circ. 2,500. **Document type:** academic/scholarly publication.
Description: Introduces the development and management of all aspects of Japanese economy: industry, agriculture, transportation, finance and foreign trade.

330 CC
XIANGGANG JINGJI RIBAO/HONG KONG ECONOMIC TIMES. (Supplements avail.: H K Money Times (bi-m.); H K Information Technology Times (w.)) (Text in Chinese) 1988. d. (Mon.-Sat.). HK.$1800. 5F Kodak House II, 321 Java Rd., North Point, Hong Kong, People's Republic of China. TEL 2880-2888. FAX 2565-0676. Ed. Lawrence Fung. adv.: B&W page HK.$34560, color page HK.$69760; trim 208 x 140; adv. contact: Peter Man. film rev.; music rev.; play rev.; illus.; circ. 59,806 (paid). **Document type:** newspaper.
Description: Business newspaper that concentrates on economic news and reports. Also covers a diverse range of political, social and cultural topics.

330 CC
XINWEN BAO. (Text in Chinese) d. $157.40. 930 Jiangning Lu, Shanghai 200041, People's Republic of China. TEL 3252863. (Dist. in U.S. by: China Books & Periodicals, Inc., 2929 24th St., San Francisco, CA 94110) **Document type:** newspaper.

330 US
YALE UNIVERSITY. ECONOMIC GROWTH CENTER. THREE YEAR REPORT. 1961. every 3 yrs. free. Yale University, Economic Growth Center, Box 208269, New Haven, CT 06520-8269. TEL 203-432-3610. FAX 203-432-3898. circ. 500. circ. (controlled).
Former titles: Yale University. Economic Growth Center. Five Year Report & Yale University. Economic Growth Center. Annual Report.

330   IS
YARCHON CHESEV; prices and economic information. (Text in Hebrew) m. Cheshev Ltd., P.O. Box 40021, Tel Aviv 61 400, Israel.

330   CC   ISSN 1000-6052
HC411
YATAI JINGJI/ECONOMY OF ASIA AND PACIFIC RIM. (Text in Chinese) bi-m. Y6. Fujian Sheng Shehui Kexueyuan, Yatai Jingji Yanjiusuo - Fujian Academy of Social Sciences, Institute of Economy of Asia and Pacific Rim, Xiaoliucun, Huanchenglu, Fuzhou, Fujian 350001, People's Republic of China. TEL 552835. (Dist. overseas by: Jiangsu Publications Import & Export Corp., 56 Gao Yun Ling, Nanjing, Jiangsu, P.R.C.)
—BLDSC (1742.260330).
Description: Discusses issues in the developing Pacific Rim regional economy, including economic situations and problems, the open-door policy, management of joint ventures, and economic relationships between mainland China and Hong Kong, Taiwan, and Macao.

YEDA LEMEIDA; journal on taxation, law and economics. see BUSINESS AND ECONOMICS — Public Finance, Taxation

YOUR (YEAR) GUIDE TO SOCIAL SECURITY BENEFITS. see SOCIAL SERVICES AND WELFARE

330   GW
ZAHLEN ZUR WIRTSCHAFTLICHEN ENTWICKLUNG DER BUNDESREPUBLIK DEUTSCHLAND. 1962. a. DM.11.30. Deutscher Instituts Verlag GmbH, Postfach 510670, 50942 Cologne, Germany. TEL 49-221-4981452. FAX 49-221-4981592. Ed. Waltraut Peter. circ. 100,000. **Document type:** bulletin.

330   NE
ZAKENREISNIEUWS. 10/yr. free. Holland International Travel Group, Afdeling Reisbureaus, Treubstraat 16, 2288 EJ Rijswijk, Netherlands. circ. 12,000.

330   ZA
ZAMBIA. MINISTRY OF DECENTRALISATION. DISTRICT COUNCILS REVENUE AND CAPITAL ESTIMATES. a. Zambia Government Printing Department, P.O. Box 30316, Lusaka, Zambia. TEL 260-1-228724. circ. 900. **Document type:** government publication.

330 020   ZA
ZAMBIA. MINISTRY OF LEGAL AFFAIRS. ANNUAL REPORT. (Text in English) a. Zambia Government Printing Department, P.O. Box 30136, Lusaka, Zambia. FAX 260-1-228724. circ. 750. **Document type:** government publication.
Description: Reports on the year's news at the Ministry of Legal Affairs in Zambia.

330   GW   ISSN 0936-8787
HD28
ZEITSCHRIFT FUER PLANUNG/JOURNAL OF PLANNING. 1990. q. DM.431.60 (foreign DM.435.20) (effective 1998). Physica-Verlag GmbH und Co. (Subsidiary of: Springer-Verlag), Postfach 105280, 69042 Heidelberg, Germany. TEL 49-6221-487492. FAX 49-6221-487177. E-mail: physica@springer.de; URL: http://www.springer.de. (Subscr. to: Springer Verlag GmbH, Postfach 311340, 10643 Berlin, Germany. TEL 49-30-82787-0. FAX 49-30-82787448; Dist. in N. America by: Springer-Verlag New York Inc., Box 2485, Secaucus, NJ 07096-2485. TEL 212-460-1500. FAX 212-473-6272) Ed.Bd. circ. 700. (also avail. in microform from UMI) **Document type:** academic/scholarly publication.
—BLDSC (9484.245000); UMI. **CCC.**

330 300   GW   ISSN 0342-1783
HB5
ZEITSCHRIFT FUER WIRTSCHAFTS- UND SOZIALWISSENSCHAFTEN. (Supplements avail.) (Text and summaries in English and German) 1880. q. DM.148. (Gesellschaft fuer Wirtschafts- und Sozialwissenschaften) Duncker und Humblot GmbH, Postfach 410329, 12113 Berlin, Germany. TEL 49-30-7900060. FAX 49-30-7900631. E-mail: duh-werbung@t-online.de. Ed. Artur Woll. adv.; bk.rev.; index. circ. 2,400. (reprint service avail. from SCH) **Indexed:** A.B.C.Pol.Sci., ELLIS, IBR, Int.Polit.Sci.Abstr., J.of Econ.Lit., P.A.I.S.For.Lang.Ind., P.A.I.S. **Document type:** academic/scholarly publication.
—SWETS. **CCC.**
Formerly: Schmollers Jahrbuch fuer Wirtschafts- und Sozialwissenschaften (ISSN 0036-6234)

330   GW   ISSN 0936-8566
ZENTRALER STELLENANZEIGER MARKT UND CHANCE. 1955. w. free. Zentralstelle fuer Arbeitsvermittlung, Postfach 170545, 60079 Frankfurt a.M., Germany. TEL 49-69-71110. FAX 49-69-7111653. (looseleaf format) **Document type:** government publication.
Formerly: Markt und Chance.

330   CC
ZHEJIANG JINGJI/ZHEJIANG ECONOMICS. (Text in Chinese) m. Zhejiang Sheng Jihua Jingji Weiyuanhui - Zhejiang Provincial Committee of Planned Economics, No.31-1, Tianmushan Lu, Hangzhou, Zhejiang 310007, People's Republic of China. TEL 554997. Ed. Zhu Jialiang.

330   CC
ZHONGGUO JIHUA GUANLI/CHINESE JOURNAL OF PLANNED MANAGEMENT. (Text in Chinese) m. Guojia Jihua Weiyuanhui, Zhongguo Jihua Guanli Bianjibu, Sanlihe, Beijing 100824, People's Republic of China. TEL 8091803. Ed. Fang Weizhong.

330   CC
ZHONGGUO WUZI JINGJI/CHINESE COMMODITY ECONOMICS. (Text in Chinese) m. Wuzi Bu, 25, Yuetan Beijie, Beijing 100834, People's Republic of China. TEL 8392749. Ed. Liu Suinian.

330 951.104   CC   ISSN 1004-9835
ZHONGGUO XINAN/SOUTHWEST CHINA. (Text in Chinese, English) bi-m. Sichuan Waishi Bangongshi, 4th Fl., No. 72, Renmin Nanlu 2 Duan, Chengdu, Sichuan 610016, People's Republic of China. TEL 86-28-6635186. FAX 86-28-6635194. TELEX 60168 SCFAO CN. (Dist. overseas by: China International Book Trading Corp., P.O. Box 399, Beijing 100044, P.R. China)
Description: Covers Southwest China's economy and natural resources, investment environment and policies; introduces the area's beautiful sceneries, culture and customs.

ZHONGGUO YIYAO SHANGQING XINXI BAN/CHINA PHARMACEUTICAL BUSINESS INFORMATION. see PHARMACY AND PHARMACOLOGY

330   SZ
ZUGER GEWERBE AKTUELL. m. Kuendig Druck AG, Bundesplatz 10, CH-6304 Zug, Switzerland. TEL 042-212353. circ. 1,500.

330 630   PL   ISSN 0137-7299
ZYCIE GOSPODARCZE; tygodnik spoleczno-gospodarczy. (Supplement avail.: Srodowisko i Zycie) 1945. w. $240 (effective 1998). Oferta dla Kazdego, Spolka z o.o., Wiejska 12, 00-490 Warsaw, Poland. TEL 48-22-628-06-28. FAX 48-22-628-83-92. (Dist. by: Mezhdunarodnaya Kniga, B. Yakimanka 39, 117049 Moscow, Russia. TEL 7-095-2384967. FAX 7-095-2384634) Ed. Marzanna Witek. adv. contact: Adriana Blach. bk.rev.; charts; illus.; stat.; index. circ. 45,000. (also avail. in microfilm from UMI; back issues avail.) **Indexed:** AgroLibrex. **Document type:** newspaper.
Description: Presents economic situation and conditions for professional readers.

330   US
128 NEWS. 1986. m. $18. Reider Communications, 328 Lowell St., Wakefield, MA 01880. TEL 617-246-3883. FAX 617-246-5722. Ed. Sandie Horwitz; Pub. Martin Reider. R&P contact: Martin Reider. TEL 508-525-3081. adv. circ. 25,000. **Document type:** newspaper.
Description: Publishes articles on business issues, high technology, and lifestyle concerns of Massachusetts route 128.

BUSINESS AND ECONOMICS —
Abstracting, Bibliographies, Statistics

A B C BLUE BOOK: CANADIAN PERIODICALS. (Audit Bureau of Circulations) see PUBLISHING AND BOOK TRADE

A B C BLUE BOOK: U S AND CANADIAN BUSINESS PUBLICATIONS. (Audit Bureau of Circulations) see PUBLISHING AND BOOK TRADE

A B C BLUE BOOK: U S AND CANADIAN FARM PUBLICATIONS. (Audit Bureau of Circulations) see PUBLISHING AND BOOK TRADE

A B C BLUE BOOK: U S AND CANADIAN MAGAZINES. (Audit Bureau of Circulations) see PUBLISHING AND BOOK TRADE

016   US   ISSN 1062-5127
Z7164.C81
A B I - INFORM. (American Business Information) (Not avail. in printed format) 1971. m. U M I (Subsidiary of: Bell & Howell Company), 300 N. Zeeb Rd., Ann Arbor, MI 48106. TEL 313-761-4700; 800-521-0600. FAX 800-864-0019. URL: http://wwww.umi.com. (also avail. in magnetic tape) **Document type:** abstracting/indexing.
●Also available online. Vendor(s): Data-Star (INFO), European Space Agency (File no.30), Knight-Ridder Information, Inc. (File no.15), Lexis-Nexis (ABI), Ovid Technologies, Inc. (INFO), Questel Orbit Inc. (INFO), STN International (STN), UMI.
Also available on CD-ROM. Producer(s): UMI.
Description: Indexes and abstracts 1,300 business and management journals. Full-text articles are available from 600 journals.

330 011   AT
A B I X: AUSTRALASIAN BUSINESS INTELLIGENCE; the key to Australasian business, industry and trade information. 1981. every 4 wks. Aus.$3500 for CD-ROM. Business Intelligence Australia Pty. Ltd., McConnell Dowell House, 627 Chapel St., S. Yarra, Vic. 3141, Australia. TEL 61-3-98279088. FAX 61-3-98279099. URL: http://www.abix.com.au. Ed. Janet E. Thompson. R&P contact: Janet E. Thompson. adv. contact: Janet E. Thompson. (also avail. in diskette format; back issues avail.) **Document type:** abstracting/indexing.
●Also available online. Vendor(s): AUSINET, Kiwinet. Also available on CD-ROM.
Formerly: Australian Business Index (ISSN 0725-3109)
Description: Features Australian and New Zealand business, company news, finance, investment, industry news, and Reuters bussiness briefing.

330.9   UK
A B R E E S. (Abstracts Russian and East European Series) (Former name of issuing body: British Association for Slavonic and East European Studies) 1970. 4/yr. $699. A B R E E S Ltd., St. Andrews House, 77c Roupell St., London SE1 8SS, England. Ed. Ray Hutchings; Pub. Dan Re'em. adv.; abstr.; bibl.; index. circ. 200. (also avail. in microfiche) **Indexed:** Curr.Cont., PROMT. **Document type:** abstracting/indexing, academic/scholarly publication.
—**CCC.**
Formerly (until 1993): A B S E E S (Abstracts Soviet and East European Series) (ISSN 0044-5622); Incorporates: C R E E S Soviet Press Abstracts; Soviet Studies. Information Supplement (ISSN 0584-567X)
Description: Contains economic and business information covering Eastern Europe and Russia abstracted from newspapers and periodicals.

BUSINESS AND ECONOMICS — ABSTRACTING, BIBLIOGRAPHIES, STATISTICS

339 US ISSN 1070-9169
HB235.U6 CODEN: CLIIEX
A C C R A COST OF LIVING INDEX.* 1968. q. $100. American Chamber of Commerce Researchers Association, 4232 King St., Alexandria, VA 22302-1507. TEL 502-897-2890. FAX 502-894-9917. (Subscr. to: Box 6749, Louisville, KY 40206-6749) Ed. C.A. Kasdorf III. index; circ. 2,900 (paid). Indexed: SRI. **Document type**: abstracting/indexing.
   Former titles (until 1992): Cost of Living Index (ISSN 1048-2830) & A C C R A Inter-City Cost of Living Index (ISSN 0740-7130); Inter-City Cost of Living Indicators; Formed by the merger of: Cost of Living Indicators: Inter-City Index Report; Cost of Living Indicators: Price Report.
   Description: Data for 280-310 urban areas. Includes a composite index, six component indexes and average prices for 59 goods or services items.

338.9 016 US ISSN 0096-1507
HD82
A I D RESEARCH AND DEVELOPMENT ABSTRACTS. 1973. q. $10 (foreign $25). U.S. Agency for International Development, Policy Directorate, Center for Development Information and Evaluation, POL-CDIE-DI, Dept. of State, Washington, DC 20523-1802. TEL 202-875-4818. FAX 703-351-4039. circ. 5,000 (controlled). (also avail. in microfiche) Indexed: Rural Recreat.Tour.Abstr., Soils & Fert., World Agri.Econ.& Rural Sociol.Abstr. **Document type**: abstracting/indexing.
   Formerly: A I D Research Abstracts.

ABSTRACTS IN BIOCOMMERCE. see *BIOLOGY — Abstracting, Bibliographies, Statistics*

016 338 690 BU ISSN 0204-577X
Z7911 CODEN: ASLTD5
ABSTRACTS OF BULGARIAN SCIENTIFIC LITERATURE. INDUSTRY, BUILDING AND TRANSPORT.* (Editions in English and Russian) 1957. q. 6 lv. per no. (effective Jan. 1991). Central Technological Library, 52A, G.M. Dimitrov, ld., 1040 Sofia, Bulgaria. TEL 7-12-91. TELEX 22404. (Dist. by: Hemus, 6 Rouski Blvd., 1000 Sofia, Bulgaria) Ed. B. Balev. abstr. circ. 46. Indexed: Chem.Abstr. **Document type**: abstracting/indexing.
   —Linda Hall.

ABSTRACTS OF PUBLIC ADMINISTRATION, DEVELOPMENT AND ENVIRONMENT. see *PUBLIC ADMINISTRATION — Abstracting, Bibliographies, Statistics*

330 016 UK ISSN 0951-0079
HB1
ABSTRACTS OF WORKING PAPERS IN ECONOMICS. 1986. 5/yr. £166($250) (effective 1998). Cambridge University Press, Edinburgh Bldg., Shaftesbury Rd., Cambridge CB2 2RU, England. TEL 44-1223-312393. FAX 44-1223-315052. E-mail: information@cup.cam.ac.uk; URL: http://www.cup.org/journals/CUPJNLS.html. (N. America addr.: Cambridge University Press, Journals Dept., 40 W. 20th St., New York, NY 10011. TEL 212-924-3900. FAX 212-691-3239) Ed. Halbert White. R&P contact: Linda Nicol. adv. contact: Rebecca Symons. (also avail. in diskette format; back issues avail.; reprint service avail. from SWZ) **Document type**: abstracting/indexing, academic/scholarly publication.
   ●Also available online.
   Also available on CD-ROM.
   —UMI.
   Description: Publishes research in economics, finance, and econometrics; complete bibliographic information on recent working papers produced by scholars at more than 70 research institutions worldwide.

330 TS
ABU DHABI. DA'IRAT AL-TAKHTIT. AL-NASHRAH AL-SANAWIYYAH LI-AS'AR AL-TAJZI'AH/ABU DHABI. PLANNING ADMINISTRATION. ANNUAL BULLETIN OF RETAIL PRICES. (Text in Arabic, English) 1978. a. Planning Administration, Statistical Department - Da'irat al-Takhtit, Al-Sha'abah al-Ihsa'iyyah, P.O. Box 12, Abu Dhabi, United Arab Emirates. TEL 727200. circ. 500 (controlled).

330 TS
ABU DHABI. DA'IRAT AL-TAKHTIT. AL-NASHRAH AL-SHAHRIYYAH LI-AS'AR AL-TAJZI'AH/ABU DHABI. PLANNING ADMINISTRATION. MONTHLY BULLETIN OF RETAIL PRICES. (Text in Arabic, English) 1977. m. Planning Administration, Statistical Department - Da'irat al-Takhtit, Al-Sha'abah al-Ihsa'iyyah, P.O. Box 12, Abu Dhabi, United Arab Emirates. TEL 727200. circ. controlled.
   Description: Provides a comprehensive overview of all consumer prices in Abu Dhabi markets.

330 TS
ABU DHABI. FOREIGN TRADE STATISTICS/ABU DHABI. IHSA'IYYAT AL-TIJARAH AL-KHARIJIYYAH. (Text in English) 1978. m. Government of Abu Dhabi, P.O. Box 255, Abu Dhabi, United Arab Emirates. TEL 720700. circ. controlled.
   Description: Comprehensive statistical information on trade between Abu Dhabi and the world, based upon customs declarations.

ACCOUNTING & FINANCE ABSTRACTS. see *COMPUTERS — Abstracting, Bibliographies, Statistics*

657 US ISSN 1063-0287
Z7164.C81
ACCOUNTING AND TAX INDEX. 1920. q. (plus a. cumulation). U M I (Subsidiary of: Bell & Howell Company), 300 N. Zeeb Rd., Ann Arbor, MI 48106. TEL 313-761-4700; 800-521-0600. FAX 800-864-0019. URL: http://wwww.umi.com. Ed. Paula McCoy. (also avail. in microform from UMI) **Document type**: abstracting/indexing.
   ●Also available online. Vendor(s): Knight-Ridder Information, Inc. (File no. 485), UMI.
   Also available on CD-ROM.
   —UMI.
   Formerly (until 1992): Accountants' Index (ISSN 0748-7975)

657 016 US ISSN 0007-7992
ACCOUNTING ARTICLES. 1965. m. $533. C C H Incorporated, 2700 Lake Cook Rd., Riverwoods, IL 60015. TEL 847-267-7000; 800-835-5224. FAX 800-224-8299. bk.rev.; abstr.; bibl.; cum.index. (looseleaf format)
   Formerly: C C H Accounting Articles.

657 808.0666 US
ACCOUNTING WRITING; A P W C bibliography series. 1993. irreg. $5 to non-members; members $3. Association of Professional Communication Consultants, 3924 S. Troost, Tulsa, OK 74105. TEL 918-743-4793. (Subscr. to: Reva Daniel, 1301 Post Rd., Clinton, MS 39056) Ed. Dana Gulling Mead. (looseleaf format) **Document type**: bibliography.
   Description: Helps accountants write effectively for a variety of audiences.

ACROSS AMERICA. see *GEOGRAPHY*

AFFAERSBANKERNA; samtliga bankaktiebolag. see *BUSINESS AND ECONOMICS — Banking And Finance*

353.001 US
AFFIRMATIVE EMPLOYMENT STATISTICS. 1976. biennial. $35. U.S. Office of Personnel Management, Personnel Systems and Oversight Group, Statistical Analysis and Services Division, 1900 E. St., N.W., Washington, DC 20415. TEL 703-487-4650. FAX 202-606-1719. (Subscr. to: NTIS, 5285 Port Royal Rd., Springfield, VA 22161) (also avail. in microfiche) **Document type**: government publication.
   Formerly (until 1980): Equal Employment Opportunity Statistics (ISSN 0161-245X); **Supersedes**: Minority Group Employment in the Federal Government (ISSN 0090-3531); (1966-1975): Study of Employment of Women in the Federal Government (ISSN 0097-7764)

338.91 332 IV
AFRICAN DEVELOPMENT BANK. COMPENDIUM OF STATISTICS/BANQUE AFRICAINE DE DEVELOPPEMENT. COMPENDIUM DE STATISTIQUES. (Text in English, French) a. African Development Bank, B.P. 1387, Abidjan 01, Ivory Coast. TEL 225-20-44-44. FAX 225-20-49-48. TELEX 225-23717.

338.91 332 IV
AFRICAN DEVELOPMENT BANK. SELECTED STATISTICS ON REGIONAL MEMBER COUNTRIES/BANQUE AFRICAINE DE DEVELOPPEMENT. STATISTIQUES CHOISIES SUR LES PAYS-MEMBRES REGIONAUX. (Text in English, French) a. African Development Bank, B.P. 1387, Abidjan 01, Ivory Coast. TEL 225-20-44-44. FAX 225-20-49-48. TELEX 225-23717.

310 US
ALABAMA SUBSTATE LABOR MARKET NEWS. 1954. m. free. Department of Industrial Relations, Research and Statistics Division, Industrial Relations Bldg., Rm. 427, 649 Monroe St., Montgomery, AL 36131. TEL 334-242-8855. FAX 334-242-2543. E-mail: hliittlej@dsmd.dsmd.state.al.us; URL: http://129.66.172.4/dir/alalmi.htm; http://webserver.dsmd.state.al.us. Ed.Bd. circ. 3,400. **Document type**: government publication.
   Formerly: Alabama Labor Market News.
   Description: Provides information on non-agricultural wage and salary for the State of Alabama.

331 US ISSN 1063-3782
HD5725.A4
ALASKA EMPLOYMENT AND EARNINGS REPORT. 1959. a. free. Department of Labor, Research and Analysis Section, Box 25501, Juneau, AK 99802-5501. TEL 907-465-4520. FAX 907-465-2101. stat. circ. 600. **Document type**: government publication.
   Formerly: Alaska Statistical Quarterly.

330 CN ISSN 0319-4264
HC117.A6
ALBERTA ECONOMIC ACCOUNTS.* 1976. a. Bureau of Statistics, Alberta Treasury, 9515-107 St., Edmonton, AB T5K 2C3, Canada. TEL 403-427-3058. FAX 403-427-0409. TELEX 037-43237. **Document type**: government publication.

316 AE
ALGERIA. OFFICE NATIONAL DES STATISTIQUES. INDICES DES PRIX A LA CONSOMMATION. (Subseries of: Algeria. Office National des Statistiques. Donnees Statistiques (ISSN 1111-5939)) (Text in French) m. 500 din. Office National des Statistiques - Al-Diwan al-Watani lil-Ihsa'iyat, 8 & 10 rue des Moussebiline, B.P. 202 Ferhat Boussad, Algiers, Algeria. TEL 213-64-77-90. (back issues avail.) **Document type**: government publication.

332.1 016 US
AMERICAN BANKER INDEX. Variant title: Index to the American Banker. 1971. m. U M I (Subsidiary of: Bell & Howell Company), 300 N. Zeeb Rd., Ann Arbor, MI 48106. TEL 313-761-4700; 800-521-0600. FAX 800-864-0019. URL: http://www.umi.com. cum.index. (also avail. in microform from UMI; magnetic tape) **Document type**: abstracting/indexing.
   ●Also available online. Vendor(s): Knight-Ridder Information, Inc., UMI.
   Former titles (until 1982): Bell and Howell Newspaper Index to the American Banker (ISSN 0195-6426); (until 1979): Index to the American Banker (ISSN 0046-8916)

330 UK
▼**AMERICAN COMPANIES: GUIDE TO SOURCES OF INFORMATION/SOCIETES AMERICAINES: REPERTOIRE DES SOURCES DE DOCUMENTATION/AMERICANISCHE HANDELSGESELLSCHAFTEN: HANDBUCH DER INFORMATIONSQUELLEN.** 1996. irreg. £78($163) C.B.D. Research Ltd., 15 Wickham Rd., Beckenham, Kent BR3 2JS, England. TEL 44-181-650-7745. FAX 44-181-650-0768. **Document type**: directory.
   Description: Lists and describes in detail 1,500 information sources.

330 US
AMERICAN COST OF LIVING SURVEY. 1993. irreg., 2nd ed., 1995. $149 (effective 1997). Gale Research, 835 Penobscot Bldg., 645 Griswold St., Detroit, MI 48226-4094. TEL 313-961-2242; 800-877-4253. FAX 800-414-5043. E-mail: daniel_snyder@gale.com.

BUSINESS AND ECONOMICS — ABSTRACTING, BIBLIOGRAPHIES, STATISTICS

331.11 US ISSN 1055-7628
HD4973
AMERICAN SALARIES AND WAGES SURVEY. a. 4th ed., 1997. $105 (effective 1997). Gale Research, 835 Penobscot Bldg., 645 Griswold St., Detroit, MI 48226-4094. TEL 313-961-2242; 800-877-4253. FAX 800-414-5043. E-mail: daniel_snyder@gale.com. Ed. Helen S. Fisher. (also avail. in diskette format; magnetic tape)

330 317 US ISSN 0066-0736
HA1
AMERICAN STATISTICAL ASSOCIATION. BUSINESS AND ECONOMIC STATISTICS SECTION. PROCEEDINGS. 1954. a. price varies. American Statistical Association, 1429 Duke St., Alexandria, VA 22314-3415. TEL 703-684-1221. FAX 703-684-2037. (also avail. in microform from UMI) **Indexed:** Curr.Ind.Stat. **Document type:** proceedings.
—BLDSC (6636.200000); UMI.

338 US
AMERICAN STATISTICAL ASSOCIATION. SECTION ON QUALITY AND PRODUCTIVITY. PROCEEDINGS. 1992. a. prie varies. American Statistical Association, 1429 Duke St., Alexandria, VA 22314-3415. TEL 703-684-1221. FAX 703-684-2037. **Indexed:** Curr.Ind.Stat. **Document type:** proceedings.

382 CU
ANALISIS ANUAL DEL MERCADO DEL AZUCAR. 1981. a. C.$14. (Ministerio del Comercio Exterior (MINCEX) Empresa Cubazucar, Calle 23 No. 55, Vedado, Havana, Cuba. TEL 70-9742. TELEX 51-1147.
Description: Covers market, prices and statistics on sugar. Analyzes present and future developments.

330 UK ISSN 1351-3044
ANBAR MANAGEMENT OF QUALITY ABSTRACTS. 1994. bi-m. £699($1099) (foreign Aus.$1399) (effective 1998). M C B University Press Ltd., Anbar Electronic Intelligence, 60-62 Toller Ln., Bradford, W. Yorks BD8 9BY, England. TEL 44-1274-499821. FAX 44-1274-547143. E-mail: spuesey@anbar.co.uk; URL: http://www.anbar.co.uk/anbar.htm. (N. American subscr. to: M C B University Press Ltd., Box 1943, Birmingham, AL 35201) Ed. Eric Sandelands. **Document type:** academic/scholarly publication.
—BLDSC (0900.180000).

382 316 AO ISSN 0066-1848
ANGOLA. DIRECCAO DOS SERVICOS DE ESTATISTICA. ESTATISTICAS DO COMERCIO EXTERNO. (Text in Portuguese) 1938. irreg. Direccao dos Servicos de Estatistica, C.P. 1215, Luanda, Angola. stat. circ. 750.

382 316 TG
ANNUAIRE DES STATISTIQUES DU COMMERCE EXTERIEUR DU TOGO. a. latest 1977. 4000 Fr.CFA. Direction de la Statistique, Boite Postale 118, Lome, Togo.

338 US ISSN 0082-9307
HD9724
ANNUAL SURVEY OF MANUFACTURES. 1949. a. (except for years ending in "2" or "7". price varies. U.S. Bureau of the Census, Customer Services, Washington, DC 20233. TEL 301-457-4100. FAX 301-457-4714. URL: http://www.census.gov/. (Orders to: Superintendent of Documents, U.S. Government Printing Office, Box 371954, Pittsburgh, PA 15250-7954. TEL 202-512-1800. FAX 202-512-2233) **Document type:** government publication.
●Also available online. Vendor(s): CompuServe, Inc., Knight-Ridder Information, Inc.

330 IT
ANNUARIO GEOECONOMICO MONDIALE; commercio e produzioni. a. Istituto Geografico de Agostini, Corso dela Vittoria 91, 28100 Novara, Italy. TEL 0321-422439. FAX 0321-422460. Ed. Roberto Besana.

330 IT
ANNUARIO KOMPASS REPERTORIO GENERALE DELL'ECONOMIA ITALIANA. 1961. a. L.500000. Kompass Italia s.p.a., Via G. Servais 125, 10146 Turin, Italy. Ed. Filiberto Dani. adv.: color page L.5150000. circ. 15,000.

332 MX ISSN 0188-3860
HG5161
ANUARIO BURSATIL. English edition: Annual Stock Exchange Statistics Report. a. $40 (effective May 1996). Bolsa Mexicana de Valores, S.A. de C.V. - Mexican Stock Exchange, Paseo de la Reforma 255, 06500 Mexico D.F., Mexico. TEL 525-726-6791. FAX 525-591-05-34.
Description: Contains facts and figures, statistical data of brokerage firms, international markets, foreign investment, price trends, corporate actions, and dividends. Includes information on Mexican securities listed on foreign markets.

382 UY ISSN 0797-8243
ANUARIO DE IMPORTACION - EXPORTACION DEL URUGUAY. 1957. a. $130 (effective 1996). Centro de Estadisticas Nacionales y Comercio Internacional del Uruguay, Misiones 1361, Casilla de Correo 1510, 11000 Montevideo, Uruguay. TEL 598-2-952930. FAX 598-2-954578. Ed. C. Vetesi. adv. circ. 2,500. **Document type:** trade publication.

382.09 318 VE ISSN 1013-3771
ANUARIO DEL COMERCIO EXTERIOR DE VENEZUELA. (In 2 vols.: Exportaciones and Importaciones) a. Bs.1000 (for 1992 ed.). Oficina Central de Estadistica e Informatica, Apdo. de Correos 4593, Carmelitas, Caracas 1010A, Venezuela. TEL 58-2-782-11-33. FAX 58-2-781-13-80. TELEX 21241.
Former titles: Estadisticas del Comercio Exterior de Venezuela. Periodicidad Anual; Estadisticas del Comercio Exterior de Venezuela. Boletin.
Description: Covers import-export statistics, international trade and manufacturing of products.

382 318 GT ISSN 0570-426X
ANUARIO ESTADISTICO CENTROAMERICANO DE COMERCIO EXTERIOR. 1964. a. $15. Secretaria Permanente del Tratado General de Integracion Economica Centroamericana - Permanent Secretariat of the General Treaty of Central American Economic Integration, 4a Avda. 10-25, Zona 14, Apdo. 1237, 01901 Guatemala, Guatemala.

382 318 MX
ANUARIO ESTADISTICO DE COMERCIO EXTERIOR DE LOS ESTADOS UNIDOS MEXICANOS. 1941-1979; resumed. a. Mex.$49.50($17) Instituto Nacional de Estadistica, Geografia e Informatica, Secretaria de Programacion y Presupuesto, Prol. Heroe de Nacozari 2301 Sur, Puerto 11, Acceso, 20270 Aguascalientes Ags., Mexico. TEL 49-18-19-48. FAX 491-807-39. circ. 500.

ANUARIO ESTADISTICO - SEGUROS Y PREVISION SOCIAL. see INSURANCE — Abstracting, Bibliographies, Statistics

330.9 US ISSN 1045-4195
HA241
ARIZONA STATISTICAL ABSTRACT. 1976. irreg., latest 1993 edition. $27.95 (foreign $36). University of Arizona, College of Business and Public Administration, Economic and Business Research Program, McClelland Hall 204K, Tucson, AZ 85721. TEL 520-621-2155. FAX 520-621-2150. E-mail: pmontoya@bpa.arizona.edu.
Description: Aims to develop and disseminate economic and socioeconomic data on the state of Arizona in quantitative terms over time; to permit comparison of the economic and social attainments of subareas of the state: cities, counties and metropolitan areas; and to relate Arizona's activities to those of neighboring southwestern states and to the nation as a whole.

310 US
ARKANSAS. EMPLOYMENT SECURITY DEPARTMENT. STATISTICAL REVIEW. q. free. Employment Security Department, Research and Information Section, Box 2981, Little Rock, AR 72203. TEL 501-682-3119.
Formerly: Arkansas. Department of Labor. Employment Security Division. Statistical Review.

330 II ISSN 0970-8162
ARTHA SUCHI. 1983. q. Rs.300 (foreign $30). National Council of Applied Economic Research, Publication Division, Parisila Bhawan, 11, Indraprastha Estate, New Delhi 110 002, India. TEL 91-11-3317861. FAX 91-11-3327164. Ed. N.J. Sebastian. index, cum.index. circ. 120. **Document type:** abstracting/indexing.
Description: A computerized index to government reports, journal articles and newspaper writeups in the field of Indian economics.

338.025 016 UK ISSN 1352-3198
HF5381.A1
ASIAN AND AUSTRALASIAN COMPANIES. 1993. irreg. £87($174) C.B.D. Research Ltd., 15 Wickham Rd., Beckenham, Kent BR3 2JS, England. TEL 44-181-650-7745. FAX 44-181-650-0768. (Dist. in the U.S. by: Hoover's Inc., 6448 Hwy. 290 E., Ste. E. 104, Austin, TX 78723) **Document type:** directory.
Description: Compiles 2,000 sources of company information available in Asia, Australia, and Oceania.

332.1 PH ISSN 0116-2799
HC411
ASIAN DEVELOPMENT BANK. STATISTICAL REPORT SERIES. (Text in English) irreg., no. 15, 1991. Asian Development Bank, Economics and Development Resource Center, P.O. Box 789, 1099 Manila, Philippines. TEL 632-711-3851. FAX 632-741-7961. TELEX 29066 ADB PH. **Indexed:** IDA.

338.91 UK ISSN 0818-9935
HC411 CODEN: AELIEB
ASIAN-PACIFIC ECONOMIC LITERATURE. 1987. s-a. £57($90) (foreign £57) (effective 1997). (Australian National University, Research School of Pacific and Asian Studies, Economics Division) Blackwell Publishers Ltd., 108 Cowley Rd., Oxford OX4 1JF, England. TEL 44-1865-791100. FAX 44-1865-791347. E-mail: jnlinfo@blackwellpublishers.co.uk; URL: http://www.blackwellpublishers.co.uk. Ed. H.W. Arndt. bk.rev.; index. **Indexed:** CLOSS, Geo.Abstr., IDA. **Document type:** bibliography.
—BLDSC (1742.705210); SWETS. **CCC.**
Description: Covers economic and related development topics in Hong Kong, Indonesia, Taiwan, mainland China, and other countries of the region.

330 310 AT
AUSTRALIA. BUREAU OF STATISTICS. A GUIDE TO THE AUSTRALIAN NATIONAL ACCOUNTS. 1990. irreg., latest 1994. Aus.$10. Australian Bureau of Statistics, P.O. Box 10, Belconnen, A.C.T. 2616, Australia. **Document type:** government publication.
Description: Contains a brief outline of the most important features of the national accounts.

339 310 AT
AUSTRALIA. BUREAU OF STATISTICS. A GUIDE TO THE CONSUMER INDEX. 1978. irreg., latest 1993. Aus.$10. Australian Bureau of Statistics, P.O. Box 10, Belconnen, A.C.T. 2616, Australia. **Document type:** government publication.

AUSTRALIA. BUREAU OF STATISTICS. AGRICULTURAL INDUSTRIES, FINANCIAL STATISTICS, AUSTRALIA. see AGRICULTURE — Abstracting, Bibliographies, Statistics

AUSTRALIA. BUREAU OF STATISTICS. AGRICULTURAL INDUSTRIES, FINANCIAL STATISTICS, AUSTRALIA, PRELIMINARY ESTIMATES. see AGRICULTURE — Abstracting, Bibliographies, Statistics

332 310 AT
AUSTRALIA. BUREAU OF STATISTICS. ANNUAL STATISTICS ON FINANCIAL INSTITUTIONS. 1990. a. Australian Bureau of Statistics, P.O. Box 10, Belconnen, A.C.T. 2616, Australia. **Document type:** government publication.

332.6 AT ISSN 1035-7378
AUSTRALIA. BUREAU OF STATISTICS. ASSETS OF SUPERANNUATION FUNDS AND APPROVED DEPOSIT FUNDS. 1989. q. Aus.$11 per no. Australian Bureau of Statistics, P.O. Box 10, Belconnen, A.C.T. 2616, Australia. **Document type:** government publication.
Description: Provides data on the assets of the superannuation industry.

BUSINESS AND ECONOMICS — ABSTRACTING, BIBLIOGRAPHIES, STATISTICS

330 310 — AT — ISSN 1320-811X
AUSTRALIA. BUREAU OF STATISTICS. AUSTRALIAN BUSINESS EXPECTATIONS. 1993. q. Aus.$25 per no. Australian Bureau of Statistics, P.O. Box 10, Belconnen, A.C.T. 2616, Australia. **Document type:** government publication.
  Description: Estimates of percentage change in key business performance indicators obtained from a sample survey of business in all industries except general government and agriculture.

330 — AT — ISSN 1320-808X
AUSTRALIA. BUREAU OF STATISTICS. AUSTRALIAN CAPITAL TERRITORY BUSINESS INDICATORS. 1993. m. Aus.$13 per no. Australian Bureau of Statistics, P.O. Box 10, Belconnen, A.C.T. 2616, Australia. **Document type:** government publication.
  Description: A monthly summary of business related statistics for the Australian Capital Territory, with Australian and other State comparisons.

330 310 — AT
AUSTRALIA. BUREAU OF STATISTICS. AUSTRALIAN CONSUMER PRICE INDEX: CONCEPTS, SOURCES AND METHODS. 1984. irreg., latest 1995. Aus.$30. Australian Bureau of Statistics, P.O. Box 10, Belconnen, A.C.T. 2616, Australia. **Document type:** government publication.

330 — HC601 — ISSN 1035-865X
AUSTRALIA. BUREAU OF STATISTICS. AUSTRALIAN ECONOMIC INDICATORS. 1991. m. Aus.$26 per no. Australian Bureau of Statistics, P.O. Box 10, Belconnen, A.C.T. 2616, Australia. **Document type:** government publication.
  Description: Presents a statistical summary of recent developments in the Australian economy.

331.11 310 — AT — ISSN 1038-927X
AUSTRALIA. BUREAU OF STATISTICS. AUSTRALIAN LABOUR MARKET. 1992. a. Aus.$17.50. Australian Bureau of Statistics, P.O. Box 10, Belconnen, A.C.T. 2616, Australia. **Document type:** government publication.
  Description: Contains a series of articles based on data primarily released from the labor household survey program in the previous year.

330 — AT — ISSN 1033-3010
AUSTRALIA. BUREAU OF STATISTICS. AUSTRALIAN NATIONAL ACCOUNTS: CAPITAL STOCK. 1985. a. Aus.$24. Australian Bureau of Statistics, P.O. Box 10, Belconnen, A.C.T. 2616, Australia. **Document type:** government publication.
  Formerly: Australian National Accounts: Estimates of Capital Stock.
  Description: Estimates consumption of fixed capital, gross and net capital stock and gross fixed capital expenditure.

332 310 — AT — ISSN 1038-4286
AUSTRALIA. BUREAU OF STATISTICS. AUSTRALIAN NATIONAL ACCOUNTS: FINANCIAL ACCOUNTS. 1989. q. Aus.$51. Australian Bureau of Statistics, P.O. Box 10, Belconnen, A.C.T. 2616, Australia. **Document type:** government publication.
  Description: Contains information about the level (stock) of financial assets and liabilities of each sector of the economy, as well as information about financial transactions between the sectors.

330 — AT — ISSN 0727-9434
AUSTRALIA. BUREAU OF STATISTICS. AUSTRALIAN NATIONAL ACCOUNTS: INPUT-OUTPUT TABLES. 1958. triennial. Aus.$50 per no. Australian Bureau of Statistics, P.O. Box 10, Belconnen, A.C.T. 2616, Australia. **Document type:** government publication.
  Formerly: Australian National Accounts: Input-Output Multipliers.
  Description: Provides input by industry and output by commodity group, industry by industry flow matrices, direct and total requirement coefficient matrices.

330 — AT — ISSN 0727-1476
AUSTRALIA. BUREAU OF STATISTICS. AUSTRALIAN NATIONAL ACCOUNTS: INPUT-OUTPUT TABLES (COMMODITY DETAILS). 1968. triennial. Aus.$50 per no. Australian Bureau of Statistics, P.O. Box 10, Belconnen, A.C.T. 2616, Australia. **Document type:** government publication.
  Description: Provides detailed information about the input-output commodity classification, value of Australian production, and imports and exports for over 1,000 commodities.

330 — AT — ISSN 1036-1324
AUSTRALIA. BUREAU OF STATISTICS. AUSTRALIAN NATIONAL ACCOUNTS: MULTIFACTOR PRODUCTIVITY. 1989. a. Aus.$16.50. Australian Bureau of Statistics, P.O. Box 10, Belconnen, A.C.T. 2616, Australia. **Document type:** government publication.
  Description: Presents average annual growth rates over growth-cycle periods of estimates of multifactor productivity for the market and non-farm market sectors of the Australian economy.

339.394 — AT — ISSN 0067-1983
HC610.I5
AUSTRALIA. BUREAU OF STATISTICS. AUSTRALIAN NATIONAL ACCOUNTS: NATIONAL INCOME AND EXPENDITURE (ANNUAL). 1948. a. Aus.$35. Australian Bureau of Statistics, P.O. Box 10, Belconnen, A.C.T. 2616, Australia. TEL 062-527911. FAX 062-516009. illus. circ. 676. **Document type:** government publication.
  Description: Presents detailed information about Australian national accounts, including income components of gross domestic product, corporate trading enterprises, and financial enterprises.

339 319 — AT — ISSN 1322-2902
AUSTRALIA. BUREAU OF STATISTICS. AUSTRALIAN NATIONAL ACCOUNTS: NATIONAL INCOME AND EXPENDITURE AND PRODUCT. 1960. q. Aus.$29 per no. Australian Bureau of Statistics, P.O. Box 10, Belconnen, A.C.T. 2616, Australia. TEL 062-527911. FAX 062-516009. charts. circ. 786. (processed) **Document type:** government publication.
  Incorporates (1988-1992): Australian National Accounts: Gross Product, Employment and Hours Worked (ISSN 1030-9047); Former titles: Australian National Accounts: National Income and Expenditure (Quarterly) (ISSN 1031-5128); Quarterly Estimates of National Income and Expenditure, Australia (ISSN 1030-0988); National Income and Expenditure, Quarterly Estimates (ISSN 0004-8577)
  Description: Presents detailed quarterly national accounts at both current prices and average prices in both original and seasonally adjusted terms.

330 310 — AT — ISSN 0819-7423
AUSTRALIA. BUREAU OF STATISTICS. AUSTRALIAN NATIONAL ACCOUNTS: STATE ACCOUNTS (ANNUAL). 1985. a. Aus.$29. Australian Bureau of Statistics, P.O. Box 10, Belconnen, A.C.T. 2616, Australia. **Document type:** government publication.
  Description: Contains dissections for the last 12 years of various national accounting aggregates by state and territory, including household income, private consumption expenditure, farm income, prices, wages and gross operating surplus by industry.

330 310 — AT — ISSN 1039-2610
AUSTRALIA. BUREAU OF STATISTICS. AUSTRALIAN NATIONAL ACCOUNTS: STATE ACCOUNTS (QUARTERLY). 1992. q. Aus.$29 per no. Australian Bureau of Statistics, P.O. Box 10, Belconnen, A.C.T. 2616, Australia. **Document type:** government publication.

332 310 — AT
AUSTRALIA. BUREAU OF STATISTICS. AVERAGE MONTHLY EXCHANGE RATES. 1990. m. Australian Bureau of Statistics, P.O. Box 10, Belconnen, A.C.T. 2616, Australia. **Document type:** government publication.
  Description: Covers averages of daily exchange rates for about 35 currencies, including both the telegraphic transfer buying rate and selling rate, and final trading day values against the major currencies.

332 — AT — ISSN 0812-5546
AUSTRALIA. BUREAU OF STATISTICS. AVERAGE RETAIL PRICES OF SELECTED ITEMS, EIGHT CAPITAL CITIES. 1962. q. Aus.$10 per no. Australian Bureau of Statistics, P.O. Box 10, Belconnen, A.C.T. 2616, Australia. **Document type:** government publication.
  Description: Contains average retail prices of selected items for each of the six state capitals, and Canberra and Darwin.

331.2 — AT — ISSN 1031-0584
AUSTRALIA. BUREAU OF STATISTICS. AVERAGE WEEKLY EARNING, AUSTRALIA, PRELIMINARY. 1975. q. Aus.$11 per no. Australian Bureau of Statistics, P.O. Box 10, Belconnen, A.C.T. 2616, Australia. **Document type:** government publication.
  Description: Contains preliminary estimates for Australia of average weekly ordinary time earnings and average weekly total earnings for full-time adult employees and average weekly total earnings for all employees.

331 — AT
AUSTRALIA. BUREAU OF STATISTICS. AVERAGE WEEKLY EARNINGS, STATE AND AUSTRALIA. 1967. q. Aus.$15 per no. Australian Bureau of Statistics, P.O. Box 10, Belconnen, A.C.T. 2616, Australia. **Document type:** government publication.

331.2 319 — AT — ISSN 0812-0137
AUSTRALIA. BUREAU OF STATISTICS. AWARD RATES OF PAY INDEXES, AUSTRALIA. 1962. m. Aus.$15 per no. Australian Bureau of Statistics, P.O. Box 10, Belconnen, A.C.T. 2616, Australia. TEL 062-527911. FAX 062-516009. stat. circ. 977. (processed) **Document type:** government publication.
  Formed by the 1982 merger of: Wage Rates, Indexes, Australia, Preliminary (ISSN 0812-0145); Which was formerly (until 1979): Wage Rates Indexes, Preliminary (ISSN 0812-0382); Wage Rates, Australia (ISSN 0812-0153); Which was formerly (until 1979): Wage Rates.
  Description: Provides index numbers of weighted average minimum weekly and hourly award rates of pay for wage and salary earners, classified by sex, industry and occupation group.

336 — AT
HF275
AUSTRALIA. BUREAU OF STATISTICS. BALANCE OF PAYMENTS, AUSTRALIA (ANNUAL). 1946. a. Aus.$36 (foreign Aus.$42.10). Australian Bureau of Statistics, P.O. Box 10, Belconnen, A.C.T. 2616, Australia. TEL 062-527911. FAX 062-516009. circ. 471. **Document type:** government publication.
  Former titles: Balance of Payments (Canberra, 1963) (ISSN 0045-0111); (until 1963): Australian Balance of Payments.
  Description: Provides detailed balance of payments tables on current and capital account transactions. Includes historical estimates classified by region, tables of related statistics, tables of reconciling foreign trade statistics, and levels of official reserve assets with balance of payments data.

336 310 — AT — ISSN 0313-2773
AUSTRALIA. BUREAU OF STATISTICS. BALANCE OF PAYMENTS, AUSTRALIA (CANBERRA, 1976). 1976. m. Aus.$16.50 per no. Australian Bureau of Statistics, P.O. Box 10, Belconnen, A.C.T. 2616, Australia. (also avail. in diskette format) **Document type:** government publication.
  Description: Provides preliminary estimates of the principal balance of payments aggregates and balances.

336 310 — AT
AUSTRALIA. BUREAU OF STATISTICS. BALANCE OF PAYMENTS, AUSTRALIA - CONCEPTS, SOURCES AND METHODS. 1981. irreg., latest 1990. Aus.$35. Australian Bureau of Statistics, P.O. Box 10, Belconnen, A.C.T. 2616, Australia. **Document type:** government publication.
  Description: Provides a comprehensive description of the concepts and structure of the Australian balance of payments and of the data sources and methods used to compile the statistics contained in Australian balance of payments publications.

336 310 — AT — ISSN 0819-114X
AUSTRALIA. BUREAU OF STATISTICS. BALANCE OF PAYMENTS, AUSTRALIA (QUARTERLY). 1961. q. Aus.$27. Australian Bureau of Statistics, P.O. Box 10, Belconnen, A.C.T. 2616, Australia. (also avail. in diskette format) **Document type:** government publication.
  Description: Provides detailed quarterly balance of payments tables on current and capital transactions.

BUSINESS AND ECONOMICS — ABSTRACTING, BIBLIOGRAPHIES, STATISTICS

336 310   AT
AUSTRALIA. BUREAU OF STATISTICS. BALANCE OF PAYMENTS, AUSTRALIA - SUMMARY OF CONCEPTS, SOURCES AND METHODS. 1988. irreg., latest 1995. Aus.$25. Australian Bureau of Statistics, P.O. Box 10, Belconnen, A.C.T. 2616, Australia. **Document type:** government publication.
   Description: Provides a summary of the conceptual framework of Australia's balance of payments accounts and of the data sources and methods used to compile the statistics contained in balance of payments publications.

330 310   AT   ISSN 1036-272X
AUSTRALIA. BUREAU OF STATISTICS. BUSINESS OPERATIONS AND INDUSTRY PERFORMANCE, AUSTRALIA. 1990. a. Aus.$35. Australian Bureau of Statistics, P.O. Box 10, Belconnen, A.C.T. 2616, Australia. **Document type:** government publication.
   Description: Economic statistics, including aggregates and ratios, based on profit and loss and balance sheet accounts of businesses in most industries of the Australian economy.

330   AT   ISSN 0818-9986
AUSTRALIA. BUREAU OF STATISTICS. COMPANY PROFITS, AUSTRALIA. 1986. q. Aus.$11.50 per no. Australian Bureau of Statistics, P.O. Box 10, Belconnen, A.C.T. 2616, Australia. **Document type:** government publication.
   Description: Contains preliminary estimates derived from a sample survey of incorporated business enterprises of company profits, depreciation and net interest paid.

338   AT   ISSN 1034-4748
AUSTRALIA. BUREAU OF STATISTICS. CONSTANT PRICE ESTIMATES OF MANUFACTURING PRODUCTION, AUSTRALIA. 1968. a. Aus.$10.50. Australian Bureau of Statistics, P.O. Box 10, Belconnen, A.C.T. 2616, Australia. **Document type:** government publication.
   Description: Contains constant price estimates of manufacturing gross product.

330   AT   ISSN 1031-0207
AUSTRALIA. BUREAU OF STATISTICS. CONSUMER PRICE INDEX. 1960. q. Aus.$13 per no. Australian Bureau of Statistics, P.O. Box 10, Belconnen, A.C.T. 2616, Australia. **Document type:** government publication.
   Description: Measures movements in retail prices of goods and services commonly purchased by metropolitan wage and salary earner households.

332.6 310   AT
AUSTRALIA. BUREAU OF STATISTICS. CONSUMER PRICE INDEX: EFFECT OF CHANGES IN PRICES OF IMPORTED ITEMS. 1985. q. Aus.$100. Australian Bureau of Statistics, P.O. Box 10, Belconnen, A.C.T. 2616, Australia. **Document type:** government publication.
   Description: Provides information on the price movements of wholly or predominantly imported items included in the CPI, together with information about their effect on the CPI as a whole.

331.1 310   AT
AUSTRALIA. BUREAU OF STATISTICS. DIRECTORY OF INDUSTRIAL RELATIONS STATISTICS. 1992. irreg., latest 1995. Aus.$10. Australian Bureau of Statistics, P.O. Box 10, Belconnen, A.C.T. 2616, Australia. **Document type:** government publication, directory.
   Description: Brief overview of the types of ABS data that are available relating to industrial relations issues and an understanding of the wide range of statistics available, and how they can be used.

331.11 310   AT
AUSTRALIA. BUREAU OF STATISTICS. DIRECTORY OF LABOUR MARKET AND SOCIAL SURVEY DATA. 1994. irreg. Aus.$10. Australian Bureau of Statistics, P.O. Box 10, Belconnen, A.C.T. 2616, Australia. **Document type:** government publication, directory.

331.2 319   AT   ISSN 1031-0231
AUSTRALIA. BUREAU OF STATISTICS. DISTRIBUTION AND COMPOSITION OF EMPLOYEE EARNINGS AND HOURS, AUSTRALIA, PRELIMINARY. 1975. a. Aus.$15. Australian Bureau of Statistics, P.O. Box 10, Belconnen, A.C.T. 2616, Australia. **Document type:** government publication.
   Formerly (until 1985): Earnings and Hours of Employees, Distribution and Composition, Preliminary (Canberra) (ISSN 0312-4460)
   Description: Contains information about the distribution of average weekly earnings of employees classified by sex.

331.2 310   AT
AUSTRALIA. BUREAU OF STATISTICS. DISTRIBUTION AND COMPOSITION OF EMPLOYEE EARNINGS AND HOURS, STATES AND AUSTRALIA - DATA SERVICE. 1983. a. Australian Bureau of Statistics, P.O. Box 10, Belconnen, A.C.T. 2616, Australia. (also avail. in diskette format) **Document type:** government publication.

331.2   AT   ISSN 0814-6195
AUSTRALIA. BUREAU OF STATISTICS. EMPLOYED WAGE AND SALARY EARNERS, AUSTRALIA. 1983. q. Aus.$18 per no. Australian Bureau of Statistics, P.O. Box 10, Belconnen, A.C.T. 2616, Australia. **Document type:** government publication.
   Description: Contains estimates of gross earnings classified by industry and sector for Australia, states and territories.

331.86 310   AT
AUSTRALIA. BUREAU OF STATISTICS. EMPLOYER TRAINING EXPENDITURE, AUSTRALIA. 1989. irreg., latest 1993. Australian Bureau of Statistics, P.O. Box 10, Belconnen, A.C.T. 2616, Australia. **Document type:** government publication.
   Description: Provides comprehensive information on employer training expenditure in Australia.

332.6   AT   ISSN 1031-0290
AUSTRALIA. BUREAU OF STATISTICS. EXPORT PRICE INDEX, AUSTRALIA. 1937. m. Aus.$10 per no. Australian Bureau of Statistics, P.O. Box 10, Belconnen, A.C.T. 2616, Australia. **Document type:** government publication.
   Description: Measures f.o.b. port of origin price movements for Australian merchandise exports.

336   AT   ISSN 1031-7104
AUSTRALIA. BUREAU OF STATISTICS. GOVERNMENT FINANCE STATISTICS, AUSTRALIA. 1989. a. Aus.$32. Australian Bureau of Statistics, P.O. Box 10, Belconnen, A.C.T. 2616, Australia. TEL 062-527911. FAX 062-516009. circ. 362. **Document type:** government publication.
   Formed by the merger of (1961-1989): Commonwealth Government Finance, Australia (ISSN 0725-3427); (1971-1989): State and Local Government Finance, Australia (ISSN 0158-9946); Which was formerly: Government Finance Statistics; Public Authority Finance. State and Local Authorities.
   Description: Provides details of the consolidated financial transactions of non-financial public enterprises of all levels of government compiled in accordance with national accounting concepts.

319.4   AT   ISSN 0159-3951
AUSTRALIA. BUREAU OF STATISTICS. GOVERNMENT FINANCIAL ESTIMATES, AUSTRALIA. 1974. a. Aus.$30. Australian Bureau of Statistics, P.O. Box 10, Belconnen, A.C.T. 2616, Australia. TEL 062-527911. FAX 062-516009. circ. 400. **Document type:** government publication.
   Formerly: Public Authority Finance. Public Authority Estimates (ISSN 0312-4479)
   Description: Shows forward estimates for state general government and public trading enterprise sectors and local authorities, compiled in accordance with national accounting concepts.

332   AT   ISSN 1031-0320
AUSTRALIA. BUREAU OF STATISTICS. HOUSING FINANCE FOR OWNER OCCUPATION, AUSTRALIA. 1975. m. Aus.$13 per no. Australian Bureau of Statistics, P.O. Box 10, Belconnen, A.C.T. 2616, Australia. **Document type:** government publication.
   Description: Contains secured finance commitments to individuals for construction of dwellings, purchase of new and established dwellings by savings and trading banks, permanent building societies and other lenders.

330   AT   ISSN 0812-7247
AUSTRALIA. BUREAU OF STATISTICS. IMPORT PRICE INDEX, AUSTRALIA. 1982. m. Aus.$13 per no. Australian Bureau of Statistics, P.O. Box 10, Belconnen, A.C.T. 2616, Australia. **Document type:** government publication.
   Description: Measures changes in f.o.b. country-of-origin price movements of imports of merchandise into Australia.

330 310   AT   ISSN 1322-9788
AUSTRALIA. BUREAU OF STATISTICS. INCOME DISTRIBUTION, AUSTRALIA. 1978. a. Aus.$32. Australian Bureau of Statistics, P.O. Box 10, Belconnen, A.C.T. 2616, Australia. **Document type:** government publication.
   Formerly: Survey of Income and Housing Costs and Amenities: Income Distribution: Income Units, Australia.

331   AT   ISSN 1031-0347
AUSTRALIA. BUREAU OF STATISTICS. INDUSTRIAL DISPUTES, AUSTRALIA (MONTHLY). 1970. m. Aus.$11 per no. Australian Bureau of Statistics, P.O. Box 10, Belconnen, A.C.T. 2616, Australia. **Document type:** government publication.
   Description: Provides information on the number of labor disputes, workers involved, working days lost in disputes involving work stoppages lasting ten working days or more.

331 310   AT
AUSTRALIA. BUREAU OF STATISTICS. INFORMATION PAPER: MEASURING EMPLOYMENT AND UNEMPLOYMENT. 1991. irreg., latest 1994. Aus.$10. Australian Bureau of Statistics, P.O. Box 10, Belconnen, A.C.T. 2616, Australia. **Document type:** government publication.
   Description: Provides information about the Monthly Labour Force Survey and discusses the Australian labor force framework.

332.6   AT   ISSN 1037-8782
HG4538
AUSTRALIA. BUREAU OF STATISTICS. INTERNATIONAL INVESTMENT POSITION, AUSTRALIA (ANNUAL). 1955. a. Aus.$41. Australian Bureau of Statistics, P.O. Box 10, Belconnen, A.C.T. 2616, Australia. **Document type:** government publication.
   Formerly: Foreign Investment, Australia (ISSN 1031-2609)
   Description: Provides comprehensive information on Australia's foreign financial assets and liabilities, including foreign debt.

332.65 310   AT
AUSTRALIA. BUREAU OF STATISTICS. INTERNATIONAL INVESTMENT POSITION. AUSTRALIA: AUSTRALIAN SECURITIES HELD BY NOMINEES ON BEHALF OF NON-RESIDENTS. 1987. a. Aus.$100. Australian Bureau of Statistics, P.O. Box 10, Belconnen, A.C.T. 2616, Australia. **Document type:** government publication.
   Formerly: Foreign Investment, Australia: Australian Securities Held by Nominees on Behalf of Non-residents.
   Description: Provides information on the value of Australian securities held by nominees on behalf of non-residents classified by type of security, institutional sector of the issuing enterprise and country of the non-resident investor.

332.65 310   AT
AUSTRALIA. BUREAU OF STATISTICS. INTERNATIONAL INVESTMENT POSITION, AUSTRALIA: PURCHASES AND SALES OF PORTFOLIO CORPORATE EQUITIES BY NON-RESIDENTS. 1989. q. Aus.$25. Australian Bureau of Statistics, P.O. Box 10, Belconnen, A.C.T. 2616, Australia. **Document type:** government publication.
   Description: Provides information on purchases and sales of shares in Australian companies by security dealers on behalf of non-residents.

332.6   AT   ISSN 1037-8774
AUSTRALIA. BUREAU OF STATISTICS. INTERNATIONAL INVESTMENT POSITION, AUSTRALIA (QUARTERLY). 1976. q. Aus.$24 per no. Australian Bureau of Statistics, P.O. Box 10, Belconnen, A.C.T. 2616, Australia. **Document type:** government publication.
   Formerly: Foreign Investment, Australia (ISSN 0819-0925); Incorporates (1976-1991): Foreign Investment, Australia, Preliminary (ISSN 0819-5900)

332.6 AT
AUSTRALIA. BUREAU OF STATISTICS. INTERNATIONAL INVESTMENT POSITION, AUSTRALIA: SUPPLEMENTARY COUNTRY STATISTICS.
(Supplement to: International Investment Position, Australia (ISSN 1037-8782)) 1988. a. Aus.$100. Australian Bureau of Statistics, P.O. Box 10, Belconnen, A.C.T. 2616, Australia. **Document type:** government publication.
Formerly: International Investment Position, Australia: Supplementary Country by Broad Industry Statistics (ISSN 1030-8997)
Description: Contains details on country and industry of investment, level of investment, investment flows and associated income.

332.6 AT ISSN 1321-3512
AUSTRALIA. BUREAU OF STATISTICS. INTERNATIONAL MERCHANDISE TRADE, AUSTRALIA. 1978. q. Aus.$30 per no. Australian Bureau of Statistics, P.O. Box 10, Belconnen, A.C.T. 2616, Australia. **Document type:** government publication.
Former titles: Foreign Trade, Australia: Merchandise Exports and Imports by Country (ISSN 1037-9061); Exports and Imports, Australia: Trade with Selected Countries and Major Country Groups (ISSN 1031-0304)

332.6 AT ISSN 1034-0505
AUSTRALIA. BUREAU OF STATISTICS. INTERNATIONAL TRADE IN SERVICES, AUSTRALIA. 1987. biennial. Aus.$23 per no. Australian Bureau of Statistics, P.O. Box 10, Belconnen, A.C.T. 2616, Australia. **Document type:** government publication.
Description: Presents detailed estimates of Australia's international trade in services and related royalties transactions.

331 AT ISSN 1038-6637
AUSTRALIA. BUREAU OF STATISTICS. LABOUR COSTS, AUSTRALIA. 1985. a. Aus.$25. Australian Bureau of Statistics, P.O. Box 10, Belconnen, A.C.T. 2616, Australia. **Document type:** government publication.
Former titles: Major Labour Costs, Australia (ISSN 1030-9020); Major Labour Costs, Private Sector, Australia (ISSN 0819-5080)
Description: Contains estimates of major labor costs for the private and public sectors, including employee earnings, employee payments for superannuation, workers' compensation, payroll tax and fringe benefits tax paid.

331 AT ISSN 1030-0996
AUSTRALIA. BUREAU OF STATISTICS. LABOUR FORCE, AUSTRALIA. 1966. m. Aus.$18 per no. Australian Bureau of Statistics, P.O. Box 10, Belconnen, A.C.T. 2616, Australia. **Document type:** government publication.
Incorporates (1979-1994): Weekly Earnings of Employees (Distribution), Australia (ISSN 1031-0819); (1969-1994): Labour Force Experience, Australia (ISSN 1031-0398); Labour Mobility, Australia (ISSN 0729-364X); Persons Not in the Labour Force, Australia (ISSN 0819-9914); Job Search Experience of Unemployed Persons, Australia (ISSN 0815-9971); Labour Force Status and Other Characteristics of Families, Australia (ISSN 1031-0401); Retirement and Retirement Intentions, Australia (ISSN 0819-2855); Successful and Unsuccessful Job Search Experience, Australia (ISSN 0818-9978); Underemployed Workers, Australia (ISSN 1032-4941); Persons Who Have Left the Labour Force, Australia (ISSN 0818-8033); Multiple Jobholding, Australia.
Description: Provides information on the civilian population aged 15 and over, classified by sex, labor force status, age, marital status, education, birthplace, occupation and hours worked.

331 AT ISSN 1031-038X
AUSTRALIA. BUREAU OF STATISTICS. LABOUR FORCE, AUSTRALIA, PRELIMINARY. 1972. m. Aus.$15 per no. Australian Bureau of Statistics, P.O. Box 10, Belconnen, A.C.T. 2616, Australia. **Document type:** government publication.
Description: Provides information on the civilian population aged 15 and over, classified by sex, labor force status, and full-time and part-time status and other items.

331 319 AT ISSN 0314-2779
HD8841
AUSTRALIA. BUREAU OF STATISTICS. LABOUR STATISTICS, AUSTRALIA. 1912. a. Aus.$39. Australian Bureau of Statistics, P.O. Box 10, Belconnen, A.C.T. 2616, Australia. TEL 062-527911. FAX 062-516009. circ. 718. **Document type:** government publication.
Formerly: Labour Report (ISSN 0067-0812)
Description: Gives a wide coverage of labor statistics: labor force, earnings and award rates of pay, income and labor costs, non-wage benefits, work patterns and hours of work, job satisfaction and work preferences, industrial disputes, and trade unions, etc.

331 AT ISSN 1031-041X
AUSTRALIA. BUREAU OF STATISTICS. LABOUR STATISTICS IN BRIEF, AUSTRALIA. 1986. a. Aus.$1. Australian Bureau of Statistics, P.O. Box 10, Belconnen, A.C.T. 2616, Australia. **Document type:** government publication.
Description: Presents a range of summary statistics with an emphasis on simple tabular and graphical presentations.

332 AT ISSN 1037-7786
AUSTRALIA. BUREAU OF STATISTICS. MANAGED FUNDS, AUSTRALIA. 1992. q. Aus.$25 per no. Australian Bureau of Statistics, P.O. Box 10, Belconnen, A.C.T. 2616, Australia. **Document type:** government publication.
Incorporates (1989-1993): Assets and Liabilities of Friendly Societies, Australia (ISSN 1036-8299); (1989-1993): Common Funds, Australia (ISSN 1037-2857); (1985-1993): Public Unit Trusts, Australia (ISSN 0818-9722); (1983-1994): Cash Management Trusts, Australia (ISSN 0813-1139)
Description: Provides information about money pooled for investment purposes on a consolidated basis for a range of institutions, classified according to type of fund and type of asset.

330 AT ISSN 1036-2738
HD9738.A8
AUSTRALIA. BUREAU OF STATISTICS. MANUFACTURING INDUSTRY, AUSTRALIA. 1968. a. Aus.$33. Australian Bureau of Statistics, P.O. Box 10, Belconnen, A.C.T. 2616, Australia. **Document type:** government publication.
Formerly (until 1989): Manufacturing Industry: Details of Operations, Australia (ISSN 0312-1607)
Description: Presents final results from the manufacturing census, including the number of establishments, employment, and wages and salaries.

330 AT ISSN 1033-4033
AUSTRALIA. BUREAU OF STATISTICS. MANUFACTURING INDUSTRY, AUSTRALIA, PRELIMINARY. 1968. a. Aus.$10.50. Australian Bureau of Statistics, P.O. Box 10, Belconnen, A.C.T. 2616, Australia. **Document type:** government publication.
Formerly: Census of Manufacturing Establishments, Australia, Preliminary.
Description: Contains statistics on the Australian manufacturing sector, including number of establishments, employment, wages and salaries, and turnover.

338 AT ISSN 1035-9311
AUSTRALIA. BUREAU OF STATISTICS. MANUFACTURING PRODUCTION, AUSTRALIA, PRELIMINARY. 1961. m. Aus.$10.50 per no. Australian Bureau of Statistics, P.O. Box 10, Belconnen, A.C.T. 2616, Australia. **Document type:** government publication.
Supersedes in part (in 1994): Manufacturing Production, Australia: Metal Products (ISSN 1035-9184); **Formerly:** Production Statistics, Australia, Preliminary.
Description: Contains estimates of production for 27 major indicators, including metals and textiles.

310 338 AT ISSN 0157-9703
AUSTRALIA. BUREAU OF STATISTICS. MANUFACTURING PRODUCTION, AUSTRALIA: PRINCIPAL COMMODITIES PRODUCED. 1975. triennial. Aus.$15 per no. Australian Bureau of Statistics, P.O. Box 10, Belconnen, A.C.T. 2616, Australia. **Document type:** government publication.
Formerly: Manufacturing Commodities: Selected Principal Articles Produced, Australia, Preliminary.
Description: Provides statistics of quantities produced, value of sales of about 400 selected principal manufacturing commodities.

332.6 310 AT ISSN 1321-8271
AUSTRALIA. BUREAU OF STATISTICS. MERCHANDISE IMPORTS, AUSTRALIA: BALANCE OF PAYMENTS BASIS. 1994. m. Aus.$10 per no. Australian Bureau of Statistics, P.O. Box 10, Belconnen, A.C.T. 2616, Australia. **Document type:** government publication.
Description: Provides the earliest release of preliminary aggregate measures of merchandise imports on a balance of payments basis (including seasonally adjusted and trend estimates).

332 310 AT
AUSTRALIA. BUREAU OF STATISTICS. MONTHLY STATISTICS FOR CORPORATIONS REGISTERED UNDER THE FINANCIAL CORPORATIONS ACT. 1990. m. Australian Bureau of Statistics, P.O. Box 10, Belconnen, A.C.T. 2616, Australia. (also avail. in diskette format) **Document type:** government publication.

339 310 AT ISSN 1031-2641
AUSTRALIA. BUREAU OF STATISTICS. N I F - 10S MODEL DATA BASE MANUAL. (National Income Forecasting) 1989. q. Aus.$40. Australian Bureau of Statistics, P.O. Box 10, Belconnen, A.C.T. 2616, Australia. (also avail. in magnetic tape; diskette format; microfiche) **Document type:** government publication.
Description: Provides over 300 time series forming the data base for the National Income Forecasting Model of the Australian economy.

330 AT ISSN 1031-8534
AUSTRALIA. BUREAU OF STATISTICS. NEW SOUTH WALES OFFICE. ECONOMIC INDICATORS, NEW SOUTH WALES. 1988. m. Aus.$10 per no. Australian Bureau of Statistics, New South Wales Office, St. Andrews House, Sydney Square, George St., Sydney, N.S.W. 2000, Australia. **Document type:** government publication.
Description: Provides an up-to-date overview of economic trends in N.S.W.

658 310 AT
AUSTRALIA. BUREAU OF STATISTICS. NEW SOUTH WALES OFFICE. RETAILING IN NEW SOUTH WALES. 1968. irreg., latest 1991. Aus.$15. Australian Bureau of Statistics, New South Wales Office, St. Andrews House, Sydney Square, George St., Sydney, N.S.W. 2000, Australia. **Document type:** government publication.
Formerly: Retail Industry, Small Area Statistics, New South Wales.
Description: Contains details by industry group and statistical local area of number of retail locations, employment, wages and salaries, turnover and floorspace.

331 AT ISSN 1322-0179
AUSTRALIA. BUREAU OF STATISTICS. NEW SOUTH WALES OFFICE. THE LABOUR FORCE, NEW SOUTH WALES AND AUSTRALIAN CAPITAL TERRITORY. 1974. q. Aus.$18 per no. Australian Bureau of Statistics, New South Wales Office, St. Andrews House, Sydney Square, George St., Sydney, N.S.W. 2000, Australia. **Document type:** government publication.
Former titles: Labour Force, New South Wales (ISSN 1031-7686); Labour Force (Including Regional Estimates), New South Wales.
Description: Provides statistics on the labour force status of the civilian population aged 15 and over.

330 AT ISSN 1031-0029
AUSTRALIA. BUREAU OF STATISTICS. PRICE INDEXES OF ARTICLES PRODUCED BY MANUFACTURING INDUSTRY, AUSTRALIA. 1976. m. Aus.$11.50 per no. Australian Bureau of Statistics, P.O. Box 10, Belconnen, A.C.T. 2616, Australia.
Description: Measures price movements of articles produced by manufacturers for sale.

330 AT ISSN 1031-0649
AUSTRALIA. BUREAU OF STATISTICS. PRICE INDEXES OF MATERIALS USED IN MANUFACTURING INDUSTRIES, AUSTRALIA. 1975. m. Aus.$12 per no. Australian Bureau of Statistics, P.O. Box 10, Belconnen, A.C.T. 2616, Australia. **Document type:** government publication.
Formerly: Price Indexes of Materials Used in Manufacturing Industry, Australia.
Description: Measures price movements of materials and fuels used by industrial establishments.

BUSINESS AND ECONOMICS — ABSTRACTING, BIBLIOGRAPHIES, STATISTICS

332 AT ISSN 1033-5048
AUSTRALIA. BUREAU OF STATISTICS. PRIVATE NEW CAPITAL EXPENDITURE, AUSTRALIA, ACTUAL AND EXPECTED EXPENDITURE, PRELIMINARY. 1947. q. Aus.$10.50 per no. Australian Bureau of Statistics, P.O. Box 10, Belconnen, A.C.T. 2616, Australia. **Document type:** government publication.
Formerly: Private New Capital Expenditure, Australia, Preliminary.
Description: Contains preliminary estimates of actual and expected new capital expenditure by type of asset.

332 AT ISSN 1323-2568
AUSTRALIA. BUREAU OF STATISTICS. PRIVATE NEW CAPITAL EXPENDITURE AND EXPECTED EXPENDITURE, AUSTRALIA. 1963. q. Aus.$13 per no. Australian Bureau of Statistics, P.O. Box 10, Belconnen, A.C.T. 2616, Australia. **Document type:** government publication.
Former titles: Private New Capital Expenditure, Australia, Actual and Expected Expenditure (ISSN 0819-002X); New Fixed Capital Expenditure by Private Enterprises in Selected Industries, Australia.
Description: Contains detailed statistics on new capital expenditure in current price and constant prices and in original and seasonally adjusted terms.

332.6 310 AT
AUSTRALIA. BUREAU OF STATISTICS. PRODUCER AND FOREIGN TRADE PRICE INDEXES: CONCEPTS, SOURCES AND METHODS. 1991. irreg., latest 1995. Aus.$30. Australian Bureau of Statistics, P.O. Box 10, Belconnen, A.C.T. 2616, Australia. **Document type:** government publication.

330 310 AT ISSN 1036-3785
AUSTRALIA. BUREAU OF STATISTICS. PROFILES OF AUSTRALIAN BUSINESS. 1992. irreg., latest 1995. Aus.$23. Australian Bureau of Statistics, P.O. Box 10, Belconnen, A.C.T. 2616, Australia. **Document type:** government publication.
Description: Contains statistical information extracted from the ABS Business Register.

336 AT ISSN 1320-6184
AUSTRALIA. BUREAU OF STATISTICS. PUBLIC SECTOR FINANCIAL ASSETS AND LIABILITIES, AUSTRALIA. 1987. a. Aus.$13. Australian Bureau of Statistics, P.O. Box 10, Belconnen, A.C.T. 2616, Australia. **Document type:** government publication.
Formerly: Public Sector Debt, Australia (ISSN 1031-7112)
Description: Contains statistics on the financial assets and liabilities of the Australian non-financial public sector.

338 AT ISSN 1035-9613
AUSTRALIA. BUREAU OF STATISTICS. QUARTERLY INDEXES OF INDUSTRIAL PRODUCTION, AUSTRALIA. 1990. q. Aus.$14 per no. Australian Bureau of Statistics, P.O. Box 10, Belconnen, A.C.T. 2616, Australia. **Document type:** government publication.
Incorporates (1987-1990): Quarterly Indexes of Manufacturing Production, Australia (ISSN 0812-2075)
Description: Contains indexes of gross product at constant prices for the industrial sector and each of its major component industries -- mining, manufacturing, electricity, and gas and water.

330 AT ISSN 0819-2928
AUSTRALIA. BUREAU OF STATISTICS. QUEENSLAND OFFICE. ECONOMIC INDICATORS, QUEENSLAND. 1987. m. Aus.$10 per no. Australian Bureau of Statistics, Queensland Office, 313 Adelaide St., Brisbane, Qld. 4000, Australia. TEL 07-222-6022. FAX 07-229-6171. TELEX AA 40271. **Document type:** government publication.
Description: Provides tables and diagrams of the latest available Queensland and Australian information on a wide range of economic indicators.

331.11 AT ISSN 0313-1912
AUSTRALIA. BUREAU OF STATISTICS. QUEENSLAND OFFICE. LABOUR FORCE, QUEENSLAND. 1975. q. Aus.$18 per no. Australian Bureau of Statistics, Queensland Office, 313 Adelaide St., Brisbane, Qld. 4000, Australia. TEL 07-222-6022. FAX 07-229-6171. TELEX AA 40271. **Document type:** government publication.
Description: Provides information on labor force status of the civilian population aged 15 and over for Queensland and each region of Queensland.

AUSTRALIA. BUREAU OF STATISTICS. QUEENSLAND OFFICE. LOCAL GOVERNMENT, QUEENSLAND. see PUBLIC ADMINISTRATION — Abstracting, Bibliographies, Statistics

330 AT ISSN 1036-2762
AUSTRALIA. BUREAU OF STATISTICS. QUEENSLAND OFFICE. MANUFACTURING INDUSTRY, QUEENSLAND. 1968. a. Aus.$18. Australian Bureau of Statistics, Queensland Office, 313 Adelaide St., Brisbane, Qld. 4000, Australia. TEL 07-222-6022. FAX 07-229-6171. TELEX AA 40271. **Document type:** government publication.
Formerly (until 1990): Manufacturing Establishments: Details of Operations, Queensland (ISSN 0818-7185)
Description: Presents final detailed results from the manufacturing census for structural variables: number of establishments, employment, wages and salaries, turnover, stocks, purchases and more, value added and fixed capital expenditure by industry group.

330 AT
AUSTRALIA. BUREAU OF STATISTICS. QUEENSLAND OFFICE. RETAIL INDUSTRY: SMALL AREA STATISTICS, QUEENSLAND. 1969. every 5 yrs. Aus.$10.50. Australian Bureau of Statistics, Queensland Office, 313 Adelaide St., Brisbane, Qld. 4000, Australia. TEL 07-222-6022. FAX 07-229-6171. TELEX AA 40271. (also avail. in diskette format)
Census of Retail Establishments and Selected Service Establishments: Industry Details for Statistical Retail Areas.
Description: Presents retail establishments: number of establishments, employment, trading hours, turnover and total floor space by statistical retail areas, statistical divisions and industry class; establishments, employment, wages and salaries, turnover and total floor space by statistical local areas, statistical divisions and statistical districts.

330 AT ISSN 0819-9876
AUSTRALIA. BUREAU OF STATISTICS. RESEARCH AND EXPERIMENTAL DEVELOPMENT, ALL SECTOR SUMMARY (INTER-YEAR SURVEY), AUSTRALIA. 1985. biennial. Aus.$10 per no. Australian Bureau of Statistics, P.O. Box 10, Belconnen, A.C.T. 2616, Australia. **Document type:** government publication.
Description: Contains estimates of the level of distribution of expenditure and human resources devoted to research and experimental development carried out by business enterprises, government, higher education and private non-profit sectors in Australia.

330 AT ISSN 0728-5140
AUSTRALIA. BUREAU OF STATISTICS. RESEARCH AND EXPERIMENTAL DEVELOPMENT, BUSINESS ENTERPRISES, AUSTRALIA. 1976. biennial. Aus.$22 per no. Australian Bureau of Statistics, P.O. Box 10, Belconnen, A.C.T. 2616, Australia. **Document type:** government publication.
Description: Covers expenditure and human enterprises devoted to research and experimental development carried out by business enterprises in Australia.

330 AT ISSN 0159-1584
AUSTRALIA. BUREAU OF STATISTICS. RESEARCH AND EXPERIMENTAL DEVELOPMENT, BUSINESS ENTERPRISES, AUSTRALIA, PRELIMINARY. 1978. biennial. Australian Bureau of Statistics, P.O. Box 10, Belconnen, A.C.T. 2616, Australia. **Document type:** government publication.
Description: Covers expenditure and human resources devoted to research and experimental development carried out in Australia by business enterprises, classified by broad industry group.

330 AT ISSN 1032-6219
AUSTRALIA. BUREAU OF STATISTICS. RESEARCH AND EXPERIMENTAL DEVELOPMENT, GENERAL GOVERNMENT AND PRIVATE NON-PROFIT ORGANISATIONS, AUSTRALIA. 1978. biennial. Aus.$22 per no. Australian Bureau of Statistics, P.O. Box 10, Belconnen, A.C.T. 2616, Australia. **Document type:** government publication.
Description: Provides statistics on expenditure and human resources devoted to research and experimental development carried out by general government organizations.

658 310 AT
AUSTRALIA. BUREAU OF STATISTICS. RETAIL INDUSTRY, AUSTRALIA. 1968. irreg., latest 1992. Aus.$15. Australian Bureau of Statistics, P.O. Box 10, Belconnen, A.C.T. 2616, Australia. **Document type:** government publication.
Formerly: Retail Industry: Details of Operations, Australia.
Description: Contains details by industry of number of business units, employment, wages and salaries, income and expenditure, operating profit, gross product and selected performance measures.

330 AT ISSN 1032-3651
AUSTRALIA. BUREAU OF STATISTICS. RETAIL TRADE, AUSTRALIA. 1961. m. Aus.$10.50 per no. Australian Bureau of Statistics, P.O. Box 10, Belconnen, A.C.T. 2616, Australia. **Document type:** government publication.
Description: Contains monthly estimates of turnover for retail and selected service establishments.

658 310 AT ISSN 1031-8046
AUSTRALIA. BUREAU OF STATISTICS. RETAIL TRADE, AUSTRALIA: COMMODITY DETAILS. 1988. irreg. Aus.$18. Australian Bureau of Statistics, P.O. Box 10, Belconnen, A.C.T. 2616, Australia. **Document type:** government publication.
Description: Annual sales for major commodity groups for Australia, each State and Territory.

658 330 AT
AUSTRALIA. BUREAU OF STATISTICS. RETAILING IN AUSTRALIA. 1979. irreg., latest 1992. Aus.$10. Australian Bureau of Statistics, P.O. Box 10, Belconnen, A.C.T. 2616, Australia. **Document type:** government publication.
Description: Presents results from the retail industry location census.

AUSTRALIA. BUREAU OF STATISTICS. SALES OF AUSTRALIAN WINE AND BRANDY BY WINEMAKERS. see BEVERAGES — Abstracting, Bibliographies, Statistics

338 310 AT
AUSTRALIA. BUREAU OF STATISTICS. SMALL BUSINESS IN AUSTRALIA. 1983. irreg., latest 1995. Aus.$42. Australian Bureau of Statistics, P.O. Box 10, Belconnen, A.C.T. 2616, Australia. **Document type:** government publication.
Description: Contains statistics on the number and employment of small businesses on a national, state and industry basis. Also contains statistics on bankruptcy, earnings, labour costs and research and development for small businesses and compares these with other businesses.

338 AT ISSN 1036-2770
AUSTRALIA. BUREAU OF STATISTICS. SOUTH AUSTRALIAN OFFICE. MANUFACTURING INDUSTRY, SOUTH AUSTRALIA. 1987. a. Aus.$17.50. Australian Bureau of Statistics, South Australian Office, G.P.O. Box 2272, Adelaide, S.A. 5001, Australia. FAX 61-8-82377566. **Document type:** government publication.
Formerly (until 1989): Manufacturing, South Australia (ISSN 1034-4004)
Description: Contains statistics on employment, wages and salaries paid and turnover.

330 310 AT ISSN 1039-8880
AUSTRALIA. BUREAU OF STATISTICS. SOUTH AUSTRALIAN OFFICE. SOUTH AUSTRALIAN ECONOMIC INDICATORS. 1993. m. Aus.$17.50 per no. Australian Bureau of Statistics, South Australian Office, G.P.O. Box 2272, Adelaide, S.A. 5001, Australia. FAX 61-8-82377566. **Document type:** government publication.
Description: Provides an up-to-date overview of the South Australian economy.

332 AT ISSN 0819-0909
AUSTRALIA. BUREAU OF STATISTICS. STATE ESTIMATES OF PRIVATE NEW CAPITAL EXPENDITURE. 1982. q. Aus.$13 per no. Australian Bureau of Statistics, P.O. Box 10, Belconnen, A.C.T. 2616, Australia. **Document type:** government publication.
Formerly: State Estimates of Actual and Expected New Fixed Capital Expenditure by Private Enterprises in Selected Industries, Australia.
Description: Contains state estimates of new capital expenditure in current price and constant prices and in original and seasonally adjusted terms.

BUSINESS AND ECONOMICS — ABSTRACTING, BIBLIOGRAPHIES, STATISTICS

332   AT   ISSN 1323-2614
AUSTRALIA. BUREAU OF STATISTICS. STOCKS, SELECTED INDUSTRY SALES AND EXPECTED SALES, AUSTRALIA. 1974. q. Aus.$13 per no. Australian Bureau of Statistics, P.O. Box 10, Belconnen, A.C.T. 2616, Australia. **Document type:** government publication.
 Former titles: Stocks, Manufacturers' Sales and Expected Sales, Australia (ISSN 1033-551X); Stocks and Manufacturers' Sales, Australia.
 Description: Contains preliminary estimates of stocks owned by private enterprises in selected industries, together with manufacturers' sales and expected sales.

336   AT   ISSN 1034-7321
AUSTRALIA. BUREAU OF STATISTICS. TASMANIAN OFFICE. GOVERNMENT FINANCE STATISTICS, TASMANIA. 1971. a. Aus.$16. Australian Bureau of Statistics, Tasmanian Office, G.P.O. Box 66A, Hobart, Tas. 7001, Australia. **Document type:** government publication.
 Formerly: Local Government Finance, Tasmania.
 Description: Provides state and local government finance statistics.

336   AT   ISSN 0819-9361
AUSTRALIA. BUREAU OF STATISTICS. TAXATION REVENUE, AUSTRALIA. 1969. a. Aus.$18. Australian Bureau of Statistics, P.O. Box 10, Belconnen, A.C.T. 2616, Australia. **Document type:** government publication.
 Description: Details the revenue from taxation of Commonwealth, state and local authorities in Australia.

331.86 310   AT
AUSTRALIA. BUREAU OF STATISTICS. TRAINING AND EDUCATION EXPERIENCE, AUSTRALIA. 1989. irreg., latest 1993. Aus.$30. Australian Bureau of Statistics, P.O. Box 10, Belconnen, A.C.t. 2616, Australia. **Document type:** government publication.
 Formerly: How Workers Get Their Training, Australia.
 Description: Provides details of the training and education experiences of persons who had worked as wage and salary earners in the last twelve months, as well as those who are employers, self-employed, unemployed or marginally attached to the labour force.

331.1 310   AT   ISSN 1030-536X
AUSTRALIA. BUREAU OF STATISTICS. VICTORIAN OFFICE. LABOUR FORCE, VICTORIA. 1978. q. Aus.$18 per no. Australian Bureau of Statistics, Victorian Office, G.P.O. Box 2796Y, Melbourne, Vic. 3001, Australia. charts; stat. circ. 340. **Document type:** government publication.
 Formerly (until 1984): Labour Force, Victorian Region (ISSN 0156-9732)
 Description: Covers civilian population by labor force status for Victoria and each of the twelve Victorian regions.

388   AT   ISSN 1036-2754
AUSTRALIA. BUREAU OF STATISTICS. VICTORIAN OFFICE. MANUFACTURING INDUSTRY, VICTORIA. 1986. a. Aus.$16.30. Australian Bureau of Statistics, Victorian Office, G.P.O. Box 2796Y, Melbourne, Vic. 3001, Australia. **Document type:** government publication.
 Supersedes (in 1989): Manufacturing, Victoria (ISSN 1033-7784)
 Description: Contains statistics on the number of establishments, employment, wages and salaries, and turnover.

330   AT   ISSN 1032-4429
AUSTRALIA. BUREAU OF STATISTICS. VICTORIAN OFFICE. RETAIL INDUSTRY: DETAILS OF OPERATIONS, VICTORIA. 1968. irreg., latest 1986. Aus.$15 per no. Australian Bureau of Statistics, Victorian Office, G.P.O. Box 2796Y, Melbourne, Vic. 3001, Australia. **Document type:** government publication.
 Formerly: Census of Retail Establishments and Selected Service Establishments: Details of Operations by Industry Class, Victoria.
 Description: Contains number of establishments, employment, wages, turnover, stocks, purchases and expenses for Victoria.

330   AT   ISSN 1036-2789
AUSTRALIA. BUREAU OF STATISTICS. WESTERN AUSTRALIAN OFFICE. MANUFACTURING INDUSTRY, WESTERN AUSTRALIA. 1988. a. Aus.$15.50 per no. (effective 1996). Australian Bureau of Statistics, Western Australian Office, 30 Terrace Rd., E. Perth, W.A. 6004, Australia. **Document type:** government publication.
 Formerly (until 1989): Manufacturing, Western Australia (ISSN 1036-5753)
 Description: Presents final results for Western Australia from the manufacturing census.

658 310   AT
AUSTRALIA. BUREAU OF STATISTICS. WHOLESALE INDUSTRY, AUSTRALIA. 1981. irreg., latest 1992. Aus.$15. Australian Bureau of Statistics, P.O. Box 10, Belconnen, A.C.T. 2616, Australia. **Document type:** government publication.
 Description: Estimates of the number of wholesale business units; employment; wages and salaries; turnover; profit; gross product and selected operating ratios - classified by industry.

330 310   AT   ISSN 1320-5099
AUSTRALIA. BUREAU OF STATISTICS. WORKING PAPERS IN ECONOMETRICS AND APPLIED STATISTICS. 1993. irreg. Aus.$11. Australian Bureau of Statistics, P.O. Box 10, Belconnen, A.C.T. 2616, Australia. **Document type:** government publication.
 Description: Contains working papers drawn from ABS research in the fields of econometrics, time series and statistics.

330.9 319   AT
AUSTRALIA. DEPARTMENT OF THE TREASURY. ECONOMIC ROUND-UP. q. Aus.$40. Australian Government Publishing Service, G.P.O. Box 84, Canberra, A.C.T. 2601, Australia. TEL 61-6-295-4411. FAX 61-6-295-4455. TELEX AA62013. **Document type:** government publication.
 Former titles: Australia. Department of the Treasury. Round-Up (ISSN 0815-1881); (until 1985): Australia. Department of the Treasury. Round-Up of Economic Statistics (ISSN 0310-4230)
 Description: Contains an overview of recent economic conditions, which ties together the statistics on the economy.

332 310   AT   ISSN 1034-9685
AUSTRALIAN BANKING STATISTICS. 1990. m. Aus.$15 (effective Sep. 1994). Reserve Bank of Australia, 65 Martin Pl., G.P.O. Box 3947, Sydney, N.S.W. 2001, Australia. TEL 61-2-5518111. FAX 61-2-5518000. circ. 300. (also avail. in diskette format) **Document type:** bulletin.
 Description: Presents selected liabilities and assets recorded on Banks' Australian Books as at close of business on Wednesdays.

330   AT   ISSN 1325-8109
HD9049.W3
AUSTRALIAN BUREAU OF AGRICULTURAL AND RESOURCE ECONOMICS. AUSTRALIAN COMMODITY STATISTICS (YEAR). 1986. a. Aus.$90 (effective 1997). Australian Bureau of Agricultural and Resource Economics, G.P.O. Box 1563, Canberra, A.C.T. 2601, Australia. TEL 61-2-2722211. FAX 61-2-2722330. E-mail: deniseflamia@abare.gov.au. Ed. Andrew Wright. index. **Document type:** government publication, bulletin.
 Formerly: Australian Bureau of Agricultural and Resource Economics. Commodity Statistical Bulletin (Year) (ISSN 0817-685X); Formed by the merger of (1949-1986): Wool Situation and Outlook (ISSN 0311-8797), Which was formerly (until 1974): Wool Outlook (ISSN 0314-1306); (1972-1986): Meat Situation and Outlook (ISSN 0311-0885), Which was formerly (until 1974): Meat Situation (ISSN 0310-0685); (1953-1986): Dairy Products Situation and Outlook (ISSN 0311-8843), Which was formerly (until 1974): Diary Situation (ISSN 0084-7038); (1951-1986): Wheat Situation and Outlook (ISSN 0310-9917), Which was formerly (until 1974): Wheat Situation (ISSN 0043-4736); (1955-1986): Eggs Situation and Outlook (ISSN 0311-8843), Which was formerly (until 1974): Egg Situation (ISSN 0084-7046); (1974-1986): Coarse Grains Situation and Outlook (ISSN 0311-0788); (1974-1986): Oilseeds Situation and Outlook (ISSN 0310-9917).
 Description: Covers all aspects of Australian economics: agriculture, minerals, energy, forestry and fishing industries.

331.2 319   AT   ISSN 1031-024X
AUSTRALIAN BUREAU OF STATISTICS. DISTRIBUTION AND COMPOSITION OF EMPLOYEE EARNINGS AND HOURS, AUSTRALIA. a. Aus.$23. Australian Bureau of Statistics, P.O. Box 10, Belconnen, A.C.T. 2616, Australia. TEL 062-527911. FAX 062-516009. circ. 349. **Document type:** government publication.
 Formerly (until 1985): Earnings and Hours of Employees, Distribution and Composition, Australia.
 Description: Contains survey results about the distribution and composition of average weekly earnings and hours of employees, classified by sex, adult-junior, industry, occupation, type of employment, and composition of earnings and hours.

330 310 028.5   AT   ISSN 1035-6142
AUSTRALIA'S ECONOMIC STATISTICS; a student guide to recent Australian experience. 1989. a. Aus.$10.95. Warringal Publications, 114 Argyle St., Fitzroy, Vic. 3065, Australia. TEL 61-3-94160200. FAX 61-3-94160402. Ed. Ted Kramer; Pub. Jane Arter. charts. circ. 2,000. (back issues avail.)
 Description: Presents economic statistics relating to the Australian economy of the past year for 12 grade students.

382 314   AU
AUSTRIA. STATISTISCHES ZENTRALAMT. AUSSENHANDEL OESTERREICHS. (In three series: 1A; 1B; 2) 1947. 8/yr. S.2000 (series 1A S.1350; series 1B S.500; series 2 S.400). Oesterreichisches Statistisches Zentralamt, Hintere Zollamtsstr. 2b, A-1033 Vienna, Austria. TEL 43-1-71128-0. FAX 43-1-7156828. adv.; bk.rev.; stat. (back issues avail.) **Document type:** government publication.
 Formerly: Statistik des Aussenhandels Oesterreichs (ISSN 0004-816X)
 Description: Export and import data, classification in goods and countries.

338 314   AU
AUSTRIA. STATISTISCHES ZENTRALAMT. GEWERBESTATISTIK PART 2. (Subseries of its Beitraege zur Oesterreichischen Statistik) 1969. a. S.560. Oesterreichisches Statistisches Zentralamt, Hintere Zollamtsstr. 2b, A-1033 Vienna, Austria. TEL 43-1-71128-0. FAX 43-1-7156828. **Document type:** government publication.
 Description: Data on structure and success in small scale manufacturing industries and services.

338 314   AU
AUSTRIA. STATISTISCHES ZENTRALAMT. INDUSTRIE UND GEWERBESTATISTIK PART 1. (Subseries of its Beitraege zur Oesterreichischen Statistik) 1954. a. S.370. Oesterreichisches Statistisches Zentralamt, Hintere Zollamtsstr. 2b, A-1033 Vienna, Austria. TEL 43-1-71128-0. FAX 43-1-7156828. **Document type:** government publication.
 Former titles: Austria. Statistisches Zentralamt. Industrie Statistik und Gewerb; Austria. Statistisches Zentralamt. Industrie Statistik.
 Description: Data on amount and value of industrial goods with data on energy consumption on the establishments and persons engaged.

338.7 314   AU   ISSN 0081-5233
AUSTRIA. STATISTISCHES ZENTRALAMT. STATISTIK DER AKTIENGESELLSCHAFTEN IN OESTERREICH. 1961. a. S.250. Oesterreichisches Statistisches Zentralamt, Hintere Zollamtsstr. 2b, A-1033 Vienna, Austria. TEL 43-1-71128-0. FAX 43-1-7156828. **Document type:** government publication.

330.9   GW   ISSN 0005-0598
AUSZUEGE AUS PRESSEARTIKELN. 1948. s-w. free. Deutsche Bundesbank, Postfach 100602, 60006 Frankfurt a.M., Germany. TEL 49-69-9566-1. FAX 49-69-5601071. URL: http://www.bundesbank.de. circ. 16,800. (looseleaf format) **Indexed:** ELLIS. **Document type:** abstracting/indexing. –CCC.
 Description: Includes excerpts from published articles and press releases of the Bundesbank.

AUTOMATED OFFICE ABSTRACTS. see *COMPUTERS — Abstracting, Bibliographies, Statistics*

BUSINESS AND ECONOMICS — ABSTRACTING, BIBLIOGRAPHIES, STATISTICS

382 MX ISSN 0187-4942
HF3231
AVANCE DE INFORMACION ECONOMICA. BALANZA COMERCIAL. 1986. m. Mex.$77($26) Instituto Nacional de Estadistica, Geografia e Informatica, Secretaria de Programacion y Presupuesto, Prol. Heroe de Nacozari 2301 Sur, Puerta 11, Acceso, 20270 Aguascalientes Ags., Mexico. TEL 49-18-19-48. FAX 491-807-39. circ. 950.

331 MX ISSN 0187-4969
HD5731
AVANCE DE INFORMACION ECONOMICA. EMPLEO. 1986. m. Mex.$77($26) Instituto Nacional de Estadistica, Geografia e Informatica, Secretaria de Programacion y Presupuesto, Prol. Heroe de Nacozari 2301 Sur, Puerta 11, Acceso, 20270 Aguascalientes Ags., Mexico. TEL 49-18-19-48. FAX 491-807-39. circ. 900.

381 MX
AVANCE DE INFORMACION ECONOMICA. ENCUESTA SOBRE ESTABLECIMIENTOS COMERCIALES. CIUDADES DE: MEXICO, GUADALAJARA Y MONTERREY. 1986. m. Mex.$420($140) Instituto Nacional de Estadistica, Geografia e Informatica, Secretaria de Programacion y Presupuesto, Prol. Heroe de Nacozari 2301 Sur, Puerta 11, Acceso, 20270 Aguascalientes Ags., Mexico. TEL 49-18-19-48. FAX 49-18-07-39. circ. 800.
Formed by the 1991 merger of: Avance de Informacion Economica. Encuesta sobre Establecimientos Comerciales. Cuidad de Mexico (ISSN 0187-4985) & Avance de Informacion Economica. Encuesta sobre Establecimientos Comerciales. Cuidad de Guadalajara (ISSN 0187-6708) & Avance de Informacion Economica. Encuesta sobre Establecimientos Comerciales. Ciudad de Monterrey (ISSN 0187-5000)

338 MX
AVANCE DE INFORMACION ECONOMICA. INDICADORES DE LA ACTIVIDAD INDUSTRIAL. 1986. m. Mex.$77($26) Instituto Nacional de Estadistica, Geografia e Informatica, Secretaria de Programacion y Presupuesto, Prol. Heroe de Nacozari 2301 Sur, Puerta 11, Acceso, 20270 Aguascalientes Ags., Mexico. TEL 49-18-19-48. FAX 491-807-39. circ. 1,050.

338 MX ISSN 0187-4977
HD9734.M4
AVANCE DE INFORMACION ECONOMICA. INDICADORES DEL SECTOR MANUFACTURERO; 145 clases de actividad. 1986. m. Mex.$77($26) Instituto Nacional de Estadistica, Geografia e Informatica, Secretaria de Programacion y Presupuesto, Prol. Heroe de Nacozari 2301 Sur, Puerta 11, Acceso, 20270 Aguascalientes Ags., Mexico. TEL 49-18-19-48. FAX 491-807-39. circ. 900.

382 MX ISSN 0187-5019
AVANCE DE INFORMACION ECONOMICA. INDUSTRIA MAQUILADORA DE EXPORTACION. 1986. m. Mex.$77($26) Instituto Nacional de Estadistica, Geografia e Informatica, Secretaria de Programacion y Presupuesto, Prol. Heroe de Nacozari 2301 Sur, Puerta 11, Acceso, 20270 Aguascalientes Ags., Mexico. TEL 49-18-19-48. FAX 491-807-39. circ. 800.

330.9 MX
AVANCE DE INFORMACION ECONOMICA. PRODUCTO INTERNO BRUTO TRIMESTRAL. 1986. q. Mex.$48($16) Instituto Nacional de Estadistica, Geografia e Informatica, Secretaria de Programacion y Presupuesto, Prol. Heroe de Nacozari 2301 Sur, Puerta 11, Acceso, 20270 Aguascalientes Ags., Mexico. TEL 49-18-19-48. FAX 491-807-39. circ. 800.

650 016 US ISSN 0005-318X
B I T S. (Business Industry Technology Service) 1954. m. (except July & Aug.). free. Dayton & Montgomery County Public Library, 215 E. Third St., Dayton, OH 45402. TEL 513-227-9500. Ed. Rita White. bk.rev. circ. 1,500. (processed)
Description: Previews of new books in the business and technology fields.

330 BF
BAHAMAS. DEPARTMENT OF STATISTICS. ANNUAL REVIEW OF PRICES: REPORT. 1974. a. $2. Department of Statistics, P.O. Box N 3904, Nassau, Bahamas.

318 382 BF
BAHAMAS. DEPARTMENT OF STATISTICS. EXTERNAL TRADE. a. $6. Department of Statistics, P.O. Box N 3904, Nassau, Bahamas.

331.1 339 318 BF
BAHAMAS. DEPARTMENT OF STATISTICS. HOUSEHOLD INCOME REPORT. 1973. irreg. $5. Department of Statistics, P.O. Box N 3904, Nassau, Bahamas. illus.
Incorporates (in 1975): Bahamas. Department of Statistics. Labour Force and Income Distribution.

318 382 BF
BAHAMAS. DEPARTMENT OF STATISTICS. SUMMARY OF EXTERNAL TRADE STATISTICS. 1970. q. $2. Department of Statistics, P.O. Box N 3904, Nassau, Bahamas.

336 BA
BAHRAIN. MONETARY AGENCY. QUARTERLY STATISTICAL BULLETIN. 1975. q. Monetary Agency, P.O. Box 27, Manama, Bahrain. TEL 535535. FAX 533342. TELEX BN9191. charts; stat.
Document type: government publication, bulletin.
Formerly: Bahrain. Monetary Agency. Quarterly Statement of Affairs and Statistical Bulletin.

336 382 TR ISSN 0067-3005
BALANCE OF PAYMENTS OF TRINIDAD AND TOBAGO. a. T.T.$15($7.50) Central Statistical Office, 35-41 Queen St., P.O. Box 98, Port-of-Spain, Trinidad & Tobago, W.I. TEL 809-623-7069. **Document type:** government publication.

332.1 315 PK
BALANCE SHEET ANALYSIS OF JOINT STOCK COMPANIES. (Text in English) a. Rs.82($13) State Bank of Pakistan, Central Directorate, Public Relations Department, I.I. Chundrigar Rd., P.O. Box 4456, Karachi, Pakistan. TEL 92-2414141. FAX 92-2417865. TELEX 2754 SBPK PK. **Document type:** government publication.

330 314 GR ISSN 1105-2511
BALANCE SHEETS. (Supplement to: Epilogi) 1987. a. Dr.4000. Electra Press, 4 Stadiou St., 105 64 Athens, Greece. TEL 323-3203. FAX 323-5160. TELEX 210564. Ed. Christos Papaioannou. adv.; stat. circ. 11,000.
Description: Analyzes the finances of private, public, industrial, and service sectors of Greece with particular attention to banking and insurance companies.

332 BO
BANCO CENTRAL DE BOLIVIA. BOLETIN DEL SECTOR EXTERNO. 1989. s-a. Bs.20. Banco Central de Bolivia, Casilla 3118, La Paz, Bolivia. Ed. Luis Alberto Arce Catacora. **Document type:** bulletin.

332 BO ISSN 0522-0939
HG185.B6
BANCO CENTRAL DE BOLIVIA. BOLETIN ESTADISTICO. 1967. q. Bs.20. Banco Central de Bolivia, Casilla 3118, La Paz, Bolivia. Ed. Luis Alberto Arce Catacora. charts; stat. **Indexed:** P.A.I.S.For.Lang.Ind. **Document type:** bulletin.

332 BO ISSN 1023-361X
BANCO CENTRAL DE BOLIVIA. MEMORIA. 1929. a. Bs.50. Banco Central de Bolivia, Casilla 3118, La Paz, Bolivia. Ed. Luis Alberto Arce Catacora. **Document type:** corporate report.

330.9 318 HO ISSN 1012-9510
BANCO CENTRAL DE HONDURAS. DEPARTAMENTO DE ESTUDIOS ECONOMICOS. BOLETIN ESTADISTICO MENSUAL. 1950. m. Banco Central de Honduras, Departamento de Estudios Economicos, 6a y 7a Avda., 1a Calle, Tegucigalpa D.C., Honduras. TEL 22-2270. charts; stat. **Indexed:** P.A.I.S.For.Lang.Ind.
Formerly: Banco Central de Honduras. Departamento de Estudios Economicos. Boletin Estadistico (ISSN 0252-9033)
Description: Provides statistics on banking and the economy in Honduras, with emphasis on the Central Bank of Honduras.

BANCO CENTRAL DE HONDURAS. DIVISION DE SEGUROS. BOLETIN DE ESTADISTICAS DE SEGUROS. see *INSURANCE — Abstracting, Bibliographies, Statistics*

332 318 AG ISSN 0005-4674
HA943
BANCO CENTRAL DE LA REPUBLICA ARGENTINA. BOLETIN ESTADISTICO. 1958. m. free. Banco Central de la Republica Argentina, Centro de Estudios Monetarios y Bancarios, Reconquista 266-78, Buenos Aires, Argentina. **Indexed:** P.A.I.S.For.Lang.Ind.

332 VE
BANCO CENTRAL DE VENEZUELA. ANUARIO DE BALANZA DE PAGOS. a. $3 (effective 1994). Banco Central de Venezuela, Avda. Urdaneta Esq. de las Carmelitas, Caracas 1010, Venezuela. TEL 58-2-8015111.

332.1 VE
BANCO CENTRAL DE VENEZUELA. ANUARIO DE ESTADISTICAS INTERNACIONALES. a. $2 (effective 1994). Banco Central de Venezuela, Avda. Urdaneta esq. de las Carmelitas, Caracas 1010, Venezuela. TEL 58-2-8015111.

330 VE
BANCO CENTRAL DE VENEZUELA. ANUARIO DE ESTADISTICAS PRECIOS Y MERCADO LABORAL. a. $6 (effective 1994). Banco Central de Estadistica, Avda. Urdaneta Esq. de las Carmelitas, Caracas 1010, Venezuela. TEL 58-2-8015111.

332 VE
BANCO CENTRAL DE VENEZUELA. ANUARIO DE ESTADISTICAS SECTOR FINANCIERO. a. $9 (effective 1994). Banco Central de Venezuela, Avda. Urdaneta Esq. de las Carmelitas, Caracas 1010, Venezuela. TEL 58-2-8015111.

332.1 330 EC
BANCO CENTRAL DEL ECUADOR. BALANZA DE PAGOS. (Text in English and Spanish) a. free. Banco Central del Ecuador, Casilla 29C, Sucursal No.15, Quito, Ecuador. TEL 561-521. (Dist. by: Libreria Economica y Cultural, Ave. 10 de Agosto, No. 600 y Checa, Quito, Ecuador) circ. 15,000.

332 011 EC
BANCO CENTRAL DEL ECUADOR. INFORMACION ESTADISTICA QUINCENAL. fortn. Banco Central del Ecuador, Casilla 29C, Sucursal No.15, Quito, Ecuador. TEL 561-521. (Dist. by: Libreria Economia y Cultura, Av. 10 de Agosto, No. 600 y Checa, Quito, Ecuador) charts; stat. circ. 6,000.
Former titles: Banco Central de Ecuador. Informacion Estadistica Mensual; Banco Central del Ecuador. Informacion Estadistica.

330.9 UY
BANCO CENTRAL DEL URUGUAY. DEPARTAMENTO DE ESTADISTICAS ECONOMICAS. BOLETIN ESTADISTICO. (Includes q.: Endeudamiento Externo del Uruguay) 1942. m. free. Banco Central del Uruguay, Departamento de Estadisticas Economicas, Casilla 1467, Paysando y Florida, Montevideo, Uruguay. FAX 598-2-921782. TELEX 26939 BACENUR UY. charts; stat. **Indexed:** P.A.I.S.For.Lang.Ind.
Former titles: Banco Central del Uruguay. Departamento de Investigaciones Economicas. Boletin Estadistico & Banco Central del Uruguay. Boletin Estadistico Mensual (ISSN 0005-4747); Supersedes: Banco de la Republica Oriental del Uruguay. Revista.

BANCO DE ESPANA. BOLETIN ESTADISTICO. see *BUSINESS AND ECONOMICS — Banking And Finance*

BANCO DE GUATEMALA. BOLETIN ESTADISTICO. see *BUSINESS AND ECONOMICS — Banking And Finance*

332.6 MX
BANCO DE MEXICO. INDICADORES DEL SECTOR EXTERNO. m. Mex.$800 (US $240; Europe $300; elsewhere $360) (effective Aug. 1996). Banco de Mexico, Subdireccion de Investigacion Economica y Bancaria, Av. Juarez 90, Col. Centro, Del. Cuauhtemoc, 06059 Mexico DF, Mexico. TEL 525-761-8588.

330 MX
BANCO DE MEXICO. INDICE DE PRECIOS. m. Mex.$800 (US $240; Europe $300; elsewhere $360) (effective Aug. 1996). Banco de Mexico, Subdireccion de Investigacion Economica y Bancaria, Av. Juarez 90, Col. Centro, Del. Cuauhtemoc, 06059 Mexico DF, Mexico. TEL 525-761-8588.

BUSINESS AND ECONOMICS — ABSTRACTING, BIBLIOGRAPHIES, STATISTICS

330 318   PO
BANCO DE PORTUGAL. ESTATISTICA E ESTUDOS ECONOMICOS. m. Banco de Portugal, Departamento de Estatisticas e Estudos Economicos, Rua Febo Moniz no. 4, 6 andar, 1100 Lisbon, Portugal. (Dist. by: Gabinete de Informacao e Documentacao.)

330.9 318   UY
BANCO HIPOTECARIO DEL URUGUAY. BOLETIN ESTADISTICO. s-a. Banco Hipotecario del Uruguay, Departamento de Planificacion y Metodos, Montevideo, Uruguay. charts; illus.; stat.

BANCOS CENTRALES DE LOS PAISES DEL ACUERDO DE CARTAGENA. BOLETIN ESTADISTICO. see *BUSINESS AND ECONOMICS — Banking And Finance*

332 310   BG
BANGLADESH BANK. STATISTICS DEPARTMENT. ANNUAL BALANCE OF PAYMENTS. (Text in English) 1974. a. Bangladesh Bank, Department of Public Relations and Publications, Motijheel Commercial Area, Dhaka 2, Bangladesh. stat.

382 316   BG
BANGLADESH BANK. STATISTICS DEPARTMENT. ANNUAL IMPORT PAYMENTS. (Text in English) 1973. a. Bangladesh Bank, Department of Public Relations and Publications, Motijheel Commercial Area, Dhaka 2, Bangladesh. stat.

332 336   BG
BANGLADESH BANK. STATISTICS DEPARTMENT. BALANCE OF PAYMENTS. (Text in English) 1974. q. Bangladesh Bank, Department of Public Relations and Publications, Motijheel Commercial Area, Dhaka 2, Bangladesh.

332.1 316   BG
BANGLADESH BANK. STATISTICS DEPARTMENT. QUARTERLY SCHEDULED BANKS STATISTICS. (Text in English) 1977. q. Bangladesh Bank, Department of Public Relations and Publications, Motijheel Commercial Area, Dhaka 2, Bangladesh.

330.9   MY
BANK NEGARA MALAYSIA. STATISTICAL BULLETIN. (Text in English, Malay) m. $80 in Asia & Australasia; Europe $99; Africa & America $108. Bank Negara Malaysia - Central Bank of Malaysia, P.O. Box 10922, Jalan Dato'onn, 50480 Kuala Lumpur, Malaysia. TEL 2988044. FAX 2912990. TELEX MA 30201. Ed.Bd. charts, stat.; circ. controlled. (back issues avail.) **Document type:** bulletin.
Description: Reports the monetary, banking, liquidity, capital market and macroeconomic situations.

332 317   CN   ISSN 0005-5158
BANK OF CANADA. WEEKLY FINANCIAL STATISTICS/BANQUE DU CANADA. BULLETIN HEBDOMADAIRE DE STATISTIQUES FINANCIERES. 1954. w. Can.$55. Bank of Canada - Banque du Canada, Publications Distribution, Communications Services, 234 Wellington St., Ottawa, ON K1A OG9, Canada. TEL 613-782-8248. FAX 613-782-8874. E-mail: publications@bank-banque-canada.ca; URL: http://www.bank-banque-canada.ca. circ. 1,600. pp./issue: 16. (processed) **Document type:** government publication, bulletin.
Description: Shows banking statistics and economic indicators in Canada.

332 314   GR   ISSN 1105-0519
HG3066
BANK OF GREECE. MONTHLY STATISTICAL BULLETIN. (Text in English and Greek) 1932. m. $30 (foreign $55). Bank of Greece, Economic Research Division, 21 Panepistimiou St., 102 50 Athens, Greece. FAX 30-1-323-3025. TELEX 30-1-215-102. charts; mkt.; stat. circ. 2,500. **Document type:** bulletin.

332.1   IS   ISSN 0334-4541
HG3260
BANK OF ISRAEL. ANNUAL STATISTICS OF ISRAEL'S BANKING SYSTEM. 1978. a. IS.20. Bank of Israel, Kiryat Ben Gurion, P.O. Box 780, Jerusalem 91007, Israel.

332.1   IS
BANK OF ISRAEL. CURRENT BANKING STATISTICS. (Text in English, Hebrew) m. IS.120. Bank of Israel, Publications Unit, Kiryath Ben Gurion, P.O. Box 780, Jerusalem 91007, Israel. (processed)
Formerly: Bank of Israel. Banking Statistics (ISSN 0039-0607)

332   IS
BANK OF ISRAEL. EXCHANGE RATES. (Text in English, Hebrew) w. IS.145. Bank of Israel, Publications Unit, Kiryat Ben Gurion, P.O. Box 780, Jerusalem 91007, Israel.

332   IS
BANK OF ISRAEL. MAIN ISRAELI ECONOMIC DATA. (Text in English, Hebrew) s-m. IS.150 (effective 1992). Bank of Israel, Publications Unit, Kiryat Ben Gurion, P.O. Box 780, Jerusalem 91007, Israel.

330.9 315   JM   ISSN 1018-9084
HG185.J3
BANK OF JAMAICA. ECONOMIC STATISTICS. 1991. m. free. Bank of Jamaica, Research & Economic Programming Division, P.O. Box 621, King St., Kingston, Jamaica, W.I. TEL 809-922-0750. FAX 809-967-4265. TELEX 2165. illus.; stat.; circ. 1,200. (controlled)

330   JA
BANK OF JAPAN. COMMODITY GROUPS, WEIGHTS, ITEMS OF COMMODITY GROUPS AND LINKED INDEXES. (Text in English, Japanese) every 5 yrs. 1700 Yen. Bank of Japan - Nippon Ginko, c/o Public Relations Department, 2-1-1 Hongoku-cho, Nihonbashi, Chuo-ku, Tokyo 103, Japan. TEL 81-3-3279-1111. FAX 81-3-5209-8703. (Dist. by: Tokiwa Sohgoh Service Co., Ltd., Kyodo Bldg., 2-4, 3-chome, Hongokucho, Nihonbashi, Chuo-ku, Tokyo 103, Japan. TEL 81-3-3270-5713. FAX 81-3-3270-5710; Dist. overseas by: Japan Publications Trading Co., Ltd., Book Export No.2 Department, P.O. Box 5030 Tokyo International, Tokyo 100-31, Japan. TEL 81-3-3292-3753. FAX 81-3-3292-0410)

310   JA
▼**BANK OF JAPAN. ECONOMIC AND FINANCIAL DATA ON C D - R O M.** (Text in English, Japanese) 1997. a. 3420 Yen. Bank of Japan, Research and Statistics Department, c/o Public Relations Department, 1-1, 2-chome, Hongokucho, Nihonbashi, Chuo-ku, Tokyo 103, Japan. TELEX JPTCO J27161. (Dist. by: Tokiwa Sohgoh Service Co., Ltd., Publications and Research Dept., Kyodo Bldg., 2-4, 3-chome, Hongokucho, Nihonbashi, Chuo-ku, Tokyo 103, Japan. TEL 81-3-3270-5713; Dist. overseas by: Japan Publications Trading Co., Ltd., Book Export No.2 Dept., P.O. Box 5030 Tokyo International, Tokyo 100-31, Japan. TEL 81-3-3292-3753. FAX 81-3-3292-0410)
●Available only on CD-ROM.
Description: Provides annual statistics on money and banking, public finance, balance of payments, foreign exchange, industry, labor, prices, household economy, and national accounts.

330 315   JA   ISSN 0910-6006
BANK OF JAPAN. ECONOMIC STATISTICS ANNUAL/NIPPON GINKO. KEIZAI TOKET NENPO. (Text in English, Japanese) 1919. a. 3260 Yen. Bank of Japan, Research and Statistics Department - Nippon Ginko, c/o Public Relations Department, 1-1, 2-chome Hongoku-cho, Nihonbashi, Chuo-ku, Tokyo 103, Japan. TEL 81-3-3292-3753. FAX 81-3-3292-0410. (Dist. by: Tokiwa Sohgoh Service Co., Ltd., Publication and Research Department, Kyodo Bldg., 2-4, 3-chome, Hongokucho, Nihonbashi, Chuo-ku, Tokyo 103, Japan. TEL 81-3-3270-5713. FAX 81-3-3270-5710; Overseas dist. by: Japan Publications Trading Co., Ltd., Book Export No. 2 Dept., P.O. Box 5030 Tokyo International, Tokyo 100-31, Japan) pp./issue: 380.
Formerly (until 1967): Bank of Japan. Economic Statistics of Japan (ISSN 0910-5999)
Description: Annual statistics on money and banking, public finance, balance of payments, foreign exchange, industry, labor, prices, household economy, national accounts and economic prospects.

330.9 315   JA   ISSN 0005-5247
BANK OF JAPAN. ECONOMIC STATISTICS MONTHLY. (Text in English, Japanese) 1946. m. 1050 Yen per no. Bank of Japan, Research and Statistics Department - Nippon Ginko, c/o Public Relations Department, 2-1-1 Hongoku-cho, Nihonbashi, Chuo-ku, Tokyo 103, Japan. TEL 81-3-3292-3753. FAX 81-3-3292-0410. (Dist. by: Tokiwa Sohgoh Service Co., Ltd., Publication and Research Dept., Kyodo Bldg., 2-4, 3-chome, Hongokucho, Nihonbashi, Chuo-ku, Tokyo 103, Japan. TEL 81-3-3270-5713; Overseas dist. by: Japan Publications Trading Co., Ltd., Book Export No. 2 Dept., P.O. Box 5030 Tokyo International, Tokyo 100-31, Japan) charts; mkt.; stat. pp./issue: 250.
Description: Monthly statistics on money and banking, public finance, balance of payments, foreign exchange, industry, labor, prices, household economy, national income, and overseas key statistics.

382   JA
BANK OF JAPAN. PRICE INDEXES ANNUAL. (Appendix avail.) (Text in English, Japanese) a. 4100 Yen. Bank of Japan, Research and Statistics Department - Nippon Ginko, c/o Public Relations Department, 2-1-1 Hongoku-Cho, Nihonbashi, Chuo-ku, Tokyo 103, Japan. TEL 81-3-3292-3753. FAX 81-3-3292-0410. (Dist. by: Tokiwa Sohgoh Service Co., Ltd., Kyodo Bldg., 2-4, 3-chome, Hongokucho, Nihonbashi, Chuo-ku, Tokyo 103, Japan. TEL 81-3-3270-5713. FAX 81-3-3270-5710; Overseas dist. by: Japan Publications Trading Co., Ltd., Book Export No. 2 Dept., P.O. Box 5030 Tokyo International, Tokyo 100-31, Japan) pp./issue: 525.
Description: Wholesale price indexes, export and import price indexes, corporate service price index, and input-output price indexes of manufacturing industry by sector.

330   JA
BANK OF JAPAN. STATISTICS HANDBOOK/TOKEI BINRAN. (Text in Japanese) m. 830 Yen per no. Bank of Japan, Research and Statistics Department - Nippon Ginko, c/o Public Relations Department, 2-1-1 Hongoku-Cho, Nihonbashi, Chuo-ku, Tokyo 103, Japan. TEL 81-3-3292-3753. FAX 81-3-3292-0410. (Dist. by: Tokiwa Sohgoh Service Co., Ltd., Publication & Research Dept., Kyodo Bldg., 2-4, 3-chome, Hongokucho, Nihonbashi, Chuo-ku, Tokyo 103, Japan. TEL 81-3-3270-5713; Overseas dist. by: Japan Publications Trading Co., Ltd., Book Export No. 2 Dept., P.O. Box 5030 Tokyo International, Tokyo 100-31, Japan) pp./issue: 160.
Description: Covers money and banking, public finance, foreign trade, foreign exchange, balance of payments, industries, consumption, prices, labor, national income, overseas key statistics and more.

382 316   SJ   ISSN 0522-246X
HF273.S8
BANK OF SUDAN. FOREIGN TRADE STATISTICAL DIGEST. (Text in English) 1968. q. Bank of Sudan, Statistics Department, Box 313, Khartoum, Sudan. TEL 78064. TELEX 22559 ELBNK SD.
Description: Documents the foreign trade statistics and balance of payments covering all exports and imports through Port Sudan.

BANKING ABSTRACTS; idee e tecniche di management bancario selezionate dalla stampa italiana ed estera. see *BUSINESS AND ECONOMICS — Banking And Finance*

332   US   ISSN 0736-5659
Z7164.F5
BANKING LITERATURE INDEX. Cover title: American Bankers Association. Banking Literature Index. 1982. m. (plus a. cumulation). U M I (Subsidiary of: Bell & Howell Company), 300 N. Zeeb Rd., Ann Arbor, MI 48106. TEL 313-761-4700; 800-521-0600. FAX 800-864-0019. Ed. Elinor Dumont. circ. 450 (paid). (back issues avail.)
Document type: abstracting/indexing.
Description: Information tracking system for new developments in the banking and financial services industry. Provides subject access to more than 185 journals, magazines, newspapers, and newsletters.

BUSINESS AND ECONOMICS — ABSTRACTING, BIBLIOGRAPHIES, STATISTICS

332   FR
BANQUE DE FRANCE. CAHIER DES TITRES DE CREANCES NEGOCIABLES. m. 1200 F. Banque de France, Service de l'Information, 48 rue Croix des Petits Champs, 75001 Paris, France. TEL 42-92-39-31. FAX 42-92-39-40.
Description: Covers certificates of deposit and treasury bills.

332   FR
BANQUE DE FRANCE. ENQUETE FINANCIERE. m. 120 F. Banque de France, Service de l'Information, 48 rue Croix des Petits Champs, 75001 Paris, France. TEL 42-92-39-08. FAX 42-92-39-40.

332   FR
BANQUE DE FRANCE. MOYENS DE PAIEMENT ET CIRCUITS DE RECOUVREMENT. a. 60 F. Banque de France, Service de l'Information, 48 rue Croix des Petits Champs, 75001 Paris, France. TEL 43-92-39-08. FAX 42-92-39-40.

332   FR
BANQUE DE FRANCE. SITUATION DU SYSTEME PRODUCTIF EN (YEAR). a. 100 F. Banque de France, Service de l'Information, 48 rue Croix des Petits Champs, B.P. 140-01, 75001 Paris, France. TEL 42-92-39-08. FAX 42-92-39-40.

332   FR   ISSN 1142-8651
BANQUE DE FRANCE. STATISTIQUES MONETAIRES ET FINANCIERES ANNUELLES. 1982. a. 120 F. Banque de France, Service de l'Information, 48 rue Croix des Petits Champs, 75001 Paris, France. TEL 42-92-39-31. FAX 42-92-39-40.
Formerly (until 1987): Banque de France. Statistiques Monetaires Annuelles (ISSN 0767-6565)
Description: Presents statistical information on money, credit, capital markets and the activities of financial institutions.

332   CM   ISSN 0014-2069
HG3409.E65
BANQUE DES ETATS DE L'AFRIQUE CENTRALE. ETUDES ET STATISTIQUES; bulletin mensuel. 1956. 10/yr. Banque des Etats de l'Afrique Centrale, Direction des Etudes et de la Documentation, Services Centraux, B.P. 1917, Yaounde, Cameroon. TEL 22-25-05. FAX 23-33-29. TELEX 8343. stat. circ. 1,500. **Indexed:** Documentatieblad, P.A.I.S.For.Lang.Ind. **Document type:** bulletin.

330.9 316   CG
BANQUE DU ZAIRE. BULLETIN MENSUEL DE LA STATISTIQUE. m. K.5.23 per no. Banque du Zaire, B.P. 2697, Kinshasa, Democratic Republic of the Congo. **Document type:** bulletin.

310   BB
BARBADOS. STATISTICAL SERVICE. BULLETIN. OVERSEAS TRADE. 1983. m. free. Statistical Service, National Insurance Bldg., 3rd Fl., Fairchild St., Bridgetown, Barbados, W.I. stat. circ. 200. **Document type:** government publication.
Description: Detailed figures on imports and exports of CARICOM countries.

011   US   ISSN 0360-8379
HG1
BARRON'S INDEX. Issued with (after 1981): Wall Street Journal Index (ISSN 0083-7075) (Availability: 1975-1980) irreg. U M I (Subsidiary of: Bell & Howell Company), 300 N. Zeeb Rd., Ann Arbor, MI 48106. TEL 313-761-4700; 800-521-0600. FAX 800-864-0019. **Indexed:** Hlth.Ind. **Document type:** abstracting/indexing.

339 314   BE
BELGIUM. INSTITUT NATIONAL DE STATISTIQUE. COMPTES NATIONAUX DE LA BELGIQUE. Issued with: Belgium. Institut National de Statistique. Etudes Statistiques (ISSN 0069-8075) (Editions in Dutch, French) a. 240 BEF (foreign 300 BEF). Institut National de Statistique, 44 rue de Louvain, 1000 Brussels, Belgium. TEL 32-2-5486211. FAX 32-2-5486367. **Document type:** government publication.
Description: Provides historical data on Belgian national accounts during the preceding 8-10 years.

332 314   BE   ISSN 0771-6184
BELGIUM. INSTITUT NATIONAL DE STATISTIQUE. STATISTIQUES FINANCIERES. (Text in Dutch, French) 1972. irreg. (3-4/yr.), no.61, 1993. 660 BEF for 3 nos. (foreign 830 BEF) (effective 1997). Institut National de Statistique, 44 rue de Louvain, 1000 Brussels, Belgium. TEL 32-2-5486211. FAX 32-2-5486367. charts; stat. **Document type:** government publication.

314.93   BE   ISSN 0772-7704
HC311
BELGIUM. INSTITUT NATIONAL DE STATISTIQUE. STATISTIQUES INDUSTRIELLES. Key Title: Statistiques Industrielles (Brussels). Dutch edition: Industriele Statistieken (ISSN 0772-7690) (Text in Dutch, French) 1967. 11/yr. 1600 BEF (foreign 2000 BEF) (effective 1997). Institut National de Statistique, 44 rue de Louvain, 1000 Brussels, Belgium. TEL 32-2-548-6211. FAX 32-2-5486367. charts; stat. **Indexed:** P.A.I.S.For.Lang.Ind. **Document type:** government publication.

658.3   MX
BENEFITS SURVEY. (Text in English, Spanish) a. $112. American Chamber of Commerce of Mexico, A.C., Lucerna 78, Col. Juarez, Del. Cuauhtemoc, 06600 Mexico DF, Mexico. TEL 52-5-724-3800. FAX 52-5-703-2911. TELEX 177-7609 ACHAME. R&P contact: Diana H. de Hernandez. **Document type:** corporate report.
Description: Provides information on fringe benefits received by executives, other high-level personnel and salespeople by company size, location and industrial sector within Mexico.

331 320   BL   ISSN 0103-2038
Z7165.B7
BIBLIOGRAFIA DE POLITICA INDUSTRIAL. 1987. a. Confederacao Nacional da Industria, Av. Nilo Pecanha, 50, S-3204, 20044-900 Rio de Janeiro RJ, Brazil.

330   PL
BIBLIOGRAFIA PUBLIKACJI PRACOWNIKOW NAUKOWYCH AKADEMII EKONOMICZNEJ W KRAKOWIE. a. price varies. Akademia Ekonomiczna, Krakow, Ul. Rakowicka 27, 31-510 Krakow, Poland. FAX 48-12-210536. Ed.Bd. index. **Document type:** bibliography.
Description: Announcement of publications issued by the Krakow Academy of Economics.

330 015   MX   ISSN 0188-6673
Z7165.M45
BIBLIOGRAFIA SOBRE LA ECONOMIA MEXICANA. LIBROS. 1955. irreg., latest 1990-1992 ed. Mex.$70 (America $20; Europe $25) (effective Aug. 1996). Banco de Mexico, Subdireccion de Investigacion Economica y Bancaria, Av. Juarez 90, Col. Centro, Del. Cuauhtemoc, 06059 Mexico DF, Mexico. TEL 525-761-8588. bibl. circ. 200.
Formerly (until 1981): Bibliografia Economica de Mexico (ISSN 0006-100X)
Description: Covers publications from Mexico and about Mexico.

330   US   ISSN 0360-2702
Z7164.C81
BIBLIOGRAPHIC GUIDE TO BUSINESS AND ECONOMICS. 1974. a. $715 (effective 1997). G.K. Hall & Co., MacMillan Library Reference USA, Box 159, Thorndike, ME 04986. TEL 212-654-8452; 800-223-6121. FAX 207-948-2863. URL: http://www.mir.com/thordike. (Subscr. to: Simon & Schuster, Library Reference Order Processing, 200 Old Tappan Rd., Old Tappan, NJ 07675. TEL 800-223-2336) **Document type:** abstracting/indexing, bibliography.
Description: Covers books, reports, conference papers and miscellaneous publications in the New York Public Library, with additional entries covering all aspects of business and economics: theory, history, population, demography, land-agriculture, industry, labor, transportation, communication, commerce, business administration, finance, foreign exchange, insurance, taxation, statistics.

330 016   GW   ISSN 0006-1417
Z7164.E2
BIBLIOGRAPHIE DER WIRTSCHAFTSPRESSE. 1949. m. DM.210. H W W A - Institut fuer Wirtschaftsforschung Hamburg, Informationszentrum, Neuer Jungfernstieg 21, 20347 Hamburg, Germany. TEL 040-3562260. (reprint service avail. from ISI) **Indexed:** Key to Econ.Sci., P.A.I.S.For.Lang.Ind. **Document type:** bibliography.
—CCC.

016   US   ISSN 0749-1786
BIBLIOGRAPHIES AND INDEXES IN ECONOMICS AND ECONOMIC HISTORY. 1984. irreg. price varies. Greenwood Press, Inc. (Subsidiary of: Greenwood Publishing Group Inc.), 88 Post Rd. W., Box 5007, Westport, CT 06881-5007. TEL 203-226-3571. FAX 203-222-1502. **Document type:** bibliography.

658   US
BIBLIOGRAPHY OF BUSINESS - COMPETITIVE AND BENCHMARKING LITERATURE. irreg. $275 (effective 1997). Washington Researchers, Ltd., Box 19005, 20th St. Sta., Washington, DC 20036-9005. TEL 202-333-3499. FAX 202-625-0656. Ed. M. Newman. R&P contact: Ellen O'Kane. **Document type:** directory.
Description: Lists books, journal articles, conference proceedings, research reports, and audio and videotapes that cover business intelligence and the use of benchmarking techniques.

330   CE
BIBLIOGRAPHY OF ECONOMIC AND SOCIAL DEVELOPMENT SRI LANKA. (Text in English) 1982. irreg. Rs.200($25) Ministry of Policy Planning & Implementation, National Planning Dept., Centre for Development Information, Treasury Bldg., Columbo 01, Sri Lanka. FAX 549823. TELEX 21409-FINMIN-CE. circ. 250. (back issues avail.) **Document type:** bibliography.
Description: Provides bibliographical data on development information related to Sri Lanka from various government, non-governmental, private, and international agencies.

330 016.3309   TZ
BIBLIOGRAPHY OF ECONOMIC AND STATISTICAL PUBLICATIONS ON TANZANIA. 1967. irreg. Bureau of Statistics, P.O. Box 796, Dar es Salaam, Tanzania. (Orders to: Government Publications Agency, P.O. Box 1801, Dar es Salaam, Tanzania) **Document type:** bibliography, government publication.

330 315   II
BIBLIOGRAPHY OF PUBLICATIONS FROM ECONOMIC RESEARCH CENTRES IN INDIA. (Supplements avail. annually) 1973. irreg., latest 1988. Rs.250($75) Information Research Academy, 37 Amir Ali Ave., Calcutta 700019, India. Ed. Partha Subir Guha. adv. circ. 1,900. **Document type:** bibliography.

658.8 011   US
BIBLIOGRAPHY ON LOGISTICS MANAGEMENT. 1967. a. $35. Council of Logistics Management, 2803 Butterfield Rd., Ste. 380, Oak Brook, IL 60521. TEL 630-574-0985. FAX 630-574-0989. **Document type:** bibliography.
Description: Covers materials published during the previous year.

650 329   YU   ISSN 0351-4048
BILTEN DOKUMENTACIJE. SAVREMENA ORGANIZACIJA I EKONOMIJA ORGANIZACIJA UDRUZENOG RADA. 1964. bi-m. $264. Jugoslovenski Centar za Tehnicku i Naucnu Dokumentaciju - Yugoslav Center for Technical and Scientific Documentation (YCTSD), Sl. Penezica-Krcuna 29-31, Box 724, 11000 Belgrade, Yugoslavia. Ed. Ljiljana Kojic-Bogdanovic.
Formerly: Bilten Dokumentacije. Savremena Organizacija i Ekonomija Radnih Organizacija (ISSN 0303-223X)

332   US   ISSN 1063-3197
BIO-BIBLIOGRAPHIES IN ECONOMICS. 1992. irreg. price varies. Greenwood Press, Inc. (Subsidiary of: Greenwood Publishing Group Inc.), 88 Post Rd. W., Box 5007, Westport, CT 06881-5007. TEL 203-226-3571. FAX 203-222-1502. **Document type:** bibliography, monographic series.

BIOCOMMERCE FINANCIAL ABSTRACTS. see *BIOLOGY — Abstracting, Bibliographies, Statistics*

BUSINESS AND ECONOMICS — ABSTRACTING, BIBLIOGRAPHIES, STATISTICS

330.9   **BL**   ISSN 0104-5458
BOLETIM CONJUNTURAL DO NORDESTE DO BRASIL. 1993. irreg. donation. Superintendencia do Desenvolvimento do Nordeste, Praca Ministro J. Goncalves de Souza, Edf. Sudene, Cidade Universitaria, 50670-900 Recife PE, Brazil. TEL 55-81-4162222. FAX 55-81-4531277. **Document type:** government publication.

330.9 332   **GT**
BOLETIN DE ESTADISTICAS BANCARIAS. 1951. q. free. Superintendencia de Bancos, Departamento Tecnico, Seccion de Estadistica, 7a. Av. 22-01, Zona 1, Edificio Bco. de Guatemala, 10 Nivel, Guatemala, Guatemala. TEL 53-42-43. charts; illus.; stat.; index. (back issues avail.) **Document type:** bulletin.
Description: Statistics on the 60 institutions under the supervision of Superintendencia de Bancos.

331   **SP**   ISSN 0212-7180
HD8581
BOLETIN DE ESTADISTICAS LABORALES. m. 12000 ptas. (effective 1997). Ministerio de Trabajo y Asuntos Sociales, Centro de Publicaciones, Agustin de Bethencourt 11, 28003 Madrid, Spain. TEL 34-1-5543400. FAX 34-1-5540813. E-mail: libreria@mundiprensa.es. (Subscr. to: Mundi-Prensa Libros, S.A., Castello 37, 28001 Madrid, Spain. TEL 34-1-4313222. FAX 34-1-5753998) **Document type:** government publication.

310 382   **BO**
BOLIVIA. INSTITUTO NACIONAL DE ESTADISTICA. ANUARIO DE COMERCIO EXTERIOR. 1910. a. $12. Instituto Nacional de Estadistica, Casilla de Correo No. 6129, La Paz, Bolivia.

310 338   **BO**
BOLIVIA. INSTITUTO NACIONAL DE ESTADISTICA. ANUARIO DE ESTADISTICAS INDUSTRIALES. 1939. a. $15. Instituto Nacional de Estadistica, Casilla de Correo No. 6129, La Paz, Bolivia.

339 318   **BO**
BOLIVIA. INSTITUTO NACIONAL DE ESTADISTICA. INDICE DE PRECIOS AL CONSUMIDOR. (Cum. edition avail.: Resumen Anual 1974. m. $43. Instituto Nacional de Estadistica, Casilla de Correo No. 6129, La Paz, Bolivia.

332   **MX**   ISSN 0188-3879
HC131
BOLSA MEXICANA DE VALORES. ANUARIO FINANCIERO (YEAR). English edition: Mexican Stock Exchange. Annual Financial Facts and Figures (Year). a. $40 (effective May 1996). Bolsa Mexicana de Valores, S.A. de C.V. - Mexican Stock Exchange, Paseo de la Reforma 255, 06500 Mexico D.F., Mexico. TEL 525-726-67-91. FAX 525-591-05-34.
Description: Contains individual and sectorial financial data of companies listed on the Mexican Stock Exchange. Includes 4 years historical information, Board of Directors' report, general company information and basic data.

332   **MX**   ISSN 0188-3925
HG5161
BOLSA MEXICANA DE VALORES. INDICADORES FINANCIEROS/MEXICAN STOCK EXCHANGE. FINANCIAL FACTS AND FIGURES. q. $75 (effective May 1996). Bolsa Mexicana de Valores, S.A. de C.V. - Mexican Stock Exchange, Paseo de la Reforma 255, 06500 Mexico D.F., Mexico. TEL 525-726-67-91. FAX 525-591-05-34.
Incorporates: Bolsa Mexicana de Valores. Financial Studies.
Description: Contains balance sheets, income statements and financial ratios, by sector and by issuer.

332.6   **MX**   ISSN 1405-230X
BOLSA MEXICANA DE VALORES. RESUMEN BURSATIL/MEXICAN STOCK EXCHANGE. STATISTICS SUMMARY. m. $35 (effective May 1996). Bolsa Mexicana de Valores, S.A. de C.V. - Mexican Stock Exchange, Paseo de la Reforma 255, 06500 Mexico DF, Mexico. TEL 525-7266791. FAX 525-591-0534.
Description: Summarizes securities market activity.

330   **BS**
BOTSWANA. CENTRAL STATISTICS OFFICE. DEMOGRAPHIC AND HEALTH SURVEY. a. Central Statistics Office, Ministry of Finance and Development Planning, Private Bag 0024, Gaborone, Botswana. TEL 267-352200. (Orders to: Government Printer, P.O. Box 87, Gaborone, Botswana) Ed. G.M. Charumbira; Pub. J.G. Segwe. **Document type:** government publication.
Description: Provides demographic profiles of family planning, pregnancy, infant and childhood mortality, and child care.

330.9 332.6   **BS**   ISSN 1013-5707
HF3906
BOTSWANA. CENTRAL STATISTICS OFFICE. EXTERNAL TRADE STATISTICS. a. P.20. Central Statistics Office, Ministry of Finance and Development Planning, Private Bag 0024, Gaborone, Botswana. TEL 267-352200. (Orders to: Government Printer, P.O. Box 87, Gaborone, Botswana) Ed. G.M. Charumbira; Pub. J.G. Segwe. **Document type:** government publication.

330   **BS**
BOTSWANA. CENTRAL STATISTICS OFFICE. HOUSEHOLD INCOME AND EXPENDITURE SURVEY. irreg. P.10. Central Statistics Office, Ministry of Finance and Development Planning, Private Bag 0024, Gaborone, Botswana. TEL 267-352200. (Orders to: Government Printer, P.O. Box 87, Gaborone, Botswana) Ed. G.M. Charumbira; Pub. J.G. Segwe. charts; stat. **Document type:** government publication.
Description: Analyzes household income and expenditure data for Botswana.

331.1 316   **BS**
BOTSWANA. CENTRAL STATISTICS OFFICE. LABOUR STATISTICS. (Text in English) a. P.5. Central Statistics Office, Ministry of Finance and Development Planning, Private Bag 0024, Gaborone, Botswana. TEL 267-352200. (Orders to: Government Printer, P.O. Box 87, Gaborone, Botswana) Ed. G.M. Charumbira; Pub. J.G. Segwe. **Document type:** government publication.
Formerly: Botswana. Central Statistics Office. Employment Survey.
Description: Provides information on number of persons employed and their earnings broken down by industry.

316.8   **BS**   ISSN 1013-5693
BOTSWANA. CENTRAL STATISTICS OFFICE. STATISTICAL BULLETIN. q. P.5. Central Statistics Office, Ministry of Finance and Development Planning, Private Bag 0024, Gaborone, Botswana. TEL 267-352200. (Orders to: Government Printer, P.O. Box 87, Gaborone, Botswana) Ed. G.M. Charumbira; Pub. J.G. Segwe. illus. **Document type:** government publication.
Formerly: Botswana. Central Statistical Office. Statistical Newsletter.
Description: Compiles economic and social statistics.

332.6   **FR**
BOURSE DE PARIS. INDICES. m. 3800 F. Bourse de Paris, 39 rue Cambon, 75001 Paris, France. TEL 49-27-10-00. FAX 49-27-14-33. TELEX 215 561 F.
Description: Studies the composition of the French CAC40 index and its evolution.

338.91 314   **UK**   ISSN 0068-1210
HC60
BRITISH AID STATISTICS; statistics of U.K. economic aid to developing countries and countries of Central and Eastern Europe, and the former Soviet Union. 1966. a. £9.50 (effective 1996). Overseas Development Administration, Publications Section, Abercrombie House, Eaglesham Rd., East Kilbride, Glasgow G75 8EA, Scotland. TEL 44-1355-843246. FAX 44-1355-844099. (also avail. in microfiche from CHL) **Document type:** government publication. —BLDSC (2286.970000). **CCC.**

330   **CN**   ISSN 1184-9207
BRITISH COLUMBIA BUSINESS INDICATORS. 1991. m. Can.$60 (effective 1997). Ministry of Finance and Corporate Relations, B C Stats, P.O. Box 9410, Stn. Prov. Govt., Victoria, BC V8W 9V1, Canada. TEL 250-387-0359. FAX 250-387-0380. E-mail: bcstats@fincc04.fin.gov.bc.ca; URL: http://www.bcstats.gov.bc.ca. **Document type:** government publication.
Description: Provides a range of up-to-date economic and financial data, including production and shipments for British Columbia's major industries.

382   **CN**   ISSN 1186-2920
BRITISH COLUMBIA ORIGIN EXPORTS. 12/yr. Can.$60 (effective 1997). Ministry of Finance and Corporate Relations, B C Stats, P.O. Box 9410, Stn. Prov. Govt., Victoria, BC V8W 9V1, Canada. TEL 250-387-1502. FAX 250-387-0329. E-mail: bcstats@fincc04.fin.gov.bc.ca; URL: http://www.bcstats.gov.bc.ca. **Document type:** government publication.
Description: Reports on the latest British Columbia exports to major trading partners and blocs. Contains commodity detail.

330.9 312   **CN**
BRITISH COLUMBIA REGIONAL INDEX. irreg. Can.$40 (effective 1997). Ministry of Finance and Corporate Relations, B C Stats, P.O. Box 9410, Stn. Prov. Govt., Victoria, BC V8W 9V1, Canada. TEL 250-387-1502. FAX 250-387-0329. E-mail: bcstats@fincc04.fin.gov.bc.ca; URL: http://www.bcstats.gov.bc.ca. **Document type:** government publication.
Description: Provides detailed demographic and economic data by eight development regions and 73 sub-areas in B.C.

319   **VB**
BRITISH VIRGIN ISLANDS. STATISTICS OFFICE. BALANCE OF PAYMENTS. irreg. Statistics Office, Finance Department, Road Town, Tortola, British Virgin Islands, W.I.

319   **VB**
BRITISH VIRGIN ISLANDS. STATISTICS OFFICE. NATIONAL INCOME AND EXPENDITURE. irreg. $3.50. Statistics Office, Finance Department, Road Town, Tortola, British Virgin Islands, W.I.

330   **HU**
Z7164.E2
BUDAPESTI KOZGAZDASAGTUDOMANYI EGYETEM: DOKTORI ERTEKEZESEK. (Print format ceased in 1989.) 1969. biennial. exchange basis. Budapesti Kozgazdasagtudomanyi Egyetem - Budapest University of Economic Sciences, Fovam Ter 8, II-268, 1093 Budapest IX, Hungary. TEL 2179-377. FAX 2174-910. (Subscr. to: B K E Kozponti Konyvtara, Zsil u. 2, 1093 Budapest, Hungary) index. circ. 300. (diskette format; also avail. in microfilm; back issues avail.) **Document type:** bibliography.
Formerly (until 1989): Marx Karoly Kozgazdasagtudomanyi Egyetem: Doktori Ertekezesek (ISSN 0521-4211)
Description: Bibliography of doctoral theses accepted at the university.

330   **HU**
Z7164.E2
BUDAPESTI KOZGAZDASAGTUDOMANYI EGYETEM OKTATOINAK SZAKIRODALMI MUNKASSAGA. (Print format ceased in 1988.) 1968. biennial. exchange basis. Budapesti Kozgazdasagtudomanyi Egyetem - Budapest University of Economic Sciences, Fovam Ter 8, II-268, 1093 Budapest IX, Hungary. TEL 2179-377. FAX 2174-910. (Subscr. to: B K E Kozponti Konyvtara, Zsil u. 2, Budapest, Hungary) index; circ. 300 (controlled). (diskette format; also avail. in microfilm) **Document type:** bibliography. —BLDSC (5383.285000).
Formerly (until 1989): Marx Karoly Kozgazdasagtudomanyi Egyetem Oktatoinak Szakirodalmi Munkassaga (ISSN 0133-5162)
Description: Bibliography of publications and typescripts by teachers and staff of the university.

BUSINESS AND ECONOMICS — ABSTRACTING, BIBLIOGRAPHIES, STATISTICS

331   UN   ISSN 0007-4950
HD4826
BULLETIN OF LABOUR STATISTICS; supplementing the annual data presented in the Year Book of Labour Statistics. (Text in English, French and Spanish) 1965. 4/yr. (plus 5 supplements). 105 SFr.($84) (International Labour Office) I L O Publications, CH-1211 Geneva 22, Switzerland. TEL 41-22-799-6111. FAX 41-22-798-6358. TELEX 415-647-ILOCH. (Dist. in US by: I L O Publications Center, 49 Sheridan Ave., Albany, NY 12210. TEL 518-436-9686. FAX 518-436-7433) stat. (also avail. in microform from ILO,CIS) **Indexed:** IIS, P.A.I.S. **Document type:** bulletin.
—UnCover. **CCC.**
   Description: Contains articles on methodology and special topics. Includes trilingual tables of current statistics on employment, unemployment, wages, hours of work and consumer prices.

330.9 316   UV
BURKINA FASO. INSTITUT NATIONAL DE LA STATISTIQUE ET DE LA DEMOGRAPHIE. BULLETIN D'INFORMATION STATISTIQUE ET ECONOMIQUE. no.16, 1975. a. Institut National de la Statistique et de la Demographie, Ouagadougou, Burkina Faso. **Document type:** bulletin.
   Former titles: Burkina Faso. Institut National de la Statistique et de la Demographie. Bulletin Annuaire d'Information Statistique et Economique; Upper Volta. Institut National de la Statistique et de la Demographie. Bulletin Annuaire d'Information Statistique et Economique; Supersedes: Upper Volta. Direction de la Statistique et de la Mecanographie. Bulletin Mensuel d'Information Statistique et Economique; Upper Volta. Directions de la Statistique et de la Mecanographie. Bulletin Annuaire Statistique et Economique.

381   BD
BURUNDI. INSTITUT DE STATISTIQUES ET D'ETUDES ECONOMIQUES. COMPTES ECONOMIQUES. a. $30. Institut de Statistiques et d'Etudes Economiques, B.P. 1156, Bujumbura, Burundi. **Document type:** monographic series.

BUSINESS AND ENVIRONMENTAL ABSTRACTS. see ENVIRONMENTAL STUDIES — Abstracting, Bibliographies, Statistics

BUSINESS EDUCATION INDEX. see EDUCATION — Abstracting, Bibliographies, Statistics

330 016   US   ISSN 0273-3684
BUSINESS INDEX. m. $3500 on CD-ROM. Information Access Company (Subsidiary of: Thomson Corporation), 362 Lakeside Dr., Foster City, CA 94404. TEL 415-378-5200; 800-227-8431. FAX 415-378-5369. (Or: Predicasts Europe, 8-10 Denman St., London W1V 7RF, England. TEL 44-171-494-3817) (microform) **Document type:** abstracting/indexing.
●Also available online. Vendor(s): Knight-Ridder Information, Inc. (File no.148), Lexis-Nexis, Ovid Technologies, Inc.
   Description: Provides comprehensive guide to more than 800 business, trade and management journals, including the Wall Street Journal and the business-finance sections of the New York Times.

330.9   UK
BUSINESS MONITOR. RETAIL PRICES INDEX. (Part of the Miscellaneous Monitors series) m. £70 (effective 1993). Office for National Statistics, Government Bldgs., Cardiff Rd., Newport, Gwent NP9 1XG, Wales. TEL 44-1633-812973. FAX 44-1633-812599. TELEX 497121 ALBBSONPT G. E-mail: library@ons.gov.uk. (Subscr. to: Stationery Office Publications Centre, P.O. Box 276, London SW8 5DT, England. TEL 44-171-873-9090. FAX 44-171-873-8200) charts; stat. **Document type:** government publication.

332   UK
BUSINESS MONITOR: ASSETS AND LIABILITIES OF FINANCE HOUSES AND OTHER CONSUMER CREDIT COMPANIES. (Part of the Service and Distributive Monitors series) q. Office for National Statistics, Government Bldgs., Cardiff Rd., Newport, Gwent NP9 1XG, Wales. TEL 44-1633-812973. FAX 44-1633-812599. TELEX 497121 ALBBSONPT G. E-mail: library@ons.gov.uk. (Subscr. to: Stationery Office Publications Centre, P.O. Box 276, London SW8 5DT, England. TEL 44-171-873-9090. FAX 44-171-873-8200) charts. (back issues avail.) **Document type:** consumer publication.

BUSINESS MONITOR: CATERING AND ALLIED TRADES. see HOTELS AND RESTAURANTS — Abstracting, Bibliographies, Statistics

332   UK
BUSINESS MONITOR: COMPANY FINANCE. (Part of the Miscellaneous Monitors series) a. Office for National Statistics, Government Buildings, 551 Cardiff Rd., Newport. Gwent NP9 1XG, Wales. TEL 44-1633-812973. FAX 44-1633-812599. TELEX 497121 ALBBSONPT G. E-mail: library@ons.gov.uk. (Dist. by: Stationery Office Publications Office, Box 276, London SW8 5DT, England. TEL 44-171-873-9090. FAX 44-171-873-8200) charts. (back issues avail.) **Indexed:** Int.Packag.Abstr., Paper & Bd.Abstr. **Document type:** government publication.
   Formerly: Business Monitor: Miscellaneous Series. M3 Company Finance (ISSN 0068-4457)

BUSINESS MONITOR: COMPUTER SERVICES. see COMPUTERS — Computer Industry

332   UK   ISSN 0957-2813
BUSINESS MONITOR: CREDIT BUSINESS. (Part of the Service and Distributive Monitors series) 198? m. Office for National Statistics, Government Bldgs., Cardiff Rd., Newport, Gwent NP9 1XG, Wales. TEL 44-1633-812973. FAX 44-1633-812599. E-mail: library@ons.gov.uk. (Subscr. to: Stationery Office Publications Centre, P.O. Box 276, London SW8 5DT, England. TEL 44-171-873-9090. FAX 44-171-873-8200) charts; stat. (back issues avail.) **Document type:** government publication.

332.6   UK   ISSN 0958-4838
BUSINESS MONITOR: GUIDE TO THE CLASSIFICATION OF OVERSEAS TRADE STATISTICS. (Part of the Miscellaneous Monitors series) 1989. a. Office for National Statistics, Government Bldgs., Cardiff Rd., Newport, Gwent NP9 1XG, Wales. TEL 44-1633-812973. FAX 44-1633-812599. TELEX 497121 ALBBSONPT G. E-mail: library@ons.govk. (Subscr. to: Stationery Office Publications Centre, P.O. Box 276, London SW8 5DT, England. TEL 44-171-873-9090. FAX 44-171-873-8200) charts; stat. (back issues avail.) **Document type:** government publication.
—BLDSC (2934.326300).

BUSINESS MONITOR: MOTOR TRADES. see TRANSPORTATION — Abstracting, Bibliographies, Statistics

382   UK
BUSINESS MONITOR: OVERSEAS DIRECT INVESTMENT. (Part of the Miscellaneous Monitors Series) a. £23.95. Office of National Statistics, Government Bldgs., 551 Cardiff Rd., Newport, Gwent NP9 1XG, Wales. TEL 44-1633-812973. FAX 44-1633-512799. TELEX 497121 ALBBSONPT G. E-mail: libraryons@gov.uk. (Dist. by: Stationery Office, P.O. Box 276, London SW8 5DT, England. TEL 44-171-273-9090. FAX 44-171-273-8200) (back issues avail.) **Indexed:** Paper & Bd.Abstr. **Document type:** government publication.
   Formerly (until 1992): Business Monitor: Overseas Transactions (ISSN 0068-4465)

332.6 314   UK   ISSN 0436-3574
HF3501
BUSINESS MONITOR: OVERSEAS TRADE STATISTICS OF THE UNITED KINGDOM (ANNUAL REVISION). (Part of Miscellaneous Monitors series) a. £50. Office for National Statistics, Government Bldgs., Cardiff Rd., Newport, Gwent NP9 1XG, Wales. TEL 44-1633-812973. FAX 44-1633-812599. TELEX 497121 ALBBSONPT G613. E-mail: library@ons.gov.uk. (Orders to: Stationery Office Publications Centre, P.O. Box 276, London SW8 5DT, England. TEL 44-171-873-9090. FAX 44-171-873-8200) charts; stat. circ. 1,375. (also avail. in microfiche from CHL; back issues avail.) **Document type:** government publication.
   Description: Provides statistical information on U.K. manufacturing and other economic activity.

332.6   UK   ISSN 1353-0208
BUSINESS MONITOR: OVERSEAS TRADE STATISTICS OF THE UNITED KINGDOM (QUARTERLY REVISION). (Part of the Miscellaneous Monitors series) 1993. q. Office for National Statistics, Cardiff Rd., Newport, Gwent NP9 1XG, Wales. TEL 44-1633-512973. FAX 44-1633-812599. TELEX 497121 ALB BSONPT G. E-mail: library@ons.gov.uk. (Dist. by: Stationery Office Publications Centre, P.O. Box 276, London SW8 5DT, England. TEL 44-171-873-9090. FAX 44-171-873-8200) charts; stat. (also avail. in microfiche from CHL; back issues avail.) **Indexed:** Print.Abstr. **Document type:** government publication.
   Description: Provides statistical information on U.K. manufacturing and other economic activity.

BUSINESS MONITOR: OVERSEAS TRAVEL AND TOURISM. see TRAVEL AND TOURISM — Abstracting, Bibliographies, Statistics

658.8   UK   ISSN 0264-3979
BUSINESS MONITOR: RETAIL SALES. (Part of Service and Distributive Monitors series) 1980. m. Office for National Statistics, Government Bldgs., Cardiff Rd., Newport, Gwent NP9 1XG, Wales. TEL 44-1633-812973. FAX 44-1633-812599. TELEX 497121 ALBBSONPT G. E-mail: library@ons.gov.uk. (Subscr. to: Stationery Office Publications Centre, P.O. Box 276, London SW8 5DT, England. TEL 44-171-873-9090. FAX 44-171-873-8200) charts; stat. (back issues avail.) **Document type:** government publication.

658   UK
BUSINESS MONITOR: RETAILING. (Part of the Service and Distributive Monitors series) a. Office for National Statistics, Government Bldgs., Cardiff Rd., Newport, Gwent NP9 1XG, England. TEL 44-1633-812973. FAX 44-1633-812599. TELEX 497121 ALBBSONPT G. (Subscr. to: Stationery Office Publications Centre, P.O. Box 276, London SW8 5DT, England. TEL 44-171-873-9090. FAX 44-171-873-8200) charts; stat. (back issues avail.) **Document type:** government publication.

338   UK   ISSN 0957-5758
BUSINESS MONITOR: SERVICE TRADES. (Part of the Service and Distributive Monitors series) a. Office for National Statistics, Government Bldgs., Cardiff Rd., Newport, Gwent NP9 1XG, Wales. TEL 44-1633-812973. FAX 44-1633-812599. TELEX 497121 ALBBSONPT G. E-mail: library@ons.gov.uk. (Subscr. to: Stationery Office Publications Centre, P.O. Box 276, London SW8 5DT, England. TEL 44-171-873-9090. FAX 44-171-873-8200) charts; stat. (back issues avail.) **Document type:** government publication.
—BLDSC (2934.430500).

658   UK
BUSINESS MONITOR: WHOLESALING. (Part of the Service and Distributive Monitors series) a. Office for National Statistics, Government Bldgs., Cardiff Rd., Newport, Gwent NP9 1XG, Wales. TEL 44-1633-812973. FAX 44-1633-812599. TELEX 497121 ALBBSONPT G. E-mail: library@ons.gov.uk. (Subscr. to: Stationery Office Publications Centre, P.O. Box 276, London SW8 5DT, England. TEL 44-171-873-9090. FAX 44-171-873-8200) charts; stat. (back issues avail.) **Document type:** government publication.

BUSINESS AND ECONOMICS — ABSTRACTING, BIBLIOGRAPHIES, STATISTICS 1027

016.33 US ISSN 0007-6961
Z7164.C81
BUSINESS PERIODICALS INDEX. CD-ROM edition (US ISSN 1076-7053) 1958. m. (except Aug.) (plus q. and a. cumulations); m. on CD-ROM. service basis for print version; $1495 for CD-ROM. H.W. Wilson Co., 950 University Ave., Bronx, NY 10452. TEL 718-588-8400; 800-367-6770. FAX 718-590-1617. TELEX 4990003HWILSON. Ed. Hiyol Yang. (also avail. in magnetic tape) Document type: abstracting/indexing.
●Also available online. Vendor(s): Knight-Ridder Information, Inc., OCLC, Ovid Technologies, Inc., Wilsonline (File BPI).
Also available on CD-ROM. Producer(s): SilverPlatter Information, Inc., H.W. Wilson (WILSONDISC).
—BLDSC (2934.555000); CISTI; Linda Hall.
Supersedes in part: Industrial Arts Index (ISSN 0275-1682)
Description: Cumulative subject index to English-language periodicals in the fields of accounting, advertising and public relations, automation, banking, communications, economics, finance and investments, insurance, labor, management and specific businesses and trades. Indexes the Wall Street Journal and the business section of the New York Times.

330 US ISSN 1043-7908
HG4050
BUSINESS RANKINGS ANNUAL. a., latest 1997. $175 (effective 1997). (Brooklyn Public Library, Business Library) Gale Research, 835 Penobscot Bldg., 645 Griswold St., Detroit, MI 48266-4094. TEL 313-961-2242; 800-877-4253. FAX 800-414-5043. E-mail: daniel_snyder@gale.com.

330 UK
BUSINESS SPAIN QUARTERLY INDEX. (Supplement to: Business Spain (ISSN 0957-7939)) (Text primarily in Spanish) q. £395 (outside Europe £405) (includes Business Spain). 5 Newton Rd., Wimbledon, London SW19 3PJ, England. TEL 0181-540-8520. FAX 0181-542-9185. Ed. Graham Faiella; Pub. Graham Faiella. Document type: abstracting/indexing.
Description: Informs subscribers to Business Spain of new and existing resources at the Business Spain library concerning business developments in Spain.

368.4 FR
CAISSES CENTRALES DE MUTUALITE SOCIALE AGRICOLE. STATISTIQUES. (In two parts: Resultats d'Ensemble; Resultats Detailles) 1969. a. 75 F. Union des Caisses Centrales de la Mutualite Agricole, 8-10 rue d'Astorg, 75380 Paris Cedex 8, France. stat.

310 US ISSN 1050-303X
HC107.C23
CALIFORNIA COUNTY PROJECTIONS (YEAR). 1987. a. $225. Center for Continuing Study of the California Economy, 610 University Ave., Palo Alto, CA 94301. TEL 415-321-8550. E-mail: calecon@aol.com. Ed. Stephen Levy. R&P contact: Nanacy Levy. adv. contact: Nancy Leuy.
Description: Projections for each of California's 58 counties are included for population, households, per capita income, average household income, total personal income, taxable retail sales, and total taxable sales. Includes recent historical data and projections to 2005.

310 US ISSN 1053-7252
HC107.C23
CALIFORNIA ECONOMIC GROWTH (YEAR). 1988. a. $225. Center for Continuing Study of the California Economy, 610 University Ave., Palo Alto, CA 94301. TEL 415-321-8550. Ed. Stephen Levy.
Description: Economic growth in California and 5 regions in 1990 and projected to 2005. Regional projections focus on jobs, construction trends and income and spending. Analysis and discussion of the main trends and issues in California.

CAMEROON. DIRECTION DE LA STATISTIQUE ET DE LA COMPTABILITE NATIONAL. BULLETIN TRIMESTRIEL DE CONJONCTURE. see PUBLIC ADMINISTRATION — Abstracting, Bibliographies, Statistics

316.7 CM
CAMEROON. DIRECTION DE LA STATISTIQUE ET DE LA COMPTABILITE NATIONALE. NOTE ANNUELLE DE STATISTIQUE. 1974. a. 4000 Fr.CFA. Direction de la Statistique et de la Comptabilite Nationale - Department of Statistics and National Accounts, B.P. 660, Yaounde, Cameroon. stat. (also avail. in microfiche from CHL)

338 317 CN ISSN 0317-7882
HC120.L3
CANADA. STATISTICS CANADA. AGGREGATE PRODUCTIVITY MEASURES. French edition: Mesures Globales de Productivite. (Editions in English and French) 1946. a. Can.$46 (foreign $46) (effective 1998). Statistics Canada, Operations and Integration Division, Circulation Management, Jean Talon Bldg., 2-C12, Tunney's Pasture, Ottawa, ON K1A 0T6, Canada. TEL 613-951-7277; 800-267-6677. FAX 613-951-1584. URL: http://www.statcan.ca. (also avail. in microform from MML) Document type: government publication.
Former titles: Canada. Statistics Canada. Aggregate Productivity Trends - Tendances de la Productivite des Agregats (ISSN 0068-7073); Indexes of Output per Person Employed and per Man-Hour in Canada, Commercial Industries (ISSN 0073-6082)
Description: Shows output per person employed and per person-hour, and unit labor costs for all commercial industries as well as industry groupings. Provides corresponding US official measures where available.

332.64 CN ISSN 1183-4315
HG4503
CANADA. STATISTICS CANADA. CANADA'S INTERNATIONAL TRANSACTIONS IN SECURITIES/OPERATIONS INTERNATIONALES DU CANADA EN VALEURS MOBILIERES. (Text in English and French) 1935. m. Can.$176 (foreign $176) (effective 1998). Statistics Canada, Operations and Integration Division, Circulation Management, Jean Talon Bldg., 2-C12, Tunney's Pasture, Ottawa, ON K1A 0T6, Canada. TEL 613-951-7277; 800-267-6677. FAX 613-951-1584. URL: http://www.statcan.ca. (also avail. in microform from MML) Document type: government publication.
Formerly: Canada. Statistics Canada. Security Transactions with Non-Residents (ISSN 0702-6587)
Description: Presents trading in Canadian and foreign bonds and stocks with non-residents.

339 317 CN ISSN 0380-691X
HB235.C2
CANADA. STATISTICS CANADA. CONSUMER PRICES AND PRICE INDEXES/PRIX A LA CONSOMMATION ET INDICES DES PRIX. (Text in English and French) 1975. q. Can.$83 (foreign $103) (effective 1998). Statistics Canada, Operations and Integration Division, Circulation Management, Jean Talon Bldg., 2-C12, Tunney's Pasture, Ottawa, ON K1A 0T6, Canada. TEL 613-951-7277; 800-267-6677. FAX 613-951-1584. URL: http://statcan.ca:80/cgi-bin/downpub/downpub.cgi. (also avail. in microform from MML) Document type: government publication.
●Also available online.
—CISTI.
Description: Highlights the current and historical statistics on consumer prices and related price indexes.

658.8 317 CN ISSN 0590-5702
HF5429.6.C3
CANADA. STATISTICS CANADA. DIRECT SELLING IN CANADA/LA VENTE DIRECTE AU CANADA. (Text in English and French) 1966. a. Can.$25 (foreign $25) (effective 1998). Statistics Canada, Operations and Integration Division, Circulation Management, Jean Talon Bldg., 2-C12, Tunney's Pasture, Ottawa, ON K1A 0T6, Canada. TEL 613-951-7277; 800-267-6677. FAX 613-951-1584. URL: http://www.statcan.ca. (also avail. in microform from MML) Document type: government publication.
Description: Presents non-store retail sales for Canada, giving data on commodities sold and breakdowns by methods of distribution.

331.2 317 CN ISSN 0380-6936
HD5727
CANADA. STATISTICS CANADA. EMPLOYMENT, EARNINGS AND HOURS/EMPLOI, GAINS ET DUREE DU TRAVAIL. (Text in English and French) 1922. m. Can.$320 (foreign $320) (effective 1998). Statistics Canada, Operations and Integration Division, Circulation Management, Jean Talon Bldg., 2-C12, Tunney's Pasture, Ottawa, ON K1A 0T6, Canada. TEL 613-951-7277; 800-267-6677. FAX 613-951-1584. URL: http://www.statcan.ca. (also avail. in microform from MML) Document type: government publication.
Description: Provides detailed industrial and geographical data on employment, average weekly earnings, hours and hourly earnings by types of employees for firms of all sizes and take-all firms.

382 CN ISSN 1181-6732
HF129
CANADA. STATISTICS CANADA. EXPORTS BY COMMODITY/EXPORTATIONS PAR MARCHANDISES. (Text in English and French) 1944. m. Can.$773 (foreign $773) (effective 1998). Statistics Canada, Operations and Integration Division, Circulation Management, Jean Talon Bldg., 2-C12, Tunney's Pasture, Ottawa, ON K1A 0T6, Canada. TEL 613-651-7277; 800-267-6677. FAX 613-951-1584. URL: http://www.statcan.ca. (also avail. in microform from MML) Document type: government publication.
Description: Presents detailed export trade data, quantity and value by commodity and country according to the harmonized system at the six digit level and summarized data by country, section and province of origin.

382 CN ISSN 0317-5375
HF3221
CANADA. STATISTICS CANADA. EXPORTS, MERCHANDISE TRADE/EXPORTATIONS, COMMERCE DE MARCHANDISES. (Text in English and French) 1939. a. Can.$258 (foreign $258) (effective 1998). Statistics Canada, Operations and Integration Division, Circulation Management, Jean Talon Bldg., 2-C12, Tunney's Pasture, Ottawa, ON K1A 0T6, Canada. TEL 613-951-7277; 800-267-6677. FAX 613-951-1584. URL: http://www.statcan.ca. (also avail. in microform from MML) Document type: government publication.
Description: Provides detailed annual export data for the current year (quantity and value) by commodity and country according to the Harmonized System at the six-digit level.

304.6 CN ISSN 0703-7368
HC120.I5
CANADA. STATISTICS CANADA. FAMILY INCOMES, CENSUS FAMILIES/REVENUS DES FAMILLES, FAMILLES DE RECENSEMENT. (Text in English and French) 1971. a. Can.$28 (foreign $28) (effective 1998). Statistics Canada, Operations and Integration Division, Circulation Management, Jean Talon Bldg., 2-C12, Tunney's Pasture, Ottawa, ON K1A 0T6, Canada. TEL 613-951-7277; 800-267-6677. FAX 613-951-1584. URL: http://www.statcan.ca. (also avail. in microform from MML) Document type: government publication.
Description: Demonstrates the distribution of census families and persons not in families by size of income, major source of income, region - province, age, sex and other characteristics.

331.11 317 CN ISSN 1181-957X
HD5727
CANADA. STATISTICS CANADA. HISTORICAL LABOUR FORCE STATISTICS/STATISTIQUES CHRONOLOGIQUES SUR LA POPULATION ACTIVE. (Text in English and French) 1953. a. Can.$114 (foreign $114) (effective 1998). Statistics Canada, Operations and Integration Division, Circulation Management, Jean Talon Bldg., 2-C12, Tunney's Pasture, Ottawa, ON K1A 0T6, Canada. TEL 613-951-7277; 800-267-6677. FAX 613-951-1584. URL: http://www.statcan.ca. (also avail. in microform from MML) Document type: government publication.
Formerly: Canada. Statistics Canada. Historical Labour Force Statistics, Actual Data, Seasonal Factors, Seasonally Adjusted Data (ISSN 0703-2684)
Description: Presents historical labor force statistics and related seasonal adjustment information. Contains time series from the monthly Labour Force Survey.

BUSINESS AND ECONOMICS — ABSTRACTING, BIBLIOGRAPHIES, STATISTICS

382 CN ISSN 0380-1349
HF3221
CANADA. STATISTICS CANADA. IMPORTS, MERCHANDISE TRADE/IMPORTATIONS, COMMERCE DE MARCHANDISES. (Text in English and French) 1939. a. Can.$258 (foreign $258) (effective 1998). Statistics Canada, Operations and Integration Division, Circulation Management, Jean Talon Bldg., 2-C12, Tunney's Pasture, Ottawa, ON K1A 0T6, Canada. TEL 613-951-7277; 800-267-6677. FAX 613-951-1584. URL: http://www.statcan.ca. (also avail. in microform from MML) **Document type:** government publication.
Description: Provides detailed annual import data for the current year, showing values only by commodity and country according to the Harmonized System at the six-digit level.

331.1 317 CN ISSN 0708-3157
HD5727
CANADA. STATISTICS CANADA. LABOUR FORCE INFORMATION/INFORMATION POPULATION ACTIVE. (Text in English and French) 1945. m. Can.$103 (foreign $103) (effective 1998). Statistics Canada, Operations and Integration Division, Circulation Management, Jean Talon Bldg., 2-C12, Tunney's Pasture, Ottawa, ON K1A 0T6, Canada. TEL 613-651-7277; 800-267-6677. FAX 613-951-1584. URL: http://www.statcan.ca. (also avail. in microform from MML) **Document type:** government publication.
Formerly: Canada. Statistics Canada. The Labour Force (ISSN 0380-6804)
Description: Presents seasonally adjusted and unadjusted estimates of labour force, employment and unemployment, with unemployment and participation rates analyzed by selected geographic, demographic and occupational variables.

658 CN ISSN 0590-9325
HC111
CANADA. STATISTICS CANADA. MARKET RESEARCH HANDBOOK/MANUEL STATISTIQUE POUR ETUDES DE MARCHE. (Text in English and French) 1975. a. Can.$114 (foreign $114) (effective 1998). Statistics Canada, Operations and Integration Division, Circulation Management, Jean Talon Bldg., 2-C12, Tunney's Pasture, Ottawa, ON K1A 0T6, Canada. TEL 613-951-7277; 800-267-6677. FAX 613-951-1584. URL: http://www.statcan.ca. (also avail. in microform from MML)
—CISTI.
Description: Source of socio-economic statistics for market researchers, strategists, product planners and sales leaders.

339 317 CN ISSN 1201-6772
CANADA. STATISTICS CANADA. NATIONAL ECONOMIC AND FINANCIAL ACCOUNTS, QUARTERLY ESTIMATES/COMPTES ECONOMIQUES ET FINANCIERS NATIONAUX, ESTIMATIONS TRIMESTRIELLES. (Text in English and French) 1953. q. Can.$145 (foreign $145) (effective 1998). Statistics Canada, Operations and Integration Division, Circulation Management, Jean Talon Bldg., 2-C12, Tunney's Pasture, Ottawa, ON K1A 0T6, Canada. TEL 613-951-7277; 800-267-6677. FAX 613-951-1584. URL: http://www.statcan.ca. (also avail. in diskette format; microform from MML) **Document type:** government publication.
Former titles: Canada. Statistics Canada. National Income and Expenditure Accounts; Canada. Statistics Canada. System of National Accounts, National Income and Expenditure Accounts; Canada. Statistics Canada. National Income and Expenditure Accounts - Comptes Nationaux des Revenus et des Depenses (ISSN 0318-708X)
Description: Gives a comprehensive statistical picture of Canadian economic developments.

338 CN ISSN 0835-0191
HD9734.C2
CANADA. STATISTICS CANADA. OTHER MANUFACTURING INDUSTRIES/AUTRES INDUSTRIES MANUFACTURIERES. (Text in English and French) 1930. a. Can.$40 (foreign $40) (effective 1998). Statistics Canada, Operations and Integration Division, Circulation Management, Jean Talon Bldg., 2-C12, Tunney's Pasture, Ottawa, ON K1A 0T6, Canada. TEL 613-951-7277; 800-267-6677. FAX 613-951-1584. URL: http://www.statcan.ca. (also avail. in microform from MML) **Document type:** government publication.
Former titles: Canada. Statistics Canada. Miscellaneous Manufacturing Industries (ISSN 0575-9021); Sporting Goods and Toy Industries (ISSN 0575-979X); Scientific and Professional Equipment Industries (ISSN 0384-4242); Jewellery and Precious Metal Industries (ISSN 0828-9832)

339 317 CN ISSN 0823-065X
HG5151
CANADA. STATISTICS CANADA. PRIVATE AND PUBLIC INVESTMENT IN CANADA, INTENTIONS/INVESTISSEMENTS PRIVES ET PUBLICS AU CANADA, PERSPECTIVE. (Text in English and French) 1946. a. Can.$47 (foreign $47) (effective 1998). Statistics Canada, Operations and Integration Division, Circulation Management, Jean Talon Bldg., 2-C12, Tunney's Pasture, Ottawa, ON K1A 0T6, Canada. TEL 613-951-7277; 800-267-6677. FAX 613-951-1584. URL: http://www.statcan.ca. (also avail. in microform from MML) **Document type:** government publication.
Formerly: Canada. Statistics Canada. Private and Public Investment in Canada. Outlook (ISSN 0318-2274)
Description: Presents capital and repair expenditures on construction and machinery and equipment for all sectors of the Canadian economy and by province for selected industry groups.

339 317 CN ISSN 0823-0668
HC120.C3
CANADA. STATISTICS CANADA. PRIVATE AND PUBLIC INVESTMENT IN CANADA. REVISED INTENTIONS/INVESTISSEMENTS PRIVES ET PUBLICS AU CANADA, PERSPECTIVE REVISEE. (Text in English and French) 1968. a. Can.$44 (foreign $44) (effective 1998). Statistics Canada, Operations and Integration Division, Circulation Management, Jean Talon Bldg., 2-C12, Tunney's Pasture, Ottawa, ON K1A 0T6, Canada. TEL 613-951-7277; 800-267-6677. FAX 613-951-1584. URL: http://www.statcan.ca. (also avail. in microform from MML) **Document type:** government publication.
Formerly: Canada. Statistics Canada. Private and Public Investment in Canada, Mid-Year Review (ISSN 0707-9559)
Description: Presents capital and repair expenditures on construction and machinery and equipment for all sectors of the Canadian economy and by province for selected industry groups.

338.4 317 CN ISSN 0575-9455
HD9734.C2
CANADA. STATISTICS CANADA. PRODUCTS SHIPPED BY CANADIAN MANUFACTURERS/PRODUITS LIVRES PAR LES FABRICANTS CANADIENS. (Text in English and French) 1961. a. Can.$67 (foreign $67) (effective 1998). Statistics Canada, Operations and Integration Division, Circulation Management, Jean Talon Bldg., 2-C12, Tunney's Pasture, Ottawa, ON K1A 0T6, Canada. TEL 613-951-7277; 800-267-6677. FAX 613-951-1584. URL: http://www.statcan.ca. (also avail. in microform from MML) **Document type:** government publication.
Description: Presents value and quantity of products shipped by manufacturers, classified by commodity according to the Industrial Commodity Classification for Canada and the provinces.

331.2 CN ISSN 1201-8481
JL106
CANADA. STATISTICS CANADA. PUBLIC SECTOR EMPLOYMENT AND WAGES AND SALARIES/CANADA. STATISTIQUE CANADA. EMPLOI ET SALAIRES ET TRAITEMENTS DANS LE SECTEUR PUBLIQUE. (Text in English and French) 1990. a. Can.$44 (foreign $44) (effective 1998). Statistics Canada, Operations and Integration Division, Circulation Management, Jean Talon Bldg., 2-C12, Tunney's Pasture, Ottawa, ON K1A 0T6, Canada. TEL 613-951-7277; 800-267-6677. FAX 613-951-1584. URL: http://www.statcan.ca. (also avail. in microform from MML) **Document type:** government publication.
Formerly: Canada. Statistics Canada. Public Sector Employment and Renumeration (Year) (ISSN 1188-0619)
Description: Presents employment and remuneration data for federal, provincial and territorial, and local governments, as well as data for federal, provincial and territorial, and local government business enterprises.

331 317 CN ISSN 0700-205X
CANADA. STATISTICS CANADA. QUARTERLY ESTIMATES OF TRUSTEED PENSION FUNDS/ESTIMATIONS TRIMESTRIELLES SUR LES REGIMES DE PENSIONS EN FIDUCIE. (Text in English and French) 1973. q. Can.$62 (foreign $62) (effective 1998). Statistics Canada, Operations and Integration Division, Circulation Management, Jean Talon Bldg., 2-C12, Tunney's Pasture, Ottawa, ON K1A 0T6, Canada. TEL 613-951-7277; 800-267-6677. FAX 613-951-1584. URL: http://www.statcan.ca. (also avail. in microform from MML) **Document type:** government publication.
Description: Provides estimates for Canada of the income, expenditures and asset portfolios of trusteed pension funds, as well as advance estimates of the annual survey of Trusteed Pension Funds.

658.8 317 CN ISSN 0227-017X
HF5468
CANADA. STATISTICS CANADA. RETAIL CHAIN AND DEPARTMENT STORES/MAGASINS DE DETAIL A SUCCURSALES ET LES GRANDS MAGASINS. (Text in English and French) 1933. a. Can.$39 (foreign $39) (effective 1998). Statistics Canada, Operations and Integration Division, Circulation Management, Jean Talon Bldg., 2-C12, Tunney's Pasture, Ottawa, ON K1A 0T6, Canada. TEL 613-951-7277; 800-267-6677. FAX 613-951-1584. URL: http://www.statcan.ca. (also avail. in microform from MML) **Document type:** government publication.
Formerly: Canada. Statistics Canada. Retail Chain Stores (ISSN 0380-7878)
Description: Presents retail sales of chain and department store organizations by kind of business, province, selected localities, number of stores operated and by annual sales volume.

658 CN ISSN 0380-6146
HF5429.6.C3
CANADA. STATISTICS CANADA. RETAIL TRADE/COMMERCE DE DETAIL. (Text in English and French) 1929. m. Can.$206 (foreign $206) (effective 1998). Statistics Canada, Operations and Integration Division, Circulation Management, Jean Talon Bldg., 2-C12, Tunney's Pasture, Ottawa, ON K1A 0T6, Canada. TEL 613-951-7277; 800-267-6677. FAX 613-951-1584. URL: http://www.statcan.ca. (also avail. in microform from MML) **Document type:** government publication.
Description: Presents data on retail sales, for chain and independent stores; seasonally adjusted sales. Includes data analysis, definitions, methodology, data reliability and bibliography.

BUSINESS AND ECONOMICS — ABSTRACTING, BIBLIOGRAPHIES, STATISTICS

332.6 317   CN
CANADA. STATISTICS CANADA. SYSTEM OF NATIONAL ACCOUNTS, CANADA'S INTERNATIONAL INVESTMENT POSITION/BILAN DES INVESTISSEMENTS INTERNATIONAUX DU CANADA. (Text in English and French) 1926. a. Can.$52 (foreign $52) (effective 1998). Statistics Canada, Operations and Integration Division, Circulation Management, Jean Talon Bldg., 2-C12, Tunney's Pasture, Ottawa, ON K1A 0T6, Canada. TEL 613-951-7277; 800-267-6677. FAX 613-951-1584. URL: http://www.statcan.ca. (also avail. in microform from MML) **Document type:** government publication.
 Formerly: Canada's International Investment Position (ISSN 0318-8868)
 Description: Presents the external financial position of Canada in terms of foreign investments in Canada and Canadian investments abroad at year end.

331 317   CN   ISSN 0835-4634
HD7106.C2
CANADA. STATISTICS CANADA. TRUSTEED PENSION FUNDS - FINANCIAL STATISTICS/CAISSES DE RETRAITE EN FIDUCIE, STATISTIQUES FINANCIERES. (Text in English and French) 1957. biennial. Can.$42($51) (foreign $59) (effective 1998). Statistics Canada, Operations and Integration Division, Circulation Management, Jean Talon Bldg., 2-C12, Tunney's Pasture, Ottawa, ON K1A 0T6, Canada. TEL 613-951-7277; 800-267-6677. FAX 613-951-1584. URL: http://www.statcan.ca. (also avail. in microform from MML) **Document type:** government publication.
 Formerly (until 1984): Canada. Statistics Canada. Trusteed Pension Plans - Financial Statistics (ISSN 0575-9978); Which incorporates: Canada. Statistics Canada. Regimes de Pensions en Fiducie - Statistiques Financieres (ISSN 0825-3781)
 Description: Presents information on the income, expenditure and assets of all trusteed pension funds in both the public and private sectors at the national level.

380 317   CN   ISSN 0380-7894
HF5421.5.C3
CANADA. STATISTICS CANADA. WHOLESALE TRADE/COMMERCE DE GROS. (Text in English and French) 1935. m. Can.$186 (foreign $186) (effective 1998). Statistics Canada, Operations and Integration Division, Circulation Management, Jean Talon Bldg., 2-C12, Tunney's Pasture, Ottawa, ON K1A 0T6, Canada. TEL 613-951-7277; 800-267-6677. FAX 613-951-1584. URL: http://www.statcan.ca. (also avail. in microform from MML) **Document type:** government publication.
 Description: Presents data on wholesale trade: percentage changes for sales and inventors and stocks-sales ratios of wholesale merchants.

317   CN   ISSN 0835-9148
HC111
CANADIAN ECONOMIC OBSERVER/OBSERVATEUR ECONOMIQUE CANADIEN. (Text in English and French) 1926. m. Can.$227 (foreign $227) (effective 1998). Statistics Canada, Operations and Integration Division, Circulation Management, Jean Talon Bldg., 2-C12, Tunney's Pasture, Ottawa, ON K1A 0T6, Canada. TEL 613-951-7277; 800-267-6677. FAX 613-951-1584. URL: http://www.statcan.ca. (also avail. in microform from MML) **Indexed:** Can.B.P.I., P.A.I.S. **Document type:** government publication.
 —CISTI; SWETS.
 Supersedes (in 1988): Canadian Statistical Review (ISSN 0008-509X); Canada. Statistics Canada. Current Economic Indicators (ISSN 0828-0851); Canada. Statistics Canada. Quarterly Economic Summary (ISSN 0828-086X); Canada. Statistics Canada. Quarterly Economic Summary. Statistical Supplement (ISSN 0828-0878)
 Description: Contains a monthly summary of the economy, major economic and statistical events, a feature article and a technical note.

336 340   CN
CANADIAN INCOME TAX RESEARCH INDEX. q. Can.$345. C C H Canadian Ltd., 6 Garamond Ct., North York, ON M3C 1Z5, Canada. TEL 416-441-2992; 800-268-4522. FAX 416-444-9011. **Document type:** trade publication.
 Description: Indexes of interpretive articles, court decisions and other references relating to federal income tax.

016 338   CN   ISSN 1192-4160
AI3
CANADIAN INDEX. 1975. m. (plus a. cumulation). price varies. Micromedia Ltd., 20 Victoria St., Toronto, ON M5C 2N8, Canada. TEL 416-362-5211. FAX 416-362-6161. Ed. Lucy Lemieux. R&P contact: Gail Dykstra. index. **Document type:** abstracting/indexing.
 ●Also available online. Vendor(s): Data-Star, IST-INFORMATHEQUE, Inc., Knight-Ridder Information, Inc. (File no.262), QL Systems Ltd. Also available on CD-ROM. Producer(s): Knight-Ridder, Inc.
 Formed by the merger of: Canadian Magazine Index (ISSN 0829-8777) & Canadian News Index (ISSN 0225-7459); Which was formerly: Canadian Newspaper Index (ISSN 0384-983X) & Canadian Business Index (ISSN 0227-8669); Which was formerly: Canadian Business Periodicals Index (ISSN 0318-6717)

382   CN   ISSN 1198-7391
HF3221
CANADIAN INTERNATIONAL MERCHANDISE TRADE/LE COMMERCE INTERNATIONAL DE MARCHANDISE DU CANADA. (Text in English and French) 1947. m. Can.$188 (foreign $188) (effective 1998). Statistics Canada, Operations and Integration Division, Circulation Management, Jean Talon Bldg., 2-C12, Tunney's Pasture, Ottawa, ON K1A 0T6, Canada. TEL 613-951-7277; 800-267-6677. FAX 613-951-1584. URL: http://statcan.ca:80/cgi-bin/downpub/downpub.cgi. charts. (also avail. in diskette format; microform from MML) **Document type:** government publication.
 ●Also available online.
 Formerly (until 1994): Canadian International Merchandise Trade (ISSN 0828-1556); Incorporates in part (in 1994): Preliminary Statement of Canadian International Trade (ISSN 0828-1998); Which was previously (until 1985): Canada. Statistics Canada. Summary of External Trade (ISSN 0318-2347); Which was formed by the 1975 merger of: Canada. Statistics Canada. Summary of Foreign Trade (ISSN 0575-9951); Which was formerly (until 1962): Canada. Statistics Canada. Monthly Summary of Foreign Trade (ISSN 0318-2355); (1935-1947): Canada. Statistics Canada. Trade of Canada by Months (ISSN 0840-3414); And: Canada. Statistics Canada. Summary of Imports (ISSN 0527-6330); Which, in turn, was formed by the merger of (1934-1947): Canada. Statistics Canada. Imports into Canada for Consumption by Countries (ISSN 0844-6539); And: Canada. Statistics Canada. Summary of Canada's Imports for Consumption (ISSN 0840-3430); Which was previously (1931-1945): Canada. Statistics Canada. Summary of Canada's Imports (ISSN 0840-3422).
 Description: Contains a series of summary tables and charts showing monthly, quarterly and annual trade data.

CARACTERIZACAO DAS EMPRESAS PORTUGUESAS. see BUSINESS AND ECONOMICS — Banking And Finance

330   CK   ISSN 0120-4564
Z7165.C64
CATALOGO COLECTIVO DE LIBROS Y MONOGRAFIAS ECONOMICAS. (Text in English, French, Portuguese, Spanish) 1979. 3/yr. Col.$1500($15) Camara de Comercio de Bogota, Carrera 9, No. 16-21, Piso 8, Apdo. Aereo 29824, Bogota, Colombia. TEL 2-847528. Eds. Fabiola de Briceno, Rubby Angel Giraldo. circ. 300.

331   UN   ISSN 1011-0569
CATALOGUE OF I L O PUBLICATIONS IN PRINT. French edition: Catalogue des Publications du B I T (ISSN 0259-3726) a. (International Labour Office) I L O Publications, 4 route des Morillons, CH-1211 Geneva 22, Switzerland. TEL 41-22-799-6111. FAX 41-22-798-6358. TELEX 415647-ILO-CH. **Document type:** catalog.

330   BL   ISSN 0103-5312
CENSO COMERCIAL. 1940. quinquennial. Fundacao Instituto Brasileiro de Geografia e Estatistica, Centro de Documentacao e Disseminacao de Informacoes, Rua General Canabarro 706, 2o andar, Maracana 20271-201 Rio de Janeiro, Brazil. TEL 55-21-2645424. FAX 55-21-2841959. **Document type:** government publication.

338   BL   ISSN 0103-5320
CENSO DOS SERVICOS. 1940. quinquennial. Fundacao Instituto Brasileiro de Geografia e Estatistica, Centro de Documentacao e Disseminacao de Informacoes, Rua General Canabarro 706, 2o andar, Maracana 20271-201 Rio de Janeiro, Brazil. TEL 55-21-2645424. FAX 55-21-2841959. **Document type:** government publication.
 Description: Contains data on number of service establishments, employed persons, salaries and wages, receipts and more.

338   BL   ISSN 0103-6165
CENSO INDUSTRIAL. 1940. quinquennial. Fundacao Instituto Brasileiro de Geografia e Estatistica, Centro de Documentacao e Disseminacao de Informacoes, Rua General Canabarro 706, 2o andar, Maracana 20271-201 Rio de Janeiro, Brazil. TEL 55-21-2645424. FAX 55-21-2841959. **Document type:** government publication.
 Description: Presents data on the establishments, employed persons, salaries and wages, gross value of industrial production, industrial operation costs etc.

338 316   ZA   ISSN 0069-1429
CENSUS OF INDUSTRIAL PRODUCTION IN ZAMBIA. 1962. a., latest 1980. K3. Central Statistical Office, P.O. Box 31908, Lusaka, Zambia. TEL 211-231.

338   US   ISSN 0082-9374
CENSUS OF MANUFACTURES: FINAL REPORTS. (Issued in 3 series: Geographic Area Series, Industry Series, and Subject Series) 1810. quinquennial, latest 1992. $210 for Geographic Area Series (foreign $262.50); Industry Series $341 (foreign $426.25). U.S. Bureau of the Census, Customer Services, Washington, DC 20233. TEL 301-457-4100. FAX 301-457-4714. URL: http://www.census.gov/. (Subscr. to: Superintendent of Documents, Box 317954, Pittsburgh, PA 15250-7954. TEL 202-512-1800. FAX 202-512-2250; Or: Bernan, 4611-F Assembly Dr., Lanham, MD 20706. TEL 301-459-7666. FAX 301-459-0056) **Document type:** government publication.
 ●Also available online.
 Also available on CD-ROM.

338   US
CENSUS OF MANUFACTURES: PRELIMINARY REPORTS. quinquennial, latest 1992. $162 for Industry Series (foreign $202.50); United States Summary Report $5. U.S. Bureau of the Census, Customer Services, Washington, DC 20233. TEL 301-457-4100. FAX 301-457-4714. URL: http://www.census.gov/. (Subscr. to: Superintendent of Documents, U.S. Government Printing Office, Box 371954, Pittsburgh, PA 15250-7954. TEL 202-512-1800. FAX 202-512-2250; Or: Bernan, 4611-F Assembly Dr., Lanham, MD 20706. TEL 301-459-7666. FAX 301-459-0056) **Document type:** government publication.
 ●Also available on CD-ROM.

310   FJ
CENSUS OF PRIVATE NON-PROFIT MAKING INSTITUTIONS IN FIJI. A REPORT. irreg., latest 1990. $5 per no. (effective 1997). Bureau of Statistics, P.O. Box 2221, Suva, Fiji. **Document type:** government publication.

650   US
CENSUS OF RETAIL TRADE: FINAL REPORTS. (Issued in 3 series: Geographic Area Series, Industry Series, and Subject Series) 1929. quinquennial, latest 1992. $253 for Geographic Area Series (foreign $316.25). U.S. Bureau of the Census, Customer Services, Washington, DC 20233. TEL 301-457-4100. FAX 301-457-4714. URL: http://www.census.gov/. (Subscr. to: Superintendent of Documents, U.S. Government Printing Office, Box 371954, Pittsburgh, PA 15250-7954. TEL 202-512-1800. FAX 202-512-2250; Or: Bernan, 4611-F Assembly Dr., Lanham, MD 20706. TEL 301-459-7666. FAX 301-459-0056) **Document type:** government publication.
 ●Also available on CD-ROM.
 Supersedes in part: U.S. Bureau of the Census. Census of Retail Trade, Wholesale Trade and Selected Service Industries; Which was formerly: U.S. Bureau of the Census. Census of Business (ISSN 0082-9323)

BUSINESS AND ECONOMICS — ABSTRACTING, BIBLIOGRAPHIES, STATISTICS

330.9   US
CENSUS OF SERVICE INDUSTRIES: FINAL REPORTS. (Issued in 3 series: Geographic Area Series, Industry Series, and Subject Series) 1933. quinquennial, latest 1992. $321 for Geographic Area Series (foreign $401.25). U.S. Bureau of the Census, Customer Services, Washington, DC 20233. TEL 301-457-4100. FAX 301-457-4714. URL: http://www.census.gov/. (Subscr. to: Superintendent of Documents, U.S. Government Printing Office, Box 371954, Pittsburgh, PA 15250-7954. TEL 202-512-1800. FAX 202-512-2250; Or: Bernan, 4611-F Assembly Dr., Lanham, MD 20706. TEL 301-459-7666. FAX 301-459-0056) **Document type:** government publication.
● Also available on CD-ROM.
Supersedes in part: U.S. Bureau of the Census. Census of Retail Trade, Wholesale Trade and Selected Service Industries; Which was formerly: U.S. Bureau of the Census. Census of Business (ISSN 0082-9323)

381   CY
CENSUS OF WHOLESALE AND RETAIL TRADE. (Text in English) 1981. irreg. £5. Ministry of Finance, Department of Statistics and Research, 13 Lord Byron Ave., Nicosia, Cyprus. TEL 357-2-302349. FAX 357-2-456712. **Document type:** government publication.
Formerly: Census of Distribution.
Description: Enumeration of trade establishments, with data on the number of establishments by size of employment, persons engaged, sales, stocks, costs and gross margins.

330.9   US
CENSUS OF WHOLESALE TRADE: FINAL REPORTS. (Issued in 3 series: Geographic Area Series, Industry Series, and Subject Series.) quinquennial, latest 1992. $216 for Geographic Area Series (foreign $270). U.S. Bureau of the Census, Customer Services, Washington, DC 20233. TEL 301-457-4100. FAX 301-457-4714. (Subscr. to: Superintendent of Documents, U.S. Government Printing Office, Box 317954, Pittsburgh, PA 15250-7954. TEL 202-512-1800. FAX 202-512-2250; Or: Bernan, 4611-F Assembly Dr., Lanham, MD 20706. TEL 301-459-7666. FAX 301-459-0056) **Document type:** government publication.
● Also available on CD-ROM.
Supersedes in part: U.S. Bureau of the Census. Census of Retail Trade, Wholesale Trade and Service Industries; Which was formerly: U.S. Bureau of the Census. Census of Business (ISSN 0082-9323)

319   BB   ISSN 0255-8432
HG3883.B35
CENTRAL BANK OF BARBADOS. BALANCE OF PAYMENTS. Variant title: Balance of Payments of Barbados. (Formerly issued by Barbados Statistical Service) 1976. a. free. Central Bank of Barbados, Research Department, P.O. Box 1016, Spry St., Bridgetown, Barbados, W.I. TEL 246-436-6870. FAX 246-427-1431. TELEX CENBANK 2251. E-mail: cbb.libr@caribsurf.com. Ed.Bd. R&P contact: Neville Pollard. adv. contact: Neville Pollard. circ. 2,000 (controlled). **Document type:** corporate report.

CENTRAL BANK OF BARBADOS. ECONOMIC AND FINANCIAL STATISTICS. see BUSINESS AND ECONOMICS — Banking And Finance

336   BH   ISSN 1025-1642
CENTRAL BANK OF BELIZE. ANNUAL STATISTICAL DIGEST. 1982. a. free. Central Bank of Belize, P.O. Box 852, Belize City, Belize. TEL 501-2-77216. FAX 501-2-76383. TELEX 225 MONETARY BZ. E-mail: orlanda@cenbank.gov.bz.
Formerly: Monetary Authority of Belize. Statistical Digest.

310   IC   ISSN 0256-193X
CENTRAL BANK OF ICELAND. ECONOMIC STATISTICS. (Text in English) 1932. q. free. Sedlabanki Islands, Hagfraedideild - Central Bank of Iceland, Department of Economics, Kalkofnsvegur 1, IS-150 Reykjavik, Iceland. TEL 354-569-9600. FAX 354-569-9608. TELEX 2020 CENTBK IS. Ed. Stefan Johann Stefansson. circ. 1,500. **Document type:** government publication, bulletin.
—BLDSC (3655.669000).
Supersedes (in 1980): Iceland. Statistical Bureau. Statistical Bulletin (ISSN 0019-1086)
Description: Contains an abbreviated version of the Icelandic economy information found in Hagtoelur Manadarins published monthly by the Central Bank.

332   IE   ISSN 0332-2696
CENTRAL BANK OF IRELAND. IRISH ECONOMIC STATISTICS. 1973. a. free. Central Bank of Ireland, P.O. Box 559, Dame St., Dublin 2, Ireland. TEL 353-1-6716666. FAX 353-1-6716561. stat. circ. 7,000. **Document type:** corporate report.
Description: Pocket-sized compendium of Irish economic statistics.

330.9   JO
CENTRAL BANK OF JORDAN. MONTHLY STATISTICAL BULLETIN. (Text in Arabic, English) 1965. m. free. Central Bank of Jordan, Department of Research and Studies, P.O. Box 37, Amman, Jordan. stat. **Document type:** bulletin.
Formerly: Central Bank of Jordan. Quarterly Bulletin (ISSN 0008-9265)
Description: Statistical tables and graphic charts covering all aspects of money and banking activities, public finance, external trade and balance of payments, production and price indexes of the Central Bank of Jordan.

332 330.9   KU
CENTRAL BANK OF KUWAIT. MONTHLY MONETARY STATISTICS. (Text in Arabic, English) 1979. m. free. Central Bank of Kuwait, Economic Research Department, P.O. Box 526, Safat 13006, Kuwait. TEL 965-2449200. FAX 965-2440887. E-mail: cbk@cbk.gov.kw; URL: http://www.cbk.gov.kw. charts; stat.
Former titles: Central Bank of Kuwait. Monthly Monetary Review & Central Bank of Kuwait. Monthly Monetary Tables.

332 330.9   KU   ISSN 1012-4209
CENTRAL BANK OF KUWAIT. QUARTERLY STATISTICAL BULLETIN/BANK AL-KUWAYT AL-MARKAZI. AL-NASHRAH AL-IHSA'IYYAH AL-FASLIYYAH. (Text in Arabic, English) 1974. q. free. Central Bank of Kuwait, Economic Research Department - Bank al-Kuwayt al-Markazi, Idarat al-Buhuth al-ektsadia, P.O. Box 526, 13006 Safat, Kuwait. TEL 965-2449200. FAX 965-2440887. TELEX 22101. E-mail: cbk@cbk.gov.kw; URL: http://www.cbk.gov.kw. charts; stat. circ. 900. **Document type:** government publication.

330   CE
CENTRAL BANK OF SRI LANKA. SOCIO ECONOMIC DATA. (Text in English) 1979. irreg., latest 1995. $3. Central Bank of Sri Lanka, Janadhipathi Mawatha, P.O. Box 590, Colombo 1, Sri Lanka. TEL 94-1-421191. FAX 94-1-445127.

332.1   BF
CENTRAL BANK OF THE BAHAMAS. QUARTERLY STATISTICAL DIGEST. 1992. q. free. Central Bank of the Bahamas, Research Department, P.O. Box N4868, Nassau, Bahamas. FAX 809-322-4321. TELEX CENTRALBANK 20115. Ed.Bd. charts. circ. 1,300. (back issues avail.) **Document type:** government publication.

332.1   TR   ISSN 1011-6338
CENTRAL BANK OF TRINIDAD AND TOBAGO. MONTHLY STATISTICAL DIGEST. vol.7, 1974. m. $40 (effective 1997). Central Bank of Trinidad and Tobago, Eric Williams Plaza, Independence Sq., P.O. Box 1250, Port-of-Spain, Trinidad & Tobago, W.I. TEL 868-625-4835. FAX 868-627-4696. TELEX 386-270. circ. 350. (processed) **Document type:** bulletin, corporate report.
Supersedes in part: Central Bank of Trinidad and Tobago. Statistical Digest.

332.1   TR   ISSN 1011-6362
CENTRAL BANK OF TRINIDAD AND TOBAGO. QUARTERLY STATISTICAL DIGEST. q. $55 includes Annual Economic Survey, Quarterly Economic Bulletin, and Quarterly Statistical Digest (effective 1997). Central Bank of Trinidad and Tobago, Eric Williams Plaza, Independence Sq., P.O. Box 1250, Port-of-Spain, Trinidad & Tobago, W.I. TEL 868-625-4835. FAX 868-627-4696. TELEX 386-270. circ. 850. **Document type:** bulletin, corporate report.
Supersedes in part: Central Bank of Trinidad and Tobago. Statistical Digest.

380   UK   ISSN 0958-7322
CENTRE RANKINGS. 1990. a. £195. Chas E. Goad Ltd., 8-12 Salisbury Square, Old Hatfield, Herts AL9 5BJ, England. TEL 0707-271171. FAX 0707-274641. TELEX 83147 TEMCOL. Eds. Jonathan Reynolds, Trevor Wood.
Description: An authoritative guide to shopping centre retailing in the UK.

CENTRES, BUREAUS & RESEARCH INSTITUTES; the directory of UK concentrations of effort, information, and expertise. see BUSINESS AND ECONOMICS — Trade And Industrial Directories

381   CD
CHAD. BULLETIN MENSUEL DE STATISTIQUES. m. Commission for Trade and Industry, B.P. 453, N'djamena, Chad. **Document type:** bulletin.

330   UK   ISSN 0955-1034
CD1040
CHARTERED INSTITUTE OF PUBLIC FINANCE AND ACCOUNTANCY. ARCHIVES STATISTICS. ESTIMATES. 1988. a. £55. Chartered Institute of Public Finance and Accountancy, Statistical Information Service, 3 Robert St., London WC2N 6BH, England. TEL 44-171-543-5600. FAX 44-171-543-5700. (back issues avail.) **Document type:** bulletin.

310 330   UK   ISSN 0263-2985
HJ9431
CHARTERED INSTITUTE OF PUBLIC FINANCE AND ACCOUNTANCY. CAPITAL EXPENDITURE AND DEBT FINANCING STATISTICS. ACTUALS. 1946. a. £105. Chartered Institute of Public Finance and Accountancy, Statistical Information Service, 3 Robert St., London WC2N 6BH, England. TEL 44-171-543-5600. FAX 44-171-543-5700. stat. (back issues avail.)
Formerly: Return of Outstanding Debt (ISSN 0143-103X)
Description: Analyzes local authority debt in England, Wales, Scotland, and Northern Ireland.

336.2   UK
CHARTERED INSTITUTE OF PUBLIC FINANCE AND ACCOUNTANCY. COUNCIL TAX STATISTICS. ESTIMATES. a. £55. Chartered Institute of Public Finance and Accountancy, Statistical Information Service, 3 Robert St., London WC2N 6BH, England. TEL 44-171-543-5600. FAX 44-171-543-5700. (back issues avail.)

CHARTERED INSTITUTE OF PUBLIC FINANCE AND ACCOUNTANCY. EDUCATION STATISTICS. ESTIMATES. see EDUCATION — Abstracting, Bibliographies, Statistics

332 310   UK
CHARTERED INSTITUTE OF PUBLIC FINANCE AND ACCOUNTANCY. FINANCE AND GENERAL STATISTICS. ESTIMATES. 1978. a. £105. Chartered Institute of Public Finance and Accountancy, Statistical Information Service, 3 Robert St., London WC2N 6BH, England. TEL 44-171-543-5600. FAX 44-171-543-5700. (back issues avail.)
—BLDSC (3926.866800).
Former titles: Chartered Institute of Public Finance and Accountancy. Financial General and Rating Statistics; Chartered Institute of Public Finance and Accountancy. Return of Rates (ISSN 0263-2276)

CHARTERED INSTITUTE OF PUBLIC FINANCE AND ACCOUNTANCY. LEISURE CHARGES STATISTICS. ACTUALS. see SPORTS AND GAMES — Abstracting, Bibliographies, Statistics

336   UK
CHARTERED INSTITUTE OF PUBLIC FINANCE AND ACCOUNTANCY. RATING REVIEW (SCOTLAND). ACTUALS. a. £8. Chartered Institute of Public Finance and Accountancy, Statistical Information Service, 3 Robert St., London WC2N 6BH, England. TEL 44-171-543-5600. FAX 44-171-543-5700. (back issues avail.)

336   UK
CHARTERED INSTITUTE OF PUBLIC FINANCE AND ACCOUNTANCY. RATING REVIEW (SCOTLAND) STATISTICS. ESTIMATES. a. £8. Chartered Institute of Public Finance and Accountancy, Statistical Information Service, 3 Robert St., London WC2N 6BH, England. TEL 44-171-543-5600. FAX 44-171-543-5700. (back issues avail.)

336.2 310   UK   ISSN 0260-5546
CHARTERED INSTITUTE OF PUBLIC FINANCE AND ACCOUNTANCY. REVENUE COLLECTION STATISTICS. ACTUALS. 1945. a. £80. Chartered Institute of Public Finance and Accountancy, Statistical Information Service, 3 Robert St., London WC2N 6BH, England. TEL 44-171-543-5600. FAX 44-171-543-5700. (back issues avail.)

BUSINESS AND ECONOMICS — ABSTRACTING, BIBLIOGRAPHIES, STATISTICS

330.9 UK
CHARTERED INSTITUTE OF PUBLIC FINANCE AND ACCOUNTANCY. TRADING STANDARDS STATISTICS. ACTUALS & ESTIMATES. 1994. a. £55. Chartered Institute of Public Finance and Accountancy, Statistical Information Service, 3 Robert Street, London WC2N 6BH, England. TEL 44-171-543-5600. FAX 44-171-543-5700. circ. 1,500.
Formed by the merger of (1984-1994): Chartered Institute of Public Finance and Accountancy. Trading Standards Statistics. Estimates (ISSN 0954-1853); (1984-1994): Chartered Institute of Public Finance and Accountancy. Trading Standards Statistics. Actuals (ISSN 0954-1780)

381 CL
CHILE. INSTITUTO NACIONAL DE ESTADISTICAS. ANUARIO DE COMERCIO INTERIOR Y SERVICIOS. 1970. a. Ch.$2000 (US $13.50; elsewhere $15.90) (effective 1995). Instituto Nacional de Estadisticas, Av. Bulnes 418, Casilla 498, Correo 3 Santiago, Chile. TEL 56-2-6991441. FAX 56-2-6712169. (also avail. in diskette format)

381 CL
CHILE. INSTITUTO NACIONAL DE ESTADISTICAS. ANUARIO DE PRECIOS. 1983. a. Ch.$2000 (US $13.50; elsewhere $15.90) (effective 1995). Instituto Nacional de Estadisticas, Av. Bulnes 418, Casilla 498, Correo 3 Santiago, Chile. TEL 56-2-6991441. FAX 56-2-6712169.

330 318 CL
CHILE. INSTITUTO NACIONAL DE ESTADISTICAS. ENCUESTA NACIONAL DEL EMPLEO. m. Ch.$3010 (fax subscr. Ch.$20410) (effective 1995). Instituto Nacional de Estadisticas, Av. Bulnes 418, Casilla 498, Correo 3 Santiago, Chile. TEL 56-2-6991441. FAX 56-2-6712169. (processed; also avail. in diskette format)

331.2 318 CL
CHILE. INSTITUTO NACIONAL DE ESTADISTICAS. ESTADISTICAS E INDICE DE REMUNERACIONES. 1959. m. Ch.$1550 (US $10.10; elsewhere $12.30) (effective 1995). Instituto Nacional de Estadisticas, Av. Bulnes 418, Casilla 498, Correo 3 Santiago, Chile. TEL 56-2-6991441. FAX 56-2-6712169.
Formerly (until 1983): Chile. Instituto Nacional de Estadisticas. Indice de Sueldos y Salarios.

332 CL
CHILE. INSTITUTO NACIONAL DE ESTADISTICAS. FINANZAS. 1912. a. Ch.$1200 (US $8.20; elsewhere $9.40) (effective 1995). Instituto Nacional de Estadisticas, Av. Bulnes 418, Casilla 498, Correo 3 Santiago, Chile. TEL 56-2-6991441. FAX 56-2-6712169. stat. circ. controlled. (processed)
Formerly (until 1958): Finanzas, Bancos y Cajas Sociales.

330 CL
CHILE. INSTITUTO NACIONAL DE ESTADISTICAS. INDICADORES DE EMPLEO, POR SEXO Y GRUPOS DE EDAD, TOTAL NACIONAL. 1985. a. Ch.$1200 (US $8.20; elsewhere $9.40) (effective 1995). Instituto Nacional de Estadisticas, Av. Bulnes 418, Casilla 498, Correo 3 Santiago, Chile. TEL 56-2-6991441. FAX 56-2-6712169. (also avail. in diskette format)

339 318 CL
CHILE. INSTITUTO NACIONAL DE ESTADISTICAS. INDICE DE PRECIOS AL CONSUMIDOR. (With 2 m. subseries: Series, Informe) 1928. m. Ch.$1790 (fax subscr. Ch.$12490) (effective 1995). Instituto Nacional de Estadisticas, Av. Bulnes 418, Casilla 498, Correo 3 Santiago, Chile. TEL 56-2-6991441. FAX 56-2-6712169. (also avail. in diskette format)

330 318 CL
CHILE. INSTITUTO NACIONAL DE ESTADISTICAS. INDICE DE PRECIOS AL POR MAYOR. (With 2 subseries: Series, Informe) 1974. m. Instituto Nacional de Estadisticas, Av. Bulnes 418, Casilla 498, Correo 3 Santiago, Chile. (also avail. in diskette format) **Document type:** government publication.

338 CL
CHILE. INSTITUTO NACIONAL DE ESTADISTICAS. INDICE DE PRODUCCION Y VENTA FISICA DE INDUSTRIAS MANUFACTURERAS. 1983. q. Ch.$2250 (US $14.90; elsewhere $17.90) (effective 1995). Instituto Nacional de Estadisticas, Av. Bulnes 418, Casilla 498, Correo 3 Santiago, Chile. TEL 56-2-6991441. FAX 56-2-6712169. **Document type:** government publication.

658.3 CL
CHILE. INSTITUTO NACIONAL DE ESTADISTICAS. INDICE DE RENUMERACIONES. 1983. m. Instituto Nacional de Estadisticas, Av. Bulnes 418, Casilla 498, Correo 3 Santiago, Chile. (processed) **Document type:** government publication.

338 CL ISSN 0716-842X
CHILE. INSTITUTO NACIONAL DE ESTADISTICAS. INDUSTRIAS MANUFACTURERAS. 1960. a. Ch.$2700 (US $18.60; elsewhere $23.60) (effective 1995). Instituto Nacional de Estadisticas, Av. Bulnes 418, Casilla 498, Correo 3 Santiago, Chile. TEL 56-2-6991441. FAX 56-2-6712169.

332 658 CL
CHILE MARKETING AND FINANCIAL STATISTICS. 1990. a. Time - America Economia, Galvarino Gallardo 1576, Casilla 113, Correo 35, Santiago, Chile. TEL 02-2237913. FAX 02-223-1903.

339 310 CC
CHINA MONTHLY STATISTICS. (Text in English) m. Y2040($240) China Statistical Information and Consultancy Service Center, 38 Yuetan Nanjie, Sanlihe, Beijing 100826, People's Republic of China. TEL 86-10-8515076. FAX 86-10-8515078. (Co-sponsor: International Centre for the Advancement of Science and Technology Ltd.) Ed. Zhang Shu.
Description: Contains statistics on China's social and economic situations.

338 CH ISSN 0257-5671
CHINA, REPUBLIC. EXECUTIVE YUAN. DIRECTORATE-GENERAL OF BUDGET, ACCOUNTING & STATISTICS. NATIONAL INCOME IN TAIWAN AREA, R. O.C. Key Title: National Income in Taiwan Area, Republic of China. (Text and summaries in English) 1969. a. NT.$500. Executive Yuan, Directorate-General of Budget, Accounting & Statistics, 2 Kwangchow St., Taipei, Taiwan, Republic of China. TEL 886-2-381-4910. (Subscr. to: Chen Chung Book Co., 3F, 20 Heng-Yang Rd., Taipei, Taiwan, R.O.C.. TEL 886-2-381-3980) circ. 350.
Description: Provides information about GNP, economic growth, and the main statistical data on Taiwan's economy.

382 315 CH
CHINA, REPUBLIC. MINISTRY OF FINANCE. DEPARTMENT OF STATISTICS. MONTHLY STATISTICS OF EXPORTS AND IMPORTS/CHIN CH'U K'OU MAO I T'UNG CHI YUEH PAO. (Text in Chinese and English) 1965. m. Ministry of Finance, Department of Statistics, Taipei, Taiwan, Republic of China. charts; stat.
Description: Covers goods exported to and imported from foreign countries.

336.2 315 CH
CHINA, REPUBLIC. MINISTRY OF FINANCE. DEPARTMENT OF STATISTICS. YEARBOOK OF TAX STATISTICS.* (Text in Chinese and English) 1974. a. Ministry of Finance, Department of Statistics, Taipei, Taiwan, Republic of China.

381 338.91 CC ISSN 0258-3046
CHINA'S CUSTOMS STATISTICS. (Text in English) 1982. m. HK.$648($135) Economic Information & Agency, 342 Hennessy Rd., 10th Fl., Wanchai, Hong Kong, People's Republic of China. TEL 852-573-8217. FAX 852-838-8304. TELEX 86990 EIA HX. (back issues avail.)

355.6 US ISSN 0882-8857
UA23.2
CIVILIAN MANPOWER STATISTICS. 1980. q. $12 (foreign $15). U.S. Department of Defense, Washington Headquarters Services, (Subsidiary of: Directorate for Information, Operations and Reports), The Pentagon, Washington, DC 20301-1155. (Subscr. to: Superintendent of Documents, U.S. Government Printing Office, Box 371954, Pittsburgh, PA 15250-7954. TEL 202-512-1800. FAX 202-512-2250) (back issues avail.) **Document type:** government publication.
Description: Comprises tables containing official summary data on Department of Defense civilian employment levels. Includes selected data on trends on civilian employment and accession and separation rates.

353.83 331 US
CLASSIFIED INDEX OF N.L.R.B. AND RELATED COURT DECISIONS. bi-m. price varies. U.S. National Labor Relations Board, 1099 14th St., N.W., Washington, DC 20570-0001. TEL 202-273-1991. FAX 202-273-1789. (Subscr. to: Superintendent of Documents, U.S. Government Printing Office, Washington, DC 20402. TEL 202-512-1800) **Document type:** government publication.
—UMI.
Former titles: Classified Index of National Labor Relations Board Decisions and Related Court Decisions (ISSN 0092-4962); U.S. National Labor Relations Board. Digest of Decisions of the National Labor Relations Board (ISSN 0012-2734)

651 AT
CLERICAL SALARY REVIEW. 1970. 2/yr. Aus.$1500. Cullen Egan Dell, Level 8, 50 Bridge St., Sydney, N.S.W. 2000, Australia. TEL 61-2-93759800. FAX 61-2-92336800. Ed. Colin Hickling. charts; stat. circ. 150. (looseleaf format)
Description: Salary data on clerical positions in Australia.

COLOMBIA. DEPARTAMENTO ADMINISTRATIVO NACIONAL DE ESTADISTICA. ANUARIO DE COMERCIO EXTERIOR. see *BUSINESS AND ECONOMICS — International Commerce*

332 336 318 CK
COLOMBIA. DEPARTAMENTO ADMINISTRATIVO NACIONAL DE ESTADISTICA. ANUARIO DE ESTADISTICAS FISCALES Y FINANCIERAS. 1960. a. $5. Departamento Administrativo Nacional de Estadistica, Banco Nacional de Datos, Centro Administrativo Nacional, Avda. El Dorado, Apdo. Aereo 80043, Bogota D.E., Colombia. Ed. Dr. Saul Ojeda Gomez. adv.; bk.rev.

338 CK
COLOMBIA. DEPARTAMENTO ADMINISTRATIVO NACIONAL DE ESTADISTICA. ANUARIO DE ESTADISTICAS INDUSTRIALES. 1972. a. Departamento Administrativo Nacional de Estadistica, Banco Nacional de Datos, Centro Administrativo Nacional, Avda. El Dorado, Apdo. Aereo 80043, Bogota D.E., Colombia.
Supersedes: Colombia. Departamento Administrativo Nacional de Estadistica. Industria Manufacturera Nacional.

330 CK
COLOMBIA. SUPERINTENDENCIA BANCARIA. INFORMACION ESTADISTICA POR CIUDADES. 1976. q. free. Superintendencia Bancaria, Apdo. Aereo 3460, Bogota DC, Colombia. TEL 57-1-2804060. FAX 57-1-2800864. circ. 500.

310 330 MX ISSN 0186-0496
COMERCIO EXTERIOR DE MEXICO. INFORMACION PRELIMINAR. 1977. m. Mex.$2200($150) Instituto Nacional de Estadistica, Geografia e Informatica, Secretaria de Programacion y Presupuesto, Prol. Heroe de Nacozari 2301 Sur, Puerta 11, Acceso, 20270 Aguascalientes Ags., Mexico. TEL 91-49-18-19-48. FAX 91-491-80739. circ. 900. **Document type:** government publication.

BUSINESS AND ECONOMICS — ABSTRACTING, BIBLIOGRAPHIES, STATISTICS

382   RM   ISSN 1223-5636
HF3741
COMERTUL EXTERIOR AL ROMANIEI/FOREIGN TRADE OF ROMANIA. (Text in English, Rumanian) biennial. 10000 lei (foreing $25) (effective 1997). Comisia Nationala pentru Statistica - National Commission for Statistics, Bd. Libertatii 16, Sector 5, 70542 Bucharest, Rumania. TEL 40-1-6143371. FAX 40-1-3124873. **Document type:** government publication.
    Description: Presents data regarding Rumania's exports and imports structured by sections and chapters, according to the harmonized system of products classification by origin and destination countries.

382 314   GR   ISSN 0071-738X
HF197
COMMERCE EXTERIEUR DE LA GRECE/EXOTERIKON EMPORION TES ELLADOS. (Text in French and Greek) 1953. a. $60. National Statistical Service of Greece, Statistical Information and Publications Division - Ethniki Statistiki Yperesia tes Ellados, 14-16 Lykourgou, 101 66 Athens, Greece. TEL 30-1-3289-397. FAX 30-1-3221-102. TELEX 216734 ESYE GR. (back issues avail.) **Document type:** government publication.
    Formerly (until 1965): Foreign Trade of Greece.

338 315   CH   ISSN 0257-5728
COMMODITY PRICE STATISTICS MONTHLY IN TAIWAN AREA. Key Title: Wujia Tongji Yuebao. (Text in Chinese and English; summaries in Chinese) 1971. m. NT.$100. Executive Yuan, Directorate-General of Budget, Accounting & Statistics, 2 Kwangchow St., Taipei, Taiwan, Republic of China. TEL 886-2-371-1521. FAX 886-2-381-8246. (Subscr. to: Chen Chung Book Co., 3F, 20 Heng-Yang Rd., Taipei, Taiwan, R.O.C.. TEL 886-2-381-3980) index, cum.index. circ. 1,300. (microfilm)
    Description: Provides statistics on recent changing conditions of commodity prices in the Taiwan area of the Republic of China. Includes export and import price indices.

339 310   UN   ISSN 0010-3233
HF1
COMMODITY TRADE STATISTICS; according to the Standard International Trade Classification. (Text in English) 1950. 28/yr. $225. United Nations Publications, Supscription Office, P.O. Box 361, Birmingham, AL 35201-0361. (Or: Distribution and Sales Section, Palais des Nations, CH-1211 Geneva 10, Switzerland) (also avail. in microfiche from CIS) **Indexed:** IIS.
—SWETS.
    Description: Analyzes more than 150 groups of commodities exported or imported by the world's principal trading nations.

330.9   JA   ISSN 0918-7057
COMPARATIVE ECONOMIC AND FINANCIAL STATISTICS - JAPAN AND OTHER MAJOR COUNTRIES. Key Title: Nihon Keizai Ochushin Tosuru Kokusai Hikaku Tokei. (Text in English, Japanese) 1964. a. 2600 Yen. Bank of Japan, International Department - Nippon Ginko, c/o Public Relations Department, 2-1-1 Hongoku-Cho, Nihonbashi, Chuo-ku, Tokyo 103, Japan. TEL 81-3-3279-1111. FAX 81-3-5203-8703. TELEX JPTCO J27161. (Dist. by: Tokiwa Sohgoh Service, 3-2-4 Hongoku-cho, Nihonbashi Chuo-ku, Tokyo 103, Japan. TEL 81-3-3270-5713; Overseas dist. by: Japan Publications Trading Co., Ltd., Book Export No.2 Dept., P.O. Box 5030 Tokyo International, Tokyo 100-31, Japan) pp./issue: 350.
    Formerly: International Comparative Statistics Centering on the Japanese Economy.
    Description: Various economic statistics of major countries compiled through systematic processing and classification in order to clarify Japan's international position and competitiveness. Indispensable to business operations and research in this era of internationalization.

COMPENDIUM OF HOUSING FINANCE STATISTICS. see HOUSING AND URBAN PLANNING — Abstracting, Bibliographies, Statistics

658 016   UK   ISSN 1361-4959
▼**COMPENSATION AND BENEFITS ABSTRACTS.** 1996. q. M C B University Press Ltd., Anbar Electronic Intelligence, 60-62 Toller Ln., Bradford, W. Yorks BD8 9BY, England. TEL 44-1274-480916. FAX 44-1274-543576. E-mail: spuesey@anbar.co.uk; URL: http://www.anbar.co.uk/anbar.htm. **Document type:** abstracting/indexing.

658   UK
HD28
COMPLEAT ANBAR. 1972. a. M C B University Press Ltd., Anbar Electronic Intelligence, 60-62 Toller Ln., Bradford, W. Yorks BD8 9BY, England. URL: http://www.mcb.co.uk. Ed. Eric Sandelands. **Document type:** abstracting/indexing.
—BLDSC (0900.308000).
    Formerly: Anbar Yearbook (ISSN 0307-0409)

COMPOSITES INDUSTRY ABSTRACTS. see PLASTICS — Abstracting, Bibliographies, Statistics

330   CF
COMPTE DE LA NATION. 1970. a. 8000 Fr.CFA. Centre National de la Statistique et des Etudes Economiques, B.P. 2031, Brazzaville, Congo. TEL 83-36-94.

330   GP
COMPTES ECONOMIQUES DE LA GUADELOUPE. 1968. a. 5 F. Institut National de la Statistique et des Etudes Economiques, Service Regional Guadeloupe, Ave. Paul-Lacave, B.P. 96, 97102 Basse-Terre Cedex, Guadeloupe. stat. circ. 530.

330 318   MQ   ISSN 0532-4785
COMPTES ECONOMIQUES DE LA MARTINIQUE. 1968. irreg., latest 1987. price varies. Institut National de la Statistique et des Etudes Economiques, Pointe de Jaham, B.P. 7212, 97233 Schoelcher Cedex, Martinique. TEL 61-60-88. FAX 61-27-22. TELEX 912394 MR. adv. circ. 600. **Document type:** government publication.

330   NG
COMPTES ECONOMIQUES DE LA NATION. (Text in French) s-a. 5000 Fr.CFA. Direction de la Statistique et de l'Informatique, B.P. 862, Niamey, Niger. TEL 227-72-34-44. stat. circ. 200.

381   RW   ISSN 1013-6118
COMPTES ECONOMIQUES NATIONAUX DU RWANDA. 1976. a. $17 (effective Aug. 1991). Direction Generale de la Statistique, B.P. 46, Kigali, Rwanda. **Document type:** government publication.

CONFERENCE BOARD OF CANADA. INDEX OF BUSINESS CONFIDENCE. see BUSINESS AND ECONOMICS — Investments

CONFERENCE BOARD OF CANADA. INDEX OF CONSUMER ATTITUDES. see BUSINESS AND ECONOMICS — Marketing And Purchasing

CONGO. CENTRE NATIONAL DE LA STATISTIQUE ET DES ETUDES ECONOMIQUES. BULLETIN TRIMESTRIEL DE LA CONJONCTURE. see PUBLIC ADMINISTRATION — Abstracting, Bibliographies, Statistics

330   CF
CONGO. CENTRE NATIONAL DE LA STATISTIQUE ET DES ETUDES ECONOMIQUES. CADRE COMPTABLE NATIONAL. 1977. a. 5000 Fr.CFA. Centre National de la Statistique et des Etudes Economiques, B.P. 2031, Brazzaville, Congo. TEL 83-36-94.

330   CF
CONGO. CENTRE NATIONAL DE LA STATISTIQUE ET DES ETUDES ECONOMIQUES. CADRE MACRO-ECONOMIQUE. 1983. a. 8000 Fr.CFA. Centre National de la Statistique et des Etudes Economiques, B.P. 2031, Brazzaville, Congo. TEL 83-36-94.

381   BH
CONSUMER PRICE INDEX OF BELIZE. q. free. Ministry of Finance, Central Statistical Office, New Administration Bldg., Belmopan, Belize. TEL 501-8-22352. FAX 501-8-23206. E-mail: csogob@blt.net. **Document type:** government publication, bulletin.
    Description: Measures inflation in the 7 geographic districts of Belize. Includes 7 index tables.

330   US
CONSUMER PRODUCT AND MANUFACTURER RATING ANNUAL. 1993. base vol. plus a. update. $195 (base vol. $395). Gale Research, 835 Penobscot Bldg., 645 Griswold St., Detroit, Mi 48226-4094. TEL 313-961-2242; 800-877-4253. FAX 800-414-5043. E-mail: daniel__snyder@gale.com.
    Description: Source of comparative ratings for consumer goods offered by over 1800 manufacturers worldwide.

330 016   UK   ISSN 0045-8368
CONTENTS OF RECENT ECONOMICS JOURNALS. Abbreviated title: C R E J. 1971. 50/yr. £90. H.M.S.O., 51 Nine Elms Ln., London SW8 5DR, England. TEL 44-171-873-0011. FAX 44-171-873-8247. Ed. J.M. Titcombe. circ. 600. (reprint service avail. from UMI) **Document type:** government publication.
—BLDSC (3425.360000).

650 016   UK   ISSN 0306-3224
CONTENTS PAGES IN MANAGEMENT. 1972. fortn. £130 (effective 1997). Manchester Business School, Booth St. W., Manchester M15 6PB, England. TEL 44-161-275-6504. FAX 44-161-275-6505. E-mail: d.ross@fsz.mbs.ac.uk. Ed. Dorothy Ross. circ. 250. **Document type:** abstracting/indexing.
    Formerly: Current Contents in Management.

330   IT
CONTI ECONOMICI TRIMESTRALI. q. L.13000 (foreign L.18000) (effective 1995). Istituto Nazionale di Statistica, Via Cesare Balbo 16, 00100 Rome, Italy. FAX 39-6-46735198. **Document type:** government publication.

318 331.11   CR   ISSN 1409-0198
HD5734
COSTA RICA. DIRECCION GENERAL DE ESTADISTICA Y CENSOS. ENCUESTA DE HOGARES DE PROPOSITOS MULTIPLES MODULO DE EMPLEO. 1976. a. Direccion General de Estadistica y Censos, Apdo. 10163, 1000 San Jose, Costa Rica.

COUNCIL OF EUROPE. DOCUMENTATION SECTION. BIBLIO BULLETIN. SERIES: POLITICAL, ECONOMIC AND SOCIAL AFFAIRS. see POLITICAL SCIENCE — Abstracting, Bibliographies, Statistics

650   US   ISSN 1064-539X
HC101
COUNTY BUSINESS PATTERNS. (Consists of 1 report per state and a U.S. summary) 1946. a. $283 for complete set (foreign $328.75); United States Summary $7; prices of reports of individual states vary. U.S. Bureau of the Census, Customer Services, Washington, DC 20233. TEL 301-457-4100. FAX 301-457-4714. URL: http://www.census.gov/. (Subscr. to: Superintendent of Documents, U.S. Government Printing Office, Box 371954, Pittsburgh, PA 15250-7954. TEL 202-512-1800. FAX 202-512-2250; Or: Bernan, 4611-F Assembly Dr., Lanham, MD 20706. TEL 301-459-7666. FAX 301-459-0056) **Document type:** government publication.
●Also available online.
Also available on CD-ROM.

330.9 310   CU
CUBA EN CIFRAS. a. Comite Estatal de Estadisticas, Centro de Informacion Cientifico-Tecnica, Almendares No. 156, esq. a Desague, Gaveta Postal 6016, Havana, Cuba. charts; stat.

310   CU   ISSN 0138-7766
HC152.5.A1
CUBA QUARTERLY ECONOMIC REPORT. (Text in English) q. Banco Nacional de Cuba, Comite Estatal de Estadisticas, Almendares No. 156, esq. a Desague, Gaveta Postal 6016, Havana, Cuba.

016.33   PH
CURRENT AWARENESS BULLETIN. (Text in English) 1988. m. free. Department of Trade and Industry, Trade & Industry Information Center, 4th Fl., Industry & Investment Bldg., 385 Sen. Gil J. Puyat Ave., Makati, Metro Manila 3117, Philippines. TEL 863611. FAX 856487. TELEX 14830 MTIPS. Ed. Minerva R. Fajardo. R&P contact: Remedios Abing. circ. 800. **Document type:** abstracting/indexing, government publication.
    Description: Provides a list of current acquisitions of TIIC and their abstracts.

BUSINESS AND ECONOMICS — ABSTRACTING, BIBLIOGRAPHIES, STATISTICS

658 016   JA   ISSN 0011-3328
CURRENT BIBLIOGRAPHY ON SCIENCE AND TECHNOLOGY: MANAGEMENT SCIENCE AND SYSTEMS ENGINEERING/KAGAKU GIJUTSU BUNKEN SOKUHO. KANRI SHISUTEMU GIJUTSU-HEN. (Text in Japanese) 1963. m. $1090. Japan Science and Technology Corporation, Information Center for Science and Technology - Kagaku Gijutsu Shinko Jigyodan, 5-3, Yonbancho, Chiyoda-ku, Tokyo 102, Japan. TEL 81-3-5214-8413. FAX 81-3-5214-8410. index. circ. 500. **Document type:** bibliography.
● Also available online. Vendor(s): JICST. Also available on CD-ROM.

016   UK   ISSN 0070-1858
CURRENT BRITISH DIRECTORIES. 1953. irreg., no. 12, 1993. £140($280) C.B.D. Research Ltd., 15 Wickham Rd., Beckenham, Kent BR3 2JS, England. TEL 44-181-650-7745. FAX 44-181-650-0768. Ed. C.A.P. Henderson. adv.; index. circ. 4,000. **Document type:** directory.
—BLDSC (3494.670000); Linda Hall.
Description: Lists alphabetically some 4,000 directories published in the U.K.

381 317   US   ISSN 1073-0087
HF5429.3
CURRENT BUSINESS REPORTS: MONTHLY RETAIL TRADE: SALES AND INVENTORIES. (Supplement avail: Current Business Reports: Combined Annual and Revised Monthly Trade) m. (plus m. Advance Reports and a. supplement). $57 (foreign $71.25). U.S. Bureau of the Census, Customer Services, Washington, DC 20233. TEL 301-457-4100. FAX 301-457-4714. URL: http://www.census.gov/. (Subscr. to: Superintendent of Documents, U.S. Government Printing Office, Box 371954, Pittsburgh, PA 15250-7954. TEL 202-512-1800. FAX 202-512-2250) stat. (diskette format; back issues avail.; reprint service avail.) **Indexed:** Amer.Stat.Ind. (1973-), PROMT. **Document type:** government publication.
● Also available online. Vendor(s): CompuServe, Inc., Knight-Ridder Information, Inc.
Formed by the 1991 merger of: Current Business Reports. Revised Monthly Retail Sales and Inventories (ISSN 0272-443X); Current Business Reports: Retail Trade, Annual Sales, Year-End Inventories, Purchases, Gross Margin, and Accounts Receivable by Kind of Retail Store (ISSN 0899-028X); Which was formerly (until 1983): Current Business Reports: Retail Trade, Annual Sales, Year-End Inventories and Accounts Receivable, by Kind of Retail Store (ISSN 0734-3477); (until 1978): Current Business Reports: Monthly Retail Trade, Annual Sales and Purchases, Year-End Inventories, and Accounts Receivable by Kind of Retail Store (ISSN 0194-3995)

016 658 330   KO
CURRENT CONTENTS OF FOREIGN JOURNALS: MANAGEMENT & ECONOMICS. (Text in language of original article) 1972. m. $62. Korea Institute for Economics and Technology, P.O. Box 205, 206-9 Cheongryangri-Dong, Dongdaimun-Ku, Seoul, S. Korea. Ed. Moon Shin Hong. circ. 300. (reprint service avail. from UMI) **Document type:** abstracting/indexing.
Formerly: Current Contents of Journals in Managerial Sciences.

011   UK   ISSN 0070-1955
CURRENT EUROPEAN DIRECTORIES/REPERTOIRE DES ANNUAIRES EUROPEENS/HANDBUCH DER EUROPAEISCHEN ADRESSBUECHER. 1969-198?; resumed. irreg., 3rd. edition, 1994. £140($280) C.B.D. Research Ltd., 15 Wickham Rd., Beckenham, Kent BR3 2JS, England. TEL 44-181-650-7745. FAX 44-181-650-0768. (Dist. in U.S. by: Gale Research Co., Penobscot Bldg., Detroit, MI 48226) adv.; index. circ. 2,000. **Document type:** directory.
Description: Lists 3,000 directories printed in European countries, along with extensive descriptions and an index of publishers with full addresses.

331.1   US   ISSN 0091-9209
HD8011.A1
CURRENT GOVERNMENTS REPORTS: CITY EMPLOYMENT. Key Title: City Employment. (Series GE-2) 1948. a. price varies. U.S. Bureau of the Census, Governments Division, Washington, DC 20233. TEL 301-457-1523. (also avail. in microfiche) **Document type:** government publication.
● Available only online. Vendor(s): CompuServe, Inc., Knight-Ridder Information, Inc.

336.73 317   US   ISSN 0090-5895
HJ275
CURRENT GOVERNMENTS REPORTS: STATE GOVERNMENT FINANCES. Key Title: State Government Finances. (Series GF-3) a. U.S. Bureau of the Census, Governments Division, Washington, DC 20233. TEL 202-457-1586. (also avail. in microfiche) **Document type:** government publication.
● Available only online.
Formerly: U.S. Bureau of the Census. State Finances.

658 016   II   ISSN 0376-7604
Z7164.07
CURRENT MANAGEMENT LITERATURE. (Text in English) m. Rs.60($20) Administrative Staff College of India, Bella Vista, Box 4, Hyderabad 500049, India. Ed. P.R.K. Murthy. **Document type:** abstracting/indexing.

310   CY
CYPRUS. DEPARTMENT OF STATISTICS AND RESEARCH. CENSUS OF COTTAGE INDUSTRY. (Text in English, Greek) 1967. irreg. £C5. Ministry of Finance, Department of Statistics and Research, 13 Lord Byron Ave., Nicosia, Cyprus. TEL 357-2-302349. FAX 357-2-456712. **Document type:** government publication.
Description: Compiles data on establishments, employment, output, investments, structure and regional distribution of cottage industry.

310   CY
CYPRUS. DEPARTMENT OF STATISTICS AND RESEARCH. CENSUS OF INDUSTRIAL PRODUCTION. (Text in English) 1954. quinquennial. £C5. Ministry of Finance, Department of Statistics and Research, 13 Lord Byron Ave., Nicosia, Cyprus. TEL 357-2-302349. FAX 357-2-456712. **Document type:** government publication.
Description: Compiles data on the number of enterprises, employment, labor costs and other expenses, output, sales, stocks, fixed assets and capacity of mining and quarrying, manufacturing, electricity, gas and water.

330 314   CY   ISSN 0070-2412
CYPRUS. DEPARTMENT OF STATISTICS AND RESEARCH. ECONOMIC REPORT. (Title varies: 1955-1962 - Economic Review) (Text in English, Greek) 1954. a. £C6. Ministry of Finance, Department of Statistics and Research, 13 Lord Byron Ave., Nicosia, Cyprus. TEL 357-2-302349. FAX 357-2-456712. **Document type:** government publication.
Description: Provides comprehensive information on the Cypriot economy.

310   CY
CYPRUS. DEPARTMENT OF STATISTICS AND RESEARCH. HOUSEHOLD INCOME AND EXPENDITURE SURVEY. (Text in English) 1971. quinquennial. £C10. Ministry of Finance, Department of Statistics and Research, 13 Lord Byron Ave., Nicosia, Cyprus. TEL 357-2-302349. FAX 357-2-456712. **Document type:** government publication.
Formerly: Cyprus. Department of Statistics and Research. Household Expenditure Survey.
Description: Covers both urban and rural households residing in the government-controlled area.

382 314   CY   ISSN 0253-858X
HF259.C9
CYPRUS. DEPARTMENT OF STATISTICS AND RESEARCH. IMPORTS AND EXPORTS STATISTICS. (Text in English) q. £C3. Ministry of Finance, Department of Statistics and Research, 13 Lord Byron Ave., Nicosia, Cyprus. TEL 357-2-302349. FAX 357-2-456712. abstr.; bibl.; mkt.; index, cum.index. (processed) **Document type:** government publication.
Description: Supplies detailed statistics of imports and exports by commodity.

331   CY   ISSN 1010-1160
HC497.C9
CYPRUS. DEPARTMENT OF STATISTICS AND RESEARCH. INDUSTRIAL STATISTICS. (Text in English, Greek) a. £C5 per no. Ministry of Finance, Department of Statistics and Research, 13 Lord Byron Ave., Nicosia, Cyprus. TEL 357-2-303208. FAX 357-2-456712. **Document type:** government publication.
Incorporates (1976-1984): Employment, Output and Capital Formation in the Industrial Sector; Industrial Production Survey; Sales of Vine Products; Price Index for the Manufacturing Sector.
Description: Provides a broad account of industrial statistics in Cyprus.

331   CY
CYPRUS. DEPARTMENT OF STATISTICS AND RESEARCH. LABOUR STATISTICS. (Text in English, Greek) a. £C6. Ministry of Finance, Department of Statistics and Research, 13 Lord Byron Ave., Nicosia, Cyprus. TEL 357-2-302349. FAX 357-2-456712. **Document type:** government publication.
Formerly: Labour Statistics Report (ISSN 0255-8386); Which supersedes: Annual Report on Unemployment.
Description: Presents annual statistics on employment, unemployment, vacancies and government labor force.

382 310   CY   ISSN 0070-2420
HF3757
CYPRUS. DEPARTMENT OF STATISTICS AND RESEARCH. STATISTICS OF IMPORTS AND EXPORTS. (Text in English) 1961. a. £C20. Ministry of Finance, Department of Statistics and Research, 13 Lord Byron Ave., Nicosia, Cyprus. TEL 357-2-302349. FAX 357-2-456712. **Document type:** government publication.
Description: Presents detailed statistics of imports and exports by commodity and by country.

330   XR
CZECH REPUBLIC. CESKY STATISTICKY URAD. STATISTICKY BULLETIN. m. $110. Cesky Statisticky Urad - Czech Statistical Office, Sokolovska 142, 186 04 Prague 8, Czech Republic. TEL 42-2-6604-2451. FAX 42-2-6631-0429.
Description: Contains reports on the development of the national economy.

330   XR
CZECH REPUBLIC. CZECH STATISTICAL OFFICE. BULLETIN. (Text in English) q. $36. Cesky Statisticky Urad, Sokolovska 142, 186 04 Prague 8, Czech Republic. TEL 42-2-6604-2451. FAX 42-2-6631-0429.
Description: Jointly issued by the central statistical bodies of the Czech Republic, Slovakia, Hungary and Poland. Intended for experts and the general public, both in the CR and abroad.

382.094 314   DK   ISSN 0070-2781
HF3641
DANMARKS VAREINDFOERSEL OG UDFOERSEL/EXTERNAL TRADE OF DENMARK. (Text in Danish; notes in English) 1883. a. DKK 289.60 (effective 1997). Danmarks Statistik, Sejroegade 11, DK-2100 Copenhagen OE, Denmark. TEL 45-39-17-39-17. FAX 45-31-18-48-01. **Document type:** government publication.

331 314   DK   ISSN 0909-0347
HD5049
DANSK ARBEJDSGIVERFORENING. D A LOENSTATISTIK. 1953. q. DKK 325 (effective 1997). Dansk Arbejdsgiverforening - Danish Employers Confederation, Vester Voldgade 113, DK-1790 Copenhagen V, Denmark. TEL 45-33-93-40-00. FAX 45-33-12-29-76. Ed. Fini Beilin. charts.
Formed by the 1993 merger of: Dansk Arbejdsgiverforening. Statistikken. Funktionaerloen (ISSN 0107-086X) & Dansk Arbejdsgiverforening. Statistikken. Arbejderloen (ISSN 0107-0851); Which supersedes in part (in 1978): Dansk Arbejdsgiverforening. Statistikken (ISSN 0011-619X)

330   MX   ISSN 0187-6163
DATOS BASICOS SOBRE LA ECONOMIA DE MEXICO. irreg., latest 1988. Instituto Nacional de Estadistica, Geografia e Informatica, Secretaria de Programacion y Presupuesto, Prol. Heroe de Nacozari 2301 Sur, Puerta 11, Acceso, 20270 Aguascalientes Ags., Mexico. TEL 49-18-19-48. FAX 491-807-39.

DELTA PI EPSILON. INDEX TO DOCTORAL DISSERTATIONS IN BUSINESS EDUCATION. see EDUCATION — Abstracting, Bibliographies, Statistics

339.2209489   DK   ISSN 0107-105X
HC360.I5
DENMARK. DANMARKS STATISTIK. INDKOMSTER OG FORMUER. (Text in Danish; notes in English) 1975. a. DKK 212 (effective 1997). Danmarks Statistik, Sejroegade 11, DK-2100 Copenhagen OE, Denmark. TEL 45-39-173917. FAX 45-31-184801. TELEX 16236. **Document type:** government publication.
Supersedes: Denmark. Danmarks Statistik. Indkomster og Formuer Ved Slutligningen; Denmark. Danmarks Statistik. Indkomstansaettelser til Staten (ISSN 0070-3524)

BUSINESS AND ECONOMICS — ABSTRACTING, BIBLIOGRAPHIES, STATISTICS

338.09489 314   DK   ISSN 0070-3532
HC351
DENMARK. DANMARKS STATISTIK. INDUSTRISTATISTIK. (Text in Danish; notes in English) 1905. a. DKK 81. Danmarks Statistik, Sejroegade 11, 2100 Copenhagen OE, Denmark. TEL 45-39-173917. FAX 45-31-184801. TELEX 16236. **Document type:** government publication.

330.9048   DK   ISSN 0109-1271
DENMARK. DANMARKS STATISTIK. KONJUNKTURTENDENSER I UDVALGTE LANDE. (Text in Danish; summaries in English) 1983. s-m. DKK 499.20 (effective 1997); newsstand price: DKK 54.40. Danmarks Statistik, Sejroegade 11, 2100 Copenhagen OE, Denmark. TEL 45-39-17-39-17. FAX 45-31-18-48-01. TELEX 16236.
Description: Contains the most important short-term indicators for selected European countries as well as the USA and Japan.

339.3489   DK   ISSN 0107-8771
HD5049
DENMARK. DANMARKS STATISTIK. LOEN- OG INDKOMSTATISTIK/STATISTICS OF EARNINGS AND INCOMES. 1982. irreg. (4-6/yr.). DKK 256 (effective 1997); newsstand price: DKK 23.20 (4-22pp), 119.20 (76-88pp). Danmarks Statistik, Sejroegade 11, 2100 Copenhagen OE, Denmark. TEL 45-39-173917. FAX 45-31-184801. TELEX 16236. **Document type:** government publication.
Description: Contains detailed statistics of indexes of hourly wage costs and monthly salary costs.

331.09489   DK   ISSN 0105-1083
HD5049
DENMARK. DANMARKS STATISTIK. MAANEDLIG BESKAEFTIGELSES- OG LOENSTATISTIK FOR INDUSTRI/MONTHLY STATISTICS OF INDUSTRIAL EMPLOYMENT AND LABOUR COSTS. (Text in Danish; notes in English) m. DKK 216.39. Danmarks Statistik, Sejroegade 11, 2100 Copenhagen OE, Denmark. TEL 45-39-173917. FAX 45-31-184801. TELEX 16236. **Document type:** government publication.

338.09489   DK   ISSN 0105-0877
DENMARK. DANMARKS STATISTIK. MAANEDLIG ORDRE- OG OMSAETNINGSSTATISTIK FOR INDUSTRI/MONTHLY STATISTICS OF INDUSTRIAL SALES AND ORDER BOOKS. (Text in Danish; notes in English) m. DKK 340 (effective 1997); newsstand price: 54.40. Danmarks Statistik, Sejroegade 11, 2100 Copenhagen OE, Denmark. TEL 45-39-17-39-17. FAX 45-31-18-48-01. TELEX 16236. **Document type:** government publication.

332.09489   DK   ISSN 0108-5476
HG27
DENMARK. DANMARKS STATISTIK. PENGE- OG KAPITALMARKED/MONEY AND CAPITAL MARKET. irreg. DKK 297.60 (effective 1997); newsstand price: DKK 23.20. Danmarks Statistik, Sejroegade 11, 2100 Copenhagen OE, Denmark. TEL 45-39-17-39-17. FAX 45-31-18-48-01. TELEX 16236. **Document type:** government publication.
Formerly: Denmark. Danmarks Statistik. Kreditmarkedsstatistik (ISSN 0107-3095).
Description: Liquidity, bank balances, mortgage registrations, bond issues, insolvencies. Insurance, pension funds and fires damages.

338.528   DK   ISSN 0106-6684
HB235.D4
DENMARK. DANMARKS STATISTIK. PRISSTATISTIK. (Text in Danish; notes in English) 1980. m. DKK 468. Danmarks Statistik, Sejroegade 11, DK-2100 Copenhagen OE, Denmark. TEL 45-39-173917. FAX 45-31-184801. TELEX 16238. **Document type:** government publication.

338.09489   DK   ISSN 0108-738X
HC360.F55
DENMARK. DANMARKS STATISTIK. REGNSKABSSTATISTIK FOR INDUSTRI/DENMARK. DANMARKS STATISTIK. INDUSTRIAL ACCOUNTS STATISTICS. (Text in Danish and English) 1981. a. DKK 136.80 (effective 1997). Danmarks Statistik, Sejroegade 11, DK-2100 Copenhagen OE, Denmark. TEL 45-39-17-39-17. FAX 45-31-18-48-01. TELEX 16236. **Document type:** government publication.
Formerly (until 1981): Denmark. Danmarks Statistik. Driftsregnskabsstatistik for Industrien.

366.2009489   DK   ISSN 0105-1164
HJ4369
DENMARK. DANMARKS STATISTIK. SKATTER OG AFGIFTER. OVERSIGT (YEAR)/TAXES AND DUTIES. (Text in Danish; notes in English) a. DKK 236 (effective 1997). Danmarks Statistik, Sejroegade 11, DK-2100 Copenhagen OE, Denmark. TEL 45-39-17-39-17. FAX 45-31-18-48-01. TELEX 16236. **Document type:** government publication.
Supersedes in part: Denmark. Danmarks Statistik. Ejendoms- og Selskabsbeskatningen i Skatteaaret.

382.09489   DK   ISSN 0108-5506
HF3641
DENMARK. DANMARKS STATISTIK. UDENRIGSHANDEL/DENMARK. DANMARKS STATISTIK. EXTERNAL TRADE. (Text in Danish; notes in English) 1980. a. DKK 512 (effective 1997). Danmarks Statistik, Sejroegade 11, DK-2100 Copenhagen OE, Denmark. TEL 45-39-17-39-17. FAX 45-31-18-48-01. TELEX 16236. **Document type:** government publication.
Formerly: Denmark. Danmarks Statistik. Handelsstatistiske Meddelelser. Maanedsstatistik over Udenrigshandelen (ISSN 0017-7342)
Description: Imports, exports, current-value indexes, quantity indexes, the terms of trade, distributions by countries, by commodity groups and by modes of transport. EU export subsidies and external trade of Greenland.

338.476   DK   ISSN 0107-0967
DENMARK. DANMARKS STATISTIK. VARESTATISTIK FOR INDUSTRI. SERIES A. 1970. q. DKK 136.80 (effective 1997); newsstand price: DKK 37.60. Danmarks Statistik, Sejroegade 11, DK-2100 Copenhagen OE, Denmark. TEL 45-39-173917. FAX 45-31-184801. TELEX 16236. **Document type:** government publication.
Supersedes in part (in 1980): Denmark. Danmarks Statistik. Kvartalsstatistik for Industrien.

338.476   DK   ISSN 0107-0975
DENMARK. DANMARKS STATISTIK. VARESTATISTIK FOR INDUSTRI. SERIES B. 1970. q. DKK 176 (effective 1997); newsstand price: DKK 48. Danmarks Statistik, Sejroegade 11, DK-2100 Copenhagen OE, Denmark. TEL 45-39-173917. FAX 45-31-184801. TELEX 16236. **Document type:** government publication.
Supersedes in part (in 1980): Denmark. Danmarks Statistik. Kvartalsstatistik for Industrien.

338.476   DK   ISSN 0107-0983
DENMARK. DANMARKS STATISTIK. VARESTATISTIK FOR INDUSTRI. SERIES C. 1970. q. DKK 113.60 (effective 1997); newsstand price: DKK 32. Danmarks Statistik, Sejroegade 11, DK-2100 Copenhagen OE, Denmark. TEL 45-39-173917. FAX 45-31-184801. TELEX 16236. **Document type:** government publication.
Supersedes in part (in 1980): Denmark. Danmarks Statistik. Kvartalsstatistik for Industrien.

338.476   DK   ISSN 0107-0991
DENMARK. DANMARKS STATISTIK. VARESTATISTIK FOR INDUSTRI. SERIES D. 1970. q. DKK 202.40 (effective 1997); newsstand price: DKK 56. Danmarks Statistik, Sejroegade 11, DK-2100 Copenhagen OE, Denmark. TEL 45-39-173917. FAX 45-31-184801. TELEX 16236. **Document type:** government publication.
Supersedes in part (in 1980): Denmark. Danmarks Statistik. Kvartalsstatistik for Industrien.

658   CN   ISSN 0380-7045
HF5465.C3
DEPARTMENT STORE SALES & STOCKS. 1938. m. Can.$144($173) (foreign $202). Statistics Canada, Operations and Integration Division, Circulation Management, Jean Talon Bldg., 2-C12, Tunney's Pasture, Ottawa, ON K1A 0T6, Canada. TEL 613-951-7277; 800-267-6677. FAX 613-951-1584. URL: http://www.statcan.ca.
Description: Presents data on department stores: sales, stocks and number of outlets. Includes data analysis, definitions, methodology, data reliability, list of department store organizations and bibliography.

338   SZ
DETAILHANDELSUMSAETZE/CHIFFRES D'AFFAIRES DU COMMERCE DE DETAIL. (Text in French and German) 1988. m. 32 SFr. Bundesamt fuer Statistik, Schwarztorstr. 96, CH-3003 Bern, Switzerland. TEL 41-31-3236011. FAX 41-31-3236061. URL: http://www.admin.ch/bfs. **Document type:** government publication.

322.1   GW   ISSN 0419-9014
HG3051
DEUTSCHE BUNDESBANK. MONATSBERICHTE. STATISTISCHE BEIHEFTE. REIHE 1: BANKENSTATISTIK NACH BANKENGRUPPEN. (Text in German; summaries in English) 1969. m. Deutsche Bundesbank, Postfach 100602, 60006 Frankfurt a.M., Germany. TEL 49-69-9566-1. FAX 49-69-5601071. URL: http://www.bundesbank.de. **Document type:** bulletin.

332.4   GW   ISSN 0341-8928
DEUTSCHE BUNDESBANK. MONATSBERICHTE. STATISTISCHE BEIHEFTE. REIHE 5: DEVISENKURSSTATISTIK. (Text in German; summaries in English) 1968. q. Deutsche Bundesbank, Postfach 100602, 60006 Frankfurt a.M., Germany. TEL 49-69-9566-1. FAX 49-69-5601071. URL: http://www.bundesbank.de. **Document type:** bulletin.
Formerly: Deutsche Bundesbank. Monatsberichte. Statistische Beihefte. Reihe 5: Waehrungen der Welt (ISSN 0341-9029)

332.1   GW
HG5491
DEUTSCHE BUNDESBANK. MONATSBERICHTE. STATISTISCHE BEIHEFTE. REIHE 2: KAPITALMARKTSTATISTIK. (Text in German; summaries in English) 1968. m. Deutsche Bundesbank, Postfach 100602, 60006 Frankfurt a.M., Germany. TEL 49-69-9566-1. FAX 49-69-5601071. URL: http://www.bundesbank.de. **Document type:** bulletin.
Formerly: Deutsche Bundesbank. Monatsberichte. Statistische Beihefte. Reihe 2: Wertpapierstatistik (ISSN 0418-8314)

332.1   GW   ISSN 0418-8330
HC290.5.I5
DEUTSCHE BUNDESBANK. MONATSBERICHTE. STATISTISCHE BEIHEFTE. REIHE 4: SAISONBEREINIGTE WIRTSCHAFTSZAHLEN. (Text in German; summaries in English) m. Deutsche Bundesbank, Postfach 100602, 60006 Frankfurt a.M., Germany. TEL 49-69-9566-1. FAX 49-69-5601071. URL: http://www.bundesbank.de. **Document type:** bulletin.

332.1   GW   ISSN 0418-8322
HG3883.G3
DEUTSCHE BUNDESBANK. MONATSBERICHTE. STATISTISCHE BEIHEFTE. REIHE 3: ZAHLUNGSBILANZSTATISTIK. (Text in German; summaries in English) 1968. m. Deutsche Bundesbank, Postfach 100602, 60006 Frankfurt a.M., Germany. TEL 49-69-9566-1. FAX 49-69-5601071. URL: http://www.bundesbank.de. **Document type:** bulletin.

334 310   GW
DIE DEUTSCHEN GENOSSENSCHAFTEN. STATISTIK. 1977. biennial. DM.22. D G Bank - Deutsche Genossenschaftsbank, Am Platz der Republik, 60325 Frankfurt a.M., Germany. TEL 49-69-744701. FAX 49-69-74471685. URL: http://www.dgbank.de. stat. circ. 2,000. **Document type:** trade publication.
Formerly: Genossenschaften in der Bundesrepublik Deutschland. Statistik.
Description: Statistical changes in the German cooperative system.

338.91   UN   ISSN 0254-2412
DEVELOPMENT INFORMATION ABSTRACTS/BULLETIN ANALYTIQUE SUR LE DEVELOPPEMENT/RESUMENES DE INFORMACION SOBRE EL DESARROLLO. (Text in English, French, Spanish; summaries in English) 1981. bi-m. free. United Nations, Department of Economic and Social Development, Development Information, Room DC1-1090, New York, NY 10017. TEL 212-963-4296. Ed. Letitia N. Mutter. abstr.; bibl. circ. 1,800. (back issues avail.) **Document type:** abstracting/indexing.
Description: Covers unpublished material by or for the United Nations in the field of economic and social development.

BUSINESS AND ECONOMICS — ABSTRACTING, BIBLIOGRAPHIES, STATISTICS

382 310   UN   ISSN 0252-306X
HF1016
DIRECTION OF TRADE STATISTICS. Yearbook issue (ISSN 0252-3019) 1958. q. (plus yearbook). $96 ($48 to university faculty and students). International Monetary Fund, Publication Services, 700 19th St., N.W., Ste. C-100, Washington, DC 20431. TEL 202-623-7430. FAX 202-623-7201. Ed. John B. McLenaghan. charts; mkt. circ. 6,000. (also avail. in microfilm from UMI; microfiche from CIS; magnetic tape; reprint service avail. from UMI) Indexed: IIS.
●Also available online.
— BLDSC (3590.351830); UMI.
Formerly (until 1980): Direction of Trade (ISSN 0012-3226)
Description: Provides data on the country and area distribution of countries' exports and imports as reported by themselves or by their partners.

DIRECTORY OF BUSINESS INFORMATION RESOURCES. see *BUSINESS AND ECONOMICS — Trade And Industrial Directories*

DIRECTORY OF EUROPEAN MEDICAL ORGANISATIONS. see *MEDICAL SCIENCES — Abstracting, Bibliographies, Statistics*

DIRECTORY OF EUROPEAN SPORTS ORGANISATIONS. see *SPORTS AND GAMES — Abstracting, Bibliographies, Statistics*

336   SZ
DIREKTE BUNDESSTEUER, STEUERERTRAEGE UND KOPFQUOTEN DER VERANLAGUNGSPERIODE/IMPOT FEDERAL DIRECT, RENDEMENTS DE L'IMPOT ET COTES PAR TETE DE LA PERIODE DE TAXATION. (Text in French and German) 1983. biennial. 10 SFr. Bundesamt fuer Statistik, Schwarztorstr. 96, CH-3003 Bern, Switzerland. TEL 41-31-3236060. FAX 41-31-3236061. URL: http://www.admin.ch/bfs. **Document type:** government publication.

331   US
DISPLACED WORKERS. (Subseries of: B L S Bulletins) irreg. $2.50. U.S. Bureau of Labor Statistics, 2 Massachusetts Ave., N.E., Washington, DC 20212. TEL 202-655-4000. (Subscr. to: Superintendent of Documents, U.S. Government Printing Office, Box 371954, Pittsburgh, PA 15250-7954. TEL 202-512-1800. FAX 202-512-2250; Or: Bureau of Labor Statistics Publications Sales Center, Box 2145, Chicago, IL 06090) **Document type:** government publication.
Description: Provides information on workers who lost their jobs to cutbacks or plant closings.

314   NE
DISTRIBUTIVE TRADES IN E C COUNTRIES. (Text in English) a. Hoofdbedrijfsschap Detailhandel, Postbus 90703, 2509 LS The Hague, Netherlands. TEL 31-70-3529800. **Document type:** government publication.

336.2 382 316   CX
DIVISION D'AIDE ET DE COOPERATION FRANCAISE. BULLETIN TRIMESTRIEL DE STATISTIQUE. 1963. q. 21660 Fr.CFA($81) Division d'Aide et de Cooperation Francaise, Departement des Statistiques, B.P. 1418, Bangui, Central African Republic. TEL 614574. (Subscr. to: Division des Statistiques et des Etudes Economiques, B.P. 696, Bangui, Central African Republic) charts. **Document type:** bulletin.
Former titles: Union Douaniere et Economique de l'Afrique Centrale. Bulletin des Statistiques Generales (ISSN 0041-6851); Union Douaniere Equatoriale. Bulletin des Statistiques Generales.

382   DQ   ISSN 0417-9382
DOMINICA. MINISTRY OF FINANCE. CENTRAL STATISTICAL OFFICE. ANNUAL OVERSEAS TRADE REPORT. a. $9.30. Ministry of Finance, Central Statistical Office, Kennedy Ave., Roseau, Dominica, W.I. Ed. Michael Murphy. **Document type:** government publication.
Formerly: Dominica. Ministry of Finance and Development. Annual Overseas Trade Report.

330   DQ
DOMINICA. MINISTRY OF FINANCE. CENTRAL STATISTICAL OFFICE. CONSUMER PRICE INDICES. a. $13.50. Ministry of Finance, Central Statistical Office, Kennedy Ave., Roseau, Dominica, W.I. Ed. Michael Murphy. **Document type:** government publication.

330   DQ
DOMINICA. MINISTRY OF FINANCE. CENTRAL STATISTICAL OFFICE. NATIONAL ACCOUNTS AND BALANCE OF PAYMENTS. a. $13.50. Ministry of Finance, Central Statistical Office, Kennedy Ave., Roseau, Dominica, W.I. Ed. Michael Murphy. **Document type:** government publication.

330   DQ
DOMINICA. MINISTRY OF FINANCE. CENTRAL STATISTICAL OFFICE. QUARTERLY ECONOMIC INDICATORS. q. free. Ministry of Finance, Central Statistical Office, Kennedy Ave., Roseau, Dominica, W.I. Ed. Michael Murphy. **Document type:** government publication.

DOMINICAN REPUBLIC. CENTRO DOMINICANO DE PROMOCION DE EXPORTACIONES. BOLETIN ESTADISTICO. see *BUSINESS AND ECONOMICS — International Commerce*

339 314   YU   ISSN 0300-2527
DRUSTVENI PROIZVOD I NARODNI DOHODAK. (Subseries of Statisticki Bilten) 1969. a. 30 din.($1.67) Savezni Zavod za Statistiku, Kneza Milosa 20, Belgrade, Yugoslavia. TEL 681-999. stat.

330   TS
DUBAI EXTERNAL TRADE STATISTICS/IHSA'IYYAT DUBAI LIL-TIJARAH AL-KHARIJIYYAH. (Text in English) 1979. a. Central Accounting Administration, Statistics Section - Idarat al-Hisabat al-Markazi, Qism al-Ihsa', P.O. Box 516, Dubai, United Arab Emirates. TEL 531074. FAX 531959. TELEX 47470 HISAB EM. circ. 500 (controlled).
Description: Covers imports, exports and re-exports, with statistics for fuel supplied to ships and aircraft, and Free Zone Port Rashid activity reports.

330 016   SW   ISSN 0348-968X
E F I - NYTT/E F I NEWS. (Text in Swedish; summaries in English) 1968. irreg. free. Handelshoegskolan i Stockholm, Ekonomiska Forskningsinstitutet (EFI) - Economic Research Institute at the Stockholm School of Economics, P.O. Box 6501, 113 83 Stockholm, Sweden. Ed. Rune Castenaes. bk.rev. circ. 4,000. **Document type:** newsletter.
— BLDSC (3664.130000).

331   CN
EARNINGS AND EMPLOYMENT TRENDS. 12/yr. Can.$60 (effective 1997). Ministry of Finance and Corporate Relations, B C Stats, P.O. Box 9410, Stn. Prov. Govt., Victoria, BC V8W 9V1, Canada. TEL 250-387-1502. FAX 250-387-0329. E-mail: bcstats@fincc04.fin.gov.bc.ca; URL: http://www.bcstats.gov.bc.ca. Ed. Anne Kittredge. **Document type:** directory.
Description: Provides sectoral analysis of the B.C. labor force and its wage structure.

314   EI   ISSN 0259-0492
HD5014.5
EARNINGS - INDUSTRY AND SERVICES. (Text in English, French, German, Italian, Spanish) s-a. $71. Statistical Office of the European Communities, Rue Alcide de Gasperi, 2920 Luxembourg, Luxembourg. (Dist. in the U.S. by: Unipub, 4611-F Assembly Dr., Lanham, MD 20706-4391. TEL 800-274-4888. FAX 301-459-0056) (also avail. in microfiche from CIS) **Indexed:** IIS.
— BLDSC (0747.750000).

316 316   KE   ISSN 0012-9992
EAST AFRICAN COMMUNITY. ECONOMIC AND STATISTICAL REVIEW. 1948. q. EAs.10. East African Community, Statistical Department, P.O. Box 30462, Nairobi, Kenya. bibl.; charts. circ. 1,000.
Formerly: East African Quarterly Economic and Statistical Bulletin.

330 011   UK
EAST ASIA BIBLIOGRAPHY; a review of new publications on China & the Far East. 1979. irreg. £8 for 4 nos. East Asia Co., 103 Camden High St., London NW1 7JN, England. adv.; bk.rev. circ. 2,000. **Document type:** bibliography.

330.9   US
ECONOMIC ABSTRACT OF ALABAMA. Variant title: Alabama Economic Abstract. a.? $25 (effective 1995). Center for Business and Economic Research, University of Alabama, Box 870221, Tuscaloosa, AL 35487-0221. TEL 205-348-6191. FAX 205-348-2951. **Document type:** directory.
Description: Comprehensive source of demographic and economic information available about Alabama and its counties.

381   CN   ISSN 0229-1665
HC117.B8
ECONOMIC ACCOUNTS. a. Can.$20 (effective 1997). Ministry of Finance and Corporate Relations, B C Stats, P.O. Box 9410, Stn. Prov. Govt., Victoria, BC V8W 9V1, Canada. TEL 250-387-0359. FAX 250-387-0380. E-mail: bcstats@fincc04.fin.gov.bc.ca; URL: http://www.bcstats.gov.bc.ca. charts. **Document type:** government publication.
Description: Presents the principal estimates of aggregate economic activity in the province.

310   CE
ECONOMIC AND SOCIAL STATISTICS OF SRI LANKA. 1978. irreg., latest 1993. $7. Central Bank of Sri Lanka, Janadhipathi Mawatha, P.O. Box 590, Colombo 1, Sri Lanka. TEL 94-1-421191. FAX 94-1-445127. circ. 1,500. **Document type:** academic/scholarly publication.
Description: Provides statistical information on population, labor force, employment, national accounts, agriculture, industry, trade, finance and transporation in Sri Lanka.

352.7   UK
ECONOMIC DEVELOPMENT TODAY. 1984. m. £95 to non-members (foreign £145); members £85 (effective 1997). Planning Exchange, Tontine House, 8 Gordon St., Glasgow G1 3PL, Scotland. TEL 44-141-248-8541. FAX 44-141-248-8277. Ed. Chris McAuley. adv. contact: Michelle Buchan. **Document type:** abstracting/indexing.
Formerly (until 1996): Economic Development Digest (ISSN 0266-4194)
Description: Abstracts of literature on local and regional economic development.

339   PH
ECONOMIC INDICATORS. m. $279 in Asia (Australia & New Zealand $345; US & Canada $399; Europe $447; elsewhere $555). National Statistical Coordination Board, c/o National Statistical Information Center, Midland-Buendia Bldg., 403 Sen. Gil Puyat Ave., Makati City, Philippines. TEL 63-2-890-9405. FAX 63-2-890-9408. E-mail: nscb__nsic@mozcom.com. **Document type:** government publication.
Former titles: N E D A Philippine Economic Indicators; N E D A Economic Indicators.
Description: Presents statistical indicators of the levels and trends of economic activities and performance. Covers production and consumption, transportation and tourism, external sector, employment, prices, money and banking, and public finance.

330   US
ECONOMIC INDICATORS HANDBOOK; time series, conversions, documentation. 1992. biennial. $166.75. Gale Research, 835 Penobscot Bldg., 645 Griswold St., Detroit, MI 48226-4094. TEL 313-961-2242; 800-877-4253. FAX 800-414-5043. E-mail: daniel__snyder@gale.com.
Description: Presents aggregate national economic indicators in 175 different statistical series.

ECONOMIST. ANNUAL INDEX. see *BUSINESS AND ECONOMICS — Economic Situation And Conditions*

330   EC
ECUADOR. DEPARTAMENTO DE ESTADISTICAS FISCALES. ESTADISTICAS FISCALES. irreg. Departamento de Estadisticas Fiscales, Subsecretaria de Presupuesto y Credito Publico, Quito, Ecuador.

381   EC
ECUADOR. INSTITUTO NACIONAL DE ESTADISTICA Y CENSOS. ENCUESTA ANUAL DE COMERCIO INTERNO. a. Esc.33000($88) (effective 1994). Instituto Nacional de Estadistica y Censos, Av. 10 de Agosto 229, Quito, Ecuador. TEL 593-2-581900. FAX 593-2-580041. **Document type:** government publication.

BUSINESS AND ECONOMICS — ABSTRACTING, BIBLIOGRAPHIES, STATISTICS

338 318   EC   ISSN 0302-5233
ECUADOR. INSTITUTO NACIONAL DE ESTADISTICA Y CENSOS. ENCUESTA ANUAL DE MANUFACTURA Y MINERIA. a. $187. Instituto Nacional de Estadistica y Censos, Av. 10 de Agosto 229, Quito, Ecuador. TEL 593-2-581900. FAX 593-2-580041. charts; stat.

331.11 318   EC   ISSN 0070-8917
ECUADOR. INSTITUTO NACIONAL DE ESTADISTICA Y CENSOS. ESTADISTICA DEL TRABAJO; INDICE DE EMPLEO Y REMUNERACIONES. 1985? q. Esc.10000($79) Instituto Nacional de Estadistica y Censos, Av. 10 de Agosto 229, Quito, Ecuador. TEL 593-2-581900. FAX 593-2-580041.

382 316   UA   ISSN 0027-0237
EGYPT. CENTRAL AGENCY FOR PUBLIC MOBILISATION AND STATISTICS. MONTHLY BULLETIN OF FOREIGN TRADE. (Text in Arabic & English) 1964. m. £E60. Central Agency for Public Mobilisation & Statistics, Box 2086, Nasr City, Cairo, Egypt. stat. **Document type:** bulletin.

330 310   UA   ISSN 0013-239X
HC531
L'EGYPTE CONTEMPORAINE. (Text in Arabic, English, French) 1910. q. P.T.225($12) Egyptian Society of Political Economy, Statistics and Legislation - Societe Egyptienne d'Economie Politique, de Statistique et de Legislation, 16 Sharia Ramses, P.O. Box 732, Cairo, Egypt. TEL 02-750797. Ed. M.H. Ghanem. bk.rev.; bibl.; cum.index: 1910-1959. circ. 1,500. **Indexed:** Documentatieblad, IBR, IDA, Int.Lab.Doc., Int.Polit.Sci.Abstr.

330   RU
EKONOMIKA: OTECHESTVENNAYA I ZARUBEZHNAYA LITERATURA; referativnyi zhurnal. 1992. q. $64. Rossiiskaya Akademiya Nauk, Institut Nauchnoi Informatsii po Obshchestvennym Naukam, Ul. Krasikova 28-21, 117418 Moscow V-418, Russia. Ed. I.M. Osadchaya. **Document type:** abstracting/indexing.
    Formed by the merger of (1973-1992): Obshchestvennye Nauki v S.S.S.R. Ekonomika (ISSN 0202-2044); (1972-1992): Obshchestvennye Nauki za Rubezhom. Ekonomika (ISSN 0132-7372)

658 016   RU   ISSN 0321-3668
EKSPRESS-INFORMATSIYA. PROMYSHLENNYI ORGANICHESKII SINTEZ. 1960. 48/yr. 38 Rub. Vsesoyuznyi Institut Nauchno-Tekhnicheskoi Informatsii (VINITI), Baltiiskaya ul., 14, Moscow A-219, Russia. (Subscr. to: Mezhdunarodnaya Kniga, Dimitrova ul. 39, 113095 Moscow, Russia)

382   ES
EL SALVADOR. MINISTERIO DE COMERCIO EXTERIOR. ESTADISTICAS. a. Ministerio de Comercio Exterior - Ministry of Foreign Trade of El Salvador, San Salvador, El Salvador.

331.11 318   ES
EL SALVADOR. MINISTERIO DE TRABAJO Y PREVISION SOCIAL. ESTADISTICAS DEL TRABAJO. a. Ministerio de Trabajo y Prevision Social, Avda. Norte 428, Edif. 2A, San Salvador, El Salvador. TEL 77-1250.

334.11 350.6   US
EMPLOYMENT AND PAYROLLS IN WASHINGTON STATE BY COUNTY AND INDUSTRY; industries covered by the Employment Security Act and federal employment covered by Title 5, U.S.C. 85. q. (plus a. summary). $20 (diskette version $25; annual summary only $6). Employment Security Department, Box 9046, Olympia, WA 98507-9046. charts. (also avail. in diskette format; back issues avail.) **Document type:** government publication.
    Description: Contains employment and wage data for businesses and organizations subject to the Washington State Employment Security Act.

EMPLOYMENT AND VACANCIES STATISTICS. SERIES B: WHOLESALE, RETAIL TRADES, RESTAURANTS AND HOTELS. see *OCCUPATIONS AND CAREERS — Abstracting, Bibliographies, Statistics*

330.9   CC
EMPLOYMENT AND VACANCIES STATISTICS. SERIES C: INDUSTRIAL SECTOR. (Text in Chinese, English) 1985. a. HK.$108. Census and Statistics Department, Wanchai Tower, 12 Harbour Rd., Central, Hong Kong, People's Republic of China. TEL 852-2598-8197. FAX 852-2598-7482. (Subscr. to: Director of Information Services, Information Services Dept., 28-F Sui On Centre, 188 Lockhart Rd., Wanchai, Hong Kong; People's Republic of China) Ed.Bd. charts. **Document type:** government publication.
    Formerly: Employment and Vacancy Statistics: Manufacturing, Mining and Quarrying, Electricity and Gas.

331   US
EMPLOYMENT AND WAGES ANNUAL AVERAGES. (Subseries of: B L S Bulletins) a. $32. U.S. Bureau of Labor Statistics, 2 Massachusetts Ave., N.E., Washington, DC 20212. TEL 202-655-4000. (Subscr. to: Superintendent of Documents, U.S. Government Printing Office, Box 371954, Pittsburgh, PA 15250-7954. TEL 202-512-1800. FAX 202-512-2250; Or: Bureau of Labor Statistics Publications Sales Center, Box 2145, Chicago, IL 60690) **Document type:** government publication.
    Description: Provides a complete count of employment and wages for workers covered by state unemployment programs; national employment and wage totals are given for specific industries.

331.1   US
EMPLOYMENT IN PERSPECTIVE: MINORITY WORKERS. (Subseries of: B L S Reports) q. U.S. Bureau of Labor Statistics, 2 Massachusetts Ave., N.E., Washington, DC 20212. TEL 202-655-4000. (Subscr. to: Superintendent of Documents, U.S. Government Printing Office, Box 371954, Pittsburgh, PA 15250-7954. TEL 202-512-1800. FAX 202-512-2250; Or: Bureau of Labor Statistics Publications Sales Center, Box 2145, Chicago, IL 60690) **Document type:** government publication.
    Description: Examines the extent of nonagricultural self-employment among minority workers.

330   VE   ISSN 0798-8648
ENCUESTA CUANTITATIVA DE COMERCIO AL DETAL. 1985. a. Bs.150 (for 1991-92 ed.). Oficina Central de Estadistica e Informatica, Apdo. de Correos 4593, Carmelitas, Caracas 1010A, Venezuela. TEL 58-2-782-11-33. FAX 58-2-781-13-80. **Document type:** government publication.

338 318   VE   ISSN 0259-515X
ENCUESTA INDUSTRIAL: RESULTADOS NACIONALES. 1974. a. Bs.250 (for 1991 ed.). Oficina Central de Estadistica e Informatica, Apdo. de Correos 4593, Carmelitas, Caracas 1010A, Venezuela. TEL 58-2-782-11-33. FAX 58-2-781-13-80. TELEX 21241. stat.
    Formerly: Encuesta Industrial de Venezuela.
    Description: Covers accounting and labor issues.

338.91 610 551   GW   ISSN 0722-0111
Z7164.U5
ENTWICKLUNGSLAENDER-STUDIEN; Bibliographie entwicklungslaenderbezogener Forschungsarbeiten. 1966. a. Deutsche Stiftung fuer Internationale Entwicklung, Zentrale Dokumentation - German Foundation for International Development, Hans-Boeckler-Str. 5, 53225 Bonn, Germany. TEL 49-228-4001-0. FAX 49-228-4001-111. Ed. Herbert Henselek. index. (back issues avail.) **Document type:** bibliography.
—BLDSC (3791.040000).

ERHVERVSUDDANNELSERNE. see *EDUCATION — Abstracting, Bibliographies, Statistics*

338   PR
ESTABLECIMIENTOS MANUFACTURERAS EN PUERTO RICO. a. free. Department of Labor, Bureau of Labor Statistics, 505 Munoz Rivera Ave., Hato Rey, PR 00918. TEL 787-754-5348. Ed. Myrta Olmos Quinones. index. circ. 775. **Document type:** government publication.

382   MX   ISSN 0187-4845
HD9734.M4
ESTADISTICA DE LA INDUSTRIA MAQUILADORA DE EXPORTACION. 1981. a. Instituto Nacional de Estadistica, Geografia e Informatica, Secretaria de Programacion y Presupuesto, Prol. Heroe de Nacozari 2301 Sur, Puerta 11, Acceso, 20270 Aguascalientes Ags., Mexico. TEL 49-18-19-48. FAX 491-807-39.

382 314   SP   ISSN 0071-1527
ESTADISTICA DEL COMERCIO EXTERIOR DE ESPANA. ceased. m. (with a. summary). 50000 ptas. Agencia Tributaria, Servicio de Publicaciones, C. Guzman El Bueno 137, 28071 Madrid, Spain. TEL 39-1-5543200 ext. 570. FAX 39-1-5536189. (also avail. in diskette format)

318 338   PN   ISSN 0378-2557
HC147
ESTADISTICA PANAMENA. SITUACION ECONOMICA. SECCION 314, 323, 324, 325, 353. INDUSTRIA. 1958. s-a. Bl.0.50 (effective 1997). Direccion de Estadistica y Censo, Contraloria General, Apdo. 5213, Panama 5, Panama. FAX 507-269-7294. circ. 800. **Document type:** government publication, bulletin.
    Description: Offers data on fishing, manufacturing, construction, and energy, gas, and water usage and production on a national level.

330 318   PN   ISSN 0379-4245
ESTADISTICA PANAMENA. SITUACION ECONOMICA. SECCION 321. INDUSTRIA ENCUESTA. 1957. a. Bl.0.50 (effective 1997). Direccion de Estadistica y Censo, Contraloria General, Apdo. 5213, Panama 5, Panama. FAX 507-269-7294. circ. 800. **Document type:** government publication, bulletin.
    Formerly: Panama. Direccion de Estadistica y Censo. Estadistica Panamena. Serie F. Industrias - Encuestas (ISSN 0078-8937)
    Description: Presents information on establishments dedicated to the manufacturing industry.

318   PN   ISSN 0378-4983
HF142
ESTADISTICA PANAMENA. SITUACION ECONOMICA. SECCION 331. COMERCIO. ANUARIO DE COMERCIO EXTERIOR. (In 4 vols.; vol.1: Importacion, vol.2: Exportacion, vol.3: Zona Libre de Colon, vol.4: Reexportacion) 1953. a. Bl.6.50 (effective 1997). Direccion de Estadistica y Censo, Contraloria General, Apdo. 5213, Panama 5, Panama. FAX 507-69-7294. charts. circ. 800. **Document type:** government publication, bulletin.
    Formerly: Estadistica Panamena. Situacion Economica. Seccion 331. Comercio. Comercio Exterior. (Anual).
    Description: Presents information on the movement of commercial goods.

318   PN   ISSN 1017-4273
HJ21
ESTADISTICA PANAMENA. SITUACION ECONOMICA. SECCION 343. HACIENDA PUBLICA. 1958. a. Bl.0.75 (effective 1997). Direccion de Estadistica y Censo, Contraloria General, Apdo. 5213, Panama 5, Panama. FAX 507-269-7294. circ. 750. **Document type:** government publication, bulletin.
    Supersedes in part (in 1988): Estadistica Panamena. Situacion Economica. Seccion 343-344. Hacienda Publica y Finanzas (ISSN 0378-6730)
    Description: Presents information on budgets, revenues, expenditures, and debts of the public sector.

318   PN   ISSN 0378-2522
HB235.P35
ESTADISTICA PANAMENA. SITUACION ECONOMICA. SECCION 351. INDICE DE PRECIOS AL POR MAYOR Y AL CONSUMIDOR. 1957. q. Bl.2 (effective 1997). Direccion de Estadistica y Censo, Contraloria General, Apdo. 5213, Panama 5, Panama. FAX 507-269-7294. circ. 900. **Document type:** government publication, bulletin.
    Description: Presents indexes of prices from the import, industrial, and agricultural sectors.

338 318   PN
ESTADISTICA PANAMENA. SITUACION SOCIAL. SECCION 441. ESTADISTICAS DEL TRABAJO. (In 2 vols.: Vol.1 Encuesta Continua de Hogares, Vol.2 Empleo en los Sectores Publico y Privado) 1963. a. Bl.0.75 (effective 1997). Direccion de Estadistica y Censo, Contraloria General, Apdo. 5213, Panama 5, Panama. FAX 507-269-7294. circ. 750. **Document type:** government publication, bulletin.
    Formerly: Estadistica Panamena. Situacion Social. Seccion 441 - Trabajo y Salarios. Estadisticas del Trabajo (ISSN 0379-072X); **Supersedes:** Estadistica Panamena. Serie M. Empleo.
    Description: Presents data from the census of housing and employment.

339   GT
ESTADISTICAS MACROECONOMICAS DE CENTROAMERICA. a. $10. Secretaria Permanente del Tratado General de Integracion Economica Centroamericana - Permanent Secretariat of the General Treaty on Central American Economic Integration, 4a Avda. 10-25, Zona 14, Apdo. 1237, 01901 Guatemala, Guatemala. TEL 2-682151. FAX 2-681071. TELEX 5676.

387   CN
ESTIMATES OF REVENUE AND EXPENDITURE. (Supplement avail.) a. Can.$16.70. Ministry of Finance and Corporate Relations, 1405 Douglas St., 2nd Fl., Victoria, BC V8V 1X4, Canada. TEL 604-387-1502. FAX 604-387-0329. (Subscr. to: Crown Publications, 546 Yates St., Victoria, BC V8W 1K8, Canada. TEL 604-386-4636)
     Description: Outlines the revenue and expenditure intentions of the government for the next fiscal year.

382 316   ET   ISSN 0425-4309
ETHIOPIA. CUSTOMS HEAD OFFICE. EXTERNAL TRADE STATISTICS. (Text in English) 1946. a. $21. Customs Head Office, Box 3248, Addis Ababa, Ethiopia. TELEX 21177. charts.

330
EUROPEAN BUSINESS RANKINGS ANNUAL. 1992. a. $160. Gale Research, 835 Penobscot Bldg., 645 Griswold St., Detroit, MI 48226-4094. TEL 313-961-2242; 800-877-4253. FAX 800-414-5043. E-mail: daniel_snyder@gale.com.
     Description: Displays over 2250 business statistics from throughout Europe. Covers products, institutions, industries, companies, services, demographics and economic trends.

338 016   UK   ISSN 0071-2582
EUROPEAN COMPANIES; guide to sources of information. 1962. irreg., no. 4, 1992. £80($160) C B D Research Ltd., 15 Wickham Rd., Beckenham, Kent BR3 2JS, England. TEL 44-181-650-7745. FAX 44-181-650-0768. (Dist. in the U.S. by: Hoover, Inc., 6448 Hwy. 290 E., Ste. E-104, Austin, TX 78723) Ed. R Rickson. adv. circ. 2,000.
     Document type: directory.
     Description: Compiles 1,400 sources of company information available in all European countries.

330 384   UK   ISSN 0966-7458
THE EUROPEAN JOURNAL OF TELEWORKING. 1993. q. £50 to individuals (N. America $99; elsewhere £60); institutions £99 (N. America $175; elsewhere £110). (National Association of Teleworkers) Addico Cornix Ltd., 70 Causeway Head, Penzance, Cornwall TR18 2SR, England. TEL 44-1736-332736. FAX 44-1736-69477. E-mail: srs@cornix.co.uk; 100021,2563@compuserve.com. Ed. Stephen Simmons. R&P contact: S. White. adv. contact: Nicki Groves. **Document type:** trade publication.
     —BLDSC (3829.746300).
     Description: Covers research on all aspects of teleworking from academic, industrial, and commercial sources. Aimed at policymakers and practitioners interested in cutting-edge developments in the field.

330   US
EUROPEAN MARKET SHARE REPORTER. 1993. biennial. $152. Gale Research, 835 Penobscot Bldg., 645 Griswold St., Detroit, MI 48226-4094. TEL 313-961-2242; 800-877-4253. FAX 800-414-5043. E-mail: daniel_snyder@gale.com. Ed. Oksana Newman.
     Description: Provides statistics on European products, markets, and services.

658.8   UK   ISSN 0071-2930
HC79.C6
EUROPEAN MARKETING DATA AND STATISTICS (YEAR). 1962. a. £175($350) (effective 1997). Euromonitor, 60-61 Britton St., London EC1M 5NA, England. TEL 44-171-251-8024. FAX 44-171-608-3149. E-mail: info@euromonitor.com; URL: http://www.euromonitor.com. (Addr. in N. America: Euromonitor International, 122 S. Michigan Ave., Ste. 1220, Chicago, IL 60603. TEL 800-577-3876. FAX 312-922-1157) **Document type:** trade publication, directory.
     —CISTI.
     Description: Contains more than 100,000 statistics on a wide range of business, economic, and social topics covering 30 European countries.

332.6   EI   ISSN 1026-9150
EUROSTAT. E U EXTERNAL TRADE INDICES/INDICES DU COMMERCE EXTERIEUR DE L'U E. Key Title: Eurostat. Aussenhandelsindizes der E.U. (Text in English, French, and German) a. Statistical Office of the European Communities, Eurostat, L-2920 Luxembourg, Luxembourg. TEL 352-4301-34526. FAX 352-4301-33415. (Dist. in the U.S. by: Unipub, 4611 Assembly Dr., Lanham, MD 20706. TEL 800-274-4888. FAX 301-459-0056) charts.
     Document type: government publication.
     —BLDSC (3823.622200).
     Supersedes (in 1993): Eurostat. E C External Trade Indices (ISSN 1015-9622)

EUROSTAT. GAS PRICES. see *ENERGY — Abstracting, Bibliographies, Statistics*

330.9   EI   ISSN 1024-4298
EUROSTAT. STATISTICS IN FOCUS. ECONOMY AND FINANCE. French edition: Eurostat. Statistiques en Bref. Economie et Finances (ISSN 1024-4301); German edition: Eurostat. Statistik Kurzgefasst. Wirtschaft und Finanzen (ISSN 1024-431X) (Text in English) m. Statistical Office of the European Communities, Eurostat, L-2920 Luxembourg, Luxembourg. TEL 352-4301-34526. FAX 352-4301-33415. (Dist. in the U.S. by: Unipub, 4611-F Assembly Dr., Lanham, MD 20706. TEL 800-274-4888. FAX 301-459-0056) charts.
     Document type: government publication.
     —BLDSC (8453.536750).
     Formerly (until 1994): Eurostat. Rapid Reports. Economy and Finance (ISSN 1016-0213)

330.9 333.79   EI   ISSN 1024-4328
EUROSTAT. STATISTICS IN FOCUS. ENERGY AND INDUSTRY. French edition: Eurostat. Statistiques en Bref. Energie et Industrie (ISSN 1024-4336); German edition: Eurostat. Statistik Kurzgefasst. Energie und Industrie (ISSN 1024-4344) (Text in English) 1987. m. Statistical Office of the European Communities, Eurostat, L-2920 Luxembourg, Luxembourg. TEL 352-4301-34526. FAX 352-4301-33415. (Dist. in the U.S. by: Unipub, 4611-F Assembly Dr., Lanham, MD 20706. TEL 800-274-4888. FAX 301-459-0056) charts.
     Document type: government publication.
     —BLDSC (8453.536760).
     Former titles (until 1994): Eurostat. Rapid Reports. Energy and Industry (ISSN 1016-0191); Eurostat. Rapid Reports. Energy (ISSN 1013-0403)

332.6   EI   ISSN 1024-6878
EUROSTAT. STATISTICS IN FOCUS. EXTERNAL TRADE. French edition: Eurostat. Statistiques Rapides. Commerce Exterieur (ISSN 1016-5762); German edition: Eurostat. Schnellberichte. Aussenhandel (ISSN 1017-5806) (Text in English) 1991. m. Statistical Office of the European Communities, Eurostat, L-2920 Luxembourg, Luxembourg. TEL 352-4301-34526. FAX 352-4301-33415. (Dist. in the U.S. by: Bernan Associates, 4611-F Assembly Dr., Lanham, MD 20706. TEL 800-274-4888. FAX 301-459-0056) charts.
     Document type: government publication.
     —BLDSC (8453.536765).
     Formerly (until 1995): Eurostat. Rapid Reports. Foreign Trade (ISSN 1017-5792)

330.9 312   EI   ISSN 1024-4352
EUROSTAT. STATISTICS IN FOCUS. POPULATION AND SOCIAL CONDITIONS. French edition: Eurostat. Statistiques en Bref. Population et Conditions Sociales (ISSN 1024-4360); German edition: Eurostat. Statistik Kurzgefasst. Bevoelkerung und Soziale Bedingungen (ISSN 1024-4379) (Text in English) m. Statistical Office of the European Communities, Eurostat, L-2920 Luxembourg, Luxembourg. TEL 352-4301-32526. FAX 352-4301-33415. (Dist. in the U.S. by: Unipub, 4611-F Assembly Dr., Lanham, MD 20706. TEL 800-274-4888. FAX 301-459-0056) charts.
     Document type: government publication.
     —BLDSC (8453.536770).
     Formerly (until 1994): Eurostat. Rapid Reports. Population and Social Conditions (ISSN 1016-0205)

330.9   EI   ISSN 1024-6886
EUROSTAT. STATISTICS IN FOCUS. REGIONS. French edition: Eurostat. Statistiques Rapides. Regions (ISSN 1015-8936); German edition: Eurostat. Schnellberichte. Regionen (ISSN 1017-5873) (Text in English) m. Statistical Office of the European Communities, Eurostat, L-2920 Luxembourg, Luxembourg. TEL 352-4301-34526. FAX 352-4301-33415. (Dist. in the U.S. by: Unipub, 4611-F Assembly Dr., Lanham, MD 20706. TEL 800-274-4888. FAX 301-459-0056) charts.
     Document type: government publication.
     —BLDSC (8453.536775).
     Formerly (until 1995): Eurostat. Rapid Reports. Regions (ISSN 1013-0535)

330   EI   ISSN 1024-7971
▼**EUROSTAT. STATISTICS IN FOCUS. RESEARCH AND DEVELOPMENT.** French edition: Eurostat. Statistiques en Bref. Recherche et Developpement (ISSN 1024-7963); German edition: Eurostat. Statistik Kurzgefasst. Forschung und Entwicklung (ISSN 1024-798X) (Text in English) 1995. m. Statistical Office of the European Communities, Eurostat, L-2920 Luxembourg, Luxembourg. TEL 352-4301-34526. FAX 352-4301-33415. (Dist. in the U.S. by: Unipub, 4611-F Assembly Dr., Lanham, MD 20706. TEL 800-274-4888. FAX 301-459-0056) charts. **Document type:** government publication.
     —BLDSC (8453.536778).

330.9 312   EI   ISSN 1024-4379
EUROSTAT. STATISTIK KURZGEFASST. BEVOELKERUNG UND SOZIALE BEDINGUNGEN. English edition: Eurostat. Statistics in Focus. Populations and Social Conditions (ISSN 1024-4352); French edition: Eurostat. Statistiques en Bref. Population et Conditions Sociales (ISSN 1024-4360) (Text in German) m. Statistical Office of the European Communities, Eurostat, Rue Alcide de Gasperi, L-2920 Luxembourg, Luxembourg. TEL 352-4301-34526. FAX 352-4301-34415. (Dist. in the U.S. by: Unipub, 4611-F Assembly Dr., Lanham, MD 20706. TEL 800-274-4888. FAX 301-459-0056) charts. **Document type:** government publication.
     Formerly (until 1994): Eurostat. Schnellberichte. Bevoelkerung und Soziale Bedingungen (ISSN 1017-5865)

330.9 333.79   EI   ISSN 1024-4344
EUROSTAT. STATISTIK KURZGEFASST. ENERGIE UND INDUSTRIE. English edition: Eurostat. Statistics in Focus. Energy and Industry (ISSN 1024-4328); French edition: Eurostat. Statistiques en Bref. Energie et Industrie (ISSN 1024-4336) (Text in German) m. Statistical Office of the European Communities, Eurostat, L-2920 Luxembourg, Luxembourg. TEL 352-4301-34526. FAX 352-4301-34415. (Dist. in the U.S. by: Unipub, 4611-F Assembly Dr., Lanham, MD 20706. TEL 800-274-4888. FAX 301-459-0056) charts.
     Document type: government publication.
     Formerly (until 1994): Eurostat. Schnellberichte. Energie und Industrie (ISSN 1017-5822)

330   EI   ISSN 1024-798X
▼**EUROSTAT. STATISTIK KURZGEFASST. FORSCHUNG UND ENTWICKLUNG.** English edition: Eurostat. Statistics in Focus. Research and Development. French edition: Eurostat. Statistiques en Bref. Recherche et Developpement (ISSN 1024-7963) (Text in German) 1995. m. Statistical Office of the European Communities, Eurostat, Rue Alcide Gasperi, L-2920 Luxembourg, Luxembourg. TEL 352-4301-34526. FAX 352-4301-34415. (Dist. in the U.S by: Unipub, 4611-F Assembly Dr., Lanham, MD 20706. TEL 800-274-4888. FAX 301-459-0056) charts. **Document type:** government publication.

330.9   EI   ISSN 1024-431X
EUROSTAT. STATISTIK KURZGEFASST. WIRTSCHAFT UND FINANZEN. English edition: Eurostat. Statistics in Focus. Economy and Finance (ISSN 1024-4298); French edition: Eurostat. Statistiques en Bref. Economie et Finances (ISSN 1024-4301) (Text in German) m. Statistical Office of the European Communities, Eurostat, L-2920 Luxembourg, Luxembourg. TEL 352-4301-34526. FAX 352-4301-33415. (Dist. in the U.S. by: Unipub, 4611-F Assembly Dr., Lanham, MD 20706. TEL 800-274-4888. FAX 301-459-0056) charts.
     Document type: government publication.
     Formerly (until 1994): Eurostat. Schnellberichte. Wirtschaft und Finanzen (ISSN 1017-5814)

BUSINESS AND ECONOMICS — ABSTRACTING, BIBLIOGRAPHIES, STATISTICS

330.9   EI   ISSN 1024-4301
EUROSTAT. STATISTIQUES EN BREF. ECONOMIE ET FINANCES. English edition: Eurostat. Statistics in Focus. Economy and Finance (ISSN 1024-4298); German edition: Eurostat. Statistik Kurzgefasst. Wirtschaft und Finanzen (ISSN 1024-431X) (Text in French) m. Statistical Office of the European Communities, Eurostat, L-2920 Luxembourg, Luxembourg. TEL 352-4301-34526. FAX 352-4301-33415. (Dist. in the U.S. by: Unipub, 4611-F Assembly Dr., Lanham, MD 20706. TEL 800-274-4888. FAX 301-459-0056) charts. **Document type:** government publication.
    Formerly (until 1994): Eurostat. Statistiques Rapides. Economie et Finances (ISSN 1015-8944)

330.9 333.79   EI   ISSN 1024-4336
EUROSTAT. STATISTIQUES EN BREF. ENERGIE ET INDUSTRIE. English edition: Eurostat. Statistics in Focus. Energy and Industry (ISSN 1024-4328); German edition: Eurostat. Statistik Kurzgefasst. Energie und Industrie (ISSN 1024-4344) (Text in French) m. Statistical Office of the European Communities, Eurostat, L-2920 Luxembourg, Luxembourg. TEL 352-4301-34526. FAX 352-4301-33415. (Dist. in the U.S. by: Unipub, 4611-F Assembly Dr., Lanham, MD 20706. TEL 800-274-4888. FAX 301-459-0056) charts. **Document type:** government publication.
    Formerly (until 1994): Eurostat. Statistiques Rapides. Energie et Industrie (ISSN 1015-891X)

330.9 312   EI   ISSN 1024-4360
EUROSTAT. STATISTIQUES EN BREF. POPULATION ET CONDITIONS SOCIALES. English edition: Eurostat. Statistics in Focus. Population and Social Conditions (ISSN 1024-4352); German edition: Eurostat. Statistik Kurzgefasst. Bevoelkerung und Soziale Bedingungen (ISSN 1024-4379) (Text in French) m. Statistical Office of the European Communities, Eurostat, L-2920 Luxembourg, Luxembourg. TEL 352-4301-34526. FAX 352-4301-34415. (Dist. in the U.S. by: Unipub, 4611-F Assembly Dr., Lanham, MD 20706. TEL 800-274-4888. FAX 301-459-0056) charts. **Document type:** government publication.
    Formerly (until 1994): Eurostat. Statistiques Rapides. Population et Conditions Sociales (ISSN 1015-3306)

330   EI   ISSN 1024-7963
▼**EUROSTAT. STATISTIQUES EN BREF. RECHERCHE ET DEVELOPPEMENT.** English edition: Eurostat. Statistics in Focus. Research and Development (ISSN 1024-7971); German edition: Eurostat. Statistik Kurzgefasst. Forschung und Entwicklung (ISSN 1024-798X) (Text in French) 1995. m. Statistical Office of the European Communities, L-2920 Luxembourg, Luxembourg. TEL 352-4301-34526. FAX 352-4301-33415. (Dist. in the U.S. by: Unipub, 4611-F Assembly Dr., Lanham, MD 20706. TEL 800-274-4888. FAX 301-459-0056) charts. **Document type:** government publication.

330   EI   ISSN 0252-8266
HC241.2.A1
EUROSTATISTICS DATA FOR SHORT TERM ECONOMIC ANALYSIS. m. $165. (Statistical Office of the European Communities) Office for Official Publications of the European Communities, Rue Alcide de Gasperi, 2920 Luxembourg, Luxembourg. (Subscr. in U.S. to: Unipub, 4611-F Assembly Dr., Lanham, MD 20706-4391. TEL 800-274-4888. FAX 301-459-0056) (also avail. in microfiche from CIS) **Indexed:** IIS.
 ●Also available online. Vendor(s): Commission of the European Communities.
  —BLDSC (3830.445000).
    Formerly: Eurostatistics.
    Description: Enables the reader to keep a close watch on general economic and social trends in the European Community.

EXPORT STATISTICAL SCHEDULE OF JAPAN (YEAR). see BUSINESS AND ECONOMICS — International Commerce

310   AF
EXPORT STATISTICS OF AFGHANISTAN/IHSA'IYAH-I AMUAL-I SADIRATI-I AFGHANISTAN. (Text in English or Persian) a. $20. Central Statistical Office, Nader Shah Minah, Block No. 4, Box 2002, Kabul, Afghanistan. stat.

382   GM   ISSN 0303-9277
HF266.G27
EXTERNAL TRADE STATISTICS OF GAMBIA. Variant title: Gambia. Central Statistics Department. Annual Report of External Trade Statistics. (Formerly issued by Central Statistics Division) 1973. a. D.25. Central Statistics Department, Wellington St., Banjul, Gambia.

332.6   GH   ISSN 0435-8805
HF266.G6
EXTERNAL TRADE STATISTICS OF GHANA (ANNUAL). 1951. a. $60. Statistical Service, Information Section, P.O. Box 1098, Accra, Ghana. TEL 233-21-663758. FAX 233-21-667069. TELEX 2205 MIFAEP GH. **Document type:** trade publication, government publication.

332.6   GH
EXTERNAL TRADE STATISTICS OF GHANA (HALF-YEARLY). s-a. $30. Statistical Service, Information Section, P.O. Box 1098, Accra, Ghana. TEL 233-21-663758. FAX 233-21-667069. TELEX 2205 MIFAEP GH. **Document type:** government publication.

382   GH   ISSN 0855-1049
HF266.G6
EXTERNAL TRADE STATISTICS OF GHANA (QUARTERLY). 1993. q. $30. Statistical Service, Information Section, P.O. Box 1098, Accra, Ghana. TEL 233-21-663758. FAX 233-21-667069. TELEX 2205 MIFAEP GH. **Document type:** government publication, trade publication.

338 016   NR
F I I R O INDUSTRIAL ABSTRACTS. 1976. q. £N100. Federal Institute of Industrial Research, Oshodi, P.M.B. 21023, Ikeja, Lagos State, Nigeria. Ed.Bd. circ. 200. **Document type:** abstracting/indexing, government publication.

658 016   FR   ISSN 1157-3783
Z7164.A2
F R A N C I S. 528: BIBLIOGRAPHIE INTERNATIONALE DE SCIENCE ADMINISTRATIVE. (Printed format ceased Jan. 1995) (Text in French, English) 1971. q. Centre National de la Recherche Scientifique, Institut de l'Information Scientifique et Technique, 2 allee du Parc de Brabois, 54514 Vandoeuvre-les-Nancy Cedex, France. TEL 83-50-46-00. FAX 83-50-46-50. adv. contact: Veronique Guinvarc'h. cum.index. **Indexed:** E.I. **Document type:** bibliography.
 ●Also available online. Vendor(s): Telesystemes - Questel.
 Also available on CD-ROM.
    Former titles: Bulletin Signaletique. Part 528: Bibliographie Internationale de Science Administrative (ISSN 0150-8695); Bulletin Signaletique. Part 528: Science Administrative (ISSN 0007-5639)

330 011   FR   ISSN 1157-383X
Z7163
F R A N C I S. 617: E C O D O C; documentation automatisee en economie generale. (Printed format ceased Jan. 1995) 1982. q. Centre National de la Recherche Scientifique, Institut de l'Information Scientifique et Technique, 2 allee du Parc de Brabois, 54514 Vandoeuvre-les-Nancy Cedex, France. TEL 83-50-46-00. FAX 83-50-46-50. (Subscr. to: Documentation Francaise, 124 rue Henri Barbusse, 93308 Aubervilliers Cedex, France) Ed. Claude Patou. adv. contact: Veronique Guinvarc'h. circ. 500. (also avail. in magnetic tape; back issues avail.; reprint service avail. from SCH) **Indexed:** P.A.I.S.For.Lang.Ind. **Document type:** bibliography.
 ●Also available online. Vendor(s): Telesystemes - Questel.
 Also available on CD-ROM.
    Former titles: E C O D O C (ISSN 0292-1782); Documentation Economique (ISSN 0012-4648)

330   GW
FACHBUCHVERZEICHNIS WIRTSCHAFTSWISSENSCHAFTEN. a. Rossipaul Kommunikation GmbH, Menzingerstr. 37, 80638 Munich, Germany. TEL 49-89-179106-0. FAX 49-89-17910622. Ed. Angela Sendlinger. circ. 25,000. **Document type:** bibliography.

384.6 651   US   ISSN 1079-5359
FACSIMILE FACTS AND FIGURES. 1989. a. (plus irreg. updates). $1500. International Facsimile Consultative Council, 4019 Lake View Dr., Lake Havasu City, AZ 86406. TEL 520-453-3850. FAX 520-453-9234. Ed. David Day. stat.; index. (looseleaf format; also avail. in diskette format; back issues avail.)
    Description: Includes global installed base figures, OEM study, official import and export figures, manufacturers market share percentages, dealer numbers, public fax transmission numbers.

330   CN   ISSN 0838-3715
FAMILY EXPENDITURE IN CANADA. 1982. irreg. Can.$38 (foreign $46). Statistics Canada, Operations and Integration Division, Circulation Management, Jean Talon Bldg., 2-C12, Tunney's Pasture, Ottawa, ON K1A 0T6, Canada. TEL 613-951-7277; 800-267-6677. FAX 613-951-1584. URL: http://www.statcan.ca.
    Description: Offers a comprehensive look at the budgets of families and unattached individuals belonging to variety of demographic and economic groups.

330   CN   ISSN 0838-3898
FAMILY FOOD EXPENDITURE IN CANADA. 1982. biennial. Can.$28 (foreign $29). Statistics Canada, Operations and Integration Division, Circulation Management, Jean Talon Bldg., 2-C12, Tunney's Pasture, Ottawa, ON K1A 0T6, Canada. TEL 613-951-7277; 800-267-6677. FAX 613-951-1584. URL: http://www.statcan.ca.
    Description: Offers a comprehensive look at food expenditure detail of families and unattached individuals living in both urban and rural areas of Canada classified by a variety of demographic and economic groups.

330 310   JA   ISSN 0448-7109
HD7057
FAMILY SAVING SURVEY (YEAR). 1989. a. 4078 Yen. Nihon Tokei Kyokai - Japan Statistical Association, Crest 21, 6-21 Yocho-machi, Shinjuku-ku, Tokyo 162, Japan. TEL 81-3-5269-3051. FAX 81-3-5269-3058. (Co-sponsor: Somu-cho Tokei-kyoku - Statistics Bureau, Management and Coordination Agency) Ed. Hideshi Honda. R&P contact: Hideshi Honda. adv. contact: Hideshi Honda. **Document type:** government publication.

332   US   ISSN 0891-2769
Z7164.F5
FED IN PRINT; economics and banking topics. 1969. s-a. free. Federal Reserve Bank of Philadelphia, 10 Independence Mall, Philadelphia, PA 19106. TEL 215-574-6540. FAX 215-574-3847. URL: http://www.phil.frb.org. Ed. Deborah Naulty. circ. 2,400. **Document type:** abstracting/indexing.

331.11   US
FEDERAL CIVILIAN WORK FORCE STATISTICS. AFFIRMATIVE EMPLOYMENT STATISTICS. 1965. biennial. U.S. Office of Personnel Management, Personnel Systems and Oversight Group, Statistical Analysis and Services Division, Washington, DC 20415. TEL 202-655-4000. (Dist. by: Supt. of Docs., Govt. Printing Office, Washington, DC 20402) circ. 2,000. (also avail. in microfiche) **Indexed:** C.I.S. Ind. **Document type:** government publication.
    Former titles: Federal Civilian Work Force Statistics Equal Employment Opportunity Statistics; Federal Civilian Work Force Statistics. Minority Group Employment in the Federal Government; Federal Civilian Manpower Statistics. Minority Group Employment in the Federal Government; Minority Group Employment in the Federal Government; Study of Minority Group Employment in the Federal Government.

331.2   US
FEDERAL CIVILIAN WORK FORCE STATISTICS. PAY STRUCTURE OF THE FEDERAL CIVIL SERVICE. 1947. a. $15.95. U.S. Office of Personnel Management, Personnel Systems and Oversight Group, Office of Workforce Information, Washington, DC 20415. TEL 703-487-4650. FAX 202-606-1719. (Subscr. to: National Technical Information Service, 5285 Port Royal Rd., Springfield, VA 22161) charts; circ. 900 (controlled). (also avail. in microfiche) **Indexed:** C.I.S. Ind. **Document type:** government publication.
    Former titles: Federal Civilian Manpower Statistics Pay Structure of the Federal Civil Service; Pay Structure of the Federal Civil Service.

BUSINESS AND ECONOMICS — ABSTRACTING, BIBLIOGRAPHIES, STATISTICS

331   US   ISSN 0277-3325
JK776
FEDERAL CIVILIAN WORK FORCE STATISTICS. WORK YEARS AND PERSONNEL COSTS. EXECUTIVE BRANCH, UNITED STATES GOVERNMENT. 1970. a. $17. U.S. Office of Personnel Management, Personnel Systems and Oversight Group, Office of Workforce Information, 1900 E St., N.W., Washington, DC 20415. TEL 703-487-4650. (Subscr. to: National Technical Information Service, 5285 Port Royal Rd., Springfield, VA 22161) charts; circ. 400 (controlled). (also avail. in microfiche) **Document type:** government publication.
    Former titles: Work-Years and Personnel Costs. Executive Branch of the United States Government; Work-Years and Personnel Costs. Executive Branch, U.S. Government; Man-Years and Personnel Costs. Executive Branch, U.S. Government.

351.1 317   US
FEDERAL CIVILIAN WORKFORCE STATISTICS. EMPLOYMENT AND TRENDS. 1969. bi-m. $11 (foreign $13.75). U.S. Office of Personnel Management, Personnel Systems and Oversight Group, Office of Workforce Information, 1900 E St., N.W., Washington, DC 20415. TEL 202-606-1178. (Subscr. to: Superintendent of Documents, U.S. Government Printing Office, Box 371954, Pittsburgh, PA 15250-7954. TEL 202-512-1800. FAX 202-512-2250) circ. 950 (controlled). (also avail. in microfiche from CIS; back issues avail.; reprint service avail. from CIS) **Indexed:** Amer.Stat.Ind. (1973-), C.I.S. Ind. **Document type:** government publication.
    Former titles: Federal Civilian Workforce Statistics. Monthly Release (ISSN 0163-8270); (until 1976): Federal Civilian Manpower Statistics. Monthly Release (ISSN 0090-7227)
    Description: Presents employment information on civilians working for the federal government on the basis of reports received from each department and agency.

331   US
FEDERAL CIVILIAN WORKFORCE STATISTICS. OCCUPATIONS OF FEDERAL WHITE-COLLAR AND BLUE-COLLAR WORKERS. 1956. biennial. $29. U.S. Office of Personnel Management, Personnel Systems and Oversight Group, Office of Workforce Information, 1900 E St., N.W., Washington, DC 20415. TEL 703-487-4650. (Subscr. to: National Technical Information Service, 5285 Port Royal Rd., Springfield, VA 22161. TEL 703-487-4650. FAX 703-321-8547) Ed.Bd. (also avail. in microfiche) **Indexed:** C.I.S. Ind. **Document type:** government publication.
    Former titles: Federal Civilian Workforce Statistics. Occupations of Federal White-Collar Workers (ISSN 0146-4906); Occupations of Federal White-Collar Workers; Federal White-Collar Workers. Their Occupations and Salaries.

332.3   US
FEDERAL HOME LOAN BANK OF DALLAS. FINANCIAL STATEMENTS. a. Federal Home Loan Bank of Dallas, Office of the Corporate Secretary, Box 619026, Dallas-Ft. Worth, TX 75261-9026. TEL 214-541-8500.

338 319   FJ   ISSN 0259-6024
FIJI. BUREAU OF STATISTICS. CENSUS OF DISTRIBUTION AND SERVICES. 1971. irreg. $5 per no. (effective 1997). Bureau of Statistics, P.O. Box 2221, Suva, Fiji. **Document type:** government publication.

338   FJ
FIJI. BUREAU OF STATISTICS. CENSUS OF INDUSTRIES. 1968. a., latest 1992. $5 (effective 1997). Bureau of Statistics, P.O. Box 2221, Suva, Fiji. **Document type:** government publication.
    Formerly: Fiji. Bureau of Statistics. Census of Industrial Production (ISSN 0259-6032)

330 319   FJ   ISSN 0015-0894
FIJI. BUREAU OF STATISTICS. CURRENT ECONOMIC STATISTICS. (Text in English) 1969. q. $5 per no. (effective 1997). Bureau of Statistics, P.O. Box 2221, Suva, Fiji. charts. circ. 580. (processed) **Document type:** government publication.
    Supersedes: Fiji. Bureau of Statistics. Quarterly Statistical Summary.

336   FJ
FIJI. BUREAU OF STATISTICS. ECONOMIC AND FUNCTIONAL CLASSIFICATION OF GOVERNMENT ACCOUNTS. 1968. irreg., latest 1986. $5 per no. (effective 1997). Bureau of Statistics, P.O. Box 2221, Suva, Fiji. **Document type:** government publication.

331.11   FJ
FIJI. BUREAU OF STATISTICS. EMPLOYMENT SURVEY OF FIJI. 1969. a.; latest 1989. $5 (effective 1997). Bureau of Statistics, P.O. Box 2221, Suva, Fiji. **Document type:** government publication.

315 339   FJ
FIJI. BUREAU OF STATISTICS. FIJI HOUSEHOLD INCOME AND EXPENDITURE SURVEY. 1973. irreg., latest 1977. $5 (effective 1997). Bureau of Statistics, P.O. Box 2221, Suva, Fiji. stat. **Document type:** government publication.

331   FJ
FIJI. BUREAU OF STATISTICS. NATIONWIDE UNEMPLOYMENT SURVEY. 1973. irreg. $5 per no. (effective 1997). Bureau of Statistics, P.O. Box 2221, Suva, Fiji. **Document type:** government publication.

380   FJ
FIJI. BUREAU OF STATISTICS. SURVEY OF DISTRIBUTIVE TRADE. (Text in English) irreg., latest 1993. $5 (effective 1997). Bureau of Statistics, P.O. Box 2221, Suva, Fiji. **Document type:** government publication.

382   FJ
FIJI. BUREAU OF STATISTICS. TRADE REPORT. 1939. a., latest 1988. $15 (effective 1997). Bureau of Statistics, P.O. Box 2221, Suva, Fiji. **Document type:** government publication.

330.9   FJ
FIJI. BUREAU OF STATISTICS. VITAL STATISTICS. 1976. irreg., latest 1988. $5 (effective 1997). Bureau of Statistics, P.O. Box 2221, Suva, Fiji. **Document type:** government publication.

330   FJ
FIJI FACTS AND FIGURES. 1975. a., latest 1995. free. Bureau of Statistics, P.O. Box 2221, Suva, Fiji. **Document type:** government publication.

332.1 368 333.33   US   ISSN 1066-7350
HG181
FINANCE, INSURANCE AND REAL ESTATE U S A. 1993. biennial. $169. Gale Research, 835 Penobscot Bldg., 645 Griswold St., Detroit, MI 48226-4094. TEL 313-961-2242; 800-877-4253. FAX 800-414-5043. E-mail: daniel_snyder@gale.com. Ed. Arsen J. Darnay. **Document type:** trade publication.
    Description: Contains statistics in these areas of the American economy.

330   CN   ISSN 0380-075X
HG185.C2
FINANCIAL INSTITUTIONS, FINANCIAL STATISTICS. 1963. q. Can.$176($211). (foreign $246). Statistics Canada, Operations and Integration Division, Circulation Management, Jean Talon Bldg., 2-C12, Tunney's Pasture, Ottawa, ON K1A 0T6, Canada. TEL 613-951-7277; 800-267-6677. FAX 613-951-1584. URL: http://www.statcan.ca.
    Description: Focuses on the financial position and operations of financial institutions, financial intermediaries and investment funds operating in Canada.

332   UK
FINANCIAL JOURNALS INDEX. 1995. m. Legal Information Resources Ltd., The Hatcheries, Hall Bank Ln., Mytholmroyd, Hebden Bridge, W. Yorkshire HX7 5HQ, England. TEL 44-1422-888000. FAX 44-1422-888001. E-mail: julie.lord@itps.co.uk. Ed.Bd. cum.index. (also avail. in magnetic tape; back issues avail.) **Document type:** abstracting/indexing.
    Formed by the merger of (1992-1995): Pensions Journals Index (ISSN 0966-825X); (1992-1995): Insurance Journals Index (ISSN 0966-8241); (1993-1995): Banking Journals Index.

332 315   CH
FINANCIAL STATISTICS MONTHLY, TAIWAN DISTRICT, REPUBLIC OF CHINA. (Text in Chinese and English) 1951. m. $40. Central Bank of China, 2 Roosevelt Rd., Sec. 1, Taipei, Taiwan 107, Republic of China. FAX 02-397-3768. Ed.Bd. circ. 2,250.
    Formerly: Taiwan Financial Statistics Monthly (ISSN 0496-7046)

336.52   JA   ISSN 0289-1522
HG41
FINANCIAL STATISTICS OF JAPAN. 1952. a. free. Ministry of Finance, Institute of Fiscal and Monetary Policy - Okura-sho, 3-1-1 Kasumigaseki, Chiyoda-ku, Tokyo 100, Japan. **Document type:** government publication.
    Formerly (until 1983): Japan. Finance Department. Quarterly Bulletin of Financial Statistics (ISSN 0447-4740)

336   MX   ISSN 0187-4853
HJ15
FINANZAS PUBLICAS ESTATALES Y MUNICIPALES DE MEXICO. 1984. irreg., latest 1988. Mex.$36($10) Instituto Nacional de Estadistica, Geografia e Informatica, Secretaria de Programacion y Presupuesto, Prol. Heroe de Nacozari 2301 Sur, Puerta 11, Acceso, 20270 Aguascalientes Ags., Mexico. TEL 49-18-19-48. FAX 491-807-39. circ. 1,500.

658.8   UK   ISSN 0273-4125
HF5415.2
FINDEX (YEAR); the worldwide directory of market research reports, studies & surveys. 1979. a. £295($590) Euromonitor, 60-61 Britton St., London EC1M 5NA, England. TEL 44-171-251-8024. FAX 44-171-608-3149. E-mail: info@euromonitor.com; URL: http://www.euromonitor.com. (N. American addr.: Euromonitor International, 122 S. Michigan Ave., Ste. 1200, Chicago, IL 60603. TEL 800-577-3876. FAX 312-922-1157) Ed. Edward Reid. index. circ. 2,000. **Document type:** directory, abstracting/indexing.
    ●Also available online. Vendor(s): Knight-Ridder Information, Inc. (File no.196).
Also available on CD-ROM. Producer(s): SilverPlatter Information, Inc.
—BLDSC (3927.732000).
    Incorporates (1976-1986): Directory of U.S. and Canadian Marketing Surveys and Services (ISSN 0364-8966)
    Description: Abstracts and indexes more than 8,500 market research and company reports. Entries are organized by 12 major categories.

330.021 610   FI   ISSN 0355-2144
FINLAND. TILASTOKESKUS. KUOLEMANSYYT/FINLAND. STATISTIKCENTRALEN. DOEDSORSAKER/FINLAND. STATISTICS FINLAND. CAUSES OF DEATH IN FINLAND. (Text in English, Finnish and Swedish) 1939. a. FIM 145. Tilastokeskus, P.O. Box 2B, SF-00022 Tilastokeskus, Finland. **Document type:** government publication.

314 332   FI   ISSN 0784-8382
FINLAND. TILASTOKESKUS. RAHOITUS/FINLAND. STATISTIKCENTRALEN. FINANSIERING/FINLAND. STATISTICS FINLAND. FINANCING. (Text in English, Finnish, Swedish) 1974. irreg. FIM 1970. Tilastokeskus, P.O. Box 2B, SF-00022 Tilastokeskus, Finland. TEL 358-0-17341. FAX 358-01734-2279. (Subscr. to: Government Printing Centre, Box 516, SF-00100 Helsinki 10, Finland) **Document type:** government publication.
    Formerly: Tilastokeskus. Pankit (ISSN 0355-2454); Formed by the merger of: Finland. Tilastokeskus. Osuuspankkitilasto; Finland. Tilastokeskus. Saastopankkitilasto; Finland. Tilastokeskus. Liikepankit ja Kiinnitys Luottolaitokset.

310   FI   ISSN 0784-8374
HD5047.3
FINLAND. TILASTOKESKUS. TILASTOTIEDOTUS. PALKAT LONER/FINLAND. CENTRAL STATISTICAL OFFICE. WAGES AND SALARIES. a. FIM 666. Tilastotiedotus, Annankatu 44, SF-00100 Helsinki, Finland. TEL 358-0-17341. FAX 358-01734-2279. TELEX 1002111 TILASTO SF.
    Formerly: Tilastotiedotus P A (ISSN 0355-2306)

BUSINESS AND ECONOMICS — ABSTRACTING, BIBLIOGRAPHIES, STATISTICS

331   FI   ISSN 0784-8420
FINLAND. TILASTOKESKUS. TULOT JA KULUTUS/FINLAND. STATISTIKCENTRALEN. IMKOMST OCH KONSOMTION/FINLAND. STATISTICS FINLAND. INCOME AND CONSUMPTION. (Text in English, Finnish, Swedish) 1980. irreg. FIM 320. Tilastokeskus, P.O. Box 2B, SF-00022 Tilastokeskus, Finland. (Subscr. to: Government Printing Centre, Box 516, SF-00101 Helsinki 10, Finland) **Document type:** government publication.
    Formerly: Tilastokeskus. Tulonjakotilasto (ISSN 0358-2825)

314 338   FI   ISSN 0355-2071
HC337.F5
FINLAND. TILASTOKESKUS. TUTKIMUKSIA/FINLAND. STATISTIKCENTRALEN. UNDERSOEKNINGAR/FINLAND. STATISTICS FINLAND. STUDIES. 1966. irreg. price varies. Tilastokeskus, P.O. Box 2B, SF-00022 Tilastokeskus, Finland. **Document type:** government publication.

382 314   FI   ISSN 0789-743X
FINLAND. TULLIHALLITUS. ULKOMAANKAUPPA/FINLAND. NATIONAL BOARD OF CUSTOMS. FOREIGN TRADE/FINLAND. TULLSTYRELSEN. UTRIKESHANDEL. (Section I A of Official Statistics of Finland) (Text in English, Finnish and Swedish) 1904. m. FIM 700 (effective 1997). Tullihallitus - National Board of Customs, Box 512, FIN-00101 Helsinki, Finland. TEL 0-6141. FAX 0-6142813. TELEX 121559-TUHLS-SF. (Dist. by: Edita Ltd., Annankatu 44, FIN-00100 Helsinki 10, Finland) Ed. Tuomo Jaerveinheimo. charts. circ. 1,170. **Document type:** government publication.
    Formerly: Finland. Tullihallituksen Tilastotoimisto. Ulkomaankauppa-Kuukausijulkaisu - Foreign Trade Monthly Bulletin (ISSN 0041-6177)

975   US
FLORIDA AND THE OTHER FORTY-NINE. 1976. irreg. (approx. a.). free. Department of Commerce, Bureau of Economic Analysis, 107 W. Gaines St., Tallahassee, FL 32399-2000. TEL 904-487-2971. TELEX 510-6002141 FL TRADE TAS. stat.; circ. controlled.
    Description: National and state comparisons of demographic and business climates; statistical tables.

975   US   ISSN 0734-8045
HC107.F6
FLORIDA COUNTY COMPARISONS. 1980. a. free. Department of Commerce, Bureau of Economic Analysis, 107 W. Gaines St., Tallahassee, FL 32399-2000. TEL 904-487-2971. TELEX 510-6002141 FL TRADE TAS. circ. controlled.
    Description: Statistical tables comparing and ranking Florida's 67 counties in terms of business climate.

318   US
FLORIDA LONG-TERM ECONOMIC FORECAST. a. (in 2 vol.). $49 (diskette $39; both versions $69). University of Florida, College of Business Administration, Bureau of Economic and Business Research, Box 117145, 221 Matherly Hall, Gainesville, FL 32611-7145. TEL 352-392-0171. FAX 352-392-4739. Ed. David Lenze. (also avail. in diskette format) **Document type:** bulletin.
    Description: Provides a long-range economic forecast for the state of Florida, its metropolitan statistical areas, and counties.

318   US   ISSN 0071-6022
HA311
FLORIDA STATISTICAL ABSTRACT. Variant title: Florida Statistical Abstracts Annual. 1967. a. for paperbound edition; hardcover $44.95; diskette $60. (University of Florida, College of Business Administration, Bureau of Economic and Business Research) University Press of Florida, Box 117145, 221 Matherly Hall, Gainesville, FL 32611-7145. TEL 352-392-0171. FAX 352-392-4739. Ed. Ann Pierce. circ. 3,700. (also avail. in microfiche from BHP,CIS; diskette format) **Indexed:** SRI. **Document type:** abstracting/indexing.
    —BLDSC (3956.160000).
    Description: Contains more than 800 pages of current and historical information about the economy and demography of Florida, its counties, and metropolitan areas.

330 304.6   US
FORECAST (NEW YORK); the magazine of demographics and business statistics. 1993. bi-m. $99 (foreign $129) (effective 1995). Faulkner & Gray, Inc. (New York), 11 Penn Plaza, New York, NY 10117-0373. TEL 212-631-1420. FAX 212-629-7885. Ed. Beth Enslow. adv. contact: Lynn Carannante. **Document type:** consumer publication.

330.9   JA
FOREIGN ECONOMIC STATISTICS ANNUAL/GAIKOKU KEIZAI TOKEI NENPO. (Text in Japanese) a. 3100 Yen. Bank of Japan, International Department - Nippon Ginko, c/o Public Relations Department, 2-1-1 Hongoku-Cho, Nihonbashi, Chuo-ku, Tokyo 103, Japan. TEL 81-3-3279-1111. FAX 81-3-5203-8111. TELEX JPTCO J27161. (Dist. by: Tokiwa Sohgoh Service Co., Ltd., 3-2-4 Hongoku-cho, Nihonbashi Chuo-ku, Tokyo 103, Japan. TEL 81-3-3270-5713; Overseas dist. by: Japan Publications Trading Co., Ltd., Book Export No. 2 Dept., P.O. Box 5030 Tokyo International, Tokyo 100-31, Japan) pp./issue: 370.
    Description: Presents excellent research material for seeing economic trends in various countries. Incorporates information and economic statistics from foreign sources.

382 316   UN   ISSN 0071-7398
FOREIGN TRADE STATISTICS OF AFRICA. SERIES A: DIRECTION OF TRADE. (Text in English and French) 1962. irreg., no.25, 1977. price varies. United Nations Economic Commission for Africa - Commission Economique pour l'Afrique, P.O. Box 3001, Addis Ababa, Ethiopia. (Dist. by: United Nations Sales Section, Palais des Nations, CH-1211 Geneva 10, Switzerland; or: Unipub, 4611-F Assembly Dr., Lanham, MD 20706) charts. (also avail. in microfiche from CIS) **Indexed:** IIS. **Document type:** government publication.
    Description: Presents statistical data for northern, southern, central, western, and eastern Africa.

382   UN   ISSN 0252-2012
FOREIGN TRADE STATISTICS OF AFRICA. SERIES C: SUMMARY TABLES/STATISTIQUES AFRICAINES DU COMMERCE EXTERIEUR. SERIE C: TABLEAUX RECAPITULATIFS. 1977. irreg., no.3, 1980. United Nations Economic Commission for Africa, P.O. Box 3001, Addis Ababa, Ethiopia. (Dist. by: United Nations Sales Section, Palais des Nations, 1211 Geneva 10, Switzerland; or: Unipub, 4611-F Assembly Dr., Lanham, MD 20706) (also avail. in microfiche from CIS) **Indexed:** IIS. **Document type:** government publication.
    Description: Presents statistical summaries for foreign trades for northern, southern, central, western, and eastern Africa.

382 315   UN   ISSN 1011-4858
JX1977
FOREIGN TRADE STATISTICS OF ASIA AND THE PACIFIC. (Series A (1969-1983 vol.22); Series B (1977-1984 vol.17)) (Text in English and French) 1987 N.S. a. $45. United Nations Economic and Social Commission for Asia and the Pacific (ESCAP), United Nations Bldg., Rajadamnern Ave., Bangkok 10200, Thailand. (Dist. by: United Nations Publications, Rm. DC2-0853, New York, NY 10017; or Distribution and Sales Section, Palais des Nations, CH-1211 Geneva 10, Switzerland; or Conference Services Unit, E.S.C.A.P., Bangkok) (also avail. in microfiche from CIS; back issues avail.) **Indexed:** IIS.
    Formed by the 1987 merger of: Foreign Trade Statistics of Asia and the Pacific. Series A (ISSN 0252-4538); Which was formerly: Foreign Trade Statistics of Asia and the Far East. Series A; Foreign Trade Statistics of Asia and the Pacific. Series B (ISSN 0252-4546); Which was formerly: Foreign Trade Statistics of Asia and the Far East. Series B.

315   BG
FOREIGN TRADE STATISTICS OF BANGLADESH. (Text in English) 1961. a. Tk.150($35) Bureau of Statistics, Secretariat, Dhaka 2, Bangladesh.
    Formerly: Annual Foreign Trade Statistics of Bangladesh (ISSN 0071-7371)
    Description: Articles and data on export, import and balance of trade in Bangladesh.

382 315   IR
FOREIGN TRADE STATISTICS OF IRAN/AMAR-E BAZARGANI-YE KHAREJI-YE IRAN. (Text in Persian, English) 1900. q. Rs.100 per no. Ministry of Finance and Economic Affairs, Naser Khosrow Ave, Teheran, Iran.

382 315   IR   ISSN 0075-0492
FOREIGN TRADE STATISTICS OF IRAN. YEARBOOK.* (Text in Arabic and English) a. Ministry of Finance and Economic Affairs, Naser Khosrow Ave., Teheran, Iran.

382 315   PH   ISSN 0116-1822
FOREIGN TRADE STATISTICS OF THE PHILIPPINES. (In 2 vols.: Vol. 1: Imports; Vol. 2: Exports) a. $110 for Vol. 1; Vol. 2 $80. National Statistics Office, Ramon Magsaysay Blvd., Box 779, Manila, Philippines. TEL 63-2-606-909. FAX 63-2-716-0247. circ. 250. (also avail. in diskette format)
    Description: Focuses on the quality and value of Philippine trade with other countries for the calendar year.

382 315   YE   ISSN 0376-5695
HF235
FOREIGN TRADE STATISTICS OF YEMEN ARAB REPUBLIC. (Text in English) a. Central Bank of Yemen, Research Department, Box 59, Sana'a, Republic of Yemen.

FORSCHUNGSDOKUMENTATION ZUR ARBEITSMARKT- UND BERUFSFORSCHUNG, see BUSINESS AND ECONOMICS — Labor And Industrial Relations

332.7 314   FR
FRANCE. CONSEIL NATIONAL DU CREDIT. STATISTIQUES MENSUELLES. m. free. Banque de France, Service de l'Information, 48, rue Croix des Petits Champs, 75001 Paris, France. TEL 1-42-92-39-08. FAX 1-42-92-39-40. circ. controlled.
    ●Also available online. Vendor(s): GSI-ECO.

332.7 314   FR
FRANCE. CONSEIL NATIONAL DU CREDIT. STATISTIQUES TRIMESTRIELLES. q. free. Banque de France, Service de l'Information, 48, Croix des Petits Champs, 75001 Paris, France. TEL 1-42-92-39-08. FAX 1-42-92-39-40. circ. controlled.
    ●Also available online. Vendor(s): GSI-ECO.

330 310   FR   ISSN 1268-6484
FRANCE. DIRECTION DE L'ANIMATION DE LA RECHERCHE, DES ETUDES ET DES STATISTIQUES. DOSSIERS. Key Title: Premieres Informations. Dossiers Statistiques. Short title: Dossiers de la D A R E S. 10/yr. 800 F. (Europe 840 F.; elsewhere 905 F.) (effective 1997). (Direction de l'Animation de la Recherche, des Etudes et des Statistiques) Documentation Francaise, 29-31 quai Voltaire, 75344 Paris Cedex 07, France. TEL 33-1-40157000. FAX 33-1-40157230. (Subscr. to: 124 rue Henri Barbusse, 93308 Aubervilliers Cedex, France. TEL 33-1-48395600. FAX 33-1-48395601) **Document type:** government publication.

382 314   FR   ISSN 0071-8688
FRANCE. DIRECTION GENERALE DES DOUANES ET DROITS INDIRECTS. STATISTIQUES DU COMMERCE EXTERIEUR: IMPORTATIONS - EXPORTATIONS. NOMENCLATURE: N.G.P. (NOMENCLATURE GENERALE DES PRODUITS). a. 135 F. Imprimerie Nationale, B.P. 514, 59505 Douai Cedex, France. TEL 37-93-70-70. FAX 27-93-70-96. TELEX 120 389 F.
    Description: Presents total of imports and exports by principal country of origin and destination.

331.1 314   FR   ISSN 1161-8205
FRANCE. MINISTERE DU TRAVAIL, DE L'EMPLOI ET DE LA FORMATION PROFESSIONNELLE. BULLETIN MENSUEL DES STATISTIQUES DU TRAVAIL. Short title: B M S T. (Supplements accompany some issues) m. 450 F. (Europe 465 F.; elsewhere 530 F.) (effective 1997). Documentation Francaise, 29-31 quai Voltaire, 75344 Paris Cedex 07, France. TEL 33-1-40157000. FAX 33-1-40157230. TELEX 215 666 DOCFRAN. (Subscr. to: 124 rue Henri Barbusse, 93308 Aubervilliers Cedex, France. TEL 33-1-48395600. FAX 33-1-48395601) adv. circ. 3,800. (also avail. in microfiche) **Indexed:** P.A.I.S.For.Lang.Ind. **Document type:** government publication.
    Former titles: France. Ministere du Travail. Statistiques du Travail (ISSN 0338-4284); France. Ministere du Travail. Bulletin Mensuel des Statistiques du Travail (ISSN 0338-4276)

BUSINESS AND ECONOMICS — ABSTRACTING, BIBLIOGRAPHIES, STATISTICS

338 314 — FR
FRANCE. SERVICE D'ETUDE DES STRATEGIES ET DES STATISTIQUES INDUSTRIELLES. ANNUAIRE DE STATISTIQUE INDUSTRIELLE. 1947. a. 400 F. (foreign 480 F.)(effective 1991). Service d'Etude des Strategies et des Statistiques Industrielles (SESSI), 85, Bd. du Montparnasse, 75270 Paris Cedex 06, France. TEL 45-56-42-34. FAX 45-56-40-71.
Former titles: France. Service du Traitement de l'Information et des Statistiques Industrielles. Annuaire de Statistique Industrielle (ISSN 0071-8211); France. Bureau Centrale de Statistique Industrielle. Annuaire de Statistique Industrielle.
Description: Statistics on industry: production and sales figures.

338 314 — FR — ISSN 0151-0770
HC271
FRANCE. SERVICE D'ETUDE DES STRATEGIES ET DES STATISTIQUES INDUSTRIELLES. BULLETIN MENSUEL DE STATISTIQUE INDUSTRIELLE. 1944. m. 400 F. (foreign 480 F.) (effective 1991). Service d'Etude des Strategies et des Statistiques Industrielles (SESSI), 85 Bd. du Montparnasse, 75270 Paris Cedex 06, France. TEL 45-56-42-34. FAX 45-56-40-71. **Indexed:** P.A.I.S.For.Lang.Ind.
Former titles: France. Service du Traitement de l'Information et des Statistiques Industrielles. Bulletin Mensuel de Statistique Industrielle & France. Ministere de l'Industrie. Bulletin Mensuel de Statistique Industrielle.
Description: Follows more than 700 products through production, invoicing and delivery.

338 311 — FR — ISSN 0244-7118
TL159
FRANCE. SERVICE D'ETUDE DES STRATEGIES ET DES STATISTIQUES INDUSTRIELLES. COLLECTIONS: TRAITS FONDAMENTAUX DU SYSTEME INDUSTRIEL FRANCAIS. 1974. irreg., no.14, 1977. 90 F. Service d'Etude des Strategies et des Statistiques Industrielles (SESSI), 85 Bd. du Montparnasse, 75270 Paris Cedex 06, France. TEL 45-56-42-34. FAX 45-56-40-71.
Former titles: France. Service d'Etude des Strategies et des Statistiques Industrielles. Recueil Statistiques; France. Service du Traitement de l'Information et des Statistiques Industrielles. Recueil Statistiques.
Description: Statistics on industry, detailed by sector.

381 — FR — ISSN 1240-747X
FRANCE. SERVICE D'ETUDE DES STRATEGIES ET DES STATISTIQUES INDUSTRIELLES. LES CHIFFRES CLES DE L'INDUSTRIE. a. 120 F. (foreign 150 F.) (effective 1991). Service d'Etude des Strategies et des Statistiques Industrielles (SESSI), 85 Bd. du Montparnasse, 75270 Paris Cedex 06, France. TEL 45-56-42-34. FAX 45-56-40-71. bibl.; charts.
Description: Presents essential statistics on 85 industrial activities.

381 — FR
FRANCE. SERVICE D'ETUDE DES STRATEGIES ET DES STATISTIQUES INDUSTRIELLES. LES CHIFFRES CLES DE L'INDUSTRIE DANS LES REGIONS. a. 170 F. (foreign 210 F.) (effective 1991). Service d'Etude des Strategies et des Statistiques Industrielles (SESSI), 85 Bd. du Montparnasse, 75270 Paris Cedex 06, France. TEL 45-56-42-34. FAX 45-56-40-71. charts.
Description: Permits regional comparison of principal industrial characteristics.

381 — FR
FRANCE. SERVICE D'ETUDE DES STRATEGIES ET DES STATISTIQUES INDUSTRIELLES. LA DISPERSION DES PERFORMANCES DES ENTREPRISES. a. 300 F. (foreign 350 F.) (effective 1991). Service d'Etude des Strategies et des Statistiques Industrielles (SESSI), 85 Bd. du Montparnasse, 75270 Paris Cedex 06, France. TEL 45-56-42-34. FAX 45-56-40-71. (also avail. in diskette format)
Description: Analyzes performance in 300 industrial categories.

381 338 — FR
FRANCE. SERVICE D'ETUDE DES STRATEGIES ET DES STATISTIQUES INDUSTRIELLES. L'IMPLANTATION ETRANGERE DANS L'INDUSTRIE. a. 85 F. (foreign 110 F.) (effective 1991). Service d'Etude des Strategies et des Statistiques Industrielles (SESSI), 85 Bd. du Montparnasse, 75270 Paris Cedex 06, France. TEL 45-56-42-34. FAX 45-56-40-71.
Description: Covers foreign-controlled industrial activity in France. Lists by sector, origin of investment, and location in France.

338 310 — FR — ISSN 0998-4208
FRANCE. SERVICE D'ETUDE DES STRATEGIES ET DES STATISTIQUES INDUSTRIELLES. LA SITUATION DE L'INDUSTRIE. PREMIERS RESULTATS. 1968. a. 50 F. (foreign 60 F.) (effective 1991). Service d'Etude des Strategies et des Statistiques Industrielles (SESSI), 85 bd. Montparnasse, 75270 Paris Cedex 06, France. TEL 45-56-42-34. FAX 45-56-40-71.
Supersedes in part: France. Ministere de l'Industrie, des P & T et du Tourisme. Enquete Annuelle d'Entreprise; Which was formerly: France. Ministere de Redeploiement Industriel et du Commerce Exterieur. Enquete Annuelle.

330.9 381 — FR
FRANCE. SERVICE D'ETUDE DES STRATEGIES ET DES STATISTIQUES INDUSTRIELLES. LA SITUATION DE L'INDUSTRIE: RESULTATS AGREGES. a. 85 F. (foreign 110 F.) (effective 1991). Service d'Etude des Strategies et des Statistiques Industrielles (SESSI), 85 Bd. du Montparnasse, 75270 Paris Cedex 06, France. TEL 45-56-42-34. FAX 45-56-40-71.
Supersedes in part: France. Ministere de l'Industrie, des P & T et du Tourisme. Enquete Annuelle d'Entreprise; Which was formerly: France. Ministere de Redeploiement Industriel et du Commerce Exterieur. Enquete Annuelle.
Description: Analyzes recent growth, net results, employment, investments and exports in 40 sectors of industry. Data presented by size of business.

330.9 381 — FR
FRANCE. SERVICE D'ETUDE DES STRATEGIES ET DES STATISTIQUES INDUSTRIELLES. LA SITUATION DE L'INDUSTRIE: RESULTATS DETAILEES. a. 85 F. (foreign 110 F.) (effective 1991). Service d'Etude des Strategies et des Statistiques Industrielles (SESSI), 85 Bd. du Montparnasse, 75270 Paris Cedex 06, France. TEL 45-56-42-34. FAX 45-56-40-71.
Supersedes in part: France. Ministere de l'Industrie, des P & T et du Tourisme. Enquete Annuelle d'Entreprise; Which was formerly: France. Ministere de Redeploiement Industriel et du Commerce Exterieur. Enquete Annuelle.
Description: Complete analysis of 250 industrial sectors. Data by branch, size and region.

FRITZ-HUESER-INSTITUT FUER DEUTSCHE UND AUSLAENDISCHE ARBEITERLITERATUR. INFORMATIONEN. see *LITERATURE — Abstracting, Bibliographies, Statistics*

316 916.6 — GM
GAMBIA. CENTRAL STATISTICS DEPARTMENT. CONSUMER PRICE INDEX. (Formerly issued by Central Statistics Division) m. D.12. Central Statistics Department, Wellington St., Banjul, Gambia. **Document type:** government publication.

382 — GM
GAMBIA. CENTRAL STATISTICS DEPARTMENT. MONTHLY SUMMARY OF EXTERNAL TRADE STATISTICS. m. Central Statistics Department, Wellington St., Banjul, Gambia. **Document type:** government publication.

331.11 316 — GM
GAMBIA. CENTRAL STATISTICS DEPARTMENT. QUARTERLY SURVEY OF EMPLOYMENT AND EARNINGS. (Formerly issued by Central Statistics Division) q. D.7.50. Central Statistics Department, Wellington St., Banjul, Gambia.

330.9 — GH
GAZETTEER; alphabetical list of localities with statistics on population, number of houses and main source of water supply. (Issued in 2 vols.: Gazeteer 1 (AA-KU); Gazeteer 2 (KW-ZU) irreg. (in 2 vols.); latest 1984. $35 for both vols. Statistical Service, Information Section, P.O. Box 1098, Accra, Ghana. TEL 233-21-336758. FAX 233-21-667069. TELEX 2205 MIFAEP GH. **Document type:** government publication.

317 — US — ISSN 0085-1043
HA321
GEORGIA STATISTICAL ABSTRACT. 1951. biennial. $25. University of Georgia, Terry College of Business, Selig Center for Economic Growth, Athens, GA 30602. TEL 706-542-4085. FAX 706-542-3835. Ed. Lorena Akioka. circ. 1,000. (also avail. in microfiche from BHP) **Document type:** academic/scholarly publication.

331.11 314 — GW
GERMANY. BUNDESANSTALT FUER ARBEIT. BERUFSBERATUNG. ERGEBNISSE DER BERUFSBERATUNGSSTATISTIK. 1953. a. DM.7. Bundesanstalt fuer Arbeit, Regensburgerstr. 104, 90478 Nuernberg, Germany. TEL 49-911-1795034. FAX 49-911-1792123. index. **Document type:** government publication.

331 314 — GW — ISSN 0341-7840
HD8441
GERMANY. BUNDESMINISTERIUM FUER ARBEIT UND SOZIALORDNUNG. HAUPTERGEBNISSE DER ARBEITS- UND SOZIALSTATISTIK. 1952. a. DM.25. Bundesministerium fuer Arbeit und Sozialordnung, Postfach 140280, 5300 Bonn 1, Germany. TEL 0228-5271130. Ed.Bd. bk.rev. circ. 2,000. **Document type:** government publication.

382 310 — GW — ISSN 0072-1638
GERMANY. STATISTISCHES BUNDESAMT. ALPHABETISCHES LAENDERVERZEICHNIS FUER DIE AUSSENHANDELSSTATISTIK. irreg. DM.9.30 per no. 65180 Wiesbaden, Germany. TEL 49-611-75-1. FAX 49-611-724000. TELEX 61186-STBA-D. URL: http://www.statistik-bund.de. **Document type:** government publication.

331 314 — GW — ISSN 0072-1832
GERMANY. STATISTISCHES BUNDESAMT. FACHSERIE 1, BEVOELKERUNG UND ERWERBSTAETIGKEIT, REIHE 4: ERWERBSTAETIGKEIT. irreg. price varies. 65180 Wiesbaden, Germany. TEL 49-611-75-1. FAX 49-611-724000. TELEX 61186-STBA-D. URL: http://www.statistik-bund.de. **Document type:** government publication.

338 314 — GW
GERMANY. STATISTISCHES BUNDESAMT. FACHSERIE 2, UNTERNEHMEN UND ARBEITSSTAETTEN, REIHE 3: ABSCHLUESSE DER OEFFENTLICHEN VERSORGUNGS-, ENTSORGUNGS- UND VERKEHRSUNTERNEHMEN. 1959. a. DM.12.70. Statistisches Bundesamt, 65180 Wiesbaden, Germany. TEL 49-611-75-1. FAX 49-611-724000. TELEX 61186-STBA-D. URL: http://www.statistik-bund.de. **Document type:** government publication.
Formerly: Germany (Federal Republic, 1949-). Statistisches Bundesamt. Fachserie 2, Unternehmen und Arbeitsstaetten, Reihe 3: Abschluesse der Oeffentlichen Versorgungs- und Verkehrsunternehmen.

332.1 314 — GW
GERMANY. STATISTISCHES BUNDESAMT. FACHSERIE 2, UNTERNEHMEN UND ARBEITSSTAETTEN, REIHE 4.1: INSOLVENZVERFAHREN. (Consists of two subseries) m. DM.92.40 (effective 1997). 65180 Wiesbaden, Germany. TEL 49-611-75-1. FAX 49-611-724000. TELEX 61186-STBA-D. URL: http://www.statistik-bund.de. **Document type:** government publication.
Formerly: Germany. Statistisches Bundesamt. Fachserie 2, Unternehmen und Arbeitsstaetten, Reihe 4: Zahlungsschwierigkeiten (ISSN 0072-2030)

338 314 — GW
GERMANY. STATISTISCHES BUNDESAMT. FACHSERIE 4, PRODUZIERENDES GEWERBE, REIHE 2.1: INDIZES DER PRODUKTION UND PRODUKTION AUSGEWAEHLTER ERZEUGNISSE IM PRODUZIERENDEN GEWERBE. (Consists of several subseries) 1951. m. DM.163.20 (effective 1997). 65180 Wiesbaden, Germany. TEL 49-611-75-1. FAX 49-611-724000. TELEX 61186-STBA-D. URL: http://www.statistik-bund.de. **Document type:** government publication.
Formerly: Germany. Statistisches Bundesamt. Fachserie 4, Produzierendes Gewerbe, Reihe 2: Indices fuer das Produzierende Gewerbe.

BUSINESS AND ECONOMICS — ABSTRACTING, BIBLIOGRAPHIES, STATISTICS

338 314 GW
GERMANY. STATISTISCHES BUNDESAMT. FACHSERIE 4, PRODUZIERENDES GEWERBE, REIHE 2.2: AUFTRAGSEINGANG UND UMSATZ IM VERARBEITENDEN GEWERBE, AUFTRAGSEINGANG UND AUFTRAGSBESTAND IM BAUHAUPTGEWERBE. INDICES. m. DM.286.80 (effective 1997). Statistisches Bundesamt, 65180 Wiesbaden, Germany. TEL 49-611-75-1. FAX 49-611-724000. TELEX 61186-STBA-D. URL: http://www.statistik-bund.de. **Document type:** government publication.
Formerly: Germany (Federal Republic, 1949-). Statistisches Bundesamt. Fachserie 4, Produzierendes Gewerbe, Reihe 2.2: Indices des Auftragseingangs, des Umsatzes und des Auftragsbestands fuer das Verarbeitende Gewerbe und fuer das Bauhauptgewerbe; Which superseded: Germany (Federal Republic, 1949-) Statistisches Bundesamt. Fachserie 4, Reihe 2: Indices des Auftragseingangs in Ausgewaehlten Industriezweigen und im Bauhauptgewerbe (ISSN 0072-209X)

338 314 GW
GERMANY. STATISTISCHES BUNDESAMT. FACHSERIE 4, PRODUZIERENDES GEWERBE, REIHE 3.1: PRODUKTION IM PRODUZIERENDEN GEWERBE. (Consists of several subseries) 1951. q. (plus a.). DM.126.80 (a. DM.30.50) (effective 1997). Statistisches Bundesamt, 65180 Wiesbaden, Germany. TEL 49-611-75-1. FAX 49-611-724000. TELEX 61186-STBA-D. URL: http://www.statistik-bund.de. **Document type:** government publication.
Formerly (until 1991): Germany (Federal Republic, 1949-). Statistisches Bundesamt. Fachserie 4, Produzierendes Gewerbe, Reihe 3.1: Produktion Gewerbe des In- und Auslandes.

338 314 GW
GERMANY. STATISTISCHES BUNDESAMT. FACHSERIE 4, PRODUZIERENDES GEWERBE, REIHE 7.1: HANDWERK. BESCHAEFTIGTE UND UMSATZ IM HANDWERK. q. DM.29.60. Statistisches Bundesamt, 65180 Wiesbaden, Germany. TEL 49-611-75-1. FAX 49-611-724000. TELEX 61186-STBA-D. URL: http://www.statistik-bund.de. **Document type:** government publication.
Formerly: Germany (Federal Republic, 1949-). Statistisches Bundesamt. Fachserie 4, Produzierende Gastgewerbe, Reihe 7.1: Handwerk. Beschaeftigte um Umsatz im Handwerk (ISSN 0072-2103)

380 314 GW
GERMANY. STATISTISCHES BUNDESAMT. FACHSERIE 6, BINNENHANDEL, GASTGEWERBE, TOURISMUS; REIHE 1: GROSSHANDEL. irreg. price varies. 65180 Wiesbaden, Germany. TEL 49-611-75-1. FAX 49-611-724000. TELEX 61186-STBA-D. URL: http://www.statistik-bund.de. **Document type:** government publication.
Formerly: Germany. Statistisches Bundesamt. Fachserie 6, Handel, Gastgewerbe, Reiseverkehr; Reihe 1: Grosshandel (ISSN 0072-1964)

380 314 GW
GERMANY. STATISTISCHES BUNDESAMT. FACHSERIE 6, BINNENHANDEL, GASTGEWERBE, TOURISMUS; REIHE 3: EINZELHANDEL. (Consists of several subseries) irreg. price varies. 65180 Wiesbaden, Germany. TEL 49-611-75-1. FAX 49-611-724000. TELEX 61186-STBA-D. URL: http://www.statistik-bund.de. **Document type:** government publication.
Formerly: Germany. Statistisches Bundesamt. Fachserie 6, Handel, Gastgewerbe, Reiseverkehr; Reihe 3: Einzelhandel (ISSN 0072-1972)

382 314 GW
GERMANY. STATISTISCHES BUNDESAMT. FACHSERIE 7, AUSSENHANDEL, REIHE 4. AUSSENHANDEL MIT AUSGEWAEHLTEN WAREN; Reihe 4.1: Ein- und Ausfuhr von Mineraloel (Generalhandel). m. (plus a. cum.). DM.163.20 (effective 1997). 65180 Wiesbaden, Germany. TEL 49-611-75-1. FAX 49-611-724000. TELEX 61186-STBA-D. URL: http://www.statistik-bund.de. **Document type:** government publication.

382 314 GW
GERMANY. STATISTISCHES BUNDESAMT. FACHSERIE 7, AUSSENHANDEL, REIHE 7: AUSSENHANDEL NACH LAENDERN UND GUETERGRUPPEN DER PRODUKTIONSSTATISTIKEN (SPEZIALHANDEL). a. DM.20.50. 65180 Wiesbaden, Germany. TEL 49-611-75-1. FAX 49-611-724000. TELEX 61186-STBA-D. URL: http://www.statistik-bund.de. **Document type:** government publication.
Formerly: Germany (Federal Republic, 1949-). Statisches Bundesamt. Fachserie 7, Aussenhandel, Reihe 7: Sonderbeitraege (ISSN 0072-1700)

382 314 GW ISSN 0072-1662
GERMANY. STATISTISCHES BUNDESAMT. FACHSERIE 7, AUSSENHANDEL, REIHE 3: AUSSENHANDEL NACH LAENDERN UND WARENGRUPPEN (SPEZIALHANDEL). s-a. DM.68.20. 65180 Wiesbaden, Germany. TEL 49-611-75-1. FAX 49-611-724000. TELEX 61186-STBA-D. URL: http://www.statistik-bund.de. **Document type:** government publication.

382 314 GW ISSN 0072-1654
GERMANY. STATISTISCHES BUNDESAMT. FACHSERIE 7, AUSSENHANDEL, REIHE 2: AUSSENHANDEL NACH WAREN UND LAENDERN (SPEZIALHANDEL). m. (plus a. cumulation). DM.526.80 (effective 1997). 65180 Wiesbaden, Germany. TEL 49-611-75-1. FAX 49-611-724000. TELEX 61186-STBA-D. URL: http://www.statistik-bund.de. **Document type:** government publication.

382 314 GW ISSN 0072-1646
GERMANY. STATISTISCHES BUNDESAMT. FACHSERIE 7, AUSSENHANDEL, REIHE 1: ZUSAMMENFASSENDE UEBERSICHTEN FUER DEN AUSSENHANDEL. m. DM.141.60 (effective 1997). 65180 Wiesbaden, Germany. TEL 49-611-75-1. FAX 49-611-724000. TELEX 61186-STBA-D. URL: http://www.statistik-bund.de. **Document type:** government publication.

336 314 GW
GERMANY. STATISTISCHES BUNDESAMT. FACHSERIE 14: FINANZEN UND STEUERN. (Consists of several subseries) 1959. irreg. price varies. 65180 Wiesbaden, Germany. TEL 49-611-75-1. FAX 49-611-724000. TELEX 61186-STBA-D. URL: http://www.statistik-bund.de. **Document type:** government publication.

339.42 314 GW ISSN 0176-9405
GERMANY. STATISTISCHES BUNDESAMT. FACHSERIE 15, WIRTSCHAFTSRECHNUNGEN, REIHE 1: EINNAHMEN UND AUSGABEN AUSGEWAEHLTER PRIVATER HAUSHALTE. 1954. q. DM.29.60. Statistisches Bundesamt, 65180 Wiesbaden, Germany. TEL 49-611-75-1. FAX 49-611-724000. TELEX 61186-STBA-D. URL: http://www.statistik-bund.de. **Document type:** government publication.
Supersedes: Germany (Federal Republic, 1949-) Statistisches Bundesamt. Fachserie 15, Reihe 1: Wirtschaftsrechnungen (ISSN 0072-386X)

331.2 338.1 314 GW ISSN 0176-7445
GERMANY. STATISTISCHES BUNDESAMT. FACHSERIE 16, LOEHNE UND GEHAELTER, REIHE 1: ARBEITERVERDIENSTE IN DER LANDWIRTSCHAFT. a. DM.4.40 (effective 1997). Statistisches Bundesamt, 65180 Wiesbaden, Germany. TEL 49-611-75-1. FAX 49-611-724000. TELEX 61186-STBA-D. URL: http://www.statistik-bund.de. **Document type:** government publication.
Supersedes: Germany (Federal Republic, 1949-). Statistisches Bundesamt. Loehne und Gehaelter. Reihe 1: Arbeiterverdienste in der Landwirtschaft.

331.2 314 GW ISSN 0177-2473
GERMANY. STATISTISCHES BUNDESAMT. FACHSERIE 16, LOEHNE UND GEHAELTER, REIHE 2.1: ARBEITERVERDIENSTE IN DER INDUSTRIE. q. DM.82 (effective 1997). Statistisches Bundesamt, 65180 Wiesbaden, Germany. TEL 49-611-75-1. FAX 49-611-724000. TELEX 61186-STBA-D. URL: http://www.statistik-bund.de. **Document type:** government publication.
Formerly: Germany (Federal Republic, 1949-). Statistisches Bundesamt. Fachserie 16, Reihe 2: Angestelltenverdienste in Industrie und Handel (ISSN 0072-3789)

331.2 GW
GERMANY. STATISTISCHES BUNDESAMT. FACHSERIE 16, LOEHNE UND GEHAELTER, REIHE 2.2: ANGESTELLTENVERDIENST IN INDUSTRIE UND HANDEL. 1959. q. price varies. Metzler - Poeschel Verlag, Postfach 1152, 72125 Kusterdingen, Germany. TEL 49-7071-935350. FAX 49-7071-935393. adv. **Document type:** government publication.

331.2 314 GW ISSN 0072-3797
GERMANY. STATISTISCHES BUNDESAMT. FACHSERIE 16, LOEHNE UND GEHAELTER, REIHE 3: ARBEITERVERDIENSTE IM HANDWERK. 1957. a. DM.7.70 (effective 1997). 65180 Wiesbaden, Germany. TEL 49-611-75-1. FAX 49-611-724000. TELEX 61186-STBA-D. URL: http://www.statistik-bund.de. **Document type:** government publication.

336 314 GW ISSN 0072-3843
GERMANY. STATISTISCHES BUNDESAMT. FACHSERIE 16, LOEHNE UND GEHAELTER, REIHE 4: TARIFLOEHNE UND TARIFGEHAELTER. irreg. price varies. 65180 Wiesbaden, Germany. TEL 49-611-75-1. FAX 49-611-724000. TELEX 61186-STBA-D. URL: http://www.statistik-bund.de. **Document type:** government publication.

331.2 310 GW ISSN 0941-3685
GERMANY. STATISTISCHES BUNDESAMT. FACHSERIE 16, LOEHNE UND GEHAELTER, REIHE 5: LOEHNE, GEHAELTER UND ARBEITSKOSTEN IM AUSLAND. 1950. a. DM.17.70. Statistisches Bundesamt, 65180 Wiesbaden, Germany. TEL 49-611-75-1. FAX 49-611-724000. TELEX 61186-STBA-D. URL: http://www.statistik-bund.de. **Document type:** government publication.
Formerly: Germany (Federal Republic, 1949-). Statistisches Bundesamt. Fachserie 16, Loehne und Gehaelter, Reihe 5.2: Tarifloehne und Gehaelter des Auslandes.

338.5 314 GW ISSN 0721-121X
GERMANY. STATISTISCHES BUNDESAMT. FACHSERIE 17, PREISE, REIHE 2: PREISE UND PREISINDIZES FUER GEWERBLICHE PRODUKTE. ERZEUGERPREISE. m. DM.141.60. Statistisches Bundesamt, 65180 Wiesbaden, Germany. TEL 49-611-75-1. FAX 49-611-724000. TELEX 61186-STBA-D. URL: http://www.statistik-bund.de. **Document type:** government publication.
Formerly: Germany (Federal Republic, 1949-). Statistisches Bundesamt. Fachserie 17, Reihe 2: Preise und Preisindizes fuer Industrielle Produkte. Erzeugerpreise (ISSN 0072-3886)

338.5 314 GW ISSN 0940-3949
GERMANY. STATISTISCHES BUNDESAMT. FACHSERIE 17, PREISE, REIHE 3: PREISINDEX FUER DEN WARENEINGANG DES PRODUZIERENDEN GEWERBES. 1955. m. DM.88.80. Statistisches Bundesamt, 65180 Wiesbaden, Germany. TEL 49-611-75-1. FAX 49-611-724000. TELEX 61186-STBA-D. URL: http://www.statistik-bund.de. **Document type:** government publication.
Formerly: Germany (Federal Republic, 1949-). Statistisches Bundesamt. Fachserie 17, Preise, Reihe 3: Index der Grundstoffepreise (ISSN 0072-3878)

380 314 GW ISSN 0720-4221
GERMANY. STATISTISCHES BUNDESAMT. FACHSERIE 17 PREISE, REIHE 4: MESSZAHLEN FUER BAULEISTUNGSPREISE UND PREISINDIZES FUER BAUWERKE. q. DM.47.20 (effective 1997). Statistisches Bundesamt, 65180 Wiesbaden, Germany. TEL 49-611-75-1. FAX 49-611-724000. TELEX 61186-STBA-D. URL: http://www.statistik-bund.de. **Document type:** government publication.

339 314 GW
GERMANY. STATISTISCHES BUNDESAMT. FACHSERIE 17, PREISE, REIHE 7: PREISINDICES FUER DIE LEBENSHALTUNG. m. DM.220.80 (effective 1997). Statistisches Bundesamt, 65180 Wiesbaden, Germany. TEL 49-611-75-1. FAX 49-611-724000. TELEX 61186-STBA-D. URL: http://www.statistik-bund.de. **Document type:** government publication.
Formerly: Germany. Statistisches Bundesamt. Fachserie 17, Preise, Reihe 7: Preise und Preisindizes fuer die Lebenshaltung (ISSN 0072-3916)

BUSINESS AND ECONOMICS — ABSTRACTING, BIBLIOGRAPHIES, STATISTICS

382 314   GW
GERMANY. STATISTISCHES BUNDESAMT. FACHSERIE 17, PREISE, REIHE 8: PREISINDIZES FUER DIE EIN- UND AUSFUHR. 1955. m. DM.116.40 (effective 1997). Statistisches Bundesamt, 65180 Wiesbaden, Germany. TEL 49-611-75-1. FAX 49-611-724000. TELEX 61186-STBA-D. URL: http://www.statistik-bund.de. **Document type:** government publication.
  Formerly: Germany. Statistisches Bundesamt. Fachserie 17, Preise, Reihe 8: Preise und Preisindizes fuer die Ein- und Ausfuhr (ISSN 0177-1787)

339 310   GW   ISSN 0072-3827
GERMANY. STATISTISCHES BUNDESAMT. FACHSERIE 17, PREISE, REIHE 10: INTERNATIONALER VERGLEICH DER PREISE FUER DIE LEBENSHALTUNG. 1960. m. DM.55.20 (effective 1997). 65180 Wiesbaden, Germany. TEL 49-611-75-1. FAX 49-611-724000. TELEX 61186-STBA-D. URL: http://www.statistik-bund.de. **Document type:** government publication.

382 310   GW   ISSN 0072-3940
GERMANY. STATISTISCHES BUNDESAMT. FACHSERIE 17, PREISE, REIHE 11: PREISE UND PREISINDIZES IM AUSLAND. m. DM.92.40 (effective 1997). 65180 Wiesbaden, Germany. TEL 49-611-75-1. FAX 49-611-724000. TELEX 61186-STBA-D. URL: http://www.statistik-bund.de. **Document type:** government publication.

330 314   GW   ISSN 0072-4009
GERMANY. STATISTISCHES BUNDESAMT. FACHSERIE 18, VOLKSWIRTSCHAFTLICHE GESAMTRECHNUNGEN, REIHE 1: KONTEN UND STANDARDTABELLEN. a. price varies. 65180 Wiesbaden, Germany. TEL 49-611-75-1. FAX 49-611-724000. TELEX 61186-STBA-D. URL: http://www.statistik-bund.de. **Document type:** government publication.

382 314   GW
GERMANY. STATISTISCHES BUNDESAMT. FREMDSPRACHIGE VEROEFFENTLICHUNGEN NR. 6370010: FOREIGN TRADE ACCORDING TO STANDARD INTERNATIONAL TRADE CLASSIFICATION (SITC) - SPECIAL TRADE. a. DM.30.50 (effective 1997). 65180 Wiesbaden, Germany. TEL 49-611-75-1. FAX 49-611-724000. TELEX 61186-STBA-D. URL: http://www.statistik-bund.de. **Document type:** government publication.

314   GW   ISSN 0072-4106
GERMANY. STATISTISCHES BUNDESAMT. WARENVERZEICHNIS FUER DIE AUSSENHANDELSSTATISTIK. a. DM.62. 65180 Wiesbaden, Germany. TEL 49-611-75-1. FAX 49-611-724000. TELEX 61186-STBA-D. URL: http://www.statistik-bund.de. **Document type:** government publication.

338   SZ
GESCHAEFTSGANG IN DER SCHWEIZER INDUSTRIE. PRODUKTIONS-, AUFTRAGS-, UMSATZ- UND LAGERINDIZES/EVOLUTION DE LA SITUATION DAUS L'INDUSTRIE SUISSE. INDICES DE LA PRODUCTION, DES COMMANDES, DES CHIFFRES D'AFFAIRES ET DES STOCKS. (Text in French and German) 1987. a. 20 SFr. Bundesamt fuer Statistik, Schwarzstorstr. 96, CH-3003 Bern, Switzerland. TEL 41-31-3236060. FAX 41-31-3236012. URL: http://www.admin.ch/bfs. **Document type:** government publication.
  Formerly: Auftrags-, Produktions-, Umsatz- und Lagerverhaeltnisse in der Industrie und im Bauhauptgewerbe.

330   FR   ISSN 1243-3470
LA GESTION EN RESUMES/ABSTRACT BUSINESS. (Text in English, French) 10/yr. (plus supplements). 980 F. (foreign 1048 F.) (effective 1995). Editions E S K A, 27 rue Dunois, 75013 Paris, France. TEL 33-1-44-06-80-42. FAX 33-1-44-24-06-94. **Document type:** abstracting/indexing.
  Description: Abstracts selected important articles by specialists, professionals, and instructors of economics and business administration.

330.9   GH
GHANA. STATISTICAL SERVICE. CONSUMER PRICE INDEX NUMBERS. m. $24. Statistical Service, Information Section, P.O. Box 1098, Accra, Ghana. TEL 233-21-663578. FAX 233-21-667069. TELEX 2205 MIFAEP GH. **Document type:** government publication.
  Formerly: Ghana. Central Bureau of Statistics. Consumer Price Index.

330.9 316   GH   ISSN 0855-0247
GHANA. STATISTICAL SERVICE. ECONOMIC SURVEY. 1951. irreg., latest 1982. $20. Statistical Service, Information Section, P.O. Box 1098, Accra, Ghana. TEL 233-21-663578. FAX 233-21-667069. TELEX 2205 MIFAEP GH. **Document type:** government publication.
  Formerly: Ghana. Central Bureau of Statistics. Economic Survey (ISSN 0072-4335)

330.9   GH
GHANA INDUSTRIAL CENSUS. DIRECTORY OF INDUSTRIAL ESTABLISHMENTS. irreg., latest 1988. $15. Statistical Service, Information Section, P.O. Box 1098, Accra, Ghana. TEL 233-21-663578. FAX 233-21-667069. TELEX 2205 MIFAEP GH. **Document type:** government publication, directory.

330.9   GH
GHANA INDUSTRIAL CENSUS. PHASE II REPORT. irreg., latest 1987. $9. Statistical Service, Information Section, P.O. Box 1098, Accra, Ghana. TEL 233-21-663578. FAX 233-21-337069. TELEX 2205 MIFAEP GH. **Document type:** government publication.

330.9 304.6   GH
GHANA LIVING STANDARDS SURVEY. ROUND REPORT. 1988. irreg., no.3, 1992. $30 (includes all Round Reports and Rural Communities in Ghana). Statistical Service, Information Section, P.O. Box 1098, Accra, Ghana. TEL 233-21-663578. FAX 223-21-667069. TELEX 2205 MIFAEP GH. **Document type:** government publication.

330.9 304.6   GH
GHANA LIVING STANDARDS SURVEY. RURAL COMMUNITIES IN GHANA. irreg. $9. Statistical Service, Information Section, P.O. Box 1098, Accra, Ghana. TEL 233-21-663578. FAX 233-21-667069. TELEX 2205 MIFAEP GH. **Document type:** government publication.

657   US   ISSN 1055-3940
GLOBAL COMMUNIQUE. 6/yr. membership. Information Systems Audit & Control Association, 3701 Algonquin Rd., Ste. 1010, Rolling Meadows, IL 60008. TEL 847-253-1545. FAX 847-253-1443. E-mail: publication@isaca.org; URL: http://www.isaca.org. Ed. Patricia Dahlberg. circ. 15,000. **Document type:** newsletter.
—CCC.
  Formerly (until 1990): E D P Auditor Update (ISSN 0885-9450)

382 314   NE   ISSN 1383-5777
GOEDERENNAALIJST. 1969. a. Centraal Bureau voor de Statistiek, Prinses Beatrixlaan 428, Voorburg, Netherlands. (Subscr. to: SDU - Publishers, Christoffel Plantijnstraat, The Hague, Netherlands) **Document type:** government publication.
  Formerly (until 1993): Netherlands. Central Bureau voor de Statistiek. Naamlijsten voor de Statistieken van de Buitenlandse Handel (ISSN 0168-4094)

338 314   UK
GREAT BRITAIN. CENTRAL STATISTICAL OFFICE. ANNUAL CENSUS OF PRODUCTION REPORTS. (Issued in parts. Subseries of the Business Monitor) 1970. a. price varies. Office for National Statistics, Government Bldgs., 155 Cardiff Rd., Newport, Gwent NP9 1XG. TEL 44-1633-812973. FAX 44-1633-812599. TELEX 497121 BSO NPT G. E-mail: library@ons.gov.uk. (Orders to: Stationery Office Publications Centre, P.O. Box 276, London SW8 5DT, England. TEL 44-171-873-9090. FAX 44-171-873-8200) stat. **Document type:** government publication.
  Former titles: Great Britain. Department of Trade and Industry. Business Statistics Office Report on the Census of Production; Great Britain. Department of Industry. Business Statistics Office Report on the Census of Production; Great Britain. Department of Trade and Industry. Business Statistics Office. Report on the Census of Production.
  Description: Compiles statistical information on UK manufacturing and other economic activities.

GREAT BRITAIN. CENTRAL STATISTICAL OFFICE. KEY DATA. see *STATISTICS*

330.9 314   UK
GREAT BRITAIN. CENTRAL STATISTICAL OFFICE. STANDARD INDUSTRIAL CLASSIFICATION OF ECONOMIC ACTIVITIES (YEAR). a. £18. Office for National Statistics, Government Bldgs., 155 Cardiff Rd., Newport, Gwent NP9 1XG, Wales. TEL 44-1633-812973. FAX 44-1633-812599. TELEX 497121 BSO NPT G. (Orders to: Stationery Office Publications Centre, P.O. Box 276, London SW8 5DT, England. TEL 44-171-873-9090. FAX 44-171-873-8200) stat.; index. **Document type:** government publication.
  Description: Classifies U.K. industries and cross-indexes them with the E.U. system.

332.152   UK   ISSN 0950-7558
HF3501
GREAT BRITAIN. CENTRAL STATISTICAL OFFICE. UNITED KINGDOM BALANCE OF PAYMENTS. Variant title: Pink Book. 1948. a. £13.25. Office for National Statistics, Government Bldgs., 155 Cardiff Rd., Newport, Gwent NP9 1XG, Wales. TEL 44-1633-812973. FAX 44-1633-812599. TELEX 497121 BSO NPT G. E-mail: library@ons.gov.uk. (Orders to: Stationery Office Publications Centre, P.O. Box 276, London SW8 5DT, England. TEL 44-171-873-9090. FAX 44-171-873-8200) stat. (back issues avail.) **Document type:** government publication.
—BLDSC (9093.500000).
  Description: Gives detailed balance-of-payments data for a range of areas, including foreign trade.

339.341   UK   ISSN 0267-8691
HC260.I5
GREAT BRITAIN. CENTRAL STATISTICAL OFFICE. UNITED KINGDOM NATIONAL ACCOUNTS. Variant title: Blue Book. 1984. a. £15.50. Office for National Statistics, Government Bldgs., 155 Cardiff Rd., Newport, Gwent NP9 1XG, Wales. TEL 44-1633-812973. FAX 44-1633-812599. TELEX 497121 BSO NPT G. E-mail: library@ons.gov.uk. (Orders to: Stationery Office Publications Centre, P.O. Box 276, London SW8 5DT, England. TEL 44-171-873-9090. FAX 44-171-873-8200) stat. (back issues avail.) **Document type:** government publication.
—BLDSC (6963.501000).
  Description: Examines all aspects of the UK economy.

GREAT BRITAIN. DEPARTMENT OF THE ENVIRONMENT. LOCAL GOVERNMENT FINANCIAL STATISTICS: ENGLAND AND WALES. see *PUBLIC ADMINISTRATION — Abstracting, Bibliographies, Statistics*

332 314   UK
HG186.G7
GREAT BRITAIN. OFFICE FOR NATIONAL STATISTICS. FINANCIAL STATISTICS. 1962. m. £255 (includes a. supplement) (effective 1996). Office for National Statistics, Great George St., London SWIP 3AQ, England. TEL 44-171-270-6182. FAX 44-171-270-6019. TELEX 497121 BSO NPT G. E-mail: library@ons.gov.uk. (Subscr. to: Stationery Office Publications Centre, P.O. Box 267, London SW8 5DT, England. TEL 44-171-873-9090. FAX 44-171-873-8200) Ed. Natu Patel. stat. (reprint service avail. from SCH) **Document type:** government publication.
—BLDSC (3926.990220). CCC.
  Formerly (until Apr. 1996): Great Britain. Central Statistical Office. Financial Statistics (ISSN 0015-203X)
  Description: Provides data on topics including financial accounts for sectors of the economy, government income and expenditure, public sector borrowing, banking statistics, money supply, institutional investment, company finance and liquidity, security prices and exchange rates.

338 314   GR   ISSN 0072-7393
HC291
GREECE. NATIONAL STATISTICAL SERVICE. ANNUAL INDUSTRIAL SURVEY. (Text in English and Greek) 1958. a. $12. National Statistical Service of Greece, Statistical Information and Publications Division - Ethniki Statistiki Yperesia tes Ellados, 14-16 Lykourgou, 101 66 Athens, Greece. TEL 30-1-3289-397. FAX 30-1-3241-102. TELEX 216734 ESYE GR. (back issues avail.) **Document type:** government publication.
  Formerly (until 1963): Greece. National Statistical Service. Results of the Annual Industrial Survey.

BUSINESS AND ECONOMICS — ABSTRACTING, BIBLIOGRAPHIES, STATISTICS

330.9   GR   ISSN 1012-2397
GREECE. NATIONAL STATISTICAL SERVICE. HOUSEHOLD EXPENDITURE SURVEY. (Text in English, Greek) 1957. irreg. $12. National Statistical Service of Greece, Statistical Information and Publications Division - Ethniki Statistiki Yperesia tes Ellados, 14-16 Lykourgou, 101 66 Athens, Greece. TEL 30-1-3289-397. FAX 30-1-3241-102. TELEX 216734 ESYE GR. (back issues avail.) **Document type:** government publication.

331.1   GR   ISSN 0256-3576
HB2722.5.A3
GREECE. NATIONAL STATISTICAL SERVICE. LABOUR FORCE SURVEY. 1974. a. $12. National Statistical Service of Greece, Statistical Information and Publications Division - Ethniki Statistiki Yperesia tes Ellados, 14-16 Lykourgou, 101 66 Athens, Greece. TEL 30-1-3289-397. FAX 30-1-3241-102. TELEX 216734 ESYE GR. (back issues avail.)
    Formerly (until 1980): Greece. National Statistical Service. Employment Survey Conducted in Urban and Semi-Urban Areas (ISSN 0256-8004)

338   GR
GREECE. NATIONAL STATISTICAL SERVICE. PRODUCTION OF MANUFACTURED ITEMS. (Text in Greek) 1987. trienial. $5. National Statistical Service of Greece, Statistical Information and Publications Division - Ethniki Statistiki Yperesia tes Ellados, 14-16 Lykourgou, 101 66 Athens, Greece. TEL 30-1-3289-397. FAX 30-1-3241-102. TELEX 216 ESYE GR. (back issues avail.) **Document type:** government publication.

236   GR   ISSN 0259-997X
GREECE. NATIONAL STATISTICAL SERVICE. PROVISIONAL NATIONAL ACCOUNTS OF GREECE. (Text in English and Greek) 1980. a. $13. National Statistical Service of Greece, Statistical Information and Publications Division - Ethniki Statistiki Yperesia tes Ellados, 14-16 Lykourgou, 101 66 Athens, Greece. TEL 30-1-3289-397. FAX 30-1-3241-102. TELEX 216734 ESYE GR. (back issues avail.) **Document type:** government publication.

336 314   GR   ISSN 0256-3568
HJ50
GREECE. NATIONAL STATISTICAL SERVICE. PUBLIC FINANCE STATISTICS. (Text in English and Greek) 1973. a. $15. National Statistical Service of Greece, Statistical Information and Publications Division - Ethniki Statistiki Yperesia tes Ellados, 14-16 Lykourgou, 101 66 Athens, Greece. TEL 30-1-3289-397. FAX 30-1-3241-102. TELEX 216734 ESYE GR. (back issues avail.) **Document type:** government publication.
    —BLDSC (3661.317630).
    Formerly (until 1974): Greece. National Statistical Service. Statistical Yearbook of Public Finance (ISSN 0072-7431)

336   GR   ISSN 1105-2147
GREECE. NATIONAL STATISTICAL SERVICE. QUARTERLY NATIONAL ACCOUNTS OF GREECE. (Text in Greek, English) 1984. q. $3 per no. National Statistical Service of Greece, Statistical Information and Publications Division - Ethniki Statistiki Yperesia tes Ellados, 14-16 Lykourgou, 101 66 Athens, Greece. TEL 30-1-3289-397. FAX 30-1-3241-102. TELEX 216734 ESYE GR. (back issues avail.) **Document type:** government publication.

338   GR
GREECE. NATIONAL STATISTICAL SERVICE. REVISED CONSUMER PRICE INDEX. (Text in English and Greek) 1960. irreg. $4. National Statistical Service of Greece, Statistical Information and Publications Division - Ethniki Statistiki Yperesia tes Ellados, 14-16 Lykourgou, 101 66 Athens, Greece. TEL 30-1-3244-748. FAX 30-1-3241-102. TELEX 216734 ESYE GR. (back issues avail.) **Document type:** government publication.

GREECE. NATIONAL STATISTICAL SERVICE. REVISED PRICE INDICES OF NEW BUILDING DWELLINGS CONSTRUCTION (YEAR). see BUILDING AND CONSTRUCTION — Abstracting, Bibliographies, Statistics

381   GR
GREECE. NATIONAL STATISTICAL SERVICE. STANDARD CLASSIFICATION OF THE BRANCHES OF ECONOMIC ACTIVITY. Variant title: Greece. National Statistical Service. Greek Industrial Classification. (Text in Greek) 1975. irreg., latest 1991. $4. National Statistical Service of Greece, Statistical Information and Publications Division - Ethniki Statistiki Yperesia tes Ellados, 14-16 Lykourgou, 101 66 Athens, Greece. TEL 30-1-3289-397. FAX 30-1-3241-102. TELEX 216734 ESYE GR. **Document type:** government publication.

336 314   GR   ISSN 0256-3592
GREECE. NATIONAL STATISTICAL SERVICE. STATISTICAL BULLETIN OF PUBLIC FINANCE. (Text in English and Greek) q. $9. National Statistical Service of Greece, Statistical Information and Publications Division - Ethniki Statistiki Yperesia tes Ellados, 14-16 Lykourgou, 101 66 Athens, Greece. TEL 30-1-3289-397. FAX 30-1-3241-102. TELEX 216734 ESYE GR. (back issues avail.) **Document type:** bulletin, government publication.
    Formerly (until 1973): Greece. National Statistical Service. Monthly Statistical Bulletin of Public Finance (ISSN 0028-0259)

336   GR   ISSN 0302-1416
GREECE. NATIONAL STATISTICAL SERVICE. STATISTICS OF THE DECLARED INCOME OF LEGAL ENTITIES AND ITS TAXATION. (Text in Greek) 1959. a. $4. National Statistical Service of Greece, Statistical Information and Publications Division - Ethniki Statistiki Yperesia tes Ellados, 14-16 Lykourgou, 101 66 Athens, Greece. TEL 30-1-3289-397. FAX 30-1-3241-102. TELEX 216734 ESYE GR. (back issues avail.) **Document type:** government publication.

336   GR   ISSN 0302-1114
GREECE. NATIONAL STATISTICAL SERVICE. STATISTICS ON THE DECLARED INCOME OF PHYSICAL PERSONS AND ITS TAXATION. (Text in Greek) 1960. a. $12. National Statistical Service of Greece, Statistical Information and Publications Division - Ethniki Statistiki Yperesia tes Ellados, 14-16 Lykourgou, 101 66 Athens, Greece. TEL 30-1-3289-397. FAX 30-1-3241-102. TELEX 216734 ESYE GR. (back issues avail.) **Document type:** government publication.

331.1   GR
GREECE. NATIONAL STATISTICAL SERVICE. STATISTIQUES DU TRAVAIL. Key Title: Statistikes Ergasias - Ethnike Statistike Upersia tes Ellados. (Text in French, Greek) 1967. q. $7 per no. National Statistical Service of Greece, Statistical Information and Publications Division - Ethniki Statistiki Yperesia tes Ellados, 14-16 Lykourgou, 101 66 Athens, Greece. TEL 30-1-3289-397. FAX 30-1-3241-102. TELEX 216734 ESYE GR. **Document type:** bulletin, government publication.

330 314   GR   ISSN 0257-7240
GREEK ECONOMY IN FIGURES (YEAR). (Text in English, Greek) 1980. a. $180. Electra Press, 4 Stadiou St., 10564 Athens, Greece. TEL 01-32-33-203. FAX 01-32-35-160. TELEX 210564. Ed. Christos Papaioannou. adv.; stat. circ. 6,000.
    Description: Statistical guide to Greece concerning information about Greece and other EEC economies, demographics, national accounts, industrial production and capacity, public finance, money and credit prices. Provides comparative tables and diagrams with commentary about data and trends of the Greek, major OECD, EC and neighboring economies.

330.1   US
GROSS REPORT; a summary of key economic statistics. 1992. m. $225. John E. Gross, Ed. & Pub., 355 New York Ave., Huntington, NY 11743. TEL 516-271-9457. stat.; illus. Indexed: Alloys Ind., Eng.Mat.Abstr., Met.Abstr.Ind., Met.Abstr., Nonfer.Met.Alert, PCC Alert, Steels Alert, World Alum.Abstr. **Document type:** newsletter.
    Formerly: Economy at a Glance (ISSN 1063-1208)
    Description: Provides a quick overview of the economy structured in a unique and easy to read format.
    Refereed Serial

330   CC
GUANGDONG SOCIOECONOMIC STATISTICS MONTHLY. (Text in Chinese, English) m. HK.$1200($185) Economic Information & Agency, 342 Hennessy Rd., 10th Fl., Wanchai, Hong Kong, People's Republic of China. TEL 852-573-8217. FAX 852-838-8304. TELEX 86990 EIA HX.

338 318   GT
GUATEMALA. INSTITUTO NACIONAL DE ESTADISTICA. DIRECTORIO NACIONAL DE ESTABLECIMIENTOS INDUSTRIALES. (Former name of issuing body: Direccion General de Estadistica) a. $15 (effective 1993 ed.). Instituto Nacional de Estadistica, Ministerio de Economia, 8A Calle no. 9-55, Zona 1, Guatemala, Guatemala. TEL 502-26136. **Document type:** directory.

382   US   ISSN 0565-0933
HF105
GUIDE TO FOREIGN TRADE STATISTICS. irreg. price varies. U.S. Bureau of the Census, Foreign Trade Division, Washington, DC 20233-8300. TEL 301-763-5140. (Subscr. to: Superintendent of Documents, U.S. Government Printing Office, Box 371954, Pittsburgh, PA 15250-7954. TEL 202-783-3238. FAX 202-512-2233) stat. (also avail. in microfiche) **Document type:** government publication.

382 339 016   UN   ISSN 0255-9358
GUIDE TO U N C T A D PUBLICATIONS. (Supplement avail.) (Text in English, French, and Spanish) 1968. a. free. United Nations Conference on Trade and Development (UNCTAD), Reference Unit, Palais des Nations, 1211 Geneva 10, Switzerland. TEL 734-6011. FAX 733-9879. **Document type:** bibliography.
    Formerly: U N C T A D Guide to Publications (ISSN 0041-5227)

336   GY   ISSN 0301-7168
GUYANA. AUDITOR GENERAL. REPORT ON THE PUBLIC ACCOUNTS. Key Title: Public Accounts of the Government of Guyana. a. Auditor General, P.O. Box 10002, Georgetown, Guyana. Dir. Anand Goolsarran.

382   GY   ISSN 0533-991X
HF172.G88
GUYANA. STATISTICAL BUREAU. ANNUAL ACCOUNT RELATING TO EXTERNAL TRADE. 1954. a. $3. Statistical Bureau, Georgetown, Guyana.

658 016   US   ISSN 1042-654X
HD30.4
H B S CATALOG OF TEACHING MATERIALS. a. $15 to individuals; academics $7.50. Harvard University, Graduate School of Business Administration, Soldiers Field Rd., Boston, MA 02163. TEL 617-495-6117. FAX 617-495-6985. bibl. circ. 5,000. (back issues avail.; reprint service avail.) **Document type:** catalog.
    Formerly: H B S Case Bibliography; Supersedes (1975-1980): Intercollegiate Bibliography. New Cases in Administration (ISSN 0095-490X)
    Description: Contains annotated listings and comprehensive indexes of teaching materials available for purchase from the Harvard Business School.

H I A'S NATIONWIDE CRAFT & HOBBY INDUSTRY CONSUMER SURVEY (YEAR). (Hobby Industry Association) see HOBBIES — Abstracting, Bibliographies, Statistics

310   IC   ISSN 0256-7288
HAGTOELUR MANADARINS. 1973. m. Sedlabanki Islands, Hagfraedideild - Central Bank of Iceland, Department of Economics, Kalkofnsvegur 3, IS-150 Reykjavik, Iceland. TEL 354-569-9600. FAX 354-569-9608. TELEX 220 CENTBK IS. Ed. Stefan Johann Stefansson. **Document type:** government publication.
    Description: Contains economic statistics in tables, short articles on the latest economic developments, an overview of various aspects of the Icelandic economy, and announcements from the Central Bank of Iceland.

310   CC
HAIGUAN TONGJI/CUSTOMS STATISTICS. (Text in Chinese) q. Haiguan Zongshu, Zonghe Tongji-si, No. 4, Taipingqiao Dajie, Beijing 100810, People's Republic of China. TEL 6011155. Ed. Wang Shunli.

BUSINESS AND ECONOMICS — ABSTRACTING, BIBLIOGRAPHIES, STATISTICS

330.021   US   ISSN 0017-7199
HC101
HANDBOOK OF BASIC ECONOMIC STATISTICS;* a manual of basic economic data on industry, commerce, labor and agriculture in the United States. 1947. m. $132 or q. with m. supp., $66; or a. with m. supp., $33. Economic Statistics Bureau of Washington, D.C., 4550 N. Park Ave., Apt. T106, Chevy Chase, MD 20815-7233.
TEL 202-393-5070. Ed. Charles L. Franklin. mkt.; index.

382   UN   ISSN 0251-9461
HANDBOOK OF INTERNATIONAL TRADE AND DEVELOPMENT STATISTICS - UNITED NATIONS/MANUEL DE STATISTIQUES DU COMMERCE INTERNATIONAL ET DU DEVELOPMENT - NATIONS UNIES. (Text in English and French) 1969. a. $80. United Nations Conference on Trade and Development, Palais des Nations, CH-1211 Geneva 10, Switzerland. (Dist. by: United Nations Publications, Rm. DC2-853, New York, NY 10017. TEL 212-963-8302. FAX 212-963-6489; Also dist. in N. America by: Unipub, 4611-F Assembly Dr., Lanham, MD 20706. TEL 310-459-7666. FAX 310-459-0056) Ed. Juergen Richtering. circ. 5,200. (back issues avail.) **Indexed:** IIS. **Document type:** bulletin.
—BLDSC (4250.560000).
Description: Analyzes world trade and development through statistical data. Includes data on world financial transactions and indebtedness to foreign countries.

331 317   US
HANDBOOK OF OKLAHOMA EMPLOYMENT STATISTICS. 1952. a. (in 2 vols.). free. Employment Security Commission, Research Department, Will Rogers Bldg., 2401 N. Lincoln Blvd., Oklahoma City, OK 73105. Ed. Brenda Beed. circ. 750. **Document type:** government publication.

382   UN   ISSN 0256-2189
HANDBOOK OF STATE TRADING ORGANIZATIONS OF DEVELOPING COUNTRIES/REPERTOIRE DES ORGANISMES DE COMMERCE D'ETAT DES PAYS EN DEVELOPPEMENT/REPERTORIO DE LAS ORGANIZACIONES COMERCIALES ESTATALES DE PAISES EN DESARROLLO/DALIL AL-HAY'AT AL-TIGANIYYA AL-HUKUMIYYA FI AL-BULDAN AN-NAMIYA. (Text in Arabic, English, French, Spanish) 1983. irreg. (in 2 vols.); latest 1990. price varies. United Nations Conference on Trade and Development, Palais des Nations, 1211 Geneva 10, Switzerland. (Dist. by: United Nations Publications, Rm. DC2-853, New York, NY 10017. TEL 212-963-8302. FAX 212-963-3489; Also dist. in N. America by: Unipub, 4611-F Assembly Dr., Lanham, MD 20706. TEL 310-459-7666. FAX 310-459-0056) **Document type:** government publication.
Description: Conveys relevant information on state trading organizations in developing nations.

330   US
HARVARD BUSINESS REVIEW CATALOG (YEAR). a. $10 to individuals; academic institutions $5. (Harvard University. Graduate School of Business Administration) Harvard Business School Publishing Corporation, Soldier's Field Rd., Boston, MA 02163. TEL 617-495-6192. FAX 617-495-6985. index, cum.index.
Description: Includes indexes of all Harvard Business Review articles published between 1985 and 1990 and best-selling articles published between 1952 and 1985.

330 016   US   ISSN 0735-2336
HARVARD BUSINESS SCHOOL. BAKER LIBRARY. RECENT ADDITIONS TO BAKER LIBRARY. Key Title: Recent Additions to Baker Library. vol.13, 1973. m. $45 (foreign $60) (effective 1997). Harvard Business School, Baker Library, Soldiers Field, Boston, MA 02163. TEL 617-495-6405. circ. 1,000. (processed) **Document type:** bibliography.
Former titles: Harvard University. Graduate School of Business Administration. Baker Library. Recent Additions to Baker Library; (until 1979): New Books in Business and Economics (ISSN 0028-4319)
Description: New titles listed by broad subject areas.

650 016   US   ISSN 1044-2111
Z7164.C81
HARVARD BUSINESS SCHOOL. CORE COLLECTION, AN AUTHOR, TITLE AND SUBJECT GUIDE. Key Title: Harvard Business School Core Collection. 1969. a. $65. Harvard Business School, 60 Harvard Way, Boston, MA 02163. TEL 617-495-6192.
FAX 617-495-6985. E-mail: custserv@hbsp.harvard.edu; URL: http://www.hbsp.harvard.edu. R&P contact: R. Krout. adv. contact: Carol Concannon. **Document type:** bibliography.
Former titles: Harvard Business School. Publishing Division. Core Collection, An Author and Subject Guide; (until 1988): Harvard Business School. Baker Library. Core Collection, an Author, Title and Subject Guide (ISSN 0730-6121); Harvard University. Graduate School of Business Administration. Baker Library. Core Collection, an Author, Title and Subject Guide.
Description: Index to Harvard reading room collection updated with best and most recent titles.

330 016.33   FI   ISSN 0356-8164
HELSINGIN KAUPPAKORKEAKOULU. JULKAISUSARJA D.. (Text in English and Finnish) 1975. irreg. price varies. Helsingin Kauppakorkeakoulu - Helsinki School of Economics, Runeberginkatu 22-24, FIN-00100 Helsinki 10, Finland. Ed.Bd. bibl. circ. 300.
—BLDSC (4286.718100).

330.9 352   GW
HERNE IN ZAHLEN. JAHRBUCH (YEAR). 1956. a. DM.35. Stadt Herne, Amt fuer Informationsverarbeitung und Stadtforschung, Postfach 101820, 44621 Herne, Germany.
TEL 49-2323-162100. FAX 49-2323-162311. stat. circ. 450. **Document type:** government publication.
Formerly: Herne in Zahlen. Jahresheft (Year).

330.9 352   GW
HERNE IN ZAHLEN. MONATSBERICHT. 1992. m. DM.5. Stadt Herne, Amt fuer Informationsverarbeitung und Stadtforschung, Postfach 101820, 44621 Herne, Germany. TEL 49-2323-162100.
FAX 49-2323-162311. circ. 100. **Document type:** government publication.

330.9 352   GW
HERNE IN ZAHLEN. VIERTELJAHRESBERICHTE. 1956. q. DM.10. Stadt Herne, Amt fuer Informationsverarbeitung und Stadtforschung, Postfach 101820, 44621 Herne, Germany. TEL 49-2323-162100. FAX 49-2323-162311. circ. 450. **Document type:** government publication.

HONG KONG. CENSUS AND STATISTICS DEPARTMENT. CONSUMER PRICE INDEX. ANNUAL REPORT. see *STATISTICS*

HONG KONG. CENSUS AND STATISTICS DEPARTMENT. CONSUMER PRICE INDEX. REPORT. see *STATISTICS*

339 315   CC
HONG KONG. CENSUS AND STATISTICS DEPARTMENT. ESTIMATES OF GROSS DOMESTIC PRODUCT. (Text in English) 1966. a. HK.$64. Census and Statistics Department, Wanchai Tower, 12 Harbour Rd., Central, Hong Kong, People's Republic of China. TEL 852-2598-8197. FAX 852-2598-7482.
(Subscr. to: Director of Information Services, Information Services Department, 28-F Siu On Centre, 188 Lockhart Rd., Wanchai, Hong Kong; People's Republic of China) **Document type:** government publication.

331   CC
HONG KONG. CENSUS AND STATISTICS DEPARTMENT. HALF-YEARLY REPORT OF WAGE STATISTICS. (Text in English) 1982. s-a. HK.$57. Census and Statistics Department, Wanchai Tower, 12 Harbour Rd., Central, Hong Kong, People's Republic of China. TEL 852-2598-8197. FAX 852-2598-7482.
(Subscr. to: Director of Information Services, Information Services Department, 28-F Siu On Centre, 188 Lockhart Rd., Wanchai, Hong Kong; People's Republic of China) **Document type:** government publication.
Former titles: Hong Kong. Census and Statistics Department. Report on Half-Yearly Survey of Wages, Salaries and Employee Benefits. Volume 1; Hong Kong. Census and Statistics Department. Quarterly Report of Wages, Salaries and Employee Benefits Statistics. Volume 1; Hong Kong. Census and Statistics Department. Wage Statistics Report.

HONG KONG. CENSUS AND STATISTICS DEPARTMENT. MONTHLY SURVEY OF RETAIL SALES. REPORT. see *STATISTICS*

331   CC
HONG KONG. CENSUS AND STATISTICS DEPARTMENT. QUARTERLY REPORT ON GENERAL HOUSEHOLD SURVEY. 1981. q. HK.$53. Census and Statistics Department, Wanchai Tower, 12 Harbour Rd., Central, Hong Kong, People's Republic of China. TEL 852-2598-8197. FAX 852-2598-7482.
(Subscr. to: Director of Information Services, Information Services Department, 28-F Siu On Centre, 188 Lockhart Rd., Wanchai, Hong Kong; People's Republic of China) **Document type:** government publication.
Former titles: Hong Kong. Census and Statistics Department. General Household Survey Labour Force Characteristics; (until 1981): Hong Kong. Census and Statistics Department. Labour Force Survey Report.

331   CC
HONG KONG. CENSUS AND STATISTICS DEPARTMENT. SALARIES AND EMPLOYEE BENEFITS STATISTICS. REPORT. MANAGERIAL AND PROFESSIONAL EMPLOYEES (EXCLUDING TOP MANAGEMENT). (Text in Chinese, English) 1985. a. HK.$25. Census and Statistics Department, Wanchai Tower, 12 Harbour Rd., Central, Hong Kong, People's Republic of China. TEL 852-2598-8197. FAX 852-2598-7482.
(Subscr. to: Director of Information Services, Information Services Dept., 28-F Siu On Centre, 188 Lockhart Rd., Wanchai, Hong Kong; People's Republic of China) Ed.Bd. **Document type:** government publication.

382   CC
HONG KONG. CENSUS AND STATISTICS DEPARTMENT. TRADE INDEX NUMBERS. (Text in Chinese, English) m. HK.$14. Census and Statistics Department, Wanchai Tower, 12 Harbour Rd., Central, Hong Kong, People's Republic of China.
TEL 852-2598-8197. FAX 852-2598-7482.
(Subscr. to: Director of Information Services, Information Services Dept., 28-F Siu On Centre, 188 Lockhart Rd., Wanchai, Hong Kong; People's Republic of China) Ed.Bd. (back issues avail.) **Document type:** government publication.

382   CC
HONG KONG. CENSUS AND STATISTICS DEPARTMENT. WHOLESALE, RETAIL AND IMPORT - EXPORT TRADES, RESTAURANTS AND HOTELS. SURVEY. (Text in Chinese, English) 1984. a. HK.$34. Census and Statistics Department, Wanchai Tower, 12 Harbour Rd., Central, Hong Kong, People's Republic of China. TEL 852-2598-8197. FAX 852-2598-7482.
(Subscr. to: Director of Information Services, Information Serivces Dept., 28-F Siu On Centre, 188 Lockhart Rd., Wanchai, Hong Kong; People's Republic of China) Ed.Bd. **Document type:** government publication.

332.1   CC
HONG KONG. COMMISSIONER OF BANKING. ANNUAL REPORT. (Editions in Chinese, English) a. HK.$20. Government Publication Centre, G.P.O. Bldg., Ground Fl., Connaught Pl., Hong Kong, People's Republic of China. TEL 852-842-8801. (Subscr. to: Director of Information Services, Information Services Dept., 1 Battery Path, G-F, Central, Hong Kong; People's Republic of China) Ed.Bd. **Document type:** government publication.

330 315   CC
HONG KONG ECONOMIC TRENDS. 1977. m. HK.$4. Census and Statistics Department, Wanchai Tower, 12 Harbour Rd., Central, Hong Kong, People's Republic of China. TEL 852-2598-8197.
FAX 852-2598-7482. (Subscr. to: Director of Information Services, Information Services Department, 28-F Siu On Centre, 188 Lockhart Rd., Wanchai, Hong Kong; People's Republic of China) charts. circ. 500. **Document type:** government publication.
Former titles: Hong Kong Economic Trends and Indexes; Hong Kong Economic Indicators.

BUSINESS AND ECONOMICS — ABSTRACTING, BIBLIOGRAPHIES, STATISTICS

382   CC
HONG KONG EXTERNAL TRADE. 1968. m. HK.$129. Census and Statistics Department, Trade Statistics Dissemination Section, Wanchai Tower, 12 Harbour Rd., Central, Hong Kong, People's Republic of China. TEL 852-2598-8197. FAX 852-2598-7482. (Subscr. to: Director of Information Services, Information Services Department, 28-F Siu On Centre, 188 Lockhart Rd., Wanchai, Hong Kong; People's Republic of China) charts; circ. 700 (controlled). (back issues avail.) **Document type:** government publication.
   Incorporates (1968-1989): Hong Kong Trade Statistics. Summary.
   Description: Contains summary tables on external trade performance, information on important changes in direction and content of trade, trade statistics analyzed by principal products and main markets, and statistics on airborne and seaborne trade.

382 315   CC
HONG KONG TRADE STATISTICS. 1954. m. HK.$7280 (including a. supplement). Census and Statistics Department, Wanchai Tower, 12 Harbour Rd., Central, Hong Kong, People's Republic of China. TEL 852-2598-8197. FAX 852-2598-7482. (Subscr. to: Director of Information Services, Information Services Department, 28-F Siu On Centre, 188 Lockhart Rd., Wanchai, Hong Kong; People's Republic of China) circ. 900. **Document type:** government publication.

330.9 352.7   US   ISSN 1056-5132
HOUSING MARKET STATISTICS. m. $105. National Association of Home Builders of the United States, Economics Mortgage Finance and Housing Policy Division, 1201 15th St., N.W., Washington, DC 20005-2800. TEL 202-822-0245. FAX 202-822-0559. charts. circ. 700. (back issues avail.)
   Formerly (until 1991): Current Housing Situation.
   Description: Compilation of national and regional statistics on housing related indicators.

381 314   HU   ISSN 0866-1146
HF192.H8
HUNGARY. KOZPONTI STATISZTIKAI HIVATAL. BELKERESKEDELM. a. 321 Ft. Statisztikai Kiado Vallalat, Kaszasdulo u. 2, P.O. Box 99, 1300 Budapest 3, Hungary. TEL 36-1-180-3311. FAX 36-1-168-8635. TELEX 22-6699. (Subscr. to: Kultura, Box 149, H-1389 Budapest, Hungary) circ. 1,200. **Document type:** government publication.
   Formed by the 1989 merger of: Hungary. Kozponti Statisztikai Hivatal. A Kiskereskedem es a Fogyasztasi Szolgalt (ISSN 0865-0926) & Hungary. Kozponti Statisztikai Hivatal. Belkereskedelmi Statisztikai Evkonyv (ISSN 0238-9916); Which was formerly: Hungary. Kozponti Statisztikai Hivatal. Belkereskedelmi Evkonyv (ISSN 0134-1138).

331.2 314   HU   ISSN 0133-543X
HD5022.H8
HUNGARY. KOZPONTI STATISZTIKAI HIVATAL. FOGLALKOZTATOTTSAG ES KERESETI ARANYOK. a. Statisztikai Kiado Vallalat, Kaszasdulo u. 2, P.O. Box 99, 1300 Budapest 3, Hungary. TEL 36-1-180-3311. FAX 36-1-168-8635. TELEX 22-6699. (Subscr. to: Kultura, Box 149, H-1389 Budapest, Hungary) stat. circ. 900. **Document type:** government publication.
—BLDSC (3964.277000).

338 690 314   HU   ISSN 0239-1589
HUNGARY. KOZPONTI STATISZTIKAI HIVATAL. GAZDASAG ES STATISZTIKA. (Text in Hungarian; contents page in English, German, Russian) 1949. bi-m. 480 Ft.($14.30) Statisztikai Kiado Vallalat, Kaszasdulo u. 2, P.O. Box 99, 1300 Budapest 3, Hungary. TEL 36-1-180-3311. FAX 36-1-168-8635. TELEX 22-6699. (Subscr. to: Kultura, Box 149, H-1389 Budapest, Hungary) Ed. Albert Kiss. bk.rev.; charts; stat. circ. 1,000. **Document type:** government publication.
—BLDSC (4090.395000).
   Formerly: Hungary. Kozponti Statisztikai Hivatal. Ipari es Epitoipari Statisztikai Ertesito (ISSN 0018-7801)

314 338   HU   ISSN 0133-8684
HUNGARY. KOZPONTI STATISZTIKAI HIVATAL. IPARI ZSEBKONYV. a. 82 Ft. Statisztikai Kiado Vallalat, Kaszasdulo u. 2, P.O. Box 99, 1300 Budapest 3, Hungary. TEL 36-1-180-3311. FAX 36-1-168-8635. TELEX 22-6699. (Subscr. to: Kultura, Box 149, H-1389 Budapest, Hungary) stat. circ. 1,900. **Document type:** government publication.

338 314   HU   ISSN 0209-4002
HC300.2
HUNGARY. KOZPONTI STATISZTIKAI HIVATAL. IPARSTATISZTIKAI EVKONYV. a. 348 Ft. Statisztikai Kiado Vallalat, Kaszasdulo u. 2, P.O. Box 99, 1300 Budapest 3, Hungary. TEL 36-1-180-3311. FAX 36-1-168-8635. TELEX 22-6699. (Subscr. to: Kultura, Box 149, H-1389 Budapest, Hungary) stat. circ. 1,200. **Document type:** government publication.

382 314   HU   ISSN 0139-3634
HF192.5
HUNGARY. KOZPONTI STATISZTIKAI HIVATAL. KULKERESKEDELMI STATISZTIKAI EVKONYV. 1971. a. 411 Ft. (Kozponti Statisztikai Hivatal) Statisztikai Kiado Vallalat, Kaszasdulo u. 2, P.O. Box 99, 1300 Budapest 3, Hungary. TEL 36-1-180-3311. FAX 36-1-168-8635. TELEX 22-6699. (Subscr. to: Kultura, Box 149, H-1389 Budapest, Hungary) stat. circ. 1,200. **Document type:** government publication.

330   HU   ISSN 0455-1923
HC267.A23
HUNGARY. KOZPONTI STATISZTIKAI HIVATAL. LAKOSSAG JOVEDELME ES FOGYASZTASA. 1960. irreg., latest 1987. (Kozponti Statisztikai Hivatal) Statisztikai Kiado Vallalat, Kaszasulo u. 2, P.O. Box 99, 1300 Budapest 3, Hungary. TEL 36-1-180-3311. FAX 36-1-168-8635. TELEX 22-6699. stat. **Document type:** government publication.
   Formerly (until 1965): Lakossag Fogyasztasa (ISSN 0200-7037)

330.9   AT   ISSN 1030-0856
HUNTER REGION ECONOMIC INDICATORS. 1980. q. Hunter Valley Research Foundation, P.O. Box 323, Hamilton DC, N.S.W. 2303, Australia. TEL 61-49-69-4566. FAX 61-49-614981. E-mail: oukhvrf@cc.newcastle.edu.au. charts. circ. 600. (back issues avail.)
   Formerly: Hunter Region Quarterly Economic Indicators (ISSN 0725-6809)

330   UK
I A L DIRECTORY OF EUROPEAN MARKET REPORTS. a. £150. I A L Consultants, 109 Uxbridge Rd., Ealing, London W5 5TL, England. TEL 44-181-810-0919. FAX 44-181-566-4931. **Document type:** directory.
   Formerly: I A L Directory of Industrial and Business Market Reports.
   Description: Compiles listings of reports from more than 100 leading European and US market research consultancies.

330   II   ISSN 0250-9695
I C S S R JOURNAL OF ABSTRACTS AND REVIEWS: ECONOMICS. (Text in English) 1971. q. Rs.30 to individuals; institutions Rs.50. Indian Council of Social Science Research, 35 Ferozshah Rd., New Delhi 110 001, India. TEL 91-11-388-3091. FAX 91-11-338-8037. TELEX 31-61083-ISSR-IN. (Co-sponsor: Giri Institute of Development Studies) Ed. A.K. Singh. adv.; bk.rev. circ. 550. (back issues avail.) **Document type:** abstracting/indexing.
—BLDSC (4362.091600).
   Description: Abstracts of articles in Indian economics periodicals.

332 016   UN   ISSN 0047-083X
HG3881
I M F SURVEY. French edition: Bulletin du F M I (ISSN 0250-7412); Spanish edition: Boletin del F M I (ISSN 0250-7420) (Editions in English, French, and Spanish) s-m. (23/yr.). $79. International Monetary Fund, Publication Services, 700 19th St., N.W., Ste. C-100, Washington, DC 20431. TEL 202-623-7430. FAX 202-623-7201. Ed. David M. Cheney. abstr.; index. circ. 22,000. (also avail. in microfilm from UMI,CIS; reprint service avail. from UMI) **Indexed:** IIS, Ind.Per.Art.Relat.Law, Key to Econ.Sci., PROMT, World Bank.Abstr.
—UMI.
   Supersedes: International Financial News Survey (ISSN 0020-6717)
   Description: Covers all IMF activities (including all press releases, communiques and major speeches, and SDR valuation) presented in the broader context of developments in the world economy, economic research and policy, national economies, and international finance.

330.9 310   FR   ISSN 1249-4399
I N S E E PICARDIE DOSSIERS. 1994. 4/yr. 200 F. to individuals (Europe 250 F.; elsewhere 290 F.); institutions 170 F. (Europe 212.50 F.); elsewhere 246.50 F.) (effective 1997). Institut National de la Statistique et des Etudes Economiques, Observatoire Regional de Picardie, 1 rue Vincent Auriol, 80040 Amiens Cedex 1, France. TEL 33-3-22973210. FAX 33-3-22973204. TELEX 140 818. Ed. Victor-Pierre Morales; Pub. Christian Gabet. **Document type:** newsletter.

330.9 310   FR   ISSN 1261-3797
▼**I N S E E PICARDIE PREMIERE.** 1995. m. (11/yr.). 100 F. to individuals (Europe 125 F.; elsewhere 155 F.); institutions 85 F. (Europe 106.25 F.; elsewhere 131.75 F.) (effective 1997). Institut National de la Statistique et des Etudes Economiques, Observatoire Regional de Picardie, 1 rue Vincent Auriol, 80040 Amiens Cedex 1, France. TEL 33-3-22973210. FAX 33-3-22973204. TELEX 140 818. Ed. Victor-Pierre Morales; Pub. Christian Gabet. **Document type:** newsletter.

330.9 310   FR   ISSN 0396-3128
HC277.P5
I N S E E PICARDIE RELAIS. Key Title: Relais. 1977. m. (11/yr.). 120 F. to individuals (Europe 150 F.; elsewhere 170 F.); institutions 102 F. (Europe 127.50 F.; elsewhere 144.50 F.) (effective 1997). Institut National de la Statistique et des Etudes Economiques, Observatoire Economique Regional de Picardie, 1 rue Vincent Auriol, 80040 Amiens Cedex 1, France. TEL 33-3-22973210. FAX 33-3-22973204. TELEX 140 818. Ed. Victor-Pierre Morales; Pub. Christian Gabet. (back issues avail.) **Document type:** newsletter.

382   IC   ISSN 1024-7475
▼**ICELANDIC EXTERNAL TRADE;** commodities and countries. Icelandic edition: Utanrikisverslun (ISSN 1024-7483) (Text in English) 1995. a. $22 (effective 1997). Hagstofa Islands - Statistics Iceland, Skuggasund 3, IS-150 Reykjavik, Iceland. FAX 354-562-8865. E-mail: hagstofa@hag.stjr.is. Dir. Hallgrimur Snorrason. (back issues avail.) **Document type:** government publication.

330   FR   ISSN 0984-4724
ILE DE FRANCE A LA PAGE. 1987. m. 173 F. (foreign 216 F.) (effective 1997). Institut National de la Statistique et des Etudes Economiques (INSEE), Direction Regionale d'Ile-de-France, 7 rue Stephenson, Montigny-le-Bretonneux, 78188 Saint-Quentin-en-Yvelines Cedex, France. TEL 33-1-30969000. FAX 33-1-30969001. Ed. Annie Etienne. adv. contact: Jacqueline Riou. bk.rev. circ. 800.
   Description: Statistics and economic articles about l'Ile-de-France.

336   US
ILLINOIS PROPERTY TAX STATISTICS. 1940. a. free. Department of Revenue, Office of Local Government Services, 101 W. Jefferson St., Mail Code 3-520, Springfield, IL 62702. FAX 217-524-0526. Ed. Sharon Logsdon. stat. circ. 1,400. **Document type:** government publication.

BUSINESS AND ECONOMICS — ABSTRACTING, BIBLIOGRAPHIES, STATISTICS

310   AF
IMPORTS STATISTICS OF AFGHANISTAN/IHSA'IYAH-I AMUAL-I VARIDATI-I AFGHANISTAN. (Text in English or Persian) a. $20. Central Statistical Office, Nader Shah Minah, Block No. 4, Box 2002, Kabul, Afghanistan. stat. **Document type:** government publication.

016 330   MR
INDEX ANALYTIQUE SIGNALETIQUE BIBLIOGRAPHIQUE. (Text in French) 1972. irreg. (4-6/yr.). DH.120 per issue. Ministere de la Population, Centre National de Documentation, Charii Ahmed Cherkaoui - Haut Agdal, B.P. 826 - 10004, Rabat, Morocco. TEL 212-7-774944. FAX 212-7-773134. TELEX CND 310-52 M. E-mail: maghridoc@wizarat-sukkan.sukkan.gov.ma; URL: http://wizarat-sukkan.sukkan.gov.ma. Ed. Ahmed Fassi Fihri. adv.; bk.rev. circ. 1,000. (also avail. in microfiche) **Document type:** bibliography, government publication.
● Also available online.
Formerly (until 1994, no.48): I D E S T (Index Documentation - Economie - Science - Technique) (ISSN 0851-0016)
Description: Multi-disciplinary periodical bibliography which includes documents published in Morocco and about Morocco.

330 016   US   ISSN 0536-647X
Z7164.E2
INDEX OF ECONOMIC ARTICLES IN JOURNALS AND COLLECTIVE VOLUMES. 1961. irreg., latest 1992. $110. American Economic Association, 2014 Broadway, Ste. 305, Nashville, TN 37203. TEL 615-322-2595. (Subscr. to: JEL, 4615 Fifth Ave., Pittsburgh, PA 15213) (back issues avail.) **Document type:** abstracting/indexing.
● Also available online. Vendor(s): Knight-Ridder Information, Inc. (File no.139).
Description: Lists by subject category and by author, articles in economic journals and in collective volumes published during a specific year.

382   UK   ISSN 0266-0180
INDEX TO BUSINESS REPORTS. 1978. 2/yr. £19.95 (Europe £24.95) (effective 1997). University of Bradford, Management Centre Library, Emm Ln., Bradford BD9 4JL, England. TEL 44-1274-384306. Ed. Jenny Finder. circ. 400. **Document type:** abstracting/indexing.
—BLDSC (4377.343000).
Description: Provides access to about 800 major special reports on a wide range of topics: industrial, commercial, financial and economic subjects.

353 016   US   ISSN 0149-6166
INDEX TO FEDERAL TAX ARTICLES (SUPPLEMENT). q. $425 (effective 1997). Warren, Gorham & Lamont, 395 Hudson St., New York, NY 10014. TEL 212-367-3000. FAX 212-367-5113. (Subscr. to: The Park Square Bldg., 31 St. James Ave., Boston, MA 02116-4112. TEL 800-950-1207) (looseleaf format) **Document type:** abstracting/indexing.
—UnCover.
Description: Lists every significant article on federal income, estate, and gift taxation since 1913, including information by professionals about various tax issues.

330 016   II   ISSN 0019-4026
Z7164.E2
INDEX TO INDIAN ECONOMIC JOURNALS. 1966. m. Rs.350($150) Information Research Academy, 37 Amir Ali Ave., Calcutta 700019, India. Ed. Partha Subir Guha. adv.; bk.rev.; cum.index. circ. 2,100. (also avail. in microfilm) **Document type:** abstracting/indexing.
Description: Indexes all economic and allied periodicals published in India.

330   II
INDIA. CENTRAL STATISTICAL ORGANIZATION. NATIONAL ACCOUNTS STATISTICS: SOURCES AND METHODS. 1980. irreg. Rs.16.50($5.94) Central Statistical Organisation, Sardar Patel Bhavan, Sansad Marg, New Delhi 110001, India. **Document type:** government publication.

331 315   II
INDIA. LABOUR BUREAU. POCKET BOOK OF LABOUR STATISTICS. 1959. a. Rs.15($5.40) Labour Bureau, Simla 171004, India. (Subscr. to: Controller of Publications, Government of India, Civil Lines, Delhi 110054, India) circ. 2,700. **Document type:** government publication.

331 016   II
INDIA. MINISTRY OF LABOUR. BULLETIN OF CURRENT AWARENESS. Ministry of Labour, Library, Sharam Shakti Bhavan, Rafi Marg, New Delhi, India. (processed) **Document type:** government publication.
Formerly: Labour Bulletin of Current Awareness; Which superseded: India. Department of Labour and Employment. Library. Documentation of Labour.

INDIAN DEOILED CAKES EXPORTERS' PERFORMANCE MONITOR. see AGRICULTURE — Abstracting, Bibliographies, Statistics

INDIAN GRANITE EXPORTERS' PERFORMANCE MONITOR. see MINES AND MINING INDUSTRY — Abstracting, Bibliographies, Statistics

658 016   II   ISSN 0019-5820
INDIAN MANAGEMENT ABSTRACTS. 1972. q. Rs.350($150) Information Research Academy, 37 Amir Ali Ave., Calcutta 700019, India. Ed. Partha Subir Guha. adv.; bk.rev.; abstr.; cum.index. circ. 2,050. **Document type:** abstracting/indexing.
Description: Abstracts articles on management and allied topics published in India.

INDIAN RICE EXPORTERS' PERFORMANCE MONITOR. see FOOD AND FOOD INDUSTRIES — Abstracting, Bibliographies, Statistics

INDIAN SPICES EXPORTERS' PERFORMANCE MONITOR. see FOOD AND FOOD INDUSTRIES — Abstracting, Bibliographies, Statistics

INDIAN TEA EXPORTERS' PERFORMANCE MONITOR. see FOOD AND FOOD INDUSTRIES — Abstracting, Bibliographies, Statistics

INDIANA. DEPARTMENT OF EMPLOYMENT AND TRAINING SERVICES. UNEMPLOYMENT INSURANCE CLAIMS BY AREA. see INSURANCE — Abstracting, Bibliographies, Statistics

INDIANA. DEPARTMENT OF EMPLOYMENT AND TRAINING SERVICES. UNEMPLOYMENT INSURANCE PAYMENTS BY INDUSTRY. see INSURANCE — Abstracting, Bibliographies, Statistics

332   MX   ISSN 0188-3909
INDICADORES BURSATILES. English edition: Mexican Stock Exchange. Facts and Figures. m. $227 (effective May 1996). Bolsa Mexicana de Valores, S.A. de C.V. - Mexican Stock Exchange, Paseo de la Reforma 255, 06500 Mexico D.F., Mexico. TEL 525-726-67-91. FAX 525-591-05-34.
Description: Contains information on the securities market, trading by issue and series, foreign investment in stocks, trading summary by brokerage firm, methodological notes and member directory.

331.11   VE   ISSN 0798-8796
INDICADORES DE LA FUERZA DE TRABAJO; total nacional y por regiones. 1967. s-a. Bs.400 (for 1992 vols.). Oficina Central de Estadistica e Informatica, Apdo. de Correos 4593, Carmelitas, Caracas 1010A, Venezuela. TEL 58-2-782-11-33. FAX 58-2-781-13-80. **Document type:** government publication.
Formerly (until 1983): Encuesta de Hogares por Muestreo.

339 318   EC   ISSN 0019-7025
INDICE DE PRECIOS AL CONSUMIDOR; area urbana. 1953. m. S/140($8) per no. Instituto Nacional de Estadistica y Censos, Av. 10 de Agosto 229, Quito, Ecuador. TEL 519320. FAX 513557. charts; index. circ. 1,000. (processed)

339 318   ES
INDICE DE PRECIOS AL CONSUMIDOR. 1954. m. free or exchange basis. Direccion General de Estadistica y Censos, 1 Calle Poniente y 43 Avenida Sur, San Salvador, El Salvador. stat. **Document type:** government publication.
Formerly (until 1979): Indice de Precios al Consumidor para San Salvador, Mejicanos y Villa Delgado (ISSN 0019-7009)

330 301 320   SP   ISSN 0213-0521
INDICE ESPANOL DE CIENCIAS SOCIALES. SERIES B: ECONOMICS, SOCIOLOGY AND POLITICAL SCIENCE. 1979. a. 9000 ptas. or exchange basis (effective 1997). Centro de Informacion y Documentacion Cientifica (Cindoc), Joaquin Costa 22, 28002 Madrid, Spain. TEL 34-1-4111098. FAX 34-1-5645069. E-mail: sdi@cindoc.csic.es. Ed. Angel Villagra. (also avail. in diskette format) **Document type:** abstracting/indexing.
● Also available online.
Also available on CD-ROM.
Supersedes in part (in 1982): Indice Espanol de Ciencias Sociales (ISSN 0211-1373)

330.9   US
INDIVIDUAL BANK REPORTS. m. $2800 for 1600 bpi in US, Canada, Mexico; elsewhere $5600. (Federal Reserve System) U.S. National Technical Information Service, 5825 Port Royal Rd., Springfield, VA 22161. TEL 703-487-4630. (magnetic tape)
Description: Balance sheet and income statement for insured commercial banks, mutual savings banks, Banking Edge Act and Agreement Corporations, branches and agencies of foreign banks, and New York State investment companies.

339   IO   ISSN 0126-2319
INDONESIA. CENTRAL BUREAU OF STATISTICS. ECONOMIC INDICATOR BULLETIN. (Text in English, Indonesian) 1970. m. Rps.12000($5.25) Central Bureau of Statistics - Biro Pusat Statistik, Jalan Dr. Sutomo No. 8, Box 3, Jakarta Pusat, Indonesia. TEL 62-21-372808. charts; illus. circ. 900. **Document type:** government publication, bulletin.

315.98   IO   ISSN 0376-9984
HA1815
INDONESIA STATISTICS. (Text in English) a. First National City Bank, Jl. Thamrin 45, Box 2463, Jakarta, Indonesia.

331 016   US   ISSN 0070-0142
INDUSTRIAL AND LABOR RELATIONS BIBLIOGRAPHY SERIES. 1952. irreg., no.17, 1994. price varies. (New York State School of Industrial and Labor Relations) I L R Press, Cornell University Press, 512 E. State St., Ithaca, NY 14850. TEL 607-277-2338; 800-666-2211. Ed. Frances Benson. R&P contact: Clare Wellnitz. adv. contact: Heidi Marschner. **Indexed:** Curr.Cont., E.I. **Document type:** monographic series.

330 310   UN
HC59
INDUSTRIAL COMMODITY STATISTICS YEARBOOK. 1950. a. $110 (effective 1997). (United Nations, Department of Economic and Social Affairs) United Nations Publications, Sales and Marketing Section, Room DC2-0853, New York, NY 10017. TEL 212-963-8300; 800-253-9646. FAX 212-963-3489. E-mail: publications@un.org; URL: http://www.un.org/publications. (also avail. in microfiche from CIS) **Indexed:** IIS.
—CISTI.
Former titles (until 1992): Industrial Statistics Yearbook (ISSN 0257-7208); (until 1981): Yearbook of Industrial Statistics (ISSN 0250-9873); (until 1973): Growth of World Industry.

330 016   US
INDUSTRIAL LITERATURE REVIEW. 1976. s-a. Thomas Publishing Company, Five Penn Plaza, New York, New York, NY 10001. TEL 212-629-1551. adv.; bibl. circ. 202,146.

330.9   US
INDUSTRIAL PRODUCTION INDEX. m. $200 per no. (outside N. America $400). (Federal Reserve System) U.S. National Technical Information Service, 5825 Port Royal Rd., Springfield, VA 22161. TEL 703-487-4630. stat. (magnetic tape; also avail. in microfiche from CIS; reprint service avail. from CIS) **Indexed:** Amer.Stat.Ind. (1974-). **Document type:** government publication.
Description: Measures the physical output of US factories, mines, and electric and gas utilities expressed as a percentage of production in the base period (currently 1967). Both seasonally adjusted and not seasonally adjusted data are shown.

BUSINESS AND ECONOMICS — ABSTRACTING, BIBLIOGRAPHIES, STATISTICS

314
HC241.2 — EI — ISSN 0258-1922
INDUSTRIAL TRENDS. m. $140. (Statistical Office of the European Communities) Office for Official Publications of the European Communities, Rue Alcide de Gasperi, 2920 Luxembourg, Luxembourg. (Dist. in U.S. by: Unipub 4611-F Assembly Dr., Lanham, MD 20706-4391. TEL 800-274-4888. FAX 301-459-0056) (also avail. in microfiche from CIS) **Indexed:** IIS.
—BLDSC (4462.758000).
Description: Information on industrial activity in the European Community.

338 314 — YU
INDUSTRIJSKI PROIZVODI. (Subseries of: Statisticki Bilten) a. 30 din.($1.67) Savezni Zavod za Statistiku, Kneza Milosa 20, Belgrade, Yugoslavia. TEL 38-681-999. circ. 1,000. **Document type:** government publication.

330
HB235.C2 — CN — ISSN 0700-2033
INDUSTRY PRICE INDEXES. 1971. m. Can.$182($218) (foreign $255). Statistics Canada, Operations and Integration Division, Circulation Management, Jean Talon Bldg., 2-C12, Tunney's Pasture, Ottawa, ON K1A 0T6, Canada. TEL 613-951-7277; 800-267-6677. FAX 613-951-1584. URL: http://www.statcan.ca. **Document type:** government publication.
Description: Indexes of industry selling prices for manufacturing industries, with commodity detail.

310 332.6
HG4961 — US — ISSN 1047-3114
INDUSTRY REVIEW. s-a. $495. Moody's Investors Service, (Subsidiary of: Dun & Bradstreet Corporation), 99 Church St., New York, NY 10007. TEL 212-553-0300. FAX 212-553-4700. stat.
—CCC.
Description: Covers comparative statistics and rankings of 4,000 leading corporations in 139 industry groups.

382 — SP
INFORMACION COMERCIAL ESPANOLA. SECTOR EXTERIOR (YEAR). 1986. a. 2100 ptas. Ministerio de Comercio y Turismo, Paseo de la Castellana 162, pl. 16, 28046 Madrid, Spain. TEL 34-1-349-36-47. FAX 34-1-349-36-34. circ. 1,500. **Document type:** government publication.

THE INFORMATION REPORT. see *BIBLIOGRAPHIES*

331 — BL
INFORME P E D. (Pesquisa de Emprego e Desemprego) 1991. m. free in Brazil. Fundacao de Economia e Estatistica, Rua Duque de Caxias 1691, 90010-283 Porto Alegre RG, Brazil. TEL 55-512-259455. FAX 55-512-25006. Ed. Calino Pacheco Filho. **Document type:** newsletter.
Description: Presents data on employment, unemployment and earnings in the metropolitan region.

330.9
HA1037 — FG — ISSN 0751-7599
INSTITUT NATIONAL DE LA STATISTIQUE ET DES ETUDES ECONOMIQUES. SERVICE DEPARTEMENTAL DE LA GUYANE. BULLETIN TRIMESTRIEL DE STATISTIQUES. 1981. 4/yr. Institut National de la Statistique et des Etudes Economiques, 1 rue Maillard Dumesle, B.P. 6017, 97306 Cayenne Cedex, French Guyana.

INSTITUT ZA MEDUNARODNU POLITIKU I PRIVREDU. BILTEN DOKUMENTACIJE. see *POLITICAL SCIENCE — Abstracting, Bibliographies, Statistics*

338.9
HC59.69 — UK — ISSN 0955-0569
INSTITUTE OF DEVELOPMENT STUDIES. DEVELOPMENT BIBLIOGRAPHY SERIES. 1988. irreg. (1-3/yr.). price varies. Institute of Development Studies, University of Sussex, Brighton, Sussex BN1 9RE, England. TEL 44-1273-606261. FAX 44-1273-678420. TELEX 877997 IDS BTN G. Ed. Katherine Henry. circ. 500. **Document type:** bibliography.
Description: Contains bibliographies devoted to a key theme in development studies.

330 310 — NZ — ISSN 0110-7321
INTER-INDUSTRY STUDY OF THE NEW ZEALAND ECONOMY. 1957. quinquennial. NZ.$49.50. Department of Statistics, P.O. Box 2922, Wellington, New Zealand. **Document type:** government publication.

330 016 — UK — ISSN 0085-204X
Z7164.E2
INTERNATIONAL BIBLIOGRAPHY OF THE SOCIAL SCIENCES. ECONOMICS. Title page also reads: International Bibliography of Economics. 1952. a. £125($230) throughout Europe. (British Library of Political and Economic Science) Routledge, 11 New Fetter Ln., London EC4P 4EE, England. TEL 44-171-583-9855. FAX 44-171-583-0701. TELEX 263398 ROUT G. URL: http://www.routledge.com/routledge/journal/journals.html. Ed. Lynne J. Brindley. adv. circ. 2,000. (reprint service avail. from KTO) **Document type:** academic/scholarly publication, abstracting/indexing, bibliography.
●Also available online. Vendor(s): QL Systems Ltd.
—BLDSC (4537.111000).
Description: Indexes monographs and the contents of more than 2,000 journals in the social sciences from a selective bibliography by subject, geographical terms, and author.

INTERNATIONAL DEVELOPMENT ABSTRACTS. see *GEOGRAPHY — Abstracting, Bibliographies, Statistics*

332 310 — UN — ISSN 0020-6725
HG3881
INTERNATIONAL FINANCIAL STATISTICS. French edition: Statistiques Financieres Internationales (ISSN 0252-2977); Spanish edition: Estadisticas Financieras Internacionales (ISSN 0252-3078) 1948. m. (plus annual issue). $218 ($109 to university faculty and students). International Monetary Fund, Publications Unit, 700 19th St., N.W., Washington, DC 20431. TEL 202-623-7430. FAX 202-623-7201. Ed. John B. McLenaghan. mkt.; charts. circ. 12,500. (also avail. in microfilm from UMI,BHP,PMC; microfiche from CIS; magnetic tape; reprint service avail. from UMI) **Indexed:** Cadscan, IIS, Intl.Mgmt.Info., Key to Econ.Sci., Lead Abstr., Mid.East: Abstr.& Ind., P.A.I.S., PROMT, Zincscan.
●Also available online. Vendor(s): National Data Corp.
Also available on CD-ROM.
—UMI.
Description: Covers all aspects of international and domestic finance.

332 — UN — ISSN 0250-7463
HG61
INTERNATIONAL FINANCIAL STATISTICS YEARBOOK. French edition: Statistiques Financieres Internationales Annuaire (ISSN 0252-029X); Spanish edition: Estadisticas Financieras Internacionales Anuario (ISSN 0252-3043) 1976. a. $50. International Monetary Fund, Publication Services, 700 19th St., N.W., Washington, DC 20431. TEL 202-623-7430. FAX 202-623-7201. (also avail. in microfiche from CIS; reprint service avail. from UMI) **Indexed:** IIS.
—BLDSC (4540.201200).
Description: Cumulates over 35 years of annual data, by country, from the monthly issues of IFS including some additional time series in country tables and some additional tables of area and world aggregates.

331 — UN — ISSN 1010-8106
INTERNATIONAL INSTITUTE FOR LABOUR STUDIES. BIBLIOGRAPHY SERIES. 1979. irreg., latest no.17, 1993. price varies. International Institute for Labour Studies, P.O. Box 6, CH-1211 Geneva 22, Switzerland. TEL 41-22-799-6128. FAX 41-22-788-0950. (back issues avail.) **Document type:** bibliography.
Description: Bibliographic references and analyses of the literature covering recent and emerging labour and social questions.

382 016 — US — ISSN 0020-7004
INTERNATIONAL INTERTRADE INDEX; new foreign products-marketing techniques. (Supplement avail.: Foreign Trade Fairs New Products) 1955. m. $45 (effective 1998). Box 636, Federal Sq., Newark, NJ 07101. TEL 908-686-2382. FAX 201-622-1740. Ed. John E. Felber. abstr.; pat. (looseleaf format) **Document type:** catalog.
Formerly: International Import Index.
Description: Lists new imported products available from foreign manufacturers for import into the U.S.

INTERNATIONAL JOURNAL OF INFORMATION AND MANAGEMENT SCIENCES. see *BUSINESS AND ECONOMICS — Management*

331 016 — UN — ISSN 0020-7756
Z7164.L1
INTERNATIONAL LABOUR DOCUMENTATION. (Supplementary list for internal use only) 1965. m. 100 SFr.($80) (International Labour Office) I L O Publications, CH-1211 Geneva 22, Switzerland. TEL 41-22-799-6111. FAX 41-22-798-6358. TELEX 415647-ILO-CH. (Dist. in US by: I L O Publications Center, 49 Sheridan Ave., Albany, NY 12210. TEL 518-436-9686. FAX 518-436-7433) abstr.; cum.index. circ. 1,300. (also avail. in microfiche from ILO) **Indexed:** HR Rep., Popul.Ind. **Document type:** bulletin.
●Also available online. Vendor(s): European Space Agency (File no.53/LABORDOC), Human Resources Information Network, Questel Orbit Inc. (LDOC).
—BLDSC (4542.750000). **CCC.**

310 658.8 — UK — ISSN 0308-2938
HA42
INTERNATIONAL MARKETING DATA AND STATISTICS (YEAR). 1975. a. £175($350) for print edition; CD-ROM edition £695 ($1390) (effective 1997). Euromonitor, 60-61 Britton St., London EC1M 5QU, England. TEL 44-171-251-8024. FAX 44-171-608-3149. E-mail: info@euromonitor.com; URL: http://www.euromonitor.com. (Addr. in N. America: Euromonitor International, 122 S. Michigan Ave., Ste. 1200, Chicago, IL 60603. TEL 800-577-3876. FAX 312-922-1157) **Document type:** directory.
●Also available on CD-ROM.
—CISTI.
Description: Provides statistical information for over 160 countries outside Europe, on employment, health, and education.

332 — UN — ISSN 0252-3035
HG3882
INTERNATIONAL MONETARY FUND. BALANCE OF PAYMENTS STATISTICS YEARBOOK. (Balance of Payments Statistics (ISSN 0252-3051) m. edition ceased) 1949. a. $56. International Monetary Fund, Publication Services, 700 19th St., N.W., Washington, DC 20431. TEL 202-623-7430. FAX 202-623-7201. Ed. John B. McLeneghan. circ. 4,000. (also avail. in microform from CIS,IIS; microfiche from CIS; microfilm from BHP; magnetic tape; reprint service avail. from UMI) **Indexed:** IIS.
●Also available online.
—UMI.
Supersedes (in 1981): Balance of Payments Yearbook (ISSN 0378-2662)

332.1 — UN — ISSN 0250-7374
HJ101 — CODEN: GFSYEV
INTERNATIONAL MONETARY FUND. GOVERNMENT FINANCE STATISTICS YEARBOOK. 1977. a. $54. International Monetary Fund, Publication Services, 700 19th St., N.W., Washington, DC 20431. TEL 202-623-7430. FAX 202-623-7201. Ed. Werner Dannemann. charts. circ. 3,000. (also avail. in microform from UMI,CIS; back issues avail.) **Indexed:** IIS, World Bank.Abstr.
—BLDSC (4204.103000).
Description: Provides information on the various units of government, government accounts, the enterprises and financial institutions that governments own and control, and the national sources of data on government operations.

INTERNATIONAL PETROLEUM STATISTICS REPORT. see *STATISTICS*

382 310 — UN — ISSN 1010-447X
INTERNATIONAL TRADE STATISTICS YEARBOOK. 1950. a. (in 2 vols.). $135 (effective 1997). (United Nations Statistical Office) United Nations Publications, Sales and Marketing Section, Room DC2-0853, New York, NY 10017. TEL 212-963-8302; 800-253-9646. FAX 212-963-3489. E-mail: publications@un.org; URL: http://www.un.org/publications. (Or: Distribution and Sales Section, CH-1211 Geneva 10 Switzerland) (also avail. in microfiche from CIS) **Indexed:** IIS.
Formerly (until 1983): United Nations. Yearbook of International Trade Statistics (ISSN 0084-3822)
Description: Covers commodity trade, internationa trade, trade statistics.

330 310   UK
INTERNATIONAL YEARBOOK OF INDUSTRIAL STATISTICS. a. £175 (effective 1997). (United Nations Industrial Development Organization, UN) Edward Elgar Publishing Ltd., Box 330, Lyme, NH 03768. TEL 603-795-2282. FAX 603-795-2818. URL: http://www.e-elgar.co.uk. (US subscr. to: Edward Elgar Publishing, Box 574, Illiston, VT 95495. TEL 800-390-3149. FAX 802-864-7626) stat. circ. 5,000. (tabloid format) **Document type:** trade publication.
    Supersedes (1982-1995): Handbook of Industrial Statistics (ISSN 1014-4641); Incorporates (in 1995): Industrial Statistics Yearbook, Volume 1. General Industrial Statistics; Which was formerly (until 1981): Yearbook of Industrial Statistics (ISSN 0250-9873); (until 1973): Growth of World Industry.
    Description: Presents up-to-date internationally comparable statistics for more than 120 countries at different levels of detail in industry-product specification.

330   GW
INTERNATIONALE WIRTSCHAFTSZAHLEN/INTERNATIONAL ECONOMIC INDICATORS. (Text in English, German) 1980. a. DM.15.80. (Institut der Deutschen Wirtschaft) Deutscher Instituts Verlag GmbH, Postfach 510670, 50942 Cologne, Germany. TEL 49-221-4981452. FAX 49-221-4981592. TELEX 8882768-IWKD. Ed. Joerg Beyfuss. circ. 5,000. **Document type:** trade publication.

332.67 314   YU   ISSN 0351-4129
INVESTICIJE. (Subseries of Statisticki Bilten) 1966. a. 100 din.($3.24) Savezni Zavod za Statistiku, Kneza Milosa 20, Belgrade, Yugoslavia. TEL 38-681-999. circ. 1,000. **Document type:** government publication.

INVESTMENT AND OPERATING COST IN THE PHILIPPINES. see BUSINESS AND ECONOMICS — Investments

330 315   IR
IRAN. MINISTRY OF ECONOMY. BUREAU OF STATISTICS. SERIES. no.49, 1969. irreg. Ministry of Finance and Economic Affairs, Bureau of Statistics, Tehran, Iran. Ed. A. Sh. Shaheen. charts. **Document type:** government publication.

381 315   IR
IRAN. MINISTRY OF ECONOMY. INTERNAL WHOLESALE TRADE STATISTICS.* (Text in English) a. free. Ministry of Finance and Economic Affairs, Bureau of Statistics, Teheran, Iran. circ. controlled. (also avail. in record) **Document type:** government publication.

382 315   IR
IRAN. MINISTRY OF ECONOMY. INTERNATIONAL TRADE STATISTICS.* (Text in English) irreg. (approx. 1/yr.). free. Ministry of Finance and Economic Affairs, Bureau of Statistics, Teheran, Iran. circ. controlled. (also avail. in record) **Document type:** government publication.

338 315   IR   ISSN 0075-0506
IRANIAN INDUSTRIAL STATISTICS. (Text in English and Persian) 1962. a. free. Ministry of Finance and Economic Affairs, Bureau of Statistics, Tehran, Iran. **Document type:** government publication.

382 315   IQ
IRAQ. CENTRAL STATISTICAL ORGANIZATION. QUARTERLY BULLETIN OF FOREIGN TRADE STATISTICS.* (Text in Arabic and English) 1969. q. ID.750. Central Statistical Organization, Nr. an Nusoor Sq., Baghdad, Iraq. circ. 400. **Document type:** government publication.
    Formerly: Iraq. Central Statistical Organization. Monthly Bulletin of Foreign Trade Statistics (ISSN 0027-0245).

338 315   IQ
IRAQ. CENTRAL STATISTICAL ORGANIZATION. RESULTS OF THE INDUSTRIAL SURVEY OF LARGE ESTABLISHMENTS IN IRAQ.* (Text in Arabic and English) 1957. a. ID.1500. Central Statistical Organization, Nr. an Nusoor Sq., Baghdad, Iraq. **Document type:** government publication.

382 315   IQ   ISSN 0021-0900
IRAQ. CENTRAL STATISTICAL ORGANIZATION. SUMMARY OF FOREIGN TRADE STATISTICS.* (Text and title in Arabic and English) 1960. a. ID.250. Central Statistical Organization, Nr an Nusoor Sq., Baghdad, Iraq. circ. 500. **Document type:** government publication.

330   IE   ISSN 1393-0583
IRELAND. CENTRAL STATISTICS OFFICE. ANNUAL SERVICES INQUIRY. 1994. a. I£7. Central Statistics Office, Skehard Rd., Cork, Ireland. TEL 353-21-359000. FAX 353-21-359090. E-mail: information@cso.ie; URL: http://www.cso.ie. **Document type:** government publication.
    Description: Provides estimates of accounting and employment variables based on a sample survey of services firms.

336   IE   ISSN 0791-3370
IRELAND. CENTRAL STATISTICS OFFICE. BALANCE OF INTERNATIONAL PAYMENTS. q. I£8. Central Statistics Office, Skehard Rd., Cork, Ireland. TEL 353-21-359000. FAX 353-21-359090. E-mail: information@cso.ie; URL: http://www.cso.ie. (processed) **Document type:** government publication.
    Description: Estimates of the balance of international payments on current and capital accounts.

330   IE   ISSN 0791-3168
IRELAND. CENTRAL STATISTICS OFFICE. BANKING, INSURANCE AND BUILDING SOCIETIES. EMPLOYMENT AND EARNINGS. q. I£8. Central Statistics Office, Skehard Rd., Cork, Ireland. TEL 353-21-359000. FAX 353-21-359090. E-mail: information@cso.ie; URL: http://www.cso.ie. **Document type:** government publication.
    Description: Monitors employment levels and earnings trends in banks, insurance companies and building societies.

IRELAND. CENTRAL STATISTICS OFFICE. BUILDING AND CONSTRUCTION: AVERAGE EARNINGS AND HOURS WORKED. see BUILDING AND CONSTRUCTION — Abstracting, Bibliographies, Statistics

IRELAND. CENTRAL STATISTICS OFFICE. BUILDING AND CONSTRUCTION. MONTHLY INDEX OF EMPLOYMENT IN PRIVATE FIRMS WITH FIVE OR MORE PERSONS ENGAGED. see BUILDING AND CONSTRUCTION — Abstracting, Bibliographies, Statistics

IRELAND. CENTRAL STATISTICS OFFICE. BUILDING AND CONSTRUCTION PLANNING PERMISSIONS. see BUILDING AND CONSTRUCTION — Abstracting, Bibliographies, Statistics

IRELAND. CENTRAL STATISTICS OFFICE. CENSUS OF BUILDING AND CONSTRUCTION. RESULTS FOR PRIVATE FIRMS WITH 20 OR MORE PERSONS ENGAGED. see BUILDING AND CONSTRUCTION — Abstracting, Bibliographies, Statistics

330 310   IE   ISSN 0790-6080
HC257.I6
IRELAND. CENTRAL STATISTICS OFFICE. CENSUS OF INDUSTRIAL PRODUCTION. 1979. a. £15. Central Statistics Office, Skehard Rd., Cork, Ireland. TEL 353-21-359000. FAX 353-21-359090. E-mail: information@cso.ie; URL: http://www.cso.ie. (Subscr. to: Government Publications Sale Office, Sun Alliance House, Moleswort St., Dublin 2, Ireland. TEL 353-1-6710309) **Document type:** government publication.

330   IE
IRELAND. CENTRAL STATISTICS OFFICE. CENSUS OF INDUSTRIAL PRODUCTION. OVERALL RESULTS FOR LOCAL UNITS. a. I£2. Central Statistics Office, Skehard Rd., Cork, Ireland. TEL 353-21-359000. FAX 353-21-359090. **Document type:** government publication.
    Formerly: Ireland. Central Statistics Office. Census of Industrial Production. Overall Results for Industrial Establishments (ISSN 0790-6099).

330   IE   ISSN 1393-3523
IRELAND. CENTRAL STATISTICS OFFICE. CENSUS OF INDUSTRIAL PRODUCTION, PROVISIONAL OVERALL RESULTS FOR INDUSTRIAL ENTERPRISES AND INDUSTRIAL LOCAL UNITS. 1997. a. I£2. Central Statistics Office, Skehard Rd., Cork, Ireland. TEL 353-21-359000. FAX 353-21-359090. E-mail: information@cso.ie; URL: http://www.cso.ie. **Document type:** government publication.
    Formed by the 1997 merger of: Ireland. Central Statistics Office. Census of Industrial Production, Provisional Overall Results for Industrial Enterprises (ISSN 1393-2578); Which was formerly: Ireland. Central Statistics Office. Census of Industrial Production, Overall Results for Industrial Enterprises (ISSN 0791-2897) & Ireland. Central Statistics Office. Census of Industrial Production, Provisional Overall Results for Industrial Local Units (ISSN 1393-2535); Which was formerly: Ireland. Central Statistics Office. Census of Industrial Production, Provisional Overall Results for Industrial Establishments (ISSN 1393-2586).

IRELAND. CENTRAL STATISTICS OFFICE. CONSUMER PRICE INDEX. see BUSINESS AND ECONOMICS — Marketing And Purchasing

331   IE   ISSN 0791-329X
IRELAND. CENTRAL STATISTICS OFFICE. INDUSTRIAL DISPUTES. q. I£8. Central Statistics Office, Skehard Rd., Cork, Ireland. TEL 353-21-359000. FAX 353-21-359090. E-mail: information@cso.ie; URL: http://www.cso.ie. **Document type:** government publication.
    Formerly: Ireland. Central Statistics Office. Strikes or Lock-outs Reported during the Quarter.

330   IE   ISSN 0791-2900
IRELAND. CENTRAL STATISTICS OFFICE. INDUSTRIAL EARNINGS AND HOURS WORKED. q. I£8. Central Statistics Office, Skehard Rd., Cork, Ireland. TEL 353-21-359000. FAX 353-21-359090. E-mail: information@cso.ie; URL: http://www.cso.ie. **Document type:** government publication.
    Superseded in part: Ireland. Central Statistics Office. Industrial Employment Earnings and Hours Worked.

330   IE   ISSN 0791-2919
IRELAND. CENTRAL STATISTICS OFFICE. INDUSTRIAL EMPLOYMENT. q. I£8. Central Statistics Office, Skehard Rd., Cork, Ireland. TEL 353-21-359000. FAX 353-21-359090. E-mail: information@cso.ie; URL: http://www.cso.ie. **Document type:** government publication.
    Superseded in part: Ireland. Central Statistics Office. Industrial Employment Earnings and Hours Worked.

330   IE   ISSN 0791-2927
IRELAND. CENTRAL STATISTICS OFFICE. INDUSTRIAL EMPLOYMENT EARNINGS AND HOURS WORKED: DETAILS FOR SUPPLEMENTARY N A C E SUB-SECTORS. q. I£8. Central Statistics Office, Skehard Rd., Cork, Ireland. TEL 353-21-359000. FAX 353-21-359090. E-mail: information@cso.ie; URL: http://www.cso.ie. (processed) **Document type:** government publication.
    Formerly: Ireland. Central Statistics Office. Industrial Employment Earnings and Hours Worked: Details for Supplementary N A C E Sub-Groups.

330   IE   ISSN 0790-5130
IRELAND. CENTRAL STATISTICS OFFICE. INDUSTRIAL PRODUCTION INDEX. m. I£24. Central Statistics Office, Skehard Rd., Cork, Ireland. TEL 353-21-359000. FAX 353-21-359090. E-mail: information@cso.ie; URL: http://www.cso.ie. (processed) **Document type:** government publication.
    Description: Monitors current trends in the volume of production of industrial establishments with three or more persons engaged.

330   IE   ISSN 0791-2889
IRELAND. CENTRAL STATISTICS OFFICE. INDUSTRIAL TURNOVER INDEX. m. I£24. Central Statistics Office, Skehard Rd., Cork, Ireland. TEL 353-21-359000. FAX 353-21-359090. E-mail: information@cso.ie; URL: http://www.cso.ie. (processed) **Document type:** government publication.
    Description: Covers industrial establishments with 20 or more persons engaged, measures the change in the level of sales of industrial products irrespective of whether manufactured during the month in question or in previous periods.

BUSINESS AND ECONOMICS — ABSTRACTING, BIBLIOGRAPHIES, STATISTICS

330   IE   ISSN 0791-3176
IRELAND. CENTRAL STATISTICS OFFICE. LABOUR FORCE, PRELIMINARY ESTIMATES. a. I£2. Central Statistics Office, Skehard Rd., Cork, Ireland. TEL 353-21-359000. FAX 353-21-359090. E-mail: information@cso.ie; URL: http://www.cso.ie.
Document type: government publication.
Description: Preliminary estimates of labour force at mid-April.

331   IE   ISSN 0791-0533
IRELAND. CENTRAL STATISTICS OFFICE. LABOUR FORCE SURVEY. a. I£10. Central Statistics Office, Skehard Rd., Cork, Ireland. TEL 353-21-359000. FAX 353-21-359090. E-mail: information@cso.ie; URL: http://www.cso.ie. (Subscr. to: Government Supplies Agency, Trade and Postal Sales, 4-5 Harcourt Rd., Dublin 2, Ireland) **Document type:** government publication.
Formerly: Ireland. Central Statistics Office. Labour Force Survey. First Results (ISSN 0790-5866)
Description: Provides estimates of the total population classified by age, sex and planning region and of the population aged 15 and over classified by principal economic status, industrial group, occupational group, marital status, etc.

331   IE   ISSN 0791-394X
IRELAND. CENTRAL STATISTICS OFFICE. LIVE REGISTER AGE BY DURATION ANALYSIS. s-a. I£4. Central Statistics Office, Skehard Rd., Cork, Ireland. TEL 353-21-359000. FAX 353-21-359090. E-mail: information@cso.ie; URL: http://www.cso.ie.
Document type: government publication.
Formerly: Ireland. Central Statistics Office. Age-by-Duration Analysis of the Live Register.

331   IE   ISSN 0791-3206
IRELAND. CENTRAL STATISTICS OFFICE. LIVE REGISTER AREA ANALYSIS. m. I£24. Central Statistics Office, Skehard Rd., Cork, Ireland. TEL 353-21-359000. FAX 353-21-359090. E-mail: information@cso.ie; URL: http://www.cso.ie. **Document type:** government publication.
Formerly: Ireland. Central Statistics Office. Analysis of the Live Register According to Area of Residence.

330   IE   ISSN 0791-3192
IRELAND. CENTRAL STATISTICS OFFICE. LIVE REGISTER, MONTHLY FLOW ANALYSIS. m. I£24. Central Statistics Office, Skehard Rd., Cork, Ireland. TEL 353-21-359000. FAX 353-21-359090. E-mail: information@cso.ie; URL: http://www.cso.ie.
Document type: government publication.
Description: Information on flows on/off the live register.

331   IE   ISSN 0791-3222
IRELAND. CENTRAL STATISTICS OFFICE. LIVE REGISTER STATEMENT. m. I£24. Central Statistics Office, Skehard Rd., Cork, Ireland. TEL 353-21-359000. FAX 353-21-359090. E-mail: information@cso.ie; URL: http://www.cso.ie. **Document type:** government publication.
Former titles (until 1989): Ireland. Central Statistical Office. Live Register, Monthly Statement (ISSN 0791-3230); (until 1987): Ireland. Central Statistics Office. Monthly Live Register Statement (ISSN 0791-3249)
Description: Provides both seasonally adjusted and unadjusted data on the number of males and females registered at local employment offices on the last Friday of each month.

336   IE   ISSN 0075-0603
IRELAND. CENTRAL STATISTICS OFFICE. NATIONAL INCOME AND EXPENDITURE. 1958. a. I£10. Central Statistics Office, Skehard Rd., Cork, Ireland. TEL 353-21-539000. FAX 353-21-359090. E-mail: information@cso.ie; URL: http://www.cso.ie. (Subscr. to: Government Supplies Agency, 4-5 Harcourt Rd., Dublin 2, Ireland) circ. 2,000. **Document type:** government publication.
Supersedes in part: Irish Statistical Survey.

330   IE   ISSN 0791-8682
IRELAND. CENTRAL STATISTICS OFFICE. PARTICULARS OF VEHICLES LICENSED FOR THE FIRST TIME IN EACH COUNTY AND COUNTY BOROUGH DURING THE MONTH. m. I£24. Central Statistics Office, Skehard Rd., Cork, Ireland. TEL 353-21-359000. FAX 353-21-359090. E-mail: information@cso.ie; URL: http://www.cso.ie. **Document type:** government publication.
Formerly: Ireland. Central Statistics Office. Particulars of Vehicles Registered and Licensed for the First Time in Each County and County Borough During the Month (ISSN 0791-3427)
Description: Final detailed data on motor registrations.

330   IE   ISSN 1393-2896
IRELAND. CENTRAL STATISTICS OFFICE. PUBLIC SECTOR EMPLOYMENT. q. I£8. Central Statistics Office, Skehard Rd., Cork, Ireland. TEL 353-21-359000. FAX 353-21-359090. E-mail: information@cso.ie; URL: http://www.cso.ie. **Document type:** government publication.

IRELAND. CENTRAL STATISTICS OFFICE. RETAIL SALES INDEX. see BUSINESS AND ECONOMICS — Marketing And Purchasing

330   IE   ISSN 0790-9934
IRELAND. CENTRAL STATISTICS OFFICE. ROAD FREIGHT TRANSPORT SURVEY. 1980. a. I£5. Central Statistics Office, Skehard Rd., Cork, Ireland. TEL 353-21-359000. FAX 353-21-359090. E-mail: information@cso.ie; URL: http://www.cso.ie. (Subscr. to: Government Supplies Agency, 4-5 Harcourt Rd., Dublin 2, Ireland) **Document type:** government publication.
Description: Contains the results of the National Road Freight Transport Survey.

330   IE   ISSN 0791-8984
IRELAND. CENTRAL STATISTICS OFFICE. TOTAL EXTERNAL TRADE. PROVISIONAL ESTIMATES. m. I£24. Central Statistics Office, Skehard Rd., Cork, Ireland. TEL 353-21-359000. FAX 353-21-359090. E-mail: information@cso.ie; URL: http://www.cso.ie. **Document type:** government publication.
Formerly (until 1994): Ireland. Central Statistics Office. External Trade Provisional Figures (ISSN 0791-3478)

330   IE   ISSN 0791-3443
IRELAND. CENTRAL STATISTICS OFFICE. TOURISM AND TRAVEL. a. I£2. Central Statistics Office, Skehard Rd., Cork, Ireland. TEL 353-21-359000. FAX 353-21-359090. E-mail: information@cso.ie; URL: http://www.cso.ie. (processed) **Document type:** government publication.
Formerly: Ireland. Central Statistics Office. Estimated Numbers and Expenditures of Visitors to Ireland and Irish Visitors Abroad.

330   IE   ISSN 0791-3656
IRELAND. CENTRAL STATISTICS OFFICE. TOURISM AND TRAVEL QUARTERLY. q. I£8. Central Statistics Office, Skehard Rd., Cork, Ireland. TEL 353-21-359000. FAX 353-21-359090. E-mail: information@cso.ie; URL: http://www.cso.ie. **Document type:** government publication.
Description: Estimated numbers and expenditures of visitors to Ireland.

330   IE   ISSN 0791-8976
IRELAND. CENTRAL STATISTICS OFFICE. TRADE WITH NON - E C COUNTRIES. PROVISIONAL. m. I£24. Central Statistics Office, Skehard Rd., Cork, Ireland. TEL 353-21-359000. FAX 353-21-359090. **Document type:** government publication.

331 314   IE   ISSN 0075-0638
IRELAND. CENTRAL STATISTICS OFFICE. TREND OF EMPLOYMENT AND UNEMPLOYMENT. 1935. irreg., latest 1991. I£3.55. Central Statistics Office, Skehard Rd., Cork, Ireland. TEL 353-21-359000. FAX 353-21-359090. E-mail: information@cso.ie; URL: http://www.cso.ie. (Subscr. to: Government Supplies Agency, Bishop St., Dublin 8, Ireland) **Document type:** government publication.

330   IE   ISSN 0791-8453
IRELAND. CENTRAL STATISTICS OFFICE. VEHICLE LICENSING - PROVISIONAL RESULTS. m. I£24. Central Statistics Office, Skehard Rd., Cork, Ireland. TEL 353-21-359000. FAX 353-21-359090. E-mail: information@cso.ie; URL: http://www.cso.ie.
Document type: government publication.
Formerly (until 1993): Ireland. Central Statistics Office. Motor Registrations - Provisional Results (ISSN 0791-3435)
Description: Provisional data for motor registrations.

658   IE   ISSN 0791-3311
IRELAND. CENTRAL STATISTICS OFFICE. WHOLESALE PRICE INDEX. m. I£24. Central Statistics Office, Skehard Rd., Cork, Ireland. TEL 353-21-359000. FAX 353-21-359090. E-mail: information@cso.ie; URL: http://www.cso.ie. **Document type:** government publication.

310   IE   ISSN 0790-8407
IRELAND. STATIONERY OFFICE. ECONOMIC SERIES. m. I£50. Stationery Office, Dublin, Ireland. TEL 353-1-6613111. FAX 353-1-4752760. (Subscr. to: Government Supplies Agency, Publications Section, 4-5 Harcourt Rd., Dublin 2, Ireland) (processed) **Document type:** government publication.
Formerly: Ireland. Central Statistics Office. Economic Series.
Description: Provides details for 142 principal short term economic series with five years retrospection. Up to ten years retrospection is given in the December issue.

382 315   IS   ISSN 0333-8436
ISRAEL. CENTRAL BUREAU OF STATISTICS. FOREIGN TRADE STATISTICS (ANNUAL) - EXPORTS. (Text in English, Hebrew) 1951. a. IS.190 price varies. Central Bureau of Statistics, P.O. Box 13015, Jerusalem 91130, Israel. TEL 972-2-6553400. FAX 972-2-6553325. (also avail. in diskette format) **Document type:** government publication.

382 315   IS   ISSN 0333-8487
ISRAEL. CENTRAL BUREAU OF STATISTICS. FOREIGN TRADE STATISTICS (ANNUAL) - IMPORTS. (Text in English, Hebrew) 1974. a. IS.270. Central Bureau of Statistics, P.O. Box 13015, Jerusalem 91130, Israel. TEL 972-2-6553400. FAX 972-2-6553325. (also avail. in diskette format) **Document type:** government publication.
—CCC.

382 315   IS   ISSN 0334-2972
ISRAEL. CENTRAL BUREAU OF STATISTICS. FOREIGN TRADE STATISTICS QUARTERLY. (Text in English, Hebrew) 1980. q. $30. Central Bureau of Statistics, P.O. Box 13015, Jerusalem 91130, Israel. TEL 972-2-653400. FAX 972-2-6553325.
Document type: government publication.
Supersedes: Israel's Foreign Trade (ISSN 0075-1421); Israel. Central Bureau of Statistics. Foreign Trade Statistics Quarterly (ISSN 0021-1990); Israel. Central Bureau of Statistics. Monthly Foreign Trade Statistics.

338   IS   ISSN 0578-8420
ISRAEL. CENTRAL BUREAU OF STATISTICS. INDUSTRY AND CRAFTS SURVEY. (Text in English and Hebrew) irreg., latest 1993. price varies. Central Bureau of Statistics, P.O. Box 13015, Jerusalem 91130, Israel. TEL 972-2-6553400. FAX 972-2-6553325. **Document type:** government publication.

331 315   IS   ISSN 0075-1049
ISRAEL. CENTRAL BUREAU OF STATISTICS. LABOUR FORCE SURVEYS. (Text in English and Hebrew) 1954. irreg., latest 1994. price varies. Central Bureau of Statistics, P.O. Box 13015, Jerusalem 91130, Israel. TEL 972-2-6553400. FAX 972-2-6553325. (also avail. in diskette format) **Document type:** government publication.

331   IS
ISRAEL. CENTRAL BUREAU OF STATISTICS. LABOUR MOBILITY SURVEY. (Text in English, Hebrew) 1977. irreg. Central Bureau of Statistics, P.O. Box 13015, Jerusalem 91130, Israel. TEL 972-2-6553400. FAX 972-2-6553325. **Document type:** government publication.
Formerly: Israel. Central Bureau of Statistics. Labour Force Mobility Survey (ISSN 0333-9599)

BUSINESS AND ECONOMICS — ABSTRACTING, BIBLIOGRAPHIES, STATISTICS

336   IS   ISSN 0333-886X
ISRAEL. CENTRAL BUREAU OF STATISTICS. LOCAL AUTHORITIES IN ISRAEL: FINANCIAL DATA. (Text in Hebrew) irreg., latest 1992. IS.100. Central Bureau of Statistics, P.O. Box 13015, Jerusalem 91130, Israel. TEL 972-2-6553400. FAX 972-2-6553325. (also avail. in diskette format) **Document type:** government publication.

338 315   IS   ISSN 0021-2008
ISRAEL. CENTRAL BUREAU OF STATISTICS. MONTHLY PRICE STATISTICS. (Text in Hebrew) 1949. m. $140. Central Bureau of Statistics, P.O. Box 13015, Jerusalem 91130, Israel. TEL 972-2-6553400. FAX 972-2-6553325. (also avail. in diskette format) **Document type:** government publication.

332   IS   ISSN 0793-2235
ISRAEL. CENTRAL BUREAU OF STATISTICS. NATIONAL ACCOUNTS OF ISRAEL. (Text in English, Hebrew) 1994. irreg., latest for years 1950-1995. IS.100. Central Bureau of Statistics, P.O. Box 13015, Jerusalem 91130, Israel. TEL 972-2-6553400. FAX 972-2-6553325. (also avail. in diskette format) **Document type:** government publication.

332   IS   ISSN 0333-9440
ISRAEL. CENTRAL BUREAU OF STATISTICS. NATIONAL ACCOUNTS OF JUDEA, SAMARIA, AND THE GAZA AREA. (Text in English, Hebrew) 1979. irreg., latest covers 1968-1993. IS.35. Central Bureau of Statistics, P.O. Box 13015, Jerusalem 91130, Israel. TEL 972-2-6553400. FAX 972-2-6553325. (also avail. in diskette format) **Document type:** government publication.

330   IS   ISSN 0333-9793
ISRAEL. CENTRAL BUREAU OF STATISTICS. SURVEY ON RESEARCH AND DEVELOPMENT IN INDUSTRY. (Text in English and Hebrew) irreg. IS.35. Central Bureau of Statistics, P.O. Box 13015, Jerusalem 91130, Israel. TEL 972-2-6553400. FAX 972-2-6553325. **Document type:** government publication.

382 314   IT
ITALY. ISTITUTO NAZIONALE DI STATISTICA. NOTIZIARIO. Short title: Notiziari I S T A T. (In 4 series: Serie 1: Demografiche e Sociali; Serie 2: Attivita Produttive; Serie 3: Lavoro, Retribuzione, Prezzi; Serie 4: Argomenti Vari) vol.22, 1970. m. L.106000 (foreign L.144000) (effective 1991). Istituto Centrale di Statistica, Via Cesare Balbo 16, 00100 Rome, Italy. FAX 39-6-46735198. charts. **Document type:** government publication.
    Formerly: Italy. Istituto Centrale di Statistica. Notiziario (ISSN 0029-4381).

382 314   IT   ISSN 0390-6566
ITALY. ISTITUTO NAZIONALE DI STATISTICA. STATISTICA ANNUALE DEL COMMERCIO CON L'ESTERO. TOMO 2: MERCI PER PAESI. 1953. a. L.109300. Istituto Nazionale di Statistica, Via Cesare Balbo 16, 00100 Rome, Italy. FAX 39-6-46735198. circ. 1,100. **Document type:** government publication.
    Supersedes in part (in 1963): Italy. Istituto Centrale di Statistica. Statistica Annuale del Commercio con l'Estero (ISSN 0075-1871).

382 314   IT
ITALY. ISTITUTO NAZIONALE DI STATISTICA. STATISTICA TRIMESTRALE DEL COMMERCIO CON L'ESTERO. q. L.105000 (foreign L.126000) (effective 1995). Istituto Nazionale di Statistica, Via Cesare Balbo 16, 00100 Rome, Italy. FAX 39-6-46735198. circ. 1,900. Indexed: P.A.I.S.For.Lang.Ind. **Document type:** government publication.
    Former titles: Italy. Istituto Centrale di Statistica. Statistica Mensile del Commercio con l'Estero (ISSN 0535-9821); (until 1955): Italy. Istituto Centrale di Statistica. Statistica Mensile del Commercio Speciale di Importazione e d'Esportazione.

382 314   IT
ITALY. ISTITUTO NAZIONALE DI STATISTICA. STATISTICA TRIMESTRALE DEL COMMERCIO CON L'ESTERO. DATI GENERALI E RIASSUNTIVI. 1953. q. L.38000. Istituto Nazionale di Statistica, Via Cesare Balbo 16, 00100 Rome, Italy. FAX 39-6-46735198. circ. 1,100. **Document type:** government publication.
    Formerly: Italy. Istituto Nazionale di Statistica. Statistica Annuale del Commercio con l'Estero. Tomo 1. Dati Generali e Riassuntivi (ISSN 0390-6558); Supersedes in part (in 1963): Italy. Istituto Centrale di Statistica. Statistica Annuale del Commercio con l'Estero (ISSN 0075-1871).

381 314   IT
ITALY. ISTITUTO NAZIONALE DI STATISTICA. STATISTICHE DEL COMMERCIO INTERNO. 1957. a. L.15000 (effective 1992). Istituto Nazionale di Statistica, Via Cesare Balbo 16, 00100 Rome, Italy. FAX 39-6-46735198. circ. 1,200. **Document type:** government publication.
    Supersedes in part: Italy. Istituto Centrale di Statistica. Annuario Statistico del Commercio Interno e del Turismo; Which was formerly: Italy. Istituto Centrale di Statistica. Annuario Statistico del Commercio Interno (ISSN 0075-1782)

330 314   IT
HC301
ITALY. ISTITUTO NAZIONALE DI STATISTICA. STATISTICHE INDUSTRIALI. 1956. a. L.41000 (effective 1986-87 ed.). Istituto Nazionale di Statistica, Via Cesare Balbo 16, 00184 Rome, Italy. TEL 39-6-46732380. FAX 39-6-46735198. charts; illus. circ. 1,500. **Document type:** government publication.
    Formerly: Italy. Istituto Centrale di Statistica. Annuario di Statistiche Industriali (ISSN 0075-1723)

331 314   IT
ITALY. MINISTERO DEL LAVORO E DELLA PREVIDENZA SOCIALE. NOTIZIARIO MENSILE. STATISTICHE DEL LAVORO. 1972. m. Ministero del Lavoro e della Previdenza Sociale, Rome, Italy. **Document type:** government publication.

338 310   MY   ISSN 0128-973X
HC445.5.A1
JABATAN PERANGKAAN MALAYSIA. PENYIASATAN TAHUNAN INDUSTRI PEMBUATAN/MALAYSIA. DEPARTMENT OF STATISTICS. ANNUAL SURVEY OF MANUFACTURING INDUSTRIES. (Text in English, Malay) a. Department of Statistics - Jabatan Perangkaan, Wisma Statistik, Jalan Cenderasary, 50514 Kuala Lumpur, Malaysia. TEL 60-3-2922133. **Document type:** government publication.
    Former titles (until 1992): Penyiasatan Perusahaan Malaysia (ISSN 0126-6993); (until 1981): Penyiasatan Perusahaan Semenjung Malaysia.

651   GW   ISSN 0932-3635
JAHRBUCH DER BUEROKOMMUNIKATION. 1985. a. DM.28. F B O - Fachverlag fuer Buero- und Organisationstechnik GmbH, Hermannstr. 2, 76530 Baden-Baden, Germany. TEL 49-7221-271066. adv. (back issues avail.) **Document type:** trade publication.
    Description: Articles collected from the journal "Office Management."

300 016   GW   ISSN 0948-5139
H9
JAHRBUCH FUER WIRTSCHAFTSWISSENSCHAFTEN; review of economics. (Text in English, German) 1950. 3/yr. DM.175. Vandenhoeck und Ruprecht, Robert-Bosch-Breite 6, 37079 Goettingen, Germany. TEL 49-551-6959-26. FAX 49-551-695917. (Subscr. to: 37070 Goettingen, Germany) Ed.Bd. adv.; index. circ. 600. Indexed: ASCA, Curr.Cont., ELLIS, Int.Polit.Sci.Abstr., Key to Econ.Sci., P.A.I.S.For.Lang.Ind., Risk Abstr., SSCI. **Document type:** academic/scholarly publication.
    —BLDSC (4632.667000); Genuine Article; SWETS; UnCover. **CCC.**
    Formerly (until 1995): Jahrbuch fuer Sozialwissenschaft (ISSN 0075-2770)

331.11 315   JA
JAPAN. MANAGEMENT AND COORDINATION AGENCY. STATISTICS BUREAU. EMPLOYMENT STATUS SURVEY. (Includes: Employment Statistics) 1956. quinquennial. price varies. Somucho, Tokeikyoku - Management and Coordination Agency, Statistics Bureau, 19-1 Wakamatsu-cho, Shinjuku-ku, Tokyo 162, Japan. TEL 81-3-3203-1111. FAX 81-3-5273-1180. (Subscr. to: Government Publications Service Centre, 2-1 Kasumigaseki 1-chome, Chiyoda-ku, Tokyo 100, Japan) **Document type:** government publication.

331 315   JA
JAPAN. MINISTRY OF LABOUR. YEARBOOK OF LABOUR STATISTICS. (Text in English and Japanese) 1948. a. 8000 Yen. Ministry of Labour, Statistics and Information Department - Nihon Rodosho, Minister's Secretariat, Tokyo 100, Japan. charts. circ. 800. **Document type:** government publication.

332.6   JA   ISSN 0910-3007
HF251
JAPAN EXPORTS & IMPORTS: COMMODITY BY COUNTRY. (Text in Japanese, English) m. $27184. Japan Tariff Association, c/o Jibiki Daini Bldg., 4-7-8 Kojimachi, Chiyoda-ku, Tokyo, Japan. (Dist. by: Intercontinental Marketing Corp., I.P.O. Box 5056, Tokyo 100-30, Japan. TEL 81-3-3661-7458. FAX 81-3-3667-9646) **Document type:** government publication.

331   JA   ISSN 0289-1344
JAPAN STATISTICAL ASSOCIATION. ANNUAL REPORT ON THE LABOUR FORCE SURVEY. (Text in English, Japanese) a. 3885 Yen. Nihon Tokei Kyokai - Japan Statistical Association, Crest 21, 6-21, Yocho-machi, Shinjuku-ku, Tokyo 162, Japan. TEL 81-3-5269-3051. FAX 81-3-5269-3058. (Subscr. to: Government Publications Service Center, 2-1 Kasumigaseki 1-chome, Chiyoda-ku, Tokyo 100, Japan) Ed. Hideshi Honda. R&P contact: Hideshi Honda. **Document type:** government publication.

331   JA   ISSN 0289-1301
JAPAN STATISTICAL ASSOCIATION. ANNUAL REPORT ON THE RETAIL PRICE SURVEY. (Text in English, Japanese) a. 7340 Yen. Nihon Tokei Kyokai - Japan Statistical Association, Crest 21, 6-21, Yocho-machi, Shinjuku-ku, Tokyo 162, Japan. TEL 81-3-5269-3051. FAX 81-3-5269-3058. (Subscr. to: Government Publications Service Center, 2-1 Kasumigaseki 1-chome, Chiyoda-ku, Tokyo 100, Japan) Ed. Hideshi Honda. R&P contact: Hideshi Honda. **Document type:** government publication.

331   JA   ISSN 0448-7141
JAPAN STATISTICAL ASSOCIATION. ANNUAL REPORT ON THE UNINCORPORATED ENTERPRISE SURVEY. (Text in English, Japanese) a. 3364 Yen. Nihon Tokei Kyokai - Japan Statistical Association, Crest 21, 6-21, Yocho-machi, Shinjuku-ku, Tokyo 162, Japan. TEL 81-3-5269-3051. FAX 81-3-5269-3058. (Subscr. to: Government Publications Center, 2-1 Kasumigaseki 1-chome, Chiyoda-ku, Tokyo 100, Japan) Ed. Hideshi/Honda. R&P contact: Hideshi Honda. **Document type:** government publication.

658 310   JA
JAPAN STATISTICAL ASSOCIATION. MONTHLY REPORT OF RETAIL PRICES. CONSUMER PRICE INDEX. (Text in English, Japanese) m. 740 Yen per no. Nihon Tokei Kyokai, Crest 21, 6-21, Yocho-machi, Shinjuku-ku, Tokyo 162, Japan. TEL 81-3-5269-3051. FAX 81-3-5269-3058. Ed. Hideshi Honda. R&P contact: Hideshi Honda. **Document type:** government publication.

658 310   JA
JAPAN STATISTICAL ASSOCIATION. MONTHLY REPORT OF RETAIL PRICES. PRICES OF CONSUMER GOODS AND SERVICES. (Text in English, Japanese) m. 650 Yen per no. Nihon Tokei Kyokai, Crest 21, 6-21, Yocho-machi, Shinjuku-ku, Tokyo 162, Japan. TEL 81-3-5269-3051. FAX 81-3-5269-3058. Ed. Hideshi Honda. R&P contact: Hideshi Honda. **Document type:** government publication.

339 310   JA
JAPAN STATISTICAL ASSOCIATION. MONTHLY REPORT ON THE FAMILY INCOME AND EXPENDITURE SURVEY. (Text in English, Japanese) m. 870 Yen per no. Nihon Tokei Kyokai, Crest 21, 6-21, Yocho-machi, Shinjuku-ku, Tokyo 162, Japan. TEL 81-3-5269-3051. FAX 81-3-5269-3058. Ed. Hideshi Honda. R&P contact: Hideshi Honda. **Document type:** government publication.

BUSINESS AND ECONOMICS — ABSTRACTING, BIBLIOGRAPHIES, STATISTICS

331.11   JA
JAPAN STATISTICAL ASSOCIATION. MONTHLY REPORT ON THE LABOUR FORCE SURVEY. (Text in English, Japanese) m. 550 Yen per no. Nihon Tokei Kyokai, Crest 21, 6-21, Yocho-machi, Shinjuku-ku, Tokyo 162, Japan. TEL 81-3-5269-3051. FAX 81-3-5269-3058. Ed. Hideshi Honda. R&P contact: Hideshi Honda. **Document type:** government publication.

331.2   US
JOINT GOVERNMENTAL SALARY AND BENEFITS SURVEY: ARIZONA. 1974. a. $50. Department of Administration, Personnel Division, 1831 W. Jefferson, Phoenix, AZ 85007-3204. TEL 602-542-5250. Ed. Joan Toner. charts; circ. controlled. **Document type:** government publication.
   Formerly: Joint Governmental Salary Survey: Arizona; **Supersedes:** Survey of Salaries and Employee Benefits of Private and Public Employers in Arizona. (ISSN 0091-5599)

331.11   JO
JORDAN. DEPARTMENT OF STATISTICS. EMPLOYMENT SURVEY FOR ESTABLISHMENTS ENGAGING FIVE PERSONS OR MORE. (Text in Arabic and English) 1967. a. $15. Department of Statistics, P.O. Box 2015, Amman, Jordan. TEL 962-6-842171. FAX 962-6-833518. TELEX 24117 STATIS JO. **Document type:** government publication.

310   JO
JORDAN. DEPARTMENT OF STATISTICS. EMPLOYMENT, UNEMPLOYMENT AND INCOME SURVEY. (Text in Arabic, English) 1988. a. $25 (effective 1997). Department of Statistics, P.O. Box 2105, Amman, Jordan. TEL 962-6-842171. FAX 962-6-833518. TELEX 24117 STATIS JO. **Document type:** government publication.
   Formerly: Jordan. Department of Statistics. Services Survey.

382 315   JO   ISSN 0075-4021
HF259.J6
JORDAN. DEPARTMENT OF STATISTICS. EXTERNAL TRADE STATISTICS. 1965. a. $105. Department of Statistics, P.O. Box 2015, Amman, Jordan. TEL 962-6-842171. FAX 962-6-833518. TELEX 24117 STATIS JO. **Document type:** government publication.

330   JO
JORDAN. DEPARTMENT OF STATISTICS. INDUSTRIAL SURVEY. (Text in Arabic, English) 1965. a. $15. Department of Statistics, P.O. Box 2015, Amman, Jordan. TEL 962-6-842171. FAX 962-6-833518. TELEX 24117 STATIS JO. **Document type:** government publication.

381   JO
JORDAN. DEPARTMENT OF STATISTICS. WHOLESALE & RETAIL TRADE SURVEY. (Text in Arabic, English) 1985. a. $15. Department of Statistics, P.O. Box 2015, Amman, Jordan. TEL 962-6-842171. FAX 962-6-833518. TELEX 24117 STATIS JO. **Document type:** government publication.
   Formerly: Jordan. Department of Statistics. Internal Trade Survey.

658   UK   ISSN 0142-5951
JOURNAL CONTENTS IN QUANTITATIVE METHODS. 1979. m. £175 in Europe (N. America $295; elsewhere £185) (effective 1997). University of Manchester, Institute of Science and Technology, School of Management, P.O. Box 88, Manchester M60 1QD, England. FAX 44-161-200-3505. Ed. Simon Conrad. **Document type:** abstracting/indexing.
   Description: Contains tables of contents of more than 150 journals in statistics and operations research, and quantitative journals in the different functional areas of management.

330.9 310   US   ISSN 0735-0015
HB137
JOURNAL OF BUSINESS AND ECONOMIC STATISTICS. 1983. q. $72 to libraries. American Statistical Association, 1429 Duke St., Alexandria, VA 22314-3415. TEL 703-684-1221. FAX 703-684-2037. E-mail: asainfo@amstat.org. URL: http://www.amstat.org/publications/index.html. Indexed: ABI Inform., ASCA, B.P.I., Cont.Pg.Manage., Curr.Cont.(1983-), Curr.Ind.Stat., J.Cont.Quant.Meth., J.of Econ.Lit., Oper.Res.Manage.Sci., Qual.Contr.Appl.Stat., SSCI, Stat.Theor.Meth.Abstr. (1983-), Triticale Abstr., World Agri.Econ.& Rural Sociol.Abstr.
—BLDSC (4954.661000); Genuine Article; KR SourceOne; SWETS; UMI; UnCover. **CCC.**

JOURNAL OF ECONOMIC AND SOCIAL MEASUREMENT. see *STATISTICS*

330 016   US   ISSN 0022-0515
HB1   CODEN: JECLB3
JOURNAL OF ECONOMIC LITERATURE. 1963. q. $130 (includes American Economic Review and Journal of Economic Perspectives). American Economic Association, 2014 Broadway, Ste. 305, Nashville, TN 37203. TEL 615-322-2595. Ed. John Pencavel. R&P contact: Dana Ragan. adv.; bk.rev.; index. circ. 27,000. (also avail. in microform from UMI; reprint service avail. from UMI, SCH,WSH) Indexed: ABI Inform., Acad.Ind., Amer.Bibl.Slavic & E.Eur.Stud., Amer.Hist.& Life (1969-), Arts & Hum.Cit.Ind., ASCA, Asian-Pac.Econ.Lit., Bk.Rev.Dig., Bk.Rev.Ind. (1974-), BPIA, Bus.Ind., C.R.E.J., Child.Bk.Rev.Ind. (1974-), Curr.Cont., Curr.Lit.Fam.Plan., Hist.Abstr. (1969-), Int.Lab.Doc., J.of Econ.Abstr., Key to Econ.Sci., Manage.Cont., Mgmt.& Market.Abstr., Mid.East: Abstr.& Ind., Oper.Res.Manage.Sci., Popul.Ind., PROMT, Pub.Admin.Abstr., Qual.Contr.Appl.Stat., Rural Recreat.Tour.Abstr., SCIMP (1978-), Soc.Sci.Ind., SSCI, World Agri.Econ.& Rural Sociol.Abstr., World Bank.Abstr. **Document type:** abstracting/indexing.
● Also available online. Vendor(s): Knight-Ridder Information, Inc. (Economic Literature Index File no. 139).
Also available on CD-ROM. Producer(s): SilverPlatter Information, Inc.
—BLDSC (4973.053000); Genuine Article; KR SourceOne; SWETS; UMI; UnCover.
   Incorporates: Journal of Economic Abstracts.
   Description: Designed to provide economists with a guide to ongoing research and publications. Includes index of articles on economic subjects in English-language journals. Focuses on academic and research topics rather than on popular literature.

332.6   US   ISSN 0893-2700
P92.U5
KAGAN MEDIA INDEX. 1987. m. $675 (effective 1997). Paul Kagan Associates, Inc., 126 Clock Tower Pl., Carmel, CA 93923. TEL 408-624-1536. FAX 408-625-3225. Ed. Paul Kagan.

330.9   NR
KANO (STATE). LOCAL GOVERNMENT SURVEY OF TOWNS, VILLAGES AND HAMLETS. 1993. quinquennial. $30 (effective 1996). Budget & Economic Planning Directorate, Ministry of Finance, Audu Bako Secretariat, P.M.B. 3291, Kano, Nigeria. **Document type:** government publication.

331   NR
KANO (STATE) MANPOWER STATISTICS. 1984. biennial. $30 (effective 1996). Budget & Economic Planning Directorate, Department of Manpower Statistics, Ministry of Finance, Audu Bako Secretariat, P.M.B. 3291, Kano, Nigeria. stat. **Document type:** government publication.

330.9   NR
KANO (STATE). PRICES OF SELECTED COMMODITIES IN SOME TOWNS IN KANO STATE. 1981. q. $30 (effective 1996). Budget & Economic Planning Directorate, Ministry of Finance, Audu Bako Secretariat, P.M.B. 3291, Kano, Nigeria. stat. **Document type:** government publication, consumer publication.

336   NR
KANO (STATE) PUBLIC FINANCE STATISTICS OF KANO STATE & LOCAL GOVERNMENT COUNCILS. 1991. biennial. $30 (effective 1996). Budget & Economic Planning Directorate, Ministry of Finance, Audu Bako Secretariat, P.M.B. 3291, Kano, Nigeria. stat. **Document type:** government publication.

316.69 330.9   NR
KANO (STATE). STATISTICAL YEAR-BOOK. 1970. biennial. $30 (effective 1996). Budget & Economic Planning Directorate, Ministry of Finance, Audu Bako Secretariat, P.M.B. 3291, Kano, Nigeria. bk.rev. **Document type:** government publication.
   Supersedes: Northern Nigeria. Ministry of Economic Planning. Statistical Year Book.

330.9 317   US   ISSN 0361-591X
HC107.K4
KENTUCKY DESKBOOK OF ECONOMIC STATISTICS. 1952. a. $10 per no. Cabinet for Economic Development, Division of Research, 500 Mero St., Ste. 2300, Frankfort, KY 40601. TEL 502-564-4886. FAX 502-564-3256. Ed. Ron Decker. circ. 1,000. Indexed: SRI. **Document type:** government publication.
   Formerly: Deskbook of Kentucky Economic Statistics (ISSN 0363-7301)
   Description: Contains a compilation of statistics of population, employment, unemployment, labor force characteristics, wages, income and other selected data.

338.9   KE
KENYA. CENTRAL BUREAU OF STATISTICS. DEVELOPMENT ESTIMATES. (Former name of issuing body: Kenya. Ministry of Planning and National Development) a. Ministry of Finance and Planning, Central Bureau of Statistics, P.O. Box 30266, Nairobi, Kenya. (Subscr. to: Government Press, Haile Selaissie Ave., P.O. Box 30128, Nairobi, Kenya. TEL 254-2-334075) stat. **Document type:** government publication.
   Formerly: Kenya. Ministry of Economic Planning and Development. Statistics Division. Development Estimates (ISSN 0075-5818)

316 331   KE   ISSN 0376-8864
HD5841.K4
KENYA. CENTRAL BUREAU OF STATISTICS. EMPLOYMENT AND EARNINGS IN THE MODERN SECTOR. Key Title: Employment and Earnings in the Modern Sector. (Former name of issuing body: Ministry of Planning and National Development) 1971. irreg., latest 1981. KShs.50. Ministry of Finance and Planning, Central Bureau of Statistics, P.O. Box 30266, Nairobi, Kenya. (Subscr. to: Government Press, Haile Selaissie Ave., P.O. Box 30128, Nairobi, Kenya. TEL 254-2-334075) stat. **Document type:** government publication.

338.9   KE   ISSN 0075-5834
KENYA. CENTRAL BUREAU OF STATISTICS. ESTIMATES OF RECURRENT EXPENDITURES. (Former name of issuing body: Kenya. Ministry of Economic Planning and Development) 1959. a. Ministry of Finance and Planning, Central Bureau of Statistics, P.O. Box 30266, Nairobi, Kenya. (Subscr. to: Government Press, Haile Selaissie Ave., P.O. Box 30128, Nairobi, Kenya. TEL 254-2-334075) stat. **Document type:** government publication.

338.9   KE
KENYA. CENTRAL BUREAU OF STATISTICS. ESTIMATES OF REVENUE EXPENDITURES. (Former name of issuing body: Kenya. Ministry of Planning and National Development) 1959. a. Ministry of Finance and Planning, Central Bureau of Statistics, P.O. Box 30266, Nairobi, Kenya. (Subscr. to: Government Press, Haile Selaissie Ave., P.O. Box 30128, Nairobi, Kenya. TEL 254-2-334075) stat. **Document type:** government publication.
   Formerly: Kenya. Ministry of Economic Planning and Development. Estimates of Revenue Expenditures (ISSN 0075-5826)

338 316   KE
KENYA. CENTRAL BUREAU OF STATISTICS. REGISTER OF MANUFACTURING FIRMS. (Former name of issuing body: Kenya. Ministry of Planning and National Development) 1970. irreg. Ministry of Finance and Planning, Central Bureau of Statistics, P.O. Box 30266, Nairobi, Kenya. (Subscr. to: Government Press, Haile Selaissie Ave., P.O. Box 30128, Nairobi, Kenya. TEL 254-2-334075) stat. **Document type:** government publication.
   Formerly: Kenya. Ministry of Finance and Economic Planning. Statistics Division. Register of Manufacturing Firms.

BUSINESS AND ECONOMICS — ABSTRACTING, BIBLIOGRAPHIES, STATISTICS

338   KE
KENYA. CENTRAL BUREAU OF STATISTICS. SURVEYS OF INDUSTRIAL PRODUCTION. (Former name of issuing body: Kenya. Ministry of Planning and National Development) irreg. Ministry of Finance and Planning, Central Bureau of Statistics, P.O. Box 30266, Nairobi, Kenya. (Subscr. to: Government Press, Haile Selaissie Ave., P.O. Box 30128, Nairobi, Kenya. TEL 254-2-334075) **Document type:** government publication.

330   GW
KIELER BIBLIOGRAPHIEN ZU AKTUELLEN OEKONOMISCHEN THEMEN. irreg., vol.15, 1996. DM.20. Institut fuer Weltwirtschaft, Duesternbrooker Weg 120, 24105 Kiel, Germany. TEL 49-431-8814305. FAX 49-431-8814527. E-mail: info@ifw.uni-kiel.de; URL: http://www.uni-kiel.de:8080/ifw/. **Document type:** bibliography.
Formerly: Kieler Schnellbibliographien zu Aktuellen Wirtschaftsthemen.
Refereed Serial

KONINKLIJK INSTITUUT VOR DE TROPEN. ANNOTATED BIBLIOGRAPHIES SERIES. see *AGRICULTURE — Abstracting, Bibliographies, Statistics*

331   KO
KOREA (REPUBLIC). NATIONAL STATISTICAL OFFICE. ANNUAL REPORT ON THE ECONOMICALLY ACTIVE POPULATION SURVEY. (Text in English and Korean) 1963. a. 6500 Won($15) National Statistical Office, Hanta Bldg., 647-15, Yoksam-dong, Kangnam-gu, Seoul 135-080, S. Korea. TEL 82-2-222-1971. (Subscr. to: the Korean Statistical Association, Room 302, Chungok Building, 561-30, Sinsa-dong, Gangnam-gu, Seoul 135-120, S. Korea. TEL 82-2-725-4344. FAX 82-2-725-4347) circ. 800. **Document type:** government publication.
Formerly: Korea (Republic). Economic Planning Board. Annual Report on the Economically Active Population Survey (ISSN 0454-7543)

339 315   KO   ISSN 1011-6222
KOREA (REPUBLIC). NATIONAL STATISTICAL OFFICE. ANNUAL REPORT ON THE FAMILY INCOME AND EXPENDITURE SURVEY. (Text in English and Korean) 1963. a. 8500 Won($15) National Statistical Office, Hanta Bldg., 647-15, Yoksam-dong, Kangnam-gu, Seoul 135-080, S. Korea. TEL 82-2-222-1971. (Subscr. to: the Korean Statistical Association, Room 302, Chungok Building, 561-30, Sinsa-dong, Gangnam-gu, Seoul 135-120, S. Korea. TEL 82-2-517-0382. FAX 82-2-725-4347) circ. 600. **Document type:** government publication.
Formerly: Korea (Republic). National Bureau of Statistics. Annual Report on the Family Income and Expenditure Survey (ISSN 0075-6822)

338.9 315   KO
KOREA (REPUBLIC). NATIONAL STATISTICAL OFFICE. ANNUAL REPORT ON THE PRICE SURVEY/MULGA YONBO. (Text in English and Korean) 1965. a. 16000 Won($18) National Statistical Office, Hanta Bldg., 647-15, Yoksam-dong, Kangnam-gu, Seoul 135-080, S. Korea. TEL 82-2-222-1971. (Subscr. to: the Korean Statistical Association, Room 302, Chungok Building, 561-30, Sinsa-dong, Gangnam-gu, Seoul 135-120, S. Korea. TEL 82-2-517-0382. FAX 82-2-725-4347) circ. 960. **Document type:** government publication.
Formerly: Korea (Republic). National Bureau of Statistics. Annual Report on the Price Survey (ISSN 0075-6830)

KOREA (REPUBLIC). NATIONAL STATISTICAL OFFICE. REPORT ON MINING AND MANUFACTURING SURVEY. see *MINES AND MINING INDUSTRY — Abstracting, Bibliographies, Statistics*

332.6   KU
KUWAIT. CENTRAL STATISTICAL OFFICE. ANNUAL BULLETIN OF FOREIGN TRADE STATISTICS/KUWAIT. AL-IDARAH AL-MARKAZIYYAH AL-NASHRAH AL-SANAWIYYAH LI-IHSA'AT AL-TIJARAH AL-KHARIJIYYAH. (Text in Arabic, English) 1964. a., latest 1995. 1 din. Central Statistical Office - Al-Idarah al-Markaziyyah lil-Ihsa', P.O. Box 26188, Safat 13122, Kuwait. TEL 965-2428200. FAX 965-2430464. TELEX 22468 TAKHTET KT. **Document type:** government publication.
Description: Provides statistics on commodity imports and exports and commercial exchanges between Kuwait and foreign countries.

KUWAIT. CENTRAL STATISTICAL OFFICE. ANNUAL SURVEY OF ESTABLISHMENTS - CONSTRUCTION/KUWAIT. AL-IDARAH AL-MARKAZIYYAH LIL-IHSA'. AL-BAHTH AL-SANAWI LIL-MANSHAAT - AL-TASHYID WAL-BINA'. see *BUILDING AND CONSTRUCTION — Abstracting, Bibliographies, Statistics*

338   KU
KUWAIT. CENTRAL STATISTICAL OFFICE. ANNUAL SURVEY OF ESTABLISHMENTS - INDUSTRIAL/KUWAIT. AL-IDARAH AL-MARKAZIYYAH LIL-IHSA'. AL-BAHTH AL-SANAWI LIL-MANSHAAT - AL-SINA'AH. (Text in Arabic, English) 1983. a., latest 1993. Central Statistical Office - Al-Idarah al-Markaziyyah lil-Ihsa', P.O. Box 26188, Safat 13122, Kuwait. TEL 965-2428200. FAX 965-2430464. TELEX 22468 TAKHTET KT. **Document type:** government publication.

338   KU
KUWAIT. CENTRAL STATISTICAL OFFICE. ANNUAL SURVEY OF ESTABLISHMENTS - SERVICES/KUWAIT. AL-IDARAH AL-MARKAZIYYAH LIL-IHSA'. AL-BAHTH AL-SANAWI LIL-MANSHAAT - AL-KHADAMAT. (Text in Arabic, English) 1982. a., latest 1993. Central Statistical Office - Al-Idarah al-Markaziyyah lil-Ihsa', P.O. Box 26188, Safat 13122, Kuwait. TEL 965-2428200. FAX 965-2430464. TELEX 22468 TAKHTET KT. **Document type:** government publication.

338   KU
KUWAIT. CENTRAL STATISTICAL OFFICE. ANNUAL SURVEY OF ESTABLISHMENTS - WHOLESALE & RETAIL TRADE/KUWAIT. AL-IDARAH AL-MARKAZIYYAH LIL-IHSA'. AL-BAHTH AL-SANAWI LIL-MANSHAAT - TIJARAH AL-JUMLAH WAL-TAJZI'AH. (Text in Arabic, English) 1983. a., latest 1993. Central Statistical Office - Al-Idarah al-Markaziyyah lil-Ihsa', P.O. Box 26188, Safat 13122, Kuwait. TEL 965-2428200. FAX 965-2430464. TELEX 22468 TAKHTET KT. **Document type:** government publication.

330   KU
KUWAIT. CENTRAL STATISTICAL OFFICE. BUILDINGS AND DWELLINGS CENSUS/KUWAIT. AL-IDARAH AL-MARKAZIYYAH LIL-IHSA'. TA'DAD AL-MABANI WAL-MASAKIN. (Text in Arabic) 1957. irreg., 7th, 1985. Central Statistical Office - Al-Idarah al-Markaziyyah lil-Ihsa', P.O. Box 26188, Safat 13122, Kuwait. TEL 965-2428200. FAX 965-2430464. TELEX 22468 TAKHTET KT. **Document type:** government publication.

330   KU
KUWAIT. CENTRAL STATISTICAL OFFICE. ESTABLISHMENT CENSUS/KUWAIT. AL-IDARAH AL-MARKAZIYYAH LIL-IHSA'. TA'DAD AL-MUNSHAAT. (Text in Arabic) 1957. irreg., 7th, 1985. Central Statistical Office - Al-Idarah al-Markaziyyah lil-Ihsa', P.O. Box 26188, Safat 13122, Kuwait. TEL 965-2428200. FAX 965-2430464. TELEX 22468 TAKHTET KT. **Document type:** government publication.

330   KU
KUWAIT. CENTRAL STATISTICAL OFFICE. FAMILY BUDGET SURVEY - FINAL RESULTS/KUWAIT. AL-IDARAH AL-MARKAZIYYAH LIL-IHSA'. MIZANIYYAT AL-USRAH - AL-NATA'IJ AL-TAJMI'IYYAH AL-NIHA'IYYAH. (Text in Arabic, English) 1973. irreg., latest 1987. Central Statistical Office - Al-Idarah al-Markaziyyah lil-Ihsa', P.O. Box 26188, Safat 13122, Kuwait. TEL 965-2428200. FAX 965-2430464. TELEX 22468 TAKHTET KT. **Document type:** government publication.

330   KU
KUWAIT. CENTRAL STATISTICAL OFFICE. FINANCIAL STATISTICS/KUWAIT. AL-IDARAH AL-MARKAZIYYAH LIL-IHSA'. AL-IHSA'AT AL-MAALIYYAH. (Text in Arabic, English) 1975. a., latest 1995. Central Statistical Office - Al-Idarah al-Markaziyyah lil-Ihsa', P.O. Box 26188, Safat 13122, Kuwait. TEL 965-2428200. FAX 965-2430464. TELEX 22468 TAKHTET KT. **Document type:** government publication.
Description: Provides statistics relating to banking and monetary activities, the insurance sector, shareholding companies, and development assistance from the Kuwait Fund for Arab Economic Development.

336   KU
KUWAIT. CENTRAL STATISTICAL OFFICE. GOVERNMENT FINANCIAL STATISTICS/KUWAIT. AL-IDARAH AL-MARKAZIYYAH LIL-IHSA'. AL-IHSA'AT AL-MAALIYYAH LIL-HUKUMAH. (Text in Arabic, English) 1975. a., latest for years 1994-1995. Central Statistical Office - Al-Idarah al-Markaziyyah lil-Ihsa', P.O. Box 26188, Safat 13122, Kuwait. TEL 965-2428200. FAX 965-2430464. TELEX 22468 TAKHTET KT. **Document type:** government publication.
Supersedes in part (in 1981): Kuwait. Al-Idarah al-Markaziyyah lil-Ihsa'. Al-Ihsa'at al-Maaliyyah.

332.6   KU   ISSN 0454-7063
KUWAIT. CENTRAL STATISTICAL OFFICE. MONTHLY BULLETIN OF FOREIGN TRADE STATISTICS/KUWAIT. AL-IDARAH AL-MARKAZIYYAH LIL-IHSA'. AL-NASHRAH AL-SHAHRIYYAH LI-IHSA'AT AL-TIJARAH AL-KHARIJIYYAH. (Text in Arabic, English) 1964. m. Central Statistical Office - Al-Idarah al-Markaziyyah lil-Ihsa', P.O. Box 26188, Safat 13122, Kuwait. TEL 965-2428200. FAX 965-2430464. TELEX 22468 TAKHTET KT. **Document type:** government publication.
Description: Provides summary statistical tables on monthly imports and exports during the preceding three years, information on imports and exports by major commodity group and country of origin or destination.

339   KU
KUWAIT. CENTRAL STATISTICAL OFFICE. MONTHLY CONSUMER PRICE INDEX NUMBERS. (Text in Arabic, English) 1973. m., latest Mar. 1996. 0.50 din. Central Statistical Office - Al-Idarah al-Markaziyyah lil-Ihsa', P.O. Box 26188, Safat 13122, Kuwait. TEL 965-2428200. FAX 965-2430464. TELEX 22468 TAKHTET KT. **Document type:** government publication.
Formerly: Kuwait. Al-Idarah al-Markaziyyah lil-Ihsa'. Al-Nashrah al-Shahriyyah lil-Arqam al-Qiyasiyyah li-As'ar al-Mustahlak; **Supersedes in part:** Kuwait. Central Statistical Office. Annual Bulletin for Prices and Index Numbers.

336   KU
KUWAIT. CENTRAL STATISTICAL OFFICE. NATIONAL ACCOUNTS STATISTICS/KUWAIT. AL-IDARAH AL-MARKAZIYYAH LIL-IHSA'. IHSA'AT AL-HISABAT AL-QAWMIYYAH. (Text in Arabic, English) 1975. a., latest for years 1977-1993. Central Statistical Office - Al-Idarah al-Markaziyyah lil-Ihsa', P.O. Box 26188, Safat 13122, Kuwait. TEL 965-2428200. FAX 965-2430464. TELEX 22468 TAKHTET KT. **Document type:** government publication.
Supersedes in part (in 1981): Kuwait. Al-Idarah al-Markaziyyah lil-Ihsa'. Al-Ihsa'at al-Maaliyyah.

330   KU
KUWAIT. CENTRAL STATISTICAL OFFICE. PRELIMINARY RESULTS OF LABOUR FORCE BY SAMPLE. (Text in Arabic) 1973. irreg., latest 1990. Central Statistical Office - Al-Idarah al-Markaziyyah lil-Ihsa', P.O. Box 26188, Safat 13122, Kuwait. TEL 965-2428200. FAX 965-2430464. TELEX 22468 TAKHTET KT. **Document type:** government publication.
Supersedes: Kuwait. Central Statistical Office. Labour Force by Sample Survey.

336   KU
KUWAIT. CENTRAL STATISTICAL OFFICE. PROVISIONAL ESTIMATES - NATIONAL ACCOUNTS. (Text in Arabic, English) 1976. a., latest for years 1989-1992. Central Statistical Office - Al-Idarah al-Markaziyyah lil-Ihsa', P.O. Box 26188, Safat 13122, Kuwait. TEL 965-2428200. FAX 965-2430464. TELEX 22468 TAKHTET KT. **Document type:** government publication.
Supersedes (in 1983): Kuwait. Al-Idarah al-Markaziyyah lil-Ihsa'. Al-Hisabat al-Qawmiyyah wa-Jadawal al-Mudkhalat wal-Mukharajat.

330   KU
KUWAIT. CENTRAL STATISTICAL OFFICE. QUARTERLY BULLETIN FOR RETAIL PRICES. (Text in Arabic, English) q. 0.50 din. per no. (effective 1996). Central Statistical Office - Al-Idarah al-Markaziyyah lil-Ihsa', P.O. Box 26188, Safat 13122, Kuwait. TEL 965-2428200. FAX 965-2430464. TELEX 22468 TAKHTET KT. **Document type:** government publication.

BUSINESS AND ECONOMICS — ABSTRACTING, BIBLIOGRAPHIES, STATISTICS

330   KU
KUWAIT. CENTRAL STATISTICAL OFFICE. QUARTERLY BULLETIN FOR WHOLESALE PRICES. (Text in Arabic, English) q. 0.50 din. per no. Central Statistical Office - Al-Idarah al-Markaziyyah lil-Ihsa', P.O. Box 26188, Safat 13122, Kuwait. TEL 965-2428200. FAX 965-2430464. TELEX 22468 TAKHTET KT. **Document type:** government publication.

330   KU
KUWAIT. CENTRAL STATISTICAL OFFICE. WHOLESALE PRICE INDEX NUMBERS/KUWAIT. AL-IDARAH AL-MARKAZIYYAH LIL-IHSA'. AL-ARQAM AL-QIYASIYYAH LI-AS'AR AL-JUMLAH. Variant title: Price Index Numbers - Wholesale. (Text in Arabic, English) 1973. m. Central Statistical Office - Al-Idarah al-Markaziyyah lil-Ihsa', P.O. Box 26188, Safat 13122, Kuwait. TEL 965-2428200. FAX 965-2430464. TELEX 22468 TAKHTET KT. **Document type:** government publication.

332.6   KU
KUWAIT. CENTRAL STATISTICAL OFFICE. YEARLY BULLETIN OF TRANSIT STATISTICS/KUWAIT. AL-IDARAH AL-MARKAZIYYAH LIL-IHSA'. NASHRAH IHSA'AT AL-TRANSIT. (Text in Arabic, English) 1981. a., latest 1989. Central Statistical Office - Al-Idarah al-Markaziyyah lil-Ihsa', P.O. Box 26188, Safat 13122, Kuwait. TEL 965-2428200. FAX 965-2430464. TELEX 22468 TAKHTET KT. **Document type:** government publication.
Description: Provides statistics on transit movement through Kuwait, listed by major commodity group, country of origin and destination.

331.11   US
LABOR FORCE AND EMPLOYMENT IN WASHINGTON STATE. m. (plus a. reports). $5. Employment Security Department, Labor Market and Economic Analysis Branch, Box 9046, Olympia, WA 98507-9046. Ed. Gary Bodeutsch. charts. **Document type:** government publication.
Description: Presents current and historical labor force and employment data for the state of Washington and each of its 12 Metropolitan Statistical Areas.

331.11   US
LABOR FORCE AND NONAGRICULTURAL EMPLOYMENT ESTIMATES. 1970. a. free. Department of Employment Security, Research and Statistics Division, 500 James Robertson Pkwy., 11th Fl., Nashville, TN 37245-1000. TEL 615-741-1729. circ. controlled. **Document type:** government publication.
Formerly: Tennessee Annual Average Labor Force Estimates; Which was formed by the merger of: Tennessee Civilian Work Force Estimates (ISSN 0085-7165); Tennessee Annual Average Work Force Estimates.

331.88   IO
LABOUR FORCE SITUATION IN INDONESIA: PRELIMINARY FIGURES/KEADAAN ANGKATAN KERJA DI INDONESIA: ANGKA SEMENTARA. (Text in English and Indonesian) 1964. a. Rps.27500($11.97) Central Bureau of Statistics - Biro Pusat Statistik, Jalan Dr. Sutomo No. 8, Box 3, Jakarta Pusat, Indonesia. TEL 62-21-372808. circ. 500. **Document type:** government publication.

331.11   CN
LABOUR FORCE SURVEY. 12/yr. Can.$60 (effective 1997). Ministry of Finance and Corporate Relations, B C Stats, P.O. Box 9410, Stn. Prov. Govt., Victoria, BC V8W 9V1, Canada. TEL 250-387-1502. FAX 250-387-0329. E-mail: bcstats@fincc04.fin.gov.bc.ca; URL: http://www.bcstats.gov.bc.ca. **Document type:** government publication.
Description: Shows employment and unemployment by age, sex, occupation and industry, with regional breakdowns.

330.9   UK   ISSN 1351-4504
LABOUR MARKET BULLETIN. 1991. m. £68 (overseas £110) (effective 1996). London Research Centre, Research Library, 81 Black Prince Rd., London SE1 7SZ, England. TEL 44-171-627-9666. FAX 44-171-627-9674. Ed. Tim Owen. adv. contact: Annabel Davies. **Document type:** abstracting/indexing.

658   SZ
LANDESINDEX DER KONSUMENTENPREISE/INDICE SUISSE DES PRIX A LA CONSOMMATION. (Text in French and German) 1988. m. 44 SFr. Bundesamt fuer Statistik, Schwarztorstr. 96, CH-3003 Bern, Switzerland. TEL 41-31-3236060. FAX 41-31-3236061. URL: http://www.admin.ch/bfs. **Document type:** government publication.

658   UK
▼**LATEST MANAGEMENT RESEARCH AND PRACTICE.** 1996. m. M C B University Press Ltd., 60-62 Toller Ln., Bradford, W. Yorks BD8 9BY, England. TEL 44-1274-777700. FAX 44-1274-785200. E-mail: mwills@mcb.co.uk; URL: http://www.mcb.co.uk/lmrp.htm. Eds. John Peters, Mathew Wills. **Document type:** abstracting/indexing.
●Available only online.
Description: Seeks to promote the widespread dissemination of current management literature.

LATIN AMERICAN INDEX. see POLITICAL SCIENCE — *Abstracting, Bibliographies, Statistics*

330   CK   ISSN 0120-2596
HC196
LECTURAS DE ECONOMIA. 1980. 2/yr. Col.$8000($80) (effective 1996). Universidad de Antioquia, Centro de Investigaciones Economicas, Apdo. Aereo 1226, Medellin, Colombia. TEL 574-210-58-42. FAX 574-2331249. E-mail: alviar@quimbaya.udea.edu.co. Ed. Mauricio Alviar. R&P contact: Mauricio Alviar. adv. contact: Ricardo Arango. bk.rev. circ. 1,000. (back issues avail.) Indexed: IBR, P.A.I.S.For.Lang.Ind. **Document type:** academic/scholarly publication.
Formerly (until no.2, 1980): Revista Temas Economicos (ISSN 0120-1794)

330 314   IT   ISSN 0024-1326
LETTERE D'AFFARI. 1946. m. L.70000. Centro per la Statistica Aziendale, Via A. Baldesi 18, 50131 Florence, Italy. TEL 39-55-576041. FAX 39-55-576265. Ed. Massimo Livi Bacci. bibl.; charts; mkt. **Document type:** monographic series.

382 316   LY
LIBYA. CENSUS AND STATISTICAL DEPARTMENT. TRENDS OF EXTERNAL TRADE. (Text in Arabic and English) 1958. m.? free. Secretariat of Planning, Census and Statistics Department, P.O. Box 600, Tripoli, Libya. **Document type:** government publication.
Formerly: Libya. Census and Statistical Department. Summary of External Trade Statistics (ISSN 0023-1622)

382   LY
LIBYA. CENSUS AND STATISTICS DEPARTMENT. EXTERNAL TRADE INDEX. (Text in Arabic, English) irreg. free. Secretariat of Planning, Census and Statistics Department, P.O. Box 600, Tripoli, Libya. **Document type:** government publication.

382 316   LY   ISSN 0075-9228
LIBYA. CENSUS AND STATISTICS DEPARTMENT. EXTERNAL TRADE STATISTICS. (Text in Arabic and English) 1954. a. free. Secretariat of Planning, Census and Statistics Department, P.O. Box 600, Tripoli, Libya. **Document type:** government publication.

338 316   LY   ISSN 0075-9244
LIBYA. CENSUS AND STATISTICS DEPARTMENT. INDUSTRIAL CENSUS. (Text in Arabic and English) 1964. decennial. free. Secretariat of Planning, Census and Statistics Department, P.O. Box 600, Tripoli, Libya. **Document type:** government publication.

338 316   LY   ISSN 0075-9252
LIBYA. CENSUS AND STATISTICS DEPARTMENT. REPORT OF THE ANNUAL SURVEY OF LARGE MANUFACTURING ESTABLISHMENTS. (Text in Arabic and English) 1965. a. free. Secretariat of Planning, Census and Statistics Department, P.O. Box 600, Tripoli, Libya. **Document type:** government publication.

330   LY
LIBYA. CENSUS AND STATISTICS DEPARTMENT. STATISTICAL HANDBOOK OF THE LIBYAN ARAB JAMAHIRIYA. (Text in Arabic and English) 1980. a. free. Secretariat of Planning, Census and Statistics Department, P.O. Box 600, Tripoli, Libya. **Document type:** government publication.

330   LY   ISSN 1013-736X
LIBYA. CENSUS AND STATISTICS DEPARTMENT. VITAL STATISTICS OF THE SOCIALIST PEOPLE'S LIBYAN ARAB JAMAHIRIYA. Key Title: Al-Ihsa'iyyat al-Hayawiyyat. (Text in Arabic and English) 1972. a. free. Secretariat of Planning, Census and Statistics Department, P.O. Box 600, Tripoli, Libya. **Document type:** government publication.

338 316   LY   ISSN 0075-9295
LIBYA. CENSUS AND STATISTICS DEPARTMENT. WHOLESALE PRICES IN TRIPOLI TOWN. (Text in Arabic and English) 1967. q. free. Secretariat of Planning, Census and Statistics Department, P.O. Box 600, Tripoli, Libya. **Document type:** government publication.

331.2 314   YU   ISSN 0300-2535
HA1631
LICNI DOHOCI. (Subseries of Statisticki Bilten) a. 30 din.($1.67) Savezni Zavod za Statistiku, Kneza Milosa 20, Belgrade, Yugoslavia. TEL 681-999. stat. circ. 1,000. **Document type:** government publication.

LIFESTYLE CHARACTERISTICS OF SPORTING GOODS CONSUMERS. see SPORTS AND GAMES — *Abstracting, Bibliographies, Statistics*

658   US   ISSN 1067-182X
HF5415.33.U6
LIFESTYLE MARKET ANALYST. a. $310 (effective 1997). S R D S (Subsidiary of: V N U U.S.A.), 1700 Higgins Rd., Des Plaines, IL 60018. TEL 847-375-5000; 800-851-7737. FAX 847-375-5001. E-mail: jlevy@srds.com; URL: http://www.srds.com. Ed. June Levy. **Document type:** trade publication.
Description: Covers national, regional, and local markets. Offers detailed demographic data, including age, income, occupation, education, and home ownership.

382   IT
LISTINO QUINDICINALE PREZZI. fortn. L.240000 (effective 1997). Camera di Commercio Industria Artigianato e Agricoltura di Torino, Via S. Francesco da Paola 24, 10123 Turin, Italy. TEL 39-11-57161. FAX 39-11-5716516.

382   IT
LISTINO SETTIMANALE PREZZI. w. L.52000 (effective 1997). Camera di Commercio Industria Artigianato e Agricoltura di Torino, Via S. Francesco da Paola 24, 10123 Turin, Italy. TEL 39-11-57161. FAX 39-11-5716516.

331 016   GW   ISSN 0935-4743
LITERATURDOKUMENTATION ZUR ARBEITSMARKT- UND BERUFSFORSCHUNG. 1972. 2/yr. DM.70. Bundesanstalt fuer Arbeit, Institut fuer Arbeitsmarkt- und Berufsforschung, Regensburgerstr. 104, 90327 Nuernberg, Germany. TEL 49-911-1793011. FAX 49-911-1793258. E-mail: iab.ba@t-online.de. circ. 3,000. Indexed: Int.Lab.Doc. **Document type:** government publication, bibliography.
Description: List of journals, monographs, and conference papers on labor market and occupational research.

330   UK
LONDON RESEARCH CENTRE. LONDON (YEAR). 1966. a. London Research Centre, 81 Black Prince Rd., London SE1 7SZ, England. TEL 44-171-735-4250. FAX 44-171-627-9606. **Document type:** abstracting/indexing.
Formerly: Annual Abstract of Greater London Statistics (ISSN 0960-9741)

314 330   LU   ISSN 0076-1575
HA1411
LUXEMBOURG. SERVICE CENTRAL DE LA STATISTIQUE ET DES ETUDES ECONOMIQUES. ANNUAIRE STATISTIQUE. 1955. a. 1100 Fr. Service Central de la Statistique et des Etudes Economiques, 6 bd. Royal, B.P. 304, 2013 Luxembourg, Luxembourg. TEL 352-478-4268. FAX 352-46-42-89. E-mail: statec.post@statec.etat.lu; URL: http://statec.gouvernement.lu. Dir. Robert Weides; Pub. Guy Zacharias. R&P contact: Guy Zacharias. TEL 352-478-4281. adv. contact: Eliane Schreurs. circ. 1,300. (also avail. in diskette format) **Document type:** government publication.
Formerly (until 1962): Luxembourg. Office de la Statistique Generale. Annuaire Statistique.
Description: Reports economic and social statistical data for Luxembourg.

BUSINESS AND ECONOMICS — ABSTRACTING, BIBLIOGRAPHIES, STATISTICS

332.6 LU
LUXEMBOURG. SERVICE CENTRAL DE LA STATISTIQUE ET DES ETUDES ECONOMIQUES. ANNUAIRE STATISTIQUE (YEAR); de la grande region Saar-Lor-Lux-Treves - Palatinat Occidental - Wallonie. (Text in French, German) biennial. 360 Fr. Service Central de la Statistique et des Etudes Economiques, 6 bd. Royal, B.P. 304, 2013 Luxembourg, Luxembourg. TEL 352-478-4268. FAX 352-464289. E-mail: statec.post@statec.etat.lu; URL: http://statec.gouvernement.lu. circ. 2,000. **Document type:** government publication.
Description: Presents and analyzes statistical data on the economic conditions and situation in the Luxembourg-Germany-France-Belgium border region.

330 314 LU ISSN 0076-1583
HC330.
LUXEMBOURG. SERVICE CENTRAL DE LA STATISTIQUE ET DES ETUDES ECONOMIQUES. BULLETIN DU STATEC. 1955. 8/yr. 900 Fr. (effective 1997). Service Central de la Statistique et des Etudes Economiques, 6 bd. Royal, B.P. 304, 2013 Luxembourg, Luxembourg. TEL 352-478-4268. FAX 352-464289. E-mail: statec.post@statec.etat.lu; URL: http://statec.gouvernement.lu. circ. 900. **Document type:** government publication, bulletin. —BLDSC (2909.300000).
Description: Contains commentaries on specific statistical surveys and studies on economic problems of Luxembourg.

332.6 LU
LUXEMBOURG. SERVICE CENTRAL DE LA STATISTIQUE ET DES ETUDES ECONOMIQUES. CONJONCTURE ACTUELLE. (Text in French, German) m. free. Service Central de la Statistique et des Etudes Economiques, 6 bd. Royal, B.P. 304, 2013 Luxembourg, Luxembourg. TEL 352-478-4268. FAX 352-464289. E-mail: statec.post@statec.etat.lu; URL: http://statec.gouvernement.lu. **Document type:** government publication.
Description: Provides a quick statistical reference to the Saar-Lor-Lux-Treves Palatinat occidental border region.

332.6 LU ISSN 0076-1605
LUXEMBOURG. SERVICE CENTRAL DE LA STATISTIQUE ET DES ETUDES ECONOMIQUES. CAHIERS ECONOMIQUES. 1951. irreg., no.85, 1995. price varies. Service Central de la Statistique et des Etudes Economiques, 6 bd. Royal, B.P. 304, 2013 Luxembourg, Luxembourg. TEL 352-478-4268. FAX 352-464289. E-mail: statec.post@statec.etat.lu; URL: http://statec.gouvernement.lu. **Document type:** monographic series, government publication.
Description: Comprises various statistical studies of the economic condition of Luxembourg.

330 LU ISSN 1012-6619
LUXEMBOURG. SERVICE CENTRAL DE LA STATISTIQUE ET DES ETUDES ECONOMIQUES. INDICATEURS RAPIDES. SERIE A1: INDICES DES PRIX A LA COMSOMMATION. 1979. m. 300 Fr. for complete series (effective 1997). Service Central de la Statistique et des Etudes Economiques, 6 bd. Royal, B.P. 304, 2013 Luxembourg, Luxembourg. TEL 352-478-4268. FAX 352-464289. E-mail: statec.post@statec.etat.lu; URL: http://statec.gouvernement.lu. (looseleaf format) **Document type:** government publication.

330 LU ISSN 1012-6589
LUXEMBOURG. SERVICE CENTRAL DE LA STATISTIQUE ET DES ETUDES ECONOMIQUES. INDICATEURS RAPIDES. SERIE A3: INDICES DES PRIX A LA PRODUCTION DES PRODUITS INDUSTRIELS. m. 1000 Fr. for complete series (effective 1997). Service Central de la Statistique et des Etudes Economiques, 6 bd. Royal, B.P. 304, 2013 Luxembourg, Luxembourg. TEL 352-478-4268. FAX 352-464289. E-mail: statec.post@statec.etat.lu; URL: http://statec.gouvernement.lu. (looseleaf format) **Document type:** government publication.

330 314 LU ISSN 0019-6916
LUXEMBOURG. SERVICE CENTRAL DE LA STATISTIQUE ET DES ETUDES ECONOMIQUES. INDICATEURS RAPIDES. SERIE B1: INDICES DE L'ACTIVITE INDUSTRIELLE. (Consists of 23 series) 1963. m. 1000 Fr. (effective 1997). Service Central de la Statistique et des Etudes Economiques, 6 bd Royal, B.P. 304, 2013 Luxembourg, Luxembourg. TEL 352-478-4268. FAX 352-464289. E-mail: statec.post@statec.etat.lu; URL: http://statec.gouvernement.lu. charts. circ. 400. (looseleaf format) **Document type:** government publication.

330 LU ISSN 1012-6627
LUXEMBOURG. SERVICE CENTRAL DE LA STATISTIQUE ET DES ETUDES ECONOMIQUES. INDICATEURS RAPIDES. SERIE C: EMPLOI ET CHOMAGE - SIDERURGIE - FINANCES - TRANSPORT ET COMMERCE. m. 1000 F. for complete series (effective 1997). Service Central de la Statistique et des Etudes Economiques, 6 bd. Royal, B.P. 304, 2013 Luxembourg, Luxembourg. TEL 352-478-4268. FAX 352-464289. E-mail: statec.post@statec.etat.lu; URL: http://statec.gouvernement.lu. (looseleaf format) **Document type:** government publication.

LUXEMBOURG. SERVICE CENTRAL DE LA STATISTIQUE ET DES ETUDES ECONOMIQUES. INDICATEURS RAPIDES. SERIE D. IMMATRICULATIONS DE VEHICULES AUTOMOTEURS. see
TRANSPORTATION — Abstracting, Bibliographies, Statistics

332.6 LU ISSN 1012-6678
LUXEMBOURG. SERVICE CENTRAL DE LA STATISTIQUE ET DES ETUDES ECONOMIQUES. INDICATEURS RAPIDES. SERIE H: COMMERCE EXTERIEUR DU LUXEMBOURG. 3/yr. 1000 F. for complete series (effective 1997). Service Central de la Statistique et des Etudes Economiques, 6 bd. Royal, B.P. 304, 2013 Luxembourg, Luxembourg. TEL 352-478-4268. FAX 382-464289. E-mail: statec.post@statec.etat.lu; URL: http://statec.gouvernement.lu. (looseleaf format) **Document type:** government publication.

330.021 LU
LUXEMBOURG. SERVICE CENTRAL DE LA STATISTIQUE ET DES ETUDES ECONOMIQUES. STATISTIQUES HISTORIQUES. (Subseries of its Annuaire Statistique) 1960. irreg., latest 1990. 1200 Fr. (effective 1997). Service Central de la Statistique et des Etudes Economiques, 6 bd. Royal, B.P. 304, 2013 Luxembourg, Luxembourg. TEL 352-478-4268. FAX 352-164289. E-mail: statec.post@statec.etat.lu; URL: http://statec.gouvernement.lu. bibl. **Document type:** government publication.
Formerly: Luxembourg. Service Central de la Statistique et des Etudes Economiques. Statistiques Retrospectif.
Description: Contains historical statistical data covering the 150 years of Luxembourg's independence.

330 016 UK
M I R A AUTOMOTIVE BUSINESS NEWS. 1979. fortn. £320. Motor Industry Research Association, Watling St., Nuneaton, Warwickshire CV10 0TU, England. FAX 44-1203-343772. Ed. Jane Stone. (back issues avail.) **Document type:** trade publication.
●Also available online. Vendor(s): European Space Agency.
Former titles: M I R A Automotive Business Index; Business News Index (ISSN 0260-194X); Business Information for the Motor Industry.
Description: Contains items from the business and technical press on commercial aspects of the motor industry.

382 310 MH
MACAO. DIRECCAO DOS SERVICOS DE ESTATISTICA E CENSOS. ANUARIO ESTATISTICO DO COMERCIO EXTERNO/MACAO. CENSUS AND STATISTICS DEPARTMENT. YEARBOOK OF EXTERNAL TRADE STATISTICS. (Text in Portuguese) 1955. a. free. Direccao dos Servicos de Estatistica e Censos, Rua Inacio Baptista, No. 4-6, P.O. Box 3022, Macao. TEL 853-3995311. FAX 853-307825. **Document type:** government publication.

381 MH
MACAO. DIRECCAO DOS SERVICOS DE ESTATISTICA E CENSOS. C A M CLASSIFICACAO DAS ACTIVIDADES ECONOMICAS DE MACAU/MACAO. CENSUS AND STATISTICS DEPARTMENT. C A M CLASSIFICATION OF ECONOMIC ACTIVITIES OF MACAO. (Text in Chinese, Portuguese) 1986. irreg. free. Direccao dos Servicos de Estatistica e Censos, Rua Inacio Baptista, No. 4-6, P.O. Box 3022, Macao. TEL 853-3995311. FAX 853-307825. **Document type:** government publication.

330 MH
MACAO. DIRECCAO DOS SERVICOS DE ESTATISTICA E CENSOS. CONTAS ECONOMICAS DO SECTOR PUBLICO NAO EMPRESARIAL/MACAO. CENSUS AND STATISTICS DEPARTMENT. ECONOMIC ACCOUNTS OF PUBLIC SECTOR. (Text in Chinese, Portuguese) 1982. a. free. Direccao dos Servicos de Estatistica e Censos, Rua Inacio Baptista, No. 4-6, P.O. Box 3022, Macao. TEL 853-3995311. FAX 853-307825. **Document type:** government publication.

382 310 MH
MACAO. DIRECCAO DOS SERVICOS DE ESTATISTICA E CENSOS. ESTATISTICAS DO COMERCIO EXTERNO/MACAO. CENSUS AND STATISTICS DEPARTMENT. STATISTICS ON EXTERNAL TRADE. (Text in Chinese, Portuguese) 1977. q. Direccao dos Servicos de Estatistica e Censos, Rua Inacio Baptista, No. 4-6, P.O. Box 3022, Macao. TEL 853-3995311. FAX 853-307825. **Document type:** government publication.
Formerly: Macao. Direccaco dos Servicos de Estatistica e Censos. Boletim Mensual do Comercio Exterior (ISSN 0872-4628)
Description: Contains a series of summary tables showing monthly and annual trade data by principal trading countries and selected commodity groupings.

330 MH
MACAO. DIRECCAO DOS SERVICOS DE ESTATISTICA E CENSOS. ESTIMATIVAS DO PRODUTO INTERNO BRUTO/MACAO. CENSUS AND STATISTICS DEPARTMENT. GROSS DOMESTIC PRODUCT ESTIMATES. (Text in Chinese and Portuguese) 1982. a. free. Direccao dos Servicos de Estatistica e Censos, Rua Inacio Baptista, No. 4-6, P.O. Box 3022, Macao. TEL 853-3995269. FAX 853-307825. **Document type:** government publication.
Description: Estimates the GDP in Macao by using the expenditure approach that covers private consumption expenditure, government consumption expenditure, gross domestic fixed capital formation, and increase in stock, exports and imports.

382 MH
MACAO. DIRECCAO DOS SERVICOS DE ESTATISTICA E CENSOS. INDICADORES DO COMERCIO EXTERNO/MACAO. CENSUS AND STATISTICS DEPARTMENT. EXTERNAL TRADE INDICATORS. (Text in Chinese and Portuguese) 1992. m. Direccao dos Servicos de Estatistica e Censos, Rua Inacio Baptista, No. 4-6, P.O. Box 3022, Macao. TEL 853-3995311. FAX 853-307825. **Document type:** government publication.

381 MH ISSN 0870-5577
MACAO. DIRECCAO DOS SERVICOS DE ESTATISTICA E CENSOS. INDICE DE PRECOS NO CONSUMIDOR/MACAO. CENSUS AND STATISTICS DEPARTMENT. CONSUMER PRICE INDEX. (Supplements avail.) (Text in Chinese, Portuguese) 1984. q. free. Direccao dos Servicos de Estatistica e Censos, Rua Inacio Baptista, No. 4-6, P.O. Box 3022, Macao. TEL 853-3995311. FAX 853-307825. **Document type:** government publication.
Description: Presents statistics on price movement of representative consumer goods and services.

381 MH ISSN 0870-5631
MACAO. DIRECCAO DOS SERVICOS DE ESTATISTICA E CENSOS. INDICE DE PRECOS NO CONSUMIDOR (RELATORIO ANUAL)/MACAO. CENSUS AND STATISTICS DEPARTMENT. CONSUMER PRICE INDEX (ANNUAL REPORT). (Text in Chinese, Portuguese) 1984. a. free. Direccao dos Servicos de Estatistica e Censos, Rua Inacio Baptista, No. 4-6, P.O. Box 3022, Macao. TEL 853-3995311. FAX 853-307825. **Document type:** government publication.
Description: Presents statistics on price movement of representative consumer goods and services in annual base.

BUSINESS AND ECONOMICS — ABSTRACTING, BIBLIOGRAPHIES, STATISTICS

331 MH
MACAO. DIRECCAO DOS SERVICOS DE ESTATISTICA E CENSOS. INDICES E SALARIOS DA CONSTRUCAO CIVIL/MACAO. CENSUS AND STATISTICS DEPARTMENT. INDEXES AND WAGES IN CIVIL CONTRUCTION. (Text in Chinese, Portuguese) 1985. q. free. Direccao dos Servicos de Estatistica e Censos, Rua Inacio Baptista, No. 4-6, P.O. Box 3022, Macao. TEL 853-3995311. FAX 853-307825. **Document type:** government publication.
  Formerly: Macao. Direccao dos Servicos de Estatistica e Censos. Inquerito ao Emprego e Salarios na Construcao Civil - Survey of Employment and Wages in the Construction Industry (ISSN 0870-5607)
  Description: Presents the salaries of construction workers engaged in private and public sectors.

331.11 MH
MACAO. DIRECCAO DOS SERVICOS DE ESTATISTICA E CENSOS. INQUERITO AO EMPREGO/MACAO. CENSUS AND STATISTICS DEPARTMENT. EMPLOYMENT SURVEY. (Text in Chinese, Portuguese) m. and q. free. Direccao dos Servicos de Estatistica e Censos, Rua Inacio Baptista, No. 4-6, P.O. Box 3022, Macao. TEL 853-3995311. FAX 853-307825. **Document type:** government publication.

332.6 MH ISSN 0870-5674
MACAO. DIRECCAO DOS SERVICOS DE ESTATISTICA E CENSOS. INQUERITO AS DESPESAS FAMILIARES/MACAO. CENSUS AND STATISTICS DEPARTMENT. HOUSEHOLD EXPENDITURE SURVEY. (Text in Chinese, Portuguese) 1981. quinquennial. free. Direccao dos Servicos de Estatistica e Censos, Rua Inacio Baptista, No. 4-6, P.O. Box 3022, Macao. TEL 853-3995311. FAX 853-307825. **Document type:** government publication.
  Description: Analyzes household structure expenditure and receipt data for the computation of the Consumer Price Index.

330 MH
MACAO. DIRECCAO DOS SERVICOS DE ESTATISTICA E CENSOS. INQUERITO INDUSTRIAL/MACAO. CENSUS AND STATISTICS DEPARTMENT. INDUSTRIAL SURVEY. (Text in Chinese, Portuguese) 1979. a. free. Direccao dos Servicos de Estatistica e Censos, Rua Inacio Baptista, No. 4-6, P.O. Box 3022, Macao. TEL 853-3995311. FAX 853-307825. **Document type:** government publication.
  Formerly: Macao Direccao dos Servicos de Estatistica e Censos. Recesamento Industrial & Macao. Direccao dos Servicos de Estatistica e Censos. Inquerito Industrial (ISSN 0870-5666)

330 MH
MACAO. DIRECCAO DOS SERVICOS DE ESTATISTICA E CENSOS. INQUERITOS AS NECESSIDADES DE MAO-DE-OBRA E AS REMUNERACOES/MACAO. CENSUS AND STATISTICS DEPARTMENT. MANPOWER NEEDS AND WAGES SURVEY. (Text in Chinese, Portuguese) q. free. Direccao dos Servicos de Estatistica e Censos, Rua Inacio Baptista, No. 4-6, P.O. Box 3022, Macao. TEL 853-3995311. FAX 853-307825. **Document type:** government publication.
  Formerly: Macao. Direccao dos Servicos de Estatistica e Censos. Avaliacao das Necessidades de Mao-de-Obra.

381 MH
MACAO. DIRECCAO DOS SERVICOS DE ESTATISTICA E CENSOS. METODOLOGIA DO INDICE DE PRECOS NO CONSUMIDOR/MACAO. CENSUS AND STATISTICS DEPARTMENT. CONSUMER PRICE INDEX METHODOLOGY. (Text in Chinese, Portuguese) 1984. irreg. free. Direccao dos Servicos de Estatistica e Censos, Rua Inacio Baptista, No. 4-6, P.O. Box 3022, Macao. TEL 853-3995311. FAX 853-307825. **Document type:** government publication.

381 MG
MADAGASCAR. DIRECTION GENERALE DE L'INSTITUT NATIONAL DE LA STATISTIQUE. ANALYSE DES DONNEES. 1994. a. FMG.9909. Direction Generale de l'Institut National de la Statistique, B.P. 485, Antananarivo 101, Madagascar. TEL 261-2-200-70. FAX 261-2-200-80. Ed. Daniel Ramarokoto; Pub. Daniel Ramarokoto. adv. contact: Daniel Ramarokoto. **Document type:** government publication.

381 MG
MADAGASCAR. DIRECTION GENERALE DE L'INSTITUT NATIONAL DE LA STATISTIQUE. BULLETIN MENSUEL DE STATISTIQUE. s-a. FMG.13200. Direction Generale de l'Institut National de la Statistique, Ministere de l'Economie et du Plan, B.P. 485, Antananarivo 101, Madagascar. TEL 261-2-200-70. FAX 261-2-200-80. **Document type:** government publication, bulletin.
  Formerly: Malagasy Republic. Direction Generale de la Banque des Donnees de l'Etat. Bulletin Mensuel de Statistique.

381 MG
MADAGASCAR. DIRECTION GENERALE DE L'INSTITUT NATIONAL DE LA STATISTIQUE. INVENTAIRE SOCIO-ECONOMIQUE. 1988. every 5 yrs. FMG.18290. Direction Generale de l'Institut National de la Statistique, B.P. 485, Antananarivo 101, Madagascar. TEL 261-2-200-70. FAX 261-2-200-80. Ed. Daniel Ramarokoto; Pub. Daniel Ramarokoto. adv. contact: Daniel Ramarokoto. **Document type:** government publication.

330 315 II ISSN 0025-0481
MAHARASHTRA QUARTERLY BULLETIN OF ECONOMICS AND STATISTICS. 1960. q. Rs.200. Directorate of Economics and Statistics, MHADA Bldg., Kalanagar, Bandra (E), Bombay 400051, India. (Subscr. to: Government Printing and Stationery, Charni Rd. Gardens, Bombay 400 004, India) charts; mkt.; stat. **Indexed:** Rural Devel.Abstr. **Document type:** government publication, bulletin.
  Formerly: Quarterly Bulletin of Economics and Statistics.

330.9 331.8 US
MAJOR COLLECTIVE BARGAINING SETTLEMENTS IN PRIVATE INDUSTRY. (Subseries of: National Office News Releases) q. U.S. Bureau of Labor Statistics, 2 Massachusetts Ave., N.E., Washington, DC 20212. TEL 202-655-4000. (Subscr. to: Superintendent of Documents, U.S. Government Printing Office, Box 371954, Pittsburgh, PA 15250-7954. TEL 202-512-1800. FAX 202-512-2250; Or: Bureau of Labor Statistics Publications Sales Center, Box 2145, Chicago, IL 60690) **Document type:** government publication.

MAJOR U K COMPANIES HANDBOOK. see **BUSINESS AND ECONOMICS** — Investments

382 316 MW ISSN 0076-325X
MALAWI. NATIONAL STATISTICAL OFFICE. ANNUAL STATEMENT OF EXTERNAL TRADE. 1964. a. K.250. National Statistical Office, Commissioner for Census and Statistics, P.O. Box 333, Zomba, Malawi. TEL 265-50-522377. FAX 265-50-523130. TELEX 44015 CENSUS MI. **Document type:** government publication.

330 316 MW ISSN 0076-3241
MALAWI. NATIONAL STATISTICAL OFFICE. ANNUAL SURVEY OF ECONOMIC ACTIVITIES. (Issued in 1966 as: Census of Industrial Production) 1966. a. K.170. National Statistical Office, Commissioner for Census and Statistics, P.O. Box 333, Zomba, Malawi. TEL 265-50-522377. FAX 265-50-523130. TELEX 44015 CENSUS MI. **Document type:** government publication.

336 382 MW ISSN 0085-3003
MALAWI. NATIONAL STATISTICAL OFFICE. BALANCE OF PAYMENTS. 1964. a. K.200. National Statistical Office, Commissioner for Census and Statistics, P.O. Box 333, Zomba, Malawi. TEL 265-50-522377. FAX 265-50-523130. TELEX 44015 CENSUS MI. **Document type:** government publication.

331 316 MW
MALAWI. NATIONAL STATISTICAL OFFICE. EMPLOYMENT AND EARNINGS: ANNUAL REPORT. a. K.150. National Statistical Office, Commissioner for Census and Statistics, P.O. Box 333, Zomba, Malawi. TEL 265-50-522377. FAX 265-50-523130. TELEX 44015 CENSUS MI. **Document type:** government publication.
  Formerly: Malawi. National Statistical Office. Reported Employment and Earnings: Annual Report.

382 315 MY ISSN 0127-8533
HF3800.6
MALAYSIA. DEPARTMENT OF STATISTICS. EXTERNAL TRADE STATISTICS, MALAYSIA. (Issued in 2 vols.) (Text in English, Malay) 1962. a. price varies. Department of Statistics - Jabatan Perangkaan, Wisma Statistik, Jalan Cenderasari, 50514 Kuala Lumpur, Malaysia. TEL 60-3-2922133. FAX 60-3-2937018. circ. 1,400. **Document type:** government publication.
  Formerly (until 1981): West Malaysia Annual Statistics of External Trade (ISSN 0085-8080)

382 MY ISSN 0127-9637
MALAYSIA. DEPARTMENT OF STATISTICS. EXTERNAL TRADE SUMMARY MALAYSIA. (Text in English) m. M.$10 per no. Department of Statistics, Wisma Statistik, Jalan Cenderasari, 50514 Kuala Lumpur, Malaysia. TEL 60-3-2922133. FAX 60-3-2937018. **Document type:** government publication.

338 MY
MALAYSIA. DEPARTMENT OF STATISTICS. INDEX OF INDUSTRIAL PRODUCTION, MALAYSIA. (Text in English) 1989. m. M.$5 per no. Department of Statistics, Wisma Statistik, Jalan Cenderasari, 50514 Kuala Lumpur, Malaysia. TEL 60-3-2922133. FAX 60-3-2937018. **Document type:** government publication.

338 MY ISSN 0128-3499
HC447.5
MALAYSIA. DEPARTMENT OF STATISTICS. MONTHLY MANUFACTURING STATISTICS, MALAYSIA. (Text in English) 1989. m. M.$7 per no. Department of Statistics, Wisma Statistik, Jalan Cenderasari, 50514 Kuala Lumpur, Malaysia. TEL 60-3-2922133. FAX 60-3-2937018. **Document type:** government publication.

382 315 MY ISSN 0127-0451
MALAYSIA. DEPARTMENT OF STATISTICS. STATISTICS OF EXTERNAL TRADE SARAWAK. (Text in English) 1954. a. M.$60. Department of Statistics, Wisma Statistik, Jalan Cenderasari, 50514 Kuala Lumpur, Malaysia. TEL 60-3-2922133. FAX 60-3-2937018. (Subscr. to: Department of Statistics, Malaysia (Sarawak Branch), 5th Fl., Bangunan Tun Datuk, Patinggi Tuanku Hj. Bujang, 93514 Kuching, Sarawak, Malaysia) **Document type:** government publication.
  Formerly: Sarawak External Trade Statistics (ISSN 0080-6455)

330 MY
MALAYSIAN ECONOMY IN BRIEF. (Text in English) m. M.$5 per no. Department of Statistics - Jabatan Perangkaan, Wisma Statistik, Jalan Cenderasari, 50514 Kuala Lumpur, Malaysia. TEL 03-2922133. FAX 03-2937018. **Document type:** government publication.

330 316 ML
MALI. DIRECTION NATIONALE DE LA STATISTIQUE ET DE L'INFORMATIQUE. ANNUAIRE STATISTIQUE.* 1962. a. price varies. Direction Nationale de la Statistique et de l'Informatique, B.P. 12, Bamako, Mali. index. (also avail. in microfiche from CHL) **Document type:** government publication.
  Former titles: Mali. Service de la Statistique Generale, de la Comptabilite Nationale et de la Mecanographie. Annuaire Statistique (ISSN 0076-3411); Supersedes (in 1962): Chambre de Commerce, d'Agriculture et d'Industrie de Bamako, Mali. Annuaire Statistique (ISSN 0069-2522)

336 316 ML
MALI. SERVICE DE LA STATISTIQUE GENERALE, DE LA COMPTABILITE NATIONALE ET DE LA MECANOGRAPHIE. STATISTIQUES DOUANIERES DU COMMERCE EXTERIEUR.* irreg. Direction Nationale de la Statistique et de l'Informatique, B.P. 12, Bamako, Mali. **Document type:** government publication.

338 314 MM
MALTA. CENTRAL OFFICE OF STATISTICS. INDUSTRIAL STATISTICS. a. L.2. Central Office of Statistics, Auberge d'Italie, Merchants' St., Valletta, Malta. FAX 356-248483. (Subscr. to: Publications Bookshop, Auberge de Castille, Valletta, Malta) **Document type:** government publication.
  Former titles: Malta. Central Office of Statistics. Census of Industrial Production Report (ISSN 0076-3462); Incorporates: Malta. Central Office of Statistics. Census of Industrial Production Summary Report; Malta. Central Office of Statistics. Census of Production Report.

BUSINESS AND ECONOMICS — ABSTRACTING, BIBLIOGRAPHIES, STATISTICS

330 — MM
MALTA'S ECONOMIC INDICATORS. 1955. a. free. Central Office of Statistics, Auberge d'Italie, Merchants' St., Valletta, Malta. FAX 356-248483. **Document type:** government publication.
  Formerly: Malta. Central Office of Statistics. Economic Trends.

658 629.13 — US — ISSN 0565-7199
Z7914.A2
MANAGEMENT (BALTIMORE); a bibliography for N A S A managers. 1968. a. U.S. National Aeronautics and Space Administration, National Technology Transfer Center, Information Collection and Management, 800 Elkridge Landing Rd., Linthicum Heights, MD 21090-2934. E-mail: help@sti.nasa.gov; URL: http://www.sti.nasa.gov. index. **Document type:** government publication, bibliography.

658.8 016 — UK — ISSN 0308-2172
HD28
MANAGEMENT AND MARKETING ABSTRACTS. 1976. m. £617($987) (effective 1997). Pira International, Randalls Rd., Leatherhead, Surrey KT22 7RU, England. TEL 44-1372-802050. FAX 44-1372-802239. E-mail: publications@pira.co.uk; URL: http://www.pira.co.uk/. Ed. Paul Taylor; Pub. Marie Rushton. bk.rev.; index. **Document type:** abstracting/indexing.
  ●Also available online. Vendor(s): Data-Star, GBI.
  —BLDSC (5359.008800). **CCC.**
  Formerly: Marketing Abstracts (ISSN 0307-0794)

658 016 — UK — ISSN 0309-0582
HD28
MANAGEMENT BIBLIOGRAPHIES AND REVIEWS. 1975. bi-m. £3999($6399) (foreign Aus.$7999) (effective 1998). M C B University Press Ltd., 60-62 Toller Ln., Bradford, W. Yorks BD8 9BY, England. TEL 44-1274-777700. FAX 44-1274-785200. TELEX 51317-MCBUNI-G. URL: http://www.mcb.co.uk. Ed. C. Richmond. index. (back issues avail.; reprint service avail. from SWZ) **Indexed:** Bus.Ind. **Document type:** bibliography.
  —CCC.
  Incorporates: Business Education (ISSN 0144-2813).
  Description: Provides up-to-date information on new developments and thinking in management practice and serves as an invaluable resource for the research worker and practicing manager.

011 658 — US — ISSN 1046-9524
MANAGEMENT CONSULTING;* annotated bibliography of selected references. biennial. $45. Association of Management Consulting Firms, 521 Fifth Ave., 35th Fl., New York, NY 10175-3599. TEL 212-697-9693. **Document type:** bibliography.
  Description: Disseminates information on where to find current published information covering the scope of management consulting.

016 658 — US — ISSN 0360-2400
Z7164.07
MANAGEMENT CONTENTS; semi-monthly compilation of tables of contents from more than 320 business magazines and journals. 1975. m. $102 per hour Dialog; $80 BRS; $97.80 Data-Star. Information Access Company (Subsidiary of: Thomson Corporation), 362 Lakeside Dr., Foster City, CA 94409. TEL 415-378-5200; 800-227-8431. FAX 415-378-5369. (Or: Predicasts Europe, 8-10 Denman St., London W1V 7RF, England. TEL 44-171-494-3817) Ed. Karen O'Connor. adv.; bk.rev. circ. 2,000. (back issues avail.) **Document type:** abstracting/indexing.
  ●Available only online. Vendor(s): Data-Star (MGMT), Knight-Ridder Information, Inc. (File no.75), Ovid Technologies, Inc. (MGMT).

658 016 — UK — ISSN 1361-4932
HD28
▼**MANAGEMENT DEVELOPMENT ABSTRACTS.** 1996. m. M C B University Press Ltd., Anbar Electronic Intelligence, 60-62 Toller Ln., Bradford, W. Yorks BD8 9BY, England. TEL 44-1274-480916. FAX 44-1274-543576. E-mail: dkavanagh@mcb.co.uk; URL: http://www.anbar.co.uk/anbar.htm. Ed. David Pollitt. **Document type:** abstracting/indexing.
  —BLDSC (5359.019367).

658 016 — UK — ISSN 1361-4924
HD28
▼**MANAGEMENT OF CHANGE ABSTRACTS.** 1996. bi-m. M C B University Press Ltd., Anbar Electronic Intelligence, 60-62 Toller Ln., Bradford, W. Yorks BD8 9BY, England. TEL 44-1274-480916. FAX 44-1274-543576. E-mail: spuesey@anbar.co.uk; URL: http://www.anbar.co.uk/anbar.htm. Ed. David Pollitt; Pub. Carol Fellingham Webb. **Document type:** abstracting/indexing.
  —BLDSC (5359.013220).

658 — GW — ISSN 0935-9915
MANAGEMENT REVUE. 1990. q. DM.104. Rainer Hampp Verlag, Meringerzellerstr. 16, 86415 Mering, Germany. TEL 49-8233-4783. FAX 49-8233-30755. E-mail: rainer_hampp_verlag@t-online.de. Ed.Bd. **Document type:** bibliography.

332.6 — LU
LE MARCHE DES EMPRUNTS OBLIGATAIRES EN E C U/BOND MARKET IN E C U. (European Currency Unit) (Text in English, French) 1983. a. free. Societe de la Bourse de Luxembourg - Luxembourg Stock Exchange, P.O. Box 165, 11 av. de la Porte-Neuve, L-2011 Luxembourg, Luxembourg. TEL 352-4779361. FAX 352-473298. TELEX 2559-STOEX-LU. circ. 600.
  Supersedes in part: Bond Market in Luxembourg Francs and E C U; Which was formed by the merger of: Marche des Emprunts Obligataires; Marche National des Emprunts Obligataires.
  Description: Contains statistical information on the bond market in ECU regarding listings, trading volumes.

332.6 — LU
LE MARCHE DES EMPRUNTS OBLIGATAIRES EN FRANCS LUXEMBOURGEOIS/BOND MARKET IN LUXEMBOURG FRANCS. (Text in English, French) 1984. a. free. Societe de la Bourse de Luxembourg - Luxembourg Stock Exchange, P.O. Box 165, 11 av. de la Porte-Neuve, L-2011 Luxembourg, Luxembourg. TEL 352-4779361. FAX 352-473298. TELEX 2559-STOEX-LU. circ. 600.
  Supersedes in part: Bond Market in Luxembourg Francs and in E C U; Formed by the merger of: Marche des Emprunts Internationaux en E C U; Marche National des Emprunts Obligataires.
  Description: Contains statistical information on the bond market in LUF regarding listings, trading volume.

332.6 — LU
LE MARCHE EURO-OBLIGATAIRE EN E C U - STATISTIQUES MENSUELLES/EUROBOND MARKET IN E C U - MONTHLY STATISTICS. (European Currency Unit) (Text in English, French) 1991. m. free. Societe de la Bourse de Luxembourg - Luxembourg Stock Exchange, P.O. Box 165, 11 av. de la Porte-Neuve, L-2011 Luxembourg, Luxembourg. TEL 352-4779361. FAX 352-473298. TELEX 2559-STOEX-LU. E-mail: info@bourse.lu. circ. 250.
  Formerly: E C U.
  Description: Tracks the main trends of the E C U Eurobond market.

658.8 016 — UK — ISSN 0025-3596
HF5415.2
MARKET RESEARCH ABSTRACTS. 1963. s-a. £95 (foreign £105) (effective 1998). Market Research Society, 15 Northburgh St., London EC1V 0AH, England. TEL 44-171-490-4911. FAX 44-171-490-0608. (Subscr. to: NTC Publications Ltd., P.O. Box 69, Henley-on-Thames, Oxon RG9 1GB, England. TEL 44-1491-411000) Ed. P. Vangelder; Pub. Peter Greenwood. R&P contact: Nicola Potts. circ. 700. (also avail. in microfilm from UMI; reprint service avail. from SCH) **Document type:** abstracting/indexing.
  ●Also available online. Vendor(s): Data-Star, Knight-Ridder Information, Inc.
  —BLDSC (5381.560000); UMI.
  Description: Covers all fields of marketing and advertising research, as well as relevant papers in statistics, psychology, economics, sociology and other fields relevant to market researchers.

330 — US — ISSN 1052-9578
HF5410
MARKET SHARE REPORTER; an annual compilation of reported market share data on companies, products, and services. a. $170. Gale Research, 835 Penobscot Bldg., 645 Griswold St., Detroit, MI 48226-4094. TEL 313-961-2242; 800-877-4253. FAX 800-414-5043. E-mail: daniel_snyder@gale.com. Ed. Arsen J. Darnay.

658.8 016 — UK — ISSN 0305-0661
HF5415
MARKETING & DISTRIBUTION ABSTRACTS. 1971. bi-m. £3199($4999) (foreign Aus.$6499) (effective 1998). M C B University Press Ltd., Anbar Electronic Intelligence, 60-62 Toller Ln., Bradford, W. Yorks BD8 9BY, England. TEL 44-1274-480916. FAX 44-1274-543576. TELEX 51317-MCBUNI-G. URL: http://www.mcb.co.uk. Ed. Eric Sandelands. (looseleaf format) **Document type:** abstracting/indexing.
  —BLDSC (0900.290000).
  Description: Contains abstracts of articles selected from over 300 international management journals. Covers topics such as: market planning, the retail trade, advertising, new product development, logistics, direct marketing, design and stock control.

016 658.8 — US — ISSN 0732-555X
MARKETING UPDATE. w. $225 (foreign $250). Information Access Company (Subsidiary of: Thomson Corporation), 362 Lakeside Dr., Foster City, CA 94404. TEL 415-378-5200; 800-227-8431. FAX 415-378-5369. (Or: Predicasts Europe, 8-10 Denman St., London W1V 7RF, England. TEL 44-171-494-3817) (also avail. in microform from UMI) **Document type:** abstracting/indexing.
  —CCC.
  Formerly: Marketing Ideas.
  Description: Provides abstracts on marketing and communications activities, including advertising, market research, new products, sales techniques, and related topics.

658.8 — UK — ISSN 0952-2581
MARKETSEARCH. 1976. a. £189 (foreign $295) (effective 1997). Arlington Management Publications, 1 Hay Hill, Berkeley Sq., London W1X 7LF, England. TEL 44-171-495-1940. FAX 44-171-409-2557. E-mail: 106076.2024@compuserve.com. (Dist. in the U.S. by: Box 5228, Evanston, IL 60204) Ed. Kathleen Mann. **Document type:** directory.
  ●Also available online.
  Also available on CD-ROM.
  —BLDSC (5381.698600).
  Formerly: International Directory of Published Market Research.
  Description: Lists 20,000 published market research studies. Each listing includes title, a brief summary, countries covered, page count, price, date of publication, and author reference. Other sections include a publishers directory and a directory of report titles by author.

331 — US
MASSACHUSETTS. DEPARTMENT OF EMPLOYMENT AND TRAINING. EMPLOYMENT AND WAGES STATE SUMMARY. 1970. a. free. Department of Employment and Training, Charles F. Hurley Bldg., Government Center, Boston, MA 02114. TEL 617-727-6360. circ. 700. **Document type:** government publication.
  Former titles: Massachusetts. Division of Employment Security. Employment and Wages in Establishments Subject to the Massachusetts Employment Security Law. State Summary (ISSN 0076-4922); Massachusetts. Division of Employment Security. Employment and Wages in the Establishments Subject to the Massachusetts Employment Security Law. (ISSN 0360-8301); Massachusetts. Division of Employment Security. Employment and Wages for the Year.

330.9 350 310 — US
MASSACHUSETTS TAXPAYERS FOUNDATION. STATE BUDGET TRENDS. 1973. a. $3.50. Massachusetts Taxpayers Foundation, Inc., 24 Province St., Boston, MA 02108. TEL 617-720-1000. FAX 617-720-0799. (back issues avail.)
  Description: Analysis of Governor's proposed budget, with 10-year comparisons.

MAURITIUS. CENTRAL STATISTICAL OFFICE. ANNUAL DIGEST OF STATISTICS. see *STATISTICS*

BUSINESS AND ECONOMICS — ABSTRACTING, BIBLIOGRAPHIES, STATISTICS

330 MF
MAURITIUS. CENTRAL STATISTICAL OFFICE. DIGEST OF INDUSTRIAL STATISTICS. 1985. a. Rs.75 (effective Jun. 1995). Central Statistical Office, Toorawa Centre, Cr. S.S. R & J. Mosque Sts., Port Louis, Mauritius. (Subscr. to: Government Printing Office, Ramtoolah Bldg., Sir S. Ramgoolam St., Port Louis, Mauritius) TEL 230-234-5294. FAX 230-208-4011) **Document type:** government publication.
Description: Contains latest available statistical information on the industrial sector. Topics covered include quarrying, manufacturing, electricity, gas and water, and construction.

331.2 MF
MAURITIUS. CENTRAL STATISTICAL OFFICE. DIGEST OF LABOUR STATISTICS. 1966. a. Rs.50 (effective Jun. 1995). Central Statistical Office, Toorawa Centre, Cr. S.S. R & J. Mosque Sts., Port Louis, Mauritius. TEL 230-234-5294. FAX 230-208-4011. (Subscr. to: Government Printing Office, Ramtoolah Bldg., Sir S. Ramgoolam St., Port Louis, Mauritius) **Document type:** government publication.
Formerly: Mauritius. Central Statistical Office. Bi-Annual Survey of Employment and Earnings (ISSN 1013-6053)

336 MF
MAURITIUS. CENTRAL STATISTICAL OFFICE. DIGEST OF PUBLIC FINANCE STATISTICS. (Text in English) a. Rs.50 (effective Jun. 1995). Central Statistical Office, Toorawa Centre, Cr. S.S. R & J. Mosque Sts., Port Louis, Mauritius. (Subscr. to: Government Printing Office, Ramtoolah Bldg., Ramgoolam St., Port Louis, Mauritius. TEL 230-234-5294. FAX 230-208-4011) **Document type:** government publication.

382 MF
MAURITIUS. CENTRAL STATISTICAL OFFICE. EXTERNAL TRADE STATISTICS. 1977. s-a. Rs.100 (effective Jun. 1995). Central Statistical Office, Toorawa Centre, Cr. S.S. R & J. Mosque Sts., Port Louis, Mauritius. (Subscr. to; Government Printing Office, Ramtoolah Bldg., Sir S. Ramgoolam St., Port Louis, Mauritius. TEL 230-234-5294. FAX 230-208-4011) **Document type:** government publication.
Former titles (until 1989): Mauritius. Central Statistical Office. External Trade Statistics (Annual); (until 1986): Mauritius. Central Statistical Office. Quarterly External Trade Statistics; (until 1985): Mauritius. Central Statistical Office. External Trade Statistics.

381 MF
MAURITIUS. CENTRAL STATISTICAL OFFICE. NATIONAL ACCOUNTS OF MAURITIUS. 1983. a. Rs.100 (effective June 1995). Central Statistical Office, Toorawa Centre, Cr. S.S. R & J. Mosque Sts., Port Louis, Mauritius. TEL 230-234-5294. FAX 230-208-4011. (Subscr. to: Ramtoolah Bldg., Sir S. Ramgoolam St., Port Louis, Mauritius) **Document type:** government publication.

657 US
MEMBER FIRM CONFIDENTIAL STATISTICS REPORT. irreg. American Group of C P A Firms, 1910 S. Highland Ave., Ste. 210, Lombard, IL 60148. TEL 708-916-0300. **Document type:** bulletin.

330 BL ISSN 1021-7398
MERCOSUL: SINOPSE ESTATISTICA/MERCOSUR: SINOPSIS ESTADISTICA. 1992. a. R.19.30($50) Fundacao Instituto Brasileiro de Geografia e Estatistica, Rua General Canabarro 666, 2o andar, Maracana 20271-201 Rio de Janeiro, Brazil. TEL 55-21-2645424. FAX 55-21-2289575. **Document type:** government publication.
Description: Provides information on the main characteristics of the population, housing, labor force, and economic affairs. Provides analysis of Latin American integration.

MEXICO. COMISION NACIONAL BANCARIA. BOLETIN ESTADISTICO. see *BUSINESS AND ECONOMICS — Banking And Finance*

338 318 MX ISSN 0186-0488
MEXICO. INSTITUTO NACIONAL DE ESTADISTICA, GEOGRAFIA E INFORMATICA. ENCUESTA INDUSTRIAL MENSUAL; 129 clases de actividad. 1964. m. free. Instituto Nacional de Estadistica, Geografia e Informatica, Secretaria de Programacion y Presupuesto, Prol. Heroe de Nacozari 2301 Sur, Puerta 11, Acceso, 20270 Aguascalientes Ags., Mexico. TEL 49-18-19-48. FAX 491-807-39. charts. **Document type:** government publication.
Formerly (until 1978): Mexico. Direccion General de Estadistica. Estadistica Industrial Mensual.

MEXICO. INSTITUTO NACIONAL DE ESTADISTICA, GEOGRAFIA E INFORMATICA. ENCUESTA NACIONAL DE EDUCACION CAPACITACION Y EMPLEO. see *EDUCATION — Abstracting, Bibliographies, Statistics*

330 MX
MEXICO DATA BANK/MEXICO BANCO DE DATOS. (Text in English, Spanish) 1982. a. $298 (outside N. America $330). Inversionista Mexicano, S.A. de C.V., Felix Cuevas 301-204, Col. del Valle, Deleg. Benito Juarez, 03100 Mexico DF, Mexico. TEL 52-5-524-3131. FAX 52-5-5243794. circ. 1,200 (paid). **Document type:** trade publication.
Description: Yearbook on Mexican economy and finances for business and research purposes.

651.2 UK ISSN 0953-3737
CODEN: MMPLEO
MICROGRAPHICS MARKET PLACE; news of the microfilm industry. 1986. 6/yr. £20 in U.K. & Europe; rest of world £35($50) (effective 1997). Themeprint Ltd., 65 Winchester Dr., Burbage, Leics. LE10 2BA, England. TEL 44-1203-382328. FAX 44-1203-382319. Ed. Tim Nixon. adv. contact: Tim Nixon. bk.rev. circ. 2,700. (back issues avail.) **Indexed:** Info.Media & Tech., INSPEC. **Document type:** trade publication.
—AskIEEE; KR SourceOne.
Description: Includes new products, trade news, letters, application studies and relevant articles.

330.9 NA
MODUS STATISTISCH MAGAZINE. (Text and summaries in Dutch) 1979; N.S. 1995. q. fl.25. Centraal Bureau voor de Statistiek, Fort Amsterdam z/n, Willemstad, Curacao, Netherlands Antilles. TEL 599-9-611031. FAX 599-9-611696. E-mail: ank0004@ibm.net. circ. 450. **Document type:** government publication.
Formerly (until 1995): Economisch Profiel Nederlandse Antillen.

315 330.9 BG
MONTHLY INDICATORS OF CURRENT ECONOMIC SITUATION OF BANGLADESH. (Text in English) 1974. m. Tk.480($120) Bureau of Statistics, Secretariat, Dhaka 2, Bangladesh. circ. 250. **Document type:** government publication.
Formed by the merger of: Monthly Economic Situation of Bangladesh; Monthly Economic Indicators of Bangladesh; Which was formerly: Economic Indicators of Bangladesh; Quarterly Economic Indicators of Bangladesh.
Description: Economic trends, such as money and banking, foreign aid and trade protocols, agriculture and the food situation in Bangladesh.

330.9 US ISSN 0098-1818
HD8051
MONTHLY LABOR REVIEW. 1915. m. $29 (effective 1996). U.S. Bureau of Labor Statistics, 2 Massachusetts Ave., N.E., Washington, DC 20212. TEL 202-606-5902. (Subscr. to: Superintendent of Documents, U.S. Government Printing Office, Box 371954, Pittsburgh, PA 15250-7954. TEL 202-512-1800. FAX 202-512-2250; Or: Bureau of Labor Statistics Publications Sales Center, Box 2145, Chicago, IL 60690) Ed. Deborah Klein. bk.rev.; index, cum.index every 12 yrs. circ. 14,000. (also avail. in microform from PMC; microfiche from CIS; back issues avail.; reprint service avail. from CIS,KTO,WSH) **Indexed:** ABI Inform., Abstr.Health Care Manage.Stud., Acad.Ind., Account.Ind. (1975-), Amer.Hist.& Life (1968-1995), Amer.Stat.Ind. (1973-), ASCA, B.P.I., Bk.Rev.Dig., Bk.Rev.Ind. (1975-), BPIA, C.I.J.E., C.L.I., Chic.Per.Ind., Child.Bk.Rev.Ind. (1975-), CLOA, Curr.Cont., Hist.Abstr. (1968-1995), Ind.U.S.Gov.Per., Int.Lab.Doc., J.of Econ.Lit., L.R.I., Mag.Ind., P.A.I.S., Popul.Ind., Poult.Abstr., R.G.Abstr., R.G., Soc.Sci.Ind., Soc.Work Res.& Abstr., SSCI, Tech.Educ.Abstr., Tr.& Indus.Ind., Work Rel.Abstr., World Agri.Econ.& Rural Sociol.Abstr. **Document type:** government publication.
●Also available online. Vendor(s): Information Access Co., Knight-Ridder Information, Inc., UMI. Also available on CD-ROM.
—BLDSC (5938.700000); Genuine Article; KR SourceOne; SWETS; UMI; UnCover.
Supersedes: U.S. Bureau of Labor Statistics. Monthly Review (ISSN 0027-044X)
Description: Contains articles on the labor force, wages, prices, productivity, economic growth, and occupational injuries and illnesses.

382 315 II ISSN 0027-0547
MONTHLY STATISTICS OF FOREIGN TRADE OF INDIA. (Issued in two vols.: Export and Re-Export; Imports) 1957. m. Rs.1160($417.60) for vol.1; vol.2 Rs.760 ($273.60). Government of India, Department of Publications, Civil Lanes, Delhi 110 054, India. stat. circ. 6,181. **Document type:** government publication.

382 MJ
MONTSERRAT. STATISTICS OFFICE. DIGEST OF STATISTICS. no.2, 1975. a. $10. Statistics Office, Government Headquarters, Plymouth, Montserrat. **Document type:** government publication.
Formerly: Montserrat. Statistics Office. Digest of Overseas Trade Statistics.

338 MR ISSN 0851-0954
MOROCCO. DIRECTION DE LA STATISTIQUE. INDICE DES PRIX A LA PRODUCTION INDUSTRIELLE, ENERGETIQUE ET MINIERE. (Text in Arabic, French) q. DH.165 for all 3 Indices. Direction de la Statistique, B.P. 178, Rabat, Morocco. TEL 212-7-77-36-06. FAX 212-7-77-32-17. **Document type:** government publication.

338 MR ISSN 0851-0970
HB235.M68
MOROCCO. DIRECTION DE LA STATISTIQUE. INDICE DES PRIX DE GROS. (Text in Arabic, French) m. DH.165 for all 3 Indices. Direction de la Statistique, B.P. 178, Rabat, Morocco. TEL 212-7-77-36-06. FAX 212-7-77-32-17. **Document type:** government publication.

338 MR ISSN 0851-0962
MOROCCO. DIRECTION DE LA STATISTIQUE. INDICE DU COUT DE LA VIE. (Text in Arabic, French) m. DH.165 for all 3 Indices. Direction de la Statistique, B.P. 178, Rabat, Morocco. TEL 212-7-77-36-06. FAX 212-7-77-32-17. (also avail. in microfiche) **Document type:** government publication.

330 016 620 HU ISSN 0238-9878
MUSZAKI-GAZDASAGI MAGAZIN/TECHNICAL ECONOMIC DIGEST. (Text in Hungarian; table of contents in English, Russian and German) 1960. m. 6000 Ft.($100) Orszagos Muszaki Informacios Kozpont es Konyvtar (O.M.I.K.K.) - National Technica Information Centre and Library, Muzeum u. 17, P.O. Box 12, 1428 Budapest, Hungary. (Subscr. to: Kultura, Box 149, 1389 Budapest, Hungary) Ed. Schonviszkyne Anna Galdi. adv.; bk.rev.; charts; illus.; mkt.; index. circ. 1,400.
Formerly (until 1989): Muszaki-Gazdasagi Tajekoztato (ISSN 0027-4933)

N A B E INDUSTRY SURVEY. (National Association of Business Economists) see *BUSINESS AND ECONOMICS — Economic Situation And Conditions*

BUSINESS AND ECONOMICS — ABSTRACTING, BIBLIOGRAPHIES, STATISTICS

N A B E OUTLOOK & POLICY SURVEY. (National Association of Business Economists) see BUSINESS AND ECONOMICS — Economic Situation And Conditions

650 330 016   US   ISSN 1074-1674
N T I S ALERTS: BUSINESS & ECONOMICS. w. $135 (foreign $195). U.S. National Technical Information Service, 5285 Port Royal Rd., Springfield, VA 22161. TEL 703-487-4630. FAX 703-321-8547. TELEX 64617. index. (also avail. in microform from NTI; back issues avail.) **Document type:** abstracting/indexing.
Former titles: Abstract Newsletter: Business and Economics; Weekly Abstract Newsletter: Business and Economics; Weekly Government Abstracts. Business and Economics (ISSN 0364-7978)

330 322   FR   ISSN 0256-758X
NATIONAL ACCOUNTS OF O E C D COUNTRIES. VOLUME 1 MAIN AGGREGATES. Key Title: National Accounts. Main Aggregates. O E C D Department of Economics and Statistics. a. price varies. Organization for Economic Cooperation and Development, 2 rue Andre-Pascal, 75775 Paris Cedex 16, France. (U.S. orders to: O.E.C.D. Publications and Information Center, 2001 L St., N.W., Ste. 650, Washington, DC 20036-4922. TEL 202-785-6323) **Indexed:** IIS.
Supersedes in part (in 1976): National Accounts of O E C D Countries (ISSN 0304-3401)

330 322   FR   ISSN 0256-7571
HC79.I5
NATIONAL ACCOUNTS OF O E C D COUNTRIES. VOLUME 2 DETAILED TABLES. Key Title: National Accounts. Detailed Tables. O E C D Department of Economics and Statistics. a. price varies. Organization for Economic Cooperation and Development, 2 rue Andre-Pascal, 75775 Paris Cedex 16, France. (U.S. orders to: O.E.C.D. Publications and Information Center, 2001 L St., N.W., Ste. 650, Washington, DC 20036-4922. TEL 202-785-6323) **Indexed:** IIS.
Supersedes in part (in 1976): National Accounts of O E C D Countries (ISSN 0304-3401)

336   MM   ISSN 0077-295X
NATIONAL ACCOUNTS OF THE MALTESE ISLANDS. 1957. a. L.0.75. Central Office of Statistics, Auberge d'Italie, Merchants' St., Valletta, Malta. FAX 356-248483. (Subscr. to: Publications Bookshop, Auberge de Castille, Valletta, Malta) **Document type:** government publication.

657.75 331.252   UK   ISSN 0309-0078
NATIONAL ASSOCIATION OF PENSION FUNDS. ANNUAL SURVEY. 1975. a. £96 to non-members; members £48. National Association of Pension Funds, 12-18 Grosvenor Gardens, London SW1W 0DH, England. TEL 0171-730-0585. FAX 0171-730-2595. Ed. Mike Brown. **Document type:** bulletin.

657.75 331.252   UK   ISSN 0144-2589
NATIONAL ASSOCIATION OF PENSION FUNDS. YEAR BOOK. 1979. a. £50 to non-members; members £27.50. National Association of Pension Funds, 12-18 Grosvenor Gardens, London SW1W 0DH, England. TEL 44-171-730-0585. FAX 44-171-730-2595. Ed. Richard Fairclough. circ. 4,000. **Document type:** directory.
—BLDSC (9390.730000).

338.4   US
NATIONAL HOUSEWARES MANUFACTURERS ASSOCIATION. STATE OF THE INDUSTRY REPORT. a. $200 (effective 1995). National Housewares Manufacturers Association, 6400 Shafer Ct., Ste. 650, Rosemont, IL 60018-4914. TEL 847-292-4200. FAX 847-292-4211. URL: http://www.housewares.org. Pub. Philip Brandle. R&P contact: Debora Teschele. TEL 847-692-0110.
Supersedes: Marketing Research Study of the Housewares Industry.

339 315   TH
NATIONAL INCOME OF THAILAND. (Text in English, Thai) 1964. a. free. National Economic and Social Development Board, National Accounts Division, Office of the Prime Minister, Bangkok 10100, Thailand. TEL 662-2829156. FAX 662-2810946. charts. **Document type:** government publication.
Formerly: National Income Statistics of Thailand (ISSN 0077-4723)

338 314   YU   ISSN 0300-2497
NEKI POKAZATELJI TEHNICKOG RAZVOJA PRIVREDE JUGOSLAVIJE. (Subseries of Statisticki Bilten. Continues Statistika Nove Tehniki) (Editions in English, Serbian) a. 10 din.($1.11) Savezni Zavod za Statistiku, Kneza Milosa 20, Belgrade, Yugoslavia. TEL 681-999. circ. 1,000. **Document type:** government publication.

330
NEPAL BANK LIMITED. TATHYANK BIBARAN. (Text in Nepali) s-a. Nepal Bank Limited, Dharma Path, Kathmandu, Nepal.

016 338.9   NP
NEPAL DOCUMENTATION; occasional bibliography. (Text in English and Nepali) 1972. irreg. Rs.10($4) Centre for Economic Development and Administration, Publications and Information Services Division, P.O. Box 797, Kirtipur Campus, Kathmandu, Nepal. index. (back issues avail.) **Document type:** bibliography.

338.9 315   NP   ISSN 0077-6564
NEPAL INDUSTRIAL DEVELOPMENT CORPORATION. STATISTICAL ABSTRACTS. (Text in English) irreg. Nepal Industrial Development Corporation, N.I.D.C. Bldg., Durbar Marg, Box 10, Kathmandu, Nepal.

332.75 314   NE   ISSN 0077-6793
NETHERLANDS. CENTRAAL BUREAU VOOR DE STATISTIEK. FAILLISSEMENTSSTATISTIEK/NETHERLANDS. CENTRAL BUREAU OF STATISTICS. BANKRUPTCY STATISTICS. (Text in Dutch and English) 1951. a. fl.23. Centraal Bureau voor de Statistiek, Prinses Beatrixlaan 428, Voorburg, Netherlands. (Subscr. to: SDU - Publishers, Christoffel Plantijnstraat 2, Postbus 20014, 2500 EA The Hague, Netherlands) **Document type:** government publication.

332   NE   ISSN 1381-6780
HG186.N4
NETHERLANDS. CENTRAAL BUREAU VOOR DE STATISTIEK. FINANCIELE MAANDSTATISTIEK. 1953. m. fl.20. Centraal Bureau voor de Statistiek, Prinses Beatrixlaan 428, Voorburg, Netherlands. (Subscr. to: S D U, Christoffel Plantijnstraat, The Hague, Netherlands) charts; stat.; index. **Document type:** government publication.
—SWETS.
Formerly (until 1995): Maandstatistiek van het Financiewezen (ISSN 0024-8762)

332.6 314   NE   ISSN 0168-3381
HG5561
NETHERLANDS. CENTRAAL BUREAU VOOR DE STATISTIEK. INSTITUTIONELE BELEGGERS. (Text in Dutch and English) 1966. a. fl.21.25. Centraal Bureau voor de Statistiek, Prinses Beatrixlaan 428, Voorburg, Netherlands. (Orders to: SDU - Publishers, Christoffel Plantijnstraat, The Hague, Netherlands) **Document type:** government publication.
Formerly: Netherlands. Centraal Bureau voor de Statistiek. Beleggingen van Institutionele Beleggers.

336   NE   ISSN 0168-3489
HG186.N4
NETHERLANDS. CENTRAAL BUREAU VOOR DE STATISTIEK. NATIONALE REKENINGEN/NETHERLANDS. CENTRAL BUREAU OF STATISTICS. NATIONAL ACCOUNTS. (Text in Dutch and English) 1948. a. fl.175. Centraal Bureau voor de Statistiek, Prinses Beatrixlaan 428, Voorburg, Netherlands. (Orders to: SDU - Publishers, Christoffel Plantijnstraat 2, Postbus 20014, 2500 EA The Hague, Netherlands) **Document type:** government publication.

336   NE   ISSN 0168-373X
HJ54
NETHERLANDS. CENTRAAL BUREAU VOOR DE STATISTIEK. STATISTIEK DER RIJKSFINANCIEN/NETHERLANDS. CENTRAL BUREAU OF STATISTICS. STATISTICS OF THE STATE FINANCES OF THE NETHERLANDS. (Text in Dutch and English) 1944. irreg. fl.39. Centraal Bureau voor de Statistiek, Prinses Beatrixlaan 428, Voorburg, Netherlands. (Subscr. to: SDU- Publishers, Christoffel Plantijnstraat 2, Postbus 20014, 2500 EA The Hague, Netherlands) **Document type:** government publication.

332   NE   ISSN 0168-7956
NETHERLANDS. CENTRAAL BUREAU VOOR DE STATISTIEK. STATISTIEK VAN DE INVESTERINGEN IN VASTE ACTIVA IN DE NIJVERHEID/NETHERLANDS. CENTRAL BUREAU OF STATISTICS. STATISTICS ON FIXED CAPITAL FORMATION IN INDUSTRY. (Text in Dutch and English) 1952. a. fl.29.50. Centraal Bureau voor de Statistiek, Prinses Beatrixlaan 428, Voorburg, Netherlands. (Subscr. to: SDU - Publishers, Christoffel Plantijnstraat 2, Postbus 20014, 2500 EA The Hague, Netherlands) **Document type:** government publication.
Formerly: Netherlands. Centraal Bureau voor de Statistiek. Statistiek van de Investeringen in Vaste Activa in de Industrie (ISSN 0077-7110)

332 314   NE   ISSN 0168-3330
NETHERLANDS. CENTRAAL BUREAU VOOR DE STATISTIEK. STATISTIEK VAN DE SPAARGELDEN/NETHERLANDS. CENTRAL BUREAU OF STATISTICS. STATISTICS OF SAVINGS. (Text in Dutch and English) 1965. a. fl.15.50 price varies. Centraal Bureau voor de Statistiek, Prinses Beatrixlaan 428, Voorburg, Netherlands. (Subscr. to: SDU - Publishers, Christoffel Plantijnstraat 2, Postbus 20014, 2500 EA The Hague, Netherlands) **Document type:** government publication.

330 310   NL   ISSN 0757-9888
NEW CALEDONIA. INSTITUT TERRITORIAL DE LA STATISTIQUE ET DES ETUDES ECONOMIQUES. BULLETIN DE CONJONCTURE. q. CFPF2500 (foreign CFPF3500). Institut Territorial de la Statistique et des Etudes Economiques, P.O. Box 823, Noumea, New Caledonia. TEL 687-275481. FAX 687-288148. E-mail: itsee@cipac.nc. Ed. Gerard Baudchon. **Document type:** government publication.

330 310   NL   ISSN 0988-3215
HD9715.N36
NEW CALEDONIA. INSTITUT TERRITORIAL DE LA STATISTIQUE ET DES ETUDES ECONOMIQUES. INDICES DES PRIX A LA CONSOMMATION. 1986. m. CFPF1500 (foreign CFPF2500) (effective 1997). Institut Territorial de la Statistique et des Etudes Economiques, P.O. Box 823, Noumea, New Caledonia. TEL 687-275481. FAX 687-288148. E-mail: itsee@cipac.nc. Ed. Gerard Baudochon. **Document type:** government publication.
Formerly (until 1989): New Caledonia. Institut Territorial de la Statistique et des Etudes Economiques. Indice Mensuel des Prix de Detail a la Consommation des Menages (ISSN 0758-0339)

NEW CALEDONIA. INSTITUT TERRITORIAL DE LA STATISTIQUE ET DES ETUDES ECONOMIQUES. INDICE ET INDEX DU B T P. see BUILDING AND CONSTRUCTION — Abstracting, Bibliographies, Statistics

330 310   NL
HC684.5.Z9
NEW CALEDONIA. INSTITUT TERRITORIAL DE LA STATISTIQUE ET DES ETUDES ECONOMIQUES. TABLEAUX DE L'ECONOMIE CALEDONIENNE. Short title: T E C. (Editions in English, French) 3/yr. price varies. Institut Territorial de la Statistique et des Etudes Economiques, P.O. Box 823, Noumea, New Caledonia. TEL 687-275481. FAX 687-288148. E-mail: itsee@cipac.nc. Ed. Gerard Baudchon. **Document type:** government publication.
Incorporates: New Caledonia. Institut Territorial de la Statistique et des Etudes Economiques. Annuaires Statistiques.

331.1   US   ISSN 0093-5034
HD5725.N7
NEW YORK (STATE). DEPARTMENT OF LABOR. DIVISION OF RESEARCH AND STATISTICS. LABOR RESEARCH REPORT. Key Title: Labor Research Report (Albany). irreg. Department of Labor, Division of Research and Statistics, 1 Main St., 9th Fl., Brooklyn, NY 11201. TEL 718-797-7703. (Subscr. to: Division of Research and Statistics, State Campus, Albany, NY 12240) Ed. Eileen DeVeau. stat. **Document type:** government publication.
Formerly: New York (State). Division of Employment. Research and Statistics Office. Research Bulletin.

BUSINESS AND ECONOMICS — ABSTRACTING, BIBLIOGRAPHIES, STATISTICS

331.1 317 US ISSN 0550-6638
NEW YORK (STATE). DEPARTMENT OF LABOR. STATISTICS ON OPERATIONS. ANNUAL REPORT. a. Department of Labor, Division of Research and Statistics, 1 Main St., 9th Fl., Brooklyn, NY 11201. TEL 718-797-7703. (Subscr. to: Office of Communications, State Campus, Albany, NY 12240) Ed. Eileen DeVeau. illus.; stat. **Document type:** government publication.

319 339 NZ ISSN 1170-747X
HD7707.5
NEW ZEALAND. DEPARTMENT OF STATISTICS. CONSUMER EXPENDITURE. 1974. a. NZ.$34.95. Department of Statistics, P.O. Box 2922, Wellington, New Zealand. **Document type:** government publication.
  Supersedes in part: New Zealand Household Expenditure and Income Survey (ISSN 0112-6601); Which was formerly: New Zealand Household Survey (ISSN 0110-392X); New Zealand. Department of Statistics. Household Sample Survey.

330 310 NZ ISSN 1170-8271
HC670.I5
NEW ZEALAND. DEPARTMENT OF STATISTICS. INCOMES. 1974. a. NZ.$29.95. Department of Statistics, P.O. Box 2922, Wellington, New Zealand. **Document type:** government publication.
  Supersedes in part: New Zealand Household Expenditure and Income Survey (ISSN 0112-6601); Which was formerly: New Zealand Household Survey (ISSN 0110-392X); New Zealand. Department of Statistics. Household Sample Survey.

382 NZ ISSN 0114-2607
NEW ZEALAND. DEPARTMENT OF STATISTICS. OVERSEAS TRADE. 1989. a. NZ.$49.95. Department of Statistics, P.O. Box 2922, Wellington, New Zealand. **Document type:** government publication.
  Formed by the 1989 merger of: New Zealand. Department of Statistics. Exports (ISSN 0110-2184) & New Zealand. Department of Statistics. Imports (ISSN 0110-3741) & New Zealand. Department of Statistics. Report and Analysis of External Trade (ISSN 0077-9806) & New Zealand. Department of Statistics. External Trade Price and Volume Indexes & New Zealand. Department of Statistics. Shipping and Cargo (ISSN 0110-5698)

332.6 US ISSN 0733-432X
NEWSLETTER DIGEST. 1979. s-m. $75. 2201 Big Cove Rd., Huntsville, AL 35801. TEL 205-534-1535. FAX 205-533-4871. Ed. Al Owen. bk.rev.; charts. circ. 1,500. (looseleaf format; back issues avail.) **Document type:** abstracting/indexing.
  Description: Selected abstracts from reviewed investment newsletters worldwide, with editorial commentary.

338 NQ
NICARAGUA. INSTITUTO NACIONAL DE ESTADISTICAS Y CENSOS. ENCUESTA ANUAL INDUSTRIA MANUFACTURERA. a. Instituto Nacional de Estadisticas y Censos, Apdo. Postal 4031, Managua, Nicaragua. **Document type:** government publication.

316 382 NR ISSN 0078-0634
NIGERIA. FEDERAL OFFICE OF STATISTICS. REVIEW OF EXTERNAL TRADE. (Text in English) 1964. a. £N5. Federal Office of Statistics, Dissemination Division, c/o Mrs. M.T. Osita, P.M.B. 12528, 36-38 Broad St., Lagos, Nigeria. **Document type:** government publication.

338 310 NR ISSN 0331-1570
NIGERIA. NATIONAL INTEGRATED SURVEY OF HOUSEHOLDS. INDUSTRIAL SURVEY. Key Title: Industrial Survey of Nigeria. a. Federal Office of Statistics, Dissemination Division, National Integrated Survey of Households, c/o Mrs. M.T. Osita, P.M.B. 12528, 36-38 Broad St., Lagos, Nigeria. TEL 234-1-2601710-4. **Document type:** government publication.
  Supersedes: Nigeria. Federal Office of Statistics. Industrial Survey.

658 310 NR
NIGERIA. NATIONAL INTEGRATED SURVEY OF HOUSEHOLDS. REPORT ON GENERAL CONSUMER SURVEY. a. £N2. Federal Office of Statistics, Dissemination Division, National Integrated Survey of Households, c/o Mrs. M.T. Osita, P.M.B. 12528, 36-38 Broad St., Lagos, Nigeria. TEL 234-1-2601710-4. **Document type:** government publication.
  Supersedes: Nigeria. Federal Office of Statistics. Report on General Consumer Survey; Which incorporated in part: Nigeria. Federal Office of Statistics. Report on Rural Household Survey; Nigeria. Federal Office of Statistics. Report on Rural Economic Survey; Nigeria. Federal Office of Statistics. Report on Rural Consumer Survey; Nigeria. Federal Office of Statistics. Report on Consumer Survey; Nigeria. Federal Office of Statistics. Report on Urban Household Survey.

330.9 310 NR
NIGERIA. NATIONAL INTEGRATED SURVEY OF HOUSEHOLDS. REPORT ON GENERAL HOUSEHOLD. a. Federal Office of Statistics, Dissemination Division, National Integated Survey of Households, c/o Mrs. M.T. Osita, P.M.B. 12528, 36-38 Broad St., Lagos, Nigeria. TEL 234-1-2601710-4. **Document type:** government publication.
  Supersedes: Nigeria. Federal Office of Statistics. Report on General Household; Which incorporated in part: Nigeria. Federal Office of Statistics. Report on Rural Household Survey; Nigeria. Federal Office of Statistics. Report on Rural Economic Survey; Nigeria. Federal Office of Statistics. Report on Rural Consumer Survey; Nigeria. Federal Office of Statistics. Report on Consumer Survey; Nigeria. Federal Office of Statistics. Report on Urban Household Survey.

658 310 NR ISSN 0189-336X
HA4731
NIGERIA. NATIONAL INTEGRATED SURVEY OF HOUSEHOLDS. REPORT ON NATIONAL CONSUMER SURVEY. Key Title: Report on National Consumer Survey. a. £N10($10) Federal Office of Statistics, Dissemination Division, National Integrated Survey of Households, c/o Mrs. M.T. Osita, P.M.B. 12528, 36-38 Broad St., Lagos, Nigeria. TEL 234-1-2601710-4. **Document type:** government publication.
  Supersedes: Nigeria. Federal Office of Statistics. Report on National Consumer Survey; Which incorporated in part: Nigeria. Federal Office of Statistics. Report on Rural Household Survey; Nigeria. Federal Office of Statistics. Report on Rural Economic Survey; Nigeria. Federal Office of Statistics. Report on Rural Consumer Survey; Nigeria. Federal Office of Statistics. Report on Consumer Survey; Nigeria. Federal Office of Statistics. Report on Urban Household Survey.

330 JA ISSN 0389-5602
HA1
NIHON TOKEI GAKKAISHI (TOKYO, 1971)/JAPAN STATISTICAL SOCIETY. JOURNAL. (Text in English and Japanese) 1971. s-a. 6000 Yen($40) Nihon Tokei Gakkai - Japan Statistical Society, c/o Tokei Suri Kenkyujo - Institute of Statistical Mathematics, 6-7, Minami-Azabu 4-chome, Minato-ku, Tokyo 106, Japan. TEL 03-3442-5801. FAX 03-3442-5924. Ed. Akimichi Takemura. adv.; bk.rev. circ. 1,500. (back issues avail.) **Indexed:** Curr.Cont. (1970-), Curr.Ind.Stat., Stat.Theor.Meth.Abstr. (1970-), Zent.Math. **Document type:** academic/scholarly publication.

NONFERROUS METALS ALERT. see METALLURGY — Abstracting, Bibliographies, Statistics

943 310 GW
NORDRHEIN-WESTFAELISCHEN INDUSTRIE- UND HANDELSKAMMER. STATISTISCHES JAHRBUCH. 1954. a. DM.32. Gemeinsame Statistische Stelle der Nordrhein-Westfaelischen Industrie- und Handelskammer, Postfach 105035, 44047 Dortmund, Germany. TEL 0231-5417231. FAX 0231-5417109. circ. 1,000. (back issues avail.)

331.1021 314 NO ISSN 0804-8894
HA1501
NORWAY. STATISTISK SENTRALBYRAA. ARBEIDSMARKEDSTATISTIKK. HEFTE I: HOVEDTALL. (Subseries of its Norges Offisielle Statistikk) (Text in English and Norwegian) 1967. a. NOK 95 (effective 1997). Statistisk Sentralbyraa, P.O. Box 8131 Dep., N-0033 Oslo, Norway. TEL 47-22-864500. FAX 47-22-864976. circ. 1,100. **Document type:** government publication.
  Supersedes in part (in 1993): Norway. Statistisk Sentralbyraa. Arbeidsmarkedstatistikk - Labor Market Statistics (ISSN 0078-1878)

332.1 332.7 NO ISSN 0333-1504
NORWAY. STATISTISK SENTRALBYRAA. BANK- OG KREDITTSTATISTIKK. AKTUELLE TALL. 1981. irreg. NOK 350 (effective 1997); newsstand price: NOK 35. Statistisk Sentralbyraa, Box 8131 Dep., N-0033 Oslo, Norway. TEL 47-22-86-45-00. FAX 47-22-86-49-76. URL: http://www.ssb.no. circ. 13,200. **Document type:** government publication.

339 314 NO ISSN 0807-4763
HA1501 subser.
NORWAY. STATISTISK SENTRALBYRAA. INDUSTRISTATISTIKK. NAERINGSTALL/STATISTICS NORWAY. MANUFACTURING STATISTICS. INDUSTRIAL FIGURES. (Subseries of its Norges Offisielle Statistikk) (Text in English and Norwegian) 1961. a. NOK 80. Statistisk Sentralbyraa, P.O. Box 8131 Dep., N-0033 Oslo, Norway. TEL 47-22-864500. FAX 47-22-864973. circ. 1,150. **Document type:** government publication.
  Formerly (until 1992): Norway. Statistisk Sentralbyraa. Industrialstatistikk. Hefte 1: Naeringstall (ISSN 0800-580X); Supersedes in part (in 1982): Norway. Statistisk Sentralbyraa. Industrialstatistikk (ISSN 0078-1886)

331.2 314 NO ISSN 0078-1916
HA1501
NORWAY. STATISTISK SENTRALBYRAA. LOENNSSTATISTIKK/STATISTICS NORWAY. WAGE STATISTICS. (Subseries of its Norges Offisielle Statistikk) (Text in English and Norwegian) 1950. a. NOK 80 (effective 1997). Statistisk Sentralbyraa, P.O. Box 8131 Dep., N-0033 Oslo, Norway. TEL 47-22-864500. FAX 47-22-864976. circ. 900. **Document type:** government publication.

339.3 NO
HA1501
NORWAY. STATISTISK SENTRALBYRAA. NASJONALREGNSKAPSSTATISTIKK. (Subseries of its Norges Offisielle Statistikk) 1900. a. NOK 125 (effective 1997). Statistisk Sentralbyraa, P.O. Box 8131 Dep., N-0033 Oslo, Norway. TEL 47-22-864500. FAX 47-22-864976. circ. 1,700. **Document type:** government publication.
  Formerly (until 1987): Norway. Statistisk Sentralbyraa. Nasjonalregnskap - National Accounts Statistics (ISSN 0550-0494)

338.5 330.9481 NO ISSN 0800-4110
NORWAY. STATISTISK SENTRALBYRAA. OEKONOMISKE ANALYSER. English edition: Norway. Statistisk Sentralbyraa. Economic Survey (ISSN 0801-8324) 1976. 9/yr. NOK 440 (effective 1997); newsstand price: NOK 60. Statistisk Sentralbyraa, Forskningsavdelingen, Box 8131 Dep., N-0033 Oslo, Norway. TEL 47-2286-45-00. FAX 47-22-86-49-76. URL: http://www.ssb.no. circ. 22,250; Economic Survey 4,175. **Document type:** government publication.
  Formerly (until 1982): Norway. Statistisk Sentralbyraa. Konjunkturtendensene (ISSN 0800-160X)

314.81 NO ISSN 0800-7500
NORWAY. STATISTISK SENTRALBYRAA. REPRINTS - R E P R. (Text in various languages) 1985. irreg. free. Statistisk Sentralbyraa - Statistics Norway, P.O. Box 8131, N-0033 Oslo, Norway. TEL 47-22-00-44-80. FAX 47-22-86-49-76. Eds. Erling Holmoey, Haakon Vennemo.
  Description: Reprints of articles from various journals.

NORWAY. STATISTISK SENTRALBYRAA. SOSIALE OG OEKONOMISKE STUDIER. see SOCIOLOGY — Abstracting, Bibliographies, Statistics

BUSINESS AND ECONOMICS — ABSTRACTING, BIBLIOGRAPHIES, STATISTICS

314.81 NO ISSN 0333-2888
NORWAY. STATISTISK SENTRALBYRAA. STATISTISK VAREFORTEGNELSE FOR MAANEDSSTATISTIKK OVER UTENRIKSHANDELEN. English edition: Norway. Central Bureau of Statistics. Commodity List for Monthly Bulletin for External Trade (ISSN 0333-2896) 1913. m. NOK 400 (effective 1997); newsstand price: NOK 40. Statistisk Sentralbyraa, Box 8131 Dep., N-0033 Oslo, Norway. TEL 47-22-86-45-00. FAX 47-22-86--49-76. URL: http://www.ssb.no. circ. 13,200. **Document type:** government publication.
Formerly (until 1982): Norway. Statistisk Sentralbyraa. Maanedsstatistikk over Utenrikshandelen (ISSN 0332-6403).

382.09481 NO ISSN 0802-9571
NORWAY. STATISTISK SENTRALBYRAA. UTENRIKSHANDEL/STATISTICS NORWAY. EXTERNAL TRADE. (Subseries of its Norges Offisielle Statistikk) (Text in English and Norwegian) 1961. a. NOK 140 (effective 1997). Statistisk Sentralbyraa, P.O. Box 8131 Dep., N-0033 Oslo, Norway. TEL 47-22-864500. FAX 47-22-864976. circ. 1,300. **Document type:** government publication.

381.021 314 NO ISSN 0078-1959
HA1501
NORWAY. STATISTISK SENTRALBYRAA. VAREHANDELSSTATISTIKK/STATISTICS NORWAY. WHOLESALE AND RETAIL TRADE STATISTICS. (Subseries of its Norges Offisielle Statistikk) (Text in English, Norwegian) 1966. a. NOK 70 (effective 1997). Statistisk Sentralbyraa, P.O. Box 8131 Dep., N-0033 Oslo, Norway. TEL 47-22-864500. FAX 47-22-864976. circ. 900. **Document type:** government publication.

330 011 RU
NOVAYA LITERATURA PO SOTSIAL'NYM I GUMANITARNYM NAUKAM. EKONOMIKA; bibliograficheskii ukazatel' 1992. m. $109. Rossiiskaya Akademiya Nauk, Institut Nauchnoi Informatsii po Obshchestvennym Naukam, Krasikova 28-21, 117418 Moscow V-418, Russia. Ed. V.A. Arkhangel'skaya. **Document type:** bibliography.
Formed by the merger of (1951-1992): Novaya Inostrannaya Literatura po Obshchestvennym Naukam. Ekonomika (ISSN 0134-2835); (1934-1992): Novaya Sovetskaya Literatura po Obshchestvennym Naukam. Ekonomika (ISSN 0134-272X).

338.91 UK ISSN 0954-190X
O D I INDEX TO DEVELOPMENT LITERATURE. 1989. bi-m. £25. Overseas Development Institute, Regent's College, Inner Circle, Regent's Park, London NW1 4NS, England. TEL 44-171-487-7413. FAX 44-171-487-7590. E-mail: odi@odi.org.uk. circ. 200 (controlled). **Document type:** abstracting/indexing.
Description: Reference guide which covers the selected contents of over 300 journals, working papers and research reports.

330 011 FR
O E C D ECONOMIC OUTLOOK HISTORICAL STATISTICS. a. price varies. Organization for Economic Cooperation and Development, 2 rue Andre-Pascal, 75775 Paris Cedex 16, France. (U.S. orders to: O.E.C.D. Publications and Information Center, 2001 L St., N.W., Ste. 650, Washington, DC 20036-4922. TEL 202-785-6323)

336 FR ISSN 1015-4159
HJ8899
O E C D EXTERNAL DEBT STATISTICS. French edition: O C D E Statistiques de la Dette Exterieure (ISSN 1018-7049) a. price varies. Organization for Economic Cooperation and Development, 2 rue Andre-Pascal, 75775 Paris Cedex 16, France. (U.S. orders to: O.E.C.D. Publications and Information Center, 2001 L St., N.W., Ste. 650, Washington, DC 20036-4922. TEL 202-785-6323) **Indexed:** IIS.

332 310 FR ISSN 0304-3371
HG186.N6
O E C D FINANCIAL STATISTICS/STATISTIQUES FINANCIERES DE L'O C D E. (In 3 parts plus the Methodological Supplement; Part 1: Monthly Financial Statistics; Part 2: Financial Accounts (ISSN 0255-6979); Part 3: Non-Financial Enterprises Financial Statements (Text in English, French) 1971. m.(Part 1); 3/yr.(Part 2); a.(Part 3 and supplement). $320 (Part 1 combined with Financial Market Trends $240). Organization for Economic Cooperation and Development, 2 rue Andre-Pascal, 75775 Paris Cedex 16, France. (US orders to: O E C D Publications and Information Center, 2001 L St., N.W., Ste. 650, Washington, DC 20036-4922. TEL 202-785-6323) **Indexed:** IIS, World Bank.Abstr.
Description: Contains figures on the preceding month's operations in international financial markets. Also addresses domestic financial markets and interest rates in international and domestic markets.

332 310 FR ISSN 0256-7342
O E C D FINANCIAL STATISTICS. PART 1: MONTHLY FINANCIAL STATISTICS. (In 3 parts plus the Methodological Statement; Part 1: Monthly Financial Statistics; Part 2: Financial Accounts (ISSN 0255-6979); Part 3: Non-Financial Enterprises Financial Statements (Text in English, French) m. Organization for Economic Cooperation and Development, 2 rue Andre-Pascal, 75775 Paris Cedex 16, France. (U.S. orders to: O E C D Publications and Information Center, 2001 L St., N.W., Ste. 650, Washington DC 20036-4922. TEL 202-785-6323)

332 310 FR ISSN 0255-6979
HG176
O E C D FINANCIAL STATISTICS. PART 2: FINANCIAL ACCOUNTS. (In 3 parts plus the Methodological Statement; Part 1: Monthly Financial Statistics; Part 2: Financial Accounts; Part 3: Non-Financial Enterprises Financial Statements) (Text in English, French) 3/yr. Organization for Economic Cooperation and Development, 2 rue Andre-Pascal, 75775 Paris Cedex 16, France. (US orders to: O E C D Publications and Information Center, 2001 L St., N.W., Ste. 650, Washington, DC 20036-4922. TEL 202-785-6323) **Indexed:** IIS.

332 310 FR ISSN 0255-6987
O E C D FINANCIAL STATISTICS. PART 3: NON-FINANCIAL ENTERPRISES FINANCIAL STATEMENTS. (In 3 parts plus the Methodological Statement; Part 1: Monthly Financial Statistics; Part 2: Financial Accounts (ISSN 0255-6979); Part 3: Non-Financial Enterprises Financial Statements) (Text in English, French) a. Organization for Economic Cooperation and Development, 2 rue Andre-Pascal, 75775 Paris Cedex 16, France. (U.S. orders to: O E C D Publications and Information Center, 2001 L St., N.W., Ste. 650, Washington, DC 20036-4922. TEL 202-785-6323) **Indexed:** IIS.

382 FR ISSN 0474-540X
O E C D FOREIGN TRADE BY COMMODITIES. SERIES C. (Editions in English, French) 1975. a. 1800 F.($425) Organization for Economic Cooperation and Development, 2 rue Andre-Pascal, 75775 Paris Cedex 16, France. (U.S. orders to: O.E.C.D. Publications and Information Center, 2001 L St., N.W., Ste. 650, Washington, DC 20036-4922. TEL 202-785-6323) **Indexed:** IIS.
Former titles: Organization for Economic Cooperation and Development. Statistics of Foreign Trade. Series C: Tables by Commodities. - Imports and Exports - Statistiques du Commerce Exterieur. Serie C: Tableaux par Produits; Organization for Economic Cooperation and Development. Statistics of Foreign Trade. Series C: Trade by Commodities. Market Summaries. Imports and Exports - Statistiques du Commerce Exterieur. Serie C: Exchange Par Produits. Resume Par Marches. Importations et Exportations; O E C D Foreign Trade Statistics. Serie C.
Description: Matrix tables show trade between OECD countries and partner countries for commodity groups defined at 1 and 2-digit levels of the standard international trade classification.

338 FR ISSN 0250-4278
HC10
O E C D INDICATORS OF INDUSTRIAL ACTIVITY. q. $64. Organization for Economic Cooperation and Development, 2 rue Andre Pascal, 75775 Paris Cedex 16, France. (U.S. orders to: O.E.C.D. Publications and Information Center, 2001 L St., N.W., Ste. 650, Washington, DC 20036-4922. TEL 202-785-6323) **Indexed:** IIS.
—CISTI.
Formed by the 1978 merger of: Industrial Production (ISSN 0474-5450); Indications Economiques a Court Terme pour les Industries Manufacturieres (ISSN 0378-7303)
Description: Provides an overall view of short-term economic developments in different industries for all OECD member countries.

330 310 FR ISSN 0256-3142
O E C D INDUSTRIAL STRUCTURE STATISTICS. 1984. a. price varies. Organization for Economic Cooperation and Development, 2 rue Andre-Pascal, 75775 Paris Cedex 16, France. (U.S. orders to: O.E.C.D. Publications and Information Center, 2001 L St., N.W., Ste. 650, Washington, DC 20026-4922. TEL 202-785-6323) **Indexed:** IIS.
—BLDSC (4462.585000).

O E C D LABOUR FORCE STATISTICS/O C D E STATISTIQUES DE LA POPULATION ACTIVE. see BUSINESS AND ECONOMICS — Labor And Industrial Relations

338.9 310 FR ISSN 0258-2325
O E C D MAIN ECONOMIC INDICATORS. HISTORICAL STATISTICS/O C D E PRINCIPAUX INDICATEURS ECONOMIQUES. STATISTIQUES RETROSPECTIVES. (Supplement avail. (ISSN 0258-2333)) (Text in English, French) 1966. irreg. price varies. Organization for Economic Cooperation and Development, 2 rue Andre-Pascal, 75775 Paris Cedex 16, France. (U.S. orders to: O.E.C.D. Publications and Information Center, 2001 L St., N.W., Ste. 650, Washington, DC 20036-4922. TEL 202-785-6323) **Indexed:** IIS.
Formerly: Organization for Economic Cooperation and Development. Historical Statistics. Statistiques Retrospectives (ISSN 0474-5442)

382 FR ISSN 0474-5388
O E C D MONTHLY STATISTICS OF FOREIGN TRADE SERIES A/O C D E STATISTIQUES MENSUEL DU COMMERCE EXTERIEUR. (Text in English, French) 1974. m. $158. Organization for Economic Cooperation and Development, 2 rue Andre-Pascal, 75775 Paris Cedex 16, France. (U.S. orders to: O.E.C.D. Publications and Information Center, 2001 L St., N.W., Ste. 650, Washington, D.C. 20036-4922. TEL 202-785-6323) (magnetic tape; diskette format) **Indexed:** IIS.
Formerly: O E C D Foreign Trade Statistics. Series A (ISSN 0029-702X)
Description: Shows the trade of individual OECD member countries and main country groupings with most of their partner countries.

330 669 FR ISSN 0254-3885
O E C D STEEL MARKET IN (YEAR) AND OUTLOOK FOR (YEAR). French edition avail.: Marche de l'Acier en (Year) et les Perspectives pour (Year) (ISSN 1017-0049) a. price varies. Organization for Economic Cooperation and Development, 2 rue Andre-Pascal, 75775 Paris Cedex 16, France. (U.S. orders to: O.E.C.D. Publications and Information Center, 2001 L St., N.W., Ste. 650, Washington, DC 20036-4922. TEL 202-785-6323)
—BLDSC (8463.720000).

310 330.9 AQ ISSN 1021-7320
O E C S DIGEST OF EXTERNAL TRADE STATISTICS. 1984. irreg. EC$160($60) Organisation of Eastern Caribbean States, Economic Affairs Secretariat, P.O. Box 822, St. John's, Antigua, W.I. TEL 809-462-3500. FAX 809-462-1537. E-mail: economico@candw.ag. stat. **Document type:** trade publication.
Formerly: O E C S Trade Digest.
Description: Provides a statistical picture of trade relations of the OECS countries locally and internationally.

OCCUPATIONAL OUTLOOK HANDBOOK. see OCCUPATIONS AND CAREERS — Abstracting, Bibliographies, Statistics

BUSINESS AND ECONOMICS — ABSTRACTING, BIBLIOGRAPHIES, STATISTICS

OCCUPATIONAL OUTLOOK QUARTERLY. see OCCUPATIONS AND CAREERS — Abstracting, Bibliographies, Statistics

314.3 331.7 AU
OESTERREICHISCHES STATISTISCHES ZENTRALAMT. LAND- UND FORSTWIRTSCHAFTLICHE ARBEITSKRAEFTE. irreg. S.270. Oesterreichisches Statistisches Zentralamt, Hintere Zollamtsstr. 2b, A-1033 Vienna, Austria. TEL 43-1-71128-7654. FAX 43-1-7156828. **Document type:** government publication.
   Formerly: Austria. Statistisches Zentralamt. Erhebung der Land und Forstwirtschaftlichen Arbeitskraefte.
   Description: Census of agricultural and forestry laborers.

339 314 AU ISSN 0085-4433
OESTERREICHS VOLKSEINKOMMEN. 1952. a. S.320. Oesterreichisches Statistisches Zentralamt, Hintere Zollamtsstr. 2b, A-1033 Vienna, Austria. TEL 43-1-71128-0. FAX 43-1-7156828. circ. 550. **Document type:** government publication.
   Description: Data on national accounts, gross domestic production and national income.

016.72 UK
OFFICIAL INDEX TO THE FINANCIAL TIMES. m. $1181.90 (effective 1996). Primary Source Media, P.O. Box 45, Reading RG1 8HF, England. TEL 44-1734-583247. FAX 44-1734-591325. (In the Western hemisphere: 12 Lunar Dr., Drawer AB, Woodbridge, CT 06525. TEL 800-444-0799. FAX 203-397-3893) **Document type:** abstracting/indexing.
   ●Also available on CD-ROM.

382 665.5 US
OIL IMPORTS INTO THE UNITED STATES AND PUERTO RICO (E I A 814). m. $240 per no. in N. America; elsewhere $480. (U.S. Department of Energy, Energy Information Administration) U.S. National Technical Information Service, 5825 Port Royal Rd., Springfield, VA 22161. TEL 703-487-4630. (magnetic tape)
   Description: Surveys firms importing crude oil, unfinished oil, and finished petroleum products in the United States and Puerto Rico. Collects data on port of entry, country of origin, location of refinery, quantity of crude or products in barrels, and sulfur content.

331 US
OKLAHOMA. EMPLOYMENT SECURITY COMMISSION. RESEARCH DEPARTMENT. COUNTY EMPLOYMENT AND WAGE DATA. 1952. a. free. Employment Security Commission, Research Department, Will Rogers Bldg., 2401 N. Lincoln Blvd., Oklahoma City, OK 73105. Ed. George Bethke. stat. circ. 600. **Document type:** government publication.
   Formerly: Oklahoma. Employment Security Commission. Research and Planning Division. County Employment and Wage Data.

650 US ISSN 0030-1671
HC107.O5
OKLAHOMA BUSINESS BULLETIN. 1928. m. $10. University of Oklahoma, Center for Economic and Management Research, College of Business Administration, 307 W. Brooks St., Rm. 4, Norman, OK 73019. TEL 405-325-2931. FAX 405-325-7688. Ed. John McCraw. charts; mkt. circ. 600. (also avail. in microform from UMI; microfiche from CIS; back issues avail.; reprint service avail. from UMI) **Indexed:** ABI Inform., SRI. **Document type:** bulletin.
   —UMI; UnCover.

016.658 658 UK ISSN 1353-5498
TS155.A1
OPERATIONS & PRODUCTION MANAGEMENT ABSTRACTS. 1973. m. £3199($4999) (includes 3 CD-ROM issues) (effective 1997). (Institute of Management Services) M C B University Press Ltd., Anbar Electronic Intelligence, 60-62 Toller Ln., Bradford, W. Yorks BD8 9BY, England. TEL 44-1274-480916. FAX 44-1274-543576. TELEX 51317-MCBUNI-G. URL: http://www.mcb.co.uk. Ed. Eric Sandelands. (looseleaf format) **Document type:** abstracting/indexing.
   ●Also available on CD-ROM.
   —BLDSC (0900.303000).
   Former titles (until 1994): Management Services & Production Abstracts (ISSN 0952-4614); Work Study and O and M Abstracts (ISSN 0305-0653); Which supersedes in part: Anbar Management Services Abstracts (ISSN 0003-2794)
   Description: Contains abstracts of articles selected from over 300 international management journals. Covers topics such as: productivity, industrial engineering, work measurement, operational research, safety, production methods.

658.4 016 US ISSN 0030-3658
OPERATIONS RESEARCH - MANAGEMENT SCIENCE; international literature digest service. 1961. bi-m. $165 (foreign $199) (effective 1998). Executive Sciences Institute, 1005 Mississippi Ave., Davenport, IA 52803. TEL 319-324-4463. Ed. Bruce Brocka. abstr.; charts; illus.; stat.; index. **Document type:** abstracting/indexing.
   —CISTI; SWETS; UnCover.

003 658.4 US ISSN 0473-0496
HD20
OPERATIONS RESEARCH - MANAGEMENT SCIENCE YEARBOOK. a. $151. Executive Sciences Institute, 1005 Mississippi Ave., Davenport, IA 52803. TEL 319-324-4463. **Document type:** abstracting/indexing.

336 US
OREGON DEPARTMENT OF REVENUE. INCOME AND INHERITANCE TAX LAW ABSTRACTS. biennial. $10. Department of Revenue, Revenue Bldg., Salem, OR 97310. TEL 503-945-8635. FAX 503-945-8738. cum.index. **Document type:** government publication.
   Description: Abstracts of formal and informal opinions of Oregon Department of Revenue, attorney general and court decisions.

336.2 US
OREGON PERSONAL INCOME TAX STATISTICS. 1969. a. $5. Department of Revenue, Revenue Bldg., Salem, OR 97310. TEL 503-945-8635. FAX 503-945-8738. **Document type:** government publication.
   Former titles: Analysis of Oregon Personal Income; Personal Income Tax Analysis (ISSN 0092-6655); Analysis of Oregon's Personal Income Tax Returns.
   Description: Statistical breakdown of Oregon personal income tax data by income levels, filer types, counties and other measures.

336.2 US ISSN 0145-4269
HJ4121.O7
OREGON PROPERTY TAX STATISTICS. 1970. a. $5. Department of Revenue, Revenue Bldg., Salem, OR 97310. TEL 503-945-8635. FAX 503-945-8738. **Document type:** government publication.
   Formerly: Oregon. Department of Revenue. Summary of Levies and Statistics.
   Description: Contains tables of property values and tax levies for counties and cities in Oregon.

OXFORD BULLETIN OF ECONOMICS AND STATISTICS. see BUSINESS AND ECONOMICS

332 US ISSN 1057-8900
HG1710
P S I ABSTRACTS. m. $500. Payment Systems Incorporated, 3030 N. Rocky Point Dr. W., Ste. 800, Tampa, FL 33607. TEL 813-287-2774. FAX 813-286-7377. E-mail: mbrod@psi-nfo.com; URL: http://www.psi-nfo.com. Ed. Mark A. Broderick. R&P contact: Mark A. Broderick. circ. 450. **Document type:** abstracting/indexing.

336 PK
PAKISTAN. FINANCE DIVISION. PUBLIC FINANCE STATISTICS. (Text in English) 1975. a. Finance Division, Islamabad, Pakistan. **Document type:** government publication.

338.9 315 PK
PAKISTAN INSTITUTE OF DEVELOPMENT ECONOMICS. STATISTICAL PAPERS SERIES. 1980. irreg. price varies. Pakistan Institute of Development Economics, P.O. Box 1091, Islamabad 44000, Pakistan. TEL 92-51-9206610. FAX 92-51-9210886. Ed.Bd. stat. circ. 1,000. **Document type:** monographic series.

338 315 PP ISSN 1023-6481
PAPUA NEW GUINEA. NATIONAL STATISTICAL OFFICE. ANNUAL BUSINESS CENSUS. 1994. a. K.7 (foreign K.12). National Statistical Office, P.O. Box 337, Waigani, N.C.D., Papua New Guinea. TEL 675-3011226. FAX 675-3251869. TELEX FINANCE 22312. Ed. Francis K. Kasau. **Document type:** government publication.
   Formed by the 1994 merger of: Rural Industries (ISSN 0078-7701); Agriculture Largeholdings (Preliminary) (ISSN 0078-9321); Secondary Industries (ISSN 0078-933X); Secondary Industries (Preliminary) (ISSN 0078-9313); Capital Expenditure by Private Businesses (ISSN 0078-9259); Census of Retail Sales and Selected Services (ISSN 1017-6470); Census of Employment (ISSN 1017-6489).

339 PP ISSN 1017-6403
PAPUA NEW GUINEA. NATIONAL STATISTICAL OFFICE. DOMESTIC FACTOR INCOMES, BY REGION AND PROVINCE. a. K.1.50. National Statistical Office, P.O. Box 337, Waigani, N.C.D., Papua New Guinea. TEL 675-3011226. FAX 675-3251869. TELEX FINANCE NE 22312. Ed. Francis K. Kasau. **Document type:** government publication.
   Description: Contains estimates of domestic factor incomes for each of the four regions and 20 provinces, including the National Capital District.

330 PP ISSN 1017-6381
PAPUA NEW GUINEA. NATIONAL STATISTICAL OFFICE. ECONOMIC INDICATORS. 1976. m. K.12 (foreign K.18). National Statistical Office, P.O. Box 337, Waigani, N.C.D., Papua New Guinea. TEL 675-3011226. FAX 675-3251869. TELEX FINANCE NE 22312. **Document type:** government publication.
   Description: Provides the latest available figures on a wide range of economic indicators, including banking, balance of payments, international trade, export prices, consumer price indices, and international arrivals and departures.

382 PP ISSN 1017-6527
PAPUA NEW GUINEA. NATIONAL STATISTICAL OFFICE. EXPORT PRICE INDEXES. q. K.7 (foreign K.12). National Statistical Office, P.O. Box 337, Papua New Guinea, Papua New Guinea. TEL 675-3011226. FAX 675-3251869. TELEX FINANCE NE 22312. Ed. Francis K. Kasau. **Document type:** government publication.
   Description: Covers price indices of all major domestic exports.

339 PP ISSN 1017-6411
PAPUA NEW GUINEA. NATIONAL STATISTICAL OFFICE. GOVERNMENT FINANCE STATISTICS. a. K.2.50. National Statistical Office, P.O. Box 337, Waigani, N.C.D., Papua New Guinea. TEL 675-3011226. FAX 675-3251869. TELEX FINANCE NE 22312. Ed. Francis K. Kasau. **Document type:** government publication.

319 330 PP ISSN 1017-639X
HC683.5.Z9
PAPUA NEW GUINEA. NATIONAL STATISTICAL OFFICE. GROSS DOMESTIC PRODUCT AND EXPENDITURE. (Text in English) a. K.2. National Statistical Office, P.O. Box 337, Waigani, N.C.D., Papua New Guinea. TEL 675-3011226. FAX 675-3251869. TELEX FINANCE NE 22312. Ed. Francis K. Kasau. **Document type:** government publication.
   Formed by the merger of: Papua New Guinea. Bureau of Statistics. Gross Domestic Product and Domestic Factor Incomes by Kind of Economic Activity & Papua New Guinea. Bureau of Statistics. Consolidated National Economic Accounts & Papua New Guinea. Bureau of Statistics. Gross Domestic Product at Constant Prices; Which was formerly: Papua New Guinea. Bureau of Statistics. National Accounts Statistics: Expenditure of Gross Domestic Product at Constant Purchasers' Values.
   Description: Provides a summary of all economic activity in Papua New Guinea.

BUSINESS AND ECONOMICS — ABSTRACTING, BIBLIOGRAPHIES, STATISTICS

382   PP   ISSN 1017-6543
PAPUA NEW GUINEA. NATIONAL STATISTICAL OFFICE. IMPORT PRICE INDEXES. a. K.1.50. National Statistical Office, P.O. Box 337, Waigani, N.C.D., Papua New Guinea. TEL 675-3011226. FAX 675-3251869. TELEX FINANCE NE 22312. Ed. Francis K. Kasau. **Document type:** government publication.
   Description: Contains price indexes for imports in each of Sections 0-8 of the Standard International Trade Classification.

382   PP   ISSN 1017-6519
PAPUA NEW GUINEA. NATIONAL STATISTICAL OFFICE. INTERNATIONAL TRADE - EXPORTS. q. K.7 (foreign K.12). National Statistical Office, P.O. Box 337, Waigani, N.C.D., Papua New Guinea. TEL 675-3011226. FAX 675-3251869. TELEX FINANCE NE 22312. Ed. Francis K. Kasau. **Document type:** government publication.
   Description: Includes summaries of export values classified by port of shipment and country of destination, along with quantities and values of major exports, classified by country of destination and commodity.

382   PP   ISSN 1017-6535
PAPUA NEW GUINEA. NATIONAL STATISTICAL OFFICE. INTERNATIONAL TRADE - IMPORTS. q. K.7 (foreign K.12). National Statistical Office, P.O. Box 337, Waigani, N.C.D., Papua New Guinea. TEL 675-3011226. FAX 675-325869. TELEX FINANCE NE 22312. Ed. Francis K. Kasau. **Document type:** government publication.
   Description: Summarizes values of imports, by statistical section and group, port of entry, country of origin, and broad economic category.

330 310   AT
PAPUA NEW GUINEA HANDBOOK. 1954. irreg. (plus a. updates). Aus.$500. Australian National University, National Centre for Development Studies, Canberra, A.C.T. 0200, Australia. TEL 61-6-2494705. FAX 61-6-2572886. (Subscr. to: Bibliotech, Canberra, A.C.T. 0200, Australia) Ed. Maree Tait. adv.; index.
   Formerly (until 1990): Handbook of Papua and New Guinea (ISSN 0072-9868)
   Description: A comprehensive survey of the Papua New Guinea economy.

338 318   PY   ISSN 0085-4743
PARAGUAY. MINISTERIO DE INDUSTRIA Y COMERCIO. DIVISION DE REGISTRO Y ESTADISTICA INDUSTRIAL. ENCUESTA INDUSTRIAL. Formerly issued by the Ministry's Departamento de Estadística y Censos. irreg. free. Ministerio de Industria y Comercio, Division de Registro y Estadística Industrial, Avda. España 374, C.C. 1772, Asuncion, Paraguay. stat. (processed)

330.9 318   BL
PARANA, BRAZIL. SECRETARIA DE ESTADO DA FAZENDA. ESTATISTICA ECONOMICO-FINANCEIRA. 1972. irreg., latest 1989. free. Secretaria de Estado da Fazenda, Av. Vicente Machado 445, 1oo andar, 80420-010 Curitiba, PA, Brazil. TEL 041-223-2216. FAX 041-222-3505. TELEX 41-6007 SFIN. Dir. Everlindo Henklein. illus. circ. 1,000. **Document type:** government publication.

658.3 016   UK   ISSN 0305-067X
HF5549.A2
PERSONNEL & TRAINING ABSTRACTS. 1971. bi-m. £3199($4999) (foreign Aus.$6499) (effective 1998). (Institute of Personnel Management) M C B University Press Ltd., Anbar Electronic Intelligence, 60-62 Toller Ln., Bradford, W. Yorks BD8 9BY, England. TEL 44-1274-480916. FAX 44-1274-543576. TELEX 935779. Ed. Eric Sandelands. (looseleaf format) **Document type:** abstracting/indexing.
   —BLDSC (0900.305000).
   Supersedes in part: Anbar Management Services Abstracts (ISSN 0003-2794)
   Description: Contains abstracts of articles selected from over 300 international management journals. Covers such topics as health and safety, management development, industrial relations.

658.3 016   US   ISSN 0031-577X
HF5549
PERSONNEL MANAGEMENT ABSTRACTS. 1955. q. $180 (includes a. cumulation) (foreign $186) (effective 1998). Personnel Management Abstracts, 704 Island Lake Rd., Chelsea, MI 48118. TEL 313-475-1979. Ed. Gloria Reo; Pub. Gloria Reo. adv.; bk.rev.; abstr.; index, cum.index. circ. 850. (also avail. in microform from UMI; reprint service avail. from UMI) **Indexed:** P.A.I.S. **Document type:** abstracting/indexing.
   —BLDSC (6428.077000); UMI.

331.2   CN   ISSN 0840-8750
HD5727   CODEN: PLAIEY
PERSPECTIVES ON LABOUR AND INCOME. French edition: L'Emploi et le Revenu en Perspective (ISSN 0843-4565) 1989. q. Can.$56($68) (foreign $80). Statistics Canada, Operations and Integration Division, Circulation Management, Jean Talon Bldg., 2-C12, Tunney's Pasture, Ottawa, ON K1A 0T6, Canada. TEL 613-951-7277; 800-267-6677. FAX 613-951-1584. URL: http://www.statcan.ca. index. **Indexed:** Can.B.P.I. **Document type:** government publication.
   —CCC.
   Description: Brings together and analyzes a wide range of data.

339   PE
PERU. INSTITUTO NACIONAL DE ESTADISTICA. BOLETIN ANUAL. 1983. irreg. Instituto Nacional de Estadistica y Informatica, Oficina Regional de Estadistica del Cusco, Direccion General de Indicadores Economicos y Sociales, Av. 28 de Julio 1056, Lima, Peru. Ed.Bd. circ. 500.

338   BL   ISSN 0100-5138
HC186
PESQUISA INDUSTRIAL. 1952. a. Fundacao Instituto Brasileiro de Geografia e Estatistica, Centro de Documentacao e Disseminacao de Informacoes, Rua General Canabarro 706, 2o andar, Maracana 20271-201 Rio de Janeiro, Brazil. TEL 55-21-2645424. FAX 55-21-2841959. **Document type:** government publication.
   Formerly (until 1972): Producao Industrial (ISSN 0525-3969)

330 630 016   PH   ISSN 0115-4192
PHILIPPINE BUSINESS AND INDUSTRY INDEX. (Text in English) 1980. a. $200. Library Integrated Services Cooperative, P.O. Box 192, U.P. Campus, 1101 Quezon City, Philippines. TEL 921-9231. Ed. Vidal E. Santos. bk.rev. circ. 500. **Document type:** abstracting/indexing.

330 310   PH
PHILIPPINE STATISTICAL DEVELOPMENT PROGRAM. (Text in English) every 5 yrs., latest 1993. $56 in Asia (Australia & New Zealand $64; US, Canada & Europe $75; Latin America $88; elsewhere $108). National Statistical Coordination Board, c/o National Statistical Information Center, Midland-Buendia Bldg., 403 Sen. Gil Puyat Ave., Makati City, Philippines. TEL 63-2-890-9405. FAX 63-2-890-9408. E-mail: nscb__nsic@mozcom.com. **Document type:** government publication.
   Description: Analyzes the major developments in the Philippine Statistical System during the preceding planning period; sets objectives, strategies and statistical programs for the next six years.

315 336   PH
PHILIPPINE STATISTICAL YEARBOOK. (Text in English) 1974. a. $142 in Asia (Australia & New Zealand $153; US & Canada $163; Europe $165; Latin America $185; elsewhere $213). National Statistical Coordination Board, c/o National Statistical Information Center, Midland-Buendia Bldg., 403 Sen. Gil Puyat Ave., Makati City, Philippines. TEL 63-2-890-9405. FAX 63-2-890-9408. E-mail: nscb__nsic@mozcom.com. **Document type:** government publication.
   Formerly: N E D A Statistical Yearbook of the Philippines.
   Description: Contains a comprehensive compilation of major economic and social statistical information about the Philippines, its people and environment, and selected countries of the world produced by various government agencies, and international organization.

331   PH
PHILIPPINES. BUREAU OF LABOR AND EMPLOYMENT STATISTICS. CURRENT LABOR STATISTICS. (Text in English) 1980. m. P.636. Bureau of Labor and Employment Statistics, Department of Labor and Employment, DOLE Bldg., Intramuros, Manila, Philippines. TEL 63-2-408896. stat. circ. 400. **Document type:** government publication.
   Description: Statistical compendium; data presented in monthly and quarterly breakdown for current year.

331   PH
PHILIPPINES. BUREAU OF LABOR AND EMPLOYMENT STATISTICS. LABOR AND EMPLOYMENT STATISTICAL REPORT. (Text in English) 1989. q. P.128. Bureau of Labor and Employment Statistics, Department of Labor and Employment, DOLE Bldg., Intramuros, Manila, Philippines. TEL 63-2-408896. charts; stat. circ. 300. **Document type:** government publication.
   Description: Descriptive analysis of quarterly labor and employment statistics compared to previous year.

331 310   PH
PHILIPPINES. BUREAU OF LABOR AND EMPLOYMENT STATISTICS. OCCUPATIONAL WAGES SURVEY. (Text in English) 1990. a. free. Bureau of Labor and Employment Statistics, Department of Labor and Employment, DOLE Bldg., Intramuros, Manila, Philippines. TEL 63-2-408896. circ. 500. **Document type:** government publication.

331.1 315   PH
HD8713
PHILIPPINES. BUREAU OF LABOR AND EMPLOYMENT STATISTICS. YEARBOOK OF LABOR STATISTICS. (Text in English) 1973. a. P.160. Bureau of Labor and Employment Statistics, Department of Labor and Employment, DOLE Bldg., Intramuros, Manila, Philippines. TEL 63-2-408896. stat. circ. 500. **Document type:** government publication.
   Formerly: Philippines. Labor Statistics Service. Yearbook of Labor Statistics (ISSN 0115-1851)
   Description: Statistical compendium containing some historical data series.

330 310   PH
PHILIPPINES. NATIONAL STATISTICAL COORDINATION BOARD. ECONOMIC AND SOCIAL INDICATORS. (Text in English) a. $127 in Asia (Australia & New Zealand $138; US & Canada $148; Europe $150; Latin America $170; elsewhere $198). National Statistical Coordination Board, c/o National Statistical Information Center, Midland-Buendia Bldg., 403 Sen. Gil Puyat Ave., Makati City, Philippines. TEL 63-2-890-9405. FAX 63-2-890-9408. E-mail: nscb__nsic@mozcom.com. **Document type:** government publication.
   Description: Contains about 100 indicators grouped into 13 developmental goal areas and subareas: production, finance, foreign trade, natural and energy resources, employment, household income, expenditures and prices, population, health and nutrition, housing, education, social welfare and community development, public order, safety and justice.

330 310   PH
PHILIPPINES. NATIONAL STATISTICAL COORDINATION BOARD. REGIONAL SOCIAL AND ECONOMIC TRENDS SERIES. (Separate regional issues avail.) (Text in English) 1993. a. $102 in Asia (Australia & New Zealand $113; US & Canada $123; Europe $125; Latin America $145; elsewhere $173). National Statistical Coordination Board, c/o National Statistical Information Center, Midland-Buendia Bldg., 403 Sen. Gil Puyat Ave., Makati City, Philippines. TEL 63-2-890-9405. FAX 63-2-890-9408. E-mail: nscb__nsic@mozcom.com. **Document type:** government publication.
   Description: Presents major social and economic developments at the regional and subregional levels in data series with textual analysis and graphical illustration.

BUSINESS AND ECONOMICS — ABSTRACTING, BIBLIOGRAPHIES, STATISTICS

381   PH   ISSN 0116-2659
HF5421.5.P6
PHILIPPINES. NATIONAL STATISTICS OFFICE. ANNUAL SURVEY OF ESTABLISHMENTS. (In 11 parts) 1973. a., latest 1992. $50. National Statistics Office, Ramon Magsaysay Blvd., Box 779, Manila, Philippines. FAX 63-2-610794. (also avail. in diskette format) **Document type:** government publication.
    Formerly: Philippines. National Census and Statistics Office. Annual Survey of Establishments.
    Description: Presents the final results of the survey on the structure, trends, and levels of economic activity in the country.

330 310   PH
PHILIPPINES. NATIONAL STATISTICS OFFICE. CENSUS OF ESTABLISHMENTS. (In 11 vols.: Vol.1: Agriculture and Forestry; Vol. 2.: Fishery; Vol. 3: Manufacturing - Large; Vol. 3-A: Manufacturing - Small; Vol. 4: Electricity, Gas, and Water; Vol. 5: Construction; Vol. 6: Mining and Quarrying; Vol. 7: Wholesale and Retail Trade - Large; Vol. 7-A: Wholesale and Retail Trade - Small; Vol. 8: Transportation, Communication and Storage; Vol. 9: Financing, Insurance, Real Estate, and Business Services - Large; Vol. 9-A: Financing, Insurance, Real Estate, and Business Services - Small; Vol. 10: Community, Social, and Personal Services - Large; Vol. 10-A: Community, Social, and Personal Services - Small; Vol. 11: Public Education and Health Services) every 5 yrs. National Statistics Office, Ramon Magsaysay Blvd., Box 779, Manila, Philippines. FAX 63-2-610794. (also avail. in diskette format) **Document type:** government publication.
    Description: A nationwide comprehensive collection and compilation of statistical information pertaining to business operations of establishments at any time or the whole year.

330 310   PH   ISSN 0117-9772
PHILIPPINES. NATIONAL STATISTICS OFFICE. CONSUMER PRICE INDEX IN THE PHILIPPINES. a. National Statistics Office, Ramon Magsaysay Blvd., Box 779, Manila, Philippines. FAX 63-2-610794. illus. (also avail. in diskette format) **Document type:** government publication.
    Description: Presents changes in the price level of goods and services that most people buy for day-to-day consumption. Also reports inflation rates and the purchasing power of the peso, and includes a textual analysis.

330 310   PH
PHILIPPINES. NATIONAL STATISTICS OFFICE. DIRECTORY OF LARGE ESTABLISHMENTS. irreg., latest 1983. $90. National Statistics Office, Ramon Magsaysay Blvd., Box 779, Manila, Philippines. FAX 63-2-610794. **Document type:** government publication, directory.

330   US
PLAYBOY ENTERPRISES. ANNUAL REPORT. a. Playboy Enterprises, Inc., 680 N. Lake Shore Dr., Chicago, IL 60611. TEL 312-751-8000. FAX 312-751-2818. **Document type:** corporate report.

330   PL
POLAND. GLOWNY URZAD STATYSTYCZNY. STATYSTYKA POLSKI. SERIA: MATERIALY STATYSTYCZNE. WARUNKI MIESZKANIOWE GOSPODARSTW DOMOWYCH ORAZ WYDADKI NA MIESZKANIE (YEAR). irreg., latest 1987. Zaklad Wydawnictw Statystycznych, Al. Niepodleglosci 208, 00-925 Warsaw, Poland. Ed. Tadeusz Kania. **Document type:** government publication.

331 314   PL   ISSN 0079-2896
HD6167.7.A6
POLAND. GLOWNY URZAD STATYSTYCZNY. ZATRUDNIENIE W GOSPODARCE NARODOWEJ. (Subseries of its: Statystyka Polski) 1969. a. 24 ZI. Zaklad Wydawnictw Statystycznych, Al. Niepodleglosci 208, 00-925 Warsaw, Poland. TEL 48 22 25-03-45. **Document type:** government publication.

330   PL   ISSN 1230-5782
POLAND. GLOWNY URZAD STATYSTYCZNY. ZMIANY CEN W GOSPODARCE NARODOWEJ. 1971. irreg. Zaklad Wydawnictw Statystycznych, Al. Niepodleglosci 208, 00-925 Warsaw, Poland. **Document type:** government publication.
    Formerly (until 1989): Poland. Glowny Urzad Statystyczny. Ceny Detaliczne (ISSN 0860-6730)

POLYMERS, CERAMICS, COMPOSITES ALERT. see PLASTICS — Abstracting, Bibliographies, Statistics

338 314   PO   ISSN 0377-2314
HC391
PORTUGAL. ESTATISTICAS INDUSTRIAIS: CONTINENTE, ACORES E MADEIRA. VOLUME 1: INDUSTRIAS EXTRACTIVAS, ELECTRICIDADE, GAS, AGUA/PORTUGAL. STATISTIQUES INDUSTRIELLES: CONTINENT, ACORES ET MADERE. VOLUME 1: INDUSTRIES EXTRACTIVES, ELECTRICITE, GAZ, EAU.. (Text in French and Portuguese) 1943. a. Esc.2000. Instituto Nacional de Estatistica, Ave. Antonio Jose de Almeida, 1078 Lisbon, Portugal. TEL 351-1-8470050. FAX 351-1-8478578. TELEX 351-63738 PCDINE P. **Document type:** government publication.
    Former titles (until 1971): Portugal. Estatisticas Industrias. Continente e Ilhas Adjacentes; Portugal. Instituto Nacional de Estatistica. Estatistica Industrial.

330   PO   ISSN 0079-418X
PORTUGAL. ESTATISTICAS INDUSTRIAIS: CONTINENTE, ACORES E MADEIRA. VOLUME 2: INDUSTRIAS TRANSFORMADORAS/PORTUGAL. STATISTIQUES INDUSTRIELLES: CONTINENT, ACORES ET MADERE. VOLUME 2: INDUSTRIES MANUFACTURIERES. 1971. a. Esc.6700. Instituto Nacional de Estatistica, Ave. Antonio Jose de Almeida, 1078 Lisbon Codex, Portugal. (Subscr. to: Impresa Nacional, Casada da Moeda, Direccao Comercial, Rua D. Francisco Manuel de Melo 5, 1000 Lisbon, Portugal) **Document type:** government publication.
    Former titles: Portugal. Estatisticas Industriais: Continente e Ilhas Adjacentes; Portugal. Instituto Nacional de Estatistica. Estatistica Industrial.

310 382   PO   ISSN 0873-092X
PORTUGAL. INSTITUTO NACIONAL DE ESTATISTICA. COMERCIO EXTRACOMUNITARIO. (Text in French, Portuguese) 1975. m. Esc.10000. Instituto Nacional de Estatistica, Ave. Antonio Jose de Almeida, 1078 Lisbon, Portugal. TEL 351-1-8470050. FAX 351-1-8478578. TELEX 351-1-63738-PCDINE. stat.; index. circ. 1,000. (also avail. in microfiche; back issues avail.) **Document type:** bulletin, government publication.
    Former titles (until 1991): Portugal. Instituto Nacional de Estatistica. Boletim Mensal das Estatisticas do Comercio Externo (ISSN 0377-2160); (until 1995): Portugal. Instituto Nacional de Estatistica. Indicadores do Comercio Externo (ISSN 0871-9179)

PORTUGAL. INSTITUTO NACIONAL DE ESTATISTICA. CONTAS NACIONAIS. see BUSINESS AND ECONOMICS — Macroeconomics

PORTUGAL. INSTITUTO NACIONAL DE ESTATISTICA. CONTAS NACIONAIS TRIMESTRAIS. see BUSINESS AND ECONOMICS — Macroeconomics

336.2 314   PO
PORTUGAL. INSTITUTO NACIONAL DE ESTATISTICA. ESTATISTICAS DAS CONTRIBUICOES E IMPOSTOS. CONTINENTE, ACORES E MADEIRA. 1877. a. Esc.1100. Instituto Nacional de Estatistica, Ave. Antonio Jose de Almeida, 1078 Lisbon, Portugal. TEL 351-1-8470050. FAX 351-1-8478578. TELEX 351-63738 PCDINE P. **Document type:** government publication.
    Formerly: Portugal. Instituto Nacional de Estatistica. Estatisticas das Contribuicoes e Impostos (ISSN 0079-4120)
    Description: Provides statistical data on income tax, liquidation and taxes in general for the mainland and autonomous regions.

336 314   PO
PORTUGAL. INSTITUTO NACIONAL DE ESTATISTICA. ESTATISTICAS DAS FINANCAS PUBLICAS. CONTINENTE, ACORES E MADEIRA. (Text in French and Portuguese) 1968. a. Esc.3650. Instituto Nacional de Estatistica, Ave. Antonio Jose de Almeida, 1078 Lisbon, Portugal. TEL 351-1-8470050. FAX 351-1-8478578. TELEX 351-63738 PCDINE P. **Document type:** government publication.
    Formerly: Portugal. Instituto Nacional de Estatistica. Estatisticas das Financas Publicas (ISSN 0377-2276)
    Description: Provides information on public sector divided into three categories: Central Government, Local Government and Social Security.

382 314   PO   ISSN 0873-0687
PORTUGAL. INSTITUTO NACIONAL DE ESTATISTICA. ESTATISTICAS DO COMERCIO INTERNACIONAL. 1914. a. Esc.10500 (effective 1997). Instituto Nacional de Estatistica, Ave. Antonio Jose de Almeida, 1078 Lisbon, Portugal. TEL 351-1-8470050. FAX 351-1-8478578. TELEX 351-63738 PCDINE P. Dir. C. Correa Gago. circ. 650. **Document type:** government publication.
    Former titles (until 1993): Portugal. Instituto Nacional de Estatistica. Estatisticas do Comercio Externo. Continente Acores e Madeira; Portugal. Instituto Nacional de Estatistica. Estatisticas do Comercio Externo (ISSN 0079-4147)
    Description: Provides statistical data on imports and exports divided by goods and countries.

PORTUGAL. INSTITUTO NACIONAL DE ESTATISTICA. ESTATISTICAS MONETARIAS E FINANCIERAS. see BUSINESS AND ECONOMICS — Banking And Finance

PORTUGAL. INSTITUTO NACIONAL DE ESTATISTICA. INDICE DA PRODUCAO INDUSTRIAL. see MINES AND MINING INDUSTRY

PORTUGAL. INSTITUTO NACIONAL DE ESTATISTICA. INDICE DE PRECOS NO CONSUMIDOR. see BUSINESS AND ECONOMICS — Domestic Commerce

PORTUGAL. INSTITUTO NACIONAL DE ESTATISTICA. INDICE DO COMERCIO EXTERNO. see BUSINESS AND ECONOMICS — International Commerce

PORTUGAL. INSTITUTO NACIONAL DE ESTATISTICA. INQUERITO AO EMPREGO. see BUSINESS AND ECONOMICS — Small Business

PORTUGAL. INSTITUTO NACIONAL DE ESTATISTICA. INQUERITO DE CONJUNTURA AO INVESTIMENTO. see BUSINESS AND ECONOMICS — Investments

331.11 314   PO
PORTUGAL. MINISTERIO DO TRABALHO. SERVICO DE ESTATISTICAS. ESTATISTICAS DO TRABALHO. (Text in Portuguese; summaries in English, French) 1975. irreg. Ministerio do Trabalho, Servico de Informacao Cientifica e Tecnica, Praca de Londres 2 r-c, 1000 Lisbon, Portugal. **Document type:** government publication.

338 016   US   ISSN 0551-9276
PREDI-BRIEFS. (Available in 29 industry topics) 1961. m. $225 (foreign $250). Information Access Company (Subsidiary of: Thomson Corporation), 362 Lakeside Dr., Foster City, CA 94404. TEL 415-378-5200; 800-227-8431. FAX 415-358-4759. (Or: Predicasts Europe, 8-10 Denman St., London W1V 7RF, England. TEL 44-171-494-3817) **Indexed:** Resour.Ctr.Ind. **Document type:** abstracting/indexing.
—CCC.
    Description: Provides industry-specific abstracts from business and trade publications.

338   US   ISSN 0738-9906
HA214
PREDICASTS BASEBOOK. 1973. a. $600 (foreign $700). Information Access Company (Subsidiary of: Thomson Corporation), 362 Lakeside Dr., Foster City, CA 94404. TEL 415-378-5200; 800-227-8431. FAX 415-358-4759. (Or: Predicasts Europe, 8-10 Denman St., London W1V 7RF, England. TEL 44-171-494-3817) **Document type:** abstracting/indexing.
    ●Also available online. Vendor(s): Data-Star, Knight-Ridder Information, Inc.
—CCC.
    Description: Provides industry- and product-specific statistics covering aspects of US demographics, economics, industry, finance, and other business activities.

330   US   ISSN 0739-1862
HC10
PREDICASTS COMPANY THESAURUS. (In 3 vols.) a. $300 (foreign $325). Information Access Company (Subsidiary of: Thomson Corporation), 362 Lakeside Dr., Foster City, CA 94404. TEL 415-378-5200; 800-227-8431. FAX 415-358-4759. (Or: Predicasts Europe, 8-10 Denman St., London W1V 7RF, England. TEL 44-171-494-3817) **Document type:** abstracting/indexing, directory.
    Formerly: Corporate Thesaurus.
    Description: Lists all company names appearing in Predicasts' databases and publications, ordered by company and by database code.

BUSINESS AND ECONOMICS — ABSTRACTING, BIBLIOGRAPHIES, STATISTICS

338 016 US ISSN 0270-4536
HC240.A1
PREDICASTS F & S INDEX EUROPE. (Annual edition avail. (ISSN 0277-9684)) 1978. m. with q. and a. cumulations. $975 (foreign $1050). Information Access Company (Subsidiary of: Thomson Corporation), 362 Lakeside Dr., Foster City, CA 94404. TEL 415-378-5200; 800-227-8431. FAX 415-358-4759. (Or: Predicasts Europe, 8-10 Denman St., London W1V 7RF, England. TEL 44-171-494-3817) bibl.; stat.; tr.lit. **Document type:** abstracting/indexing.
●Also available online. Vendor(s): Data-Star, Knight-Ridder Information, Inc., Ovid Technologies, Inc. (PTSI).
—CCC.
Former titles: F and S Index Europe (ISSN 0199-5219); F and S Europe (ISSN 0193-1229)
Description: Covers business and economic data, providing an index to product, company, industry, and market activities reported in business publications.

338 016 US ISSN 0270-4528
Z7164.C81
PREDICASTS F & S INDEX INTERNATIONAL. (Annual edition avail. (ISSN 0277-9692)) 1967. m. with q. and a. cumulations. $975 (foreign $1050) ($3500 on CD-ROM). Information Access Company (Subsidiary of: Thomson Corporation), 362 Lakeside Dr., Foster City, CA 94404. TEL 415-378-5200; 800-227-8431. FAX 415-358-5369. (Or: Predicasts Europe, 8-10 Denman St., London W1V 7RF, England. TEL 44-171-494-3817) **Document type:** abstracting/indexing.
●Also available online. Vendor(s): Data-Star, Knight-Ridder Information, Inc., Ovid Technologies, Inc. (PTSI).
Also available on CD-ROM.
—CCC.
Formerly: F and S International (ISSN 0014-5661)
Description: Covers business and economic data in Canada, Latin America, Africa, Asia, and Oceania. Provides an index to product, company, industry, and market activities reported in business publications.

338 US ISSN 0744-2785
HD2741
PREDICASTS F & S INDEX OF CORPORATE CHANGE. 1972. q. with a. cumulation. $300 (foreign $325). Information Access Company (Subsidiary of: Thomson Corporation), 362 Lakeside Dr., Foster City, CA 94404. TEL 415-378-5200; 800-227-8431. FAX 415-358-4759. (Or: Predicasts Europe, 8-10 Denman St., London W1V 7RF, England. TEL 44-171-494-3817) abstr.; bibl.; index. **Document type:** abstracting/indexing.
●Also available online. Vendor(s): Knight-Ridder Information, Inc., Ovid Technologies, Inc. (PTSI).
—CCC.
Former titles (until 1981): Predicasts Index of Corporate Change (ISSN 0273-3994); F and S Index of Corporate Change (ISSN 0163-6693)
Description: Index to business literature covering changes in ownership of US-based corporations, including company formations, mergers and acquisitions, bankruptcies, liquidations, reorganizations, joint ventures, and name and subsidiary changes.

338 016 US ISSN 0270-4544
Z7165.U5
PREDICASTS F & S INDEX UNITED STATES. (Annual edition avail. (ISSN 0277-9676)) 1960. m. with q. and a. cumulations. $975 ($1100 with w. supplements) ($3500 on CD-ROM). Information Access Company (Subsidiary of: Thomson Corporation), 362 Lakeside Dr., Foster City, CA 94404. TEL 415-378-5200. FAX 415-378-5369. (Or: Predicasts Europe, 8-10 Denman St., London W1V 7RF, England. TEL 44-171-494-3817) index. (back issues avail.) **Document type:** abstracting/indexing.
●Also available online. Vendor(s): Data-Star, Knight-Ridder Information, Inc., Ovid Technologies, Inc. (PTSI).
—CCC.
Formerly: F and S Index of Corporations and Industries (ISSN 0014-567X)
Description: Covers business and economic data in the U.S. Provides an index to product, company, industry, and market activities reported in business publications.

338 016 US ISSN 0278-0135
HC101
PREDICASTS FORECASTS. 1960. q. with a. cumulation. $850 (foreign $900) (effective 1992). Information Access Company (Subsidiary of: Thomson Corporation), 362 Lakeside Dr., Foster City, CA 94404. TEL 415-378-5200; 800-227-8431. FAX 415-358-4759. (Or: Predicasts Europe, 8-10 Denman St., London W1V 7RF, England. TEL 44-171-494-3817) Ed. Eileen Gazzuolo. charts; mkt.; tr.lit.; index. **Document type:** abstracting/indexing.
●Also available online. Vendor(s): Data-Star (PTFC), Knight-Ridder Information, Inc.
—CCC.
Formerly: Predicasts (ISSN 0032-7166)
Description: Provides statistical abstracts of forecasts published in international trade and business literature. Covers production, sales, exports, for specific industries and product areas.

338 016 US ISSN 0092-7767
Z7164.C81
PREDICASTS SOURCE DIRECTORY. Key Title: Source Directory of Predicasts, Inc. (Supplement avail.) 1973. a. $200 includes supplement (foreign $225). Information Access Company (Subsidiary of: Thomson Corporation), 362 Lakeside Dr., Foster City, CA 94404. TEL 415-378-5200; 800-227-8431. FAX 415-358-4759. (Or: Predicasts Europe, 8-10 Denman St., London W1V 7RF, England. TEL 44-171-494-3817) bibl. **Document type:** abstracting/indexing, directory.
Description: Lists all publications abstracted and indexed by Predicasts.

310 CE
PRICE AND WAGE STATISTICS OF SRI LANKA. (Text in English) 1982. irreg., latest 1993. $8. Central Bank of Sri Lanka, Janadhipathi Mawatha, P.O. Box 590, Colombo 1, Sri Lanka. TEL 94-1-421191. FAX 94-1-445127.

330 332.1 JA ISSN 0386-6297
PRICE INDEXES MONTHLY. (Text in English and Japanese) m. 900 Yen per no. Bank of Japan, Research and Statistics Department - Nippon Ginko, c/o Public Relations Department, 2-1-1 Hongoku-Cho, Nihonbashi, Chuo-ku, Tokyo 103, Japan. TEL 81-3-3292-3753. FAX 81-3-3292-0410. TELEX JPTCO J27161. (Dist. by: Tokiwa Sohgoh Service Co., Ltd., Kyodo Bldg., 2-4, 3-chome, Hogokucho, Nihonbashi Chuo-ku, Tokyo 103, Japan. TEL 81-3-3270-5713. FAX 81-3-3292-0410; Overseas dist. by: Japan Publications Trading Co., Ltd., Book Export No.2 Dept., P.O. Box 5030, Tokyo International, Tokyo 100-31, Japan) pp./issue: 130.
Description: Contains wholesale price indexes, export and import price indexes, corporate service price index, input-output price indexes of manufacturing industry by sector, and monthly percentage change for all commodities.

331 016 US ISSN 0037-1351
Z7164.L1
PRINCETON UNIVERSITY. INDUSTRIAL RELATIONS SECTION. SELECTED REFERENCES. 1969. 5/yr. Princeton University, Industrial Relations Section, Firestone Library, Princeton, NJ 08544. TEL 609-258-4040. circ. 1,500. **Indexed:** P.A.I.S. **Document type:** academic/scholarly publication.

330 GW ISSN 0342-0922
PROARBEIT; Informationssystem zu Arbeit, Beruf, Berufsbildung und Arbeitswissenschaft. 2/yr. DM.350. Bundesanstalt fuer Arbeit, Institut fuer Arbeitsmarkt- und Berufsforschung, Regensburgerstr. 104, 90327 Nuernberg, Germany. TEL 49-911-1793011. FAX 49-911-1791147. (Dist. by: Landesarbeitsamt Nordbayern, Geschaeftsstelle fuer Veroeffentlichungen, Regensburgerstr. 100, 90328 Nuernberg, Germany. TEL 49-911-1794162) **Document type:** abstracting/indexing, government publication.
●Also available online.
Also available on CD-ROM.

PRODUCTION AND DISPOSITION OF TOBACCO PRODUCTS/PRODUCTION ET DISPOSITION DES PRODUITS DU TABAC. see TOBACCO — Abstracting, Bibliographies, Statistics

338 310 JA ISSN 1342-338X
HC415.L3
PRODUCTIVITY STATISTICS; productivity indexes and levels in APO member countries. 1984. a. free. Asian Productivity Organization, 8-4-14 Akasaka, Minato-ku, Tokyo 107, Japan. FAX 81-3-3408-7220. E-mail: apo@gol.com; URL: http://www.apo-tokyo.com. circ. 1,000.

330.9 SZ
PRODUKTIONS- UND WERTSCHOEPFUNGSSTATISTIK. BUCHHALTUNGSERGEBNISSE SCHWEIZERISCHER UNTERNEHMUNGEN/STATISTIQUE DE LA PRODUCTION ET DE LA VALEUR AJOUTEE. LES RESULTATS COMPTABLES DES ENTREPRISES SUISSES. (Text in French and German) 1980. a. 16 SFr. Bundesamt fuer Statistik, Schwarztorstr. 96, CH-3003 Bern, Switzerland. TEL 41-31-3236060. FAX 41-31-3236061. URL: http://www.admin.ch/bfs. **Document type:** government publication.
Formerly: Buchhaltungsergebnisse Schweizerische Unternehmungen.

380 SZ
PRODUZENTEN- UND IMPORTPREISINDEX/INDICE DES PRIX A LA PRODUCTION ET A L'IMPORTATION. (Text in French and German) 1988. m. 44 SFr. Bundesamt fuer Statistik, Schwarztorstr. 96, CH-3003 Bern, Switzerland. TEL 41-31-3236060. FAX 41-31-3236061. URL: http://www.admin.ch/bfs. **Document type:** government publication.
Formerly: Grosshandelspreisindes.

314 CY
PROFILES OF EARNINGS IN CYPRUS: BY EDUCATION, OCCUPATION, EXPERIENCE, AGE, SEX AND SECTOR. (Text in English) 1979. irreg. £C0.50. Ministry of Finance, Department of Statistics and Research, 13 Lord Byron Ave., Nicosia, Cyprus. TEL 357-2-302349. FAX 357-2-156712. **Document type:** government publication.
Description: Analyzes earnings by education, occupational experience, age, sex, and sector.

658 016 UK ISSN 1361-4940
▼**PROMOTIONAL STRATEGIES AND TACTICS ABSTRACTS.** 1996. q. M C B University Press Ltd., Anbar Electronic Intelligence, 60-62 Toller Ln., Bradford, W. Yorks BD8 9BY, England. TEL 44-1274-480916. FAX 44-1274-543576. E-mail: spuesey@anbar.co.uk; URL: http://www.anbar.co.uk/anbar.htm. **Document type:** abstracting/indexing.

PUBLIC RELATIONS REVIEW; journal of research and comment. see ADVERTISING AND PUBLIC RELATIONS

331 317 PR
PUERTO RICO. DEPARTMENT OF LABOR. EMPLEO, ASALARIADO NO AGRICOLA EN PUERTO RICO. (Text in English, Spanish) m. Department of Labor, Bureau of Labor Statistics, 505 Munoz Rivera Ave., Hato Rey, PR 00918. TEL 787-754-5351. Ed. Antonio Padilla Torres. **Document type:** government publication.
Former titles: Puerto Rico. Department of Labor. Empleo, Horas y Salarios en las Industrias Manufactureras - Employment, Hours and Earnings in the Manufacturing Industries; Puerto Rico. Bureau of Labor Statistics. Salarios, Horas Semanales Trabajadas y Otras Condiciones de Trabajo.

330.9 PR
PUERTO RICO ECONOMIC INDICATORS. bi-m. Government Development Bank for Puerto Rico, P.O. Box 42001, Minillas Sta., San Juan, PR 00940-2001. TEL 787-729-6433. FAX 787-728-0975. (US addr.: 140 Broadway, 38th Fl., New York, NY 10005. TEL 212-422-6420) charts; stat.
Description: Compiles basic economic and statistical information from various sources.

BUSINESS AND ECONOMICS — ABSTRACTING, BIBLIOGRAPHIES, STATISTICS

331 012   UK   ISSN 0965-8521
HF5549.2.G7
QUALITY OF WORKING LIFE NEWS & ABSTRACTS. Key Title: Q W L News & Abstracts. 1978. q. free. Advisory Conciliation Arbitration Service, Brandon House, 180 Borough High St., London SE1 1LW, England. TEL 44-171-210-3613. FAX 44-171-210-3615. Ed. Brian Chaney. adv.; bk.rev. circ. 2,000. (back issues avail.) **Indexed:** Mgmt.& Market.Abstr. **Document type:** abstracting/indexing.
—BLDSC (7218.276800). **CCC.**
    Former titles (until 1992): Great Britain. Advisory Conciliation Arbitration Service. Work Research Unit. News and Abstracts (ISSN 0960-2615); (until 1990): Information Service News and Abstracts (ISSN 0951-0524); (until 1986): Information System News and Abstracts (ISSN 0267-873X); (until 1984): Information System Abstract (ISSN 0142-4602)
    Description: Covers quality of working life, job satisfaction, job design, effects of new technology on employees.

330   IE   ISSN 0791-4857
QUANTITY SURVEYORS INQUIRY. q. £8. Central Statistics Office, Skehard Rd., Cork, Ireland. TEL 353-21-359000. FAX 353-21-359090. E-mail: information@cso.ie; URL: http://www.cso.ie.
Document type: government publication.
    Description: Provides a short-term indicator of output in the non-residential building sector.

330   XR
QUARTERLY STATISTICAL BULLETIN/BULLETIN STATISTIQUE TRIMESTRIEL. (Text in English, French) q. $32. Cesky Statisticky Urad, Sokolovska 142, 186 04 Prague 8, Czech Republic. TEL 42-2-6604-2451. FAX 42-2-6631-0429.
    Description: Provides statistical analysis and tabulation covering the development of the Czech economy and its gradual shift to a free market system.

310   CN   ISSN 0832-8544
HD5729.Q4
QUEBEC (PROVINCE). BUREAU DE STATISTIQUE. DONNEES SUR LA POPULATION ACTIVE.* 1979. m. Ministere de la Culture et Communications, Direction Generale des Publications Gouvernementales, 225 Grand Allee est., Quebec, PQ G1R 5G5, Canada. TEL 418-643-2183. **Document type:** government publication.

331.1 016   CN   ISSN 0075-613X
QUEEN'S UNIVERSITY AT KINGSTON. INDUSTRIAL RELATIONS CENTRE. BIBLIOGRAPHY SERIES. 1965. irreg., no. 8, 1991. price varies. Queen's University, Industrial Relations Centre, Kingston, ON K7L 3N6, Canada. TEL 613-545-6709. FAX 613-545-6812. E-mail: ircpress@post.queensu.ca; URL: http://qsilver.queensu.ca/irl/ircpress/. Ed. Carol Williams. **Document type:** bibliography.

310 330   II   ISSN 0079-9564
HA1728.R3
RAJASTHAN, INDIA. DIRECTORATE OF ECONOMICS AND STATISTICS. BASIC STATISTICS. (Text in English) 1956. a. Rs.50. Directorate of Economics and Statistics, Tilak Marg, Jaipur, Rajasthan, India. **Document type:** government publication.

330   CF
RAPPORT D'ACTIVITES DES ENTREPRISES DU SECTEUR MODERNE. 1974. a. 5000 Fr.CFA. Centre National de la Statistique et des Etudes Economiques, B.P. 2031, Brazzaville, Congo. TEL 242-83-36-94. **Document type:** government publication.

330 016   RU   ISSN 0203-6223
HC10
REFERATIVNYI ZHURNAL. EKONOMIKA PROMYSHLENNOSTI. 1960. m. $933 (effective 1998). Vsesoyuznyi Institut Nauchno-Tekhnicheskoi Informatsii (VINITI), Baltiiskaya ul., 14, Moscow A-219, Russia. (Subscr. to: Mezhdunarodnaya Kniga, Dimitrova ul. 39, 113095 Moscow, Russia) **Document type:** abstracting/indexing.
—Linda Hall.

677 016   RU   ISSN 0034-2432
REFERATIVNYI ZHURNAL. LEGKAYA PROMYSHLENNOST'. 1956. m. $429 (effective 1998). Vsesoyuznyi Institut Nauchno-Tekhnicheskoi Informatsii (VINITI), Baltiiskaya ul., 14, Moscow A-219, Russia. (Subscr. to: Mezhdunarodnaya Kniga, Dimitrova ul. 39, 113095 Moscow, Russia) **Indexed:** Chem.Abstr. **Document type:** abstracting/indexing.
—Linda Hall.

658 016   RU   ISSN 0132-5639
HD28   CODEN: RZOUEM
REFERATIVNYI ZHURNAL. ORGANIZATSIYA UPRAVLENIYA. 1965. m. $396 (effective 1998). Vsesoyuznyi Institut Nauchno-Tekhnicheskoi Informatsii (VINITI), Baltiiskaya ul., 14, Moscow A-219, Russia. (Subscr. to: Mezhdunarodnaya Kniga, Dimitrova ul. 39, 113095 Moscow, Russia) **Document type:** abstracting/indexing.
    Formerly: Referativnyi Zhurnal. Organizatsiya Upravleniya Promyshlennost'yu (ISSN 0034-253X)

REGULATORY REVIEW (YEAR). see *PUBLIC ADMINISTRATION — Abstracting, Bibliographies, Statistics*

332.1 319 330.9   AT   ISSN 0725-0320
HG189
RESERVE BANK OF AUSTRALIA. BULLETIN. 1937. m. Aus.$25. Reserve Bank of Australia, 65 Martin Pl., G.P.O. Box 3974, Sydney, N.S.W. 2001, Australia. TEL 61-2-551-8111. FAX 61-2-551-8000. Ed.Bd. charts; stat.; cum.index. circ. 4,400. **Indexed:** Key to Econ.Sci., P.A.I.S. **Document type:** bulletin.
    Formerly (until Jul. 1981): Reserve Bank of Australia. Statistical Bulletin (ISSN 0034-5504)

651.2   US
RESOURCE CENTER INDEX. (Former name of issuing body: National Micrographics Association) 1974. s-a. $100 (members $75). Association for Information and Image Management, Resource Center, 1100 Wayne Ave., Ste. 1100, Silver Spring, MD 20910. TEL 301-587-8202. FAX 301-587-2711. E-mail: rescntr@capcon.net. bk.rev. (also avail. in microfiche from UMI) **Document type:** abstracting/indexing.
    Formerly: Micrographics Index.
    Description: Key to the Resource Center's database contains over 26,000 items, including bibliographic information on all aspects of document management, image processing, including micrographics, record management, CAD-CAM, optical and interactive multimedia technology, CD-ROM, and office automation.

382   SP
RESUMENES ESTADISTICOS DE IMPORTACION. 1991. a. 5000 ptas. Ministerio de Comercio y Turismo, Paseo de la Castellana 162, 28046 Madrid, Spain. TEL 34-1-349-39-65. FAX 34-1-349-36-34. circ. 1,000. (also avail. in diskette format) **Document type:** government publication.

336.2   FR   ISSN 0259-5249
REVENUE STATISTICS OF O E C D MEMBER COUNTRIES. (Text in English, French) 1965. a. price varies. Organization for Economic Cooperation and Development, 2 rue Andre-Pascal, 75775 Paris Cedex 16, France. (U.S. orders to: O.E.C.D. Publications and Information Center, 2001 L St., N.W., Ste. 650, Washington, DC 20036-4922. TEL 202-785-6323) **Indexed:** IIS.
—BLDSC (7785.820000).

330 016   AG   ISSN 0034-7825
REVISTA DE COMPENDIOS DE ARTICULOS DE ECONOMIA. 1964. s-a. exchange basis. Universidad Nacional de Cordoba, Facultad de Ciencias Economicas, Instituto de Economia y Finanzas, Ciudad Universitaria, Estafeta 32, 5000 Cordoba, Argentina. TELEX BUCOR - AR 51822. circ. 500. **Document type:** academic/scholarly publication.
    Description: Covers brief summaries of articles on economics.

REVISTA DE ECONOMIA Y ESTADISTICA. see *BUSINESS AND ECONOMICS*

RIVISTA ITALIANA DI ECONOMIA DEMOGRAFIA E STATISTICA. see *POPULATION STUDIES — Abstracting, Bibliographies, Statistics*

330   RM   ISSN 1221-7050
HB235.R8
RUMANIA. COMISIA NATIONALA PENTRU STATISTICA. BULETIN STATISTIC DE PRETURI/RUMANIA. NATIONAL COMMISSION FOR STATISTICS. PRICES STATISTICAL BULLETIN. (Text in English, Rumanian) m. 36000 lei (foreign $72) (effective 1997). Comisia Nationala pentru Statistica - National Commission for Statistics, Bd. Libertatii 16, Sector 5, 70542 Bucharest, Rumania. TEL 40-1-614-3371. FAX 40-1-3124873. **Document type:** government publication.
    Description: Presents consumer price indices of the population by total, grouped by goods and services, industrial output, prices indices per total, sections and branches.

382   RM   ISSN 1223-0510
RUMANIA. COMISIA NATIONALA PENTRU STATISTICA. BULETIN STATISTIC DE COMERT EXTERIOR/RUMANIA. NATIONAL COMMISSION FOR STATISTICS. FOREIGN TRADE STATISTICS. (Text in English and Rumanian) m. 36000 lei (foreign $72) (effective 1997). Comisia Nationala pentru Statistica - National Commission for Statistics, Bd. Libertatii 16, Sector 5, 70542 Bucharest, Rumania. TEL 40-1-6143371. FAX 40-1-3124873. **Document type:** government publication.
    Description: Presents data on foreign trade by exports, imports, trade balance, and destination and origin countries.

338   RM   ISSN 1223-0502
HC405.A1
RUMANIA. COMISIA NATIONALA PENTRU STATISTICA. BULETIN STATISTIC INDUSTRIE/RUMANIA. NATIONAL COMMISSION FOR STATISTICS. STATISTICAL BULLETIN - INDUSTRY. (Text in English and Rumanian) m. 36000 lei (foreign $72) (effective 1997). Comisia Nationala pentru Statistica - National Commission for Statistics, Bd. Libertatii 16, Sector 5, 70542 Bucharest, Rumania. TEL 40-1-6143371. FAX 40-1-3124873. **Document type:** government publication.
    Description: Presents data and comments referring to the level and evolution of industrial production, per total and by branches, the power resources from own production and import.

330   RM   ISSN 1224-290X
RUMANIA. NATIONAL COMMISSION FOR STATISTICS. NATIONAL ACCOUNTS. (Text in English) a. 5000 lei (foreign $12) (effective 1997). Comisia Nationala pentru Statistica - National Commission for Statistics, 16 Bd. Libertatii, Sector 5, 70542 Bucharest, Rumania. TEL 40-1-6143371. FAX 40-1-3124873. **Document type:** government publication.
    Description: Analyzes the evolution of main macroeconomic aggregates and their structure by sectors and branches. Covers the tables system data specific to national accounts.

S R D S: BULLET; the latest in list activity. (Standard Rate and Data Service) see *ADVERTISING AND PUBLIC RELATIONS — Abstracting, Bibliographies, Statistics*

382   XK
ST. LUCIA. STATISTICAL DEPARTMENT. ANNUAL OVERSEAS TRADE REPORT: PART 2. 1960. a. EC$20. Statistical Department, New Government Bldg., Block C, 2nd Fl., Conway, Castries, St. Lucia, W.I. TEL 758-45-22697. FAX 758-45-31648. TELEX 6394 FORAFF. Ed. Bryan Boxill. **Document type:** government publication.

382   XK
ST. LUCIA. STATISTICAL DEPARTMENT. QUARTERLY OVERSEAS TRADE REPORTS. 1960. q. EC$20. Statistical Department, New Government Bldg., Block C, 2nd Fl., Conway, Castries, St. Lucia, W.I. TEL 758-45-22697. FAX 758-45-31648. TELEX 6394 FORAFF. Ed. Brian Bixill. **Document type:** government publication.

BUSINESS AND ECONOMICS — ABSTRACTING, BIBLIOGRAPHIES, STATISTICS

658.8 310   US
SALES & MARKETING MANAGEMENT SURVEY OF BUYING POWER (PART I). 1929. a. $95 (with part II $125) (effective 1993). Bill Communications, Inc., 355 Park Ave. S., 5th Fl., New York, NY 10010-1789. TEL 212-592-6200. FAX 212-892-6339. (Subscr. to: Bill Communications, Inc. 200 S. Rte 130, Cinnaminson, NJ 08077. TEL 800-253-6708) Ed. Richard P. Kern. adv.; charts; stat. circ. 65,000. (reprint service avail. from UMI) **Document type:** trade publication.
    Formerly: Sales Management Survey of Buying Power (Part I).
    Description: Metro market county and city data on population income and retail sales.

658.8 310   US
SALES & MARKETING MANAGEMENT SURVEY OF BUYING POWER (PART II). 1973. a. $55 (effective 1993). Bill Communications, Inc., 355 Park Ave. S., 5th Fl., New York, NY 10010-1789. TEL 212-592-6200. FAX 212-592-6339. (Subscr. to: Bill Communications, Inc., 200 S. Rte. 130, Cinnaminson, NJ 08077. TEL 800-253-6708) Ed. Richard P. Kern. adv.; charts; stat. circ. 65,000. (reprint service avail. from UMI) **Document type:** trade publication.
    Formerly: Sales Management Survey of Buying Power (Part II).
    Description: Surveys U.S. buying power by covering merchandise line sales, projections for metro markets and current newspaper and TV market data.

658.8 310   US
SALES & MARKETING MANAGEMENT SURVEY OF SELLING COSTS. 1973. a. $35. Bill Communications, Inc., 355 Park Ave. S., 5th Fl., New York, NY 10010-1789. TEL 212-592-6200. FAX 212-592-6339. Ed. Richard P. Kern. adv.; charts; stat. circ. 57,000. (reprint service avail. from UMI)
    Formerly: Sales Management Survey of Selling Costs.
    Description: Annual compendium of selling cost surveys, giving statistics on cost-per-call, compensation, meetings, incentives and transportation.

SARDIUS; bibliography of southern African politics and economics. see POLITICAL SCIENCE — Abstracting, Bibliographies, Statistics

338 310   CN   ISSN 0837-8649
HA747.S3
SASKATCHEWAN. BUREAU OF STATISTICS. MONTHLY STATISTICAL REVIEW. 1975. m. free. Bureau of Statistics, 5th Fl., 2350 Albert St., Regina, SK S4P 4A6, Canada. TEL 306-787-6327. FAX 306-787-6311. charts; stat. **Indexed:** CS Ind. **Document type:** government publication.
    Former titles (until 1975): Saskatchewan. Bureau of Statistics. Monthly Statistical Review (ISSN 0706-7836); (until 1977): Saskatchewan Monthly Statistical Review (ISSN 0837-8630)

382 319   SU
SAUDI ARABIA. CENTRAL DEPARTMENT OF STATISTICS. FOREIGN TRADE STATISTICS. (Text in Arabic, English) a. s.R.100. Central Department of Statistics, P.O. Box 3735, Riyadh 11118, Saudi Arabia. **Document type:** government publication.

382 319   SU
SAUDI ARABIA. CENTRAL DEPARTMENT OF STATISTICS. QUARTERLY DIGEST OF FOREIGN TRADE STATISTICS. (Text in Arabic, English) q. Central Department of Statistics, P.O. Box 3735, Riyadh 11118, Saudi Arabia. **Document type:** government publication.

330 315.6   SU
SAUDI ARABIA. CENTRAL DEPARTMENT OF STATISTICS. STATISTICAL INDICATOR. (Text in Arabic, English) 1976. a. free. Central Department of Statistics, P.O. Box 3735, Riyadh 11118, Saudi Arabia. charts; stat. **Document type:** government publication.

SAUDI ARABIAN MONETARY AGENCY. STATISTICAL SUMMARY. see BUSINESS AND ECONOMICS — Banking And Finance

016.33 016.56   FI   ISSN 0358-0520
SCANP. Key Title: Scandinavian Periodicals Index in Economics and Business. (Text in Danish, English, Norwegian, Swedish) 1977. q. FIM 640. Helsinki School of Economics, Runeberginkatu 22-24, FIN-00100 Helsinki, Finland. Ed. Benita Rinne. circ. 150. (back issues avail.) **Document type:** abstracting/indexing.
    ●Also available online. Vendor(s): Helsinki School of Economics.

658   SZ
SCHLATTER GESCHAEFTSBERICHT (YEAR). a. H.A. Schlatter AG, Brandstr. 24, CH-8952 Schlieren, Switzerland. TEL 41-1-7327111. FAX 41-1-7309476. TELEX 827790-HAS-CH. **Document type:** corporate report.

330   SG
SENEGAL. MINISTERE DE L'ECONOMIE ET DES FINANCES. BANQUE DE DONNEES ECONOMIQUES ET FINANCIERES. a. 20000 Fr.CFA (foreign 30000 Fr.CFA). Ministere de l'Economie et des Finances, Direction de la Statistique, B.P. 116, Dakar, Senegal. TEL 221-21-03-01. **Document type:** government publication.

330   SG
SENEGAL. MINISTERE DE L'ECONOMIE ET DES FINANCES. BULLETIN ECONOMIQUE STATISTIQUE. a. 2000 Fr.CFA (foreign 4000 Fr.CFA). Ministere de l'Economie et des Finances, Direction de la Statistique, B.P. 116, Dakar, Senegal. TEL 221-21-03-01. **Document type:** government publication.

316.63 330.9   SG
SENEGAL. MINISTERE DE L'ECONOMIE ET DES FINANCES. BULLETIN STATISTIQUE ET ECONOMIQUE. bi-m. 4000 Fr.CFA. Ministere de l'Economie et des Finances, Direction de la Statistique, B.P. 116, Dakar, Senegal. TEL 221-21-03-01. charts; mkt.; stat. **Indexed:** P.A.I.S.For.Lang.Ind. **Document type:** government publication.
    Former titles: Senegal. Ministere de l'Economie et des Finances. Bulletin Statistique Mensuel; Senegal. Direction de la Statistique. Bulletin Statistique et Economique Mensuel (ISSN 0037-2153)

330.9   SG
SENEGAL. MINISTERE DE L'ECONOMIE ET DES FINANCES. DOSSIERS DOCUMENTAIRES. irreg. 7000 Fr.CFA per no. Ministere de l'Economie et des Finances, Direction de la Statistique, B.P. 116, Dakar, Senegal. Ed. Jean N'Dong. stat. **Document type:** government publication.

330   SG
SENEGAL. MINISTERE DE L'ECONOMIE ET DES FINANCES. EVOLUTION CONJONCTURELLE. q. 2000 Fr.CFA (foreign 4000 Fr.CFA). Ministere de l'Economie et des Finances, Direction de la Statistique, B.P. 116, Dakar, Senegal. TEL 221-21-03-01. **Document type:** government publication.

SENEGAL. MINISTERE DE L'ECONOMIE ET DES FINANCES. INDICE DES PRIX. see BUSINESS AND ECONOMICS — Production Of Goods And Services

SENEGAL. MINISTERE DE L'ECONOMIE ET DES FINANCES. INDICE ET LA PRODUCTION INDUSTRIELLE. see BUSINESS AND ECONOMICS — Production Of Goods And Services

330   GT
SERIES ESTADISTICAS SELECCIONADAS DE CENTROAMERICA Y PANAMA. a. $10. Secretaria Permanente del Tratado General de Integracion Economica Centroamericana - Permanent Secretariat of the General Treaty on Central American Economic Integration, 4a Avda. 10-25, Zona 14, Apdo. 1237, 01901 Guatemala, Guatemala. TEL 502-2-682151. FAX 502-2-681071. TELEX 5676. **Document type:** government publication.

330.1   CN   ISSN 1188-6293
SERVICE INDUSTRIES IN THE CANADIAN INPUT - OUTPUT ACCOUNTS: CURRENT PRICES, SOURCES OF DATA AND METHODS OF ESTIMATION/INDUSTRIES DE SERVICES DANS LES COMPTES D'ENTREES - SORTIES DU CANADA: EN PRIX COURANTS, SOURCES DE DONNEES ET METHODES D'ESTIMATION. (Subseries of: Input - Output Accounts Sources and Methods) (Text in English and French) irreg. Can.$45 (US $54; elsewhere $63) (effective 1998). Statistics Canada, Operations and Integration Division, Circulation Management, Jean Talon Bldg., 2-C12, Tunney's Pasture, Ottawa, ON K1A 0T6, Canada. TEL 613-951-7277; 800-267-6677. FAX 613-951-1584. URL: http://www.statcan.ca. (also avail. in microform from MML) **Document type:** government publication.
    Description: Outlines the conceptual and statistical framework of the services sector in the Canadian input-output accounts.

658   UK
SERVICE SECTOR RETAIL SALES. m. Office for National Statistics, Government Offices, Rm. 65c-3, Great George St., London SW1P 3AQ, England. TEL 44-171-396-2828. FAX 44-171-270-6019. **Document type:** government publication.
    Formerly (until 1996): U K Service Sector Retail Sales.

330 319   SE
SEYCHELLES. DEPARTMENT OF FINANCE. ECONOMIC INDICATORS. q. R.1.50. Department of Finance, Statistics Division, P.O. Box 206, Independence House, Victoria, Seychelles. **Document type:** government publication.

330.9 310   SE
SEYCHELLES. PRESIDENT'S OFFICE. STATISTICS DIVISION. EMPLOYMENT & EARNINGS. 1982. q. Rs.5.00. President's Office, Department of Finance, Statistics Division, PO Box 206, Mahe, Seychelles. **Document type:** government publication.

382 310   SE
SEYCHELLES. PRESIDENT'S OFFICE. STATISTICS DIVISION. EXTERNAL TRADE. 1982. q. Rs.5.00. President's Office, Department of Finance, Statistics Division, PO Box 206, Mahe, Seychelles. **Document type:** government publication.

310   SE
SEYCHELLES. PRESIDENT'S OFFICE. STATISTICS DIVISION. HOUSEHOLD EXPENDITURE SURVEY. irreg., latest 1984. Rs.45. President's Private Office, Statistics Division, P.O. Box 206, Mahe, Seychelles. stat. **Document type:** government publication.

338 310   SE
SEYCHELLES. PRESIDENT'S OFFICE. STATISTICS DIVISION. PRODUCTION INDICATORS. 1982. q. Rs.2.50. President's Office, Department of Finance, Statistics Division, PO Box 206, Mahe, Seychelles. **Document type:** government publication.

658 310   SE
SEYCHELLES. PRESIDENT'S OFFICE. STATISTICS DIVISION. RETAIL PRICES. 1982. m. Rs.2.50. President's Office, Department of Finance, Statistics Division, PO Box 206, Mahe, Seychelles. **Document type:** government publication.

316   SE
SEYCHELLES. PRESIDENT'S OFFICE. STATISTICS DIVISION. STATISTICAL ABSTRACT. a. Rs.60. President's Office, Statistics Division, PO Box 206, Mahe, Seychelles. **Document type:** government publication.

SEYCHELLES. STATISTICS DIVISION. STATISTICAL BULLETIN. VISITOR SURVEY. see TRAVEL AND TOURISM — Abstracting, Bibliographies, Statistics

330   CC
SHANTOU SPECIAL ECONOMIC ZONE YEARBOOK (YEAR). (Text in Chinese) 1992. a. HK.$240($55) Economic Information & Agency, 342 Hennessy Rd., 10th Fl., Wanchai, Hong Kong, People's Republic of China. TEL 852-573-8217. FAX 852-838-8304. TELEX 86990 EIA HX.

BUSINESS AND ECONOMICS — ABSTRACTING, BIBLIOGRAPHIES, STATISTICS

330   CC
SHENZHEN TONGJI NIANJIAN (YEAR)/SHENZHEN STATISTICAL YEARBOOK. (Text in Chinese) 1992. a. HK.$200($45) Economic Information & Agency, 342 Hennessy Rd., 10th Fl., Wanchai, Hong Kong, People's Republic of China. TEL 852-573-8217. FAX 852-838-8304. TELEX 86990 EIA HX.

338 315   SI   ISSN 0080-9675
SINGAPORE. ECONOMIC DEVELOPMENT BOARD. REPORT ON THE CENSUS OF INDUSTRIAL PRODUCTION. a. S.$16. Economic Development Board, 250 N. Bridge Rd., 24-00 Raffles City Tower, Singapore 0617, Singapore.

381   SI   ISSN 0129-7414
SINGAPORE MONTHLY TRADE STATISTICS: IMPORTS & EXPORTS. m. S.$555 (foreign S.$708). Trade Statistics, 303 Upper Serangoon Rd., P.O. Box 485, Singapore 1334, Singapore. (U.S. subscr. to: I.S.B.S., Inc., 5602 N.E. Hassalo St., Portland, OR 97213. TEL 800-547-7734. FAX 503-284-8858)
● Also available on CD-ROM.
Description: Provides detailed information on the imports and exports of Singapore, classified by commodity, country of origin and country of destination.

330 016   AG   ISSN 0080-9772
SINTESIS BIBLIOGRAFICA. 1964. irreg., no.9, 1972. free. Universidad Nacional de la Plata, Facultad de Ciencias Economicas, Biblioteca, 6 Esq. 47, La Plata, Argentina.
Formerly: Boletin Hemerografico.

330   CL   ISSN 0716-2472
HG185.C5
SINTESIS MONETARIA Y FINANCIERA. 1979. m. Ch.$56000($300) Banco Central de Chile, Casilla 967, Santiago, Chile. TEL 56-2-6702000. FAX 56-2-6984847. TELEX 40569 CENBC CL. circ. 130 (paid).

330   CL   ISSN 0716-2480
HG185.C5
SINTESIS MONETARIA Y FINANCIERA, EN PROMEDIOS. 1980. a. Ch.$19200($70) (effective 1997). Banco Central de Chile, Casilla 967, Santiago, Chile. TEL 56-2-6702000. FAX 56-2-6984847. circ. 150.

330   CL   ISSN 0716-2499
HG185.C5
SINTESIS MONETARIA Y FINANCIERA, EN SALDOS. 1984. a. Ch.$19200($70) Banco Central de Chile, Casilla 967, Santiago, Chile. TEL 56-2-670-2000. FAX 56-2-698-4847. circ. 150.

SIZE OF THE CRAFT - HOBBY INDUSTRY SURVEY. see HOBBIES — Abstracting, Bibliographies, Statistics

338   US   ISSN 1049-9636
HD2346.U5
SMALL BUSINESS START-UP INDEX. 1990. s-a. (plus a. cum.). $130. Gale Research, 835 Penobscot Bldg., 645 Griswold St., Detroit, MI 48226-4094. TEL 313-961-2242; 800-877-4253. FAX 800-414-5043. E-mail: daniel_snyder@gale.com. Ed. Michael Madden. **Document type:** bibliography.
Description: Offers a current index to a wide range of publications containing practical advice and information related to starting and running hundreds of types of small businesses, ranging from accounting services to gas stations to word processing services.

332.6   LU
SOCIETE DE LA BOURSE DE LUXEMBOURG. FAITS ET CHIFFRES/LUXEMBOURG STOCK EXCHANGE. FACTS AND FIGURES. (Text in English, French) 1983. s-a. free. Societe de la Bourse de Luxembourg - Luxembourg Stock Exchange, P.O. Box 165, 11 av. de la Porte-Neuve, L-2011 Luxembourg, Luxembourg. TEL 352-4779361. FAX 352-473298. TELEX 2559-STOEX-LU. circ. 10,000 (5,000 English ed.; 5,000 French ed.).
Description: Contains general statistical and organizational information.

338.4 316.8   SA
SOUTH AFRICA. CENTRAL STATISTICAL SERVICE. CENSUS OF BUSINESS SERVICES - ACCOUNTING, AUDITING AND BOOKKEEPING SERVICES. (Report No. 83-11-01) irreg., latest 1987. R.4.40 (foreign R.4.80). Central Statistical Service - Sentral Statistiekdiens, Private Bag X44, Pretoria 0001, South Africa. TEL 27-12-310-8911. FAX 27-12-310-8500. (Orders to: Government Printing Works, Private Bag X85, Pretoria 0001, South Africa) **Document type:** government publication.

338.4 316.8   SA
SOUTH AFRICA. CENTRAL STATISTICAL SERVICE. CENSUS OF BUSINESS SERVICES - CONSULTING ENGINEERS. (Report No. 83-14-01) irreg., latest 1987. R.4.40 (foreign R.4.80). Central Statistical Service - Sentral Statistiekdiens, Private Bag X44, Pretoria 0001, South Africa. TEL 27-12-310-8911. FAX 27-12-310-8500. (Orders to: Government Printing Works, Private Bag X85, Pretoria 0001, South Africa) **Document type:** government publication.

338.4 316.8   SA
SOUTH AFRICA. CENTRAL STATISTICAL SERVICE. CENSUS OF BUSINESS SERVICES - DATA PROCESSING SERVICES. (Report No. 83-16-01) irreg., latest 1987. R.4.40 (foreign R.5.50). Central Statistical Service - Sentrale.Statistiekdiens, Private Bag X44, Pretoria 0001, South Africa. TEL 27-12-310-8911. FAX 27-12-310-8500. (Orders to: Government Printing Works, Private Bag X85, Pretoria 0001, South Africa) **Document type:** government publication.

338.4 316.8   SA
SOUTH AFRICA. CENTRAL STATISTICAL SERVICE. CENSUS OF BUSINESS SERVICES - EMPLOYMENT PLACEMENT AGENCIES, RECRUITING ORGANISATIONS AND LABOUR BROKERS SERVICES. (Report No. 83-15-01) irreg., latest 1987. R.4.40 (foreign R.4.80). Central Statistical Service - Sentrale Statistiekdiens, Private Bag X44, Pretoria 0001, South Africa. TEL 27-12-310-8911. FAX 27-12-310-8500. (Orders to: Government Printing Works, Private Bag X85, Pretoria 0001, South Africa) **Document type:** government publication.

338.4 316.8   SA
SOUTH AFRICA. CENTRAL STATISTICAL SERVICE. CENSUS OF BUSINESS SERVICES - LEGAL SERVICES. (Report No. 83-12-01) irreg., latest 1987. R.4.40 (foreign R.4.80). Central Statistical Service - Sentrale Statistiekdiens, Private Bag X44, Pretoria 0001, South Africa. TEL 27-12-310-8911. FAX 27-12-310-8500. (Orders to: Government Printing Works, Private Bag X85, Pretoria 0001, South Africa) **Document type:** government publication.

338.4 316.8   SA
SOUTH AFRICA. CENTRAL STATISTICAL SERVICE. CENSUS OF MANUFACTURING - MATERIALS PURCHASED AND MANUFACTURES SOLD. (Report No. 30-01-03) triennial, latest 1985. R.6.60 (foreign R.7.20). Central Statistical Service - Sentrale Statistiekdiens, Private Bag X44, Pretoria 0001, South Africa. TEL 27-12-310-8911. FAX 27-12-310-8500. (Orders to: Government Printing Works, Private Bag X85, Pretoria 0001, South Africa) **Document type:** government publication.
Supersedes in part: South Africa. Department of Statistics. Census of Manufacturing (ISSN 0259-5303)

338.4 316.8   SA
SOUTH AFRICA. CENTRAL STATISTICAL SERVICE. CENSUS OF MANUFACTURING - PRINCIPAL STATISTICS ON A REGIONAL BASIS. (Report No. 30-01-02) triennial, latest 1988. R.40 (foreign R.43.90). Central Statistical Service - Sentrale Statistiekdiens, Private Bag X44, Pretoria 0001, South Africa. TEL 27-12-310-8911. FAX 27-12-310-8500. (Orders to: Government Printing Works, Private Bag X85, Pretoria 0001, South Africa) **Document type:** government publication.
Supersedes in part: South Africa. Department of Statistics. Census of Manufacturing (ISSN 0259-5303)

338.4   SA
SOUTH AFRICA. CENTRAL STATISTICAL SERVICE. CENSUS OF MANUFACTURING - REGISTER OF MANUFACTURERS ACCORDING TO PRODUCTS MANUFACTURED IN SOUTH AFRICA. (Report No. 30-01-04) triennial, latest 1989. R.25 (foreign R.27). Central Statistical Service - Sentrale Statistiekdiens, Private Bag X44, Pretoria 0001, South Africa. TEL 27-12-310-8911. FAX 27-12-310-8500. (Orders to: Government Printing Works, Private Bag X85, Pretoria 0001, South Africa) **Document type:** government publication.
Formerly: South Africa. Central Statistical Service. Register of Products Manufactured in South Africa.

338.4 316.8   SA
SOUTH AFRICA. CENTRAL STATISTICAL SERVICE. CENSUS OF MANUFACTURING - STATISTICS ACCORDING TO MAJOR GROUPS AND SUBGROUPS. (Report No. 30-01-01) triennial, latest 1988. R.25 (foreign R.27.40). Central Statistical Service - Sentrale Statistiekdiens, Private Bag X44, Pretoria 0001, South Africa. TEL 27-12-310-8911. FAX 27-12-310-8500. (Orders to: Government Printing Works, Private Bag X85, Pretoria 0001, South Africa) **Document type:** government publication.
Supersedes in part: South Africa. Department of Statistics. Census of Manufacturing (ISSN 0259-5303)

381 316.8   SA
SOUTH AFRICA. CENTRAL STATISTICAL SERVICE. CENSUS OF MOTOR TRADE AND REPAIR SERVICES. (Report No. 62-11-01) irreg., latest 1983. R.4.40 (foreign R.4.80). Central Statistical Service - Sentrale Statistiekdiens, Private Bag X44, Pretoria 0001, South Africa. TEL 27-12-310-8911. FAX 27-12-310-8500. (Orders to: Government Printing Works, Private Bag X85, Pretoria 0001, South Africa) **Document type:** government publication.

381 316.8   SA
SOUTH AFRICA. CENTRAL STATISTICAL SERVICE. CENSUS OF RETAIL TRADE. (Report No. 62-01-01) irreg., latest 1983. R.4.40 (foreign R.5.50). Central Statistical Service - Sentrale Statistiekdiens, Private Bag X44, Pretoria 0001, South Africa. TEL 27-12-310-8911. FAX 27-12-310-8500. (Orders to: Government Printing Works, Private Bag X85, Pretoria 0001, South Africa) **Document type:** government publication.

381 316.8   SA
SOUTH AFRICA. CENTRAL STATISTICAL SERVICE. CENSUS OF WHOLESALE TRADE, COMMERCIAL AGENTS AND ALLIED SERVICES. (Report No. 61-01-01) irreg., latest 1983. R.4.40 (foreign R.4.80). Central Statistical Service - Sentrale Statistiekdiens, Private Bag X44, Pretoria 0001, South Africa. TEL 27-12-310-8911. FAX 27-12-310-8500. (Orders to: Government Printing Works, Private Bag X85, Pretoria 0001, South Africa) **Document type:** government publication.

332 316.8   SA   ISSN 1013-7289
SOUTH AFRICA. CENTRAL STATISTICAL SERVICE. FINANCIAL STATISTICS OF COMPANIES (YEAR). (Report No. 17-01-03) irreg., latest 1980. R.2.31 (foreign R.2.89). Central Statistical Service - Sentrale Statistiekdiens, Private Bag X44, Pretoria 0001, South Africa. TEL 27-12-310-8911. FAX 27-12-310-8500. (Orders to: Government Printing Works, Private Bag X85, Pretoria 0001, South Africa) **Document type:** government publication.

351.7 316.8   SA   ISSN 0259-6075
SOUTH AFRICA. CENTRAL STATISTICAL SERVICE. INPUT OUTPUT TABLES. (Report No. 04-02-01 (Final)) irreg., latest 1988. R.21.40 (foreign R.25); diskette version R.15 (foreign R.18.75). Central Statistical Service - Sentrale Statistiekdiens, Private Bag X44, Pretoria 0001, South Africa. TEL 27-12-310-8911. FAX 27-12-310-8500. (also avail. in diskette format) **Document type:** government publication.

331 316.8   SA   ISSN 1018-2306
SOUTH AFRICA. CENTRAL STATISTICAL SERVICE. MANPOWER SURVEY (OCCUPATIONAL INFORMATION). (Report No. 02-01-01) a., latest 1991. R.8 (foreign R.10). Central Statistical Service - Sentrale Statistiekdiens, Private Bag X44, Pretoria 0001, South Africa. TEL 27-12-310-8911. FAX 27-12-310-8500. (Orders to: Government Printing Works, Private Bag X85, Pretoria 0001, South Africa) **Document type:** government publication

BUSINESS AND ECONOMICS — ABSTRACTING, BIBLIOGRAPHIES, STATISTICS

336 316.8 SA
SOUTH AFRICA. CENTRAL STATISTICAL SERVICE. STATISTICAL RELEASE. ACTUAL AND ANTICIPATED CAPITAL EXPENDITURE OF THE PUBLIC SECTOR. (No. P9101.1) a. free. Central Statistical Service - Sentral Statistiekdiens, Private Bag X44, Pretoria 0001, South Africa. TEL 27-12-310-8911. FAX 27-12-310-8500. **Document type:** government publication.

336 316.8 SA
SOUTH AFRICA. CENTRAL STATISTICAL SERVICE. STATISTICAL RELEASE. ACTUAL AND ANTICIPATED CONSTRUCTION EXPENDITURE OF THE PUBLIC SECTOR BY REGION. (No. P9101.2) a. free. Central Statistical Service - Sentrale Statistiekdiens, Private Bag X44, Pretoria 0001, South Africa. TEL 27-12-310-8911. FAX 27-12-310-8500. **Document type:** government publication.

339 316.8 SA
SOUTH AFRICA. CENTRAL STATISTICAL SERVICE. STATISTICAL RELEASE. AVERAGE RETAIL PRICES OF FOOD. (No. P0141.2) m. free. Central Statistical Service - Sentrale Statistiekdiens, Private Bag X44, Pretoria 0001, South Africa. TEL 27-12-310-8911. FAX 27-12-310-8500. **Document type:** government publication.

338.4 316.8 SA
SOUTH AFRICA. CENTRAL STATISTICAL SERVICE. STATISTICAL RELEASE. CENSUS OF ACCOUNTING, AUDITING AND BOOKKEEPING SERVICES (YEAR). (No. P8311) irreg., latest 1987. free. Central Statistical Service - Sentral Statistiekdiens, Private Bag X44, Pretoria 0001, South Africa. TEL 27-12-310-8911. FAX 27-12-310-8500. **Document type:** government publication.

338.4 316.8 SA
SOUTH AFRICA. CENTRAL STATISTICAL SERVICE. STATISTICAL RELEASE. CENSUS OF BUSINESS SERVICES - LEGAL SERVICES (YEAR). (No. P8312) irreg., latest 1987. free. Central Statistical Service - Sentrale Statistiekdiens, Private Bag X44, Pretoria 0001, South Africa. TEL 27-12-310-8911. FAX 27-12-310-8500. **Document type:** government publication.

338.4 316.8 SA
SOUTH AFRICA. CENTRAL STATISTICAL SERVICE. STATISTICAL RELEASE. CENSUS OF CONSULTING ENGINEERING SERVICES (YEAR). (No. P8314) irreg., latest 1987. free. Central Statistical Service - Sentrale Statistiekdiens, Private Bag X44, Pretoria 0001, South Africa. TEL 27-12-310-8911. FAX 27-12-310-8500. **Document type:** government publication.

338.4 316.8 SA
SOUTH AFRICA. CENTRAL STATISTICAL SERVICE. STATISTICAL RELEASE. CENSUS OF DATA PROCESSING SERVICES (YEAR). (No. P8316) irreg., latest 1987. free. Central Statistical Service - Sentrale Statistiekdiens, Private Bag X44, Pretoria 0001, South Africa. TEL 27-12-310-8911. FAX 27-12-310-8500. **Document type:** government publication.

338.4 316.8 SA
SOUTH AFRICA. CENTRAL STATISTICAL SERVICE. STATISTICAL RELEASE. CENSUS OF EMPLOYMENT PLACEMENT AGENCIES, RECRUITING ORGANISATIONS AND LABOUR BROKERS SERVICES. (No. P8315) irreg., latest 1987. free. Central Statistical Service - Sentrale Statistiekdiens, Private Bag X44, Pretoria 0001, South Africa. TEL 27-12-310-8911. FAX 27-12-310-8500. **Document type:** government publication.

338.4 316.8 SA
SOUTH AFRICA. CENTRAL STATISTICAL SERVICE. STATISTICAL RELEASE. CENSUS OF MANUFACTURING. (No. P3001) irreg. free. Central Statistical Service - Sentrale Statistiekdiens, Private Bag X44, Pretoria 0001, South Africa. TEL 27-12-310-8911. FAX 27-12-310-8500. **Document type:** government publication.

339 316.8 SA
SOUTH AFRICA. CENTRAL STATISTICAL SERVICE. STATISTICAL RELEASE. CONSUMER PRICE INDEX. (No. P0141.1) m. free. Central Statistical Service - Sentrale Statistiekdiens, Private Bag X44, Pretoria 0001, South Africa. TEL 27-12-310-8911. FAX 27-12-310-8500. **Document type:** government publication.

339 316.8 SA
SOUTH AFRICA. CENTRAL STATISTICAL SERVICE. STATISTICAL RELEASE. CONSUMER PRICE INDEX BASE. (No. P0141.4) irreg., latest for 1990. free. Central Statistical Service - Sentrale Statistiekdiens, Private Bag X44, Pretoria 0001, South Africa. TEL 27-12-310-8911. FAX 27-12-310-8500. **Document type:** government publication.
Description: Cumulative information, with conversion factors.

339 316.8 SA
SOUTH AFRICA. CENTRAL STATISTICAL SERVICE. STATISTICAL RELEASE. CONSUMER PRICE INDEX WEIGHTS. (No. P0141.5) irreg., latest for 1990. free. Central Statistical Service - Sentrale Statistiekdiens, Private Bag X44, Pretoria 0001, South Africa. TEL 27-12-310-8911. FAX 27-12-310-8500. **Document type:** government publication.

332 316.8 SA
SOUTH AFRICA. CENTRAL STATISTICAL SERVICE. STATISTICAL RELEASE. FINANCIAL STATISTICS OF COMPANIES. (No. P0002) (Text in Afrikaans, English) irreg. free. Central Statistical Service - Sentrale Statistiekdiens, Private Bag X44, Pretoria 0001, South Africa. TEL 27-12-310-8911. FAX 27-12-310-8500. **Document type:** government publication.

336 316.8 SA
SOUTH AFRICA. CENTRAL STATISTICAL SERVICE. STATISTICAL RELEASE. FINANCIAL STATISTICS OF EXTRABUDGETARY ACCOUNTS AND FUNDS. (No. P9102.2) a. free. Central Statistical Service - Sentrale Statistiekdiens, Private Bag X44, Pretoria 0001, South Africa. TEL 27-12-310-8911. FAX 27-12-310-8500. **Document type:** government publication.

380.1 316.8 SA
SOUTH AFRICA. CENTRAL STATISTICAL SERVICE. STATISTICAL RELEASE. FOREIGN TRADE STATISTICS. (No. P6161) m. free. Central Statistical Service - Sentrale Statistiekdiens, Private Bag X44, Pretoria 0001, South Africa. TEL 27-12-310-8911. FAX 27-12-310-8500. **Document type:** government publication.

339 316.8 SA
SOUTH AFRICA. CENTRAL STATISTICAL SERVICE. STATISTICAL RELEASE. GROSS DOMESTIC PRODUCT AT CONSTANT PRICES. (No. P0441 (Economic Activity); No. P0441.2 (Kind of Economic Activity)) q. free. Central Statistical Service - Sentrale Statistiekdiens, Private Bag X44, Pretoria 0001, South Africa. TEL 27-12-310-8911. FAX 27-12-310-8500. **Document type:** government publication.

339 316.8 SA
SOUTH AFRICA. CENTRAL STATISTICAL SERVICE. STATISTICAL RELEASE. GROSS GEOGRAPHIC PRODUCT AT FACTOR INCOMES. (No. P0401) irreg., latest 1988. free. Central Statistical Service - Sentrale Statistiekdiens, Private Bag X44, Pretoria 0001, South Africa. TEL 27-12-310-8911. FAX 27-12-310-8500. **Document type:** government publication.

339 316.8 SA
SOUTH AFRICA. CENTRAL STATISTICAL SERVICE. STATISTICAL RELEASE. HOUSEHOLD EXPENDITURE. (No. P0111) irreg., latest 1985. free. Central Statistical Service - Sentrale Statistiekdiens, Private Bag X44, Pretoria 0001, South Africa. TEL 27-12-310-8911. FAX 27-12-310-8500. **Document type:** government publication.
Description: Income and expenditure data for households.

338.4 316.8 SA
SOUTH AFRICA. CENTRAL STATISTICAL SERVICE. STATISTICAL RELEASE. INDICES OF THE PHYSICAL VOLUME OF MANUFACTURING PRODUCTION - PRELIMINARY. (No. P3041.1) m. free. Central Statistical Service - Sentrale Statistiekdiens, Private Bag X44, Pretoria 0001, South Africa. TEL 27-12-310-8911. FAX 27-12-310-8500. **Document type:** government publication.

332 316.8 SA
SOUTH AFRICA. CENTRAL STATISTICAL SERVICE. STATISTICAL RELEASE. LABOUR STATISTICS: BUILDING SOCIETIES, BANKING INSTITUTIONS AND INSURANCE COMPANIES. (No. P0262) q. free. Central Statistical Service - Sentrale Statistiekdiens, Private Bag X44, Pretoria 0001, South Africa. TEL 27-12-310-8911. FAX 27-12-310-8500. **Document type:** government publication.

331 316.8 SA
SOUTH AFRICA. CENTRAL STATISTICAL SERVICE. STATISTICAL RELEASE. LABOUR STATISTICS: EMPLOYMENT AND SALARIES AND WAGES - WHOLESALE, RETAIL, MOTOR TRADE AND HOTELS. (No. P0244) q. free. Central Statistical Service - Sentrale Statistiekdiens, Private Bag X44, Pretoria 0001, South Africa. TEL 27-12-310-8911. FAX 27-12-310-8500. **Document type:** government publication.

332 316.8 SA
SOUTH AFRICA. CENTRAL STATISTICAL SERVICE. STATISTICAL RELEASE. LABOUR STATISTICS: INDICES OF WAGE RATES AND LABOUR COSTS IN THE METAL AND ENGINEERING INDUSTRIES. (No. P0283) q. free. Central Statistical Service - Sentrale Statistiekdiens, Private Bag X44, Pretoria 0001, South Africa. TEL 27-12-310-8911. FAX 27-12-310-8500. **Document type:** government publication.
Description: Calculations by the Steel and Engineering Industries Federation of South Africa, based upon sample surveys.

331 316.8 SA
SOUTH AFRICA. CENTRAL STATISTICAL SERVICE. STATISTICAL RELEASE. MANUFACTURING AND CONSTRUCTION (EMPLOYMENT AND EARNINGS). (No. P0242.2) irreg. free. Central Statistical Service - Sentrale Statistiekdiens, Private Bag X44, Pretoria 0001, South Africa. TEL 27-12-310-8911. FAX 27-12-310-8500. **Document type:** government publication.

338.4 316.8 SA
SOUTH AFRICA. CENTRAL STATISTICAL SERVICE. STATISTICAL RELEASE. MANUFACTURING - CAPITAL EXPENDITURE ON NEW ASSETS. (No. P3042.3) irreg., latest covers 1977-1990. free. Central Statistical Service - Sentrale Statistiekdiens, Private Bag X44, Pretoria 0001, South Africa. TEL 27-12-310-8911. FAX 27-12-310-8500. **Document type:** government publication.

338.4 316.8 SA
SOUTH AFRICA. CENTRAL STATISTICAL SERVICE. STATISTICAL RELEASE. MANUFACTURING - FINANCIAL STATISTICS. (No. P3042.2) irreg. free. Central Statistical Service - Sentrale Statistiekdiens, Private Bag X44, Pretoria 0001, South Africa. TEL 27-12-310-8911. FAX 27-12-310-8500. **Document type:** government publication.

338.4 316.8 SA
SOUTH AFRICA. CENTRAL STATISTICAL SERVICE. STATISTICAL RELEASE. MANUFACTURING - FINANCIAL STATISTICS (QUARTERLY). (No. P3042.1) q. free. Central Statistical Service - Sentrale Statistiekdiens, Private Bag X44, Pretoria 0001, South Africa. TEL 27-12-310-8911. FAX 27-12-310-8500. **Document type:** government publication.

338.4 316.8 SA
SOUTH AFRICA. CENTRAL STATISTICAL SERVICE. STATISTICAL RELEASE. MANUFACTURING PRODUCTION. (No. P3041,3) irreg. free. Central Statistical Service - Sentrale Statistiekdiens, Private Bag X44, Pretoria 0001, South Africa. TEL 27-12-310-8911. FAX 27-12-310-8500. **Document type:** government publication.
Description: Historical data of production indices and value of sales and unfilled orders by subgroup of Standard Industrial Classification.

338.4 316.8 SA
SOUTH AFRICA. CENTRAL STATISTICAL SERVICE. STATISTICAL RELEASE. MANUFACTURING - PRODUCTION AND SALES. (No. P3041.2) m. free. Central Statistical Service - Sentrale Statistiekdiens, Private Bag X44, Pretoria 0001, South Africa. TEL 27-12-310-8911. FAX 27-12-3108500. **Document type:** government publication.

BUSINESS AND ECONOMICS — ABSTRACTING, BIBLIOGRAPHIES, STATISTICS

338.4 316.8   SA
SOUTH AFRICA. CENTRAL STATISTICAL SERVICE. STATISTICAL RELEASE. MANUFACTURING STATISTICS: BASIC METAL AND FABRICATED METAL PRODUCTS, MACHINERY AND EQUIPMENT, MOTOR VEHICLES AND PARTS AND MISCELLANEOUS PRODUCTS. (No. P3051.4) bi-m. free. Central Statistical Service - Sentrale Statistiekdiens, Private Bag X44, Pretoria 0001, South Africa. TEL 27-12-310-8911. FAX 27-12-310-8500. **Document type:** government publication.

338.4 316.8   SA
SOUTH AFRICA. CENTRAL STATISTICAL SERVICE. STATISTICAL RELEASE. MANUFACTURING STATISTICS: CHEMICAL, RUBBER, PLASTIC, GLASS AND NON-METALLIC MINERAL PRODUCTS. (No. P3051.3) bi-m. free. Central Statistical Service - Sentrale Statistiekdiens, Private Bag X44, Pretoria 0001, South Africa. TEL 27-12-310-8911. FAX 27-12-310-8500. **Document type:** government publication.

338.4 316.8   SA
SOUTH AFRICA. CENTRAL STATISTICAL SERVICE. STATISTICAL RELEASE. MANUFACTURING STATISTICS: PRODUCTS MANUFACTURED: FOODS, BEVERAGES AND TOBACCO PRODUCTS. (No. P3051.1) bi-m. free. Central Statistical Service - Sentrale Statistiekdiens, Private Bag X44, Pretoria 0001, South Africa. TEL 27-12-310-8911. FAX 27-12-310-8500. **Document type:** government publication.

338.4 316.8   SA
SOUTH AFRICA. CENTRAL STATISTICAL SERVICE. STATISTICAL RELEASE. MANUFACTURING STATISTICS: PRODUCTS MANUFACTURED: TEXTILES, CLOTHING, LEATHER AND LEATHER PRODUCTS, WOOD AND WOOD PRODUCTS, PAPER AND PAPER PRODUCTS AND PRINTING. (No. P3051.2) bi-m. free. Central Statistical Service - Sentrale Statistiekdiens, Private Bag X44, Pretoria 0001, South Africa. TEL 27-12-310-8911. FAX 27-12-310-8500. **Document type:** government publication.

331 316.8   SA
SOUTH AFRICA. CENTRAL STATISTICAL SERVICE. STATISTICAL RELEASE. MINING, QUARRYING, MANUFACTURING, CONSTRUCTION, ELECTRICITY (EMPLOYMENT AND EARNINGS). (No. P0242.1) m. free. Central Statistical Service - Sentrale Statistiekdiens, Private Bag X44, Pretoria 0001, South Africa. TEL 27-12-310-8911. FAX 27-12-310-8500. **Document type:** government publication.

380.1 316.8   SA
SOUTH AFRICA. CENTRAL STATISTICAL SERVICE. STATISTICAL RELEASE. MOTOR TRADE - FINANCIAL STATISTICS. (No. P6344) q. free. Central Statistical Service - Sentrale Statistiekdiens, Private Bag X44, Pretoria 0001, South Africa. TEL 27-12-310-8911. FAX 27-12-310-8500. **Document type:** government publication.

339 316.8   SA
SOUTH AFRICA. CENTRAL STATISTICAL SERVICE. STATISTICAL RELEASE. PRICE INDICES FOR THE CIVIL ENGINEERING INDUSTRY. (No. P0142.2) m. free. Central Statistical Service - Sentrale Statistiekdiens, Private Bag X44, Pretoria 0001, South Africa. TEL 27-12-310-8911. FAX 27-12-310-8500. **Document type:** government publication.

339 316.8   SA
SOUTH AFRICA. CENTRAL STATISTICAL SERVICE. STATISTICAL RELEASE. PRODUCTION PRICES - ALL ITEMS. (No. P0142.3) a. free. Central Statistical Service - Sentrale Statistiekdiens, Private Bag X44, Pretoria 0001, South Africa. TEL 27-12-310-8911. FAX 27-12-310-8500. **Document type:** government publication.

339 316.8   SA
SOUTH AFRICA. CENTRAL STATISTICAL SERVICE. STATISTICAL RELEASE. PRODUCTION PRICE INDEX. (No. P0142.1) m. free. Central Statistical Service - Sentrale Statistiekdiens, Private Bag X44, Pretoria 0001, South Africa. TEL 27-12-310-8911. FAX 27-12-310-8500. **Document type:** government publication.
Description: Price indices of commodities for South African consumption, of output of South Africa industry groups and of selected materials.

339 316.8   SA
SOUTH AFRICA. CENTRAL STATISTICAL SERVICE. STATISTICAL RELEASE. PRODUCTION PRICE INDEX BASE (YEAR). (No. P0142.4) irreg., latest for years 1971-1991. Central Statistical Service - Sentrale Statistiekdiens, Private Bag X44, Pretoria 0001, South Africa. TEL 27-12-310-8911. FAX 27-12-310-8500. **Document type:** government publication.
Description: Price indices of commodities for South African consumption, of output of South African industry groups and of certain selected materials. 1990 is used as the base year.

331 316.8   SA
SOUTH AFRICA. CENTRAL STATISTICAL SERVICE. STATISTICAL RELEASE. PUBLIC SECTOR (EMPLOYMENT AND EARNINGS). (No. P0251) q. free. Central Statistical Service - Sentrale Statistiekdiens, Private Bag X44, Pretoria 0001, South Africa. TEL 27-12-310-8911. FAX 27-12-310-8500. **Document type:** government publication.

380.1 316.8   SA
SOUTH AFRICA. CENTRAL STATISTICAL SERVICE. STATISTICAL RELEASE. RETAILERS IN MOTOR VEHICLES AND ACCESSORIES - TRADING REVENUE: EXPECTED VALUES. (No. P6343.1) m. free. Central Statistical Service - Sentrale Statistiekdiens, Private Bag X44, Pretoria 0001, South Africa. TEL 27-12-310-8911. FAX 27-12-310-8500. **Document type:** government publication.

339 316.8   SA
SOUTH AFRICA. CENTRAL STATISTICAL SERVICE. STATISTICAL RELEASE. RETAIL PRICES - ALL ITEMS. (No. P0141.3) a. Central Statistical Service - Sentrale Statistiekdiens, Private Bag X44, Pretoria 0001, South Africa. TEL 27-12-310-8911. FAX 27-12-310-8500. **Document type:** government publication.
Former titles (until 1985): South Africa. Central Statistical Service. Report on Prices; South Africa. Department of Statistics. Report on Prices.

380.1 316.8   SA
SOUTH AFRICA. CENTRAL STATISTICAL SERVICE. STATISTICAL RELEASE. RETAIL TRADE - FINANCIAL STATISTICS. (No. P6243) q. free. Central Statistical Service - Sentrale Statistiekdiens, Private Bag X44, Pretoria 0001, South Africa. TEL 27-12-310-8911. FAX 27-12-310-8500. **Document type:** government publication.

380.1 316.8   SA
SOUTH AFRICA. CENTRAL STATISTICAL SERVICE. STATISTICAL RELEASE. RETAIL TRADE IN MOTOR VEHICLES AND ACCESSORIES - TRADING REVENUE (FINAL). (No. P6343.2) m. free. Central Statistical Service - Sentrale Statistiekdiens, Private Bag X44, Pretoria 0001, South Africa. TEL 27-12-310-8911. FAX 27-12-310-8500. **Document type:** government publication.

380.1 316.8   SA
SOUTH AFRICA. CENTRAL STATISTICAL SERVICE. STATISTICAL RELEASE. RETAIL TRADE SALES. (No. P6242.3) irreg., latest covers 1977-1991. free. Central Statistical Service - Sentrale Statistiekdiens, Private Bag X44, Pretoria 0001, South Africa. TEL 27-12-310-8911. FAX 27-12-310-8500. **Document type:** government publication.
Description: Cumulative statistics on retail trade sales by kind of business, economic regions, kind of merchandise, and kind of sales, at national and provincial level.

380.1 316.8   SA
SOUTH AFRICA. CENTRAL STATISTICAL SERVICE. STATISTICAL RELEASE. RETAIL TRADE SALES - EXPECTED SALES. (No. P6241) m. free. Central Statistical Service - Sentrale Statistiekdiens, Private Bag X44, Pretoria 0001, South Africa. TEL 27-12-310-8911. FAX 27-12-310-8500. **Document type:** government publication.

380.1 316.8   SA
SOUTH AFRICA. CENTRAL STATISTICAL SERVICE. STATISTICAL RELEASE. RETAIL TRADE SALES (FINAL). (No. P6242.2) m. free. Central Statistical Service - Sentrale Statistiekdiens, Private Bag X44, Pretoria 0001, South Africa. TEL 27-12-310-8911. FAX 27-12-310-8500. **Document type:** government publication.

380.1 316.8   SA
SOUTH AFRICA. CENTRAL STATISTICAL SERVICE. STATISTICAL RELEASE. RETAIL TRADE SALES - PRELIMINARY. (No. P6242.1) m. free. Central Statistical Service - Sentrale Statistiekdiens, Private Bag X44, Pretoria 0001, South Africa. TEL 27-12-310-8911. FAX 27-12-310-800. **Document type:** government publication.

331 316.8   SA
SOUTH AFRICA. CENTRAL STATISTICAL SERVICE. STATISTICAL RELEASE. STATISTICALLY UNRECORDED ACTIVITIES OF COLOUREDS, INDIANS AND BLACKS. (No. P0315) a., latest 1990. free. Central Statistical Service - Sentrale Statistiekdiens, Private Bag X44, Pretoria 0001, South Africa. TEL 27-12-310-8911. FAX 27-12-3108500. **Document type:** government publication.
Description: Covers persons active in the informal sector.

331 316.8   SA
SOUTH AFRICA. CENTRAL STATISTICAL SERVICE. STATISTICAL RELEASE. SUMMARY LABOUR STATISTICS. (No. P0200) q. free. Central Statistical Service - Sentrale Statistiekdiens, Private Bag X44, Pretoria 0001, South Africa. TEL 27-12-310-8911. FAX 27-12-310-8500. **Document type:** government publication.
Description: Summary data covering a large proportion of the economically active population.

338.4 316.8   SA
SOUTH AFRICA. CENTRAL STATISTICAL SERVICE. STATISTICAL RELEASE. SURVEY OF ARCHITECTS AND QUANTITY SURVEYORS. (No. P8301) irreg. free. Central Statistical Service - Sentrale Statistiekdiens, Private Bag X44, Pretoria 0001, South Africa. TEL 27-12-310-8911. FAX 27-12-310-8500. **Document type:** government publication.

380.1 316.8   SA
SOUTH AFRICA. CENTRAL STATISTICAL SERVICE. STATISTICAL RELEASE. TOTAL VALUE OF WHOLESALE TRADE SALES - EXPECTED SALES. (No. P6141.1) m. free. Central Statistical Service - Sentrale Statistiekdiens, Private Bag X44, Pretoria 0001, South Africa. TEL 27-12-310-8911. FAX 27-12-310-8500. **Document type:** government publication.

338.4 316.8   SA
SOUTH AFRICA. CENTRAL STATISTICAL SERVICE. STATISTICAL RELEASE. UTILIZATION OF PRODUCTION CAPACITY. (No. P3043) q. free. Central Statistical Service - Sentrale Statistiekdiens, Private Bag X44, Pretoria 0001, South Africa. TEL 27-12-310-8911. FAX 27-12-310-8500. **Document type:** government publication.
Description: Indicates percentage utilization and reasons for under-utilization by major group of Standard Industrial Classification.

332 316.8   SA
SOUTH AFRICA. CENTRAL STATISTICAL SERVICE. STATISTICAL RELEASE. WAGE RATES: BUILDING INDUSTRY. (No. P0281) q. free. Central Statistical Service - Sentrale Statistiekdiens, Private Bag X44, Pretoria 0001, South Africa. TEL 27-12-310-8911. FAX 27-12-310-8500. **Document type:** government publication.

332 316.8   SA
SOUTH AFRICA. CENTRAL STATISTICAL SERVICE. STATISTICAL RELEASE. WAGE RATES: CIVIL ENGINEERING INDUSTRY. (No. P0282) q. free. Central Statistical Service - Sentrale Statistiekdiens, Private Bag X44, Pretoria 0001, South Africa. TEL 27-12-310-8911. FAX 27-12-310-8500. **Document type:** government publication.

380.1 316.8   SA
SOUTH AFRICA. CENTRAL STATISTICAL SERVICE. STATISTICAL RELEASE. WHOLESALE TRADE - FINANCIAL STATISTICS. (No. P6142) q. free. Central Statistical Service - Sentrale Statistiekdiens, Private Bag X44, Pretoria 0001, South Africa. TEL 27-12-310-8911. FAX 27-12-310-8500. **Document type:** government publication.

380.1 316.8   SA
SOUTH AFRICA. CENTRAL STATISTICAL SERVICE. STATISTICAL RELEASE. WHOLESALE TRADE SALES. (No. P6141.2) m. free. Central Statistical Service - Sentrale Statistiekdiens, Private Bag X44, Pretoria 0001, South Africa. TEL 27-12-310-8911. FAX 27-12-310-8500. **Document type:** government publication.

330 316.8   SA
SOUTH AFRICA. CENTRAL STATISTICAL SERVICE. SURVEY OF HOUSEHOLD EXPENDITURE. (Report No. 01-11-01) irreg., latest 1990. R.7 (foreign R.8.75). Central Statistical Service - Sentrale Statistiekdiens, Private Bag X44, Pretoria 0001, South Africa. TEL 27-12-310-8911. FAX 27-12-310-8500. **Document type:** government publication.
 Supersedes (in 1985): South Africa. Central Statistical Service. Survey of Household Expenditure (According to Area and Type of Dwelling - Whites).

338.23   SA
SOUTH AFRICA. CENTRAL STATISTICAL SERVICE. SURVEY OF THE ACCOUNTS OF COMPANIES.. (Report No. 00-05-01. Consists of 1 vol.: Part 1: Secondary and Tertiary Industries; Part 2: Investment Companies; Part 3: Mining) a., latest for years 1991-1992. R.15 (foreign R.18.75). Central Statistical Service - Sentrale Statistiekdiens, Bag X44, Pretoria 0001, South Africa. TEL 27-12-310-8911. FAX 27-12-310-8500. (Orders to: Government Printing Works, Private Bag X85, Pretoria 0001, South Africa) **Document type:** government publication.
 Supersedes: South Africa. Department of Statistics. Survey of the Accounts of Companies in Secondary and Tertiary Industries (ISSN 0258-7769); Incorporates: South Africa. Department of Statistics. Survey of the Accounts of Mining Companies.

382 316   SA
SOUTH AFRICA. COMMISSIONER FOR CUSTOMS AND EXCISE. FOREIGN TRADE STATISTICS. a. price varies. Commissioner for Customs and Excise, Private Bag X47, Pretoria 0001, South Africa. (Subscr. to: Government Printing Works, Private Bag X85, Pretoria 0001, South Africa) Ed. J.M. Heyns. **Document type:** government publication.
 Formerly: South Africa. Department of Customs and Excise. Foreign Trade Statistics (ISSN 0081-2196)

382   SA
SOUTH AFRICA. COMMISSIONER FOR CUSTOMS AND EXCISE. MONTHLY ABSTRACT OF TRADE STATISTICS. m. R.100. Commissioner for Customs and Excise, Private Bag X47, Pretoria 0001, South Africa. (Subscr. to: Government Printing Works, Private Bag X85, Pretoria 0001, South Africa) Ed. J.M. Heyns. **Document type:** government publication.
 Formerly: South Africa. Department of Customs and Excise. Monthly Abstract of Trade Statistics.

331 316.8   SA
SOUTH AFRICAN LABOUR STATISTICS. a., latest 1994. R.60 (foreign R.64.50) (effective 1994). Central Statistical Service - Sentrale Statistiekdiens, Private Bag X44, Pretoria 0001, South Africa. TEL 27-12-310-8911. FAX 27-12-310-8500. (Orders to: Government Printing Works, Private Bag X85, Pretoria 0001, South Africa) **Document type:** government publication.

332 316   SA
SOUTH AFRICAN RESERVE BANK. MONTHLY RELEASE OF SELECTED DATA/SUID-AFRIKAANSE RESERWEBANK. MAANDELIKSE VRYSTELLING VAN UITGESOEKTE GEGEWENS. (Text in Afrikaans and English) 1966. m. free. South African Reserve Bank, P.O. Box 427, Pretoria 0001, South Africa. TEL 27-12-3133911. FAX 27-12-3133197. E-mail: info@gwisel.resbank. co.za; URL: http://www.resbank.co.za. circ. 750.
 Formerly: South African Reserve Bank. Monthly Release of Money and Banking Statistics (ISSN 0584-3073)

SOUTH AFRICAN RESERVE BANK. QUARTERLY BULLETIN/SUID-AFRIKAANSE RESERWEBANK. KWARTAALBLAD. see *BUSINESS AND ECONOMICS — Banking And Finance*

336.2 317   US   ISSN 0085-6460
HJ11
SOUTH DAKOTA. DEPARTMENT OF REVENUE. ANNUAL STATISTICAL REPORT. 1952. a. Department of Revenue, Kneip Bldg., Pierre, SD 57501. TEL 605-773-3311. FAX 605-773-5129. Ed. Laurie Bonrud. charts. circ. 450. (processed; also avail. in microfiche from CIS) **Indexed:** SRI. **Document type:** government publication.
 Formerly: South Dakota. Department of Revenue. Annual Report.

330 310   NL   ISSN 1018-0958
SOUTH PACIFIC ECONOMIES: STATISTICAL SUMMARY. (Text in English, French) 1978. a. South Pacific Commission, B.P. D5, 98848 Noumea Cedex, New Caledonia. TEL 687-262000. FAX 687-263818. E-mail: spc@spc.org.nc. (also avail. in microfiche from CIS) **Indexed:** IIS.

331 314   SP   ISSN 0212-6532
SPAIN. INSTITUTO NACIONAL DE ESTADISTICA. ENCUESTA DE POBLACION ACTIVA. PRINCIPALES RESULTADOS. q. Instituto Nacional de Estadistica, P. de la Castellana, 183, 28071 Madrid, Spain. **Indexed:** P.A.I.S.For.Lang.Ind. **Document type:** government publication.
 Former titles: Spain. Instituto Nacional de Estadistica. Encuesta de la Poblacion Activa; Spain. Instituto Nacional de Estadistica. Poblacion Activa (ISSN 0081-3389)

331   SP   ISSN 0212-6990
SPAIN. INSTITUTO NACIONAL DE ESTADISTICA. ENCUESTA DE POBLACION ACTIVA. RESULTADOS DETALLADOS. q. Instituto Nacional de Estadistica, P. de la Castellana, 183, 28071 Madrid, Spain. **Indexed:** P.A.I.S.For.Lang.Ind. **Document type:** government publication.

338 314   SP
SPAIN. INSTITUTO NACIONAL DE ESTADISTICA. ENCUESTA INDUSTRIAL. a. Instituto Nacional de Estadistica, P. de la Castellana, 183, 28071 Madrid, Spain. **Document type:** government publication.
 Formerly (until 1978): Spain. Instituto Nacional de Estadistica. Estadistica Industrial (ISSN 0081-3354)

336 314   SP
SPAIN. MINISTERIO DE ECONOMIA Y HACIENDA. ESTADISTICAS PRESUPUESTARIAS Y FISCALES. a. 2575 ptas. Ministerio de Economia y Hacienda, Secretaria General Tecnica, Centro de Publicaciones, Plaza del Campillo del Mundo Nuevo, 3, 28005 Madrid, Spain. TEL 34-1-5271437. **Document type:** government publication.
 Former titles (until 1973): Spain. Ministerio de Economia y Hacienda. Informacion Estadistica; Spain. Ministerio de Hacienda. Informacion Estadistica (ISSN 0081-3435)

SPORT CLOTHING EXPENDITURES IN (YEAR). see *SPORTS AND GAMES — Abstracting, Bibliographies, Statistics*

SPORTING GOODS MARKET. see *SPORTS AND GAMES — Abstracting, Bibliographies, Statistics*

SPORTS EQUIPMENT EXPENDITURES. see *SPORTS AND GAMES — Abstracting, Bibliographies, Statistics*

SPORTS PARTICIPATION IN (YEAR): LIFECYCLE DEMOGRAPHICS. see *SPORTS AND GAMES — Abstracting, Bibliographies, Statistics*

SPORTS PARTICIPATION IN (YEAR): SERIES II. see *SPORTS AND GAMES — Abstracting, Bibliographies, Statistics*

SPORTS PARTICIPATION IN (YEAR): STATE BY STATE. see *SPORTS AND GAMES — Abstracting, Bibliographies, Statistics*

330.9   CE   ISSN 0256-808X
DS488
SRI LANKA YEARBOOK. (Text in English, Sinhala, Tamil) 1948. irreg., latest 1982. Rs.21. Department of Census and Statistics, P.O. Box 563, 15-12, Maitland Crescent, Colombo 07, Sri Lanka. TEL 94-1-695291. FAX 94-1-695291. (Subscr. to: Superintendent, Government Publications Bureau, Colombo, Sri Lanka) circ. 4,640. **Document type:** government publication.
 Formerly: Ceylon Yearbook.

330.9 352   GW
STADT HERNE. ARBEITSMARKTBERICHT. 1989. q. DM.10. Stadt Herne, Amt fuer Informationsverarbeitung und Stadtforschung, Postfach 101820, 44621 Herne, Germany. TEL 49-2323-162100. FAX 49-2323-162311. circ. 150. **Document type:** government publication.

330 011   GW
STAEDTE- UND KREISSTATISTIK RUHRGEBIET. 1976. a. DM.16. Kommunalverband Ruhrgebiet, Kronprinzenstr. 35, 45128 Essen, Germany. TEL 49-201-2069-0. FAX 49-201-2069-500. Ed.Bd. circ. 1,000. **Document type:** trade publication.

332   US   ISSN 1054-7282
HG1501
STANDARD & POOR'S FINANCIAL INSTITUTIONS RATINGS (QUARTERLY EDITION). q. Standard & Poor's Corporation (Subsidiary of: McGraw-Hill, Inc.), 25 Broadway, New York, NY 10004. TEL 212-208-8000. **Document type:** trade publication.

332.1 315   PK
STATE BANK OF PAKISTAN. EQUITY YIELDS ON ORDINARY SHARES. a. Rs.14($4) State Bank of Pakistan, Central Directorate, Public Relations Department, I.I. Chundrigar Rd., P.O. Box 4456, Karachi, Pakistan. TEL 92-2414141. FAX 92-2417865. TELEX 2754 SBPK PK. **Document type:** government publication.

332.6   PK   ISSN 0081-4466
STATE BANK OF PAKISTAN. INDEX NUMBERS OF STOCK EXCHANGE SECURITIES. (Text in English) 1963. a. Rs.17($3.50) State Bank of Pakistan, Central Directorate, Public Relations Department, I.I. Chundrigar Rd., P.O. Box 4456, Karachi, Pakistan. TEL 92-2414141. FAX 92-2417865. TELEX 2754 SBPK PK. **Document type:** government publication.
 Description: Includes an index of share prices.

334.2 315   PK   ISSN 0039-0569
STATE BANK OF PAKISTAN. STATISTICS ON CO-OPERATIVE BANKS. (Text in English) 1965-1976; resumed. q. Rs.32($12) State Bank of Pakistan, Central Directorate, Public Relations Department, I.I. Chundrigar Rd., P.O. Box 4456, Karachi, Pakistan. TEL 92-2414141. FAX 92-2417865. TELEX 2754 SBPK PK. **Document type:** government publication.

332.1 315   PK   ISSN 0039-0577
STATE BANK OF PAKISTAN. STATISTICS ON SCHEDULED BANKS. (Text in English) 1961. q. Rs.80($22) State Bank of Pakistan, Central Directorate, Public Relations Department, I.I. Chundrigar Rd., P.O. Box 4456, Karachi, Pakistan. TEL 92-2414141. FAX 92-2417865. TELEX 2754 SBPK PK. **Document type:** government publication.
 Description: Includes information on deposits.

350 336   II
STATE DOMESTIC PRODUCT OF HIMACHAL PRADESH. (Text in English) 1963. a. Directorate of Economics and Statistics, Simla, Himachal Pradesh, India. circ. 700. **Document type:** government publication.
 Supersedes: State Income of Himachal Pradesh.

338.9   US   ISSN 0073-1080
HA329.1
STATE OF HAWAII DATA BOOK. 1962. a. $19. Department of Business, Economic Development and Tourism, Business Resource Center, Box 2359, Honolulu, HI 96804. TEL 808-586-2423. FAX 808-586-2452. Ed. Glenn Ifuku. stat. circ. 2,500. (also avail. in microfiche from CIS) **Indexed:** SRI. **Document type:** government publication.
 Formerly: Statistical Abstract of Hawaii.

338.91 312   FR   ISSN 0224-098X
HA37.A33
STATECO. 1972. q. free. Institut National de la Statistique et des Etudes Economiques, Division Etudes et Methodes Statistiques pour le Developpement, 18 bd. Adolphe Pinard, 75675 Paris Cedex 14, France. TEL 33-1-41175313. FAX 33-1-41176644. Ed. Philippe Brion. **Document type:** government publication.
 Description: Methodological presentation of the work of statisticians and economists working in developing countries.

BUSINESS AND ECONOMICS — ABSTRACTING, BIBLIOGRAPHIES, STATISTICS

330 317   US   ISSN 0081-4695
HA401
STATISTICAL ABSTRACT OF LOUISIANA. 1965. irreg., latest 1994. $30. University of New Orleans, Division of Business and Economic Research, New Orleans, LA 70148. TEL 504-280-6240. FAX 504-280-6094. E-mail: vlmdb@uno.edu. Ed. Vincent Maruggi. circ. 1,000 (paid). (also avail. in diskette format) **Indexed:** SRI. **Document type:** bibliography.

317 650   US   ISSN 0191-0310
HA581
STATISTICAL ABSTRACT OF OKLAHOMA. 1956. a. $22. University of Oklahoma, Center for Economic and Management Research, College of Business Administration, 307 W. Brooks St., Rm. 4, Norman, OK 73019. TEL 405-325-2931. FAX 405-325-7688. Eds. John McCraw, Patricia Wickham. illus. circ. 1,000. **Indexed:** SRI. **Document type:** academic/scholarly publication.

STATISTICAL ABSTRACT OF UTAH. see *STATISTICS*

332.1 315   TH
STATISTICAL DATA ON COMMERCIAL BANKS IN THAILAND. (Text in English) 1964. a. free. Bangkok Bank Ltd., Economic Research Division, 9 Suapa Rd., Bangkok, Thailand. illus.

315   UN   ISSN 0252-4457
STATISTICAL INDICATORS FOR ASIA AND THE PACIFIC. (Text in English) 1971. q. $17.50. United Nations Economic and Social Commission for Asia and the Pacific (ESCAP), United Nations Bldg., Rajadamnern Ave., Bangkok 10200, Thailand. (Dist. by: United Nations Publications, Rm. DC2-0853, New York, NY 10017; or Distribution and Sales Section, Palais des Nations, CH-1211 Geneva 10, Switzerland; or Conference Services Unit, E.S.C.A.P., Bangkok) (also avail. in microfiche from CIS; back issues avail.) **Indexed:** IIS.
    Former titles (until 1977): Statistical Indicators in E S C A P Countries (ISSN 1010-5131); (until 1974): Statistical Indicators in E C A F E Countries (ISSN 1010-5123)

960   UN   ISSN 0253-4002
STATISTICAL INFORMATION BULLETIN FOR AFRICA/BULLETIN D'INFORMATION STATISTIQUE POUR L'AFRIQUE. (Text in English or French) irreg., no.13, 1980. United Nations Economic Commission for Africa, P.O. Box 3001, Addis Ababa, Ethiopia. **Indexed:** IIS.
    Continues: Statistical and Economic Information Bulletin for Africa (ISSN 0252-5046)

339 318   JM
STATISTICAL INSTITUTE OF JAMAICA. CONSUMER PRICE INDICES BULLETIN. 1957. m. $42. Statistical Institute of Jamaica, 9 Swallowfield Rd., Kingston 5, Jamaica, W.I. FAX 809-92-64859. stat. circ. 709. (processed) **Document type:** bulletin.
    Former titles (until 1976): Statistical Institute of Jamaica. Consumer Price Indices; Jamaica. Department of Statistics. Consumer Price Indices (ISSN 0302-9336); Jamaica. Department of Statistics. Rural Retail Price Index (ISSN 0021-4108)

318 382   JM
STATISTICAL INSTITUTE OF JAMAICA. EXTERNAL TRADE. q. $15.50 per no. Statistical Institute of Jamaica, 9 Swallowfield Rd., Kingston 5, Jamaica, W.I. FAX 809-92-64859. circ. 11.
    Formerly: Jamaica. Department of Statistics. External Trade.

382 318   JM
STATISTICAL INSTITUTE OF JAMAICA. EXTERNAL TRADE ANNUAL REVIEW. 1936. a. $47.50. Statistical Institute of Jamaica, 9 Swallowfield Rd., Kingston 5, Jamaica, W.I. FAX 809-92-64859. stat. circ. 150.
    Formerly (until 1969): Jamaica. Department of Statistics. External Trade Annual Review.

382   JM
STATISTICAL INSTITUTE OF JAMAICA. EXTERNAL TRADE MONTHLY BULLETIN. 1949. m. $42. Statistical Institute of Jamaica, 9 Swallowfield Rd., Kingston 5, Jamaica, W.I. FAX 809-92-64859. stat. circ. 303. (processed)
    Former titles (until 1975): Statistical Institute of Jamaica. External Trade Summary Tables; (until 1968): Jamaica. Department of Statistics. External Trade Summary Tables; Jamaica. Department of Statistics. Monthly Trade Bulletin (ISSN 0027-0628)

318 330   JM
STATISTICAL INSTITUTE OF JAMAICA. NATIONAL INCOME AND PRODUCT. 1950. a. $41. Statistical Institute of Jamaica, 9 Swallowfield Rd., Kingston 5, Jamaica, W.I. FAX 809-92-64859.
    Formerly (until 1975): Jamaica. Department of Statistics. National Income and Product.

339 314   EI   ISSN 0081-4911
STATISTICAL OFFICE OF THE EUROPEAN COMMUNITIES. NATIONAL ACCOUNTS YEARBOOK. (Text in Dutch, English, French, German, Italian) a. price varies. Rue Alcide de Gasperi, 2920 Luxembourg, Luxembourg. (Dist. in the U.S. by: Unipub, 4611-F Assembly Dr., Lanham, MD 20706-4391. TEL 800-274-4888. FAX 301-459-0056)

657   EI   ISSN 1010-1764
STATISTICAL OFFICE OF THE EUROPEAN COMMUNITIES. QUARTERLY NATIONAL ACCOUNTS. (Text in English, French, German) q. Statistical Office of the European Communities, Rue Alcide de Gasperi, 2920 Luxembourg, Luxembourg. (Dist. in the U.S. by: Unipub, 4611-F Assembly Dr., Lanham, MD 20706-4391. TEL 800-274-4888. FAX 301-459-0056) (also avail. in microfiche from CIS) **Indexed:** IIS.
    —BLDSC (7196.627000).

338 314   EI
STATISTICAL OFFICE OF THE EUROPEAN COMMUNITIES. STATISTICAL STUDIES AND SURVEYS. 4/yr. $120. Statistical Office of the European Communities, Rue Alcide de Gasperi, 2920 Luxembourg, Luxembourg. (Dist. in the U.S. by: Unipub, 4611-F Assembly Dr., Lanham, MD 20706-4391. TEL 800-274-4888. FAX 301-459-0056)

338.9 316   KE   ISSN 0377-5712
STATISTICAL SURVEY OF THE EAST AFRICAN COMMUNITY INSTITUTIONS. 1973. a. East African Community, Statistical Department, P.O. Box 30462, Nairobi, Kenya.

330   CL   ISSN 0716-2464
HA992
STATISTICAL SYNTHESIS OF CHILE. 1978. a. Ch.$5300($20) Banco Central de Chile, Casilla 967, Santiago, Chile. TEL 56-2-6702000. FAX 56-2-6984847. TELEX 405 69 CENBC. circ. 2,000. **Document type:** government publication.
    Description: General and economic statistics of Chile.

300.8   UN   ISSN 0252-3655
STATISTICAL YEARBOOK FOR ASIA AND THE PACIFIC/ANNUAIRE STATISTIQUE POUR L'ASIE ET LE PACIFIQUE. (Text in English and French) 1968. a. $80. United Nations Economic and Social Commission for Asia and the Pacific (ESCAP), United Nations Bldg., Rajadamnern Ave., Bangkok 10200, Thailand. (Dist. by: United Nations Publications, Rm. DC2-0853, New York, NY 10017; or Distribution and Sales Section, Palais des Nations, CH-1211 Geneva 10, Switzerland; or Conference Services Unit, E.S.C.A.P., Bangkok) (also avail. in microfiche from CIS) **Indexed:** IIS.
    —BLDSC (8452.832000).
    Formerly: Statistical Yearbook for Asia and the Far East (ISSN 0085-6711)

330   CC
STATISTICAL YEARBOOK OF GUANGDONG (YEAR). (Text in Chinese) 1992. a. HK.$300($58) Economic Information & Agency, 342 Hennessy Rd., 10th Fl., Wanchai, Hong Kong, People's Republic of China. TEL 852-573-8217. FAX 852-838-8304. TELEX 86990 EIA HX.

336 315   CH   ISSN 0256-7857
HA1710.5
STATISTICAL YEARBOOK OF THE REPUBLIC OF CHINA. (Text in English) 1975. a. NT.$350. Executive Yuan, Directorate-General of Budget, Accounting & Statistics, 2 Kwangchow St., Taipei, Taiwan, Republic of China. TEL 886-2-381-4910. (Subscr. to: Chen Chung Book Co., 3F, 20 Heng-Yang Rd., Taipei, Taiwan, R.O.C.. TEL 886-2-381-3980) stat. **Document type:** government publication.
    —BLDSC (8452.919500).

330 947   XR
STATISTICKA ROCENKA CESKE REPUBLIKY. (Text in Czech, English) 1957. approx. a. $60 per no. Cesky Statisticky Urad, Sokolovska 142, 186 04 Prague 8, Czech Republic. TEL 42-2-6604-2451. FAX 42-2-6631-0429. (Subscr. to Cesky Spisovatel, Obchodni Oddeleni, Narodni trida 9, 111 47 Prague 1, Czech Republic) circ. 13,300. (also avail. in microfiche from CHL)
    Former titles (until 1992): Statisticka Rocenka Ceske a Slovenske Federalni Republiky (ISSN 0862-7843); (until 1990): Statisticka Rocenka Ceskoslovenske Socialisticke Republiki (ISSN 0139-6196)
    Description: Presents an aggregative statistical survey of all branches of the national economy.

314   UK   ISSN 0081-5101
STATISTICS - EUROPE; sources for market research. 1968. irreg., no. 6, 1997. £97.50($195) C.B.D. Research Ltd., 15 Wickham Rd., Beckenham, Kent BR3 2JS, England. TEL 44-181-650-7745. FAX 44-181-650-0768. Ed. Joan M. Harvey. index.; stat. circ. 2,000. **Document type:** directory.
    Description: Contains 1,250 sources for social, economic, and market research in each European country.

382 315   SY   ISSN 0081-5136
STATISTICS OF FOREIGN TRADE OF SYRIA; classified according to United Nations standard international trade classification revised. (Text in Arabic, English) 1964. a. $50 in Arab countries; elsewhere $75 (effective 1997). Central Bureau of Statistics, Damascus, Syria. FAX 963-11-3322292. TELEX STC 411093 SY. **Document type:** government publication.

382 679   II   ISSN 0971-3204
STATISTICS OF MARINE PRODUCTS EXPORTS. (Text in English) 1973. a. $5. Marine Products Export Development Authority, MPEDA House, Panampilly Avenue Rd., Cochin 682 036, India. TEL 311979. TELEX 0885-6288. charts; illus.; stat. **Document type:** trade publication.
    Formerly: Marine Products Export Review.

338 315   JA   ISSN 0081-5209
STATISTICS ON JAPANESE INDUSTRIES.* (Text in English) 1965. a. 1500 Yen. Ministry of International Trade and Industry, Research and Statistics Division - Tsusho Sangyo Chosakai, 1-3-1 Kasumigaseki, Chiyoda-ku, Tokyo 100, Japan. TEL 03-501-1511. circ. 1,000. **Document type:** government publication.

330.9 310   MX
STATISTICS ON THE MEXICAN ECONOMY/ECONOMIA MEXICANA EN CIFRAS. 1977. biennial. Mex.$90 (effective Jan. 1996). Nacional Financiera, S.N.C., Subdireccion de Informacion Tecnica y Publicaciones, Insurgentes Sur 1971, Nivel Fuente, Col. Guadalupe Inn, 01020 Mexico, D.F., Mexico. TEL 52-5-3256047. **Document type:** government publication.

332 315   IO   ISSN 0126-3846
HG188.I7
STATISTIK EKONOMI-KEUANGAN INDONESIA/INDONESIAN FINANCIAL STATISTICS. (Text in English, Indonesian) 1968-1975; resumed Nov. 1976. m. $84. Bank Indonesia, Urusan Ekonomi dan Statistik - Bank Indonesia, Economics & Statistics Department, Kantor Pusat, Jl. Kebon Sirih No. 82-84, Teromol Pos 422, Jakarta, Indonesia. bk.rev.; stat. circ. 1,000.

314.37 330   XR   ISSN 0322-788X
STATISTIKA. (Text in Czech; summaries in English) 1962. m. $76.50. Cesky Statisticky Urad, Sokolovska 142, 186 04 Prague 8, Czech Republic. TEL 42-2-6604-2451. FAX 42-2-6631-0429. Ed. J. Jilek. bk.rev.; charts; stat.; index. circ. 4,000. **Indexed:** Curr.Cont. (1992)-, Stat.Theor.Meth.Abstr. (1992-).
    —BLDSC (8453.840000).
    Supersedes in part: Statistika a Demografie.
    Description: Presents statistical theory, methodology as well as statistical experience and practice.

382 314   YU   ISSN 0084-4373
STATISTIKA SPOLJNE TRGOVINE S F R JUGOSLAVIJE. 1949. a. 500 din.($22.22) Savezni Zavod za Statistiku, Kneza Milosa 20, Belgrade, Yugoslavia. TEL 381-681-999. circ. 1,500. **Document type:** government publication.

BUSINESS AND ECONOMICS — ABSTRACTING, BIBLIOGRAPHIES, STATISTICS

332.6   FR   ISSN 1163-5614
STATISTIQUES ANNUELLES DES BOURSES FRANCAISES DE VALEURS. a. 450 F. Bourse de Paris, 39 rue Cambon, 75001 Paris, France. TEL 33-1-49-27-10-00. FAX 33-1-49-27-14-33. TELEX 215 561 F.
  Formerly (until 1989): Annee Boursiere (ISSN 0570-1945)
  Description: Studies stock and bond performance for the year.

382 316   AE
STATISTIQUES DU COMMERCE EXTERIEUR DE L'ALGERIE. (Text in French) 1963. m. (plus q. and a. cumulations). price varies. Direction des Douanes, 19, rue du Docteur Saadane, Algiers, Algeria. (Dist. in US by: African Imprint Library Service, Box 350, West Falmouth, MA 02574. TEL 508-540-5378)
  Document type: government publication.

382   BE   ISSN 0772-6694
HF3601
STATISTIQUES DU COMMERCE EXTERIEUR DE L'UNION ECONOMIQUE BELGO-LUXEMBOURGEOISE. Dutch edition: Statistieken over de Buitenlandes Handel van de Belgische-Luxemburgse Economische Unie (ISSN 0772-6686) 1984. m. 4130 BEF (foreign 5160 BEF) (effective 1993). Institut National de Statistique, 44 rue de Louvain, 1000 Brussels, Belgium. TEL 32-2-5486211. FAX 32-2-5486367. **Indexed:** P.A.I.S.For.Lang.Ind. **Document type:** government publication.
  Supersedes (1967-1983): Bulletin Mensuel du Commerce Exterieur de l'Union Economique Belgo-Luxembourgeoise (ISSN 0566-5272)

382 316   TI   ISSN 0081-5292
STATISTIQUES DU COMMERCE EXTERIEUR DE LA TUNISIE. a. 15000 din. Institut National de la Statistique, 70 rue Echcham, Tunis, Tunisia.
  Document type: government publication.

330 310   CN   ISSN 0835-409X
STATISTIQUES FINANCIERES DES INSTITUTIONS DE DEPOT. 1987. q. Can.$65. Bureau de la Statistique, 5800 rue St. Denis, Ste. 1605, Montreal, PQ H2S 3L5, Canada. TEL 514-272-1373. Ed. James O'Connor. adv. contact: James O'Connor. circ. 200. pp./issue: 36. **Document type:** government publication.
  Description: Shows market shares of the deposit taking institutions, by type of institution, in Quebec and the rest of Canada.

STATS - MONTHLY STATISTICAL AND MARKETING DIGEST. see *STATISTICS*

STEELS ALERT. see *METALLURGY — Abstracting, Bibliographies, Statistics*

336.2 016   AU   ISSN 1025-806X
STEUER UND WIRTSCHAFT INTERNATIONAL. 1991. m. S.1220. Linde Verlag Wien GmbH, Scheydgasse 24, A-1210 Vienna, Austria. TEL 43-1-2780526. FAX 43-1-278052623. URL: http://www.telecom.at/wkims/linde. R&P contact: Heidelinde Langmayr. **Document type:** consumer publication.

336.2 016   AU   ISSN 1025-8078
STEUER UND WIRTSCHAFTSKARTEI. 1925. 3/m. S.2376. Linde Verlag Wien GmbH, Scheydgasse 24, A-1210 Vienna, Austria. TEL 43-1-2780526. FAX 43-1-278052623. URL: http://www.telecom.at/wkims/linde. R&P contact: Heidelinde Langmayr. **Document type:** consumer publication.
  Formerly (until 1983): Oesterreichische Steuer und Wirtschaftskarei (ISSN 0029-9510)

336   SZ
STEUERBELASTUNG IN DER SCHWEIZ - NATUERLICHE PERSONEN NACH GEMEINDEN/CHARGE FISCALE EN SUISSE - PERSONNES PHYSIQUES PAR COMMUNES. (Text in French and German) 1931. a. 8 SFr. Bundesamt fuer Statistik, Schwarztorstr. 96, CH-3003 Bern, Switzerland. TEL 41-31-3236060. FAX 41-31-3236061. URL: http://www.admin.ch/bfs. **Document type:** government publication.

382 310   SJ   ISSN 0585-8488
SUDAN. DEPARTMENT OF STATISTICS. FOREIGN TRADE STATISTICS. (Text in Arabic, English) q. Department of Statistics, Box 700, Khartoum, Sudan. **Document type:** government publication.

310 381   SJ   ISSN 0377-0125
HF273.S8
SUDAN. DEPARTMENT OF STATISTICS. INTERNAL TRADE AND OTHER STATISTICS. (Text in English) a. Department of Statistics, Box 700, Khartoum, Sudan. **Document type:** government publication.

330 370   SJ
SUDAN. NATIONAL COUNCIL FOR RESEARCH. ECONOMIC AND SOCIAL RESEARCH COUNCIL. BIBLIOGRAPHIES. (Text in Arabic, English) 1974. irreg., no.10, 1985. National Council for Research, Economic and Social Research Council, P.O. Box 1166, Khartoum, Sudan. TEL 78805. TELEX 22342 ILIMI. **Document type:** government publication, bibliography.

336   FI   ISSN 0789-9955
HG5581
SUOMEN PANKKI. TILASTOKATSAUS. RAHOITUSMARKKINAT/FINLANDS BANK. STATISTISK OEVERSIKT. FINANSMARKNADEN/BANK OF FINLAND. STATISTICAL REVIEW. FINANCIAL MARKETS. (Text in English, Finnish, Swedish) 1987. m. FIM 200 (effective 1997). Suomen Pankki, Tiedotus, P.O. Box 160, FIN-00101 Helsinki, Finland. TEL 358-0-1831. FAX 358-0-174-872. Ed.Bd.
  Formerly (until 1992): Suomen Pankki. Tiedote. Raha- ja Valuuttamarkkinatilastoja (ISSN 0784-0462)

318.8 388   SR   ISSN 0585-9913
HA1037.S8
SURINAM. ALGEMEEN BUREAU VOOR DE STATISTIEK. KWARTAAL STATISTIEK VAN DE INDUSTRIELE PRODUKTIE. (Text in Dutch) irreg. Algemeen Bureau voor de Statistiek, Paramaribo, Surinam. **Document type:** government publication.
  Description: Contains collected statistics of industrial production.

658.3   MX
SURVEY OF SALARIES. (Text in English, Spanish) a. $188. American Chamber of Commerce of Mexico, A.C., Lucerna 78, Col. Juarez, Del. Cuauhtemoc, 06600 Mexico DF, Mexico. TEL 52-5-724-3800. FAX 52-5-703-2911. TELEX 177-7609 ACHAME. R&P contact: Diana H. de Hernandez. **Document type:** trade publication.
  Formerly: Salary Survey.
  Description: Lists salary rates of executives and other high-level personnel by company size, location and industrial sector within Mexico.

352.1   IC   ISSN 1017-6357
SVEITARSJODAREIKNINGAR/LOCAL GOVERNMENT FINANCE. (Text in Icelandic; table headings in English) 1959. a. $30 (effective 1997). Hagstofa Islands - Statistics Iceland, Skuggasund 3, IS-150 Reykjavik, Iceland. TEL 354-1-560-9800. FAX 354-1-562-8865. E-mail: hagstofa@hag.stjr.is. Dir. Hallgrimur Snorrason. (back issues avail.) **Document type:** government publication.

SVERIGES RIKSBANK. STATISTISK AARSBOK/SVERIGES RIKSBANK - SWEDISH CENTRAL BANK. STATISTICAL YEARBOOK. see *BUSINESS AND ECONOMICS — Banking And Finance*

338 316   SQ
SWAZILAND. CENTRAL STATISTICAL OFFICE. CENSUS OF INDUSTRIES. (Not published in 1968, 1969, 1974, 1975) 1967. a. free. Central Statistical Office, P.O. Box 456, Mbabane, Swaziland. TEL 268-43765. circ. 500. **Document type:** government publication.
  Formerly: Swaziland. Central Statistical Office. Census of Industrial Production.

382 314   SW   ISSN 0281-0050
HF3671
SWEDEN. STATISTISKA CENTRALBYRAAN. FOREIGN TRADE: IMPORT-EXPORT. DISTRIBUTION BY COUNTRY - COMMODITY ACCORDING TO THE S I T C. (Text in Swedish; summaries in English) 1964. a. SEK 280. Statistiska Centralbyraan, Publishing Unit, S-701 89 Oerebro, Sweden. circ. 1,500. **Document type:** government publication.
  Supersedes: Sweden. Statistika Centralbyraan. Utrikeshandel - Foreign Trade (ISSN 0082-0369)

338 314   SW
SWEDEN. STATISTISKA CENTRALBYRAAN. INDUSTRI. (In 2 parts: Part 1 (ISSN 0348-3797); Part 2 (ISSN 0348-3835)) (Text in Swedish; summaries in English) 1911. a. SEK 560 for 2 vols. Statistiska Centralbyraan, Publishing Unit, S-701 89 Oerebro, Sweden. circ. 1,500. **Document type:** government publication.
  Supersedes (in 1970): Industri (ISSN 0082-0172)

658.3 314   SW
SWEDEN. STATISTISKA CENTRALBYRAAN. LOENER OCH SYSSELSATTNING INOM OFFENTLIG SEKTOR. (In 2 parts: Part 1: Statsaellda (ISSN 0283-8141); Part 2: Kommunal Personal (ISSN 0283-815X)) (Text in Swedish; title heads in English) 1968. a. SEK 320 for both vols. Statistiska Centralbyraan, Publishing Unit, S-701 89 Oerebro, Sweden. circ. 600. **Document type:** government publication.

314 331   SW   ISSN 0082-0237
SWEDEN. STATISTISKA CENTRALBYRAAN. STATISTISKA MEDDELANDEN. SERIE AM, ARBETSMARKNAD. (Text in Swedish; table heads and summaries in English) N.S. 1964. irreg. SEK 2400. Statistiska Centralbyraan, Publishing Unit, S-701 89 Oerebro, Sweden. circ. 1,250. **Document type:** government publication.

338 314   SW   ISSN 1100-1038
HC371
SWEDEN. STATISTISKA CENTRALBYRAAN. STATISTISKA MEDDELANDEN. SERIE I, INDUSTRI. (Text in Swedish; table heads and summaries in English) N.S. 1963. irreg. SEK 300. Statistiska Centralbyraan, Publishing Unit, S-701 89 Oerebro, Sweden. circ. 1,300. **Document type:** government publication.

338 334   SW   ISSN 0346-6078
SWEDEN. STATISTISKA CENTRALBYRAAN. STATISTISKA MEDDELANDEN. SERIE K, KREDITMARKNAD. (Text in Swedish; summaries in English) 1976. irreg. SEK 1160 (effective 1992). Statistiska Centralbyraan, Publishing Unit, S-701 89 Oerebro, Sweden. **Document type:** government publication, abstracting/indexing.

336 314   SW   ISSN 0282-3489
SWEDEN. STATISTISKA CENTRALBYRAAN. STATISTISKA MEDDELANDEN. SERIE N, NATIONALRAEKENSKAPERNA. (Text in Swedish; table heads and summaries in English) 1963. irreg. SEK 500 (effective 1991). Statistiska Centralbyraan, Publishing Unit, S-701 89 Oerebro, Sweden. circ. 1,500. **Document type:** government publication.
  Supersedes in part (in 1986): Sweden. Statiska Centralybraan. Statiska Meddelanden. Serie N, Nationalraekenskaper och Offentliga Finanser.

336   SW   ISSN 0282-3497
HJ59
SWEDEN. STATISTISKA CENTRALBYRAAN. STATISTISKA MEDDELANDEN. SERIE O, OFFTENTLIGA FINANSER. (Text in Swedish; summaries in English) 1985. irreg. SEK 300 (effective 1992). Statistiska Centralbyraan, Publishing Unit, S-701 89 Oerebro, Sweden. **Document type:** government publication, abstracting/indexing.

330 314   SW   ISSN 0082-030X
SWEDEN. STATISTISKA CENTRALBYRAAN. STATISTISKA MEDDELANDEN. SERIE P, PRISER OCH KONSUMTION. (Text in Swedish; table heads and summaries in English) N.S. 1963. irreg. SEK 1550. Statistiska Centralbyraan, Publishing Unit, S-701 89 Oerebro, Sweden. circ. 2,150. **Document type:** government publication.
  Incorporates (in 1976): Sweden. Statistiska Centralbyraan. Statistiska Meddelanden. Serie Pa, Konsumentprisindex.

380.1 338 314   SW   ISSN 1100-9373
HF31
SWEDEN. STATISTISKA CENTRALBYRAAN. STATISTISKA MEDDELANDEN. SERIE SE, SERVICENAERINGAR. (Text in Swedish; table heads and summaries in English) N.S. 1963. 28/yr. SEK 500 (effective 1991). Statistiska Centralbyraan, Publishing Unit, S-701 89 Oerebro, Sweden. circ. 2,000. **Document type:** government publication.
  Supersedes in part (in 1990): Sweden. Statistiska Centralbyraan. Statistiska Meddelanden. Serie H, Handel (ISSN 0082-0261)

BUSINESS AND ECONOMICS — ABSTRACTING, BIBLIOGRAPHIES, STATISTICS

381   SW   ISSN 1100-9381
SWEDEN. STATISTISKA CENTRALBYRAAN. STATISTISKA MEDDELANDEN. SERIE UH, UTRIKESHANDEL. (Text in Swedish; table heads and summaries in English) N.S. 1963. 14/yr. SEK 1900 (effective 1991). Statistiska Centralbyraan, Publishing Unit, S-701 89 Oerebro, Sweden. **Document type:** government publication.
   Supersedes in part (in 1990): Sweden. Statistiska Centralbyraan. Statistiska Meddelanden. Serie H, Handel (ISSN 0082-0261)

338 314   SW   ISSN 0346-606X
HC371
SWEDEN. STATISTISKA CENTRALBYRAAN. STATISTISKA MEDDELANDEN. SUBGROUP F (ENTREPRISES). (Text in Swedish; summaries in English) 1976. irreg. SEK 400 (effective 1992). Statistiska Centralbyraan, Publishing Unit, S-701 89 Oerebro, Sweden. **Document type:** government publication, abstracting/indexing.

336   SZ
SWITZERLAND. BUNDESAMT FUER STATISTIK. DIREKTE BUNDESSTEUER. EINSCHAETZUNGSERGEBNISSE DER NATUERLICHEN UND JURISTISCHEN PERSONEN. VERANLAGUNGSPERIODE/IMPOT FEDERAL DIRECT. RESULTATS DE LA TAXATION DES PERSONNES PHYSIQUES ET MORALES. PERIODE DE TAXATION. (Text in French and German) 1983. biennial. 9 SFr. Bundesamt fuer Statistik, Schwarztorstr. 96, CH-3003 Bern, Switzerland. TEL 41-31-3236060. FAX 41-31-3236061. URL: http://www.admin.ch/bfs. **Document type:** government publication.
   Formerly (until 1994): Switzerland. Bundesamt fuer Statistik. Direkte Bundessteuer - Statistik der Veranlagungsperiode (Year).

382 314   SZ
SWITZERLAND. DIRECTORATE GENERAL OF CUSTOMS. ANNUAL REPORT. (Text in French, German) a. 29.60 SFr. (foreign 34 SFr.). Directorate General of Customs, Section Statistics, Monbijoustr. 40, CH-3003 Bern, Switzerland. TEL 41-31-3226610. FAX 41-31-3227872. TELEX 911100-OZD-CH. **Document type:** government publication.

382 314   SZ   ISSN 0081-525X
SWITZERLAND. DIRECTORATE GENERAL OF CUSTOMS. ANNUAL STATISTICS. (Text in French, German) 1885. a. (3 vols.). 199.90 SFr. (foreign 231 SFr.). Directorate General of Customs, Section Statistics, Monbijoustr. 40, CH-3003 Bern, Switzerland. TEL 41-31-3226610. FAX 41-31-3227872. TELEX 911100-OZD-CH. **Document type:** government publication.

382 314   SZ   ISSN 0049-2183
SWITZERLAND. DIRECTORATE GENERAL OF CUSTOMS. MONTHLY STATISTICS. (Text in French, German) 1885. m. 218.30 SFr. (foreign 248 SFr.). Directorate General of Customs, Section Statistics, Monbijoustr. 40, CH-3003 Bern, Switzerland. TEL 41-31-3226610. FAX 41-31-3227872. TELEX 911100-OZD-CH. stat. **Document type:** government publication.

382 315   SY
SYRIA. CENTRAL BUREAU OF STATISTICS. SUMMARY OF FOREIGN TRADE. (Text in Arabic, English) 1958. 2/yr. $40 per vol. in Arab countries; elsewhere $75 (effective 1997). Central Bureau of Statistics, Damascus, Syria. FAX 963-11-3322292. TELEX STC 411093 SY. mkt.; stat. **Document type:** government publication.
   Former titles: Syria. Central Bureau of Statistics. Monthly Summary of Foreign Trade; Syria. Central Bureau of Statistics. Summary of Foreign Trade Statistics (ISSN 0039-7954)
   Description: Includes tables of imports and exports by sections and chapters, lists important items and main countries by item of import, export, and transit under the code of unified Arab classification.

330   FP   ISSN 0765-1104
HC688.A1
TABLEAUX DE L'ECONOMIE POLYNESIENNE. 1985. a. 2000 FCFP (foreign 3000 FCFP). Institut Territorial de la Statistique, B.P. 395, Papeete, Tahiti, French Polynesia. TEL 689-43-71-96. FAX 689-42-72-52. TELEX 537 FP. Ed. Charles Durand.

330   FR   ISSN 0291-8692
TABLEAUX ECONOMIQUES DE MIDI-PYRENEES. 1981. biennial. 80 F. per issue. Institut National de la Statistique et des Etudes Economiques (INSEE - Midi-Pyrenees), 36 rue des 36 Ponts, 31054 Toulouse Cedex, France. TEL 33-61366136. FAX 33-61366200. Ed. Francois Limet.
   Description: Offers important statistical information concerning the Midi-Pyrenees region.

330   GP   ISSN 0999-1271
TABLEAUX ECONOMIQUES REGIONAUX: GUADELOUPE. 1988. q. Institut National de la Statistique et des Etudes Economiques, Service Regional Guadeloupe, Ave. Paul-Lacave, B.P. 96, 97102 Basse-Terre Cedex, Guadeloupe. TEL 590-81-42-50. **Document type:** government publication.

330   FG   ISSN 0999-128X
TABLEAUX ECONOMIQUES REGIONAUX: GUYANE. 1988. biennial. 60 F. Institut National de la Statistique et des Etudes Economiques, Service Regional Guyane, 1 rue Maillard-Dumesle, B.P. 6017, 97306 Cayenne Cedex, French Guiana. TEL 19-594-31-56-03. FAX 19-594-30-87-89. (back issues avail.)

330   MQ   ISSN 0999-1409
TABLEAUX ECONOMIQUES REGIONAUX: MARTINIQUE. 1988. a. 4.79 F. Institut Nationale de la Statistique et des Etudes Economiques, Service Regional de Martinique, Pointe de Jaham, B.P. 7212, 97233 Schoelcher Cedex, Martinique. TEL 590-915980. FAX 590-838925. **Document type:** government publication.

330.9   CH   ISSN 1016-2224
HA1710.5
TAIWAN STATISTICAL DATA BOOK. (Text in English) 1960. a. NT.$250($12) Council for Economic Planning and Development, 9-F, 87 Nanking E. Rd. Sec. 2, Taipei, Taiwan 10408, Republic of China. TEL 866-2-522-5404. FAX 866-2-562-2950. Dir. W.P. Chang. R&P contact: W.P. Chang. circ. 4,000. **Document type:** government publication.
—BLDSC (8598.649000).

331 316   TZ
TANZANIA. BUREAU OF STATISTICS. SURVEY OF EMPLOYMENT. 1961. irreg. (approx. a.). Bureau of Statistics, P.O. Box 796, Dar es Salaam, Tanzania. (Subscr. to: Government Publications Agency, P.O. Box 1801, Dar es Salaam, Tanzania) **Document type:** government publication.
   Formerly: Tanzania. Bureau of Statistics. Employment and Earnings (ISSN 0049-2973)

338 316   TZ
TANZANIA. BUREAU OF STATISTICS. SURVEY OF INDUSTRIAL PRODUCTION. 1965. a. Bureau of Statistics, P.O. Box 796, Dar es Salaam, Tanzania. (Subscr. to: Government Publications Agency, P.O. Box 1801, Dar es Salaam, Tanzania) **Document type:** government publication.
   Formerly: Tanzania. Central Statistical Bureau. Survey of Industrial Production (ISSN 0564-6545)

TECHNOLOGY MEDIA SOURCE. see *ADVERTISING AND PUBLIC RELATIONS — Abstracting, Bibliographies, Statistics*

TENNESSEE. LABOR MARKET INFORMATION DIRECTORY. see *BUSINESS AND ECONOMICS — Labor And Industrial Relations*

TENNESSEE. THE LABOR MARKET REPORT. see *BUSINESS AND ECONOMICS — Labor And Industrial Relations*

382   TH
THAILAND'S FOREIGN TRADE STATISTICS. (Text mainly in English, Thai; occasionally in Chinese) irreg. B.250. Interstate Publications, P.O. Box 5-85, Pathumwan, Bangkok 5, Thailand.

330.9 310   TG
TOGO. MINISTRY OF ECONOMY AND FINANCE. BULLETIN DE STATISTIQUES. m. Ministry of Economy and Finance, Service de la Statistique Generale, B.P. 118, Lome, Togo. **Document type:** government publication, bulletin.

658 016   UK   ISSN 0049-4100
HD28
TOP MANAGEMENT ABSTRACTS. 1971. bi-m. £3199($4999) (foreign Aus.$6499) (effective 1998). (British Institute of Management) M C B University Press Ltd., Anbar Electronic Intelligence, 60-62 Toller Ln., Bradford, W. Yorks BD8 9BY, England. TEL 44-1274-480916. FAX 44-1274-543576. TELEX 51317-MCBUNI-G. URL: http://www.mcb.co.uk. Ed. Eric Sandelands. (looseleaf format) **Indexed:** AESIS. **Document type:** abstracting/indexing.
—BLDSC (0900.307000).
   Supersedes in part: Anbar Management Services Abstracts (ISSN 0003-2794)
   Description: Contains abstracts of articles selected from 300 or more international management journals, on topics of interest to senior management.

TOPICATOR; classified article guide to the advertising/communications/marketing periodical press. see *ADVERTISING AND PUBLIC RELATIONS — Abstracting, Bibliographies, Statistics*

330   US
TRADE & INDUSTRY INDEX. m. Information Access Company (Subsidiary of: Thomson Corporation), 362 Lakeside Dr., Foster City, CA 94404. TEL 415-378-5200; 800-227-8431. FAX 415-358-4759. (Or: Predicasts Europe, 8-10 Denman St., London W1V 7RF, England. TEL 44-171-494-3817) **Document type:** abstracting/indexing.
● Available only online. Vendor(s): Knight-Ridder Information, Inc. (File no.148), Ovid Technologies, Inc. (TSAP).

382 314   IE   ISSN 0790-9381
TRADE STATISTICS. 1924. m. I£130. Central Statistics Office, Skehard Rd., Cork, Ireland. TEL 353-21-359000. FAX 353-21-359090. E-mail: information@cso.ie; URL: http://www.cso.ie. circ. 600. **Document type:** government publication.
   Former titles: Trade Statistics of Ireland; Ireland (Eire) Central Statistics Office. External Trade Statistics (ISSN 0075-0565)

330 658.3   US   ISSN 1049-3875
HF5549.5.T7
TRAINING AND DEVELOPMENT YEARBOOK. 1990. a. $79.95. (Advanced Personnel Systems) Prentice Hall, 270 Sylvan Ave., Englewood Cliffs, NJ 07632. TEL 201-592-2000. Ed. Richard B. Frantzreb.
   Description: Consists of reprint articles and abstracts from training literature of the previous year. Case studies and research summaries are highlighted.

330.9   IT
TRIBUNA ECONOMICA. 1972. m. free. Camera di Commercio, Industria, Artigianato e Agricoltura di Livorno, Piazza Municipio 48, 57100 Livorno, Italy. TEL 30-586-231111. FAX 39-586-886689. TELEX 500486 CCIA LI. circ. 10,000.
   Description: Covers economics, statistics and information on business.

318 330.9   TR
TRINIDAD AND TOBAGO. CENTRAL STATISTICAL OFFICE. BUSINESS SURVEYS. irreg., latest 1990. T.T.$4. Central Statistical Office, 35-41 Queen St., P.O. Box 98, Port-of-Spain, Trinidad & Tobago, W.I. TEL 809-623-7069. **Document type:** government publication.

330.9 318   TR
TRINIDAD AND TOBAGO. CENTRAL STATISTICAL OFFICE. ECONOMIC INDICATORS. 1974. biennial. T.T.$15. Central Statistical Office, 35-41 Queen St., P.O. Box 98, Port-of-Spain, Trinidad & Tobago, W.I. TEL 809-623-7069. **Document type:** government publication.

317.29 331.1   TR
TRINIDAD AND TOBAGO. CENTRAL STATISTICAL OFFICE. LABOUR FORCE BY SEX. (Subseries of: Continuous Sample Survey of Population (ISSN 0564-2612)) q T.T.$3. Central Statistical Office, 35-41 Queen St., P.O. Box 98, Port-of-Spain, Trinidad & Tobago, W.I. TEL 809-623-7069. illus.; stat. **Document type:** government publication.

BUSINESS AND ECONOMICS — ABSTRACTING, BIBLIOGRAPHIES, STATISTICS

382 318　　　　　TR　　ISSN 0082-6545
TRINIDAD AND TOBAGO. CENTRAL STATISTICAL OFFICE. OVERSEAS TRADE. ANNUAL REPORT. (Issued in three parts) 1951. a. $40 for Part A; Part B $10; Part C $20. Central Statistical Office, 35-41 Queen St., P.O. Box 98, Port-of-Spain, Trinidad & Tobago, W.I. TEL 809-623-7069. **Document type:** government publication.

382 318　　　　　TR　　ISSN 0030-7505
TRINIDAD AND TOBAGO. CENTRAL STATISTICAL OFFICE. OVERSEAS TRADE. BI-MONTHLY REPORT. 1951. m. T.T.$24. Central Statistical Office, 35-41 Queen St., P.O. Box 98, Port-of-Spain, Trinidad & Tobago, W.I. TEL 809-623-7069. mkt.; stat. circ. 650. **Document type:** government publication.
　　Formerly: Trinidad and Tobago. Statistical Office. Overseas Trade Report.

330　　　　　　　TR　　ISSN 0041-3046
HC157.T8
TRINIDAD AND TOBAGO. CENTRAL STATISTICAL OFFICE. QUARTERLY ECONOMIC REPORT. 1950. biennial. T.T.$15($7.50) Central Statistical Office, 35-41 Queen St., P.O. Box 98, Port-of-Spain, Trinidad & Tobago, W.I. TEL 809-623-7069. charts; stat. circ. 700. **Document type:** government publication.

338.5 314　　　　BU
TSENI. 1969. m. $120. Tsentralno Statistichesko Upravlenie, c/o Distributor: Foreign Trade Co. "Hemus", 1B Raiko Daskalov Sq., 1000 Sofia, Bulgaria. TEL 359-2-871686. FAX 359-2-9803319. stat. circ. 280.

315.61　　　　　TU　　ISSN 1300-0802
TURKEY. DEVLET ISTATISTIK ENSTITUSU. AYLIK DIS TICARET OZETI/TURKEY. STATE INSTITUTE OF STATISTICS. MONTHLY SUMMARY OF FOREIGN TRADE. Key Title: Aylik Dis Ticaret Ozeti. (Text in English, Turkish) 1964. m. $20. Devlet Istatistik Enstitusu - State Institute of Statistics, Necatibey Caddesi No. 114, 06100 Ankara, Turkey. TEL 90-312-4185027. FAX 90-312-4170432. circ. 2,100. (also avail. in diskette format) **Document type:** government publication.

315.61　　　　　TU
TURKEY. DEVLET ISTATISTIK ENSTITUSU. AYLIK EKONOMIK GOSTERGELER/TURKEY. STATE INSTITUTE OF STATISTICS. MONTHLY ECONOMIC INDICATORS. (Text in English, Turkish) 1980. m. $8.80. Devlet Istatistik Enstitusu - State Institute of Statistics, Necatibey Caddesi No. 114, 06100 Ankara, Turkey. TEL 90-312-4185027. FAX 90-312-4170432. circ. 2,000. **Document type:** government publication.

315.61　　　　　TU　　ISSN 0259-5338
TURKEY. DEVLET ISTATISTIK ENSTITUSU. DIS TICARET ISTATISTIKLERI/TURKEY. STATE INSTITUTE OF STATISTICS. FOREIGN TRADE STATISTICS. Key Title: Dis Ticaret Istatistikleri. (Text in English, Turkish) 1926. a. $65 (effective 1996). Devlet Istatistik Enstitusu - State Institute of Statistics, Necatibey Caddesi No. 114, 06100 Ankara, Turkey. TEL 90-312-4185027. FAX 90-312-4170432. circ. 800. (also avail. in diskette format) **Document type:** government publication.
　　Formerly: Turkey. Devlet Istatistik Enstitusu. Dis Ticaret Yillik Istatistik - Annual Foreign Trade Statistics (ISSN 0082-6901)

315.61　　　　　TU　　ISSN 1300-090X
TURKEY. DEVLET ISTATISTIK ENSTITUSU. DONEMLER ITIBARIYLE IMALAT SANAYII: ISTIHDAM - ODEMELER - URETIM EGILIM (GECICI SONUCLAR)/TURKEY. STATE INSTITUTE OF STATISTICS. MANUFACTURING INDUSTRY (QUARTERLY) EMPLOYMENT - PAYMENTS - PRODUCTION - EXPECTATIONS (PROVISIONAL RESULTS). (Text in English, Turkish) q. $50 (effective 1996). Devlet Istatistik Enstitusu - State Institute of Statistics, Necatibey Caddesi No. 114, 06100 Ankara, Turkey. TEL 90-312-4185027. FAX 90-312-4170432. (also avail. in diskette format) **Document type:** government publication.

315.61　　　　　TU
TURKEY. DEVLET ISTATISTIK ENSTITUSU. GAYRI SAFI MILLI HASILA, HABER BULTENI/TURKEY. STATE INSTITUTE OF STATISTICS. GROSS NATIONAL PRODUCT RESULTS, NEWS BULLETIN. (Text in English, Turkish) 1947. q. (with a. cumulation). Devlet Istatistik Enstitusu - State Institute of Statistics, Necatibey Caddesi No. 114, 06100 Ankara, Turkey. TEL 90-312-4185027. FAX 90-312-4170432. **Document type:** government publication, bulletin.

338.528　　　　　TU　　ISSN 1300-1035
TURKEY. DEVLET ISTATISTIK ENSTITUSU. PERAKENDE FIYAT ISTATISTIKLERI/TURKEY. STATE INSTITUTE OF STATISTICS. RETAIL PRICE STATISTICS. Key Title: Perakende Fiyat Istatistikleri. (Text in English, Turkish) 1972. a., latest for years 1992-1994. $60 (effective 1996). Devlet Istatistik Enstitusu - State Institute of Statistics, Necatibey Caddesi No. 114, 06100 Ankara, Turkey. TEL 90-312-4185027. FAX 90-312-4170432. (also avail. in diskette format) **Document type:** government publication.

315.61　　　　　TU
TURKEY. DEVLET ISTATISTIK ENSTITUSU. SANAYI URETIM INDEKSI (DONEMLER ITIBARIYLE)/TURKEY. STATE INSTITUTE OF STATISTICS. INDUSTRIAL PRODUCTION INDEXES (QUARTERLY). (Text in English, Turkish) 1984. q. $45. Devlet Istatistik Enstitusu - State Institute of Statistics, Necatibey Caddesi No. 114, 06100 Ankara, Turkey. TEL 90-312-4185027. FAX 90-312-4170432. circ. 1,242. (also avail. in diskette format) **Document type:** government publication.

338.7021　　　　TU　　ISSN 1300-1124
HA1911
TURKEY. DEVLET ISTATISTIK ENSTITUSU. SIRKETLER KOOPERATIFLER VE FIRMA ISTATISTIKLERI/TURKEY. STATE INSTITUTE OF STATISTICS. COMPANIES, COOPERATIVES AND FIRMS STATISTICS. Key Title: Sirketler Kooperatifler ve Firma Istatistikleri. (Text in English, Turkish) 1967. a., latest 1994. $45 (effective 1996). Devlet Istatistik Enstitusu - State Institute of Statistics, Necatibey Caddesi No. 114, 06100 Ankara, Turkey. TEL 90-312-4085027. FAX 90-312-4170432. circ. 1,200. **Document type:** government publication.

381　　　　　　　TU　　ISSN 1300-3992
TURKEY. DEVLET ISTATISTIK ENSTITUSU. TASIMACELIK ACISINDAN TURKIYE'NIN DIS TICAETI/TURKEY. STATE INSTITUTE OF STATISTICS. FOREIGN TRADE BY TRANSPORT SYSTEM. (Text in English, Turkish) 1994. a. $45 (effective 1996). Devlet Istatistik Enstitusu, Necatibey Caddesi No. 114, 06100 Ankara, Turkey. TEL 90-312-4185027. FAX 90-312-4170432. **Document type:** newspaper.

315.61　　　　　TU　　ISSN 1012-6376
TURKEY. DEVLET ISTATISTIK ENSTITUSU. TOPTAN ESYA VE TUKETICI FIYATLARI AYLIK INDEKS BULTENI/TURKEY. STATE INSTITUTE OF STATISTICS. WHOLESALE AND CONSUMER PRICE INDEXES MONTHLY BULLETIN. Key Title: Toptan Esya ve Tuketici Fiyatlari Aylik Indeks Bulteni. (Text in English, Turkish) 1963. m. $25. Devlet Istatistik Enstitusu - State Institute of Statistics, Necatibey Caddesi No. 114, 06100 Ankara, Turkey. TEL 90-312-4185027. FAX 90-312-4170432. circ. 2,000. (also avail. in diskette format) **Document type:** government publication.

315.61　　　　　TU　　ISSN 1300-1140
TURKEY. DEVLET ISTATISTIK ENSTITUSU. TOPTAN FIYAT ISTATISTIKLERI/TURKEY. STATE INSTITUTE OF STATISTICS. WHOLESALE PRICE STATISTICS. Key Title: Toptan Fiyat Istatistikleri. (Text in English, Turkish) 1974. a., latest for years 1991-1995. $45 (effective 1996). Devlet Istatistik Enstitusu - State Institute of Statistics, Necatibey Caddesi No. 114, 06100 Ankara, Turkey. TEL 90-312-4185027. FAX 90-312-4170432. index, cum.index; circ. 500 (controlled). (also avail. in diskette format) **Document type:** government publication.

315.61　　　　　TU　　ISSN 1300-1264
HC491
TURKEY. DEVLET ISTATISTIK ENSTITUSU. TURKIYE EKONOMISI ISTATISTIK VE YORUMLAR/TURKEY. STATE INSTITUTE OF STATISTICS. TURKISH ECONOMY STATISTICS AND EVALUATIONS. (Text in Turkish) 1990. m. $75 (effective 1996). Devlet Istatistik Enstitusu - State Institute of Statistics, Necatibey Caddesi No. 114, 06100 Ankara, Turkey. TEL 90-312-4185027. FAX 90-312-4170432. (also avail. in diskette format) **Document type:** government publication.
　　Description: Provides statistical information on price fluctuations, GNP, household income and consumption, foreign trade, labor force and industry, mining, construction, agriculture, as well as the environment, education, social and economic characteristics of the population.

315.61　　　　　TU
TURKEY. DEVLET ISTATISTIK ENSTITUSU. YAYINLAY VE ELEKTRONIK HIZMETLER KATALOGU. English edition: Turkey. State Institute of Statistics. Publications and Electronic Services Catalogue. 1994. irreg. free. Devlet Istatistik Enstitusu, Necatibey Caddesi No. 114, 06100 Ankara, Turkey. TEL 90-312-4185027. FAX 90-312-4170432. illus. **Document type:** government publication, catalog.
　　Description: Presents information on available statistical publications covering social and economic conditions in Turkey.

315.61　　　　　TU　　ISSN 0259-5141
TURKEY. DEVLET ISTATISTIK ENSTITUSU. YILLIK IMALAT SANAYI ISTATISTIKLERI/TURKEY. STATE INSTITUTE OF STATISTICS. ANNUAL MANUFACTURING INDUSTRY STATISTICS. Key Title: Yillik Imalat Sanayi Istatistikleri. (Text in English, Turkish) 1974. a., latest 1991. $65 (effective 1996). Devlet Istatistik Enstitusu - State Institute of Statistics, Necatibey Caddesi No. 114, 06100 Ankara, Turkey. TEL 90-312-4185027. FAX 90-312-4170432. circ. 1,100. (also avail. in diskette format) **Document type:** government publication.
　　Description: Provides detailed information about all aspects of the Turkish manufacturing sector.

315.61　　　　　TU　　ISSN 1300-7173
TURKEY. STATE INSTITUTE OF STATISTICS. CENSUS OF INDUSTRY AND BUSINESS ESTABLISHMENTS - 1ST STAGE RESULTS. (Text in English, Turkish) 1974. irreg., latest 1992. $65 (effective 1996). Devlet Istatistik Enstitusu - State Institute of Statistics, Necatibey Caddesi No. 114, 06100 Ankara, Turkey. TEL 90-4-4176440. FAX 90-4-4253387. circ. 550. **Document type:** government publication.

315.61　　　　　TU
TURKEY. STATE INSTITUTE OF STATISTICS. CENSUS OF INDUSTRY AND BUSINESS ESTABLISHMENTS - 2ND STAGE RESULTS, LARGE SCALE MANUFACTURING INDUSTRIES. (Text in English, Turkish) 1976. irreg., latest 1985. Devlet Istatistik Enstitusu - State Institute of Statistics, Necatibey Caddesi No. 114, 06100 Ankara, Turkey. TEL 90-4-4176440. FAX 90-4-4253387. circ. 1,350. **Document type:** government publication.

315.61　　　　　TU
TURKEY. STATE INSTITUTE OF STATISTICS. CENSUS OF INDUSTRY AND BUSINESS ESTABLISHMENTS - 2ND STAGE RESULTS, SERVICE, HOTEL, RESTAURANT, GUEST HOUSE, CAFE. (Text in English, Turkish) 1974. irreg., latest 1985. Devlet Istatistik Enstitusu - State Institute of Statistics, Necatibey Caddesi No. 114, 06100 Ankara, Turkey. TEL 90-4-4176440. FAX 90-4-4253387. **Document type:** government publication.

315.61　　　　　TU
TURKEY. STATE INSTITUTE OF STATISTICS. CENSUS OF INDUSTRY AND BUSINESS ESTABLISHMENTS - 2ND STAGE RESULTS, SMALL-SCALE MANUFACTURING INDUSTRIES. (Text in English, Turkish) 1975. irreg., latest 1985. Devlet Istatistik Enstitusu - State Institute of Statistics, Necatibey Caddesi No. 114, 06100 Ankara, Turkey. TEL 90-4-4176440. FAX 90-4-4253387. circ. 1,350. **Document type:** government publication.

315.61　　　　　TU
TURKEY. STATE INSTITUTE OF STATISTICS. CENSUS OF INDUSTRY AND BUSINESS ESTABLISHMENTS - 2ND STAGE RESULTS, TRADE. (Text in English, Turkish) 1974. irreg., latest 1985. Devlet Istatistik Enstitusu - State Institute of Statistics, Necatibey Caddesi No. 114, 06100 Ankara, Turkey. TEL 90-4-4176440. FAX 90-4-4253387. circ. 1,350. **Document type:** government publication.

315.61　　　　　TU
TURKEY. STATE INSTITUTE OF STATISTICS. CONSUMPTION EXPENDITURES. (Text in English, Turkish) 1979. a., latest 1987. Devlet Istatistik Enstitusu - State Institute of Statistics, Necatibey Caddesi No. 114, 06100 Ankara, Turkey. TEL 90-4-4176440. FAX 90-4-4253387. circ. 1,350. **Document type:** government publication.

BUSINESS AND ECONOMICS — ABSTRACTING, BIBLIOGRAPHIES, STATISTICS

315.61 TU ISSN 0259-5036
TURKEY. STATE INSTITUTE OF STATISTICS. HOUSEHOLD LABOR FORCE SURVEY RESULTS. (Text in English, Turkish) 1968. irreg., latest 1994. $60 (effective 1996). Devlet Istatistik Enstitusu - State Institute of Statistics, Necatibey Caddesi No. 114, 06100 Ankara, Turkey. TEL 90-4-4176440. FAX 90-4-4253387. circ. 1,150. **Document type:** government publication.

315.61 TU
TURKEY. STATE INSTITUTE OF STATISTICS. INCOME DISTRIBUTION. (Text in English, Turkish) a., latest 1987. Devlet Istatistik Enstitusu - State Institute of Statistics, Necatibey Caddesi No. 114, 06100 Ankara, Turkey. TEL 90-4-4176440. FAX 90-4-4253387. **Document type:** government publication.

315.61 TU
TURKEY. STATE INSTITUTE OF STATISTICS. METHODOLOGY EXPLANATION OF TRADE PRICE AND QUANTITY INDEXES. (Text in English) 1992. irreg. free. Devlet Istatistik Enstitusu - State Institute of Statistics, Necatibey Caddesi No. 114, 06100 Ankara, Turkey. TEL 90-4-4176440. FAX 90-4-4253387. **Document type:** government publication.

363.6 310 363.7 UK ISSN 1353-6702
THE U K REGULATED INDUSTRIES: FINANCIAL FACTS (YEAR). (Subseries of: C R I Statistics Series) 1992. a. £25 to non-members; members £20. Chartered Institute of Public Finance and Accountancy, Centre for the Study of Regulated Industries, 3 Robert St., London WC2N 6BH, England. TEL 44-171-543-5600. FAX 44-171-543-5700. **Document type:** trade publication. **Description:** Disseminates financial statistics on regulated industries in the U.K.

330 310 UN ISSN 1012-0793
HF1040
U N C T A D COMMODITY YEARBOOK. 1984. a. $52. (United Nations Conference on Trade and Development) United Nations Publications, Sales and Marketing Section, Room DC2-0853, New York, NY 10017. TEL 212-963-8302; 800-253-9646. FAX 212-963-3489. E-mail: publications@un.org; URL: http://www.un.org/publications. (also avail. in microfiche from CIS) **Indexed:** IIS.
Formerly (until 1987): Yearbook of International Commodity Statistics (ISSN 0257-1870)

332.6 US ISSN 1059-4418
HA4551
U S AND ASIA STATISTICAL HANDBOOK. a. $8 (effective 1995). Heritage Foundation, 214 Massachusetts Ave., N.E., Washington, DC 20002. TEL 202-546-4400. FAX 202-543-9647. Eds. William J. Bonde, Richard D. Fisher. **Description:** Contains information on political, military, economic and social conditions in 34 countries and territories in Asia.

382.09489 DK ISSN 0109-5420
HF211
UDENRIGSHANDELEN FORDELT PAA VARER OG LANDE/EXTERNAL TRADE BY COMMODITIES AND COUNTRIES. (Text in Danish; notes in English) 1969. q. DKK 2060 (effective 1997); newsstand price: DKK 604.80. Danmarks Statistik, Sejroegade 11, DK-2100 Copenhagen OE, Denmark. TEL 45-39-17-39-17. FAX 45-31-18-48-01. TELEX 16236. (back issues avail.) **Document type:** government publication.
Formerly (until 1984): Denmark. Danmarks Statistik. Kvartalsstatistik over Udenrigshandelen (ISSN 0106-9780)
Description: Contains detailed statistics of imports and exports by Working Tariff items and countries.

330 XR
UKAZATELEU SOCIALNIHO A HOSPODARSKEHO VYVOJE CESKE REPUBLIKY/INDICATORS OF SOCIAL AND ECONOMIC DEVELOPMENT IN THE CZECH REPUBLIC. q. $24. Cesky Statisticky Urad, Sokolovska 142, 186 04 Prague 8, Czech Republic. TEL 42-2-6604-2451. FAX 42-2-6631-0429.
Formed by the merger of: Ciselne Zrcadlo Ceske Ekonomiky & Prahled Ukazatelu Ekonomickeho a Socialniho Rozvoje Ceske Republiky. **Description:** Provides basic data characterizing the development of the economy and living standards since 1985.

UNESCO. STATISTICS ON SCIENCE AND TECHNOLOGY/STATISTIQUES RELATIVES AUX SCIENCE ET A LA TECHNOLOGIE/ESTADISTICAS RELATIVAS A LA CIENCIA Y A LA TECNOLOGIA. see SCIENCES: COMPREHENSIVE WORKS — Abstracting, Bibliographies, Statistics

UNIFORM COMMERCIAL CODE LAW JOURNAL. see LAW — Abstracting, Bibliographies, Statistics

336 330 CX
UNITE - DIGNITE - TRAVAIL: PROGRAMME TRIENNAL D'INVESTISSEMENT DE L'ETAT. 1988. a. $80. Ministry of Economics, Division of Programs and Projects, Bangui, Central African Republic. FAX 236-61-73-97. TELEX 5208 RC. **Document type:** government publication.

330 TS
UNITED ARAB EMIRATES. AL-MASRAF AL-MARKAZI. AL-MULHIQ AL-IHSA'I/UNITED ARAB EMIRATES. CENTRAL BANK. STATISTICAL SUPPLEMENT. (Text in Arabic, English) 1979. q. Central Bank, P.O. Box 854, Abu Dhabi, United Arab Emirates. TEL 652220. FAX 668483. TELEX 24173 MARKAZI EM. circ. 500 (controlled). **Document type:** government publication.
Description: Statistical information on Central Bank activities, the petroleum industries, and external trade of the U.A.E.

339 UN ISSN 0259-3017
UNITED NATIONS. NATIONAL ACCOUNTS STATISTICS. ANALYSIS OF MAIN AGGREGATES. (Text in English) 1958. a. $125. United Nations Publications, Sales and Marketing Section, Room DC2-0853, New York, NY 10017. TEL 212-963-8302; 800-253-9646. FAX 212-963-3489. E-mail: publications@un.org; URL: http://www.un.org/publications. (Or: Distribution and Sales Section, CH-1211 Geneva 10, Switzerland) (also avail. in microfiche from CIS) **Indexed:** IIS.
Supersedes in part (in 1985): Yearbook of National Account Statistics (ISSN 0084-3881)

339 UN ISSN 0259-3009
UNITED NATIONS. NATIONAL ACCOUNTS STATISTICS. GOVERNMENT ACCOUNTS AND TABLES. (Text in English) 1958. a. United Nations Publications, Sales and Marketing Section, Room DC2-0853, New York, NY 10017. TEL 212-963-8302; 800-253-9646. FAX 212-963-3489. E-mail: publications@un.org; URL: http://www.un.org/publications. (Or: Distribution and Sales Section, CH-1211 Geneva 10, Switzerland)
Supersedes in part (in 1985): Yearbook of National Account Statistics (ISSN 0084-3881)

339 UN ISSN 0259-3025
UNITED NATIONS. NATIONAL ACCOUNTS STATISTICS. MAIN AGGREGATES AND DETAILED TABLES. (Text in English) 1958. a. United Nations Publications, Sales and Marketing Section, Room DC2-0853, New York, NY 10017. TEL 212-963-8302; 800-253-9646. FAX 212-963-3489. E-mail: publications@un.org; URL: http://www.un.org/publications. (Or: Distribution and Sales Section, CH-1211 Geneva 10, Switzerland) (also avail. in microfiche from CIS) **Indexed:** IIS.
●Also available online.
—BLDSC (6015.780500).
Supersedes in part (in 1985): Yearbook of National Account Statistics (ISSN 0084-3881)

310 UN ISSN 0252-3647
HA37
UNITED NATIONS ECONOMIC AND SOCIAL COMMISSION FOR ASIA AND THE PACIFIC. STATISTICAL NEWSLETTER. q. United Nations Economic and Social Commission for Asia and the Pacific (ESCAP), United Nations Bldg., Rajadamnern Ave., Bangkok 10200, Thailand. stat. (also avail. in microfiche from CIS) **Indexed:** IIS.

316 UN
UNITED NATIONS ECONOMIC COMMISSION FOR AFRICA. STATISTICAL NEWSLETTER. (Text in Arabic, English, French) a. United Nations Economic Commission for Africa, P.O. Box 3001, Addis Ababa, Ethiopia. (also avail. in microfiche from CIS) **Indexed:** IIS.

330.9 US
U.S. BUREAU OF LABOR STATISTICS. SOUTHWEST STATISTICAL SUMMARY. m. free. U.S. Bureau of Labor Statistics, Southwest Regional Office, 525 Griffin St., Rm. 221, Dallas, TX 75202. TEL 214-767-6970. Ed. Bill Luker, Jr. circ. 10,000. (also avail. in microfiche from CIS; reprint service avail. from CIS) **Indexed:** Amer.Stat.Ind. (1975-). **Document type:** government publication.
Formerly (until 1985): U.S. Bureau of Labor Statistics. Southwest Employment and Earnings.

U.S. FEDERAL RESERVE SYSTEM. ANNUAL STATISTICAL DIGEST. see BUSINESS AND ECONOMICS — Banking And Finance

U.S. FOREIGN AGRICULTURAL TRADE AND AGRICULTURAL TRADE UPDATES STATISTICAL REPORT. see AGRICULTURE — Abstracting, Bibliographies, Statistics

U.S. FOREIGN AGRICULTURAL TRADE STATISTICAL REPORT. FISCAL YEAR. see AGRICULTURE — Abstracting, Bibliographies, Statistics

336 310 US
U.S. INTERNAL REVENUE SERVICE. STATISTICS OF INCOME, FINAL CORPORATION INCOME TAX RETURNS. irreg. $13. U.S. Internal Revenue Service, I R S Bldg., 1111 Constitution Ave., N.W., Washington, DC 20224. (Dist. by: Bernan, 4611-F, Assembly Dr., Lanham, MD 20706-4391. TEL 800-274-4447. FAX 301-459-0056; And: Superintendent of Documents, U.S. Government Printing Office, Box 371954, Pittsburgh, PA 15250-7954. TEL 202-512-1800. FAX 202-512-2250) (also avail. in microfiche from BHP) **Document type:** government publication.

336 US
U.S. INTERNAL REVENUE SERVICE. STATISTICS OF INCOME, FINAL INDIVIDUAL INCOME TAX RETURNS. irreg. $8.50. U.S. Internal Revenue Service, I R S Bldg., 1111 Constitution Ave., N.W., Washington, DC 20224. (Dist. by: Bernan, 4611-F Assembly Dr., Lanham, MD 20706-4391. TEL 800-274-4447. FAX 301-459-0056; And: Superintendent of Documents, U.S. Government Printing Office, Box 371954, Pittsburgh, PA 15250-7954. TEL 202-512-1800. FAX 202-512-2250) (also avail. in microfiche from BHP) **Document type:** government publication.

332.6 US
HD7116.R118
U.S. RAILROAD RETIREMENT BOARD. QUARTERLY BENEFIT STATISTICS. 1968. q. free. U.S. Railroad Retirement Board, 844 N. Rush St., Chicago, IL 60611-2092. TEL 312-751-4776. Ed. W. Poulos. circ. 1,500. (also avail. in microfiche from CIS; reprint service avail. from CIS) **Indexed:** Amer.Stat.Ind. (1973-). **Document type:** government publication.
Formerly (until 1997): U.S. Railroad Retirement Board. Monthly Benefit Statistics (ISSN 0364-7129)

330 016 CL
UNIVERSIDAD DE CHILE. FACULTAD DE CIENCIAS ECONOMICAS Y ADMINISTRATIVAS. BIBLIOTECA. LISTA DE MEMORIAS Y LIBROS SELECCIONADOS. libros y folletos recibidos, articulos seleccionados. (Text in English, French, Spanish) 1964. bi-m. Universidad de Chile, Facultad de Ciencias Economicas y Administrativas, Av. Ranacagua 257, Santiago, Chile. Ed. Mariela Morales Piderit. circ. 300.
Supersedes (since 1978): Universidad de Chile. Instituto de Economia. Biblioteca. Boletin (ISSN 0041-8366)

658.4 016 GW
UNIVERSITAET BONN. INSTITUT FUER OEKONOMETRIE UND OPERATIONS RESEARCH. NEUANSCHAFFUNGSLISTEN. 1963. q. free. Universitaet Bonn, Institut fuer Oekonometrie und Operations Research, Nassestr. 2, 53113 Bonn, Germany. circ. 150.

UNIVERSITAET HOHENHEIM. FORSCHUNGSBERICHT. see SCIENCES: COMPREHENSIVE WORKS — Abstracting, Bibliographies, Statistics

BUSINESS AND ECONOMICS — ABSTRACTING, BIBLIOGRAPHIES, STATISTICS

330 310   GH
UNIVERSITY OF GHANA. INSTITUTE OF STATISTICAL, SOCIAL AND ECONOMIC RESEARCH. TECHNICAL PUBLICATION SERIES. 1966. irreg., no.57, 1993. University of Ghana, Institute of Statistical, Social and Economic Research, P.O. Box 74, Legon, Ghana. **Document type:** monographic series.
   Formerly: University of Ghana. Institute of Statistical, Social and Economic Research. Technical Research Monographs (ISSN 0072-4416)
   Description: Addresses social structure and poverty in selected rural communities in Ghana.

318   UY   ISSN 0797-258X
URUGUAY. DIRECCION GENERAL DE ESTADISTICA Y CENSOS. INDICE MEDIO DE SALARIOS. q. Direccion General de Estadistica y Censos, Montevideo, Uruguay. **Document type:** government publication.

382   IC   ISSN 1024-7483
▼**UTANRIKISVERSLUN/EXTERNAL TRADE**; voeruflokkar og vidskiptaloend. English edition: Icelandic External Trade (ISSN 1024-7475) 1995. a. $22 (effective 1997). Hagstofa Islands - Statistics Iceland, Skuggasund 3, IS-150 Reykjavik, Iceland. TEL 354-560-9800. FAX 354-562-8865. E-mail: hagstofa@hag.stjr.is. Dir. Hallgrimur Snorrason. (back issues avail.) **Document type:** government publication.

382   IC   ISSN 1024-7467
▼**UTANRIKISVERSLUN EFTIR TOLLSKRARNUMERUM/EXTERNAL TRADE BY HS-NUMBERS.** (Text in Icelandic; tableheadings in English) 1995. a. $40 (effective 1997). Hagstofa Islands - Statistics Iceland, Skuggasund 3, IS-150 Reykjavik, Iceland. TEL 354-560-9800. FAX 354-562-8865. E-mail: hagstofa@hag.stjr.is. Dir. Hallgrimur Snorrason. (back issues avail.) **Document type:** government publication.

330   HU   ISSN 1219-7793
HG4149.5
VALLALATOK PENZUGYI ADATAI/FINANCIAL DATA OF NON-FINANCIAL CORPORATIONS. irreg. Kozponti Statistikai Hivatal, Keleti Karoly u. 10, 1024 Budapest II, Hungary. TEL 40-0-2124348.
   Supersedes in part (in 1992): Gazdasagstatisztikai Evkonyv (ISSN 1215-6728)

658 016   HU   ISSN 0231-0759
Z7164.07
VALLALATSZERVEZESI ES IPARGAZDASAGI SZAKIRODALMI TAJEKOZTATO/INDUSTRIAL MANAGEMENT ABSTRACTS. 1950. m. 9900 Ft. Orszagos Muszaki Informacios Kozpont es Konyvtar (O.M.I.K.K.) - National Technical Information Centre and Library, Muzeum u. 17, P.O. Box 12, 1428 Budapest, Hungary. (Subscr. to: Kultura, PO Box 149, 1389 Budapest, Hungary) Ed. Ernone Huszar. circ. 750.
   Supersedes (in 1982): Muszaki Lapszemle. Uzemszervezes, Ipargazdasag - Technical Abstracts. Business Organization, Industrial Economics (ISSN 0027-4941)

382   NN
VANUATU. STATISTICS OFFICE. ANNUAL SUMMARY OF OVERSEAS TRADE. (Text in English, French) 1971. a. 500 vatu($5) (effective 1996). Statistics Office, Private Mail Bag 19, Port-Vila, Vanuatu. TEL 678-22110. FAX 678-24583. Ed. Jacob Isaiah. adv. contact: Tali Saurei. circ. 400. **Document type:** government publication.
   Former titles: Vanuatu. Statistics Office. Overseas Trade (ISSN 1013-6088); Vanuatu. National Planning and Statistics Office. Overseas Trade; Vanuatu. Bureau of Statistics. Overseas Trade.

331.11   NN
VANUATU. STATISTICS OFFICE. MANPOWER AND EMPLOYMENT SURVEYS. (Text in English, French) 1973. irreg. $19. Statistics Office, Private Mail Bag 19, Port-Vila, Vanuatu. TEL 678-22110. FAX 678-24583. Ed. Jacob Isaiah. adv. contact: Tali Saurei. stat. circ. 500. **Document type:** government publication.
   Former titles: Vanuatu. National Planning and Statistics Office. Manpower and Employment Survey. Final Results; (until 1984): Vanuatu. Bureau of Statistics. Manpower and Employment Survey. Final Results.

332   NN
VANUATU. STATISTICS OFFICE. MONETARY AND BANKING STATISTICS. (Text in English, French) 1982. q. 100 vatu($10) (effective 1996). Statistics Office, Private Mail Bag 19, Port-Vila, Vanuatu. TEL 678-22110. FAX 678-24583. Ed. Jacob Isaiah. adv. contact: Tali Saurei. circ. 300. **Document type:** government publication, bulletin.
   Formerly: Vanuatu. National Planning and Statistics Office. Monetary and Banking Statistics.
   Description: Provides the latest statistics on major monetary indicators, money supply, foreign currency liquidity, bank assets, and bank loans.

657   NN
VANUATU. STATISTICS OFFICE. NATIONAL ACCOUNTS OF VANUATU. irreg., latest 1985-1989 ed. 500 vatu($5) (effective 1996). Statistics Office, Private Mail Bag 19, Port-Vila, Vanuatu. TEL 678-22110. FAX 678-24583. Ed. Jacob Isaiah. adv. contact: Tali Saurei. circ. 300. **Document type:** government publication.
   Description: Highlights the Vanuatu economy, including data on the gross domestic product and expenditure, national disposable income and its appropriation, household income and outlay account and more.

330   NN
VANUATU. STATISTICS OFFICE. SECOND NATIONAL DEVELOPMENT PLAN. (In 2 vols.) every 5 yrs. $40. Statistics Office, Private Mail Bag 19, Port-Vila, Vanuatu. TEL 678-22110. FAX 678-24583. Ed. Jacob Isaiah. adv. contact: Tali Saurei. **Document type:** government publication.

330.9   NN
VANUATU. STATISTICS OFFICE. STATISTICAL INDICATORS. (Text in English, French) 1976. q. 300 vatu($13) (effective 1996). Statistics Office, Private Mail Bag 19, Port-Vila, Vanuatu. TEL 678-22110. FAX 678-24583. Ed. Jacob Isaiah. adv. contact: Tali Saurei. charts; stat. circ. 350. **Document type:** government publication.
   Former titles: Vanuatu. National Planning and Statistics Office. Statistical Indicators; Vanuatu. Bureau of Statistics. Statistical Indicators.
   Description: Provides statistics on overseas trade, consumer prices, migration, tourism, monetary and banking, transport, energy consumption, construction and employment.

330 318   VE   ISSN 0798-1546
VENEZUELA. OFICINA CENTRAL DE ESTADISTICA E INFORMATICA. COYUNTURA ECONOMICA. no. 2, 1975. q. Bs.270 (for 1992 vols.). Oficina Central de Estadistica e Informatica, Apdo. de Correos 4593, Carmelitas, Caracas 1010A, Venezuela. TEL 58-2-7821133. FAX 58-2-7811380. TELEX 21241. circ. 1,000. (also avail. in diskette format) **Indexed:** P.A.I.S.For.Lang.Ind. **Document type:** government publication.
   Former titles: Boletin de Indicadores de Coyuntura; Indicadores Socioeconomicos y de Coyuntura.

330   VE   ISSN 0798-8761
VENEZUELA. OFICINA CENTRAL DE ESTADISTICA E INFORMATICA. ENCUESTA CUALITATIVA. 1984. a. Bs.400 (for 1992 ed.) Oficina Central de Estadistica e Informatica, Apdo. de Correos 4593, Carmelitas, Caracas 1010A, Venezuela. TEL 58-2-782-11-33. FAX 58-2-781-13-80. TELEX 21241. circ. controlled. **Document type:** government publication.

658   SZ
VERBRAUCHSERHEBUNG. AUSGABEN UND EINNAHMEN DER PRIVATEN HAUSHALTE/ENQUETE SUR LA CONSOMMATION LES DEPENSES ET LES REVENUS DES MENAGES PRIVES. (Editions in French, German) 1987. a. 10 SFr. Bundesamt fuer Statistik, Schwarztorstr. 96, CH-3003 Bern, Switzerland. TEL 41-31-3236060. FAX 41-31-3236061. URL: http://www.admin.ch/bfs. **Document type:** government publication.
   Formerly: Verbraucherhebung. Ausgaben und Einnahmen.

331   US
VERMONT. DEPARTMENT OF EMPLOYMENT & TRAINING. LABOR MARKET BULLETIN. q. Department of Employment & Training, Box 488, Montpelier, VT 05602. TEL 802-828-4000. Ed. Susan Auld. **Document type:** bulletin, government publication.

382   IC   ISSN 1017-6365
HA1491
VERSLUNARSKYRSLUR/EXTERNAL TRADE. (Text in Icelandic; tableheadings in English) 1914. a. $40 (effective 1997). Hagstofa Islands - Statistics Iceland, Skuggasund 3, IS-150 Reykjavik, Iceland. TEL 354-560-9800. FAX 354-562-8865. E-mail: hagstofa@hag.stjr.is. Dir. Hallgrimur Snorrason. (back issues avail.) **Document type:** government publication.
   Description: Presents external trade statistics of Iceland.

331.12   IC   ISSN 1024-0020
▼**VINNUMARKADUR/LABOR MARKET STATISTICS.** (Text in Icelandic; tableheadings in English) 1994. a. $20 (effective 1997). Hagstofa Islands - Statistics Iceland, Skuggasund 3, IS-150 Reykjavik, Iceland. TEL 354-560-9800. FAX 354-562-8865. Dir. Hallgrimur Snorrason. (back issues avail.)

310   US   ISSN 0081-475X
VIRGINIA STATISTICAL ABSTRACT (YEAR).* 1966. a. University of Virginia, Center for Public Service, 918 Emmet St., N., Ste. 300, Charlottesville, VA 22903-4832. TEL 804-924-4871. FAX 804-924-4538. (also avail. in microfiche from BHP)

338   US   ISSN 1081-0846
HD4973
▼**WAGES AND COST OF LIVING.** 1995. biennial. $60 (academic institutions $40) (effective 1996). Research Associates of Washington, 2605 Klingle Rd., N.W., Washington, DC 20008. TEL 202-966-3326. FAX 202-966-0309. Ed. D. Kent Halstead. R&P contact: Marjorie Halstead. (also avail. in diskette format) **Document type:** academic/scholarly publication.
   Description: Presents earnings data and cost of living information for 507 counties in the U.S.

336.2   US
WASHINGTON (STATE). DEPARTMENT OF REVENUE. RESEARCH DIVISION. PROPERTY TAX STATISTICS. 1970. a. Department of Revenue, Research Division, Box 47459, Olympia, WA 98504-7459. TEL 360-753-2087. FAX 360-664-0972. stat.; circ. controlled. (tabloid format) **Document type:** government publication.
   Former titles: Washington (State). Department of Revenue. Research Section. Property Tax Levy and Collection Statistics; Washington (State). Department of Revenue. Research and Information Division. Property Tax Levy and Collection Statistics.

336.2   US
WASHINGTON (STATE). DEPARTMENT OF REVENUE. RESEARCH DIVISION. TAX STATISTICS. 1973. a. Department of Revenue, Research Division, Box 47459, Olympia, WA 98504-7459. TEL 360-753-2087. FAX 360-664-0972. circ. 1,000. **Indexed:** SRI. **Document type:** government publication.

WASHINGTON (STATE). EMPLOYMENT SECURITY DEPARTMENT. MONTHLY JOB SERVICE STATISTICS. see OCCUPATIONS AND CAREERS — Abstracting, Bibliographies, Statistics

WASHINGTON (STATE). EMPLOYMENT SECURITY DEPARTMENT. OCCUPATIONAL PROFILES. see OCCUPATIONS AND CAREERS — Abstracting, Bibliographies, Statistics

WASHINGTON (STATE). EMPLOYMENT SECURITY DEPARTMENT. WEEKLY INSURED UNEMPLOYMENT REPORT. see INSURANCE — Abstracting, Bibliographies, Statistics

BUSINESS AND ECONOMICS — ABSTRACTING, BIBLIOGRAPHIES, STATISTICS

331.11   US
WASHINGTON LABOR MARKET. (Separate reports avail. for state and areas) 1942. m. free. Employment Security Department, Labor Market and Economic Analysis Branch, Box 9046, Olympia, WA 98507-9046. TEL 360-438-4820. FAX 360-438-4846. charts. circ. 1,700. (also avail. in microfiche from CIS; back issues avail.) **Indexed:** SRI. **Document type:** government publication, newsletter.
  Former titles (until 1974): Washington (State). Employment Security Department. Labor Area Summary Reports; Washington (State) Employment Security Department. Local Labor Market Developments.
  Description: Provides a broad picture of economic conditions in Washington State and individual counties and regions. Contains nonagricultural wage and salary employment data by industry, employment and unemployment data by state and county, figures on hours worked and wages earned among nonsupervisory workers in various nonmanufacturing industries, and economic information such as consumer price index and per capita income.

332   NZ
WEEKLY STATISTICAL RELEASE. w. NZ.$90 (Australia NZ.$150; elsewhere NZ.$218) (effective 1996-97). Reserve Bank of New Zealand, Corporate Services, 2 The Terrace, P.O. Box 2498, Wellington, New Zealand. TEL 64-4-472-2029. FAX 64-4-473-8554. TELEX NZ 3368.
  Description: New Zealand statistical data updating bulletin tables.

338   UK
WELSH ECONOMIC STATISTICS MONTHLY. m. Welsh Office, Statistical Directorate, Publication Unit, Cathays Park, Cardiff CF1 4NQ, Wales. TEL 44-1222-825054. FAX 44-1222-825350. E-mail: statswales@gtnet.gov.uk. **Document type:** government publication.

338   UK   ISSN 0262-8309
WELSH ECONOMIC TRENDS. 1974. a. £10. Welsh Office, Statistical Directorate, Publication Unit, Cathays Park, Cardiff CF1 4NQ, Wales. TEL 44-1222-825054. FAX 44-1222-825350. E-mail: statswales@gtnet.gov.uk. circ. 550. **Document type:** government publication.
—BLDSC (9294.420000). **CCC.**
  Description: Contains specifics on industrial activity, earnings, working population, capital and public expenditure, employment, unemployment and regional income.

336 310   II
WEST BENGAL. ANNUAL FINANCIAL STATEMENT (BUDGET). a. West Bengal Government Press, Publication Branch, 38 Gopal Nagar Rd., Alipore, Calcutta 27, India. **Document type:** government publication.

315.4 330   II   ISSN 0511-5493
WEST BENGAL. BUREAU OF APPLIED ECONOMICS AND STATISTICS. STATISTICAL HANDBOOK. (Issuing body varies) (Text in English) 1960. a. price varies. Bureau of Applied Economics and Statistics, 1 Kiron Sankar Roy Rd., Calcutta 700001, India. **Document type:** government publication.

WHAT'S NEW IN ADVERTISING AND MARKETING. see *ADVERTISING AND PUBLIC RELATIONS — Abstracting, Bibliographies, Statistics*

339   IR
WHOLESALE PRICE INDEX IN IRAN. m. Bank Markazi Jomhouri Islami Iran, Economic Statistics Department - Central Bank of the Islamic Republic of Iran, P.O. Box 11365-8531, Tehran, Iran. FAX 982-21-390323. TELEX 216219.

016.33
WILSON BUSINESS ABSTRACTS. (Not avail. in print format) 1990. m., 9/yr., and q. versions avail. $2495 for m.; 9/yr. $1875; q. $1245. H.W. Wilson Co., 950 University Ave., Bronx, NY 10452. TEL 718-588-8400; 800-367-6770. FAX 718-590-1617. TELEX 4990003HWILSON. **Document type:** abstracting/indexing.
●Also available online. Vendor(s): Knight-Ridder Information, Inc., OCLC, Ovid Technologies, Inc., Wilsonline (File WBA).
Also available on CD-ROM. Producer(s): SilverPlatter Information, Inc., H.W. Wilson (WILSONDISC).

658 011   US   ISSN 0149-8703
WORK IN AMERICA INSTITUTE: HIGHLIGHTS OF THE LITERATURE. (Subseries of: Work in America Institute Studies in Productivity (ISSN 0149-869X)) 1978. 6/yr. $180. Work in America Institute, 700 White Plains Rd., Scarsdale, NY 10583. TEL 914-472-9600. Ed. Jerome M. Rosow. (also avail. in microform)
—CCC.

338.9   UN   ISSN 0258-3143
HC60
WORLD BANK RESEARCH PROGRAM. 1974. a. World Bank, 1818 H St., N.W., Washington, DC 20433. TEL 202-473-1155. FAX 202-522-2627. E-mail: books@worldbank.org. (U.S. orders to: Box 7247-8619, Philadelphia, PA 19170-8619; Also avail. from: 66 av. D'lena, 75116 Paris, France. TEL 33-1-40-69-30-55. FAX 33-1-40-69-30-68) **Document type:** abstracting/indexing.
  Former titles (until 1986): World Bank. Abstracts of Current Studies (ISSN 0253-9535); (until 1981): World Bank Research Program (ISSN 1010-3023)

WORLD BANKING ABSTRACTS. see *BUSINESS AND ECONOMICS — Banking And Finance*

WORLD COUNCIL OF CREDIT UNIONS. ANNUAL AND STATISTICAL REPORT. see *BUSINESS AND ECONOMICS — Banking And Finance*

WORLD DIRECTORY OF NON-OFFICIAL STATISTICAL SOURCES. see *STATISTICS*

382   UK
WORLD DIRECTORY OF NON-OFFICIAL STATISTICS SOURCES. 1990. irreg. £275($550) Euromonitor, 60-61 Britton St., London EC1M 5NA, England. TEL 44-171-251-8024. FAX 44-171-608-3149. E-mail: info@euromonitor.com; URL: http://www.euromonitor.com. (Address in N. America: Euromonitor International, 122 S. Michigan Ave., Ste. 1200, Chicago, IL 60603. TEL 800-577-3876. FAX 312-922-1157) **Document type:** directory.
  Formerly: International Directory of Non-Official Statistics Sources (ISSN 0959-5139)
  Description: Contains descriptions of more than 3,000 important business periodicals, trade association publications, economic research journals, statistical database newsletters, and other current reference sources spanning a broad range of products. Entries provide complete bibliographical details.

330   UK
WORLD ECONOMIC FACTBOOK. 1993. a. £195($390) (effective 1997). Euromonitor, 87-88 Turnmill St., London EC1M 5QU, England. TEL 44-171-251-8024. FAX 44-171-608-3149. E-mail: info@euromonitor.com; URL: http://www.euromonitor.com. (Addr. in N. America: Euromonitor International, 122 S. Michigan Ave., Ste. 1200, Chicago, IL 60603. TEL 800-577-3876. FAX 312-922-1157) stat. **Document type:** trade publication.
  Description: Supplies demographic and political information on 200 countries worldwide.

330   US   ISSN 1078-6783
▼**WORLD MARKET SHARE REPORTER.** 1996. biennial. Gale Research, 835 Penobscot Bldg., 645 Griswold St., Detroit, MI 48226-4094. TEL 313-961-2242; 800-877-4253. FAX 800-414-5043. E-mail: daniel__snyder@gale.com. Eds. Marlita A. Reddy, Robert Lazich.
—CISTI.

382   US   ISSN 0512-3739
HF53
WORLD TRADE ANNUAL. 1963. a. price varies. (United Nations Statistical Office, UN) Walker & Co., 435 Hudson St., New York, NY 10014-3941. TEL 212-727-8300. FAX 212-727-0984. **Document type:** directory.
—BLDSC (9360.152000).
  Description: Provides complete statistical data on world trade.

382   US   ISSN 0512-3747
WORLD TRADE ANNUAL SUPPLEMENT. 1964. a. price varies. (United Nations Statistical Office, UN) Walker & Co., 435 Hudson St., New York, NY 10014-3941. TEL 212-727-8300. FAX 212-727-0984. **Document type:** directory.
  Description: Provides comprehensive statistical data on world trade.

338 016   US   ISSN 0163-6723
HF1040
WORLDCASTS: PRODUCT EDITION. 1964. q. $900 (foreign $925); with Regional Edition $1300 (foreign $1375). Information Access Company (Subsidiary of: Thomson Corporation), 362 Lakeside Dr., Foster City, CA 94404. TEL 415-378-5200; 800-227-8431. FAX 415-358-4759. (Or: Predicasts Europe, 8-10 Denman St., London W1V 7RF, England. TEL 44-171-494-3817) charts. **Document type:** abstracting/indexing.
●Also available online. Vendor(s): Data-Star, Knight-Ridder Information, Inc.
—CCC.
  Formerly: World-Product-Casts (ISSN 0043-8898)
  Description: Contains statistical abstracts of forecasts published in international business and trade literature, covering production, sales, exports, for specific industries and product areas.

338 016   US   ISSN 0163-6731
HF1040
WORLDCASTS: REGIONAL EDITION. 1964. q. $900 (foreign $925); with Product Edition $1300 (foreign $1375). Information Access Company (Subsidiary of: Thomson Corporation), 362 Lakeside Dr., Foster City, CA 94404. TEL 415-378-5200; 800-227-8431. FAX 415-358-4759. (Or: Predicasts Europe, 8-10 Denman St., London W1V 7RF, England. TEL 44-171-494-3817) Ed. Eileen Gazzuolo. charts. **Document type:** abstracting/indexing.
●Also available online. Vendor(s): Data-Star, Knight-Ridder Information, Inc.
—CCC.
  Formerly: World-Regional Casts (ISSN 0043-8936)
  Description: Provides statistical abstracts of forecasts published in international business and trade literature. Covers production, sales, exports, for specific industries and product areas.

331.11021   BH
BELIZE LABOUR FORCE INDICATORS. a. Ministry of Finance, Central Statistical Office, Belmopan, Belize. TEL 501-8-22352. FAX 501-8-23206. E-mail: csogob@btl.net.

382 387   IS   ISSN 0084-3830
YEARBOOK OF ISRAEL PORTS STATISTICS/SHENATON STATISTI: LE NEMLEI ISRAEL. (Absorbed its English edition Yearbook of Israel Ports Statistics with no.3, 1965-66) (Text in English, Hebrew) 1963. a. Israel Ports & Railways Authority, P.O. Box 20121, Tel-Aviv, Israel.

331 310   UN   ISSN 0084-3857
HD4826
YEAR BOOK OF LABOUR STATISTICS/ANNUAIRE DES STATISTIQUES DU TRAVAIL/ANUARIO DE ESTADISTICAS DEL TRABAJO. (In 2 volumes: Sources and Methods; Labour Statistics) (Text in English, French and Spanish) 1935/36. a. 210 SFr.($168) (International Labour Office) I L O Publications, CH-1211 Geneva 22, Switzerland. TEL 41-22-799-6111. FAX 41-22-798-6358. TELEX 415647-ILO-CH. (Dist. in US by: I L O Publications Center, 49 Sheridan Ave., Albany, NY 12210. TEL 518-436-9686. FAX 518-436-7433) stat. circ. 5,600. (also avail. in microfiche from ILO) **Indexed:** IIS. **Document type:** bulletin.
—BLDSC (9414.300000). **CCC.**
  Description: Contains essential statistical information for following the evolution of labor and of living and working conditions throughout the world.

331.1 314   YU
YUGOSLAVIA. SAVEZNI ZAVOD ZA STATISTIKU. ANKETA O OSTVARIVANJU PRAVA RADNIKA IZ RADNOG ODNOSA. (Subseries of Statisticki Bilten) irreg. 10 din.($0.60) Savezni Zavod za Statistiku, Kneza Milosa 20, Belgrade, Yugoslavia. TEL 38-11-681999. **Document type:** government publication.

339.4 314   YU
YUGOSLAVIA. SAVEZNI ZAVOD ZA STATISTIKU. ANKETA O PORODICNIM BUDZETIMA RADNICKIH DOMACINSTAVA. (Subseries of: Yugoslavia. Savezni Zavod Statistiki. Statisticki Bilten) (Editions in Serbian, English) irreg. Savezni Zavod za Statistiku, Kneza Milosa 20, Belgrade, Yugoslavia. TEL 38-11-681999. **Document type:** government publication.

314 338 YU
YUGOSLAVIA. SAVEZNI ZAVOD ZA STATISTIKU. INDUSTRIJSKE ORGANIZACIJE. (Subseries of: Yugoslavia. Savezni Zavod za Statistiku. Statisticki Bilten) irreg. Savezni Zavod za Statistiku, Kneza Milosa 20, Belgrade, Yugoslavia. TEL 38-11-681999. stat. **Document type:** government publication.

331 314 YU
YUGOSLAVIA. SAVEZNI ZAVOD ZA STATISTIKU. SAMOUPRAVLJANJE U PRIVREDI. (Subseries of: Statisticki Bilten) irreg. Savezni Zavod za Statistiku, Kneza Milosa 20, Belgrade, Yugoslavia. TEL 38-11-681999. circ. 1,000. **Document type:** government publication.

658 331 314 YU
YUGOSLAVIA. SAVEZNI ZAVOD ZA STATISTIKU. SAMOUPRAVLJANJE U USTANOVAMA DRUSTVENIH SLUZBI. (Subseries of: Yugoslavia. Savezni Zavod za Statistiku. Statisticki Bilten) irreg. Savezni Zavod za Statistiku, Kneza Milosa 20, Belgrade, Yugoslavia. TEL 38-11-681999. **Document type:** government publication.

331 314 YU ISSN 0513-0883
YUGOSLAVIA. SAVEZNI ZAVOD ZA STATISTIKU. ZAPOSLENO OSOBLJE. (Subseries of: Statisticki Bilten) irreg. Savezni Zavod za Statistiku, Kneza Milosa 20, Belgrade, Yugoslavia. TEL 38-11-681999. circ. 1,000. **Document type:** government publication.

331.11 314 YU
YUGOSLAVIA. SAVEZNI ZAVOD ZA STATISTIKU. ZAPOSLENO OSOBLJE I NETO LICNI DOHOCI PO GRUPAMA DELATNOSTI. (Subseries of: Statisticki Bilten) s-a. Savezni Zavod za Statistiku, Kneza Milosa 20, Belgrade, Yugoslavia. TEL 38-11-681999. circ. 1,000. **Document type:** government publication.

331.11 314 YU ISSN 0513-0891
YUGOSLAVIA. SAVEZNI ZAVOD ZA STATISTIKU. ZAPOSLENOST. (Subseries of: Statisticki Bilten) 1956. s-a. Savezni Zavod za Statistiku, Kneza Milosa 20, Belgrade, Yugoslavia. TEL 33-11-681999. **Document type:** government publication.

382 316 ZA ISSN 0084-4489
HF3903
ZAMBIA. CENTRAL STATISTICAL OFFICE. ANNUAL STATEMENT OF EXTERNAL TRADE. (Published in 2 vols: Vol. 1, Imports, Exports and Re-Exports by S.I.T.C. Grouping; Vol. 2, Major Country Analysis) 1964. a. $5. Central Statistical Office, P.O. Box 31908, Lusaka, Zambia. TEL 260-1-211231. **Document type:** government publication.

382.1 336 ZA
ZAMBIA. CENTRAL STATISTICAL OFFICE. BALANCE OF PAYMENTS STATISTICS. a. $3. Central Statistical Office, P.O. Box 31908, Lusaka, Zambia. TEL 260-1-211231. **Document type:** government publication.

658 ZA
ZAMBIA. CENTRAL STATISTICAL OFFICE. CONSUMER PRICE STATISTICS. 1980. q. $4. Central Statistical Office, P.O. Box 31908, Lusaka, Zambia. TEL 260-1-211231. **Document type:** government publication.

316 331 ZA ISSN 0084-4500
ZAMBIA. CENTRAL STATISTICAL OFFICE. EMPLOYMENT AND EARNINGS. 1969. irreg., latest 1980. K.3. Central Statistical Office, P.O. Box 31908, Lusaka, Zambia. TEL 260-1-211231. **Document type:** government publication.

316 650 ZA ISSN 0084-4519
ZAMBIA. CENTRAL STATISTICAL OFFICE. FINANCIAL STATISTICS OF PUBLIC CORPORATIONS. 1965. a. $2.50. Central Statistical Office, P.O. Box 31908, Lusaka, Zambia. TEL 260-1-211231. **Document type:** government publication.

330 ZA
ZAMBIA. CENTRAL STATISTICAL OFFICE. INDUSTRY MONOGRAPHS. irreg. K.4. Central Statistical Office, P.O. Box 31908, Lusaka, Zambia. TEL 260-1-211231. **Document type:** monographic series, government publication.

331.11 ZA
ZAMBIA. CENTRAL STATISTICAL OFFICE. MANPOWER SURVEY. (Text in English) 1975. a. $3. Central Statistical Office, P.O. Box 31908, Lusaka, Zambia. TEL 260-1-211231. **Document type:** government publication.

336 ZA
ZAMBIA. CENTRAL STATISTICAL OFFICE. NATIONAL ACCOUNTS. 1965. a. K.5. Central Statistical Office, P.O. Box 31908, Lusaka, Zambia. TEL 260-1-211231. **Document type:** government publication.

330 CC
ZHUHAI TONGJI NIANJIAN (YEAR)/ZHUHAI STATISTICAL YEARBOOK. (Text in Chinese) 1992. a. HK.$220($50) Economic Information & Agency, 342 Hennessy Rd., 10th Fl., Wanchai, Hong Kong, People's Republic of China. TEL 852-573-8217. FAX 852-838-8304. TELEX 86990 EIA HX.

338 330 RH
ZIMBABWE. CENTRAL STATISTICAL OFFICE. CENSUS OF PRODUCTION. 1962. a. Z.$53 in Africa; Europe Z.$64; Aisa Z.$67; North & South America Z.$72. Central Statistical Office, P.O. Box 8063, Causeway, Harare, Zimbabwe. circ. 220. **Document type:** government publication.

BUSINESS AND ECONOMICS — Accounting

657 US
A A C P A NEWSLETTER.* bi-m. Asian American Certified Public Accountants, 110 Pacific Ave., Box 264, San Francisco, CA 94111. TEL 415-393-4300. **Document type:** newsletter.
Description: Covers activities and events. Includes membership list.

657 UK
A A MAGAZINE. 1969. w. £100 (foreign £120) (effective 1996). V N U Business Publications BV, VNU House, 32-34 Broadwick St., London W1A 2HG, England. TEL 44-171-439-4242. FAX 44-171-437-7001. Ed. Yvette Page; Pub. Melanie Williams. adv. contact: Chris Willis. bk.rev.; charts; illus.; stat.; circ. 62,202 (controlled). (tabloid format; also avail. in microform from UMI) **Indexed:** Account.& Data Proc.Abstr., Anbar. **Document type:** trade publication.
●Also available online.
—BLDSC (0573.545000); UMI.
Formerly (until 1994): Accountancy Age (ISSN 0001-4672)

A A S B ACCOUNTING STANDARDS. (Australian Accounting Standards Board) see LAW — Corporate Law

150 332 AT ISSN 0728-4969
A F M EXPLANATORY SERIES (NO.). irreg., latest no.2. University of New England, Department of Accounting and Financial Management, Armidale, N.S.W. 2351, Australia. TEL 61-67-732201. FAX 61-67-711778. R&P contact: J.J. Staunton. TEL 61-67-733276. **Document type:** academic/scholarly publication.

657 AT ISSN 0155-1221
A F M EXPLORATORY SERIES. 1975. irreg., latest no.4. University of New England, Department of Accounting and Financial Management, Armidale, N.S.W. 2351, Australia. TEL 61-67-733333. FAX 61-67-733122. R&P contact: J.J. Staunton. TEL 61-67-733276. circ. 500. **Document type:** academic/scholarly publication.

657 US ISSN 1058-9198
HF5691
A I C P A VEST-POCKET ACCOUNTING AND AUDITING REFERENCE. 1991. a. American Institute of Certified Public Accountants, Harborside Financial Ctr., 201 Plaza Three, Jersey City, NJ 07311-9801. TEL 201-938-3796; 800-862-4272. FAX 201-329-1112. URL: http://www.aicpa.org. (Alt. addr.: 1211 Ave. of the Americas, New York, NY 10036. TEL 212-596-6200) **Document type:** directory.

657 US ISSN 0883-2102
A P I ACCOUNT. 1974. q. $35 (effective 1997). Accountants for the Public Interest, 1012 14th St. N.W., Ste.906, Washington, DC 20005. TEL 202-347-1668. FAX 202-347-1663. adv. circ. 3,000. **Indexed:** Account.Ind. (1978-). **Document type:** newsletter.
Description: Includes reports on national and affiliate volunteer activities, and on issues relating to volunteer accounting.

657 US
A P I AFFILIATE NEWSBRIEF. 3/yr. Accountants for the Public Interest, 1012 14th St., Ste. 906, Washington, DC 20005. TEL 202-347-1668. FAX 202-347-1663. URL: http://www.accountingnet.com. **Document type:** bulletin.

657 US
A R A F MARKETING UPDATE. bi-m. membership only. Associated Regional Accounting Firms, 3700 Crestwood Pky. N.W., Duluth, GA 30136-5599. TEL 770-279-4560. **Document type:** newsletter.

657 US
A R A F QUARTERLY REPORT. q. membership only. Associated Regional Accounting Firms, 3700 Crestwood Pky. N.W., Duluth, GA 30136-5599. TEL 770-279-4560. **Document type:** newsletter.

657 US
A W S C P A NEWSLETTER. bi-m. membership. American Women's Society of Certified Public Accountants, 401 N. Michigan Ave., Chicago, IL 60611. TEL 312-644-6610. E-mail: awscoa_hq@sba.com. Ed. Christine Stevens. R&P contact: Patrick Nolan. circ. 5,000. **Document type:** newsletter.

657 US
A W T A O ANNUAL REPORT. a. Association of Water Transportation Accounting Officers, Box 53, Bowling Green Sta., New York, NY 10004. TEL 212-264-1384. **Document type:** corporate report.

657 US
A W T A O BULLETIN. bi-m. Association of Water Transportation Accounting Officers, Box 53, Bowling Green Sta., New York, NY 10004. TEL 212-264-1384. **Document type:** bulletin.

657 UK ISSN 0001-3072
HF5601 CODEN: ABACAF
ABACUS; a journal of accounting and business studies. 1964. s-a. £66($119) (foreign £75) (effective 1997). (Accounting and Finance Foundation, AT) Blackwell Publishers Ltd., 108 Cowley Rd., Oxford OX4 1JF, England. TEL 44-1865-791100. FAX 44-1865-791347. E-mail: jnlinfo@blackwellpublishers.co.uk; URL: http://www.blackwellpublishers.co.uk. Ed. G. Dean. adv.; bk.rev.; cum.index every 4 yrs. circ. 1,200. (also avail. in microfilm; back issues avail.; reprint service avail. from SWZ,UMI) **Indexed:** AAR, ABI Inform., Account.& Data Proc.Abstr., Account.Ind. (1974-), Anbar., Aus.P.A.I.S., BPIA, Bus.Ind., Cont.Pg.Manage., Curr.Cont., Manage.Cont., Mgmt.& Market.Abstr., P.A.I.S., SSCI, World Bank.Abstr. **Document type:** academic/scholarly publication.
—BLDSC (0537.724000); Genuine Article; SWETS; UMI; UnCover. **CCC**.

657.6 332.1 UK
ABERDEEN PAPERS IN ACCOUNTANCY AND FINANCE. 1991. irreg. £5. University of Aberdeen, Department of Accountancy, Edward Wright Bldg., Dunbar St., Aberdeen AB24 3QY, Scotland. TEL 44-1224-272205. FAX 44-1224-272214. (Co-sponsor: University of Aberdeen, Department of Economics) Ed. Patricia Fraser. R&P contact: Patricia Fraser. circ. 200. **Document type:** monographic series.
—BLDSC (0537.946920).
Formerly: Aberdeen Papers in Accountancy, Finance and Management (ISSN 0962-4627)
Description: Stimulates debate on financial and accounting issues.

657 US ISSN 1054-3619
HF5611
ACADEMY OF ACCOUNTING HISTORIANS. DIRECTORY. 1990. a. Academy of Accounting Historians, c/o William D. Samson, Ed., Culvershouse School of Accountancy, University of Alabama, Tuscaloosa, AL 35487. TEL 205-348-2903. R&P contact: William D. Samson. **Document type:** directory.

BUSINESS AND ECONOMICS — ACCOUNTING

657   NE   ISSN 0924-4182
ACCOUNT. 1988. 8/yr. fl.102 (foreign fl.140) (effective 1998). B.V. Uitgeversmaatschappij Bonaventura (Subsidiary of: Elsevier N.V.), Postbus 2158, 1000 CD Amsterdam, Netherlands. TEL 31-20-6914111. FAX 31-20-5674398. adv. circ. 52,000.

657   UK   ISSN 0001-4664
HF5601   CODEN: ACTYAD
ACCOUNTANCY. International editio. 1889. m. (plus a. CD-ROM). £45 (rest of Europe £58; elsewhere £63); CD-ROM edition £47 (foreign £50). Institute of Chartered Accountants in England and Wales, P.O. Box 433, Moorgate Pl., London EC2P 2BJ, England. TEL 44-171-833-3291. E-mail: postmaster@thebg. demon.co.uk; URL: http://www.accountancymag. demon.co.uk/. (Subscr. to: 40 Bernard St., London WC1N 1LD, England. TEL 44-1800-592361) Ed. Brian Singleton Green. adv. contact: Karen Glaseby. bk.rev.; charts; illus.; index. circ. 71,000. (also avail. in microform from UMI; reprint service avail. from KTO) **Indexed:** AAR, ABI Inform., Account.& Data Proc.Abstr., Account.Ind. (1974-), ASEAN Manage.Abstr., B.P.I., BPIA, Bus.Ind., Cont.Pg.Manage., Euro.LJI, Excerp.Med., High.Educ.Curr.Aware.Bull., INSPEC, LJI, Manage.Cont., Mgmt.& Market.Abstr., PROMT, PSI, SCIMP (1979-), Tr.& Indus.Ind., World Bank.Abstr. **Document type:** trade publication.
●Also available online. Vendor(s): UMI.
Also available on CD-ROM.
—BLDSC (0573.540000); AskIEEE; KR SourceOne; SWETS; UMI; UnCover.
Description: Covers both the technical and business aspects of the profession, along with international issues. UK edition concentrates on UK developments. International edition includes both UK and international events.

657 368   UA   ISSN 0001-4680
ACCOUNTANCY, BUSINESS & INSURANCE REVIEW. (Text in Arabic, English, French) 1961. 2/yr. £E20. University of Cairo, Faculty of Commerce, Cairo, Egypt. Ed. Mahmoud Bazaraa. bk.rev.; charts. circ. 500.

657   IE   ISSN 0001-4699
ACCOUNTANCY IRELAND. 1969. bi-m. I£20 (U.K. £20; elsewhere $60) (effective 1997). Institute of Chartered Accountants in Ireland, Chartered Accountants House, 87-89 Pembroke Rd., Dublin 4, Ireland. TEL 353-1-6680400. FAX 353-1-6680842. Ed. Charles O'Rourke. adv.: B&W page I£1100, color page I£1600; trim 184 x 267; adv. contact: Geraldine Kane. bk.rev.; bibl.; charts; illus.; index. circ. 17,592. **Indexed:** Account.& Data Proc.Abstr., Account.Ind. (1974-), Anbar, Intl.Mgmt.Info. **Document type:** newsletter.
—BLDSC (0573.547000); UMI.

340   US
ACCOUNTANCY LAW REPORTS. 1938. m. $675. C C H Incorporated, 2700 Lake Cook Rd., Riverwoods, IL 60015. TEL 847-267-7000; 800-248-3248. FAX 800-224-8299.

657   SA   ISSN 0258-7254
HF5601
ACCOUNTANCY S A/REKENINGKUNDE S A. (Includes Employment Supplement) (Text in Afrikaans, English) 1914. m. R.120 (foreign R.150) (effective 1997). South African Institute of Chartered Accountants, P.O. Box 59875, Kengray 2100, South Africa. TEL 27-11-622-6655. FAX 27-11-622-3321. E-mail: journal@saica.co.za; URL: http://www.saica.co.za. Ed. Donna Stofberg. R&P contact: Donna Stofberg. adv. contact: Donna Stofberg. bk.rev.; index; circ. 22,244 (controlled). (also avail. in microform from UMI; back issues avail.; reprint service avail. from UMI) **Indexed:** Account.Ind. (1974-), Anbar, Ind.S.A.Per. **Document type:** trade publication.
—BLDSC (0573.549000); UMI.
Formerly (until 1983): South African Chartered Accountant - Suid-Afrikaanse Geoktrooieerde Rekenmeester (ISSN 0038-206X)
Description: Covers news and developments affecting the accounting profession in South Africa and to a lesser extent, internationally.
Refereed Serial

657   NE   ISSN 0001-4729
ACCOUNTANT. 1895. 11/yr. fl.145. Nederlands Instituut van Registeraccountants, Postbus 7984, 1008 AD Amsterdam, Netherlands. Ed. W.P. Moleveld. adv. contact: R. de Vries. bk.rev.; charts; index. circ. 18,000. **Indexed:** Account.& Data Proc.Abstr., Bus.Ind., ELLIS, Key to Econ.Sci. **Document type:** academic/scholarly publication.
—SWETS.

657   IE   ISSN 0001-4710
HF5601
THE ACCOUNTANT. 1874. m. I£349. Lafferty Publications Ltd., The Tower, IDA Enterprise Centre, Pearse St., Dublin 2, Ireland. TEL 353-1-6718022. FAX 353-1-6718240. E-mail: cvserv@lafferty.ie; URL: http://www.unm.lafferty.co.uk/newsletters/ iaccount.html. (Subscr. in US to: Lafferty Publications (USA), 420 Lexington Ave., Ste. 1745, New York, NY 10170. TEL 212-557-6726) Ed. Ciaran Hancock. R&P contact: David Barr. adv.; bk.rev. **Indexed:** AAR, Account.& Data Proc.Abstr., Account.Ind. (1974-), Anbar, BPIA, INSPEC (1983-1988), Intl.Mgmt.Info., Key to Econ.Sci. **Document type:** trade publication.
—BLDSC (0573.560000); SWETS; UMI; UnCover. CCC.
Description: Provides professional intelligence for accountants.

657   KE   ISSN 1010-4135
THE ACCOUNTANT. 1983. q. KShs.250($6) (foreign $15). Institute of Certified Public Accountants of Kenya, P.O. Box 59963, Nairobi, Kenya. TEL 254-2-224629. FAX 254-2-211563. E-mail: icpak@form-net.com. Ed. J.K. Njiraini. adv.; bk.rev.; circ. 18,000 (controlled). **Indexed:** Account.Ind. (1983-). **Document type:** trade publication.
Refereed Serial

657   NE   ISSN 0165-2729
ACCOUNTANT ADVISEUR. Key Title: A A. Accountant Adviseur. 1966. 10/yr. fl.185 (effective 1996). (Nederlandse Orde van Accountants-Administratieconsultenten) Kluwer Bedrijfswetenschappen B.V. (Subsidiary of: Wolters Kluwer N.V.), Postbus 23, 7400 GA Deventer, Netherlands. TEL 31-5700-48999. FAX 31-5700-11504. (Subscr. to: Intermedia bv, Postbus 4, 2400 MA Alphen aan den Rijn, Netherlands. TEL 31-172-466321. FAX 31-172-435527) adv.; bk.rev.; stat.; index. circ. 6,500. **Document type:** trade publication.
—SWETS.

657   AT   ISSN 0044-5916
ACCOUNTANTS AND SECRETARIES EDUCATIONAL JOURNAL. 1954. m. membership. Accountants and Secretaries Educational Society, PO Box 1883, Brisbane, Queensland 4001, Australia.

346.73033
347.30633   US   ISSN 8756-4262
ACCOUNTANT'S LIABILITY. base vol. (plus a. updates). $125 (effective 1996). Practising Law institute, 810 Seventh Ave., New York, NY 10019. TEL 212-824-5700; 800-260-4754. FAX 800-321-0093. E-mail: info@pli.edu; URL: http://www.pli.edu. Eds. Dan L. Goldwasser, Thomas Arnold. (looseleaf format)

657 368.5   US
KF2920.3.A15
ACCOUNTANTS' LIABILITY QUARTERLY. 1987. q. $225. Versus Law, Inc., Box 1435, Bellevue, WA 98009. TEL 425-250-0142. FAX 425-250-0157. Ed. Ruth G. Bernhardt; Pub. Joe Acton. R&P contact: Ruth Bernhardt. index. (back issues avail.) **Document type:** trade publication.
Formerly: Accountants' Liability Review (ISSN 1048-9967)
Description: Covers issues relating to accountant malpractice and professional responsibility.

657 332.6   US
ACCOUNTANTS S E C PRACTICE MANUAL. 1976. m. $607. C C H Incorporated, 2700 Lake Cook Rd., Riverwoods, IL 60015. TEL 847-267-7000; 800-835-5224. FAX 800-224-8299. (looseleaf format)

ACCOUNTANT'S TAX WEEKLY. see *BUSINESS AND ECONOMICS — Public Finance, Taxation*

657.6   US   ISSN 0737-3325
HF5658
THE ACCOUNTING & AUDITING DISCLOSURE MANUAL.
a. $134.95 (overseas $200.45) (effective 1995). Warren, Gorham & Lamont, One Penn Plaza, New York, NY 10119. TEL 212-971-5000. (Subscr. to: The Park Square Bldg., 31 St. James Ave., Boston, MA 02116-4112. TEL 800-950-1207) Eds. Allan B. Afterman, Rowan H. Jones. **Document type:** trade publication.
Description: Compiles all relevant G.A.A.P. and G.A.A.S. requirements.

657.6 658.3   US
ACCOUNTING AND AUDITING FOR EMPLOYEE BENEFITS.
base vol. (plus a. supplements). $164.95 (overseas $243.55) (effective 1995). Warren, Gorham & Lamont, One Penn Plaza, New York, NY 10119. TEL 212-971-5000. FAX 212-971-5113. (Subscr. to: The Park Square Bldg., 31 St. James Ave., Boston, MA 02116-4112. TEL 800-950-1207) Ed. Paul Rosenfield. (looseleaf format) **Document type:** trade publication.
Formerly: Accounting and Auditing for Employee Benefit Plans.
Description: Guides personnel managers through the complex array of laws and accounting and auditing standards.

657   US   ISSN 1045-1447
ACCOUNTING AND AUDITING UPDATE SERVICE. 1984. 48/yr. $266.50 (overseas $356.45) (effective 1995). Warren, Gorham & Lamont, One Penn Plaza, New York, NY 10119. TEL 212-971-5000. FAX 212-971-5113. (Subscr. to: The Park Square Bldg., 31 St. James Ave., Boston, MA 02116-4112. TEL 800-950-1207) Ed. Allan B. Afterman. **Document type:** newsletter.
—CCC.
Description: Analyzes and interprets all F.A.S.B. and A.I.C.P.A. pronouncements as they are issued.

657   UK   ISSN 0001-4788
ACCOUNTING AND BUSINESS RESEARCH. 1970. q. £32 to individuals (foreign £38); institutions £80 (foreign £90). Institute of Chartered Accountants in England and Wales, P.O. Box 433, Moorgate Pl., London EC2P 2BJ, England. TEL 44-171-920-8899. E-mail: postmaster@theabg.demon.co.uk; URL: http://www. accountancymag.demonn.co.uk/home/abr. (Subscr. to: 40 Bernard St., London WC1N 1LD, England. TEL 44-1800-592361) Ed. K.V. Peasnell. adv.; bk.rev.; index. circ. 1,500. (also avail. in microform from UMI; microfilm from WMP; back issues avail.; reprint service avail. from SCH,SWZ) **Indexed:** ABI Inform., Account.& Data Proc.Abstr., Account.Ind. (1974-), Anbar, B.P.I., BPIA, Bus.Ind., C.R.E.J., Cont.Pg.Manage., Excerp.Med., High.Educ.Curr.Aware.Bull., Manage.Cont., Mgmt.& Market.Abstr., P.A.I.S, SCIMP (1978-), Tr.& Indus.Ind., World Bank.Abstr. **Document type:** academic/scholarly publication.
—BLDSC (0573.588000); KR SourceOne; SWETS; UMI; UnCover.
Formerly (until 1970): Accounting Research.
Description: Academic articles on issues affecting the profession.
Refereed Serial

657   SI   ISSN 0218-5563
ACCOUNTING AND BUSINESS REVIEW. Abbreviated title S A B R E. (Text in English) 1994. s-a. $69. World Scientific Publishing Co. Pte. Ltd., Farrer Rd., P.O. Box 128, Singapore 9128, Singapore. TEL 65-3825663. FAX 65-3825919. TELEX RS-28561-WSPC. E-mail: wspcsl@singnet.com.sg; sales@wspc2.demon.co.uk; wspc@wspc.com; URL: http://www.singnet.com.sg/~wspclib/. (UK addr.: 5 Shelton St., Covent Garden, WC2H 9HE, England. TEL 44-171-836-0888. FAX 44-171-836-2020; US addr.: 1060 Main St., Ste. 1B, River Edge, NJ 07661. TEL 800-227-7562. FAX 201-487-9656 Ed. Pang Yang Hoong. **Indexed:** Asian-Pac.Econ.Lit. —BLDSC (0573.588300).

657 378 AT ISSN 0810-5391
ACCOUNTING AND FINANCE. 1960. s-a. Aus.$65 to individuals; institutions, libraries Aus.$100. Accounting Association of Australia and New Zealand, 4th Fl., CPA House, 170 Queen St., Melbourne, Vic. 3000, Australia. FAX 61-3-96420227. E-mail: effiem@clyde.its. unimelb.edu.au; URL: http://www.ecom.unimelb.edu. au/accwww/aaanz/. Ed. Jilnaught Wong. adv. contact: Effie Margiolis. bk.rev. circ. 900. (also avail. in microform from UMI; back issues avail.; reprint service avail. from SCH) **Indexed:** AAR, ABI Inform., Account.Ind. (1979-), BPIA, Bus.Ind., Manage.Cont., Res.High.Educ.Abstr., Tr.& Indus.Ind. **Document type:** academic/scholarly publication.
●Also available online. Vendor(s): Information Access Co., UMI.
—SWETS; UnCover.
  Former titles: Accounting Education; Australasian Association of University Teachers of Accounting. New Bulletin.
  Description: Research articles in accounting, finance and cognate fields.

657 UK ISSN 0951-3574
ACCOUNTING, AUDITING AND ACCOUNTABILITY. 5/yr. £689($999) (effective 1998). M C B University Press Ltd., 60-62 Toller Ln., Bradford, W. Yorks BD8 9BY, England. TEL 44-1274-499821. FAX 44-1274-547143. TELEX 51317 MCBUNI G. URL: http://www.mcb.co. org. (N. American subscr. to: MCB University Press Ltd., Box 10812, Birmingham, AL 35201-0812. TEL 205-995-1567. FAX 205-995-1588) Eds. Lee Parker, James Guthrie. index. (reprint service avail. from SWZ) **Indexed:** Account.Ind. (1988-), Cont.Pg.Manage., SCIMP (1991-). **Document type:** academic/scholarly publication.
—SWETS; UMI. **CCC.**
  Description: Covers accounting practice, policy and trends.

657 US ISSN 1042-928X
ACCOUNTING DEPARTMENT MANAGEMENT & ADMINISTRATION REPORT. Abbreviated title: ADMAR. 1988. m. $249 in U.S. & Canada; elsewhere $273. Institute of Management & Administration, Inc., 29 W. 35th St., 5th Fl., New York, NY 10001-2299. TEL 212-244-0360. FAX 212-564-0465. URL: http://www.ioma.com. Ed. Tim Harris; Pub. Perry Patterson. R&P contact: Sofie Kourkoutakis. index. (looseleaf format; back issues avail.) **Document type:** newsletter.
—CCC.
  Description: Covers how to manage corporate accounting departments more effectively, including actionable strategies on streamlining operations, getting the most out of PCs, software, current data on salaries and compensation.

657 378 UK ISSN 0963-9284
HF5630
ACCOUNTING EDUCATION. 1992. q. £60 (foreign $100) to individuals; institutions £195 (foreign $325); print & online eds. combined £235 (foreign $390) (effective 1998). Thomson Professional (Subsidiary of: International Thomson Publishing Group), 2-6 Boundary Row, London SE1 8HN, England. TEL 44-171-8650066. FAX 44-171-8659623. TELEX 290164 CHAPMA G. E-mail: journal@rapidcom.co.uk; URL: http://ae. thomsonprofessional.com. (Dist. by: International Thomson Publishing Services Ltd., Cheriton House, North Way, Andover, Hants. SP10 5BE, England. TEL 44-1264-342713. FAX 44-1264-342807; Subscr. in US & Canada to: 400 Market St., Philadelphia, PA 19106. TEL 800-552-5866) Ed. Richard M.S. Wilson. adv. contact: Gemma Heiser. (back issues avail.; reprint service avail.) **Indexed:** Cont.Pg.Educ., Cont.Pg.Manage., Educ.Tech.Abstr., Tech.Educ.Abstr. **Document type:** academic/scholarly publication.
●Also available online.
—BLDSC (0573.593000); SWETS. **CCC.**
  Description: Covers research and key issues of accounting education and training.
  Refereed Serial

657.07 US ISSN 1085-4622
HF5630
▼**ACCOUNTING EDUCATION.** 1996. s-a. $70 to individuals (foreign $90); institutions $145 (foreign $165) (effective 1998). J A I Press Inc., 55 Old Post Rd., No. 2, Box 1678, Greenwich, CT 06836-1678. TEL 203-661-7602. FAX 203-661-0792. E-mail: jai@jaipress.com; URL: http://www.jaipress.com. (In Europe: J A I Press Ltd., 38 Tavistock St., Covent Garden, London WC2E 7PB, England. TEL 44-171-379-8834. FAX 44-171-379-8835) Eds. Bill N. Schwartz, David E. Stout. **Document type:** academic/scholarly publication.
—BLDSC (0573.592700).
  Description: Meets the needs of individuals interested in the education process in the field of accounting.
  Refereed Serial

657 370 US ISSN 0882-956X
ACCOUNTING EDUCATION NEWS. 1973. 6/yr. membership. American Accounting Association, 5717 Bessie Dr., Sarasota, FL 34233-2399. TEL 941-921-7747. FAX 941-923-4093. R&P contact: Mary Cole. **Document type:** newsletter.
●Also available online. Vendor(s): UMI.
—UMI.

657 332 US
ACCOUNTING FOR BANKS. (Issued in 1 vol. with supplements) 1982. irreg. $185. Matthew Bender & Co., Inc., 2 Park Ave., New York, NY 10016. TEL 212-448-2000. E-mail: international@bender. com; URL: http://www.bender.com. Ed. Ken Halajian. (looseleaf format) **Document type:** trade publication.
  Description: Discusses accounting principles applicable to banks within the framework of their operations.

657 350 US
ACCOUNTING FOR GOVERNMENT CONTRACTS: COST ACCOUNTING STANDARDS. (Issued in 1 vol. with supplements) 1981. irreg. $190. Matthew Bender & Co., Inc., 2 Park Ave., New York, NY 10016. TEL 212-448-2000. E-mail: international@bender. com; URL: http://www.bender.com.
  Description: Provides detailed analysis for implementing and complying with cost accounting standards for federal government procurement contracts.

657 350 US
ACCOUNTING FOR GOVERNMENT CONTRACTS: FEDERAL ACQUISITION REGULATION. (Issued in 1 vol. with supplements) 1985. base vol. plus q. updates; CD-ROM version q. $190 for print edition (foreign $200); CD-ROM $80 (foreign $100) (effective 1996). (U.S. General Services Administration) Matthew Bender & Co., Inc., 2 Park Ave., New York, NY 10016. TEL 212-448-2000. E-mail: international@bender.com; URL: http://www.bender. com. (Subscr. to: Superintendent of Documents, U.S. Government Printing Office, Box 371954, Pittsburgh, PA 15250-7954. TEL 202-512-1800. FAX 202-512-2250) (looseleaf format) **Document type:** government publication.
●Also available on CD-ROM.
  Description: Covers all aspects of government contract accounting, with particular emphasis on the Federal Acquisition Regulation.

657 US ISSN 0898-8102
KF320.A2
ACCOUNTING FOR LAW FIRMS. 1988. m. $195. New York Law Publishing Co., 345 Park Ave. S., New York, NY 10010. TEL 212-545-6170. FAX 212-696-1848. URL: http://www.ljx.com. Ed. Mark Hopkins. index. (looseleaf format) **Document type:** newsletter.
  Description: Provides analyses of new and pending statutes, regulations and cases, as well as practical strategies for increasing firms' profitability to law firm partners, chief financial officers, administrators, accountants and financial planners.

657.834 US ISSN 0730-7721
ACCOUNTING FOR LAWYERS. a. $99 (effective 1996). Practising Law Institute, 810 Seventh Ave., New York, NY 10019. TEL 212-824-5700; 800-260-4754. FAX 800-321-0093. E-mail: info@ pli.edu; URL: http://www.pli.edu.

657 363.6 US
ACCOUNTING FOR PUBLIC UTILITIES. 1983. irreg. $185. Matthew Bender & Co., Inc., 2 Park Ave., New York, NY 10016. TEL 212-448-2000. E-mail: international@bender.com; URL: http://www.bender. com. (looseleaf format) **Document type:** trade publication.
  Description: Provides analysis of public utility accounting for anyone involved in rate-making and utility accounting.

657 338 AT ISSN 0155-9982
ACCOUNTING FORUM. 1978. 4/yr. Aus.$45 to individuals; institutions Aus.$55; libraries Aus.$80; students Aus.$30 (effective 1997). University of South Australia, School of Accounting, Faculty of Business and Management, G.P.O. Box 2471, Adelaide, S.A. 5001, Australia. TEL 61-8-3022293. FAX 61-8-3022102. E-mail: Glen.Lehman@UniSA. edu.au. Eds. Glen Lehman, Tony Tinker. adv. contact: Bev Schutt. bk.rev.; cum.index. (back issues avail.) **Indexed:** Aus.P.A.I.S. **Document type:** academic/scholarly publication.
—BLDSC (0573.594500); UMI; UnCover.
  Description: Covers accounting education and practice with regard to accounting theory, practice and policy; small business topics.

657 AT ISSN 1031-3109
ACCOUNTING GUIDANCE RELEASE. 1985. irreg. Aus.$6 per issue. Australian Accounting Research Foundation, 211 Hawthorn Rd., Caulfield, Vic. 3162, Australia. TEL 61-3-95238111. FAX 61-3-95235499. E-mail: standard@aarf.asn. au. (Co-sponsors: Australian Society of Certified Practising Accountants; Institute of Chartered Accountants in Australia) circ. 1,400. **Document type:** newsletter.

657 US ISSN 0148-4184
HF5601
ACCOUNTING HISTORIANS JOURNAL. 1974. s-a. $40 to individuals; institutions $50 (effective 1997). Academy of Accounting Historians, c/o William D. Samson, Culverhouse School of Accountancy, University of Alabama, Tuscaloosa, AL 35487. TEL 205-348-2903. URL: http://nexxus.som.cwru. edu/Accounting. Eds. Barbara Marino, Patti Millsn. R&P contact: Barbara Marino. adv.; bk.rev.; bibl.; index. circ. 900. (back issues avail.) **Indexed:** AAR, Account.Ind. (1977-), Amer.Hist.& Life (1989-), Hist.Abstr. (1989-). **Document type:** academic/scholarly publication.
●Also available online. Vendor(s): UMI.
—BLDSC (0573.595200); SWETS; UMI; UnCover.
  Formerly (until 1977): Accounting Historian.
  Description: Features articles on accounting history.
  Refereed Serial

657 US
ACCOUNTING HISTORIANS NOTEBOOK. s-a. membership. Academy of Accounting Historians, c/o William D. Samson, Culurhouse School of Accountancy, University of Alabama, Tuscaloosa, AR 35487. TEL 205-348-2903. **Document type:** academic/scholarly publication, newsletter.
  Description: Contains short articles and observations on accounting history.

657 AT ISSN 1032-3732
▼**ACCOUNTING HISTORY.** 1996. s-a. Aus.$60 (foreign Aus.$72). Garry Carnegie, Ed. & Pub., c/o School of Accounting and Finance, Faculty of Business and Law, Deakin University, Geelong, Vic. 3217, Australia. TEL 61-3-52272733. FAX 61-3-52272264. E-mail: carnegie@deakin.edu. au. bibl.; charts; illus.; stat.; index. (back issues avail.)
●Also available online.
  Refereed Serial

657 US ISSN 0888-7993
HF5616.U5
ACCOUNTING HORIZONS. 1987. q. $60 to non-members. American Accounting Association, 5717 Bessie Dr., Sarasota, FL 34233. TEL 941-921-7747. FAX 941-923-4093. URL: http://www.rutgers.edu/Accounting/raw/aaa/ publish/aaaind.htm. Ed. Helen Gernon. R&P contact: Mary Cole. **Indexed:** ABI Inform., Account.Ind. (1987-), B.P.I.
—BLDSC (0573.595400); KR SourceOne; SWETS; UMI; UnCover.

BUSINESS AND ECONOMICS — ACCOUNTING

657   MY   ISSN 0126-625X
HF5601
ACCOUNTING JOURNAL. (Text in English) 1971. a. M.$4. University of Malaya, Faculty of Economics & Administration, Lembah Pantai, 59100 Kuala Lumpur, Malaysia. Ed.Bd. adv.; bibl.; charts. circ. 750.

657   UK   ISSN 0959-8022
HF5679   CODEN: ACMTEZ
ACCOUNTING, MANAGEMENT AND INFORMATION TECHNOLOGIES. 1991. q. fl.736($423) (effective 1998). Elsevier Science Ltd., Pergamon, P.O. Box 800, Kidlington, Oxford OX5 1DX, England. TEL 44-1865-843000. FAX 44-1865-843010. E-mail: nlinfo-f@elsevier.nl; usinfo-f@elsevier.com; forinfo-kyf04035@niftyserve.or.jp; URL: http://www.elsevier.nl/. (Subscr. to: Elsevier Science, Regional Sales Office, P.O. Box 211, 1000 AE Amsterdam, Netherlands. TEL 31-20-4853757. FAX 31-20-4853432; Subscr. in the Americas to: Elsevier Science, Regional Sales Office, Box 945, New York, NY 10159-0945. TEL 212-633-3730. FAX 212-633-3680; Subscr. in Australasia and the Far East to: Elsevier Science (Singapore) Pte Ltd, No.1 Temasek Ave., No.17-01 Millenia Tower, Singapore 039192, Singapore. TEL 65-434-3727. FAX 65-337-2230) Ed. Richard J. Boland. index. (also avail. in microform from UMI; back issues avail.) **Document type:** academic/scholarly publication.
—BLDSC (0573.597500); SWETS; UMI. **CCC.**
Description: Offers a forum for research on the interrelations of information technologies with accounting and control systems and with management practices and policies.
Refereed Serial

658   US   ISSN 0749-2928
ACCOUNTING OFFICE MANAGEMENT & ADMINISTRATION REPORT. Abbreviated title: A O M A R. 1983. m. $249 in U.S. & Canada; elsewhere $273. Institute of Management & Administration, Inc., 29 W. 35th St., 5th Fl., New York, NY 10001-2299. TEL 212-244-0360. FAX 212-564-0465. URL: http://www.ioma.com. Ed. Sue Sandler; Pub. Lee Rath. R&P contact: Sofie Kourkoutakis. index. (looseleaf format; back issues avail.) **Document type:** newsletter.
—**CCC.**
Description: Presents strategies for increasing accounting office efficiency and profitability. Offers practical guidance on fees and billing rates, compensation levels and benefits for CPAs and staff, firm performance, benchmarks.

657   UK   ISSN 0361-3682
HF5601
ACCOUNTING, ORGANIZATIONS AND SOCIETY. 1976. 8/yr. fl.1926($1107) (effective 1998). Elsevier Science Ltd., Pergamon, P.O. Box 800, Kidlington, Oxford OX5 1DX, England. TEL 44-1865-843000. FAX 44-1865-843010. E-mail: nlinfo-f@elsevier.nl; usinfo-f@elsevier.com; forinfo-kyf04035@niftyserve.or.jp; URL: http://www.elsevier.nl:80/inca/publications/store/4/8/6/. (Subscr. to: Elsevier Science, Regional Sales Office, P.O. Box 211, 1000 AE Amsterdam, Netherlands. TEL 31-20-4853757. FAX 31-20-4853432; Subscr. in the Americas to: Elsevier Science, Regional Sales Office, Box 945, New York, NY 10159-0945. TEL 212-633-3730. FAX 212-633-3680; Subscr. in Australasia and the Far East to: Elsevier Science (Singapore) Pte Ltd, No.1 Temasek Ave., No.17-01 Millenia Tower, Singapore 039192, Singapore. TEL 65-434-3727. FAX 65-337-2230) Ed. Anthony Hopwood. adv.: B&W page $550, color page $1350; trim 7 1/4 x 9 3/4. abstr.; charts; index. (also avail. in microform from UMI) **Indexed:** Account.& Data Proc.Abstr., Account.Ind. (1976-), Arts & Hum.Cit.Ind., ASCA, BPIA, Bus.Ind., Cont.Pg.Manage., Curr.Cont., Int.Lab.Doc., Manage.Cont., Mid.East: Abstr.& Ind., Risk Abstr., SCIMP (1979-), SSCI, World Bank.Abstr. **Document type:** academic/scholarly publication.
—BLDSC (0573.598000); Genuine Article; SWETS; UMI; UnCover. **CCC.**
Description: Concerned with all aspects of the relationship between accounting and human behavior, organizational structures and processes and the changing social and political environment of the enterprise.
Refereed Serial

637   US
ACCOUNTING PROFESSIONALS PRODUCT NEWS. 1992. bi-m. free. Accounting Professional Product News, Inc., 4210 W. Vickery Blvd., Ft. Worth, TX 76107. TEL 817-738-3371. FAX 817-731-9704. Ed. Hawk Chud. R&P contact: Hawk Chud. adv.: B&W page $2200; trim 9 13/16 x 14 1/4; adv. contact: Hawk Chud. circ. 40,000 (controlled). **Document type:** trade publication.

657 332   AT   ISSN 1030-9616
ACCOUNTING RESEARCH JOURNAL. 1988. s-a. Aus.$30. Royal Melbourne Institute of Technology, Department of Economics and Finance, G.P.O. Box 2476V, Melbourne, Vic. 3001, Australia. E-mail: robertf@bf.rmit.edu.au; URL: http://www.bf.rmit.edu.au/Ecofin.arj.html. Ed. Robert Faff. R&P contact: Robert Faff. adv. contact: Robert Faff. bk.rev.; cum.index. circ. 200. **Document type:** academic/scholarly publication.
—UnCover.
Description: Covers research and practice of accounting, finance, auditing, commercial law and cognate disciplines.
Refereed Serial

657   US   ISSN 0001-4826
HF5601   CODEN: ACRVAS
ACCOUNTING REVIEW. 1926. q. $100 to non-members. American Accounting Association, 5717 Bessie Dr., Sarasota, FL 34233. TEL 941-921-7747. FAX 941-923-4093. URL: http://www.rutgers.edu/Accounting/raw/aaa/publish/aaaind.htm. Ed. Gerry Salamon. R&P contact: Mary Cole. adv. contact: Gordon Cox. bk.rev.; charts; index. circ. 18,500. (also avail. in microform from UMI; reprint service avail. from KTO) **Indexed:** AAR, Account.& Data Proc.Abstr., Account.Ind. (1974-), Anbar, ASCA, ASEAN Manage.Abstr., B.P.I., BPIA, Bus.Ind., C.R.E.J., Child.Bk.Rev.Ind. (1965-), Comput.Abstr., Comput.Lit.Ind., Cont.Pg.Manage., Curr.Cont., High.Educ.Curr.Aware.Bull., Ind.Per.Art.Relat.Law, Intl.Mgmt.Info., J.of Econ.Lit., Manage.Cont., Mgmt.& Market.Abstr., Mid.East: Abstr.& Ind., PROMT, Risk Abstr., SCIMP (1978-), SSCI, World Bank.Abstr.
—BLDSC (0573.700000); KR SourceOne; SWETS; UMI; UnCover.

657   US   ISSN 1043-7940
HF5616.U5
ACCOUNTING STANDARDS. STATEMENTS OF FINANCIAL ACCOUNTING CONCEPTS.* a. Financial Accounting Standards Board, 401 Merritt 7, Box 5116, Norwalk, CT 06856-5116.

657 340   US
ACCOUNTING SYSTEMS FOR LAW OFFICES. (Issued in 1 vol. with supplements) 1978. irreg. $190. Matthew Bender & Co., Inc., 2 Park Ave., New York, NY 10016. TEL 212-448-2000. E-mail: international@bender.com; URL: http://www.bender.com. (looseleaf format)
Description: Provides details on financial and accounting systems for law offices.

657   US   ISSN 1049-5401
HF5601
THE ACCOUNTING SYSTEMS JOURNAL. 1989. s-a. Memphis State University, Fogelman College of Business and Economics, School of Accountancy, Memphis, TN 38152.

657   UK
ACCOUNTING TECHNICIAN. 1981. m. £1.95 per no. (Association of Accounting Technicians) Reed Business Information (Subsidiary of: Reed Elsevier group), Quadrant House, The Quadrant, Sutton, Surrey SM2 5AS, England. TEL 44-181-652-4800. FAX 44-181-652-4748. Ed. Claire Melvin; Pub. Jerry Cosney. R&P contact: Claire Melvin. adv. contact: Gary Eversfield. bk.rev. circ. 82,403. **Document type:** trade publication.
Description: Covers areas of accounting: standards, taxation, public sector, and data management.

657   US   ISSN 1068-6452
HF5679   CODEN: ACCTEJ
ACCOUNTING TECHNOLOGY. 1987. m. (except Feb.-Mar. & Apr.-May combined). Faulkner & Gray, Inc. (New York), 11 Penn Plaza, 17th Fl., New York, NY 10001. TEL 212-967-7000. FAX 212-967-7155. Ed. Ted Needleman. adv.; illus. circ. 20,000. (back issues avail.) **Indexed:** INSPEC (1993-). **Document type:** trade publication.
●Also available online. Vendor(s): UMI.
—BLDSC (0573.702500); AskIEEE; KR SourceOne; UMI; UnCover. **CCC.**
Formerly (until 1993): Computers in Accounting (ISSN 0883-1866)
Description: Covers technology issues for the accounting profession, including hardware, software and office equipment.

657   AT   ISSN 0818-9412
ACCOUNTING THEORY MONOGRAPH. 1982. irreg. price varies. Australian Accounting Research Foundation, 211 Hawthorn Rd., Caulfield, Vic. 3162, Australia. TEL 61-3-95238111. FAX 61-3-95235499. E-mail: standard@aarf.asn.au. (Co-sponsors: Australian Society of Certified Practising Accountants; Institute of Chartered Accountants in Australia) circ. 1,400. **Document type:** monographic series.

657   PH   ISSN 0028-9418
ACCOUNTING TIMES. 1950. m. $21 in Asia (Middle East $23; elsewhere $25). Philippine Institute of Certified Public Accountants, PICPA House, 700 Shaw Blvd., Mandaluyong City, Metro-Manila, Philippines. TEL 63-2-701166. FAX 63-2-796787. Ed. Gayla C. Carreon. adv. contact: Emelita P. Agustin. charts; illus. circ. 27,500.
Formerly (until 1981): Newsette.
Description: Covers news and activities of PICPA, technical advisory on cooperatives and other inquiries related to accountancy.

657   US   ISSN 1044-5714
HF5601
ACCOUNTING TODAY; the newspaper for the accounting professional. 1987. bi-w. (except Apr., Aug.). $96. Faulkner and Gray, Inc. (New York), 11 Penn Plaza, 17th Fl., New York, NY 10001. TEL 212-967-7000. FAX 212-967-7155. URL: http://www.faulknergray.com/account/today.htm. Ed. Rick Telberg. adv.: B&W page $3075, color page $4400. bk.rev.; tr.lit. circ. 32,000. (tabloid format; back issues avail.) **Document type:** newspaper.
●Also available online. Vendor(s): Information Access Co., UMI.
—KR SourceOne; UMI. **CCC.**
Description: Reports the news of the profession, emphasizing the people, organizations, technology, emerging issues and competitive strategies that influence the field's direction.

ACCOUNTING WRITING; A P W C bibliography series. see BUSINESS AND ECONOMICS — *Abstracting, Bibliographies, Statistics*

657   US
ACCREDITATION COUNCIL FOR ACCOUNTANCY AND TAXATION. ACTION LETTER. q. membership. Accreditation Council for Accountancy and Taxation, 1010 N. Fairfax St., Alexandria, VA 22314-1574. TEL 703-549-6400. FAX 703-549-2984. circ. 6,000 (controlled). **Document type:** newsletter.
Formerly: Accreditation Council for Accountancy. Action Letter.

ACTUARIAL UPDATE. see *INSURANCE*

ADMINISTRATIE EN BEHEER. see *RELIGIONS AND THEOLOGY — Protestant*

657   US   ISSN 0882-6110
HF5601
ADVANCES IN ACCOUNTING. (Supplement avail.: Advances in Accounting. Supplement (ISSN 1046-5715)) 1984. a. $73.25 (effective 1998). J A I Press Inc., 55 Old Post Rd., No. 2, Box 1678, Greenwich, CT 06836-1678. TEL 203-661-7602. FAX 203-661-0792. E-mail: jai@jaipress.com. (Addr. in the UK and the rest of Europe: J A I Press Ltd., 38 Tavistock St., Covent Garden, London WC2 7PB, England. TEL 44-171-379-8834. FAX 44-171-379-8835) Ed. Philip Reckers. **Document type:** trade publication.
—BLDSC (0697.220000); UnCover. **CCC.**

BUSINESS AND ECONOMICS — ACCOUNTING

657 US ISSN 1046-5715
HF5601
ADVANCES IN ACCOUNTING. SUPPLEMENT. 1989. irreg. J A I Press Inc., 55 Old Post Rd., No. 2, Box 1678, Greenwich, CT 06836-1678. TEL 203-661-7602. FAX 203-661-0792. E-mail: jai@jaipress.com. (Addr. in UK: J A I Press Ltd., 38 Tavistock Rd., Covent Garden, London WC2E 7PB, England. TEL 44-171-379-8834. FAX 44-171-379-8835) **Document type:** trade publication.

657 003 US
ADVANCES IN ACCOUNTING INFORMATION SYSTEMS. 1992. irreg., vol.4, 1996. $73.25. J A I Press Inc., 55 Old Post Rd., No. 2, Box 1678, Greenwich, CT 06836-1678. TEL 203-661-7602. FAX 203-661-0792. E-mail: jai@jaipress.com. (Addr. in Europe: JAI Press Ltd., 38 Tavistock St., Covent Garden, London WC2E 7PB, England. TEL 44-171-379-8834. FAX 44-171-379-8835) Ed. Steve Sutton. **Document type:** trade publication.

657 US
ADVANCES IN MANAGEMENT ACCOUNTING. 1992. irreg., vol.5, 1996. $73.25. J A I Press Inc., 55 Old Post Rd., No. 2, Greenwich, CT 06830-1678. TEL 203-661-7602. FAX 203-661-0792. E-mail: jai@jaipress.com. (Addr. in the UK: J A I Press Ltd., 38 Tavistock St., Covent Garden, London WC2E 7PB, England. TEL 44-171-379-8834. FAX 44-171-379-8835) Ed. Marc Epstein. **Document type:** academic/scholarly publication.

657 NE ISSN 0928-0685
ADVIES. 1992. 10/yr. fl.175 (effective 1996). (Federatie Advieserende Beroepen) Uitgeverij Fed bv (Subsidiary of: Wolters Kluwer N.V.), Postbus 23, 7400 GA Deventer, Netherlands. TEL 31-570-633155. FAX 31-570-633834. Ed. L.G.M. Stevens. adv. circ. 1,600. (back issues avail.) **Document type:** trade publication.

657 IO ISSN 0002-3892
AKUNTANSI & ADMINISTRASI;* Indonesian journal of accountancy. (Text in English and Indonesian) 1962. m. Rps.3000. Ikatan Akuntan Indonesia, Jalan Tosari 26, Jakarta, Indonesia. Ed. B. Soenasto. adv. circ. 2,000. (processed)

657 336 BE ISSN 0772-6465
ALGEMEEN FISKAAL TIJDSCHRIFT; informatie voor de belastingkundige en de administratieve en financiele managers. Short title: A F T. French edition: Revue Generale de Fiscalite (ISSN 0772-6473) (Supplement avail.: Newsletter) (Text in Flemish) 1949. m. (except Jul. & Aug.) 8586 BEF. C E D Samsom (Subsidiary of: Wolters Samsom Belgie n.v.), Kouterveld 14, B-1831 Diegem, Belgium. TEL 32-2-7231111. Ed. A. Tiberghein. index.
Description: Details trends in national and local taxation.

657 US ISSN 0732-6815
HF5601
AMERICAN ACCOUNTING ASSOCIATION. COLLECTED ABSTRACTS OF THE ANNUAL MEETING. 1975. a. American Accounting Association, Paul F. Gerhardt Bldg., 5717 Bessie Dr., Sarasota, FL 34233. TEL 941-921-7747. FAX 941-923-4093. R&P contact: Mary Cole. illus.
—BLDSC (3300.550000).
Formerly (until 1980): American Accounting Association. Collected Papers of the Annual Meeting (ISSN 0270-6059)

657 US
AMERICAN GROUP DIRECTORY OF SPECIALIZED KNOWLEDGE. irreg. American Group of C P A Firms, 1910 N. Highland Ave., Ste. 210, Lombard, IL 60148. TEL 708-916-0300. **Document type:** directory.

657 US
AMERICAN GROUP OF C P A FIRMS. CHRONICLE. (Certified Public Accountant) irreg. American Group of C P A Firms, 1910 S. Highland Ave., Ste. 210, Lombard, IL 60148. TEL 708-916-0300. **Document type:** trade publication.

657.84 US
AMERICAN INSTITUTE OF CERTIFIED PUBLIC ACCOUNTANTS. PUBLIC OVERSIGHT BOARD. ANNUAL REPORT. 1979. a. American Institute of Certified Public Accountants, Public Oversight Board, 1 Station Pl., Stamford, CT 06902-6800. TEL 203-353-5300. URL: http://www.aicpa.org. Ed. Jerry D. Sullivan. circ. 8,000. **Document type:** corporate report.

657 US
APPLYING G A A P AND G A A S. (Generally Accepted Accounting Principles and Generally Accepted Accounting Standards) (Issued in 2 base vols. with supplements) 1985. irreg. $310. Matthew Bender & Co., Inc., 2 Park Ave., New York, NY 10016. TEL 212-448-2000. FAX 518-462-3788. E-mail: international@bender.com; URL: http://www.bender.com. (looseleaf format)
Description: Provides information on how to handle all aspects of financial reporting, including debt, equity, operations, income taxes, investments, pensions and leases. Covers the interrelationship of accounting and auditing.

657 378 UK ISSN 0263-1768
APPROVED COURSES FOR ACCOUNTANCY EDUCATION. 1981. a. Board of Accreditation of Educational Courses, P.O. Box 686, Central Milton Keynes, London MK9 2PB, England.
Formerly: Degree Studies and the Accountancy Profession.

ART LAW & ACCOUNTING REPORTER. see *LAW*

657 US ISSN 0883-7384
ASSET. 1952. m. $25. Missouri Society of Certified Public Accountants, 275 N. Lindbergh Blvd., Ste. 10, St. Louis, MO 63141. TEL 314-997-7966. FAX 314-997-2592. Ed. Kristen M. Bequette. adv. circ. 7,066. **Indexed:** Account.Ind. (1974-).
Document type: newsletter.
Description: Covers news of the accounting profession, educational seminars and technical information.

657 333.33 US ISSN 1083-6322
ASSISTED HOUSING FINANCIAL MANAGEMENT INSIDER. bi-m. $195 (effective 1996). Brownstone Publishers, Inc., 149 Fifth Ave., New York, NY 10010-6801. TEL 212-473-8200. FAX 212-473-8786. Ed. George Schaeffer; Pub. John M. Striker.
Formerly: Assisted Housing Accounts and Audits Insider.
Description: Explains how to comply with regulatory STET requirements for accounting and auditing for federally assisted housing.

657 US
ASSOCIATED ACCOUNTING FIRMS INTERNATIONAL NEWSLETTER. 1969. s-a. membership. Associated Accounting Firms International, 1000 Connecticut Ave., N.W., Ste. 1006, Washington, DC 20036-5302. TEL 202-463-7900. FAX 202-296-0741. E-mail: aafi@aafi.org; URL: http://www.aafi.org. Ed. Gregory Hickman. R&P contact: Gregory Hickman. circ. 3,500. (controlled). **Document type:** newsletter.
Description: Provides a summary of the association's meetings, plans for the future, and updates on members and the profession.

657 FR
ASSOCIATION DES COMPTABLES. BULLETIN. q. Association des Comptables, Societe Mutualiste Professionnelle, 81 rue St. Lazare, 75009 Paris, France.

657 US
ASSOCIATION OF INSOLVENCY ACCOUNTANTS NEWSLETTER. q. membership. Association of Insolvency Accountants, 31360 Via Colinas, Ste. 108, Westlake Village, CA 91362-3916. TEL 818-889-8317. FAX 818-889-5107. adv.; bk.rev. circ. 620. **Document type:** newsletter.

ATTORNEY - C P A. see *LAW — Corporate Law*

ATTORNEY'S HANDBOOK OF ACCOUNTING. see *LAW — Corporate Law*

657 US
ATTORNEY'S REPORT. q. membership only. Associated Regional Accounting Firms, 3700 Crestwood Pky., N.W., Duluth, GA 30136-5599. TEL 770-279-4560. **Document type:** newsletter.

657 IE ISSN 0961-124X
AUDIT; the audit automation magazine. 1990. bi-m. I£95 in E.U.; elsewhere I£117/($187) (effective 1997). Cork Publishing Ltd., 19 Rutland St., Cork, Ireland. TEL 353-21-313855.
FAX 353-21-313496. Ed. Ken Ebbage; Pub. Brian O'Kane. R&P contact: Brian O'Kane. adv. contact: Terry Homan. bk.rev.; circ. 500 (paid). **Document type:** trade publication.
—BLDSC (1789.645000). **CCC.**
Description: Addresses the issues raised by the application of technology to the audit process.
Refereed Serial

657 UK ISSN 0958-367X
AUDIT BRIEFING. 1989. m. £79 (foreign £92). Tolley Publishing Co. Ltd., Tolley House, 2 Addiscombe Rd., Croydon, Surrey CR9 5AF, England. TEL 44-181-686-9141. FAX 44-181-686-3155. Ed. Claire Melvin. bk.rev. **Document type:** trade publication.

657 AT ISSN 0816-4746
AUDIT GUIDE. 1985. irreg. price varies. Australian Accounting Research Foundation, 211 Hawthorn Rd., Caulfield, Vic. 3162, Australia. TEL 61-3-95238111. FAX 61-3-95235499. E-mail: standard@aarf.asn.au. (Co-sponsors: Australian Society of Certified Practising Accountants; Institute of Chartered Accountants in Australia) circ. 1,000. **Document type:** monographic series.

657 AT ISSN 1034-3423
AUDIT MONOGRAPH. 1990. irreg. price varies. Australian Accounting Research Foundation, 211 Hawthorn Rd., Caulfield, Vic. 3162, Australia. TEL 61-3-95238111. FAX 61-3-95235499. E-mail: standard@aarf.asn.au. (Co-sponsors: Australian Society of Certified Practising Accountants; Institute of Chartered Accountants in Australia) circ. 1,000. **Document type:** monographic series.

657.6 US ISSN 0278-0380
HF5667
AUDITING. 1981. s-a. $25 to non-members. American Accounting Association, 5717 Bessie Dr., Sarasota, FL 34233. TEL 941-921-7747. FAX 941-923-4093. URL: http://www.indiana.edu/!audsec/newjc.html. Ed. Theodore J. Mock. adv. contact: Mary Cole. circ. 2,000. **Indexed:** Account.Ind. (1981-), ASCA, Curr.Cont., SSCI.
—BLDSC (1789.680000); Genuine Article; SWETS; UMI.
Description: Contains technical articles as well as news and reports on current activities of the association.
Refereed Serial

657 AT ISSN 0818-8122
AUDITING DISCUSSION PAPER. 1986. irreg. price varies. Australian Accounting Research Foundation, 211 Hawthorn Rd., Caulfield, Vic. 3162, Australia. TEL 61-3-95238111. FAX 61-3-95235499. E-mail: standard@aarf.asn.au. (Co-sponsors: Australian Society of Certified Practising Accountants; Institute of Chartered Accountants in Australia) circ. 1,000. **Document type:** monographic series.

657 AT
AUDITING GUIDANCE STATEMENTS. 1985. irreg. Aus.$6 per issue. Australian Accounting Research Foundation, 211 Hawthorn Rd., Caulfield, Vic. 3162, Australia. TEL 61-3-95238111.
FAX 61-3-95235499. E-mail: standard@aarf.asn.au. (Co-sponsors: Australian Society of Certified Practising Accountants; Institute of Chartered Accountants in Australia) circ. 1,000.
Formerly: Auditing Guidance Relsease (ISSN 1031-3117)

657 IR
AUDITOR. q. 77 Ferdowsi Ave., N., Teheran, Iran.

ULRICH'S INTERNATIONAL PERIODICALS DIRECTORY 1998

BUSINESS AND ECONOMICS — ACCOUNTING

657 US ISSN 1063-4053
HF5686.C7
AUDITOR-TRAK. 1992. q. $492 (Canada $522; elsewhere $547) (effective Aug. 1996). Strafford Publications, Inc., Specialized Information Services, 590 Dutch Valley Rd., N.E., Drawer 13729, Atlanta, GA 30324. TEL 404-881-1140. FAX 404-881-0074. E-mail: editors@straffordpub.com. Ed. Brian P. McGregory; Pub. Richard M. Ossoff. (back issues avail.) **Document type:** trade publication, academic/scholarly publication.
  Description: Allows for the tracking of SEC auditor changes. Includes comprehensive gains and losses analysis and additional commentary on many changes.

657 AT ISSN 0004-8631
HF5601 CODEN: AUACAC
AUSTRALIAN ACCOUNTANT. (Supplement avail.: Australian Society of Certified Practising Accountants. Annual Report) 1936. m. (except Jan.) (effective 1997). Aus.$75 (foreign Aus.$95). Australian Society of Certified Practising Accountants, 170 Queen St., Melbourne, Vic. 3000, Australia. TEL 61-3-96069606. FAX 61-3-96708901. (Subscr. addr.: G.P.O. Box 2820 AA, Melbourne, Vic. 3000, Australia) Ed. Derek Parker. adv.; bk.rev.; index. circ. 90,146. (back issues avail.) **Indexed:** AAR, ABI Inform., Account.& Data Proc.Abstr., Account.Ind. (1974-), AESIS, Anbar, Aus.P.A.I.S. **Document type:** trade publication.
  ●Also available online. Vendor(s): UMI.
  —BLDSC (1796.700000); SWETS; UMI; UnCover. **CCC.**
  Incorporates: Financial Forum.
  Description: Accounting, finance, investment, taxation, legal issues, financial reporting, auditing, professional development, and general articles of interest to accountants.

657 AT ISSN 1037-5570
AUSTRALIAN ACCOUNTING RESEARCH FOUNDATION. ACCOUNTING RESEARCH STUDY. 1970. irreg. price varies. Australian Accounting Research Foundation, 211 Hawthorn Rd., Caulfield, Vic. 3162, Australia. TEL 61-3-95238111. FAX 61-3-95235499. E-mail: standard@aarf.asn.au. (Co-sponsors: Australian Society of Certified Practising Accountants; Institute of Chartered Accountants in Australia) Ed.Bd. circ. 1,000. **Document type:** academic/scholarly publication, monographic series.
  Formerly: Accountancy Research Foundation, Melbourne. Accounting and Auditing Research Committee. Research Studies (ISSN 0084-5884)

657 AT ISSN 0818-9404
AUSTRALIAN ACCOUNTING RESEARCH FOUNDATION. DISCUSSION PAPER (ACCOUNTING). 1979. irreg. price varies. Australian Accounting Research Foundation, 211 Hawthorn Rd., Caulfield, Vic. 3162, Australia. TEL 61-3-95238111. FAX 61-3-95235499. E-mail: standard@aarf.asn.au. (Co-sponsors: Australian Society of Certified Practising Accountants; Institute of Chartered Accountants in Australia) circ. 1,000. **Document type:** monographic series.

657 AT ISSN 1035-6908
HF5601
AUSTRALIAN ACCOUNTING REVIEW. Abbreviated title: A A R. 1991. 2/yr. Aus.$35 to non-members; institutions and libraries Aus.$40 (effective 1997). Australian Society of Certified Practising Accountants, 170 Queen St., Melbourne, Vic. 3000, Australia. TEL 61-3-96069606. FAX 61-3-96708901. (Subscr. addr.: G.P.O. Box 2820 AA, Melbourne, Vic. 3000, Australia) (Co-sponsor: Monash University, Victoria, Faculty of Business and Economics) Ed. Linda M. English. adv. contact: Jan Fraser. circ. 3,000. **Document type:** academic/scholarly publication.
  —BLDSC (1796.710000).
  Description: Resource for academics, students and all those accountants interested in the theoretical side of their profession.
  Refereed Serial

657 AT ISSN 1034-3717
AUSTRALIAN ACCOUNTING STANDARD. 1989. irreg. Aus.$6 per issue. Australian Accounting Research Foundation, 211 Hawthorn Rd., Caulfield, Vic. 3162, Australia. TEL 61-3-95238111. FAX 61-3-95235499. E-mail: standard@aarf.asn.au. (Co-sponsors: Australian Society of Certified Practising Accountants; Institute of Chartered Accountants in Australia) circ. 1,400.

657 AT
▼**AUSTRALIAN ACCOUNTING STANDARDS SOURCE MATERIALS.** 1995. q. C C H Australia Ltd., P.O. Box 230, North Ryde, N.S.W. 2113, Australia. TEL 61-1-300300224. FAX 61-1-330306224. (looseleaf format)
  Description: Contains the full text of Australian Accounting Standards, Statements of Accounting Concepts, Accounting Guidance Releases, Exposure Drafts, AASB Accounting Standards and International Accounting Standards.

657 AT
AUSTRALIAN ACCOUNTS PREPARATION MANUAL. (In 4 vols.) 1985. m. C C H Australia Ltd., P.O. Box 230, North Ryde, N.S.W. 2113, Australia. TEL 61-1-300300224. FAX 61-1-300306224. (looseleaf format)
  Description: Designed to answer, in practical manner, problems in relation to preparing and presenting financial statements for all types of entities. includes accounting standards, legislation, checklist, precedents and year-end information.

657 AT
AUSTRALIAN AUDIT MANUAL. 1993. s-a. C C H Australia Ltd., P.O. Box 230, North Ryde, N.S.W. 2113, Australia. TEL 61-1-300300224. FAX 61-1-300306224. (looseleaf format)
  Description: Aims at assisting practitioners in the proper conduct of an audit for a variety of reporting and non-reporting entities, including superannuation plans.

657 AT
AUSTRALIAN SOCIETY OF CERTIFIED PRACTISING ACCOUNTANTS. ANNUAL REPORT. (Supplement to: Australian Accountant) a. members only. Australian Society of Certified Practising Accountants, 170 Queen St., Melbourne, Vic. 3000, Australia. TEL 61-3-96069606. FAX 61-3-96708901. **Document type:** corporate report.
  Formerly: Australian Society of Accountants. Annual Report.

657 SW ISSN 1103-5765
B F N INFORMERAR. 1987. irreg. (2-5/yr.). SEK 275 (effective 1996). (Bokfoereningsnaemnden) Fritzes, S-106 47 Stockholm, Sweden. TEL 46-8-6909090. FAX 46-8-205021. Ed. Soerin Wallin. **Document type:** government publication.
  Description: Publishes information on new accounting standards.

657 AU ISSN 0005-3465
B Z; Fachzeitschrift fuer Wirtschaft-Steuer-Datentechnik. 1945. m. S.1628. Verlag Dr. Herta Ranner, Zeismannsbrunngasse 1, A-1070 Vienna, Austria. TEL 43-1-935387. adv.; bk.rev. **Document type:** bulletin.

657 BE ISSN 0772-4853
BALANS; nieuwsbrief voor accountancy en financieel management. French Edition: Bilan (ISSN 0772-4861) (Text in Dutch) 1982. s-m. 7230 BEF (in Europe 7380 BEF; elsewhere 7550 BEF). Biblo N.V., Brasschaatsteenweg 308, 2920 Kalmthout, Belgium. Ed. Jan Van Dijck. index. (also avail. in microfiche; back issues avail.) **Document type:** newsletter.

657 SW ISSN 0346-8208
BALANS. 1975. m. SEK 545 (effective 1991). Foereningen Autoriserade Revisorer (FAR), P.O. Box 6417, S-113 82 Stockholm, Sweden.

657 332 US ISSN 0894-3958
HG1707
BANK ACCOUNTING & FINANCE. 1987. q. $195 (foreign $225) (effective 1996). Institutional Investor Journals, 488 Madison Ave., New York, NY 10022. TEL 212-224-3185. FAX 212-224-3527. Ed. Claire Greene. adv.; B&W page $1900; color page $2500. **Indexed:** Account.Ind. (1987-).
  —BLDSC (1861.753500); SWETS; UMI. **CCC.**
  Description: Peer research articles on all financial, legislative, and corporate aspects of operating a bank.

BANK AUDITING & ACCOUNTING REPORT. see BUSINESS AND ECONOMICS — Banking And Finance

BANK INTERNAL AUDIT: A WORKING GUIDE TO REGULATORY COMPLIANCE. see BUSINESS AND ECONOMICS — Banking And Finance

BANKRUPTCY LAW REVIEW. see LAW — Corporate Law

657 150 US ISSN 1050-4753
HF5601
BEHAVIORAL RESEARCH IN ACCOUNTING. 1989. a. $20. American Accounting Association, 5717 Bessie Dr., Sarasota, FL 34233. TEL 941-921-7747. FAX 941-923-4093. Ed. Jacob G. Birnberg. R&P contact: Mary Cole. (also avail. in microform from UMI; back issues avail.)
  —BLDSC (1877.780000); SWETS; UMI.
  Description: Publishes original research related to accounting and how it affects and is affected by individuals and organizations.

657 CC
BEIJING CAIKUAI/BEIJING ACCOUNTING. (Text in Chinese) bi-m. Beijing Caizheng Xuehui, 6 Chegongzhuang Dajie, Xicheng-qu, Beijing 100044, People's Republic of China. TEL 8314043. Ed. Gao Xuezeng.

BESTUUR EN BELEID V Z W. see BUSINESS AND ECONOMICS

657 YU ISSN 0354-6195
BILANSIRANJE I POSLOVNE FINANSIJE; casopis za unapredenje organizacije preduzeca, racuvodstva i poslovnih finasija. Short title: BilPof. m.? P.P. Bilanisranje Preduzeca, Nisefora Niepsa 9, Belgrade, Yugoslavia. Ed. Olivera Mijatovic.

657 GW ISSN 0930-0597
BILANZ- UND BUCHHALTUNG; Zeitschrift fuer Rechnungswesen und Steuern. 1955. 11/yr. DM.138 (foreign DM.160) (effective 1997). Betriebswirtschaftlicher Verlag Dr. Th. Gabler GmbH, Abraham-Lincoln-Str. 46, 65189 Wiesbaden, Germany. TEL 49-611-7878129. FAX 49-611-7878423. Ed.Bd. adv.; bk.rev.; abstr.; stat.; index. circ. 11,166. **Document type:** trade publication.
  —CCC.
  Formerly: Bilanz- und Buchhaltungspraxis (ISSN 0006-2359)

657 GW ISSN 0940-8851
BILANZBUCHHALTER; Zeitschrift fuer Fuehrungskraefte im Finanz- und Rechnungswesen und Controlling. 1977. m. DM.92 (foreign DM.184; students DM.62) (effective 1996). (Bundesverband der Bilanzbuchhalter e.V.) Verlag C.H. Beck, 80791 Munich, Germany. TEL 49-89-38189-338. FAX 49-89-38189-398. adv.; B&W page DM.2500, color page DM.4375; trim 260 x 186. bk.rev. circ. 6,500. (back issues avail.) **Document type:** trade publication.
  Description: Covers management of financial and accounting affairs.

657 US
BOLETIN INTERAMERICANO DE CONTABILIDAD/INTERAMERICAN BULLETIN. 1968. bi-m. $50 includes Revista Interamericana. Asociacion Interamericana de Contabilidad - Interamerican Accounting Association, c/o Exec. Dir. Victor Abreu Paez, Fontainebleau Exec. Center, 275 Fountainebleau Blvd., Ste. 245, Miami, FL 33172. TEL 305-225-1991. FAX 305-225-2011. circ. 2,000 (paid). **Document type:** bulletin.

657 II
BOMBAY CHARTERED ACCOUNTANT JOURNAL. (Supplements accompany some issues) (Text in English) 1958. m. Rs.500 (effective 1995). Bombay Chartered Accountants' Society, Churchgate Mansion, 1st Fl., A Road, Churchgate, Bombay 400 020, India. TEL 91-22-2043359. Eds. A.A. Thakkar, Nayan Parikh. adv.; bk.rev.; index. circ. 9,000. **Document type:** trade publication.

657.2 US
BOOKKEEPER'S TAX LETTER. 1991. m. $131.40. ProPub Inc., Box 102, Wyckoff, NJ 07481-0102. TEL 201-447-6485. FAX 201-447-9356. Pub. Randy Cochran. **Document type:** newsletter.

657 US
BOTTOM LINE (LOUISVILLE). vol.23, 1970. bi-m. membership. Kentucky Society of Certified Public Accountants, 1735 Alliant Ave., Louisville, KY 40299. TEL 502-266-5272. Ed. Dianna Ott. adv. contact: Diana Ott. charts; illus. circ. 4,400. **Indexed:** AAR. **Document type:** trade publication.
  Formerly (until Aug. 1979): Kentucky Accountant (ISSN 0023-009X)

BUSINESS AND ECONOMICS — ACCOUNTING

657 001.6 621.381   US   ISSN 0279-1889
BOTTOMLINE (AUSTIN). 1982. bi-m. $50 (free to members, educational institutions and libraries.). International Association of Hospitality Accountants, Box 203008, Austin, TX 78720-3008. TEL 512-346-5680. FAX 512-346-5760. Eds. Jennifer Carr, Audra Johnson. R&P contact: Audra Johnson. adv. contact: Audra Johnson. bk.rev. circ. 3,600. **Indexed**: Art.Hosp.& Tour., Lod.Restr.& Tour.Ind. **Document type**: trade publication.
—BLDSC (2264.027000); UMI; UnCover.
Description: Provides information to accountants, controllers and financial officers on hospitality accounting, management, technology, law and more.

657   US   ISSN 0897-3482
HD30.27
BOWMAN'S ACCOUNTING REPORT. 1987. m. $215 (foreign $275). Hudson Sawyer Professional Services Marketing, Inc., 905 E. Paces Ferry Rd., Ste. 2425, Atlanta, GA 30326-9868. TEL 404-264-9977. FAX 404-264-9968. E-mail: awbowman@cris.com. Ed. Arthur W. Bowman. R&P contact: Arthur Bowman. bk.rev. (looseleaf format; also avail. in microform from UMI; back issues avail.) **Indexed**: Account.Ind. (1987-). **Document type**: newsletter.
—UMI.
Description: News, analysis and commentary of events, trends, strategies, and politics in the accounting profession, analysis of fiscal performance and ranking of one hundred largest US firms and Big Six firms.

657   UK   ISSN 0890-8389
HF5601
BRITISH ACCOUNTING REVIEW. bi-m. £203 (effective 1998). (British Accounting Association) Academic Press Ltd. (Subsidiary of: Harcourt Brace & Company Ltd.), 24-28 Oval Rd., London NW1 7DX, England. TEL 44-171-267-4466. FAX 44-171-482-2293. TELEX 25775 ACPRES G. E-mail: apsubs@acad.com; URL: http://www.hbuk.co.uk/ap/bar; http://www.europe.idealibrary.com/. (Subscr. to: Harcourt Brace & Company Ltd., Foots Cray High St., Sidcup, Kent DA14 5HP, England. TEL 44-181-300-3322) Eds. M.J. Scherer, A. Stark. R&P contact: Catherine John. adv. contact: Nik Screen. bk.rev. (reprint service avail. from SCH,SWZ) **Indexed**: Account.Ind. (1987-), Cont.Pg.Manage. **Document type**: academic/scholarly publication.
●Also available online.
—BLDSC (2286.864000); SWETS. **CCC**.
Description: Provides a forum for communication throughout the world between members of the academic and professional communities concerned with the research and teaching, at degree level and above, of accounting, finance, and cognate disciplines.

BUILDING SOCIETY ANNUAL ACCOUNTS MANUAL. see BUILDING AND CONSTRUCTION

657   RU   ISSN 0321-0154
BUKHGALTERSKII UCHET. 1937. m. $259 (effective 1998). (Ministerstvo Finansov) Izdatel'stvo Finansy i Statistika, Ul. Chernyshevskogo, 7, 101000 Moscow, Russia. (Dist. by: Mezhdunarodnaya Kniga, B. Yakimanka 39, 117049 Moscow, Russia) index.

657   FR   ISSN 0220-2352
BULLETIN COMPTABLE & FINANCIER. 1978. m. 380 F. (effective 1997). Editions Francis Lefebvre, 42 rue de Villiers, 92300 Levallois, France. TEL 41-05-22-00. FAX 41-05-22-30.

657   FR   ISSN 0984-9114
BULLETIN OFFICIEL DE LA COMPTABILITE PUBLIQUE. 1981. m. 1100 F. Imprimerie Nationale, B.P. 514, 59505 Douai Cedex, France. TEL 27-93-70-70. FAX 27-93-70-96. TELEX 120 389 F.

657 346   US   ISSN 0885-1034
KF1357.A15
BUSINESS ACCOUNTING FOR LAWYERS NEWSLETTER; summary, analysis, and application of current accounting concepts in the practice of law. 1984. 8/yr. $110. Practising Law Institute, 810 Seventh Ave., New York, NY 10019. TEL 212-824-5700; 800-260-4754. FAX 800-321-0093. E-mail: info@pli.edu; URL: http://www.pli.edu. Ed. Samuel P. Gunther. (reprint service avail. from UMI) **Document type**: newsletter.

657   US
BUSINESS ADVISORY CLIENT NEWSLETTER. q. C P A Associates International, Inc., Meadows Office Complex, 201 Rte. 17 N., Rutherford, NJ 07070-2574. TEL 212-804-8686.
Description: Promotes role of members as consultants to business.

BUSINESS MONEY. see BUSINESS AND ECONOMICS — Banking And Finance

657 346   UK
BUTTERWORTHS ACCOUNTING INTELLIGENCE. m. £85. Butterworth & Co. (Publishers) Ltd., Part of the Reed Elsevier group, Halsbury House, 35 Chancery Ln., London WC2A 1EL, England. TEL 44-171-400-2500. FAX 44-171-400-2842.
Description: Compiles the latest information on accounting, financial reporting, auditing and relevant company law issues.

657   CN   ISSN 0317-6878
HF5601   CODEN: CAMADJ
C A MAGAZINE. (Chartered Accountant) French edition (ISSN 0832-9117) 1911. 10/yr. Can.$47 (foreign Can.$72) (effective 1997); newsstand price: Can.$4.75. Canadian Institute of Chartered Accountants, 277 Wellington St., W., Toronto, Ont. M5V 3H2, Canada. TEL 416-204-3222. FAX 416-204-3409. TELEX 062-22835. URL: http://www.cica.ca/new/index.htm. Ed. Christian Bellavance; Pub. Randall T. Pearce. adv.: B&W page Can.$2980, color page Can.$3975; trim 8 1/8 x 10 7/8; adv. contact: Louis D'Souza. bk.rev.; charts; illus.; index; circ. 68,000 (paid). (also avail. in microform from UMI; back issues avail.; reprint service avail. from UMI) **Indexed**: AAR, ABI Inform., Abstr.Health Care Manage.Stud., Account.Ind. (1974-), Anbar, B.P.I., BPIA, Bus.Ind., Can.B.P.I., Can.Per.Ind., Data Process.Dig., Ind.Can.L.P.L., INSPEC (1974-), Manage.Cont., P.A.I.S., PSI, Tr.& Indus.Ind., World Bank.Abstr. **Document type**: trade publication.
—BLDSC (2943.183000); AskIEEE; KR SourceOne; SWETS; UMI; UnCover. **CCC**.
Incorporates: C I C A Dialogue (ISSN 0045-4982); Formerly: Canadian Chartered Accountant (ISSN 0008-316X)
Description: Covers developments in areas of accounting, auditing, financial management, tax legislation and EDP.

657   UK   ISSN 1352-9021
HF5601
C A MAGAZINE. (Chartered Accountant's) 1897. m. £23 (foreign £58); newsstand price: £2. Institute of Chartered Accountants of Scotland, 27 Queen St., Edinburgh EH2 1LA, Scotland. TEL 44-131-225-5673. FAX 44-131-225-3813. URL: http://www.commarts.com/cm_home.html. Ed. John Hatfield; Pub. David McMurray. R&P contact: John Hatfield. adv.: B&W page £1939, color page £2723; trim 297 x 210; adv. contact: Laura Houston. illus.; index. circ. 23,419. (also avail. in microform from UMI,WDS; back issues avail.) **Indexed**: AAR, Account.& Data Proc.Abstr., Account.Ind. (1974-), BPIA, Bus.Ind., Cont.Pg.Manage., Excerp.Med., INSPEC (1991-), Intl.Mgmt.Info., Manage.Cont., Tr.& Indus.Ind. **Document type**: trade publication.
—AskIEEE; KR SourceOne; SWETS; UMI; UnCover. **CCC**.
Incorporates (in 1990): Accountants Magazine (ISSN 0001-4761)
Description: Contains features on technology, personal finance, management, legal developments, and accountancy.

657 382   CN
C G A - CANADA RESEARCH FOUNDATION. STUDY PAPERS. (Text in English, French) 1981. irreg. price varies. Certified General Accountants' Association of Canada, C G A - Canada Research Foundation, 700-1188 W. Georgia St., Ste. 700, Vancouver, BC V6A 4A2, Canada. TEL 604-669-3555. FAX 604-689-5845. circ. 700. (back issues avail.) **Document type**: monographic series, academic/scholarly publication.
Formerly: Canadian Certified General Accountants' Research Foundation. Study Papers.

657   CN   ISSN 0318-742X
HF5616.C2
C G A MAGAZINE. 1967. 11/yr. Can.$30 (foreign Can.$45). Certified General Accountants' Association of Canada, 1188 W. Georgia St., Ste. 700, Vancouver, BC V6E 4A2, Canada. TEL 604-669-3555. FAX 604-689-5845. Ed. Lesley Wood; Pub. Lesley Wood. adv.: B&W page Can.$2465, color page Can.$3645; trim 8 3/8 x 10 7/8; adv. contact: Gordon W. Smart. bk.rev.; illus. circ. 48,000. (also avail. in microform from MML) **Indexed**: Account.Ind. (1974-), Can.B.P.I., Can.Per.Ind.
—BLDSC (3128.541000); SWETS.
Former titles: Certified General Accountant (ISSN 0009-0425); Canadian Certified Accountant (ISSN 0008-3151)
Description: Covers accounting, auditing, taxation, computers and law for Canadian professional accountants and financial executives.

657   CN   ISSN 0068-8983
C I C A HANDBOOK. (Editions in English, French) 1968. irreg. Can.$65 (base vol.) Can.$48 (supplements). Canadian Institute of Chartered Accountants, 277 Wellington St. W., Toronto, ON M5V 3H2, Canada. TEL 416-977-3222. FAX 416-977-8585. circ. 84,000. (looseleaf format) **Document type**: trade publication.

657   UK
C I M A QUESTIONS AND SUGGESTED ANSWERS. 1987. s-a. (in 4 vols.). £7.50 per vol. Chartered Institute of Management Accountants, 63 Portland Pl., London W1N 4AB, England. TEL 44-171-917-9229. FAX 44-171-323-1487. E-mail: pubs@cima.org.uk. R&P contact: R. Hawkins. adv. contact: T. Walter. (back issues avail.) **Document type**: academic/scholarly publication.
Description: Offers assistance to students studying for their accounting certification exams.
Refereed Serial

657 658   CN
HF5601   CODEN: CMAAEA
C M A MAGAZINE. (Certified Management Accountant); for better management decisions. (Text in English, French) 1926. 10/yr. Can.$40($45) (foreign Can.$60) (effective 1997). Society of Management Accountants of Canada, 120 King St. W., Box 176 M.P.O., Hamilton, ON L8N 3C3, Canada. TEL 905-525-4100. FAX 905-525-4533. Pub. Dan R. Hicks. adv. contact: Kevin Graham. bk.rev.; charts; illus.; index. circ. 75,000. (also avail. in microform from UMI; reprint service avail. from UMI) **Indexed**: ABI Inform., Account.& Data Proc.Abstr., Account.Ind. (1974-), Anbar, ASEAN Manage.Abstr., BPIA, Can.B.P.I., Can.Per.Ind., Data Process.Dig., INSPEC (1985-), Key to Econ.Sci., Manage.Cont., Pers.Manage.Abstr., PROMT, SSCI, Tr.& Indus.Ind., Work Rel.Abstr. **Document type**: trade publication.
●Also available online. Vendor(s): Information Access Co.
—AskIEEE; KR SourceOne; SWETS; UMI; UnCover. **CCC**.
Former titles (until June 1995): C M A (ISSN 0831-3881); Cost and Management (ISSN 0010-9592)
Description: Information for practitioners of accounting and management.

C P A ADMINISTRATOR'S REPORT & MANAGER'S REPORT; the resource successful CPA firms use in firm administration. see BUSINESS AND ECONOMICS — Personnel Management

657   US
C P A ASSOCIATES. UPDATE. (Certified Public Accountant) bi-m. membership. C P A Associates International, Inc., Meadows Office Complex, 201 Rte. 17 N., Rutherford, NJ 07070-2574. TEL 212-804-8686. circ. 1,600.
Description: Updates professional staff of members on relevant association changes and developments.

BUSINESS AND ECONOMICS — ACCOUNTING

336 338 US
C P A CLIENT BULLETIN. 1976. m. $182 without imprinting; with imprinting $280 (membership only). American Institute of Certified Public Accountants, Harborside Financial Ctr., 201 Plaza Three, Jersey City, NJ 07311-3881. TEL 201-938-3201; 800-862-4272. FAX 201-938-3329. URL: http://www.aicpa.org. (Alt addr.: 1211 Ave. of the Americas, New York, NY 10036. TEL 212-596-6200) Ed. Anne Waggenbrenner. circ. 950,000 (controlled). (also avail. in diskette format) **Document type:** newsletter, bulletin.
● Also available online. Vendor(s): UMI.
Description: Covers the range of topics a CPA would discuss with small business and tax clients.

657 336 US ISSN 0741-3610
C P A DIGEST; ideas for the busy C P A. 1979. m. $194 (effective 1997). Harcourt Brace Professional Publishing, 525 B St., Ste 1900, San Diego, CA 92101-4495. TEL 619-699-6716. FAX 619-699-6593. Ed. David Cottle; Pub. Ken Rethmeier. R&P contact: Jenna Lake. TEL 619-699-6265. bk.rev.; charts; illus.; stat.; tr.lit.; index. (back issues avail.) **Document type:** newsletter.
Incorporates: Accounting Practices and Regulation (ISSN 8756-3061); C P A Seminar Report.
Description: Covers tax, accounting, auditing, finance, economics, computing, and practice management.

657 US ISSN 1052-7362
HF5681.B2
C P A FIRM PRACTICE MANUAL (YEAR). (Certified Public Accountant) a. $139.95 (overseas $237.95) (effective 1995). Warren, Gorham & Lamont, One Penn Plaza, New York, NY 10119. TEL 212-971-5000. FAX 212-971-5113. (Subscr. to: The Park Square Bldg., 31 St. James Ave., Boston, MA 02116-4112. TEL 800-950-1207) **Document type:** trade publication.

657 US ISSN 1069-7403
C P A GOVERNMENT AND NONPROFIT REPORT. (Certified Public Accountant) m. $216 (effective 1997). Harcourt Brace Professional Publishing, 525 B St., Ste. 1900, San Diego, CA 92101-4495. TEL 619-699-6716. FAX 619-699-6593. Ed. Rhett Harrell. **Document type:** newsletter.
Description: Provides guidance on governmental and nonprofit accounting and auditing.

657 US ISSN 1047-580X
C P A HEALTH NICHE ADVISOR. 1989. m. $214 (effective 1997). Harcourt Brace Professional Publishing, 525 B St., Ste. 1900, San Diego, CA 92101-4495. TEL 619-699-6716. FAX 619-699-6593. Ed. Rick Hammonds; Pub. Ken Rethmeier. R&P contact: Jenna Lake. TEL 619-699-6265. (back issues avail.) **Document type:** newsletter.
Description: Provides information and specialized techniques and strategies for CPAs seeking to develop a health care practice.

657 IE
C P A JOURNAL OF ACCOUNTANCY. 1941. q. Institute of Certified Public Accountants in Ireland, 9 Ely Pl., Dublin 2, Ireland. TEL 353-1-6767353. FAX 353-1-6612367. Ed. Deirdre McDonnell. adv. contact: Deirdre McDonnell. bk.rev. circ. 2,900. **Document type:** trade publication.
Formerly: C P A Newsletter.
Description: Features include legislation, finance and banking, insurance, taxation, education, computing, business and management.

657 US ISSN 0094-792X
HF5601
C P A LETTER; a news report to members. 1920. s-m. (except July-Aug. & Feb.-Mar. combined); membership. American Institute of Certified Public Accountants, Public Relations - Communications, Harborside Financial Center, 201 Plaza Three, Jersey City, NJ 07311-9801. TEL 201-938-3796; 800-862-4272. FAX 800-329-1112. E-mail: egoldstein@aicpa.org; URL: http://www.aicpa.org/pubs/cpaltr/index.htm. (Alt. addr.: AICPA, 1211 Ave. of the Americas, New York, NY 10036. TEL 212-596-6200) Ed. Ellen J. Goldstein. bk.rev.; bibl. circ. 290,000. **Document type:** trade publication, trade publication.
● Also available online. Vendor(s): UMI.
—UMI.

C P A LITIGATION SERVICE COUNSELOR. see *LAW*

657 658 US ISSN 0894-1815
C P A MANAGING PARTNER REPORT; management news for accounting executives. 1986. m. $297 (Canada $327; elsewhere $352) (effective Oct. 1996). Strafford Publications, Inc., Specialized Information Services, 590 Dutch Valley Rd., N.E., Drawer 13729, Atlanta, GA 30324-0729. TEL 404-881-1141. FAX 404-881-0074. E-mail: custserv@straffordpub.com. Ed. Suzanne Verity; Pub. Richard M. Ossoff. (looseleaf format; back issues avail. **Document type:** newsletter.
Description: Provides partners with problem-solving tactics and management methods that can help the firm maintain stability and enhance profitability as it strives to achieve short-term and long-range goals.

C P A MARKETING REPORT. see *BUSINESS AND ECONOMICS — Marketing And Purchasing*

C P A PERSONNEL REPORT. see *BUSINESS AND ECONOMICS — Personnel Management*

657 US ISSN 1080-5745
C P A PROFITABILITY MONTHLY. m. $185 (foreign $132) (effective 1997). Harcourt Brace Professional Publishing, 525 B St., Ste.1900, San Diego, CA 92101-4495. TEL 619-699-6716. FAX 619-699-6593. Ed. Allan Boress; Pub. Ken Rethmeier. R&P contact: Jenna Lake. TEL 619-699-6265. charts; illus. **Document type:** newsletter.
Former titles: C P A Profitability Report; (until 1995): C P A Quality Client Service (ISSN 1047-5842)
Description: Provides advice on improving the quality of client service, those helping CPA firms to retains their existing clients and gain new ones.

C P A SOFTWARE NEWS. see *BUSINESS AND ECONOMICS — Computer Applications*

C R I DISCUSSION PAPERS. (Centre for the Study of Regulated Industries) see *PUBLIC ADMINISTRATION*

C R I PROCEEDINGS SERIES. (Centre for the Study of Regulated Industries) see *PUBLIC ADMINISTRATION*

C R I REGULATORY BRIEFS. (Centre for the Study of Regulated Industries) see *PUBLIC ADMINISTRATION*

657 346 US ISSN 0884-7282
C S C P A NEWSLETTER. 1961. 10/yr. membership. Connecticut Society of Certified Public Accountants, 179 Allyn St., Ste. 201, Hartford, CT 06103-1491. TEL 860-549-3596. FAX 860-525-1153. URL: http://www.cs-cpa.org. Ed. Mark Zampino. R&P contact: Mark Zampino. adv. contact: Lisa Trescot. (looseleaf format) **Document type:** newsletter.
Description: Provides members with news of events of interest to the profession of accountancy in Connecticut. Covers legislation, ethics, regulations, firm news; and profiles members in public service.

657 CC ISSN 1001-3172
CAIWU YU KUAIJI. (Text in Chinese) 1978. m. Zhongguo Caizheng Zazhishe, C-27 Wanshou Lu, Beijing 100036, People's Republic of China. TEL 813952. Ed. Qian Duling.

657 US
CALIFORNIA ACCOUNTANCY ACT WITH RULES AND REGULATIONS. 1901. quadrennial. $4.50. Department of Consumer Affairs, Board of Accountancy, 2000 Evergreen St., Ste. 250, Sacramento, CA 95815-3832. TEL 916-263-3680. FAX 916-263-3975. Ed. Carol Sigmann; Pub. Carol Sigmann. circ. 45,000 (controlled). **Document type:** government publication.

657 CN ISSN 0713-357X
HF5616.C2
CANADIAN INSTITUTE OF CHARTERED ACCOUNTANTS. UNIFORM FINAL EXAMINATION REPORT. French edition (ISSN 0820-0386) (Editions in English and French) a. price varies. Canadian Institute of Chartered Accountants, 277 Wellington St. W., Toronto, ON M5V 3H2, Canada. TEL 416-977-3222. FAX 416-977-8585. circ. 10,000. **Document type:** trade publication.
Former titles: Canadian Institute of Chartered Accountants. Uniform Final Examination Handbook; Canadian Institute of Chartered Accountants. Intermediate and Final Examinations.
Description: Contains UFE questions and approaches to answering the uniform final examination, as well as the report of the Board of Governors to the Provincial Institutes of Chartered Accountants.

657 IE ISSN 0306-2406
HF5601
CERTIFIED ACCOUNTANT. 1905. m. £42 in U.K. and Ireland (students £25); elsewhere £85 (students £50) (effective 1997); newsstand price: $3.50. (Chartered Association of Certified Accountants) Cork Publishing Ltd., Granary House, 19 Rutland St., Cork, Ireland. TEL 353-21-313855. FAX 353-21-313496. E-mail: mail@cork-publishing.com; bokane@cork-publishing.com; URL: http://www.silk.ie//cork/certacc.html. Ed. Brian O'Kane. R&P contact: Brian O'Kane. adv. contact: Terry Homan. bk.rev.; illus.; stat.; index. circ. 59,450. (also avail. in microform) **Indexed:** Account.& Data Proc.Abstr., Account.Ind. (1974-), Anbar, ASEAN Manage.Abstr., BPIA, World Bank.Abstr. **Document type:** trade publication.
—BLDSC (3120.192000); SWETS.
Formerly: Certified Accountants Journal (ISSN 0009-0417)
Description: Covers news, features and developments of interest to certified accounts in the U.K. and elsewhere, as well as association news.

657 CN
CERTIFIED MANAGEMENT ACCOUNTANTS SOCIETY OF BRITISH COLUMBIA. UPDATE. bi-m. free. Certified Management Accountants of British Columbia, 1575 - 650 W. Georgia St., Box 11548, Vancouver, BC V6B 4W7, Canada. TEL 604-687-5891; 800-663-9646. FAX 604-687-6688. E-mail: cmabc@cmabc.com; URL: http://www.cmabc.com. Ed. Heather Treleaven; Pub. Heather Treleaven. R&P contact: Heather Treleaven. adv. contact: Heather Treleaven. (back issues avail.) **Document type:** newsletter.
Formerly: Society of Management Accountants of British Columbia. Update.
Description: For certified management accountants in British Columbia

657 AT ISSN 1037-6267
CHARTAC ACCOUNTANCY NEWS. 1976. m. Aus.$397. Professional Information Pty. Ltd., 196 Drummond St., Carlton, Vic. 3053, Australia. TEL 61-3-662-2822. FAX 61-3-662-3191. Ed. Ashley Gordon McKeon. (back issues avail.) **Document type:** newsletter.
Formerly: Chartac Accounting Report (ISSN 0814-8074)

657 AT
CHARTAC TAX PLANNING NEWS. 1982. m. Aus.$397. Professional Information Pty. Ltd., 196 Drummond St., Carlton, Vic. 3053, Australia. TEL 61-3-662-2822. FAX 61-3-662-3191. Ed. Ashley Gordon McKeon. (looseleaf format; back issues avail.) **Document type:** newsletter.
Former titles: Chartac Tax Practice Ideas; Chartac Tax Planning News (ISSN 1037-6275); Chartac Taxation Report (ISSN 0814-8120); Tax Action Report.

657 AT ISSN 1035-0748
HF5601
CHARTER. 1930. 11/yr. Aus.$60 (foreign Aus.$70) (effective 1996). Institute of Chartered Accountants in Australia, Box 3921, Sydney, N.S.W. 2001, Australia. TEL 61-2-92901344. FAX 61-2-92623953. Ed. Ian Hay. R&P contact: Ian Hay. adv. contact: Craig Hodges. bk.rev.; tr.lit.; index. circ. 36,500. Indexed: AAR, Account.& Data Proc.Abstr., Account.Ind. (1974-), Anbar, Aus.P.A.I.S., Comput.Rev.
—BLDSC (3129.969300); SWETS; UMI; UnCover.
 Former titles (until 1990): Chartered Accountant; (until 1989): Chartered Accountant in Australia (ISSN 0009-1898)
 Description: Provides topical, in-depth coverage on areas of concern to the business professional.

657 II ISSN 0009-188X
HF5601
CHARTERED ACCOUNTANT. (Text and summaries in English) 1952. m. Rs.400 (foreign $75). Institute of Chartered Accountants of India, Indraprastha Marg, P.O. Box 7100, New Delhi 2, India. TEL 91-11-3312055. TELEX 031-62236 CICA IN. Ed. K.M. Agarwal. adv.; bk.rev.; index; circ. 28,000 (paid); 75,000 (controlled). Indexed: Account.Ind. (1974-). **Document type**: trade publication.
—BLDSC (3129.973000); UnCover.
 Description: Provides information on corporate finance, corporate practices, economy, and news of interest to accounting, finance professionals.

657 CE
CHARTERED ACCOUNTANTS. (Text in English, Sinhalese, Tamil) 1966. s-a. Rs.85. Institute of Chartered Accountants of Sri Lanka, 30A Malalasekera Mawatha, Colombo 7, Sri Lanka. Ed.Bd. adv.; bk.rev. circ. 1,000. (tabloid format) Indexed: Account.Ind. (1978-).
 Former titles (until 1987): Institute of Chartered Accountants of Sri Lanka. Journal (ISSN 1015-0005); (until 1977): Accountant; (until 1973): Accountant Journal (ISSN 0001-4702)

657 NZ ISSN 1172-9929
HF5601
CHARTERED ACCOUNTANTS JOURNAL OF NEW ZEALAND. 1922. m. NZ.$77.70. Institute of Chartered Accountants, Cigna House, 40 Mercer St., Wellington, New Zealand. TEL 64-4-4747842. FAX 64-4-4998033. E-mail: angus__m@icanz.co.nz. Ed. Angus McLeod. R&P contact: Angus McLeod. adv.; bk.rev.; bibl.; charts; illus.; index. circ. 13,000. Indexed: Account.& Data Proc.Abstr., Account.Ind. (1974-), Anbar, B.P.I. **Document type**: trade publication.
—BLDSC (3129.976950); KR SourceOne; UnCover. CCC.
 Formerly: Accountants' Journal (ISSN 0001-4745)
 Refereed Serial

657 UK
CHARTERED INSTITUTE OF MANAGEMENT ACCOUNTANTS. ADVANCED MANAGEMENT ACCOUNTING & FINANCE SERIES. irreg. £7.95 per vol. Academic Press Ltd. (Subsidiary of: Harcourt Brace & Company Ltd.), 24-28 Oval Rd., London NW1 7DX, England. TEL 44-171-267-4466. FAX 44-171-482-2293. TELEX 2775 ACPRES G. (Orders to: C.I.M.A., Publishing Sales Department, 63 Portland Pl., London W1N 4AB, England. TEL 44-171-917-9229. FAX 44-171-631-5309; Or: Harcourt Brace & Company Ltd., Foots Cray High St., Sidcup, Kent DA14, England. TEL 44-181-300-3322. FAX 44-181-309-0807) Ed. David Otley. (back issues avail.) **Document type**: monographic series, trade publication.
 Description: Treats a specific area of management accounting in depth and aims to assist undergraduate and postgraduate students in their courses and certification.

657 UK
CHARTERED INSTITUTE OF MANAGEMENT ACCOUNTANTS. FINANCIAL SKILLS SERIES. 1994. irreg. price varies. (Chartered Institute of Management Accountants) Kogan Page Ltd., 120 Pentonville Rd., London N1 9JN, England. TEL 44-171-278-0433. FAX 44-171-837-6348. TELEX 263088 KOGAN G. (Orders to: C.I.M.A., Publishing Sales Department, 63 Portland Pl., London W1N 4AB, England. TEL 44-171-917-9229. FAX 44-171-631-5309) R&P contact: Linda Batman. **Document type**: monographic series.
 Description: Provides up-to-the-minute advice on a variety of specific occupational skills.

657 UK
CHARTERED INSTITUTE OF MANAGEMENT ACCOUNTANTS. FRAMEWORK SERIES IN ACCOUNTING. 1983. irreg. price varies. Chartered Institute of Management Accountants, 63 Portland Pl., London W1N 4AB, England. TEL 44-171-917-9229. FAX 44-171-323-1487. (back issues avail.) **Document type**: monographic series.
 Formerly: Institute of Cost and Management Accountants. Framework Series in Accounting.
 Description: Contains news of accounting from various industries and commercial sectors.

657 UK
CHARTERED INSTITUTE OF MANAGEMENT ACCOUNTANTS. OCCASIONAL PAPERS SERIES. (Subseries of: Research Studies Series) irreg. price varies. Chartered Institute of Management Accountants, 63 Portland Pl., London W1N 4AB, England. TEL 44-171-917-9229. FAX 44-171-323-1487. (back issues avail.) **Document type**: monographic series.
 Formerly: Institute of Cost and Management Accountants. Occasional Papers Series.
 Description: Findings of research carried out under the auspices of the Chartered Institute of Management Accountants Research and Technical Committee.

657 UK
CHARTERED INSTITUTE OF MANAGEMENT ACCOUNTANTS. PROFESSIONAL HANDBOOK SERIES. irreg. price varies. Butterworth - Heinemann, Part of the Reed Elsevier group, Linacre House, Jordan Hill, Oxford OX2 8DP, England. TEL 44-1865-310366. FAX 44-1865-310898. TELEX 8311 BHPOXF G. (Orders to: C.I.M.A., Publishing Sales Department, 63 Portland Pl., London W1N 4AB, England. TEL 44-171-917-9229. FAX 44-171-631-5309; Or: Elsevier Science Ltd., P.O. Box 800, Kidlington, Oxford OX5 1DX, England. TEL 44-1865-843000. FAX 44-1865-843010; Orders in N. America to: Elsevier Science, 660 White Plains Rd., Tarrytown, NY 10591-5153. TEL 914-524-9200. FAX 914-333-2444) (back issues avail.) **Document type**: monographic series, trade publication.
 Description: Helps management accountants keep abreast of key developments in the profession.

657 UK
CHARTERED INSTITUTE OF MANAGEMENT ACCOUNTANTS. RESEARCH STUDIES. irreg. price varies. Chartered Institute of Management Accountants, 63 Portland Pl., London W1N 4AB, England. TEL 44-171-917-9229. FAX 44-171-323-1487. **Document type**: monographic series.

657 UK
CHARTERED INSTITUTE OF PUBLIC FINANCE AND ACCOUNTANCY. CONFERENCE HANDBOOK. 1890. a. membership. Chartered Institute of Public Finance and Accountancy, 3 Robert St., London WC2N 6BH, England. TEL 44-171-543-5600. FAX 44-171-543-5700. circ. controlled.

657 UK
CHARTERED INSTITUTE OF PUBLIC FINANCE AND ACCOUNTANCY. MEMBERS' YEARBOOK (YEAR). a. membership. Chartered Institute of Public Finance and Accountancy, 3 Robert St., London WC2N 6BH, England. TEL 44-171-543-5600. FAX 44-171-543-5700.

657 US ISSN 1056-134X
HF5686.O5
CHECKLIST FOR DEFINED BENEFIT PENSION PLANS AND ILLUSTRATIVE FINANCIAL STATEMENTS. 1990. a. American Institute of Certified Public Accountants, Harborside Financial Ctr., 201 Plaza Three, Jersey City, NJ 07311-9801. TEL 201-938-3796; 800-862-4272. FAX 201-329-1112. URL: http://www.aicpa.org. (Alt. addr.: 1211 Ave. of the Americas, New ork, NY 10036. TEL 212-596-6200) **Document type**: bulletin.

657 692.8 US ISSN 1056-1331
HF5686.B7
CHECKLIST SUPPLEMENT AND ILLUSTRATIVE FINANCIAL STATEMENTS FOR CONSTRUCTION CONTRACTORS. 1990. a. American Institute of Certified Public Accountants, Harborside Financial Ctr., 201 Plaza Three, Jersey City, NJ 07311-9801. TEL 201-938-3796; 800-862-4272. FAX 201-329-1112. URL: http://www.aicpa.org. (Alt. addr: 1211 Ave. of the Americas, New York, NY 10036. TEL 212-596-6200) **Document type**: bulletin.

657 332 US ISSN 1056-5183
HG1708
CHECKLISTS AND ILLUSTRATIVE FINANCIAL STATEMENTS FOR BANKS. 1989. a. American Institute of Certified Public Accountants, Harborside Financial Ctr., 201 Plaza Three, Jersey City, NJ 07311-9801. TEL 201-938-3796; 800-862-4272. FAX 201-329-1112. URL: http://www.aicpa.org. (Alt. addr.: 1211 Ave. of the Americas, New York, NY 10036. TEL 212-596-6200) **Document type**: trade publication.
 Formerly (until 1989): Disclosure Checklists and Illustrative Financial Statements for Banks (ISSN 1046-428X)

657 US ISSN 1055-9558
HF5686.C7
CHECKLISTS AND ILLUSTRATIVE FINANCIAL STATEMENTS FOR CORPORATIONS. 1990. a. American Institute of Certified Public Accountants, Harboside Financial Ctr., 201 Plaza Three, NJ 07311-9801. TEL 201-938-3796; 800-862-4272. FAX 201-329-1112. URL: http://www.aicpa.org. (Alt. addr.: 1211 Ave. of the Americas, New York, NY 10036. TEL 212-596-6200) **Document type**: trade publication.

657 334 US ISSN 1056-0572
HF5686.C92
CHECKLISTS AND ILLUSTRATIVE FINANCIAL STATEMENTS FOR CREDIT UNIONS. 1990. a. American Institute of Certified Public Accountants, Harborside Financial Ctr., 201 Plaza Three, Jersey City, NJ 07311-9801. TEL 201-938-3796; 800-862-4272. FAX 201-329-1112. URL: http://www.aicpa.org. (Alt. addr.: 1211 Ave. of the Americas, New York, NY 10036. TEL 212-596-6200) **Document type**: trade publication.

657 332 US ISSN 1056-0580
HF5686.C495
CHECKLISTS AND ILLUSTRATIVE FINANCIAL STATEMENTS FOR FINANCE COMPANIES. 1990. a. American Institute of Certified Public Accountants, Harborside Financial Ctr., 201 Plaza Three, Jersey City, NJ 07311-9801. TEL 201-938-3796; 800-862-4272. FAX 201-329-1112. URL: http://www.aicpa.org. (Alt. addr.: 1211 Ave. of the Americas, New York, NY 10036. TEL 212-596-6200) **Document type**: trade publication.

657.3 360 US ISSN 1059-2679
HF5686.N56
CHECKLISTS AND ILLUSTRATIVE FINANCIAL STATEMENTS FOR NONPROFIT ORGANIZATIONS. 1989. irreg. American Institute of Certified Public Accountants, Harborside Financial Ctr., 201 Plaza Three, Jersey City, NJ 07311-3881. TEL 201-938-3796; 800-862-4272. FAX 201-329-1112. URL: http://www.aicpa.org. (Alt addr.: 1211 Ave. of the Americas, New York, NY 10036. TEL 212-596-6200) **Document type**: trade publication.
 Formerly (until 1990): Disclosure Checklists and Illustrative Financial Statements for Nonprofit Organizations (ISSN 1046-4271)

657 336 US
CLIENT TAX NEWSLETTER. s-a. American Group of C P A Firms, 1910 S. Highland Ave., Ste. 210, Lombard, IL 60148. TEL 708-916-0300. **Document type**: newsletter.

336.2 658.153 US
CLIENT'S MONTHLY ALERT; monthly roundup of significant business & tax developments. 1971. m. Faulkner and Gray, Inc. (New York), 11 Penn Plaza, 17th Fl., New York, NY 10001. TEL 212-967-7000. FAX 212-967-7155. Ed. Richard Kantz. circ. 400.
 Description: For small practices to major accounting firms to help them build and strengthen their accounting practice.

BUSINESS AND ECONOMICS — ACCOUNTING

657.450285 US ISSN 0738-4270
COM - A N D. (Computer Audit News and Developments) 1983. 6/yr. $70 (foreign $85) (effective 1997). Management Advisory Publications, 57 Greylock Rd., Box 81151, Wellesley Hills, MA 02181. TEL 617-235-2895. Ed. J.F. Kuong. **Document type:** trade publication.
Description: Analysis of developments in computer technology and its impact on auditing procedures for audit managers, auditors, EDP auditors, security and computer control experts. Also of use to information security and systems managers who must review their computer systems.

657 UK
COMPANY ACCOUNTANT. 1928. bi-m. £20 (foreign £22.90) (effective 1997). The Institute of Company Accountants, 40 Tyndalls Park Rd., Bristol BS8 1PL, England. TEL 44-117-973-8261. FAX 44-117-923-8292. Ed. B.T. Banks. R&P contact: B.T. Banks. adv. contact: J.S. Slade. bk.rev. circ. 10,000. **Indexed:** Account.Ind. (1977-).
Document type: trade publication, academic/scholarly publication.
—BLDSC (3363.734000).
Incorporates: Accountants Record (ISSN 0954-8106)

COMPENSATION IN THE ACCOUNTING - FINANCIAL FIELD. see *BUSINESS AND ECONOMICS — Labor And Industrial Relations*

657 FR
COMPTABILITE ET MECANOGRAPHIE. (Includes 3 annual supplements) 11/yr. 14 rue de la Somme, 94000 Cachan, France. Ed. Jean Deit.

COMPUTER ACCOUNTING LETTER. see *BUSINESS AND ECONOMICS — Computer Applications*

COMPUTER AUDIT UPDATE. see *COMPUTERS — Computer Security*

COMPUTER DIGEST AND DATA PROCESSING. see *COMPUTERS — Electronic Data Processing*

657 336 US
CONSTRUCTION ACCOUNTING MANUAL. base vol. (plus a. supplement). $160.95 (overseas $235.95) (effective 1995). Warren, Gorham & Lamont, One Penn Plaza, New York, NY 10119. TEL 212-971-5000. FAX 212-971-5113. (Subscr. to: The Park Square Bldg., 31 St. James Ave., Boston, MA 02116-4112. TEL 800-950-1207) Eds. John L. Callan, Hugh L. Rice. (looseleaf format) **Document type:** trade publication.
Description: Provides accounting professionals in the construction industry with accounting, auditing, tax, and financial guidance.

657 US
CONSTRUCTION CLIENT NEWSLETTER. q. C P A Associates International, Inc., Meadows Office Complex, 201 Rte. 17 N., Rutherford, NJ 07070-2574. TEL 212-804-8686. **Document type:** newsletter.
Description: Focuses on services for members' clients.

657 CL
CONTABILIDAD, TEORIA Y PRACTICA. 1986. q. Esc.4000. Universidad de Chile, Facultad de Ciencias Economicas y Administrativas, Av. Ranacagua 257, Santiago, Chile. TEL 56-2-2220704. FAX 56-2-2220309. Ed. Jorge Nino.

657 MX ISSN 0186-1042
CONTADURIA Y ADMINISTRACION. 1957. q. Mex.$80 (effective 1997). Universidad Nacional Autonoma de Mexico, Facultad de Contaduria y Administracion, Apartado Postal 70-287, Edificio de la Direccion, 2o. Piso, Cub. 21, Circuito Exterior, Ciudad Universitaria, 04510 Mexico, D.F., Mexico. TEL 52-5-6228396. FAX 52-5-6161355. E-mail: publica@server.contad.unam.mx. Ed. Arturo Diaz Alonso. charts; stat. (back issues avail.)
Formerly (until 1972): Contabilidad Administracion (ISSN 0010-7212)
Description: Publishes original articles about accounting, management and computer applications on those fields.

657 CN ISSN 0823-9150
CONTEMPORARY ACCOUNTING RESEARCH. (Text in English; abstracts in French) 1984. q. $75 to individuals; institutions $90 (effective 1997). Canadian Academic Accounting Association, 223 Scurfield Hall, Faculty of Management, University of Calgary, Calgary, AB T2N 1N4, Canada. TEL 403-220-8517. FAX 403-282-0095. E-mail: CARProduction@compuserve.com; URL: http://www.tcel.com/~car/ads/aos.htm. Eds. Jerry Feltham, Dan Simunic; Pub. Jane Flower. R&P contact: Jane Flower. adv. contact: Jane Flower. bk.rev.; circ. 1,400 (paid). (also avail. in microform from UMI; reprint service avail. from SWZ) **Indexed:** Account.Ind. (1984-). **Document type:** academic/scholarly publication.
—BLDSC (3425.168950); SWETS; UMI; UnCover. **CCC.**
Description: Presents scholarly and practical research in the field of accounting.
Refereed Serial

657 694 US ISSN 1058-9260
CONTRACTOR'S BUSINESS MANAGEMENT REPORT. 1991. m. $249 in U.S. & Canada; elsewhere $273. Institute of Management & Administration, Inc., 29 W. 35th St., 5th Fl., New York, NY 10001-2299. TEL 212-244-0360. FAX 212-564-0465. URL: http://www.ioma.com. Ed. Kneeland Godfrey; Pub. Lee Rath. R&P contact: Sofie Kourkoutakis. index. (looseleaf format; back issues avail.) **Document type:** newsletter.
—**CCC.**
Description: Offers practical guidance on salary levels for management staff, construction bonds, purchasing equipment.

657 UK
CONTROLLER'S BUSINESS ADVISOR. a. $116.45 (overseas $175.45) (effective 1995). Warren Gorham Lamont, One Penn Plaza, New York, NY 10119. TEL 212-971-5000. (Subscr. to: The Park Square Bldg., 31 St. James Ave., Boston, MA 02116-4112. TEL 800-950-1207) **Document type:** trade publication.

657 US ISSN 0895-2787
THE CONTROLLER'S REPORT. 1986. m. $249 in U.S. & Canada; elsewhere $273. Institute of Management & Administration, Inc., 29 W. 35th St., 5th Fl., New York, NY 10001-2299. TEL 212-244-0360. FAX 212-564-0465. URL: http://www.ioma.com. Ed. Tim Harris; Pub. Perry Patterson. R&P contact: Sofie Kourkoutakis. index. (looseleaf format; back issues avail.) **Document type:** newsletter.
—**CCC.**
Incorporates: Building Corporate Cash.
Description: Contains actionable strategies for corporate controllers, including cost benchmarks broken down by industry, region and company size. Exclusive surveys describe cost-cutting measures for workers' compensation, 401(k) plans.

657 US ISSN 8756-5676
CONTROLLERS UPDATE. 1985. m. $75. Institute of Management Accountants, 10 Paragon Dr., Montvale, NJ 07645-1760. TEL 201-573-9000. FAX 201-573-8185. Ed. Karen Sanders. bk.rev.; tr.lit. circ. 2,000. (back issues avail.)
●Also available online. Vendor(s): UMI.
—UMI. **CCC.**

657 NE ISSN 1380-3344
CONTROLLERSVIZIER. 1989. 4/yr. fl.120 (effective 1996). (Vereniging van Registercontrollers) Kluwer Bedrijfswetenschappen B.V. (Subsidiary of: Wolters Kluwer N.V.), Postbus 23, 7400 GA Deventer, Netherlands. TEL 31-5700-48999. FAX 31-5700-11504. (Subscr. to: Intermedia bv, Postbus 4, 2400 MA Alphen aan den Rijn, Netherlands. TEL 31-172-466321. FAX 31-172-435527) **Document type:** trade publication.

657 334 US ISSN 0010-8391
COOPERATIVE ACCOUNTANT. 1947. q. $60 (foreign $70). National Society of Accountants for Cooperatives (NSAC), 6320 Augusta Dr., Ste. 800, Springfield, VA 22150. TEL 703-569-3088. FAX 703-569-0235. Ed. James L. Evans. index. circ. 2,000. **Indexed:** AAR, Account.Ind. (1974-).
—UnCover.
Description: For accountants, auditors, bankers, attorneys and others actively involved in the financial planning and management of cooperative businesses.

657 US ISSN 0279-6163
COORDINATOR (MEMPHIS). 1953. m. $12 to non-members. American Society of Women Accountants, 1255 Lynnfield Rd., Ste. 257, Memphis, TN 38119-7235. TEL 901-680-0470. FAX 901-680-0505. Ed. Allison Conte. adv.: B&W page $500. bk.rev. circ. 7,500. **Document type:** newsletter.

657 IE ISSN 0791-2471
HF5686.C7
CORPORATE ACCOUNTING INTERNATIONAL. 10/yr. I£599. Lafferty Publications Ltd., The Tower, IDA Enterprise Centre, Pearse St., Dublin 2, Ireland. TEL 353-1-6718022. FAX 353-1-6718520. E-mail: cvserv@lafferty.ie; URL: http://www.unm.lafferty.co.uk. (US subscr. to: 420 Lexington Ave., Ste. 1745, New York, NY 10170. TEL 212-557-6726) Ed. Ciaran Hancock. R&P contact: David Barr. **Document type:** trade publication.
Description: Provides news on developments and trends in corporate accounting, reporting, and auditing worldwide.

657 US ISSN 0899-0174
HF5686.C7
CORPORATE CONTROLLER (NEW YORK, 1988). 1988. bi-m. $115 (foreign $140). Faulkner & Gray, Inc. (New York), 11 Penn Plaza, 17th Fl., New York, NY 10001. TEL 212-967-7000. FAX 212-967-7155. Ed. Pam Goett. adv.: B&W page $1300, color page $2175; trim 8 1/2 x 10 7/8. circ. 1,200. **Indexed:** Account.Ind. (1988-).
—UMI.
Description: Shows how successful companies use today's most advanced accounting systems, cost control programs and new auditing procedures.

657 US
HG4001
CORPORATE CONTROLLER (NEW YORK, 1997). 1983. q. $125 in U.S. and Canada; elsewhere $162 (effective 1997). Warren, Gorham & Lamont, One Penn Plaza, New York, NY 10119. TEL 212-971-5000. FAX 212-971-5113. (Subscr. to: The Park Square Bldg., 31 St. James Ave., Boston, MA 02116-4112. TEL 800-950-1207) circ. 15,000. (also avail. in microform from UMI) **Document type:** trade publication.
—BLDSC (3472.060755); KR SourceOne; SWETS; UMI; UnCover. **CCC.**
Former titles (until 1996): Small Business Controller (ISSN 1053-766X); (until 1990): Financial Manager (New York) (ISSN 1040-0842); (until 1988): Corporate Accounting (ISSN 0745-5119)
Description: Offers practical business guidance for increasing efficiency, controlling costs, and improving profitability.

CORPORATE MONEY; the newsletter of corporate financings and transactions. see *BUSINESS AND ECONOMICS — Banking And Finance*

657 US ISSN 0162-1165
COST ACCOUNTING STANDARDS GUIDE. 1972. m. $320. C C H Incorporated, 2700 Lake Cook Rd., Riverwoods, IL 60015. TEL 847-267-7000; 800-835-5224. FAX 800-224-8299.
—**CCC.**

COST ENGINEERS' NOTEBOOK. see *ENGINEERING*

657 SZ
COURRIER DU COMPTABLE. (Text in French) bi-m. Society of Swiss Accountants, Av. Victor Ruffy 34, CH-1012 Lausanne, Switzerland. TEL 021-6521837. Ed. Claude Montandon. circ. 2,000.

CREDIT UNION ACCOUNTANT. see *BUSINESS AND ECONOMICS — Banking And Finance*

657 US
CREDIT UNION AUDITOR. q. membership only. Associated Regional Accounting Firms, 3700 Crestwood Pky., N.W., Duluth, GA 30136-5599. TEL 770-279-4560. **Document type:** newsletter.

657　　　　　　UK　ISSN 1045-2354
HF5601
CRITICAL PERSPECTIVES ON ACCOUNTING; an international journal for social and organizational accountability. 1990. bi-m. £103($169) to individuals; institutions £227 (effective 1998). Academic Press Ltd. (Subsidiary of: Harcourt Brace & Company Ltd.), 24-28 Oval Rd., London NW1 7DX, England. TEL 44-171-267-4466. FAX 44-171-482-2293. TELEX 25775 ACPRES G. E-mail: apsubs@acad.com; URL: http://www.hbuk.co.uk/ap/cpa; http://www.europe.idealibrary.com/. (Subscr. to: Harcourt Brace & Company Ltd., Foots Cray High St., Sidcup, Kent DA14 5HP, England. TEL 44-181-300-3322. FAX 44-181-309-0807) Eds. David Cooper, A.M. Tinker. R&P contact: Catherine John. adv. contact: Nik Screen. (reprint service avail. from SWZ) **Indexed:** Account.Ind. (1990-). **Document type:** academic/scholarly publication.
●Also available online.
—BLDSC (3487.457100); SWETS; UnCover. **CCC**.
    Description: Provides a forum for the growing number of accounting researchers and practitioners who realize that conventional theory and practice is ill suited to the challenges of the modern environment, and that accounting practices and corporate behavior are inextricably connected with many allocative, distributive, social, and ecological problems of our era.
    Refereed Serial

657 086　　　　　　US
LA CUENTA. q. membership. American Association of Hispanic C P A's, 19726 E. Colima Rd., Ste. 270, Rowland Heights, CA 91748. Ed. John Hernandez. **Document type:** newsletter.

657 332.1　　　　　　US
CURRENT ISSUES IN THE FINANCIAL SERVICES INDUSTRIES. 1983. a. free. Ernst & Young, 787 Seventh Ave., New York, NY 10019. TEL 212-773-6000. Ed. Richard Brezover. stat. circ. 55,000. (back issues avail.)
    Former titles: Current Issues in the Financial Securities Industry; Current Issues in Banks and Thrift Institutions; Current Issues in Banking; Supersedes: Current Issues in Savings Institutions.
    Description: Review of accounting and regulatory issues influencing the industry.

657　　　　　　US
HF5601.A1D36
DELOITTE & TOUCHE REVIEW. s-m. free. Deloitte & Touche, 10 Westport Rd., C-2 N., Box 820, Wilton, CT 06897. TEL 203-761-3280. FAX 203-834-2200. Ed. R. Eugene Marion. circ. 85,000. **Document type:** newsletter.
    Formerly: Week in Review.

657.025　　CN　ISSN 0527-9275
HF5616.C2
DIRECTORY OF CANADIAN CHARTERED ACCOUNTANTS. a. Can.$39.50 members; to non-members Can.$125. Canadian Institute of Chartered Accountants, 277 Wellington St. W., Toronto, ON M5V 3H2, Canada. TEL 416-977-3222. FAX 416-977-8585. circ. 4,000. **Document type:** directory.
    Description: Contains a list of all CICA members (with addresses, year of graduation, and province), as well as a list of all Canadian Chartered Accountancy Firms (with addresses, telephone numbers and partners).

657　　　　　　IT
ECONOMIA D'AZIENDA E BILANCI. 1989. irreg., no.3, 1993. price varies. Liguori Editore s.r.l., Via Posillipo 394, 80123 Naples, Italy. TEL 39-81-7206111. FAX 39-81-7206244. Pub. Guido Liguori. adv. contact: Maria Liguori. **Document type:** monographic series.

657　　US　ISSN 1073-2888
EDWARDS DIRECTORY OF AMERICAN FACTORS; a guide to commercial accounts receivable factoring in the United States. 1994. a. $249. Edwards Research Group, Inc., Box 95101, Newton, MA 02195. TEL 617-244-8414; 800-963-1993. FAX 617-964-5333. E-mail: info@edwardsresearch.com. Ed. Mace Edwards. adv. contact: Mace Edwards. **Document type:** directory.

657　　　　　　US
EMERGING PRACTICES IN COST MANAGEMENT. a. $149.95 (overseas $220.95) (effective 1995). Warren Gorham Lamont, One Penn Plaza, New York, NY 10119. TEL 212-971-5000. FAX 212-971-5113. (Subscr. to: The Park Square Bldg., 31 St. James Ave., Boston, MA 02116-4112. TEL 800-950-1207) Ed. Barry J. Brinker. **Document type:** trade publication.
    Description: Enables managers to carry out cost-management programs more efficiently.

EMERSON'S DIRECTORY OF LEADING ACCOUNTING FIRMS WORLDWIDE. see *BUSINESS AND ECONOMICS — Trade And Industrial Directories*

657　　US　ISSN 1060-8729
EMERSON'S PROFESSIONAL SERVICE REVIEW. 1983. bi-m. $295. Emerson Company, 12356 Northup Way, Ste. 103, Bellevue, WA 98005. TEL 206-869-0655. FAX 206-869-0746. Ed. James C. Emerson. circ. 2,500. (back issues avail.) **Document type:** trade publication.
    Formerly (until 1990): Big Eight Review (ISSN 0748-4763)
    Description: Includes special features and commentary on current events involving the "Big Six" accounting - consulting firms.

ENROLLED ACTUARIES REPORT. see *INSURANCE*

ENVIRONMENTAL ACCOUNTING AND AUDITING REPORTER. see *ENVIRONMENTAL STUDIES*

ENVIRONMENTAL TAXATION AND ACCOUNTING. see *BUSINESS AND ECONOMICS — Public Finance, Taxation*

657　　IE　ISSN 0791-3664
EUROPEAN ACCOUNTANT. 10/yr. £549. Lafferty Publications Ltd., The Tower, IDA Enterprise Centre, Pearse St., Dublin 2, Ireland. TEL 353-1-6718022. FAX 353-1-6718520. E-mail: cvserv@lafferty.ie; URL: http://www.unm.lafferty.co.uk. (US subscr. to: 420 Lexington Ave., Ste. 1745, New York, NY 10170. TEL 212-557-6726) Ed. David Porter. R&P contact: David Barr. **Document type:** trade publication.
    Description: Offers informative and in-depth coverage of the European accounting profession.

657　　UK　ISSN 0955-4882
EUROPEAN ACCOUNTING FOCUS. 1989. 10/yr. £350($602) (effective Jan. 1997). Armstrong International Ltd., The Courtyard, 12 Hill St., Jersey JE2 4UB, Channel Islands. TEL 44-1534-613650. FAX 44-1534-613651. E-mail: 106001.446@compuserve.com. Ed. Ingrid Tighe; Pub. Richard Armstrong. adv. contact: Emma Sherry. stat. (back issues avail.) **Document type:** newsletter.
    Description: Profiles accounting firms in the U.K. and abroad, covers accounting trends and legislation in various countries around the world, and reports news in the field.

657　　UK　ISSN 0963-8180
HF5616.E8
THE EUROPEAN ACCOUNTING REVIEW. 1992. q. £165 to institutions (foreign £275); print & online eds. combined £200 (foreign $330) (effective 1998). (European Accounting Association - Association Europeenne de Comptabilite) Thomson Professional (Subsidiary of: International Thomson Publishing Group), 2-6 Boundary Row, London SE1 8HN, England. TEL 44-171-865-0066. FAX 44-171-522-9621. E-mail: journal@rapidcom.co.uk; URL: http://ear.thomsonprofessional.com. (Subscr. to: ITPS Ltd., Cheriton House, North Way, Andover, Hants. SP10 5BE, England. TEL 44-1264-342919. FAX 44-1264-342807; Membership addr.: Gerry Van Dyck, c/o EIASM, Rue D'Egmont 13, B-1050 Brussels, Belgium. TEL 32-2-5119116. FAX 32-2-5121929) Ed. Anne Loft. adv. contact: Gemma Heiser. (back issues avail.) **Document type:** academic/scholarly publication.
●Also available online.
—BLDSC (3829.482940); SWETS. **CCC**.
    Supersedes (1989-1992): European Accounting Association. Newsletter (ISSN 1015-5686)
    Description: Provides a European forum for the reporting of accounting research and developments, including analytical, empirical and policy-oriented scholarship.
    Refereed Serial

657.6　　US　ISSN 0190-2733
THE EXAMINER (RALEIGH). vol.5, 1980. q. $65 to non-members. Society of Financial Examiners, 4101 Lake Boone Trail, No. 201, Raleigh, NC 27607. TEL 919-787-5181. FAX 919-787-4961. E-mail: 104753.1062@compuserve.com. Ed. Chris Gerhard. R&P contact: Chris Gerhard. circ. 2,400. **Document type:** academic/scholarly publication.
    Description: Includes articles about the regulation of insurance companies, financial institutions and credit unions.
    Refereed Serial

657　　　　　　UK
EXECUTIVE ACCOUNTANT. 1974. q. £15. Institute of Cost and Executive Accountants Educational Trust, 141-149 Fonthill Rd., London N4 3HF, England. TEL 44-171-272-3925. FAX 44-171-281-5723. Ed. Rowland W. J. Godden. adv. contact: Rowland W. J. Godden. bk.rev. circ. 5,000. **Indexed:** Account.Ind. (1986-).
●Also available online. Vendor(s): UMI.

657　　　　　　FR
EXPERT COMPTABLE DE DEMAIN. 6/yr. National Association of Probationary Chartered Accountants, 92 rue de Rivoli, 75004 Paris, France. TEL 42-72-73-72. FAX 42-78-20-26. Ed. Valerie Hervouet. circ. 7,000.

657　　AT　ISSN 1030-5882
EXPOSURE DRAFT (ACCOUNTING STANDARDS). 1990. irreg. Aus.$6 per issue. Australian Accounting Research Foundation, 211 Hawthorn Rd., Caulfield, Vic. 3162, Australia. TEL 61-3-95238111. FAX 61-3-95235499. E-mail: standard@aarf.asn.au. (Co-sponsors: Australian Society of Certified Practising Accountants; Institute of Chartered Accountants in Australia) circ. 1,000.
    Formed by the merger of (1989-1990): Invitation to Comment (ISSN 1032-660X); (1989-1990): Proposed Approved Accounting Standard and Proposed Australian Accounting Standard (ISSN 1033-9191); (1989-1990): Proposed Australian Accounting Standard (ISSN 1034-3415); Which was formerly (1971-1989): Proposed Statement of Accounting Standards.

657　　AT　ISSN 1030-603X
EXPOSURE DRAFT (AUDITING PRACTICE). 1990. irreg. Aus.$6 per issue. Australian Accounting Research Foundation, 211 Hawthorn Rd., Caulfield, Vic. 3162, Australia. TEL 61-3-95238111. FAX 61-3-95235499. E-mail: standard@aarf.asn.au. (Co-sponsors: Australian Society of Certified Practising Accountants; Institute of Chartered Accountants in Australia) circ. 1,000.
    Formed by the merger of (1989-1990): Proposed Statement on Applicability; (1980-1990): Proposed Statement of Auditing Practice.

EXTEL DIVIDEND & INTEREST RECORD. see *BUSINESS AND ECONOMICS — Banking And Finance*

657　　　　　　US
F A E UPDATE.* m. Foundation for Accounting Education, 5530 Fifth Ave., 5th Fl., New York, NY 10036-5101. TEL 212-973-8300.

657 350　　　　　　US
F A R FASTSEARCH; Federal Acquisition regulations. 1990. q. (plus m. updates). $299. FastSearch Corporation, Box 421057, Plymouth, MN 55442-0057. TEL 800-232-4590. FAX 612-595-0229. Ed. Alan Rosenauer. circ. 3,750.

657.6　　　　　　US
FEDERAL AUDIT GUIDES. 4 base vols. (plus irreg. updates). $593. C C H Incorporated, 2700 Lake Cook Rd., Riverwoods, IL 60015. TEL 847-267-7000; 800-835-5224. FAX 800-224-8299.

FINANCE INDIA. see *BUSINESS AND ECONOMICS — Banking And Finance*

657　　US　ISSN 0196-9692
FINANCIAL ACCOUNTING FOUNDATION. ANNUAL REPORT. a. Financial Accounting Foundation, 401 Merritt 7, Box 5116, Norwalk, CT 06856-5116.

BUSINESS AND ECONOMICS — ACCOUNTING

657 US
FINANCIAL INFORMATION SYSTEMS MANUAL. base vol. (plus a. supplement). $172.95 (overseas $233.95) (effective 1995). Warren, Gorham & Lamont, One Penn Plaza, New York, NY 10119. TEL 212-971-5000. FAX 212-971-5113. (Subscr. to: The Park Square Bldg., 31 St. James Ave., Boston, MA 02116-4112. TEL 800-950-1207) Ed. S.W. Barcus. (looseleaf format) **Document type:** trade publication.
Description: Focuses on how technology can be used to obtain important financial information.

657 US
FINANCIAL LENDING NOTES. q. membership only. Associated Regional Accounting Firms, 3700 Crestwood Pky. N.W., Duluth, GA 30136-5599. TEL 770-279-4560. **Document type:** newsletter.

657 690 US
FINANCIAL MANAGEMENT AND ACCOUNTING FOR THE CONSTRUCTION INDUSTRY. (Issued in 1 vol. with supplements) 1988. irreg. $165. (Construction Financial Management Association) Matthew Bender & Co., Inc., 2 Park Ave., New York, NY 10016. TEL 212-448-2000. E-mail: international@bender.com; URL: http://www.bender.com. (looseleaf format)
Description: Exclusively for the construction industry. Covers such vital topics as how to recognize income and expenses, plan for income taxation, and prepare bids and estimates.

657.305 UK ISSN 0969-1545
FINANCIAL REPORTING & AUDITING NEWSLETTER. 1993. m. £90. Butterworth & Co. (Publishers) Ltd., Halsbury House, 35 Chancery Ln., London WC2A 1EL, England. TEL 44-171-400-2500. FAX 44-171-400-2842. (Addr. in US: Butterworth Legal Publishers, 90 Stiles Rd., Salem, NH 03079-9981. TEL 603-898-9664) Ed. Richard Derwent. **Document type:** newsletter.
Description: Provides commentary on current events and new regulations affecting the accounting and auditing professions.

657 CN ISSN 0071-5115
FINANCIAL REPORTING IN CANADA. 1953. biennial. price varies. Canadian Institute of Chartered Accountants, 277 Wellington St. W., Toronto, ON M5V 3H2, Canada. TEL 416-977-3222. FAX 416-977-8585. Ed. G. Lew. circ. 3,500. **Document type:** trade publication.
Description: Studies 300 Canadian companies with annual sales revenues of Can.$1 million to Can.$1 billion. Covers the preparation of their financial statements, the terminology, and the techniques.

657 UK
FINANCIAL SERVICES SOCIETY NEWSLETTER. (Former name of issuing body: Association of Certified and Corporate Accountants) bi-m. Chartered Association of Certified Accountants, 29 Lincolns Inn Fields, London WC2A 3EE, England. TEL 44-171-396-5900. FAX 44-171-396-5959. Ed. Paul Norkett. bk.rev. circ. 3,000. (back issues avail.) **Document type:** newsletter.
Description: Covers issues of concern to members in the financial services sector.

657 336 RU
FINANSOVYE BUKHALTERSKIE KONSYL'TATSII. (Text in Russian) 1993. m. $168 (effective 1998). Myasnitskaya ul., 44-1, 101000 Moscow, Russia. TEL 7-095-9249271. FAX 7-095-9212214. (Dist. by: Mezhdunarodnaya Kniga, B. Yakimanka 39, 117049 Moscow, Russia. TEL 7-095-2384967. FAX 7-095-2384634) Ed. S. Shapigonzor. adv.: 1000000 Rub. index. circ. 9,000. (back issues avail.)
Refereed Serial

657 US
FLORIDA INDEPENDENT ACCOUNTANT. 1986. q. Florida Association of Independent Accountants, Box 13089, Tallahassee, FL 32317. TEL 904-878-3134. FAX 904-878-1291. adv.; circ. 900 (controlled). **Document type:** trade publication.
Description: Covers association activities and legislative concerns.

657 US
FOCUS (MONTVALE). bi-m. Institute of Management Accountants, 10 Paragon Dr., Montvale, NJ 07645-1760. TEL 201-573-9000; 800-638-4427. FAX 201-573-8601. Ed. Kathy Williams; Pub. Gary Scopes. R&P contact: Robert F. Randall. adv. contact: Jim Hart. circ. 60,000. **Document type:** newsletter.
Former titles: Leader (Montvale); Association Leader (Montvale) (ISSN 0896-2847)
Description: Focuses on improving communication between members and the national office. Includes calendar of events and conference information.

FORENSIC ACCOUNTING REVIEW. see BUSINESS AND ECONOMICS

657 US
FORESIGHT. q. membership only. Associated Regional Accounting Firms, 3700 Crestwood Pky. N.W., Duluth, GA 30136-5599. TEL 770-279-4560. Ed. Missy Patrick. **Document type:** newsletter.
Formerly: Foresight Client Newsletter.

G A O DAYBOOK. (U.S. General Accounting Office) see PUBLIC ADMINISTRATION

657 US
G A O DOCUMENTS. vol.4, 1979. m. U.S. General Accounting Office, Office of Public Affairs, Box 6015, Gaithersburg, MD 20884-6015. TEL 202-512-6000. FAX 301-258-4066. E-mail: info@www.gao.gov. bibl.; index. **Indexed:** MEDOC. **Document type:** government publication.

G A O REVIEW. (U.S. General Accounting Office) see PUBLIC ADMINISTRATION

657 346 BE
GIDS VOOR ACCOUNTANTS EN BEDRIJFSREVISOREN. (Text in Dutch) 1989. a. 8500 BEF. Kluwer Rechtswetenschappen Belgie (Subsidiary of: Wolters Kluwer N.V.), Santvoortbeeklaan 21-25, 2100 Antwerp, Belgium. FAX 32-3-3600467. Eds. Andre Chiau, Jo Van den Bossche. **Document type:** trade publication.
Formerly: Gids voor Accountants (ISSN 0776-9148)

GILBERT LAW SUMMARIES. BASIC ACCOUNTING FOR LAWYERS. see LAW — Corporate Law

GLOBAL COMMUNIQUE. see BUSINESS AND ECONOMICS — Abstracting, Bibliographies, Statistics

657 US ISSN 0883-1483
HJ9801
GOVERNMENT ACCOUNTANTS JOURNAL. 1952. q. $60 (foreign $65). Association of Government Accountants, 2200 Mount Vernon Ave., Alexandria, VA 22301-1314. TEL 703-684-6931. FAX 703-548-9367. E-mail: agapubs@aol.com. Ed. Marie S. Force. R&P contact: Marie S. Force. adv. contact: Jennifer Grace. bk.rev.; charts; index, cum.index. circ. 15,000. (also avail. in microform from UMI; reprint service avail. from SCH,UMI) **Indexed:** ABI Inform., Account.& Data Proc.Abstr., Account.Ind. (1974-), BPIA, Bus.Ind., Manage.Cont., P.A.I.S, Pers.Lit. **Document type:** trade publication, academic/scholarly publication.
—BLDSC (4203.840000); SWETS; UMI; UnCover.
Formerly (until vol.25, 1976): Federal Accountant (ISSN 0014-9004)
Refereed Serial

657 350 US ISSN 1048-1389
GOVERNMENT ACCOUNTING AND AUDITING UPDATE. 1990. m. $172.25 (overseas $239.45) (effective 1995). Warren, Gorham & Lamont, One Penn Plaza, New York, NY 10119. TEL 212-971-5000. FAX 212-971-5113. (Subscr. to: The Park Square Bldg., 31 St. James Ave., Boston, MA 02116-4112. TEL 800-950-1207) **Document type:** newsletter.
—UMI. CCC.
Description: Informs readers on changes in government accounting and financial reporting and how they affect their businesses.

657 350.6 US
GOVERNMENT ACCOUNTING AND FINANCIAL REPORTING MANUAL. base vol. (plus a. supplement). $172.95 (overseas $246.95) (effective 1995). Warren, Gorham & Lamont, One Penn Plaza, New York, NY 10119. TEL 212-971-5000. FAX 212-971-5113. (Subscr. to: The Park Square Bldg., 31 St. James Ave., Boston, MA 02116-4112. TEL 800-950-1207) Ed. William J. Raftery. (looseleaf format) **Document type:** trade publication.
Description: Guides in all areas of government accounting and financial reporting.

657 US ISSN 0886-2982
HJ9701
GOVERNMENTAL ACCOUNTING STANDARDS BOARD. ACTION REPORT. 1984. m. $68 (effective Dec. 1996 to Nov. 1997). Governmental Accounting Standards Board, 401 Merritt 7, Box 5116, Norwalk, CT 06856-5116. TEL 203-847-0700. FAX 203-849-9714. Ed. Deborah Harrington. circ. 10,125. **Document type:** newsletter.

657 FR ISSN 1144-5777
GUIDE DES DECLARATIONS FISCALES. (Supplements avail.) 1989. a. 970 F. (with supplements 1310 F.) (effective 1993). Lamy S.A., 187-189 quai de Valmy, 75490 Paris Cedex 10, France. TEL 33-1-44721343. FAX 33-1-44721395. (looseleaf format) **Document type:** trade publication.
Description: Provides instructions to aid in filling out fiscal forms.

657 US
HANDBOOK FOR INTERNAL AUDITORS. (Issued in 2 base vols. with supplements) 1985. irreg. $315. Matthew Bender & Co., Inc., 2 Park Ave., New York, NY 10016. TEL 212-448-2000. FAX 518-462-3788. E-mail: international@bender.com; URL: http://www.bender.com. Eds. William E. Perry, Keagle W. Davis. (looseleaf format)
Description: Provides guidance on every aspect of internal auditing - from establishing an internal auditing function within a company, to managing an internal auditing department, to performing audit fieldwork.

657 658 US
HANDBOOK OF COST MANAGEMENT. 1993. base vol. (plus a. supplement). $157.95 (overseas $227.95) (effective 1995). Warren Gorham Lamont, One Penn Plaza, New York, NY 10119. TEL 212-971-5000. FAX 212-971-5113. (Subscr. to: The Park Square Bldg., 31 St. James Ave., Boston, MA 02116-4112. TEL 800-950-1207) Ed. Barry J. Brinker. **Document type:** trade publication.
Description: Enables managers to implement and improve cost-management programs for every phase of their operations.

657 332 US ISSN 1046-3534
HF5686.C7
HANDBOOK OF S E C ACCOUNTING AND DISCLOSURE. (Securities and Exchange Commission) 1988. a. $184.95 (overseas $262.55) (effective 1995). Warren, Gorham & Lamont, One Penn Plaza, New York, NY 10119. TEL 212-971-5000. FAX 212-971-5113. (Subscr. to: The Park Square Bldg., 31 St. James Ave., Boston, MA 02116-4112. TEL 800-950-1207) Ed. Allan B. Afterman. **Document type:** trade publication.
—CCC.
Description: Guides public accountants in all steps of preparing disclosure statements for the Securities and Exchange Commission.

657 CC ISSN 1003-0131
HEBEI CAIKUAI/HEBEI FINANCE AND ACCOUNTING. (Text in Chinese) m. Hebei Sheng Caizheng Ting, Fu 9, Kangle Jie, Shijiazhuang, Hebei 050051, People's Republic of China. TEL 744621. Ed. Lu Baorui. circ. controlled.

HORSE OWNERS AND BREEDERS TAX MANUAL. see SPORTS AND GAMES — Horses And Horsemanship

657 GW ISSN 0937-4019
I D W FACHNACHRICHTEN. 1947. m. Institut der Wirtschaftspruefer in Deutschland e.V., Tersteegenstr. 14, Postfach 320580, 40474 Duesseldorf, Germany. TEL 49-211-4561. FAX 49-211-4541097. Ed. Horst Kaminski. bk.rev circ. 16,500. (back issues avail.) **Document type:** trade publication.

BUSINESS AND ECONOMICS — ACCOUNTING

657 US
I F A ANNUAL REPORT.* a. International Federation of Accountants, 114 W. 47th St., Ste. 2410, New York, NY 10036-1510. TEL 212-486-2446.

I F A C INTERNATIONAL PUBLIC SECTOR GUIDELINE (NO.). see BUSINESS AND ECONOMICS — Public Finance, Taxation

I F A C PUBLIC SECTOR COMMITTEE STUDY REPORT (NO.). see BUSINESS AND ECONOMICS — Public Finance, Taxation

657 US
I F A NEWSLETTER.* q. International Federation of Accountants, 114 W. 47th St., Ste. 2410, New York, NY 10036-1510. TEL 212-486-2446.

657.6 US ISSN 0744-1223
I I A TODAY. 1981. bi-m. membership. Institute of Internal Auditors, Inc., 249 Maitland Ave., Altamonte Springs, FL 32701-4201. TEL 407-830-7600. FAX 407-831-5171. Ed. Leah Miller. R&P contact: Gretchen Gorfine. adv. contact: JoAn Shultz. bk.rev.; charts; illus.; stat.; tr.lit. circ. 40,000. (back issues avail.) **Document type:** newsletter.
Supersedes (1980-1981): Internos (ISSN 0199-9249)

I R S LETTER RULINGS. (Internal Revenue Service) see BUSINESS AND ECONOMICS — Public Finance, Taxation

657 US
INCOME AND FEES OF ACCOUNTANTS IN PUBLIC PRACTICE. triennial. $50 to non-members; members $35. National Society of Public Accountants, 1010 N. Fairfax St., Alexandria, VA 22314. TEL 703-549-6400. circ. 23,000. **Indexed:** SRI. **Document type:** trade publication.

657 US
INDEPENDENT ACCOUNTANTS INTERNATIONAL. UPDATE. 1979. m. membership. Independent Accountants International, 9200 S. Dadeland Blvd., Ste. 510, Miami, FL 33156-2703. TEL 305-670-0580. FAX 305-670-3818. Ed. Dorothy J. Biederman. R&P contact: Julia Gray. adv. contact: Arthur D. Goessel. bk.rev. circ. 700. (looseleaf format) **Document type:** newsletter, trade publication.
Formerly: International Affiliation of Independent Accounting Firms. Update.

637 US ISSN 1053-8542
INSIGHT (CHICAGO). 1947. 10/yr. $20. Illinois C P A Society, 222 S. Riverside Plaza, 16th Fl., Chicago, IL 60606. TEL 312-993-0393. FAX 312-993-7713. Ed. Julia Winn. R&P contact: Julia Winn. adv.: B&W page $1095, color page $1645; trim 8 3/8 x 10 7/8; adv. contact: Ilene Zurla. circ. 26,000 (controlled). (also avail. in microfilm) **Document type:** trade publication.
Formerly (until 1990): Newsjournal (ISSN 1043-7215)
Description: Contains analyses of issues that affect the working lives of public and non-public CPAs.

657 AT
INSTITUTE OF CHARTERED ACCOUNTANTS IN AUSTRALIA. ANNUAL REPORT AND ACCOUNTS. a. Institute of Chartered Accountants in Australia, P.O. Box 3921, Sydney, N.S.W. 2001, Australia. TEL 61-2-92901344. FAX 61-2-92623953. R&P contact: Ian Hay. **Document type:** corporate report.

657 UK
INSTITUTE OF CHARTERED ACCOUNTANTS IN ENGLAND AND WALES. ACCOUNTING STANDARDS BOARD. PAPERS. (Subseries avail.: Financial Reporting Standards, Exposure Drafts, Discussion Papers) irreg. price varies. Institute of Chartered Accountants in England and Wales, P.O. Box 620, Central Milton Keynes, Bucks. MK9 2JX, England. (back issues avail.) **Document type:** monographic series.
Former titles: Institute of Chartered Accountants in England and Wales. Exposure Drafts and Statements of Standard Accounting Practice; Institute of Chartered Accountants in England and Wales. Practice Administration Series, Exposure Drafts and Statements of Standard Accounting Practice (ISSN 0073-9049)

657 UK
INSTITUTE OF CHARTERED ACCOUNTANTS IN ENGLAND AND WALES. INTERNATIONAL ACCOUNTING STANDARDS COMMITTEE. PAPERS. 1975. irreg., latest Jan. 1993. $5. Institute of Chartered Accountants in England and Wales, P.O. Box 620, Central Milton Keynes, Bucks. MK9 2JX, England. **Document type:** monographic series.

657 UK
INSTITUTE OF CHARTERED ACCOUNTANTS IN ENGLAND AND WALES. UPDATE. 1979. m. £75 (overseas £85.50). Accountancy Books, 399 Silbury Blvd., Central Milton Keynes, Bucks. MK9 2HL, England. TEL 44-1908-248000. FAX 44-1908-248001. TELEX 827502. **Document type:** trade publication.
Formerly (until 1984): Institute of Chartered Accountants in England and Wales. Technical Bulletin (ISSN 0143-9758)

657 CN
INSTITUTE OF CHARTERED ACCOUNTANTS OF ALBERTA. C A MONTHLY STATEMENT. 1968. m. membership. Institute of Chartered Accountants of Alberta, 580 Manulife Pl., 10180 - 101 St., Edmonton, AB T5J 4R2, Canada. TEL 403-424-7391. FAX 403-425-8766. Ed. Karin Holmgren. R&P contact: Karin Holmgren. bk.rev. circ. 7,200. **Document type:** newsletter.
Formerly: Institute of Chartered Accountants of Alberta. Monthly Statement (ISSN 0316-6546)

657 CN
INSTITUTE OF CHARTERED ACCOUNTANTS OF BRITISH COLUMBIA. BEYOND NUMBERS. 1945. 10/yr. membership. Institute of Chartered Accountants of British Columbia, 1133 Melville St., 6th Fl., Vancouver, BC V6E 4E5, Canada. TEL 604-681-3264. FAX 604-681-1523. Ed. Karen McCluskey; Pub. Penelope Noble. R&P contact: Karen McCluskey. adv.: B&W page Can.$1000, color page Can.$2280; adv. contact: Sotos Petrides. bk.rev. circ. 8,000. **Document type:** trade publication.
Former titles (until 1996): Institute of Chartered Accountants of British Columbia. Communication (ISSN 0834-0188); (until 1986): Institute of Chartered Accountants of British Columbia. News and Views (ISSN 0380-4011)
Description: Information for chartered accountants in British Columbia.

657 UK ISSN 0073-9057
INSTITUTE OF CHARTERED ACCOUNTANTS OF SCOTLAND. OFFICIAL DIRECTORY. 1896. a. £58. Institute of Chartered Accountants of Scotland, 27 Queen St., Edinburgh, EH2 1LA, Scotland. TEL 44-131-225-5673. FAX 44-131-225-3813. Ed. Peter Johnston; Pub. David McMurray. R&P contact: John Hatfield. adv. contact: Laura Houston. circ. 1,500. **Document type:** directory.

657 SP
INSTITUTO DE CENSORES JURADOS DE CUENTAS DE ESPAGNA. REVISTA TECHNICA. fortn. Instituto de Censores Jurados de Cuentas de Espagna, c/o General Arrando 9, 28010 Madrid, Spain. TEL 91-445-03-54.

INSURANCE ACCOUNTANT. see INSURANCE

657 US ISSN 0897-0378
HF5668
INTERNAL AUDITING. 1985. q. $108.98 (overseas $179.15) (effective 1995). Warren, Gorham & Lamont, One Penn Plaza, New York, NY 10119. TEL 212-971-5000. FAX 212-971-5113. URL: http://www.wgl.com/acct.inta.html. (Subscr. to: The Park Square Bldg., 31 St. James Ave., Boston, MA 02116-4112. TEL 800-950-1207) **Indexed:** ABI Inform., Account.Ind. (1985-). **Document type:** trade publication.
—BLDSC (4534.678070); UMI. **CCC.**
Description: Provides timely information and ideas that show the practitioner how to devise an overall internal auditing approach and develop strategic plans.

657.6 US ISSN 0744-2947
INTERNAL AUDITING ALERT. 1981. m. $141.50 (overseas $200.45) (effective 1995). Warren, Gorham & Lamont, One Penn Plaza, New York, NY 10119. TEL 212-971-5000. FAX 212-971-5113. URL: http://www.wgl.com/acct.iaa.html. (Subscr. to: The Park Square Bldg., 31 St. James Ave., Boston, MA 02116-4112. TEL 800-950-1207) (also avail. in microform from UMI; back issues avail.) **Document type:** newsletter.
—UMI. **CCC.**
Description: Focuses on the means of monitoring and controlling the accounting system used by any enterprise or organization.

657 US ISSN 0020-5745
HF5667 CODEN: ITAUA
INTERNAL AUDITOR. 1944. bi-m. $60. Institute of Internal Auditors, Inc., 249 Maitland Ave., Altamonte Springs, FL 32701-4201. TEL 407-830-7600. FAX 407-831-5171. URL: http://www.rutgers.edu/Accounting/raw/iia. Ed. Anne Graham. R&P contact: Gretchen Gorfine. adv.: B&W page $1812, color page $3279; trim 8 3/8 x 10 7/8; adv. contact: JoAn Shultz. bk.rev.; illus.; index. circ. 50,000. (also avail. in microform from UMI; reprint service avail. from SCH) **Indexed:** ABI Inform., Account.& Data Proc.Abstr., Account.Ind. (1974-), Anbar, B.P.I., BPIA, Bus.Ind., Comput.Lit.Ind., Excerp.Med., INSPEC (1983-), Intl.Mgmt.Info., Manage.Cont., Tr.& Indus.Ind. **Document type:** trade publication.
●Also available online. Vendor(s): Information Access Co., UMI.
—BLDSC (4534.680000); AskIEEE; KR SourceOne; SWETS; UMI; UnCover. **CCC.**
Formerly: I I A Research Reports.
Description: For internal auditors, mid- to high-level corporate executives and board members.

657 UK
HF5601
INTERNATIONAL ACCOUNTANT. 1928. q. £2 per no. Association of International Accountants, South Bank Bldg., Kingsway, Team Valley, Gateshead, Tyne and Wear NE11 OJS, England. Ed. Philip J. Turnbull. adv.; bk.rev.; charts; index. **Indexed:** Account.Ind. (1974-).
—BLDSC (4535.593000).
Supersedes: Student Accounting Review (ISSN 1353-5609); **Former titles** (until 1993): Association of International Accountants. Newsreview (ISSN 0969-4935); (until 1992): Association of International Accountants. Newsletter (ISSN 0969-4897); (until 1990): International Accountant (ISSN 0020-5826); (until 1967): International Accountants' Journal.
Description: Serves as offcial journal for the association. Covers subjects of particular interest to students as well as accounting in general. Includes articles on such topics as passing exams, accounting and auditing standards, accounting in developing countries, etc.

657 US ISSN 1058-272X
HF5601
INTERNATIONAL ACCOUNTING AND AUDITING TRENDS. 1991. a. C I F A R Publications, Inc., 3490 US Hwy. 1, BL012, Princeton, NJ 08540-5920. TEL 609-520-9333. FAX 609-520-0905. Ed. Vinod Bavishi.

657 UN ISSN 1014-4633
INTERNATIONAL ACCOUNTING AND REPORTING ISSUES. 1984. a. United Nations Centre on Transnational Corporations, Room DC2-0853, New York, NY 10017. FAX 212-963-4116.

657 IE ISSN 0265-0223
INTERNATIONAL ACCOUNTING BULLETIN. 1983. 23/yr. I£679. Lafferty Publications Ltd., The Tower, IDA Enterprise Centre, Pearse St., Dublin 2, Ireland. TEL 353-1-6718022. FAX 353-1-6718520. E-mail: cvserv@lafferty.ie; URL: http://www.unm.lafferty.co.uk. (US subscr. addr.: Lafferty Publications (USA), 420 Lexington Ave., Ste. 1745, New York, NY 10170. TEL 212-557-6726) Ed. Ciaran Hancock. R&P contact: David Barr. (back issues avail.) **Indexed:** Account.Ind. (1983-). **Document type:** bulletin.
—SWETS.
Description: Provides news, analysis and reports in the world accounting market.

BUSINESS AND ECONOMICS — ACCOUNTING

657 US ISSN 1056-2583
HF5601
INTERNATIONAL ACCOUNTING SUMMARIES. 1991. a. (Coopers & Lybrand) John Wiley & Sons, Inc., 605 Third Ave., New York, NY 10158.

657 378 US ISSN 0020-7063
HF5601
THE INTERNATIONAL JOURNAL OF ACCOUNTING EDUCATION AND RESEARCH. 1965. 5/yr. $95 to individuals (foreign $120); institutions $225 (foreign $250) (effective 1998). J A I Press Inc., 55 Old Post Rd., No.2, Box 1678, Greenwich, CT 06830-1678. TEL 203-661-7602. FAX 203-661-0792. E-mail: jai@jaipress.com; URL: http://www.cba.uiuc.edu/accy/intl/journal.html. (In Europe: J A I Press Ltd., 38 Tavistock St., Covent Garden, London WC2E 7PB, England. TEL 44-171-379-8834. FAX 44-171-379-8835) cum.index every 2 yrs. (reprint service avail. from SWZ) **Indexed:** Account.Ind. (1974-), Asian-Pac.Econ.Lit., Cont.Pg.Manage., Mid.East: Abstr.& Ind., P.A.I.S., SCIMP, World Bank.Abstr. **Document type:** academic/scholarly publication.
—BLDSC (4541.525000); SWETS; UnCover. **CCC.**

657 UK ISSN 1090-6738
▼**INTERNATIONAL JOURNAL OF AUDITING.** 1997. 3/yr. $225 (effective 1998). John Wiley & Sons Ltd., Journals, Baffins Ln., Chichester, W. Sussex PO19 1UD, England. TEL 44-1243-779777. FAX 44-1243-843232. E-mail: cs-journals@wiley.co.uk; URL: http://www.wiley.co.uk. (Subscr. in the Americas to: John Wiley & Sons, Inc., 605 Third Ave., New York, NY 10158. TEL 212-850-6645. FAX 212-850-6021) Ed. Andrew Chambers. **Document type:** academic/scholarly publication.

INTERNATIONAL JOURNAL OF INTELLIGENT SYSTEMS IN ACCOUNTING, FINANCE & MANAGEMENT. see BUSINESS AND ECONOMICS — Computer Applications

INTERNATIONAL JOURNAL OF MANAGEMENT. see BUSINESS AND ECONOMICS — Management

657 510 US
INTERNATIONAL SOCIETY OF PARAMETRIC ANALYSTS. CONFERENCE PROCEEDINGS. 1983. a. $75 membership (effective 1997). (International Society of Parametric Analysts, Inc. (ISPA)) J. Clyde Perry and Associates, Box 6402, Chesterfield, MO 63006-6402. TEL 314-527-2955. FAX 314-256-8358. Ed. Darryl Webb. R&P contact: Clyde Perry. adv. contact: Clyde Perry. circ. 400. **Document type:** proceedings.

657 UK ISSN 1350-6242
IRISH COMPANY REPORTING. 1993. irreg. £30. University of Ulster, School of Management, Coleraine BT52 1SA, N. Ireland. TEL 44-1232-365131. FAX 44-1232-366805. E-mail: rj.kirk@ulst.ac.uk. Ed. Robert Kirk. R&P contact: Robert Kirk. circ. 100. **Document type:** monographic series.

657 370 US ISSN 0739-3172
HF5630
ISSUES IN ACCOUNTING EDUCATION. 1983. s-a. $30. American Accounting Association, 5717 Bessie Dr., Sarasota, FL 33583-2399. TEL 941-921-7747. FAX 941-923-4093. URL: http://www.rutgers.edu/Accounting/raw/aaa/publish/aaaind.htm. Ed. Wanda Wallace. R&P contact: Mary Cole. adv. contact: Gordon Cox. bk.rev.; illus. **Indexed:** Account.Ind. (1986-).
—BLDSC (4584.065000); SWETS; UMI; UnCover.
Description: Contains research articles for accounting faculty that describe or discuss aspects of accounting education.
Refereed Serial

657 IS
JERUSALEM CONFERENCE ON ACCOUNTANCY. (Text in English) 1971. triennial. price varies. Institute of Certified Public Accountants in Israel, P.O. Box 29281, 1 Montefiore St., Tel Aviv, Israel. TEL 972-3-5161114. FAX 972-3-5103105.

657 PO ISSN 0870-8789
JORNAL DE CONTABILIDADE. 1977. m. Esc.6000 (effective 1997). Associacao Portuguesa de Tecnicos de Contas, Rua Rodrigues Sampaio 50-3o Esq., 1150 Lisbon, Portugal. TEL 351-1-3140413. FAX 351-1-3156068. E-mail: apotec@mail.telepac.pt; URL: http://www.apotec.pt. Ed. Dr. Severo Praxedes Soares. adv. contact: Antonio Lopes Reis. bk.rev.; index. circ. 10,200. (back issues avail.) **Document type:** trade publication.
Description: For accountants and business managers.

657 US ISSN 0021-8448
HF5601 CODEN: JACYAD
JOURNAL OF ACCOUNTANCY. 1905. m. $56 (foreign $81) (effective 1997). American Institute of Certified Public Accountants, Harborside Financial Ctr., 201 Plaza Three, Jersey City, NJ 07311-9801. TEL 201-938-3796; 800-862-4272. FAX 201-329-1112. E-mail: journal@aicpa.org; URL: http://www.aicpa.org/pubs/jofa/index.htm. (Alt. addr.: AICPA, 1211 Ave. of the Americas, New York,NY 10036. TEL 212-596-6200) Ed. Collen Katz. R&P contact: Marie MacBryde. adv. contact: Cecilia Robin. bk.rev.; bibl.; charts; illus.; s-a. index. circ. 320,000. (also avail. in microform from MIM,UMI; reprint service avail. from SCH,UMI) **Indexed:** ABI Inform., Abstr.Bk.Rev.Curr.Leg.Per., Account.Ind. (1974-), Anbar, B.P.I, BPIA, Bus.Educ.Ind., Bus.Ind., C.L.I., Comput.Lit.Ind., Cont.Pg.Manage., Curr.Cont., Data Process.Dig., High.Educ.Curr.Aware.Bull., Intl.Mgmt.Info., L.R.I., Law Ofc.Info.Svc., Manage.Cont., Mgmt.& Market.Abstr., Oper.Res.Manage.Sci., P.A.I.S., PROMT, PSI, Risk Abstr., SCIMP, SSCI, Tr.& Indus.Ind., World Bank.Abstr. **Document type:** trade publication.
● Also available online. Vendor(s): Information Access Co., UMI.
—BLDSC (4918.860000); CASDDS; Genuine Article; KR SourceOne; SWETS; UMI; UnCover. **CCC.**
Description: Reports on developments, trends, management advisory services, taxation, education, professional subjects.
Refereed Serial

657 330.9 NE ISSN 0165-4101
CODEN: JAECDS
JOURNAL OF ACCOUNTING AND ECONOMICS. (Text in English) 1979. bi-m. fl.1150($661) (effective 1998). North-Holland (Subsidiary of: Elsevier Science B.V.), P.O. Box 211, 1000 AE Amsterdam, Netherlands. TEL 31-20-4853911. FAX 31-20-4853598. TELEX 18582 ESPA NL. URL: http://www.elsevier.nl:80/inca/publications/store/5/0/5/5/5/6/505556.pub.shtml. (Subscr. in the Americas to: Elsevier Science, Regional Sales Office, Box 945, New York, NY 10159-0945. TEL 212-633-3730. FAX 212-633-3680; Subscr. in Australasia and the Far East to: Elsevier Science (Singapore) Pte Ltd, No.1 Temasek Ave., No.17-01 Millenia Tower, Singapore 039192, Singapore. TEL 65-434-3727. FAX 65-337-2230; Subscr. in Japan to: Elsevier Science Japan, 9-15 Higashi-Azabu 1-chome, Minato-ku, Tokyo 106, Japan. TEL 81-3-5561-5033. FAX 81-3-5561-5047) Ed.Bd. bibl.; illus. (also avail. in microform from UMI; back issues avail.; reprint service avail. from SWZ) **Indexed:** ABI Inform., Account.Ind. (1979-), ASCA, BPIA, Bus.Ind., C.R.E.J., Curr.Cont., J.Cont.Quant.Meth., J.of Econ.Lit., Manage.Cont., SSCI, Tr.& Indus.Ind., World Bank.Abstr. **Document type:** academic/scholarly publication.
—BLDSC (4918.866000); Genuine Article; SWETS; UMI; UnCover. **CCC.**
Description: Provides a forum for the publication of economic analyses of accounting problems.
Refereed Serial

657 US ISSN 0278-4254
H97 CODEN: JACPDN
JOURNAL OF ACCOUNTING AND PUBLIC POLICY. 1982. q. fl.651($374) (effective 1998). Elsevier Science Inc., Box 945, New York, NY 10159-0945. TEL 212-633-3730. FAX 212-633-3680. TELEX 420643 AEP. E-mail: usinfo-f@elsevier.com; URL: http://www.elsevier.nl:80/inca/publications/store/5/0/5/7/2/1/505721.pub.shtml. (Subscr. outside the Americas to: Elsevier Science, Regional Sales Office, P.O. Box 211, 1000 AE Amsterdam, Netherlands. TEL 31-20-4853757. FAX 31-20-4853432; Subscr. in Australasia and the Far East to: Elsevier Science (Singapore) Pte Ltd, No.1 Temasek Ave., No.17-01 Millenia Tower, Singapore 039192, Singapore. TEL 65-434-3727. FAX 65-337-2230; Subscr. in Japan to: Elsevier Science Japan, 9-15 Higashi-Azabu 1-chome, Minato-ku, Tokyo 106, Japan. TEL 81-3-5561-5033. FAX 81-3-5561-5047) Eds. L.A. Gordon, S.E. Loeb. bibl. (also avail. in microform from UMI; reprint service avail. from SWZ) **Indexed:** ABI Inform., Account.Ind. (1982-), ASCA, BPIA, Cont.Pg.Manage., Curr.Cont., P.A.I.S., Risk Abstr., Sage Pub.Admin.Abstr., SSCI, World Bank.Abstr. **Document type:** academic/scholarly publication.
—BLDSC (4918.868000); Genuine Article; SWETS; UMI; UnCover. **CCC.**
Description: Publishes articles exploring the interaction of accounting with a wide range of disciplines including economics, public administration, political science, social psychology, policy science, and the law.
Refereed Serial

657 US ISSN 0148-558X
HF5601
JOURNAL OF ACCOUNTING, AUDITING & FINANCE. 1977-1985; N.S. 1986. q. $135 (foreign $145) (effective 1998). (New York University, Vincent C. Ross Institute of Accounting Research) Greenwood Press, Inc., Subscription Publications (Subsidiary of: Greenwood Publishing Group Inc.), 88 Post Rd. W., Box 5007, Westport, CT 06881-5007. TEL 203-226-3571. FAX 203-222-1502. URL: http://www.stern.nyu.edu/-ymcnair/jaaf.html. Ed. Jeffrey L. Callen. circ. 3,000. (also avail. in microform from UMI; reprint service avail. from RRI,WSH) **Indexed:** ABI Inform., Account.Ind. (1977-), B.P.I, Bank.Lit.Ind., BPIA, Bus.Ind., C.L.I., Cont.Pg.Manage., L.I.I., Leg.Per., Manage.Cont. **Document type:** academic/scholarly publication.
—BLDSC (4918.870000); KR SourceOne; SWETS; UnCover. **CCC.**

657 378 UK ISSN 0748-5751
HF5630
JOURNAL OF ACCOUNTING EDUCATION. 1982. q. fl.557($320) (effective 1998). (James Madison University, School of Accounting, US) Elsevier Science Ltd., Pergamon, P.O. Box 800, Kidlington, Oxford OX5 1DX, England. TEL 44-1865-843000. FAX 44-1865-843010. E-mail: nlinfo-f@elsevier.nl; usinfo-f@elsevier.com; forinfo-kyf04035@niftyserve.or.jp; URL: http://www.elsevier.nl:80/inca/publicaions/store/8/4/6/840.pub.shtml. (Subscr. to: Elsevier Science, Regional Sales Office, P.O. Box 211, 1000 AE Amsterdam, Netherlands. TEL 31-20-4853757. FAX 31-20-4853432; Subscr. in the Americas to: Elsevier Science, Regional Sales Office, Box 945, New York, NY 10159-0945. TEL 212-633-3730. FAX 212-633-3680; Subscr. in Australasia and the Far East to: Elsevier Science (Singapore) Pte Ltd, No.1 Temasek Ave., No.17-01 Millenia Tower, Singapore 039192, Singapore. TEL 65-434-3727. FAX 65-337-2230) Ed. E. Kent St. Pierre. adv. circ. 1,500. (also avail. in microform from UMI; back issues avail.) **Indexed:** Account.Ind. (1983-), Cont.Pg.Educ., Educ.Tech.Abstr., Tech.Educ.Abstr. **Document type:** academic/scholarly publication.
—BLDSC (4918.875000); SWETS; UMI; UnCover. **CCC.**
Description: Provides a forum for the exchange of ideas, opinion and research results among accounting educators.
Refereed Serial

BUSINESS AND ECONOMICS — ACCOUNTING

657 US ISSN 0737-4607
HF5601
JOURNAL OF ACCOUNTING LITERATURE. 1982. a. $22 to individuals; students $12; institutions $32 (effective 1997). University of Florida, Accounting Research Center, Fisher School of Accounting-267 BUS, College of Business Administration, Gainsville, FL 32611. TEL 904-392-0155. Eds. Bipin B. Ajinkya, William F. Messier, Jr. illus. **Indexed:** Account.Ind. (1982-). **Document type:** academic/scholarly publication.
●Also available online. Vendor(s): UMI.
—BLDSC (4918.877000); SWETS; UMI; UnCover.
Description: Provides in-depth review articles on accounting topics, as well as research on accounting and auditing standards.
Refereed Serial

657 US ISSN 0021-8456
HF5601 CODEN: JACRBR
JOURNAL OF ACCOUNTING RESEARCH. 1963. s-a plus a. supplement. $70 to academicians and students; others $86 (subscr. includes a. supplement) (effective 1997). University of Chicago, Graduate School of Business, Institute of Professional Accounting, c/o Marjorie E. Holme, Managing, 1101 E. 58th St., Chicago, IL 60637. TEL 312-702-7460. FAX 312-702-0458. Ed. Katherine Schipper. bk.rev.; charts; stat.; index. circ. 2,800. (also avail. in microform from MIM,UMI; reprint service avail. from SCH,UMI) **Indexed:** ABI Inform., Account.& Data Proc.Abstr., Account.Ind. (1974-), Anbar, ASCA, B.P.I., BPIA, Bus.Ind., C.R.E.J., Cont.Pg.Manage., Curr.Cont., J.Cont.Quant.Meth., J.of Econ.Lit., Manage.Cont., Oper.Res.Manage.Sci., SCIMP (1978-), SSCI, Tr.& Indus.Ind., World Bank.Abstr. **Document type:** academic/scholarly publication.
—BLDSC (4918.880000); KR SourceOne; SWETS; UMI; UnCover.
Description: Unpublished original research in the fields of empirical, analytic and experimental accounting.

657 US
JOURNAL OF ACCOUNTING RESEARCH. SUPPLEMENT. (Supplement to: Journal of Accounting Research) 1963. a. University of Chicago, Graduate School of Business, Institute of Professional Accounting, 1101 E. 58th St., Chicago, IL 60637. TEL 312-702-7460. FAX 312-702-0458. Eds. Nicholas Dopuch, Katherine Schipper. charts. (also avail. in microfiche from UMI) **Indexed:** Cont.Pg.Manage. **Document type:** academic/scholarly publication.
Formerly (until 1973): Empirical Research in Accounting, Selected Studies (ISSN 0424-9283)

JOURNAL OF ACTUARIAL PRACTICE. see *INSURANCE*

657.072 UK ISSN 0967-5426
JOURNAL OF APPLIED ACCOUNTING RESEARCH. 1992. 3/yr. De Montfort University, Leicester Business School, Department of Accounting & Finance, The Gateway, Leicester LE1 9BH, England. TEL 44-116-2511551. FAX 44-116-2517548. Ed. Leigh Holland. **Document type:** academic/scholarly publication.

332.1 340 US ISSN 0895-853X
HG1707
JOURNAL OF BANK ACCOUNTING & AUDITING. 1987. q. $125. (Bank Administration Institute) Faulkner & Gray, Inc. (New York), 11 Penn Plaza, 17th Fl., New York, NY 10001. TEL 212-967-7000. FAX 212-967-7155. Ed. Pamela Goett. circ. 2,000. **Indexed:** Account.Ind. (1988-).
—UMI.
Description: Discusses compliance with government standards, recent legislation, and staff and computer management topics.

JOURNAL OF BANK COST & MANAGEMENT ACCOUNTING. see *BUSINESS AND ECONOMICS — Banking And Finance*

657 338 UK ISSN 0306-686X
HG11
JOURNAL OF BUSINESS FINANCE & ACCOUNTING. 1974. 10/yr. £232($434) (foreign £280) (effective 1997). Blackwell Publishers Ltd., 108 Cowley Rd., Oxford OX4 1JF, England. TEL 44-1865-791100. FAX 44-1865-791347. E-mail: jnlinfo@blackwellpublishers.co.uk; URL: http://www.blackwellpublishers.co.uk. Ed. Richard Briston. adv. circ. 1,350. (reprint service avail. from SWZ,UMI) **Indexed:** ABI Inform., Account.& Data Proc.Abstr., Account.Ind. (1974-), BPIA, Bus.Ind., C.R.E.J., Cont.Pg.Manage., J.Cont.Quant.Meth., Manage.Cont., Mgmt.& Market.Abstr., SCIMP (1978-), Tr.& Indus.Ind., World Bank.Abstr. **Document type:** academic/scholarly publication.
—BLDSC (4954.693000); SWETS; UMI; UnCover. CCC.
Refereed Serial

657 336 US ISSN 1054-3007
HF5686.B7
JOURNAL OF CONSTRUCTION ACCOUNTING AND TAXATION. 1991. q. $125.98 (overseas $199.95) (effective 1995). Warren, Gorham & Lamont, One Penn Plaza, New York, NY 10119. TEL 212-971-5000. FAX 212-971-5113. (Subscr. to: The Park Square Bldg., 31 St. James Ave., Boston, MA 02116-4112. TEL 800-950-1207) Ed. Gersham Goldstein. (also avail. in microform from UMI; reprint service avail. from WSH) **Document type:** trade publication.
—UMI. CCC.
Description: Provides in-depth coverage of accounting, tax, and financial problems encountered in the construction industry.

657 US ISSN 1044-8136
HF5686.C7 CODEN: JCAFFX
JOURNAL OF CORPORATE ACCOUNTING AND FINANCE. 1979. q. $249 (foreign $273) (effective 1998). John Wiley & Sons, Inc., Journals, 605 Third Ave., New York, NY 10158. TEL 212-850-6645. FAX 212-850-6021. E-mail: subinfo@jwiley.com; URL: http://www.wiley.co.uk. Ed. Paul Munter. adv.: B&W page £640, color page £1515; trim 279 x 210. (also avail. in microfiche from WSH; reprint service avail. from WSH) **Indexed:** Account.Ind. (1989-), B.P.I., BPIA. **Document type:** trade publication.
—BLDSC (4965.333000); KR SourceOne; SWETS; UMI. CCC.
Former titles (until 1989): Financial Accounting Reporter (ISSN 0890-3484); (until 1986): Corporate Accounting Reporter (ISSN 0199-0683); Financial Regulation Report.
Description: Provides advice on dealing with current issues. Examines corporate accounting practices and policies and analyzes existing and proposed professional regulatory and tax law developments.

657 US ISSN 0882-3871
HF5686.C8
JOURNAL OF COST ANALYSIS. 1984. a. $40 (foreign $50) (effective 1995). Society of Cost Estimating and Analysis, 101 S. Whiting St., Ste. 201, Alexandria, VA 22304. TEL 703-751-8069. FAX 703-461-7328. Ed. Roland Kankey. R&P contact: Leroy Baseman. abstr.; bibl.; illus. circ. 2,500. **Indexed:** Account.Ind. (1984-). **Document type:** academic/scholarly publication.
Refereed Serial

JOURNAL OF FINANCIAL PLANNING. see *BUSINESS AND ECONOMICS — Investments*

JOURNAL OF I S FINANCIAL MANAGEMENT. see *COMPUTERS — Electronic Data Processing*

THE JOURNAL OF INFORMATION SYSTEMS. see *COMPUTERS — Information Science And Information Theory*

657 336 US ISSN 1061-9518
HF5601
JOURNAL OF INTERNATIONAL ACCOUNTING, AUDITING AND TAXATION. 1992. s-a. $75 to individuals (foreign $95); institutions $205 (foreign $225) (effective 1998). J A I Press Inc., 55 Old Post Rd., No. 2, Box 1678, Greenwich, CT 06830-1678. TEL 203-661-7602. FAX 203-661-0792. E-mail: jai@jaipress.com; URL: http://www.jaipress.com/jiaat.htm. (Addr. in Europe: J A I Press Ltd., 38 Tavistock St., Covent Garden, London WC2E 7PB, England. TEL 44-171-379-8834. FAX 44-171-379-8835) Ed.Bd. (also avail. in microform from UMI; back issues avail.) **Document type:** trade publication.
—BLDSC (5007.548900); SWETS; UnCover. CCC.

JOURNAL OF INTERNATIONAL FINANCIAL MANAGEMENT AND ACCOUNTING. see *BUSINESS AND ECONOMICS — Banking And Finance*

657 658 US ISSN 1049-2127
HF5657.4
JOURNAL OF MANAGEMENT ACCOUNTING RESEARCH. 1989. a. $15. American Accounting Association, 5717 Bessie Dr., Sarasota, FL 34233. TEL 941-921-7747. FAX 941-923-4093. URL: http://www.nan.shh.fi/raw/aaa/aaa.htm. R&P contact: Mary Cole. **Document type:** academic/scholarly publication.
●Also available online. Vendor(s): UMI.
—BLDSC (5011.130000); SWETS; UMI.

657 510 US ISSN 1015-7891
JOURNAL OF PARAMETRICS. 1981. s-a. $45 membership (effective 1997). (International Society of Parametric Analysts, Inc. (ISPA)) J. Clyde Perry and Associates, Box 6402, Chesterfield, MO 63006-6402. TEL 314-527-2955. FAX 314-256-8358. Eds. Glenn Boyce, Jr., Dimitri Mavris. R&P contact: Clyde Perry. adv. contact: Clyde Perry. circ. 400. **Document type:** trade publication.
—BLDSC (5028.650000).
Description: Covers cost estimating and analysis.

657 IC
▼**K P M G FRETTIR/K P M G NEWS.** 1995. irreg. free to qualified personnel. Klynveld, Peat Marwick, Goerdeler Endurskodun hf., Vegmuli 3, IS-108 Reykjavik, Iceland. TEL 354-533-5555. FAX 354-533-5550. Ed. Saemundur Valdimarsson; Pub. Olafur Nilsson. illus. circ. 2,000. **Document type:** newsletter, trade publication.
Description: Contains news and other material of interest to public accountants and their clients in Iceland and elsewhere.

K R P; Zeitschrift fuer Controlling. (Kostenrechnungspraxis) see *BUSINESS AND ECONOMICS — Management*

657 UK
▼**KEY NOTE MARKET REPORT: ACCOUNTANCY.** Variant title: Accountancy. 1995. irreg. £205. Key Note Ltd., Field House, 72 Oldfield Rd., Hampton, Middlesex TW12 2HQ, England. TEL 44-181-783-0755. FAX 44-181-783-0049. **Document type:** trade publication.
●Also available online.
Also available on CD-ROM.
Formerly: Key Note Report: Accountancy.

657 YU ISSN 0023-2394
KNJIGOVODSTVO; casopis za pitanja knjigovodstva. 1956. fortn. 750 din. Udruzenje Knjigovoda Srbije, Njegoseva 19, PO Box 403, Belgrade, Yugoslavia. Ed. Sergije Djurovic.

657 GW ISSN 0172-7400
KREDITPRAXIS. bi-m. DM.139 (student DM.98) (foreign DM.150) (effective 1997). Betriebswirtschaftlicher Verlag Dr. Th. Gabler GmbH, Abraham-Lincoln-Str. 46, 65189 Wiesbaden, Germany. TEL 49-611-7878129. FAX 49-611-7878423. **Document type:** trade publication.
—CCC.

LAWYERS' AND ACCOUNTANTS' GUIDE TO PURCHASE - SALE OF SMALL BUSINESS. see *LAW*

LEDGER QUARTERLY. see *BUSINESS AND ECONOMICS — Banking And Finance*

LEGAL ABACUS. see *LAW*

BUSINESS AND ECONOMICS — ACCOUNTING

LEGISLATIVE POLICY DISCUSSION PAPER. see *LAW — Corporate Law*

657   UK
LIBRA. 1974. q. free to members. Chartered Accountant Students' Society of London (CASSL), Friendly House, 52 Tabernacle St., London EC2A 4NB, England. TEL 44-171-250-3072. FAX 44-171-253-4630. Ed. Janet P. Brown. R&P contact: Janet P. Brown. adv. contact: Lesley Wyper. bk.rev.; circ. 6,500 (controlled). **Document type:** newsletter.

657   UK
▼**LONDON ACCOUNTANT.** 1995. 10/yr. £60 (outside Europe £64). (London Society of Chartered Accountants) Angel Business Communications Ltd., Kingsland House, 361-373 City Rd., London EC1V 1LR, England. TEL 44-171-417-7400. FAX 44-171-417-7500. Ed. Peter Williams. circ. 21,041 (controlled). (back issues avail.) **Document type:** trade publication.
 Description: Official publication of the society. Features a wide range of topics from IT to factoring & discounting, and tax to education.

657   NE   ISSN 0924-6304
M A B - MAANDBLAD VOOR ACCOUNTANCY EN BEDRIJFSECONOMIE. Key Title: M A B. (Text mainly in Dutch; occasionally in English) 1924. 10/yr. fl.130. Delwel Uitgeverij B.V., Postbus 19110, 2500 CC The Hague, Netherlands. TEL 31-70-3624800. FAX 31-70-3605606. Ed.Bd. adv.; bk.rev.; abstr.; charts; stat.; index. circ. 5,000. **Indexed:** Key to Econ.Sci. **Document type:** academic/scholarly publication.
 —BLDSC (5318.914000); SWETS; UMI.
 Formerly (until 1989): Maandblad voor Accountancy en Bedrijfshuishoudkunde (ISSN 0024-8622)
 Description: Forum for practical and scholarly debate of issues of interest to the accounting profession.

657   US
M A N A BUSINESS & TAX STRATEGIES.* (Includes: Business Owner) 1991. bi-m. membership. Business Owner, 16 Fox Ln., Locust Valley, NY 11560-1119. TEL 516-681-2111. circ. 10,000.

657   II   ISSN 0025-1674
HF5686.C8
MANAGEMENT ACCOUNTANT. (Text in English) 1955. m. Rs.300($150) Institute of Cost and Works Accountants of India, 12 Sudder St., Calcutta 700 016, India. TEL 91-33-244-1031. FAX 91-33-244-0993. TELEX 215503 ICWA IN. Ed. Siddhartha Sen. adv.; B&W page Rs.8000; 260 x 200. bk.rev.; charts; illus.; stat.; index. circ. 45,000. (also avail. in microfiche from UMI) **Indexed:** Account.Ind. (1974-), Intl.Mgmt.Info, Pub.Admin.Abstr. **Document type:** academic/scholarly publication.
 —BLDSC (5359.003000); UMI.
 Supersedes: Cost and Works Accountant.

657   PK
HD47
MANAGEMENT ACCOUNTANT. (Text in English) 1962; N.S. 1992. q. $10 to non-members. Institute of Cost and Management Accountants of Pakistan, ST-18 C, Block 6, Gulshan-e-Iqbal, Karachi 75300, Pakistan. TEL 92-21-460900. FAX 92-21-462702. Ed. M.H. Asif. adv.; bk.rev.; illus. circ. 5,000. (also avail. in microform from UMI; reprint service avail. from UMI) **Indexed:** Account.Ind. (1975-).
 —UMI; UnCover.
 Formerly (until 1992): Industrial Accountant (ISSN 0019-7793)

657   CN   ISSN 1182-8951
MANAGEMENT ACCOUNTER. q. free to members. Society of Management Accountants of Alberta, 1800-125 Ninth Ave., S.E., Calgary, AB T2G 0P6, Canada. TEL 403-269-5341. FAX 403-262-5477. E-mail: socmanaa@ccinet.ab.ca. Ed. Barbara Warburton. adv. contact: Joan Bedard. bk.rev.; circ. 7,000 (controlled). **Document type:** newsletter.
 Formerly: Accounter (ISSN 0702-5300)

657   UK   ISSN 0025-1682
HF5686.C8   CODEN: MATGBA
MANAGEMENT ACCOUNTING. 1921. m. £30. Chartered Institute of Management Accountants, c/o Management Accounting, 63 Portland Pl., London W1N 4AB. TEL 44-171-637-2311. FAX 44-171-495-6098. E-mail: journal@cima.org.uk; URL: http://www.cima.org.uk/inst.htm. Ed. John Hillary. adv.; bk.rev.; charts; illus.; stat.; index. circ. 100,000. (reprint service avail. from SCH) **Indexed:** ABI Inform., Account.Ind. (1974-), ANBAR, ASEAN Manage.Abstr., BMT, BPIA, Build.Manage.Abstr., Bus.Ind., Cont.Pg.Manage., Data Process.Dig., Intl.Mgmt.Info., Key to Econ.Sci., Manage.Cont., Mgmt.& Market.Abstr., SCIMP (1979-), Tr.& Indus.Ind., World Bank.Abstr. **Document type:** trade publication.
 ●Also available online. Vendor(s): UMI.
 —BLDSC (5359.005000); AskIEEE; KR SourceOne; SWETS; UMI; UnCover.
 Formerly: Cost Accountant.

657   US   ISSN 0025-1690
HF5686.C8   CODEN: MGACBD
MANAGEMENT ACCOUNTING. 1919. m. $135 (effective Sep. 1997). Institute of Management Accountants, 10 Paragon Dr., Montvale, NJ 07645-1760. TEL 201-573-9000; 800-638-4427. FAX 201-573-0639. E-mail: mgtacct@imanet.org; URL: http://www.imanet.org; http://www.rutgers.edu/Accounting/raw/ima/maraw.htm. Ed. Kathy Williams; Pub. Gary Scopes. R&P contact: Robert F. Randall. adv. contact: Jim Hart. bk.rev.; charts; illus.; index, cum.index: 1920-1990, 1990-1995. circ. 85,000. (also avail. in microform from KTO,UMI; back issues avail.; reprint service avail. from SCH,UMI) **Indexed:** ABI Inform., Account.Ind. (1974-), Anbar, ASEAN Manage.Abstr., B.P.I., BPIA, Bus.Ind., Comput.Lit.Ind., Cont.Pg.Manage., Data Process.Dig., Eng.Ind., INSPEC, Intl.Mgmt.Info., Key to Econ.Sci., Manage.Cont., P.A.I.S., PSI, SCIMP, Tr.& Indus.Ind. **Document type:** trade publication.
 ●Also available online. Vendor(s): Information Access Co., UMI.
 —BLDSC (5359.006000); AskIEEE; KR SourceOne; SWETS; UMI. CCC.
 Formerly: N A A Bulletin-Management Accounting.

657   UK   ISSN 1044-5005
HF5657.4
MANAGEMENT ACCOUNTING RESEARCH. Short title: M A R. 1983. q. £64($120) to individuals; institutions £139 (effective 1998). (Chartered Institute of Management Accountants) Academic Press Ltd. (Subsidiary of: Harcourt Brace & Company Ltd.), 24-28 Oval Rd., London NW1 7DX, England. TEL 44-171-267-4466. FAX 44-171-482-2293. TELEX 25775 ACPRES G. E-mail: apsubs@acad.com; URL: http://www.hbuk.co.uk/ap/mar; http://www.europe.idealibrary.com/. (Subscr. to: Harcourt Brace & Company Ltd., Foots Cray High St., Sidcup, Kent DA14 5HP, England. TEL 44-181-300-3322. FAX 44-181-309-0807) Eds. M. Bromwich, R.W. Scapens. R&P contact: Catherine John. adv. contact: Nik Screen. circ. 400. (reprint service avail. from SWZ) **Cont.Pg.Manage. Document type:** academic/scholarly publication.
 ●Also available online.
 —BLDSC (5359.006370); SWETS; UnCover. CCC.
 Supersedes: I C M A Abstracts Bulletin.
 Description: Aims to encourage scholarship and empirical research in management accounting by providing a vehicle for publishing original research in the field.

657   US   ISSN 1080-5753
▼**MANAGING ACCOUNTS PAYABLE.** 1995. m. $249 (outside N. America $273). Institute of Management & Administration, Inc., 29 W. 35th St., 5th fl., New York, NY 10001-2299. TEL 212-244-0360. FAX 212-564-0465. URL: http://www.ioma.com. Ed. Lisa Isom; Pub. Lee Rath. R&P contact: Sofie Kourkoutakis. **Document type:** newsletter.

658   US
MANAGING YOUR ACCOUNTING AND CONSULTING PRACTICE. (Issued as 1 base vol. with supplements) 1978. irreg. Matthew Bender & Co., Inc., 2 Park Ave., New York, NY 10016. TEL 212-448-2000. FAX 518-462-3788. E-mail: international@bender.com; URL: http://www.bender.com. Eds. Mary Ann Altman, Robert I. Weil. (looseleaf format)
 Description: Comprehensive guidebook for accountants and consultants, including management consultants and engineers, on applying sound management principles to their own practices.

657.04   SA
MANEO. (Text in Afrikaans, English) 1993. bi-m. membership. Public Accountants' and Auditors' Board - Openbare Rekenmeesters- en Ouditeursraad, P.O. Box 59783, Kengray 2100, South Africa. illus. **Document type:** newsletter.

657   US   ISSN 0025-4770
MASSACHUSETTS C P A REVIEW. 1928. 4/yr. $20 to non-members. Massachusetts Society of Certified Public Accountants, Inc., 105 Chauncy St., 10th Fl., Boston, MA 02111-1742. TEL 617-556-4000. FAX 617-556-4126. E-mail: 75270,3256@compuserve.com; 103146,2144@compuserve.com. Ed. Cheryl McCloud; Pub. Theodore J. Flynn. R&P contact: Christina Baltzer. adv.: B&W page $1035, color page $1655; trim 7 x 9 1/2; adv. contact: Wendy Devine. bk.rev.; cum.index. circ. 8,500. (reprint service avail. from SCH) **Indexed:** ABI Inform., Account.Ind. (1974-), BPIA, Bus.Ind. **Document type:** trade publication.
 ●Also available online. Vendor(s): UMI.
 —BLDSC (5388.630000); UMI.
 Formerly: Massachusetts Society of Certified Public Accountants, Inc. News Bulletin.

657   NZ   ISSN 1172-1065
MASSEY UNIVERSITY. DEPARTMENT OF ACCOUNTANCY. DISCUSSION PAPER SERIES. 1972. irreg., no.165, 1996. NZ.$10 per no. Massey University, Department of Accountancy and Business Law, Private Bag 11222, Palmerston North, New Zealand. TEL 64-6-3505259. FAX 64-6-3505617. E-mail: K.Dixon@massey.ac.nz. Ed. Kieth Dixon. R&P contact: M.H.B. Perera. adv.; bk.rev. circ. 90. **Document type:** academic/scholarly publication.
 —BLDSC (3597.966350). CCC.
 Former titles (until 1990): Massey University. Division of Accountancy. Discussion Paper Series (ISSN 1170-6902); Massey University. Department of Accountancy. Discussion Paper Series (ISSN 0114-5932); Massey University. Department of Accounting and Finance. Discussion Paper Series (ISSN 0111-7874); (until 1981): Massey University. Faculty of Business Studies. Occasional Paper Series.
 Description: Intends to provide staff and postgraduate students working in the Department of Accountancy with a means of communication for new and partly developed ideas in order to facilitate academic debate.

657   US
MEDICAL CLIENT NEWSLETTER. q. C P A Associates International, Inc., Meadows Office Complex, 201 Rte. 17 N., Rutherford, NJ 07070-2574. TEL 212-804-8686.
 Description: Information on members' services to clients.

657   SA   ISSN 1022-2529
MEDITARI. (Text in Afrikaans, English) 1993. a. R.40. University of Pretoria, School of Accounting Sciences, Brooklyn, Pretoria 0002, South Africa. **Indexed:** Ind.S.A.Per. **Document type:** academic/scholarly publication.

657   US   ISSN 0026-2064
MICHIGAN C P A. 1901. q. $6. Michigan Association of C P A, Box 9054, 28116 Orchard Lake Rd., Farmington Hills, MI 48333. TEL 248-855-2288. FAX 248-855-9122. Eds. Marla Jannes, Gwen McRae. R&P contact: Chris Sheldon. adv.: B&W page $635; trim 8 1/4 x 11; adv. contact: Carmen Hernandez. circ. 5,000. **Document type:** trade publication.
 ●Also available online. Vendor(s): Information Access Co., UMI.
 —UMI.

BUSINESS AND ECONOMICS — ACCOUNTING

657 US ISSN 1077-8489
HF5616.U5
MILLER G A A P GUIDE; a comprehensive restatement of all current promulgated generally accepted accounting principles. 1980. a. (plus m. Update Service). $59 (disk $65; CD-ROM $65; updates $189) (effective 1997). Harcourt Brace Professional Publishing, 525 B St., Ste. 1900, San Diego, CA 92101-4495. TEL 619-699-6716. FAX 619-699-6542. Ed. Jan R. Williams. (also avail. in diskette format) **Document type:** trade publication.
●Also available on CD-ROM.
Former titles (until 1994): H B J Miller Comprehensive G A A P Guide (ISSN 1077-8470); (until 1992): Miller's Comprehensive G A A P Guide (ISSN 0734-8355)
Description: Restates accounting pronouncements in clear, easy-to-understand language along with examples, illustrations and expert analyses.

657.6 US
MILLER G A A S GUIDE; a comprehensive restatement of standards for auditing, attestation, compilation and review and the code of professional conduct. a. (plus m. update service). $59 (CD-ROM $65; updates $189) (effective 1997). Harcourt Brace Professional Publishing, 525 B St., Ste. 1900, San Diego, CA 92101-4495. TEL 619-699-6716. FAX 619-699-6593. Ed. Larry P. Bailey. **Document type:** trade publication.
●Also available on CD-ROM.
Description: Contains comprehensive analysis of all auditing standards. Also includes sections on auditing in a microcomputer environment, compliance auditing, new guidance on completing the audit and litigation support service.

657.2 US
MILLER GOVERNMENTAL G A A P GUIDE; a comprehensive interpretation of current promulgated governmental generally accepted accounting principles for state and local governments. a. (plus m. update service). $59 (CD-ROM $65; updates $189) (effective 1997). Harcourt Brace Professional Publishing, 525 B St., Ste. 1900, San Diego, CA 92101-4495. TEL 619-699-6716. FAX 619-699-6593. Ed. Larry P. Bailey.

657 US ISSN 1076-660X
KF1357
MODERN ACCOUNTING AND AUDITING CHECKLISTS. 2 base vols., plus s-a. updates. $169.95 (foreign $261.45) (effective 1995). Warren, Gorham & Lamont, One Penn Plaza, New York, NY 10119. TEL 212-970-5000. FAX 212-971-5113. (Subscr. to: The Park Square Bldg., 31 St. James Ave., Boston, MA 02116-4112. TEL 800-950-1207) (also avail. in looseleaf format) **Document type:** trade publication.

657 US
N O S A UPDATE. 1982. m. $76 to non-members. National Office Systems Association, Box 8187, Silver Spring, MD 20907-8187. TEL 301-589-8125. FAX 301-589-0564. **Document type:** bulletin, newsletter.
Formerly: National One-Write Systems Association Newsletter.

657 US ISSN 0469-3922
N S P A WASHINGTON REPORTER. 1947. m. membership. National Society of Public Accountants, 1010 N. Fairfax St., Alexandria, VA 22314. TEL 703-549-6400. Ed. Susan Cappitelli. circ. 22,000.
Description: Newsletter featuring updates on the activities of NSPA, Congress and the IRS.

657 336 AT ISSN 1039-608X
NATIONAL ACCOUNTANT. 1985. bi-m. Aus.$30 (foreign Aus.$60). (National Institute of Accountants) Hassel, Hunt & Moore Media Pty. Ltd., 1st Fl., 5 Vuko Pl., Warriewood, N.S.W. 2102, Australia. TEL 61-2-99706688. FAX 61-2-99706979. E-mail: hhm@franchise.net.au. Ed. Geoff Hill. R&P contact: Geoff Hill. adv.: B&W page Aus.$1925, color page Aus.$2585; trim 275 x 205; adv. contact: Ken Lane. bk.rev.; software rev. circ. 14,701. (back issues avail.)
Formerly (until 1993): Counting House (ISSN 0816-5599)
Description: Contains technical accounting, management and taxation articles.

657 305.896073 US
NATIONAL ASSOCIATION OF BLACK ACCOUNTANTS. CHAPTER TO CHAPTER. 3/yr. National Association of Black Accountants, 7249A Hanover Pkwy., Greenbelt, MD 20770-3653. TEL 301-474-6222. circ. 2,500. **Document type:** newsletter.
Formerly: National Association of Black Accountants. Student News Plus.

657 305.896073 US
NATIONAL ASSOCIATION OF BLACK ACCOUNTANTS. NEWS PLUS. q. $15. National Association of Black Accountants, 7249A Hanover Pkwy, Greenbelt, MD 20770-3653. TEL 301-474-6222. circ. 3,000. **Document type:** newsletter.

657 340 US ISSN 0889-3500
NATIONAL ASSOCIATION OF STATE BOARDS OF ACCOUNTANCY. STATE BOARD REPORT.* vol.21, 1992. m. $40. National Association of State Boards of Accountancy, 150 4th Ave., N., Ste. 700, Nashville, TN 37219-2421. Ed. James E. Thomashower. index. circ. 1,400. (tabloid format; back issues avail.)
Description: Digest of current developments affecting state accountancy regulation.

657 US
NATIONAL C P A GROUP. NEWSLETTER.* (Certified Public Accountant) bi-m. National C P A Group, c/o BKR Int'l, 40 Exchange Pl. No. 1100, New York, NY 10005-2701. TEL 212-766-4260.

657 US ISSN 0027-9978
HF5601 CODEN: NPACAI
NATIONAL PUBLIC ACCOUNTANT. 1949. m. $18 to non-members. National Society of Public Accountants, 1010 N. Fairfax St., Alexandria, VA 22314. TEL 703-549-6400. URL: http://www.nspa.org/. Ed. Mary Beth Loutinsky. adv.; bk.rev.; index. circ. 22,000. (also avail. in microfilm from UMI; reprint service avail. from UMI) **Indexed:** ABI Inform., Account.Ind. (1974-), B.P.I., BPIA, Bus.Ind., Manage.Cont., P.A.I.S., PSI, Tr.& Indus.Ind.
●Also available online. Vendor(s): UMI.
—BLDSC (6029.900000); KR SourceOne; SWETS; UMI; UnCover.
Description: For accounting and tax practitioners.

657 SZ
DIE NATIONALE BUCHHALTUNG DER SCHWEIZ/COMPTES NATIONAUX DE LA SUISSE. (Text in French and German) 1984. a. 9 SFr. Bundesamt fuer Statistik, Schwarztorstr. 96, CH-3003 Bern, Switzerland. TEL 41-31-3236060. FAX 41-31-3236061. URL: http://www.admin.ch/bfs. **Document type:** government publication.

657 NE
NEDERLANDSE ORDE VAN ACCOUNTANTS - ADMINISTRATIECONSULTENTEN. LEDEN - INFO. bi-m. Nederlandse Orde van Accountants - Administratieconsulenten, Nieuwe Parklaan 25, 2597 LA The Hague, Netherlands. TEL 31-70-3383600. FAX 31-70-3512836.

657 US ISSN 0882-8067
NEW ACCOUNTANT. 1985. 8/yr. (m. Sep.-Apr.). $85 to individuals; libraries $25. Real Estate News Corp., 3525 W. Petersen Ave., Chicago, IL 60659. Ed. Morrie Helitzer. adv.; bk.rev.; stat.; index; circ. 64,632. (controlled). (back issues avail.) **Indexed:** Account.Ind. (1985-). **Document type:** trade publication.
●Also available online. Vendor(s): UMI.
—BLDSC (6081.671000); UMI.
Description: Covers business news with special focus on careers, issues, and developments in accounting and finance.

657 CN
NEW BRUNSWICK INSTITUTE OF CHARTERED ACCOUNTANTS. NEWSLETTER. q. New Brunswick Institute of Chartered Accountants - Institut des Comptables Agrees du Nouveau-Brunswick, 93 Prince William St., 4th Fl., Saint John, N.B. E2L 2B2, Canada. TEL 506-634-1558.

150 332 AT ISSN 0155-123X
NEW ENGLAND ACCOUNTING RESEARCH STUDIES (NO.). irreg., latest no.13. University of New England, Department of Accounting and Financial Management, Armindale, N.S.W. 2351, Australia. TEL 61-67-73221. FAX 61-67-711778. R&P contact: J.J. Staunton. TEL 61-67-733276.

657 US
NEW WORKS IN ACCOUNTING HISTORY. irreg. Garland Publishing, Inc., 1000A Sherman Ave., Hamden, CT 06514. TEL 203-281-4487; 800-627-6273. FAX 203-230-1186. E-mail: info@garland.com. (And: 717 Fifth Ave., New York, NY 10022. TEL 212-751-7447) Ed. Richard P. Brief. **Document type:** monographic series.
Formerly: Academy of Accounting Historians. Monograph Series.

NEW ZEALAND COMPANY LAW GUIDE. see *LAW — Corporate Law*

657 NZ
NEW ZEALAND FINANCIAL REPORTING MANUAL. 1987. q. NZ.$716 (effective 1997). C C H New Zealand Limited, P.O. Box 2378, Auckland, New Zealand. TEL 64-9-483-9179. FAX 64-9-483-4009. (looseleaf format)
Formerly: New Zealand Accounts Preparation Manual.
Description: A comprehensive service providing detailed coverage of the preparation of financial statements by business entities in New Zealand. Includes full text of New Zealand Accounting Standards with commentary and new draft proposals.

657 US
NEWS & VIEWS (LAKE SUCCESS). m. National Conference of C P A Practitioners, 3000 Marcus Ave., Lake Success, NY 11042. TEL 516-488-5400. FAX 516-488-5549. Ed. Brenda Mahler. R&P contact: Brenda Mahler. circ. 1,200.
Formerly: National Conference of C P A Practitioners. Newsletter.

657 CC ISSN 1002-5588
NONGCUN CAIWU KUAIJI/RURAL FINANCE AND ACCOUNTING. (Text in Chinese) m. Y12. Nongye Bu, Hezuo Jingji Jingying Guanli Zongzhan, 11, Nongzhanguan Nanli, Beijing 100026, People's Republic of China. TEL 86-1-5005773. FAX 86-1-5002448. TELEX 22233 MAGR CN. Ed. Gaorang Shi; Pub. Jianfeng Hu. adv. contact: Jun Dai.

657 US
NONPROFIT ACCOUNTING AND AUDITING DISCLOSURE MANUAL. base vol. (plus a. supplement). $145.95 (overseas $214.45) (effective 1995). Warren, Gorham & Lamont, One Penn Plaza, New York, NY 10119. TEL 212-971-5000. FAX 212-971-5113. (Subscr. to: The Park Square Bldg., 31 St. James Ave., Boston, MA 02116-4112. TEL 800-950-1207) Eds. Allan B. Afterman, Rowan H. Jones. (looseleaf format) **Document type:** trade publication.
Description: Outlines all G.A.A.P. and G.A.A.S. disclosure requirements for nonprofit organizations.

657 US ISSN 1056-5094
HF5686.N56
THE NONPROFIT REPORT; accounting, taxation & management. 1991. m. $117.98 (overseas $170.55) (effective 1995). Warren, Gorham & Lamont, One Penn Plaza, New York, NY 10119. TEL 212-971-5000. FAX 212-971-5113. (Subscr. to: The Park Square Bldg., 31 St. James Ave., Boston, MA 02116-4112. TEL 800-950-1207) Ed. Murray Dropkin. (also avail. in microform from UMI) **Document type:** newsletter.
—UMI. **CCC.**
Description: Offers certified public accountants working with nonprofit organizations insight into key financial and tax legislation.

657 AU ISSN 1018-3779
OESTERREICHISCHE ZEITSCHRIFT FUER RECHNUNGSWESEN. m. S.1600. Verlag Orac GesmbH & Co. KG, Graben 17, A-1010 Vienna, Austria. TEL 43-1-53452-0. FAX 43-1-53452141. adv.: B&W page S.14500; trim 167 x 249; adv. contact: Christian Braun. circ. 5,200. **Document type:** trade publication.

BUSINESS AND ECONOMICS — ACCOUNTING

657 US ISSN 0749-8284
HF5601 CODEN: OCPAA7
THE OHIO C P A JOURNAL. 1941. q. $20 (foreign $35). Ohio Society of Certified Public Accountants, 535 Metro Place S., Box 1810, Dublin, OH 43017-7810. TEL 614-764-2727. FAX 614-764-5880. Ed. James Meddaugh; Pub. Clarke Price. R&P contact: Angela Jacobsen. adv. contact: Mike Domke. bk.rev.; charts; stat.; index. circ. 19,000. (also avail. in microform from UMI; reprint service avail. from UMI) **Indexed:** ABI Inform., Account.& Data Proc.Abstr., Account.Ind. (1974-), Anbar, BPIA, INSPEC (1983-), Manage.Cont., Tr.& Indus.Ind. **Document type:** trade publication.
● Also available online. Vendor(s): Information Access Co., UMI.
—BLDSC (6245.582000); AskIEEE; KR SourceOne; UMI; UnCover.
Former titles (until 1979): Ohio C P A (ISSN 0737-7371); (until 1958): Ohio Certified Public Accountant.
Description: Professional advice, technical and educational materials, and issues relevant to members of the O S C P A, accounting educators, business and finance professionals.

657 665.5 US ISSN 1059-6003
HF5686.P3
OIL AND GAS ACCOUNTING. 1978. a. $140. (Southwestern Legal Foundation) Matthew Bender & Co., Inc., 2 Park Ave., New York, NY 10016. TEL 212-448-2000. E-mail: international@bender.com; URL: http://www.bender.com. (looseleaf format)
Description: Provides analysis of recent developments in oil and gas accounting, including tax issues in the petroleum industry, trends in capital formation, financing innovations and current developments of FASB.

OIL & GAS FINANCE AND ACCOUNTING. see PETROLEUM AND GAS

657 CN
ORDRE DES COMPTABLES AGREES DU QUEBEC. BILAN. (Text in English, French) 1953. 6/yr. Can.$18 to individuals; students Can.$10 (effective 1997). Ordre des Comptables Agrees du Quebec, 680 Sherbrooke St. W., 7th Fl., Montreal, PQ H3A 2S3, Canada. TEL 514-982-4620. FAX 514-843-8375. E-mail: pm.adam@ocaq.qc.ca; URL: http://www.ocaq.qc.ca. Ed. Maryse Parant. adv.: B&W page Can.$1220, color page Can.$2545; trim 8 1/4 x 11. bk.rev.; illus. circ. 19,000. **Document type:** newsletter.
Former titles: Ordre des Comptables Agrees du Quebec. Bilans (ISSN 0828-6833); (until Mar. 1983): Ordre des Comptables Agrees du Quebec. Journal (ISSN 0711-3560); Order of Chartered Accountants of Quebec. Newsletter.
Description: Includes articles on accounting, business, economy, taxation and new technology.

657 US ISSN 0273-835X
HF5601
OUTLOOK (REDWOOD CITY). 1925. q. $30 to non-members (Canada $35; Europe, S. America, and North Africa $40). California Society of Certified Public Accountants, 275 Shoreline Dr., Redwood City, CA 94065. TEL 415-802-2427. FAX 415-802-2300. E-mail: 74140.3614@compuserve.com. Ed. David MacFarlane; Pub. Jim Kurtz. adv. contact: Larry Peters. circ. 29,000. (also avail. in microform from UMI; reprint service avail. from UMI) **Indexed:** AAR, Account.Ind. (1974-), Anbar, BPIA, Bus.Ind., Bus.Ind., Tr.& Indus.Ind. **Document type:** trade publication.
● Also available online. Vendor(s): Information Access Co.
—UMI; UnCover.
Former titles (until 1980): California C P A Quarterly (ISSN 0008-0934); California Certified Public Accountant.

OVERHEIDSMANAGEMENT; vakblad voor financien automatisering en personeel & organisatie. see BUSINESS AND ECONOMICS — Banking And Finance

657 UK ISSN 1352-8645
P A S S. (Professional Accountancy Student Service); the first choice for Rart Qualified Accountants. 1984. m. £30 (foreign £35). Reed Business Information, Quadrant House, The Quadrant, Sutton, Surrey SM2 5AS, England. TEL 44-181-652-4720. FAX 44-181-652-4748. Ed. Graham Hambly. adv.; bk.rev.; bibl.; charts; illus.; stat. circ. 25,000. (tabloid format; back issues avail.) **Document type:** trade publication.

657 510 US ISSN 1072-3803
PARAMETRIC WORLD. 1981. bi-m. $15 to non-members (effective 1997). International Society of Parametric Analysts Inc. (ISPA), Box 6402, Chesterfield, MO 63006-6402. TEL 314-527-2955. FAX 314-256-8358. Eds. Nina Tahir, Gary Constantine. circ. 500. **Document type:** trade publication.
Description: Newsletter which discusses parametrics, with emphasis on cost estimating.

657 SP ISSN 1133-7869
PARTIDA DOBLE. 1990. 11/yr. 21700 ptas. (effective 1996). Grupo Especial Directivos, C. Orense 39 2o D, 28020 Madrid, Spain. TEL 34-1-5556411. FAX 34-1-5554148. Ed. Francisco Serrano. adv.: B&W page 230000 ptas., color page 275000 ptas.; trim 185 x 272; adv. contact: Ricardo Zavala. circ. 7,500.

657 US ISSN 1043-7428
PARTNER'S REPORT, THE MONTHLY UPDATE FOR CPA FIRM OWNERS. 1989. m. $259 (outside N. America $283). Institute of Management & Administration, Inc., 29 W. 35th St., 5th Fl., New York, NY 10001-2299. TEL 212-244-0360. FAX 212-564-0465. URL: http://www.ioma.com. Ed. Sue Sandler; Pub. Lee Rath. R&P contact: Sofie Kourkoutakis. index. (looseleaf format; back issues avail.) **Document type:** newsletter.
—CCC.
Description: Offers management advice for owners of CPA firms to help them enhance profits. Practical guidance on compensation and benefits, retirement plan alternatives, professional liability coverage, "rainmaking".

657 AT ISSN 1037-7093
PASSWORD. 1982. q. membership. Information Systems Audit and Control Association, Melbourne Chapter, G.P.O. Box 451C, Melbourne, Vic. 3001, Australia. TEL 61-3-96333889. FAX 61-3-96333460. E-mail: marlin.silcock@colybrand.com.au. Ed. G. Breydon. adv.; bk.rev. circ. 900. **Document type:** newsletter.

PATIENT ACCOUNTS. see HOSPITALS

PAYMENTS SYSTEM REPORT. see BUSINESS AND ECONOMICS — Banking And Finance — Computer Applications

657 336 US ISSN 1063-3200
KF6436
PAYROLL PRACTITIONER'S COMPLIANCE HANDBOOK; year-end and quarterly reporting. base vol. (plus a. update). $99 (foreign $163.70). Warren, Gorham & Lamont, One Penn Plaza, New York, NY 10119. TEL 212-971-5000. FAX 212-971-5113. (Subscr. to: The Park Square Bldg., 31 St. James Ave., Boston, MA 02116-4112. TEL 800-950-1207) Eds. Howard Freedman, Debera J. Salam. charts. (looseleaf format) **Document type:** trade publication.
Description: Training manual that includes all payroll essentials with clear explanations of laws and accounting procedures.

657 US ISSN 0746-1062
PENNSYLVANIA C P A JOURNAL. 1931. q. $3 to non-members. Pennsylvania Institute of Certified Public Accountants, 1608 Walnut St., 3rd Fl., Philadelphia, PA 19103. TEL 215-735-2635; 888-272-2001. FAX 215-735-3694. E-mail: picpa@ix.netcom.comrve.com; URL: http://www.picpa.com. Ed. Ross Wladis. R&P contact: Laurel Webster. adv. contact: Christine Sullivan. index. circ. 20,000. **Indexed:** ABI Inform., Account.Ind. (1974-). **Document type:** trade publication.
● Also available online. Vendor(s): UMI.
—BLDSC (6421.704000); UMI; UnCover.
Formerly (until June 1983): Pennsylvania C P A Spokesman (ISSN 0031-4390)
Description: Focuses on information and developments that affect the day-to-day operations of CPAs in Pennsylvania.

PENSION COORDINATOR. see BUSINESS AND ECONOMICS — Personnel Management

657 US
PERSONAL FINANCE PLANNING QUARTERLY.* q. National C P A Group, c/o BKR Int'l, 40 Exchange Pl., No. 1100, New York, NY 10005-2701. TEL 212-766-4260.

PEYRON TAX ACCOUNTANT'S COMMUNIQUE. see BUSINESS AND ECONOMICS — Public Finance, Taxation

657 US
PISTAS DE AUDITORIA. (Text in Spanish) 1986. bi-m. membership. Institute of Internal Auditors, 249 Maitland Ave., Altamonte Springs, FL 32701. TEL 407-830-7600. FAX 407-831-5171. R&P contact: J. Burke. circ. 3,500. **Document type:** newsletter.

DER PLATOW BRIEF. see BUSINESS AND ECONOMICS — Economic Situation And Conditions

657 336.2 US ISSN 0032-6321
HF5601 CODEN: PACNBD
THE PRACTICAL ACCOUNTANT; accounting and taxes in everyday practice. 1967. m. $60. Faulkner and Gray, Inc. (New York), 11 Penn Plaza, 17th Fl., New York, NY 10001. TEL 212-967-7000. FAX 212-967-7155. URL: http://www.faulknergray.com/account/prac.htm. adv.; bk.rev.; charts; illus.; stat.; index. circ. 45,422. (also avail. in microform from UMI; reprint service avail. from UMI) **Indexed:** ABI Inform., Account.Ind. (1986-), B.P.I, BPIA, Bus.Ind., Law Ofc.Info.Svc., Leg.Cont., Manage.Cont., PROMT, PSI, Tr.& Indus.Ind. **Document type:** trade publication.
● Also available online. Vendor(s): Information Access Co., UMI.
—BLDSC (6593.870000); KR SourceOne; SWETS; UMI; UnCover. **CCC.**
Formerly: Practical Accounting.
Description: Forum covering every facet of accounting and taxes.

657 336.2 US ISSN 1055-7717
KF6314.A15
PRACTICAL ACCOUNTANT ALERT. 24/yr. $98. Faulkner and Gray, Inc. (New York), 11 Penn Plaza, 17th Fl., New York, NY 10001. TEL 212-967-7000. FAX 212-967-7155. (also avail. in microform from UMI)
—UMI.
Description: Covers taxes, IRS highlights, computers, practice management, accounting, auditing, government contracts and more.

PRACTICAL CASH MANAGEMENT. see BUSINESS AND ECONOMICS — Banking And Finance

657 US
PRACTICE STRATEGIES. q. membership only. Associated Regional Accounting Firms, 3700 Crestwood Pky., N.W., Duluth, GA 30136-5599. TEL 770-279-4560. **Document type:** newsletter.

657 US ISSN 0885-6931
PRACTICING C P A. 1991. m. membership only. American Institute of Certified Public Accountants, Private Companies Practice Section, Harborside Financial Ctr., 201 Plaza Three, Jersey City, NJ 07311-3881. TEL 201-938-3796; 800-862-4272. FAX 800-329-1112. URL: http://www.aicpa.org. (Alt. addr.: AICPA, 1211 Ave. of the Americas, New York, NY 10036. TEL 212-596-6200) Ed. Graham G. Goddard. circ. controlled. (back issues avail.) **Indexed:** Account.Ind. (1978-). **Document type:** trade publication.
● Also available online. Vendor(s): UMI.
—UMI.

657 NE ISSN 1380-0256
PRAKTIJK REGISTER ACCOUNTANTS (YEAR). Variant title: N I V R A Gids. a. fl.110. Delwel Uitgeverij B.V., Postbus 19110, 2500 CC The Hague, Netherlands. TEL 31-70-3624800. FAX 31-70-3605606. **Document type:** directory.
Description: Discusses significant developments in the accounting profession, and provides current information on practicing accountants in the Netherlands, as well as information on accounting divisions of government agencies at a national, regional and local level.

PRAKTIJKBOEK VOOR VENNOOTSCHAPPEN; juridisch, boekhoudkundig, fiscaal. see LAW — Corporate Law

BUSINESS AND ECONOMICS — ACCOUNTING

657 658 IT
PRATICA AZIENDALE. 1979. m. L.160000($100) Pirola Editore S.p.A., Via Parabiago 19, Casella Postale 10444, 20110 Milan, Italy. TEL 2-30-221. FAX 2-380-11-205. Ed.Bd. bk.rev. circ. 3,500.

PRINCIPLES OF PAYROLL ADMINISTRATION; the complete learning and reference guide. see *BUSINESS AND ECONOMICS — Management*

657 AT ISSN 1030-5890
PROPOSED STATEMENT OF ACCOUNTING CONCEPTS. 1987. irreg. Aus.$6 per issue. Australian Accounting Research Foundation, 211 Hawthorn Rd., Caulfield, Vic. 3162, Australia. TEL 61-3-95238111. FAX 61-3-95235499. E-mail: standard@aarf.asn.au. (Co-sponsors: Australian Society of Certified Practising Accountants; Institute of Chartered Accountants in Australia) circ. 1,400.

657 US ISSN 0160-3094
CODEN: NRATBG
PUBLIC ACCOUNTING REPORT. 1978. 23/yr. $267 (Canada $297; elsewhere $322) (effective Oct. 1996). Strafford Publications, Inc., Specialized Information Services, 590 Dutch Valley Rd., N.E., Drawer 13729, Atlanta, GA 30324-0729. TEL 404-881-1141. FAX 404-881-0074. E-mail: custserv@straffordpub.com. Ed. Suzanne Verity; Pub. Richard M. Ossoff. R&P contact: Marianne Mueller. (looseleaf format; back issues avail.) Indexed: Account.Ind. (1981-). **Document type:** newsletter.
Description: Provides firms with authoritative news and analysis of developments in the profession today, as well as trends.

PUBLIC MONEY. see *BUSINESS AND ECONOMICS — Public Finance, Taxation*

657 005.3 US ISSN 1055-0208
QUANTUM P C REPORT FOR C P AS. 1986. m. $235. Quantum Professional Publishing, 700 Larkspur Landing Cir., Ste. 199, Larkspur, CA 94939. TEL 415-789-8800. FAX 415-435-3851. Ed. Jack C. McClure. circ. 1,000 (paid). **Document type:** newsletter.
—KR SourceOne.
Description: Articles by CPAs to help CPAs become more proficient with PCs.

QUESTION BUDGET, INCOME TAX LAW FOR ACCOUNTANTS, INCOME TAX LAW FOR TAX AGENTS. ANSWERS TO QUESTIONS (YEAR). see *BUSINESS AND ECONOMICS — Public Finance, Taxation*

657 PL ISSN 0481-5475
RACHUNKOWOSC. 1949. m. 9.50 (foreign $6) per issue (effective 1996 & 1997). (Stowarzyszenie Ksiegowych w Polsce) Rachunkowosc Sp. z o.o., Ul. Tamka 18, lokal 29, 00-349 Warsaw, Poland. TEL 48-22-265621. FAX 48-22-265621. (Dist. by: Centrala Kolportazy "Ruch", Towarowa 28, 00-958 Warsaw, Poland) Ed. Zdzislaw Fedak. adv.; bk.rev.; bibl.; index. circ. 36,000.
Refereed Serial

RAILWAY ACCOUNTING RULES. see *TRANSPORTATION — Railroads*

657 UK
RECOMMENDATION FOR ACCOUNTANTS AND AUDITORS. 1980. irreg. £4.50. Marcus Tobias & Co., 65 Shakespeare Dr., Shirley, Solihull B90 2AN, England. TEL 0121-744-2912. FAX 0121-733-2902. **Document type:** monographic series.

657 US ISSN 1052-0457
K18
RESEARCH IN ACCOUNTING REGULATION. 1987. irreg., vol.11, 1997. $73.25. J A I Press Inc., 55 Old Post Rd., No. 2, Box 1678, Greenwich, CT 06830-1678. TEL 203-661-7602. FAX 203-661-0792. E-mail: jai@jaipress.com. (Subscr. in the UK and Europe to: JAI Press Ltd., 38 Tavistock St., Covent Garden, London WC2E 7PB, England. TEL 44-171-379-8834. FAX 44-171-379-8835) Ed. Gary John Previts. **Document type:** monographic series.
—BLDSC (7714.305000).

657 US ISSN 0884-0741
HJ9701
RESEARCH IN GOVERNMENTAL AND NON-PROFIT ACCOUNTING. 1985. irreg., vol.10, 1997. $78.50. J A I Press Inc., 55 Old Post Rd., No.2, Box 1678, Greenwich, CT 06830-1678. TEL 203-661-7602. FAX 203-661-0792. E-mail: jai@jaipress.com. (Subscr. in the UK and Europe to: JAI Press Ltd., 38 Tavistock St., Covent Garden, London WC2E 7PB, England. TEL 44-171-379-8834. FAX 44-171-379-8835) Ed. James L. Chan. **Document type:** monographic series.
—BLDSC (7741.146000).

657 UK ISSN 1058-1995
HF5616.D44
RESEARCH IN THIRD WORLD ACCOUNTING. 1990. a. J A I Press Ltd., The Courtyard, 28 High St., Hampton Hill, Mddx. TW12 1PD, England. TEL 44-181-943-9296. FAX 44-181-943-9317. E-mail: jai@cix.compulink.co.uk. (U.S. addr.: JAI Press, Inc., 55 Old Press Rd., No.2, Greenwich, CT 06836-1678. TEL 203-661-7602. FAX 203-661-0792) Ed.Bd. **Document type:** academic/scholarly publication.
—BLDSC (7773.718000).

657 US
RESEARCH INSTITUTE OF AMERICA. SPECIAL STUDIES. m. $125. Research Institute of America, Inc., 90 Fifth Ave., New York, NY 10011. TEL 212-645-4800. FAX 212-337-4279. (Subscr. to: 117 E. Stevens Ave., Valhalla, NY 10595. TEL 800-431-9025) **Document type:** academic/scholarly publication.
Description: Provides in-depth discussions of key tax developments.

657 170 US
▼**RESEARCH ON ACCOUNTING ETHICS.** 1995. irreg., vol.3, 1997. $73.25. J A I Press Inc., 55 Old Post Rd., No. 2, Box 1678, Greenwich, CT 06830-1678. TEL 203-661-7602. FAX 203-661-0792. E-mail: jai@jaipress.com. (Addr. in Europe: J A I Press Ltd., 38 Tavistock St., Covent Garden, London WC2E 7PB, England. TEL 44-171-379-8834. FAX 44-171-379-8835) Ed. Lawrence Ponemon. **Document type:** monographic series.

REVENUE ACCOUNTING MANUAL. see *TRANSPORTATION — Air Transport*

657 330 US ISSN 1089-8670
HF5679
▼**REVIEW OF ACCOUNTING INFORMATION SYSTEMS.** 1997. q. $186 (effective 1997). Western Academic Press, Box 620760, Littleton, CO 80162. TEL 303-904-4750. FAX 303-978-0413. E-mail: cluter@wapress.com; URL: http://www.cluter@wapress.com. Ed. Ronald C. Clute. circ. 600. **Document type:** academic/scholarly publication.
Description: Provides a forum for research and debate for all areas of accounting information systems.
Refereed Serial

657 US ISSN 1380-6653
HF5601
▼**REVIEW OF ACCOUNTING STUDIES.** 1996. q. fl.500 to institutions; $256.50 to institutions in U.S. (effective 1998). Kluwer Academic Publishers Boston, Box 358, Accord Sta., Hingham, MA 02018-0358. TEL 617-871-6600. FAX 617-871-6528. E-mail: services@wkap.nl; URL: http://kapis.www.wkap.nl/kapis/CGI-BIN/WORLD/journalhome.html. (Dist outside N. America by: Kluwer Academic Publishers Group, P.O. Box 322, 3300 AH Dordrecht, Netherlands. TEL 31-78-6392392. FAX 31-78-6546474) Ed. John S. Hughes. **Document type:** academic/scholarly publication.
—BLDSC (7786.740500). **CCC.**
Description: Publishes academic research on all aspects of the theory and practice of accounting.
Refereed Serial

330 US ISSN 0924-865X
HG173 CODEN: RQFAEO
REVIEW OF QUANTITATIVE FINANCE AND ACCOUNTING. (Text in English) 1991. bi-m. fl.820 to institutions; $421 to institutions in U.S. (effective 1998). Kluwer Academic Publishers Boston, Box 358, Accord Sta., Hingham, MA 02018-0358. FAX 617-871-6528. TELEX 200190. E-mail: services@wkap.nl; URL: http://www.wkap.nl. (Dist. outside N. America by: Kluwer Academic Publishers Group, P.O. Box 322, 3300 AH Dordrecht, Netherlands. TEL 31-78-6392392. FAX 31-78-6546474) Ed. Cheng-few Lee. (also avail. in microform from UMI; back issues avail.; reprint service avail. from SWZ) **Document type:** academic/scholarly publication.
—BLDSC (7794.183500); SWETS; UMI. **CCC.**
Description: Deals with research involving the interaction of finance with accounting, economics and quantitative methods. Publishes theoretical and methodological research as well as empirical applications.
Refereed Serial

657 DK ISSN 0034-6918
REVISION & REGNSKABSVAESEN; tidsskrift for erhvervsoekonomi og skatteforhold. 1932. m. DKK 685($66) Foreningen af Statsautoriserede Revisorer, Kronprinsessegade 8, DK-1306 Copenhagen K, Denmark. TEL 33-93-91-91. FAX 33-11-09-13. TELEX 22491. Ed. Bent Hansen. adv.; bk.rev.; charts; illus.; index. circ. 7,200. **Document type:** trade publication.

657 NO ISSN 0332-7795
REVISJON OG REGNSKAP. 1931. 8/yr. NOK 430 (foreign NOK 550) (effective 1997). Norges Statsautoriserte Revisorers Forening, Pilestredet 75 D, P.O. Box 5864 Majorstuen, N-0308 Oslo, Norway. TEL 47-22-69-59-10. FAX 47-22-69-05-55. E-mail: revregn.red@nsrf.telemax.no. Ed. Terje Groenn. adv. contact: Else-Marie Lindeman. circ. 8,025. **Document type:** academic/scholarly publication.
Formerly: Tidsskrift for Revisjon og Regnskapsvesen (ISSN 0040-7151)

657 DK ISSN 0108-9196
REVISOR POSTEN. 1983. 3/yr. DKK 8 membership only. Foreningen af Statsautoriserede Revisorer, Kronprinsessegade 8, 1306 Copenhagen K, Denmark. TEL 33-93-91-91. FAX 33-11-09-13. TELEX 22491. **Document type:** trade publication.

657 DK ISSN 0106-5203
REVISORBLADET. 1940. 8/yr. DKK 440. Foreningen af Registrerede Revisorer, Flintholm Alle 8, 2000 Copenhagen F, Denmark. TEL 38-33-13-18. Ed. Henning Moelgaard. adv.; bk.rev. circ. 4,500. (reprint service avail.) **Document type:** trade publication.

657 DK ISSN 0108-3716
REVISORHAANDBOGEN. 1982. biennial. DKK 250. Foreningen af Statsautoriserede Revisorer, Revisorernes Hus, Kronprinsessegade 8, 1306 Copenhagen K, Denmark. TEL 33-93-91-91. FAX 33-11-09-13. TELEX 22491. **Document type:** trade publication.

657 332.1 AG
REVISTA DE CIENCIAS ECONOMICAS. 1987. bi-m. free. Consejo Profesional de Ciencias Economicas de la Provincia de Santa Fe, Camara 1, Colegio de Graduados en Ciencias Economicas de Santa Fe, San Lorenzo, 1849, 3000 Santa Fe, Argentina. TEL 042-31924. (back issues avail.)
Description: Covers accounting, banking, domestic commerce and economic situation.

657 AG ISSN 0327-022X
REVISTA DE INVESTIGACION CONTABLE (TEUKEN). (Abstracts in English, French, Portuguese, Spanish) 1987. q. $120. Universidad Nacional de la Patagonia San Juan Bosca, Facultad de Ciencias Economicas, Sarmiento 553 Casilla de Correo 172, 9000 C. Rivadavia, Argentina. TEL 0967-24463. FAX 54-96724463. TELEX 86022 UNPCR. Ed. Jorge Manuel Gil. bk.rev.; bibl.; charts. circ. 700. **Document type:** academic/scholarly publication.
●Also available on CD-ROM.

BUSINESS AND ECONOMICS — ACCOUNTING

657   US
REVISTA INTERAMERICANA/INTER-AMERICAN NEWSLETTER. 1980. q. $50 includes Boletin Interamericano. Asociacion Interamericana de Contabilidad - Interamerican Accounting Association, Fontainebleau Exec. Ctr., 275 Fontainebleau Blvd., Ste. 245, Miami, FL 33172. TEL 305-225-1991. FAX 305-225-2011. Ed. Victor Abreu Paez. circ. 1,500 (paid). **Indexed:** Amer.Hist.& Life, Hist.Abstr. **Document type:** newsletter.

657 336   FR   ISSN 0035-2713
REVUE DU TRESOR; organe d'etudes et d'informations professionnelles. 1921. m. (except Mar.-Apr. and Aug.-Sep. combined). 328.50 F. (foreign 384.30 F.) (effective 1997). S.A.R.L. des Editions du Tresor, 26 rue de Lille, 75007 Paris, France. TEL 33-2-40497011. bk.rev.; bibl.; charts; illus.; index. **Indexed:** P.A.I.S.For.Lang.Ind.
—BLDSC (7956.620000).

657   FR   ISSN 0484-8764
HF5601
REVUE FRANCAISE DE COMPTABILITE. (Text in French; summaries in English, German, Spanish) 1955. m. 550 F. (foreign 830 F.) (effective 1996). (Societe d'Edition de l'Ordre des Experts Comptables, Conseil Superieur) Editions Comptables Malesherbes, 88 rue de Courcelles, 75008 Paris, France. TEL 44-15-95-95. FAX 44-15-90-76. TELEX 640 994 ORDREXP. Ed. G. Nicol. adv. contact: Georges Gelly. bk.rev.; index. circ. 17,000. (reprint service avail. from SCH) **Indexed:** SCIMP (1979-).
—BLDSC (7902.800000); SWETS.
Description: Covers accounting, tax and business law, management, tax control and more.

657   FR   ISSN 0762-4301
REVUE FRANCAISE DE L'AUDIT INTERNE. 1971. 5/yr. 530 F. (effective 1996). Institut Francais des Auditeurs Consultants Internes, 40 Ave. Hoche, 75008 Paris, France. TEL 42-56-19-39. FAX 42-62-40-89. Ed. Claude Parent. adv.; bk.rev. circ. 1,000. **Document type:** bulletin.

657 336   BE   ISSN 0772-6473
REVUE GENERALE DE FISCALITE; information a l'usage des conseillers fiscaux, gestionnaires administratifs et financiers. Flemish edition: Algemeen Fiskaal Tijdschrift (ISSN 0772-6465) (Supplement avail.: Newsletter) 1970. w. 8586 BEF. C E D Samsom (Subsidiary of: Wolters Samsom Belgie n.v.), Kouterveld 14, B-1831 Diegem, Belgium. TEL 32-2-7231111. Ed. A. Tiberghien.
Description: Trends in national and local taxation.

657   IS   ISSN 0035-7790
ROEH HACHESHBON. (Text in Hebrew) 1950. m. Institute of Certified Public Accountants in Israel, P.O. Box 29281, 1 Montefiore St., Tel Aviv, Israel. TEL 972-3-5161114. FAX 972-3-5103105. Ed. Yoram Eden. adv.; bk.rev.; abstr.; bibl.; charts; illus.; index; circ. 2,700 (controlled). **Indexed:** Ind.Heb.Per.

657   US   ISSN 1045-1439
S E C ACCOUNTING AND REPORTING UPDATE SERVICE. (Securities and Exchange Commission) 1984. 48/yr. $341.50 (overseas $453.95) (effective 1995). Warren, Gorham & Lamont, One Penn Plaza, New York, NY 10119. TEL 212-971-5000. FAX 212-971-5113. (Subscr. to: The Park Square Bldg., 31 St. James Ave., Boston, MA 02116-4112. TEL 800-950-1207) Eds. Allan B. Afterman, Charles Maurer. **Document type:** newsletter.
—CCC.
Description: Reports on S.E.C. pronouncements within three weeks, including detailed analysis and practical examples.

657   US   ISSN 0146-485X
KF1446.A15
S E C ACCOUNTING REPORT. (Securities and Exchange Commission) 1974. m. $224.75 (overseas $304.45) (effective 1995). Warren, Gorham & Lamont, One Penn Plaza, New York, NY 10119. TEL 212-971-5000. FAX 212-971-5113. (Subscr. to: The Park Square Bldg., 31 St. James Ave., Boston, MA 02116-4112. TEL 800-950-1207) Ed. Paul J. Wendell. (also avail. in microfilm; microform from UMI) **Indexed:** Account.Ind. (1975-). **Document type:** newsletter.
—UMI. **CCC.**
Description: Covers S.E.C., F.A.S.B., and related financial reporting matters. Offers up-to-date information on new S.E.C. developments and federal regulations.

S E C ACCOUNTING RULES. (Securities and Exchange Commission) see BUSINESS AND ECONOMICS — *Investments*

S E C FINANCIAL REPORTING: ANNUAL REPORTS TO SHAREHOLDERS, FORM 10-K, QUARTERLY FINANCIAL REPORTING. see BUSINESS AND ECONOMICS — *Investments*

657   US   ISSN 0745-2667
S E C TODAY. (Securities Exchange Commission) 1982. 250/yr. $760. Washington Service Bureau, Inc., 655 15th St., N.W., Washington, DC 20005. TEL 202-508-0600. FAX 202-659-3655. URL: http://www.wsb.com/sectoday. Ed. Jacquelyn Lumb; Pub. Lawrence Hamm. R&P contact: Jaquelyn Lumb. adv. contact: John Stricklett. (back issues avail.) **Document type:** newsletter.
—CCC.

657   FR
S I C. 1983. m. (11/yr.). 400 F. Ordre des Experts Comptables, 153 rue de Courcelles, 75017 Paris, France. TEL 33-1-45156000. FAX 33-1-45159005. Ed. Rene Ricol. R&P contact: G. Gelly. circ. 20,500. **Document type:** bulletin.
Description: Covers the French accountancy profession.

657 336   BE   ISSN 0776-0590
SAMSOM ACTUALITE COMPTABLE; lettre bimensuelle a l'usage des experts-comptables, reviseurs d'enterprises, directeurs financiers et administratifs. Flemish edition: Samsom Accountancy Actualiteit (ISSN 0773-2155) (Supplement avail.) (Text in French) 1984. s-m. 6042 BEF. C E D Samsom (Subsidiary of: Wolters Samsom Belgie n.v.), Kouterveld 14, B-1831 Diegem, Belgium. TEL 32-2-7231111. index.
Description: Articles on all aspects of accountancy, including financial analysis.

657.6   BE   ISSN 0773-8625
SAMSOM AUDIT & REVISORAAT. (Supplement avail.) (Text in Flemish) s-m. 4134 BEF. (Instituut der Interne Auditors) C E D Samsom (Subsidiary of: Wolters Samsom Belgie n.v.), Kouterveld 14, B-1831 Diegem, Belgium. TEL 32-2-7231111.
Description: Consists of professional information on internal audits, controls, enterprise laws.

SAMSOM BESLOTEN VENNOOTSCHAPPEN MET BEPERKTE AANSPRAKELIJKHEID. see BUSINESS AND ECONOMICS

SAMSOM COOPERATIEVE VENNOOTSCHAPPEN. see BUSINESS AND ECONOMICS

SAMSOM GELD EN ONDERNEMING. see BUSINESS AND ECONOMICS — *Banking And Finance*

657   SZ   ISSN 0036-746X
DER SCHWEIZER TREUHAENDER/EXPERT-COMPTABLE SUISSE. (Text and in French and German) 1926. 10/yr. 145 SFr. (includes CD-ROM) (effective 1997). Treuhand-Kammer - Chambre Fiduciaire, Postfach 892, CH-8025 Zurich, Switzerland. TEL 41-1-2677575. FAX 41-1-2677555. Ed. Kurt Schuele. adv.; bk.rev.; circ. 10,465. **Document type:** trade publication.
●Also available on CD-ROM.
Refereed Serial

657 690   UK
SCOPE (YEAR).* a. B A A S, Fortern House, 23 Savile Rd., London W1X 1AB, England.

657   CC
SHANDONG SHENJI/SHANDONG AUDITING. (Text in Chinese) bi-m. Shandong Shenji Xuehui - Shandong Auditing Society, No. 117, Wenhua Xilu, Jinan, Shandong 250012, People's Republic of China. TEL 26263. Ed. Wang Zeqing.

657   CC   ISSN 1007-5135
SHANGHAI KUAIJI/SHANGHAI ACCOUNTING. (Text in Chinese) 1979. m. Y51.60 (effective 1998). Shanghai Kuaiji Xuehui - Shanghai Accounting Association, 2230 Zhongshan Xilu, Room 1415, Shanghai 200233, People's Republic of China. TEL 86-21-6438-0194. Ed. Zhonghua Ouyang. R&P contact: Zhonghua Ouyang. adv. contact: Yizhong Wang. circ. 57,000. **Document type:** academic/scholarly publication.
Description: Provides information on the financial policies and laws in China and introduces advanced accounting knowledge to accountants, accounting faculty and students.

657.6   CC   ISSN 1002-3739
SHENJI LILUN YU SHIJIAN/AUDITING THEORY AND PRACTICE. (Text in Chinese) 1986. m. newsstand price: Y2.90. Beijing Shenji Yanjiusuo, 69 Xibianmennei Dajie, Beijing 100053, People's Republic of China. TEL 86-10-6303-4849. Ed. Daxian Liu. R&P contact: Daxian Liu. bk.rev.; circ. 45,000 (paid). **Document type:** academic/scholarly publication.
Description: Covers basic auditing theories, methods, practice, experience, case analysis, professional auditing and directory of laws and regulations.
Refereed Serial

657   CC   ISSN 1002-4239
SHENJI YANJIU/AUDITING STUDIES. (Text in Chinese) 1985. bi-m. Y15 (foreign $10). Zhongguo Shenji Xuehui - Chinese Auditing Society, A-4 Baishiqiao Lu, Beijing 100086, People's Republic of China. TEL 2170223. (Co-sponsor: Chinese Internal Auditing Society) Ed. Yang Shuzi. **Document type:** academic/scholarly publication.

657   CC   ISSN 1003-2452
SICHUAN KUAIJI/SICHUAN ACCOUNTANTS. (Text in Chinese) 1981. m. Y21 (effective 1994). Sichuan Kuaiji Xuehui - Sichuan Accountants Association, 37 Nanxin Jie, Chengdu, Sichuan 610016, People's Republic of China. TEL 665220. (Dist. overseas by: China National Publishing Industry Trading Corp., Serials Export Dept., P.o. Box 782, Beijing, P.R. China. TEL 4215031. FAX 4214540) (Co-sponsor: Sichuan Caiwu Chengben Yanjiuhui) Ed. Tao Sipu. adv. contact: Benqian Zhang. circ. 30,000. **Document type:** academic/scholarly publication.

657 340   SI   ISSN 0217-4456
SINGAPORE ACCOUNTANT. 1984. bi-m. S.$86. Longman Singapore Publishers (Pte) Ltd., 25 First Lok Yang Rd., Singapore 2262, Singapore. TEL 2682666. FAX 2641740. TELEX LMS-RS-24268. (Or: P.O. Box 267, Jurong Town Post Office, Singapore 9161, Singapore) Ed. June Oei. adv.; bk.rev. circ. 8,000. **Indexed:** Account.Ind. (1974-).
—BLDSC (8285.430000).
Description: Covers accounting, legal, management and computer information services with reports on case law, new legislation and other local and international developments.

657   XN   ISSN 0351-9643
SMETKOVODSTVENO FINANSISKA REVIJA; spisanie za smetkovodstveno-finansiska i organizaciona problematika na rabotnite organizacii. (Text in Macedonian) 1958. bi-m. Zdruzenie na Smetkovodstveno-Finansiskite Rabotnici na Makedonija, Box 267, Skopje, Macedonia. Ed. Boris Stojmenov. adv.; bk.rev. circ. 1,000.
Formerly (until 1981): Sovremeno Pretprijatie (ISSN 0038-5964)

657   PO
SOCIEDADE PORTUGUESA DE CONTABILIDADE. BOLETIM. 4/yr. Sociedade Portuguesa de Contabilidade, Rua Barata Salguiero 1-2o, Lisbon, Portugal. TEL 57-18-44. **Document type:** bulletin.

657   IT   ISSN 0394-3631
SOCIETA BILANCIO E CONTABILITA. 11/yr. De Lillo Editore, Via Mecenate 76, 3, 20138 Milan, Italy. TEL 2-50-64-741. FAX 2-506-48-18. Ed. Pietro de Lillo. circ. 14,000.

BUSINESS AND ECONOMICS — ACCOUNTING 1099

657.6   US   ISSN 1067-8689
SOCIETY OF DEPRECIATION PROFESSIONALS. JOURNAL. 1989. a. $15. Society of Depreciation Professionals, 5505 Connecticut Ave. N.W., No. 280, Washington, DC 20015-2601. TEL 202-362-0680. FAX 202-866-2283. URL: http://www.depr.org. Ed. Rod Daniel; Pub. Rod Daniel. R&P contact: Rod Daniel. adv. contact: Jerry Houck. circ. 400 (controlled). (back issues avail.) **Document type:** monographic series.
   Description: Promotes professional developments and ethics, recognizes the field of depreciation, and collects and exchanges information.
   Refereed Serial

657 658   CN
SOCIETY OF MANAGEMENT ACCOUNTANTS OF CANADA. ANNUAL REPORT. a. Society of Management Accountants of Canada, 120 King St. W., Box 176 M.P.O., Hamilton, ON L8N 3C3, Canada. TEL 905-525-4100. FAX 905-525-4533. **Document type:** corporate report.

657 305.896073   US
SPECTRUM (GREENBELT). 1972. a. $20. National Association of Black Accountants, 7249A Hanover Pkwy., Greenbelt, MD 20770-3653. TEL 301-474-6222. circ. 3,000. **Indexed:** Account.Ind. (1986-). **Document type:** proceedings.
   Description: Educational and technical information for minorities in the accounting profession.
   Refereed Serial

657   AT
THE STANDARD. 1989. irreg. price varies. Australian Accounting Research Foundation, 211 Hawthorn Rd., Caulfield, Vic. 3162, Australia. TEL 61-3-95238111. FAX 61-3-95235499. E-mail: standard@aarf.asn.au. (Co-sponsors: Australian Society of Certified Practising Accountants; Institute of Chartered Accountants in Australia) circ. 1,400. **Document type:** monographic series.
   Supersedes (in 1966): A A R F Report (ISSN 1034-2060)

657   US
STATE TAX ACTION COORDINATOR. 6 base vols. (irreg. supplements). $725. Research Institute of America, Inc., 90 Fifth Ave., New York, NY 10011. TEL 212-645-4800. FAX 212-337-4279. (Subscr. to: 117 E. Stevens Ave., Valhalla, NY 10595) (looseleaf format)

657   AT   ISSN 1035-3631
STATEMENT OF ACCOUNTING CONCEPTS. 1990. irreg. Aus.$6 per issue. Australian Accounting Research Foundation, 211 Hawthorn Rd., Caulfield, Vic. 3162, Australia. TEL 61-3-95238111. FAX 61-3-95235499. E-mail: standard@aarf.asn.au. (Co-sponsors: Australian Society of Certified Practising Accountants; Institute of Chartered Accountants in Australia) circ. 1,400. **Document type:** academic/scholarly publication.

657   AT   ISSN 1034-859X
STATEMENT OF AUDITING PRACTICE. 1990. irreg. Aus.$6 per issue. Australian Accounting Research Foundation, 211 Hawthorn Rd., Caulfield, Vic. 3162, Australia. TEL 61-3-95238111. FAX 61-3-95235499. E-mail: standard@aarf.asn.au. (Co-sponsors: Australian Society of Certified Practising Accountants; Institute of Chartered Accountants in Australia) circ. 1,000. **Document type:** trade publication.

657   AT
STATEMENT OF AUDITING PRACTICE - RELATED SERVICES. 1990. irreg. Aus.$6 per issue. Australian Accounting Research Foundation, 211 Hawthorn Rd., Caulfield, Vic. 3162, Australia. TEL 61-3-95238111. FAX 61-3-95235499. E-mail: standard@aarf.asn.au. (Co-sponsors: Australian Society Certified Practising of Accountants; Institute of Chartered Accountants in Australia) circ. 1,000. **Document type:** trade publication.
   Formerly (until 1992): Statement of Auditing Standards (ISSN 1034-8203)

657   US   ISSN 0586-5050
HF5601
STUDIES IN ACCOUNTING RESEARCH. 1969. irreg., no.31, 1990. price varies. American Accounting Association, Paul F. Gerhardt Bldg., 5717 Bessie Dr., Sarasota, FL 34233. TEL 941-921-7747. FAX 941-923-4093. R&P contact: Mary Cole. **Document type:** academic/scholarly publication.
   —BLDSC (8488.917000).

657   US   ISSN 1078-0106
HF5616.U62
THE SUCCESSFUL CALIFORNIA ACCOUNTANT. 1946. q. (plus m. updates) $30 to non-members. Society of California Accountants, 2131 Capitol Ave., Ste. 305, Sacramento, CA 95816. TEL 916-443-2057. FAX 916-443-0486. Ed.Bd. adv. contact: Diana Granger. circ. 1,550. (back issues avail.) **Document type:** trade publication.
   Formerly (until 1994): California Accountant (ISSN 0744-9895)
   Description: Examines various accounting subjects, the upgrading of computer systems, spreadsheet formats for accountants, and continuing education seminars.

657 378   US
SUM NEWS. 1990. bi-m. membership. Massachusetts Society of Certified Public Accountants, Inc., 105 Chauncy St., 10th Fl., Boston, MA 02111-1726. TEL 617-556-4000. FAX 617-556-4126. Ed. Cheryl A. McClowd; Pub. Theodore J. Flynn. R&P contact: Christina E. Baltzer. adv.: B&W page $980; trim 8 x 10 1/2; adv. contact: Wendy Devine. circ. 7,800. (also avail. in microform from UMI; back issues avail.) **Document type:** trade publication, newsletter.
   Formerly: Sum Monthly News.

657   IT
SUMMA (ROME).* 6/yr. National Association of Accountants and Commercial Experts, Via Paisiello 24, 00198 Rome, Italy. TEL 824761.

657   AT   ISSN 1034-8298
SUPPLEMENTARY STATEMENT TO STATEMENT OF AUDITING PRACTICE. 1990. irreg. Aus.$6 per issue. Australian Accounting Research Foundation, 211 Hawthorn Rd., Caulfield, Vic. 3162, Australia. TEL 61-3-95238111. FAX 61-3-95235499. E-mail: standard@aarf.asn.au. (Co-sponsors: Australian Society of Certified Practising Accountants; Institute of Chartered Accountants in Australia) circ. 1,000. **Document type:** academic/scholarly publication.

657 371.42   AT
SURVEY OF FINAL YEAR ACCOUNTING STUDENTS. irreg. Monash University, Careers and Appointment Service, Wellington Rd., Clayton, Vic. 3168, Australia. TEL 03-565-3150. Ed. Lionel Parrott.
   Description: Surveys success rates of accounting students in securing offers of employment.

657 332   NE   ISSN 0920-0428
T A C. (Tijdschrift voor Administrateurs en Controllers); tijdschrift voor controlling. 1986. 10/yr. fl.195 (effective 1996). (N G A Vereniging van Financieel-Administratieve Managers) Kluwer Bedrijfswetenschappen B.V. (Subsidiary of: Wolters Kluwer N.V.), Postbus 23, 7400 GA Deventer, Netherlands. TEL 31-570-648902. FAX 31-570-611504. (Subscr to: Intermedia bv, Postbus 4, 2400 MA Alphen aan den Rijn, Netherlands. TEL 31-172-466321. FAX 31-172-435527) Ed. J. Roos; Pub. K.A. Lagerwerf. adv.: B&W page fl.2765, color page fl.4915; trim 297 x 210; adv. contact: Ad Nuesink. circ. 7,500. **Document type:** trade publication.
   —SWETS.
   Description: Provides practical information for controllers and administrators.

657 336   US
TAX ACCOUNTING. (Issued in 2 base vols. with supplements) 1982. irreg. $380. Matthew Bender & Co., Inc., 2 Park Ave., New York, NY 10016. TEL 212-448-2000. E-mail: international@bender.com; URL: http://www.bender.com. (looseleaf format)
   Description: Provides a comprehensive analysis of the accounting methods and periods available for tax purposes, with explanation of their tax advantages and disadvantages. Details the requirements for electing, using, or changing a method to ensure effective tax planning.

657 336   US
TAX & BUSINESS ADVISER. 1982. bi-m. free to clients. 800 One Prudential Plaza, Chicago, IL 60601. TEL 312-856-0001. FAX 312-861-1340. Eds. Mary Jaspers, Lee O'Connor. circ. 60,000. **Document type:** newsletter.
   Formerly (until Jan. 1990): Tax Planner - Scan; Incorporates: Tax Planner and Business Scan.

TAX AND BUSINESS PLANNING OF LIMITED LIABILITY COMPANIES. see *BUSINESS AND ECONOMICS — Public Finance, Taxation*

657 336   UK
TAX FILE. 1980. w. £245. TaxFile 2000 Ltd., Briar House, Spinfield Lane, Marlow, Bucks. SL7 2JT, England. TEL 44-1622-757032. FAX 44-1622-690802. Ed. Joe Watson. R&P contact: Joe Watson. adv. contact: Joe Watson. bk.rev.; index. circ. 2,000. (looseleaf format; back issues avail.) **Document type:** trade publication.
   Description: Offers tax information and advice for businessmen and their advisers.

657   US
TAX OUTLOOK. q. membership. C P A Associates International, Inc., Meadows Office Complex, 201 Rte. 17 N., Rutherford, NJ 07070-2574. TEL 212-804-8686. circ. 20,000.
   Description: Concerned with the federal tax law changes, from both individual and corporate perspectives.

TAXATION FOR ACCOUNTANTS. see *BUSINESS AND ECONOMICS — Public Finance, Taxation*

TEACHER'S TAX GUIDE. see *BUSINESS AND ECONOMICS — Public Finance, Taxation*

657 332   US
THRIFT ACCOUNTANT. 48/yr. $645 for new subscr. (foreign $695); renewal $715 (foreign $765). American Banker - Bond Buyer, Newsletter Division (Subsidiary of: Thomson Financial Services Company), One State St. Plaza, New York, NY 10004-1549. TEL 800-733-4371. FAX 212-943-2224. (Subscr. to: Box 28315, Washington, DC 20038-8315. TEL 202-347-2665) Ed. Dave Postal. adv. (back issues avail.) **Document type:** newsletter.
   Description: Analyses and interpretations and regulatory changes of new examination standards, market value disclosure notations and other developments affecting accounting for thrift institutions.

TIJDSCHRIFT FINANCIEEL MANAGEMENT. see *BUSINESS AND ECONOMICS — Banking And Finance*

TIJDSCHRIFT VOOR BEDRIJFSADMINISTRATIE. see *BUSINESS AND ECONOMICS — Management*

657   US   ISSN 0889-4337
TODAY'S C P A.* 1927. bi-m. $24. Texas Society of C P A's, 14860 Montfort Dr., Ste. 150, Dallas, TX 75240-6718. TEL 214-689-6000. FAX 214-689-6046. Ed. Mr. Brux Austin. adv.; charts; illus.; stat.; tr.lit.; index. circ. 30,000. (back issues avail.) **Indexed:** Account.Ind. (1983-). **Document type:** trade publication.
   —UnCover.
   Formerly: C P A (Year).
   Refereed Serial

TODAY'S LAWYER. see *LAW*

UGESKRIFT FOR RETSVAESEN. see *LAW*

657   US
U.S. GENERAL ACCOUNTING OFFICE. ABSTRACTS OF REPORTS AND TESTIMONY: FISCAL YEAR (YEAR). a. U.S. General Accounting Office, Office of Public Affairs, Box 6015, Gaithersburg, MD 20884-6015. TEL 202-512-6000. FAX 301-258-4066. E-mail: info@www.gao.gov. **Document type:** government publication.

657   US   ISSN 0071-6065
UNIVERSITY OF FLORIDA. DEPARTMENT OF ACCOUNTING. ACCOUNTING SERIES. 1963. irreg., no.12, 1982. price varies. University Press of Florida, 15 N.W. 15th St., Gainesville, FL 32611. FAX 904-392-7302. Ed. A. Rashad Abdel-Khalik. **Document type:** monographic series.

BUSINESS AND ECONOMICS — BANKING AND FINANCE

657   US   ISSN 0073-5191
UNIVERSITY OF ILLINOIS AT URBANA-CHAMPAIGN. CENTER FOR INTERNATIONAL EDUCATION AND RESEARCH IN ACCOUNTING. MONOGRAPHS. 1964. irreg., latest no.11. price varies. University of Illinois at Urbana-Champaign, Center for International Education and Research in Accounting, 320 Commerce West Bldg., Box 109, 1206 S. Sixth St., Champaign, IL 61820-6271. TEL 217-333-4545. FAX 217-244-6565. TELEX 5106015276 COL COMM UI. E-mail: bsmith2@commerce.cba.uiuc.edu; URL: http://www.cba.uiuc.edu/accy/intl/intro.htm. Ed. Andrew D. Bailey Jr. adv. circ. 700. **Document type:** monographic series, academic/scholarly publication.

657 332   AT   ISSN 0814-9372
UNIVERSITY OF NEW ENGLAND. DEPARTMENT OF ACCOUNTING & FINANCIAL MANAGEMENT. WORKING PAPERS. 1985. irreg. free. University of New England, Department of Accounting & Financial Management, Armidale, N.S.W. 2351, Australia. TEL 61-67-732178. FAX 61-67-733122. TELEX 166050. Ed. Jim Psaros. R&P contact: J.J. Staunton. TEL 61-67-733276. circ. 150. (back issues avail.) **Document type:** academic/scholarly publication.

VANUATU. STATISTICS OFFICE. NATIONAL ACCOUNTS OF VANUATU. see BUSINESS AND ECONOMICS — Abstracting, Bibliographies, Statistics

657   US   ISSN 0043-3217
WEST VIRGINIA C.P.A. vol.15, 1970. bi-m. membership. West Virginia Society of Certified Public Accountants, Box 1142, Charleston, WV 25324. FAX 304-344-4636. Ed. Patricia M. Moyers. adv. contact: Patricia A. Moyers. illus. circ. 3,500. (tabloid format) **Document type:** newsletter.

THE WHITE PAPER. see CRIMINOLOGY AND LAW ENFORCEMENT — Security

657   GW   ISSN 0936-5117
WIRTSCHAFTSPRUEFERKAMMER. MITTEILUNGEN; Zeitschrift fuer Berufspolitik, Berufsrecht und berufliche Praxis. 1961. q. DM.40 (effective 1997). Verlag Dr. Otto Schmidt KG, Unter den Ulmen 96-98, 50968 Cologne, Germany. TEL 49-221-9373801. FAX 49-221-93738943. E-mail: dr.otto.schmidt@t-online.de. index. circ. 15,500. (reprint service avail. from SCH) **Document type:** bulletin.

657   GW   ISSN 0340-9031
DIE WIRTSCHAFTSPRUEFUNG. 1948. s-m. DM.315 (effective 1996). (German Institute of Accountants) I D W Verlag GmbH, Tersteegenstr. 14, 40474 Duesseldorf, Germany. TEL 49-211-4561-0. FAX 49-211-4561206. Ed. Guenter Siepe. adv.; bk.rev.; charts; tr.lit.; index. circ. 12,500. (back issues avail.) **Indexed:** Account.& Data Proc.Abstr., ELLIS, IBR. **Document type:** academic/scholarly publication.
—BLDSC (9325.600000); SWETS.

657   AU   ISSN 0043-6321
DER WIRTSCHAFTSTREUHAENDER. 1949. 6/yr. S.600. Vereinigung Oesterreichischer Wirtschaftstreuhaender, Postfach 17, A-3434 Tulbing, Austria. TEL 02273-2594. adv.; bk.rev. circ. 4,100. (processed) **Document type:** trade publication.

657   US   ISSN 0043-6402
HJ9701
THE WISCONSIN C P A. 1952. 12/yr. Wisconsin Institute of Certified Public Accountants, 235 N. Executive Dr., Brookfield, WI 53008-1010. TEL 414-785-0445; 800-772-6939. FAX 414-785-0838. URL: http://www.wicpa.org. (Subscr. to: Box 1010, Brookfield, WI 53008-1010) Ed. Marcia Tillett. R&P contact: Marcia Tillett. adv. contact: Kandra Maxwell. bk.rev.; illus.; circ. 8,100 (controlled). **Indexed:** Account.Ind. (1974-). **Document type:** trade publication.
Formerly: Wisconsin Society of Certified Public Accountants. Newsletter.

657 346   US
WORLD ACCOUNTING. 1986. 3 base vols. (plus updates 2/yr.). $510 for base vols.; updates $213. Matthew Bender & Co., Inc., 2 Park Ave., New York, NY 10016. TEL 212-448-2000. E-mail: international@bender.com; URL: http://www.bender.com.
Description: Practical guide to accounting standards of the thirty most important trading partners of the U.S. Coverage includes for each jurisdiction financial statement requirements, standard setting bodies, chart of accounts, differences in treatment for financial statements and tax purposes.

657   UK   ISSN 0308-4965
WORLD ACCOUNTING REPORT. Abbreviated title: W A R. m. £335($525) (overseas £350) (effective 1995). Financial Times Professional Publishing, Newsletters (Subsidiary of: Financial Times Group), Maple House, 149 Tottenham Court Rd., London W1P 9LL, England. TEL 44-171-896-2222. FAX 44-171-896-2276. Ed. Kate Atchley; Pub. John McLachlan. (also avail. in microform from UMI) **Indexed:** Account.Ind. (1981-). **Document type:** newsletter.
●Also available online. Vendor(s): Data-Star, Information Access Co., Lexis-Nexis (WAR).
—BLDSC (9352.370000); SWETS; UMI.
Description: Provides coverage and analysis of accounting developments worldwide. Activities of the national and international accounting committees and regulatory bodies, new accounting laws, regulations and auditing standards, and in-depth surveys on the accounting profession in individual countries.

657   US
YEAR-END TAX PLANNING GUIDE. a. membership. C P A Associates International, Inc., Meadows Office Complex, 201 Rte. 17 N., Rutherford, NJ 07070-2574. TEL 212-804-8686. circ. 30,000.
Description: Examines legislative and financial developments. Provides tax information for planning.

657   GW   ISSN 0044-3816
HF5667   CODEN: ZIREAM
ZEITSCHRIFT INTERNE REVISION; Fachzeitschrift fuer Wissenschaft und Praxis. 1966. 6/yr. DM.96. (Institut fuer Interne Revision e.V.) Erich Schmidt Verlag GmbH & Co. (Berlin), Genthiner Str. 30G, 10785 Berlin, Germany. TEL 49-30-250085-0. FAX 49-30-25008521. adv.; bk.rev.; charts; stat.; tr.lit.; index. **Indexed:** Account.& Data Proc.Abstr., SCIMP. **Document type:** academic/scholarly publication.
—SWETS. **CCC.**

657.6   CC   ISSN 1002-5049
ZHONGGUO SHENJI/AUDITING IN CHINA. (Text in Chinese) 1983. m. $33.20. (Guojia Shenjishu - National Audit Office of the People's Republic of China) Zhongguo Shenji Bianjibu, A-4 Baishiqiao Lu, Beijing 100086, People's Republic of China. TEL 86-10-217-0321. (Dist. in U.S. by: China Books & Periodicals, Inc., 2929 24th St., San Francisco, CA 94110. TEL 415-282-2994) Ed. Qihan Yu; Pub. Yingqing Zeng. R&P contact: Qihan Yu. adv. contact: Qihan Yu. bk.rev. **Document type:** trade publication.

657   RH
ZIMBABWE CHARTERED ACCOUNTANT. 1987. bi-m. Z.$165 (foreign Z.$171.30) (effective 1997). (Institute of Chartered Accountants of Zimbabwe) Thomson Publications Zimbabwe (Pvt) Ltd., Thomson House, P.O. Box 1683, Harare, Zimbabwe. TEL 263-4-736835. FAX 263-4-752390. **Indexed:** P.L.E.S.A. **Document type:** trade publication.
Formerly: Zimbabwe Quarterly; **Supersedes:** Zimbabwe Commercial and Legal Quarterly.

BUSINESS AND ECONOMICS — Banking And Finance

see also Business and Economics–Economic Situation and Conditions; Business and Economics–Investments; Insurance

332.1   US   ISSN 0887-0187
KF967
A B A BANK COMPLIANCE. (Suppl. avail: Legislative and Regulatory Update) 1980. m. $295 to non-members; members $195 (includes suppl.). American Bankers Association, Compliance Division, 1120 Connecticut Ave., N.W., Washington, DC 20036. TEL 202-663-5497. FAX 202-663-7543. (Subscr. to: Customer Service Center, Box 630544, Baltimore, MD 21263-0544. TEL 800-338-0626) Ed. Robert Rowe. circ. 4,500. (also avail. in microform from UMI) **Indexed:** ABI Inform., Bank.Lit.Ind. **Document type:** trade publication.
●Also available online. Vendor(s): UMI.
—BLDSC (0537.720900); UMI.
Formerly: Bank Compliance (ISSN 0276-4253)
Description: Provides information on legislative and regulatory changes, what they mean for your bank, and how to satisfy new requirements.

332.1   US   ISSN 1069-5907
A B A BANKERS NEWS. 1981. bi-w. $96 to non-members; members $48. American Bankers Association, Member Communications, 1120 Connecticut Ave., N.W., Washington, DC 20036. TEL 202-663-5445. FAX 202-296-9258. Ed. Laura Keefe. adv. circ. 22,000. (tabloid format) **Indexed:** Bank.Lit.Ind. **Document type:** trade publication, newspaper.
—UMI.
Former titles (until 1993): A B A Bankers Weekly (ISSN 0889-7662); Which incorporated: Agricultural Banker; (until 1986): A B A Bankers News Weekly (ISSN 0746-3367); (until 1983): Bankers News Weekly (ISSN 0744-2688); **Supersedes** (as of Feb. 1982): Capital (ISSN 0195-444X)
Description: Covers current legislative and regulatory information, association stance and news for CEOs of most U.S. banks.

332.1   US   ISSN 0194-5947
HG1501   CODEN: ABAJD5
A B A BANKING JOURNAL. 1908. m. $25. (American Bankers Association, Member Communications) Simmons - Boardman Publishing Corp., 345 Hudson St., New York, NY 10014-4502. TEL 212-620-7200. FAX 212-633-1165. (Addr. in Netherlands: Nijverheidsweg 46, 3340 Henrik Ido Ambacht, Netherlands) Ed. William W. Streeter; Pub. Russell S. Selover. adv.; bk.rev.; charts; illus.; stat.; index. circ. 34,652. (also avail. in microform from UMI) **Indexed:** ABI Inform., Account.Ind. (1974-), B.P.I., Bank.Lit.Ind., BPIA, Chic.Per.Ind., Comput.Lit.Ind., Data Process.Dig., INSPEC (1982-), Manage.Cont., Mid.East: Abstr.& Ind., P.A.I.S., Tr.& Dev.Alert, Tr.& Indus.Ind., World Bank.Abstr. **Document type:** trade publication.
●Also available online. Vendor(s): Dow Jones News Retrieval, Information Access Co., Knight-Ridder Information, Inc. (File no.648), Lexis-Nexis, Ovid Technologies, Inc. (TSAP), UMI.
—BLDSC (0537.721000); AskIEEE; KR SourceOne; SWETS; UMI; UnCover. **CCC.**
Incorporates: Banking Buying Guide; **Former titles** (until 1979): Banking (ISSN 0005-5492); American Bankers Association. Journal.
Description: Provides current look at trends, products, and developments in financial services.

332.1 640.73   US
A B A CONSUMER BANKING DIGEST. 1982. 6/yr. $115 to non-members; members $75 (effective Sep. 1990). American Bankers Association, Retail Services Center, 1120 Connecticut Ave., N.W., Washington, DC 20036. TEL 202-663-5094. FAX 202-828-4544. Ed. Craig Sablosky. circ. 800. (also avail. in microform from UMI)
Description: Features articles on treatment of key consumer banking issues including industry trends, innovative programs, organizational issues, and changing market conditions.

BUSINESS AND ECONOMICS — BANKING AND FINANCE

332.1   US
A B A MANAGEMENT UPDATE OF PERSONAL TRUST & PRIVATE BANKING. Short title: Management Update. 6/yr. $200 to non-members; members $135. American Bankers Association, Trust and Private Banking Center, 1120 Connecticut Ave., N.W., Washington, DC 20036. TEL 202-663-5087. FAX 202-663-7543. (Subscr. to: Customer Service Center, Box 630538, Baltimore, MD 21623-0538. TEL 800-338-0626) circ. 800. (also avail. in microform from UMI) **Document type:** newsletter.
   Description: Compendium of articles written by industry leaders, academicians, and management consultants, providing information on management issues, industry trends, and reports on innovative bank programs in trust and private banking.

332 346   US
KF1507.A24
A B I JOURNAL. 1983. 10/yr. membership. American Bankruptcy Institute, 44 Canal Center Plz, Ste. 404, Alexandria, VA 22314-1592. TEL 703-739-0800. FAX 703-739-1060. URL: http://www.abiworld.org. Ed. Samuel J. Gerdano. adv. contact: Jon Woodward. bk.rev. circ. 5,700. (reprint service avail.) **Document type:** trade publication.
   Formerly: A B I Newsletter.

332   KE
A C C O S C A NEWSLETTER. (Text in English and French) q. free. African Confederation of Savings and Credit Cooperatives - Association des Cooperatives d'Epargne et de Credit d'Afrique, P.O. Box 43278, Nairobi, Kenya. TEL 254-2-721944. FAX 254-2-721274. TELEX 23176 ACCOSCA NAIROBI KE. **Document type:** newsletter.
   Formerly: A C C O S C A News.

332.2   KE
A C O S C A NEWS. (Text in English and French) 1980. q. EAs.5 per no. Africa Cooperative Savings and Credit Association, P.O. Box 43278, Nairobi, Kenya. FAX 254-2-721274. TELEX 23176-ACCOSCA-N. Ed. Mr. Gicheri Kimaru. circ. 1,000. **Document type:** newsletter.
   Formerly (until 1982): A C O S C A Eastern Regional Newsletter.

332.1   IV
A D B NEWS. m. African Development Bank, Information and Public Relations Division, B.P. 1387, Abidjan 01, Ivory Coast. **Document type:** newsletter.

332.1   UY   ISSN 0001-1010
A E B U.* vol.20, 1967. m. Asociacion de Bancos del Uruguay, Rincon 468, 2o, Montevideo, Uruguay. TEL 2-965051. Ed. Felix Duarte. adv.; charts; stat.

A F M EXPLANATORY SERIES (NO.). (Department of Accounting and Financial Management) see BUSINESS AND ECONOMICS — Accounting

332   IE
A I B REVIEW. m. Allied Irish Banks Ltd., Bank Centre, Ballsbridge, Dublin 4, Ireland. TEL 353-1-600311. FAX 353-1-609508. **Document type:** bulletin.

332   US
A I M R NEWSLETTER. (Former issuing body: Institute of Chartered Financial Analysts) q. $25. Association for Investment Management and Research, Box 3668, Charlottesville, VA 22903. TEL 804-980-3668. FAX 804-980-9755.
   Formerly: C F A Newsletter.
   Description: Provides updates on the activities of the association and its members. Includes information about programs, publications, and candidate activities, as well as the AIMR Board of Trustees and AIMR policy decisions.

332   GW
A LA CARD EURO-NEWS. (Text in English, German) 1991. m. DM.650. Steinau Verlag GmbH, Am Kurgarten 1, 23879 Moelln, Germany. TEL 49-4542-8461-0. FAX 49-4542-846111. E-mail: 100637.610@compuserve.com; URL: http://www.alacard.de. Ed. Meike Wolff. adv. contact: Sabine Pohlmeyer. circ. 4,000 (paid) **Document type:** trade publication.
   Description: Provides the latest news on card applications, card-based payment systems and international card management.

332   IT
A S E F I. 1984. a. L.150000. Annuario Servizi Finanziari, Via S. Sempliciano, 2, 20121 Milan, Italy. TEL 39-2-86463056. FAX 39-2-804179. Ed. Gianfranco Monti. adv.: B&W page L.5400000, color page L.9700000; adv. contact: Donatella Joan.

ABERDEEN PAPERS IN ACCOUNTANCY AND FINANCE. see BUSINESS AND ECONOMICS — Accounting

381 332   CN
ABSTRACT OF AMERICAN ECONOMIC TREND ANALYSIS. 1980. q. Can.$60 membership; newsstand price: Can.$25. Maxiplan Financial Club, 12687 52nd Ave., Montreal, PQ H1E 2H6, Canada. Ed. Marcel Wistaff. **Document type:** newsletter.
   Description: Provides an economic activity outlook, development strategy, future confidence survey, investment strength, potential output, productivity growth, US financial market timing.

ABSTRACT OF INTERNATIONAL ECONOMIC TREND ANALYSIS. see BUSINESS AND ECONOMICS — International Commerce

332   US
ACCESS (GREENWOOD). 1945. q. membership only. American Safe Deposit Association, 330 W. Main St., Greenwood, IN 46142. TEL 317-888-1118. FAX 317-888-1787. E-mail: jmclin@Aol.com. Ed. Joyce A. McLin; Pub. Joyce A. McLin. R&P contact: Joyce A. McLin. adv. contact: Joyce A. McLin. circ. 3,900. **Document type:** trade publication.
   Formerly: National News.

ACCOUNTING FOR BANKS. see BUSINESS AND ECONOMICS — Accounting

ACCOUNTING RESEARCH JOURNAL. see BUSINESS AND ECONOMICS — Accounting

332   US
ACTIONS OF THE BOARD: APPLICATIONS AND REPORTS RECEIVED. w. $55. U.S. Federal Reserve System, Board of Governors, Publications Services, Rm. MS-138, Washington, DC 20551. TEL 202-452-3244. FAX 202-728-5886. **Document type:** government publication.

332   FR
ACTUALITES ECONOMIQUES. 1953. w. 3800 F. (foreign 4080 F.) (effective 1997). Societe Generale de Presse et d'Editions, 13 av. de l'Opera, 75001 Paris, France. TEL 40-15-17-89. FAX 40-15-17-15. TELEX SOGPRES 230023. Ed. Marianne Berard-Quelin. adv. circ. 3,000.
   Description: Contains economic, social and financial news and data.

AD IDEAS. see ADVERTISING AND PUBLIC RELATIONS

ADVANCES IN FINANCE, INVESTMENT AND BANKING. see BUSINESS AND ECONOMICS — Investments

332   US
ADVANCES IN FINANCIAL PLANNING AND FORECASTING. 1985. irreg., vol.7, 1997. $90.25. J A I Press Inc., 55 Old Post Rd., No. 2, Box 1678, Greenwich, CT 06830-1678. TEL 203-661-7602. FAX 203-661-0792. E-mail: jai@jaipress.com. (Subscr. in UK and Europe to: JAI Press Ltd., 38 Tavistock St., Covent Garden, London WC2E 7PB, England. TEL 44-171-379-8834. FAX 44-171-379-8835) Ed. Cheng-Few Lee. **Document type:** monographic series.

ADVANCES IN FINANCIAL PLANNING AND FORECASTING. SUPPLEMENT. see BUSINESS AND ECONOMICS — Management

332.1   SW   ISSN 0281-787X
AFFAERSBANKERNA; samtliga bankaktiebolag. 1912. m. SEK 400 (effective 1990). Statistiska Centralbyraan, Bankinspektionen, S-701 89 Oerebro, Sweden.
   Former titles (until 1984): Bankerna; (until 1954): Statistiska Meddelanden. Ser. E, Uppgifter om Bankerna.

332   CN   ISSN 0229-3404
LES AFFAIRES. 1928. w. (50/yr.) Can.$54.95. Publications Transcontinental Inc., 1100 boul. Rene Levesque W., 24th Fl., Montreal, PQ H3B 4X9, Canada. TEL 514-392-9000. FAX 514-392-4723. Ed. Jean-Paul Gagne; Pub. Suzanne Paquet. adv. contact: Yvon Tremblay. bk.rev. circ. 86,550. (tabloid format) **Indexed:** Can.B.P.I., Can.Per.Ind., Pt.de Rep. (1990-).
   ●Also available online. Vendor(s): Southam Electronic Publishing.
   Former titles (until 1979): Journal les Affaires (ISSN 0705-1859); (until 1978): Affaires (ISSN 0044-6459)

AFFAIRES ET GENS D'AFFAIRES. see HISTORY — History Of Europe

332 352.7   US   ISSN 1080-2177
HD7288.78.U5
AFFORDABLE HOUSING FINANCE. 1993. bi-m. $95. Business Communication Services, 657 Mission St., Ste. 502, San Francisco, CA 94105-4118. TEL 415-546-7255. FAX 415-546-0954. E-mail: ahf@housingfinance.com; URL: http://www.housingfinance.com. Ed. Andre Shashaty. R&P contact: Andre Shashaty. adv.: page $1857; 7 1/2 x 10. circ. 6,000. **Document type:** trade publication.
   Description: Provides news and in-depth information on sources of financing for affordable multifamily housing for developer, real estate and financial professionals, and government officials.

AFRICA ANALYSIS; fortnightly bulletin on financial and political trends. see BUSINESS AND ECONOMICS — Economic Situation And Conditions

332   KE
AFRICAN CONFEDERATION OF SAVINGS AND CREDIT COOPERATIVES. ANNUAL REPORT. (Text in English, French) a. African Confederation of Savings and Credit Cooperatives, P.O. Box 43278, Nairobi, Kenya. **Document type:** corporate report.
   Formerly: Africa Cooperative Savings and Credit Association. Annual Report.

AFRICAN DEVELOPMENT BANK. COMPENDIUM OF STATISTICS/BANQUE AFRICAINE DE DEVELOPPEMENT. COMPENDIUM DE STATISTIQUES. see BUSINESS AND ECONOMICS — Abstracting, Bibliographies, Statistics

AFRICAN DEVELOPMENT BANK. SELECTED STATISTICS ON REGIONAL MEMBER COUNTRIES/BANQUE AFRICAINE DE DEVELOPPEMENT. STATISTIQUES CHOISIES SUR LES PAYS-MEMBRES REGIONAUX. see BUSINESS AND ECONOMICS — Abstracting, Bibliographies, Statistics

AFRICAN DEVELOPMENT REPORT/RAPPORT SUR LE DEVELOPPEMENT EN AFRIQUE. see BUSINESS AND ECONOMICS — International Development And Assistance

AFRICAN DEVELOPMENT REVIEW/REVUE AFRICAINE DE DEVELOPPEMENT. see BUSINESS AND ECONOMICS — International Development And Assistance

332.1   FR   ISSN 0755-1940
AGENCE ECONOMIQUE ET FINANCIERE. (Supplement avail.: A G E F I Magazine (ISSN 0982-832X)) 1911. d. (5/w.) 9405 F. 48 rue Notre Dame des Victoires, 75002 Paris, France. TEL 44-88-46-46. FAX 44-88-47253. Ed. Henri-Paul Vanel; Pub. Philippe Micouleau. adv. contact: Xavier Ginoux. (back issues avail.) **Document type:** newspaper.

332   US   ISSN 0749-9035
AGGREGATE RESERVES OF DEPOSITORY INSTITUTIONS AND THE MONETARY BASE. w. $15. U.S. Federal Reserve System, Board of Governors, Publications Services, Rm. MS-138, Washington, DC 20551. TEL 202-452-3244. FAX 202-728-5886. **Document type:** government publication.

332   US
AGGREGATE SUMMARIES OF ANNUAL SURVEYS OF SECURITIES CREDIT EXTENSION. a. $5. U.S. Federal Reserve System, Board of Governors, Publications Services, Rm. MS-138, Washington, DC 20551. TEL 202-452-3244. FAX 202-728-5886. (also avail. in diskette format) **Document type:** government publication.

BUSINESS AND ECONOMICS — BANKING AND FINANCE

AGRICULTURAL CREDIT. see *AGRICULTURE — Agricultural Economics*

332   US   ISSN 1070-6755
AGRICULTURAL FINANCE DATABOOK. q. $5. U.S. Federal Reserve System, Board of Governors, Publications Services, Rm. MS-138, Washington, DC 20551. TEL 202-452-3244. FAX 202-728-5886. **Document type:** government publication.
    Formerly (until 1989): Agricultural Finance Databook. Quarterly Series.

332   YU
AGROBANKA. 1988. bi-m. Agrobanka, Sremska 5, Belgrade, Yugoslavia. Ed. Miroslava Polic.

332   SP
AGRUPACION SINDICAL NACIONAL DE EMPRESAS DE FINANCIACION. CENSO. irreg. Agrupacion Sindical Nacional de Empresa de Financiacion, Paseo del Prado 18 y 20, Madrid, Spain.

332.6 387.7   UK   ISSN 0266-2132
HD9711.A1
AIR FINANCE ANNUAL. 1984. a. £95 (foreign $170) (effective 1996). Euromoney Publications plc., Nestor House, Playhouse Yard, London EC4V 5EX, England. TEL 44-171-779-8935. FAX 44-171-779-8541. (Orders to: Plymbridge Distributors Ltd., Estover, Plymouth, Devon PL6 7PZ, England. TEL 44-1752-695668; Dist. in US by: American Educational Systems, 173 W. 81st St., New York, NY 10024. TEL 800-717-2669. FAX 212-501-8926) Ed.Bd. adv. circ. 5,000. (back issues avail.) **Document type:** trade publication.
    Description: Includes articles on all aspects of aircraft financing techniques.

AIRCRAFT VALUE JOURNAL. see *AERONAUTICS AND SPACE FLIGHT*

AIRFINANCE JOURNAL. see *TRANSPORTATION — Air Transport*

332   KU
ALAHLI BANK OF KUWAIT K.S.C. ANNUAL REPORT AND BALANCE SHEET. a. Alahli Bank of Kuwait K.S.C., Mubarak Al-Kabir Street, P.O. Box 1387, Safat, Kuwait. charts; illus.; stat. **Document type:** corporate report.

332   CN   ISSN 0318-3971
HC120.P63
ALBERTA OPPORTUNITY COMPANY. ANNUAL REPORT. 1974. a. Alberta Opportunity Co., P.O. Box 1860, Ponoka, AB T0C 2H0, Canada. TEL 403-427-2140. **Document type:** corporate report.

332   AU
ALLGEMEINE SPARKASSE. KURZ NOTIERT. 1960. m. free. Allgemeine Sparkasse, Promenade 11-13, A-4041 Linz, Austria. FAX 0732-23912802. Ed. Kurt Mueller. bk.rev. circ. 8,000. **Document type:** bulletin.
    Formerly: Allgemeine Sparkasse Linz. Kurz Notiert (ISSN 0002-5933)

332.1   IE   ISSN 0332-320X
ALLIED IRISH BANK REVIEW. 1973. q. free. Allied Irish Banks Ltd., Bankcentre, Ballsbridge, Dublin 4, Ireland. TEL 353-1-6600311. FAX 353-1-6604715. Ed. John Beggs. circ. 7,000. **Indexed:** P.A.I.S., World Bank.Abstr. **Document type:** bulletin.

332   US   ISSN 0747-9107
HF5681.R25
ALMANAC OF BUSINESS AND INDUSTRIAL FINANCIAL RATIOS. 1971. a. $89.95. Prentice Hall, Inc., Englewood Cliffs, NJ 07632. TEL 201-592-2000. Ed. Dr. Leo Troy. charts; stat.; index. circ. 5,000. **Indexed:** SRI.

332   LE
ALMANACH OF BANKS IN LEBANON. (Text in French) 1980. a? Association of Banks in Lebanon, DORA, Centre Moucarri, P.O. Box 80536, Lebanon. TELEX ASSOBLE 43069 LE. circ. 1,000. **Document type:** directory.
    Description: Provides information on addresses, branches and management of all banks operating in Lebanon.

332.1   US   ISSN 0569-292X
HG2441
AMERICAN BANK DIRECTORY. a. $255. Thomson Financial Publishing, 4709 W. Golf Rd., Skokie, IL 60076-7565. TEL 847-676-9600; 800-321-3373. FAX 847-933-8101. Ed. Beth Swann. adv. circ. 57,773. **Document type:** directory.

332.1   US   ISSN 0002-7561
HG1501
AMERICAN BANKER. 1836. d.(5/wk.). $750. American Banker - Bond Buyer, Newsletter Division (Subsidiary of: Thomson Financial Services Company), One State St. Plaza, New York, NY 10004-1549. TEL 800-733-4371. FAX 212-843-9600. (Subscr. to: Box 28315, Washington, DC 20038-8315. TEL 202-347-2665) Ed. Je Mysak. adv.; bk.rev.; mkt.; stat.; cum.index. circ. 24,000. (also avail. in microform from UMI; reprint service avail. from UMI) **Indexed:** Bank.Lit.Ind., Bus.Ind., PROMT, SRI (until 1993), Tr.& Indus.Ind., World Bank.Abstr. **Document type:** newspaper, trade publication.
    ●Also available online. Vendor(s): Data-Star (BANK), Information Access Co., Knight-Ridder Information, Inc. (File no.625), Lexis-Nexis, NewsNet (FI10), Ovid Technologies, Inc.
    —UMI. **CCC.**

332.1   US   ISSN 1064-5349
HG2441
AMERICAN BANKERS ASSOCIATION KEY TO ROUTING NUMBERS. 1911. a. $95. Thomson Financial Publishing, 4709 W. Golf Rd., Skokie, IL 60076. TEL 847-676-9600; 800-321-3373. FAX 847-933-8101. Ed. Beth Swann. R&P contact: Beth Swann. adv. contact: Hugh Boyd. (also avail. in magnetic tape) **Document type:** directory.
    Description: Is the official registry of the A.B.A. routing and transit number system. Includes all routing numbers, both active and retired, assigned to banks, institutions and credit unions. Listings are cross-referenced by city, state and federal district.

332   US
AMERICAN BANKER'S WASHINGTON WATCH. 48/yr. $695 (foreign $725). American Banker - Bond Buyer, Newsletter Division (Subsidiary of: Thomson Financial Services Company), One State St. Plaza, New York, NY 10004-1549. TEL 800-733-4371. FAX 212-943-2224. (Subscr. to: Box 28315, Washington, DC 20038-8315. TEL 202-347-2665) Ed. Miles Maguire. adv. **Document type:** newsletter.
    ●Also available online. Vendor(s): Information Access Co., Knight-Ridder Information, Inc., Lexis-Nexis, NewsNet (FI05).
    Formerly: F D I C Watch; Incorporates: Central Bank Watch; Savings and Loan Reporter; Which was formerly: Banking Reporter.
    Description: Analysis of the developing regulatory and legislative initiative affecting insured financial institutions. Covers events at the FDIC, the Federal Reserve Board, and the Office of the Comptroller of the Currency.

332.7 346   US   ISSN 1068-0861
AMERICAN BANKRUPTCY INSTITUTE LAW REVIEW. 1993. biennial. $48.50 (effective 1997). L R P Publications, 580 Village Blvd., Ste. 140, West Palm Beach, FL 33409-1904. TEL 407-687-1220. FAX 407-687-1220. URL: http://www.lrp.com. Ed. Joanne Fiore. (back issues avail.) **Indexed:** L.R.I., Leg.Per.
    —KR SourceOne. **CCC.**

AMERICAN BANKRUPTCY LAW JOURNAL. see *LAW*

332 338.025   US
AMERICAN FINANCIAL DIRECTORY. a. $395. Thomson Financial Publishing, 4709 W. Golf Rd., Skokie, IL 60076. TEL 847-676-9600; 800-321-3373. FAX 847-933-8101. Ed. Beth Swann. **Document type:** directory.

332.1   US
AMERICAN INSTITUTE OF BANKING. LEADERS LETTER. 1965. q. $15 to non-members. American Bankers Association, Bank Programs & Professional Development, 1120 Connecticut Ave., N.W., Washington, DC 20036. TEL 202-663-5391. FAX 202-828-4544. Ed. Hunter Moss. bk.rev.; stat.; index. circ. 7,200. **Document type:** newsletter.
    Description: Focuses on organizational, administrative, and educational issues affecting AIB units, and features articles on new educational programs, courses and seminars, and chapter activities.

332 380.1   US
AMERICAN RECOVERY ASSOCIATION. NEWS AND VIEWS.* Short title: A R A. 1962. m. free. American Recovery Association, Inc., 1 Seine Ct., Ste. 505, New Orleans, LA 70114-6553. TEL 504-392-0672. FAX 504-392-2612. (Subscr. to: Box 6788, New Orleans, LA 70174) Ed. Huey Mayronne. circ. 32,000.
    Description: News for banks, credit unions, finance companies and leasing companies dealing with repossessions.

332.2   US
AMERICAN SAVINGS DIRECTORY. 1981. a. $169. Thomson Financial Publishing, 4709 W. Golf Rd., Skokie, IL 60076. TEL 847-676-9600; 800-321-3373. FAX 847-933-8101. Ed. Beth Swann. adv. circ. 5,200. **Document type:** directory.

333 332 368   US
AMERICAN SOCIETY OF APPRAISERS. NEWSLINE. 1984. m. $20. American Society of Appraisers, Box 17265, Washington, DC 20041-0265. TEL 703-478-2228. FAX 703-742-8471. E-mail: asainfo@apo.com. Ed. Rebecca Ewing. R&P contact: Rebecca Ewing. TEL 703-733-2103. adv.: page $800; adv. contact: Amy Starliper. circ. 7,000. **Document type:** newsletter.
    Description: Provides information on appraisal related issues and society activities.

332   US
AMERICAN STOCK EXCHANGE GUIDE. 1960. m. $416. C C H Incorporated, 2700 Lake Cook Rd., Riverwoods, IL 60015. TEL 847-267-7000; 800-835-5224. FAX 800-224-8299. (looseleaf format)

332.2   US
HG1921
AMERICA'S COMMUNITY BANKER. m. $65 to non-members; members $49 (effective 1997). America's Community Bankers, 900 19th St., N.W., Ste. 400, Washington, DC 20006. TEL 202-857-3100. FAX 202-857-5581. URL: http://www.acbankers.org. Ed. Brian Nixon; Pub. William T. Marshall. adv.: B&W page $2640, color page $3790; trim 8 1/2 x 10 7/8. charts; illus.; index. circ. 12,000. (also avail. in microform from UMI; back issues avail.) **Indexed:** B.P.I. **Document type:** trade publication.
    ●Also available online. Vendor(s): Information Access Co., UMI.
    —BLDSC (0858.544000); KR SourceOne; UMI; UnCover. **CCC.**
    Formerly (until Apr. 1995): Savings and Community Banker (ISSN 1067-1757); Which was formed by the 1993 merger of: Savings Institution Magazine (ISSN 0746-1321); Which was formerly (1952-1983): Savings and Loan News (ISSN 0036-5114); And: Bottomline (Washington) (ISSN 0740-5464); Which was formed by the merger of (1921-1983): Savings Bank Journal (ISSN 0036-5130); (1974-1983): National Savings and Community League Journal; And incorporates: National League Journal of Insured Savings Associations (ISSN 0027-9617).
    Description: Provides analysis of the latest legislative and regulatory developments, in-depth coverage of economic trends and guidance for meeting managerial concerns and challenges.

332.2   US
AMERICA'S COMMUNITY BANKERS. REGULATORY REPORT. m. $549 to non-members; members $325. America's Community Bankers, 900 19th St. N.W., Ste. 400, Washington, DC 20006. TEL 202-857-3100. FAX 202-296-8716. Ed. William T. Marshall. circ. 3,000. (back issues avail.) **Document type:** newsletter.
    Former titles: Savings & Community Bankers of America. Regulatory Report; National Council of Savings Institutions. Regulatory Update.
    Description: Provides in-depth information on regulations affecting the operations of savings and community banking institutions.

AMERICA'S CORPORATE FINANCE DIRECTORY. see *BUSINESS AND ECONOMICS — Trade And Industrial Directories*

BUSINESS AND ECONOMICS — BANKING AND FINANCE

332 IT
AMMINISTRAZIONE E FINANZA. 1986. s-m. L.255000 (foreign L.510000). I P S O A s.r.l. (Subsidiary of: Wolters Kluwer N.V.), Strada 1, Palazzo F6, 20090 Assago (Milan), Italy. TEL 39-2-824761. Ed. Massimiliano Galioni. adv.: B&W page L.4200000. circ. 20,500.

332 IT ISSN 1121-2438
AMMINISTRAZIONE E FINANZA ORO. 1990. 4/yr. L.100000 (foreign L.200000). I P S O A s.r.l. (Subsidiary of: Wolters Kluwer N.V.), Strada 1, Palazzo F6, 20090 Assago (Milan), Italy. TEL 39-2-824-761. Ed. Massimiliano Galioni. adv.: B&W page L.3800000. circ. 8,815. **Document type:** consumer publication.

332 341 NE
AMSTERDAM FINANCIAL SERIES. BANKING AND E E C LAW: COMMENTARY. (Text in English) 1992. base vol. (plus s-a. updates). fl.270($169) (effective 1996). Kluwer Law International (Subsidiary of: Wolters Kluwer N.V.), Postbus 85889, 2508 CN The Hague, Netherlands. TEL 31-70-3081511. FAX 31-70-3081515. (Dist. by: Libresso Distribution Centre, P.O. Box 23, 7400 GA Deventer, Netherlands. TEL 31-570-633155. FAX 31-570-633834; In N. America: Kluwer Law International, 675 Massachusetts Ave., Cambridge, MA 02139. TEL 617-354-0140. FAX 617-354-8595) Eds. Martijn van Empel, Rene Smits. (looseleaf format)
Description: Covers the impact of EC directives on intracommunity traffic of money and day-to-day business.

332 341 NE
AMSTERDAM FINANCIAL SERIES. FINANCIAL SERVICES AND E E C LAW: MATERIALS AND CASES. (Text in English) 1991. 2 base vols. (plus s-a. updates). fl.525($328) (effective 1994). Kluwer Law International (Subsidiary of: Wolters Kluwer N.V.), Postbus 85889, 2508 CN The Hague, Netherlands. TEL 31-70-3081511. FAX 31-70-3081515. (Dist. by: Libresso Distribution Center, P.O. Box 23, 7400 GA Deventer, Netherlands. TEL 31-570-633155. FAX 31-570-633834; In N. America: Kluwer Law International, 675 Massachusetts Ave., Cambridge, MA 02139. TEL 617-354-0140. FAX 617-354-8595) Eds. Martijn van Empel, Patrick Pearson. (looseleaf format)
Description: Provides comprehensive and practical coverage of EEC legislation, case law and decisions of the European Commission relating to capital movements, banking, securities and stock exchanges.

332.1 NE ISSN 0066-1309
AMSTERDAM-ROTTERDAM BANK. ANNUAL REPORT. 1964. a. (Amsterdam-Rotterdam Bank N.V.) A B N Amro Bank N.V., P.O. Box 283, 1000 EA Amsterdam, Netherlands. **Document type:** corporate report.

332 GW ISSN 0172-7419
ANLAGEPRAXIS. 1977. m. DM.192 (foreign DM.210) (effective 1997). Betriebswirtschaftlicher Verlag Dr. Th. Gabler GmbH, Abraham-Lincoln-Str. 46, 65189 Wiesbaden, Germany. TEL 49-611-7878129. FAX 49-611-7878423. circ. 3,500. (back issues avail.) **Document type:** trade publication.
—CCC.

332.1 332.6 CN ISSN 1198-1180
HG4090
ANNUAL DIVIDEND RECORD - TEN YEAR PRICE RANGE. 1979. a. Can.$49.95. Financial Post Data Group, 333 King St. E., Toronto, ON M5A 4N2, Canada. TEL 416-350-6507; 800-661-POST. FAX 416-350-6501. Ed. Joanne Bryant; Pub. Doug Knight.
Former titles: Financial Post Ten Year Price Range (ISSN 0844-1774); Financial Post Eight Year Price Range (ISSN 0828-153X); Financial Post Corporation Service. Eight Year Price Range.
Description: A 10 year "snapshot" of price history for all securities listed on the Toronto, Montreal, Vancouver and Alberta stock exchanges.

332.1 US
ANNUAL EDITIONS: MONEY AND BANKING. 1990. a. $12.95. Dushkin Publishing Group, Sluice Dock, Guilford, CT 06437-9989. TEL 203-453-4351. FAX 203-453-6000. Ed. James P. Egan; Pub. Ian Nielsen. illus. **Document type:** academic/scholarly publication.
Refereed Serial

ANNUAL INSTITUTE ON MUNICIPAL FINANCE. see LAW — Corporate Law

332 334 US ISSN 0195-5756
KF1440
ANNUAL INSTITUTE ON SECURITIES REGULATION. 1969. a. $99. Practising Law Institute, 810 Seventh Ave., New York, NY 10019. TEL 212-824-5700; 800-260-4754. FAX 800-321-0093. E-mail: info@pli.edu; URL: http://www.pli.edu. Ed.Bd. (back issues avail.; reprint service avail. from UMI) **Indexed:** L.R.I.
—KR SourceOne.

332.1 340 US ISSN 0739-2451
K1
ANNUAL REVIEW OF BANKING LAW. 1982. a. $110. (Boston University, School of Law) Butterworth Legal Publishers (Salem) (Subsidiary of: Reed Elsevier plc), 8 Industrial Way, Bldg. C, Salem, NH 03079. TEL 800-548-4001. FAX 603-898-9858. (also avail. in microfiche from WSH; reprint service avail. from WSH) **Indexed:** C.L.I., L.R.I., Leg.Per.
—KR SourceOne; UnCover. **CCC**.
Description: Covers national and international banking law developments.

332.1 SP
ANNUARIO ESTADISTICO DE LA BANCA PRIVADA. 1974. a. Consejo Superior Bancario, Jose Abascal 57, 28003 Madrid, Spain. TEL 91-441-06-11. FAX 91-441-27-20. circ. 1,500.

332 AQ
ANTIGUA COMMERCIAL BANK. ANNUAL REPORT. a. Antigua Commercial Bank, Thames and St. Mary Sts., P.O. Box 95, St. John's, Antigua, W.I. TEL 809-462-1217. FAX 809-462-1220. **Document type:** corporate report.

332 340 US ISSN 1070-8472
KF1644
ANTITRUST LITIGATION REPORTER. 1993. m. $750. Andrews Publications, 175 Strafford Ave., Bldg. 4, Ste. 140, Wayne, PA 19087. TEL 610-225-0510. FAX 610-225-0501. Ed. Gerry Matics; Pub. John Backe Jr. R&P contact: Robert Maroldo. adv. contact: Melissa Webber. (back issues avail.) **Document type:** newsletter.
●Also available online. Vendor(s): Lexis-Nexis.
Description: Offers comprehensive coverage of significant litigation brought under the federal and state antitrust statutes.

ANUARIO BURSATIL. see BUSINESS AND ECONOMICS — Abstracting, Bibliographies, Statistics

ANUARIO ESTADISTICO - SEGUROS Y PREVISION SOCIAL. see INSURANCE — Abstracting, Bibliographies, Statistics

ANUARIO FINANCIERO Y DE SOCIEDADES ANONIMAS DE ESPANA. see BUSINESS AND ECONOMICS — Production Of Goods And Services

APPLIED FINANCIAL ECONOMICS. see BUSINESS AND ECONOMICS — Economic Situation And Conditions

APPLIED MATHEMATICAL FINANCE. see MATHEMATICS

338.91 330 SJ
ARAB BANK FOR ECONOMIC DEVELOPMENT IN AFRICA. ANNUAL REPORT. 1975. a. Arab Bank for Economic Development in Africa, P.O. Box 2640, Khartoum, Sudan. FAX 22248. TELEX 22739 BADEA SD. Ed.Bd. charts; illus.; stat. **Document type:** corporate report.

332.1 SJ
ARAB BANK FOR ECONOMIC DEVELOPMENT IN AFRICA. QUARTERLY REVIEW. Running title: B A D E A Quarterly Review. (Editions in Arabic, English and French) q. Arab Bank for Economic Development in Africa - Banque Arabe pour le Developpement Economique en Afrique, P.O. Box 2640, Khartoum, Sudan. FAX 22248. TELEX 22739 BADEA SD.

332.1 BA
ARAB BANKING AND FINANCE DIRECTORY. (Text in English) 1983. a. $56. Tele-Gulf Directory Publications W L L, Bahrain Tower, 3rd Fl., P.O. Box 2738, Manama, Bahrain. TEL 973-213301. FAX 973-210503. Ed. V.N. Gopalakrishnan. adv.: B&W page $2280, color page $2896; trim 170 x 240; adv. contact: Hazel Irving. stat. circ. 10,000. **Document type:** directory.
Formerly: Arab Banking and Finance Handbook.
Description: Covers banking in the Arab countries, with an economic overview, and information on the principal banks, insurance companies and more.

332.1 US ISSN 0004-1726
ARKANSAS BANKER. 1917. m. $19.95. Arkansas Bankers Association, 1220 W. 3rd St., Little Rock, AR 72201-1904. TEL 501-376-3741. FAX 501-376-9243. Ed. H.G. "Tres" Williams, III. adv.: bk.rev.; illus. circ. 2,400. **Document type:** trade publication.

ARREARS MANAGEMENT MANUAL. see REAL ESTATE

332 II
ARTH CHETNA. (Text in Hindi) 1991. w. newsstand price: Rs.3.50. Kasyap Publication Pvt. Ltd., 13, Press Complex, A.B. Rd., Indore 452 008, India. Ed. Prakash Bohra. adv. contact: J.K. Bandi. circ. 24,260. cols./p.: 8; pp./issue: 12.

332 II
ARTHIK JAGAT. (Text in Hindi) 1956. w. Rs.60; newsstand price: Rs.1.50. Arvind Vajpeyi, Ed. & Pub., 4-2B, Leonard Rd., Hastings, Calcutta 700 022, India. TEL 2420651. adv.: page Rs.2500; trim 250 x 200. circ. 11,248.

384 332 US ISSN 1074-1127
ASIA PACIFIC MEDIA INVESTOR. 1993. m. $795 (effective 1997). Kagan World Media, Ltd., 126 Clock Tower Pl., Carmel, CA 93923. TEL 408-624-1536. FAX 408-625-3225. E-mail: info@kagan.com. Ed. Robin Flynn. adv. contact: Lorraine Yglesias. **Document type:** trade publication.
Description: Analyzes the names, numbers and values needed to understand the regulations and alliances involved in media in Asia and the Pacific Rim countries. Covers pay-cable TV penetration, media convergence, TV programming, broadcast operations, satellite growth, mergers and acquisitions, regulatory developments.

332 CC
ASIABANKING.* 1980. m. c/o Intercontinental Marketing Corp., I.P.O. Box 5056, Tokyo 100-30, Japan. Ed. Steven Thompson. adv.; bk.rev. circ. 10,000. **Indexed:** World Bank.Abstr.
Former titles (until 1984): Asian Banking and Corporate Finance (ISSN 0250-9717); (until 1983): Asian Banking.

332 CC
ASIAMONEY. 1989. 10/yr. £195 (foreign $295) (effective 1996). Euromoney Publications plc., 20th Fl., Trust Tower, 68 Johnston Road, Wanchai, Hong Kong, People's Republic of China. TEL 852-529-5009. FAX 852-866-9046. (Subscr. addr.: c/o Amanda Barretto, Asia Money, Singapore Airlines Bldg., 5th fl., 138 HV Del A Costa, Salcepo Village, Makati, Metro Manila, Philippines. TEL (632) 867-3491. FAX (632) 896-8232; Subscr. in US to: American Educational Systems, 173 W. 81st St., New York, NY 10024. TEL 800-717-2669. FAX 212-501-8926) Ed. Sarah Sargent. adv. contact: Karen Chambers. bk.rev. circ. 25,000. **Indexed:** B.P.I., HongKongiana. **Document type:** trade publication.
●Also available online. Vendor(s): UMI.
—BLDSC (1742.269750); KR SourceOne; SWETS; UMI.
Former titles: Asia Money and Finance; (until Nov. 1991): Asiamoney (ISSN 0958-9309); Which incorporates: Billion and Asian Finance.
Description: Covers financial market and investment developments in Asia and the Pacific Rim.

332.1 338.9 PH ISSN 0116-1164
HG4517
ASIAN DEVELOPMENT BANK. ANNUAL REPORT. (Text in English) 1967. a. free. Asian Development Bank, P.O. Box 789, 1099 Manila, Philippines. TEL 632-711-3851. FAX 632-741-7961. TELEX 29066 ADB PH. **Indexed:** IIS.
—BLDSC (1109.527500).

BUSINESS AND ECONOMICS — BANKING AND FINANCE

ASIAN DEVELOPMENT BANK. BOARD OF GOVERNORS. SUMMARY OF PROCEEDINGS.. see BUSINESS AND ECONOMICS — International Development And Assistance

332.1 338.9   PH   ISSN 0116-3000
HC411
ASIAN DEVELOPMENT BANK. KEY INDICATORS OF DEVELOPING ASIAN AND PACIFIC COUNTRIES. (Text in English) 1969. a. Asian Development Bank, Economics and Development Resource Center, P.O. Box 789, 1099 Manila, Philippines. TEL 632-711-3851. FAX 632-741-7961. TELEX 23103 ADB PH. stat. Indexed: IIS.
—BLDSC (5091.822945).
   Formerly: Asian Development Bank. Key Indicators of Developing Member Countries of A D B.
   Description: Presents the latest statistical data and socioeconomic indicators from the ADB member countries.

ASIAN DEVELOPMENT BANK. STATISTICAL REPORT SERIES. see BUSINESS AND ECONOMICS — Abstracting, Bibliographies, Statistics

332   CC   ISSN 0377-9920
CODEN: AWSJD4
THE ASIAN WALL STREET JOURNAL. 1976. d. (Mon.-Fri.). $850 (effective Jan. 1996). Dow Jones Publishing Company (Asia) Inc., G.P.O. Box 9825, 1 Stubbs Rd., A1A Bldg., 2nd Fl., Hong Kong, People's Republic of China. TEL 852-2573-7121. FAX 852-2834-5291. TELEX 83828 AWSJ HX. Ed. Urban C. Lehner. adv. contact: Robert Stone. circ. 51,009. (also avail. in microfilm from UMI)
Document type: newspaper.
—CASDDS.
   Description: Regional business and financial daily newspaper.

332   UK
ASIA'S 7500 LARGEST COMPANIES. (Text in English) 1985. a. £160. E L C Publishing Ltd., 109 Uxbridge Rd., Ealing, London W5 STL, England. TEL 0181-566-2288. FAX 0181-566-4931. Ed. D. Wildey. circ. 1,000.
   Description: Describes general activities and financial data for each of the top 7,500 companies in Southeast Asia.

ASSET-BASED FINANCING. see LAW — Civil Law

332 340   US
ASSET BASED FINANCING: A TRANSACTIONAL GUIDE. (Issued in 4 base vols. with supplements) irreg. $485. Matthew Bender & Co., Inc., 2 Park Ave., New York, NY 10016. TEL 212-448-2000. E-mail: international@bender.com; URL: http://www.bender.com. Ed. Howard Ruda. (looseleaf format)
   Description: For commercial banks, commercial finance companies, thrift institutions, and attorneys representing corporations engaged in asset based borrowing. Provides how-to information on structuring the loan transaction, monitoring the security underlying the loan, and proceeding in case of default.

332   US
ASSETS AND LIABILITIES OF INSURED DOMESTICALLY CHARTERED AND FOREIGN RELATED BANKING INSTITUTIONS. w. $30. U.S. Federal Reserve System, Board of Governors, Publications Services, Rm. MS-138, Washington, DC 20551. TEL 202-452-3244. FAX 202-728-5886. Document type: government publication.

332.1   LE
ASSOCIATION DES BANQUES DU LIBAN. BILANS DES BANQUES.* irreg. Association of Banks in Lebanon, DORA, Centre Moucarri, P.O. Box 80536, Beirut, Lebanon. stat.

332   US
ASSOCIATION FOR INVESTMENT MANAGEMENT AND RESEARCH. SEMINAR PROCEEDINGS. irreg. (approx. 8/yr.). $100. Association for Investment Management and Research, Box 3668, Charlottesville, VA 22903. TEL 804-980-3668. FAX 804-980-9755. Document type: proceedings.
   Formerly: Institute of Chartered Financial Analysts. Seminar Proceedings.

ASSOCIATION OF WINE SUPPLIERS. BANKRUPTCY UPDATE. see BEVERAGES

332.1 352   UK   ISSN 1353-2979
AUDIT COMMISSION. HEALTH & PERSONAL SOCIAL SERVICES. BULLETIN. 1993. a. $6. Audit Commission for Local Authorities and the National Health Service in England and Wales, 1 Vincent Sq., London SW1P 2PN, England. (Dist. by: H.M.S.O. Publications Centre, P.O. Box 276, London SW8 5DT, England. TEL 0171-873-9090. FAX 0171-873-8200) Document type: government publication, bulletin.
—BLDSC (4274.827000).

332.1 352   UK   ISSN 1353-2987
AUDIT COMMISSION. LOCAL GOVERNMENT BULLETIN. 1993. irreg. Audit Commission for Local Authorities in the National Health Service in England and Wales, 1 Vincent Sq., London SW1P, England. (Orders to: Bookpaint, 39 Milon Pak, Abingdon, Oxon. OX14 4TD, England. TEL 44-1235-400400. FAX 44-1235-400454) Document type: monographic series, government publication.
—BLDSC (5290.012800).

332.1 352   UK
AUDIT COMMISSION. LOCAL GOVERNMENT REPORTS. irreg., approx. 35-50/yr. £550. Audit Commission for Local Authorities in the National Health Service in England and Wales, 1 Vincent Sq., London SW1P, England. (Orders to: Bookpaint, 39 Milton Park, Abingdon, Oxon. OX14 4TD, England. TEL 44-1235-400400. FAX 44-1235-404454)
Document type: government publication, monographic series.

332.1 352   UK   ISSN 0959-2571
AUDIT COMMISSION. OCCASIONAL PAPERS. irreg. price varies. Audit Commission for Local Authorities in the National Health Service in England and Wales, 1 Vincent Sq., London SW1P, England. (Orders to: Bookpaint, 39 Milton Pk., Abingdon, Oxon. OX14 4TD, England. TEL 44-1235-400400. FAX 44-1235-400454) adv. contact: B. Dewar.
Document type: government publication, monographic series.

332.1 352   UK
AUDIT COMMISSION. REPORT & ACCOUNTS (YEAR). 1981. a. £9. Audit Commission for Local Authorities and the National Health Service in England and Wales, 1 Vincent Sq., London SW1P 2PN, England. (Dist. by: H.M.S.O. Publications Centre, P.O. Box 276, London SW8 5DT, England. TEL 0171-873-9090. FAX 0171-873-8200) Document type: government publication.

AUSTRALIA. BUREAU OF STATISTICS. AGRICULTURAL INDUSTRIES, FINANCIAL STATISTICS, AUSTRALIA, PRELIMINARY ESTIMATES. see AGRICULTURE — Abstracting, Bibliographies, Statistics

AUSTRALIA. BUREAU OF STATISTICS. ANNUAL STATISTICS ON FINANCIAL INSTITUTIONS. see BUSINESS AND ECONOMICS — Abstracting, Bibliographies, Statistics

AUSTRALIA. BUREAU OF STATISTICS. AUSTRALIAN NATIONAL ACCOUNTS: FINANCIAL ACCOUNTS. see BUSINESS AND ECONOMICS — Abstracting, Bibliographies, Statistics

AUSTRALIA. BUREAU OF STATISTICS. AVERAGE MONTHLY EXCHANGE RATES. see BUSINESS AND ECONOMICS — Abstracting, Bibliographies, Statistics

AUSTRALIA. BUREAU OF STATISTICS. HOUSING FINANCE FOR OWNER OCCUPATION, AUSTRALIA. see BUSINESS AND ECONOMICS — Abstracting, Bibliographies, Statistics

AUSTRALIA. BUREAU OF STATISTICS. MANAGED FUNDS, AUSTRALIA. see BUSINESS AND ECONOMICS — Abstracting, Bibliographies, Statistics

AUSTRALIA. BUREAU OF STATISTICS. MONTHLY STATISTICS FOR CORPORATIONS REGISTERED UNDER THE FINANCIAL CORPORATIONS ACT. see BUSINESS AND ECONOMICS — Abstracting, Bibliographies, Statistics

AUSTRALIA. BUREAU OF STATISTICS. NEW SOUTH WALES OFFICE. MONTHLY SUMMARY OF STATISTICS, NEW SOUTH WALES. see POPULATION STUDIES — Abstracting, Bibliographies, Statistics

AUSTRALIA. BUREAU OF STATISTICS. PRIVATE NEW CAPITAL EXPENDITURE, AUSTRALIA, ACTUAL AND EXPECTED EXPENDITURE, PRELIMINARY. see BUSINESS AND ECONOMICS — Abstracting, Bibliographies, Statistics

AUSTRALIA. BUREAU OF STATISTICS. PRIVATE NEW CAPITAL EXPENDITURE AND EXPECTED EXPENDITURE, AUSTRALIA. see BUSINESS AND ECONOMICS — Abstracting, Bibliographies, Statistics

AUSTRALIA. BUREAU OF STATISTICS. STATE ESTIMATES OF PRIVATE NEW CAPITAL EXPENDITURE. see BUSINESS AND ECONOMICS — Abstracting, Bibliographies, Statistics

AUSTRALIA. BUREAU OF STATISTICS. STOCKS, SELECTED INDUSTRY SALES AND EXPECTED SALES, AUSTRALIA. see BUSINESS AND ECONOMICS — Abstracting, Bibliographies, Statistics

332.1   AT   ISSN 0814-2912
HG1503
AUSTRALIAN BANKER. 1886. bi-m. Aus.$85 (foreign Aus.$110) (effective Feb. 1997). Australian Institute of Banking and Finance, Level 19, 385 Bourke St., Melbourne, Vic. 300, Australia. TEL 61-3-96025811. FAX 61-3-6023923. E-mail: info@aibf.com.au. Ed. Mark Sheehan. R&P contact: Mark Sheehan. adv.: B&W page Aus.$2500, color page Aus.Aus.$3500; trim 275 x 210; adv. contact: Carmel Lococo. bk.rev.; index. circ. 15,919. Indexed: Aus.P.A.I.S., P.A.I.S., World Bank.Abstr. Document type: academic/scholarly publication.
—BLDSC (1797.657000); UnCover.
   Supersedes: Bankers' Magazine of Australasia (ISSN 0005-5468)

AUSTRALIAN BANKING STATISTICS. see BUSINESS AND ECONOMICS — Abstracting, Bibliographies, Statistics

AUSTRALIAN CONSUMER CREDIT LAW. see LAW

332   AT
AUSTRALIAN CONSUMER CREDIT LAW GUIDE. 1994. q. C C H Australia Ltd., P.O. Box 230, North Ryde, N.S.W. 2113, Australia. TEL 61-1-300300224. FAX 61-1-300306224. (looseleaf format)
   Description: Contains an outline of the Consumer Credit Code together with the text of Bills that have been introduced by each state pursuant to the "Credit Laws Reform: Agreed Policy".

332.7   AT   ISSN 0725-0665
AUSTRALIAN CREDIT UNIONS MAGAZINE. 1980. q. Aus.$45 (foreign Aus.$60). (Credit Union Services Corporation (Australia) Ltd.) Australian Credit Unions Magazine, Level 6, 51 Druitt St., Sydney, N.S.W. 2000, Australia. TEL 61-2-333-7539. FAX 61-2-333-7762. Ed. Adam Milgate. R&P contact: Sue Wood. adv. contact: Jacqui Martin. bk.rev.; circ. 2,100 (paid). Document type: trade publication.
   Description: Covers items of specific interest to credit unions operating in Australia; touching on many areas of business management.

332   AT   ISSN 0404-2018
AUSTRALIAN FINANCIAL REVIEW. 1951. d. John Fairfax & Sons Ltd., 235 Jones St., Broadway, Sydney, N.S.W. 2007, Australia. TEL 02-282-2833. FAX 02-282-2484. TELEX 24851. Ed. Peter Robinson. circ. 74,000. Document type: newspaper.
   Description: National economic newspaper with financial and business articles.

332.7 346   AT   ISSN 1033-9345
AUSTRALIAN INSOLVENCY BULLETIN. 1933. q. Aus.$150 (effective 1997). Insolvency Practitioners Association of Australia, G.P.O. Box 3921, Sydney, N.S.W. 2001, Australia. TEL 61-2-92905700. FAX 61-2-92902820. Ed. David E.W. Blackwell. R&P contact: David E.W. Blackwell. adv.; bk.rev.; circ. 860 (paid). (also avail. in microfilm from UMI)
Document type: academic/scholarly publication, corporate report.
   Formerly (until 1989): Australian Bankruptcy Bulletin (ISSN 0045-0286)

BUSINESS AND ECONOMICS — BANKING AND FINANCE 1105

332 330.9   FR
AVIS ET DECISIONS DU CONSEIL DE LA CONCURRENCE. (Supplements avail.) a. 1760 F. (effective 1993). Lamy S.A., 187-189 quai de Valmy, 75490 Paris Cedex 10, France. TEL 33-1-44721343. FAX 33-1-44721395. index. (looseleaf format) **Description:** A guide to the decisions, actions, and economic and financial sanctions of the council.

332.1 368   UK
B I F U REPORT. bi-m. £5. Banking Insurance & Finance Union, Sheffield House, 1B Amity Grove, Raynes Park, London SW20 OLG, England. TEL 44-181-946-9151. FAX 44-181-879-3728. Ed. Noel Howell. R&P contact: Noel Howell. TEL 44-181-947-9879. adv.; bk.rev.; illus.; circ. 112,000 (controlled). (tabloid format) **Document type:** newspaper.
Formerly: N U B E News (ISSN 0027-7088)
Description: Information for union members.

332   MR
B M C E INFORMATION REVIEW. (Editions in English and French) 1976. m. free. Banque Marocaine du Commerce Exterieur, 140 Ave. Hassan II, Casablanca, Morocco. adv.; bk.rev. circ. 8,000 French Ed.; 4,000 English Ed. **Indexed:** ELLIS, P.A.I.S.
Formerly: B M C E Monthly Information Review; Formed by the (1976) merger of: Banque Marocaine du Commerce Exterieur. Revue Bimensuelle; Banque Marocaine du Commerce Exterieur. Monthly Bulletin of Information (ISSN 0522-327X)

332   IT
B P M. bi-m. Banco Popolare di Milano, Piazza Meda 4, 20121 Milan, Italy. Ed. Enrico Falcetti.

332   HT   ISSN 1012-3326
B R H MAGAZINE. q. Gde.80($20) Banque de la Republique d'Haiti, Direction Administrative, B.P. 1570, Port-au-Prince, Haiti. TEL 23-1944. FAX 22-2607. TELEX BRH DGA 2030537.

B S A DIRECTORY OF MEMBERS. see *REAL ESTATE*

332 387.7   CN
B S P DATA INTERCHANGE SPECIFICATIONS HANDBOOK. a. $35 (effective 1997). International Air Transport Association, 2000 Peel St., Montreal, PQ H3A 2R4, Canada. TEL 514-844-6311. FAX 514-844-5286. E-mail: sales@iata.org; URL: http://www.iata.org. ●Also available online.
Description: Contains specifications for data interchange for BSP operations including: reporting tape; hand-off tape; agent transaction tape; credit sales invoicing tape; ticket inventory tape.

332   GW
B V - EUROLETTER; E G-Binnenmarkt: Tips, Trends, Termine. 1989. m. free. Bayerische Vereinsbank AG, Kardinal-Faulhaber-Str. 1, 80333 Munich, Germany. TEL 089-2132-5530. FAX 089-2132-5699. circ. 24,000. (back issues avail.)
Description: News and trends in the European Common Market.

332   UI   ISSN 1355-7793
BACK OFFICE FOCUS. 1994. m. £395($600) (effective Jan. 1997). Armstrong International Ltd., The Courtyard, 12 Hill St., St. Helier, Jersey JE2 4UB, Channel Islands. TEL 44-1534-613650. FAX 44-1534-613651. E-mail: 106001.446@compuserve.com. Ed. Natasha Dabrowski; Pub. Richard Armstrong. adv. contact: Sarah Witts. (back issues avail.) **Document type:** newsletter.
Description: Covers global issues relating to post-trade activity in the securities industry, for heads of IT, electronic settlements and operations, and fund managers in brokerage houses and banks.

332.1   CH   ISSN 0256-3169
HG3883.T28
BALANCE OF PAYMENTS, TAIWAN DISTRICT, REPUBLIC OF CHINA. (Text in English) 1981. q. $5. Central Bank of China - Chung Yang Yin Hang, 2 Roosevelt Rd., Sec. 1, Taipei, Taiwan 107, Republic of China. FAX 02-397-3768. circ. 2,000.

332   UK   ISSN 0965-7967
BALANCE SHEET; strategies and policies for financial institutions. 1991. q. £199($299) (effective 1997). Financial Engineering Ltd., Risk Publications, 104-112 Marylebone Ln., London W1M 5FU, England. TEL 44-171-487-5326. FAX 44-171-486-0879. Ed. Graham Cooper; Pub. Peter Field. adv.: B&W page £1815; trim 297 x 210; adv. contact: Simon Turner. software rev.; charts. circ. 2,000. (back issues avail.) **Document type:** newsletter.
Description: Covers asset and liability management and its integration with overall strategy, profitability goals, new product development, and risk management. Aimed at bank treasurers, finance directors in banks, mortgage officers, insurance professionals, and regulators.

BALANCE SHEET ANALYSIS OF JOINT STOCK COMPANIES. see *BUSINESS AND ECONOMICS — Abstracting, Bibliographies, Statistics*

332   US
BALANCE SHEETS FOR THE U.S. ECONOMY. s-a. $5. U.S. Federal Reserve System, Board of Governors, Publications Services, Rm. MS-138, Washington, DC 20551. TEL 202-452-3244. FAX 202-728-5886. **Document type:** government publication.

332.1   SP
BALANCES Y ESTADISTICAS DE LA BANCA EN ESPANA. 1924. m. Consejo Superior Bancario, Jose Abascal 57, 28003 Madrid, Spain. TEL 91-441-06-11. FAX 91-441-27-20. circ. 1,500. (also avail. in magnetic tape; diskette format; back issues avail.)
Formerly: Balances y Estadisticas de la Banca Privada.

332 340.5   IT
BANCA BORSA E TITOLI DI CREDITO; rivista di dottrina e giurisprudenza. 1934. bi-m. Lit.190000 (foreign Lit.285000) (effective 1997). Casa Editrice Dott. A. Giuffre, Via Busto Arsizio 40, 20151 Milan, Italy. TEL 39-2-3807820. FAX 39-2-38009582. Ed. Federico Martorano. adv. circ. 3,900. **Indexed:** IBR.

332.1   IT   ISSN 0067-3161
BANCA D'ITALIA. ASSEMBLEA GENERALE ORDINARIA DEI PARTECIPANTI. (Editions in English, Italian) 1894. a. free. Banca d'Italia, Servizio Studi, Via Nazionale, 91, Rome, Italy. TEL 39-6-47922333. FAX 39-6-4747820. circ. 12,000. (back issues avail.) **Document type:** corporate report.

332   IT
BANCA D'ITALIA. BOLLETTINO DI VIGILANZA. 1962. m. free. Banca d'Italia, Servizio Normativa e Affari Generali di Vigilanza, Via Nazionale, 187, 00184 Rome, Italy. TEL 39-6-47924317. FAX 39-6-47924460. Ed. Giovanni Castaldi. circ. 3,000. **Document type:** bulletin.
Formerly (until 1994): Banca d'Italia. Bollettino - Vigilanza delle Azeinde di Credito (ISSN 0005-4593); Supersedes (1936-1943): Ispettorato per la Difesa del Risparmio e per l'Esercizio del Credito. Bollettino.

332   IT
HG3084
BANCA D'ITALIA. BOLLETTINO STATISTICO. STATISTICHE ANALITICHE MONETARIE E FINANZIARIE. NUOVA SERIE. 1945-1988; N.S. 1991. q. free. Banca d'Italia, Servizio Studi, Via Nazionale, 91, 00184 Rome, Italy. TEL 39-6-47921. FAX 39-6-4747820. Ed. Claudio Conigliani. charts; mkt.; stat.; index. circ. 7,800. (back issues avail.) **Indexed:** P.A.I.S.For.Lang.Ind. **Document type:** bulletin.
Former titles (until 1988): Banca d'Italia. Bollettino Statistico - Servizio Studi (ISSN 0393-604X); (until 1983): Banca d'Italia. Bollettino - Servizio Studi (ISSN 0393-6090); (until 1978): Banca d'Italia. Bollettino (ISSN 0392-467X); (until 1950): Banca d'Italia. Bollettino del Servizio Studi Economici (ISSN 0391-4720); (until 1947): Bollettino Mensile del Servizio Studi Economici.

332   IT
BANCA D'ITALIA. SERVIZIO STUDI. TEMI DI DISCUSSIONE. 1979. irreg. free. Banca d'Italia, Servizio Studi, Via Nazionale, 91, 00184 Rome, Italy. TEL 39-6-47922333. FAX 39-6-4747820. circ. 5,000. (back issues avail.) **Document type:** monographic series.

332   SP   ISSN 0210-1688
BANCA ESPANOLA. 1970. m. 3030 ptas. (foreign $45). Justo de la Mota, Ed. & Pub., Avda. de Alfonso XIII, 15, bajo B, 28002 Madrid, Spain. TEL 91-5191799. FAX 91-5191795. adv. circ. 6,500.
—CINDOC.

332.1   IT   ISSN 1120-9453
BANCA IMPRESA SOCIETA. 1983. 3/yr. Lit.110000 (foreign Lit.180000) (effective 1997). Societa Editrice Il Mulino, Strada Maggiore, 37, 40125 Bologna, Italy. TEL 39-51-256011. FAX 39-51-256034. E-mail: riviste@mulino.it. Ed.Bd. adv. contact: M. Luisa Vezzali. index. circ. 3,500. (back issues avail.)

332   IT
BANCA NAZIONALE DEL LAVORO. PREVISIONI. a. B N L Edizioni S.p.A., Via Lucullo 7, 00187 Rome, Italy. TEL 39-6-4884380. FAX 39-6-4745272.

332   IT
BANCA NAZIONALE DEL LAVORO. PROBLEMI E ANALISI. irreg. (6-8/yr.). L.100000 (effective 1995). B N L Edizioni S.p.A., Via Lucullo 7, 00187 Rome, Italy. TEL 39-6-4884380. FAX 39-6-4745272. **Document type:** monographic series.

332.1   IT
BANCA NAZIONALE DEL LAVORO. QUADERNI DI RICERCA. a. B N L Edizioni S.p.A., Via Lucullo 7, 00187 Rome, Italy. TEL 39-6-4884380. FAX 39-6-4745272.
Description: Reports on savings institutions.

330   IT   ISSN 0005-4607
HC301
BANCA NAZIONALE DEL LAVORO QUARTERLY REVIEW. 1947. q. L.80000 (effective 1995). B N L Edizioni S.p.A., Via Lucullo 7, 00187 Rome, Italy. TEL 39-6-4884380. FAX 39-6-4745272. Ed. Alessandro Roncaglia. adv. contact: Filippo Cucuccio. index. circ. 3,500. (reprint service avail. from UMI,SCH) **Indexed:** BPIA, Bus.Ind., C.R.E.J., ELLIS, J.of Econ.Lit., Key to Econ.Sci., P.A.I.S., Tr.& Indus.Ind., World Bank.Abstr. **Document type:** academic/scholarly publication.
—BLDSC (7203.525000); SWETS; UMI.
Description: Articles by leading economists on macroeconomic theory and policy, international trade and finance, the evolution of national monetary and financial institutions and allied topics.

332.1   IT
BANCA OGGI. bi-m. L.45000. Systems Comunicazioni, Via Orlanda, 6, 20083 Gaggiano (MI), Italy. TEL 39-2-90841814. FAX 39-2-90841682. adv.: B&W page L.2100000, color page L.3000000; trim 180 x 240. circ. 9,812.

332 330   IT
BANCA SANTO PAULO DI BRESCIA. NOTIZIARIO ECONOMICO. 1975. q. Ufficio Studi, Corso Martiri della Liberta, 13, 25100 Brescia, Italy. FAX 030-2992515. Ed.Bd. circ. 3,500.
Formerly: Notiziario Economico Bresciano.

332.1   MX   ISSN 0005-4615
BANCA Y COMERCIO. 1936. q. Mex.$3750($8) Escuela Bancaria y Comercial, Paseo de la Reforma 202, Mexico 06600 D.F., Mexico. FAX 905-546-0326. Ed. Carlos Prieto Sierra. adv.; bk.rev.; circ. 6,500 (controlled).

332   CK   ISSN 0120-7040
BANCA Y FINANZAS. 1976. q. $70 (effective 1998). Asociacion Bancaria y de Entidades Financieras, Apdo. Aereo 13994, Bogota D.C., Colombia. TEL 57-1-2114811. FAX 57-1-2119915. E-mail: info@asobancaria.com; URL: http://www.asobancaria.com.
Description: Provides articles on economic theory and policy, and comprehensive financial analyses.

331   IT   ISSN 0393-7062
BANCAMATICA. 10/yr. Edizioni di Protezione Civile s.r.l., Via dell'Acqua Traversa 187-189, 00135 Rome, Italy. TEL 39-6-3313000. FAX 39-6-3313212. TELEX 626462 EPCINF I. Ed. Adalberto Biasiotti; Pub. Pier Roberto Pais. adv.: B&W page L.2700000, color page L.3000000; adv. contact: Roberto Barberini. circ. 7,500. **Document type:** trade publication.

BUSINESS AND ECONOMICS — BANKING AND FINANCE

332.1   IT   ISSN 0005-4623
HG19
BANCARIA. 1945. m. L.130000 (foreign L.240000) (effective 1995). (Associazione Bancaria Italiana) Bancaria Editrice S.p.A., Piazza del Gesu 49, 00186 Rome, Italy. TEL 39-6-6767394. FAX 39-6-6767435. Ed. Tancredi Bianchi. adv.: B&W page L.2000000, color page L.2600000. bk.rev.; abstr.; bibl.; charts; stat.; index, cum.index. circ. 7,000. **Indexed:** IBR, Key to Econ.Sci., P.A.I.S.For.Lang.Ind.

BANCASSURANCE REPORT. see *INSURANCE*

332   IT   ISSN 0390-1378
BANCHE E BANCHIERI. 1974. bi-m. L.100000 (effective 1997). (Private Banks Association) Iniziative Culturali ed Editoriali Bancarie, Via Domenichino 5, 20149 Milan, Italy. TEL 39-2-48013830. FAX 39-2-48016164. Ed. Angelo Gersandi. R&P contact: Angelo Gersandi. adv.: B&W page L.2200000, color page L.3000000; adv. contact: Anna Consonni. bk.rev. circ. 2,500. (processed) **Indexed:** P.A.I.S.For.Lang.Ind. **Document type:** academic/scholarly publication.
Description: Covers research articles on areas related to the institutional aspects of credit systems and their management technique.

332.1   XV   ISSN 0005-4631
HG3234.S5
BANCNI VESTNIK; revija za denarnistvo in bancnistvo. (Text in Slovenian; summaries in English) 1951. m. 4410 SLT. Zdruzenje Bank Slovenije, Subiceva 2, 61001 Ljubljana, Slovenia. TEL 061-215-076. FAX 061-212-180. Ed. Ivo Graul. adv. circ. 2,150.

332.1   CL   ISSN 0716-2901
HG2896
BANCO CENTRAL DE CHILE. ANNUAL REPORT. (Text in English) 1983. a. free. Banco Central de Chile, Casilla 967, Santiago, Chile. TEL 56-2-6702000. FAX 56-2-6984847. TELEX 405 69 CENBC CL. circ. 600. **Document type:** corporate report.
Description: Balance sheet and financial statements, with summary of Chilean economic development during the year.

332 330.9   CL   ISSN 0716-2367
HG2900.S3
BANCO CENTRAL DE CHILE. BOLETIN MENSUAL. 1928. m. Ch.$82000($300) Banco Central de Chile, Casilla 967, Santiago, Chile. TEL 56-2-6702000. FAX 56-2-6984847. TELEX 405 69 CENBC CL. illus.; mkt.; stat.; index, cum.index: 1928-1992. circ. 1,350. **Indexed:** P.A.I.S.For.Lang.Ind. **Document type:** corporate report.
Description: Presents statistical charts of all economic and external sectors with articles on Chilean economic policy.

332.1 330.9   CL   ISSN 0716-2448
HG2900.S3
BANCO CENTRAL DE CHILE. MEMORIA ANUAL. (Editions in English, Spanish) 1926. a. free. Banco Central de Chile, Casilla 967, Santiago, Chile. TEL 56-2-6702000. FAX 56-2-6984847. TELEX 40569 CENBC CL. circ. 800. **Document type:** corporate report.
Description: Balance sheet and financial statement, with summary of Chilean economic development during the year.

332   DR
BANCO CENTRAL DE LA REPUBLICA DOMINICANA. BOLETIN TRIMESTRAL. 1947. q. $48. Banco Central de la Republica Dominicana, Departamento de Estudios Economicos, Apdo. Postal 1347, Santo Domingo, Dominican Republic. charts; stat. circ. 1,000. **Indexed:** P.A.I.S.For.Lang.Ind. **Document type:** bulletin.
Formerly: Banco Central de la Republica Dominicana. Boletin Mensual (ISSN 0005-4682)

332   DR
BANCO CENTRAL DE LA REPUBLICA DOMINICANA. MEMORIA. a. Banco Central de la Republica Dominicana, Apdo. Postal 1347, Santo Domingo, Dominican Republic.

332   DR
BANCO CENTRAL DE LA REPUBLICA DOMINICANA. PRINCIPALES INDICADORES ECONOMICOS. 1992. m. Banco Central de la Republica Dominicana, Apdo. Postal 1347, Santo Domingo, Dominican Republic.

332   ES
BANCO CENTRAL DE RESERVA DE EL SALVADOR. BOLETIN ECONOMICO. 1988. m. free. Banco Central de Reserva de El Salvador, Subgerencia de Politica Economica, Calle Ruben Dario y 17 Avda. Sur, Apdo. Postal (06) 106, San Salvador, El Salvador. TEL 22-5022. Ed.Bd. stat. circ. 2,000.
Description: Articles and analysis on money and banking, trade, public finance, commerce and production.

332.1   ES
BANCO CENTRAL DE RESERVA DE EL SALVADOR. MEMORIA DE LABORES. 1934. a. Banco Central de Reserva de El Salvador, Subgerencia de Politica Economica, Calle Ruben Dario y 17 Avda. Sur, Apdo. Postal (06) 106, San Salvador, El Salvador. TEL 503-22-5022. stat. circ. 3,100. (also avail. in microfilm from OMN)
Formerly (until 1993): Banco Central de Reserva de El Salvador. Memoria.
Description: Compares current economic and financial performance to the previous year. Covers the GNP, inflation, balance of payments, fiscal and monetary sectors, exchange rate, and monetary and credit policies and measures.

332   ES
HF6
BANCO CENTRAL DE RESERVA DE EL SALVADOR. REVISTA TRIMESTRAL. 1934. q. donation. Banco Central de Reserva de El Salvador, Subgerencia de Politica Economica, Calle Ruben Dario y 17 Avda. Sur, Apdo. Postal (06) 106, San Salvador, El Salvador. TEL 22-5022. Ed.Bd. stat. circ. 3,100. (also avail. in microfilm from OMN) **Indexed:** P.A.I.S.For.Lang.Ind., PROMT.
Formerly: Banco Central de Reserva de El Salvador. Revista Mensual (ISSN 0005-4704)
Description: Covers the statistics of money and banking, balance of payments, public finance, and prices and production of goods and services.

332   PE   ISSN 0005-4712
HG2946
BANCO CENTRAL DE RESERVA DEL PERU. BOLETIN. 1931. m. free. Banco Central de Reserva del Peru, Seccion Publicaciones, Apdo. 1958, Lima, Peru. charts; mkt.; stat. circ. 4,200. **Indexed:** P.A.I.S.For.Lang.Ind.

332   PE
BANCO CENTRAL DE RESERVA DEL PERU. MEMORIA. 1922. a. Banco Central de Reserva del Peru, Seccion Publicaciones, Apdo. 1958, Lima, Peru. charts; stat.

332   VE
BANCO CENTRAL DE VENEZUELA. ANUARIO DE CUENTAS NACIONALES. a. $13 (effective 1994). Banco Central de Venezuela, Avda. Urdaneta Esq. de las Carmelitas, Caracas 1010, Venezuela. TEL 58-2-8015111.

332   VE
BANCO CENTRAL DE VENEZUELA. BOLETIN DE INDICADORES SEMANALES. 1981. w. $78 (effective 1996). Banco Central de Venezuela, Avda. Urdaneta esq. de las Carmelitas, Caracas 1010, Venezuela. TEL 58-2-8015111.

332   VE
BANCO CENTRAL DE VENEZUELA. BOLETIN MENSUAL. 1944. m. $60 (effective 1996). Banco Central de Venezuela, Avda. Urdaneta esq. de las Carmelitas, Caracas 1010, Venezuela. TEL 58-2-8015111. **Indexed:** P.A.I.S.For.Lang.Ind.

332.1   VE   ISSN 0067-3269
HG2966
BANCO CENTRAL DE VENEZUELA. MEMORIA. 1940. a. $5 (effective 1993). Banco Central de Venezuela, Avda. Urdaneta Esq. de las Carmelitas, Caracas 1010, Venezuela. TEL 58-2-8015111. circ. 2,000.

332   VE   ISSN 0005-4720
HG1505
BANCO CENTRAL DE VENEZUELA. REVISTA. 1941-1975 (no.370); resumed 1986. s-a. $10 (effective 1996). Banco Central de Venezuela, Avda. Urdaneta Esq. de las Carmelitas, Caracas 1010, Venezuela. TEL 58-2-8015111. charts; mkt.; stat. circ. 4,500.

BANCO CENTRAL DEL ECUADOR. BALANZA DE PAGOS. see *BUSINESS AND ECONOMICS — Abstracting, Bibliographies, Statistics*

332   EC   ISSN 0005-4739
BANCO CENTRAL DEL ECUADOR. BOLETIN. (Text in Spanish) 1927. s-a. free. Banco Central del Ecuador, Division Tecnica, Casilla 29C, Sucursal No.15, Quito, Ecuador. TEL 210-340. (Distr. by: Libreria Economia y Cultura, Av. 10 de Agosto, No. 660 y Chec, Quito, Ecuador) charts; stat.; cum.index: 1927-1976. circ. 6,000. **Indexed:** P.A.I.S.For.Lang.Ind.
Description: Provides statistics on public and private banking in Ecuador.

332.1   EC   ISSN 0067-3277
BANCO CENTRAL DEL ECUADOR. MEMORIA DEL GERENTE GENERAL. 1948. irreg. free. Banco Central del Ecuador, Casilla 29C, Sucursal No.15, Quito, Ecuador. TEL 561-521. (Distr. by: Libreria Economia y Cultura, Av. 10 de Agosto, No. 600 y Checa, Quito, Ecuador) charts; illus.; stat. circ. 4,000.

332.1   PY   ISSN 0067-3285
BANCO CENTRAL DEL PARAGUAY. MEMORIA. 1952. a. free. Banco Central del Paraguay, Avda. Pablo VI y Avda. Sgt. Marecos, Asuncion, Paraguay. TEL 21-60-8019. FAX 21-60-8150.

332.1   UY
BANCO CENTRAL DEL URUGUAY. RESENA DE LA ACTIVIDAD ECONOMICO-FINANCIERA. irreg. Banco Central del Uruguay, Departamento de Estadisticas Economicas, Casilla 1467, Paysando y Florida, Montevideo, Uruguay. stat.

332   BL   ISSN 0101-4668
HG2886
BANCO CENTRAL DO BRASIL. BOLETIM. (Includes: Relatorio Anual do Banco Central do Brasil) 1965. m. (plus 2 a. supplements). R.721($801.11) Banco Central do Brasil, Departamento Economico, Ed. Sede, 10 Andar, 70074-900 Brasilia D.F., Brazil. TEL 226-2082. (Subscr. to: DEBRA-RESUP, SIG, Quadra 8, Lote 2025, 70610-400 Brasilia DF, Brazil. TEL 55-61-3441554. FAX 55-61-344-2982) stat. circ. 3,000.

332.1   HO
BANCO CENTROAMERICANO DE INTEGRACION ECONOMICA. MEMORIA ANUAL. (Text in English, Spanish) 1962. a. Banco Centroamericano de Integracion Economica, Apdo. Postal 772, Tegucigalpa D.C., Honduras. TEL 504-222230. Dir. Carlos Guillermo Herrera. index. circ. 1,200. (back issues avail.) **Document type:** corporate report.

332.1   SP
BANCO DE BILBAO. AGENDA FINANCIERA. vol.14, 1975. a. Banco de Bilbao, Servicio de Estudios, Gran Via 12, Bilbao 1, Spain.

332   SP
BANCO DE BILBAO. INFORME - MEMORIA. a. Banco de Bilbao, Servicio de Estudios, Gran Via 12, Bilbao, Spain. charts; illus.; stat.
Formerly: Banco de Bilbao. Memoria.

332   SP   ISSN 0005-4798
BANCO DE ESPANA. BOLETIN ESTADISTICO. (Supplement included: Boletin Estadistico: Notas; Includes: Informe Anual; Cuentas Financieras de la Economia Espanola) 1960. m. 22472 ptas. in Europe 36000 ptas.; America 51500 ptas.; elsewhere 58000 ptas.(includes Boletin Economico). Banco de Espana, Seccion de Publicaciones, Negociado de Distribucion y Gestion, Alcala 50, 28014 Madrid, Spain. TEL 338-51-80. bk.rev. (also avail. in magnetic tape) **Indexed:** P.A.I.S.For.Lang.Ind.

332   SP
BANCO DE ESPANA. DOCUMENTO DE TRABAJO. (Text mainly in Spanish; occasionally in English) irreg., no.9506, 1995. Banco de Espana, Seccion de Publicaciones, Negociado de Distribucion e Gestion, Alcala 50, 28014 Madrid, Spain. TEL 34-1-3385180.

332.1   SP   ISSN 0067-3315
HC381
BANCO DE ESPANA. INFORME ANUAL. (Editions in English, Spanish) 1962. a. 1590 ptas. in Europe 2500 ptas.; America 3000 ptas.; elsewhere 4000 ptas. Banco de Espana, Seccion de Publicaciones, Negociado de Distribucion y Gestion, Alcala 50, Madrid 28014, Spain. TEL 3385180. FAX 5310059. charts; stat.
Description: Provides information on economic and financial institutions; includes a separate statistical appendix.

BUSINESS AND ECONOMICS — BANKING AND FINANCE

332   GT   ISSN 0005-481X
HG2746
BANCO DE GUATEMALA. BOLETIN ESTADISTICO. 1947. q. free. Banco de Guatemala, 7a Av. 22-01, Zona 1, C.P. 01001 Guatemala, Guatemala. TEL 53-4053. charts; stat. **Indexed:** P.A.I.S.For.Lang.Ind.
   Description: Statistics from the National Bank on money and banking, public finance, commerce, and tourism.

332   GT
BANCO DE GUATEMALA. BOLETIN INFORMATIVO. m. free. Banco de Guatemala, 7a Av. 22-01, Zona 1, C.P. 01001 Guatemala, Guatemala. TEL 535932. Ed. Francisco Albiurez Palma. charts; illus.; stat.
   Description: Covers financial and economic news.

332   GT
BANCO DE GUATEMALA. ESTUDIO ECONOMICO Y MEMORIA DE LABORES. 1945. a. Banco de Guatemala, Departamento de Relaciones Publicas, 7a Av. 22-01, Zona 1, C.P. 01001 Guatemala, Guatemala. TEL 535932.
   Formerly (until 1967): Banco de Guatemala. Memoria.

332 330.9   CK   ISSN 0005-4828
HG2906
BANCO DE LA REPUBLICA. REVISTA. 1927. m. Col.$15000($60) Banco de la Republica, Departamento Editorial, Calle 13 No. 35-51, Bogota, Colombia. bk.rev.; charts; mkt.; stat.; index, cum.index: 1927-1991. circ. 4,500. **Indexed:** Key to Econ.Sci., P.A.I.S.For.Lang.Ind.
   Description: Includes articles on economics and related topics.

332.1 330.9   MX   ISSN 0067-3374
BANCO DE MEXICO. INFORME ANUAL. a. Mex.$80 (America $20; Europe $25; elsewhere $30) (effective Aug. 1996). Banco de Mexico, Subdireccion de Investigacion Economica y Bancaria, Av. Juarez 90, Col. Centro, Del. Cuauhtemoc, 06059 Mexico DF, Mexico. TEL 525-761-8588. charts. (also avail. in microfiche)

332.1   MX
BANCO DE MEXICO. SERIE DOCUMENTOS DE INVESTIGACION. 1978-1991; N.S. 1995. irreg., no.9604, 1996. Mex.$70 (America $20; Europe $25) (effective Aug. 1996). Banco de Mexico, Subdireccion de Investigacion Economica y Bancaria, Av. Juarez 90, Col. Centro, Del. Cuauhtemoc, 06059 Mexico DF, Mexico. TEL 525-761-8588.

BANCO DE PORTUGAL. ESTATISTICA E ESTUDOS ECONOMICOS. see BUSINESS AND ECONOMICS — Abstracting, Bibliographies, Statistics

332   PO
BANCO DE PORTUGAL. REPORT OF THE DIRECTORS AND ECONOMIC AND FINANCIAL SURVEY. a. Banco de Portugal, Rua do Comercio 148, 1000 Lisbon, Portugal.

332   VE
BANCO DE VENEZUELA. INFORME SEMESTRAL. 1974. s-a. Banco de Venezuela, Apdo. Postal 6268, Caracas 1010, Venezuela. charts; illus.; stat.

332.1   BL   ISSN 0101-0646
BANCO DO BRASIL. ANNUAL REPORT. (Text in English) a. free. Banco do Brasil S.A., Setor Bancario Sul, Quadra 4, Bloco C, Lote 32, 70089-900 Brasilia, DF, Brazil. TEL 55-61-3103774. FAX 55-61-3103531. URL: http://www.bbnet.com.br. Ed.Bd. charts; illus.; stat. **Document type:** corporate report.

332.1   BL
BANCO DO BRASIL. BOLETIM DE INFORMACAO AO PESSOAL. 1978. fortn. free to qualified personnel. Banco do Brasil S.A., Departamento Geral de Selecao e Desenvolvimento do Pessoal, Setor Bancario Sul, Lote 23, Bloco C, C.P. 562, Brasilia, D.F., Brazil. Ed.Bd. charts; illus.; stat.; circ. 100,000 (controlled).
   Description: Internal organization of bank.

332.1   BL
BANCO DO ESTADO DE PERNAMBUCO. BANDEPE RELATORIO. (Summary in English) 1969. a. free. Banco do Estado de Pernambuco, Cais do Apolo, 222, Recife, Brazil. illus.; stat. circ. 3,000.

332   BO
BANCO MINERO DE BOLIVIA. MEMORIA. a. Banco Minero de Bolivia, Casilla 1410, La Paz, Bolivia.

332   MX
BANCO NACIONAL DE COMERCIO EXTERIOR, MEXICO. ANNUAL REPORT. Spanish edition: Informe Anual. (Text in English) 1938. a. free. Banco Nacional de Comercio Exterior S.A., Gerencia de Publicaciones, Periferico Sur 4333, 4o Pte., Jardines de la Montana, 14210 Mexico D.F., Mexico. illus.; stat. **Indexed:** Key to Econ.Sci.

332.1   HO
BANCO NACIONAL DE DESARROLLO AGRICOLA. MEMORIA ANUAL. 1950. a. free. Banco National de Desarrollo Agricola, Unidad de Estudios Economicos, Tegucigalpa D.C., Honduras. FAX 37-5187. Ed. Cesar Marini. charts; illus.; stat. circ. 2,000. **Document type:** corporate report.
   Formerly (until 1979): Banco Nacional de Fomento, Tegucigalpa. Memoria Anual (ISSN 0067-3390)
   Description: Covers all areas of agriculture as it relates to banking and the economy of Honduras.

332   EC
BANCO NACIONAL DE FOMENTO. BOLETIN. 1975. bi-m. free. Banco Nacional de Fomento, Departamento de Divulgacion Tecnica, Apdo. 685, Quito, Ecuador. illus.

332   PN
BANCO NACIONAL DE PANAMA. INFORME DEL GERENTE GENERAL. 1904. a.? Banco Nacional de Panama, Apdo. 5220, Panama 5, Panama.

332.1   PN
BANCO NACIONAL DE PANAMA. MEMORIA ANUAL. 1904. a. free. Banco Nacional de Panama, Gerencia de Mercadotecnia y Comunicacion Social, Apdo. 5220, Panama 5, Panama. FAX 507-69-2529. circ. 1,500.
   Formerly: Banco Nacional de Panama. Asesoria Economica. Memoria Anual.

332.1   CK
BANCOS CENTRALES DE LOS PAISES DEL ACUERDO DE CARTAGENA. BOLETIN ESTADISTICO. N.S. 1984. q. free. Latin American Reserve Fund - Fondo Latinoamericano de Reservas, Apdo. Aereo 241523, Bogota, Colombia. FAX 2881117. TELEX 45586. charts; stat. circ. 1,200.

332   CK   ISSN 0120-5226
HG1505
BANCOS Y BANCARIOS DE COLOMBIA. 1957. q. Col.$10000($30) (effective 1995). Av. Jimenez No. 4-03, Edificio Lerner, Oficina 1003, Apdo. 9418, Bogota, Colombia. TEL 57-911-2831262. FAX 57-911-342-9453. Ed. Arcesio Ramirez Jaramillo. adv.: B&W page $1000, color page $1200; trim 165 x 240. bk.rev.; charts; illus.; stat.; circ. 19,700 (paid). **Document type:** trade publication.
   Description: Covers economics, banking, business administration and people who work in the financial sector.

330.9   PH
HC451
BANGKO SENTRAL REVIEW. (Text in English) 1949. m. $25. Central Bank of the Philippines, A. Mabini corner Vito Cruz Streets, Manila, Philippines. FAX 632-597363. Ed. Mercedes B. Suleik. charts; mkt.; stat. circ. 5,500. **Indexed:** Ind.Phil.Per., Key to Econ.Sci., P.A.I.S., PROMT, World Bank.Abstr. —UnCover.
   Former titles (until Jul. 1993): C B Review (ISSN 0115-1401); Central Bank News Digest (ISSN 0008-9214)

332   TH   ISSN 0005-4984
BANGKOK BANK. MONTHLY REVIEW. (Text in English) 1960. m. free. Bangkok Bank Ltd., Research Office, 333 Silom Rd., Bangkok, Thailand. Ed. Viraphong Vachratit. charts; stat.; index. circ. 5,500. **Indexed:** Asian-Pac.Econ.Lit., Cott.& Trop.Fibr.Abstr., Key to Econ.Sci., Maize Abstr., P.A.I.S., Poult.Abstr., Rural Recreat.Tour.Abstr., World Agri.Econ.& Rural Sociol.Abstr.

332.1   BG
BANGLADESH BANK. ANNUAL REPORT. (Text in English) a. Bangladesh Bank, Department of Public Relations and Publications, Motijheel Commercial Area, Dhaka 2, Bangladesh.

BANGLADESH BANK. STATISTICS DEPARTMENT. ANNUAL BALANCE OF PAYMENTS. see BUSINESS AND ECONOMICS — Abstracting, Bibliographies, Statistics

BANGLADESH BANK. STATISTICS DEPARTMENT. BALANCE OF PAYMENTS. see BUSINESS AND ECONOMICS — Abstracting, Bibliographies, Statistics

332.1   GW
DIE BANK; Zeitschrift fuer Bankpolitik und Bankpraxis. 1961. m. DM.95. (Bundesverband Deutscher Banken e.V.) Bank-Verlag GmbH, Melatenguertel 113, 50825 Cologne, Germany. TEL 49-221-5490-0. FAX 49-221-5490120. Ed. Werner Karsch. adv.; bk.rev.; bibl.; charts. circ. 10,700. **Indexed:** P.A.I.S.For.Lang.Ind. **Document type:** trade publication.
   Formerly (until 1976): Bank-Betrieb (ISSN 0005-5034)

BANK ACCOUNTING & FINANCE. see BUSINESS AND ECONOMICS — Accounting

332 659.1   US   ISSN 0274-7111
HG1616.M3
BANK ADVERTISING NEWS; the independent national newspaper of financial marketing. w. $398. Advertising News Service, Inc., 11811 Federal Highway One, Box 088888, N. Palm Beach, FL 33408-8888. TEL 407-627-7330. FAX 407-627-7335. URL: http://www.bankrate.com. Ed. Linda Green. **Document type:** trade publication.
   Description: Provides coverage of bank, thrift and credit union promotions, marketing efforts and advertising campaigns in the nation's top 100 markets, as well as financial marketing related conferences.

332.1   MR
BANK AL-MAGHRIB. RAPPORT ANNUEL. 1959. a. free. Bank Al-Maghrib, 277 Ave. Mohammed V, Rabat, Morocco.
   Formerly: Banque du Maroc. Rapport Annuel (ISSN 0067-396X)

332   AU   ISSN 1015-1516
BANK ARCHIV; Zeitschrift fuer das gesamte Bank- und Boersenwesen. m. S.1670. (Oesterreichische Bankwissenschaftliche Gesellschaft) Verlag Orac GesmbH & Co. KG, Graben 17, A-1010 Vienna, Austria. TEL 43-1-53452-0. FAX 43-1-53452141. adv.: B&W page S.12000; trim 170 x 253; adv. contact: Christian Braun. circ. 3,000. **Document type:** trade publication.
   —BLDSC (1861.762830).

332 658   US   ISSN 0896-6230
HG1615.25
BANK ASSET - LIABILITY MANAGEMENT. 1985. m. $193.75 (overseas $265.45) (effective 1995). Warren, Gorham & Lamont, One Penn Plaza, New York, NY 10119. TEL 212-971-5000. FAX 212-971-5113. (Subscr. to: The Park Square Bldg., 31 St. James Ave., Boston, MA 02116-4112. TEL 800-950-1207) (also avail. in microform from UMI) **Document type:** newsletter.
   —UMI. **CCC.**
   Description: For bankers concerned with balancing an asset and liability portfolio. Helps bankers reduce exposure to interest rate volatility.

332.1 657   US   ISSN 0522-2478
BANK AUDITING & ACCOUNTING REPORT. 1967. m. $168 (overseas $232.95) (effective 1995). Warren, Gorham & Lamont, One Penn Plaza, New York, NY 10119. TEL 212-971-5000. FAX 212-971-5113. (Subscr. to: The Park Square Bldg., 31 St. James Ave., Boston, MA 02116-4112. TEL 800-950-1207) Eds. K. Gary Gibbs, Brent E. Olney. (also avail. in microform from UMI) **Indexed:** Bank.Lit.Ind. **Document type:** newsletter.
   —UMI. **CCC.**
   Description: Covers developments in regard to government regulations, practices and techniques in bank accounting, and financial controls surrounding the industry.

BUSINESS AND ECONOMICS — BANKING AND FINANCE

332 346.066　　US　　ISSN 1047-5133
KF967
BANK BAILOUT LITIGATION NEWS. 1989. bi-w. $645 (foreign $667) (effective 1997). L R P Publications, 747 Dresher Rd., Box 980, Horsham, PA 19044-0980. TEL 215-784-0941; 800-341-7874. FAX 215-784-9639. URL: http://www.lrp.com. Ed. Damarie Sanjurjo. **Document type:** newsletter.
—CCC.
　　Incorporates: Bank - Thrift Litigation and Enforcement News (ISSN 1047-1502).
　　Description: Washington-based lawyer-written newsletter on failed bank and thrift liquidation issues. Includes in-depth analysis of the latest news in the transactional, professional liability, enforcement and other areas of failed bank law.

332.1　　US　　ISSN 0005-5042
BANK BOARD LETTER. 1969. m. $52. Bank News, Inc., 912 Baltimore, Ste. 900, Kansas City, MO 64105. TEL 314-421-5445. Ed. R.W. Doquette. **Document type:** newsletter.

332　　US
HG1643
BANK CARD INDUSTRY REPORT. Key Title: A B A Bank Card Industry Report. a. $230 to non-members; members $153. American Bankers Association, Retail Services Center, 1120 Connecticut Ave., N.W., Washington, DC 20036. TEL 202-663-5430. FAX 301-843-8405. (Subscr. to: Order Processing Department, Box 630544, Baltimore, MD 21263-0544. TEL 800-338-0626) charts.
　　Formerly: Bank Card Credit Report (ISSN 1043-9196); Which supersedes in part (in 1987): Retail Bank Credit Report (ISSN 0276-9093)
　　Description: Contains current data on every aspect of bank card operations and marketing.

332　　US
BANK DIGEST. 1988. d. $650. Washington Service Bureau, Inc., 655 15th St., N.W., Washington, DC 20005. TEL 202-508-0600. FAX 202-508-0694. URL: http://www.wsb.com/sectoday. (back issues avail.) **Document type:** newsletter.

332　　US
BANK DIRECTOR. 1991. q. $105. Bank Director, Box 3468, Brentwood, TN 37024. TEL 615-371-0406. FAX 615-371-0899. E-mail: bankdirector@nashville.com. Ed. Deborah Scally; Pub. L.William Seidman. R&P contact: Deborah Scally. adv. contact: Joan Susie. bk.rev. circ. 43,000. **Indexed:** Bank.Lit.Ind. **Document type:** trade publication.
　　Description: For directors of financial institutions. Addresses concerns of bank boards, including issues of banking leadership, corporate governance and personal liability.
　　Refereed Serial

332　　US
BANK DIRECTOR'S BRIEFING. 1979. m. $28. (American Bankers Association, Member Communications) Simmons - Boardman Publishing Corp., 345 Hudson St., New York, NY 10014-4502. TEL 212-620-7200. FAX 212-633-1165. (Addr. in Netherlands: Nijverheidsweg 46, 3340 Henrick Ido Ambacht, Netherlands) Ed. Steven Cocheo; Pub. Russell S. Selover. **Document type:** newsletter.
　　Description: Provides a concise and readable summary of events in banking for outside directors of community banks.

330.9　　IO　　ISSN 0302-6795
HG3310.J34
BANK EKSPORT IMPORT INDONESIA. ANNUAL REPORT. (Text in English and Indonesian) a. Bank Eksport Import Indonesia, Jl. Lapagan Setasium 1, Box 32, Jakarta, Indonesia. illus.; stat.

332.1　　NE　　ISSN 0005-5018
BANK- EN EFFECTENBEDRIJF. 1952. 10/yr. fl.163 (effective 1996). Nederlands Instituut voor het Bank- en Effectenbedrijf, Herengracht 205, 1016 BE Amsterdam, Netherlands. FAX 31-20-5208603. Ed. A.R.A. Koning. adv.; bk.rev.; abstr.; stat.; index. circ. 6,000. **Document type:** bulletin.
—SWETS.

332.1　　CN　　ISSN 0711-6497
BANK FACTS. (Editions in English and French) 1968. a. free. Canadian Bankers Association, P.O. Box 348, Commerce Ct. W., Ste. 3000, 199 Bay St., Toronto, ON M5L 1G2, Canada. TEL 416-362-6092. R&P contact: Karen Bentley. circ. 64,000. **Document type:** trade publication.
　　Formerly: Factbook: Chartered Banks of Canada.

BANK FAILURE LITIGATION NEWS. see *LAW — Civil Law*

332　　US
BANK FINANCIAL QUARTERLY (HARTLAND). q. $389 (effective 1997). I D C Financial Publishing, Inc., Box 140, Hartland, WI 53029. TEL 414-367-7231; 800-525-5457. Ed. John E. Rickmeier. R&P contact: John E. Rickmeier. (back issues avail.) **Document type:** trade publication.

332.1　　US
BANK FINANCIAL QUARTERLY (ROCKVILLE). 1986. 4/yr. $349. United Communications Group, 11300 Rockville Pike, Ste. 1100, Rockville, MD 20852-3030. TEL 301-816-8950. FAX 301-816-8945. Ed. Daniel Brown.
　　Description: Gives 30 key financial indicators on most of the commercial banks in the U.S.. Also rates safety and soundness.

332.1　　SZ　　ISSN 0067-3560
HG1997.I6
BANK FOR INTERNATIONAL SETTLEMENTS. ANNUAL REPORT. (Text in English, French, German and Italian) a. avail. to limited qualified personnel only. Bank for International Settlements, 7 Centralbahnstr., Case Postale 262, CH-4002 Basel, Switzerland. charts; stat.; index; circ. controlled. (reprint service avail. from SCH)

332　　US　　ISSN 1065-8165
BANK FRAUD. 1986. m. $174 (foreign $189) (effective 1997). Bank Administration Institute Foundation, 1 N. Franklin St., Chicago, IL 60606. TEL 312-683-2248. FAX 312-683-2373. Ed. Richard G. Kemmer. **Document type:** newsletter.
—CCC.
　　Formerly: Bank Fraud Alert.
　　Description: Covers fraud and risk management, including typical fraud cases, telling what happened, how it was handled, the final outcome, and preventative measures.

332　　US
BANK GOVERNANCE LAW LETTER. 1992. m. $1000. Law Reporters, 1519 Connecticut Ave., N.W., Ste. 200, Washington, DC 20036. TEL 202-462-5755. FAX 202-328-2430. Ed. John Noble. s-a. index. (looseleaf format) **Document type:** newsletter.

332.1　　US
BANK HOLDING COMPANY (Y-9). q. $1440 in U.S., Canada, Mexico; elsewhere $2800. (Federal Reserve System) U.S. National Technical Information Service, 5825 Port Royal Rd., Springfield, VA 22161. TEL 703-487-4630. (magnetic tape)

BANK HOLDING COMPANY COMPLIANCE MANUAL. see *LAW*

332　　PL　　ISSN 0137-5520
BANK I KREDYT. 1945. m. 8.50 Zl. (foreign 17). Narodowy Bank Polski, Promotion and Information Division, Ul. Swietokrzyska 11-21, 00-919 Warsaw, Poland. TEL 48-22-6532335. FAX 48-22-6531321. Ed. Boguslaw Pietrzak. R&P contact: Elzbieta Lyszkowska. TEL 48-22-6532797. **Indexed:** AgroLibrex. **Document type:** bulletin.
　　Formerly (until 1970): Narodowy Bank Polski. Wiadomosci.

332.1 336　　US　　ISSN 0734-8037
KF6495.B2
THE BANK INCOME TAX RETURN MANUAL. 1983. a. $170.95 (overseas $246.95) (effective 1997). Warren, Gorham & Lamont, 395 Hudson St., New York, NY 10014. TEL 212-367-6300. FAX 212-367-6718. (Subscr. to: The Park Square Bldg., 31 St. James Ave., Boston, MA 02116-4112. TEL 800-950-1207) Eds. Charles W. Wheeler, Jack B. Wilson, Jr. (LL) **Document type:** trade publication.
　　Description: Enables bank tax professionals to prepare bank income tax return schedules accurately, reducing the possibility of an I.R.S. audit.

332 368　　US
BANK INSURANCE AND PROTECTION BULLETIN. m. American Bankers Association, 1120 Connecticut Ave., N.W., Washington, DC 20036. TEL 202-663-5305. Ed. Gregg Broomfield. (looseleaf format; also avail. in microform from UMI) **Document type:** newsletter.

BANK INSURANCE AND RISK MANAGEMENT. see *INSURANCE*

332 657.2　　US
BANK INTERNAL AUDIT: A WORKING GUIDE TO REGULATORY COMPLIANCE. (Subseries of: Compliance and Law series) 1991. base vol. (plus a. updates). $275 (updates $125). Sheshunoff Information Services Inc., 505 Barton Springs Rd., Ste. 1100, Austin, TX 78704. TEL 512-472-2244; 800-456-2340. (looseleaf format) **Document type:** trade publication.
　　Description: Enables bank audit personnel to implement and run effective audit programs.

332　　US　　ISSN 1055-3193
HG1616.I5
BANK INVESTMENT REPRESENTATIVE;* the magazine of investment marketing and investment program management. 1991. m. $60. Quantum Communications, Inc., 40 W. 57th St., 11th Fl., New York, NY 10019-4001. Ed. Jeffrey H. Champlin; Pub. Jeffrey H. Champlin. adv. contact: Lyn Fisher. illus.; circ. 31,209 (controlled). (back issues avail.) **Document type:** trade publication.
　　Description: Presents successful strategies and ideas in management, marketing, sales, motivation and service for managers and sales representatives in financial institutions.

BANK KARAMCHARI. see *LABOR UNIONS*

BANK LAWYER LIABILITY. see *LAW — Corporate Law*

332　　US
BANK LETTER; newsletter of commercial and institutional banking. 1977. w. $1495 (Canada $1525; elsewhere $1570). Institutional Investor Newsletters, 477 Madison Ave., New York, NY 10022. TEL 212-224-3233. FAX 212-224-3353. Ed. Tom Lamont. adv. (also avail. in microfiche; reprint service avail. from UMI) **Document type:** newsletter.
●Also available on CD-ROM.
　　Description: Examines the news events, key issues and trends at both money center and middle market banks. The emphasis is on regulatory affairs, new products, corporate borrowings, marketing, trusts, strategy shifts and senior personnel moves.

332.1　　US
BANK LOAN REPORT. w. $3500 (effective 1997). Investment Dealers' Digest, 2 World Trade Center, 18th Fl., New York, NY 10048-0638. TEL 212-227-1200. FAX 212-321-2336. Ed. Mark Kollar. R&P contact: Denise Robbins. adv. contact: Todd Miller. **Document type:** newsletter.
●Also available online. Vendor(s): Information Access Co., UMI.

332.1　　GW
BANK MAGAZIN. 1952. m. DM.149 (foreign DM.165) (students DM.98) (effective 1997). Betriebswirtschaftlicher Verlag Dr. Th. Gabler GmbH, Abraham-Lincoln-Str. 46, 65189 Wiesbaden, Germany. TEL 49-611-7878129. FAX 49-611-7878423. Ed.Bd. adv.; bk.rev.; abstr.; tr.lit. **Document type:** trade publication.
—CCC.
　　Formerly: Bankkaufmann (ISSN 0005-5085)

332 330.9　　IR　　ISSN 0256-5323
HC471
BANK MARKAZI JOMHOURI ISLAMI IRAN. BULLETIN. Key Title: Bulletin - Bank Markazi Islamic Republic of Iran 1962. q. free. Bank Markazi Jomhouri Islami Irani, Economic Research Department - Central Bank of the Islamic Republic of Iran, P.O. Box 11365-8531, Tehran, Iran. FAX 98-21-390323. TELEX 216219. charts; stat.; index. circ. 1,800. **Indexed:** Key to Econ.Sci., PROMT. **Document type:** bulletin.
—BLDSC (2435.160000).
　　Formerly (until 1983): Bank Markazi Iran Bulletin (ISSN 0005-5093)

BUSINESS AND ECONOMICS — BANKING AND FINANCE

332.1 658.8 US ISSN 0888-3149
HG1501 CODEN: BAMAFA
BANK MARKETING. 1915. m. $98 to non-members; members $80; foreign $125. Bank Marketing Association, 1120 Connecticut Ave., N.W., Washington, DC 20036-3902. TEL 202-663-5268. FAX 202-828-4540. E-mail: ksherida@aba.com. Ed. Kevin Sheridan; Pub. Laurence Price. R&P contact: George McGuinn. TEL 202-663-5032. adv. contact: Laurence Price. bk.rev.; circ. 4,015 (paid). (also avail. in microfilm from UMI) **Indexed:** ABI Inform., B.P.I., BPIA, Bus.Ind., INSPEC (1983-), Manage.Cont., Tr.& Indus.Ind., World Bank.Abstr. **Document type:** trade publication.
—BLDSC (1861.818000); AskIEEE; KR SourceOne; SWETS; UMI; UnCover.
Formerly (until 1972): Bank Marketing Management (ISSN 0572-595X)
Description: Explores all aspects of retail and corporate bank marketing. Feature articles include informative how-tos, banker-written case histories, and updates on "hot topics" in bank marketing.

332 IE ISSN 0791-2765
BANK MARKETING INTERNATIONAL. 1990. m. I£479. Lafferty Publications Ltd., The Tower, IDA Enterprise Centre, Pearse St., Dublin 2, Ireland. TEL 353-1-6718022. FAX 353-1-6718520. E-mail: cvserv@lafferty.ie; URL: http://www.unm.lafferty.co.uk. (US subscr. to: Lafferty Publications (USA), 420 Lexington Ave., Ste. 1745, New York, NY 10170. TEL 212-557-6726) Ed. Ann O'Dea. R&P contact: David Barr. **Document type:** trade publication.
Description: Market intelligence for the financial services industry.

332 US
BANK MERGERS & ACQUISITIONS. m. $795. S N L Securities, LP, 410 E. Main St., Box 2124, Charlottesville, VA 22902. TEL 804-977-1600. FAX 804-977-4466. Ed. Reid Nagle. (also avail. in diskette format; back issues avail.) **Document type:** newsletter.
●Also available online. Vendor(s): NewsNet (FI59).

332 US
BANK MUTUAL FUND REPORT. 1994. 48/yr. $795 for new subscr. (foreign $845); renewal $995 (foreign $1045). (American Bankers Association) American Banker Newsletters, One State Street Plaza, 26th Fl., New York, NY 10004-1505. TEL 212-803-8300; 800-407-8241. FAX 212-843-9620. Ed. John J. Jedlicka; Pub. David G. Schutt. adv.: page $1400; trime 8 1/2 x 11; adv. contact: Peter B. Jacobs. **Document type:** newsletter.
●Also available online. Vendor(s): Data-Star, Knight-Ridder Information, Inc., Lexis-Nexis, NewsNet.
Description: Covers bank mergers and acquisitions, technological innovations and market leader's strategies. Also provides weekly analysis of legal issues, legal rulings and litigation affecting all investement management practices of depository institutions.

332 MY
BANK NEGARA MALAYSIA. DIRECTOR GENERAL OF INSURANCE ANNUAL REPORT. (Text in English, Malay) a. Bank Negara Malaysia - Central Bank of Malaysia, P.O. Box 10922, Jalan Dato'Onn, 50480 Kuala Lumpur, Malaysia. TEL 03-2988044. FAX 03-2912990. TELEX MA 30201.

332 MY
BANK NEGARA MALAYSIA. DISCUSSION PAPERS. (Text in English) 1986. irreg., latest no.33. Bank Negara Malaysia - Central Bank of Malaysia, P.O. Box 10922, Jalan Dato'Onn, 50480 Kuala Lumpur, Malaysia. TEL 03-2988044. FAX 03-2912990. TELEX MA 30201.
Description: Contains papers prepared by Bank Negara staff on various topics.

332 MY
BANK NEGARA MALAYSIA. OCCASIONAL PAPERS. (Text in English) 1984. irreg., latest no.4. Bank Negara Malaysia - Central Bank of Malaysia, P.O. Box 10922, Jalan Dato'Onn, 50480 Kuala Lumpur, Malaysia. TEL 03-2988044. FAX 03-2912990. TELEX MA 30201.
Description: Contains studies on a variety of economic and financial subjects by Bank Negara staff.

BANK NEGARA MALAYSIA. STATISTICAL BULLETIN. see BUSINESS AND ECONOMICS — Abstracting, Bibliographies, Statistics

332.1 US ISSN 0005-5123
HG1501
BANK NEWS. 1901. m. $54 includes weekly newsletter supplement. Bank News, Inc., 912 Baltimore Ave., Ste. 900, Kansas City, MO 64105. TEL 816-421-7941. Ed. R.W. Poquette. adv.; bk.rev.; charts; illus.; stat.; tr.lit. circ. 8,000. (also avail. in microform from UMI) **Indexed:** P.A.I.S. **Document type:** trade publication.
●Also available online. Vendor(s): UMI.
—UMI; UnCover.
Incorporating (1919-1984): Mountain States Banker (ISSN 0027-2590)

330 332 BS
BANK OF BOTSWANA. BULLETIN. (Text in English) 1983. q. $2. Bank of Botswana, P.O. Box 712, Gaborone, Botswana. circ. 600. (back issues avail.) **Document type:** bulletin.

332.1 CN ISSN 0067-3587
HG2706
BANK OF CANADA. ANNUAL REPORT. 1935. a. free. Bank of Canada, Publications Distribution, Communications Services, 234 Wellington St., Ottawa, ON K1A 0G9, Canada. TEL 613-782-8248. FAX 613-782-8874. E-mail: publications@bank-banque-canada.ca; URL: http://www.bank-banque-canada.ca. **Document type:** corporate report.

332.1 CN ISSN 0045-1460
HC111
BANK OF CANADA. REVIEW/BANQUE DU CANADA. REVUE. (Text in English and French) 1971. q. Can.$40 (US Can.$50; foreign Can.$55) includes supplements (effective 1997). Bank of Canada, Publications Distribution, Communications Services, 234 Wellington St., Ottawa, On K1A 0G9, Canada. TEL 613-782-8248. FAX 613-782-8874. E-mail: publications@bank-banque-canada.ca; URL: http://www.bank-banque-canada.ca. index. circ. 4,600. (also avail. in microform from UMI) **Indexed:** Can.B.P.I., Can.B.P.I., Can.Per.Ind., Pt.de Rep. (1979-). **Document type:** corporate report.
●Also available online. Vendor(s): UMI.
—UMI.
Supersedes: Bank of Canada Statistical Summary (ISSN 0005-514X)

332.1 CN ISSN 0713-7931
HC111
BANK OF CANADA. TECHNICAL REPORTS. 1969. irreg. free. Bank of Canada, Publications Distribution, Communications Services, Ottawa, ON K1A 0G9, Canada. TEL 613-782-8248. FAX 613-782-8874. E-mail: publications@bank-banque-canada.ca; URL: http://www.bank-banque-canada.ca. **Document type:** corporate report.
—BLDSC (8711.940000).
Formerly (until 1973): Bank of Canada. Staff Research Studies (ISSN 0067-3595)

332 CN
BANK OF CANADA. WORKING PAPERS/BANQUE DU CANADA. DOCUMENT DE TRAVAIL. irreg. Bank of Canada, Publication Distribution, Communications Services, 234 Wellington St., Ottawa, ON K1A 0G9, Canada. TEL 613-782-8248. FAX 613-782-8874. E-mail: publications@bank-banque-canada.ca; URL: http://www.bank-banque-canada.ca.

330.9 CE
BANK OF CEYLON. ANNUAL REPORT AND ACCOUNTS. (Text in English) 1939. a. free to institutions. Bank of Ceylon, 4, Bank of Ceylon Mawatha, Colombo 1, Sri Lanka. TEL 348878. FAX 445798. illus. circ. 3,500.
Formerly (until 1965): Bank of Ceylon. Annual Report.

332.1 UK
BANK OF ENGLAND. BANK BRIEFING. q. Bank of England, Publications Group, Public Enquiries, Threadneedle St., London EC2R 8AH, England. TEL 44-171-601-4878. FAX 44-171-601-5460. circ. 16,000. **Document type:** bulletin.
Description: Provides a digest of the Bank of England Inflation Report.

332.1 UK ISSN 0308-5279
HG2994
BANK OF ENGLAND. REPORT AND ACCOUNTS. a. free. Bank of England, Press Office, London EC2R 8AH, England. TEL 44-171-601-3904. FAX 44-171-601-5460. (reprint service avail. from UMI) **Document type:** corporate report.
—BLDSC (7637.918000).
Formerly: Bank of England. Report (ISSN 0067-3625)
Description: Contains the annual report of the bank on the exercise of functions conferred on it by the Banking Act of 1979.

332 UK ISSN 0307-8175
BANK OF ENGLAND. STATISTICAL ABSTRACT. (Avail. in 2 parts) a. £40 worldwide (effective 1997). Bank of England, Publications Group, Inflation Report Division, Threadneedle St., London EC2R 8AH, England. TEL 44-171-601-4030. FAX 44-171-601-5196. **Document type:** trade publication.
—BLDSC (1861.785000).

332 UK
BANK OF ENGLAND. WORKING PAPER SERIES. 1991. irreg. free. Bank of England, Publications Group, Threadneedle St., London EC2R 8AH, England. TEL 44-171-601-4030. FAX 44-171-601-5196. (back issues avail.; reprint service avail. from UMI) **Document type:** monographic series.
Formed by the merger of (1978-1991): Bank of England. Discussion Papers (ISSN 0142-6753); (1982-1991): Bank of England. Technical Series.
Description: Working papers written by the bank on topics of general interest.

332 FI
BANK OF FINLAND. STATEMENT; the balance sheet and the statement of note issue. w. Bank of Finland, Accounting Department, P.O. Box 160, FIN-00101 Helsinki, Finland. TEL 358-0-1832566. FAX 358-0-174872. E-mail: publications@bofnet.mailnet.fi.

332 FI ISSN 1239-9345
HG3133
BANK OF FINLAND ANNUAL REPORT (ENGLISH EDITION). Finnish edition: Suomen Pankin Vuosikertomus (ISSN 1239-9329); Swedish edition: Finlands Banks Aarsbraettelse (ISSN 1239-9337) 1914. a. FIM 75. Suomen Pankki - Bank of Finland, Publication and Language Services, P.O. Box 160, FIN-00101 Helsinki, Finland. TEL 358-0-1832566. FAX 358-0-174872. E-mail: publications@bofnet.mailnet.fi. circ. 8,000.
Formerly (until 1996): Bank of Finland Year Book (ISSN 0081-9468); **Incorporates** (1866-1987): Bank of Finland. Annual Statement (ISSN 0081-945X)
Description: Covers economic developments, monetary policy, payment systems and maintenance of currency supply, international relations, balance sheet, charts, tables and more.

332 FI ISSN 0784-6509
HC337.F5
BANK OF FINLAND BULLETIN. (Text in English) 1921. m. free. Suomen Pankki - Bank of Finland, Publication and Language Services, P.O. Box 160, FIN-00101 Helsinki, Finland. TEL 358-9-1831. FAX 358-9-174872. TELEX 121224 SPBF FI. E-mail: publications@bof.fi. Ed. Sirkka Harnalainen. charts; mkt.; stat.; index, cum.index. circ. 5,600. (reprint service avail. from UMI) **Indexed:** Key to Econ.Sci., P.A.I.S., World Bank.Abstr. **Document type:** bulletin.
—BLDSC (2409.683500); UMI; UnCover.
Formerly (unil 1987): Bank of Finland Monthly Bulletin (ISSN 0005-5174)
Description: Covers topics relating to the banking industry, including monetary policy and financial market analysis.

332 FI ISSN 0785-3572
HG37.F5
BANK OF FINLAND DISCUSSIONS PAPERS. (Text in English, Finnish, Swedish) irreg. free. Suomen Pankki - Bank of Finland, P.O. Box 160, FIN-00101 Helsinki, Finland. TEL 358-9-1832566. FAX 358-9-174872. E-mail: publications@bof.fi. circ. 500. (reprint service avail.)
—BLDSC (1861.797000).

BUSINESS AND ECONOMICS — BANKING AND FINANCE

332   **GR**   ISSN 1107-5287
BANK OF GREECE. BULLETIN OF CONJUNCTURAL INDICATORS. 1997. m. free. Bank of Greece, Economic Research Division, 21 Panepistimiou St., 102 50 Athens, Greece. FAX 30-1-323-3025. TELEX 215102. E-mail: boglibr@ath.forthnet.gr. charts, stat. **Document type:** bulletin.

332   **GR**   ISSN 1105-9729
BANK OF GREECE. ECONOMIC BULLETIN. 1993. s-a. free. Bank of Greece. Economic Bulletin, Economic Research Division, 21 Panepistimiou St., 102 50 Athens, Greece. FAX 30-1-323-3025. TELEX 215102. E-mail: boglibr@ath.forthnet.gr. charts; stat. **Document type:** bulletin.

BANK OF GREECE. MONTHLY STATISTICAL BULLETIN. see *BUSINESS AND ECONOMICS — Abstracting, Bibliographies, Statistics*

332   **GR**
BANK OF GREECE. REPORT OF THE GOVERNOR. 1928. a. free. Bank of Greece, Economic Research Division, 21 Panepistimiou St., 102 50 Athens, Greece. FAX 30-1-323-3025. TELEX 215102. E-mail: boglibr@ath.forthnet.gr. charts; stat. **Document type:** corporate report.

BANK OF INDIA. BULLETIN. see *BUSINESS AND ECONOMICS — Economic Situation And Conditions*

332.1   **IS**   ISSN 0067-365X
HG3361.P22
BANK OF ISRAEL. ANNUAL REPORT. (Editions in English and Hebrew) a. IS.50. Bank of Israel, Kiryath Ben Gurion, P.O. Box 780, Jerusalem 91007, Israel. **Document type:** corporate report.

BANK OF ISRAEL. ANNUAL STATISTICS OF ISRAEL'S BANKING SYSTEM. see *BUSINESS AND ECONOMICS — Abstracting, Bibliographies, Statistics*

BANK OF ISRAEL. CURRENT BANKING STATISTICS. see *BUSINESS AND ECONOMICS — Abstracting, Bibliographies, Statistics*

BANK OF ISRAEL. ECONOMIC REVIEW. see *BUSINESS AND ECONOMICS — Economic Situation And Conditions*

BANK OF JAMAICA. ECONOMIC STATISTICS. see *BUSINESS AND ECONOMICS — Abstracting, Bibliographies, Statistics*

332   **JM**   ISSN 0067-3668
HG2826
BANK OF JAMAICA. REPORT AND STATEMENT OF ACCOUNTS. a. free. Bank of Jamaica, P.O. Box 621, King St., Kingston, Jamaica, W.I. TEL 809-922-0750. FAX 809-967-4265. TELEX 2165. circ. 1,200.

332   **JM**   ISSN 0572-5968
HG185.J3
BANK OF JAMAICA. STATISTICAL DIGEST. 1969. m. free. Bank of Jamaica, P.O. Box 621, King St., Kingston, Jamaica, W.I. TEL 809-922-0750. FAX 809-967-4265. TELEX 2165. stat. circ. 990.

332   **JA**
BANK OF JAPAN. ANNUAL REVIEW. (Text in English) a. free. Bank of Japan, c/o Public Relations Department, 2-1-1 Hongoku-cho, Nihombashi, Chuo-ku, Tokyo 103, Japan. TEL 81-3-3279-1111. FAX 81-3-5203-8703. pp./issue: 120.
Description: Contains reviews of monetary and economic developments of the previous fiscal year, an outline of the Bank's policy measures and financial statements, and more.

332   **JA**   ISSN 0919-1380
HC461
BANK OF JAPAN QUARTERLY BULLETIN. (Text in English) q. 550 Yen per no. Bank of Japan - Nippon Ginko, c/o Public Relations Department, 2-1-1 Hongoku-cho, Nihonbashi, Chuo-ku, Tokyo 103, Japan. TEL 81-3-3279-1111. FAX 81-3-5203-8703. (Dist. by: Tokiwa Sohgoh Service Co. Ltd., Kyodo Bldg., 2-4-3, Hongoku-cho, Nihonbashi, Chuo-ku, Tokyo 103, Japan. TEL 81-3-32709-5713; Overseas dist. by: Japan Publications Trading Co., Ltd., Book Export No.2 Department, P.O. Box 5030 Tokyo International, Tokyo 100-31, Japan) pp./issue: 130.
—BLDSC (7171.421000).
Description: Contains research papers on finance and the economy of Japan.

332.1   **MF**   ISSN 0067-3722
BANK OF MAURITIUS. ANNUAL REPORT. (Text in English) 1968. a. free. Bank of Mauritius, P.O. Box 29, Port Louis, Mauritius. TEL 230-208-4164. FAX 230-208-9204. TELEX 4253 MAUBNK IW. charts; stat. circ. 1,000. **Document type:** corporate report.

332   **MF**   ISSN 0005-5301
HC517.M5
BANK OF MAURITIUS. QUARTERLY REVIEW. 1968. q. free. Bank of Mauritius, P.O. Box 29, Port Louis, Mauritius. TEL 230-208-4164. FAX 230-208-9204. TELEX 4253 MAUBNK IW. charts; stat. circ. 600. **Indexed:** World Bank.Abstr. **Document type:** trade publication.

332.1   **PP**
BANK OF PAPUA NEW GUINEA. QUARTERLY ECONOMIC BULLETIN. q. free. Bank of Papua New Guinea, Economics Department, P.O. Box 121, Port Moresby, Papua New Guinea. TEL 227200. FAX 211617. TELEX NE 22128. Ed. E.W. Malori. **Indexed:** Key to Econ.Sci., P.A.I.S. **Document type:** bulletin.
Description: Reviews economic conditions for the past quarter and contains a comprehensive set of updated statistical tables. The bank staff also includes special articles related to current economic policy.

332.1   **PP**
BANK OF PAPUA NEW GUINEA. REPORT AND FINANCIAL STATEMENTS. (Text in English) 1974. a. free. Bank of Papua New Guinea, Economics Department, P.O. Box 121, Port Moresby, Papua New Guinea. TEL 22-7200. FAX 21-1617. TELEX NE 22128. illus.; stat. circ. 2,000.

332   **KO**
BANK OF SEOUL AND TRUST COMPANY. ECONOMIC REVIEW. no.5,6, 1977. irreg. Bank of Seoul and Trust Company, Seoul, S. Korea.

332.1   **SJ**   ISSN 0067-3749
HG3387.A7
BANK OF SUDAN. REPORT. a. free. Bank of Sudan, P.O. Box 313, Khartoum, Sudan.
Description: Provides annual coverage for all economic and financial developments, starting with the world economic situation, agricultural and industrial production and ending with the accounts of the bank.

BANK OF TAIWAN QUARTERLY. see *BUSINESS AND ECONOMICS — Economic Situation And Conditions*

BANK OF TANZANIA. ECONOMIC AND OPERATIONS REPORT (YEAR). see *BUSINESS AND ECONOMICS — Economic Situation And Conditions*

332   **JA**
BANK OF TOKYO. ANNUAL REPORT. 1978. a. Bank of Tokyo Ltd., 1-6-3 Hongokucho, Nihombashi, Chuo-ku, Tokyo 103, Japan. charts; cum.index every 2 yrs. circ. 12,000.
Formerly: Bank of Tokyo. Semiannual Report (ISSN 0005-5360)

332.1   **TO**
BANK OF TONGA. ANNUAL REPORT. a. Bank of Tonga, Head Office, P.O. Box 924, Nuku'alofa, Tonga.

332   **ZA**
BANK OF ZAMBIA. QUARTERLY FINANCIAL AND STATISTICAL REVIEW. 1971. 3/yr. free. Bank of Zambia, c/o Librarian, P.O. Box 30080, Lusaka 10101, Zambia. charts. circ. 1,500. **Indexed:** World Bank.Abstr.
Formerly: Bank of Zambia. Quarterly Statistical Review.

332.1   **ZA**
BANK OF ZAMBIA. REPORT AND STATEMENT OF ACCOUNTS. (Text in English) a. Bank of Zambia, c/o Librarian, P.O. Box 30080, Lusaka 10101, Zambia.

332   **IO**   ISSN 0408-4632
BANK PEMBANGUNAN INDONESIA. ANNUAL REPORT. (Text in English) 1960. a. free. Bank Pembangunan Indonesia - Development Bank of Indonesia, 2-4 Jalan Gondangdia Lama, P.O. Box 140, Jakarta, Indonesia. Ed.Bd. charts; illus.; stat.

332.1   **IO**   ISSN 0045-1495
BANK PEMBANGUNAN INDONESIA. NEWSLETTER. (Text in English and Indonesian) q. free. Bank Pembangunan Indonesia - Development Bank of Indonesia, 2-4 Jalan Gondangdia Lama, P.O. Box 140, Jakarta, Indonesia. Ed.Bd. charts; stat. **Document type:** newsletter.

332   **IO**
BANK PEMBANGUNAN INDONESIA. OPERATIONS OF BAPINDO. s-a. Bank Pembangunan Indonesia - Development Bank of Indonesia, 2-4 Jalan Gondangdia Lama, P.O. Box 140, Jakarta, Indonesia.

658.3 332.1   **US**   ISSN 0272-3271
BANK PERSONNEL NEWS. m. $150 to non-members; members $100. American Bankers Association, Human Resource Division, 1120 Connecticut Ave., N.W., Washington, DC 20036. TEL 202-663-5090. FAX 301-828-4540. (Subscr. to: Order Processing Department, 10 Jay Gould Ct, Waldorf, MD 20602-2725. TEL 800-338-0626) (also avail. in microform from UMI)
●Also available online. Vendor(s): UMI.
—UMI.
Description: Reports on developments in banking, private industry, and the Equal Employment Opportunity Commission, National Labor Relations Board, Congress, the federal courts, and other government agencies.

332   **US**
BANK RATE MONITOR; the weekly financial rate reporter. w. $895. Advertising News Service, Inc., 11811 Federal Highway One, Box 088888, N. Palm Beach, FL 33408-8888. TEL 407-627-7330. FAX 407-627-7335. URL: www.bankrate.com. Ed. Gail Liberman. **Document type:** trade publication.
Description: Covers deposit and loan rates set by banks and thrifts. Special surveys list rates, fees, and balance requirements on the hottest products of the week.

332   **US**
BANK SECURITIES MONTHLY. m. S N L Securities, 410 E. Main St., Charlottesville, VA 22901. TEL 804-977-1600. FAX 804-977-4466. Ed. Reid Nagle.

BANK SECURITY REPORT. see *CRIMINOLOGY AND LAW ENFORCEMENT — Security*

332 387.7   **CN**
BANK SETTLEMENT PLAN QUICK REFERENCE HANDBOOK. a. $58. International Air Transport Association, 2000 Peel St., Montreal, PQ H3A 2R4, Canada. TEL 514-844-6311. FAX 514-844-5286. E-mail: sales@iata.org; URL: http://www.iata.org.
Description: Provides information on each operating BSP as well as those that have been endorsed and are in the process of implementation.

332.1   **US**
BANK STRUCTURE FILE TAPE. q. $1200 in US, Canada, Mexico; elsewhere $2400. (Federal Reserve System) U.S. National Technical Information Service, 5825 Port Royal Rd., Springfield, VA 22161. TEL 703-487-4630. (magnetic tape)

BUSINESS AND ECONOMICS — BANKING AND FINANCE

332.1   US   ISSN 1045-9472
CODEN: BSEQD6
BANK SYSTEMS & TECHNOLOGY; for senior-level executives in perations and technology management. 1964. 13/yr. $65 (Canada $67; elsewhere $90). Miller Freeman Inc. (New York) (Subsidiary of: United News & Media), One Penn Plaza, New York, NY 10119. TEL 212-714-1300. FAX 212-302-6273. (Subscr. to: Box 1052, Skokie, IL 60076-8052. TEL 800-255-2824. FAX 708-647-5972) Ed. Holly Sraeel; Pub. Annie Feldman. adv.; bk.rev.; illus.; tr.lit.; index; circ. 23,400 (controlled). (also avail. in microform from UMI; back issues avail.) **Indexed:** ABI Inform., BPIA, Comput.Lit.Ind., Data Process.Dig., INSPEC (1989-), Resour.Ctr.Ind. **Document type:** trade publication.
●Also available online. Vendor(s): UMI.
—BLDSC (1861.833100); AskIEEE; KR SourceOne; UMI. **CCC.**
  Former titles (until 1989): Bank Systems and Equipment; Bank Equipment News (ISSN 0146-0900)
  Description: For senior-level banking executives interested in emerging technologies and products that reshaping the future of banking.

332   US   ISSN 1060-3506
BANK TECHNOLOGY NEWS. 1987. m. $59 (effective 1995). Faulkner & Gray, Inc. (New York), 11 Penn Plaza, 17th Fl., New York, NY 10001. TEL 212-967-7000. Ed. Chris Costanzo. circ. 25,000. (also avail. in microform from UMI) **Document type:** trade publication.
●Also available online. Vendor(s): Information Access Co., NewsNet (FI70), UMI.
—KR SourceOne; UMI. **CCC.**
  Formerly (until 1991): Bank New Product News (ISSN 0895-9293)

332.1   US   ISSN 0162-7473
BANK TELLER'S REPORT. 1969. m. $110.98 (overseas $161.45). Warren, Gorham & Lamont, 395 Hudson St., New York, NY 10119. TEL 212-367-6300. FAX 212-367-6718. (Subscr. to: The Park Square Bldg., 31 St. James Ave., Boston, MA 02116-4112. TEL 800-950-1207) (also avail. in microform from UMI) **Document type:** newsletter.
—UMI. **CCC.**
  Incorporates (in Sep. 1975): Teller's Marketing Bulletin.
  Description: Provides bank tellers with practical advice on all phases of banking: cross-selling, security, operations, money-handling techniques, and customer relations.

332 658.8   GW   ISSN 0933-3770
BANK UND MARKT UND TECHNIK; Zeitschrift fuer Management, Marketing und Organisation. (Supplement to: Zeitschrift fuer das Gesamte Kreditwesen) 1972. m. DM.294.48 (foreign DM.304.80) (effective 1996). Fritz Knapp Verlag GmbH, Postfach 111151, 60046 Frankfurt a.M., Germany. TEL 49-69-970833-0. FAX 49-69-7078400. Ed. Anja Haak. adv. contact: Werner Scholz. bk.rev.; illus.; index. circ. 3,683. **Document type:** trade publication.
—BLDSC (1861.837000); SWETS. **CCC.**
  Formerly: Bank und Markt (ISSN 0341-3667); Which incorporated: Ausgabe Technik.

332   TU
BANKA VE EKONOMIK YORUMLAR. 1964. m. Banka va Ekonomik, P.K. 769, Karakoy, Istanbul, Turkey. Ed. Oztin Akgue. adv. circ. 5,000.

BANKA VE TICARET HUKUKU DERGISI. see *LAW*

332 640.73   US
BANKCARD BAROMETER. 1989. m. $995. Card Management Information Services, Box 1700, Frederick, MD 21702. TEL 301-695-4660. FAX 301-695-0160. Ed. Robert B. McKinley; Pub. Robert B. McKinley. R&P contact: Joan Gassman. adv. contact: Joan Gassman. circ. 1,000. **Document type:** trade publication.
  Former titles: R A M Research Bank Card Barometer (ISSN 1040-6905); (until 1990): R A M Research Bank Credit Card Issuers Yearbook.
  Description: Provides broad proprietary data on approximately 500 U.S. card portfolios. Covers all aspects of the bank credit card industry: card base, cardmix, accounts receivables, interest rates, transaction volume, outstandings, attrition, yields, delinquency, charge-offs and market share.

332.1   US
BANKCARD CONSUMER NEWS. 1986. bi-m. $24. Bankcard Holders of America, 524 Branch Dr., Salem, VA 24153-4119. TEL 703-389-5445. FAX 703-481-6037. Ed. Ruth Susswein. bk.rev. circ. 100,000. **Document type:** consumer publication.

332 640.73   US
BANKCARD UPDATE. 1987. m. $995. Card Management Information Services, Box 1700, Frederick, MD 21702. TEL 301-695-4660. FAX 301-695-0160. Ed. Robert B. McKinley; Pub. Robert B. McKinley. R&P contact: Joan Gassman. adv. contact: Joan Gassman. circ. 1,000. **Document type:** newsletter, trade publication.
  Former titles: R A M Research Bankcard Update (ISSN 1040-8959) & R A M Bankcard Update (ISSN 0894-2390)
  Description: Covers pricing, management benchmarks, marketing trends and data on bank credit card industry.

332   US   ISSN 1087-7304
BANKCHECK. 1990. q. $25 to individuals & non-profit organizations; institutions $50 (effective 1997). International Rivers Network, 1847 Berkeley Way, Berkeley, CA 94703. TEL 510-848-1155. FAX 510-848-1008. E-mail: irn@irn.org; URL: http://www.irn.org. Ed. Juliette Majot. bk.rev. (back issues avail.) **Indexed:** Alt.Press Ind. (1991-). **Document type:** newsletter.
  Description: Monitors international financing of development projects.

332   GW   ISSN 0722-2424
BANKEN-JAHRBUCH. 1982. a. DM.658. Verlag Hoppenstedt GmbH, Havelstr. 9, 64295 Darmstadt, Germany. TEL 49-6151-380-0. FAX 49-6151-380-360. **Document type:** trade publication.

332.1   UK   ISSN 0005-5395
CODEN: BNKRB2
THE BANKER. (Includes supplement) 1926. m. £57($197) (Europe £94; elsewhere £143). Financial Times Business Information, Magazines (Subsidiary of: Financial Times Group), 2 Greystoke Pl., Fetter Ln., London EC4A 1ND, England. TEL 0171-405-6969. FAX 0171-405-5276. TELEX 296926 BUSINF G. (Subscr. to: 126 Jermyn St., London SW1Y 4UJ, England) Ed. Gavin Shreeve. adv.; bk.rev.; stat.; index. circ. 12,500. (also avail. in microfilm from UMI; back issues avail.; reprint service avail. from SCH) **Indexed:** ABI Inform, B.P.I., BPIA, Br.Hum.Ind., Bus.Ind., C.R.E.J., Cont.Pg.Manage., ELLIS, Ind.Bus.Rep., Key to Econ.Sci., Mgmt.& Market.Abstr., P.A.I.S., Rural Recreat.Tour.Abstr., SCIMP (1978-), Tr. & Indus.Ind., World Agri.Econ.& Rural Sociol.Abstr., World Bank.Abstr. **Document type:** trade publication.
●Also available online. Vendor(s): UMI.
—BLDSC (1861.850000); KR SourceOne; SWETS; UMI; UnCover.
  Description: Includes articles and editorials covering key aspects of banking, capital markets, country economical situations, trade finance, risk analysis, and interviews.

332   II   ISSN 0522-2931
BANKER. (Text in English) 1954. m. $50. Rajesh Suneja, Ed. & Pub., 24/90 Connaught Circus, New Delhi 110 001, India. TEL 345501. FAX 91-11-345501. TELEX 31-61184 GNS IN. adv.: B&W page Rs.4500, color page Rs.9900; trim 20 x 16; adv. contact: Rajesh Suneja. bk.rev. circ. 4,736. (reprint service avail. from SCH) **Indexed:** B.P.I., Tr. & Indus.Ind.
  Description: Information about the public, private and co-operative sectors of banking, as well as economy, business and finance.

332 332.6   FR
BANKERS/BUNUK. (Text in Arabic) 1965. m. $100. Mideast Press, 116, av. des Champs Elysees, 75008 Paris, France. TEL 47-50-62-83. FAX 47-50-24-63. TELEX 649447. Ed. Samir Hakim. circ. 22,000. (back issues avail.) **Document type:** trade publication.
  Description: Middle East business magazine.

332.1   UK
BANKERS' ALMANAC. 1866. s-a. (in 4 vols.). £285($456) Reed Information Services Ltd., Division of Reed Telepublishing Ltd. (Subsidiary of: Reed Elsevier group), Windsor Ct., E. Grinstead House, E. Grinstead, W. Sussex RH19 1XA, England. TEL 44-1342-326972. FAX 44-1342-335612. TELEX 95127 INFSER G. Ed. R. Phelps. adv. circ. 20,000. **Document type:** directory.
  Formerly: Bankers' Almanac and Year Book (ISSN 0067-379X)
  Description: Covers more than 27,000 financial institutions that have the legal status of banks in their country of registration.

321.1   UK
BANKERS' ALMANAC WORLD RANKING. a. £145 (foreign $229). Reed Information Services Ltd., Division of Reed Telepublishing Ltd. (Subsidiary of: Reed Elsevier group), Windsor Ct., E. Grinstead House, E. Grinstead, W. Sussex RH19 1XA, England. TEL 01342-335962. FAX 01342-335977. TELEX 95127 INFSER G. Ed. R. Phelps. **Document type:** directory.
  Description: Covers the world's leading 3,000 international banks, providing reference to the standing of a bank both internationally and within its own country.

332.1   US
BANKERS DIARY AND GUIDE. a. $40.95. Warren, Gorham & Lamont, One Penn Plaza, New York, NY 10119. TEL 212-971-5000. FAX 212-971-5113. (Subscr. to: The Park Square Bldg., 21 St. James Ave., Boston, MA 02116-4112. TEL 800-950-1207) **Document type:** trade publication.

332.1   US   ISSN 0005-5425
BANKERS DIGEST; a weekly news magazine devoted to Southwest bank news. 1942. w. $24 (effective 1995). Bonnie Jamison Blackman, Ed. & Pub., 7515 Greenville Ave., Ste. 901, Dallas, TX 75231-3890. TEL 214-373-4544. adv.; bk.rev.; tr.lit. circ. 3,200. **Document type:** trade publication.

332   CC   ISSN 1012-9952
BANKERS HANDBOOK FOR ASIA. 1976. a. $140. Dataline Asia - Pacific Ltd., 3rd Fl. Hollywood Centre, 233 Hollywood Rd., Hong Kong, People's Republic of China. TEL 8155221. FAX 8542794. Ed. Amitabha Chowdhury. adv.; charts; illus. circ. 10,000.

332.1 340   US   ISSN 0005-5433
BANKER'S LETTER OF THE LAW. 1967. m. $188.75 (overseas $258.95) (effective 1995). Warren, Gorham & Lamont, One Penn Plaza, New York, NY 10119. TEL 212-971-5000. FAX 212-971-5113. (Subscr. to: The Park Square Bldg., 31 St. James Ave., Boston, MA 02116-4112. TEL 800-950-1207) (looseleaf format; also avail. in microform from UMI) **Indexed:** Bank.Lit.Ind. **Document type:** newsletter.
—UMI. **CCC.**
  Description: Alerts bank attorneys to the latest rulings involving federal and state banking issues. Cites specific cases and translates "legalese" into everyday language.

332.1   US   ISSN 0005-545X
HG1501   CODEN: BNMGBD
BANKERS' MAGAZINE. 1886. bi-m. $134.98 (overseas $212.95) (effective 1995). Warren, Gorham & Lamont, One Penn Plaza, New York, NY 10119. TEL 212-971-5000. FAX 212-971-5113. (Subscr. to: The Park Square Bldg., 31 St. James Ave., Boston, MA 02116-4112. TEL 800-950-1207) Eds. Natalie Baumer, Margaret Murray. adv.; bk.rev.; illus. (also avail. in microform from UMI; reprint service avail. from SCH) **Indexed:** AAR, ABI Inform, Account.Ind. (1974-), B.P.I., BPIA, Comput.Lit.Ind., Cont.Pg.Manage., Manage.Cont., P.A.I.S., Tr.& Indus.Ind., World Bank.Abstr. **Document type:** trade publication.
—BLDSC (1861.870000); KR SourceOne; SWETS; UMI; UnCover. **CCC.**
  Description: Influential bankers contribute editorial insight, strategies and real-life perspectives that help the reader understand a wide range of current banking issues.

BUSINESS AND ECONOMICS — BANKING AND FINANCE

332   **US**
BANKERS RESEARCH. m. $326 (foreign $361) (effective 1997). Bankers Research, Inc., Box 431, Westport, CT 06881-0431. TEL 203-227-1237. Ed. Theodore W. Volckhausen; Pub. Theodore G. Volckhausen. R&P contact: Theodore W. Volckhausen. (also avail. in microform from UMI) **Document type:** newsletter.
● Also available online. Vendor(s): UMI.
Incorporates: Funds Transfer Report.

332.1   **II**   **ISSN 0067-3803**
BANKERS' WHO'S WHO. (Text in English) 1962. irreg. £15. Business Publications International, United India Life Building, Box 548, F-Block, Connaught Place, New Delhi 1, India. Ed. K.L. Sahgal. adv.; bk.rev. circ. 10,000. (back issues avail.)

332.1   **GW**   **ISSN 0341-6208**
BANKHISTORISCHES ARCHIV. 1975. s-a. DM.86.50 (foreign DM.87) (effective 1996). Fritz Knapp Verlag GmbH, Postfach 111151, 60046 Frankfurt a.M., Germany. TEL 49-69-970833-0. FAX 49-69-7078400. Ed. Gabriele Jachmich. adv. contact: Werner Scholz. bk.rev. (reprint service avail. from SCH) **Indexed:** Amer.Hist.& Life (1990-), Hist.Abstr. (1990-), IBR. **Document type:** trade publication.
—SWETS. **CCC.**
Description: Covers banking history.

332.1   **IT**
BANKING ABSTRACTS; idee e tecniche di management bancario selezionate dalla stampa italiana ed estera. (Text in Italian) 1984. m. L.160000 (effective 1995). Iniziative Culturali ed Editoriale Bancarie, Via Domenichino 5, 20149 Milan, Italy. TEL 39-2-48013830. FAX 39-2-48016164. Ed. Laura Pirovano. bk.rev. circ. 800. **Document type:** academic/scholarly publication.
Description: Contains abstracts on banking and finance selected from Italian and foreign periodicals.

332   **NR**   **ISSN 0795-932X**
BANKING & FINANCE DIGEST. 1989. q. £N560 (effective Jan. 1994). Research & Data Services Ltd., 54-55 Taiwo St. (off Abibu Oki St.), P.O. Box 2720, Marina, Lagos, Nigeria. TEL 234-2-664639. FAX 234-2-660926. Ed. Chike Uchime. (back issues avail.) **Document type:** trade publication.

332.1 340   **CN**   **ISSN 0832-8722**
K2
BANKING AND FINANCE LAW REVIEW/REVUE DE DROIT BANCAIRE ET DE FINANCE. (Text and summaries in English, French) 1986. 3/yr. (plus 1 bound vol.). Can.$180 per vol. Carswell, One Corporate Plaza, 2075 Kennedy Rd., Scarborough, ON M1T 3V4, Canada. TEL 416-609-8000. FAX 416-298-5094. Ed. Benjamin Geva. adv. contact: M. Lalani. bk.rev. **Indexed:** C.L.I., Ind.Can.L.P.L., L.R.I.
—BLDSC (1861.924300). **CCC.**
Description: Provides discussion and insight into issues and problems which confront both the legal and financial communities in Canada. Information is arranged in four sections: articles, commentaries on recent developments in banking in Canada and internationally, case notes and book reviews.

332   **SA**
BANKING & FINANCE WERKS. 1992. irreg. Werksmans, P.O. Box 927, Johannesburg 2000, South Africa. illus.

332   **UK**   **ISSN 0265-7988**
BANKING & FINANCIAL TRAINING. 1985. 10/yr. £245($385) (effective Jan. 1997). Armstrong International Ltd., The Courtyard, 12 Hill St., St. Helier, Jersey JE2 4UB, Channel Islands. TEL 44-1534-613650. FAX 44-1534-613650. E-mail: 106001.446@compuserve.com. Ed. Nicky Farrington; Pub. Richard Armstrong. adv. contact: Sarah Witts. bk.rev.; film rev. circ. 2,100. (back issues avail.) **Indexed:** Cont.Pg.Educ. **Document type:** trade publication.
—BLDSC (1861.925000).
Description: Provides information about training products and techniques in banking and finance.

332.1   **US**
BANKING GUIDES - ASIA, AUSTRALIA, NEW ZEALAND WITH PRINCIPAL HOTELS AND BANK HOLIDAYS.* Cover title: Asian Banking Guide. a. Manufacturers Hanover Trust Co., International Division, 270 Park Ave., New York, NY 10022.

332   **UK**
BANKING IN THE E C. (European Community); structures and sources of finance. irreg., latest Apr. 1991. £175($315) (overseas £185). Financial Times Business Information, Management Reports (Subsidiary of: Financial Times Group), 102 Clerkenwell Rd., London EC1M 5SA, England. TEL 44-171-251-9321. FAX 44-171-251-4686. (Orders to: F T B I, 126 Jermyn St., London SW1Y 4UJ, England. TEL 44-1209-612193. FAX 44-1209-612811) **Document type:** trade publication.
Formerly: Banking Structures and Sources of Finance in the European Community.
Description: Explains the operation, supervision, and regulation of the national financial systems of each E.C. member state.

332.1   **UK**
BANKING IN THE E U AND SWITZERLAND (YEAR). 1987? a. £250($416) (foreign £260). Financial Times Business Information, Management Reports (Subsidiary of: Financial Times Group), 102 Clerkenwell Rd., London EC1M 5SA, England. TEL 44-171-814-9770. FAX 44-171-814-9778. (Orders to: F T B I, 126 Jermyn St., London SW1Y 4UJ, England. TEL 44-1209-612493. FAX 44-1209-612811) charts. **Document type:** trade publication.
Description: Covers important banking developments in the nations of the European Union.

332   **UK**
BANKING IN THE FAR EAST. 1986. irreg., latest 1993. £186($333) (foreign £196). Financial Times Business Information, Management Reports (Subsidiary of: Financial Times Group), 102 Clerkenwell Rd., London EC1M 5SA, England. TEL 44-171-251-9321. FAX 44-171-251-4686. (Subscr. to: F T B I, 126 Jermyn St., London SW1Y 4UJ, England. TEL 44-1209-612493. FAX 44-1209-612811) **Document type:** trade publication.
Formerly (until 1986): Banking Structures and Sources of Finance in the Far East.
Description: Covers the operation, supervision, and regulation of the financial systems of 12 major Pacific Rim nations.

332.1   **US**
BANKING INSURANCE AND PROTECTION NEWSLETTER. m. $36 to non-members; members $24. American Bankers Association, Security and Risk Management, 1120 Connecticut Ave., N.W., Washington, DC 20036. TEL 202-663-5497.
—UMI.
Former titles: Banking Insurance and Protection Bulletin (ISSN 0091-0392)
Description: Reports on the latest trends in risk management, insurance, and security, for officers responsible for these activities.

332.1   **US**
BANKING ISSUES AND INNOVATIONS IN PRODUCTS, MARKETING AND TECHNOLOGY.* m. $120. (Bank Administration Institute) Probus & Bankers Publishing, 1333 Burr Ridge Pkwy., Burr Ridge, IL 60521-6489. TEL 312-868-1100. Ed. Phyllis L. van Holland. **Indexed:** Bank.Lit.Ind.
Former titles: Issues and Innovations; Ideas and Innovations in Banking; Banking Issues and Innovations.

332   **US**
BANKING: LATIN AMERICAN INDUSTRIAL REPORT. (Avail. for each of 22 Latin American countries) 1985. a. $435 per country report. Aquino Productions, Box 125, Rochester, VT 05767. Ed. Andres C. Aquino.

BANKING LAW. see *LAW*

BANKING LAW ANTHOLOGY. see *LAW*

BANKING LAW IN THE UNITED STATES. see *LAW*

332.1 340   **US**   **ISSN 0005-5506**
K2
BANKING LAW JOURNAL. 1889. bi-m. $135.98 (overseas $212.95) (effective 1995). Warren, Gorham & Lamont, One Penn Plaza, New York, NY 10119. TEL 212-971-5000. FAX 212-971-5113. (Subscr. to: The Park Square Bldg., 31 St. James Ave., Boston, MA 02116-4112. TEL 800-950-1207) Ed. Gerald T. Dunne. bk.rev. (also avail. in microform from UMI,MIM; microfiche from WSH; reprint service avail. from RRI,WSH) **Indexed:** ABI Inform, ASCA, Bank.Lit.Ind., BPIA, Bus.Ind., C.L.I., Curr.Cont., L.R.I., Leg.Cont., Leg.Per., P.A.I.S., SSCI, World Bank.Abstr. **Document type:** trade publication.
—BLDSC (1861.930000); Genuine Article; KR SourceOne; SWETS; UMI; UnCover. **CCC.**
Description: Covers every area of major interest to bankers and bank attorneys, with practical material for bank counsel use.
Refereed Serial

332.1 340   **US**   **ISSN 0271-6909**
KF971.3
BANKING LAW JOURNAL DIGEST (SUPPLEMENT). base vol. (plus a. updates). $185 (for base vol.) (foreign $173.45) (effective 1997). Warren, Gorham & Lamont, 395 Hudson St., New York, NY 10014. TEL 212-367-6300. FAX 212-367-6718. (Subscr. to: The Park Square Bldg., 31 St. James Ave., Boston, MA 02116-4112. TEL 800-950-1207) **Document type:** trade publication.

BANKING LAW MANUAL: LEGAL GUIDE TO COMMERCIAL BANKS, THRIFT INSTITUTIONS AND CREDIT UNIONS. see *LAW*

346 341.7   **UK**   **ISSN 0961-7256**
K2
BANKING LAW REPORTS. 1991. 10/yr. (plus a. cumulation). £240($370) includes cumulation (effective 1997). L L P Ltd., 69-77 Paul St., London EC2A 4LQ, England. TEL 44-171-553-1000. FAX 44-171-553-1115. **Document type:** academic/scholarly publication.

332 340   **US**   **ISSN 0898-7998**
KF967
BANKING LAW REVIEW; practical legal guidance for bankers and their attorneys. 1988. q. $125. Faulkner & Gray, Inc. (New York), 11 Penn Plaza, 17th Fl., New York, NY 10001. TEL 212-967-7000. FAX 212-967-7155. Ed. Patricia L. Hogan. **Indexed:** Leg.Per.
—KR SourceOne; UMI.
Description: Provides in-depth coverage of landmark cases, critical legal issues in banking, new laws and regulations, and protective strategies.

332.1   **US**   **ISSN 1059-1257**
KF967
BANKING POLICY REPORT. 1982. s-m. $345. Law and Business, Inc. (Subsidiary of: Prentice Hall), 1185 Avenue of the Americas, New York, NY 10036-2601. TEL 201-894-8484. FAX 201-894-8666. Eds. Steven & Lynn Glasser. index. circ. 2,000. (looseleaf format) **Indexed:** Bank.Lit.Ind.
● Also available online. Vendor(s): Lexis-Nexis.
Formerly (until 1991): Banking Expansion Reporter (ISSN 0730-689X)

332.1   **PK**   **ISSN 0067-3811**
BANKING STATISTICS OF PAKISTAN. (Text in English) 1948. a. Rs.51($11) State Bank of Pakistan, Central Directorate, Public Relations Department, I.I. Chundrigar Rd., P.O. Box 4456, Karachi, Pakistan. TEL 92-2414141. FAX 92-2417865. TELEX 2754 SBPK PK. circ. 470. **Document type:** government publication.
Description: Includes scheduled advances of the bank.

BUSINESS AND ECONOMICS — BANKING AND FINANCE

332.1 US ISSN 1091-6385
HG1501 CODEN: BASTFT
BANKING STRATEGIES. 1925. m. $59 (foreign $89) (effective 1997). Bank Administration Institute, One N. Franklin St., Chicago, IL 60606. TEL 312-683-2248. FAX 312-683-2373. Ed. Ronald G. Burke. adv.; illus.; tr.lit.; index. circ. 40,481. (also avail. in microform from UMI; reprint service avail. from UMI) **Indexed:** AAR, ABI Inform., Account.Ind. (1974-), B.P.I., Bank.Lit.Ind., BPIA, Bus.Ind., Comput.Lit.Ind., INSPEC (1990-), Manage.Cont., P.A.I.S., So.Pac.Per.Ind., World Bank.Abstr.
●Also available online. Vendor(s): Information Access Co., Lexis-Nexis, UMI.
—AskIEEE; KR SourceOne; SWETS; UMI; UnCover.
    Former titles (until 1996): Bank Management (ISSN 1049-1775); (until 1990): Bank Administration (ISSN 0024-9823); Auditgram.
    Description: Deals exclusively with the strategic planning and thinking of upper management in financial institutions worldwide.

332.1 UK ISSN 0737-6413
HG1503
BANKING WORLD.* 1844. m. £42 (overseas £52) (effective 1995); newsstand price: £3.50. (Chartered Institute of Bankers) Headway House & Law, Premier Mags c/o Katharine Buckley, Haymarket House, 1 Oxendon St., London SW1Y 4EE, England. TEL 44-171-388-3171. (Membership to: Emmanuel House, Canterbury, Kent, England. TEL 44-1227-762600. FAX 44-1227-763788) Ed. Garth Hewitt; Pub. Andrew Sculthorpe. adv.; bk.rev.; mkt.; stat.; index. circ. 128,146. **Indexed:** ABI Inform, Bank.Lit.Ind., Bus.Ind., Comput.Lit.Ind., Cont.Pg.Manage., INSPEC (1983-), Mid.East: Abstr.& Ind., P.A.I.S., PSI, Rural Recreat.Tour.Abstr., World Agri.Econ.& Rural Sociol.Abstr., World Bank.Abstr. **Document type:** trade publication.
●Also available online. Vendor(s): UMI.
—AskIEEE; KR SourceOne; UMI. **CCC.**
    Formerly: Bankers' Magazine (London) (ISSN 0005-5441)
    Description: Discusses issues that affect bankers; profiles noteworthy persons and innovations.

332.1 MG
BANKIN'NY INDOSTRIA. RAPPORT ANNUEL. 1964. a. free. Bankin'Ny Indostria - Bank Nationale pour le Developpement Industriel, B.P. 174, 101 Antananarivo, Madagascar. TEL 239-51. FAX 33749. TELEX 22205 BNI MG Ed.Bd. circ. 1,500.
    Formerly (until 1977): Banque Nationale Malagasy de Developpement. Rapport d'Activite (ISSN 0067-401X)

332.1 368 PK ISSN 0005-5522
BANKINSURANCE NEWS. (Text in English) 1971. w. Rs.150($35) Tareen & Tareen Ltd., 4 Amil St. off Robson Rd., Karachi 1, Pakistan. Ed. Naushad Shamimul Haq. adv.; bk.rev. circ. 9,000.

332.1 NO ISSN 0333-0079
BANKOEKONOMEN.* 1971. bi-m. Bankoekonomisk Forening og Bankakademiet, Postboks 729, 0105 Oslo 1, Norway. adv. circ. 3,000.

BANKRUPTCY COURT DECISIONS. see LAW — Corporate Law

332 US ISSN 0744-7671
KF1507
BANKRUPTCY LAW LETTER. 1981. m. $156.25 (overseas $218.65) (effective 1997). Warren, Gorham & Lamont, 395 Hudson St., New York, NY 10114. TEL 212-367-6300. FAX 212-367-6718. (Subscr. to: The Park Square Bldg., 31 St. James Ave., Boston, MA 02116-4112. TEL 800-950-1207) Ed. Charles J. Tabb. (also avail. in microform from UMI; back issues avail.) **Document type:** trade publication.
—UMI. **CCC.**
    Description: Covers recent developments in bankruptcy law; includes involuntary position, adequate positions, automatic stay, use, sale, and lease of property.

332 US ISSN 0747-8917
KF1507
BANKRUPTCY STRATEGIST. 1983. m. $245. New York Law Publishing Co., 345 Park Ave. S., New York, NY 10010. TEL 212-545-6170. FAX 212-696-1848. URL: http://www.ljx.com. Ed. Herbert S. Schlagman. bk.rev. **Document type:** newsletter.
    Description: Devoted to practical tips and viable solutions for practitioners of bankruptcy law. Reports on legislative developments, fee awards, procedural techniques and judicial rulings.

332 US ISSN 1054-9463
KF1507.5
BANKRUPTCY YEARBOOK AND ALMANAC. 1991. a. New Generation Research, Inc., 225 Friend St., Ste. 801, Boston, MA 02114. TEL 617-573-9550. Ed. Christopher McHugh; Pub. George Putnam, III. R&P contact: Christopher McHugh. TEL 617-573-9552. **Document type:** trade publication.

332 SI ISSN 0217-7730
BANKS AND FINANCIAL INSTITUTIONS IN INDONESIA. (Text in English) 1985. a. S.$89.50($56) R.A. Communications and Trading Pte. Ltd., 10 New Industrial Rd., No. 02-02, Singapore 1953, Singapore. Ed. Andrew Chan. circ. 2,000. (back issues avail.)

332 368 US ISSN 8756-6079
KF1167.A15
BANKS IN INSURANCE REPORT. 1985. m. $499 (foreign $571) (effective 1998). John Wiley & Sons, Inc., Journals, 605 Third Ave., New York, NY 10158. TEL 212-850-6645. FAX 212-850-6021. E-mail: subinfo@jwiley.com; URL: http://www.wiley.co.uk. Ed. Edward J. Stone. adv.— B&W page £640, color page £1515; trim 279 x 210. **Document type:** newsletter.
—CCC.
    Description: Provides specific information on bank expansion into insurance. Covers techniques banks are using to increase their share of the financial products and services market. Includes legal, legislative and regulatory developments, business strategies and selling tactics.

332.1 GR
BANKS, INVESTMENT & STOCKMARKET. (Supplement to: Epilogi) 1990. a. Dr.1500. Electra Press, 4 Stadiou, 105 64 Athens, Greece. TEL 30-1-3233-203. FAX 30-1-3235-160. TELEX 210564. Ed. Christos Papaioannou. adv. circ. 11,000. **Document type:** trade publication.
    Formerly: Banking Sector.

332.1 SZ ISSN 0067-382X
BANKWIRTSCHAFTLICHE FORSCHUNGEN. 1969. irreg., no.242, 1996. price varies. (Universitaet Zuerich, Institut fuer Schweizerisches Bankwesen) Paul Haupt AG, Falkenplatz 14, CH-3001 Bern, Switzerland. TEL 41-31-3012345. FAX 41-31-3014669. (Co-sponsor: Hochschule St. Gallen fuer Wirtschafts- und Sozialwissenschaften, Institut fuer Bankwirtschaft) **Document type:** monographic series.
—CCC.

332 FR ISSN 0005-5581
HG1505
BANQUE; revue du banquier, de son personnel et de sa clientele. 1926. m. 470 F. 18 rue la Fayette, 75009 Paris, France. TEL 42-47-17-80. TELEX 660 282 F. Ed. F. de Juvigny. adv.; bk.rev.; stat.; index. circ. 20,000. **Indexed:** ELLIS, P.A.I.S.For.Lang.Ind., SCIMP (1986-).
—BLDSC (1861.950000); SWETS. **CCC.**

332.1 BE
BANQUE BRUXELLES LAMBERT. RAPPORTS DE L'EXERCICE/BANQUE BRUSSELS LAMBERT. ANNUAL REPORTS/BANQUE BRUSSEL LAMBERT. JAARVERSLAG. (Editions in Dutch, English, French) 1935. a. free. Banque Bruxelles Lambert s.a., Ave. Marnix 24, B-1050 Brussels, Belgium. TEL 32-2-5472111. FAX 32-2-5473844. Ed. Daniel Cardon. circ. 27,000. **Document type:** corporate report.
    Formerly: Banque de Bruxelles. Rapport Annuel (ISSN 0067-3919)

332.1 TI ISSN 0067-3854
BANQUE CENTRALE DE TUNISIE. BULLETIN. 1959-1971 (no.43); resumed 1986. irreg. Banque Centrale de Tunisie, Rue de la Monnaie, 1001 Tunis, Tunisia. TEL 254000. **Document type:** bulletin.

332.1 TI ISSN 0067-3862
BANQUE CENTRALE DE TUNISIE. RAPPORT D'ACTIVITE. (Title varies: Rapport Annuel) 1959. a. Banque Centrale de Tunisie, Rue de la Monnaie, 1001 Tunis, Tunisia. TEL 254000. TELEX 13309.

332 TI
BANQUE CENTRALE DE TUNISIE. STATISTIQUES FINANCIERES. (Text in French) 1972. q. Banque Centrale de Tunisie, Rue de la Monnaie, 1001 Tunis, Tunisia. charts; stat. **Indexed:** P.A.I.S.For.Lang.Ind.

332 SG ISSN 0005-559X
BANQUE CENTRALE DES ETATS DE L'AFRIQUE DE L'OUEST. NOTES D'INFORMATION ET STATISTIQUES. 1956. m. 10000 Fr.CFA($40) (effective 1997). Banque Centrale des Etats de l'Afrique de l'Ouest-Siege, Ave. Abdoulaye Fadiga, B.P. 3108, Dakar, Senegal. TEL 23-10-42. TELEX BCEAO 21833 SG. bk.rev.; bibl.; charts; illus.; stat.; index. circ. 600. (looseleaf format) **Indexed:** Documentatieblad, Key to Econ.Sci., P.A.I.S.For.Lang.Ind.

332 SG ISSN 0067-3889
BANQUE CENTRALE DES ETATS DE L'AFRIQUE DE L'OUEST. RAPPORT ANNUEL. 1955. a. 10000 Fr.CFA($40) (effective 1997). Banque Centrale des Etats de l'Afrique de l'Ouest-Siege, Ave. Abdoulaye Fadiga, B.P. 3108, Dakar, Senegal. TEL 23-10-42. TELEX BCEAO 21833 SG. circ. 2,000. **Indexed:** P.A.I.S.For.Lang.Ind.

332.1 SG ISSN 0067-3897
HG3421.A7
BANQUE CENTRALE DES ETATS DE L'AFRIQUE DE L'OUEST. RAPPORT D'ACTIVITE.. 1955. a. Banque Centrale des Etats de l'Afrique de l'Ouest-Siege, Ave. Abdoulaye Fadiga, B.P. 3108, Dakar, Senegal. TEL 23-10-42. TELEX BCEAO 21833 SG.

332.1 CG
BANQUE COMMERCIALE ZAIROISE. RAPPORTS ET BILANS ANNUELS/BANQUE COMMERCIALE ZAIROISE. REPORTS AND BALANCE SHEETS. a. Banque Commerciale Zairoise, B.P. 2798, Kinshasa, Democratic Republic of the Congo. Dir. Kitoko Pene-Kiyayo.

332.3 BD
BANQUE DE CREDIT DE BUJUMBURA. RAPPORTS ET BILAN. (Text in French) 1965. a. free. Banque de Credit de Bujumbura, B.P. 300, Bujumbura, Burundi. circ. 700.

332.1 FR ISSN 1167-5128
BANQUE DE FRANCE. ANALYSES COMPARATIVES. (In 2 vols.: Vol.1: Activite des Etablissements de Credit; Vol.2: Resultats des Etablissements de Credit) 1988. a. 220 F. Banque de France, Service de l'Information, 48 rue Croix des Petits Champs, B.P. 140-01, 75001 Paris, France. TEL 1-42-92-39-31. FAX 1-42-92-39-40.
    Former titles (until 1991): France. Commission Bancaire. Etudes et Analyses Comparatives; (until 1989): France. Commission Bancaire. Resultats des Etablissements de Credit et des Maisons de Titres (ISSN 0992-5635)

332.1 330.9 FR ISSN 1250-5765
HG3021
BANQUE DE FRANCE. BULLETIN. (Supplements avail.: Statistiques (ISSN 1250-5846), Etudes (ISSN 1250-5854)) 1971. m. (plus supplements 8/yr.). 500 F. (outside Europe 1400 F.). Banque de France, Service de l'Information, 48, rue Croix des Petits Champs, 75001 Paris, France. TEL 1-42-92-39-31. FAX 1-42-92-39-40. stat. circ. 7,200. (back issues avail.) **Indexed:** ELLIS, Key to Econ.Sci., P.A.I.S.For.Lang.Ind., P.A.I.S. **Document type:** bulletin.
    Formed by the merger of (1967-1994): Banque de France. Situation Economique a l'Etranger (ISSN 0242-5904); (1990-1994): Banque de France. Bulletin Mensuel (ISSN 1145-5535); (1971-1994): Banque de France. Bulletin Trimestriel (ISSN 0150-7583) & Banque de France. Statistiques Monetaires et Financieres (ISSN 1161-2967); Which was (1984-1991): Banque de France. Statistiques Monetaires Definitives (ISSN 0999-1085)
    Description: Analyzes monetary developments and their economic environment in France and abroad.

BUSINESS AND ECONOMICS — BANKING AND FINANCE

332.1 FR ISSN 1250-5862
BANQUE DE FRANCE. BULLETIN DIGEST. (English abridged supplement to: Banque de France. Bulletin (ISSN 1250-5765)) (Text in English) 1994. 8/yr. 500 F. (foreign 1400 F.) includes m. French Bulletin. Banque de France, Service de l'Information, 48 rue Croix-Des-Petits-Champs, 75001 Paris, France. TEL 33-1-42923931. FAX 33-1-42923940.
 Description: Reference work on economic, monetary, and financial issues.

332.1 FR
BANQUE DE FRANCE. CENTRALE DE BILANS. ETUDES. a. 500 F. Banque de France, Service de l'Information, 48 rue Croix-Des-Petits-Champs, 75001 Paris, France. TEL 1-42-92-39-31. FAX 1-42-92-39-40.

332.1 FR
BANQUE DE FRANCE. CENTRALE DE BILANS. FASCICULES DE RESULTATS. a. 1900 F. Banque de France, Service de l'Information, 48 rue Croix des Petits Champs, B.P. 140-01, 75001 Paris, France. TEL 1-42-92-39-08. FAX 1-42-92-39-40. (also avail. in diskette format)
 Description: Allows businesses to compare their professional results with data from the sample taken by the Centrale de Bilans.

332.1 FR
BANQUE DE FRANCE. CENTRALE DE BILANS. FASCICULES DE RESULTATS SECTORIELS. a. price varies. Banque de France, Service de l'Information, 48 rue Croix-Des-Petits-Champs, 75001 Paris, France. TEL 1-42-92-39-31. FAX 1-42-92-39-40.

332.1 FR
BANQUE DE FRANCE. CENTRALE DE BILANS. SELECTION D'INDICATEURS; fiches sectorielles. a. 1500 F. Banque de France, Service de l'Information, 48 rue Croix des Petits Champs, B.P. 140-01, 75001 Paris, France. TEL 1-42-92-39-08. FAX 1-42-92-39-40.

332.1 FR ISSN 1161-0522
BANQUE DE FRANCE. COLLECTION ENTERPRISES. 1988. irreg. 100 F. Banque de France, Service de l'Information, 48 rue Croix-Des-Petits-Champs, 75001 Paris, France. TEL 1-42-92-39-31. FAX 1-42-92-39-40.

332.1 FR
BANQUE DE FRANCE. COLLECTION ETUDES. SYSTEMES DE PAIEMENT DANS LES ETATS MEMBRES DE LA C E E. base vol. (plus a. updates). 180 F. for base vol.; updates free. Banque de France, Service de l'Information, 48 rue Croix-Des-Petits-Champs, 75001 Paris, France. TEL 1-42-92-39-31. FAX 1-42-92-39-40. **Document type:** government publication.

332.1 FR
BANQUE DE FRANCE. COLLECTION ETUDES. SYSTEMES DE PAIEMENT DANS ONZE PAYS DEVELOPPES. base vol. (plus a. updates). 100 F. for base vol.; updates free. Banque de France, Service de l'Information, 48 rue Croix-Des-Petits-Champs, 75001 Paris, France. TEL 1-42-92-39-31. FAX 1-42-92-39-40.

332 FR ISSN 1169-8489
BANQUE DE FRANCE. COMITE CONSULTATIF. RAPPORT. 1987? a. 80 F. (effective 1995). Banque de France, Service de l'Information, 48 rue Croix des Petits Champs, 75001 Paris, France. TEL 42-92-39-09. FAX 42-92-39-40. (Co-sponsor: Conseil National du Credit)
 Description: Studies the problems in the relationship between credit institutions and their clientele.

332 FR ISSN 1169-8462
BANQUE DE FRANCE. COMITE DE LA REGLEMENTATION BANCAIRE. RAPPORT. 1989. a. 120 F. (effective 1995). Banque de France, Service de l'Information, 48 rue Croix des Petits Champs, 75001 Paris, France. TEL 42-92-39-08. FAX 42-92-39-40.

332 FR ISSN 1153-2785
BANQUE DE FRANCE. COMITE DES ETABLISSEMENTS DE CREDIT. RAPPORT. a. 120 F. (effective 1995). Banque de France, Service de l'Information, 48 rue Croix des Petits Champs, 75001 Paris, France. TEL 42-92-39-08. FAX 42-92-39-40.

332.1 FR
BANQUE DE FRANCE. CONSEIL NATIONAL DU CREDIT. RAPPORTS DES GROUPES DE TRAVAIL. 1986. irreg. 100 F. Banque de France, Service de l'Information, 48 rue Croix des Petits Champs, B.P. 140-01, 75001 Paris, France. TEL 1-42-92-39-08. FAX 1-42-92-39-40. (back issues avail.)
 Description: Covers developments affecting the financial system.

332.1 FR ISSN 0242-5866
BANQUE DE FRANCE. LA MONNAIE EN (YEAR). Variant title: La Monnaie et les Systemes de Paiement en (Year). English edition: Money in (Year). 1970. a. 80 F. (English ed. 50 F.). Banque de France, Service de l'Information, 48 rue Croix-Des-Petits-Champs, 75001 Paris, France. TEL 33-1-42923908. FAX 33-1-42923940. charts; stat.
 Description: Summarizes main data relating to monetary policy as well as developments in money, credit and financial investment.

332.1 FR
BANQUE DE FRANCE. LETTRE MENSUELLE REGIONALE. (In 22 series: Auvergne (ISSN 0767-7995), Lorraine (ISSN 0180-8591), Champagne-Ardenne (ISSN 1158-1484), Alsace (ISSN 0758-7155), Aquitaine (ISSN 0247-4093), Basse-Normandie (ISSN 0182-6042), Bourgogne (ISSN 0242-2700), Bretagne (ISSN 0182-5992), Centre (ISSN 0222-9099), Franche-Comte (ISSN 0183-6625), Haute-Normandie (ISSN 0181-7590), Ile-de-France (ISSN 0294-0191), Languedoc-Roussillon (ISSN 0223-7245), Limousin (ISSN 0183-7184), Midi-Pyrenees (ISSN 0249-8626), Nord-Pas-de-Calais (ISSN 0249-6232), Pays de la Lorraine (ISSN 0183-7141), Picardie (ISSN 0182-6069), Poitou-Charentes (ISSN 0183-7486), Provence-Alpes (ISSN 0294-1961), Corse (ISSN 0997-7260), Rhone-Alpes (ISSN 0221-4083)) m. (10/yr.). 200 F. Banque de France, Service de l'Information, 48 rue Croix des Petits Champs, B.P. 140-01, 75001 Paris, France. TEL 1-42-92-39-31. FAX 1-42-92-39-40.

332.1 FR
BANQUE DE FRANCE. NOTE FINANCIERE ANNUELLE. a. 45 F. Banque de France, Service de l'Information, 48 rue Croix des Petits Champs, B.P. 140-01, 75001 Paris, France. TEL 1-42-92-39-08. FAX 1-42-92-39-40.

332.1 FR
BANQUE DE FRANCE. NOTES D'INFORMATION. 1971. irreg. free. Banque de France, Service de l'Information, 48, rue Croix des Petits Champs, 75001 Paris, France. TEL 1-42-92-39-08. FAX 1-42-92-39-40.

332.1 FR ISSN 1161-0263
BANQUE DE FRANCE. PRINCIPALES BRANCHES D'ACTIVITE EN (YEAR). 1984. a. 120 F. Banque de France, Service de l'Information, 48 rue Croix des Petits Champs, B.P. 140-01, 75001 Paris, France. TEL 1-42-92-39-31. FAX 1-42-92-39-40.
 Formerly (until 1991): Banque de France. Revue Annuelle de l'Evolution des Principales Branches d'Activite en (Year) (ISSN 0762-1779)
 Description: Provides statistics for professional organizations as well as commentaries on their activities, employment and structures.

332.1 FR ISSN 1250-5242
BANQUE DE FRANCE. RAPPORT. a. free. Banque de France, Service de l'Information, 48, rue Croix des Petits Champs, 75001 Paris, France. TEL 1-42-92-39-08. FAX 1-42-92-39-40.
 Former titles (until 1994): Banque de France. Compte Rendu (ISSN 0242-5890); (until 1973): Banque de France. Compte Rendu des Operations (ISSN 0067-3927)
 Description: Describes the banks activities, its balance sheet and income statements and presents the Governor's comments on the economic and monetary situation.

332 FR ISSN 1250-5242
HG3034
BANQUE DE FRANCE. RAPPORT ANNUEL. English edition: Banque de France. Annual Report (ISSN 1240-6813) (Text in English) 1992. a. free. Banque de France, Service de l'Information, 48 rue Croix des Petits Champs, 75001 Paris, France. TEL 33-1-42923908. FAX 33-1-42923940. **Document type:** corporate report.

332 FR
BANQUE DE FRANCE. RECUEIL DES TEXTES RELATIFS A L'EXERCICE DES ACTIVITES BANCAIRES. English edition: French Banking Act and Selected Banking Regulations. a. 300 F. Banque de France, Service de l'Information, 48 rue Crois des Petits Champs, 75001 Paris, France. TEL 42-92-39-31. FAX 42-92-39-40.
 Formerly: Banque de France. Recueil des Textes Applicables a l'Exercice des Activites Bancaires.

332.1 FR
BANQUE DE FRANCE. SITUATION DU SYSTEME PRODUCTIF. a. 100 F. Banque de France, Service de l'Information, 48 rue Croix-Des-Petits-Champs, 75001 Paris, France. TEL 1-42-92-39-31. FAX 1-42-92-39-40.

332.1 FR
BANQUE DE FRANCE ET LA MONNAIE. (Subseries of: Collection Documentation et Information (ISSN 1152-538X)) irreg., 5th ed., 1995. 120 F. Banque de France, Service de l'Information, 48 rue Croix-Des-Petits-Champs, 75001 Paris, France. TEL 1-42-92-39-31. FAX 1-42-92-39-40.

332 HT ISSN 0257-4349
HG2813
BANQUE DE LA REPUBLIQUE D'HAITI. BULLETIN. s-a. Gde.50($12) Banque de la Republique d'Haiti, Direction Administrative, B.P. 1570, Port-au-Prince, Haiti. TEL 23-1944. FAX 22-2607. TELEX BRH DGA 2030537.

332.1 HT ISSN 0257-4357
BANQUE DE LA REPUBLIQUE D'HAITI. RAPPORT ANNUEL. a. Gde.25($6) Banque de la Republique d'Haiti, Direction Administrative, B.P. 1570, Port-au-Prince, Haiti.
 Formerly: Banque Nationale de la Republique d'Haiti. Rapport du Departement Fiscal.

332.1 BD ISSN 1013-5332
HC880.A1
BANQUE DE LA REPUBLIQUE DU BURUNDI. BULLETIN MENSUEL. 1978. m. 4200 Fr. to individuals; Africa $55; Europe $65; elsewhere $75 (effective 1996). Banque de la Republique du Burundi, Service des Etudes, B.P. 705, Bujumbura, Burundi. TEL 225142. FAX 257-22-3128. TELEX BDI 5071. **Indexed:** P.A.I.S.For.Lang.Ind. **Document type:** bulletin.
 Description: Covers industrial production statistics on the monetary situation.

332.1 BD ISSN 1013-5359
BANQUE DE LA REPUBLIQUE DU BURUNDI. RAPPORT ANNUEL. (Text in French) 1964. a. $9 in Africa; Europe $10; Asia & America $11. Banque de la Republique du Burundi, Service des Etudes, B.P. 705, Bujumbura, Burundi. TEL 225142. FAX 257-22-3128. TELEX BDI 5071. circ. 500. **Document type:** corporate report.
 Description: Discusses numerous sectors in the economy such as major import-exported products, employment conditions, the budget, political events influencing the economy, balance sheet and other financial documents.

BANQUE DES ETATS DE L'AFRIQUE CENTRALE. ETUDES ET STATISTIQUES; bulletin mensuel. see BUSINESS AND ECONOMICS — Abstracting, Bibliographies, Statistics

332.1 CM ISSN 0067-3900
BANQUE DES ETATS DE L'AFRIQUE CENTRALE. RAPPORT D'ACTIVITE. (Former name of issuing body: Banque Centrale des Etats de l'Afrique Equatoriale et du Cameroun) 1973. a. free. Banque des Etats de l'Afrique Centrale, Direction des Etudes et de la Documentation, Services Centraux, B.P. 1917, Yaounde, Cameroon. circ. 1,500.

332.1 CG ISSN 0300-1172
BANQUE DU ZAIRE. RAPPORT ANNUEL. a. 66.85 Fr.CFA per no. Banque du Zaire, B.P. 2697, Kinshasa, Democratic Republic of the Congo.
 Formerly: Banque Nationale du Congo. Rapport Annuel (ISSN 0067-4001)

BUSINESS AND ECONOMICS — BANKING AND FINANCE

332.1   **LU**
BANQUE ET CAISSE D'EPARGNE DE L'ETAT, LUXEMBOURG. RAPPORTS ET BILAN. English edition: Banque et Caisse d'Epargne de l'Etat, Luxembourg. Annual Report. 1901. a. free. Banque et Caisse d'Epargne de l'Etat, Luxembourg, 2 pl. de Metz, L-2954 Luxembourg, Luxembourg. TEL 352-40-15-1. FAX 352-40-15-42-84. TELEX 3417 SWIFTL BCEELULL. Ed.Bd. circ. 3,000. Document type: corporate report.
   Formerly: Caisse d'Epargne de l'Etat du Grand-Duche de Luxembourg. Rapports et Bilans.
   Description: Presents statistics and charts summarizing the all bank's financial activities, including income and expenditures.

332   **SZ**
BANQUE & FINANCE. 3/yr. Promoedition SA, 2 rue Bovy-Lysberg, Case postale 5615, CH-1211 Geneva 11, Switzerland. TEL 022-3215466. FAX 022-3219862. Ed. Marian Stepczynski. circ. 15,000. Document type: bulletin.

332.1   **MR**
BANQUE MAROCAINE DU COMMERCE EXTERIEUR. ANNUAL REPORT. (Editions in Arabic, English, French) 1961. a. Banque Marocaine du Commerce Exterieur, 140 Avenue Hassan II, Casablanca, Morocco. circ. 6,000 French ed.; 3,000 English ed.

332 330.9   **BE**   **ISSN 0005-5611**
HC311
BANQUE NATIONALE DE BELGIQUE. BULLETIN. (Editions in Flemish, French) 1926 (French edition); 1938 (Flemish edition). m. (plus s-a. supplements). 750 BEF (foreign 1550 BEF). Banque Nationale de Belgique, Service de la documentation, Bd. de Berlaimont 14, B-1000 Brussels, Belgium. TEL 32-2-2212033. FAX 32-2-2213163. bibl.; charts; stat. Indexed: P.A.I.S.For.Lang.Ind. Document type: bulletin.

332.1   **BE**   **ISSN 0067-3978**
BANQUE NATIONALE DE BELGIQUE. RAPPORT SUR LES OPERATIONS. (Editions in Dutch, English, French) 1852. a. free. Banque Nationale de Belgique, Bd. de Berlaimont 14, 1000 Brussels, Belgium. TEL 32-2-2212111. FAX 32-2-2213100. TELEX 21105 BNBSG B. E-mail: secritariat@bnbb.be. Document type: corporate report.
   Description: Information on the Belgian economy and business outlook.

332.1   **BD**
BANQUE NATIONALE DE DEVELOPPEMENT ECONOMIQUE DU BURUNDI. RAPPORT ANNUEL. a. $30. Banque Nationale de Developpement Economique du Burundi, B.P. 1620, Bujumbura, Burundi.
   Description: Contains message from the president, economic history of Burundi, functions within the organizations, financial standing, numerous documents detailing the balance of payments.

332.1   **RW**
BANQUE NATIONALE DU RWANDA. BULLETIN. (Text in French) s-a. 1500 F.($60) Banque Nationale du Rwanda, B.P. 531, Kigali, Rwanda. FAX 250-72551. TELEX 508-589. Indexed: P.A.I.S.For.Lang.Ind. Document type: bulletin.
   Formerly: Banque Nationale du Rwanda. Bulletin Trimestriel.

332.1   **RW**
BANQUE NATIONALE DU RWANDA. RAPPORT SUR L'EVOLUTION ECONOMIQUE ET MONETAIRE DU RWANDA. a. 1000 F. (foreign $35). Banque Nationale du Rwanda, B.P. 531, Kigali, Rwanda. stat.
   Former titles: Banque Nationale du Rwanda. Rapport d'Activites; (until 1986): Banque Nationale du Rwanda. Rapport Annuel.

332.1   **MG**
BANQUE NATIONALE POUR LE DEVELOPPEMENT RURAL. RAPPORT ANNUEL. a. free. Banque Nationale pour le Developpement Rural, B.P. 183, Antananarivo, Madagascar. FAX 21398. TELEX 22208 BTM MG.

332   **SZ**   **ISSN 0005-4240**
BANQUE POPULAIRE SUISSE. BALANCE SHEET PROSPECTUS. (Editions in English, French, German and Italian) s-a. free. Banque Populaire Suisse, Weltpostrasse 5, Case Postale 2620, CH-3001 Berne, Switzerland. circ. 30,000 (combined).

332.1   **SZ**   **ISSN 0067-4028**
BANQUE POPULAIRE SUISSE. INFORMATION. (Editions in French and German; occasionally in English) 3/yr. free. Banque Populaire Suisse, Weltpostrasse 5, Case Postale 2620, CH-3001 Berne, Switzerland. circ. 80,000.

332
BANQUE POPULAIRE SUISSE. JOURNAL. (Editions in French, German, Italian) 4/yr. free. Banque Populaire Suisse, Weltpostrasse 5, Case Postale 2620, CH-3001 Berne, Switzerland.
   Supersedes (1962-1977): Fragments (ISSN 0015-9336).

332.1   **RW**
BANQUE RWANDAISE DE DEVELOPPEMENT. RAPPORT ANNUEL. (Text in French) a. Banque Rwandaise de Developpement, B.P. 1341, Kigali, Rwanda. TEL 75079. FAX 22563. TELEX 73569. charts; stat.

332.1   **TG**
BANQUE TOGOLAISE DE DEVELOPPEMENT. RAPPORT D'ACTIVITES. (Text in French) a. Banque Togolaise de Developpement, B.P. 65, Lome, Togo.
   Formerly: Banque Togolaise de Developpement. Rapport Annuel (ISSN 0067-4036).
   Description: Consists of reports concerning financial operations, deposits and external relations.

332   **FR**   **ISSN 1168-0377**
BANQUES DES ENTREPRISES. 1992. m. 3450 F. (foreign 3700 F.). Publi-News, 3 ave. Gallieni, 92000 Nanterre, France. TEL 33-47-29-88-11. FAX 33-47-29-88-18. Ed. Ange Galula. Document type: newsletter.

332   **FR**   **ISSN 1163-7773**
BANQUES DES PARTICULIERS. 1992. m. (14/yr.). 3720 F. (foreign 3850 F.). Publi-News, 3 ave. Gallieni, 92000 Nanterre, France. TEL 33 47-29-88-11. FAX 33-47-29-88-18. Ed. Ange Galula. Document type: newsletter.

332 338   **FR**   **ISSN 1148-1978**
BANQUES DES PROFESSIONNELS. 1991. m. 3220 F. (foreign 3700 F.). Publi-News, 3 ave. Gallieni, 92000 Nanterre, France. TEL 47-29-88-11. FAX 47-29-88-18. Ed. Ange Galula. Document type: newsletter.
   Description: Covers banks' strategies for small sized companies, shops, newly created companies, shopkeepers as well as doctors and lawyers.

332 330   **MR**   **ISSN 0851-2167**
BANQUES ET ENTREPRISES AU MAROC. (Text in French) 1985. q. Revue Banques et Entreprises au Maroc, 8 rue 4 Guise, Roches Noires, Casablanca 05, Morocco. Ed. Ibnou-Zahir Abdelwahab.

332 658.3   **FR**   **ISSN 1162-1516**
BANQUES RESSOURCES HUMAINES. 1991. m. 3150 F. (foreign 3350 F.). Publi-News, 3 ave. Gallieni, 9200 Nanterre, France. TEL 47-29-88-11. FAX 47-29-88-18. Ed. Ange Galula. Document type: newsletter.
   Description: Covers training, human resources management, motivation, recruiting and more.

332.1   **CN**   **ISSN 0822-6849**
LE BANQUIER. English edition: Canadian Banker (ISSN 0822-6830) (Text in French) 1974. bi-m. Can.$35 (foreign $28) (effective 1998). Canadian Bankers Association (Montreal), Tour Scotia, 1002, rue Sherbrooke Ouest, Bur. 900, Montreal, PQ H3A 3M5, Canada. TEL 514-840-8747. FAX 514-282-7551. Ed. Jacques Hebert. adv. contact: Bob Dumouchel. bk.rev./; index. circ. 8,855. (also avail. in microfilm) Indexed: Pt.de Rep. (1983-).

332.1   **BB**
BARBADOS NATIONAL BANK. ANNUAL REPORT & STATEMENT OF ACCOUNTS. a. Barbados National Bank, James St., Bridgetown, Barbados, W.I.

332   **UK**
BARCLAYS BANK. GLOBAL CURRENCIES OUTLOOK. (Part of Foreign Exchange Reports series) m. £150 (academic institutions and students £75); full set of Foreign Exchange Reports £300 (academic institutions and students £150). Barclays Bank plc., Economics Department, P.O. Box 12, Barclays House, 1 Wimborne Rd., Poole, Dorset BH15 2BB, England. TEL 01202-344023. FAX 01202-402303.
   Description: Forecasts the currencies of 20 nations and gives the outlook for their interest rates.

BARCLAYS BANK. INDUSTRY BRIEFINGS. see *BUSINESS AND ECONOMICS — Economic Situation And Conditions*

332   **UK**
BARCLAY'S BANK. MONTHLY FINANCIAL OUTLOOK. (Part of Foreign Exchange Reports series) m. £150 (academic institutions and students £75); full set of Foreign Exchange Reports £300 (academic institutions and students £150). Barclays Bank plc., Economics Department, P.O. Box 12, Barclays House, 1 Wimborne Rd., Poole, Dorset BH15 2BB, England. TEL 01202-344023. FAX 01202-402303.

332   **UK**
BARCLAYS BANK. WEEKLY EXCHANGE & INTEREST RATE OUTLOOK. (Part of the Foreign Exchange Reports series). w. £150 (academic institutions and students £75); full set of Foreign Exchange Reports £300 (academic institutions and students £150). Barclays Bank plc., Economics Department, P.O. Box 12, Barclays House, 1 Wimborne Rd., Poole, Dorset BH15 2BB, England. TEL 01202-344023. FAX 01202-402303.
   Description: Forecasts the exchange and interest rates for the U.S. Dollar, Japanese Yen, Deutschemark, and British Pound Sterling.

332   **UK**   **ISSN 0956-5574**
HG3000.L84
BARCLAYS ECONOMIC REVIEW. 1919. q. £60 (academic institutions and students £30). Barclays Bank plc., Economics Department, P.O. Box 12, Barclays House, 1 Wimborne Rd., Poole, Dorset BH15 2BB, England. TEL 01202-344023. FAX 01202-402303. circ. 12,500. (reprint service avail. from SCH) Indexed: ABI Inform, Br.Hum.Ind., Cont.Pg.Manage., Mgmt.& Market.Abstr., P.A.I.S., SCIMP (1978-), World Bank.Abstr. Document type: academic/scholarly publication.
   ●Also available online. Vendor(s): Data-Star, Knight-Ridder Information, Inc., UMI.
   —BLDSC (1863.602500); UMI.
   Former titles (until 1989): Barclays Review (ISSN 0269-7009); (until 1971): Barclays Bank Review (ISSN 0005-5905)

332 790.1   **UK**
▼**BARCLAYS PREMIER WORLD MAGAZINE.** 1995. q. membership. (Barclays Premier Card) The Publishing Team, Exmouth House, 3-11 Pine St., London EC1R 0JH, England. TEL 44-171-923-5400. FAX 44-171-923-5401. Ed. Kate Edwards; Pub. Neil O'Brien. adv.: color page £2500; adv. contact: Daniel Squirrell. circ. 70,000. (back issues avail.) Document type: consumer publication.

332.1   **US**
BARNETT ACTION. 1966. q. Barnett Banks, Inc., Box 40789, Jacksonville, FL 32231. TEL 904-791-7651. FAX 904-791-5382. Ed. Sherry McGlamory. R&P contact: Sherry McGlamory. illus. circ. 23,500. Document type: newsletter.
   Formerly: Action.

332   **YU**
BEOBANKA. 1976. w. (Beogradska Banka) Beobanka, Trg Nikole Pasica 5, Beograd, Yugoslavia. Ed. Zoran Pavlovic.

332.6   **GW**   **ISSN 0172-0236**
BERLINER BANK. BOERSENBRIEF. Key Title: Boersenbrief. 1950. fortn. free. Berliner Bank Aktiengesellschaft, Hardenbergstr. 32, 10890 Berlin, Germany. TEL 49-30-3109-0. FAX 49-30-31092165. circ. 12,500. Document type: bulletin.

BUSINESS AND ECONOMICS — BANKING AND FINANCE

332   BM
BERMUDA MONETARY AUTHORITY. REPORTS & ACCOUNTS. 1969. a. free. Bermuda Monetary Authority, Burnaby House, 26 Burnaby St., P.O. Box HM 2447, Hamilton HM 11, Bermuda. TEL 441-295-5278. FAX 441-292-7471. E-mail: info@bma.bm; URL: http://www.bma.bm. Ed.Bd. circ. 1,000.

332 368   US
BEST OF THE YEAR.* a. (Banking Law Institute) Executive Enterprises Publications Co., Inc., 21 W. 31st St., New York, NY 10001-2727. TEL 212-645-7880; 800-223-0787.
   Description: Informs readers about banking regulations.

BETRIEBSWIRTSCHAFTLICHE BLAETTER. see *BUSINESS AND ECONOMICS — Management*

332   YU   ISSN 0354-3242
BILTEN - SLUZBENA OBJASNJENJA I STRUCNA MISLJENJA ZA PRIMENU FINANSIJSKIH PROPISA. (Supplement to: Finansije (ISSN 0015-2145)) 1961. m. (Poslovni Sistem "Grmec") Privredni Pregled, Marsala Birjuzova 3-5, 11000 Belgrade, Yugoslavia. Ed. Viden Pancic.
   Former titles: Bilten Objasnjenja za Primenu Propisa iz Oblasti Finansija i Strucna Misljenja (ISSN 0354-2688); (until 1992): Bilten Objasnjenja za Primenu Propisa iz Oblasti Finansija (ISSN 0523-6125)

BIOWORLD FINANCIAL WATCH. see *BIOLOGY*

332.1   IT
▼ **BIREL NEWSLETTER.** 1996. irreg. (Banca d'Italia, Servizio Anticipazioni Sconti e Compensazioni, Divisione Riserve e Regolamenti) Canca d'Italia, Via Milano, 60 g, 00184 Rome, Italy. TEL 39-6-47925341. FAX 39-6-47925148. (Co-sponsor: Associacione Bancaria Italiana, Servizio Mercati Finaziari)
   Description: Addresses managers in the areas where change will be farthest-reaching, in particular those responsible for treasury and organizational matters as well as marketing and credit managers.

BLAY'S COMMERCIAL MORTGAGEMATCH. see *REAL ESTATE*

BOERSE. see *BUSINESS AND ECONOMICS — Investments*

BOERSE ONLINE; Wochenzeitung fuer moderne Kapitalanlage. see *BUSINESS AND ECONOMICS — Investments*

332   DK
BOERSEN. (Supplement avail.: Boersen Informatik (ISSN 0906-8317)) 1895. d. DKK 1870 (effective 1997). Dagbladet Boersen A-S, Moentergade 19, DK-1140 Copenhagen K, Denmark. TEL 45-33-32-01-02. FAX 45-33-12-24-45. Ed.Bd. circ. 43,455. **Document type:** newspaper.

BOLETIN DE ESTADISTICAS BANCARIAS. see *BUSINESS AND ECONOMICS — Abstracting, Bibliographies, Statistics*

332   CK   ISSN 0121-0629
BOLETIN JURIDICO Y FINANCIERO. 1988. w. $170 (effective 1998). Asociacion Bancaria y de Entidades Financieras, Apdo. Aereo 13994, Bogota D.C., Colombia. TEL 57-1-2114811. FAX 57-1-2119915. E-mail: info@asobancaria.com; URL: http://www.asobancaria.com.
   Description: Compiles all legislation pertaining to the financial sector and the country's monetary, credit and foreign exchange policies.

332   UY
BOLSA DE VALORES DE MONTEVIDEO. ESTUDIOS ESTADISTICOS. 1976. q. Bolsa de Valores de Montevideo, Misiones 1400, Montevideo, Uruguay.

BOLSA MEXICANA DE VALORES. ANUARIO FINANCIERO (YEAR). see *BUSINESS AND ECONOMICS — Abstracting, Bibliographies, Statistics*

BOLSA MEXICANA DE VALORES. INDICADORES FINANCIEROS/MEXICAN STOCK EXCHANGE. FINANCIAL FACTS AND FIGURES. see *BUSINESS AND ECONOMICS — Abstracting, Bibliographies, Statistics*

332   FR   ISSN 1161-9430
BOTTIN DE LA FINANCE. a. Bottin S A, 4 rue Andre Boulle, 94961 Creteil Cedex 9, France. TEL 49-81-56-56. FAX 49-81-56-76. (also avail. in diskette format; magnetic tape) **Document type:** directory.

BOWNE DIGEST FOR CORPORATE & SECURITIES LAWYERS; abstracts of current articles from more than 280 legal periodicals. see *LAW — Abstracting, Bibliographies, Statistics*

332   US   ISSN 1047-6172
BOWNE REVIEW FOR C F OS AND INVESTMENT BANKERS. 1989. m. free. Brumberg Publications, Inc., 124 Harvard St., Brookline, MA 02146. TEL 617-734-1979. FAX 617-734-1989. E-mail: brumberg@compuserve.com. Ed. Susan Koffman; Pub. Bruce Brumberg. (looseleaf format; back issues avail.) **Document type:** newsletter.

332   US
BRANCH OPERATIONS MANAGEMENT SERVICE. (Part of the Financial Management series) base vol. (plus s-a. updates). $295. Sheshunoff Information Services Inc., 505 Barton Springs Rd., Ste. 1100, Austin, TX 78704. TEL 512-472-2244; 800-456-2340. (looseleaf format) **Document type:** trade publication.

332   US
BRANCHES OF NEW YORK. m. Sheshunoff Information Services Inc., Box 13203, Capitol Sta., Austin, TX 78711-3203. TEL 512-472-2244; 800-456-2340. charts; stat. **Document type:** trade publication.
   Description: Contains competitive analyses of New York banks by county and city, along with a historical growth overview and information on bank holding companies and their subsidiaries.

332   CN
BRITISH COLUMBIA MAJOR PROJECTS INVENTORY. q. Can.$75 (effective 1997). Ministry of Finance and Corporate Relations, B C Stats, P.O. Box 9410, Stn. Prov. Govt., Victoria, BC V8W 9V1, Canada. TEL 250-387-1502. FAX 250-387-0329. E-mail: bcstats@fincc04.fin.gov.bc.ca; URL: http://www.bcstats.gov.bc.ca. circ. 500. **Document type:** government publication.
   Description: Covers major capital projects. For developers, suppliers of goods and services, retailers, transportation providers, planners and other government officials.

332.63 384   US   ISSN 0889-2644
BROADCAST BANKER - BROKER. 1984. m. $675 (effective 1997). Paul Kagan Associates, Inc., 126 Clock Tower Pl., Carmel, CA 93923. TEL 408-624-1536. TELEX 408-625-3225. Eds. Paul Kagan, Sharon Armbrust.
   Formerly: Broadcast Banking.
   Description: Covers equity and debt financing for radio and TV. Includes an analysis of interest rates and cashflow.

332   UK   ISSN 0068-3566
BUILDING SOCIETIES. YEAR BOOK. 1927. a. £63. Franey and Co. Ltd., South Quay Plaza, 183 Marsh Wall, London E14 9FS, England. adv. **Document type:** trade publication.
   —BLDSC (2365.760000).

BUILDING SOCIETIES YEARBOOK. see *REAL ESTATE*

BUILDING SOCIETY ANNUAL ACCOUNTS DATA. see *REAL ESTATE*

BUILDING SOCIETY LEAGUE TABLES (FINANCIAL). see *REAL ESTATE*

332   UK
BUILDING SOCIETY MORTGAGE ARREARS AND LOSSES REPORT. a. £195 to non-members; members £136 (effective 1996-97). Building Societies Association, 3 Savile Row, London W1X 1AF, England. TEL 44-171-437-0655. FAX 44-171-287-0109. (Co-sponsor: Council of Mortgage Lenders) **Document type:** trade publication.
   Description: Contains a detailed analysis of arrears, provisions, and losses for each U.K. building society, along with commentary and accounting policy statements as reported by each society in its annual report.

BUILDING SOCIETY PEER GROUPS (FINANCIAL). see *REAL ESTATE*

332   SZ   ISSN 1024-1663
BULLETIN I F S/BULLETIN I T M S/BULLETIN I R M S. (Text in French, German, Italian) 1994. a. 10 SFr. Inventar der Fundmuenzen der Schweiz - Inventaire des Trouvailles Monetaires Suisses - Inventario dei Ritrovamenti Monetali Svizzeri, Hardturmstr. 185, CH-8005 Zurich, Switzerland. TEL 41-1-2729310. FAX 41-1-2729458. **Document type:** bulletin.

332.1 330   CK
BULLETIN L A R F. (Editions in English, Spanish) 1982. q. free. Latin American Reserve Fund, Apdo. Aereo 241523, Bogota, Colombia. FAX 2881117. TELEX 45586.
   Former titles: Bulletin A R F; Andean Reserve Fund. Bulletin.
   Description: Covers quarterly economic summaries of the member countries: Bolivia, Colombia, Ecuador, Peru and Venezuela.

330.9   KU
BURGAN BANK S.A.K. ANNUAL REPORT. 1977. a. Burgan Bank S.A.K., Ahmed Al-Jaber St., P.O. Box 5389, Safat 13054, Kuwait. **Document type:** corporate report.

332 330   US
BUSINESS ADVICE AND FINANCIAL PLANNING. 1987. q. $18 to members; non-members $68. Illinois State Bar Association, Illinois Bar Center, Springfield, IL 62701. TEL 217-525-1760. FAX 217-525-0712. Ed. Malcolm L. Morris. **Document type:** newsletter.

332   US   ISSN 0738-7253
BUSINESS & ACQUISITION NEWSLETTER. 1966. m. $300. Newsletters International, Inc., 2600 S. Gessner Rd., Houston, TX 77063. TEL 713-783-0100. Ed. Len Fox. bk.rev. **Document type:** newsletter.
   Former titles: Acquisition Newsletter International; Acquisition Newsletter.
   Description: Covers acquisitions and merger opportunities.

650 332   IE   ISSN 0007-6473
HF5001
BUSINESS AND FINANCE. 1964. w. I£102.20 (England I£104.70; Europe I£146; rest of world I£144.10) (effective 1996 & 1997). Belenos Publications Ltd., 50 Fitzwilliam Sq. W., Dublin 2, Ireland. TEL 353-1-6764587. FAX 353-1-6619781. Ed. Dan White. adv.; illus. circ. 11,526. **Indexed:** ELLIS, Key to Econ.Sci., P.A.I.S., PROMT, World Bank.Abstr. **Document type:** newspaper, trade publication.

332.7 658   US   ISSN 0897-0181
HF5565
BUSINESS CREDIT. 1898. m. $34. National Association of Credit Management, 8815 Centre Park Dr., Ste. 200, Columbia, MD 21045. TEL 410-740-5560. FAX 410-740-5574. Ed. Cindy Tursman. adv.; charts; illus.; stat.; index. circ. 37,000. (also avail. in microform from UMI; back issues avail.; reprint service avail. from UMI) **Indexed:** AAR, ABI Inform., Account.Ind. (1974-), B.P.I., BPIA, Bus.Ind., Data Process.Dig., Intl.Mgmt.Info., Manage.Cont., PROMT, Tr.& Indus.Ind. **Document type:** trade publication.
   ●Also available online. Vendor(s): Information Access Co., UMI.
   —BLDSC (2933.419200); KR SourceOne; SWETS; UMI; UnCover. CCC.
   Formerly: Credit and Financial Management (ISSN 0011-0973)
   Description: For corporate credit and financial professionals.

332   CN
HG2708.F4
BUSINESS DEVELOPMENT BANK OF CANADA. ANNUAL REPORT. 1945. a. free. Business Development Bank of Canada, 5 Place Ville Marie, Bureau 400, Montreal, PQ H3B 5E7, Canada. TEL 514-283-5904. FAX 514-283-7838. URL: http://www.bdc.ca. Ed. Peter Stewart. circ. 15,000. **Document type:** corporate report.
   Formerly: Federal Business Development Bank. Annual Report (ISSN 0703-0347)

BUSINESS AND ECONOMICS — BANKING AND FINANCE

332   NE   ISSN 1045-7798
HG1   CODEN: BLRVE4
BUSINESS LIBRARY REVIEW; an international journal. 1973. q. $105 (effective 1998). Gordon and Breach - Harwood Academic, Amsteldisk 166, 1st Fl., 1079 LH Amsterdam, Netherlands. (Subscr. to: International Publishers Distributor, Box 32160, Newark, NJ 07102. TEL 800-545-8398. FAX 215-750-6343) Eds. David & Beth Whitten. adv.; bk.rev.; bibl.; index. (also avail. in microform; reprint service avail. from UMI) **Indexed:** Bk.Rev.Ind. (1975-), Child.Bk.Rev.Ind. (1975-), Manage.Cont. **Document type:** academic/scholarly publication.
—BLDSC (2934.188000). CCC.
Formed by the 1990 merger of: Wall Street Review of Books (ISSN 0091-1526) & Economics and Business (ISSN 0884-8335); Which was formerly (1976-1984): Economics Selections (ISSN 0140-7635)
Description: Reviews leading publications, computer software, film and video in finance, economics, insurance, and international commerce.
Refereed Serial

332 346   UK   ISSN 1350-1038
BUSINESS MONEY. 1993. m. £95($225) Business Money Ltd, Srobe House, 10 Leigh Rd., Somerset BA16 OHA. TEL 44-1458-841112. FAX 44-1458-841286. E-mail: editor@business-money.com; URL: http://www.business-money.com. (Subscr. to: P.O. Box 1658, Street, Somers. BA6 9FE, England. TEL 44-1458-841112; Alt. addr.: 8 Irving Rd., Keinton, Mandeville, Somerton, Somers. TA11 6ET, England. TEL 44-1458-223048) Ed. Robert Lefroy. R&P contact: Robert Lefroy. adv.: B&W page £1250, color £2000; adv. contact: Helen Palmer. circ. 7,000. circ. 7,000. (controlled). (back issues avail.) **Document type:** trade publication, directory.
Description: Serves as the trade magazine for the UK business funding industry. Aimed at accountants, lawyers, bankers, financial advisers, and brokers.

BUSINESS MONITOR: ASSETS AND LIABILITIES OF FINANCE HOUSES AND OTHER CONSUMER CREDIT COMPANIES. see *BUSINESS AND ECONOMICS — Abstracting, Bibliographies, Statistics*

BUSINESS MONITOR: COMPANY FINANCE. see *BUSINESS AND ECONOMICS — Abstracting, Bibliographies, Statistics*

BUSINESS MONITOR: CREDIT BUSINESS. see *BUSINESS AND ECONOMICS — Abstracting, Bibliographies, Statistics*

BUSINESS NEWS FROM POLAND. see *BUSINESS AND ECONOMICS*

332 658.8   UK
BUSINESS RATIO PLUS: FINANCE HOUSES. 1979. a. I C C Business Publications Ltd., Field House, 72 Oldfield Rd., Hampton, Mddx. TW12 2HQ, England. TEL 44-181-783-0922. FAX 44-181-783-1940. charts; stat. **Document type:** trade publication.
Formerly (until 1994): Business Ratio Report: Finance Houses (ISSN 0261-8087)

333.33   US   ISSN 0897-1781
BUSINESS VALUATION REVIEW. 1982. q. $50 to non-members (foreign $65). American Society of Appraisers, Business Valuation Committee, Box 101923, Denver, CO 80250. TEL 303-758-6148. Ed. James H. Schilt; Pub. John E. Bakker. R&P contact: Shelly Chamberlain. cum.index. circ. 2,500. **Document type:** trade publication.
Formerly (until 1987): Business Valuation News (ISSN 0882-2875)
Description: Provides up-to-date information for all persons who have an interest in the valuation of businesses, professional practices, corporate stock, and tangible and intangible assets.
Refereed Serial

BUTTERWORTHS JOURNAL OF INTERNATIONAL BANKING AND FINANCIAL LAW. see *LAW*

332 338   AT
BUYING AND SELLING BUSINESSES - PERSONAL PROPERTY. 1991. q. C C H Australia Ltd., P.O. Box 230, North Ryde, N.S.W. 2113, Australia. TEL 61-1-300300224. FAX 61-1-300306224. (looseleaf format)
Description: Covers the principles and practice of buying and selling the assets of a business, the shares in a company which conducts and business and items of personal property.

332 658   UK
C C A NEWS. 1980. q. £30 to non-members. (Consumer Credit Association) C C A (U.K.) Advisory Services Ltd., Queens House, Queens Rd., Chester CH1 3BQ, England. TEL 44-1244-312044. FAX 44-1244-318035. Ed. Bill Williams. R&P contact: Steve Yong. TEL 44-1244-505906. adv. contact: Steve Yong. circ. 1,400. (back issues avail.)
Description: In-house magazine for members of the largest U.K. Trade Association for the unsecured lending industry.

332   US
C C H FINANCIAL AND ESTATE PLANNING. (Commerce Clearing House) 1980. 4 base vols. (plus s-m. reports). $802. C C H Incorporated, 2700 Lake Cook Rd., Riverwoods, IL 60015. TEL 847-267-7000; 800-835-5224. FAX 800-224-8299. (looseleaf format)
●Also available on CD-ROM.

C C I A NEWSLETTER. (Consumer Credit Insurance Association) see *INSURANCE*

332   BB   ISSN 0257-6090
C D B NEWS. 1983. q. free. Caribbean Development Bank, P.O. Box 408, Wildey, St. Michael, Barbados, W.I. TEL 246-431-1600. FAX 246-426-7269. TELEX WB 2287. Ed. Hubert S. Williams. bk.rev. circ. 5,000. (reprint service avail.) **Document type:** newsletter.
Description: Gives general information about the Bank's activities and serves as an aid in project design & equipment selection by potential investors.

332   US
C D RATE WATCH. (Certificate of Deposit) 1983. m. $99. Bauer Communications, Inc., 2655 LeJeune Rd., PH-1A, Drawer 145510, Coral Gables, FL 33114-5510. TEL 305-445-9500; 800-388-6686. FAX 305-445-6775. Ed. Caroline P. Jervey. circ. 3,250.
Former titles: Rate Watch; Tiered Rate Watch (ISSN 8750-3727)

332   US   ISSN 1056-1722
HG4928.5
C F A CANDIDATE STUDY AND EXAMINATION PROGRAM REVIEW. 1983. a. $20. Association for Investment Management and Research, Box 3668, Charlottesville, VA 22903. TEL 804-980-3668. FAX 804-980-9755. circ. 19,000. (back issues avail.)

332   US   ISSN 0046-9777
HG4501
C F A DIGEST. (Chartered Financial Analyst) 1971. q. $40. Association for Investment Management and Research, Box 3668, Charlottesville, VA 22903. TEL 804-977-3668. FAX 804-980-9755. circ. 19,000 (controlled).
—UnCover.

C F M A BUILDING PROFITS. (Construction Financial Management Association) see *BUILDING AND CONSTRUCTION*

332   US
C F O ALERT (WEEKLY). (Chief Financial Officer) 1994. 48/yr. $625 (foreign $675) (effective 1996). (American Bankers Association) American Banker Newsletters, One State Street Plaza, 26th Fl., New York, NY 10004-1505. TEL 212-803-8300; 800-407-8241. FAX 212-843-9620. Ed. John Hintze; Pub. David G. Schutt. adv.: page $1400; trim 8 1/2 x 11; adv. contact: Cynthia Colvin. **Document type:** newsletter.
●Also available online. Vendor(s): Data-Star, Knight-Ridder Information, Inc., Lexis-Nexis, NewsNet.
Description: Covers regulatory and accounting changes, capital markets, bank funding news and strategies, asset and liability management, automation techniques and new banking products. Also features CFO interviews.

C M L ANNUAL REPORT. (Council of Mortgage Lenders) see *REAL ESTATE*

C M L DIRECTORY OF MEMBERS. see *REAL ESTATE*

C M L LIBRARY BULLETIN. see *REAL ESTATE*

C M L MARKET BRIEFING. see *REAL ESTATE*

C M L PARLIAMENTARY CUTTING SERVICE. see *REAL ESTATE*

332   US   ISSN 0734-0486
C M R E MONOGRAPHS. 1971. irreg., latest no.53. $5 per no. Committee for Monetary Research and Education, Inc., 10004 Greenwood Ct., Charlotte, NC 28215-9621. TEL 704-598-3717. FAX 704-599-7036. circ. 3,000. **Document type:** monographs series.
Former titles: C M R E Monetary Tracts; C M R E Money Tracts.

332.1   EC
C O F I E C. INFORME ANUAL. a. Compania Financiera Ecuatoriana de Desarrollo, Box 411, Quito, Ecuador. FAX 564224. TELEX 22131. illus.; stat. circ. 3,000.

332 340   US
C S B S EXAMINER. 1969. w. membership. Conference of State Bank Supervisors, 1015 18th St., N.W., Ste. 1000, Washington, DC 20036-5278. TEL 202-296-2840. FAX 202-296-1928. Ed. Ellen Lamb. R&P contact: Ellen Lamb. **Document type:** newsletter.
Formerly: Capitol Comments.

334.2   US   ISSN 1087-108X
C U E S - F Y I. (For Your Information) m. $456 includes membership. Credit Union Executives Society, Box 14167, Madison, WI 53714-0167. TEL 608-271-2664. FAX 608-271-2303. E-mail: cues@cues.org. circ. 3,500. **Document type:** newsletter.
Formerly: F Y I Management Memo.

334.2   US
C U I S. (Credit Union Information Service) (Supplement avail: CUIS Special Reports) 1973. bi-w. $277. United Communications Group, 11300 Rockville Pike, Rockville, MD 20852-3030. TEL 301-816-8950. FAX 301-816-8945. Ed. Jonathan Stern.
Description: Gives the latest innovations in credit union management, asseses investment options, and provides industry news.

332 384   US   ISSN 1062-3515
CABLE NETWORK INVESTOR. 1991. m. $795 (effective 1997). Paul Kagan Associates, Inc., 126 Clock Tower Pl., Carmel, CA 93923. TEL 408-624-1536. FAX 408-625-3225. Ed. Paul Kagan. **Document type:** trade publication.
Description: Presents data on public stock offerings, growth projections, analysis of balance sheet leverage and equity, rankings of competitors and insight into corporate financings.

CABLE T V FINANCE; newsletter on bank, insurance, commercial loans to cable operators. see *COMMUNICATIONS — Television And Cable*

332   FR   ISSN 0395-8175
CAHIERS DU CREDIT MUTUEL; presse professionnelle et bancaire. 1963. 5/yr. 210 F. (foreign 235 F.) (effective 1997). 34 rue du Wacken, 67000 Strasbourg, France. TEL 33-3-88147241. FAX 33-3-88147239. Ed. Bernard Sadoun. adv.; bk.rev. circ. 10,000. **Indexed:** ELLIS.
Formerly: Eurepargne.

332   CC   ISSN 1000-8306
HB9
CAIJING KEXUE/FINANCE AND ECONOMICS. (Text in Chinese) 1957. bi-m. $18.50. Xinan Caijing Daxue - Southwestern University of Finance and Economics, Guanghua Cun, Chengdu Xijiao, Sichuan 610074, People's Republic of China. (Dist. in US by: China Books & Periodicals, Inc., 2929 24th St., San Francisco, CA 94110. TEL 415-282-2994) Ed. Lei Qiquan. adv. contact: Fu Xianqing. **Document type:** academic/scholarly publication.

332   CC   ISSN 1000-176X
HB9
CAIJING WENTI YANJIU/RESEARCH ON FINANCIAL AND ECONOMIC PROBLEMS. (Text in Chinese) 1979. m. Y66. Dongbei Caijing Daxue - Northeast University of Finance and Economics, Dalian, Liaoning 116025, People's Republic of China. TEL 467-1101. Ed. Jian He. R&P contact: Jian He. **Document type:** academic/scholarly publication.

332   US
CAIJING YANJIU/STUDY OF FINANCE & ECONOMICS. (Text in Chinese) m. $36.80. China Books & Periodicals, Inc., 2929 24th St., San Francisco, CA 94110. TEL 415-282-2994. FAX 415-282-0994.

BUSINESS AND ECONOMICS — BANKING AND FINANCE

332   **CC**   **ISSN 1004-0994**
CAIKUAI YUEKAN/MONTHLY OF FINANCE AND ACCOUNTING. (Text in Chinese) 1980. m. Y48 (effective 1997). Wuhan Shi Caizheng Ju - Wuhan Finance Bureau, No. 19, Wansongyuan Rd., Wuhan, Hubei 430022, People's Republic of China. TEL 86-27-5792958. FAX 86-27-5792844. Ed. Xingbang Liu. adv. B&W page Y2000, color page Y4000; adv. contact: Xingbang Liu. bk.rev. circ. 190,000. **Document type:** trade publication.
    Formerly (until 1991): Hubei Caikua.
    Description: Covers finance and accounting, tax and auditing, as well as economic and financial policies.

332 382   **CC**
CAIMAO JINGJI/FINANCE AND TRADE ECONOMICS. (Text in Chinese; table of contents in English) m. Y18($48.60) (Zhongguo Shehui Kexueyuan, Caimao Wuzi Jingji Yanjiusuo - Chinese Academy of Social Sciences, Finance Economics Institute) Caimao Jingji Zazhishe, 2, Yuetan Beixiaojie, Fuwai, Beijing 100836, People's Republic of China. TEL 8312198. (Dist. outside China by: China International Book Trading Corp., P.O. Box 399, Beijing, P.R.C.; Dist. in US by: China Books & Periodicals, Inc., 2929 24th St., San Francisco, CA 94110) Ed. Zhang Zhuoyuan. adv.

332 640.73   **CN**   **ISSN 0225-4700**
MA CAISSE; revue d'information des caisses populaires et des caisses d'economie Desjardins. 1963. bi-m. (plus special issue). Can.$6.50. Confederation des Caisses Populaires et d'Economie Desjardins du Quebec, Direction Information et Affaires Publiques, 100 ave. des Commandeurs, Levis, PQ G6V 7N5, Canada. TEL 800-463-4810. FAX 418-833-5873. Ed. Pierre Goulet. adv. circ. 130,000. (back issues avail.) **Indexed:** Periodex, RADAR.

332   **CC**   **ISSN 0496-3318**
CAIZHENG/FINANCE. (Text in Chinese) m. $36.80. Zhongguo Caizheng Zazhishe, C-27 Wanshou Lu, Beijing 100036, People's Republic of China. TEL 813952. (Dist. in US by: China Books & Periodicals, Inc., 2929 24th St., San Francisco, CA 94110. TEL 415-282-2994) Qian Duling.

332   **CC**   **ISSN 1003-2878**
CAIZHENG YANJIU/PUBLIC FINANCE RESEARCH. (Text in Chinese) 1980. m. Caizheng-bu, Caizheng Kexue Yanjiusuo - Ministry of Finance, Financial Science Institute, Sanlihe, Beijing 100820, People's Republic of China. TEL 86-10-6818-1225. FAX 86-10-6818-9001. E-mail: ckswcs@public3.bta.net.cn. Ed. Kang Jia. adv. contact: Kang Jia. **Document type:** academic/scholarly publication.

332   **US**
CALLAHAN'S CREDIT UNION REPORT. 1985. m. $149. 1001 Connecticut Ave., N.W., Ste. 1022, Washington, DC 20036. TEL 202-223-3920. FAX 202-223-1311. E-mail: callahan@creditnnions.com; URL: http://www.creditunions.com/callahan. Ed. Brooke Stoddard. adv. contact: Jeremy D. Birch. circ. 1,000. **Document type:** newsletter.

CAMPO; boletin de informacion agraria. see *AGRICULTURE*

CANADA. DEPARTMENT OF INSURANCE. REPORT. CO-OPERATIVE CREDIT ASSOCIATIONS. see *INSURANCE*

CANADA. DEPARTMENT OF INSURANCE. REPORT. SMALL LOANS COMPANIES AND MONEY-LENDERS. see *INSURANCE*

CANADA. DEPARTMENT OF INSURANCE. REPORT. TRUST AND LOAN COMPANIES. see *INSURANCE*

332   **CN**
CANADA. TREASURY BOARD. ACCESS REGISTER. (Editions in English, French) a. Can.$10. (Treasury Board) Supply and Services Canada, Ottawa, ON K1A 0S9, Canada. TEL 613-997-2560.
    Supersedes in part: Canada. Treasury Board. Index of Federal Information Banks.

332   **CN**
CANADA. TREASURY BOARD. INDEX TO PERSONAL INFORMATION. (Editions in English, French) a. Can.$10. (Treasury Board) Supply and Services Canada, Ottawa, ON K1A 0S9, Canada. TEL 613-997-2560. **Document type:** government publication.
    Supersedes in part: Canada. Treasury Board. Index of Federal Information Banks.

332.1   **CN**   **ISSN 0822-6830**
HG1507
CANADIAN BANKER. French edition: Banquier (ISSN 0822-6849) 1893. bi-m. Can.$35 (foreign $28) (effective 1998). Canadian Bankers Association, P.O. Box 348, Commerce Ct. W., Ste. 3000, 199 Bay St., Toronto, ON M5L 1G2, Canada. TEL 416-362-6092. FAX 416-362-5658. Ed. Simon Hally. R&P contact: Karen Bentley. adv. contact: Karen Bentley. bk.rev.; illus.; index. circ. 34,000. (also avail. in microform from UMI; reprint service avail. from UMI) **Indexed:** ABI Inform., B.P.I., Bank.Lit.Ind., BPIA, Bus.Ind., Can.B.P.I., Can.Per.Ind., Ind.Can.L.P.L., Manage.Cont., P.A.I.S., Tr.& Indus.Ind., World Bank.Abstr. **Document type:** trade publication.
    ●Also available online. **Vendor(s):** Information Access Co., UMI.
    —BLDSC (3017.610000); KR SourceOne; UMI; UnCover.
    Formerly: Canadian Banker and I C B Review (ISSN 0315-6230); Which was formed by the merger of: Canadian Banker (ISSN 0008-297X); I C B Review (Institute of Canadian Bankers) (ISSN 0046-9769)
    Description: Provides a forum for the presentation of authoritative and stimulating information about banking and other subjects pertinent to the industry.

332.1   **CN**   **ISSN 0068-8347**
CANADIAN BANKRUPTCY REPORTS. (3RD SERIES). 1921; N.S. 1960. 7 vols./yr. Can.$118 per vol. Carswell, One Corporate Plaza, 2075 Kennedy Rd., Scarborough, ON M1T 3V4, Canada. TEL 416-609-8000. FAX 416-298-5094. Ed.Bd. adv. contact: M. Lalani. cum.index. **Indexed:** C.L.I., Ind.Can.L.P.L., L.R.I.
    —CCC.
    Description: Includes all important bankruptcy decisions across Canada, as well as extensive notes, commentaries and annotations.

332.1   **CN**
CANADIAN PAYMENTS DIRECTORIES. (In three volumes: Volume 1: Banks; Volume 2: Credit Unions and Caisses Populaires; Volume 3: Trust Companies, Loan Companies and Other Deposit-Taking Financial Institutions.) 1981. a. Can.$105.60 (U.S. Can.$127.94, elsewhere Can.$146.39). (Canadian Payments Association) Bowne of Canada, Ltd., 60 Gervais Drive, Toronto, Ont. M3C 1Z3, Canada. TEL 416-449-6400. FAX 416-449-7114. circ. 9,000. **Document type:** directory.
    Formerly: Bank Directory of Canada (ISSN 0045-1436)

332   **CN**   **ISSN 0845-7328**
CANADIAN TREASURER. 1985. 6/yr. Can.$37.50. Treasury Management Association of Canada, 8 King St. E., Ste. 1010, Toronto, ON M5C 1B5, Canada. FAX 416-367-3240. E-mail: mcdouga@ecf.toronto.edu; URL: http://www.tmac.ca. Ed. Bruce McDougall. R&P contact: Bruce McDougall. adv. contact: Ted Gittings. bk.rev. circ. 4,500. **Indexed:** Can.B.P.I. **Document type:** trade publication.
    Former titles: T M A C Journal (ISSN 1041-9020); (until 1988): Cash Management Association of Canada. Journal (ISSN 0888-6474)

332   **CN**   **ISSN 0829-4003**
CANADIAN TREASURY MANAGEMENT REVIEW. (French edition: Revue Canadienne de Gestion de Tresorerie (ISSN 0829-4011) ceased 1990) 1980. bi-m. Can.$75. Royal Bank of Canada, S. Tower, 9th Fl., Royal Bank Plaza, Toronto, ON M5J 2J5, Canada. TEL 416-974-2274. FAX 416-974-0365. Ed. Colleen Killeavy. circ. 4,000. (also avail. in microform from UMI)
    ●Also available online. **Vendor(s):** UMI.
    —UMI.
    Description: Provides news about cash and treasury management for corporate treasurers.

332.1   **US**
CAPACITY UTILIZATION TAPE. m. $200 per no. in U.S., Canada, Mexico; elsewhere $400. (Federal Reserve System) U.S. National Technical Information Service, 5825 Port Royal Rd., Springfield, VA 22161. TEL 703-487-4630. (magnetic tape; also avail. in microfiche from CIS; reprint service avail. from CIS) **Indexed:** Amer.Stat.Ind. (1976-).
    Description: Discusses manufacturing, mining, and utilities industries. Rates are derived by dividing the capacity indices into the associated production indices.

332   **II**
CAPITAL MARKET.* (Text in English) 1986. fortn. newsstand price: Rs.14. Investwel Publishers Pvt. Ltd., c/o S. Anatharaman, Pub. & Ed., 401 Swastic Chambers, Sion-Trombay Rd., Chembur, Bombay 400 071, India. TEL 2043430. TELEX 011-6890 FICS IN. adv.: B&W page Rs.17500, color page Rs.42000; adv. contact: Ruby Anand.

332   **UK**
CAPITAL MARKET STRATEGIES. 1987. q. £295($443) l F R Publishing (Subsidiary of: Thomson Financial Services Ltd.), 11 New Fetter Ln., London EC4A 1JN, England. TEL 0171-815-3800. FAX 0171-315-3850. Ed. Julie Davis; Pub. Anne O'Brien. **Indexed:** ELLIS. **Document type:** trade publication.
    Formerly (until Jul. 1994): Journal of International Securities Markets (ISSN 0952-7486)
    Description: Discusses finance and investment strategies.

332.1021   **PO**   **ISSN 0871-8709**
CARACTERIZACAO DAS EMPRESAS PORTUGUESAS. 1991. a. Instituto Nacional de Estatistica, Ave. Antonio Jose de Almeida, 1078 Lisbon, Portugal. TEL 351-1-8470050. FAX 351-1-8477863. TELEX 351-63738 PCDINE P. **Document type:** trade publication.
    Description: Describes the Portuguese business sector and provides a companies classification by district, type of business and activities.

332   **US**
CARD FAX. 1990. w. $695. Faulkner & Gray, Inc. (New York), 11 Penn Plaza, 17th Fl., New York, NY 10001. TEL 212-967-7000. FAX 212-967-7155. Ed. Peter Lucas. (also avail. by fax) **Document type:** trade publication.
    ●Also available online. **Vendor(s):** Information Access Co., NewsNet (FI67).
    Description: Contains critical news, deals, trade talk, and competitive developments.

332.7   **US**   **ISSN 1051-6778**
HG3756.U54
CARD INDUSTRY DIRECTORY. 1989. a. $395. Faulkner & Gray, Inc. (New York), 11 Penn Plaza, 17th Fl., New York, NY 10001. TEL 212-967-7000. FAX 212-967-7155. Ed. Kathy Morrall. **Document type:** directory.
    Description: Contains revised rankings of the top 250 credit cards and the top 300 debit card issuers.

332.1   **US**   **ISSN 0894-0797**
CARD NEWS. bi-w. $695 (foreign $730) (effective 1997). Phillips Business Information, Inc., 1201 Seven Locks Rd., Potomac, MD 20854. TEL 301-424-3338. FAX 301-309-3847. E-mail: pbi@phillips.com. Ed. Lurdes da Maia-Abruscato. **Document type:** newsletter.
    ●Also available online. **Vendor(s):** Data-Star, Information Access Co., Knight-Ridder Information, Inc., NewsNet (FI24).
    —CCC.
    Incorporates (in 1992): Credit Card Insider.
    Description: Provides information on developments affecting credit card issuers and manufacturers of equipment for credit card transactions and management.

332.7   **UK**   **ISSN 0954-8564**
CARD WORLD INDEPENDENT; international journal for the plastic card, financial and retail services industries. 1988. m. £395($665) C & M Publications Ltd., P.O. Box 28, Corby, Northants NN17 5LY, England. TEL 44-1536-403648. FAX 44-1536-406888. Ed. Annich McIntosh. circ. 5,000. (tabloid format; back issues avail.) **Document type:** newsletter.

332.7　　　　　　UK　ISSN 0967-8026
CARD WORLD USER GUIDE. 1990. a. £25. C & M Publications Ltd., P.O. Box 28, Corby, Northants NN17 5LY, England. TEL 44-1536-403648. FAX 44-1536-406888. Ed. Annich McIntosh. adv.: color page £3350; adv. contact: Jane Davidson. circ. 10,000. (back issues avail.) **Document type:** directory.
Description: Review of the plastic card, financial, and retail services industries.

332.1　　　　　　UK　ISSN 0966-6656
CARDIFF BUSINESS SCHOOL. DISCUSSION PAPER SERIES IN FINANCIAL AND BANKING ECONOMICS. 1992. q. Cardiff Business School, University of Wales, Aberconway Bldg., Colum Dr., Cardiff CF1 3EU, Wales. TEL 44-1222-874417. FAX 44-1222-874419. Ed. Victor Murinde. **Document type:** monographic series.
—BLDSC (3597.983300).
Description: Publishes research papers, short articles, notes, and commentary on financial economics and banking and monetary economics, with emphasis on practical aspects and applied topics.
Refereed Serial

332 640.73　　　　　US
CARDSEARCH. 1989. a. $50. Cardtrak of America, Box 1700, Frederick, MD 21702. TEL 301-695-4660. FAX 301-695-0160. Ed. Robert B. McKinley. circ. 100,000.
Former titles: R A M Research Cardsearch (ISSN 1040-6662); (until 1990): R A M Research Consumer Credit Card Yearbook.
Description: Guide to cards available to U.S. consumers. Provides comprehensive data on over 400 bank credit card issuers, including roundup of industry developments directly affecting consumers.

332 640.73　　　　　US
CARDTRAK. 1991. m. $59. Cardtrak of America, Box 1700, Frederick, MD 21702. TEL 301-695-4660. FAX 301-695-0160. circ. 500,000. **Document type:** newsletter, consumer publication.
Formerly: R A M Research Cardtrak (ISSN 1053-9719)
Description: Covers developments affecting credit card users.

332　　　　　　　BB　ISSN 0257-6120
CARIBBEAN DEVELOPMENT BANK. ANNUAL REPORT. a. Caribbean Development Bank, P.O. Box 408, Wildey, St. Michael, Barbados, W.I. TEL 246-431-1600. FAX 246-426-7269. TELEX WB 2287. E-mail: william@caribank.com. Ed. Hubert S. Williams. charts; stat. circ. 2,750. (also avail. in microfiche from CIS; reprint service avail.) **Indexed:** IIS. **Document type:** corporate report.
Description: Provides a detailed summary of economic developments, policies, and financial statements for the preceding year.

332.1　　　　　　BB
CARIBBEAN DEVELOPMENT BANK. BOARD OF GOVERNORS. ANNUAL MEETING OF THE BOARD OF GOVERNORS: SUMMARY OF PROCEEDINGS. (Text in English) 1971. a. Caribbean Development Bank, Board of Governors, P.O. Box 408, Wildey, St. Michael, Barbados, W.I. TEL 246-431-1600. FAX 246-426-7269. TELEX WB 2287. Ed. Hubert S. Williams. circ. 300. (reprint service avail.) **Document type:** proceedings.

CARRIER REPORTS. see *TRANSPORTATION — Abstracting, Bibliographies, Statistics*

332　　　　　　　SZ
CASH; die Wirtschaftszeitung der Schweiz. (Text in German) 1989. w. 155 SFr. Ringier AG, Hehlstr. 192, CH-8040 Zurich, Switzerland. TEL 01-2982888. FAX 01-2982899. bibl.; charts; illus.; stat. circ. 45,000. (tabloid format; back issues avail.) **Document type:** newspaper.
Description: Reports on economic and financial subjects.

332　　　　　　　BB　ISSN 0255-8440
HG185.B35
CENTRAL BANK OF BARBADOS. ANNUAL STATISTICAL DIGEST. 1975. a. free. Central Bank of Barbados, Research Department, P.O. Box 1016, Spry St., Bridgetown, Barbados, W.I. TEL 246-436-6870. FAX 246-427-1431. TELEX 2251 CENBANK. E-mail: cbb.libr@caribsurf.com. Ed.Bd. R&P contact: Neville Pollard. adv. contact: Neville Pollard. charts; stat. circ. 1,200. **Document type:** bulletin, corporate report.

332　　　　　　　BB　ISSN 0378-178X
HC157.B35
CENTRAL BANK OF BARBADOS. ECONOMIC AND FINANCIAL STATISTICS. 1973. m. free. Central Bank of Barbados, Research Department, P.O. Box 1016, Spry St., Bridgetown, Barbados, W.I. TEL 246-436-6870. FAX 246-427-1431. TELEX 2251 CENBANK. E-mail: cbb.libr@caribsurf.com. Ed.Bd. R&P contact: Neville Pollard. circ. 500. **Document type:** bulletin, corporate report.

332　　　　　　　BB　ISSN 0255-7460
HC157.B35
CENTRAL BANK OF BARBADOS. ECONOMIC REVIEW. 1975. 3/yr. free. Central Bank of Barbados, Research Department, P.O. Box 1016, Spry St., Bridgetown, Barbados, W.I. TEL 246-436-6870. FAX 246-427-1431. TELEX 2251 CENBANK. E-mail: cvv.libr@caribsurf.com. Ed.Bd. R&P contact: Neville Pollard. adv. contact: Neville Pollard. bk.rev.; bibl.; charts; stat. circ. 600. **Indexed:** Key to Econ.Sci., World Bank.Abstr. **Document type:** bulletin, corporate report.
Formerly: Central Bank of Barbados. Quarterly Report.

332.1　　　　　　CH　ISSN 0069-150X
CENTRAL BANK OF CHINA. ANNUAL REPORT. (Editions in Chinese and English) 1962. a. $5. Central Bank of China, 2 Roosevelt Rd., Sec. 1, Taipei, Taiwan 107, Republic of China. FAX 02-397-3768. circ. 3,500 (Chinese edition); 2,000 (English edition). **Document type:** corporate report.

332.1　　　　　　CH
CENTRAL BANK OF CHINA. QUARTERLY. (Text in Chinese) 1979. q. $20. Central Bank of China - Chung Yang Yin Hang, 2 Roosevelt Rd., Sec. 1, Taipei, Taiwan 107, Republic of China. FAX 02-397-3768. circ. 2,500.

332.1　　　　　　CY　ISSN 0069-1518
HG3257.A7
CENTRAL BANK OF CYPRUS. ANNUAL REPORT. (Text in English) 1965. a. free. Central Bank of Cyprus, P.O. Box 5529, Nicosia, Cyprus. circ. 940. **Document type:** corporate report.

332.1　　　　　　CY　ISSN 0008-9230
HG3361.C93
CENTRAL BANK OF CYPRUS. BULLETIN. 1964. q. free. Central Bank of Cyprus, P.O. Box 5529, Nicosia, Cyprus. **Indexed:** Key to Econ.Sci., World Bank.Abstr. **Document type:** bulletin.

332.1　　　　　　UA　ISSN 0258-8706
CENTRAL BANK OF EGYPT. ANNUAL REPORT. (Editions in Arabic, English) 1961. a. free. Central Bank of Egypt, Research Department, 31 Sharia Kasr-el Nil, Cairo, Egypt. Eds. Mohamed Saad Badr, Mahasen Abdel Rehim. circ. 2,500. **Document type:** corporate report.
—BLDSC (1141.240000).
Former titles: Central Bank of Egypt. Report of the Board of Directors for the Year (ISSN 1012-5604); Central Bank of Egypt. Board of Directors. Report (ISSN 0069-1526).

332 330.9　　　　　IQ　ISSN 0008-9257
CENTRAL BANK OF IRAQ. QUARTERLY BULLETIN. (Text in Arabic and English) 1952. q. and monthly statement of accounts. free. Central Bank of Iraq, Statistics and Research Department, Box 64, Baghdad, Iraq. charts; stat. circ. 2,000. **Document type:** bulletin.

332　　　　　　　IQ　ISSN 0069-1534
CENTRAL BANK OF IRAQ, BAGHDAD. REPORT. (Text in Arabic and English) 1951. a. free. Central Bank of Iraq, Statistics and Research Department, P.O. Box 64, Baghdad, Iraq. circ. 2,000.

332.1　　　　　　IE　ISSN 0069-1542
CENTRAL BANK OF IRELAND. ANNUAL REPORT. (Includes Summer Quarterly Bulletin) 1943. a. free. Central Bank of Ireland, P.O. Box 559, Dame St., Dublin 2, Ireland. TEL 353-1-6716666. FAX 353-1-6716561. circ. 4,500. **Document type:** corporate report.
—BLDSC (2435.155000).
Description: Review of Irish economy, monetary developments in Ireland and international developments. Articles on current financial and economic topics. Statistical appendix.

332　　　　　　　IE
CENTRAL BANK OF IRELAND. BULLETIN. 1943. q. Central Bank of Ireland, P.O. Box 559, Dame St., Dublin 2, Ireland. TEL 353-1-6716666. FAX 353-1-6716561. stat. circ. 4,000. **Indexed:** C.R.E.J., Cont.Pg.Manage., ELLIS, Key to Econ.Sci., P.A.I.S., World Bank.Abstr. **Document type:** bulletin.
Former titles: Central Bank of Ireland. Quarterly Bulletin (ISSN 0332-2645); (until 1962): Central Bank of Ireland. Quarterly Statistical Bulletin (ISSN 0332-2599); (until 1943): Currency Commission. Quarterly Statistical Bulletin (ISSN 0332-2823)
Description: Review of Irish economy, monetary developments in Ireland, international developments and articles on current financial and economic topics. Statistical appendix.

CENTRAL BANK OF IRELAND. IRISH ECONOMIC STATISTICS. see *BUSINESS AND ECONOMICS — Abstracting, Bibliographies, Statistics*

332　　　　　　　IE　ISSN 0791-1785
CENTRAL BANK OF IRELAND. MONTHLY STATISTICS. 1965. m. free. Central Bank of Ireland, P.O. Box 559, Dame St., Dublin 2, Ireland. TEL 353-1-6716666. FAX 353-1-6716561. stat. circ. 850. **Document type:** bulletin.
Former titles (until Mar. 1989): Central Bank of Ireland. Statistical Supplement (ISSN 0790-3979); (until 1983): Central Bank of Ireland. Statistical Supplement to the Quarterly Bulletin (ISSN 0332-2742); (Until 1968): Central Bank of Ireland. Statistical Tables of the Quarterly Bulletin (ISSN 0332-2793)

332　　　　　　　JO　ISSN 0069-1550
CENTRAL BANK OF JORDAN. ANNUAL REPORT/BANK AL-MARKAZI AL-URDUNI. ANNUAL REPORT. a. Central Bank of Jordan, Department of Research and Studies, Box 37, Amman, Jordan. charts; stat.
Description: Details monetary and economic developments, public finance, external trade and balance of payments.

332.1　　　　　　KE
CENTRAL BANK OF KENYA. ANNUAL ECONOMIC REPORT. 1966. a. Central Bank of Kenya, P.O. Box 60000, Nairobi, Kenya. **Document type:** corporate report.
Formerly: Central Bank of Kenya. Annual Report (ISSN 0069-1569)

332　　　　　　　KU
CENTRAL BANK OF KUWAIT. ANNUAL REPORT. (Editions in Arabic, English) 1970. a. free. Central Bank of Kuwait, Economic Research Department, P.O. Box 526, Safat 13006, Kuwait. TEL 965-2403257. FAX 965-2440887. E-mail: cbk@cbk.gov.kw; URL: http://www.cbk.gov.kw. circ. 2,000. **Document type:** corporate report.

CENTRAL BANK OF KUWAIT. QUARTERLY STATISTICAL BULLETIN/BANK AL-KUWAYT AL-MARKAZI. AL-NASHRAH AL-IHSA'IYYAH AL-FASLIYYAH. see *BUSINESS AND ECONOMICS — Abstracting, Bibliographies, Statistics*

332　　　　　　　MM　ISSN 0577-0653
CENTRAL BANK OF MALTA. ANNUAL REPORT. 1968. a. free. Central Bank of Malta, Economics and Research Department, Castille Square, Valletta CMR 01, Malta. circ. 2,000. **Document type:** corporate report.

332　　　　　　　MM　ISSN 0008-9273
HG3090.5.A7
CENTRAL BANK OF MALTA. QUARTERLY REVIEW. 1968. q. free. Central Bank of Malta, Economics and Research Department, Castille Square, Valletta CMR 01, Malta. charts; stat. circ. 2,000. **Indexed:** Key to Econ.Sci., P.A.I.S., World Bank.Abstr.
—BLDSC (7203.545000).

BUSINESS AND ECONOMICS — BANKING AND FINANCE

332.1   NR   ISSN 0069-1577
CENTRAL BANK OF NIGERIA. ANNUAL REPORT AND STATEMENT OF ACCOUNTS. 1960. a. Central Bank of Nigeria, P.M.B. 12194, Tinubu Sq., Lagos, Nigeria. circ. 4,000. **Document type:** corporate report.
—BLDSC (1505.500000).

332   NR   ISSN 0008-929X
CENTRAL BANK OF NIGERIA. MONTHLY REPORT. m. Central Bank of Nigeria, P.M.B. 12194, Tinubu Sq., Lagos, Nigeria. Ed.Bd. charts; stat. circ. 2,000. (processed) **Indexed:** World Bank.Abstr.

332.1   CE
CENTRAL BANK OF SRI LANKA. ANNUAL REPORT. (Text in English, Sinhalese, Tamil) 1950. a. $15. Central Bank of Sri Lanka, Janadhipathi Mawatha, P.O. Box 590, Colombo 1, Sri Lanka. TEL 94-1-421191. FAX 94-1-445127. **Document type:** corporate report.
Formerly (until 1972): Central Bank of Ceylon. Annual Report (ISSN 0069-1496)

332   CE
CENTRAL BANK OF SRI LANKA. NEWS SURVEY. (Text in English) m. $30 (foreign $50). Central Bank of Sri Lanka, Janadhipathi Mawatha, P.O. Box 590, Colombo 1, Sri Lanka. TEL 94-1-421191. FAX 94-1-445127.

332   CE
CENTRAL BANK OF SRI LANKA. OCCASIONAL PAPERS. (Text in English) irreg., latest no. 24. $2. Central Bank of Sri Lanka, Janadhipathi Mawatha, P.O. Box 590, Colombo 1, Sri Lanka. TEL 94-1-421191. FAX 94-1-445127.

332   CE
CENTRAL BANK OF SRI LANKA. SURVEY REPORTS. (Text in English) irreg. price varies. Central Bank of Sri Lanka, Janadhipathi Mawatha, P.O. Box 590, Colombo 1, Sri Lanka. TEL 94-1-421191. FAX 94-1-445127.

332.1   SQ
CENTRAL BANK OF SWAZILAND. ANNUAL REPORT. 1974. a. Central Bank of Swaziland, Research Department, P.O. Box 546, Mbabane, Swaziland. illus. circ. 400. **Document type:** corporate report.
Description: Presents a copy of financial accounts for the year, reports of operations and affairs, general review of the economy.

332   SQ   ISSN 0378-1593
HG3405.A7
CENTRAL BANK OF SWAZILAND. QUARTERLY REVIEW. 1975. q. free. Central Bank of Swaziland, Research Department, P.O. Box 546, Mbabane, Swaziland. FAX 45417. TELEX 2029 WD. charts; stat. circ. 500.
Description: Information on the Central Bank's monetary position.

CENTRAL BANK OF SYRIA. QUARTERLY BULLETIN. see BUSINESS AND ECONOMICS — Economic Situation And Conditions

354   BF
CENTRAL BANK OF THE BAHAMAS. ANNUAL REPORT AND STATEMENT OF ACCOUNTS. 1974. a. free. Central Bank of the Bahamas, Research Department, P.O. Box N4868, Nassau, Bahamas. FAX 809-322-4321. TELEX 20-115. Ed. Wendy Craigg. illus.; stat. circ. 1,400. (back issues avail.) **Document type:** directory.

332   BF
CENTRAL BANK OF THE BAHAMAS. ECONOMIC REVIEW. 1974. q. free. Central Bank of the Bahamas, Research Department, P.O. Box N4868, Nassau, Bahamas. FAX 809-322-4321. TELEX CENTRALBANK 20115. Ed.Bd. charts; stat. circ. 1,300. (back issues avail.) **Indexed:** Key to Econ.Sci., World Bank.Abstr.
Supersedes (in 1992): Central Bank of the Bahamas. Quarterly Review.

CENTRAL BANK OF THE BAHAMAS. QUARTERLY STATISTICAL DIGEST. see BUSINESS AND ECONOMICS — Abstracting, Bibliographies, Statistics

332.1   GM   ISSN 0796-1049
CENTRAL BANK OF THE GAMBIA. ANNUAL REPORT. 1971. a. free. Central Bank of the Gambia, Economic Research Department, 1-2 Buckle St., Banjul, Gambia. TEL 228103. FAX 226969. TELEX 2218 GAMBANK GV. Ed. Buah Saidy. circ. 200. **Document type:** bulletin.

332   TU   ISSN 1013-6193
CENTRAL BANK OF THE REPUBLIC OF TURKEY. ANNUAL REPORT. Key Title: Annual Report - Central Bank of the Republic of Turkey. (Text in English) 1931. a. Central Bank of the Republic of Turkey - Turkiye Cumhuriyet Merkez Bankasi, General Directorate of Planning and Research, Directorate of Documentation, Ankara, Turkey. FAX 90-312-3116685. stat. circ. 2,000. **Document type:** government publication, corporate report.
Description: Covers the results of the Central Bank's accounting year. Contains a detailed study of those international economic developments which relate to similar economic developments at home.

332   TU
CENTRAL BANK OF THE REPUBLIC OF TURKEY. MONTHLY STATISTICAL AND EVALUATION BULLETIN. 1986. m. free. Central Bank of the Republic of Turkey, General Directorate of Planning and Research, Directorate of Documentation, Ankara, Turkey. FAX 324-23-03. circ. 2,000. **Document type:** bulletin.
Description: Publishes the data used by the research staff of the Central Bank.

332   TR   ISSN 1011-6311
HC157.A1
CENTRAL BANK OF TRINIDAD AND TOBAGO. ANNUAL ECONOMIC SURVEY. 1986. a. $12 (effective 1996). Central Bank of Trinidad and Tobago, Eric Williams Plaza, Independence Sq., P.O. Box 1250, Port-of-Spain, Trinidad & Tobago, W.I. TEL 868-625-4835. FAX 868-627-4696. TELEX 386-270. **Document type:** bulletin, corporate report.
—UMI.

332.1   TR   ISSN 0069-1593
HC157.T8
CENTRAL BANK OF TRINIDAD AND TOBAGO. ANNUAL REPORT. 1965. a. free. Central Bank of Trinidad and Tobago, Eric Williams Plaza, Independence Sq., P.O. Box 1250, Port-of-Spain, Trinidad & Tobago, W.I. TEL 868-625-4835. FAX 868-627-4696. TELEX 386-270. circ. 1,000. **Document type:** bulletin, corporate report.

332   YE   ISSN 0301-6625
CENTRAL BANK OF YEMEN. ANNUAL REPORT. (Text in Arabic and English) 1971/72. a. free. Central Bank of Yemen, Box 59, San'a, Republic of Yemen.

332   UK   ISSN 0960-6319
CENTRAL BANKING; policy markets supervision. 1990. q. £220 (foreign $350) (effective 1997). Central Bankig Publications Ltd., Chancery Lane, London WC2A 1PA, England. TEL 44-171-404-6435. FAX 44-171-404-6436. E-mail: centralbank@easynet.co.uk; URL: http://www.easyweb.easynet.co.uk/centralbank/. (Dist. in N. America by: European Business Publications Inc., Box 891, Darien, CT 06820-9859. TEL 203-656-2701. FAX 203-655-8332) Ed. Robert Pringle. **Document type:** trade publication.
—BLDSC (3105.982000).
Description: Offers a wide variety of features and topical reports on central banking policies and their impact on banking and money markets.

332.1   UK   ISSN 0962-2543
HF3500.7
CENTRAL EUROPEAN. 1991. 10/yr. £240 (foreign $435) (effective 1997). Euromoney Publications plc., Nestor House, Playhouse Yard, London EC4V 5EX, England. TEL 44-171-779-8535. FAX 44-171-779-8541. (Dist. in US by: American Educational Systems, 173 W. 81st St., New York, NY 10024. TEL 800-717-2669. FAX 212-501-8926) Ed. Helena Frith Powell. adv.: B&W page £4950; trim 297 x 210; adv. contact: Paul Gallerani. bk.rev. circ. 10,000. (back issues avail.) **Indexed:** B.P.I. **Document type:** trade publication.
●Also available online. Vendor(s): UMI.
—BLDSC (3106.135000); UMI.
Description: Covers the stock and bond markets, as well as other financial news, in Central Europe.

332   BE
CENTRE FOR EUROPEAN POLICY STUDIES. FINANCIAL MARKETS UNIT. RESEARCH REPORT. (Text in English) irreg., no.20, 1996. 1800 BEF per no. Centre for European Policy Studies, Place du Congres 1, B-1000 Brussels, Belgium. TEL 32-2-2293911. FAX 32-2-2194151. (back issues avail.) **Document type:** monographic series.
Refereed Serial

CENTRES, BUREAUX & RESEARCH INSTITUTES; the directory of UK concentrations of effort, information, and expertise. see BUSINESS AND ECONOMICS — Trade And Industrial Directories

332.4   MX   ISSN 0186-7229
HG6
CENTRO DE ESTUDIOS MONETARIOS LATINOAMERICANOS. BOLETIN BIMENSUAL. Variant title: C E M L A Boletin Bimensual. 1955. 7/yr. $70. Centro de Estudios Monetarios Latinoamericanos, A.C., Durango 54, 06700 Mexico D.F., Mexico. TEL 915-533030. FAX 514-6554. TELEX 0177 1229 CEMLME. Ed. Juan Manuel Rodriguez. charts; index. circ. 1,000. **Document type:** bulletin.
Formerly: Centro de Estudios Monetarios Latinoamericanos. Boletin Mensual (ISSN 0008-9958)

332.1   MX   ISSN 0577-2451
CENTRO DE ESTUDIOS MONETARIOS LATINOAMERICANOS. ENSAYOS. 1963. irreg. price varies. Centro de Estudios Monetarios Latinoamericanos, A.C., Durango 54, 06700 Mexico D.F., Mexico. TEL 915-533030O. FAX 514-6554. TELEX 0177-1229 CEMLME. Ed. Juan Manuel Rodriguez. circ. 1,000. **Document type:** monographic series.

332   UK
▼**CHARTERED BANKER.** 1995. m. (Chartered Institute of Bankers) Financial & Business Publications, 4 Cavendish Sq., London W1M 9HA, England. TEL 44-171-637-1115. FAX 44-171-637-1117. Ed. Michael Imeson. adv. contact: Peter Keith. circ. 44,700. **Document type:** trade publication.

332.04   US
CHASE REVIEW. 1982. 4/yr. $125. Chase Manhattan Bank, 1211 Ave. of the Americas, 34th Fl., New York, NY 10036. TEL 212-787-5311. FAX 212-789-5352. Ed. Jonathan Blattmachr. bk.rev. circ. 1,000. (looseleaf format; back issues avail.) **Document type:** newsletter.

CHECKLISTS AND ILLUSTRATIVE FINANCIAL STATEMENTS FOR BANKS. see BUSINESS AND ECONOMICS — Accounting

CHECKLISTS AND ILLUSTRATIVE FINANCIAL STATEMENTS FOR FINANCE COMPANIES. see BUSINESS AND ECONOMICS — Accounting

332   US   ISSN 1046-4956
CHECKS & CHECKING; the insider's report on checks and the checking business. 1990. m. $295 in U.S., Canada, Mexico; elsewhere $335. Faulkner & Gray, Inc., 300 S. Wacker Dr., 18th Fl., Chicago, IL 60606. TEL 212-967-7000. FAX 212-967-7155. Ed. Patricia A. Murphy. (also avail. in microform from UMI) **Document type:** trade publication.
—UMI.

332.1   US   ISSN 1066-3029
HG1704
CHEKLIST. 1989. q. $25. B K B Publications Inc., 98 Greenwich Ave., No. 1 FL, New York, NY 10011-7743. TEL 212-807-0148. FAX 212-807-1821. Ed. Charlene Komar Storey; Pub. Brian K. Burkart. R&P contact: Brian K. Burkart. adv.: B&W page $1450, color page $2390; trim 8 1/2 x 11. circ. 6,000. **Document type:** trade publication.
Description: Helps executives in the check-cashing industry manage their business for continued growth. Includes general news, feature articles, legislative updates, reports on trends, marketing tips, product information and news of state and national association activities.

332   CC
CHENGSHI JINRONG/URBAN FINANCE. (Text in Chinese) m. Hebei Sheng Gongshang Yinhang, 60, Gongnong Xilu, Shijiazhuang, Hebei 050051, People's Republic of China. TEL 34961. Ed. Chang Ruiming.

BUSINESS AND ECONOMICS — BANKING AND FINANCE

332   CC   ISSN 1007-0346
▼**CHENGSHI JINRONG LUNTAN/URBAN FINANCE FORUM.** (Text in Chinese) 1996. Y84 (Hong Kong HK.$120; foreign $72). (Industrial and Commercial Bank of China) Chengshi Jinrong Luntan Bianjibu, 15 Cuiwei Rd., Haidian, Beijing 100036, People's Republic of China. TEL 86-10-8185253. FAX 86-10-8217853. TELEX 22770 LCBHO CN. (Co-sponsors: Urban Finance Research Institute of China; Urban Finance Association of China) Ed. Dazhi Xun; Pub. Jingen Pan. R&P contact: Yi Yian. adv. contact: Jingen Pan. circ. 25,000. **Document type:** academic/scholarly publication.
    Description: Covers all aspects of Chinese urban finance, including theory, research, administration, macroeconomy analysis, financial market, and much more.
    Refereed Serial

332   CH
CHIAO TUNG BANK. ANNUAL REPORT. (Text in English) 1961. a. free. Chiao Tung Bank, 91 Heng Yang Road, Taipei, Taiwan, Republic of China. TEL 886-2-361-3000. FAX 886-2-361-2046. TELEX 11341 CHIAOTUNG. Ed. H.L. Huang. **Document type:** government publication, corporate report.
    Formerly (until Mar. 1992): Bank of Communications. Annual Report.

332.1   US
CHIEF FINANCIAL OFFICER NEWSBRIEF.* m. $127 to non-members; members $97. (American Bankers Association, Chief Financial Officer) American Banker Newsletters, One State Street Plaza, 26th Fl., New York, NY 10004-1505. TEL 212-803-8300; 800-407-8241. FAX 212-843-9620.
    Description: Provides current summaries of regulatory, legislative, accounting issues which affect the Chief Financial Officer.

CHILE. INSTITUTO NACIONAL DE ESTADISTICAS. FINANZAS. see BUSINESS AND ECONOMICS — Abstracting, Bibliographies, Statistics

CHILE MARKETING AND FINANCIAL STATISTICS. see BUSINESS AND ECONOMICS — Abstracting, Bibliographies, Statistics

332 340   CC   ISSN 1012-6732
CHINA BANKING & FINANCE. (Text in English) 1988. 10/yr. HK.$3450 (foreign $465) (effective 1996). Asia Law & Practice Ltd., 2-F, 29 Hollywood Rd., Central, Hong Kong, People's Republic of China. TEL 852-544-9918. FAX 852-543-7617. (Dist. in US by: American Educational Systems, 173 W. 81st St., New York, NY 10024. TEL 800-717-2669. FAX 212-501-8926) Ed. Chris Hunter. index. circ. 3,000. (back issues avail.)
    Description: Contains in-depth updates on regulatory developments affecting banking and finance in the People's Republic of China for foreign investors.

332   UK   ISSN 1024-1167
▼**CHINA JOINT VENTURER.** 1995. 10/yr. $440. Euromoney Publications plc., Nestor House, Playhouse Yard, London EC4V 5EX, England. TEL 44-171-779-8935. FAX 44-171-779-8541. (Dist. in US by: American Educational Systems, 173 W. 81st St., New York, NY 10024. TEL 800-717-2669. FAX 212-501-8926) **Document type:** trade publication.

332 658.8 380.1   UK   ISSN 1362-3672
CITYFILE. 1985. 6/yr. £230 (effective 1997). PIMS (UK) Ltd., PIMS House, Mildmay Ave., London N1 4RS, England. TEL 44-171-226-1000. FAX 44-171-354-7053. (Co-publisher: Edinburgh Financial Publishing) **Document type:** directory.
    Former titles (until 1996): Pims Business, Investor and Government Relations Directory (ISSN 0963-6978); Pims Financial Directory (ISSN 0268-2117)
    Description: Provides details on key U.K. based financial media and stockbroking houses and their analysts.

332   US   ISSN 1063-2220
CLARK'S BANK DEPOSITS AND PAYMENTS MONTHLY. 1992. m. $172.25 (overseas $239.45) (effective 1997). Warren, Gorham & Lamont, 395 Hudson St., New York, NY 10014. TEL 212-367-6300. FAX 212-367-6718. (Subscr. to: The Park Square Bldg., 31 St. James Ave., Boston, MA 02116-4112. TEL 800-950-1207) Eds. Barkley Clark, Barbara Brewer Clark. (also avail. in microform from UMI) **Document type:** newsletter.
—UMI. CCC.
    Description: Reports on legal developments affecting bank deposits, collections, and credit cards.

332   US   ISSN 1063-5289
CLARK'S SECURED TRANSACTIONS MONTHLY. 1984. m. $151.50 (overseas $213.45) (effective 1997). Warren, Gorham & Lamont, 395 Hudson St., New York, NY 10014. TEL 212-367-6300. FAX 212-367-6718. (Subscr. to: The Park Square Bldg., 31 St. James Ave., Boston, MA 02116-4112. TEL 800-950-1207) Eds. Barkley Clark, Barbara Brewer Clark. (back issues avail.) **Document type:** newsletter.
—CCC.
    Formerly (until 1992): Secured Lending Alert (ISSN 0895-5492)
    Description: Provides "how-to" guidance on drafting air-tight lending agreements.

332   US   ISSN 1052-4029
COLLECTION AGENCY REPORT. 1990. m. $420. First Detroit Corp., Box 520, Warren, MI 48090-5025. TEL 810-573-0045. FAX 810-573-9219. Ed. Albert W. Scace; Pub. Albert W. Scace. R&P contact: Albert W. Scace. bk.rev.; index. (back issues avail.) **Document type:** newsletter, trade publication.
    Description: News and advisory service for collection agency executives and major credit grantors.
    Refereed Serial

332.7
COLLECTIONS AND CREDIT RISK; the monthly magazine for collections and credit policy professionals. m. $95 US & Canada; elsewhere $125. Faulkner & Gray, Inc (New York), 11 Penn Plaza, 17th Fl., New York, NY 10001-2006. TEL 312-983-6146; 800-535-8403. E-mail: Faulknergray@MSN.com; URL: http://www.Faulknergray.com. Ed. John Stewart.

332.7   US   ISSN 0010-082X
COLLECTOR. 1939. m. $60 to non-members; members $30. American Collectors Association, Inc., Box 39106, 4040 W. 70th St., Minneapolis, MN 55435. TEL 612-926-6547. FAX 612-926-1624. Ed. Timothy Dressen. R&P contact: Timothy Dressen. adv.; bk.rev.; charts; illus.; index. circ. 5,000. **Document type:** trade publication.
    Description: Covers collection techniques, legislation and management issues in the customer debt collection industry.

332   US   ISSN 0099-1848
KF1515.A2
COLLIER BANKRUPTCY CASES. 1979. 5 base vols. (with bi-m. supplements). $710. Matthew Bender & Co., Inc., 2 Park Ave., New York, NY 10016. TEL 212-448-2000. E-mail: international@bender.com; URL: http://www.bender.com. Ed.Bd. (back issues avail.)
—CCC.

332 340   US
COLLIER BANKRUPTCY COMPENSATION GUIDE. (Issued as 1 base vol. with supplements) 1988. irreg. $195. Matthew Bender & Co., Inc., 2 Park Ave., New York, NY 10016. TEL 212-448-2000. FAX 518-462-3788. E-mail: international@bender.com; URL: http://www.bender.com. Ed. Lawrence P. King. (looseleaf format)
    Description: Examines the Bankruptcy Code's provisions, case law, and current practice trends relevant to the compensation of attorneys, trustees and other professionals involved in bankruptcy cases. Contains substantive analysis as well as strategic and practical guidance.

332 340   US
COLLIER BANKRUPTCY MANUAL. (Issued in 3 base vols. with supplements) 1979. irreg. 3rd ed. $460. Matthew Bender & Co., Inc., 2 Park Ave., New York, NY 10016. TEL 212-448-2000. E-mail: international@bender.com; URL: http://www.bender.com. Ed.Bd. (looseleaf format) **Document type:** trade publication.
    Description: Provides substantive analysis necessary for handling a case under the Bankruptcy Code, keyed to the section numbers of the 1978 Code.

332   US   ISSN 1044-0917
KF1544
COLLIER HANDBOOK FOR CREDITORS' COMMITTEES. 1988. base vol. (with a. supplement). $85 for base vol. (supplements $85/yr.). Matthew Bender & Co., Inc., 2 Park Ave., New York, NY 10016. TEL 212-448-2000. E-mail: international@bender.com; URL: http://www.bender.co. Ed. Lawrence P. King.
    Description: Covers the role of Chapter 11 creditors' committees, fiduciary responsibilities and Chapter 11 plan negotiations.

332 340   US
COLLIER LENDING INSTITUTIONS AND THE BANKRUPTCY CODE. (Issued as 1 base vol. with supplements) 1986. irreg. $200. Matthew Bender & Co., Inc., 2 Park Ave., New York, NY 10016. TEL 212-448-2000. E-mail: international@bender.com; URL: http://www.bender.com. Ed.Bd. (looseleaf format)
    Description: Practice-oriented guide to the impact of bankruptcy on lending transactions.

332 340   US
COLLIER ON BANKRUPTCY. (Issued in 16 vols. with 4 updates per year) 1979. irreg. $2360. Matthew Bender & Co., Inc., 2 Park Ave., New York, NY 10016. TEL 212-448-2000. E-mail: international@bender.com; URL: http://www.bender.com. Ed. Lawrence P. King. (looseleaf format; also avail. in microfiche from WSH; microform from WSH)
    Description: Provides detailed discussion, by the leading bankruptcy authorities, of the Bankruptcy Code as amended. Includes coverage of the bankruptcy judges, United States trustees, and Family Farmer Bankruptcy Act of 1986.

332 333.33   US
COLLIER REAL ESTATE TRANSACTIONS AND THE BANKRUPTCY CODE. (Issued as 1 base vol. with supplements) 1984. irreg. $200. Matthew Bender & Co., Inc., 2 Park Ave., New York, NY 10016. TEL 212-448-2000. E-mail: international@bender.com; URL: http://www.bender.com. Ed. Laurence D. Cherkis. (looseleaf format)
    Description: Practice-oriented guide to the impact of bankruptcy on real estate transactions, for both the general practitioner and the real estate specialist.

332   CK
COLOMBIA. SUPERINTENDENCIA BANCARIA. INFORME DE LABORES. 1924. a. free. Superintendencia Bancaria, Apdo. Aereo 3460, Bogota DC, Colombia. TEL 57-1-2804060. FAX 57-1-2800864. circ. 1,400.

332   CK   ISSN 0120-4017
HG2901
COLOMBIA. SUPERINTENDENCIA BANCARIA. REVISTA. 1935. q. free. Superintendencia Bancaria, Apdo. Aereo 3460, Bogota DC, Colombia. TEL 57-1-2804060. FAX 57-1-2800864. circ. 1,600.

332   ET   ISSN 0588-6694
COMMERCIAL BANK OF ETHIOPIA. ANNUAL REPORT. a. free. Commercial Bank of Ethiopia, P.O. Box 255, Addis Ababa, Ethiopia. TEL 251-1-515000. TELEX 21037A. charts; illus.; stat. **Document type:** corporate report.

332   ET   ISSN 0045-7574
COMMERCIAL BANK OF ETHIOPIA. MARKET REPORT. 1964. 6/yr. Commercial Bank of Ethiopia, Market Research Department, P.O. Box 255, Addis Ababa, Ethiopia. Ed. Leikun Berhanu. adv. circ. 1,000.

BUSINESS AND ECONOMICS — BANKING AND FINANCE

332.1   GR
COMMERCIAL BANK OF GREECE. REPORT. a. Commercial Bank of Greece, 11 Sophocleous St., 102 35 Athens, Greece. **Document type:** corporate report.
  Description: Covers the performance, developments and long-term strategic options of the bank.

332.1   GR   ISSN 0424-9402
COMMERCIAL BANK OF GREECE. REPORT OF THE CHAIRMAN OF THE BOARD OF DIRECTORS. (Text in English) a. free. Commercial Bank of Greece, Public Relations Department, 11 Sophocleous St., 102 35 Athens, Greece. illus. stat.; charts. **Document type:** corporate report.

332   KU
COMMERCIAL BANK OF KUWAIT. ANNUAL REPORT. a. free. Commercial Bank of Kuwait S.A.K., Mubarak al-Kabir St., P.O. Box 2861 Safat, 13029 Safat, Kuwait. TEL 965-2411001. FAX 965-2450150. TELEX 22004 CBK KT. **Document type:** corporate report.
  Formerly: Commercial Bank of Kuwait. Annual Report & Accounts (ISSN 0257-4454); Supersedes: Commercial Bank of Kuwait. Annual Report of the Board of Directors and Accounts.

COMMERCIAL LENDING LITIGATIONS NEWS. see LAW — Corporate Law

332.1   US   ISSN 1040-3426
COMMERCIAL LENDING NEWSLETTER. 1969. m. $35. Robert Morris Associates, One Liberty Place, Ste. 2300, 1650 Market St., Philadelphia, PA 19103. TEL 215-851-9100. FAX 215-851-9206. Ed. Kathleen Beans. tr.lit.; index. circ. 21,000. (tabloid format; back issues avail.) **Indexed:** World Bank.Abstr. **Document type:** newsletter.
—UMI. **CCC.**
  Description: Presents articles on commercial lending-related topics, including loan officer productivity, management issues, statistical data and problem loans.

332   US   ISSN 0886-8204
HG1641
COMMERCIAL LENDING REVIEW. 1985. q. $140 (foreign $170) (effective 1996). (American Bankers Association, Commercial Lending) Institutional Investor Journals, 488 Madison Ave., New York, NY 10022. TEL 212-224-3185. FAX 212-224-3527. Ed. Claire M. Greene. adv.: B&W page $1000. bk.rev. **Indexed:** ABI Inform, Account.Ind. (1986-).
—BLDSC (3336.969800); UMI. **CCC.**
  Description: Articles and statistical information on loans for acquisitions and buy-outs for commercial bankers, with regular columns on strategies, accounting practices, and training techniques.

332.1   US
COMMERCIAL LOAN DOCUMENTATION GUIDE. (Issued as 1 base vol. with supplements) 1988. irreg. $120. Matthew Bender & Co., Inc., 2 Park Ave., New York, NY 10016. TEL 212-448-2000. E-mail: international@bender.com; URL: http://www.bender.com.
  Description: Covers the full spectrum of loan documentation; includes forms, checklists and useful hints for both borrowers and lenders.

COMMERSANT WEEKLY. see BUSINESS AND ECONOMICS — Economic Situation And Conditions

332   GW
COMMERZBANK JOURNAL. 1989. q. Commerzbank AG, Neue-Mainzer-Str. 32-36, 60311 Frankfurt a.M., Germany. TEL 49-69-1362-0.
FAX 49-69-13629336. Ed. Ulrich Ramm. adv.: color page DM.22000; trim 272 x 280. bk.rev.; circ. 260,000. (back issues avail.) **Document type:** bulletin.

332.7   US
COMMUNICATOR (WASHINGTON, 1953). 1953. m. membership. Associated Credit Bureaus, Inc., 1090 Vermont Ave., N.W., Ste. 200, Washington, DC 20005-4905. TEL 202-371-0910.
FAX 202-371-0134. Ed. Jennifer M. Mclean. adv.; illus. circ. 3,000. **Document type:** newsletter, trade publication.
  Formerly (until 1973): A C B Management (ISSN 0001-0596)
  Description: Keeps owners and managers of credit bureaus, collection agencies and related services throughout the US, Canada, and Mexico abreast of the latest developments affecting the credit reporting industry.

332   US   ISSN 0276-0908
THE COMMUNITY BANK PRESIDENT. 1980. m. $319 (effective 1997). Siefer Consultants, Inc., Box 1384, Storm Lake, IA 50588. TEL 712-732-7340.
FAX 712-732-7906. Ed. Jow Sheller; Pub. Dan R. Siefer. index. circ. 1,750. (back issues avail.) **Document type:** newsletter.
  Description: Offers profit-making ideas for community banks.

323.3 333.33   US
COMMUNITY ENTERPRISE. q. free. Federal Home Loan Bank of Atlanta, 1475 Peachtree St., Atlanta, GA 30309. TEL 404-888-8000.

COMMUNITY INVESTMENT AND AFFORDABLE HOUSING. see BUSINESS AND ECONOMICS — Investments

332   US   ISSN 1058-5931
COMMUNITY REINVESTMENT ACT BULLETIN. 1991. m. $172.25 (foreign $239.45) (effective 1997). Warren, Gorham & Lamont, 395 Hudson St., New York, NY 10014. TEL 212-367-6300.
FAX 212-367-6718. (Subscr. to: The Park Square Bldg., 31 St. James Ave., Boston, MA 02116-4112. TEL 800-950-1207) Eds. Jerome D. & Nina Groskind. (looseleaf format; back issues avail.) **Document type:** bulletin, newsletter.
—UMI. **CCC.**
  Description: Covers developments related to the Community Reinvestment Act and discusses compliance issues.

COMPANY LAW INSTITUTE OF INDIA. REPORTS OF COMPANY CASES INCLUDING BANKING & INSURANCE. see LAW — Corporate Law

332   UK   ISSN 1356-255X
COMPANY R E F S. 1994. m. and q. versions avail. £675 for m. (Europe £750; elsewhere £795); q. £250 (Europe £275; elsewhere £295) (effective 1997). Hemmington Scott Publishing Ltd., City Innovation Centre, 26-31 Wiskin St., London EC1R OBP, England. TEL 44-171-278-7769.
FAX 44-171-278-9808. (back issues avail.) **Document type:** consumer publication.

COMPLETING THE INTERNAL MARKET OF THE EUROPEAN COMMUNITY: 1992 LEGISLATION - FINANCIAL SERVICES AND CAPITAL MOVEMENTS. see LAW — International Law

332   US
COMPLIANCE ALERT. 1988. 26/yr. $385 (foreign $420) (effective 1997). Bank Administration Institute Foundation, 1 N. Franklin St., Chicago, IL 60606. TEL 312-683-2248; 800-323-8552.
FAX 312-683-2273. **Document type:** newsletter.
  Description: Provides immediate and specific analyses of federal laws and rules complete with impact statements, and exploration of long-term implications.

COMPLIANCE EXAMINATIONS UPDATE. see LAW

332.1 346 657   US
COMPLIANCE OFFICER'S MANAGEMENT MANUAL. (Part of the Compliance and Law series.) s-a. (q. on diskette and CD-ROM). $345 (electronic editions $595). Sheshunoff Information Services Inc., 505 Barton Springs Rd., Ste. 1100, Austin, TX 78704. TEL 512-472-2244; 800-456-2340. (looseleaf format; also avail. in diskette format) **Document type:** trade publication.
●Also available on CD-ROM.
  Description: Enables bank managers to develop, implement, and maintain effective compliance audit and training programs.

332   US
COMPLIANCE REPORTER. bi-w. $1395 (Canada $1425; elsewhere $1470). Institutional Investor Newsletters, 477 Madison Ave., New York, NY 10022. TEL 212-224-3233. FAX 212-224-3353. **Document type:** newsletter.
  Description: Presents information for brokers, dealers and investment advisors.

COMPTROLLER'S HANDBOOK. see BUSINESS AND ECONOMICS — Public Finance, Taxation

332.1   US   ISSN 0084-9154
CONFERENCE ON BANK STRUCTURE AND COMPETITION. PROCEEDINGS. 1964. a. price varies. Federal Reserve Bank of Chicago, Public Information Center, Research Dept., Box 834, Chicago, IL 60690. TEL 312-322-5112. (reprint service avail.) **Document type:** proceedings.

CONSEILLER DES ASSURANCES ET DE LA FINANCE. see INSURANCE

CONSTRUCTION INDUSTRY ANNUAL FINANCIAL SURVEY. see BUILDING AND CONSTRUCTION

381.3   UK
CONSUMER CONCERNS (YEAR). 1990. a. National Consumer Council, 20 Grosvenor Gardens, London SW1W 0DH, England. TEL 44-171-730-3469. FAX 44-171-730-0191. E-mail: admin@nccuk.demon.co.uk. Ed. Liz Dunbar. R&P contact: Liz Dunbar. **Document type:** monographic series.
  Description: Contains a series of market research surveys identifying consumers' current concerns in particular topic areas.

332.7   UK
CONSUMER CREDIT. 1947. bi-m. £30 (overseas £36) (effective 1997). Consumer Credit Trade Association, 1st Fl., Tennyson House, 159-163 Great Portland St., London W1N 5FD, England. TEL 44-171-636-7564. FAX 44-171-323-0096. Ed. P.J. Patrick. R&P contact: P.J. Patrick. adv. contact: P.J. Patrick. bk.rev. circ. 1,300. **Document type:** trade publication.
  Formerly: Hire Trading.
  Description: Covers news of relevance to credit grantors' and consumers' rights, business trends and innovations, and related topics.

CONSUMER CREDIT & TRUTH IN LENDING COMPLIANCE REPORT. see LAW

332.1   US   ISSN 1058-8841
CONSUMER CREDIT DELINQUENCY BULLETIN. m. $200 to non-members; members $135. American Bankers Association, Retail Services Center, 1120 Connecticut Ave., N.W., Washington, DC 20036. TEL 202-663-5493. (also avail. in microform from UMI) **Indexed:** SRI.
—UMI.
  Formerly: Consumer Credit Delinquency Rates.
  Description: For the consumer credit manager; features tables and graphs reporting delinquency rates and repossession ratios.

332 640.73   US
CONSUMER FINANCE BULLETIN. 1947. m. $95. American Financial Services, 919 18th St. N.W., Ste. 300, Washington, DC 20006. TEL 202-296-5544. FAX 202-223-0321. Eds. Robert E. McKew, Christian T. Jones. s-a. index. circ. 500. (looseleaf format)

332   US   ISSN 0364-2844
CONSUMER INSTALLMENT CREDIT. m. $5. U.S. Federal Reserve System, Board of Governors, Publications Services, Rm. MS-138, Washington, DC 20551. TEL 202-452-3244. FAX 202-728-5886. (also avail. in diskette format) **Document type:** government publication.
  Formerly: Consumer Credit (ISSN 0196-5379)

332   US   ISSN 1077-0445
CONSUMER LENDING NEWS. 1993. m. $319 (effective 1997). Siefer Consultants, Inc., Box 1384, Storm Lake, IA 50588. TEL 712-732-7340.
FAX 712-732-7906. Ed. Joe Sheller. index. circ. 1,000. (back issues avail.) **Document type:** newsletter.
  Description: Strategies to improve loan quality, growth and collections.

BUSINESS AND ECONOMICS — BANKING AND FINANCE

332 US
CONSUMER TRENDS; an independent newsletter on credit issues and financial affairs. 1963. m. $100. International Credit Association, Box 419057, St. Louis, MO 63141-1757. TEL 314-991-3030. FAX 314-991-3029. Ed. Janet Lipkind. R&P contact: Janet Lipkind. stat. circ. 7,000. (also avail. in microform from UMI) **Document type:** newsletter.
Description: Forecasts and statistics, system information, outlooks, and legislation pertaining to consumer credit and financial affairs.

CONTEMPORARY STUDIES IN ECONOMIC AND FINANCIAL ANALYSIS; an international series of monographs. see BUSINESS AND ECONOMICS

332 CK
CONVENCION BANCARIA Y DE ENTIDADES FINANCIERAS. MEMORIA. a. free ($8 effective 1991). Asociacion Bancaria de Colombia, Carrera 7, No. 17-01, Piso 3, Bogota D.E., Colombia. TEL 57-1-281-3501. FAX 57-1-281-3017.

332.1 TZ
COOPERATIVE AND RURAL DEVELOPMENT BANK. ANNUAL REPORT AND ACCOUNTS. (Text in English, Swahili) 1972. a. free. Cooperative and Rural Development Bank, P.O. Box 268, Dar es Salaam, Tanzania. TEL 255-51-26511. TELEX 41643 TARDEB TZ. **Document type:** corporate report.
Formerly: Tanzania Rural Development Bank. Annual Report and Accounts.

332.1 KE
CO-OPERATIVE BANK OF KENYA. ANNUAL REPORT & ACCOUNTS. 1969. a. free. (Co-operative Bank of Kenya Ltd.) MS. Autolitho Ltd., P.O. Box 73467, Nairobi, Kenya, Box 48231, Nairobi, Kenya. TEL 254-2-228453. FAX 254-2-336073. TELEX 22938. Ed. L.C. Karissa. R&P contact: L.C. Karissa. circ. 3,000. **Document type:** corporate report.
Formerly: Co-operative Bank of Kenya. Annual Report and Statement of Accounts.

332.1 CH
COOPERATIVE BANK OF TAIWAN. ANNUAL REPORT/TAI-WAN SHENG HO-TSO CHIN-K'U. ANNUAL REPORT.. 1957. a. free. Cooperative Bank of Taiwan, 75-1 Kuan Chien Rd., Taipei, Taiwan, Republic of China. illus.; stat.

CORPORATE ACQUISITIONS & MERGERS. see LAW

CORPORATE BRIEF. see BUSINESS AND ECONOMICS — Economic Situation And Conditions

332 US ISSN 1040-0311
HG4028.C45 CODEN: CCASES
CORPORATE CASHFLOW; the magazine of treasury management. 1980. m. (plus a. Directory). $78 (foreign $138). Intertec Publishing Corp. (Atlanta), 6151 Powers Ferry Rd., N.W., Atlanta, GA 30339-2941. TEL 770-955-2500. FAX 770-955-0400. Ed. Richard H. Gamble. adv. contact: Wayne Cloutier. bk.rev.; s-a. index. circ. 40,627. (also avail. in microform from UMI; back issues avail.; reprint service avail. from UMI) **Indexed:** ABI Inform., BPIA, Bus.Ind., Manage.Cont., P.A.I.S., PROMT, Tr.& Indus.Ind. **Document type:** trade publication.
●Also available online. Vendor(s): Information Access Co., UMI.
—BLDSC (3472.060680); CASDDS; UMI; UnCover. CCC.
Formerly (until 1988): Cashflow (ISSN 0196-6227)
Description: Geared towards treasury finance decision-makers. Covers corporate financing, cash and risk management, credits and accounts receivable, investments and benefits, insurance and international finance.

332 US
CORPORATE CASHFLOW DIRECTORY OF TREASURY SERVICES. 1990. a. $54.95. Intertec Publishing Corp. (Atlanta), 6151 Powers Ferry Rd., N.W., Atlanta, GA 30339-2941. TEL 770-955-2500. FAX 770-955-0400. Ed. Barbara Katinsky. circ. 40,100. **Document type:** directory.

332 US ISSN 0272-0299
CORPORATE E F T REPORT. (Electronic Funds Transfer) 1983. bi-w. $595 (foreign $630) (effective 1997). Phillips Business Information, Inc., 1201 Seven Locks Rd., Potomac, MD 20854. TEL 301-424-3338. FAX 301-424-4297. E-mail: pbi@phillips.com. Ed. Lurdes de Maia-Abruscato. **Document type:** newsletter.
●Also available online. Vendor(s): Information Access Co., Knight-Ridder Information, Inc., Lexis-Nexis, NewsNet (FI12).
—CCC.
Incorporates (in Mar. 1993): Treasury Watch; Which incorporated (in Dec. 1992): Treasury Manager (ISSN 0896-2987); Which was formerly: Cash Manager (ISSN 0197-7075)

CORPORATE EXAMINER. see BUSINESS AND ECONOMICS

332 UK ISSN 0958-2053
HG3810
CORPORATE FINANCE. 1984. m. £255 (foreign $465) (effective 1997). Euromoney Publications plc., Nestor House, Playhouse Yard, London EC4V 5EX, England. TEL 44-171-779-8935. FAX 44-171-779-8541. (Dist. in US by: American Educational Systems, 173 W. 81st St., New York, NY 10024. TEL 800-717-2669. FAX 212-501-8926) circ. 11,200. **Indexed:** B.P.I. **Document type:** trade publication.
—BLDSC (3472.062500); KR SourceOne; SWETS; UMI.
Formerly: Euromoney Corporate Finance (ISSN 0266-7002)
Description: Provides information and analysis of mergers and acquisitions, risk management and derivatives, debt offerings and county capital.

332 US ISSN 1064-1912
HG4050
CORPORATE FINANCING WEEK; the newsweekly of corporate finance, investment banking and M & A. 1975. w. $1595 (Canada $1625; foreign $1670). Institutional Investor Newsletters, 477 Madison Ave., New York, NY 10022. TEL 212-224-3233. FAX 212-224-3353. Ed. Tom Lamont. adv. (also avail. in microfiche) **Indexed:** Bus.Ind. **Document type:** newsletter.
●Also available on CD-ROM.
—CCC.
Supersedes: Corporation Finance and New Issue Weekly (ISSN 0090-919X)
Description: Informs finance executives at corporations about innovations, trends, and ways to save money on new debt and equity issues, private placements, mergers and acquisitions, leveraged buyouts, venture capital and tax and accounting issues.

332 657 UK
CORPORATE MONEY; the newsletter of corporate financings and transactions. 1987. bi-w. Centaur Communications Ltd., St. Giles House, 50 Poland St., London W1V 4AX, England.
TEL 44-171-287-9800. FAX 44-171-439-1480. Ed. Jonathan Isaacs. adv. contact: Phil Dwyer. (also avail. in diskette format; back issues) **Document type:** newsletter.
●Also available online. Vendor(s): Information Access Co.
Description: Contains news and features on corporate deals and financings.

CORPORATE REPORT MINNESOTA. see BUSINESS AND ECONOMICS — Management

332 II
CORPORATE RUPEE. (Text in English) 1988. fortn. Rs.90; newsstand price: Rs.4. Promilla Kapoor, Ed. & Pub., 252-E, Sant Nagar, East of Kailash, New Delhi 110 065, India. TEL 6431256. adv. contact: Mohan Sontakay. cols./p.: 8; pp./issue: 8.

CORPORATION, BANKING & BUSINESS LAW NEWSLETTER. see LAW — Corporate Law

332.1 US
CORRESPONDENT (TOPEKA). 1991. q. free. Federal Home Loan Bank of Topeka, 2 Townsite Plaza, Box 176, Topeka, KS 66601. FAX 913-234-1797. Ed. Kim Gronniger.
Former titles (until 1996): Banking News; (until 1993): Correspondent (Topeka).
Description: Contains member and industry news and information about bank products and services.

332 US
THE COST CONTROLLER FOR FINANCIAL INSTITUTIONS. 1990. m. $319 (effective 1997). Siefer Consultants, Inc., Box 1384, Storm Lake, IA 50588. TEL 712-732-7340. FAX 712-732-7906. Ed. Marty Gallagher. index. circ. 600. (back issues avail.) **Document type:** newsletter.
Formerly: Cost Controller News (ISSN 1050-0677)
Description: Practical ways to reduce overhead and operating costs at financial institutions.

332.1 US ISSN 0091-3855
HG1628
COST OF PERSONAL BORROWING IN THE UNITED STATES.. 1971. a. $175 (effective 1997). Financial Publishing Company, Box 15698, 520 Commmwealth Ave., Ste. 420, Boston, MA 02215. TEL 617-262-4040. FAX 617-247-0136. Ed. Jeff Buysse. charts. circ. 625.

332 US ISSN 1067-4349
HG2040.5.U5
THE COST STUDY; income & cost for origination & servicing of 1-4 to 4-unit residential loans. 1977. a. $300 to non-members; members $150. Mortgage Bankers Association of America, Economics Department, 1125 15th St., N.W., Washington, DC 20005. TEL 202-861-8157. Ed. David Lereah. (back issues avail.)

332.1 333.33 UK
▼**COUNCIL OF MORTGAGE LENDERS. RESEARCH PAPERS**. 1995. irreg., latest no.4. £20 per no. Council of Mortgage Lenders, 3 Savile Row, London W1X 1AF, England. TEL 44-171-437-0075. FAX 44-171-734-6416. (back issues avail.) **Document type:** monographic series.
Description: Covers topics in housing and housing finance issues. Helps agencies involved in providing housing and housing finance focus on and make informed decisions across a range of subjects.

332 US
COUNTRY EXPOSURE LENDING SURVEY. q. $5. U.S. Federal Reserve System, Board of Governors, Publications Services, Rm. MS-138, Washington, DC 20551. TEL 202-452-3244. FAX 202-728-5886. **Document type:** government publication.

COUNTRY FORECASTS (SYRACUSE). see BUSINESS AND ECONOMICS

COUNTRY RISK SERVICE. see BUSINESS AND ECONOMICS — Economic Situation And Conditions

COUNTRY RISK SERVICE. ALGERIA. see BUSINESS AND ECONOMICS — Economic Situation And Conditions

COUNTRY RISK SERVICE. ANGOLA. see BUSINESS AND ECONOMICS — Economic Situation And Conditions

COUNTRY RISK SERVICE. ARGENTINA. see BUSINESS AND ECONOMICS — Economic Situation And Conditions

COUNTRY RISK SERVICE. AUSTRALIA. see BUSINESS AND ECONOMICS — Economic Situation And Conditions

COUNTRY RISK SERVICE. BAHRAIN. see BUSINESS AND ECONOMICS — Economic Situation And Conditions

COUNTRY RISK SERVICE. BANGLADESH. see BUSINESS AND ECONOMICS — Economic Situation And Conditions

COUNTRY RISK SERVICE. BOLIVIA. see BUSINESS AND ECONOMICS — Economic Situation And Conditions

COUNTRY RISK SERVICE. BOTSWANA. see BUSINESS AND ECONOMICS — Economic Situation And Conditions

COUNTRY RISK SERVICE. BRAZIL. see BUSINESS AND ECONOMICS — Economic Situation And Conditions

COUNTRY RISK SERVICE. BULGARIA. see BUSINESS AND ECONOMICS — Economic Situation And Conditions

COUNTRY RISK SERVICE. CAMEROON. see BUSINESS AND ECONOMICS — Economic Situation And Conditions

COUNTRY RISK SERVICE. CHILE. see BUSINESS AND ECONOMICS — Economic Situation And Conditions

BUSINESS AND ECONOMICS — BANKING AND FINANCE

COUNTRY RISK SERVICE. CHINA. see *BUSINESS AND ECONOMICS — Economic Situation And Conditions*

COUNTRY RISK SERVICE. COLOMBIA. see *BUSINESS AND ECONOMICS — Economic Situation And Conditions*

COUNTRY RISK SERVICE. CONGO. see *BUSINESS AND ECONOMICS — Economic Situation And Conditions*

COUNTRY RISK SERVICE. COSTA RICA. see *BUSINESS AND ECONOMICS — Economic Situation And Conditions*

COUNTRY RISK SERVICE. COTE D'IVOIRE. see *BUSINESS AND ECONOMICS — Economic Situation And Conditions*

COUNTRY RISK SERVICE. CYPRUS. see *BUSINESS AND ECONOMICS — Economic Situation And Conditions*

COUNTRY RISK SERVICE. CZECH REPUBLIC. see *BUSINESS AND ECONOMICS — Economic Situation And Conditions*

COUNTRY RISK SERVICE. DOMINICAN REPUBLIC. see *BUSINESS AND ECONOMICS — Economic Situation And Conditions*

COUNTRY RISK SERVICE. ECUADOR. see *BUSINESS AND ECONOMICS — Economic Situation And Conditions*

COUNTRY RISK SERVICE. EGYPT. see *BUSINESS AND ECONOMICS — Economic Situation And Conditions*

COUNTRY RISK SERVICE. EL SALVADOR. see *BUSINESS AND ECONOMICS — Economic Situation And Conditions*

COUNTRY RISK SERVICE. FORMER YUGOSLAV REPUBLICS: SERBIA, MONTENEGRO, MACEDONIA. see *BUSINESS AND ECONOMICS — Economic Situation And Conditions*

COUNTRY RISK SERVICE. GABON. see *BUSINESS AND ECONOMICS — Economic Situation And Conditions*

COUNTRY RISK SERVICE. GHANA. see *BUSINESS AND ECONOMICS — Economic Situation And Conditions*

COUNTRY RISK SERVICE. GREECE. see *BUSINESS AND ECONOMICS — Economic Situation And Conditions*

COUNTRY RISK SERVICE. GUATEMALA. see *BUSINESS AND ECONOMICS — Economic Situation And Conditions*

COUNTRY RISK SERVICE. HONDURAS. see *BUSINESS AND ECONOMICS — Economic Situation And Conditions*

COUNTRY RISK SERVICE. HONG KONG. see *BUSINESS AND ECONOMICS — Economic Situation And Conditions*

COUNTRY RISK SERVICE. HUNGARY. see *BUSINESS AND ECONOMICS — Economic Situation And Conditions*

COUNTRY RISK SERVICE. INDIA. see *BUSINESS AND ECONOMICS — Economic Situation And Conditions*

COUNTRY RISK SERVICE. INDONESIA. see *BUSINESS AND ECONOMICS — Economic Situation And Conditions*

COUNTRY RISK SERVICE. IRAN. see *BUSINESS AND ECONOMICS — Economic Situation And Conditions*

COUNTRY RISK SERVICE. IRAQ. see *BUSINESS AND ECONOMICS — Economic Situation And Conditions*

COUNTRY RISK SERVICE. ISRAEL. see *BUSINESS AND ECONOMICS — Economic Situation And Conditions*

COUNTRY RISK SERVICE. JAMAICA. see *BUSINESS AND ECONOMICS — Economic Situation And Conditions*

COUNTRY RISK SERVICE. JORDAN. see *BUSINESS AND ECONOMICS — Economic Situation And Conditions*

COUNTRY RISK SERVICE. KAZAKHSTAN. see *BUSINESS AND ECONOMICS — Economic Situation And Conditions*

COUNTRY RISK SERVICE. KENYA. see *BUSINESS AND ECONOMICS — Economic Situation And Conditions*

COUNTRY RISK SERVICE. KUWAIT. see *BUSINESS AND ECONOMICS — Economic Situation And Conditions*

COUNTRY RISK SERVICE. LIBYA. see *BUSINESS AND ECONOMICS — Economic Situation And Conditions*

COUNTRY RISK SERVICE. MALAWI. see *BUSINESS AND ECONOMICS — Economic Situation And Conditions*

COUNTRY RISK SERVICE. MALAYSIA. see *BUSINESS AND ECONOMICS — Economic Situation And Conditions*

COUNTRY RISK SERVICE. MEXICO. see *BUSINESS AND ECONOMICS — Economic Situation And Conditions*

COUNTRY RISK SERVICE. MOROCCO. see *BUSINESS AND ECONOMICS — Economic Situation And Conditions*

COUNTRY RISK SERVICE. NAMIBIA. see *BUSINESS AND ECONOMICS — Economic Situation And Conditions*

COUNTRY RISK SERVICE. NEW ZEALAND. see *BUSINESS AND ECONOMICS — Economic Situation And Conditions*

COUNTRY RISK SERVICE. NICARAGUA. see *BUSINESS AND ECONOMICS — Economic Situation And Conditions*

COUNTRY RISK SERVICE. NIGERIA. see *BUSINESS AND ECONOMICS — Economic Situation And Conditions*

COUNTRY RISK SERVICE. OMAN. see *BUSINESS AND ECONOMICS — Economic Situation And Conditions*

COUNTRY RISK SERVICE. PAKISTAN. see *BUSINESS AND ECONOMICS — Economic Situation And Conditions*

COUNTRY RISK SERVICE. PANAMA. see *BUSINESS AND ECONOMICS — Economic Situation And Conditions*

COUNTRY RISK SERVICE. PAPUA NEW GUINEA. see *BUSINESS AND ECONOMICS — Economic Situation And Conditions*

COUNTRY RISK SERVICE. PARAGUAY. see *BUSINESS AND ECONOMICS — Economic Situation And Conditions*

COUNTRY RISK SERVICE. PERU. see *BUSINESS AND ECONOMICS — Economic Situation And Conditions*

COUNTRY RISK SERVICE. PHILIPPINES. see *BUSINESS AND ECONOMICS — Economic Situation And Conditions*

COUNTRY RISK SERVICE. POLAND. see *BUSINESS AND ECONOMICS — Economic Situation And Conditions*

COUNTRY RISK SERVICE. PORTUGAL. see *BUSINESS AND ECONOMICS — Economic Situation And Conditions*

COUNTRY RISK SERVICE. QATAR. see *BUSINESS AND ECONOMICS — Economic Situation And Conditions*

COUNTRY RISK SERVICE. ROMANIA. see *BUSINESS AND ECONOMICS — Economic Situation And Conditions*

COUNTRY RISK SERVICE. RUSSIA. see *BUSINESS AND ECONOMICS — Economic Situation And Conditions*

COUNTRY RISK SERVICE. SAUDI ARABIA. see *BUSINESS AND ECONOMICS — Economic Situation And Conditions*

COUNTRY RISK SERVICE. SENEGAL. see *BUSINESS AND ECONOMICS — Economic Situation And Conditions*

COUNTRY RISK SERVICE. SINGAPORE. see *BUSINESS AND ECONOMICS — Economic Situation And Conditions*

COUNTRY RISK SERVICE. SLOVENIA. see *BUSINESS AND ECONOMICS — Economic Situation And Conditions*

COUNTRY RISK SERVICE. SOUTH AFRICA. see *BUSINESS AND ECONOMICS — Economic Situation And Conditions*

COUNTRY RISK SERVICE. SOUTH KOREA. see *BUSINESS AND ECONOMICS — Economic Situation And Conditions*

COUNTRY RISK SERVICE. SPAIN. see *BUSINESS AND ECONOMICS — Economic Situation And Conditions*

COUNTRY RISK SERVICE. SRI LANKA. see *BUSINESS AND ECONOMICS — Economic Situation And Conditions*

COUNTRY RISK SERVICE. SUDAN. see *BUSINESS AND ECONOMICS — Economic Situation And Conditions*

COUNTRY RISK SERVICE. SYRIA. see *BUSINESS AND ECONOMICS — Economic Situation And Conditions*

COUNTRY RISK SERVICE. TAIWAN. see *BUSINESS AND ECONOMICS — Economic Situation And Conditions*

COUNTRY RISK SERVICE. THAILAND. see *BUSINESS AND ECONOMICS — Economic Situation And Conditions*

COUNTRY RISK SERVICE. THE BALTIC REPUBLICS: LATVIA, ESTONIA, LITHUANIA. see *BUSINESS AND ECONOMICS — Economic Situation And Conditions*

COUNTRY RISK SERVICE. TRINIDAD AND TOBAGO. see *BUSINESS AND ECONOMICS — Economic Situation And Conditions*

COUNTRY RISK SERVICE. TUNISIA. see *BUSINESS AND ECONOMICS — Economic Situation And Conditions*

COUNTRY RISK SERVICE. TURKEY. see *BUSINESS AND ECONOMICS — Economic Situation And Conditions*

COUNTRY RISK SERVICE. UKRAINE. see *BUSINESS AND ECONOMICS — Economic Situation And Conditions*

COUNTRY RISK SERVICE. UNITED ARAB EMIRATES. see *BUSINESS AND ECONOMICS — Economic Situation And Conditions*

COUNTRY RISK SERVICE. URUGUAY. see *BUSINESS AND ECONOMICS — Economic Situation And Conditions*

COUNTRY RISK SERVICE. VENEZUELA. see *BUSINESS AND ECONOMICS — Economic Situation And Conditions*

COUNTRY RISK SERVICE. VIETNAM. see *BUSINESS AND ECONOMICS — Economic Situation And Conditions*

COUNTRY RISK SERVICE. YEMEN. see *BUSINESS AND ECONOMICS — Economic Situation And Conditions*

COUNTRY RISK SERVICE. ZAIRE. see *BUSINESS AND ECONOMICS — Economic Situation And Conditions*

COUNTRY RISK SERVICE. ZAMBIA. see *BUSINESS AND ECONOMICS — Economic Situation And Conditions*

COUNTRY RISK SERVICE. ZIMBABWE. see *BUSINESS AND ECONOMICS — Economic Situation And Conditions*

332.1   PH   ISSN 0115-0693
HG3311
COUNTRYSIDE BANKING. (Text in English) bi-m. $1 per no. Central Bank of the Philippines, A. Mabini corner Vito Cruz Streets, Manila, Philippines. Ed. Celine A. Quinio. charts; illus. circ. 4,000. **Indexed:** Ind.Phil.Per.

332   UK   ISSN 0953-8089
CRAWFORD'S DIRECTORY OF CITY CONNECTIONS. 1973 a. (plus 5/yr. updates). £229.50 (Europe £242; rest of world £250) (with updates U.K. £251.50; Europe £264; rest of world £272) (CD-ROM U.K. £599.50; Europe £612; rest of world £620) (effective 1997). Miller Freeman Information Services (Subsidiary of: United News & Media), Riverbank House, Angel Ln., Tonbridge, Kent TN9 1SE, England. TEL 44-1732-362666. FAX 44-1732-367301. Ed. Gwen Young. adv. contact: Elaine Soni. (also avail. in diskette format) **Document type:** directory.
●Also available on CD-ROM.
—BLDSC (3593.285000).
 Description: Lists U.K. companies and their advisers, with full contact details, names, addresses and telephone numbers of senior directors, major shareholders, and corporate advisers.

BUSINESS AND ECONOMICS — BANKING AND FINANCE

332.3 336 US
CRED-ALERT. 1972. m. $36 to non-members; members $18. American Collectors Association, Inc., Box 39106, 4040 W. 70th St. Minneapolis, MN 55439. TEL 612-926-6547. FAX 612-926-1624. circ. 3,600 (paid). (back issues avail.) **Document type:** newsletter, trade publication.
Description: Covers state and federal legislation that affects credit and the collection industry.

332.7 UK
CREDIT AND CHARGE CARDS: THE INTERNATIONAL MARKET. (Subseries of: Market Direction reports) a. £1595($3190) (effective 1997). Euromonitor, 60-61 Britton St., London EC1M 5NA, England. TEL 44-171-251-8024. FAX 44-171-608-3149. E-mail: info@euromonitor.com; URL: http://www.euromonitor.com. (Addr. in N. America: Euromonitor International, 122 S. Michigan Ave., Ste. 1200, Chicago, IL 60603. TEL 800-577-3876. FAX 312-922-1157) (looseleaf format) **Document type:** trade publication.
●Also available online. Vendor(s): Data-Star, Knight-Ridder Information, Inc.
Description: Analyzes the credit and charge card markets for France, Germany, Italy, Spain, the U.K., the U.S., and Japan.

332 658 US ISSN 1060-2739
CREDIT & COLLECTION MANAGER'S LETTER. 1967. s-m. $159.36. Bureau of Business Practice, 24 Rope Ferry Rd., Waterford, CT 06386. TEL 860-442-4365. FAX 860-437-3555. URL: http://www.bbpnews.com. Ed. Wayne Muller; Pub. Peter Garabedian. R&P contact: Debra Ferraro. **Document type:** newsletter.
Formerly: Credit and Collection Management Bulletin (ISSN 0273-9623)
Description: Provides business and consumer lenders and creditors with up-to-date information on credit procedures, collection practices, legal problems, financial analyses and bankruptcy proceedings.

CREDIT & FINANCE LAW. see LAW

332 658 US ISSN 0896-9329
CREDIT CARD MANAGEMENT. (Supplements avail.: Card Technology Review, Debit Card Directory) 1988. m. $98 (outside N. America $113). Faulkner & Gray, Inc., 300 S. Wacker Dr., 18th Fl., Chicago, IL 60606. TEL 312-913-1334; 800-535-8403. E-mail: faulknerygray@msn.com. Ed. James L. Daly; Pub. John Stewart. **Document type:** trade publication.
●Also available online. Vendor(s): Information Access Co., Lexis-Nexis, NewsNet, UMI.
—BLDSC (3487.280300); UMI.
Incorporates (in 1991): Journal of Consumer Lending.
Description: Shows new ideas, products and strategies from successful credit card programs. Covers all aspects of the business from finance to marketing to new technology.

332.7 US
CREDIT CARD NEWS. 1989. fortn. $345. Faulkner & Gray, Inc. (New York), 11 Penn Plaza, 17th Fl., New York, NY 10001. TEL 212-967-7000. FAX 212-967-7155. Ed. Kurt Peters. **Document type:** trade publication.
●Also available online. Vendor(s): Information Access Co., UMI.
Description: Covers card programs and people who are profiting in the business. Reports on credit card marketing wars, newcomers, credit economics, technology and profitability.

332 BE ISSN 0011-099X
CREDIT COMMUNAL DE BELGIQUE. BULLETIN TRIMESTRIEL. Dutch edition: Gemeentekrediet van Belgie. Driemaandelijks Tijdschrift (ISSN 0773-9273) (Text in French) 1947. q. free. Credit Communal de Belgique - Gemeentekrediet van Belgie, 44 bd. Pacheco, 1000 Brussels, Belgium. TEL 32-2-2224112. FAX 32-2-2225752. Ed. G. Helbig. bk.rev.; charts; illus. circ. 16,000 (8,000 French ed.; 8,000 Dutch ed.). **Indexed:** P.A.I.S.For.Lang.Ind. **Document type:** bulletin.

332.3 UK ISSN 0143-5329
CREDIT CONTROL. 1979. m. £259.95 (foreign £455.35). House of Words Ltd., 7 Greding Walk, Hutton, Brentwood, Essex CM13 2UF, England. TEL 44-1277-225402. FAX 44-1277-201554. Ed. Carol Baker; Pub. Gareth Price. adv. contact: Carol Baker. bk.rev.; index; illus.; circ. 1,000 (paid). (back issues avail.) **Document type:** trade publication, academic/scholarly publication.
●Also available online. Vendor(s): UMI.
—BLDSC (3487.282000); UMI.
Description: Addresses key issues facing credit controllers, managers, analysts, financial directors, and corporate vice presidents through news; legal, technical, and management articles; and reviews, maintaining a balance of theory and practice.
Refereed Serial

332 US ISSN 1078-0149
CREDIT LINE; concise advise for the credit & collection staff. 1994. m. $83.88. Bureau of Business Practice, 24 Rope Ferry Rd., Waterford, CT 06386. TEL 860-442-4365. FAX 860-437-3555. URL: http://www.bbpnews.com. Ed. Joyce Ann Grabel; Pub. Peter Garabedian. R&P contact: Debra Ferraro. **Document type:** newsletter.
Description: Covers a variety of topics of interest to credit and collection staffers including credit checks, telephone collections, where to turn for in-depth credit information, UCC law, collection tips, dealing with angry customers, dealing with stress, and teamwork.

658.15 US ISSN 0070-1467
CREDIT MANUAL OF COMMERCIAL LAWS. 1898. a. $81 to non-members. National Association of Credit Management, 8815 Centre Park Dr., Ste. 200, Columbia, MD 21045. TEL 410-740-5560. FAX 410-740-5574. **Document type:** trade publication.
—CCC.

332.7 658 US
THE CREDIT MEMO. 1907; N.S. 1994. bi-m. membership. New York Credit & Financial Management Association, 49 W. 45th St., 5th Fl., New York, NY 10036-4603. TEL 212-944-2400. FAX 212-944-2663. Ed. J. Robert Murray; Pub. Kim J. Zablocky. adv.: B&W page $500; adv. contact: Judy Parker-Markowitz. bk.rev.; illus. circ. 3,500. **Indexed:** World Bank.Abstr. **Document type:** newsletter.
Supersedes: Credit Executive (ISSN 0011-1007)

332 UK ISSN 0965-9331
CREDIT RATINGS INTERNATIONAL. q. £546($907) (overseas £567) (effective 1993). Financial Times Business Information, Newsletters (Subsidiary of: Financial Times Group), 126 Jermyn St., London SW1Y 4UJ, England. TEL 0171-411-4414. FAX 0171-411-4415. **Document type:** newsletter.
Description: Provides ratings assigned by the world's most influential credit ratings agencies to more than 6,000 issuers of internationally traded debt.

332.1 US ISSN 1054-5069
CREDIT RISK MANAGEMENT. 1990. bi-w. $595 (foreign $630) (effective 1997). Phillips Business Information, Inc., 1201 Seven Locks Rd., Potomac, MD 20854. TEL 301-424-3338. FAX 301-309-3847. E-mail: pbi@phillips.com. Ed. Meredith Jordan. **Document type:** newsletter.
●Also available online. Vendor(s): NewsNet (FI57).
—CCC.

332.7 330.9 SZ ISSN 0011-1023
HC395
CREDIT SUISSE. BULLETIN. (Editions in English, French, German and Italian) 1895. 6/yr. (French and German eds.); q. (English and Italian eds.). free. Credit Suisse, Corporate Affairs Division, Paradeplatz 8, CH-8070 Zurich, Switzerland. Ed.Bd. charts; mkt.; stat.; index. circ. 140,000 (combined). **Indexed:** World Bank.Abstr. **Document type:** bulletin.

332 US
CREDIT UNION ACCOUNTANT. 48/yr. $625 for new subscr. (foreign $675); renewal $695 (foreign $745). American Banker - Bond Buyer, Newsletter Division (Subsidiary of: Thomson Financial Services Company), One State St. Plaza, New York, NY 10004-1549. TEL 800-733-4371. FAX 212-943-2224. (Subscr. to: Box 28315, Washington, DC 20038-8315. TEL 202-347-2665) **Document type:** newsletter.
●Also available online. Vendor(s): Information Access Co.
Description: Focuses on accounting policy changes for credit unions emanating from government agencies. Includes a ledger summarizing the most critical developments in legal and regulatory issues affecting how the books of credit unions are kept as well as the latest actions being considered by the FASB, the AICPA and the National Credit Union Administration.

332.3 US ISSN 1040-9246
CREDIT UNION DIRECTOR. 1983. q. $60 to non-members; members $35. Credit Union Executives Society, Box 14167, Madison, WI 53714. TEL 608-271-2664. FAX 608-271-2303. E-mail: cues@cues.org; URL: http://www.cues.org. Ed. Ron Jooss; Pub. Mary Arnold. R&P contact: Mary Arnold. adv.: B&W page $1180, color page $2180; trim 8 1/2 x 11; adv. contact: Frank Ostendorf. index. circ. 4,630. (back issues avail.; reprint service avail.) **Document type:** trade publication.
Formerly: Credit Union Volunteer.
Description: Features articles, departments for legal issues, making financial policy decisions, and for board committee members.

332.3 US ISSN 1058-1561
CREDIT UNION DIRECTORS NEWSLETTER. m. $65. Credit Union National Association, Inc., 5710 Mineral Point Rd., Box 431, Madison, WI 53701. TEL 608-231-4082. FAX 608-231-4370. Ed. Gene Johnson; Pub. Mark Condon. adv. contact: Philip Heckman. circ. 8,118. **Document type:** newsletter.
—CCC.
Former titles: Credit Union Board C E O Newsletter; Credit Union President Newsletter.

334.2 US ISSN 0011-1058
HG2035
CREDIT UNION EXECUTIVE; for active leaders and managers of credit unions. 1962. bi-m. $99. (Credit Union National Association, Inc., Communications Division) C U N A Publications, Box 431, Madison, WI 53701. TEL 608-231-4000. FAX 608-231-4370. Ed. Leigh Gregg; Pub. Mark Condon. R&P contact: Philip Heckman. adv. contact: Rick Sheridan. bk.rev.; charts; tr.lit.; index. circ. 2,700. (back issues avail.) **Indexed:** ABI Inform, BPIA, Bus.Ind., Tr.& Indus.Ind. **Document type:** trade publication.
●Also available online. Vendor(s): Information Access Co.
—UMI. CCC.

332 US ISSN 1043-1888
HG2037
CREDIT UNION FINANCIAL PROFILES. q., s-a. $389 for q.; s-a $224 (effective 1997). I D C Financial Publishing, Inc., Box 140, Hartland, WI 53029. TEL 414-367-7231; 800-525-7231. Ed. John E. Rickmeier. R&P contact: John E. Rickmeier. charts; illus.; stat. (back issues avail.) **Document type:** trade publication.
Description: Covers the world of banking and finance with special attention to credit and credit unions.

334.2 US ISSN 0011-1066
HG2033
CREDIT UNION MAGAZINE; for credit union elected officials, managers and employees. 1924. m. $36. Credit Union National Association, Inc., Publications Department, Box 431, Madison, WI 53701. TEL 608-231-4079. FAX 608-231-4370. Ed. Steve Rodgers; Pub. Mark Condon. adv. contact: Philip Heckman. charts; illus.; tr.lit.; index. circ. 40,161. (also avail. in microform from UMI; reprint service avail. from UMI) **Indexed:** ABI Inform, BPIA, P.A.I.S., World Bank.Abstr. **Document type:** trade publication.
—BLDSC (3487.290000); UMI; UnCover. CCC.
Formerly: Credit Union Bridge.

BUSINESS AND ECONOMICS — BANKING AND FINANCE

332   US   ISSN 0273-9267
HG2032
CREDIT UNION MANAGEMENT. 1978. m. $90 to non-members; members $54. Credit Union Executives Society, Box 14167, Madison, WI 53714-0167. TEL 608-271-2664. FAX 608-271-2303. E-mail: cues@cues.org; URL: http://www.cues.org. Ed. Mary Auestad Arnold. adv. contact: Paula Ostendorf. bk.rev.; charts; illus.; index. circ. 5,405. (reprint service avail.) **Indexed:** ABI Inform, P.A.I.S. **Document type:** trade publication.
●Also available online. Vendor(s): UMI.
—BLDSC (3487.290500); UMI.
  Incorporates (1986-1990): Financial Operations; (1979-1990): Credit Union Marketing.
  Description: Feature articles, departments, classifieds, regular sections devoted to general management, operations, marketing, and human resources issues.

332.3   US   ISSN 1068-2120
CREDIT UNION MANAGER NEWSLETTER. 1975. fortn. $145. Credit Union National Association, Inc., 5710 Mineral Point Rd., Box 431, Madison, WI 53701. TEL 608-231-4082. FAX 608-231-4370. Ed. Gene Johnson; Pub. Mark Condon. adv. contact: Philip Heckman. circ. 2,174. **Document type:** newsletter.
—CCC.

332.7   US   ISSN 0199-9311
CREDIT UNION NEWS. 1981. 24/yr. $99. B K B Publications Inc., 98 Greenwich Ave., No. 1 FL, New York, NY 10011-7743. TEL 212-807-6995. FAX 212-807-1821. Ed. Charlene Komar Storey; Pub. Brian K. Burkart. R&P contact: Brian K. Burkart. adv.; bk.rev. circ. 7,000. **Document type:** newspaper, trade publication.
—UMI.
  Description: Provides management of credit unions with timely reports of regulatory and technical matters. Contains news of conventions, government activities, personnel changes.

332   US   ISSN 0889-5597
CREDIT UNION NEWSWATCH. 1981. w. $125. Credit Union National Association, Inc., 5710 Mineral Point Rd., Box 431, Madison, WI 53701. TEL 608-231-4042. FAX 608-231-4858. Ed. Jack E. Blake; Pub. Mark Condon. adv. contact: Philip Heckman. circ. 17,000. (looseleaf format; back issues avail.) **Document type:** newsletter.
—CCC.
  Supersedes (1972-1981): Credit Union Leadership Letter.

310   US   ISSN 0894-752X
HG2037
CREDIT UNION REPORT. a. $25. Credit Union National Association, Inc., 5710 Mineral Point Rd., Box 431, Madison, WI 53701. TEL 608-231-4043. FAX 608-231-4858. Ed. Paul Thompson. circ. 9,000. (back issues avail.) **Indexed:** SRI. **Document type:** monographic series.

332.3 334   IE   ISSN 0790-505X
CREDIT UNION REVIEW. 1980. bi-m. I£0.30. Irish League of Credit Unions, Castleside Dr., Rathfarnham, Dublin 14, Ireland. TEL 353-1-4908911. FAX 353-1-4908915. Ed. Grace Perrott. adv. contact: Roger Cole. bk.rev.; illus. circ. 10,000. **Document type:** trade publication.

332   US   ISSN 1058-7764
HG2037
CREDIT UNION TIMES. w. $120 (foreign $169). Credit Union Times, Inc., Box 3828, West Palm Beach, FL 33402-3828. TEL 561-683-8515. FAX 561-683-8514. Ed. Carol Anne Burger; Pub. Mike Welch. adv. contact: Julie Idle. circ. 9,500 (paid). **Document type:** trade publication.

332 334   CN   ISSN 0829-2175
CREDIT UNION WAY. 1948. m. (10/yr.). Can.$35($35) (foreign Can.$43). Credit Union Central of Saskatchewan, P.O. Box 3030, 2055 Albert St., Regina, SK S4P 3G8, Canada. TEL 306-566-1360. FAX 306-566-1847. Ed. James Duggleby; Pub. Eric Eggertson. adv. contact: Kelly Lee. bk.rev.; index. circ. 5,600. (back issues avail.) **Indexed:** Can.B.P.I. **Document type:** trade publication.
  Description: For directors, employees and members of Canadian credit unions and co-operatives.

332.7   US   ISSN 0011-1074
HF5565
CREDIT WORLD. 1912. bi-m. $50 to non-members. International Credit Association, 243 N. Lindbergh Blvd., Box 419057, St. Louis, MO 63141-1757. TEL 314-991-3030. FAX 314-991-3029. Ed. Janet Lipkind. R&P contact: Janet Lipkind. adv.; B&W page $1230, color page $2420; trim 8 1/8 X 10 7/8; adv. contact: Laura Diamond. bk.rev.; charts; illus.; mkt.; stat.; tr.lit. circ. 7,100. (also avail. in microform from UMI; reprint service avail from UMI) **Indexed:** ABI Inform., B.P.I., BPIA, Bus.Ind., Data Process.Dig., Manage.Cont., P.A.I.S., World Bank.Abstr. **Document type:** trade publication.
●Also available online. Vendor(s): UMI.
—BLDSC (3487.293000); KR SourceOne; UMI; UnCover.
  Description: Covers consumer credit and financial affairs.

332.3   AU   ISSN 0304-6915
HG3020.V54
CREDITANSTALT-BANKVEREIN. ANNUAL REPORT. (Text in English) a. Creditanstalt-Bankverein, Schottengasse 6, A-1010 Vienna, Austria.
  Formerly: Creditanstalt-Bankverein. Report.

332.7   NO   ISSN 0802-4138
CREDITINFORM. 1914. s-m. NOK 890. Creditinform a-s, Postboks 5275 Majorstua, Oslo 3, Norway. FAX 47-22-46-53-90. TELEX 11093 CINFO N. Ed. Bjoern Oestgaard. adv.; stat. circ. 7,000.
—CCC.
  Former titles (until 1989): Creditreform (ISSN 0011-1104); (until 1926): Kredittidende (ISSN 0801-1567)

CRITTENDEN REPORT REAL ESTATE FINANCING. see REAL ESTATE

332   US   ISSN 1066-6419
CROSS SALES REPORT. 1992. m. $319 (effective 1997). Siefer Consultants, Inc., Box 1384, Storm Lake, IA 50588. TEL 712-732-7340. FAX 712-732-7906. Ed. Joe Sheller. index. (back issues avail.) **Document type:** newsletter.
  Description: Provides cross-sales and customer service tips for banks.

332   UK   ISSN 1354-0904
CROSS-SHAREHOLDINGS IN EUROPE. 1994. irreg. £195. O X E R A Press, Blue Boar Ct., Alfred St., Oxford OX1 4EH, England. TEL 44-1865-251142. FAX 44-1865-201080. **Document type:** academic/scholarly publication.
  Description: Provides an evaluation of the use of cross-shareholdings, particularly as a form of proactive takeover defense.

332   CL   ISSN 0716-2383
CUENTAS NACIONALES DE CHILE. 1981. a. Ch.$9800($50) Banco Central de Chile, Casilla 967, Santiago, Chile. TEL 56-2-6702000. FAX 56-2-6984847. TELEX 40569 CENBC CL. circ. 700 (paid).

330.9   EC   ISSN 0252-8673
CUESTIONES ECONOMICAS. 1979. 3/yr. Banco Central del Ecuador, Departamento de Publicaciones Tecnicas, Casilla 29C, Sucursal No.15, Quito, Ecuador. TEL 561-521. (Dist. by: Libreria Economia y Cultura, Av. 10 de Agosto, No. 600 y Checa, Quito, Ecuador) circ. 2,000.

332   EC   ISSN 0252-8657
F3710
CULTURA (QUITO). 1978. 3/yr. $14. Banco Central del Ecuador, Casilla 29C, Sucursal No.15, Quito, Ecuador. TEL 561-521. (Dist. by: Libreria Economia y Cultura, Av. 10 de Agosto, No.600 y Checa, Quito, Ecuador)

CURIERUL NATIONAL. see BUSINESS AND ECONOMICS — Economic Situation And Conditions

332   UK   ISSN 0955-6656
CURRENCY AND INTEREST RATE OUTLOOK. 1987. m. £295($495) Corporate Treasury Consultants Ltd., 111 Promenade, Cheltenham, Glos. GL50 1NW, England. TEL 44-1242-232356. FAX 44-1242-260793. Ed. Bob Steiner. **Document type:** newsletter.
  Description: Provides forecasting details on currency and interest rate movements for the next six months, with analysis and summaries based on economic and other fundamentals and market factors.

332   UK   ISSN 0143-0769
CURRENCY PROFILES.* 1977. m. £850. Henley Centre for Forecasting Ltd., 9 Bridewell Pl., London EC4Y 6AY, England. Ed. Filippo Dell'Osso. illus.
  Incorporates: Forecasts of Exchange Rate Movements (ISSN 0305-9944); Former titles: Forecasts of Exchange Rate Movements (Dollar Edition) (ISSN 0140-9247); Forecasts of Exchange Rate Movements (Overseas Edition) (ISSN 0140-9255)
  Description: Short- and medium-range analysis of prospects for international currencies against the pound and the dollar.

CURRENT ISSUES IN REAL ESTATE FINANCE & ECONOMICS. see REAL ESTATE

CURRENT ISSUES IN THE FINANCIAL SERVICES INDUSTRIES. see BUSINESS AND ECONOMICS — Accounting

332   US   ISSN 1055-1700
CYCLE PROJECTIONS. 1990. m. $125. Foundation for the Study of Cycles, 900 W. Valley Rd., Ste. 502, Wayne, PA 19087-1821. TEL 610-995-2120. FAX 610-995-2130. E-mail: cycles@cycles.org; URL: http://www.cycles.org/~cycles. Ed. Chester Joy. **Document type:** newsletter.
  Description: Offers timely projections in a variety of markets. Covers short, intermediate and long term cycles.

332   CY
CYPRUS DEVELOPMENT BANK. ANNUAL REPORT. 1963. a. free. Cyprus Development Bank, Nicosia, Cyprus. TEL 357-2-457575. FAX 357-2-464322. TELEX 2797 DEBANK CY. circ. 1,100. **Document type:** corporate report.

332   GW
CZERWENSKY INTERN. 1988. 2/wk. DM.625. Kronberger Verlags GmbH, Eschersheimer Landstr. 9, 60322 Frankfurt a.M., Germany. TEL 069-550002. FAX 069-550006. Ed. Gerhard Czerwensky. (tabloid format) **Document type:** newsletter.

384.5 332   US   ISSN 1054-0814
THE D B S REPORT. (Direct Broadcast Satellite) 1990. m. $695 (effective 1997). Paul Kagan Associates, Inc., 126 Clock Tower Place, Carmel, CA 93923. TEL 408-624-1536. FAX 408-625-3225. Ed. Larry Gerbrandt.
  Description: Analysis of direct-to-home satellite ventures. Projects future scenarios, costs and values.

332.1   GW   ISSN 0722-5334
HD3500.A1
D G BANK DEUTSCHE GENOSSENSCHAFTSBANK. BERICHT UEBER DAS GESCHAEFTSJAHR. (Editions in English, French, German and Spanish) 1951. a. D G Bank - Deutsche Genossenschaftsbank, Am Platz der Republik, 60325 Frankfurt a.M., Germany. TEL 49-69-744701. FAX 49-69-74471685. URL: http://www.dgbank.de. charts; stat. **Document type:** corporate report.
  Formerly (until 1976): Deutsche Genossenschaftsbank. Bericht (ISSN 0417-1888)

332   DK   ISSN 0109-7644
DAGENS DANMARK. 1984. q. membership. Kreditforeningen Danmark, Jarmers Plads 2, 1590 Copenhagen V, Denmark. illus.

DAILY REPORTER (SIOUX CITY). see LAW

332   SA   ISSN 0258-8986
DAILY TENDER BULLETIN. 1938. d. Trade Information Services (Subsidiary of: Times Media Ltd.), P.O. Box 56311, Pinegowrie 2123, South Africa. TEL 27-11-886-3166.
  Formerly (until 1976): Daily Bulletin.

332   II
DALAL STREET JOURNAL. (Text in English) 1986. fortn. Rs.330; newsstand price: Rs.20. Dalal Street Communications Pvt. Ltd., 31-A, Noble Chambers, 4th Fl., Janmabhoomi Marg, Bombay 400 001, India. TEL 2870287. FAX 2872779. TELEX 011-81130. E-mail: dsj@hotmail.com; URL: http://www.cyberindia.net/DSJ/home.htm. Ed. Pratap V. Padode. adv.: B&W page Rs.48000, color page Rs.62000; trim 240 x 180; adv. contact: T.N. Streekrishna. circ. 74,302.
●Also available online.

BUSINESS AND ECONOMICS — BANKING AND FINANCE

332.632   DK   ISSN 0909-0487
DANISH GOVERNMENT SECURITIES. Danish edition: Statens Laantagning og Gaeld (ISSN 0902-6681) (Text in English) 1994. a. free. Danmarks Nationalbank, Havnegade 5, DK-1093 Copenhagen K, Denmark. FAX 45-33-14-14-04. circ. 2,000.

332.1109489   DK   ISSN 0108-6979
DANMARKS NATIONALBANK. BERETNING OG REGNSKAB (DANSK UDGAVE). English edition: Danmarks Nationalbank. Report and Accounts for the Year (ISSN 0108-6995) 1819. a. free. Danmarks Nationalbank, Havnegade 5, DK-1093 Copenhagen K, Denmark. illus. circ. 13,200 (Danish ed. 11,000, English ed. 200).

330.9489   DK   ISSN 0011-6149
DANMARKS NATIONALBANK. MONETARY REVIEW. (Editions in Danish, English) 1962. q. free. Danmarks Nationalbank, 5 Havnegade, 1093 Copenhagen K, Denmark. FAX 01145902. TELEX 27051. charts; stat. circ. 7,100 (2,100 English ed., 5,000 Danish ed.). Indexed: ELLIS, World Bank.Abstr.

332.1109489   DK   ISSN 0108-6995
DANMARKS NATIONALBANK. REPORT AND ACCOUNTS FOR THE YEAR. 1945. a. Danmarks Nationalbank, Havnegade 5, DK-1093 Copenhagen K, Denmark.

332.1   DK
DEN DANSKE BANK. ANNUAL REPORT. (Text in English) 1871. a. Danske Bank, c/o Library, Holmens Kanal 12, DK-1092 Copenhagen, Denmark. TEL 45-33-15-65-00. FAX 45-33-44-37-78. TELEX 27000. illus.
    Former titles: Danske Bank af 1871. Annual Report; (until 1976): Danske Landmandsbank. Annual Report (ISSN 0070-2838)

332.1   DK
DEN DANSKE BANK AKTIESELSKAB. REPORT AND ACCOUNTS. (Editions in Danish, English) s-a. (free to qualified personnel). Danske Bank Aktieselskab, Information Department, 2-12 Holmens Kanal, DK-1092 Copenhagen K, Denmark. TEL 45-33-44-00-00. FAX 45-31-18-58-73. charts; stat.
    Formerly (until 1990): Copenhagen HandelsBank. Report and Accounts.

332   CH   ISSN 1011-2189
HG41
DATA BANK REVIEW.* Key Title: Caijing Jishi. (Text in Chinese) 1987. m. NT.$1500 in ROC; Hong Kong NT.$1620 ($60); elsewhere NT.$1730 ($64). 5F, No. 189, Yen-Ping S. Rd., Taipei, Taiwan, Republic of China. TEL 02-565-2480. FAX 02-563-6357. adv.
    Description: Covers international market trends.

336.3409489   DK   ISSN 0906-6993
DATA ON DANISH PUBLIC FOREIGN BORROWING. 1988. biennial. free. Danmarks Nationalbank, Havnegade 5, DK-1093 Copenhagen K, Denmark. FAX 45-33-32-46-27. circ. 700.
    Formerly (until 1991): Danish Data on the Public Foreign Borrowing and the Economy (ISSN 0905-1473)

332   US
DEBIT CARD NEWS; newsletter for retail electronic payments. (Includes 3 special issues.) 1984. m. $245. Faulkner & Gray, Inc., 300 S. Wacker Dr., 18th Fl., Chicago, IL 60606. TEL 312-913-1334. Ed. Lori Giesen. index. (back issues avail.) **Document type:** newsletter.
    ●Also available online. Vendor(s): Information Access Co., UMI.
    Formerly: P O S News (Point of Sale).
    Description: Covers developments affecting debit card marketing, economics and pricing issues, technology and operations and new POS applications.

332   US   ISSN 0731-0536
DEBITS AND DEPOSIT TURNOVER AT COMMERCIAL BANKS. m. $5. U.S. Federal Reserve System, Board of Governors, Publications Services, Rm. MS-138, Washington, DC 20551. TEL 202-452-3244. FAX 202-728-5886. **Document type:** government publication.
    Formerly (until 1977): Bank Debits, Deposits, and Deposit Turnover (ISSN 0730-4900)

332   US   ISSN 1076-9676
DEBT-FREE AND PROSPEROUS LIVING. 1992. m. $69 (effective Jan. 1995). Financial Independence Network Limited, Inc., 310 Second St., Boscobel, WI 53805-1164. TEL 608-675-3100. Ed. John M. Cummuta. circ. 3,000 (paid). (looseleaf format) **Document type:** consumer publication, newsletter.
    Formerly: Personal Financial Success.
    Description: Helps middle class baby boomers reclaim their incomes instead of transfering their lives' wealth to credit companies.

332   US
DEBTZAPPER. m. free. E-mail: pbalweirz@earthlink.net; URL: http://www.gen.com/debtzapper/tour/2044. **Document type:** newsletter.
    ●Available only online.
    Description: Designed to inform and educate the average individual in the art of financial management.

332   US
DELUXE; ideas for the business of living. 1985. q. (Deluxe Check Printers, Inc.) Maxwell Custom Publishing, 1999 Shepard Rd., St. Paul, MN 55116. TEL 612-690-7200. FAX 612-690-7357. Ed. George Ashfield. circ. controlled.

332   RU   ISSN 0130-3090
DEN'GI I KREDIT. 1932. m. $82 (effective 1998). Neglinnaya ul. 12, 103016 Moscow, Russia. TEL 095-925-4503. (Dist. by: Mezhdunarodnaya Kniga, B. Yakimanka 39, 117049 Moscow, Russia; Dist. in U.S. by: Victor Kamkin Inc., Boiling Brook Pkwy., Rockville, MD 20852. TEL 301-881-5973. FAX 301-881-1637) Ed. Y.G. Dmitriev. bk.rev.; charts; illus.; stat.; index. circ. 30,000. Indexed: Rural Recreat.Tour.Abstr., World Agri.Econ.& Rural Sociol.Abstr.
    —BLDSC (0052.700000).

332   DK   ISSN 0905-0965
HG8655
DENMARK. FINANSTILSYNET. BERETNING. 1989. a. DKK 50 (effective 1996). Finanstilsynet, Gl. Kongevej 74 A, DK-1850 Frederiksberg C, Denmark. TEL 45-33-55-82-82. FAX 45-33-55-82-00. (Dist. by: D B K Bogdistribution, Siljangade 2-8, DK-2300 Copenhagen S, Denmark)
    Formed by the merger of (1975-1989): Denmark. Finanstilsynet. Banker og Sparekasser (ISSN 0108-9129); (1988-1989): Denmark. Finanstilsynet. Fondsboersen og Boersmaeglerselskaber (ISSN 0904-437X); (1984-1989): Denmark. Finanstilsynet. Investeringsforeninger (ISSN 0109-9426); (1988-1989): Denmark. Finanstilsynet. Forsikringsselskaber og Pensionskasser m.v. (ISSN 0904-4361); Which was formerly (1982-1988): Denmark. Forsikringstilsynet. Beretning (ISSN 0108-7304); Incorporated (1983-1989): Denmark. Tilsynet med Realkreditinstitutter. Beretning (ISSN 0108-819X).

332   DK   ISSN 0907-3744
HG5594.3
DENMARK. FINANSTILSYNET. STATISTISK MATERIALE: BOERSOMRAADET. 1989. a. DKK 25. Finanstilsynet, Gl. Kongevej 74A, DK-1850 Frederiksberg C, Denmark. TEL 45-33-55-82-82. FAX 45-33-55-82-00. (Dist. by: D B K Bogdistribution, Siljangade 2-8, DK-2300 Copenhagen S, Denmark)
    Formerly (until 1991): Denmark. Finanstilsynet. Beretning. Bilag 4: Boersomraadet.

332   DK   ISSN 0907-3736
HG8655
DENMARK. FINANSTILSYNET. STATISTISK MATERIALE: SKADESFORSIKRINGSSELSKABER M.V. 1989. a. DKK 50. Finanstilsynet, Gl. Kongevej 74, 5, DK-1850 Frederiksberg C, Denmark. TEL 45-33-55-82-82. FAX 45-33-55-82-00. (Dist. by: D B K Bogdistribution, Siljangade 2-8, DK-2300 Copenhagen S, Denmark) circ. 3,500.
    Formerly (until 1991): Denmark. Finanstilsynet. Beretning. Bilag 3: Skadesforsikringsselskaber.

332.3   DK   ISSN 0906-5563
DENMARK. FINANSTILSYNET. TILSYNET MED REALKREDITINSTITUTTER. BERETNING. (Text in Danish, English and French) 1983. a. DKK 45. Finanstilsynet, Gl. Kongevej 7 A, DK-1850 Frederiksberg C, Denmark. TEL 45-33-55-82-82. FAX 45-33-55-82-00. (Dist. by: D B K Bogdistribution, Siljangade 2-8, DK-2300 Copenhagen S, Denmark) **Document type:** government publication.
    Formerly (until 1991): Denmark. Boligstyrelsen. Finanstilsynet. Tilsynet med Realkreditinstitutter. Beretning (ISSN 0108-819X)

332   US   ISSN 1082-8605
DEPOSIT GROWTH STRATEGIES. 1994. m. $319 (effective 1997). Siefer Consultants, Inc., Box 1384, Storm Lake, IA 50588. TEL 712-732-7340. FAX 712-732-7906. Ed. Joe Sheller. circ. 1,000 (paid). (back issues avail.) **Document type:** newsletter.
    Description: Discusses strategies for financial institutions to increase profits with deposits.

332   US   ISSN 1081-3268
DERIVATIVES QUARTERLY. q. $290 (foreign $365) (effective 1996). Institutional Investor Journals, 488 Madison Ave., New York, NY 10022. TEL 212-224-3185. FAX 212-224-3527.
    Formerly (until 1994): Derivatives Review.
    Description: Devoted to educating the financial professional on derivatives, explaining their use, defining risks and benefits, and providing practical strategies and applications.

DEUDA EXTERNA DE CHILE. see BUSINESS AND ECONOMICS

332   GW   ISSN 0722-3250
DEUTSCHE BANK BULLETIN; current economic and monetary issues. (Text in English) 1982. q. DM.20. Deutsche Bank Research, Guiollettstr. 48, 60325 Frankfurt a.M., Germany. TEL 49-69-7150-4732. Ed. Dieter Brauninger. **Document type:** bulletin.
    Description: Analyses of German and international business activity, financial markets, monetary policy, and industries reports.

332.1   GW   ISSN 0070-394X
HG3054
DEUTSCHE BUNDESBANK. GESCHAEFTSBERICHT. English Edition: Deutsche Bundesbank. Report (ISSN 0418-8306) (Editions in English, German) 1948. a. Deutsche Bundesbank, Postfach 100602, 60006 Frankfurt a.M., Germany. TEL 49-69-9566-1. FAX 49-69-5601071. URL: http://www.bundesbank.de. charts; stat. circ. 70,500 (63,000 German ed.; 7,500 English ed.). **Document type:** corporate report.
    Description: Covers economic developments and bank policy, international monetary developments and policy, annual accounts.

332   GW   ISSN 0011-9997
DEUTSCHE BUNDESBANK. MITTEILUNGEN. 1966. w. DM.28 per quarter (effective 1994). Druck- und Verlagshaus Frankfurt am Main GmbH, Grosse Eschenheimer Str. 16-18, 60313 Frankfurt a.M., Germany. TEL 49-69-2199-1. FAX 49-69-2199421. **Document type:** corporate report.

332   GW   ISSN 0012-0006
HC281
DEUTSCHE BUNDESBANK. MONATSBERICHTE. English edition: Deutsche Bundesbank. Monthly Report. (ISSN 0418-8292) (Editions in English, German) 1948. m. free. Deutsche Bundesbank, Postfach 100602, 60006 Frankfurt a.M., Germany. TEL 49-69-9566-1. FAX 49-69-5601071. URL: http://www.bundesbank.de. charts; mkt.; stat.; index. circ. 58,000 (controlled)(52,500 German ed.; 5,500 English ed.) Indexed: ELLIS, Key to Econ.Sci., P.A.I.S., World Bank.Abstr. **Document type:** bulletin.
    Description: Covers economic and financial situation in Germany.

DEUTSCHE BUNDESBANK. MONATSBERICHTE. STATISTISCHE BEIHEFTE. REIHE 1: BANKENSTATISTIK NACH BANKENGRUPPEN. see BUSINESS AND ECONOMICS — Abstracting, Bibliographies, Statistics

DEUTSCHE BUNDESBANK. MONATSBERICHTE. STATISTISCHE BEIHEFTE. REIHE 5: DEVISENKURSSTATISTIK. see BUSINESS AND ECONOMICS — Abstracting, Bibliographies, Statistics

BUSINESS AND ECONOMICS — BANKING AND FINANCE

DEUTSCHE BUNDESBANK. MONATSBERICHTE. STATISTISCHE BEIHEFTE. REIHE 2: KAPITALMARKTSTATISTIK. see *BUSINESS AND ECONOMICS — Abstracting, Bibliographies, Statistics*

DEUTSCHE BUNDESBANK. MONATSBERICHTE. STATISTISCHE BEIHEFTE. REIHE 4: SAISONBEREINIGTE WIRTSCHAFTSZAHLEN. see *BUSINESS AND ECONOMICS — Abstracting, Bibliographies, Statistics*

DEUTSCHE BUNDESBANK. MONATSBERICHTE. STATISTISCHE BEIHEFTE. REIHE 3: ZAHLUNGSBILANZSTATISTIK. see *BUSINESS AND ECONOMICS — Abstracting, Bibliographies, Statistics*

332 GW
DEUTSCHE GELD- UND KREDITINSTITUTE. BANKEN-ORTSLEXIKON. 1950. base vol. (plus m. updates). DM.915 (CD-ROM DM.1280) (effective 1997). Verlag Hoppenstedt GmbH, Havelstr. 9, 64295 Darmstadt, Germany. TEL 49-6151-380-0. FAX 49-6151-380-360. (looseleaf format) **Document type:** directory.
●Also available on CD-ROM.

332 GW
DEUTSCHE POSTBANK AG GESCHAEFTSBERICHT. 1990. a. Deutsche Postbank AG, Postfach 4000, 53105 Bonn, Germany. TEL 49-228-920-1101. FAX 49-228-920-1810. URL: http://www.postbank.de. **Document type:** corporate report.

332.1 GW ISSN 0012-0766
DEUTSCHE SPARKASSENZEITUNG. 1924. 2/w. DM.138 (effective 1996). (Deutscher Sparkassen- und Giroverband e.V.) Deutscher Sparkassenverlag GmbH, Am Wallgraben 115, 70565 Stuttgart, Germany. Ed. George Clegg. adv.; charts; illus.; stat.; index, cum.index. circ. 23,000. **Document type:** newsletter.
—CCC.

332 331.8 GW
DEUTSCHES BANKEN-HANDBUCH. irreg. (approx. 3/yr.). DM.78. Walhalla Fachverlag, Haus an der Eisernen Bruecke, 93059 Regensburg, Germany. TEL 49-941-5684-0. FAX 49-941-5684111. E-mail: walhalla@walhalla.de; URL: http://www.walhalla.de. adv.; bk.rev. circ. 5,500. (looseleaf format) **Document type:** bulletin.
Formerly: Bankangestellte (ISSN 0067-3781)

332 GW
DEUTSCHES SPARKASSEN HANDBUCH. irreg. (approx. 3/yr.). DM.78. Walhalla Fachverlag, Haus an der Eisernen Bruecke, 93059 Regensburg, Germany. TEL 49-941-5684-0. FAX 49-941-5684111. E-mail: walhalla@walhalla.de; URL: http://www.walhalla.de. adv. circ. 5,800. (looseleaf format) **Document type:** bulletin.

332 SA ISSN 1018-6026
DEVELOPER. (Text in English) 1982. 3/yr. free. Kwazulu Finance and Investment Corporation Ltd., P.O. Box 2801, Durban 4000, South Africa. TEL 27-31-9078612. FAX 27-31-9073292. Ed. Michael Phillips. adv.; circ. 10,000. (controlled). (back issues avail.)
—BLDSC (3578.541500).
Description: Covers topics relevant to the economic, industrial, agricultural and social development of Kwazulu-Natal.
Refereed Serial

332.1 MF
DEVELOPMENT BANK OF MAURITIUS. REPORT AND ACCOUNTS. (Text in English) 1965. a. Development Bank of Mauritius, Box 157, Port Louis, Mauritius.

DEVELOPMENT BANK OF SOUTHERN AFRICA. DEVELOPMENT PAPERS. see *BUSINESS AND ECONOMICS — International Development And Assistance*

332.1 ZA
DEVELOPMENT BANK OF ZAMBIA. ANNUAL REPORT. (Text in English) a. Development Bank of Zambia, P.O. Box 33955, Lusaka, Zambia. TEL 260-1-228576. FAX 260-1-222426. TELEX ZA 45040. **Document type:** corporate report.

332 KE
DEVELOPMENT FINANCE COMPANY OF KENYA. ANNUAL REPORT AND STATEMENT OF ACCOUNTS. (Text in English) a. Development Finance Company of Kenya Ltd., P.O. Box 30483, Finance House, Loitta St., Nairobi, Kenya. **Document type:** corporate report.

332 FR
DICTIONNAIRE PERMANENT: EPARGNE ET PRODUITS FINANCIERS. 2 base vols. plus m. updates. 1590 F. for base vol. (updates 400 F.) (effective 1995). Editions Legislatives et Administratives, 80 ave. de la Marne, 92546 Montrouge Cedex, France. TEL 40-92-68-68. FAX 46-56-00-15. TELEX 632 855 F. (looseleaf format)
Description: Examines financial, legal and fiscal problems pertaining to savings and investments.

332 333.33 340 CN ISSN 0315-811X
DIGEST, BUSINESS & LAW JOURNAL. 1971. w. Can.$250 (effective 1997). Wa-Bowden Real Estate Reports Ltd., 826 Erin St., Winnipeg, MB R3G 2W4, Canada. TEL 204-775-8918. FAX 204-788-4322. Pub. W.G. Bowden. adv.; bk.rev. circ. 1,800. (back issues avail.)

332 US
DIGEST OF CHANGES IN C U S I P. (Committee on Uniform Security Procedures) a. $225. (American Bankers Association, Committee on Uniform Security Identification Procedures) Standard & Poor's Corporation (Subsidiary of: McGraw-Hill, Inc.), 25 Broadway, New York, NY 10004. TEL 212-208-8000. Ed. John Frei. **Document type:** trade publication.

332 368 IE
▼**DIRECT DELIVERY INTERNATIONAL.** 1995. 10/yr. I£360. Lafferty Publications Ltd., The Tower, IDA Enterprise Centre, Pearse St., Dublin 2, Ireland. TEL 353-1-6718022. FAX 353-1-6718520. E-mail: cvserv@lafferty.ie; URL: http://www.unm.lafferty.co.uk. (US subscr. to: 420 Lexington Ave., Ste. 1745, New York, NY 10170. TEL 212-557-6726) Ed. Peter Kinahan. R&P contact: David Barry. **Document type:** trade publication.
Description: Provides information on new developments, strategies and trends in international banking and insurance.

332 CK
DIRECTORIO DE INSTITUCIONES FINANCIERAS. a. Col.$3000($10) Corporacion Editorial Interamericana, Avda. Jimenez 403 (of 907), Apdo. 14965, Bogota 1, Colombia.

DIRECTORIO DEL SECTOR FINANCIERO. see *BUSINESS AND ECONOMICS — Trade And Industrial Directories*

DIRECTORIO Y SERVICIOS DE INSTITUCIONES DEL SISTEMA FINANCIERO DE EL SALVADOR. see *BUSINESS AND ECONOMICS — Trade And Industrial Directories*

332.2 US ISSN 1068-6460
HG2150
DIRECTORS & TRUSTEES DIGEST. 198? m. $70 to non-members; members $32. America's Community Bankers, 900 19th St., N.W., Ste. 400, Washington, DC 20006. TEL 202-857-3100. FAX 202-296-8716. URL: http://www.acbankers.org. Ed. Peter Faletti. circ. 11,080. (back issues avail.) **Document type:** newsletter.
Formed by the 1992 merger of: Directors Digest & Trustees and Directors Letter.
Description: Provides the latest details on board-management relations, legislation and regulations and corporate governance challenges facing savings and community bankers.

332 UK
▼**DIRECTORY OF FINANCIAL REGULATORY AGENCIES.** 1996. a. $180 (effective 1997). Central Banking Publications Ltd., 27 Chancery Lane, London WC2A 1PA, England. TEL 44-171-404-6435. FAX 4-171-404-6436. E-mail: centralbank@easynet.co.uk; URL: http://easyweb.easynet.co.uk/centralbank/. (Dist. in N. America by: European Business Publications, Box 391, Darien, CT 06820. TEL 203-656-2701. FAX 203-655-8332) Ed. Robert Pringle. **Document type:** directory.

332.1 US ISSN 0093-951X
HG4347.A1
DIRECTORY OF TRUST INSTITUTIONS. 1962. a. $69.95. Intertec Publishing Corp. (Atlanta), 6151 Powers Ferry Rd., N.W., Atlanta, GA 30339-2941. TEL 770-955-2500. FAX 770-955-0400. Ed. Barbara Katinsky. adv.; illus. circ. 12,583. **Document type:** directory.
Formerly: Directory of Trust Institutions of United States and Canada.

332 IT
DIRITTO DELLA BANCA E DEL MERCATO FINANZIARIO. 1987. q. L.160000 (foreign L.220000) (effective 1997). (Centro Studi di Diritto e Legislazione Bancaria) Casa Editrice Dott. Antonio Milani, Via Jappelli 5-6, 35121 Padua, Italy. TEL 39-49-656677. FAX 39-49-8752900. Ed. Alessandro Nigro. circ. 1,000.

DOLLARS & CENTS. see *BUSINESS AND ECONOMICS — Management*

332 US ISSN 0194-8490
DOLLARSENSE; your money management magazine. 1977. q. $12 to qualified personnel. E.F. Baumer & Company, 401 Shatto Pl., Ste. 105, Los Angeles, CA 90020. TEL 213-386-2111. FAX 213-386-6470. E-mail: efbandco@aol.com. Ed. Richard Baumer. R&P contact: Aaron P. Gill. adv. contact: Aaron P. Gill. bk.rev.; circ. 800,000 (controlled). (back issues avail.) **Document type:** consumer publication.
●Also available online.
Also available on CD-ROM.
Description: Addresses personal financial planning, estate planning and retirement planning for the general reader.

332.1 DR ISSN 0302-5241
DOMINICAN REPUBLIC. SUPERINTENDENCIA DE BANCOS. ANUARIO ESTADISTICO. 1971. a. Superintendencia de Bancos, Avda. Mexico, esq. L. Navarro, Apdo. 1326, Santo Domingo, Dominican Republic. **Document type:** government publication.

332 DR
DOMINICAN REPUBLIC. SUPERINTENDENCIA DE BANCOS. INFORME ESTADISTICO TRIMESTRAL. q. Superintendencia de Bancos, Avda. Mexico, esq. L. Navarro, Apdo. 1326, Santo Domingo, Dominican Republic. **Document type:** government publication.

334.2 CN ISSN 0012-6934
DUCA POST. (Text in English) 1960. 8/yr. membership Duca Community Credit Union Ltd., Box 1100, Willowdale, ON M2N 5W5, Canada. TEL 416-223-8502. FAX 416-223-2575. E-mail: duca.into@duca.com; URL: http://www.duca.com. Ed. Jack Vanderkooy. R&P contact: Jack Vanderkooy. adv. contact: Jack Vanderkooy. bk.rev.; circ. 11,000 (controlled). **Document type:** newsletter.
Refereed Serial

332 658.3 US
E B QUARTERLY. (Employee Benefits) 1989. q. $200 to non-members; members $135. American Bankers Association, Trust and Private Banking Center, 1120 Connecticut Ave., N.W., Washington, DC 20036. TEL 202-663-5087. FAX 202-663-7543. (Subscr. to: Customer Service Center, Box 630538, Baltimore, MD 21623-0538. TEL 800-338-0626) (also avail. in microform from UMI; back issues avail.) **Document type:** newsletter.
●Also available online. Vendor(s): UMI.
Description: Provides information on pension and tax law changes, DOL and IRS regulations, court rulings, liability developments, and reporting and participant recordkeeping requirements.

332.1 340 UK ISSN 1356-9147
▼**E U BANKING AND FINANCE LAW.** 1995. base vol. (plus updates). £375 worldwide. Agra Europe (London) Ltd., 25 Frant Rd., Tunbridge Wells, Kent TN2 5JT, England. TEL 44-1892-833813. FAX 44-1892-544895. TELEX 95114 AGRATW G. E-mail: 100637.3460@compuserve.com. (looseleaf format) **Document type:** trade publication.

332 UK
EARNINGS GUIDE; weekly analysis of profits and earnings estimates. (Also avail. direct via modem) 1978. m. £270. Box 1, Horsham, W. Sussex RH12 3YY, England. TEL 0403-791155. FAX 0403-701152. Ed. R. Finch-Hatton. adv. (back issues avail.) **Document type:** trade publication.

BUSINESS AND ECONOMICS — BANKING AND FINANCE

332   UK
EARNINGS GUIDE ON P C. (Not avail. in printed format) w. £1,200. Box 1, Horsham, W. Sussex RH12 3YY, England. TEL 0403-791155. FAX 0403-701152. Ed. R. Finch-Hatton. (diskette format; DOS and Windows versions avail.)
●Also available online.

332.1   UG   ISSN 1015-0676
EAST AFRICAN DEVELOPMENT BANK. ANNUAL REPORT. (Text in English) 1968. a. East African Development Bank, Box 7128, Kampala, Uganda.

EAST EUROPE & THE REPUBLICS: A POLITICAL RISK ANNUAL. see *BUSINESS AND ECONOMICS — Economic Situation And Conditions*

332   IE   ISSN 0791-3931
EAST EUROPEAN BANKER. 1990. 10/yr. I£549. Lafferty Publications Ltd., The Tower, IDA Enterprise Centre, Pearse St., Dublin 2, Ireland. TEL 353-1-6718022. FAX 353-1-6718520. E-mail: cvserv@lafferty.ie; URL: http://www.unm.lafferty.co.uk. (US subscr. to: 420 Lexington Ave., Ste. 1745, New York, NY 10170. TEL 212-557-6726) Ed. Ciaran Brennan. R&P contact: David Barr. **Document type:** bulletin.
Description: Specialist intelligence monitor on East and Central European financial affairs.

EAST EUROPEAN MARKETS; the East European business and financial briefing. see *BUSINESS AND ECONOMICS — Marketing And Purchasing*

EAST - WEST COMMERSANT. see *BUSINESS AND ECONOMICS — Economic Situation And Conditions*

332   XI
EASTERN CARIBBEAN CENTRAL BANK. QUARTERLY COMMERCIAL BANKING STATISTICS. q. free. Eastern Caribbean Central Bank, Research Department, P.O. Box 89, Basseterre, St. Kitts, W.I. TEL 869-465-2537. **Document type:** bulletin.

332   BE
ECHO (VINDERHOUTE). (Text in Flemish, French) 1964. s-a. membership. Association Nationale des Comptables de Belgique, Kasteellaan 8, 9921 Vinderhoute, Belgium. TEL 91-267916. adv.

332   BE
ECHO DES TIRAGES. (Text in French) m. 700 BEF. Agefi Luxembourg, 131 rue de Birmingham, B-1070 Brussels, Belgium. adv. circ. 18,000.

332   MR   ISSN 0851-1470
LES ECHOS AFRICAINS; mensuel marocain d'informations economiques et financieres. (Text in French) 1972. m. DH.150. Immeuble SONIR, Rue d'Anjou angle rue Mohamed Smiha, B.P. 1340, Casablanca, Morocco. TEL 30-72-71. TELEX 27905. Ed. Mohamed Chouffani El-Fassi. adv. circ. 2,000. **Document type:** newspaper.
Description: Covers international and domestic business and government news affecting Morocco.

332   IT   ISSN 0393-9243
ECONOMIA E BANCA. 1978. q. L.50000($36) (Banca di Trento e Bolzano) Manfrini Editori, Via Brennero 2, 38060 Calliano (TN), Italy. index. circ. 15,000. (back issues avail.)

ECONOMIC & FINANCIAL QUARTERLY. see *BUSINESS AND ECONOMICS — Economic Situation And Conditions*

332.1   CL   ISSN 0716-2421
ECONOMIC AND FINANCIAL REPORT. (Text in English) 1982. m. Ch.$31000($150) Banco Central de Chile, Casilla 967, Santiago, Chile. TEL 56-2-6702000. FAX 56-2-6984847. TELEX 405 69 CENBC CL. circ. 300. **Document type:** government publication.
Description: Chilean economic survey with statistical charts.

ECONOMIC COMMENTARY. see *BUSINESS AND ECONOMICS*

332   CH
ECONOMIC NEWS DAILY BULLETIN. 5/w. price varies. China Economic News Service, 561 Chunghsiao E. Rd. Sec. 4, Taipei, Taiwan 10516, Republic of China. TEL 02-642-2629. FAX 02-642-7422. TELEX 27710-CENSPC. **Document type:** bulletin.

ECONOMIC OUTLOOK. see *BUSINESS AND ECONOMICS — Economic Situation And Conditions*

332.2   US
ECONOMIC OUTLOOK; a newsletter on economic issues for financial institutions. 1991. m. $212 to non-members; members $106. American Community Bankers, 900 19th St., N.W., Ste. 400, Washington, DC 20006. TEL 202-857-3126. FAX 202-296-8716. Ed. Robert Davis. charts. circ. 4,500. (back issues avail.) **Document type:** newsletter.
Formerly (until 1993): Economic Insight.
Description: Tracks the changes in interest rates, the housing market and the U.S. economy.

332   US   ISSN 0013-0281
HC107.03   CODEN: ERFCBR
ECONOMIC REVIEW. 1919. q. free. Federal Reserve Bank of Cleveland, Box 6387, Cleveland, OH 44101. TEL 216-579-3079. FAX 216-579-2477. Eds. Robin Ratliff, Tess Ferg. R&P contact: Kathy Popovich. charts; stat. circ. 12,100. (also avail. in microfiche from CIS; back issues avail.; reprint service avail. from CIS) **Indexed:** ABI Inform., Amer.Stat.Ind. (1980-), C.R.E.J., Fed Print, P.A.I.S., PROMT. **Document type:** academic/scholarly publication.
●Also available online. Vendor(s): UMI.
—BLDSC (3654.930000); UMI; UnCover.
Supersedes: Monthly Business Review.

330   II   ISSN 0013-0389
HC424.A1
ECONOMIC TIMES. (Text in English) 1961. d. $200. Bennett, Coleman & Co. Ltd. (Bombay), Times Bldg., Dr. D.N. Rd., Bombay 400 001, India. TEL 4150271. URL: http://www.economictimes.com. (U.S. subscr. addr.: M-s. Kalpana, 42-75 Main St., Flushing, NY 11355) Ed. Hannan Ezekiel. adv.; bk.rev.; charts; illus.; stat. circ. 45,300. (also avail. in microfilm; microfiche) **Document type:** newspaper.

332   CE
ECONOMIC TIMES. (Text in English) 1970. fortn. $16. Albion Publications, 146-54 Aramaya Rd., Colombo 9, Sri Lanka. TEL 686337. Ed. Thimsy Fahim. R&P contact: Al Haj M.A.C.M. Fahim. adv.: page $286; adv. contact: Al Haj M.A.C.M. Fahim. bk.rev. circ. 10,000. **Indexed:** Sri Lanka Sci.Ind. **Document type:** newspaper.

332   US
ECONOMIC TOPICS.* m. $100 to non-members. United States League of Savings Institutions, 900 19th St., N.W., No. 900, Washington, DC 20006-2105. TEL 312-644-3100. FAX 312-644-9358. Ed. James Christian. circ. 11,000.
Formerly: Economic Topics for Savings and Loan Management.
Description: Contains analysis and forecasting of major market trends to determine their impact on the savings institution business.

332   PH   ISSN 0117-0511
HC411
ECONOMICS AND DEVELOPMENT RESOURCE CENTER. REPORT SERIES. (Text in English) irreg., no. 55, 1991. Asian Development Bank, Economics and Development Resource Center, P.O. Box 789, 1099 Manila, Philippines. TEL 632-711-3851. FAX 632-741-7961. TELEX 29066 ADB PH.

332   FR
ECONOMIES ET SOCIETES. SERIE MO. ECONOMIE MONETAIRE. 1978. irreg. 350 F. Presses Universitaires de Grenoble, B.P. 47, 38040 Grenoble Cedex 9, France. Dir. C. de Boissieu.

330   AG   ISSN 0013-0648
ECONOMISTA; semanario economico-financiero. 1951. w. Arg.$5800. Empresa Editorial el Economista s.r.l., Avda. Cordoba 632, 2o, 1054 Buenos Aires, Argentina. TEL 322-3308. FAX 322-8157. TELEX 23542. Dir. D. Radonjic. adv.; bk.rev.; stat.; tr.lit. circ. 37,800. **Document type:** newspaper.

332   SP   ISSN 0013-0656
ECONOMISTA; revista financiera. 1886. w. 1590 ptas. Calle del Conde de Aranda 8, Apdo. 1024, Madrid 28001, Spain. TEL 91-4350462. Dir. Jose Luis Elorriaga. adv.; bk.rev.; charts; mkt.; pat.; tr.lit.; tr.mk. circ. 21,000.

332   EC
ECUADOR. SUPERINTENDENCIA DE BANCOS. BOLETIN ESTADISTICO. 1938. a. S/2000. Superintendencia de Bancos, Avda. 12 de Octubre 1561, Apdo. de Correos 17-17-770, Quito, Ecuador. FAX 563-652. TELEX 21102 SUPBAN ED. charts; stat. **Document type:** government publication, bulletin.
Formerly: Ecuador. Superintendencia de Bancos. Boletin.

332   EC
ECUADOR. SUPERINTENDENCIA DE BANCOS. MEMORIA. a. S/18000 for 1992 ed. Superintendencia de Bancos, Avda. 12 de Octubre 1561, Apdo. de Correos 17-17-770, Quito, Ecuador. FAX 563-652. TELEX 21102 SUPBAN ED. charts; stat.

332.1   VE
EKARE. 1976-198? bi-m. $10. Banco del Libro, Unidad de Divulgacion y Relaciones Institucionales, Apdo. 5893, Caracas 1010A, Venezuela.

332.024 305.26   US
ELDERCARE FORUM. 1994. q. $14. ElderCare Financial Management, Inc., 170 Elaine Dr., Roswell, GA 30075. TEL 770-518-2767. E-mail: hwlj87a@prodigy.com; URL: http://www.mindspung.com/~eldercare/elderweb.htm. Ed. Laura Beller. R&P contact: Laura Beller. circ. 15,000 (paid). **Document type:** trade publication.
●Also available online.
Description: Educates and informs caregivers about issues related to aging and taking care of an aging parent. Focuses on personal financial management, health and medical issues, housing, government programs, and resources for caregivers.

332   US
▼**ELECTRONIC COMMERCE REPORT.** 1996. m. $175. Treasury Management Association, 7315 Wisconsin Ave., Ste. 600 W., Bethesda, MD 20814. TEL 301-307-2862. FAX 301-307-2864. Ed. Ayo I. Mseka; Pub. Donald E. Manger. R&P contact: Jessica Ripper. adv. contact: Maria C. DeRyke. circ. 450. **Document type:** newsletter.

332   UN   ISSN 1012-8115
HG5993
EMERGING STOCK MARKETS FACTBOOK. 1986. a. $100. International Finance Corporation, Capital Market Dept., 1818 H St., N.W., Washington, DC 20433. TEL 202-478-0611. FAX 202-676-9299. E-mail: emdb@ifc.org; URL: http://www.ifc.org. circ. 5,000. (also avail. in microfiche from CIS) **Indexed:** IIS.
Description: Provides both fundamental economic information and vital data on market size, liquidity, and valuations.

332   BL
EMPRESAS NA BOLSA.* a. (Ascor Dealer Sociedade Financeira de Corretagem) Texto Editora, Lda., Alto de Bela Vista, Casal de Vale Mourao, 2735 Cacem, Portugal. TEL 1-9180208. Eds. Alvaro Mendonca, Ana Paula Saude.

ENCYCLOPEDIA OF BANKING LAW. see *LAW*

332.1 334   US
END POINT EXPRESS; exclusive report for bank operations professionals. 1984. fortn. $247. United Communications Group, 11300 Rockville Pike, Ste. 1100, Rockville, MD 20852-3030. TEL 301-816-8950. FAX 301-816-8945. Ed. Martin Zook. bk.rev.
Former titles: Back-Office Bulletin; Executive Automation Report for the Community Banker.
Description: Covers changing technologies, new approaches and cost-saving ideas.

332 333.79   UK   ISSN 1362-5403
ENERGY & POWER RISK MANAGEMENT. 1994. 10/yr. £199($299) (effective 1997). Financial Engineering Ltd., Risk Publications, 104-112 Marylebone Ln., London W1M 5FU, England. TEL 44-171-487-5326. FAX 44-171-486-0879. Ed. Graham Cooper; Pub. Peter Field. adv.: B&W page £2250, color page £2670; trim 297 x 210; adv. contact: Simon Turner. circ. 4,000. **Document type:** trade publication.
Formerly (until 1996): Energy Risk (ISSN 1352-0768).
Description: Delivers comprehensive, cutting-edge analysis of financial risk management in the world's energy and power markets.

BUSINESS AND ECONOMICS — BANKING AND FINANCE

332   IT
ENNEPI. 1987. m. L.52000. Edisek di Puccinelli GianCarlo, Via V. Veneto 124, 56025 Pontedera, Italy. TEL 39-587-56-647. FAX 39-587-550-30. TELEX 590180 SECINF I. Ed. Gianluca Puccinelli. adv.: B&W page L.920000, color page L.1656000. circ. 5,000.

332   GW   ISSN 0421-2991
ENTSCHEIDUNGEN DER FINANZGERICHTE. 1953. s-m. DM.368 (effective 1997). Stollfuss Verlag Bonn, Postfach 2428, 53014 Bonn, Germany. TEL 49-228-724-0. FAX 49-228-659223. Ed. Eckart Ranft. (back issues avail.) **Document type:** bulletin.
—CCC.

332.1   FR   ISSN 1157-6472
EPARGNE ET FINANCE; le magazine de l'actualite et des mutations bancaires. 1882. bi-m. 120 F. (foreign 200 F.) (effective 1995). Journal des Caisses d'Epargne, SARL, 29 rue de la Tombe-Issoire, 75673 Paris Cedex 14, France. TEL 40-78-41-01. FAX 40-78-40-10. TELEX 200 668. Ed. Nicolas de Bourgies. adv.: B&W page 8700 F., color page 13900 F.; trim 297 x 199. bk.rev.; charts; illus.; stat. circ. 15,000. **Indexed:** ELLIS, P.A.I.S.For.Lang.Ind.
Formerly (until 1992): Journal des Caisses d'Epargne (ISSN 0047-2182)
Description: For bank managers, financiers and economists.

332   GR   ISSN 1105-2503
HC291
EPILOGI/CHOICE; oikonomiki epitheorisi. (Supplement to: Shipping and Tourism) (Text in Greek; statistics & summaries in English) 1963. m. $150 (subscr. includes 7 supplements). Electra Press, 4 Stadiou, 105 64 Athens, Greece. TEL 30-1-323-3203. FAX 323-5160. TELEX 210564. Ed. Christos Papaioannou. adv.; bk.rev.; stat. circ. 9,000. **Indexed:** Lib.Lit.
Description: Economic reviews of banking, the financial markets, management, and international and domestic business. Examines the impact of current domestic and international developments.

332   US   ISSN 0071-142X
HG136
ESSAYS IN INTERNATIONAL FINANCE. 1943. irreg., no.201, 1996. $40 (includes Studies in International Finance; Reprints in International Finance; Special Papers in International Economics) (effective 1996 & 1997). Princeton University, International Finance Section, c/o Margaret B. Riccardi, Ed., Department of Economics, Fisher Hall, Princeton, NJ 08544-1021. TEL 609-258-4048. FAX 609-258-6419. R&P contact: Margaret B. Riccardi. circ. 2,000. (also avail. in microfilm from UMI; back issues avail.; reprint service avail. from UMI) **Document type:** monographic series.
—BLDSC (3811.698000); UMI.
Description: Nontechnical accounts of international finance for professional economists and laypersons.

332   PN   ISSN 1017-4281
HJ21
ESTADISTICA PANAMENA. SITUACION ECONOMICA. SECCION 344. FINANZAS. 1958. a. Bl.0.50 (effective 1997). Direccion de Estadistica y Censo, Contraloria General, Apdo. 5213, Panama 5, Panama. FAX 507-269-7294. circ. 700. **Document type:** government publication, bulletin.
Supersedes in part (in 1988): Estadistica Panamena. Situacion Economica. Seccion 343-344. Hacienda Publica y Finanzas (ISSN 0378-6730)
Description: Contains statistics on the banking system and the International Bank of Panama. Presents information on credit institutions, savings and loan associations, and cooperatives.

ESTATE TAX FREEZE: TOOLS AND TECHNIQUES. see REAL ESTATE

332   CL   ISSN 0716-1255
ESTRATEGIA. 1978. d. (5/w.). Ch.$89900 (foreign $700) (effective 1997). Editorial Gestion, Ltda., Rafael Canas 114, Casilla 16485, Correo 9, Santiago, Chile. TEL 56-2-2361313. FAX 56-2-2361114. E-mail: estrategia@edgestion. cl. Ed. Victor Manuel Ojeda. adv. contact: Rodrigo Sepulveda. charts; mkt.; stat. circ. 42,000. (tabloid format)

332   SP   ISSN 1130-8753
ESTRATEGIA FINANCIERA. 1987. 11/yr. 26500 ptas. (effective 1996). Grupo Especial Directivos, C. Orense 39 2o D, 28020 Madrid, Spain. TEL 34-1-5566411. FAX 34-1-5554118. Ed. Juan Jose Gonzalez Ortiz. adv.: B&W page 365000 ptas., color page 450000 ptas.; trim 187 x 272; adv. contact: Ricardo Zavala. circ. 8,000 (controlled).
—CINDOC.

332.1   SP
ESTUDIA Y AHORRA. 1966. q. free. Caja de Ahorros de Ronda, Virgen de la Paz, 18, Ronda (Malaga), Spain. bk.rev.

332.1 338   US   ISSN 1083-8880
EUROMEDIA ACQUISITIONS & FINANCE. 1992. m. $795 (effective 1997). Kagan World Media, Ltd., 126 Clock Tower Pl., Carmel, CA 93923. TEL 408-624-1536. FAX 408-625-3225. E-mail: info@kagan.com. Ed. Paul Kagan. adv. contact: Lorraine Yglesias. **Document type:** trade publication.
Formed by the merger of: Euromedia Acquisitions (ISSN 1061-2874) & Euromedia Finance (ISSN 1070-3233)

332.4 382   UK   ISSN 0014-2433
HG3881
EUROMONEY; the monthly journal of international money and capital markets. (Supplement avail.: Guide to World Equity Markets) 1969. 12. £195 (Europe, US & Canada $395; elsewhere $420) (effective 1997). Euromoney Publications plc., Nestor House, Playhouse Yard, London EC4V 5EX, England. TEL 44-171-779-8935. FAX 44-171-779-8541. E-mail: gevans@pobox. com; URL: http://www.emwl.com/contents/ publications/euromoney/. (Subscr. to: Quadrant Subscription Services, Stuart House, Parrymount Rd., Haywards Heath, W. Sussex RH16 3BN, England; Dist. in US by: American Educational Systems, 173 W. 81st St., New York, NY 10024. TEL 800-717-2669. FAX 212-501-8926) Ed. Chris Garnet. bk.rev.; index. circ. 20,674. (also avail. in microform from UMI; reprint service avail. from UMI) **Indexed:** ABI Inform., B.P.I., Bank.Lit.Ind., BPIA, Bus.Ind., C.R.E.J., ELLIS, Euro.LJI, Ind.Bus.Rep., Ind.Per.Art.Relat.Law, Key to Econ.Sci., LJI, Manage.Cont., Mid.East: Abstr.& Ind., P.A.I.S., PROMT, SCIMP (1980-), Tr.& Indus.Ind., World Bank.Abstr. **Document type:** trade publication.
●Also available online. Vendor(s): Information Access Co., Knight-Ridder Information, Inc., UMI. Also available on CD-ROM.
—BLDSC (3829.286000); KR SourceOne; SWETS; UMI; UnCover.
Description: Covers the world of international finance.

332.4   UK
EUROMONEY CAPITAL MARKETS GUIDE; the complete data service on syndicated loans and Eurobonds. 1980. m. £1950 (foreign $3125) (effective 1997). Euromoney Publications plc., Nestor House, Playhouse Yard, London EC4V 5EX, England. TEL 44-171-779-8935. FAX 44-171-779-8541. (Dist. in US by: American Educational Systems, 173 W. 81st St., New York, NY 10024. TEL 800-717-2669. FAX 212-501-8926) Ed. Nick Evans. **Document type:** trade publication.
Formerly: Euromoney Syndication Guide (ISSN 0260-6747)

332   UK
EUROMONEY JAPANESE DIGEST. (Text and summaries in Japanese) 1986. q. £125 (Japan 29000 Yen; elsewhere $225) (effective 1997). Euromoney Publications plc., Nestor House, Playhouse Yard, London EC4V 5EX, England. TEL 44-171-779-8888. FAX 44-171-779-8617. (Subscr. to: Quadrant Subscription Services, Stuart House, Perrymount Rd., Haywards Heath, W. Sussex RH16 3BN, England; Dist. in US by: American Educational Systems, 173 W. 81st St., New York, NY 10024. TEL 800-717-2669. FAX 212-501-8926) Ed. Mika Ishiwata. circ. 7,500. **Document type:** trade publication.
Description: Covers current affairs in the world of finance.

332   IT   ISSN 0390-2102
HF3581
EUROPA DOMANI. 1974. m. L.70000 (foreign L.120000) (effective 1996). Stampa Economica s.r.l., Viale Lombardia 22, 20131 Milan, Italy. TEL 39-2-70635233. FAX 39-2-70635364. Ed. Goffredo Giovannetti. adv.: B&W page L.6500000, color page L.7800000; adv. contact: Diana Giani. circ. 15,000 (paid). **Indexed:** PROMT.

332   IE   ISSN 0953-8399
EUROPEAN BANKER. 1989. 10/yr. I£679. Lafferty Publications Ltd., The Tower, IDA Enterprise Centre, Pearse St., Dublin 2, Ireland. TEL 353-1-6718022. FAX 353-1-6718520. E-mail: cvserv@lafferty.ie; URL: http://www.unm.lafferty.co.uk. (US subscr. to: 420 Lexington Ave., Ste. 1745, New York, NY 10170. TEL 212-557-6726) Ed. Aine Coffey. R&P contact: David Barr. **Document type:** newsletter.
Description: Gives news and market intelligence on national and cross-border developments in European banking, insurance and finance.

332.1   BE   ISSN 0071-2787
EUROPEAN FEDERATION OF FINANCE HOUSE ASSOCIATIONS. ANNUAL REPORT. Short title: Eurofinas. Annual Report. (Text in English, French, German) 1963. a. free. European Federation of Finance House Associations, 267 av. de Tervuren, 1150 Brussels, Belgium. FAX 32-2-7780579. Ed. M. Baert. circ. controlled.

332   BE   ISSN 0300-4252
EUROPEAN FEDERATION OF FINANCE HOUSE ASSOCIATIONS. NEWSLETTER. Short title: Eurofinas. Newsletter. (Text in English, French, German) 1961. 6/yr. free. European Federation of Finance House Associations, 267 av. de Tervuren, 1150 Brussels, Belgium. FAX 32-2-7780579. Ed. M. Baert. circ. controlled. **Document type:** newsletter.

332   UK   ISSN 0955-4033
EUROPEAN FINANCE DIRECTOR. 1987. q. £38. Harrington Kilbride plc., The Publishing House, Highbury Station Rd., Islington, London N1 1SE, England. TEL 071-226-2222. FAX 071-226-1255. TELEX 263174 HKP G. Ed. Alan Spence. (back issues avail.)
Description: Contains articles of interest to political leaders, civil servants, financial company senior management, attorneys, and accountants.

332 341   US   ISSN 1382-6662
▼**EUROPEAN FINANCE REVIEW**. Announced for publication in 1997. 3/yr. fl.400 to institutions; $205.50 to institutions in U.S. (effective 1998). Kluwer Academic Publishers Boston, Box 358, Accord Sta., Hingham, MA 02018-0358. TEL 617-871-6600. FAX 617-871-6528. E-mail: services@wkap.nl; URL: http://www.wkap.nl. (Dist. outside N. America by: Kluwer Academic Publishers Group, P.O. Box 322, 3300 AH Dordrecht, Netherlands. TEL 31-78-6392392. FAX 31-78-6546474) **Document type:** academic/scholarly publication.
Refereed Serial

332   UK
EUROPEAN FINANCIAL INSTITUTIONS AND MARKETS SERIES. 1993. irreg. Routledge, 11 New Fetter Ln., London EC4P 4EE, England. TEL 44-171-583-9855. FAX 44-171-583-0701. E-mail: sample.journals@routledge.com; URL: http:// www.routledge.com/routledge/journal/journals.html Eds. Jack Revell, Richard Harrington. **Document type:** monographic series.

332   UK   ISSN 1354-7798
▼**EUROPEAN FINANCIAL MANAGEMENT**. 1995. 3/yr. £145($218) (foreign £145) (effective 1997). (European Financial Management Association) Blackwell Publishers Ltd., 108 Cowley Rd., Oxford OX4 1JF, England. TEL 44-1865-791100. FAX 44-1865-791347. E-mail: jnlinfo@ blackwellpublishers.co.uk; URL: http://www. blackwellpublishers.co.uk. Ed. John Doukas. **Document type:** academic/scholarly publication.
—BLDSC (3829.711530); SWETS. **CCC.**
Description: Discusses issues in financial management.
Refereed Serial

BUSINESS AND ECONOMICS — BANKING AND FINANCE

332 341   NE   ISSN 1350-2018
EUROPEAN FINANCIAL SERVICES LAW. (Text in English) 1994. 11/yr. fl.665 to institutions; $341.50 to institutions in U.S. (effective 1998). Kluwer Law International (Subsidiary of: Wolters Kluwer N.V.), Postbus 85889, 2508 CN The Hague, Netherlands. TEL 31-70-30815003. FAX 31-70-3081515. E-mail: services@kwap.nl; URL: http://www.wkap.nl. (Dist. by: Kluwer Academic Publishers Group, P.O. Box 332, 3300 AH Dordrecht, Netherlands. TEL 31-78-6392392. FAX 31-78-6546474; In N. America: Kluwer Law International, 675 Massachusetts Ave., Cambridge, MA 02139. TEL 617-354-0140. FAX 617-354-8595) Ed. Nicholas Goldman. (back issues avail.; reprint service avail. from SWZ) **Document type:** trade publication.
—BLDSC (3829.712250). **CCC.**
Description: Provides compliance management within financial institutions, their legal advisers, and regulatory officials with information on developments in European law and regulation affecting the financial services industry.
Refereed Serial

EUROPEAN INTERACTIVE MULLTIMEDIA. see *COMMUNICATIONS*

332.6   EI   ISSN 0071-2868
HG3881
EUROPEAN INVESTMENT BANK. ANNUAL REPORT. (Editions in Danish, Dutch, English, Finnish, French, German, Greek, Italian, Portuguese, Spanish, Swedish) 1958. a. free. European Investment Bank - Banque Europeenne d'Investissement, 100 bd. Konrad Adenauer, L-2950 Luxembourg, Luxembourg. TEL 43791. FAX 437704. TELEX 3530 BNKEU LU. (Dist. in U.S. by: European Community Information Service, 2100 M St., N.W., Ste. 707, Washington, DC 20037) charts; illus.; stat. **Indexed:** IIS. **Document type:** corporate report.
—BLDSC (1245.465000).
Description: Reviews the European Investment Bank's borrowing and lending during the calendar year.

332.6   LU
EUROPEAN INVESTMENT BANK IN (YEAR). (Text in Danish, Dutch, English, French, Finish, German, Greek, Italian, Portuguese, Spanish, Swedish) 1987. a. free. European Investment Bank - Banque Europeenne d'Investissement, 100 bd. Konrad Adenauer, L-2950 Luxembourg, Luxembourg. TEL 352-4379-3215. FAX 352-4379-3289. TELEX 3530 BNKEU LU. (Dist. in U.S. by: European Community Information Service, 2100 M St., N.W., Washington, DC 20037) **Document type:** corporate report.
Description: Presents a general description and key figures of the bank for the previous year.

332   UK   ISSN 1351-847X
HG11
▼**THE EUROPEAN JOURNAL OF FINANCE.** 1995. q. £213 (foreign $360) (effective 1998). Thomson Professional (Subsidiary of: International Thomson Publishing Group), 2-6 Boundary Row, London SE1 8HN, England. TEL 44-171-8650066. FAX 44-171-5229623. TELEX 290164 CHAPMA G. E-mail: journal@rapidcom.co.uk; URL: http://www.thomsonprofessional.com. (Subscr. to: International Thomson Publishing Services Ltd., Cheriton House, North Way, Andover, Hants. SP10 5BE, England. TEL 44-1264-342713. FAX 44-1264-342807; Subscr. in US & Canada to: 400 Market St., Philadelphia, PA 19106. TEL 800-552-5866) Eds. Christopher Adcock, Eve Hicks. adv. (reprint service avail.) **Indexed:** Cont.Pg.Manage. **Document type:** academic/scholarly publication.
●Also available online.
—BLDSC (3829.728960). **CCC.**
Description: Devoted to theoretical, practical, and empirical issues in finance.
Refereed Serial

332   UK   ISSN 1071-1570
EUROPEAN MEDIA BUSINESS & FINANCE. 1993. bi-w. $895 (effective 1996). Omnicom P B I, Rosemount House, Rosemount Ave., W. Byfleet, Surrey KT14 6NP, England. TEL 44-1932-355515. FAX 44-1932-355962. (back issues avail.) **Document type:** newsletter.
●Also available online. Vendor(s): Information Access Co.
—**CCC.**

332.2   EI
EUROPEAN SAVINGS BANK. REPORT. (Editions in English, French, German) 1966. a. European Savings Banks Group - Groupement Europeen des Caisses d'Epargne, Ave. de la Renaissance, 12, B-1000 Brussels, Belgium. TEL 02-739-16-11. FAX 02-736-09-55. Ed. C. De Noose. circ. 3,000.

332   EI   ISSN 0255-6510
HG930.5
EUROSTAT. MONEY AND FINANCE. (Editions in English, French) q. $80. Statistical Office of the European Communities, Eurostat, Rue Alcide de Gasperi, 2920 Luxembourg, Luxembourg. FAX 352-4301-34526. FAX 352-4301-34415. (Dist. in the U.S. by: Unipub, 4611-F Assembly Dr., Lanham, MD 20706-4391. TEL 800-274-4888. FAX 301-459-0056) stat. (also avail. in microfiche from CIS) **Indexed:** IIS.
—BLDSC (5908.360600).
Description: Collection of various statistics relating to the European Communities, Japan and the United States. A detailed methodological introduction presents the numerical data, which are in three sections: structural indicators, European monetary system, and current statistics.

EUROSTAT. STATISTICS IN FOCUS. ECONOMY AND FINANCE. see *BUSINESS AND ECONOMICS — Abstracting, Bibliographies, Statistics*

EUROSTAT. STATISTIK KURZGEFASST. WIRTSCHAFT UND FINANZEN. see *BUSINESS AND ECONOMICS — Abstracting, Bibliographies, Statistics*

EUROSTAT. STATISTIQUES EN BREF. ECONOMIE ET FINANCES. see *BUSINESS AND ECONOMICS — Abstracting, Bibliographies, Statistics*

332   UK   ISSN 0952-7036
HG3879
EUROWEEK. 1987. w. £1950 (foreign $3350) (effective 1997). Euromoney Publications plc., Nestor House, Playhouse Yard, London EC4V 5EX, England. TEL 44-171-779-8935. FAX 44-171-779-8541. (Subscr. to: Quadrant Subscription Services, Stuart House, Perrymount Rd., Haywards Heath, W. Sussex RH16 3BN, England; Dist. in US by: American Educational Systems, 173 W. 81st St., New York, NY 10024. TEL 800-717-2669. FAX 212-501-8926) Ed. Nigel Pavay. **Document type:** newspaper.
●Also available online. Vendor(s): UMI.
—UMI.
Description: Compiles financial market news, Forex forecasts, data on deals, and league tables.

334.2   US   ISSN 0423-8710
EVERYBODY'S MONEY; a guide to family finance and consumer action. 1961. q. $99 for 100 bulk copies. Credit Union National Association, Inc., Box 431, Madison, WI 53701. TEL 608-231-4000. FAX 608-231-4370. Ed. Susan Tiffany. bk.rev. circ. 436,500. (also avail. in microform from UMI; reprint service avail. from UMI; back issues avail.) **Indexed:** Consum.Ind. **Document type:** consumer publication.
—UMI. **CCC.**

332   UK   ISSN 0142-6044
EXCHANGE RATE OUTLOOK. 1978. m. £495 (foreign £537). Ashgate Publishing Ltd. (Subsidiary of: Gower Publishing Co. Ltd.), Gower House, Croft Rd., Aldershot, Hants. GU11 3HR, England. TEL 44-1252-331551. FAX 44-1252-344405. TELEX 337210 BUREAU G.

332   UK   ISSN 0954-2760
EXPAT INVESTOR. 1991. bi-m. free. Tolley Publishing Co. Ltd., Tolley House, 2 Addiscombe Rd., Croydon, Surrey CR9 5AF, England. TEL 44-181-686-9141. FAX 44-181-760-0588. Ed. Peter Jolly. adv.: page £3000; adv. contact: Alison Almery. circ. 30,000. **Document type:** bulletin.

EXPORT - IMPORT BANK OF JAPAN. ANNUAL REPORT. see *BUSINESS AND ECONOMICS — International Commerce*

332.1   US   ISSN 0270-5109
HG3754.U5
EXPORT-IMPORT BANK OF THE UNITED STATES. ANNUAL REPORT. 1945. a. free. Export-Import Bank of the United States, 811 Vermont Ave., N.W., Washington, DC 20571. TEL 202-566-8990. FAX 202-566-7524. TELEX (TRT) 197681 EXIMUT. circ. 10,000. **Document type:** corporate report.
Former titles: Export-Import Bank of the United States. Statement of Condition (ISSN 0270-5087); Export-Import Bank of the United States. Summary of Operations (ISSN 0071-3511); Export-Import Bank of the United States. Report to Congress.

332.1   US
EXPORT-IMPORT BANK OF THE UNITED STATES. REPORT TO CONGRESS ON EXPORT CREDIT COMPETITION AND THE EXPORT-IMPORT BANK OF THE UNITED STATES. 1972. a. free. Export-Import Bank of the United States, 811 Vermont Ave., N.W., Washington, DC 20571. TEL 202-566-8861. FAX 202-566-7524. TELEX (TRT) 197681 EXIMUT. circ. 1,250. **Document type:** corporate report.
Formerly: Export-Import Bank of the United States. Semiannual Report to Congress on Export Credit Competition and the Export-Import Bank of the United States.

332   FR   ISSN 0014-5289
EXPRESS DOCUMENTS; juridique fiscal & social. vol.27, 1967. 45/yr. 2200 F. Groupe Revenu Francais, 1 bis av. de la Republique, 75011 Paris, France. TEL 49-29-30-00. FAX 43-55-91-41. (Subscr. to: B. 522, 60732 Ste. Genevieve Cedex, France. TEL 44-07-45-56. FAX 44-07-43-36) Ed. Robert Monteux. adv.; charts; illus. circ. 15,000.

332 336   UK   ISSN 1362-007X
EXTEL DIVIDEND & INTEREST RECORD. 1967. a. vol. (plus supplements 3/yr.). £165 for bound a. vol.; with supplements £205. Financial Times Information Ltd., Extel, Fitzroy House, 13-17 Epworth St., London EC2A 4DL, England. TEL 44-171-825-8000. FAX 44-171-608-2032. TELEX 884319. E-mail: eic@ft.com; URL: http://www.info.ft.com/.
Formerly (until 1995): UK Dividend and Interest Record (ISSN 0959-5775); Which was formed by the 1982 merger of: Extel Dividend Record (ISSN 0141-8327) & Extel Fixed Interest Record (ISSN 0141-8653)
Description: Covers dividend and fixed payments made by UK equities and unit trusts.

332   SA
F & T WEEKLY. (Text in English) 1984. w. (Fri.). R.240 (effective 1997). Nasionale Media, P.O. Box 53171, Troyeville 2139, South Africa. TEL 27-11-4026372. FAX 27-11-4041701. Ed. G.J. Basson; Pub. G.L. Marais. R&P contact: G.L. Marais. adv. contact: Willis du Plessis. circ. 12,377 (paid). **Indexed:** Ind.S.A.Per.
Formerly (until 1995): Finansies en Tegniek (ISSN 0256-470X)
Description: Covers business, financial and related issues.

332   US
▼**F & T WEEKLY.** (Text in English) 1995. w. (Fri.). R.240 (effective April 1996). Nasionale Media, P.O. Box 53171, Troyeville 2139, South Africa. TEL 27-11-4026372. FAX 27-11-4041701. Ed. Deon Basson; Pub. G.L. Marais. R&P contact: G.L. Marais. adv. contact: Willis du Plessis. circ. 12,377 (paid).

332.7 320   US
F C I B COUNTRY CREDIT REPORT.* 1982. m. $100 to non-members; members $80. (Finance, Credit and International Business - National Association of Credit Management) F C I B - N A C M Corp., 485 US Hwy. 1 A-100, Iselin, NJ 08830-3009. TEL 212-947-5368. FAX 212-465-8360. Ed. Raymond J. Schweitzer.

332.7   US
F C I B INTERNATIONAL BULLETIN.* 1919. m. $200. (Finance, Credit and International Business - National Association of Credit Management) F C I B - N A C M Corp., 485 US Hwy. 1 A-100, Iselin, NJ 08830-3009. TEL 212-947-5368. FAX 212-465-8360. Ed. Raymond J. Schweitzer. adv. circ. 1,000. **Document type:** bulletin.
Formerly: F C I B Bulletin (ISSN 0014-5718)

BUSINESS AND ECONOMICS — BANKING AND FINANCE

332.7 320   US
F C I B - N A C M. MINUTES OF ROUND TABLE CONFERENCE.* m. $500. (Finance, Credit and International Business - National Association of Credit Management) F C I B - N A C M Corp., 485 US Hwy. 1 A-100, Iselin, NJ 08830-3009. TEL 212-947-5368. FAX 212-465-8360. Ed. Gerd-Peter E. Lota.

332   NE   ISSN 0165-5655
F E M. (Financieel Economisch Magazine) Key Title: FEM. Financieel Economisch Magazine. 1969. bi-w. fl.355 (foreign fl.416) (effective 1998). B.V. Uitgeversmaatschappij Bonaventura (Subsidiary of: Elsevier N.V.), Postbus 2158, 1000 CD Amsterdam, Netherlands. TEL 31-20-6914111. FAX 31-20-5674398. Ed. P. de Hen. adv.; bk.rev.; illus. circ. 13,000. Indexed: ELLIS, Key to Econ.Sci. —SWETS.

332.1   US
THE F E R C REPORT. 1980. bi-w. $276. United Communications Group, 11300 Rockville Pike, Ste. 1100, Rockville, MD 20852-3030. TEL 301-816-8950. Ed. Jason Huffman.
    Former titles: Bank President's Letter; Community Banker.
    Description: Offers news and guidance on financial enforcement, regulation and compliance for CEO's and compliance officers in banks, thrifts and credit unions.

658   US
F R M WEEKLY. (Fund Raising Management) w. $115 (foreign $165) (effective 1996). Hoke Communications, Inc., 224 Seventh St., Garden City, NY 11530. TEL 516-746-6700. Ed. Bill Olcott; Pub. Henry R. Hoke, III. adv. circ. 300. (back issues avail.) **Document type:** newsletter.

332   US   ISSN 1080-0808
HG4050
F W'S CORPORATE FINANCE. (Financial World); the magazine for the financing strategist. (During 1990-1991 was incorporated in: Financial World (ISSN 0015-2064)) 1986. q. $50. Financial World Partners, 1328 Broadway, New York, NY 10001. TEL 212-594-5030. FAX 212-629-0026. Ed. Anthony Baldo. adv.; circ. 60,000 (controlled). (also avail. in microform from UMI) **Indexed:** Account.Ind. (1986-). **Document type:** consumer publication. —UMI. **CCC.**
    Formerly (until Oct. 1993): Corporate Finance (New York, 1986) (ISSN 0894-6817)

332   UK
F X MANAGER. (Foreign Exchange) 1982. m. £485 (foreign £790) (effective 1997). Euromoney Publications plc., Nestor House, Playhouse Yard, London EC4V 5EX, England. TEL 44-171-779-8532. FAX 44-171-779-8934. (Subscr. to: Quadrant Subscription Services Ltd., 41-43 Perrymount Rd., Haywards Heath, Sussex RH16 3DH, England. TEL 44-1444-445353. FAX 44-1444-445599; Dist. in US by: American Educational Systems, 173 W. 81st St., New York, NY 10024. TEL 800-717-2669. FAX 212-501-8926) Ed. M. Halls; Pub. Christopher Brown. circ. 1,500. (back issues avail.) **Document type:** trade publication.
    Formerly: Euromoney Treasury Manager.
    Description: Covers foreign-exchange markets.

332 658   NE   ISSN 0926-4078
FACT; feiten, cijfers, trends voor financieel en administratief management. (Text and summaries in Dutch) 1991. fortn. fl.385 (effective 1996). Kluwer Bedrijfswetenschappen B.V. (Subsidiary of: Wolters Kluwer N.V.), Postbus 23, 7400 GA Deventer, Netherlands. TEL 31-5700-48954. FAX 31-5700-11504. (Subscr. to: Intermedia bv, Postbus 4, 2400 MA Alphen aan den Rijn, Netherlands. TEL 31-172-466321. FAX 31-172-435527) Ed. E. Meyerink. bk.rev.; abstr.; index; circ. 2,000 (paid). **Document type:** newsletter.
    Description: Financial and economic information for managers, advisors and consultants.

332 332.1   PH
FACTBOOK ON THE PHILIPPINE FINANCIAL SYSTEM.* (Text and summaries in English) 1976. a. P.80. Central Bank of the Philippines, A. Mabini corner Vito Cruz Streets, Manila, Philippines. circ. 500. (back issues avail.)

332   US   ISSN 8755-1624
FACTORS AFFECTING RESERVES OF DEPOSITORY INSTITUTIONS AND CONDITION STATEMENT OF FEDERAL RESERVE BANKS. w. $20. U.S. Federal Reserve System, Board of Governors, Publications Services, Rm. MS-138, Washington, DC 20551. TEL 202-452-3244. FAX 202-728-5886. **Document type:** government publication.

332   CN   ISSN 0071-3864
FARM CREDIT CORPORATION CANADA. ANNUAL REPORT. 1960. a. free. Farm Credit Corporation Canada, Box 4320, 1800 Hamilton St., Regina, SK S4P 4L3, Canada. TEL 306-780-8100. FAX 306-780-5456. **Document type:** corporate report.

332 340   US   ISSN 0162-1157
FEDERAL BANKING LAW REPORTS. 1914. w. $1323. C H Incorporated, 2700 Lake Cook Rd., Riverwoods, IL 60015. TEL 847-267-7000; 800-835-5224. FAX 800-224-8299. (looseleaf format)
    ●Also available on CD-ROM.
    Description: Provides full text of all federal banking statutes and regulations as well as analysis and explanation. Also includes full text of relevant court decisions.

332   US   ISSN 1043-7789
HG2037
FEDERAL CREDIT UNION. 1976. bi-m. $100. National Association of Federal Credit Unions, 3138 N. Tenth St., Arlington, VA 22201. TEL 703-522-4770. FAX 703-524-1082. Ed. Patrick M. Keefe. adv. circ. 8,418. **Document type:** trade publication.

332 352   US   ISSN 0195-5330
FEDERAL ELECTION CAMPAIGN FINANCING GUIDE. 1976. m. $465. C C H Incorporated, 2700 Lake Cook Rd., Riverwoods, IL 60015. TEL 847-267-7000; 800-835-5224. FAX 800-224-8299.
—**CCC.**

332.1 333.33   US
FEDERAL HOME LOAN BANK OF ATLANTA. ANNUAL REPORT. a. free. Federal Home Loan Bank of Atlanta, 1475 Peachtree St., Atlanta, GA 30309. TEL 404-888-8000. illus.; stat. **Document type:** corporate report.

332.1   US
FEDERAL HOME LOAN BANK OF CHICAGO. ANNUAL REPORT. 1933. a. Federal Home Loan Bank of Chicago, 111 E. Wacker Dr., Chicago, IL 60601. Ed. Michael O'Malley. adv. contact: Charles Huston. circ. 2,000. **Document type:** corporate report.

332.1   US
FEDERAL HOME LOAN BANK OF DALLAS. ANNUAL REPORT. 1932. a. Federal Home Loan Bank of Dallas, Office of the Corporate Secretary, Box 619026, Dallas-Ft. Worth, TX 75261-9026. TEL 214-541-8500. Ed. Karen A. Krug. **Document type:** corporate report.

FEDERAL HOME LOAN BANK OF DALLAS. FINANCIAL STATEMENTS. see BUSINESS AND ECONOMICS — Abstracting, Bibliographies, Statistics

332.1   US
FEDERAL HOME LOAN BANK OF DES MOINES. ANNUAL REPORT. a. free. Federal Home Loan Bank of Des Moines, 907 Walnut St., Des Moines, IA 50309. TEL 515-281-1101. FAX 515-281-1022. Ed. Nichola Schissel. circ. 2,000. **Document type:** corporate report.

332.1   US
FEDERAL HOME LOAN BANK OF DES MOINES. WEEKLY FINANCIAL BULLETIN. w. free. Federal Home Loan Bank of Des Moines, 907 Walnut St., Des Moines, IA 50309. TEL 515-281-1101. FAX 515-281-1022. **Document type:** bulletin.

332.1   US
FEDERAL HOME LOAN BANK OF INDIANAPOLIS. ANNUAL REPORT. 1934. a. free. Federal Home Loan Bank of Indianapolis, Library, Box 60, Indianapolis, IN 46206-0060. Ed. Mike Barker. **Document type:** corporate report.

332.1   US
FEDERAL HOME LOAN BANK OF LITTLE ROCK. ANNUAL REPORT.* a. Federal Home Loan Bank of Little Rock, 500 Broadway St.. Apt. 300, Little Rock, AR 72201-3342. TEL 501-372-7141. **Document type:** corporate report.

332.3   US   ISSN 0098-2830
HG2626.S3
FEDERAL HOME LOAN BANK OF SAN FRANCISCO. ANNUAL REPORT.. Key Title: Annual Report - Federal Home Loan Bank of San Francisco. a. free. Federal Home Loan Bank of San Francisco, Box 7948, San Francisco, CA 94120. TEL 415-616-2610. illus. **Document type:** corporate report.

332.1   US
FEDERAL HOME LOAN BANK OF SEATTLE. ANNUAL REPORT. a. free. Federal Home Loan Bank of Seattle, 1501 Fourth Ave., Ste. 1900, Seattle, WA 98101-1693. TEL 206-340-2300. FAX 206-340-2485. Ed. Mary Grace Helsper. **Document type:** corporate report.

332.1   US
FEDERAL HOME LOAN BANK OF TOPEKA. ANNUAL REPORT. a. free. Federal Home Loan Bank of Topeka, 2 Townsite Plaza, Box 176, Topeka, KS 66601-0176. FAX 913-234-1797. Ed. Kim Gronniger. **Document type:** corporate report.
    Description: Contains member and industry news and information about bank products and services.

332.1   US   ISSN 0094-7156
HG2040.5.U5
FEDERAL HOME LOAN MORTGAGE CORPORATION. REPORT. Key Title: Report of the Federal Home Loan Mortgage Corporation. Variant title: Federal Home Loan Mortgage Corporation. Annual Report. a. Federal Home Loan Mortgage Corporation, 8200 Jones Branch Dr., McLean, VA 22102-3107. TEL 703-903-2000. FAX 703-759-8069. illus.; stat. **Document type:** corporate report.

FEDERAL INCOME TAXATION OF BANKS AND FINANCIAL INSTITUTIONS (SUPPLEMENT). see BUSINESS AND ECONOMICS — Public Finance, Taxation

332   US   ISSN 0899-6563
FEDERAL RESERVE BANK OF ATLANTA. FINANCIAL UPDATE. 1988. q. free. Federal Reserve Bank of Atlanta, 104 Marietta St., N.W., Atlanta, GA 30303-2713. TEL 404-521-8020. FAX 404-521-8050. URL: http://www.frbatlanta. org. Ed. David Sutton. bk.rev.; charts, stat, tr.lit. 7,000. **Document type:** newsletter.
    ●Also available online.

330   US
FEDERAL RESERVE BANK OF ATLANTA. WORKING PAPER SERIES. 1976. irreg. free. Federal Reserve Bank of Atlanta, 104 Marietta N.W., Atlanta, GA 30303-2713. TEL 404-521-8020. circ. 3,400. (back issues avail.) **Indexed:** Fed Print. **Document type:** academic/scholarly publication.

332.1   US
FEDERAL RESERVE BANK OF BOSTON. WORKING PAPER SERIES. irreg. Federal Reserve Bank of Boston, Research Department, 600 Atlantic Ave., Box 2076, Boston, MA 06100. TEL 617-973-3397. FAX 617-973-4292. URL: http://www.bos.frb.org. Ed. Ann Eggleston.

332 368   US
FEDERAL RESERVE BANK OF CLEVELAND. WORKING PAPER. 1976. irreg. (approx. 12/yr.). free. Federal Reserve Bank of Cleveland, Research Department, Box 6387, Cleveland, OH 44101. TEL 216-579-2380. FAX 216-579-3050. Eds. Tes Ferg, Robin Ratliff. R&P contact: Kathy Popovich. circ. 233. **Indexed:** Fed Print. **Document type:** academic/scholarly publication.
    ●Available only online.

BUSINESS AND ECONOMICS — BANKING AND FINANCE

332.1   US
HG2609
FEDERAL RESERVE BANK OF KANSAS CITY. FINANCIAL INDUSTRY TRENDS AND PERSPECTIVES. (Includes an annual statistical supplement) 1983. a. free. Federal Reserve Bank of Kansas City, Division of Bank Supervision and Structure, 925 Grand Blvd., Kansas City, MO 64198-0001. TEL 816-881-2934. Ed. John Yorke. circ. 5,500. **Indexed:** World Bank.Abstr. **Document type:** academic/scholarly publication.
   Formerly (until 1991): Federal Reserve Bank of Kansas City. Banking Studies (ISSN 0743-6351)
   Description: Provides index of bank control share prices, financial facts and structure statistics.

332 338.1   US   ISSN 0737-948X
FEDERAL RESERVE BANK OF MINNEAPOLIS. AGRICULTURAL CREDIT CONDITIONS SURVEY. Bound with: Fedgazette (ISSN 1045-3334) 1968. q. free. Federal Reserve Bank of Minneapolis, Public Affairs Department, 250 Marquette Ave., Minneapolis, MN 55401-2171. TEL 612-340-2446. FAX 612-340-7757. circ. 5,000. (also avail. in microfiche from CIS; reprint service avail. from CIS) **Indexed:** Amer.Stat.Ind. (1975-).
   Description: Analysis of farm credit conditions based on a survey of rural bankers in the Ninth Federal Reserve District.

332.4   US   ISSN 0361-8013
HG2613.M64
FEDERAL RESERVE BANK OF MINNEAPOLIS. ANNUAL REPORT. a. free. Federal Reserve Bank of Minneapolis, Public Affairs Department, Box 291, Minneapolis, MN 55480-0291. TEL 612-340-2446. FAX 612-335-2855. E-mail: webmaster@res.mpls.frb.fed.us; URL: http://woodrow.mpls.frb.fed.us. **Document type:** corporate report.
—BLDSC (1250.798000).
   Description: Statement of financial condition of the Federal Reserve Bank of Minneapolis.

330   US   ISSN 0271-5287
HG2559
FEDERAL RESERVE BANK OF MINNEAPOLIS. QUARTERLY REVIEW. 1977. q. free. Federal Reserve Bank of Minneapolis, Research Department, Minneapolis, MN 55480-0291. TEL 612-240-6455. FAX 612-204-5515. E-mail: err@res.mpls.frb.fed.us; URL: http://woodrow.mpls.frb.fed.us. stat. circ. 12,000. (also avail. in microform from UMI,MIM; microfiche from CIS; reprint service avail. from CIS,UMI) **Indexed:** ABI Inform., Amer.Stat.Ind. (1973-), B.P.I., Bank.Lit.Ind., BPIA, C.R.E.J., Fed.Print, J.of Econ.Lit., P.A.I.S., PROMT, World Bank.Abstr. **Document type:** academic/scholarly publication.
●Also available online. Vendor(s): UMI.
—BLDSC (3901.934300); KR SourceOne; UMI; UnCover.
   Former titles (until 1977): Ninth District Quarterly (ISSN 0364-4529); Ninth District Conditions (ISSN 0029-0580); Federal Reserve Bank of Minneapolis. Monthly Review.
   Description: Economic research aimed at improving policymaking by the Federal Reserve System and other governmental authorities.
   Refereed Serial

332.1   US   ISSN 0361-7998
HG2613.N54
FEDERAL RESERVE BANK OF NEW YORK. ANNUAL REPORT. 1942. a. Federal Reserve Bank of New York, Public Information, 33 Liberty St., New York, NY 10045-0001. TEL 212-720-6150. Ed.Bd. charts; stat. circ. 38,000. (back issues avail.) **Document type:** corporate report.
—BLDSC (1250.800000).

FEDERAL RESERVE BANK OF PHILADELPHIA. BUSINESS REVIEW. see *BUSINESS AND ECONOMICS — Economic Situation And Conditions*

332   US   ISSN 0164-0798
HG2613.R54
FEDERAL RESERVE BANK OF RICHMOND. ANNUAL REPORT. 1916. a. Federal Reserve Bank of Richmond, Research Department, 701 E. Byrd St., Richmond, VA 23219. TEL 804-697-8785. FAX 804-697-8287. E-mail: eg@rich.frb.org; URL: http://www.rich.frb.org. (Subscr. to: Public Affairs, Box 27622, Richmond, VA 23261. TEL 804-697-8111) R&P contact: Elaine Mandaleris. TEL 804-697-8144. **Document type:** corporate report, academic/scholarly publication.

332   US   ISSN 0014-9209
HG2401   CODEN: FDRBAU
FEDERAL RESERVE BULLETIN. 1915. m. $25 (foreign $35). U.S. Federal Reserve System, Board of Governors, Publications Services, Rm. MS-138, Washington, DC 20551. TEL 202-452-3244. FAX 202-728-5886. Ed.Bd. charts; mkt.; stat.; index. circ. 26,000. (also avail. in microform from MIM,UMI,PMC; microfiche from CIS; reprint service avail. from CIS,KTO,UMI,WSH) **Indexed:** ABI Inform., Acad.Ind., Amer.Stat.Ind. (1974-), B.P.I., Bank.Lit.Ind., BPIA, Bus.Ind., C.L.I., C.R.E.J., Fed Print, Ind.U.S.Gov.Per., J.of Econ.Lit., Key to Econ.Sci., Leg.Per., Manage.Cont., Mid.East: Abstr.& Ind., P.A.I.S., PROMT, Tr.& Indus.Ind., World Bank.Abstr. **Document type:** government publication.
●Also available online. Vendor(s): Information Access Co., Knight-Ridder Information, Inc., Lexis-Nexis, UMI.
—BLDSC (3901.935000); KR SourceOne; SWETS; UMI; UnCover.

332.1   US
FEDERAL RESERVE REGULATORY SERVICE. (Includes 4 handbooks updated at least monthly: Consumer and Community Affairs; Monetary Policy and Reserve Requirements; Securities Credit Transactions; Payment System) 4 base vols. plus irreg. supplements. $75 per handbook (foreign $90); set $200 (foreign $250). Federal Reserve System, Board of Governors, Publications Services, Rm. MS-127, 20th and Constitution Ave., N.W., Washington, DC 20551. TEL 202-452-3244. FAX 202-728-5886. (looseleaf format; also avail. in diskette format) **Document type:** government publication.

332   FR   ISSN 0071-4380
FEDERATION NATIONALE DU CREDIT AGRICOLE. ANNUAIRE DU CREDIT AGRICOLE MUTUEL.* 1960. a., 3rd ed. Federation Nationale du Credit Agricole, 48 rue la Boetie, 75008 Paris, France.

332 334   SW
FEDERATION OF SWEDISH CO-OPERATIVE BANKS. ANNUAL REPORT. a. Sveriges Foereningsbankers Foerbund, Box 30144, S-104 25 Stockholm, Sweden. (Co-sponsor: Foereningsbankernas Bank)

FIELD GUIDE TO ESTATE PLANNING, BUSINESS PLANNING & EMPLOYEE BENEFITS. see *INSURANCE*

332   JA   ISSN 0448-6072
FINANCE/FAINANSU.* (Text in Japanese) 1965. m. 5400 Yen. Ministry of Finance, General Coordination Division - Okura-sho, Minister's Secretariat, 3-1-1 Kasumigaseki, Chiyoda-ku, Tokyo 100, Japan. Ed. Toshiyuki Tsukazaki. adv.; bk.rev. circ. 13,000.

332   FR   ISSN 0752-6180
FINANCE. 1980. s-a. 580 F. to individuals (foreign 720 F.); agencies 522 F. (foreign 648 F.) (effective 1998). (Association Francaise de Finance) Presses Universitaires de France, Departement des Revues, 14 av. du Bois-de-l'Epine, 91003 Evry Cedex, France. TEL 33-1-60778205. FAX 33-1-60792045. TELEX PUF 600 474 F. Ed.Bd.
—BLDSC (3926.853000).
   Formerly (until 1982): Association Francaise de Finance. Revue (ISSN 0248-0107)
   Description: Covers management, market equilibrium, taxes, investments, the balance of payments, and exchange rates.

330   XR   ISSN 0015-1920
FINANCE A UVER.* 1950. m. $46.80. (Federalni Ministerstvo Financi) Economia, a.s., Na Florenci 3, 115 43 Prague 1, Czech Republic. (Dist. by: Artia, Ve Smeckach 30, 111 27 Prague 1, Czech Republic) Ed. Ivan Kocarnik. bk.rev.; bibl.; illus.; index.

FINANCE AND ACCOUNTING JOBS REPORT. see *OCCUPATIONS AND CAREERS*

332   US   ISSN 8750-6149
FINANCE AND COMMERCE. 1896. d. $129 (effective 1995). Finance and Commerce, Inc., 615 S. 7th St., Minneapolis, MN 55415. FAX 612-333-4244. Ed. Dave Elmstrom. adv.; circ. 4,500 (paid). (back issues avail.) **Document type:** newspaper.
   Description: Covers business and legal matters in the city of Minneapolis and Hennepin County.

332.1 338.9   UN   ISSN 0145-1707
HG3881   CODEN: FNDVAM
FINANCE AND DEVELOPMENT. Arabic edition: Al-Tamwil wal-Tanmiya (ISSN 0250-7455); French edition: Finances et Developpement (ISSN 0430-473X); German edition: Finanzierung und Entwicklung (ISSN 0250-7439); Portuguese edition: Financas e Desenvolvimento (ISSN 0255-7622); Spanish edition: Finanzas y Desarrollo (ISSN 0250-7447) (Text in English) 1964. q. free. International Monetary Fund, Publication Services, 700 19th St., N.W., Washington, DC 20431. TEL 202-623-7430. FAX 202-623-7201. (Co-sponsor: International Bank for Reconstruction and Development (World Bank)) bk.rev.; charts; illus.; index. circ. 121,000. (also avail. in microform from UMI,CIS; reprint service avail. from SCH,UMI) **Indexed:** ABI Inform., Account.Ind. (1974-), AESIS, Amer.Hist.& Life (1967-1973), Asian-Pac.Econ.Lit., B.P.I., BPIA, Bus.Ind., E.I., Geo.Abstr.H.G., Hist.Abstr. (1967-1973), IBR, IDA, Ind.Free Per., Ind.Free Per., Ind.Per.Art.Relat.Law, J.of Econ.Lit., Key to Econ.Sci., Manage.Cont., Mid.East: Abstr.& Ind., P.A.I.S., Per.Islam (1991-), Polit.Sci.Abstr., PROMT, PSI, Rural Devel.Abstr., Rural Ext.Educ.& Tr.Abstr., Sage Pub.Admin.Abstr., Soc.Sci.Ind., Tr.& Indus.Ind., World Agri.Econ.& Rural Sociol.Abstr.
●Also available online. Vendor(s): Information Access Co., UMI.
   Formerly: Fund and Bank Review.
   Description: Publishes articles of an informative or analytical character on the policies and activities of the institutions, emphasizing new aspects of approaches as they arise, as well as general pieces on financial and development issues.

332 510   GW   ISSN 0949-2984
FINANCE AND STOCHASTICS. Online edition (GW ISSN 1432-1122) (Text in English) q. DM.356 (foreign DM.360.60) (effective 1998). Springer-Verlag, Heidelberger Platz 3, 14197 Berlin, Germany. TEL 49-30-82787-0. FAX 49-30-82787448. E-mail: subscriptions@springer.de; URL: http://link.springer.de. (Subscr. in N. America to: Springer-Verlag New York, Inc., 333 Meadowlands Pkwy., Secaucus, NJ 07094. TEL 212-460-1500. FAX 212-473-6272) Ed. D. Sondermann. (back issues avail.) **Document type:** academic/scholarly publication.
●Also available online.
—BLDSC (3926.910000). CCC.
   Refereed Serial

332 382   US
FINANCE & TREASURY. 50/yr. $995 (foreign $1045). WorldTrade Executive, Inc., Box 761, Concord, MA 01742. TEL 508-287-0301. FAX 508-287-0302. Ed. George Cassidy; Pub. Gary A. Brown. adv.; page $975; 7 1/2 x 9 1/2.
   Description: For international treasury managers. Demonstrates cash management techniques to manage worldwide financial resources, such as cross-border pooling, multilateral netting, regional invoicing, and the use of various electronic applications.

332   US   ISSN 0364-0132
FINANCE COMPANIES. m. $5. U.S. Federal Reserve System, Board of Governors, Publications Services, Rm. MS-138, Washington, DC 20551. TEL 202-452-3244. FAX 202-728-5886. **Document type:** government publication.

332   UK   ISSN 0268-8581
FINANCE DIRECTOR INTERNATIONAL. 1986. a. £55. Sterling Publications Ltd., 86-88 Edgware Rd., London W2 2YW, England. TEL 44-171-915-9600. FAX 44-171-915-9619. R&P contact: Sandy Tucker. circ. 10,000. **Document type:** trade publication.

332   UK   ISSN 0260-1176
FINANCE DIRECTOR'S REVIEW. 1980. m. £165 (foreign £181). Tolley Publishing Co. Ltd., Tolley House, 2 Addiscombe Rd., Croydon, Surrey CR9 5AX, England. TEL 44-181-686-9111. FAX 44-181-686-3155. Ed. Claire Melvin. circ. 650. **Document type:** trade publication.

BUSINESS AND ECONOMICS — BANKING AND FINANCE

332   UK   ISSN 0965-9560
FINANCE EAST EUROPE. fortn. £395($696) (overseas £435) (effective 1993). Financial Times Business Information, Newsletters (Subsidiary of: Financial Times Group), 126 Jermyn St., London SW1Y 4UJ, England. TEL 44-171-411-4414. FAX 44-171-411-4415. (also avail. in microform from UMI) **Document type:** newsletter.
● Also available online. Vendor(s): Information Access Co.
Description: Contains East European finance, banking, and investment briefings.

332 657   II   ISSN 0970-3772
HG41
FINANCE INDIA. (Text in English) 1987. q. Rs.600 to individuals (foreign $60); Institutions Rs.800 (foreign $80). Indian Institute of Finance, P.O. Box 8486, Ashok Vihar, Delhi 110 052, India. TEL 91-11-7125791. FAX 91-11-7454128. E-mail: iif.instofin@gems.vsnl.net.in. Ed. J.D. Agarwal. adv.: page Rs.10000; 8 x 4 1/2. bk.rev.; abstr.; bibl.; stat.; circ. 1,700 (paid). **Document type:** academic/scholarly publication.
Description: Provides a forum for intradisciplinary study of finance, accounting and related areas. *Refereed Serial*

FINANCE, INSURANCE AND REAL ESTATE U S A. see BUSINESS AND ECONOMICS — *Abstracting, Bibliographies, Statistics*

332   US
FINANCE: LATIN AMERICAN INDUSTRIAL REPORT. (Avail. for each of 20 Latin American countries) 1985. a. $235 per country report. Aquino Productions, Box 125, Rochester, VT 05767. Ed. Andres C. Aquino.

332   SA   ISSN 0256-0321
HG46
FINANCE WEEK. 1979. w. R.195. Finance Week Ltd., Private Bag 78816, Sandton 2146, South Africa. TEL 27-11-444-0555. FAX 27-11-444-0424. Ed. Allan Greenblo. adv. contact: Carole Shill. bk.rev.; circ. 18,000 (paid). **Indexed:** Ind.S.A.Per., INIS Atomind. **Document type:** trade publication.

332   FR
FINANCEMENTS DES PARTICULIERS. 1993. m. 3300 F. (foreign 3500 F.). Publi-News, 3 ave. Gallieni, 9200 Nanterre, France. TEL 477-29-88-11. FAX 47-29-88-18. Ed. Ange Galula. **Document type:** newsletter.
Description: Covers mortgage loans, revolving credit, consumer financing, and auto financing.

FINANCIAL ADVERTISING REVIEW; creative forum for the people who plan and create financial advertising programs. see ADVERTISING AND PUBLIC RELATIONS

332   II
FINANCIAL ANALYSIS. (Text in English) 1991. m. Rs.7 per no. Quick Data Organization Pvt. Ltd., 306, Jyoti Bhawan, Commercial Complex, Dr. Mukherjee Nagar, New Delhi 110 009, India. Ed. J.R. Gupta.

FINANCIAL AND ESTATE PLANNING FOR THE MATURE CLIENT IN ONTARIO. see LAW — *Estate Planning*

FINANCIAL & INVESTMENT YEARBOOK R O C. see BUSINESS AND ECONOMICS — *Investments*

336.74   NE   ISSN 0921-8580
FINANCIAL AND MONETARY POLICY STUDIES. 1974. irreg., vol.25, 1992. price varies. (Societe Universitaire Europeenne de Recherches Financieres) Kluwer Academic Publishers, Postbus 17, 3300 AA Dordrecht, Netherlands. TEL 31-78-6392392. FAX 31-78-6392254. TELEX 29245 KAPG NL. E-mail: services@wkap.nl; URL: http://www.wkap.nl. (Dist. by: Kluwer Academic Publishers Group, P.O. Box 322, 3300 AH Dordrecht, Netherlands. TEL 31-78-6392392. FAX 31-78-6546474; N, America dist. addr.: Box 358, Accord Sta., Hingham, MA 02018-0358. TEL 617-871-6600) (back issues avail.) **Document type:** monographic series, proceedings.
—BLDSC (3926.946400).
Formerly: Financial and Monetary Studies.
Description: In depth analysis and discussion of European and international issues relating to fiscal, taxation and monetary policy, financial integration, financial institutions. Certain volumes constitute lectures presented at SUERF Colloquia.
Refereed Serial

FINANCIAL CONDITION OF COLORADO MUNICIPALITIES. see PUBLIC ADMINISTRATION — *Municipal Government*

332   US
FINANCIAL CONNECTION. 1991. q. free. U.S. Dept. of the Treasury, Financial Management Service, 401 14th St., S.W., Washington, DC 20227.

332   US
FINANCIAL CONSULTANT. q.? $300 (foreign $375) (effective 1996). Institutional Investor Journals, 488 Madison Ave., New York, NY 10022. TEL 212-224-3185. FAX 212-224-3527.

332.024   US   ISSN 1052-3073
HG179
FINANCIAL COUNSELING AND PLANNING. 1990. s-a. $60 individual membership; institutional membership $100; libraries $60 (effective 1997). Association for Financial Counseling and Planning Education, c/o Sherman Hanna, Ed., Consumer and Textile Sciences Dept., Ohio State University, 1787 Neil Ave., Columbus, OH 43210-1295. TEL 614-292-4584. FAX 614-292-7536. E-mail: hanna.1@osu.edu; URL: http://www.hec.ohio-state.edu/hanna/. (Subscr. to: Ruth Helein, The Administrator's Inc., 3900 E. Camelback Rd., Ste. 200, Phoenix, AZ 85018. TEL 602-912-5331. FAX 602-957-4828) R&P contact: Sherman Hanna.
Indexed: Bus.Educ.Ind. **Document type:** academic/scholarly publication.
—BLDSC (3926.952160).
Description: Disseminates scholarly research related to financial counseling and planning education.
Refereed Serial

332   UK   ISSN 0961-2556
FINANCIAL DIRECTOR. 1984. m. £35 (foreign £55) (effective 1996). V N U Business Publications BV, VNU House, 32-34 Broadwick St., London W1A 2HG, England. TEL 44-171-439-4242. FAX 44-171-437-4841. **Indexed:** INSPEC (1990-). **Document type:** trade publication.
—BLDSC (3926.952280); AskIEEE; KR SourceOne.
Formerly (until 1989): Financial Decisions (ISSN 0267-4785)

332   II   ISSN 0015-2005
FINANCIAL EXPRESS. (Regional editions avail. for Bangalore, Bombay, Calcutta, Madras, and New Delhi) (Text in English) 1961. d. Rs.145. Indian Express Newspapers (Mumbai) Pvt. Ltd., Express Towers, Nariman Point, Box 867, Mumbai 400 021, India. TEL 91-22-2022627. FAX 91-22-2022139. TELEX 011-82585 INEX IN. Ed. A.M. Khusro. bk.rev.; stat.; tr.lit. circ. 20,000. **Document type:** newspaper.

332   US
FINANCIAL FAX. w. D R I - McGraw-Hill, 24 Hartwell Ave., Lexington, MA 02173. TEL 617-863-5100. FAX 617-860-6332. TELEX 200 284. Ed. Cynthia Latta. (also avail. by fax)
● Also available online.
Formerly: Comments on Money and Credit.

FINANCIAL FRAUD. see LAW — *Corporate Law*

332 333.33   US   ISSN 1065-5816
FINANCIAL FREEDOM REPORT QUARTERLY; the magazine for high profit investors. 1976. q. $160. American Home Business Association, 4505 Wasatch Blvd., Salt Lake City, UT 84124-4709. TEL 801-273-5301. FAX 801-273-5422. Ed. Carolyn Tice; Pub. Mark O. Haroldsen. R&P contact: Carolyn Tice. adv.; tr.lit.; index. circ. 3,500. **Document type:** trade publication.
Former titles (until 1992): Financial Freedom Report (ISSN 0196-514X); (until 1979): How To Master Your Financial Destiny Financial Freedom Report (ISSN 0164-5641)

FINANCIAL HANDBOOK FOR BANKRUPTCY PROFESSIONALS. see LAW

332   UK   ISSN 0968-5650
HG171
FINANCIAL HISTORY REVIEW. 1994. s-a. £48($88) (effective 1998). (European Association for Banking History) Cambridge University Press, The Edinburgh Bldg., Shaftesbury Rd., Cambridge CB2 2RU, England. TEL 44-1223-312393. FAX 44-1223-315052. TELEX 851817256. E-mail: information@cup.cam.ac.uk; URL: http://www.cup.cam.ac.uk. (N. American addr.: Cambridge University Press, Journals Division, 40 W. 20th St., New York, NY 10011. TEL 212-924-3900. FAX 212-691-3239) Eds. Youssef Cassis, Philip Cottrell. R&P contact: Linda Nicol. adv. contact: Rebecca Symons. bk.rev. (back issues avail.; reprint service avail. from ISI) **Indexed:** Amer.Hist.& Life (1995-), Hist.Abstr. (1995-). **Document type:** academic/scholarly publication.
—BLDSC (3926.956230); SWETS; UMI; UnCover. CCC.
Description: Provides an international forum for scholars interested in the development of banking, finance and other monetary matters.
Refereed Serial

332   US
FINANCIAL INDUSTRY ISSUES. 1991. q. free. Federal Reserve Bank of Dallas, Box 655906, Dallas, TX 75265-5906. TEL 214-922-5254. FAX 214-922-5268. Ed. Tara Barrett. circ. 10,000. (back issues avail.) **Document type:** newsletter.
Description: Presents research about the financial industry in the eleventh district.

332.1   US   ISSN 0362-1405
HG4512
FINANCIAL INDUSTRY NUMBER STANDARD DIRECTORY. 1976. irreg. Depository Trust Company, 55 Water St., New York, NY 10041. TEL 212-558-8000. **Document type:** directory.

332   US
FINANCIAL INDUSTRY STUDIES. 1988. s-a. free. Federal Reserve Bank of Dallas, Box 655906, Dallas, TX 75265-5906. TEL 214-922-5254. FAX 214-922-5268. Ed. Tara Barrett. circ. 15,000.
Description: Presents research on economic and financial topics, with emphasis on the financial industry at regional, national and international levels.

332   US
FINANCIAL INDUSTRY STUDIES WORKING PAPERS. irreg. free. Federal Reserve Bank of Dallas, Sta. K, Dallas, TX 75222. TEL 214-651-6289. circ. 1,100. (back issues avail.)

332   US
FINANCIAL INSTITUTIONS DIRECTORY OF NEW ENGLAND. 1913. a. $32. Shawmut Bank, N.A., Correspondent Banking Group, One Federal St., Boston, MA 02211. TEL 617-292-3823. FAX 617-292-4417. (Dist. by: R.L. Polk Co., Box 305100, Nashville, TN 37230-5100. TEL 800-788-2230) circ. controlled. **Document type:** directory.
Formerly: Bank Directory of New England.

332   US   ISSN 1055-8675
HG1
FINANCIAL LEADERSHIP SPEAKS; * the journal and index of financial speeches. 1991. bi-m. $125 (foreign $132). Forum Two, Inc., c/o 110 E. 42nd St., Ste. 224, New York, NY 10017-5611. TEL 212-922-0791. FAX 212-922-0874. Ed. Richard Cook. **Document type:** trade publication.
Description: Contains 10 full-text speeches, 15-20 abstracts, a speaker index with addresses and an in-depth subject index.

332   SA   ISSN 0015-2013
HG46
FINANCIAL MAIL. (Text in English) 1959. w. R.175.24 (foreign R.315.64) (effective 1993). Times Media Limited, P.O. Box 1138, Johannesburg 2000, South Africa. TEL 27-11-497-2711. FAX 27-11-834-1408. (Subscr. to: Circulation Manager, P.O. Box 10493, Johannesburg 2000, South Africa) Ed. Nigel Bruce. adv.; bk.rev.; charts; illus.; stat.; index; circ. 32,500 (paid). (also avail. in microfilm) **Indexed:** Ind.S.A.Per., INIS Atomind., Key to Econ.Sci., P.A.I.S., PROMT.
Description: Covers the economy and financial markets, companies and investment, business and current affairs in South Africa and the world, providing a broad spectrum of news, information and comment.

BUSINESS AND ECONOMICS — BANKING AND FINANCE 1135

FINANCIAL MANAGER FOR THE MEDIA PROFESSIONAL. see *COMMUNICATIONS — Television And Cable*

332 US
FINANCIAL MANAGERS UPDATE. bi-w. $305 to non-members (effective 1995). Financial Managers Society, Inc., 230 W. Monroe St., Ste. 2205, Chicago, IL 60606-4703. TEL 312-578-1306. FAX 312-578-1308. Ed. Beatrice McLean. adv.: B&W page $700; 7 1/2 x 10; adv. contact: Laurie Kaczmar. circ. 2,100 (paid). **Document type:** newsletter.
Former titles (until 1994): F M S Update & Update Newsletter; Printout (ISSN 8755-5751)
Description: Covers the latest accounting and regulatory information related to financial institutions, as well as trends relating to financial management practice.

332 FR ISSN 0378-651X
HG136 CODEN: FMTRDI
FINANCIAL MARKET TRENDS. French edition: Tendances des Marches des Capitaux (ISSN 0378-6528) (Text in English) 1977. 3/yr. $67 (combined subscription with Part 1 of O E C D Financial Statistics $240). Organization for Economic Cooperation and Development, 2 rue Andre-Pascal, 75775 Paris Cedex 16, France. (U.S. orders to: O.E.C.D. Publications and Information Center, 2001 L St., N.W., Ste. 650, Washington, DC 20036-4922. TEL 202-785-6323) (back issues avail.) **Indexed:** ABI Inform., BPIA, IIS, Key to Econ.Sci., P.A.I.S., Tr.& Indus.Ind.
●Also available online. Vendor(s): Information Access Co., UMI.
—SWETS; UMI; UnCover.
Description: Provides an assessment of trends and prospects in the international and major domestic financial markets of the OECD area.

332 658.8 US ISSN 0746-245X
FINANCIAL MARKETING. 1965. m. (10/yr.). $110 (effective 1994). Financial Institutions Marketing Association, 401 N. Michigan Ave., Ste. 2200, Chicago, IL 60611-4267. TEL 312-644-6610. FAX 312-321-6869. E-mail: fima@sba.com. Ed. Charles E. Bartling. adv.: page $800; trim 8 1/2 x 11. bk.rev.; circ. 1,000 (paid). (also avail. in microfilm) **Document type:** newsletter, trade publication.
—CCC.
Formerly (until 1983): S I M S A News (ISSN 0162-718X)
Description: Provides marketing executives of banks, credit unions, and savings institutions with relevant information on trends and developments in financial services.

332 US ISSN 0963-8008
HG173
FINANCIAL MARKETS, INSTITUTIONS AND INSTRUMENTS. 1928; N.S. 1975. 5/yr. $78 to individuals (foreign $94); institutions $151.50 (foreign $176) (effective 1997). (New York University, Salomon Center) Blackwell Publishers, 238 Main St., Cambridge, MA 02142. TEL 617-547-7110. FAX 617-547-0789. E-mail: subscript@blackwellpub.com. Ed. Anthony Saunders. adv. **Document type:** academic/scholarly publication.
●Also available online. Vendor(s): UMI.
—BLDSC (3926.962550); SWETS; UMI; UnCover.
CCC.
Former titles (until 1992): Monograph Series in Finance and Economics (ISSN 0276-2021); (until 1990): Salomon Brothers Center for the Study of Financial Institutions. Monograph Series; New York University Institute of Finance. Bulletin.
Description: Provides in-depth coverage of topics of current interest in the areas of financial markets, institutions and instruments.

332 US
FINANCIAL NEWS AND DAILY RECORD. 1912. d. (Mon.-Fri.). $89.46. Financial News Corporation, 10 N. Newnan St., Jacksonville, FL 32202. TEL 904-356-2466. FAX 904-353-2628. Ed. Stewart Verney; Pub. James F. Bailey, Jr. adv. contact: Neil O'Donnell. bk.rev. circ. 4,200. (tabloid format) **Document type:** newspaper.

332 US
FINANCIAL PLANNERS AND PLANNING ORGANIZATIONS DIRECTORY. 1987. irreg. $195. Gale Research, 835 Penobscot Bldg., 645 Griswold St., Detroit, MI 48226-4094. TEL 313-961-2242; 800-877-4253. FAX 800-414-5043. E-mail: daniel__snyder@gale.com. Ed.Bd. **Document type:** directory.
Description: More than 2,400 financial planners and 1,650 planning organizations are profiled in this directory.

FINANCIAL PLANNING (NEW YORK). see *BUSINESS AND ECONOMICS — Management*

332 US ISSN 1076-6324
FINANCIAL PLANNING DIGEST. m. $120 (effective 1997). Harcourt Brace Professional Publishing, 525 B St., Ste. 1900, San Diego, CA 92101-4495. TEL 619-699-6716. FAX 619-699-6593. Ed. Bill Teague; Pub. Ken Rethmeier. R&P contact: Jenna Lake. TEL 619-699-6265. **Document type:** newsletter.
Description: Covers all facets of financial planning: retirement, insurance, income tax, estate planning, and investment.

332 CN ISSN 0015-2021
FINANCIAL POST; Canada's business voice. (Supplement avail.: Financial Post 500) 1907. d. (plus a. suppl.). Can.$219.78. Financial Post Co., Ltd., 333 King St. E., Toronto, ON M5A 4N2, Canada. TEL 416-350-6500; 800-387-9011. FAX 416-350-6601. Ed. Diane Francis; Pub. Douglas W. Knight. adv. contact: Bill Neill. bk.rev.; charts; illus.; mkt.; stat. circ. 180,000. (also avail. in microfilm from UMI; reprint service avail. from MML) **Indexed:** CAD CAM Abstr., Can.B.P.I., Can.B.P.I., Can.Lit.Ind., Can.Per.Ind., CMI, Key to Econ.Sci., PROMT, Sportsearch (1977-), Telegen, World Bank.Abstr. **Document type:** newspaper.
●Also available online. Vendor(s): Information Access Co., Southam Electronic Publishing.
—CCC.
Incorporates: Your Money & Moneywise.

332 332.6 CN ISSN 1184-7824
FINANCIAL POST MAGAZINE. (Includes a. special issue: Financial Post Moneyplanner) 11/yr. Financial Post Co., Ltd., 333 King St. E., Toronto, ON M5A 4N2, Canada. TEL 416-350-6516. FAX 416-350-6501. Ed. David Bailey. adv. contact: Bill Neill. **Indexed:** Can.B.P.I.
●Also available online.
Formerly (until Jun. 1990): Financial Post Moneywise (ISSN 1182-0713)
Description: Tells how to get your financial life in order. Covers investment, taxation, retirement and the basic aspects of intelligent financial planning. Includes special worksheets and a directory of services.

332 US
FINANCIAL PRACTICE AND EDUCATION. 1991. s-a. $80. Financial Management Association, Univ. of South Florida, College of Bus. Admin. 3331, Tampa, FL 33620. TEL 813-974-2084. FAX 813-974-3318. E-mail: fma@bsn01.bsn.usf.edu; URL: http://www.webspace.com/~fma/. Ed. Raj Aggrawal. circ. 4,500. **Document type:** academic/scholarly publication.
Description: Covers topics relevant to both financial practice and financial education in the fields of financial management, investments, and financial institutions and markets.
Refereed Serial

332.024 323.4 US ISSN 1059-0013
FINANCIAL PRIVACY REPORT. 1991. m. $144 (foreign $164) (effective 1997). 12254 Nicollet Ave., Burnsville, MN 55337. TEL 612-895-8757. FAX 612-895-5526. Ed. Michael Ketcher; Pub. Daniel Rosenthal. bk.rev.; circ. 7,000 (paid). (back issues avail.) **Document type:** newsletter.
Description: How to protect your personal and financial privacy.

332.1 US
FINANCIAL READING REVIEW. 1984. q. $248. Advisory Board Company, 600 New Hampshire Ave., N.W., Washington, DC 20037-2403. TEL 202-544-5900. FAX 202-543-6054. Ed. Kevin J. Donahve. bk.rev. circ. 4,000. (back issues avail.) **Document type:** newsletter.
Formerly (until 1992): Bank Reading Review.
Description: Contains reviews of articles, surveys, government publications concerning the financial services industry.

332 UK ISSN 0192-088X
KF1428.A15
FINANCIAL REGULATION REPORT. m. £414($702) (overseas £439) (effective 1993). Financial Times Business Information, Newsletters (Subsidiary of: Financial Times Group), 126 Jermyn St., London SW1Y 4UJ, England. TEL 0171-441-4414. FAX 0171-441-4415. Ed. Peter Mayo Elstob. (also avail. in microform from UMI) **Document type:** newsletter.
●Also available online. Vendor(s): Data-Star, Lexis-Nexis.
—CCC.
Description: Provides a service on regulatory developments and their market implications in the global financial industry.

332 UK ISSN 1362-7511
▼**THE FINANCIAL REGULATOR;** the journal of global issues. 1996. q. £220 (foreign $350) (effective 1997). Central Banking Publications Ltd., 27 Chancery Lane, London WC2A 1PA, England. TEL 44-171-404-6435. FAX 44-171-404-6436. E-mail: centralbank@easynet.co.uk; URL: http://www.easyweb.easynet.co.uk/centralbank/. (Dist. in N. America by: European Business Publications Inc., Box 891, Darien, CT 06820) Ed. Michael Taylor.
Description: Dedicated to reporting and commenting on the activities of the world's financial regulators. It reports and analyses new regulations issued by agencies and central banks in the major capital markets. Aims to cover the personalities, institutions and policies which will shape financial regulation in the future.

332.1 NO ISSN 0800-3564
HG29
FINANCIAL REVIEW. 1925. 4/yr. NOK 450. Norske Bankforening - Norwegian Bankers' Association, Dronning Maudsgt. 15, P.O. Box 1489, Vika, N-0116 Oslo, Norway. FAX 47-22-83-07-43. Ed. Knut Toensberg. charts; stat. circ. 270. **Indexed:** P.A.I.S.
Formerly: Norwegian Commercial Banks Financial Review (ISSN 0029-3660)

332 US ISSN 0732-8516
HG181
FINANCIAL REVIEW (STATESBORO). 1966. q. $25 to individuals; institutions $75 (effective 1997). Eastern Finance Association, c/o Univ. of Tennessee, 426 Stokley Management Ctr., Knoxville, TN 37996-0540. TEL 423-974-1713. FAX 423-974-1716. E-mail: finrev@utkux.utcc.utk.edu. Eds. G.C. Philippatos, H.A. Black. adv.; bk.rev.; index. circ. 2,000. (also avail. in microform from UMI; back issues avail.; reprint service avail.) **Indexed:** B.P.I., BPIA, J.of Econ.Lit., P.A.I.S., PROMT. **Document type:** academic/scholarly publication.
●Also available online. Vendor(s): Information Access Co.
—BLDSC (3926.979800); KR SourceOne; SWETS; UMI; UnCover.
Incorporates: Eastern Finance Association. Proceedings of the Annual Meeting (ISSN 0163-6855)
Description: Publishes empirical, theoretical and methodological articles on topics of micro- and macrofinance.
Refereed Serial

332 US
FINANCIAL SERVICES ALERT. 1986. w. $525. Institute for Strategy Development, 1150 18th St., N.W., Washington, DC 20036. TEL 202-296-5240. FAX 202-452-6816. circ. 250. (back issues avail.) **Document type:** newsletter.
Formerly: Bankalert.

332 US
FINANCIAL SERVICES DOCUMENT WATCH - BANKING EDITION. (Consists of 4 eds.: Banking; Insurance; Public Finance; Thrift) m. $180. American Banker - Bond Buyer, Newsletter Division (Subsidiary of: Thomson Financial Services Company), One State St. Plaza, New York, NY 10004-1549. TEL 800-733-4371. FAX 212-943-2224. (Subscr. to: Box 28315, Washington, DC 20038-8315. TEL 202-347-2665) **Document type:** newsletter.
Supersedes in part: Insurance Document Watch.
Description: Real-time delivery of key documents in the banking sector.

FINANCIAL SERVICES DOCUMENT WATCH - INSURANCE EDITION. see *INSURANCE*

ULRICH'S INTERNATIONAL PERIODICALS DIRECTORY 1998

BUSINESS AND ECONOMICS — BANKING AND FINANCE

FINANCIAL SERVICES DOCUMENT WATCH - PUBLIC FINANCE EDITION. see BUSINESS AND ECONOMICS — Public Finance, Taxation

332 US
FINANCIAL SERVICES DOCUMENT WATCH - THRIFT EDITION. (Consists of 4 eds.: Banking; Insurance; Public Finance; Thrift) m. $180. American Banker - Bond Buyer, Newsletter Division (Subsidiary of: Thomson Financial Services Company), One State St. Plaza, New York, NY 10004-1549. TEL 800-733-4371. FAX 212-943-2224. (Subscr. to: Box 28315, Washington, DC 20038-8315. TEL 202-347-2665) **Document type:** newsletter.
  Supersedes in part: Insurance Document Watch.
  Description: Real-time delivery of key documents in the thrift sector.

332 UK ISSN 1363-9005
▼**FINANCIAL SERVICES IN LEEDS;** a survey of the financial services industry. 1996. a. Yorkshire and Humberside Regional Research Observatory, University of Leeds, School of Geography, Leeds LS2 9JT, England. TEL 44-113-233-3336. FAX 44-113-233-3308. E-mail: chris@goeg.leeds.ac.uk. **Document type:** trade publication.
—BLDSC (3926.985332).

FINANCIAL SERVICES - LAW & PRACTICE. see LAW

332 US
FINANCIAL SERVICES REGULATION AND LEGISLATION. 1986. 26/yr. $1250. Institute for Strategy Development, 1150 18th St., N.W., Washington, DC 20036. TEL 202-296-5240. FAX 202-452-6816. Ed. Theodore B. Dolmatch. s-a. index. circ. 200. **Document type:** newsletter.
  Formerly: Bank Regulation and Legislation Review.

332 US ISSN 1057-0810
HG179
FINANCIAL SERVICES REVIEW; the journal of individual financial management. 1991. q. $80 to individuals (foreign $100); institutions $225 (foreign $245) (effective 1998). (Academy of Financial Services) J A I Press Inc., 55 Old Post Rd., No. 2, Box 1678, Greenwich, CT 06830-1678. TEL 203-661-7602. FAX 203-661-0792. E-mail: jai@jaipress.com. (Addr. in Europe: J A I Press Ltd., 38 Tavistock St., Covent Garden, London WC2E 7PB, England. TEL 44-171-379-8834. FAX 44-171-379-8835) Ed. Karen Eilers Lahey. (also avail. in microform from UMI; back issues avail.) **Document type:** trade publication, academic/scholarly publication.
—BLDSC (3926.986030); UnCover. **CCC**.
  Description: Disseminates scientific research in the financial services field.

332 UK
FINANCIAL STABILITY REVIEW. 1997. irreg. £10. Bank of England, HO-3, Threadneedle St., London EC2R 8AH, England. TEL 44-171-601-5191. FAX 44-171-601-3217. (Co-sponsor: Securities and Investments Board)
  Description: Aims to promote the latest thinking on risk, regulation and financial markets, to facilitate discussion of issues that might affect risks in the UK financial system, and to provide a forum for debate among practitioners, policy makers, and academics.

332.1 US ISSN 0363-8987
HD2346.U5
FINANCIAL STUDIES OF THE SMALL BUSINESS. 1976. a. $104 (diskette $136; both $178) (effective Oct. 1996). Financial Research Associates, 510 Ave. J, S.E., Winter Haven, FL 33880-3781. TEL 941-299-3969. FAX 941-299-2131. Ed. Karen Goodman; Pub. Karen Goodman. R&P contact: Grant Lacerte. stat. circ. 6,000. (also avail. in diskette format) **Document type:** academic/scholarly publication.
  Description: Presents financial ratios and statistics for small businesses capitalized 1 million and under. Includes 5-year trends.

FINANCIAL SURVEY. COMMODITY BROKERS. ENGLAND AND WALES; company data for success. see BUSINESS AND ECONOMICS — Trade And Industrial Directories

FINANCIAL SURVEY. INSTALLMENT, CREDIT, AND FINANCE; company data for success. see BUSINESS AND ECONOMICS — Trade And Industrial Directories

FINANCIAL TECHNOLOGY REVIEW. see BUSINESS AND ECONOMICS — Investments

330 GW ISSN 0174-7363
CODEN: FITIBT
FINANCIAL TIMES (FRANKFURT EDITION). (Text in English) 1888. d. Financial Times (Europe) GmbH, Nibelungenplatz 3, 60318 Frankfurt a.M., Germany. TEL 069-156850. FAX 069-5964481. adv. circ. 70,000. **Document type:** newspaper.
●Also available on CD-ROM. Producer(s): Chadwyck-Healey Inc.
—CASDDS.

332 320 UK ISSN 0307-1766
FINANCIAL TIMES (LONDON, 1888). Frankfurt edition (ISSN 0174-7363); North American edition (ISSN 0884-6782) (Editions also printed in Leeds, Paris, Stockholm, Tokyo) 1888. d. (Mon.-Sat.). £409.64 (foreign £572.88) (effective 1997); newsstand price: £1.33. Financial Times, One Southwark Bridge, London SE1 9HL, England. TEL 44-171-873-3514. FAX 44-171-263-9764. URL: http://www.ft.com. (Subscr. to: Johnsons International Media Services, 43 Millharbour, London E14 9TR, England. TEL 44-171-538-8288. FAX 44-171-537-3594) Ed. Richard Lambert. adv.; bk.rev.; m. index. circ. 326,676. (also avail. in microfilm from RPI) **Indexed:** Alloys Ind., BNI (1990-), Eng.Mat.Abstr., GeoRef., Ind.Bus.Rep., Int.Packag.Abstr., Intl.Polym.Sci.& Tech., Met.Abstr.Ind., Mgmt.& Market.Abstr., Nonfer.Met.Alert, Paper & Bd.Abstr., PCC Alert, Print.Abstr., PROMT, RAPRA, Steels Alert, World Alum.Abstr., World Surf.Coat. **Document type:** newspaper.
●Also available on CD-ROM. Producer(s): Chadwyck-Healey Inc.

332 320 US ISSN 0884-6782
CODEN: FITIEW
FINANCIAL TIMES (NORTH AMERICAN EDITION). 1985. d. (Mon.-Sat.). $450 (Canada Can.$485) (effective Aug. 1995). F T Publications Inc., 14 E. 60th St., New York, NY 10022. TEL 212-752-7400; 800-628-8088. FAX 212-319-0704. E-mail: circulation@financialtimes.com; URL: http://www.ft.com.cum.index. (also avail. in microform from RPI) **Document type:** newspaper.
●Also available on CD-ROM. Producer(s): Chadwyck-Healey Inc.
—CASDDS.

332 CE
FINANCIAL TIMES OF CEYLON. (Text in English) 1961. q. Union Co. Ltd., 323 Union Place, P.O. Box 330, Colombo 2, Sri Lanka. Ed. Cyril Gardiner. adv. circ. 2,800.

332 320 UK
FINANCIAL TIMES ON C D - R O M. 1990. q. $1600 (effective 1996). (Financial Times Information) Chadwyck-Healey Ltd., The Quorum, Barnwell Rd., Cambridge CB5 8SW, England. TEL 44-1223-215512. FAX 44-1223-215514. (In N. America: Chadwyck-Healey Inc., 1101 King St., Alexandria, VA 22314. TEL 800-752-0515. FAX 703-683-7589)
●Available only on CD-ROM. Producer(s): Chadwyck-Healey Inc.

332 II
FINANCIAL WIZARD. (Text in English) 1990. w. newsstand price: Rs.5. Digital Finance & Investment Consultancy Pvt. Ltd., 24-B, Rajabahadur Compound, Ambalal Doshi Marg, Bombay 400 023, India. Ed. Ravi Shankar. circ. 42,135.

332.1 US ISSN 1059-3950
HG181
FINANCIAL WOMAN TODAY. 1985. 7/yr. $24 to non-members. Financial Women International, 200 N. Glebe Rd, Ste. 814, Arlington, VA 22203-3728. TEL 703-807-2007. FAX 703-807-0111. Ed. Megan Eisel. R&P contact: Valette Piper. adv.: page $1000; adv. contact: Truby Chiaviello. bk.rev.; illus. circ. 10,000. **Indexed:** ABI Inform., Bank.Lit.Ind., BPIA. **Document type:** newsletter.
  Formerly (until 1990): Executive Financial Women (ISSN 0886-540X); **Which supersedes** (1924-1985): N A B W Journal (ISSN 0885-5080)
  Description: Empowers women in the financial services industry to attain professional, economic, and personal goals, and to influence the future shape of the industry.

332 US
FINANCIAL WOMEN'S ASSOCIATION OF NEW YORK NEWSLETTER. 1956. m. $75. Financial Women's Association of New York, 215 Park Ave., S., Ste. 2010, New York, NY 10003. TEL 212-533-2141. FAX 212-982-3008. Ed. Nancy Sellar. adv. circ. 1,500. (tabloid format) **Document type:** newsletter.
  Description: Provides information about the organization, its programs and members.

332 US ISSN 0015-2064
HG4501 CODEN: FIWOAR
FINANCIAL WORLD. (During 1990-1991 incorporated: Corporate Finance (ISSN 0894-6817)) 1902. bi-w. $39. Financial World Partners, 1328 Broadway, New York, NY 10001. TEL 212-594-5030. FAX 212-629-0021. Ed. Geof Smith. adv. contact: Robert Meagher. bk.rev.; charts; illus.; mkt.; stat.; q. index. circ. 500,000. (also avail. in microform from UMI,MIM; reprint service avail. from UMI) **Indexed:** ABI Inform., B.P.I., BPIA, Bus.Ind., CAD CAM Abstr., Energy Info.Abstr., Environ.Abstr., INSPEC, Mag.Ind., Manage.Cont., Mid.East: Abstr.& Ind., P.A.I.S., PROMT, Tel.Abstr., Telegen, Tr.& Indus.Ind. **Document type:** consumer publication.
●Also available online. Vendor(s): Data-Star, Information Access Co., Knight-Ridder Information, Inc., Lexis-Nexis, UMI.
—BLDSC (3927.150000); AskIEEE; CASDDS; KR SourceOne; SWETS; UMI; UnCover. **CCC**.

332 NE ISSN 0005-8343
FINANCIEEL ECONOMISCH WEEKBLAD BELEGGERS BELANGEN. Key Title: Beleggers Belangen. 1956. w. fl.335 (foreign fl.416) (effective 1998). B.V. Uitgeversmaatschappij Bonaventura (Subsidiary of: Elsevier N.V.), Postbus 2158, 1000 CD Amsterdam, Netherlands. TEL 31-20-6914111. FAX 31-20-5674398. adv.; bk.rev. circ. 10,800. **Indexed:** Key to Econ.Sci.
  Incorporates (1980-1992): Geldactief (ISSN 1380-4626)

332 658 NE ISSN 0926-1753
FINANCIEEL MANAGEMENT SECLECT; het beste uit de international vakpers. 1991. 4/yr. fl.280 (effective 1996). Kluwer Bedrijfswetenschappen B.V. (Subsidiary of: Wolters Kluwer N.V.), Postbus 23, 7400 GA Deventer, Netherlands. TEL 31-5700-48999. FAX 31-5700-11504. (Subscr. to: Intermedia bv, Postbus 4, 2400 MA Alphen aan den Rijn, Netherlands. TEL 31-172-466321. FAX 31-172-435527) adv. **Document type:** trade publication.
—SWETS.

332 NE ISSN 1383-7656
FINANCIELE & MONETAIRE STUDIES. 1982. q. fl.49.50 to individuals; corporations fl.99 (effective 1996). WoltersgroepGroningen b.v. (Subsidiary of: Wolters Kluwer N.V.), Postbus 58, 9700 MB Groningen, Netherlands. TEL 31-50-5226524. FAX 31-50-5264866. Ed. Mrs. C.H. Zwansweg. **Document type:** academic/scholarly publication.
  Formerly (until 1996): Rotterdamse Monetaire Studies (ISSN 1381-0650)

332 NE ISSN 0015-2099
FINANCIELE KOERIER; weekblad voor beleggers. 1942. w. fl.271. Uitgeverij Lexico B.V., Herengracht 503, 1017 BV Amsterdam, Netherlands. TEL 31-20-6391536. FAX 31-20-6392969. Ed. F.W.J. Baijens. adv.: B&W page fl.2450; trim 210 x 298. circ. 6,700. **Indexed:** Key to Econ.Sci. **Document type:** trade publication.

332 US ISSN 1073-7340
HG181
FINANCIER: ANALYSES OF CAPITAL AND MONEY MARKET TRANSACTIONS. 1977; N.S. 1994. 5/yr. $125 (foreign $160) (effective 1997). Financier, Inc., 220 Locust St., Apt. 3-E, Philadelphia, PA 19106-3928. TEL 215-829-1354. FAX 215-829-1376. E-mail: zfinance@interserv.com; URL: http://www.the-financier.com. Ed. Charles Stone. R&P contact: Charles Stone. adv. contact: Anne Zissu. bk.rev. circ. 2,000. **Indexed:** ABI Inform, P.A.I.S. **Document type:** trade publication.
●Also available online.
—UMI. **CCC**.
  Formerly: Financier (ISSN 0745-242X)
  Description: Composed of analyses that examine how public authorities and private enterprises raise capital.
  Refereed Serial

BUSINESS AND ECONOMICS — BANKING AND FINANCE

332   SP   ISSN 0015-2102
FINANCIERO; revista internacional de economia, comercio e industria. 1959. m. 25000 ptas. Maldonado 55, 1a, Edif. 1, Ofc. 116, 28006 Madrid, Spain. TEL 411-06-53. FAX 411-07-52. Dir. Francisco Bermejo. adv.; bk.rev.; charts; illus.; stat. circ. 46,000.

332   MX
EL FINANCIERO INTERNATIONAL EDITION. (Text in English) vol.4, no.51, 1995. w. $180. El Financiero International, Inc., Lago Bolsena 176, Col. Anahuac, 11320 Mexico DF, Mexico. TEL 525-227-7600. FAX 525-227-7634. URL: http://basic.attis.com.mx/wwwFinanNews.html. (US addr.: 2300 S. Broadway, Los Angeles, CA 90007-2714. TEL 213-747-7547. FAX 213-747-2489) Ed. Alejandro Ramos; Pub. Rogelio Cardenas. R&P contact: Jane Johnson. adv. contact: Laura Knapp. bk.rev.; mkt.; stat. (tabloid format) **Document type:** newspaper.
●Also available online.
Also available on CD-ROM.
   Description: Contains in-depth news and analysis on Mexican business, trade and politics.

FINANCING AGRICULTURE. see *AGRICULTURE*

332.1   US
FINANCING AND INSURING EXPORTS: A USER'S GUIDE TO EXIMBANK AND F.C.I.A. PROGRAMS. 1985. a. $55. Export-Import Bank of the United States, 811 Vermont Ave., N.W., Washington, DC 20571. TEL 202-566-8990. FAX 202-566-7524. TELEX (TRT) 197681 EXIMUT. circ. 2,100.

332   US
FINANCING OPERATIONS. AFRICA. (Includes Nigeria, Saudi Arabia, South Africa, and Turkey) base vol. (plus s-a. updates). Economist Intelligence Unit, 111 W. 57th St., New York, NY 10019. TEL 212-554-0600; 800-938-4685. FAX 212-586-1181. TELEX 1755677. URL: http://www.eiu.com. (UK addr.: Economist Intelligence Unit Ltd., Subscriptions Dept., P.O. Box 200, Harold Hill, Romford, Essex RM3 8UX, England. TEL 44-1708-381-444. FAX 44-1708-371-850)
●Also available online. Vendor(s): Knight-Ridder Information, Inc., Lexis-Nexis.
   Former titles (until 1997): Financing Foreign Operations. Middle East - Africa & Financing Foreign Operations. Europe - Middle East - Africa.

332   US
FINANCING OPERATIONS. ARGENTINA. base vol. (plus q. updates). £195($295) Economist Intelligence Unit, 111 W. 57th St., New York, NY 10019. TEL 212-554-0600; 800-938-4685. FAX 212-586-1181. TELEX 175567. URL: http://www.eiu.com. (UK addr.: Economist Intelligence Unit Ltd., Subscriptions Dept., P.O. Box 200, Harold Hill, Romford, Essex RM3 8UX, England. TEL 44-1708-381444) (looseleaf format)
●Also available online. Vendor(s): Knight-Ridder Information, Inc., Lexis-Nexis.
   Formerly (until 1997): Financing Foreign Operations. Argentina (ISSN 1353-596X)
   Description: Provides details on critical areas such as exchange controls, sources of funding, financial markets, cash management and trade credit facilities for Argentina.

332   US
FINANCING OPERATIONS. AUSTRALIA. base vol. (plus s-a. updates). £195($295) Economist Intelligence Unit, 111 W. 57th St., New York, NY 10019. TEL 212-554-0600; 800-938-4685. FAX 212-586-1181. TELEX 175567. URL: http://www.eiu.com. (UK addr.: Economist Intelligence Unit Ltd., Subscriptions Dept., P.O. Box 200, Harold Hill, Romford, Essex RM3 8UX, England. TEL 44-1708-381-444. FAX 44-1708-371-850) (looseleaf format)
●Also available online. Vendor(s): Knight-Ridder Information, Inc., Lexis-Nexis.
   Formerly (until 1997): Financing Foreign Operations. Australia (ISSN 1353-5986)
   Description: Provides details on such critical areas as exchange controls, sources of funding, financial markets, cash management and trade credit facilities for Australia.

332   US
FINANCING OPERATIONS. BELGIUM. base vol. (plus s-a. updates). £195($295) Economist Intelligence Unit, 111 W. 57th St., New York, NY 10019. TEL 212-554-0600; 800-938-4685. FAX 212-586-1181. TELEX 175567. URL: http://www.eiu.com. (UK addr.: Economist Intelligence Unit Ltd., Subscriptions Dept., P.O. Box 200, Harold Hill, Romford, Essex RM3 8UX, England. TEL 44-1708-381-444. FAX 44-1708-371-850) (looseleaf format)
●Also available online. Vendor(s): Knight-Ridder Information, Inc., Lexis-Nexis.
   Formerly (until 1997): Financing Foreign Operations. Belgium (ISSN 1352-5875)
   Description: Provides details on critical areas such as exchange controls, sources of funding, financial markets, cash management and trade credit facilities for Belgium.

332   US
FINANCING OPERATIONS. BRAZIL. base vol. (plus q. updates). £195($295) Economist Intelligence Unit, 111 W. 57th St., New York, NY 10019. TEL 212-554-0600; 800-938-4685. FAX 212-586-1181. TELEX 175567. URL: http://www.eiu.com. (UK addr.: Economist Intelligence Unit Ltd., Subscriptions Dept., P.O. Box 200, Harold Hill, Romford, Essex RM3 8UX, England. TEL 44-1708-381-444. FAX 44-1708-371-850) (looseleaf format)
●Also available online. Vendor(s): Knight-Ridder Information, Inc., Lexis-Nexis.
   Formerly (until 1997): Financing Foreign Operations. Brazil (ISSN 1352-5883)
   Description: Provides details on critical areas such as exchange controls, sources of funding, financial markets, cash management and trade credit facilities for Brazil.

332   US
FINANCING OPERATIONS. CANADA. base vol. (plus s-a. updates). £195($295) Economist Intelligence Unit, 111 W. 57th St., New York, NY 10019. TEL 212-554-0600; 800-938-4685. FAX 212-586-1181. TELEX 175567. URL: http://www.eiu.com. (UK addr.: Economist Intelligence Unit Ltd., Subscriptions Dept., P.O. Box 200, Harold Hill, Romford, Essex RM3 8UX, England. TEL 44-1708-381-444. FAX 44-1708-371-850) (looseleaf format)
●Also available online. Vendor(s): Knight-Ridder Information, Inc., Lexis-Nexis.
   Formerly (until 1997): Financing Foreign Operations. Canada (ISSN 1352-5951)
   Description: Provides details on critical areas such as exchange controls, sources of funding, financial markets, cash management and trade credit facilities for Canada.

332   US
FINANCING OPERATIONS. CHILE. base vol. (plus s-a. updates). £195($295) Economist Intelligence Unit, 111 W. 57th St., New York, NY 10019. TEL 212-554-0600; 800-938-4685. FAX 212-586-1181. TELEX 175567. (UK addr.: Economist Intelligence Unit Ltd., Subscriptions Dept., P.O. Box 200, Harold Hill, Romford, Essex RM3 8UX, England. TEL 44-1708-381-444. FAX 44-1708-371-850) (looseleaf format)
●Also available online. Vendor(s): Knight-Ridder Information, Inc., Lexis-Nexis.
   Formerly (until 1997): Financing Foreign Operations. Chile.
   Description: Provides details on critical areas such as exchange controls, sources of funding, financial markets, cash management and trade credit facilities for Chile.

332   US
FINANCING OPERATIONS. CHINA. 1993. base vol. (plus q. updates). £195($295) Economist Intelligence Unit, 111 W. 57th St., New York, NY 10019. TEL 212-554-0600; 800-938-4685. FAX 212-586-1181. TELEX 175567. URL: http://www.eiu.com. (U.K. addr.: Economist Intelligence Unit Ltd., Subscriptions Dept., P.O. Box 200, Harold Hill, Romford, Essex RM3 8UX, England. TEL 44-1708-381444. FAX 44-1708-371850) **Document type:** trade publication.
   Formerly (until 1997): Financing Foreign Operations. China (ISSN 1353-5943)
   Description: Provides details on such critical areas as exchange controls, sources of funding, financial markets, cash management and trade credit facilities for China.

332   US
FINANCING OPERATIONS. COLOMBIA. base vol. (plus s-a. updates). £195($295) Economist Intelligence Unit, 111 W. 57th St., New York, NY 10019. TEL 212-554-0600; 800-938-4685. FAX 212-586-1181. TELEX 175567. URL: http://www.eiu.com. (UK addr.: Economist Intelligence Unit Ltd., Subscriptions Dept., P.O. Box 200, Harold Hill, Romford, Essex RM3 8UX, England. TEL 44-1708-381-444. FAX 44-1708-371-850) (looseleaf format)
●Also available online. Vendor(s): Knight-Ridder Information, Inc., Lexis-Nexis.
   Formerly (until 1997): Financing Foreign Operations. Colombia (ISSN 1352-5905)
   Description: Provides details on critical areas such as exchange controls, sources of funding, financial markets, cash management and trade credit facilities for Colombia.

332   US
FINANCING OPERATIONS. COSTA RICA. base vol. (plus s-a. updates). £195($295) Economist Intelligence Unit, 111 W. 57th St., New York, NY 10019. TEL 212-554-0600; 800-938-4685. FAX 212-586-1181. TELEX 175567. URL: http://www.eiu.com. (UK addr.: Economist Intelligence Unit Ltd., Subscriptions Dept., P.O. Box 200, Harold Hill, Romford, Essex RM3 8UX, England. TEL 44-1708-381-444. FAX 44-1708-371-850) (looseleaf format)
●Also available online. Vendor(s): Knight-Ridder Information, Inc., Lexis-Nexis.
   Formerly (until 1997): Financing Foreign Operations. Costa Rica.
   Description: Provides details on critical areas such as exchange controls, sources of funding, financial markets, cash management and trade credit facilities for the covered countries.

332   US
FINANCING OPERATIONS. CZECH REPUBLIC. base vol. (plus q. updates). £195($295) Economist Intelligence Unit, 111 W. 57th St., New York, NY 10019. TEL 212-554-0600; 800-938-4685. FAX 212-586-1181. TELEX 175567. URL: http://www.eiu.com. (UK addr.: Economist Intelligence Unit Ltd., Subscriptions Dept., P.O. Box 200, Harold Hill, Romford, Essex RM3 8UX, England. TEL 44-1708-381-444. FAX 44-1708-371-850) (looseleaf format)
●Also available online. Vendor(s): Knight-Ridder Information, Inc., Lexis-Nexis.
   Former titles (until 1997): Financing Foreign Operations. Czech Republic; (until Apr. 1995): Financing Foreign Operations. Czech Republic and Slovakia; Financing Foreign Operations. Czechoslovakia (ISSN 1352-5735)
   Description: Provides details on critical areas such as exchange controls, sources of funding, financial markets, cash management and trade credit facilities for the Czech Republic and Slovakia.

332   US
FINANCING OPERATIONS. EL SALVADOR. £195($295) Economist Intelligence Unit, 111 W. 57th St., New York, NY 10019. TEL 212-554-0600; 800-938-4685. FAX 212-586-1182. TELEX 175567. URL: http://www.eiu.com. (UK addr.: Economist Intelligence Unit Ltd., Subscriptions Dept., P.O. Box 200 Harold Hill, Romford, Essex RM3 8UX, England. TEL 44-1708-381-444. FAX 44-1708-371-850) (looseleaf format)
●Also available online. Vendor(s): Knight-Ridder Information, Inc., Lexis-Nexis.
   Formerly (until 1997): Financing Foreign Operations. El Salvador.
   Description: Provides details on critical areas such as exchange controls, sources of funding, financial markets, cash management and trade credit facilities for El Salvador.

BUSINESS AND ECONOMICS — BANKING AND FINANCE

332 US
FINANCING OPERATIONS. FRANCE. base vol. (plus s-a. updates). £175($295) Economist Intelligence Unit, 111 W. 57th St., New York, NY 10019. TEL 212-554-0600; 800-938-4685. FAX 212-586-1181. TELEX 175567. URL: http://www.eiu.com. (UK addr.: Economist Intelligence Unit Ltd., Subscriptions Dept., P.O. Box 200, Harold Hill, Romford, Essex RM3 8UX, England. TEL 44-1708-381-444. FAX 44-1708-371-850) (looseleaf format)
●Also available online. Vendor(s): Knight-Ridder Information, Inc., Lexis-Nexis.
Formerly (until 1997): Financing Foreign Operations. France (ISSN 1353-6311)
Description: Provides details on critical areas such as exchange controls, sources of funding, financial markets, cash management and trade credit facilities for France.

332 US
FINANCING OPERATIONS. GERMANY. base vol. (plus s-a. updates). £175($295) Economist Intelligence Unit, 111 W. 57th St., New York, NY 10019. TEL 212-554-0600; 800-938-4685. FAX 212-586-1181. TELEX 175567. URL: http://www.eiu.com. (UK addr.: Economist Intelligence Unit Ltd., Subscriptions Dept., P.O. Box 200, Harold Hill, Romford, Essex RM3 8UX, England. TEL 444-1708-381-444. FAX 44-1708-371-850) (looseleaf format)
●Also available online. Vendor(s): Knight-Ridder Information, Inc., Lexis-Nexis.
Formerly (until 1997): Financing Foreign Operations. Germany (ISSN 1352-5743)
Description: Provides details on critical areas such as exchange controls, sources of funding, financial markets, cash management and trade credit facilities for Germany.

332 US
FINANCING OPERATIONS. GREECE. base vol. (plus s-a. updates). £175($295) Economist Intelligence Unit, 111 W. 57th St., New York, NY 10019. TEL 212-554-0600; 800-938-4685. FAX 212-586-1181. TELEX 175567. URL: http://www.eiu.com. (UK addr.: Economist Intelligence Unit Ltd., Subscriptions Dept., P.O. Box 200, Harold Hill, Romford, Essex RM3 8UX, England. TEL 44-1708-381-444. FAX 44-1708-371-850) (looseleaf format)
●Also available online. Vendor(s): Knight-Ridder Information, Inc., Lexis-Nexis.
Formerly (until 1997): Financing Foreign Operations. Greece (ISSN 1366-3070)
Description: Provides details on critical areas such as exchange controls, sources of funding, financial markets, cash management and trade credit facilities for Greece.

332 US
FINANCING OPERATIONS. GUATEMALA. base vol. (plus s-a. updates). £195($295) Economist Intelligence Unit, 111 W. 57th St., New York, NY 10019. TEL 212-554-0600; 800-938-4685. FAX 212-586-1182. TELEX 175567. URL: http://www.eiu.com. (UK addr.: Economist Intelligence Unit Ltd., Subscriptions Dept., P.O. Box 200, Harold Hill, Romford, Essex RM3 8UX, England. TEL 44-1708-381-444. FAX 44-1708-371-850) (looseleaf format)
●Also available online. Vendor(s): Knight-Ridder Information, Inc., Lexis-Nexis.
Formerly (until 1997): Financing Foreign Operations. Guatemala.
Description: Provides details on critical areas such as exchange controls, sources of funding, financial markets, cash management and trade credit facilities for Guatemala.

332 US
FINANCING OPERATIONS. HONDURAS. base vol. (plus s-a. updates). £195($295) Economist Intelligence Unit, 111 W. 57th St., New York, NY 10019. TEL 212-554-0600; 800-938-4685. FAX 212-586-1182. TELEX 175567. URL: http://www.eiu.com. (UK addr.: Economist Intelligence Unit Ltd., Subscriptions Dept., P.O. Box 200, Harold Hill, Romford, Essex RM3 8UX, England. TEL 44-1708-381-444. FAX 44-1708-371-850) (looseleaf format)
●Also available online. Vendor(s): Knight-Ridder Information, Inc., Lexis-Nexis.
Formerly (until 1997): Financing Foreign Operations. Honduras.
Description: Provides details on critical areas such as exchange controls, sources of funding, financial markets, cash management and trade credit facilities for Honduras.

332 US
FINANCING OPERATIONS. HONG KONG. base vol. (plus s-a. updates). £195($295) Economist Intelligence Unit, 111 W. 57th St., New York, NY 10019. TEL 212-554-0600; 800-938-4685. FAX 212-586-1181. TELEX 175567. URL: http://www.eiu.com. (UK addr.: Economist Intelligence Unit Ltd., Subscriptions Dept., P.O. Box 200, Harold Hill, Romford, Essex RM3 8UX, England. TEL 44-1708-381-444. FAX 44-1708-371-850) (looseleaf format)
●Also available online. Vendor(s): Knight-Ridder Information, Inc., Lexis-Nexis.
Formerly (until 1997): Financing Foreign Operations. Hong Kong (ISSN 1352-5751)
Description: Provides details on critical areas such as exchange controls, sources of funding, financial markets, cash management and trade credit facilities for Hong Kong.

332 US
FINANCING OPERATIONS. HUNGARY. base vol. (plus q. updates). £195($295) Economist Intelligence Unit, 111 W. 57th St., New York, NY 10019. TEL 212-554-0600; 800-938-4685. FAX 212-586-1181. TELEX 175567. URL: http://www.eiu.com. (UK addr.: Economist Intelligence Unit Ltd., Subscriptions Dept., P.O. Box 200, Harold Hill, Romford, Essex RM3 8UX, England. TEL 44-1708-381-444. FAX 44-1708-371-850) (looseleaf format)
●Also available online. Vendor(s): Knight-Ridder Information, Inc., Lexis-Nexis.
Formerly (until 1997): Financing Foreign Operations. Hungary (ISSN 1366-0225)
Description: Provides details on critical areas such as exchange controls, sources of funding, financial markets, cash management and trade credit facilities for Hungary.

332 US
FINANCING OPERATIONS. INDIA. base vol. (plus q. update). £195($295) Economist Intelligence Unit, 111 W. 57th St., New York, NY 10019. TEL 212-554-0600; 800-938-4685. FAX 212-586-1181. TELEX 175567. URL: http://www.eiu.com. (UK addr.: Economist Intelligence Unit Ltd., Subscriptions Dept., P.O. Box 200, Harold Hill, Romford, Essex RM3 8UX, England. TEL 44-1708-371-444. FAX 44-1708-371-850) (looseleaf format)
●Also available online. Vendor(s): Knight-Ridder Information, Inc., Lexis-Nexis.
Formerly (until 1997): Financing Foreign Operations. India (ISSN 1366-364X)
Description: Provides details on critical areas such as exchange controls, sources of funding, financial markets, cash management and trade credit facilities for India.

332 US
FINANCING OPERATIONS. INDONESIA. 1993. base vol. (plus s-a. updates). £195($295) Economist Intelligence Unit, 111 W. 57th St., New York, NY 10019. TEL 212-554-0600; 800-938-4685. FAX 212-586-1181. TELEX 175567. URL: http://www.eiu.com. (U.K. addr.: Economist Intelligence Unit Ltd., Subscriptions Dept., P.O. Box 200, Harold Hill, Romford, Essex RM3 8UX, England. TEL 44-1708-381444. FAX 44-1708-371850)
Document type: trade publication.
Formerly (until 1997): Financing Foreign Operations. Indonesia (ISSN 1352-576X)
Description: Provides details on such critical areas such as exchange controls, sources of funding, financial markets, cash management and trade credit facilities for Indonesia.

332 US
FINANCING OPERATIONS. ITALY. base vol. (plus s-a. updates). £195($295) Economist Intelligence Unit, 111 W. 57th St., New York, NY 10019. TEL 212-554-0600; 800-938-4685. FAX 212-586-1181. TELEX 175567. URL: http://www.eiu.com. (UK addr.: Economist Intelligence Unit Ltd., Subscriptions Dept., P.O. Box 200, Harold Hill, Romford, Essex RM3 8UX, England. TEL 44-1708-381-444. FAX 44-1708-371-850) (looseleaf format)
●Also available online. Vendor(s): Knight-Ridder Information, Inc., Lexis-Nexis.
Formerly (until 1997): Financing Foreign Operations. Italy (ISSN 1366-3054)
Description: Provides details on critical areas such as exchange controls, sources of funding, financial markets, cash management and trade credit facilities for Italy.

332 US
FINANCING OPERATIONS. JAPAN. base vol. (plus s-a. updates). £195($295) Economist Intelligence Unit, 111 W. 57th St., New York, NY 10019. TEL 212-554-0600; 800-938-1181. FAX 212-586-1182. TELEX 175567. URL: http://www.eiu.com. (UK addr.: Economist Intelligence Unit Ltd., Subscriptions Dept., P.O. Box 200, Harold Hill, Romford, Essex RM3 8UX, England. TEL 44-1708-381-444. FAX 44-1708-371-850) (looseleaf format)
●Also available online. Vendor(s): Knight-Ridder Information, Inc., Lexis-Nexis.
Formerly (until 1997): Financing Foreign Operations. Japan (ISSN 1353-632X)
Description: Provides details on critical areas such as exchange controls, sources of funding, financial markets, cash management and trade credit facilities for Japan.

332 US
FINANCING OPERATIONS. MALAYSIA. base vol. (plus q. updates). £195($295) Economist Intelligence Unit, 111 W. 57th St., New York, NY 10019. TEL 212-554-0600; 800-938-4685. FAX 212-586-1181. TELEX 175567. URL: http://www.eiu.com. (UK addr.: Economist Intelligence Unit Ltd., Subscriptions Dept., P.O. Box 200, Harold Hill, Romford, Essex RM3 8UX, England. TEL 44-1708-381-444. FAX 44-1708-371-850) (looseleaf format)
●Also available online. Vendor(s): Knight-Ridder Information, Inc., Lexis-Nexis.
Formerly (until 1997): Financing Foreign Operations. Malaysia (ISSN 1352-5778)
Description: Provides details on critical areas such as exchange controls, sources of funding, financial markets, cash management and trade credit facilities for Malaysia.

332 US
FINANCING OPERATIONS. MEXICO. base vol. (plus q. updates). £195($295) Economist Intelligence Unit, 111 W. 57th St., New York, NY 10019. TEL 212-554-0600; 800-938-4685. FAX 212-586-1181. TELEX 175567. URL: http://www.eiu.com. (UK addr.: Economist Intelligence Unit Ltd., Subscriptions Dept., P.O. Box 200, Harold Hill, Romford, Essex RM3 8UX, England. TEL 44-1708-381-444. FAX 44-1708-371-850) (looseleaf format)
●Also available online. Vendor(s): Knight-Ridder Information, Inc., Lexis-Nexis.
Formerly (until 1997): Financing Foreign Operations. Mexico (ISSN 1352-5786)
Description: Provides details on critical areas such as exchange controls, sources of funding, financial markets, cash management and trade credit facilities for Mexico.

BUSINESS AND ECONOMICS — BANKING AND FINANCE

332 — US
FINANCING OPERATIONS. NETHERLANDS. base vol. (plus s-a. updates). £195($295) Economist Intelligence Unit, 111 W. 57th St., New York, NY 10019. TEL 212-554-0600; 800-938-4685. FAX 212-586-1181. TELEX 175567. URL: http://www.eiu.com. (UK addr.: Economist Intelligence Unit, Subscriptions Dept., P.O. Box 200, Harold Hill, Romford, Essex RM3 8UX, England. TEL 44-1708-381-444. FAX 44-1708-371-850) (looseleaf format)
● Also available online. Vendor(s): Knight-Ridder Information, Inc., Lexis-Nexis.
Formerly (until 1997): Financing Foreign Operations. Netherlands (ISSN 1353-5846)
Description: Provides details on critical areas such as exchange controls, sources of funding, financial markets, cash management and trade credit facilities for the Netherlands.

382.0993 — US
FINANCING OPERATIONS. NEW ZEALAND. 1993. base vol. (plus s-a. updates). £195($295) Economist Intelligence Unit, 111 W. 57th St., New York, NY 10019. TEL 212-554-0600; 800-938-4685. FAX 212-586-1181. TELEX 175567. URL: http://www.eiu.com. (U.K. addr.: Economist Intelligence Unit Ltd., Subscriptions Dept., P.O. Box 200, Harold Hill, Romford, Essex RM3 8UX, England. TEL 44-1708-381444. FAX 44-1708-371850)
Document type: trade publication.
Formerly (until 1997): Financing Foreign Operations. New Zealand (ISSN 1352-5794)
Description: Provides details on such critical areas as exchange controls, sources of funding, financial markets, cash management and trade credit facilities for New Zealand.

332 — US
FINANCING OPERATIONS. NICARAGUA. base vol. (plus s-a. updates). £195($295) Economist Intelligence Unit, 111 W. 57th St., New York, NY 10019. TEL 212-554-0600; 800-938-4685. FAX 212-586-1182. TELEX 175567. URL: http://www.eiu.com. (UK addr.: Economist Intelligence Unit Ltd., Subscriptions Dept., P.O. Box 200, Harold Hill, Romford, Essex RM3 8UX, England. TEL 44-1708-381-444. FAX 44-1708-371-850) (looseleaf format)
● Also available online. Vendor(s): Knight-Ridder Information, Inc., Lexis-Nexis.
Formerly (until 1997): Financing Foreign Operations. Nicaragua.
Description: Provides details on critical areas such as exchange controls, sources of funding, financial markets, cash management and trade credit facilities for Nicaragua.

332 — US
FINANCING OPERATIONS. NIGERIA. base vol. (plus s-a. updates). £195($295) Economist Intelligence Unit, 111 W. 57th St., New York, NY 10019. TEL 212-554-0600; 800-938-4685. FAX 212-586-1181. TELEX 175567. URL: http://www.eiu.com. (UK addr.: Economist Intelligence Unit Ltd., Subscriptions Dept., P.O. Box 200, Harold Hill, Romford, Essex RM3 8UX, England. TEL 44-1708-381-444. FAX 44-1708-371-850) (looseleaf format)
● Also available online. Vendor(s): Knight-Ridder Information, Inc., Lexis-Nexis.
Formerly (until 1997): Financing Foreign Operations. Nigeria (ISSN 1353-582X)
Description: Details areas such as exchange control, source of funding, financial markets, cash management and trade credit facilities.

332 — US
FINANCING OPERATIONS. NORWAY. base vol. (plus s-a. updates). £195($295) Economist Intelligence Unit, 111 W. 57th St., New York, NY 10019. TEL 212-554-0600; 800-938-4685. FAX 212-586-1181. TELEX 175567. URL: http://www.eiu.com. (UK addr.: Economist Intelligence Unit Ltd., Subscriptions Dept., P.O. Box 200, Harold Hill, Romford, Essex RM3 8UX, England. TEL 44-1708-381-444. FAX 44-1708-371-850) (looseleaf format)
● Also available online. Vendor(s): Knight-Ridder Information, Inc., Lexis-Nexis.
Formerly (until 1997): Financing Foreign Operations. Norway (ISSN 1352-5808)
Description: Provides details on critical areas such as exchange controls, sources of funding, financial markets, cash management and trade credit facilities for Norway.

332 — US
FINANCING OPERATIONS. PANAMA. base vol. (plus s-a. updates). £195($295) Economist Intelligence Unit, 111 W. 57th St., New York, NY 10019. TEL 212-554-0600; 800-938-4685. FAX 212-586-1181. TELEX 175567. URL: http://www.eiu.com. (UK addr.: Economist Intelligence Unit Ltd., Subscriptions Dept., P.O. Box 200, Harold Hill, Romford, Essex RM3 8UX, England. TEL 44-1708-381-444. FAX 44-1708-371-850) (looseleaf format)
● Also available online. Vendor(s): Knight-Ridder Information, Inc., Lexis-Nexis.
Formerly (until 1997): Financing Foreign Operations. Panama (ISSN 1366-3097)
Description: Provides details on critical areas such as exchange controls, sources of funding, financial markets, cash management and trade credit facilities for Panama.

332 — US
FINANCING OPERATIONS. PHILIPPINES. base vol. (plus s-a. updates). £195($295) Economist Intelligence Unit, 111 W. 57th St., New York, NY 10019. TEL 212-554-0600; 800-938-4685. FAX 212-586-1181. TELEX 175567. URL: http://www.eiu.com. (UK addr.: Economist Intelligence Unit Ltd., Subscriptions Dept., P.O. Box 200, Harold Hill, Romford, Essex RM3 8UX, England. TEL 44-1708-381-444. FAX 44-1708-371-850) (looseleaf format)
● Also available online. Vendor(s): Knight-Ridder Information, Inc., Lexis-Nexis.
Formerly (until 1997): Financing Foreign Operations. Philippines.
Description: Provides details on critical areas such as exchange controls, sources of funding, financial markets, cash management and trade credit facilities for the Philippines.

332 — US
FINANCING OPERATIONS. POLAND. base vol. (plus q. updates). £195($295) Economist Intelligence Unit, 111 W. 57th St., New York, NY 10019. TEL 212-554-0600; 800-938-4685. FAX 212-586-1181. TELEX 175567. URL: http://www.eiu.com. (UK addr.: Economist Intelligence Unit Ltd., Subscriptions Dept., P.O. Box 200, Harold Hill, Romford, Essex RM3 8UX, England. TEL 44-1708-381-444. FAX 44-1708-371-850) (looseleaf format)
● Also available online. Vendor(s): Knight-Ridder Information, Inc., Lexis-Nexis.
Formerly (until 1997): Financing Foreign Operations. Poland (ISSN 1352-5816)
Description: Provides details on critical areas such as exchange controls, sources of funding, financial markets, cash management and trade credit facilities for Poland.

332.6 382 — US
FINANCING OPERATIONS. PORTUGAL. base vol. (plus s-a. updates). £195($295) Economist Intelligence Unit, 111 W. 57th St., New York, NY 10019. TEL 212-554-0600; 800-938-4685. FAX 212-586-1181. TELEX 175567. URL: http://www.eiu.com. (UK addr.: Economist Intelligence Unit Ltd., Subscriptions Dept., P.O. Box 200, Harold Hill, Romford, Essex RM3 8UX, England. TEL 44-1708-381-444. FAX 44-1708-371-850)
Formerly (until 1997): Financing Foreign Operations. Portugal (ISSN 1353-5811)
Description: Provides details on critical areas such as exchange controls, sources of funding, financial markets, cash management and trade credit facilities for Portugal.

332 — US
FINANCING OPERATIONS. RUSSIA. base vol. (plus q. updates). £195($295) Economist Intelligence Unit, 111 W. 57th St., New York, NY 10019. TEL 212-554-0600; 800-938-4685. FAX 212-586-1181. TELEX 175567. URL: http://www.eiu.com. (UK addr.: Economist Intelligence Unit Ltd., Subscriptions Dept., P.O. Box 200, Harold Hill, Romford, Essex RM3 8UX, England. TEL 44-1708-381-444. FAX 44-1708-371-850) (looseleaf format)
● Also available online. Vendor(s): Knight-Ridder Information, Inc., Lexis-Nexis.
Former titles (until 1997): Financing Foreign Operations. Russia (ISSN 1352-5824); (until 1993): Financing Foreign Operations. Commonwealth of Independent States.
Description: Provides details on critical areas such as exchange controls, sources of funding, financial markets, cash management and trade credit facilities for Russia.

332 — US
FINANCING OPERATIONS. SAUDI ARABIA. base vol. (plus s-a. updates). £195($295) Economist Intelligence Unit, 111 W. 57th St., New York, NY 10019. TEL 212-554-0600; 800-938-4685. FAX 212-586-1181. TELEX 175567. URL: http://www.eiu.com. (UK addr.: Economist Intelligence Unit Ltd., Subscriptions Dept., P.O. Box 200, Harold Hill, Romford, Essex RM3 8UX, England. TEL 44-1708-381-444. FAX 44-1708-371-850) (looseleaf format)
● Also available online. Vendor(s): Knight-Ridder Information, Inc., Lexis-Nexis.
Formerly (until 1997): Financing Foreign Operations. Saudi Arabia.
Description: Provides details on critical areas such as exchange controls, sources of funding, financial markets, cash management and trade credit facilities for Saudi Arabia.

332 — US
FINANCING OPERATIONS. SINGAPORE. base vol. (plus s-a. updates). £195($295) Economist Intelligence Unit, 111 W. 57th St., New York, NY 10019. TEL 212-554-0600; 800-938-4685. FAX 212-586-1181. TELEX 175567. URL: http://www.eiu.com. (UK addr.: Economist Intelligence Unit Ltd., Subscriptions Dept., P.O. Box 200, Harold Hill, Romford, Essex RM3 8UX, England. TEL 44-1708-381-444. FAX 44-1708-371-850) (looseleaf format)
● Also available online. Vendor(s): Knight-Ridder Information, Inc., Lexis-Nexis.
Formerly (until 1997): Financing Foreign Operations. Singapore (ISSN 1353-5862)
Description: Provides details on critical areas such as exchange controls, sources of funding, financial markets, cash management and trade credit facilities for Singapore.

332 — US
FINANCING OPERATIONS. SOUTH AFRICA. base vol. (plus s-a. updates). £195($295) Economist Intelligence Unit, 111 W. 57th St., New York, NY 10019. TEL 212-586-1181. TELEX 175567. URL: http://www.eiu.com. (UK addr.: Economist Intelligence Unit Ltd., Subscriptions Dept., P.O. Box 200, Harold Hill, Romford, Essex RM3 8UX, England. TEL 44-1708-381-444. FAX 44-1708-371-850) (looseleaf format)
● Also available online. Vendor(s): Knight-Ridder Information, Inc., Lexis-Nexis.
Formerly (until 1997): Financing Foreign Operations. South Africa (ISSN 1353-5854)
Description: Provides details on critical areas such as exchange controls, sources of funding, financial markets, cash management and trade credit facilities for South Africa.

BUSINESS AND ECONOMICS — BANKING AND FINANCE

332   **US**
FINANCING OPERATIONS. SOUTH KOREA. base vol. (plus s-a. updates). £195($295) Economist Intelligence Unit, 111 W. 57th St., New York, NY 10019. TEL 212-554-0600; 800-938-4685. FAX 212-586-1181. TELEX 175567. URL: http://www.eiu.com. (UK addr.: Economist Intelligence Unit Ltd., Subscriptions Dept., P.O. Box 200, Harold Hill, Romford, Essex RM3 8UX, England. TEL 44-1708-381-444. FAX 44-1708-371-850) (looseleaf format)
●Also available online. Vendor(s): Knight-Ridder Information, Inc., Lexis-Nexis.
Former titles (until 1997): Financing Foreign Operations. South Korea (ISSN 1365-9634) & Financing Foreign Operations. Korea.
Description: Provides details on critical areas such as exchange controls, sources of funding, financial markets, cash management and trade credit facilities for Korea.

332   **US**
FINANCING OPERATIONS. TAIWAN. base vol. (plus s-a. updates). £195($295) Economist Intelligence Unit, 111 W. 57th St., New York, NY 10019. TEL 212-554-0600; 800-938-4685. FAX 212-586-1181. TELEX 175567. URL: http://www.eiu.com. (UK addr.: Economist Intelligence Unit Ltd., Subscriptions Dept., P.O. Box 200, Harold Hill, Romford, Essex RM3 8UX, England. TEL 44-1708-381-444. FAX 44-1708-371-850) (looseleaf format)
●Also available online. Vendor(s): Knight-Ridder Information, Inc., Lexis-Nexis.
Formerly (until 1997): Financing Foreign Operations. Taiwan.
Description: Provides details on critical areas such as exchange controls, sources of funding, financial markets, cash management and trade credit facilities for Taiwan.

332   **US**
FINANCING OPERATIONS. UNITED STATES OF AMERICA. base vol. (plus q. updates). £195($295) Economist Intelligence Unit, 111 W. 57th St., New York, NY 10019. TEL 212-554-0600; 800-938-4685. FAX 212-586-1181. TELEX 175567. URL: http://www.eiu.com. (UK addr.: Economist Intelligence Unit Ltd., Subscriptions Dept., P.O. Box 200, Harold Hill, Romford, Essex RM3 8UX, England. TEL 44-1708-381-444. FAX 44-1708-371-850) (looseleaf format)
●Also available online. Vendor(s): Knight-Ridder Information, Inc., Lexis-Nexis.
Formerly (until 1997): Financing Foreign Operations. United States of America (ISSN 1352-5867)
Description: Provides details on critical areas such as exchange controls, sources of funding, financial markets, cash management and trade credit facilities for the US.

332   **US**
FINANCING OPERATIONS. VENEZUELA. base vol. (plus q. updates). £195($295) Economist Intelligence Unit, 111 W. 57th St., New York, NY 10019. TEL 212-554-0600; 800-938-4685. FAX 212-586-1181. TELEX 175567. URL: http://www.eiu.com. (UK addr.: Economist Intelligence Unit Ltd., Subscriptions Dept., P.O. Box 200, Harold Hill, Romford, Essex RM3 8UX, England. TEL 44-1708-381-444. FAX 44-1708-371-850) (looseleaf format)
●Also available online. Vendor(s): Knight-Ridder Information, Inc., Lexis-Nexis.
Formerly (until 1997): Financing Foreign Operations. Venezuela (ISSN 1353-5897)
Description: Provides details on critical areas such as exchange controls, sources of funding, financial markets, cash management and trade credit facilities for Venezuela.

332   **US**
FINANCING OPERATIONS. SPAIN. base vol. (plus s-a. updates). £195($295) Economist Intelligence Unit, 111 W. 57th St., New York, NY 10019. TEL 212-554-0600; 800-938-4685. FAX 212-586-1181. TELEX 175567. URL: http://www.eiu.com. (UK addr.: Economist Intelligence Unit Ltd., Subscriptions Dept., P.O. Box 200, Harold Hill, Romford, Essex RM3 8UX, England. TEL 44-1708-381-444. FAX 44-1708-371-850) (looseleaf format)
●Also available online. Vendor(s): Knight-Ridder Information, Inc., Lexis-Nexis.
Formerly (until 1997): Financing Foreign Operations. Spain (ISSN 1352-5859)
Description: Provides details on critical areas such as exchange controls, sources of funding, financial markets, cash management and trade credit facilities for Spain.

332   **US**
FINANCING OPERATIONS. THAILAND. base vol. (plus q. updates). £195($295) Economist Intelligence Unit, 111 W. 57th St., New York, NY 10019. TEL 212-554-0600; 800-938-4685. FAX 212-586-1181. TELEX 175567. URL: http://www.eiu.com. (UK addr.: Economist Intelligence Unit Ltd., Subscriptions Dept., P.O. Box 200, Harold Hill, Romford, Essex RM3 8UX, England. TEL 44-1708-381-444. FAX 44-1708-371-850) (looseleaf format)
●Also available online. Vendor(s): Knight-Ridder Information, Inc., Lexis-Nexis.
Formerly (until 1997): Financing Foreign Operations. Thailand (ISSN 1353-5900)
Description: Provides details on critical areas such as exchange controls, sources of funding, financial markets, cash management and trade credit facilities for Thailand.

332   **XR**   ISSN 0322-9653
FINANCNI ZPRAVODAJ. 1956. irreg. (approx. 12/yr.). 60 Kc. for 5 nos. Ministerstvo Financi Ceske Republiky, Letenska 15, 118 10 Prague 1, Czech Republic. Ed. Alena Sauerova. charts; illus.; index.
Formerly: Federalni Ministerstvo Financi. Vestnik (ISSN 0042-4641)

331.881   **DK**   ISSN 0907-0192
FINANS. 1992. 20/yr. Finansforbundet, Langebrohus, Langebrogade 5, Appelbys Plads, DK-1411 Copenhagen, Denmark. Ed. Kjelo Jacobsen. adv. circ. 37,500.
Formed by the merger of (1942-1992): Sparekassestanden (ISSN 0108-612X); (1938-1992): Bankstanden (ISSN 0901-3385)

332   **US**
FINANCING OPERATIONS. SWEDEN. base vol. (plus s-a. updates). £195($295) Economist Intelligence Unit, 111 W. 57th St., New York, NY 10019. TEL 212-554-0600; 800-938-4685. FAX 212-586-1181. TELEX 175567. URL: http://www.eiu.com. (UK addr.: Economist Intelligence Unit Ltd., Subscriptions Dept., P.O. Box 200, Harold Hill, Romford, Essex RM3 8UX, England. TEL 44-1708-381-444. FAX 44-1708-371-850) (looseleaf format)
●Also available online. Vendor(s): Knight-Ridder Information, Inc., Lexis-Nexis.
Formerly (until 1997): Financing Foreign Operations. Sweden.
Description: Provides details on critical areas such as funding, financial markets, cash management and trade credit facilities for Sweden.

332.67   **US**
FINANCING OPERATIONS. TURKEY. 1993. base vol. (plus. s-a. updates). £195($295) Economist Intelligence Unit, 111 W. 57th St., New York, NY 10019. TEL 212-554-0600; 800-938-4685. FAX 212-586-1181. TELEX 175567. URL: http://www.eiu.com. (U.K. addr.: Economist Intelligence Unit Ltd., Subscriptions Dept., P.O. Box 200, Harold Hill, Romford, Essex RM3 8UX, England. TEL 44-1708-381444. FAX 44-1708-371850)
Document type: trade publication.
Formerly (until 1997): Financing Foreign Operations. Turkey (ISSN 1352-5840)
Description: Provides details on such critical areas as exchange controls, sources of funding, financial markets, cash management and trade credit facilities for Turkey.

332.1   **DK**   ISSN 0905-9415
FINANS OG SAMFUND. 1900. m. DKK 300 (effective 1997). Finansraadet, Finansraadets Hus, Amaliegade 7, DK-1256 Copenhagen K, Denmark. Ed. Henrik Theil. adv.; bk.rev.; charts; illus.; stat. circ. 5,000. **Document type:** trade publication.
Former titles (until 1990): Sparekassen (ISSN 0107-9530); Sparekassetidende (ISSN 0038-6529)

332.1   **DK**   ISSN 0909-1025
FINANSFOKUS. Key Title: Finansfokus (Koebenhavn). bi-m. Finansforbundet, Langebrogade 5, DK-1411 Copenhagen K, Denmark. TEL 45-31-42-59-49. FAX 45-35-26-47-37. Ed. Christian Clausen. adv. circ. 4,000. **Indexed:** ELLIS.
Former titles (until 1994): Fagskrift for Finansvaesen (ISSN 0907-659X); (until 1993): Fagskrift for Bankvaesen (ISSN 0106-178X)

332   **US**
FINANCING OPERATIONS. SWITZERLAND. base vol. (plus s-a. updates). £195($295) Economist Intelligence Unit, 111 W. 57th St., New York, NY 10019. TEL 212-554-0600; 800-938-4685. FAX 212-586-1181. TELEX 175567. URL: http://www.eiu.com. (UK addr.: Economist Intelligence Unit Ltd., Subscriptions Dept., P.O. Box 200, Harold Hill, Romford, Essex RM3 8UX, England. TEL 44-1708-381-444. FAX 44-1708-371-850) (looseleaf format)
●Also available online. Vendor(s): Knight-Ridder Information, Inc., Lexis-Nexis.
Formerly (until 1997): Financing Foreign Operations. Switzerland.
Description: Provides details on critical areas such as exchange controls, sources of funding, financial markets, cash management and trade credit facilities for Switzerland.

332   **US**
FINANCING OPERATIONS. UNITED KINGDOM. base vol. (plus s-a. updates). £195($295) Economist Intelligence Unit, 111 W. 57th St., New York, NY 10019. TEL 212-554-0600; 800-938-4685. FAX 212-586-1181. TELEX 175567. URL: http://www.eiu.com. (UK addr.: Economist Intelligence Unit Ltd., Subscriptions Dept., P.O. Box 200, Harold Hill, Romford, Essex RM3 8UX, England. TEL 44-1708-381-444. FAX 44-1708-371-850) (looseleaf format)
●Also available online. Vendor(s): Knight-Ridder Information, Inc., Lexis-Nexis.
Formerly (until 1997): Financing Foreign Operations. United Kingdom.
Description: Provides details on critical areas such as exchange controls, sources of funding, financial markets, cash management and trade credit facilities for the United Kingdom.

332   **YU**   ISSN 0015-2145
FINANSIJE; casopis za teoriju i praksu iz oblasti finansija. (Supplement avail.: Bilten - Sluzebna Objasnjenja i Slrocna Misljenja za Primenu Finansijskih Propisa (ISSN 0354-2688)) 1946. bi-m. Privredni Pregled, Marsala Birjuzova 3-5, 11000 Belgrade, Yugoslavia. Ed. Vuk Ognjanovicevic.
Description: Covers the theory and practice from the field of finance.

332.7 658.8   **SW**   ISSN 1104-7348
FINANSMARKNADET. English edition: Swedish Financial Market (ISSN 1104-7356) 1985. a. free. Sveriges Riksbank, Financial Statistics Department - Swedish Central Bank, S-103 37 Stockholm, Sweden.
Formerly (until 1994): Kredit- och Valutamarknaden (ISSN 0282-8111)

332   SW   ISSN 1100-682X
FINANSTIDNINGEN. 1989. 235/yr. SEK 1790 (effective 1990). Sveriges Finansnyheter AB, P.O. Box 70347, S-107 23 Stockholm, Sweden. TEL 46-8-677-4500. FAX 46-8-14-99-30. Ed. Raoul Gruenthal. adv.: B&W page SEK 21800, color page SEK 32500; trim 280 x 385; adv. contact: Haakan Kjellstroem. circ. 6,700 (paid); 250 (controlled). (tabloid format)

332.1 331.8   SW
FINANSVAERLDEN. 1911. 12/yr. SEK 250. Finansfoerbundet, P.O. Box 7375, 103 91 Stockholm, Sweden. TEL 46-8-614-03-08. FAX 46-8-678-67-13. Ed. Anna Calissendorff. adv.: B&W page SEK 12500, color page SEK 19500; trim 186 x 264. bk.rev.; abstr.; charts; illus.; stat.; index. circ. 49,800. (also avail. in audio cassette)
   Former titles: Bankvaerlden (ISSN 0005-5549); (until 1920): Svenska Bankmannafoereningens Tidskrift.

332   RU   ISSN 0869-446X
FINANSY. 1954. m. $79. Ul. Tverskaya 22B, 103050 Moscow, Russia. TEL 095-299-4333. FAX 095-299-9306. (Subscr. to: Mezhdunarodnaya Kniga, ul. Dimitrova 39, Moscow G-200, Russia; Dist. in U.S. by: Victor Kamkin Inc., 4956 Boiling Brook Pkwy., Rockville, MD 20852. TEL 301-881-5973) Ed. Yu.M. Artemov. bk.rev.; bibl.; stat.; tr.lit.; index. circ. 50,000. **Indexed:** Amer.Hist.& Life, Curr.Dig.Sov.Press, Hist.Abstr., Rural Recreat.Tour.Abstr., World Agri.Econ.& Rural Sociol.Abstr.
   Former titles: Finansy S.S.S.R. (ISSN 0130-576X); Sovetskie Finansy.
   Description: Covers theory and information on finances; compiling and execution of the state budget, insurance, lending, taxation etc.

332   AU
FINANZ AKTUELL. 6/yr. Bohmann Druck und Verlag GmbH & Co. KG, Leberstr. 122, A-1110 Vienna, Austria. TEL 43-1-74095464. FAX 43-1-74095491. Ed. Georg Karp. circ. 19,500. **Document type:** bulletin.

332   AU
FINANZ-COMPASS. a. S.2500. Compass Verlag, Matznergasse 17, A-1141 Vienna, Austria. TEL 43-1-98116-0. FAX 43-1-9811698. E-mail: office@compass.co.at; URL: http://www.compass.co.at. Ed. Werner Futter. R&P contact: Werner Futter. adv. contact: Michael Bayer. **Document type:** trade publication.
   Description: Information on banks, savings banks, credit associations, insurance institutes.

332   AU   ISSN 1017-5695
FINANZ JOURNAL; die umfassende Fachinformation fuer Steuerrechtsthemen. 1961. m. S.1550. Grenz Verlag, Flossgasse 6, A-1025 Vienna, Austria. TEL 43-1-2141715. FAX 43-1-214171530. Ed. H. Reinold. adv.; bk.rev. **Indexed:** P.A.I.S.For.Lang.Ind. **Document type:** trade publication.

332   IT
FINANZA E MERCATO. bi-m. L.80000 (effective 1995). (Banca Nazionale del Lavoro) B N L Edizioni S.p.A., Via Lucillo 7, 00187 Rome, Italy. TEL 39-6-4884380. FAX 39-6-4745272.

332   GW
DER FINANZBERATER. (Text in English, German) 1984. q. DM.10. Akademie fuer Finanz-Marketing, Postfach 102143, 40745 Langenfeld, Germany. TEL 02173-23048. FAX 02173-235754. Ed. Harold Kraemer. index; circ. 18,000. **Document type:** academic/scholarly publication.

332   GW   ISSN 0944-0968
FINANZEN; das Wirtschafts Magazin fuer Kapitalanleger. m. DM.108 (Europe DM.132; elsewhere DM.162) (effective 1997). Finanzen Verlagsgesellschaft mbH, Keltenring 12, 82041 Oberhaching, Germany. TEL 49-89-613796-0. FAX 49-89-61379699. Ed. Frank-Bernhard Werner; Pub. Michael Koelmel. adv.: B&W page DM.7500, color page DM.11400; trim 213 x 303; adv. contact: Hans Rainer Lindner. index. circ. 88,000. (back issues avail.) **Document type:** trade publication.

332   GW   ISSN 0939-7825
FINANZIERUNGS BERATER. 1991. q. DM.298. Verlag Norman Rentrop, Theodor-Heuss-Str. 4, 53177 Bonn, Germany. TEL 49-228-8205-0. FAX 49-228-364411. Ed. Hans Joachim Oberhettinger. (looseleaf format) **Document type:** bulletin.

332   AU   ISSN 0015-2269
FINANZNACHRICHTEN. 1924. w. S.4090. Liechtensteinstr. 63-3, A-1090 Vienna, Austria. TEL 43-1-3109620-0. FAX 43-1-310962022. Ed. Christoph Hartmann; Pub. Christoph Hartmann. adv.; bk.rev.; abstr.; charts; stat.; index. circ. 1,000. (looseleaf format) **Document type:** newspaper.

332   GW
FINANZWIRTSCHAFT (MUNICH). m. DM.156. Verlagsgruppe Jehle Rehm GmbH, Einsteinstr. 172, 81675 Munich, Germany. TEL 49-89-41979-0. FAX 49-89-4706998. Ed. Wolfgang Bergs. **Document type:** trade publication.

330   IT   ISSN 0391-6405
FIORINO; quotidiano del mattino e finanza e economia e actualita. 1969. d. L.145000 (foreign L.280000)(effective 1992). Societa Editrice Esedra s.r.l., Via Parigi 11, 00185 Rome, Italy. TEL 06-474901. FAX 06-4883435. Ed. Luigi d'Amato. circ. 30,000. **Document type:** newspaper.

332.1   US
FIRST EMPIRE STATE CORPORATION. ANNUAL REPORT. a. First Empire State Corporation, One M & T Plaza, Buffalo, NY 14240. TEL 716-842-5138. FAX 716-842-5021. **Document type:** corporate report.

332.1   US
FIRST EMPIRE STATE CORPORATION. INTERIM REPORT. q. First Empire State Corporation, One M & T Plaza, Buffalo, NY 14240. TEL 716-842-5138. FAX 716-842-5021.

332.1   LB
FIRST NATIONAL CITY BANK, LIBERIA. ANNUAL REPORT.* a. First National City Bank, P.O. Box 280, Monrovia, Liberia. illus.; stat.

FISC; fiscale nieuwsbrief voor de onderneming. see *BUSINESS AND ECONOMICS — Management*

332   BE
FISCALITEIT. MONOGRAFIEEN. (Text in Flemish) irreg. price varies. C E D Samsom (Subsidiary of: Wolters Samsom Belgie n.v.), Kouterveld 14, B-1831 Diegem, Belgium. TEL 32-2-7231111. Ed. Bd. **Document type:** monographic series.

FIVE YEAR FORECASTS. see *BUSINESS AND ECONOMICS — Economic Situation And Conditions*

332   IC   ISSN 0015-3346
HC360.5
FJARMALATIDINDI; timarit um efnahagsmal. 1954. s-a. free. Sedlabanki Islands - Central Bank of Iceland, Kalkofnsvegur 1, IS-150 Reykjavik, Iceland. TEL 354-569-9600. FAX 354-569-9608. TELEX 220 CENTBK IS. Eds. Birgir Isl. Gunnarsson, Stefan Johann Stefansson. charts; stat.; index; circ. 2,200 (controlled). **Document type:** government publication. —BLDSC (3949.680000).
   Description: Covers economics in general and Icelandic economy in particular.

332.1   US   ISSN 1064-0673
FLORIDA BANKING; for Florida banking industry. 1974. bi-m. $18. Florida Bankers Association, Box 1360, Tallahassee, FL 32302-1360. TEL 904-224-2265. FAX 904-224-2423. Ed. Wendy Barager; Pub. John Milstead. R&P contact: Wendy Barager. adv. contact: Fellis Carnley. bk.rev.; illus. circ. 6,200. (back issues avail.; reprint service avail.) **Indexed:** World Bank.Abstr. **Document type:** trade publication.
   Former titles: (until 1987): Banking Today (ISSN 1052-0562); (until 1984): Florida Banker (ISSN 0147-1961)

332.7   US
FLORIDA MORTGAGE BROKER. 1965. q. membership. Florida Association of Mortgage Brokers, Box 6477, Tallahassee, FL 32314-6477. TEL 904-942-6411. FAX 904-942-4654. Ed. Carolyn Devonshire. R&P contact: Carolyn Devonshire. adv. contact: Carolyn Devonshire. circ. 2,000. **Document type:** trade publication.
   Description: Covers legislative concerns and association activities.

332   US
FLOW OF FUNDS ACCOUNTS: SEASONALLY ADJUSTED AND UNADJUSTED. q. $25. U.S. Federal Reserve System, Board of Governors, Publications Services, Rm. MS-138, Washington, DC 20551. TEL 202-452-3244. FAX 202-728-5886. (also avail. in diskette format) **Document type:** government publication.

332.1   CH   ISSN 1017-9658
FLOW OF FUNDS IN TAIWAN DISTRICT, REPUBLIC OF CHINA. (Text in Chinese and English) 1968. a. $5. Central Bank of China, 2 Roosevelt Rd., Sec. 1, Taipei, Taiwan 107, Republic of China. FAX 02-397-3768. circ. 1,200.

332   US
FLOW OF FUNDS SUMMARY STATISTICS. q. $5. U.S. Federal Reserve System, Board of Governors, Publications Services, Rm. MS-138, Washington, DC 20551. TEL 202-452-3244. FAX 202-728-5886. **Document type:** government publication.

332.1   US
FOCUS WEST (PHOENIX). 1969. bi-m. free. Valley National Corporation, Communication Services (4-646), Box 71, Phoenix, AZ 85001. TEL 602-221-4840. FAX 602-221-4899. Ed. Steven J. Henden. charts; illus.; stat.; circ. 9,500.
   Former titles: Eagle (Phoenix); Valley National Eagle; Eagle; Valley Bank Eagle.

332.1   BL   ISSN 0015-5446
FOLHA BANCARIA. 1924. bi-m. free. Sindicato dos Empregados em Estabelecimentos Bancarios de Sao Paulo, Rua Sao Bento, 365, Sao Paulo, Brazil. Ed. Rui Sa Silva Barros. charts; illus.; stat. circ. 80,000. (tabloid format)

332   EC
FOMENTO Y PRODUCCION. 1983. s-a. Banco Nacional de Fomento, Apdo. 685, Quito, Ecuador. Ed. Hernan Luna Ponce.

332   BE   ISSN 0779-9411
FONDS ET SICAV. Dutch edition: Fondsen en Sicav (ISSN 0779-942X) (Text in French) 1993. m. (11/yr.). 3300 BEF in Belgium and Luxemburg (elsewhere 3544 BEF). Association des Consommateurs - Verbruikersunie, Rue de Hollande 13, 1060 Brussels, Belgium. TEL 32-2-5423211. FAX 32-2-5423250. TELEX 26771. **Document type:** consumer publication.

332   UK
FORCES NEWS. 1976. bi-m. free. Mandrake Associates Ltd., 6 North Brink, Wisbech, Cambs PE13 1JR, England. TEL 01945-65177. FAX 01945-64712. Ed. Douglas Nicholson. adv.; bk.rev.; circ. 35,000. **Document type:** newsletter.
   Formerly: Forces Financial News.

332   US   ISSN 0364-1341
FOREIGN EXCHANGE RATES. w. & m. $20 for w.; m. release $5. U.S. Federal Reserve System, Board of Governors, Publications Services, Rm. MS-138, Washington, DC 20551. TEL 202-452-3244. FAX 202-728-5886. **Document type:** government publication.

332.31   FR   ISSN 0071-8254
FRANCE. CAISSE NATIONALE DE CREDIT AGRICOLE. RAPPORT SUR LE CREDIT AGRICOLE MUTUEL. English edition: Credit Agricole Annual Report. 1975. a. free. Caisse Nationale de Credit Agricole, 91-93 Boulevard Pasteur, 75015 Paris, France. circ. 5,710 (4,000 French ed.; 1,710 English ed.).

BUSINESS AND ECONOMICS — BANKING AND FINANCE

332.1 FR ISSN 1142-3110
FRANCE. COMMISSION BANCAIRE. ANNUAL REPORT. French edition: France. Commission Bancaire. Rapport Annuel (ISSN 0984-5585) (Text in English) a. 80 F. Banque de France, Service de l'Information, 48 rue Croix-Des-Petits-Champs, 75001 Paris, France. TEL 1-42-92-39-31. FAX 1-42-92-39-40.
Description: Reference book about French banking system.

332.1 FR ISSN 1142-2858
FRANCE. COMMISSION BANCAIRE. BULLETIN. 1989. s-a. 220 F. (effective 1995). Banque de France, Service de l'Information, 48 rue Croix des Petits Champs, B.P. 140-01, 75001 Paris, France. TEL 1-42-92-39-31. FAX 1-42-92-39-40.
Description: Examines the role of the commission and the decisions it makes.

332.1 FR ISSN 0767-9505
FRANCE. COMMISSION BANCAIRE. COMPTES ANNUELS DES ETABLISSEMENTS DE CREDIT. 1949. a. 400 F. Banque de France, Service de l'Information, 48 rue Croix des Petits Champs, B.P. 140-01, 75001 Paris, France. TEL 1-42-92-39-31. FAX 1-42-92-39-40.
Formerly (until 1987): France. Commission Bancaire. Bilans des Banques.

332.1 FR ISSN 0984-5585
FRANCE. COMMISSION BANCAIRE. RAPPORT ANNUEL. English edition: France. Banking Commission. Annual Report (ISSN 1142-3110) a. 210 F. Banque de France, Service de l'Information, 48, rue Croix des Petits Champs, 75001 Paris, France. TEL 1-42-92-39-31. FAX 1-42-92-39-40. (Or: Commission Bancaire, 73 rue de Richelieu, 75002 Paris, France)
Formerly: Commission de Controle des Banques. Rapport Annuel (ISSN 0984-5631)
Description: Provides a summary of the activities of the commission as well as reviews legislation and new rules governing credit institutions.

332.7 FR ISSN 0980-0107
FRANCE. CONSEIL NATIONAL DU CREDIT. RAPPORT ANNUEL. English edition: France. National Counsel of Credit. Annual Report (ISSN 1249-528X) a. 120 F. (effective 1995). (Conseil National du Credit) Banque de France, Service de l'Information, 48, rue Croix des Petits Champs, 75001 Paris, France. TEL 1-42-92-39-08. FAX 1-42-92-39-40.

332 GW
FRANKFURT FINANCE. (Text in English) m. DM.595. Frankfurter Allgemeine Zeitung GmbH, Information Services, Hellerhofstr. 2-4, 60327 Frankfurt a.M., Germany. TEL 49-69-75912219. FAX 49-69-75912188. (Dist. in U.S. by: European Business Publications, Inc., Box 891, Darien, CT 06820. TEL 203-656-2701. FAX 203-655-8332) **Document type:** newsletter.
Formerly: Old Continent.
Description: Provides a look at the inner workings of the Bundesbank and analyzes its decision making process.

332.1 GW
FRANKFURTER FINANZMARKT BERICHT. 1990. bi-m. Landeszentralbank in Hessen, Hauptverwaltung der Deutschen Bundesbank, Taunusanlage 5, 60329 Frankfurt a.M., Germany. TEL 069-2388-0. FAX 069-2388-2130.

332 UK ISSN 0966-7334
FRAUD WATCH. 1992. q. £160($300) C & M Publications Ltd., P.O. Box 28, Corby, Northants NN17 5LY, England. TEL 44-1536-403648. FAX 44-1536-406888. Ed. Annich McIntosh. circ. 5,000. (back issues avail.) **Document type:** newsletter.

332.1 FR ISSN 1240-6694
FRENCH BANKING ACT AND SELECTED BANKING REGULATIONS. (Text in English) 1992. a. 200 F. Banque de France, Service de l'Information, 48 rue Croix-Des-Petits-Champs, 75001 Paris, France. TEL 1-42-92-39-31. FAX 1-42-92-39-40.
Description: Contains the Banking Act, together with the main legal, accounting, prudential and monetary provisions applicable to credit institutions doing business in France.

332 973 US ISSN 0278-8861
HG4633
FRIENDS OF FINANCIAL HISTORY. 1978. q. $25. Museum of American Financial History, 26 Broadway, New York, NY 10004. TEL 212-908-4519. FAX 212-908-4600. Ed. Patrick Harris. adv. contact: Diane Boone. bk.rev.; circ. 2,000 (paid).
—UnCover.

332 CC ISSN 1002-2740
FUJIAN JINRONG/FUJIAN FINANCE. (Text in Chinese) 1986. m. Y12. Fujian Jingrong Zazhishe, No.21, Guping Lu, Fuzhou, Fujian 350003, People's Republic of China. TEL 557778. (Dist. overseas by: Jiangsu Publications Import & Export Corp., 56 Gao Yun Ling, Nanjing, Jiangsu, P.R.C.) Ed. Wang Liangyuan.
Description: Provides information on the flexible financial policies applicable in the special economic zones of Fujian Province.

332 US
FUND ACTION. 1989. w. $1295 (Canada $1325; elsewhere $1370). Institutional Investor Newsletters, 477 Madison Ave., New York, NY 10022. TEL 212-224-3233. FAX 212-224-3353. Ed. Molly Butler Hart; Pub. Michael D. Briffin. adv. contact: Ed O'Farrell. **Document type:** newsletter.

658 US ISSN 0016-268X
HV41
FUND RAISING MANAGEMENT. 1969. m. $58 (foreign $98) (effective 1996). Hoke Communications, Inc., 224 Seventh St., Garden City, NY 11530. TEL 516-746-6700. FAX 516-294-8141. Ed. Bill Olcott. adv.: B&W page $1295, color page $2045; trim 8 1/4 x 10 7/8. bk.rev.; illus. circ. 8,000. (also avail. in microform from UMI) **Indexed:** ABI Inform., BPIA, Bus.Ind., PSI, Tr.& Indus.Ind. **Document type:** trade publication.
●Also available online. **Vendor(s):** Information Access Co., Knight-Ridder Information, Inc., UMI.
—BLDSC (4055.955000); UMI; UnCover. **CCC.**
Description: Features articles on fund raising and related activities among academic religious, health, civic and cultural groups.

332 IE ISSN 1393-0486
FUNDS INTERNATIONAL. 1994. m. I£599. Lafferty Publications Ltd., The Tower, IDA Enterprise Centre, Pearse St., Dublin 2, Ireland. TEL 353-1-6718022. FAX 353-1-6718520. E-mail: cvserv@lafferty.ie; URL: http://www.unm.lafferty.co.uk. (US subscr. to: 420 Lexington Ave., Ste. 1745, New York, NY 10170. TEL 212-557-6726) R&P contact: David Barr. **Document type:** trade publication.
Description: Gives news, information and advice on the fund management industry worldwide.

FUTURES AND OPTIONS. see BUSINESS AND ECONOMICS — Investments

332 PL ISSN 0860-7613
HG3136
GAZETA BANKOWA. 1988. w. $30 (foreign $130). Pankiewicza 3, 00-696 Warsaw, Poland. TEL 48-2-6287272. FAX 48-2-6212653. TELEX 813439. Ed. Andrzej Wroblewski. adv. contact: Nina Tyszkiewicz. circ. 45,000. **Document type:** newspaper.
Description: Covers economy and finance.

GELD (YEAR). see CONSUMER EDUCATION AND PROTECTION

332 GW ISSN 0175-9469
DAS GELD A B C. 1984. a. DM.58. Verlag Wirtschaft Recht und Steuern, Fraunhoferstr. 5, 82152 Planegg, Germany. TEL 49-89-89517-0. FAX 49-89-89517250. (Subscr. to: Postfach 1363, 82142 Planegg, Germany) **Document type:** trade publication.

332 GW
GELDANLAGE UND STEUERN. 1984. a. DM.48. Betriebswirtschaftlicher Verlag Dr. Th. Gabler GmbH, Abraham-Lincoln-Str. 46, 65189 Wiesbaden, Germany. TEL 49-611-7878129. FAX 49-611-7878423. adv.; index. circ. 4,500. **Document type:** bulletin.

332.1 GW ISSN 0343-8740
GELDINSTITUTE. 1969. 8/yr. DM.174 (foreign DM.192). Hans Holzmann Verlag GmbH, Gewerbestr. 2, 86825 Bad Woerishofen, Germany. TEL 08247-35401. FAX 08247-354170. Ed. Erwin Stroebele. adv. circ. 6,062. **Document type:** consumer publication.

332 BE
GENERALE BANK. BULLETIN. (Text in Dutch, French) 1963. m. 600 BEF students 200BEF. Generale Bank, Montagne du Parc 3, B-1000 Brussels, Belgium. TEL 32-2-5162266. FAX 32-2-5163283. TELEX 21283 GEBA B. Ed. Anne Vleminckx. **Indexed:** ELLIS. **Document type:** bulletin.
Formerly: Societe Generale de Banque. Bulletin.

332.1 BE
GENERALE BANK. REPORT. (Text in Dutch, English, French, German) a. Generale Bank, Montagne du Parc 3, B-1000 Brussels, Belgium. TEL 32-2-565111. FAX 32-2-5654222. TELEX 21283 GEBA B. Ed. Anne Vleminckx.
Formerly: Societe Generale de Banque. Rapport.

332 US
GEOGRAPHICAL DISTRIBUTION OF ASSETS AND LIABILITIES OF MAJOR FOREIGN BRANCHES OF U.S. BANKS. q. $5. U.S. Federal Reserve System, Board of Governors, Publications Services, Rm. MS-138, Washington, DC 20551. TEL 202-452-3244. FAX 202-728-5886. **Document type:** government publication.

332 US ISSN 0882-5971
HC107.G4
GEORGIA TREND;* magazine of Georgia business & finance. 1985. m. $27. Grimes Publications, Inc., Box 1266, Athens, GA 30603. TEL 404-354-0463. FAX 404-354-6824. adv.; illus.; circ. 39,400 (controlled). **Document type:** trade publication.
●Also available online. **Vendor(s):** Information Access Co., Knight-Ridder Information, Inc., Lexis-Nexis, UMI. —UMI.
Incorporates: Business Atlanta (ISSN 0192-0855); Which was formerly: Real Estate and Business Atlanta; Real Estate Atlanta.
Description: Covers issues relating to Georgia business and finance.

332 CL ISSN 0716-1239
GESTION. 1975. m. Ch.$37524 (foreign $260) (effective 1997). Editorial Gestion, Ltda., Rafael Canas 114, Casilla 16485, Correo 9, Santiago, Chile. TEL 56-2-2361313. FAX 56-2-2361114. E-mail: estrategia@edgestion.cl. Ed. Victor Manuel Ojeda. adv. contact: Rodrigo Sepulveda. circ. 38,000. **Indexed:** Pt.de Rep., RADAR.

331 IT ISSN 1120-5091
GIORNALE DELLA BANCA. 1989. 11/yr. L.10000 per no. Arnoldo Mondadori Editore S.p.A., Casella Postale 17135, 20170 Milan, Italy. TEL 2-75-42-1. adv.: B&W page L.5500000, color page L.8800000. circ. 11,000.

GIURISPRUDENZA COMMERCIALE. see LAW — Corporate Law

GLOBAL ASSET ALLOCATION. see BUSINESS AND ECONOMICS — Investments

GLOBAL BUSINESS AND FINANCE REVIEW. see BUSINESS AND ECONOMICS — International Commerce

GLOBAL COMPANY HANDBOOK. see BUSINESS AND ECONOMICS — International Commerce

GLOBAL ECONOMIC FORECASTS. see BUSINESS AND ECONOMICS — Economic Situation And Conditions

332 US ISSN 1044-0283
HG3879
GLOBAL FINANCE JOURNAL. 1989. s-a. $80 to individuals (foreign $100); institutions $205 (foreign $225) (effective 1998). J A I Press Inc., 55 Old Post Rd., No.2, Box 1678, Greenwich, CT 06830-1678. TEL 203-661-7602. FAX 203-661-0792. E-mail: jai@jaipress.com. (Addr. in Europe: J A I Press Ltd., 38 Tavistock St., Covent Garden, London WC2E 7PB, England. TEL 44-171-379-8834. FAX 44-171-379-8835) Ed. Manucher Shahrokhi. (also avail. in microform from UMI; back issues avail.) **Document type:** trade publication.
—BLDSC (4195.398000); SWETS; UnCover. **CCC.**

BUSINESS AND ECONOMICS — BANKING AND FINANCE

332   US   ISSN 1058-3920
BAL INVESTMENT TECHNOLOGY. 1991. bi-w. $595 foreign $675) (effective 1997). Investment Media, nc., 909 Third Ave., 6th Fl., New York, NY 10022. TEL 212-888-5810. FAX 212-888-6145. Ed. Pavan Sahgal; Pub. Michael Horton. adv. contact: Michael Horton. circ. 1,900. **Document type:** newsletter.
   Description: Addresses strategic business issues affecting US and non-US investment institutions and pension plan sponsors. Contains key insights on systems solutions to current business needs, including reports on innovative software applications and electronic services.

332 330.9   UK   ISSN 0951-3604
HG4502
BAL INVESTOR. (Text in English and Japanese) 1987. m. (10/yr.). £230 (foreign $425) (effective 1997). Euromoney Publications plc., Nestor House, Playhouse Yard, London EC4V 5EX, England. TEL 44-171-779-8935. FAX 44-171-779-8541. (Dist. in US by: American Educational Systems, 173 W. 81st St., New York, NY 10024. TEL 800-717-2669. FAX 212-501-8926) Ed. Andrew Capon. circ. 10,000. **Document type:** trade publication.
   ● Also available online. Vendor(s): UMI.
   —UMI; UnCover.

332   UK   ISSN 1355-7866
BAL M & A AND CORPORATE STRATEGY. q. £115 (Europe and U.S. $170) (effective 1996). Euromoney Publications plc., Nestor House, Playhouse Yard, London EC4V 5EX, England. TEL 44-171-779-8935. FAX 44-171-779-8541. (Dist. in US by: American Educational Systems, 173 W. 81st St., New York, NY 10024. TEL 800-717-2669. FAX 212-501-8926) **Document type:** trade publication.

332   US
BAL PRIVATE BANKING. bi-w. $1595 (Canada $1625; elsewhere $1670). Institutional Investor Newsletters, 477 Madison Ave., New York, NY 10022. TEL 212-224-3233. FAX 212-224-3353. **Document type:** newsletter.
   Description: Provides information on the secretive high-net-worth management business worldwide.

OS. see *ETHNIC INTERESTS*

332   US   ISSN 0278-0038
HG4050
ING PUBLIC - THE I P O REPORTER. (Initial Public Offering) 1977. w. $1195 (effective 1997). Investment Dealers' Digest, 2 World Trade Ctr., 18th Fl., New York, NY 10048. TEL 212-432-0045. Ed. Mark Kollar. bk.rev.; bibl.; charts; stat.
   —UMI. CCC.
   Former titles: Going Public; Business Borrower.

332   UK   ISSN 0196-3546
OLD & SILVER SURVEY; world gold & silver prices. 1980. 10/yr. £215($525) World Reports Ltd., 108 Horseferry Rd., Westminster, London SW1P 2EF, England. TEL 44-171-222-3836. FAX 44-171-233-0185. (U.S. subscr. to: World Reports Ltd., 280 Madison Ave., Ste. 1209, New York, NY 10016-0802. TEL 212-599-4560) Ed. Christopher Story. (back issues avail.) **Document type:** trade publication.

332 338.025   US
OLDEN STATES FINANCIAL DIRECTORY. a. $89. Thomson Financial Publishing, 4709 W. Golf Rd., Skokie, IL 60076. TEL 847-676-9600; 800-321-3373. FAX 847-933-8101. **Document type:** directory.

332.1   UK   ISSN 1353-6923
OLDMAN SACHS FOREIGN EXCHANGE HANDBOOK (YEAR). 1992. a. (in 2 vols.). £135($250) Euromoney Publications plc., Books, Nestor House, Playhouse Yard, London EC4V 5EX, England. TEL 0171-779-8935. FAX 0171-779-8541. (Orders to: Plymbridge Distributors Ltd., Estover, Plymouth, Devon PL6 7PZ, England. TEL 0171-779-8610. FAX 01752-695668) **Document type:** trade publication.
   Description: Lists more than 2,500 institutions and 35,000 personnel in foreign exchange.

332   PR   ISSN 0093-7479
HG2838
GOVERNMENT DEVELOPMENT BANK FOR PUERTO RICO. ANNUAL REPORT. Key Title: Banco Gubernamental de Fomento para Puerto Rico Informe Anual. (Includes: G D B Financial Review) 1978. a. Government Development Bank for Puerto Rico, P.O. Box 42001, Minillas Sta., San Juan, PR 00940-2001. TEL 787-729-6433. FAX 787-728-0975. (U.S. addr.: 140 Broadway, 38th Fl., New York, NY 10005. TEL 212-422-6420) Ed. Anne W. Chevako. charts; illus.; stat. circ. 7,500. **Document type:** corporate report.
   Formerly: Government Development Bank for Puerto Rico. Report of Activities.

332   UK
GREAT BRITAIN. DEPARTMENT OF TRADE. INSOLVENCY: GENERAL ANNUAL REPORT. a. H.M.S.O., 51 Nine Elms Ln., London SW8 5DR, England. TEL 44-171-873-0011. FAX 44-171-873-8247. (Co-sponsor: Department of Trade) (reprint service avail. from UMI) **Document type:** government publication.
   Formerly: Great Britain. Department of Trade. Bankruptcy: General Annual Report (ISSN 0072-5633)

332   US
GREEN MONEY JOURNAL. 1992. q. $35 (effective 1996). W. 608 Glass Ave., Spokane, WA 99205. TEL 509-328-1741. URL: http://www.greenmoney.com. Ed. Tom Kliewer; Pub. Cliff Feigerbaum. adv.: page $1500. bk.rev. circ. 7,000. (back issues avail.) **Document type:** consumer publication, newsletter.
   Description: Covers ethical spending, investing, and business practices.

322   GW   ISSN 0340-9392
GRUNDLAGEN UND PRAXIS DES BANK- UND BOERSENWESENS. 1976. irreg. price varies. Erich Schmidt Verlag GmbH & Co. (Bielefeld), Viktoriastr. 44A, 33602 Bielefeld, Germany. TEL 49-521-583080. (Subscr. to: Postfach 102451, 33524 Bielefeld, Germany) **Document type:** monographic series.

322   CC
GUANGDONG JINRONG/GUANGDONG FINANCE. (Text in Chinese) m. Guangdong Sheng Jinrong Xuehui, No. 137 Changti, Guangzhou, Guangdong 510120, People's Republic of China. TEL 884316. Ed. Li Dan'er.

332   US
GUARANTOR (NEW YORK). 48/yr. $895 (foreign $945). American Banker - Bond Buyer, Newsletter Division (Subsidiary of: Thomson Financial Services Company), One State St. Plaza, New York, NY 10004-1549. TEL 800-733-4371. FAX 212-943-2224. **Document type:** newsletter.
   ● Also available online. Vendor(s): Information Access Co.
   Formerly: Global Guarantee.

332   EC
GUIA DEL SECTOR FINANCIERO ECUATORIANO. 1991. a. Dinediciones S.A., Av. Gonzalez Suarez 335 y San Ignacio, Quito, Ecuador. TEL 565-477.

332   UY   ISSN 0797-1176
GUIA FINANCIERA. Key Title: Guia Financiera Magui. 1977. w. Miguel Malis, Pub., Nicaragua 1579, Montevideo, Uruguay. TEL 202689. Ed. Romeo Guida. circ. 5,000.

GUIDE TO THE CANADIAN FINANCIAL SERVICES INDUSTRY. see *BUSINESS AND ECONOMICS — Trade And Industrial Directories*

332   CC
GUOJI JINRONG DAOKAN/INTERNATIONAL FINANCIAL HERALD. (Text in Chinese) bi-m. (Nanfang Guoji Jinrong Xuehui) Guoji Jinrong Daokan Bianjibu, Guangzhou Gyoji Jinrong Dasha, 197 Dongfeng Xilu, Guangzhou, Guangdong 510130, People's Republic of China. TEL 3338080. (For domestic sale only; For distr. overseas by: China International Book Trading Corp., P.O. Box 399, Beijing 100044, P.R. China) Ed. Wu Runjing. pp./issue: 56.

332   AT
H W W RATE CHECK BOOK: AT CALL DEPOSITS. 1988. d., w., m. Aus.$2000. H W W Pty. Ltd. (Horan Wall & Walker), 15-19 Prospect St., P.O. Box 8, Surry Hills, N.S.W. 2010, Australia. TEL 61-2-93609360. FAX 61-2-93805533. URL: http://www.hww.com.au. **Document type:** trade publication.
   Formerly: Retail Banking Products Survey: At Call Deposits (ISSN 1032-870X); Supersedes in part: H W W Retail Banking Products Survey (ISSN 1031-4148)

332   AT
H W W RATE CHECK BOOK: BUSINESS CHEQUE ACCOUNTS IN CREDIT AND DEBIT. 1992. m. Aus.$2000. H W W Pty. Ltd. (Horan Wall & Walker), 15-19 Prospect St., P.O. Box 8, Surry Hills, N.S.W. 2010, Australia. TEL 61-2-93609360. FAX 61-2-93805533. URL: http://www.hww.com.au. **Document type:** trade publication.
   Former titles: H W W Rate Check Book: Business Cheque Accounts; Commercial Banking Products Surveys: Business Cheque Accounts (ISSN 1038-6505)

332   AT
H W W RATE CHECK BOOK: COMMERCIAL LOANS. 1992. m. Aus.$2000. H W W Pty. Ltd. (Horan Wall & Walker), 15-19 Prospect St., P.O. Box 8, Surry Hills, N.S.W. 2010, Australia. TEL 61-2-93609360. FAX 61-2-93805533. URL: http://www.hww.com.au. **Document type:** trade publication.
   Formerly: Commercial Banking Products Surveys: Commercial Loans (ISSN 1038-6491)

332   AT
H W W RATE CHECK BOOK: CONTINUING CREDIT. 1988. d., w., m. Aus.$2000. H W W Pty. Ltd. (Horan Wall & Walker), 15-19 Prospect St., Surry Hills, N.S.W. 2010, Australia. TEL 61-2-93609360. FAX 61-2-93805533. **Document type:** trade publication.
   Formerly: Retail Banking Products Survey: Continuing Credit (ISSN 1032-8726)

332   AT
H W W RATE CHECK BOOK: CREDIT CARDS. 1988. m. Aus.$2000. H W W Pty. Ltd. (Horan Wall & Walker), 15-19 Prospect St., Surry Hills, N.S.W. 2010, Australia. TEL 61-2-93609360. FAX 61-2-93805533. URL: http://www.hww.com.au. **Document type:** trade publication.
   Formerly: Retail Banking Products Survey: Credit Cards (ISSN 1032-8742); Supersedes in part: H W W Retail Banking Products Survey (ISSN 1031-4148)

332   AT
H W W RATE CHECK BOOK: TERM DEPOSITS. 1988. d., w., m. Aus.$2000. H W W Pty. Ltd. (Horan Wall & Walker), 15-19 Prospect St., Surry Hills, N.S.W. 2010, Australia. TEL 61-2-93609360. FAX 61-2-93805533. URL: http://www.hww.com.au. **Document type:** trade publication.
   Formerly: Retail Banking Products Survey: Term Deposits (ISSN 1032-8718); Supersedes in part: H W W Retail Banking Products Survey (ISSN 1031-4148)

332   AT
H W W RATE CHECK BOOK: TERM LOANS. 1988. d., w., m. Aus.$2000. H W W Pty. Ltd. (Horan Wall & Walker), 15-19 Prospect St., Surry Hills, N.S.W. 2010, Australia. TEL 61-2-93609360. FAX 61-2-93805533. URL: http://www.hww.com.au. **Document type:** trade publication.
   Formerly: Retail Banking Products Survey: Term Loans (ISSN 1032-8734); Supersedes in part: H W W Retail Banking Products Survey (ISSN 1031-4148)

332   CC
HAINAN JINRONG/HAINAN FINANCE. (Text in Chinese) m. Hainan Sheng Jinrong Xuehui - Hainan Society of Finance, Sheng Renmin Yinhang, Binhai Dadao, Haikou, Hainan 570005, People's Republic of China. TEL 74205. Ed. Wu Qiping.

HALLO SPAREFROH; Freund der Sparjugend. see *CHILDREN AND YOUTH — For*

BUSINESS AND ECONOMICS — BANKING AND FINANCE

332 **UK** **ISSN 0144-2015**
THE HAMBRO COMPANY GUIDE; a detailed guide to U.K. stockmarket companies. 1978. q. £125 (Europe £165; Far East and Australia £191; elsewhere £181). Hemmington Scott Publishing Ltd., City Innovation Centre, 26-31 Whiskin St., London EC1R OBP, England. TEL 44-171-278-7769. FAX 44-171-278-9808. Ed. Jill Meiring. **Document type:** directory.
Description: Provides financial details for all U.K. listed companies.

HAMBROS DEALERS DIRECTORY (YEAR); foreign exchange treasury and bullion. see *BUSINESS AND ECONOMICS — Trade And Industrial Directories*

HANDBOOK OF S E C ACCOUNTING AND DISCLOSURE. see *BUSINESS AND ECONOMICS — Accounting*

332 **DK** **ISSN 0105-4058**
HANDELSHOEJSKOLEN I AARHUS. INSTITUT FOR FINANSIERING OG KREDITVAESEN. KOMPENDIUM D. no. 8, 1981. irreg. Handelshoejskolen i Aarhus, Institut for Finansiering og Kreditvaesen, Aarhus, Denmark. illus.

HARVARD BUSINESS SCHOOL CAREER GUIDE. FINANCE. see *OCCUPATIONS AND CAREERS*

HARVARD COLLEGE ECONOMIST. see *BUSINESS AND ECONOMICS — Macroeconomics*

332.1 **AU**
HAUPTVERBAND DER OESTERREICHISCHEN SPARKASSEN. JAHRESBERICHT. (Text in German; summaries in English, French and German) 1912. a. free. Hauptverband der Oesterreichischen Sparkassen, Postfach 256, A-1011 Vienna, Austria. TEL 0222-71169. FAX 0222-7138926. charts; stat. circ. 4,000. **Document type:** corporate report.

HEALTH CITY SUN. see *LAW*

332 **CC** **ISSN 1003-3793**
HEBEI CAIJING XUEYUAN XUEBAO/HEBEI INSTITUTE OF FINANCE AND ECONOMICS. JOURNAL. (Text in Chinese) 1978. bi-m. $18. Hebei Caijing Xueyuan, Xuebao Bianjibu, 106 Hongqi Dajie, Shijiazhuang, Hebei 050091, People's Republic of China. TEL 0311-333427. FAX 0311-614039. Ed. Chen Jinlung. adv.: page $100; adv. contact: Liu Wenming. **Document type:** academic/scholarly publication.
Description: Covers theories, policies and practices in the field of finance and economics.

332 **CC**
HEILONGJIANG CHENGSHI JINRONG/HEILONGJIANG URBAN FINANCE. (Text in Chinese) m. Zhongguo Gongshang Yinhang, Heilongjiang Fenhang, 75, Zhongshan Lu, Xiangfang-qu, Harbin, Heilongjiang 150036, People's Republic of China. TEL 228797. Ed. Zhang Dexin.

332 **CC** **ISSN 1001-0432**
HEILONGJIANG JINGRONG/HEILONGJIANG FINANCE. (Text in Chinese) 1981. m. Y1.50 per no. Heilongjiang Jinrong Yanjiusuo - Heilongjiang Institute of Finance, 75, Zhongshan Lu, Xiangfang-qu, Harbin, Heilongjiang 150036, People's Republic of China. TEL 0451-2623247. FAX 0451-2623247. Ed. Li Qingshan. circ. 12,000. **Document type:** academic/scholarly publication.

332 **US** **ISSN 0885-2138**
HIGH SPOTS. 1960. m. $25. Ohio Credit Union League, 1201 Dublin Rd., Columbus, OH 43215. TEL 614-486-2917. FAX 614-486-6044. Ed. Jeannine M. Seitz. circ. 16,000. (tabloid format; back issues avail.)

332 **US**
HIGH YIELD REPORT. w. $705 for new subscr. (foreign $755); renewal $795 (foreign $845). American Banker - Bond Buyer, Newsletter Division (Subsidiary of: Thomson Financial Services Company), One State St. Plaza, New York, NY 10004-1549. TEL 800-733-4371. FAX 212-943-2224. (Subscr. to: Box 28315, Washington, DC 20038-8315. TEL 202-347-2665) Ed. Ken Hunter. **Document type:** newsletter.
●Also available online. Vendor(s): Information Access Co., Knight-Ridder Information, Inc., Lexis-Nexis, NewsNet.
Formed by the merger of: Junk Bond Reporter; Distressed Debt Report.
Description: Reports on high-yield bond market, workouts, bankruptcies and distressed securities. Includes pricing information for both primary and secondary markets, and analysis of the high-yield sector.

332 **II**
HINDU BUSINESS LINE. (Text in English) 1994. d. Rs.395; newsstand price: Rs.4. Kasturi & Sons Ltd., Kasuri Bldgs., 859-860 Anna Salai, Chennai 600 002, India. TEL 91-44-835067. FAX 91-44-835325. TELEX 416655. Ed. N. Ram; Pub. S. Rangarajan. adv. contact: K.V. Balasubramaniam. circ. 24,073. cols./p.: 6. **Document type:** newsletter.

332.7 **US** **ISSN 1051-4902**
HG2040.45
HOME EQUITY LINES OF CREDIT REPORT. a. $90 to non-members; members $60. American Bankers Association, Retail Services Center, 1120 Connecticut Ave. N.W., Washington, DC 20036. TEL 202-663-5430. FAX 301-843-8405.
Formerly (until 1989): Home Equity Credit Report (ISSN 1043-6499); Which supersedes in part (in 1987): Retail Bank Credit Report (ISSN 0276-9093)

HONG KONG. COMMISSIONER OF BANKING. ANNUAL REPORT. see *BUSINESS AND ECONOMICS — Abstracting, Bibliographies, Statistics*

332.7 **CC**
HONG KONG EXPORT CREDIT INSURANCE CORPORATION. ANNUAL REPORT. a. Hong Kong Export Credit Insurance Corporation, South Seas Centre, Tower 1, 2nd Floor, 75 Mody Rd., Tsimshatsui East, Kowloon, Hong Kong, People's Republic of China.

332.1 **US** **ISSN 0018-473X**
HOOSIER BANKER. 1916. m. $27 to non-members; members $18 (effective 1997). Indiana Bankers Association, 3135 N. Meridian St., Indianapolis, IN 46208-4717. TEL 317-921-3135. FAX 317-921-3131. E-mail: lwilson@inbankers.org. Ed. Laura Wilson; Pub. William King. R&P contact: Laura Wilson. TEL 317-254-1477. adv. contact: Peggy Trieloff. bk.rev.; illus. circ. 2,500. (also avail. in microform from UMI) **Indexed:** Bank.Lit.Ind. **Document type:** trade publication.
●Also available online. Vendor(s): UMI.
—UMI.

332 **GW** **ISSN 0171-5658**
HOPPENSTEDT BOERSENFUEHRER. (Text in German; summaries in English) q. DM.379 (effective 1997). Verlag Hoppenstedt GmbH, Havelstr. 9, 64295 Darmstadt, Germany. TEL 49-6151-380-0. FAX 49-6151-380-360. Ed. Friederike Mueller. circ. 3,000. **Document type:** trade publication.

332 332.65 **GW**
HOPPENSTEDT CHARTS. 1970. w. price varies. Verlag Hoppenstedt GmbH, Havelstr. 9, 64295 Darmstadt, Germany. TEL 49-6151-380-0. FAX 49-6151-380-360. **Document type:** bulletin.

332.3 **US**
HOTLINE (LOS ANGELES). 1927. s-m. $40 to non-members. Western League of Savings Institutions, 1960 E. Grand Ave., Ste. 1000, El Segundo, CA 90245. TEL 310-414-8300. FAX 310-414-8399. Ed. Kathleen Wedeking. bk.rev. circ. 3,600. (looseleaf format) **Document type:** newsletter.
Former titles: California Hotline; California Savings and Loan Hotline; (until 1981): California Savings and Loan Journal (ISSN 0008-1485)
Description: General membership newsletter covering industry trends, federal and state legislation, and activities in California.

HOUSING FINANCE. see *REAL ESTATE*

HOUSING FINANCE COMPANY OF KENYA. ANNUAL REPORT AND ACCOUNTS. see *HOUSING AND URBAN PLANNING*

332 **US**
HOUSING FINANCE INTERNATIONAL. 1986. q. $125. International Union of Housing Finance Institutions, 111 E. Wacker Dr., Ste. 400, Chicago, IL 60601-4389. TEL 312-946-8200. FAX 312-946-8202. Ed. Michael Lia.
Description: Items of interest to both the developed, as well as the developing world with emphasis on thematic content.

HOUSING LEGISLATION MANUAL. see *PUBLIC ADMINISTRATION*

HOW TO AVOID FINANCIAL TANGLES. see *BUSINESS AND ECONOMICS — Management*

332 **US** **ISSN 1052-2654**
HG4061
HOW TO FIND FINANCIAL INFORMATION ABOUT COMPANIES. 1990. irreg. Washington Researcher Ltd., Box 19005, 20th St. Sta., Washington, DC 20036-9005. TEL 202-333-3499. FAX 202-625-0656. E-mail: research@researcher.com; URL: http://www.researchers.com/pub/businetl/researchers.html. Ed. M. Newman. R&P contact: Ellen O'Kane. **Document type:** directory.

I B C'S MONEY FUND REPORT. see *BUSINESS AND ECONOMICS — Investments*

332 **UK**
HG4534
I C B. (International Correspondent Banker); the magazine for global transactions services. 1984. bi-m. £140 (foreign £150) (effective 1996). Reactions Publishing Group Ltd., 39-41 North Rd. London N7 9DP, England. TEL 44-171-6098661 FAX 44-171-6090139. (Dist. in US by: American Educational Systems, 173 W. 81st St., New York, NY 10024. TEL 800-717-2669. FAX 212-501-8926) Ed. John Lee. adv. contact: Francoise Cesar. circ. 10,576. (back issues avail.) **Document type:** trade publication.
—BLDSC (4360.289000); UMI.
Former titles (until 1995): I C B Magazine (ISSN 0968-6118); I C B (ISSN 0953-5632); (until 1987): International Correspondent Banker (ISSN 0952-9888)

332.1 **UK** **ISSN 1355-8447**
I C B NEWSLETTER. (International Correspondent Banker) m. £445 (foreign £895) (effective 1996). Euromoney Publications plc., Nestor House, Playhouse Yard, London EC4V 5EX, England. TEL 44-171-779-8935. FAX 44-171-779-8541. (Dist. in US by: American Educational Systems, 17 W. 81st St., New York, NY 10024. TEL 800-717-2669. FAX 212-501-8926) **Document type:** newsletter.
—BLDSC (4360.293000).
Description: Dedicated to covering banks' transaction processing-related business.

332 338.9 **US**
THE I D B. (Includes supplement: IDB Extra) (Editions in English, Spanish) 1974. 10/yr. free. Inter-American Development Bank, 1300 New York Ave., N.W., Washington, DC 20577. TEL 202-623-1000. Ed. Roger Hamilton. illus.; stat. (also avail. in microfiche from CIS) **Indexed:** IIS, World Bank.Abstr.
Description: Reports on economic and social trends in Latin America and the Caribbean and on the activities of the Bank.

332 **GW** **ISSN 0081-7279**
I F O STUDIEN ZUR FINANZPOLITIK. 1964. irreg., vol.62, 1996. price varies. I F O Institut fuer Wirtschaftsforschung, Poschingerstr. 5, 81679 Munich, Germany. TEL 49-89-9224-0. FAX 49-89-985369. circ. 400. **Document type:** monographic series.

332 **GW**
I K REPORT; Zeitschrift zum Informationswesen der Kreditwirtschaft. 1987. a. Informationsring Kreditwirtschaft e.V., Merkurhaus, Am Hauptbahnhof 12, 60429 Frankfurt a.M., Germany. TEL 069-27100217. FAX 069-27100210. Ed. Rolf Weigand. **Document type:** trade publication.

BUSINESS AND ECONOMICS — BANKING AND FINANCE

332   US
I O M A'S REPORT ON DEFINED CONTRIBUTION PLAN INVESTING. Key Title: I O M A's Report on D C Plan Investing. 1989. s-m. $1089 (outside N. America $1137). Institute of Management & Administration, Inc., 29 W. 35th St., 5th Fl., New York, NY 10001-2299. TEL 212-244-0360. FAX 212-564-0465. URL: http://www.ioma.com. Ed. Sean Hanna; Pub. Perry Patterson. R&P contact: Sofie Kourkoutakis. index. (looseleaf format; back issues avail.) **Document type:** newsletter.
—CCC.
   Formerly (until Jan. 1992): I O M A's G I C - B I C Yields and Market Report (Guaranteed Investment Contracts - Bank Investment Contracts) (ISSN 1047-9244)
   Description: Ratings of money managers and bundled service providers, with risk-return benchmarks. Current asset allocation trends for participants in the DC plan marketplace. Also includes GIC yields.

I O M A'S REPORT ON MANAGING 401K PLANS. (Institute of Management & Administration, Inc.) see BUSINESS AND ECONOMICS — Personnel Management

332   BU   ISSN 0204-711X
HC403.A1
IKONOMIKA. 10/yr. $10. Ministerstvo na Finansite, Rakovski St. 102, 1000 Sofia, Bulgaria. (Dist. by: Hemus, 6, Rouski Blvd., 1000 Sofia, Bulgaria) (Co-sponsor: Bulgarska Narodna Banka) bibl.; charts; stat. circ. 5,000. **Indexed:** BSL Econ.
   Formerly: Finansi i Kredit.

332.1   US   ISSN 0019-185X
ILLINOIS BANKER. 1916. m. $75 (members $37.50). Illinois Bankers Association, 111 N. Canal, Ste. 1111, Chicago, IL 60606. TEL 312-876-9900. FAX 312-876-3826. Ed. Kathleen C. Gill; Pub. William J. Hocter. adv.: B&W page $915, color page $1590; trim 8 3/8 x 10 7/8; adv. contact: Cindy L. Altman. bk.rev. circ. 2,600. **Indexed:** BPIA, World Bank.Abstr. **Document type:** trade publication.

332
ILLINOIS BANKING ACT AND RELATED LAWS. a. $32.50. Michie, A Division of Reed Elsevier Inc., Box 7587, Charlottesville, VA 22906-7587. TEL 804-972-7566; 800-562-1197. FAX 800-643-1280. E-mail: custserv@michie.com; URL: http://www.michie.com. Ed. George Harley. pp./issue: 569.

332   US
ILLINOIS BANKNEWS. fortn. $70 to non-members; members $35. Illinois Bankers Association, 111 N. Canal St., Ste. 1111, Chicago, IL 60606-4299. TEL 312-876-9900. FAX 312-876-3826. Ed. Kathleen C. Grill. R&P contact: Kathleen C. Grill. adv.: B&W page $650, color page $1000; 7 1/16 x 10 9/16; adv. contact: Cind L. Altman. circ. 2,200. (tabloid format; back issues avail.) **Document type:** newsletter, trade publication.

332   US
ILLINOIS REPORTER. bi-m. Illinois League of Financial Institutions, 133 S. 4th St., Ste. 206, Springfield, IL 62701-1203. TEL 217-522-5575. Ed. Norma Altman. circ. 1,000.

332.1   US   ISSN 0019-3674
INDEPENDENT BANKER. 1950. m. $35 for nonmembers; members $25. Independent Bankers Association of America, Box 267, Sauk Centre, MN 56378. TEL 612-352-6546. Ed. David C. Bordewyk. adv.; illus. circ. 10,000. (also avail. in microfiche from UMI; back issues avail.) **Indexed:** Bank.Lit.Ind., BPIA, P.A.I.S. **Document type:** trade publication.
● Also available online. Vendor(s): UMI.
—UMI; UnCover.
   Description: Focuses on the nation's independent banks, mostly the small to medium-size commercial banks.

332   II   ISSN 0019-4204
INDIA. MINISTRY OF FINANCE. FINANCE LIBRARY. WEEKLY BULLETIN. 1954. w. free. Ministry of Finance, Finance Library, North Block, New Delhi 110001, India. TEL 3013852. Ed. H.S. Pooji. circ. controlled. (processed) **Document type:** government publication, bulletin.

332   II
INDIAN BANK TODAY AND TOMORROW. (Text in English) 1976. m. Rs.116. S.R. Suneja, Ed. & Pub., B4-29 Safdarjang Enclave, New Delhi 110 029, India.

332.1   II   ISSN 0019-4921
HG1505
INDIAN INSTITUTE OF BANKERS. JOURNAL. (Text in English) 1929. q. Rs.24. Indian Institute of Bankers, World Trade Centre, 2nd Fl., East Wing, Cuffe Parade Branch, Mumbai 400 005, India. TEL 91-22-217073. TELEX 11-3524 IIB IN. Ed. R.D. Pandya. circ. 300,000. **Indexed:** Pub.Admin.Abstr., World Bank.Abstr. **Document type:** academic/scholarly publication.
—UnCover.

332   II   ISSN 0971-0566
HG4001
INDIAN JOURNAL OF FINANCE AND RESEARCH. (Text in English) 1991. s-a. $30 (effective 1995). Indian Financial Management Association, 116-D Pocket IV, Mayur Vihar, New Delhi 110 091, India. TEL 2250164. Ed. Mohinder N. Kaura. adv. contact: D. Jagananthan. bk.rev. circ. 500. **Document type:** academic/scholarly publication.
   Description: Publishes research articles on finance, especially corporate finance, to bridge the gap between theory and practice.
   Refereed Serial

INDICADORES BURSATILES. see BUSINESS AND ECONOMICS — Abstracting, Bibliographies, Statistics

332.1   KO
INDUSTRIAL BANK OF KOREA. ANNUAL REPORT. (Text in English) 1962. a. free. Industrial Bank of Korea, 50 Ulchiro 2-ga, Chung-gu, Seoul, S. Korea. TEL 02-729-6114. FAX 02-729-7095. TELEX K-23932. Ed. Jhoh Dong-Hweh. charts; stat.; illus. circ. 4,000.
   Former titles: Small and Medium Industry Bank, Seoul. Annual Report; Medium Industry Bank, Seoul. Report (ISSN 0076-6143)
   Description: Covers the financial and economic performance of the Industrial Bank of Korea, as well as its management and organization.

332.3   KU
INDUSTRIAL BANK OF KUWAIT. ANNUAL REPORT. (Text in English) 1975. a. free. Industrial Bank of Kuwait - Bank al-Kuwayt al-Sinai, Box 3146, Safat, Kuwait. circ. 1,500.

332.1   SJ   ISSN 0073-7356
INDUSTRIAL BANK OF SUDAN. BOARD OF DIRECTORS. ANNUAL REPORT. (Text in Arabic and English) 1962. a. free. Industrial Bank of Sudan, Research Department, P.O. Box 1722, Khartoum, Sudan. TELEX 22456 SINAI SD. Ed. Mohamed Amara. **Document type:** corporate report.

332.1   JO
INDUSTRIAL DEVELOPMENT BANK. ANNUAL REPORT AND BALANCE SHEET/BANK AL-INMA AL-SINAI. ANNUAL REPORT AND BALANCE SHEET. 1967. a. free. Industrial Development Bank, Schools of the Islamic College St., P.O. Box 1982, Amman, Jordan. TEL 06-642216. FAX 06-647821. TELEX 21349 IDB JO. charts; illus. circ. 2,000.

332.1   KE
INDUSTRIAL DEVELOPMENT BANK LIMITED. ANNUAL REPORT AND ACCOUNTS. 1974. a. Industrial Development Bank Ltd., National Bank Bldg., P.O. Box 44036, Nairobi, Kenya. FAX 254-2-334594. illus.; stat. **Document type:** corporate report.

332.1   II   ISSN 0073-7372
INDUSTRIAL DEVELOPMENT BANK OF INDIA. ANNUAL REPORT. (Text in English; occasionally in Hindi) 1965. a. free. Industrial Development Bank of India, 227 Backbay Reclamation, Nariman Bhavan, Nariman Point, Bombay 400 021, India. **Document type:** corporate report.

INDUSTRIAL ECONOMIST. see BUSINESS AND ECONOMICS — Production Of Goods And Services

332   US
INDUSTRIAL PRODUCTION AND CAPACITY UTILIZATION. m. $15. U.S. Federal Reserve System, Board of Governors, Publications Services, Rm. MS-138, Washington, DC 20551. TEL 202-452-3244. FAX 202-728-5886. (also avail. in diskette format) **Document type:** government publication.

INFORMACOES F I P E. see BUSINESS AND ECONOMICS

332   AU
INFORMATIONEN AUS DER WIRTSCHAFT. 1965. m. S.5. Zentralsparkasse und Kommerzialbank, Vordere Zollamtsstr. 13, A-1030 Vienna, Austria. TEL 0222-71191-0. FAX 0222-71191-2807. Ed.Bd. bibl.; mkt.; stat.; tr.lit.; tr.mk.; index. circ. 68,000.
   Formerly: Zentralsparkasse der Gemeinde Wien. Information (ISSN 0044-4316)

332   BL   ISSN 0020-0654
INFORMATIVO BAMERINDUS. 1970. m. free. Banco Bamerindus do Brazil, Avenida Kennedy 3080, 80000 Curitiba, Parana, Brazil. bk.rev.; charts; stat.
   Formerly: Bamerindus.

INFORMAZIONE MEDITERRANEA. see BUSINESS AND ECONOMICS — Economic Situation And Conditions

332.7   CK
INFORME COYUNTURA ESTABLECIMIENTOS DE CREDITO. 1992. q. free. Superintendencia Bancaria, Apdo. Aereo 3460, Bogota DC, Colombia. TEL 57-1-2804060. FAX 57-1-2800864. circ. 500.

332 368   CK
INFORME COYUNTURA SEGUROS Y CAPITALIZACION. 1992. q. free. Superintendencia Bancaria, Apdo. Aereo 3460, Bogota DC, Colombia. TEL 57-1-2804060. FAX 57-1-2800864. circ. 500.

332   CK
INFORME COYUNTURA SERVICIOS FINANCIEROS. 1992. q. free. Superintendencia Bancaria, Apdo. Aereo 3460, Bogota DC, Colombia. TEL 57-1-2804060. FAX 57-1-2800864. circ. 500.

332.1   CL   ISSN 0716-243X
HC191
INFORME ECONOMICO Y FINANCIERO. 1982. s-m. Ch.$78000($300) Banco Central de Chile, Casilla 967, Santiago, Chile. TEL 56-2-6702000. FAX 56-2-6984847. TELEX 405 69 CENBC CL. circ. 780. **Document type:** government publication.
   Description: Chilean economic survey with statistical charts.

332   CK
INFORME FINANCIERO SEMANAL. 1988. w. Superintendencia Bancaria, Apdo. Aereo 3460, Bogota DC, Colombia. TEL 57-1-2804060. FAX 57-1-2800864. circ. 450.

332   US
▼**INSIDE B & C LENDING.** 1996. bi-w. $495 (effective 1997). Inside Mortgage Finance Publications, Box 42387, Washington, DC 20015. TEL 301-951-1240. FAX 301-656-1709. URL: http://users.aol.com/imfpubs. Ed. Guy D. Cecala; Pub. Guy D. Cecala. R&P contact: Didi Parks. **Document type:** trade publication.
   Description: Focuses on the business of lending to borrowers with less than perfect credit ratings. Explains loan grading approaches, regulatory developments and activity among the top market players.

332   US
HG2040.5.U5
INSIDE FAIR LENDING. 1990. m. $395 (effective 1997). Inside Mortgage Finance Publications, Box 42387, Washington, DC 20015. TEL 301-951-1240. FAX 301-656-1709. URL: http://users.aol.com/imfpubs. Ed. Guy D. Cecala; Pub. Guy D. Cecala. R&P contact: Didi Parks. **Document type:** newsletter.
   Formerly: C R A - H M D A Update (ISSN 1059-1400)
   Description: Coverage and analysis of fair lending and compliance issues as well as legislative developments.

BUSINESS AND ECONOMICS — BANKING AND FINANCE

332   US
INSIDE M B S & A B S. 1985. w. (48/yr.) $895 (effective 1997). Inside Mortgage Finance Publications, Box 42387, Washington, DC 20015. TEL 301-951-1240. FAX 301-656-1709. URL: http://users.aol.com/imfpubs. Ed. Guy D. Cecala; Pub. Guy D. Cecala. R&P contact: Didi Parks. charts; stat. (back issues avail.)
    Former titles: Inside Mortgage Securities; Inside Mortgage Capital Markets (ISSN 1059-1397)
    Description: Covers mortgage-related and asset-backed securities as well as the secondary mortgage market. Focuses on market, regulatory and legislative developments.

332   US
INSIDERS' QUARTERLY.* q. $250. Thomson Financial Services, One State St. Plaza, New York, NY 10004. TEL 800-733-4371. FAX 301-654-1678.

332.7 346   UK
INSOLVENCY BULLETIN. 10/yr. £245($385) Intellectual Property Publishing Ltd. (Subsidiary of: Armstrong Group Ltd.), Third Fl., Brigade House, Parson's Green, London SW6 4TH, England. TEL 44-171-736-7111. FAX 44-171-371-7806. Ed. Laura Strong; Pub. Richard Armstrong. (back issues avail.) **Document type:** trade publication.

332   US   ISSN 1041-6390
HG1642.U5
INSTALLMENT CREDIT REPORT. a. $190 to non-members; members $127. American Bankers Association, Retail Services Center, 1120 Connecticut Ave., N.W., Washington, DC 20036. TEL 202-663-5430. FAX 301-843-8405. (Subscr. to: Order Processing Department, 10 Jay Gould Court, Waldorf, MD 20602-2725. TEL 800-338-0626) charts.
    Supersedes in part (in 1987): Retail Bank Credit Report (ISSN 0276-9093)
    Description: Provides comprehensive data on installment loans, ordered by bank size. Covers variable rate loans, loan delinquencies and losses, and expense elements.

332   DK
INSTITUT FOR FINANSIERING OG KREDITVAESEN. KOMPENDIUM. irreg., no.10, 1982. price varies. Institut for Finansiering og Kreditvaesen, Handelshoejskolen i Aarhus, Aarhus, Denmark. (Dist. by: Handelsvidenskabelig Boghandel, Fuglesangs Alle 4, 8210 Aarhus V, Denmark) illus.

332 346.066   SZ
INSTITUT FUER FINANZWIRTSCHAFT UND FINANZRECHT. SCHRIFTENREIHE. 1970. irreg., no.85, 1996. price varies. Paul Haupt AG, Falkenplatz 14, CH-3001 Bern, Switzerland. TEL 41-31-3012345. FAX 41-31-3014669. **Document type:** monographic series.
    Formerly: Schriftenreihe Finanzwirtschaft und Finanzrecht.

INSTITUT FUER FINANZWISSENSCHAFT UND STEUERRECHT. GELBE BRIEFE. see BUSINESS AND ECONOMICS — Public Finance, Taxation

INSTITUT FUER FINANZWISSENSCHAFT UND STEUERRECHT. MITTEILUNGSBLATT. see BUSINESS AND ECONOMICS — Public Finance, Taxation

332.1   PK   ISSN 0073-8999
INSTITUTE OF BANKERS IN PAKISTAN. COUNCIL. REPORT AND ACCOUNTS. (Text in English) s-a. Institute of Bankers in Pakistan, Karachi, Pakistan. **Indexed:** World Bank.Abstr.

INSTITUTE OF BANKERS OF SRI LANKA. JOURNAL. see OCCUPATIONS AND CAREERS

332   UK   ISSN 0269-3933
INSTITUTE OF EUROPEAN FINANCE. SCHOOL OF ACCOUNTING, BANKING AND ECONOMICS. RESEARCH PAPERS IN BANKING AND FINANCE. 1986. irreg. £100. Institute of European Finance, School of Accounting, Banking and Economics, University of Wales, Bangor, Gwynedd, Wales. TEL 44-1248-382277. FAX 1248-364760. E-mail: ief@bangor.ac.uk. Eds. E.P.M. Gardener, P. Molyneux. **Document type:** academic/scholarly publication, monographic series.

332   US
INSTITUTIONAL BROKERS ESTIMATE SYSTEM. Short title: I-B-E-S. 1971. d. price varies. I-B-E-S Inc., 345 Hudson St., New York, NY 10014. TEL 212-243-3335. FAX 212-727-1386. circ. 900. (also avail. in magnetic tape; back issues avail.)

INSURANCE AND FINANCIAL SERVICES CAREERS. see OCCUPATIONS AND CAREERS

INSURANCE FINANCE AND INVESTMENT. see INSURANCE

332.1 338.9   US
INTER-AMERICAN DEVELOPMENT BANK. ANNUAL REPORT. Spanish edition: Inter-American Development Bank. Informe Anual. (Editions in English, French and Portuguese) 1960. a. Inter-American Development Bank, 1300 New York Ave., N.W., Washington, DC 20577. TEL 202-623-1000. (also avail. in microfiche from CIS) **Indexed:** IIS. **Document type:** corporate report.
    Formerly: Inter-American Development Bank. Report (ISSN 0074-087X); **Incorporates:** Inter-American Development Bank. Statement of Loans.
    Description: Reports on the bank's activities.

332.1 338.9   US   ISSN 0074-0861
INTER-AMERICAN DEVELOPMENT BANK. BOARD OF GOVERNORS. PROCEEDINGS OF THE MEETING. Spanish edition: Inter-American Development Bank. Board of Governors. Anales (de la) Reunion (ISSN 0538-3102) (Editions in English, Portuguese, Spanish and French) 1960. a. Inter-American Development Bank, 1300 New York Ave., N.W., Washington, DC 20577. TEL 202-623-1000. **Document type:** proceedings.
    Description: Minutes of the bank's annual meetings.

332   SP
INTERCOGUI; boletin internacional. 1973. m. free. Banco Guipuzcoano, Departamento Internacional, Avda. de la Libertad, 21, 20004 San Sebastian, Spain. FAX 43-426828. TELEX 36369. circ. 2,500. **Document type:** bulletin.

332.4   UK   ISSN 0308-9002
INTEREST RATE SERVICE. 10/yr. £450($950) (effective 1996). World Reports Ltd., 108 Horseferry Rd., Westminster, London SW1P 2EF, England. TEL 44-171-222-3826. FAX 44-171-233-0185. (U.S. subscr. to: World Reports Ltd., 280 Madison Ave., Ste. 1209, New York, NY 10016-0802. TEL 212-599-4560. FAX 212-679-1094) Ed. Christopher Story. (back issues avail.) **Document type:** trade publication.
    Description: Surveys global interest rates and monetary developments for investors.

332   AT   ISSN 0813-6491
INTEREST RATES SURVEY. 1979. q. Aus.$540($500) Investment and Econometrics Research Pty. Ltd., 5 Powell St., Neutral Bay, N.S.W. 2089, Australia. Ed. R.R. Taylor. (back issues avail.)
    Description: Lists risk premiums on public and corporate borrowings, interest rates, and promissory notes.

330   NE   ISSN 0020-5605
INTERMEDIAIR. 1965. w. fl.350 (effective 1993). V N U Business Publications B.V., Postbus 9194, 1006 CC Amsterdam, Netherlands. TEL 31-206175137. TELEX 14407 PUBLI NL. Ed.Bd. adv.; bk.rev.; bibl.; illus.; stat.; index; circ. 20,000 (paid); 195,000 (controlled). **Indexed:** ELLIS, Excerp.Med., Key to Econ.Sci. —SWETS.
    Description: Covers current developments affecting the world of business and industry, including scientific, political, economic and management issues.

332.1   CN   ISSN 0020-6113
HG3
INTERNATIONAL BANK CREDIT ANALYST. 1962. m. $795. B C A Publications Ltd., 1002 Sherbrooke St. W., 16th Fl., Montreal, PQ H3A 3L6, Canada. TEL 514-499-9706. FAX 514-499-9709. Ed.Bd. abstr.; charts.
    Description: Provides a forecast and analysis for the principal countries of interest rates, equity markets, gold and commodity prices, economic trends and currency movements.

INTERNATIONAL BANKING AND FINANCIAL LAW. see LAW — International Law

332 346   US   ISSN 0958-353X
K1066.A13
INTERNATIONAL BANKING REGULATOR. Cover title: Thomson's International Banking Regulator. 48/yr. $765 for new subscr.; renewal $850. American Banker - Bond Buyer, Newsletter Division (Subsidiary of: Thomson Financial Services Company), One State St. Plaza, New York, NY 10004-1549. TEL 800-733-4371. FAX 212-943-2224. (Subscr. to: Box 28315, Washington, DC 20038-8315. TEL 202-347-2665) **Document type:** newsletter.
    ●Also available online. Vendor(s): Information Access Co., NewsNet (IT36).
    Formerly: International Banking Regulator - International Banking Report; **Incorporates:** E C Banking Regulator; Financial Compliance Watch.
    Description: Provides analysis detailing the imperative regulatory and legislative decisions being made in key international financial centers, and insights on debates in the US on banking and securities deregulation.

332   UK   ISSN 0965-674X
INTERNATIONAL BANKING SYSTEMS. 1991. 10/yr. £260 in UK & Europe; U.S. $450; elsewhere £275. I B S Publishing, St. Catherine's House, Cliff Rd, Hythe, Kent CT21 5XW, England. TEL 44-181-467-1079. FAX 44-181-467-1079. E-mail: 106151.1125@compuserve.com; URL: http://www.intbksys.co.uk. Ed. Martin Whybrow. index. (back issues avail.) **Document type:** newsletter.

332   UK
INTERNATIONAL BONDS SERVICE. w. £1495 (foreign £1725). Financial Times Information Ltd., Extel, Fitzroy House, 13-17 Epworth St., London EC2A 4DL, England. TEL 44-171-825-8000. FAX 44-171-608-2032. TELEX 884319. E-mail: eic@ft.com; URL: http://www.info.ft.com/.
    Description: Summary details of every international and Eurobond.

332.1   CH
INTERNATIONAL COMMERCIAL BANK OF CHINA. ANNUAL REPORT. (Text in English) 1960. a. free. International Commercial Bank of China, Head Office-Economic Research Department, 100 Chilin Rd., Taipei, Taiwan 10424, Republic of China. FAX 02-5611216. TELEX 11300 INCOBK. Ed. Hun-Ming Cheng. stat. circ. 4,500. **Document type:** corporate report.
    Formerly: Chung-Kuo Yin Hang. Annual Report.

332   UK   ISSN 1361-6048
INTERNATIONAL CORRESPONDENT BANKING REVIEW. a. £95($170) (effective 1997). Euromoney Publications plc., Books, Nestor House, Playhouse Yard, London EC4V 5EX, England. TEL 44-171-779-8935. FAX 44-171-779-8541.
    Description: Covers international correspondent banking market with country reviews contributed by leading banking experts worldwide.

INTERNATIONAL COUNTRY RISK GUIDE. see BUSINESS AND ECONOMICS — Economic Situation And Conditions

332.4   UK   ISSN 0020-6490
HG3881
INTERNATIONAL CURRENCY REVIEW. 1969. q. £225($465) (effective 1996). World Reports Ltd., 108 Horseferry Rd., Westminster, London SW1P 2EF, England. TEL 44-171-222-3826. FAX 44-171-233-0185. (U.S. subscr. to: World Reports Ltd., 280 Madison Ave., Ste. 1209, New York, NY 10016-0802. TEL 212-679-0095. FAX 212-679-1094) Ed. Christopher Story. (back issues avail.) **Indexed:** C.R.E.J., Key to Econ.Sci., P.A.I.S., World Bank.Abstr. **Document type:** trade publication. —BLDSC (4539.500500); SWETS.
    Description: Reviews global financial and economic affairs.

332.024 333.33   US
INTERNATIONAL ESTATE PLANNING. 1992. base vol. (plus a. update). $110 for base vol.; update $68. Matthew Bender & Co., Inc., 2 Park Ave., New York, NY 10016. TEL 212-448-2000. E-mail: international@bender.com; URL: http://www.bender.com.
    Description: A guide to assist clients with assets in more than one country; either U.S. citizens living abroad or foreign citizens with U.S. property.

BUSINESS AND ECONOMICS — BANKING AND FINANCE

332 UN ISSN 0074-6061
HG3881
INTERNATIONAL FINANCE CORPORATION. REPORT. 1957. a. International Finance Corporation, 1818 H St., N.W., Washington, DC 20433. Ed. Carol Rosen. (also avail. in microfiche from CIS) **Indexed:** IIS.

INTERNATIONAL FINANCIAL LAW REVIEW. see *LAW — International Law*

332 US ISSN 0271-2423
INTERNATIONAL FINANCIER. 1979. m. $1000 includes membership. International Society of Financiers, Box 18508, Asheville, NC 28814. TEL 704-252-5907. FAX 704-251-5061. Ed. Ronald I. Gershen. adv.; bk.rev.; circ. 500 (controlled).
Description: Covers major domestic and international financial projects and transactions.

332 UK ISSN 0953-0223
HG3879
INTERNATIONAL FINANCING REVIEW. 1974. w. £1950 in the U.K.; rest of Europe £2140; N. America $3500. I F R Publishing (Subsidiary of: Thomson Financial Services Ltd.), 11 New Fetter Ln., London EC4A 1JN, England. TEL 0171-815-3800. FAX 0171-315-3850. Ed. Peter Krijgsman. adv.; index.
Description: Provides financial information for the global capital markets. Reports on all international primary market transactions.

332.7 346.066 UK ISSN 1180-0518
CODEN: IINRES
INTERNATIONAL INSOLVENCY REVIEW. Variant title: Insol International Review. 1992. 3/yr. $375 (foreign $375) (effective 1998). (International Association of Insolvency Practitioners) John Wiley & Sons Ltd., Journals, Baffins Ln., Chichester, W. Sussex PO19 1UD, England. TEL 44-1243-779777. FAX 44-1243-775878. E-mail: info-assets@wiley.co.uk. (Subscr. in the Americas to: John Wiley & Sons, Inc., 605 Third Ave., New York, NY 10158-0012. TEL 212-850-6645. FAX 212-850-6021) Ed. Ian F. Fletcher; Pub. David Wilson. adv.: B&W page £595, color page £1495; trim 235 x 160; adv. contact: Bob Kern. (also avail. in microform from UMI; back issues avail.) **Indexed:** L.R.I. **Document type:** academic/scholarly publication.
—BLDSC (4541.305000); SWETS. **CCC.**
Description: Provides analysis and commentary on key insolvency issues across major jurisdictions in Europe and the EC, Eastern Europe, the US, the Far East, Asia and Australia.

330 UK ISSN 0265-2323
CODEN: IJBMES
INTERNATIONAL JOURNAL OF BANK MARKETING. 1982. 7/yr. £3839($5939) (foreign Aus.$7489) (effective 1998). M C B University Press Ltd., 60-62 Toller Ln., Bradford, W. Yorks BD8 9BY, England. TEL 44-1274-777700. FAX 44-1274-785200. TELEX 51317-MCBUNI-G. URL: http://www.mcb.co.uk. Ed. Trevor Watkins. (reprint service avail. from SWZ) **Indexed:** ABI Inform, Cont.Pg.Manage., INSPEC (1986-), World Bank.Abstr. **Document type:** academic/scholarly publication.
●Also available on CD-ROM.
—BLDSC (4542.127000); AskIEEE; KR SourceOne; UMI. **CCC.**
Description: Aims to present the latest innovations and research findings on all the issues of concern for bank marketers. Focuses on the adoption and implementation of marketing planning and management in personal, corporate and international banking.

INTERNATIONAL JOURNAL OF DEVELOPMENT BANKING. see *BUSINESS AND ECONOMICS — International Development And Assistance*

332 US ISSN 1041-2743
INTERNATIONAL JOURNAL OF FINANCE. 1988. 4/yr. $40 to individuals (foreign $45); institutions $125 (foreign $140). 206 Rabbit Run Dr., Cherry Hill, NJ 08003-1427. TEL 609-424-2262. FAX 609-424-6007. E-mail: int.journalfin@juno.com. Ed. Dilip Ghosh. **Document type:** academic/scholarly publication.
—BLDSC (4542.251000).
Description: Publishes original contributions, theoretical, as well as empirical, in the field of corporate finance, investment, financial institutions, international finance and financial economics.
Refereed Serial

332 UK ISSN 1076-9307
HG3879 CODEN: IJFEEO
▼**INTERNATIONAL JOURNAL OF FINANCE AND ECONOMICS.** 1996. q. $285 (foreign $285) (effective 1998). John Wiley & Sons Ltd., Journals, Baffins Ln., Chichester, W. Sussex PO19 1UD, England. TEL 44-1243-779777. FAX 44-1243-775878. E-mail: info-assets@wiley.co.uk; URL: http://www.wiley.co.uk. (Subscr. in the Americas to: John Wiley & Sons, Inc., 605 Third Ave., New York, NY 10158. TEL 212-850-6645. FAX 212-850-6021) Ed.Bd.; Pub. Richard Baggeley. adv.: B&W page £595, color page £1495; trim 260 x 200; adv. contact: Bob Kern. **Document type:** academic/scholarly publication.
—BLDSC (4542.251200). **CCC.**

332 330.9 CN
INTERNATIONAL MARKET REVIEW. 1985. m. free. Bank of Montreal, Economics Department, First Canadian Place, 21st Fl., Toronto, ON M5X 1A1, Canada. TEL 416-867-7842. FAX 416-867-5401. charts; stat. **Document type:** newsletter.
Description: Covers expected short-term financial and exchange rate developments in the principal industrial countries.

332 UN ISSN 0250-7498
HG3881
INTERNATIONAL MONETARY FUND. ANNUAL REPORT OF THE EXECUTIVE BOARD. French edition: Fonds Monetaire International. Rapport Annuel du Conseil d'Administration (ISSN 0250-7501); German edition: Internationaler Waehrungsfonds. Jahresbericht der Exekutivdirektoren (ISSN 0250-7528); Spanish edition: Fondo Monetario Internacional. Informe Anual del Directorio Ejecutivo (ISSN 0250-751X) (Text in English) 1947. a. free. International Monetary Fund, Publication Services, 700 19th St., N.W., Washington, DC 20431. TEL 202-623-7430. FAX 202-623-7201. (also avail. in microfilm from BHP; microfiche from WSH; microfiche from CIS; reprint service avail. from UMI) **Indexed:** IIS, World Bank.Abstr.
—BLDSC (1311.550000); UMI.
Formerly: International Monetary Fund. Annual Report of the Executive Directors (ISSN 0085-2171)
Description: Reviews the fund's activities, policies, organization, and administration and surveys the world economy, with special emphasis on balance of payments problems, exchange rates, world trade, international liquidity, and developments in the international monetary system.

332 UN ISSN 0250-7366
K4440.A13
INTERNATIONAL MONETARY FUND. ANNUAL REPORT ON EXCHANGE ARRANGEMENTS AND EXCHANGE RESTRICTIONS. 1950. a. $70 ($35 to university faculty and students). International Monetary Fund, Publication Services, 700 19th St., N.W., Washington, DC 20431. TEL 202-623-7430. FAX 202-623-7201. (also avail. in microform from UMI; reprint service avail. from UMI)
—UMI.
Formerly: International Monetary Fund. Annual Report on Exchange Restrictions (ISSN 0085-2163)
Description: Contains country-by-country descriptions of the exchange systems and related measures in operation in all Fund member countries.

332 UN ISSN 0251-6365
INTERNATIONAL MONETARY FUND. OCCASIONAL PAPERS. 1980. irreg., no.110, 1993. $15 ($12 to university faculty and students). International Monetary Fund, Publication Services, 700 19th St., N.W., Washington, DC 20431. TEL 202-623-7430. FAX 202-623-7201. (also avail. in microform from UMI; back issues avail.) **Indexed:** Geo.Abstr.H.G.
—BLDSC (6217.477500); EMDOCS; KR SourceOne.
Description: Contains studies on a variety of economic and financial subjects of importance to the work of the Fund.

332 UN ISSN 0538-8759
INTERNATIONAL MONETARY FUND. PAMPHLET SERIES. French edition: Fonds Monetaire International. Serie des Brochures (ISSN 0252-2985); Spanish edition: Fondo Monetario Internacional. Serie de Folletos (ISSN 0252-2993) 1964. irreg., no.46, 1992. free. International Monetary Fund, Publications Unit, 700 19th St., N.W., Washington, DC 20431. TEL 202-623-7430. FAX 202-623-7201. Ed. Ian S. McDonald. (also avail. in microform from UMI; reprint service avail. from UMI)

332.1 UN ISSN 0094-1735
HG3881
INTERNATIONAL MONETARY FUND. SELECTED DECISIONS OF THE INTERNATIONAL MONETARY FUND AND SELECTED DOCUMENTS. 1972. irreg. free. International Monetary Fund, Publication Services, 700 19th St., N.W., Washington, DC 20431. TEL 202-623-7430. FAX 202-623-7201. index. (reprint service avail. from UMI)
Formerly: International Monetary Fund. Selected Decisions of the Executive Directors and Selected Documents.

332.4 UN ISSN 0020-8027
HG3810
INTERNATIONAL MONETARY FUND. STAFF PAPERS. 1950. q. $50 ($25 to university faculty and students). International Monetary Fund, Publication Services, 700 19th St., N.W., Ste. C-100, Washington, DC 20431. TEL 202-623-7430. FAX 202-623-7201. Ed. Ian S. McDonald. charts; index, cum.index. circ. 5,000. (also avail. in microform from UMI,CIS; reprint service avail. from SCH,UMI) **Indexed:** Amer.Hist.& Life (1963-1969), ASCA, B.P.I., Bus.Ind., Cont.Pg.Manage., Curr.Cont., ELLIS, Hist.Abstr. (1963-1969), IBR, IIS, J.of Econ.Lit., Mid.East: Abstr.& Ind., P.A.I.S., Pub.Admin.Abstr., Risk Abstr., Rural Recreat.Tour.Abstr., Soc.Sci.Ind., SSCI, Tr.& Indus.Ind., World Agri.Econ.& Rural Sociol.Abstr., World Bank.Abstr. **Document type:** academic/scholarly publication.
●Also available online. Vendor(s): Information Access Co., UMI.
—BLDSC (8426.350000); Genuine Article; KR SourceOne; SWETS; UMI; UnCover.
Description: Contains theoretical studies on monetary and financial problems prepared by Fund staff. Subjects covered include balance of payments and exchange rates, monetary systems and analysis, national monetary and fiscal policies, and international liquidity.

330 UN ISSN 0074-7025
HG3881.5.I58
INTERNATIONAL MONETARY FUND. SUMMARY PROCEEDINGS OF THE ANNUAL MEETING OF THE BOARD OF GOVERNORS. (Includes list of members of delegations) 1946. a. free. International Monetary Fund, Publication Services, 700 19th St., N.W., Ste. C-100, Washington, DC 20431. TEL 202-623-7430. FAX 202-623-7201. (also avail. in microform from UMI,BHP; microfilm from BHP; reprint service avail. from UMI) **Document type:** proceedings.
—BLDSC (8531.160000); UMI.
Description: Contains the opening and closing addresses of the Chairman of the Board of Governors, presentation of the Annual Report by the Managing Director, statements of Governors, committee reports, resolutions, and a list of delegates.

332.1 338.9 UN ISSN 0258-7440
INTERNATIONAL MONETARY FUND. WORLD ECONOMIC AND FINANCIAL SURVEYS. (Subseries of: International Monetary Fund. Occasional Papers (ISSN 0251-6365)) irreg. (8-9/yr.) price varies. International Monetary Fund, Publication Services, 700 19th St., N.W., Washington, DC 20431. TEL 202-623-6639. FAX 202-623-7201. (also avail. in microfiche from CIS) **Indexed:** IIS.

332 SA
INTERNATIONAL PERSONAL FINANCE. 1985. m. $205 (effective through Oct. 1997). Prescon Publishing Corporation (Pty) Ltd., P.O. Box 84004, Greenside 2034, South Africa. TEL 27-11-646-9750. FAX 27-11-646-4617. E-mail: prescon@aztec.co.za. Ed. Martin C. Spring. R&P contact: Liz Spring. TEL 27-11-646-9046. **Document type:** newsletter.
Description: Provides international investment information for individuals with particular focus for South Africans and others still subject to exchange control.

INTERNATIONAL PETROLEUM FINANCE; earnings, finances and management strategies in the petroleum industry. see *PETROLEUM AND GAS*

BUSINESS AND ECONOMICS — BANKING AND FINANCE

332 UK ISSN 1367-6512
INTERNATIONAL POWER FINANCE REVIEW. a. £95($170) Euromoney Publications plc., Books, Nestor House, Playhouse Yard, London EC4V 5EX, England. TEL 44-171-779-8935. FAX 44-171-779-8541.
 Description: Aimed at the international power finance market, featuring contributions from experts within the field of project and power finance.

INTERNATIONAL PRESS CUTTING SERVICE: TAXATION - FINANCE - COMPANY LAW. see BUSINESS AND ECONOMICS — Public Finance, Taxation

INTERNATIONAL REVIEW OF ECONOMICS AND FINANCE. see BUSINESS AND ECONOMICS — Economic Situation And Conditions

332
HG1 US ISSN 1057-5219
INTERNATIONAL REVIEW OF FINANCIAL ANALYSIS. 1991. 3/yr. $80 to individuals (foreign $100); institutions $205 (foreign $225) (effective 1998). J A I Press Inc., 55 Old Post Rd., No. 2, Box 1678, Greenwich, CT 06830-1678. TEL 203-661-7602. FAX 203-661-0792. E-mail: jai@jaipress.com. (Addr. in Europe: J A I Press Ltd., 38 Tavistock St., Covent Garden, London WC2E 7PB, England. TEL 44-171-379-8834. FAX 44-171-379-8835) Eds. George M. Frankfurter, George C. Philippatos. (also avail. in microform from UMI; back issues avail.) **Document type:** trade publication.
—BLDSC (4547.160000); SWETS. **CCC.**
 Refereed Serial

INTERNATIONAL RISK MANAGEMENT. see BUSINESS AND ECONOMICS

332 UK ISSN 0964-9301
INTERNATIONAL SECURITIES LENDING. 1992. q. £125 (foreign $220) (effective 1997). Euromoney Publications plc., Nestor House, Playhouse Yard, London EC4V 5EX, England. TEL 44-171-779-8674. FAX 44-171-779-8595. TELEX 290706 EURMON G. (Subscr. to: Quadrant Subscription Services Ltd., Oakfield House, Perrymount Rd., Haywards Heath, Sussex RH16 3DH, England. TEL 44-1444-445353; Dist. in Us by: American Educational Systems, 173 W. 81st St., New York, NY 10024. TEL 800-717-2669. FAX 212-501-8926) Ed. Andrew Capon. adv. **Document type:** trade publication.
—BLDSC (4548.895300).

INTERNATIONAL SMART CARD INDUSTRY GUIDE. see COMPUTERS — Computer Industry

332.7 382 UK ISSN 0968-4026
INTERNATIONAL TRADE FINANCE. s-m. £435($781) (overseas £488) (effective 1993). Financial Times Business Information, Newsletters (Subsidiary of: Financial Times Group), 126 Jermyn St., London SW1Y 4UJ, England. TEL 44-171-411-4414. FAX 44-171-441-4415. (also avail. in microform from UMI) **Document type:** newsletter.
●Also available online. Vendor(s): Information Access Co.
 Description: Covers all aspects on international trade finance and insurance, including coverage of export credit insurance and detailed analysis of major project finance packages. Includes regular assessments of country risk and an annual survey of export finance and insurance conditions in ten key exporting nations.

332 NE
INTERNATIONAL TRANSFER PRICING JOURNAL. (Text in English) 1993. bi-m. $375 (effective 1997). I B F D Publications B.V., P.O. Box 20237, 1000 HE Amsterdam, Netherlands. TEL 31-20-6267726. FAX 31-20-6228658. TELEX 13217 INTAX NL. (In US: IBFD Publications USA, Inc., 4 Maple Ln., Valatie, NY 12184. TEL 800-299-6330. FAX 518-758-2246) **Indexed:** Euro.LJI, LJI.
 Description: Covers major current issues in international transfer pricing, including case reports and news of worldwide developments.

332 SA
INTERNATIONAL WERKS. 1993. irreg. Werksmans, P.O. Box 927, Johannesburg 2000, South Africa. Ed. Charles Butler. R&P contact: Kandy Wright. adv. contact: Kandy Wright. **Document type:** bulletin.
 Description: Discusses issues relating to foreign investment in South Africa.

332 YU
INVESTBANKA; list radne zajednice investbanka. 1964. m. free. Investbanka, Terazije 9, Box 152, 11001 Belgrade, Yugoslavia. TEL 011 658-582. FAX 320-617. TELEX 11147. Ed. Ljubisa Stojiljkovic. adv.; charts; illus.

332 YU
INVESTBANKA. ANNUAL REPORT. 1956. a. free. Investbanka, Terazije 9, Box 152, 11001 Belgrade, Yugoslavia. TEL 38-11-656-842. FAX 38-11-320-617. TELEX 11147. Ed. Ljubisa K. Plavsic. circ. 1,200. **Document type:** corporate report.
 Formerly: Yugoslovenska Investiciona Banka. Annual Report (ISSN 0075-4536)

332 FR ISSN 0759-7673
INVESTIR. 1974. w. 595 F. (outside Europe 855 F.). Societe d'Information Economique et Financiere, Investir Publications, 48 rue Notre-Dame des Victoires, 75002 Paris, France. TEL 1-44-88-48-00. FAX 1-44-88-48-01. Ed. Jean-Claude Regnier. adv. contact: Frederic Huignard. circ. 120,000 (controlled). **Document type:** newspaper.

332.1 MW
INVESTMENT AND DEVELOPMENT BANK OF MALAWI. ANNUAL REPORT AND ACCOUNTS. (Text in English) 1973. a. Investment and Development Bank of Malawi Ltd., P.O. Box 358, Blantyre, Malawi. TEL 265-620055. FAX 265-623353. TELEX 45201 MI. E-mail: indebank@malawi.net. Ed. Webster Nyengo. circ. 500. **Document type:** corporate report.

332 332.62 UK ISSN 0267-3770
INVESTMENT MANAGEMENT. 1985. 10/yr. £40 (foreign £90). Mitre House Publishing Ltd., The Clifton Centre, 110 Clifton St., London EC2A 4HD, England. TEL 071-729-6644. Ed. Richard Blausten. adv. contact: Joseph Gaydecki. circ. 8,000. (back issues avail.) **Document type:** trade publication.

332 UK ISSN 1319-0830
AL-IQTISADIYYAH; jaridat al-arab al-iqtisadiyyah al-duwaliyyah - the international Arab business daily. Variant title: Al Eqtisadiah. (Text in Arabic) 1992. d. £150 (effective 1997). Saudi Research and Marketing, Arab Press House, 184 High Holborn, London WC1V 7AP, England. TEL 44-171-831-8181. FAX 44-171-404-6311. (And: P.O. Box 4556, Jeddah 21441, Saudi Arabia. TEL 966-2-6691888. FAX 966-2-6671650; Subscr. in U.S. and Canada to: Attache International, 3050 Broadway, Ste. 300, Boulder, CO 80304-3154. TEL 303-442-8900. FAX 303-442-7979) Ed. Mohammad Tunsi. adv.: B&W page $7893; 14 x 21 3/16. bk.rev. cols./p.: 8; pp./issue: 12. (broadsheet format) **Document type:** newspaper.
 Description: Covers business and investment opportunities, market trends, financial issues, with a particular focus on the Gulf region.

332 IE ISSN 0790-066X
IRISH BANK OFFICIALS ASSOCIATION NEWSHEET. 1919. m. $25. Irish Bank Officials Association, 93 St. Stephen's Green, Dublin 2, Ireland. TEL 353-1-8722255. FAX 353-1-4780567. Ed. Ken Doyle. R&P contact: Ken Doyle. adv. contact: Joan McSwiney. bk.rev.; circ. 11,000. **Document type:** newsletter.

332.1 IE ISSN 0021-1060
HC257.I6
IRISH BANKING REVIEW. 1957. q. Irish Bankers' Federation, Nassau House, 40 Nassau St., Dublin 2, Ireland. TEL 353-1-6715311. FAX 353-1-6796680. TELEX 93957. Ed. F. O'Regan. circ. 4,000. **Indexed:** C.R.E.J., Key to Econ.Sci., LJI, P.A.I.S., Rural Recreat.Tour.Abstr., World Agri.Econ.& Rural Sociol.Abstr., World Bank.Abstr. **Document type:** trade publication.
—BLDSC (4569.500000).
 Description: Encourages discussion of economic and development issues, including monetary systems, private sector projects and macro-economic policies.

332.153 SU ISSN 1319-1314
ISLAMIC DEVELOPMENT BANK. ANNUAL REPORT. (Editions in Arabic, English and French) 1975. a. free. Islamic Development Bank, P.O. Box 5925, 21432 Jeddah, Saudi Arabia. TEL 966-2-6361400. FAX 966-2-6366871. TELEX 601137 ISDB SJ. circ. 15,000. (also avail. in microfilm) **Document type:** corporate report.
 Description: Covers world economic developments and their impacts, economic cooperation, major policy developments and operations.

332.1 IS ISSN 0334-2093
HG3260.A5
ISRAEL'S BANKING SYSTEM. (Editions in English and Hebrew) is.33. Bank of Israel, Kiryath Ben Gurion, P.O. Box 780, Jerusalem 91007, Israel.

J A S S A. see BUSINESS AND ECONOMICS — Investments

332 SZ
JAHRBUCH ZUM FINANZ- UND RECHNUNGSWESEN. a. Weka Verlag AG, Hermetschloostr. 77, CH-8010 Zurich, Switzerland. TEL 41-1-4348888. FAX 41-1-4328201. Ed. Hans Siegwart. **Document type:** bulletin.

332 338 JA ISSN 0385-2369
HG41
JAPANESE FINANCE AND INDUSTRY: QUARTERLY SURVEY. (Text in English) 1949. q. free. Industrial Bank of Japan, Reference and Statistics Center - Nippon Kogyo Ginko, 1-3-3 Marunouchi, Chiyoda-ku, Tokyo, Japan. charts; stat. **Indexed:** Key to Econ.Sci., P.A.I.S.
—BLDSC (4650.765800); UnCover.
 Formerly: Quarterly Survey of Japanese Finance and Industry (ISSN 0039-6249)

332 CC
JIANGXI CHENGSHI JINRONG/JIANGXI URBAN FINANCE. (Text in Chinese) m. Jiangxi Sheng Chengshi Jinrong Xuehui - Jiangxi Urban Finance Society, No. 23, Tie Jie, Nanchang, Jiangxi 330008, People's Republic of China. TEL 51918. Ed. Tu Yide.

332 US
JINRONG SHIBAO/FINANCIAL NEWS. (Text in Chinese) d. $314.70. China Books & Periodicals, Inc., 2929 24th St., San Francisco, CA 94110. TEL 415-282-2994. FAX 415-282-0994. **Document type:** newspaper.

332 CC ISSN 0529-2794
JINRONG YANJIU/BANKING AND FINANCE STUDIES. (Text in Chinese) m. Zhongguo Jinrong Xuehui - Chinese Society of Banking and Finance, 1 Baiguanglu Toutiao, Beijing 100053, People's Republic of China. TEL 6014422. Ed. Zhao Haixian.

332 368 CC ISSN 1005-4383
JINRONG YU BAOXIAN/FINANCE AND INSURANCE. (Subseries of: Fuyin Baokan Ziliao) (Text in Chinese) m. $162.01. Zhongguo Renmin Daxue, Shubao Ziliao Zhongxin - China People's University, Book & Newspaper Information Center, 3 Zhang Zizhong Rd., P.O. Box 1122, Beijing 100007, People's Republic of China. TEL 86-10-4015080. (Dist. in US by: China Publications Service, Box 49614, Chicago, IL 60649. TEL 312-288-3291. FAX 312-288-8570)
 Description: Covers Chinese currency, banking and finance, insurance, investment and security issues.

332 FR ISSN 0021-8049
JOURNAL DES FINANCES.* 1867. w. 1160 F. 10 Place du General Catroux, 75858 Paris Cedex, France. TEL 45-08-42-75. FAX 42-36-49-98. TELEX 215 760 F. Ed. C. Pophillat. adv.; bk.rev.; abstr.; bibl.; stat.; index. circ. 103,000.
—CCC.

332.1 630 US
JOURNAL OF AGRICULTURAL LENDING. q. $190 non-members; members $125. American Bankers Association, Agricultural Banking Division, 1120 Connecticut Ave., N.W., Washington, DC 20036. TEL 202-663-5378. FAX 202-828-4540. (also avail. in microform from UMI)
●Also available online. Vendor(s): UMI.
 Description: Supplies current information on agricultural lending, including annual Farm Credit Situation Survey results; and profiles of prominent industry figures.

BUSINESS AND ECONOMICS — BANKING AND FINANCE

332.1 US ISSN 1078-1196
HG4001
JOURNAL OF APPLIED CORPORATE FINANCE. 1988. q. $95 to professionals (foreign $125); institutions $125 (foreign $145); students and professors $35 (foreign $50). (Bank of America) Stern Stewart Management Services, Inc., 40 W. 57th St., New York, NY 10019-4001. TEL 212-261-0600. FAX 212-581-6420. Ed. Donald H. Chew, Jr. R&P contact: Donald H. Chew. cum. index. **Indexed:** Account.Ind. (1988-). **Document type:** academic/scholarly publication, trade publication.
—BLDSC (4942.375000); SWETS; UMI; UnCover. **CCC.**
Formerly: Continental Bank Journal of Applied Corporate Finance (ISSN 0898-4484)
Refereed Serial

JOURNAL OF BANK ACCOUNTING & AUDITING. see BUSINESS AND ECONOMICS — Accounting

332 657 US ISSN 1070-941X
JOURNAL OF BANK COST & MANAGEMENT ACCOUNTING. 1985. 3/yr. $90 in US and Canada; elsewhere $100 (effective 1997 & 1998). National Association of Bank Cost and Management Accounting, 2385 Castilian Cir., Box 458, Northbrook, IL 60062-7614. TEL 847-272-4233. FAX 847-272-6445. Ed. Albert E. Schneider, Jr. R&P contact: Nancy Basinger. circ. 500. (also avail. in microform from UMI) **Document type:** academic/scholarly publication.
● Also available online. Vendor(s): UMI.
Description: Covers issues and practice advances affecting cost and management accounting in the financial services industry.

332 336 US ISSN 0895-4720
KF6495.B2
JOURNAL OF BANK TAXATION. (Former pub.: Faulkner & Gray) 1987. q. $151.50 (overseas $232.45) (effective 1995). Warren, Gorham & Lamont, One Penn Plaza, New York, NY 10119. TEL 212-971-5000. FAX 212-971-5113. (Subscr. to: The Park Square Bldg., 31 St. James Ave., Boston, MA 02116-4112. TEL 800-950-1252) Ed. John W. Alexander; Pub. Thomas J. Kelly. circ. 1,500. **Document type:** trade publication.
—BLDSC (4951.111000); UMI. **CCC.**
Description: Covers important developments for tax professionals dealing with banks.

332 NE ISSN 0378-4266
HG23 CODEN: JBFIDO
JOURNAL OF BANKING AND FINANCE. (Text in English) 1977. m. fl.2500($1437) (effective 1998). (Universita degli Studi di Bergamo, IT) North-Holland (Subsidiary of: Elsevier Science B.V.), P.O. Box 211, 1000 AE Amsterdam, Netherlands. TEL 31-20-4853911. FAX 31-20-4853598. TELEX 18582 ESPA NL. (Subscr. in the Americas to: Elsevier Science, Regional Sales Office, Box 945, New York, NY 10159-0945. TEL 212-633-3730. FAX 212-633-3680; Subscr. in Australasia and the Far East to: Elsevier Science (Singapore) Pte Ltd, No.1 Temasek Ave., No.17-01 Millenia Tower, Singapore 039192, Singapore. TEL 65-434-3727. FAX 65-337-2230; Subscr. in Japan to: Elsevier Science Japan, 9-15 Higashi-Azabu 1-chome, Minato-ku, Tokyo 106, Japan. TEL 81-3-5561-5033. FAX 81-3-5561-5047) Ed. E.I. Altman. adv.; bk.rev.; charts; illus.; index. (also avail. in microform from UMI; back issues avail.; reprint service avail. from SWZ) **Indexed:** ABI Inform., ASCA, B.P.I., BPIA, Bus.Ind., C.R.E.J., Cont.Pg.Manage., Curr.Cont., ELLIS, J.Cont.Quant.Meth., J.of Econ.Lit., Manage.Cont., P.A.I.S., Risk Abstr., SSCI, Tr.& Indus.Ind., World Bank.Abstr. **Document type:** academic/scholarly publication.
—BLDSC (4951.112000); Genuine Article; KR SourceOne; SWETS; UMI; UnCover. **CCC.**
Incorporates (1985-1989): Studies in Banking and Finance (ISSN 0169-6319)
Description: Provides an outlet for the increasing flow of scholarly research concerning financial institutions and the money and capital markets within which they function.
Refereed Serial

332 346 AT ISSN 1034-3040
JOURNAL OF BANKING AND FINANCE - LAW AND PRACTICE. 4/yr. Aus.$245. (Banking Law Association) L B C Information Services, 50 Waterloo Rd., N. Ryde, N.S.W. 2113, Australia. TEL 61-2-99366444. FAX 61-2-98889706. TELEX ASBOOK 27995. Ed. Gregory Burton, R. Baxt. **Indexed:** L.R.I. **Document type:** trade publication.
—BLDSC (4951.113000); UnCover.
Description: Contains articles of topical interest on legislative and case law developments affecting banking and finance law and practice.

332 US
JOURNAL OF BUSINESS (SPOKANE). Variant title: Spokane Journal of Business. (Includes supplement: Spokane Woman) 1986. 24/yr. $22. Northwest Business Press, Inc., 112 E. First Ave., Spokane, WA 99202. TEL 509-456-5257. Ed. Richard Ripley. R&P contact: Paul Read. adv. circ. 15,000. (also avail. in microform from UMI; reprint service avail. from SCH) **Indexed:** Acad.Ind., Curr.Cont., Manage.Cont. **Document type:** newspaper.
● Also available online. Vendor(s): UMI.
Description: Covers local business news for Spokane, Washington, Coeur d'Alene and other north Idaho and eastern Washington markets.

332 NE ISSN 0929-1199
HG4001
JOURNAL OF CORPORATE FINANCE; contracting, governance and organization. (Text in English) 1994. q. fl.375($216) (effective 1998). North-Holland (Subsidiary of: Elsevier Science B.V.), P.O. Box 211, 1000 AE Amsterdam, Netherlands. TEL 31-20-4853911. FAX 31-20-4853598. (Subscr. in the Americas to: Elsevier Science, Regional Sales Office, Box 945, New York, NY 10159-0945. TEL 212-633-3730. FAX 212-633-3680; Subscr. in Australasia and the Far East to: Elsevier Science (Singapore) Pte Ltd, No.1 Temasek Ave., No.17-01 Millenia Tower, Singapore 039192, Singapore. TEL 65-434-3727. FAX 63-337-2230; Subscr. in Japan to: Elsevier Science Japan, 9-15 Higashi-Azabu 1-chome, Minato-ku Tokyo 106, Japan. TEL 81-3-5561-5033. FAX 81-3-5561-5047) Eds. Kenneth Lehn, Wayne Marr. adv.; abstr.; index. (also avail. in microform from UMI; back issues avail.) **Document type:** academic/scholarly publication.
—BLDSC (4965.336300); SWETS; UnCover. **CCC.**
Description: Publishes empirical and theoretical papers that combine the disciplines of financial economics, industrial organization, corporate law, accounting, and applied econometrics in analyzing the contractual underpinnings of firms.
Refereed Serial

332.7 US
HG1507
THE JOURNAL OF CREDIT & RISK MANAGEMENT. 1918. m. $60. Robert Morris Associates, One Liberty Place, Ste. 2300, 1650 Market St., Philadelphia, PA 19107. TEL 215-851-9100. Ed. Elizabeth Bond. bk.rev.; charts; illus.; stat.; index, cum.index. circ. 27,000. (also avail. in microfilm from UMI; microfiche from CIS; reprint service avail.) **Indexed:** ABI Inform., Account.Ind. (1974-), B.P.I., Bank.Lit.Ind., BPIA, Bus.Ind., Cont.Pg.Manage., Curr.Cont., Ind.Per.Art.Relat.Law, Manage.Cont., P.A.I.S., SRI, Tr.& Indus.Ind., World Bank.Abstr. **Document type:** trade publication.
● Also available online. Vendor(s): Information Access Co., UMI.
—BLDSC (5010.290000); KR SourceOne; UMI; UnCover. **CCC.**
Former titles (until 1996): Journal of Commercial Lending (ISSN 1062-6271); (until 1992): Journal of Commercial Bank Lending (ISSN 0021-986X); (until 1968): Robert Morris Associates Bulletin.
Description: Covers issues relating to commercial lending, risk management and related topics.

332 US ISSN 1074-1240
HG6024.A3
JOURNAL OF DERIVATIVES. 1993. q. $280 (foreign $355) (effective 1996). Institutional Investor Journals, 488 Madison Ave., New York, NY 10022. TEL 212-224-3185. FAX 212-224-3527. Ed. Stephen Figlewski; Pub. Gauri Goyal. adv.; B&W page $4500, color page $7700; adv. contact: Robin DuCharme.
—BLDSC (4968.758000); SWETS. **CCC.**
Description: Bridges the gap between academic theory and practical application. Includes analysis of the market.

332 341 US ISSN 1083-9798
▼**JOURNAL OF EMERGING MARKETS.** 1996. 3/yr. $45 to individuals; institutions $95; libraries $75 (effective 1996-97). (Emerging Markets Traders Association) Center for Global Education, St. John's University, 8000 Utopia Pkwy., Jamaica, New York, NY 11439. TEL 718-990-1951. FAX 718-380-8934. Eds. Maximo Eng, Francis Lees. adv.: page $195; adv. contact: Gregory Reisert. bk.rev. circ. 140. (back issues avail.) **Document type:** academic/scholarly publication.
Refereed Serial

332 519 NE ISSN 0927-5398
HG23 CODEN: JEFIEC
JOURNAL OF EMPIRICAL FINANCE. (Text in English) 1993. q. fl.400($230) (effective 1998). North-Holland (Subsidiary of: Elsevier Science B.V.), P.O. Box 211, 1000 AE Amsterdam, Netherlands. TEL 31-20-4853911. FAX 31-20-4853598. TELEX 18582 ESPA NL. (Subscr. in the Americas to: Elsevier Science, Regional Sales Office, Box 945, New York, NY 10159-0945. TEL 212-633-3730. FAX 212-633-3680; Subscr. in Australasia and the Far East to: Elsevier Science (Singapore) Pte Ltd, No.1 Temasek Ave., No.17-01 Millenia Tower, Singapore 039192, Singapore. TEL 65-434-3727. FAX 65-337-2230; Subscr. in Japan to: Elsevier Science Japan, 9-15 Higashi-Azabu 1-chome, Minato-ku Tokyo 106, Japan. TEL 81-3-5561-5033. FAX 81-3-5561-5047) Ed.Bd. adv.; stat. (also avail. in microform from UMI; back issues avail.) **Document type:** academic/scholarly publication.
—BLDSC (4977.630000); SWETS. **CCC.**
Description: Publishes empirical studies dealing with econometric analyses of financial markets and data, including forecasting, risk measurement, nonlinear dynamic models, and applications in corporate finance, asset pricing, bond markets.
Refereed Serial

332 US
JOURNAL OF ENTERTAINMENT FINANCE.* 1993. bi-m. $225. A E R Publications, Box 13392, Arlington, VA 22219-3392. TEL 202-342-0526. adv.: B&W page $2500. circ. 6,500. **Document type:** trade publication.

THE JOURNAL OF ENTREPRENEURIAL AND SMALL FIRM FINANCE. see BUSINESS AND ECONOMICS — Small Business

332 US ISSN 0022-1082
HG1 CODEN: JLFIAN
JOURNAL OF FINANCE. 1946. 5/yr. $43 to individuals; institutions $59. American Finance Association, c/o W. Michael Keenan, Stern School of Business, New York University, 44 W. 4th St., Ste. 9-190, New York, NY 10012. TEL 212-998-0355. (Subscr. to: Fulco, Box 3000, Denville, NJ 07843. TEL 800-875-2997. FAX 201-627-5872) Ed. Rene Stulz. adv.; bk.rev.; index. circ. 7,500. (also avail. in microform from MIM,UMI; reprint service avail. from UMI,KTO) **Indexed:** ABI Inform., Account.Ind. (1974-), ASCA, B.P.I., Bank.Lit.Ind., Bk.Rev.Ind. (1976-1982), BPIA, Bus.Ind., C.R.E.J., Child.Bk.Rev.Ind. (1976-1982), Cont.Pg.Manage., Curr.Cont., IBR, J.Cont.Quant.Meth., J.of Econ.Lit., Key to Econ.Sci., Manage.Cont., Math.R., Mgmt.& Market.Abstr., P.A.I.S., Risk Abstr., SCIMP (1978-), SSCI, Tr.& Indus.Ind., World Bank.Abstr. **Document type:** academic/scholarly publication.
● Also available online. Vendor(s): Information Access Co.
—BLDSC (4984.220000); Genuine Article; KR SourceOne; SWETS; UMI; UnCover. **CCC.**

BUSINESS AND ECONOMICS — BANKING AND FINANCE

658 US ISSN 0022-1090
HG1 CODEN: JFQAAC
JOURNAL OF FINANCIAL AND QUANTITATIVE ANALYSIS. 1966. 4/yr. $40 to individuals; libraries $85; students $25 (effective 1997). University of Washington, Graduate School of Business Administration, 326 Lewis Hall, Box 353200, Seattle, WA 98195. FAX 206-543-6872. Eds. Jonathan Karpoff, Paul Malatesta. adv.; charts; stat.; index; circ. 3,200 (paid). (also avail. in microform from UMI; reprint service avail. from SCH,UMI) Indexed: ABI Inform., Account.Ind. (1974-), ASCA, B.P.I., Bank.Lit.Ind., BPIA, C.R.E.J., Cont.Pg.Manage., Curr.Cont., IBR, J. of Econ.Lit., J.Cont.Quant.Meth., Lib.Lit., Manage.Cont., Oper.Res.Manage.Sci., Qual.Contr.Appl.Stat., Risk Abstr., SSCI, Tr.& Indus.Ind., World Bank.Abstr. **Document type:** academic/scholarly publication.
—BLDSC (4984.230000); Genuine Article; KR SourceOne; SWETS; UMI; UnCover.
  Description: Furthers advanced research in finance.
  Refereed Serial

JOURNAL OF FINANCIAL CRIME. see *LAW — Criminal Law*

332 378 US ISSN 0093-3961
HG174
JOURNAL OF FINANCIAL EDUCATION. 1972. s-a. $15 to individuals; institutions $25. c/o Jean L. Heck, Ed., Dept. of Finance, Villanova University, Villanova, PA 19085. TEL 610-519-4325. adv. circ. 800. (back issues avail.) **Document type:** academic/scholarly publication.
  Formerly: Financial Education (ISSN 0190-7654)

332 US ISSN 1062-8924
HG176.7
JOURNAL OF FINANCIAL ENGINEERING.* q. membership. (International Association of Financial Engineers) Kolb Publishing Company, 9638 Mountain Ridge Pl., Boulder, CO 80302-9336.
—BLDSC (4984.259200); SWETS.

332 II ISSN 0970-4205
HG4001 CODEN: JFANE9
JOURNAL OF FINANCIAL MANAGEMENT AND ANALYSIS; international review of finance. (Text in English) 1988. s-a. $85. Om Sai Ram Centre for Financial Management Research, 15 Prakash Co-operative Housing Society, Relief Rd., Santacruz (W.), Mumbai 400 054, India. TEL 91-22-6121715. Ed. M.R.K. Swamy. adv.; bk.rev.; charts; stat. circ. 2,500. (back issues avail.) Indexed: Geo.Abstr.P.G., IDA. **Document type:** academic/scholarly publication.
●Also available online.
—BLDSC (4984.260000); SWETS.
  Description: Offers techniques and new concepts backed up by case studies. Provides a bridge between financial management theory and practice in line with demands of today's techno-economic corporate, cooperative and public-sector business environments to find solutions to critical issues in financial management.
  Refereed Serial

332 US ISSN 0892-3159
JOURNAL OF FINANCIAL PLANNING TODAY. 1977. q. $100 (effective 1996 & 1997). New Directions Publications, Inc., Box 6097, W. Palm Beach, FL 33405. TEL 407-434-0100. FAX 407-641-4801. Ed. B.E. Newmark. adv.; bk.rev.; circ. 500 (controlled). Indexed: Account.Ind. (1979-), BPIA, Bus.Ind., C.L.I., L.R.I., Leg.Per., Tr.& Indus.Ind. **Document type:** academic/scholarly publication.
●Also available online. Vendor(s): UMI.
—BLDSC (3926.963500). **CCC.**
  Former titles: Financial Planning Today (ISSN 0164-9698); Journal of Financial Planning (ISSN 0195-9948)
  Refereed Serial

332 340 UK
JOURNAL OF FINANCIAL REGULATION AND COMPLIANCE. 1992. q. £205 to European Union; U.S. & Canada $320; rest of world £220. Henry Stewart Publications, Russell House, 28-30 Little Russell St., London WC1A 2HN, England. TEL 44-171-404-3040. FAX 44-171-404-2081. E-mail: 100622.3264@compuserve.com. (Subscr. in US and Canada to: 810 E. 10th St., Box 1897, Lawrence, KS 66044. TEL 913-843-1221. FAX 913-843-1274) Ed. Daryn Moody. adv. contact: Fraser Tant. **Document type:** trade publication.
  Formerly (until 1993): Regulatory Law and Practice (ISSN 0968-087X)
  Description: Publishes articles and notes that enhance an understanding of, and thinking on, the practice, systems, and theory of financial regulation and compliance.
  Refereed Serial

JOURNAL OF FINANCIAL RESEARCH. see *BUSINESS AND ECONOMICS*

332 368 US ISSN 0920-8550
HG1 CODEN: JFSRE9
JOURNAL OF FINANCIAL SERVICES RESEARCH. 1987. bi-m. fl.800 to institutions; $411 to institutions in U.S. (effective 1998). Kluwer Academic Publishers Boston, Box 358, Accord Sta., Hingham, MA 02018-0358. TEL 617-871-6300. FAX 617-871-6528. TELEX 200190. E-mail: services@wkap.nl; URL: http://www.wkap.nl. (Dist. outside N. America by: Kluwer Academic Publishers Group, P.O. Box 322, 3300 AH Dordrecht, Netherlands. TEL 31-78-6392392. FAX 31-78-6546474) Ed. Robert Eisenbeis. (also avail. in microform from UMI; reprint service avail. from SWZ,UMI) Indexed: ASCA, Curr.Cont., J.of Econ.Lit., SSCI. **Document type:** academic/scholarly publication.
—BLDSC (4984.266000); Genuine Article; SWETS; UMI; UnCover. **CCC.**
  Description: Publishes original research dealing with private and public policy questions arising from the evolution of the financial services sector.
  Refereed Serial

332 US
JOURNAL OF FINANCIAL STATEMENT ANALYSIS. q. $200 (foreign $275) (effective 1996). Institutional Investor Journals, 488 Madison Ave., New York, NY 10022. TEL 212-224-3185. FAX 212-224-3527.
  Description: Explains how to better analyze and interpret financial statements, combining both accounting and finance disciplines.

JOURNAL OF INTERNATIONAL BANKING LAW. see *LAW — Corporate Law*

332 UK ISSN 0954-1314
HG4027.5
JOURNAL OF INTERNATIONAL FINANCIAL MANAGEMENT AND ACCOUNTING. 1988. 3/yr. £91($153) (foreign £105) (effective 1997). Blackwell Publishers Ltd., 108 Cowley Rd., Oxford OX4 1JF, England. TEL 44-1865-791100. E-mail: jnlinfo@blackwellpublishers.co.uk; URL: http://www.blackwellpublishers.co.uk. Ed. Frederick Choi. circ. 600. (reprint service avail. from SWZ) Indexed: Account.Ind. (1989-), B.P.I. **Document type:** academic/scholarly publication.
—BLDSC (5007.661200); KR SourceOne; SWETS; UMI. **CCC.**
  Refereed Serial

332.04505 UK ISSN 1042-4431
HG3879
JOURNAL OF INTERNATIONAL FINANCIAL MARKETS, INSTITUTIONS & MONEY. 1991. q. fl.350($201) (effective 1998). Elsevier Science Ltd., Pergamon, P.O. Box 800, Kidlington, Oxford OX5 1DX. TEL 44-1865-843000. FAX 44-1865-843010. E-mail: nlinfo-f@elsevier.nl; usinfo-f@elsevier.com; URL: http://www.elsevier.nl/. (Subscr. to: Elsevier Science, Regional Sales Office, P.O. Box 211, 1000 AE Amsterdam, Netherlands. TEL 31-20-4853757. FAX 31-20-4853432; Subscr. in the Americas to: Elsevier Science, Regional Sales Office, Box 945, New York, NY 10159-0945. TEL 212-633-3730. FAX 212-633-3680; Subscr. in Australasia and the Far East to: Elsevier Science (Singapore) Pte Ltd, No.1 Temasek Ave., No.17-01 Millenia Tower, Singapore 039192, Singapore. TEL 65-434-3727. FAX 65-337-2230) (also avail. in microform from UMI; reprint service avail.) Indexed: Cont.Pg.Mana **Document type:** academic/scholarly publication.
—BLDSC (5007.661300); SWETS. **CCC.**
  Description: Includes original articles dealing with the international aspects of financial markets, institutions, and money.
  Refereed Serial

332 UK ISSN 0261-5606
HG3879
JOURNAL OF INTERNATIONAL MONEY AND FINANCE. 1982. bi-m. fl.1142($656) (effective 1998). Elsevier Science Ltd., Pergamon, P.O. Box 800, Kidlington, Oxford OX5 1DX, England. TEL 44-1865-843000. FAX 44-1865-843010. TELEX 83111 BHPOXF G. E-mail: nlinfo-f@elsevier.nl; usinfo-f@elsevier.com; forinfo-kyf04035@niftyserve.or.jp; URL: http://www.elsevier.nl/. (Subscr. to: Elsevier Science, Regional Sales Office, P.O. Box 211, 10009 AE Amsterdam, Netherlands. TEL 31-20-4853757. FAX 31-20-4853432; Subscr. in the Americas to: Elsevier Science, Regional Sales Office, Box 945, New York, NY 10159-0945. TEL 212-633-3730. FAX 212-633-3680; Subscr. in Australasia and the Far East to: Elsevier Science (Singapore) Pte Ltd, No.1 Temasek Ave., No.17-10 Millenia Tower, Singapore 039192, Singapore. TEL 65-434-3727. FAX 65-337-2230) Eds. James R. Lothian, Michael T. Melvin. bk.rev.; index. (also avail. in microform from UMI; back issues avail.) Indexed: ABI Inform., ASCA, Asian-Pac.Econ.Lit., BPIA, Cont.Pg.Manage., Curr.Cont., J.of Econ.Lit., Risk Abstr., SSCI. **Document type:** academic/scholarly publication.
—BLDSC (5007.677000); Genuine Article; SWETS; UMI; UnCover. **CCC.**
  Description: Covers foreign exchange, balance of payments, international interactions of prices, incomes and money, multinational corporate finance, foreign aid, and international economic institutions.
  Refereed Serial

JOURNAL OF INTERNATIONAL TRUST AND CORPORATE PLANNING. see *LAW — Corporate Law*

JOURNAL OF MANAGEMENT & GOVERNANCE. see *BUSINESS AND ECONOMICS — Management*

BUSINESS AND ECONOMICS — BANKING AND FINANCE

332   NE   ISSN 0304-3932
HG201   CODEN: JMOEDW
JOURNAL OF MONETARY ECONOMICS. (Text in English) 1975. bi-m. fl.1430($822) (effective 1998). North-Holland (Subsidiary of: Elsevier Science B.V.), P.O. Box 211, 1000 AE Amsterdam, Netherlands. TEL 31-20-4853911. FAX 31-20-4853598. TELEX 18582 ESPA NL. (Subscr. in the Americas to: Elsevier Science, Regional Sales Office, Box 945, New York, NY 10159-0945. TEL 212-633-3730. FAX 212-633-3680; Subscr. in Australasia and the Far East to: Elsevier Science (Singapore) Pte Ltd, No.1 Temasek Ave., No.17-01 Millenia Tower, Singapore 039192, Singapore. TEL 65-434-3727. FAX 65-337-2230; Subscr. in Japan to: Elsevier Science Japan, 9-15 Higashi-Azabu 1-chome, Minato-ku, Tokyo 106, Japan. TEL 81-3-5561-5033. FAX 81-3-5561-5047) Eds. Robert King, Charles Plosser. (also avail. in microform from UMI; back issues avail.; reprint service avail. from ISI,SWZ) **Indexed:** ABI Inform., ASCA, BPIA, Bus.Ind., C.R.E.J., Cont.Pg.Manage., Curr.Cont., ELLIS, J.of Econ.Lit., Manage.Cont., P.A.I.S., SSCI, Tr.& Indus.Ind., World Bank.Abstr. **Document type:** academic/scholarly publication.
—BLDSC (5020.860000); Genuine Article; SWETS; UMI; UnCover. **CCC.**
  Description: Discusses problems in the broader field of monetary economics, with particular emphasis on monetary analysis.
Refereed Serial

332   US   ISSN 0022-2879
HG201   CODEN: JMCBBT
JOURNAL OF MONEY, CREDIT & BANKING. 1969. q. $45 to individuals (Canada $54.65; elsewhere $51.50); institutions $100 (Canada $113.50; elsewhere $106.50); electronic version $90; print and electronic versions $125 to institutions (Canada $140.25; elsewhere $131.50) (effective 1998). Ohio State University Press, 1070 Carmack Rd., Columbus, OH 43210. TEL 614-292-6930. FAX 614-292-2065. E-mail: mcgrothers.1@osu.edu; jstor-info@umich.edu; URL: http://www.jstor.org/journals/00222879.html. Eds. Stephen G. Cecchetti, Paul D. Evans. adv.; bk.rev.; index; circ. 3,700 (paid). (also avail. in microfiche from UMI; back issues avail., reprint service avail. from ISI,SCH,UMI) **Indexed:** ABI Inform., ASCA, Asian-Pac.Econ.Lit., B.P.I., Bank.Lit.Ind., BPIA, Bus.Ind., C.R.E.J., Cont.Pg.Manage., Curr.Cont., J. of Econ.Lit., Manage.Cont., P.A.I.S., Risk Abstr., Soc.Sci.Ind., SSCI, World Bank.Abstr. **Document type:** academic/scholarly publication.
●Also available online. Vendor(s): Information Access Co.
Also available on CD-ROM. Producer(s): UMI.
—BLDSC (5020.880000); Genuine Article; KR SourceOne; SWETS; UMI; UnCover. **CCC.**
  Description: Reports major findings in the study of financial institutions, financial markets, monetary and fiscal policy, credit markets, money and banking.
Refereed Serial

JOURNAL OF MULTINATIONAL FINANCIAL MANAGEMENT. see BUSINESS AND ECONOMICS — Management

332   US   ISSN 1071-846X
HG4930
JOURNAL OF MUTUAL FUND SERVICES. 8/yr. $795 (foreign $895). Dalbar Inc., 600 Atlantic Ave., T-30, Boston, MA 02110-2226. TEL 617-723-6400. FAX 617-624-7200. E-mail: tjmfs@dalbar.com. Ed. Elizabeth Pease. adv. contact: Kelly Doherty. (back issues avail.) **Document type:** trade publication.
  Formerly (until 1993): F A C S - Funds Agents, Custodians, Suppliers (ISSN 0887-8161)

332   US   ISSN 1082-3220
HG5993
▼**JOURNAL OF PROJECT FINANCE.** 1995. q. $290 (foreign $365) (effective 1996). Institutional Investor Journals, 488 Madison Ave., New York, NY 10022. TEL 212-224-3185. FAX 212-224-3527. —**CCC.**
  Description: Provides articles and case studies on specific aspects of project finance deals.

JOURNAL OF REAL ESTATE FINANCE AND ECONOMICS. see REAL ESTATE

332   US   ISSN 0195-2064
HG1501
JOURNAL OF RETAIL BANKING. 1979. q. $97. American Banker - Bond Buyer, Newsletter Division (Subsidiary of: Thomson Financial Services Company), One State St. Plaza, New York, NY 10004-1549. TEL 212-943-5908. Ed. Leonard Berry. adv. circ. 2,800. (also avail. in microform from SCH, UMI) **Indexed:** ABI Inform., B.P.I., Bank.Lit.Ind., BPIA, Bus.Ind., Manage.Cont., P.A.I.S., Tr.& Indus.Ind., World Bank.Abstr. **Document type:** trade publication.
●Also available online. Vendor(s): Information Access Co.
—KR SourceOne; SWETS; UMI; UnCover. **CCC.**

332   YU   ISSN 0350-4077
JUGOSLOVENSKO BANKARSTVO. 1972. m. $30. Udruzenje Banka Jugoslavije, Masarikova 5, Belgrade, Yugoslavia. Ed. Dr. Milovan Milutinovic. bk.rev. circ. 2,100.

JUMBO FLASH REPORT. see BUSINESS AND ECONOMICS — Investments

332 332.6   US   ISSN 8756-2332
JUMBO RATE NEWS. 1983. w. $445. Bauer Communications, Inc., 2655 LeJeune Rd., PH-1A, Drawer 145510, Coral Gables, FL 33114-5510. TEL 305-445-9500; 800-388-6686. FAX 305-445-6775. Ed. Paul A. Bauer. bk.rev.; stat. circ. 3,500. (also avail. in diskette format; back issues avail.) **Document type:** newsletter.
  Description: Investments at pre-screened credit worthy banks and thrifts for jumbo CD ($95,000-100,000) investors.

K D B REPORT. (Korea Development Bank) see BUSINESS AND ECONOMICS

332 340   GW   ISSN 0932-6782
K F R - KOMMENTIERTE FINANZ RECHTSPRECHUNG. 1987. m. DM.15.75 per mo. (effective 1996). Verlag Neue Wirtschafts-Briefe GmbH, Eschstr. 22, 44629 Herne, Germany. **Document type:** academic/scholarly publication.

332   SW   ISSN 0283-6408
KAERVEN; Foereningsbankens tidning. 1940. bi-m. Foereningsbanken, Grev Tureg. 30, S-114 91 Stockholm, Sweden. illus.
  Incorporates (1975-1982): Foereningsbankerna (Tidskrift) (ISSN 0346-9670); Formerly (until 1975): Jordbrukskasseroerelsen (ISSN 0021-745X)

332.1   US   ISSN 0022-8478
KANSAS BANKER. 1910. m. $4. Kansas Bankers Association, 707 Merchants National Bank Bldg., Topeka, KS 66612. TEL 913-232-3444. Ed. Roger D. Kirkwood. adv. circ. 1,500.

332   GW   ISSN 0937-597X
KARTEN/CARDS/CARTES. (Supplement to: Bank und Markt und Technik (ISSN 0933-3770)) 1990. q. DM.109.80 (foreign DM.137) (effective 1996). Fritz Knapp Verlag GmbH, Postfach 111151, 60046 Frankfurt a.M., Germany. TEL 49-69-970833-0. FAX 49-69-7078400. Ed. Anje Haak. **Document type:** consumer publication.

332.1   US   ISSN 0023-0111
KENTUCKY BANKER. no.151, 1938. bi-m. $30 (effective 1997). Kentucky Bankers Association, Ste. 1000, Waterfront Plaza, 325 W. Main St., Louisville, KY 40202. TEL 502-582-2453. FAX 502-584-6390. E-mail: slambert@kybanks.com. Ed. Steve Lambert. R&P contact: Steve Lambert. illus. circ. 900. **Document type:** trade publication.
●Also available online. Vendor(s): UMI.
—UMI.
  Description: Contains financial related articles on compliance, accounting, legal and legislative issues related to the banking industry.

332.1   US
KENTUCKY BANKING AND RELATED LAWS AND RULES ANNOTATED. a. (Kentucky Banker's Association) Michie, A Division of Reed Elsevier Inc., Box 7587, Charlottesville, VA 22906-7587. TEL 804-972-7566; 800-562-1197. FAX 800-643-1280. E-mail: custserv@michie.com; URL: http://www.michie.com. Ed. George Harley. pp./issue: 366.
●Also available online.

332   KE
KENYA COMMERCIAL BANK. DIRECTOR'S REPORT AND ACCOUNTS AND EXECUTIVE CHAIRMAN'S STATEMENT. a. Kenya Commercial Bank, P.O. Box 48400, Nairobi, Kenya.

332   UK
KEY NOTE MARKET REPORT: C T N'S. Variant title: C T N's. irreg., no.7, 1994. £205. Key Note Ltd., Field House, 72 Oldfield Rd., Hampton, Middlesex TW12 2HQ, England. TEL 44-181-783-0755. FAX 44-181-783-0049. **Document type:** trade publication.
●Also available online.
Also available on CD-ROM.
  Formerly: Key Note Report: C T N's (ISSN 0957-7319)

332   UK
KEY NOTE MARKET REPORT: CREDIT & OTHER FINANCE CARDS. Variant title: Credit & Other Finance Cards. irreg., no.10, 1995. £205. Key Note Ltd., Field House, 72 Oldfield Rd., Hampton, Middlesex TW12 2HQ, England. TEL 44-181-783-0755. FAX 44-181-783-0049. **Document type:** trade publication.
●Also available online.
Also available on CD-ROM.
  Formerly (until 1995): Key Note Report: Credit and Other Finance Cards (ISSN 1352-6545)

332   UK
KEY NOTE MARKET REPORT: DEBT MANAGEMENT & FACTORING. Variant title: Debt Management & Factoring. irreg., no.9, 1995. £205. Key Note Ltd., Field House, 72 Oldfield Rd., Hampton, Middlesex TW12 2HQ, England. TEL 44-181-783-0755. FAX 44-181-783-0049. **Document type:** trade publication.
●Also available online.
Also available on CD-ROM.
  Formerly: Key Note Report: Debt Management and Factoring.

332   UK
KEY NOTE MARKET REPORT: FINANCE HOUSES. Variant title: Finance Houses. 1984. irreg., no.9, 1993. £205. Key Note Ltd., Field House, 72 Oldfield Rd., Hampton, Middlesex TW12 2HQ, England. TEL 44-181-783-0755. FAX 44-181-783-0049. **Document type:** trade publication.
●Also available online.
Also available on CD-ROM.
  Formerly: Key Note Report: Finance Houses (ISSN 0951-6689)

332 658.8   UK
KEY NOTE MARKET REPORT: MORTGAGE FINANCE. Variant title: Mortgage Finance. 1994. irreg. £205. Key Note Ltd., Field House, 72 Oldfield Rd., Hampton, Middlesex TW12 2HQ, England. TEL 44-181-783-0755. FAX 44-181-783-0049. Ed. Eleanor Hughes. **Document type:** trade publication.
●Also available online.
Also available on CD-ROM.
  Formerly: Key Note Report: Mortgage Finance (ISSN 1354-2141)

332   UK
KEY NOTE MARKET REPORT: RETAIL BRANCH BANKING. Variant title: Retail Branch Banking. irreg., no.8, 1993. £205. Key Note Ltd., Field House, 72 Oldfield Rd., Hampton, Middlesex TW12 2HQ, England. TEL 44-181-783-0755. FAX 44-181-783-0049. **Document type:** trade publication.
●Also available online.
Also available on CD-ROM.
  Formerly: Key Note Report: Retail Branch Banking (ISSN 1352-6987)

332   UK
KEY NOTE MARKET REVIEW: PERSONAL FINANCE IN THE U K. Variant title: Personal Finance in the U K. irreg., no.6, 1996. £410. Key Note Ltd., Field House, 72 Oldfield Rd., Hampton, Middlesex TW12 2HQ, England. TEL 44-181-783-0755. FAX 44-181-783-0049. **Document type:** trade publication.
●Also available online.
Also available on CD-ROM.

BUSINESS AND ECONOMICS — BANKING AND FINANCE

332   JA
KIN'YU ZAISEI JIJO/FINANCIAL ECONOMIST WEEKLY. (Text in Japanese) 1950. w. 24000 Yen. Institute for Financial Affairs, Inc., 19 Minami-Moto-machi, Shinjuku-ku, Tokyo 160, Japan. TEL 81-3-3355-1711. FAX 81-3-3357-7416. Ed. M. Kato; Pub. H. Arima. R&P contact: M. Kato. adv. contact: M. Inukai. bk.rev. circ. 63,000. (back issues avail.) **Document type:** trade publication.

332.024   US   ISSN 1056-697X
HC101   CODEN: KPFMEA
KIPLINGER'S PERSONAL FINANCE MAGAZINE. Abbreviated title: K P F. 1947. m. $19.95. Kiplinger Washington Editors, Inc., 1729 H St., N.W., Washington, DC 20006. TEL 202-887-6400. FAX 202-331-1206. Ed. Theodore J. Miller. bk.rev.; rec.rev.; charts; illus.; mkt.; stat.; tr.lit.; index. circ. 1,350,000. (also avail. in microfiche from NBI,UMI; reprint service avail. from UMI) **Indexed:** Abr.R.G., Acad.Ind., B.P.I., Bank.Lit.Ind., Bk.Rev.Ind. (1977-), Child.Bk.Rev.Ind. (1977-), CHNI, CINAHL, Consum.Ind., Curr.Pack.Abstr., Hlth.Ind., Jun.High.Mag.Abstr., Mag.Ind., P.A.I.S., R.G.Abstr., R.G., Rehabil.Lit., TOM. **Document type:** trade publication.
•Also available online. Vendor(s): Information Access Co., Knight-Ridder Information, Inc., UMI.
Also available on CD-ROM. Producer(s): UMI.
—Genuine Article; KR SourceOne; UMI; UnCover.
Formerly (until 1991): Changing Times (ISSN 0009-143X)
Description: Contains advice on personal finance, including home, job, and health.

332   FR
KOMPASS FINANCE. 1993. a. 980 F. (effective 1997). Kompass France, 66 quai du Marechal Joffre, 92415 Courbevoie Cedex, France. Ed. Bertrand Macabeo; Pub. Bertrand Macabeo. R&P contact: Bertrand Macabeo. adv. contact: Mireille Girault. **Document type:** directory.
Description: Covers business activity, workforce, summarized balance sheets for the last three financial years and its main financial links.

332.1   KO   ISSN 0075-6806
KOREA DEVELOPMENT BANK: ITS FUNCTIONS AND ACTIVITIES. (Text in English) 1965. a. free. Korea Development Bank, 10-2 Kwanch'ol-dong, Chongno-gu, C.P.O. Box 28, Seoul, S. Korea. Ed. Min Beoung Yun.

332   KO
KOREA EXCHANGE BANK. QUARTERLY REVIEW. (Text in English) 1967. q. free. Korea Exchange Bank, 1 Ulgiro, Chung-ku, Seoul 100, S. Korea. Ed. Jong-Mo Yun; Pub. Myung-Sun Chang. charts; mkt.; stat. circ. 5,500. **Indexed:** Key to Econ.Sci., P.A.I.S., World Bank.Abstr. **Document type:** bulletin.
—UnCover.
Former titles (until 1991): Korea Exchange Bank. Monthly Review (ISSN 0023-3889); Foreign Exchange Bank of Korea.

332   BE   ISSN 0778-421X
KREDIETBANK. MONTHLY BULLETIN. French edition: Bulletin Mensuel (ISSN 0778-3582) (Text in English) 1988. m. (11/yr.). 200 BEF (in Europe 10 ECU; outside Europe $15) (effective 1996). Kredietbank, Economics and Statistics Department, Arenbergstraat 7, B-1000 Brussels, Belgium. Ed. D. Geerts. index. **Document type:** bulletin.

332   BE   ISSN 0772-3318
HC311
KREDIETBANK. WEEKBERICHTEN. French edition: Bulletin Hebdomadaire (ISSN 0772-330X) (French edition avail. in Belgium only) (Text in Dutch) 1946. w. (35/yr.) 800 BEF (in Europe 40 ECU; outside Europe $60) (effective 1996). Kredietbank, Economics and Statistics Department, Arenbergstraat 7, B-1000 Brussels, Belgium. Ed. D. Geerts. mkt.; index. circ. 30,000. **Indexed:** Key to Econ.Sci., P.A.I.S., World Bank.Abstr.
Formerly: Kredietbank. Weekly Bulletin (ISSN 0023-4583)

332   GW   ISSN 0023-4591
HG999.5
KREDIT UND KAPITAL. (Supplements avail.) (Text in English and German; summaries in English, French and German) 1968. q. DM.112. Duncker und Humblot GmbH, Postfach 410329, 12113 Berlin, Germany. TEL 49-30-7900060. FAX 49-30-79000631. E-mail: duh-werbung@t-online. adv.; bk.rev.; abstr.; stat.; index. circ. 1,000. **Indexed:** C.R.E.J., ELLIS, IBR, J.of Econ.Lit., P.A.I.S.For.Lang.Ind. **Document type:** academic/scholarly publication.
—BLDSC (5118.151000); SWETS. **CCC.**

332.7   SW   ISSN 1103-0895
KREDITGUIDE; kreditinformation foer penningmarknaden. 1990. q. SEK 2600 (effective 1997). Standard & Poor's AB, P.O. Box 1753, S-111 87 Stockholm, Sweden.

332   GW   ISSN 0939-3722
KREDITWESENGESETZ. 1963. irreg. DM.248. Erich Schmidt Verlag GmbH & Co. (Berlin), Genthiner Str. 30G, 10785 Berlin, Germany. TEL 49-30-250085-0. FAX 49-30-25008521. (looseleaf format) **Document type:** bulletin.

332   KU
KUWAIT INTERIM ECONOMIC AND FINANCIAL REPORT. q. National Bank of Kuwait, Economic Research and Planning Division, Box 95, 13001 Safat, Kuwait. TEL 2422011. FAX 2429442. TELEX 2204322451-NATBANK-KT.

332   KU
KUWAIT INVESTMENT COMPANY (REPORT). a. Kuwait Investment Company, Box 1005, Safat, Kuwait.

332   FI   ISSN 0023-5989
KYMPPI. 1955. m. FIM 90. Skopbank, Postilokero 47, 00101 Helsinki 10, Finland. Ed. V.M. Hepoluhta. film rev.; play rev.; illus.; mkt. circ. 194,426. (avail. on records)

L A R F REPORT. ANNUAL. (Latin American Reserve Fund) see BUSINESS AND ECONOMICS

332   US
L D C DEBT REPORT. (Lesser Developed Countries) 48/yr. $775 for new subscr. (foreign $825); renewal $850 (foreign $900). American Banker - Bond Buyer, Newsletter Division (Subsidiary of: Thomson Financial Services Company), One State St. Plaza, New York, NY 10004-1549. TEL 800-733-4371. FAX 212-943-2224. (Subscr. to: Box 28315, Washington, DC 20038-8315. TEL 202-347-2665) Ed. Mary D'Ambrosio. **Document type:** newsletter.
•Also available online. Vendor(s): Information Access Co., Knight-Ridder Information, Inc., Lexis-Nexis, NewsNet (FI42).
Formerly: L D C Debt Report - Latin American Markets; Incorporates (in 1992): North American Report on Free Trade.
Description: Devoted exclusively to the subject of less-developed-country debt. Reports on all aspects of LCD debt, including the latest debt reduction programs; developments at the World Bank and the IMF; and the impact that Third World borrowers have on bank earnings.

L I M R A'S VISION; effective strategy for tomorrow's leaders. see BUSINESS AND ECONOMICS — Management

LAGNIAPPE LETTER; bi-weekly report of issues affecting business in Latin America. see BUSINESS AND ECONOMICS — International Commerce

LAGNIAPPE MONTHLY ON LATIN AMERICAN PROJECTS & FINANCE; monthly report on project and infrastructure development opportunities in Latin America. see BUSINESS AND ECONOMICS — International Commerce

332   FR
LAMY DROIT DU FINANCEMENT; haut de bilan, tresorerie, relations banque entreprise. (Supplement avail.) a. 2070 F. (effective 1994). Lamy S.A., 187-189 quai de Valmy, 75490 Paris Cedex 10, France. TEL 33-1-44721343. FAX 33-1-44721393.

332   FR
LAMY FINANCEMENTS DES ENTREPRISES; haut de bilan, tresorie, relation banque-entreprise. a. 1500 F. (effective 1990). Lamy S.A., 187-189 quai de Valmy, 75490 Paris Cedex 10, France. TEL 33-1-44721343. FAX 33-1-44721395. index.
Description: Covers finances, fixed assets, debt, credit and international finance of corporations.

LAMY FISCAL; l'outil pratique pour connaitre et exploiter la reglementation fiscale. see LAW

LAMY SOCIETE COMMERCIALES. see LAW — Corporate Law

332.1   II   ISSN 0970-8472
LAND BANK JOURNAL. 1963. q. Rs.25. National Cooperative Agriculture and Rural Development Banks' Federation, Shivshakti, 2nd Fl., B.G. Kher Rd., Worli, Bombay 400 018, India. TEL 22-4934349. Ed. P.V. Prabhu. adv.; bk.rev. circ. 2,000.
Former titles (until 1975): All India Central Land Development Bank Cooperative Union. Journal (ISSN 0569-0196); (until 1966): All India Central Land Mortgage Bank Cooperative Union. Journal.

332   GW
LANDESZENTRALBANK IN HESSEN. VIERTELJAHRESBERICHTE. 1949. q. Landeszentralbank in Hessen, Taunusanlage 5, 60329 Frankfurt a.M., Germany.

332   GW   ISSN 0342-0930
DER LANGFRISTIGE KRED1T; Zeitschrift fuer Finanzierung und Vermoegensanlage. 1950. s-m. DM.337.68 (foreign DM.389.28) (effective 1997). Helmut Richardi Verlag GmbH, Postfach 111151, 60046 Frankfurt a.M., Germany. TEL 49-69-970833-0. FAX 49-69-7078400. Ed. Klaus Friedrich Otto. adv.; bk.rev.; charts; stat. circ. 2,150. **Document type:** trade publication.
—CCC.

LATIN AMERICAN FINANCE & CAPITAL MARKETS. see BUSINESS AND ECONOMICS — Investments

LATIN AMERICAN INFORMES ESPECIALES. see BUSINESS AND ECONOMICS — Investments

LATIN AMERICAN SPECIAL REPORTS. see BUSINESS AND ECONOMICS — Investments

332   US   ISSN 1048-535X
HG185.L3
LATINFINANCE. (Supplement avail.: Latin Banking Guide & Directory) 1988. m. $195 (foreign $225). Latin American Financial Publications, Inc., 2121 Ponce de Leon Blvd., Ste. 1020, Coral Gables, FL 33134. TEL 305-448-6593. FAX 305-448-0718. (Dist. by: American Educational Systems, 173 W. 81st St., New York, NY 10024. TEL 800-717-2669. FAX 212-501-8926) Ed. Richard Burns; Pub. Peter Conway. R&P contact: Scott Weeks. adv. contact: Rosemary Winters. circ. 30,000. **Indexed:** B.P.I. **Document type:** trade publication.
•Also available online. Vendor(s): Information Access Co.
—KR SourceOne; UnCover.
Description: Covers Latin bonds, equities, money market instruments, derivatives, funds, infrastructure project finance and privatization, as well as other evolving forms of creative financial engineering being developed in Latin America.

332.1 340   US
THE LAW AND REGULATION OF FINANCIAL INSTITUTIONS. a. $115 (for 2 vols.) (foreign $166.95) (effective 1997). Warren, Gorham & Lamont, 395 Hudson St., New York, NY 10014. TEL 212-367-6300. FAX 212-367-6178. (Subscr. to: The Park Square Bldg., 31 St. James Ave., Boston, MA 02116-4112. TEL 800-950-1207) **Document type:** trade publication.
Formerly: Bank Officers Handbook of Commercial Banking Law.

332 340   US
LAW OF BANK DEPOSITS, COLLECTIONS AND CREDIT CARDS (SUPPLEMENT). base vol. (plus s-a. updates). $115 (foreign $166.95) (effective 1995). Warren, Gorham & Lamont, One Penn Plaza, New York, NY 10119. TEL 212-971-5000. FAX 212-971-5113. (Subscr. to: The Park Square Bldg., 31 St. James Ave., Boston, MA 02116-4112. TEL 800-950-1207) **Document type:** trade publication.

BUSINESS AND ECONOMICS — BANKING AND FINANCE

LAW RELATING TO BANKER AND CUSTOMER IN AUSTRALIA. see *LAW*

LAWS OF VIRGINIA RELATED TO FINANCIAL INSTITUTIONS. see *LAW — Corporate Law*

332 US ISSN 1045-2508
HD9800.4.U6
LEASING SOURCEBOOK; the directory of the U.S. capital equipment leasing industry. 1986. irreg. (approx. every 12-18 m.). $135 (effective 1997-98 ed.). Bibliotechnology Systems & Publishing Co., Box 657, Lincoln, MA 01773. TEL 617-259-0524. FAX 617-259-9861. Ed. Barbara B. Low; Pub. Barbara B. Low. (back issues avail.) Document type: trade publication.
Description: Directory of firms engaged in capital equipment leasing or providing services to the capital equipment leasing industry.

332 657 US ISSN 1058-7101
LEDGER QUARTERLY. q. $55 to non-members; members $40 (effective 1996). Community Associations Institute, 1630 Duke St., Alexandria, VA 22314. TEL 703-548-8600. FAX 703-684-1581. URL: http://www.caionline.com. (Subscr. to: Box 26506, Richmond, VA 23260-6506) Ed. Gary Porter. circ. 2,650. Document type: newsletter.
Description: Provides financial and accounting information to community associations.

332 US
LEGISLATIVE AND REGULATORY UPDATE. (Suppl. to: A B A Bank Compliance) 12/yr. $395 (foreign $474) (effective until Sep. 1997). American Bankers Association, Compliance Division, 1120 Connecticut Ave., N.W., Washington, DC 20036. TEL 202-663-5497. FAX 202-663-7543. (Subscr. to: Customer Service Center, Box 630544, Baltimore, MD 21263-0544. TEL 202-663-5087) Ed. Cynthia Baltverra. adv. contact: Larry Price. circ. 4,000 (paid). Document type: trade publication, newsletter.

LENDER LIABILITY LAW REPORT. see *LAW — Corporate Law*

332.1 LO
LESOTHO BANK. ANNUAL REPORT. a. Lesotho Bank, Lesotho Development Bank, Lesotho Bank Centre, Kingways St., P.O. Box 999, Maseru 100, Lesotho. TEL 266-314333. FAX 266-326119. TELEX LESBANK 4366 LO. Ed.Bd. charts. Document type: corporate report.
Description: Reports on financial highlights, international economic scene, past and present financial performance, and financial statements.

332 IT ISSN 0391-7711
LETTERA FINANZIARIA. 52/yr. Via de Alessandri 11, 20155 Milan, Italy. TEL 2-4986250. FAX 2-4982226. TELEX 334104 EXPRESS. Ed. Antonio Calabro.

LETTERS OF CREDIT. see *LAW*

332.7 340 US ISSN 0886-0459
LETTERS OF CREDIT REPORT; bank guaranties and acceptances. 1986. bi-m. $299 (foreign $335) (effective 1998). John Wiley & Sons, Inc., Journals, 605 Third Ave., New York, NY 10158. TEL 212-850-6645. FAX 212-850-6021. E-mail: subinfo@jwiley.com; URL: http://www.wiley.co.uk. Ed. Gerard T. McLaughlin. adv.: B&W page £640, color page £1515; tirm 279 x 210. Document type: newsletter.
—CCC.
Description: For bankers, lawyers, and foreign correspondents on domestic and foreign legal developments impacting letters of credit, bank acceptances, and guarantees.

LETTRE DE L'EXPANSION. see *BUSINESS AND ECONOMICS — Production Of Goods And Services*

332 FR ISSN 0395-0905
LETTRE FINANCIERE; hebdomadaire d'information et de documentation professionnelles sur la banque et le credit. 1976. w. 4950 F. (foreign 5230 F.) (effective 1997). Societe Generale de Presse et d'Editions, 13 av. de l'Opera, 75001 Paris, France. TEL 40-15-17-89. FAX 40-15-17-15. TELEX SOGPRES 230023.

332.6 658 FR ISSN 1261-7709
▼**LETTRES INTERNATIONALES DU MARKETING BANCAIRE.** 1995. m. 4300 F. (foreign 4600 F.). Publi-News, 3 ave. Gallieni, 92000 Nanterre, France. TEL 33-47-29-88-11. FAX 33-47-29-88-18. Ed. Ange Galula. Document type: newsletter.

332 FR
LES LIAISONS FINANCIERES. 1966. a. 5477 F. D A F S A, 42 rue Emeriau, 75015 Paris, France. FAX 40-60-51-51. TELEX 206 065. adv.
Former titles: Collection Radiographie du Capital - Les Liaisons Financieres; Liaisons Financieres en France (ISSN 0075-8957)

332.1 UK ISSN 0953-5004
HC10
LLOYDS BANK ANNUAL REVIEW. 1930. a. £37.50. Lloyds Bank plc., Economics Department, P.O. Box 19, Hays Lane House, 1 Hays Ln., London SE1 2HA, England. TEL 44-171-407-1000. FAX 44-171-357-4378. Ed. Christopher Johnson. charts; circ. controlled. (also avail. in microform from UMI; reprint service avail. from SCH) Indexed: BPIA, Br.Hum.Ind., Bus.Ind., C.R.E.J., Cont.Pg.Manage., Geo.Abstr., IBR, IDA, INSPEC, Int.Lab.Doc., J.of Econ.Lit., Key to Econ.Sci., Manage.Cont., Mgmt.& Market.Abstr., P.A.I.S., PROMT, SCIMP, SSCI, Tr.& Indus.Ind., World Bank.Abstr., World Text.Abstr. Document type: corporate report.
●Also available online. Vendor(s): Information Access Co.
—UMI.
Formerly (until 1988): Lloyds Bank Review Quarterly (ISSN 0024-547X)
Description: Annual thematic volumes that deal with major current economic topics.

332 UK ISSN 0261-0175
LLOYDS BANK ECONOMIC BULLETIN. 1979. m. £12. Lloyds Bank plc., Economics Department, P.O. Box 19, Hays Lane House, 1 Hays Ln., London SE1 2HA, England. TEL 0171-407-1000. FAX 0171-357-4378. Ed. Patrick Foley. circ. 32,000. Indexed: World Bank.Abstr. Document type: bulletin.

332 UK
LLOYDS BANK NEWS. 1966. m. Lloyds Bank plc., Economics Department, P.O. Box 19, Hays Lane House, 1 Hays Ln., London SE1 2HA, England. TEL 0171-407-1000. FAX 0171-357-4378. Ed. Peter Dyball. circ. 38,000. Document type: newsletter.

332 US ISSN 1049-2240
THE LOAN INVESTOR.* fortn. Loan Pricing Corporation, 135 W. 50th St., 13 Fl., New York, NY 10020-1201. TEL 212-489-5455. Ed. Floyd Loomis.

332 US
LOANS AND SECURITIES AT ALL COMMERCIAL BANKS. m. $5. U.S. Federal Reserve System, Board of Governors, Publications Services, Rm. MS-138, Washington, DC 20551. TEL 202-452-3244. FAX 202-728-5886. Document type: government publication.

332 IT
LOMBARD. 1987. bi-m. L.140000 (Europe L.150000; America & Asia L.170000; Africa L.162000; elsewhere L.185000). Lombard Editori s.r.l., Via Marco Burigozzo 5, 20122 Milan, Italy. TEL 39-2-58219286. FAX 39-2-167822196. Ed. Ettore Mazzotti. adv.: B&W page L.21900000, color page L.25400000; adv. contact: Danilo Della Mura. circ. 21,851.

332 UK ISSN 0307-0360
LONDON CURRENCY REPORT. 1972. 10/yr. £450($950) (effective 1996). World Reports Ltd., 108 Horseferry Rd., Westminster, London SW1P 2EF, England. TEL 44-171-222-3836. FAX 44-171-233-0185. (U.S. subscr. to: World Reports Ltd., 280 Madison Ave., Ste. 1209, New York, NY 10016-0802. TEL 212-679-0095. FAX 212-679-1094) Ed. Christopher Story. (back issues avail.) Document type: trade publication.
Description: Surveys global currency and economic developments.

332 US
A LONG CYCLE OBSERVER. m. $36. Box 4132, White River Junction, VT 05001. Ed. Andrew Ralph. Document type: newsletter.
Description: Provides financial advice and discusses issues relating to financial markets.

332.1 US ISSN 0895-1640
LOUISIANA BANKER. 1934. s-m. $15. Louisiana Bankers Association, Box 2871, Baton Rouge, LA 70821. TEL 504-387-3282. FAX 504-343-3159. Ed. Heidi Picard. adv. circ. 2,000. Indexed: Bank.Lit.Ind. Document type: trade publication.
Formerly: L B A Banker.

LUMBERMENS RED BOOK; reference book of the Lumbermens Credit Association. see *FORESTS AND FORESTRY — Lumber And Wood*

332 FR ISSN 1163-8427
LUNDI FISCAL. (Subscription is by fax only) 1991. w. (46/yr.). 1200 F. (effective 1994). Lamy S.A., 187-189 quai de Valmy, 75490 Paris Cedex 10, France. TEL 33-1-44721343. FAX 33-1-44721395.
Description: Provides fiscal information for the week.

332 UK ISSN 0968-4239
M & A JAPAN. (Mergers & Acquisitions); international journal of Japanese mergers and acquisitions. (Text in English; summaries in Japanese) 1990. 10/yr. £290($550) M & A Japan Ltd., P.O. Box 3581, London NW10 6TP, England. TEL 0181-838-2889. FAX 0181-838-2840. Ed. R.A. Amlot. circ. 170. (back issues avail.) Document type: trade publication.

332 GW ISSN 0941-1089
M & A REVIEW. (Mergers & Acquisitions) (Text in English, German) 1990. m. DM.780. Verlagsgruppe Handelsblatt Fachverlag, Kasernenstr. 67, 40213 Duesseldorf, Germany. TEL 49-211-8870. FAX 49-211-8871400. Document type: trade publication.

333.33 UK
M I R A S LENDERS MANUAL. base vol. (plus irreg. updates). £200 to non-members; members £85 (effective 1996-97). Council of Mortgage Lenders, 3 Savile Row, London W1X 1AF, England. TEL 44-171-437-0075. FAX 44-171-287-0109. (Co-sponsor: Building Societies Association) (looseleaf format)
Description: Covers practical and legal aspects of mortgage lending and borrowing.

332 SA
M L S BANK NEWSLETTER. (Text in Afrikaans, English) irreg. M L S Bank, P.O. Box 87175, Houghton 2041, South Africa.
Former titles: M L S Bank. News - Nuus; M L S Bank. News.

M P T REVIEW; specializing in modern portfolio theory. see *BUSINESS AND ECONOMICS — Investments*

332 737 US ISSN 1055-3851
HG353
M R I BANKERS' GUIDE TO FOREIGN CURRENCY. (Text in English, French, German, Portuguese and Spanish) 1991. q. $200 to individuals; institutions $150 (effective 1997). Monetary Research Institute, 1223 Witte Rd., P.O. Box 3174, Houston, TX 77253-3174. TEL 713-827-1796. FAX 713-827-8665. E-mail: aefron@mriguide.com; URL: http://www.miguide.com. Ed. Arnoldo Efron. adv. circ. 5,000. Document type: trade publication.
Description: Provides information on the monetary units and currency regulations, along with description and full color illustration of all current banknotes of all countries of the world.

MAGAZINE P M E; le magazine de l'entrepreneurship du Quebec. see *BUSINESS AND ECONOMICS — Small Business*

332.1 II ISSN 0076-2563
MAHARASHTRA STATE FINANCIAL CORPORATION. ANNUAL REPORT. (Text in English) 1963. a. free. Maharashtra State Financial Corporation, New Excelsior Bldg., 7, 8 & 9th Floors, Amrit Keshav Nayak Marg, Fort, Bombay 400001, India. charts; stat. Document type: corporate report.

MAJOR FINANCIAL INSTITUTIONS OF CONTINENTAL EUROPE (YEAR). see *BUSINESS AND ECONOMICS — Trade And Industrial Directories*

BUSINESS AND ECONOMICS — BANKING AND FINANCE

332 US
MAJOR NONDEPOSIT FUNDS OF COMMERCIAL BANKS. m. $5. U.S. Federal Reserve System, Board of Governors, Publications Services, Rm. MS-138, Washington, DC 20551. TEL 202-452-3244. FAX 202-728-5886. **Document type:** government publication.

332.1 MW ISSN 0076-3322
MALAWI. POST OFFICE SAVINGS BANK. ANNUAL REPORT. 1964. a. Post Office Savings Bank, P.O. Box 521, Blantyre, Malawi. circ. 300. **Document type:** government publication, corporate report.

332 US ISSN 1074-8903
MANAGING CREDIT, RECEIVABLES & COLLECTIONS. Abbreviated title: M C R C. 1994. m. $249 (outside N. America $273). Institute of Management & Administration, Inc., 29 W. 35th St., 5th Fl., New York, NY 10001-2299. TEL 212-244-0360. FAX 212-564-0465. URL: http://www.ioma.com. Ed. Mary S. Ludwig; Pub. Perry Patterson. R&P contact: Sofie Kourkoutakis. index. (looseleaf format) **Document type:** newsletter.
—CCC.
Description: Helps credit and receivables managers set credit policies and accelerate receivables.

332 CN ISSN 0848-5542
MANITOBA. CO-OPERATIVE LOANS AND LOANS GUARANTEE BOARD. ANNUAL REPORT. 1971. a. free. Co-Operative Loans and Loans Guarantee Board, 155 Carlton St., 7th Fl., Winnipeg, MB R3C 3H8, Canada. FAX 204-945-2302. Ed.Bd. circ. 100. **Document type:** government publication.

332.1 IS ISSN 0076-4515
MARITIME BANK OF ISRAEL. ANNUAL REPORT/BANK HA-SAPANUT LE-YISRAEL. ANNUAL REPORT.* (Text in English and Hebrew) a. free. Maritime Bank of Israel, Ltd., P.O. Box 29373, 16 Ahad Ha'an St., Tel Aviv 65142, Israel. **Document type:** corporate report.

332.1 MK
AL-MARKAZI. (Text in Arabic, English) 1975. bi-m. free. Central Bank of Oman, P.O. Box 1161, 112 Muscat, Sultanate of Oman. TEL 702222. FAX 707913. TELEX 3794. Ed. Omar Zein. **Document type:** newspaper.
Description: Highlights current economic and banking issues and economic activities in Oman.

332 US
THE MARKET DATA INDUSTRY. q. $4995 (Europe £3330). Waters Information Services, Inc., Box 2248, Binghamton, NY 13902-2248. TEL 607-770-9242; 800-947-7947. FAX 607-770-9435. (European and Asian subscr. to: Waters Information Services Ltd., 57-58 Neal St., London EC2H 9PJ, England. TEL 44-171-240-2090. FAX 44-171-240-2076) **Document type:** trade publication.
Description: Contains facts and analyses on the strategies and positioning of the major market data vendors.

332 330.9 UK
THE MARKET FOR PERSONAL FINANCE IN CHINA. (Subseries of: Emerging Market Reports) irreg. £895 (U.S. $1,790). Euromonitor, 60-61 Britton St., London EC1M 5NA, England. TEL 44-1711-251-0985; 800-577-3876. FAX 44-171-251-0985. E-mail: info@euromonitor.com; URL: http://www.euromonitor.com. (Addr. in Americas: Euromonitor International, 122 S. Michigan Ave., Ste. 1200, Chicago, IL 60603. TEL 312-922-1115. FAX 312-922-1157) charts; stat.

332 330.9 UK
THE MARKET FOR PERSONAL FINANCE IN LATIN AMERICA. (Subseries of: Emerging Market Reports) 1996. irreg. £1950 (U.S. $3,900). Euromonitor, 60-61 Britton St., London EC1M 5NA, England. TEL 44-171-251-1105; 800-577-3876. FAX 44-171-251-1105. E-mail: info@euromonitor.com; URL: http://www.euromonitor.com. (Addr. in Americas: Euromonitor International, 122 S. Michigan Ave., Ste. 1200, Chicago, IL 60603. TEL 312-922-1115. FAX 312-922-1157) charts; stat.
Description: Analyses the performance and prospects of the personal finance sector including retail banking, credit and charge cards, and mortgage finances.

332.45 UK ISSN 1358-0779
MARKET INSIGHT. EMERGING MARKETS SERVICE. 1993. 3/m. £395($595) for fax edition. Markets International Ltd., 111 The Promenade, Cheltenham, Glos. GL50 1NW, England. TEL 44-1242-232356. FAX 44-1242-260793. **Document type:** newsletter.
Supersedes in part (in 1995): Market Insight.
Description: Provides forecasts of emerging market currencies and interest rates for the following six months, with analysis and summaries based on economic and other fundamentals and market factors.

332.45 UK ISSN 1358-0787
MARKET INSIGHT. WEEKLY MAJOR MARKETS SERVICE. 1993. w. £395($595) for fax edition. Markets International Ltd., 111 The Promenade, Cheltenham, Glos. GL50 1NW, England. TEL 44-1242-232356. FAX 44-1242-260793. **Document type:** newsletter.
Supersedes in part (in 1995): Marketing Insight.
Description: Provides forecasts of major currencies and interest rates for the coming six months, with analysis and summaries based on economic and other fundamental factors.

332 SI
MARKETWATCH. 1926. m. free. Fraser Roach & Co. Pte. Ltd., Maxwell Rd., P.O. Box 789, Singapore 9015, Singapore. FAX 65-5351745. TELEX RS21433-FRASA. stat. circ. 2,250. **Indexed:** World Bank.Abstr.
Formerly (until 1987): Fraser's Circular (ISSN 0016-0083)

332 FI ISSN 1236-4231
MARKKA & TALOUS. (Text in Finnish, occasionally in Swedish) 1993. q. free. Suomen Pankki - Bank of Finland, Publication and Language Services, P.O. Box 160, FIN-00101 Helsinki, Finland. TEL 358-9-1832566. FAX 358-9-174872. E-mail: publications@bofnet.mailnet.fi. Ed.Bd. circ. 6,600.

MASSEY UNIVERSITY. DEPARTMENT OF ACCOUNTANCY. DISCUSSION PAPER SERIES. see BUSINESS AND ECONOMICS — Accounting

332 368.6 IT ISSN 0394-9214
MATECON; materiali di finanza, credito e assicurazioni. 1982. m. L.150000. (Centro di Ricerche Economiche Finanziare) Liocorno Editori, Via Collina 48, 00187 Rome, Italy. TEL 39-6-4746100. FAX 39-6-4743639. Ed. Renzo Stefanelli. adv.; bk.rev.; index. circ. 3,000. **Indexed:** P.A.I.S.For.Lang.Ind.

510 US ISSN 0960-1627
HF5691
MATHEMATICAL FINANCE; an international journal of mathematics, statistics and financial economics. 1991. q. $95 to individuals (foreign $110); institutions $224 (foreign $256) (effective 1997). Blackwell Publishers, 238 Main St., Cambridge, MA 02142. TEL 617-547-7110. FAX 617-547-0789. E-mail: subscript@blackwellpub.com. Ed. Stanley R. Pliska. adv. circ. 800. **Indexed:** Curr.Cont. (1991)-, Stat.Theor.Meth.Abstr. (1991-). **Document type:** academic/scholarly publication.
—BLDSC (5401.975000); SWETS; UMI. CCC.
Description: Presents the latest theoretical studies, focusing on finance theory, finance engineering, and the related mathematical and statistical techniques.

MEDIUM COMPANIES OF EUROPE. VOLUME 1. MEDIUM COMPANIES OF THE CONTINENTAL EUROPEAN ECONOMIC COMMUNITY. see BUSINESS AND ECONOMICS — Trade And Industrial Directories

MEDIUM COMPANIES OF EUROPE. VOLUME 2. MEDIUM COMPANIES OF THE UNITED KINGDOM. see BUSINESS AND ECONOMICS — Trade And Industrial Directories

MEDIUM COMPANIES OF EUROPE. VOLUME 3. MEDIUM COMPANIES OF WESTERN EUROPE OUTSIDE THE EUROPEAN ECONOMIC COMMUNITY. see BUSINESS AND ECONOMICS — Trade And Industrial Directories

332.7 GW ISSN 0025-8792
MEIN EIGENHEIM. 1924. 4/yr. free. (Bausparkasse Wuestenrot) Kundenzeitschriften und Service Verlagsgesellschaft mbH, Griegstr. 75, 22763 Hamburg, Germany. TEL 49-40-88303480. FAX 49-40-88303472. Ed. Regine Scourtelis. adv.; bk.rev.; illus.; index. circ. 1,850,000. **Document type:** bulletin.

332 BL
MENSAGEM ECONOMICA/ECONOMIC MESSAGE. 1952. m. Associacao Comercial de Minas, Av. Afonso Pena 172, Belo Horizonte, Brazil. adv. circ. 6,000.

MERGERS & ACQUISITIONS CONSULTANT; the management report and information resource. see BUSINESS AND ECONOMICS — Management

332 MX
MEXICAN FINANCIAL REPORT.* (Text in English) 1974. m. Mex.$375($30) Publicaciones Marynka, S.A., Salaverry 1204, Col. Zacatenco, 07360 Mexico D.F., Mexico. Ed.Bd. charts; stat.

332.1 MX ISSN 0185-1675
HG2711
MEXICO. COMISION NACIONAL BANCARIA. BOLETIN ESTADISTICO. 1925. m. Comision Nacional Bancaria, Secretaria de Hacienda y Credito Publico, Av. de los Insurgentes 1971, Plaza Inn Torre 2 Norte, Piso 10, 01020 Mexico D.F., Mexico. **Document type:** government publication, bulletin.

332 UK ISSN 0307-0387
MIDDLE EAST CURRENCY REPORTS. 6/yr. £235($550) (effective 1996). World Reports Ltd., 108 Horseferry Rd., Westminster, London SW1P 2EF, England. TEL 44-171-222-3836. FAX 44-171-233-0185. (U.S. subscr. to: World Reports Ltd., 280 Madison Ave., Ste. 1209, New York, NY 10016-0802. TEL 212-679-0095. FAX 212-679-1094) Ed. Christopher Story. (back issues avail.) **Document type:** trade publication.
Description: Reports on the currencies, economies and socio-political background of Middle East nations.

332 UK ISSN 0266-2094
HG3256.A5
MIDDLE EAST FINANCIAL DIRECTORY. a. £120 (effective 1997). M E E D Publications, 21 John St., London WC1N 2BP, England. TEL 44-171-470-6406. FAX 44-171-430-0337. adv.; index. (back issues avail.) **Document type:** directory.
Description: Country by country listing of financial institutions in the Middle East.

332 UK
MIDLAND GROUP NEWS. 1971. 12/yr. free. Midland Bank, 79 Hoyle St., Sheffield S3 7EW, England. TEL 0742 528620. Ed. Eric Walker. adv. circ. 60,500. (tabloid format; back issues avail.)
Formerly: Midland Bank Group Newspaper.

MIDWEST CLEARING CORPORATION AND MIDWEST SECURITIES TRUST COMPANY. DIRECTORY OF PARTICIPANTS. see BUSINESS AND ECONOMICS — Trade And Industrial Directories

332.1 US ISSN 0026-6159
MISSISSIPPI BANKER. 1914. m. $25. Mississippi Bankers Association, Box 37, 640 N. State St., Jackson, MS 39205. TEL 601-948-6366. Ed. Kristen/Phillips. adv. contact: Kristen Phillips. bk.rev.; illus. circ. 1,000. **Document type:** trade publication.

332 SW ISSN 1100-4738
MODERN BANKING; tidskrift foer anstaellda inom bank- och finansindustrin. 1988. q. Eventor Konsult, P.O. Box 6911, S-102 39 Stockholm, Sweden.

332.1 US
MODERN BANKING CHECKLISTS (SUPPLEMENT). base vols. (s-a. updates). $165 (foreign $231.95) (effective 1995). Warren, Gorham & Lamont, One Penn Plaza, New York, NY 10119. TEL 212-971-5000. FAX 212-971-5113. (Subscr. to: The Park Square Bldg., 31 St. James Ave., Boston, MA 02116-4112. TEL 800-950-1207) **Document type:** trade publication.

332.024 333.33 US
MODERN ESTATE PLANNING. 1981. 7 base vols. (plus updates 2/yr.). $1065 for base vols.; updates $829. Matthew Bender & Co., Inc., 2 Park Ave., New York, NY 10016. TEL 212-448-2000. E-mail: international@bender.com; URL: http://www.bender.com.
●Also available on CD-ROM.
Description: A unified, transactional approach to estate and financial planning covering estate, gift, and income taxes.

BUSINESS AND ECONOMICS — BANKING AND FINANCE

332.1   IT   ISSN 0026-9506
MONDO BANCARIO; rassegna bimestrale illustrata di cultura, di studi e di documentazione. 1959. bi-m. L.75000 (foreign L.120000) (effective 1996). Futura 2000 S.p.A., Via J. Sannazzaro 6-8, 00141 Rome, Italy. TEL 39-6-8260326. FAX 39-6-8260270. Ed. G. Girardi. adv.; bk.rev.; bibl.; charts; illus.; mkt.; maps; stat.; tr.lit.; index; circ. 9,000 (paid). **Indexed:** P.A.I.S.For.Lang.Ind. **Document type:** academic/scholarly publication, monographic series.

330.9   PR
MONEDA. 1978. bi-w. $20. Moneda Inc., 1614 San Mateo, Santurce, PR 00912. TEL 787-721-7977. FAX 787-721-7991. Ed. Martha Dreyer Duperray. adv. circ. 30,000. (back issues avail.)

332   AG
MONEDA Y FINANZAS DEL CONO SUR. CUADERNOS. q. Arg.$24 (foreign $13). Universidad Nacional de Lujan, C.C. 221, 6700 Lujan, Argentina. Ed. Jose Luis Moreno.
Description: Covers research and analysis of various aspects in banking, business and finance.

332   IT   ISSN 0026-9611
HG19
MONETA E CREDITO. 1948. q. L.80000 (effective 1995). (Banca Nazionale del Lavoro) B N L Edizioni S.p.A., Via Lucullo 7, 00187 Rome, Italy. TEL 39-6-4884380. FAX 39-6-4745272. Ed. Alessandro Roncaglia. adv. contact: Filippo Cucuccio. bk.rev.; charts; index. circ. 5,000. **Indexed:** ELLIS, P.A.I.S.For.Lang.Ind. **Document type:** academic/scholarly publication.
Description: Articles by leading economists on macroeconomic theory and policy, international trade and finance, the evolution of national monetary and financial institutions and allied topics.

332.1   MX   ISSN 0185-1136
HG185.L3
MONETARIA. 1978. q. $60. Centro de Estudios Monetarios Latinoamericanos, A.C., Durango 54, 06700 Mexico D.F., Mexico. TEL 905-5330-300. FAX 514-6554. TELEX 0177 1229 CEMLME. Ed. Juan Manuel Rodriguez Sierra. adv.; bk.rev.; index. circ. 1,000. **Indexed:** IBR. **Document type:** bulletin.
—SWETS.

332.1   JA   ISSN 0287-5306
MONETARY AND ECONOMIC STUDIES. (Text in Japanese) 4/yr. 1030 Yen per no. Bank of Japan, Institute for Monetary and Economic Studies - Nippon Ginko, c/o Public Relations Department, 2-1-1 Hongoku-Cho, Nihonbashi, Chuo-ku, Tokyo 103, Japan. TEL 81-3-3270-5913. FAX 81-3-3292-0410. TELEX JPTCO J27161. (Dist. by: Tokiwa Sohgoh Service Co., Ltd., Kyodo Bldg., 3-2-4 Hongoku-cho, Nihonbashi Chuo-ku, Tokyo 103, Japan. TEL 81-3-3270-5913; Overseas Dist. by: Japan Publications Trading Co., Ltd., Book Export No. 2 Dept., P.O. Box 5030 Tokyo International, Tokyo 100-31, Japan) **Indexed:** J.of Econ.Lit.
Description: Theses regarding monetary and economic theory, system and historical developments written by the staff of the Institute for Monetary and Economic Studies and by visiting scholars both from Japan and abroad.

332   US
MONETARY POLICY AND RESERVE REQUIREMENTS HANDBOOK. a. $75. U.S. Federal Reserve System, Board of Governors, Publications Services, Rm. MS-137, 20th and Constitution Ave., N.W., Washington, DC 20551. TEL 202-752-3244. FAX 202-728-5886. **Document type:** government publication.

332   NE   ISSN 0925-4129
MONEY. (Text in Dutch) 1990. 7/yr. fl.59.50 (foreign fl.96.50) (effective 1998). Reed Elsevier plc, Postbus 4, 7000 BA Doetinchem, Netherlands. TEL 31-8340-49911. FAX 31-8340-43839. **Document type:** consumer publication.

332   US   ISSN 0149-4953
HG179   CODEN: MNEYAB
MONEY (NEW YORK). 1972. m. $39.95. Time Inc. (Subsidiary of: Time Warner, Inc.), Time & Life Bldg., Rockefeller Center, 1271 Ave. of the Americas, New York, NY 10020. TEL 212-522-1212. URL: http://pathfinder.com/. (Subscr. to: Money, Box 60001, Tampa, FL 33630-0001. TEL 800-633-9970) Ed. Frank Lalli; Pub. Geoff Dodge. R&P contact: Marilyn Downs. adv. contact: Geoff Dodge. bk.rev.; s-a. index; circ. 1,993,119 (paid). (also avail. in microform from UMI,MCE) **Indexed:** ABI Inform., Account.Ind. (1974-), B.P.I., Bank.Lit.Ind., Bk.Rev.Ind. (1972-), BPIA, Bus.Ind., Child.Bk.Rev.Ind. (1972-), Consum.Ind., Environ.Abstr., Mag.Ind., P.A.I.S., PMR, PSI, R.G.Abstr., R.G., TOM, Tr.& Indus.Ind. **Document type:** consumer publication.
● Also available online. Vendor(s): Information Access Co., Knight-Ridder Information, Inc., Lexis-Nexis, MediaStream, UMI.
Also available on CD-ROM. Producer(s): UMI.
—BLDSC (5908.358000); KR SourceOne; SWETS; UMI; UnCover.

332   MX   ISSN 0187-7615
MONEY AFFAIRS. 1988. s-a. $20. Centro de Estudios Monetarios Latinoamericanos, A.C., Durango 54, 06700 Mexico D.F., Mexico. TEL 905-5330-300. FAX 514-6554. TELEX 0177 1229 CEMLME. Ed. Juan Manuel Rodriguez Sierra. adv.; bk.rev.; index. circ. 300. **Document type:** bulletin.

332   JA   ISSN 0911-9353
MONEY JAPAN. (Supplements avail.) (Text in English) 1985. m. 600 Yen per no. S.S. Communications Inc., SSC Bldg., 11 Niban-cho, Chiyoda-ku, Tokyo 102, Japan. TEL 81-3-5276-2140. FAX 81-3-5276-2159. Ed. Kenji Morita. adv. circ. 400,000.
Description: Offers the latest financial information. Topics include shopping, travel, marriage, educational expenses, mortgages, health and retirement funds.

MONEY LAUNDERING ALERT. see *CRIMINOLOGY AND LAW ENFORCEMENT*

MONEY LAUNDERING LAW REPORT. see *LAW — Corporate Law*

332   US
MONEY LINES MAGAZINE. 1988. q. $4.95 per no. Lifetime Periodicals, Inc., 2131 Hollywood Blvd., Hollywood, FL 33020. TEL 305-925-5242. FAX 305-925-5244. E-mail: lifetime@shadow.net; URL: http://www.lifetime books.com. Ed. Brian Feinblum; Pub. Donald Lessne. circ. 50,000. (back issues avail.) **Document type:** consumer publication.
Formerly: Financial Planning Series.
Description: Covers a range of investment opportunities, from how to get rich to mutual funds to tips on selling; provides the reader with information on what, where, how and why.

332   UK
MONEY MANAGEMENT. m. £59 in the U.K. and Ireland; elsewhere £103. Financial Times Business Information, Magazines (Subsidiary of: Financial Times Group), 2 Greystoke Pl., Fetter Ln., London EC4A 1ND, England. TEL 0171-405-6969. FAX 0171-405-5276. TELEX 296926 BUSINF G. (Subscr. to: 126 Jermyn St., London SW1Y 4UJ, England) stat. (also avail. in microform from UMI) **Document type:** trade publication.
Description: Publishes in-depth surveys covering transfer plans, P.E.P.s, I.F.A. training, and long-term care insurance. Also covers every aspect of the intermediary and insurance markets and financial news.

MONEY MANAGEMENT LETTER; bi-weekly newsletter covering the pensions & money management industry. see *BUSINESS AND ECONOMICS — Investments*

332   US   ISSN 0736-6051
HG4509
MONEY MARKET DIRECTORY OF PENSION FUNDS AND THEIR INVESTMENT MANAGERS. 1970. a. $975. Money Market Directories, Inc., Box 1608, Charlottesville, VA 22902. TEL 804-977-1450; 800-446-2810. FAX 804-979-9962. Ed. Jehu Martin; Pub. Thomas McQueeney. adv.; index. circ. 8,500. (magnetic tape) **Document type:** directory.
Former titles: Money Market Directory of Pension Funds and Their Investment Advisors; Money Market Directory (ISSN 0077-0388)

332   UK
MONEY MARKETING UNIT TRUST INDEX. 1987. q. $40. Centaur Communications Ltd., St. Giles House, 50 Poland St., London W1V 4AX, England. TEL 44-171-287-9800. FAX 44-171-439-1480. Ed. Jane Green. adv. circ. 4,419. (also avail. in microform from UMI) **Document type:** trade publication.
Description: For investment intermediaries in the U.K. Lists fund management groups.

332   SA
MONEY NEWSLETTER. 1984. m. $100 (effective through Oct. 1997). Prescon Publishing Corporation (Pty) Ltd, P.O. Box 84004, Greenside 2034, South Africa. TEL 27-11-646-9750. FAX 27-11-646-4617. E-mail: prescon@aztec.co.za. Ed. Leon J. Kok. **Document type:** newsletter.
Formerly: Money Magazine.
Description: Provides personal financial advice for middle income individuals.

332   II
MONEY OPPORTUNITIES. (Text in English) 1985. w. newsstand price: Rs.5. Ross Murarka Finance Ltd., Sterling Centre, 2nd Fl., Dr. Annie Besant Rd., Worli, Bombay 400 018, India. TEL 4949766. FAX 4932134. TELEX 011 76884. Ed. Lynn Deas. adv. contact: Nimal Parekh. circ. 53,186. cols./p.: 8.

332   US
MONEY STOCK, LIQUID ASSETS, AND DEBT MEASURES. w. $35. U.S. Federal Reserve System, Board of Governors, Publications Services, Rm. MS-138, Washington, DC 20551. TEL 202-452-3244. FAX 202-728-5886. **Document type:** government publication.

MONEYLETTER (ASHLAND). see *BUSINESS AND ECONOMICS — Investments*

332   UK   ISSN 1357-0676
MONKS U.K. BOARD EARNINGS (YEAR). a. Monks Partnership Ltd., The Mill House, Wendens Ambo, Saffron Walden, Essex CB11 4JX, England. TEL 44-1799-542222. FAX 44-1799-541805. Ed. Alsion Smith. R&P contact: David Atkins. **Document type:** corporate report.
—BLDSC (9093.530000).

332   US
MONTEREY BAY AREA LOCALE. 1960. q. free to qualified personnel. (Monterey Savings and Loan Association) Locale Publishing Co., 1948 Riverside Dr., Los Angeles, CA 90039. TEL 213-666-5661. Ed. Wil Goodrich. charts; illus. circ. 55,000.

332   JA   ISSN 0388-0605
HG41
MONTHLY FINANCE REVIEW. (Text in English) 1973. m. free. Ministry of Finance, Institute of Fiscal and Monetary Policy - Okura-sho, 3-1-1, Kasumigaseki, Chiyoda-ku, Tokyo 100, Japan. circ. 1,060. **Document type:** government publication.

332   US   ISSN 0545-0152
HG4961
MOODY'S BANK AND FINANCE MANUAL. a. $1395 (includes s-w. Moody's Bank & Finance News Reports). Moody's Investors Service (Subsidiary of: Dun & Bradstreet Corporation), 99 Church St., New York, NY 10007. TEL 212-553-0300. FAX 212-553-4700. Ed. Robert Hanson. (also avail. in microfiche from MIS)
—CCC.
Description: Full financial and operating data on 18,000 institutions in the U.S.

MOODY'S BANK AND FINANCE NEWS REPORTS. see *BUSINESS AND ECONOMICS — Investments*

MORGAN STANLEY CENTRAL BANK DIRECTORY (YEAR). see *BUSINESS AND ECONOMICS — Trade And Industrial Directories*

332   US
MORTGAGE-BACKED SECURITIES; developments and trends in the secondary mortgage market. a. $140. Clark - Boardman - Callaghan, 375 Hudson St., New York, NY 10014. TEL 212-929-7500; 800-422-2101. FAX 212-924-0460. Ed. Kenneth G. Lore.
Description: Covers the legal, tax, and business considerations affecting the sale of mortgage-backed securities.

BUSINESS AND ECONOMICS — BANKING AND FINANCE

332.7   US   ISSN 0730-0212
HG2051.U5   CODEN: MOBAAX
MORTGAGE BANKING. 1939. m. $40. Mortgage Bankers Association of America, 1125 15th St., N.W., Washington, DC 20005-2766. TEL 202-861-1930. FAX 202-861-1930. E-mail: janet__hewitt@mbaa.org. Ed. Janet Hewitt. R&P contact: Susan Edgar. adv.; illus. circ. 10,023. (also avail. in microform from UMI; microfiche from CIS) Indexed: ABI Inform., Account.Ind. (1974-), B.P.I., Bank.Lit.Ind., BPIA, Bus.Ind., Manage.Cont., P.A.I.S., SRI, Tr.& Indus.Ind. **Document type:** trade publication.
●Also available online. Vendor(s): Information Access Co.
—BLDSC (5967.465000); KR SourceOne; UMI; UnCover. **CCC.**
   Former titles (until 1981): Mortgage Banker (ISSN 0027-1241); M B A News Review.

332.1   333.333   UK   ISSN 0964-7988
MORTGAGE FINANCE GAZETTE. 1869. m. £65. Franey and Co. Ltd., South Quay Plaza, 183 Marsh Wall, London E14 9FS, England. Ed. Neil Madden. adv.; bk.rev.; illus.; stat.; tr.lit.; index. circ. 5,000. **Indexed:** RICS, World Bank.Abstr. **Document type:** trade publication.
—BLDSC (5967.466300).
   Formerly (until 1990): Building Societies' Gazette (ISSN 0007-3652)

MORTGAGE LAW AND PRACTICE MANUAL. see *LAW*

332   US   ISSN 1055-4696
KF695
MORTGAGE LOAN DISCLOSURE HANDBOOK; a step-by-step guide with forms. 1987. a. $145. Clark - Boardman - Callaghan, 375 Hudson St., New York, NY 10014. TEL 212-929-7500; 800-422-2101. FAX 212-924-0460. Ed. Kenneth F. Hall.
   Description: Provides sample forms and detailed information on the disclosure requirements lenders must meet under federal laws and regulations.

MORTGAGE NEWS. see *REAL ESTATE*

332   SP   ISSN 0300-3884
HC381
EL MUNDO FINANCIERO; gran revista grafica de economia y finanzas. 1946. m. 3500 ptas.($28) C. Hermosilla 93, 1o Izq., Apdo. de Correo 6119, 28080 Madrid, Spain. TEL 34-1-5773376. E-mail: mundofinanciero@nauta.es; URL: http://www.nauta.es/mundof/. Ed. Jose Luis Barcelo; Pub. Miguel A. Martinez. R&P contact: Jose Luis Barcelo. adv. contact: Pilar Vicente. bk.rev.; bibl.; illus.; stat. circ. 100,000. (also avail. in microfilm) **Document type:** newsletter.

332   346.078   US
N A B TALK. q. National Association of Bankruptcy Trustees, 3008 Milwood Ave., Columbia, SC 29205. TEL 803-252-5646. **Document type:** newsletter.
   Description: Discusses bankruptcy issues and ways to manage a bankruptcy practice more efficiently.

332.1   II
N A F S C O B BULLETIN. 1973-1977; resumed 1982. q. free. National Federation of State Cooperative Banks Ltd., Garment House, Dr. Annie Besant Rd. Worli, Bombay 400018, India. Ed. B. Subrahmanyam. bk.rev. circ. 600. **Document type:** bulletin.
   Formerly: Cooperative Banker.

N A S D A Q FACT BOOK. (National Association of Securities Dealers Automated Quotations) see *BUSINESS AND ECONOMICS — Investments*

N A S D A Q SUBSCRIBER BULLETIN. (National Association of Securities Dealers Automated Quotations) see *BUSINESS AND ECONOMICS — Investments*

N A S D ANNUAL REPORT. (National Association of Securities Dealers, Inc.) see *BUSINESS AND ECONOMICS — Investments*

N A S D REGULATORY AND COMPLIANCE ALERT. (National Association of Securities Dealers, Inc.) see *BUSINESS AND ECONOMICS — Investments*

332   LB
N B L REVIEW. 1984. q. National Bank of Liberia, E.G. King Plaza, Broad St., P.O. Box 2048, Monrovia, Liberia. TEL 231-222580. TELEX NATBANK, 44215 MONROVIA. Ed. James Monxhwedey.
   Description: Covers news of the National Bank of Liberia and the events it sponsors.

N C F E MOTIVATOR. (National Center for Financial Education) see *CONSUMER EDUCATION AND PROTECTION*

332.3   US
N C U A WATCH. (National Credit Union Administration) 1983. 48/yr. $595 for new subscr. (foreign $645); renewal $675 (foreign $725). American Banker - Bond Buyer, Newsletter Division (Subsidiary of: Thomson Financial Services Company), One State St. Plaza, New York, NY 10004-1549. TEL 800-733-4371. FAX 212-943-2224. (Subscr. to: Box 28315, Washington, DC 20038-8315. TEL 202-347-2665) Ed. Ed Roberts. **Document type:** newsletter.
   Description: Covers policy and expected policy, as well as action such as lawsuits, pertaining to the activities of the NCUA.

332   US   ISSN 1066-0283
N E F E DIGEST. 1984. m. National Endowment for Financial Education, 4695 S. Monaco St., Denver, CO 80237-3403. TEL 303-220-1200. FAX 303-220-1810. URL: http://insweb.com/carriers/nefe/. Ed. Barbara Munson. R&P contact: Helen Mulhern. circ. 70,000 (controlled).
   Formerly: College for Financial Planning. Digest.

332   US
N I B E S A NEWS. 1980. m. membership. National Independent Bank Equipment & Systems Association, 1411 Peterson Ave., Ste. 101, Park Ridge, IL 60068. TEL 708-825-8419; 800-843-6082. FAX 708-825-8445. Ed. Ann Walk. adv. contact: Ann Walk. circ. 400. **Document type:** newsletter.

332   MX   ISSN 0185-4968
NACIONAL FINANCIERA. ANNUAL REPORT. a. Nacional Financiera, S.N.C., Subdireccion de Informacion Tecnica y Publicaciones, Insurgentes Sur 1971, Nivel Fuente, Col. Guadalupe Inn, 01020 Mexico, D.F., Mexico. TEL 52-5-3256047. **Document type:** corporate report.

332.09   YU   ISSN 0351-3211
NARODNA BANKA JUGOSLAVIJE. BILTEN. English edition: National Bank of Yugoslavia. Quarterly Bulletin (ISSN 0350-4484) (Text in Serbo-Croatian) 1973. m. (English ed. q.). Narodna Banka Jugoslavije, Bulevar Revolucije 15, P.O. Box 1010, 11001 Belgrade, Yugoslavia. TEL 332-001. Ed. Jovan Petrovic. circ. 1,200. **Indexed:** Key to Econ.Sci.
   Description: Economic and monetary developments.

NARODNA BANKA JUGOSLAVIJE. GODISNJI IZVESTAJ. see *BUSINESS AND ECONOMICS — Economic Situation And Conditions*

332   PL   ISSN 1230-0020
NARODOWY BANK POLSKI. BIULETYN INFORMACYJNY. English edition: National Bank of Poland. Information Bulletin (ISSN 1230-0101) (Text in Polish) 1990. m. free. Narodowy Bank Polski, Promotion and Information Division, Ul. Swietokrzyska 11-21, 00-919 Warsaw, Poland. TEL 48-22-6531000. FAX 48-22-6531321. circ. 1,200. **Document type:** bulletin.
   Formerly (until 1991): Narodowy Bank Polski. Miesieczny Biuletyn Informacyjny (ISSN 0867-2423)
   Description: Covers the economic and financial situation of Polish economy and monetary policy.

332.1   TZ
NATIONAL BANK OF COMMERCE. ANNUAL REPORT AND ACCOUNTS. (Text in English and Swahili) 1967. a. free. National Bank of Commerce, P.O. Box 1863, Dar es Salaam, Tanzania. circ. 3,000. **Document type:** corporate report.

NATIONAL BANK OF EGYPT. ECONOMIC BULLETIN. see *BUSINESS AND ECONOMICS — Economic Situation And Conditions*

332   ET   ISSN 1015-2717
NATIONAL BANK OF ETHIOPIA. ANNUAL REPORT. 1964. a. $2.50 (airmail $5). National Bank of Ethiopia, c/o Documentation Division, P.O. Box 5550, Addis Ababa, Ethiopia. **Document type:** government publication.

330.9   ET   ISSN 0027-8750
HC845.A1
NATIONAL BANK OF ETHIOPIA. QUARTERLY BULLETIN. 1964. q. $20. National Bank of Ethiopia, Economic Research and Planning Division, c/o Documentation Division, P.O. Box 5550, Addis Ababa, Ethiopia. charts; mkt. **Document type:** government publication, bulletin.
   Supersedes: State Bank of Ethiopia. Report on Economic Conditions and Market Trends.

332.1   GR   ISSN 0077-3514
NATIONAL BANK OF GREECE. ANNUAL REPORT/ETHNIKE TRAPEZA TES HELLADOS. APOLOGISMOS. (Editions in English and Greek) 1843. a. free. National Bank of Greece, Economic Research and Planning Department, 86 Eolou St., Athens 102 32, Greece. circ. 21,000 (12,500 Greek ed.; 8,500 English ed.). **Document type:** corporate report.

332   KU
NATIONAL BANK OF KUWAIT. ANNUAL REPORT OF THE BOARD OF DIRECTORS AND ACCOUNTS. 1953. a. free. National Bank of Kuwait S.A.K., Economic Research & Planning Division, Abdullah al-Salim St., P.O. Box 95, Kuwait. **Document type:** corporate report.
   Description: Covers the international economy as it applies to Kuwait, proceedings of the Gulf Corporation Council, economic developments in Kuwait as well as all other financial reports.

332.1   LB
NATIONAL BANK OF LIBERIA. ANNUAL REPORT. 1974. a. National Bank of Liberia, E.G. King Plaza, Broad St., P.O. Box 2048, Monrovia, Liberia. TEL 231-222580. TELEX NATBANK, 44215 MONROVIA. charts; stat. **Document type:** corporate report.

332   LB
NATIONAL BANK OF LIBERIA. QUARTERLY STATISTICAL BULLETIN. q. National Bank of Liberia, Research Department, E.G. King Plaza, Broad St., P.O. Box 2048, Monrovia, Liberia. TEL 231-222580. TELEX NATBANK, 44215 MONROVIA. **Document type:** bulletin.

332   PK
NATIONAL BANK OF PAKISTAN. ANNUAL REPORT. (Text in English) a. National Bank of Pakistan, I.I. Chundrigar Rd., Karachi 2, Pakistan. **Document type:** corporate report.

332   PK
NATIONAL BANK OF PAKISTAN. MONTHLY ECONOMIC LETTER. (Text in English) 1975. m. free. National Bank of Pakistan, Planning & Research Division, I.I. Chundrigar Rd., P.O. Box 4973, Karachi, Pakistan. TEL 021-2416171. FAX 021-2416157. TELEX 23732 NBPPK. Ed. Muhammad Naeemuddin. circ. 2,700. **Indexed:** Key to Econ.Sci., World Bank.Abstr.

332.1   PK   ISSN 0077-3522
NATIONAL BANK OF PAKISTAN. REPORT AND STATEMENT OF ACCOUNTS. (Text in English) a. National Bank of Pakistan, I.I. Chundrigar Rd., Karachi 2, Pakistan. **Document type:** corporate report.

332.1   CN   ISSN 0822-1081
NATIONAL BANKING LAW REVIEW; banking business and the law. 1982. bi-m. Can.$220. Butterworths Canada Ltd., Part of the Reed Elsevier group, 75 Clegg Rd., Markham, ON L6G 1A1, Canada. TEL 905-479-2665. FAX 905-479-2826. (back issues avail.) **Indexed:** Ind.Can.L.P.L. **Document type:** trade publication.
   Description: Provides information and comments on recent developments of interest to lenders and clients.

BUSINESS AND ECONOMICS — BANKING AND FINANCE

332   US   ISSN 0275-0252
KF1519
NATIONAL BANKRUPTCY REPORTER; reports new business bankruptcies. 1974. w. $1800. Andrews Publications, 175 Strafford Ave., Bldg. 4, Ste. 140, Wayne, PA 19087. TEL 215-225-0510; 800-345-1101. FAX 215-225-0501. Ed. Rose MacDonald; Pub. John Backe Jr. R&P contact: Robert Maroldo. adv. contact: Melissa Webber. (looseleaf format; back issues avail.) **Document type:** newsletter.

332.3   DQ
NATIONAL COMMERCIAL & DEVELOPMENT BANK. ANNUAL REPORT AND FINANCIAL STATEMENTS. a. National Commercial & Development Bank, 64 Hillsborough St., Roseau, Dominica, W.I. (Affiliate: A I D Bank) illus. **Document type:** corporate report.
Formerly: Dominica Agricultural and Industrial Development Bank. Annual Report and Financial Statements.

332.7   CN   ISSN 0829-2019
NATIONAL CREDITOR-DEBTOR REVIEW; a journal of creditor-debtor relations. 1986. q. Can.$170. Butterworths Canada Ltd., Part of the Reed Elsevier group, 75 Clegg Rd., Markham, ON L6G 1A1, Canada. TEL 905-479-2665. FAX 905-479-2826. (back issues avail.) **Indexed:** Ind.Can.L.P.L. **Document type:** trade publication.
Description: Reviews recent laws and cases in the area of creditors' and debtors' obligations and rights.

332.1   SL
NATIONAL DEVELOPMENT BANK. ANNUAL REPORT AND ACCOUNTS. (Text in English) 1969. a. free. National Development Bank, Leone House, 21-23 Siaka Stevens St., Freetown, Sierra Leone. FAX 232-22-24468. TELEX 3589 NATDEV. stat. circ. 450. **Document type:** corporate report.

332 340   US   ISSN 1073-953X
NATIONAL FINANCING LAW DIGEST. 1989. m. $367 (Canada $397; elsewhere $422) (effective Oct. 1996). Strafford Publications, Inc., Specialized Information Services, 590 Dutch Valley Rd., N.E., Drawer 13729, Atlanta, GA 30324-0729. TEL 404-881-1141. FAX 404-881-0074. E-mail: custserv@straffordpub.com. Ed. Jennifer F. Vaughan; Pub. Richard M. Ossoff. index. (back issues avail.) **Document type:** newsletter.
Description: Offers complete coverage of workouts, bankruptcy, lender's liability, and the growing number of court decisions related to the changing economic situation.

332   CN   ISSN 0822-2584
NATIONAL INSOLVENCY REVIEW. bi-m. Can.$220. Butterworths Canada Ltd., Part of the Reed Elsevier group, 75 Clegg Rd., Markham, ON L6G 1A1, Canada. TEL 905-479-2665. FAX 905-479-2826. (back issues avail.) **Indexed:** Ind.Can.L.P.L. **Document type:** trade publication.
Description: Reviews recent laws and cases in the area of insolvency, bankruptcy and creditors' rights.

332.1   GH
NATIONAL INVESTMENT BANK, GHANA. ANNUAL REPORT.* Short title: N I B Annual Report. 1963. a. National Investment Bank, 37 Kwame Nkrumah Ave., P.O. Box 3726, Accra, Ghana. TELEX 2161 MIBGH. Ed. H.Y. Annan. illus.; stat.; circ. controlled. **Document type:** corporate report.
Formerly: National Investment Bank, Ghana. Report of the Directors (ISSN 0077-5061)

332 797.1   US
NATIONAL MARINE BANKERS ASSOCIATION. SUMMARY ANNUAL REPORT.* a. membership. National Marine Bankers Association, 200 E. Randolph St., Ste. 5100, Chicago, IL 60601-6436. **Document type:** corporate report.
Description: Describes activities, programs and trends in the recreational boat loan marketplace and includes statistics on delinquencies, charge-offs, average transactions, terms, turnover.

NATIONAL MORTGAGE BROKER. see *REAL ESTATE*

332.3   US   ISSN 1050-3331
HG2150
NATIONAL MORTGAGE NEWS. 1976. w. $198 (effective Jan. 1994). Faulkner & Gray, 22nd Fl., 11 Penn Plaza, New York, NY 10001. TEL 212-967-7000. FAX 212-564-8879. Ed. Mark Fogarty; Pub. Tim Murphy. R&P contact: Mark Fogarty. adv. contact: Steve Schloss. bk.rev. circ. 12,000. (tabloid format; also avail. in microfiche from UMI; back issues avail.) **Indexed:** Bank.Lit.Ind. **Document type:** newspaper.
● Also available online. Vendor(s): UMI.
—UMI. CCC.
Former titles (until 1990): National Thrift and Mortgage News (ISSN 1045-9766); (until 1989): National Thrift News (ISSN 0193-287X)
Description: News of developments in the banking, finance and real estate sectors for an executive audience.

332   US   ISSN 0097-6202
NATIONAL REVIEW OF CORPORATE ACQUISITIONS.* 1974. w. $295 (foreign $345). Acquisition Resource Corp., 55 Main St., Belvedere Tiburon, CA 94920-2507. TEL 415-435-2175. FAX 415-435-6310. Pub. Frederick H. Potts. adv.; bk.rev.; index. (looseleaf format; back issues avail.) **Document type:** newsletter.

333.33   US
NATIONAL SECOND MORTGAGE ASSOCIATION. LEGISLATIVE REPORT.* 1980. 2/yr. membership. National Second Mortgage Association, 3833 Schaefer Ave., Ste. K, Chino, CA 91710-5456. TEL 909-941-2080. FAX 909-941-8248. Ed. Jeffrey Zeltzer. circ. 350. (looseleaf format; back issues avail.)
Description: Covers legislative activity at the state level regarding mortgage lending, mortgage insurance, and relevant developments in consumer protection.

332   NE   ISSN 0169-0922
DE NEDERLANDSCHE BANK N.V. ANNUAL REPORT. 1981. a. free. (Nederlandsche Bank N.V. - Dutch Central Bank) Kluwer Academic Publishers, Postbus 17, 3300 AA Dordrecht, Netherlands. TEL 31-78-6392392. FAX 31-78-6392254. TELEX 29245 KAPG NL. E-mail: services@wkap.nl; URL: http://www.wkap.nl. (Dist. by: Kluwer Academic Publishers Group, P.O. Box 322, 3300 AH Dordrecht, Netherlands. TEL 31-78-6392392. FAX 31-78-6546474; N. America dist. addr.: Box 358, Accord Sta., Hingham, MA 02018-0358. TEL 617-871-6600. FAX 617-871-6528) **Document type:** corporate report.
—CCC.
Formerly: Nederlandsche Bank. Report (ISSN 0167-3998)

332   NE   ISSN 0922-6184
DE NEDERLANDSCHE BANK N.V. QUARTERLY BULLETIN/DUTCH CENTRAL BANK. QUARTERLY BULLETIN. Dutch edition: Nederlandsche Bank N.V. Kwartaalbericht (ISSN 0166-915X) 1972. q. free. (Nederlandsche Bank N.V. - Dutch Central Bank) Kluwer Academic Publishers, Postbus 17, 3300 AA Dordrecht, Netherlands. TEL 31-78-6392392. FAX 31-78-6392254. TELEX 29245 KAPG NL. E-mail: services@wkap.nl; URL: http://www.wkap.nl. (Dist. by: Kluwer Academic Publishers Group, P.O. Box 322, 3300 AH Dordrecht, Netherlands. TEL 31-78-6392392. FAX 31-78-6546474; N. America dist. addr.: Box 358, Accord Sta., Hingham, MA 02018-0358. TEL 617-871-6600. FAX 617-871-6528) **Document type:** bulletin.
—CCC.
Formerly (until 1983): Nederlandsche Bank N.V. Quarterly Statistics (ISSN 0166-9400)

332   MX   ISSN 0028-2456
NEGOCIOS Y BANCOS. Short title: Negobancos. 1951. 24/yr. $60. Publicaciones Importantes, S.A., Bolivar 8-601, Apdo. Postal 1907, 06000 Mexico, D.F., Mexico. TEL 5-510-1884. FAX 5-512-9411. Ed. Alfredo Farrugia Reed. adv.: B&W page $3000, color page $3750. illus.; stat. circ. 18,000.

NELSON'S DIRECTORY OF INVESTMENT MANAGERS. see *BUSINESS AND ECONOMICS — Trade And Industrial Directories*

NELSON'S DIRECTORY OF INVESTMENT RESEARCH. see *BUSINESS AND ECONOMICS — Trade And Industrial Directories*

332   NP
NEPAL BANK LIMITED. ANNUAL REPORT AND BALANCE SHEET. (Text in English, Nepali) a. Nepal Bank Limited, Dharma Path, Kathmandu, Nepal. charts; stat. **Document type:** corporate report.

332   NP
NEPAL BANK PATRIKA/NEPAL BANK BULLETIN. (Editions in English and Nepali) 1968. m. free. Nepal Bank Limited, Dharma Path, Kathmandu, Nepal. Ed. Chiranjivi Dutt. charts; illus.; stat. circ. 2,500. **Document type:** bulletin.

332.1   NP   ISSN 1016-7544
NEPAL RASTRA BANK. ANNUAL REPORT. (Text in English) 1957. a. free. Nepal Rastra Bank, Research Department, Baluwatar, Kathmandu, Nepal. **Document type:** corporate report.
Formerly: Nepal Rastra Bank. Report of the Board of Directors (ISSN 0077-6580)
Description: Financial report of the bank.

332   NE
NETHERLANDS INSTITUTE OF BANKERS AND STOCK BROKERS. PUBLICATIONS. vol. 31, 1977. irreg. price varies. Kluwer Academic Publishers, Postbus 17, 3300 AA Dordrecht, Netherlands. TEL 31-78-6392392. FAX 31-78-6392254. E-mail: services@wkap.nl; URL: http://www.wkap.nl. (Dist. by: Kluwer Academic Publishers Group, P.O. Box 322, 3300 AH Dordrecht, Netherlands. TEL 31-78-6392392. FAX 31-78-6546474; N. America dist. addr.: Box 358, Accord Sta., Hingham, MA 02018-0358. TEL 617-871-6600. FAX 617-871-6528) **Document type:** monographic series.

332.1 338.9   NE
NETHERLANDS INVESTMENT BANK FOR DEVELOPING COUNTRIES. REPORT/NEDERLANDSE INVESTERINGSBANK VOOR ONTWIKKELINGSLANDEN. VERSLAG. (Text in Dutch and English) 1965. a. free. Netherlands Investment Bank for Developing Countries - Nederlandse Investeringsbank voor Ontwikkelingslanden N.V., SE Carmegicplcin, P.O. Box 380, 2501 BH The Hague, Netherlands. TEL 31-70-3425425. FAX 31-70-3657815. TELEX 32089 NIO NL. circ. 2,000. **Document type:** corporate report.
Formerly: Netherlands Investment Bank for Developing Countries. Annual Report (ISSN 0077-7560)
Description: Includes development aid budget, list of bank loans and grants to the different countries, funding, profit and loss account as well as a balance sheet.

NEW ENGLAND ACCOUNTING RESEARCH STUDIES (NO.). see *BUSINESS AND ECONOMICS — Accounting*

332   US
NEW ENGLAND BANKING TRENDS. 1992. q. free. Federal Reserve Bank of Boston, Research Department, 600 Atlantic Ave., Box 2076, Boston, MA 02106-2076. TEL 617-973-3397. FAX 617-973-4292. Ed. Peggy Gilligan. circ. 2,000.

332   US
NEW ENGLAND FISCAL FACTS. 1991. 3/yr. free. Federal Reserve Bank of Boston, Research Department, 600 Atlantic Ave., Box 2076, Boston, MA 02106-2076. TEL 617-973-3397. FAX 617-973-4292. URL: http://www.bos.fsb.org. Ed. Robert Tannenwald. circ. 2,500.

332.1 368   UK   ISSN 0955-095X
NEW HORIZON. 1975. m. £30 (Europe £36; rest of world £45) (effective 1996 & 1997). Institute of Islamic Banking & Insurance, 144-146 King's Cross Rd., London WC1X 9DH, England. TEL 44-171-833-8275. FAX 44-171-278-4797. E-mail: icis@iibi.demon.co.uk. Ed. S. Ghazanfar Ali. adv.: B&W page £500, color page £600; trim 294 x 210. bk.rev./; circ. 7,000 (paid). (back issues avail.) **Indexed:** Per.Islam.
—BLDSC (6084.237910).
Description: Concerns the interests and activities of those involved with Islamic (interest-free) banking and insurance.

BUSINESS AND ECONOMICS — BANKING AND FINANCE

332.1   US
NEW JERSEY. DEPARTMENT OF BANKING. ANNUAL REPORT. 1895. a. $10. Department of Banking, Box CN040, Trenton, NJ 08625. TEL 609-984-2772. FAX 609-292-5455. Ed. Gerald Trimble. circ. 1,300. (also avail. in microfiche from CIS) **Document type:** government publication.
  Formed by the merger of: New Jersey. Division of Savings and Loan Associations. Annual Report (ISSN 0098-8073); New Jersey. Division of Banking. Annual Report (ISSN 0098-7409)

332.1   US
NEW JERSEY LEAGUE NEWS. 1922. 3/yr. New Jersey Community & Savings League Bankers League, 411 North Ave. E., Cranford, NJ 07016. TEL 908-272-8500. FAX 908-272-6626. Ed. Samuel J. Damiano. adv. contact: James Meredith. stat.; circ. 1,200 (controlled). **Document type:** newsletter.
  Former titles: New Jersey Savings League News; New Jersey Savings League Guide (ISSN 0300-6115)

332   US
NEW JERSEY STATE BAR ASSOCIATION. BANKING LAW SECTION. NEWSLETTER. 1977. irreg. membership. New Jersey State Bar Association, Banking Law Section, One Constitution Sq., New Brunswick, NJ 08901-1500. TEL 908-249-5000. FAX 908-828-0034. Ed. Barbara Sheehan. bk.rev. circ. 800. (back issues avail.) **Document type:** newsletter.

332 340   US
NEW JERSEY STATE BAR ASSOCIATION. CREDITOR AND DEBTOR RELATIONS SECTION NEWSLETTER. 1966. irreg. free to members. New Jersey State Bar Association, Creditor and Debtor Relations Section, One Constitution Sq., New Brunswick, NJ 08901-1500. TEL 908-249-5000. FAX 908-828-0034. Ed. Barbara Sheehan. **Document type:** newsletter.

332.1 340   US
NEW YORK BANKING LAW. a. $50. New York Legal Publishing Corp., 6 Charles Park, Guilderland, NY 12084. TEL 800-541-2681. FAX 518-456-0828.

332   US
NEW YORK UNIVERSITY. SALOMON CENTER. NEWSLETTER. 1971. q. New York University, Salomon Center, Stern School of Business, 44 W. Fourth St., New York, NY 10012. TEL 212-998-0700. Dir. Ingo Walter. bibl. **Document type:** newsletter.
  Formerly (until 1990): New York University Salomon Brothers Center for the Study of Financial Institutions. Newsletter.
  Description: Focuses on research projects, conferences and the Center's objectives. Lists recent business monographs, working papers and occasional papers.

332   US
NEW YORK UNIVERSITY. SALOMON CENTER. OCCASIONAL PAPERS. 1979. irreg., no.9, 1989. price varies. New York University, Salomon Center, Stern School of Business, 44 W. Fourth St., New York, NY 10012. TEL 212-998-0700. Ed. Ingo Walter. circ. 1,000.
  Formerly (until 1990): Salomon Brothers Center for the Study of Financial Institutions. Occasional Papers.
  Description: Series devoted to work-in-progress that has important current applications.

332   US   ISSN 0884-318X
HG1
NEW YORK UNIVERSITY. SALOMON CENTER. OCCASIONAL PAPERS IN BUSINESS AND FINANCE. irreg. $10 per no. New York University, Salomon Center, Stern School of Business, 44 W. Fourth St., New York, NY 10012. TEL 212-998-0700.
  Former titles (until 1990): Salomon Brothers Center for the Study of Financial Institutions. Occasional Papers in Business and Finance; Occasional Papers in Metropolitan Business and Finance.

332   US
NEW YORK UNIVERSITY. SALOMON CENTER. WORKING PAPERS SERIES. 1971. irreg. $100. New York University, Salomon Center, Stern School of Business, 44 W. Fourth St., New York, NY 10012. TEL 212-998-0700. Ed. Ingo Walter. circ. 500. **Document type:** monographic series.
  Formerly (until 1990): Salomon Brothers Center for the Study of Financial Institutions. Working Paper Series.

332   NZ
NEW ZEALAND BANKERS' ASSOCIATION ANNUAL REVIEW. a. free. New Zealand Bankers' Association, P.O. Box 3043, Wellington, New Zealand. Ed. Margaret Syles. circ. 1,000. **Document type:** corporate report.
  Formerly: New Zealand Bankers' Association Annual Report.
  Description: Reports association's activities and concerns.

332   NR   ISSN 0794-6430
HG3431
NIGERIA BANKING, FINANCE & COMMERCE. (Text in English) 1985. a. £N500. Research & Data Services Ltd., 54-55 Taiwo St. (off Abibu Oki St.), P.O. Box 2720, Marina, Lagos, Nigeria. TEL 234-2-664639. FAX 234-2-660926. Ed. Amade Abalaka. adv.: page £N17500. **Document type:** directory.
  Description: Lists Nigerian banks and nonbank financial institutions, as well as regulatory bodies. Profiles companies and compiles financial statistics.

332 336   NR
NIGERIA FINANCE YEAR-BOOK. 1992. £N350. Goldstar Publishers (Nigeria) Ltd., 13-15 Osolo Way, Ajao Estate, Isolo, P.O. Box 51699, Ikoyi, Lagos, Nigeria. TEL 234-1-522530.
  Description: Contains essential facts and information on the companies, institutions, and activities in the finance sector.

332.1   NR   ISSN 0549-2734
HG3399.N53
NIGERIAN INDUSTRIAL DEVELOPMENT BANK. ANNUAL REPORT AND ACCOUNTS. 1963. a. free. Nigerian Industrial Development Bank, 63-71 Broad St., P.O. Box 2357, Lagos, Nigeria. TELEX 21774. illus. circ. 2,000. **Document type:** corporate report.

333   NR   ISSN 0189-3319
NIGERIAN JOURNAL OF FINANCIAL MANAGEMENT; international review of finance. s-a. £N25($40) Centre for Financial Management and Research, Institute of Management and Technology, P.M.B. 1079, Nsukka, Enugu State, Nigeria. Ed. M.R.K. Swamy. adv.; bk.rev. circ. 1,500. **Document type:** academic/scholarly publication.

332   JA   ISSN 0285-5887
NIHON KAIHATSU GINKO. CHOSABU. CHOSA. 1973. irreg. free. Japan Development Bank - Nihon Kaihatsu Ginko, 1-9-1 Otemachi, 1-chome, Chiyoda-ku, Tokyo 100, Japan. TEL 03-3244-1770. FAX 03-3245-0954. TELEX J24342. circ. 3,000. —BLDSC (6112.717000).

332   JA
NIKKEI. ANNUAL CORPORATION REPORTS (LISTED COMPANIES). a. Nihon Keizai Shimbun, Inc., 1-9-5 Ote-machi, Chiyoda-ku, Tokyo 100-66, Japan. TEL 81-3-3270-0251. FAX 81-3-5255-2661. TELEX J22308 NIKKEI. **Document type:** trade publication, corporate report.
  Description: Contains entries on all companies listed on Japan's eight stock exchanges and major extracts from financial statements, including balance sheets and statements of profit and loss.

332   JA
NIKKEI. ANNUAL CORPORATION REPORTS (UNLISTED COMPANIES). a. Nihon Keizai Shimbun, Inc., 1-9-5 Ote-machi, Chiyoda-ku, Tokyo 100-66, Japan. TEL 81-3-3270-0251. FAX 81-3-5255-2661. TELEX J22308 NIKKEI. **Document type:** trade publication, corporate report.
  Description: Covers more than 18,000 unlisted companies. Provides information on finance, financial indices, profitability, and capital formation.

332   JA
NIKKEI ANNUAL FINANCIAL REPORT. a. Nihon Keizai Shimbun, Inc., 1-9-5 Ote-machi, Chiyoda-ku, Tokyo 100-66, Japan. TEL 81-3-3270-0251. FAX 81-3-5255-2661. TELEX J22308 NIKKEI. **Document type:** corporate report.
  Description: Publishes rankings and management indices for 1,600 leading financial and securities institutions.

332   JA
NIKKEI COUNTRY RISK REPORT. m.? Nihon Keizai Shimbun, Inc., Japan Bond Research Institute, 1-9-5 Ote-machi, Chiyoda-ku, Tokyo 100-66, Japan. TEL 81-3-3270-0251. FAX 81-3-5255-2661. TELEX J22308 NIKKEI. **Document type:** newsletter.
  Description: Covers financial statuses and risk levels of various countries.

332   JA
NIKKEI FINANCIAL ANALYSIS (LISTED COMPANIES). a. Nihon Keizai Shimbun, Inc., 1-9-5 Ote-machi, Chiyoda-ku, Tokyo 100-66, Japan. TEL 81-3-3270-0251. FAX 81-3-5255-2661. TELEX J22308 NIKKEI. **Document type:** trade publication.
  Description: Analysis of various data and 107 indices for 2,100 nonfinancial companies listed on Japan's eight stock exchanges.

332   JA
NIKKEI FINANCIAL ANALYSIS (UNLISTED COMPANIES). a. Nihon Keizai Shimbun, Inc., 1-9-5 Ote-machi, Chiyoda-ku, Tokyo 100-66, Japan. TEL 81-3-3270-0251. FAX 81-3-5255-2661. TELEX J22308 NIKKEI. **Document type:** trade publication.
  Description: Analysis of 4,900 leading unlisted Japanese companies.

332   JA
NIKKEI KINYU SHIMBUN/NIKKEI FINANCIAL DAILY. (Text in Japanese) 1987. 6/w. Nihon Keizai Shimbun, Inc., 1-9-5 Ote-machi, Chiyoda-ku, Tokyo 100, Japan. TEL 81-3-3270-0251. FAX 81-3-5255-2661. TELEX J22308 NIKKEI. Ed. Fumio Tateiwa. adv.: B&W page 1095000 Yen; trim 385 x 533; adv. contact: Masahiro Matsui. circ. 61,864. **Document type:** newspaper.
  Description: Covers the international capital and money markets. Provides in-depth analysis of the strategies and financial performances of both Japanese and foreign companies.

332   JA
NIKKEI MONEY. (Text in Japanese) m. Nikkei Home Publishing, Inc. (Subsidiary of: Nihon Keizai Shimbun, Inc.), 2-2-7 Kanda Tsukasa-cho, Chiyoda-ku, Tokyo 101, Japan. TEL 03-3258-7818.
  Description: Contains savings, bonds, stocks, pension funds, and other financial information.

332   JA
NIKKEI NEWSLETTER ON BOND & MONEY. w. Japan Bond Research Institute, 2-6-1 Nihonbashi Kayaba-cho, Chuo-ku, Tokyo 103, Japan. TEL 03-3639-2840. FAX 03-3639-2848. **Document type:** newsletter.
  Description: Contains news on bond issues and other financial matters.

332   JA   ISSN 0917-2165
NIPPON GINKO GEPPO/BANK OF JAPAN MONTHLY BULLETIN. m. 780 Yen per no. Bank of Japan - Nippon Ginko, c/o Public Relations Department, 2-1-1 Hongoku-Cho, Nihonbashi, Chuo-ku, Tokyo 103, Japan. TEL 81-3-3279-1111. FAX 81-3-5203-8703. (Dist. by: Tokiwa Sohgoh Service Co., Ltd., Kyodo Bldg., 2-4, 3-chome, Hongokucho, Nihonbashi Chuo-ku, Tokyo 103, Japan. TEL 81-3-3270-5713. FAX 81-3-3270-5710; Overseas dist. by: Japan Publications Trading Co., Ltd., Book Export No.2 Dept., P.O. Box 5030 Tokyo International, Tokyo 100-31, Japan) pp./issue: 130. **Document type:** bulletin.
  Description: Contains research papers on finance and the economy of Japan.

NORDRHEIN-WESTFALEN. FINANZMINISTERIUM. FINANZ REPORT. see *PUBLIC ADMINISTRATION*

BUSINESS AND ECONOMICS — BANKING AND FINANCE

332.1   NO   ISSN 0078-1185
NORGES BANK. REPORT AND ACCOUNTS. Cover title: Norges Bank. Annual Report. Norwegian edition: Norges Bank. Beretning og Regnskap (ISSN 0800-8507) (Text in English) 1955. a. Norges Bank, Information Department - Central Bank of Norway, P.O. Box 1179 Sentrum, N-0107 Oslo, Norway. TEL 47-22-31-60-00. FAX 47-22-41-31-05. TELEX 56-71-369 NBANK N. Pub. Kjell Storvik. **Document type:** corporate report.

THE NORTH AMERICAN JOURNAL OF ECONOMICS AND FINANCE; a journal of theory and practice. see BUSINESS AND ECONOMICS — Economic Situation And Conditions

NORTH SEA LETTER. see PETROLEUM AND GAS

332   US   ISSN 1042-1254
HF1
NORTHWESTERN FINANCIAL REVIEW. 1894. w. $75. 3407 W. 44th St., Minneapolis, MN 55410-1439. TEL 612-929-8110. FAX 612-929-8146. E-mail: cp_casserly@tcilink.com; URL: http://www.nfrcom.com. Ed. Tom Bengtson; Pub. Tom Bengtson. R&P contact: Tom Bengtson. adv. contact: Robert Cronin. illus.; mkt.; circ. 3,000 (paid). **Indexed:** Bank.Lit.Ind. **Document type:** trade publication.
Incorporates: Commercial West; Which was formerly (until 1988): Northwestern Banker (ISSN 0010-3144); Incorporates (1902-1980): Michigan Investor; Northwest Banker.
Description: For the banking and finance industry in the Upper Midwest.

338.47   UK
NORWAY FINANCIAL ANALYSIS SERVICE. s-a. £7500 for single users (renewals £4800); network £9000 (renewals £6000). Arthur Andersen, Petroleum Services Group, 1 Surrey St., London WC2R 2PS, England. TEL 44-171-438-3888. FAX 44-171-438-3881. TELEX 8812711. Eds. Mike Coulten, Gary Howorth. (diskette format) **Document type:** trade publication.
Description: Calculates discounted pre- and post-tax cashflow by field and company for Norway.

332   FR   ISSN 0399-1636
NOUVELLES FISCALES. 1957. bi-m. 1660 F. (effective 1992). Groupe Liaisons S.A., 1 av. Edouard Belin, 92856 Rueil Malmaison, France. TEL 33-1-48059105. FAX 33-1-43550233. **Document type:** trade publication.
Formerly (until 1973): Aide - Memoire Fiscal (ISSN 0995-9106)

332   XV
NOVICE; glasilo delovne skupnosti Jugobanke. (Text in Slovenian) 1974. m. 7.30 din. per no. Banka D.D. Ljubljana, Titova 32, Ljubljana, Slovenia. Ed. Maja Tejkal. circ. 500.

O C C BULLETINS. (U.S. Office of the Comptroller of the Currency) see BUSINESS AND ECONOMICS — Public Finance, Taxation

382 332   FR   ISSN 0474-5655
O E C D CODE OF LIBERALIZATION OF CAPITAL MOVEMENTS/O C D E CODE DE LA LIBERATION DES MOUVEMENTS DE CAPITAUX. (Editions in English, French) irreg. price varies. Organization for Economic Cooperation and Development, 2 rue Andre Pascal, 75775 Paris 16, France. (U.S. orders to: O.E.C.D. Publications and Information Center, 2001 L St., N.W., Ste. 650, Washington, DC 20036-4922. TEL 202-785-6323)

332.1   US
OBERWEIS REPORT: A MONTHLY REVIEW. 1976. m. $139 (Fax $249) (effective 1997). Oberweis Asset Management, Inc., 951 Ice Cream Dr., Ste. 200, North Aurora, IL 60542-1472. TEL 800-323-6166. FAX 630-896-5282. Ed. James D. Oberweis. circ. 6,000 (paid); 4,000 (controlled). (also avail. by fax; back issues avail.)
Former titles: Oberweis Securities Monthly Review; Oberweis Management Monthly Review.

332   NO   ISSN 0030-1914
OEKONOMISK REVY. 1918. 6/yr. NOK 430 (foreign NOK 490). Norske Bankforening - Dronning Maudsgt, 15, P.O. Box 1489, Vika, N-0116 Oslo, Norway. FAX 47-22-83-07-43. TELEX 77218. Ed. Johan Joergen Thorsen. adv.; bk.rev.; mkt.; stat.; index. circ. 1,800.

332.1   AU
OESTERREICHISCHE BANKWISSENSCHAFTLICHE GESELLSCHAFT. BANKWISSENSCHAFTLICHE SCHRIFTENREIHE. 1953. irreg., vol.82, 1996. price varies. Bank Verlag, Wallnerstr. 1, A-1010 Vienna, Austria. TEL 43-1-5335050. FAX 43-1-53127247. Ed. Otto Lucius. **Document type:** monographic series.

332   AU
OESTERREICHISCHE NATIONALBANK. BERICHTE UND STUDIEN. (Editions in English and German) 1990. q. free. Oesterreichische Nationalbank, Otto-Wagner-Platz 3, A-1090 Vienna, Austria. Ed. Peter Achleitner. circ. 2,500. **Document type:** bulletin.

332.1   AU
OESTERREICHISCHE NATIONALBANK. GESCHAEFTSBERICHT UEBER DAS GESCHAEFTSJAHR MIT JAHRESABSCHLUSS - ANNUAL REPORT. (Editions in English and German) 1956. a. free. Oesterreichische Nationalbank, Otto-Wagner-Platz 3, A-1090 Vienna, Austria. Ed. Peter Achleitner. circ. 2,500. **Document type:** corporate report.
Formerly: Oesterreichische Nationalbank, Bericht ueber das Geschaeftsjahr mit Rechnungsabschluss - Annual Report (ISSN 0078-3528)
Description: Covers the Austrian and international economy. Includes balance sheet, profit and loss account, tables, and graphs.

332.4   AU
HG3014
OESTERREICHISCHE NATIONALBANK. STATISTISCHES MONATSHEFT. 1926. m. S.1000. Oesterreichische Nationalbank, Otto-Wagner-Platz 3, A-1090 Vienna, Austria. Ed. Peter Achleitner. charts; index. **Indexed:** PROMT.
Formerly: Oesterreichische Nationalbank. Mitteilungen des Direktoriums (ISSN 0029-9332)
Description: Statistics on the Austrian Central Bank, Austria's money and credit market, interest rates, capital markets, notes and coin, public finance, economic development, etc.

332.2   AU
OESTERREICHISCHE SPARKASSENZEITUNG. fortn. Hauptverband der Oesterreichischen Sparkassen, Postfach 256, A-1011 Vienna, Austria. TEL 0222-71169. FAX 0222-7138926. **Document type:** bulletin.

332   AU   ISSN 0472-5859
OESTERREICHISCHES FORSCHUNGSINSTITUT FUER SPARKASSENWESEN. SCHRIFTENREIHE. 1961. q. S.180. Sparkassenverlag GmbH, Grimmelshausengasse 1, A-1030 Vienna, Austria. TEL 43-1-71170-0. FAX 43-1-71170310. Ed. Dr. Gustav Raab. charts; stat. circ. 550. **Indexed:** P.A.I.S.For.Lang.Ind. **Document type:** academic/scholarly publication.

OESTERREICHISCHES UND EUROPAEISCHES WIRTSCHAFTSPRIVATRECHT. see LAW

332   BF
OFFSHORE; an e - journal. 1991. 26/yr. $20 donation. Global Group Ltd., P.O. Box CB13039, Nassau, Bahamas. E-mail: offshore@bahamas.net.bs; URL: http://www.dnai.com/offshore/offshore.html. Ed. Arnold L. Cornez. bk.rev.
● Available only online.
Description: Discusses tax havens, scam alerts, offshore banking, offshore trusts, asset protection, annuities, foundations and more.
Refereed Serial

332.1   UK   ISSN 1353-422X
OFFSHORE FINANCE YEARBOOK (YEAR). 1993. a. £130($235) Euromoney Publications plc., Books, Nestor House, Playhouse Yard, London EC4V 5EX, England. TEL 0171-779-8935. FAX 0171-779-8541. (Orders to: Plymbridge Distributors Ltd., Estover, Plymouth, Devon PL6 7PZ, England. TEL 0171-779-8610. FAX 01752-695668) **Document type:** directory.
Description: Lists 400 companies active in the offshore finance market.

332   UK   ISSN 0954-0628
OFFSHORE INVESTMENT. 1986. 10/yr. £150($270) (outside Europe £210 ($378)) (effective 1997). European Magazine Services Ltd., 62 Brompton Rd., Knightsbridge, London SW3 1BW, England. TEL 44-171-225-0550. FAX 44-171-584-1093. E-mail: http://www.offshoreinvestment.com/offshore. Ed. Charles A. Cain; Pub. Barry C. Bingham. adv. contact: Colin Martin. bk.rev.; charts; illus.; tr.lit.; index. circ. 12,000. (back issues avail.) **Document type:** trade publication.
Description: Presents current information regarding offshore incorporation, investment, domicile, and tax issues.
Refereed Serial

332.1   US   ISSN 0030-0802
OHIO BANKER. 1908. m. $25. Ohio Bankers Association, 37 W. Broad St., Ste. 1001, Columbus, OH 43215-4162. TEL 614-221-5121. FAX 614-221-3421. Ed. Melea Wachtman. adv. circ. 3,400. **Indexed:** Bank.Lit.Ind. **Document type:** newsletter.

332   NE
ONDERNEMINGSANALYSES BANKEN. a. fl.89.50. Delwel Uitgeverij B.V., Postbus 19110, 2500 CC The Hague, Netherlands. TEL 31-70-3624800. FAX 31-70-3605606.
Description: Provides information on the financial performance of the banking and finance sectors in the Netherlands.

332.1   US
OPERATING BANKS AND BRANCHES. DATA BOOK: UNITED STATES, STATES, COUNTIES, OTHER AREAS; summary of deposits in all FDIC BIF-insured commercial and savings banks and US branches of foreign banks. Spine title: F D I C Data Book - United States, States, Counties, Other Areas. a. free. U.S. Federal Deposit Insurance Corporation, Division of Accounting and Corporate Services, Management Information Services Branch, Bank Financial Reporting Section, 550 17th St., N.W., Washington, DC 20429-9990. TEL 202-393-8400.

332.1   US
OPERATING BANKS AND BRANCHES. DATA BOOK 1: CONNECTICUT, MAINE, MASSACHUSETTS, NEW HAMPSHIRE, NEW JERSEY, NEW YORK, PENNSYLVANIA, RHODE ISLAND, VERMONT, PUERTO RICO, VIRGIN ISLANDS; summary of deposits in all FDIC BIF-insured commercial and savings banks and US branches of foreign banks. Spine title: F D I C Data Book 1 - CT, ME, MA, NH, NJ, NY, PA, RI, VT, PR, VI. a. free. U.S. Federal Deposit Insurance Corporation, Division of Accounting and Corporate Services, Management Information Services Branch, Bank Financial Reporting Section, 1550 17th St., N.W., Washington, DC 20429-9990. TEL 202-393-8400.

332.1   US
OPERATING BANKS AND BRANCHES. DATA BOOK 2: DELAWARE, DISTRICT OF COLUMBIA, FLORIDA, GEORGIA, MARYLAND, NORTH CAROLINA, SOUTH CAROLINA, VIRGINIA, WEST VIRGINIA; summary of deposits in all FDIC BIF-insured commercial and savings banks and US branches of foreign banks. Spine title: F D I C Data Book 2 - DE, DC, FL, GA, MD, NC, SC, VA, WV. a. free. U.S. Federal Deposit Insurance Corporation, Division of Accounting and Corporate Services, Management Information Services Branch, Bank Financial Reporting Section, 550 17th St., N.W., Washington, DC 20429-9990. TEL 202-393-8400.

332.1   US
OPERATING BANKS AND BRANCHES. DATA BOOK 3: ILLINOIS, INDIANA, KENTUCKY, MICHIGAN, OHIO, WISCONSIN; summary of deposits in all FDIC BIF-insured commercial and savings banks and US branches of foreign banks. Spine title: F D I C Data Book 3 - IL, IN, KY, MI, OH, WI. a. free. U.S. Federal Deposit Insurance Corporation, Division of Accounting and Corporate Services, Management Information Services Branch, Bank Financial Reporting Section, 550 17th St., N.W., Washington, DC 20429-9990. TEL 202-393-8400.

BUSINESS AND ECONOMICS — BANKING AND FINANCE

332.1 US
OPERATING BANKS AND BRANCHES. DATA BOOK 4: ALABAMA, ARKANSAS, LOUISIANA, MISSISSIPPI, OKLAHOMA, TENNESSEE, TEXAS; summary of deposits in all FDIC BIF-insured commercial and savings banks and US branches of foreign banks. Spine title: F D I C Data Book 4 - AL, AR, LA, MS, OK, TN, TX. a. free. U.S. Federal Deposit Insurance Corporation, Division of Accounting and Corporate Services, Management Information Services Branch, Bank Financial Reporting Section, 550 17th St., N.W., Washington, DC 20429-9990. TEL 202-393-8400.

332.1 US
OPERATING BANKS AND BRANCHES. DATA BOOK 5: IOWA, KANSAS, MINNESOTA, MISSOURI, NEBRASKA, NORTH DAKOTA, SOUTH DAKOTA; summary of deposits in all FDIC BIF-insured commercial and savings banks and US branches of foreign banks. Spine title: F D I C Data Book 5 - IA, KS, MN, MO, NE, ND, SD. a. free. U.S. Federal Deposit Insurance Corporation, Division of Accounting and Corporate Services, Management Information Services Branch, Bank Financial Reporting Section, 550 17th St., N.W., Washington, DC 20429-9990. TEL 202-393-8400.

332.1 US
OPERATING BANKS AND BRANCHES. DATA BOOK 6: ALASKA, ARIZONA, CALIFORNIA, COLORADO, HAWAII, IDAHO, MONTANA, NEVADA, NEW MEXICO, OREGON, UTAH, WASHINGTON, WYOMING, PACIFIC ISLANDS; summary of deposits in all FDIC BIF-insured commercial and savings banks and US branches of foreign banks. Spine title: F D I C Data Book 6 - AK, AZ, CA, CO, HI, ID, MT, NV, NM, OR, UT, WA, WY, PI. a. free. U.S. Federal Deposit Insurance Corporation, Division of Accounting and Corporate Services, Management Information Services Branch, Bank Financial Reporting Section, 550 17th St., N.W., Washington, DC 20429-9990. TEL 202-393-8400.

332 US
OPERATIONS ALERT (CHICAGO).* 1981. bi-w. $200 to non-members. United States League of Savings Institutions, 900 19th St. N.W., No. 900, Washington, DC 20006-2105. TEL 312-644-3100. Eds. William T. Marshall, Edward T. Maney. circ. 9,000.
  Description: Covers information on the latest operating developments and practices in the savings institution business.

332 US
OPERATIONS MANAGEMENT REPORT. 1986. m. $319 (effective 1997). Siefer Consultants, Inc., Box 1384, Storm Lake, IA 50588. TEL 712-732-7340. FAX 712-732-7906. Ed. Steve Herron. index. circ. 2,300. (back issues avail.) Document type: newsletter.
  Formerly: Fee Income Report (ISSN 0892-7383)
  Description: Bank-tested ideas to increase fees, service charges, and commission income.

330 FR ISSN 0989-1900
OPTION FINANCE. w. (48/yr.). 1500 F. 1 rue du Colonel Pierre Avia, 75503 Paris Cedex 15, France. TEL 33-01-46-48-48-48. FAX 33-01-46-48-49-66. (Subscr. to: Subscr. Dept. B310, 60732 Ste. Genevieve Cedex, France. TEL 33-03-44074452) Ed. Valerie Nau; Pub. Francois Fahys. R&P contact: Francois Fahys. adv. contact: Michele Fenetre. circ. 20,000.

332.7 IL
OPTIONS. (Text in English) 1994. q. free. Magna Publishing Company Ltd., Magna House, 100E Old Prabhadevi Rd., Prabhadevi, Bombay 400 025, India. TEL 91-22-4362270. FAX 91-22-4306523. TELEX 11-73288 MAG IN. Ed. Ashvina Vakil. adv.: B&W page Rs.15000, color page Rs.30000; trim 267 x 203. circ. 106,250.

332.3 333.33 US ISSN 1083-8481
ORIGINATION NEWS MONTHLY. 1990. m. $56. Faulkner & Gray, 22nd Fl., 11 Penn Plaza, New York, NY 10001. TEL 212-967-7000. Ed. Mark Fogarty; Pub. Tim Murphy. R&P contact: Mark Fogarty. adv. circ. 18,998. (tabloid format; also avail. in microform from UMI; back issues avail.) Document type: newspaper.
  ●Also available online. Vendor(s): UMI.
  —UMI. CCC.
  Formerly: Managing Mortgages (ISSN 1060-9318).
  Description: General management publication for mortgage brokers, wholesale lenders, and managers.

332 NE ISSN 0928-8503
HJ54
OVERHEIDSMANAGEMENT; vakblad voor financien automatisering en personeel & organisatie. 1925. 11/yr. fl.112. Vuga Uitgeverij B.V., Postbus 16400, 2500 BK The Hague, Netherlands. TEL 31-70-3614011. FAX 31-70-3625468. Ed. Gea Boschma. adv.: B&W page fl.2680, color page fl.4755; trim 215 x 285. bk.rev.; stat.; illus. circ. 2,700. Indexed: Key to Econ.Sci. Document type: trade publication.
  —SWETS.
  Former titles (until 1992): Financieel Overheidsmanagement (ISSN 0922-1026); (until 1988): Financieel Overheidsbeheer (ISSN 0015-2072)
  Description: Covers developments in finance, computers, personnel and management of interest to management at all levels.

332 320 UK ISSN 0032-3284
P & M. (Politics & Money) 1970. m. £3.80($12.80) to individuals; students £3.10 ($10.80). Politics and Money Publishing Co., 14 South Hill Park Gardens, London N.W.3, England. Ed.Bd. bk.rev.

330.9 PH
P N B INTERNATIONAL. q. free. Philippine National Bank, Public Information Office, PNB Head Office Bldg., 9th Fl., Escolta, Manila, Philippines. Ed. E.P. Patanne. illus.

332.1 US ISSN 8750-6718
HG2609
PACIFIC BANKER. 1902. m. $15. Faulkner & Gray, Inc. (New York), 11 Penn Plaza, 17th Fl., New York, NY 10001. TEL 212-967-7000. FAX 212-967-7155. adv.; charts; illus. circ. 8,663. Indexed: ABI Inform., Bank.Lit.Ind.
  —UMI.
  Formerly (until 1985): Pacific Banker and Business (ISSN 0030-8536)

332 NE ISSN 0927-538X
HG5980.7.A2 CODEN: PBFJEQ
PACIFIC BASIN FINANCE JOURNAL. (Text in English) 1993. 5/yr. fl.600($345) (effective 1998). North-Holland (Subsidiary of: Elsevier Science B.V.), P.O. Box 211, 1000 AE Amsterdam, Netherlands. TEL 31-20-4853911. FAX 31-20-4853598. TELEX 18582 ESPA NL. (Subscr. in the Americas to: Elsevier Science, Regional Sales Office, Box 945, New York, NY 10159-0945. TEL 212-633-3730. FAX 212-633-3680; Subscr. in Australasia and the Far East to: Elsevier Science (Singapore) Pte Ltd, No.1 Temasek Ave., No.17-01 Millenia Tower, Singapore 039192, Singapore. TEL 65-434-3727. FAX 65-337-2230; Subscr. in Japan to: Elsevier Science Japan, 9-15 Higashi-Azabu 1-chome, Minato-ku Tokyo 106, Japan. TEL 81-3-5561-5033. FAX 81-3-5561-5047) Ed. S. Ghon Rhee. (also avail. in microform from UMI; back issues avail.) Indexed: Asian-Pac.Econ.Lit. Document type: academic/scholarly publication.
  —BLDSC (6328.784000); SWETS. CCC.
  Description: Publishes original empirical and theoretical research on capital markets of the Asia Pacific countries.
  Refereed Serial

THE PAINE WEBBER EUROMONEY DIRECTORY. see BUSINESS AND ECONOMICS — Trade And Industrial Directories

332 YU
PANONSKA BANKA NOVI SAD. BILTEN. m. Panonska Banka, Novi Sad, Yugoslavia. Ed. Milan Popovic.
  Formerly: Vojvodanska Banka - Osnovna Banka. Bilten.

332.1 BL
PANORAMA ESTATISTICO DE SETOR BANCARIA. 1971. q. Sindicato dos Bancos do Estado da Guanabara, Assessoria Economica, Av. Rio Branco, 81, Rio de Janeiro, Brazil. stat.

332 PP
PAPUA NEW GUINEA BANKING CORPORATION. ANNUAL REPORT. a. Papua New Guinea Banking Corporation, Cnr. Musgrave & Douglas St., Port Moresby, Papua New Guinea. TEL 675-211999. FAX 675-222867. TELEX BACKCOR 22160. Document type: corporate report.

332 UK
PARIBAS CENTRAL BANK AND MINISTRY OF FINANCE YEARBOOK (YEAR). a. £95($170) (Paribas Capital Markets) Euromoney Publications plc., Nestor House, Playhouse Yard, London EC4V 5EX, England. TEL 0171-779-8935. FAX 0171-779-8541. Ed. Guy Norton; Pub. Chris Brown. Document type: corporate report.

PARKER'S (YEAR) TEXAS UNIFORM COMMERCIAL CODE. see LAW — Corporate Law

PARTNERS IN BUSINESS. see BUSINESS AND ECONOMICS — Management

332 US
THE PAYMENT SYSTEM HANDBOOK. a. $75. U.S. Federal Reserve System, Board of Governors, Publications Services, Rm. MS-127, 20th and Constitution Ave., N.W., Washington, DC 20551. TEL 202-452-3244. FAX 202-728-5886. Document type: government publication.

332 US ISSN 1051-7359
PAYMENT SYSTEMS WORLDWIDE. 1990. q. $96 (effective 1995 & 1996). F.I.A. Financial Publishing Co., 582 Oakwood Ave., Ste. 203, Lake Forest, IL 60045. TEL 708-615-0405. FAX 708-615-0416. Ed. R. Gerald Fox. Document type: trade publication.
  ●Also available online. Vendor(s): UMI.
  —BLDSC (6413.109880).

332 US ISSN 0162-1610
PAYROLL MANAGEMENT GUIDE. 1943. w. $527. C C H Incorporated, 2700 Lake Cook Rd., Riverwoods, IL 60015. TEL 847-267-7000; 800-835-5224. FAX 800-224-8299. (looseleaf format) Document type: trade publication.
  ●Also available on CD-ROM.
  —CCC.

332 NO ISSN 0332-5598
PENGER OG KREDITT. 1973. q. NOK 150. Norges Bank, Information Department, P.O. Box 1179 Sentrum, N-0107 Oslo, Norway. TEL 47-22-31-60-00. FAX 47-22-41-31-05. TELEX 71-369 NBANK N. Ed. Kjell Storvik. Document type: academic/scholarly publication.

332 US ISSN 0252-3108
PER JACOBSSON FOUNDATION. LECTURES. (Editions in English, French, Spanish) 1964. a. free. Per Jacobsson Foundation, International Monetary Fund Bldg., Washington, DC 20431. TEL 202-477-3366. FAX 202-623-4661. (Affiliate: International Monetary Fund) circ. 13,000 (10,000 English ed.; 2,000 French ed.; 1,000 Spanish ed.). Document type: academic/scholarly publication.
  Former titles: Per Jacobsson Foundation. Proceedings (ISSN 0079-0761); Per Jacobsson Memorial Lecture (ISSN 0079-077X)

332.3 US
PERCEPTIONS (DULUTH). q. Georgia Credit Union Affiliates, 2400 Pleasant Hill Rd., Ste. 300, Duluth, GA 30136-5200. TEL 404-476-9625. Ed. Sherrie Futch. adv. circ. 3,200.

332 SA
PERSONAL FINANCE. 1980. m. $250 (effective through Oct. 1997). Prescon Publishing Corporation (Pty) Ltd, P.O. Box 84004, Greenside 2034, South Africa. TEL 27-11-646-9750. FAX 27-11-646-4617. E-mail: prescon@aztec.co.za. Ed. Martin C. Spring. bk.rev. Document type: newsletter.
  Incorporates (in 1993): Business Success; Which was formerly (until 1989): Independent Business.
  Description: Gives specific advice on all aspects of personal finance for upper-income individuals, including investments, taxation, insurance, retirement planning and more.

BUSINESS AND ECONOMICS — BANKING AND FINANCE

332   **UK**
PERSONAL FINANCE INTELLIGENCE. 1985. q. £1495 (effective 1996). Mintel International Group Ltd., 18-19 Long Ln., London EC1A 9HE, England. TEL 44-171-606-4533. FAX 44-171-606-5932. Ed. Paul Hersey. (back issues avail.) **Document type:** trade publication.
●Also available online.
Also available on CD-ROM.
Description: Contains reports aiming to provide insight into consumer attitudes towards developments in financial services and institutions.

332   **US**   **ISSN 0883-5608**
PERSONAL IDENTIFICATION NEWS. Abbreviated title: P I N. 1985. m. $345 (foreign $370). Warfel & Miller, Inc., 7101 Wisconsin Ave., Ste. 1100, Bethesda, MD 20814-4805. Ed. Ben Miller. bk.rev.; index. (back issues avail.) **Document type:** newsletter.
Description: Publishes executive-level summaries of business developments in smart card and advanced security technology.

332   **AU**
PERSONEN-COMPASS. a. S.1500 (effective 1996). Compass Verlag, Matznergasse 17, A-1141 Vienna, Austria. TEL 43-1-98116-0. FAX 43-1-9811698. E-mail: office@compass.co.at; URL: http://www.compass.co.at. Ed. Werner Futter. R&P contact: Werner Futter. adv. contact: Michael Bayer. **Document type:** trade publication.

332   **SP**   **ISSN 1132-9564**
PERSPECTIVAS DEL SISTEMA FINANCIERO. 1983. q. 7000 ptas. (foreign 8000 ptas.) (effective 1997). Fundacion de las Cajas de Ahorros Confederadas para la Investigacion Economica y Social, Padre Damian, 48, 28036 Madrid, Spain. TEL 34-1-3596158. FAX 34-1-3504959. (Subscr. to: Juan Hurtado de Mendoza 19, 28036 Madrid, Spain. TEL 34-1-3504400. FAX 34-1-3508040) Ed. Fernando Gonzalez Olivares; Pub. Victorio Valle Sanchez. R&P contact: Fernando Gonzalez Olivares. circ. 3,500. (also avail. in microfiche) **Document type:** monographic series.
—CINDOC.
Formerly (until 1992): Papeles de Economia Espanola. Suplementos sobre el Sistema Financiero (ISSN 0212-5994)

332   **EI**
PERSPECTIVES. (Text English, French, German) 1970. irreg. (approx. 8-12/yr.). European Savings Banks Group - Groupement Europeen des Caisses d'Epargne, Ave. de la Renaissance, 12, B-1000 Brussels, Belgium. TEL 32-2-7391611. FAX 32-2-7360955. (Co-sponsor: World Savings Bank Institute - Institut Mondial des Caisses d'Epargnes) Ed. Gael du Bouetiez; Pub. C. De Noose. R&P contact: Gael du Bouetiez. circ. 3,000. **Indexed:** World Bank.Abstr. **Document type:** monographic series.
Supersedes (in 1995): E U F I Journal; **Incorporates** (in Oct. 1991): E E (Epargne Europe) (ISSN 0046-0869)
Description: Discusses economic issues affecting the EU.

332 338.91   **US**
PERSPECTIVES (MADISON). 1991. bi-m. free. World Council of Credit Unions, Box 2982, Madison, WI 53701. TEL 608-231-7130. FAX 608-238-8020. TELEX 467918. Ed. Karen Kaplan. circ. 4,200. (looseleaf format; back issues avail.) **Document type:** newsletter.

332   **US**
PETER DAG PORTFOLIO STRATEGY AND MANAGEMENT. 1977. 24/yr. $195. Peter Dag & Associates, Inc., 65 Lakefront Dr., Akron, OH 44319-3698. TEL 216-644-2782; 800-833-2782. FAX 216-644-2798. Ed. George Dagnino. bk.rev.; charts; stat. circ. 2,000. (back issues avail.) **Document type:** newsletter.
—CCC.
Formerly (until Jan. 1995): Peter Dag Investment Letter (ISSN 0196-9323)
Description: Provides stock market forecasts, outlook for short-term interest rates, bonds, foreign equity markets, gold and energy stocks and US dollar. Includes a model portfolio of no-load mutual funds (Vanguard) and exclusive Equity-10 portfolio of 10 stocks.

332.1   **PH**
PHILIPPINE NATIONAL BANK. ECONOMIC BRIEF. m. Philippine National Bank, Public Information Office, PNB Head Office Bldg., 9th Fl., Escolta; Manila, Philippines. charts; illus.; stat.

332 380 320   **PH**   **ISSN 0115-3005**
PHILIPPINES YEARBOOK OF THE FOOKIEN TIMES. (Text in English) 1936. a. $65. Star Group of Publications, P.O. Box 747, Port Area, Manila, Philippines. TEL 632-527-5818. FAX 632-527-2411. Ed. Vernon Go; Pub. Grace Glory Go. adv.: B&W page P.36000, color page P.48000; trim 315 x 250; adv. contact: Rose Fernandez. circ. 50,000. (back issues avail.) **Indexed:** Ind.Phil.Per.
Description: Includes annual reports of all major government offices; economic analyses; special features on the country's leading corporations; environment; health; science and technology; education.

332   **UK**   **ISSN 0032-0668**
PLANNED SAVINGS; a review of personal finance & saving. 1968. m. £54 (foreign £75). E M A P - Finance & Freight Ltd., 33-39 Bowling Green Ln., London EC1R 0DA, England. TEL 44-171-505-8000. FAX 44-171-505-8187. Ed. Julia Dodd. adv.; bk.rev.; charts; illus. circ. 6,386. **Indexed:** World Bank.Abstr. **Document type:** trade publication.
—BLDSC (6508.800000).

PLUNKETT'S FINANCIAL SERVICES INDUSTRY ALMANAC. see BUSINESS AND ECONOMICS — Trade And Industrial Directories

332.1   **C**   **ISSN 0350-4387**
PODUZECE BANKA. 1969. m. Instruktivni Biro, Zagreb, Tkalciceva 48-50, Zagreb, Croatia. Ed. Mladen Canadjija.

POLITICAL FINANCE & LOBBY REPORTER. see POLITICAL SCIENCE

POLITICAL RISK LETTER. see BUSINESS AND ECONOMICS — International Commerce

332 382   **US**
JQ1871.A1
POLITICAL RISK YEARBOOK. (Consists of 6 vols; Vol. I: North & Central America (ISSN 0897-8557); Vol. II: Middle East & North Africa (ISSN 0897-8530); Vol. III: South America (ISSN 0897-8549); Vol. IV: Sub-Saharan Africa (ISSN 0889-2725); Vol. V: Asia & the Pacific (ISSN 0897-8565); Vol. VI: Europe (ISSN 1053-8771)) 1987. a. $1000 for 6 vols. (effective 1994). The P R S Group, Box 248, East Syracuse, NY 13057-0248. TEL 315-431-0511. FAX 315-431-0200. Eds. William D. Coplin, Michael K. O'Leary.
●Also available online. Vendor(s): Data-Star (FSRI), Lexis-Nexis.
Also available on CD-ROM.
Description: Contains complete reports on 100 countries.

332 382   **US**   **ISSN 0897-8557**
JL1416
POLITICAL RISK YEARBOOK. VOLUME 1: NORTH & CENTRAL AMERICA. 1987. a. $250. The P R S Group, Box 248, East Syracuse, NY 13057-0248. TEL 315-431-0511. FAX 315-431-0200.
●Also available online. Vendor(s): Data-Star (FSRI), Lexis-Nexis.

332 382   **US**   **ISSN 0897-8530**
JQ1758.A1
POLITICAL RISK YEARBOOK. VOLUME 2: MIDDLE EAST & NORTH AFRICA. 1987. a. $250. The P R S Group, Box 248, East Syracuse, NY 13057-0248. TEL 315-431-0511. FAX 315-431-0200.
●Also available online. Vendor(s): Data-Star (FSRI), Lexis-Nexis.

332 382   **US**   **ISSN 0897-8549**
JL1866
POLITICAL RISK YEARBOOK. VOLUME 3: SOUTH AMERICA. 1987. a. $250. The P R S Group, Box 248, East Syracuse, NY 13057-0248. TEL 315-431-0511. FAX 315-431-0200.
●Also available online. Vendor(s): Data-Star (FSRI), Lexis-Nexis.

332 382   **US**   **ISSN 0889-2725**
JQ1871.A1
POLITICAL RISK YEARBOOK. VOLUME 4: SUB-SAHARAN AFRICA. 1987. a. $250. The P R S Group, Box 248, East Syracuse, NY 13057-0248. TEL 315-431-0511. FAX 315-431-0200.
●Also available online. Vendor(s): Data-Star (FSRI), Lexis-Nexis.

332 382   **US**   **ISSN 0897-8565**
JQ21.A1
POLITICAL RISK YEARBOOK. VOLUME 5: ASIA & THE PACIFIC. 1987. a. $250. The P R S Group, Box 248, East Syracuse, NY 13057-0248. TEL 315-431-0511. FAX 315-431-0200.
●Also available online. Vendor(s): Data-Star (FSRI), Lexis-Nexis.

332 382   **US**
JN12
POLITICAL RISK YEARBOOK. VOLUME 6: EUROPE. 1987. a. $250 (effective 1995). The P R S Group, Box 248, East Syracuse, NY 13057-0248. TEL 315-431-0511. FAX 315-431-0200.
●Also available online. Vendor(s): Data-Star (FSRI), Lexis-Nexis.
Formed by the merger of: Political Risk Yearbook. Volume 6: Europe - Countries of the European Union (ISSN 1080-0174); Which was formerly (until 1995): Political Risk Yearbook. Volume 6 - Countries of the E C (ISSN 1053-8771); (until 1991): Political Risk Yearbook. Volume 6 - Western Europe (ISSN 0897-8522); Political Risk Yearbook. Volume 7: Europe - Outside the European Union (ISSN 1080-0182); Which was formerly (until 1995): Political Risk Yearbook. Volume 7: Europe - Outside the E C (ISSN 1053-878X); (until 1991): Political Risk Yearbook. Volume 7: Eastern Europe (ISSN 0897-8514).

POLK BANK DIRECTORY. INTERNATIONAL EDITION. see BUSINESS AND ECONOMICS — Trade And Industrial Directories

POLK BANK DIRECTORY. NORTH AMERICAN EDITION. see BUSINESS AND ECONOMICS — Trade And Industrial Directories

POLK'S FINANCIAL INSTITUTIONS BUYER'S GUIDE AND SERVICES DIRECTORY. see BUSINESS AND ECONOMICS — Trade And Industrial Directories

332.1021   **PO**   **ISSN 0377-2322**
PORTUGAL. INSTITUTO NACIONAL DE ESTATISTICA. ESTATISTICAS MONETARIAS E FINANCIERAS. 1930. a. Esc.8100 (effective 1997). Instituto Nacional de Estatistica, Ave. Antonio Jose de Almeida, 1078 Lisbon, Portugal. TEL 351-1-8470050. FAX 351-1-8478578. TELEX 351-63738 PCDINE P. **Document type:** government publication.
Description: Provides statistical data on banking, financial institutions, insurance companies and mutual aid societies.

332.1   **MF**
POST OFFICE SAVINGS BANK. ANNUAL REPORT. (Text in English) a. Government Printing Office, Elizabeth II Ave., Port Louis, Mauritius. **Document type:** corporate report.

332 657   **US**
PRACTICAL CASH MANAGEMENT. m. $327 (foreign $362) (effective 1997). Bankers Research, Inc., Box 431, Westport, CT 06881-0431. TEL 203-227-1237. Ed. Theodore W. Volckhausen; Pub. Theodore G. Volckhausen. R&P contact: Theodore W. Volckhausen. **Document type:** newsletter.

332.1 658   **II**   **ISSN 0970-8448**
PRAJNAN (PUNE); journal of social and management sciences. 1972. q. Rs.150 (foreign $40 or £30), National Institute of Bank Management, NIBM Post Office, Kondhwe Khurd, Pune 411 048, India. TEL 91-212-673080. FAX 91-212-674478. TELEX 145 7256 NIBM IN. Ed. T.S. Ravisankar. adv.: page Rs.2500 or $125. bk.rev.; film rev.; software rev.; bibl.; illus.; index, cum.index: 1972-1987. (reprint service avail.) **Document type:** academic/scholarly publication.
Description: Encourages new thinking on concepts and theoretical frameworks in the various disciplines of social, administrative and management sciences, which have relevance to the workings and development of banking and financial institutions.
Refereed Serial

BUSINESS AND ECONOMICS — BANKING AND FINANCE

332.1 US ISSN 1049-3883
HG2401
PRENTICE HALL BANKING YEARBOOK. 1990. a. Prentice Hall, Business & Professional Division, Englewood Cliffs, NJ 07632.

PREVISIONS GLISSANTES DETAILLEES EN PERSPECTIVES SECTORIELLES (VOL.33): BANQUES. see BUSINESS AND ECONOMICS — Economic Situation And Conditions

PRICE INDEXES MONTHLY. see BUSINESS AND ECONOMICS — Abstracting, Bibliographies, Statistics

PRIME TIMES MAGAZINE. see CONSUMER EDUCATION AND PROTECTION

332.7 FR
PRINCIPALES PROCEDURES DE FINANCEMENT DES BESOINS DES ENTREPRISES ET DES MENAGES. (Subseries of: Collection Documentation et Information (ISSN 1152-538X)) 1989. irreg., latest 1993. 90 F. (effective 1995). Banque de France, Service de l'Information, 48, Croix des Petits Champs, 75001 Paris, France. TEL 1-42-92-39-31. FAX 1-42-92-39-40.
Formerly: Principaux Mecanismes de Distribution de Credit.

332 IE ISSN 0953-7031
PRIVATE BANKER INTERNATIONAL. 1987. m. If649. Lafferty Publications Ltd., The Tower, IDA Enterprise Centre, Pearse St., Dublin 2, Ireland. TEL 353-1-6718022. FAX 353-1-6718520. E-mail: cvserv@lafferty.ie; URL: http://www.unm.lafferty.co.uk. (US subscr. to: 420 Lexington Ave., Ste. 1745, New York, NY 10170. TEL 212-557-6726) Ed. Ian Orton. R&P contact: David Barr. **Document type:** bulletin.
Description: Gives news, information and advice on maintaining affluent client relationships.

332 US ISSN 1053-1963
PRIVATE BANKING REPORT. 1988. m. $345. Faulkner & Gray, Inc., 300 S. Wacker Dr., 18th Fl., Chicago, IL 60606. TEL 312-913-1334. Ed. Pam Goett.
Description: Contains the latest trends, data and analyses of the affluent banking market.

332 US
PRIVATE EQUITY WEEK. w. $980 (foreign $1080) (effective 1997). Investment Dealers' Digest, 2 World Trade Center, 18th Fl., New York, NY 10048-0638. TEL 212-432-0045. FAX 212-321-2336. Ed. Michele Stibgen. R&P contact: Denise Robbins. adv. contact: Todd Miller.

332.1 US
PRIVATE PLACEMENT LETTER. 1982. w. $1190 (foreign $1290) (effective 1997). Investment Dealers' Digest, 2 World Trade Ctr., 18th Fl., New York, NY 10048. TEL 212-432-0045. Ed. Mark Kollar. R&P contact: Denise Robbins. adv. contact: Todd Miller.
Formerly: Private Placements (ISSN 0735-9950)

332 US
PRIVATE PLACEMENT REPORTER. 48/yr. $705 for new subscr. (foreign $755); renewal $795 (foreign $845). American Banker - Bond Buyer, Newsletter Division (Subsidiary of: Thomson Financial Services Company), One State St. Plaza, New York, NY 10004-1549. TEL 800-733-4371. FAX 212-943-2224. (Subscr. to: Box 28315, Washington, DC 20038-8315. TEL 202-347-2665) Ed. Dwight Cass. **Document type:** newsletter.
●Also available online. Vendor(s): Information Access Co., Knight-Ridder Information, Inc., Lexis-Nexis, NewsNet (Fl61).
Description: Covers buying, selling and trading unregistered securities. Includes deal structure and pricing, covenant packages and spreads; surveillance and the "new" private placement market in post-144A environment; stories affecting the marketplace.

332 YU
PRIVREDNA BANKA PANCEVO. BILTEN. 1977. m. Osnovna Privredna Banka, Trg Slobode 6, Pancevo, Yugoslavia. Ed. Koviljka Martic.

332 336.2 UK
PROFESSIONAL PRACTICE MANAGEMENT; the business monthly for the professions. 1982. m. £159 (foreign $318) (effective 1997). Monitor Press Ltd., Suffolk House, Church Field Rd., Sudbury, Suffolk CO10, England. TEL 44-1787-378607. FAX 44-1787-881147. Ed. Susannah Lear. (back issues avail.) **Document type:** newsletter.
Formerly: Partnership Management (ISSN 0263-7928)
Description: Takes an objective look at issues affecting efficient management today and provides helpful advice and information on how to do things better.

332 340 US ISSN 0734-6638
HG2573
PROFILE OF STATE CHARTERED BANKING. 1965. a. Conference of State Bank Supervisors, 1015 18th St., N.W., Ste. 1000, Washington, DC 20036-5275. TEL 202-296-2840. FAX 202-296-1928. Ed. Ellen Lamb. R&P contact: Ellen Lamb. **Document type:** academic/scholarly publication.

332.1 PR
PROGRESS IN PUERTO RICO/PROGRESO EN PUERTO RICO. (Text in English and Spanish) 1965. q. free. Banco Popular de Puerto Rico, Strategic Planning Division, P.O. Box 362708, Banco Popular Center, San Juan, PR 00936-2708. TEL 787-754-7639. FAX 787-758-2714. E-mail: bpprplan@caribe.net. Ed. Ginoris Lopez-Lay. circ. 5,000. **Document type:** newsletter.
Description: Reports economic and financial data related to Puerto Rico and the U.S.

332 382 UK ISSN 1350-2700
PROJECT & TRADE FINANCE. (Fax service avail. w.) 1983. m. £365 (foreign $625) (w. fax service $840(foreign $1450)) (effective 1997). Euromoney Publications plc., Nestor House, Playhouse Yard, London EC4V 5EX, England. TEL 44-171-779-8935. FAX 44-171-779-8541. Ed. Rupert Sayer. charts; stat.; index. circ. 6,000. (also avail. in microform from UMI) **Indexed:** BPIA, World Bank.Abstr. **Document type:** trade publication. —BLDSC (6924.840800); SWETS; UMI.
Former titles (until 1991): Trade Finance and Banker International (ISSN 0960-1740); (until 1989): Banker International (ISSN 0951-5739); (until 1987): Euromoney Trade Finance Report (ISSN 0264-6706)
Description: Keeps exporters and their bankers worldwide informed of the major trends in the provision of term financing for domestic and overseas projects and for wholesale trade deals.

332 UK ISSN 0967-5914
PROJECT FINANCE INTERNATIONAL. 1989. fortn. £795. I F R Publishing (Subsidiary of: Thomson Financial Services Ltd.), 11 New Fetter Ln., London EC4A 1JN, England. TEL 44-171-815-3900. FAX 44-171-815-3856. Ed. Rod Morrison. adv.: page £1500; adv. contact: Diane Bush. circ. 2,500. (back issues avail.) **Document type:** trade publication.
●Also available on CD-ROM.
—CCC.
Formerly (until 1992): Project Finance (ISSN 0961-818X)

332 UK ISSN 1352-4062
PROJECT FINANCE INTERNATIONAL DIRECTORY. 1993. a. I F R Publishing (Subsidiary of: Thomson Financial Services Ltd.), 11 New Fetter Ln., London EC4A 1JN, England. TEL 44-171-815-3900. FAX 44-171-815-3856. **Document type:** directory.

332 UK ISSN 0968-2279
HD75.8
PROJECT FINANCE YEARBOOK (YEAR). a. £95 (foreign $170) (effective 1996). Euromoney Publications plc., Books, Nestor House, Playhouse Yard, London EC4V 5EX, England. TEL 44-171-779-8935. FAX 44-171-779-8541. (Orders to: Plymbridge Distributors Ltd., Estover, Plymouth, Devon PL6 7PZ, England. TEL 44-171-779-8610. FAX 44-1752-695668; Dist. in US by: American Educational Systems, 173 W. 81st St., New York, NY 10024. TEL 800-717-2669. FAX 212-501-8926) Ed. Adrian Hornbrook. **Document type:** trade publication, directory.
Description: Examines ways in which projects can be financed in the current market, listing more than 600 firms that provide financing or advice.

332 AT ISSN 0729-2910
PROMISSORY NOTE SURVEY. 1981. q. Aus.$495($500) Investment and Econometrics Research Pty. Ltd., 5 Powell St., Neutral Bay, N.S.W. 2089, Australia. TEL 02-909-8843. Ed. R.R. Taylor. (back issues avail.)
Description: Lists risk premiums on public and corporate borrowings, interest rates, promissory notes.

332 MX
PRONTUARIO INTERNACIONAL. d. Mex.$250 in Mexico only (effective Aug. 1996). Banco de Mexico, Subdireccion de Investigacion Economica y Bancaria, Av. Juarez 90, Col. Centro, Del. Cuauhtemoc, 06059 Mexico DF, Mexico. TEL 525-761-8588.

332 US
PUBLIC UTILITY FINANCING TRACKER. 1950. w., q., and a. $625 for all 3 issues; q. & a. $475; a. $375; w. $375. P U F T, Inc., 2408 Durango Ln., Naperville, IL 60564. TEL 630-904-3503. Ed. Sherri Jepsen. **Document type:** trade publication.
Formerly: Analysis of Public Utility Financing (ISSN 0421-9910)
Description: Comprehensive analysis of money costs and other financing data for each new utility security issue.

332 PR ISSN 0270-126X
HC154.5.A1
PUERTO RICO BUSINESS REVIEW. (Supplement avail.: Economic Indicators) (Text in English) 1976. q. free. Government Development Bank for Puerto Rico - Banco Gubernamental de Fomento para Puerto Rico, P.O. Box 42001, Minillas Sta., San Juan, PR 00940-2001. TEL 787-729-6433. FAX 787-728-0975. (U.S. addr.: 140 Broadway, New York, NY 10005. TEL 212-422-6420) Ed. Eunice A. Pagan-Vega. charts; illus.; stat.; cum.index: 1976-1988. circ. 11,000.
Description: Provides business-related articles of interest to the financial community, economists, and the private and public sectors.

332.1 II ISSN 0304-8101
HG3290.D44
PUNJAB NATIONAL BANK. ANNUAL REPORT. Key Title: Annual Report - Punjab National Bank. (Text in English) a. Punjab National Bank, Ltd., 5 Parliament St., New Delhi 10001, India. **Document type:** corporate report.

332 QA
QATAR NATIONAL BANK (S.A.Q.). REPORT OF THE DIRECTORS AND BALANCE SHEET. a. Qatar National Bank (S.A.Q.), Box 1000, Doha, Qatar. **Document type:** corporate report.

QUALIFIED RETIREMENT AND OTHER EMPLOYEE BENEFIT PLANS. see BUSINESS AND ECONOMICS — Personnel Management

332 US ISSN 1089-1900
▼**QUALITY CUSTOMER SERVICE.** 1995. m. $319 (effective 1997). Siefer Consultants, Inc., Box 1384, Storm Lake, IA 50588. TEL 712-732-7340. FAX 712-732-7906. (back issues avail.) **Document type:** newsletter.
Description: Manager's guide to building long-term customer relationships.

332 US
QUARTERLY BANK DIGEST. m. S N L Securities, LP, 410 E. Main St., Box 2124, Charlottesville, VA 22902. TEL 804-977-1600. FAX 804-977-4466. Ed. Elisabeth Todaro.
Formerly: Bank Portfolio Strategist.
Description: Data publication for commercial banks.

QUARTERLY BUSINESS FAILURES. see BUSINESS AND ECONOMICS — Economic Situation And Conditions

BUSINESS AND ECONOMICS — BANKING AND FINANCE

332.10973   US
QUARTERLY FINANCIAL INSTITUTION RATINGS.
Abbreviated title: Q F I R. 1989. q. $324.95. L A C E Financial Corp., 118 N. Court St., Frederick, MD 21701. TEL 301-662-1011. Ed. Barron Putnam; Pub. Clara Smith. (also avail. in diskette format)
●Also available on CD-ROM.
Formerly: Quarterly Bank, Savings and Loan Rating Service (ISSN 1051-8010)
Description: Features comprehensive coverage of 12,000 commercial and savings banks, 2,600 savings and loans, 2,500 credit unions and the 100 largest bank holding companies, including information on assets, income, liquidity, asset quality, capital and earnings.

332   II   ISSN 0536-8014
QUARTERLY STATISTICS OF THE WORKING OF CAPITAL ISSUES CONTROL. (Text in English) q. Rs.6($2.16) Government of India, Department of Publications, Civil Lines, Delhi 110 054, India. TEL 2517409. charts; stat.

332   SP
R E S.* (Relacion de Empresas Suspensas en Pagos, Embargos y Subastas) 1977-199? w. 22700 ptas. (foreign 27000 ptas.). Tecnipublicaciones S.A., Fernando VI 27-1, 28004 Madrid, Spain. TEL 91-319-7889. FAX 91-410-1069. stat.; circ. 5,000 (controlled). (processed)

332 650   US   ISSN 0080-3340
HF5681.B2
R M A ANNUAL STATEMENT STUDIES. 1923. a. $119 to non-members; members $19. Robert Morris Associates, One Liberty Place, Ste. 2300, 1650 Market St., Philadelphia, PA 19107. TEL 215-851-9100. FAX 215-851-9206. Ed. Susan Kelsay. index. circ. 40,000. (also avail. in microfiche from CIS) **Indexed:** SRI. **Document type:** corporate report.
—CCC.
Description: Contains corporate balance sheets, income data and ratios on over 400 different industries. Includes trend data for the past five years for most of these industries.

332   US
R T C WATCH.* w. $465 for new subscr. (foreign $495); renewal $645 (foreign $675). Thomson Financial Services, One State St. Plaza, New York, NY 10004. TEL 800-733-4371. FAX 301-654-1678.
●Also available online. Vendor(s): NewsNet (FI03).

332   US   ISSN 0898-1515
R T F I: THE REAL-TIME FINANCIAL INFORMATION INDEX. 1988. base vol. (plus updates 4/yr.) $2495 (Europe £1695). Waters Information Services, Inc., Box 2248, Binghamton, NY 13902-2248. TEL 607-770-9242; 800-947-7947. FAX 607-770-9435. URL: http://www.watersinfo.com. (European and Asian subscr. to: Waters Information Services Ltd., 57-59 Neal St., London WC2H 9PJ, England. TEL 44-171-240-2090. FAX 44-171-240-2076) **Document type:** directory.
Description: Documents key features and data coverage of real-time market data services in North America and Europe; reviews key financial services vendors.

R UND V REPORT. see *INSURANCE*

630 332.7   NE
RABOBANK. 1906. m. fl.37. Rabobank Nederland, Croeselaan 18, Utrecht, Netherlands. TELEX 47700 NL. bk.rev.; illus.; stat.; index. circ. 33,000. **Indexed:** Key to Econ.Sci., World Bank.Abstr.
Supersedes: Boerenleenbank (ISSN 0006-5625)

332   SZ
RAIFFEISEN. m. Schweizer Verband der Raiffeisenkassen, Vadianstr. 17, CH-9001 Sankt Gallen, Switzerland. TEL 219111.

332   IS
RASHUT NEYAROT EREKH. ANNUAL REPORT/ISRAEL SECURITIES AUTHORITY. ANNUAL REPORT. (Text in Hebrew) a. free. Rashut Neyarot Erekh - Israel Securities Authority, 3 Kanfe Nesharim St., Jerusalem 95464, Israel. TEL 972-2-314011. FAX 972-2-513939. circ. 1,000. **Document type:** corporate report.

332.1   US   ISSN 0887-7408
RATEGRAM.* 1982. bi-w. $395 to individuals (foreign $430); libraries $195 (foreign $230). Bradshaw Group, Limited, Box 3517, San Rafael, CA 94912-3517. TEL 415-479-3815. Ed. Martin G. Bradshaw. circ. 8,500. (back issues avail.)
●Also available online. Vendor(s): NewsNet (IV61).
Description: Standard reference for savers and investors who require highest CD and money market yields; includes highest bank, S and L, and money fund yields.

332 333.33   US
RATES AND TERMS ON CONVENTIONAL HOME MORTGAGES. a. free. U.S. Federal Housing Finance Board, 1777 F St., N.W., Washington, DC 20006. TEL 202-408-2967. **Document type:** government publication.

REAL ESTATE FINANCE AND INVESTMENT. see *REAL ESTATE*

REAL ESTATE FINANCE JOURNAL. see *REAL ESTATE*

REAL ESTATE FINANCING - TEXT, FORMS, TAX ANALYSIS, REAL ESTATE TRANSACTION SERIES. see *REAL ESTATE*

RECENT BANKRUPTCY DECISIONS. see *LAW — Corporate Law*

332   US
RECENT DEVELOPMENTS IN INTERNATIONAL BANKING AND FINANCE.* a. Blackwell Publishers, 350 Main St., Malden, MA 02148-3018. TEL 617-547-7110. FAX 617-547-0782. E-mail: subscript@blackwellpub.com. (UK addr.: 108 Cowley Rd., Oxford OX4 1JF, England) **Document type:** monographic series.

332   GW
RECHT DER KREDITWIRTSCHAFT. 2-3/yr. DM.88. Walhalla Fachverlag, Haus an der Eisernen Bruecke, 93059 Regensburg, Germany. TEL 49-941-5684-0. FAX 49-941-5684111. E-mail: walhalla@walhalla.de; URL: http://www.walhalla.de. Eds. Wolfgang Grill, Hannelore Grill. adv. circ. 1,500. (looseleaf format) **Document type:** trade publication.

332   US   ISSN 1045-3369
THE REGION MAGAZINE. 1987. q. free. Federal Reserve Bank of Minneapolis, 250 Marquette Ave., Minneapolis, MN 55401-2171. TEL 612-340-2446. FAX 612-335-2855. URL: http://woodrow.mpls.frb.fed.us. Ed. David Fettig.
—UMI.
Description: Explores banking and economic policy issues that relate to Federal Reserve activities.

332.1   US   ISSN 1049-5339
HC107.A165
REGIONAL ECONOMIC DIGEST. 1974. q. free. Federal Reserve Bank of Kansas City, 925 Grand Blvd., Kansas City, MO 64198. TEL 816-881-2000. Ed. Craig S. Hakkio. circ. 8,000. **Indexed:** Amer.Stat.Ind. (1975-), Fed Print. **Document type:** academic/scholarly publication.
—UMI; UnCover.
Formerly (until 1990): Federal Reserve Bank of Kansas City. Financial Letter (ISSN 0739-5299)

REGULATION OF FOREIGN BANKS; United States and international. see *LAW — International Law*

332   US   ISSN 1064-4342
KF967
REGULATORY COMPLIANCE WATCH. 48/yr. $595 for new subscr. (foreign $645); renewal $695 (foreign $745). American Banker - Bond Buyer, Newsletter Division (Subsidiary of: Thomson Financial Services Company), One State St. Plaza, New York, NY 10004-1549. TEL 800-733-4371. FAX 212-943-2224. (Subscr. to: Box 28315, Washington, DC 20038-8315. TEL 202-347-2665) Ed. Anthony Kimmery. **Document type:** newsletter.
●Also available online. Vendor(s): Information Access Co., NewsNet (FI04).
Incorporates: C R A Alert.
Description: Covers the legal, regulatory, and legislative developments in Washington, affecting the nation's banks, S&L's, and credit unions. Contains analyses and interpretations of all the critical regulatory changes in progress.

REIMBURSEMENT ADVISOR. see *HOSPITALS*

332   SP   ISSN 0034-4184
REMANSO. 1958. bi-m. free. Caja de Ahorros y Monte de Piedad de Zaragoza, Aragon y Rioja, Calle San Jorge No. 8, Zaragoza, Spain. Ed. Manuel Cabeza Munoz. circ. 1,500.

332   LU
REPERES. 1984. q. Banque Internationale a Luxembourg, L-2953 Luxembourg, Luxembourg. TEL 4590-2248. FAX 4590-3850. TELEX 3626 BIL LU. charts; stat. circ. 4,000. **Document type:** bulletin.

332   US
REPORT ON THE TERMS OF CREDIT CARD PLAN. s-a. $5. U.S. Federal Reserve System, Board of Governors, Publications Services, Rm. MS-138, Washington, DC 20551. TEL 202-452-3244. FAX 202-728-5886. **Document type:** government publication.

332   US   ISSN 0080-1380
REPRINTS IN INTERNATIONAL FINANCE. 1965. irreg., no.29, 1996. $40 (includes Essays in International Finance; Studies in International Finance; Special Papers in International Economics) (effective 1996 & 1997). Princeton University, International Finance Section, c/o Margaret B. Riccardi, Ed., Department of Economics, Fisher Hall, Princeton, NJ 08544-1021. TEL 609-258-4048. FAX 609-258-6419. R&P contact: Margaret B. Riccardi. circ. 2,000. (back issues avail.; reprint service avail. from UMI) **Document type:** monographic series.
Description: Reprints of articles and essays by staff members of the International Finance Section that have appeared in other publications.

332   CH
REPUBLIC OF CHINA. MINISTRY OF FINANCE. BUREAU OF MONETARY AFFAIRS. ANNUAL REPORT. (Text in Chinese, English) a. Ministry of Finance, Bureau of Monetary Affairs, 4th Fl., 1 Nanhai Rd., Taipei, Taiwan, Republic of China. TEL 886-2-3055000. FAX 886-2-3977506. Ed. Mu-Tsai Chen.

332   US   ISSN 0196-3821
HG1
RESEARCH IN FINANCE. (Supplement avail.: Management Under Government Intervention: The View from Mount Scopus) 1979. irreg., vol.14, 1996. $73.25. J A I Press Inc., 55 Old Post Rd., No. 2, Box 1678, Greenwich, CT 06830-1678. TEL 203-661-7602. FAX 203-661-0792. E-mail: jai@jaipress.com. (Subscr. in the UK and Europe to: JAI Press Ltd., 38 Tavistock St., Covent Garden, London WC2E 7PB, England. TEL 44-171-379-8834. FAX 44-171-379-8835) Ed. Andrew Chen. **Document type:** monographic series.
—BLDSC (7741.035000). CCC.

332   CN   ISSN 0833-1677
RESEARCH MONEY. 1987. 20/yr. Can.$475. Evert Communications Ltd., 1296 Carling Ave., Ottawa, ON K1Z 7K8, Canada. TEL 613-728-4621. FAX 613-728-0385. E-mail: service@evert.com; URL: http://www.evert.com. Ed. Mark Henderson. **Document type:** directory.
—CISTI.
Description: Covers funding issues in industry, university and government programs.

332.1 330.9   NZ   ISSN 0112-871X
HC621
RESERVE BANK BULLETIN. 1938. q. NZ.$62 (Australia NZ.$82; elsewhere NZ.$117) (effective 1996-97). Reserve Bank of New Zealand, Corporate Services, 2 The Terrace, P.O. Box 2498, Wellington, New Zealand. TEL 4-64-472-2029. FAX 64-4-473-8554. TELEX NZ 3368. charts; stat.; index, cum.index: 1950-1959, 1969-1979. circ. 1,500. **Indexed:** Key to Econ.Sci., P.A.I.S. **Document type:** bulletin.
—UnCover. CCC.
Formerly (until 1982): Reserve Bank of New Zealand. Bulletin (ISSN 0034-5539)

332.1   AT   ISSN 0484-5412
HG3446
RESERVE BANK OF AUSTRALIA. ANNUAL REPORT. 1960. a. free. Reserve Bank of Australia, 65 Martin Place, G.P.O. Box 3947, Sydney, N.S.W. 2001, Australia. TEL 61-2-551-8111. FAX 61-2-551-8000. circ. 12,000. **Document type:** corporate report.

RESERVE BANK OF AUSTRALIA. BULLETIN. see *BUSINESS AND ECONOMICS — Abstracting, Bibliographies, Statistics*

BUSINESS AND ECONOMICS — BANKING AND FINANCE

332.1 330.9   AT   ISSN 0080-178X
RESERVE BANK OF AUSTRALIA. OCCASIONAL PAPERS. 1970. irreg. price varies. Reserve Bank of Australia, 65 Martin Place, G.P.O. Box 3947, Sydney, N.S.W. 2001, Australia. TEL 61-2-551-8111. FAX 61-2-551-8000.

332 330.9   AT   ISSN 1320-7229
RESERVE BANK OF AUSTRALIA. RESEARCH DISCUSSION PAPER. 1969. irreg., approx. 15/yr. Reserve Bank of Australia, 65 Martin Pl., G.P.O. Box 3947, Sydney, N.S.W. 2001, Australia. TEL 61-2-5518111. FAX 61-2-5518000. abstr.; bibl. circ. 500. (back issues avail.) **Document type:** academic/scholarly publication.
—BLDSC (7738.874000).
Description: Presents preliminary results of economic research.

RESERVE BANK OF FIJI. ANNUAL REPORT. see BUSINESS AND ECONOMICS — Economic Situation And Conditions

RESERVE BANK OF FIJI. MONTHLY ECONOMIC BULLETIN. see BUSINESS AND ECONOMICS — Economic Situation And Conditions

RESERVE BANK OF FIJI. NEWS REVIEW. see BUSINESS AND ECONOMICS — Economic Situation And Conditions

RESERVE BANK OF FIJI. QUARTERLY REVIEW. see BUSINESS AND ECONOMICS — Economic Situation And Conditions

332   II   ISSN 0080-1801
RESERVE BANK OF INDIA. ANNUAL REPORT. Short title: R B I Annual Report. (Text in English and Hindi) 1936. a. free. Reserve Bank of India, Department of Economic Analysis & Policy, Division of Reports, Reviews & Publications, New Central Office Bldg., 9th Fl., Shahid Bhagat Singh Rd., P.O. Box 1036, Bombay 400 023, India. TEL 22-2862524. Ed. A. Seshan. circ. 8,500. **Document type:** corporate report.

332   II   ISSN 0034-5512
HG188.I6
RESERVE BANK OF INDIA. BULLETIN. (Text in English and Hindi) 1947. m. Rs.300($100) Reserve Bank of India, Department of Economic Analysis & Policy, Division of Reports, Reviews & Publications, New Central Office Bldg., Shahid Bhagat Singh Rd., Post Box 1036, Bombay 400 023, India. TEL 22-2862524. Ed. M.P. Nair. adv.; charts; index. circ. 5,300. **Indexed:** Key to Econ.Sci., P.A.I.S. **Document type:** bulletin.

332   II
RESERVE BANK OF INDIA. BULLETIN. WEEKLY STATISTICAL SUPPLEMENT. (Text in English) 1949. w. Rs.50($17) Reserve Bank of India, Department of Economic Analysis & Policy, Division of Reports, Reviews & Publications, New Central Office Bldg., Shahid Bhagat Singh Rd., Post Box 1036, Bombay 400 023, India. TEL 22-2862524. charts; stat. circ. 1,400. **Document type:** bulletin.

332.1   II
RESERVE BANK OF INDIA. OCCASIONAL PAPERS. (Text in English) 1980. 4/yr. Rs.40($14) Reserve Bank of India, Department of Economic Analysis & Policy, Division of Reports, Reviews & Publications, New Central Office Bldg., Shahid Bhagat Singh Rd., P.O. Box 1036, Mumbai 400 023, India. TEL 91-22-2862524. Ed. S.H. Shetty. adv. circ. 1,000. **Indexed:** Pub.Admin.Abstr. **Document type:** government publication, monographic series.

332   II
RESERVE BANK OF INDIA. REPORT ON CURRENCY AND FINANCE. (Issued in two sections: Economic Reviews; Statistical Statements) (Text in English and Hindi) 1936. a. Rs.100($40) for Economic Reviews; Statistical Statements Rs.60($25). Reserve Bank of India, Department of Economic Analysis & Policy, Division of Reports, Reviews & Publications, P.B. 1036, New Central Office Bldg., Shahid Bhagat Singh Rd., Bombay 400 023, India. TEL 22-2862524. Ed. S.J. Salvi. circ. 3,000.

RESERVE BANK OF MALAWI. FINANCIAL AND ECONOMIC REVIEW. see BUSINESS AND ECONOMICS — Economic Situation And Conditions

332   MW   ISSN 0486-5383
HG3407.A7
RESERVE BANK OF MALAWI. REPORT AND ACCOUNTS. a. free. Reserve Bank of Malawi, Research Department, P.O. Box 30063, Lilongwe 3, Malawi. TEL 265-780600. charts; stat.; maps. **Document type:** corporate report.
Formerly: Reserve Bank of Malawi. Annual Report and Statement of Account.
Description: Analyzes the financial and economic performance of various sectors of the economy.

332.1   NZ   ISSN 0110-7070
HG3466
RESERVE BANK OF NEW ZEALAND. ANNUAL REPORT. a. free. Reserve Bank of New Zealand, Corporate Services, 2 The Terrace, P.O. Box 2498, Wellington, New Zealand. TEL 64-4-472-2029. FAX 64-4-472-8554. TELEX NZ 2268. **Document type:** corporate report.

332   RH   ISSN 1024-2732
RESERVE BANK OF ZIMBABWE. ANNUAL REPORT. Key Title: Reserve Bank of Zimbabwe. Annual Report and Statements of Accounts for the Year. (Text in English) 1994. a. Z.$25 (rest of Africa $5.50; rest of world $6.50). Reserve Bank of Zimbabwe, Economic Research and Policy Division, P.O. Box 1283, Harare, Zimbabwe. TEL 263-4-703000. FAX 263-4-707800.

332   RH   ISSN 1024-2740
RESERVE BANK OF ZIMBABWE. MONTHLY BULLETIN. (Text in English) 1980. m. Z.$100 (rest of Africa $26; rest of world $32) (effective 1997). Reserve Bank of Zimbabwe, Economic Research and Policy Division, P.O. Box 1283, Harare, Zimbabwe. TEL 263-4-703000. FAX 263-4-707800. TELEX 26033 RESZIM ZW. **Document type:** bulletin.

332   RH   ISSN 0251-1819
RESERVE BANK OF ZIMBABWE. QUARTERLY ECONOMIC AND STATISTICAL REVIEW. (Text in English) 1980. q. Z.$70 (rest of Africa $17; rest of world $20). Reserve Bank of Zimbabwe, Economic Research and Policy Division, P.O. Box 1283, Harare, Zimbabwe. TEL 263-4-703000. FAX 263-4-707800.

332   IE   ISSN 0261-1740
RETAIL BANKER INTERNATIONAL. 1981. bi-w. I£699. Lafferty Publications Ltd., The Tower, IDA Enterprise Centre, Pearse St., Dublin 2, Ireland. TEL 353-1-6718022. FAX 353-1-6718520. E-mail: cvserv@lafferty.ie; URL: http://www.unm.lafferty.co.uk. (US subscr. addr.: Lafferty Publications (USA), 420 Lexington Ave., Ste. 1745, New York, NY 10170. TEL 212-557-6726) Ed. Peter Kinahan. R&P contact: David Barr. (back issues avail.) **Document type:** trade publication.
Description: Directed to senior management in the consumer financial services industry.

332   US   ISSN 1058-885X
HG1660.U5
RETAIL BANKING REPORT. a. $173 to non-members; members $115 (effective 1992). American Bankers Association, Retail Services Center, 1120 Connecticut Ave., N.W., Washington, DC 20036. TEL 202-663-5430. FAX 301-843-8405. (Subscr. to: Box 630544, Baltimore, MD 21263-0544. TEL 800-338-0626)
Formerly (until 1991): Retail Deposit Services Report (ISSN 0270-2762)

332   US   ISSN 0093-5352
HG179
RETIREMENT LETTER; the money newsletter for mature people. 1973. m. $49. Phillips Publishing, Inc., Consumer Publishing, 7811 Montrose Rd., Potomac, MD 20854. TEL 301-340-2100. FAX 301-424-7034. Ed. Peter A. Dickinson. circ. 10,000.
—CCC.
Incorporates: Retirement Digest; Communique.

332.1   US
REVIEW OF BANK PERFORMANCE. a. Salomon Brothers, Inc., Marketing Department, 7 World Trade Center, New York, NY 10048. TEL 212-747-7000.

332   US   ISSN 1051-1741
KF967
THE REVIEW OF BANKING AND FINANCIAL SERVICES; an analysis of current laws and regulations affecting banking and related industries. 1985. s-m. (22/yr.). $495. Standard & Poor's Corporation (Subsidiary of: McGraw-Hill, Inc.), 25 Broadway, New York, NY 10004. TEL 212-208-8000. Ed. Michael O. Finkelstein. index. **Document type:** newsletter.
●Also available online. Vendor(s): Dow Jones News Retrieval (RBFS), Knight-Ridder Information, Inc. (BFS), Lexis-Nexis (RBFS), NewsNet (FI17).
Formerly (until 1989): Review of Financial Services Regulation (ISSN 0897-1196)
Description: Focuses on practical analyses of regulations in banking and related fields, discussing the strengths and weaknesses of recent legislation and how they affect attorneys' clients and pracice.

332   US   ISSN 1380-6645
CODEN: RDREF6
▼**REVIEW OF DERIVATIVES RESEARCH.** (Text in English) 1996. q. fl.460 to institutions; $236 to institutions in U.S. (effective 1998). Kluwer Academic Publishers Boston, Box 358, Accord Sta., Hingham, MA 02018-0358. TEL 617-871-6600. FAX 617-871-6528. E-mail: services@wkap.nl; URL: http://www.wkap.nl. (Dist. outside N. America by: Kluwer Academic Publishers Group, P.O. Box 322, 3300 AH Dordrecht, Netherlands. TEL 31-78-6392392. FAX 31-78-6546474) Eds. Menachem Brenner, Marti Subrahmanyam. **Document type:** academic/scholarly publication.
—BLDSC (7790.161600). CCC.
Description: Publishes academic research articles dealing with the pricing and hedging of derivative assets on any underlying asset.
Refereed Serial

332   SI   ISSN 0218-9283
▼**REVIEW OF FINANCIAL MARKETS.** (Text in English) 1997. s-a. S.$98 (foreign $70). John Wiley & Sons (Asia) Pte. Ltd., 2 Clementi Loop 02-01, Jin Xing Distripark, Singapore 129809, Singapore. TEL 65-4632400. FAX 65-4634605. E-mail: csd_ord@wiley.com.sg. Ed. Wong Kie Ann. adv.: B&W page £640, color page £1515. **Document type:** trade publication.
Description: Publishes original manuscripts that analyze issues of concern to scholars and practitioners in the Asia Pacific region.
Refereed Serial

332   US   ISSN 0893-9454
HG1
THE REVIEW OF FINANCIAL STUDIES. 1988. q. $55 to individuals; academic institutions $180; corporate institutions $265; students $10 (effective 1998). Oxford University Press, Journals, 2001 Evans Rd., Cary, NC 27513. TEL 919-677-0977; 800-852-7323. FAX 919-677-1714. E-mail: jnlorders@oup-usa.org; URL: http://www.oup-usa.org/. (Subscr. outside N. America to: Oxford University Press, Journals, Great Clarendon St., Oxford OX2 6DP, England. TEL 44-1865-267907. FAX 44-1865-267485) Ed. Franklin Allen. adv.; bibl. circ. 1,420. **Indexed:** ASCA, Curr.Cont., J.of Econ.Lit., SSCI. **Document type:** academic/scholarly publication.
—BLDSC (7790.565000); Genuine Article; SWETS; UMI; UnCover. **CCC.**
Description: Covers new research in financial economics. Strives to maintain a balance between theoretical and empirical studies.
Refereed Serial

REVIEW OF QUANTITATIVE FINANCE AND ACCOUNTING. see BUSINESS AND ECONOMICS — Accounting

332.1   GT
REVISTA BANCA CENTRAL. q. Banco de Guatemala, 7a Av. 22-01, Zona 1, C.P. 01001 Guatemala, Guatemala. TEL 535932. Ed. Francisco Albizurez. adv.; charts; illus.; stat.

332.1   BL   ISSN 0034-706X
REVISTA BANCARIA BRASILEIRA. 1933. m. $150. Caixa Postal 2291, ZC-00 Rio de Janeiro, Brazil. TEL 55-21-2407275. Ed. Oyama Pereira Teixeira. adv.: B&W page Cr.500, color page Cr.900; 185 x 260; adv. contact: Ronaldo Boucas. stat. circ. 15,000. **Indexed:** P.A.I.S.For.Lang.Ind.

REVISTA DE CIENCIAS ECONOMICAS. see BUSINESS AND ECONOMICS — Accounting

BUSINESS AND ECONOMICS — BANKING AND FINANCE

REVISTA DE DERECHO FINANCIERO Y DE HACIENDA PUBLICA. see *LAW*

336   SP   ISSN 0212-4610
REVISTA DE HACIENDA AUTONOMICA Y LOCAL. 1971. 3/yr. 10000 ptas.($98) Editoriales de Derecho Reunidas, S.A., Valverde 32, 1o izda., 28004 Madrid, Spain. TEL 521-0246. FAX 521-0539. Ed. Julio Banacloche.
    Formerly (until 1982): Revista de Economia y Hacienda Local (ISSN 0210-2404)

REVISTA ECUATORIANA DE HISTORIA ECONOMICA. see *BUSINESS AND ECONOMICS*

332   SP   ISSN 0210-2412
REVISTA ESPANOLA DE FINANCIACION Y CONTABILIDAD. 1972. q. 12000 ptas.($118) Editoriales de Derecho Reunidas, S.A., Valverde 32, 1o izda., 28004 Madrid, Spain. TEL 521-02-46. FAX 521-05-39. index. (back issues avail.)
—CINDOC.

332   MX   ISSN 0556-6835
HG6
REVISTA MEXICANA DE FIANZAS. 1964. a. Mex.$10($7) (Mexican Bond Companies and Bancomer, S.N.C.) Fernando Castaneda Alatorre, Ed. & Pub., Puebla 383, Col. Roma, Deleg. Cuauhtemoc, 06700 Mexico, D.F., Mexico. adv. circ. 1,000.

332   MX
REVISTA MEXICANA DE SEGUROS FIANZAS Y FINANZAS. 1948. m. $75. Revista Mexicana de Seguros y Fianzas, S.A. de C.V., Box 19-193, 03910 Mexico, D.F., Mexico. FAX 511-1133. Ed. Marivel Campos. adv.; bk.rev. circ. 15,000.

332   FR   ISSN 0987-3368
HG15
REVUE D'ECONOMIE FINANCIERE. 1987. 6/yr. 750 F. (foreign 1000 F.) (effective 1997). (Association d'Economie Financiere) Editions Juridiques Associees, 14 rue Pierre et Marie Curie, 75005 Paris, France. TEL 33-1-44419710. FAX 33-1-43547821. TELEX EJA203918F. Ed. Youssef Achour. **Indexed**: ELLIS.
    Description: Promotes analytical studies of economic finance.

332   BE   ISSN 0772-7798
REVUE DE LA BANQUE. (Supplements avail.: Revue de la Banque. Cahier (ISSN 0772-7801); Centre d'Etudes Financieres. Newsletter (ISSN 0772-7798)) (Text in Dutch, English, French) 1936. 10/yr. 2400 BEF. (Studie Centrum voor het Financiewezen) Belgische Vereniging van Banken, Ravensteinstraat 36 B-5, 1000 Brussels, Belgium. FAX 32-2-5111951. adv.; bk.rev. circ. 4,000. **Indexed**: ELLIS, Key to Econ.Sci., Numis.Lit., Pt.de Rep., World Bank.Abstr.

332.1   FR   ISSN 0035-1938
REVUE DES CAISSES D'EPARGNE. 1919. m. 40 F. Societe Mutualiste du Personnel des Caisses d'Epargne, 6 rue de la Grosse-Ecritoire, B.P. 2747, 51062 Reims Cedex, France. Ed. Pierre Giffo. index. circ. 5,800.

332   CN   ISSN 0035-2284
REVUE DESJARDINS. 1935. 5/yr. Can.$14. Confederation des Caisses Populaires et d'Economie Desjardins du Quebec, 100 Ave. des Commandeurs, Levis, PQ G6V 7N5, Canada. TEL 418-835-2203. FAX 418-835-3809. Ed. Pierre Goulet. adv. contact: Yvan Forest. bk.rev.; charts; illus.; index. circ. 25,000. **Indexed**: Pt.de Rep. (1981-). **Document type**: trade publication, catalog.

332   UK   ISSN 0952-8776
HG4502
RISK. 1987. £279($469) (effective 1997). Financial Engineering Ltd., Risk Publications, 104-112 Marylebone Ln., London W1M 5FU, England. TEL 44-171-487-5326. FAX 44-171-486-0879. Ed. Graham Cooper; Pub. Peter Field. R&P contact: Peter Field. adv.: B&W page £5895, color page £6995; trim 297 x 230; adv. contact: Celine Connell. bk.rev. **Document type**: trade publication.
—BLDSC (7972.581300); SWETS.
    Description: An international journal of financial risk management covering currencies, interest rates, equities, commodities and credit.

332   US   ISSN 0194-1038
RISK MANAGEMENT NEWS. 1975. m. $80. James E. Mooney & Company, Inc., Box 50, 262 Mountain Ave., Springfield, NJ 07081. Ed. James E. Mooney. (looseleaf format; back issues avail.)

332   UK   ISSN 0261-3344
RISK MEASUREMENT SERVICE. 1979. q. £350 corporate; institutions £175. (London Business School) L B S Financial Services, Sussex Pl., Regent's Park, London NW1 4SA, England. TEL 44-171-262-5050. FAX 44-171-724-3317. TELEX 27461. E-mail: rms@lbs.ac.uk; URL: http://www.lbs.ac.uk/lfa/rms.htm. Eds. Elroy Dimson, Paul Marsh. R&P contact: Russell Lloyd. adv. contact: Anna Bousfield. illus. circ. 180. (also avail. in diskette format) **Document type**: bulletin.
    Description: Provides the information used by investment professionals and corporate executives to analyze the risks of UK shares and portfolios.

332   IT   ISSN 0035-5615
RISPARMIO. (Titles in English, French and German) 1953. bi-m. Lit.150000 (foreign Lit.225000) (effective 1997). (Associazione fra le Casse di Risparmio Italiane) Casa Editrice Dott. A. Giuffre, Via Busto Arsizio 40, Milan 20151, Italy. TEL 39-2-38089200. FAX 39-2-38009582. Ed. M. Talamona. bk.rev.; bibl.; charts; stat.; index. circ. 3,400. **Indexed**: ELLIS, P.A.I.S.For.Lang.Ind.

332   IS
RIVEON LEBANKAUT/QUARTERLY BANKING REVIEW. 1962. q. IS.90. Association of Banks in Israel, P.O. Box 2258, Tel Aviv 61021, Israel. TEL 972-3-5609019. FAX 972-3-5660317. Ed. Freddy Wieder. bk.rev.; circ. 2,000 (paid). **Document type**: academic/scholarly publication.
    Formerly: Revon Lebankaut - Banking Quarterly (ISSN 0557-1480)
    Refereed Serial

332   IT   ISSN 0035-578X
RIVISTA BANCARIA - MINERVA BANCARIA. 1936. bi-m. L.75000 (foreign L.150000). Istituto di Cultura Bancaria Milano, Via Montevideo 18, 00198 Rome, Italy. (And: Via Silvio Pellico 12, 20121 Milan, Italy) Ed. Francesco Parrillo.
—BLDSC (7981.700000).
    Formed by the merger of (1926-1935): Rivista Bancaria (ISSN 0392-8802); (1928-1935): Minerva Bancaria (ISSN 0392-8799)

332 340   IT   ISSN 0035-6131
RIVISTA DI DIRITTO FINANZIARIO E SCIENZA DELLE FINANZE. 1942. q. Lit.120000 (foreign Lit.18000) (effective 1997). Casa Editrice Dott. A. Giuffre, Via Busto Arsizio 40, 20151 Milan, Italy. TEL 39-2-38089200. FAX 39-2-38009852. Eds. Emilio Gerelli, Enrico Allorio. bk.rev.; bibl.; charts; index. circ. 1,300. **Indexed**: ELLIS, IBR.
—SWETS.

332   IT   ISSN 0035-676X
H7
RIVISTA INTERNAZIONALE DI SCIENZE SOCIALI. (Text in English, French, Italian) 1893. q. Lit.111000 (foreign Lit.166000 ($120)) (effective 1997); newsstand price: Lit.33000. (Universita Cattolica del Sacro Cuore, Istituto di Economia) Vita e Pensiero, Largo Gemelli 1, 20123 Milan, Italy. TEL 39-2-72342370. FAX 39-2-72342974. TELEX 321033-UCATHI-1. Ed. Dr. Gian Carlo Mazzocchi. adv.: B&W page Lit.2500000. bk.rev.; bibl.; charts; illus.; stat.; index. circ. 1,050. **Indexed**: Amer.Hist.& Life (1973-1985), Hist.Abstr. (1973-1985), Int.Polit.Sci.Abstr., Lang.& Lang.Behav.Abstr. **Document type**: academic/scholarly publication.
—SWETS.
    Description: Covers various areas in social sciences, with emphasis on economics.

RIVON CHESHEV. see *BUSINESS AND ECONOMICS — Marketing And Purchasing*

332.1 330.9   CN   ISSN 0229-0243
HC111
ROYAL BANK LETTER. French edition (ISSN 0227-5961) 1920. q. free. Royal Bank of Canada, Public Affairs Department, One Place Ville Marie, 7th Fl. W., Box 6001, Montreal, PQ H3C 3A9, Canada. TEL 514-874-2110. FAX 514-874-5891. URL: http://www.royalbank.com/. Ed. Robert Stewart. R&P contact: Gilda Derouin. circ. 150,000 (controlled). **Indexed**: Can.B.P.I., Can.Per.Ind., Ind.Free Per., P.A.I.S. **Document type**: newsletter.
—BLDSC (8028.620000).
    Formerly (until July 1980): Royal Bank of Canada. Monthly Letter (ISSN 0035-8770)
    Description: Presents subjects of general interest; instruction, self betterment, history and economics have been key areas.

332   TR
ROYAL BANK OF TRINIDAD AND TOBAGO. ANNUAL REPORT. a. Royal Bank of Trinidad and Tobago, 36 Chancery Lane, Port-of-Spain, Trinidad & Tobago, W.I. **Document type**: corporate report.

336   US
ROYALTY RATE REPORT FOR THE PHARMACEUTICAL & BIOTECHNOLOGY INDUSTRIES. a. $895 (renewals $250). Intellectual Property Research Associates, 1004 Buckingham Way, Yardley, PA 19067. TEL 215-428-1163. FAX 215-428-1163. Ed. Russell L. Parr.
    Description: Contains financial information about technology transfers. Presents financial details about pharmaceutical and biotechnology intellectual-property strategic alliances, primarily focusing on license fees and royalty rates.

RYNOK TSENNYKH BUMAG/SECURITIES MARKET; analiticheskii zhurnal. see *BUSINESS AND ECONOMICS — Investments*

332.1   SA
S A S B O NEWS/S A S B O NUUS. (Text in Afrikaans and English) m. South African Society of Bank Officials, S A S B O House, 97 Simmonds Str., Braamfontein, Johannesburg, South Africa. Ed. B.J. Smith. adv.; illus. circ. 39,000.

332.2 332.3   US
S & L QUARTERLY. (Savings and Loan) 1986. q. $349. United Communications Group, 11300 Rockville Pike, Ste. 1100, Rockville, MD 20852-3030. TEL 301-816-8950. FAX 301-816-8945. Ed. Martin Zook.
    Description: Lists 30 key figures and ratios for every federally insured savings and loan, and federal savings bank in America.

S B I C DIRECTORY AND HANDBOOK OF SMALL BUSINESS FINANCE. see *BUSINESS AND ECONOMICS — Small Business*

332   AU
S - GESUENDER LEBEN. 6/yr. S P V Printmedien GmbH, Talgasse 15, A-2753 Markt Piesting, Austria. TEL 43-1-71170-0. FAX 43-1-71170310. Ed. Ingeborg Plaschka. circ. 100,000. **Document type**: bulletin.
    Formerly: S Kontakt.

332   AU
S JOURNAL. q. Sparkassenverlag GmbH, Grimmelshausengasse 1, A-1030 Vienna, Austria. TEL 43-1-711700. FAX 43-1-71170310. Ed. Paul Holy. circ. 24,000. **Document type**: bulletin.

332   SP   ISSN 0409-9192
"SA NOSTRA" CAIXA DE BALEARS. MEMORIA. irreg. "Sa Nostra" Caixa de Balears, C. Ramon Llull 2, Palma de Mallorca, Spain. Dir. Pedro Batle Mayol. illus.; charts; stat.
    Formerly: Caja de Ahorros y Monte de Piedad de las Baleares. Memoria.

332   FI   ISSN 0036-2123
SAASTOPANKKI. 1904. m. FIM 250. Saastopankkiliitto, Postilokero 47, SF-00101 Helsinki 10, Finland. FAX 0-1334935. Ed. Risto Partanen. adv.; abstr.; charts; illus.; stat.; cum.index; circ. 27,188 (controlled). **Document type**: trade publication.

332.1   US   ISSN 0036-2379
SAFE DEPOSIT BULLETIN. 1911. q. membership. New York State Safe Deposit Association, c/o Paul Sanchez, Ed., Box 5074, Rockefeller Center, New York, NY 10185. TEL 212-484-2260. bk.rev. **Document type**: bulletin.

BUSINESS AND ECONOMICS — BANKING AND FINANCE

332 XI
ST. KITTS NEVIS ANGUILLA NATIONAL BANK LIMITED AND ITS SUBSIDIARIES. ANNUAL REPORT AND ACCOUNTS. a. St. Kitts Nevis Anguilla National Bank Limited, Church St., Basseterre, St. Kitts, W.I. **Document type:** corporate report.

332 BE ISSN 0778-1288
SAMSOM GELD EN ONDERNEMING. Variant title: Geld en Onderneming. (Supplement avail.) (Text in Flemish) 1986. s-m. 4770 BEF. C E D Samsom (Subsidiary of: Wolters Samsom Belgie n.v.), Kouterveld 14, B-1831 Diegem, Belgium. TEL 32-2-7231111.
   Description: For financial directors, chief accountants and banking houses. Examines business transactions from a fiscal perspective.

332 US
SAN GABRIEL VALLEY BUSINESS JOURNAL. 1993. m. $29.95. Southwest Business Publishing Co., 1274 E. Center Court Dr., No. 207, Covina, CA 91724. TEL 818-858-3351. FAX 818-339-3783. Ed. Mike Seiler. adv.: B&W page $1360; color page $1760; adv. contact: Richard Lawrence. charts; illus.; stat. circ. 10,000. (tabloid format; back issues avail.) **Document type:** trade publication.
   Description: Provides business news and information for corporate executives in eastern Los Angeles County, including economic data, company profiles, regional economic statistics, and special reports on selected industries.

SAN JOSE POST-RECORD; daily legal, & commercial real estate & financial news. see LAW

332.1 JA
SANWA BANK. CORPORATE COMMUNICATIONS DEPARTMENT. ANNUAL REPORT. a. Sanwa Bank Ltd., Corporate Communications Department, 1-1-1 Otemachi, Chiyoda-ku, Tokyo 100, Japan. TEL 03-216-3111. **Document type:** corporate report.

332 SU ISSN 0581-8672
SAUDI ARABIAN MONETARY AGENCY. STATISTICAL SUMMARY. a. Saudi Arabian Monetary Agency, Research and Statistics Department, P.O. Box 2992, Riyadh 11169, Saudi Arabia. TEL 966-1-463-3000. TELEX 401734. charts; stat. **Document type:** government publication.
   Description: Reviews major economic developments in Saudi Arabia such as money and banking, cost of living, government budget and oil developments.

332 IT ISSN 0393-4551
HG46
SAVINGS AND DEVELOPMENT. (Supplement included: African Review of Money, Finance and Banking) (Text in English; summaries in French) 1977. q. L.115000($80) (foreign L.160000($105)) (effective 1996). Giordano dell'Amore Foundation, Via San Vigilio 10, 20142 Milan, Italy. TEL 39-2-8135341. FAX 39-2-8137481. TELEX 313223 FINAFR I. Ed. Arnaldo Mauri; Pub. Felice Tambussi. R&P contact: Cinzia Raimondi. adv. contact: Cinzia Raimondi. bk.rev.; charts; stat.; index, cum.index. circ. 2,500. (back issues avail.) **Indexed:** Abstr.Rural Dev.Trop., Documentatieblad, Geo.Abstr.P.G., IDA, Int.Lab.Doc., Per.Islam. (1991-), Rural Devel.Abstr., Rural Recreat.Tour.Abstr., World Agri.Econ.& Rural Sociol.Abstr., World Bank.Abstr. **Document type:** academic/scholarly publication.
   —BLDSC (8077.254000); SWETS; UnCover.
   Formerly (until 1977): Finafrica Bulletin (ISSN 0393-456X)

332 US ISSN 1054-3805
HG1921
SAVINGS BANKS OF AMERICA. 1989. a. Sheshunoff Information Services Inc., Box 13203, Capitol Sta., Austin, TX 78711-3203. TEL 512-472-2244; 800-456-2340. **Document type:** trade publication.

332 US ISSN 0882-3197
HG2151
SAVINGS INSTITUTIONS SOURCEBOOK. 1954. a. $2.50. United States League of Savings Institutions, 900 19th St. N.W., No. 900, Washington, DC 20006-2105. TEL 312-644-3100. Ed. Diana S. Cheseldine. circ. 24,000. **Indexed:** SRI.
   Formerly: Savings and Loan Sourcebook (ISSN 0731-0935); Which supersedes in part (in 1980): Savings and Loan Fact Book (ISSN 0581-8761)
   Description: Includes research data and background information on the savings institution business.

SCHOLARSHIPS, FELLOWSHIPS AND LOANS. see EDUCATION — Higher Education

332 SZ ISSN 1010-5808
SCHWEIZER BANK. (Text in German) 1986. m. 96 SFr. (foreign 135 SFr.). S H Z Fachverlag AG, Alte Landstr. 43, CH-8700 Kuesnacht, Switzerland. TEL 01-9108022. FAX 01-9105155. Ed. Brigitte Strebel. adv. circ. 24,000. **Document type:** trade publication.
   Description: For executives in the banking and financial business.

332 SZ
SCHWEIZERISCHE BANKPERSONAL ZEITUNG. 22/yr. Zentralsekretariat, Postfach 8235, CH-3001 Bern, Switzerland. TEL 031-454311. FAX 031-459874. Ed. Urs Tschumi. circ. 30,000.

332.1 SZ
SCHWEIZERISCHE BANKWESEN. (Text in German) a. 24.30 (Europe 27 SFr.; overseas 30.50 SFr.). (Schweizerische Nationalbank) Zuerichsee Medien AG, Seestr. 86, CH-7612 Staefa, Switzerland. TEL 01-9285611. FAX 01-9285600. stat. **Document type:** corporate report.

332 SZ ISSN 0036-7729
HC395
SCHWEIZERISCHE NATIONALBANK. MONATSBERICHT. (Text in French and German) 1926. m. 40 SFr. (Europe 70 SFr.; overseas 136 SFr.). Zuerichsee Medien AG, Seestr. 86, CH-7612 Staefa, Switzerland. TEL 01-9285611. FAX 01-9285600. charts; mkt.; stat. circ. 3,600. **Document type:** bulletin.

332 SZ
SCHWEIZERISCHE NATIONALBANK. QUARTALSHEFT. q. 25 SFr. (Europe 30 SFr.; overseas 55 SFr.). Zuerichsee Medien AG, Seestr. 86, CH-8712 Staefa, Switzerland. TEL 01-9285611. FAX 01-9285600. **Document type:** bulletin.

332 CN
SCOTIABANKER. 12/yr. free. 44 King St. W., Scotia Plaza, Toronto, ON M5H 1H1, Canada. TEL 416-866-3999. FAX 416-866-4988. Ed. Sue LaVigne. circ. 35,000. **Document type:** newsletter.

332.1 UK
SCOTTISH BANKER. 1909. q. £18. The Chartered Institute of Bankers in Scotland, 19 Rutland Sq., Edinburgh EH1 2DE, Scotland. TEL 0131-229-9869. FAX 0131-229-1852. Ed. Charles W. Munn. adv.; bk.rev.; illus.; index. circ. 12,000. **Indexed:** Br.Hum.Ind., Cont.Pg.Manage., P.A.I.S., World Bank.Abstr. **Document type:** trade publication.
   Formerly: Scottish Bankers Magazine (ISSN 0036-9128)

332 332.6 658 UK ISSN 0952-1488
SCOTTISH BUSINESS INSIDER. Variant title: Insider. 1984. m. £36 (rest of Europe £552 U.S. £59); newsstand price: £3. Insider Publications Ltd., 43 Queensferry Street Ln., Edinburgh EH2 4PF, Scotland. TEL 0131-225-8323. FAX 0131-220-1203. E-mail: 100732.1772@compuserve.com. Ed. Bill Millar. adv. contact: David Roulstone. circ. 20,000 (paid). (back issues avail.) **Document type:** trade publication.
   Description: Covers the major sectors of business, commerce and industry in Scotland.

SCREEN FINANCE. see MOTION PICTURES

332 US ISSN 0891-2947
SECONDARY MARKETING EXECUTIVE. 1986. m. $48. L D J Corporation, 70 Edwin Ave., Box 2330, Waterbury, CT 06722-2330. TEL 203-755-0158. FAX 203-755-3480. Ed. Ruth G. Field. R&P contact: Neil Morse. adv. contact: Linda Herrmann. charts; illus.; tr.lit.; index. circ. 23,000. (tabloid format; back issues avail.) **Document type:** trade publication, newspaper.
   Description: Provides how-to information and trends analysis for buyers and sellers of mortgage loans and servicing rights on the secondary market.

333.33 US ISSN 0740-4271
HG2040.25
SECONDARY MORTGAGE MARKETS. 1984. q. free. Federal Home Loan Mortgage Corporation, 8200 Jones Branch Dr., McLean, VA 22102-3107. TEL 703-903-2343. FAX 703-903-4045. Ed. Jane Lehmans. circ. 5,300. (also avail. in microform from UMI) **Indexed:** ABI Inform., Bank.Lit.Ind., BPIA, World Bank.Abstr. **Document type:** trade publication.
   —UMI.

332 US ISSN 0888-255X
HF5565
SECURED LENDER. 1945. bi-m. $48 to non-members; members $24. Commercial Finance Association, 225 W. 34th St., Rm. 1815, New York, NY 10122-0008. TEL 212-594-3480. Ed. Bruce H. Jones; Pub. Bruce H. Jones. adv. contact: Bruce H. Jones. bk.rev. circ. 5,400. **Indexed:** ABI Inform., World Bank.Abstr. **Document type:** trade publication.
   ●Also available online. Vendor(s): UMI.
   —BLDSC (8216.988000); UMI.
   Former titles (until 1986): Journal: Asset-Based Financial Services Industry (ISSN 0278-9353); (until 1980): Commercial Finance Journal (ISSN 0160-5178); Incorporates: National Commercial Finance Association. Journal.

332 658.4 FR ISSN 0297-9101
SECURITE INFORMATIQUE. 1986. m. (11/yr.). 3200 F. (foreign 3350 F.). Publi-News, 3 ave. Gallieni, 92000 Nanterre, France. TEL 47-29-88-11. FAX 47-29-88-18. Ed. Ange Galula. **Document type:** newsletter.
   Description: Contains information on technology products, trends, users, security strategy and law.

332 340 US ISSN 0080-8474
KF1066.A32
SECURITIES LAW REVIEW. 1969. a. $130. Clark - Boardman - Callaghan, 375 Hudson St., New York, NY 10014. TEL 212-929-7500; 800-221-9428. FAX 212-924-0460. Ed. Donald C. Langevoort. (reprint service avail. from WSH) **Indexed:** C.L.I., L.R.I., Leg.Per.
   —UnCover.
   Description: Covers the latest developments in securities law.

332 US
SECURITIES TRANSACTIONS HANDBOOK. a. $75. U.S. Federal Reserve System, Board of Governors, Publications Services, Rm. MS-127, 20th and Constitution Ave., N.W., Washington, DC 20551. TEL 202-452-3244. FAX 202-728-5886. **Document type:** government publication.

332 340 US
SECURITIZATION: ASSET-BACKED AND MORTGAGE-BACKED SECURITIES. 1991. base vol. (plus a. supplements). $90. Butterworth Legal Publishers (Salem) (Subsidiary of: Reed Elsevier plc), 8 Industrial Way, Bldg. C, Salem, NH 03079. TEL 800-548-4001. FAX 603-898-9858. Ed. Ronald S. Borod. (looseleaf format)
   Description: Covers all federal and state regulatory and tax provisions governing securitized transactions, including rules of accounting and rating agency requirements.

332 JA
SEISAKU IINKAI GEPPO. (Text in Japanese) m. free. Bank of Japan - Nippon Ginko, c/o Public Relations Department, 2-1-1 Hongoko-cho, Nihonbashi, Chuo-ku, Tokyo 103, Japan. TEL 81-3-3292-3753. FAX 81-3-3292-0410.

332 US
SELECTED BORROWINGS IN IMMEDIATELY AVAILABLE FUNDS OF LARGE COMMERCIAL BANKS. w. $20. U.S. Federal Reserve System, Board of Governors, Publications Services, Rm. MS-138, Washington, DC 20551. TEL 202-452-3244. FAX 202-728-5886. **Document type:** government publication.

332 US
SELECTED INTEREST RATES. w. and m. releases. $20 for w. release; m. release $5. U.S. Federal Reserve System, Board of Governors, Publications Services, Rm. MS-138, Washington, DC 20551. TEL 202-452-3244. FAX 202-728-5886. **Document type:** government publication.

SELECTED LAWS AND REGULATIONS OF TENNESSEE FINANCIAL INSTITUTIONS. see LAW — Corporate Law

BUSINESS AND ECONOMICS — BANKING AND FINANCE

SENTINEL INVESTMENT LETTER. see *BUSINESS AND ECONOMICS* — *Investments*

332   FR   ISSN 0037-2595
SERVICE ECONOMIQUE & FINANCIER "SECOFI". 1942. w. 160 F. (Express Documents) Groupe Revenue Francais, 1 bis av. de la Republique, 75011 Paris, France. TEL 49-29-30-00. FAX 43-55-91-41. Ed. Robert Monteux. adv.; bibl.; stat.; index, cum.index. circ. 15,000.

332   US   ISSN 1044-1077
SERVICING MANAGEMENT. m. L D J Corporation, Box 2330, Waterbury, CT 06722-2330. TEL 203-755-0158. FAX 203-755-3480. Ed. Ruth G. Fields. R&P contact: Ruth G. Fields. adv. contact: Joyce Rubinstein. charts; illus.; tr.lit.; index. circ. 22,000. (tabloid format; back issues avail.)
Document type: trade publication.
Description: Provides how-to information and trends analysis for executives and managers of mortgage servicing operations.

332   CC
SHANGHAI JINRONG/SHANGHAI FINANCE. (Text in Chinese) m. Shanghai Jinrong Xuehui - Shanghai Financial Association, Jia San Lou (Building A-3), Zhongshan Dong 2 Lu, Shanghai 200002, People's Republic of China. TEL 3287836. Ed. Sheng Mujie.

332.1
SHAREHOLDERS, FORM 10-K. BANKING SUPPLEMENT. 1983. s-a. free. Ernst & Young, 787 Seventh Ave., New York, NY 10019. TEL 212-773-6000. stat. circ. 3,675.
Former titles (until 1988): S E C Annual Reports. Banking Supplement; S E C Annual Reports.

332.7   US   ISSN 0730-1936
KF1515.5
SHEPARD'S BANKRUPTCY CITATIONS. 1985. bi-m. $490. Shepard's (Subsidiary of: Reed Elsevier plc & The Times Mirror Company), Box 35300, Colorado Springs, CO 80935-3530. TEL 800-525-2474.

332 340   US
SHESHUNOFF COMPLIANCE AND LAW SERIES. 1989? a. (plus irreg. updates). $1950. Sheshunoff Information Services Inc., 505 Barton Springs Rd., Ste. 1100, Austin, TX 78704. TEL 512-472-2244; 800-456-2340. index. (looseleaf format; back issues avail.) **Document type:** trade publication.
Description: Provides important reference data for compliance managers at banks.

332   US
SHESHUNOFF FINANCIAL MANAGEMENT SERIES. irreg. price varies. Sheshunoff Information Services Inc., 505 Barton Springs Rd., Ste. 1100, Austin, TX 78704. TEL 512-472-2244; 800-456-2340. (back issues avail.) **Document type:** trade publication.

332   US
SHESHUNOFF REGULATORY REPORTING SERIES. irreg. price varies. Sheshunoff Information Services Inc., 505 Barton Springs Rd., Ste. 1100, Austin, TX 78704. TEL 512-472-2244; 800-456-2340.
Document type: trade publication.
Description: Offers bank management guidance in regulations governing disclosure.

332   US
SHESHUNOFF TRAINING SERIES. irreg. price varies. Sheshunoff Information Services Inc., 505 Barton Springs Rd., Ste. 1100, Austin, TX 78704. TEL 512-472-2340; 800-456-2340. (back issues avail.) **Document type:** trade publication.

332   CC
SICHUAN CAIZHENG YANJIU/SICHUAN FINANCE RESEARCH. (Text in Chinese) m. Sichuan Caizheng Ting - Sichuan Bureau of Finance, 37 Nanxin Jie, Chengdu, Sichuan 610016, People's Republic of China. TEL 22353.

332   CC
SICHUAN JINRONG/SICHUAN FINANCE. (Text in Chinese) m. Sichuan Finance Society, Yinhang Dasha (Bank Building), Shudu Dadao, Chengdu, Sichuan 610016, People's Republic of China. TEL 554360. (Co-sponsor: Chinese People's Bank, Sichuan Branch)

332   CK
SIMPOSIO SOBRE MERCADO DE CAPITALES. no.3, 1974. a. $11 (effective 1990). Asociacion Bancaria de Colombia, Carrera 7, No. 17-01, Piso 3, Bogota D.E., Colombia. TEL 57-1-281-3501. FAX 57-1-281-3017.

332.4   SI
SINGAPORE. BOARD OF COMMISSIONERS OF CURRENCY. ANNUAL REPORT AND ACCOUNTS. 1967. a. Board of Commissioners of Currency, 79 Robinson Rd., No.01-01, Singapore 0106, Singapore. TEL 2222211. FAX 2257671. TELEX SINWANG RS 24722. circ. 800.
Formerly: Singapore. Board of Commissioners of Currency. Annual Report.

332   CK
SISTEMA FINANCIERO INFORME TRIMESTRAL. 1990. q. free. Superintendencia Bancaria, Apdo. Aereo 3460, Bogota DC, Colombia. TEL 57-1-2804060. FAX 57-1-2800864. circ. 500.

332   UK
SMALL BUSINESSES AND THEIR BANKS. 1988. biennial. Forum of Private Business, Ruskin Chambers, Drury Ln., Knutsford, Ches. WA6 6HA, England. TEL 44-1565-634467. FAX 44-1565-650059. **Document type:** academic/scholarly publication.

332   US   ISSN 1069-2851
HG179
SMARTMONEY; the Wall Street Journal magazine of personal business. 1992. m. $24 (Canada $39) (effective 1997). Hearst Corporation and Dow Jones & Company, Inc., SmartMoney Magazine, 1790 Broadway, New York, NY 10019. TEL 212-492-1300. E-mail: editors@smartmoney.com; URL: http://hearstcorp.com. (Subscr. to: Box 7538, Red Oak, IA 51591. TEL 800-444-4204) Ed. Steven Swartz; Pub. Christopher L. Lambiase. R&P contact: Nikki Frost. adv.: B&W page $31,290, color page $42,900; adv. contact: Susan Stewart. bk.rev.; illus.; circ. 650,000 (paid). Indexed: B.P.I. **Document type:** consumer publication.
—KR SourceOne; UnCover.
Description: Covers a variety of personal finance topics for upscale readers, including retirement planning, investment strategies, financial planning for education, and related life-style issues.

332   BE   ISSN 0081-1114
SOCIETE GENERALE DE BELGIQUE. RAPPORT - REPORT. (Editions in English, French) 1822. a. free. Societe Generale de Belgique, Communications Department, 30 rue Royale, B-1000 Brussels, Belgium.

332.1   UK
SORTING CODE NUMBERS; directory of bank branches and other financial institutions to which code numbers have been allocated. 1967. a. £3.20. (Association for Payment Clearing Services) Reed Information Services Ltd., Division of Reed Telepublishing Ltd. (Subsidiary of: Reed Elsevier group), Windsor Court, E. Grinstead House, E. Grinstead, W. Sussex RH19 1XA, England. TEL 01342-326962. FAX 01342-335977. TELEX 95127-INFSER-G. Ed. R. Phelps. circ. 155,000. (also avail. in magnetic tape) **Document type:** directory.

332.1   SA   ISSN 0038-2000
HG3399.S7
SOUTH AFRICAN BANKER/SUID-AFRIKAANSE BANKIER. 1904. q. R.48 (foreign R.64.50) (effective 1997). Institute of Bankers in South Africa, P.O. Box 61420, Marshalltown 2107, South Africa. TEL 27-11-8321371. Ed. Mrs. J.E. Hodges. adv.; bk.rev.; illus.; index. circ. 16,000. Indexed: Ind.S.A.Per., P.A.I.S., World Bank.Abstr. **Document type:** academic/scholarly publication.
Formerly (until 1968): South African Banker's Journal.
Refereed Serial

332   SA   ISSN 0049-1403
SOUTH AFRICAN FINANCIAL GAZETTE. Cover title: Financial Gazette. 1964. w. R.18. South African Financial Gazette Ltd., P.O. Box 8161, Johannesburg 2000, South Africa. Ed. Otto Krause. adv.; film rev.; play rev.; charts; stat. circ. 15,000.

332   SA   ISSN 0038-2620
HG3399.S7
SOUTH AFRICAN RESERVE BANK. QUARTERLY BULLETIN/SUID-AFRIKAANSE RESERWEBANK. KWARTAALBLAD. (Text and title in Afrikaans, English) 1946. q. R.75 (overseas free) (effective 1996). South African Reserve Bank, P.O. Box 427, Pretoria 0001, South Africa. TEL 27-12-3133911. FAX 27-12-3133197. E-mail: info@gwisel.resbank.oc.za; URL: http://www.resbank.co.za. charts; stat. circ. 3,000. Indexed: PROMT, World Bank.Abstr. **Document type:** bulletin.
Formerly: South African Reserve Bank. Quarterly Bulletin of Statistics.

332.1   SA
SOUTH AFRICAN RESERVE BANK. REPORT OF THE ORDINARY GENERAL MEETING/SUID-AFRIKAANSE RESERWEBANK. VERSLAG VAN DIE GEWONE ALGEMENE VERGADERING. (Text in Afrikaans, English) 1922. a. free. South African Reserve Bank, P.O. Box 427, Pretoria 0001, South Africa. TEL 27-12-3133911. FAX 27-12-3133197. E-mail: info@gwisel.resbank.co.za; URL: http://www.resbank.co.za. circ. 3,120. **Document type:** corporate report.

THE SOUTHERN AFRICA EXCLUSIVE; bulletin covering financial and political trends for southern Africa. see *BUSINESS AND ECONOMICS* — *Economic Situation And Conditions*

332.1   US
SOUTHWEST ECONOMY. 1982. bi-m. free. Federal Reserve Bank of Dallas, Box 655906, Dallas, TX 75265-5906. TEL 214-922-5254. FAX 214-922-5268. Ed. Rhonda Harris. circ. 11,000. (back issues avail.) Indexed: Amer.Hist.& Life (1978-1984), Hist.Abstr. (1978-1984).
Formerly (until 1988): Roundup (Dallas).
Description: Covers economic conditions and business developments in the Southwest, including agriculture, banking, energy, high technology, manufacturing and international trade.

SOVEREIGN ASSESSMENT MONTHLY. see *BUSINESS AND ECONOMICS* — *Investments*

332.1   NO   ISSN 0038-6502
SPAREBANKBLADET/NORWEGIAN SAVINGS BANK NEWS. 1917. m. NOK 210 (effective 1997). Sparebankforeningens Publikasjoner AS, P.O. Box 6772, St. Olavs Plass, N-0130 Oslo, Norway. TEL 47-22-11-00-75. FAX 47-22-36-25-33. Ed. Ragnar Falck. adv.; bk.rev.; charts; stat.; circ. 7,500 (controlled).
—CCC.

332   AU
SPAREN - BAUEN - WOHNEN. 3/yr. Orac Zeitschriftenverlag GmbH, Brunner Feldstr. 45, A-2380 Perchtoldsdorf, Austria. TEL 43-1-8696536. FAX 43-1-8696536. adv.: B&W page S.117200, color page S.142984; trim 185 x 250. circ. 908,000. **Document type:** bulletin.

332.1   GW   ISSN 0038-6561
HG1939.G2
SPARKASSE. 1881. m. DM.210 (effective 1996). (Deutscher Sparkassen- und Giroverband e.V.) Deutscher Sparkassenverlag GmbH, Am Wallgraben 115, 70565 Stuttgart, Germany. Ed. Arnulf Sauter. adv.; bk.rev.; charts; illus.; stat.; index. circ. 7,000. Indexed: P.A.I.S.For.Lang.Ind. **Document type:** bulletin.
—BLDSC (8361.742000). CCC.

332.1   GW
SPARKASSENFACHBUCH (YEAR). a. Deutscher Sparkassenverlag GmbH, Am Wallgraben 115, 70565 Stuttgart, Germany. **Document type:** trade publication.

SPECIAL PAPERS IN INTERNATIONAL ECONOMICS. see *BUSINESS AND ECONOMICS*

332   US
STANDARD & POOR'S DIVIDEND RECORD (ANNUAL). q. $26. Standard & Poor's Corporation (Subsidiary of: McGraw-Hill, Inc.), 25 Broadway, New York, NY 10004. Ed. Anthony Onofrio. (looseleaf format; also avail. in microfiche)

STANDARD & POOR'S FINANCIAL INSTITUTIONS RATINGS (QUARTERLY EDITION). see *BUSINESS AND ECONOMICS* — *Abstracting, Bibliographies, Statistics*

BUSINESS AND ECONOMICS — BANKING AND FINANCE

332 II
STATE BANK OF INDIA. ANNUAL REPORT. (Text in English) 1955. a. State Bank of India, Economic Research Department, Central Office, New Administration Bldg., Backbay Reclamation, Bombay 400021, India. **Document type:** corporate report.
   Supersedes: State Bank of India. Report of the Central Board of Directors (ISSN 0585-0991); Report for the Half Year of the Imperial Bank of India.

332.1 PK ISSN 0081-444X
STATE BANK OF PAKISTAN. ANNUAL REPORT. (Text in English) 1949. a. free. State Bank of Pakistan, Central Directorate, Public Relations Department, I.I. Chundrigar Rd., P.O. Box 4456, Karachi, Pakistan. TEL 92-2414141. FAX 92-2417865. TELEX 2754 SBPK PK. circ. 2,500. **Document type:** government publication.

332 PK ISSN 0039-0011
HC440.5
STATE BANK OF PAKISTAN. BULLETIN. (Text in English) 1950. m. Rs.288($48) State Bank of Pakistan, Central Directorate, Public Relations Department, I.I. Chundrigar Rd., P.O. Box 4456, Karachi, Pakistan. TEL 92-2414141. FAX 92-2417865. TELEX 2754 SBPK PK. Ed.Bd. circ. 727. **Indexed:** World Bank.Abstr. **Document type:** government publication, bulletin.
   Description: Provides information on prices, labor, and national accounts in Pakistan.

332 PK ISSN 0561-8738
STATE BANK OF PAKISTAN. STATE BANK NEWS. (Text in English) 1963. s-m. State Bank of Pakistan, Central Directorate, Public Relations Department, I.I. Chundrigar Rd., P.O. Box 4456, Karachi, Pakistan. TEL 92-2414141. FAX 92-2417865. TELEX 2754 SBPK PK. **Document type:** government publication, newsletter.
   Description: Provides information of relevance to bank employees.

332 US
STATE OF DELAWARE. LAWS RELATING TO FINANCIAL INSTITUTIONS. a. $30. Michie, A Division of Reed Elsevier Inc., Box 7587, Charlottesville, VA 22906-7587. TEL 804-972-7566; 800-562-1197. FAX 800-643-1280. E-mail: custserv@michie.com; URL: http://www.michie.com. Ed. George Harley. pp./issue: 30.

332.1 US ISSN 1053-3435
HG2571
STATE OF THE STATE BANKING SYSTEM. 1965. a, 15th ed., 1994. $60. Conference of State Bank Supervisors, 1015 18th St., N.W., Ste. 1100, Washington, DC 20036-5275. TEL 202-296-2840. FAX 202-296-1928. Ed. Ellen Lamb. R&P contact: Ellen Lamb.

334.2 US
STATELINE. 1975. m. National Association of State Credit Union Supervisors, 1901 N. Ft. Myer Dr., Ste. 201, Arlington, VA 22209-1604. Ed. Mary Martha Fortney. circ. 650.
   Description: Covers the credit union financial industry.

332 CC
STOCK EXCHANGE OF HONG KONG. DAILY QUOTATIONS. (Text in English) d. HK.$190 (Asia HK.$350; elsewhere HK.$400). Stock Exchange of Hong Kong, Distribution Centre, 1-F One & Two Exchange Sq., Central, Hong Kong, People's Republic of China. TEL 852-2522-1122. FAX 852-2845-3554. TELEX 86839 STOEX HX.
   Formerly: Stock Exchange of Hong Kong. Market Summary.

332 CC
STOCK EXCHANGE OF HONG KONG. FACT BOOK (YEAR). (Text in English) a. HK.$88 (Asia HK.$128; elsewhere HK.$132). Stock Exchange of Hong Kong, Distribution Centre, 1-F One & Two Exchange Sq., Central, Hong Kong, People's Republic of China. TEL 852-2522-1122. FAX 852-2845-3554. TELEX 86839 STOEX HX.

332 CC
STOCK EXCHANGE OF HONG KONG. FACT SHEET. (Text in English) 1987. q. HK.$10 (Asia HK.$13; elsewhere HK.$14). Stock Exchange of Hong Kong, Distribution Centre, 1-F One & Two Exchange Sq., Central, Hong Kong, People's Republic of China. TEL 852-2522-1122. FAX 852-2845-3554. TELEX 86839 STOEX HX.

332 CC
STOCK EXCHANGE OF HONG KONG. MEMBER LIST. (Text in English) q. HK.$70 (Asia HK.$129; elsewhere HK.$134). Stock Exchange of Hong Kong, Distribution Centre, 1-F One & Two Exchange Sq., Central, Hong Kong, People's Republic of China. TEL 852-2522-1122. FAX 852-2845-3554. TELEX 86839 STOEX HX.

332 CC
STOCK EXCHANGE OF HONG KONG. MONTHLY MARKET STATISTICS. (Text in English) m. Stock Exchange of Hong Kong, Distribution Centre, 1-F One & Two Exchange Sq., Central, Hong Kong, People's Republic of China. TEL 852-2522-1122. FAX 852-2845-3554. TELEX 86839 STOEX HX.

332 CC
STOCK EXCHANGE OF HONG KONG. WEEKLY QUOTATIONS. (Text in English) w. HK.$200 (Asia HK.$475; elsewhere HK.$600). Stock Exchange of Hong Kong, Distribution Centre, 1-F One & Two Exchange Sq., Central, Hong Kong, People's Republic of China. TEL 852-2522-1122. FAX 852-2845-3554. TELEX 86839 STOEX HX.
   Formerly: Stock Exchange of Hong Kong. Weekly Report.

332 II
STOCK MARKET YEARBOOK; an easy reference to 200 companies. (Text in English) 1989. a. Rs.150. Quantum Financial Services Pvt. Ltd., 2 Jay Mahal, A Road, Mumbai 400 020, India. TEL 91-22-283-0322. FAX 91-22-285-4318. TELEX 011-4529 MCTC IN. Ed. Ajit Dayal. R&P contact: Ajit Dayal.

STOCK SUMMARY (MONTHLY EDITION). see *BUSINESS AND ECONOMICS — Investments*

332 GW
STUDIEN ZU FUNDMUENZEN DER ANTIKE. irreg., vol.11, 1996. DM.134. Gebr. Mann Verlag GmbH, Charlottenstr. 13, 10969 Berlin, Germany. TEL 49-30-2591-3589. FAX 49-30-2591-3537. Ed. Aleksander Bursche. **Document type:** academic/scholarly publication, monographic series.

332 US ISSN 0081-8070
STUDIES IN INTERNATIONAL FINANCE. 1950. irreg., no.78, 1995. $40 (includes Essays in International Finance; Reprints in International Finance; Special Papers in International Economics) (effective 1996 & 1997). Princeton University, International Finance Section, c/o Margaret B. Riccardi, Ed., Department of Economics, Fisher Hall, Princeton, NJ 08544-1021. TEL 609-258-4048. FAX 609-258-6419. R&P contact: Margaret B. Riccardi. circ. 2,000. (back issues avail.; reprint service avail. from UMI) **Document type:** monographic series.
—CCC.
   Description: Research studies in the field of international finance problems that are too technical or too specialized to appear in "Essays in International Finance".

332 NE
STUDIES IN MONETARY ECONOMICS. 1976. irreg., vol.7, 1981. price varies. Elsevier Science B.V., Books Division, P.O. Box 211, 1000 AE Amsterdam, Netherlands. TEL 31-20-4853911. FAX 31-20-4853705. TELEX 18582 ESPA NL. E-mail: nlinfo-f@elsevier.nl; usinfo-f@elsevier.com; forinfo-kyf04035@niftyserve.or.jp; URL: http://www.elsevier.nl/. (Subscr. in the Americas to: Elsevier Science, Regional Sales Office, Box 945, New York, NY 10159-0945. TEL 212-633-3730. FAX 212-633-3680; Subscr. in Australasia and the Far East to: Elsevier Science (Singapore) Pte Ltd, No.1 Temasek Ave., No.17-01 Millenia Tower, Singapore 039192, Singapore. TEL 65-434-3727. FAX 65-337-2230; Subscr. in Japan to: Elsevier Science Japan, 9-15 Higashi-Azabu 1-chome, Minato-ku, Tokyo 106, Japan. TEL 81-3-5561-5033. FAX 81-3-5561-5047) Ed. Karl Brunner. charts; stat. **Document type:** monographic series.
   Refereed Serial

SUARA N U B E. see *LABOR UNIONS*

332 SJ
SUDAN COMMERCIAL BANK. REPORT OF THE BOARD OF DIRECTORS. irreg. Sudan Commercial Bank, Box 1116, Khartoum, Sudan. **Document type:** corporate report.

332 JA ISSN 0910-1403
SUMITOMO BANK. ANNUAL REPORT. (Text in English) 1951. a. free. Sumitomo Bank, Ltd., Economic Department, C.P.O. Box 4, Tokyo 100-91, Japan. **Document type:** corporate report.
   Formerly (until 1968): Sumitomo Bank. Half-yearly Report (ISSN 0910-139X)

332 AT ISSN 1324-5295
SUPER REVIEW. 1986. m. Aus.$99($132) (effective 1996). Reed Business Publishing Pty. Ltd. (Subsidiary of: Reed International PLC), P.O. Box 5487, W. Chatswood, N.S.W. 2057, Australia. TEL 61-2-372-5222. FAX 61-2-419-7399. circ. 4,500. **Document type:** trade publication.
   Formerly (until 1994): Australian Super Review (ISSN 0819-341X)
   Description: Provides in-depth coverage of superannuation policy, compliance, administration and investment issues.

SUPER REVIEW TOP 1500 DIRECTORY. see *BUSINESS AND ECONOMICS — Trade And Industrial Directories*

332 US
SURVEY OF TERMS OF BANK LENDING. q. $5. U.S. Federal Reserve System, Board of Governors, Publications Services, Rm. MS-138, Washington, DC 20551. TEL 202-452-3244. FAX 202-728-5886. **Document type:** government publication.

332 SW
SVENSK OBLIGATIONSBOK. 1913. a. SEK 575. Svenska Bankfoereningen - Swedish Bankers Association, P.O. Box 7603, S-103 94 Stockholm, Sweden. Ed. Sture Braasjoe.

332.1 SW ISSN 0081-9913
SVENSKA HANDELSBANKEN. ANNUAL REPORT. Variant title: Svenska Handelsbanken. Annual Report and Auditors' Report. 1871 Swedish ed.; 1955 English ed. a. free. Svenska Handelsbanken, S-106 70 Stockholm, Sweden. TEL 46-8-701-2408. FAX 46-8-701-2345. TELEX 11090-HANDST-S. circ. 8,000. **Document type:** corporate report.
—BLDSC (1464.300000).

332.1 SW ISSN 0347-3198
SVERIGES RIKSBANK. FOERVALTNINGSBERAETTELSE. a. free. Sveriges Riksbank, S-103 37 Stockholm, Sweden. TEL 46-8-787-00-00. FAX 46-8-21-05-31. Dir. Michael Wallin. **Document type:** government publication, corporate report.

332.1 SW ISSN 1100-5815
SVERIGES RIKSBANK. PENNING- OCH VALUTAPOLITIK. English edition: Sveriges Riksbank - Swedish Central Bank. Quarterly Review (ISSN 0348-6583) 1979. q. free. Sveriges Riksbank, Informationssekretariatet, S-103 37 Stockholm, Sweden. TEL 46-8-787-01-50. FAX 46-8-787-05-26. E-mail: kerstin.wallmark@riskbank.se; URL: http://www.riskbank.se. (Subscr. to: Quarterly Review - Sveriges Riksbank, Information Secretariat, S-103 37 Stockholm, Sweden) Ed. Kerstin Wallmark. circ. 1,200. **Indexed:** ELLIS. **Document type:** academic/scholarly publication.
   Formerly (until 1989): Sveriges Riksbank. Kredit- och Valutaoeversikt (ISSN 0348-5153)

332.1 SW ISSN 0348-7342
HG3176
SVERIGES RIKSBANK. STATISTISK AARSBOK/SVERIGES RIKSBANK - SWEDISH CENTRAL BANK. STATISTICAL YEARBOOK. (Tables in English and Swedish) 1908. a. Sveriges Riksbank, S-103 37 Stockholm, Sweden. TEL 46-8-787-00-00. FAX 46-8-21-05-31. Dir. Michael Wallin. **Document type:** abstracting/indexing.
   Formerly (until 1979): Sveriges Riksbank. Aarsbok.

332 SQ
SWAZILAND. MINISTRY OF FINANCE. CAPITAL FUND ESTIMATES. a. free. Ministry of Finance, P.O. Box 456, Mbabane, Swaziland. TEL 268-43765. **Document type:** government publication.
   Formerly: Swaziland. Central Statistical Office. Capital Fund Estimates.

BUSINESS AND ECONOMICS — BANKING AND FINANCE

332   SZ
SWISS BANK CORPORATION. REPORT OF THE BOARD OF DIRECTORS TO THE ANNUAL GENERAL MEETING OF SHAREHOLDERS. a. Schweizerischer Bankverein - Swiss Bank Corporation, 6 Aeschenplatz, CH-4002 Basel, Switzerland. TEL 41-61-2882020. FAX 41-61-2883708. Ed. Rainer Skierka. R&P contact: Rainer Skierka. **Indexed**: World Bank.Abstr. **Document type**: corporate report.

332   FR   ISSN 1261-7733
▼**SYSTEMES DE PAIEMENT**. 1995. m. 3450 F. (foreign 3500 F.). Publi-News, 3 ave. Gallieni, 92000 Nanterre, France. TEL 33-47-29-88-11. FAX 33-47-29-88-18. Ed. Ange Galula. **Document type**: newsletter.
    Description: Covers the marketing of credit and debit cards.

T A C; tijdschrift voor controlling. (Tijdschrift voor Administrateurs en Controllers) see *BUSINESS AND ECONOMICS — Accounting*

332   US
HG4028.C45
T M A JOURNAL. 1981. bi-m. $90 (Canada & Mexico $100; elsewhere $120). Treasury Management Association, 7315 Wisconsin Ave., Ste. 600 W., Bethesda, MD 20814. TEL 301-907-2862. FAX 301-907-2864. URL: http://www.tma-net.org/treasury. Ed. Ayo I. Mseka; Pub. Donald E. Manger. adv.: B&W page $2500; trim 8 1/2 x 11; adv. contact: Maria C. DeRyke. bk.rev. circ. 10,000. (reprint service avail.) **Indexed**: ABI Inform., B.P.I., Bank.Lit.Ind. **Document type**: trade publication.
—SWETS; UMI; UnCover. **CCC**.
    Formerly (until Jan. 1994): Journal of Cash Management (ISSN 0731-1281)
    Description: Publishes in-depth articles on the latest developments in the treasury field. Includes columns on banking, international trends and short-term investments and the industry's most comprehensive calendar of events.
    Refereed Serial

332   US
T M A NEWS. (Former name of issuing body: National Corporate Cash Management Association) m. membership only. Treasury Management Association, 7315 Wisconsin Ave., Ste. 600 W., Bethesda, MD 20814. TEL 301-907-2862. FAX 301-907-2864. URL: http://www.tma-net.org/treasury. Ed. Ayo I. Mseka; Pub. Donald E. Manger. **Document type**: newsletter.
    Formerly: N C C M A News.

332.1   TZ   ISSN 0856-2687
TANZANIA HOUSING BANK. ANNUAL REPORT AND STATEMENT OF ACCOUNTS/BENKI YA NYUMBA TANZANIA. RIPOTI YA MWAKA. (Text in English, Swahili) 1974. a. Tanzania Housing Bank, Planning and Research Department, P.O. Box 1723, Dar es Salaam, Tanzania. TEL 255-51-3112. FAX 255-51-3119. TELEX 41831. Ed.Bd. circ. 600. **Document type**: corporate report.
    Description: Aims to provide the public with information to give them confidence in continuing to invest in the bank.

332.1   TZ   ISSN 0856-2423
TANZANIA INVESTMENT BANK. ANNUAL REPORT. (Text in English, Swahili) 1971. a. Tanzania Investment Bank, P.O. Box 9373, Dar es Salaam, Tanzania. **Document type**: corporate report.

332   TZ
TANZANIAN BANKERS JOURNAL. 1986. irreg., no.3, 1990. National Bank of Commerce, P.O. Box 1863, Dar es Salaam, Tanzania. **Indexed**: P.L.E.S.A.

332   CC
TARGET FINANCIAL SERVICE. (Text in English) 1973. 5/w. HK.$7000 (Asia $1500; elsewhere $1700) includes Target Intelligence Report, and Data Compilation Report. Target Newspapers Ltd., 4-F, Wah Tao Bldg., 42 Wood Rd., Wanchai, Hong Kong, People's Republic of China. TEL 852-2573-0379. FAX 852-2838-1597. adv. contact: Cecilia Lee. **Document type**: newspaper.
    Description: Covers the financial and industrial situation in Hong Kong, with company reports, industry surveys, stock market reviews and a list of court cases and property transactions.

332   CC
TARGET INTELLIGENCE REPORT. (Text in English) 1973. m. HK.$7000 (Asia $1500; elsewhere $1700) includes Target Financial Service, and Data Compilation Report. Target Newspapers Ltd., 4-F, Wah Tao Bldg., 42 Wood Rd., Wanchai, Hong Kong, People's Republic of China. TEL 852-2573-0379. FAX 852-2838-1597. circ. 120,000. **Document type**: corporate report.
    Description: Presents financial analysis, investigations and surveys.

TAX & BUSINESS ADVISER. see *BUSINESS AND ECONOMICS — Accounting*

TAX, ESTATE & FINANCIAL PLANNING FOR THE ELDERLY. see *GERONTOLOGY AND GERIATRICS*

TAX, ESTATE & FINANCIAL PLANNING FOR THE ELDERLY: FORMS AND PRACTICE. see *GERONTOLOGY AND GERIATRICS*

332   US   ISSN 8756-1360
KF6296.A15
TAX MANAGEMENT FINANCIAL PLANNING JOURNAL. (Supplement avail.; Subseries of: Tax Management Financial Planning Series) 1985. m. $327. Tax Management, Inc. (Subsidiary of: The Bureau of National Affairs, Inc.), 1250 23rd St., N.W., Washington, DC 20037. TEL 202-833-7240. FAX 202-833-7297. TELEX 285656-BNAI-WSH. (Subscr. to: 9435 Key West Ave., Rockville, MD 20850. TEL 800-372-1033) Ed. Glenn B. Davis. index. (back issues avail.) **Indexed**: Account.Ind. (1985-), C.L.I., L.R.I. **Document type**: trade publication.
●Also available online. Vendor(s): UMI.
—UMI. **CCC**.
    Description: Provides coverage on the state of financial planning today, including legislative, regulatory, and economic developments.

332 380   CC   ISSN 1004-9339
TAXATION AND ECONOMY. (Text in Chinese; table of contents in English) 1979. bi-m. Y35($30) Changchun Institute of Taxation, Journal Editorial Department, 102 Renmin St., Changchun, Jilin 130021, People's Republic of China. TEL 86-431-8919931-340. (Dist. outside China by: China Educational Books Import & Export Corporation, 15 Xueyuan Lu, Haidian Qu, Beijing, P.R.C.) Ed. Shangguan Shuyan. circ. 4,000. (back issues avail.) **Document type**: academic/scholarly publication.
    Formerly (until Jan. 1993): Jilin Caimao Xueyuan Xuebao - Jilin Institute of Finance and Trade. Journal (ISSN 1001-4586)
    Description: Contains papers on taxation theory, financial strategy and policy, enterprise management, relations between state and private enterprise, financial regulation and reform, joint ventures, accounting principles, and related topics.

332 658.15   CN   ISSN 0829-917X
TEACHERS' MONEY MATTERS. 1983. 8/yr. Can.$20. Teachers' Money Matters Ltd., 70 Scriven Rd., Bailieboro, Ont. K0L 1B0, Canada. TEL 705-939-1203. FAX 705-939-1179. Ed. Michael Pengelley. adv.: B&W page Can.$1900; trim 8 1/8 x 10 3/4; adv. contact: Paul Cramp. bk.rev.; circ. 1,000 (paid); 33,000 (controlled).

332   UK
TECHNICAL TAX PROPOSALS. a. £20. Confederation of British Industry, Centre Point, 103 New Oxford St., London WC1A 1DU, England. TEL 44-71-379-7400. FAX 44-71-240-1578. TELEX 21332.
    Formerly: Technical Budget Representations.

332   FR   ISSN 0765-3069
TECHNOLOGIES BANCAIRES. 1984. m. 3470 F. (foreign 3600 F.). Publi-News, 3 ave. Gallieni, 92000 Nanterre, France. TEL 33-47-29-88-11. FAX 33-47-29-88-18. Ed. Ange Galula. **Document type**: newsletter.
    Description: Presents information technology in the banking sector.

332.1   FR   ISSN 0768-7702
TECHNOLOGIES BANCAIRES MAGAZINE. 1986. bi-m. 465 F. (foreign 540 F.). Publi-News, 3 av. Gallieni, 92000 Nanterre, France. TEL 47-29-88-11. FAX 47-29-88-18. TELEX 613 505. Ed. Ange Galula; Pub. Ange Galula. adv. contact: Ziva Galula. circ. 10,000. **Document type**: trade publication.
    Description: Contains information on technology in the banking market: software applications, financial markets, dealing markets, back office, home banking, cash management, EDI, payment systems.

332 600   US   ISSN 1089-1927
▼**TECHNOLOGY NEWS AND TRENDS**. 1995. m. $319 (effective 1997). Siefer Consultants, Inc., Box 1384, Storm Lake, IA 50588. TEL 712-732-7340. FAX 712-732-7906. (back issues avail.) **Document type**: newsletter.
    Description: Real-life examples of how bankers are using cutting-edge technology to improve their bottom lines.

332.1   UK   ISSN 0955-4327
TELERATE - DOW JONES BANK REGISTER (YEAR). 1986. a. £170($300) (includes index). Euromoney Publications plc., Books, Nestor House, Playhouse Yard, London EC4V 5EX, England. TEL 0171-779-8935. FAX 0171-779-8541. (Orders to: Plymbridge Distributors Ltd., Estover, Plymouth, Devon PL6 7PZ, England. TEL 0171-779-8610. FAX 01752-695668) Ed.Bd. index. circ. 5,000. (back issues avail.) **Document type**: directory.
    Formerly: Telerate Bank Register (Year).
    Description: Gives full contact details on more than 12,000 institutions in 180 countries, as well as information on correspondent banks, subsidiaries, and ownership.

332   US   ISSN 1077-4343
TELLER SENSE. 1970. s-m. $45.84. Bureau of Business Practice, 24 Rope Ferry Rd., Waterford, CT 06386. TEL 860-442-4365. FAX 860-437-3555. URL: http://www.bbpnews.com. Ed. Michele Dunaj; Pub. Peter Garabedian. R&P contact: Debra Ferraro.
    Description: Includes tips and techniques tellers can apply to their own jobs.

332   US   ISSN 0895-1039
TELLER VISION. 1984. s-m. $69.84. Bureau of Business Practice, 24 Rope Ferry Rd., Waterford, CT 06386. TEL 860-442-4365. FAX 860-437-3555. URL: http://www.bbpnews.com. Ed. Michele Dunaj; Pub. Peter Garabedian. R&P contact: Debra Ferraro. s-a. index. (back issues avail.) **Document type**: newsletter.
    Description: Features interviews with banking or training experts who offer practical information and techniques tellers can easily apply to their own jobs.

332.1   US   ISSN 0040-3199
TENNESSEE BANKER. 1913. m. $20 to members; non-members $30. Tennessee Bankers Association, 201 Venture Cir., Nashville, TN 37228-1603. TEL 615-244-4871. FAX 615-244-0995. Ed. Bradley L. Barrett. adv.: B&W page $435; trim 8 1/2 x 11; adv. contact: Dianne Martin. illus.; circ. 2,300 (paid). **Document type**: trade publication.
    Description: Educates, informs, and guides readers about the activities and projects of their banks, fellow bankers, and the T.B.A.

332   US   ISSN 0885-6907
HG1507
TEXAS BANKING. 1911. m. $35 to non-members; members $25. 912 Baltimore, Ste. 900, Kansas City, MO 64105. TEL 512-472-8388. FAX 512-473-2560. Eds. Steve Scurlock, William F. Baker. adv.; bk.rev. circ. 5,000. **Indexed**: ABI Inform. **Document type**: trade publication.
●Also available online. Vendor(s): UMI.
—BLDSC (8798.672700); UMI.
    Formerly (until 1985): Texas Bankers Record (ISSN 0738-7652)

332.1   US
TEXAS BANKING RED BOOK. 1946. s-a. $26. Texas Red Book, Inc., 912 Baltimore, Ste. 900, Kansas City, MO 64105. TEL 800-336-1120. Ed. William Baker. adv. circ. 20,000. (looseleaf format; also avail. in diskette format)

332   US   ISSN 1063-0376
TEXAS FINANCE REPORT. 1956. w. $60. Report Publications, Inc., Box 12368, Austin, TX 78711. TEL 512-478-5663. FAX 512-478-2345. Ed. Bill Kidd. circ. 290.

BUSINESS AND ECONOMICS — BANKING AND FINANCE

THOMSON BANK DIRECTORY. see *BUSINESS AND ECONOMICS — Trade And Industrial Directories*

332.3   US   ISSN 1061-1681
HG2037
THOMSON CREDIT UNION DIRECTORY. 1986. a. $119. Thomson Financial Publishing, 4709 Golf Rd., Skokie, IL 60076-1253. TEL 847-676-9600; 800-321-3373. FAX 847-933-8101. Ed. Beth Swann. R&P contact: Beth Swann. adv. contact: Hugh Boyd. stat. **Document type:** directory.
  Formerly: Rand McNally Credit Union Directory.
  Description: Lists all credit unions in the U.S., including routing numbers, wire transfer information and key personnel.

332   US
THOMSON REGULATION C C DIRECTORY. 1988. a. 65. Thomson Financial Publishing, 4709 W. Golf Rd., Skokie, IL 60076. TEL 847-676-9600; 800-321-3373. FAX 847-933-8101. Ed. Beth Swann. R&P contact: Beth Swann. adv. contact: Hugh Boyd. **Document type:** directory.
  Description: Matches bank routing numbers with direct telephone numbers for checks and return-items contacts.

THOMSON SAVINGS DIRECTORY. see *BUSINESS AND ECONOMICS — Trade And Industrial Directories*

332   US   ISSN 0196-7762
HG1626
THORNDIKE ENCYCLOPEDIA OF BANKING AND FINANCIAL TABLES. a. $175.95 (overseas $253.45) (effective 1995). Warren, Gorham & Lamont, One Penn Plaza, New York, NY 10119. TEL 212-971-5000. FAX 212-971-5113. (Subscr. to: The Park Square Bldg., 31 St. James Ave., Boston, MA 02116-4112. TEL 800-950-1207) Ed. David Thorndike. **Document type:** trade publication.
  Description: Covers all aspects of interest rate calculation.

THRIFT ACCOUNTANT. see *BUSINESS AND ECONOMICS — Accounting*

332 657   NE   ISSN 0167-0581
TIJDSCHRIFT FINANCIEEL MANAGEMENT. 1980. bi-m. fl.246($164) (effective 1995). Bocaal Business Press, Stolbergstraat 14, 2012 EP Haarlem, Netherlands. TEL 31-23-319014. FAX 31-23-317974. Ed. A.P. van de Bovenkamp. adv.; circ. 3,200 (paid). **Document type:** academic/scholarly publication.
  —SWETS.
  Description: Practical articles for the top financial executive.

332   CN   ISSN 0838-5769
TIMELY DISCLOSURE. 1987. m. Can.$20($30) Timely Disclosure Inc., 5027 Cenabar Crt., Burlington, Ont. L7L 4Y6, Canada. TEL 416-847-1617. Ed. Mario Carr. circ. 13,455.
  Description: News affecting Canada's securities industry.

332   US
TIMELY TIPS MAGAZINE. 1925. m. $10 (Canada $12) (effective 1997). Mc Enterprises, Box 603, Marshall, MI 49068. TEL 616-945-6008. Pub. Carl Eisenlord. adv.: B&W page $160. (back issues avail.) **Document type:** trade publication.

332   JA   ISSN 0387-6896
TOKYO FINANCIAL REVIEW. 1976. w. free. Bank of Tokyo, Ltd., 3-26 Kanda Nishikicho, Chiyoda-ku, Toyko 101, Japan. Ed. Iwao Takesada. charts; cum.index covering 3 yrs. circ. 9,200. **Indexed:** Key to Econ.Sci., PROMT.
  ●Also available online.
  Formerly: Bank of Tokyo Weekly Review (ISSN 0005-5379)

332   US   ISSN 0894-7295
HG4928.5
TRADERS MAGAZINE; the magazine for the professional securities trader. 1987. m. $60 in Canada and Mexico $79; elsewhere $99. (Security Traders Association) Securities Data Publishing, 40 W. 57th St., 11th Fl., New York, NY 10106. TEL 212-765-5311. FAX 212-765-6123. Ed. John Byrne. adv.; bk.rev.; charts; stat.; tr.lit.; circ. 4,000 (controlled). (back issues avail.) **Document type:** trade publication.
  —CCC.
  Description: Directed to the investment community with profiles of individuals, reports on conventions, securities laws, and news.

332   US   ISSN 1071-8532
TREASURY MANAGER'S REPORT. 1993. bi-w. $595 (foreign $630) (effective 1997). Phillips Business Information, Inc., 1201 Seven Locks Rd., Potomac, MD 20854. TEL 301-424-3338. FAX 301-309-3847. E-mail: pbi@phillips.com. Ed. Gary Crowse. (back issues avail.) **Document type:** newsletter.
  ●Also available online. Vendor(s): Information Access Co.
  —CCC.
  Incorporates in part (1987-1997): Financial Services Report (ISSN 0894-7260); **Incorporates** (in 1995): Securities Marketing News (ISSN 1074-8385); Which was formerly (until 1994): Bank Securities Report (ISSN 1071-2038); (1993-1994): Bank Securities News (ISSN 1068-3763); Financial Services Law Report; Financial Services Week (Potomac).

332   AU
TREASURYLOG. 1991. 5/yr. Go Public Relations, Badnerstr. 3-21, A-2500 Baden, Austria. E-mail: sabina.schwabe@go-public.com; URL: http://www.go-public.com/treasurylog. Ed. Sabina Schwabe. circ. 14,000. **Document type:** bulletin.
  ●Also available online.
  Description: Information, experiences and contributions for and from treasury professionals. *Refereed Serial*

332.1   US
TRENDS (WASHINGTON, 1987); a resource for strategic decisions. 1987. bi-m. $200 to non-members; members $135. American Bankers Association, Fiduciary and Securities Operations, 1120 Connecticut Ave., N.W., Washington, DC 20036. TEL 202-663-5301. FAX 202-828-4544. bk.rev. circ. 630.
  Description: Reports on trends in securities processing, corporate securities services, and trust operations. Covers global custody services, Group of Thirty recommendations for securities clearance and settlement, new investment types.

332   SZ   ISSN 1021-9978
DER TREUHANDEXPERTE. 1987. bi-m. 135 SFr. (Europe 148 SFr.; rest of world 155 SFr.) (effective 1996). Helbing und Lichtenhahn Verlag AG, Freie Str. 84, CH-4051 Basel, Switzerland. TEL 41-61-2721116. FAX 41-61-2721150. (Subscr. to: Sauerlaender AG, Laurenzenvorstadt 89, CH-5001 Aarau, Switzerland. TEL 41-64-268626. FAX 41-64-245780) Ed. Rene Huessy. adv.: B&W page 1000 SFr., color page 2200 SFr.; trim 168 x 270. **Document type:** trade publication.
  Incorporates (in 1993): Treuhand und Praxis (ISSN 1016-8516)

332   IT
TRIBUNA DEI DOTTORI COMMERCIALISTI.* 1973. 6/yr. Unione Nazionale Giovani Dottori Commercialisti - Union of Young Economics Graduates, Via Venezia 24, 20122 Milan, Italy. TEL 2-82476328. FAX 2-82476609. Ed. Antonio Ortolani. adv.: Luciano/Alcaro Menichini. circ. 25,670.

332.1   US
TRUST LETTER. no.97, 1976. 12/yr. $210 to non-members; members $140. American Bankers Association, Trust and Private Banking Center, 1120 Connecticut Ave., N.W., Washington, DC 20036. TEL 202-663-5087. FAX 202-663-7543. (Subscr. to: Customer Service Center, Box 630538, Baltimore, MD 21623-0538. TEL 800-338-0626) Ed. Susan Johnston; Pub. Larry Price. R&P contact: Carole McGuinn. TEL 202-663-5032. (also avail. in microform from UMI) **Document type:** newsletter.
  ●Also available online. Vendor(s): UMI.
  Description: Provides current information on national legislation and regulation that impact trust and investment businesses.

332.1   US   ISSN 1068-4301
TRUST REGULATORY NEWS. 1992. m. $395 (effective 1997). A.M. Publishing, Inc., Box 1110, Chicago, IL 60690-1110. TEL 773-784-1818. FAX 773-561-2462. E-mail: trustnews@aol.com. Ed. Bernard Garbo; Pub. Bernard Garbo. index, cum.index every 5 yrs. (looseleaf format) **Document type:** newsletter.
  Description: Covers regulatory, legal and legislative issues: federal banking regulators, Department of Labor, and state and federal courts. Of interest to fiduciaries: primarily trust bankers, attorneys, and auditors, but also insurance and securities executives.

332   US
TRUTH-IN-LENDING MANUAL. base vol. (plus s-a. updates). $185.95 (foreign $287.45) (effective 1995). Warren, Gorham & Lamont, 395 Hudson St., New York, NY 10014. TEL 212-367-6300. FAX 212-367-6718. (Subscr. to: The Park Square Bldg., 31 St. James Ave., Boston, MA 02116-4112. TEL 800-950-1205) **Document type:** trade publication.

332   FI   ISSN 0359-9108
TULOSUUNTA. 8/yr. Erikoislehdet Oy Business Publications, P.O. Box 16, SF-00381 Helsinki, Finland. Ed. Jukka Miettinen. circ. 75,000.

332   TU   ISSN 0041-4336
TURKIYE CUMHURIYET MERKEZ BANKASI. AYLIK BULTEN/CENTRAL BANK OF THE REPUBLIC OF TURKEY. QUARTERLY BULLETIN. (Text in English, Turkish) 1931. bi-m. free. Central Bank of the Republic of Turkey, General Directorate of Planning and Research, Directorate of Documentation, Ankara, Turkey. FAX 90-312-3116685. mkt.; stat. **Indexed:** PROMT. **Document type:** government publication, bulletin.
  Description: Covers credit statistics of the Central Bank of Turkey.

332.1   TU   ISSN 0073-7402
HG3729.T82
TURKIYE SINAI KALKINMA BANKASI. ANNUAL STATEMENT/INDUSTRIAL DEVELOPMENT BANK OF TURKEY. ANNUAL STATEMENT. Cover title: Turkiye Sinai Kalkinma Bankasi Annual Report. (Text in English) a. Turkiye Sinai Kalkinma Bankasi A.S. - Industrial Development Bank of Turkey, Meclisi Mebusan Cad. No. 137, 80040 Findikli - Istanbul, Turkey. TEL 90-212-2512792. FAX 90-212-2432975. TELEX 24344 TSKB TR. illus.; stat. **Document type:** corporate report.
  Description: Reports on the financial status of the bank, with a review of the economic environment and operations in different sectors of activity.

332   PL   ISSN 1231-3955
TWOJ BANK. 1994. m. free. Powszechny Bank Kredytowy S.A., Nowy Swiat 6-12, 00-400 Warsaw, Poland. TEL 48-22-6617733. FAX 48-22-6617658. Ed. Marek Ryczkowski. **Document type:** consumer publication.

332   SZ
U B S INTERNATIONAL FINANCE. (Text in English) q. free. Union Bank of Switzerland, Bahnhofstr. 45, CH-8021 Zurich, Switzerland. TEL 41-1-2346544. FAX 41-1-2346190. circ. 25,000. **Document type:** bulletin.

U C B INVESTOR'S HANDBOOK. (Uganda Commercial Bank) see *BUSINESS AND ECONOMICS — Investments*

U K BUSINESS FINANCE DIRECTORY (YEAR); the guide to sources of U K corporate finance. see *BUSINESS AND ECONOMICS — Trade And Industrial Directories*

BUSINESS AND ECONOMICS — BANKING AND FINANCE

U K DIRECTORY OF PROPERTY DEVELOPERS, INVESTORS & FINANCIERS. see *REAL ESTATE*

332   UK
THE U K'S 10000 LARGEST COMPANIES. 1985. a. £165. E L C Publishing Ltd., 109 Uxbridge Rd., Ealing, London W5 STL, England. TEL 0181-998-8812. FAX 0181-998-8318. Ed. D. Wildey. circ. 1,000.
   Description: General, financial and business activity information on each of the top 10,000 companies in the UK.

U S BANKER. see *BUSINESS AND ECONOMICS — Investments*

332   US
U S INTERNATIONAL TRANSFER PRICING. 15/yr. $295 (foreign $408.45) (effective 1995). Warren, Gorham & Lamont, One Penn Plaza, New York, NY 10119. TEL 212-971-5000. FAX 212-971-5113. (Subscr. to: The Park Square Bldg., 31 St. James Ave., Boston, MA 02116-4112. TEL 800-950-1207) **Document type:** newsletter.

332.1   UG
UGANDA COMMERCIAL BANK. ANNUAL REPORT. (Text in English) 1966. a. Uganda Commercial Bank, Box 973, Kampala, Uganda. circ. 2,000. **Document type:** corporate report.
   Description: Facts of the Ugandan economy and how it affects the banking industry there. Gives the environment in which banking activities are carried out, disclosing the final accounts to shareholders, depositors and borrowers.

332   UG
UGANDA COMMERCIAL BANK. QUARTERLY ECONOMIC REVIEW. 1983. q. Uganda Commercial Bank, P.O. Box 973, Kampala, Uganda. TEL 234710. FAX 259012. circ. 2,000. **Indexed:** Documentatieblad.
   Description: Presents analytic data on Uganda's economy. Attempts to promote public consciousness of the factors that influence the economy.

332   MR
UNION BANCARIA HISPANO MARROQUI. ASSEMBLEE GENERALE ORDINAIRE DES ACTIONNAIRES. RAPPORT. a. Union Bancaria Hispano Marroqui, Assemblee Generale Ordinaire des Actionnaires, 69 rue du Prince Moulay Abdallah, Casablanca, Morocco.

332   FI   ISSN 0355-0133
UNION BANK OF FINLAND. ANNUAL REPORT. 1952. a. Union Bank of Finland, FIN-00020 UBF, Finland. FAX 358-0-1652648. TELEX 124407 UNIT FI. **Document type:** corporate report.

332   UK   ISSN 0503-2628
UNIT TRUST YEAR BOOK (YEAR). 1964. a. £97($152) (overseas £110) (effective 1994). (Association of Unit Trust and Investment Funds) Financial Times Business Information, Management Reports (Subsidiary of: Financial Times Group), 102-108 Clerkenwell Rd., London EC1M 5SA, England. TEL 44-171-215-9321. FAX 44-171-251-9321. (Orders to: F T B I, 126 Jermyn St., London SW1Y 4UJ, England. TEL 44-1209-612493. FAX 44-1209-612811) Ed. Christine Stopp. adv.: B&W page £2150; color page £2600; adv. contact: Colin Clarke. circ. 3,500. (tabloid format) **Document type:** academic/scholarly publication.
   Supersedes: Directory of Unit Trusts.
   Description: Contains a comprehensive listing of U.K. authorized units and editorials on industry and legislative changes.

UNITE DE PROGRAMMATION DU MINISTERE. BULLETIN DE CONJONCTURE. see *BUSINESS AND ECONOMICS — Economic Situation And Conditions*

332.6   TS
UNITED ARAB EMIRATES. AL-MASRAF AL-MARKAZI. AL-NASHRAH AL-IQTISADIYYAH/UNITED ARAB EMIRATES. CENTRAL BANK. ECONOMIC BULLETIN. (Text in Arabic) 1974. a. Central Bank, P.O. Box 854, Abu Dhabi, United Arab Emirates. TEL 652220. FAX 668483. TELEX 24173 MARKAZI EM. charts; stat.; circ. controlled.
   Formerly: United Arab Emirates. Central Bank. Publication.

332.4   US   ISSN 0041-2155
HJ10
U.S. DEPARTMENT OF THE TREASURY. FINANCIAL MANAGEMENT SERVICE. BUDGET REPORTS BRANCH. TREASURY BULLETIN. 1939. q. $31 (foreign $38.75) (effective 1995). U.S. Department of the Treasury, Financial Management Service, Washington, DC 20227. TEL 202-208-1709. FAX 202-208-1633. (Subscr. to: Superintendent of Documents, U.S. Government Printing Office, Box 371954, Pittsburgh, PA 15250-7954. TEL 202-512-1800. FAX 202-512-2250) charts; stat. circ. 1,900. (also avail. in microform from PMC; microfiche from CIS; back issues avail.; reprint service avail. from CIS) **Indexed:** Amer.Stat.Ind. (1974-). **Document type:** bulletin, government publication.
   —UMI; UnCover.
   Description: Contains a mix of narrative, tables, and charts on Treasury issues, federal financial operations, international statistics, and special reports on liabilities currency and coins in circulation.

332.4   US   ISSN 0364-1007
U.S. DEPARTMENT OF THE TREASURY. FINANCIAL MANAGEMENT SERVICE. MONTHLY TREASURY STATEMENT OF RECEIPTS AND OUTLAYS OF THE UNITED STATES GOVERNMENT. m. $27 (foreign $33.73). U.S. Department of the Treasury, Financial Management Service, Budget Reports Branch, 941 N. Capitol St., Rm. 749, Washington, DC 20227. TEL 202-208-1434. (Subscr. to: Supt. of Documents, Washington, DC 20402) (also avail. in microfiche from CIS; reprint service avail. from CIS) **Indexed:** Amer.Stat.Ind. (1976-). **Document type:** government publication.
   Former titles: U.S. Department of the Treasury. Bureau of Government Financial Operations. Monthly Treasury Statement of Receipts and Outlays of the United States Government; U.S. Department of the Treasury. Bureau of Government Financial Operations. Monthly Statement of Receipts and Outlays of the United States Government.

U.S. FEDERAL DEPOSIT INSURANCE CORPORATION. ANNUAL REPORT. see *INSURANCE*

332   US
U.S. FEDERAL DEPOSIT INSURANCE CORPORATION. NEWS RELEASES. irreg. U.S. Federal Deposit Insurance Corporation, 550 17th St. N.W., Washington, DC 20429. TEL 202-393-8400.

332   US   ISSN 0278-5692
HG4345
U.S. FEDERAL DEPOSIT INSURANCE CORPORATION. TRUST ASSETS OF BANKS AND TRUST COMPANIES. a. U.S. Federal Deposit Insurance Corporation, 550 17th St., N.W., Washington, DC 20429. TEL 202-389-4221.
   Formerly: U.S. Federal Deposit Insurance Corporation. Trust Assets of Insured Commercial Banks (ISSN 0149-8274)

332.1   US   ISSN 0083-0887
U.S. FEDERAL RESERVE SYSTEM. ANNUAL REPORT. 1914. a. price varies. U.S. Federal Reserve System, Board of Governors, Publications Services, Rm. MS-138, Washington, DC 20551. TEL 202-452-3244. FAX 202-728-5886. circ. 10,000. (back issues avail.) **Document type:** government publication, corporate report.

332.1   US   ISSN 0148-4338
HG181.A1
U.S. FEDERAL RESERVE SYSTEM. ANNUAL STATISTICAL DIGEST. Key Title: Annual Statistical Digest - Board of Governors of the Federal Reserve System. 1981. a. price varies. U.S. Federal Reserve System, Board of Governors, Publications Services, Rm. MS-138, Washington, DC 20551. TEL 202-452-3244. FAX 202-728-5886. **Document type:** government publication.

U.S. FEDERAL RESERVE SYSTEM. RESEARCH LIBRARY - RECENT ACQUISITIONS. see *BIBLIOGRAPHIES*

332.1   US   ISSN 0364-8370
U.S. FEDERAL RESERVE SYSTEM. SELECTED INTEREST AND EXCHANGE RATES. WEEKLY SERIES OF CHARTS. w. $30 (foreign $35). U.S. Federal Reserve System, Board of Governors, Publications Services, Rm. MS-138, Washington, DC 20551. TEL 202-452-3244. FAX 202-728-5886. (also avail. in microfiche from CIS; reprint service avail. from CIS) **Indexed:** Amer.Stat.Ind. (1974-). **Document type:** government publication.

332   US
U.S. FEDERAL RESERVE SYSTEM. STAFF STUDIES. vol.146, 1985. irreg. (approx. 1-4/yr.). U.S. Federal Reserve System, Board of Governors, Publications Services, Rm. MS-138, Washington, DC 20551. TEL 202-452-3244. FAX 202-728-5886. **Document type:** monographic series, government publication.
   Description: Examines economic and financial matters of general interest.

U.S. OFFICE OF THE COMPTROLLER OF THE CURRENCY. INTERPRETATIONS AND ACTIONS. see *BUSINESS AND ECONOMICS — Public Finance, Taxation*

U.S. OFFICE OF THE COMPTROLLER OF THE CURRENCY. QUARTERLY JOURNAL. see *BUSINESS AND ECONOMICS — Public Finance, Taxation*

332.2   US
UNITED STATES LEAGUE OF SAVINGS INSTITUTIONS. MEMBERSHIP BULLETIN. bi-m. membership. United States League of Savings Institutions, 900 19th St. N.W., No. 900, Washington, DC 20006-2105. TEL 312-644-3100. **Document type:** bulletin.

332.4   US   ISSN 0160-1210
HG451
UNITED STATES MINT. ANNUAL REPORT OF THE DIRECTOR OF THE MINT. 1873. a. $3. United States Mint, 633 Third St., N.W., Washington, DC 20220. TEL 202-566-2000. (Subscr. to: Superintendent of Documents, U.S. Government Printing Office, Box 371954, Pittsburgh, PA 15250-7954. TEL 202-512-1800. FAX 202-512-2250) **Document type:** government publication.
   Formerly: U.S. Department of the Treasury. Bureau of the Mint. Annual Report of the Director of the Mint.

332   AU
UNIVERSITAET INNSBRUCK. FINANZWISSENSCHAFTLICHE STUDIEN. (Subseries of: Universitaet Innsbruck. Veroeffentlichungen) 1969. irreg., vol.9, 1970. price varies. Oesterreichische Kommissionsbuchhandlung, Maximilianstr. 17, A-6020 Innsbruck, Austria. Ed. Clemens August Andreae.

UNIVERSITY OF NEW ENGLAND. DEPARTMENT OF ACCOUNTING & FINANCIAL MANAGEMENT. WORKING PAPERS. see *BUSINESS AND ECONOMICS — Accounting*

V W D - FINANZ- UND WIRTSCHAFTSSPIEGEL. see *BUSINESS AND ECONOMICS — Investments*

333.33 368   US   ISSN 0042-238X
VALUATION. 1942. s-a. $15 per no. American Society of Appraisers, Box 17265, Washington, DC 20041-0265. TEL 703-478-2228. FAX 703-742-8471. E-mail: asainfo@apo.com. Ed. Rebecca Ewing. R&P contact: Rebecca Ewing. TEL 703-733-2103. adv.: page $700; adv. contact: Amy Starliper. bk.rev.; charts. circ. 7,000. **Indexed:** Account.Ind. (1974-), BPIA, Bus.Ind. **Document type:** trade publication.
   —BLDSC (9142.057000); UnCover.
   Description: Technical journal covering appraisal of all types of property.
   Refereed Serial

VANUATU. STATISTICS OFFICE. MONETARY AND BANKING STATISTICS. see *BUSINESS AND ECONOMICS — Abstracting, Bibliographies, Statistics*

332   NE
VENTURE CAPITAL GIDS - N V P JAARBOEK. a. fl.49.35. (Nederlandse Vereniging van Participatiemaatschappijen) Delwel Uitgeverij B.V., Postbus 19110, 2500 CC The Hague, Netherlands. TEL 31-70-3624800. FAX 31-70-3605606.
   Formerly: Nederlandse Venture Capital Gids - N V P Jaarboek.
   Description: Provides an overview of developments in the venture capital sector of the banking industry in the Netherlands.

BUSINESS AND ECONOMICS — BANKING AND FINANCE

332.1 US
HG2411
VERMONT. COMMISSIONER OF BANKING INSURANCE AND SECURITIES. ANNUAL REPORT OF THE BANK COMMISSIONER. 1880. a. free. Department of Banking Insurance and Securities, Division of Banking, 89 Main St., Drawer 20, Montpelier, VT 05620. TEL 802-828-3301. Ed. Thomas J. Candon. circ. 1,700 (controlled). (also avail. in microfiche from CIS). **Indexed:** SRI. **Document type:** government publication.
 Formerly: Vermont. Commissioner of Banking and Insurance. Annual Reports of the Bank Commissioner (ISSN 0083-5730)

332 YU ISSN 0351-6245
VESNIK; specialized banking & finance review. (Text mainly in Serbo-Croatian; some articles and summaries in English) 1957. m. 6000 din.($20) (Investbanka) Terazije 7-9, P.O. Box 152, 11000 Belgrade, Yugoslavia. TEL 011-656-842. FAX 320-617. TELEX 11147 YUINV. Ed. Ljubisa K. Plavsic. adv.; bk.rev. circ. 1,500. (also avail. in microform)

332 MR ISSN 0505-4885
VIE ECONOMIQUE. (Text in French) 1921. w. $60. Societe Fermiere de Presse et Publicite, 5 bd. Abdellah ben Yacine, Casablanca, Morocco. TEL 307332. FAX 304542. TELEX 28045. Ed. Marcel Herzog. adv. circ. 22,000. **Indexed:** Key to Econ.Sci., P.A.I.S.For.Lang.Ind., World Bibl.Soc.Sec.

332.1 II ISSN 0970-8456
VINIMAYA/BANK MANAGEMENT EDUCATION. 1979. q. Rs.50 (foreign $8). National Institute of Bank Management, NIBM P. O., Kondhwe Khurd, Pune 411 048, India. TEL 91-212-673080. FAX 91-212-674478. TELEX 145 7256 NIBM IN. Ed. K. Swarup. **Document type:** academic/scholarly publication.
 Description: Presents conceptual and practical viewpoints of both the bankers and management educationists on bank management which has relevance to the workings and development of banking and financial institutions.

332 YU
VOJVODANSKA BANKA. ANNUAL REPORT. (Editions in Russian and Serbo-Croatian) 1994. a. Vojvodanska Banka, Trg Slobode 7, Novi Sad, Yugoslavia.

332 330.9 GW ISSN 0172-2530
VORTEILHAFTE GELDANLAGEN; Handbuch fuer Anleger, Berater und Vermittler. 1978. m. DM.280. Rudolf Haufe Verlag GmbH & Co. KG, Hindenburgstr. 64, 79102 Freiburg, Germany. TEL 49-761-3683-0. FAX 49-761-3683-195. Ed.Bd. **Document type:** trade publication.

332 AU
W I F - WIRTSCHAFT, INFORMATION, FORTBILDUNG. 4/yr. Sparkassenverlag GmbH, Grimmelshausengasse 1, A-1030 Vienna, Austria. TEL 43-1-71170-0. FAX 43-1-71170310. Ed. Klaus Orthaber. circ. 15,000. **Document type:** bulletin.
 Formerly: Wirtschaft in Form.

W I K. see *CRIMINOLOGY AND LAW ENFORCEMENT*

332 GW ISSN 0342-6874
W M ALLGEMEINE VERLOSUNGSTABELLE. (Wertpapier-Mitteilungen) w. DM.257.95. Herausgebergemeinschaft Wertpapier-Mitteilungen Keppler, Lehmann GmbH & Co., Postfach 110932, 60044 Frankfurt a.M., Germany. TEL 49-69-2732-0. FAX 49-69-232264. TELEX 412066-BZFFM. index. (looseleaf format; also avail. in magnetic tape; back issues avail.) **Document type:** bulletin.

332 GW
W M TEIL I: SAMMELLISTE MIT OPPOSITION BELEGTE WERTPAPIERE. (Wertpapier-Mitteilungen) d. DM.216.90. Herausgebergemeinschaft Wertpapier-Mitteilungen Keppler, Lehmann GmbH & Co., Postfach 110932, 60044 Frankfurt a.M., Germany. TEL 49-69-2732-0. FAX 49-69-232264. TELEX 412066-BZFFM. **Document type:** bulletin.

332 GW ISSN 0342-6939
W M TEIL II: NACHRICHTEN UEBER DEUTSCHE FESTVERZINSLICHE WERTE. (Wertpapier-Mitteilungen) w. DM.242.15. Herausgebergemeinschaft Wertpapier-Mitteilungen Keppler, Lehmann GmbH & Co., Postfach 110932, 60044 Frankfurt a.M., Germany. TEL 49-69-2732-0. FAX 49-69-232264. TELEX 412066-BZFFM. **Document type:** bulletin.

332 GW
W M TEIL IIA: NEUEMISSIONEN - SCHNELLDIENST. (Wertpapier-Mitteilungen) d. DM.118.70. Herausgebergemeinschaft Wertpapier-Mitteilungen Keppler, Lehmann GmbH & Co., Postfach 110932, 60044 Frankfurt a.M., Germany. TEL 49-69-2732-0. FAX 49-69-232264. TELEX 412066-BZFFM. index. (looseleaf format) **Document type:** bulletin.

332 GW ISSN 0170-5458
W M TEIL IIB: SAMMELLISTE GEKUENDIGTER UND VERLOSTER WERTPAPIERE. (Wertpapier-Mitteilungen) w. DM.141.05. Herausgebergemeinschaft Wertpapier-Mitteilungen Keppler, Lehmann GmbH & Co., Postfach 110932, 60044 Frankfurt a.M., Germany. TEL 49-69-2732-0. FAX 49-69-232264. TELEX 412066-BZFFM. index. (looseleaf format; back issues avail.) **Document type:** bulletin.

332 GW ISSN 0342-6955
W M TEIL III: NACHRICHTEN UEBER DEUTSCHE AKTIEN, ANTEILE, GENUSSSCHEINE, KUXE. (Wertpapier-Mitteilungen) w. DM.203.25. Herausgebergemeinschaft Wertpapier-Mitteilungen Keppler, Lehmann GmbH & Co., Postfach 110932, 60044 Frankfurt a.M., Germany. TEL 49-69-2732-0. FAX 49-69-232264. TELEX 412066-BZFFM. index. (looseleaf format; also avail. in magnetic tape; back issues avail.) **Document type:** bulletin.

W M TEIL IV: ZEITSCHRIFT FUER WIRTSCHAFTS- UND BANKRECHT. (Wertpapier-Mitteilungen) see *LAW*

332 GW ISSN 0342-6998
W M TEIL VA: NACHRICHTEN UEBER AUSLAENDISCHE AKTIEN UND AKTIENAEHNLICHE WERTE. (Wertpapier-Mitteilungen) w. DM.397.35. Herausgebergemeinschaft Wertpapier-Mitteilungen Keppler, Lehmann GmbH & Co., Postfach 110932, 60044 Frankfurt a.M., Germany. TEL 49-69-2732-0. FAX 49-69-232264. TELEX 412066-BZFFM. index. (looseleaf format; also avail. in magnetic tape; back issues avail.) **Document type:** bulletin.

332 GW
W M TEIL VB: NACHRICHTEN UEBER AUSLAENDISCHE FESTVERZINSLICHE WERTPAPIERE. (Wertpapier Mitteilungen) w. DM.325.25. Herausgebergemeinschaft Wertpapier-Mitteilungen Keppler, Lehmann GmbH & Co., Postfach 110932, 60044 Frankfurt a.M., Germany. TEL 49-69-2732-0. FAX 49-69-232264. TELEX 4123-066-BZFFM. **Document type:** bulletin.

332 GW ISSN 0937-4108
W M TEIL VI: NACHRICHTEN UEBER OPTIONEN UND FUTURES. (Wertpapier Mitteilungen) w. DM.109.25. Herausgebergemeinschaft Wertpapier-Mitteilungen Keppler, Lehmann GmbH & Co., Postfach 110932, 60044 Frankfurt a.M., Germany. TEL 49-69-2732-0. FAX 49-69-232264. **Document type:** bulletin.

332 GW ISSN 0342-6882
W M: WERTPAPIERBERATUNG. w. DM.234.15. Herausgebergemeinschaft Wertpapier-Mitteilungen Keppler, Lehmann GmbH & Co., Postfach 110932, 6044 Frankfurt a.M., Germany. TEL 49-69-2732-0. FAX 49-69-232264. TELEX 412066-BZFFM. index. (looseleaf format; also avail. in magnetic tape; back issues avail.) **Document type:** bulletin.

332 330.9 US ISSN 0899-0530
WALL STREET DIGEST. 1977. m. $150. Wall Street Digest, Inc., 2 N. Tamiami Trail, Ste. 602, Sarasota, FL 34236. TEL 813-954-5500. FAX 813-364-8447. Ed. Donald H. Rowe. bk.rev. circ. 25,000. (back issues avail.)

332 US ISSN 0099-9660
CODEN: WSJOAF
WALL STREET JOURNAL (EASTERN EDITION). Midwest edition (ISSN 0163-089X); Southwest edition (ISSN 0193-225X); Western edition (ISSN 0193-2241) Online edition: Wall Street Journal Interactive Edition. 1889. d. (Mon.-Fri.). $164 (Interactive Edition $49) (effective 1996); newsstand price: $0.75. Dow Jones & Co., Inc., 200 Liberty St., New York, NY 10281. TEL 212-416-2000. URL: http://www.wsj.com. (Subscr. to: 200 Burnett Rd., Chicopee, MA 01020. TEL 800-568-7625) Ed. Robert L. Bartley; Peter R. Kann. adv.; circ. 1,841,188 (paid). (broadsheet format; reprint service avail. from UMI) **Indexed:** B.P.I., Bank.Lit.Ind., Bk.Rev.Ind. (1965-), CAD CAM Abstr., Chem.Abstr., Child.Bk.Rev.Ind. (1965-), CHNI, CHNI, Comput.Indus.Up., Energy Info.Abstr., F.R., Fut.Surv., Gard.Lit. (1992-), Hlth.Ind., Med.Care Rev., Music Ind., Oper.Res.Manage.Sci., P.A.I.S., PCR2, Pers.Lit., Qual.Contr.Appl.Stat., Tel.Abstr., Tel.Alert, Telegen, Text.Tech.Dig. **Document type:** newspaper.
 ●Also available online. Vendor(s): Dow Jones News Retrieval.
 —CASDDS; KR SourceOne. **CCC.**
 Supersedes (in 1959): Wall Street Journal.

332.6 US ISSN 0163-089X
CODEN: WSJEDM
WALL STREET JOURNAL (MIDWEST EDITION). 5/wk. $175 (effective 1997). Dow Jones & Company, Inc. (Chicago), One S. Wacker Dr., 21st Fl., Chicago, IL 60606-3388. TEL 312-750-4100. FAX 312-750-4153. (Subscr. to: Box 300, Princeton, NJ 08543-0300. TEL 800-628-9320) Ed. Kevin Helliker; Pub. Peter Kann. R&P contact: Linda Arnold. adv. contact: Robert Ross. bk.rev.; circ. 651,189 (paid). **Document type:** newspaper.
 —CASDDS. **CCC.**

332.6 US ISSN 0193-225X
WALL STREET JOURNAL (SOUTHWEST EDITION). 5/wk. $139 (effective 1992). Dow Jones & Company, Inc. (Dallas), 1233 Regal Row, Dallas, TX 75247-3644. TEL 214-631-7520. FAX 214-631-5387. (Subscr. to: Box 300, Princeton, NJ 08543-0300. TEL 800-628-9320) Ed. Hal Lancaster. circ. 209,177. **Document type:** newspaper.
 —**CCC.**

332.6 US ISSN 0193-2241
WALL STREET JOURNAL (WESTERN EDITION). 5/wk. $175 (effective 1997). Dow Jones & Company, Inc. (San Francisco), 201 California St., Ste. 1300, San Francisco, CA 94111-5077. TEL 415-986-6886. FAX 415-391-4534. (Subscr. to: Box 300, Princeton, NJ 08543-0300. TEL 800-628-9320) Ed. Robert Bartley. adv.: B&W page 33548.64. circ. 380.312 (paid). **Document type:** newspaper.
 —**CCC.**

332 BE ISSN 0921-9986
WALL STREET JOURNAL EUROPE. (Text in English) 1983. d. 14300 BEF (in UK £250; Germany DM.795; E. Europe $300) (effective 1996). Dow Jones Publishing Co., Europe, 87 Bd. Brand Whitlock, 1200 Brussels, Belgium. TEL 32-2-7411211. FAX 32-2-7321102. (Subscr. to: Circulation Department, P.O. Box 2845, In de Cramer 37, 6401 DH Heerlen, Netherlands. TEL 31-45-5761222. FAX 31-45-5714722) Ed. Philip Revzin. adv. contact: Anne Renton. bk.rev.; circ. 61,500 (paid). (also avail. in microfilm from UMI) **Indexed:** ABC, Mgmt.& Market.Abstr., WPM. **Document type:** newspaper.
 —**CCC.**

332 US ISSN 0083-7075
HG1
THE WALL STREET JOURNAL INDEX. 1958. a. (plus m. updates). U M I (Subsidiary of: Bell & Howell Company), 300 N. Zeeb Rd., Ann Arbor, MI 48106. TEL 313-761-4700; 800-521-0600. FAX 800-864-0019. (also avail. in diskette format) **Document type:** abstracting/indexing.
 ●Also available online.
 Also available on CD-ROM.
 Description: Abstracts and indexes articles and columns from the Wall Street Journal.

BUSINESS AND ECONOMICS — BANKING AND FINANCE

332   US
WASHINGTON PERSPECTIVE. 1983. w. $450 to non-members; members $195. America's Community Bankers, 900 19th St., N.W., Ste. 400, Washington, DC 20006. TEL 202-857-3100. FAX 202-296-8716. URL: http://www.acbankers.org. circ. 6,590. (back issues avail.) **Document type:** newsletter.
    Formed by the 1992 merger of: Washington Notes (ISSN 0195-525X) & Washington Memo (Washington) (ISSN 0882-2247)
    Description: Provides up-to-date coverage of new laws and final regulations that affect savings and commercial banking institutions.

332 340   US
WASHINGTON STATE BAR ASSOCIATION. CREDITOR - DEBTOR LAW SECTION NEWSLETTER.* 1974. q. $17.50. Washington State Bar Association, 2101 Fourth Ave., Ste. 400, Seattle, WA 98121-2330. TEL 206-727-8239. FAX 206-727-8320. circ. 680. **Document type:** newsletter.

332   US
▼**WEB FINANCE.** 1996. w. free. Investment Dealers' Digest, E-mail: webfinance@iddis.com; URL: http://nestegg.iddis.com/webfinance. Ed. Hal Lux. **Document type:** trade publication.
    ●Available only online.
    Description: Covers online financial services and the use of the internet by financial services companies. For financial professionals.

THE WEBSTER AGRICULTURAL LETTER. see *AGRICULTURE*

332   US
WEEKLY CONSOLIDATED CONDITION REPORT OF LARGE COMMERCIAL BANKS AND DOMESTIC SUBSIDIARIES. w. $14. U.S. Federal Reserve System, Board of Governors, Publications Services, Rm. MS-138, Washington, DC 20551. TEL 202-452-3244. FAX 202-728-5886. **Document type:** government publication.

WEEKLY STATISTICAL RELEASE. see *BUSINESS AND ECONOMICS — Abstracting, Bibliographies, Statistics*

332   US   ISSN 1049-5673
WEISS BANK SAFETY DIRECTORY. q. $438 (effective 1997). Weiss Ratings, Inc., 4176 Burns Rd., Palm Beach Gardens, FL 33410. TEL 407-627-3300. FAX 407-625-6685. E-mail: tom-r@weiss.com; URL: http://www.weissinc.com. Pub. Martin Weiss. R&P contact: Steve H. Ackerman. pp./issue: 330. **Document type:** directory.
    Description: Guide to the financial strength of U.S. banks, including their safety ratings.

332   US   ISSN 1080-000X
WEISS SAVINGS & LOAN SAFETY DIRECTORY. q. $438 (effective 1997). Weiss Ratings, Inc., 4176 Burns Rd., Palm Beach Gardens, FL 33410. TEL 407-627-3300. FAX 407-625-6685. E-mail: tom-r@weiss.com; URL: http://www.weissinc.com. Pub. Martin Weiss. R&P contact: Steve H. Ackerman. pp./issue: 90. **Document type:** directory.
    Former titles (until 1994): Weiss Research's Savings and Loan Safety Directory (ISSN 1074-2131); (until 1992): S and L Safety Directory (ISSN 1058-1979)

322 346.066   US
WESTERN LEAGUE OF SAVINGS INSTITUTIONS. REGULATORY CHECKLIST. s-m. $35 to non-members; members $25. Western League of Savings Institutions, 1960 E. Grand Ave., Ste. 1000, El Segundo, CA 90245. TEL 310-414-8300. FAX 310-414-8399. Ed. Cathy Moran. circ. 700. (looseleaf format) **Document type:** newsletter.
    Former titles (until 1994): California League of Savings Institutions. Regulatory Checklist; (until 1992): California League of Savings Institutions. Legislation and Regulation Update.
    Description: Informs employees of savings and loans industry in California of changes in regulations that affect the operating of their financial institution.

WETBOEK ECONOMISCH EN FINANCIEEL RECHT - DEEL FINANCIEEL RECHT. see *LAW — Corporate Law*

332   UK
WHAT FINANCE.* 1983. bi-m. £9. Chartherhouse Communications Ltd., 4 Tabernacle St., London ECXA 4LU, England. circ. 30,000.

323   UK   ISSN 0305-3954
WHO OWNS WHAT IN WORLD BANKING. 1971. a. £192($309) (foreign £202) (effective 1994). Financial Times Business Information, Management Reports (Subsidiary of: Financial Times Group), 102 Clerkenwell Rd., London EC1M 5SA, England. TEL 44-171-251-9321. FAX 44-171-251-4686. (Orders to: F T B I, 126 Jermyn St., London SW1Y 4UJ, England. TEL 44-1209-612493. FAX 44-1209-612811) adv.; stat. **Document type:** trade publication.
    Description: Summarizes recent events in world banking, enumerates main parent banks worldwide with their subsidiaries and affiliates, and lists consortium banks and their participants.

WHO'S WHO IN INTERNATIONAL BANKING. see *BIOGRAPHY*

WHO'S WHO IN MORTGAGE FINANCE. see *BUSINESS AND ECONOMICS — Trade And Industrial Directories*

332.1   US
WILMINGTON TRUST BRIEFINGS. q. Wilmington Trust Company, Trust Department, Wilmington, DE 19890.

332   UK   ISSN 1360-9165
▼**WINDOWS ON FINANCE.** 1995. q. £95 (foreign $145) (effective 1996). Euromoney Publications plc., Nestor House, Playhouse Yard, London EC4V 5EX, England. TEL 44-171-779-8935. FAX 44-171-779-8541. (Dist. in US by: American Educational Systems, 173 W. 81st St., New York, NY 10024. TEL 800-717-2669. FAX 212-501-8926) **Document type:** trade publication.

332   AU
WIRTSCHAFT HEUTE. q. Landesverband der Sparkassen Oberoesterreichs, Promenade 11-13, A-4041 Linz, Austria. TEL 0732-2391-2500.

332.1   US
WISCONSIN BANKING NEWS. 1971. m. $92.50 (effective 1996). Public Relations Enterprises, Inc., Box 12236, Lansing, MI 48901-2236. TEL 517-484-0775. Ed. Jerome H. O'Neil; Pub. Jerome H. O'Neil. R&P contact: Jerome H. O'Neil. adv. contact: Jerome H. O'Neil. circ. 590 (paid). **Document type:** trade publication.

WORLD BANK. E D I DEVELOPMENT STUDY. (Economic Development Institute) see *BUSINESS AND ECONOMICS — International Development And Assistance*

332   UN
WORLD BANK GROUP DIRECTORY. 2/yr. $9.95 per no. World Bank, 1818 H St., N.W., Washington, DC 20433. TEL 202-473-1155. FAX 202-522-2627. E-mail: books@worldbank.org. (U.S. orders to: Box 7247-8619, Philadelphia, PA 19170-8619; Also avail. from: 66 av. D'lena, 75116 Paris, France. TEL 33-1-40-69-30-55. FAX 33-1-40-69-30-68) **Document type:** directory.

332.1   UN   ISSN 0257-3032
HD72
WORLD BANK RESEARCH OBSERVER. 1986. s-a. $20 to individuals; institutions $35. World Bank, 1818 H St., N.W., Washington, DC 20433. TEL 202-473-1155. FAX 202-522-2627. E-mail: books@worldbank.org. (Subscr. to: Box 7247-7956, Philadelphia, PA 19170-7956. TEL 201-476-2192. FAX 201-476-2197) Ed. Moshe Syrquin. circ. 5,000. (also avail. in microfiche from CIS; microform from UMI) **Indexed:** ABI Inform., Abstr.Anthropol., ASCA, Asian-Pac.Econ.Lit., Curr.Cont., Geo.Abstr.P.G., IIS, J.of Econ.Lit., Pub.Admin.Abstr., Rural Devel.Abstr., Rural Ext.Educ.& Tr.Abstr., Triticale Abstr. **Document type:** academic/scholarly publication.
    ●Also available online. Vendor(s): Knight-Ridder Information, Inc., UMI.
    —BLDSC (9352.928500); Genuine Article; SWETS; UMI; UnCover.
    Description: Covers policy-relevant development economics for noneconomists.
    Refereed Serial

332.1   UK   ISSN 0265-9484
HG1505
WORLD BANKING ABSTRACTS. 1984. bi-m. £450($590) (effective 1997). (Institute of European Finance) Blackwell Publishers Ltd., 108 Cowley Rd., Oxford OX4 1JF, England. TEL 44-1865-791100. FAX 44-1865-791347. E-mail: jnlinfo@blackwellpublishers.co.uk; URL: http://www.blackwellpublishers.co.uk. Ed. E.P.M. Gardener. (also avail. in microform from UMI) **Document type:** abstracting/indexing.
    —BLDSC (9352.938200); UMI. CCC.

332   US
WORLD COUNCIL OF CREDIT UNIONS. ANNUAL AND STATISTICAL REPORT. (Text in English, French, Spanish) a. World Council of Credit Unions, 5710 Mineral Pt. Rd., Box 2982, Madison, WI 53701. TEL 608-231-7130. FAX 608-238-8020. Ed. Karen Kaplan. charts; stat. circ. 4,000. **Document type:** corporate report.
    Former titles: World Council of Credit Unions. International Annual Report; World Council of Credit Unions Yearbook.

332   US   ISSN 0743-5363
HG219
WORLD CURRENCY YEARBOOK.* 1955. a. $250. International Currency Analysis, Inc., 7595 aymeadows Circle W., Ste 2714, Jacksonville, FL 32256-1864. TEL 718-531-3685. Ed. Philip Cowitt; Pub. Georgette Cowitt. charts; stat.; index. circ. 1,000. (also avail. in microform) **Indexed:** SRI. **Document type:** academic/scholarly publication.
    —BLDSC (9354.060000).
    Formerly: Pick's Currency Yearbook (ISSN 0079-2063)

WORLD LEASING YEARBOOK (YEAR). see *BUSINESS AND ECONOMICS — Economic Situation And Conditions*

332.1   US   ISSN 0730-8736
HG1501   CODEN: WOBADA
WORLD OF BANKING; the international magazine of bank management. 1981. bi-m. $80 (effective 1995). 582 Oakwood, Ste. 203, Lake Forest, IL 60045. TEL 708-615-0405. FAX 708-615-0416. Ed. R. Gerald Fox; Pub. R. Gerald Fox. adv.; bk.rev. **Indexed:** ABI Inform., Bank.Lit.Ind., INSPEC, P.A.I.S., World Bank.Abstr. **Document type:** trade publication.
    —BLDSC (9352.936000); UMI; UnCover. CCC.

332   AU
WUESTENROT MAGAZIN. 1930. 3/yr. free. Bausparkasse Wuestenrot, Postfach 155, Alpenstr. 70, A-5033 Salzburg, Austria. TEL 43-662-6386. FAX 43-662-6386577. E-mail: wuestenrot-presse@mail.apenet.at; URL: http://www.wuestenrot.co.at. Ed. Hannes Rosner. adv.; bk.rev.; illus.; stat. circ. 900,000. **Document type:** bulletin.
    Formerly: Wuestenrot-Heim (ISSN 0043-9622)

332   CC
XIN JINRONG/NEW FINANCE. (Text in Chinese; abstracts in English) 1988. m. Y280($50) Bank of Communications, c/o Head Office, 18 Xianxia Rd., Shanghai 200335, People's Republic of China. TEL 86-21-6275-7261. FAX 86-21-6275-5462. Ed. Feng Song; Pub. Yiming Lin. adv. contact: Cuiting Wang. circ. 17,000. **Document type:** academic/scholarly publication.
    Description: Covers the theory and practice of banking and finance, and the administration and operation of Chinese commercial banks.

332.1   TU
YAPI VE KREDI BANKASI. ANNUAL REPORT. (Text in English) a. Yapi ve Kredi Bankasi, Istiklal Caddesi, Korsan Cikmazi 1, Box 250, Beyoglu, Istanbul, Turkey.

BUSINESS AND ECONOMICS — BANKING AND FINANCE–COMPUTER APPLICATIONS

332   UK   ISSN 1357-4353
YOUR MORTGAGE. 1986. m. £27; newsstand price: £2.25. Brass Tacks Publishing Company Ltd., 62-68 Rosebery Ave., London EC1R 4RR, England. TEL 44-171-833-5566. FAX 44-171-833-8050. E-mail: 1006001.2172@compuserve.com; URL: http://www.mmcltd.co.uk/ym. Ed. Andrew Stuart; Pub. Andrew Stuart. adv.: B&W page £3680; color page £5040; adv. contact: Philip Harding. charts. circ. 18,000. (back issues avail.; reprint service avail.) **Document type:** consumer publication.
    Formerly (until 1995): Which Mortgage (ISSN 0963-7044)
    Description: Contains all information consumers need to purchase and finance a home. Lists mortgage interest rates.

332 333.33   AT   ISSN 1039-0081
YOUR MORTGAGE MAGAZINE. 1993. 4/yr. Aus.$45. H W W Pty. Ltd. (Horan Wall & Walker), 15-19 Prospect Dr., P.O. Box 8, Surry Hills, N.S.W. 2010, Australia. TEL 61-2-93609360. FAX 61-2-93805533. URL: http://www.hww.com.au. Ed. Gregan McMahon. **Document type:** consumer publication.
    Description: For home buyers and owners.

332   JA
ZAIKAI/FINANCIAL WORLD. 1953. fortn. Zaikai Kenkyujo, Akasaka-Tokyu Bldg., 2-14-3 Nagato-cho, Chiyoda-ku, Tokyo 100, Japan. TEL 81-3-3582-6771. FAX 81-3-3581-6777. Dir. Akira Kanemitsu. circ. 120,000.

332.1   GW   ISSN 0936-2800
KK2188.A13
ZEITSCHRIFT FUER BANKRECHT UND BANKWIRTSCHAFT. q. DM.65.75 per no. Verlag Kommunikationsforum GmbH Recht Wirtschaft Steuern, Aachener Str. 217, 50931 Cologne, Germany. TEL 0221-40088-0. FAX 0221-4008828. **Indexed:** IBr.

332.7   GW   ISSN 0340-8485
HG17
ZEITSCHRIFT FUER DAS GESAMTE KREDITWESEN. 1948. s-m. DM.379.80 (foreign DM.394.80) (effective 1996). Fritz Knapp Verlag GmbH, Postfach 111151, 60046 Frankfurt a.M., Germany. TEL 49-69-970833-0. FAX 49-69-7078400. Ed. Berthold Morschhaeuser. adv. contact: Werner Scholz. bk.rev.; charts; stat.; s-a. index, cum.index: 1948-1967. circ. 3,869. **Indexed:** ELLIS, IBR, Key to Econ.Sci., P.A.I.S.For.Lang.Ind. **Document type:** trade publication.
    —CCC.

332 340   AU   ISSN 1024-6096
▼**ZEITSCHRIFT FUER INSOLVENZRECHT UND KREDITSCHUTZ.** 1995. m. S.900. Verlag Orac GesmbH & Co. KG, Graben 17, A-1010 Vienna, Austria. TEL 43-1-53452-0. FAX 43-1-53452141. adv.: B&W page S.10000; trim 167 x 249; adv. contact: Christian Braun. circ. 3,000 (paid). **Document type:** trade publication.

ZEITSCHRIFT FUER WIRTSCHAFTSRECHT - Z I P. see *LAW*

332   CC   ISSN 0578-1485
ZHONGGUO JINRONG/CHINA FINANCE. (Text in Chinese; table of contents in English) m. Y19.20($45.80) (Zhongguo Renmin Yinhang Zonghang - Head Office of China People's Bank) Zhongguo Jinrong Chubanshe, 17 Xijiaomin Xiang, Beijing 100031, People's Republic of China. TEL 653858. (Dist. outside China by: China International Book Trading Corp., P.O. Box 399, Beijing, P.R.C.; Dist. in US by: China Books & Periodicals, Inc., 2929 24th St., San Francisco, CA 94110. TEL 415-282-2994) Ed. Xu Shuxin. adv.; charts; illus.

332   CC   ISSN 1001-5841
HG3331
ZHONGGUO JINRONG NIANJIAN/CHINA FINANCE YEAR BOOK. (Text in Chinese) a. Zhongguo Jinrong Xuehui - Chinese Society of Banking and Finance, 1 Baiguanglu Toutiao, Beijing 100053, People's Republic of China. TEL 363428. Ed. Chen Yuan.

332 630   CC
ZHONGGUO NONGCUN JINRONG/CHINA RURAL FINANCE. (Text in Chinese) m. Zhongguo Nongcun Jinrong Zazhishe, 25, Fuxing Lu, Beijing 100036, People's Republic of China. TEL 8211639. Ed. Zhang Fan.

ZHONGNAN CAIJING DAXUE XUEBAO/CENTRAL-SOUTH UNIVERSITY OF FINANCE AND ECONOMICS. JOURNAL. see *BUSINESS AND ECONOMICS — Economic Systems And Theories, Economic History*

332   RH
ZIMBABWE FINANCIAL HOLDINGS LIMITED. ANNUAL REPORT. 1967. a. Zimbabwe Financial Holdings Limited, P.O. Box 3198, Harare, Zimbabwe. TEL 263-4-735011. FAX 263-4-735600. TELEX 24163 ZW. **Document type:** corporate report.
    Supersedes (in 1993): Zimbabwe Banking Corporation. Group Annual Report.
    Description: Reports on group corporate activities in the commercial and merchant banking fields in Zimbabwe and Botswana.

332   SZ
ZUERCHER BANKANGESTELLTE. bi-m. Zuercher Bankpersonalverband, Schanzeneggstr. 1, CH-8002 Zurich, Switzerland. TEL 01-2012421. circ. 5,500.

20-20 INSIGHT. see *BUSINESS AND ECONOMICS — Investments*

332.1   US   ISSN 0885-4777
100 HIGHEST YIELDS. 1984. w. $124. Advertising News Service, Inc., 11811 Federal Highway One, Box 088888, N. Palm Beach, FL 33408-8888. TEL 407-627-7330. FAX 407-627-7335. URL: www.bankrate.com. Ed. Linda Green; Pub. Bob Heady. charts.
    Description: Lists high-yielding CD's and money markets offered by federally-insured institutions nationwide.

BUSINESS AND ECONOMICS — Banking And Finance–computer Applications

ADVANCES IN MATHEMATICAL PROGRAMMING AND FINANCIAL PLANNING. see *MATHEMATICS — Computer Applications*

THE AIRLINE INDUSTRY: AN INDUSTRY OVERVIEW. see *TRANSPORTATION — Air Transport*

332.1 001.64   US   ISSN 0095-5396
HG1709
AMERICAN BANKERS ASSOCIATION. NATIONAL OPERATIONS & AUTOMATION CONFERENCE. PROCEEDINGS. 1963. a. price varies. American Bankers Association, Operations and Automation Division, 1120 Connecticut Ave., N.W., Washington, DC 20036. TEL 202-663-5087. FAX 301-843-8405. (Subscr. to: Order Processing Department, Box 630544, Baltimore, MD 21263-0544. TEL 800-338-0626) **Document type:** proceedings.
    Formerly: American Bankers Association. National Automation Conference. Proceedings (ISSN 0065-7441)
    Description: A collection of abstracts of presentations. Topics may include microcomputers, protection of software and data, return item automation, productivity improvement and automatic banking hardware.

332.1 001.64   US
AMERICAN BANKERS ASSOCIATION. OPERATIONS AND AUTOMATION DIVISION. CHECK PROCESSING. triennial. $120 to non-members. American Bankers Association, Operations and Automation Division, 1120 Connecticut Ave., N.W., Washington, DC 20036. TEL 202-663-5087. FAX 301-843-8405. TELEX 892787 ABA-WASH. (Subscr. to: Order Processing Department, Box 630544, Baltimore, MD 21236. TEL 800-338-0626)
    Supersedes in part: American Bankers Association. Operations and Automation Division. Results of the National Operations and Automation Survey (ISSN 0363-2539)
    Description: Responses to over 500 questions from over 700 banks on check processing.

332.1 001.64   US
AMERICAN BANKERS ASSOCIATION. OPERATIONS AND AUTOMATION DIVISION. DATA PROCESSING - TELECOMMUNICATIONS. irreg. $19.90. American Bankers Association, Operations and Automation Division, 1120 Connecticut Ave., N.W., Washington, DC 20036. TEL 202-663-5087. FAX 301-843-8405. TELEX 892787 ABA-WASH. (Subscr. to: Order Processing Department, Box 630544, Baltimore, MD 21263-0554. TEL 800-338-0626)
    Supersedes in part: American Bankers Association. Operations and Automation Division. Results of the National Operations and Automation Survey (ISSN 0363-2539)
    Description: Responses to over 500 questions from over 700 banks on data processing and telecommunications.

332.1 001.64   US
TC425.M7
AMERICAN BANKERS ASSOCIATION. OPERATIONS AND AUTOMATION DIVISION. RETAIL OPERATIONS. 1975. triennial. $255 to non-members; members $169. American Bankers Association, Operations and Automation Division, 1120 Connecticut Ave., N.W., Washington, DC 20036. TEL 202-663-5087. FAX 301-843-8405. TELEX 892787 ABA-WASH. (Subscr. to: Order Processing Department, Box 630544, Baltimore, MD 21263-0544. TEL 800-338-0626)
    Supersedes in part: American Bankers Association. Operations and Automation Division. Results of the National Operations and Automation Survey (ISSN 0363-2539); Formerly: American Bankers Association. Operations and Automation Division. Results of the National Automation Survey.
    Description: Responses to over 500 questions from over 700 banks on retail operations.

332.1   UK   ISSN 0965-4380
ASSOCIATION FOR GLOBAL STRATEGIC INFORMATION. JOURNAL. 1992. 3/yr. £85($175) to non-members. (A G S I) Infonortics, Ltd., 15 Market Place, Tetbury, Gloucestershire GL8 8DD, England. TEL 44-1666-505772. FAX 44-1666-505774. E-mail: contact@infonortics.com; URL: http://www.infonortics.com. Ed. Harry Collier. adv. contact: S. Davis. **Document type:** academic/scholarly publication.
    —BLDSC (4682.100000).
    Description: Brings together facts, ideas, and a theoretical background of computer-applicated information for corporations.
    Refereed Serial

332.1   US
BANK AUTOMATION NEWS. 1989. bi-w. $595 (foreign $630) (effective 1997). Phillips Business Information, Inc., 1201 Seven Locks Rd., Potomac, MD 20854. TEL 301-424-3338. FAX 301-309-3847. E-mail: pbi@phillips.com. **Document type:** newsletter.
    ●Also available online. Vendor(s): Data-Star, Information Access Co., Knight-Ridder Information, Inc., NewsNet.
    —CCC.
    Incorporates: Bank Automation Contract Watch & Bank Outsourcing Report & Bank Disaster and Contingency Planner; Formerly: Branch Automation News (ISSN 1044-145X)
    Description: Covers new products and technology, and selection and implementation of automated banking systems.

332.1   US
BANK DATA PROCESSING POLICIES AND PROCEDURES. (Part of the Compliance and Law series) 1991. base vol. (plus a. updates). $285 (updates $125). Sheshunoff Information Services Inc., 505 Barton Springs Rd., Ste. 1100, Austin, TX 78704. TEL 512-472-2244; 800-456-2340. (looseleaf format)
    Description: Informs bank data personnel about regulations and assists them in implementing policies in security and risk management, short- and long-range planning, internal and external audits, and computer operations.

BUSINESS AND ECONOMICS — BANKING AND FINANCE–COMPUTER APPLICATIONS

332.1 US ISSN 1063-4428
HG1710
BANK NETWORK NEWS; news and analysis of shared E F T networks. 1982. s-m. $395. Faulkner & Gray, Inc., 300 S. Wacker Dr., 18th Fl., Chicago, IL 60606. TEL 312-913-1334. (Subscr. to: Box 87271, Chicago, IL 60680) Eds. Mark Bohan, Richard Mitchell. index. (back issues avail.) **Document type:** trade publication.
●Also available online. Vendor(s): Information Access Co., NewsNet (FI71).
Description: News and analysis of electronic banking and automated retail payments.

001.64 332 US
BANK OPERATIONS BULLETIN. 1984. m. $150 to non-members; members $100. American Bankers Association, Operations and Automation Division, 1120 Connecticut Ave. N.W., Washington, DC 20036. TEL 202-663-5430. FAX 302-834-8405. (Subscr. to: Order Processing Department, Box 630538, Baltimore, MD 22163-0538. TEL 800-338-0626) (also avail. in microform from UMI) **Document type:** newsletter.
●Also available online. Vendor(s): UMI.
Formerly: Thruput.
Description: Provides current information on the multitude of industry developments and changes in regulations, operational techniques, systems and procedures, and standards.

BANK WAGE-HOUR & PERSONNEL REPORT. see *LAW — Corporate Law*

332.1 FR ISSN 0248-9708
BANQUE ET INFORMATIQUE. 1981. m. 500 F. (effective 1997). Bi-Magazines, 14 rue du Champ de Mars, 75007 Paris, France. TEL 33-1-45556052. FAX 33-1-45561576. Ed. Lylianne Heise. adv. circ. 10,000. **Document type:** consumer publication.

332.1 US
A BETTER CHANNEL.* 1985. m. A B C D: The Microcomputer Industry Association, 450 E. 22nd St., Ste. 230, Lombard, IL 60148-6158. TEL 708-240-1818. FAX 708-240-1384. Ed. Averil Reisman. adv.: B&W page $1125, color page $1500. circ. 2,800.
Formerly: Association of Better Computer Dealers Newsletter.
Description: Provides articles on how to manage a microcomputer or software sales organization more efficiently and effectively.

BIOTECH BUSINESS. see *BIOLOGY — Genetics*

C A A S NEWS; newsletter on computer-assisted appraisal. (Computer-Assisted Appraisal Section) see *REAL ESTATE*

332.1 US
C P A TECHNOLOGY ADVISOR. (Certified Public Accountant); profitable strategies and practical solutions for managing technology. 1981. m. $214 (effective 1997). Harcourt Brace Professional Publishing, 525 B St., Ste. 1900, San Diego, CA 92101-4495. TEL 619-699-6716. FAX 619-699-6593. (Subscr. to: Journal Fulfillment, 6277 Sea Harbor Dr., Orlando, FL 32887-4600. TEL 800-831-7799. FAX 407-363-9661) Ed. Bill Teague; Pub. Ken Rethmeier. R&P contact: Jenna Lake. TEL 619-699-6264. bk.rev.; index, cum.index: 1981-1988. (looseleaf format; back issues avail.) **Document type:** newsletter.
Formerly: C P A Technology Report; Which incorporated (1991-1995): C P A's P C Network Advisor (ISSN 1059-4590); Formerly (until 1993): C P A Micro Report (ISSN 1047-5826); Incorporates (1983-198?): P C Accounting Trends (ISSN 0742-6704).
Description: Provides profitable strategies and practical solutions for managing technology.

332 IE ISSN 0956-5558
CARDS INTERNATIONAL. 1989. fortn. I£699. Lafferty Publications Ltd., The Tower, IDA Enterprise Centre, Pearse St., Dublin 2, Ireland. TEL 353-1-6718022. FAX 353-1-6718520. E-mail: cvserv@lafferty.ie; URL: http://www.unm.lafferty.co.uk. (US subscr. to: 420 Lexington Ave., Ste. 1745, New York, NY 10170. TEL 212-557-6726) Ed. Richard Martin. R&P contact: David Barr. **Document type:** trade publication.
Description: Worldwide briefing on the plastic card industry.

CORPORATE E F T REPORT. see *BUSINESS AND ECONOMICS — Banking And Finance*

332.1 US
CREDIT UNION TECHNOLOGY; the magazine for credit union technology decision makers. 1991. bi-m. $36. Credit Union Technology, Inc., 110-64 Queens Blvd., Ste. 106, Forest Hills, NY 11375-6347. TEL 718-793-9400. FAX 718-793-9414. Ed. Andrew B. Mallon. adv.; bk.rev.; index. circ. 6,000. (back issues avail.) **Document type:** trade publication.

001.64 US ISSN 0730-8809
DATAPRO REPORTS ON BANKING AUTOMATION. m. $1066 to new subscr.; renewals $926 (effective 1996). Datapro Information Services Group (Subsidiary of: McGraw-Hill, Inc.), 600 Delran Pkwy., Delran, NJ 08075. TEL 609-764-0100. FAX 609-764-8953. (looseleaf format; back issues avail.)
—CCC.
Description: Offers information on banking automation products, software and systems. Topics covered include automated tellers, communication systems, plastic card technology, credit authorization, security systems and voice response.

332.1 US ISSN 0955-2138
DEALING WITH TECHNOLOGY. 1988. bi-w. $995 (Europe £545). Waters Information Services, Inc., Box 2248, Binghamton, NY 13902-2248. TEL 607-770-9242; 800-947-7947. FAX 607-770-9435. URL: http://www.watersinfo.com. (European and Asian subscr. to: Waters Information Services Ltd., 57-59 Neal St., London EC2H 9PJ, England. TEL 44-171-240-2090. FAX 44-171-240-2076) Ed. Peter Harris. **Document type:** trade publication.
Description: Aimed at those involved with dealing with technology, both vendors and users.

332.1 US
DERIVATIVES ENGINEERING AND TECHNOLOGY. bi-w. $795 (Europe £545). Waters Information Services, Inc., Box 2248, Binghamton, NY 13902-2248. TEL 607-770-9242; 800-947-7947. FAX 607-770-9435. URL: http://www.watersinfo.com. (European and Asian subscr. to: Waters Information Services Ltd., 57-59 Neal St., London WC2H 9PJ, England. TEL 44-171-240-2090. FAX 44-171-240-2076) **Document type:** newsletter.
Description: Delivers behind-the-scenes reports on the latest software, systems, and networks supporting leading-edge financial engineering and risk management.

E D I YELLOW PAGES. (Electronic Data Interchange) see *BUSINESS AND ECONOMICS — Trade And Industrial Directories*

332.1 US ISSN 0195-7287
E F T REPORT. (Electronic Funds Transfer) 1978. bi-w. $595 (foreign $630) (effective 1997). Phillips Business Information, Inc., 1201 Seven Locks Rd., Potomac, MD 20854. TEL 301-424-3338. FAX 301-309-3847. E-mail: pbi@phillips.com. Ed. Lurdes da Maia-Abruscato. (back issues avail.) **Indexed:** PROMT. **Document type:** newsletter.
●Also available online. Vendor(s): Information Access Co., Knight-Ridder Information, Inc., Lexis-Nexis, NewsNet (FI11).
—CCC.
Description: For administrators and bankers interested in the electronic funds transfer market. Contains reports on automated teller machine systems, personal identification systems, home banking, home security, and regional and national networks.

332.1 IE ISSN 0954-0393
ELECTRONIC PAYMENTS INTERNATIONAL. 10/yr. I£649. Lafferty Publications Ltd., The Tower, IDA Enterprise Centre, Pearse St., Dublin 2, Ireland. TEL 353-1-6718022. FAX 353-1-6718520. E-mail: cvserv@lafferty.ie; URL: http://www.unm.lafferty.co.uk. (US subscr. to: 420 Lexington Ave., Ste. 1745, New York, NY 10170. TEL 212-557-6726) Ed. Richard Martin. R&P contact: David Barr. **Document type:** bulletin.
Description: Global intelligence on the electronic payments industry, covering marketplace and technology developments in retail EFT services, EDI, homebanking and interbank payment systems.

330.9 NE ISSN 1380-2011
HG41 CODEN: FEJMEY
FINANCIAL ENGINEERING AND THE JAPANESE MARKETS. (Text in English) 1994. 3/yr. fl.400 to institutions; $205.50 to institutions in U.S. (effective 1998). (Japanese Association of Financial Econometrics and Engineering) Kluwer Academic Publishers, Postbus 17, 3300 AA Dordrecht, Netherlands. TEL 31-78-6392392. FAX 31-78-6392254. E-mail: services@wkap.nl; URL: http://www.wkap.nl. (Dist. by: Kluwer Academic Publishers Group, P.O. Box 322, 3300 AH Dordrecht, Netherlands. TEL 31-78-6392392. FAX 31-78-6546474; N. America dist. addr.: Box 358, Accord Sta., Hingham, MA 02018-0358. TEL 617-871-6600. FAX 617-871-6528) Ed. Takeaki Kariya. (back issues avail.; reprint service avail. from SWZ) **Document type:** academic/scholarly publication.
—BLDSC (3926.953200). CCC.
Description: Publishes empirical and theoretical research on the Japanese financial markets, in all areas of financial econometrics and financial engineering.
Refereed Serial

FINANCIAL SOFTWARE AND SYSTEMS GUIDE. see *COMPUTERS — Software*

FINANCIAL TECHNOLOGY INSIGHT. see *BUSINESS AND ECONOMICS — Computer Applications*

332.64 US ISSN 1070-1826
FINANCIAL TRADER. 1993. 11/yr. $160 in U.S. and Canada; elsewhere $200 (effective 1996). Miller Freeman, Inc. (Subsidiary of: United News & Media), 600 Harrison St., San Francisco, CA 94107. TEL 415-905-2200. FAX 415-905-2233. (Subscr. to: Box 1177, Skokie, IL 60076-8177. TEL 800-255-2824. FAX 708-647-5972)
—CCC.

332.1 005 US
GUIDE TO REAL ESTATE & MORTGAGE BANKING SOFTWARE. 1984. biennial, 8th ed., 1995. $89.95. Real Estate Solutions, Inc., 1125 15th St., N.W., Ste. 503, Washington, DC 20005-2715. TEL 202-293-2240. FAX 202-293-2243. Ed. Ina S. Bechhoefer. R&P contact: Ina S. Bechhoefer. **Document type:** directory.
Description: Provides detailed descriptions of more than 600 real estate and-or mortgage banking software products.

001.6 332.1 FR ISSN 0241-2640
CODEN: NFTCDC
INFOTECTURE; bimensuel d'actualite des banques de donnees. 1979. bi-m. 2800 F. A Jour, 11 rue du Marche St. Honore, 75001 Paris, France. TEL 42-96-67-22. FAX 40-20-07-75. TELEX TELEXEL 615887F. Ed. Nathalie Bloch-Sitbon. bk.rev. (back issues avail.) **Indexed:** Comput.Cont.
—CASDDS. CCC.

332.1 621.381 US ISSN 1047-2908
INSIDE MARKET DATA; the newsletter of real-time market data. 1985. s-m. $995 (Europe £645). Waters Information Services, Inc., Box 2248, Binghamton, NY 13902-2248. TEL 607-770-9242; 800-947-7947. FAX 607-770-9435. URL: http://www.watersinfo.com. (European and Asian subscr. to: 57-59 Neal St., London WC2H 9PJ, England. TEL 44-171-240-2090. FAX 44-171-240-2076) Ed. Mary Schroeder. **Document type:** newsletter.
Formerly: Micro Ticker Report (ISSN 0885-2510)
Description: Reports news and analysis on electronic information services and databases used by financial market professionals.

INTERNATIONAL JOURNAL OF INTELLIGENT SYSTEMS IN ACCOUNTING, FINANCE & MANAGEMENT. see *BUSINESS AND ECONOMICS — Computer Applications*

332.1 332.6 US ISSN 1057-5626
INVESTMENT MANAGEMENT TECHNOLOGY. 1991. bi-w. $695 (Europe £445). Waters Information Services, Inc., Box 2248, Binghamton, NY 13902-2248. TEL 607-770-9242; 800-947-7947. FAX 607-770-9435. URL: http://www.watersinfo.com. (European and Asian subscr. to: Waters Information Services Ltd., 57-59 Neal St., London WC2H 9PJ, England. TEL 44-171-240-2090. FAX 44-171-240-2076) **Document type:** newsletter.
Description: Provides focused, in-depth coverage of the information technology demands of the institutional investor marketplace.

BUSINESS AND ECONOMICS — CHAMBER OF COMMERCE PUBLICATIONS

006.3 332.1   US
JOURNAL OF COMPUTATIONAL INTELLIGENCE IN FINANCE; advanced technology in finance. 1993. 6/yr. $90 (Canada & Mexico $100; elsewhere $110) (effective 1996). Finance & Technology Publishing, Box 764, Haymarket, VA 20168. TEL 703-754-0696. FAX 703-753-2634. E-mail: 72672.261@compuserve.com; URL: http://ourworld.compuserve.com/homepages/ftpub. Ed. Randall Caldwell. R&P contact: Randall Caldwell. adv. contact: Agnes Caldwell. bk.rev. **Document type:** academic/scholarly publication.
●Also available online.
Formerly (until 1997): NeuroVest Journal (ISSN 1074-5637)
Description: Focuses on applications of neural networks and emerging technologies to investing and trading in the financial markets. Discusses products, tools, and techniques involving the use of neural networks and computational intelligence and finance for profitable investment.

LAW AND ELECTRONIC COMMERCE. see LAW

330   US
M I C - TECH-RETAIL AND BANKING. 1989. m. $905. Management Information Corporation, 1111 Marlkress Rd., Box 5062, Cherry Hill, NJ 08003-5602. TEL 609-424-1100. FAX 609-424-1999. (diskette format)
Description: Provides product references, specifications, performance and prices on retail and banking terminals, ATMs and document processors.

332.1 621.381   US   ISSN 0738-7156
MICROBANKER; the research letter on financial end-user computing. 1981. 14/yr. $395 (effective 1997). Microbanker, Inc., Box 708, Lake George, NY 12845. TEL 518-745-7071. FAX 518-745-7009. E-mail: http://www.microbanker.com. Ed. Nancy Davis. bk.rev. circ. 2,000. (also avail. in microform from UMI; back issues avail.) **Document type:** newsletter.
—UMI.
Description: For bankers using microcomputers. Articles cover banking operations, related programs and software packages.

332.1   US
NEWSLINE NEWSLETTER. m. $16 to members; non-members $32. Western Independent Bankers, 100 Spear St., Ste. 1505, San Francisco, CA 94105. TEL 415-543-1001. FAX 415-543-1744. Ed. Nancy Jennings. adv. circ. 1,300. (looseleaf format; back issues avail.) **Document type:** newsletter.
Description: Contains banking and finance news for CEOs and CFOs of independent and community banks.

332.1   US
P C BUSINESS PRODUCTS. 1989. m. $150 (outside N. America $165). Worldwide Videotex, Box 3273, Bounton Beach, FL 33424-3273. TEL 508-477-8979. Ed. Mark Wright; Pub. Mark Wright. bk.rev. (back issues avail.) **Document type:** newsletter.
●Also available online. Vendor(s): Data-Star, Information Access Co., Knight-Ridder Information, Inc., NewsNet (EC94).
Description: Provides the latest news and information on software, hardware, supplies, and services for individuals and companies using microcomputers for business applications. Contains detailed product information, prices, and evaluations to help microcomputer users select products that will best meet their needs.

332.1   US   ISSN 0731-4396
P S I MONITOR; the monthly review of financial service industry developments. 1981. m. $95 (foreign $155). Payment Systems, Inc., 3030 N. Rocky Pt. Dr. W., Ste. 670, Tampa, FL 33607. TEL 813-287-2774. FAX 813-286-7377. Ed. Fonda Anderson. circ. 300.
Description: Summary of significant developments in the financial services market.

332.1 657   US
PAYMENTS SYSTEM REPORT. m. $150 to non-members; members $95. National Automated Clearing House Association, 607 Herndon Pkwy., Ste. 200, Herndon, VA 20170. TEL 703-742-9190. FAX 703-787-0996. E-mail: psr@nacha.org. Ed. Brian Ragan. R&P contact: Brian Ragan. adv. contact: Geirgie Goldston. circ. 3,500. (also avail. in microform from UMI) **Document type:** newsletter.
●Also available online. Vendor(s): UMI.
—UMI.
Formerly: Automated Payments Update (ISSN 0897-6457)

332.1   US   ISSN 0892-5542
TRADING SYSTEMS TECHNOLOGY. 1987. bi-w. $895 (Europe £645). Waters Information Services, Inc., Box 2248, Binghamton, NY 13902-2248. TEL 607-770-9242; 800-947-7947. FAX 607-770-9435. URL: http://www.watersinfo.com. (European and Asian subscr. to: Waters Information Services Ltd., 57-59 Neal St., London WC2H 9PJ, England. TEL 44-171-240-2090. FAX 44-171-240-2076) Ed. Eugene Grygo. **Document type:** trade publication.
Incorporates (1992-1994): Wall Street Network News (ISSN 1063-3839)

332.1   US   ISSN 1060-989X
HG4515.5   CODEN: WSTEE5
WALL STREET & TECHNOLOGY; for senior-level executives in technology and information management in securities and investment firms. 1983. 14/yr. $85 (Canada $105; elsewhere $125) (effective 1996). United News & Media, One Penn Plaza, New York, NY 10119. TEL 212-869-1300; 800-255-2824. Ed. Sharon Schwartzman. adv.: B&W page $5170; trim 8 1/2 x 10 7/8. bk.rev.; circ. 25,200. (controlled). Indexed: ABI Inform., Comput.Cont., Comput.Dtbs., INSPEC, Microcomp.Ind., PCR2.
●Also available online. Vendor(s): Information Access Co., UMI.
—BLDSC (9261.479300); AskIEEE; KR SourceOne; SWETS; UMI. **CCC**.
Formerly (until 1992): Wall Street Computer Review (ISSN 0738-4343); Which incorporated (in 1991): Wall Street Computer Review. Buyer's Guide (ISSN 1042-7171).
Description: Provides vital and authoritative information on new and emerging technologies that are driving the global securities and investment management industries.

BUSINESS AND ECONOMICS — Chamber Of Commerce Publications

A C C R A COST OF LIVING INDEX. (American Chamber of Commerce Researchers Association) see BUSINESS AND ECONOMICS — Abstracting, Bibliographies, Statistics

330.9   US   ISSN 0899-2304
A C C R A NEWSLETTER;* promoting excellence in research for community & economic development. 1968. bi-m. $75. American Chamber of Commerce Researchers Association, 4232 King St., Alexandria, VA 22302-1507. TEL 502-897-2890. FAX 502-894-9917. Ed. Daryl McKee. bk.rev.; software rev. circ. 450. (looseleaf format) **Document type:** newsletter.
Description: Covers community and economic development research techniques, and association membership news.

380.14   AT
A C M BULLETIN. 1973. m. Aus.$80 membership. Australian Chamber of Manufactures, 380 St. Kilda Rd., Melbourne, Vic. 3004, Australia. TEL 61-3-96894111. FAX 61-3-96991729. Ed. H. Leek. adv. contact: H. Leek. (back issues avail.) **Document type:** trade publication.
Former titles (until 1991): A C M Bulletin (Victorian Edition) (ISSN 1035-395X); (until 1990): File; (until 1984): V.C.M. File (ISSN 0311-127X)

330   IT   ISSN 0001-1339
A G I E S. 1963. m. membership. Camara Oficial de Comercio de Espana in Italia, Via Rugabella 1, 20122 Milan, Italy. Ed. F.M. Granata. circ. 3,000.

380   TS
ABU DHABI. (Text in Arabic, English) 1969. m. DH.100. Abu Dhabi Chamber of Commerce and Industry - Ghurfat Tijarah wa-Sina'ah Abu Dhabi, P.O. Box 662, Abu Dhabi, United Arab Emirates. TEL 2-214000. FAX 2-215867. TELEX 22449 TIJARA EM. Ed. Salem Hamdan al-Amiri.
Formerly: Abu Dhabi Chamber of Commerce and Industry. Review.
Description: Covers local, Arab, and international economic affairs.

953   TS
ABU DHABI CHAMBER OF COMMERCE AND INDUSTRY. ANNUAL REPORT/GHURFAT TIJARAH WA-SINA'AH ABU DHABI. AL-TAQRIR AL-SANAWI. (Text in Arabic, English) 1969. a. Abu Dhabi Chamber of Commerce and Industry - Ghurfat Tijarah wa-Sina'ah Abu Dhabi, P.O. Box 662, Abu Dhabi, United Arab Emirates. TEL 2-214000. FAX 2-215867. TELEX 22449 TIJARAH EM. Ed. Salem Hamdan al-Amiri. circ. 500 (controlled).
Description: Covers news and activities of the chamber, with an overview of the economic situation in Abu Dhabi.

382   CN   ISSN 0318-7306
ACTION CANADA FRANCE. 1976. 4/yr. Can.$10 (foreign Can.$15). Chambre De Commerce Francaise, Ste. 360, rue St. Francois Xavier, Montreal, PQ H2Y 2S8, Canada. TEL 514-281-1246. FAX 514-289-9594. adv. contact: Stephane Narchal. bk.rev.; charts; illus. circ. 4,500. **Document type:** trade publication.
Supersedes: Chambre de Commerce Francaise au Canada. Revue (ISSN 0045-6306)
Description: Deals with commercial, industrial and financial exchanges between France and Canada.

963   ET
ADDIS ABABA CHAMBER OF COMMERCE. CHAMBER NEWS. (Text in Amharic, English) 1981. irreg. free. Addis Ababa Chamber of Commerce, c/o Ethiopian Chamber of Commerce, P.O. Box 517, Addis Ababa, Ethiopia. Ed. Solomon Asfaow. adv. circ. 2,500.

382   TS   ISSN 1024-266X
AFAQ IQTISADIYYAH/ECONOMIC HORIZONS. (Text and summaries in Arabic, English) 1980. q. 50DH. to individuals (foreign $25); institutions 80DH. (foreign $45). Federation of U A E Chambers of Commerce and Industry - Ittihad Ghuraf al-Tijarah wal-Sina'ah fi Dawlat al-Imarat al-Arabiyyah al-Muttahidah, P.O. Box 3014, Abu Dhabi, United Arab Emirates. TEL 971-2-214144. FAX 971-2-339210. TELEX 23883 GHURFA EM. (Dubai addr.: F.C.C.I., P.O. Box 8886, Dubai, United Arab Emirates. TEL 971-4-212977) Ed. Mohammed Ibrahim Rabooy. adv.; bk.rev.; abstr.; bibl. circ. 750. **Document type:** academic/scholarly publication.
Description: Covers U.A.E. and regional business matters, economic cooperation and development, and chamber activities.
Refereed Serial

381   US
AGENDA (MEMPHIS); the magazine of Memphis success. 1990. bi-m. free; newsstand price: $1.95. (Memphis Area Chamber of Commerce) Towery Publishing, Inc., 1835 Union Ave., No. 142, Memphis, TN 38104. TEL 901-725-2400. FAX 901-725-2401. E-mail: agenda@towery.com; URL: http://www.towery.c. Ed. Richard Banks; Pub. Robert Towery. R&P contact: J. RObert Towery. TEL 901-725-2450. adv. contact: Gigi Phillips. circ. 20,000 (controlled). (back issues avail.) **Document type:** consumer publication.
●Also available online.
Formerly: Memphis Business.
Description: Contains business profiles, pen portraits, stories and reviews designed to highlight noteworthy businesses, organizations, and individuals in Memphis and the Mid-South.

953   TS
AJMAN. q. Ajman Chamber of Commerce and Industry, P.O. Box 662, Ajman, United Arab Emirates. TEL 422177. TELEX 69523 TIJARA EM. Ed. Naeim Ahmed Jumaa. circ. 1,000 (controlled).
Formerly: Ajman Chamber of Commerce and Industry. Magazine.
Description: Covers chamber news and activities and examines local and international economic issues.

BUSINESS AND ECONOMICS — CHAMBER OF COMMERCE PUBLICATIONS

917.6 346.066 US ISSN 0745-5771
ALABAMA TODAY. 1986. m. membership. Business Council of Alabama, 2 N. Jackson St., Ste. 500, Box 76, Montgomery, AL 36101-0276. TEL 334-834-6000. FAX 334-262-7371. Ed. Renee LeMaire. circ. 3,500. (tabloid format) **Document type:** directory.
Description: Informs members of the council of legislative and regulatory actions, reports on BCA events, membership news, chamber of commerce news, calendar of events, and new member listings.

976.8 US
ALASKA ACTION. m. free. Alaska State Chamber of Commerce, 217 Second St., Ste. 201, Juneau, AK 99801. TEL 586-2323. Ed. Pamela LaBolle. **Document type:** newsletter.

381 CN ISSN 0709-5333
ALBERTA CHAMBER OF COMMERCE. LEGISLATIVE REPORT. 1979. 8/yr. Can.$125. Alberta Chamber of Commerce, 2105 T.D. Tower, Edmonton Centre, Edmonton, AB T5J 2Z1, Canada. TEL 403-425-4180. FAX 403-429-1061. Ed. Martin Salloum. circ. 300.

382 382 BE ISSN 0778-2624
AMCHAM. (Text in English) 1959. 10/yr. 4000 BEF. American Chamber of Commerce in Belgium, 50 av. des Arts, 1040 Brussels, Belgium. FAX 2-513-79-28. Ed. Carole Hazlewood. adv.; bk.rev. circ. 2,500. **Indexed:** ELLIS, HongKongiana, Key to Econ.Sci.
Formerly (until Dec. 1990): Commerce in Belgium.

382 CC
AMCHAM MAGAZINE. (Text in English) m. $90; newsstand price: $9. American Chamber of Commerce in Hong Kong, G.P.O. Box 355, Hong Kong, People's Republic of China. TEL 852-2525-0165. FAX 852-2810-1289. URL: http://www.amcham.org.hk. Ed. Fred Armentrout. adv.: B&W page HK.$11300, color page HK.$15600; trim 215 x 280; adv. contact: Susan Abraham. circ. 8,169.

382 MR ISSN 0065-7689
AMCHAM MOROCCO.* Cover title: American Chamber of Commerce in Morocco. Annual Review. (Text in English, French) 1966. a. free. American Chamber of Commerce in Morocco, c/o Fed. des Chambres de Commerce du Maroc, 6 rue d'Erfoud, Rabat Agdal, Morocco. adv.

382 NE ISSN 0001-1878
AMCHAM NEWSLETTER. (Text in English) 1962. m. membership. American Chamber of Commerce in the Netherlands, Burg. van Karnebeeklaan 14, 2585 BB The Hague, Netherlands. TEL 31-70-3659808. FAX 31-70-3646992. E-mail: amchamnl@worldaccess.nl; URL: http://www.unisys.nl/amcham/. Ed. S Paul. bk.rev.; bibl.; charts; illus.; stat. circ. 1,700. **Document type:** newsletter.
Description: Consists of updates on upcoming events, new publications, seminars and conferences of relevance to members.

382 BL ISSN 0065-7662
AMERICAN CHAMBER OF COMMERCE FOR BRAZIL. ANNUAL DIRECTORY. 1917. a. membership. American Chamber of Commerce for Brazil, Praca Pio X No. 15, 5th Fl., Caixa Postal 916, 20040-020 Rio de Janeiro, Brazil. FAX 55-21-2032477. E-mail: achambr@amchamrio.com.br; URL: http://www.amchamrio.br. Ed. Ronaldo Lapa. adv. contact: Mario Simoes. circ. 2,200. **Document type:** directory.

382 FR ISSN 0065-7670
AMERICAN CHAMBER OF COMMERCE IN FRANCE. DIRECTORY. 1894. biennial. 500 F. American Chamber of Commerce in France, 21 Av. George V, 75008 Paris, France. TEL 47-23-80-26. FAX 47-20-18-62. Ed. Anne L. Salvan; Pub. Barrett Dower. adv. circ. 1,800. **Document type:** directory.
Incorporates: List of American Firms in France.

382 US ISSN 0172-9799
AMERICAN CHAMBER OF COMMERCE IN GERMANY. MEMBERSHIP DIRECTORY AND YEARBOOK. a. $190. European Business Publications, Inc., Box 891, Darien, CT 06820-9859. TEL 203-656-2701. **Document type:** directory.
Former titles (until 1978): American Chamber of Commerce in Germany. Directory and Yearbook (ISSN 0173-2641); (until 1970): American Chamber of Commerce in Germany. Annual Report and Directory (ISSN 0569-3640); (until 1967): American Chamber of Commerce in Germany. Yearbook (ISSN 0569-3659)

382 IT ISSN 0569-3667
AMERICAN CHAMBER OF COMMERCE IN ITALY. DIRECTORY. 1964. a. L.180000($175) American Chamber of Commerce in Italy, Via Cantu 1, 20123 Milan, Italy. adv. circ. 3,000. **Document type:** directory.
Description: Covers American trade in Italy and Italian trade in the US.

382 IT
AMERICAN CHAMBER OF COMMERCE IN ITALY. NEWSLETTER. (Text in English, Italian) 1964. m. American Chamber of Commerce in Italy, Via Cantu 1, 20123 Milan, Italy. adv. circ. 4,000. **Document type:** newsletter.
Description: News of upcoming events and American Chamber of Commerce activities in Italy.

382 JA ISSN 0002-7847
HF41
AMERICAN CHAMBER OF COMMERCE IN JAPAN. JOURNAL. 1964. m. 8000 Yen($64) (American Chamber of Commerce in Japan) Paradigm, Kamiyama Ambassador, Ste. 209, 18-6 Kamiyama-cho, Shibuya-ku, Tokyo 150, Japan. TEL 03-5478-7941. FAX 03-5478-7942. Ed. Glenn Davis. adv.; bk.rev.; charts; illus.; stat. circ. 4,500. **Indexed:** Key to Econ.Sci., P.A.I.S. **Document type:** trade publication.
—BLDSC (4684.400000); UnCover.
Description: Monthly business magazine.

382 MR
AMERICAN CHAMBER OF COMMERCE IN MOROCCO. BULLETIN.* (Text in English, French) m. American Chamber of Commerce in Morocco, c/o Fed. des Chambres de Commerce du Maroc, 6 rue d'Erfoud, Rabat Agdal, Morocco. **Document type:** bulletin.

993.1 NZ ISSN 0113-9495
AMERICAN CHAMBER OF COMMERCE IN NEW ZEALAND. ANNUAL DIRECTORY. a. $130. American Chamber of Commerce in New Zealand, P.O. Box 106-002, Downtown Auckland, New Zealand. TEL 64-9-3099140. FAX 64-9-3091090. **Document type:** directory.
Description: Listing of members, who's who in US business in New Zealand.

993.1 NZ
AMERICAN CHAMBER OF COMMERCE IN NEW ZEALAND. NEWSLETTER. 8/yr. $150 membership only. American Chamber of Commerce in New Zealand, P.O. Box 106-002, Downtown Auckland, New Zealand. TEL 64-9-3099140. FAX 64-9-3091090. **Document type:** newsletter.
Description: Covers US-New Zealand trade topics.

382 TH
AMERICAN CHAMBER OF COMMERCE IN THAILAND. HANDBOOK DIRECTORY. biennial. $20. American Chamber of Commerce in Thailand, 140 Wireless Rd., Bangkok, Thailand. **Document type:** directory.

381 PH ISSN 0115-3188
AMERICAN CHAMBER OF COMMERCE OF THE PHILIPPINES. WEEKLY EXECUTIVE UPDATE. Variant title: AmCham W E U. Short title: Weekly Executive Update (W E U). w. $165. American Chamber of Commerce of the Philippines, C.P.O. Box 2562, Makati City 1299, Philippines. TEL 818-79-11. FAX 816-63-59. Ed. L.P. Gonzaga. R&P contact: Robert M. Sears. adv. contact: Lynn A. Acejas. circ. 5,000. **Document type:** consumer publication.
Formerly: American Chamber of Commerce of the Philippines. Weekly Business Letter.

382 BL
AMERICAN CHAMBER OF COMMERCE - SAO PAULO. UPDATE/CAMARA AMERICANA DE COMERCIO - SAO PAULO. UPDATE. (Text in English, Portuguese) 1945. bi-w. $80 (foreign $125). American Chamber of Commerce - Sao Paulo, Rua Alexandre Dumas 1976, 04717-004 Sao Paulo, Brazil. TEL 011-2469199. FAX 0055-2469080. TELEX 1157059 AMCH BR. Ed. Brian Nicholson. adv.; stat. circ. 4,800.
Former titles: AmCham News Update; Brazilian News Briefs (ISSN 0006-9507); Sao Paulo Letter.

382 GR ISSN 0065-8529
AMERICAN - HELLENIC CHAMBER OF COMMERCE. BUSINESS DIRECTORY/ELLINOAMERIKANIKON EMBORIKON EPIMELITIRION. BUSINESS DIRECTORY. (Includes supplement: Special Issue (ISSN: 0065-8537)) every 18 mos. $250. American - Hellenic Chamber of Commerce - Ellinoamerikanikon Emborikon Epimelitirion, 16 Kanari St., 106 74 Athens, Greece. TEL 363-6407. Ed. Sotiris Yannopoulos; Pub. Sotiris Yannopoulos. **Document type:** directory, trade publication.

338 US ISSN 0272-1953
HG4057
AMERICAN SUBSIDIARIES OF GERMAN FIRMS/AMERIKANSICHE TOCHTERGESELLSCHAFTEN DEUTSCHER UNTERNEHMEN. 1968. biennial. $100 to non-members; members $80. German American Chamber of Commerce, Publication Services, 40 W. 57th St., 31st Fl., New York, NY 10019. TEL 212-974-8830. FAX 212-974-8867. Ed. Sven Oehme. adv. contact: Benigna Kirsten. circ. 1,500. **Document type:** directory.

382 AU
AMERIKANISCHE HANDELSKAMMER IN OESTERREICH. NEWSLETTER. 1960. m. Amerikansische Handelskammer in Oesterreich - American Chamber of Commerce in Austria, Porzellangasse 35, A-1090 Vienna, Austria. TEL 43-1-3195751. FAX 43-1-3195151. E-mail: amcham@netway.at; URL: http://www.amcham.or.at. Ed. Patricia Helletzgruber. adv.: B&W page S.12000. bk.rev. circ. 700. **Document type:** newsletter.
Formerly: Magazine Oesterreich - U S A.

941 UK ISSN 0066-1813
HF54.G7
ANGLO - AMERICAN TRADE DIRECTORY (YEAR). 1916. a. £90($170) American Chamber of Commerce (UK), 75 Brook St., London W1Y 2EB, England. TEL 44-171-493-0381. FAX 44-171-493-2394. TELEX 23675 AMCHAM G. E-mail: acc@amcham.demon.co.uk. Ed. Shahpari Dolatshahi. adv. **Document type:** directory.
—BLDSC (0902.805000).
Description: Lists more than 18,000 British and American companies that have transatlantic business links with each other.

382 UK ISSN 0003-3375
ANGLO-NORWEGIAN TRADE JOURNAL. 1915. bi-m. membership. Norwegian Chamber of Commerce (London) Inc., Norway House, 21-24 Cockspur St., London S.W.1, England. Ed. Oeystein Graham-Flateboe. adv.; bk.rev.; bibl.; stat. circ. 1,800.

382 UK
ANGLO-SPANISH TRADE DIRECTORY/DIRECTORIO COMERCIAL HISPANO BRITANICO. a. (Spanish Chamber of Commerce in Great Britain - Camara Oficial de Comercio de Espana en Gran Bretana) Kogan Page Ltd., 120 Pentonville Rd., London N1 9JN, England. TEL 44-171-278-0433. FAX 44-171-837-6348. R&P contact: Linda Batman. **Document type:** directory.

330.9 FR
ANJOU ECONOMIQUE. 1966. 5/yr. 80 F. Chambre de Commerce et d'Industrie d'Angers, 8, bd. du Roi-Rene, B.P. 626, 49006 Angers Cedex, France. TEL 33-2-41205420. FAX 33-2-41205414. Ed. Alain Ratour. adv. contact: Eve Narquin. circ. 12,000. **Document type:** trade publication.

381 FR ISSN 0066-2798
ANNUAIRE DES CHAMBRES DE COMMERCE ET D'INDUSTRIE. 1963. triennial. 500 F. Assemblee des Chambres Francaises de Commerce et d'Industrie (ACFCI), 45 av. d'Iena, 75116 Paris, France. FAX 1-47-20-61-28. TELEX 610-396. adv. **Document type:** directory.

BUSINESS AND ECONOMICS — CHAMBER OF COMMERCE PUBLICATIONS

382　　　　　　　　CG
ANNUAIRE DES ENTREPRISES DU ZAIRE. (Text in French) 1984. a. Association Nationale des Entreprises du Zaire, 10 av. des Aviateurs, B.P. 7247, Kinshasa, Democratic Republic of the Congo. TEL 22286. Ed.Bd. adv. circ. 3,000.
　　Description: Provides information on Zairean economic agents: names, addresses, telex, fax and telephone numbers, business, number of employees, name of top executives, some official addresses and the Zaire investment code.

382　　　　　　FR　　ISSN 0066-3115
ANNUAIRE FRANCO-ITALIEN. 1964. biennial. 150 F. Chambre de Commerce Italienne de Paris, 134 rue du Faubourg Saint-Honore, 75008 Paris, France. adv. circ. 2,000.

944 330　　　　　　FR
ANNUAIRE TELEXPORT; les exportateurs et importateurs francais. (Text in English, French, German or Spanish) 1990. a. 900 F. (effective 1997). (Association Telexport) Chambre de Commerce et d'Industrie de Paris (CEDIP), 27 av. de Friedland, 75008 Paris, France.
TEL 33-1-42897240. FAX 33-1-42897281.
●Also available online. Vendor(s): Data-Star.
Also available on CD-ROM.
　　Description: Provides address, telephone, fax and telex numbers, top management, exports and imports and geographic ranges for 38000 French companies.

946　　　　　　　　SP
ANUARIO INDUSTRIAL DE LA PROVINCIA. a. Camara Oficial de Comercio, Industria y Navegacion de Tarragona, Av. de Colon, 2, Tarragona, Spain. TEL 219676.

382　　　　　　　　SZ
ARAB - SWISS CHAMBER OF COMMERCE AND INDUSTRY. ANNUAL DIRECTORY. a. 120 SFr. Arab - Swiss Chamber of Commerce and Industry, 70 route de Florissant, P.O. Box 304, CH-1211 Geneva 12, Switzerland. TEL 41-22-3473202.
FAX 41-22-3473870. TELEX 427119-CHAM-CH. Ed. Elias Attia. adv.: B&W page 2900 SFr., color page 5200 SFr.; trim 270 x 185; adv. contact: Elias Ettia. **Document type:** directory.

382　　　　　　　　SZ
ARAB - SWISS CO-OPERATION. 1975. q. free. Arab - Swiss Chamber of Commerce and Industry, 70 route de Florissant, P.O. Box 304, CH-1211 Geneva 12, Switzerland. TEL 41-22-3473202.
FAX 41-22-3473870. TELEX 427119-CHAM-CH. Ed. Elias Attia. adv.: B&W page 2450 SFr., color page 3100 SFr.; trim 270 x 185; adv. contact: Elias Attia. circ. 6,000. **Document type:** trade publication.

944　　　　　　FR　　ISSN 0335-0088
ARDENNE ECONOMIQUE. 1966. 4/yr. 18A av. G. Corneau, B.P. 389, 08106 Carleville-Mezieres, France. TEL 24-56-62-62. FAX 24-56-62-22. TELEX 840 016 CHAMCO. Ed. B. Lebeau. circ. 6,000.

330　　　　　　IT　　ISSN 0004-363X
ARTI E MERCATURE. 1866. bi-m. L.15000. Camera di Commercio Industria e Agricoltura di Firenze, Piazza dei Giudici, 3 Florence, Italy. FAX 2795259. TELEX 570406. Ed. Santi Semplici. adv.; illus.

967 338.1　　　　　　TZ
ARUSHA CHAMBER OF COMMERCE AND AGRICULTURE. BULLETIN TO MEMBERS. (Text in English) bi-m. Arusha Chamber of Commerce and Agriculture, P.O. Box 141, Arusha, Tanzania. TEL 255-3722.
Document type: bulletin.

956　　　　　　　　IS
ASAKIM & KALKALA. 1973. q. Igud Lishkot Hamischar Be-Israel - Federation of Israeli Chambers of Commerce, P.O. Box 20027, Tel Aviv 61200, Israel. TEL 972-3-5631010. FAX 972-3-5612614. TELEX 33484. Ed. Zvi Amit. adv. circ. 5,000.
　　Former titles (until May 1993): Kalkala Umischar (ISSN 0334-7753); (until 1985): Bakalkalah Umischar (ISSN 0334-3006)

381　　　　　　　　US
ASHEVILLE REPORT. 1943. bi-m. $12. Asheville Area Chamber of Commerce, Box 1010, Asheville, NC 28802. TEL 704-258-6131. FAX 704-251-0926. URL: http://www.ashevillechamber.org. Ed. Lynn Schroeder; Pub. Jay Garner. R&P contact: Lynn Schroeder. adv. contact: Lynn Schroeder. illus.; circ. 2,500 (controlled). **Document type:** newsletter.
　　Former titles: Asheville Area Chamber of Commerce. Report; Sky News Report.
　　Description: Covers chamber news, industry spotlights, education and local government.

382　　　　　　FR　　ISSN 0004-4725
ASIE NOUVELLE. 1951. w. 2500 F. Chambre de Commerce Franco-Asiatique, 94 rue St. Lazare, 75009 Paris, France. adv.; illus.; index. **Document type:** newspaper, newsletter.

381　　　　　　　　EA
ASMARA CHAMBER OF COMMERCE. TRADE AND DEVELOPMENT BULLETIN. (Text in English, Tigrinya) 1979. q. $16. Asmara Chamber of Commerce, P.O. Box 856, Asmara, Eritrea. TEL 110814. TELEX 42079. Ed. Taame Foto. adv.; stat. circ. 1,500.
Document type: bulletin.
　　Supersedes (1972 - Dec. 1977): Chamber of Commerce, Industry and Agriculture of Eritrea. Trade and Development Bulletin.

382　　　　　　　　II
ASSO CHAM BULLETIN. m. Rs.500. Associated Chambers of Commerce and Industry of India, Allahabad Bank Bldg., 2nd Fl., 17 Parliament St., New Delhi 110 001, India. TEL 91-11-3360704. FAX 91-11-3342193. E-mail: assocham@ibis.delhi. nic.in. circ. 1,500. **Document type:** bulletin.

382　　　　　　　　II
ASSO CHAM NEWS & VIEWS. (Text in English) w. Rs.1000. Associated Chambers of Commerce and Industry of India, Allahabad Bank Bldg., 2nd Fl., 17 Parliament St., New Delhi 110 001, India.
TEL 91-11-3360704. FAX 91-11-3342193. E-mail: assocham@ibis.delhi.nic.in. circ. 1,500.

382　　　　　　　　II
ASSO CHAM PARLIAMENTARY DIGEST. w. Rs.2500. Associated Chambers of Commerce and Industry of India, Allahabad Bank Bldg., 2nd Fl., 17 Parliament St., New Delhi 110 001, India.
TEL 91-11-3360704. FAX 91-11-3342193. E-mail: assocham@ibis.delhi.nic.in. circ. 1,000.

380　　　　　　BL　　ISSN 0004-5217
ASSOCIACAO COMERCIAL DO AMAZONAS. BOLETIM.* 1968. s-m. free. Associacao Comercial do Amazonas, Rua Guilherme Moreira 281, Manaus, Amazonas, Brazil. mkt.; stat. (processed) **Document type:** bulletin.

946.9　　　　　　　　PO
ASSOCIACAO DOS MUNICIPIOS DO DISTRITO DE SETUBAL. REVISTA. 12/yr. Associacao dos Municipios do Distrito de Setubal, Av. Dr. Manuel de Arriaga 6-2o Esq., 2900 Setubal, Portugal.
TEL 34221. TELEX 40164. Ed. Joao Neves. circ. 12,500.

967　　　　　　　　MW
ASSOCIATED CHAMBERS OF COMMERCE AND INDUSTRY OF MALAWI. NEWSLETTER. (Text in English) m. Associated Chamber of Commerce and Industry of Malawi, P.O. Box 258, Blantyre, Malawi.
TEL 265-671988. FAX 265-671147. TELEX 43992. **Document type:** newsletter.

968.91　　　　　　　　RH
ASSOCIATED CHAMBERS OF COMMERCE OF ZIMBABWE. COMMERCE. m. Associated Chambers of Commerce of Zimbabwe, Equity House, Rezende St, P.O. Box 1934, Harare, Zimbabwe.

382　　　　　　　　MY
ASSOCIATED CHINESE CHAMBER OF COMMERCE. TRADE DIRECTORY. Associated Chinese Chamber of Commerce, 24th 1st Fl., Jalan Green Hill, 93100 Kuching, Sarawak, Malaysia. FAX 082-429950.
Document type: directory.

330　　　　　　　　CG
ASSOCIATION NATIONALE DES ENTREPRISES DU ZAIRE. CIRCULAIRE D'INFORMATION. 1959. m. $85 to non-members; members $75 (effective 1996-1997). Association Nationale des Entreprises du Zaire, 10 av. des Aviateurs, B.P. 7247, Kinshasa, Democratic Republic of the Congo. TEL 22286. Ed. Edouard Luboya Diyoka. adv. circ. 1,000.
　　Former titles: Association Nationale des Entreprises Zairoises. Circulaire d'Information; Federation Nationale des Chambres de Commerce, d'Industrie et d'Agriculture de la Republique du Zaire. Circulaire d'Information (ISSN 0085-0497)
　　Description: Reprints, entirely or in abstracts, any laws, regulations, rules or decisions relating to business or trade carried out in Zaire. Provides tenders for joint ventures and bids.

330　　　　　　IT　　ISSN 0004-6078
ASTI INFORMAZIONI ECONOMICHE. 1946. m. L.80000. Camera di Commercio, Industria, Artigianato e Agricoltura di Asti, Piazza Medici No. 8, 14100 Asti, Italy. Ed. stat. circ. 1,200.
　　Description: Features economic news.

380 338　　　　　　GR　　ISSN 0004-6612
ATHENS CHAMBER OF COMMERCE AND INDUSTRY. MONTHLY BULLETIN. (Text in Greek) 1920. m. free. Athens Chamber of Commerce and Industry, 7 Acadimias St., 106 71 Athens, Greece. charts; mkt.; pat.; tr.lit.; tr.mk.; index, cum.index covering 42 yrs. circ. 4,500. **Document type:** bulletin.

382　　　　　　　　UK
ATLANTIC. vol.17, 1978. m. £40($88) American Chamber of Commerce (UK), 75 Brook St., London W1Y 2EB, England. TEL 071-493-0381.
FAX 071-493-2394. TELEX 23675-AMCHAM-G. Ed. Mara Papathedorou. adv.; bk.rev. circ. 5,000.
Indexed: Acad.Ind., Can.B.P.I., Deep Sea Res.& Oceanogr.Abstr., Ind.Per.Art.Relat.Law, Mag.Ind., Mid.East: Abstr.& Ind., P.A.I.S., PMR.
●Also available online. Vendor(s): Knight-Ridder Information, Inc.
　　Formerly: Anglo American Trade News (ISSN 0003-3316)
　　Description: Contains a broad-ranging review of transatlantic business for directors of UK and US companies in Britain.

330　　　　　　FR　　ISSN 0989-697X
ATOUT CAMBRESIS; bulletin economique. 1947. q. 88 F. (effective 1995). Chambre de Commerce et d'Industrie de Cambrai, Place de la Republique, B.P. 367, 59407 Cambrai, France. TEL 27-72-10-10. FAX 27-72-10-05. TELEX 820 211. Ed. M. Tome. adv.; bk.rev.; illus.; mkt. circ. 6,000. **Document type:** trade publication.
　　Formerly: Bulletin Economique du Cambresis (ISSN 0007-4578)

382　　　　　　　　IT
ATTUALITA ITALIA - AUSTRALIA. 1988. 6/yr. L.20000. Italian - Australian Chamber of Commerce, Via Barberini 86, 00187 Rome, Italy.
TEL 39-6-4743565. FAX 39-6-4817813. E-mail: austral@flashnet.it. Ed. Massimo Cerofolini; Pub. Vincenzo Romiti. adv.: B&W page Aus.$1000, color page Aus.$1300; trim 265 x 190; adv. contact: Vincenzo Romiti. circ. 80,000 (controlled). **Document type:** trade publication.
　　Description: Covers Australian culture, industry, business, finance, art, science, and fashion.

943　　　　　　　　GW
AUSSENWIRTSCHAFT AKTUELL. 1947. s-m. membership. Industrie- und Handelskammer Nuernberg, Hauptmarkt 25-27, 90403 Nuernberg, Germany. TEL 0911-1335-0. FAX 0911-1335488 bk.rev. circ. 860.
　　Formerly (until 1986): Aussenhandelsrundschreiben.
　　Description: Chamber of Commerce publication concerned with foreign trade worldwide. Includes lis of fairs and exhibitions.

382 332.6　　　　　　UK
AUSTRALIA IN BRITAIN. a. £25 to non-members. Australian British Chamber of Commerce (UK), Morley House, Ste. 10-16, 3rd Fl., 314-322 Reger St., London W1R 5AE, England.
TEL 44-171-636-4525. Pub. Nick Came. **Documen type:** directory.
　　Description: Lists Australian and U.K. governmen agencies, Australian companies and their subsidiaries in the UK.

BUSINESS AND ECONOMICS — CHAMBER OF COMMERCE PUBLICATIONS

382 US
AUSTRIAN BUSINESS. vol.27, 1975. q. $28. United States Austrian Chamber of Commerce, 165 W. 46th St., New York, NY 10036. TEL 212-819-0117. FAX 212-819-0117. Ed. Erika N. Borozan. adv.; illus.

330 IQ
BAGHDAD CHAMBER OF COMMERCE & INDUSTRY. MONTHLY BULLETIN. (Text in Arabic, English) 1950. m. ID.7000. Baghdad Chamber of Commerce & Industry, Studies and Statistics Department, Mustansir St., Baghdad, Iraq. TELEX 212821 GHURFA IK. adv.; bk.rev. circ. 5,000. Document type: bulletin.
Formerly: Baghdad Chamber of Commerce. Weekly Bulletin (ISSN 0005-3899)
Description: Covers trade and economic news, index prices, and laws and regulations.

970 BF
BAHAMAS. CHAMBER OF COMMERCE. ANNUAL DIRECTORY. (Text in English) 1960. a. $8. Chamber of Commerce, Attn: Executive Dir., P.O. Box N665, Nassau, Bahamas. TEL 242-322-2145. FAX 242-322-4649. Ed. Ruby Lee/Sweeting. adv. contact: Ruby Lee Sweeting. circ. 10,000 (controlled). Document type: directory.

380 BA
BAHRAIN CHAMBER OF COMMERCE AND INDUSTRY. COMMERCE REVIEW/AL-HAYA AL-TIJARIYA. (Text in Arabic, English) 1961. m. 10 din. Bahrain Chamber of Commerce and Industry, P.O. Box 248, Manama, Bahrain. TEL 233193. FAX 241294. TELEX 8691 GHURFA BN. Ed. Khalil Yousuf. adv. circ. 3,500.

949.4 SZ
BASLER HANDELSKAMMER. INFO AND B H K NEWS. 1976. m. membership. Basler Handelskammer, Postfach 1548, CH-4001 Basel, Switzerland. TEL 41-61-2721888. FAX 41-61-2726228. E-mail: 101320,3471@compuserve.com. Document type: bulletin.
Formerly: Basler Handelskammer. Info and Bulletin.

381 US
BATON ROUGE'S COMMERCE. 1951. q. $12. Greater Baton Rouge Chamber of Commerce, Box 3217, Baton Rouge, LA 70821. TEL 504-381-7125. Ed. Jace Dobrowlski. adv.; illus.; stat. circ. 3,400. (tabloid format)
Former titles: Action Newsletter (Baton Rouge); Baton Rouge (ISSN 0005-6324)

381 GW ISSN 0171-9416
BAYERISCH-SCHWAEBISCHE WIRTSCHAFT. 1945. m. DM.89. Industrie- und Handelskammer fuer Augsburg und Schwaben, Stettenstr. 1-3, 86150 Augsburg, Germany. TEL 49-821-3162-0. FAX 49-821-3162180. TELEX 53815. E-mail: bsw@augsburg.ihk.de. Ed. Hans-Ulrich Rohde. adv.; B&W page DM.7100, color page DM.9060; trim 185 x 260; adv. contact: Gerald Beranek. bk.rev.; film rev.; bibl.; charts; stat.; index; circ. 87,500 (controlled). (back issues avail.) Document type: trade publication.
Description: Concerned with industry, retail trade and services, business and regional economic development.

382 US ISSN 0196-4631
HF21
BELGIAN AMERICAN TRADE REVIEW.* 1946. a. $75. Belgian - American Chamber of Commerce in the U S, 1350 Ave. of the Americas, No. 26, New York, NY 10119-5400. TEL 212-967-9898. Ed. Claire F. Raick. adv.; bk.rev.; charts; illus.; index. circ. 4,000. Indexed: PROMT.
Formerly: Belgian Trade Review (ISSN 0005-8394)

382 UK ISSN 1357-6879
BELGO-LUXEMBOURG CHAMBER OF COMMERCE IN GREAT BRITAIN. JOURNAL. 1978. 6/yr. membership. Belgo-Luxembourg Chamber of Commerce in Great Britain, Berkeley House, 73 Upper Richmond Rd., 2nd Fl., London SW15 2SZ, England. TEL 0181-877-3025. FAX 0181-877-3961. Ed. D. Maeremans. adv.: B&W page £515, color page £710; adv. contact: Annelies Van Gysegem. bk.rev.; charts; illus.; tr.lit. circ. 3,500.
Former titles: Business Contact; Belgian Chamber of Commerce in Great Britain Journal (ISSN 0005-8378)
Description: Interviews with business leaders, embassy news and events, new member profiles, and a list of trade fairs.

382 GW ISSN 0939-4443
BERLIN - BRANDENBURGISCHE HANDWERK. 1986. fortn. DM.60. (Handwerkskammer Berlin) Westkreuz Druckerei und Verlag, Toepchiner Weg 198-200, 12309 Berlin, Germany. TEL 49-30-7452047. FAX 49-30-7453066. Ed. Christian Schmaling. adv. contact: Erika Broeschke. Document type: academic/scholarly publication.
Formerly (until 1990): Berliner Handwerk (ISSN 0931-3206)

943 GW ISSN 0405-5756
DIE BERLINER WIRTSCHAFT. 1950. m. DM.78. Industrie- und Handelskammer, Hardenbergstr. 16-18, 10623 Berlin, Germany. TEL 030-31510276. FAX 030-31510344. Ed. Egbert Steinke. adv.; charts; illus.; index. circ. 53,000. Document type: trade publication.

943 GW
BERUFSBILDUNGSBRIEF. 1965. q. free. Industrie- und Handelskammer zu Dortmund, 44127 Dortmund, Germany. TEL 49-231-5417260. FAX 49-231-5417329. E-mail: weibert@dortmund.ihk.de. Ed. Claus-Dieter Weibert. circ. 7,000. (back issues avail.) Document type: bulletin.
Description: Information on vocational training affairs.

382 PO
BILATERAL. (Text in English, Portuguese) 1951. q. Esc.4200 (outside Europe Esc.10000) (effective 1997). British-Portuguese Chamber of Commerce, Rua da Estrela 8, 1200 Lisbon, Portugal. TEL 351-1-3961586. FAX 351-1-601513. Ed. Ralph Vaz. adv.: color page Esc.110000; trim 200 x 285; adv. contact: Apolonia Barton. bk.rev.; charts; illus.; stat. circ. 3,000. Document type: trade publication.
Former titles (until 1994): Camara de Comercio Luso-Britanica. Revista Bimestral (ISSN 0872-1572); (until 1986): British-Portuguese Chamber of Commerce Magazine (ISSN 0872-9832); British-Portuguese Chamber of Commerce. Monthly Bulletin (ISSN 0007-165X)

976 US ISSN 0006-369X
BIRMINGHAM. 1961. m. $15. Birmingham Area Chamber of Commerce, 2027 First Ave. N., Birmingham, AL 35203. TEL 205-323-5461. (Subscr. to: Box 10127, Birmingham, AL 35202) Ed. Joe O'Donnell. adv.; bk.rev. circ. 10,000.
Description: General interest city magazine.

381 UK ISSN 0307-0158
HF302
BIRMINGHAM & WEST MIDLANDS CHAMBERS OF COMMERCE DIRECTORY. 1905. a. £75. (Birmingham Chamber of Industry & Commerce) Kemps Publishing Ltd., 11 The Swan Courtyard, Charles Edward Rd., Birmingham B26 1BU, England. TEL 44-121-765-4144. FAX 44-121-706-6210. Document type: directory.

917.6 US ISSN 0888-403X
BIRMINGHAM BUSINESS. m. $6 to non-members. Birmingham Area Chamber of Commerce, 2027 First Ave. N., Birmingham, AL 35203. TEL 205-323-5461. FAX 205-250-7669. Ed. Kristi Gilmore. circ. 5,000. (back issues avail.)
●Also available online. Vendor(s): UMI.
Description: Reports on chamber activities and programs; provides calendar of events.

943 GW
BLICKPUNKT WIRTSCHAFT. 1956. m. membership. Industrie- und Handelskammer Giessen, Chamber of Industry and Commerce Giessen, Lonystr. 7, P.O. Box 111220, 35390 Giessen, Germany. Ed.Bd. adv.; bk.rev. circ. 6,300.

382 UY
BOLEBU. m. DM.120. Camara de Comercio Uruguayo-Alemana - Deutsch-Uruguayische Handelskammer, Zabala 1379, Casilla de Correo 1499, 11000 Montevideo, Uruguay. TEL 598-2-953521. FAX 598-2-963281. Ed. Klaus Roessler. Document type: newsletter.

380 SP ISSN 0211-1268
BOLETIN DE COYUNTURA Y ESTADISTICA DEL PAIS VASCO. (Text in Spanish and Basque) 1969-1978; resumed. 3/yr. 3500 ptas. Camara Oficial de Comercio y Industria de Alava, Dato 38, 01005 Vitoria, Spain. TEL 34-45-141800. FAX 34-45-143156. TELEX 35515. Dir. Lorenzo Bergareche Capa. charts. circ. 2,000.
Formed by the merger of: Camaras Oficiales de Comercio, Industria y Navegacion de la Region Vasconavarra. Coyuntura Industrial Regional; Utilizacion de la Capacidad Productiva Regional.

986 CK
BOLETIN INTERNACIONAL DE OPORTUNIDADES. 1971. w. $60. Camara de Comercio de Bogota, Carrera 9, No. 16-21, Piso 8, Apdo. Aereo 5609, Bogota, Colombia. circ. 800.

BOLLETTINO COMMERCIO ESTERO. see BUSINESS AND ECONOMICS — International Commerce

945 IT
BOLLETTINO DEI PROTESTI. fortn. Camera di Commercio, Industria, Artigianato e Agricoltura di Vicenza, Corso Antonio Fogazzaro 37, 36100 Vicenza, Italy. TEL 39-444-994811. FAX 39-444-994834.

330 IT ISSN 0006-6796
BOLLETTINO ECONOMICO. 1946. m. free. Camera di Commercio, Industria, Artigianato e Agricoltura di Ancona, 1 Piazza 24 Maggio, Ancona, Italy. TEL 071-58981. Ed. Roberto Ronchitelli. adv. circ. 600. Indexed: Numis.Lit. Document type: bulletin, government publication.

380 AG ISSN 0325-4984
BOLSA. (Supplements avail.: Bolsa. Supplemento (ISSN 0325-4992); Bolsa. Supplemento Semanal (ISSN 0325-500X)) 1905. irreg. $3 per no. Bolsa de Comercio de Buenos Aires, Sarmiento 299, Buenos Aires, Argentina. adv.; illus.; mkt.; stat.
Formerly (until 1968): Bolsa de Comercio de Buenos Aires. Boletin (ISSN 0006-6923)

982
BOLSA DE COMERCIO DE MENDOZA. CENTRO DE INFORMACIONES. BOLETIN. no.152, 1975. m. Arg.$100. Bolsa de Comercio de Mendoza, Sarmiento 199, Mendoza, Argentina. Ed. Ernesto Diez Miralles. adv.; bk.rev. Document type: bulletin.

380 AG ISSN 0006-6931
BOLSA DE COMERCIO DE ROSARIO. REVISTA. 1913. 3/yr. free. Bolsa de Comercio de Rosario, Cordoba 1402, 2000 Rosario, Santa Fe, Argentina. TEL 54-41-213472. FAX 54-41-241019. TELEX 41894 BOROS AR. adv. contact: Cristian Amuchastegui. mkt.; stat. circ. 5,000. Document type: trade publication.

381 FR ISSN 0988-9590
BOULOGNE INFORMATIONS. 1951. 2/m. 60 F. (effective 1997). Chambre de Commerce et d'Industrie de Boulogne, 98 quai Gambetta, B.P. 269, 62204 Boulogne, France. FAX 33-3-21996201. Ed. Michel Baillieu. adv.: B&W page 4547.27 F., color page 6820.38 F.; trim 190 x 250; adv. contact: Bruno Leleu. bk.rev. circ. 9,000. Document type: trade publication.
Formerly (until 1970): Revue de Bologne et de la Region (ISSN 0988-9582)

382 US ISSN 0300-7464
BRAZILIAN AMERICAN CHAMBER OF COMMERCE NEWS BULLETIN. (Text in English) vol.7, 1977. m. $120. Brazilian - American Chamber of Commerce, 22 W. 48th St., Ste. 404, New York, NY 10036-1886. TEL 212-575-9030. FAX 212-921-1078. Ed. Sueli Christina Bonaperte. adv. contact: Brooke Novick Weinstein. stat. circ. 1,200. (processed) Document type: newsletter.

BUSINESS AND ECONOMICS — CHAMBER OF COMMERCE PUBLICATIONS

944 **FR** ISSN 0153-6028
BRETAGNE ECONOMIQUE. 1979. 10/yr. 250 F. (effective 1996). Edition Bretagne Economique, 1 rue du General Guillaudot, 35044 Rennes Cedex, France. TEL 33-2-99254137. FAX 33-2-99633528. TELEX 730 020. Ed. Elizabeth Pantou Vincent. adv. contact: Jean-Claude Crocq. circ. 15,000.
Refereed Serial

382 **TH**
BRITISH CHAMBER OF COMMERCE. MONTHLY INFORMATION SERVICE. British Chamber of Commerce, Bangkok Insurance Bldg., 302 Silom Rd., Bangkok 10500, Thailand. TEL 2341140.

382 **BL**
BRITISH CHAMBER OF COMMERCE IN BRAZIL. NEWS & VIEWS. 1916. m. £15. British Chamber of Commerce in Brazil, Box 1621, Sao Paulo, Brazil. Ed. S.J.A. Allen. adv.; stat. circ. 1,000. (processed)
Formerly (until 1981): British Chamber of Commerce in Brazil. Information Circular (ISSN 0007-0408)

382 **AG**
BRITISH CHAMBER OF COMMERCE IN THE ARGENTINE REPUBLIC. BULLETIN. 1914. w. $120 to non-members (effective 1996). British Chamber of Commerce in the Argentine Republic, Av. Corrientes, 457, 1043 Buenos Aires, Argentina. TEL 54-1-3942318. Ed. Charles Lagrange. adv. circ. 500. **Document type:** bulletin.
Description: Provides data on new members, bilateral commerce data, news of members and general business news. Includes a calendar of coming activities and trade shows.

382 **TU** ISSN 0007-0416
BRITISH CHAMBER OF COMMERCE OF TURKEY. TRADE JOURNAL. 1908. m. $61. British Chamber of Commerce of Turkey, P.K. 190, Karakoy, Istanbul, Turkey. FAX 152-55-51. TELEX 24-881 ITOD TR. Ed. Ilter Koral. adv.; mkt.; stat.; index. circ. 700.

382 **UK** ISSN 0260-3985
BRITISH-ISRAEL TRADE. 1957. 5/yr. membership. British-Israel Chamber of Commerce, 14-15 Rodmarton St., London W1H 3FW, England. TEL 071-486-2371. FAX 071-224-1783. Ed. Walter Nelson. adv.; abstr.; circ. 2,800 (controlled).
Formerly (until vol.23, no.5, 1980): Anglo-Israel Trade Journal (ISSN 0003-3359)

381 **AG**
BUENOS AIRES. CAMARA DE COMERCIO. INFORMATIVO MENSUAL. 1913. m. free. Camara de Comercio, Florida, piso 4, Buenos Aires, Argentina. bk.rev.; illus. circ. 1,000.

381 **UV**
BULLETIN ECONOMIQUE ET FISCAL DU BURKINA FASO. 1971. bi-m. 16000 Fr.CFA. Chambre de Commerce, d'Industrie et d'Artisanat, 01 Box 502, Ouagadougou 01, Burkina Faso. TEL 30-61-15. FAX 30-61-16. TELEX 5268 BF. stat.; cum.index. circ. 350. (back issues avail.)
Former titles: Bulletin Economique et Fiscal de la Haute Volta; (until 1975): Chambre de Commerce, d'Agriculture et d'Industrie de Haute-Volta. Bulletin Douanier et Fiscal.
Description: Contains legislative and statutory notices.

382 **AU**
BURGENLANDS WIRTSCHAFT. w. S.300. Wirtschaftskammer Burgenland, Julius-Raab-Str. 1, A-7001 Eisenstadt, Austria. TEL 43-268-2695. **Document type:** newspaper.
Formerly: Burgenlandischer Wirtschaftsdienst.

381 **US** ISSN 0887-7904
BUSINESS (LITTLE ROCK). (Publishing body formed by the merger of the Chambers of Commerce of Little Rock and North Little Rock) 1977. m. $225 to non-members; members $1. Greater Little Rock Chamber of Commerce, 1 Spring Bldg., Little Rock, AR 72201. TEL 501-374-4871. Ed. Gary Newton. adv.; stat. circ. 2,430. (back issues avail.)
Superseded: Little Rock Currents.

381 **IE** ISSN 0791-9182
BUSINESS CONTACT. 10/yr. Dyflin Publications, Hogan House, Grand Canal St., Dublin, Ireland. Ed. Karen Hesse. circ. 4,500.

381 **US**
BUSINESS DESK REFERENCE. a. $53.95 to non-members (effective 1997). Hampton Roads Chamber of Commerce, 420 Bank St., Norfolk, VA 23510. TEL 757-622-2312. FAX 757-622-5563. Ed. Amy Bull; Pub. John A. Hornbeck Jr. R&P contact: Amy Bull. TEL 757-664-2530. adv. contact: Amy Bull. circ. 10,000. **Document type:** directory.
Description: Includes 3000 business listings with contact name, title, business address, phone and fax. Organized alphabetically and by type of business.

382 **HT**
BUSINESS HAITI. q. $10. Haitian-American Chamber of Commerce and Industry, Scotiabank Bldg., 82, Rte. de Delmas, P.O. Box 13486 Delmas, Port-au-Prince, Haiti.

974 **US**
BUSINESS INSIDER. m. $25. Niagara Falls Area Chamber of Commerce, 345 Third St., Niagara Falls, NY 14303-1117. TEL 716-285-9141. FAX 716-285-0941. Ed. Fred Caso, Jr. R&P contact: Fred Caso, Jr. adv. contact: Fred Caso, Jr. circ. 3,000. (back issues avail.) **Document type:** newsletter.
Description: Journal for the business community of the Niagara Falls area.

382 **PH** ISSN 0116-452X
HC451
BUSINESS JOURNAL. 1921. m. P.385 (foreign $27). American Chamber of Commerce of the Philippines, C.P.O. Box 2562, Makati City 1299, Philippines. TEL 63-818-79-11. FAX 63-816-63-59. Ed. Katherine D. Mayo. adv.; B&W page $350; 7 1/2 x 10; adv. contact: Linda A. Acejas. circ. 5,000. **Indexed:** Ind.Phil.Per., P.A.I.S., PROMT. **Document type:** trade publication.
—BLDSC (0809.229820); UnCover.

THE BUSINESS LINK. see *BUSINESS AND ECONOMICS — International Commerce*

338 **US** ISSN 0007-6945
BUSINESS MEMO FROM BELGIUM. 1957. q. free. Embassy of Belgium, Investments Office, 3330 Garfield St. N.W., Washington, DC 20008. TEL 202-625-5888. FAX 202-625-7567. TELEX 440139. E-mail: usa@belgium__emb.orb; URL: http://www.belgium__emb.orb. Ed. Water Stevens. circ. 50,000 (controlled). (processed) **Indexed:** PROMT. **Document type:** newsletter.
—UMI.
Description: Focuses on Belgium's legal and economic environment, available investment opportunities, and foreign companies operating in the country.

382 **MX** ISSN 0187-1455
HF3231
BUSINESS MEXICO. (Text in English) 1922. 11/yr. $134. American Chamber of Commerce of Mexico, A.C., Lucerna 78, Col. Juarez, Del. Cuauhtemoc, 0600 Mexico DF, Mexico. TEL 52-5-724-3800. FAX 52-5-703-2911. TELEX 177-7609 ACHAME. Ed. Kate Sheehy. R&P contact: Diana H. de Hernandez. adv. contact: Cristina Bustos. bk.rev.; charts; illus.; index. circ. 10,000. (also avail. in microform from UMI) **Indexed:** B.P.I., Hisp.Amer.Per.Ind., Key to Econ.Sci., P.A.I.S. **Document type:** corporate report.
●Also available online. Vendor(s): Lexis-Nexis, UMI. Also available on CD-ROM. Producer(s): UMI.
—BLDSC (2934.286000); KR SourceOne; UMI.
Formed by the 1983 merger of: American Chamber of Commerce of Mexico. Quarterly Economic Report; Mexican-American Review (ISSN 0026-1696)
Description: Comprehensive view of Mexico's economics, investment, trade, environment and industries.

974 **US** ISSN 1051-7510
BUSINESS PHILADELPHIA. 1990. m. $38.50. Penn Communications Group, Inc., 260 S. Broad St., Philadelphia, PA 19102. TEL 215-735-6969. FAX 215-735-6965. Ed. Julide Liedman. R&P contact: Shawn Hart. adv.; B&W page $3200, color page $4800; trim 8 x 10 7/8; adv. contact: Tom Curry. circ. 25,150 (paid); 29,000 (controlled). (also avail. in microform from UMI) **Document type:** consumer publication.
—UMI.
Description: Features personality profiles, with information about the business, community and recreational lives of the city's business leaders.

382 **MX**
BUSINESS PLANNING. (Text in English, Spanish) a. $150. American Chamber of Commerce of Mexico, A.C., Lucerna 78, Col. Juarez, Del. Cuauhtemoc, 06600 Mexico DF, Mexico. TEL 52-5-724-3800. FAX 52-5-703-2911. TELEX 177-7609 ACHAME. R&P contact: Diana H. de Hernandez. **Document type:** trade publication.
Formerly: Strategic Planning.
Description: Includes macroeconomic overview, alternative economic scenarios, survey of business perspectives, sectoral analysis and historic data.

381 **US**
BUSINESS REVIEW - DIRECTORY. a. $50. Brazilian-American Chamber of Commerce, Inc., 22 W. 48th St., Ste. 404, New York, NY 10036-1886. FAX 212-921-1078. circ. 1,000. **Document type:** directory.
Description: Listing of Chamber members and economic-statistical information on Brazil.

382 **BL**
BUSINESS ROUND-UP. m. American Chamber of Commerce for Brazil - Camara de Comercio Americana, Praca Pio X No. 15, 5th Fl., Caixa Postal 916, 20040-020 Rio de Janeiro, Brazil. TEL 55-21-2032477. E-mail: achambr@amchamrio.com.br; URL: http://www.amchamrio.com.br.

382 **US**
BUSINESS SOUTHWEST.* q. German - American Chamber of Commerce (Houston), 5599 San Felipe St., Ste. 510, Houston, TX 77056-2720.

380.1 **US** ISSN 1043-5336
BUSINESS TODAY (ST. PAUL).* 1975. bi-m. $20. St. Paul Area Chamber of Commerce, 332 Minnesota St., Ste. N205, St. Paul, MN 55101-2701. TEL 612-223-5000. FAX 612-223-5119. bk.rev. circ. 3,000. **Document type:** newsletter.
Former titles (until 1989): Chamberview (ISSN 0885-0828); Saint Paul Area Chamber of Commerce Dialogue.

382 **VE** ISSN 0045-3641
BUSINESS VENEZUELA. (Text in English) 1968. m. $80 (foreign $140). Venezuelan - American Chamber of Commerce and Industry - Camara Venezolano Americana de Comercio e Industria, Apdo. 5181, Caracas 1010A, Venezuela. TEL 58-2-2630833. FAX 58-2-2631829. TELEX 28399. Ed. George Soules. adv. circ. 10,000. (also avail. in microform from UMI; reprint service avail. from UMI) **Indexed:** Hisp.Amer.Per.Ind. (1994-1996), Key to Econ.Sci.
—UMI.

960 **SA**
C C I ANNUAL REPORT. (Membership Directory avail.) 1940. a. membership. Cape Chamber of Industries, Broadway Industries Centre, Heerengracht, P.O. Box 1536, Cape Town 8000, South Africa. TEL 27-21-215180. FAX 27-21-4195982. TELEX 5-27409. Ed. C.E. McCarthy. adv. circ. 1,200. **Document type:** corporate report.
Supersedes in part (in 1987): C C I Year Book and Directory.

944 **FR**
C C I MAGAZINE. 4/yr. Chambre de Commerce et d'Industrie de Cherbourg-Cotentin, Hotel Atlantique, Bd. Felix Amiot, B.P. 839, 50108 Cherbourg Cedex, France. TEL 33-2-33233200. FAX 33-2-33233228. TELEX 170 849 F. Ed. Rene Moirand. circ. 5,000. **Document type:** bulletin.

380 **UA**
CAIRO CHAMBER OF COMMERCE. JOURNAL/GHURFAT AL-TIGARA AL-QAHIRA. MAGALLA. m. Cairo Chamber of Commerce - Ghurfat al-Tigara al-Qahira, 4 Midan al-Falaky, Cairo, Egypt. TEL 02-3558261. FAX 02-3563603. TELEX 92453.

979.4 **US** ISSN 0882-0929
CALIFORNIA CHAMBER OF COMMERCE ALERT. 1972. 34/yr. membership only. California Chamber of Commerce, Box 1736, Sacramento, CA 95812-1736. TEL 916-444-6670. FAX 916-444-6685. E-mail: alert@calchamber.com; URL: http://www.calchamber.com. Ed. Ann S. Amioka; Pub. Kirk West. R&P contact: Ann S. Amioka. circ. 22,000. **Document type:** newsletter.
Formerly: Pacific Alert (ISSN 0048-2617)
Description: Provides updates on legislation, regulations and policy issues of concern to California employers.

BUSINESS AND ECONOMICS — CHAMBER OF COMMERCE PUBLICATIONS

975.9 US
CAMACOL NEWS. m. Latin Chamber of Commerce - Camara de Comercio Latina, 1417 W. Flagler, Miami, FL 33135.

380.1 SP ISSN 1130-832X
LA CAMARA. 1944. m. 3000 ptas. Camara Oficial de Comercio Industria y Navegacion de Valencia, Poeta Querol 15, 46002 Valencia, Spain. TEL 34-6-3511301. FAX 34-6-3516349. Ed. Jose M. Gil Suay. adv.; bk.rev.; illus. circ. 15,000.
    Formerly (until Dec. 1989): Comercio Industria y Navegacion (ISSN 0211-1578)

382 CL
CAMARA CHILENO - ALEMANA DE COMERCIO E INDUSTRIA. ANNUAL REPORT. a. Camara Chileno - Alemana de Comercio e Industria - Deutsch - Chilenische Industrie- und Handelskammer, Ahumada 131, Oficina 808-815, Casilla 9980, Santiago, Chile. TEL 2-6964494. TELEX 240503.

382 CL
CAMARA CHILENO - SUIZA DE COMERCIO. BOLETIN NUEVO. q. Camara Chileno - Suiza de Comercio, Clasificador 1368, Santiago, Chile. TEL 6980808.

382 PO
CAMARA DE COMERCIO AMERICANA. BOLETIM. (Membership Directory avail.) 1956. 9/yr. Esc.67500($500) Camara de Comercio Americana, Rua Dona Estefania 155-5 Esq., 1000 Lisbon, Portugal. TEL 578208. FAX 572580. adv.; charts; illus.; index. circ. 2,000. **Document type:** bulletin.
    Former titles: Camara de Comercio Luso-Americana. Boletim (ISSN 0008-1906); Camara de Comercio dos Estados Unidos da America do Norte em Portugal. Boletim.

330 CK ISSN 0008-185X
CAMARA DE COMERCIO DE BOGOTA. BOLETIN. 1916. fortn. $38. Camara de Comercio de Bogota, Carrera 9, No. 16-21, Piso 8, Apdo. Aereo 29824, Bogota, Colombia. Dir. Mario Suarez Melo. adv. **Document type:** bulletin.

338 980 CK ISSN 0120-4289
HF6
CAMARA DE COMERCIO DE BOGOTA. REVISTA. 1970. q. $50. Camara de Comercio de Bogota, Carrera 9, No. 16-21, Piso 8, Apdo. Aereo 29824, Bogota, Colombia. Ed. Mario Suarez Melo. bk.rev.; bibl. **Indexed:** Key to Econ.Sci., P.A.I.S.For.Lang.Ind.

381 CK
CAMARA DE COMERCIO DE BOGOTA. SERVICIO INFORMATIVO. 1969. m? Camara de Comercio de Bogota, Carrera 9, No. 16-21, Piso 8, Apdo. Aereo 29824, Bogota, Colombia. Ed. Mario Suarez.
    Former titles: Camara de Comercio de Bogota. Servicio Informativo Mensual; Camara de Comercio de Bogota. Servicio Informativo Quincenal.

972.86 CR
CAMARA DE COMERCIO DE COSTA RICA. MAGAZINE. Camara de Comercio de Costa Rica, Barrio Tournon, Apdo. 1114, San Jose, Costa Rica.

330 NQ
CAMARA DE COMERCIO DE NICARAGUA. BOLETIN COMERCIAL. 1928. m. C.$42($6) Camara de Comercio de Nicaragua, Apdo. Postal 135-C001, Managua, Nicaragua. adv.; charts; mkt. circ. 2,500. **Document type:** bulletin.
    Former titles: Camara Nacional de Comercio de Managua. Boletin (ISSN 0008-1922); Camara Nacional de Comercio e Industrias de Managua. Boletin.

381 EC
CAMARA DE COMERCIO DE QUITO. BOLETIN DE INFORMACION COMERCIAL. no.78, 1977. m. Camara de Comercio de Quito, Avenidas Amazonas y de la Republica, Apdo. 202, Quito, Ecuador. TEL 453-011. **Document type:** bulletin.

382 BO
CAMARA DE COMERCIO E INDUSTRIA BOLIVIANO - ALEMANA. BULLETIN BOLIVIA - GERMANY. q. Camara de Comercio e Industria Boliviano - Alemana - Deutsch - Bolivianische Industrie- und Handelskammer, Av. Villazon 1966, Casilla 2722, La Paz, Bolivia. TEL 327596. TELEX 2298 CA CAMBOLAL.

382 BO
CAMARA DE COMERCIO E INDUSTRIA BOLIVIANO - ALEMANA. CARTA DE INFORMACION. m. Camara de Comercio e Industria Boliviano - Alemana - Deutsch - Bolivianische Industrie- und Handelskammer, Av. Villazon 1966, Casilla 2722, La Paz, Bolivia. TEL 327596. TELEX 2298 CA CAMBOLAL.

382 PO
CAMARA DE COMERCIO E INDUSTRIA LUSO - ALEMA. INFORMATIONEN.* m. Camara de Comercio e Industria Luso - Alema, c/o Camara de Comercio e Industria Portuguesa, Rua das Portas de Santo Antao 89, 1194 Lisbon, Portugal. TEL 1-772587. TELEX 16469.

380 SP
CAMARA DE COMERCIO HISPANO-SUECA DE MADRID. INFO. (Text in Spanish and Swedish) 1949. 10/yr. membership. Camara de Comercio Hispano-Sueca de Madrid, Caracas, 23, 28010 Madrid, Spain. illus.; pat.; stat.; tr.lit.; circ. 500 (controlled). (back issues avail.)
    Former titles: Comite Hispano-Sueco. Camara de Comercio de Suecia en Espana. Circular Informativa & Asociacion Comercial Hispano-Sueca. Circula Informativa; Camara de Comercio de Sueca. Circular Informativa.

987 VE
CAMARA DE COMERCIO, INDUSTRIA Y AGRICULTURA VENEZOLANO-ITALIANO. 1954. q. $50. Av. Andres Bello, Centro Andres Bello, Torre Oeste, p. 14, Ofs. 143-144, Apdo. 14204, Caracas 1050, Venezuela.

382 PY
CAMARA DE COMERCIO PARAGUAYO - ALEMANA. 8/yr. Camara de Comercio Paraguayo - Alemana - Deutsch - Paraguayische Handelskammern, J.E. O'Leary 409, Oficina 316, P.O. Box 919, Asuncion, Paraguay. TEL 21-46594.

382 AG
CAMARA DE COMERCIO SUIZA-ARGENTINA. BULLETIN. m. Av. Leandro N. Alem 1074, 1001 Buenos Aires, Argentina. TEL 3117187. **Document type:** bulletin.

989 UY
CAMARA DE COMERCIO URUGUAY - U S A. REVISTA. s-a. Camara de Comercio Uruguay - USA - Chamber of Commerce of the USA in Uruguay, Casilla 809, Montevideo, Uruguay. TEL 2-986934.

382 AG ISSN 0008-2112
CAMARA DE INDUSTRIA Y COMERCIO ARGENTINO-ALEMANA. BOLETIN/DEUTSCH-ARGENTINISCHE INDUSTRIE- UND HANDELSKAMMER. MITTEILUNGEN. (Text in German, Spanish) 1951. 6/yr. Arg.$30000($36) (in Germany DM.60). Camara de Industria y Comercio Argentino-Alemana, Florida 547, p. 19, 1005 Buenos Aires, Argentina. TEL 322-0173. FAX 00541-118167. adv.; bk.rev.; bibl. circ. 800. **Indexed:** Key to Econ.Sci.

382 FR ISSN 0762-6339
CAMARA INFORMA. m. Camara de Comercio de Espana, 32 av. de l'Opera, 75002 Paris, France. TEL 7424574. TELEX 212259.

989 UY ISSN 0797-5686
CAMARA NACIONAL DE COMERCIO. INFORME ANUAL. a. Camara Nacional de Comercio, Misiones 1400, 11000 Montevideo, Uruguay. TEL 961277. FAX 5982-961243. **Document type:** corporate report.

989 UY
CAMARA NACIONAL DE COMERCIO. PUBLICACIONES. irreg. Camara Nacional de Comercio, Misiones 1400, 11000 Montevideo, Uruguay. TEL 961277. FAX 5982-961243. **Document type:** monographic series.

989 UY ISSN 0797-2989
HF300.U8
CAMARA NACIONAL DE COMERCIO. REVISTA. 1979. bi-m. membership. Camara Nacional de Comercio, Misiones 1400, 11000 Montevideo, Uruguay. TEL 96-12-77. FAX 5982-961243. charts; stat. **Document type:** bulletin.

983 CL
CAMARA NACIONAL DE COMERCIO DE CHILE. BOLETIN DE INFORMES COMERCIALES. w. Camara Nacional de Comercio de Chile, Santa Lucia 302, Santiago, Chile. TEL 394744. TELEX 560264.

983 CL
CAMARA NACIONAL DE COMERCIO DE CHILE. INFORMATIVO. w. Camara Nacional de Comercio de Chile, Santa Lucia 302, Santiago, Chile. TEL 396639.

381 SP
CAMARA OFICIAL DE COMERCIO E INDUSTRIA DE ALAVA. BOLETIN INFORMATIVO. (Supplement avail.: Suplemento de Coyuntura) m. free. Camara Oficial de Comercio e Industria de Alava, Dato 38, 01005 Vitoria, Spain. TEL 34-45-141800. FAX 34-45-143156. TELEX 35515. Dir. Lorenzo Bergareche Capa. adv.; charts; illus.; stat. circ. 4,000.

380 338 SP ISSN 0008-1930
CAMARA OFICIAL DE COMERCIO, INDUSTRIA Y NAVEGACION DE BARCELONA. BOLETIN/CAMBRA OFICIAL DE COMERC, INDUSTRIA I NAVEGACIO DE BARCELONA. BUTLLETI. 1967. 4/yr. free. Cambra Oficial de Comerc, Industria i Navegacio de Barcelona, Avda. Diagonal, 452, 08006 Barcelona, Spain. TEL 34-3-4169300. FAX 34-3-4169311. Ed. Carles Castells i Oliveres. adv.; bk.rev.; charts; mkt.; stat. circ. 25,000. **Document type:** bulletin.
    Formed by the merger of (1918-1966): Comercio y Navegacion (ISSN 0210-8216); (1916-1966): Camara Oficial de la Industria. Boletin Informativo (ISSN 0404-9241); Which was formerly (until 1955): Industria Espanola (Barcelona) (ISSN 1131-5547)

946 SP
CAMARA OFICIAL DE COMERCIO, INDUSTRIA Y NAVEGACION DE SANTA CRUZ DE TENERIFE. BOLETIN INFORMATIVO. 1954. 12/yr. 3500 ptas. Camara Oficial de Comercio, Industria y Navegacion de Santa Cruz de Tenerife, Plaza Candelaria 6, 4o, 38003 Santa Cruz de Tenerife, Spain. TEL 34-22-245384. FAX 34-22-240364. Ed. Rafael Espejo Castro. adv. contact: Adela Sosa Santana. circ. 1,500. **Document type:** bulletin.

382 VE
CAMARA VENEZOLANO BRITANICA DE COMERCIO E INDUSTRIA. ANUARIO. (Text in English, Spanish) 1972. a. Bs.900. Camara Venezolano Britanica de Comercio e Industria, Torre Britanica, piso 10, Altamar Sur, Caracas 1062, Venezuela. TEL 58-2-2673112. FAX 58-2-2630362. Dir. Tim Duhan. adv. circ. 2,000.
    Formerly: Asociacion Venezolano Britanica de Comercio e Industria. Anuario (ISSN 0084-6848)

381 UK
CAMBRIDGESHIRE BUSINESS. 1970. m. (Cambridgeshire Chamber of Commerce) E C N Special Publications, Unit D8, Pinetrees Rd., Salhouse Rd., Norwich, Norfolk NR1 1TB, England. FAX 0603-700006. adv.; bk.rev. circ. 9,500.
    Description: Covers commercial and industrial news, finance, property, high-tech, motoring, people in business plus regular business features.

338 338.1 IT ISSN 0008-2147
CAMERA DI COMMERCIO, INDUSTRIA, ARTIGIANATO E AGRICOLTURA DI BELLUNO. RASSEGNA ECONOMICA. 1953. bi-m. L.30000 (foreign L.35000). Camera di Commercio Industria Artigianato e Agricoltura di Belluno, Via S. Stefano 19, 32100 Belluno, Italy. TEL 0437-940016. Dir. Armando Mosca. adv.; illus.; stat. circ. 500. (back issues avail.)

338 IT ISSN 0391-7436
CAMERA DI COMMERCIO, INDUSTRIA, ARTIGIANATO E AGRICOLTURA DI CUNEO. NOTIZIARIO ECONOMICO. 1946. bi-m. L.30000. Camera di Commercio Industria Artigianato e Agricoltura di Cuneo, Via Emanuele Filiberto 3, Cuneo, Italy. TEL 0171-318711. FAX 0171-696581. Ed. Rinaldo Chiabra. adv.; charts; illus.; stat. circ. 4,250.
    Description: Covers the tourism and agricultural industries and climate of Cuneo.

945 IT ISSN 1120-3900
CAMERA DI COMMERCIO, INDUSTRIA, ARTIGIANATO E AGRICOLTURA DI FERRARA. LISTINO DEI PREZZI ALL'INGROSSO. 1954. w. L.65000 (effective 1997). Camera di Commercio, Industria, Artigianato e Agricoltura di Ferrara, Via Borgoleoni, 11, 44100 Ferrara, Italy. TEL 39-532-783711. FAX 39-532-240204. Dir. Pietro Cocurullo.

BUSINESS AND ECONOMICS — CHAMBER OF COMMERCE PUBLICATIONS

338   IT   ISSN 1120-3943
CAMERA DI COMMERCIO, INDUSTRIA, ARTIGIANATO E AGRICOLTURA DI FERRARA. NOTIZIARIO MENSILE. 1981. m. L.210000 (effective 1997). Camera di Commercio, Industria, Artigianato e Agricoltura di Ferrara, Via Borgoleoni 11, 44100 Ferrara, Italy. TEL 39-532-783711. FAX 39-532-240204. Dir. Luigi Litardi.

CAMERA DI COMMERCIO, INDUSTRIA, ARTIGIANATO E AGRICOLTURA DI FORLI. LISTINO SETTIMANALE PREZZI. see BUSINESS AND ECONOMICS — Domestic Commerce

381   IT
CAMERA DI COMMERCIO, INDUSTRIA, ARTIGIANATO E AGRICOLTURA DI PADOVA. RAPPORTI. 1983. 3/yr. free. Camera di Commercio, Industria, Artigianato e Agricoltura di Padova, Via E. Filiberto 34, Padua, Italy. TEL 39-49-8208111. TELEX 430047 CCIA PD I. Ed. Giampaolo Redivo. circ. 280. **Document type:** monographic series.

382   BL
CAMERA DI COMMERCIO ITALIANA DI RIO DE JANEIRO. QUARTERLY REVIEW. q. Camera di Commercio Italiana di Rio de Janeiro, Av. Presidente Antonio Carlos, 40, 20020 Rio de Janeiro, Brazil. TEL 2208417.

382   CN   ISSN 0045-4214
CANADA JAPAN TRADE COUNCIL. NEWSLETTER. 1963. bi-m. free. Canada Japan Trade Council, Fuller Bldg., Ste. 903, 75 Albert St., Ottawa, ON K1P 5E7, Canada. TEL 613-233-4047. Ed. K.H. Pringsheim. circ. 3,000. (also avail. in microform from UMI) **Document type:** newsletter.
—UMI.

382   UK   ISSN 1361-7494
CANADA U.K. LINK. 1921. bi-m. membership. Canada - United Kingdom Chamber of Commerce, 3 Regent St., London SW1Y 4NZ, England. TEL 44-171-930-7711. FAX 44-171-930-9703. Ed. C. Lengyel. adv. circ. 1,600. **Document type:** newsletter.
   Former titles (until 1995): Can - U.K. Link (ISSN 0267-4319); (Until 1984): Canada - U.K. Trade News (ISSN 0045-4281); (until 1971): Canada - United Kingdom Trade News (ISSN 0591-0897)

382   UK   ISSN 0309-0329
CANADA - U.K. YEAR BOOK. 1925. a. £10.60. (Canada-United Kingdom Chamber of Commerce) Rank Zerox Ltd., 2 Brewers Green, Victoria SW1H 0RH, England. Ed. G.F. Bacon. circ. 550.

944   FR
CANTALE ECO. 8/yr. Chambre de Commerce & d'Industrie d'Aurillac et du Cantal, 44 bd. du Pont Rouge, 15013 Aurillac Cedex, France. TEL 71-45-40-40. FAX 71-48-48-12. TELEX 393 160. Ed. M. Delzangles. adv. contact: Robert Lafeuille. circ. 6,000. **Document type:** newspaper.

382   SP   ISSN 0213-9286
CATALUNYA EXPORTA - CATALUNYA IMPORTA. 1964. a. 4500 ptas. Cambra Oficial de Comerc, Industria i Navegacio de Barcelona, Diagonal, 452, 08006 Barcelona, Spain. circ. 1,000.
   Formerly (until 1984): Catalunya Exporta (ISSN 0069-1178)

972.9   CJ
CAYMAN ISLANDS CHAMBER OF COMMERCE DIRECTORY. 1984. a. $25 to non-members. Chamber of Commerce, P.O. Box 1000, George Town, Grand Cayman, British W.I. TEL 809-949-8090. FAX 809-949-0220. Ed.Bd. adv. circ. 5,000. **Document type:** directory.

972.9   CJ
CAYMAN ISLANDS CHAMBER OF COMMERCE NEWSLETTER. 1986. m. $100. Chamber of Commerce, P.O. Box 1000, George Town, Grand Cayman, British W.I. TEL 809-949-8090. FAX 809-949-0220. Ed.Bd. adv. circ. 1,300. **Document type:** newsletter.

330   UK
CENTRAL MIDLAND ENTERPRISE. 1978. m. free. Coventry Chamber of Commerce and Industry, 57 Nicholas St., Coventry CV1 4FD, England. Ed. Brian Willis. adv.

971   CN
CENTRAL NOVA BUSINESS NEWS. m. (Truro and District Chamber of Commerce) Gordon Publishing and Printing, 228 Main St., Bible Hill, NS B2N 4H2, Canada. TEL 902-895-7948. FAX 902-893-1427. (Subscr. to: Box 946, Truro, N.S. B2N 5G7, Canada) Ed. Peter Heckbert. adv.: B&W page Can.$180. circ. 2,200.

381   UK
CENTRAL SCOTLAND CHAMBER OF COMMERCE QUARTERLY BULLETIN.* vol.15, 1973. q. 50p. Central Scotland Chamber of Commerce, Ste. A, Haypark, Marchmont Av., Polmont, Stirlingshire FK2 0NZ, Scotland. Ed. H.B. Johnson. adv. circ. 900.
   Formerly: Forth Valley Chamber of Commerce Quarterly Bulletin (ISSN 0015-8100)

944   FR
CENTRE ECONOMIQUE MAGAZINE. 1955. 6/yr. 4500 F. 15 bd. Carnot, B.P. 3248, 03106 Montlucon Cedex, France. TEL 33-4-70025000. FAX 33-4-70025059. TELEX CHAMCO 990 029 F. Ed. Bruno Paugam. circ. 10,000. **Document type:** bulletin.

381   CE
CEYLON CHAMBER OF COMMERCE. ANNUAL REVIEW OF BUSINESS AND TRADE (YEAR). (Text in English) 1839. a., latest 1991. $30. Ceylon Chamber of Commerce, Chamber of Commerce Bldg., Box 274, Colombo 2, Sri Lanka. FAX 941-449352. Ed.Bd. charts; stat.

381   CE
CEYLON CHAMBER OF COMMERCE. REGISTER OF MEMBERS. (Text in English) 1981. biennial. $30. Ceylon Chamber of Commerce, Chamber of Commerce Bldg., Box 274, Colombo 2, Sri Lanka. FAX 941-449352.

381   UK   ISSN 0266-4127
CHACOM. (Chamber of Commerce) 1984. m. £18 membership. Central & West Lancashire Chamber of Commerce and Industry, 9-10 Eastway Business Village, Oliver's Pl., Fulwood, Preston PR2 9WT, England. TEL 44-1772-653000. FAX 44-1772-655544. Ed. Habiba Bhayat. adv. contact: Nick Wilson. bk.rev. circ. 3,500. **Document type:** trade publication.
   Formerly: Forum for Commerce and Industry.

914.4   FR
CHAMBER DE COMMERCE ET D'INDUSTRIE DE MEURTHE ET MOSELLE. DOSSIERS. q. Chambre de Commerce et d'Industrie de Meurthe et Moselle, 40 Ave. Henri Poincare, 54042 Nancy, France. Ed. Gerard Barthier.
   Description: Covers activities in the import-export industry and international commerce.

973   US   ISSN 0884-8114
CHAMBER EXECUTIVE. m. $87 (foreign $135). American Chamber of Commerce Executives, 4232 King St., Alexandria, VA 22302-9950. TEL 703-998-0072. FAX 703-931-5624. Ed. Marlies Mulckhuyse. adv. circ. 5,100. (also avail. in microform)
—UMI.
   Description: Covers official news of the Chamber of Commerce and its executives.

977   US   ISSN 1070-2342
CHAMBER EXECUTIVE NETWORK. 1984. m. $110. Hakes Publications, Box 603, Storm Lake, IA 50588. TEL 712-732-7718. E-mail: hakes@bvu.edu. Ed. Richard L. Hakes; Pub. Richard L. Hakes. R&P contact: Richard L. Hakes. circ. 800 (paid). (looseleaf format; back issues avail.) **Document type:** newsletter.
   Formerly: Community Development Executive (ISSN 0747-7503)
   Description: Advisory newsletter for Chamber of Commerce managers in U.S. and Canada.

380 338   UK
CHAMBER IMPACT. 1970. m. membership. South Essex Chamber of Commerce, Trade & Industry Ltd., 845 London Rd., Westcliff-on-Sea, Essex SS0 9SZ, England. TEL 44-1702-77090. FAX 44-1702-77161. Ed. D.J. Horsley. adv.; illus.; index. circ. 700. **Document type:** directory.
   Former titles: South Essex Chamber of Commerce, Trade and Industry. Southend. Monthly Journal; Southend-on-Sea and District Chamber of Commerce, Trade and Industry. Monthly Journal; Southend-on-Sea and District Chamber of Trade and Industry. Monthly Journal (ISSN 0038-3724)

973   US
CHAMBER JOBWATCH. s-m. $80 to non-members; members $40. American Chamber of Commerce Executives, 4232 King St., Alexandria, VA 22302-9950. TEL 703-998-0072. FAX 703-931-5624. Ed. Lisa Raspino. bk.rev.; circ. 250 (paid). (back issues avail.)
   ●Also available online.
   Description: Lists chamber of commerce job openings across the United States.

381   US   ISSN 0897-7917
CHAMBER JOURNAL. bi-m. membership. New Orleans Area Chamber of Commerce, New Orleans and the River Region, 601 Poydras St., Ste. 1700, New Orleans, LA 70130. TEL 504-527-6921. FAX 504-527-6970. E-mail: journal@www.gnofn.org. (Alt. addr.: Box 30240, New Orleans, LA 70190) Ed. Sarah Shaw. adv. contact: Sarah Shaw. index. (tabloid format; also avail. in diskette format; microfilm from BHP; back issues avail.) **Document type:** newsletter.
   Formerly: New Orleans Area Chamber of Commerce. Journal.
   Description: Informs businesspeople of the New Orleans region about Chamber events. Includes items of interest and general news.

975   US
CHAMBER NEWS. 1986. m. membership. Greater Hartsville Chamber of Commerce, Box 578, Hartsville, SC 29551. TEL 803-332-6401. FAX 803-332-8017. Ed. Nancy Truesdale. circ. 600 (controlled). **Document type:** newsletter.
   Formerly: Greater Hartsville Chamber of Commerce Newsletter.
   Description: News items, information, and announcements on the members and activities of the Chamber of Commerce of Greater Hartsville, South Carolina.

954.9   PK
CHAMBER OF COMMERCE AND INDUSTRY. TRADE JOURNAL. bi-w. Chamber of Commerce and Industry Nicol Rd., P.O. Box 4158, Karachi, Pakistan.

380.1   IO
CHAMBER OF COMMERCE AND INDUSTRY IN WEST JAVA. MEMBER LIST/KAMAR DAGANG DAN INDUSTRI DI JAWA BARAT. DAFTAR ANGGOTA. (Text in English, Indonesian) a. Chamber of Commerce and Industry in West Java, Jl. Sunaiaraja 3, Bandung, West Java, Indonesia.

381   SL   ISSN 0080-9527
CHAMBER OF COMMERCE OF SIERRA LEONE. JOURNAL. (Text in English) 1965. m. Le.1.50. Chamber of Commerce of Sierra Leone, Industry & Agriculture Dept., Guma Bldg., Lamina Sankoh St., 5th Fl., Freetown, Sierra Leone. TEL 26305. Ed. F. Iscandar adv. circ. 1,000.

989   UY
CHAMBER OF COMMERCE OF THE U S A IN URUGUAY. NEWSLETTER. bi-m. Camara de Comercio Uruguay USA, Casilla 809, Montevideo, Uruguay. TEL 986934. TELEX 853. **Document type:** newsletter.

382   YU
CHAMBER OF ECONOMY OF VOJVODINA. BUSINESS INFORMATION. m. Chamber of Economy of Vojvodina - Privredna Komora Vojvodina, Bulevar Marsala Tita 25, 21000 Novi Sad, Yugoslavia. TEL 021-57022 TELEX 14107.

BUSINESS AND ECONOMICS — CHAMBER OF COMMERCE PUBLICATIONS

950 NP
CHAMBER PATRIKA; economic and business affairs in Nepal. fortn. Nepal Chamber of Commerce (N.C.C.), Kantipath, Kathmandu, P.O. Box 198, Kathmandu, Nepal. TEL 977-1-222890. FAX 977-1-229998. Ed. Yagya Narayan Shrestha. adv.: page Rs.1800. charts.
Description: Covers economic and business news in Nepal, as it affects both domestic and international trade.

330 US ISSN 0279-0785
THE CHAMBER TODAY. 1916. m. $12. Greater San Antonio Chamber of Commerce, 602 E. Commerce, Box 1628, San Antonio, TX 78296. TEL 210-229-2108. FAX 210-229-1600. Ed. Joseph R. Krier. illus. circ. 7,000. **Document type**: newsletter.
Formerly (until 1980): San Antonian (ISSN 0036-3952).

380.1 US
CHAMBER UPDATE. 1965. m. $12. Greater Yakima Chamber of Commerce, Box 1490, Yakima, WA 98907-1490. TEL 509-248-2021. FAX 509-248-0601. Ed. Jennifer Fix. adv. circ. 1,500. (tabloid format) **Document type**: newsletter.
Supersedes (in 197?): Working Together for a Greater Yakima.

380.106 US
CHAMBERWAY GERMANY-MIDWEST. (Ed. Christian J. Roehr) 1982. bi-m. $25 (effective 1997). German American Chamber of Commerce of the Midwest, 401 N. Michigan Ave., Ste. 2525, Chicago, IL 60611-4212. TEL 312-644-2662. FAX 312-644-0738. Pub. Christian J. Roehr. adv.: page $920; trim 8 1/2 x 11; adv. contact: Katherine A. Bender. bk.rev. circ. 6,000. (back issues avail.) **Document type**: newsletter.
Former titles (until 1996): German American Business Journal Midwest; (until 1995): Focus Germany-Midwest.
Description: Features business, market and product developments, economic commentaries, company profiles, statistics on Germany and the U.S. as well as the European Union.

966.1 MU
CHAMBRE DE COMMERCE, D'AGRICULTURE, D'ELEVAGE, D'INDUSTRIE ET DES MINES DE LA REPUBLIQUE ISLAMIQUE DE MAURITANIE. BULLETIN. m. Chambre de Commerce, d'Agriculture, d'Elevage, d'Industrie et des Mines de la Republique Islamique de Mauritanie, BP 215, Nouakchott, Mauritania. **Document type**: bulletin.

964.26 NG
CHAMBRE DE COMMERCE, D'AGRICULTURE, D'INDUSTRIE ET D'ARTISANAT DU NIGER. WEEKLY BULLETIN. 1960. w. 30000 Fr.CFA (Europe 40000 Fr.CFA; US 50000 Fr.CFA). Chambre de Commerce, d'Agriculture, d'Industrie et d'Artisanat du Niger, B.P. 209, Niamey, Niger. TELEX 5242 NI. adv.; circ. 170. **Document type**: bulletin.

967.2 GO ISSN 0045-6276
CHAMBRE DE COMMERCE, D'AGRICULTURE, D'INDUSTRIE ET DES MINES DU GABON. BULLETIN. m. 25000 Fr.CFA. Chambre de Commerce, d'Agriculture, d'Industrie, et des Mines du Gabon, B.P. 2234, Libreville, Gabon. TEL 72-20-64. TELEX 5554. adv.; charts; stat. (processed)

960 CD
CHAMBRE DE COMMERCE, D'AGRICULTURE ET D'INDUSTRIE. INFORMATIONS ECONOMIQUES. w. Chambre de Commerce, d'Agriculture et d'Industrie, B.P. 458, N'djamena, Chad.

960 CG
CHAMBRE DE COMMERCE, D'INDUSTRIE ET D'AGRICULTURE DE LITTURI. BULLETIN. (Text in French) m. Chambre de Commerce, d'Industrie et d'Agriculture, B.P. 38, Bunia, Democratic Republic of the Congo. adv. **Document type**: bulletin.

960 CG
CHAMBRE DE COMMERCE, D'INDUSTRIE ET D'AGRICULTURE DU KISAI. BULLETIN. (Text in French) m. Chambre de Commerce, d'Industrie et d'Agriculture du Kisai Occidental, Av. Commandant Michaux, B.P. 194, Luluabourg, Democratic Republic of the Congo. adv. **Document type**: bulletin.

382 UV
CHAMBRE DE COMMERCE, D'INDUSTRIE ET D'ARTISANAT. REPERTOIRE NATIONAL DES ENTREPRISES. a. Chambre de Commerce, d'Industrie et d'Artisanat, Direction des Etudes et de l'Information, 01 B.P. 502, Ouagadougou 01, Burkina Faso. TEL 30-61-14. FAX 30-61-16. TELEX 5268 BF.

381 UV
CHAMBRE DE COMMERCE, D'INDUSTRIE ET D'ARTISANAT DU BURKINA FASO. ANNUAIRE DES ENTREPRISES. 1980. a. 10000 Fr.CFA. Chambre de Commerce, d'Industrie et d'Artisanat, 01 Box 502, Ouagadougou 01, Burkina Faso. FAX 306116. TELEX 5268 BF. adv.; bk.rev. circ. 2,500. **Document type**: directory.
Former titles: Chambre de Commerce, d'Industrie et d'Artisanat du Burkina Faso. Annuaire & Chambre de Commerce, d'Artisanat et d'Industrie de Haute-Volta. Annuaire.

916.4 338 CM ISSN 0008-2198
CHAMBRE DE COMMERCE, D'INDUSTRIE ET DES MINES DU CAMEROUN. BULLETIN D'INFORMATION. 1967-1975; resumed 1980. m. 100 Fr.CFA per no. Chambre de Commerce, d'Industrie et des Mines du Cameroun, B.P. 4011, Douala, Cameroon. TEL 42-28-88. FAX 42-55-96. TELEX 5616. Ed. Saidou A. Bobboy. adv.; illus.; stat. **Document type**: bulletin.

380.1 CM
CHAMBRE DE COMMERCE, D'INDUSTRIE ET DES MINES DU CAMEROUN. COMPTE-RENDU D'ACTIVITES. irreg. Chambre de Commerce, d'Industrie et des Mines du Cameroun, B.P. 4011, Douala, Cameroon. TEL 42-36-90. FAX 42-55-96. TELEX 5948 KN. Ed. Saidou A. Bobboy. **Document type**: corporate report.

966.11 CM
CHAMBRE DE COMMERCE, D'INDUSTRIE ET DES MINES DU CAMEROUN. IMPORT EXPORT.* m. Chambre de Commerce, d'Industrie et des Mines du Cameroun (Victoria) - Chamber of Commerce, Industry and Mines of Cameroon, BP 211, Victoria, Cameroon. TEL 332430.

960 CF
CHAMBRE DE COMMERCE DE BRAZZAVILLE. BULLETIN MENSUEL. m. Chambre de Commerce de Brazzaville, B.P. 92, Brazzaville, Congo.

381 TI
CHAMBRE DE COMMERCE DE TUNIS. BULLETIN. (Text in Arabic, English) m. 1 din. Chambre de Commerce de Tunis, 1 rue des Entrepreneurs, Tunis, Tunisia. charts; stat. **Indexed**: Key to Econ.Sci. **Document type**: bulletin.

382 BE
CHAMBRE DE COMMERCE ESPAGNOLE EN BELGIQUE. BULLETIN.* m. Chambre de Commerce Espagnole en Belgique, c/o Chambre de Commerce et d'Industrie de Bruxelles, 500 av. Louise, 1050 Brussels, Belgium. TEL 2302192. TELEX 26306. **Document type**: bulletin.

382 BE
CHAMBRE DE COMMERCE ESPAGNOLE EN BELGIQUE. REVUE.* q. Chambre de Commerce Espagnole en Belgique, c/o Chambre de Commerce et d'Industrie de Bruxelles, 500 av. Louise, 1050 Brussels, Belgium. TEL 2302192. TELEX 26306.

944 FR
CHAMBRE DE COMMERCE ET D'INDUSTRIE. LETTRE. 11/yr. Chambre de Commerce et d'Industrie, B.P. 84, 58004 Nevers Cedex, France. TEL 86-60-61-62. FAX 86-60-61-14. TELEX 800 426. Ed. Berard Moncomble. circ. 7,500.

944 FR ISSN 1247-4312
CHAMBRE DE COMMERCE ET D'INDUSTRIE D'AUXERRE. ACTION CONSULAIRE. 1964. 6/yr. 60 F. Chambre de Commerce et d'Industrie d'Auxerre, Informations Economiques, 26 rue Etienne Dolet, 89015 Auxerre Cedex, France. TEL 33-3-86494000. FAX 33-3-86494009. Ed. Guido Ruffinoni; Pub. Patrick Ardisson. R&P contact: Patrick Ardisson. adv. contact: Guido Ruffinoni. bk.rev. circ. 8,500. **Document type**: bulletin.
Formerly (until 1993): Chambre de Commerce et d'Industrie d'Auxerre. Documentation Economique (ISSN 0183-4037).

961 MR
CHAMBRE DE COMMERCE ET D'INDUSTRIE DE CASABLANCA. REVUE MENSUELLE. (Text in French) m. Chambre de Commerce et d'Industrie de Casablanca, B.P. 423, Casablanca, Morocco. Ed. Abdlah Souiri. adv.

966.68 IV
CHAMBRE DE COMMERCE ET D'INDUSTRIE DE LA REPUBLIQUE DE COTE D'IVOIRE. BULLETIN. 1928. m. 25000 Fr.CFA. Chambre de Commerce de la Republique de Cote d'Ivoire, 6 av. Joseph Anoma, B.P. 1399, Abidjan 01, Ivory Coast. TEL 32-46-79. FAX 32-39-42. TELEX 23 224 CHACOM-CI. **Document type**: bulletin.
Formerly (until 1992): Chambre de Commerce de la Republique de Cote d'Ivoire. Bulletin.

380 DM
CHAMBRE DE COMMERCE ET D'INDUSTRIE DE LA REPUBLIQUE POPULAIRE DE BENIN. NOTE HEBDOMADAIRE. w. 12000 Fr.CFA. Chambre de Commerce et d'Industrie de la Republique Populaire de Benin, Avenue du General de Gaulle, B.P. 31, Cotonou, Benin. stat. **Indexed**: Key to Econ.Sci.
Formerly: Chambre de Commerce et d'Industrie du Dahomey. Note Hebdomadaire; Chambre de Commerce, d'Agriculture et d'Industrie du Dahomey. Note Hebdomadaire.

944 FR
CHAMBRE DE COMMERCE ET D'INDUSTRIE DE MEAUX. REVUE. 4/yr. Chambre de Commerce et d'Industrie de Meaux, 12 bd. Jean Rose, B.P. 216, 77104 Meaux Cedex, France. TEL 64-34-20-13. FAX 64-33-41-15. TELEX 691 142 F.

944 FR
CHAMBRE DE COMMERCE ET D'INDUSTRIE DE PARIS. LE NOUVEAU COURRIER. 9/yr. Chambre de Commerce et d'Industrie de Paris (CEDIP), 27 av. de Friedland, 75008 Paris, France. TEL 33-1-42897240. FAX 33-1-42897281. circ. 250,000.
Formerly: Chambre de Commerce et d'Industrie de Paris. Courrier.

381 GP ISSN 1141-7978
CHAMBRE DE COMMERCE ET D'INDUSTRIE DE POINTE-A-PITRE. LETTRE. irreg. Chambre de Commerce et d'Industrie de Pointe-a-Pitre, B.P. 64, 97152 Pointe-a-Pitre Cedex, Guadeloupe. TEL 90-08-08. FAX 90-21-87. TELEX 919 780 GL. Ed. Patricia Merino.
Formerly (until 1989): Chambre de Commerce et d'Industrie de Pointe-a-Pitre. Lettre d'Information (ISSN 0750-4233).

380 338 FR ISSN 0009-1227
CHAMBRE DE COMMERCE ET D'INDUSTRIE DE ROUEN. BULLETIN ECONOMIQUE. 1948. m. 250 F. (effective 1997). Chambre de Commerce et d'Industrie de Rouen, B.P. 641, 76000 Rouen, France. TEL 33-2-35143737. FAX 33-2-35708092. E-mail: http://www.rouen.cci.fr. Ed. Yves Poyeton. adv.: B&W page 7700 F., color page 10300 F.; adv. contact: Annaick Seve. bk.rev.; charts; illus.; stat. circ. 17,500. **Document type**: bulletin.

943 BE
CHAMBRE DE COMMERCE ET D'INDUSTRIE DU CENTRE. BULLETIN. 1928. bi-m. membership. Chambre de Commerce et d'Industrie du Centre, Av. des Croix du Feu 9, 7100 la Louviere, Belgium. TEL 064-222349. FAX 064-282382. **Document type**: bulletin.

381 TI ISSN 0330-9584
HC547.T8
CHAMBRE DE COMMERCE ET D'INDUSTRIE DU SUD. BULLETIN. 1949. s-m. 15 din. Chambre de Commerce et d'Industrie du Sud - Chamber of Commerce and Industry of the South, 127 Rue Haffouz, B.P. 794, 3018 Sfax, Tunisia. TEL 04-96-120. FAX 04-96-121. TELEX 40767. Ed. Mohamed Amous. adv. circ. 720. (also avail. in microform) **Document type**: bulletin.
Formerly: Chambre de Commerce du Sud de la Tunisie. Bulletin Economique (ISSN 0045-6292).
Description: Covers activities of the Chamber as well as supply, demands and proposals of societies.

BUSINESS AND ECONOMICS — CHAMBER OF COMMERCE PUBLICATIONS

382   BE
CHAMBRE DE COMMERCE ET D'INDUSTRIE FRANCAISE POUR LA BELGIQUE ET LE GRAND-DUCHE LUXEMBOURG COMMERCE EXTERIEUR.* m. Chambre de Commerce et d'Industrie Francaise pour la Belgique et le Grand-Duche de Luxembourg, c/o Chambre de Commerce et d'Industrie de Bruxelles, 500 av. Louise, 1050 Brussels, Belgium. TEL 02-2302250.

944   FR
CHAMBRE DE COMMERCE ET INDUSTRIE. LETTRE. 10/yr. Chambre de Commerce et Industrie (Chartres), B.P. 62, 1 rue de l'Etroit Degre, 28002 Chartres Cedex, France. TEL 33-2-37842828. FAX 33-2-37842829. Ed. Jean-Paul Vidal. circ. 11,000.

382   FR   ISSN 0069-2557
CHAMBRE DE COMMERCE FRANCO-ASIATIQUE. ANNUAIRE DES MEMBRES. (Special number of: Asie Nouvelle) 1968. a. Chambre de Commerce Franco-Asiatique, 94 rue St. Lazare, 75009 Paris, France. **Document type:** directory.

382   IS
CHAMBRE DE COMMERCE ISRAEL - FRANCE. BULLETIN. m. free. Chambre de Commerce Israel - France, 28 Siderot David Hamelech, Tel Aviv 64954, Israel. TEL 972-3-6960816. FAX 972-3-6960825. TELEX 342315 PCENT IL. circ. 1,000. **Document type:** bulletin.
Description: News about bilateral trade, chamber activities, business proposals and more.

382   FR   ISSN 0069-2565
CHAMBRE DE COMMERCE JAPONAISE EN FRANCE. ANNUAIRE.* 1968. a. Chambre de Commerce Japonaise en France, 1 av. Friedland, 75008 Paris, France.

944   FR
CHAMBRE DE METIERS DE L'AIN. BULLETIN. 6/yr. Chambre de Metiers de l'Ain, 3 rue Paul-Ploda, 01000 Bourg-en-Bresse, France. TEL 74-23-33-01. FAX 74-23-24-18. Ed. Jean Garcia. circ. 13,000.

381   MR   ISSN 0528-8231
CHAMBRE FRANCAISE DE COMMERCE ET D'INDUSTRIE DU MAROC. REVUE CONJONCTURE. 1962. s-m. $54. Chambre Francaise de Commerce et d'Industrie du Maroc, 15 Av. Mers Sultan, Casablanca, Morocco. FAX 27-37-86. TELEX 24652 M. adv.; bk.rev. circ. 2,000.

382   AE
CHAMBRE FRANCAISE DE COMMERCE ET D'INDUSTRIE EN ALGERIE. ECONOMIC NEWS BULLETIN. 1968. m. 1 Rue du Languedoc, Alger, Algeria. TEL 632525. TELEX 53719. **Document type:** bulletin.

382   FR
CHAMBRE FRANCO ALLEMANDE DE COMMERCE ET D'INDUSTRIE. LISTE DES MEMBRES. 1966. a. 240 F. Chambre Franco Allemande de Commerce et d'Industrie, 18 rue Balard, 75015 Paris, France. TEL 40-58-35-35. FAX 45-75-47-39. TELEX 203-738 CFACI.
Formerly: Chambre Officielle Franco Allemande de Commerce et d'Industrie. Liste des Membres (ISSN 0069-2581).

967   FT
CHAMBRE INTERNATIONALE DE COMMERCE ET D'INDUSTRIE DE DJIBOUTI. BULLETIN PERIODIQUE. (Text in French) m. Chambre Internationale de Commerce et d'Industrie de Djibouti, B.P. 84, Djibouti, Djibouti.
Formerly (until 1979): Chambre de Commerce et d'Industrie de Djibouti. Bulletin Periodique.

381   FR
CHAMBRE REGIONALE DE COMMERCE ET D'INDUSTRIE D'ALSACE. RAPPORT SUR LES ACTIVITES. a. Chambre Regionale de Commerce et d'Industrie d'Alsace, 42 rue Schweighaeuser, 67000 Strasbourg, France. TEL 33-3-88607475. FAX 33-3-88615354.

944   FR   ISSN 0220-9241
CHAMBRE REGIONALE DE COMMERCE ET D'INDUSTRIE PROVENCE - ALPES - COTE D'AZUR - CORSE. CONJONCTURE. 1973. q. 180 F. Chambre Regionale de Commerce et d'Industrie Provence - Alpes - Cote d'Azur - Corse, 8 rue Neuve St. Martin, BP 1880, 13222 Marseille Cedex 1, France. TEL 33-4-91144200. FAX 33-4-91144245.
Formerly (until 1978): Chambre Regionale de Commerce et d'Industrie de la Provence - Cote d'Azur - Corse. Conjoncture (ISSN 0220-9233).

382 961.1   TI
CHAMBRE TUNISO-FRANCAISE DE COMMERCE ET D'INDUSTRIE. BULLETIN D'INFORMATION. q. Chambre Tuniso - Francaise de Commerce et d'Industrie (CTFCI), 14 Rue de la Monnaie, 1001 Tunis, Tunisia. TEL 01-253545. TELEX 14463.

384   FR   ISSN 1146-8599
LA CHAMPAGNE ECONOMIQUE; magazine mensuel d'information economique des Chambres de Commerce et d'Industrie de la Marne. 1946. 9/yr. 160 F.; newsstand price: 25 F. Chambre de Commerce et d'Industrie de Reims et d'Epernay, 5 rue des Marmouzets, B.P. 2511, 51070 Reims Cedex, France. TEL 33-3-26506200. FAX 33-3-26506289. E-mail: info@reims.cci.fr. (Alt. addr.: 2 rue de Chastillon, B.P. 533, 51010 Chalons-en-Champagne Cedex, France. TEL 33-3-26211133. FAX 33-3-26684707) Ed. Michel Clary; Pub. Jean-Pierre Appert. adv.; pap 10000 F. bk.rev. circ. 17,000. (back issues avail.) **Document type:** trade publication, monographic series.
Description: Contains practical information on various industrial, commercial and service businesses in the Marne region. Includes contributions on the organization's financial status.

381   UK
CITY AND COUNTY.* 1934. m. 50p. Leicester & County Chamber of Commerce, 4-6 New St., Leicester LE1 5HT, England. Ed. A.H. Green. adv.; bk.rev.; illus.; stat.; index. circ. 2,000.
Formerly: Leicester and County Chamber of Commerce Journal (ISSN 0024-0648).

380   EC   ISSN 0008-1868
COMERCIANTE.* 1965. m. S/100($10.) Av. Olmedo 414, Guayaquil, Ecuador. adv.; abstr.; illus.; stat. (microform)
Supersedes: Camara de Comercio de Guayaquil. Revista.

330   CR
COMERCIO. 1975. q. free. Camara de Comercio de Costa Rica, Barrio Tournon, Apdo. 1114, San Jose, Costa Rica.
Formerly: Camara de Comercio. Boletin Informativo (ISSN 0010-9630).

380   HO   ISSN 0010-2245
COMERCIO. 1970. m. free. (Camara de Comercio e Industrias de Tegucigalpa) Honduras Industrial, S. A., Apdo. Postal No. 17-G, Tegucigalpa, D.C., Honduras. TEL 32-8210. FAX 31-2049. Ed. Jorge Mejia Ortega. adv.; bk.rev. circ. 3,500.

380   EC   ISSN 0010-2296
COMERCIO ECUATORIANO. 1906. m. S/300($10) membership. Camara de Comercio de Quito, Avenidas Amazonas y de la Republica, Apdo. 202, Quito, Ecuador. TEL 453-011. TELEX 2638. Ed. Marcelo Eguez Toro. adv.; stat.

946.9   SP
COMERCIO EXTERIOR DE LA COMUNIDAD VALENCIANA. 1973. a. Camara Oficial de Comercio, Industria y Navegacion de Valencia, Poeta Querol 15, 46002 Valencia, Spain. TEL 34-6-3511301. FAX 34-6-3516349. (Co-sponsors: Camaras Oficiales de Comercio, Industria y Navegacion de Alcoy, Alicante, Castellon, Orihuela)
Formerly (until 1986): Region Exporta (ISSN 0211-8866)

382   UK   ISSN 0010-2326
COMERCIO HISPANO BRITANICO. (Text in English, Spanish) 1908. 6/yr. free. Spanish Chamber of Commerce in Great Britain, 5 Cavendish Sq., London WIM 0DP, England. TEL 44-171-637-9061. FAX 44-171-436-7188. TELEX 8811583-CAMCOE-G. Eds. Helen Beasley, J. Fernandez Bragado. R&P contact: Helen Beasley. adv. contact: Helen Beasley. bk.rev.; stat.; circ. 1,500 (controlled). **Document type:** trade publication.

380   PO
COMERCIO, INDUSTRIA, SERVICOS. 1939. 4/yrn. membership. Associacao Comercial de Lisboa, Camara de Comercio e Industria Portuguesa, Rua das Portas de Santo Antao 89, 1194 Lisbon Codex, Portugal. TEL 363355. Ed. Sergio Teixeira de Queiroz. adv.; illus.; stat. circ. 3,000.
Formerly (until 1975): Comercio Portugues (ISSN 0010-2334)

380 338   DR   ISSN 0010-2342
COMERCIO Y PRODUCCION. 1943. m. RD.$3.60. Camara de Comercio Agricultura e Industria del Distrito Nacional, Inc., Calle Arzobispo Nouel 206, Apdo. Postal 815, Santo Domingo, Dominican Republic. Ed. Virgilio Hoepelman. adv.; bk.rev. circ. 1,500.

380 338   PE   ISSN 0008-1892
COMERCIO Y PRODUCCION. 1929. w. Camara de Comercio de Lima, Av. Gregorio Escobedo 398, Lima 11, Peru. TEL 51-14619864. FAX 51-14633686. Ed. Pedro A. Flores Polo. adv.; mkt.; stat.; index. circ. 2,500.
Incorporates: Camara de Comercio de Lima. Boletin Semanal - Informativo Legal; Which was formed by the merger of: Camara de Comercio de Lima. Boletin Semanal (ISSN 0008-1884); Camara de Comercio de Lima. Informativo Legal; Formerly: Camara de Comercio de Lima. Revista Mensual.

380 338   PR   ISSN 0010-2350
COMERCIO Y PRODUCCION. (Text in English, Spanish) 1960. bi-m. $15. Chamber of Commerce of Puerto Rico, Box 3789, San Juan, PR 00904. Ed. Sixto Toro Cintron. adv.; charts; illus.; stat.; tr.lit.; circ. 1,500 (controlled). (processed)

382   AG   ISSN 0010-2660
COMMENTS ON ARGENTINE TRADE. (Text in English) 1919. bi-m. $35 (foreign $75). American Chamber of Commerce in Argentina, Viamonte 1133, p. 8, 1053 Buenos Aires, Argentina. TEL 54-1-3714500. FAX 54-1-3718400. Ed. Antonio Lofeudo. R&P contact: Antonio Lofeudo. adv. contact: Mariana Urrestarazu. bk.rev.; illus.; stat.; tr.lit.; index. circ. 2,500. **Indexed:** P.A.I.S. **Document type:** trade publication.
Formerly: AmCham Weekly News.

380   CN
COMMERCE COMMENTS. 1968. m. Can.$25.68. Calgary Chamber of Commerce, 517 Center St. S., Calgary, AB T2G 2C4, Canada. TEL 403-750-0400. FAX 403-266-3413. Ed. R. Glenn Tackaberry. adv. contact: Yasmin Irani. illus. circ. 15,000. **Document type:** consumer publication.
Former titles: Calgary Commerce (ISSN 0707-8064); Calgary Business; Calgary Chamber of Commerce. Business News (ISSN 0382-7887).
Description: Dedicated to the support of orderly community development and the promotion of fair and honest practice of private competitive enterprise.

382   FR   ISSN 0222-6618
COMMERCE ET COOPERATION. 1970. 4/yr. 200 F. Chambre de Commerce Franco-Rousse, 22 av. F.D. Roosevelt, 75008 Paris, France. TEL 42-25-97-10. FAX 43-59-74-73. TELEX 280 909. Ed. Benedicte Martin. adv. circ. 500.

944   FR   ISSN 0996-1860
COMMERCE ET INDUSTRIE DE L'INDRE. 1952. 5/yr. 24 place Gambetta, 36028 Chateauroux Cedex, France. TEL 54-53-52-51. FAX 54-34-17-77. TELEX 750 534. Ed. Andre Blanc-Bernard. circ. 8,000.

382   FR
COMMERCE EXTERIEUR DES REGIONS PROVENCE, COTE D'AZUR ET CORSE. 1968. a. 115 F. per no. Chambre de Commerce et d'Industrie de Marseille, Immeuble CMCI, 2 rue Henri Barbasse, 13241 Marseille Cedex 1, France. Ed. Rene Delboy. illus. circ. 600.

382   SZ   ISSN 0010-2830
COMMERCE FRANCO-SUISSE. 1894. 4/yr. membership. Chambre France-Suisse Pour le Commerce et l'Industrie, 32 Av. de Frontenex, 1211 Geneva 6, Switzerland. adv.; bk.rev.; bibl.; illus.; pat.; stat.; tr.lit. tr.mk.; index. circ. 5,000. **Indexed:** Key to Econ.Sci.

BUSINESS AND ECONOMICS — CHAMBER OF COMMERCE PUBLICATIONS

382 RH
COMMERCE - ZIMBABWE. m. Z.$106.80 (foreign Z.$128.40) (effective 1997). (Zimbabwe National Chamber of Commerce) Thomson Publications Zimbabwe (Pvt) Ltd., Thomson House, P.O. Box 1683, Harare, Zimbabwe. TEL 263-4-736835. FAX 263-4-752390. adv. **Document type:** trade publication.
Formerly: Commerce - Rhodesia.

380 MM ISSN 0010-2938
COMMERCIAL COURIER. (Text in English) 1947. m. Malta Chamber of Commerce, The Exchange, Republic St., Valletta VLT 05, Malta. FAX 356-245223. Ed. Kevin J. Borg. R&P contact: Kevin J. Borg. adv.; bk.rev. circ. 1,500. **Indexed:** Key to Econ.Sci. **Document type:** bulletin.
Description: Official organ of the Malta Chamber of Commerce.

977 US
▼**COMMUNITY IMPROVEMENT PROJECTS & FUNDING.** 1995. m. $119. Hakes Publications, Box 343, Storm Lake, IA 50588. TEL 712-732-7718. E-mail: hakes@bvu.edu. Ed. Richard L. Hakes; Pub. Richard L. Hakes. R&P contact: Richard L. Hakes. circ. 250 (paid). (looseleaf format; back issues avail.) **Document type:** newsletter.
Description: For mayors, city administrators, chamber of commerce executives and other community leaders.

381 CK
CONFEDERACION COLOMBIANA DE CAMARAS DE COMERCIO. ASAMBLEA GENERAL. INFORME FINAL.* 1970. irreg. free. Confederacion Colombiana de Camaras de Comercio, Carrera 13, no. 27-47, Oficina 502, Apdo. 29750, Bogota, Colombia. circ. 1,000.

380 CK
CONFEDERACION COLOMBIANA DE CAMARAS DE COMERCIO. SINTESIS MENSUAL.* 1969. m. Col.$400($10) Confederacion Colombiana de Camaras de Comercio, Carrera 13, no. 27-47, Oficina 502, Apdo. 29750, Bogota, Colombia. Ed. Alvaro Garcia. illus. circ. 8,000.

382 381 FR
CONTACT; economie franco-allemande. (Text in French, German) 10/yr. 450 F. Chambre Franco-Allemande de Commerce et d'Industrie, 18 rue Balard, 75015 Paris, France. TEL 40-58-35-35. FAX 45-75-47-39. TELEX 203738. adv.; bk.rev.; bibl.; pat.; stat. circ. 3,000.

382 IT
CONTACTS FRANCO-ITALIENS. (Text in French, Italian) 1885. bi-m. L.120000. Chambre Francaise de Commerce et d'Industrie a Milan - Camera Francese di Commercio ed Industria in Italia, Via Borgonuovo 18, 20121 Milan, Italy. TEL 39-2-6575847. Ed. Eric Sauvaire. adv.; B&W page L.1150000, color page L.1550000. bk.rev. circ. 1,500.
Description: Forum covering articles on the economic life in Italy and France. Includes monthly letters, French subsidiaries and a list of members.

945 IT
CORRIERE DEL COMMERCIO. 20/yr. Associazione Commercianti della Provincia di Bologna, Strada Maggiore 23, Bologna, Italy. Ed. Franco Fabbri. adv. circ. 20,000.

338 916 UV ISSN 0574-3370
COURRIER CONSULAIRE DU BURKINA FASO. (Text in French) 1960. m. 14000 Fr.CFA. Chambre de Commerce, d'Industrie et d'Artisanat, 01 Box 502, Ouagadougou 01, Burkina Faso. TEL 30-61-14. FAX 30-61-16. TELEX 5268 BF. charts; stat.
Formerly: Courrier Consulaire de la Haute Volta.
Description: Contains legislative and statutory notices.

946 SP
COYUNTURA INDUSTRIAL. BOLETIN. m. Camara Oficial de Comercio, Industria y Navegacion de Tarragona, Av. de Colon, 2, Tarragona, Spain. **Document type:** bulletin.

382 FR
CROSS CHANNEL. 1952. bi-m. 250 F. Franco-British Chamber of Commerce and Industry, 31 rue Boissy d'Anglas, 75008 Paris, France. TEL 33-1-53308130. FAX 33-1-53308135. Ed. Catherine Le Yaouanc. adv.; bk.rev. circ. 2,000.
Formerly (until 1992): Cross Channel Trade (ISSN 0983-1487)

338 UK
CROYDON AND SOUTH LONDON CHAMBER OF COMMERCE AND INDUSTRY DIRECTORY. a. £35. Kemps Publishing Ltd., 11 The Swan Courtyard, Charles Edward Rd., Birmingham B26 1BU, England. TEL 44-121-765-4144. FAX 44-121-706-6210. **Document type:** directory.
Former titles: Croydon Chamber of Commerce Directory; Southern Home Counties Chamber of Commerce Directory; Southern Home Counties Directory; Croydon Chamber of Commerce and Industry Directory (ISSN 0144-2996)

382 CU ISSN 0864-3857
HF300.C9
CUBA FOREIGN TRADE. (Text in English and Spanish) 1963-1972; resumed 1987. q. $16 in America; Europe $20; elsewhere $24 (effective 1992). Camara de Comercio - Chamber of Commerce, Calle 21 No. 661, esq. A, Casilla 4237, Vedado, Havana, Cuba. TEL 809-30-3356. FAX 809-333042. TELEX 51-1752. adv.; B&W page $700, color page $1035; trim 215 x 280; adv. contact: Sandra Gonzalez. illus.; index. circ. 6,000. **Document type:** trade publication.

954 380 II
D C C TRADE DIRECTORY. 1982. a. free to members, chamber of commerce and trade associations. Delhi Chamber of Commerce, Sodhbans Chambers, 9104 D.B. Gupta Rd., Paharganj 110 055, New Delhi, India. TEL 91-11-7516421. FAX 91-11-7528847. TELEX 31-61826 DCC IN. adv. circ. 3,000. **Document type:** directory.
Description: Readers service to importers and exporters in the world.

382 AU
D H K WIRTSCHAFTSSPIEGEL. 1964. 10/yr. membership. Deutsche Handelskammer in Oesterreich, Wiedner Hauptstr. 142, A-1050 Vienna, Austria. TEL 01-5451417. FAX 01-5452259. Ed. Florien Hoeland. adv.; B&W page S.18000, color page S.27000; trim 185 x 250; adv. contact: Corina Kaltenhauser. bk.rev.; charts; illus.; stat.; tr.lit. circ. 9,000. (tabloid format; also avail. in cards) **Document type:** trade publication.
Formerly: Deutsche Handelskammer in Oesterreich. Bulletin (ISSN 0012-0251)

972 MX ISSN 0185-1985
DECISION; comercio, servicios y turismo. 1979. m. Mex.$100 (America $50; elsewhere $55). Confederacion de Camaras Nacionales de Comercio, Servicios y Turismo, Balderas 144, 2o Piso, Apdo. Postal 113, 06079 Mexico, D.F., Mexico. TEL 709-15-59 ext. 249. FAX 709-11-52. Ed. Carlos Arrieta Davila. adv. contact: Nelia Sanchez Mendez. bk.rev. circ. 30,000.
Description: Publishes economic, political, commercial, and tourism and service industry information.

954
DELHI CHAMBER OF COMMERCE. BULLETIN. bi-w. free to members, chamber of commerce and trade associations. Delhi Chamber of Commerce, Sodhbans Chambers, 9104 D.B. Gupta Rd., Paharganj, New Delhi 10 055, India. TEL 91-11-7516421. FAX 91-11-7528847. TELEX 31-61826 DCC IN. adv. circ. 1,200. **Document type:** bulletin.
Description: Renders service to importers and exporters world wide.

381 US ISSN 0011-9709
DETROITER. 1910. m. $18 to non-members; members $18 (effective 1997). Greater Detroit Chamber Communications Inc., 600 W. Lafayette, Box 33840, Detroit, MI 48232-0840. TEL 313-596-0373. E-mail: cmead@detroitchamber.com; vbollin@detroitchamber.com; URL: http://www.detroitchamber.com. Ed. Chris Mead; Pub. Richard E. Blouse Jr. adv. contact: Valerie Bollinn. bk.rev.; illus. circ. 17,000. (also avail. in microform from UMI; reprint service avail.) **Indexed:** Mich.Mag.Ind.
●Also available online. Vendor(s): UMI.
—UMI.
Incorporates: Chamber Business News (ISSN 1061-1649); **Formerly:** Detroiter Business News.
Description: Covers business in Greater Detroit.

944 FR ISSN 0184-878X
DIEPPE INFO. q. free. 4 bd. du General-de-Gaulle, 76374 Dieppe Cedex, France. TEL 35-06-50-50. FAX 35-06-50-51. TELEX 180 770 CHAMLOM. Ed. Corinne Emo; Pub. Christophe Maurel. circ. 3,800.
Former titles (until 1977): Doc Info (ISSN 0184-8771); (until 1975): Via Dieppe (ISSN 0335-2935)

980 ES
DIRECTORIO COMERCIAL E INDUSTRIAL. (Text and summaries in English, Spanish) 1970. a. $12. (Camara de Comercio e Industria de El Salvador) Ediciones Culturales Publicitarias, S.A., 57 Avenida Norte No. 114, Colonia Escalon, San Salvador, El Salvador. (Subscr. to: 9a Avenida Norte y 5a, Calle Poniente, San Salvador, El Salvador) adv.; index. circ. 2,000.

382 MX
DIRECTORY OF AMERICAN COMPANIES. (Text in English, Spanish) irreg. $200. American Chamber of Commerce of Mexico, A.C., Lucerna 78, Col. Juarez, Del. Cuauhtemoc, 06600 Mexico DF, Mexico. TEL 52-5-724-3800. FAX 52-5-703-2911. TELEX 177-7609 ACHAME. R&P contact: Mariana Prado. **Document type:** trade publication.
Description: Supplies details on 2900 US firms operating in Mexico, Mexican companies, products and services manufactured, sold or offered by representative firms, and US locations.

381 CE
DIRECTORY OF EXPORTERS. (Text in English) 1975. biennial. $25. Ceylon Chamber of Commerce, Export Section, Chamber of Commerce Bldg., Box 274, Colombo 2, Sri Lanka. FAX 941-449352. adv. **Document type:** directory.

DIRECTORY OF INDUSTRIAL PRODUCTS: MADE IN SHARJAH, UNITED ARAB EMIRATES/DALEEL AL MONTAJAT AL SINA'IAH: SON'I FI AL SHARIQAH. see BUSINESS AND ECONOMICS — Trade And Industrial Directories

941 UK
DIRECTORY OF THE BRISTOL AND WESTERN CHAMBERS OF COMMERCE. a. £50. (Bristol Chamber of Commerce & Industry) Kemps Publishing Ltd., 11 The Swan Courtyard, Charles Edward Rd., Birmingham B26 1BU, England. TEL 44-121-765-4144. FAX 44-121-706-6210. adv. **Document type:** directory.
Former titles: Bristol Business Reference Book; (until 1993): Bristol Chamber of Commerce and Industry Directory.

940 UK
DIRECTORY OF U.S. SUBSIDIARIES OF BRITISH COMPANIES. 1976. a. $95 (diskette $299; CD-ROM $299). British - American Chamber of Commerce, 52 Vanderbilt Ave., Ste. 20, New York, NY 10017-3808. TEL 212-661-4060. URL: http://www.bacc.org. R&P contact: Molly Hayes. adv. contact: Molly Hayes. circ. 1,200. (also avail. in diskette format) **Document type:** directory.
●Also available on CD-ROM.
Description: Lists British firms and their subsidiaries in the US, Canada and Mexico, as well as American firms and their subsidiaries in Britain.

986.1 CK
DOCTRINA MERCANTIL. a. Camara de Comercio de Bogota, Carrera 9, No. 16-21, Piso 8, Apdo. Aereo 29824, Bogota, Colombia.

BUSINESS AND ECONOMICS — CHAMBER OF COMMERCE PUBLICATIONS

381   US   ISSN 0012-7116
DULUTHIAN. 1965. bi-m. free to members. Duluth Area Chamber of Commerce, 118 E. Superior St., Duluth, MN 55802. TEL 218-722-5501. Ed. Gina Chiodi Greene; Pub. Gina Chiodi Greene. adv.; bk.rev.; charts; illus.; tr.lit.; index. circ. 2,000. (also avail. in microform from UMI) **Document type:** newsletter.
●Also available online. Vendor(s): UMI.
—UMI.

381   UK
DUNDEE AND TAYSIDE CHAMBER OF COMMERCE AND INDUSTRY. BUYER'S GUIDE AND TRADE DIRECTORY. 1958. a. £7.50. Dundee and Tayside Chamber of Commerce and Industry, Panmure St., Dundee DD1 1ED, Scotland. Ed. W.D. Shaw. adv. circ. 1,800 (controlled). **Document type:** directory.
Formerly: Dundee Chamber of Commerce. Buyer's Guide and Trade Directory.

338   UK   ISSN 0306-0241
DUNDEE TAYSIDE; industry in the Tayside region. 1958. q. £1.50. Dundee and Tayside Chamber of Commerce and Industry, Chamber of Commerce Bldgs, Panmure St., Dundee DD1 1ED, Scotland. Ed. W.D. Shaw. adv. circ. controlled. **Document type:** trade publication.
—BLDSC (3631.125300).
Formerly: Dundee Chamber of Commerce Journal (ISSN 0012-7124)

944   FR   ISSN 0243-2633
DUNKERQUE EXPANSION. 36/yr. Dunkerque Expansion, 1 rue du Rempart, 59140 Dunkerque, France. TEL 33-3-28664761. FAX 33-3-28662104. TELEX 820 970. Ed. Laurence Desbischop. adv. contact: Laurence Desbischop. circ. 6,000. **Document type:** newspaper.

381   SA
DURBAN CHAMBER OF COMMERCE AND INDUSTRY. CHAMBER DIGEST. 1953. fortn. Durban Chamber of Commerce and Industry, P.O. Box 1506, Durban 4000, South Africa. TEL 27-31-3013692. E-mail: chambers@iafrica.com; URL: http://www.durban.org.za/chamber/. Ed. N. Thomson; Pub. Lorraine Wheal. R&P contact: N. Thomson. adv. contact: Lorraine Wheal. Indexed: Ind.S.A.Per. **Document type:** bulletin.
Formerly (until 1993): Durban Regional Chamber of Business. Information Digest (ISSN 0250-1740)

EAST MERCIA CHAMBER OF COMMERCE & INDUSTRY DIRECTORY. see BUSINESS AND ECONOMICS — Trade And Industrial Directories

381   US   ISSN 0012-8538
EAST SIDE CHAMBER OF COMMERCE NEWSLETTER. 1956. bi-m. free. East Side Chamber of Commerce, Box 3380, New York, NY 10008-3380. TEL 212-233-2470. FAX 212-233-1965. Ed. Sidney Baumgarten. adv. contact: Sidney Baumgarten. charts. circ. 500. **Document type:** newsletter.

974 346   US
EAST - WEST LEGAL UPDATE. s-a. $125 to non-members. United States Council for International Business, 1212 Ave. of the Americas, New York, NY 10036-1689. TEL 212-354-4480. FAX 212-575-0327. Ed. Melinda Hanisch. **Document type:** newsletter.

382   GW   ISSN 0723-2179
ECONOMIA; Zeitschrift der Italienischen Handelskammer fuer Deutschland. (Text in German, Italian) 1950. q. DM.50 (effective 1997). Italienische Handelskammer fuer Deutschland - Camera di Commercio Italiana per la Germania, Bockenheimer Landstr. 59, 60325 Frankfurt a.M., Germany. TEL 49-69-97145101. FAX 49-69-97145299. E-mail: ccigermany@ithk.ccmail.compuserve.com. adv.: B&W page DM.2000; trim 178 x 260; adv. contact: Kathrin Walter. bk.rev.; circ. 3,000. Indexed: ELLIS. **Document type:** bulletin.

330.9   SP   ISSN 0568-8876
HC387.A53
ECONOMIA ALAVESA. a. 2000 ptas. Camara Oficial de Comercio e Industria de Alava, Dato 38, 01005 Vitoria, Spain. TEL 34-45-141800. FAX 34-45-143156. TELEX 35515. Ed. D. Lorenzo Bergareche Capa. index. circ. 1,000.

330   IT   ISSN 0012-9747
ECONOMIA ARETINA. 1922. m. L.30000. Camera di Commercio Industria Artigianato e Agricoltura di Arezzo, Viale Giotto 4, Arezzo, Italy. Ed. Ludovico Loslovichi. adv. contact: Piero Innocenti. bk.rev.; charts; illus.; mkt.; stat. circ. 1,400. **Document type:** bulletin.
—BLDSC (3650.300000).
Formerly: Rassegna Economica (Arezzo).

330   IT   ISSN 0391-6332
ECONOMIA BRINDISINA. 1975. bi-m. L.10000. Camera di Commercio, Industria, Artigianato e Agricoltura di Brindisi, Via Congregazione, Brindisi, Italy. charts; illus.; stat.

330   IT
ECONOMIA DELLA MARCA TREVIGIANA. 1903. w. free. Camera di Commercio Industria Artigianato e Agricoltura di Treviso, Piazza della Borsa, 31100 Treviso, Italy. TEL 39-422-5951. FAX 39-422-412625. TELEX 410672 TVCAM I. Ed. Armando Mosca. adv. circ. 5,200. (tabloid format)

330   SP   ISSN 0211-4763
ECONOMIA GUIPUZCOANA. 1965. 4/yr. free. Camara Oficial de Comercio, Industria y Navegacion de Guipuzcoa, Ramon Maria Lili, 6, San Sebastian, Spain. TEL 43-27-2100. FAX 43-29-3105. TELEX 36529 CAMIN E. Ed. Felix Iraola. adv.; abstr.; illus.; stat.; circ. 12,000 (controlled). **Document type:** bulletin.

945   IT
ECONOMIA ISONTINA. 1960. m. L.20000. Camera di Commercio, Industria, Artigianato, Agricoltura (Gorizia), Via Francesco Crispi, 10, 34170 Gorizia, Italy. TEL 39-481-3841. FAX 39-481-533176. Dir. Renato Chahinian. adv. **Document type:** bulletin.
Description: Covers the Chamber's activities, domestic economic system, and economic relations with Eastern European countries.

330   IT   ISSN 0391-6359
ECONOMIA PESARESE. 1948. bi-m. L.45000 (effective 1993). Camera di Commercio Industria, Artigianato e Agricoltura di Pesaro e Urbino, Corso XI Settembre 116, 61100 Pesaro, Italy. TEL 0721-3571. FAX 0721-31015. TELEX 560229 CAMCOM. Ed. Paolo Lamaro. adv. circ. 1,500. **Document type:** bulletin, monographic series.
Description: Includes articles on economic subjects and activities of the organization.

330   IT   ISSN 0012-9879
ECONOMIA TRENTINA. 1952. q. L.37000 (effective Jan. 1992). Camera di Commercio, Industria, Artigianato e Agricoltura di Trento, Via Calepina 13, 38100 Trento, Italy. TEL 39-461-887111. FAX 39-461-986356. TELEX 400469. Ed. Ezio Marco Tomasi. adv. contact: Giorgio Baldi. circ. 1,100. Indexed: P.A.I.S.For.Lang.Ind.
—BLDSC (3651.130000).
Formerly: Economia Atesina.

330   II   ISSN 0970-6453
ECONOMIC TRENDS. (Supplement avail.: Parliament News) (Text in English) 1970. q. Rs.1000($90) Federation of Indian Chambers of Commerce and Industry, Federation House, Tansen Marg, New Delhi 110 001, India. TEL 11-3319251. FAX 11-3320714. TELEX 031-61768. Ed. Joseph Thachil. adv.; bk.rev.; bibl.; charts; stat.; tr.lit. circ. 3,000. (processed; reprint service avail. from SCH)
Formerly: Federation of Indian Chambers of Commerce and Industry. Fortnightly Review (ISSN 0014-9470)

381   SZ
ECONOMIE LAUSANNOISE. q. Case Postale 62, CH-1018 Lausanne, Switzerland. TEL 021-361704. circ. 2,500.

330   LE   ISSN 0013-0540
ECONOMIE LIBANAISE ET ARABE.* vol.19, 1970. bi-m. £40($20) Chambre de Commerce et d'Industrie de Beyrouth, Rue Allenby, P.O.B. 1801, Immeuble Avass, Beirut, Lebanon. Ed. Sami N. Atiyeh. adv.; charts; illus.; stat.
Description: Survey of economic developments in Lebanon.

969.82   MF
ECONOMY IN FIGURES. a. free. Mauritius Chamber of Commerce and Industry, 3 Royal St., Port Louis, Mauritius. TEL 230-208-3301. FAX 230-208-0076. E-mail: mccipl@bow.intnet.mu. circ. 1,200. **Document type:** trade publication.
Formerly: Facts and Figures.

382   EC
ECUADOR BUSINESS & COMMERCE. m. $3 per no. Ecuadorian - American Chamber of Commerce, Edif. Multicentro, 4P, La Nina y 6 Diciembre, Quito, Ecuador. TEL 5932-507-450. FAX 5932-504-571. circ. 2,000. **Document type:** consumer publication.
Formerly: Comercio Ecuatoriano Americano - Ecuadorian American Business.

382   EC
ECUADORIAN - AMERICAN CHAMBER OF COMMERCE. ANNUAL DIRECTORY. a. $40. Ecuadorian - American Chamber of Commerce, Edif. Multicentro, 4P, La Nina y 6 Diciembre, Quito, Ecuador. TEL 5932-507-450. FAX 5932-504-571. circ. 1,000. **Document type:** directory.

381   UK
EDINBURGH CHAMBER OF COMMERCE AND MANUFACTURES JOURNAL. 1918. q. Edinburgh Chamber of Commerce and Manufactures, 3 Randolph Crescent, Edinburgh EH3 7UD, Scotland.

381   CN   ISSN 0704-8017
EDMONTON CHAMBER OF COMMERCE. COMMERCE NEWS. 1976. m. Can.$1 per no. Edmonton Chamber of Commerce, Suite 600, 10123-99 St., Edmonton, AB T5J 3G9, Canada. TEL 403-426-4620. FAX 403-424-7946. Ed. Gary Slywchuk; Pub. Martin Salloum. adv.: B&W page Can.$1695, color page $2190; trim 11 1/4 x 13 1/2; adv. contact: Rita Boyce. bk.rev.; illus.; circ. 54,000 (controlled). **Document type:** newspaper.
●Also available online. Vendor(s): UMI.
—UMI.

380   UA
EGYPTIAN CHAMBER OF COMMERCE. BULLETIN. (Text in English) m. Egyptian Chamber of Commerce, 4 Midan Falaki, Cairo, Egypt. **Document type:** bulletin.

956.1   TU
EKONOMI/ECONOMY. 1978. w. Turkish Cypriot Chamber of Commerce, Bedrettin Demirel Ave., P.O. Box 718, Lefkosa, Mersin 10, Turkey. TEL 90-392-2283760. FAX 90-392-2283089. TELEX 57511. circ. 3,000. **Document type:** newspaper.

945   IT   ISSN 1120-3951
ELENCO UFFICIALE DEI PROTESTI CAMBIARI. 1955. s-m. L.30000 (effective 1997). Camera di Commercio, Industria, Artigianato e Agricoltura di Ferrara, Via Borgoleoni, 11, 44100 Ferrara, Italy. TEL 39-532-783711. FAX 39-532-240204. Dir. Pietro Cocurullo.
Formerly: Elenco dei Protesti Cambiari.

332   IT   ISSN 0013-6050
ELENCO UFFICIALE DEI PROTESTI CAMBIARI LEVATI NELLA PROVINCIA DI TORINO. 1955. fortn. L.240000 (effective 1997). Camera di Commercio Industria Artigianato e Agricoltura di Torino, Via. S. Francesco da Paola 24, 10123 Turin, Italy. TEL 39-11-57161. FAX 39-11-5716516. Ed. Franco Alunno. circ. 1,300.

EMPLOYEE BENEFITS; survey data from benefit (year). see BUSINESS AND ECONOMICS — Personnel Management

382   SI
ENQUIRES. bi-w. Singapore Indian Chamber of Commerce, 101 Cecil St., 23-01 Tong Eng Bldg., Singapore 0106, Singapore. FAX 65-223-1707.

338 974   US
ENRICH; information bank briefings for network members. 1985. m. $60. National Chamber of Commerce for Women, 10 Waterside Plaza, Ste. 6H New York, NY 10010. TEL 212-685-3454. Ed. Teresa Lauren; Pub. R. Wright. R&P contact: Teresa Lauren. adv. contact: R. Wright. bk.rev.; charts; illus. circ. 4,700. (back issues avail.)
Description: Provides business plan formats, results and analysis, plus next-step guidelines for women in business, and pay range reports for women in salaried positions.

BUSINESS AND ECONOMICS — CHAMBER OF COMMERCE PUBLICATIONS

381   CN   ISSN 0046-2136
ENTERPRISER. 1969. q. membership. Alberta Chamber of Commerce, 2105 T.D. Tower, Edmonton Centre, Edmonton, AB T5J 2Z1, Canada. TEL 403-425-4180. FAX 403-429-1061. Ed. Patrick J. McKenna. adv.; bk.rev. circ. 1,000.

330   BE   ISSN 0770-2264
ENTREPRENDRE. 1875. m. membership. Chambre de Commerce de Bruxelles, 500 av. Louise, Brussels, Belgium. Ed. Philippe D'Houdt. adv. contact: Robert Demarche. bibl.; charts; index. circ. 10,000. **Indexed:** Pt.de Rep. Document type: trade publication.
Formerly (until vol.106, no.3, 1980): Chambre de Commerce de Bruxelles. Bulletin Officiel (ISSN 0009-1197)

960   IV
L'ENTREPRISE IVOIRIENNE. a. Chambre d'Industrie de Cote d'Ivoire, B.P. 1758, Abidjan, Ivory Coast.

381   SZ   ISSN 1013-3089
ENTREPRISE ROMANDE. 1933. 46/yr. 98 Rue de St. Jean, CH-1211 Geneva 11, Switzerland. TEL 022-7153244. FAX 022-7313642. Ed. Didier Fleck. circ. 19,937.
Formerly (until 1983): Ordre Professionnel (ISSN 1013-3070)

944   FR   ISSN 0755-6306
ENTREPRISES MIDI-PYRENEES. 1983. 11/yr. 11 bd. des Recollets, 31078 Toulouse Cedex, France. TEL 61-52-75-92. FAX 61-55-59-20. TELEX 520 267. Ed. Emma Bao. circ. 10,000.

382   FR   ISSN 0758-6671
L'ESPAGNE. 1960. m. Camara de Comercio de Espana, 32 av. de l'Opera, 75002 Paris, France. TEL 74245574. TELEX 212259.

ETHIOPIAN TRADE DIRECTORY. see *BUSINESS AND ECONOMICS — Trade And Industrial Directories*

963   ET
ETHIOPIAN TRADE JOURNAL. (Not published 1970-1980) (Text in English) vol.5, 1967. q. $16. Ethiopian Chamber of Commerce, P.O. Box 517, Addis Ababa, Ethiopia. Ed. Getachew Zicke. circ. 3,000. Document type: trade publication.

974   US
EUROPEAN COMMUNITY AFFAIRS. bi-m. United States Council for International Business, 1212 Ave. of the Americas, New York, NY 10036. TEL 212-354-4480.
Formerly: Enterprise and Development.

382   SI   ISSN 0129-5225
EXPATRIATE LIVING COSTS IN SINGAPORE. (Text in English) 1970. a. S.$10 per no. Singapore International Chamber of Commerce, 6 Raffles Quay, No. 10-01, John Hancock Tower, Singapore 048580, Singapore. TEL 65-2241255. FAX 65-2242785. TELEX RS 25235 INTCHAM. E-mail: singicc@asianconnect.com; URL: http://www.sicc.com.sg. circ. 8,000 (paid). Document type: consumer publication.
Description: Regularly updated guide on the cost of living of expatriate families in Singapore.

382   UK   ISSN 1351-4601
EXPORT HANDBOOK (YEAR). 1992. a. £30. (London Chamber of Commerce and Industry) Kogan Page Ltd., 120 Pentonville Rd., London N1 9JN, England. TEL 44-171-278-0433. FAX 44-171-837-6348. TELEX 263088 KOGAN G. R&P contact: Linda Batman. Document type: directory.

944   FR   ISSN 0985-0074
FACE. 9/yr. 350 F. Chambre de Commerce et Industrie de Lille, Place du Theatre, B.P. 121, 59001 Lille Cedex, France. TEL 33-3-20637866. FAX 33-3-20637863. Ed. Dominique Louvet. circ. 35,000.

956.45   CY
FAMAGUSTA CHAMBER OF COMMERCE AND INDUSTRY. TRADE INFORMATION BULLETIN. q. Famagusta Chamber of Commerce and Industry, Stylianides Bldg., 3rd Fl., P.O. Box 347, Koumandarias St., Limassol, Cyprus. TEL 357-5-170165. Document type: bulletin.

381   BG
FEDERATION OF BANGLADESH CHAMBERS OF COMMERCE AND INDUSTRY. FEDERATION JOURNAL.* (Text in English) q. Federation of Bangladesh Chambers of Commerce and Industry, 60 Motijheel Commercial Area, Dhaka 2, Bangladesh.

956.95   JO
FEDERATION OF JORDANIAN CHAMBERS OF COMMERCE. MAGAZINE. q. Federation of Jordanian Chambers of Commerce, P.O. Box 7029, Amman, Jordan. TEL 65492. TELEX 21543 CA CHAMBERS.

381   NP
FEDERATION OF NEPALESE CHAMBERS OF COMMERCE AND INDUSTRY. NEWSLETTER. (Text in Nepali) 1992. m. $6. Federation of Nepalese Chambers of Commerce and Industry, P.O. Box 269, Teku, Kathmandu, Nepal. TEL 977-1-233196. FAX 977-1-227322. Ed. Rameshwor Acharya. R&P contact: Rameswar Acharya. bk.rev. Document type: newsletter.

954.9   PK
FEDERATION OF PAKISTAN CHAMBERS OF COMMERCE AND INDUSTRY. ANNUAL REPORT. a. Federation of Pakistan Chambers of Commerce and Industry, St-28, Block 5, Scheme-V, Share-Firdousi-Kehkashan, Clifton, Karachi, Pakistan. TEL 534621. TELEX 25370 FEDCOMERC.

381   PK   ISSN 0071-4429
FEDERATION OF PAKISTAN CHAMBERS OF COMMERCE AND INDUSTRY. BRIEF REPORT OF ACTIVITIES. (Text in English) a. Rs.100. Federation of Pakistan Chambers of Commerce and Industry, St-28, Block 5, Scheme-V, Share-Firdousi Kehkashan, Clifton, Karachi, Pakistan.

FEDERATION OF PAKISTAN CHAMBERS OF COMMERCE AND INDUSTRY. DIRECTORY OF EXPORTERS. see *BUSINESS AND ECONOMICS — Trade And Industrial Directories*

954.9   PK
FEDERATION OF PAKISTAN CHAMBERS OF COMMERCE AND INDUSTRY. TRADE BULLETIN. bi-w. Federation of Pakistan Chambers of Commerce and Industry, St-28, Block 5, Scheme-V, Share-Firdousi-Kehkashan, Clifton, Karachi, Pakistan. TEL 534621. TELEX 25370 FEDCOMERC.

945   IT   ISSN 1120-396X
FERRARA ECONOMICA. 1987. bi-m. free. Camera di Commercio, Industria, Artigianato e Agricoltura di Ferrara, Via Borgoleoni, 11, 44100 Ferrara, Italy. TEL 39-532-783711. FAX 39-532-240204. Dir. Pietro Cocurullo.

330   IT
IL FILUGELLO. 1945. q. plus 1 monthly supplement. L.25000 (includes: Osservatorio Economico - Selezione Notizie). Camera di Commercio, Industria, Artigianato e Agricoltura, Piazza della Vittoria, 42100 Reggio Emilia, Italy. TEL 0522-7961. FAX 0522-433750. adv.; illus.; charts; stat. circ. 1,000.

382   SZ
FLASH INFORMATION.* bi-m. Chambre de Commerce Belgo-Luxembourgeoise en Suisse - Belgisch-Luxemburgische Handelskammer, Boersengebaeude, Bleicherweg 5, Postfach 4031, CH-8022 Zurich, Switzerland.

FLORIDA AND THE OTHER FORTY-NINE. see *BUSINESS AND ECONOMICS — Abstracting, Bibliographies, Statistics*

FLORIDA COUNTY COMPARISONS. see *BUSINESS AND ECONOMICS — Abstracting, Bibliographies, Statistics*

975   US
FLORIDA COUNTY PROFILES. 1979. a. free. Department of Commerce, Bureau of Economic Analysis, 107 W. Gaines St., Tallahassee, FL 32399-2000. TEL 904-487-2971. TELEX 510-6002141 FL TRADE TAS. stat.; circ. controlled.
Formerly: Florida Community-County Comparison.
Description: Sixty-seven individual Florida county profiles concerning business climate information.

338 380   UK
FOCUS (STOKE-ON-TRENT). 1952. bi-m. £30. (North Staffordshire Chamber of Commerce and Industry) Tudored Publishing Ltd., Brook St., Leek, Staffs ST13 5JL, England. TEL 44-1538-399998. FAX 44-1538-399967. Ed. David Cliffe. adv.: B&W page £600, color page £900; 275 x 185; adv. contact: Angela Smith. bk.rev.; illus. circ. 3,500. (tabloid format) Document type: newsletter.
Former titles: Focus on Industry and Commerce (ISSN 0015-5098); North Staffordshire Focus on Industry and Commerce.

382   FR   ISSN 0752-1537
FRANCE, BELGIQUE, LUXEMBOURG. Short title: F.B.L. 1949. q. Chambre de Commerce Belgo - Luxembourgeoise en France, 174 Blvd. Haussman, 75008 Paris, France. TEL 5621531.
Formerly (until 1982): Revue France - Belge (ISSN 0752-1529)

382   JA   ISSN 1342-369X
FRANCE JAPON ECO; vie et affaires au Japon. (Text in French) q. 240 F. (students 200 F.). Chambre de Commerce et d'Industrie Francaise du Japon - Zai-Nichi Furansu Shoko Kaigisho, IIDA Bldg., 5-5, Rokubancho, Chiyoda-ku, Tokyo 102, Japan. TEL 81-3-3288-9621. FAX 81-3288-9558. TELEX J32383-CCIFJ. E-mail: lemait_c@ccifj.or.jp; URL: http://www.ccifj.or.jp/. Ed. Catherine Lemaitre Tsukui. adv. contact: Laurence Fabre. bk.rev.; circ. 6,000 (paid). Document type: trade publication.
Refereed Serial

382   NE   ISSN 1023-7666
FRANCE PAYS-BAS; le magazine des relations commerciales franco-neerlandaises. (Text in Dutch, French) 1960. 6/yr. fl.100. Nederlands - Franse Kamer van Koophandel - Chambre de Commerce Franco-Neerlandaise, Postbus 90852, 2509 LW The Hague, Netherlands. TEL 31-70-3820551. FAX 31-70-3477975. adv.; bk.rev.; circ. 2,500 (controlled). **Indexed:** Key to Econ.Sci. Document type: bulletin.
Former titles (until 1993): France Pays-Bas Korte Berichten (ISSN 0766-379X); France Pays-Bas Informations Rapides (ISSN 0154-1536); (until 1977): France Pays-Bas (ISSN 0046-4945)
Description: Publishes the latest news relating to French-Dutch commercial relations and the activities of the chamber.

382   FR   ISSN 0995-2209
FRANCO-BRITISH CHAMBER OF COMMERCE AND INDUSTRY. TRADE DIRECTORY. 1874. a. 375 F. Franco-British Chamber of Commerce and Industry, 31 rue Boissy d'Anglas, 75008 Paris, France. adv. circ. 1,500.
Former titles: Franco-British Chamber of Commerce and Industry. Year Book (ISSN 0766-7000); British Chamber of Commerce in France. Year Book (ISSN 0068-1415)

FRANCO-BRITISH TRADE DIRECTORY. see *BUSINESS AND ECONOMICS — Trade And Industrial Directories*

974   US
FRENCH - AMERICAN NEWS. bi-m. membership. French - American Chamber of Commerce, 1350 Ave. of the Americas, 6th Fl., New York, NY 10019-4702. TEL 212-765-4460. FAX 212-765-4650. Ed. Serge Bellanger. R&P contact: Vicki Banner. adv. contact: Jean Choi. bk.rev.; circ. 650 (controlled). (looseleaf format) Document type: newsletter.
Description: Covers business and other news of interest to the French - American business community.

946   SP
FULLS INFORMATIUS. m. Camara Oficial de Comercio, Industria y Navegacion de Tarragona, Av. de Colon, 2, Tarragona, Spain.

381   UK
FUTURE. m. Leeds Junior Chamber of Commerce, Mill Hill, Leeds, W. Yorks LS1 5DQ, England. Ed. Nora Harrigan. adv. Document type: bulletin.

338.025   US
FUTURE 50 LIST. a. free. Metropolitan Milwaukee Association of Commerce, Council of Small Business Executives, 756 N. Milwaukee St., Milwaukee, WI 53202. TEL 414-287-4100.
Description: Lists 50 young and growing companies in the metro Milwaukee area, including a description of the businesses.

BUSINESS AND ECONOMICS — CHAMBER OF COMMERCE PUBLICATIONS

381   **GD**
G C I C ANNUAL REPORT. 1986. a. $5. Grenada Chamber of Industry and Commerce, Mt. Gay, St. George's, Grenada, W.I. TEL 809-440-2937. FAX 809-440-6627. E-mail: gcic@caribsurf.com. Ed. Cheryl Kirton. R&P contact: Cheryl Kirton. circ. 200. **Document type:** corporate report.

GERMAN AMERICAN TRADE. see *BUSINESS AND ECONOMICS — International Commerce*

382   **UA**   ISSN 0072-1433
GERMAN ARAB TRADE. irreg. membership. Deutsch-Arabische Handelskammer - German-Arab Chamber of Commerce, 2 Sherif St., Cairo, Egypt.

382 380   **TH**
GERMAN-THAI CHAMBER OF COMMERCE HANDBOOK AND DIRECTORY. 1978. a. $140. (German-Thai Chamber of Commerce) Chamber Publications LP, 699 Silom Rd., Kongboonma Bldg., Bangkok 10500, Thailand. TEL 02-236-2396. FAX 02-236-4711. TELEX 82836-GTCC-TH. Ed. Derek D. Enscoe. adv. circ. 2,500. **Document type:** directory.
    Formerly: German-Thai Chamber of Commerce Handbook.

382   **SZ**
GESCHAEFTE MIT OESTERREICH.* 1977. 9/yr. Oesterreichischer Handelsdelegierter fuer die Schweiz und Liechtenstein, Talstr. 65, CH-8039 Zurich, Switzerland. Ed. Peter Schneider.

966.7   **GH**
GHANA NATIONAL CHAMBER OF COMMERCE. ANNUAL REPORT. 1962. a. $10. Ghana National Chamber of Commerce, P.O. Box 2325, Accra, Ghana. TEL 233-21-662427. FAX 233-21-662210. TELEX 2687 GH. Ed. John B.K. Amanfu. adv. contact: Daniel Armah. **Document type:** corporate report.

381   **GH**
GHANA NATIONAL CHAMBER OF COMMERCE. BUSINESS DIRECTORY. 1992. biennial. $55. Ghana National Chamber of Commerce, P.O. Box 2325, Accra, Ghana. TEL 233-21-662427. FAX 233-21-662210. TELEX 2687-GH. Ed. John B.K. Amanfu. adv. contact: Daniel Armah. **Document type:** directory.

330 915.357   **TS**
AL-GHURFA. 1971. 4/yr. exchange basis. Ras al-Khaimah Chamber of Commerce, Industry and Agriculture, P.O. Box 87, Ras al-Khaimah, United Arab Emirates. TEL 33511. FAX 30233. TELEX 99140 TEJARA EM. Ed. Zaki Hassan Saqr. circ. 500.
    Description: Covers local business and agricultural news, provides official listings of company registrations and business legislation.

382   **MK**
AL-GHURFAH/OMAN COMMERCE. q. Oman Chamber of Commerce and Industry, P.O. Box 4400, Muscat, Sultanate of Oman. TEL 707674. TELEX 3389. Ed. Maqboul bin Ali bin Sultan.

945   **IT**
GIORNALE DEI GELATIERI. 1966. m. (11/yr.). Association of Dairy, Ice Cream and Allied Machinery, Corso Venezia 47-49, 20121 Milan, Italy. TEL 2-77-50. Ed. Francesco Colucci. adv. circ. 148,000.

330   **IT**   ISSN 0017-0429
GIORNALE ECONOMICO. no.78, 1966. bi-m. L.6500. Camera di Commercio Industria Artigianato e Agricoltura di Venezia, Via 22 Marzo 2032, Venice, Italy. Ed. Filippo Lo Torto. adv.; charts; illus.; stat.

380   **UK**
GLASGOW CHAMBER OF COMMERCE. ANNUAL REPORT. a. Glasgow Chamber of Commerce, 30 George Sq., Glasgow G2 1EQ, Scotland. TEL 0141-204-2121. FAX 0141-221-2336. TELEX 777967 CHACOM G. Ed.Bd. charts; illus. **Document type:** corporate report.

380   **UK**
GLASGOW CHAMBER OF COMMERCE. INFORMATION NEWSLETTER. m. Glasgow Chamber of Commerce, 30 George Sq., Glasgow G2 1EQ, Scotland. TEL 0141-204-2121. FAX 0141-221-2336. TELEX 777967 CHACOM G. **Document type:** newsletter.

380   **UK**   ISSN 0017-0860
GLASGOW CHAMBER OF COMMERCE. JOURNAL. 1918. m. £30. Glasgow Chamber of Commerce, 30 George Sq., Glasgow G2 1EQ, Scotland. TEL 44-141-204-2121. FAX 44-141-221-2336. TELEX 777967 CHACOM G. Ed. James Carson. adv.; bk.rev.; illus. circ. 5,000.

954   **II**
GOA CHAMBER OF COMMERCE AND INDUSTRY. BULLETIN. m. Goa Chamber of Commerce and Industry, Ormuz Rd., P.O. Box 59, Punjim 403 001, India. TEL 3420-4223. **Document type:** bulletin.

968   **SA**
GOING CONCERNS. (Text in English) 1975. fortn. membership. Johannesburg Chamber of Commerce & Industry, JCC House, Auckland Park, Private Bag 34, Auckland Park 2006, Johannesburg, South Africa. TEL 27-11-726-5300. FAX 27-11-726-8421. Ed. Ric Beattie. adv. circ. 6,800.
    Former titles: Chamber Bulletin; J C C Bulletin; J C C News.

GREATER BATON ROUGE MANUFACTURERS DIRECTORY. see *BUSINESS AND ECONOMICS — Trade And Industrial Directories*

975   **US**
GREATER WASHINGTON BOARD OF TRADE PROGRESS REPORT. Bound with: Greater Washington Board of Trade News. a. membership. Greater Washington Board of Trade, 1129 20th St., N.W., Ste. 200, Washington, DC 20036. TEL 202-857-5900. FAX 202-223-2648. Ed. Moira Saucer. circ. 6,700 (controlled). (back issues avail.)
    Description: Outlines goals for the year and how they were met. Lists board of directors and staff. Describes each committee and its purpose.

382   **GR**   ISSN 0046-6379
GREEK - AMERICAN TRADE. 1966. bi-m. $100. American - Hellenic Chamber of Commerce, 16 Kanari St., 106 74 Athens, Greece. TEL 363-6407. Ed. Sotiris Yannopoulos; Pub. Sotiris Yannopoulos. adv.; charts. circ. 2,500.

949.5   **GR**
GREEK EXPORT DIRECTORY. (Text in English) 1970. triennial. free. Athens Chamber of Commerce and Industry, 7 Acadimias St., 106 71 Athens, Greece. adv.; illus. circ. 5,000. **Document type:** directory.

990   **GP**   ISSN 0397-703X
HC158.5.A1
GUADELOUPE ECONOMIQUE. 1971. bi-m. 200 F. Chambre de Commerce et d'Industrie de Pointe-a-Pitre, B.P. 64, 97152 Pointe-a-Pitre Cedex, Guadeloupe. TEL 19-590-90-08-08. FAX 19-590-90-21-87. TELEX CCI PAP 919 780 GL. adv. circ. 4,000. (back issues avail.)
    Formerly (until 1978): Chambre de Commerce et d'Industrie de Pointe-a-Pitre. Bulletin (ISSN 0335-1580)

380   **SP**   ISSN 0211-4917
GUIA DEL COMERCIO Y DE LA INDUSTRIA (YEAR). 1960. biennial. 5000 ptas.($31) Camara Oficial de Comercio e Industria de Madrid, Huertas 13, 28012 Madrid, Spain. adv. circ. 2,000.
    Former titles (until 1980): Guia del Comercio y de la Industria de Madrid; Catalogo de la Industria de Madrid y Su Provincia (ISSN 0528-2438)

382   **FR**   ISSN 1023-8336
GUIDE DES AFFAIRES FRANCO-CANADIENNES. a. 430 F. (effective 1997). Chambre de Commerce France-Canada, 9-11 av. Franklin D. Roosevelt, 75008 Paris, France. TEL 33-1-43593238. Pub. Philippe Guerin. adv. contact: Francoise Labbe. **Document type:** directory.
    Description: Provides data on business professionals in both countries.

954   **II**
GUJARAT CHAMBER OF COMMERCE AND INDUSTRY. ANNUAL REPORT. a. Gujarat Chamber of Commerce and Industry, Ranchhodlal Marg, Navarangpura, P.O. Box 4045, Ahmedabad 380 009, India. TEL 402301.

954   **II**
GUJARAT CHAMBER OF COMMERCE AND INDUSTRY. BULLETIN. m. Gujarat Chamber of Commerce and Industry, Ranchhodlal Marg, Navrangpura, P.O. Box 4045, Ahmedabad 380 009, India. TEL 402301. **Document type:** bulletin.

330   **GW**   ISSN 0935-0594
HAMBURGER WIRTSCHAFT; Mitteilungen der Handelskammer Hamburg. 1946. m. DM.60 to non-members. (Handelskammer Hamburg) Continentale Werbung GmbH, Rabiosen 16, 20095 Hamburg, Germany. adv.; illus.; stat.; tr.list.; index. circ. 33,400. **Document type:** newspaper.
    ●Also available online. Vendor(s): GBI.
    Formerly: Handelskammer Hamburg. Mitteilungen (ISSN 0017-730X)

330   **SW**   ISSN 0345-4495
HANDELSKAMMARTIDNINGEN. Abbreviated title: H K T. 1917. 8/yr. SEK 350. Stockholms Handelskammare - Stockholm Chamber of Commerce, Vaestra Traedgaardsgatan 9, P.O. Box 16050, S-103 22 Stockholm, Sweden. TEL 46-8-613-18-00. FAX 46-8-241317. E-mail: lena.lindstedt@chamber.se. Ed. Lena Lindstedt. adv. contact: Susanne Karlsson. bk.rev.; charts; illus.; index. circ. 5,000.
    Formerly (until vol.3, 1973): Meddelanden fraan Stockholms Handelskammare (ISSN 0039-1654)

382   **SZ**
HANDELSKAMMER FINNLAND-SCHWEIZ. BULLETIN.* q. Handelskammer Finnland - Schweiz - Chambre de Commerce Finno - Suisse, Forchstr. 45, 8032 Zurich, Switzerland. TEL 2023630. **Document type:** bulletin.

944   **FR**
HAUTE LOIRE ECONOMIQUE. 5/yr. Chambre de Commerce et d'Industrie le Puy-en-Velay - Yssingeaux, B.P. 127, 43004 Le Puy en Velay Cedex, France. TEL 71-02-11-46. FAX 71-02-77-58. TELEX 393 934 F. Ed. Guy Quemener. circ. 8,000.

382   **US**
HAWAII'S INTERNATIONAL FESTIVAL OF THE PACIFIC. a. Japanese Chamber of Commerce and Industry of Hawaii, 400 Hualani St., Ste. 20 B, Hilo, HI 96720. TEL 808-949-5531.

381   **US**   ISSN 0894-6434
JK5601
HERE IS YOUR INDIANA GOVERNMENT.* 1944. biennial. $5. Indiana State Chamber of Commerce, 115 W. Washington St., No. 8505, Indianapolis, IN 46204-3407. TEL 317-264-3110. FAX 317-264-6855. Ed. Carl Henn, Jr. circ. 25,000.
    Description: Covers form and function of state and local government.

382   **SA**
HILITE. 1977. m. R.2 per issue to non-members. (Border Chamber of Business) Moonieya & Associates CC, 10 St. Georges Road, Southernwood 5213, South Africa. TEL 27-431-438438. FAX 27-431-432249. Ed. P.M. Miles. adv. contact: Kim van Rooyen. bk.rev.; stat.; index. circ. 1,200. (back issues avail.) **Document type:** bulletin.

330   **II**   ISSN 0971-1066
HINDUSTAN CHAMBER REVIEW. (Text in English) 1965. m. free. Hindustan Chamber of Commerce, 8 Kondi Chetty St., Madras 600 001, India. TEL 583134. FAX 568063. Ed. P. Gopalakrishna. bk.rev.; film rev.; play rev.; circ. controlled.
    Description: Covers Indian policies relating to trade, industry and commerce as well as important labor and consumer cases.

382   **SZ**
HOLLAND - SCHWEIZ. 1917. bi-m. free. Handelskammer Holland-Schweiz, Hornergasse 13, Postfach 7040, CH-8023 Zurich, Switzerland. FAX 41-1-2116517. Ed. Rezio Blass. adv. contact: Rezio Blass. circ. 2,000. **Document type:** newsletter.

BUSINESS AND ECONOMICS — CHAMBER OF COMMERCE PUBLICATIONS

382   US
HOLLAND - U S A. 1942. 4/yr. free. Netherlands Chamber of Commerce in U.S., 303 E. Wacker Dr., Ste. 412, Chicago, IL 60601. TEL 312-938-9050. FAX 312-938-8949. Ed. Michael Donahue. adv.; bk.rev.; charts; stat.; index, cum.index. circ. 7,000.
 Indexed: Key to Econ.Sci. Document type: newsletter.
 Formerly: Holland - U S A and Netherlands News; Supersedes: Netherlands - American Trade (ISSN 0028-2855)
 Description: Focuses on economics, commercial legislation, cultural events and historical buildings and estates.

951.25   CC
HONG KONG GENERAL CHAMBER OF COMMERCE. ANNUAL REPORT. a. Hong Kong General Chamber of Commerce, United Centre, 22nd Fl., 95 Queensway, G.P.O. Box 852, Hong Kong, People's Republic of China. TEL 852-2529-9229. FAX 852-2527-9843. TELEX 83535-TRIND-HK. Ed. Raymond Cheung.
 Document type: corporate report.

950   CC
HONG KONG GENERAL CHAMBER OF COMMERCE BULLETIN. 1970. m. HK.$360($30) to non-members. Hong Kong General Chamber of Commerce, United Centre, 22nd Fl., 95 Queensway, G.P.O. Box 852, Hong Kong, People's Republic of China. TEL 852-2529-9229. FAX 852-2527-9843. TELEX 83535-TRIND-HK. Ed. Raymond Cheng. adv.: B&W page HK.$8240, color page HK.$12760; trim 210 x 286; adv. contact: Connie Kwok. circ. 7,000. Document type: trade publication.

949.2   NE
I C C NEDERLAND. PUBLICATIES. a. I C C Nederland - Nederlandse Organisatie voor de Internationale Kamer van Koophandel, Prinses Beatrixlaan 5, 2595 AK The Hague, Netherlands. TEL 836646.

380   TU   ISSN 1300-3720
I C O C. Key Title: ICOC. (Text in English) 1881. q. free. Istanbul Chamber of Commerce, P.O. Box 377, Istanbul, Turkey. Ed. Cengiz Ersun. adv. circ. 5,000. —BLDSC (4362.053000).
 Formerly (until 1982): Istanbul Ticaret Odasi Mecmuasi - Istanbul Chamber of Commerce. Journal.
 Description: Covers the Turkish economy and Turkish industries, including textiles, mining, marble, ceramics.

943   GW   ISSN 0946-4557
I H K AKTUELL. 1948. m. DM.32. Industrie- und Handelskammer zu Luebeck, Breitestr. 6-8, 23552 Luebeck, Germany. FAX 49-451-7085284. Ed. Hans-Jochen Arndt. R&P contact: Hans-Jochen Arndt. adv. contact: Christiane Kermel. bk.rev.; index. circ. 47,500. (back issues avail.) Document type: newsletter.

943.1   GW
I H K LIPPE INFO. m. DM.48. Industrie- und Handelskammer Lippe zu Detmold, Willi-Hofmann-Str. 5, 32756 Detmold, Germany. TEL 05231-76010. FAX 05231-760157. Ed. Michael Swoboda. adv. Document type: bulletin.
 Formerly: Informationen fuer die Lippische Wirtschaft.

382   GW
I H K REPORT SUEDHESSEN. 1947. 11/yr. DM.24. (Industrie- und Handelskammer Darmstadt) Eduard Roether KG, Postfach 101205, 64212 Darmstadt, Germany. TEL 49-6151-3001-0. FAX 49-6151-314026. URL: http://www.darmstadt.gmd.de/ihk/. Ed. Martin Proba. adv.: B&W page DM.4850, color page DM.7640; trim 185 x 260; adv. contact: Kristina Ross. bk.rev.; circ. 41,500. (back issues avail.) Document type: bulletin.
 Former titles (until 1996): Starkenburger Wirtschaft (ISSN 0722-4249); (until 1982): Industrie- und Handelskammer Darmstadt. Nachrichten (ISSN 0722-4230)

382   GW
I H K WIRTSCHAFTSSPIEGEL. m. DM.36. (Industrie- und Handelskammer Muenster) Verlag Aschendorff, Soesterstr. 13, 48155 Muenster, Germany. TEL 49-251-690570. FAX 49-251-690578. Ed. Anne Pinnekamp. adv.: B&W page DM.5900; trim 185 x 252; adv. contact: Inge Schaefer. circ. 76,000. Document type: bulletin.

380   GW
I H K WUPPERTAL. BERGISCHE WIRTSCHAFT. s-m. DM.24. Industrie- und Handelskammer Wuppertal - Solingen - Remscheid, Heinrich-Kamp-Platz 2, 42013 Wuppertal, Germany. adv.; bk.rev.; abstr.; pat.; stat.; tr.lit.; tr.mk.; index. Document type: bulletin.
 Formerly: I H K Wuppertal. Wirtschaftliche Mitteilungen (ISSN 0018-9839)

382   NE   ISSN 0921-2701
I N F.* (Information Nederland France) (Text in Dutch, French) 1980. q. fl.35 (effective 1994). Chambre Francaise de Commerce et d'Industrie aux Pays-Bas - French Chamber of Commerce and Industry in the Netherlands, Wibaustraat 129 11th, 1091 GL Amsterdam, Netherlands. Ed. Josee Focke. adv. circ. 5,000. Document type: bulletin.
 Description: Covers French and Dutch economy, exhibitions, technology and scientific research, and commercial exchange between the two countries.

382   US
▼**ILLINOIS BUSINESS.** 1995. q. (Illinois Chamber of Commerce) Progressive Publishing, Inc., Box 354, Bloomingdale, IL 60108. TEL 630-582-8888. FAX 630-582-8895. E-mail: Almanac123@aol.com; profiles@mindspring.com. Ed. Juli Bridgers; Pub. Dan Nugara. adv. contact: Joseph Nugara. circ. 25,000. (controlled).
 Description: Contains news, columns, and feature stories about Illinois businesses and state chamber members; legislative and business issues affecting large and small businesses in Illinois.

974.1   US   ISSN 1055-3029
IMPACT (AUGUSTA). 1989. w. $25 (effective 1997). Maine Chamber and Business Alliance, 7 Community Dr., Augusta, ME 04330-9412. TEL 207-623-4568. FAX 207-622-7723. E-mail: impact@mainechamber.org; URL: http://www.mainechamber.org. Ed. RoJean Tulk; Pub. Dana F. Connors. R&P contact: RoJean Tulk. adv. contact: Diane Andrews. circ. 1,700. Document type: newsletter.
 Former titles: Maine Chamber of Commerce and Industry. Newsletter (ISSN 1045-6902); Maine Business Newsletter (ISSN 8750-8443)
 Description: Deals with legislative and regulatory issues facing Maine business.

381   IT   ISSN 1123-5519
IMPRESA & STATO. 1988. q. L.60000 (foreign L.90000). Camera di Commercio, Industria, Artiganato e Agricoltura di Milano, Via Meravigli 9-B, 20123 Milan, Italy. TEL 39-2-85154206. URL: http://www.mi.camcom.it/impresa.htm. Ed. Piero Bassetti. R&P contact: Patrizio Surace. adv.: B&W page L.3000000, color page L.4000000; adv. contact: Patrizio Surace. circ. 4,000. Document type: monographic series.
 ●Also available online.

944   FR   ISSN 1152-3263
IMPULSION. 1966. 4/yr. Chambre de Commerce et d'Industrie de Bolbec-Lillebonne, 16 bis, av. Foch, B.P. 11, 76210 Bolbec, France. TEL 35-31-00-78. FAX 35-31-20-55. Ed. Annie Lemasurier. circ. 2,000.
 Former titles (until 1989): Info C C I (ISSN 1148-7283); (until 1983): Bulletin Economique de la Valle du Commerce (ISSN 0338-3601); (until 1974): Chambre de Commerce et d'Industrie de Bolbec, Lillebonne et Notre Dame de Gravenvchon. Bulletin de Liaison (ISSN 0338-3598)

954   II
INDO-AMERICAN CHAMBER OF COMMERCE. NEWSLETTER. m. Indo-American Chamber of Commerce, Vulcan Insurance Bldg., Veer Nariman Rd., P.O. Box 11057, Bombay 400 020, India. Document type: newsletter.

382   II
INDO - U S BUSINESS. (Text in English) 1970. m. Indo-American Chamber of Commerce, Vulcan Insurance Bldg., Veer Nariman Rd., Churchgate, Bombay 400 020, India. Ed. V. Rangaraj. adv.; bk.rev.; circ. 1,800. (controlled).
 Formerly (until 1987): I A C C Newsletter.

989.5   UY
INDUSTRIA EN EL URUGUAY. a. Camara de Industrias del Uruguay, Departamento de Estudios Economicos, Av. Lib. Brig. Gral. Lavalleja 1672, Montevideo, Uruguay.

338   UK   ISSN 0019-8579
INDUSTRIAL NOTTINGHAMSHIRE. 1917. m. £40. Nottinghamshire Chamber of Commerce and Industry, 395 Mansfield Rd., Nottingham NG5 2DL, England. TEL 0602-624624. FAX 0602-605981. TELEX 37605-COMIND-G. Ed. Gillian Dodd. adv.; bk.rev.; illus.; tr.lit.; index; circ. 2,500. (controlled)

338 380   GW   ISSN 0019-8986
INDUSTRIE- UND HANDELSKAMMER FRANKFURT AM MAIN. MITTEILUNGEN. 1878. 19/yr. DM.38. Industrie- und Handelskammer Frankfurt am Main, Boersenplatz 4, 60313 Frankfurt a.M., Germany. FAX 069-2197488. Ed. Wolfgang Weber. adv.: B&W page 8 1/2 x 11; adv. contact: Berndt Holthaus. bk.rev.; charts; illus.; index. circ. 27,000. Document type: proceedings.

338 380   GW
INDUSTRIE- UND HANDELSKAMMER HANNOVER-HILDESHEIM. YEARBOOK - STATISTICS. 1949. a. free. Industrie- und Handelskammer Hannover-Hildesheim, Schiffgraben 49, 30175 Hannover, Germany. TEL 0511-3107-268. Ed. Martin Rudolph. adv.; bk.rev.; stat.; tr.lit.; index. circ. 8,000. Document type: corporate report.
 Former titles: Industrie- und Handelskammer Hannover-Hildesheim. Yearbook - Information Kommentaire; Industrie- und Handelskammer Hannover-Hildesheim. Information-Kommentaire (ISSN 0171-1016)

943.1   GW
INDUSTRIE- UND HANDELSKAMMER LUENEBURG-WOLFSBURG. MITTEILUNGEN. m. Industrie- und Handelskammer Lueneburg-Wolfsburg, Am Sande 1, 21335 Luneburg, Germany. TEL 7090. FAX 709180.

943   GW
INDUSTRIE- UND HANDELSKAMMER ZU AACHEN. WIRTSCHAFTLICHE NACHRICHTEN. 1919. m. DM.72. Georgi GmbH, Theaterstr. 77, 52062 Aachen, Germany. TEL 0241-4779116. FAX 0241-4779160. Ed. Heinz Heiliger. adv. contact: Liane Wilden. bk.rev. circ. 32,500. Document type: trade publication.

943   GW
INDUSTRIE- UND HANDELSKAMMER ZU DUESSELDORF. SCHNELLDIENST.* w. DM.12.60. Bergische Verlagsgesellschaft Menzel KG, Islandufer 21, D-5600 Wuppertal, Germany. Ed. M. Kranenberg. adv. circ. 11,000.

382   UK
INFO. (Text and summaries in English, French) bi-m. £35. French Chamber of Commerce in Great Britain, 197 Knightsbridge, London SW7, England. Ed. Ms. T. Penketh. index, cum.index. circ. 2,000.
 Former titles: Franco - British Trade Journal; Franco-British Trade Review (ISSN 0015-9867)
 Description: Promoting Franco-British business relations.

330   BU   ISSN 1310-9332
INFOBUSINESS - ECONOMIC NEWS OF BULGARIA. (Text in English) 1959. m. $24. Bulgarian Chamber of Commerce and Industry, 42 Parchevich Str., Sofia, Bulgaria. TEL 359-2-872631. FAX 359-2-873209. TELEX 22374. Ed. L Mikhailov. illus. circ. 3,000.
 Indexed: Key to Econ.Sci., PROMT.
 Formerly (until 1996): Economic News of Bulgaria (ISSN 0205-1400)
 Description: Presents Bulgaria's export, import and customs regulations, taxation, banking, foreign investment, privatization as well as individual firms, and offers for business contacts.

944   FR   ISSN 0992-7514
L'INFORMATEUR. 1956. a. 150 F. Chambre de Commerce et Industrie (Cholet), 34 rue Nationale, B.P. 2116, 49321 Cholet Cedex, France. TEL 02-41-49-10-00. FAX 02-41-49-10-10. Ed. Samuel Leblond. circ. 5,000. Document type: corporate report.
 Formerly (until 1988): Informateur Economique du Choletais (ISSN 0995-6735)

944   FR   ISSN 0996-1488
INFORMATION ECONOMIQUE DU LOIRET. 1945. 9/yr. 190 F. 23 place du Martroi, 45044 Orleans Cedex 01, France. TEL 33-2-38777777. FAX 33-2-38530978. TELEX 760 912. Ed. Alain Souche; Pub. Jean-Pierre Marty. adv. contact: Martine Charlet. circ. 15,000. Document type: newspaper.

BUSINESS AND ECONOMICS — CHAMBER OF COMMERCE PUBLICATIONS

943 GW
INFORMATIONEN FUER DIE WIRTSCHAFT. m. Industrie- und Handelskammer Nordschwarzwald, Dr.-Brandenburg-Str. 6, Postfach 920, 75173 Pforsheim, Germany. TEL 07231-2010. TELEX 783803.

382 FR ISSN 0020-0433
INFORMATIONS CANADIENNES; les relations economiques Franco-Canadiennes. 1955. 11/yr. 225 F. (effective 1997). Chambre de Commerce France-Canada, 9-11 av. Franklin D. Roosevelt, 75008 Paris, France. TEL 33-1-43593238. FAX 33-1-42562562. Ed. Helene Cledat; Pub. Philippe Guerin. adv. contact: Francoise Labbe. bk.rev.; stat. circ. 1,350. **Document type**: newsletter.
Description: Provides information on investing, starting businesses, creating joint ventures and licensing policies in Canada and France.

945 IT
INFORMATORE DEI COMMERCIANTI. m., (11/yr.). Unione del Commercio e del Turismo della Provincia di Milano, Corso Venezia 47-49, 20121 Milan, Italy. Ed. Giuseppe Orlando. adv. circ. 25,000.

330.9 SP ISSN 0211-5468
HC387.A68
INFORME ECONOMICO DE ARAGON. 1980. a. 2000 ptas. Consejo de Camaras de Comercio e Industria de Aragon, Paseo Isabel 1a Catolica, 2, 50009 Zaragoza, Spain. FAX 35-79-45. TELEX 58-072 CACIN E. circ. 1,000.
Former titles (until 1978): Provincia de Zaragoza. Informe Economico; (until 1976): Desarrollo Industrial y Mercantil en la Provincia de Zaragoza.
Description: Contains economic information on the region of Aragon. Includes general information, national and international, about the preceding year.

946.9 SP ISSN 0211-8734
INFORME ECONOMICO REGIONAL. a. Camara Oficial de Comercio, Industria y Navegacion de Valencia, Poeta Querol 15, 46002 Valencia, Spain. TEL 34-6-3511301. FAX 34-6-3516349. TELEX 62243 COCIN E. (Co-sponsors: Camaras de Comercio, Industria y Navegacion de Alcoy, Alicante, Castellon, Orihuela) bk.rev. circ. 1,000.
Formerly (until 1972): Camara Oficial de Comercio, Industria y Navegacion de Valencia (ISSN 0211-8750)

382 GW ISSN 0940-2330
INTERCAMARA. bi-m. Amtliche Spanische Handelskammer fuer Deutschland, Schaumainkai 83, 60596 Frankfurt a.M., Germany. TEL 069-638031. FAX 069-638047. TELEX 414472. adv.; bk.rev. circ. 1,500.
Formerly: Amtliche Spanische Handelskammer fuer Deutschland. Informationsblatt.

382 MX ISSN 0020-5192
INTER-CAMBIO. (Text in English) 1943. 4/yr. $16 to non-members. Camara de Comercio Britanica, A.C. - British Chamber of Commerce, Rio de la Plata 30, Col. Cuauhtemoc, 06500 Mexico, D.F., Mexico. TEL 52-5-2560901. FAX 52-5-2115451. Ed. Rachel Taplin. R&P contact: Lourdes G. Loyola. TEL 52-5-2560901. adv.; B&W page Mex.$4800, color page Mex.$6600; trim 215 x 280; adv. contact: Lourdes G. Loyola. bk.rev.; illus.; pat.; index. circ. 1,000. **Document type**: corporate report, trade publication.
Description: Covers Anglo-Mexican business topics.

381 FR ISSN 0988-5838
INTERCONSULAIRE FRANCE REGIONS. 1973. m. Chambres de Commerce et d'Industrie, 45 Av d'Iena, 75116 Paris, France. Ed. Francois de la Maisonneuve. illus.; stat.
Formerly (until 1987): France Regions (ISSN 0988-582X)

941 AT
INTERNATIONAL BUSINESS JOURNAL. q. Aus.$30 to non-members (foreign Aus.$70); members free. (Australian British Chamber of Commerce) Verandah Press Pty. Ltd., P.O. Box 835, Epping, N.S.W 2121, Australia. TEL 02-876-5046. FAX 02-867-4059. Ed. Richard Stanton. adv.: page Aus.$975. **Document type**: newsletter, trade publication.
Formerly: A B C C Newsletter.

974 US
INTERNATIONAL LABOR AFFAIRS REPORT. bi-m. United States Council for International Business, 1212 Ave. of the Americas, New York, NY 10036-1689. TEL 212-354-4480. FAX 212-575-0327. Ed. William J. Sibravy. **Document type**: newsletter.

INVESTOR'S GUIDE TO SINGAPORE. see BUSINESS AND ECONOMICS — Investments

382 IR
IRAN CHAMBER OF COMMERCE, INDUSTRIES AND MINES. DIRECTORY. discontinued; resumed. biennial. $75 (diskette $35). Iran Chamber of Commerce, Industries and Mines, Public Relations, 254 Taleghanni Ave., P.O. Box 15875-4671, Tehran, Iran. TEL 98-21-8846031. FAX 98-21-8825111. TELEX 213382 TCIM. adv.: B&W page $1000; color page $1750. (also avail. in diskette format) **Document type**: directory.

330 IR ISSN 1023-1838
IRAN COMMERCE. (Text in English) q. $30. Iran Chamber of Commerce, Industries and Mines, 254 Taleghani Ave., P.O. Box 15875-4671, Tehran, Iran. TEL 98-21-8846031. FAX 98-21-8825111. TELEX 213382 TCIM. adv.: B&W page $750, color page $1750.

330.9561 TU ISSN 1300-3712
ISTANBUL CHAMBER OF COMMERCE. ECONOMIC REPORT. Key Title: Economic Report. Turkish edition: Ekonomik Rapor (ISSN 1300-3704) (Text in English) 1983. a. Istanbul Chamber of Commerce - Istanbul Ticaret Odasi, Ragip Gumuspala Cad, Eminonu, P.K. 377, Istanbul, Turkey. TEL 0901-5266215. TELEX 22682.

956.1 TU
ISTANBUL CHAMBER OF COMMERCE. MAGAZINE. q. Istanbul Chamber of Commerce, Ragip Gumuspala Cad, Eminonu, P.K. 377, Istanbul, Turkey. TEL 0901-5266215. TELEX 22682 ODA TR.

381 TU ISSN 1300-3666
ISTANBUL TICARET GAZETESI. 1958. w. Istanbul Chamber of Commerce - Istanbul Ticaret Odasi, Ragip Gumuspala Cad, Eminonu, P.K. 377, Istanbul, Turkey. TELEX 22682 ODA TR.

380 CN ISSN 0225-1140
ITALCOMMERCE. (Text in English, French, Italian) 1964. 6/yr. Can.$18 to non-members. Italian Chamber of Commerce of Montreal, 550 Sherbrooke Ouest, No. 980, Montreal, PQ H3A 1B9, Canada. TEL 514-844-4249; 800-263-4372. FAX 514-844-4875. E-mail: camit@magnet.ca; URL: http://www.emporion.it/montreal. Ed. Giuseppe Mancini. adv.: B&W page Can.$1200, color page Can.$1500. bk.rev. circ. 6,000. **Document type**: trade publication.
Formerly: Italian Chamber of Commerce Bulletin (ISSN 0318-7985)
Description: Canada-Italy business exchanges magazine and guide.

382 IT ISSN 0021-2873
ITALIAN AMERICAN BUSINESS. (Text in English, Italian) 1956. bi-m. membership. American Chamber of Commerce in Italy, Via Cesare Cantu 1, 20123 Milan, Italy. TEL 39-2-869-0661. FAX 39-2-8057737. Ed. Gabriella Gabet. adv.: B&W page L.1400000. charts; illus.; mkt. circ. 4,000.
Indexed: P.A.I.S.
Description: News from the United States, the EEC and Italy on the legal, economic and fiscal aspects of doing business in Italy and the United States.

382 US ISSN 0021-2903
ITALIAN AMERICAN CHAMBER OF COMMERCE OF CHICAGO. BULLETIN. 1907. bi-m. $24. Italian American Chamber of Commerce, 30 S. Michigan Ave., Ste. 504, Chicago, IL 60603. TEL 312-553-9137. FAX 312-553-9142. E-mail: italchgo@interaccess.com; URL: http:www.italy-america-chamber.com. Ed. Leonora LiPuma. adv.; bibl.; illus.; stat. circ. 1,600. **Document type**: bulletin.

382 CN ISSN 0021-3098
ITALY CANADA TRADE. (Text in English, Italian; summaries in English) 1964. q. free to qualified personnel. Italian Chamber of Commerce of Toronto, 901 Lawrence Ave. W., Ste. 306, Toronto, ON M6A 1C3, Canada. TEL 416-789-7169. FAX 416-789-7160. E-mail: mail@italchamber-tor.on.ca; URL: http://www.italchamber-tor.on.ca. Ed. Arturo Pelliccione. adv.; illus. circ. 10,000. **Document type**: trade publication.

382 UK
ITALY - U K - TRADE - MONTHLY PUBLICATION. m. membership. Italian Chamber of Commerce and Industry for the U.K., Walmar House, 296 Regent St., London WIR 6AE, England. TEL 44-171-637-3153. FAX 44-171-436-6037. Ed. Antonino Leone. R&P contact: Antonino Leone. TEL 44-171-436-4742. adv. contact: Antonino Leone. stat. circ. 1,000. **Document type**: newsletter.
Formerly: Italian Chamber of Commerce for Great Britain. Information Bulletin.
Description: Contains economic information, business contacts, chamber news, and statistics.

382 TU ISSN 0021-3357
IZMIR TICARET ODASI DERGISI/IZMIR CHAMBER OF COMMERCE REVIEW. (Text in Turkish) 1926. bi-m. $11.50. Izmir Ticaret Odasi - Izmir Chamber of Commerce, Ataturk Cad. no.126, Izmir, Turkey. TEL 90-232-4417777. FAX 90-232-4837853. TELEX 52331 IODA TR. Ed. Cengiz/Ural. adv. contact: Cengiz Ural. bk.rev.; charts; illus.; mkt.; stat.; tr.lit.; index. circ. 2,000. **Document type**: trade publication.
Description: Promotes commercial relations with other countries. Examines Turkey's import-export activities.

382 TU
IZMIR TICARET ODASI HABER GAZETESI. (Text in Turkish) 1989. m. free. Izmir Ticaret Odasi - Izmir Chamber of Commerce, Ataturk Cad., no. 126, Izmir, Turkey. TEL 90-232-4417777. FAX 90-232-4837853. TELEX 134119. Ed. Cengiz Ural. adv. contact: Cengiz Ural. **Document type**: newspaper.
Supersedes: Izmir Ticaret Odasi Bulten.
Description: Provides news of foreign trade and domestic trade.

381 US ISSN 0891-1428
JACKSONVILLE MAGAZINE (LONGWOOD).* 1963. 12/yr. $17.75. (Jacksonville Chamber of Commerce) White Publishing Company, 1650 Prudential Dr., Ste. 300, Jacksonville, FL 32207. TEL 904-725-7505. FAX 904-725-8221. TELEX 904-353-0300. Ed. Kathy Blum. adv.; charts; illus. circ. 15,000.
Formerly (until 1985): Jacksonville (ISSN 0021-3861)
Description: Covers business trends, important people and companies, as well as general-interest articles. Includes local events and dining guide.

330 JM ISSN 0021-4094
JAMAICA CHAMBER OF COMMERCE JOURNAL. vol.29, 1973. s-a. free. Jamaica Chamber of Commerce, 7-8 E. Parade, P.O. Box 172, Kingston, Jamaica, W.I. TEL 809-922-0150. FAX 809-924-9056. Ed. Chester Burgess. adv.; bk.rev.; illus. circ. 2,000.

382 US
JAPANESE CHAMBER OF COMMERCE AND INDUSTRY OF HAWAII. NEWSBULLETIN. m. Japanese Chamber of Commerce and Industry of Hawaii, 400 Hualani St, Ste. 20 B, Hilo, HI 96720. TEL 808-949-5531.

330 UK ISSN 1353-5552
THE JOURNAL; business magazine of Leeds & Bradford chambers of commerce and industry. 1924. m. £30. Leeds & Bradford Chamber Services Ltd., Park House, Cote Ln., Farsley, Leeds LS28 5XZ, England. TEL 0532-363136. FAX 0532-363128. Ed. Sue Harper. adv. contact: Barbara Hartley-Quin. bk.rev.; stat. circ. 4,200. **Document type**: trade publication. —BLDSC (4674.931435).
Former titles (until 1994): Leeds & Bradford Journal (ISSN 1351-0584); (until 1993): Leeds Journal (ISSN 0024-0273)

944 FR ISSN 1246-8576
JOURNAL DES ENTREPRISES DE SAINT-DENIS. 4/yr. 2 place Victor-Hugo, 93200 Saint-Denis, France. TEL 48-20-63-83. FAX 48-09-02-39. Ed. Dominique Sanchez. circ. 50,000.

BUSINESS AND ECONOMICS — CHAMBER OF COMMERCE PUBLICATIONS

951.9   KO
K C C I BUSINESS JOURNAL. (Text in English) 1986. q. free. Korea Chamber of Commerce and Industry, 45, Namdaemunno 4-ga, Chung-gu, C.P.O. Box 25, Seoul 100-743, S. Korea. TEL 82-2-3163-114. FAX 82-2-757-9475. Ed. Kim Chung-Tai. **Document type:** newsletter.
    Former titles (until 1996): K C C I Quarterly Review; Korea Chamber of Commerce and Industry. News.

381   NE
KAMER VAN KOOPHANDEL EN FABRIEKEN VOOR AMSTERDAM. JAARREDE. 1812. a. Kamer van Koophandel en Fabrieken voor Amsterdam - Chamber of Commerce, De Ruyterkade 5, 1013 AA Amsterdam, Netherlands. TEL 31-20-5236600. FAX 31-20-5236677. TELEX 18888AMTRA. circ. 5,000.

949.2   NE   ISSN 0167-1138
KAMER VAN KOOPHANDEL EN FABRIEKEN VOOR EEMLAND. KAMER VAN KOOPHANDEL. m. Kamer van Koophandel en Fabrieken voor Eemland, Stationsplein 25, 3818 LE Amersfoort, Netherlands. TEL 12964.

381   BE   ISSN 0022-8087
KAMER VAN KOOPHANDEL EN NIJVERHEID VAN ANTWERPEN. BULLETIN. Key Title: Bulletin - Kamer van Koophandel en Nijverheid van Antwerpen. French edition: Chambre de Commerce et d'Industrie d'Anvers. Bulletin. (Text in Dutch) 1969. m. 2500 BEF. Kamer van Koophandel en Nijverheid van Antwerpen - Antwerp Chamber of Commerce and Industry, Markgravestraat 12, 2000 Antwerp, Belgium. FAX 32-3-2336442. Eds. Luc Luwel, Lieve Noels; Pub. Luc Luwel. R&P contact: Lieve Noels. adv. contact: Liesbeth De Taevernier. bk.rev.; illus. circ. 2,500. Indexed: ELLIS, Key to Econ.Sci. **Document type:** bulletin.
    Formed by the merger of: Chambre de Commerce, Antwerp. Bulletin; Chambre d'Industrie, Antwerp. Bulletin.

381   NE
KAMERKRANT (LANDELIJKE EDITIE); informatiekrant van de Kamer van Koophandel. (26 regional editions also avail.: Amersfoort; Amsterdam - Haarlem; Apeldoorn; Arnhem - Nijmegen - Doetinchem - Ede; Den Bosch; Breda; Dordrecht; Drenthe; Eindhoven; Enschede; Flevoland; Gouda; Groningen; The Hague - Delft; Hilversum; Leiden; Middelburg; Noordwest Holland; Roermond; Terneuzen; Tiel; Tilburg; Utrecht; Venlo; Zuid-Limburg; Zwolle) 1979. 11/yr. free to qualified personnel. Stichting K v K Media, Postbus 181, 3440 AD Woerden, Netherlands. TEL 31-348-430252. FAX 31-348-430543. E-mail: info@kvk-media.kvk.nl; URL: http://www.kvk.nl. Dir. J.C. Boersma. adv.: B&W page (Landelijke editie) fl.53460, color page fl.90060; trim 315 x 418; adv. contact: Ms. H.W.M. Rutger. circ. 110,000. (tabloid format) **Document type:** newspaper.
    Formerly (until 1994): Kamer van Koophandel.

330   AU   ISSN 0022-8184
KAMMER NACHRICHTEN. 1947. w. S.600 (effective 1997). Wirtschaftskammer Oberoesterreich, Hessenplatz 3, A-4010 Linz, Austria. TEL 43-732-7800-361. FAX 43-732-7800-395. Ed. Johann Grosswindhager. adv.: B&W page S.43000, color page S.57000; trim 192 x 258. bk.rev.; abstr.; charts; illus.; stat.; index. circ. 56,000. (tabloid format) **Document type:** newspaper.

381   II   ISSN 0300-4074
KANARA CHAMBER OF COMMERCE & INDUSTRY JOURNAL. (Text in English, Kannada) 1971. m. Rs.96 (effective 1997). Kanara Chamber of Commerce & Industry, Box 116, Bunder, Mangalore 575 001, India. TEL 420128. Ed. Sri G. Giridhar Prahu. adv. contact: H.S. Kamath. bk.rev.; illus.; stat. circ. 6,600. **Document type:** trade publication.
    Description: Provides information on latest government notifications, clarifications, laws and rules, and amendments. Also contains export statistics and market reports, and discusses current issues.
    Refereed Serial

978   US   ISSN 0274-9912
KANSAS CITIAN. 1910. s-m. $50 to non-members; members $25. Greater Kansas City Chamber of Commerce, 911 Main, 2600 Commerce Tower, Kansas City, MO 64105. TEL 816-221-2424. FAX 816-221-7440. URL: http://www.kcity.com. Ed. Pamela Kingsolver. R&P contact: Pamela Kingsolver. adv. contact: Liz Wheeler. circ. 6,200. **Document type:** newsletter.
    Description: Contains articles on activities, events, and issues relevant to the Chamber.

338   PK   ISSN 0075-5079
KARACHI. CHAMBER OF COMMERCE AND INDUSTRY. ANNUAL REPORT. (Text in English) a. free. Chamber of Commerce and Industry, Aiwan-e-Tijarat, Box 4158, Nicol Rd., Karachi 2, Pakistan.
    Formerly: Karachi. Chamber of Commerce and Industry. Report.

954   PK
KARACHI. CHAMBER OF COMMERCE AND INDUSTRY. NEWS BULLETIN. (Text in English) fortn. free for members. Karachi Chamber of Commerce and Industry, Aiwan-e-Tijarat, Box 4158, Nicol Rd., Karachi 2, Pakistan. **Document type:** bulletin.

948.97   FI   ISSN 0781-6375
HF37.F5
KAUPPAKAMARILEHTI. 1920. 8/yr. FIM 250 (effective 1997). Keskuskauppakamari - Central Chamber of Commerce of Finland, P.O. Box 1000, FIN-00101 Helsinki 10, Finland. TEL 358-9-696969. FAX 358-9-650303. E-mail: keskuskauppakamari@wtc.fi; URL: http://www.keskuskauppakamari.fi/uutisia/kauppakamarilehti.html. Ed. Sampsa Saralehto. adv. contact: Heidi Puonti-Nuhari. bk.rev.; circ. 20,000. (controlled). **Document type:** newspaper.

380.1   KE
KENYA NATIONAL CHAMBER OF COMMERCE AND INDUSTRY. TRADE AND INDUSTRY GUIDE. a. KShs.50. Kenya National Chamber of Commerce and Industry, Nairobi, Kenya. TEL 254-2-220867. FAX 254-2-340664. Ed. Peter G. Muiruri. stat. circ. 9,000. **Document type:** directory.
    Formerly: Kenya National Chamber of Commerce and Industry. Annual Report.

952   JA
KYOTO BUSINESS DIRECTORY. s-a. Kyoto Chamber of Commerce and Industry, 240 Shoshoi-cho, Karasuma-dori Ebisugawaagaru, Nakakyo-ku, Kyoto 604, Japan. TEL 075-231-0181. **Document type:** directory.

954   PK
LAHORE CHAMBER OF COMMERCE & INDUSTRY. WEEKLY CHAMBER CIRCULAR. (Text in English, Urdu) 1972. w. Lahore Chamber of Commerce & Industry, P.O. Box 597, 11 Aiwan-i-Tijarat, Lahore, Pakistan. Ed. M.A. Hameed. circ. 5,000.

975.9   US
LATIN CHAMBER OF COMMERCE. DIRECTORIO COMERCIAL. a. Latin Chamber of Commerce, 1417 W. Flagler, Miami, FL 33135.

382 340   BL
LAW AND YOU. m. American Chamber of Commerce for Brazil - Camara de Comercio Americana, Praca Pio X No. 15, 5th Fl., Caixa Postal 916, 20040-020 Rio de Janeiro, Brazil. TEL 55-21-2032477. E-mail: achambr@amchamrio.com.br; URL: http://www.amchamrio.com.br.

338   UK
LEICESTERSHIRE CHAMBER OF COMMERCE & INDUSTRY DIRECTORY. a. £35. Kemps Publishing Ltd., 11 The Swan Courtyard, Charles Edward Rd., Birmingham B26 1BU, England. TEL 44-121-765-4144. FAX 44-121-706-6210. **Document type:** directory.
    Formerly: Leicester & County Chamber of Commerce & Industry Directory.
    Description: Lists all Chamber members and many others within the county of Leicestershire.

382   GW
LEIPZIGER WIRTSCHAFT. 1990. m. DM.56. (Industrie- und Handelskammer zu Leipzig) Schluetersche GmbH und Co. KG, Hans-Boeckler-Allee 7, 30173 Hannover, Germany. TEL 49-511-8550-0. FAX 49-511-8550402. adv. contact: Heinz Buse. circ. 38,000. (back issues avail.) **Document type:** bulletin.

944   FR   ISSN 1150-4706
LA LETTRE D'ACTIVITES EN PAYS BASQUE. 9/yr. free. Bayonne and Basque country's Chamber of Commerce, 50-51 allees Marines, B.P. 215, 64102 Bayonne Cedex, France. TEL 33-5-59465999. FAX 33-5-59594279. TELEX 570 001 CHAMCO. Ed. Gerard Eder. bk.rev.; circ. 11,000 (controlled). **Document type:** newsletter.
    Formerly (until 1990): Activites en Pays Basque (ISSN 0400-4450)

966.62   LB
LIBERIAN TRADE TOPICS AND NEWSLETTER AND FORECASTS. m. Liberia Chamber of Commerce, P.O. Box 92, Monrovia, Liberia.

943   LH
LIECHTENSTEINISCHE INDUSTRIE- UND HANDELSKAMMER. ANNUAL REPORT. bi-m. Liechtensteinische Industrie- und Handelskammer, Josef-Rheinberger-Str. 11, Postfach 232, FL-9490 Vaduz, Liechtenstein. TEL 41-75-2375511. **Document type:** corporate report.

943   LH
LIECHTENSTEINISCHE INDUSTRIE- UND HANDELSKAMMER. BULLETIN. bi-m. Liechtensteinische Industrie- und Handelskammer, Josef-Rheinberger-Str. 11, Postfach 232, FL-9490 Vaduz, Liechtenstein. TEL 41-75-2375511. **Document type:** bulletin.

945   IT
LIGURIA TRE - RAPPORTO ANNUALE; andamento socio economico della regione. 1972. a. free. Unioncamere Liguri, Via San Lorenzo, 15, 16123 Genova, Italy. FAX 39-10-290422. bk.rev. circ. 2,000.
    Formerly: Liguria Tre.

382   EC
LIVING IN ECUADOR. a. $40. Ecuadorian - American Chamber of Commerce, Edif. Multicentro, 4P, La Nina y 6 Diciembre, Quito, Ecuador. TEL 5932-507-450. FAX 5932-504-571. circ. 1,000.

LIVING IN VENEZUELA. see *TRAVEL AND TOURISM*

381   UK
LONDON CHAMBER OF COMMERCE AND INDUSTRY. ANNUAL REVIEW. 1882. a. membership. London Chamber of Commerce and Industry, 33 Queen St., London EC4R 1AP, England. TEL 44-171-248-4444. adv. circ. 4,000. **Document type:** trade publication.
    Former titles: London Chamber of Commerce. Annual Review; London Chamber of Commerce and Industry. Annual Review.

381   UK   ISSN 0142-9728
LONDON CHAMBER OF COMMERCE AND INDUSTRY. DIRECTORY. 1882. a. £50. Kemps Publishing Ltd., 11 The Swan Courtyard, Charles Edward Rd., Birmingham B26 1BU, England. TEL 44-121-765-4144. FAX 44-121-706-6210. adv. **Document type:** directory.
    Incorporates: Westminster Chamber of Commerce and Industry; **Formerly:** London Chamber of Commerce and Industry. Annual Report and Annual Directory (ISSN 0076-0528)

381   SZ
LUZERNER GEWERBE ZEITUNG. 8/yr. Burgerstr. 17, Postfach 272, CH-6000 Luzern 7, Switzerland. TEL 041-231838. circ. 5,300.

382   MY   ISSN 0127-5739
M I C C I DIGEST. m. free. Malaysian International Chamber of Commerce and Industry - Dewan Perniagaan dan Perindustrian Antarabangsa, P.O. Box 12921, 10th Fl. Wisma Damansara, Jalan Semantan, 50792 Kuala Lumpur, Malaysia. TEL 60-3-254-2677. FAX 60-3-255-4946. Ed. Keith Sargeant. **Document type:** newsletter.

382   IT   ISSN 0394-347X
MADE IN ITALY; rivista del commercio estero. (Text in English, French, German, Italian and Spanish) 1946. m. $60. Camera di Commercio Italiana per l'Estero, Corso Vittorio Emanuele 15, 20122 Milan, Italy. TEL 2-76-02-02-69. FAX 2-76-00-49-82. Ed. Marco Polenghi. adv.; illus.

974 US
MADISON, CONNECTICUT - A PICTORIAL GUIDE.* 1982. biennial. Madison Chamber of Commerce, Inc., P.O. Box 706, Madison, CT 06443-0906. TEL 203-245-7394. FAX 203-245-3419. Ed. Nancy C. Sullivan. adv.; illus. circ. 13,750.
  Description: Directory designed to serve as a direct guide for shopping and as a survey of opportunities for community involvement.

943.1 GW
MAGAZIN WIRTSCHAFT. 1972. m. DM.45. Industrie- und Handelskammer Region Stuttgart, Postfach 102444, 70020 Stuttgart, Germany. TEL 0711-2005-0. FAX 0711-2005327. Ed. Guenter Huhndorf. adv. contact: Peter Schmidt. circ. 98,000. **Document type:** trade publication.
  Formerly: Mittlerer Neckar.

954 II
MAHARASHTRA CHAMBER PATRIKA. bi-w. Maharashtra Chamber of Commerce, 12 Rampart Row, Bombay 400 023, India. TEL 22-244548.

944 FR
MAINE ECONOMIE. 11/yr. 12 place de la Republique, 72000 Le Mans, France. TEL 43-24-52-41. FAX 43-28-16-58. TELEX CHAMCO MANS 720 015. circ. 12,000.

976 US
MAJOR EMPLOYERS DIRECTORY. a. $20. Birmingham Area Chamber of Commerce, 2027 First Ave., Birmingham, AL 35203. TEL 205-323-5461. **Document type:** directory.
  Description: Lists companies in the Birmingham MSA that employ 100 or more people.

914 IT ISSN 0025-2506
MANTOVA. 1905. q. L.3000. Camera di Commercio Industria e Agricoltura di Mantova, Via P.F. Calvi 28, Mantua, Italy. TEL 76-322371. FAX 76-361883. TELEX 300686. adv.; bk.rev.

382 FR ISSN 0249-5430
MARCHE DES DECHETS INDUSTRIELS. q. Chambre Regionale de Commerce et d'Industrie d'Alsace, 42 rue Schweighaeuser, 67000 Strasbourg, France. TEL 33-3-88607475. FAX 33-3-88615354.

381 GW ISSN 0721-9148
MARKT & WIRTSCHAFT. m. DM.36. Industrie- und Handelskammer Koeln, Unter Sachsenhausen 10-26, 50667 Cologne, Germany. TEL 0221-1640-0. FAX 0221-1640123. (Dist. by: Greven & Bechtold GmbH, Sigurd-Greven-Str., 50354 Huerth, Germany. TEL 02233-6900-0. FAX 02233-690055) Ed. Christian Knull. adv.: page DM.8215; trim 184 x 265. **Document type:** bulletin.
  ●Also available online.
  Formerly (until 1981): I H K Mitteilungen (ISSN 0341-146X).

975.2 US
THE MARYLAND AGENDA. m. membership. Maryland Chamber of Commerce, 60 West St., Ste. 1000, Annapolis, MD 21401-2434. TEL 301-269-0642. FAX 301-269-5247. Ed. Gene Bracken. adv. circ. 5,200. **Document type:** newspaper.
  Formerly: Maryland State Chamber of Commerce. Newsletter.

968.91 RH
MASHONALAND CHAMBER OF INDUSTRIES. ANNUAL REPORT. Mashonaland Chamber of Industries (MCI), 109 Rotten Row, P.O. Box 3794, Harare, Zimbabwe. TEL 702431. TELEX 2073.

945 IT
MATERA. bi-m. Camera di Commercio, Industria e Agricoltura di Matera, Matera, Italy.

967 MF
MAURITIUS CHAMBER OF COMMERCE AND INDUSTRY. ANNUAL REPORT. (Text in English) 1950. a. free. Mauritius Chamber of Commerce and Industry, 3 Royal St., Port Louis, Mauritius. TEL 230-208-3301. FAX 230-208-0076. E-mail: mccipl@bow.intnet.mu. Ed.Bd. circ. 800. **Document type:** corporate report.

382 UY ISSN 0797-2733
MERCADO. (Text mainly in Spanish; occasionally in German) 1987. q. Camara de Comercio Uruguayo-Alemana - Deutsch-Uruguayische Handelskammer, Zabala 1379, Casilla de Correo 1499, 11000 Montevideo, Uruguay. TEL 598-2-970307. FAX 598-2-963281. adv.: B&W page DM.1000, color page DM.1200. circ. 800.

380.1 US ISSN 0194-9101
HF1
MERCER BUSINESS MAGAZINE. 1924. m. $22 (effective 1997). Mercer County Chamber of Commerce, 2550 Kuser Rd., Box 8307, Trenton, NJ 08650. TEL 609-586-2056. FAX 609-586-8052. Ed. Gene J. Sayko. adv. contact: Donna Krupa. bk.rev.; stat. circ. 8,500. (also avail. in microform from UMI.) Indexed: P.A.I.S. **Document type:** trade publication.
  ●Also available online. Vendor(s): Knight-Ridder Information, Inc., UMI.
  —UMI.
  Formerly (until 1979): Trenton (ISSN 0041-2449).
  Description: A monthly business features magazine covering activities in the Princeton-Trenton, New Jersey metro-market.

944 FR ISSN 1248-9468
METIERS REUSSITE 01. 1959. bi-m. 2 F. Chambre de Metiers de l'Ain, 3, rue P.-Piola, Bourg (Ain), France. adv. circ. 7,800.
  Former titles (until 1993): Metiers (ISSN 1248-945X); (until 1972): Chambre de Metiers de l'Ain. Bulletin (ISSN 1248-9441)

381 BG
METROPOLITAN CHAMBER OF COMMERCE AND INDUSTRY, DHAKA. CHAMBER NEWS. (Text in English) 1978. m. Tk.50. Metropolitan Chamber of Commerce and Industry, Chamber Bldg., 4th Fl., 122-124, Motijheel C.A., Dhaka 1000, Bangladesh. adv.; bk.rev. circ. 400. Indexed: Key to Econ.Sci.
  Formerly: Narayanganj Chambers of Commerce & Industry. Chamber News.

METROPOLITAN MILWAUKEE ASSOCIATION OF COMMERCE. MEMBERSHIP DIRECTORY & BUYERS' GUIDE (YEAR). see BUSINESS AND ECONOMICS — Trade And Industrial Directories

944 FR ISSN 0755-7078
MEUSE ECONOMIQUE. q. 120 F. (effective 1997). Chambre de Commerce et d'Industrie de la Meuse, 6 Parc Bradfer, 55000 Bar-le-Duc, France. TEL 33-3-29768300. FAX 33-3-29454742. Ed. Francois Godinot. adv. contact: Marie-Claude Bertaud. circ. 4,800. **Document type:** bulletin.

053.1 GW
MITTEILUNGEN "BERUFSBILDUNG". 1959. m. Industrie- und Handelskammer zu Muenster, Sentmaringer Weg 61, 48151 Muenster, Germany. TEL 0251-707-261. FAX 0251-707-325. circ. 10,700. **Document type:** bulletin.

381 GW ISSN 0949-4677
MITTELFRAENKISCHE WIRTSCHAFT. 1944. m. DM.40 (effective 1996). (Industrie- und Handelskammer Nuernberg) Hofmann Druck Nuernberg, Postfach 120260, 90109 Nuernberg, Germany. TEL 49-911-5203-0. FAX 49-911-5203148. E-mail: 100415.1125@compuserve.com; URL: http://ihk-nuernberg.de. Ed. Kurt Hesse; Pub. Guenter Hofmann. R&P contact: Dieter Goessner. adv.: B&W page DM.6300, color page DM.9600; trim 188 x 260; adv. contact: Ruediger Sander. bk.rev.; circ. 70,000. **Document type:** trade publication.

382 US
MOBILE AREA CHAMBER OF COMMERCE MEMBERSHIP DIRECTORY AND BUYER'S GUIDE. a. $20 to non-members. Mobile Area Chamber of Commerce, Box 2187, Mobile, AL 36652. TEL 205-433-6951. FAX 205-431-8608. Ed. Walter A. Underwood. adv. circ. 5,000. **Document type:** directory.
  Formerly (since 1979): Who's Who in the Mobile Area.

330 IT ISSN 0391-6626
MODENA ECONOMICA. 1892. 9/yr. Camera di Commercio, Industria, Artigianato e Agricoltura di Modena, Via Ganaceto 134, 41100 Modena, Italy. TEL 208111. FAX 211035. Ed. Giorgio Bertolani. adv.; bk.rev.; illus, mkt, stat. circ. 7,000.
  Formerly: Modena (ISSN 0026-7430)

914 320 IT
MONDO PADANO. 1981. w. L.88000 (effective 1997). Societa Editrice Lombarda S.r.l., Via Aporti 17, 26100 Cremona, Italy. TEL 39-372-411731. Ed. Antonio Leoni. adv. circ. 22,000. **Document type:** newspaper.

949.4 SZ
MONTAGNA. (Text in French, German and Italian) 1990. m. 51 SFr. Schweizerische Arbeitsgemeinschaft fuer die Berggebiete, Laurstr. 10, CH-5200 Brugg, Switzerland. TEL 056-423012. FAX 056-413642. adv.; bk.rev. circ. 6,000. (back issues avail.) **Document type:** newsletter.

382 954 PK
MONTHLY EXPORT TRENDS; monitor of Pakistan's export trade. 1986. m. Rs.180. Readers' Publications Pvt. Ltd., Shaheen Chambers, A-4, Commercial Area, Block 7-8, K.C.H.S, Karachi, Pakistan. TEL 435804. TELEX 23862 DABH PK. (Co-sponsor: Federation of Pakistan Chambers of Commerce and Industry) Ed. Agha Masood. adv.; bk.rev. circ. 5,000.

381 CN ISSN 1196-1651
MONTREAL PLUS. (Text in English, French) 1992. 7/yr. Can.$20. Board of Trade of Metropolitan Montreal - Chambre de Commerce du Montreal Metropolitain, 5 Ville Marie Place, Ste. 12500, Plaza Level, Montreal, PQ H3B 4Y2, Canada. TEL 514-871-4000. FAX 514-871-1255. Ed. Joelle Ganguillet. R&P contact: Joelle Ganguillet. adv.: B&W page Can.$1400; adv. contact: Johanne Gagne. circ. 10,000. **Document type:** trade publication.

945 IT
MOVIMENTO ANAGRAFE DITTE. 1991. m. L.35000 (effective 1993). Camera di Commercio Industria, Artigianato e Agricoltura di Pesaro e Urbino, Corso XI Settembre, 116, 61100 Pesaro, Italy. TEL 0721-3571. FAX 0721-31015. TELEX 560229 CAMCOM. Ed. Paolo Lamaro. circ. 720 (controlled). **Document type:** government publication, directory.
  Description: Lists new and ceased firms in the province of Pesaro.

381 US
MT. OLIVE TODAY. 1991. q. free. Mt. Olive Area Chamber of Commerce, 100 Rt. 46, Village Green Annex, Budd Lake, NJ 07828-9998. TEL 201-691-0109. FAX 201-691-0110. Ed. Dolores Ortiz. adv. **Document type:** newsletter.
  Description: Discusses the Chamber's activities and ambitions; promotes active participation in the organization.

380 II ISSN 0027-559X
MYSORE COMMERCE. 1944. m. Rs.6. Federation of Karnataka Chambers of Commerce & Industry, Post Box 9996, K.G. Rd., Bangalore 560009, India. Ed. B.N. Narayan. adv.; bk.rev.; bibl.; charts; illus.; pat.; stat. circ. 2,000.

382 NE ISSN 0927-703X
HF3611
N C H TRADELETTER. 1948. 8/yr. fl.90($45) Nederlands Centrum voor Handelsbevordering, Postbus 10, 2501 CA The Hague, Netherlands. Ed. W.F. van der Hooft. abstr.; pat.; stat.; tr.lit. circ. 400. Indexed: Key to Econ.Sci. **Document type:** newsletter.
  Formerly (until 1992): Newsletter - N C H (ISSN 0923-3911); Incorporates (in 1992): Oost Europa - U S S R Bulletin (ISSN 0924-3410); Which was formed by the 1988 merger of: Oost Europa (ISSN 0924-3429) & Nederland - U S S R Instituut. Maandberichten (ISSN 0028-2022); Incorporates (in 1992): Afrika - Midden-Oosten Bulletin (ISSN 0923-3377); Israel Bulletin (ISSN 0924-2821); Latijns-Amerika Bulletin (ISSN 0923-3431); West-Europa Bulletin (ISSN 0924-3380).

381 338 SA
N.T.C.I. CURRENT AFFAIRS UPDATE. 1993. 7/yr. Northern Transvaal Chamber of Industries, P.O. Box 933, Pretoria 0001, South Africa. Indexed: Ind.S.A.Per.

BUSINESS AND ECONOMICS — CHAMBER OF COMMERCE PUBLICATIONS

330   IR   ISSN 1024-3011
NAMAH-'I UTAQ-I BAZARGANI. m. $50. Iran Chamber of Commerce, Industry and Mines, 254 Taleghani Ave., P.O. Box 15875-4671, Tehran, Iran. TEL 98-21-8846031. FAX 98-21-8825111. TELEX 213382 TCIM. adv.: B&W page $500, color page $1500.

382   US   ISSN 1064-9913
HF1009.5
NATIONAL TRADE DATA BANK. 1990. m. $575 (foreign $775). Department of Commerce, Office of Business Analysis, Economics and Statistics Administration, c/o U.S. National Technical Information Service, 5825 Port Royal Rd., Springfield, VA 22161. —CISTI.

338   US   ISSN 0028-047X
HF1   CODEN: NBUSAY
NATION'S BUSINESS. 1912. m. $22; newsstand price: $2.50. U.S. Chamber of Commerce, 1615 H St., N.W., Washington, DC 20062-2000. TEL 202-463-5650. FAX 202-887-3437. URL: http://www.uschamber.org/publications/index.html. Ed. Mary McElveen; Pub. David A. Roe. adv. contact: Pete McCutchen. illus.; index. circ. 850,000. (also avail. in microfiche from NBI,UMI; reprint service avail. from UMI) Indexed: ABI Inform., Acad.Ind., B.P.I., Bank.Lit.Ind., BPIA, Bus.Ind., Hlth.Ind., Mag.Ind., Manage.Cont., Microcomp.Ind., Mid.East: Abstr.& Ind., Pers.Lit., PMR, PROMT, R.G., R.G.Abstr., TOM, Tr.& Indus.Ind., Work Rel.Abstr. **Document type:** trade publication.
●Also available online. Vendor(s): Information Access Co., UMI.
Also available on CD-ROM. Producer(s): UMI.
—BLDSC (6033.600000); KR SourceOne; SWETS; UMI; UnCover. **CCC.**
Description: Provides small and mid-sized business executives with strategies, personality profiles and insight into government actions that affect the business community.

382   NE
NETHERLANDS-AMERICAN TRADE DIRECTORY. (Text in English) 1969. biennial. fl.190($130) to non-members; members free. American Chamber of Commerce in the Netherlands, Burg. van Karnebeeklaan 14, 2585 BB The Hague, Netherlands. TEL 31-70-3659808. FAX 31-70-3646992. E-mail: amchamnl@worldaccess.nl; URL: http://www.unisys.nl/amcham/. Ed. M. van den Berg. stat. **Document type:** directory.
Description: Listings of members, US firms with Netherlands subsidiaries, Netherlands firms with US subsidiaries, classification of firms by SIC-code, state or region. Includes related organizations in US and Netherlands, and statistical information on trade between the US and the Netherlands.

NETHERLANDS-BRITISH TRADE DIRECTORY. see BUSINESS AND ECONOMICS — *Trade And Industrial Directories*

382   FR   ISSN 1021-1144
NEW I C C WORLD DIRECTORY OF CHAMBERS OF COMMERCE/NOUVEL ANNUAIRE MONDIAL C C I DES CHAMBRES DE COMMERCE. 1981. a. (International Chamber of Commerce - Chambre de Commerce Internationale) I C C Publishing, 38 Cours Albert 1er, 75008 Paris, France. TEL 49-53-28-28. FAX 42-25-36-23. TELEX 650 770. **Document type:** directory.
Formerly: I C C World Directory of Chambers of Commerce (ISSN 0256-6214)

381   NP
NEWS & NEWS. 1992. m. $2. Federation of Nepalese Chambers of Commerce and Industry, P.O. Box 269, Teku, Kathmandu, Nepal. TEL 977-1-233196. adv.; bk.rev.

381   US
NEWTON - NEEDHAM BUSINESS. 1959. 10/yr. $25. Newton - Needham Chamber of Commerce, Inc., Box 268, Newton, MA 02159-0002. TEL 617-244-5300. FAX 617-244-5302. Ed. Martin Cohn. **Document type:** newsletter.
Description: Covers news and issues of interest to the local business community.

974   US
NIAGARA FALLS AREA CHAMBER OF COMMERCE. MEMBERSHIP DIRECTORY & BUYERS' GUIDE. a. $25. Niagara Falls Area Chamber of Commerce, 345 Third St., Niagara Falls, NY 14303-1117. TEL 716-285-9141. FAX 716-285-0941. Ed. Fred Caso, Jr. R&P contact: Fred Caso, Jr. adv. circ. 2,500. **Document type:** directory.
Formerly: Niagara Falls Area Chamber of Commerce. Business - Industrial Directory.
Description: Listing of Chamber members, contact personnel, financial institutions and local industry.

943.1   GW
NIEDERBAYERISCHE WIRTSCHAFT. 1947. m. DM.42. Industrie- und Handelskammer fuer Niederbayern in Passau, Nibelungenstr. 15, 94032 Passau, Germany. TEL 0851-507-0. FAX 0851-507280. Ed. Juergen Karl. adv.: B&W page DM.2600, color DM.3800; trim 250 x 185; abs. adv. contact: Martin Brunner. circ. 13,200. **Document type:** bulletin.

380   NR   ISSN 0189-5036
NIGERIAN BUSINESS JOURNAL. (Text in English) 1950. a. £N.10. Lagos Chamber of Commerce and Industry, 1 Idowu Taylor St., P.O. Box 109, Victoria Island. Lagos State, Nigeria. Ed. S.B. Akande. adv.; bk.rev. circ. 5,000. **Document type:** trade publication.
Formerly: Commerce in Nigeria (ISSN 0069-6633)

944   FR   ISSN 0243-8860
NORD SEINE ET MARNE INFORMATIONS. 1960. 4/yr. Chambre de Commerce et d'Industrie de Meaux, 12 bd. Jean-Rose, B.P. 216, 77104 Meaux, France. TEL 64-34-20-13. FAX 64-33-41-15. TELEX 691 142 F. Ed. Yves Kahn.
Formerly (until 1980): Chambre de Commerce et d'Industrie de Meaux-Coulommiers. Bulletin Trimestriel (ISSN 0243-8739)

941.6   UK
NORTHERN IRELAND CHAMBER OF COMMERCE AND INDUSTRY YEARBOOK. a. Northern Ireland Chamber of Commerce and Industry, 22 Great Victoria St., Belfast Bl2 7BJ, N. Ireland.

380.1   UK
HF302
NORTH WEST ENGLAND AND NORTH WALES CHAMBER OF COMMERCE AND INDUSTRY DIRECTORY. a. £60. (Manchester Chamber of Commerce and Industry) Kemps Publishing Ltd., 11 The Swan Courtyard, Charles Edward Rd., Birmingham B26 1BU, England. TEL 44-121-765-4144. FAX 44-121-706-6210. illus. **Document type:** directory.
Former titles: North West Chambers of Commerce Business Directory; Manchester Regional Business Directory; Manchester Chamber of Commerce and Industry. Yearbook (ISSN 0306-5758)

382   US   ISSN 0803-1134
NORWAY AT YOUR SERVICE. 2/yr. membership. Norwegian American Chamber of Commerce, Inc., 800 Third Ave., New York, NY 10022. TEL 212-421-9210.

382   UK   ISSN 0305-0998
HF302
NORWEGIAN CHAMBER OF COMMERCE. YEAR BOOK AND DIRECTORY OF MEMBERS. (Text in English) 1908. a. free to members. Norwegian Chamber of Commerce (London) Inc., 21-24 Cockspur St., London S.W.1, England. Ed. Oeystein Grahamm-Flateboe. adv. circ. 1,800. **Document type:** directory.

382   US   ISSN 0891-2890
NORWEGIAN TRADE BULLETIN. 8/yr. free. Norwegian American Chamber of Commerce, Inc., 800 Third Ave., New York, NY 10022. TEL 212-421-9210. **Document type:** bulletin.

941   UK   ISSN 0953-5470
NORWICH AND NORFOLK CHAMBER OF COMMERCE AND INDUSTRY. DIRECTORY. (Editions in English, French, German) 1981. a. £35 to non-members; members free. Norwich and Norfolk Chamber of Commerce, 112 Barrack St., Norwich, Norfolk NR3 1UB, England. TEL 0603-625977. FAX 0603-633032. TELEX CHACOM-G-975247. Ed. Deb Jackson. adv.; illus. circ. 3,500. **Document type:** directory.
Description: Gives current data on the region with membership listings under alphabetical and classified headings.

381   IT
NOTE SULLA CONGIUNTURA. 1984. s-a. free. Camera di Commercio, Industria, Artigianato e Agricoltura di Padova, Via E. Filiberto 34, Padua, Italy. TEL 39-49-8208111. TELEX 430047 CCIA PD I. Ed. Giampaolo Redivo. circ. 280. **Document type:** monographic series.
Description: Covers the economic trends in the district of Padua.

380.1   CK   ISSN 0120-615X
NOTICIA COMERCIAL DEL ORIENTE. 1979. m. $17. Camara de Comercio de Bogota, Carrera 9, No. 16-21, Piso 8, Apdo. Aereo 29824, Bogota, Colombia. Ed. Alba Maria Rueda Vasquez. adv.; charts; illus.; stat. circ. 1,000.
Supersedes: Noticiero Mercantil; Organizacion Mercantil (ISSN 0030-5049)

945   IT
NOTIZIARIO COMMERCIO ESTERO. 1960. m. free. Camera di Commercio, Industria, Artigianato e Agricoltura di Vincenza, Corso Antonio Fogazzaro, 37, 36100 Vicenza, Italy. TEL 39-444-994811. FAX 39-444-994834. TELEX 480496 VICAM I. Ed. Antonio Bellin. circ. 3,800. **Document type:** trade publication.
Description: Contains articles on international trade and business opportunities.

330   IT
NOTIZIE DELL'ECONOMIA TERAMANA. 1945. m. L.6000. Camera di Commercio Industria Artigianato e Agricoltura di Teramo, Piazza Martiri della Liberta, 64100 Teramo, Italy. Ed. Luciotti R. Gianni. adv.

330   IT   ISSN 0029-6171
NUOVA ECONOMIA. m. Camera di Commercio Industria, Artigianato e Agricoltura di Perugia, 1 Piazza Italia, 06100 Perugia, Italy. abstr.; bibl.; charts; illus.; stat. circ. 1,000.

945   IT
NUOVO COMMERCIO. 1963. m. Confesercenti del Comprensorio di Cesena, Via Roverella 1, Cesena (FO), Italy. TEL 547-22771. Ed. Dino Amadori. adv. circ. 9,000.

338   GW   ISSN 0029-7496
OBERFRAENKISCHE WIRTSCHAFT. 1910. m. DM.5. Industrie- und Handelskammer fuer Oberfranken, Bahnhofstr. 25-27, 95444 Bayreuth, Germany. Ed. Bodo Schultheiss. adv. contact: Monika Oberst. bk.rev.; charts; illus.; stat.; tr.lit. circ. 38,000. **Document type:** consumer publication.

382   AU   ISSN 0029-8751
OESTERREICH-NEDERLAND. 1961. irreg. (approx. 5/yr.). membership. Niederlaendische Handelskammer fuer Oesterreich, Schwarzenbergplatz 10, Postfach 160, A-1041 Vienna, Austria. TEL 0222-5055708. FAX 0222-5055700. adv.; bk.rev.; abstr.; bibl.; charts; illus.; stat.; tr.lit. circ. 3,000.

382   NE
OOSTENRIJKSE ECONOMISCHE BERICHTEN. 1950. m. free. Oostenrijkse Handelsdelegatie in Nederland - Oesterreichische Aussenhandelsstelle in den Niederlanden, Lange Voorhout 58a, 2514 EG The Hague, Netherlands. (Affiliate: Bundeshandelskammer, Vienna) adv.; illus.; tr.lit. circ. 3,000.
Supersedes: Oostenrijkse Handelsdelegatie in Nederland (ISSN 0030-3291)

382   FR   ISSN 0249-5163
OPPORTUNITES INDUSTRIELLES BULLETIN. q. Chambre Regionale de Commerce et d'Industrie d'Alsace, 42 rue Schweighaeuser, 67000 Strasbourg, France. TEL 33-3-88607475. FAX 33-3-88615354. **Document type:** bulletin.

945   IT
OSSERVATORIO ECONOMICO. (Supplement to: Il Filugello) 1966. m. Camera di Commercio, Industria, Artigianato e Agricoltura, Piazza della Vittoria 4, 42100 Reggio Emilia, Italy. TEL 0522-7961. FAX 0522-433750. Ed. Franco Moleterni. adv. circ. 4,000.

BUSINESS AND ECONOMICS — CHAMBER OF COMMERCE PUBLICATIONS

330 GW ISSN 0720-4868
OSTSEEJAHRBUCH. 1934. a. price varies. Industrie- und Handelskammer zu Luebeck, Breitestr. 6-8, 23552 Luebeck, Germany. FAX 49-451-7085284. Ed. Hans-Jochen Arndt. R&P contact: Hans-Jochen Arndt. circ. 1,200. **Document type:** bulletin.
   Former title: Wirtschaft im Ostseeraum (ISSN 0084-0483)

943 GW
OSTWESTFAELISCHE WIRTSCHAFT. m. Industrie- und Handelskammer Ostwestfalen zu Bielefeld, Elsa-Braendstroem-Str. 1-3, 33602 Bielefeld, Germany. TEL 0521-5540. FAX 0521-554219. TELEX 175218182. adv.; bk.rev. **Document type:** bulletin.

330 IT ISSN 0030-9206
PADOVA ECONOMICA. 1963-1985; resumed 1989. bi-m. L.50000 (effective 1997). Camera di Commercio, Industria, Artigianato e Agricoltura di Padova, Via E. Filiberto 34, Padua, Italy. Ed. Bruno Geromin. adv.; bibl.; illus.; stat.; index; circ. 2,000 (controlled). **Document type:** bulletin.

338 PK
PAKISTAN DIRECTORY OF TRADE AND INDUSTRY. (Text in English) 1976. a. Lahore Chamber of Commerce and Industry, P.O. Box 597, 11 Aiwan-i-Tijarat, Lahore, Pakistan. **Document type:** directory.

380.1 US
PARTNERSHIP PROGRESS. 1955. m. (membership). Regional Business Partnership, 1 Newark Center, 22nd Fl., Newark, NJ 07102. TEL 201-242-6237. FAX 201-824-6587. Ed. Lori Garofalo. adv.; charts; illus. circ. 10,000. (tabloid format) **Document type:** newsletter.
   Former titles (until 1994): Metro Courier (Newark); (until 1989): Metro-Newark; Newark.

330 IT ISSN 0391-8319
PAVIA ECONOMICA. 1946. 3/yr. L.25000. Camera di Commercio Industria Artigianato e Agricoltura di Pavia, Via Mentana 27, 27100 Pavia, Italy. TEL 39-382-3931. FAX 39-382-304559. TELEX 310-033 CAMPV I. Ed. G. Pallavicini. adv.; page L.800000. bk.rev.; index. **Document type:** trade publication.
   Formerly (until 1961): Informazioni Economiche.

381 US
PENNSYLVANIA CHAMBER OF BUSINESS AND INDUSTRY. STATE & REGIONAL DIRECTORY.* a. $40 to non-members; members $25. Pennsylvania Chamber of Business and Industry, 417 Walnut St., Harrisburg, PA 17101. TEL 717-255-3252. FAX 717-255-3298. Ed. John Eichorn. circ. 650. **Document type:** directory.
   Former titles: Pennsylvania Chamber of Commerce. State and Regional Directory; Pennsylvania Chamber of Commerce. Directory of State, Regional and Commercial Organizations (ISSN 0098-5368)

982 AG ISSN 0325-5069
PENSAMIENTO ECONOMICO. 1925. q. Camara Argentina de Comercio, Avda. Leandro N. Alem 36, 1003 Buenos Aires, Argentina. TEL 331-8051. TELEX 18542. Dir. Pedro Naon Argerich.
   Formerly (until 1975): Camara Argentina de Comercio. Revista.

382 SP ISSN 1135-5891
PERSPECTIVES. 1969. 6/yr. 1000 F. (effective 1995). Chambre Francaise de Commerce et d'Industrie de Madrid - Camara Francesa de Comercio e Industria de Madrid, C. Ruiz de Alarcon, 7, 28014 Madrid, Spain. TEL 34-1-5226742. FAX 34-1-5233642. (Subscr. to: Chambre de Commerce et d'Industrie Francaise, Passeig de Gracia 2, 08007 Barcelona, Spain. TEL 34-3-3176738. FAX 34-3-3171139) Ed. B. Barthelemy. adv.; circ. 2,200 (controlled). **Document type:** monographic series.
   Description: Each issue presents a complete approach to a theme of Spanish economy, with concrete examples, written by Spanish and French professionals.

338 IT ISSN 0031-9570
LA PIANURA. 1964. 3/yr. free. Camera di Commercio, Industria, Artigianato e Agricoltura di Ferrara, Via Borgoleoni 11, 44100 Ferrara, Italy. TEL 39-532-783711. FAX 39-532-240204. Dir. Pietro Cocurullo. adv.; charts; illus.; stat.

944 FR ISSN 0180-6084
PLEIN OUEST; informations economiques Nantes Atlantique. 1977. bi-m. 120 F. Chambres de Commerce et d'Industrie de Nantes et de Saint-Nazaire, Centre de Salorges, 16 Quai Ernest-Renaud, 44040 Nantes Cedex, France. TEL 33-2-40446347. FAX 33-2-40446090. (Subscr. to: B.P. 718, 44027 Nantes Cedex 04, France) Ed. Philippe Hervouet. adv.; illus. circ. 26,000. **Document type:** consumer publication.
   Description: Covers the economic news of the Pays de la Loire.

PLYMOUTH COUNTY BUSINESS REVIEW. see BUSINESS AND ECONOMICS — Domestic Commerce

381 US
THE POINT! 1916. s-m. $25. Oklahoma City Chamber of Commerce, 123 Park Ave., Oklahoma City, OK 73102-9031. TEL 405-297-8900. FAX 405-297-8916. Ed. Kelly Brooks. R&P contact: Kelly Brooks. adv. contact: Kelly Brooks. charts; illus. circ. 5,000. (also avail. in microform from UMI; reprint service avail. from UMI) **Document type:** trade publication.
   —UMI.
   Former titles (until 1994): O K C Action (ISSN 1043-4259); (until 1989): Oklahoma (ISSN 0030-1639)

380.1 FR ISSN 0758-573X
POINT ECONOMIQUE. 1971. 8/yr. 110 F. (effective 1997). Chambre de Commerce et d'Industrie de Strasbourg et du Bas-Rhin, 10 place Gutenberg, 67081 Strasbourg Cedex, France. TEL 33-3-88752525. FAX 33-3-33223120. TELEX 870068 F CHAMCO. Ed. Philippe Grillault Laroche. adv.; bk.rev. circ. 25,000.

382 SZ
POINT ECONOMIQUE. 10/yr. Chambre France - Suisse pour le Commerce et l'Industrie, 32 Av. de Frontenex, CP 229, 1211 Geneva, Switzerland.

944 FR ISSN 0981-1869
PRESENCES. 1987. 10/yr. 150 F. (effective 1996). 1 place Andre-Malraux, B.P. 297, 38016 Grenoble Cedex, France. TEL 76-28-28-76. FAX 76-28-28-60. TELEX CECOMEX 320 824 F. Ed. Jacques Baillieux; Pub. Catherine Ledoux. adv. contact: Catherine Ledoux. circ. 40,000. **Document type:** newspaper.

382 VE
PRESENZA ECONOMICA. m? Camara de Comercio, Industria y Agricultura Venezolano-Italiana, Av. Andres Bello, Centro Andres Bello, Torre Oeste, p. 14, Ofs. 143-144, Apdo. 14204, Caracas 1050, Venezuela. TEL 02-781-5213. FAX 7813731. TELEX 28676 CAMCO VC. adv.; charts;illus.

382 IT ISSN 1120-3919
PREZZI DEI MATERIALI E DELLE OPERE EDILI IN FERRARA. 1968. q. L.40000. Camera di Commercio, Industria, Artigianato e Agricoltura di Ferrara, Via Borgoleoni, 11, Ferrara 44100, Italy. TEL 39-532-783711. FAX 39-532-240204. Dir. Luigi Litardi. adv.
   Formerly: Inserite Nuove Voci e Miglioramenti Tipografici.

330 CI ISSN 0350-9427
PRIVREDA (OSIJEK); casopis za privredna pitanja Slavonije i Baranje. 1957. m. Privredna Komora Slavonije i Baranje, Bulevar JNA 13, 54000 Osijek, Croatia. Ed. Petar Djidara. circ. 1,100.
   Formerly: Privreda Kotara Osijek (ISSN 0032-8960)

382 CI ISSN 0350-4476
PRIVREDA DALMACIJE. m. Privredna Komora Dalmacije, Saveznicka Obala 4, 58000 Split, Croatia.

381 US ISSN 1048-2989
PROFILE (LOS ANGELES). 1925. bi-m. $1 to members only. Los Angeles Junior Chamber of Commerce, 404 S. Bixel St., Los Angeles, CA 90017. TEL 213-482-1311. FAX 213-482-0865. Ed. Bob Levey. illus. circ. 1,500. **Document type:** newsletter.
   Formerly (until 1989): Headlines (ISSN 0300-7782)

380.1 US ISSN 0162-5241
PROFILE (OMAHA). vol.33, 1973. s-m. $40 to non-members; members $20. Greater Omaha Chamber of Commerce, 1301 Harney, Omaha, NE 68102-1832. TEL 402-346-5000. FAX 402-346-7050. Ed. Vicki Krecek. adv.; illus. circ. 3,800. **Document type:** newsletter.
   Formerly: Omaha Profile (ISSN 0030-221X)
   Description: News items, information, and announcements of the activities and issues pertaining to the Chamber of Commerce.

338 UK ISSN 0019-8854
PROGRESS WALES.* 1946. q. free. Development Corporation for Wales, Pearl Assurance House, Greyfriars Rd., Cardiff CF1 3AG, Wales. Ed. N. Granville Davies. adv.; bk.rev.; illus. circ. 4,500.
   Formerly: Industrial Wales.

381 US ISSN 0033-6068
HF296
QUEENSBOROUGH. 1914. a. $175 membership. Queens Chamber of Commerce, 75-20 Astoria Blvd., Ste. 140, Jackson Heights, NY 11370. TEL 718-898-8500. FAX 718-898-8599. Ed. Eric P. Robinson; Pub. Lucy Nunziato. R&P contact: Eric P. Robinson. adv. contact: Marilyn McAndrews. illus. circ. 1,500. **Document type:** newsletter.

R C G A'S DIRECTORY OF ST. LOUIS LARGE EMPLOYERS. (St. Louis Regional Commerce and Growth Association) see BUSINESS AND ECONOMICS — Trade And Industrial Directories

945 IT
RASSEGNA ECONOMICA DELLA PROVINCIA DI SONDRIO. 1948. bi-m. L.24000. Camera di Commercio, Industria, Artigianato e Agricoltura di Sondrio, 23100 Sondrio, Italy. adv.; bk.rev. circ. 7,000.

380.1 FR ISSN 0223-5730
REALITES FRANC-COMTOISES. 1957. m. 340 F. (effective 1997). Chambre de Commerce et d'Industrie du Doubs, 46 av. Villarceau, 25042 Besancon Cedex, France. TEL 33-3-81252525. FAX 33-3-81252502. URL: http://www.tjts.com/f/realfrco.htm. Ed. Gerard Bassand. adv. circ. 3,500. **Indexed:** P.A.I.S. **Document type:** trade publication.

REGISTER & BUYERS GUIDE. (Confederation of Zimbabwe Industries) see BUSINESS AND ECONOMICS — Trade And Industrial Directories

650 FR ISSN 1147-8217
REPERTOIRE D'ANNUAIRES FRANCAIS. 1974. irreg., 13th ed., 1997. 450 F. (effective 1997). Chambre de Commerce et d'Industrie de Paris (CEDIP), 27 av. de Friedland, 75382 Paris Cedex 08, France. TEL 33-1-53845353. FAX 33-1-53845351.
   Formerly (until 1986): Repertoire d'Annuaires Francais et Listes d'Adresses Susceptibles d'Interesser le Commerce et l'Industrie (ISSN 0996-3227); Supersedes (in 1969): Annuaires Francais et Listes d'Adresses Susceptibles d'Interesser le Commerce et l'Industrie (ISSN 0066-3743)
   Description: Listing of 1400 trade guides representing French businesses, industries and economic associations.

946.9 SP
REPERTORIO DE EXPORTADORES. 1942. s-a. Camara Oficial de Comercio, Industria y Navegacion de Valencia, Poeta Querol 15, 46002 Valencia, Spain. adv.
   Formerly: Catalogo de Exportadores.

946.9 SP
REPERTORIO DE IMPORTADORES. 1982. s-a. Camara Oficial de Comercio, Industria y Navegacion de Valencia, Poeta Querol 15, 46002 Valencia, Spain. TEL 34-6-3511301. FAX 34-6-3516349.
   Formerly: Catalogo de Importadores.

931 CH
REPUBLIC OF CHINA. CHAMBER OF COMMERCE BULLETIN. q. General Chamber of Commerce of the Republic of China, 162 Hsin Yi Rd., Sec. 3, Rose Mansion, 7th Fl., Taipei, Taiwan, Republic of China. TEL 02-7080350. TELEX 11396. **Document type:** bulletin.

BUSINESS AND ECONOMICS — CHAMBER OF COMMERCE PUBLICATIONS

382 CK
RVISTA SUIZA. (Text in French, German, Spanish) 1985. q. Col.$30000. Camara de Comercio Colombo Suiza, Apdo. Aereo 11232, Bogota, Colombia. TEL 2885079. FAX 2885459. Ed. Roland Grobli. adv. **Document type:** trade publication.
Former titles (until 1993): Bitacora Colombo Suizo; Circulo Colombo Suizo. Boletin Informativo.
Description: Covers the economic situations of Switzerland and Colombia.

382 BE ISSN 0017-7334
VUE COMMERCIALE - HANDELSOVERZICHT. (Text in Dutch, French) 1917. bi-m. 2400 BEF membership. Chambre de Commerce Neerlandaise pour la Belgique et le Luxembourg - Nederlandse Kamer van Koophandel voor Belgie en Luxemburg, 18 rue du Congres, B-1000 Brussels, Belgium.
TEL 32-2-2191174. FAX 32-2-2187821. TELEX 63174. Ed. L.A.A. van den Hamer. adv.; bk.rev. circ. 4,000. **Indexed:** ELLIS. **Document type:** bulletin.

944 FR ISSN 0980-2282
VUE DE PRESSE CHAMPAGNE-ARDENNE ACTUALITES. w. (48/yr.) 540 F. (effective 1997). Chambre Regionale de Commerce et d'Industrie de Champagne - Ardenne, 10 rue de Chastillon, B.P. 537, 51011 Chalons-en-Champagne Cedex, France. TEL 33-3-26693340. FAX 33-3-26693369. Ed. Pierre Dellon. **Document type:** newsletter.
Description: Reviews over 125 economic periodicals.

382 FR ISSN 0753-3098
RVUE DE PRESSE ET DE DOCUMENTATION ALLEMANDE. m. Chambre Regionale de Commerce et d'Industrie d'Alsace, 42 rue Schweighaeuser, 67000 Strasbourg, France. TEL 33-3-88607475. FAX 33-3-88615354.

971 CN
RVUE ECONOMIQUE. 1984. 3/yr. Chambre de Commerce de Laval, 1555 Chomedy Blvd., Ste. 200, Laval, Que. H7V 3Z1, Canada.
TEL 514-682-5255. FAX 514-682-5735. Ed. Roger Desautels. adv.; B&W page Can.$1150, color page Can.$1400. circ. 17,712. (reprint service avail. from SCH)

382 FR
RVUE ECONOMIQUE SUISSE EN FRANCE. 1920. q. 220 F. Chambre de Commerce Suisse en France, 10 rue des Messageries, 75010 Paris, France. TEL 33-1-48010077. FAX 33-1-48010575. Ed. Olivier Julliard. adv. contact: Dominique Barue. bibl.; illus.; index. **Indexed:** ELLIS.
Formerly (until 1996): Revue Economique Franco Suisse (ISSN 0035-2799)

338.9 FR ISSN 0080-2506
RVUE FRANCAISE DE COOPERATION ECONOMIQUE AVEC ISRAEL. 1969. bi-m. 1000 F. (effective 1997). Chambre de Commerce France-Israel, 64 av. Marceau, 75008 Paris, France.
TEL 33-1-44433506. Dir. L. Stoleru. adv.; bk.rev. circ. 5,000. **Document type:** trade publication, directory, bulletin.
Formerly (until 1969): Revue Economique France-Israel.

338 GW ISSN 0035-4449
RHEINHESSISCHE WIRTSCHAFT. 1910. m. DM.30. Industrie- und Handelskammer fuer Rheinhessen, Schillerplatz 7, 55116 Mainz, Germany.
TEL 06131-262-0. FAX 06131-262169. Ed. Ernst Thoene, Wolfgang Holdschuh. adv.; bk.rev. circ. 26,000. **Document type:** corporate report.

338
RIO (SAN ANTONIO); the official magazine of the River Walk. 1968. m. $12 (free to qualified personnel). Paseo del Rio Association of San Antonio, 213 Broadway, Ste. 5, San Antonio, TX 78205-1923. TEL 210-227-4262. FAX 210-212-7602. Ed. Cybele Bolado; Pub. Sam Gorena. R&P contact: Lori Tafolla. adv. contact: Lori Tafolla. charts; illus.; circ. 50,000 (controlled). **Document type:** consumer publication.
Former titles: Reflexiones - Reflections; Paseo del Rio Showboat (ISSN 0301-2592)
Description: Tourist information and resources for visitors to the River Walk in San Antonio.

956.95 JO
RISALAT AL SINA'A/AMMAN CHAMBER OF INDUSTRY. BIMONTHLY INDUSTRIAL BULLETIN. (Text in Arabic) bi-m. $24. Amman Chamber of Industry, P.O. Box 1800, Amman, Jordan. TEL 643001. FAX 647852. TELEX 22079 INDUST JO. adv. circ. 1,750.
Description: Reviews legislation, regulations, statistics, and information concerning industry and trade opportunities.

382 SZ
RIVISTA DEGLI SCAMBI ITALO-SVIZZERI.* m. Zuericher Handelskammer, Boersengebaeude, Bleicherweg 5, Postfach 4031, 8022 Zuerich, Switzerland.
TEL 1-471080. TELEX 57509 COMITALIA.

381 US
ROANOKE REGIONAL CHAMBER OF COMMERCE. BUSINESS AGENDA. vol.8, 1970. m. $15. Roanoke Regional Chamber of Commerce, 212 S. Jefferson St., Roanoke, VA 24011. TEL 540-983-0700. Ed. Patti Dunbar. adv.; illus.; stat. circ. 3,200. **Document type:** newsletter.
Former titles: Agenda (Roanoke) (ISSN 1056-3733); (until 1990): Valley Commerce (ISSN 1043-1969); Roanoke Valley Chamber of Commerce (ISSN 0884-3155); (until 1984): New Directions (ISSN 0028-4629); Business Direction.

975 670 US
ROANOKE REGIONAL CHAMBER OF COMMERCE. INDUSTRIAL DIRECTORY. biennial. $20. Roanoke Regional Chamber of Commerce, 212 S. Jefferson St., Roanoke, VA 24011. TEL 540-983-0700. FAX 540-983-0723. circ. 2,000. **Document type:** directory.
Formerly: Roanoke Valley Chamber of Commerce. Industrial Directory.

380 US ISSN 0036-293X
HC108.S2
ST. LOUIS COMMERCE. 1926. m. $36. (St. Louis Regional Commerce and Growth Association) Commerce Magazine, Inc., 1 Metropolitan Sq., Ste. 1300, St. Louis, MO 63102-2733.
TEL 314-231-5555. FAX 314-206-3222. E-mail: cswab@stlrcga.org. Ed. Carol Schwab; Pub. Richard C.D. Fleming. R&P contact: Laura S. Barlow. adv. contact: Gloria Jarvis. illus. circ. 11,000. (also avail. in microform from UMI; reprint service avail. from UMI) **Indexed:** P.A.I.S. **Document type:** consumer publication, directory.
●Also available online. Vendor(s): Lexis-Nexis, UMI. —UMI.

330 AU ISSN 0036-3677
SALZBURGER WIRTSCHAFT. 1947. w. S.260. Kammer der Gewerblichen Wirtschaft fuer Salzburg, Julius-Raab-Platz 1, A-5027 Salzburg, Austria. FAX 0662-78513. Ed. Ernst Holfeld-Weitlof. adv.; bk.rev. circ. 28,000.

954 II
SAMRUDDHI. m. Southern Gujarat Chamber of Commerce and Industry, Samruddhi, Nanpura, Surat 395 001, India.

SAN FRANCISCO COUNTY COMMERCE AND INDUSTRY DIRECTORY. see BUSINESS AND ECONOMICS — Trade And Industrial Directories

SAN MATEO COUNTY COMMERCE AND INDUSTRY DIRECTORY. see BUSINESS AND ECONOMICS — Trade And Industrial Directories

SANTA CLARA COUNTY COMMERCE AND INDUSTRY DIRECTORY. see BUSINESS AND ECONOMICS — Trade And Industrial Directories

382 BL
SAO PAULO YEARBOOK. 1946. a. $175 (effective 1997). American Chamber of Commerce for Brazil, Praca Pio X No. 15, 5th Fl., Caixa Postal 916, 20040-020 Rio de Janeiro, Brazil.
TEL 55-21-2032477. E-mail: achambr@amchamrio.com.br; URL: http://www.amchamrio.com.br. Ed. Elizabeth Mortlock. adv. circ. 4,500.

330 IT ISSN 0036-4770
SARDEGNA ECONOMICA.* 1963. m. L.8000. Camera di Commercio Industria e Agricoltura di Cagliari, Cagliari, Sardinia, Italy. Ed. A. Petti. adv.; illus.

380 UK
SCOTLAND CHAMBERS OF COMMERCE. NATIONAL DIRECTORY. a. £48. Glasgow Chamber of Commerce, 30 George Sq., Glasgow G2 1EQ, Scotland. TEL 0141-204-2121.
FAX 0141-221-2336. TELEX 777967 CHACOM G. adv.; index. circ. 10,000. **Document type:** directory.
Former titles: Glasgow Chamber of Commerce. Directory & Glasgow Chamber of Commerce. Regional Directory; Glasgow Chamber of Commerce. Industrial Index to Glasgow and West of Scotland.

941 UK
SCOTTISH CHAMBERS OF COMMERCE NATIONAL DIRECTORY. 1948. a. £50. (Scottish Chambers of Commerce) Kemps Publishing Ltd., 11 The Swan Courtyard, Charles Edward Rd., Birmingham B26 1BU, England. TEL 44-121-765-4144.
FAX 44-121-706-6210. **Document type:** directory.
Formerly (until 1984): Glasgow Chamber of Commerce and Manufactures Regional Directory (ISSN 0260-0641)

382 UK
SCOTTISH COUNCIL DEVELOPMENT AND INDUSTRY. ANNUAL REPORT AND ACCOUNTS. a. Scottish Council Development and Industry, 23 Chester St., Edinburgh EH3 7ET, Scotland.
TEL 44-131-225-7911. FAX 44-131-220-2116.
Document type: corporate report.
Formerly: Scottish Council Development and Industry. Annual Report.

SHARJAH COMMERCIAL DIRECTORY/DALIL AL-SHARQAH AL-TIJARI. see BUSINESS AND ECONOMICS — Trade And Industrial Directories

SHARJAH EXPORTER - IMPORTER DIRECTORY/DALEEL AL SARIQAH LIL MOSADDIREEN WA AL-MOSTAWRIDEEN. see BUSINESS AND ECONOMICS — Trade And Industrial Directories

954.9 PK
SHIPPERS' DIGEST. bi-w. Federation of Pakistan Chambers of Commerce and Industry, Main Clifton, Karachi, 6, Pakistan. TEL 534621. TELEX 25370 FEDCOMERC.

959.52 SI ISSN 0129-5179
SHOWCASE. 1975. a. Hagley & Hoyle Pte. Ltd., 70 Shenton Way 03-03, Marina House, Singapore 0207, Singapore. TEL 2240688. FAX 2246998.

382 SI
SINGAPORE INDIAN CHAMBER OF COMMERCE. CIRCULARS. m. Singapore Indian Chamber of Commerce, 101 Cecil St., 23-01 Tong Eng Bldg., Singapore 0106, Singapore. FAX 65-223-1707.

382 SI ISSN 0037-5659
HC445.8.A1
SINGAPORE INTERNATIONAL CHAMBER OF COMMERCE. ECONOMIC BULLETIN. (Text in English) 1960. m. S.$3 per no. Singapore International Chamber of Commerce, 6 Raffles Quay, No. 10-01, John Hancock Tower, Singapore 048580, Singapore. TEL 65-2241255. FAX 65-2242785. E-mail: singicc@asianconnect.com; URL: http://www.sicc.com.sg. adv.; charts; mkt.; stat.; tr.lit. circ. 3,200. **Indexed:** Asian-Pac.Econ.Lit., P.A.I.S. **Document type:** bulletin.
Description: Provides business features and regional news of interest as well as the latest available trade statistics and trade enquiries to businessmen and industrialists.

382 SI ISSN 0377-449X
HF331.S58
SINGAPORE INTERNATIONAL CHAMBER OF COMMERCE. REPORT. 1837. a. S.$20 per no. Singapore International Chamber of Commerce, 6 Raffles Quay, No. 10-01, John Hancock Tower, Singapore 048580, Singapore. TEL 65-2241255.
FAX 65-2242785. E-mail: singicc@asianconnect.com; URL: http://www.sicc.com.sg. stat. circ. 1,400. **Document type:** corporate report.
Description: Reviews the performance of various sectors of the Singapore economy each year.

BUSINESS AND ECONOMICS — CHAMBER OF COMMERCE PUBLICATIONS

381   SA
SMALL BUSINESS FORUM; an extract of articles published. (Text in English) 1993. a. R.57. Durban Chamber of Commerce and Industry, P.O. Box 1506, Durban 4000, South Africa. TEL 27-31-3013692. FAX 27-31-3045255. Ed. B. Poulsom; Pub. B. Poulsom. R&P contact: B. Poulsom. **Document type:** trade publication.
   Description: Collects articles on small business published in issues of the preceding year's digest.

949.4   SZ
SOLOTHURNISCHE HANDELSKAMMER. JAHRESBERICHT. a. Solothurnische Handelskammer, Grabackerstr. 6, CH-4502 Solothurn, Switzerland. TEL 41-32-6262424. FAX 41-32-6262426. **Document type:** bulletin.

949.4   SZ
SOLOTHURNISCHE HANDELSKAMMER. MITTEILUNGEN. bi-m. Solothurnische Handelskammer, Grabackerstr. 6, CH-4502 Solothurn, Switzerland. TEL 41-32-6262424. FAX 41-32-6262426. **Document type:** bulletin.

338   AT   ISSN 0818-4674
SOUTH AUSTRALIA IN BUSINESS. 1911. m. Aus.$30. Chamber of Commerce & Industry S.A. Inc., Entreprise House, 136 Greenhill Rd., Unley, S.A. 5061, Australia. TEL 08-373-1422. FAX 08-272-9662. Ed. Ian Dove. adv.; bk.rev.; illus. circ. 4,500. Indexed: C.I.S. Abstr.
   Formerly: Journal of Industry (ISSN 0022-1872)

338   UK
SOUTHAMPTON AND FAREFIAM CHAMBER OF COMMERCE AND INDUSTRY DIRECTORY. a. £50. Kemps Publishing Ltd., 11 The Swan Courtyard, Charles Edward Rd., Birmingham B26 1BU, England. TEL 44-121-765-4144. FAX 44-121-706-6210. **Document type:** directory.
   Former titles: Confederation of Chambers of Commerce Central Southern England Directory; Southampton Chamber of Commerce Regional Directory.
   Description: Directory of business in the Southampton area. Includes local chamber news, membership lists and classified section.

380.1   US   ISSN 0038-3880
SOUTHERN CALIFORNIA BUSINESS. 1923. m. $17.34 (foreign $35) (effective 1997). Los Angeles Area Chamber of Commerce, 350 S. Bixel St., Los Angeles, CA 90017. TEL 213-580-7571. FAX 213-580-7586. Ed. Christopher J. Volker. adv. contact: Diane Wiggins. bk.rev.; charts; illus.; stat.; circ. 10,000 (controlled). (also avail. in microfilm from LIB) **Document type:** newspaper.
● Also available online. Vendor(s): Information Access Co., UMI.
— UMI.

SOUTHERN CALIFORNIA BUSINESS DIRECTORY AND BUYERS GUIDE. see BUSINESS AND ECONOMICS — Trade And Industrial Directories

381   UK
SOUTH WEST CHAMBER OF COMMERCE YEAR BOOK. a. £20. Plymouth Chamber of Commerce and Industry, 29 Looe St., Plymouth PL4 0EA, England. TEL 01752-221151. FAX -1752-222589. adv. **Document type:** directory.

382   AT
SPANISH OFFICIAL CHAMBER OF COMMERCE IN AUSTRALIA. SPANISH - AUSTRALIAN TRADE. q. Aus.$150. Spanish Official Chamber of Commerce in Australia, Ste. 205, Edgecliff Centre, 203 New South Head Rd., Edgecliff, N.S.W. 2027, Australia. TEL 61-2-3623168. FAX 61-2-3624074. Ed. Sara/Lopez; Pub. Sara Lopez. R&P contact: Sara Lopez. adv. contact: Sara Lopez. **Document type:** newsletter.

380   IT   ISSN 0391-7983
SPEZIA OGGI. 1973. m. L.10000. Camera di Commercio, Industria, Artigianato e Agricoltura della Spezia, Via Veneto 28, 19100 La Spezia, Italy. Dir. Pier E. Macchiavelli. bk.rev.; stat. circ. 1,200.
   Formerly: Camera di Commercio della Spezia. Rassegna Commerciale (ISSN 0033-9350)

380.1   US
SPOKANE AREA CHAMBER OF COMMERCE. DIRECTORY OF ORGANIZATIONS. a. $20 to non-members; members $12. Spokane Area Chamber of Commerce, W. 1020 Riverside, Box 2147, Spokane, WA 99210. TEL 509-624-1393. FAX 509-747-0077. URL: http://www.spokane.org. **Document type:** directory.
   Description: Lists more than 400 social, fraternal, patriotic, and service organizations in Spokane, WA.

380.1   US   ISSN 1074-3065
SPOKANE BUSINESS INTERACTION. 1924. m. $25 to non-members. Spokane Area Chamber of Commerce, Marketing Department, W. 1020 Riverside, Box 2147, Spokane, WA 99210. TEL 509-624-1393. FAX 509-747-0077. URL: http://www.spokane.org. Ed. Stacy Baker. adv.; bk.rev.; illus.; stat. circ. 4,000. **Document type:** newsletter.
   Formerly (until 1994): Spokane Affairs (ISSN 0038-7681)
   Description: Focuses on public meetings, business affairs seminars, political issues and new members.

381   CE
SRI LANKA IN BRIEF. (Text in English) 1977. a. $8. Ceylon Chamber of Commerce, Chamber of Commerce Bldg., Box 274, Colombo 2, Sri Lanka. FAX 941-449352.

STANDARD TRADE INDEX OF JAPAN. see BUSINESS AND ECONOMICS — Trade And Industrial Directories

382   GW
SUEDTHUERINGISCHE WIRTSCHAFT. 1990. m. (Industrie- und Handelskammer Suedthueringen) V H I Verlagsgesellschaft fuer Handel und Industrie, Klostergasse 2, 98617 Meiningen, Germany. TEL 03693-43108. adv. **Document type:** bulletin.

330   GW   ISSN 0039-4637
SUEDWESTFAELISCHE WIRTSCHAFT. 1964. m. DM.32. (Suedwestfaelische Industrie- und Handelskammer zu Hagen) V.D. Linnepe Verlagsgesellschaft KG, Bahnhofstr. 28, 58119 Hagen, Germany. TEL 02331-32078. FAX 02331-32090. adv.; bk.rev.; abstr.; bibl.; charts; illus.; stat.; index. circ. 1,000.

990   AT   ISSN 1039-4761
SURVEY OF AUSTRALIAN MANUFACTURING. 1980. q. Aus.$150 to non-members; members Aus.$130. Australian Chamber of Manufactures, 380 St. Kilda Rd., Melbourne, Vic. 3004, Australia. TEL 61-3-96894358. FAX 61-3-96991729. Ed. Tony Pensabene. circ. 250. (back issues avail.) **Document type:** trade publication.
   Former titles: Survey of Victorian Manufacturing (ISSN 1033-9094); (until 1988): Pulse Survey of Victorian Manufacturing (ISSN 0158-9857)
   Description: Trends in Australian manufacturing.

380   US   ISSN 0069-2441
HF284
SURVEY OF LOCAL CHAMBERS OF COMMERCE. a. $35. Chamber of Commerce of the U.S., 1615 H St., N.W., Washington, DC 20062. TEL 800-638-6582. Ed. Richard Loomis. Indexed: SRI.
   Description: Examines income sources, staff salaries and staff benefits.

382   IT
SVIZZERA INDUSTRIALE E COMMERCIALE. 1938. m. (11/yr.). membership. Camera di Commercio Svizzera in Italia - Swiss Chamber of Commerce in Italy, Via Palestro 2, 20121 Milan, Italy. TEL 39-2-76003606. Ed. Bernardo Cerutti. adv.: B&W page L.950000, color page L.1200000. circ. 2,500. **Document type:** consumer publication.

382   JA
SWISS CHAMBER OF COMMERCE AND INDUSTRY IN JAPAN. NEWSLETTER. 5/yr. membership only. Swiss Chamber of Commerce and Industry in Japan - Zainichi Suisu Shoko Kaigisho, C S Tower, 1-11-30, Akasaka, Minato-ku, Tokyo 107, Japan. TEL 03-3587-1122. FAX 03-3587-2266. **Document type:** newsletter.

949.2   NE
SWISS MATE. q. Zwitserse Kamer van Koophandel in Nederland, Koningsplein 11, 1017 BB, Amsterdam, Netherlands. TEL 249436.

380.1   US
TACOMA - PIERCE COUNTY CHAMBER OF COMMERCE UPDATE. 1926. m. $25. Tacoma-Pierce County Chamber of Commerce, 950 Pacific Ave., Ste. 300, Box 1933, Tacoma, WA 98401. TEL 206-627-2175. FAX 206-597-7305. Ed. Denise Ploof. adv.; bk.rev.; circ. 3,500 (controlled). **Document type:** newsletter.
   Formerly: Tacoma Area Progress.
   Description: Features information of community and business issues as well as chamber programs and activities.

951.9   KO
TAEGU CHAMBER OF COMMERCE AND INDUSTRY. MONTHLY. m. Taegu Chamber of Commerce and Industry, 107, 3-gu Sincheon-dong, Dong-gu, Taegu 635, S. Korea. TEL 053-730041-6. TELEX 54343.

954   II
TAMIL CHAMBER OF COMMERCE. JOURNAL. bi-m. Tamil Chamber of Commerce, Caithness Hall, 157 Linghi Chetty St., P.O. Box 1661, Madras 600 001, India. TEL 21799.

382   AT
TASMANIAN BUSINESS REPORTER. 1981. m. Tasmanian Chamber of Commerce and Industry, G.P.O. Box 793H, Hobart, Tas. 7001, Australia. TEL 61-3-62345933. FAX 61-3-62311278. E-mail: admin@tcci.org.au. Ed. Heidi Murphy. R&P contact: Heidi Murphy. adv. contact: Dong Williams. circ. 16,400 (controlled). **Document type:** newspaper.
   Formerly: T C I News.
   Description: Aims to accurately inform business management about current trends, government action affecting business, new products, marketing trends, overseas news, real estate, the computer world, trade appointments, people in the news, import-export opportunities, transport and travel.

382   TH   ISSN 0125-0191
THAI-AMERICAN BUSINESS. 1967. bi-m. B.400($20) American Chamber of Commerce in Thailand, 140 Wireless Rd., Bangkok, Thailand. Ed. Tom Seale. adv.; illus. circ. 3,000.
   Formerly: American Chamber of Commerce in Thailand. Review (ISSN 0002-7855)

382   TH
THAI CHAMBER OF COMMERCE. DIRECTORY (YEAR). (Text in English) a. $40 per no. Cosmic Group of Companies, 4th Fl., Phyathai Bldg., 31 Phyathai Rd., Rajthevi, Bangkok 10400, Thailand. TEL 662-2453850. FAX 662-2461710. adv.: color page $1200. illus.; circ. 5,000 (controlled). **Document type:** directory.
   Former titles: Thai Chamber of Commerce. Handbook (Year); (until 1983): Thai Chamber of Commerce. Business Directory (ISSN 0563-3400)
   Description: Covers the member companies of Thai Chamber of Commerce, including company profiles and a view on Thai economy.

954   TH
THAI CHAMBER OF COMMERCE. JOURNAL. (Text in Thai and English) m. Bamrung Nukoulkit Press, 83 Bamrung Muang Rd., Bangkok, Thailand. Ed. L. Chara.

382 959.3   TH
THAI - CHINESE CHAMBER OF COMMERCE. NEWS. Variant title: Chamber News. q. Thai - Chinese Chamber of Commerce, 233 South Sathorn Rd., Bangkok, Thailand.

382.025 338.025   TH
▼**THAI-KOREAN CHAMBER OF COMMERCE HANDBOOK & DIRECTORY.** (Text in English) 1995. a. 20. Cosmic Group of Companies, 4th Fl., Phyathai Bldg., 31 Phyathai Rd., Rajthevi, Bangkok 10400, Thailand. TEL 662-2453850. FAX 662-2461710. adv.: color page $1000. illus.; circ. 2,000 (controlled). **Document type:** directory.
   Description: Covers the member companies of Thai-Korean Chamber of Commerce, including company profiles and a view on the Thai and Korean economies.

THAMES VALLEY BUSINESS DIRECTORY. see BUSINESS AND ECONOMICS — Trade And Industrial Directories

BUSINESS AND ECONOMICS — CHAMBER OF COMMERCE PUBLICATIONS

338 380   GW   ISSN 0945-2397
THEMA WIRTSCHAFT. 1945. m. DM.54. (Niederrheinische Industrie- und Handelskammer Duisburg - Wesel - Kleve zu Duisburg) L.N. Schaffrath GmbH and Co. KG, Hartstr. 4-6, 47594 Geldern, Germany. TEL 02831-396229. FAX 02831-396110. Ed. Alfred Kilian. adv.: B&W page DM.3200; trim 185 x 260; adv. contact: Inge Giesen. bk.rev.; charts; illus.; stat.; index. circ. 38,400. **Document type:** trade publication.
    Former titles (until 1993): NiederrheinKammer (ISSN 0174-5700); (until 19&&): Niederrheinishe Industrie- und Handelskammer Duisberg Wesel zu Duisberg. Wirtschaftliche Mitteilungen (ISSN 0028-9752); Niederrheinishe Industrie- und Handelskammer Duisberg Wesel. Mitteilungen (ISSN 0174-5719)

953   TS
AL-TIJARAH. (Text in Arabic, English) 1971. m. $85 in Arab countries; elsewhere $145. Sharjah Chamber of Commerce and Industry, P.O. Box 580, Sharjah, United Arab Emirates. TEL 971-6-541444. FAX 971-6-541119. Ed. Hassan Abdullah Al Noman. R&P contact: Saeed O. Al Jarwan. adv. contact: Saeed Al Najjar. circ. 50,000.
    Description: Discusses chamber activities and related news affecting economic development in Sharjah, al-Dhaid, Khor Fakkan and Kalba, as well as regional and international development issues.

382   SU
AL-TIJARAH (JEDDAH). 1960. m. Jeddah Chamber of Commerce and Industry, P.O. Box 1264, Jeddah, Saudi Arabia. TEL 966-2-4711000. FAX 966-2-6484603. Ed. Abdullah S. Dahlan. circ. 8,000.

330.9   TG
TOGO. CHAMBRE DE COMMERCE, D'AGRICULTURE ET D'INDUSTRIE. BULLETIN BIMESTRIEL. bi-m. 17000 Fr.CFA in Lome (rest of Togo 20000 Fr.CFA; rest of Africa and France 25000 Fr.CFA; elsewhere in Europe 27000 Fr.CFA; N. America 30000 Fr.CFA; Asia and Oceania 35000 Fr.CFA) (effective Apr. 1996). Chambre de Commerce, d'Agriculture et d'Industrie du Togo, Angle Av. de La Presidence et Av. Georges Pompidou, Lome, Togo. TEL 228-21-70-65. FAX 228-21-47-30. TELEX 5023 TG. (Subscr. to: B.P. 360, Lome, Togo) bk.rev. circ. 450.
    Formerly: Chambre de Commerce, d'Agriculture et d'Industrie du Togo. Bulletin Mensuel.
    Description: News of commercial, agricultural and industrial activities of the chamber.

944   FR
TOURAINE ECONOMIQUE. 9/yr. 180 F. (effective 1997). Chambre du Commerce et d'Industrie de Touraine, B.P. 1028, 37010 Tours Cedex 1, France. TEL 33-2-47472022. TELEX CHAMCO-TOURS 750 020. Ed. Laurent Blain; Pub. Pascal Rivet. adv.; illus. circ. 16,000. **Document type:** trade publication.

953   TS
TRADE AND INDUSTRY/MAJALLAT AL-TIJARA WAL-SINA'A. (Text in Arabic) 1975. m. Dubai Chamber of Commerce and Industry, P.O. Box 1457, Dubai, United Arab Emirates. TEL 4-221181. FAX 211646. TELEX 45997 TIJARA EM. Ed. Abdul Rahman G. al-Mutawee. circ. 7,500.
    Description: Covers the business and economic situation in Dubai, the Gulf, and the Arab world.

961   ET
TRADE FOCUS. (Text in English) q. Addis Ababa Chamber of Commerce, c/o Ethiopian Chamber of Commerce, P.O. Box 517, Addis Ababa, Ethiopia. Ed. Solomon Asfaon.

382 931   CH
TRADE OPPORTUNITY. 35/yr. Chinese National Association of Industry and Commerce, 4th Fl., No. 7 Roosevelt Rd., Sec. 1, Taipei, Taiwan, Republic of China.

TRADE UNIONS INTERNATIONAL OF CHEMICAL, OIL AND ALLIED WORKERS. INFORMATION BULLETIN. see *LABOR UNIONS*

382   GR   ISSN 0041-0543
HF37.G7
TRADE WITH GREECE. (Text in English) 1959. s-a. free. Athens Chamber of Commerce and Industry, 7 Acadimias St., 106 71 Athens, Greece. Ed. J. Fotinias. adv.; illus.; tr.lit.; index, cum.index every 7 yrs. circ. 7,500. **Indexed:** Key to Econ.Sci., PROMT.
    Incorporates: Data from the Greek Economic Life (ISSN 0007-4462)

382   US   ISSN 0041-0551
TRADE WITH ITALY. 1946. bi-m. $48. Italy - America Chamber of Commerce, Inc., 730 Fifth Ave., New York, NY 10019. TEL 212-459-0044. FAX 212-459-0090. Ed. Franco DeAngelis. adv.; bk.rev.; charts; illus.; mkt.; index. circ. 4,000.

974   US   ISSN 0893-2107
U K & U S A; the British-American magazine. 1987. q. $30. British - American Chamber of Commerce, 52 Vanderbilt Ave., Ste. 20, New York, NY 10017-3808. TEL 212-661-4060. URL: http://bacc.org. Ed. Charles Burck. R&P contact: Nicola Lewis. adv. contact: Nicola Lewis. bk.rev. circ. 12,000. **Document type:** newsletter.
    Description: Subjects of interest to Anglo-American business people.

U S FIRMS IN GERMANY/AMERIKANISCHE UNTERNEHMEN IN DEUTSCHLAND. see *BUSINESS AND ECONOMICS — Trade And Industrial Directories*

950   NP
UDYOG BANIHYA PATRIKA. 1967. s-a. $3.50. Federation of Nepalese Chambers of Commerce and Industry, P.O. Box 269, Teku, Kathmandu, Nepal. TEL 977-1-233196. FAX 977-1-227322. Ed. Rameshwor Acharya. R&P contact: Rameswar Acharya. adv.; bk.rev. circ. 1,000. **Document type:** newsletter.

381   US
U.S. CHAMBER OF COMMERCE. ASSOCIATION AGENDA. 1958. m. U.S. Chamber of Commerce, 1615 H St., N.W., Washington, DC 20062. TEL 202-463-5560. FAX 202-463-3190. Ed. Gary A. LaBranche. circ. 1,200 (controlled). **Document type:** newsletter.
    Formerly: U.S. Chamber of Commerce. Chamber Memo.
    Description: Contains news and information of interest to members.

974   US
UNITED STATES COUNCIL FOR INTERNATIONAL BUSINESS. NEWSLETTER. bi-m. United States Council for International Business, 1212 Ave. of the Americas, New York, NY 10036-1689. TEL 212-354-4480. FAX 212-575-0327. Ed. Christina Stenchik. **Document type:** newsletter.

382   US
UNITED STATES - GERMAN ECONOMIC YEARBOOK (YEAR). German edition: Deutsch - Amerikanisches Wirtschaftsjahrbuch (Year). a. DM.75($45) (effective 1994). German American Chamber of Commerce, Publication Services, 40 W. 57th St., 31st Fl., New York, NY 10019. TEL 212-974-8830. FAX 212-974-8867. Ed. Richard Jacob. adv. contact: Benigna Kirsten. **Indexed:** SRI.
    Description: PRovides an in-depth view of U.S.-German politics, economics and finance.

UNITED STATES - ITALY TRADE DIRECTORY. see *BUSINESS AND ECONOMICS — Trade And Industrial Directories*

977   US
UPDATE (LACROSSE). 1980. fortn. $3. Greater LaCrosse Area Chamber of Commerce, Box 219, LaCrosse, WI 54602-0219. TEL 608-784-4880. Ed. Bill Sorenson. circ. 1,480.

330   US   ISSN 0732-3115
UPPER MIDWEST REPORT. vol.2, 1981. bi-m. free. Upper Midwest Council, Federal Reserve Bank Bldg., 250 Marquette Ave., Minneapolis, MN 55480. TEL 612-340-9666. Ed. Molly MacGregor.

989   UY
URUGUAY - INFO. m. Camara de Comercio Uruguayo-Alemana - Deutsch-Uruguayische Handelskammer, Zabala 1379, Casilla de Correo 1499, 11000 Montevideo, Uruguay. TEL 598-2-970307. FAX 598-2-963281. Ed. Klaus Roessler.

330   IR
UTAQ-I BAZARGANI VA SANAYI' VA MA'ADIN-I IRAN. HAFTAH'NAMAH. (Text in English, Persian) 1970. w. Iranian Chamber of Commerce, Industries and Mines, P.O. Box 15875-4671, Tehran, Iran. **Document type:** trade publication.

943   GW
V D C - NACHRICHTEN. s-a. Verband Deutscher Chemo Techniker und Chemisch - Technischer Association, Mulhauser Str. 61, 47906 Kempen, Germany. TEL 02152 3503.

954   II
VAIBHAV. m. Maharashtra Chamber of Commerce, 12 Rampart Row, Bombay 400 023, India. TEL 22-244548.

947   BU   ISSN 0323-9152
HF3721
VANSHNA TARGOVIA. English edition: Foreign Trade - Bulgaria. (Text in Bulgarian) 1952. 10/yr. $36 for Bulgarian ed.; English ed. $48. (Bulgarian Chamber of Commerce and Industry) Vanshna Targovia, P.O. Box 21, 1408 Sofia, Bulgaria. TEL 359-2-719136. FAX 359-2-512293. Ed. Lilia Karakasheva. adv.; illus.; tr.lit. circ. 13,200. **Indexed:** BSL Econ., Key to Econ.Sci., Mid.East: Abstr.& Ind.
—BLDSC (3987.223400).
    Description: Organ of the Bulgarian foreign-economic complex, with information on trade, industrial cooperation and joint ventures with the Bulgarian economy.

944   FR   ISSN 0994-1258
VENDEE MAGAZINE. 1988. 11/yr. P A M, 4 rue Marechal-Foch, 85000 La-Roche-sur-Yon, France. TEL 51-36-34-37. FAX 51-46-03-56. Ed. Claude Grimaud. circ. 11,000.

382   VE
VENEZUELAN - AMERICAN CHAMBER OF COMMERCE AND INDUSTRY. YEARBOOK AND MEMBERSHIP DIRECTORY. 1961. a. $75. Venezuelan - American Chamber of Commerce and Industry - Camara Venezolano-Americana de Comercio e Industria, Apdo. 5181, Caracas 1010A, Venezuela. TEL 58-2-2630833. FAX 58-2-2631829. TELEX 28399. adv. circ. 5,000. (reprint service avail. from UMI) **Document type:** directory.
    Formerly: American Chamber of Commerce of Venezuela. Yearbook and Membership Directory (ISSN 0065-7697)

943   GW
VERBAND ANGESTELLTER AKADEMIKER UND LEITENDER ANGESTELLTER DER CHEMISCHEN INDUSTRIE. INFO. Short title: Info. 8/yr. Verband Angestellter Akademiker und Leitender Angestellter der Chemischen Industrie, Kattenburg 2, 50667 Cologne, Germany.

945   IT
VICENZA ECONOMICA. m. Camera di Commercio, Industria, Artigianato e Agricoltura di Vicenza, Corso Antonio Fogazzaro, 37, 36100 Vicenza, Italy. TEL 39-444-994811. FAX 39-444-994834.

944   FR
VIE ECO SAONE ET LOIRE. 8/yr. J.P. Doiteau et Associes, 42 Quai Joseph-Gillet, 69004 Lyon, France. TEL 78-29-18-33. FAX 78-29-66-14. circ. 8,000.

WALES BUSINESS DIRECTORY (SOLIHULL). see *BUSINESS AND ECONOMICS — Trade And Industrial Directories*

941.5   IE
WATERFORD CHAMBER OF COMMERCE. NEWS LETTER. q. Waterford Chamber of Commerce, George's St. Waterford, Ireland. TEL 051-72639. FAX 051-76002. **Document type:** newsletter.

975   US
WEST VIRGINIA: AN ECONOMIC-STATISTICAL PROFILE. 1982. irreg. (every 3-4 yrs). $26.19. West Virginia Chamber of Commerce, Box 2789, Charleston, WV 25330. TEL 304-342-1115. stat. circ. 1,500. (back issues avail.) **Document type:** trade publication.

BUSINESS AND ECONOMICS — COMPUTER APPLICATIONS

380.1   SW
WESTERN SWEDEN CHAMBER OF COMMERCE. MEMBERSHIP DIRECTORY. 1953. biennial. latest 1990. free. Western Sweden Chamber of Commerce - Vaestsvenska Handelskammaren, Box 5253, S-402 25 Goeteborg, Sweden. TEL 46-31-835900. FAX 46-31-835936. TELEX 27430 GOTCHAM. adv. circ. 5,000. **Document type:** directory.
    Former titles: Gothenburg and Western Sweden Chamber of Commerce. Membership Directory; Trade Directory of Western Sweden.

382   CK
WHO'S WHO OF COLOMBIAN - AMERICAN BUSINESS. (Text in English, Spanish) 1956. a. $50. Camara de Comercio Colombo-Americana, Apdo. Aereo 8008, Bogota, Colombia. **Document type:** directory.
    Description: Lists members with relevant data, organizations in Colombia, Latin America and the U.S. that are useful contacts, and general economic and visa information for both countries.

943   GW   ISSN 0173-329X
WIRTSCHAFT AM BAYERISCHEN UNTERMAIN. 1946. m. DM.36. Industrie- und Handelskammer Aschaffenburg, Kerschensteinerstr. 9, 63741 Aschaffenburg, Germany. TEL 06021-880-117. FAX 06021-87981. TELEX 04188867. Ed. Juergen Parr. adv.; bk.rev. circ. 15,000. (back issues avail.) **Document type:** corporate report.

382   CL
DIE WIRTSCHAFT CHILES. m. Camara Chileno - Suiza de Comercio, Clasificador 1368, Santiago, Chile. TEL 6980808.

943.1   GW
WIRTSCHAFT IM RAUM HANAU KINZIGTAL. m. Industrie- und Handelskammer Hanau - Gelnhausen - Schluchtern, Am Pedro-Jung-Park 14, 63450 Hanau, Germany. TEL 24387. TELEX 184738.

943.1   GW
WIRTSCHAFT IM SUEDOESTLICHEN WESTFALEN. m. DM.30. Industrie- und Handelskammer fuer das Suedostliche Westfalen zu Arnsberg, Koenigstr. 18-20, 59821 Arnsberg, Germany. TEL 02931-878154. FAX 02931-21427. Ed. Ralf Huess. adv.; bk.rev. circ. 11,500. **Document type:** newsletter.
    Formerly (until 1993): Wirtschaft in Suedostwestfalen.

943   GW   ISSN 0931-2196
WIRTSCHAFT IN BREMEN. 1948. m. DM.45. (Handelskammer Bremen) Carl Ed. Schuenemann KG, Postfach 106067, 28060 Bremen, Germany. TEL 49-421-369-03-72. FAX 49-421-36903-34. Ed. Christine Backhaus. circ. 13,983. **Document type:** bulletin.

380   GW   ISSN 0938-8230
WIRTSCHAFT IN OSTWUERTTEMBERG. 1970. m. free to members. (Industrie- und Handelskammer Ostwuerttemberg) C.F. Rees GmbH, Postfach, 7920 Heidenheim, Germany. adv.; bk.rev. circ. 8,000.
    Formerly (until 1973): Ostschwaebische Wirtschaft (ISSN 0019-8994)

330   GW
WIRTSCHAFT - NECKAR - ALB. 1946. m. DM.60. Industrie- und Handelskammer Reutlingen, Postfach 1944, 72709 Reutlingen, Germany. TEL 49-7121-201-0. Ed. Ulrike Fleischle. adv. contact: Ingeborg Moench. bk.rev.; illus.; stat. circ. 24,000. **Document type:** trade publication.
    Formerly (until 1980): Industrie- und Handelskammer Reutlingen. Mitteilungen (ISSN 0026-6892)

941.1   GW   ISSN 0940-4449
WIRTSCHAFT NORDHESSEN. 1946. m. DM.72. Industrie- und Handelskammer Kassel, Kurfuerstenstr. 9, 34117 Kassel, Germany. TEL 49-561-78910. FAX 49-561-7891290. E-mail: marschelke@kassel.ihk.de. Ed. Herbert Marschelke. adv.; bk.rev.; circ. 50,000 (controlled). **Document type:** bulletin.
    Formerly: Kurhessische Wirtschaft.
    Description: Provides reports and information about general and regional economic and other affairs for the owners and managers of enterprises in the area of North Hesse.

943.1   GW   ISSN 0178-8337
WIRTSCHAFT UND KAMMER. m. Industrie- und Handelskammer fuer Essen, Muelheim an der Ruhr, Oberhausen zu Essen, Am Waldthausenpark 2, 45127 Essen, Germany. TEL 49-201-18920. FAX 49-201-207866. Ed. Veronika Luehl. adv. contact: Felix Nyga. **Document type:** bulletin.

943   GW
WIRTSCHAFTSMAGAZIN PFALZ. m. Industrie- und Handelskammer fuer die Pfalz, Ludwigstr. 2-3, 67059 Ludwigshafen, Germany. TEL 0621-59040. adv.: B&W page DM.5023, color page DM.8623; trim 185 x 250. circ. 45,000. **Document type:** bulletin.
    Formerly: I H K Magazin.

943   GW
WIRTSCHAFTSMAGAZIN RHEIN-NECKAR. m. DM.55. Industrie- und Handelskammer Rhein-Neckar, Postfach 101661, 68016 Mannheim, Germany. TEL 49-621-1709-0. FAX 49-621-1709100. Eds. Andrea Kiefer, Christa Bender. adv.: B&W page DM.4800; trim 185 x 250. bk.rev. circ. 42,000. **Document type:** trade publication.
    Formerly: Wirtschaft.

330   AU   ISSN 0043-6291
HC261
WIRTSCHAFTSPOLITISCHE BLAETTER. 1954. bi-m. S.348. (Bundeskammer der Gewerblichen Wirtschaft) Oesterreichischer Wirtschaftsverlag, Nikolsdorfergasse 7-11, A-1051 Vienna, Austria. TEL 0222-555585. TELEX 1-11669. Ed. Ernst Hofbauer. circ. 4,200. (reprint service avail. from SCH) **Indexed:** ELLIS.

382   AU
WIRTSCHAFTSRUNDSCHAU. m. Schweizerische Handelskammer in Oesterreich, Neuer Markt, 4, A-1010 Vienna, Austria. TEL 0222-525959.

382   AU
WIRTSCHAFTSRUNDSCHAU ITALIA - OESTERREICH. q. Italienische Handelskammer fuer Oesterreich, Reisnerstr. 20, A-1030 Vienna, Austria. TEL 0222-7158782. FAX 0222-7158789.

380   US   ISSN 1048-2849
HF294   CODEN: WCCDE9
WORLD CHAMBER OF COMMERCE DIRECTORY. 1967. a. $35. Box 1029, Loveland, CO 80539. TEL 970-663-3231. FAX 970-663-6187. E-mail: 104406.3326@compuserve.com. Ed. Jan Pierce. circ. 12,000. **Document type:** directory.
—CASDDS; CISTI.
    Formerly: Worldwide Chamber of Commerce Directory (ISSN 0893-326X)
    Description: Lists addresses, phone numbers, and the name of person in charge; population; and the number of members of chambers of commerce throughout the world. Includes embassies.

966.9   NR
WORLD TRADE CENTER OF NIGERIA. NEWSLETTER. (Text in English) 1988. q. $10. Apple Academy Press, 63 Coker St., Ilupeju, P.O. Box 3445, Lagos, Nigeria. Ed. John Adeyemi Adeleke. charts; stat.; tr.lit. circ. 4,500. (back issues avail.) **Document type:** newsletter.

968.9   RH
Z N C C NEWSLETTER. 1981. m. free. Zimbabwe National Chamber of Commerce, P. O. Box 1934, Harare, Zimbabwe. Ed. E. Mpundu. adv.; bk.rev. circ. 2,000. (back issues avail.) **Document type:** newsletter.
    Formerly: A C C O Z News.

ZIMBABWE NATIONAL CHAMBER OF COMMERCE DIRECTORY. see BUSINESS AND ECONOMICS — Trade And Industrial Directories

381   SZ
ZUERI-GWERB. 11/yr. Gewerbeverbaende von Kanton und Stadt Zuerich, Wiesenstr. 7, Postfach, CH-8032 Zurich, Switzerland. TEL 01-3832370. FAX 01-3832593. Ed. Ursula Speich-Hochstrasser. circ. 18,495.

968   SA
ZULULAND CHAMBER OF COMMERCE AND INDUSTRY. NEWS. Variant title: Chamber News. m. Zululand Chamber of Commerce and Industry, P.O. Box 1133, Empangeni, Zululand, South Africa. TEL 0351-25335.

BUSINESS AND ECONOMICS — Computer Applications

A B S E L NEWS & VIEWS. (Association for Business Simulation and Experiential Learning) see COMPUTERS — Computer Simulation

ACCOUNTING, MANAGEMENT AND INFORMATION TECHNOLOGIES. see BUSINESS AND ECONOMICS — Accounting

ACCOUNTING TECHNOLOGY. see BUSINESS AND ECONOMICS — Accounting

330 510   NE
ADVANCES IN COMPUTATIONAL ECONOMICS. (Text in English) 1993. irreg., vol.4, 1994. price varies. Kluwer Academic Publishers, Postbus 17, 3300 AA Dordrecht, Netherlands. TEL 31-78-6392392. FAX 31-78-6392254. TELEX 29245 KAPG NL. E-mail: services@wkap.nl; URL: http://www.wkap.nl. (Dist. by: Kluwer Academic Publishers Group, P.O. Box 332, 3300 AH Dordrecht, Netherlands. TEL 31-78-6392392. FAX 31-78-6546474; N. America dist. addr.: Box 358, Accord Sta., Hingham, MA 02018-0358. TEL 617-871-6600) (back issues avail.) **Indexed:** Zent.Math. **Document type:** monographic series.
Refereed Serial

330   US   ISSN 1040-6034
ATLANTA COMPUTER CURRENTS; regional guide to technology products and services. 1989. m. Computer Currents Publishing, Inc., 5720 Hollis St., Emeryville, CA 94608. TEL 510-547-6800; 800-365-7773. FAX 510-547-4613. E-mail: editorial@compcurr.com; URL: http://www.currnets.net. (Atlanta Office: Jaye Communications, Inc., 550 Interstate N. Pkwy., Ste. 150, Atlanta, GA 30339-5008. TEL 770-984-9444. FAX 770-613-0760) Ed. Mike Adkinsan; Pub. Mike Adkinsan. R&P contact: Colleen Canny. adv.: B&W page $2320, color page $3070; trim 10 1/2 x 12 1/4; adv. contact: Alexis Caldwell. circ. 50,000. **Document type:** trade publication.
    Description: Covers computing and computer products for the business community.

AUTOMOTIVE MANAGEMENT INFORMATION SYSTEMS COUNCIL NEWSLETTER. see BUSINESS AND ECONOMICS — Office Equipment And Services

B I T. (Buero und Informations Technik) see BUSINESS AND ECONOMICS — Office Equipment And Services

BANK SYSTEMS & TECHNOLOGY; for senior-level executives in perations and technology management. see BUSINESS AND ECONOMICS — Banking And Finance

658 004   US   ISSN 0178-5001
BETRIEBS- UND WIRTSCHAFTSINFORMATIK. 1982. irreg. price varies. Springer-Verlag, 175 Fifth Ave., New York, NY 10010. TEL 212-460-1500. FAX 212-473-6272. (Also: Berlin, Heidelberg, Tokyo and Vienna) Ed.Bd. **Document type:** academic/scholarly publication.

651.3   AU   ISSN 1019-4096
BUERO UND COMPUTER REPORT; das Kennziffer-Fachmagazin fuer Bueroorganisation, Kommunikation und EDV. 1979. m. S.540. Verlag Technik - Report GmbH, Markgraf-Ruediger-Str. 8, A-1150 Vienna, Austria. TEL 01-98170-0. FAX 01-9817033. TELEX 135041. Ed. Roman Moertel. adv. circ. 19,110. **Document type:** consumer publication.
    Incorporates: P C Report; **Formerly:** Bueroreport.
    Description: Austrian specialist magazine for office organization, communication and data.

BUEROSWISS; Fachzeitschrift fuer Buero und Automation. see COMPUTERS — Electronic Data Processing

BUEROTECHNIK IM TEST; Fachzeitschrift fuer Automation, Buerotechnik, Datentechnik, EDV-Zubehoer. see BUSINESS AND ECONOMICS — Office Equipment And Services

BUILDERS' COMPUTER NEWSLETTER. see BUILDING AND CONSTRUCTION

BUSINESS AND ECONOMICS — COMPUTER APPLICATIONS

330 UK ISSN 1351-3680
BUSINESS & TECHNOLOGY MAGAZINE. 1993. m. £48($120) Cromwell Media Ltd., 5-6 Glenthorne Mews, Glenthorne Rd., London W6 0LJ, England. TEL 44-181-563-1000. FAX 44-181-563-1010. Ed. Magnus MacIntyre. adv.: color page £3300; adv. contact: Tom Bureau. circ. 30,000. (back issues avail.) **Document type:** trade publication.

330 II
BUSINESS COMPUTER. (Text in English) 1986. m. Nariman Point Building Services & Trading Pvt. Ltd., 920 Tulsiani Chambers, Nariman Point, Bombay 400 021, India. Ed. Maneck Davar. adv.: B&W page Rs.9000, color page Rs.18000; trim 240 x 165.

330 UK ISSN 1350-5092
BUSINESS COMPUTING BRIEF. 1984. s-m. £279($418) (effective 1993). Financial Times Telecoms & Media Publishing (Subsidiary of: Financial Times Group), Maple House, 149 Tottenham Court Rd., London W1P 9LL, England. TEL 44-171-896-2234. FAX 44-171-896-2256. Pub. Helen Nicol. (also avail. in microform from UMI) **Document type:** newsletter.
●Also available online. Vendor(s): Data-Star, Information Access Co., Lexis-Nexis.
Formerly (until 1993): FinTech. 2, Electronic Office (ISSN 0266-7797)
Description: Covers office technology, vendors, equipment, systems, international standards, and attitudes. Contains case studies on automation successes and failures.

330 GW
▼**BUSINESS ONLINE.** 1996. m. DM.168 (foreign DM.178.80) (effective 1997). Konradin Verlag Robert Kohlhammer GmbH, Ernst-Mey-Str. 8, 70771 Leinfelden-Echterdingen, Germany. TEL 49-711-7594-0. FAX 49-711-7594390. Ed. Juergen Janik. adv.: B&W page DM.6900; trim 190 x 270; adv. contact: Dietmar Buettner. circ. 25,000 (paid). (back issues avail.) **Document type:** trade publication.
Description: Deals with the professional use of worldwide data networks and reports on all aspects of the online market.

330 US
BUSINESS - PROFESSIONAL ONLINE SERVICES: REVIEW, TRENDS & FORECAST. 1991? a. $995. Cowles - SIMBA Information (Subsidiary of: Cowles Business Media), 11 Riverbend Dr. S., Box 4949, Stamford, CT 06907-0949. TEL 203-358-9900; 800-307-2529. FAX 203-358-5811. E-mail: info@simbanet.com; URL: http://www.simbanet.com.
Description: Analyzes and forecasts the business and professional online publishing industry.

330 US ISSN 0894-9301
T58.6 CODEN: CIOOEQ
C I O. (Chief Information Officer); the magazine for information executives. 1987. 21/yr. $98. C I O Communications, 492 Old Connecticut Path, Box 9208, Framingham, MA 01701-9208. TEL 508-872-0080. FAX 508-872-0618. URL: http://www.cio.com. Ed. Abbie Lundberg; Pub. Joseph Levy. R&P contact: Bill Kerber. adv.: B&W page $9000; adv. contact: Michael Masters. bk.rev. (also avail. in microform; back issues avail.) **Document type:** trade publication.
—BLDSC (3198.667000); AskIEEE; KR SourceOne; SWETS. **CCC.**
Description: Business publication covering information technology for top-level information executives.

330 657 US ISSN 1068-8285
C P A SOFTWARE NEWS. 1991. 8/yr. $39.95. Software News Publishing, 110 N. Bell, Ste. 300, Shawnee, OK 74801. TEL 405-275-3100. FAX 405-275-3101. E-mail: tawn@ezin.net. Ed. T. Allen Rose; Pub. T. Allen Rose. R&P contact: T. Allen Rose. adv.: B&W page $5495, color page $6995; trim 11 1/2 x 14; adv. contact: Shari Dodgen. bk.rev. circ. 52,314. (tabloid format; back issues avail.) **Document type:** trade publication.
Formerly: N S P A Software News.
Description: Includes articles to assist CPAs with computer software, installing computers, client write-up, tax software, spreadsheets, and accounting software.

338 001.6 FR ISSN 0985-0791
CENTRE D'INFORMATION DES UTILISATEURS DE PROGICIELS. CATALOGUE. 1976. a. 500 F.($120) (effective 1996). Centre d'Experimentation des Progiciels (CXP), 19-21 rue du Rocher, 75008 Paris, France. TEL 43-87-90-28. FAX 44-70-91-10. Eds. Alain Pauly, Isabelle Jahn. adv. circ. 8,000. **Document type:** catalog, directory.
Former titles: Guide Europeen des Progiciels (ISSN 0294-0701); Guide Europeen des Produits Logiciels (ISSN 0395-2061)
Description: Provides information on 14000 software packages available in a database on Minitel.

CHRISTIAN MANAGEMENT REPORT. see BUSINESS AND ECONOMICS — Management

COM - A N D. (Computer Audit News and Developments) see BUSINESS AND ECONOMICS — Accounting

330 US
COMPENSATION & BENEFITS SOFTWARE CENSUS.* 1993. a. $79.95. Advanced Personnel Systems, 1873-Hidden View Ln., Roseville, CA 95661-5819. TEL 916-781-2900. FAX 916-781-2901. E-mail: frantz@hrcensus.com; URL: http://www.hrcensus.com. Ed. Richard B. Frantzreb. circ. 2,000 (paid). **Document type:** directory.
●Also available online. Vendor(s): Human Resources Information Network.
Formerly: Compensation and Benefits Software Locator (ISSN 1072-1428)
Description: Covers compensation and employee benefits software with listings for over 800 products. Includes 50-word feature descriptions, platform information, price, and vendor contact information.

330 NE ISSN 0927-7099
HB143.5 CODEN: CNOMEL
COMPUTATIONAL ECONOMICS. (Text in English) 1988. bi-m. fl.760 to institutions; $390 to institutions in U.S. (effective 1998). Kluwer Academic Publishers, Postbus 17, 3300 AA Dordrecht, Netherlands. TEL 31-78-6392392. FAX 31-78-6392254. TELEX 29245 KAPG NL. E-mail: services@wkap.nl; URL: http://www.wkap.nl. (Dist. by: Kluwer Academic Publishers Group, P.O. Box 322, 3300 AH Dordrecht. TEL 31-78-6392392. FAX 31-78-6546424; N. American dist. addr.: Box 358, Accord Sta., Hingham, MA 02018-0358. TEL 617-871-6600. FAX 617-871-6528) Ed. H.M. Amman. (also avail. in microform from UMI; reprint service avail. from SWZ) **Indexed:** Comput.& Info.Sys., Comput.Lit.Ind., Comput.Rev., Eng.Ind., IDA, INSPEC (1988-), J.of Econ.Lit., Math.R., Zent.Math. **Document type:** academic/scholarly publication.
—BLDSC (3390.585000); AskIEEE; Ei; KR SourceOne; SWETS; UMI; UnCover. **CCC.**
Formerly (until vol.6, 1993): Computer Science in Economics and Management (ISSN 0921-2736)
Description: Serves as an interface for work which integrates computer science with economic or management science.
Refereed Serial

330 657 CN ISSN 0843-8072
COMPUTER ACCOUNTING LETTER. 1989. q. Can.$25. Morochove & Associates Inc., 390 Bay St., Ste. 2000, Toronto, ON M5H 2Y2, Canada. TEL 416-947-1427. FAX 416-923-3938. Ed. Richard Morochove. circ. 2,000.
Description: Aimed at the end-user of financial applications such as accounting, tax and financial analysis; provides news, reviews and strategies.

COMPUTER AND COMMUNICATIONS. see COMPUTERS — Electronic Data Processing

COMPUTER INDUSTRY REPORT. see COMPUTERS — Electronic Data Processing

330 US
COMPUTER STUDIES: COMPUTERS IN BUSINESS. 1987. irreg. $12.95. Dushkin Publishing Group, Sluice Dock, Guilford, CT 06437-9989. TEL 203-453-4351. FAX 203-453-6000. Ed. Louis J. Zivic; Pub. Ian Nielsen. illus. **Document type:** academic/scholarly publication.

330 621.381 US
COMPUTERLAND MAGAZINE. 1985. 8/yr. free to qualified personnel. ComputerLand Corporation, 5964 W. Las Positas, Pleasanton, CA 94588-8575. TEL 510-734-4087. FAX 510-734-4802. Ed. David Gancher. adv. circ. 270,000 (controlled). (microfiche; back issues avail.)
Description: Presents innovative applications of computers - hardware and software.

330 621.381 US ISSN 0740-7270
COMPUTERS IN ACCOUNTING. 1984. 10/yr. $58. Faulkner and Gray, Inc. (New York), 11 Penn Plaza, 17th Fl., New York, NY 10001. TEL 212-967-7000. FAX 212-967-7155. Ed. Jules H. Gilder. adv.: B&W page $1300; trim 8 1/2 x 11. **Indexed:** A.I.Abstr., ABI Inform., Account.Ind. (1984-), Comput.Lit.Ind., PCR2, PSI.
—**CCC.**
Description: For accounting and financial executives. Features articles on software selections (including electronic spreadsheets, charts and graphics), hardware, peripherals and user groups.

004 621.39 NE ISSN 0166-3615
TS155.A1 CODEN: CINUD4
COMPUTERS IN INDUSTRY; a new international journal of experience and practice on computer applications in industrial and technological processes. (Text in English) 1980. 9/yr. fl.1287($740) (effective 1998). North-Holland (Subsidiary of: Elsevier Science B.V.), P.O. Box 211, 1000 AE Amsterdam, Netherlands. TEL 31-20-4853911. FAX 31-20-4853598. TELEX 18582 ESPA NL. E-mail: information@elsevier.nl; URL: http://www.elsevier.nl:80/inca/publications/store/5/0/6/4/6/505646.pub.shtml. (Subscr. in the Americas to: Elsevier Science, Regional Sales Office, Box 945, New York, NY 10159-0945. TEL 212-633-3730. FAX 212-633-3680; Subscr. in Australasia and the Far East to: Elsevier Science (Singapore) Pte Ltd, No.1 Temasek Ave., No.17-01 Millenia Tower, Singapore 039192, Singapore. TEL 65-434-3727. FAX 65-337-2230; Subscr. in Japan to: Elsevier Science Japan, 9-15 Higashi-Azabu 1-chome, Minato-ku, Tokyo 106, Japan. TEL 81-3-5561-5033. FAX 81-3-5561-5047) Ed. G. Karlmark. adv.; bk.rev.; illus.; index. (also avail. in microform from UMI; back issues avail.) **Indexed:** A.I.Abstr., A.S.& T.Ind., ABI Inform., ASCA, CAD CAM Abstr., Chem.Eng.Abstr., Compumath, Comput.Abstr., Comput.Cont., Comput.Lit.Ind., Curr.Cont., Energy Info.Abstr., Ind.Sci.Rev., INSPEC, Int.Packag.Abstr., Intl.Civil Eng.Abstr., Oper.Res.Manage.Sci., Qual.Contr.Appl.Stat., Robomat., Soft.Abstr.Eng., SSCI. **Document type:** academic/scholarly publication.
—BLDSC (3394.923000); AskIEEE; CISTI; Ei; Genuine Article; KR SourceOne; Linda Hall; SWETS; UMI; UnCover. **CCC.**
Description: Contains case studies, reviews and survey papers on computer applications and computing techniques in industry. Focuses on computer-aided design and manufacturing, production planning and control, and material and control management.
Refereed Serial

330 IE ISSN 0790-7281
COMPUTERSCOPE. 1985. m. ComputerScope, Ltd., Prospect House, 1 Prospect Rd., Glasnevin, Ireland. TEL 353-1-8303455. FAX 353-1-8300888. E-mail: info@scope.ie. Ed. David D'Arcy; Pub. Frank Quinn. adv.: B&W page I£2300, color page I£2650; trim 405 x 280; adv. contact: Paul Byrne. circ. 7,800. **Document type:** trade publication.
Description: Covers PCs, minis, mainframes, datacomms, networks and trade news and analysis for business computer usersand professionals.

COMPUTING & CONTROL ENGINEERING JOURNAL. see ENGINEERING — Computer Applications

CONFERENCE ON ARTIFICIAL INTELLIGENCE APPLICATIONS. PROCEEDINGS. see COMPUTERS — Artificial Intelligence

330 UK ISSN 0266-2493
CONTROL SYSTEMS. 1983. m. £65 in the UK; Europe £85; elsewhere £120. I M L Group plc, Blair House, High St., Tonbridge, Kent TN9 1BQ, England. TEL 01732-359990. FAX 01732-770049. Ed. Les Hunt; Pub. Peter Whitfield. R&P contact: M.T. Croucher. adv. contact: Miles Bossom. circ. 19,950. **Indexed:** Cyb.Abstr., INSPEC (1992-). **Document type:** trade publication.
—BLDSC (3463.003000); AskIEEE; KR SourceOne.

ULRICH'S INTERNATIONAL PERIODICALS DIRECTORY 1998

BUSINESS AND ECONOMICS — COMPUTER APPLICATIONS

330   US   ISSN 0955-209X
CODEN: CORCED
CORPORATE COMPUTING;* the magazine of the reengineering age. 1992. m. free to qualified personnel. Ziff-Davis Publishing (San Francisco), 50 Beale St., 14th Fl., San Francisco, CA 94105-1813. TEL 415-578-7600; 800-827-7556. FAX 415-578-7799. Ed. Jon Zilber; Pub. Robert J. Nolan. adv.; illus.; circ. 155,000 (controlled). **Indexed:** Comput.Ind.
—CCC.
  Formerly: Business Software Review (U.K. edition).
  Description: Helps senior executives responsible for corporate computer systems to select, purchase and maintain equipment.

330   US
CORPORATE SOFTWARE & SOLUTIONS (INTERNATIONAL). 2 base vols. (plus m. updates). $1116 to new subscr.; renewals $958 (effective 1996). Datapro Information Services Group (Subsidiary of: McGraw-Hill, Inc.), 600 Delran Pkwy., Delran, NJ 08075. TEL 609-764-0100; 800-328-2776. FAX 609-764-8953.

D B. (Diablo Business) see BUSINESS AND ECONOMICS — Domestic Commerce

DATA COMMUNICATIONS. see COMPUTERS — Data Communications And Data Transmission Systems

DATA ENTRY MANAGEMENT ASSOCIATION. NEWSLETTER. see COMPUTERS — Electronic Data Processing

330 001.64   US   ISSN 0730-8817
DATAPRO REPORTS ON RETAIL AUTOMATION. base vol. (plus bi-m. updates). $1008 to new subscr.; renewals $914 (effective 1996). Datapro Information Services Group (Subsidiary of: McGraw-Hill, Inc.), 600 Delran Pkwy., Delran, NJ 08075. TEL 609-764-0100; 800-328-2776. FAX 609-764-2814.
—CCC.
  Description: For buyers, product planners, merchandisers, specifiers, marketers and system designers. Covers electronic cash registers, credit and payment systems, specialized industry systems, software, hardware, weighing and packaging, and recognition equipment.

DECISION SUPPORT SYSTEMS; an international journal. see BUSINESS AND ECONOMICS — Management

DEVELOPMENTS IN BUSINESS SIMULATION & EXPERIENTIAL EXERCISES. see COMPUTERS — Computer Simulation

330   GW   ISSN 0341-3683
DIEBOLD MANAGEMENT REPORT. 1971. m. DM.295. Diebold Deutschland GmbH, Frankfurterstr. 27, 65760 Eschborn, Germany. TEL 06196-9030. FAX 06196-903465. (Subscr. to: FBO-Verlag, Postfach 316, 76482 Baden-Baden, Germany. TEL 07221-271066. FAX 07221-33228) Ed. Hans-Joachim Grobe. adv. contact: Karin Schlicke. circ. 2,200 (paid). **Document type:** trade publication.
—SWETS.

330 621.381   US
DUN'S DATALINE. q. for online subscribers. Dun's Marketing Services, Online Department (Subsidiary of: Dun & Bradstreet, Inc.), 3 Sylvan Way, Parsippany, NJ 07054-9978. TEL 800-223-1026. Ed. Tom Croarkin.
  Description: For Dun's online database users. Includes articles featuring individual databases, new product developments and enhancements as well as user tips.

330   AU
E A N AUSTRIA INFORMATION. q. E A N Austria Gesellschaft fuer Kooperative Logistik GmbH, Mayerhofgasse 1-15, A-1040 Vienna, Austria. TEL 01-5058601. Ed. Peter Franzmair. adv. contact: Renate Pardatscher. circ. 6,000. **Document type:** bulletin.

E D I FORUM; the journal of electronic data interchange. see COMPUTERS — Data Communications And Data Transmission Systems

330   GW   ISSN 0943-4542
E D V BERATER. 1993. m. DM.199.80. Verlag Norman Rentrop, Theodor-Heuss-Str. 4, 53177 Bonn, Germany. TEL 49-228-82050. FAX 49-228-364411. TELEX 17228309. Ed. Eduard Altmann. (looseleaf format) **Document type:** bulletin.
  Incorporates: Telekommunikations-Berater (ISSN 0943-9110)
  Description: Information related to computers for office use.

330   UK   ISSN 0962-2780
HB143.5
ECONOMIC & FINANCIAL COMPUTING; a quarterly international journal. 1991. q. £1 (outside Europe £190). European Economics and Financial Centre, Publications Department, P.O. Box 2498, London W2 4LE, England. TEL 0171-229-0402. FAX 0171-221-5118. Ed. H.M. Scobie. adv. contact: Nigel Olsen. bk.rev. **Document type:** academic/scholarly publication.
—BLDSC (3651.446500); SWETS. CCC.
  Description: Provides a forum to present recent advances on the measurement aspects of economic and financial problems. Focuses on both the methodological and practical facets of quantitative and computational techniques.
Refereed Serial

330   UK   ISSN 1350-7419
ECONOMIC & FINANCIAL MODELLING. 1994. q. £180 (outside Europe £195). European Economics and Financial Centre, Publications Department, P.O. Box 2498, London W2 4LE, England. TEL 44-171-229-0402. FAX 44-171-221-5118. Ed. H.M. Scobie. **Document type:** academic/scholarly publication.
—BLDSC (3651.447500).
  Description: Presents recent advances in all aspects of economic modelling.
Refereed Serial

381   US   ISSN 1092-0366
HF5548.33
ELECTRONIC COMMERCE WORLD; business solutions through technology integration. 1991. m. $45 (Canada & Mexico $55, elsewhere $90). E D I World, Inc., 2021 Coolidge St., Hollywood, FL 33020. TEL 954-925-5900; 954-336-4887. FAX 305-925-7533. Ed. Michael S. McGarr; Pub. Rick D'Allesandro. R&P contact: Rick D'Allesandro. adv.: Rachel/Sessa. **Document type:** trade publication.
—KR SourceOne.
  Formerly: E D I World (ISSN 1055-0399)

THE ELECTRONIC MARKETPLACE (YEAR): STRATEGIES FOR CONNECTING BUYERS & SELLERS. see COMPUTERS — Computer Networks

001.6   US   ISSN 0735-8423
ELECTRONIC OFFICE; management and technology. 1980. 2 base vols. (plus m. updates). $990 (effective 1993). Faulkner Information Services, Inc., 114 Cooper Center, 7905 Browning Rd., Pennsauken, NJ 08109-4319. TEL 609-662-2070. FAX 609-662-3380. Ed. Janet Mann. (looseleaf format)
  Description: Covers all office system technologies and related management issues.

332.6 658   UK
ELECTRONIC TRADER. 1990. m. £75. Edicom, 10 Fourways, Canning Rd., Croydon, Surrey CR0 6QB, England. TEL 44-181-655-4354. FAX 44-181-662-1715. E-mail: johnkav@cix.compulink.co.uk. (Dist. by: Edicom, 21 rue Tournefort, 75005 Paris, France. TEL 33-1-47-07-29-29) Ed. John Kavanagh; Pub. Richard Bricaire. adv.; bk.rev. circ. 1,000.
  Description: Covers electronic commerce and electronic data interchange, helping business and information technology managers evaluate, install, and use their systems.

EUROPEAN COMMUNICATIONS NEWSFILE. see COMPUTERS — Data Communications And Data Transmission Systems

330   UK   ISSN 0268-6872
CODEN: EXEEE5
EXE; software developers magazine. 1986. m. £35 (E.C. £50; elsewhere £70). Centaur Communications Ltd., St. Giles House, 50 Poland St., London W1V 4AX, England. TEL 44-171-287-5000. FAX 44-171-437-1350. E-mail: editorial@dotexe.demon.co.uk. Ed. David Mery; Pub. Declan Gough. R&P contact: Declan Gough. adv.: B&W page £1450, color page £2050; adv. contact: Mark Parker. bk.rev. circ. 10,000. (back issues avail.) **Document type:** trade publication.
—BLDSC (3836.208500); SWETS.

330 621.381   US   ISSN 0741-0050
EXECUTIVE COMPUTING; ideas you can use about small computers. 1975. m. $99 membership. Association of Computer Users, 1250 45th St., Ste. 200, Emeryville, CA 94608-2924. TEL 510-596-9300. Ed. Eric Adams. R&P contact: James Sinkinson. adv. contact: J.B. Downey. circ. 10,000 (paid). **Document type:** newsletter.
—CCC.
  Formerly (until 1983): Interactive Computing.
  Description: For members of the Association of Computer Users. A newsletter featuring timely articles on software, programs, programming and business applications.
Refereed Serial

330   UK   ISSN 0968-8803
EXECUTIVE SYSTEMS INTERNATIONAL; the newsletter for management support professionals. 1989. fortn. £295 (rest of Europe £315; N. America £325; elsewhere £345). Business Intelligence Publishing, 25 Prospect Rd., Southborough, Tunbridge Wells, Kent TN4 0EL, England. TEL 01892-517340. FAX 01892-517476. E-mail: clivec@cix.compulink.co.uk; 100030,121@compuserve.com. (Subscr. to: Forum House, 1 Graham Rd., London SW19 3SW, England. TEL 0181-544-1830. FAX 0181-544-9020) Ed. Clive Couldwell; Pub. Ian Meiklejohn. software rev.; charts; stat. **Document type:** newsletter.
  Description: Provides research for users and vendors and programmers of management-support systems (e.g., executive information systems, decision-support systems, and business-intelligence systems).
Refereed Serial

300   US   ISSN 1053-234X
FAXREPORTER. m. $385. Buyers Laboratory Inc., 20 Railroad Ave., Hackensack, NJ 07601. TEL 201-488-0404. FAX 201-488-0461. E-mail: 76311.1067@compuserve.com; URL: http://www.buyers-lab.com. Ed. Daria Hoffman; Pub. Burt Meerow. R&P contact: Jane Lyons. adv. contact: John Ahrens. circ. 2,000. (looseleaf format) **Document type:** newsletter.
  Description: Provides news and analysis of fax machines, new products, new technologies, market trends, and options for fax units.

330 UK ISSN 0961-5342
HG1709
FINANCIAL TECHNOLOGY INSIGHT. 1984. m. £300($447) (effective 1995). Elsevier Science Ltd., P.O. Box 800, Kidlington, Oxford OX5 1DX, England. TEL 44-1865-843000. FAX 44-1865-843010. E-mail: nlinfo-f@elsevier.nl; usinfo-f@elsevier.com; forinfo-kyf04035@niftyserve.or.jp; URL: http://www.elsevier.nl/. (Subscr. to: Elsevier Science, Regional Sales Office, P.O. Box 211, 1000 AE Amsterdam, Netherlands. TEL 31-20-4853757. FAX 31-20-4853432; Subscr. in the Americas to: Elsevier Science, Regional Sales Office, Box 945, New York, NY 10159-0945. TEL 212-633-3730. FAX 212-633-3680; Subscr. in Australasia and the Far East to: Elsevier Science (Singapore) Pte Ltd, No.1 Temasek Ave., No.17-01 Millenia Tower, Singapore 039192, Singapore TEL 65-434-3727. FAX 65-337-2230) Ed. J. Meyer. bk.rev.; charts; stat. (also avail. in microform from UMI; back issues avail.) **Indexed:** INSPEC (1984-). **Document type:** bulletin, newsletter.
●Also available online. **Vendor(s):** Data-Star, Information Access Co., Knight-Ridder Information, Inc.
—AskIEEE; KR SourceOne. **CCC.**
 Incorporates (1991-1993): E D I in Finance Newsletter (ISSN 0960-4634); **Formerly** (until 1992): Electronic Banking and Finance (ISSN 0265-9239)
 Description: Provides information on the latest technology and policy implications of advanced automation and the globalization of banking and financial services.

330 US
FORBES A S A P. (Supplement to: Forbes (ISSN 0015-6914)) 1992. q. included with Forbes subscr. Forbes, Inc., 60 Fifth Ave., New York, NY 10011. TEL 212-620-2200. URL: http://www.forbes.com/. Ed. Rich Karlgaard. adv.; circ. 760,000 (controlled).
 Description: Covers the impact of information technology on the business world.

330 658.3 US
H R IN REVIEW.* (Human Resource Information Network); the human resource information network newsletter. 1987. bi-m. free. E T S I: Executive Telecom System International, Box 3370, Gaithersburg, MD 20885-3370. TEL 800-638-8044. FAX 301-990-8378. Ed. Ramsey G. Perry. (back issues avail.) **Document type:** newsletter.
 Former titles: H R Update; (until 1988): H R Power.
 Description: For users of the Human Resource Information Network.

330 658.3 US ISSN 0884-9129
HD9696.C63
H R - P C; computer technology for human resource management. 1985. 4/yr. $125. D G M Associates, Box 10639, Marina Del Rey, CA 90295-6639. TEL 310-578-1428. Ed. David G. Mahal. adv.; bk.rev.; index. **Document type:** trade publication.

HANDBOOK OF I S MANAGEMENT. see BUSINESS AND ECONOMICS — Management

330 658 US
HANDBOOK OF SYSTEMS MANAGEMENT; development and support. base vol. (plus a. update). $156. Auerbach Publishers (Subsidiary of: Warren, Gorham & Lamont), One Penn Plaza, New York, NY 10119. TEL 212-971-5000. FAX 212-971-5024. (Subscr. to: 31 St. James Ave., Boston, MA 02116-4112. TEL 800-950-1218. FAX 617-423-1914) Ed. Paul Tinnirello. **Document type:** trade publication.
 Description: Provides practical advice and analysis to help bridge the gap between the traditional, technical role of management and newer managerial challenges.

HANDELSHOCHSCHULE LEIPZIG. WISSENSCHAFTLICHE ZEITSCHRIFT. see BUSINESS AND ECONOMICS

330 US ISSN 1043-6146
HARLOW REPORT: GEOGRAPHIC INFORMATION SYSTEMS. 1978. m. $190 (effective 1995). Advanced Information Management Group, Inc., 905 Thistledown Ln., Hoover, AL 35244-3361. TEL 305-213-0053. Ed. Chris Harlow; Pub. Chris Harlow. bk.rev.; illus. (looseleaf format; back issues avail.) **Document type:** newsletter.
 Formerly: F - M Automation Newsletter (Facilities Management) (ISSN 0742-468X)
 Description: Presents current reports on the use of computers and computer graphics for managing geographic information systems. Written for engineers, planners, systems developers, cartographers, and others interested in the management of geographic information systems and facilities.

HIGH TECHNOLOGY AND OTHER GROWTH STOCKS. see BUSINESS AND ECONOMICS — Investments

330 UK CODEN: ICLTEG
I D G NEWS SERVICE. 1985. m. free. I.D.G. Communications Ltd., 2 Stone Rd., Bromley, Kent BR2 9AU, England. TEL 0181-460-0944. Ed. Ron Condon. bk.rev.; illus. circ. 16,000. (back issues avail.) **Indexed:** INSPEC (1987-).
—AskIEEE; KR SourceOne.
 Formerly: I C L Today (ISSN 0268-5957)

330 001.6 US ISSN 0892-676X
HF5416 CODEN: IDSYE5
I D SYSTEMS; the magazine of automated data collection. 1981. m. $55 (effective 1997) (free to qualified personnel). Helmers Publishing, Inc., 174 Concord St., Box 874, Peterborough, NH 03458-0874. TEL 603-924-9631. FAX 603-924-7408. Ed. Mark Reynolds; Pub. Dan Rodrigues. adv. circ. 75,000. **Indexed:** Abstr.Bull.Inst.Pap.Chem., INSPEC (1993-), Int.Packag.Abstr., Print.Abstr. **Document type:** trade publication.
—BLDSC (4362.225000); CASDDS; Ei; KR SourceOne. **CCC.**
 Formerly: Bar Code News.
 Description: Provides technical information to users of bar codes and automated data collection.

330 001.6 US ISSN 1043-8319
HD9801.6.P763
I D SYSTEMS BUYERS GUIDE. 1983. a. Helmers Publishing, Inc., 174 Concord St., Box 874, Peterborough, NH 03458. TEL 603-924-9631. FAX 603-924-7408. Ed. Mark Reynolds; Pub. Dan Rodrigues. adv.: B&W page $4795; trim 8 1/8 x 10 7/8. circ. 75,000. **Document type:** directory.
 Former titles (until 1989): Automatic Identification Manufacturers and Services Directory (ISSN 1042-4512); (until 1987): Bar Code Manufacturers and Services Directory (ISSN 8755-7851)
 Description: Lists companies and products for the automated data collection industry.

330 001.6 US ISSN 1081-275X
I D SYSTEMS EUROPEAN EDITION. (Text in English; summaries in French, German) 1993. 9/yr. $30 (free to qualified Western European personnel). Helmers Publishing, Inc., 174 Concord St., Box 874, Peterborough, NH 03458-0874. TEL 603-924-9631. FAX 603-924-7408. (Subscr. to: Helmers Publishing, Inc., The ACTE Business Center, 304 av. Louise, 5th Fl., 1050 Brussels, Belgium) Ed. Susan R. Beale.
—BLDSC (4362.225005); AskIEEE; KR SourceOne.

I E E E SYMPOSIUM ON MASS STORAGE SYSTEMS. DIGEST OF PAPERS. see COMPUTERS

I N T I X NEWSLETTER. (International Ticketing Association) see BUSINESS AND ECONOMICS — Marketing And Purchasing

658.5 001.6 UK ISSN 0263-5577
HD28 CODEN: IMDSD8
INDUSTRIAL MANAGEMENT & DATA SYSTEMS. 8/yr. £2499($3879) (foreign Aus.$4879) (effective 1998). M C B University Press Ltd., 60-62 Toller Ln., Bradford, W. Yorks BD8 9BY, England. TEL 44-1274-777700. FAX 44-1274-785200. TELEX 51317-MCBUNI-G. URL: http://www.mcb.co.uk. Eds. Sue de Verteuil, Len Williams. bk.rev.; illus.; abstr. (back issues avail.; reprint service avail. SWZ) **Indexed:** A.I.Abstr., Account.& Data Proc.Abstr., ASCA, ASEAN Manage.Abstr., B.P.I., BMT, Br.Tech.Ind., Comput.Cont., Comput.Lit.Ind., Cont.Pg.Manage., Educ.Tech.Abstr., Ergon.Abstr., INSPEC, Mgmt.& Market.Abstr., Tr.& Indus.Ind. **Document type:** academic/scholarly publication.
●Also available on CD-ROM.
—BLDSC (4457.715000); AskIEEE; Ei; Genuine Article; KR SourceOne; SWETS; UMI; UnCover. **CCC.**
 Formed by 1980 merger of: Data Systems (ISSN 0011-6912); Industrial Management (ISSN 0007-6929)
 Description: Aims to improve skills by promoting awareness of new products, processes, training techniques and management concepts. Covers the full range of managerial activity: personnel, production, communications, marketing.

330 CN ISSN 1189-6515
INFO-TECH MAGAZINE; informatique & technologie. 1980. m. (11/yr.) Can.$31.13. Publications Transcontinental Inc., 1100 Boul. Rene Levesque W., 24th Fl., Montreal, PQ H3B 4X9, Canada. TEL 514-288-8875. FAX 514-288-6931. Ed. Alain Thibault. adv. contact: Carole Caron. circ. 19,351. (back issues avail.) **Indexed:** Can.B.P.I., Can.Per.Ind., Pt.de Rep. (1983-).
—AskIEEE; CISTI; KR SourceOne.
 Formed by the 1993 merger of: Informatique et Bureautique (ISSN 0227-8332) & Info-Log Magazine (ISSN 0847-4915); Which was formerly (until 1990): Informations - Logiciel (ISSN 0832-638X)

330 US ISSN 1040-2179
INFOCUS (PORTLAND); the newsletter on products, services and trends in forms and systems. 1988. m. (10/yr.) $50 (foreign $65). Business Forms Management Association, Inc., 319 S.W. Washington St., Ste. 710, Portland, OR 97204-2604. TEL 503-227-3393. FAX 503-274-7667. E-mail: Paul@bfma.org; URL: http://www.bfma.org/~bfma/. Ed. Paul Telles. R&P contact: Paul Telles. adv. contact: Paul Telles. bk.rev. circ. 2,000. (back issues avail.) **Document type:** newsletter.
 Description: Covers industry news, events and hardware and software for forms and records design. Includes tips on ways of improving forms and systems.

THE INFORMATION ADVISOR. see LIBRARY AND INFORMATION SCIENCES — Computer Applications

INFORMATION SYSTEMS AUDIT & CONTROL ASSOCIATION. CONTROL OBJECTIVES; for information and related technology. see COMPUTERS — Electronic Data Processing

INPUT - OUTPUT STUDIEN. see BUSINESS AND ECONOMICS

330 US ISSN 1042-4296
INTELLIGENCE: THE FUTURE OF COMPUTING. 1984. m. $395 (foreign $450) (effective 1998). Intelligence, Box 20008, New York, NY 10025-1510. TEL 212-222-1123. FAX 212-222-1123. E-mail: i@businesstech.com; URL: http://businesstech.com/intelligence/. Ed. Edward Rosenfeld; Pub. Edward Rosenfeld. R&P contact: Edward Rosenfeld. adv. contact: Edward Rosenfeld. bk.rev. (back issues avail.) **Document type:** newsletter.
 Description: Provides news about neurocomputing, artificial intelligence, nanotechnology and other technologies that will impact the future of computing.

INTERACTIVE MARKETING & P R NEWS. see BUSINESS AND ECONOMICS — Marketing And Purchasing

BUSINESS AND ECONOMICS — COMPUTER APPLICATIONS

006 338   UK   ISSN 0951-192X
TS155.6
INTERNATIONAL JOURNAL OF COMPUTER INTEGRATED MANUFACTURING. Online edition (UK ISSN 1362-3052) 1988. bi-m. £273($451) to institutions (£328($541) with online ed.) (effective 1998). Taylor & Francis Ltd., 1 Gunpowder Sq., London EC4A 3DE, England. TEL 44-171-583-0490. FAX 44-171-583-0585. TELEX 858540. E-mail: info@tandf.co.uk; URL: http://www.tandfco.uk/jnls/cim.htm. (Subscr. in N. America to: Taylor & Francis Inc., 1900 Frost Rd., Bristol, PA 19007-1598. TEL 800-821-8312. FAX 215-785-5515) Ed. David Williams. **Indexed:** A.I.Abstr., Abstr.Hum.Comp.Inter., ASCA, CAD CAM Abstr., Compumath, Curr.Cont., INSPEC (1987-), Robomat. (until 1992), SSCI. **Document type:** academic/scholarly publication.
●Also available online.
—BLDSC (4542.174700); AskIEEE; CISTI; Ei; Genuine Article; KR SourceOne; SWETS; UnCover. **CCC.**
Description: Presents papers related to CIM in a wide variety of manufacturing environments: mechanical, electronic, process and automotive.
Refereed Serial

380.10285   US   ISSN 1086-4415
HF5548.32
▼**INTERNATIONAL JOURNAL OF ELECTRONIC COMMERCE.** 1996. q. $64 to individuals (foreign $76.80); institutions $260 (foreign $290) (effective Jan. 1997). M.E. Sharpe, Inc., 80 Business Park Dr., Armonk, NY 10504. TEL 914-273-1800; 800-541-6563. FAX 914-273-2106. Ed. Vladimir Zwass. adv.: $300; trim 6 x 9; adv. contact: Barbara Ladd. **Document type:** academic/scholarly publication.
—BLDSC (4542.231000).
Description: Offers an integrated view of the field covering the areas of management information systems, computer science, economics, sociology, and related disciplines.
Refereed Serial

330 657   UK   ISSN 1055-615X
HF5679   CODEN: IJAMEN
INTERNATIONAL JOURNAL OF INTELLIGENT SYSTEMS IN ACCOUNTING, FINANCE & MANAGEMENT. 198? q. $350 (foreign $350) (effective 1998). John Wiley & Sons Ltd., Journals, Baffins Ln., Chichester, W. Sussex PO19 1UD, England. TEL 44-1243-779777. FAX 44-1243-775878. E-mail: info-assets@wiley.co.uk; URL: http://www.wiley.co.uk. (Subscr. in the Americas to: John Wiley & Sons, Inc., 605 Third Ave., New York, NY 10158. TEL 212-850-6645. FAX 212-850-6021) Ed. Daniel E. O'Leary. R&P contact: Sally Morris. adv.: B&W page £595, color page £1495; trim 260 x 200; adv. contact: Bob Kern. (also avail. in microform from UMI; back issues avail.; reprint service avail. from SWZ) **Indexed:** INSPEC (1993-). **Document type:** academic/scholarly publication.
—BLDSC (4542.310700); AskIEEE; KR SourceOne; SWETS; UMI. **CCC.**
Formerly (until 1992): Expert Systems Review for Business & Accounting (ISSN 1059-3640)
Description: Publishes original material concerned with all aspects of intelligent systems in business-based applications with an aim of providing a forum for advancing theory and application of intelligent systems in business theory.
Refereed Serial

338 658   UK   ISSN 0263-7863
T56.8
INTERNATIONAL JOURNAL OF PROJECT MANAGEMENT. 1983. bi-m. fl.917($527) (effective 1998). (International Project Management Association (INTERNET)) Elsevier Science Ltd., Pergamon, P.O. Box 800, Kidlington, Oxford OX5 1DX, England. TEL 44-1865-843000. FAX 44-1865-843010. TELEX 83111 BHPOXF G. E-mail: nlinfo-f@elsevier.nl; usinfo-f@elsevier.com; forinfo-kyf04035@niftyserve.or.jp; URL: http://www.elsevier.nl/. (Subscr. to: Elsevier Science, Regional Sales Office, P.O. Box 211, 1000 AE Amsterdam, Netherlands. TEL 31-20-4853757. FAX 31-20-4853432; Subscr. in the Americas to: Elsevier Science, Regional Sales Office, Box 945, New York, NY 10159-0945. TEL 212-633-3730. FAX 212-633-3680; Subscr. in Australasia and the Far East to: Elsevier Science (Singapore) Pte Ltd, No.1 Temasek Ave., No.17-01 Millenia Tower, Singapore 039192, Singapore. TEL 65-434-3727. FAX 65-337-2230) Ed. B. Curtis. bk.rev.; index. (also avail. in microform from UMI; back issues avail.) **Indexed:** BPIA, Excerp.Med., INSPEC (1985-), Oper.Res.Manage.Sci., Qual.Contr.Appl.Stat., SCIMP (1986-). **Document type:** academic/scholarly publication.
—BLDSC (4542.487100); AskIEEE; CISTI; Ei; KR SourceOne; SWETS; UMI; UnCover. **CCC.**
Description: Offers guidance to practicing managers striving to complete projects on time, to meet project requirements and to stay within budget.
Refereed Serial

330.1   NE   ISSN 0924-5835
INTERNATIONAL SERIES IN ECONOMIC MODELING. (Text in English) 1986. irreg. price varies. Kluwer Academic Publishers, Postbus 17, 3300 AA Dordrecht, Netherlands. TEL 31-78-6392392. FAX 31-78-6392254. TELEX 29245 KAPG NL. E-mail: services@wkap.nl; URL: http://www.wkap.nl. (Dist. by: Kluwer Academic Publishers Group, P.O. Box 322, 3300 AH Dordrecht, Netherlands. TEL 31-78-6392392. FAX 31-78-6546474; N. America dist. addr.: Box 358, Accord Sta., Hingham, MA 02018-0358. TEL 617-871-6600. FAX 617-871-6528) **Document type:** monographic series.
Refereed Serial

330   US   ISSN 1091-4293
▼**INTERNET BUSINESS AND TECHNOLOGY REPORT.** 1997. m. $390. Computer Technology Research Group, 6 N. Atlantic Wharf, Charleston, SC 29401-2993. TEL 803-853-6460. Ed. Stacy Evangelist.
Description: Examines tools and technologies for businesses.

INTERNET FOR BUSINESS. see *COMPUTERS — Computer Networks*

338.025 658   US
INTERNET YELLOW PAGES: BUSINESS MODELS AND MARKET OPPORTUNITIES. a. $1995 (Canada and Mexico $2015; elsewhere $2035) (effective 1997). Cowles - SIMBA Information (Subsidiary of: Cowles Business Media), 11 Riverbend Dr. S., Box 4949, Stamford, CT 06907-0949. TEL 203-358-9900; 800-307-2529. FAX 203-358-5811. E-mail: info@simbanet.com; URL: http://www.simbanet.com. **Document type:** trade publication.
Formerly: Electronic Yellow and White Pages: Review, Trends and Forecast.
Description: Helps users sort through online services and identify the potential risks and rewards of venturing onto the internet.

330   US
INTRANET AND NETWORKING STRATEGIES REPORT. 1996. m. $395 (effective 1997). Computer Economics, Inc., 5841 Edison Pl., Carlsbad, CA 92008-6519. TEL 760-438-8100; 800-326-8100. FAX 760-431-1126. E-mail: editor@compecon.com; URL: http://www.computereconomics.com. **Document type:** newsletter.
●Also available on CD-ROM.
—AskIEEE; KR SourceOne. **CCC.**
Formed by the merger of (1994-1996): Open Systems Economics Letter (ISSN 1071-6394); (1993-1996): Network Economics Letter (ISSN 1069-126X).
Description: Enables readers to maximize enterprise network investments by aligning intranet, networking, and open systems strategies with business objectives.

658   UK   ISSN 1350-2328
THE JOURNAL OF DATABASE MARKETING. 1993. q. £130($210) (outside Europe £145) (effective 1996). Henry Stewart Publications, Russell House, 28-30 Little Russell St., London WC1A 2HN, England. TEL 44-171-404-3040. FAX 44-171-404-2081. (Addr. in N. America: Box 1897, Lawrence, KS 66044-8897. TEL 913-843-1221. FAX 913-843-1274) Ed. May Corfield. adv.; bk.rev.; charts; illus.; software rev.; circ. 600 (paid). (back issues avail.) **Document type:** academic/scholarly publication.
—BLDSC (4967.816000). **CCC.**
Description: Explores the use of databases in marketing for business professionals and academics alike.
Refereed Serial

330 658   US   ISSN 1047-8310
HD62.37   CODEN: JTMRE9
JOURNAL OF HIGH TECHNOLOGY MANAGEMENT RESEARCH. 1990. s-a. $80 to individuals (foreign $100); institutions $205 (foreign $225) (effective 1998). J A I Press Inc., 55 Old Post Rd., No. 2, Box 1678, Greenwich, CT 06830-1678. TEL 203-661-7602. FAX 203-661-0792. E-mail: jai@jaipress.com. (Addr. in Europe: J A I Press Ltd., 38 Tavistock St., Covent Garden, London WC2E 7PB, England. TEL 44-171-379-8834. FAX 44-171-379-8835) Ed. Luis R. Gomez-Mejia. (also avail. in microform from UMI; back issues avail.) **Document type:** academic/scholarly publication.
—BLDSC (4998.565000); SWETS; UnCover. **CCC.**
Description: Promotes interdisciplinary research regarding special problems and opportunities related to marketing and managing emerging technologies, their products, services, and companies.

JOURNAL OF MANAGEMENT INFORMATION SYSTEMS. see *COMPUTERS — Information Science And Information Theory*

JYVASKYLA STUDIES IN COMPUTER SCIENCE, ECONOMICS AND STATISTICS. see *COMPUTERS*

330   GW
KOMPETENZ. q. (Diebold Deutschland GmbH) Vereinigte Verlagsanstalten GmbH, Hoehenweg 278, 40231 Duesseldorf, Germany. TEL 49-211-7357-0. FAX 49-211-7357223. circ. 10,000. **Document type:** newsletter.

330   JA   ISSN 0913-5545
KOSHIEN UNIVERSITY. COLLEGE OF BUSINESS ADMINISTRATION AND INFORMATION SCIENCE. BULLETIN. (Text in English, Japanese; summaries in English) no.14, 1986. a. Koshien University, College of Business Administration and Information Science, 10-1 Momiji-ga-oka, Takarazuka 665, Japan. TEL 0797-87-5111. Ed. Hiroyuki Masutani. circ. 500. **Indexed:** Zent.Math. **Document type:** bulletin.

332.1   GW   ISSN 0173-6213
LOGISTIK HEUTE. 1979. 10/yr. DM.180. (Bundesvereinigung Logistik e.V.) Huss-Verlag GmbH, Joseph-Dollinger-Bogen 5, 80807 Munich, Germany. TEL 49-89-32391-260. FAX 49-89-32391-416. Ed. Karin Eberhardt. adv.: B&W page DM.9480, color page DM.14700; trim 185 x 270; adv. contact: Erika Sammetinger. bk.rev.; index. circ. 42,000. (back issues avail.)
—SWETS.
Description: Methods and plans for using computers and communications to build chains of goods and material flow.

MANAGEMENT UND COMPUTER. see *BUSINESS AND ECONOMICS — Management*

330   US
MARKETSCAN INTERNATIONAL. 4/yr. $395 in N. America; elsewhere $450 (effective 1996). Miller Freeman, Inc. (Subsidiary of: United News & Media), 600 Harrison St., San Francisco, CA 94107. TEL 415-905-2200. FAX 415-905-2233. (Subscr. to: Box 7703, San Francisco, CA 94120-7703. TEL 415-905-2308. FAX 415-905-2562)

330   US
MICROCOMPUTER INVESTOR. 1977. 2/yr. MicroComputer Investors Association, 902 Anderson Dr., Fredericksburg, VA 22405. TEL 703-371-5474. Ed. Jack M. Williams. bk.rev. (looseleaf format; back issues avail.) **Document type:** trade publication, newsletter.

BUSINESS AND ECONOMICS — COMPUTER APPLICATIONS 1203

MICROVIEW; journal for micro users in business. see COMPUTERS — Microcomputers

MIND YOUR OWN BUSINESS. see BUSINESS AND ECONOMICS — Office Equipment And Services

001.642 US
MOODY'S COMPANY DATA. Short title: Moody's C D. m. $6,000. Moody's Investors Service (Subsidiary of: Dun & Bradstreet Corporation), 99 Church St., New York, NY 10007-0300. TEL 212-553-0300. FAX 212-553-4700. (also avail. in microform from MIS)
● Available only on CD-ROM.
Incorporates: Moody's 5000 Plus & Moody's O T C Plus.
Description: Allows access to in-depth information on more than 10,000 public companies listed in NYSE, AMEX, NASDAQ-NMS, NASDAQ, OTC and Regional exchanges.

330 658 UK
▼**MULTIMEDIA NETWORKS NEWSFILE.** 1995. fortn. (Communications and Information Technology Research Ltd.) C I T Publications, 3 Colleton Cresc., Exeter, Devon EX2 4DG, England. TEL 44-1392-493444. FAX 44-1392-493626. E-mail: talk2us@citpubs.zynet.co.uk; URL: http://www.telecoms-data.com. Ed. Simon Sherrington. charts. **Document type:** bulletin, newsletter.
Description: Focuses on networked multimedia services. Includes company profiles, studies of the interactive services, interviews with industry pioneers, and analysis.

629.8 GW ISSN 0936-5052
OFFICE BANKING. 4/yr. DM.60. F B O - Fachverlag fuer Buero- und Organisationstechnik GmbH, Hermannstr. 2, 76530 Baden-Baden, Germany. TEL 07221-271066. FAX 07221-33228. **Document type:** bulletin.

629.8 651.8 GW ISSN 0343-2319
HF5547.A2 CODEN: BUERDN
OFFICE MANAGEMENT; information, organization, communication. 1971. 10/yr. DM.252 (foreign DM.263) (effective 1996). F B O - Fachverlag fuer Buero- und Organisationstechnik GmbH, Taunusstr. 54, 65183 Wiesbaden, Germany. TEL 49-611-534-0. FAX 49-611-534430. Ed. Heinz Scharfenberg. adv.; bk.rev.; abstr.; charts; illus.; index. circ. 12,000. (back issues avail.; reprint service avail. from SCH,UMI) **Indexed:** Account.& Data Proc.Abstr., INSPEC, PROMT. **Document type:** trade publication.
—BLDSC (6237.447000); AskIEEE; KR SourceOne; SWETS; UMI.
Formerly: Buerotechnik Automation und Organisation; Which was formed by the merger of: B T A - Buerotechnik und Automation (ISSN 0005-3368); B T O - Buerotechnik und Organisation (ISSN 0007-6325)

330 UK ISSN 1352-0490
CODEN: OBINE8
▼**ONLINE - C D - R O M BUSINESS INFORMATION.** 1985. m. (11/yr., plus directory supplement). £235($435) (effective 1997). Headland Business Information, Customer Services Department, Maypole House, Maypole Rd., E. Grinstead, W. Sussex RH19 1HU, England. TEL 44-1342-330100. FAX 44-1342-330191. (Subscr. to : Worldwide Subscription Services, Unit 4, Gibbs Reed Farm, Ticehurst, E. Sussex TN5 74E, England) Ed. Pamela Foster. adv.; bk.rev.; software rev.; cum.index. circ. 500. (back issues avail.) **Indexed:** INSPEC (1993-). **Document type:** newsletter.
—BLDSC (6260.761480); AskIEEE; KR SourceOne.
Formerly (until 1994): Online Business Information (ISSN 0267-9515)
Description: Evaluates electronic databases for business.

330 US ISSN 1085-5068
▼**ONLINE TACTICS.** 1995. m. $345. Cowles - SIMBA Information (Subsidiary of: Cowles Business Media), 11 Riverbend Dr. S., Box 4949, Stamford, CT 06907-0949. TEL 203-358-9900; 800-307-2529. FAX 203-358-5811. E-mail: info@simbanet.com; URL: http://www.simbanet.com.
Description: Explores online activities of leading media industries, including magazine, book and newspaper publishers, advertisers and their agencies, and cable and radio broadcasters.

ORGANIZACJA I KIEROWANIE/ORGANIZATION AND MANAGEMENT. see BUSINESS AND ECONOMICS — Management

330 US
HD30.2
ORGANIZATIONAL COMPUTING AND ELECTRONIC COMMERCE. 1991. q. $50 to individuals; institutions $150 (effective 1997). (Association for Information Systems) Ablex Publishing Corporation, Box 5297, Greenwich, CT 06831-0504. TEL 203-661-7602. FAX 203-661-0792. E-mail: abw@uts.cc.utexas.edu. Ed. Andrew B. Whinston. adv.; abstr.; bibl. **Indexed:** INSPEC (1991-). **Document type:** academic/scholarly publication.
—AskIEEE; KR SourceOne; SWETS; UnCover.
Formerly: Journal of Organizational Computing (ISSN 1054-1721)
Description: Publishes original research articles concerned with the impact of computer and communication technology on organizational design, operations, and performance.

330 IE
P C LIVE. m. ComputerScope, Ltd., Prospect House, 1 Prospect Rd., Glasnevin, Ireland. TEL 353-1-8303455. FAX 353-1-8300888. E-mail: info@scope.ie. Ed. John Collins; Pub. Frank Quinn. adv. contact: Paul Byrne. circ. 13,000. **Document type:** consumer publication.
Description: Consumer and small business computer magazine.

P C MANAGEMENT; corporate strategy, connectivity and analysis. see COMPUTERS — Personal Computers

330 001.642 US
P M S TODAY.* 1977. 12/yr. free to qualified personnel. Policy Management Systems Corp., Box 10, Columbia, SC 29202. TEL 803-748-2000. Ed. John Hutto. circ. 6,000.

PERSONNEL SOFTWARE CENSUS. see BUSINESS AND ECONOMICS — Personnel Management

PROCESS EQUIPMENT NEWS; new products for busy managers. see ENGINEERING

QUICK SOLUTIONS. see BUSINESS AND ECONOMICS — Small Business

RAGAN'S INTERACTIVE PUBLIC RELATIONS. see ADVERTISING AND PUBLIC RELATIONS

REPERTOIRE DES BANQUES DE DONNEES TELETEL POUR L'ENTREPRISE. see COMMUNICATIONS — Computer Applications

332.1 658 FR ISSN 0982-3085
HF5415.125
REPERTOIRE INTERNATIONAL DES BANQUES DE DONNEES POUR LE MARKETING ET LES ETUDES. 1987. irreg., no.2, 1994. 620 F. (effective 1997). Editions F L A Consultants, 27 rue de la Vistule, 75013 Paris, France. TEL 33-1-45827575. FAX 33-1-45824604. E-mail: flabases@iway.fr; URL: http://www.fla-consultants.fr. Eds. Anne-Sophie Kandel, Francois Libmann. adv. contact: Beatrice Riou. **Document type:** directory.
Description: Lists databases useful for marketing and studies.

650.0285 004 US ISSN 1060-3808
RETAIL INFO SYSTEMS NEWS; strategic solutions for growth. Variant title: R I S News. 1988. 10/yr. $50 to non-qualified readers. Edgell Communications, Inc., Ten W. Hanover Ave., Ste. 107, Randolph, NJ 07869. TEL 973-895-3300. FAX 973-895-7711. Ed. Mark Frantz; Pub. Doug Edgell. R&P contact: Mark Frantz. adv.: page $5200; adv. contact: Doug Edgell. circ. 18,500. (tabloid format) **Document type:** trade publication.
Formerly: R I S (ISSN 1044-6796)
Description: Examines computer applications in retail for corporate operations and financial functions.

658.8 330
RETAIL INFO SYSTEMS NEWS DIRECTORY. 1989. a. Edgell Enterprises, Inc., Ten W. Hanover Ave., Ste. 107, Randolph, NJ 07869. TEL 201-895-3300. FAX 201-895-7711. Ed. Georgia Colicchio; Pub. Douglas C. Edgell. **Document type:** directory, trade publication.
Description: Provides systems solutions for corporate management, operations and MIS management functions at retail.

REVIEW OF ACCOUNTING INFORMATION SYSTEMS. see BUSINESS AND ECONOMICS — Accounting

003 658.4 IT ISSN 0390-8127
RICERCA OPERATIVA. (Text in Italian; summaries in English, Italian) 1970. q. L.95000 (foreign L.130000) (effective 1993). (Associazione Italiana de Ricerca Operativa - Italian Association of Operations Research) Franco Angeli Editore, Viale Monza 106, 20127 Milan, Italy. TEL 02-28-27-651. Ed. Bruno Martinoli. adv.: B&W page L.750000. bk.rev. circ. 800.

RUTGERS COMPUTER & TECHNOLOGY LAW JOURNAL. see LAW — Computer Applications

S C I M A. (Society of Management Science and Applied Cybernetics) see COMPUTERS — Cybernetics

SAMSOM PERSONAL COMPUTER (EDITION FRANCAISE). see COMPUTERS — Personal Computers

SAMSOM PERSONAL COMPUTER (VLAAMSE EDITIE). see COMPUTERS — Personal Computers

658 JA ISSN 0916-8192
SENRYAKU KONPYUTA/CREATIVE MANAGEMENT BY I T SENRYAKU COMPUTER. (Text in Japanese) 1962. m. 860 Yen per no. Industrial Daily News Ltd. - Nikkan Kogyo Shinbunsha, 1-8-10 Kudan Kita, Chiyoda-ku, Tokyo 102, Japan. circ. 30,000. **Indexed:** JCT, JTA.
Formerly (until 1991): Administrative Management (Jimu Kanri) (ISSN 0386-9962)

SIMULATION & GAMING; an international journal of theory, design and research. see COMPUTERS — Computer Simulation

330 US
▼**THE SMALL BUSINESS ADVISOR: SOFTWARE NEWS.** 1996. 8/yr. Software News Publishing, 110 N. Bell, Ste. 300, Shawnee, OK 74801. TEL 405-275-3100; 800-456-0864. FAX 405-275-3101. E-mail: tawn@ezin.net. Ed. T. Allen Rose; Pub. T. Allen Rose. R&P contact: T. Allen Rose. **Document type:** trade publication.

330 MX ISSN 0188-8048
SOLUCIONES AVANZADAS; tecnologias de informacion y estrategias de negocios. 1993. m. Mex.$150($100) (effective 1995-96). Xview, S.A. de C.V., Tuxpan 2, Desp. 603, Col. Roma Sur, 06760 Mexico DF, Mexico. TEL 574-5316. FAX 574-5318. E-mail: mvs@solucion.internet.com.mx. (In U.S.: 9297 Siempreviva Rd., Ste. 76-475, San Diego, CA 92173-3628) Ed. Carlos Vizcaino. adv. contact: Oscar Guerrero B. bk.rev. circ. 5,000. **Document type:** trade publication.
● Also available online.
Refereed Serial

SOUTHERN BUSINESS & ECONOMIC JOURNAL. see BUSINESS AND ECONOMICS

330 US
STANDARD FOR AUDITING COMPUTER APPLICATIONS. base vol. (plus s-a. updates). $172. Auerbach Publishers (Subsidiary of: Warren, Gorham & Lamont), One Penn Plaza, New York, NY 10119. TEL 212-971-5000. FAX 212-971-5024. (Subscr. to: 31 St. James Ave., Boston, MA 02116-4112. TEL 800-950-1218. FAX 617-423-1914) Ed. William E. Perry. **Document type:** trade publication.
Description: Offers information systems auditors a structured, cost-effective methodology for increasing the efficiency and productivity of information systems audits.

330 640.73 US
SURVIVE & WIN.* 1988. m. $50. Consumertronics, Box 23097, Albuquerque, NM 87192-1097. TEL 505-434-0234. Ed. John Williams. adv.; bk.rev. circ. 21,000. (back issues avail.)
Description: Survival information and tips using hi-tech tactics and strategies.

651.3 GW ISSN 0341-2024
T B REPORT. (Technische Buero) Archivierung und Datensicherung im Technischen Buero. 1970. q. DM.52 (foreign DM.84) (effective 1997). B I T Verlag Weinbrenner GmbH & Co. KG, Fasanenweg 18, 70771 Leinfelden-Echterdingen, Germany. TEL 49-711-7591-0. FAX 49-711-7591368. **Document type:** trade publication.

BUSINESS AND ECONOMICS — COOPERATIVES

658   NE   ISSN 0378-3766
T I M S STUDIES IN THE MANAGEMENT SCIENCES. (Text in English) 1975. irreg., vol.22, 1986. price varies. Elsevier Science B.V., Books Division, P.O. Box 211, 1000 AE Amsterdam, Netherlands. TEL 31-20-4853911. FAX 31-20-4853705. TELEX 18582 ESPA NL. E-mail: nlinfo-f@elsevier.nl; usinfo-f@elsevier.com; forinfo-kyf04035@niftyserve.or.jp; URL: http://www.elsevier.nl/. (Subscr. in the Americas to: Elsevier Science, Regional Sales Office, Box 945, New York, NY 10159-0945. TEL 212-633-3730. FAX 212-633-3680; Subscr. in Australasia and the Far East to: Elsevier Science (Singapore) Pte Ltd, No.1 Temasek Ave., No.17-01 Millenia Tower, Singapore 039192, Singapore. TEL 65-434-3727. FAX 65-337-2230; Subscr. in Japan to: Elsevier Science Japan, 9-15 Higashi-Azabu 1-chome, Minato-ku, Tokyo 106, Japan. TEL 81-3-5561-5033. FAX 81-3-5561-5047) Ed. R.E. Machol. bibl.; charts. (also avail. in microform from UMI) **Indexed:** Int.Abstr.Oper.Res., Zent.Math. **Document type:** monographic series.
—CCC.
Refereed Serial

330 380.3   US   ISSN 1054-979X
TECHSCAN NEWSLETTER; the manager's guide to technology. 1990. m. $87.50 (foreign $111.50). Richmond Research, Inc., Box 537, Village Sta., New York, NY 10014-0537. TEL 212-741-0045. FAX 212-243-7356. E-mail: techscan@pipeline.com. Ed. Louis Giacalone. R&P contact: Louis Giacalone. bk.rev.; bibl.; charts; illus.; stat.; circ. 2,500 (paid). (back issues avail.) **Document type:** newsletter.
Formerly: Intelligent Systems.
Description: Informs business professionals about technological developments and applications, design techniques, and products used to solve business problems.

TEL-COM - BRIEF; Telekommunikation, Datenverarbeitung und Organisation. see *BUSINESS AND ECONOMICS — Office Equipment And Services*

THEORY AND DECISION LIBRARY. SERIES C: GAME THEORY, MATHEMATICAL PROGRAMMING AND OPERATIONS RESEARCH. see *MATHEMATICS — Computer Applications*

330   US   ISSN 1046-8188
HF5548.2   CODEN: ATISET
TRANSACTIONS ON INFORMATION SYSTEMS. Short title: T O I S. 1983. q. $110 to non-members. Association for Computing Machinery, 1515 Broadway, 17th Fl., New York, NY 10036-5701. TEL 212-869-7440. FAX 212-944-1318. TELEX 421686. Ed. Robert B. Allen. circ. 5,800. **Indexed:** Abstr.Hum.Comp.Inter., Arts & Hum.Cit.Ind., ASCA, CAD CAM Abstr., Compumath, Comput Dtbs., Comput.Lit.Ind., Curr.Cont., INSPEC (1989-), J.of Ferroc., LISA, SSCI, Tel.Abstr.
—BLDSC (0578.668000); AskIEEE; CASDDS; CISTI; Ei; Genuine Article; KR SourceOne; SWETS; UMI; UnCover. **CCC**.
Formerly (until 1988): Transactions on Office Information Systems (ISSN 0734-2047).
Description: Serves corporate and academic researchers who have broad interests in information systems.

330   NE   ISSN 0169-4766
TRANSNATIONAL CORPORATIONS AND TRANSBORDER DATA FLOWS. 1983. irreg., vol.5, 1984. price varies. (United Nations Centre on Transnational Corporations) Elsevier Science B.V., Books Division, P.O. Box 211, 1000 AE Amsterdam, Netherlands. TEL 31-20-4853911. FAX 31-20-4853705. TELEX 18582 ESPA NL. E-mail: nlinfo-f@elsevier.nl; usinfo-f@elsevier.com; forinfo-kyf04035@niftyserve.or.jp; URL: http://www.elsevier.nl/. (Subscr. in the Americas to: Elsevier Science, Regional Sales Office, Box 945, New York, NY 10159-0945. TEL 212-633-3730. FAX 212-633-3680; Subscr. in Australasia and the Far East to: Elsevier Science (Singapore) Pte Ltd, No.1 Temasek Ave., No.17-01 Millenia Tower, Singapore 039192, Singapore. TEL 65-434-3727. FAX 65-337-2230; Subscr. in Japan to: Elsevier Science Japan, 9-15 Higashi-Azabu 1-chome, Minato-ku, Tokyo 106, Japan. TEL 81-3-5561-5033. FAX 81-3-5561-5047)
Document type: monographic series.
Refereed Serial

UNIGRAM.X; the weekly information newsletter for the UNIX community worldwide. see *COMPUTERS — Software*

UNISYS WORLD; an independent news monthly for Unisys system users. see *COMPUTERS — Microcomputers*

004.6   US
WEB - ONLINE SERVICES (YEAR): CONSUMER MARKET ANALYSIS & FORECAST. a. $1295 (effective 1997). Cowles - SIMBA Information (Subsidiary of: Cowles Business Media), 11 River Bend Dr., S., Box 4949, Stamford, CT 06907-0949. TEL 203-358-9900; 800-307-2529. FAX 203-358-5811. E-mail: info@simbanet.com; URL: http://www.simbanet.com.

330   US
▼**WEB PUBLISHING (YEAR): CONSUMER MARKET STRATEGIES & STATISTICS.** 1997. a. $1295. Cowles - SIMBA Information (Subsidiary of: Cowles Business Media), 11 Riverbend Dr. S., Box 4949, Stamford, CT 06907-0949. TEL 203-358-9900; 800-307-2529. FAX 203-358-5811. E-mail: info@simbanet.com; URL: http://www.simbanet.com. Ed. Karen Burka.
—CCC.
Supersedes in part (in 1997): Online Services: Review, Trends and Forecast (ISSN 1057-3666)
Description: Provides tactical data and exclusive statistics and forecasts on the rapidly changing web and online consumer market.

005   US   ISSN 1053-9638
WORDPERFECT REPORT. 1987. q. free to registered users of WordPerfect products. WordPerfect Corporation, 1555 N. Technology Way, Orem, UT 84057. TEL 801-225-5000. FAX 801-222-5077. circ. 2,000,000. **Document type:** newsletter.
—Linda Hall.
Formerly (until 1990): WPCorp Report.
Description: Covers WordPerfect applications. Includes conference, seminar, and training program schedules.

BUSINESS AND ECONOMICS — Cooperatives

334   HU   ISSN 1217-7040
A F E S Z MAGAZIN. 1922. w. Altalanos Fogyasztasi es Ertekesito Szovetkezetek - National Council of Consumers' Cooperative Societies, Szabadsag ter 14, 1054 Budapest, Hungary. TEL 36-1-131-3132. TELEX 224862. Ed. Attila Kovacs. circ. 85,000. **Document type:** newspaper.
Former titles (until 1993): Uj Szovetkezet (ISSN 0865-6940); (until 1989): Szovetkezet (ISSN 0133-1612); (until 1948): Magyar Szovetkezes (ISSN 0324-2641); (until 1922): Orszagos Kozponti Hitelszovetkezeti Ertesito (ISSN 0324-3990)

A G P MITTEILUNGEN; Zeitschrift fuer Partnerschaft in der Wirtschaft. (Arbeitsgemeinschaft zur Foerderung der Partnerschaft in der Wirtschaft e.V.) see *BUSINESS AND ECONOMICS — Labor And Industrial Relations*

334   NE
AALSMEER NIEUWS. fortn. fl.35 (free to qualified personnel). Bloemenveiling Aalsmeer, Legmeerdijk 313, 1431 GB Aalsmeer, Netherlands. TEL 31-297-393939. FAX 31-297-390021. circ. 12,500. **Document type:** newspaper.
Formerly: V B A Bode (Verenigde Bloemveilingen Aalsmeer).

630   GR   ISSN 1105-1213
AGROTICOS SYNERGATISMOS. 1945. m. Dr.1200($20) Panhellenic Confederation of Unions of Agricultural Cooperatives, 16 Kifissias Ave., 115 26 Athens, Greece. TEL 30-1-7704079. FAX 30-1-7779313. TELEX 21-83-43 PASE GR. Ed. Nikolaos G. Gotsinas. adv.; bk.rev. circ. 8,000.
Former titles (until 1982): Agroticos Cosmos K Synergatismos; (until 1979): Voice of the Cooperatives.

334   GW
AKTUELLES FUER DEN LANDWIRT. m. Genossenschaftsverband Bayern e.V., Tuerkenstr. 16, 80333 Munich, Germany. TEL 089-21342925. FAX 089-21342928. **Document type:** trade publication.

ALTERNATIVE TRADING NEWS. see *BUSINESS AND ECONOMICS — International Development And Assistance*

334   CK
AMERICA COOPERATIVA. 1964. 3/yr. $20. Organization of the Cooperatives of America - Organizacion de las Cooperativas de America, Carrera 11 No. 86-32 Ofc. 101, 241263 Bogota, D.E., Colombia. TEL 2181295. FAX 057-1-610-19-12. TELEX 45103 FICOP-CO. OCA. Dir. Carlos Julio Pineda Suarez. adv.: B&W page Col.$70000, color page Col.$150000; trim 210 x 280. illus.; circ. 5,000 (controlled). (looseleaf format)
Formerly: Cooperative America (ISSN 0002-7057)

334   US   ISSN 0065-793X
HD3443
AMERICAN COOPERATION YEARBOOK. 1925. a. $35 hardcover; softcover $30. National Council of Farmer Cooperatives, 50 F St., N.W., Ste. 900, Washington, DC 20001. TEL 202-626-8700. FAX 202-626-8722. Ed. Lisa Keller. index. circ. 1,800. **Document type:** trade publication.
—BLDSC (0812.623000).
Description: Presents a current and comprehensive picture of what American farmer cooperatives are doing today and planning for tomorrow.

334   IS
AMUDIM; bulletin of the religious kibbutzim. (Text in Hebrew) m. IS.68($24.50) Religious Kibbutz Movement - Ha'Kibbutz Hadati, 7 Dubnov St., Tel Aviv 64732, Israel. TEL 972-3-6957231. FAX 972-3-6957039. Ed. Chana Amit. bk.rev. circ. 4,000. **Document type:** bulletin.

334   DK   ISSN 0003-2913
ANDELSBLADET. 1900. fortn. DKK 300. Federation of Danish Co-operatives, FDC, Vesterbrogade 4A 2, DK-1620 Copenhagen V, Denmark. TEL 45-33-12-14-19. FAX 45-33-11-45-12. E-mail: fedecoop@inet.uni-c.dk. Ed. Torsten Buhl; Pub. H. Hasle Nielsen. adv.; bk.rev.; index. circ. 12,000. **Indexed:** Dairy Sci.Abstr. **Document type:** corporate report, newsletter.

334   UK   ISSN 1370-4788
ANNALS OF PUBLIC AND COOPERATIVE ECONOMICS. (Text in English, French, German) 1908. q. £84($141) (foreign £89) (effective 1997). (International Centre of Research and Information on Public and Cooperative Economy, Universite de Liege au Sart-Tilman) Blackwell Publishers Ltd., 108 Cowley Rd., Oxford OX4 1JF, England. TEL 44-1865-791100. FAX 44-1865-791347. E-mail: jnlinfo@blackwellpublishers.co.uk; URL: http://www.blackwellpublishers.co.uk. Ed. B. Thiry. bk.rev.; bibl. (back issues avail.; reprint service avail. from SWZ) **Indexed:** C.R.E.J., ELLIS, IBR, Int.Lab.Doc., J.of Econ.Lit., Mid.East: Abstr.& Ind., P.A.I.S.For.Lang.Ind., P.A.I.S., Rural Recreat.Tour.Abstr., SSCI, World Agri.Econ.& Rural Sociol.Abstr. **Document type:** academic/scholarly publication.
—SWETS; UnCover. **CCC**.
Former titles (until 1989): Annals of Public and Co-operative Economy (ISSN 0770-8548); Annales de l'Economie Publique, Sociale et Cooperative (ISSN 0379-3699); (until 1964): Annales de l'Economie Collective (ISSN 0003-407X)

ANNOTATED BIBLIOGRAPHY OF LITERATURE ON COOPERATIVE MOVEMENTS IN SOUTH-EAST ASIA. see *BIBLIOGRAPHIES*

ANNUAIRE GENERAL DES COOPERATIVES ET DE LEURS FOURNISSEURS: FRANCE, OUTRE-MER ET MARCHE EUROPEEN. see *BUSINESS AND ECONOMICS — Domestic Commerce*

BANQUES DE DONNEES UTILES AUX COLLECTIVITES LOCALES ET TERRITORIALES. see *PUBLIC ADMINISTRATION — Computer Applications*

334   GW
BAYERISCHES RAIFFEISENBLATT. m. Genossenschaftsverband Bayern e.V., Tuerkenstr. 22-24, 80333 Munich, Germany.

334   SP   ISSN 0006-6273
BOLETIN DE FORMACION COOPERATIVA.* no. 67, 1972 bi-m. Asociacion de Estudios Cooperativos, Heroes del 10 de Agosto 5, 4 Andar, Madrid-1, Spain. Dir. Rafael Monge Simon. bk.rev.; charts; illus.

BUSINESS AND ECONOMICS — COOPERATIVES

334   BS
BOTSWANA. MINISTRY OF AGRICULTURE. DIVISION OF CO-OPERATIVE DEVELOPMENT. ANNUAL REPORT (YEAR). (Includes: Cooperative Statistic of Cooperative Societies in the last three years 1986-1988) a. Ministry of Agriculture, Division of Co-Operative Development, Private Bag 033, Gaborone, Botswana. illus.; stat.

C U E S - F Y I. (Credit Union Executives Society) see BUSINESS AND ECONOMICS — Banking And Finance

C U I S. (Credit Union Information Service) see BUSINESS AND ECONOMICS — Banking And Finance

334   FR
CAISSE FRANCAISE DE DEVELOPPEMENT. RAPPORT ANNUEL. (Text in English and French) 1947. a. free. Caisse Francaise de Developpement, Cite du Retiro, 35-37 rue Boissy d'Anglas, 75379 Paris Cedex 08, France. FAX 40-06-40-85. TELEX 212 632 F. adv. contact: Denis Castaing. illus. circ. 8,000.
   Former titles: Caisse Centrale de Cooperation Economique. Rapport Annuel; Caisse Centrale de Cooperation Economique. Rapport d'Activite (ISSN 0575-1632)

334   US   ISSN 0743-605X
JK1
CATO POLICY REPORT. 1977. 6/yr. membership only. Cato Institute, 1000 Massachusetts Ave, N.W., Washington, DC 20001-5403. TEL 202-842-0200. FAX 202-842-3490. Ed. David Boaz. R&P contact: Aaron Lukas. bk.rev. circ. 12,000. Indexed: P.A.I.S. —SWETS.
   Formerly: Policy Report (ISSN 0190-325X)
   Description: Contains original articles on public policy issues.

CHECKLISTS AND ILLUSTRATIVE FINANCIAL STATEMENTS FOR CREDIT UNIONS. see BUSINESS AND ECONOMICS — Accounting

334 647.9   FR   ISSN 1242-2126
COLLECTIVITES HOTELLERIE ET RESTAURATION. 1953. 9/yr. 340 F. (foreign 510 F.) (effective 1993). Editions Max Brezol, 9 rue Labie, 75838 Paris Cedex 17, France. TEL 45-74-21-62. FAX 45-74-01-03. Ed. Georges Golan. adv.
   Formerly (until 1992): Collectivites - Express (ISSN 0010-0811)
   Description: Details administration of collective institutions.

334   IT   ISSN 1120-639X
COLLETTIVITA - CONVIVENZE. 1962. 19/yr. L.115000 (Europe L.160000) (effective 1997). Via A. Pestalozza 31, 20131 Milan, Italy. TEL 39-2-70630022. FAX 39-2-26680516. Ed. Luigi Porro. adv. circ. 19,000. Document type: trade publication.
   Description: For stewards, superintendents, managers of institutes, colleges, boarding schools, national health offices, hospitals, and nursing homes.

COMMUNITIES; journal of cooperative living. see SOCIAL SCIENCES: COMPREHENSIVE WORKS

COMMUNITY ASSOCIATION LAW REPORTER. see HOUSING AND URBAN PLANNING

334 332.6 352.7   US   ISSN 1045-4322
COMMUNITY ECONOMICS. 1983. 3/yr. $25 to institutions (effective Nov.1991). Institute for Community Economics, 57 School St., Springfield, MA 01105-1331. TEL 413-746-8660. FAX 413-746-8862. Ed. Kirby White. bk.rev. circ. 6,500.
   Description: Covers community based developments, land reform, community land trusts, preserving permanently affordable housing and community investing.

334   IT   ISSN 0391-6278
COOP ITALIA. 1966. bi-m. Viale Famagosta 75, 20142 Milan, Italy. Ed. Bruno Cremascoli. adv. circ. 5,000.

334   JA
CO-OP JAPAN INFORMATION. q. free. Japanese Consumers Cooperative Union - Nihon Seikatsu Kyodokumiai Rengokai, Seikyo Kaikan, 4-1-13 Sendagaya, Shibuya-ku, Tokyo, Japan. TEL 81-3-3497-9103. FAX 81-3-3497-0722. E-mail: jccu-int@mxb.meshnet.or.jp. Ed. Boku Nakano. circ. 400. **Document type:** newsletter.
   Description: Provides information about current situation of consumer co-ops in Japan.

334   NR   ISSN 0794-7763
COOP NEWS. 1985. m. £N36 (effective 1991). Co-operative Federation of Nigeria, P.M.B. 5533, Ibadan, Oyo State, Nigeria. TEL 234-22-711276. TELEX 31621 COEDPRO NG. Ed. 'Sola Osola. adv.; bk.rev. circ. 4,000.

334   SZ
COOP - ZEITUNG. 1902. w. 39 SFr. Coop Schweiz, Thiersteineralle 12, Postfach 2550, CH-4002 Basel, Switzerland. TEL 41-61-3367118. FAX 41-61-3367072. Ed. Urs Knapp. adv. contact: Karl Voegeli. circ. 1,031,921. **Document type:** newspaper.

334   AG   ISSN 0010-8316
COOPERACION LIBRE. 1913. m.(except Jan. & Feb.). free. Cooperativa el Hogar Obrero, Moreno 1729, Buenos Aires, Argentina. Ed. Arturo Vainstok. adv.; bk.rev.; film rev.; play rev.; illus. circ. 200,000.

334   NE
COOPERATIE. 1935. q. fl.35. Nationale Cooperatieve Raad voor Land- en Tuinbouw - National Co-operative Council for Agriculture and Horticulture, Postbus 29774, 2502 LT The Hague, Netherlands. TEL 31-70-3382780. FAX 31-70-3546643. E-mail: ncr@xs4all.nl. Ed. G. van Dyk. bk.rev.; abstr.; bibl.; stat.; index. circ. 3,200. Indexed: Key to Econ.Sci.
   Former titles (until 1996): Cooperatie Magazine (ISSN 0928-3048); (until 1991): Cooperatie (ISSN 0009-9783)

334   SZ
COOPERATION. w. Coop Schweiz, Thiersteinerallee 12, Postfach 2550, CH-4002 Basel, Switzerland. TEL 41-61-3367117. FAX 41-61-3367072. Ed. L. Rebeaud. adv. contact: Karl Voegeli. circ. 281,821. **Document type:** newspaper.

334   TU   ISSN 1300-1477
COOPERATION IN TURKIYE. (Text in English, German) 1984. 2/yr. $12. Turk Kooperatifcilik Kurumu - Turkish Cooperative Association, Mithatpasa Caddesi, 38-A, 06420 Kizilay - Ankara, Turkey. TEL 90-312-4316125. FAX 90-312-4340646. Ed. Celal Er. adv.; charts; illus.; stat.
   Formerly (until 1991): Cooperation in Turkey.
   Description: Covers activities of economic cooperative organizations in Turkey, including legislative issues and historical discussions.

COOPERATIVE ACCOUNTANT. see BUSINESS AND ECONOMICS — Accounting

334   US   ISSN 0893-3391
COOPERATIVE BUSINESS JOURNAL. 1987. 10/yr. $15 (foreign $25) (effective 1997). National Cooperative Business Association, Communications Department, 1401 New York Ave., N.W., Ste. 1100, Washington, DC 20005. TEL 202-638-6222. FAX 202-638-1374. E-mail: ncba@ncba.org; URL: http://www.cooperative.org. Ed. Leta M. Mach; Pub. Leta Mach. R&P contact: Leta Mach. adv. contact: Leta Mach. bk.rev. circ. 6,000. (tabloid format; back issues avail.) **Document type:** newspaper.
   Description: Deals with cooperative businesses of all types.

334   UK   ISSN 0009-9821
HD2951
CO-OPERATIVE NEWS; official organ of the Co-operative Movement. 1871. w. (51/yr.) £43 (rest of Europe £65; elsewhere £86) (effective 1997). Co-Operative Press Ltd., Chester Rd., Manchester M16 9HP, England. TEL 44-161-872-2991. FAX 44-161-872-6366. Ed. Geoffrey Whiteley. R&P contact: Geoffrey Whiteley. adv. contact: Keith Sidebotham. bk.rev.; illus. **Document type:** newspaper.
   Incorporates: Co-Operative News (Scottish Edition); Which was formerly: Scottish Cooperator (ISSN 0048-976X)
   Description: Organ of Britain's coop movement.

COOPERATIVE NEWS INTERNATIONAL. see BUSINESS AND ECONOMICS — International Development And Assistance

334   US   ISSN 0896-9426
COOPERATIVE PARTNERS. 1925. 8/yr. $5. Cenex - Land O'Lakes, Box 64089, St. Paul, MN 55164-0089. TEL 612-451-5035. FAX 612-451-4310. Ed. Linda Tank. adv.; charts; illus. circ. 230,000. (also avail. in microfilm)
   Formerly (until 1987): Cooperative Builder (ISSN 0010-8413)
   Description: Communicates innovative thinking that contributes to Land O'Lakes and Cenex customers' profitability and the quality of rural life.

334   UK
CO-OPERATIVE STATISTICS. 1879. a. £79. Co-operative Union Ltd., Holyoake House, Hanover St., Manchester M60 0AS, England. TEL 44-161-832-4300. FAX 44-161-831-7684. E-mail: info@co-opu.demon.co.uk; URL: http://www.co-op.co.uk/UKCM/Union/index.html. Ed. I.V. Williamson. circ. 400.
   Description: Statistics of all British co-operative societies showing membership, sources and uses of funds, and other information.

334   II
COOPERATIVE SUGAR PRESS NEWS. w. National Federation of Co-operative Sugar Factories, 82 Nehru Pl., New Delhi 110 019, India. TEL 011-6412868. TELEX 314561.

334   II   ISSN 0069-9837
COOPERATIVE TRADE DIRECTORY FOR SOUTHEAST ASIA. (Text in English) 1964. irreg., 3rd ed., 1970. supplement. Rs.20($3) per set. International Cooperative Alliance, Regional Office and Education Centre for South-East Asia, Box 3312, 43 Friends Colony, New Delhi 110014, India. Ed. M.V. Madane. circ. 300. **Document type:** directory.

334   UK
CO-OPERATIVE UNION. ANNUAL REPORT. 1869. a. £5. Co-operative Union Ltd., Holyoake House, Hanover St., Manchester M60 0AS, England. TEL 44-0161-832-4300. FAX 44-0161-831-7684. E-mail: info@co-opu.demon.co.uk; URL: http://www.co-op.co.uk/UKCM/Union/index.html. Ed. I.V. Williamson. circ. 1,200. (back issues avail.) **Document type:** corporate report.
   Supersedes in part: Co-operative Union. Annual Report and Financial Statements.
   Description: Publishes the reports and transactions of committees and departments of the British Co-operative Union.

334   UK
CO-OPERATIVE UNION. FINANCIAL STATEMENTS. 1869. a. £5. Co-operative Union Ltd., Holyoake House, Hanover St., Manchester M60 0AS, England. FAX 0161-831-7684. E-mail: info@co-opu.demon.co.uk; URL: http://www.co-op.co.uk/UKCM/Union/index.html. Ed. I.V. Williamson. circ. 1,200. (back issues avail.) **Document type:** corporate report.
   Supersedes in part: Co-operative Union. Annual Report and Financial Statements.
   Description: Publishes the transactions of committees and departments of the British Co-operative Union.

334   CN   ISSN 0712-2748
HD3450.A3   CODEN: CDEVEU
COOPERATIVES ET DEVELOPPEMENT. (Text mainly in French; occasionally in English) 1968. s-a. Can.$28($36) (effective 1995). Centre Interuniversitaire de Recherche d'Information et d'Enseignement sur les Cooperatives, 5255 av. Decelles, Montreal, PQ H3T 1V6, Canada. TEL 514-340-6016. FAX 514-340-6995. Ed. Benoit Levesque. bk.rev.; bibl.; charts; stat. circ. 1,000. (back issues avail.) Indexed: Pt.de Rep. (1990-).
   Description: Studies the characteristics of cooperatives, their role as agent of socio-economic development, their economy, management and the main sectors of activity where they are involved.
   Refereed Serial

334   CH   ISSN 0009-9856
CO-OPERATIVES QUARTERLY.* (Text in Chinese and English) vol. 7, 1969. q. Cooperative Bank of Taiwan, 75-1 Kuan Chien Rd., Taipei, Taiwan, Republic of China. Ed.Bd. charts; stat.

BUSINESS AND ECONOMICS — COOPERATIVES

334 — II — ISSN 0010-8464
COOPERATOR. (Text in English) 1963. m. Rs.150($50) National Cooperative Union of India, 3-Siri Institutional Area, Panchshila Marg (Behind Hauz Khas), New Delhi 110016, India. Ed. M.L. Sharma. adv.; charts; illus. circ. 2,700.

334 — SZ
COOPERAZIONE. w. Coop Schweiz, Thiersteinerallee 12, Postfach 2550, CH-4002 Basel, Switzerland. TEL 41-61-3367149. FAX 41-61-3367072. Ed. Orazio Martinetti. adv. contact: Karl Voegeli. circ. 53,950. **Document type:** newspaper.

334 — IT — ISSN 0010-8510
COOPERAZIONE ITALIANA. 1887. m. L.70000. (Lega Nazionale delle Cooperative e Mutue) Editrice Cooperativa, Via G. Tomassetti 12, 00161 Rome, Italy. TEL 6-8844942. FAX 6-84439406. Ed. Maria Costanza Fanelli. adv.: B&W page L.2500000, color page L.4500000. bk.rev.; index; circ. 20,000 (controlled). (tabloid format)

CO-OPSERVATIONS. see HOUSING AND URBAN PLANNING

334 621.393 — US — ISSN 0747-0592
COUNTRY LIVING (COLUMBUS). (Published in 25 regional editions) 1958. m. $5. Ohio Rural Electric Cooperatives, Inc., 6677 Busch Blvd., Box 26036, Columbus, OH 43226-0036. TEL 614-846-5757. FAX 614-846-7108. Ed. Jeff Brehm. adv. circ. 241,000. (back issues avail.) **Document type:** consumer publication.
Description: For members of consumer-owned electric cooperatives. Publishes energy-related articles, columns, and rural life features.

CREDIT UNION EXECUTIVE; for active leaders and managers of credit unions. see BUSINESS AND ECONOMICS — Banking And Finance

CREDIT UNION MAGAZINE; for credit union elected officials, managers and employees. see BUSINESS AND ECONOMICS — Banking And Finance

CREDIT UNION REPORT. see BUSINESS AND ECONOMICS — Banking And Finance

CREDIT UNION REVIEW. see BUSINESS AND ECONOMICS — Banking And Finance

CREDIT UNION WAY. see BUSINESS AND ECONOMICS — Banking And Finance

334.2 — IT
CREDITO COOPERATIVO; rivista di cultura cooperativa. 1948. m. L.60000. (Federazione Nazionale delle Casse Rurali e Artigiane) Edizioni E.C.R.A., Via Massimo D'Azeglio 33, 00184 Rome, Italy. TEL 39-6-48295485. FAX 39-6-48903080. URL: http://www.bcc.it. Dir. Giuseppe Vannucci. adv.: B&W page L.2750000, color page L.4500000. bk.rev.; stat.; index. circ. 34,000.
Former titles: Credito e Cooperazione; Cooperazione di Credito (ISSN 0010-8480)
Description: Includes technical and general articles about the Italian system of BCC - credit cooperative banks.

334 — SP
CUADERNOS DE ESTUDIOS COOPERATIVOS. 1958. 4/yr. Instituto Sindical de Formacion Cooperativa, Paseo del Prado, 18, Madrid, Spain. bibl.

330.9 — UN — ISSN 0252-2195
CUADERNOS DE LA C E P A L. (Text in Spanish; occasionally in English) 1981. irreg., no.70, 1993. price varies. Comision Economica para America Latina y el Caribe, Casilla 179-D, Santiago, Chile. (Subscr. to: United Nations Publications, Sales Section, Rm. DC2-0853, New York, NY 10017; or Distribution and Sales Section, Palais des Nations, 1211 Geneva 10, Switzerland) (back issues avail.)

334 — GW
DIE DEUTSCHEN GENOSSENSCHAFTEN. 1965. biennial. DM.35. D G Bank - Deutsche Genossenschaftsbank, Am Platz der Republik, 60325 Frankfurt a.M., Germany. TEL 49-69-744701. FAX 49-69-74471685. URL: http://www.dgbank.de. illus.; stat. circ. 2,000. **Document type:** trade publication.
Formerly: Genossenschaften in der Bundesrepublik Deutschland.
Description: Reports of changes in the German cooperative system (i.e. banks, merchandise, cooperatives).

DIE DEUTSCHEN GENOSSENSCHAFTEN. STATISTIK. see BUSINESS AND ECONOMICS — Abstracting, Bibliographies, Statistics

334 — CK
DIRECTORIO NACIONAL DE ENTIDADES COOPERATIVOS. irreg. Departamento Administrativo Nacional de Estadistica, Banco Nacional de Datos, Centro Administrativo Nacional, Avda. El Dorado, Apdo. Aereo 80043, Bogota D.E., Colombia.

DIRECTORY OF INTENTIONAL COMMUNITIES. see BUSINESS AND ECONOMICS — Trade And Industrial Directories

DOCUMENTATION BULLETIN FOR SOUTH-EAST ASIA. see BIBLIOGRAPHIES

DUCA POST. see BUSINESS AND ECONOMICS — Banking And Finance

334 — FI
ELANTO. 9/yr. (Elanto Cooperative Society) Oy Kaupparengas AB, Hameentie 11, 00530 Helsinki 53, Finland. adv.

334 — GW
EMSCHERGENOSSENSCHAFT. JAHRESBERICHTE. 1906. a. Emschergenossenschaft, Kronprinzenstr. 24, 45128 Essen, Germany. TEL 0201-1042216. **Document type:** corporate report.

EVERYBODY'S MONEY; a guide to family finance and consumer action. see BUSINESS AND ECONOMICS — Banking And Finance

334 — JA
FACTS AND FIGURES. a. Japanese Consumers Cooperative Union - Nihon Seikatsu Kyodokumiai Rengokai, Seikyo Kaikan, 4-1-13 Sendagaya, Shibuya-ku, Tokyo 151, Japan. TEL 81-3-3497-9103. FAX 81-3-3470-2924. TELEX 2423380 NCOOP J. E-mail: jccu-int@mxb.meshnet.or.jp. Ed. Syakagori Katuyuki. **Document type:** corporate report.
Description: Provides statistics on consumer co-ops in Japan.

FARM CREDIT ADMINISTRATION. ANNUAL REPORT. see AGRICULTURE — Agricultural Economics

334 658.8 — SZ
FEDERATION OF MIGROS COOPERATIVES. DOCUMENTATION AND INFORMATION; report of the Board of Directors to the Assembly of Delegates. (Editions in English, French, German, Italian) 1941 French and German eds.; 1956 English eds.; 1982 Italian eds. a. free. Federation of Migros Cooperatives, Limmatstr. 152, Postfach 266, CH-8031 Zurich, Switzerland. TEL 41-1-2772111. FAX 41-1-2772525. URL: http://www.mgb.ch. adv.; bk.rev. circ. 6,000. (tabloid format) **Document type:** corporate report.
Formerly: Federation of Migros Cooperatives. Annual Report (ISSN 0071-4410)

FEDERATION OF SWEDISH CO-OPERATIVE BANKS. ANNUAL REPORT. see BUSINESS AND ECONOMICS — Banking And Finance

334.2 — US — ISSN 0094-0240
FIRST FRIDAY. 1973. m. $35. A S C U, Box 5488, Madison, WI 53705. Ed. Walter Polner. bk.rev.; charts; stat. circ. 1,450. (back issues avail.)

G E O: GRASSROOTS ECONOMIC ORGANIZING NEWSLETTER. see OCCUPATIONS AND CAREERS

334 — GW — ISSN 0933-9477
GENOSSENSCHAFTS-HANDBUCH. 1973. irreg. DM.168. Erich Schmidt Verlag GmbH & Co. (Berlin), Genthiner Str. 30G, 10785 Berlin, Germany. TEL 49-30-250085-0. FAX 49-30-25008521. (looseleaf format) **Document type:** bulletin.

334 — GW
GENOSSENSCHAFTSVERBAND HANNOVER. MITTEILUNGEN. q. Genossenschaftsverband Hannover e.V., Kaiserallee 9, 30175 Hannover, Germany. TEL 0511-81190. FAX 0511-8119348.
Formerly: Genossenschaftsverband Niedersachsen. Mitteilungen.

334 — GW — ISSN 0942-847X
GESUND UND SICHER. Key Title: G & S. Gesund und Sicher. m. Norddeutsche Metall-Berufsgenossenschaft, Hans-Bokler-Allee 26, 30173 Hannover, Germany. TEL 81180. FAX 8118200. TELEX 23357. bk.rev.
Formerly (until 1991): Nordwestliche (ISSN 0176-3652)

334 — AU
GEWERBLICHE GENOSSENSCHAFT. q. Oesterreichischer Genossenschaftsverband, Schottengasse 10, A-1010 Vienna, Austria. TELEX 114268.

334 — IS
HAIFA UNIVERSITY. INSTITUTE FOR STUDY AND RESEARCH OF THE KIBBUTZ AND THE COOPERATIVE IDEA. DISCUSSION PAPERS. (Text in English and Hebrew) irreg. Haifa University, Institute for Study and Research of the Kibbutz and the Cooperative Idea, Hacarmel, Haifa 31 999, Israel. FAX 4-342104. TELEX 46660-UVIH.

334 — IS
HAMESHEK HASHITUFI. 1916. bi-m. free. Hamashbir Hamerkazi, P.O. Box 130, Tel Aviv, Israel. TEL 03-389333. Ed. Pini Goldman. circ. 7,000.

334 — KE
HARAMBEE. q. Harambee Co-operative Savings and Credit Society Ltd., Shankardas House, Moi Ave., P.O. Box 47815, Nairobi, Kenya. Ed.Bd.

HARVEST STATES AGRIVISIONS. see AGRICULTURE

334 — II — ISSN 0017-8233
HARYANA COOPERATION. (Text in English and Hindi) vol.4, 1970. a. Rs.6. Haryana Cooperative Union Ltd., No. 96, Sector 18-A, Chandigarh, India. Ed. Prem Singh. adv.; charts.

334 — GW
HILF MIT!. 1962. q. free. Landwirtschaftliche Berufsgenossenschaft Oberfranken und Mittelfranken, Dammwaeldchen 4, 95444 Bayreuth, Germany. TEL 49-921-6030. FAX 49-921-603-386. Ed. Friedhard Pfeiffer; Pub. Friedhard Pfeiffer. R&P contact: Friedhard Pfeiffer. adv. contact: Friedhard Pfeiffer. bk.rev.; charts; illus.; stat. circ. 150,000. **Document type:** trade publication.
Description: Information about compulsory accident insurance, medical insurance, and pension funds for farmers.

334 — II
I C A REGIONAL BULLETIN. (Text in English) 1968. q. free. International Cooperative Alliance, Regional Office and Education Centre for South-East Asia, Box 3312, 43 Friends Colony, New Delhi 110014, India. Ed. A.H. Ganesan. bk.rev. circ. 2,000.
Formerly: I C A Information Bulletin (ISSN 0018-8743)

334 — II
IMPLANTER. (Text in English) vol.6, 1974. bi-w. $3.50. North East Industrial Cooperative Society Ltd., Mawkhar, Shillong 793001, India. TEL 26243. Ed. Dellymoore Wankhar. adv.; bk.rev. circ. 800.

334 301 — UK — ISSN 0309-3298
IN THE MAKING; directory of radical cooperation. 1973. biennial. £1($6) 44 Albion Rd., Sutton, Surrey SM2 5TF, England. Ed. D. Bollen. bk.rev. circ. 2,000.

334 — II — ISSN 0019-4581
INDIAN COOPERATIVE REVIEW. (Text in English) 1963. q. Rs.40($10) National Cooperative Union of India, 3-Siri Institutional Area, Panchshila Marg, New Delhi 110016, India. Ed. M.L. Sharma. adv.; bk.rev.; bibl.; index. circ. 2,000. **Indexed:** Abstr.Rural Dev.Trop., Rice Abstr.

BUSINESS AND ECONOMICS — COOPERATIVES

334 BL
INSTITUTO NACIONAL DE COLONIZACAO E REFORMA AGRARIA. COORDENADORIA REGIONAL DO PARANA. SINOPSE DO COOPERATIVISMO NO PARANA. 1970. irreg. Instituto Nacional de Colonizacao e Reforma Agraria, Coordenadoria Regional do Parana, Curitiba, Brazil. illus.

334 NG ISSN 0534-4697
INTER-AFRICAN CONFERENCE ON CO-OPERATIVE SOCIETIES MEETING. REUNION.* irreg. (Commission for Technical Co-Operation in Africa, South of the Sahara) Maison de l'Afrique, B.P. 878, Niamey, Niger.

334 II ISSN 0074-4255
INTERNATIONAL COOPERATIVE ALLIANCE. COOPERATIVE SERIES.* (Text in English) 1965. irreg. International Cooperative Alliance, Regional Office and Education Centre for South-East Asia, Box 3312, 43 Friends' Colony, New Delhi 110014, India. circ. 2,000.

334 IS ISSN 0080-1313
ISRAEL. MINISTRY OF LABOUR. REGISTRAR OF COOPERATIVE SOCIETIES. REPORT ON THE COOPERATIVE MOVEMENT IN ISRAEL. (Text in English) 1964. a. Ministry of Labour and Social Affairs, Registrar of Cooperative Societies, 10 Yad Harutzim St., Talpiot, P.O. Box 1260, Jerusalem 91012, Israel. (Co-sponsor: Women's Society & Welfare League of Israel) circ. 1,200.

334 IT ISSN 0391-7150
ITALIA COOPERATIVA. 1946. fortn. L.40000. (Confederazione Cooperativa Italiana) Editrice Tecnostudi s.r.l., Piazza della Citta Leonina 9, 00193 Rome, Italy. TEL 39-6-6879907. FAX 39-6-6540212. Ed. Dario Mengozzi. adv.: page L.5300000. circ. 65,000.

334 JA
J A - ZENCHU NEWS. 1961. bi-m. free. Central Union of Agricultural Co-operatives - Zen-chu, 1-8-3 Ote-machi, Chiyoda-ku, Tokyo 100, Japan. TEL 03-245-7565. FAX 03-525-7358. TELEX CUAC-J33809. **Document type:** newsletter.
Former titles (until Jun. 1995): J A - Zenchu Farm News & Zenchu Farm News; Japan Agricultural Coop News (ISSN 0447-5240)

334 UK ISSN 0961-5784
JOURNAL OF CO-OPERATIVE STUDIES. 3/yr. £15 (rest of world £18). Society for Co-operative Studies, 29 Dantzic St., Manchester M4 4BA, England. TEL 44-161-832-8152. FAX 44-161-958-1411. Ed. J. Birchall. circ. 600. **Document type:** academic/scholarly publication.

334 630 IS ISSN 0377-7480
HD1491.A1 CODEN: JRCOE4
JOURNAL OF RURAL COOPERATION. (Text in English) 1973. s-a. $25. International Research Center on Rural Cooperative Communities (CIRCOM), Yad Tabenkin, Ramat-Efal 52960, Israel. FAX 972-3-5346376. Ed. Dr. Yair Levi. adv.; bk.rev.; bibl. circ. 450. **Indexed:** Geo.Abstr., Rice Abstr., Rural Devel.Abstr., Rural Recreat.Tour.Abstr., World Agri.Econ.& Rural Sociol.Abstr. **Document type:** academic/scholarly publication.
—BLDSC (5052.127000).
Description: Focuses on subjects relating to the study of rural cooperatives, particularly the dynamics of cooperative-community reciprocity and relations.

334 TU
KARINCA; Kooperatif Postasi. 1931. m. $24. Turk Kooperatifcilik Kurumu - Turkish Cooperative Association, Mithatpasa Caddesi no.38-A, 06420 Kizilay, Ankara, Turkey. TEL 90-312-4316125. FAX 90-312-4340646. Ed. Celal Er. circ. 5,000.
Description: Information on cooperatives and related subjects.

334.683 II
KERALA CO-OPERATIVE JOURNAL. (Text in English and Malayalam) 1959. m. Rs.12. State Co-Operative Union, Box 35, Trivandrum 695001, Kerala, India. Ed. C.K. Mani. adv.; charts. circ. 4,500.

334 GW ISSN 0721-4596
KERAMIK UND GLAS. q. membership. Berufsgenossenschaft der Keramischen und Glas-Industrie, Postfach 5349, 97003 Wurzburg, Germany. TEL 49-931-30810. Ed. Friedrich Muenzer. **Document type:** newsletter.

334 US
KIBBUTZ JOURNAL (NEW YORK). 1983. a. donation. Kibbutz Aliya Desk, 110 E. 59th St., 3 Fl., New York, NY 10022-1304. TEL 212-255-1338. FAX 212-929-3459. circ. 14,000. (back issues avail.) **Document type:** academic/scholarly publication, newsletter.

334 IS ISSN 0333-6379
HX742.2.A3
KIBBUTZ STUDIEN. (Text in German) 1979. q. $10. Yad Tabenkin, Efal 52960, Israel. TEL 972-3-5343311. FAX 972-3-5346376. Eds. H. Seligmann, G. Madar. circ. 600. **Document type:** academic/scholarly publication.

334 IS ISSN 0792-7290
KIBBUTZ TRENDS. (Text in English) 1974. q. $24. Yad Tabenkin, Efal 52960, Israel. TEL 972-3-5343311. FAX 972-3-5346376. Eds. Idit Paz, Ruth Lacey. circ. 1,200. **Document type:** academic/scholarly publication.
Former titles (until 1991): K C. Kibbutz Currents (ISSN 0792-3163); (until 1987): Shdemot (ISSN 0334-4363)

334 DK ISSN 0023-382X
KOOPERATIONEN. 1923. m. (10/yr.). DKK 245. Kooperative Faellesforbund i Danmark, Reventlowsgade 14, 2, 1651 Copenhagen V, Denmark. TEL 31 31 22 62. FAX 31-313041. Ed.Bd. adv.; bk.rev.; charts; illus.; index. circ. 5,800.

334 SW ISSN 0023-3846
HD2951
KOOPERATOEREN. 1914. 40/yr. SEK 469. Kooperativa Foerbundet - Swedish Co-Op Union and Wholesale Society, c/o Margareta Wangius, Library, S-10465 Stockholm, Sweden. Ed. Ingrid Isakson. adv.; bk.rev.; abstr.; illus.; stat.; index. circ. 40,000.

334 SW ISSN 0024-015X
LEDARFORUM. 1925. 10/yr. SEK 550. Kooperativa Ledares Foerbund, P.O. 5200, 104 65 Stockholm, Sweden. adv.; bk.rev.; illus.; tr.lit.; index. circ. 8,000.
Former titles (until 1971): K F F; (until 1944): K F F Medlemsblad (ISSN 0023-3838)

334.008 FR ISSN 1019-1518
LETTRE DE LA FRANCOPHONIE. 1990. m. Agence de Cooperation Culturelle et Technique, 13 quai Andre-Citroen, 75015 Paris, France. TEL 33-1-44-37-33-00. Ed. Jean-Louis Roy.
Description: Covers the various activities of the Agency in the fields of education, culture and communications, technical cooperation and economic development, judicial cooperation in Francophone countries.

334 BE
LINK; lettre d'information et de liaison. (Editions in Dutch, French) 1978. bi-m. 700 BEF (foreign 1200 BEF). Centre Cooperatif de la Consommation, 28 rue Haute, 1000 Brussels, Belgium. FAX 02-514-54-43. Ed. Pierre Dejemeppe. adv.; bk.rev. circ. 7,000. **Document type:** consumer publication.
Former titles (until 1996): Forum de l'Economie Sociale (ISSN 0778-9246); (until 1992): Cooperation (ISSN 0770-7223)

334 IS
MAANIT. q. Union of Moshavim of Hapoal Hamizrachi, 166 Even Giverol St., Tel Aviv, Israel. TEL 03-441224. Ed. Shlomo Zis.

334 II ISSN 0025-0430
HD2951
MAHARASHTRA CO-OPERATIVE QUARTERLY. (Text in English) 1917. q. Rs.80 (foreign $10). Maharashtra Rajya Sahakari Sangh Maryadit - Maharashtra State Co-Operative Union, 5 B J Rd., Pune 411 001, India. TEL 91-212-629584. FAX 91-212-622640. Ed. Krishna L. Fale. adv.; bk.rev.; charts; stat.; index. circ. 800.

334 MF
MAURITIUS. MINISTRY OF CO-OPERATIVES AND CO-OPERATIVE DEVELOPMENT. ANNUAL REPORT. (Text in English) irreg. Government Printing Office, Elizabeth II Ave., Port Louis, Mauritius.

658.7 FI ISSN 0025-6269
AP80
ME. 1917. 12/yr. FIM 200 (effective 1997). Tradeka Oy, Hameentie 19, P.O. Box 71, FIN-00501 Helsinki, Finland. TEL 358-0-733-2204. FAX 385-0-733-2120. Ed. Riitta Raasakka-Niklander. adv.; bk.rev.; circ. 340,000 (controlled). **Document type:** consumer publication.
Formerly: Me Kuluttajat.

334 II ISSN 0027-6278
N C D C BULLETIN. (Text in English, Hindi) 1967. bi-m. free. National Cooperative Development Corporation, 4, Siri Institutional Area, Hauz Khas, New Delhi 110 016, India. TEL 91-11-669246. FAX 91-11-6962370. TELEX 31-73059 NCDC IN. Ed. Archna Sood; Pub. Archna Sood. bk.rev.; bibl.; charts; stat. circ. 7,000. **Document type:** bulletin.

334 CK
O C A NEWS. m. Organization of the Cooperatives of America, Carrera 11 No. 86-32 Ofc. 101, 241263 Bogota, D.E., Colombia. TEL 2181295. FAX 057-1-610-19-12.

334 AU
OE G W AKTUELL. bi-m. Anschuetzgasse 1, Postfach 80, A-1153 Vienna, Austria. TEL 01-812051791. FAX 01-812051727. Ed. Gerhard Greiner. circ. 9,000.

334 GW ISSN 0341-2016
DER OEFFENTLICH BESTELLTE UND VEREIDIGTE SACHVERSTAENDIGE. 1974. m. DM.114. Verlag Recht und Wirtschaft GmbH, Haeusserstr. 14, 69115 Heidelberg, Germany. TEL 06221-906-1. (Subscr. to: Postfach 105960, 69049 Heidelberg, Germany) adv.; bk.rev. circ. 3,172.

334 FI ISSN 0039-5609
HD3517.3
OSUUSTOIMINTALEHTI. 1908. 8/yr. FIM 300. Finn Coop Pellervo, P.O. Box 77, Simonkatu 6, FIN-00101 Helsinki, Finland. TEL 358-0-4767501. FAX 358-0-6948845. Ed. Risto Volanen. adv.: color page FIM7800. illus.; index. circ. 13,000.

PELLERVO. see *AGRICULTURE*

334 IS
PERSPECTIVES. (Text in French) 1983. s-a. $15. Yad Tabenkin, Efal 52960, Israel. TEL 972-3-5343311. FAX 972-3-5346376. Ed. R. Cohen. circ. 1,200. **Document type:** academic/scholarly publication.
Formerly: Kibbutz (Efal).

334 AT
PRIMARY PRODUCERS' GUIDE. a. Primac Association Limited, 109 Melbourne St., South Brisbane, Qld. 4001, Australia. TEL 07-840-5555. FAX 07-844-7530. TELEX AA41889.

334 PK
PUNJAB COOPERATIVE UNION. REVIEW. (Text in English) 1963. q. Rs.15($3.25) Punjab Cooperative Union, 5 Court St., Lahore, Pakistan. Ed. Khalida Saeed.
Formerly: Pakistan Cooperative Review; Supersedes (vol. 6, July 1974): West Pakistan Cooperative Review (ISSN 0511-6147)

R UND V REPORT. see *INSURANCE*

334 GW
RAIFFEISEN; Informationen des Deutschen Raiffeisenverbandes. bi-m. Deutscher Raiffeisenverband e.V., Adenauerallee 127, 53113 Bonn, Germany. TEL 0228-106-0. FAX 0228-106266. **Document type:** bulletin.

334 AU
RAIFFEISENZEITUNG. 1904. w. S.220. Oesterreichischer Raiffeisenverband, Hollandstr. 2, A-1020 Vienna, Austria. TEL 0222-236112584. FAX 0222-236112551. Ed. Kurt Ceipek. adv.; bk.rev. circ. 48,000. **Document type:** newspaper.

334 PE
REVISTA DE ASESORIA PARA COOPERATIVAS. fortn. $220. Asesorandina Publicaciones, Av. Salaverry 674, Of. 403 Jesus Maria, Lima, Peru. Ed. Carlos Torres y Torres-Lara.

1208 BUSINESS AND ECONOMICS — DOMESTIC COMMERCE

334   FR   ISSN 0299-1624
REVUE DES ETUDES COOPERATIVES, MUTUALISTES ET ASSOCIATIVES. 1921. q. 420 F. (foreign 490 F.) (effective 1997 & 1998). R.E.C.M.A., 33 rue des Trois Fontanot, B.P. 211, 92002 Nanterre, France. TEL 33-1-47248597. FAX 33-1-47248838. Ed. Jean-Francois Draperi; Pub. Jean-Louis Girodot. R&P contact: Eric Bidet. TEL 33-1-47248970. adv.; bk.rev.; index. circ. 1,200. Indexed: Geo.Abstr., P.A.I.S.For.Lang.Ind., Rural Devel.Abstr., Rural Recreat.Tour.Abstr., World Agri.Econ.& Rural Sociol.Abstr. **Document type:** academic/scholarly publication.
—BLDSC (7900.160200).
   Formerly (until 1986): Revue des Etudes Cooperatives (ISSN 0035-2020); Which supersedes in part (in 1950): Annee Politique, Economique et Cooperative (ISSN 1149-8064); Which was formerly (until 1949): Annee Politique et Revue des Etudes Cooperatives, Res Publica (ISSN 1149-8072); Formed by the 1947 merger of: Revue des Etudes Cooperatives (ISSN 1149-8056); Annee Politique Francaise et Etrangere (ISSN 1149-0152); Res Publica (ISSN 1153-5911).
   Description: Covers cooperatives, economic systems and theories.

RURAL COOPERATIVES. see AGRICULTURE

334   US   ISSN 0164-8578
RURAL MISSOURI. 1948. m. $4.99. Association of Missouri Electric Cooperatives, Inc., Box 1645, 2722 E. McCarty, Jefferson City, MO 65102. TEL 314-659-3423. Ed. Jim McCarty; Pub. Frank Stork. R&P contact: Jeff Joiner. TEL 573-659-3425. adv.: B&W page $4353, color page $5253; adv. contact: Mary Davis. bk.rev.; illus.; circ. 374,000 (paid). (tabloid format) **Document type:** consumer publication.
   Formerly: Rural Electric Missourian (ISSN 0048-8801)
   Description: Includes news items pertaining to electrification and regional issues, as well as general articles, recipes and classifieds.

334   CE
SAMUPAKARA VIGRAHAYA. (Text in Sinhalese) 3/yr. National Cooperation Board, 455 Galle Rd., Colombo 3, Sri Lanka.

334   IS
HA-SHAVUA. w. membership. Ha-Kibbutz ha-Artzi, P.O. Box 40009, Tel Aviv 61 400, Israel. TEL 03-435328. Ed. Mira Narkis. bk.rev.

334   IS   ISSN 0037-4008
SHITUF/COOPERATION. (Text in Hebrew) 1948. bi-m. $8. Central Union of Industrial Transport & Services Co-Operative Societies in Israel, 24 Haarbaa St., Box 7151, (Hakirya), Tel-Aviv, Israel. Ed. L. Losh. bk.rev.; charts; illus.; stat. circ. 12,500.

334   GW
SICHERHEIT FUER HAUS UND HOF. 1966. q. free. Landwirtschaftliche Berufsgenossenschaft Oberbayern, Unterfranken und Niederbayern - Oberpfalz, Neumarkter Str. 35, 81673 Munich, Germany. TEL 49-89-45480-0. FAX 49-89-436639813. E-mail: bernhard.richter@lsv-obb.de. Ed. Norbert Gradl. **Document type:** bulletin.

334   US   ISSN 0038-4003
SOUTHERN COOPERATOR.* 1970. irreg. $5. Federation of Southern Cooperatives, Education Dept., Box 95, Epes, AL 35460. Ed. Alice Paris. adv.; charts; illus. circ. 6,000.

STATELINE. see BUSINESS AND ECONOMICS — Banking And Finance

334   II   ISSN 0377-8002
HD3577
TAMIL NADU JOURNAL OF CO-OPERATION. (Text in English) 1909. m. Rs.30. Tamil Nadu Co-operative Union, TNCU Bldg., Near Walajah Bridge, Madras 600009, India. Ed. Thiru C.M. Rajan. adv.; bk.rev. circ. 3,000. Indexed: Int.Lab.Doc.
   Continues: Madras Journal of Co-operation.

334   IS
TELEMIM; bulletin of the Moshav movement. 1933. s-a. free. United Moshav Movement, Leonardo da Vinci St. 19, Tel Aviv, Israel. Ed. Yitzhak Lav-Tov. bk.rev. circ. 1,500.

334 333.79   US
TEXAS CO-OP POWER. 1944. m. $6. Association of Texas Electric Cooperatives, 8140 Burnet Rd., Box 9589, Austin, TX 78766. TEL 512-454-0311. FAX 512-454-0311. Ed. Janet Hunter. R&P contact: Janet Hunter. adv. contact: Beverly Anderson. circ. 465,000. **Document type:** consumer publication, trade publication.
   Description: Covers primarily general interest with features on Texas and Texans. Includes news about electric industry issues, electrotechnology and electric co-ops.

334   SP   ISSN 0210-7295
TRIBUNA COOPERATIVA. 1966. 3/yr. 750 ptas. (Escuela de Gerentes de Cooperativas) Centro Nacional de Educacion Cooperativa, Palacio de la Cooperacion, Apdo. de Correos 15, San Felix 9, Zaragoza, Spain. (Affiliate: Federacion Nacional de Cooperativas de Espana) Ed. Joaquin Mateo Blanco. adv.; bk.rev.; bibl.; illus.; stat. circ. 1,000.
   Incorporates (since 1978): Documentos de Educacion Cooperativa (ISSN 0046-0486)

334   DK   ISSN 0109-1328
UDDELERBLADET. 1901. 50/yr. DKK 220. Danmarks Uddelerforening, Markvangen 3, 8260 Viby J, Denmark. TEL 45-86-14-74-00. FAX 45-86-147992. Ed. Joergen Nielsen. adv.; bk.rev. circ. 7,500.
   Formerly (until 1983): Brugslederen.

330   CN
UNIVERSITE DE SHERBROOKE. I R E C U S. CAHIERS DE LA COOPERATION. 1969. irreg. no.6, 1992. price varies. Universite de Sherbrooke, Institut de Recherche et d'Enseignement pour les Cooperatives, Sherbrooke, PQ J1K 2R1, Canada. TEL 819-821-7220. FAX 819-821-7213. Ed.Bd.

330   CN
UNIVERSITE DE SHERBROOKE. I R E C U S. DOSSIERS SUR LES COOPERATIVES. 1973. irreg. no.5, 1985. price varies. Universite de Sherbrooke, Institut de Recherche et d'Enseignement pour les Cooperatives, Sherbrooke, PQ J1K 2R1, Canada. TEL 819-821-7220. FAX 819-821-7213. circ. 200.

330   CN
UNIVERSITE DE SHERBROOKE. I R E C U S. ESSAIS. irreg. no.23, 1991. price varies. Universite de Sherbrooke, Institut de Recherche et d'Enseignement pour les Cooperatives, Sherbrooke, PQ J1K 2R1, Canada. TEL 819-821-7220. FAX 819-821-7213.

334   FI   ISSN 0356-1364
UNIVERSITY OF HELSINKI. INSTITUTE FOR CO-OPERATIVE STUDIES. PUBLICATIONS. (Text in English, Finnish and German) 1967. irreg. price varies. University of Helsinki, Institute for Co-operative Studies, P.O. Box 25, Franseninkatu 13, FIN-00014 University of Helsinki, Finland. TEL 358-0-1911. FAX 358-0-191-7000. circ. 150.

334   NO   ISSN 0509-5409
VAART BLAD. 1905. 11/yr. NOK 60. Norges Kooperative Landsforening - Norwegian Co-Operative Union and Wholesale Society, Kirkegt. 4, 0107 Oslo 1, Norway. TEL 22-89-95-00. FAX 22-41-11-38. Ed. Tor Hansen. adv.; bk.rev.; circ. 253,355. (also avail. in microfilm) **Document type:** consumer publication.

VAIKUNTH MEHTA NATIONAL INSTITUTE OF COOPERATIVE MANAGEMENT. PUBLICATIONS. see BUSINESS AND ECONOMICS — Management

334   JO
VOICE OF COOPERATION/SAWT UL-TA'WUN. (Text in Arabic) 1957. m. free to qualified personnel. Jordan Cooperative Organization, Box 1343, Amman, Jordan. Ed. Marwan A. Dudin. adv.; bk.rev. circ. 1,000.

334   UK   ISSN 1354-7151
HD2951
WORLD OF CO-OPERATIVE ENTERPRISE. 1927. a. £16.95. Plunkett Foundation, 23 Hanborough Business Park, Long Hanborough, Oxford OX8 8LH, England. TEL 44-1993-883636. FAX 44-1993-883576. E-mail: plunkett@gn.apc.org. Ed.Bd. circ. 700. Indexed: Int.Lab.Doc., World Agri.Econ.& Rural Sociol.Abstr. **Document type:** monographic series.
—BLDSC (9353.623000); Linda Hall.
   Former titles (until 1993): Year Book of Co-Operative Enterprise (ISSN 0952-5556); (until 1987): Year Book of Agricultural Co-Operation (ISSN 0142-498X)
   Description: Articles on co-operative themes of interest worldwide, plus an annual review of all co-operative sectors in the U.K. (worker, agriculture, consumer credit union, fishery, housing, community). Refereed Serial

WUERTTEMBERGISCHE BAU-BERUFSGENOSSENSCHAFT. JAHRESBERICHT. see BUILDING AND CONSTRUCTION

334   IS
YACHAD. bi-m. Meuchad Kibbutz Movement, Rehov Dubnov 10, Tel Aviv 64 732, Israel. TEL 03-250231. Ed. Doit Tzameret.

334 334   ZA
ZAMBIA. MINISTRY OF COOPERATIVES. ANNUAL REPORT. a. K.100. Zambia Government Printing Department, P.O. Box 30136, Lusaka, Zambia. stat. **Document type:** government publication.
   Formerly: Zambia. Department of Cooperatives. Annual Report (ISSN 0514-5430)
   Description: Annual paper on the coordination of agricultural input supply services.

334   GW
ZEITSCHRIFT FUER KOMMUNALFINANZEN. m. DM.298 (effective 1997). Stollfuss Verlag Bonn, Postfach 2428, 53014 Bonn, Germany. TEL 49-228-724-0. FAX 49-228-659223. **Document type:** bulletin.

ZEITSCHRIFT FUER OEFFENTLICHE UND GEMEINWIRTSCHAFTLICHE UNTERNEHMEN. see PUBLIC ADMINISTRATION

BUSINESS AND ECONOMICS — Domestic Commerce

380 635.2   NE   ISSN 0165-6031
AARDAPPELWERELD. 1948. m. fl.92.50. Aardappelwereld B.V., Van Stolkweg 31, Postbus 84102, 2508 AC The Hague, Netherlands. FAX 31-70-3544290. Ed. M. van Delft. adv.; bk.rev.; charts; illus.; stat. circ. 5,000. Indexed: Field Crop Abstr., Key to Econ.Sci., Potato Abstr. **Document type:** trade publication.
   Former titles: Pootaardappelwereld; (until 1974): Pootaardappelhandel (ISSN 0032-4337)

381   FR   ISSN 1141-7102
ACTUALITES COMMERCE. 1964. 3/yr. 15 F. Ecole des Cadres, 70 Galerie des Damiers, La Defense 1, 92400 Courbevoie, France. TEL 46-93-02-93. FAX 47-75-99-80. Ed. Alexis Saccardo; Pub. Christian Regnier. adv. circ. 35,000. **Document type:** academic/scholarly publication.
   Former titles (until 1971): Contact (ISSN 1141-7110); (until 1967): Actualites Commerce (ISSN 0567-8684)

380   FR   ISSN 0002-0826
AGENT COMMERCIAL.* 1929. 6/yr. 130 F. (Federation Nationale des Agents Commerciaux) Editions de l' Agent Commercial, 23 rue de Rome, 75008 Paris, France. TEL 42-93-61-24. FAX 42-93-11-27. Dir. Jean Pataut. adv.; bk.rev.; bibl.; index. circ. 3,500. (tabloid format)

381   US   ISSN 0271-3276
ALASKA JOURNAL OF COMMERCE & PACIFIC RIM REPORTER;* the newsweekly for Alaska's business. Variant title: Alaska Journal of Commerce. 1977. w. $49. Pacific Rim Publishing Co., Box 201894, Anchorage, AK 99520-1894. TEL 907-272-7500. FAX 907-279-1037. Ed. Imreth Nemeth. adv.; bk.rev. circ. 5,000. (tabloid format; back issues avail.)
   ●Also available online. Vendor(s): Knight-Ridder Information, Inc., UMI.
—UMI.
   Description: Covers all major industries in Alaska.

BUSINESS AND ECONOMICS — DOMESTIC COMMERCE

381 SP
ALMERIA ECONOMICA. 12/yr. Paseo de Almeria 59, 1o, 04001 Almeria, Spain. TEL 51-23-44-33. FAX 51-23-48-50. Ed. J.M. Cosano Perez.

381 362.18 616.02 US ISSN 0891-0812
AMBULANCE INDUSTRY JOURNAL. 1981. bi-m. $25. American Ambulance Association, 3800 Auburn Blvd., Ste. C, Sacramento, CA 95821-2102. TEL 916-483-3827. FAX 916-482-5473. Ed. Johnna Crowe. R&P contact: Johnna Crowe. adv. contact: Johnna Crowe. bk.rev. circ. 2,500.
Document type: trade publication.
Formerly (until 1986): Ambulance Industry Digest (A I D).
Description: Covers industry trends, critical regulatory changes, and news for the industry.

AMCHAM. see BUSINESS AND ECONOMICS — Chamber Of Commerce Publications

381 FR
ANNUAIRE GENERAL DES COOPERATIVES ET DE LEURS FOURNISSEURS: FRANCE, OUTRE-MER ET MARCHE EUROPEEN. 1956. a. 860 F. Office des Cooperatives et des Collectivites, 49 rue de Richelieu, 75001 Paris, France. TEL 1-42-96-68-34. FAX 42-96-03-57. adv.
Formerly: Annuaire General des Cooperatives Francaises et de leurs Fournisseurs: France, Afrique et Marche Commun (ISSN 0066-3182)
Description: Classifies geographically and by activity about 8,000 agricultural, manufacturing, retail and trading cooperatives. Suppliers classified by products.

381 IT ISSN 1122-8504
ANNUARIO GENERALE ITALIANO. 1871. a. L.600000 (effective 1997). Guida Monaci S.p.A., Via Vitorchiano 107, 00189 Rome, Italy. TEL 39-6-3288805. FAX 39-6-3275693. TELEX 623324 MONACI. URL: http://italybygm.it. adv.: B&W page L.15000000. index.
●Also available on CD-ROM.
Description: Directory of Italian commercial and industrial activities.

L'ANTENNE; seul quotidien francais des transports. see TRANSPORTATION — Ships And Shipping

381 FR
ARDENNE ECONOMIQUE. q. 60 F. Chambre Regionale de Commerce et d'Industrie Champagne - Ardenne, Direction de la Communication, 10 rue de Chastillon, B.P. 537, 51011 Chalons-sur-Marne Cedex, France. TEL 33-3-26693340. FAX 33-3-26693369.

381 SP
ASTURIAS. 12/yr. membership only. Centro Asturiano de Madrid, Farmacia 2, 28004 Madrid, Spain. TEL 34-1-5328245. FAX 34-1-5328256. Ed. Cosme Sordo Obeso. circ. 100,000.

381 CN ISSN 1184-051X
ATLANTIC LIFESTYLE BUSINESS. 1990. bi-m. Can.$16.05 (US Can.$23, elsewhere Can.$32). Communications Ten Ltd., 197 Water St., P.O. Box 2356, Sta. C, St. John's, NF A1C 6E7, Canada. TEL 709-726-9300. FAX 709-726-3013. Ed. Edwina Hutton. R&P contact: Edwina Hutton. adv. contact: Hubert F. Hutton. circ. 25,000. **Document type:** consumer publication.

AVANCE DE INFORMACION ECONOMICA. ENCUESTA SOBRE ESTABLECIMIENTOS COMERCIALES. CIUDADES DE: MEXICO, GUADALAJARA Y MONTERREY. see BUSINESS AND ECONOMICS — Abstracting, Bibliographies, Statistics

658.8 **380** GW
B A G - HANDELSMAGAZIN. 1961. m. DM.98. Bundes Arbeitsgemeinschaft der Mittel- und Grossbetriebe des Einzelhandels e.V., Lindenallee 41, 50968 Cologne, Germany. TEL 0221-37679-0. FAX 0221-37679-88. Ed. Walter Deuss. adv.; bk.rev.; illus.; stat. circ. 10,000.
Formerly (until 1992): B A G - Nachrichten (ISSN 0005-2639)

B I A NEWSLINE. (Billiard and Bowling Institute of America) see SPORTS AND GAMES — Ball Games

381 CN ISSN 0704-6278
B C MANUFACTURER'S DIRECTORY. a. Can.$45 (effective 1997). Ministry of Finance and Corporate Relations, B C Stats, P.O. Box 9410, Stn. Prov. Govt., Victoria, BC V8W 9V1, Canada. TEL 250-387-0359. FAX 250-387-0380. E-mail: bcstats@fincc04.fin.gov.bc.ca; URL: http://www.bcstats.gov.bc.ca. stat. **Document type:** government publication.
Description: Publicizes the availability of locally manufactured products for the benefit of buyers and sellers.

BARGAIN SHOPPER'S GUIDE TO MELBOURNE. see CONSUMER EDUCATION AND PROTECTION

BARGAIN SHOPPERS GUIDE TO SYDNEY. see CONSUMER EDUCATION AND PROTECTION

381 SP
BASQUE ENTERPRISE. 4/yr. Spri S.A., Gran Via 35, 3o, 48009 Bilbao, Spain. TEL 4-415-82-88. FAX 4-416-96-23. Ed. Mikel Pulgarin.

381 GW ISSN 0722-4893
BAYERISCHER EINZELHANDEL. m. Wirtschaftshilfe des Bayerischen Einzelhandels, Briennen Str. 45, 80333 Munich, Germany. circ. 21,027.

381 UY
BOLETIN COMERCIAL. 1935. m. Colorn 1580, Montevideo, Uruguay. Dir. Antonio Benvenuto. adv. circ. 2,500.

381 SP
BOLETIN DE INFORMACION ECONOMICA ALTOARAGONES. 11/yr. Angel de la Guarda 7, 22005 Huesca, Spain. TEL 74-21-27-46.

BRITAIN'S DIRECT MARKETING INDUSTRY (YEAR). see BUSINESS AND ECONOMICS — Trade And Industrial Directories

BRITAIN'S FRANCHISING INDUSTRY. see BUSINESS AND ECONOMICS — Trade And Industrial Directories

BRITAIN'S PAINT INDUSTRY. see BUSINESS AND ECONOMICS — Trade And Industrial Directories

BRITAIN'S SPORTING GOODS INDUSTRY: INTO THE 1990'S. see BUSINESS AND ECONOMICS — Trade And Industrial Directories

BRITAIN'S TOP 1000 MOTOR DISTRIBUTORS. see BUSINESS AND ECONOMICS — Trade And Industrial Directories

BRITAIN'S TOP 300 PRINTERS. see BUSINESS AND ECONOMICS — Trade And Industrial Directories

381 910.09 IO ISSN 0216-0412
BULLETIN EKONOMI INDONESIA. 1970. 2/w. $50 per month. Gabungan Importir Nasional Seluruh Indonesia - National Importers Association of Indonesia, Jl. Kesejahteraan No. 98 APRJ, Jakarta 10110, Indonesia. TEL 021-360-643. FAX 62-021-367269. circ. 20,000.

380 UK ISSN 1360-1318
HD28 CODEN: BUSAB6
BUSINESS ADMINISTRATOR. 1949. q. £2.50 (foreign £3.50). Institute of Business Administration, 16 Park Crescent, London W1N 4AH, England. Ed. John Preece. adv. contact: John Smith. bk.rev.; abstr.; charts; illus.; stat.; tr.lit.; index. circ. 2,000.
Document type: trade publication.
Formerly: British Society of Commerce. Review (ISSN 0007-1781)

381 US
BUSINESS DIRECTORY. 1986. a. free. Mt. Diablo Peace Center, 65 Eckley Lane, Walnut Creek, CA 94596. TEL 415-933-7850. FAX 284-5357. Ed.Bd. adv.; circ. 5,000 (controlled).
Description: Provides opportunity to make known their goods and services to the peace center members and supporters.

658.4 II ISSN 0254-5268
HF5001
BUSINESS INDIA. (Text in English) 1978. fortn. Rs.245($110) (CD-ROM $200). Business India Group of Publications, Nirmal, Nariman Point, Mumbai 400 021, India. TEL 91-22-2009274. FAX 91-22-2875671. TELEX 118-3557-BZIN-IN. URL: http://www.indiaworld.co.in/biz/yp/bi-index.html. Pub. Ashok Advani. adv.: B&W page Rs.88000, color page Rs.125000; trim 203 x 267. bk.rev. circ. 17,508. **Indexed:** C.R.I.Abstr., C.R.I.Curr.Cont. **Document type:** trade publication.
●Also available on CD-ROM.
Description: Covers the latest business developments and economic trends worldwide.

381 US
THE BUSINESS JOURNAL (LIMA); West Central Ohio's leading business publication. 1992. m. $10. Box 388, Lima, OH 45802-0388. TEL 419-999-4762; 800-370-2351. FAX 419-991-6839. Ed. Ronald Freed; Pub. Ronald Freed. charts; stat. circ. 15,000. cols./p.: 4. (tabloid format; back issues avail.)
Document type: newspaper, trade publication.
●Also available online. Vendor(s): Information Access Co.
Formerly: Business Journal of West Central Ohio.
Description: Reports on business and management news and issues in west central Ohio.

BUSINESS LAWS OF EGYPT. see LAW — Corporate Law

BUSINESS LAWS OF IRAN. see LAW — Corporate Law

BUSINESS LAWS OF IRAQ. see LAW — Corporate Law

BUSINESS LAWS OF KUWAIT. see LAW — Corporate Law

BUSINESS LAWS OF OMAN. see LAW — Corporate Law

BUSINESS LAWS OF SAUDI ARABIA. see LAW — Corporate Law

BUSINESS LAWS OF THE UNITED ARAB EMIRATES. see LAW — Corporate Law

381 US ISSN 1046-9575
HF3161.N45
BUSINESS N H MAGAZINE. Key Title: Business New Hampshire Magazine. 1983. m. $24. Laurentian Business Publishing Inc., 404 Chestnut St., Ste. 201, Manchester, NH 03101. TEL 603-626-6354. Ed. Janet M. Phelps; Pub. B.J. Eckhardt. R&P contact: Holly Babin. adv.: B&W page $1969, color page $2670; trim 8 1/8 x 10 7/8; adv. contact: Gene Ward. circ. 13,000. **Indexed:** Tr.& Indus.Ind. **Document type:** consumer publication.
—UMI.
Former titles (until 1989): Business of New Hampshire (ISSN 1042-7511); Joliecoeur's Business N H (ISSN 0897-8093); Business N H (ISSN 0893-4800)
Description: For the N.H. business community. Covers acquisitions, marketing, banking, profiles, construction and growth trends.

381 CN ISSN 0849-3901
BUSINESS PEOPLE MAGAZINE. 1984. q. Can.$10. McCaine Davies Communications Ltd., 232 Henderson Hwy., Winnipeg, MB R2L 1L9, Canada. TEL 204-982-4000. FAX 204-982-4001. Pub. Heather McCaine-Davies. bk.rev. circ. 11,000.
Document type: trade publication.
●Also available online. Vendor(s): UMI.
Former titles (until 1990): Winnipeg's Business People (ISSN 0848-8827); (until 1989): Business People Magazine (ISSN 0838-4339); (until 1988): Business in the Information Age (ISSN 0841-2170); (until 1987): MicroSense Business in the Information Age (ISSN 0833-9384); (until 1986): MicroSense (ISSN 0831-1714); (until 1985): MicroSource (ISSN 0831-1706)
Description: Focuses on business people in Manitoba.

381 US
BUSINESS PULSE.* m. $18. Scribe Enterprises, Box 589, Burlington, WA 98233-0589. Ed. Michael Barrett. R&P contact: Michael Barrett. adv. circ. 5,000. **Document type:** newspaper.
Description: Informs Whatcom County businesspersons of the people, news, ideas, trends, and opinions affecting their businesses.

BUSINESS AND ECONOMICS — DOMESTIC COMMERCE

381 658.8   UK   ISSN 0261-8397
BUSINESS RATIO REPORT: HIGH STREET TRADING; an industry sector analysis. 1979. a. I C C Business Ratios Ltd., Freepost, Field House, Hampton, Mddx. TW12 1BR, England. TEL 081-783-0977. FAX 081-783-1940. charts; stat. Document type: trade publication.

381   UK   ISSN 0262-8597
BUSINESS SOUTH EAST. 1982. m. £12. Apple Communications Ltd., Apple Barn, Smeeth, Ashford, Kent TN25 6SR, England. TEL 44-1303-813381. FAX 44-1303-812893. TELEX 965944 ABCLTD G. Ed. Paul Smithe. adv.; bk.rev.; tr.lit. circ. 10,134. (back issues avail.)
   Description: Covers business in southeastern England.

381   CN   ISSN 1192-9332
BUSINESS TIMES; London's authoritative source for business news. 1993. m. Can.$18.95. Blackburn Magazine Group, 231 Dundas St., Ste. 203, London, ON N6A 1H1, Canada. TEL 519-679-4901. FAX 519-434-7842. Pub. Katherine Wiggett. adv.: color page Can.$2070; trim 10 3/4 x 16 1/2; adv. contact: Liane Franklin. bk.rev.; software rev.; charts; illus.; stat.; bibl. circ. 10,000. (tabloid format; back issues avail.) Document type: trade publication.
   Description: Covers the courts, bankruptcies, marketing and advertising trends, and local business news.

BUTTERWORTHS E C BRIEF. see *BUSINESS AND ECONOMICS — Economic Situation And Conditions*

CALIFORNIA CORPORATIONS CODE AND CORPORATE SECURITIES RULES. see *LAW — Corporate Law*

CAMARA DE COMERCIANTES EN ARTEFACTOS PARA EL HOGAR. REVISTA. see *INTERIOR DESIGN AND DECORATION — Furniture And House Furnishings*

381   US
CAMERA DI COMMERCIO, INDUSTRIA, ARTIGIANATO E AGRICOLTURA DI FORLI. LISTINO SETTIMANALE PREZZI. w. L.33000. Camera di Commercio, Industria, Artigianato e Agricoltura di Forli, Corso della Repubblica 5, 47100 Forli, Italy. TEL 0543-713111. FAX 0543-713416.

332.6 381   CN   ISSN 0828-0622
CANADIAN CAPITAL PROJECTS. 1981. q., plus m. supplements. Can.$622 (effective 1997). Informetrica Limited, P.O. Box 828, Stn. B, Ottawa, ON K1P 5P9, Canada. TEL 613-238-4831. FAX 613-238-7698. Ed. Stan Kustec. circ. 200. (also avail. in diskette format)
—CISTI.
   Description: Provides detailed records of major investment projects: speculative, planned or underway; classified by province and industry. Includes location, owners, value, timing, political, business or financial risks.

CANADIAN COMPETITION RECORD. see *LAW*

CANADIAN GERMAN TRADE. see *BUSINESS AND ECONOMICS — Economic Situation And Conditions*

380   UK
▼**CAPITAL BUSINESS MAGAZINE.** Variant title: Commerce Business Magazine (London Edition). 1995. m. £36; newsstand price: £3. Commerce Publications (London), 3 Southwick Mews, London W2 1JG, England. TEL 0171-402-4025. FAX 0171-402-4028. (Subscr. to: Commerce Publications, Station House, Station Rd., Newport Pagnell, Milton Keynes, Bucks. MK16 OAG, England) adv.: B&W page £950, color page £1250; trim 280 x 213. Document type: trade publication.
   Description: Examines regional and national business issues and includes personality profiles on leading figures in the business world.

381   FR   ISSN 0069-1100
CATALOGUE DES PRODUITS AGREES PAR QUALITE-FRANCE. 2nd ed., 1963. irreg. 3 F. Association Nationale pour la Promotion et le Controle de la Qualite, 18 rue Volney, 75002 Paris, France.

381   CE
CEYLON COMMERCE. (Text in English) m. $40. National Chamber of Commerce of Sri Lanka, 2nd Fl., YMBA Bldg., Main St., P.O. Box 1375, Colombo 1, Sri Lanka. TEL 94-1-689596. FAX 94-1-689596. E-mail: nccsl@slt.lk.

381   FR
CHALLENGES HAUTE-MARNE. 6/yr. 100 F. Chambre Regionale de Commerce et d'Industrie Champagne - Ardenne, Direction de la Communication, 10 rue de Chastillon, B.P. 537, 51011 Chalons-sur-Marne Cedex, France. TEL 33-3-266-3340. FAX 33-3-26693369.

CHILE. INSTITUTO NACIONAL DE ESTADISTICAS. ANUARIO DE COMERCIO INTERIOR Y SERVICIOS. see *BUSINESS AND ECONOMICS — Abstracting, Bibliographies, Statistics*

CHILE. INSTITUTO NACIONAL DE ESTADISTICAS. ANUARIO DE PRECIOS. see *BUSINESS AND ECONOMICS — Abstracting, Bibliographies, Statistics*

CHINA'S CUSTOMS STATISTICS. see *BUSINESS AND ECONOMICS — Abstracting, Bibliographies, Statistics*

381   US   ISSN 0732-071X
HF5429.4.C6
COLORADO CITY RETAIL SALES BY STANDARD INDUSTRIAL CLASSIFICATION. 1965. q. plus a. $75 (subscr. includes Colorado County and State Retail Sales). University of Colorado, Business Research Division, Campus Box 420, Boulder, CO 80309-0420. TEL 303-492-8227. FAX 303-492-3620. Ed. Cindy DiPersio.
   Supersedes in part: Colorado County and City Retail Sales by Standard Industrial Classification (ISSN 0091-4789)

381   PE   ISSN 0010-2253
COMERCIO. 1892. d. S/240($6) Empresa Editorial Cusco S.A., Casilla 70, Cusco, Peru. Dir. Abel Ramos Perea. adv.; bk.rev. circ. 60,000. Document type: newspaper.

381   PO
COMERCIO DE GAIA. 26/yr. Rua Joaquim Nicolau de Almeida 127, 4400 Vila Nova de Gaia, Portugal. TEL 2-301912.

381   SP
COMERCIO 45. 6/yr. Alameda del Recalde 50, 48008 Bilbao, Spain. TEL 4-4444054. FAX 4-4434145. TELEX 32783 CCINB. circ. 19,086.

381   SZ
LE COMMERCANT. (Text in French) bi-m. membership. Societe des Jeunes Commercants, Rue Haldimand 18, Case Postale 494, CH-1000 Lausanne 17, Switzerland. TEL 41-21-3134411. FAX 41-21-3125855. Ed. Daniel Chollet. R&P contact: F. Simons. adv.: B&W page 2200 SFr.; adv. contact: Daniel Chollet. circ. 6,000. Document type: bulletin.

380   NP
COMMERCE; English monthly. (Text in English) 1972. m. Rs.48($12) Nepal Economic and Commerce Research Centre, P.O. Box 285, 7-358 Kohity Bahal, Kathmandu, Nepal. TEL 977-1-220531. FAX 977-1-279544. TELEX 2634 ONZA NP. Ed. Manju Ratna Sakya. adv. contact: B.R. Maharjan. bk.rev.; charts; illus.; stat. circ. 15,000. Document type: trade publication, newspaper.
   Description: Covers trade, commerce, industry, and the economy.

381   CN
CODEN: WCIMEW
COMMERCE & INDUSTRY MAGAZINE. 1949. bi-m. Can.$64. Mercury Publications Ltd., 1839 Inkster Blvd., Winnipeg, MB R2X 1R3, Canada. TEL 204-697-0835. FAX 204-633-7784. Ed. Kelly Gray; Pub. Gren Yeo. adv. contact: Frank Yeo. illus. circ. 12,500. Document type: trade publication. —BLDSC (9300.199300); CISTI.
   Former titles: Western Commerce and Industry Magazine (ISSN 0043-3624); Western Construction and Building.
   Description: Trade magazine for construction, manufacturing and resource industries in Canada.

380   UK
COMMERCE BUSINESS MAGAZINE (EAST EDITION). Variant title: Commerce Magazine (East Edition). 1979. m. £36; newsstand price: £3. Commerce Publications, Station House, Station Rd., Newport Pagnell, Milton Keynes, Bucks. MK16 OAG, England. TEL 44-1908-614477. FAX 44-1908-616441. Ed. Steve Brennan; Pub. Richard Meredith. adv.: B&W page £1147, color page £1494; trim 280 x 213. circ. 6,000. Document type: trade publication.
   Description: Examines regional and national business issues and includes personality profiles on leading figures in the business world.

380   UK
COMMERCE BUSINESS MAGAZINE (MIDLANDS EDITION). Variant title: Commerce Magazine (Midlands Edition). 1981. m. £36; newsstand price: £3. Commerce Publications, Station House, Station Rd., Newport Pagnell, Milton Keynes, Bucks. MK16 OAG, England. TEL 44-1908-614477. FAX 44-1908-616441. Ed. Steve Brennan; Pub. Richard Meredith. adv.: B&W page £1147, color page £1494; trim 280 x 213. Document type: trade publication.
   Description: Examines regional and national business issues and includes personality profiles on leading figures in the business world.

380   UK
COMMERCE BUSINESS MAGAZINE (NORTH EDITION). Variant title: Commerce Magazine (North Edition). 1979. m. £36; newsstand price: £3. Commerce Publications, Station House, Station Rd., Newport Pagnell, Milton Keynes, Bucks. MK16 OAG, England. TEL 44-1908-614477. FAX 44-1908-616441. Ed. Steve Brennan; Pub. Richard Meredith. adv.: B&W page £1147, color page £1494; trim 280 x 213. Document type: trade publication.
   Description: Examines regional and national business issues and includes personality profiles on leading figures in the business world.

380   UK
COMMERCE BUSINESS MAGAZINE (SOUTH EDITION). Variant title: Commerce Magazine (South Edition). 1981. m. £36; newsstand price: £3. Commerce Publications, Station House, Station Rd., Newport Pagnell, Milton Keynes, Bucks. MK16 OAG, England. TEL 44-1908-614477. FAX 44-1908-616441. Ed. Steve Brennan; Pub. Richard Meredith. adv.: B&W page £1147, color page £1494; trim 280 x 213. Document type: trade publication.
   Description: Examines regional and national business issues and includes personality profiles on leading figures in the business world.

382   LE   ISSN 0010-2814
COMMERCE DU LEVANT. (Publication suspended 1975-1978) (Text in French) 1929. s-w. $225. Societe de la Presse Economique, Immeuble de Commerce et Financement, Rue Kantari, P.O. Box 687, Beirut, Lebanon. TEL 1-297770. Dir. Maroun Akl. adv.; charts; illus.; stat. circ. 1,500.

380   II   ISSN 0010-3012
COMMERCIAL HERALD. 1966. s-m. Rs.53. c/o Sudarshan Paul Bahri, Ed., 75-C Saheed Udhamsingh Nagar, Civil Lines, Ludhiana, India.

380   II   ISSN 0010-3039
COMMERCIAL JOURNAL. 1934. m. $50. All India Commercial Association, Daryaganj, Delhi 110 006, India. TEL 3272040. FAX 3271294. Ed. J.K. Soni. adv.; bk.rev.; stat. circ. 3,000.

380   IT
COMMERCIANTE. 1956. m. Associazione Commercianti di Reggio Emilia, Via Roma 13, 42100 Reggio Emilia, Italy. Ed. Paolo Ferraboschi. adv. circ. 7,500.

381   IT
COMMERCIO; rivista di economia e politica commerciale. 1979. q. L.66000 (foreign L.95000) (effective 1993). (Universita Commerciale Luigi Bocconi, Centro di Studi sul Commercio) Franco Angeli Editore, Viale Monza 106, 20127 Milan, Italy TEL 02-28-27-651. Ed. Aldo Spranzi.

380   IT
COMMERCIO DEL POPOLO. 1945. m. L.500. c/o E. Schiavello, Ed., Via Ponte Severso 19, Milan, Italy. adv. circ. 5,000.

BUSINESS AND ECONOMICS — DOMESTIC COMMERCE

381 910.09   IT
COMMERCIO E TURISMO ROMAGNOLO. 12/yr. Via Grado 2, 47100 Forli, Italy. TEL 543-34930. circ. 11,000.

380   IT
COMMERCIO TURISMO SERVIZI. 1948. w. (50/yr.). L.10000. Confederazione Generale Italiana del Commercio e del Turismo, Piazza Gioacchino Belli 2, Rome, Italy. TEL 6-706-701. (Subscr. to: Via Boschetti 1, Milan, Italy) Ed. Pietro Alfonsi. adv.; stat. circ. 661,473.
    Formerly: Commercio Turismo (ISSN 0017-0151)

380   II   ISSN 0010-3160
COMMERCIUM. (Text in English) vol.6, 1970. s-a. Rs.10($2.50) University of Rajasthan, School of Commerce, Gandhi Nagar, Jaipur 302004, India. Ed.Bd. adv.; bk.rev.; charts; stat. **Indexed:** Key to Econ.SCi.

381   IT
CONAD. 1970. m. L.10000. Consorzio Nazionale Dettaglianti, Via Michelino 59, 40127 Bologna, Italy. Ed. Favio Fornasari. adv.; bk.rev. circ. 23,000.

380   BL
CONFEDERACAO NACIONAL DO COMERCIO. ASSESSORIA JURIDICA. BOLETIM INFORMATIVO. vol.28, 1977. w. free. Confederacao Nacional do Comercio, Avenida General Justo 307, 6 Andar, 20221-130 Rio de Janeiro, Brazil.
    Formerly: Confederacao Nacional do Comercio. Divisao Juridico-Legislativa. Boletim.

338   BL   ISSN 0101-4315
HF6
CONFEDERACAO NACIONAL DO COMERCIO. CONSELHO TECNICO CONSULTIVO. CARTA MENSAL. 1955. m. free. Confederacao Nacional do Comercio, Ave. General Justo 307, 6 andar, 20221-130 Rio de Janeiro, Brazil. Ed. Paulo Godoy. illus. **Indexed:** P.A.I.S.For.Lang.Ind., P.A.I.S.
    Formerly: Confederacao Nacional do Comercio. Divisao de Divulgacao. Carta Mensal (ISSN 0588-9979)

381   SP
CONFEDERACION DE EMPRESARIOS DE CASTELLON. 12/yr. Escultor Viciano 1, 6o, 12002 Castellon de la Plana, Spain. TEL 64-22-62-12. circ. 50,000.

381.3   FR   ISSN 1016-538X
CONSUMER POLICY IN O E C D COUNTRIES. (Text in English) biennial. price varies. Organization for Economic Cooperation and Development, 2 rue Andre-Pascal, 75775 Paris Cedex 16, France. (U.S. orders to: O.E.C.D. Publications and Information Center, 2001 L St., N.W., Ste. 650, Washington, DC 20036-4922. TEL 202-785-6323) (also avail. in microfiche from OEC)
    Formerly: Annual Reports on Consumer Policy in O E C D Member Countries (ISSN 0376-8058)

CONSUMER PRICE INDEX OF BELIZE. see BUSINESS AND ECONOMICS — Abstracting, Bibliographies, Statistics

CONTACT; economie franco-allemande. see BUSINESS AND ECONOMICS — Chamber Of Commerce Publications

CORPORATE JOBS OUTLOOK! see OCCUPATIONS AND CAREERS

688.76   US   ISSN 0736-0703
HD9992.U5
COST OF DOING BUSINESS FOR RETAIL SPORTING GOODS STORES. 1968. biennial. $100. National Sporting Goods Association, 1699 Wall St., Mt. Prospect, IL 60056-5780. TEL 847-439-4000. FAX 847-439-0111. Ed. Thomas B. Doyle. **Indexed:** SRI.
    Description: Provides key performance ratios (profitability, productivity and financial management) as well as pro forma income statements and balance sheets for various types of sporting goods stores.

CRAIN'S CLEVELAND BUSINESS. see BUSINESS AND ECONOMICS — Economic Situation And Conditions

380   HO   ISSN 0011-2836
CULTURAL COMERCIAL.* 1959. m. L.500. Apdo. Postal 239, Tegucigalpa D.C., Honduras. adv.

658.8 381   US   ISSN 0363-8553
HF105
CURRENT BUSINESS REPORTS: MONTHLY WHOLESALE TRADE, SALES AND INVENTORIES. 1936. m. (plus a. supplement.) $16 (foreign $20). U.S. Bureau of the Census, Customer Services, Washington, DC 20233. TEL 301-457-4100. FAX 301-457-4714. URL: http://www.census.gov/. (Subscr. to: Superintendent of Documents, U.S. Government Printing Office, Box 371954, Pittsburgh, PA 15250-7954. TEL 202-512-1800. FAX 202-512-2250) (also avail. in microfiche from CIS; back issues avail.; reprint service avail. from CIS) **Indexed:** Amer.Stat.Ind. (1973-), PROMT. **Document type:** government publication.
• Also available online.
    Description: Compiles monthly wholesalers' sales and inventories, by type of business and geographic area.

381   US   ISSN 1055-7431
D B. (Diablo Business) 1989. 4/yr. Diablo Publications, 2520 Camino Diablo, Walnut Creek, CA 94596. TEL 510-943-1111. FAX 510-943-1045. Ed. Grant Opperman; Pub. Steven J. Rivera. circ. 20,000. **Document type:** consumer publication.
• Also available online. Vendor(s): Lexis-Nexis, UMI. —UMI.
    Description: Covers real estate, area economic trends, computer applications, telecommunications, banking, investments, health and fitness in the work place, and community issues.

338   US   ISSN 0896-8012
DAILY JOURNAL OF COMMERCE. 1872. d. $111. Box 10127, Portland, OR 97210. TEL 503-226-1311. circ. 3,850. (tabloid format; back issues avail.)

381   UK
THE DEALER. 1990. m. Maze Media Ltd., Castle House, 97 High St., Colchester, Essex C01 1TH, England. TEL 01206-795640. FAX 01206-795640. Ed. Ted Rowe. adv. (back issues avail.) **Document type:** consumer publication.
    Former titles: Trading Place; Trading Post.
    Description: Features trading information about the following items of interest: jewelry, watches, toys and fancy goods, electrical notions, clothing, plus business opportunities.

381   JA   ISSN 0385-7360
DIAMOND INDUSTRIA; Japan's economic journal. (Text in English) 1971. m. 9960 Yen($55) Diamond Lead Co. Ltd., 4-2 Kasumigaseki, 1-chome, Chiyoda-ku, Tokyo 100, Japan. TEL 03-504-6791. FAX 03-504-6798. TELEX J-26145 DLED. Ed. Natsuki Mori. circ. 47,000. (back issues avail.)
    Formerly: Diamond's Industria.
    Description: Devoted to business and economy and of interest to business people and investors. Includes articles on companies, their activities, industry trends and newly developed products.

DIRECTORY OF BUILDING PRODUCTS & HARDLINES DISTRIBUTORS. see BUSINESS AND ECONOMICS — Trade And Industrial Directories

381   IT
DISCIPLINA DEL COMMERCIO. 1981. 3/yr. L.78000 (foreign L.95000) (effective 1993). Franco Angeli Editore, Viale Monza 106, 20127 Milan, Italy. TEL 02-28-27-651. Ed. V. Macchitella.

DISCOVER HAWAII SALES PLANNER; the travel professional's guide to the island. see TRAVEL AND TOURISM

381   US   ISSN 1057-8684
KF390.B84
DOING BUSINESS IN THE UNITED STATES. 1980. irreg. Price Waterhouse, 1521 Ave. of the Americas, New York, NY 10020. TEL 212-819-5000.
—CISTI.

DOMESTIC WATERBORNE TRADE OF THE UNITED STATES. see TRANSPORTATION — Ships And Shipping

381 338   DR
DOMINICAN REPUBLIC. SECRETARIA DE ESTADO DE INDUSTRIA Y COMERCIO. REVISTA. 1948. 2/yr. Secretaria de Estado de Industria y Comercio, Santo Domingo, Dominican Republic. charts; stat.
    Former titles (until 1954): Dominican Republic. Secretaria de Estado de Trabajo, Economia y Comercio. Revista; (until 1952): Dominican Republic. Secretaria de Estado de Economia y Comercio. Revista; (until 1950): Dominican Republic. Secretaria de Estado de Economia Nacional. Revista.

381   UK
ECONOMIC BRIEFING. 1993. m. H M Treasury, Information Division, Parliament St., London SW1P 3AG, England. **Indexed:** Mgmt.& Market.Abstr. **Document type:** government publication.

ECUADOR. INSTITUTO NACIONAL DE ESTADISTICA Y CENSOS. ENCUESTA ANUAL DE COMERCIO INTERNO. see BUSINESS AND ECONOMICS — Abstracting, Bibliographies, Statistics

381   EC
ECUADOR. MINISTERIO DE INDUSTRIAS, COMERCIO E INTEGRACION. DOCUMENTO. 1975. a. Ministerio de Industrias, Comercio e Integracion, Quito, Ecuador.

381   EC
ECUADOR. MINISTERIO DE INDUSTRIAS, COMERCIO E INTEGRACION. INFORME A LA NACION. 1974. a. Ministerio de Industrias, Comercio e Integracion, Quito, Ecuador. illus.

381   CN   ISSN 0702-7435
EDMONTON COMMERCE AND INDUSTRY. 1974. m. Can.$5 (in US Can.$10; elsewhere Can.$12). Homershaw Advertising Agency, 214-11802 124th St., Edmonton, AB T5L OM3, Canada. TEL 403-454-5625. FAX 403-453-2553. Ed. Doug Homershaw. adv. contact: Colleen McCullough. illus. circ. 4,300. (tabloid format)
    Formerly (until 1976): Edmonton Commerce (ISSN 0702-7443)
    Description: Contains up-to-date reports on transportation, mining, construction and building developments, as well as articles and reports on local, regional and national economic, legislative and business trends.

ELECTRICAL MACHINERY: LATIN AMERICAN INDUSTRIAL REPORT. see ENGINEERING — Electrical Engineering

381 332   US
ENERGY IN THE NEWS. 1978. q. free. New York Mercantile Exchange, Corporate Communications Department, One North End Ave., World Financial Center, New York, NY 10282-1101. TEL 212-299-2777. FAX 212-301-4700. E-mail: marketing@nymex.com; URL: http://www.nymex.com. adv. contact: Karen Gleason. circ. 12,000 (controlled). **Document type:** trade publication.
    Description: Devoted to fundamental and technical energy market conditions, and futures and options trading strategies.
    Refereed Serial

380.1   TG
ENQUETE SUR LES ENTREPRISES INDUSTRIELLES ET COMMERCIALES DU TOGO. a. 5000 Fr.CFA. Direction de la Statistique, B.P. 118, Lome, Togo. stat.

381   AT   ISSN 0085-0268
ENTERPRISE (KENSINGTON).* 1963. a. free. University of New South Wales, Commerce Society, P.O. Box 1, Kensington, N.S.W. 2033, Australia.

381   JA
ENVIRONMENTAL BUSINESSES IN JAPAN: INDUSTRIAL & COMPANY NEWS (YEAR). 1990. w. 300000 Yen. Yano Research Institute Ltd., Pola Ebisu Bldg., 3-9-19 Higashi, Shibuya-ku, Tokyo 150, Japan. TEL 03-548-5461. FAX 03-548-5468.
    Description: Addresses problems and opportunities in environmental business: air pollution control, waste water treatment, waste management, recycling, and recent developments. Includes company index by product categories.

ETAGE; Chef-Informationen. see BUSINESS AND ECONOMICS

BUSINESS AND ECONOMICS — DOMESTIC COMMERCE

380   GW   ISSN 0931-5934
F F H MITTEILUNGEN. 1959. q. Forschungsstelle fuer den Handel Berlin e.V., Fehrbelliner Platz 3, 10707 Berlin, Germany. TEL 030-863094-0. FAX 030-86309444. Ed. Andrea Woelk. bk.rev.; abstr.; bibl.; index. **Document type:** bulletin.
—BLDSC (5842.190000). **CCC.**
    Formerly: F f H Mitteilungen (ISSN 0014-5831)

381   UK
FACT SHEET SERIES. s-a. £25 per no. Oxford Institute of Retail Management, Templeton College, Kennington, Oxford OX1 5NY, England. TEL 01865-735422. FAX 01865-736374. **Document type:** bulletin.

FINANCE AND COMMERCE. see *BUSINESS AND ECONOMICS — Banking And Finance*

381 658   US   ISSN 0547-8804
HF5465.U4
FINANCIAL AND OPERATING RESULTS OF DEPARTMENT AND SPECIALTY STORES. a. $100 to non-members; members $80. (National Retail Federation) John Wiley & Sons, Inc., 605 Third Ave., New York, NY 10158-0012. TEL 800-879-4539. **Indexed:** SRI.
    Description: Survey report provides expense ratios by expense center and natural divisions for department and specialty stores by volume groups. Reports profit and financial ratios, key merchandising and productivity data.

614.84 330   US   ISSN 8755-4372
FIREWORKS BUSINESS. 1983. m. $29.95 (foreign $38) (effective 1997). HC67, Box 30, Dingmans Ferry, PA 18328. TEL 717-828-8417. FAX 717-828-8695. E-mail: amerfwknws@aol.com. Ed. John M. Drewes. adv. contact: John M. Drewes. bk.rev.; circ. 500 (paid). **Document type:** newsletter.
    Description: Covers materials for the fireworks trade and fireworks enthusiasts.

381   US   ISSN 0886-2729
FLORIDA MARKET UPDATE; a newsletter and briefing service for executives with an interest in Florida. m. $100 (foreign $135). Mentor Communications, Box 290, Manhasset, NY 11030. TEL 516-741-8877. FAX 516-741-3131. Ed. Hank Boerner; Pub. Hank Boerner. **Document type:** newsletter.

FOCUS: AN ECONOMIC PROFILE OF THE APPAREL INDUSTRY. see *CLOTHING TRADE*

380   US   ISSN 0015-8097
K6
FORT WORTH COMMERCIAL RECORDER. 1903. d. (Mon.-Fri.). $150. Recorder Publishing Co., Box 11038, Ft. Worth, TX 76110. TEL 817-926-5351. FAX 817-926-5377. Ed. Genevieve Ratcliff. adv.; bk.rev.; circ. 600 (paid). **Document type:** newspaper.

380   II   ISSN 0015-864X
FORWARD MARKETS BULLETIN. (Text in English) 1959. q. Rs.20($4.70) Forward Markets Commission, Government of India, 100 Marine Drive, Bombay, India. Ed. Smt. R. M. Pavaskar. adv.; charts; stat.; index.

381   FR   ISSN 0220-9896
KJV5595.A15
FRANCE. REVUE DE LA CONCURRENCE ET DE LA CONSOMMATION. 6/yr. 360 F. (Europe 370 F., elsewhere 400 F.) (effective 1997). (Ministere de l'Economie, Direction Generale de la Concurrence, de la Consommation et de la Repression des Fraudes) Documentation Francaise, 29-31 quai Voltaire, 75344 Paris Cedex 07, France.
TEL 33-1-40157000. FAX 33-1-40157230. TELEX 215 666 DOCFRAN. (Subscr. to: 124 rue Henri Barbusse, 93308 Aubervilliers Cedex, France. TEL 33-1-48395600. FAX 33-1-48395601) (also avail. in microfiche from DFR; back issues avail.) **Indexed:** ELLIS. **Document type:** government publication.

FRANCE. SERVICE D'ETUDE DES STRATEGIES ET DES STATISTIQUES INDUSTRIELLES. L'IMPLANTATION ETRANGERE DANS L'INDUSTRIE. see *BUSINESS AND ECONOMICS — Abstracting, Bibliographies, Statistics*

381.41   SA
FRESH PRODUCE MARKET, JOHANNESBURG. REPORT OF THE DIRECTOR. (Report year ends June 30) 1913. irreg. Fresh Produce Market, P.O. Box 86007, City Deep 2049, South Africa. TEL 27-11-6132049. FAX 27-11-6135346. Dir. Daan Spengler. circ. 350. (processed)
    Supersedes: National Fresh Produce Market, Johannesburg. Annual Report of the Director.

330   US   ISSN 1045-4055
GRAND RAPIDS BUSINESS JOURNAL. 1983. w. $49. Gemini Publications, 549 Ottawa Ave. N.W., Grand Rapids, MI 49503-1444. TEL 616-459-4545. FAX 616-459-4800. Ed. Carole Valade. adv. contact: Randy Prichard. illus.; pat.; stat. circ. 7,000. (tabloid format) **Document type:** newspaper.
●Also available online. Vendor(s): Knight-Ridder Information, Inc., UMI.
—UMI. **CCC.**

380   US   ISSN 0274-5496
HC108.W3
GREATER WASHINGTON BOARD OF TRADE NEWS; a regional Chamber of Commerce for the District of Columbia, Northern Virginia and suburban Maryland. 1946. bi-m. $120. Greater Washington Board of Trade, 1129 20th St., N.W., Washington, DC 20036. TEL 202-857-5900. FAX 202-223-2648. Ed. Sandra Rubenstein. adv.: B&W page $1650; trim 10 1/2 x 15; adv. contact: Suzanne Trump. illus.; circ. 5,875 (controlled). (tabloid format)
    Formerly: Metropolitan Washington Board of Trade News (ISSN 0026-1599)
    Description: News, articles, features, editorials, and announcements pertaining to the members and activities of the Board, representing the interaction between and the integration of business and the community in the District of Columbia, Northern Virginia, and suburban Maryland.

381   UK   ISSN 0260-6526
GROCERY STORES DIRECTORIES. (Set of 4 vols.) 1980. a. £125 to non-members per vol.; members £95. Institute of Grocery Distribution, Business Publications, Letchmore Heath, Watford, Herts. WD2 8DQ, England. TEL 44-1923-857141. FAX 44-1923-852531. **Document type:** directory.
    Formerly: Large Stores Directory.

381.416 630   DK   ISSN 0106-6382
GROVVARELEDEREN. 1973. s-m. DKK 285. Viborgvej 128, Postboks 1267, DK-8210 Aarhus V, Denmark. FAX 86-151248. TELEX 64595-LAGDK. Ed. Joergen Lund Christiansen. adv.; bk.rev. circ. 2,200.

381   US
GUIDE TO LEADING TWIN CITIES COMPANIES. 1949. bi-m. $10. Prime Publications Inc., 318 Groveland Ave., Minneapolis, MN 55403. TEL 612-377-9200. Ed. Merrill J. Busch. adv.; bk.rev. circ. 6,000.
    Formerly: Greater Minneapolis (ISSN 0434-5975)

GUIDE TO SPRINGFIELD; an encyclopedia of facts and figures on the queen city of the Ozarks. see *GEOGRAPHY*

381   MX   ISSN 0533-5469
GUIDE TO THE MEXICAN MARKETS.* 1959. a. $53. Publicaciones Marynka, S.A., Salaverry 1204, Col. Zacatenco, 07360 Mexico D.F., Mexico.

380   GW   ISSN 0936-9856
H V - JOURNAL. 1949. s-m. DM.205.80 (effective 1997). (Zentralvereinigung Deutscher Handelsvertreter- und Handelsmaklerverbaende e.V.) Siegel Verlag Otto Mueller GmbH, Postfach 101937, 60019 Frankfurt a.M., Germany. TEL 49-69-759506. FAX 49-69-75952850. Ed. Dr. Paffhausen. adv.: page DM.5000; adv. contact: Peter Holzberger. bk.rev. circ. 23,000. **Document type:** bulletin.
    Formerly: Handelsvertreter und Handelsmakler (ISSN 0046-6808)

338   GW   ISSN 0017-7229
DER HANDEL; das Wirtschaftsmagazin fuer Handelsmanagement. 1951. m. DM.69 (E.U: DM.75.22; elsewhere DM.70.30) (effective 1997). Deutscher Fachverlag GmbH, Mainzer Landstr. 251, 60326 Frankfurt a.M., Germany.
TEL 49-69-7595-1832. FAX 49-69-7595-1830. Ed. Uwe Rosmanith. adv.: B&W page DM.15580, color page DM.24075; trim 179 x 243; adv. contact: Manfred Moeller. bk.rev.; illus. circ. 119,000. **Indexed:** Key to Econ.Sci. **Document type:** trade publication.
    Incorporates (in 1991): D F Z Wirtschaftsmagazin (ISSN 0341-549X); Which was formerly (1971-1976): D F Z Magazin (ISSN 0342-3727)
    Description: Business magazine for management in trade and commerce in Germany. Features retail stores, department stores, display of goods, office and communications technology, transportation, finances, personnel management, and current trends.

381   PL   ISSN 0438-5403
HF37.P6
HANDEL WEWNETRZNY. vol.20, 1974. bi-m. Wydawnictwo A.Z., Ul. Gwiazdzista 13-145, 01-651 Warsaw, Poland. Ed. M. Struzycki. bk.rev.; bibl. **Indexed:** AgroLibrex.
—BLDSC (4254.800000).

380   GW   ISSN 0017-7296
HANDELSBLATT; Deutschlands Wirtschafts- und Finanzzeitung. 1946. d. (Mon.-Fri.). DM.819. Verlagsgruppe Handelsblatt GmbH, Kasernenstr. 67, 40213 Duesseldorf, Germany. TEL 49-211-8870. FAX 49-211-329954. (Subscr. to: Postfach 102741, 40018 Duesseldorf, Germany) Ed.Bd. adv. contact: Hartmut Brendt. circ. 134,000. (also avail. in microfilm from NRP, ALP; reprint service avail. from UMI) **Indexed:** INIS Atomind., Key to Econ.Sci., PROMT. **Document type:** newspaper.
●Also available online.
—CCC.
    Incorporated: Industriekurier.

HANDELSNYTT. see *LABOR UNIONS*

381   CC
HEBEI SHANGYE YANJIU/HEBEI COMMERCE. (Text in Chinese) m. Hebei Sheng Shangye Zhuanke Xuexiao, 6, Huaibei Zhonglu, Shijiazhuang, Hebei 050011, People's Republic of China. TEL 612601. Ed. Zhong Xing.

381   CC   ISSN 1001-6066
HEILONGJIANG SHANGXUEYUAN XUEBAO/HEILONGJIANG INSTITUTE OF COMMERCE. JOURNAL. (Text in Chinese) bi-m. Heilongjiang Shangxueyuan, 50, Tongda Jie, Daoli-qu, Harbin, Heilongjiang 150076, People's Republic of China. TEL 405571. Ed. Li Liangjun.

381   LS
HENG NGAN. (Text in Lao) fortn. Lao Federation of Trade Unions, 87 ave. Lane Xang, BP 780, Vientiane, Laos. TEL 4151. Ed. Bouapheng Bounsoulinh.

381   CC
HONG KONG INDUSTRIALIST. (Text in Chinese, English) 1962. m. HK.$400($90) Federation of Hong Kong Industries, 4-F, Hankow Centre, 5-15 Hankow Rd., Tsimshatsui, Kowloon, Hong Kong, People's Republic of China. TEL 852-2732-3188.
FAX 852-2721-3494. TELEX 30101 FHKI HX. E-mail: fhki@fhki.org.hk. Ed. Sally Hopkins. adv.: B&W page HK.$7920, color page HK.$10900; trim 210 x 285. stat. circ. 35,000. **Document type:** trade publication.
    Formerly: Industrial News.
    Description: Covers investment and trade trends, economic and industrial policies, and company profiles.

381   CN   ISSN 0822-6482
HJ7662
HOW OTTAWA SPENDS. a. Can.$27.95 (effective 1997). Carleton University Press, Suite 1400, CTTC Bldg., Carleton University, 1125 Colonel By Drive, Ottawa, ON K1S 5B6, Canada. TEL 613-520-7554. FAX 613-520-2893. E-mail: jsloan@ccs.carleton.ca; URL: http://www.carleton.ca/cupress. Ed. Gene Swimmer.
    Description: Analyses 11 areas of government policy, including economic management, national unity, social policies and ethics.

BUSINESS AND ECONOMICS — DOMESTIC COMMERCE

381   IS
I B T. (Israel Business Today) (Text in English) 1986. bi-w. IS.756.70($249) International Business Communications (IBC) Ltd., P.O. Box 145, Tel Aviv 61001, Israel. TEL 972-3-6397194. FAX 972-3-6397195. Ed. Barry Davis; Pub. Ralph Kronenthal. R&P contact: Ralph Kronenthal. adv.: B&W page $1900, color page $2750; trim 245 x 178; adv. contact: Zehava Stepak. **Document type:** newsletter.
● Also available online. Vendor(s): Information Access Co., NewsNet (IT92).
Formerly: I C E N - Israel Commercial Economic Newsletter (ISSN 0792-3465)

381   KE
I C D C NEWS. (Text in English) 1975. 3/yr. Industrial and Commercial Development Corporation, P.O. Box 45519, Nairobi, Kenya.

381   GW   ISSN 0939-9909
I K; Zeitschrift fuer Industriekaufleute. m. DM.89 (foreign DM.98) (effective 1997). Betriebswirtschaftlicher Verlag Dr. Th. Gabler GmbH, Abraham-Lincoln-Str. 46, 65189 Wiesbaden, Germany. TEL 49-611-7878129. FAX 49-611-7878423. **Document type:** trade publication.
—SWETS. **CCC.**
Formerly: Industriekaufmann (ISSN 0173-6612)

381   SP
IBILTZEN. 1990. 3/yr. free. Euskal Comunicacion, S.A., Burgos 8, Trasera (Ionja), 48014 Bilbao, Spain. TEL 4-447-84-14. FAX 4-476-11-87. Ed. Javier Bustamante. circ. 21,000.

381   SP
IMAGEN VASCA ONLINE. m. Codeco, Comercial de Comunicaciones, S.L., Trasera de Burgos 8, 48014 Bilbao, Spain. FAX 34-4-4761187. E-mail: imagenvasca@codeconet.com; URL: http://www.codeconet.com/imagenvasca. Ed. Javier Bustamante. adv. contact: Rafael Vallejo. **Document type:** newspaper.
● Available only online.
Formerly: Magazine de los Negocios - Imagen Vasca.

381   IT
IMPRESA ITALIA. 1975. m. L.19500. (Confederazione Generale Italiana del Commercio e Turismo) Editore Commercio e Turismo, Via Ippolito Nievo 61, 00153 Rome, Italy. TEL 39-6-5899273. FAX 39-6-5896501. Ed. Francesco Colucci. adv. contact: Roberto Perugini. bk.rev. circ. 470,000. **Document type:** trade publication.
Formerly (until Apr. 1993): Giornale del Commercio e Turismo.

381   US   ISSN 0192-7450
IN BUSINESS (MADISON); Dane county's business magazine. 1978. m. $18. Magna Publications, Inc., 2718 Dryden Dr., Madison, WI 53704. TEL 608-246-3580. FAX 608-249-0355. E-mail: editor@magnapub.com; URL: http://www.magnapub.com. Pub. Richard Perkins. charts; illus.; stat. circ. 15,000. (back issues avail.) **Document type:** consumer publication.
Description: Dane county's source for business news targeting business decision makers.

381   II
INDEX OF WHOLESALE PRICES IN INDIA. (Text in English) m. Rs.1200($139.92) Ministry of Urban Development, Department of Publications, Civil Lines, New Delhi 110 054, India. TEL 11-2512527. **Document type:** government publication.

381   II
INDIAN INDUSTRY REVIEW. (Text in English) 1993. a. Rs.250($55) Technical Press Publications, Eucharistic Congress Bldg., No.1, 5-1 Convent St., Colaba, Mumbai 400 039, India. TEL 91-22-2021446. FAX 91-22-287-1499. TELEX 011-83479 CHEM IN. Ed. J.P. de Sousa. adv.; abstr.; charts; illus. circ. 12,000. (also avail. in microfilm from UMI; reprint service avail. from UMI) **Document type:** trade publication.

380   II   ISSN 0019-512X
HF41
INDIAN JOURNAL OF COMMERCE. (Text in English) 1960. q. Rs.33($8.) Indian Commerce Association, B.Y.K. College of Commerce, Nasik 5, Maharashtra, India. Ed. M.S. Gosavi. adv.; bk.rev.

380   II   ISSN 0019-5901
INDIAN MERCHANTS' CHAMBER. JOURNAL. (Text in English) 1907. bi-m. Rs.60($15) Indian Merchants' Chamber, Indian Merchants' Chamber Bldg., 76 Veer Nariman Rd., Churchgate, Bombay 400020, India. Ed. Shri Ramu Pandit. adv.; bk.rev.; illus. circ. 3,000.

380   II   ISSN 0019-6444
INDIAN TRADE JOURNAL. (Supplements avail.) (Text in English, Hindi) 1906. w. (except Jun.). Rs.600($216) Government of India, Department of Publications, Civil Lines, New Delhi 110 054, India. TEL 28-3111. TELEX DGCS IN 21-7902. adv.; bibl.; mkt.; stat.; index. circ. 2,322. **Indexed:** Chem.Abstr.

330   US   ISSN 0274-4929
INDIANAPOLIS BUSINESS JOURNAL. 1980. w. $64. I B J Corp., 431 N. Pennsylvania, Indianapolis, IN 46204-1806. TEL 317-634-6200. FAX 317-263-5060. Ed. Tom Harton. adv.; stat. circ. 15,500. (tabloid format; back issues avail.) **Indexed:** Tr.& Indus.Ind. **Document type:** bulletin.
● Also available online. Vendor(s): Information Access Co., UMI.
—UMI.

381   MX   ISSN 0188-4603
INDUSTRIA. 1955. m. $30. Confederacion de Camaras Industriales de los Estados Unidos Mexicanos, Manuel Ma. Contreras No. 133, 1er piso, Col. Cuauhtemoc, Del. Cuauhtemoc, 06597 Mexico D.F., Mexico. TEL 592-0529. FAX 535-6871. TELEX 1772789 CCINMEX. Dir. Andres Senosiain Ruiloba. adv.; bk.rev. circ. 25,000.
Formerly (until June 1988): ConCamIn.

381   KE
INDUSTRIAL AND COMMERCIAL DEVELOPMENT CORPORATION. ANNUAL REPORT AND ACCOUNTS. (Text in English) a. Industrial and Commercial Development Corporation, P.O. Box 45519, Nairobi, Kenya. **Document type:** corporate report.

381   JA
INDUSTRIAL GROUPINGS IN JAPAN; the anatomy of the Keiretsu. (Text in English) 1973. biennial. $800. Dodwell Marketing Consultants, Kowa no. 35 Bldg., 14-14 Akasaka 1-chome, Minato-ku, Tokyo 107, Japan. TEL 03-3589-0207. FAX 03-5570-7132. TELEX J22274 DODWELL J. index. circ. 1,000.
Description: Covers the 3,500 leading Japanese companies in 28 major industries. Provides information on annual sales, sales rankings, capital, major shareholders, and outstanding loans for 700 group companies. Classified by industry and conglomerates.

381 941.7   IE   ISSN 0791-8259
INDUSTRY & COMMERCE. 1980. m. I£25. Jude Publications Ltd., Jude House, Tara St., Dublin 2, Ireland. TEL 01-6713500. FAX 01-6713074. Ed. Kate Tammemagi. illus. **Document type:** bulletin.

381   SP
INFORMACION. 12/yr. Alda. Recalde 50, 48008 Bilbao, Spain. TEL 4-444-40-54. FAX 4-443-61-71. TELEX 32783 CCINB. Ed. Juan Carlos Landeta.

380   SP   ISSN 0213-3768
INFORMACION COMERCIAL ESPANOLA. BOLETIN ECONOMICO. 1940. w. (45/yr.). 12000 ptas. (foreign 16500 ptas.) (effective 1994). Ministerio de Industria, Comercio y Turismo, Paseo de Castellana 162, Planta 16, 28071 Madrid, Spain. TEL 34-1-349-36-47. FAX 34-1-349-36-34. Dir. Maria Eugenia Caumel. adv. circ. 6,000. **Indexed:** ELLIS, Key to Econ.Sci.
—CINDOC.
Formerly: Informacion Comercial Espanola. Boletin Semanal (ISSN 0019-9761)

380   SP
INFORMACION COMERCIAL ESPANOLA. REVISTA DE ECONOMIA. 1898. m. (11/yr.). 9000 ptas. (foreign 14000 ptas.) (effective 1995). Ministerio de Industria, Comercio y Turismo, P. Castellana 162, Planta 16, 28046 Madrid, Spain. TEL 34-1-349-36-47. FAX 34-1-349-36-34. adv.; bk.rev. circ. 8,900. **Indexed:** ELLIS, IBR, SCIMP (1989-).
—BLDSC (4478.945000); CINDOC; SWETS.
Formerly: Informacion Comercial Espanola. Revista Mensual (ISSN 0019-977X)

381   IT
INFORMATORE COMMERCIO TURISMO SERVIZI. 11/yr. Corso Venezia 47-49, 20121 Milan, Italy. TEL 2-77-50. Ed. Francesco Colucci. circ. 31,000.

381   UK
INSTITUTE OF LOGISTICS. MEMBERS' DIRECTORY. 1994. a. Institute of Logistics, Douglas House, Queen's Sq., Corby, Northants NN17 1PL, England. TEL 44-1536-205500. FAX 44-1536-400979. Ed. Gerald Fisher. adv. contact: Christine Guy.
Formerly (until 1995): Institute of Logistics. Yearbook (ISSN 1353-0267)

381   CN   ISSN 0575-8823
HD2807
INTER-CORPORATE OWNERSHIP/LIENS DE PARENTE ENTRE SOCIETES. 1975. biennial. Can.$350($420) (foreign $490) (CD-ROM Can.$3000) (effective 1998). Statistics Canada, Operations and Integration Division, Circulation Management, Jean Talon Bldg., 2-C12, Tunney's Pasture, Ottawa, ON K1A 0T6, Canada. TEL 613-951-7277; 800-267-6677. FAX 613-951-1584. URL: http://www.statcan.ca. (also avail. in microform from MML) **Document type:** government publication.
● Also available online. Vendor(s): Southam Electronic Publishing.
Also available on CD-ROM.
—CISTI.
Description: Information about Canadian corporations and subsidiaries, including foreign-controlled corporations in Canada.

381   IR   ISSN 0074-1213
INTERNAL TRADE OF IRAN. (Text in English and Persian) 1965. a. free. Ministry of Finance and Economic Affairs, Bureau of Statistics, Tehran, Iran. **Document type:** government publication.

381   US   ISSN 8750-6645
IOWA COMMERCE. 1984. m. $15 to non-members; free to members of ABI. Heartland Communications Group, 1003 Central Ave., Fort Dodge, IA 50501. TEL 515-955-1600; 800-247-2000. FAX 800-247-2000. Ed. Jeanne Lightly; Pub. Ann M. Foster. adv. contact: Ann Wahl. stat. circ. 10,000. (back issues avail.)
—UnCover.
Description: Business and industry news.

ITALY. ISTITUTO NAZIONALE DI STATISTICA. STATISTICHE DEL COMMERCIO INTERNO. see BUSINESS AND ECONOMICS — Abstracting, Bibliographies, Statistics

JORDAN'S REGIONAL DIRECTORIES OF KEY BUSINESS PROSPECTS - YORKSHIRE AND HUMBERSIDE (YEAR). see BUSINESS AND ECONOMICS — Trade And Industrial Directories

381   HT
JOURNAL DE COMMERCE. w. 49 rue Traversiere, B.P. 1569, Port-au-Prince, Haiti. TEL 1-7-3008. Ed. Gerard Allen. circ. 4,000.

380   CN   ISSN 0021-9819
JOURNAL OF COMMERCE. 1911. s-w. Can.$508 (effective 1997). Journal of Commerce Ltd., (Subsidiary of: Southam Information & Technology Group), 4285 Canada Way, Burnaby, BC V5G 1H2, Canada. TEL 604-433-8164. FAX 604-433-9549. Ed. Frank Lillquist; Pub. Brian Martin. adv. contact: Dan Gnocato. charts; illus. circ. 4,709. (tabloid format) **Indexed:** Bus.Ind., Can.B.P.I., Tr.& Indus.Ind. **Document type:** trade publication.

381 382   US   ISSN 0361-5561
CODEN: JCOCBM
JOURNAL OF COMMERCE AND COMMERCIAL. 1827. d. $365 (effective 1997). Journal of Commerce, Inc. (Subsidiary of: Economist Group), 2 World Trade Center, 27th Fl., New York, NY 10048-0203. TEL 212-837-7000. FAX 212-837-7130. (Subscr. to: 445 Marshall St., Phillipsburg, NJ 08865. TEL 800-222-0356) Ed. Donald D. Holt. adv.; charts; mkt.; circ. 22,000. (paid). (also avail. in microfilm from KTO) **Indexed:** Chem.Abstr., Hlth.Ind., Key to Econ.Sci., P.A.I.S., PROMT, Tr.& Indus.Ind. **Document type:** newspaper.
● Also available online. Vendor(s): Knight-Ridder Information, Inc., Lexis-Nexis, MediaStream.
—CASDDS. **CCC.**
Formerly: Journal of Commerce (ISSN 0021-9827)

BUSINESS AND ECONOMICS — DOMESTIC COMMERCE

380 338   LB   ISSN 0303-9293
HC591.L6
JOURNAL OF COMMERCE, INDUSTRY & TRANSPORTATION.* 1967. q. $6. Ministry of Commerce, Industry and Transportation, Box 9041, Monrovia, Liberia. (Also avail. from: African Development, Wheatsheaf House, Carmelite St., London EC4Y 0AX, England) Eds. William E. Dennis Jr., Richard M. Morris. adv.; charts; illus.; stat. circ. 7,000.
Formerly: Journal of Commerce and Industry (ISSN 0021-9843)

JOURNAL OF PHILIPPINE DEVELOPMENT. see *BUSINESS AND ECONOMICS — Public Finance, Taxation*

381   KE
K I R D I ANNUAL REPORT AND STATEMENT OF ACCOUNTS. 1982. a. Kenya Industrial Research and Development Institute, P.O. Box 30650, Nairobi, Kenya. circ. 1,000.

381   NR
KANO (STATE). MARKET CALENDAR. 1980. a. free. Budget & Economic Planning Directorate, Ministry of Finance, Audu Bako Secretariat, P.M.B. 3291, Kano, Nigeria. **Document type:** government publication, consumer publication.

THE KANSAS DIRECTORY OF COMMERCE. see *BUSINESS AND ECONOMICS — Trade And Industrial Directories*

381   GW   ISSN 0022-9474
KAUFHAUS UND WARENHAUS. 1966. q. DM.48($20) Zeitungs- und Zeitschriftenverlag Heinrichs, Brueggekamp 1, 30890 Barsinghausen, Germany. TEL 49-5105-2289. Ed. G. Heinrichs; Pub. G. Heinrichs. adv.; bk.rev.; charts; stat.; tr.lit. circ. 3,100. (tabloid format) **Document type:** trade publication.

381   US   ISSN 0279-5388
KENTUCKY JOURNAL OF COMMERCE AND INDUSTRY. 1939. fortn. $5. Associated Industries of Kentucky, 2303 Greene Way, Louisville, KY 40220-4009. TEL 502-491-4737. FAX 502-491-5322. E-mail: aik@mis.net. Ed. Larry A. Maggard. R&P contact: Larry A. Maggard. adv. contact: Larry A. Maggard. circ. 6,100 (paid). (tabloid format; back issues avail.) **Document type:** trade publication.
Description: Covers topics of interest to the business and industry community in Kentucky.

381   KE   ISSN 0304-7202
HF3899.K42
KENYA NATIONAL TRADING CORPORATION. ANNUAL REPORT. (Title varies slightly) (Text in English) a. Kenya National Trading Corporation Ltd., P.O. Box 30587, Nairobi, Kenya.

381   UK
KEY NOTE MARKET REPORT: MIXED RETAIL BUSINESSES. Variant title: Mixed Retail Businesses. irreg., no.6, 1990. £205. Key Note Ltd., Field House, 72 Oldfield Rd., Hampton, Middlesex TW12 2HQ, England. TEL 44-181-783-0755. FAX 44-181-783-0049. **Document type:** trade publication.

381   UK
KEY NOTE MARKET REPORT: NEW TRENDS IN RETAILING. Variant title: New Trends in Retailing. irreg., no.2, 1990. £185. Key Note Ltd., Field House, 72 Oldfield Rd., Hampton, Middlesex TW12 2HQ, England. TEL 44-181-783-0755. FAX 44-181-783-1940. **Document type:** trade publication.

658.87   SW   ISSN 1103-3142
KOEPMANNEN VAEST. 1941. 7/yr. SEK 100 (effective 1993). Koepmannfoerbunden i Goeteborg och Vaestergoetland, P.O. Box 53200, S-400 15 Goeteborg, Sweden.
Formerly (until 1992): Goeteborgskoepmannen.

380   YU   ISSN 0350-1019
KOMERCIJALIST; Jugoslovenski strucno informativni casopis za unapredjenje komercijalnog poslovanja. 1940. bi-m. 800 din. Udruzenje Komercijalista Jugoslavije, Zmaja od Nocaja 9, Belgrade, Yugoslavia. Ed. M. Krstovic.

381   GW
L G A NACHRICHTEN.* bi-m. Landesverband des Bayerischen Gross- und Aussenhandels, Max-Joseph-Str. 4, 8000 Munich, Germany.

381   GW   ISSN 0938-958X
LANDESVERBAND DES WESTFALISCH - LIPPISCHEN EINZELHANDELS. EINZELHANDELS - REPORT. m. Landesverband des Westfalisch - Lippischen Einzelhandels, Eisenbahnstr. 7, 48143 Muenster, Germany. TEL 43886-87.

LATIN AMERICAN METAL MECHANIC & ELECTRONIC INDUSTRY DIRECTORY. see *MACHINERY*

381   UK
LIVERPOOL COTTON ASSOCIATION. RAW COTTON REPORT AND VALUE DIFFERENCES FOR SHIPMENT CIRCULAR. fortn. £41 to non-members; members £30. Liverpool Cotton Association Ltd., 620 Cotton Exchange Bldgs., Liverpool L3 9LH, England. TEL 051-2366041. FAX 051-255-0174. TELEX 627849. circ. 300.
Formed by the merger of: Liverpool Cotton Association. Weekly Raw Cotton Report & Liverpool Cotton Association. Weekly Value Differences Circular.

LOCAL ECONOMIC DEVELOPMENT INFORMATION SERVICE. see *SOCIAL SERVICES AND WELFARE*

381   UK   ISSN 1350-6293
HF5415.7
LOGISTICS FOCUS. m. free to members. Institute of Logistics, Douglas House, Queen's Sq., Corby, Northants. NN17 1PL, England. TEL 44-1536-205500. FAX 44-1536-400979. Ed. Gerald Fisher. adv. contact: Christine J. Guy. bk.rev.; circ. 13,000 (controlled). **Indexed:** Mgmt.& Market.Abstr. **Document type:** academic/scholarly publication.
—BLDSC (5292.315700); AskIEEE; KR SourceOne.
Formed by the 1993 merger of (1982-1993): Logistics Today (ISSN 0262-4354); (1987-1993): Focus on Physical Distribution and Logistics Management (ISSN 0952-2190); Which was formerly: Focus on Logistics and Distribution Management.
Description: Explores the role of logistics in world trade.

381   BL
LOJAS & LOJISTAS. m. Sindicato dos Lojistas do Comercio de Sao Paulo, Rua Xavier de Toledo, 99-2 andar, Sao Paulo, Brazil. illus.

M D - MARKETING DIGEST; Fachbereichszeitschrift der Fachhochschule fuer Wirtschaft, Pforzheim. see *BUSINESS AND ECONOMICS — Marketing And Purchasing*

380   NZ
M.G. BUSINESS. (Mercantile Gazette) 1876. fortn. NZ.$144. Mercantile Gazette Marketing, P.O. Box 20-034, Christchurch 5, New Zealand. FAX 64-3-3584490. adv.; charts; stat. circ. 22,000. (tabloid format) **Document type:** newspaper.
Former titles: New Zealand Mercantile Gazette (ISSN 0111-3321); Mercantile Gazette of New Zealand (ISSN 0025-9799)

381   US
M M A C MILWAUKEE COMMERCE HOT-LINE ANNUAL REPORT. a. free to members. Metropolitan Milwaukee Association of Commerce, Council of Small Business Executives, 756 N. Milwaukee St., Milwaukee, WI 53202. TEL 414-287-4100.
Description: Provides yearly review of the MMAC's activities and accomplishments.

381   HU
M T I ECONEWS. (Text in English) 1988. d. (5/w.). $840 in Europe; elsewhere $1560 (effective 1998). Magyar Tavirati Iroda, Eco - Hungarian News Agency, Economic and Business News and Information Service Ltd., Pl. Naphegy ter. 8, 1016 Budapest, Hungary. TEL 36-1-1188204. FAX 36-1-2613690. TELEX 061-22-4372. E-mail: mtieco@datanet.hu. Ed. Adam Danko. R&P contact: Emese Gyuracz. adv. contact: Krisztina Segesdi. circ. 500. **Document type:** bulletin.
●Also available online.
Description: Covers the Hungarian economy, companies, banking and finance, economic trends and government economic and financial policy.

MACAO. DIRECCAO DOS SERVICOS DE ESTATISTICA E CENSOS. C A M CLASSIFICACAO DAS ACTIVIDADES ECONOMICAS DE MACAU/MACAO. CENSUS AND STATISTICS DEPARTMENT. C A M CLASSIFICATION OF ECONOMIC ACTIVITIES OF MACAO. see *BUSINESS AND ECONOMICS — Abstracting, Bibliographies, Statistics*

MACAO. DIRECCAO DOS SERVICOS DE ESTATISTICA E CENSOS. INDICE DE PRECOS NO CONSUMIDOR/MACAO. CENSUS AND STATISTICS DEPARTMENT. CONSUMER PRICE INDEX. see *BUSINESS AND ECONOMICS — Abstracting, Bibliographies, Statistics*

MACAO. DIRECCAO DOS SERVICOS DE ESTATISTICA E CENSOS. INDICE DE PRECOS NO CONSUMIDOR (RELATORIO ANUAL)/MACAO. CENSUS AND STATISTICS DEPARTMENT. CONSUMER PRICE INDEX (ANNUAL REPORT). see *BUSINESS AND ECONOMICS — Abstracting, Bibliographies, Statistics*

MACAO. DIRECCAO DOS SERVICOS DE ESTATISTICA E CENSOS. METODOLOGIA DO INDICE DE PRECOS NO CONSUMIDOR/MACAO. CENSUS AND STATISTICS DEPARTMENT. CONSUMER PRICE INDEX METHODOLOGY. see *BUSINESS AND ECONOMICS — Abstracting, Bibliographies, Statistics*

381   IT
MADE IN VARESE. 6/yr. Viale Milano 5, 21100 Varese, Italy. TEL 332-25-61-11. FAX 332-25-62-00. TELEX 316893 ASARVA I. Ed. Vito Artioli. circ. 5,000.

381   MY
MALAYSIA. DEPARTMENT OF INLAND REVENUE. ANNUAL REPORT/MALAYSIA. JABATAN HASIL DALAM NEGERI. LAPURAN TAHUNAN. (Text in Malay) 1972. a. Department of Inland Revenue, Kuala Lumpur, Malaysia.

MANAGEMENT CONSULTANCY - FINANCIAL SURVEY (YEAR). see *BUSINESS AND ECONOMICS — Trade And Industrial Directories*

381 331 658.3   GW
MANNESMANN ILLUSTRIERTE. 1970. m. Mannesmann AG, Mannesmannufer 2, D-4000 Duesseldorf, Germany. (Subscr. to: Redaktion Mannesmann-Illustrierte, Postfach 5501, D-4000 Duesseldorf, Germany) Ed. Herbert Sommer. circ. 100,000.

380   UK   ISSN 0025-2522
THE MANUFACTURERS' AGENT. 1908. bi-m. £26 (foreign £30). Manufacturers Agents Association, Somers House, 1 Somers Rd., Reigate, Surrey RH2 9DU, England. TEL 44-1737-241025. FAX 44-1737-224537. Ed. A.P. Lindsey-Renton. adv.: B&W page £190; trim 250 x 180. circ. 800. **Document type:** bulletin.

381   MX
MARYNKA: MERCADOS DE MEXICO EN ACCION. 1971. a. Publicaciones Marynka, S.A., Salaverry 1204, Col. Zacatenco, 07360 Mexico D.F., Mexico. TEL 574-13-81. circ. 5,000.

381   FR
MERCURE 10. 6/yr. 50 F. Chambre Regionale de Commerce et d'Industrie Champagne - Ardenne, Direction de la Communication, 10 rue de Chastillon, B.P. 537, France. TEL 33-3-26693340. FAX 33-3-26693369.

381   IS
MICHERON SHERUTIM FINANCIM UMISCHARIIM. (Text in Hebrew) q. Cheshev Ltd., P.O. Box 40021, Tel Aviv 61 400, Israel. TEL (03)216291.

381   US   ISSN 0746-6706
MILWAUKEE COMMERCE HOT-LINE. 1980. 3/mo. $15 to non-members. Metropolitan Milwaukee Association of Commerce, Council of Small Business Executives, 756 N. Milwaukee St., Milwaukee, WI 53202. TEL 414-287-4100. Ed. Ann Dee Allen. circ. 4,300.
Formed by the merger of (1923-1984): Milwaukee Commerce (ISSN 0026-4342); (1923-1984): Commerce Hotline (ISSN 0746-6714); Which incorporated (1980-1984): Metropolitan Milwaukee Association of Commerce. Trends in Selected Economic Indicators (ISSN 0076-7069)
Description: Provides news, and upcoming events schedules of interest to members.

BUSINESS AND ECONOMICS — DOMESTIC COMMERCE

388.044 US ISSN 0273-5822
HF5487
MINI-STORAGE MESSENGER. 1979. 12/yr. $59.95 (effective 1997); newsstand price: $5.95. Mini Co., Inc., 2531 W. Dunlap Ave., Phoenix, AZ 85021. TEL 800-824-6864. FAX 602-861-1094. E-mail: Messenger@minico.com; URL: http://www.minico.com. Ed. Tricia van Zelst; Pub. Hardy Good. R&P contact: Peter M. Conti, Jr. adv.: B&W page $1430, color page $1875; trim 8 3/8 x 10 7/8; adv. contact: Bob Rogers. circ. 6,000. **Document type:** trade publication.
  Description: Trade magazine for owners, operators and managers of self-storage facilities.

381 CN ISSN 1185-2186
MISSISSAUGA BUSINESS TIMES. 1983. 10/yr. free. (North Island Sound Ltd.) North Island Publishing, 1606 Sedlescomb Dr., Unit 8, Mississauga, ON L4X 1M6, Canada. TEL 905-625-7070. FAX 905-625-4856. Ed. A. Gutteridge; Pub. Alexander Donald. adv.: B&W page Can.$1912, color page Can.$2762; 10 x 15 1/2; adv. contact: Andrew Luke. circ. 21,055. (also avail. in microfilm from CML,SOC) **Document type:** newspaper.
  Formerly: Mississauga Business (ISSN 0826-4139)

381 IT
MODENA - MONDO. 1988. 10/yr. S.A.I.M.O. s.r.l., Via Bellinzona 27 A, 41100 Modena, Italy. TEL 39-59-448311. FAX 39-59-448310. Ed. Marzia Barbieri. adv.: B&W page L.1300000, color page L.1650000. circ. 8,000.

MONEY SAVER. see CONSUMER EDUCATION AND PROTECTION

381 658 US ISSN 1055-8268
NATIONAL AUCTIONS & SALES.* (Supplement avail.) 1991. q. $29.99. Publishing & Business Consultants, 101 W. 64th St., Unit 3-2, Inglewood, CA 90302-1255. TEL 213-732-3477. FAX 213-732-9123. (Subscr. to: Box 75392, Los Angeles, CA 90075) Ed. Andeson Napoleon Atia. adv. circ. 120,000. **Document type:** consumer publication.
  Previously announced as: Government Auctions Update.
  Description: Reviews major auctions and sales throughout the nation and provides information on upcoming events.

381 SA ISSN 0077-5894
HF3901.A48
NATIONAL TRADE-INDEX OF SOUTHERN AFRICA. 1928. a. R.190 (effective 1997). Braby's (Subsidiary of: Kohler Packaging Ltd.), P.O. Box 1426, Pinetown 3600, South Africa. TEL 27-31-7017021. FAX 27-31-7017036. Ed. A. Stagg. adv. **Document type:** directory.
  —CISTI.

381 US ISSN 0164-8152
NEW HAMPSHIRE BUSINESS REVIEW. 1978. 26/yr. $24. Business Publications, Inc. (Manchester), 150 Dow St., Manchester, NH 03101-1227. TEL 603-624-1442. FAX 603-624-1310. Ed. Don Madden. adv. contact: Shirley Meyers. bk.rev. circ. 15,000. (tabloid format; also avail. in microform from UMI) **Indexed:** Tr.& Indus.Ind. **Document type:** newspaper.
  ●Also available online. Vendor(s): Knight-Ridder Information, Inc., UMI.
  —UMI.

051 US ISSN 1059-4140
NEW MIAMI.* 1988. m. $18. New Miami, Inc., 100 N.W. 37th Ave., Miami, FL 33123-4844. TEL 305-649-0100. FAX 305-372-1669. Ed. Mike Seemuth. adv. bk.rev. circ. 20,000.
  Description: Covers community and business issues and profiles business leaders.

381 NQ ISSN 0078-0510
NICARAGUA. DIRECCION GENERAL DE ADUANAS. MEMORIA. 1918. a. $7. Direccion General de Aduanas, Managua, Nicaragua. stat. circ. 200.

NORTH AMERICAN POST/HOKUBEI HOCHI. see ETHNIC INTERESTS

381 US ISSN 1063-2875
F251
NORTH CAROLINA MAGAZINE. 1943. m. $21.20 (effective 1993). North Carolina Citizens for Business and Industry, P.O. Box 2508, Raleigh, NC 27602. TEL 919-836-1400. FAX 919-836-1425. Ed. Steve Tuttle. R&P contact: Steve Tuttle. adv. contact: Charles Couch. bk.rev.; circ. 13,374 (paid). **Document type:** trade publication.
  Formerly: We the People of North Carolina.

381 UK ISSN 0306-5650
NORTH WEST BUSINESS. 1968. m. £19.50. Business Magazine Group, Promoter House, Vale Road, Heaton Mersey, Stockport SK4 3DU, England. TEL 061-443-1113. Ed. Anabella McIntyre-Brown. adv.; bk.rev. circ. 11,818.
  Former titles: North West Business Monthly; (until 1985): North West and North Wales Industrial Review.

380 NO
NORWAY. MINISTRY OF INDUSTRY. REPORTS TO THE STORTING. irreg. price varies. Ministry of Industry, Box 8014 Dep, 0030 Oslo 1, Norway.

381 PO ISSN 0870-2047
NOTICIAS DO COMERCIO. 1938. 6/yr. Rua da Palma 284, 2o Dto., 1100 Lisbon, Portugal. TEL 860912.

381 IT
NOTIZIE F A I D. bi-m. Federazione Associazione Imprese Distribuzione, Corso Porta Nuova, 3, 20121 Milan, Italy. TEL 653333.

381 YU ISSN 0469-0281
NOVA TRGOVINA. 1948. m. 600 din. Privredni Pregled, Marsala Birjuzova 3-5, 11000 Belgrade, Yugoslavia. Ed. Ljubodrag Jozic.

381 SP
NUEVA DIMENSION. 11/yr. Lillo 1, 28041 Madrid, Spain. TEL 1-217-96-59. Ed. Fidel Astudillo. circ. 5,000.

381 IT
NUOVA DISTRIBUZIONE. m. Promodis Italia Editrice s.r.l., Via Creta 56, 25124 Brescia, Italy. TEL 39-30-220261. FAX 39-30-225868. Ed. Argentino Albori. adv.: B&W page L.6500000, color page L.11000000; trim 185 x 260. circ. 36,570.

OESTERREICHISCHES UND EUROPAEISCHES WIRTSCHAFTSPRIVATRECHT. see LAW

OFFICE - DATA PROCESSING MACHINES: LATIN AMERICAN INDUSTRIAL REPORT. see COMPUTERS — Computer Industry

381 UK
OLD BEN NEWS. 1975. q. £5. Newsvendors' Benevolent Institution, P.O. Box 306, Dunmow, Essex CM6 1HY, England. Ed. Leonard Stall. adv.; bk.rev.; circ. 46,000 (controlled).

381 333.33 US ISSN 0882-0589
ORANGE COUNTY REPORT. 1985. m. $265 (effective 1995-1996). 180 Newport Center Dr., Ste. 180, Newport Beach, CA 92660. TEL 714-720-8414. Ed. Martin Brower; Pub. Martin A. Brower. index. (back issues avail.) **Document type:** newsletter.
  Description: For business, professional, governmental and institutional leaders interested in events in Orange County, California.

OSAKA PREFECTURE UNIVERSITY. SERIES D: ECONOMICS, BUSINESS ADMINISTRATION AND LAW. see BUSINESS AND ECONOMICS

OUTSTATE BUSINESS; the magazine of Michigan business & industry. see BUSINESS AND ECONOMICS — Economic Situation And Conditions

381 918.6 PN ISSN 1011-3940
PANAMA NOW. Spanish edition: Panama Hoy (ISSN 1011-3959) 1986. biennial. $30. Focus Publications (Int.) S.A., Apdo. 6-3287, El Dorado, Panama, Panama. TEL 507-225-6638. FAX 507-225-0466. E-mail: focusint@sinfo.net; URL: http://panama.by.net. Ed. Kenneth J. Jones. adv.; index. circ. 10,000. **Document type:** consumer publication.
  Description: Portrait of the nation in yearbook form. Includes many color photos.

338 380 PY ISSN 0031-1685
PARAGUAY INDUSTRIAL Y COMERCIAL.* 1944. m. Ministerio de Industria y Comercio, Avda. Espana 374, C.C. 1772, Asuncion, Paraguay. adv.; charts; illus.

PEDDLER. see CONSUMER EDUCATION AND PROTECTION

PETROLEUM: LATIN AMERICAN INDUSTRIAL REPORT. see PETROLEUM AND GAS

PHARMACEUTICAL: LATIN AMERICAN INDUSTRIAL REPORT. see PHARMACY AND PHARMACOLOGY

PHILIPPINES. DEPARTMENT OF TRADE AND INDUSTRY. ANNUAL REPORT. see BUSINESS AND ECONOMICS — International Commerce

381 382 PH
PHILIPPINES. NATIONAL STATISTICS OFFICE. COMMODITY FLOW IN THE PHILIPPINES. a. National Statistics Office, Ramon Magsaysay Blvd., Box 779, Manila, Philippines. FAX 63-2-610794. pp./issue: 398. (also avail. in diskette format) **Document type:** government publication.
  Description: Comprehensive statistics on regional commodity flow of domestic trade by mode of transport.

381 IT ISSN 0393-9448
PIAZZA MERCATO. 1983. m. Promodis Italia Editrice s.r.l., Via Creta 56, 25124 Brescia, Italy. TEL 030-220261. FAX 030-225868. TELEX 305362 PROMED I. Ed. Argentino Albori. adv.: B&W page L.3500000, color page L.6000000; trim 184 x 260. circ. 33,640.

381 SP
PLACA GRAN. 52/yr. Roger de Lluria, 1, 08400 Granoller (Barcelona), Spain. TEL 3-870-47-09.

381 US
PLYMOUTH COUNTY BUSINESS REVIEW. 1982. s-a. $4. Plymouth County Development Council, Box 1620, Pembroke, MA 02359. TEL 617-826-3136. FAX 617-826-0444. E-mail: info@plymouth-1620.com; URL: http://www.plymouth-1620.com/. Ed. David Kindy; Pub. Brooks Kelly. adv. contact: Janet Ramsay. circ. 5,000 (controlled). (also avail. in microform from UMI)
  ●Also available online. Vendor(s): UMI.
  Description: Describes the economic climate of Plymouth County.

381 332.6 II
PONDICHERRY INDUSTRIAL PROMOTION, DEVELOPMENT AND INVESTMENT CORPORATION. ANNUAL REPORTS AND ACCOUNTS. (Text in English) 1975. a. Pondicherry Industrial Promotion, Development and Investment Corporation Ltd., 38 Romain Rolland St, Pondicherry 605001, India. circ. controlled.

381.021 PO ISSN 0870-2616
PORTUGAL. INSTITUTO NACIONAL DE ESTATISTICA. INDICE DE PRECOS NO CONSUMIDOR. 1975. m. Esc.11300. Instituto Nacional de Estatistica, Ave. Antonio Jose de Almeida, 1078 Lisbon, Portugal. TEL 351-1-8470050. FAX 351-1-8478578. TELEX 351-1-63738 PCDINE P.
  Description: Provides statistical data on inflation and price changes.

381 GW ISSN 0343-415X
POSITION. q. Deutscher Industrie- und Handelstag, Adenauerallee 148, 53113 Bonn, Germany. TEL 0228-1040. TELEX 886805.
  —CCC.

PRINTING & PUBLISHING: LATIN AMERICAN INDUSTRIAL REPORT. see PUBLISHING AND BOOK TRADE

381 II
PRODUCTION OF SELECTED INDUSTRIES IN INDIA. (Text in English) m. Rs.120($43.20) Government of India, Department of Publications, Civil Lines, Delhi 110 054, India. TEL 11-2512527.

BUSINESS AND ECONOMICS — DOMESTIC COMMERCE

381   PL   ISSN 1231-3351
PRZEGLAD HANDLOWY. English edition: Review of Commerce. 1990. w. (Polish ed.); m. (Eng.ed.). 370000 Zl. Agencja Wydawnicza Torpress, Ul. Jana H. Dabrowskiego 77, 60-529 Poznan, Poland. TEL 48-61-472669. FAX 48-61-472445. TELEX 0413214. (Also dist. by: Ruch, ul. Towarowa 28, Warsaw, Poland. TEL 48-22-201271) Ed. Przemyslaw Rejer. adv. contact: R.J. Wnukowski. cum.index: 1990-1993. circ. 50,000. (also avail. in diskette format; back issues avail.) **Document type:** newspaper.
Description: Covers business and domestic trade.

381   US
PURDUE RETAILER. 1987. q. $8.50. Purdue University, Retail Institute, 214 Matthews Hall, W. Lafayette, IN 47907. TEL 317-494-9851. FAX 317-494-0869. Ed. Holly Schrank. circ. 1,000. **Document type:** newsletter.

381   JA
RETAIL DISTRIBUTION IN JAPAN. (Text in English) irreg., latest Oct. 1991. $600 per no. Dodwell Marketing Consultants, Kowa no.35, Bldg., 14-14 Akasaka, 1-chome, Minato-ku, Tokyo 107, Japan. TEL 03-3589-0207. FAX 03-5570-7132. TELEX J22274 DODWELL J. **Document type:** directory.
Description: Information on socio-economic changes and characteristics of the Japanese distribution system. Covers retailers, wholesalers, distribution channels for imported products. Includes company profiles.

381   PO
REVISTA COMERCIO PORTUENSE. 6/yr. Av. Rodriques de Freitas 200, 4000 Porto, Portugal. TEL 57-41-48. FAX 580423. TELEX 22758 ASCOP P.

381   CU
REVISTA DEL COMERCIO. 3/yr. $15 in N. America; S. America $17; Europe $18. (Ministerio del Comercio Interior) Ediciones Cubanas, Obispo No. 527, Apdo. 605, Havana, Cuba.

380   CN   ISSN 0380-9811
HC111
REVUE COMMERCE. (Text in French) 1896. m. Can.$26.13 (foreign Can.$44) (effective 1997). Publications Transcontinental Inc., 1100 boul. Rene Levesque W., 24th Fl., Montreal, PQ H3B 4X9, Canada. TEL 514-392-9000. FAX 514-392-4726. Dir. Danielle Thibault. adv. contact: Real Curadeau. illus.; index. circ. 37,352. (also avail. in microfilm) **Indexed:** Can.B.P.I., Can.Per.Ind., Pt.de Rep. (1979-). —CISTI.
Formerly: Commerce (ISSN 0010-2725); Which incorporates (1968-1982): Point (ISSN 0316-7852)
Description: Aimed at managers in the province of Quebec.

381   MG
REVUE DE L'OCEAN INDIEN. ECONOMIE. (Text in French) 1982. q. $29. Communication et Media Ocean Indien, Rue H. Rabesahala, B.P. 46, Antsakaviro, 101 Antananarivo, Madagascar. TEL 22536. FAX 34534. TELEX 22225. Ed. Georges Ranaivosoa. adv.; bk.rev. circ. 3,000.

381 332.6   IT   ISSN 0392-064X
CODEN: RIMEDE
RIVISTA DI MERCEOLOGIA. q. L.95000 (effective 1996). Cooperativa Libraria Universitaria Editrice Bologna, Via Marsala 24, 40126 Bologna, Italy. TEL 39-51-220736. FAX 39-51-237758. —BLDSC (7990.750000); CASDDS.
Formerly (until 1978): Quaderni di Merceologia.

RIVON CHESHEV. see BUSINESS AND ECONOMICS — Marketing And Purchasing

381   US
ROUTE 202 REVIEW; serving Chester, Montgomery & Delaware County business community along the Route 202 corridor. 1984. bi-m. $42. Montgomery Newspapers, 10 Liberty Blvd., Malvern, PA 19355. TEL 610-647-8082. FAX 610-647-8180. Ed. Todd Palmer; Pub. Arthur Howe. adv. contact: Betsy Wilson. bk.rev. circ. 15,000. (tabloid format) **Document type:** newspaper.
Formerly: Great Valley Business News.
Description: News and features on lifestyles in the regional business community.

RURAL INDIA. see AGRICULTURE — Agricultural Economics

381   FR
SACHEZ-LE ENVIRONNEMENT. m. 500 F. Chambre Regionale de Commerce et d'Industrie Champagne - Ardenne, Direction de la Communication, 10 rue de Chastillon, B.P. 537, 51011 Chalons-sur-Marne Cedex. TEL 33-3-26693340. FAX 33-3-26693369.

381   SW   ISSN 0346-2560
SAELJAREN. 1965. 10/yr. membership. Saeljarnas Riksfoerbund, P.O. Box 12668, S-112 93 Stockholm, Sweden. TEL 46-8-617-02-00. FAX 46-8-652-15-10. Ed. Britt-Marie Ericson; Pub. Rolf Laurelli. adv.: B&W page SEK 7200, color page SEK 10800; trim 185 x 265. circ. 10,700. cols./p.: 3; pp./issue: 32.

381.09   CN   ISSN 1184-731X
SAINT JOHN BUSINESS TODAY. 1976. m. Saint John Board of Trade, P.O. Box 6037, 39 King St., Saint John, N.B. E2L 4R5, Canada. TEL 506-634-8111. FAX 506-632-2008. Ed. Brian McLaughlin. adv.; bk.rev. circ. 1,000.
Formerly: Saint John Today (ISSN 0705-1905)

381   US   ISSN 0890-0337
SAN FRANCISCO BUSINESS TIMES. 1986. w. $49. San Francisco Business Times, 275 Battery St., Ste. 940, San Francisco, CA 94111. TEL 415-989-2522. FAX 415-398-2494. Ed. Michael Consol. adv. circ. 16,000. (tabloid format; back issues avail.) **Document type:** trade publication.
●Also available online. Vendor(s): Information Access Co.
—UMI. **CCC.**
Formerly: California Business Times.

381   IT
SCEGLIERE COMMERCIO E CONSUMI. m. Promodis Italia Editrice, Via Creta 56, 25124 Brescia, Italy. TEL 030-220261. FAX 030-225868. TELEX 305362. adv.: B&W page L.9000000, color page L.16000000; trim 185 x 260. circ. 104,636.

380   GW   ISSN 0080-7001
SCHRIFTEN ZUR HANDELSFORSCHUNG. N.S. 1951. irreg., no.88, 1995. price varies. (Universitaet zu Koeln, Institut fuer Handelsforschung) Verlag Otto Schwartz und Co., Annastr. 7, 37075 Goettingen, Germany. TEL 49-551-31051. FAX 49-551-372812. **Document type:** monographic series.

381   SZ
SCHWEIZERISCHES HANDELSAMTSBLATT/FEUILLE OFFICIELLE SUISSE DU COMMERCE/FOGLIO UFFICIALE SVIZZERO DI COMMERCIO. (Text in French, German, Italian) 5/w. 115 SFr. (foreign 195 SFr.) (effective 1997). Bundesamt fuer Aussenwirtschaft des Eidgenoessischen Volkswirtschaftsdepartementes, Effingerstr. 1, Postfach 8164, CH-3001 Bern, Switzerland. TEL 41-31-3240992. FAX 41-31-3240961. **Document type:** newspaper.

SCOTLAND'S TOP 2000 COMPANIES (YEAR). see BUSINESS AND ECONOMICS — Trade And Industrial Directories

381   US
SEATTLE DAILY JOURNAL OF COMMERCE. 1893. d. (Mon.-Fri.). $160. Seattle Daily Journal of Commerce Inc., 83 Columbia St., Seattle, WA 98104. TEL 206-622-8272. FAX 206-622-8416. Eds. Phil Brown, Lucy Swain. adv. contact: John Mihalyo. circ. 6,544.

338.044 658.7   US
SELF-STORAGE ALMANAC. 1991. a. $49.95 (effective 1997). MiniCo, Inc., 2531 W. Dunlap Ave., Phoenix, AZ 85021. TEL 602-870-1711; 800-352-4636. FAX 602-861-1094. URL: http://www.minico.com. adv.: B&W page $1400, color page $2000. circ. 3,500.

388.044   US
SELF-STORAGE NOW. 1991. 6/yr. MiniCo, Inc., Publishing Division, 2531 W. Dunlap Ave., Phoenix, AZ 85021. TEL 602-870-1711; 800-352-4636. FAX 602-8611094. URL: http://www.minico.com. Ed. Tricia van Zelst. adv.: B&W page $1430, color page $1875; trim 7 1/2 x 9 3/4. circ. 30,000 (controlled).
Description: Each issue focuses on a particular topic linked to current events and seasonal activities in self-storage.

SENTINEL INVESTMENT LETTER. see BUSINESS AND ECONOMICS — Investments

381   CC   ISSN 1004-7808
SHANGHAI QIYE/SHANGHAI ENTERPRISE. (Text in Chinese) 1981. m. Y36 (effective 1998). (Shanghai Qiye Guanli Xiehui - Shanghai Enterprise Management Association) Shanghai Qiye Zazhishe, 988 Yan'an Zhonglu, Shanghai 200040, People's Republic of China. TEL 86-21-62477939. FAX 86-21-62472007. (Co-sponsor: China Enterprise Management Association) Ed. Tu Lianghuai. adv.: page Y5000; adv. contact: Lianghuai Tu. circ. 20,000. pp./issue: 48. **Document type:** trade publication.
Description: Covers the experiences of business management, and information on economic reform.

381 658   CC   ISSN 1005-4359
SHANGYE JINGJI, WUZI JINGJI. (Subseries of: Fuyin Baokan Ziliao) (Text in Chinese) m. $99.53. Zhongguo Renmin Daxue, Shubao Ziliao Zhongxin - China People's University, Book & Newspaper Information Center, 3 Zhang Zizhong Rd., P.O. Box 1122, Beijing 100007, People's Republic of China. TEL 86-10-4015080. (Dist. in US by: China Publications Service, Box 49614, Chicago, IL 60649. TEL 312-288-3291. FAX 312-288-8570) pp./issue: 136.
Description: Covers domestic commerce, market studies and marketing management.

381   CC
SHICHANG ZHOUBAO/MARKET WEEKLY. (Text in Chinese) 1979. w. Shichang Zhoubao Bianjibu, 2 Duan, Sanhao Jie, Heping Qu, Shenyang, Liaoning, People's Republic of China. TEL 482983. circ. 1,000,000.
Description: Includes trade, commodities and financial and economic affairs.

381   UK
SHOPPING CENTRE AND RETAIL DIRECTORY. a. £100. William Reed Publishing Ltd., Broadfield Park, Crawley, W. Sussex RH11 9RT, England. TEL 44-1293-613400. FAX 44-1293-613322. **Document type:** directory.

381   CN
SHOPPING CENTRE NEWS. s-m. Maclean-Hunter Ltd., Business Publication Division, Maclean-Hunter Bldg., 777 Bay St., Toronto, ON M5W 1A7, Canada. TEL 416-596-5000.
Description: Focuses on development plans for new centres and expansions, leasing opportunities, latest events and trends in Canada's shopping centre industry.

381   CC
SICHUAN SHANGYE JINGJI/SICHUAN COMMERCIAL ECONOMICS. (Text in Chinese) bi-m. Sichuan Sheng Shangye Jingji Xuehui, 394, Xinhua Donglu, Chengdu, Sichuan 610012, People's Republic of China. TEL 23911. Ed. Kang Shitai.

380   SL   ISSN 0037-4768
SIERRA LEONE TRADE JOURNAL. 1961. q. 30p. Ministry of Information and Broadcasting, Government Information Services, Lightfoot Boston St., Freetown, Sierra Leone. adv.; illus.; mkt.; pat.; stat. **Document type:** government publication, trade publication.

381   UK   ISSN 0264-8814
SIGNS MAGAZINE. 1981. 8/yr. £48. (British Sign Association) Angwin Associates, Leen Gate, Lenton, Notts. NG7 2LX, England. FAX 44-1602-420407. Ed. Val Hirst. adv. contact: Dawn Seager. bk.rev. circ. 4,306. (back issues avail.; reprint service avail. from SCH) **Indexed:** Acad.Ind., Deep Sea Res.& Oceanogr.Abstr., Soc.Sci.Ind. **Document type:** trade publication.

380   II   ISSN 0300-4546
SOCIETY AND COMMERCE; for balanced social change. (Text in English) 1972. m. Rs.20($8) Society & Commerce Publications (Pvt) Ltd., 2 Waterloo St., Calcutta 700069, India. Ed. Parimal Mookerjea. adv.; bk.rev.; bibl.; charts; illus. circ. 1,000.

SPACE R & D ALERT. see AERONAUTICS AND SPACE FLIGHT

BUSINESS AND ECONOMICS — DOMESTIC COMMERCE 1217

381 SP
SPAIN. DIRECCION GENERAL DE COMERCIO EXTERIOR. COLECCION CUADERNOS DE INFORMATION DEL SOIVRE. irreg., no.13, 1994. price varies. Ministerio de Comercio y Turismo, Direccion General de Comercio Exterior, P. de la Castellana 162, pl. 16, 28046 Madrid, Spain. TEL 34-1349-36-47. FAX 34-1-349-36-34.

381 SP
SPAIN. DIRECCION GENERAL DE COMERCIO INTERIOR. COLECCION ESTUDIOS. irreg., no.54, 1994. price varies. Ministerio de Comercio y Turismo, Direccion General de Comercio Interior, P. de la Castellana 162, Pl. 16, 28046 Madrid, Spain. TEL 34-1-349-36-47. FAX 34-1-349-36-34.

SUDAN. DEPARTMENT OF STATISTICS. INTERNAL TRADE AND OTHER STATISTICS. see BUSINESS AND ECONOMICS — Abstracting, Bibliographies, Statistics

381 SJ
SUDANESE BUSINESS. 1988. w. $80. P.O. Box 3219, Khartoum, Sudan. TELEX 22288 SMAGP. adv. circ. 2,000.
    Description: Concerned with business in Sudan's private sector.

381 FI ISSN 1235-8509
SUOMALAISEN TYOEN LIITTO. HYV SUOMI! 1913. 5/yr. Kotimaisen Tyoen Liitto - Association for Finnish Work, P.O. Box 429, SF-00101 Helsinki, Finland. TEL 358-9-645-733. FAX 358-9-645-252. E-mail: lars.collin@avainlippu.fi; kirsi.saukonsaari@avainlippu.fi. Ed. Mirja Ekholm. adv. **Document type:** newspaper.
    Formerly: Kotimaisen Tyon Liitto. Tuotantouutiset (ISSN 0357-4520)

SURVEY OF AUSTRALIAN MANUFACTURING. see BUSINESS AND ECONOMICS — Chamber Of Commerce Publications

381 AU
SURVEY OF THE AUSTRIAN ECONOMY/OESTERREICHS WIRTSCHAFT IM UEBERBLICK. 1972. a. S.150. Wirtschafts-Studio des Oesterreichen Gesellschafts und Wirtschaftsmuseums, Vogelsanggasse 36, A-1050 Vienna, Austria. TEL 43-1-5452551. FAX 43-1-5453209. Ed. Josef Docekal. **Document type:** bulletin.

381 SW
SWEDEN. STATENS INDUSTRIVERK. CURRENT RESEARCH PROJECTS. (Text in English) 1977. s-a. Statens Industriverk - National Industrial Board, S-117 86 Stockholm, Sweden. TEL 46-8-744-9346. FAX 46-8-744-09-80. circ. 1,000.
    Formerly: Sweden. Statens Industriverk. Research Activities.

380 AT ISSN 0011-1716
T T P I TRADE GAZETTE. 1932. fortn. Aus.$38. (Tasmanian Trade Protective Institute) Cromptons Collection Service, 84 Charles St., Launceston, Tas. 7250, Australia. Ed. Stanley A. Guy. adv.

381 SP ISSN 1130-8338
TESON. 1953. m. Alonso Quintanilla 3, 2o H, 33002 Oviedo, Spain. TEL 8-251-00-47. FAX 8-251-89-22. Ed. D. Martin Ibanez.
—CINDOC.

381 TH ISSN 0857-7277
HG4244.655
THAILAND COMPANY INFORMATION (YEAR). 1988. a. $67. A.R. Business Consultant Co., Ltd., 109 Surawong Rd., CCT Bldg., 8th Fl., Bangkok 10500, Thailand. TEL 236-2902-4. FAX 236-2900. Ed. Patchara Kiatnuntavimon.
    Description: Collection of annual balance sheets and income statements of the top 1,600 companies in Thailand, classified by business type. Also lists over 2,000 newly registered companies with over one million baht registered capital.

381 VN ISSN 0868-2712
HUONG MAI/COMMERCE. 1990. w. D.104000. Ministry of Commerce and Tourism, 100 Lo Duc St., Hanoi, Socialist Republic of Vietnam. TEL 63150. FAX 84-204696. TELEX 411 525 BNT VY. circ. 30,000.
    Description: Provides information on state policies and guidelines in commerce and trade. Also covers business experiences of local and foreign companies.

551.46 US
TIDINGS (CAMDEN). 1965. q. membership. National Marine Representatives Association, Box 969, 2742 Old Natchez Trace Trail, Camden, TN 38320-0660. TEL 901-584-0203. FAX 901-584-0420. E-mail: nmra95@aol.com; URL: http://www.nmra.com. Ed. David McCloskey. adv. circ. 400. (looseleaf format) **Document type:** newsletter.
●Also available online.
    Former titles: News Waves; N M R A Newsletter.
    Description: Covers activities of the association and industry news.

TOBACCO: LATIN AMERICAN INDUSTRIAL REPORT. see TOBACCO

381 RU ISSN 0869-5660
HF25
TORGOVLYA. (Former name of issuing body: U.S.S.R. Ministry of Trade) 1926. m. $60 (effective 1997). (Ministerstvo Torgovli i Material'nykh Resursov) Torgovlya, Ul. Berezhkovskaya nab.6, 121864 Moscow, Russia. TEL 7-95-2404837. Ed. M.M. Lysov. adv.; bk.rev.; bibl.; illus.; stat.; index. circ. 50,000. (also avail. in microform) **Indexed:** Curr.Dig.Sov.Press.
—BLDSC (0180.976500).
    Formerly (until 1992): Sovetskaya Torgovlya (ISSN 0371-1927)

381 382 US
TRADE ACTION MONITORING SYSTEM. m. $225 in US, Canada, Mexico; elsewhere $450. (Executive Office of the President, U.S. Trade Representative) U.S. National Technical Information Service, 5825 Port Royal Rd., Springfield, VA 22161. TEL 703-487-4630.
    Description: Provides the facility to trace the various petitions on the 1974 Trade Act, such as Escape Clause (Section 201,) antidumping, countervailing duties (Section 301,) and unfair trading practices (Section 337.) Illustrates the process and position of each case in the process of determining the final decision.

380 CN ISSN 0049-4321
HC111
TRADE AND COMMERCE. 1906. 5/yr. Can.$30. Sanford Evans Communications Ltd., 1700 Church Ave., Box 6900, Winnipeg, MB R3C 3B1, Canada. TEL 204-632-2606. FAX 204-694-3040. Pub. George Mitchell. adv. circ. 10,000. **Indexed:** BPIA, Can.B.P.I., P.A.I.S.

381 II
TRADE COMMERCE & INDUSTRY WEEKLY BULLETIN. (Text in English) 1951. w. membership. Indian Merchants' Chamber, Indian Merchants' Chamber Building, 76 Veer Nariman Rd., Churchgate, Bombay 400020, India. Ed. Shri S.I. Padhya. adv. circ. 3,000.

381 US ISSN 0572-9912
TRADE REGULATION REPORTS. 7 base vols. (plus w. updates). $1922. C C H Incorporated, 2700 Lake Cook Rd., Riverwoods, IL 60015. TEL 847-267-7000; 800-835-5224. FAX 800-224-8299. (looseleaf format)
—CCC.

380 NZ ISSN 1171-2961
TRANS TASMAN. 1968. w. NZ.$192($180) (Australia Aus.$215; overseas $215). Trans-Tasman News Service Ltd., Box 377, Wellington, New Zealand. FAX 04-473-8908. Ed. Ian Templeton. circ. 1,000. **Document type:** newsletter.

TRANSPORTATION: LATIN AMERICAN INDUSTRIAL REPORT. see TRANSPORTATION

381 GW
TUEBINGER VOLKSWIRTSCHAFTLICHE STUDIEN. 1991. irreg., vol.16, 1997. price varies. A. Francke Verlag GmbH, Postfach 2560, 72015 Tuebingen, Germany. TEL 49-7071-9797-0. FAX 49-7071-75288. URL: http://www.francke.de. Ed. Adolf Wagner, Alfred Ott. (back issues avail.) **Document type:** monographic series.
    Description: Studies ethnic issues from a social, cultural, or philosophic perspective.

381 PH
TULUNGAN SA KAUNLARAN/WALL NEWS. 1989. bi-m. free. Philippine Business for Social Progress, Institutional and Development Communications Unit, P.O. Box 3839, 3F Philippine Social Development Centre, Magallanes Corner, Real Sts., Intramuros, Manila, Philippines. TEL 02-498242. FAX 02-488891. Ed. Josephine Yap Roman. circ. 2,000.

346.06 380 US ISSN 0503-1966
UNIFORM COMMERCIAL CODE LAW LETTER. Variant title: U C C Law Letter. 1967. m. $183.75 (overseas $252.45) (effective 1995). Warren, Gorham & Lamont, One Penn Plaza, New York, NY 10119. TEL 212-971-5000. FAX 212-971-5113. (Subscr. to: The Park Square Bldg., 31 St. James Ave., Boston, MA 02116-4112. TEL 800-950-1207) Ed. Thomas Quinn. (also avail. in microform from UMI) **Document type:** newsletter.
—UMI. **CCC.**
    Description: Covers important state and federal case decisions and offers practical advice for conducting business under the Uniform Commercial Code.

381 US ISSN 0083-0917
HD2775
U.S. FEDERAL TRADE COMMISSION. ANNUAL REPORT. Key Title: Annual Report of the Federal Trade Commission. 1915. a. price varies. U.S. Federal Trade Commission, Office of Public Affairs, Sixth St. & Pennsylvania Ave., N.W., Washington, DC 20580. TEL 202-655-4000. (Subscr. to: Superintendent of Documents, U.S. Government Printing Office, Box 371954, Pittsburgh, PA 15250-7954. TEL 202-512-1800. FAX 202-512-2250; Or: Bernan, 4611-F Assembly Dr., Lanham, MD 20706. TEL 301-459-7666. FAX 301-459-0056) **Document type:** government publication.

381 US
U.S. FEDERAL TRADE COMMISSION. COURT DECISIONS PERTAINING TO THE FEDERAL TRADE COMMISSION. a. price varies. U.S. Federal Trade Commission, Public Reference Branch, Sixth St. & Pennsylvania Ave., N.W., Washington, DC 20580. TEL 212-655-4000. (Subscr. to: Superintendent of Documents, U.S. Government Printing Office, Box 371954, Pittsburgh, PA 15250-7954. TEL 202-783-3238. FAX 202-512-2233) **Document type:** government publication.
    Formerly: U.S. Federal Trade Commission. Statutes and Court Decisions Pertaining to the Federal Trade Commission. Supplements (ISSN 0083-0933)

381 US ISSN 0083-0925
U.S. FEDERAL TRADE COMMISSION. FEDERAL TRADE COMMISSION DECISIONS, FINDINGS, ORDERS AND STIPULATIONS. 1915. a. price varies. U.S. Federal Trade Commission, Public Reference Branch, Sixth St. & Pennsylvania Ave., N.W., Washington, DC 20580. TEL 202-655-4000. (Subscr. to: Superintendent of Documents, U.S. Government Printing Office, Box 371954, Pittsburgh, PA 15250-7954. TEL 202-783-3238. FAX 202-512-2233) (also avail. in microfilm from BHP) **Document type:** government publication.
—UMI.

380 GW ISSN 0531-030X
UNIVERSITAET ZU KOELN. INSTITUT FUER HANDELSFORSCHUNG. MITTEILUNGEN. 1949. m. DM.130. Verlag Otto Schwartz und Co., Annastr. 7, 37075 Goettingen, Germany. TEL 49-551-31051. FAX 49-551-372812. Ed. L. Mueller-Hagedom. charts; stat.; index. circ. 3,500. (back issues avail.) **Indexed:** IBR, Key to Econ.Sci., P.A.I.S.For.Lang.Ind. **Document type:** academic/scholarly publication.

381 AT ISSN 1323-787X
UNIVERSITY OF NEW SOUTH WALES. HANDBOOK: COMMERCE AND ECONOMICS. 1989. a. Aus.$5. University of New South Wales, Sydney, N.S.W. 2052, Australia. TEL 61-2-385-2840. FAX 61-2-662-2163.
    Formerly (until 1993): University of New South Wales. Faculty Handbooks: Commerce and Economics (ISSN 0811-7616)

BUSINESS AND ECONOMICS — DOMESTIC COMMERCE

381   HC905.A1   SA   ISSN 0379-6191
UNIVERSITY OF STELLENBOSCH. BUREAU FOR ECONOMIC RESEARCH. TRENDS. Key Title: Trends (Stellenbosch). q. R.575 (effective 1996 & 1997). University of Stellenbosch, Bureau for Economic Research, Private Bag 5050, University, Stellenbosch 7599, South Africa. TEL 27-21-8872810. FAX 27-21-8839225. TELEX 520-383. E-mail: odjs@maties.sun.ac.za. Ed. G.M. Pellissier. circ. 550.
Description: Presents statistical data on changes and developments in the South African economy.

381   CN   ISSN 0083-517X
VANCOUVER BOARD OF TRADE. ANNUAL REPORT. 1887. a. free. Board of Trade, World Trade Centre, Ste. 400, 999 Canada Pl., Vancouver, BC V6C 3E1, Canada. TEL 604-641-1270. FAX 604-681-0437. Ed. Davey Rezac. adv. contact: Ron Stanaitis. circ. 5,000. **Document type:** corporate report.

381   PO
VENTO NORTE. 12/yr. Pc. Marques Pombal 78, Porto, Portugal.

381   SZ
VERKAUF SCHWEIZ. w. 1.10 SFr. per no. Hungerbuelstr. 23, CH-8501 Frauenfeld, Switzerland. TEL 054-7206365. FAX 054-7207764. Eds. Christian Koepfer, Pascal Streit. circ. 15,348. **Document type:** bulletin.
Formerly: Merkur.

VICTORIAN INTERNATIONAL TRADE DIRECTORY. see BUSINESS AND ECONOMICS — Trade And Industrial Directories

381   FR   ISSN 0220-5858
VIE FRANCAISE.* 1945. w. 425 F. Opion S.A., 25 rue Leblanc, 75015 Paris, France. TEL 1-48-04-99-99. TELEX 670 092. Ed. Bruno Bertez. adv. circ. 93,475. **Indexed:** ELLIS.

381   US
VIRGINIA'S LOCAL ECONOMIES: ACCOMACK-NORTHAMPTON, P D NO. 22 (EASTERN SHORE AREA).* (Planning District) a. $7.32. University of Virginia, Center for Public Service, 918 Emmet St., N., Ste. 300, Charlottesville, VA 22903-4832. TEL 804-924-3396.

381   US
VIRGINIA'S LOCAL ECONOMIES: BRISTOL M S A.* (Metropolitan Statistical Area) a. $7.32. University of Virginia, Center for Public Service, 918 Emmet St., N., Ste 300, Charlottesville, VA 22903-4832. TEL 804-924-3396.

381   US
VIRGINIA'S LOCAL ECONOMIES: CENTRAL SHENANDOAH, P D NO. 6 (SHENANDOAH VALLEY AREA).* (Planning District) a. $7.32. University of Virginia, Center for Public Service, 918 Emmet St., N., Ste 300, Charlottesville, VA 22903-4832. TEL 804-924-3396.

381   US
VIRGINIA'S LOCAL ECONOMIES: CENTRAL VIRGINIA, P D NO. 11 (LYNCHBURG AREA).* (Planning District) a. $7.32. University of Virginia, Center for Public Service, 918 Emmet St., N., Ste 300, Charlottesville, VA 22903-4832. TEL 804-924-3396.

381   US
VIRGINIA'S LOCAL ECONOMIES: CHARLOTTESVILLE M S A.* (Metropolitan Statistical Area) a. $7.32. University of Virginia, Center for Public Service, 918 Emmet St., N., Ste. 300, Charlottesville, VA 22903-4832. TEL 804-924-3396.

381   US
VIRGINIA'S LOCAL ECONOMIES: CRATER, P D NO. 19 (PETERSBURG AREA).* (Planning District) a. $7.32. University of Virginia, Center for Public Service, 918 Emmet St., N., Ste. 300, Charlottesville, VA 22903-4832. TEL 804-924-3396.

381   US
VIRGINIA'S LOCAL ECONOMIES: CUMBERLAND PLATEAU, P D NO. 2 (TAZEWELL AREA).* (Planning District) a. $7.32. University of Virginia, Center for Public Service, 918 Emmet St., N., Ste. 300, Charlottesville, VA 22903-4832. TEL 804-924-3396.

381   US
VIRGINIA'S LOCAL ECONOMIES: DANVILLE M S A.* (Metropolitan Statistical Area) a. $7.32. University of Virginia, Center for Public Service, 918 Emmet St., N., Ste. 300, Charlottesville, VA 22903-4832. TEL 804-924-3396.

381   US
VIRGINIA'S LOCAL ECONOMIES: FIFTH, P D NO. 5 (ROANOKE AREA).* (Planning District) a. $7.32. University of Virginia, Center for Public Service, 918 Emmet St., N., Ste. 300, Charlottesville, VA 22903-4832. TEL 804-924-3396.

381   US
VIRGINIA'S LOCAL ECONOMIES: LENOWISCO, P D NO. 1 (NORTON AREA).* (Planning District) a. $7.32. University of Virginia, Center for Public Service, 918 Emmet St., N., Ste. 300, Charlottesville, VA 22903-4832. TEL 804-924-3396.

381   US
VIRGINIA'S LOCAL ECONOMIES: LORD FAIRFAX, P D NO. 7 (WINCHESTER AREA). (Planning District) a. $7.32. University of Virginia, Center for Public Service, 918 Emmet St., N., Ste. 300, Charlottesville, VA 22903-4832. TEL 804-924-3396.

381   US
VIRGINIA'S LOCAL ECONOMIES: LYNCHBURG M S A.* (Metropolitan Statistical Area) a. $7.32. University of Virginia, Center for Public Service, 918 Emmet St., N., Ste. 300, Charlottesville, VA 22903-4832. TEL 804-924-3396.

381   US
VIRGINIA'S LOCAL ECONOMIES: MIDDLE PENINSULA, P D NO. 18.* (Planning District) a. $7.32. University of Virginia, Center for Public Service, 918 Emmet St., N., Ste. 300, Charlottesville, VA 22903-4832. TEL 804-924-3396.

381   US
VIRGINIA'S LOCAL ECONOMIES: MOUNT ROGERS, P D NO. 3 (BRISTOL - GALAX AREA).* (Planning District) a. $7.32. University of Virginia, Center for Public Service, 918 Emmet St., N., Ste. 300, Charlottesville, VA 22903-4832. TEL 804-924-3396.

381   US
VIRGINIA'S LOCAL ECONOMIES: NEW RIVER VALLEY, P D NO. 4 (BLACKSBURG - REDFORD AREA).* (Planning District) a. $7.32. University of Virginia, Center for Public Service, 918 Emmet St., N., Ste. 300, Charlottesville, VA 22903-4832. TEL 804-924-3396.

381   US
VIRGINIA'S LOCAL ECONOMIES: NORFOLK - NEWPORT NEWS - VIRGINIA BEACH M S A.* (Metropolitan Statistical Area) a. $7.32. University of Virginia, Center for Public Service, 918 Emmet St., N., Ste. 300, Charlottesville, VA 22903-4832. TEL 804-924-3396.

381   US
VIRGINIA'S LOCAL ECONOMIES: NORTHERN NECK, P D NO. 17.* (Planning District) a. $7.32. University of Virginia, Center for Public Service, 918 Emmet St., N., Ste. 300, Charlottesville, VA 22903-4832. TEL 804-924-3396.

381   US
VIRGINIA'S LOCAL ECONOMIES: NORTHERN VIRGINIA M S A.* (Metropolitan Statistical Area) a. $7.32. University of Virginia, Center for Public Service, 918 Emmet St., N., Ste. 300, Charlottesville, VA 22903-4832. TEL 804-924-3396.

381   US
VIRGINIA'S LOCAL ECONOMIES: NORTHERN VIRGINIA, P D NO. 8.* (Planning District) a. $7.32. University of Virginia, Center for Public Service, 918 Emmmet St., N., Ste. 300, Charlottesville, VA 22903-4832. TEL 804-924-3396.

381   US
VIRGINIA'S LOCAL ECONOMIES: PENINSULA, P D NO. 21 (NEWPORT NEWS - HAMPTON AREA).* (Planning District) a. $7.32. University of Virginia, Center for Public Service, 918 Emmet St., N., Ste. 300, Charlottesville, VA 22903-4832. TEL 804-924-3396.

381   US
VIRGINIA'S LOCAL ECONOMIES: PIEDMONT, P D NO. 14 (FARMVILLE AREA).* (Planning District) a. $7.32. University of Virginia, Center for Public Service, 918 Emmet St., N., Ste. 300, Charlottesville, VA 22903-4832. TEL 804-924-3396.

381   US
VIRGINIA'S LOCAL ECONOMIES: RADCO, P D NO. 16 (FREDERICKSBURG AREA).* (Planning District) a. $7.32. University of Virginia, Center for Public Service, 918 Emmet St., N., Ste. 300, Charlottesville, VA 22903-4832. TEL 804-924-3396.

381   US
VIRGINIA'S LOCAL ECONOMIES: RAPPAHANNOCK - RAPIDAN, P D NO. 9 (CULPEPER AREA).* (Planning District) a. $7.32. University of Virginia, Center for Public Service, 918 Emmet St., N., Ste. 300, Charlottesville, VA 22903-4832. TEL 804-924-3396.

381   US
VIRGINIA'S LOCAL ECONOMIES: RICHMOND - PETERSBURG M S A.* (Metropolitan Statistical Area) a. $7.32. University of Virginia, Center for Public Service, 918 Emmet St., N., Ste. 300, Charlottesville, VA 22903-4832. TEL 804-924-3396.

381   US
VIRGINIA'S LOCAL ECONOMIES: RICHMOND REGIONAL, P D NO. 15.* (Planning District) a. $7.32. University of Virginia, Center for Public Service, 918 Emmet St., N., Ste. 300, Charlottesville, VA 22903-4832. TEL 804-924-3396.

381   US
VIRGINIA'S LOCAL ECONOMIES: ROANOKE M S A.* (Metropolitan Statistical Area) a. $7.32. University of Virginia, Center for Public Service, 918 Emmet St., N., Ste. 300, Charlottesville, VA 22903-4832. TEL 804-924-3396.

381   US
VIRGINIA'S LOCAL ECONOMIES: SOUTHEASTERN VIRGINIA, P D NO. 20 (NORFOLK - VIRGINIA BEACH AREA).* (Planning District) a. $7.32. University of Virginia, Center for Public Service, 918 Emmet St., N., Ste. 300, Charlottesville, VA 22903-4832. TEL 804-924-3396.

381   US
VIRGINIA'S LOCAL ECONOMIES: SOUTHSIDE, P D NO. 13 (SOUTH BOSTON AREA).* (Planning District) a. $7.32. University of Virginia, Center for Public Service, 918 Emmet St., N., Ste. 300, Charlottesville, VA 22903-4832. TEL 804-924-3396.

381   US
VIRGINIA'S LOCAL ECONOMIES: THOMAS JEFFERSON, P D NO. 10 (CHARLOTTESVILLE AREA).* (Planning District) a. $7.32. University of Virginia, Center for Public Service, 918 Emmet St., N., Ste. 300, Charlottesville, VA 22903-4832. TEL 804-924-3396.

381   US
VIRGINIA'S LOCAL ECONOMIES: WEST PIEDMONT, P D NO. 12 (DANVILLE AREA).* (Planning District) a. $7.32. University of Virginia, Center for Public Service, 918 Emmet St., N., Ste. 300, Charlottesville, VA 22903-4832. TEL 804-924-3396.

380 338   FR   ISSN 0753-0056
VOLONTE DE L'INDUSTRIE, DU COMMERCE ET DES PRESTATAIRES DE SERVICES. 1945. m. 240 F. (Confederation des Petites et Moyennes Enterprises Societe d'Edition et de Publication des P.M.E., 23 rue de Clery, 75002 Paris, France. Ed. G. Lazaro. adv.; bk.rev. circ. 125,000. (back issues avail.)
Former titles (until 1980): Volonte du Commerce, de l'Industrie et des Prestataires de Services (ISSN 0151-8631); Volonte du Commerce et de l'Industri (ISSN 0042-8612)

380 338   II
VYAVASAYA KERALAM. (Text in English or Malayalam) 1962. m. Department of Industries and Commerce Vikas Bhavan, Trivandrum 695033, India. TEL 91-471-330995. FAX 91-471-329640. Ed. K.K. Vijaya Kumar. adv.; charts; illus.
Formerly: Kerala Commerce and Industry (ISSN 0023-0499)

381   JA   ISSN 0387-3404
WASEDA SHOGAKU/WASEDA COMMERCIAL REVIEW.
(Text in Japanese) 1925. 6/yr. 400 Yen. (Waseda Shogaku Doukoulao - Waseda Commercial Study Society) Waseda Shogaku Doukoukai, 1-6-1 Nishi-waseda, Shinjuku-ku, Tokyo 169, Japan. Ed. Osamu Wishizawa. bk.rev. circ. 2,500.

381   UK
WEST COUNTRY BUSINESS REVIEW. 1987. m. £30. Herald Express Publications Ltd., Harmsworth House, Barton Hill Rd., Torquay, Devon TQ2 8JN, England. TEL 44-1803-676000. FAX 44-1803-676579. Ed. Julia Snow. adv. contact: Marc Overton. circ. 10,000. (tabloid format; back issues avail.) **Document type:** newspaper.
  Formerly: Devon Business Review.
  Description: Contains a wide variety of local business news, ideas and information relevant to industry and commerce in Devonshire.

381   AT
WESTERN AUSTRALIA. INDUSTRIAL GAZETTE. m. Aus.$243 in WA; interstate Aus.$286; foreign Aus.$406 (effective 1997). State Law Publisher, Ground Fl., 10 William St., Perth, W.A. 6000, Australia. TEL 61-9-3217688. FAX 61-9-3217536. circ. 454. **Document type:** government publication.
  Description: Serves as a medium for news and notices of an industrial relations theme from the Industrial Commission of Western Australia.

381   SZ
WIR KAUFLEUTE. 11/yr. Kaufmaennischer Verband Zuerich, Pelikanstr. 18, CH-8023 Zurich, Switzerland. TEL 01-2113322. FAX 01-2210913. Ed. Peter Volanthen. circ. 18,000.

381   GW
WIRTSCHAFT UND VERKEHR IM BAYERISCHEN DREILAENDERECK. 1947. m. DM.24. Industrie- und Handelskammer Lindau - Bodensee, Postfach 1365, 88103 Lindau, Germany. TEL 49-8382-4094. FAX 49-8382-4057. adv.; bk.rev.; stat.; tr.lit. circ. 4,000. (back issues avail.) **Document type:** bulletin.

381 338   US   ISSN 1063-6595
WORCESTER BUSINESS JOURNAL. 1990. fortn. $30; newsstand price: $1.75. Worcester Publishing Ltd., 172 Shrewsbury St., Worcester, MA 01604. TEL 508-755-8004. FAX 508-755-8860. Ed. Steven Jones-D'Agostino. adv. contact: Donna Brassard. charts; illus.; stat.; circ. 12,000. circ. Pub. Peter Stanton. cols./p.: 5; pp./issue: 32. (tabloid format; back issues avail.) **Document type:** newspaper.
  Description: Covers news and other issues of interest to owners and executives of small- and medium-sized businesses in central Massachusetts.

ZEITSCHRIFT FUER WIRTSCHAFTSRECHT - Z I P. see LAW

381   CC   ISSN 1002-9699
ZHONGGUO GONGSHANG/CHINESE INDUSTRY & COMMERCE. (Text in Chinese) m. Zhonghua Quanguo Gongshangye Lianhehui - All-China Industry and Commerce Federation, No. 93, Beiheyan Dajie, Beijing 100006, People's Republic of China. TEL 86-10-5136677. FAX 86-10-5135286. (Dist. overseas by: China International Book Trading Corp., P.O. Box 399, Beijing 100044, P.R. China) pp./issue: 48.

381   CC
ZHONGGUO MINBAN KEJI SHIYE/CHINESE PRIVATELY OWNED SCIENCE AND TECHNOLOGY ENTERPRISES. (Text in Chinese) m. Zhongguo Minban Keji Shiyejia Xiehui - Chinese Association of Private Science and Technology Entrepreneurs, Xibianmen, Bldg. 10, Rm. 1307, Xuanwu-qu, Beijing 100053, People's Republic of China. TEL 3010247. Ed. Bao Ke.

381   CC   ISSN 1002-591X
ZHONGGUO SHANGYE NIANJIAN/ALMANAC OF CHINA'S COMMERCE. (Text in Chinese) a. Y43. (Shangye-bu - Ministry of Commerce) Zhongguo Shangye Nianjian Bianjibu, 45 Fuxingmennei Dajie, Beijing 100801, People's Republic of China. TEL 6038581. adv.: B&W page Y3000, color page Y5000; adv. contact: Jinsong Li.

381   YU
ZVEZDA; list za internu upotrebu i samoupravno dogovaranje. 1976. m. Zvezda, Trgovinska i Radna Organizacija, Zona Pristanista i Skladista 66, Novi Sad, Vojvodina, Yugoslavia. Ed. Mitar Simovic.

BUSINESS AND ECONOMICS — Economic Situation And Conditions

330   UK
A B E C O R COUNTRY REPORTS. irreg. £300 for full set (academic institutions and students £150); individual reports £30 (academic institutions and students £15). Barclays Bank plc., Economics Department, P.O. Box 12, Barclays House, 1 Wimborne Rd., Poole, Dorset BH15 2BB, England. TEL 01202-344023. FAX 01202-402303. (Co-sponsor: A B E C O R) **Document type:** academic/scholarly publication.
  ●Also available online. **Vendor(s):** Data-Star, Knight-Ridder Information, Inc.
  Description: Economic reports covering developing nations.

330.9   NE   ISSN 0928-9933
A B N AMRO ECONOMIC REVIEW. (Text in English) 1967. q. free. A B N Amro Bank N.V., P.O. Box 283, 1000 EA Amsterdam, Netherlands. stat.
  —UMI.
  Incorporated (in 1991): Netherlands Economic Report (ISSN 0922-0720); Former titles (until 1991): A B N Economic Review (ISSN 0169-5363); (until 1983): Algemene Bank Netherlands. Economic Review (ISSN 0928-9992); (until 1976): A B N Economic Review (1967) (ISSN 0044-7269)

A C C R A NEWSLETTER; promoting excellence in research for community & economic development. (American Chamber of Commerce Researchers Association) see BUSINESS AND ECONOMICS — Chamber Of Commerce Publications

A G A FINANCIAL QUARTERLY REVIEW. (American Gas Association) see ENERGY

330.9   EC
A L A I SERVICIO INFORMATIVO. (Text in Spanish) 1977. 20/yr. $25 to individuals (outside Latin America $45); institutions $50 (outside Latin America $80) (effective 1996). Agencia Latino-Americana de Informacion, Casilla 17-12-877, Av. 12 de Octubre 622 y Patria, Of. 503, Quito, Ecuador. TEL 593-2-505074. FAX 593-2-505073. E-mail: info@alai.ec.ec. index. circ. 2,000. (back issues avail.) **Document type:** newsletter.
  Former titles (until Feb. 1992): A L A I Servicio Mensual de Informacion y Documentacion (ISSN 0827-5564); (until Aug. 1984): A L A I Servicio Informativo.

330.9   BL
A N D I M A RETROSPECTIVA. (Text in English, Portuguese) 1985. a. Associacao Nacional das Instituicoes do Mercado Aberto, Av. Republica do Chile 230, 12o andar, 20031-170 Rio de Janeiro RJ, Brazil. TEL 021-220-5412. FAX 021-220-7537. **Document type:** corporate report.
  Description: Records the developments of the market during the year. Includes statistics on assets, monetary indicators, price indices, the privatization program and government policies.

330.9   UK
A O N CITYSCOPE; a survey of economic & investment forecasts. 1979. m. free. Godwins Ltd., Briarcliff House, Kingsmead, Farnborough, Hants. GU14 7TE, England. TEL 01252-544484. FAX 01252-522206. Ed. Mark Chandler. circ. 200. **Document type:** bulletin.
  Former titles (until 1996): Godwins Cityscope; (until 1990): Cityscope (ISSN 0260-0293)

330   BL   ISSN 0001-2181
HC186
A P E C. (Analise e Perspectiva Economica) (Text in English and Portuguese) 1962. fortn. $200. Associacao Promotora de Estudos de Economia, Rua Sorocaba 295, Botafogo, Rio de Janeiro, Brazil. FAX 021-266-3597. Ed. Basilio Martins. bk.rev.; charts; stat. circ. 2,000.

330   CC   ISSN 0251-2521
A S E A N BRIEFING. 1978. m. $60. (Association of South East Asian Nations) Asia Letter Group, G.P.O. Box 10874, Hong Kong, People's Republic of China. TEL 852-526-2950. FAX 852-526-7131. TELEX HX-61166-HKNW. (US addr.: Box 88189, Los Angeles, CA 90009-8189) Ed. Charles R. Smith. (back issues avail.) **Document type:** newsletter.

330.9   MV
ACADEMIA DE STIINTE A REPUBLICII MOLDOVA. BULETINUL. ECONOMIE SI SOCIOLOGIE/AKADEMIYA NAUK RESPUBLIKI MOLDOVA. IZVESTIYA. EKONOMIKA I SOTSIOLOGIYA. (Text in Rumanian and Russian) 1951. 3/yr. $44 (effective 1998). Academia de Stiinte a Republicii Moldova, Biblioteca Stiinfifica Centrala, Bd. Stefan cel Mare, 1, 2001 Kishinev, Moldova. TEL 373-2-264023. (Dist. by: Mezhdunarodnaya Kniga, B. Yakimanka 39, 117049 Moscow, Russia. TEL 7-095-2384967. FAX 7-095-2384634) bk.rev. circ. 750. **Document type:** academic/scholarly publication, bulletin.
  —KNAW.
  Formerly: Academia de Stiinte a R.S.S. Moldova. Buletinul. Economie se Sociologie (ISSN 0236-3070); Supersedes in part (in 1990): Akademiya Nauk Moldavskoi S.S.R. Izvestiya. Seriya Obshchestvennykh Nauk (ISSN 0321-1681)
  Description: Devoted to the economic and social problems related to the transition to a free market economy.

330   AO   ISSN 0001-7566
ACTIVIDADE ECONOMICA DE ANGOLA;* review of economics, general survey and development. 1935. 4/yr. Esc.15 per no. Fundo de Comercializacao, Box 1338, Luanda (PWA), Angola. illus.; stat.

330   SP   ISSN 0001-7655
HC381.A1
ACTUALIDAD ECONOMICA. 1957. w. $48. Recoletos 1, 7o, 28001 Madrid, Spain. TEL 34-1-3373220. FAX 34-1-5768150. Dir. Ignacio de la Rica. adv.; bibl.; charts; illus.; mkt.; pat.; stat. circ. 39,500. **Indexed:** ELLIS, P.A.I.S.For.Lang.Ind. **Document type:** trade publication.
  ●Also available online.
  Also available on CD-ROM. **Producer(s):** Chadwyck-Healey Inc.
  —BLDSC (0677.030000); CINDOC; SWETS.

ADVANCES IN BEHAVIORAL ECONOMICS. see PSYCHOLOGY

330.9   US   ISSN 0731-9053
HB139
ADVANCES IN ECONOMETRICS. 1981. irreg., vol.11, 1996. $157. J A I Press Inc., 55 Old Post Rd., No. 2, Box 1678, Greenwich, CT 06830-1678. TEL 203-661-7602. FAX 203-661-0792. E-mail: jai@jaipress.com. (Subscr. in UK and Europe to: JAI Press Ltd., 38 Tavistock St., Covent Garden, London WC2E 7PB, England. TEL 44-171-379-8834. FAX 44-171-379-8835) Eds. Thomas Fomby, R. Carter Hill.
  —BLDSC (0704.542000). CCC.

330.9   US   ISSN 1048-4736
HB615
ADVANCES IN THE STUDY OF ENTREPRENEURSHIP, INNOVATION, AND ECONOMIC GROWTH. irreg., vol.7, 1996. $73.25. J A I Press Inc., 55 Old Post Rd., No. 2, Box 1678, Greenwich, CT 06830-1678. TEL 203-661-7602. FAX 203-661-0792. E-mail: jai@jaipress.com. (Subscr. in the UK and Europe to: JAI Press Ltd., 38 Tavistock St., Covent Garden, London WC2E 7PB, England. TEL 44-171-379-8834. FAX 44-171-379-8835) Ed. Gary Libecap. **Document type:** monographic series.
  —BLDSC (0711.593200).

ADVISOR (NEW YORK). see BUSINESS AND ECONOMICS — Marketing And Purchasing

330.9 332   UK   ISSN 0950-902X
HG46
AFRICA ANALYSIS; fortnightly bulletin on financial and political trends. 1986. fortn. £345($595) to individuals; academic institutions and charities £245 ($445). Africa Analysis Ltd., Ludgate House, 107-111 Fleet St., London EC4A 2AB, England. TEL 44-171-353-1117. FAX 44-171-353-1516. E-mail: 100321.241@compuserve.com; URL: http://www.textor.com/cms/dAAAA.html. Ed. Ahmed Rajab; Pub. Richard Hall. bk.rev. circ. 1,000. **Document type:** bulletin.
  ●Also available online.
  Incorporates: Southern Africa Business Intelligence (ISSN 0967-5019)
  Description: Explains financial and political trends of African nations, including trade and finance, contracts, currencies, exchange controls, and country-by-country statistics.

BUSINESS AND ECONOMICS — ECONOMIC SITUATION AND CONDITIONS

330   UK   ISSN 0144-8234
HC800.A1
AFRICA ECONOMIC DIGEST; weekly business news, analysis and forecast. 1980. w. £225($400) Concord Press of Nigeria, 26-32 Whistler St., London N5 1NJ, England. TEL 071-359-5335. FAX 071-359-9173. TELEX 262505. Ed. Eddie Momoh. adv.; illus. circ. 240. **Indexed:** Key to Econ.Sci.
●Also available online.
—SWETS.
Description: News articles and analysis of economic trends in the 50 member countries of the Organization of African Unity, and their relationship to domestic and international foreign and military policy, with market reports and lists of business opportunities by country.

AFRICA INSIGHT. see *HISTORY — History Of Africa*

AFRICA INSTITUTE. OCCASIONAL PUBLICATIONS. see *HISTORY — History Of Africa*

AFRICA INSTITUTE. RESEARCH PAPER. see *HISTORY — History Of Africa*

960   UK   ISSN 0001-9852
AFRICA RESEARCH BULLETIN. SERIES B: ECONOMIC, FINANCIAL AND TECHNICAL. 1964. m. £273($487) (foreign £308) (effective 1997). Blackwell Publishers Ltd., 108 Cowley Road, Oxford OX4 1JF, England. TEL 44-1865-791100. FAX 44-1865-791347. E-mail: jnlinfo@blackwellpublishers.co.uk; URL: http://www.blackwellpublishers.co.uk. Ed. Pita Adams. adv.; maps; stat.; index. **Document type:** academic/scholarly publication.
—SWETS; UMI. **CCC.**

320 338   UK   ISSN 0269-3844
HC501
AFRICA REVIEW. 1977. a. £40. Kogan Page Ltd., 120 Pentonville Rd., London N1 9JN, England. TEL 44-171-278-0433. FAX 44-171-837-6348. TELEX 263088 KOGAN G. Ed. Tony Axon. R&P contact: Linda Batman. adv.; illus.; stat. circ. 7,160. **Document type:** consumer publication.
—BLDSC (0732.186500).
Formerly (until 1985): Africa Guide (ISSN 0308-678X)
Description: Overview on the economic, commercial and political situation in every African country.

AFRICA SOUTH OF THE SAHARA (YEAR). see *POLITICAL SCIENCE*

330.9 338.91   IV
AFRICAN DEVELOPMENT BANK. ECONOMIC RESEARCH PAPERS. irreg., latest no.19. African Development Bank - Banque Africaine de Developpement, B.P. 1387, Abidjan 01, Ivory Coast. TEL 225-20-44-44. FAX 225-20-49-48. TELEX 225-23717.

330.9   KE
AFRICAN ECONOMIC DEVELOPMENT NEWS. (Text in English and French) 1984. m. P.O. Box 46854, Nairobi, Kenya. TEL 254-2-331402. Ed. Kul Bhushan.

AFRIKA SPECTRUM; Zeitschrift fuer gegenwartsbezogene Afrikaforschung. see *POLITICAL SCIENCE*

AGRICULTURAL REVIEW FOR EUROPE. see *AGRICULTURE — Agricultural Economics*

AGRICULTURAL TRADE IN EUROPE. see *AGRICULTURE — Agricultural Economics*

AGRIFACK. see *AGRICULTURE*

AIRLINE ECONOMIC RESULTS AND PROSPECTS. see *TRANSPORTATION — Air Transport*

AKTUELL EKONOMI. see *BUSINESS AND ECONOMICS — Macroeconomics*

330.9   SW   ISSN 0345-0619
AKTUELLT I HANDELSPOLITIKEN. 1971. irreg. (2-3/yr.). Utrikesdepartmentet, S-103 33 Stockholm, Sweden.

330.9   US
ALABAMA ECONOMIC OUTLOOK. 1980. a. $15. Center for Business and Economic Research, University of Alabama, Box 870221, Tuscaloosa, AL 35487-0221. TEL 205-348-6191. FAX 205-348-2951. E-mail: dhamilto@alston.cba.ua.edu; URL: http://www.cba.ua.edu/~cber. Ed. Deborah Hamilton. (also avail. in microfiche from CIS) **Indexed:** SRI.
Description: Examines current economic conditions and trends and their likely effects on the national and Alabama economies in the coming year.

650   US   ISSN 0002-4392
ALAM ATTIJARAT; the business magazine of the Arab world. (Text in Arabic) 1966. 12/yr. $60. Keller International Publishing Corporation, Mid East Publications, Inc., 150 Great Neck Rd., Great Neck, NY 11021. TEL 516-829-9210. FAX 516-829-5414. TELEX 221-574 KELLE. Ed. Nadim Makdisi. adv.; illus. circ. 25,000.

338.9   US   ISSN 1072-8139
ALASKA ECONOMIC REPORT. 1974. fortn. $245 (effective 1998). Information & Research Service, 3037 South Circle, Anchorage, AK 99507. TEL 907-349-7711. FAX 907-522-1761. Ed. Tim Bradner; Pub. Mike Bradner. R&P contact: Tim Bradner. circ. 550. **Document type:** newsletter.

330   US   ISSN 0160-3345
HD8053.A4
ALASKA ECONOMIC TRENDS. 1965. m. free. Department of Labor, Research & Analysis Section, Box 25501, Juneau, AK 99802-5501. TEL 907-465-4500. FAX 907-465-2101. Ed. J. Pennelope Goforth. charts; stat. circ. 4,000. (also avail. in microfiche from CIS) **Indexed:** P.A.I.S., SRI. **Document type:** government publication.
Former titles: Alaska Employment Trends; Trends in Alaska's Employment and Economy.
Description: Addresses the current economic and demographic conditions of Alaska including regional economic analysis, labor force data by region, nonagricultural wage and salary employment, and average hours and earnings in selected industries.

330.9   US   ISSN 0162-5403
HC107.A45
ALASKA REVIEW OF SOCIAL AND ECONOMIC CONDITIONS. 1964. irreg. free. University of Alaska, Institute of Social and Economic Research, 3211 Providence Dr., Anchorage, AK 99508-4614. TEL 907-786-7710. FAX 907-786-7739. Ed. Linda Leask. charts; illus.; index. circ. 3,000. (also avail. in microfiche from CIS) **Indexed:** P.A.I.S., Rural Recreat.Tour.Abstr., SRI, World Agri.Econ.& Rural Sociol.Abstr. **Document type:** academic/scholarly publication, government publication.
Former titles (until Dec. 1977): Alaska Review of Business and Economic Conditions (ISSN 0034-6462); Review of Business and Economic Conditions in Alaska.

330.9   US
THE ALBANY REPORT. (Print edition ceased.) 1990. free. Sawchuk, Brown Associates, 41 State St., Albany, NY 12207. TEL 518-462-0318. FAX 518-462-0688. E-mail: sawbio@eisiac.com. Ed. David P. Brown; Pub. David P. Brown. circ. 1,200 (controlled). **Document type:** newsletter, government publication.
●Available only online.

330.9   US   ISSN 1046-5480
ALL ABOUT BUSINESS IN HAWAII. 1972. a. $19.95. Crossroads Press, Inc., Box 833, Honolulu, HI 96808. TEL 808-521-0021. FAX 808-526-3273. Ed. Michelle Yamaguchi. adv. circ. 22,000.
Description: Covers life in Hawaii - its economy, people, government, market, real estate, education, taxes, labor force, agriculture, and commerce.

AMAX NEWS. see *MINES AND MINING INDUSTRY*

330.9   AG
AMERICA FINANCIERA. 1992. q.? Centro de Estudios de America Latina, Sarmiento 944, 8o Piso, Of. 18, 1041 Buenos Aires, Argentina.

AMERICA LATINA - INTERNACIONAL. see *POLITICAL SCIENCE*

330.9 336   US
AMERICA REPORT. 1994. a. $5.95. Blue Heron Press, S. Starlight Farm, Phoenix, MD 21131. TEL 410-472-4573. FAX 410-771-4213. Ed. Lyle A. Brecht. (back issues avail.) **Document type:** consumer publication.
Description: Aims to educate tax payers. Shows how the tax dollars citizens "invest" each year are being spent and what government is accomplishing with these tax dollars.

330.9   TC
AMERICAECONOMIA. (Text in Spanish; summaries in English and Spanish) 1987. m. Nanbei Ltd., Gretton House, Duke St., Grand Turk, Turks and Caicos Islands, B.W.I. (Subscr. to: Galvarino Gallardo 1576, Santiago, Chile; US addr.: c/o Dow Jones & Co., Inc., World Financial Center, 200 Liberty St., 14th Fl., New York, NY 10281) Ed. Nils Strandberg. charts, illus, stat.; index. circ. 40,000. (tabloid format; back issues avail.)

330.9   US   ISSN 0363-566X
AMERICAN BUSINESS. 1976. q. $25. Avant-Garde Media, Inc., 80 Central Park W., Ste. 16B, New York, NY 10023. Ed. Ralph Ginzburg. adv.; bk.rev. circ. 275,000. (tabloid format; back issues avail.) **Indexed:** PMR.

330.9   US
AMERICAN ECONOMIC DEVELOPMENT COUNCIL. COUNCIL NEWS. 6/yr. membership only. American Economic Development Council, 9801 W. Higgins, Ste. 540, Rosemont, IL 60018-4726. TEL 847-692-9944. FAX 847-696-2990. E-mail: aedc@interaccess.com; URL: http://www.aedc.org/hqtrs. Ed. Marion Morgan. R&P contact: Marion Morgan. circ. 2,700 (controlled). (back issues avail.) **Document type:** newsletter.

330.9   US   ISSN 0002-8282
HB1
AMERICAN ECONOMIC REVIEW. 1911. q. $130 to non-members (includes Journal of Economic Literature and Journal of Economic Perspectives). American Economic Association, 2014 Broadway, Ste. 305, Nashville, TN 37203. TEL 615-322-2595. E-mail: aeainfo@ctrvax.vanderbilt.edu; URL: http://www.vanderbilt.edu/AEA. Ed. Orley Ashenfelter. R&P contact: Dana Ragan. adv.; charts; illus.; stat.; index. circ. 27,000. (also avail. in microfiche from MIM,PMC,UMI; reprint service avail. from SCH,UMI) **Indexed:** ABI Inform., Acad.Ind., Account.Ind. (1974-), Amer.Bibl.Slavic & E.Eur.Stud., Amer.Hist.& Life (1954-1981), (1983-), Arts & Hum.Cit.Ind., ASCA, B.P.I., Bank.Lit.Ind., Bibl.Agri., Bibl.Ind., Bk.Rev.Dig., Bk.Rev.Ind. (1965-1974), BPIA, Bus.Ind., C.R.E.J., Child.Bk.Rev.Ind. (1965-1974), Cont.Pg.Manage., Curr.Cont., Deep Sea Res.& Oceanogr.Abstr., Environ.Abstr., Excerp.Med., Fam.Ind., Geo.Abstr.H.G., Hist.Abstr. (1954-1981), (1983-), IBR, IDA, Ind.Per.Art.Relat.Law, Int.Lab.Doc., J.of Econ.Lit., Key to Econ.Sci., Mag.Ind., Maize Abstr., Mgmt.& Market.Abstr., Mid.East: Abstr.& Ind., Oper.Res.Manage.Sci., P.A.I.S., Popul.Ind., Pub.Admin.Abstr., Qual.Contr.Appl.Stat., Risk Abstr., Rural Recreat.Tour.Abstr., SCIMP (1978-), Sel.Water Res.Abstr., Soc.Sci.Ind., SSCI, Tr.& Indus.Ind., World Agri.Econ.& Rural Sociol.Abstr., World Bank.Abstr. **Document type:** academic/scholarly publication.
●Also available online.
—BLDSC (0813.500000); Genuine Article; KR SourceOne; SWETS; UMI; UnCover.
Description: Contains articles and short papers on economic subjects.

330.9   US   ISSN 0569-4345
AMERICAN ECONOMIST. 1960. s-a. $20 (foreign $45). Omicron Delta Epsilon Fraternity, c/o Michael Szenberg, Ed., Graduate School of Business, Dept. of Economics, Pace University, New York, NY 10038. TEL 212-346-1921. FAX 212-346-1573. adv.; bk.rev.; abstr.; bibl.; charts; stat.; index. circ. 6,000 (paid). (also avail. in microform from UMI; reprint service avail. from KTO) **Indexed:** Amer.Bibl.Slavic & E.Eur.Stud., B.P.I., BPIA, J.of Econ.Abstr., J.of Econ.Lit., Oper.Res.Manage.Sci., P.A.I.S., Soc.Sci.Ind., SSCI, Tr.& Indus.Ind., Work Rel.Abstr. **Document type:** academic/scholarly publication.
●Also available online. Vendor(s): Information Access Co., UMI.
—BLDSC (0813.550000); KR SourceOne; SWETS; UMI; UnCover.
Refereed Serial

BUSINESS AND ECONOMICS — ECONOMIC SITUATION AND CONDITIONS

330.9 320   UK   ISSN 1351-4571
AMERICAS REVIEW. 1979. a. £40. Kogan Page Ltd., 120 Pentonville Rd., London N1 9JN, England. TEL 44-171-278-0433. FAX 44-171-837-6348. TELEX 263088 KOGAN G. Ed. Tony Axon. R&P contact: Linda Batman. adv.; illus.; stat. circ. 7,380. **Document type:** consumer publication.
  Former titles: Latin America and Caribbean Review; (until 1985): Latin America and Caribbean (ISSN 0262-5415); (until 1981): Latin America Annual Review and the Caribbean.
  Description: Overview of economic, commercial and political situations in every country in the Latin American and Caribbean regions.

AMUSEMENT BUSINESS; international newsweekly for live entertainment and amusement industry. see THEATER

330.9   EC
ANALISIS SEMANAL. English edition: Weekly Analysis of Ecuadorian Issues (ISSN 0252-2659) w. $440. Walter R. Spurrier, Ed. & Pub., P.O. Box 4925, Elizalde 119, 1oo, Guayaquil, Ecuador. FAX 4-326-842. bk.rev.; index. circ. 1,000. **Document type:** newsletter.

380 332   PE   ISSN 0251-2491
HC226
ANDEAN REPORT. (Text in English) 1908. w. $520 (e-mail deliv. $350) (effective 1997). Andean Air Mail & Peruvian Times S.A., Pasaje Los Pinos, 156, Piso B, Of. 6, Miraflores, Lima, Peru. TEL 51-14-453761. FAX 51-14-467888. E-mail: perutimes@amauta.rcp.net.pe. Pub. Eleanor Zuniga. adv. contact: Luisa Perbuli. charts; stat.; index. circ. 4,000. Indexed: PROMT. **Document type:** newsletter.
●Also available online.
  Former titles (until 1975): Peruvian Times; (until 1940): West Coast Leader; (until 1912): Peru Today.
  Description: Covers economics, finance, development and politics in Peru.

330.9   US
ANDEAN WEEKLY FAX BULLETIN. w. $495 (foreign $595) (effective 1998). Orbis Publications, LLC, 3201 New Mexico Ave., Ste. 249, Washington, DC 20016. TEL 202-237-0155. FAX 202-237-0596. E-mail: orbis@orbispub.com; URL: http://www.earthnet.net/orbis. (only avail. by fax) **Document type:** bulletin.
  Description: Reports on political, economic, and business events in Chile, Colombia, Peru, and Venezuela.

330.9   ET
ANNUAIRE ECONOMIQUE DES PAYS MEMBRES DE L'ORGANISATION DE L'UNITE AFRICAINE/ECONOMIC YEARBOOK OF MEMBER STATES OF THE ORGANIZATION OF AFRICAN UNITY.* (Text in English and French) a. Organization for African Unity, Library - Organisation de l'Unite Africaine, P.O. Box 3246, Addis Ababa, Ethiopia.

330   RH   ISSN 1012-6236
ANNUAL ECONOMIC REVIEW OF ZIMBABWE. a. Z$5. Department of Printing and Stationery, P.O. Box 8062, Causeway, Zimbabwe. **Document type:** government publication.
  Former titles (until 1981): Economic Survey of Rhodesia (ISSN 0070-8739); (until 1965): Review of the Economy of Rhodesia (ISSN 0080-1992)

330.9   JA
ANNUAL REPORT ON NATIONAL ACCOUNTS. (Text in Japanese) a. 2600 Yen. (Economic Planning Agency) Ministry of Finance, Printing Bureau, 2-2-4 Toranomon, Minato-ku, Tokyo 105, Japan. (Editorial addr.: 3-1-1, Kasumigaseki, Chiyoda-ku, Tokyo 100, Japan) **Document type:** government publication.

330.9   JM
ANNUAL REPORT ON THE JAMAICAN ECONOMY (YEAR). 1985. a. J.$805($28) Private Sector Organisation of Jamaica, 39 Hope Rd., P.O. Box 236, Kingston 10, Jamaica, W.I. TEL 809-927-6238. FAX 809-927-5137. Ed. Charles Ross. R&P contact: Charles Ross. adv. circ. 750. (back issues avail.) **Document type:** newsletter.
  Formerly (until 1990): Economic Review (Year) (ISSN 0259-9171)
  Description: Review of economic activity in the Jamaican economy during the review year. Includes sectoral activity and outcomes on GDP as well as the effects of monetary and fiscal policies on economic activity.

330.9 332   UK   ISSN 0960-3107
HG11
APPLIED FINANCIAL ECONOMICS. (Supplement to: Applied Economics (ISSN 0003-6846)) 1991. bi-m. £225 in the E.U. (N. America $385; rest of world £240) (effective 1997). Routledge, 11 New Fetter Ln., London EC4P 4EE, England. TEL 44-171-583-9855. FAX 44-171-842-2298. E-mail: info.journals@routledge.com; URL: http://www.routledge.com/routledge/journal/journals.html. (Dist. by: International Thomson Publishing Services Ltd., Cheriton House, North Way, Andover, Hants. SP10 5BE, England. TEL 44-1264-342919. FAX 44-1264-342807; Subscr. in US & Canada to: 29 W. 35th St., New York, NY 10001-2299. TEL 212-244-3336. FAX 212-564-7854) Ed. Mark Taylor. (reprint service avail.) Indexed: B.P.I., Curr.Cont. **Document type:** academic/scholarly publication.
●Also available online.
—BLDSC (1572.555000); KR SourceOne; SWETS; UnCover. **CCC.**
  Description: Provides an international forum to link the research community with financial institutes and markets.
Refereed Serial

330.9   KU   ISSN 0378-8970
HF3762
ARABIAN YEAR BOOK; commercial directory. (Includes: Who's Who in the Gulf Area) (Text in English) 1978. a. $120. Al-Muna Advertising, Publishing & Distribution, P.O. Box 42480, 70655 Shuwaikh, Kuwait. TEL 965-4834922. FAX 965-4834893. Ed. Ahmed A. Al Jarallah; Pub. Ahmed Al Talleh. adv. contact: Ahmed A. Al Talleh. circ. 15,000. **Document type:** directory.
  Formerly: Arabian Trade Digest.
  Description: Commercial directory that includes names, addresses, and full details about companies and establishments in Bahrain, Kuwait, Oman, Qatar, Saudi Arabia, and United Arab Emirates.

330.9 388   GW   ISSN 0939-8872
ARBEITSPLAETZE IN UMSCHLAG- UND LAGERANLAGEN VON SPEDITIONSUNTERNEHMEN. 1991. irreg. DM.249.80. Erich Schmidt Verlag GmbH & Co. (Berlin), Genthiner Str. 30G, 10785 Berlin, Germany. TEL 49-30-250085-0. FAX 49-30-25008521. **Document type:** bulletin.

ARCHIV DER GEGENWART; die weltweite Dokumentation fuer Politik und Wirtschaft. see POLITICAL SCIENCE

330.9   IT
AREA TERZIARIA. 1987. m. L.10000. Gedip s.r.l., Via Ippolito Nievo 61, 00153 Rome, Italy. TEL 39-6-5895215. FAX 39-6-5806396. Ed. Alessandro Sciorilli. adv.: B&W page L.3000000, color page L.4000000. circ. 14,000. **Document type:** newsletter.

330.9   AG
ARGENTINA. MINISTERIO DE ECONOMIA. ECONOMIC REPORT. SUMMARY. 1973. q. Ministerio de Economia, Servicio de Prensa, Balcarce 136 - 5 Piso, Cf. 501, Buenos Aires, Argentina. stat.
  Continues: Argentina. Ministerio de Hacienda y Finanzas. Economic Report. Summary.

330.9   AG   ISSN 0325-383X
HC171
ARGENTINA. MINISTERIO DE ECONOMIA, HACIENDA Y FINANZAS. BOLETIN SEMANAL DE ECONOMIA. no.77, 1975. w. Ministerio de Economia, Subsecretaria de Coordinacion de Informacion Economica, Direccion Nacional de Prensa y Publicaciones Economicas, Hipolito Yrigoyen 250, 6 Piso, Oficina 625, 1310 Buenos Aires, Argentina. charts; stat.
  Formerly (until no.393, Jun. 1981): Argentina. Ministerio de Economia. Boletin Semanal.

330.9   US
ARGENTINA WEEKLY FAX BULLETIN. w. $465 (foreign $565) (effective 1998). Orbis Publications, LLC, 3201 New Mexico Ave., N.W., Ste. 249, Washington, DC 20016. TEL 202-237-0155. FAX 202-237-0596. E-mail: orbis@orbispub.com; URL: http://www.earthnet.net/orbis. (only avail. by fax) **Document type:** bulletin.
  Description: Reports on political, economic, and business events in Argentina.

330.9   AG
ARGENTINE ECONOMIC DEVELOPMENT. (Text in English, French) biennial. Ministerio de Economia, Balcarce 136, Buenos Aires, Argentina.

982   AG
ARGENTINE LETTER. 1988. m. $250. Ayacucho 1370, PB "A", 1111 Buenos Aires, Argentina. FAX 54-1-311-4385. (U.S. subscr. addr.: Box 855, Bethesda, MD 20817) Eds. Javier Gonzalez Fraga, Arturo Meyer. circ. 500.

330.9   GW
ARGUMENTE ZUR WIRTSCHAFTSPOLITIK. 1985. irreg. (approx. 5/yr.) free. Frankfurter Institut Stiftung, Marktwirtschaft und Politik, Kaiser-Friedrich-Promenade 157, 61352 Bad Homburg, Germany. **Document type:** academic/scholarly publication.

330.9   US   ISSN 1042-6787
ARIZONA BLUE CHIP ECONOMIC FORECAST. (Supplement avail.: Metro Phoenix Blue Chip Economic Forecast (ISSN 1042-6825)) 1984. m. $99 (effective May 1995). Arizona State University, Economic Outlook Center, College of Business, Box 874406, Tempe, AZ 85287-4406. TEL 602-965-5543; 800-448-0432. FAX 602-965-5458. Ed. Tracy Clark. illus. circ. 790. (back issues avail.) **Document type:** newsletter.
  Description: Contains consensus economic forecasts by month for Arizona, given by 22 economists representing banks, universities, companies and state agencies.

ARIZONA STATISTICAL ABSTRACT. see BUSINESS AND ECONOMICS — Abstracting, Bibliographies, Statistics

330.9   US
ARIZONA'S ECONOMY. 1979. q. free in the U.S.; foreign $12. University of Arizona, College of Business and Public Administration, Economic and Business Research Program, McClelland Hall 204K, Tucson, AZ 85721. TEL 520-621-2155. FAX 520-621-2150. E-mail: pmontoya@bpa.arizona.edu. Ed. Diana Hunter. circ. 5,500. Indexed: P.A.I.S.
  Description: Provides current analysis of business conditions and forecasts of future economic activity in Arizona.

ARIZONA'S WORKFORCE. see BUSINESS AND ECONOMICS — Labor And Industrial Relations

AS A MATTER OF FACT. see BUSINESS AND ECONOMICS — Investments

330.9 320   UK   ISSN 1351-458X
ASIA & PACIFIC REVIEW. 1980. a. £40. Kogan Page Ltd., 120 Pentonville Rd., London N1 9JN, England. TEL 44-171-278-0433. FAX 44-171-837-6348. TELEX 263088 KOGAN G. Ed. Tony Axon. R&P contact: Linda Batman. adv.; illus.; stat. circ. 10,830. Indexed: So.Pac.Per.Ind. **Document type:** consumer publication.
  Former titles (until 1985): Asia and Pacific (ISSN 0262-5407); (until 1981): Asia and Pacific Annual Review.
  Description: Overview on the economic and political situation in the Asian and Pacific region.

330.9   CC
ASIA CORPORATE PROFILE AND NATIONAL FINANCE. a. $60. Dataline Asia - Pacific Ltd., 3rd Fl. Hollywood Centre, 223 Hollywood Rd., Hong Kong, People's Republic of China. TEL 8155221. FAX 8542794. Ed. Amitabha Chowdury.

650   CC   ISSN 0004-4466
ASIA LETTER; a weekly newsletter containing an authoritative analysis of Asian affairs. 1964. w. $175. Asia Letter Group, G.P.O. Box 10874, Hong Kong, People's Republic of China. TEL 852-526-2950. FAX 852-526-7131. TELEX HX61166-HKNW. (US addr.: Box 88189, Los Angeles, CA 90009-8189) Ed. Charles R. Smith. bk.rev. Indexed: Key to Econ.Sci. **Document type:** newsletter.

BUSINESS AND ECONOMICS — ECONOMIC SITUATION AND CONDITIONS

338   UN   ISSN 1020-1246
HC411
ASIA - PACIFIC DEVELOPMENT JOURNAL. (Text in English) 1950. 2/yr. $17.50. United Nations Economic and Social Commission for Asia and the Pacific (ESCAP), United Nations Bldg., Rajadamnern Ave., Bangkok 10200, Thailand. (Dist. by: United Nations Publications, Rm. DC2-0853, New York, NY 10017; or: Distribution and Sales Section, Palais des Nations, CH-1211 Geneva 10, Switzerland; or: Conference Services Unit, E.S.C.A.P., Bangkok) (also avail. in microfilm from UMI; microfiche from CIS; back issues avail.; reprint service avail. from UMI,SCH) **Indexed:** Asian-Pac.Econ.Lit., C.R.E.J., E.I., IIS, Int.Lab.Doc., Key to Econ.Sci., Mid.East: Abstr.& Ind., P.A.I.S., PROMT. **Document type:** government publication, bulletin.
—BLDSC (1742.260190); SWETS.
Former titles (until 1994): Economic Bulletin for Asia and the Pacific (ISSN 0378-455X); Economic Bulletin for Asia and the Far East (ISSN 0041-6371)
Description: Examines economic issues and trends affecting the Pacific Rim.

330.9   MY   ISSN 0127-3337
ASIAN AND PACIFIC DEVELOPMENT CENTRE NEWSLETTER. 1980. 3/yr. free. Asian and Pacific Development Centre, P.O. Box 12224, 50770 Kuala Lumpur, Malaysia. TEL 03-2548088. FAX 03-2550316. TELEX MA-30676-APDEC. Ed. Yap Chin Yean. bk.rev. circ. 1,600. **Document type:** newsletter.
Formerly: Asian and Pacific Development Administration Centre. Occasional Papers Series. *Refereed Serial*

330.9   CK   ISSN 0122-6657
ASOBANCARIA SEMANA ECONOMICA. w. $350 (effective 1998). Asociacion Bancaria y de Entidades Financieras, Apdo. Aereo 13994, Bogota D.C., Colombia. TEL 57-1-2114811. FAX 57-1-2119915. E-mail: info@asobancaria.com; URL: http://www.asobancaria.com/. **Description:** Follows up on the main short-term indicators of the economy.

330.9   CK
ASOCIACION NACIONAL DE INSTITUCIONES FINANCIERAS. CARTA FINANCIERA. 1974. bi-m. Col.23000 (foreign $45). Asociacion Nacional de Instituciones Financieras, Calle 70A No. 7-86, Apdo. Aereo 29677, Bogota, Colombia. TEL 57-1-2128200. FAX 57-1-2355947. adv. circ. 4,000.

ASSET FINANCE AND LEASING DIGEST. see BUSINESS AND ECONOMICS — Investments

330.9   LE
ASSOCIATION DES BANQUES DU LIBAN. RAPPORT DU CONSEIL.* Cover title: Association des Banques du Liban. Rapport Annuel. (Text in French) irreg. Association of Banks in Lebanon, DORA, Centre Moucarri, P.O. Box 80536, Beirut, Lebanon. stat. **Document type:** corporate report.

ASTUTE INVESTOR (KINGSTON). see BUSINESS AND ECONOMICS — Investments

330.9   US
AT THE HELM; investment information for Scudder shareholders. 1985. q. free to shareholders of Scudder funds. Scudder Funds, 175 Federal St., Boston, MA 02110. TEL 617-728-9431. FAX 617-728-9450. circ. 550,000. **Document type:** newsletter.
Description: Provides investment information about mutual funds, financial markets, the economy, retirement and college planning, as well as Scudder products and services.

330.9   US   ISSN 0164-8071
ATLANTA BUSINESS CHRONICLE. 1978. w. $62. American City Business Journals, 1801 Peachtree St., No. 150, Atlanta, GA 30339-1859. TEL 404-249-1000. FAX 404-249-1058. URL: http://www.amcity.com/atlanta. Ed. David Rubinger; Pub. Ed Baker. R&P contact: Bo Meyer. adv. contact: Nancy Kenerly. bk.rev.; illus.; stat.; circ. 35,000 (paid). (tabloid format) **Indexed:** Tr.& Indus.Ind. **Document type:** trade publication.
●Also available online. Vendor(s): Information Access Co., Knight-Ridder Information, Inc.
—UMI. **CCC.**

330.1   CN   ISSN 0067-0162
HC117.M35
ATLANTIC PROVINCES ECONOMIC COUNCIL. ANNUAL REPORT. 1966. a. membership. Atlantic Provinces Economic Council, 5121 Sackville St., Ste. 500, Halifax, NS B3J 1K1, Canada. TEL 902-422-6516. FAX 902-429-6803. E-mail: apec@fox.nstn.ns.ca; URL: http://ttgsba.dal.ca/apec. Ed. Elizabeth Beale. R&P contact: Elizabeth Beale. circ. 1,000. **Document type:** corporate report.

330   CN   ISSN 0004-6841
HC117.A88   **CODEN:** ATRPEV
ATLANTIC REPORT. 1966. q. membership. Atlantic Provinces Economic Council, 5121 Sackville St., Ste. 500, Halifax, NS B3J 1K1, Canada. TEL 902-422-6516. FAX 902-429-6803. E-mail: apec@fox.nstn.ns.ca; URL: http://ttg.sba.dal.ca/apec. Ed. Elizabeth Beale. charts; stat. circ. 1,300. (also avail. in microfilm from MML) **Indexed:** Can.B.P.I., CMI.

330.9 332.6   US   ISSN 1064-3184
AURA WEALTH NEWSLETTER; economic survival in perilous times. (Text in English, Spanish) 1979. s-m. $2400 includes fax service 5/w. Aura Publishing Co., 441 Central Ave., Box 1367, Scarsdale, NY 10538. TEL 914-834-2322. FAX 914-833-0930. E-mail: rsandell@aura.com. Ed. Richard A. Sandell; Pub. Arnold P. Josevie. adv. contact: Marcel Aurevie. bk.rev.; cum.index: 1979-1994; circ. 2,950 (paid); 300 (controlled). (also avail. in diskette format) **Document type:** newsletter.
Description: Covers the discovery and evolution of international wealth building opportunities and their sensitivity to taxation in the Western democracies.

AUSSENHANDEL. see BUSINESS AND ECONOMICS — International Commerce

330.9   AT   ISSN 1324-0935
HT395.A78
AUSTRALASIAN JOURNAL OF REGIONAL STUDIES. 1987. s-a. Aus.$45 to individual members; institutional members Aus.$70 (effective 1997). Regional Science Association, Australian and New Zealand Section, c/o Linda Pink, University of New England, P.O. Box U271, Armidale, N.S.W. 2351, Australia. TEL 61-67-714838. E-mail: mangan@commerce.uq.edu.au. Ed. John Mangan. R&P contact: Guy West. adv. contact: Linda Pink. bk.rev. circ. 300. **Document type:** academic/scholarly publication.
—BLDSC (1795.160000).
Formerly (until no.8, 1994): Australian Journal of Regional Studies (ISSN 1030-7923)
Description: Provides a forum for the discussion of regional development and regional policy; includes papers from the Annual Meeting.
Refereed Serial

AUSTRALIA. BUREAU OF STATISTICS. WESTERN AUSTRALIAN OFFICE. WESTERN AUSTRALIAN YEARBOOK. see HISTORY — History Of Australasia And Other Areas

350   AT   ISSN 1032-4054
AUSTRALIA. DEPARTMENT OF PRIMARY INDUSTRIES AND ENERGY. ANNUAL REPORT. 1979. a. Aus.$39.95. Department of Primary Industries and Energy, G.P.O. Box 858, Canberra, A.C.T. 2601, Australia. **Indexed:** Energy Info.Abstr.
Formerly: Australia. Department of Primary Industry. Annual Report (ISSN 0158-1309)

330.9   AT
AUSTRALIAN ECONOMIC POLICY; updated articles from the Ecodate collection. 1993. triennial. Aus.$12.95. Warringal Publications, 114 Argyle St., Fitzroy, Vic. 3065, Australia. TEL 61-3-94160200. FAX 61-3-94160402. Ed. Garry Bell; Pub. Jane Arter. charts; stat. circ. 3,000. (back issues avail.) **Document type:** academic/scholarly publication.
Description: Provides information on recent developments in Australian economics. Covers economic problems and issues, recent policy approaches, current statistics and data.

330.994   AT   ISSN 0812-2261
THE AUSTRALIAN ECONOMY; a student's guide to current economic conditions. 1982. a. Aus.$10.95. Warringal Publications, 114 Argyle St., Fitzroy, Vic. 3065, Australia. TEL 61-3-94160200. FAX 61-3-94160402. Ed. Garry Bell; Pub. Jane Arter. charts; stat. circ. 5,000. (back issues avail.) **Document type:** academic/scholarly publication.
Description: Provides commentary on developments in the economy over the past year.

330.9 338.91   AT   ISSN 0817-8038
HC681.A1   **CODEN:** PEBUEQ
AUSTRALIAN NATIONAL UNIVERSITY. NATIONAL CENTRE FOR DEVELOPMENT STUDIES. PACIFIC ECONOMIC BULLETIN. 1986. s-a. Aus.$35. Australian National University, National Centre for Development Studies, Canberra, A.C.T. 0200, Australia. TEL 61-6-2494705. FAX 61-6-2572886. (Subscr. to: Bibliotech, G.P.O. Box 4, Canberra, A.C.T. 2601, Australia. FAX 61-6-2575088) Eds. Ila Temu, Maree Tait. bk.rev.; stat. circ. 700. (back issues avail.) **Indexed:** Asian-Pac.Econ.Lit., Food Sci.& Tech.Abstr., Geo.Abstr.P.G., IDA. **Document type:** academic/scholarly publication.
—BLDSC (6329.150000); EMDOCS; KR SourceOne; UnCover.
Description: Describes the economies and economic problems of the South Pacific for public servants, academics and businesses.
Refereed Serial

330.9 028.5 375   AT   ISSN 1324-6577
AUSTRALIA'S ECONOMIC OBJECTIVES AND MANAGEMENT. 1993. a. Aus.$10.95. Warringal Publications, 114 Argyle St., Fitzroy, Vic. 3065, Australia. TEL 61-3-94160200. FAX 61-3-94160402. Ed. Jane Arter; Pub. Jane Arter. charts; stat. circ. 1,500. (back issues avail.) **Description:** Provides information on the recent performance of the following key economic objectives of the Australian government: economic growth, full employment, price stability, equity in the distribution of income, external stability. For 12 grade students.

330.9   AU   ISSN 1025-6954
▼**AUSTRIAN ECONOMIC QUARTERLY.** 1996. q. S.1000 (effective 1997 & 1998). Oesterreichisches Institut fuer Wirtschaftsforschung - Austrian Institute of Economic Research, Postfach 91, A-1103 Vienna, Austria. TEL 43-1-79826010. FAX 43-1-7989386. URL: http://www.wsr.ac.at/wifo.html/. Ed. Helmut Kramer. adv. contact: Christine Knoll. charts; mkt.stat.; index. **Document type:** bulletin.
Description: Covers all aspects of the Austrian economy and its relations with the European Union and Eastern Europe.

330.9   AU
AUSTRIAN INDUSTRIES. ANNUAL REPORT. (Text in English) a. Austrian Industries AG, Kantgasse 1, A-1015 Vienna, Austria. TEL 01-71114. FAX 01-71114-245. **Document type:** corporate report.

AUSZUEGE AUS PRESSEARTIKELN. see BUSINESS AND ECONOMICS — Abstracting, Bibliographies, Statistics

330   FR   ISSN 0045-1142
AUVERGNE ECONOMIQUE. 1968. 8/yr. 200 F. (effective 1997). Association Auvergne Economique, Aeroport de Clermont-Ferrand, Immeuble de Bureaux, 63510 Aulnat, France. TEL 33-4-73918181. FAX 33-4-73929364. Ed. Gerard Duval. adv.; bk.rev.; illus. circ. 11,000.

AVANCE DE INFORMACION ECONOMICA. PRODUCTO INTERNO BRUTO TRIMESTRAL. see BUSINESS AND ECONOMICS — Abstracting, Bibliographies, Statistics

330.9   US
AVERAGE ANNUAL PAY BY STATE AND INDUSTRY. (Subseries of: National Office News Releases) a. U.S. Bureau of Labor Statistics, 2 Massachusetts Ave., N.E., Washington, DC 20212. TEL 202-655-4000. (Subscr. to: Superintendent of Documents, U.S. Government Printing Office, Box 371954, Pittsburgh, PA 15250-7954. TEL 202-512-1800. FAX 202-512-2250; Or: Bureau of Labor Statistics Publications Sales Center, Box 2145, Chicago, IL 60690) **Document type:** government publication.

BUSINESS AND ECONOMICS — ECONOMIC SITUATION AND CONDITIONS

330.9 US
AVERAGE ANNUAL PAY LEVELS IN METROPOLITAN AREAS (YEAR). (Subseries of: National Office News Releases) a.? U.S. Bureau of Labor Statistics, 2 Massachusetts Ave., N.E., Washington, DC 20212. TEL 202-655-4000. (Subscr. to: Superintendent of Documents, U.S. Government Printing Office, Box 371954, Pittsburgh, PA 15250-7954. TEL 202-512-1800. FAX 202-512-2250; Or: Bureau of Labor Statistics Publications Sales Center, Box 2145, Chicago, IL 60690) Document type: government publication.

AVIS ET DECISIONS DU CONSEIL DE LA CONCURRENCE. see BUSINESS AND ECONOMICS — Banking And Finance

330.9 GW
B A W - MONATSBERICHT. 1978. m. free. Bremer Ausschuss fuer Wirtschaftsforschung, Schlachte 10-11, 28195 Bremen, Germany. TEL 49-421-3618804. FAX 49-421-3618810. Ed. Siegfried Loercher. circ. 1,200. (back issues avail.) Document type: bulletin.
Formerly (until 1986): Konjunkturspiegel.

330.9 CN
HC117.B8
B C FINANCIAL AND ECONOMIC REVIEW. (British Columbia Financial and Economic Review) a. Can.$25 (effective 1997). Ministry of Finance and Corporate Relations, P.O. Box 9410, Stn. Prov. Govt., Victoria, BC V8W 9V1, Canada. TEL 250-387-0359. FAX 250-387-0380. E-mail: kris__ovens@fincc04.fin.gov.bc.ca; bcstats@fincc04.fin.gov.bc.ca; URL: http://www.bcstats.gov.bc.ca. charts; maps. Document type: government publication.
Formerly: B C Economic and Statistical Review (ISSN 0847-1525); Which was formed by the merger of: British Columbia. Ministry of Finance and Corporate Relations. Financial and Economic Review; British Columbia. Ministry of Finance and Corporate Relations. Facts and Statistics.
Description: Describes BC's physical and institutional structure as well as presents information on provincial government programs and finances, economic developments and demographic trends.

318 US
B E B R MONOGRAPHS. irreg., no.8. $17. University of Florida, College of Business Administration, Bureau of Economic and Business Research, Box 11745, 221 Matherly Hall, Gainesville, FL 32611-7145. TEL 352-392-0171. FAX 352-392-4739. Document type: monographic series.
Description: Provides in-depth analyses of topics relevant to an understanding of the Florida economy and business situation.

330.9 US
B L S RELEASES: DEMOGRAPHIC DATA BOOK FOR STATES AND LARGE METROPOLITAN AREAS. (Subseries of: National Office News Releases) a. U.S. Bureau of Labor Statistics, 2 Massachusetts Ave., N.E., Washington, DC 20212. TEL 202-655-4000. (Subscr. to: Superintendent of Documents, U.S. Government Printing Office, Box 371954, Pittsburgh, PA 15250-7954. TEL 202-512-1800. FAX 202-512-2250; Or: Bureau of Labor Statistics Publications Sales Office, Box 2145, Chicago, IL 60690) Document type: government publication.

330.9 US
B L S REPORTS ON EMPLOYEE BENEFITS IN THE UNITED STATES. (Subseries of B L S Reports) biennial? U.S. Bureau of Labor Statistics, 2 Massachusetts Ave., N.E., Washington, DC 20212. TEL 202-655-4000. (Subscr. to: Superintendent of Documents, U.S. Government Printing Office, Box 371954, Pittsburgh, PA 15250-7954. TEL 202-512-1800. FAX 202-512-2250; Or: Bureau of Labor Statistics Publications Sales Center, Box 2145, Chicago, IL 60690) Document type: government publication.

330.9 US ISSN 1047-0352
HC101
L S UPDATE. q. free. U.S. Bureau of Labor Statistics, Department of Labor, 2 Massachusetts Ave., N.E., Washington, DC 20212. TEL 202-606-5886. (Subscr. to: Bureau of Labor Statistics Publications Sales Center, Box 2145, Chicago, IL 60690) bibl.; stat. Document type: catalog, government publication.
Formerly: New from B L S (ISSN 0898-1965)
Description: Lists publications issued by B.L.S. and provides news of the bureau.

330.9 US ISSN 1058-7365
KJC6411.3
B N A'S EASTERN EUROPE REPORTER. 1991. bi-w. $895. The Bureau of National Affairs, Inc., 1231 25th St., N.W., Washington, DC 20037. TEL 202-452-4200. FAX 202-822-8092. TELEX 285656 BANI WSH. URL: http://www.bna.com/. (Subscr. to: 9435 Key West Ave., Rockville, MD 20850. TEL 800-372-1033) Ed. Linda G. Botsford. (back issues avail.)
● Also available online.
—CCC.
Description: Covers legislative, regulatory, and legal developments affecting business, trade, and investment in Eastern Europe and Russia.

330.9 IT
HC301
B N L TRENDS. (Text in English and German) 1959. m. (Banca Nazionale del Lavoro, Ufficio Studi) B N L Edizioni S.p.A., Via Lucillo 7, 00187 Rome, Italy. TEL 39-6-4884380. FAX 39-6-4745272. Ed. Bruno Brovedani. charts; stat. circ. 5,600.
Formerly (until 1988): Italian Trends (ISSN 0021-3004)

330.9 SL
B S L BULLETIN. 1995. q. free. Bank of Sierra Leone, Research Department, Siaka Stevens St., P.O. Box 30, Freetown, Sierra Leone. TEL 232-22-226501. FAX 232-22-224767. TELEX 3232 FREETOWN. Ed. A.Seshan. bk.rev.; charts; stat. Indexed: P.A.I.S. Document type: bulletin.
Formed by the Jan. 1995 merger of: Bank of Sierra Leone. Economic Trends & Bank of Sierra Leone. Economic Review & Bank of Sierra Leone. Economic Report.
Description: Discusses economic issues affecting Sierra Leone. Publishes speeches on various financial topics by prominent Bank of Sierra Leone officials and contains public notices.
Refereed Serial

BAHAMAS DATELINE. see BUSINESS AND ECONOMICS — Investments

330.9 BF ISSN 0067-2912
F1650
BAHAMAS HANDBOOK AND BUSINESSMAN'S ANNUAL. 1960. a. $24.95 softcover; hardcover $30. Etienne Dupuch Jr. Publications Ltd., P.O. Box N-7513, Nassau, Bahamas. TEL 809-323-5665. FAX 809-323-5728. Ed. S.P. Dupuch. R&P contact: S.P. Dupuch. adv.; index.
Description: Leisure and vacation, business and finance in the Bahamas. Includes two A-Z listings of facts and figures.

650 BF ISSN 0005-397X
BAHAMIAN REVIEW. 1952. 10/yr. $50. Bahamian Review, Ltd., P.O. Box 494, Nassau, Bahamas. TEL 809-32-6-7416. (And: P.O. Box 1597, Nassau, Bahamas) Ed. William W. Cartwright. adv.; bk.rev.; charts; illus. circ. 50,000.

330.9 IT ISSN 0393-2400
HC301
BANCA D'ITALIA. BOLLETTINO ECONOMICO. English edition: Banca d'Italia. Economic Bulletin. 1983. 2/yr. free. Banca d'Italia, Servizio Studi, Via Nazionale 91, Rome, Italy. TEL 39-6-47922333. FAX 39-6-4747820. Ed. Ignazio Visco. circ. 15,000. Indexed: P.A.I.S.For.Lang.Ind., World Bank.Abstr. Document type: bulletin.

330.9 330.1 IT
BANCA D'ITALIA. CONTRIBUTI ALLA ANALISI ECONOMICA. 1971. a. free. Banca d'Italia, Servizio Studi, Via Nazionale 91, 00184 Rome, Italy. TEL 39-6-47922333. FAX 39-6-4747820. Ed. Ignazio Visco. circ. 5,500. Document type: monographic series.
Formerly: Banca d'Italia. Contributi alla Ricerca Economica (ISSN 0392-4661)

BANCA SANTO PAULO DI BRESCIA. NOTIZIARIO ECONOMICO. see BUSINESS AND ECONOMICS — Banking And Finance

BANCO CENTRAL DE CHILE. BOLETIN MENSUAL. see BUSINESS AND ECONOMICS — Banking And Finance

BANCO CENTRAL DE CHILE. MEMORIA ANUAL. see BUSINESS AND ECONOMICS — Banking And Finance

330 HO
BANCO CENTRAL DE HONDURAS. INFORME ECONOMICO. 1960. a. Banco Central de Honduras, Departamento de Estudios Economicos, 6a y 7a Avda., 1a Calle, Tegucigalpa, D.C., Honduras. charts; stat.

330.9 HO
BANCO CENTRAL DE HONDURAS. MEMORIA (YEAR). 1950. a. free. Banco Central de Honduras, Departamento de Estudios Economicos, 6a y 7a Avda., 1a Calle, Tegucigalpa D.C., Honduras. charts; stat.
Former titles: Banco Central de Honduras. Memoria Anual (Year); Banco Central de Honduras. Memoria (ISSN 0067-3218)

330 VE ISSN 0067-3250
HC236
BANCO CENTRAL DE VENEZUELA. INFORME ECONOMICO. 1962. s-a. $6 (effective 1994). Banco Central de Venezuela, Avda. Urdaneta Esq. de las Carmelitas, Caracas 1010, Venezuela. TEL 58-2-8015111.

330.9 EC
BANCO CENTRAL DEL ECUADOR. BOLETIN ANUARIO. 1978. a. free or exchange basis. Banco Central del Ecuador, Casilla 29C, Sucursal No.15, Quito, Ecuador. TEL 561-521. (Distr. by: Libreria Economia y Cultura, Av. 10 de Agosto, No. 600 y Checa, Quito, Ecuador) Ed. Aurelio Salas. charts; illus.; stat. circ. 3,000. Indexed: P.A.I.S.For.Lang.Ind.
Incorporates: Banco Central del Ecuador. Memoria Anual de Actividades.

330.9 918.6 EC
BANCO CENTRAL DEL ECUADOR. DIVISION TECNICA. CUENTAS NACIONALES. 1981. a. free. Banco Central del Ecuador, Division Tecnica, Gerencia de Estudios Economicos, Casilla 29C, Sucursal No.15, Quito, Ecuador. TEL 561-521. (Distr. by: Libreria Economia y Cultura, Av. 10 de Agosto, No. 600 y Checa, Quito, Ecuador) circ. 6,000.
Formerly (until 1987): Banco Central del Ecuador. Division Tecnica. Cuentas Nacionales del Ecuador.

330.9 UY
BANCO CENTRAL DEL URUGUAY. CUENTAS NACIONALES. a. free. Banco Central del Uruguay, Departamento de Estadisticas Economicas, Casilla 1467, Paysando y Florida, Montevideo, Uruguay. FAX 598-2-921782. Ed. Ariel E. Collazo.

330 UY
BANCO CENTRAL DEL URUGUAY. SELECCION DE TEMAS. q. free. Banco Central del Uruguay, Departamento de Estadisticas Economicas, Casilla 1467, Paysando y Florida, Montevideo, Uruguay. charts; stat.
Formerly: Banco Central del Uruguay. Seleccion de Temas Economicos (ISSN 0005-4755); Which superseded: Banco de la Republica Oriental del Uruguay. Boletin Mensual. Seleccion de Temas Economicos.

330.9 SP
BANCO DE BILBAO. ECONOMIC REPORT. (Text in English) a. Banco de Bilbao, Servicio de Estudios, Gran Via 12, Bilbao, Spain. charts; stat.

330.9 SP ISSN 0522-1315
HG3190.B54
BANCO DE BILBAO. INFORME ECONOMICO. 1950. a. Banco de Bilbao, Servicio de Estudios, Apartado 21, Bilbao, Spain. charts; stat.

330.9 SP ISSN 0210-3737
HC381
BANCO DE ESPANA. BOLETIN ECONOMICO. (Supplement included: Boletin Estadistico. Notas; Includes: Informe Anual; Cuentas Financieras de la Economia Espanola). m. 22472 ptas. in Europe 36000 ptas.; America 51500 ptas.; elsewhere 58000 ptas. (includes Boletin Estadistico). Banco de Espana, Seccion de Publicaciones, Negociado de Distribucion y Gestion, Alcala 50, 28014 Madrid, Spain. TEL 338-51-80. Indexed: ELLIS. Document type: bulletin.
—CINDOC.

330.9 SP ISSN 1130-4987
BANCO DE ESPANA. ECONOMIC BULLETIN. (Text in English) 1990. q. 7072 ptas. (foreign 13600 ptas.). Banco de Espana, Seccion de Publicaciones, Negociado de Distribucion y Gestion, Alcala 50, 28013 Madrid, Spain. TEL 338-51-80. FAX 34-1-3385320. charts, stat. Document type: bulletin.

1224 BUSINESS AND ECONOMICS — ECONOMIC SITUATION AND CONDITIONS

330.946 SP ISSN 0213-2699
BANCO DE ESPANA. ESTUDIOS ECONOMICOS; serie azul. 1972. irreg., no.43, 1987. 636 ptas. (foreign 1800 ptas.) per vol. Banco de Espana, Seccion de Publicaciones, Negociado de Distribucion y Gestion, Alcala 50, 28014 Madrid, Spain. TEL 34-1-3385180.

BANCO DE LA REPUBLICA. REVISTA. see *BUSINESS AND ECONOMICS — Banking And Finance*

330.9 MX
BANCO DE MEXICO. INDICADORES ECONOMICOS. 1972. m. Mex.$800 (America $240; Europe $300; elsewhere $360) (effective Aug. 1996). Banco de Mexico, Subdireccion de Investigacion Economica y Bancaria, Av. Juarez 90, Col. Centro, Del. Cuauhtemoc, 06059 Mexico DF, Mexico. TEL 525-761-8588. charts; stat.
Description: Contains statistics on monetary indicators, public finance, production, price and salary indexes.

BANCO DE MEXICO. INFORME ANUAL. see *BUSINESS AND ECONOMICS — Banking And Finance*

330.9 PO ISSN 0872-9794
▼**BANCO DE PORTUGAL. BOLETIM ECONOMICO.** English edition: Bank of Portugal. Economic Bulletin (ISSN 0872-9786) 1995. q. Banco de Portugal, Departamento de Estatistica e Estudos Economicos, Av. Almirante Reis 71, 1150 Lisbon, Portugal.

338.9 BL
BANCO DO NORDESTE DO BRASIL. SERIE ESTUDOS ECONOMICOS E SOCIAIS. 1975. irreg. Banco do Nordeste do Brasil, Celula da Administracao da Documentacao e Informacao, Av. Paranjana, 5700 Passare, 60740-000 Fortaleza CE, Brazil. TEL 55-85-2993137. FAX 55-85-2993524.

330.9 EC
BANCO NACIONAL DE FOMENTO. INFORME DE LABORES. a. Banco Nacional de Fomento, Departamento de Relaciones Publicas, Apdo. 685, Quito, Ecuador. charts; illus.; stat.

330.9 BL
BANCO REGIONAL DE DESENVOLVIMENTO DO EXTREMO SUL. ANNUAL REPORT. 1965. a. free. Banco Regional de Desenvolvimento do Extremo Sul, Caixa Postal 139, 90010-140 Porto Alegre RS, Brazil. TEL 051-228-92-00. FAX 051-228-82-83. TELEX 51-1229 BRDE BR. illus. circ. 1,000. **Document type:** corporate report.
Formed by the merger of: Banco Regional de Desenvolvimento do Extremo Sul. Relatorio da Diretoria (ISSN 0522-2079); Banco Regional de Desenvolvimento do Extremo Sul. Relatorio Annual.

BANGKO SENTRAL REVIEW. see *BUSINESS AND ECONOMICS — Banking And Finance*

338.9 BG
BANGLADESH. PLANNING COMMISSION. ANNUAL DEVELOPMENT PROGRAMME.* Bengali edition: Barshika Unnayana Karmasuci. (Text in English) a. (Planning Commission) Bangladesh Government Press, Ministry of Establishment, Teigaoh, Thaka 1209, Bangladesh.

330.9 BG ISSN 0304-9345
HC440.8.A1
BANGLADESH BANK. BULLETIN. (Text in English) 1973. m. Tk.50($36) Bangladesh Bank, Department of Public Relations and Publications, Motijheel Commercial Area, Dhaka 2, Bangladesh.

338 304.6 BG ISSN 0304-095X
HC440.8.A1
BANGLADESH DEVELOPMENT STUDIES. (Text in English) 1973. q. Tk.200($50) Bangladesh Unnayan Gobeshona Protishthan - Bangladesh Institute of Development Studies, G.P.O. Box 3854, E-17 Agargaon, Sher-e-Banglanagar, Dhaka 1207, Bangladesh. TEL 880-2-316959. FAX 880-2-833212. TELEX 642460 BHL BJ. Ed.Bd. adv.; bk.rev.; charts; illus.; index. circ. 1,500. (reprint service avail. from SCH) **Indexed:** Cott.& Trop.Fibr.Abstr., IDA, Irr.& Drain.Abstr., J.of Econ.Lit., Key to Econ.Sci., P.A.I.S., Per.Islam. (1992-), Popul.Ind., Rural Devel.Abstr., Rural Ext.Educ.& Tr.Abstr., Rural Recreat.Tour.Abstr., Soils & Fert., Triticale Abstr., World Agri.Econ.& Rural Sociol.Abstr. **Document type:** academic/scholarly publication.
—BLDSC (1861.620000); SWETS; UnCover.
Supersedes: Bangladesh Economic Review (ISSN 0304-2553)

338 BG
BANGLADESH INSTITUTE OF DEVELOPMENT STUDIES. ANNUAL REPORT. (Text in English) 1975. a. price varies. Bangladesh Unnayan Gobeshona Protishthan - Bangladesh Institute of Development Studies, G.P.O. Box 3854, E-17 Agargaon, Sher-e-Banglanagar, Dhaka 1207, Bangladesh. TEL 325401.
Formerly: Report on the Background, Current Programmes and Planned Development of the Bangladesh Institute of Development Studies.
Description: Discusses progress of current projects and plans for future research.

BANGLADESH NEWS. see *ETHNIC INTERESTS*

330 BG
BANGLADESH: SELECTED ECONOMIC INDICATORS. (Text in English) 1972. w. Bangladesh Bank, Department of Public Relations and Publications, Motijheel Commercial Area, Dhaka 2, Bangladesh.

BANK MARKAZI JOMHOURI ISLAMI IRAN. BULLETIN. see *BUSINESS AND ECONOMICS — Banking And Finance*

330.9 IR
BANK MARKAZI JOMHOURI ISLAMI IRAN. SURVEY OF THE LARGE MANUFACTURING INDUSTRIES. q. Bank Markazi Jomhouri Islami Iran, Economic Statistics Department - Central Bank of the Islamic Republic of Iran, P.O. Box 11365-8531, Tehran, Iran. FAX 98-21-390323. TELEX 216219.
Formerly (until 1983): Bank Markazi Iran. Survey of the Large Manufacturing Industries.

330.9 MY
BANK NEGARA MALAYSIA. ANNUAL REPORT. (Text in English, Malay) a. $45 in Asia & Australasia; Europe $55; African & American $60. Bank Negara Malaysia - Central Bank of Malaysia, P.O. Box 10922, Jalan Dato'Onn, 50480 Kuala Lumpur, Malaysia. TEL 2988044. FAX 2912990. TELEX MA 30201. Ed.Bd. charts, stat.; circ. controlled.
Description: Features a comprehensive material on economic developments and trends in Malaysia. Includes information on money and credit, public finance, real sector development (production, prices, wages and employment), and external sector developments (exchange rate, trade and balance of payments).

330.9 MY ISSN 0005-5115
HC445.5.A1
BANK NEGARA MALAYSIA. BULLETIN EKONOMI SUKU TAHUNAN/BANK NEGARA MALAYSIA. QUARTERLY ECONOMIC BULLETIN. (Text in English, Malay) 1968. 3/yr. $60 in Asia & Australasia; Europe $77; Africa & America $85. Bank Negara Malaysia - Central Bank of Malaysia, P.O. Box 10922, Jalan Dato'Onn, 50480 Kuala Lumpur, Malaysia. TEL 03-2988044. FAX 03-2912990. TELEX MA 30201. charts; stat.; circ. controlled. **Indexed:** Key to Econ.Sci., World Bank.Abstr. **Document type:** bulletin.
Description: Covers international economic environment and Malaysian economy with major indicators such as annual change in GDP and monetary aggregates.

BANK NEGARA MALAYSIA. STATISTICAL BULLETIN. see *BUSINESS AND ECONOMICS — Abstracting, Bibliographies, Statistics*

330.9 UK ISSN 1353-6737
HC251
BANK OF ENGLAND. INFLATION REPORT. 1993. q. £12 (rest of Europe £14; elsewhere £21-£22); with Quarterly Bulletin £40 (rest of Europe £48; elsewhere £64-£66) (effective 1997). Bank of England, Publications Group, Inflation Report Division, Threadneedle St., London EC2R 8AH, England. TEL 44-171-601-4030. FAX 44-171-601-5196. **Document type:** academic/scholarly publication.
—BLDSC (4478.846300).
Description: Seeks greater openness in explaining the basis of monetary policy. Analyzes inflationary trends and pressures and examines the range of intermediate indicators that help gauge the future path of inflation.

330.9 UK ISSN 0005-5166
HG2994
BANK OF ENGLAND QUARTERLY BULLETIN. 1960. q. £40 (rest of Europe £48; elsewhere £64-£66 (includes Inflation Report) (effective 1997). Bank of England, Publications Group, Inflation Report Division, Threadneedle St., London EC2R 8AH, England. TEL 44-171-601-4030. FAX 44-171-601-5196. abstr.; stat. (also avail. in microform from UMI; reprint service avail. from UMI, SCH) **Indexed:** BPIA, C.R.E.J., Cont.Pg.Manage., ELLIS, Key to Econ.Sci., Mgmt.& Market.Abstr., P.A.I.S., World Bank.Abstr. **Document type:** bulletin.
—BLDSC (7171.400000); SWETS; UMI.
Description: Describes and assesses recent economic and financial developments at home and abroad.

330.9 GH ISSN 0855-0964
HG517.G6
BANK OF GHANA. QUARTERLY ECONOMIC BULLETIN. 1961. q. free. Bank of Ghana, Information, Documentation and Publications Services Department, Accra, Ghana. TEL 233-21-66902-8. TELEX 2052 GHBANK. Ed.Bd. charts; stat. circ. 3,000. **Document type:** bulletin.

330.9 US ISSN 0893-0732
HC687.H3
BANK OF HAWAII BUSINESS TRENDS; a newsletter report of business and economic conditions in Hawaii. 1956. bi-m. free. Bank of Hawaii, Economics Department, Box 2900, Honolulu, HI 96846. TEL 808-537-8307. FAX 808-536-9433. URL: http://www.boh.com/econ/. Ed. Paul H. Brewbaker. stat. circ. 13,000. (back issues avail.) **Document type:** newsletter.
●Also available online.
Former titles: Bank of Hawaii. Review of Business and Economic Conditions; Bank of Hawaii Monthly Review (ISSN 0005-5204)

332 II ISSN 0005-5212
BANK OF INDIA. BULLETIN. (Text in English) 1962. m. Rs.12. Bank of India, Express Towers, Nariman Point, Bombay 400 021, India. TEL 203-3020. FAX 202-2831. TELEX 011-2281 IN. Ed. S.A. Shetty. charts; stat. circ. 6,000. **Document type:** bulletin.

332 IS
BANK OF ISRAEL. ECONOMIC REVIEW. (Editions in English and Hebrew) 1955. irreg., latest no.67. IS.22. Bank of Israel, Research Department, Kiryath Ben Gurion, P.O. Box 780, Jerusalem 91007, Israel Eds. Dorothea Shefer, Alan Hercberg. stat. circ. 1,000. **Indexed:** Ind.Heb.Per., Key to Econ.Sci., P.A.I.S., World Bank.Abstr.
Formerly: Bank of Israel. Bulletin (ISSN 0005-5220)

330 IS
BANK OF ISRAEL. RECENT ECONOMIC DEVELOPMENTS. (Text in English and Hebrew) q. IS.10. Bank of Israel Research Department, Kiryath Ben Gurion, P.O. Box 780, Jerusalem 91007, Israel. **Indexed:** World Bank.Abstr.

330.9 LY ISSN 0067-3714
BANK OF LIBYA. ANNUAL REPORT OF THE BOARD OF DIRECTORS.* (Editions in Arabic and English) 1957 a. free. Bank of Libya, Economic Research Division, P.O.B. 1103, Sharia al-Mahik Scoud, Tripoli, Libya. **Document type:** corporate report.

BUSINESS AND ECONOMICS — ECONOMIC SITUATION AND CONDITIONS

330.9   LY   ISSN 0005-5271
BANK OF LIBYA. ECONOMIC RESEARCH DIVISION. ECONOMIC BULLETIN.* (Text in Arabic and English) 1961. bi-m. free. Bank of Libya, P.O.B. 1103, Sharia al-Mahik Scoud, Tripoli, Libya. charts; mkt. circ. 2,000. **Document type:** bulletin.

332.1   SL
BANK OF SIERRA LEONE. ANNUAL REPORT AND STATEMENT OF ACCOUNTS. a. free. Bank of Sierra Leone, Siaka Stevens St., P.O. Box 30, Freetown, Sierra Leone. TEL 232-22-226501. FAX 232-22-224767. TELEX 3232 FREETOWN. **Document type:** corporate report.
     Formerly: Bank of Sierra Leone. Annual Report (ISSN 0067-3730)

332   SJ
BANK OF SUDAN. ECONOMIC AND FINANCIAL STATISTICS REVIEW. (Editions in Arabic, English) 1960. q. free. Bank of Sudan, Statistics Dept., P.O. Box 313, Khartoum, Sudan. TEL 78064. TELEX 22559 ELBNK SD. charts; stat. circ. 1,000. (processed) **Indexed:** Numis.Lit.
     Formerly (until vol.17, no.2, 1976): Bank of Sudan. Economic and Financial Bulletin (ISSN 0005-5336)
     Description: Details Sudan's economic conditions through tables showing the trade balance, balance of payments, the deficit, loans, foreign reserves, imports and exports by commodity, and industrial production and consolidation sheet.

332   CH   ISSN 0005-5344
HC430.5
BANK OF TAIWAN QUARTERLY. Key Title: Taiwan Yinhang Jikan. (Text in Chinese) 1947. q. NT.$150. Bank of Taiwan, Economic Research Department, 198 Chung-Hua Rd., Sec. 1, Taipei, 108 Taiwan, Republic of China. TEL 383211. FAX 3895294. (Dist. by: Chung-Hwa Book Co. Ltd., 94 Chungking S. Rd. Sec. 1, Taipei, Taiwan, R.O.C.) Ed. Y.T. Ting; Pub. M.S. Tsai. charts; illus.; stat.; index. circ. 1,500. **Document type:** academic/scholarly publication. —BLDSC (8600.600000).

330 332   TZ   ISSN 0067-3757
BANK OF TANZANIA. ECONOMIC AND OPERATIONS REPORT (YEAR). a. free. Bank of Tanzania, Research and Statistics Department, P.O. Box 2939, Dar es Salaam, Tanzania. TEL 255-51-21291. FAX 255-51-37485. TELEX 41024 TZ. charts; stat. circ. 3,000. **Document type:** corporate report.
     Formerly: Bank of Tanzania. Economic Report (ISSN 0067-3765)
     Description: Details economic developments and operations for the year.

330.9   TZ   ISSN 0856-101X
BANK OF TANZANIA. ECONOMIC BULLETIN. (Annual report issued in June no.) 1969. q. free or on exchange basis. Bank of Tanzania, Research and Statistics Department, P.O. Box 2939, Dar es Salaam, Tanzania. TEL 255-51-21291. FAX 255-51-37485. TELEX 41024 TZ. charts; stat. circ. 2,500. **Indexed:** Key to Econ.Sci. **Document type:** bulletin.
     Description: Discusses finance, credit, trade, and development in Tanzania.

330   TH
BANK OF THAILAND. ANNUAL ECONOMIC REPORT. a. $8.50. Bank of Thailand, Department of Economic Research, P.O. Box 154 BMC., Bangkok, Thailand. TEL 662-283-5617. FAX 662-282-5082. circ. 2,350. **Document type:** corporate report.

330.9   TH   ISSN 0125-605X
HG3300.55
BANK OF THAILAND. QUARTERLY BULLETIN. 1961. q. B.780($30) Bank of Thailand, Department of Economic Research, P.O. Box 154 BMC., Bangkok, Thailand. TEL 662-283-5617. FAX 662-282-5082. index. circ. 2,000. **Indexed:** Asian-Pac.Econ.Lit., Key to Econ.Sci., P.A.I.S., World Bank.Abstr. **Document type:** bulletin.
     Former titles (until 1981): Bank of Thailand. Monthly Bulletin (ISSN 0005-5352); Bank of Thailand Monthly Report.

330.9   IO
BANK PEMBANGUNAN INDONESIA. BULLETIN EKONOMI BAPINDO. m. Bank Pembangunan Indonesia - Development Bank of Indonesia, 2-4 Jalan Gondangdia Lama, P.O. Box 140, Jakarta, Indonesia.

330.9   GW
BANKGESELLSCHAFT BERLIN. DEVISENBRIEF. 1983. fortn. free. Bankgesellschaft Berlin AG, Alexanderplatz 2, 10178 Berlin, Germany. TEL 49-30-245500. FAX 49-30-24566333. circ. 4,600. **Document type:** bulletin.

330.9   GW
BANKGESELLSCHAFT BERLIN. KONJUNKTURBRIEF. 1977. m. free. Bankgesellschaft Berlin AG, Alexanderplatz 2, 10178 Berlin, Germany. TEL 49-30-245500. FAX 49-30-24566333. charts. circ. 9,000. **Document type:** bulletin.
     Formerly: Berliner Bank. Konjunkturbrief.

330.9   GW
BANKGESELLSCHAFT BERLIN. UNTERNEHMERBRIEF. 1992. irreg. (2-3/yr.). free. Bankgesellschaft Berlin AG, Alexanderplatz 2, 10178 Berlin, Germany. TEL 49-30-245500. FAX 49-30-24566333. circ. 1,500. **Document type:** bulletin.

330.9   GW
BANKGESELLSCHAFT BERLIN. WIRTSCHAFTSBERICHT. 1951. 2/yr. free. Bankgesellschaft Berlin AG, Alexanderplatz 2, 10178 Berlin, Germany. TEL 49-30-245500. FAX 49-30-24566333. charts; stat. circ. 12,100. **Document type:** corporate report.
     Formerly: Berliner Bank. Wirtschaftsbericht (ISSN 0005-9277)

BANQUE DE FRANCE. BULLETIN. see BUSINESS AND ECONOMICS — Banking And Finance

330.9   FR
BANQUE DE FRANCE. DIRECTION DE LA CONJONCTURE. SITUATION FINANCIERE DES REGIONS DE PROVINCE EN (YEAR); operations des residents. a. 40 F. (effective 1992). (Conseil National du Credit) Banque de France, Service de l'Information, 48, rue Croix des Petits Champs, 75001 Paris, France. TEL 1-42-92-39-08. FAX 1-42-92-39-40.
     Formerly: Etude sur la Situation Financiere des Regions.

338.9   FR
BANQUE DE FRANCE. DIRECTION DE LA CONJONCTURE. SITUATION FINANCIERE DES REGIONS EN (YEAR); operations des guichets des banques et de caisses d'epargne et de prevoyance. 1966. a. 60 F. (effective 1992). Banque de France, Service de l'Information, 48, rue Croix des Petits Champs, 75001 Paris, France. TEL 1-42-92-39-08. FAX 1-42-92-39-40. stat.
     Formerly: Banque de France. Direction de la Conjoncture. Structure et Evolution Financiere des Regions de Province (ISSN 0522-3199)

330.9   FR   ISSN 0242-5815
BANQUE DE FRANCE. ENQUETE MENSUELLE DE CONJONCTURE. (Subseries of: Collection Conjoncture (ISSN 1152-4952)) (Text in French, summaries in English) 1965. m. (11/yr.). 400 F. (effective 1995). Banque de France, Service de l'Information, 48, rue Croix des Petits Champs, 75001 Paris, France. TEL 1-42-92-39-31. FAX 1-42-92-39-40. Ed. M. Cauchi. charts; stat. (looseleaf format) **Indexed:** P.A.I.S.For.Lang.Ind.
     Formerly: Situation Economique (ISSN 0037-5926)

330.9   FR   ISSN 0245-761X
BANQUE DE L'UNION EUROPEENNE. CHIFFRES ET COMMENTAIRES. 1970. q. free. Banque de l'Union Europeenne, 4 rue Gaillon, 75002 Paris, France. TEL 42.66.20.30.
     Formerly (until 1975): Banque de l'Union Europeenne. Informations Economiques et Financieres. (ISSN 0067-3943)

330.9   UA   ISSN 0005-5603
BANQUE DE PORT-SAID. REVUE ECONOMIQUE TRIMESTRIELLE. (Editions in Arabic and French) 1929 (French ed.); 1961 (Arabic ed.). q. free. Banque de Port-Said, 18 Rue Talaat Harb, Alexandria, Egypt. Ed. Mahmoud Sami Mohamed El Adawy. charts; mkt.; stat.

332   LU
BANQUE INTERNATIONALE A LUXEMBOURG. CAHIERS DE LA BIL. 1975. irreg. free. Banque Internationale a Luxembourg, L-2953 Luxembourg, Luxembourg. TEL 4590-2248. FAX 4590-3850. TELEX 3626 BIL LU. circ. 3,500. **Indexed:** ELLIS. **Document type:** consumer publication.
     Banque Internationale a Luxembourg. Cahiers Economiques.

BANQUE NATIONALE DE BELGIQUE. BULLETIN. see BUSINESS AND ECONOMICS — Banking And Finance

330.9   FR
BANQUE SUDAMERIS. ETUDES ECONOMIQUES. (Text in French) 1954. irreg. (2-3/yr.). free. Banque SudAmeris, 4 rue Meyerbeer, 75429 Paris Cedex 09, France. TEL 48-01-78-21. FAX 48-01-79-87. TELEX SUDIR 641669. Ed. Jean-Luc Chalumeau. charts; stat. **Document type:** bulletin.
     Formerly: Banque Francaise et Italienne. Etudes Economiques (ISSN 0014-2042)
     Description: Comprises an examination of economic situations in Latin American countries.

330.9   BB
BARBADOS. MINISTRY OF FINANCE AND ECONOMIC AFFAIRS. ECONOMIC REPORT. 1977. a. $7.50 (effective 1995). Ministry of Finance and Economic Affairs, Government Printery, Bay St., St. Michael, Barbados, W.I. circ. 500. **Document type:** government publication.
     Formerly (until 1988): Barbados. Ministry of Finance and Planning. Economic Report.

BARCLAYS BANK. CONSTRUCTION SURVEY. see BUILDING AND CONSTRUCTION

330.9   UK   ISSN 0261-6351
BARCLAYS BANK. ECONOMIC SURVEYS. Key Title: Barclays Bank. International Economic Surveys. (Part of the Foreign Exchange Reports series) 1981? a. £120 (academic institutions and students £60); full set of Foreign Exchange Reports £300 (academic institutions and students £150). Barclays Bank plc., Economics Department, P.O. Box 12, Barclays House, 1 Wimborne St., Poole, Dorset BH15 2BB, England. TEL 01202-334023. FAX 01202-402303.

330.9   UK
BARCLAYS BANK. INDUSTRY BRIEFINGS. (Part of Industry Reports series) a. £300 for full set (academic institutions and students £150); individual reports £30 (academic institutions and students £15). Barclays Bank plc., Economics Department, P.O. Box 12, Barclays House, 1 Wimborne Rd., Poole, Dorset BH15 2BB, England. TEL 01202-334023. FAX 01202-402303.
     Description: Analyzes the current situation and outlook for selected manufacturing and service industries.

BARCLAYS BANK. MANUFACTURING SURVEY. see BUSINESS AND ECONOMICS — Production Of Goods And Services

330   UK   ISSN 0307-4552
BARCLAYS COUNTRY REPORTS. irreg. £300 for full set (academic institutions and students £150); individual reports £30 (academic institutions and students £15). Barclays Bank plc., Economics Department, P.O. Box 12, Barclays House, 1 Wimborne Rd., Poole, Dorset BH15 2BB, England. TEL 01202-344023. FAX 01202-402303. (looseleaf format) **Document type:** academic/scholarly publication.
     ●Also available online. Vendor(s): Data-Star, Knight-Ridder Information, Inc.
     Description: Publishes economic reports covering industrial nations.

330.9   US   ISSN 1092-3608
BARTERNEWS. 1979. q. $40 (foreign $54) (effective 1997). BarterNews Publications, Box 3024, Mission Viejo, CA 92690. TEL 714-831-0607. FAX 714-831-9378. E-mail: barter@fia.net; URL: http://www.barternews.com. Ed. Bob Meyer. adv.; bk.rev. circ. 32,500. **Document type:** trade publication.

330.9   US   ISSN 0094-1115
HC107.I2
BASIC ECONOMIC DATA FOR IDAHO. a. Department of Labor, Bureau of Research and Analysis, 317 Main St., Boise, ID 83735. TEL 208-334-6168. URL: http://www.labor.state.id.us. Ed. Katie Lamm. stat. (also avail. in microfiche from CIS) **Indexed:** SRI. **Document type:** government publication.
     Supersedes in part: Labor Force in Idaho and Basic Economic Data for Idaho.

BUSINESS AND ECONOMICS — ECONOMIC SITUATION AND CONDITIONS

330.9   GW
BERNHARD-HARMS-VORLESUNGEN. irreg., vol.17, 1996. DM.8. Institut fuer Weltwirtschaft, Duesternbrooker Weg 120, 24105 Kiel, Germany. TEL 49-431-8814305. FAX 49-431-8814520. E-mail: info@ifw.uni-kiel.de; URL: http://www.uni-kiel.de:8080/ifw/. Ed. Horst Siebert. **Document type:** monographic series.
Refereed Serial

330.9   SZ
BESCHAEFTIGUNGS- UND ERWERBSTAETIGENSTATISTIK/STATISTIQUE DE L'EMPLOI ET DE LA POPULATION ACTIVE OCCUPEE. (Text in French and German) 1986. q. 25 SFr. Bundesamt fuer Statistik, Schwarztorstr. 96, CH-3003 Bern, Switzerland. TEL 41-31-3236060. FAX 41-31-3236061. URL: http://www.admin.ch/bfs. **Document type:** government publication.

330.9   GW   ISSN 0939-415X
HJ1150.A2
BETRIEB UND WIRTSCHAFT; Zeitschrift fuer Rechnungswesen, Controlling, Steuerrechte, Wirtschaftsrecht, Arbeits- und Sozialrecht. 1947. fortn. DM.168 (foreign DM.240) (effective 1997). Verlag Die Wirtschaft GmbH, Am Friedrichshain 22, 10407 Berlin, Germany. TEL 49-30-42151421. FAX 49-30-4215123. Ed. Wolfgang Bergs. adv.; bk.rev.; index, cum.index. **Document type:** trade publication.
—BLDSC (1946.809000); SWETS.
Former titles: Sozialistische Finanzwirtschaft (ISSN 0012-0103); Deutsche Finanzwirtschaft.
Description: Covers all aspects of the financial economy in eastern Germany, such as social insurance, productivity, rationalization, financial planning, labor efficiency, and government policies.

330   II   ISSN 0006-0488
BHARAT SEVAK.* (Text in English) 1966. m. Rs.6. House No. 600, Sector 16-D, Chandigarh 17, India. Ed. B.D. Nanda. adv.; charts; illus.; stat.

330.9   SZ
BILAN; le magazine economique suisse. (Text in French) 1989. m. 97 SFr. Agedip S.A., 33 av. de la Gare, CH-1001 Lausanne, Switzerland. TEL 41-21-3494822. FAX 41-21-3494830. Ed. Max Mabillard. R&P contact: Max Mabillard. adv.: page 9280 SFr. bk.rev. circ. 25,000. **Document type:** trade publication.

330.9   SZ   ISSN 1022-3487
BILANZ; Schweizer Wirtschafts Revue. 1960. m. 116 SFr. (Europe 132 SFr.; elsewhere 151 SFr.) (effective 1996). Jean Frey AG, Edenstr. 20, CH-8021 Zurich, Switzerland. TEL 41-1-2077171. FAX 41-1-2078028. Ed. Carl M. Holliger. adv.: B&W page 10916 SFr., color page 16180 SFr.; 187 x 240. bk.rev.; illus. circ. 84,000. **Document type:** trade publication.
Supersedes (in 1977): Wirtschaftsrevue (ISSN 0510-5528); (in 1962): Schweizerische Wirtschaftszeitung.

330.9   ET
BIRRITU. (Text in Amharic, English) 1981. bi-m. exchange basis. National Bank of Ethiopia, c/o Documentation Division, P.O. Box 5550, Addis Ababa, Ethiopia. adv. circ. 6,000. **Document type:** government publication.
Supersedes: Financial Institutions Forum.
Description: Includes articles, features and news on banking and insurance. Provides a forum for intelligent informed debates.

330.9   CN   ISSN 0381-7245
HF3223
BLUE BOOK OF CANADIAN BUSINESS. 1976. a. Can.$146.95 (CD-ROM Can.$262.45; combined Can.$293.95) (effective 1997). International Press Publications Inc., 90 Nolan Ct., Ste. 21, Markham, ON L3R 4L9, Canada. TEL 905-946-9588; 800-679-2514. FAX 905-946-9590. E-mail: ipp@interlog.com; URL: http://www.interlog.com/~ipp. Ed.Bd. illus. circ. 1,000. **Document type:** directory.
●Also available on CD-ROM.
—CISTI.
Description: Provides current facts and figures on Canada's leading business enterprises.
Refereed Serial

330.9   US   ISSN 0193-4600
BLUE CHIP ECONOMIC INDICATORS; what top economists are saying about the US outlook for the year ahead. 1975. m. $545 (foreign $557) (effective 1998). Capitol Publications Inc., 1101 King St., Ste. 444, Alexandria, VA 22314. TEL 703-683-4100. FAX 703-739-6517. Ed. Robert J. Eggert. Indexed: PROMT. **Document type:** newsletter.
—CCC.
Description: Current economic forecasts for top management, corporate planners, market research directors, economists, bankers, brokers and investors.

330.9   US   ISSN 1062-9327
HD5723
BLUE CHIP JOB GROWTH UPDATE; ranking the states and MSAs. 1990. m. $79 (effective May 1995). Arizona State University, Economic Outlook Center, Box 874406, Tempe, AZ 85287-4406. TEL 602-965-5543; 800-448-0432. FAX 602-965-5458. Ed. Yolanda Strozier. circ. 135. (back issues avail.) **Document type:** newsletter.
Formerly (until 1992): Job Growth Update (ISSN 1051-5615)
Description: Presents nonagricultural establishment survey data ranked according to the percentage change in jobs for each of the major employment sectors.

330.9   US
BLUE RIDGE BUSINESS JOURNAL.* 13/yr. $22. Add, Inc. - Blue Ridge Business Journal, Box 6982, Greenville, SC 29606-6982. TEL 704-687-1442. FAX 704-687-1446. Ed. Debbie Ogden. adv. circ. 7,000. (back issues avail.)
Description: Covers business and economic news that affect business and industry in western North Carolina.

330.9   IT
BO - BOLOGNA E CIRCONDARIO. w. newsstand price: L.1000. G.M.P. s.r.l. Gestione Mezzi Pubblicitari, Via Marzabotto 31III 131, 47037 Rimini, Italy. TEL 0541-777777. Ed. Alessandro Secciani. adv.: B&W page L.300000. circ. 9,500.

330.9   UK
BOARD EARNINGS IN FT-SE 100 COMPANIES. a. Monks Partnership Ltd., The Mill House, Wendens Ambo, Saffron Walden, Essex CB11 4JX, England. TEL 44-1799-542222. FAX 44-1799-541805. Ed. Alison Smith. R&P contact: David Atkins. **Document type:** corporate report.

330.9   GW
BOERSEN JAHRBUCH. a. DM.98 (effective 1997). Verlag Hoppenstedt GmbH, Havelstr. 9, 64295 Darmstadt, Germany. TEL 49-6151-380-0. FAX 49-6151-380-360. **Document type:** trade publication.
Formerly: Wirtschaft und Boerse (ISSN 0510-5366)

BOLETIM CONJUNTURAL DO NORDESTE DO BRASIL. see BUSINESS AND ECONOMICS — *Abstracting, Bibliographies, Statistics*

330.9   CU
BOLETIN DE INFORMACION SOBRE ECONOMIA CUBANA. (Text in Spanish; table of contents in English, Spanish) 1991. q. $40 for 2 yrs. Centro de Investigaciones de la Economia Mundial, Quinta Ave., No. 2010, Esquina a 22, Miramar, Playa, Havana, Cuba. TEL 537-242507. Ed. George Carriazo Moreno. bk.rev.; bibl.; stat. circ. 300. (also avail. in diskette format) **Document type:** bulletin.
Formerly (until 1991): Boletin de Informacion sobre Estudios Cubanos.
Description: Contains feature articles on the Cuban economy.

330.9   SP   ISSN 0210-1947
BOLETIN ECONOMICO DE LA CONSTRUCCION. (Text in Catalan, Spanish) 1940. q. 7000 ptas. (effective 1994). Emancipacion 28-30, 08022 Barcelona, Spain. TEL 2112121. FAX 2112204. Ed. Balcells Gorina. **Document type:** bulletin.

338   MW
BOMA LATHU. (Text in Chichewa) 1964-1969; resumed 1973. m. free. Department of Information, P.O. Box 494, Blantyre, Malawi. TEL 265-620266. Ed. J.C. Tumbwe. adv. circ. 150,000. (tabloid format)
Formerly: Malawi Mwezi Uno-Malawi This Month (ISSN 0025-1240)
Description: Development information on the island country of Malawi.

650   II   ISSN 0006-6974
BOMBAY MARKET. (Text in English) vol.34, 1970. fortn. Rs.60. 505 Arun Chambers, Tardeo Rd., Bombay 34, India. Ed. K. Multani. adv.; illus.; mkt.; stat.

330.9   US
BOOT COVE ECONOMIC FORECAST. 1978. m. $380. Voight Industries, Inc., Box 200, Lubec, ME 04652. TEL 207-733-5593. Ed. R.O. Voight. (back issues avail.)
●Also available online. Vendor(s): NewsNet (IV29).

BOTSWANA. CENTRAL STATISTICS OFFICE. TRANSPORT STATISTICS. see *TRANSPORTATION*

BOTSWANA. MINISTRY OF AGRICULTURE. AGRICULTURAL STATISTICS. see *AGRICULTURE — Abstracting, Bibliographies, Statistics*

330.9   BL
BRAZIL. SUPERINTENDENCIA DO DESENVOLVIMENTO DO NORDESTE. RELATORIO ANUAL. irreg., latest 1986. exchange basis. Superintendencia do Desenvolvimento do Nordeste, Praca Ministro J. Goncalves de Souza, Edf. Sudene, Cidade Universitaria, 50670-900 Recife PE, Brazil. TEL 2711044. FAX 4531277. charts; stat. **Document type:** government publication.

330.9   BL   ISSN 0103-3921
HG4109.5
BRAZIL COMPANY HANDBOOK. (Text in English) 1987. a. $29.95. I M F Editora Ltda., Av. Almirante Barroso 63, Grupo 409, 20031 Rio de Janeiro RJ, Brazil. TEL 55-21-240-4347. FAX 55-21-262-7570. (Dist. worldwide by: The Reference Press, Inc., 6448 Hwy. 290 E., Ste. E-104, Austin, TX 78723. TEL 512-454-7778. FAX 512-454-9401) charts; stat. (back issues avail.) **Document type:** trade publication.
Description: Profiles 90 of Brazil's major companies and 60 money managers and investment advisors. Provides hard-to-find information on the economic conditions in Brazil.

338.9 320   UK   ISSN 0143-5272
HC186
BRAZIL REPORT. Variant title: Latin American Regional Report - Brazil Report. 1979. 10/yr. £150($195) (academic institutions £85 ($110)) (effective 1997). Lettres (U.K.) Ltd., 61 Old St., London EC1V 9HX, England. TEL 44-171-251-0012. FAX 44-171-253-8193. Ed. Colin Harding. R&P contact: Alex McHallam. (back issues avail.) **Document type:** newsletter.
●Also available online. Vendor(s): Lexis-Nexis.
—BLDSC (5160.097000).
Description: Covers in detail political, business, economic, and financial events in Brazil.

330.9   US   ISSN 0897-3067
HC186
BRAZIL WATCH. (Fax Bulletin also avail.) 1984. bi-w.; fax ed. w. $765 (fax ed. $465; foreign $565) (effective 1998). Orbis Publications, LLC, 3201 New Mexico Ave., N.W., Ste. 249, Washington, DC 20016. TEL 202-237-0155. FAX 202-237-0596. E-mail: orbis@orbispub.com; URL: http://www.earthnet.net/orbis. Ed. Richard W. Foster; Pub. Stephen Foster. R&P contact: Phillip Gonzalez. (back issues avail.) **Document type:** newsletter, bulletin.
Description: Reports on political, economic and business events in Brazil

330   FR   ISSN 0006-9566
BREF RHONE ALPES; lettre hebdomadaire d'informations economiques. 1966. 45/yr. 1750 F. Editions S.M.E., 55 Montee de Choulans, 69323 Lyon Cedex 05, France. TEL 78-42-29-53. FAX 78-42-09-14.

BRIEFING. see *POLITICAL SCIENCE*

BULLETIN L A R F. see *BUSINESS AND ECONOMICS — Banking And Finance*

BUSINESS AND ECONOMICS — ECONOMIC SITUATION AND CONDITIONS

330   AT   ISSN 0007-4918
HC446
BULLETIN OF INDONESIAN ECONOMIC STUDIES. 1965. 3/yr. Aus.$30 to individuals (foreign Aus.$35); institutions Aus.$42 (foreign Aus.$47). Australian National University, Research School of Pacific and Asian Studies, Economics Division, Indonesia Project, Canberra, A.C.T. 0200, Australia. bk.rev.; charts; illus.; stat.; cum.index. circ. 1,200. (reprint service avail. from SCH) **Indexed:** Agri.Eng.Abstr., ASCA, Asian-Pac.Econ.Lit., C.R.E.J., Curr.Cont., E.I., Energy Ind., Energy Info.Abstr., Geo.Abstr.H.G., IBR, IDA, Int.Lab.Doc., J.of Econ.Lit., Key to Econ.Sci., P.A.I.S., Per.Islam. (1993-), Popul.Ind., Ref.Zh., Rice Abstr., Rural Devel.Abstr., SSCI, World Agri.Econ.& Rural Sociol.Abstr. **Document type:** academic/scholarly publication, bulletin.
—BLDSC (2862.060000); Genuine Article; SWETS; UMI; UnCover. **CCC.**

338.9   EI   ISSN 0068-4120
BULLETIN OF THE EUROPEAN COMMUNITIES AND SUPPLEMENTS. (Text in Danish, Dutch, English, French, German, Greek, Italian, Spanish and Portuguese) 1968. 11/yr. $255. (Commission of the European Communities) Office for Official Publications of the European Communities, L-2985 Luxembourg, Luxembourg. (Dist. in U.S. by: Unipub, 4611-F Assembly Dr., Lanham, MD 20706-4391. TEL 800-274-4888. FAX 301-459-0056) (also avail. in microfiche from CIS) **Indexed:** GeoRef., IIS. **Document type:** bulletin.
Description: Features official texts adopted by the commission (communications to the council, programmes, reports, proposals).

338   EI
HC241.2   CODEN: BEUCBC
BULLETIN OF THE EUROPEAN UNION. (Supplement avail. (ISSN 1016-8702)) (Text in Danish, Dutch, English, French, German, Greek, Italian, Spanish, Portuguese) 1968. 11/yr. £210. Office for Official Publications of the European Communities, 2 rue Mercier, B.P. 1003, L-2985 Luxembourg, Luxembourg. (Dist. in the U.S. by: Unipub, 4611-F Assembly Dr., Lanham, MD 20706-4391. TEL 800-274-4888. FAX 301-459-0056) charts; tr.lit.; index. (also avail. in microfiche from CIS) **Indexed:** EC Ind., Geo.Abstr., GeoRef., IIS, Mid.East: Abstr.& Ind., Paper & Bd.Abstr., Rural Recreat.Tour.Abstr., Triticale Abstr., World Agri.Econ.& Rural Sociol.Abstr. **Document type:** bulletin.
—CISTI.
Former titles: Bulletin of the European Communities (ISSN 0378-3693); Incorporates (in 1980): Euroforum (Brussels); Industry and Society (ISSN 0304-1646); Weekly Industry Research and Technology.
Description: Covers main events, developments in community policies, external relations, financing of community activities, European political cooperation, relations between the community's institutions, and activities of the institutions.

330.9   US
BUSINESS & ECONOMIC REPORT & KANSAS ECONOMIC INDICATORS. 1971. m. $35. Wichita State University, W. Frank Barton School of Business, Center for Economic Development and Business Research, Wichita, KS 67260-0121. TEL 316-978-3225. FAX 316-978-3950. Ed. Janet Nickel. R&P contact: Janet Nickel. charts; stat. circ. 600. (processed; also avail. in microfiche from CIS) **Indexed:** P.A.I.S., SRI. **Document type:** academic/scholarly publication.
Former titles: Kansas Economic Indicators; Business and Economic Report; Kansas Business Review.
Refereed Serial

BUSINESS AND THE ENVIRONMENT; twice-monthly global news and analysis. see ENVIRONMENTAL STUDIES

382   SA
BUSINESS BRIEF. 1975. q. free. First National Bank Ltd., Economics Department, P.O. Box 1153, Johannesburg 2000, South Africa. Ed. C. Bruggemans. illus. circ. 5,000. **Indexed:** Bus.Ind., Geo.Abstr.
Former titles: Barclays Business Brief (ISSN 0250-2402); Barclays National Review (ISSN 0302-6809); Barclays Trade Review (ISSN 0005-5913)

380   US
BUSINESS CHINA; fortnightly report to managers of China operations. 1975. bi-w. £545($825) Economist Intelligence Unit, 111 W. 57th St., New York, NY 10019. TEL 212-554-0600; 800-938-4685. FAX 212-586-1182. TELEX 175567. URL: http://www.eiu.com. (UK addr.: Economist Intelligence Unit Ltd., Subscriptions Dept., P.O. Box 200, Harold Hill, Romford, Essex RM3 8UX, England. TEL 44-171-830-1007. FAX 44-1708-371850) charts; maps; stat.; index. cum.index. (also avail. in microform from UMI) **Indexed:** Key to Econ.Sci. **Document type:** newsletter.
●Also available online. Vendor(s): Knight-Ridder Information, Inc., Lexis-Nexis.
Description: Analyzes economic trends and new policies, and forecasts the effects on businesses. Identifies unfolding opportunities and competition through regular reviews of industrial sectors and reports on major transactions, joint ventures, licensing agreements and other developments in key industries.

330.9   MY   ISSN 0127-0001
BUSINESS CONDITIONS MALAYSIA. (Former name of issuing body: United Malayan Banking Corp. Berhad) (Text in English) 1980. q. free. Sime Bank Berhad, P.O. Box 12006, 50935 Kuala Lumpur, Malaysia. TEL 03-2309866. FAX 03-2322627. TELEX MA-33707 SIMEBK. Ed. Ng Goo Phai. circ. 1,500. **Document type:** newsletter.

330.9   US
▼**BUSINESS CYCLE INDICATORS.** 1996. m. $120. Conference Board, Inc., 845 Third Ave., New York, NY 10022. TEL 212-759-0900. FAX 212-980-7014. **Document type:** academic/scholarly publication.

330.9   US   ISSN 1351-8763
HF3500.7
BUSINESS EASTERN EUROPE. 1972. w. £725($1295) Economist Intelligence Unit, 111 W. 57th St., New York, NY 10019. TEL 212-554-0600; 800-938-4685. FAX 212-586-1182. TELEX 175567. URL: http://www.eiu.com. (UK addr.: Economist Intelligence Unit Ltd., Subscriptions Dept., P.O. Box 200, Harold Hill, Romford, Essex RM3 8UX, England. TEL 44-171-830-1007. FAX 44-1708-371-850) Ed. George W. Hamilton. charts; stat. (also avail. in microform from UMI) **Indexed:** Key to Econ.Sci. **Document type:** trade publication.
●Also available online. Vendor(s): Knight-Ridder Information, Inc., Lexis-Nexis.
—SWETS.
Formerly: Eastern Europe Report.
Description: Provides strategies for financing, countertrade, cooperation agreements, licensing and marketing in the six Comecon countries and Yugoslavia, from contacting foreign trade organizations to negotiating contracts, clinching deals and securing payments.

330.9 371.3   US   ISSN 1060-0663
LC1085.2
BUSINESS - EDUCATION INSIDER; how business can reform education. 1990. m. newsstand price: $3.50. Heritage Foundation, 214 Massachusetts Ave., N.E., Washington, DC 20002. TEL 202-546-4400. FAX 202-543-9647. TELEX 440235. Ed. Allyson Tucker. circ. 4,000. (back issues avail.; reprint service avail.)
●Also available online. Vendor(s): Lexis-Nexis.

330.9   US
BUSINESS FAILURE RECORD. a. free. Dun & Bradstreet, Economic Analysis Department, 220 E. 42nd St., 9th Fl., New York, NY 10017-4717. FAX 212-883-3400. (Subscr. to: Box 1861, New York, NY 10163-1861) **Indexed:** SRI.
Description: Provides number of failures and liabilities by state and region, by major industry group and by age of business, plus historical failures data.

650   US   ISSN 0007-683X
BUSINESS IN NEBRASKA. 1948. m. $10. University of Nebraska at Lincoln, Bureau of Business Research, 114 C.B.A., Lincoln, NE 68588-0406. TEL 402-472-2334. FAX 402-472-3878. Ed. F. Charles Lamphear. charts; illus.; stat. circ. 9,000. (also avail. in microfiche from CIS; reprint service avail.) **Indexed:** P.A.I.S., SRI. **Document type:** newsletter.

338   TH   ISSN 0125-0140
HF41
BUSINESS IN THAILAND. (Text in English) 1969. m. B.500($52) Business in Thailand Co. Ltd., 185 Soi Putta-O-Soth (Opp. G.P.O.), New Rd., Bangkok 10500, Thailand. TEL 2-235-6049. FAX 2-237-1517. TELEX 20932 BIT TH. (Subscr. addr.: P.O. Box 1332, Bangkok Mail Center, Bangkok 10000, Thailand) Ed. William Than; Pub. Suphat Busayapong. adv. contact: Paitoon Na Songihla. bk.rev.; charts; illus.; stat.; index. circ. 7,500. **Indexed:** Key to Econ.Sci.
—UnCover.
Description: An analysis of Thailand's business, focusing on economics, commerce, industry, and trade.

330.9   US
BUSINESS INSIGHT (AKRON). 1987. q. free. Akron-Summit County Public Library, 55 S. Main St., Akron, OH 44325. TEL 330-643-9000. circ. 2,000. **Document type:** newsletter.
Description: Informs local business community of sources and services available in Business, Labor and Government Division of the Akron-Summit County Public Library.

BUSINESS JOURNAL (PHOENIX); serving Phoenix & the Valley of the Sun. see BUSINESS AND ECONOMICS

330.9   US   ISSN 0742-6550
BUSINESS JOURNAL (PORTLAND); serving greater Portland. 1984. w. $48. American City Business Journals, Inc. (Portland), Box 14490, Portland, OR 97214. TEL 503-274-8733. FAX 503-227-2650. Ed. Steven D. Jones; Pub. Candace Clement. adv. contact: Matt Tolbert. charts; illus.; pet.; stat.; circ. 10,900 (paid); 4,100 (controlled). (tabloid format) **Document type:** newspaper.
●Also available online. Vendor(s): Information Access Co.
—UMI. **CCC.**
Description: Covers business and economics in the Portland area.

382   US   ISSN 0007-6880
BUSINESS LATIN AMERICA; weekly report to managers of Latin American operations. 1966. w. £725($1045) Economist Intelligence Unit, 111 W. 57th St., New York, NY 10019. TEL 212-554-0600; 800-938-4685. FAX 212-586-1182. TELEX 175567. E-mail: marcus@interpart.net; URL: http://www.eiu.com/2x605brid/catalog/country/samer.html. (UK addr.: Economist Intelligence Unit Ltd., Subscriptions Dept., P.O. Box 200, Harold Hill, Romford, Essex RM3 8UX, England. TEL 44-1708-381-444) Ed. Anna Szterenfeld. (also avail. in microform from UMI) **Indexed:** Key to Econ.Sci. **Document type:** newsletter.
●Also available online. Vendor(s): Knight-Ridder Information, Inc., Lexis-Nexis.
—SWETS; UMI.
Description: Interprets and evaluates changing political, economic and business-related trends, government policy changes, regulatory developments, regional integration moves and actions taken by governments and leading agencies to cope with the region's debt.

BUSINESS MONITOR. RETAIL PRICES INDEX. see BUSINESS AND ECONOMICS — Abstracting, Bibliographies, Statistics

330.9   UK
BUSINESS NEWS (SOUTH WALES EDITION). 1969. bi-m. free. Euro Publications Ltd., Euro House, 14 Pearl St., Cardiff CF2 1HD, Wales. Ed. Ray H. Zeall. adv.; bk.rev.; illus.; circ. 5,000 (controlled).

330.9   UK
BUSINESS NEWS (WEST OF ENGLAND EDITION). 1969. bi-m. free. Euro Publications Ltd., Euro House, 14 Pearl St., Cardiff CF2 1HD, Wales. Ed. R.H. Zeall. adv.; bk.rev.; illus.; circ. 5,000 (controlled).

330.9   SP
BUSINESS OPPORTUNITIES IN SPAIN. (Editions in English, French, Spanish) a. Banco de Santander, Publicidad y Estudios, Paseo de Pereda 9-12, Santander 2, Spain.

BUSINESS AND ECONOMICS — ECONOMIC SITUATION AND CONDITIONS

330.9   US   ISSN 0748-4216
BUSINESS OUTLOOK FOR WEST MICHIGAN. 1984. q. $25. W.E. Upjohn Institute for Employment Research, 300 S. Westnedge Ave., Kalamazoo, MI 49007. TEL 616-343-5541. FAX 616-343-7310. URL: httpf://www.upjohninst.org. Ed. George A. Erickcek. R&P contact: George A. Erickcek. stat. circ. 600. (back issues avail.) **Document type:** academic/scholarly publication.
    Formerly: Business Outlook.
    Description: Provides economic analysis, statistics, and forecasts for western Michigan.

330.9   US   ISSN 1064-2471
BUSINESS PICTURE. 1988. q. $240. Gilman Research Corp., Box 20567, Oakland, CA 94620. TEL 510-655-3103. Ed. George Gilman. **Document type:** newsletter.
    Description: Comprehensive collection of vital economic and financial long term charts.

BUSINESS RATIO PLUS: BUS & COACH OPERATORS. see *TRANSPORTATION*

BUSINESS RATIO PLUS: CONSTRUCTIONAL STEELWORK MANUFACTURERS. see *BUILDING AND CONSTRUCTION*

BUSINESS RATIO PLUS: ESTATE AGENCIES. see *REAL ESTATE*

BUSINESS RATIO PLUS: THE FILM & TV INDUSTRY. see *MOTION PICTURES*

BUSINESS RATIO PLUS: THE LIGHTING EQUIPMENT INDUSTRY. see *INTERIOR DESIGN AND DECORATION*

BUSINESS RATIO PLUS: MEAT PROCESSORS. see *AGRICULTURE — Poultry And Livestock*

BUSINESS RATIO PLUS: MEAT WHOLESALERS. see *AGRICULTURE — Poultry And Livestock*

330.9   TH   ISSN 0125-0477
HF5001
BUSINESS REVIEW. (Text in English) 1972. m. $60 to Southeast Asia; Europe $93; N. America $111. Nation Publishing Group Co., 44 Moo 10 Bagna-Trat Rd., Km 4.5, Bangna, Prakanong, Bangkok 10260, Thailand. TEL 317-1365. FAX 317-1384. TELEX 20326 NATION TH. (Dist. in Hong Kong by: In Group Publications Ltd., B26 Seven Seas Commercial Centre, 121 King's Rd., Hong Kong. TEL 5-887-1830) Ed. Laurie Rosenthal. adv.: page B.33000; 203 x 273. bk.rev.; illus. circ. 20,000. **Indexed:** Key to Econ.Sci., P.A.I.S., PROMT.

BUSINESS RUSSIA (CHICAGO); doing business in Russia and the newly independent states. see *BUSINESS AND ECONOMICS — International Commerce*

330.9 658   CN
BUSINESS SALES AND ACQUISITIONS DIGEST. q. Can.$195. Canadian Institute of Chartered Accountants, 277 Wellington St. W., Toronto, Ont. M5V 3H2, Canada. TEL 416-977-3222. FAX 416-977-8585. Eds. Wayne P. Albo, A. Randall Henderson. circ. 275. (looseleaf format) **Document type:** newsletter.
    Description: Provides information on mergers and acquisitions for both buyers and sellers, current trends, changes in federal and provincial tax legislation, non-tax legislation, financing.

330.9   UK   ISSN 0144-6096
HC257.S4
BUSINESS SCOTLAND; a monthly review of national and international business. 1947. m. £31.20 (foreign £37.20) (effective 1996-1997). Peebles Publishing Group Ltd., Bergius House, Clifton St., Glasgow G3 7LA, Scotland. TEL 44-141-331-1022. FAX 44-141-331-1395. Ed. Graham Lironi. adv.; bk.rev. circ. 15,000. **Document type:** trade publication.
    Formerly: Scotland (ISSN 0036-9055)

330.9   US   ISSN 0744-172X
BUSINESS TIMES. 1978. m. $36; newsstand price: $3. Choice Media, 315 Peck St., Box 580, New Haven, CT 06513-0580. TEL 203-782-1420. FAX 203-782-3793. Ed. Joel McClaren; Pub. Joel MacClaren. R&P contact: Joel McClaren. adv.: page $2400; trim 9 1/2 x 13 1/2; adv. contact: Robert Kaufman Harris. bk.rev. circ. 23,000. (back issues avail.) **Indexed:** Key to Econ.Sci., Tr.& Indus.Ind. **Document type:** newspaper.
    ●Also available online. Vendor(s): UMI.
    —UMI.
    Formerly: Connecticut Business Times (ISSN 0161-6102)
    Description: Statewide business to business publication reaching top level business executives, CFOs, presidents, business owners. Focuses on issues in banking and finance, telecommunications, healthcare, higher education and technology.

330.9   MY
BUSINESS TRENDS ASIA REPORT: INDONESIA. 1979. irreg. $30. M P R C (Asia) Sdn. Berhad, P.O. Box 10706, 50722 Kuala Lumpur, Malaysia. TEL 60-3-2217762. FAX 60-3-7564478. Ed. Paul Markandan. bk.rev.; stat.; circ. controlled.

330.9   GH
BUSINESS WEEKLY. 1966. w. Business Publication, Ring Road West Industrial Area, P.O. Box 2351, Accra, Ghana. Ed. Mark Botsio. adv. circ. 3,000. **Document type:** trade publication.

330.9   UY   ISSN 0797-2008
BUSQUEDA. 1972. w. $225. (Sociedad Interamericana de Prensa) Editorial Agora S.A., Av. Uruguay 1146, 11100 Montevideo, Uruguay. TEL 598-2-922666. FAX 598-2-922036. Ed. Danilo Arbilla Frachia. circ. 25,000.

334 381   UK   ISSN 0955-8888
BUTTERWORTHS E C BRIEF. 1989. w. £295($555) Butterworth & Co. (Publishers) Ltd., Part of the Reed Elsevier group, Halsbury House, 35 Chancery Ln., London WC2A 1EL, England. TEL 071-400-2500. FAX 071-400-2842. (U.S. addr.: Butterworth Legal Publishers, 90 Stiles Rd., Salem, NH 03079. TEL 603-898-9664) **Document type:** trade publication.
    Description: Covers E.C. directives, ComDocs, regulations and activities.

330.9   AU
C A QUARTERLY; facts and figures on Austria's economy. 1982. q. Creditanstalt-Bankverein, Schottengasse 6, A-1010 Vienna, Austria. TEL 01-53131-0. Ed. Manfred Weidmann. **Indexed:** World Bank.Abstr. **Document type:** bulletin.
    Description: Covers Austria's business cycle, Austrian economy and banking system, international economic information, and indicators of economic development.

338 331   US   ISSN 0199-686X
C B I A NEWS. 1923. m. $12 to non-members; members $9. (Connecticut Business and Industry Association) C B I A Service Corp., 370 Asylum St., Hartford, CT 06103-2022. TEL 860-244-1900. FAX 860-278-8562. Ed. Diane Friend Edwards. R&P contact: Diane Friend Edwards. adv. contact: Sally G. Piazza. bk.rev.; illus. circ. 11,500. (tabloid format) **Indexed:** P.A.I.S. **Document type:** newsletter.
    —UMI.
    Former titles: Connecticut Business and Industry; Connecticut Industry (ISSN 0010-6135)
    Description: Keeps business people informed about business trends, state politics, legislative actions, economic forecasts, regulatory changes and small-business issues. Covers basic business management skills and social changes affecting state businesses.

330.9   UK   ISSN 0142-6419
C B I ECONOMIC SITUATION REPORT. m. £320 to non-members. Confederation of British Industry, Centre Point, 103 New Oxford St., London WC1A 1DU, England. TEL 44-71-379-7400. FAX 44-71-240-1578. TELEX 21332. **Indexed:** C.R.E.J.
    —BLDSC (3655.655500).

330.9   AT
C E D A INFORMATION PAPERS (I P SERIES). 1979. irreg. price varies. Committee for Economic Development of Australia, 123 Lonsdale St., Melbourne, Vic. 3000, Australia. FAX 61-3-96637271. **Indexed:** GeoRef.

338   UN   ISSN 0251-2920
HC121
C E P A L REVIEW. Spanish edition: Revista de la C E P A L (ISSN 0252-0257) 1976. 3/yr. $30 for English ed.; Spanish ed. $16. Comision Economica para America Latina y el Caribe, Casilla 179-D, Santiago, Chile. (Subscr. to: United Nations Publications, Sales Section, Rm. DC2-0853, New York, NY 10017; or Distribution and Sales Section, Palais des Nations, 1211 Geneva 10, Switzerland) stat.; index. (also avail. in microfiche from CIS; back issues avail.) **Indexed:** Abstr.Rural Dev.Trop., C.R.E.J., Hisp.Amer.Per.Ind. (1970; 1976-), IBR, IDA, IIS, Int.Lab.Doc., J.of Econ.Lit., Key to Econ.Sci., P.A.I.S., Rural Recreat.Tour.Abstr., World Agri.Econ.& Rural Sociol.Abstr.
    —BLDSC (3113.689000); SWETS; UnCover. CCC.
    Formerly: Economic Bulletin for Latin America (ISSN 0041-6398)

330.9   FR   ISSN 0243-1947
C.E.P.I.I. LETTRE. 1979. 11/yr. 295 F. (elsewhere 305 F.) (effective 1997). (Centre d'Etudes Prospectives et d'Informations Internationales) Documentation Francaise, 29-31 quai Voltaire, 75344 Paris Cedex 07, France. TEL 33-1-40157000. FAX 33-1-40157230. (Subscr. to: 124 rue Henri Barbusse, 93308 Aubervilliers Cedex, France. TEL 33-1-48395600. FAX 33-1-48395601) (also avail. in microfiche from DFR; back issues avail.) **Document type:** bulletin.
    Description: Looks at basic economic problems from a world perspective.

330.9   CL   ISSN 0716-4467
HC121
C I E P L A N APUNTES. Key Title: Apuntes CIEPLAN. 1977. irreg. price varies. Corporacion de Investigaciones Economicas para Latinoamerica, Mac Iver 125, 5o piso, Casilla 16496, Correo 9, Santiago, Chile. TEL 56-2-6333836. FAX 56-2-6334411. E-mail: cieplan@cieplan.cl.

330.9   CL   ISSN 0716-0631
HC121
C I E P L A N COLECCION ESTUDIOS. Key Title: Coleccion Estudios CIEPLAN. 1976. 2/yr. $58 in America; Europe & Asia $70 (effective 1997). Corporacion de Investigaciones Economicas para Latinoamerica, Mac Iver 125, 5o piso, Casilla 16496, Correo 9, Santiago, Chile. TEL 56-2-6333836. FAX 56-2-6334411. E-mail: cieplan@cieplan.cl. Ed. Dagmar Raczynski. adv.; bk.rev. circ. 1,000. **Indexed:** J.of Econ.Lit., P.A.I.S.For.Lang.Ind.
    Formerly (until 1979): Estudios C I E P L A N (ISSN 0716-4963)
    Description: Focuses on Latin America economic affairs.

330.9   CL   ISSN 0716-4475
C I E P L A N NOTAS TECNICAS. Key Title: Notas Tecnicas CIEPLAN. 1977. irreg. price varies. Corporacion de Investigaciones Economicas para Latinoamerica, Mac Iver 125, 5o piso, Casilla 16496, Correo 9, Santiago, Chile. TEL 56-2-6333836. FAX 56-2-6334411. E-mail: cieplan@cieplan.cl.

C I S STEEL INFORMATION. (Commonwealth of Independent States) see *METALLURGY*

C O M E T. see *PAINTS AND PROTECTIVE COATINGS*

C R A PETROLEUM ECONOMICS MONTHLY. (Charles River Associates) see *PETROLEUM AND GAS*

330.9 300   UK
C R E S R LECTURE SERIES. irreg., no.6, 1993. Sheffield Hallam University, Centre for Regional Economic and Social Research, Pond St., Sheffield S1 1WB, England. TEL 44-114-253-3073. FAX 44-114-253-2197. **Document type:** monographic series.

330.9   UK
C R E S R PLANNING AND PROPERTY SERIES. irreg., no.5, 1996. Sheffield Hallam University, Centre for Regional Economic and Social Research, Pond St., Sheffield S1 1WB, England. TEL 44-114-253-3073. FAX 44-114-253-2197. **Document type:** monographic series.

BUSINESS AND ECONOMICS — ECONOMIC SITUATION AND CONDITIONS

330.9 300   UK
C R E S R RESEARCH PAPER. irreg., no.5, 1993. Sheffield Hallam University, Centre for Regional Economic and Social Research, Pond St., Sheffield S1 1WB, England. TEL 44-114-253-3073. FAX 44-114-253-2197. **Document type:** monographic series.

330.9   UK
C R E S R SUPERTRAM IMPACT SERIES. irreg., no.28, 1996. Sheffield Hallam University, Centre for Regional Economic and Social Research, Pond St., Sheffield S1 1WB, England. TEL 44-114-253-3073. FAX 44-114-253-2197. **Document type:** monographic series.

CAHIERS AFRICAINS/AFRIKA STUDIES. see HISTORY — History Of Africa

CAHIERS DE SOCIOLOGIE ECONOMIQUE ET CULTURELLE. see SOCIOLOGY

330.9   FR
CAHIERS REGIONAUX. (In 22 series: Ile-de-France (ISSN 0765-1708), Aquitaine (ISSN 0295-4680), Auvergne (ISSN 0764-3969), Basse-Normandie (ISS 0299-769X), Bretagne (ISSN 0298-2005), Centre (ISSN 0298-4741), Campagne-Ardenne (ISSN 0769-4792), Corse (ISSN 0299-142X), Languedoc Roussillon (ISSN 0765-2038), Nord-Pas-de-Calais (ISSN 0298-6450), Pays de la Loire (ISSN 0298-2315), Lorraine (ISSN 0767-6530), Alsace (ISSN 0982-7501), Bourgogne (ISSN 0298-9514), Franche-Comte (ISSN 0298-4733), Haute-Normandie (ISSN 0298-9506), Midi-Pyrenees (ISSN 0298-9522), Picardie (ISSN 0298-1157)) 1986. 4/yr. 400 F. (effective 1995). Banque de France, Service de l'Information, 48, rue Croix des Petits Champs, 75001 Paris, France. TEL 1-42-92-39-31. FAX 1-42-92-39-40. stat. **Indexed:** P.A.I.S.For.Lang.Ind. **Formerly:** Notes de Conjoncture Regionale.

CAIJING KEXUE/FINANCE AND ECONOMICS. see BUSINESS AND ECONOMICS — Banking And Finance

330.9   CN   ISSN 0843-0047
CALGARY IN FACT. 1977. a. Calgary Economic Development Authority, P.O. Box 2100, Sta. M, Calgary, AB T2P 2M5, Canada. TEL 403-221-7821. FAX 403-221-7837. circ. 15,000. **Document type:** trade publication. **Description:** Collection of relevant business information available on Calgary.

330.9   CN
CALGARY PICTORIAL. 1985. a. Can.$5. Calgary Economic Development Authority, P.O. Box 2100, Sta. M, Calgary, AB T2P 2M5, Canada. TEL 403-221-7821. FAX 403-221-7837. **Document type:** bulletin.

650   US   ISSN 0008-0926
HC107.C2
CALIFORNIA BUSINESS; reaching the top in California. 1965. bi-m. $18.95 (effective Sep. 1994). 1777 Rollins Rd., Burlingame, CA 95010. TEL 415-776-1472. FAX 415-776-9933. (Subscr. to: c/o Pub Data, 5615 W. Cermak Rd., Cicero, IL 60650-2290. TEL 312-762-2193. FAX 708-656-1990) Ed. Umberto Tosi; Pub. Umberto Tosi. adv. contact: Rachel Miller. illus.; stat. circ. 85,000. (also avail. in microform from UMI; reprint service avail. from UMI) **Indexed:** Cal.Per.Ind. (1978-), P.A.I.S., PMR, Tr.& Indus.Ind. **Document type:** trade publication.
●Also available online. Vendor(s): Information Access Co., Knight-Ridder Information, Inc.
—KR SourceOne; UMI; UnCover.
Description: Provides business coverage for the managers of California corporations large and small, public and private.

330.9   US   ISSN 0575-2426
CALIFORNIA ECONOMIC INDICATORS. 1968. bi-m. $8. Department of Finance, Economic Research Section, 915 L St., 8th Fl., Sacramento, CA 95814-3701. TEL 916-322-2263. FAX 916-327-0213. (Subscr. to: Box 151, Sacramento, CA 95801) charts. circ. 350. **Indexed:** SRI. **Document type:** government publication. **Description:** Summary of economic trends and data relating to the state of California.

330.9   US
CALIFORNIA LABOR MARKET BULLETIN. (Supplement avail.) 1971. m. $15 (effective 1997). Employment Development Department, Labor Market Information Division, 7000 Franklin Blvd., No. 1100, Sacramento, CA 95823. TEL 916-262-2162. FAX 916-262-2443. URL: http://www.calmis.cahwnet.gov. stat. circ. 7,000. (also avail. in microfiche from CIS) **Indexed:** SRI. **Document type:** government publication, bulletin.
●Also available online.
Description: Provides labor market information (labor force, employment and unemployment rate) for the counties and the state.

337 332.6   US   ISSN 1044-3223
E183.8.C2
CANADA - U S OUTLOOK. 1989. q. National Policy Association, 1424 16th St., N.W., Ste. 700, Washington, DC 20036. TEL 202-265-7685. FAX 202-797-5516. Ed. Danila Steinco. **Description:** Covers economic and social issues pertaining to Canada, Mexico, and the U.S.

330.9 381   CN   ISSN 0845-5171
CANADIAN GERMAN TRADE. (Text in English) 1981. m. Can.$50. (Canadian German Chamber of Industry and Commerce) Ruland Communications Inc., 12 Lawton Blvd., Toronto, ON M4V 1Z4, Canada. TEL 416-927-9129. FAX 416-927-9118. Ed. Bernd Hoegne. adv.; bk.rev. circ. 1,800. **Formerly** (until 1988): Info Germany (ISSN 0842-1609)

330   CN   ISSN 0576-5501
CANADIAN INTELLIGENCE SERVICE. m. Can.$25. Canadian Intelligence Publications, 55 Eighth Ave., High River, AB T1V 1E8, Canada. TEL 403-652-4200. FAX 403-652-7940. Ed. Ron Gostick; Pub. Ron Gostick. bk.rev. (processed) **Document type:** newsletter.

CANADIAN MANUFACTURERS ASSOCIATION. IN FOCUS. see BUSINESS AND ECONOMICS — Production Of Goods And Services

CANADIAN MARKET OUTLOOK. see BUSINESS AND ECONOMICS — Macroeconomics

330   CN   ISSN 0829-8416
CANADIAN OUTLOOK. 1974. q. Can.$2500 to non-members. Conference Board of Canada, 255 Smyth Rd., Ste. 100, Ottawa, ON K1H 8M7, Canada. TEL 613-526-3280. FAX 613-526-4857. charts. **Indexed:** CS Ind. **Document type:** bulletin.
●Also available online.
Formerly (until 1986): Conference Board of Canada. Quarterly Canadian Forecast (ISSN 0713-0406)

330   CN   ISSN 0317-0861
HC111
CANADIAN PUBLIC POLICY/ANALYSE DE POLITIQUES. (Text in English, French) 1975. q. Can.$75 to institutions (effective 1998). University of Toronto Press, Journals Department, 5201 Dufferin St., Downsview, ON M3H 5T8, Canada. TEL 416-667-7710. FAX 416-667-7881. E-mail: journals@pgu.ucc.utoronto.ca. Ed. Charles Beach. adv.; bk.rev.; charts; circ. 1,800 (paid). (also avail. in microform; back issues avail.) **Indexed:** ABI Inform., Amer.Hist.& Life (1983-), Arts & Hum.Cit.Ind., ASCA, C.R.E.J., Can.B.P.I., Can.Per.Ind., Can.Wom.Per.Ind., CMI, Curr.Cont., Energy Ind., Energy Info.Abstr., Fut.Surv., Geo.Abstr.H.G., Hist.Abstr. (1983-), Human Resour.Abstr., IDA, Ind.Can.L.P.L., Int.Polit.Sci.Abstr., J.of Econ.Lit., Lang.& Lang.Behav.Abstr., Mar.Aff.Bibl., P.A.I.S.For.Lang.Ind., P.A.I.S., Polit.Sci.Abstr., Risk Abstr., Rural Recreat.Tour.Abstr., Sage Pub.Admin.Abstr., Sage Urb.Stud.Abstr., Sociol.Abstr., SSCI, World Agri.Econ.& Rural Sociol.Abstr. **Document type:** academic/scholarly publication.
—BLDSC (3044.210000); Genuine Article; SWETS; UMI; UnCover. **CCC.**
Description: Discusses current social and economic policy issues and proposals.
Refereed Serial

994   AT   ISSN 0045-5628
CANBERRA SURVEY. 1948. fortn. Aus.$295. Australian Press Services Pty., Ltd., P.O. Box E 160, Queen Victoria Terrace, A.C.T. 2600, Australia. Ed. R.D. Chalmers. **Document type:** newsletter.

330.9   US   ISSN 0192-527X
CAPITAL DISTRICT BUSINESS REVIEW.* 1974. w. $42. Albany Business Journal, Inc., Box 15081, Albany, NY 12212-5081. TEL 518-432-1091. Ed. James C. Menneib. adv.; charts; illus. circ. 7,500. (tabloid format; also avail. in microform from UMI) **Indexed:** Tr.& Indus.Ind.
●Also available online. Vendor(s): Knight-Ridder Information, Inc.
—UMI.

338.9 320   UK
HC151.A1
CARIBBEAN & CENTRAL AMERICA REPORT. 1979. 10/yr. £150($195) (academic institutions £85 ($110)) (effective 1997). Lettres (U.K.) Ltd., 61 Old St., London EC1V 9HX, England. TEL 44-171-251-0012. FAX 44-171-253-8193. Ed. Colin Harding. R&P contact: Alex McHallam. (back issues avail.) **Document type:** newsletter.
●Also available online. Vendor(s): Lexis-Nexis.
Former titles: Latin America & Caribbean Report (ISSN 0968-2732); (until 1992): Caribbean Report (ISSN 0143-523X)

CARIBBEAN DATELINE. see BUSINESS AND ECONOMICS — Investments

CARIBBEAN NEWSLETTER. see POLITICAL SCIENCE — International Relations

CARIBBEAN UPDATE. see BUSINESS AND ECONOMICS — International Commerce

330.9   GY   ISSN 0254-962X
HC151.A1
CARICOM PERSPECTIVE. 1980. bi-m. free. Caribbean Community Secretariat, Bank of Guyana Bldg., P.O. Box 10827, Georgetown, Guyana. circ. 6,000. (back issues avail.)

330.9   BL
CARTA DA AMAZONIA. vol.6, 1978. bi-m. Banco da Amazonia S.A., Av. Presidente. Vargas 800, Belen, Para, Brazil.

CASH; die Wirtschaftszeitung der Schweiz. see BUSINESS AND ECONOMICS — Banking And Finance

330.9 332   UK
▼**CASPIAN BRIEF.** 1997. q. £35($70) Arguments and Facts Media Ltd., P.O. Box 35, Hastings, E. Sussex TN34 2UX, England. TEL 44-1424-442741. FAX 44-1424-442913. E-mail: 100104.1406@compuserve.com. **Document type:** newsletter. **Description:** Focuses on commercial and investment opportunities presented by the frontier economies of Georgia, Armenia, Uzbekistan, Kyrghizstan and Tajikistan. Provides information on growth areas such as agriculture, food-processing and packaging, and in particular, oil and gas. Includes contacts.

330.9   IT   ISSN 0008-7408
CASSA DI RISPARMIO DELLE PROVINCIE LOMBARDE QUARTERLY; bulletin on the Italian economy. (Text in English) no.16, 1970. q. free. Cassa di Risparmio delle Provincie Lombarde, Via Monte di Pieta 8, 20121 Milan, Italy. Ed. Massimo Lanza. charts; stat. **Document type:** bulletin.

330.9   US   ISSN 1040-8452
HC59.69
CENTER FOR INTERNATIONAL AND COMPARATIVE STUDIES. IOWA INTERNATIONAL PAPERS. 1989. a. price varies. University of Iowa, Center for International and Comparative Studies, 226 International Center, Iowa City, IA 52242. TEL 319-335-0368. FAX 319-335-0280. Ed. Douglas Midgett. **Document type:** academic/scholarly publication.

330.9   BB   ISSN 0304-6796
HG2846.B3
CENTRAL BANK OF BARBADOS. ANNUAL REPORT. 1973. a. free. Central Bank of Barbados, Research Department, P.O. Box 1016, Spry St., Bridgetown, Barbados, W.I. TEL 246-436-6870. FAX 246-427-1431. TELEX 2251 CENBANK. E-mail: cbblibr@caribsurf.com. Ed.Bd. R&P contact: Neville Pollard. adv. contact: Neville Pollard. charts; stat. circ. 1,400. **Document type:** bulletin, corporate report.

BUSINESS AND ECONOMICS — ECONOMIC SITUATION AND CONDITIONS

330.9   UA   ISSN 0008-9249
HF46
CENTRAL BANK OF EGYPT. ECONOMIC REVIEW. Key Title: Economic Review - Central Bank of Egypt. (Editions in Arabic, English) 1961. q. free. Central Bank of Egypt, Research Department, 31 Sharia Kasr-el Nil, Cairo, Egypt. Eds. Mahasen Abdel Rehim, Mohamed Saad Badr. charts; stat. circ. 2,500. **Indexed:** Documentatieblad, PROMT, Rural Recreat.Tour.Abstr., Soils & Fert., World Agri.Econ.& Rural Sociol.Abstr., World Bank.Abstr.
—BLDSC (3654.920000); UMI.
   Description: Deals with economic development in Egypt and abroad.

CENTRAL BANK OF IRAQ. QUARTERLY BULLETIN. see BUSINESS AND ECONOMICS — Banking And Finance

CENTRAL BANK OF JORDAN. MONTHLY STATISTICAL BULLETIN. see BUSINESS AND ECONOMICS — Abstracting, Bibliographies, Statistics

330.9   KE
CENTRAL BANK OF KENYA. QUARTERLY ECONOMIC REVIEW. 1968. q. Central Bank of Kenya, P.O. Box 60000, Nairobi, Kenya. **Indexed:** World Bank.Abstr.
   Formerly: Central Bank of Kenya. Economic and Financial Review.

330.9   KU
CENTRAL BANK OF KUWAIT. ECONOMIC REPORT. (Editions in Arabic, English) a. free. Central Bank of Kuwait, Economic Research Department - Bank al-Kuwayt al-Markazi, Idarat al-Buhuth al-ektisadia, P.O. Box 526, Safat 13006, Kuwait. TEL 965-2449200. FAX 965-2440887. TELEX 22101. E-mail: cbk@cbk.gov.kw; URL: http://www.cbk.gov.kw. charts; stat. **Document type:** government publication.

CENTRAL BANK OF KUWAIT. MONTHLY MONETARY STATISTICS. see BUSINESS AND ECONOMICS — Abstracting, Bibliographies, Statistics

CENTRAL BANK OF KUWAIT. QUARTERLY STATISTICAL BULLETIN/BANK AL-KUWAYT AL-MARKAZI. AL-NASHRAH AL-IHSA'IYYAH AL-FASLIYYAH. see BUSINESS AND ECONOMICS — Abstracting, Bibliographies, Statistics

330.9   NR   ISSN 0008-9281
CENTRAL BANK OF NIGERIA. ECONOMIC AND FINANCIAL REVIEW. 1963. irreg., vol.16, no.2, 1978. free. Central Bank of Nigeria, P.M.B. 12194, Tinubu Sq., Lagos, Nigeria. charts; stat. circ. 4,000. **Indexed:** Key to Econ.Sci.

330.9   CE
CENTRAL BANK OF SRI LANKA. BULLETIN. (Text in English) 1950. m. $30. Central Bank of Sri Lanka, Janadhipathi Mawatha, P.O. Box 590, Colombo 1, Sri Lanka. TEL 94-1-421191. FAX 94-1-445127. Ed.Bd. charts; stat.; index. circ. 875. (back issues avail.) **Indexed:** P.A.I.S. **Document type:** bulletin.
   Formerly: Central Bank of Ceylon (ISSN 0008-9222)

330.9   CE
CENTRAL BANK OF SRI LANKA. STAFF STUDIES. 1971. s-a. $5. Central Bank of Sri Lanka, Janadhipathi Mawatha, P.O. Box 590, Colombo 1, Sri Lanka. TEL 94-1-421191. FAX 94-1-445127.
   Formerly: Central Bank of Ceylon. Staff Studies.

330 332   SY   ISSN 0377-3213
CENTRAL BANK OF SYRIA. QUARTERLY BULLETIN. (Text in Arabic, English; occasionally in French) 1963. q. free. Central Bank of Syria, Research Department - Banque Centrale de Syrie, 29 Ayar Sq., Damascus, Syria. TEL 216801. FAX 2227109. TELEX 411910. charts; stat. **Indexed:** World Bank.Abstr. **Document type:** bulletin.
   Formerly: Banque Centrale de Syrie. Bulletin Periodique (ISSN 0067-3846)

330.9   GM   ISSN 0796-0220
CENTRAL BANK OF THE GAMBIA. QUARTERLY BULLETIN. 1971. q. free. Central Bank of the Gambia, Economic Research Department, 1-2 Buckle St., Banjul, Gambia. TEL 228103. FAX 226969. TELEX 2218 GAMBANK GV. Ed. Buah Saidy. circ. 200. **Document type:** bulletin.
   Supersedes: Gambia. Currency Board. Report.

330.9   TU
CENTRAL BANK OF THE REPUBLIC OF TURKEY. QUARTERLY ECONOMIC INFORMATION REPORT. q. Central Bank of the Republic of Turkey, General Directorate of Data Processing, Statistics and Economic Information, Ankara, Turkey.

330   TR   ISSN 1011-6346
CENTRAL BANK OF TRINIDAD AND TOBAGO. QUARTERLY ECONOMIC BULLETIN. 1976. q. $35 (effective 1997). Central Bank of Trinidad and Tobago, Eric Williams Plaza, Independence Sq., P.O. Box 1250, Port-of-Spain, Trinidad & Tobago, W.I. TEL 868-625-4835. FAX 868-627-4696. TELEX 386-270. circ. 750. (processed) **Indexed:** P.A.I.S., World Bank.Abstr. **Document type:** bulletin, corporate report.

330.9   NA
CENTRAL BUREAU OF STATISTICS. NATIONALE REKENINGEN. (Text and summaries in Dutch) 1980. a. fl.25. Central Bureau of Statistics, Fort Amsterdam z/n, Willemstad, Curaco, Netherlands Antilles. TEL 599-9-611031. FAX 599-9-611696. E-mail: ank0004@ibm.net. circ. 250. **Document type:** government publication.

330.943   BE
CENTRAL EUROPEAN ECONOMIC REVIEW. (Text in English) m. Dow Jones Publishing Co., Europe, 87 Bd. Brand Whitlock, 1200 Brussels, Belgium. TEL 32-2-7411211. FAX 32-2-7411600. Ed. Fred Kempe.
   Description: Covers economic changes in the countries in eastern Europe as they adapt to post-Communist conditions.

CENTRAL INTELLIGENCE AGENCY. MONOGRAPHS. see POLITICAL SCIENCE

CENTRAL INTELLIGENCE AGENCY. MONOGRAPHS. ALL COMMUNIST COUNTRIES REPORTS. see POLITICAL SCIENCE

CENTRAL INTELLIGENCE AGENCY. MONOGRAPHS. ALL COUNTRIES REPORTS. see POLITICAL SCIENCE

CENTRAL INTELLIGENCE AGENCY. MONOGRAPHS. ALL INTERNATIONAL COUNTRIES REPORTS. see POLITICAL SCIENCE

CENTRAL INTELLIGENCE AGENCY. MONOGRAPHS. CHINA REPORTS. see POLITICAL SCIENCE

CENTRAL INTELLIGENCE AGENCY. MONOGRAPHS. COMMONWEALTH OF INDEPENDENT STATES REPORT. see POLITICAL SCIENCE

CENTRAL INTELLIGENCE AGENCY. MONOGRAPHS. MAPS ONLY. see POLITICAL SCIENCE

330.9   US   ISSN 1050-3005
CENTRAL NEW YORK BUSINESS JOURNAL. vol.3, 1977. bi-w. $38. C N Y Business Journal, 231 Walton St., Syracuse, NY 13202-1226. TEL 315-472-3104. FAX 315-472-3644. Ed. Norman Poltenson; Pub. Norman Poltenson. adv. contact: James Edison. bk.rev.; illus.; stat.; index; circ. 1,300 (paid). **Indexed:** Tr.& Indus.Ind. **Document type:** newspaper.
   ●Also available online. Vendor(s): Knight-Ridder Information, Inc., UMI.
   —UMI.
   Formerly: Central New York Business Review.

330.9 340 320   CL   ISSN 0716-1123
HC591
CENTRO DE ESTUDIOS PUBLICOS. DOCUMENTO DE TRABAJO. (Text in Spanish; occasionally in English) 1981. m. Centro de Estudios Publicos, Monsenor Sotero Sanz No. 175, Providencia, Santiago 9, Chile. TEL 56-2-2315324. FAX 56-2-2335253. E-mail: cep@activa.cl; URL: http://www.iactiva.cl. Ed. Arturo Fontaine Talavera; Pub. Maria Teresa Miranda. R&P contact: Maria Teresa Miranda. adv. contact: Maria Teresa Miranda. circ. 1,000. **Document type:** academic/scholarly publication.

330.9   BO
CENTRO DE INVESTIGACION Y PROMOCION DEL CAMPESINADO. CUADERNOS DE INVESTIGACION. 1973. irreg. Centro de Investigacion y Promocion del Campesinado, Casilla 5854, La Paz, Bolivia.

330   IT   ISSN 0065-6151
CENTRO DOCUMENTAZIONE E RICERCHE ECONOMICO-SOCIALI. QUADERNI. Cover title: Quaderni Ce D R E S. 1963. irreg., no.119, 1982. free. Centro Documentazione e Ricerche Economico-Sociali, Via Galimberti 2-A, 15100 Alessandria, Italy. Ed. Carlo Beltrame. bk.rev. circ. 1,000.

CHAMBRE DE COMMERCE ET D'INDUSTRIE DE CASABLANCA. REVUE MENSUELLE. see BUSINESS AND ECONOMICS — Chamber Of Commerce Publications

CHENGSHI GAIGE YU FAZHAN/URBAN REFORM AND DEVELOPMENT. see HOUSING AND URBAN PLANNING

330.9   PK
CHIEF EXECUTIVES THINK TANK. ECONOMIC RESEARCH REPORTS. (Text in English) 1960. bi-m. Rs.1500. Shaikhconsults International, P.O. Box 8560, Saddar, Karachi 3, Pakistan. TEL 469635. Ed. S. Shaukat Ali. stat. **Indexed:** Bus.Ind., Mgmt.& Market.Abstr.
   Former titles (until 1986): Chief Executive; (until 1981): Chief Executive's Guide.

330.9   CC   ISSN 1011-2898
CHINA ECONOMIC EXPRESS (JAPANESE EDITION). Korean edition (ISSN 1013-5375) w. HK.$2900($430) Economic Information & Agency, 342 Hennessy Rd., 10th Fl., Wanchai, Hong Kong, People's Republic of China. TEL 852-573-8217. FAX 852-838-8304. TELEX 86990 EIA HX.

330.9   CC   ISSN 1013-5375
CHINA ECONOMIC EXPRESS (KOREAN EDITION). Japanese edition (ISSN 1011-2898) w. HK.$2265($310) Economic Information & Agency, 342 Hennessy Rd., 10th Fl., Wanchai, Hong Kong, People's Republic of China. TEL 852-573-8217. FAX 852-838-8304. TELEX 86990 EIA HX.

330.9   US   ISSN 1043-951X
HC426
CHINA ECONOMIC REVIEW. 1989. s-a. $90 to individuals (foreign $110); institutions $205 (foreign $225) (effective 1998). J A I Press Inc., 55 Old Post Rd., No. 2, Box 1678, Greenwich, CT 06830-1678. TEL 203-661-7602. FAX 203-661-0792. E-mail: jai@jaipress.com. (Addr. in Europe: J A I Press Ltd., 38 Tavistock St., Covent Garden, London WC2E 7PB, England. TEL 44-171-379-8834. FAX 44-171-379-8835) Eds. Bruce L. Reynolds, Mao Yu-Shi. (also avail. in microform from UMI; back issues avail.) **Indexed:** ASCA, Asian-Pac.Econ.Lit., B.P.I., Curr.Cont. **Document type:** academic/scholarly publication.
—BLDSC (3180.138100); Genuine Article; KR SourceOne; SWETS. **CCC.**
   Description: Focuses on the economic development of the People's Republic of China.

330   CC   ISSN 0379-2862
CHINA LETTER. 1971. m. $175. Asia Letter Group, G.P.O. Box 10874, Hong Kong, People's Republic of China. TEL 852-526-2950. FAX 852-526-7131. TELEX HX61166-HKNW. (US addr.: Box 88189, Los Angeles, CA 90009-8189) Ed. Charles R. Smith. bk.rev. **Document type:** newsletter.
   Description: Keeps business executives up to date on the processes of change in China and on the evolution of the China market.

330.9   CC   ISSN 0258-3054
CHINA MARKET. Variant title: China Market Monthly. (Text in English) 1982. m. HK.$300($80) Economic Information & Agency, 342 Hennessy Rd. 10th Fl., Wanchai, Hong Kong, People's Republic of China. TEL 852-573-8217. FAX 852-838-8304. TELEX 86990 EIA HX. **Indexed:** Key to Econ.Sci. —UnCover.

CHINA, REPUBLIC. EXECUTIVE YUAN. DIRECTORATE-GENERAL OF BUDGET, ACCOUNTING & STATISTICS. NATIONAL INCOME IN TAIWAN AREA, R. O.C.. see BUSINESS AND ECONOMICS — Abstracting, Bibliographies, Statistics

BUSINESS AND ECONOMICS — ECONOMIC SITUATION AND CONDITIONS

330.9   CH   ISSN 0257-5663
CHINA, REPUBLIC. EXECUTIVE YUAN. DIRECTORATE-GENERAL OF BUDGET, ACCOUNTING & STATISTICS. QUARTERLY NATIONAL ECONOMIC TRENDS, TAIWAN AREA. Key Title: Guomin Jingji Dongxiang Tongji Jibao - Zhonghua Minguo Taiwan Diqu. (Text in Chinese and English) 1978. q. NT.$200. Executive Yuan, Directorate-General of Budget, Accounting & Statistics, 2 Kwangchow St., Taipei, Taiwan, Republic of China. TEL 886-2-381-4910. (Subscr. to: Chen Chung Book Co., 3F, 20 Heng-Yang Rd., Taipei, R.O.C. TEL 886-2-381-3980) charts; stat. circ. 1,600.

330.9   US
CHINA WEEKLY FAX BULLETIN. w. $495 (foreign $595) (effective 1998). Orbis Publications, LLC, 3201 New Mexico Ave., N.W., Ste. 249, Washington, DC 20016. TEL 202-237-0155. FAX 202-237-0596. E-mail: orbis@orbispub.com; URL: http://www.earthnet.net/orbis. (only avail. by fax) **Document type:** bulletin.
   Description: Reports on political, economic, and business events in China.

330.9   US
CHINESE BUSINESS JOURNAL. 1989. fortn. $7.50. 659 S. Weller St., Seattle, WA 98104. TEL 206-624-8781. FAX 206-624-7437. Ed. Hung Szeto. adv. circ. 10,000. (tabloid format; back issues avail.) **Document type:** newspaper.
   Description: Provides information on business, finance and investment for the greater Seattle area.

330.9   KO
CHONGYONGNYON. (Text in Korean) 1976. m. free. Federation of Korean Industries, 28-1, FKI Bldg., Yoido-dong, Yong-deungpo-ku, Seoul, S. Korea. Ed. Bong-Shik Shin. adv.; bk.rev. circ. 13,000.

CHRISTLICHE DEMOKRATIE; Vierteljahresschrift fuer Zeitgeschichte, Sozial-, Kultur- und Wirtschaftsgeschichte. see HISTORY — History Of Europe

330.9   US
CITY LINE NEWS. 1985. w. $55. City Line News, Box 569, Bala Cynwyd, PA 19004. TEL 610-667-6623. FAX 610-667-6624. Ed. Joyce Engel; Pub. Carole Passman. R&P contact: Carole Passman. adv.: B&W page $1722; adv. contact: Joyce Engel. illus.; cum.index: 1985-1992; circ. 32,000 (controlled). (tabloid format; back issues avail.) **Document type:** newspaper.
   Description: Covers all facets of business, dining and entertainment, and community news.

330.9   US
CITY REPORT. m. Association of Idaho Cities, 3314 Grace St., Boise, ID 83703. TEL 208-344-8594. FAX 208-344-8677. E-mail: aic@primenet.com.

330   AG   ISSN 0009-8256
CLARIN ECONOMICO. 1960. m. $52. Arte Grafico Editorial Argentino S.A., Piedras 1743, Buenos Aires, Argentina. Ed. Ernestina Laura Herrera de Noble. charts; stat.; tr.lit.

330.9 333.33   US   ISSN 1047-6083
THE CLAYTON-FILLMORE REPORT; perspectives on economics and real estate. 1983. m. $175 (foreign $200) (effective 1995 & 1996). Clayton-Fillmore, Ltd., 2849 W. 23rd Ave., Denver, CO 80211. TEL 303-433-5323. FAX 303-433-5363. Ed. Howard Treibitz. cum.index: 1984-1992; circ. 550 (paid). (back issues avail.) **Document type:** trade publication.
   Description: Describes real estate and economic conditions in three metro areas throughout the US in each issue; contains feature articles on a particular US region.

330.9   US   ISSN 0009-8892
CLEVELANDER. 1926. m. $12. Greater Cleveland Growth Association, 200 Tower City Ctr., Cleveland, OH 44113. TEL 216-621-3300. FAX 216-621-6013. Ed. Deirdre Vodanoff. adv. circ. 17,500. Indexed: P.A.I.S. **Document type:** newsletter.

330.9   US
COBBLE HILL NEWS. w. $25. Brooklyn Journal Publications, 129 Montague St., Brooklyn, NY 11201. TEL 718-624-6033. FAX 718-875-5302.

COLABORACION INTERNACIONAL. see BUSINESS AND ECONOMICS — International Commerce

COLORADO AGRIBUSINESS ROUNDUP. see AGRICULTURE — Agricultural Economics

330.9   US   ISSN 0092-5071
HC107.C7
COLORADO BUSINESS. 1973. m. $24. Wiesner Publishing, Inc., 7009 S. Potomac St., Englewood, CO 80112. TEL 303-397-7600. FAX 303-397-7619. Ed. Bruce Goldberg; Pub. Jackie Kilfoyle. R&P contact: John Bennett. adv. contact: Susan Samford. illus.; circ. 19,469 (paid). (also avail. in microform from UMI) Indexed: Bus.Ind., Mag.Ind., Tr.& Indus.Ind. **Document type:** consumer publication.
   ●Also available online. Vendor(s): Information Access Co., Knight-Ridder Information, Inc., Lexis-Nexis.
   —UMI.

330.9   US
COLORADO SKI INDUSTRY. a. $25. University of Colorado, Business Research Division, Campus Box 420, Boulder, CO 80309-0420. Ed.Bd. **Document type:** bulletin.
   Description: Annual synopsis of the ski conditions in Colorado.

330   CL   ISSN 0716-4025
COMENTARIOS SOBRE LA SITUACION ECONOMICA. 1971. s-a. $15. Universidad de Chile, Facultad de Ciencias Economicas y Administrativas, Av. Ranacagua 257, Santiago, Chile. Ed. Luis Riveros. charts; stat. **Document type:** academic/scholarly publication.

330.9   UN
COMISION ECONOMICA PARA AMERICA LATINA Y EL CARIBE. SERIE REFORMAS DE POLITICA PUBLICA. irreg., no.35. Comision Economica para America Latina y el Caribe, Edificio Naciones Unidas, Av. Dag Hammarskjold, Casilla 197-D, Santiago, Chile. circ. (controlled). (back issues avail.)

380   SZ
COMMERCE EXTERIEUR SUISSE/SCHWEIZER AUSSENWIRTSCHAFT. (Text in French or German) 1922. m. Swiss Office for Trade Promotion, Stampfenbachstr. 85, CH-8035 Zurich, Switzerland. TEL 41-1-3655151. FAX 41-1-3655221. adv.; bk.rev.; abstr.; bibl.; stat.; tr.lit. circ. 7,000. Indexed: Key to Econ.Sci. **Document type:** trade publication.
   Former titles (until 1995): Exportation en Pratique; Marches Etrangers - Auslandsmaerkte; Wirtschaftliche Mitteilungen - Informations Economiques (ISSN 0043-6186)

330.9   GR   ISSN 0013-0028
COMMERCIAL BANK OF GREECE. ECONOMIC BULLETIN. 1954. q. free. Commercial Bank of Greece, Economic Research Department, 11 Sofokleous St., 102 35 Athens, Greece. Ed. Apostolos Theophanopoulos. stat.; charts. circ. 3,000. Indexed: ELLIS, Key to Econ.Sci., P.A.I.S., PROMT. **Document type:** bulletin.

330 332   US
COMMERSANT WEEKLY. English edition: East - West Commersant. (Text in Russian) w. $495 (foreign $545) (effective 1997). WorldTrade Executive, Inc., Box 761, Concord, MA 01742. TEL 508-287-0301. FAX 508-287-0302. Pub. Gary A. Brown. adv.: page $975; 7 1/2 x 9 1/2.
   Description: Covers business opportunities, the availability of funding, reliable local contacts, and other essential trade and investment information related to Russia and Eastern Europe.

338   UK   ISSN 0300-4406
HC241.A1
COMMON MARKET NEWS. 1971. m. $75 (outside Europe $85). European Economic Data Publishing Co., Ltd., 19 Penman Terr., Swansea SA1 6HZ, Wales. TEL 44-1792-459191. Ed. I.B.N. Evans. bk.rev.; stat.; index. circ. 2,000. **Document type:** newsletter.
   Formerly: Common Market News Letter.
   Description: Contains reports and news items on the affairs of the European Union.

COMMONWEALTH LETTERS; for investors in single family homes. see REAL ESTATE

COMMUNICATIONS MARKETS ANALYSIS. see COMMUNICATIONS

330.9 352.7   US   ISSN 0896-9159
COMMUNITY CHANGE. 1986. q. $20. Center for Community Change, 1000 Wisconsin Ave., N.W., Washington, DC 20007. TEL 202-342-0567. FAX 202-333-5462. bk.rev. circ. 2,800. (back issues avail.) **Document type:** newsletter.
   Description: For community organizations working in low-income neighborhoods and individuals concerned about poverty. Focuses on poverty and what can be done about poverty-related problems, such as the need for affordable housing.

330.9   US   ISSN 1059-0722
HD4973
COMPENSATION AND WORKING CONDITIONS. m. $23 (foreign $28.75). U.S. Bureau of Labor Statistics, 441 G St., N.W., Washington, DC 20212. TEL 202-655-4000. (Subscr. to: Superintendent of Documents, U.S. Government Printing Office, Box 371954, Pittsburgh, PA 15254-7954. TEL 202-512-1800. FAX 202-512-2250; Or: Bureau of Labor Statistics Publications Sales Center, Box 2145, Chicago, IL 60690) index. (also avail. in microform from UMI; microfiche from CIS; back issues avail.; reprint service avail. from CIS,UMI) Indexed: Amer.Stat.Ind. (1973-). **Document type:** government publication.
   ●Also available on CD-ROM.
   —UMI.
   Formerly (until 1991): Current Wage Developments (ISSN 0192-8163)
   Description: Presents information on wage and benefit changes resulting from collective bargaining settlements and unilateral management decisions.

COMPETITIVENESS REVIEW. see BUSINESS AND ECONOMICS — International Commerce

330.9   FP
COMPTES ECONOMIQUES DE LA POLYNESIE FRANCAISE. irreg. Institut Territorial de la Statistique, B.P. 395, Papeete, Tahiti, French Polynesia. TEL 689-43-71-96. FAX 689-43-72-52. **Document type:** government publication.

COMPUTATIONAL ECONOMICS. see BUSINESS AND ECONOMICS — Computer Applications

330   SP   ISSN 0210-0738
CONFEDERACION ESPANOLA DE CAJAS DE AHORROS. COYUNTURA ECONOMICA. 1977. m. 2500 ptas. Confederacion Espanola de Cajas de Ahorros, Servicio de Estudios, C. Alcala, 276, 28014 Madrid, Spain.

330   IT   ISSN 0045-8082
CONGIUNTURA ECONOMICA LOMBARDA.* vol.7, 1972. m. Cassa di Risparmio delle Provincie Lombarde, Via Monte di Pieta 8, 20121 Milan, Italy. charts; stat.

330.9   IT
CONGIUNTURA INDUSTRIALE IN EMILIA-ROMAGNA. 1984. q. Unione Regionale Camere di Commercio dell'Emilia-Romagna (C.E.R.E.S.), Via Montegrappa 4-D, 40121 Bologna, Italy. TEL 39-51-223030. FAX 39-51-234945. Dir. Claudio Pasini. circ. 6,000. **Document type:** bulletin.

330.9   TI
CONJONCTURE/AL-ALAM AL-IQTISADIY; etudes et informations economiques de Tunisie - dirasat wa mu'atiyat iqtisadiyyah 'an Tunis. (Text in Arabic, French) 1971. m. 1.50 din. per no. Ministere de l'Economie Nationale, 7 rue du Royaume d'Arabie Saoudite, Tunis, Tunisia. TEL 289-801. Eds. Kamel Gharbi, Ahmed Souibgui. adv.; bk.rev.; charts; illus.; stat. circ. 3,000. Indexed: P.A.I.S.For.Lang.Ind.

330.9   BL   ISSN 0010-5945
HC186
CONJUNTURA ECONOMICA. 1947. m. $235 (effective 1996). (Instituto Brasileiro de Economia) Fundacao Getulio Vargas, C.P. 62591, 22257-970 Rio de Janeiro, R.J., Brazil. TEL 55-21-5369196. FAX 55-21-5369155. TELEX 21-36811. Ed.Bd. adv. contact: Milton Gondim. charts; stat.; index. circ. 16,000. Indexed: Int.Lab.Doc., Key to Econ.Sci., P.A.I.S.For.Lang.Ind., P.A.I.S. **Document type:** academic/scholarly publication.
   —BLDSC (3417.565000).
   Description: Analyzes the national economy, profiles national accounts, contains price indices in different sectors, and presents the latest research in the economic area.

BUSINESS AND ECONOMICS — ECONOMIC SITUATION AND CONDITIONS

330.9   UK
HC10
CONSENSUS FORECASTS; a worldwide survey. 1984. m. £370($565) (effective 1997). Consensus Economics Inc., 53 Upper Brook St., London W17 2LT, England. TEL 44-171-491-3211. FAX 44-171-409-2331. Ed.Bd. adv. (also avail. in microform from UMI; diskette format; also avail. by fax) **Document type:** academic/scholarly publication.
Formerly: Economic Forecasts (ISSN 0169-1767)
Description: Presents and discusses individual and consensus forecasts for the G-10 countries along with historical data, analysis, foreign exchange and oil price forecasts and a special topical survey.

330.9   US
CONSUMER EXPENDITURE SURVEY. (Subseries of: B L S Bulletins) a.? $16. U.S. Bureau of Labor Statistics, 2 Massachusetts Ave., N.E., Washington, DC 20212. TEL 202-655-4000. (Subscr. to: Superintendent of Documents, U.S. Government Printing Office, Box 317594, Pittsburgh, PA 15250-7954. TEL 202-512-1800. FAX 202-512-2250; Or: Bureau of Labor Statistics Publications Sales Center, Box 2145, Chicago, IL 60690) (also avail. in diskette format) **Document type:** government publication.
Description: Presents detailed statistics on consumer spending.

331.1   US
CONSUMER EXPENDITURE SURVEY: QUARTERLY DATA FROM THE INTERVIEW SURVEY. (Subseries of: B L S Reports) q. U.S. Bureau of Labor Statistics, 2 Massachusetts Ave., N.E., Washington, DC 20212. (Subscr. to: Superintendent of Documents, U.S. Government Printing Office, Pittsburgh, PA 15250-7954. TEL 202-512-1800. FAX 202-512-2250; Or: Bureau of Labor Statistics Publications Sales Center, Box 2145, Chicago, IL 60690) **Document type:** government publication.
Description: Reports on historical consumer spending patterns.

330.9   US
CONSUMER EXPENDITURES IN (YEAR). (Subseries of: National Office News Releases) a. U.S. Bureau of Labor Statistics, 2 Massachusetts Ave., N.E., Washington, DC 20212. TEL 202-655-4000. (Subscr. to: Superintendent of Documents, U.S. Government Printing Office, Box 371954, Pittsburgh, PA 15250-7954. TEL 202-512-1800. FAX 202-512-2250; Or: Bureau of Labor Statistics Publications Sales Office, Box 2145, Chicago, IL 60690) **Document type:** government publication.

330.9   US
CONSUMER PRICE INDEX. (Subseries of: National Office News Releases) 1913. m. free. U.S. Bureau of Labor Statistics, 2 Massachusetts Ave., N.E., Washington, DC 20212. (Subscr. to: Superintendent of Documents, U.S. Government Printing Office, Box 371954, Pittsburgh, PA 15250-7954. TEL 202-512-1800. FAX 202-512-2250; Or: Bureau of Labor Statistics Publications Sales Office, Box 2145, Chicago, IL 60690) stat. circ. 5,000. (also avail. in diskette format; back issues avail.) **Document type:** government publication.

330.9   US
CONSUMER PRICE INDEX: WASHINGTON, D.C.. (Subseries of: National Office News Releases) m. free. U.S. Bureau of Labor Statistics, 2 Massachusetts Ave., N.E., Washington, DC 20212. TEL 202-655-4000. (Subscr. to: Superintendent of Documents, U.S. Government Printing Office, Box 371954, Pittsburgh, PA 15254. TEL 202-512-1800. FAX 202-512-2250; Or: Bureau of Labor Statistics Publications Sales Center, Box 2145, Chicago, IL 60690) circ. 29,000. (back issues avail.) **Document type:** government publication.

CONTEMPORARY WALES; an annual review of economic and social research. see *SOCIAL SCIENCES: COMPREHENSIVE WORKS*

330.9 320   UK   ISSN 0277-5921
HB1
CONTRIBUTIONS TO POLITICAL ECONOMY. 1980. a. £32 (foreign $55) (effective 1998). (Cambridge Political Economy Society) Oxford University Press, Academic Division, Great Clarendon St., Oxford OX2 6DP, England. TEL 44-1865-267907. FAX 44-1865-267485. E-mail: jnl.info@oup.co.uk; URL: http://www.oup.co.uk/journals. (Subscr. in U.S. to: Oxford University Press Inc., 2001 Evans Rd., Cary, NC 27513. TEL 800-852-7323. FAX 919-677-1714) Ed.Bd.; Pub. Martin Green. R&P contact: Joolz Longley. adv. contact: Jane Parker. (reprint service avail. from SWZ) **Indexed:** SSCI. **Document type:** academic/scholarly publication. —BLDSC (3461.119000); Genuine Article; UnCover. **CCC.**
Description: Publishes articles on the theory and history of political economy that fall broadly within a critical tradition in economic thought and are associated with the philosophies of the neoclassical economists, including Marx, Keynes, and Sraffa.

330.9   US
CO-OP AMERICA QUARTERLY; a magazine for building economic alternatives. 1985. q. $20 to individuals; institutions $60 (effective 1997). Co-op America Inc., 1612 K St., N.W., Ste. 600, Washington, DC 20006. TEL 202-872-5307. FAX 202-331-8166. E-mail: caq@envirolink.org; URL: http://www.coopamerica.org; http://www.eden.com/fineprint/81796.html. Ed. Rosemary J. Brown; Pub. Denise Hamler. R&P contact: Angi Moyer. adv.: B&W page $1785; 8 1/4 x 10 3/4; adv. contact: Denise Hamler. bk.rev.; circ. 60,000 (paid). (back issues avail.) **Indexed:** Alt.Press Ind. **Document type:** consumer publication.
Formerly (until 1991): Building Economic Alternatives (ISSN 0885-9930)
Description: Teaches consumers how to use their spending power to support socially and environmentally responsible businesses and promote social and economic justice.

330.9   AT
CORPORATE BRIEF. 1972. m. Aus.$545. Syntec Economic Services Pty.Ltd., G.P.O. Box 2455V, Melbourne, Vic. 3001, Australia. TEL 61-3-6621911. FAX 61-3-6621813. Ed. David Love. circ. 1,700.

CORPORATE CASHFLOW; the magazine of treasury management. see *BUSINESS AND ECONOMICS — Banking And Finance*

CORPORATE CASHFLOW DIRECTORY OF TREASURY SERVICES. see *BUSINESS AND ECONOMICS — Banking And Finance*

330   MX   ISSN 0010-9118
CORREO ECONOMICO. 1963. w. Mex.$250($25) (Informacion Nacional y Publicidad) Ediciones Correo S.A., Cadiz 53, Col. Alamos, Mexico 13, D.F., Mexico. adv.; bk.rev.; bibl.; charts; illus.; stat. circ. 19,000.

341.7   EI   ISSN 0377-466X
COUNCIL OF THE EUROPEAN COMMUNITIES. REVIEW OF THE COUNCIL'S WORK. (Text in English) a. $10. Office for Official Publications of the European Communities, L-2985 Luxembourg, Luxembourg. (Dist. in the U.S. by: Unipub, 4611-F Assembly Dr., Lanham, MD 20706-4391. TEL 800-274-4888. FAX 301-459-0056) **Indexed:** IIS.

COUNTRIES IN CRISIS. see *POLITICAL SCIENCE — International Relations*

COUNTRY FORECAST. ALGERIA. see *POLITICAL SCIENCE*

COUNTRY FORECAST. ARGENTINA. see *POLITICAL SCIENCE*

COUNTRY FORECAST. ASIA - PACIFIC. see *POLITICAL SCIENCE*

COUNTRY FORECAST. AUSTRALIA. see *POLITICAL SCIENCE*

COUNTRY FORECAST. AUSTRIA. see *POLITICAL SCIENCE*

COUNTRY FORECAST. BELGIUM. see *POLITICAL SCIENCE*

COUNTRY FORECAST. BRAZIL. see *POLITICAL SCIENCE*

COUNTRY FORECAST. BULGARIA. see *POLITICAL SCIENCE*

COUNTRY FORECAST. CANADA. see *POLITICAL SCIENCE*

COUNTRY FORECAST. CHILE. see *POLITICAL SCIENCE*

COUNTRY FORECAST. CHINA. see *POLITICAL SCIENCE*

COUNTRY FORECAST. COLOMBIA. see *POLITICAL SCIENCE*

COUNTRY FORECAST. CZECH REPUBLIC. see *POLITICAL SCIENCE*

COUNTRY FORECAST. DENMARK. see *POLITICAL SCIENCE*

COUNTRY FORECAST. EASTERN EUROPE AND THE FORMER SOVIET UNION. see *POLITICAL SCIENCE*

COUNTRY FORECAST. ECUADOR. see *POLITICAL SCIENCE*

COUNTRY FORECAST. EGYPT. see *POLITICAL SCIENCE*

COUNTRY FORECAST. EUROPE. see *POLITICAL SCIENCE*

COUNTRY FORECAST. FINLAND. see *POLITICAL SCIENCE*

COUNTRY FORECAST. FRANCE. see *POLITICAL SCIENCE*

COUNTRY FORECAST. GERMANY. see *POLITICAL SCIENCE*

COUNTRY FORECAST. GLOBAL OUTLOOK. see *POLITICAL SCIENCE*

COUNTRY FORECAST. GREECE. see *POLITICAL SCIENCE*

COUNTRY FORECAST. HONG KONG. see *POLITICAL SCIENCE*

COUNTRY FORECAST. HUNGARY. see *POLITICAL SCIENCE*

COUNTRY FORECAST. INDIA. see *POLITICAL SCIENCE*

COUNTRY FORECAST. INDONESIA. see *POLITICAL SCIENCE*

COUNTRY FORECAST. IRAN. see *POLITICAL SCIENCE*

COUNTRY FORECAST. IRAQ. see *POLITICAL SCIENCE*

COUNTRY FORECAST. IRELAND. see *POLITICAL SCIENCE*

COUNTRY FORECAST. ISRAEL. see *POLITICAL SCIENCE*

COUNTRY FORECAST. ITALY. see *POLITICAL SCIENCE*

COUNTRY FORECAST. JAPAN. see *POLITICAL SCIENCE*

COUNTRY FORECAST. LATIN AMERICA. see *POLITICAL SCIENCE*

COUNTRY FORECAST. MALAYSIA. see *POLITICAL SCIENCE*

COUNTRY FORECAST. MEXICO. see *POLITICAL SCIENCE*

COUNTRY FORECAST. MIDDLE EAST AND NORTH AFRICA. see *POLITICAL SCIENCE*

COUNTRY FORECAST. NETHERLANDS. see *POLITICAL SCIENCE*

COUNTRY FORECAST. NEW ZEALAND. see *POLITICAL SCIENCE*

COUNTRY FORECAST. NIGERIA. see *POLITICAL SCIENCE*

COUNTRY FORECAST. NORWAY. see *POLITICAL SCIENCE*

COUNTRY FORECAST. PAKISTAN. see *POLITICAL SCIENCE*

COUNTRY FORECAST. PERU. see *POLITICAL SCIENCE*

COUNTRY FORECAST. PHILIPPINES. see *POLITICAL SCIENCE*

COUNTRY FORECAST. POLAND. see *POLITICAL SCIENCE*

COUNTRY FORECAST. PORTUGAL. see *POLITICAL SCIENCE*

BUSINESS AND ECONOMICS — ECONOMIC SITUATION AND CONDITIONS

COUNTRY FORECAST. ROMANIA. see *POLITICAL SCIENCE*

COUNTRY FORECAST. RUSSIA. see *POLITICAL SCIENCE*

COUNTRY FORECAST. SAUDI ARABIA. see *POLITICAL SCIENCE*

COUNTRY FORECAST. SINGAPORE. see *POLITICAL SCIENCE*

COUNTRY FORECAST. SLOVAKIA. see *POLITICAL SCIENCE*

COUNTRY FORECAST. SOUTH AFRICA. see *POLITICAL SCIENCE*

COUNTRY FORECAST. SOUTH KOREA. see *POLITICAL SCIENCE*

COUNTRY FORECAST. SPAIN. see *POLITICAL SCIENCE*

COUNTRY FORECAST. SRI LANKA. see *POLITICAL SCIENCE*

COUNTRY FORECAST. SUB-SAHARAN AFRICA. see *POLITICAL SCIENCE*

COUNTRY FORECAST. SWEDEN. see *POLITICAL SCIENCE*

COUNTRY FORECAST. SWITZERLAND. see *POLITICAL SCIENCE*

COUNTRY FORECAST. TAIWAN. see *POLITICAL SCIENCE*

COUNTRY FORECAST. THAILAND. see *POLITICAL SCIENCE*

COUNTRY FORECAST. TURKEY. see *POLITICAL SCIENCE*

COUNTRY FORECAST. UNITED KINGDOM. see *POLITICAL SCIENCE*

COUNTRY FORECAST. UNITED STATES OF AMERICA. see *POLITICAL SCIENCE*

COUNTRY FORECAST. VENEZUELA. see *POLITICAL SCIENCE*

COUNTRY FORECAST. VIETNAM. see *POLITICAL SCIENCE*

COUNTRY FORECASTS (NEW YORK). see *POLITICAL SCIENCE*

COUNTRY PROFILE. ALBANIA; annual survey of political and economic background. see *POLITICAL SCIENCE*

COUNTRY PROFILE. ALGERIA; annual survey of political and economic background. see *POLITICAL SCIENCE*

COUNTRY PROFILE. ANGOLA; annual survey of political and economic background. see *POLITICAL SCIENCE*

COUNTRY PROFILE. ARGENTINA; annual survey of political and economic background. see *POLITICAL SCIENCE*

COUNTRY PROFILE. AUSTRALIA; annual survey of political and economic background. see *POLITICAL SCIENCE*

COUNTRY PROFILE. AUSTRIA; annual survey of political and economic background. see *POLITICAL SCIENCE*

COUNTRY PROFILE. AZERBAIJAN; annual survey of political and economic background. see *POLITICAL SCIENCE*

COUNTRY PROFILE. BAHRAIN, QATAR; annual survey of political and economic background. see *POLITICAL SCIENCE*

COUNTRY PROFILE. BALTIC REPUBLICS: LITHUANIA, LATVIA, ESTONIA; annual survey of political and economic background. see *POLITICAL SCIENCE*

COUNTRY PROFILE. BANGLADESH; annual survey of political and economic background. see *POLITICAL SCIENCE*

COUNTRY PROFILE. BELARUS, MOLDOVA; annual survey of political and economic background. see *POLITICAL SCIENCE*

COUNTRY PROFILE. BELGIUM, LUXEMBOURG; annual survey of political and economic background. see *POLITICAL SCIENCE*

COUNTRY PROFILE. BELIZE, BAHAMAS, BERMUDA; annual survey of political and economic background. see *POLITICAL SCIENCE*

COUNTRY PROFILE. BOLIVIA; annual survey of political and economic background. see *POLITICAL SCIENCE*

COUNTRY PROFILE. BOSNIA-HERCEGOVINA, CROATIA; annual survey of political and economic background. see *POLITICAL SCIENCE*

COUNTRY PROFILE. BOTSWANA, LESOTHO; annual survey of political and economic background. see *POLITICAL SCIENCE*

COUNTRY PROFILE. BRAZIL; annual survey of political and economic background. see *POLITICAL SCIENCE*

COUNTRY PROFILE. BULGARIA; annual survey of political and economic background. see *POLITICAL SCIENCE*

COUNTRY PROFILE. CAMBODIA, LAOS; annual survey of political and economic background. see *POLITICAL SCIENCE*

COUNTRY PROFILE. CAMEROON, CENTRAL AFRICAN REPUBLIC, CHAD; annual survey of political and economic background. see *POLITICAL SCIENCE*

COUNTRY PROFILE. CANADA; annual survey of political and economic background. see *POLITICAL SCIENCE*

COUNTRY PROFILE. CENTRAL ASIAN REPUBLICS: KYRGYZ REPUBLIC, TAJIKISTAN, TURKMENISTAN, UZBEKISTAN; annual survey of political and economic background. see *POLITICAL SCIENCE*

COUNTRY PROFILE. CHILE; annual survey of political and economic background. see *POLITICAL SCIENCE*

COUNTRY PROFILE. CHINA, MONGOLIA; annual survey of political and economic background. see *POLITICAL SCIENCE*

COUNTRY PROFILE. COLOMBIA; annual survey of political and economic background. see *POLITICAL SCIENCE*

COUNTRY PROFILE. CONGO; annual survey of political and economic background. see *POLITICAL SCIENCE*

COUNTRY PROFILE. COSTA RICA; annual survey of political and economic background. see *POLITICAL SCIENCE*

COUNTRY PROFILE. COTE D'IVOIRE, MALI; annual survey of political and economic background. see *POLITICAL SCIENCE*

COUNTRY PROFILE. CUBA; annual survey of political and economic background. see *POLITICAL SCIENCE*

COUNTRY PROFILE. CYPRUS, MALTA; annual survey of political and economic background. see *POLITICAL SCIENCE*

COUNTRY PROFILE. CZECH REPUBLIC; annual survey of political and economic background. see *POLITICAL SCIENCE*

COUNTRY PROFILE. DENMARK, ICELAND; annual survey of political and economic background. see *POLITICAL SCIENCE*

COUNTRY PROFILE. DOMINICAN REPUBLIC, HAITI, PUERTO RICO; annual survey of political and economic background. see *POLITICAL SCIENCE*

COUNTRY PROFILE. ECUADOR; annual survey of political and economic background. see *POLITICAL SCIENCE*

COUNTRY PROFILE. EGYPT; annual survey of political and economic background. see *POLITICAL SCIENCE*

COUNTRY PROFILE. ETHIOPIA, ERITREA, SOMALIA, DJIBOUTI; annual survey of political and economic background. see *POLITICAL SCIENCE*

COUNTRY PROFILE. FINLAND; annual survey of political and economic background. see *POLITICAL SCIENCE*

COUNTRY PROFILE. FRANCE; annual survey of political and economic background. see *POLITICAL SCIENCE*

COUNTRY PROFILE. GABON, EQUATORIAL GUINEA; annual survey of political and economic background. see *POLITICAL SCIENCE*

COUNTRY PROFILE. GEORGIA, ARMENIA; annual survey of political and economic background. see *POLITICAL SCIENCE*

COUNTRY PROFILE. GERMANY; annual survey of political and economic background. see *POLITICAL SCIENCE*

COUNTRY PROFILE. GHANA; annual survey of political and economic background. see *POLITICAL SCIENCE*

COUNTRY PROFILE. GREECE; annual survey of political and economic background. see *POLITICAL SCIENCE*

COUNTRY PROFILE. GUATEMALA, EL SALVADOR; annual survey of political and economic background. see *POLITICAL SCIENCE*

COUNTRY PROFILE. GUINEA, SIERRA LEONE, LIBERIA; annual survey of political and economic background. see *POLITICAL SCIENCE*

COUNTRY PROFILE. GUYANA, WINDWARD AND LEEWARD ISLANDS; annual survey of political and economic background. see *POLITICAL SCIENCE*

COUNTRY PROFILE. HONG KONG, MACAU; annual survey of political and economic background. see *POLITICAL SCIENCE*

COUNTRY PROFILE. HUNGARY; annual survey of political and economic background. see *POLITICAL SCIENCE*

COUNTRY PROFILE. INDIA, NEPAL; annual survey of political and economic background. see *POLITICAL SCIENCE*

COUNTRY PROFILE. INDONESIA; annual survey of political and economic background. see *POLITICAL SCIENCE*

COUNTRY PROFILE. IRAN; annual survey of political and economic background. see *POLITICAL SCIENCE*

COUNTRY PROFILE. IRAQ; annual survey of political and economic background. see *POLITICAL SCIENCE*

COUNTRY PROFILE. IRELAND; annual survey of political and economic background. see *POLITICAL SCIENCE*

COUNTRY PROFILE. ISRAEL, THE OCCUPIED TERRITORIES; annual survey of political and economic background. see *POLITICAL SCIENCE*

COUNTRY PROFILE. ITALY; annual survey of political and economic background. see *POLITICAL SCIENCE*

COUNTRY PROFILE. JAMAICA, BARBADOS; annual survey of political and economic background. see *POLITICAL SCIENCE*

COUNTRY PROFILE. JAPAN; annual survey of political and economic background. see *POLITICAL SCIENCE*

COUNTRY PROFILE. JORDAN; annual survey of political and economic background. see *POLITICAL SCIENCE*

COUNTRY PROFILE. KAZAKHSTAN; annual survey of political and economic background. see *POLITICAL SCIENCE*

COUNTRY PROFILE. KENYA; annual survey of political and economic background. see *POLITICAL SCIENCE*

COUNTRY PROFILE. KUWAIT; annual survey of political and economic background. see *POLITICAL SCIENCE*

COUNTRY PROFILE. LEBANON; annual survey of political and economic background. see *POLITICAL SCIENCE*

COUNTRY PROFILE. LIBYA; annual survey of political and economic background. see *POLITICAL SCIENCE*

COUNTRY PROFILE. MACEDONIA, SERBIA-MONTENEGRO; annual survey of political and economic background. see *POLITICAL SCIENCE*

COUNTRY PROFILE. MADAGASCAR; annual survey of political and economic background. see *POLITICAL SCIENCE*

COUNTRY PROFILE. MALAWI; annual survey of political and economic background. see *POLITICAL SCIENCE*

BUSINESS AND ECONOMICS — ECONOMIC SITUATION AND CONDITIONS

COUNTRY PROFILE. MALAYSIA, BRUNEI; annual survey of political and economic background. see *POLITICAL SCIENCE*

COUNTRY PROFILE. MAURITIUS, SEYCHELLES; annual survey of political and economic background. see *POLITICAL SCIENCE*

COUNTRY PROFILE. MEXICO; annual survey of political and economic background. see *POLITICAL SCIENCE*

COUNTRY PROFILE. MOROCCO; annual survey of political and economic background. see *POLITICAL SCIENCE*

COUNTRY PROFILE. MOZAMBIQUE; annual survey of political and economic background. see *POLITICAL SCIENCE*

COUNTRY PROFILE. MYANMAR; annual survey of political and economic background. see *POLITICAL SCIENCE*

COUNTRY PROFILE. NAMIBIA, SWAZILAND; annual survey of political and economic background. see *POLITICAL SCIENCE*

COUNTRY PROFILE. NETHERLANDS; annual survey of political and economic background. see *POLITICAL SCIENCE*

COUNTRY PROFILE. NEW ZEALAND; annual survey of political and economic background. see *POLITICAL SCIENCE*

COUNTRY PROFILE. NICARAGUA, HONDURAS; annual survey of political and economic background. see *POLITICAL SCIENCE*

COUNTRY PROFILE. NIGER, BURKINA FASO; annual survey of political and economic background. see *POLITICAL SCIENCE*

COUNTRY PROFILE. NIGERIA; annual survey of political and economic background. see *POLITICAL SCIENCE*

COUNTRY PROFILE. NORWAY; annual survey of political and economic background. see *POLITICAL SCIENCE*

COUNTRY PROFILE. OMAN; annual survey of political and economic background. see *POLITICAL SCIENCE*

COUNTRY PROFILE. PACIFIC ISLANDS: FIJI, SOLOMON ISLANDS, WESTERN SAMOA, VANUATU, TONGA AND NEW CALEDONIA; annual survey of political and economic background. see *POLITICAL SCIENCE*

COUNTRY PROFILE. PAKISTAN, AFGHANISTAN; annual survey of political and economic background. see *POLITICAL SCIENCE*

COUNTRY PROFILE. PANAMA; annual survey of political and economic background. see *POLITICAL SCIENCE*

COUNTRY PROFILE. PAPUA NEW GUINEA; annual survey of political and economic background. see *POLITICAL SCIENCE*

COUNTRY PROFILE. PERU; annual survey of political and economic background. see *POLITICAL SCIENCE*

COUNTRY PROFILE. PHILIPPINES; annual survey of political and economic background. see *POLITICAL SCIENCE*

COUNTRY PROFILE. POLAND; annual survey of political and economic background. see *POLITICAL SCIENCE*

COUNTRY PROFILE. PORTUGAL; annual survey of political and economic background. see *POLITICAL SCIENCE*

COUNTRY PROFILE. ROMANIA; annual survey of political and economic background. see *POLITICAL SCIENCE*

COUNTRY PROFILE. RUSSIA; annual survey of political and economic background. see *POLITICAL SCIENCE*

COUNTRY PROFILE. RWANDA, BURUNDI; annual survey of political and economic background. see *POLITICAL SCIENCE*

COUNTRY PROFILE. SAO TOME AND PRINCIPE, GUINEA-BISSAU, CAPE VERDE; annual survey of political and economic background. see *POLITICAL SCIENCE*

COUNTRY PROFILE. SAUDI ARABIA; annual survey of political and economic background. see *POLITICAL SCIENCE*

COUNTRY PROFILE. SENEGAL; annual survey of political and economic background. see *POLITICAL SCIENCE*

COUNTRY PROFILE. SINGAPORE; annual survey of political and economic background. see *POLITICAL SCIENCE*

COUNTRY PROFILE. SLOVAKIA; annual survey of political and economic background. see *POLITICAL SCIENCE*

COUNTRY PROFILE. SLOVENIA; annual survey of political and economic background. see *POLITICAL SCIENCE*

COUNTRY PROFILE. SOUTH AFRICA; annual survey of political and economic background. see *POLITICAL SCIENCE*

COUNTRY PROFILE. SOUTH KOREA, NORTH KOREA; annual survey of political and economic background. see *POLITICAL SCIENCE*

COUNTRY PROFILE. SPAIN; annual survey of political and economic background. see *POLITICAL SCIENCE*

COUNTRY PROFILE. SRI LANKA; annual survey of political and economic background. see *POLITICAL SCIENCE*

COUNTRY PROFILE. SUDAN; annual survey of political and economic background. see *POLITICAL SCIENCE*

COUNTRY PROFILE. SWEDEN; annual survey of political and economic background. see *POLITICAL SCIENCE*

COUNTRY PROFILE. SWITZERLAND; annual survey of political and economic background. see *POLITICAL SCIENCE*

COUNTRY PROFILE. SYRIA; annual survey of political and economic background. see *POLITICAL SCIENCE*

COUNTRY PROFILE. TAIWAN; annual survey of political and economic background. see *POLITICAL SCIENCE*

COUNTRY PROFILE. TANZANIA, COMOROS; annual survey of political and economic background. see *POLITICAL SCIENCE*

COUNTRY PROFILE. THAILAND; annual survey of political and economic background. see *POLITICAL SCIENCE*

COUNTRY PROFILE. THE GAMBIA, MAURITANIA; annual survey of political and economic background. see *POLITICAL SCIENCE*

COUNTRY PROFILE. TOGO, BENIN; annual survey of political and economic background. see *POLITICAL SCIENCE*

COUNTRY PROFILE. TRINIDAD AND TOBAGO, SURINAME, NETHERLANDS ANTILLES, ARUBA; annual survey of political and economic background. see *POLITICAL SCIENCE*

COUNTRY PROFILE. TUNISIA; annual survey of political and economic background. see *POLITICAL SCIENCE*

COUNTRY PROFILE. TURKEY; annual survey of political and economic background. see *POLITICAL SCIENCE*

COUNTRY PROFILE. UGANDA; annual survey of political and economic background. see *POLITICAL SCIENCE*

COUNTRY PROFILE. UKRAINE; annual survey of political and economic background. see *POLITICAL SCIENCE*

COUNTRY PROFILE. UNITED ARAB EMIRATES; annual survey of political and economic background. see *POLITICAL SCIENCE*

COUNTRY PROFILE. UNITED KINGDOM; annual survey of political and economic background. see *POLITICAL SCIENCE*

COUNTRY PROFILE. UNITED STATES OF AMERICA; annual survey of political and economic background. see *POLITICAL SCIENCE*

COUNTRY PROFILE. URUGUAY, PARAGUAY; annual survey of political and economic background. see *POLITICAL SCIENCE*

COUNTRY PROFILE. VENEZUELA; annual survey of political and economic background. see *POLITICAL SCIENCE*

COUNTRY PROFILE. VIETNAM; annual survey of political and economic background. see *POLITICAL SCIENCE*

COUNTRY PROFILE. YEMEN; annual survey of political and economic background. see *POLITICAL SCIENCE*

COUNTRY PROFILE. ZAIRE; annual survey of political and economic background. see *POLITICAL SCIENCE*

COUNTRY PROFILE. ZAMBIA; annual survey of political and economic background. see *POLITICAL SCIENCE*

COUNTRY PROFILE. ZIMBABWE; annual survey of political and economic background. see *POLITICAL SCIENCE*

COUNTRY PROFILES; annual survey of political and economic background. see *POLITICAL SCIENCE*

330.9 320   US   ISSN 1366-4018
COUNTRY REPORT. ALBANIA; analysis of economic and political trends every quarter. q. £225($405) Economist Intelligence Unit, 111 W. 57th St., New York, NY 10019. TEL 212-554-0600; 800-938-4685. FAX 212-586-1182. URL: http://www.eiu.com. (UK addr.: Economist Intelligence Unit Ltd., Subscriptions Dept., P.O. Box 200, Harold Hill, Romford, Essex RM3 8UX, England. TEL 44-1708-381444. FAX 44-1708-371850)
●Also available online. Vendor(s): Central Institute for Scientific & Technical Information, Knight-Ridder Information, Inc.
   Supersedes in part (in 1997): Country Report. Bulgaria, Albania (ISSN 1356-4110); Which superseded in part (in 1995): Country Report. Romania, Bulgaria, Albania (ISSN 0269-5669); Which was formerly: Quarterly Economic Review of Romania, Bulgaria, Albania (ISSN 0142-4068)
   Description: Analyzes the current political and economic climate and provides short-term economic projections.

330.9 320   US   ISSN 0269-5723
COUNTRY REPORT. ALGERIA; analysis of economic and political trends every quarter. 1952. q. £225($405) includes Country Profile. Algeria. Economist Intelligence Unit, 111 W. 57th St., New York, NY 10019. TEL 212-554-0600; 800-938-4685. FAX 212-586-1182. TELEX 175567. URL: http://www.eiu.com. (UK addr.: Economist Intelligence Unit Ltd., Subscriptions Dept., P.O. Box 200, Harold Hill, Romford, Essex RM3 8UX, England. TEL 44-1708-381-444. FAX 44-1708-371-850) illus.; stat.
●Also available online. Vendor(s): Knight-Ridder Information, Inc., Lexis-Nexis.
   Formerly: Quarterly Economic Review of Algeria (ISSN 0142-4130)
   Description: Analyzes Algeria's current political and economic climate as well as short-term economic projections.

330.9 320   US   ISSN 0969-7985
COUNTRY REPORT. ANGOLA; analysis of economic and political trends every quarter. 1952. q. £225($405) Economist Intelligence Unit, 111 W. 57th St., New York, NY 10019. TEL 212-554-0600; 800-938-4685. FAX 212-938-1182. TELEX 175567. URL: http://www.eiu.com. (UK addr.: Economist Intelligence Unit Ltd., Subscriptions Dept., P.O. Box 200, Harold Hill, Romford, Essex RM3 8UX, England. TEL 44-1708-381-444. FAX 44-1708-371-850) illus.; stat.
●Also available online. Vendor(s): Knight-Ridder Information, Inc., Lexis-Nexis.
—BLDSC (3481.897070).
   Supersedes in part (in 1994): Country Report. Angola, Botswana, Namibia, Lesotho, Swaziland; Which was formed by the 1992 merger of part of: Country Report. Angola, Sao Tome and Principe (ISSN 0269-4344); part of: Country Report. Namibia, Botswana, Lesotho, Swaziland (ISSN 0269-6746); Which was formerly: Quarterly Economic Review of Angola, Sao Tome and Principe (ISSN 0266-9781); Quarterly Economic Review of Namibia, Botswana, Lesotho, Swaziland (ISSN 0144-896X)
   Description: Analyzes the current political and economic climate as well as short-term economic projections.

BUSINESS AND ECONOMICS — ECONOMIC SITUATION AND CONDITIONS

330.9 320   US   ISSN 0269-4212
HC171
COUNTRY REPORT. ARGENTINA; analysis of economic and political trends every quarter. 1952. q. £225($405) includes Country Profile. Argentina. Economist Intelligence Unit, 111 W. 57th St., New York, NY 10019. TEL 212-554-0600; 800-938-4685. FAX 212-586-1182. TELEX 175567. URL: http://www.eiu.com. (UK addr.: Economist Intelligence Unit Ltd., Subscriptions Dept., P.O. Box 200, Harold Hill, Romford, Essex RM3 8UX, England. TEL 44-1708-381-444. FAX 44-1708-371-850) illus.; stat.
●Also available online. Vendor(s): Knight-Ridder Information, Inc., Lexis-Nexis.
—BLDSC (3481.897130).
Formerly: Quarterly Economic Review of Argentina (ISSN 0142-4149)
Description: Analyzes Argentina's current political and economic climate as well as short-term economic projections.

330.9 320   US   ISSN 0269-7106
COUNTRY REPORT. AUSTRALIA; analysis of economic and political trends every quarter. 1952. q. £225($405) includes Country Profile. Australia. Economist Intelligence Unit, 111 W. 57th St., New York, NY 10019. TEL 212-554-0600; 800-938-4685. FAX 212-586-1182. TELEX 175567. (UK addr.: Economist Intelligence Unit Ltd., Subscriptions Dept., P.O. Box 200, Harold Hill, Romford, Essex RM3 8UX, England. TEL 44-1708-381-444. FAX 44-1708-371-850) illus.; stat.
●Also available online. Vendor(s): Knight-Ridder Information, Inc., Lexis-Nexis.
Formerly: Quarterly Economic Review of Australia (ISSN 0266-9587)
Description: Analyzes Australia's current political and economic climate as well as short-term economic projections.

330.9 320   US   ISSN 0269-5170
HC261
COUNTRY REPORT. AUSTRIA; analysis of economic and political trends every quarter. 1952. q. £225($405) includes Country Profile. Austria. Economist Intelligence Unit, 111 W. 57th St., New York, NY 10019. TEL 212-554-0600; 800-938-4685. FAX 212-586-1182. TELEX 175567. URL: http://www.eiu.com. (UK addr.: Economist Intelligence Unit Ltd., Subscriptions Dept., P.O Box 200, Harold Hill, Romford, Essex RM3 8UX, England. TEL 44-1708-381-444. FAX 44-1708-371-850) illus.; stat.
●Also available online. Vendor(s): Knight-Ridder Information, Inc., Lexis-Nexis.
—BLDSC (3481.897210).
Formerly: Quarterly Economic Review of Austria (ISSN 0142-3711)
Description: Analyzes Austria's current political and economic climate as well as short-term economic projections.

330.9 320   US   ISSN 1366-4077
COUNTRY REPORT. AZERBAIJAN; analysis of economic and political trends every quarter. q. £225($405) Economist Intelligence Unit, 111 W. 57th St., New York, NY 10019. TEL 212-554-0600; 800-938-4685. FAX 212-586-1182. URL: http://www.eiu.com. (UK addr.: Economist Intelligence Unit Ltd., Subscriptions Dept., P.O. Box 200, Harold, Romford, Essex RM3 8UX, England. TEL 44-1708-381-444. FAX 44-1708-371-850)
Supersedes in part (in 1997): Country Report. Georgia, Armenia, Azerbaijan; Which superseded in part (in 1995): Country Report. Georgia, Armenia, Azerbaijan, Central Asian Republics (ISSN 1350-7206); Which superseded in part (in 1992): Country Report. Commonwealth of Independent States; Which was formerly (until 1991): Country Report. U S S R (ISSN 0269-5480); Quarterly Economic Review of U S S R (ISSN 0142-3967)
Description: Analyzes the current political and economic climate and provides short-term economic projections.

330.9 320   US   ISSN 1351-8682
HC415.38.A1
COUNTRY REPORT. BAHRAIN, QATAR; analysis of economic and political trends every quarter. 1952. q. £225($405) includes Country Profile. Bahrain, Qatar. Economist Intelligence Unit, 111 W. 57th St., New York, NY 10019. TEL 212-554-0600; 800-938-4685. FAX 212-586-1182. TELEX 175567. URL: http://www.eiu.com. (UK addr.: Economist Intelligence Unit Ltd., Subscriptions Dept., P.O. Box 200, Harold Hill, Romford, Essex RM3 8UX, England. TEL 44-1708-381-444. FAX 44-1708-371-850) illus.; stat.
●Also available online. Vendor(s): Knight-Ridder Information, Inc., Lexis-Nexis.
—BLDSC (3481.897245).
Supersedes in part (in 1992): Country Report. Bahrain, Qatar, Oman, Yemen (ISSN 0269-5707); Which was formerly: Quarterly Economic Review of Bahrain, Qatar, Oman, Yemen (ISSN 0142-4114)
Description: Analyzes Bahrain's and Qatar's current political and economic climates as well as short-term economic projections.

330.9 320   US   ISSN 1360-9459
COUNTRY REPORT. BALTIC REPUBLICS: LITHUANIA, LATVIA, ESTONIA; analysis of economic and political trends every quarter. 1952. q. £225($405) includes Country Profile. Baltic Republics: Lithuania, Latvia, Estonia. Economist Intelligence Unit, 111 W. 57th St., New York, NY 10019. TEL 212-554-0600; 800-938-4685. FAX 212-586-1182. TELEX 175567. URL: http://www.eiu.com. (UK addr.: Economist Intelligence Unit Ltd., Subscriptions Dept., P.O. Box 200, Harold Hill, Romford, Essex RM3 8UX, England. TEL 44-1708-381-444. FAX 44-1708-371-850) illus.; stat.
●Also available online. Vendor(s): Knight-Ridder Information, Inc., Lexis-Nexis.
Supersedes in part (in 1992): Country Report. Commonwealth of Independent States; Which was formerly (until 1991): Country Report. U S S R (ISSN 0269-5480); Quarterly Economic Review of U S S R (ISSN 0142-3967)
Description: Analyzes the current political and economic climate as well as short-term economic projections.

330.9 320   US   ISSN 0269-431X
HC440.8.A1
COUNTRY REPORT. BANGLADESH; analysis of economic and political trends every quarter. 1952. q. £225($405) includes Country Profile. Bangladesh. Economist Intelligence Unit, 111 W. 57th St., New York, NY 10019. TEL 212-554-0600; 800-938-4685. FAX 212-586-1182. TELEX 175567. URL: http://www.eiu.com. (UK addr.: Economist Intelligence Unit Ltd., Subscriptions Dept., P.O. Box 200, Harold Hill, Romford, Essex RM3 8UX, England. TEL 44-1708-381-444. FAX 44-1708-371-850) illus.; stat.
●Also available online. Vendor(s): Knight-Ridder Information, Inc., Lexis-Nexis.
Formerly: Quarterly Economic Review of Bangladesh (ISSN 0266-9668)
Description: Analyzes Bangladesh's current political and economic climate as well as short-term economic projections.

330.9 320   US
COUNTRY REPORT. BELARUS, MOLDOVA; analysis of economic and political trends every quarter. q. £225($405) Economist Intelligence Unit, 111 W. 57th St., New York, NY 10019. TEL 212-554-0600; 800-938-4685. FAX 212-586-1182. TELEX 175567. URL: http://www.eiu.com. (U.K. addr.: Economist Intelligence Unit Ltd., Subscription Dept., P.O. Box 200, Harold Hill, Romford, Essex RM3 8UX, England. TEL 44-1708-381440. FAX 44-1708-371850)
Supersedes in part (in 1995): Country Report. Ukraine, Belarus, Moldova (ISSN 1350-7192); Which supersedes in part (in 1992): Country Report. Commonwealth of Independent States; Which was formerly (until 1991): Country Report. U S S R (ISSN 0269-5480); Quarterly Economic Review of U S S R (ISSN 0142-3967)

330.9 320   US   ISSN 0269-4158
HC311
COUNTRY REPORT. BELGIUM, LUXEMBOURG; analysis of economic and political trends every quarter. 1952. q. £225($405) includes Country Profile. Belgium, Luxembourg. Economist Intelligence Unit, 111 W. 57th St., New York, NY 10019. TEL 212-554-0600; 800-938-4685. FAX 212-586-1182. TELEX 175567. URL: http://www.eiu.com. (UK addr.: Economist Intelligence Unit Ltd., Subscriptions Dept., P.O. Box 200, Harold Hill, Romford, Essex RM3 8UX, England. TEL 44-1708-381-444. FAX 44-1708-371-850) illus.; stat.
●Also available online. Vendor(s): Knight-Ridder Information, Inc., Lexis-Nexis.
—BLDSC (3481.897330).
Formerly: Quarterly Economic Review of Belgium, Luxembourg (ISSN 0142-372X)
Description: Analyzes Belgium's and Luxembourg's current political and economic climates as well as short-term economic projections.

330.9 320   US   ISSN 1356-4072
COUNTRY REPORT. BOLIVIA; analysis of economic and political trends every quarter. q. £225($405) Economist Intelligence Unit, 111 W. 57th St., New York, NY 10019. TEL 212-554-0600; 800-938-4685. FAX 212-586-1182. TELEX 175567. URL: http://www.eiu.com. (U.K. addr.: Economist Intelligence Unit Ltd., Subscriptions Dept., P.O. Box 200, Harold Hill, Romford, Essex RM3 8UX, England. TEL 44-1708-381444. FAX 44-1708-371850) (also avail. in microform from WMP)
●Also available online. Vendor(s): Knight-Ridder Information, Inc., Lexis-Nexis.
Also available on CD-ROM. Producer(s): Knight-Ridder, Inc., SilverPlatter Information, Inc.
Supersedes in part (in 1995): Country Report. Peru, Bolivia (ISSN 0269-543X); Which was formerly: Quarterly Economic Review of Peru, Bolivia (ISSN 0142-3916)
Description: Analyzes the current political and economic climate, as well as short-term economic projections

330.9 320   US   ISSN 1366-4123
HC407.A1
COUNTRY REPORT. BOSNIA-HERCEGOVINA, CROATIA AND SLOVENIA; analysis of economic and political trends every quarter. 1952. q. £225($405) Economist Intelligence Unit, 111 W. 57th St., New York, NY 10019. TEL 212-554-0600; 800-938-4685. FAX 212-586-1182. TELEX 175567. URL: http://www.eiu.com. (UK addr.: Economist Intelligence Unit Ltd., Subscriptions Dept., P.O. Box 200, Harold Hill, Romford, Essex RM3 8UX, England. TEL 44-1708-381-444. FAX 44-1708-371-850) illus.; stat.
●Also available online. Vendor(s): Knight-Ridder Information, Inc., Lexis-Nexis.
Supersedes in part: Country Report. Bosnia-Hercegovina, Croatia, Macedonia, Serbia-Montenegro, Slovenia (ISSN 1350-7222); Which superseded (in 1993): Country Report. Yugoslav Republics (ISSN 0968-7734); Which superseded (in 1992): Country Report. Yugoslavia (ISSN 0269-4190); Which was formerly: Quarterly Economic Review of Yugoslavia (ISSN 0142-3983)
Description: Analyzes the current political and economic climate and provides short-term economic projections.

B

BUSINESS AND ECONOMICS — ECONOMIC SITUATION AND CONDITIONS

330.9 320 US
COUNTRY REPORT. BOTSWANA, LESOTHO; analysis of economic and political trends every quarter. q. £225($405) Economist Intelligence Unit, 111 W. 57th St., New York, NY 10019. TEL 212-554-0600; 800-938-4685. FAX 212-938-1182. TELEX 175567. URL: http://www.eiu.com. (U.K. addr.: Economist Intelligence Unit Ltd., Subscriptions Dept., P.O. Box 200, Harold Hill, Romford, Essex RM3 8UX, England. TEL 44-1708-381444. FAX 44-1708-371850.
  Supersedes in part (in 1994): Country Report. Angola, Botswana, Namibia, Lesotho, Swaziland; Which was formed by the 1992 merger of part of: Country Report. Angola, Sao Tome and Principe; And part of: Country Report. Namibia, Botswana, Lesotho, Swaziland (ISSN 0269-6746); Which was formerly: Quarterly Economic Review of Angola, Sao Tome and Principe (ISSN 0266-9781); Quarterly Economic Review of Namibia, Botswana, Lesotho, Swaziland (ISSN 0144-896X)
  Description: Analyzes the current political and economic climate, as well as short-term economic projections.

330.9 320 US ISSN 0269-5731
HC186
COUNTRY REPORT. BRAZIL; analysis of economic and political trends every quarter. 1952. q. £225($405) includes Country Profile. Brazil. Economist Intelligence Unit, 111 W. 57th St., New York, NY 10019. TEL 212-554-0600; 800-938-4685. FAX 212-586-1182. TELEX 175567. URL: http://www.eiu.com. (UK addr.: Economist Intelligence Unit Ltd., Subscriptions Dept., P.O. Box 200, Harold Hill, Romford, Essex RM3 8UX, England. TEL 44-1708-381-444. FAX 44-1708-371-850) illus., stat.
  ●Also available online. Vendor(s): Knight-Ridder Information, Inc., Lexis-Nexis.
  —BLDSC (3481.897370).
  Formerly: Quarterly Economic Review of Brazil (ISSN 0142-4165)
  Description: Analyzes Brazil's current political and economic climate as well as short-term economic projections.

330.9 320 US ISSN 1366-400X
HC403.A1
COUNTRY REPORT. BULGARIA; analysis of economic and political trends every quarter. q. £225($405) Economist Intelligence Unit, 111 W. 57th St., New York, NY 10019. TEL 212-554-0600; 800-938-4685. FAX 212-586-1182. TELEX 175567. URL: http://www.eiu.com. (U.K. addr.: Economist Intelligence Unit Ltd., Subscriptions Dept., P.O. Box 200, Harold Hill, Romford, Essex RM3 8UX, England. TEL 44-1708-381444. FAX 44-1708-371850) (also avail. in microform from WMP)
  ●Also available online. Vendor(s): Knight-Ridder Information, Inc., Lexis-Nexis.
  Also available on CD-ROM. Producer(s): Knight-Ridder, Inc., SilverPlatter Information, Inc.
  Supersedes in part (in 1997): Country Report. Bulgaria, Albania (ISSN 1356-4110); Which superseded in part (in 1995): Country Report. Romania, Bulgaria, Albania (ISSN 0269-5669); Which was formerly: Quarterly Economic Review of Romania, Bulgaria, Albania (ISSN 0142-4068)
  Description: Analyzes the current political and economic climate and provides short-term economic projections.

330.9 320 US ISSN 1361-1437
HC442.A1
COUNTRY REPORT. CAMBODIA, LAOS; analysis of economic and political trends every quarter. 1952. q. £225($405) Economist Intelligence Unit, 111 W. 57th St., New York, NY 10019. TEL 212-554-0600; 800-938-4685. FAX 212-586-1182. TELEX 175567. URL: http://www.eiu.com. (UK addr.: Economist Intelligence Unit Ltd., Subscriptions Dept., P.O. Box 200, Harold Hill, Romford, Essex RM3 8UX, England. TEL 44-1708-381444. FAX 44-1708-371850) illus.; stat. (also avail. in microfiche from WMP)
  ●Also available online. Vendor(s): Knight-Ridder Information, Inc., Lexis-Nexis.
  —BLDSC (3481.897393).
  Supersedes in part: Country Report. Cambodia, Laos, Myanmar (ISSN 1356-4048); Which was formed by the 1995 merger of part of: Country Report. Indochina: Vietnam, Laos, Cambodia (ISSN 0269-5677); Which was formerly: Quarterly Economic Review of Indochina: Vietnam, Laos, Cambodia (ISSN 0142-4076); And part of: Country Report. Thailand, Myanmar (ISSN 1350-7117); Which was formerly: Country Report. Thailand, Burma (ISSN 0269-5189); Quarterly Economic Review of Thailand, Burma (ISSN 0142-3754).
  Description: Analyzes the current political and economic climate, as well as short-term economic projections.

330.9 320 US ISSN 0269-4336
HC995.A1
COUNTRY REPORT. CAMEROON, C.A.R., CHAD; analysis of economic and political trends every quarter. 1952. q. £225($405) Economist Intelligence Unit, 111 W. 57th St., New York, NY 10019. TEL 212-554-0600; 800-938-4685. FAX 212-586-1182. TELEX 175567. URL: http://www.eiu.com. (UK addr.: Economist Intelligence Unit Ltd., Subscriptions Dept., P.O. Box 200, Harold Hill, Romford, Essex RM3 8UX, England. TEL 44-1708-381-444. FAX 44-1708-371-850) illus.; stat.
  ●Also available online. Vendor(s): Knight-Ridder Information, Inc., Lexis-Nexis.
  Formerly (until 1986): Quarterly Economic Review of Cameroon, Central African Republic, Chad (ISSN 0266-9757)
  Description: Analyzes the current political and economic climate as well as short-term economic projections.

330.9 320 US ISSN 0269-4166
HC111
COUNTRY REPORT. CANADA; analysis of economic and political trends every quarter. 1952. q. £225($405) includes Country Profile. Canada. Economist Intelligence Unit, 111 W. 57th St., New York, NY 10019. TEL 212-554-0600; 800-938-4685. FAX 212-586-1182. TELEX 175567. URL: http://www.eiu.com. (UK addr.: Economist Intelligence Unit Ltd., Subscriptions Dept., P.O. Box 200, Harold Hill, Romford, Essex RM3 8UX, England. TEL 44-1708-381-444. FAX 44-1708-371-850) illus.; stat.
  ●Also available online. Vendor(s): Knight-Ridder Information, Inc., Lexis-Nexis.
  —BLDSC (3481.897450).
  Formerly: Quarterly Economic Review of Canada (ISSN 0142-3762)
  Description: Analyzes Canada's current political and economic climate as well as short-term economic projections.

330.9 320 US ISSN 0269-5197
HC191
COUNTRY REPORT. CHILE; analysis of economic and political trends every quarter. 1952. q. £225($405) includes Country Profile. Chile. Economist Intelligence Unit, 111 W. 57th St., New York, NY 10019. TEL 212-554-0600; 800-938-4685. FAX 212-586-1182. TELEX 175567. URL: http://www.eiu.com. (UK addr.: Economist Intelligence Unit Ltd., Subscriptions Dept., P.O. Box 200, Harold Hill, Romford, Essex RM3 8UX, England. TEL 44-1708-381-444. FAX 44-1708-371-850) illus.; stat.
  ●Also available online. Vendor(s): Knight-Ridder Information, Inc., Lexis-Nexis.
  —BLDSC (3481.897490).
  Formerly: Quarterly Economic Review of Chile (ISSN 0142-3789)
  Description: Analyzes Chile's current political and economic climate as well as short-term economic projections.

330.9 320 US ISSN 1350-7109
HC427.92
COUNTRY REPORT. CHINA, MONGOLIA; analysis of economic and political trends every quarter. 1952. q. £225($405) includes Country Profile. China, Mongolia. Economist Intelligence Unit, 111 W. 57th St., New York, NY 10019. TEL 212-554-0600; 800-938-4685. FAX 212-586-1182. TELEX 175567. URL: http://www.eiu.com. (UK addr.: Economist Intelligence Unit Ltd., Subscriptions Dept., P.O. Box 200, Harold Hill, Romford, Essex RM3 8UX, England. TEL 44-1708-381-444. FAX 44-3708-371-850) illus.; stat.
  ●Also available online. Vendor(s): Knight-Ridder Information, Inc., Lexis-Nexis.
  —BLDSC (3481.897500).
  Supersedes in part (in 1992): Country Report. China, North Korea (ISSN 0269-6231); Which was formerly: Quarterly Economic Review of China, North Korea (ISSN 0144-8854)
  Description: Analyzes China's and Mongolia's current political and economic climates as well as short-term economic projections.

330.9 320 US ISSN 0269-7157
HC196
COUNTRY REPORT. COLOMBIA; analysis of economic and political trends every quarter. 1952. q. £225($405) includes Country Profile. Colombia. Economist Intelligence Unit, 111 W. 57th St., New York, NY 10019. TEL 212-554-0600; 800-938-4685. FAX 212-586-1182. TELEX 175567. URL: http://www.eiu.com. (UK addr.: Economist Intelligence Unit Ltd., Subscriptions Dept., P.O. Box 200, Harold Hill, Romford, Essex RM3 8UX, England. TEL 44-1708-381-444. FAX 44-3708-371-850) illus.; stat.
  ●Also available online. Vendor(s): Knight-Ridder Information, Inc., Lexis-Nexis.
  —BLDSC (3481.897570).
  Formerly: Quarterly Economic Review of Colombia (ISSN 0266-9633)
  Description: Analyzes Colombia's current political and economic climate as well as short-term economic projections.

330.9 320 US ISSN 1350-7028
COUNTRY REPORT. CONGO, SAO TOME AND PRINCIPE, GUINEA-BISSAU, CAPE VERDE; analysis of economic and political trends every quarter. 1952. q. £225($405) includes Country Profile. Congo, Sao Tome and Principe, Guinea-Bissau, Cape Verde. Economist Intelligence Unit, 111 W. 57th St., New York, NY 10019. TEL 212-554-0600; 800-938-4685. FAX 212-586-1182. URL: http://www.eiu.com. (UK addr.: Economist Intelligence Unit Ltd., Subscriptions Dept., P.O. Box 200, Harold Hill, Romford, Essex RM3 8UX, England. TEL 44-1708-381-444. FAX 44-1708-371-850) illus.
  ●Also available online. Vendor(s): Knight-Ridder Information, Inc., Lexis-Nexis.
  Formed by the 1992 merger of part of: Country Report. Congo, Gabon, Equatorial Guinea (ISSN 0269-7246); part of: Country Report. Senegal, The Gambia, Guinea-Bissau, Cape Verde (ISSN 0269-719X); part of: Country Report. Angola, Sao Tome and Principe (ISSN 0269-4344); Which was formerly: Quarterly Economic Review of Congo, Gabon, Equatorial Guinea (ISSN 0266-9749); Quarterly Economic Review of Senegal, The Gambia, Guinea-Bissau, Cape Verde (ISSN 0266-9684); Quarterly Economic Review of Angola, Sao Tome and Principe (ISSN 0266-9781).
  Description: Analyzes the current political and economic climate as well as short-term economic projections.

BUSINESS AND ECONOMICS — ECONOMIC SITUATION AND CONDITIONS

330.9 320   US   ISSN 1366-4026
HC143.A1
COUNTRY REPORT. COSTA RICA; analysis of economic and political trends every quarter. q. £225($405) Economist Intelligence Unit, 111 W. 57th St., New York, NY 10019. TEL 212-554-0600; 800-938-4685. FAX 212-586-1182. TELEX 175567. URL: http://www.eiu.com. (UK addr.: Economist Intelligence Unit Ltd., Subscriptions Dept., P.O. Box 200, Harold Hill, Romford, Essex RM3 8UX, England. TEL 44-1708-381-444. FAX 44-1708-371-850) illus.; stat.
●Also available online. Vendor(s): Knight-Ridder Information, Inc., Lexis-Nexis.
   Supersedes in part (in 1997): Country Report. Costa Rica, Panama (ISSN 1350-7125); Which superseded in part (in 1992): Country Report. Nicaragua, Costa Rica, Panama (ISSN 0269-4247); Which was formerly: Quarterly Economic Review of Nicaragua, Costa Rica, Panama (ISSN 0142-4300)
   Description: Analyzes the current political and economic climate and provides short-term economic projections.

330.9 320   US   ISSN 0969-4730
HC1025.A1
COUNTRY REPORT. COTE D'IVOIRE, MALI; analysis of economic and political trends every quarter. 1952. q. £225($405) includes Country Profile. Cote d'Ivoire, Mali. Economist Intelligence Unit, 111 W. 57th St., New York, NY 10019. TEL 212-554-0600; 800-938-4685. FAX 212-586-1182. TELEX 175567. URL: http://eiu.com. (UK addr.: Economist Intelligence Unit Ltd., Subscriptions Dept., P.O. Box 200, Harold Hill, Romford, Essex RM3 8UX, England. TEL 44-1708-381-444. FAX 44-1708-371-850) illus.; stat.
●Also available online. Vendor(s): Knight-Ridder Information, Inc., Lexis-Nexis.
   Formed by the 1992 merger of: Country Report. Cote d'Ivoire (ISSN 0269-7254); part of: Country Report. Guinea, Mali, Mauritania (ISSN 0269-7203); Which was formerly: Quarterly Economic Review of Cote d'Ivoire (ISSN 0266-9765); Quarterly Economic Review of Guinea, Mali, Mauritania (ISSN 0266-9692)
   Description: Analyzes the current political and economic climate as well as short-term economic projections.

330.9 320   US   ISSN 0269-5251
HC152.5.A1
COUNTRY REPORT. CUBA, DOMINICAN REPUBLIC, HAITI, PUERTO RICO; analysis of economic and political trends every quarter. 1952. q. £225($405) includes Country Profile. Cuba; Country Profile. Dominican Republic, Haiti, Puerto Rico. Economist Intelligence Unit, 111 W. 57th St., New York, NY 10019. TEL 212-554-0600; 800-938-4685. FAX 212-586-1182. TELEX 175567. URL: http://www.eiu.com. (UK addr.: Economist Intelligence Unit Ltd., Subscriptions Dept., P.O. Box 200, Harold Hill, Romford, Essex RM3 8UX, England. TEL 44-1708-381-444. FAX 44-1708-371-850) illus.; stat.
●Also available online. Vendor(s): Knight-Ridder Information, Inc., Lexis-Nexis.
—BLDSC (3481.897650).
   Formerly: Quarterly Economic Review of Cuba, Dominican Republic, Haiti, Puerto Rico (ISSN 0142-3819)
   Description: Analyzes the current political and economic climate as well as short-term economic projections.

330.9 320   US   ISSN 1350-715X
COUNTRY REPORT. CYPRUS, MALTA; analysis of economic and political trends every quarter. 1952. q. £225($405) includes Country Profile. Cyprus. Economist Intelligence Unit, 111 W. 57th St., New York, NY 10019. TEL 212-554-0600; 800-938-4685. FAX 212-586-1182. TELEX 175567. URL: http://www.eiu.com. (UK addr.: Economist Intelligence Unit Ltd., Subscriptions Dept., P.O. Box 200, Harold Hill, Romford, Essex RM3 8UX, England. TEL 44-1708-381-444. FAX 44-1708-371-850) illus.; stat.
●Also available online. Vendor(s): Knight-Ridder Information, Inc., Lexis-Nexis.
   Former titles: Country Report. Cyprus; Quarterly Economic Review of Lebanon, Cyprus (ISSN 0142-4106)
   Description: Analyzes Cyprus's current political and economic climate as well as short-term economic projections.

330.9 320   US   ISSN 1366-4042
HC270.2
COUNTRY REPORT. CZECH REPUBLIC; analysis of economic and political trends every quarter. 1952. q. £225($405) Economist Intelligence Unit, 111 W. 57th St., New York, NY 10019. TEL 212-554-0600; 800-938-4685. FAX 212-586-1182. TELEX 175567. (UK addr.: Economist Intelligence Unit Ltd., Subscriptions Dept., P.O. Box 200, Harold Hill, Romford, Essex RM3 8UX, England. TEL 44-1708-381-444. FAX 44-1708-371-850) illus.; stat. (also avail. in microfilm)
●Also available online. Vendor(s): Knight-Ridder Information, Inc., Lexis-Nexis.
Also available on CD-ROM. Producer(s): Knight-Ridder, Inc., SilverPlatter Information, Inc.
—BLDSC (3481.897665).
   Supersedes in part (in 1997): Country Report. Czech Republic, Slovakia (ISSN 1350-7214); Which superseded in part (in 1992): Country Report. Czechoslovakia (ISSN 0269-4298); Which was formerly: Quarterly Economic Review of Czechoslovakia (ISSN 0144-8978)
   Description: Analyzes the current political and economic climate as well as short-term economic projections.

330.9 320   US   ISSN 0269-574X
HC351
COUNTRY REPORT. DENMARK, ICELAND; analysis of economic and political trends every quarter. 1952. q. £225($405) includes Country Profile. Denmark, Iceland. Economist Intelligence Unit, 111 W. 57th St., New York, NY 10019. TEL 212-554-0600; 800-938-4685. FAX 212-586-1182. TELEX 175567. URL: http://www.eiu.com. (UK addr.: Economist Intelligence Unit Ltd., Subscriptions Dept., P.O. Box 200, Harold Hill, Romford, Essex RM3 8UX, England. TEL 44-1708-381-444. FAX 44-1708-371-850) illus.; stat.
●Also available online. Vendor(s): Knight-Ridder Information, Inc., Lexis-Nexis.
—BLDSC (3481.897730).
   Formerly: Quarterly Economic Review of Denmark, Iceland (ISSN 0142-4181)
   Description: Analyzes the current political and economic climate as well as short-term economic projections.

330.9 320   US   ISSN 0269-7165
HC201
COUNTRY REPORT. ECUADOR; analysis of economic and political trends every quarter. 1952. q. £225($405) includes Country Profile. Ecuador. Economist Intelligence Unit, 111 W. 57th St., New York, NY 10019. TEL 212-554-0600; 800-938-4685. FAX 212-586-1182. TELEX 175567. URL: http://www.eiu.com. (UK addr.: Economist Intelligence Unit Ltd., Subscriptions Dept., P.O. Box 200, Harold Hill, Romford, Essex RM3 9UX, England. TEL 44-1708-381-444. FAX 44-1708-371-850) illus.; stat.
●Also available online. Vendor(s): Knight-Ridder Information, Inc., Lexis-Nexis.
   Formerly: Quarterly Economic Review of Ecuador (ISSN 0266-9641)
   Description: Analyzes Ecuador's current political and economic climate as well as short-term economic projections.

330.9 332   US   ISSN 0269-526X
HC830.A1
COUNTRY REPORT. EGYPT; analysis of economic and political trends every quarter. 1952. q. £225($405) includes Country Profile. Egypt. Economist Intelligence Unit, 111 W. 57th St., New York, NY 10019. TEL 212-554-0600; 800-938-4685. FAX 212-586-1182. TELEX 175567. URL: http://www.eiu.com. (UK addr.: Economist Intelligence Unit Ltd., Subscriptions Dept., P.O. Box 200, Harold Hill, Romford, Essex RM3 8UX, England. TEL 44-1708-381-444. FAX 44-1708-371-850) illus.; stat. **Indexed:** IBR.
●Also available online. Vendor(s): Knight-Ridder Information, Inc., Lexis-Nexis.
   Formerly: Quarterly Economic Review of Egypt (ISSN 0142-3827)
   Description: Analyzes Egypt's current political and economic climate as well as short-term economic projections.

330.9 320   US   ISSN 1352-2922
HC845.A1
COUNTRY REPORT. ETHIOPIA, ERITREA, SOMALIA, DJIBOUTI; analysis of economic and political trends every quarter. q. £225($405) includes Country Profile. Ethiopia, Eritrea, Somalia, Djibouti. Economist Intelligence Unit, 111 W. 57th St., New York, NY 10019. TEL 212-554-0600; 800-938-4685. FAX 212-586-1182. TELEX 175567. URL: http://www.eiu.com. (UK addr.: Economist Intelligence Unit Ltd., Subscriptions Dept., P.O. Box 200, Harold Hill, Romford, Essex RM3 8UX, England. TEL 44-1708-381-444. FAX 44-1708-371-850) illus.; stat.
●Also available online. Vendor(s): Knight-Ridder Information, Inc., Lexis-Nexis.
—BLDSC (3481.897860).
   Formerly (until 1993): Country Report. Ethiopia, Somalia, Djibouti (ISSN 1350-7036); Which superseded in part (in 1992): Country Report. Uganda, Ethiopia, Somalia, Djibouti (ISSN 0269-5685); Which was formerly: Quarterly Economic Review of Uganda, Ethiopia, Somalia, Djibouti (ISSN 0142-4092)
   Description: Analyzes the current political and economic climate as well as short-term economic projections.

330.9 320   US   ISSN 0269-5901
HC337.F5
COUNTRY REPORT. FINLAND; analysis of economic and political trends every quarter. 1952. q. £225($405) includes Country Profile. Finland. Economist Intelligence Unit, 111 W. 57th St., New York, NY 10019. TEL 212-554-0600; 800-938-4685. FAX 212-586-1182. TELEX 175567. URL: http://www.eiu.com. (UK addr.: Economist Intelligence Unit Ltd., Subscriptions Dept., P.O. Box 200, Harold Hill, Romford, Essex RM3 8UX, England. TEL 44-1708-381-444. FAX 44-1708-371-850) illus.; stat.
●Also available online. Vendor(s): Knight-Ridder Information, Inc., Lexis-Nexis.
—BLDSC (3481.897890).
   Formerly: Quarterly Economic Review of Finland (ISSN 0142-419X)
   Description: Analyzes Finland's current political and economic climate as well as short-term economic projections.

330.9 320   US   ISSN 0269-5286
HC271
COUNTRY REPORT. FRANCE; analysis of economic and political trends every quarter. 1952. q. £225($405) includes Country Profile. France. Economist Intelligence Unit, 111 W. 57th St., New York, NY 10019. TEL 212-554-0600; 800-938-4685. FAX 212-586-1182. TELEX 175567. URL: http://www.eiu.com. (UK addr.: Economist Intelligence Unit Ltd., Subscriptions Dept., P.O. Box 200, Harold Hill, Romford, Essex RM3 8UX, England. TEL 44-1708-381-444. FAX 44-1708-371-850) illus.; stat.
●Also available online. Vendor(s): Knight-Ridder Information, Inc., Lexis-Nexis.
—BLDSC (3481.897930).
   Formerly: Quarterly Economic Review of France (ISSN 0142-3843)
   Description: Analyzes France's current political and economic climate as well as short-term economic projections.

330.9 320   US
COUNTRY REPORT. GABON, EQUATORIAL GUINEA; analysis of economic and political trends every quarter. q. £225($405) includes Country Profile. Gabon, Equatorial Guinea. Economist Intelligence Unit, 111 W. 57th St., New York, NY 10019. TEL 212-554-0600; 800-938-4685. FAX 212-586-1182. TELEX 175567. URL: http://www.eiu.com. (Economist Intelligence Unit Ltd., Subscriptions Dept., P.O. Box 200, Harold Hill, Romford, Essex RM3 8UX, England. TEL 44-1708-381-444. FAX 44-1708-371-850) illus.; stat.
●Also available online. Vendor(s): Knight-Ridder Information, Inc., Lexis-Nexis.
   Supersedes in part (in 1992): Country Report. Congo, Gabon, Equatorial Guinea (ISSN 0269-7246); Which was formerly: Quarterly Economic Review of Congo, Gabon, Equatorial Guinea (ISSN 0266-9749)
   Description: Analyzes the current political and economic climate as well as short-term economic projections.

BUSINESS AND ECONOMICS — ECONOMIC SITUATION AND CONDITIONS

330.9 320 US ISSN 1366-4069
COUNTRY REPORT. GEORGIA, ARMENIA, AZERBAIJAN; analysis of economic and political trends every quarter. q. £225($405) Economist Intelligence Unit, 111 W. 57th St., New York, NY 10019. TEL 212-554-0600; 800-938-4685. FAX 212-586-1182. TELEX 175567. URL: http://www.eiu.com. (UK addr.: Economist Intelligence Unit Ltd., Subscriptions Dept., P.O. Box 200, Harold Hill, Romford, Essex RM3 8UX, England. TEL 44-1708-381-444. FAX 44-1708-371-850)
 Supersedes in part (in 1997): Country Report. Georgia, Armenia, Azerbaijan; Which superseded in part (in 1995): Country Report. Georgia, Armenia, Azerbaijan, Central Asian Republics (ISSN 1350-7206); Which superseded in part (in 1992): Country Report. Commonwealth of Independent States; Which was formerly (until 1991): Country Report. U S S R (ISSN 0269-5480); Quarterly Economic Review of U S S R (ISSN 0142-3967).
 Description: Analyzes the current political and economic climate as well as short-term economic projections.

330.9 320 US ISSN 0965-1365
COUNTRY REPORT. GERMANY; analysis of economic and political trends every quarter. 1952. q. £225($405) includes Country Profile. Germany. Economist Intelligence Unit, 111 W. 57th St., New York, NY 10019. TEL 212-554-0600; 800-938-4685. FAX 212-586-1182. TELEX 175567. URL: http://www.eiu.com. (UK addr.: Economist Intelligence Unit Ltd., Subscriptions Dept., P.O. Box 200, Harold Hill, Essex RM3 8UX, England. TEL 44-1708-381-444. FAX 44-1708-371-850) illus.; stat.
 ●Also available online. Vendor(s): Knight-Ridder Information, Inc., Lexis-Nexis.
 —BLDSC (3481.897960).
 Formerly: Quarterly Economic Review of Germany (ISSN 0142-3975); Formed by the 1990 merger of: Country Report. West Germany (ISSN 0269-5499); Country Report. East Germany (ISSN 0269-6207); Which was formerly: Quarterly Economic Review of East Germany (ISSN 0144-8889)
 Description: Analyzes Germany's current political and economic climate as well as short-term economic projections.

330.9 320 US ISSN 1350-7052
HC1060.A1
COUNTRY REPORT. GHANA; analysis of economic and political trends every quarter. q. £225($405) includes Country Profile. Ghana. Economist Intelligence Unit, 111 W. 57th St., New York, NY 10019. TEL 212-554-0600; 800-938-4685. FAX 212-586-1182. TELEX 175567. URL: http://www.eiu.com. (UK addr.: Economist Intelligence Unit Ltd., Subscriptions Dept., P.O. Box 200, Harold Hill, Romford, Essex RM3 8UX, England. TEL 44-1708-381-444. FAX 44-1708-371-850) illus.; stat.
 ●Also available online. Vendor(s): Knight-Ridder Information, Inc., Lexis-Nexis.
 —BLDSC (3481.897965).
 Supersedes in part (in 1992): Country Report. Ghana, Sierra Leone, Liberia (ISSN 0269-7181); Which was formerly: Quarterly Economic Review of Ghana, Sierra Leone, Liberia (ISSN 0266-9676).
 Description: Analyzes Ghana's current political and economic climate as well as short-term economic projections.

330.9 320 US ISSN 0269-591X
HC291
COUNTRY REPORT. GREECE; analysis of economic and political trends every quarter. 1952. q. £225($405) includes Country Profile. Greece. Economist Intelligence Unit, 111 W. 57th St., New York, NY 10019. TEL 212-554-0600; 800-938-4685. FAX 212-586-1182. TELEX 175567. URL: http://www.eiu.com. (UK addr.: Economist Intelligence Unit Ltd., Subscriptions Dept., P.O. Box 200, Harold Hill, Romford, Essex RM3 8UX, England. TEL 44-1708-381-444. FAX 44-1708-371-850) illus.; stat.
 ●Also available online. Vendor(s): Knight-Ridder Information, Inc., Lexis-Nexis.
 Formerly: Quarterly Economic Review of Greece (ISSN 0142-4203)
 Description: Analyzes Greece's current political and economic climate as well as short-term economic projections.

330.9 320 US ISSN 0969-8752
HC144.A1
COUNTRY REPORT. GUATEMALA, EL SALVADOR; analysis of economic and political trends every quarter. 1952. q. £215($395) includes Country Profile. Guatemala, El Salvador. Economist Intelligence Unit, 111 W. 57th St., New York, NY 10019. TEL 212-554-0600; 800-938-4685. FAX 212-586-1182. TELEX 175567. (UK addr.: Economist Intelligence Unit Ltd., Subscriptions Dept., P.O. Box 200, Harold Hill, Romford, Essex RM3 8UX, England. TEL 44-1708-381-444. FAX 44-1708-371-850) illus.; stat.
 ●Also available online. Vendor(s): Knight-Ridder Information, Inc., Lexis-Nexis.
 —BLDSC (3481.898030).
 Supersedes in part (in 1992): Country Report. Guatemala, El Salvador, Honduras (ISSN 0269-4220); Which was formerly: Quarterly Economic Review of Guatemala, El Salvador, Honduras (ISSN 0142-4211).
 Description: Analyzes the current political and economic climate as well as short-term economic projections.

330.9 320 US ISSN 0969-4692
HC1030.A1
COUNTRY REPORT. GUINEA, SIERRA LEONE, LIBERIA; analysis of economic and political trends every quarter. 1952. q. £225($405) includes Country Profile. Guinea, Sierra Leone, Liberia. Economist Intelligence Unit, 111 W. 57th St., New York, NY 10019. TEL 212-554-0600. FAX 212-586-1182. TELEX 175567. URL: http://www.eiu.com. (UK addr.: Economist Intelligence Unit Ltd., Subscriptions Dept., P.O. Box 200, Harold Hill, Romford, Essex RM3 8UX, England. TEL 44-1708-381-444. FAX 44-1708-371-850) illus.; stat.
 ●Also available online. Vendor(s): Knight-Ridder Information, Inc., Lexis-Nexis.
 —BLDSC (3481.898100).
 Formed by the 1992 merger of part of: Country Report. Ghana, Sierra Leone, Liberia (ISSN 0269-7181); part of: Country Report. Guinea, Mali, Mauritania (ISSN 0269-7203); Which was formerly: Quarterly Economic Review of Ghana, Sierra Leone, Liberia (ISSN 0266-9676); Quarterly Economic Review of Guinea, Mali, Mauritania (ISSN 0266-9692)
 Description: Analyzes the current political and economic current as well as short-term economic projections.

330.9 320 US ISSN 0269-6762
HC470.3.A1
COUNTRY REPORT. HONG KONG, MACAU; analysis of economic and political trends every quarter. 1952. q. £225($405) includes Country Profile. Hong Kong, Macau. Economist Intelligence Unit, 111 W. 57th St., New York, NY 10019. TEL 212-554-0600; 800-938-4685. FAX 212-586-1182. TELEX 175567. URL: http://www.eiu.com. (UK addr.: Economist Intelligence Unit Ltd., Subscriptions Dept., P.O. Box 200, Harold Hill, Romford, Essex RM3 8UX, England. TEL 44-1708-381-444. FAX 44-1708-371-850) illus.; stat.
 ●Also available online. Vendor(s): Knight-Ridder Information, Inc., Lexis-Nexis.
 Formerly: Quarterly Economic Review of Hong Kong, Macau (ISSN 0265-6906)
 Description: Analyzes the current political and economic climate as well as short-term economic projections.

330.9 320 US ISSN 0269-4301
HC300.2
COUNTRY REPORT. HUNGARY; analysis of economic and political trends every quarter. 1952. q. £225($405) includes Country Profile. Hungary. Economist Intelligence Unit, 111 W. 57th St., New York, NY 10019. TEL 212-554-0600; 800-938-4685. FAX 212-586-1182. TELEX 175567. URL: http://www.eiu.com. (UK addr.: Economist Intelligence Unit Ltd., Subscriptions Dept., P.O. Box 200, Harold Hill, Romford, Essex RM3 8UX, England. TEL 44-1708-381-444. FAX 44-1708-371-850) illus.; stat.
 ●Also available online. Vendor(s): Knight-Ridder Information, Inc., Lexis-Nexis.
 —BLDSC (3481.898170).
 Formerly: Quarterly Economic Review of Hungary (ISSN 0144-8986)
 Description: Analyzes Hungary's current political and economic climate as well as short-term economic projections.

330.9 320 US ISSN 0269-5294
HC435.2.A1
COUNTRY REPORT. INDIA, NEPAL. 1952. q. £225($405) includes Country Profile. India, Nepal. Economist Intelligence Unit, 111 W. 57th St., New York, NY 10019. TEL 212-554-0600; 800-938-4685. FAX 212-586-1182. TELEX 175567. URL: http://www.eiu.com. (UK addr.: Economist Intelligence Unit Ltd., Subscriptions Dept., P.O. Box 200, Harold Hill, Romford, Essex RM3 8UX, England. TEL 44-1708-381-444. FAX 44-1708-371-850) illus.; stat.
 ●Also available online. Vendor(s): Knight-Ridder Information, Inc., Lexis-Nexis.
 —BLDSC (3481.898210).
 Formerly: Quarterly Economic Review of India, Nepal (ISSN 0142-3851)
 Description: Analyzes the current political and economic climate as well as short-term economic projections.

330.9 320 US ISSN 0269-5413
HC446
COUNTRY REPORT. INDONESIA; analysis of economic and political trends every quarter. 1952. q. £225($405) includes Country Profile. Indonesia. Economist Intelligence Unit, 111 W. 57th St., New York, NY 10019. TEL 212-554-0600; 800-938-4685. FAX 212-586-1182. TELEX 175567. URL: http://www.eiu.com. (UK addr.: Economist Intelligence Unit Ltd., Subscriptions Dept., P.O. Box 200, Harold Hill, Romford, Essex RM3 8UX, England. TEL 44-1708-381-444. FAX 44-1708-371-850) illus.; stat.
 ●Also available online. Vendor(s): Knight-Ridder Information, Inc., Lexis-Nexis.
 —BLDSC (3481.898185).
 Formerly: Quarterly Economic Review of Indonesia (ISSN 0142-3878)
 Description: Analyzes Indonesia's current political and economic climate as well as short-term economic projections.

330.9 320 US ISSN 0269-5448
HC471
COUNTRY REPORT. IRAN; analysis of economic and political trends every quarter. 1952. q. £225($405) includes Country Profile. Iran. Economist Intelligence Unit, 111 W. 57th St., New York, NY 10019. TEL 212-554-0600; 800-938-4685. FAX 212-586-1182. TELEX 175567. URL: http://www.eiu.com. (UK addr.: Economist Intelligence Unit Ltd., Subscriptions Dept., P.O. Box 200, Harold Hill, Romford, Essex RM3 8UX, England. TEL 44-1708-381-444. FAX 44-1708-371-850) illus.; stat.
 ●Also available online. Vendor(s): Knight-Ridder Information, Inc., Lexis-Nexis.
 —BLDSC (3481.898290).
 Formerly: Quarterly Economic Review of Iran (ISSN 0142-3924)
 Description: Analyzes Iran's current political and economic climate as well as short-term economic projections.

330.9 320 US ISSN 0269-5502
HC415.4.A1
COUNTRY REPORT. IRAQ; analysis of economic and political trends every quarter. 1952. q. £225($405) includes Country Profile. Iraq. Economist Intelligence Unit, 111 W. 57th St., New York, NY 10019. TEL 212-554-0600; 800-938-4685. FAX 212-586-1182. TELEX 175567. URL: http://www.eiu.com. (UK addr.: Economist Intelligence Unit Ltd., Subscriptions Dept., P.O. Box 200, Harold Hill, Romford, Essex RM3 8UX, England. TEL 44-1708-381-444. FAX 44-1708-371-850) illus.; stat.
 ●Also available online. Vendor(s): Knight-Ridder Information, Inc., Lexis-Nexis.
 Formerly: Quarterly Economic Review of Iraq (ISSN 0142-4009)
 Description: Analyzes Iraq's current political and economic climate as well as short-term economic projections.

BUSINESS AND ECONOMICS — ECONOMIC SITUATION AND CONDITIONS

330.9 320 US ISSN 0269-5278
HC260.5.A1
COUNTRY REPORT. IRELAND; analysis of economic and political trends every quarter. 1952. q. £225($405) includes Country Profile. Ireland. Economist Intelligence Unit, 111 W. 57th St., New York, NY 10019. TEL 212-554-0600; 800-938-4685. FAX 212-586-1182. TELEX 175567. URL: http://www.eiu.com. (UK addr.: Economist Intelligence Unit Ltd., Subscriptions Dept., P.O. Box 200, Harold Hill, Romford, Essex RM3 8UX, England. TEL 44-1708-381-444. FAX 44-1708-371-850) illus.; stat.
●Also available online. Vendor(s): Knight-Ridder Information, Inc., Lexis-Nexis.
Formerly: Quarterly Economic Review of Ireland (ISSN 0142-3835)
Description: Analyzes Ireland's current political and economic climate as well as short-term economic projections.

330.9 320 US ISSN 1353-3142
HC415.25.A1
COUNTRY REPORT. ISRAEL, THE OCCUPIED TERRITORIES; analysis of economic and political trends every quarter. 1952. q. £225($405) Economist Intelligence Unit, 111 W. 57th St., New York, NY 10019. TEL 212-554-0600; 800-938-4685. FAX 212-586-1182. TELEX 175567. URL: http://www.eiu.com. (UK addr.: Economist Intelligence Unit Ltd., Subscriptions Dept., P.O. Box 200, Harold Hill, Romford, Essex RM3 8UX, England. TEL 44-1708-381-444. FAX 44-1708-371-850) illus.; stat.
●Also available online. Vendor(s): Knight-Ridder Information, Inc., Lexis-Nexis.
—BLDSC (3481.898430).
Former titles (until 1993): Country Report. Israel (ISSN 0269-5928); Quarterly Economic Review of Israel (ISSN 0142-4238)
Description: Analyzes Israel's current political and economic climate as well as short-term economic projections.

330.9 320 US ISSN 0269-5421
HC301
COUNTRY REPORT. ITALY; analysis of economic and political trends every quarter. 1952. q. £225($405) includes Country Profile. Italy. Economist Intelligence Unit, 111 W. 57th St., New York, NY 10019. TEL 212-554-0600; 800-938-4685. FAX 212-586-1182. TELEX 175567. URL: http://www.eiu.com. (UK addr.: Economist Intelligence Unit Ltd., Subscriptions Dept., P.O. Box 200, Harold Hill, Romford, Essex RM3 8UX, England. TEL 44-1708-381-444. FAX 44-1708-371-850) illus.; stat.
●Also available online. Vendor(s): Knight-Ridder Information, Inc., Lexis-Nexis.
—BLDSC (3481.898450).
Formerly: Quarterly Economic Review of Italy (ISSN 0142-3886)
Description: Analyzes Italy's current political and economic climate as well as short-term economic projections.

330.9 320 US ISSN 1351-8674
HC154.A1
COUNTRY REPORT. JAMAICA, BELIZE, BAHAMAS, BERMUDA, BARBADOS; analysis of economic and political trends every quarter. 1952. q. £225($405) includes Country Profile. Jamaica, Barbados; Country Profile. Belize, Bahamas, Bermuda. Economist Intelligence Unit, 111 W. 57th St., New York, NY 10019. TEL 212-554-0600; 800-938-4685. FAX 212-586-1182. URL: http://www.eiu.com. (UK addr.: Economist Intelligence Unit Ltd., Subscriptions Dept., P.O. Box 200, Harold Hill, Romford, Essex RM3 8UX, England. TEL 44-1708-381-444. FAX 44-1708-371-850) illus.; stat.
●Also available online. Vendor(s): Knight-Ridder Information, Inc., Lexis-Nexis.
—BLDSC (3481.898500).
Formed by the 1992 merger of part of: Country Report. Jamaica, Belize, Bahamas, Bermuda (ISSN 0269-7130); part of: Country Report. Trinidad and Tobago, Guyana, Barbados, Windward and Leeward Islands (ISSN 0269-7149); Which was formerly: Quarterly Economic Review of Jamaica, Belize, Bahamas, Bermuda (ISSN 0266-9617); Quarterly Economic Review of Trinidad and Tobago, Guyana, Barbados, Windward and Leeward Islands (ISSN 0266-9625)
Description: Analyzes the current political and economic climate as well as short-term economic projections.

330.9 320 US ISSN 0269-6681
HC461
COUNTRY REPORT. JAPAN; analysis of economic and political trends every quarter. 1952. q. £225($405) includes Country Profile. Japan. Economist Intelligence Unit, 111 W. 57th St., New York, NY 10019. TEL 212-554-0600; 800-938-4685. FAX 212-586-1182. TELEX 175567. URL: http://www.eiu.com. (UK addr.: Economist Intelligence Unit Ltd., Subscriptions Dept., P.O. Box 200, Harold Hill, Romford, Essex RM3 8UX, England. TEL 44-1708-381-444. FAX 44-1708-371-850) illus.; stat.
●Also available online. Vendor(s): Knight-Ridder Information, Inc., Lexis-Nexis.
Formerly: Quarterly Economic Review of Japan (ISSN 0144-8897)
Description: Analyzes Japan's current political and economic climate as well as short-term economic projections.

330.9 320 US ISSN 0269-722X
HC415.26.A1
COUNTRY REPORT. JORDAN; analysis of economic and political trends every quarter. 1952. q. £225($405) Economist Intelligence Unit, 111 W. 57th St., New York, NY 10019. TEL 212-554-0600; 800-938-4685. FAX 212-586-1182. TELEX 175567. URL: http://www.eiu.com. (UK addr.: Economist Intelligence Unit Ltd., Subscriptions Dept., P.O. Box 200, Harold Hill, Romford, Essex RM3 8UX, England. TEL 44-1708-381-444. FAX 44-1708-371-850) illus.; stat.
●Also available online. Vendor(s): Knight-Ridder Information, Inc., Lexis-Nexis.
Formerly: Quarterly Economic Review of Jordan (ISSN 0266-9714)
Description: Analyzes Jordan's political and economic climate as well as short-term economic projections.

330.9 320 US ISSN 1361-147X
HC420.3.A1
COUNTRY REPORT. KAZAKHSTAN. q. £225($405) Economist Intelligence Unit, 111 W. 57th St., New York, NY 10019. TEL 212-554-0600; 800-938-4685. FAX 212-586-1182. TELEX 175567. URL: http://www.eiu.com. (UK addr.: Economist Intelligence Unit Ltd., Subscriptions Dept., P.O. Box 200, Harold Hill, Romford, Essex RM3 8UX, England. TEL 44-1708-381-444. FAX 44-1708-371-850) illus.; stat.
●Also available online. Vendor(s): Knight-Ridder Information, Inc., Lexis-Nexis.
Supersedes in part: Country Report. Central Asian Republics: Kazakhstan, Kyrgyz Republic, Tajikistan, Turkmenistan, Uzbekistan; Which superseded in part (in 1995): Country Report. Georgia, Armenia, Azerbaijan, Central Asian Republics (ISSN 1350-7206); Which superseded in part (in 1992): Country Report. Commonwealth of Independent States; Which was formerly (until 1991): Country Report. U S S R (ISSN 0269-5480); Quarterly Economic Review of U S S R (ISSN 0142-3967).
Description: Analyzes the current political and economic climate as well as short-term economic projections.

330.9 320 US ISSN 0269-4239
HC865.A1
COUNTRY REPORT. KENYA; analysis of economic and political trends every quarter. 1952. q. £225($405) includes Country Profile. Kenya. Economist Intelligence Unit, 111 W. 57th St., New York, NY 10019. TEL 212-554-0600; 800-938-4685. FAX 212-586-1182. TELEX 175567. URL: http://www.eiu.com. (UK addr.: Economist Intelligence Unit Ltd., Subscriptions Dept., P.O. Box 200, Harold Hill, Romford, Essex RM3 8UX, England. TEL 44-1708-381-444. FAX 4401708-371-850) illus.; stat.
●Also available online. Vendor(s): Knight-Ridder Information, Inc., Lexis-Nexis.
—BLDSC (3481.898650).
Formerly: Quarterly Economic Review of Kenya (ISSN 0142-4254)
Description: Analyzes Kenya's current political and economic climate as well as short-term economic projections.

330.9 320 US ISSN 0269-5715
HC415.39.A1
COUNTRY REPORT. KUWAIT; analysis of economic and political trends every quarter. 1952. q. £225($405) includes Country Profile. Kuwait. Economist Intelligence Unit, 111 W. 57th St., New York, NY 10019. TEL 212-554-0600; 800-938-4685. FAX 212-586-1182. TELEX 175567. URL: http://www.eiu.com. (UK addr.: Economist Intelligence Unit Ltd., Subscriptions Dept., P.O. Box 200, Harold Hill, Romford, Essex RM3 8UX, England. TEL 44-1708-381-444. FAX 44-1708-371-850) illus.; stat.
●Also available online. Vendor(s): Knight-Ridder Information, Inc., Lexis-Nexis.
—BLDSC (3481.898690).
Formerly: Quarterly Economic Review of Kuwait
Description: Analyzes Kuwait's current political and economic climate as well as short-term economic projections.

330.9 320 US ISSN 1366-414X
COUNTRY REPORT. KYRGYZ REPUBLIC, TAJIKISTAN, TURKMENISTAN; analysis of economic and political trends every quarter. q. £225($405) Economist Intelligence Unit, 111 W. 57th St., New York, NY 10019. TEL 212-554-0600; 800-938-4685. FAX 212-586-1182. TELEX 175567. URL: http://www.eiu.com. (UK addr.: Economist Intelligence Unit Ltd., Subscriptions Dept., P.O. Box 200, Harold Hill, Romford, Essex RM3 8UX, England. TEL 44-1708-381-444. FAX 44-1708-371-850)
Supersedes in part (in 1997): Country Report. Kyrgyz Republic, Tajikistan, Turkmenistan, Uzbekistan; Which superseded in part (in 1996): Country Report. Central Asian Republics: Kazakhstan, Kyrgyz Republic, Tajikistan, Turkmenistan, Uzbekistan; Which superseded in part (in 1995): Country Report. Georgia, Armenia, Azerbaijan, Central Asian Republics; Superseded in part (in 1992): Country Report. Commonwealth of Independent States; Which was formerly (until 1991): Country Report. U S S R (ISSN 0269-5480); Quarterly Economic Review of U S S R (ISSN 0142-3967).
Description: Analyzes the current political and economic climate and provides short-term economic projections.

330.9 320 US ISSN 1350-7141
HC415.24.A1
COUNTRY REPORT. LEBANON; analysis of economic and political trends every quarter. 1952. q. £225($405) includes Country Profile. Lebanon. Economist Intelligence Unit, 111 W. 57th St., New York, NY 10019. TEL 212-554-0600; 800-938-4685. FAX 212-586-1182. TELEX 175567. URL: http://www.eiu.com. (UK addr.: Economist Intelligence Unit Ltd., Subscriptions Dept., P.O. Box 200, Harold Hill, Romford, Essex RM3 8UX, England. TEL 44-1708-381-444. FAX 44-1708-371-850) illus.; stat.
●Also available online. Vendor(s): Knight-Ridder Information, Inc., Lexis-Nexis.
—BLDSC (3481.898700).
Supersedes (in 1992): Country Report. Lebanon, Cyprus (ISSN 0269-5693); Which was formerly: Quarterly Economic Review of Lebanon, Cyprus (ISSN 0142-4106)
Description: Analyzes Lebanon's current political and economic climate as well as short-term economic projections.

330.9 320 US ISSN 0269-4328
COUNTRY REPORT. LIBYA; analysis of economic and political trends every quarter. 1952. q. £225($405) includes Country Profile. Libya. Economist Intelligence Unit, 111 W. 57th St., New York, NY 10019. TEL 212-554-0600; 800-938-4685. FAX 212-586-1182. TELEX 175567. URL: http://www.eiu.com. (UK addr.: Economist Intelligence Unit Ltd., Subscriptions Dept., P.O. Box 200, Harold Hill, Romford, Essex RM3 8UX, England. TEL 44-1708-381-444. FAX 44-1708-371-850) illus.; stat.
●Also available online. Vendor(s): Knight-Ridder Information, Inc., Lexis-Nexis.
—BLDSC (3481.898770).
Formerly: Quarterly Economic Review of Libya (ISSN 0266-9722)
Description: Analyzes Libya's current political and economic climate as well as short-term economic projections.

BUSINESS AND ECONOMICS — ECONOMIC SITUATION AND CONDITIONS

330.9 320 US ISSN 1363-4658
COUNTRY REPORT. MACEDONIA, SERBIA-MONTENEGRO; analysis of economic and political trends every quarter. q. £225($405) includes Country Profile. Macedonia, Serbia-Montenegro. Economist Intelligence Unit, 111 W. 57th St., New York, NY 10019. TEL 212-554-0600; 800-938-4685. FAX 212-586-1182. TELEX 175567. URL: http://www.eiu.com. (UK addr.: Economist Intelligence Unit Ltd., Subscriptions Dept., P.O. Box 200, Harold Hill, Romford, Essex RM3 8UX, England. TEL 44-1708-381-444. FAX 44-1708-371-850)
 Supersedes in part: Country Report. Bosnia-Hercegovina, Croatia, Macedonia, Serbia-Montenegro, Slovenia (ISSN 1350-7222); Which superseded (in 1993): Country Report. Yugoslav Republics (ISSN 0968-7734); Which superseded (in 1992): Country Report. Yugoslavia (ISSN 0269-4190); Which was formerly: Quarterly Economic Review of Yugoslavia (ISSN 0142-3983)
 Description: Analyzes the current political and economic situation as well as short-term economic projections.

330.9 320 US ISSN 0269-6703
HC445.5.A1
COUNTRY REPORT. MALAYSIA, BRUNEI; analysis of economic and political trends every quarter. 1952. q. £225($405) includes Country Profile. Malaysia, Brunei. Economist Intelligence Unit, 111 W. 57th St., New York, NY 10019. TEL 212-554-0600; 800-938-4685. FAX 212-586-1182. TELEX 175567. URL: http://www.eiu.com. (UK addr.: Economist Intelligence Unit Ltd., Subscriptions Dept., P.O. Box 200, Harold Hill, Romford, Essex RM3 8UX, England. TEL 44-1708-381-444. FAX 44-1708-371-850) illus.; stat.
 ●Also available online. Vendor(s): Knight-Ridder Information, Inc., Lexis-Nexis.
 —BLDSC (3481.898850).
 Formerly: Quarterly Economic Review of Malaysia, Brunei (ISSN 0144-8919)
 Description: Analyzes the current political and economic climate as well as short-term economic projections.

330.9 320 US ISSN 1350-7060
HC597.5.A1
COUNTRY REPORT. MAURITIUS, MADAGASCAR, SEYCHELLES; analysis of economic and political trends every quarter. 1952. q. £225($405) includes Country Profile. Mauritius; Country Profile. Madagascar, Seychelles. Economist Intelligence Unit, 111 W. 57th St., New York, NY 10019. TEL 212-554-0600; 800-938-4685. FAX 212-586-1182. TELEX 175567. URL: http://www.eiu.com. (UK addr.: Economist Intelligence Unit Ltd., Subscriptions Dept., P.O. Box 200, Harold Hill, Romford, Essex RM3 8UX, England. TEL 44-1708-381-444. FAX 44-1708-371-850) illus.; stat.
 ●Also available online. Vendor(s): Knight-Ridder Information, Inc., Lexis-Nexis.
 —BLDSC (3481.898870).
 Supersedes in part (in 1993): Country Report. Madagascar, Mauritius, Seychelles, Comoros (ISSN 0269-5154); Which was formerly: Quarterly Economic Review of Madagascar, Mauritius, Seychelles, Comoros (ISSN 0141-8092)

330.9 320 US ISSN 0269-5936
HC131
COUNTRY REPORT. MEXICO; analysis of economic and political trends every quarter. 1952. q. £225($405) includes Country Profile. Mexico. Economist Intelligence Unit, 111 W. 57th St., New York, NY 10019. TEL 212-554-0600; 800-938-4685. FAX 212-586-1182. TELEX 175567. URL: http://www.eiu.com. (UK addr.: Economist Intelligence Unit Ltd., Subscriptions Dept., P.O. Box 200, Harold Hill, Romford, Essex RM3 8UX, England. TEL 44-1708-381-444. FAX 44-1708-371-850) illus.; stat.
 ●Also available online. Vendor(s): Knight-Ridder Information, Inc., Lexis-Nexis.
 Formerly: Quarterly Economic Review of Mexico (ISSN 0142-4270)
 Description: Analyzes Mexico's current political and economic climate as well as short-term economic projections.

330.9 320 US ISSN 0269-6126
HC810.A1
COUNTRY REPORT. MOROCCO; analysis of economic and political trends every quarter. 1952. q. £225($405) includes Country Profile. Morocco. Economist Intelligence Unit, 111 W. 57th St., New York, NY 10019. TEL 212-554-0600; 800-938-4685. FAX 212-586-1182. TELEX 175567. URL: http://www.eiu.com. (UK addr.: Economist Intelligence Unit Ltd., Subscriptions Dept., P.O. Box 200, Harold Hill, Romford, Essex RM3 8UX, England. TEL 44-1708-381-444. FAX 44-1708-371-850) illus.; stat.
 ●Also available online. Vendor(s): Knight-Ridder Information, Inc., Lexis-Nexis.
 —BLDSC (3481.899910).
 Formerly: Quarterly Economic Review of Morocco (ISSN 0142-4289)
 Description: Analyzes Morocco's current political and economic climate as well as short-term economic projections.

330.9 320 US ISSN 1351-8089
COUNTRY REPORT. MOZAMBIQUE, MALAWI; analysis of economic and political trends every quarter. q. £225($405) includes Country Profile. Mozambique. Country Profile. Malawi. Economist Intelligence Unit, 111 W. 57th St., New York, NY 10019. TEL 212-554-0600; 800-938-4685. FAX 212-586-1182. TELEX 175567. URL: http://www.eiu.com. (UK addr.: Economist Intelligence Unit Ltd., Subscriptions Dept., P.O. Box 200, Harold Hill, Romford, Essex RM3 8UX, England. TEL 44-1708-381-444. FAX 44-1708-371-850) illus.; stat.
 ●Also available online. Vendor(s): Knight-Ridder Information, Inc., Lexis-Nexis.
 —BLDSC (3481.899920).
 Formed by the 1993 merger of part of: Country Report. Tanzania, Mozambique (ISSN 0269-6223); part of: Country Report. Zimbabwe, Malawi (ISSN 0269-4255); Which was formerly: Quarterly Economic Review of Tanzania, Mozambique (ISSN 0142-4505); Quarterly Economic Review of Zimbabwe, Malawi (ISSN 0266-4372)
 Description: Analyze the current political and economic climate as well as short-term economic projections.

330.9 320 US ISSN 1361-1445
HC422.A1
COUNTRY REPORT. MYANMAR (BURMA); analysis of economic and political trends every quarter. q. £225($405) Economist Intelligence Unit, 111 W. 57th St., New York, NY 10019. TEL 212-554-0600; 800-938-4685. FAX 212-586-1182. TELEX 175567. URL: http://www.eiu. (UK addr.: Economist Intelligence Unit Ltd., Subscriptions Dept., P.O. Box 200, Harold Hill, Romford, Essex RM3 8UX, England. TEL 44-1708-381444. FAX 44-1708-371850)
 —BLDSC (3481.899923).
 Supersedes in part: Country Report. Cambodia, Laos, Myanmar (ISSN 1356-4048); Which was formed by the 1995 merger of part of: Country Report. Indochina: Vietnam, Laos, Cambodia (ISSN 0269-5677); Which was formerly: Quarterly Economic Review of Indochina: Vietnam, Laos, Cambodia (ISSN 0142-4076); And part of: Country Report. Thailand, Myanmar (ISSN 1350-7117); Which was formerly: Country Report. Thailand, Burma (ISSN 0269-5189); Quarterly Economic Review of Thailand, Burma (ISSN 0142-3754).
 Description: Analyzes the current political and economic climate as well as short-term economic projections.

330.9 320 US ISSN 1356-4218
COUNTRY REPORT. NAMIBIA, SWAZILAND; analysis of economic and political trends every quarter. q. £225($405) Economist Intelligence Unit, 111 W. 57th St., New York, NY 10019. TEL 212-554-0600; 800-938-4685. FAX 212-938-1182. TELEX 175567. URL: http://www.eiu.com. (U.K. addr.: Economist Intelligence Unit Ltd., Subscriptions Dept., P.O. Box 200, Harold Hill, Romford, Essex RM3 8UX, England. TEL 44-1708-381444. FAX 44-1708-371850)
 Supersedes in part (in 1994): Country Report. Angola, Botswana, Namibia, Lesotho, Swaziland; Which was formed by the 1992 merger of part of: Country Report. Angola, Sao Tome and Principe (ISSN 0269-4344); And part of: Country Report. Namibia, Botswana, Lesotho, Swaziland (ISSN 0269-6746); Which was formerly: Quarterly Economic Review of Angola, Sao Tome and Principe (ISSN 0266-9781); Quarterly Economic Review of Namibia, Botswana, Lesotho, Swaziland (ISSN 0144-896X)
 Description: Analyzes the current political and economic climate, as well as short-term economic projections.

330.9 320 US ISSN 0269-6134
HC310.5.A1
COUNTRY REPORT. NETHERLANDS; analysis of economic and political trends every quarter. 1952. q. £225($405) includes Country Profile. Netherlands. Economist Intelligence Unit, 111 W. 57th St., New York, NY 10019. TEL 212-554-0600; 800-938-4685. FAX 212-586-1182. TELEX 175567. URL: http://www.eiu.com. (UK addr.: Economist Intelligence Unit Ltd., Subscriptions Dept., P.O. Box 200, Harold Hill, Romford, Essex RM3 8UX, England. TEL 44-1708-381-444. FAX 44-1708-371-850) illus.; stat.
 ●Also available online. Vendor(s): Knight-Ridder Information, Inc., Lexis-Nexis.
 Formerly: Quarterly Economic Review of Netherlands (ISSN 0142-4297)
 Description: Analyzes the Netherlands' current political and economic climate as well as short-term economic projections.

330.9 320 US ISSN 0269-7114
HC661
COUNTRY REPORT. NEW ZEALAND; analysis of economic and political trends every quarter. 1952. q. £225($405) includes Country Profile. New Zealand. Economist Intelligence Unit, 111 W. 57th St., New York, NY 10019. TEL 212-554-0600; 800-938-4685. FAX 212-586-1182. TELEX 175567. URL: http://www.eiu.com. (UK addr.: Economist Intelligence Unit Ltd., Subscriptions Dept., P.O. Box 200, Harold Hill, Romford, Essex RM3 8UX, England. TEL 44-1708-381-444. FAX 44-1708-371-850) illus.; stat.
 ●Also available online. Vendor(s): Knight-Ridder Information, Inc., Lexis-Nexis.
 —UMI.
 Formerly: Quarterly Economic Review of New Zealand (ISSN 0266-9595)
 Description: Analyzes New Zealand's current political and economic climate as well as short-term economic projections.

330.9 320 US ISSN 0969-8809
HC146.A1
COUNTRY REPORT. NICARAGUA, HONDURAS; analysis of economic and political trends every quarter. 1952. q. £225($405) includes Country Profile. Nicaragua, Honduras. Economist Intelligence Unit, 111 W. 57th St., New York, NY 10019. TEL 212-554-0600; 800-938-4685. FAX 212-586-1182. TELEX 175567. URL: http://www.eiu.com. (UK addr.: Economist Intelligence Unit Ltd., Subscriptions Dept., P.O. Box 200, Harold Hill, Romford, Essex RM3 8UX, England. TEL 44-1708-381-444. FAX 44-1708-371-850) illus.; stat.
 ●Also available online. Vendor(s): Knight-Ridder Information, Inc., Lexis-Nexis.
 —BLDSC (3481.900070).
 Formed by the 1992 merger of part of: Country Report. Nicaragua, Costa Rica, Panama (ISSN 0269-4247); part of: Country Report. Guatemala, El Salvador, Honduras (ISSN 0269-4220); Which was formerly: Quarterly Economic Review of Nicaragua, Costa Rica, Panama (ISSN 0142-4300); Quarterly Economic Review of Guatemala, El Salvador, Honduras (ISSN 0142-4211)
 Description: Analyzes the current political and economic climate as well as short-term economic projections.

BUSINESS AND ECONOMICS — ECONOMIC SITUATION AND CONDITIONS

330.9 320   US   ISSN 1366-4115
COUNTRY REPORT. NIGER, BURKINA FASO; analysis of economic and political trends every quarter. q. £225($405) Economist Intelligence Unit, 111 W. 57th St., New York, NY 10019. TEL 212-554-0600; 800-938-4685. FAX 212-586-1182. TELEX 175567. URL: http://www.eiu.com. (UK addr.: Economist Intelligence Unit Ltd., Subscriptions Dept., P.O. Box 200, Harold Hill, Romford, Essex RM3 8UX, England. TEL 44-1708-381-444. FAX 44-1708-371-850)
   Supersedes in part (in 1997): Country Report. Togo, Niger, Benin, Burkina Faso (ISSN 0269-7262); Which was formerly: Quarterly Economic Review of Togo, Niger, Benin, Burkina Faso (ISSN 0266-9773)
   Description: Analyzes the current political and economic climate and provides short-term economic projections.

330.9 320   US   ISSN 0269-4204
HC1055.A1
COUNTRY REPORT. NIGERIA; analysis of economic and political trends every quarter. 1952. q. £225($405) includes Country Profile. Nigeria. Economist Intelligence Unit, 111 W. 57th St., New York, NY 10019. TEL 212-554-0600; 800-938-4685. FAX 212-586-1182. TELEX 175567. URL: http://www.eiu.com. (UK addr.: Economist Intelligence Unit Ltd., Subscriptions Dept., P.O. Box 200, Harold Hill, Romford, Essex RM3 8UX, England. TEL 44-1708-381-444. FAX 44-1708-371-850) illus.; stat.
   ●Also available online. Vendor(s): Knight-Ridder Information, Inc., Lexis-Nexis.
   —BLDSC (3481.900090).
   Formerly: Quarterly Economic Review of Nigeria (ISSN 0142-4033)
   Description: Analyzes Nigeria's current political and economic climate as well as short-term economic projections.

330.9 320   US   ISSN 0269-4182
COUNTRY REPORT. NORWAY; analysis of economic and political trends every quarter. 1952. q. £225($405) includes Country Profile. Norway. Economist Intelligence Unit, 111 W. 57th St., New York, NY 10019. TEL 212-554-0600; 800-938-4685. FAX 212-586-1182. TELEX 175567. URL: http://www.eiu.com. (UK addr.: Economist Intelligence Unit Ltd., Subscriptions Dept., P.O. Box 200, Harold Hill, Romford, Essex RM3 8UX, England. TEL 44-1708-381-444. FAX 44-1708-371-850) illus.; stat.
   ●Also available online. Vendor(s): Knight-Ridder Information, Inc., Lexis-Nexis.
   —BLDSC (3481.900130).
   Formerly: Quarterly Economic Review of Norway (ISSN 0142-3908)
   Description: Analyzes Norway's current political and economic climate as well as short-term economic projections.

330.9 320   US   ISSN 1351-8690
HC415.35.A1
COUNTRY REPORT. OMAN, YEMEN; analysis of economic and political trends every quarter. q. £225($405) includes Country Profile. Oman, Yemen. Economist Intelligence Unit, 111 W. 57th St., New York, NY 10019. TEL 212-554-0600; 800-938-4685. FAX 212-586-1182. TELEX 175567. URL: http://www.eiu.com. (UK addr.: Economist Intelligence Unit Ltd., Subscriptions Dept., P.O. Box 200, Harold Hill, Romford, Essex RM3 8UX, England. TEL 44-1708-381-444. FAX 44-1708-371-850) illus.; stat.
   ●Also available online. Vendor(s): Knight-Ridder Information, Inc., Lexis-Nexis.
   —BLDSC (3481.900150).
   Supersedes in part (in 1992): Country Report. Bahrain, Qatar, Oman, Yemen (ISSN 0269-5707); Which was formerly: Quarterly Economic Review of Bahrain, Qatar, Oman, Yemen (ISSN 0142-4114)
   Description: Analyzes Oman's and Yemen's current political and economic climates as well as short-term economic projections.

330.9 320   US   ISSN 0269-7122
HC681.A1
COUNTRY REPORT. PACIFIC ISLANDS: PAPUA NEW GUINEA, FIJI, SOLOMON ISLANDS, WESTERN SAMOA, VANUATU, TONGA; analysis of economic and political trends every quarter. 1952. q. £225($405) includes Country Profile. Papua New Guinea; Country Profile. Pacific Islands: Fiji, Solomon Islands, Western Samoa, Vanuatu, Tonga. Economist Intelligence Unit, 111 W. 57th St., New York, NY 10019. TEL 212-554-0600; 800-938-4685. FAX 212-586-1827. TELEX 175567. URL: http://www.eiu.com. (UK addr.: Economist Intelligence Unit Ltd., Subscriptions Dept., P.O. Box 200, Harold Hill, Romford, Essex RM3 8UX, England. TEL 44-1708-371-850. FAX 44-1708-371-850) illus.; stat.
   ●Also available online. Vendor(s): Knight-Ridder Information, Inc., Lexis-Nexis.
   Formerly: Quarterly Economic Review of Pacific Islands: Papua New Guinea, Fiji, Solomon Islands, Western Samoa, Vanuatu, Tonga (ISSN 0266-9609)
   Description: Analyzes the current political and economic climate as well as short-term economic projections.

330.9 320   US   ISSN 0269-7173
HC440.5.A1
COUNTRY REPORT. PAKISTAN, AFGHANISTAN; analysis of economic and political trends every quarter. 1952. q. £225($405) includes Country Profile. Pakistan, Afghanistan. Economist Intelligence Unit, 111 W. 57th St., New York, NY 10019. TEL 212-554-0600; 800-938-4685. FAX 212-586-1182. TELEX 175567. URL: http://www.eiu.com. (UK addr.: Economist Intelligence Unit Ltd., Subscriptions Dept., P.O. Box 200, Harold Hill, Romford, Essex RM3 8UX, England. TEL 44-1708-381-444. FAX 44-1708-371-850) illus.; stat.
   ●Also available online. Vendor(s): Knight-Ridder Information, Inc., Lexis-Nexis.
   —BLDSC (3481.900210).
   Formerly: Quarterly Economic Review of Pakistan, Afghanistan (ISSN 0266-965X)
   Description: Analyzes the current political and economic climate as well as short-term economic projections.

330.9 320   US   ISSN 1366-4034
COUNTRY REPORT. PANAMA; analysis of economic and political trends every quarter. q. £225($405) Economist Intelligence Unit, 111 W. 57th St., New York, NY 10019. TEL 212-554-0600; 800-938-4685. FAX 212-586-1182. TELEX 175567. URL: http://www.eiu.com. (UK addr.: Economist Intelligence Unit Ltd., Subscriptions Dept., P.O. Box 200, Harold Hill, Romford, Essex RM3 8UX, England. TEL 44-1708-381-444. FAX 44-1708-371-850)
   ●Also available online. Vendor(s): Knight-Ridder Information, Inc., Lexis-Nexis.
   Supersedes in part (in 1997): Country Report. Costa Rica, Panama (ISSN 1350-7125); (in 1992): Country Report. Nicaragua, Costa Rica, Panama (ISSN 0269-4247); Which was formerly: Quarterly Economic Review of Nicaragua, Costa Rica, Panama (ISSN 0142-4300)
   Description: Analyzes the current political and economic climate and provides short-term economic projections.

330.9 320   US
HC226
COUNTRY REPORT. PERU; analysis of economic and political trends every quarter. 1952. q. £225($405) Economist Intelligence Unit, 111 W. 57th St., New York, NY 10019. TEL 212-554-0600; 800-938-4685. FAX 212-586-1182. URL: http://www.eiu.com. (UK addr.: Economist Intelligence Unit Ltd., Subscriptions Dept., P.O. Box 200, Harold Hill, Romford, Essex RM3 8UX, England. TEL 44-1708-381-444. FAX 44-1708-371-850) illus.; stat. (also avail. in microform from WMP)
   ●Also available online. Vendor(s): Knight-Ridder Information, Inc., Lexis-Nexis.
   Also available on CD-ROM. Producer(s): Knight-Ridder, Inc., SilverPlatter Information, Inc.
   Supersedes in part (in 1995): Country Report. Peru, Bolivia (ISSN 0269-543X); Which was formerly: Quarterly Economic Review of Peru, Bolivia (ISSN 0142-3916)
   Description: Analyzes the current political and economic climate, as well as short-term economic projections.

330.9 320   US   ISSN 0269-428X
HC451
COUNTRY REPORT. PHILIPPINES; analysis of economic and political trends every quarter. 1952. q. £225($405) includes Country Profile. Philippines. Economist Intelligence Unit, 111 W. 57th St., New York, NY 10019. TEL 212-554-0600; 800-938-4685. FAX 212-586-1182. TELEX 175567. URL: http://www.eiu.com. (UK addr.: Economist Intelligence Unit Ltd., Subscriptions Dept., P.O. Box 200, Harold Hill, Romford, Essex RM3 8UX, England. TEL 44-1708-381-444. FAX 44-1708-371-850) illus.; stat.
   ●Also available online. Vendor(s): Knight-Ridder Information, Inc., Lexis-Nexis.
   —BLDSC (3481.900290).
   Formerly: Quarterly Economic Review of Philippines (ISSN 0144-8935)
   Description: Analyzes Philippines' current political and economic climate as well as short-term economic projections.

330.9 320   US   ISSN 0269-6193
HC340.3.A1
COUNTRY REPORT. POLAND; analysis of economic and political trends every quarter. 1952. q. £225($405) includes Country Profile. Poland. Economist Intelligence Unit, 111 W. 57th St., New York, NY 10019. TEL 212-554-0600; 800-938-4685. FAX 212-938-4685. TELEX 175567. URL: http://www.eiu.com. (UK addr.: Economist Intelligence Unit Ltd., Subscriptions Dept., P.O. Box 200, Harold Hill, Romford, Essex RM3 8UX, England. TEL 44-1708-381-444. FAX 44-1708-371-850) illus.; stat.
   ●Also available online. Vendor(s): Knight-Ridder Information, Inc., Lexis-Nexis.
   —BLDSC (3481.900330).
   Formerly: Quarterly Economic Review of Poland (ISSN 0144-8870)
   Description: Analyzes Poland's current political and economic climate as well as short-term economic projections.

330.9 320   US   ISSN 0269-5456
HC391
COUNTRY REPORT. PORTUGAL; analysis of economic and political trends every quarter. 1952. q. £225($405) includes Country Profile. Portugal. Economist Intelligence Unit, 111 W. 57th St., New York, NY 10019. TEL 212-554-0600; 800-938-4685. FAX 212-586-1182. TELEX 175567. URL: http://www.eiu.com. (UK addr.: Economist Intelligence Unit Ltd., Subscriptions Dept., P.O. Box 200, Harold Hill, Romford, Essex RM3 8UX, England. TEL 44-1708-381-444. FAX 44-1708-371-850) illus.; stat.
   ●Also available online. Vendor(s): Knight-Ridder Information, Inc., Lexis-Nexis.
   —BLDSC (3481.900370).
   Formerly: Quarterly Economic Review of Portugal (ISSN 0142-3932)
   Description: Analyzes Portugal's current political and economic climate as well as short-term economic projections.

330.9 320   US   ISSN 1356-4102
HC405.A1
COUNTRY REPORT. ROMANIA; analysis of economic and political trends every quarter. 1952. q. £225($405) Economist Intelligence Unit, 111 W. 57th St., New York, NY 10019. TEL 212-554-0600; 800-938-4685. FAX 212-586-1182. TELEX 175567. URL: http://www.eiu.com. (UK addr.: Economist Intelligence Unit Ltd., Subscriptions Dept., P.O. Box 200, Harold Hill, Romford, Essex RM3 8UX, England. TEL 44-1708-381-444. FAX 44-1708-371-850) illus.; stat.
   ●Also available online. Vendor(s): Knight-Ridder Information, Inc., Lexis-Nexis.
   —BLDSC (3481.900390).
   Supersedes in part (in 1995): Country Report. Romania, Bulgaria, Albania (ISSN 0269-5669); Which was formerly: Quarterly Economic Review of Romania, Bulgaria, Albania (ISSN 0142-4068)
   Description: Analyzes the current political and economic climate as well as short-term economic projections.

BUSINESS AND ECONOMICS — ECONOMIC SITUATION AND CONDITIONS

330.9 320   US   ISSN 1350-7184
HC340.12.A1
COUNTRY REPORT. RUSSIA; analysis of economic and political trends every quarter. q. £225($405) includes Country Profile. Russia. Economist Intelligence Unit, 111 W. 57th St., New York, NY 10019. TEL 212-554-0600; 800-938-4685. FAX 212-586-1182. TELEX 175567. URL: http://www.eiu.com. (UK addr.: Economist Intelligence Unit Ltd., Subscriptions Dept., P.O. Box 200, Harold Hill, Romford, Essex RM3 8UX, England. TEL 44-1708-381-444. FAX 44-1708-371-850) illus.; stat.
● Also available online. Vendor(s): Knight-Ridder Information, Inc., Lexis-Nexis.
—BLDSC (3481.900430).
Supersedes in part (in 1992): Country Report. Commonwealth of Independent States; Which was formerly (until 1991): Country Report. U S S R (ISSN 0269-5480); Quarterly Economic Review of U S S R (ISSN 0142-3967)
Description: Analyzes Russia's current political and economic climate as well as short-term economic projections.

330.9 320   US   ISSN 0269-6215
HC415.33.A1
COUNTRY REPORT. SAUDI ARABIA; analysis of economic and political trends every quarter. 1952. q. £225($405) includes Country Profile. Saudi Arabia. Economist Intelligence Unit, 111 W. 57th St., New York, NY 10019. TEL 212-554-0600; 800-938-4685. FAX 212-586-1182. TELEX 175567. URL: http://www.eiu.com. (UK addr.: Economist Intelligence Unit Ltd., Subscriptions Dept., P.O. Box 200, Harold Hill, Romford, Essex RM3 8UX, England. TEL 44-1708-381-444. FAX 44-1708-371-850) illus.; stat.
● Also available online. Vendor(s): Knight-Ridder Information, Inc., Lexis-Nexis.
—BLDSC (3481.900450).
Formerly: Quarterly Economic Review of Saudi Arabia (ISSN 0142-4491)
Description: Analyzes Saudi Arabia's current political and economic climate as well as short-term economic projections.

330.9 320   US   ISSN 1350-7079
HC1045.A1
COUNTRY REPORT. SENEGAL, THE GAMBIA, MAURITANIA; analysis of economic and political trends every quarter. 1952. q. £225($405) includes Country Profile. Senegal; Country Profile. The Gambia, Mauritania. Economist Intelligence Unit, 111 W. 57th St., New York, NY 10019. TEL 212-554-0600; 800-938-4685. FAX 212-586-1182. TELEX 175567. URL: http://www.eiu.com. (UK addr.: Economist Intelligence Unit Ltd., Subscriptions Dept., P.O. Box 200, Harold Hill, Romford, Essex RM3 8UX, England. TEL 44-1708-381-444. FAX 44-1708-371-850) illus.; stat.
● Also available online. Vendor(s): Knight-Ridder Information, Inc., Lexis-Nexis.
—BLDSC (3481.900500).
Formed by the 1993 merger of part of: Country Report. Senegal, The Gambia, Guinea-Bassau, Cape Verde (ISSN 0269-719X); part of: Country Report. Guinea, Mali, Mauritania (ISSN 0269-7203); Which was formerly: Quarterly Economic Review of Senegal, The Gambia, Guinea-Bassau, Cape Verde (ISSN 0266-9684); Quarterly Economic Review of Guinea, Mali, Mauritania (ISSN 0266-9692)

330.9 320   US   ISSN 0269-6711
HC445.8.A1
COUNTRY REPORT. SINGAPORE; analysis of economic and political trends every quarter. 1952. q. £225($405) includes Country Profile. Singapore. Economist Intelligence Unit, 111 W. 57th St., New York, NY 10019. TEL 212-554-0600; 800-938-4685. FAX 212-586-1182. TELEX 175567. URL: http://www.eiu.com. (UK addr.: Economist Intelligence Unit Ltd., Subscriptions Dept., P.O. Box 200, Harold Hill, Romford, Essex RM3 8UX, England. TEL 44-1708-381-444. FAX 44-1708-371-850) illus.; stat.
● Also available online. Vendor(s): Knight-Ridder Information, Inc., Lexis-Nexis.
Formerly: Quarterly Economic Review of Singapore (ISSN 0144-8927)
Description: Analyzes Singapore's current political and economic climate as well as short-term economic projections.

330.9 320   US
COUNTRY REPORT. SLOVAKIA; analysis of economic and political trends every quarter. 1952. q. £225($405) Economist Intelligence Unit, 111 W. 57th St., New York, NY 10019. TEL 212-554-0600; 800-938-4685. FAX 212-586-1182. TELEX 175567. URL: http://www.eiu.com. (UK addr.: Economist Intelligence Unit Ltd., Subscriptions Dept., P.O. Box 200, Harold Hill, Romford, Essex RM3 8UX, England. TEL 44-1708-381-444. FAX 44-1708-371-850) illus.; stat.
● Also available online. Vendor(s): Knight-Ridder Information, Inc., Lexis-Nexis.
Supersedes in part (in 1997): Country Report. Czech Republic, Slovakia (ISSN 1350-7214); Which superseded in part (in 1992): Country Report. Czechoslovakia (ISSN 0269-4298); Which was formerly: Quarterly Economic Review of Czechoslovakia (ISSN 0144-8978)
Description: Analyzes the current political and economic climate and provides short-term economic projections.

330.9 320   US   ISSN 0269-6738
HC905.A1
COUNTRY REPORT. SOUTH AFRICA; analysis of economic and political trends every quarter. 1952. q. £225($405) includes Country Profile. South Africa. Economist Intelligence Unit, 111 W. 57th St., New York, NY 10019. TEL 212-554-0600; 800-938-4685. FAX 212-586-1182. TELEX 175567. URL: http://www.eiu.com. (UK addr.: Economist Intelligence Unit Ltd., Subscriptions Dept., P.O. Box 200, Harold Hill, Romford, Essex RM3 8UX, England. TEL 44-1708-381-444. FAX 44-1708-371-850) illus.; stat.
● Also available online. Vendor(s): Knight-Ridder Information, Inc., Lexis-Nexis.
Formerly: Quarterly Economic Review of South Africa (ISSN 0144-8951)
Description: Analyzes South Africa's current political and economic climate as well as short-term economic projections.

330.9 320   US   ISSN 1350-6900
HC466
COUNTRY REPORT. SOUTH KOREA, NORTH KOREA; analysis of economic and political trends every quarter. 1952. q. £225($405) includes Country Profile. South Korea, North Korea. Economist Intelligence Unit, 111 W. 57th St., New York, NY 10019. TEL 212-554-0600; 800-939-4685. FAX 212-586-1182. TELEX 175567. URL: http://www.eiu.com. (UK addr.: Economist Intelligence Unit Ltd., Subscriptions Dept., P.O. Box 200, Harold Hill, Romford, Essex RM3 8UX, England. TEL 44-1708-381-444. FAX 44-1708-371-850) illus.; stat.
● Also available online. Vendor(s): Knight-Ridder Information, Inc., Lexis-Nexis.
—BLDSC (3481.900630).
Formed by the 1992 merger of: Country Report. South Korea (ISSN 0269-669X); part of: Country Report. China, North Korea (ISSN 0269-6231); Which was formerly: Quarterly Economic Review of South Korea (ISSN 0144-8900); Quarterly Economic Review of China, North Korea (ISSN 0144-8854)
Description: Analyzes the current political and economic climate as well as short-term economic projections.

330.9 320   US   ISSN 0269-4263
HC381
COUNTRY REPORT. SPAIN; analysis of economic and political trends every quarter. 1952. q. £225($405) includes Country Profile. Spain. Economist Intelligence Unit, 111 W. 57th St., New York, NY 10019. TEL 212-554-0600; 800-938-4685. FAX 212-586-1182. TELEX 175567. URL: http://www.eiu.com. (UK addr.: Economist Intelligence Unit Ltd., Subscriptions Dept., P.O. Box 200, Harold Hill, Romford, Essex RM3 8UX, England. TEL 44-1708-381-444. FAX 44-1708-371-850) illus.; stat.
● Also available online. Vendor(s): Knight-Ridder Information, Inc., Lexis-Nexis.
—BLDSC (3481.900650).
Formerly: Quarterly Economic Review of Spain (ISSN 0142-4394)
Description: Analyzes Spain's current political and economic climate as well as short-term economic projections.

330.9 320   US   ISSN 0269-4174
HC424.A1
COUNTRY REPORT. SRI LANKA; analysis of economic and political trends every quarter. 1952. q. £225($405) includes Country Report. Sri Lanka. Economist Intelligence Unit, 111 W. 57th St., New York, NY 10019. TEL 212-554-0600; 800-938-4685. FAX 212-586-1182. TELEX 175567. URL: http://www.eiu.com. (UK addr.: Economist Intelligence Unit Ltd., Subscriptions Dept., P.O. Box 200, Harold Hill, Romford, Essex RM3 8UX, England. TEL 44-1708-381-444. FAX 44-1708-371-850) illus.; stat.
● Also available online. Vendor(s): Knight-Ridder Information, Inc., Lexis-Nexis.
—BLDSC (3481.900690).
Formerly: Quarterly Economic Review of Sri Lanka (ISSN 0142-3770)
Description: Analyzes Sri Lanka's current political and economic climate as well as short-term economic projections.

330.9 320   US   ISSN 0269-6150
HC835.A1
COUNTRY REPORT. SUDAN; analysis of economic and political trends every quarter. 1952. q. £225($405) includes Country Profile. Sudan. Economist Intelligence Unit, 111 W. 57th St., New York, NY 10019. TEL 212-554-0600; 800-938-4685. FAX 212-586-1182. TELEX 175567. URL: http://www.eiu.com. (UK addr.: Economist Intelligence Unit Ltd., Subscriptions Dept., P.O. Box 200, Harold Hill, Romford, Essex RM3 8UX, England. TEL 44-1708-381-444. FAX 44-1708-371-850) illus.; stat.
● Also available online. Vendor(s): Knight-Ridder Information, Inc., Lexis-Nexis.
—BLDSC (3481.900730).
Formerly: Quarterly Economic Review of Sudan (ISSN 0142-4408)
Description: Analyzes Sudan's current political and economic climate as well as short-term economic projections.

330.9 320   US   ISSN 0269-6142
HC371
COUNTRY REPORT. SWEDEN; analysis of economic and political trends every quarter. 1952. q. £225($405) includes Country Profile. Sweden. Economist Intelligence Unit, 111 W. 57th St., New York, NY 10019. TEL 212-554-0600; 800-938-4685. FAX 212-586-1182. TELEX 175567. URL: http://www.eiu.com. (UK addr.: Economist Intelligence Unit Ltd., Subscriptions Dept., P.O. Box 200, Harold Hill, Romford, Essex RM3 8UX, England. TEL 44-1708-381-444. FAX 44-1708-371-850) illus.; stat.
● Also available online. Vendor(s): Knight-Ridder Information, Inc., Lexis-Nexis.
—BLDSC (3481.900770).
Formerly: Quarterly Economic Review of Sweden (ISSN 0142-4416)
Description: Analyzes Sweden's current political and economic climate as well as short-term economic projections.

330.9 320   US   ISSN 0269-6169
HC395
COUNTRY REPORT. SWITZERLAND; analysis of economic and political trends every quarter. 1952. q. £225($405) includes Country Profile. Switzerland. Economist Intelligence Unit, 111 W. 57th St., New York, NY 10019. TEL 212-554-0600; 800-586-4685. FAX 212-586-1182. TELEX 175567. URL: http://www.eiu.com. (UK addr.: Economist Intelligence Unit Ltd., Subscriptions Dept., P.O. Box 200, Harold Hill, Romford, Essex RM3 8UX, England. TEL 44-1708-381-444. FAX 44-1708-371-850) illus.; stat.
● Also available online. Vendor(s): Knight-Ridder Information, Inc., Lexis-Nexis.
Formerly: Quarterly Economic Review of Switzerland (ISSN 0142-4424)
Description: Analyzes Switzerland's current political and economic climate as well as short-term economic projections.

BUSINESS AND ECONOMICS — ECONOMIC SITUATION AND CONDITIONS

330.9 320   US   ISSN 0269-7211
HC415.23.A1
COUNTRY REPORT. SYRIA; analysis of economic and political trends every quarter. 1952. q. £225($405) includes Country Profile. Syria. Economist Intelligence Unit, 111 W. 57th St., New York, NY 10019. TEL 212-554-0600; 800-938-4685. FAX 212-586-1182. TELEX 175567. URL: http://www.eiu.com. (UK addr.: Economist Intelligence Unit Ltd., Subscriptions Dept., P.O. Box 200, Harold Hill, Romford, Essex RM3 8UX, England. TEL 44-1708-381-444. FAX 44-1708-371-850) illus.; stat.
●Also available online. Vendor(s): Knight-Ridder Information, Inc., Lexis-Nexis.
—BLDSC (3481.900850).
  Formerly: Quarterly Economic Review of Syria (ISSN 0266-9706)
  Description: Analyzes Syria's current political and economic climate as well as short-term economic projections.

330.9 320   US   ISSN 0269-672X
HC430.5.A1
COUNTRY REPORT. TAIWAN; analysis of economic and political trends every quarter. 1952. q. £225($405) Economist Intelligence Unit, 111 W. 57th St., New York, NY 10019. TEL 212-554-0600; 800-938-4685. FAX 212-586-1182. TELEX 175567. URL: http://www.eiu.com. (UK addr.: Economist Intelligence Unit Ltd., Subscriptions Dept., P.O. Box 200, Harold Hill, Romford, Essex RM3 8UX, England. TEL 44-1708-381-444. FAX 44-1708-371-850) illus.; stat.
●Also available online. Vendor(s): Knight-Ridder Information, Inc., Lexis-Nexis.
—BLDSC (3481.900890).
  Formerly: Quarterly Economic Review of Taiwan (ISSN 0144-8943)
  Description: Analyzes Taiwan's current political and economic climate as well as short-term economic projections.

330.9 320   US   ISSN 0969-6776
COUNTRY REPORT. TANZANIA, COMOROS; analysis of economic and political trends every quarter. 1952. q. £225($405) includes Country Profile. Tanzania; Country Profile. Mozambique. Economist Intelligence Unit, 111 W. 57th St., New York, NY 10019. TEL 212-554-0600; 800-938-4685. FAX 212-586-1182. TELEX 175567. URL: http://www.eiu.com. (UK addr.: Economist Intelligence Unit Ltd., Subscriptions Dept., P.O. Box 200, Harold Hill, Romford, Essex RM3 8UX, England. TEL 44-1708-381-444. FAX 44-1708-371-850) illus.; stat. **Document type:** academic/scholarly publication.
●Also available online. Vendor(s): Knight-Ridder Information, Inc., Lexis-Nexis.
—BLDSC (3481.900900).
  Formed by the 1993 merger of part of: Country Report. Tanzania, Mozambique (ISSN 0269-6223); part of: Country Report. Madagascar, Mauritius, Seychelles, Comoros (ISSN 0269-5154); Which was formerly: Quarterly Economic Review of Tanzania, Mozambique (ISSN 0142-4505); Quarterly Economic Review of Madagascar, Mauritius, Seychelles, Comoros (ISSN 0141-8092)

330.9 320   US   ISSN 1356-4056
HC445.A1
COUNTRY REPORT. THAILAND; analysis of economic and political trends every quarter. 1952. q. £225($405) Economist Intelligence Unit, 111 W. 57th St., New York, NY 10019. TEL 212-554-0600; 800-938-4685. FAX 212-586-1182. TELEX 175567. URL: http://www.eiu.com. (UK addr.: Economist Intelligence Unit Ltd., Subscriptions Dept., P.O. Box 200, Harold Hill, Romford, Essex RM3 8UX, England. TEL 44-1708-381-444. FAX 44-1708-371-850) illus.; stat.
●Also available online. Vendor(s): Knight-Ridder Information, Inc., Lexis-Nexis.
  Supersedes in part (in 1995): Country Report. Thailand, Myanmar (ISSN 1350-7117); Formerly (until 1992): Country Report. Thailand, Burma (ISSN 0269-5189); Quarterly Economic Review of of Thailand, Burma (ISSN 0142-3754)
  Description: Analyzes the current political and economic climate as well as short-term economic projections.

330.9 320   US   ISSN 1366-4107
HC1000.A1
COUNTRY REPORT. TOGO, BENIN; analysis of economic and political trends every quarter. 1952. q. £225($405) includes Country Profile. Togo, Benin. Economist Intelligence Unit, 111 W. 57th St., New York, NY 10019. TEL 212-554-0600; 800-938-4685. FAX 212-586-1182. TELEX 175567. URL: http://www.eiu.com. (UK addr.: Economist Intelligence Unit Ltd., Subscriptions Dept., P.O. Box 200, Harold Hill, Romford, Essex RM3 8UX, England. TEL 44-1708-381-444. FAX 44-1708-371-850) illus.; stat.
●Also available online. Vendor(s): Knight-Ridder Information, Inc., Lexis-Nexis.
  Supersedes in part (in 1997): Country Report. Togo, Niger, Benin, Burkina Faso (ISSN 0269-7262); Which was formerly: Quarterly Economic Review of Togo, Niger, Benin, Burkina Faso (ISSN 0266-9773)
  Description: Analyzes the current political and economic climate and offers short-term economic projections.

330.9 320   US   ISSN 1351-1270
HC151.A1
COUNTRY REPORT. TRINIDAD & TOBAGO, GUYANA, WINDWARD & LEEWARD ISLANDS, SURINAME, NETHERLANDS ANTILLES, ARUBA; analysis of economic and political trends every quarter. 1952. q. £225($405) includes Country Profile. Trinidad & Tobago, Suriname, Netherlands Antilles, Aruba. Economist Intelligence Unit, 111 W. 57th St., New York, NY 10019. TEL 212-554-0600; 800-938-4685. FAX 212-586-1182. TELEX 175567. URL: http://www.eiu.com. (UK addr.: Economist Intelligence Unit Ltd., Subscriptions Dept., P.O. Box 200, Harold Hill, Romford, Essex RM3 8UX, England. TEL 44-1708-381-444. FAX 44-1708-371-850) illus.; stat.
●Also available online. Vendor(s): Knight-Ridder Information, Inc., Lexis-Nexis.
  Formed by the 1992 merger of part of: Country Report. Trinidad and Tobago, Guyana, Barbados, Windward and Leeward Islands (ISSN 0269-7149); part of: Country Report. Venezuela, Suriname, Netherlands Antilles (ISSN 0266-6754); Which was formerly: Quarterly Economic Review of Trinidad and Tobago, Guyana, Barbados, Windward and Leeward Islands (ISSN 0266-9625); Quarterly Economic Review of Venezuela, Suriname, Netherlands Antilles (ISSN 0264-9675)
  Description: Analyzes the current political and economic climate as well as short-term economic projections.

330.9 320   US   ISSN 1350-7168
HC820.A1
COUNTRY REPORT. TUNISIA; analysis of economic and political trends every quarter. 1952. q. £225($405) includes Country Profile. Tunisia. Economist Intelligence Unit, 111 W. 57th St., New York, NY 10019. TEL 212-554-0600; 800-938-4685. FAX 212-586-1182. TELEX 175567. URL: http://www.eiu.com. (UK addr.: Economist Intelligence Unit Ltd., Subscriptions Dept., P.O. Box 200, Harold Hill, Romford, Essex RM3 8UX, England. TEL 44-1708-381-444. FAX 44-1708-371-850) illus.; stat.
●Also available online. Vendor(s): Knight-Ridder Information, Inc., Lexis-Nexis.
  Former titles (until 1992): Country Report. Tunisia, Malta (ISSN 0269-7238); Quarterly Economic Review of Tunisia, Malta (ISSN 0266-9730)
  Description: Analyzes Tunisia's current political and economic climate as well as short-term economic projections.

330.9 320   US   ISSN 0269-5464
HC491
COUNTRY REPORT. TURKEY; analysis of economic and political trends every quarter. 1952. q. £225($405) includes Country Profile. Turkey. Economist Intelligence Unit, 111 W. 57th St., New York, NY 10019. TEL 212-554-0600; 800-938-4685. FAX 212-586-1182. TELEX 175567. URL: http://www.eiu.com. (UK addr.: Economist Intelligence Unit Ltd., Subscriptions Dept., P.O. Box 200, Harold Hill, Romford, Essex RM3 8UX, England. TEL 44-1708-381-444. FAX 44-1708-371-850) illus.; stat.
●Also available online. Vendor(s): Knight-Ridder Information, Inc., Lexis-Nexis.
  Formerly: Quarterly Economic Review of Turkey.
  Description: Analyzes Turkey's current political and economic climate as well as short-term economic projections.

330.9 320   US   ISSN 0969-8817
HC870.A1
COUNTRY REPORT. UGANDA, RWANDA, BURUNDI; analysis of economic and political trends every quarter. 1952. q. £225($405) includes Country Profile. Uganda; Country Profile. Rwanda, Burundi. Economist Intelligence Unit, 111 W. 57th St., New York, NY 10019. TEL 212-554-0600; 800-938-4685. FAX 212-586-1182. TELEX 175567. URL: http://www.eiu.com. (UK addr.: Economist Intelligence Unit Ltd., Subscriptions Dept., P.O. Box 200, Harold Hill, Romford, Essex RM3 8UX, England. TEL 44-1708-381-444. FAX 44-1708-371-850) illus.; stat.
●Also available online. Vendor(s): Knight-Ridder Information, Inc., Lexis-Nexis.
—BLDSC (3481.901172).
  Supersedes in part (in 1992): Country Report. Uganda, Ethiopia, Somalia, Djibouti (ISSN 0269-5685); Incorporates in part (in 1992): Country Report. Zaire, Rwanda, Burundi (ISSN 0269-5510); Which was formerly: Quarterly Economic Review of Uganda, Ethiopia, Somalia, Djibouti (ISSN 0142-4092); Quarterly Economic Review of Zaire, Rwanda, Burundi (ISSN 0142-4025)

330.9 320   US   ISSN 1356-4129
HC340.19.A1
COUNTRY REPORT. UKRAINE; analysis of economic and political trends every quarter. q. £225($405) includes Country Profile. Belarus, Moldova. Economist Intelligence Unit, 111 W. 57th St., New York, NY 10019. TEL 212-554-0600; 800-938-4685. FAX 212-586-1182. TELEX 175567. URL: http://www.eiu.com. (UK addr.: Economist Intelligence Unit Ltd., Subscriptions Dept., P.O. Box 200, Harold Hill, Romford, Essex RM3 8UX, England. TEL 44-1708-381-444. FAX 44-1708-371-850) illus.; stat.
●Also available online. Vendor(s): Knight-Ridder Information, Inc., Lexis-Nexis.
  Supersedes in part (in 1995): Country Report. Ukraine, Belarus, Moldova (ISSN 1350-7192); Which superseded in part (in 1992): Country Report. Commonwealth of Independent States; Which was formerly (until 1991): Country Report. U S S R (ISSN 0269-5480); Quarterly Economic Review of U S S R (ISSN 0142-3967)
  Description: Analyzes the current political and economic climate as well as short-term economic projections.

330.9 320   US   ISSN 0269-5162
HC415.36.A1
COUNTRY REPORT. UNITED ARAB EMIRATES; analysis of economic and political trends every quarter. 1952. q. £225($405) includes Country Profile. United Arab Emirates. Economist Intelligence Unit, 111 W. 57th St., New York, NY 10019. TEL 212-554-0600; 800-938-4685. FAX 212-586-1182. TELEX 175567. URL: http://www.eiu.com. (UK addr.: Economist Intelligence Unit Ltd., Subscriptions Dept., P.O. Box 200, Harold Hill, Romford, Essex RM3 8UX, England. TEL 44-1708-381-444. FAX 44-1708-371-850) illus.; stat.
●Also available online. Vendor(s): Knight-Ridder Information, Inc., Lexis-Nexis.
—BLDSC (3481.901210).
  Formerly: Quarterly Economic Review of United Arab Emirates (ISSN 0141-8416)
  Description: Analyzes the current political and economic climate as well as short-term economic projections.

330.9 320   US   ISSN 0269-5472
HC251
COUNTRY REPORT. UNITED KINGDOM; analysis of economic and political trends every quarter. 1952. q. £215($395) includes Country Profile. United Kingdom. Economist Intelligence Unit, 111 W. 57th St., New York, NY 10019. TEL 212-554-0600; 800-938-4685. FAX 212-586-1182. TELEX 175567. (UK addr.: Economist Intelligence Unit Ltd., Subscriptions Dept., P.O. Box 200, Harold Hill, Romford, Essex RM3 8UX, England. TEL 44-1708-381-444. FAX 44-1708-371-850) illus.; stat.
●Also available online. Vendor(s): Knight-Ridder Information, Inc., Lexis-Nexis.
—BLDSC (3481.901250).
  Formerly: Quarterly Economic Review of United Kingdom (ISSN 0142-3959)
  Description: Analyzes the United Kingdom's current political and economic climate as well as short-term economic projections.

BUSINESS AND ECONOMICS — ECONOMIC SITUATION AND CONDITIONS

330.9 320 US ISSN 0269-6185
HC101
COUNTRY REPORT. UNITED STATES OF AMERICA; analysis of economic and political trends every quarter. 1952. q. £225($405) includes Country Profile. United States of America. Economist Intelligence Unit, 111 W. 57th St., New York, NY 10019. TEL 212-554-0600; 800-938-4685. FAX 212-586-1182. TELEX 175567. URL: http://www.eiu.com. (UK addr.: Economist Intelligence Unit Ltd., Subscriptions Dept., P.O. Box 200, Harold Hill, Romford, Essex RM3 8UX, England. TEL 44-1708-381444. FAX 44-1708-371850) illus.; stat.
●Also available online. Vendor(s): Knight-Ridder Information, Inc., Lexis-Nexis.
Formerly: Quarterly Economic Review of United States of America (ISSN 0481-2018)
Description: Analyzes the U.S. current political and economic climate, as well as short-term economic projections.

330.9 320 US ISSN 0269-6177
HC231
COUNTRY REPORT. URUGUAY, PARAGUAY; analysis of economic and political trends every quarter. 1952. q. £225($405) includes Country Profile. Uruguay, Paraguay. Economist Intelligence Unit, 111 W. 57th St., New York, NY 10019. TEL 212-554-0600. FAX 212-586-1182. TELEX 175567. URL: http://www.eiu.com. (UK addr.: Economist Intelligence Unit Ltd., Subscriptions Dept., P.O. Box 200, Harold Hill, Romford, Essex RM3 8UX, England. TEL 44-1708-381-444. FAX 44-1708-371-850) illus.; stat.
●Also available online. Vendor(s): Knight-Ridder Information, Inc., Lexis-Nexis.
—BLDSC (3481.901290).
Formerly: Quarterly Economic Review of Uruguay, Paraguay (ISSN 0142-4440)
Description: Analyzes the current political and economic climate as well as short-term economic projections.

330.9 320 US ISSN 1366-4158
COUNTRY REPORT. UZBEKISTAN; analysis of economic and political trends every quarter. q. £225($405) Economist Intelligence Unit, 111 W. 57th St., New York, NY 10019. TEL 212-554-0600; 800-938-4685. FAX 212-586-1182. TELEX 175567. URL: http://www.eiu.com. (UK addr.: Economist Intelligence Unit Ltd., Subscriptions Dept., P.O. Box 200, Harold Hill, Romford, Essex RM3 8UX, England. TEL 44-1708-381-444. FAX 44-1708-371-850)
Supersedes in part (in 1997): Country Report. Kyrgyz Republic, Tajikistan, Turkmenistan, Uzbekistan; Which superseded in part (in 1996): Country Report. Central Asian Republics: Kazakhstan, Kyrgyz Republic, Tajikistan, Turkmenistan, Uzbekistan; Which superseded in part (in 1995): Country Report. Georgia, Armenia, Azerbaijan, Central Asian Republics; Superseded in part (in 1992): Country Report. Commonwealth of Independent States; Which was formerly (until 1991): Country Report U S S R (ISSN 0269-5480); Quarterly Economic Review of U S S R (ISSN 0142-3967).

330.9 320 US ISSN 1350-7133
HC236
COUNTRY REPORT. VENEZUELA; analysis of economic and political trends every quarter. 1952. q. £225($405) includes Country Profile. Venezuela. Economist Intelligence Unit, 111 W. 57th St., New York, NY 10019. TEL 212-554-0600; 800-938-4685. FAX 212-586-1182. TELEX 175567. URL: http://www.eiu.com. (UK addr.: Economist Intelligence Unit Ltd., Subscriptions Dept., P.O. Box 200, Harold Hill, Romford, Essex RM3 8UX, England. TEL 44-1708-381-444. FAX 44-1708-371-850) illus.; stat.
●Also available online. Vendor(s): Knight-Ridder Information, Inc., Lexis-Nexis.
—BLDSC (3481.901370).
Supersedes in part (in 1992): Country Report. Venezuela, Suriname, Netherlands Antilles (ISSN 0269-6754); Which was formerly: Quarterly Economic Review of Venezuela, Suriname, Netherlands Antilles (ISSN 0264-9675)
Description: Analyzes Venezuela's current political and economic climate as well as short-term economic projections.

330.9 320 US ISSN 1356-403X
HC444.A1
COUNTRY REPORT. VIETNAM; analysis of economic and political trends every quarter. q. £225($405) Economist Intelligence Unit, 111 W. 57th St., New York, NY 10019. TEL 212-554-0600; 800-938-4685. FAX 212-586-1182. TELEX 175567. URL: http://www.eiu.com. (U.K. addr.: Economist Intelligence Unit Ltd., Subscriptions Dept., P.O. Box 200, Harold Hill, Romford, Essex RM3 8UX, England. TEL 44-1708-381444. FAX 44-1708-371850)
—BLDSC (3481.901400).
Supersedes in part (in 1995): Country Report. Indochina: Vietnam, Laos, Cambodia (ISSN 0269-5677); Which was formerly: Quarterly Economic Review of Indochina: Vietnam, Laos, Cambodia (ISSN 0142-4076)
Description: Analyzes the current political and economic climate, as well as short-term economic projections.

330.9 320 US ISSN 1350-7087
COUNTRY REPORT. ZAMBIA, ZAIRE; analysis of economic and political trends every quarter. 1952. q. £225($405) includes Country Profile. Zambia; Country Profile. Zaire. Economist Intelligence Unit, 111 W. 57th St., New York, NY 10019. TEL 212-554-0600; 800-938-4685. FAX 212-586-1182. TELEX 175567. URL: http://www.eiu.com. (UK addr.: Economist Intelligence Unit Ltd., Subscriptions Dept., P.O. Box 200, Harold Hill, Romford, Essex RM3 8UX, England. TEL 44-1708-381-444. FAX 44-1708-371-850) illus.; stat.
●Also available online. Vendor(s): Knight-Ridder Information, Inc., Lexis-Nexis.
Supersedes (in 1992): Country Report. Zambia (ISSN 0269-4271); Incorporates in part (in 1992): Country Report. Zaire, Rwanda, Burundi (ISSN 0269-5510); Which was formerly: Quarterly Economic Review of Zambia (ISSN 0142-4467); Quarterly Economic Review of Zaire, Rwanda, Burundi (ISSN 0142-4025)
Description: Analyzes the current political and economic climate as well as short-term economic projections.

330.9 320 US ISSN 1350-7095
HC910.A1
COUNTRY REPORT. ZIMBABWE; analysis of economic and political trends every quarter. 1952. q. £225($405) includes Country Profile. Zimbabwe, Malawi. Economist Intelligence Unit, 111 W. 57th St., New York, NY 10019. TEL 212-554-0600; 800-938-4685. FAX 212-586-1182. TELEX 175567. URL: http://www.eiu.com. (UK addr. Economist Intelligence Unit Ltd., Subscriptions Dept., P.O. Box 200, Harold Hill, Romford, Essex RM3 8UX, England. TEL 44-1708-381-444. FAX 44-1708-371-850) illus.; stat.
●Also available online. Vendor(s): Knight-Ridder Information, Inc., Lexis-Nexis.
—BLDSC (3481.901550).
Supersedes in part (in 1992): Country Report. Zimbabwe, Malawi (ISSN 0269-4255); Which was formerly: Quarterly Economic Review of Zimbabwe, Malawi (ISSN 0266-4372)

330 320 US
COUNTRY REPORTS; analysis of economic and political trends every quarter. (Series consists of 99 vols. covering developments in 180 countries) 1952. q. £225($405) per vol. Economist Intelligence Unit, 111 W. 57th St., New York, NY 10019. TEL 212-554-0600; 800-938-4685. FAX 212-586-1182. TELEX 175567. URL: http://www.eiu.com. (UK addr.: Economist Intelligence Unit Ltd., Subscription Dept., P.O. Box 200, Harold Hill, Romford, Essex RM3 8UX, England. TEL 44-1708-381-444. FAX 44-1708-371-850) charts; illus.; mkt.; stat. circ. 40,000. (also avail. in microform from WMP) **Indexed:** Key to Econ.Sci., So.Pac.Per.Ind.
●Also available online. Vendor(s): Knight-Ridder Information, Inc., Lexis-Nexis.
Also available on CD-ROM.
Formerly: Quarterly Economic Reviews (ISSN 0033-5495)
Description: Analysis of international economic and political trends.

330.9 332 US
COUNTRY RISK SERVICE. (Covers 82 countries) q. £375($595) per vol. Economist Intelligence Unit, 111 W. 57th St., New York, NY 10019. TEL 212-554-0600; 800-938-4685. FAX 212-586-1182. TELEX 175567. URL: http://www.eiu.com. (UK addr.: Economist Intelligence Unit Ltd., Subscriptions Dept., P.O. Box 200, Harold Hill, Romford, Essex RM3 8UX, England. TEL 44-1708-381-444. FAX 44-1708-371-850)
●Also available online. Vendor(s): Lexis-Nexis.
Description: Two-year forecasting service assesses the solvency of 82 developing and indebted countries. Focuses on predicting growth, budget deficits, trade and current accounts, foreign financing requirements and sources, and debt service for each country.

330.9 332 US ISSN 1351-6752
HC815.A1
COUNTRY RISK SERVICE. ALGERIA. q. £375($595) Economist Intelligence Unit, 111 w. 57th St., New York, NY 10019. TEL 212-554-0600; 800-938-4685. FAX 212-586-1182. TELEX 175567. URL: http://www.eiu.com. (UK addr.: Economist Intelligence Unit Ltd., Subscriptions Dept., P.O. Box 200, Harold Hill, Romford, Essex RM3 8UX, England. TEL 44-1708-381-444. FAX 44-1708-371-850) (also avail. in diskette format)
●Also available online. Vendor(s): Lexis-Nexis.
Description: Focuses on predicting growth, budget deficits, trade and current accounts, foreign financing requirements and sources, and debt service for Algeria.

330.9 332 US ISSN 1351-6760
HC950.A1
COUNTRY RISK SERVICE. ANGOLA. q. £375($595) Economist Intelligence Unit, 111 W. 57th St., New York, NY 10019. TEL 212-554-0600; 800-938-4685. FAX 212-586-1182. TELEX 175567. URL: http://www.eiu.com. (UK addr.: Economist Intelligence Unit Ltd., Subscriptions Dept., P.O. Box 200, Harold Hill, Romford, Essex RM3 8UX, England. TEL 44-1708-381-444. FAX 44-1708-371-850) (also avail. in diskette format)
●Also available online. Vendor(s): Lexis-Nexis.
Description: Focuses on predicting growth, budget deficits, trade and current accounts, foreign financing requirements and sources, and debt service for Angola.

330.9 332 US ISSN 1351-6779
HC171
COUNTRY RISK SERVICE. ARGENTINA. q. £375($595) Economist Intelligence Unit, 111 W. 57th St., New York, NY 10019. TEL 212-554-0600; 800-938-4685. FAX 212-586-1182. TELEX 175567. URL: http://www.eiu.com. (UK addr.: Economist Intelligence Unit Ltd., Subscriptions Dept., P.O. Box 200, Harold Hill, Romford, Essex RM3 8UX, England. TEL 44-1708-381-444. FAX 44-1708-371-850) (also avail. in diskette format)
●Also available online. Vendor(s): Lexis-Nexis.
Description: Focuses on predicting growth, budget deficits, trade and current accounts, foreign financing requirements and sources, and debt service for Argentina.

330.9 332 US ISSN 1351-6787
HC601
COUNTRY RISK SERVICE. AUSTRALIA. q. £375($595) Economist Intelligence Unit, 111 W. 57th St., New York, NY 10019. TEL 212-554-0600; 800-938-4685. FAX 212-586-1182. TELEX 175567. URL: http://www.eiu.com. (UK addr.: Economist Intelligence Unit Ltd., Subscriptions Dept., P.O. Box 200, Harold Hill, Romford, Essex RM3 8UX, England. TEL 44-1708-381-444. FAX 44-1708-371-850) (also avail. in diskette format)
●Also available online. Vendor(s): Lexis-Nexis.
Description: Focuses on predicting growth, budget deficits, trade and current accounts, foreign financing requirements and sources, and debt service for Australia

BUSINESS AND ECONOMICS — ECONOMIC SITUATION AND CONDITIONS

330.9 332 US ISSN 1365-4756
COUNTRY RISK SERVICE. BAHRAIN. q. £375($595) Economist Intelligence Unit, 111 W. 57th St., New York, NY 10019. TEL 212-554-0600; 800-938-4685. FAX 212-586-1182. TELEX 175567. URL: http://www.eiu.com. (U.K. addr.: Economist Intelligence Unit Ltd., Subscriptions Dept., P.O. Box 200, Harold Hill, Romford, Essex RM3 8UX, England. TEL 44-1708-381481. FAX 44-1708-371850)
  Supersedes in part (in 1997): Country Risk Service. Bahrain, Oman, Qatar.

330.9 332 US ISSN 1351-6809
HC440.8.A1
COUNTRY RISK SERVICE. BANGLADESH. q. £375($595) Economist Intelligence Unit, 111 W. 57th St., New York, NY 10019. TEL 212-554-0600; 800-938-4685. FAX 212-586-1182. TELEX 175567. URL: http://www.eiu.com. (UK addr.: Economist Intelligence Unit Ltd., Subscriptions Dept., P.O. Box 200, Harold Hill, Romford, Essex RM3 8UX, England. TEL 44-1708-381-444. FAX 44-1708-371-850) (also avail. in diskette format)
  ●Also available online. Vendor(s): Lexis-Nexis.
  Description: Focuses on predicting growth, budget deficits, trade and current accounts, foreign financing requirements and sources, and debt service for Bangladesh.

330.9 332 US ISSN 1351-6817
HC181
COUNTRY RISK SERVICE. BOLIVIA. q. £375($595) Economist Intelligence Unit, 111 W. 57th St., New York, NY 10019. TEL 212-554-0600; 800-938-4685. FAX 212-586-1182. TELEX 175567. URL: http://www.eiu.com. (UK addr.: Economist Intelligence Unit Ltd., Subscriptions Dept., P.O. Box 200, Harold Hill, Romford, Essex RM3 8UX, England. TEL 44-1708-381-444. FAX 44-1708-371-850) (also avail. in diskette format)
  ●Also available online. Vendor(s): Lexis-Nexis.
  Description: Focuses on predicting growth, budget deficits, trade and current accounts, foreign financing requirements and sources, and debt service for Bolivia.

330.9 332 US ISSN 1354-5647
COUNTRY RISK SERVICE. BOTSWANA. 1994. q. £375($595) Economist Intelligence Unit, 111 W. 57th St., New York, NY 10019. TEL 212-554-0600; 800-938-4685. FAX 212-586-1182. TELEX 175567. URL: http://www.eiu.com. (U.K. addr.: Economist Intelligence Unit Ltd., Subscriptions Dept., P.O. Box 200, Harold Hill, Romford, Essex RM3 8UX, England. TEL 44-1708-381444. FAX 44-1708-371850)

330.9 332 US ISSN 1351-6825
HC186
COUNTRY RISK SERVICE. BRAZIL. q. £375($595) Economist Intelligence Unit, 111 W. 57th St., New York, NY 10019. TEL 212-554-0600; 800-938-4685. FAX 212-586-1182. TELEX 175567. URL: http://www.eiu.com. (UK addr.: Economist Intelligence Unit Ltd., Subscriptions Dept., P.O. Box 200, Harold Hill, Romford, Essex RM3 8UX, England. TEL 44-1708-381-444. FAX 44-1708-371-850) (also avail. in diskette format)
  ●Also available online. Vendor(s): Lexis-Nexis.
  Description: Focuses on predicting growth, budget deficits, trade and current accounts, foreign financing requirements and sources, and debt service for Brazil.

330.9 332 US ISSN 1351-6833
HC403.A1
COUNTRY RISK SERVICE. BULGARIA. q. £375($595) Economist Intelligence Unit, 111 W. 57th St., New York, NY 10019. TEL 212-554-0600; 800-938-4685. FAX 212-586-1182. TELEX 175567. URL: http://www.eiu.com. (UK addr.: Economist Intelligence Unit Ltd., Subscriptions Dept., P.O. Box 200, Harold Hill, Romford, Essex RM3 8UX, England. TEL 44-1708-381-444. FAX 44-1708-371-850) (also avail. in diskette format)
  ●Also available online. Vendor(s): Lexis-Nexis.
  Description: Focuses on predicting growth, budget deficits, trade and current accounts, foreign financing requirements and sources, and debt service for Bulgaria.

330.9 332 US ISSN 1351-6841
HC995.A1
COUNTRY RISK SERVICE. CAMEROON. q. £375($595) Economist Intelligence Unit, 111 W. 57th St., New York, NY 10019. TEL 212-554-0600; 800-938-4685. FAX 212-586-1182. TELEX 175567. URL: http://www.eiu.com. (UK addr.: Economist Intelligence Unit Ltd., Subscriptions Dept., P.O. Box 200, Harold Hill, Romford, Essex RM3 8UX, England. TEL 44-1708-381-444. FAX 44-1708-371-850) (also avail. in diskette format)
  ●Also available online. Vendor(s): Lexis-Nexis.
  Description: Focuses on predicting growth, budget deficits, trade and current accounts, foreign financing requirements and sources, and debt service for Cameroon.

330.9 332 US ISSN 1351-685X
HC191
COUNTRY RISK SERVICE. CHILE. q. £375($595) Economist Intelligence Unit, 111 W. 57th St., New York, NY 10019. TEL 212-554-0600; 800-938-4685. FAX 212-586-1182. TELEX 175567. URL: http://www.eiu.com. (UK addr.: Economist Intelligence Unit Ltd., Subscriptions Dept., P.O. Box 200, Harold Hill, Romford, Essex RM3 8UX, England. TEL 44-1708-381-444. FAX 44-1708-371-850) (also avail. in diskette format)
  ●Also available online. Vendor(s): Lexis-Nexis.
  Description: Focuses on predicting growth, budget deficits, trade and current accounts, foreign financing requirements and sources, and debt service for Chile.

330.9 332 US ISSN 1351-6868
HC426
COUNTRY RISK SERVICE. CHINA. q. £375($595) Economist Intelligence Unit, 111 W. 57th St., New York, NY 10019. TEL 212-554-0600; 800-938-4685. FAX 212-586-1182. TELEX 175567. URL: http://www.eiu.com. (UK addr.: Economist Intelligence Unit Ltd., Subscriptions Dept., P.O. Box 200, Harold Hill, Romford, Essex RM3 8UX, England. TEL 44-1708-381-444. FAX 44-1708-371-850) (also avail. in diskette format)
  ●Also available online. Vendor(s): Lexis-Nexis.
  Description: Focuses on predicting growth, budget deficits, trade and current accounts, foreign financing requirements and sources and debt service for China.

330.9 332 US ISSN 1351-6876
HC196
COUNTRY RISK SERVICE. COLOMBIA. q. £375($595) Economist Intelligence Unit, 111 W. 57th St., New York, NY 10019. TEL 212-554-0600; 800-938-4685. FAX 212-586-1182. TELEX 175567. URL: http://www.eiu.com. (UK addr.: Economist Intelligence Unit Ltd., Subscriptions Dept., P.O. Box 200, Harold Hill, Romford, Essex RM3 8UX, England. TEL 44-1708-381-444. FAX 44-1708-371-850) (also avail. in diskette format)
  ●Also available online. Vendor(s): Lexis-Nexis.
  Description: Focuses on predicting growth, budget deficits, trade and current accounts, foreign financing requirements and sources, and debt service for Colombia.

330.9 332 US ISSN 1351-6884
COUNTRY RISK SERVICE. CONGO. q. £375($595) Economist Intelligence Unit, 111 W. 57th St., New York, NY 10019. TEL 212-554-0600; 800-938-4685. FAX 212-586-1182. TELEX 175567. URL: http://www.eiu.com. (UK addr.: Economist Intelligence Unit Ltd., Subscriptions Dept., P.O. Box 200, Harold Hill, Romford, Essex RM3 8UX, England. TEL 322-289194) (also avail. in diskette format)
  ●Also available online. Vendor(s): Lexis-Nexis.
  Description: Focuses on predicting growth, budget deficits, trade and current accounts, foreign financing requirements and sources, and debt service for the Congo.

330.9 332 US ISSN 1351-6892
HC143.A1
COUNTRY RISK SERVICE. COSTA RICA. q. £375($595) Economist Intelligence Unit, 111 W. 57th St., New York, NY 10019. TEL 212-554-0600; 800-938-4685. FAX 212-586-1182. TELEX 175567. URL: http://www.eiu.com. (UK addr.: Economist Intelligence Unit Ltd., Subscriptions Dept., P.O. Box 200, Harold Hill, Romford, Essex RM3 8UX, England. TEL 44-1708-381-444. FAX 44-1708-371-850) (also avail. in diskette format)
  ●Also available online. Vendor(s): Lexis-Nexis.
  Description: Focuses on predicting growth, budget deficits, trade and current accounts, foreign financing requirements and sources, and debt service for Costa Rica.

330.9 332 US ISSN 1351-6906
HC1025.A1
COUNTRY RISK SERVICE. COTE D'IVOIRE. q. £345($545) Economist Intelligence Unit, 111 W. 57th St., New York, NY 10019. TEL 212-554-0600; 800-938-4685. FAX 212-586-1182. TELEX 175567. URL: http://www.eiu.com. (UK addr.: Economist Intelligence Unit Ltd., Subscriptions Dept., P.O. Box 200, Harold Hill, Romford, Essex RM3 8UX, England. TEL 44-1708-381-444. FAX 44-1708-371-850) (also avail. in diskette format)
  ●Also available online. Vendor(s): Lexis-Nexis.
  Description: Focuses on predicting growth, budget deficits, trade and current accounts, foreign financing requirements and sources, and debt service for Cote d'Ivoire.

330.9 332 US ISSN 1351-6914
HC415.2.A1
COUNTRY RISK SERVICE. CYPRUS. q. £375($595) Economist Intelligence Unit, 111 W. 57th St., New York, NY 10019. TEL 212-554-0600; 800-938-4685. FAX 212-586-1182. TELEX 175567. URL: http://www.eiu.com. (UK addr.: Economist Intelligence Unit Ltd., Subscriptions Dept., P.O. Box 200, Harold Hill, Romford, Essex RM3 8UX, England. TEL 44-1708-381-444. FAX 44-1708-371-850) (also avail. in diskette format)
  ●Also available online. Vendor(s): Lexis-Nexis.
  Description: Focuses on predicting growth, budget deficits, trade and current accounts, foreign financing requirements and sources, and debt service for Cyprus.

330.9 332 US ISSN 1351-6922
HC271.2
COUNTRY RISK SERVICE. CZECH REPUBLIC. q. £375($595) Economist Intelligence Unit, 111 W. 57th St., New York, NY 10019. TEL 212-554-0600; 800-938-4685. FAX 212-586-1182. TELEX 175567. URL: http://www.eiu.com. (UK addr.: Economist Intelligence Unit Ltd., Subscriptions Dept., P.O. Box 200, Harold Hill, Romford, Essex RM3 8UX, England. TEL 44-1708-381-444. FAX 44-1708-371-850) (also avail. in diskette format)
  ●Also available online. Vendor(s): Lexis-Nexis.
  Description: Focuses on predicting growth, budget deficits, trade and current accounts, foreign financing requirements and sources, and debt service for the Czech Republic.

330.9 332 US ISSN 1351-6930
HC153.5.A1
COUNTRY RISK SERVICE. DOMINICAN REPUBLIC. q. £375($595) Economist Intelligence Unit, 111 W. 57th St., New York, NY 10019. TEL 212-554-0600; 800-938-4685. FAX 212-586-1182. TELEX 175567. URL: http://www.eiu.com. (UK addr.: Economist Intelligence Unit Ltd., Subscriptions Dept., P.O. Box 200, Harold Hill, Romford, Essex RM3 8UX, England. TEL 44-1708-381-444. FAX 44-1708-371-850) (also avail. in diskette format)
  ●Also available online. Vendor(s): Lexis-Nexis.
  Description: Focuses on predicting growth, budget deficits, trade and current accounts, foreign financing requirements and sources, and debt service for the Dominican Republic.

BUSINESS AND ECONOMICS — ECONOMIC SITUATION AND CONDITIONS

330.9 332   US   ISSN 1351-6949
HC201
COUNTRY RISK SERVICE. ECUADOR. q. £375($595) Economist Intelligence Unit, 111 W. 57th St., New York, NY 10019. TEL 212-554-0600; 800-938-4685. FAX 212-586-1182. TELEX 175567. URL: http://www.eiu.com. (UK addr.: Economist Intelligence Unit Ltd., Subscriptions Dept., P.O. Box 200, Harold Hill, Romford, Essex RM3 8UX, England. TEL 44-1708-381-444. FAX 44-1708-371-850) (also avail. in diskette format)
●Also available online. Vendor(s): Lexis-Nexis.
  Description: Focuses on predicting growth, budget deficits, trade and current accounts, foreign financing requirements and sources, and debt service for Ecuador.

330.9 332   US   ISSN 1351-6981
HC291
COUNTRY RISK SERVICE. GHANA. q. £375($595) Economist Intelligence Unit, 111 W. 57th St., New York, NY 10019. TEL 212-554-0600; 800-938-4685. FAX 212-586-1182. TELEX 175567. URL: http://www.eiu.com. (UK addr.: Economist Intelligence Unit Ltd., Subscriptions Dept., P.O. Box 200, Harold Hill, Romford, Essex RM3 8UX, England. TEL 44-1708-381-444. FAX 44-1708-371-850) (also avail. in diskette format)
●Also available online. Vendor(s): Lexis-Nexis.
  Description: Focuses on predicting growth, budget deficits, trade and current accounts, foreign financing requirements and sources, and debt service for Ghana.

330.9 332   US   ISSN 1351-7031
HC300.2
COUNTRY RISK SERVICE. HUNGARY. q. £375($595) Economist Intelligence Unit, 111 W. 57th St., New York, NY 10019. TEL 212-554-0600; 800-938-4685. FAX 212-586-1182. TELEX 165567. URL: http://www.eiu.com. (UK addr.: Economist Intelligence Unit Ltd., Subscriptions Dept., P.O. Box 200, Harold Hill, Romford, Essex RM3 8UX, England. TEL 44-1708-381-444. FAX 44-1708-371-850) (also avail. in diskette format)
●Also available online. Vendor(s): Lexis-Nexis.
  Description: Focuses on predicting growth, budget deficits, trade and current accounts, foreign financing requirements and sources, and debt service for Hungary.

330.9 332   US   ISSN 1351-6957
HC830.A1
COUNTRY RISK SERVICE. EGYPT. q. £375($595) Economist Intelligence Unit, 111 W. 57th St., New York, NY 10019. TEL 212-554-0600; 800-938-4685. FAX 212-586-1182. TELEX 175567. URL: http://www.eiu.com. (UK addr.: Economist Intelligence Unit Ltd., Subscriptions Dept., P.O. Box 200, Harold Hill, Romford, Essex RM3 8UX, England. TEL 44-1708-381-444. FAX 44-1708-371-850) (also avail. in diskette format)
●Also available online. Vendor(s): Lexis-Nexis.
  Description: Focuses on predicting growth, budget deficits, trade and current accounts, foreign financing requirements and sources, and debt service for Egypt.

330.9 332   US   ISSN 1351-699X
COUNTRY RISK SERVICE. GREECE. q. £375($595) Economist Intelligence Unit, 111 W. 57th St., New York, NY 10019. TEL 212-554-0600; 800-938-4685. FAX 212-586-1182. TELEX 175567. URL: http://www.eiu.com. (UK addr.: Economist Intelligence Unit Ltd., Subscriptions Dept., P.O. Box 200, Harold Hill, Romford, Essex RM3 8UX, England. TEL 44-1708-381-444. FAX 44-1708-371-850) (also avail. in diskette format)
●Also available online. Vendor(s): Lexis-Nexis.
  Description: Focuses on predicting growth, budget deficits, trade and current accounts, foreign financing requirements and sources, and debt service for Greece.

330.9 332   US   ISSN 1351-704X
HC431
COUNTRY RISK SERVICE. INDIA. q. £375($595) Economist Intelligence Unit, 111 W. 57th St., New York, NY 10019. TEL 212-554-0600; 800-938-4685. FAX 212-586-1182. TELEX 175567. URL: http://www.eiu.com. (UK addr.: Economist Intelligence Unit Ltd., Subscriptions Dept., P.O. Box 200, Harold Hill, Romford, Essex RM3 8UX, England. TEL 44-1708-381-444. FAX 44-1708-371-850) (also avail. in diskette format)
●Also available online. Vendor(s): Lexis-Nexis.
  Description: Focuses on predicting growth, budget deficits, trade and current accounts, foreign financing requirements and sources, and debt service for India.

330.9 332   US   ISSN 1351-6965
HC148.A1
COUNTRY RISK SERVICE. EL SALVADOR. q. £375($595) Economist Intelligence Unit, 111 W. 57th St., New York, NY 10019. TEL 212-554-0600; 800-938-4685. FAX 212-586-1182. TELEX 175567. URL: http://www.eiu.com. (UK addr.: Economist Intelligence Unit Ltd., Subscriptions Dept., P.O. Box 200, Harold Hill, Romford, Essex RM3 8UX, England. TEL 44-1708-381-444. FAX 44-1708-371-850) (also avail. in diskette format)
●Also available online. Vendor(s): Lexis-Nexis.
  Description: Focuses on predicting growth, budget deficits, trade and current accounts, foreign financing requirements and sources, and debt service for El Salvador.

330.9 332   US   ISSN 1351-7007
COUNTRY RISK SERVICE. GUATEMALA. q. £375($595) Economist Intelligence Unit, 111 W. 57th St., New York, NY 10019. TEL 212-554-0600; 800-938-4685. FAX 212-586-1182. TELEX 175567. URL: http://www.eiu.com. (UK addr.: Economist Intelligence Unit Ltd., Subscriptions Dept., P.O. Box 200, Harold Hill, Romford, Essex RM3 8UX, England. TEL 44-1708-381-444. FAX 44-1708-371-850) (also avail. in diskette format)
●Also available online. Vendor(s): Lexis-Nexis.
  Description: Focuses on predicting growth, budget deficits, trade and current accounts, foreign financing requirements and sources, and debt service for Guatemala.

330.9 332   US   ISSN 1351-7058
HC446
COUNTRY RISK SERVICE. INDONESIA. q. £375($595) Economist Intelligence Unit, 111 W. 57th St., New York, NY 10019. TEL 212-554-0600; 800-938-4685. FAX 212-586-1182. TELEX 175567. URL: http://www.eiu.com. (UK addr.: Economist Intelligence Unit Ltd., Subscriptions Dept., P.O. Box 200, Harold Hill, Romford, Essex RM3 8UX, England. TEL 44-1708-381-444. FAX 44-1708-371-850) (also avail. in diskette format)
●Also available online. Vendor(s): Lexis-Nexis.
  Description: Focuses on predicting growth, budget deficits, trade and current accounts, foreign financing requirements and sources, and debt service for Indonesia.

330.9 332   US   ISSN 1366-4301
COUNTRY RISK SERVICE. FORMER YUGOSLAV REPUBLICS: SERBIA, MONTENEGRO, MACEDONIA. q. £375($595) Economist Intelligence Unit, 111 W. 57th St., New York, NY 10019. TEL 212-554-0600; 800-938-4685. FAX 212-586-1182. TELEX 175567. URL: http://www.eiu.com. (UK addr.: Economist Intelligence Unit Ltd., Subscriptions Dept., P.O. Box 200, Harold Hill, Romford, Essex RM3 8UX, England. TEL 44-1708-381-444. FAX 44-1708-371-850) (also avail. in diskette format)
●Also available online. Vendor(s): Lexis-Nexis.
  Former titles: Country Risk Service. Former Yugoslav Republics (ISSN 1351-7538) & Country Risk Service. Yugoslav Republics.
  Description: Focuses on predicting growth, budget deficits, trade and current accounts, foreign financing requirements and sources, and debt service for the former Yugoslav Republics.

330.9 332   US   ISSN 1351-7015
HC145.A1
COUNTRY RISK SERVICE. HONDURAS. q. £375($595) Economist Intelligence Unit, 111 W. 57th St., New York, NY 10019. TEL 212-554-0600; 800-938-4685. FAX 212-586-1182. TELEX 175567. URL: http://www.eiu.com. (UK addr.: Economist Intelligence Unit Ltd., Subscriptions Dept., P.O. Box 200, Harold Hill, Romford, Essex RM3 8UX, England. TEL 44-1708-381-444. FAX 44-1708-371-850) (also avail. in diskette format)
●Also available online. Vendor(s): Lexis-Nexis.
  Description: Focuses on predicting growth, budget deficits, trade and current accounts, foreign financing requirements and sources, and debt service for Honduras.

330.9 332   US   ISSN 1351-7066
HC471
COUNTRY RISK SERVICE. IRAN. q. £375($595) Economist Intelligence Unit, 111 W. 57th St., New York, NY 10019. TEL 212-554-0600; 800-938-4685. FAX 212-586-1182. TELEX 175567. URL: http://www.eiu.com. (UK addr.: Economist Intelligence Unit Ltd., Subscriptions Dept., P.O. Box 200, Harold Hill, Romford, Essex RM3 8UX, England. TEL 44-1708-381-444. FAX 44-1708-371-850) (also avail. in diskette format)
●Also available online. Vendor(s): Lexis-Nexis.
  Description: Focuses on predicting growth, budget deficits, trade and current accounts, foreign financing requirements and sources, and debt service for Iran.

330.9 332   US   ISSN 1351-6973
HC975.A1
COUNTRY RISK SERVICE. GABON. q. £375($595) Economist Intelligence Unit, 111 W. 57th St., New York, NY 10019. TEL 212-554-0600; 800-938-4685. FAX 212-538-1182. TELEX 175567. URL: http://www.eiu.com. (UK addr.: Economist Intelligence Unit Ltd., Subscriptions Dept., P.O. Box 200, Harold Hill, Romford, Essex RM3 8UX, England. TEL 44-1708-381-444. FAX 44-1708-371-850) (also avail. in diskette format)
●Also available online. Vendor(s): Lexis-Nexis.
  Description: Focuses on predicting growth, budget deficits, trade and current accounts, foreign financing requirements and sources, and debt service for Gabon.

330.9 332   US   ISSN 1351-7023
HC470.3.A1
COUNTRY RISK SERVICE. HONG KONG. q. £375($595) Economist Intelligence Unit, 111 W. 57th St., New York, NY 10019. TEL 212-554-0600; 800-938-4685. FAX 212-586-1182. TELEX 175567. URL: http://www.eiu.com. (UK addr.: Economist Intelligence Unit Ltd., Subscriptions Dept., P.O. Box 200, Harold Hill, Romford, Essex RM3 8UX, England. TEL 44-1708-381-444. FAX 44-1708-371-850) (also avail. in diskette format)
●Also available online. Vendor(s): Lexis-Nexis.
  Description: Focuses on predicting growth, budget deficits, trade and current accounts, foreign financing requirements and sources, and debt service for Hong Kong.

330.9 332   US   ISSN 1351-7074
HC415.4.A1
COUNTRY RISK SERVICE. IRAQ. q. £375($595) Economist Intelligence Unit, 111 W. 57th St., New York, NY 10019. TEL 212-554-0600; 800-938-4685. FAX 212-586-1182. TELEX 175567. URL: http://www.eiu.com. (UK addr.: Economist Intelligence Unit Ltd., Subscriptions Dept., P.O. Box 200, Harold Hill, Romford, Essex RM3 8UX, England. TEL 44-1708-381-444. FAX 44-1708-371-850) (also avail. in diskette format)
●Also available online. Vendor(s): Lexis-Nexis.
  Description: Focuses on predicting growth, budget deficits, trade and current accounts, foreign financing requirements and sources, and debt service for Iraq.

330.9 332   US   ISSN 1351-7082
HC415.25.A1
COUNTRY RISK SERVICE. ISRAEL. q. £375($595)
Economist Intelligence Unit, 111 W. 57th St., New York, NY 10019. TEL 212-554-0600; 800-938-4685. FAX 212-586-1182. TELEX 175567. URL: http://www.eiu.com. (UK addr.: Economist Intelligence Unit Ltd., Subscriptions Dept., P.O. Box 200, Harold Hill, Romford, Essex RM3 8UX, England. TEL 44-1708-381-444. FAX 44-1708-371-850) (also avail. in diskette format)
●Also available online. Vendor(s): Lexis-Nexis.
  Description: Focuses on predicting growth, budget deficits, trade and current accounts, foreign financing requirements and sources, and debt service for Israel.

330.9 332   US   ISSN 1351-7090
HC154.A1
COUNTRY RISK SERVICE. JAMAICA. q. £375($595)
Economist Intelligence Unit, 111 W. 57th St., New York, NY 10019. TEL 212-554-0600; 800-938-4685. FAX 212-586-1182. TELEX 175567. URL: http://www.eiu.com. (UK addr.: Economist Intelligence Unit Ltd., Subscriptions Dept., P.O. Box 200, Harold Hill, Romford, Essex RM3 8UX, England. TEL 44-1708-381-444. FAX 44-1708-371-850) (also avail. in diskette format)
●Also available online. Vendor(s): Lexis-Nexis.
  Description: Focuses on predicting growth, budget deficits, trade and current accounts, foreign financing requirements and sources, and debt service for Jamaica.

330.9 332   US   ISSN 1351-7104
HC415.26.A1
COUNTRY RISK SERVICE. JORDAN. q. £375($595)
Economist Intelligence Unit, 111 W. 57th St., New York, NY 10019. TEL 212-554-0600; 800-938-4685. FAX 212-586-1182. TELEX 175567. URL: http://www.eiu.com. (UK addr.: Economist Intelligence Unit Ltd., Subscriptions Dept., P.O. Box 200, Harold Hill, Romford, Essex RM3 8UX, England. TEL 44-1708-381-444. FAX 44-1708-371-850) (also avail. in diskette format)
●Also available online. Vendor(s): Lexis-Nexis.
  Description: Focuses on predicting growth, budget deficits, trade and current accounts, foreign financing requirements and sources, and debt service for Jordan.

330.9 332   US   ISSN 1351-7112
HC420.5.A1
COUNTRY RISK SERVICE. KAZAKHSTAN. q. £375($595)
Economist Intelligence Unit, 111 W. 57th St., New York, NY 10019. TEL 212-554-0600; 800-938-4685. FAX 212-586-1182. TELEX 175567. URL: http://www.eiu.com. (UK addr.: Economist Intelligence Unit Ltd., Subscriptions Dept., P.O. Box 200, Harold Hill, Romford, Essex RM3 8UX, England. TEL 44-1708-381-444. FAX 44-1708-371-850) (also avail. in diskette format)
●Also available online. Vendor(s): Lexis-Nexis.
  Description: Focuses on predicting growth, budget deficits, trade and current accounts, foreign financing requirements and sources, and debt service for Kazakhstan.

330.9 332   US   ISSN 1351-7120
HC865.A1
COUNTRY RISK SERVICE. KENYA. q. £375($595)
Economist Intelligence Unit, 111 W. 57th St., New York, NY 10019. TEL 212-554-0600; 800-938-4685. FAX 212-586-1182. TELEX 175567. URL: http://www.eiu.com. (UK addr.: Economist Intelligence Unit Ltd., Subscriptions Dept., P.O. Box 200, Harold Hill, Romford, Essex RM3 8UX, England. TEL 44-1708-381-444. FAX 44-1708-371-850) (also avail. in diskette format)
●Also available online. Vendor(s): Lexis-Nexis.
  Description: Focuses on predicting growth, budget deficits, trade and current accounts, foreign financing requirements and sources, and debt service for Kenya.

330.9 332   US   ISSN 1351-7139
HC415.39.A1
COUNTRY RISK SERVICE. KUWAIT. q. £375($595)
Economist Intelligence Unit, 111 W. 57th St., New York, NY 10019. TEL 212-554-0600; 800-938-4685. FAX 212-586-1182. TELEX 175567. URL: http://www.eiu.com. (UK addr.: Economist Intelligence Unit Ltd., Subscriptions Dept., P.O. Box 200, Harold Hill, Romford, Essex RM3 8UX, England. TEL 44-1708-381-444. FAX 44-1708-371-850) (also avail. in diskette format)
●Also available online. Vendor(s): Lexis-Nexis.
  Description: Focuses on predicting growth, budget deficits, trade and current accounts, foreign financing requirements and sources, and debt service for Kuwait.

330.9 332   US   ISSN 1351-7147
HC825.A1
COUNTRY RISK SERVICE. LIBYA. q. £375($595)
Economist Intelligence Unit, 111 W. 57th St., New York, NY 10019. TEL 212-554-0600; 800-938-4685. FAX 212-586-1182. TELEX 175567. URL: http://www.eiu.com. (UK addr.: Economist Intelligence Unit Ltd., Subscriptions Dept., P.O. Box 200, Harold Hill, Romford, Essex RM3 8UX, England. TEL 44-1708-381-444. FAX 44-1708-371-850) (also avail. in diskette format)
●Also available online. Vendor(s): Lexis-Nexis.
  Description: Focuses on predicting growth, budget deficits, trade and current accounts, foreign financing requirements and sources, and debt service for Libya.

330.9 332   US   ISSN 1351-7155
COUNTRY RISK SERVICE. MALAWI. q. £375($595)
Economist Intelligence Unit, 111 W. 57th St., New York, NY 10019. TEL 212-554-0600; 800-938-1182. FAX 212-586-1182. TELEX 175567. URL: http://www.eiu.com. (UK addr.: Economist Intelligence Unit Ltd., Subscriptions Dept., P.O. Box 200, Harold Hill, Romford, Essex RM3 8UX, England. TEL 44-1708-381-444. FAX 44-1708-371-850) (also avail. in diskette format)
●Also available online. Vendor(s): Lexis-Nexis.
  Description: Focuses on predicting growth, budget deficits, trade and current accounts, foreign financing requirements and sources, and debt service for Malawi.

330.9 332   US   ISSN 1351-7163
HC445.5.A1
COUNTRY RISK SERVICE. MALAYSIA. q. £375($595)
Economist Intelligence Unit, 111 W. 57th St., New York, NY 10019. TEL 212-554-0600; 800-938-4685. FAX 212-586-1182. TELEX 175567. URL: http://www.eiu.com. (UK addr.: Economist Intelligence Unit Ltd., Subscriptions Dept., P.O. Box 200, Harold Hill, Romford, Essex RM3 8UX, England. TEL 44-1708-381-444. FAX 44-1708-371-850) (also avail. in diskette format)
●Also available online. Vendor(s): Lexis-Nexis.
  Description: Focuses on predicting growth, budget deficits, trade and current accounts, foreign financing requirements and sources and debt service for Malaysia.

330.9 332   US   ISSN 1351-7171
HC131
COUNTRY RISK SERVICE. MEXICO. q. £375($595)
Economist Intelligence Unit, 111 W. 57th St., New York, NY 10019. TEL 212-554-0600; 800-938-4685. FAX 212-586-1182. TELEX 175567. URL: http://www.eiu.com. (UK addr.: Economist Intelligence Unit Ltd., Subscriptions Dept., P.O. Box 200, Harold Hill, Romford, Essex RM3 8UX, England. TEL 44-1708-381-444. FAX 44-1708-371-850) (also avail. in diskette format)
●Also available online. Vendor(s): Lexis-Nexis.
  Description: Focuses on predicting growth, budget deficits, trade and current accounts, foreign financing requirements and sources, and debt service for Mexico.

330.9 332   US   ISSN 1351-718X
COUNTRY RISK SERVICE. MOROCCO. q. £375($595)
Economist Intelligence Unit, 111 W. 57th St., New York, NY 10019. TEL 212-554-0600; 800-938-4685. FAX 212-586-1182. TELEX 175567. URL: http://www.eiu.com. (UK addr.: Economist Intelligence Unit Ltd., Subscriptions Dept., P.O. Box 200, Harold Hill, Romford, Essex RM3 8UX, England. TEL 44-1708-381-444. FAX 44-1708-371-850) (also avail. in diskette format)
●Also available online. Vendor(s): Lexis-Nexis.
  Description: Focuses on predicting growth, budget deficits, trade and current accounts, foreign financing requirements and sources, and debt service for Morocco.

330.9 332   US   ISSN 1351-7198
HC940.A1
COUNTRY RISK SERVICE. NAMIBIA. q. £375($595)
Economist Intelligence Unit, 111 W. 57th St., New York, NY 10019. TEL 212-586-0600; 800-938-4685. FAX 212-586-1182. TELEX 175567. URL: http://www.eiu.com. (UK addr.: Economist Intelligence Unit Ltd., Subscriptions Dept., P.O. Box 200, Harold Hill, Romford, Essex RM3 8UX, England. TEL 44-1708-381-444. FAX 44-1708-371-850) (also avail. in diskette format)
●Also available online. Vendor(s): Lexis-Nexis.
  Description: Focuses on predicting growth, budget deficits, trade and current accounts, foreign financing requirements and sources, and debt service for Namibia.

330.9 332   US   ISSN 1351-7201
HC661
COUNTRY RISK SERVICE. NEW ZEALAND. q. £375($595) Economist Intelligence Unit, 111 W. 57th St., New York, NY 10019. TEL 212-554-0600; 800-938-4685. FAX 212-586-1182. TELEX 175567. URL: http://www.eiu.com. (UK addr.: Economist Intelligence Unit Ltd., Subscriptions Dept., P.O. Box 200, Harold Hill, Romford, Essex RM3 8UX, England. TEL 44-1708-381-444. FAX 44-1708-371-850) (also avail. in diskette format)
●Also available online. Vendor(s): Lexis-Nexis.
  Description: Focuses on predicting growth, budget deficits, trade and current accounts, foreign financing requirements and sources, and debt service for New Zealand.

330.9 332   US   ISSN 1351-721X
HC146.A1
COUNTRY RISK SERVICE. NICARAGUA. q. £375($595)
Economist Intelligence Unit, 111 W. 57th St., New York, NY 10019. TEL 212-554-0600; 800-938-4685. FAX 212-586-1182. TELEX 175567. URL: http://www.eiu.com. (UK addr.: Economist Intelligence Unit Ltd., Subscriptions Dept., P.O. Box 200, Harold Hill, Romford, Essex RM3 8UX, England. TEL 44-1708-381-444. FAX 44-1708-371-850) (also avail. in diskette format)
●Also available online. Vendor(s): Lexis-Nexis.
  Description: Focuses on predicting growth, budget deficits, trade and current accounts, foreign financing requirements and sources, and debt service for Nicaragua.

330.9 332   US   ISSN 1351-7228
HC1055.A1
COUNTRY RISK SERVICE. NIGERIA. q. £375($595)
Economist Intelligence Unit, 111 W. 57th St., New York, NY 10019. TEL 212-554-0600; 800-938-4685. FAX 212-586-1182. TELEX 175567. URL: http://www.eiu.com. (UK addr.: Economist Intelligence Unit Ltd., Subscriptions Dept., P.O. Box 200, Harold Hill, Romford, Essex RM3 8UX, England. TEL 44-1708-381-444. FAX 44-1708-371-850) (also avail. in diskette format)
●Also available online. Vendor(s): Lexis-Nexis.
  Description: Focuses on predicting growth, budget deficits, trade and current accounts, foreign financing requirements and sources, and debt service for Nigeria.

330.9 332   US   ISSN 1365-4764
COUNTRY RISK SERVICE. OMAN. q. £375($595)
Economist Intelligence Unit, 111 W. 57th St., New York, NY 10019. TEL 212-554-0600; 800-938-4685. FAX 212-586-1182. URL: http://www.eiu.com. (UK addr.: Economist Intelligence Unit Ltd., Subscriptions Dept., P.O. Box 200, Harold Hill, Romford, Essex RM3 8UX, England. TEL 44-1708-381444. FAX 44-1708-371850)
  Supersedes in part (in 1997): Country Risk Service. Bahrain, Oman, Qatar.

BUSINESS AND ECONOMICS — ECONOMIC SITUATION AND CONDITIONS

330.9 332 US ISSN 1351-7236
HC440.5.A1
COUNTRY RISK SERVICE. PAKISTAN. q. £375($595) Economist Intelligence Unit, 111 W. 57th St., New York, NY 10019. TEL 212-554-0600; 800-938-4685. FAX 212-586-1182. TELEX 175567. URL: http://www.eiu.com. (UK addr.: Economist Intelligence Unit Ltd., Subscriptions Dept., P.O. Box 200, Harold Hill, Romford, Essex RM3 8UX, England. TEL 44-1708-381-444. FAX 44-1708-371-850) (also avail. in diskette format)
●Also available online. Vendor(s): Lexis-Nexis.
Description: Focuses on predicting growth, budget deficits, trade and current accounts, foreign financing requirements and sources and debt service for Pakistan.

330.9 332 US ISSN 1351-7244
HC147.A1
COUNTRY RISK SERVICE. PANAMA. q. £375($595) Economist Intelligence Unit, 111 W. 57th St., New York, NY 10019. TEL 212-554-0600; 800-938-4685. FAX 212-586-1182. TELEX 175567. URL: http://www.eiu.com. (UK addr.: Economist Intelligence Unit Ltd., Subscriptions Dept., P.O. Box 200, Harold Hill, Romford, Essex RM3 8UX, England. TEL 44-1708-381-444. FAX 44-1708-371-850) (also avail. in diskette format)
●Also available online. Vendor(s): Lexis-Nexis.
Description: Focuses on predicting growth, budget deficits, trade and current accounts, foreign financing requirements and sources, and debt service for Panama.

330.9 332 US ISSN 1351-7252
HC683.5.A1
COUNTRY RISK SERVICE. PAPUA NEW GUINEA. q. £375($595) Economist Intelligence Unit, 111 W. 57th St., New York, NY 10019. TEL 212-554-0600; 800-938-4685. FAX 212-586-1182. TELEX 175567. URL: http://www.eiu.com. (UK addr.: Economist Intelligence Unit Ltd., Subscriptions Dept., P.O. Box 200, Harold Hill, Romford, Essex RM3 8UX, England. TEL 44-1708-381-444. FAX 44-1708-371-850) (also avail. in diskette format)
●Also available online. Vendor(s): Lexis-Nexis.
Description: Focuses on predicting growth, budget deficits, trade and current accounts, foreign financing requirements and sources, and debt service for Papua New Guinea.

330.9 332 US ISSN 1351-7260
HC221
COUNTRY RISK SERVICE. PARAGUAY. q. £375($595) Economist Intelligence Unit, 111 W. 57th St., New York, NY 10019. TEL 212-554-0600; 800-938-4685. FAX 212-586-1182. TELEX 175567. URL: http://www.eiu.com. (UK addr.: Economist Intelligence Unit Ltd., Subscriptions Dept., P.O. Box 200, Harold Hill, Romford, Essex RM3 8UX, England. TEL 44-1708-381-444. FAX 44-1708-371-850) (also avail. in diskette format)
●Also available online. Vendor(s): Lexis-Nexis.
Description: Focuses on predicting growth, budget deficits, trade and current accounts, foreign financing requirements and sources, and debt service for Paraguay.

330.9 332 US ISSN 1351-7279
HC226
COUNTRY RISK SERVICE. PERU. q. £375($595) Economist Intelligence Unit, 111 W. 57th St., New York, NY 10019. TEL 212-554-0600; 800-938-4685. FAX 212-586-1182. TELEX 175567. URL: http://www.eiu.com. (UK addr.: Economist Intelligence Unit Ltd., Subscriptions Dept., P.O. Box 200, Harold Hill, Romford, Essex RM3 8UX, England. TEL 44-1708-381-444. FAX 44-1708-371-850) (also avail. in diskette format)
●Also available online. Vendor(s): Lexis-Nexis.
Description: Focuses on predicting growth, budget deficits, trade and current accounts, foreign financing requirements and sources, and debt service for Peru.

330.9 332 US ISSN 1351-7287
HC451
COUNTRY RISK SERVICE. PHILIPPINES. q. £375($595) Economist Intelligence Unit, 111 W. 57th St., New York, NY 10019. TEL 212-554-0600; 800-938-4685. FAX 212-8586-1182. TELEX 175567. URL: http://www.eiu.com. (UK addr.: Economist Intelligence Unit Ltd., Subscriptions Dept., P.O. Box 200, Harold Hill, Romford, Essex RM3 8UX, England. TEL 44-1708-381-444. FAX 44-1708-371-850) (also avail. in diskette format)
●Also available online. Vendor(s): Lexis-Nexis.
Description: Focuses on predicting growth, budget deficits, trade and current accounts, foreign financing requirements and sources and debt service for the Philippines.

330.9 332 US ISSN 1351-7295
HC340.3.A1
COUNTRY RISK SERVICE. POLAND. q. £375($595) Economist Intelligence Unit, 111 W. 57th St., New York, NY 10019. TEL 212-554-0600; 800-938-4685. FAX 212-586-1182. TELEX 175567. URL: http://www.eiu.com. (UK addr.: Economist Intelligence Unit Ltd., Subscriptions Dept., P.O. Box 200, Harold Hill, Romford, Essex RM3 8UX, England. TEL 44-1708-381-444. FAX 44-1708-371-850) (also avail. in diskette format)
●Also available online. Vendor(s): Lexis-Nexis.
Description: Focuses on predicting growth, budget deficits, trade and current accounts, foreign financing requirements and sources, and debt service for Poland.

330.9 332 US ISSN 1351-7309
HC391
COUNTRY RISK SERVICE. PORTUGAL. q. £375($595) Economist Intelligence Unit, 111 W. 57th St., New York, NY 10019. TEL 212-554-0600; 800-938-4685. FAX 212-586-1182. TELEX 175567. URL: http://www.eiu.com. (UK addr.: Economist Intelligence Unit Ltd., Subscriptions Dept., P.O. Box 200, Harold Hill, Romford, Essex RM3 8UX, England. TEL 44-1708-381-444. FAX 44-1708-371-850) (also avail. in diskette format)
●Also available online. Vendor(s): Lexis-Nexis.
Description: Focuses on predicting growth, budget deficits, trade and current accounts, foreign financing requirements and sources, and debt service for Portugal.

330.9 332 US ISSN 1365-4772
COUNTRY RISK SERVICE. QATAR. q. £375($595) Economist Intelligence Unit, 111 W. 57th St., New York, NY 10019. TEL 212-554-0600; 800-938-4685. FAX 212-586-1182. TELEX 175567. URL: http://www.eiu.com. (UK addr.: Economist Intelligence Unit Ltd., Subscriptions Dept., P.O. Box 200, Harold Hill, Romford, Essex RM3 8UX, England. TEL 44-1708-381-444. FAX 44-1708-371-850)
Supersedes in part (in 1997): Country Risk Service. Bahrain, Oman, Qatar.

330.9 332 US ISSN 1351-7317
HC405.A1
COUNTRY RISK SERVICE. ROMANIA. q. £375($595) Economist Intelligence Unit, 111 W. 57th St., New York, NY 10019. TEL 212-554-0600; 800-938-4685. FAX 212-586-1182. TELEX 175567. URL: http://www.eiu.com. (UK addr.: Economist Intelligence Unit Ltd., Subscriptions Dept., P.O. Box 200, Harold Hill, Romford, Essex RM3 8UX, England. TEL 44-1708-381-444. FAX 44-1708-371-850) (also avail. in diskette format)
●Also available online. Vendor(s): Lexis-Nexis.
Description: Focuses on predicting growth, budget deficits, trade and current accounts, foreign financing requirements and sources, and debt service for Romania.

330.9 332 US ISSN 1351-7325
HC340.12.A1
COUNTRY RISK SERVICE. RUSSIA. q. £375($595) Economist Intelligence Unit, 111 W. 57th St., New York, NY 10019. TEL 212-554-0600; 800-938-4685. FAX 212-586-1182. TELEX 175567. URL: http://www.eiu.com. (UK addr.: Economist Intelligence Unit Ltd., Subscriptions Dept., P.O. Box 200, Harold Hill, Romford, Essex RM3 8UX, England. TEL 44-1708-381-444. FAX 44-1708-371-850) (also avail. in diskette format)
●Also available online. Vendor(s): Lexis-Nexis.
Description: Focuses on predicting growth, budget deficits, trade and current accounts, foreign financing requirements and sources, and debt service for Russia.

330.9 332 US ISSN 1351-7333
HC415.33.A1
COUNTRY RISK SERVICE. SAUDI ARABIA. q. £375($595) Economist Intelligence Unit, 111 W. 57th St., New York, NY 10019. TEL 212-554-0600; 800-938-4685. FAX 212-586-1182. TELEX 175567. URL: http://www.eiu.com. (UK addr.: Economist Intelligence Unit Ltd., Subscriptions Dept., P.O. Box 200, Harold Hill, Romford, Essex RM3 8UX, England. TEL 44-1708-381-444. FAX 44-1708-371-850) (also avail. in diskette format)
●Also available online. Vendor(s): Lexis-Nexis.
Description: Focuses on predicting growth, budget deficits, trade and current accounts, foreign financing requirements and sources, and debt service for Saudi Arabia.

330.9 332 US ISSN 1351-7341
HC1045.A1
COUNTRY RISK SERVICE. SENEGAL. q. £375($595) Economist Intelligence Unit, 111 W. 57th St., New York, NY 10019. TEL 212-554-0600; 800-938-4685. FAX 212-586-1182. TELEX 175567. URL: http://www.eiu.com. (UK addr.: Economist Intelligence Unit Ltd., Subscriptions Dept., P.O. Box 200, Harold Hill, Romford, Essex RM3 8UX, England. TEL 44-1708-381-444. FAX 44-1708-371-850) (also avail. in diskette format)
●Also available online. Vendor(s): Lexis-Nexis.
Description: Focuses on predicting growth, budget deficits, trade and current accounts, foreign financing requirements and sources, and debt service for Senegal.

330.9 332 US ISSN 1351-735X
HC445.8.A1
COUNTRY RISK SERVICE. SINGAPORE. q. £375($595) Economist Intelligence Unit, 111 W. 57th St., New York, NY 10019. TEL 212-554-0600; 800-938-4685. FAX 212-586-1182. TELEX 175567. URL: http://www.eiu.com. (UK addr.: Economist Intelligence Unit Ltd., Subscriptions Dept., P.O. Box 200, Harold Hill, Romford, Essex RM3 8UX, England. TEL 44-1708-381-444. FAX 44-1708-371-850) (also avail. in diskette format)
●Also available online. Vendor(s): Lexis-Nexis.
Description: Focuses on predicting growth, budget deficits, trade and current accounts, foreign financing requirements and sources, and debt service for Singapore.

330.9 332 US ISSN 1351-7368
HC406.A1
COUNTRY RISK SERVICE. SLOVENIA. q. £375($595) Economist Intelligence Unit, 111 W. 57th St., New York, NY 10019. TEL 212-554-0600; 800-938-4685. FAX 212-586-1182. TELEX 175567. URL: http://www.eiu.com. (UK addr.: Economist Intelligence Unit Ltd., Subscriptions Dept., P.O. Box 200, Harold Hill, Romford, Essex RM3 8UX, England. TEL 44-1708-381-444. FAX 44-1708-371-850) (also avail. in diskette format)
●Also available online. Vendor(s): Lexis-Nexis.
Description: Focuses on predicting growth, budget deficits, trade and current accounts, foreign financing requirements and sources, and debt service for Slovenia.

330.9 332 US ISSN 1351-7376
HC905.A1
COUNTRY RISK SERVICE. SOUTH AFRICA. q. £375($595) Economist Intelligence Unit, 111 W. 57th St., New York, NY 10019. TEL 212-554-0600; 800-938-4685. FAX 212-586-1182. TELEX 175567. URL: http://www.eiu.com. (UK addr.: Economist Intelligence Unit Ltd., Subscriptions Dept., P.O. Box 200, Harold Hill, Romford, Essex RM3 8UX, England. TEL 44-1708-381-444. FAX 44-1708-371-850) (also avail. in diskette format)
●Also available online. Vendor(s): Lexis-Nexis.
Description: Focuses on predicting growth, budget deficits, trade and current accounts, foreign financing requirements and sources, and debt service for South Africa.

BUSINESS AND ECONOMICS — ECONOMIC SITUATION AND CONDITIONS

330.9 332   US   ISSN 1351-7384
HC466
COUNTRY RISK SERVICE. SOUTH KOREA. q. £375($595) Economist Intelligence Unit, 111 W. 57th St., New York, NY 10019. TEL 212-554-0600; 800-938-4685. FAX 212-586-1182. TELEX 175567. URL: http://www.eiu.com. (UK addr.: Economist Intelligence Unit Ltd., Subscriptions Dept., P.O. Box 200, Harold Hill, Romford, Essex RM3 8UX, England. TEL 44-1708-381-444. FAX 44-1708-371-850) (also avail. in diskette format)
●Also available online. Vendor(s): Lexis-Nexis.
   Description: Focuses on predicting growth, budget deficits, trade and current accounts, foreign financing requirements and sources, and debt service for South Korea.

330.9 332   US   ISSN 1351-7392
HC381
COUNTRY RISK SERVICE. SPAIN. q. £375($595) Economist Intelligence Unit, 111 W. 57th St., New York, NY 10019. TEL 212-554-0600; 800-938-4685. FAX 212-938-4685. TELEX 175567. URL: http://www.eiu.com. (UK addr.: Economist Intelligence Unit Ltd., Subscriptions Dept., P.O. Box 200, Harold Hill, Romford, Essex RM3 8UX, England. TEL 44-1708-381-444. FAX 44-1708-371-850) (also avail. in diskette format)
●Also available online. Vendor(s): Lexis-Nexis.
   Description: Focuses on predicting growth, budget deficits, trade and current accounts, foreign financing requirements and sources, and debt service for Spain.

330.9 332   US   ISSN 1351-7406
HC424.A1
COUNTRY RISK SERVICE. SRI LANKA. q. £375($595) Economist Intelligence Unit, 111 W. 57th St., New York, NY 10019. TEL 212-554-0600; 800-938-4685. FAX 212-586-1182. TELEX 175567. URL: http://www.eiu.com. (UK addr.: Economist Intelligence Unit Ltd., Subscriptions Dept., P.O. Box 200, Harold Hill, Romford, Essex RM3 8UX, England. TEL 44-1708-381-444. FAX 44-1708-371-850) (also avail. in diskette format)
●Also available online. Vendor(s): Lexis-Nexis.
   Description: Focuses on predicting growth, budget deficits, trade and current accounts, foreign financing requirements and sources, and debt service for Sri Lanka.

330.9 332   US   ISSN 1351-7414
HC835.A1
COUNTRY RISK SERVICE. SUDAN. q. £375($595) Economist Intelligence Unit, 111 W. 57th St., New York, NY 10019. TEL 212-554-0600; 800-938-4685. FAX 212-586-1182. TELEX 175567. URL: http://www.eiu.com. (UK addr.: Economist Intelligence Unit Ltd., Subscriptions Dept., P.O. Box 200, Harold Hill, Romford, Essex RM3 8UX, England. TEL 44-1708-381-444. FAX 44-1708-371-850) (also avail. in diskette format)
●Also available online. Vendor(s): Lexis-Nexis.
   Description: Focuses on predicting growth, budget deficits, trade and current accounts, foreign financing requirements and sources, and debt service for Sudan.

330.9 332   US   ISSN 1351-7422
HC415.23.A1
COUNTRY RISK SERVICE. SYRIA. q. £375($595) Economist Intelligence Unit, 111 W. 57th St., New York, NY 10019. TEL 212-554-0600; 800-938-4685. FAX 212-586-1182. TELEX 175567. URL: http://www.eiu.com. (UK addr.: Economist Intelligence Unit Ltd., Subscriptions Dept., P.O. Box 200, Harold Hill, Romford, Essex RM3 8UX, England. TEL 44-1708-381-444. FAX 44-1708-371-850) (also avail. in diskette format)
●Also available online. Vendor(s): Lexis-Nexis.
   Description: Focuses on predicting growth, budget deficits, trade and current accounts, foreign financing requirements and sources, and debt service for Syria.

330.9 332   US   ISSN 1351-7430
HC430.5.A1
COUNTRY RISK SERVICE. TAIWAN. q. £375($595) Economist Intelligence Unit, 111 W. 57th St., New York, NY 10019. TEL 212-554-0600; 800-938-4685. FAX 212-586-1182. TELEX 175567. URL: http://www.eiu.com. (UK addr.: Economist Intelligence Unit Ltd., Subscriptions Dept., P.O. Box 200, Harold Hill, Romford, Essex RM3 8UX, England. TEL 44-1708-381-444. FAX 44-1708-371-850) (also avail. in diskette format)
●Also available online. Vendor(s): Lexis-Nexis.
   Description: Focuses on predicting growth, budget deficits, trade and current accounts, foreign financing requirements and sources, and debt service for Taiwan.

330.9 332   US   ISSN 1351-7449
HC445.A1
COUNTRY RISK SERVICE. THAILAND. q. £375($595) Economist Intelligence Unit, 111 W. 57th St., New York, NY 10019. TEL 212-554-0600; 800-938-4685. FAX 212-586-1182. TELEX 175567. URL: http://www.eiu.com. (UK addr.: Economist Intelligence Unit Ltd., Subscriptions Dept., P.O. Box 200, Harold Hill, Romford, Essex RM3 8UX, England. TEL 44-1708-381-444. FAX 44-1708-371-850) (also avail. in diskette format)
●Also available online. Vendor(s): Lexis-Nexis.
   Description: Focuses on predicting growth, budget deficits, trade and current accounts, foreign financing requirements and sources, and debt service for Thailand.

330.9 332   US
COUNTRY RISK SERVICE. THE BALTIC REPUBLICS: LATVIA, ESTONIA, LITHUANIA. q. £375($595) Economist Intelligence Unit, 111 W. 57th St., New York, NY 10019. TEL 212-554-0600; 800-938-4685. FAX 212-586-1182. TELEX 175567. URL: http://www.eiu.com. (UK addr.: Economist Intelligence Unit Ltd., Subscriptions Dept., P.O. Box 200, Harold Hill, Romford, Essex RM3 8UX, England. TEL 44-1708-381-444. FAX 44-1708-371-850) (also avail. in diskette format)
●Also available online. Vendor(s): Lexis-Nexis.
   Formerly: Country Risk Service. Baltic Republics (ISSN 1351-6795)
   Description: Focuses on predicting growth, budget deficits, trade and current accounts, foreign financing requirements and sources, and debt service for the Baltic Republics.

330.9 332   US   ISSN 1351-7457
HC157.3.A1
COUNTRY RISK SERVICE. TRINIDAD AND TOBAGO. q. £375($595) Economist Intelligence Unit, 111 W. 57th St., New York, NY 10019. TEL 212-554-0600; 800-938-4685. FAX 212-586-1182. TELEX 175567. URL: http://www.eiu.com. (UK addr.: Economist Intelligence Unit Ltd., Subscriptions Dept., P.O. Box 200, Harold Hill, Romford, Essex RM3 8UX, England. TEL 44-1708-381-444. FAX 44-1708-371-850) (also avail. in diskette format)
●Also available online. Vendor(s): Lexis-Nexis.
   Description: Focuses on predicting growth, budget deficits, trade and current accounts, foreign financing requirements and sources, and debt service for Trinidad and Tobago.

330.9 332   US   ISSN 1351-7465
HC820.A1
COUNTRY RISK SERVICE. TUNISIA. q. £375($595) Economist Intelligence Unit, 111 W. 57th St., New York, NY 10019. TEL 212-554-0600; 800-938-4685. FAX 212-586-1182. TELEX 175567. URL: http://www.eiu.com. (UK addr.: Economist Intelligence Unit Ltd., Subscriptions Dept., P.O. Box 200, Harold Hill, Romford, Essex RM3 8UX, England. TEL 44-1708-381-444. FAX 44-1708-371-850) (also avail. in diskette format)
●Also available online. Vendor(s): Lexis-Nexis.
   Description: Focuses on predicting growth, budget deficits, trade and current accounts, foreign financing requirements and sources, and debt service for Tunisia.

330.9 332   US   ISSN 1351-7473
HC491
COUNTRY RISK SERVICE. TURKEY. q. £375($595) Economist Intelligence Unit, 111 W. 57th St., New York, NY 10019. TEL 212-554-0600; 800-938-4685. FAX 212-586-1182. TELEX 175567. URL: http://www.eiu.com. (UK addr.: Economist Intelligence Unit Ltd., Subscriptions Dept., P.O. Box 200, Harold Hill, Romford, Essex RM3 8UX, England. TEL 44-1708-381-444. FAX 44-1708-371-850) (also avail. in diskette format)
●Also available online. Vendor(s): Lexis-Nexis.
   Description: Focuses on predicting growth, budget deficits, trade and current accounts, foreign financing requirements and sources, and debt service for Turkey.

330.9 332   US   ISSN 1351-7481
HC340.19.A1
COUNTRY RISK SERVICE. UKRAINE. q. £375($595) Economist Intelligence Unit, 111 W. 57th St., New York, NY 10019. TEL 212-554-0600; 800-938-4685. FAX 212-586-1182. TELEX 175567. URL: http://www.eiu.com. (UK addr.: Economist Intelligence Unit Ltd., Subscriptions Dept., P.O. Box 200, Harold Hill, Romford, Essex RM3 8UX, England. TEL 44-1708-381-444. FAX 44-1708-371-850) (also avail. in diskette format)
●Also available online. Vendor(s): Lexis-Nexis.
   Description: Focuses on predicting growth, budget deficits, trade and current accounts, foreign financing requirements and sources, and debt service for the Ukraine.

330.9 332   US   ISSN 1351-749X
HC415.36.A1
COUNTRY RISK SERVICE. UNITED ARAB EMIRATES. q. £375($595) Economist Intelligence Unit, 111 W. 57th St., New York, NY 10019. TEL 212-554-0600; 800-938-4685. FAX 212-586-1182. TELEX 175567. URL: http://www.eiu.com. (UK addr.: Economist Intelligence Unit Ltd., Subscriptions Dept., P.O. Box 200, Harold Hill, Romford, Essex RM3 8UX, England. TEL 44-1708-381-444. FAX 44-1708-371-850) (also avail. in diskette format)
●Also available online. Vendor(s): Lexis-Nexis.
   Description: Focuses on predicting growth, budget deficits, trade and current accounts, foreign financing requirements and sources, and debt service for the United Arab Emirates.

330.9 332   US   ISSN 1351-7503
HC231
COUNTRY RISK SERVICE. URUGUAY. q. £375($595) Economist Intelligence Unit, 111 W. 57th St., New York, NY 10019. TEL 212-554-0600; 800-938-4685. FAX 212-586-1182. TELEX 175567. URL: http://www.eiu.com. (UK addr.: Economist Intelligence Unit Ltd., Subscriptions Dept., P.O. Box 200, Harold Hill, Romford, Essex RM3 8UX, England. TEL 44-1708-381-444. FAX 44-1708-371-850) (also avail. in diskette format)
●Also available online. Vendor(s): Lexis-Nexis.
   Description: Focuses on predicting growth, budget deficits, trade and current accounts, foreign financing requirements and sources, and debt service for Uruguay.

330.9 332   US   ISSN 1351-7511
HC236
COUNTRY RISK SERVICE. VENEZUELA. q. £375($595) Economist Intelligence Unit, 111 W. 57th St., New York, NY 10019. TEL 212-554-0600; 800-938-4685. FAX 212-586-1182. TELEX 175567. URL: http://www.eiu.com. (UK addr.: Economist Intelligence Unit Ltd., Subscriptions Dept., P.O. Box 200, Harold Hill, Romford, Essex RM3 8UX, England. TEL 44-1708-381-444. FAX 44-1708-371-850) (also avail. in diskette format)
●Also available online. Vendor(s): Lexis-Nexis.
   Description: Focuses on predicting growth, budget deficits, trade and current accounts, foreign financing requirements and sources, and debt service for Venezuela.

330.9 332   US
COUNTRY RISK SERVICE. VIETNAM. q. £375($595) Economist Intelligence Unit, 111 W. 57th St., New York, NY 10019. TEL 212-554-0600; 800-938-4685. FAX 212-586-1182. TELEX 175567. URL: http://www.eiu.com. (U.K. addr.: Economist Intelligence Unit Ltd., Subscriptions Dept., P.O. Box 200, Harold Hill, Romford, Essex RM3 8UX, England. TEL 44-1708381444. FAX 44-1708-371850)

BUSINESS AND ECONOMICS — ECONOMIC SITUATION AND CONDITIONS

330.9 332   US   ISSN 1351-752X
HC415.34.A1
COUNTRY RISK SERVICE. YEMEN. q. £375($595) Economist Intelligence Unit, 111 W. 57th St., New York, NY 10019. TEL 212-554-0600; 800-938-4685. FAX 212-586-1182. TELEX 175567. URL: http://www.eiu.com. (UK addr.: Economist Intelligence Unit Ltd., Subscriptions Dept., P.O. Box 200, Harold Hill, Romford, Essex RM3 8UX, England. TEL 44-1708-381-444. FAX 44-1708-371-850) (also avail. in diskette format)
●Also available online. Vendor(s): Lexis-Nexis.
Description: Focuses on predicting growth, budget deficits, trade and current accounts, foreign financing requirements and sources, and debt service for Yemen.

330.9 332   US   ISSN 1351-7546
HC955.A1
COUNTRY RISK SERVICE. ZAIRE. q. £375($595) Economist Intelligence Unit, 111 W. 57th St., New York, NY 10019. TEL 212-554-0600; 800-938-4685. FAX 212-586-1182. TELEX 175567. URL: http://www.eiu.com. (UK addr.: Economist Intelligence Unit Ltd., Subscriptions Dept., P.O. Box 200, Harold Hill, Romford, Essex RM3 8UX, England. TEL 44-1708-381-444. FAX 44-1708-371-850) (also avail. in diskette format)
●Also available online. Vendor(s): Lexis-Nexis.
Description: Focuses on predicting growth, budget deficits, trade and current accounts, foreign financing requirements and sources, and debt service for Zaire.

330.9 332   US   ISSN 1351-7554
HC915.A1
COUNTRY RISK SERVICE. ZAMBIA. q. £375($595) Economist Intelligence Unit, 111 W. 57th St., New York, NY 10019. TEL 212-554-0600; 800-938-4685. FAX 212-586-1182. TELEX 175567. URL: http://www.eiu.com. (UK addr.: Economist Intelligence Unit Ltd., Subscriptions Dept., P.O. Box 200, Harold Hill, Romford, Essex RM3 8UX, England. TEL 44-1708-381-444. FAX 44-1708-371-850) (also avail. in diskette format)
●Also available online. Vendor(s): Lexis-Nexis.
Description: Focuses on predicting growth, budget deficits, trade and current accounts, foreign financing requirements and sources, and debt service for Zambia.

330.9 332   US   ISSN 1351-7562
HC910.A1
COUNTRY RISK SERVICE. ZIMBABWE. q. £375($595) Economist Intelligence Unit, 111 W. 57th St., New York, NY 10019. TEL 212-554-0600; 800-938-4685. FAX 212-586-1182. TELEX 175567. URL: http://www.eiu.com. (UK addr.: Economist Intelligence Unit Ltd., Subscriptions Dept., P.O. Box 200, Harold Hill, Romford, Essex RM3 8UX, England. TEL 44-1708-381-444. FAX 44-1708-371-850) (also avail. in diskette format)
●Also available online. Vendor(s): Lexis-Nexis.
Description: Focuses on predicting growth, budget deficits, trade and current accounts, foreign financing requirements and sources, and debt service for Zimbabwe.

330.9   US
COUNTY ECONOMIC INDICATORS. a. $3.50. Oregon Economic Development Department, 775 Summer St., N.E., Salem, OR 97310. TEL 503-373-1290. FAX 503-581-5115. URL: http://www.econ.state.or.us/stats.htm.
●Also available online.

330.9   MR   ISSN 0752-1855
COURRIER ECONOMIQUE. (Text in French) w. 22 av. de l'Armee Royale, Casablanca, Morocco. adv.

330.9   CK   ISSN 0120-3576
HC196
COYUNTURA ECONOMICA. Fourth no. of each vol. entitled: Coyuntura Latinoamericana. 1970. q. $180 (effective 1994). Fedesarrollo - Fundacion para la Educacion Superior y el Desarrollo, Calle 78 No. 9-91, Apdo. Aereo 75074, Bogota, Colombia. TEL 3125300. FAX 212-6073. Ed. Patricia Correa. adv.; bk.rev. circ. 1,500. Indexed: Int.Lab.Doc., P.A.I.S.For.Lang.Ind., Potato Abstr., Rural Recreat.Tour.Abstr., World Agri.Econ.& Rural Sociol.Abstr. **Document type:** academic/scholarly publication.
—SWETS.

330.9   US   ISSN 0197-2375
CRAIN'S CLEVELAND BUSINESS. 1980. w. $45. Crain Communications, Inc. (Detroit), 1400 Woodbridge Ave., Detroit, MI 48207-3187. TEL 800-678-9595. FAX 216-694-4264. (Subscr. to: 965 E. Jefferson Ave., Detroit, MI 48207-9966) Ed. Mark Dodosh. adv.; bk.rev.; charts; illus. circ. 24,916. (tabloid format; also avail. in microform from UMI; reprint service avail. from UMI) Indexed: Alloys Ind., Eng.Mat.Abstr., Met.Abstr., Met.Abstr.Ind., Nonfer.Met.Alert, PCC Alert, Steels Alert, Tr.& Indus.Ind., World Alum.Abstr. **Document type:** newspaper.
●Also available online. Vendor(s): Information Access Co., Knight-Ridder Information, Inc., Lexis-Nexis. —UMI. CCC.
Description: Business newspaper concentrating its editorial coverage on Cuyahoga county and the six contiguous counties.

CRED-ALERT. see BUSINESS AND ECONOMICS — Banking And Finance

330.9   GW
CREDIT-CURIER. 1983. m. DM.96. Creditreform Neuss Frormann KG, Zollstr. 2, 41460 Neuss, Germany. TEL 49-2131-220388. FAX 49-2131-25676. TELEX 8517585. Ed. Norbert Becker-Harzheim. adv.; bk.rev. circ. 4,400. **Document type:** corporate report.

CREDIT SUISSE. BULLETIN. see BUSINESS AND ECONOMICS — Banking And Finance

CRITIQUE REGIONALE; cahiers de sociologie et d'economie regionales. see SOCIOLOGY

330.9   MX   ISSN 0186-0445
HC131
CUADERNO DE INFORMACION OPORTUNA. 1978. m. Mex.$144000($184) Instituto Nacional de Estadistica, Geografia e Informatica, Secretaria de Programacion y Presupuesto, Prol. Heroe de Nacozari 2301 Sur, Puerta 11, Acceso, 20270 Aguascalientes Ags., Mexico. TEL 91-49-18-19-48. FAX 91-491-80739. circ. 1,150.

330.9   MX   ISSN 0186-047X
CUADERNO DE INFORMACION OPORTUNA REGIONAL. 1984. q. Mex.$26($10) Instituto Nacional de Estadistica, Geografia e Informatica, Secretaria de Programacion y Presupuesto, Prol. Heroe de Nacozari 2301 Sur, Puerta 11, Acceso, 20270 Aguascalientes Ags., Mexico. TEL 91-49-18-19-48. FAX 91-491-80739. circ. 500.

330.9   AG   ISSN 0327-9693
CUADERNOS DE ECONOMIA POLITICA. 1985. 3/yr. Universidad Nacional de Lujan, C.C. 221, 6700 Lujan, Argentina. Ed. Felix Marcos.
Description: Presents research works and analysis on diverse aspects of the contemporary economic situation.

330.9   VE   ISSN 0798-5126
CUADERNOS NUEVO SUR. 1992. q. Fundacion Nuevo Sur, Apdo. 63185, Caracas 1067-A, Venezuela. TEL 58-2-9512787. Ed. Francisco Mieres.
Description: Presents analysis, information and work studies on the Latin American political and economic situation.

CUESTIONES ECONOMICAS. see BUSINESS AND ECONOMICS — Banking And Finance

381   NA
CURACAO TRADE AND INDUSTRY ASSOCIATION. NEWSLETTER. (Text in English) 1972. m. Curacao Trade and Industry Association, Pietermaai 21, Willemstad, Curacao, Netherlands Antilles. Ed. V. M. Oenes. **Document type:** newsletter.
Formerly: Trade and Industry of Curacao. Monthly Publication.

330.9   RM   ISSN 1220-4684
CURIERUL NATIONAL. (Supplement avail.: Pop Rock'n Show (ISSN 1221-1850)) 1990. d. 64296 lei (effective 1997). (Editura Presa Libera) Curierul National S.A., Ministerului St. No. 2-4, Bucharest, Romania. TEL 40-0-4016159512. FAX 40-0-4012102577. TELEX 10250. E-mail: curierul.national@logic.sprint.com. (Subscr. to: Rodipet S.A., Piata Presei Libera No. 1, Bucharest, Romania. FAX 40-0-4016153229) Ed. Valentin Paunescu. adv.: page lei4000000($4000); adv. contact: Ecaterina Rachieru. tele.rev, mkt. circ. 50,000. cols./p.: 9; pp./issue: 16. (also avail. in microfilm) **Document type:** newspaper.
Description: Covers microeconomics for private economists, businessmen, bankers and politicians.

330.9   SW   ISSN 0346-9468
CURRENT BUSINESS IN SWEDEN. (Text in English) 1973. q. SEK 250. Svenska Handelsbanken, Economic Research Dept., S-106 70 Stockholm, Sweden. FAX 46-8-6119869. Ed. Lars Heikensten. charts; stat.

CURRENT POLITICS AND ECONOMICS OF EUROPE. see POLITICAL SCIENCE

CURRENT POLITICS AND ECONOMICS OF JAPAN. see POLITICAL SCIENCE

330.9   CY   ISSN 0253-8555
HC415.2.A1
CYPRUS. DEPARTMENT OF STATISTICS AND RESEARCH. ECONOMIC INDICATORS. (Text in English) 1978. bi-m. £C4. Ministry of Finance, Department of Statistics and Research, 13 Lord Byron Ave., Nicosia, Cyprus. TEL 357-2-302349. FAX 357-2-456712. **Document type:** government publication.
Supersedes: Cyprus. Department of Statistics and Research. Short-Term Industrial Indicators.
Description: Brings together selected economic indicators to provide a picture of significant short-term developments in the Cypriot economy.

330.9   CY
CYPRUS. FIVE YEAR PLANS. Variant title: Emergency Economic Action Plans. (Text in English, Greek) 1961. quinquennial. free. Government Printing Office, Nicosia, Cyprus. TEL 357-2-302202. FAX 357-2-303175. circ. 2,000. **Document type:** government publication.

330   BL
D E S E D.* (Includes supplements) 1965. q. free. Banco do Brasil S.A., Departamento Geral de Selecao e Desenvolvimento do Pessoal, Setor Bancario Sul, Lote 23, Bloco C, C.P. 562, Brasilia D.F., Brazil. Ed.Bd. bk.rev.; illus. circ. 113,000.

332   JA   ISSN 0385-2350
D K B ECONOMIC REPORT. (Dai-Ichi Kangyo Bank) (Text in English) 1971. m. free. D K B Research Institute Corp., 1-1-5, Uchisaiwai-cho, Chiyoda-ku, Tokyo 100, Japan. FAX 81-3-3596-3198. Ed. Masato Nagasawa. R&P contact: Masato Nagasawa. charts; illus.; stat. circ. 10,500. **Document type:** newsletter, corporate report.
Formerly: N K B Research Monthly (ISSN 0027-6774)

THE D L A FINANCIAL. see ETHNIC INTERESTS

330.9   US
D R I - MCGRAW-HILL COST AND PRICE REVIEW. Key Title: Cost and Price Review. q. D R I - McGraw-Hill, 24 Hartwell Ave., Lexington, MA 02173. TEL 617-863-5100. FAX 617-860-6332. TELEX 200 284. Ed. Mark Ulmer. (back issues avail.)
Formed by the merger of: D R I McGraw-Hill Cost and Price Review: U.S. Long-Range Focus (ISSN 1052-1283); D R I - McGraw-Hill Cost and Price Review: U S Short-Range Focus (ISSN 1052-1704);
Formerly: U S Cost Forecasting Service Long-Term Review.

330.9   US   ISSN 1052-1690
HB231
D R I - MCGRAW-HILL COST AND PRICE REVIEW: INTERNATIONAL FOCUS. Key Title: Cost and Price Review: International Focus. q. D R I - McGraw-Hill, 24 Hartwell Ave., Lexington, MA 02173. TEL 617-863-5100. FAX 617-860-6332. TELEX 200 284. Ed. Mark Ulmer. **Document type:** trade publication.
Formerly: International Cost Forecasting Service Review.

BUSINESS AND ECONOMICS — ECONOMIC SITUATION AND CONDITIONS

330.9   US   ISSN 1054-495X
HD3881
D R I - MCGRAW-HILL COST AND PRICE REVIEW: UTILITY FOCUS. Key Title: Cost and Price Review: Utility Focus. q. D R I - McGraw-Hill, 24 Hartwell Ave., Lexington, MA 02173. TEL 617-863-5100. FAX 617-860-6332. TELEX 200-284. Ed. Nariman Behravesh. (back issues avail.) **Document type:** trade publication.
    Formerly: Utility Cost Forecasting Service Review.

330.9 339   US
D R I - MCGRAW-HILL COUNTRY REPORTS. q. D R I - McGraw-Hill, 24 Hartwell Ave., Lexington, MA 02173. TEL 617-863-5100. FAX 617-860-6332. TELEX 200 284. Ed. Nariman Behravesh. **Document type:** trade publication.
    Former titles (until 1992): D R I - McGraw-Hill European Review; Data Resources European Review; European Review (ISSN 0276-7430); D R I European Review (ISSN 0362-4730)

D R I - MCGRAW-HILL ENERGY REVIEW. see *ENERGY*

330.9   US
D R I - MCGRAW-HILL EUROPEAN INDUSTRY REVIEW. q. D R I - McGraw-Hill, 24 Hartwell Ave., Lexington, MA 02173. TEL 617-863-5100. FAX 617-860-6332. TELEX 200 284. Ed. Elizabeth Waelbroeck-Rocha. **Document type:** trade publication.
    Former titles (until 1992): D R I - McGraw-Hill Industry Review; European Sectoral Service Review.

330.9 339   US
D R I - MCGRAW-HILL GLOBAL RISK REPORT. s-a. D R I - McGraw-Hill, 24 Hartwell Ave., Lexington, MA 02173. TEL 617-863-5100. FAX 617-860-6332. TELEX 200 284. Ed. Eric Rice. (back issues avail.) **Document type:** trade publication.
    Former titles: D R I - McGraw-Hill Latin American Country Reports & D R I - McGraw-Hill Latin American Review; Data Resources Latin American Review.

330.9 339   US   ISSN 0743-7323
HC106.6
D R I - MCGRAW-HILL REVIEW OF THE U S ECONOMY. Key Title: Review of the U S Economy. 1972. m. D R I - McGraw-Hill, 24 Hartwell Ave., Lexington, MA 02173. TEL 617-863-5100. FAX 617-860-6332. TELEX 200 284. Ed. Cynthia Latta. **Document type:** trade publication.
    Former titles: Data Resources Review of the U S Economy (ISSN 0197-6966); (until 1979): Data Resources Review (ISSN 0092-5462)

330.9 339   US
D R I - MCGRAW-HILL REVIEW OF THE U S ECONOMY: LONG RANGE FOCUS. Key Title: Review of the U S Economy: Long Range Focus. 1976. s-a. D R I - McGraw-Hill, 24 Hartwell Ave., Lexington, MA 02173. TEL 617-863-5100. FAX 617-860-6332. TELEX 200 284. Ed. Cynthia Latta. **Document type:** trade publication.
    Former titles: D R I - McGraw-Hill U S Long-Term Review; Data Resources U S Long-Term Review; Data Resources U S Long-Term Bulletin (ISSN 0362-6199)

330.9 339   US
D R I - MCGRAW-HILL U S FORECAST SUMMARY. m. D R I - McGraw-Hill, 24 Hartwell Ave., Lexington, MA 02173. TEL 617-863-5100. FAX 617-860-6332. TELEX 200 284. Ed. Cynthia Latta. (back issues avail.) **Document type:** trade publication.
    ●Also available online.

D R I - MCGRAW-HILL U S MARKETS REVIEW: INDUSTRY FOCUS. see *BUSINESS AND ECONOMICS — Production Of Goods And Services*

D R I - MCGRAW-HILL U S MARKETS REVIEW: METRO FOCUS. see *BUSINESS AND ECONOMICS — Production Of Goods And Services*

D R I - MCGRAW-HILL U S MARKETS REVIEW: MIDWEST. STATE FOCUS. see *BUSINESS AND ECONOMICS — Production Of Goods And Services*

D R I - MCGRAW-HILL U S MARKETS REVIEW: NORTHEAST. METRO FOCUS. see *BUSINESS AND ECONOMICS — Production Of Goods And Services*

D R I - MCGRAW-HILL U S MARKETS REVIEW: NORTHEAST. STATE FOCUS. see *BUSINESS AND ECONOMICS — Production Of Goods And Services*

D R I - MCGRAW-HILL U S MARKETS REVIEW: REGIONAL FORECAST SUMMARY. see *BUSINESS AND ECONOMICS — Production Of Goods And Services*

D R I - MCGRAW-HILL U S MARKETS REVIEW: REGIONAL PREVIEW. see *BUSINESS AND ECONOMICS — Production Of Goods And Services*

D R I - MCGRAW-HILL U S MARKETS REVIEW: SOUTH. STATE FOCUS. see *BUSINESS AND ECONOMICS — Production Of Goods And Services*

D R I - MCGRAW-HILL U S MARKETS REVIEW: WEST. METRO FOCUS. see *BUSINESS AND ECONOMICS — Production Of Goods And Services*

D R I - MCGRAW-HILL U S MARKETS REVIEW: WEST. STATE FOCUS. see *BUSINESS AND ECONOMICS — Production Of Goods And Services*

DAILY BULLETIN (BROOKLYN); a daily newspaper serving professionals. see *LAW*

330.9   DK
THE DANISH ECONOMY - A QUARTERLY REVIEW. (Editions in English and German) 1938. q. free. Danske Bank Aktieselskab, Information Department, 2-12 Holmens Kanal, DK-1092 Copenhagen K, Denmark. TEL 45-33-44-00-00. FAX 45-31-18-58-73. TELEX 27000. Ed. Carsten Winkler. mkt.; stat.; index. **Indexed:** PROMT.
    Former titles: Danish Economy (ISSN 0908-3138); (until 1993): Denmark (ISSN 0906-7906); (until 1988): Denmark Quarterly Review (ISSN 0011-8427); (until 1984): Denmark (ISSN 0902-235X)

330.9   JM
DATAPAC CARIBBEAN BUSINESS TRENDS. 1983. q. J.$600($50) Data Resource Systems International Ltd., 7 Oxford Park Ave., P.O. Box 193, Kingston 5, Jamaica, W.I. TEL 809-968-0813. FAX 809-968-0826. Ed. Huntley Manhertz. adv.: B&W page J.$7000, color page J.$11000; 10 1/2 x 7 1/2. circ. 2,000. **Document type:** academic/scholarly publication.
    Formerly: DataPac Caribbean.
    Description: Contains current information on economic trends in commerce, industry and finance throughout the Caribbean.

380.102   DK   ISSN 0418-6745
DENMARK REVIEW; business news from Denmark. French edition: Realites Danoises (ISSN 0107-5810); German edition: Daenische Revue (ISSN 0107-5799); Spanish edition: Revista Danesa (ISSN 0107-5837) (Supplement avail.: Denmark Review. Special Edition (0107-5780)) 1961. q. free. Udenrigsministeriet - Ministry of Foreign Affairs, Asiatisk Plads 2, DK-1448 Copenhagen K, Denmark. TEL 45-33-92-00-00. FAX 45-31-54-05-33. TELEX 31-292. Eds. Ulrik Helweg-Larsen, Mogens Lange. **Indexed:** Key to Econ.Sci., PROMT.

330.9   US
DEPARTMENT STORE INVENTORIES. (Subseries of: National Office News Releases) m. U.S. Bureau of Labor Statistics, 2 Massachusetts Ave., N.E., Washington, DC 20212. TEL 202-655-4000. (Subscr. to: Superintendent of Documents, U.S. Government Printing Office, Box 371954, Pittsburgh, PA 15250-7954. TEL 202-512-1800. FAX 202-512-2250; Or: Bureau of Labor Statistics Publications Sales Center, Box 2145, Chicago, IL 60690) **Document type:** government publication.

330.9   CK   ISSN 0120-3584
HC196
DESARROLLO Y SOCIEDAD. Variant title: Revista Desarrollo y Sociedad. 1979. 2/yr. Col.$2800($28) (effective Jan. 1992). (Universidad de los Andes, Centro de Estudios sobre Desarrollo Economico) Tercer Mundo Editores, Calle 69, no. 6-46, Bogota DE, Colombia. TEL 57-12849911. FAX 57-12841890. (Subscr. to: Universidad de los Andes, Facultad de Economia, Apdo. Aereo 4976, Bogota, Colombia. TEL 2824800-2464) Ed. Rafael Nieves Traslavina. adv.; bk.rev. circ. 1,000. **Indexed:** IBR, P.A.I.S.For.Lang.Ind.

DEUTSCHE BANK BULLETIN; current economic and monetary issues. see *BUSINESS AND ECONOMICS — Banking And Finance*

330.9   GW
DEUTSCHER WARENHANDEL. 1966. q. DM.48. Zeitungs- und Zeitschriftenverlag Heinrichs, Brueggekamp 1, 30890 Barsinghausen, Germany. TEL 49-5105-2289. Pub. G. Heinrichs. circ. 11,000. (tabloid format) **Document type:** trade publication.

330.9   GW
DEUTSCHES INSTITUT FUER WIRTSCHAFTSFORSCHUNG. ECONOMIC BULLETIN. (Text in English) 1978. m. £180 (effective 1997). Deutsches Institut fuer Wirtschaftsforschung, Koenigin-Luise-Str. 5, 14195 Berlin, Germany. TEL 49-30-897890. FAX 49-30-89789200. E-mail: bulletin@diw-berlin.de; URL: http://www.diw-berlin.de. (Dist. by: Gower Publishing Ltd., Gower House, Croft Rd., Aldershot, Hampshire GU11 3HR, England. TEL 44-1252-331551) Ed. Dieter Teichmann. circ. 400. (back issues avail.) **Document type:** bulletin.

330.9   GW   ISSN 0012-1304
DEUTSCHES INSTITUT FUER WIRTSCHAFTSFORSCHUNG. WOCHENBERICHT. 1928. w. DM.210 (effective 1997). Duncker und Humblot GmbH, Postfach 410329, 12113 Berlin, Germany. TEL 49-30-7900060. FAX 49-30-79000361. E-mail: duh-werbung@t-online.de. Ed. Klaus Henkner. charts; stat. **Indexed:** ELLIS, INIS Atomind., Key to Econ.Sci., P.A.I.S.For.Lang.Ind. **Document type:** academic/scholarly publication.
    —BLDSC (9341.730000). CCC.

DEVELOPMENT AND INTERNATIONAL COOPERATION. see *BUSINESS AND ECONOMICS — International Development And Assistance*

330   UA
DEVELOPMENT & SOCIO-ECONOMIC PROGRESS. (Text in Arabic, English, French) 1977. q. Afro-Asian People's Solidarity Organization, 89 Abdel Aziz al Saoud St., Manial El-Roda, Cairo, Egypt. TEL 84 54 95. Ed. Nouri Abdel Razzak. bk.rev. circ. 5,000. (back issues avail.) **Indexed:** Per.Islam. (1992-).
    Description: Role is to spread awareness in Asia and Africa on the economic factor, not only with regard to building national economies, but also in consolidation of national independence.

330.9   US   ISSN 1053-3672
HC106.8
DEVELOPMENT REPORT CARD FOR THE STATES. 1987. a. $75. Corporation for Enterprise Development, 777 N. Capitol St., N.E., Ste. 410, Washington, DC 20002. TEL 202-408-9788. FAX 202-408-9793. URL: http://www.cfed.org. Ed. Daphne Clones. R&P contact: Linda Keenex. **Indexed:** SRI. **Document type:** directory.
    Formerly: Making the Grade (ISSN 1045-4691)
    Description: Comparison and ranking of each of the 50 states on 50 socio-economic indicators key to state economics and economic development. Includes brief analysis of each state, U.S. as a whole, and regions.

382   IE   ISSN 0302-7465
HC241.2
DEVELOPMENTS IN THE EUROPEAN COMMUNITIES. REPORT. 1973. irreg., latest no.40. Stationery Office, Dublin, Ireland. **Document type:** government publication.

330   BL   ISSN 0101-4218
DIGESTO ECONOMICO. 1944. bi-m. Cr.$60000. Associacao Comercial de Sao Paulo, Rua Boa Vista 51, 10 andar, CEP 01014 Sao Paulo, Brazil. TEL 11-234-3322. FAX 11-239-0067. TELEX 11-23355. Ed. Joao de Scantimburgo. adv.; bk.rev. circ. 10,000.

330.9   GW
DIREKTE AKTION; anarchosyndikalistische Zeitung. 1977. bi-m. DM.12($10) Freie Arbeiterinnen- und Arbeiter-Union (FAU), Lagerstr. 27, 20357 Hamburg, Germany. TEL 430 13 96. circ. 4,000. (back issues avail.) **Document type:** newspaper.

330.968   SA
DOING BUSINESS IN SOUTH AFRICA. (Text in English) 1994. a. Kessel Feinstein, P.O. Box 6610, Johannesburg 2000, South Africa.

BUSINESS AND ECONOMICS — ECONOMIC SITUATION AND CONDITIONS

330.9 910.03   US   ISSN 0012-5245
HC106.7
DOLLARS & SENSE. 1974. bi-m. $23 to individuals; institutions $42. Economic Affairs Bureau, Inc., One Summer St., Somerville, MA 02143. TEL 617-628-8411. FAX 617-628-2025. E-mail: dollars@igc.apc.org; URL: http://www.igc.apc.org/dollars. Eds. Marc Breslow, Abby Scher. R&P contact: Randy Divinski. adv. contact: Denise Taylor. bk.rev.; charts; illus.; stat.; index; circ. 8,417 (paid). (also avail. in microform from UMI; back issues avail.) **Indexed:** Alt.Press Ind., Chic.Per.Ind., Left Ind. (1982-), New Per.Ind., P.A.I.S., Sociol.Abstr. **Document type:** consumer publication.
●Also available online. Vendor(s): Information Access Co.
—UMI; UnCover. **CCC.**
   Description: Provides analysis of the U.S. and international economics, from health care to trade agreements, welfare reform, and environmental regulations.

DOMINICA. MINISTRY OF FINANCE. CENTRAL STATISTICAL OFFICE. CONSUMER PRICE INDICES. see BUSINESS AND ECONOMICS — Abstracting, Bibliographies, Statistics

DOMINICA. MINISTRY OF FINANCE. CENTRAL STATISTICAL OFFICE. NATIONAL ACCOUNTS AND BALANCE OF PAYMENTS. see BUSINESS AND ECONOMICS — Abstracting, Bibliographies, Statistics

DOMINICA. MINISTRY OF FINANCE. CENTRAL STATISTICAL OFFICE. QUARTERLY ECONOMIC INDICATORS. see BUSINESS AND ECONOMICS — Abstracting, Bibliographies, Statistics

330.9   DQ
DOMINICA. MINISTRY OF FINANCE. CENTRAL STATISTICAL OFFICE. STATISTICAL DIGEST. a. $14.89. Ministry of Finance, Central Statistical Office, Kennedy Ave., Roseau, Dominica, W.I. **Document type:** government publication.
   Former titles: Dominica. Ministry of Finance and Development. Statistical Division. Digest; Dominica. Ministry of Finance and Development. Statistical Digest.

330.9   GP
DOSSIERS ANTILLES GUYANE. ENQUETE ANNUELLE D'ENTREPRISE DANS LES SERVICES. a. 125 F. Institut National de la Statistique et des Etudes Economiques, Service Interregional Antilles - Guyane, Tour SECID, 7th & 8th Fls., B.P. 300, 97175 Pointe-a-Pitre, Guadeloupe. TEL 19-590-93-78-52. FAX 19-590-83-89-25. Ed. A. Tranap.

330.9   GP   ISSN 0291-8706
HD9715.G97
DOSSIERS ANTILLES GUYANE. ETUDES DIVERSES. (Text in French) 1981. irreg. price varies. Institut National de la Statistique et des Etudes Economiques, Service Interregional Antilles - Guyane, Tour SECID, 7th & 8th Fls., B.P. 300, 97175 Pointe-a-Pitre, Guadeloupe. TELEX 919912GL. Ed. Alain Tranap. adv.; bk.rev. circ. 500.

330.9   RE   ISSN 0292-6792
DOSSIERS DE L'ECONOMIE REUNIONNAISE. 1982. irreg. 360 F. (foreign 520 F.) for 8 issues. Institut National de la Statistique et des Etudes Economiques, Direction Regionale de la Reunion, 15 rue de l'Ecole, 97490 Ste. Clotilde, Reunion. TEL 29-51-57.

330.9   US   ISSN 1063-0635
CODEN: DBCEEY
DUN & BRADSTREET COMMENTS ON THE ECONOMY. irreg. free. Dun & Bradstreet, Economic Analysis Department, 220 E. 42nd St., 9th Fl., New York, NY 10017-4717. FAX 212-883-3400. (Subscr. to: Box 1861, New York, NY 10163-1861) **Document type:** newsletter.
   Description: Provides topical in-depth analyses of macro-economic conditions.

330.9   US
DUN & BRADSTREET LOOKS AT BUSINESS. irreg. free. Dun & Bradstreet, Economic Analysis Department, 220 E. 42nd St., 9th Fl., New York, NY 10017-4717. FAX 212-883-3400. (Subscr. to: Box 1861, New York, NY 10163-1861)
   Description: Business and economic highlights based on proprietary information of the Dun & Bradstreet Corporation and its divisions.

330.9   US
HG3766
DUN & BRADSTREET MONTHLY BUSINESS FAILURES. 1900. m. $30. Dun & Bradstreet, Economic Analysis Department, 220 E. 42nd St., 9th Fl., New York, NY 10163-1861. FAX 212-883-3400. (Subscr. to: Box 1861, New York, NY 10163-1861) **Indexed:** SRI.
   Former titles: Dun and Bradstreet Record of Business Closings. Monthly Business Failures (ISSN 1052-2808); (until 1986): Monthly Business Failures (ISSN 0027-027X)
   Description: Provides number of failures and liabilities in over 100 lines of business. Data is broken down by liability size, major industry group, state and region, and by selected cities.

330.9561   TU
E B A NEWSLETTER. 1969. d. Ekonomik Basin Ajansi, Bestekar Sokak 59-3, 06680 Kavaklidere - Ankara, Turkey. TEL 90-312-4685376. FAX 90-312-4684114. E-mail: ebainfo@superonline.com; URL: http://www.ebanews.com. Ed. Yavuz Tolun; Pub. Melek Tolun. R&P contact: Melek Tolun. TEL 90-312-4685380. adv. contact: Melek Tolun. **Document type:** newsletter.
   Formerly: T E B A Haber (ISSN 1300-2724)

330.9   TU
E B A REPORT. 1972. w. $560 (effective 1996 & 1997). Ekonomik Basin Ajansi, Bestekar Sokak 59-3, 06680 Kavaklidere - Ankara, Turkey. TEL 90-312-4685376. FAX 90-312-4684114. TELEX 46836 FTEB TR. E-mail: ebainfo@superonline.com; URL: http://www.ebanews.com. Ed. Yavuz Tolun; Pub. Melek Tolun. R&P contact: Melek Tolun. adv. contact: Melek Tolun. **Document type:** newsletter.
   Description: Covers business and investment, international tenders and contracts in Turkey.

330.9   PK
E I P ECONOMIC FORECASTING SERVICE. (Text in English) 1981. fortn. Rs.4000($400) Economic and Industrial Publications, Al-Masiha, 47 Abdullah Haroon Rd., P.O. Box 7843, Karachi 74400, Pakistan. Ed.Bd.; Pub. Iqbal Haidari. charts; stat. circ. 1,000. (looseleaf format) **Document type:** trade publication.
   Formerly (until 1986): E I P Labour Research Service.

330   US   ISSN 0424-3331
HC59
E I U WORLD OUTLOOK. 1969. a. £265($385) Economist Intelligence Unit, 111 W. 57th St., New York, NY 10019. TEL 212-554-0600; 800-938-4685. FAX 212-586-1182. TELEX 175567. URL: http://www.eiu.com. (UK addr.: Economist Intelligence Unit Ltd, Subscriptions Dept., P.O. Box 200, Harold Hill, Romford, Essex RM3 8UX, England. TEL 44-1708-381-444. FAX 44-1708-371-850)
—BLDSC (9356.960000); UMI.
   Description: Forecasts the political and economic trends in over 180 countries.

330.9   US
E N A. (Economic News from Austria) q. free. Austrian Press and Information Service, 3524 International Ct., N.W., Washington, DC 20008-3035. TEL 202-895-6775. FAX 202-895-6772. TELEX 440010. URL: http://www.austria.org/. **Document type:** newsletter.
●Also available online.

330.9   IE
E S R I MANPOWER FORECASTING STUDIES. irreg., no.5, 1996. I£12 (students I£6). Economic and Social Research Institute, 4 Burlington Rd., Dublin 4, Ireland. TEL 353-1-6671525. FAX 353-1-6686231. Ed.Bd. R&P contact: John Roughan. **Document type:** monographic series.

330.9   GW   ISSN 0946-7815
E U R E G/REVUE EUROPEENNE DE DEVELOPPEMENT REGIONAL/EUROPEAN JOURNAL OF REGIONAL DEVELOPMENT. Variant title: Europaeische Zeitschrift fuer Regionalentwicklung. (Text in English, French, German) 1994. 2/yr. DM.80 for 4 nos. Akademie fuer Raumforschung und Landesplanung, Hohenzollernstr. 11, 30161 Hannover, Germany. TEL 49-511-3484231. FAX 49-511-3484241. E-mail: eureg@mbox.arl.uni-hannover.de. (Co-sponsor: Association de Science Regionale de Langue Francaise) Eds. Claude Lacour, Peter Treuner. **Document type:** academic/scholarly publication.
—BLDSC (3828.770000).
   Refereed Serial

330.9   US   ISSN 0733-0138
EARLY WARNING FORECAST; business cycle outlook, industrial market forecasts. 1975. m. $259 (foreign $279). Cahners Publishing Company (Newton), Division of Reed Elsevier Inc., 275 Washington St., Newton, MA 02158-1630. TEL 800-662-7776. FAX 303-398-7691. Ed. Daryl Delano; Pub. Daryl Delano. R&P contact: Daryl Delano. circ. 500. **Document type:** newsletter.
—**CCC.**
   Description: Features forecasts of the most widely-followed economic indicators (GDP, inflation, interest rates) and industry-specific indicators (machinery, construction, electronics).

330.9   US   ISSN 0272-1589
EAST ASIAN EXECUTIVE REPORTS. 1978. m. $455 (foreign $465) (effective 1997). International Executive Reports, 717 D St., N.W., Ste. 200, Washington, DC 20004-2807. TEL 202-628-6900. FAX 202-628-6618. Ed. William Hearn. R&P contact: William Hearn. adv. contact: Lloyd Gibson. bk.rev.; index, cum.index. circ. 800. **Indexed:** ABI Inform., BPIA, C.L.I., Curr.Cont.M.E., Ind.Per.Art.Relat.Law, Key to Econ.Sci., L.R.I. **Document type:** trade publication.
●Also available online. Vendor(s): Lexis-Nexis, UMI, West Group.
—BLDSC (3645.935700); UMI. **CCC.**
   Description: Designed for international business executives involved in East Asia trade, contracting, marketing and investment.

330.9   US   ISSN 1060-6157
DJK51
EAST EUROPE & THE REPUBLICS: A POLITICAL RISK ANNUAL. 1992. a. $435 (effective 1997). The P R S Group, Box 248, East Syracuse, NY 13057-0248. TEL 315-431-0511. FAX 315-431-0200.
●Also available online. Vendor(s): Data-Star (FSRI), Lexis-Nexis (IBCRPT).
   Description: Covers the economic and political situation for investors in Eastern Europe and the former republics of the former U.S.S.R.

EAST TENNESSEE DEVELOPMENT DISTRICT ECONOMIC STATISTICS. see *STATISTICS*

330.9   US   ISSN 1065-6790
HF3626.5   CODEN: EBTREX
EAST - WEST BUSINESS AND TRADE; with news from Russia, the Baltics, Central & Eastern Europe. 1972. s-m. $367.20 to academic institutions (Canada and Mexico $377.20; elsewhere $397.20); others $459 (Canada and Mexico $469; elsewhere $489). Welt Publishing, LLC, 1413 K St, N.W., Ste. 1400, Washington, DC 20005. TEL 202-371-0555; 800-898-INTL. FAX 202-408-9369. Ed. John Justin Ford; Pub. Leo G.B. Welt. adv.; stat.; tr.lit. circ. 3,500. (looseleaf format; back issues avail.) **Indexed:** Chem.Abstr., PROMT. **Document type:** newsletter.
—CASDDS.
   Incorporates (in 1994): East - West Technology Digest (ISSN 0145-1421); Which was formerly (until 1976): Soviet Technology Digest; Formerly (until 1992): Soviet Business and Trade (ISSN 0731-7727); Which superseded in part: Business and Trade (ISSN 0196-8602); Which was formerly: Soviet Business and Trade (ISSN 0092-4695)
   Description: Provides news and analysis on business and economic developments throughout the former Soviet Union.

BUSINESS AND ECONOMICS — ECONOMIC SITUATION AND CONDITIONS

330.9 332   US
EAST - WEST COMMERSANT. Russian edition: Commersant Weekly. 22/yr. $425 (foreign $475). WorldTrade Executive Inc., Box 761, Concord, MA 01742. TEL 508-287-0301. URL: http://pages.map.com/~wtel/. Ed. Charlotte Pierce; Pub. Gary Brown. R&P contact: Gary Brown. adv.: page $975; 7 1/2 x 9 1/2; adv. contact: Ken Parker. **Document type:** newsletter.
   Formerly: East - West Business and Financial Alert.
   Description: Covers business opportunities, the availability of funding, reliable local contacts, and other trade and investment information related to Russia and Eastern Europe.

330.9
HF1532.7   US   ISSN 1067-635X
EAST - WEST EXECUTIVE GUIDE. 1992. m. $596 (foreign $646). WorldTrade Executive Inc., Box 761, Concord, MA 01742. TEL 508-287-0301. FAX 508-287-0302. URL: http://pages.map.com/~wte/. Ed. Scott Studebaker; Pub. Gary Brown. R&P contact: Gary Brown. adv.: page $975; 7 1/2 x 9 1/2; adv. contact: Ken Parker. **Document type:** newsletter.
   Incorporates: Soviet and Eastern European Report (ISSN 0963-7036); (1990-1992): East - West Business Report (ISSN 1053-7155)
   Description: Covers business and legal developments in East and Central Europe, Russia, and the Commonwealth Republics. Includes analyses of legal and practical issues from executives, lawyers, and government advisors working in the region.

330
HC431   II   ISSN 0012-8767
EASTERN ECONOMIST. 1943. w. Rs.125($30) Eastern Economist Ltd., UCO Bank Bldg., P.O. Box 34, Parliament St., New Delhi 110001, India. Ed. V. Balasubramanian. adv.; bk.rev.; mkt.stat.; index. circ. 7,000. (also avail. in microfilm from UMI; reprint service avail. from UMI) **Indexed:** Mid.East: Abstr.& Ind., P.A.I.S., PROMT, Rural Recreat.Tour.Abstr., World Agri.Econ.& Rural Sociol.Abstr.
—UMI.

EASTERN EUROPE AND THE COMMONWEALTH OF INDEPENDENT STATES (YEAR). see *POLITICAL SCIENCE*

330.9   UK   ISSN 0965-0350
EASTERN EUROPEAN ANALYST. 4/yr. £200($500) (effective 1996). World Reports Ltd., 108 Horseferry Rd., Westminster, London SW1P 2EF, England. TEL 44-171-222-3836. FAX 44-171-233-0185. (U.S. subscr. to: World Reports Ltd., 280 Madison Ave., Ste. 1209, New York, NY 10016-0802. TEL 212-599-4560. FAX 212-679-1094) Ed. Christopher Story. (back issues avail.) **Document type:** academic/scholarly publication.
   Formerly (until 1991): Comecon Reports (ISSN 0142-0763)
   Description: Economic news on the former Soviet empire and sphere of influence, the economies of Eastern European countries, and world developments in light of policy changes in Moscow.

330.9   IR
ECHO OF IRAN. m. Echo Publications, Ave. Hafez, Kuche Hurtab No. 4, P.O. Box 11365-5551, Teheran, Iran. adv.

330.9   FR
LES ECHOS; le quotidien de l'economie. 1908. 5/w. 2070 F. (foreign 3310 F.). Les Echos (Subsidiary of: Financial Times), 46, rue la Boetie, 75008 Paris, France. TEL 1-49-53-65-65. FAX 1-45-61-48-92. TELEX 640 331 F. adv. circ. 113,069. (tabloid format; also avail. in microfilm from RPI) **Indexed:** Key to Econ.Sci., PROMT. **Document type:** newspaper.
   Description: Provides concise, up-to-date news and information on business, finance and trade development at home and abroad.

ECOCENTRAL; Central America & Caribbean Sustainable Development. see *BUSINESS AND ECONOMICS — International Development And Assistance*

330.9   US   ISSN 0747-4938
HB139   CODEN: ECREEP
ECONOMETRIC REVIEWS. 1982. q. $545 (foreign $560) (effective 1998). Marcel Dekker Journals, 270 Madison Ave., New York, NY 10016. TEL 212-696-9000. FAX 212-685-4540. TELEX 421419. (Subscr. to: Box 5017, Monticello, NY 12701) Ed. Esfandiar Maasoumi. R&P contact: Julia Mulligan. adv. contact: Lourdes Barroso. (also avail. in microform from RPI; reprint service avail. from SWZ) **Indexed:** Curr.Cont.(1982-), Curr.Ind.Stat., J.Cont.Quant.Meth., J.of Econ.Lit., Math.R., Stat.Theor.Meth.Abstr. (1982-), Zent.Math. **Document type:** academic/scholarly publication.
—BLDSC (3650.080000); SWETS; UMI; UnCover. CCC.
   Formerly: Communications in Statistics. Part D: Econometric Reviews.

338.9   BL   ISSN 0424-2386
ECONOMIA BRASILEIRA E SUAS PERSPECTIVAS - A P E C A O. (Text in English and Portuguese) 1962. a. $100. Associacao Promotora de Estudos de Economia, Rua Sorocaba 295, Botafogo, Rio de Janeiro, Brazil. FAX 021-266-3597. Ed. Basilio Martins. circ. 10,000.

330.9   CK   ISSN 0422-2733
ECONOMIA COLOMBIANA. no. 115, 1976. m. $40. Contraloria General, Edificio de los Ministerios, Ofc. 126A, No. 6-40, Bogota D.E., Colombia. Ed. Bernardo Garcia. adv.; bk.rev. **Indexed:** P.A.I.S.For.Lang.Ind.

330.9   CU
ECONOMIA CUBANA. English edition: Cuban Economy. a. Comite Estatal de Estadisticas, Centro de Informacion Cientifico-Tecnica, Almendares No. 156, esq. a Desague, Gaveta Postal 6016, Havana, Cuba. stat.

330.9   MZ   ISSN 0012-9755
HC578.M6
ECONOMIA DE MOCAMBIQUE. (Text in Portuguese) m. Companhia Editoria de Mocambique, C.P. 81, Beira, Mozambique. Ed. Antonia de Almeida. adv.

330.9 301   PO   ISSN 0870-6026
ECONOMIA E SOCIOLOGIA. 1965. 2/yr. Esc.800($25) Instituto Superior Economico e Social, Rua Vasco da Gama 15, 7000 Evora, Portugal. TEL 23327. Ed. Agostinho Moreira Ferraz; Pub. Augusto da Silva. R&P contact: Manuel Ferreira da Lima Bello. bk.rev.; bibl.; illus. **Indexed:** P.A.I.S.For.Lang.Ind. **Document type:** academic/scholarly publication.
   Refereed Serial

330.9   IT
ECONOMIA EMILIA-ROMAGNA. 1994. m. free. Unione Regionale Camere di Commercio dell'Emilia-Romagna (C.E.R.E.S.), Via Montegrappa 4-D, 40121 Bologna, Italy. TEL 39-51-223030. FAX 39-51-234945. Ed. Claudio Pasini. **Document type:** trade publication.

330.9   IT   ISSN 1120-9593
ECONOMIA MARCHE. 3/yr. Lit.78000 (foreign Lit.160000) (effective 1997). (Fundazione Merloni) Societa Editrice Il Mulino, Strada Maggiore, 37, 40125 Bologna, Italy. TEL 39-51-256011. FAX 39-51-256034. E-mail: riviste@mulino.it. Ed. Gian Mario Spacca. adv. contact: M. Luisa Vezzali. index. circ. 1,800. (back issues avail.) **Indexed:** P.A.I.S.For.Lang.Ind.

338   SP   ISSN 0211-0954
ECONOMIA VASCONGADA; revista de la industria, el comercio, y la navegacion. 1945. m. 600 ptas. Enrique Vicente de Vera, Ed. & Pub., Avda. de la Libertas 7 2-H, 20004 San Sebastian (Guipuzcoa), Spain. TEL 43-42-78-85. Ed. Fermin Vega de Seoane. adv.; illus.; stat. circ. 3,400.

330   II
ECONOMIC AGE. (Text in English) vol.7, 1974. m. Rs.0.75 per no. Siba Prosad Banerjee, Ed. & Pub., P-36 India Exchange Place, 2nd Fl., Rm.40, Calcutta 700001, India. Ed. Sib Banerji. adv.; bk.rev. circ. 29,000.

338 338.9   II   ISSN 0970-0560
ECONOMIC AND COMMERCIAL NEWS. (Text in English) 1971. w. Rs.50($22) Trade Fair Authority of India, Administrative Block-Pragati Maidan, Lal Bahadur Shastri Marg, New Delhi 110 001, India. Ed. Shri N.N. Kesar. circ. 1,950. **Indexed:** Key to Econ.Sci.

ECONOMIC AND ENERGY INDICATORS. see *POLITICAL SCIENCE — International Relations*

330.9   SZ   ISSN 0256-3525
ECONOMIC AND FINANCIAL PROSPECTS. (Supplement avail.) (Text in English) 1947. bi-m. free. Schweizerischer Bankverein - Swiss Bank Corporation, 6 Aeschenplatz, CH-4002 Basel, Switzerland. TEL 41-61-288-2020. FAX 41-61-288-4424. Ed. Daniel Witschi. R&P contact: Daniel Witschi. charts; illus.; stat. circ. 30,000. (also avail. in microform from UMI; reprint service avail. from UMI) **Indexed:** P.A.I.S. **Document type:** bulletin.
—BLDSC (3651.449000); UMI.
   Formerly: Prospects.
   Description: Provides information about economic and financial issues, and issues affecting the banking community.

330.9 332   KU
ECONOMIC & FINANCIAL QUARTERLY. (Text in English) q. free. National Bank of Kuwait S.A.K., Economic Research Division, P.O. Box 95, Safat 13001, Kuwait. TEL 965-2422011. FAX 965-2465098. stat. **Document type:** bulletin.
   Description: Provides an overview of the current state of the Kuwaiti economy, information on the oil and banking sectors, foreign trade, and the outlook for the future.

338.9   CN
HJ13
ECONOMIC AND FISCAL POLICY. 1954. a. free. Saskatchewan Finance, 2350 Albert St., Regina, Sask. S4P 4S6, Canada. TEL 306-787-6768. FAX 306-787-3982. circ. 1,500.
   Formerly: Saskatchewan Economic and Finance Position (ISSN 0080-6676)

ECONOMIC & SHIPPING REVIEW. see *TRANSPORTATION — Ships And Shipping*

330.9   US   ISSN 0095-2850
HC125
ECONOMIC AND SOCIAL PROGRESS IN LATIN AMERICA. REPORT. French edition: Progres Economique et Social en Amerique Latine. Rapport (ISSN 0252-9319); Portuguese edition: Progresso Socio-Economico na America Latina. Relatorio (ISSN 0253-6021); Spanish edition: Progreso Economico y Social en America Latina. Informe (ISSN 0253-6013) (Text in English) 1961. a. $16.95 or exchange basis. Inter-American Development Bank, 1300 New York Ave., N.W., Washington, DC 20577. TEL 202-623-1000. (Dist. by: Johns Hopkins University Press, 701 W. 40th St., Ste. 275, Baltimore, MD 21211) charts. (also avail. in microfiche from CIS) **Indexed:** IIS.
—BLDSC (3651.509700).
   Formerly (until 1972): Socio-Economic Progress in Latin America. Annual Report (ISSN 0074-0888)
   Description: Regional and country-by-country survey of economic and social conditions in Latin America.

338.9   UN   ISSN 0252-5704
JX1977
ECONOMIC AND SOCIAL SURVEY OF ASIA AND THE PACIFIC. (In 2 parts) (Text in English) 1948. a. $40. United Nations Economic and Social Commission for Asia and the Pacific (ESCAP), United Nations Bldg., Rajadamnern Ave., Bangkok 10200, Thailand. (Dist. by: United Nations Publications, Rm. DC2-0853, New York, NY 10017; or Distribution and Sales Section, Palais des Nations, CH-1211 Geneva 10, Switzerland; or Conference Services Unit, E.S.C.A.P., Bangkok) (also avail. in microfiche from CIS; back issues avail.) **Indexed:** Abstr.Rural Dev.Trop., IIS. **Document type:** government publication, bulletin.
—BLDSC (3651.533000).
   Formerly: Economic Survey of Asia and the Far East (ISSN 0070-8690)
   Description: Emphasizes economic and social policy issues through an analysis of economic and social developments in the Pacific Rim.

330.9   US   ISSN 1075-8631
ECONOMIC BULLETIN (SAN DIEGO). 1953. m. $50. Greater San Diego Chamber of Commerce, 402 W. Broadway, Ste. 1000, San Diego, CA 92101-3585. TEL 619-544-1344. FAX 619-234-0571. Ed. Kelly Cuningham. circ. 5,000. (also avail. in microfilm from UMI; microfiche from UMI; reprint service avail. from UMI) **Indexed:** PROMT. **Document type:** bulletin.
   Former titles: San Diego Economic Bulletin (ISSN 0558-3918); San Diego Bulletin.

BUSINESS AND ECONOMICS — ECONOMIC SITUATION AND CONDITIONS

338   UN
HC240.A1
ECONOMIC BULLETIN FOR EUROPE (ANNUAL). (Editions in English, French and Russian) 1949. a. price varies. Economic Commission for Europe (ECE), Palais des Nations, 1211 Geneva 10, Switzerland. TEL 022-917-1234. FAX 022-917-0123. TELEX 412962. (Orders in N. America to: United Nations Publications, Rm. DC2-853, New York, NY 10017. TEL 212-963-8302. FAX 212-863-3489; Or: Unipub, 4611-F Assembly Dr., Lanham, MD 20706. TEL 301-459-7666. FAX 301-459-0056) Ed. Yves Berthelot. (also avail. in microform from MIM,UMI,CIS; reprint service avail. from UMI,SCH) **Indexed:** Amer.Bibl.Slavic & E.Eur.Stud., BPIA, Bus.Ind., C.R.E.J., Curr.Cont., IIS, Key to Econ.Sci., P.A.I.S., SSCI, Tr.& Indus.Ind. **Document type:** government publication, bulletin.
—BLDSC (3652.300000); SWETS; UMI. **CCC**.
   Supersedes in part (in 1989): Economic Bulletin for Europe (Quarterly) (ISSN 0041-638X)
   Description: Reviews economic development throughout Europe.

ECONOMIC COMMENTARY. see BUSINESS AND ECONOMICS

340   352.7   US   ISSN 0731-6941
KF5722
ECONOMIC DEVELOPMENT AND LAW CENTER REPORT. 1970. q. $25 to individuals; institutions $40. National Economic Development and Law Center, 2201 Broadway Ste. 815, Oakland, CA 94612-3024. TEL 510-251-2600. FAX 510-251-0600. Ed. Jean Wiley. bk.rev.; cum.index: 1970-1977, 1978-1982, 1983-1984. circ. 1,000. (back issues avail.)
   Former titles (until 1979): Economic Development Law Project Report; (until vol.5, 1975): Law Project Bulletin.
   Description: Analyzes the practice and trends of community and economic development, discusses policy implications, offers the nuts-and-bolts of neighborhood revitalization, often with case studies.

330.9   US
ECONOMIC DEVELOPMENT DIGEST. m. free. National Association of Development Organizations, 444 N. Capitol St., N.W., Ste. 630, Washington, DC 20001. TEL 202-624-7806. FAX 202-624-8813. E-mail: nado@sso.org. Ed. Corene Kendrick. **Document type:** newsletter.
   Description: Covers economic development issues in the U.S.

ECONOMIC DEVELOPMENT TODAY. see BUSINESS AND ECONOMICS — Abstracting, Bibliographies, Statistics

330   US   ISSN 0013-0125
HC101   CODEN: ECINA3
ECONOMIC INDICATORS (WASHINGTON). 1948. m. $33 (foreign $41.25) (effective 1995). U.S. Executive Office of the President, Council of Economic Advisers, Executive Office Bldg., Washington, DC 20500. TEL 202-395-5062. (Subscr. to: Superintendent of Documents, U.S Government Printing Office, Box 371954, Pittsburgh, PA 15250-7954. TEL 202-512-1800. FAX 202-512-2250) charts; mkt.; stat. (also avail. in microform from UMI; back issues avail.; reprint service avail. from UMI) **Indexed:** Acad.Ind., Mag.Ind., P.A.I.S., Tr.& Indus.Ind. **Document type:** government publication.
●Also available online. Vendor(s): Information Access Co., Knight-Ridder Information, Inc.
—UMI.
   Description: Publishes data on prices, wages, production, business activity, purchasing power, credit, money and federal finance.

ECONOMIC ISSUES. see BUSINESS AND ECONOMICS — Economic Systems And Theories, Economic History

ECONOMIC LOGIC. see BUSINESS AND ECONOMICS — Investments

330   PK
ECONOMIC OUTLOOK. (Text in English) 1969. m. Rs.600($60) Pakistan Press International, Press Centre, Shahrah-e-Kamal Ataturk, Karachi, Pakistan. TEL 92-21-2635751. FAX 92-21-2631125. TELEX 23868 PPI PK. Ed. Tafazzul Hussain Siddiqui. adv.; bk.rev.; charts; stat.; tr.lit. circ. 5,000. **Document type:** academic/scholarly publication.
   Description: Covers topics in economic development and technological change in Pakistan and around the world.
   Refereed Serial

332   UK   ISSN 0140-489X
ECONOMIC OUTLOOK. 1977. q. £315($488) (foreign £315) (effective 1997). (London Business School, Centre for Economic Forecasting) Blackwell Publishers Ltd., 108 Cowley Rd., Oxford OX4 1JF, England. TEL 44-1865-791100. FAX 44-1865-791347. E-mail: jnlinfo@blackwellpublishers.co.uk; URL: http://www.blackwellpublishers.co.uk. Ed.Bd. circ. 1,200. **Indexed:** Key to Econ.Sci., Mgmt.& Market.Abstr., P.A.I.S., SCiMP (1979-). **Document type:** academic/scholarly publication.
●Also available online.
—BLDSC (3653.934700); SWETS. **CCC**.
   Incorporates: International Economic Outlook (ISSN 0960-8869)
   Description: Provides a combination of independent analysis, commentary, and forecasts of the UK, as well as other major world economies previously incorporated in the International Economic Outlook. The emphasis alternates between the UK and the international economy. Designed for corporate executives, business libraries, corporate planners and government and policy-making institutions.
   Refereed Serial

ECONOMIC OUTLOOK; a newsletter on economic issues for financial institutions. see BUSINESS AND ECONOMICS — Banking And Finance

330.9   US   ISSN 1048-115X
HC107.A14
ECONOMIC PERSPECTIVES (CHICAGO). 1917. bi-m. free. Federal Reserve Bank of Chicago, Public Information Center, Box 834, Chicago, IL 60690. TEL 312-322-5112. Ed. Edward G. Nash. charts; stat.; index. circ. 39,000. (also avail. in microform from UMI; microfiche from CIS; reprint service avail. from CIS,UMI) **Indexed:** ABI Inform., Amer.Stat.Ind. (1974-), BPIA, P.A.I.S.
●Also available online. Vendor(s): Information Access Co., UMI.
—BLDSC (3654.078000); UMI; UnCover.
   Former titles (until 1989): F R B Chicago Economic Perspectives (ISSN 0884-7576); (until 1983): Economic Perspectives (ISSN 0164-0682); (until Jan. 1977): Business Conditions (ISSN 0007-6589)

330   US
ECONOMIC PROFILE OF OREGON. a. $3.50. Oregon Economic Development Department, 775 Summer St., N.E., Salem, OR 97310. TEL 503-373-1290. FAX 503-581-5115. charts. **Document type:** government publication.
   Former titles: Oregon, a Statistical Profile; Oregon, an Economic Profile.

330   US   ISSN 0193-1180
HC106.5
ECONOMIC REPORT OF THE PRESIDENT. 1947. a. $16. U.S. Executive Office of the President, Council of Economic Advisers, Washington, DC 20500. TEL 202-395-7332. E-mail: federal.bbs.gpo.gov 3001. (Subscr. to: Superintendent of Documents, U.S. Government Printing Office, Box 371954, Pittsburgh, PA 15250-7954. TEL 202-512-1800. FAX 202-512-2250) circ. 50,000. (also avail. in microfiche from BHP) **Document type:** government publication.
●Also available online.
Also available on CD-ROM.
   Formerly: U.S. Executive Office of the President. Economic Report of the President.

330.9   CH   ISSN 0013-029X
HC464.F7
ECONOMIC REVIEW. 1950. bi-m. free. International Commercial Bank of China, Head Office-Economic Research Department, 100 Chilin Rd., Taipei, Taiwan 10424, Republic of China. TEL 02-5633156. FAX 02-5611216. TELEX 11300 INCOBK. Ed. Sung-Yuen Chu. index. **Indexed:** Asian-Pac.Econ.Lit., Bus.Ind.
—BLDSC (3654.943000).
   Description: Articles on economic development, planning, and conditions in the Republic of China.

330   YU   ISSN 0013-0303
ECONOMIC REVIEW. 1955. m. 24 din.($18) Privredni Pregled, Marsala Birjuzova 3-5, 11000 Belgrade, Yugoslavia. Ed. Vladimir Kacanski. adv.; charts; illus.; stat.

330   LE   ISSN 0013-032X
ECONOMIC REVIEW OF THE ARAB WORLD; argus of Arab economy. (Text in English) 1966. m. $300 (effective 1998). Bureau of Lebanese and Arab Documentation, P.O. Box 165403, Beirut, Lebanon. TEL 961-1-219113. (Subscr. to: Marcel Tawil, Bureau of Documentation, Postfach 2142, 79514 Loerrach, Germany. TEL 49-7621-2472. FAX 49-7621-2472) charts; stat. **Indexed:** Mid.East: Abstr.& Ind., Per.Islam. (1994-). **Document type:** bulletin.
   Incorporates: Argus Pharma Report.
   Description: Round-up of economic and financial developments in the Arab world covering trade agreements, imports and exports, customs and taxation, and banking regulations.

330.9   GR   ISSN 1105-252X
ECONOMIC REVIEW OF THE YEAR - THE GREEK ECONOMY. (Supplement to: Epilogi) 1983. a. Dr.2500. Electra Press, 4 Stadiou St., 105 64 Athens, Greece. TEL 323-3203. FAX 323-5160. TELEX 210564. Ed. Christos Papaioannou. adv. circ. 11,000.
   Description: Comprehensive review and analysis of all aspects of the Greek economy, with quantitative socio-economic data for all 10 regions and 52 departments of Greece.

330.9   GW   ISSN 0431-6045
ECONOMIC SITUATION IN THE FEDERAL REPUBLIC OF GERMANY. (Text in English) m. Bundesministerium fuer Wirtschaft, 53107 Bonn, Germany. charts; illus.; stat. circ. 1,500. **Document type:** government publication.

338.9   UN   ISSN 0070-8712
ECONOMIC SURVEY OF EUROPE. (Text in English, French and Russian) 1948. a. price varies. Economic Commission for Europe (ECE), Secretariat, Palais des Nations, 1211 Geneva 10, Switzerland. TEL 022-917-2720. FAX 022-917-0036. TELEX 412962. (Orders in N. America to: United Nations Publications, Rm. DC2-853, New York, NY 10017. TEL 212-963-8302. FAX 212-963-3489; Or: Unipub, 4611-F Assembly Dr., Lanham, MD 20706. TEL 301-459-7666. FAX 301-459-0056) (also avail. in microfiche from CIS) **Indexed:** IIS. **Document type:** government publication, bulletin.
   Description: Reports on the economic condition of the E.C. nations in the world economy.

338.9   UN   ISSN 0257-2184
HC161
ECONOMIC SURVEY OF LATIN AMERICA AND THE CARIBBEAN. Spanish edition: Estudio Economico de America Latina y el Caribe (ISSN 0257-2176) (Surveys for individual countries avail.) 1948. a. $65. Comision Economica para America Latina y el Caribe, Casilla 179-D, Santiago, Chile. (Subscr. to: United Nations Publications, Sales Section, Rm. DC2-0853, New York, NY 10017; or Distribution and Sales Section, Palais des Nations, 1211 Geneva 10, Switzerland) stat.; index. (also avail. in microfiche from CIS; back issues avail.) **Indexed:** IIS.
   Formerly (until 1983): Economic Survey of Latin America (ISSN 0070-8720)

330.9   LB   ISSN 0303-853X
HA2171
ECONOMIC SURVEY OF LIBERIA.* (Text in English) a. $5. Ministry of Planning and Economic Affairs, P.O. Box 9016, Monrovia, Liberia. stat.

BUSINESS AND ECONOMICS — ECONOMIC SITUATION AND CONDITIONS

330   II
ECONOMIC SURVEY OF MAHARASHTRA. (Text in English and Marathi) 1962. a. free. Directorate of Economics and Statistics, MHADA Bldg., Kalanagar, Bandra (E), Bombay 400051, India. Ed. V.B. Mujumdar.
Former titles: Economic Survey of India; Maharashtra: An Economic Review (ISSN 0076-2539)

330.9   SI   ISSN 0376-8791
HC445.8.A1
ECONOMIC SURVEY OF SINGAPORE. (Text in English) 1974. q. S.$100 (foreign S.$150). Ministry of Trade and Industry, 8 Shenton Way, No. 49-01, Treasury Building, Singapore 0106, Singapore. TEL 2820611. FAX 2854894. TELEX SNP RS 24462. (Subscr. to: Singapore National Printers Ltd., Publications Division, 303, Upper Serangoon Road, Singapore 1334, Singapore) circ. 7,300. (back issues avail.)
Description: Provides data on the economy and reviews the effects of government policies on economic activities in Singapore.

ECONOMIC TIMES. see BUSINESS AND ECONOMICS — Banking And Finance

ECONOMIC TIMES. see BUSINESS AND ECONOMICS — Banking And Finance

330   UK   ISSN 0013-0400
HC251
ECONOMIC TRENDS. 1953. m. £196 (includes a. and q. supplements). Office for National Statistics, Government Bldgs., 155 Cardiff Rd., Newport, Gwent NP9 1XG, Wales. TEL 44-1633-812973. FAX 44-1633-812599. TELEX 497121 BSO NPT G. E-mail: library@ons.gov.uk. (Orders to: Stationery Office Publications Centre, P.O. Box 276, London SW8 5DT, England. TEL 44-171-873-9090. FAX 44-171-873-8200) charts; stat. (also avail. in microform from UMI; reprint service avail. from SCH) **Indexed:** Geo.Abstr., P.A.I.S., PROMT, Rural Recreat.Tour.Abstr., World Agri.Econ.& Rural Sociol.Abstr., World Bank.Abstr. **Document type:** government publication.
—BLDSC (3656.700000); SWETS; UMI. CCC.
Description: Brings all the main economic indicators together in graphs and statistical tables, which are analyzed in articles. Also covers quarterly national accounts and balance of payment.

330   BG
ECONOMIC TRENDS. (Text in English) 1976. m. Bangladesh Bank, Department of Public Relations and Publications, Motijheel Commercial Area, Dhaka 2, Bangladesh. (reprint service avail. from SCH)

330.9   IR
ECONOMIC TRENDS. (Text in English) q. Bank Markazi Jomhouri Islami Iran, Economic Research Department - Central Bank of the Islamic Republic of Iran, P.O. Box 11365-8531, Tehran, Iran. FAX 98-21-390323. **Document type:** bulletin.
Formerly: Central Bank of the Islamic Republic of Iran. Economic Report and Balance Sheet (ISSN 0259-9902)

330   US   ISSN 0748-2922
HC101
ECONOMIC TRENDS (CLEVELAND). 1979. m. Federal Reserve Bank of Cleveland, Box 6387, Cleveland, OH 44101. TEL 216-579-3079. FAX 216-579-2477. Eds. Robin Ratliff, Tess Ferg. R&P contact: Kathy Popovich. circ. 15,300. (also avail. in microfiche from CIS; back issues avail.; reprint service avail. from CIS,SCH) **Indexed:** Amer.Stat.Ind. (1984-). **Document type:** newsletter.
●Also available online.
—UMI.
Supersedes: Economic Presentation.
Description: Covers patterns and trends in the U.S. economy in terms of the gross national product, interest rates, capital investment, money aggregates, financial markets, and foreign exchange markets, with a specific emphasis on the economic conditions of and outlook for the state of Ohio.

330.9   JA
ECONOMIC TRENDS: JAPAN. (Text in English) s-a. Embassy of the United States in Japan, 1-10-5 Akasaka, Minato-ku, Tokyo, Japan. (reprint service avail. from SCH)

330.9   UK   ISSN 0266-2671
HB1
ECONOMICS AND PHILOSOPHY. 1985. s-a. £53($86) (effective 1998). Cambridge University Press, Edinburgh Bldg., Shaftesbury Rd., Cambridge CB2 2RU, England. TEL 44-1223-312393. FAX 44-1223-315052. TELEX 851817256. E-mail: information@cup.cam.ac.uk; journals-subscriptions@cup.org; URL: http://www.cup.org/journals/CUPJNLS.html. (N. American addr.: Cambridge University Press, Journals Dept., 40 W. 20th St., New York, NY 10011. TEL 212-924-3900. FAX 212-691-3239) Eds. John Broome, Phillipe Mongin. R&P contact: Linda Nicol. adv. contact: Rebecca Symons. bk.rev. (also avail. in microform from UMI; back issues avail.; reprint service avail. from SWZ) **Indexed:** ASCA, C.R.E.J., Curr.Cont., J.of Econ.Lit., SSCI. **Document type:** academic/scholarly publication.
—BLDSC (3656.930900); Genuine Article; SWETS; UMI; UnCover. CCC.
Description: Explores the foundations of economics as both a predictive or explanatory enterprise and a normative one.

330.9   NE   ISSN 0013-0451
HC10   CODEN: EPTPAJ
ECONOMICS OF PLANNING; an international journal devoted to the study of comparative economics. (Text in English) 1960. 3/yr. fl.375 to institutions; $192.50 to institutions in U.S. (effective 1998). Kluwer Academic Publishers, Postbus 17, 3300 AA Dordrecht, Netherlands. TEL 31-78-6392392. FAX 31-78-6392254. TELEX 29245 KAPG NL. E-mail: services@wkap.nl; URL: http://www.wkap.nl. (Dist. by: Kluwer Academic Publishers Group, P.O. Box 322, 3300 AH Dordrecht, Netherlands. TEL 31-78-6392392. FAX 31-78-6546474; N. America dist. addr.: Box 358, Accord Sta., Hingham, MA 02018-0358. TEL 617-871-6600. FAX 617-871-6528) Eds. Wojciech W. Charemza, David M. Kemme. adv.; bk.rev. (also avail. in microform from UMI; reprint service avail. from SWZ) **Indexed:** ASCA, C.R.E.J., Curr.Cont., Geo.Abstr.H.G., IBR, IDA, Int.Polit.Sci.Abstr., J.of Econ.Lit., Rural Recreat.Tour.Abstr., World Agri.Econ.& Rural Sociol.Abstr. **Document type:** academic/scholarly publication.
—BLDSC (3657.100000); Genuine Article; SWETS; UMI; UnCover. CCC.
Description: Devoted to the study of micro- and macroeconomic planning, related techniques, and analysis of recent changes in economies traditionally associated with central planning.
Refereed Serial

330   AE
ECONOMIE. (Text in French) 1962. m. D.360. Algerie Presse Service (A.P.S.), 7 bd. Che Guevara, Algiers, Algeria. TEL 2-71-24-36. FAX 2-57-85-08. TELEX 65761. Ed. B.A. Djaballah. circ. 700.
Formerly: Algerie Economique.

330.9   FR   ISSN 0151-1793
ECONOMIE CHAMPENOISE. 1979. 6/yr. 130 F. Institut National de la Statistique et des Etudes Economiques, Direction Regionale de Champagne - Ardenne, 1 rue de l'Arbalete, 51079 Reims Cedex, France. TEL 26-48-42-60. FAX 26-48-42-99. TELEX 830896. (Subscr. to: Observatoire Economique de Champagne Ardenne, 1 rue de l'Arbalete, 51079 Reims Cedex, France) Ed. L. Marciniak. bk.rev. circ. 1,000.

330.9   RE   ISSN 0750-0769
HC598.A1
L'ECONOMIE DE LA REUNION. (Text in French) 1982. bi-m. 180 F. (France 180 F.; elsewhere 300 F.). Institut National de la Statistique et des Etudes Economiques, Direction Regionale de la Reunion, 15 rue de l'Ecole, B.P. 13, 97408 St. Denis Messag Cedex 9, Reunion. TEL 48-89-00. FAX 48-89-89. Ed. Jean Claude Hautcoeur. circ. 1,600. **Indexed:** Documentatieblad.

330   TI   ISSN 0070-878X
ECONOMIE DE LA TUNISIE EN CHIFFRES. (Text in Arabic, French) 1960. a. Institut National de la Statistique, 70 rue Echcham, Tunis, Tunisia.

330.9 330.1   MR   ISSN 0851-0458
ECONOMIE ET SOCIALISME; revue morocaine de reflection et de debat. 1986. q. DH.80 to individuals (foreign DH.120); institutions DH.200 (foreign DH.300). Centre d'Etudes et de Recherches Aziz Belal, B.P. 6330, Rabat, Morocco. TEL 77-62-17. FAX 77-38-89. Ed. Thami El-Khyari. adv.; bk.rev.
Document type: academic/scholarly publication.
Description: Covers problems in economic development in Morocco, Africa and the world.
Refereed Serial

ECONOMIE RURALE. see AGRICULTURE — Agricultural Economics

300   GR   ISSN 0013-0443
ECONOMIKOS TACHYDROMOS/FINANCIAL COURIER; weekly economic and financial review. 1926. w. $159. Lambrakis Press S.A., 10 Karytsi Sq., 102 33 Athens, Greece. TEL 30-1-333-3555. FAX 30-1-323-8740. TELEX 21-0608 DOL GR. (Subscr. to: 3 Christou Lada, 102 37 Athens, Greece. TEL 30-1-333-3810) Ed. Yannis Marinos. adv. contact: Nikos Biliris. bk.rev.; abstr.; bibl.; stat. circ. 22,000.

330   NE   ISSN 0013-0583
ECONOMISCH-STATISTISCHE BERICHTEN. 1916. w. fl.190 to individuals (foreign fl.290); institutions fl.295 (foreign fl.395); students fl.125 (foreign fl.225) (effective 1995). Nederlands Economisch Instituut - Netherlands Economic Institute, P.O. Box 4224, 3006 AE Rotterdam, Netherlands. TEL 31-10-4538743. FAX 31-10-4525840. E-mail: redactie-esb@nei.nl. Ed. H.A. Keuzenkamp. R&P contact: T. van Walderveen. adv.; bk.rev.; bibl.; stat.; index. circ. 5,500. **Indexed:** Excerpt.Med., Key to Econ.Sci., SCIMP, World Bibl.Soc.Sec. **Document type:** academic/scholarly publication.
●Also available online.
—BLDSC (3658.600000); SWETS.
Description: Professional publication for economists. Covers current economic trends and information, analysis of economic issues, national and international news, business news and politics. Includes positions available.

330   JA   ISSN 0013-0621
ECONOMIST. 1923. w. 280 Yen. Mainichi Shinbun Sha, 1-1-1 Hitotsubashi, Chiyoda-ku, Tokyo 100-51, Japan. TEL 81-3-3213-3711. FAX 81-3-3213-3724. TELEX 22324. (Order from: Oversea Courier Service Inc., Osaka Branch Office, 3-28 Nozatonishi, Nishiyodogawa, Osaka 541, Japan) Ed. Saburo Zushi. adv. circ. 117,000. **Indexed:** B.P.I., Bank.Lit.Ind., Bk.Rev.Dig., Curr.Cont., Mgmt.& Market.Abstr., PROMT, Risk Abstr., Soc.Sci.Ind., SSCI, Telegen, Tr.& Indus.Ind., W.R.C.Inf.
●Also available online. Vendor(s): UMI.

BUSINESS AND ECONOMICS — ECONOMIC SITUATION AND CONDITIONS

330.9 UK ISSN 0013-0613
HG11 CODEN: EONOEH
THE ECONOMIST. (N. American, European, and English editions avail.) 1843. w. (51/yr.) £80 (academic institutions £56) ($125 in US; Mexico $145; Canada Can.$176.55; Latin America $200); newsstand price: £2; $3.50; Can.$4.50. Economist Newspaper Ltd., 25 St. James's St., London SW1A 1HG, England. TEL 44-171-830-7000. FAX 44-171-839-2968. TELEX 24344 ECON G. E-mail: gca@economist.com; URL: http://www.economist.com. (Subscr. to: P.O. Box 14, Harold Hill, Romford, Essex RM3 8EQ, England. TEL 44-1708-381555; N. American subscr. to: Box 58524, Boulder, CO 80322-8524. TEL 800-456-6086) Ed. Bill Emmott. adv. contact: David Hanger. bk.rev.; charts; illus.; stat.; q. index; a. cum.index; circ. 609,444 (paid). (also avail. in microform from UMI; reprint service avail.) **Indexed:** ABI Inform., Acad.Ind., AESIS, B.P.I., Bk.Rev.Dig., Bk.Rev.Ind. (1965-), BMT, Br.Hum.Ind., CAD CAM Abstr., Child.Bk.Rev.Ind. (1965-), Dairy Sci.Abstr., Environ.Abstr., Geo.Abstr., High.Educ.Curr.Aware.Bull., Ind.Bus.Rep., Int.Lab.Doc., Intl.Polym.Sci.& Tech., Key to Econ.Sci., Maize Abstr., Mgmt.& Market.Abstr., Mid.East: Abstr.& Ind., P.A.I.S., Polit.Sci.Abstr., PROMT, RAPRA, Robomat., So.Pac.Per.Ind., Soc.Sci.Ind., Soyabean Abstr., Tr.& Indus.Ind., W.R.C.Inf., World Agri.Econ.& Rural Sociol.Abstr., World Text.Abstr. **Document type:** consumer publication.
●Also available online. Vendor(s): Information Access Co., Lexis-Nexis, MediaStream.
Also available on CD-ROM. Producer(s): Chadwyck-Healey Inc.
—BLDSC (3659.410000); CASDDS; CISTI; Genuine Article; KR SourceOne; SWETS; UMI. **CCC.**
Description: Offers reporting, commentary, and analysis on world politics, finance, and business trends. Also covers science and technology, literature and the arts.

016.33 UK ISSN 1358-247X
ECONOMIST. ANNUAL INDEX. a. Economist Newspaper Ltd., 25 St. James's St., London SW1A 1HG, England. TEL 44-171-830-7000. FAX 44-171-839-2968. TELEX 24344 ECON G. (Subscr. to: P.O. Box 14, Harold Hill, Romford, Essex RM3 8EQ, England; N. American subscr. to: Box 58524, Boulder, CO 80322-8524. TEL 800-486-6086) (back issues avail.) **Document type:** abstracting/indexing.
●Also available on CD-ROM. Producer(s): Chadwyck-Healey Inc.

330.9 UK
THE ECONOMIST ON C D - R O M. q. $595 (effective 1996). Chadwyck-Healey Ltd., The Quorum, Barnwell Rd., Cambridge CB5 8SW, England. TEL 44-1223-215512. FAX 44-1223-215514. E-mail: marketing@chadwyck.co.uk; URL: http://www.chadwyck.com. (In N. America: Chadwyck-Healey Inc., 1101 King St., Alexandria, VA 22314. TEL 800-752-0515. FAX 703-683-7589) (back issues avail.)
●Available only on CD-ROM. Producer(s): Chadwyck-Healey Inc.
Description: Provides electronic access to the full text of The Economist magazine and its index. Archival discs cover material from 1987-1994.

330 UA ISSN 0013-0672
L'ECONOMISTE EGYPTIEN. 1901. w. Margaret & Joffre Hosni, Ed. & Pub., 11 Sharia de la Poste, P.O. Box 847, Alexandria, Egypt. adv.; mkt.; pat.; stat.; tr.lit.; tr.mk. (looseleaf format)

330.9 UG
THE ECONOMY. (Text in English) 1979. w. EAs.600. Economy Publications Ltd., POB 6787, Kampala, Uganda. Ed. Roland Mutale. circ. 25,000.

330 EC
ECUADOR; carta de noticias. 1975. w. free. Ministerio de Relaciones Exteriores, Quito, Ecuador. Ed. Abelardo Posso. charts; illus.; stat. circ. 1,200.
Description: General and economic news of Ecuador.

330 EC
ECUADOR. CORPORACION FINANCIERA NACIONAL. BOLETIN ESTADISTICO. no.6, 1978. irreg., latest 1996. Corporacion Financiera Nacional, Robles 731 y Amazonas, Apdo. de Correos 163, Quito, Ecuador. charts.
Description: Reviews statistical information from the past four years.

330.9 UK
EDINBURGH ECONOMIC REVIEW. 1986. q. free. City of Edinburgh District Council, Department of Economic Development and Estates, 375 High St., Edinburgh EH1 1QE, Scotland. TEL 44-131-5293417. FAX 44-131-5293737. Ed. G.S. Callaghan. bibl.; charts; illus.; stat. circ. 3,000. (also avail. in Braille; diskette format; large print edition avail.; back issues avail.) **Document type:** government publication.
Formerly: Edinburgh Economic and Employment Review.
Description: Stimulates debate and interest about local economic and employment issues. Includes statistical summary.

334 IO ISSN 0852-0747
EDISI CHUSUS BULLETIN KOPERASI. Variant title: Bulletin Koperasi. 1966. q. free. Department of Cooperatives, Directorate General of the Institutional Promotion for Cooperatives - Direktorat Bina Penyuluhan Koperasi, Jalan H.R. Rasuna Said Kav. 3-5, Jakarta 12940, Indonesia. TEL 5204382. Eds. Purnomo and Rosdiana Sipayung. charts; stat.; circ. 7,500 (controlled).
Description: Provides cooperative information such as government policy, operational instructions, and succsesful examples of cooperative societies to various provincial and district offices and universities in Indonesia.

330.9 CN ISSN 0824-409X
EDMONTON REPORT ON ECONOMIC DEVELOPMENT. q. free. Economic Development Edmonton, 9797 Jasper Ave., Edmonton, AB T5J 1N9, Canada. TEL 403-424-7870; 800-661-6965. FAX 403-426-0535. Ed. Janice Dewar. circ. 13,500. (back issues avail.)
Description: Responsible for the initiation of economic development programs on behalf of Edmonton.

330.9 UA
EGYPT. SPECIALISED NATIONAL COUNCILS. MAGAZINE. 1976. q. Specialised National Councils, Arab Socialist Union Bldg., Nile Corniche, Cairo, Egypt. Ed. A. Anis.

EKONOMIKA UKRAINY. see BUSINESS AND ECONOMICS — Economic Systems And Theories, Economic History

330 YU ISSN 0013-3248
HC407.Y6
EKONOMSKA POLITIKA. 1951. w. Trg Nikole Pasica 7, 11000 Belgrade, Yugoslavia. TEL 38-11-335355. TELEX 11410. Ed. Milos Markovic. adv.; bk.rev.; charts; illus.; stat. circ. 4,200. (tabloid format; back issues avail.)

330.9 ES
EL SALVADOR. MINISTERIO DE PLANIFICACION Y COORDINACION DEL DESARROLLO ECONOMICO Y SOCIAL. MEMORIA DE LABORES. 1976. irreg. Ministerio de Planificacion y Coordinacion del Desarrollo Economico y Social, Biblioteca Tecnica "Hector Humberto Zelaya", 10 Av. Sur y Calle Mexico, 1505 Barrio San Jacinto, San Salvador, El Salvador.

330.9 ES
EL SALVADOR, INFORME ECONOMICO Y SOCIAL. 1975. a. free. Ministerio de Planificacion y Coordinacion del Desarrollo Economico y Social, Biblioteca Tecnica "Hector Humberto Zelaya", 10 Av. Sur y Calle Mexico, 1505 Barrio San Jacinto, San Salvador, El Salvador. stat. circ. 88. (processed)
Formerly: Economia Salvadorena (San Salvador, 1975).
Description: Includes comparative data for previous years.

330.9 NE ISSN 0340-8744
H62.5.A9
EMPIRICA. 1974. 3/yr. fl.365 to institutions; $187.50 to institutions in U.S. (effective 1998). (Oesterreichisches Institut fuer Wirtschaftsforschung, AU - Austrian Economic Institute) Kluwer Academic Publishers, Postbus 17, 3300 AA Dordrecht, Netherlands. TEL 31-78-6392392. FAX 31-78-6392254. TELEX 29245 KAPG NL. E-mail: services@wkap.nl; URL: http://www.wkap.nl. (Dist. by: Kluwer Academic Publishers Group, P.O. Box 322, 3300 AH Dordrecht, Netherlands. TEL 31-78-6392392. FAX 31-78-6546474; N. America dist. addr.: Box 358, Accord St., Hingham, MA 02018-0358. TEL 617-871-6600. FAX 617-871-6528) (Co-sponsor: Austrian Economic Association) Ed. Peter Mooslechner. adv. circ. 800. **Indexed:** Geo.Abstr.H.G., J.of Econ.Lit., P.A.I.S.For.Lang.Ind. **Document type:** academic/scholarly publication.
—BLDSC (3737.005000); SWETS; UMI. **CCC.**
Description: Publishes applied articles and papers dealing with all kinds of problems relevant to economic policy, with particular emphasis on industrial economics, economic integration and relevant international economic issues.

330.9 US ISSN 0748-2663
HD4928.N62
EMPLOYEE BENEFITS IN MEDIUM AND LARGE FIRMS. a. $4.75. U.S. Bureau of Labor Statistics, 441 G St., N.W., Rm. 916, Washington, DC 20212. TEL 202-523-1944. (Subscr. to: Superintendent of Documents, U.S. Government Printing Office, Box 371954, Pittsburgh, PA 15150-7954. TEL 202-783-3238. FAX 202-512-2233; Or: Bureau of Labor Statistics Publications Sales Center, Box 2145, Chicago, IL 60690) Ed. Jorden N. Pfuntner. charts. circ. 3,500. (also avail. in magnetic tape; back issues avail.) **Document type:** government publication.

330.9 US
EMPLOYER COSTS FOR EMPLOYEE COMPENSATION. (Subseries of: National Office News Releases) m. U.S. Bureau of Labor Statistics, 2 Massachusetts Ave., N.E., Washington, DC 20212. TEL 202-655-4000. (Subscr. to: Superintendent of Documents, U.S. Government Printing Office, Box 371954, Pittsburgh, PA 15250-7954. TEL 202-512-1800; Or: Bureau of Labor Statistics Publications Sales Center, Box 2145, Chicago, IL 60690. FAX 202-512-2250) **Document type:** government publication.

330.9 US ISSN 0013-6840
HD5723
EMPLOYMENT AND EARNINGS. m. $31 (foreign $38.75). U.S. Bureau of Labor Statistics, 441 G St. N.W., Washington, DC 20212. TEL 202-655-4000. (Subscr. to: Superintendent of Documents, U.S. Government Printing Office, Box 371954, Pittsburgh, PA 15250-7954. TEL 202-512-1800. FAX 202-512-2250; Or: Bureau of Labor Statistics Publications Sales Center, Box 2145, Chicago, IL 60690) (also avail. in microform from UMI; microfiche from CIS; reprint service avail. from CIS,UMI) **Indexed:** Amer.Stat.Ind. (1974-), B.P.I., Ind.U.S.Gov.Per., P.A.I.S., PROMT. **Document type:** government publication.
—KR SourceOne; UMI.
Formerly: Employment and Earnings and Monthly Report on the Labor Force.
Description: Compiles national, state, and local data on unemployment, hours, and earnings.

331.1 US
EMPLOYMENT AND EARNINGS: CHARACTERISTICS OF FAMILIES. (Subseries of: National Office News Releases) q. U.S. Bureau of Labor Statistics, 2 Massachusetts Ave., N.E., Washington, DC 20212. TEL 202-655-4000. (Subscr. to: Superintendent of Documents, U.S. Government Printing Office, Box 371954, Pittsburgh, PA 15250-7954. TEL 202-512-1800. FAX 202-512-2250; Or: Bureau of Labor Statistics Publications Sales Center, Box 2145, Chicago, IL 60690) **Document type:** government publication.

BUSINESS AND ECONOMICS — ECONOMIC SITUATION AND CONDITIONS

330.9 US
EMPLOYMENT AND EARNINGS: STATES AND AREAS. (Subseries of: B L S Bulletins Series) 1939. a. U.S. Bureau of Labor Statistics, 441 G St., N.W., Washington, DC 20212. TEL 202-655-4000. (Subscr. to: Superintendent of Documents, U.S. Government Printing Office, Box 371954, Pittsburgh, PA 15250-7954. TEL 202-512-1800. FAX 202-512-2250; Or: Bureau of Labor Statistics Publications Sales Center, Box 2145, Chicago, IL 60690) **Document type:** government publication.
Formerly: Employment and Earnings Statistics for States and Areas.

330.9 US ISSN 0271-4787
HD8051
EMPLOYMENT AND EARNINGS: UNITED STATES. a. $34 (foreign $42.50). U.S. Bureau of Labor Statistics, 2 Massachusetts Ave., N.E., Washington, DC 20212. TEL 202-655-4000. (Subscr. to: Superintendent of Documents, U.S. Government Printing Office, Box 371954, Pittsburgh, PA 15250-7954. TEL 202-783-3238. FAX 202-512-2233; Or: Bureau of Labor Statistics Publications Sales Center, Box 2145, Chicago, IL 60690) (also avail. in microform from UMI) **Indexed:** Pers.Lit., PROMT, Text.Tech.Dig. **Document type:** government publication.
●Also available on CD-ROM.
Formerly: Employment and Earnings Statistics for the United States (ISSN 0071-013X)

330.9 331 US
EMPLOYMENT AND THE ECONOMY. ATLANTIC COASTAL REGION. 1969. q. free. Department of Labor, Division of Labor Market and Demographic Research, CN 057, Trenton, NJ 08625-0057. TEL 609-292-2145. Ed. Jan J. DeJong. circ. 1,300. **Document type:** government publication.
Description: Describes current labor market and economic conditions in Atlantic, Cape May, Monmouth and Ocean counties.

330.9 US
EMPLOYMENT AND THE ECONOMY. NORTHERN NEW JERSEY REGION. 1969. q. free. Department of Labor, Division of Labor Market and Demographic Research, CN 057, Trenton, NJ 08625-0057. TEL 609-292-2145. Ed. Jan J. DeJong. circ. 1,300. **Document type:** government publication.
Description: Describes current labor market and economic development conditions in Bergen, Essex, Hudson, Hunterdon, Middlesex, Morris, Passaic, Somerset, Sussex, Union, and Warren counties.

330.9 US
EMPLOYMENT AND THE ECONOMY. SOUTHERN NEW JERSEY REGION. 1969. q. free. Department of Labor, Division of Labor Market and Demographic Research, CN 057, Trenton, NJ 08625-0057. TEL 609-292-2145. Ed. Jan J. DeJong. circ. 1,300. **Document type:** government publication.
Description: Describes current labor market and economic conditions in Burlington, Camden, Cumberland, Glouster, Mercer and Salem counties.

EMPLOYMENT AND VACANCIES STATISTICS. SERIES C: INDUSTRIAL SECTOR. see BUSINESS AND ECONOMICS — Abstracting, Bibliographies, Statistics

330.9 US
EMPLOYMENT COST INDEX. (Subseries of: National Office News Releases) m. U.S. Bureau of Labor Statistics, 2 Massachusetts Ave., N.E., Washington, DC 20212. TEL 202-655-4000. (Subscr. to: Superintendent of Documents, U.S. Government Printing Office, Box 371954, Pittsburgh, PA 15250-7954. TEL 202-512-1800. FAX 202-512-2250; Or: Bureau of Labor Statistics Publications Sales Center, Box 2145, Chicago, IL 60690) **Document type:** government publication.

331.1 US
EMPLOYMENT COST INDEXES AND LEVELS. (Subseries of: B L S Bulletins) 1975. irreg. $11. U.S. Bureau of Labor Statistics, 2 Massachusetts Ave., N.E., Washington, DC 20212. TEL 202-655-4000. (Subscr. to: Superintendent of Documents, U.S. Government Printing Office, Box 371954, Pittsburgh, PA 15250-7954. TEL 202-512-1800. FAX 202-512-2250; Or: Bureau of Labor Statistics Publications Sales Center, Box 2145, Chicago, IL 60690) **Document type:** government publication.
Description: Analyzes employee compensation, using the Employment Cost Index and Employer Costs Employee Compensation data.

330.9 US
EMPLOYMENT, HOURS, AND EARNINGS: UNITED STATES. (Subseries of: B L S Bulletins) a.? $33. U.S. Bureau of Labor Statistics, 2 Massachusetts Ave., N.E., Washington, DC 20212. TEL 202-655-4000. (Subscr. to: Superintendent of Documents, U.S. Government Printing Office, Box 371954, Pittsburgh, PA 15250-7954. TEL 202-512-1800. FAX 202-512-2250; Or: Bureau of Labor Statistics Publications Sales Center, Box 2145, Chicago, IL 60690) stat. **Document type:** government publication.
Description: Presents revised monthly and annual average data on national establishment-based employment, hours, and earnings by industry.

EMPLOYMENT IN EUROPE. see BUSINESS AND ECONOMICS — Labor And Industrial Relations

330.9 US
EMPLOYMENT IN PERSPECTIVE: WOMEN IN THE LABOR FORCE. (Subseries of: B L S Reports) q. U.S. Bureau of Labor Statistics, 2 Massachusetts Ave., N.E., Washington, DC 20212. TEL 202-655-4000. (Subscr. to: Superintendent of Documents, U.S. Government Printing Office, Box 371954, Pittsburgh, PA 15250-7954. TEL 202-512-1800. FAX 202-512-2250; Or: Bureau of Labor Statistics Publications Sales Center, Box 2145, Chicago, IL 60690) **Document type:** government publication.
Description: Summarizes data about the labor force activity of older women.

EMPLOYMENT OPPORTUNITIES (WASHINGTON). see OCCUPATIONS AND CAREERS

EMPLOYMENT OUTLOOK SURVEY. see BUSINESS AND ECONOMICS — Labor And Industrial Relations

EMPLOYMENT POLICY INSTITUTE ECONOMIC REPORT. see BUSINESS AND ECONOMICS — Labor And Industrial Relations

330.9 310 US ISSN 0364-491X
HD5701
THE EMPLOYMENT SITUATION. (Subseries of: National Office News Releases) m. U.S. Bureau of Labor Statistics, 441 G St., N.W., Washington, DC 20212. TEL 202-523-1221. (Subscr. to: Superintendent of Documents, U.S. Government Printing Office, Box 371954, Pittsburgh, PA 15250-7954. TEL 202-512-1800. FAX 202-512-2250; Or: Bureau of Labor Statistics Publications Sales Center, Box 2145, Chicago, IL 60690) circ. 4,000. (also avail. in microfiche from CIS; reprint service avail. from CIS) **Indexed:** Amer.Stat.Ind. (1973-). **Document type:** government publication.

330.9 331.11 CL
ENCUESTA NACIONAL DEL EMPLEO TOTAL PAIS. 1966. irreg., latest 1986-91. $9. Instituto Nacional de Estadisticas, Av. Bulnes 418, Casilla 498, Correo 3 Santiago, Chile. circ. 700.

ENERGY ECONOMIST; an international analysis. see ENERGY

330.9861 CK ISSN 0121-117X
ENSAYOS DE ECONOMIA. 1989. s-a. Col.$12000 (foreign $60) (effective 1997). Universidad Nacional de Colombia, Facultad de Ciencias Humanas, Departamento de Economia, Apdo. Aereo 3840, Medellin, Colombia. FAX 57-4-2604451. Dir. Ramiro Restrepo Uribe.
Description: Publishes articles about Colombian economic affairs.

330.9 US
ENTERTAINMENT INDUSTRY OUTLOOK. m. $149. Cahners Publishing Company (New York), Entertainment Division, Division of Reed Elsevier Inc., 249 W. 17th St., New York, NY 10011. TEL 212-463-6500. FAX 212-463-6530. (Subscr. to: Cahners Economics, Box 59, New Town Branch, Boston, MA 02258-9908) **Document type:** newsletter.
Description: Provides economic analysis and forecasts relevant to decision makers in the entertainment industry.

330.9 GW ISSN 0177-9303
ENTSCHEIDUNGEN ZUM WIRTSCHAFTSRECHT - E W I R. 1980. s-m. DM.396. Verlag Kommunikationsforum GmbH Recht Wirtschaft Steuern, Aachener Str. 217, 50931 Cologne, Germany. TEL 0221-40088-0. Ed. Bruno M. Kuebler. adv.; bk.rev.
Formerly (until 1985): Zeitschrift fuer Wirtschaftsrecht - Z I P.

330.9 350 US
EQUALITY STATE ALMANAC. a. free. Department of Administration and Information, Economic Analysis Division, 327 E. Emerson Bldg., Cheyenne, WY 82002. TEL 307-777-7504. charts; stat. circ. 1,300. **Indexed:** SRI. **Document type:** government publication.
Formerly: Wyoming Data Handbook.
Description: Compiles detailed demographic, economic, and physical information for each county in Wyoming.

330.9 300 SJ
ESSAYS ON THE ECONOMY AND SOCIETY OF THE SUDAN. 1977. irreg., vol.2, 1986. National Council for Research, Economic and Social Research Council, P.O. Box 1166, Khartoum, Sudan. TEL 78805. TELEX 22342 ILIMI. Ed. Ali Mohamed el Hassan. bibl.

330.9 IT ISSN 0046-256X
EST - OVEST. (Text in English, French or Italian; summaries in English) 1970. 6/yr. Lit.180000 (foreign Lit.235000) (effective 1998). I S D E E - Istituto di Studi e Documentazione sull'Europa Comunitaria e l'Europa Orientale, Corso Italia, 27, 34122 Trieste, Italy. TEL 39-40-639130. FAX 39-40-634248. Ed. Tito Favaretto. R&P contact: Tito Favaretto. adv. contact: Miro Bisiach. bk.rev.; stat.; index. circ. 400. **Indexed:** A.B.C.Pol.Sci., Amer.Hist.& Life (1973-1989), Hist.Abstr. (1973-1989), Int.Lab.Doc., Int.Polit.Sci.Abstr., P.A.I.S.For.Lang.Ind. **Document type:** academic/scholarly publication.
Description: Deals with socio-economic and political-institutional aspects of Central and Eastern European countries, with particular reference to the Danubian-Balkan area and East-West relations.

330.9 PN ISSN 1023-3318
HC147
ESTADISTICA PANAMENA. INDICADORES ECONOMICOS. SECCION 011. 1965. s-a. Bl.0.50 (effective 1997). Direccion de Estadistica y Censo, Contraloria General, Apdo. 5213, Panama 5, Panama. FAX 507-269-7294. circ. 700. **Document type:** government publication, bulletin.
Supersedes in part (in 1994): Estadistica Panamena. Indicadores Economicos y Sociales. Section 011 (ISSN 0378-4940)
Description: Presents information on the economic situation of the country.

354 PN ISSN 0378-2603
HC147.Z9
ESTADISTICA PANAMENA. SITUACION ECONOMICA. SECCION 342. CUENTAS NACIONALES. 1950. a. Bl.0.50 (effective 1997). Direccion de Estadistica y Censo, Contraloria General, Apdo. 5213, Panama 5, Panama. FAX 507-269-7294. circ. 1,000. **Document type:** government publication, bulletin.
Description: Offers information on the different macroeconomic aggregates, such as national revenue, per-capita revenue, gross national product, and their means of calculation.

ESTRATEGICA SOBRE NUEVO LEON EN UNA EPOCA DE CAMBIO. see TECHNOLOGY: COMPREHENSIVE WORKS

330.9 CK ISSN 0120-0747
ESTUDIOS RURALES LATINOAMERICANOS/LATIN AMERICAN RURAL STUDIES. 1978. 3/yr. Col.750($20.40) to individuals; institutions $25.50. Fundacion Estudios Rurales Latinoamericanos, Apdo. Aereo 11386, Bogota, Colombia. TEL 2837771. Ed.Bd. adv.; bk.rev.; index. circ. 2,000. (back issues avail.) **Indexed:** Cott.& Trop.Fibr.Abstr., Hisp.Amer.Per.Ind. (1978-), IBR, Int.Lab.Doc., Rural Devel.Abstr.
●Also available online.

BUSINESS AND ECONOMICS — ECONOMIC SITUATION AND CONDITIONS

330.9   CN
ETOBICOKE BUSINESS. 10/yr. 252 Galaxy Blvd., Etobicoke, ON M9W 5R8, Canada. TEL 416-675-4390. FAX 416-675-9296. Ed. David Fuller; Pub. Betty Carr. R&P contact: Sal Bommarito. adv. contact: Dave Harvey. circ. 10,000. **Document type:** newspaper.

EURAZJA. see *POLITICAL SCIENCE — International Relations*

330.9489   DK   ISSN 0906-6039
EURO - POSTEN; Danmarks EU-avis. 1986. d. E P Erhverv, Media Huset ApS, P.O. Box 1670, Jyllingevej 57, DK-2720 Vanloese, Denmark. TEL 45-38-79-34-00. FAX 45-38-79-34-10. Ed. Ib Helge. adv.: B&W page DKK 34460, color page DKK 42100; trim 360 x 265; adv. contact: Ib Rasch. circ. 49,803. **Document type:** newspaper.
    Formerly (until 1991): Erhvervs - Posten (ISSN 0904-1486)

330.94   IT
▼**EUROMEDIA**. 1997. d. Lit.100000 (effective 1997). (Agenzia di Stampa Quotidiana e di Servizi per la Comunicazione) Mare s.r.l. Editrice, Centro Direzionale Is., G1, 80149 Naples, Italy. TEL 39-81-205948. FAX 39-81-5536574. E-mail: pisanti@mbox.vol.it. Ed. Amedeo Pisanti. **Document type:** newspaper.
    Description: Covers business and economic events in Europe and Southern Italy.

330.9   GW   ISSN 0931-5233
EUROPAEISCHE GEGENWART. (Text in English and German) 1980. bi-m. $5. Verlag fuer Wirtschaftliche Informationen, Malvenweg 4, 51061 Cologne, Germany. TEL 49-221-963564-0. FAX 49-221-96356427. circ. 10,000. **Document type:** bulletin.

EUROPAEISCHE RUNDSCHAU. see *POLITICAL SCIENCE — International Relations*

338   EI   ISSN 0191-4545
HD9525.A2   CODEN: ERPEDH
EUROPE. 1954. m. $15. (Commission of the European Communities) Office for Official Publications of the European Communities, L-2985 Luxembourg, Luxembourg. (Dist. in the U.S. by: European Community Information Service, 2100 M St., N.W., Ste. 707, Washington, DC 20037) Ed. Webster Martin. adv.; bk.rev.; illus.; stat.; index. circ. 35,000. (also avail. in microfilm from UMI; reprint service avail. from UMI) **Indexed:** B.P.I., P.A.I.S., Polit.Sci.Abstr., PROMT. **Document type:** bulletin.
●Also available online. **Vendor(s):** Information Access Co.
—BLDSC (3829.455700); KR SourceOne; SWETS; UMI; UnCover.
    Former titles: European Community (ISSN 0014-2891); Bulletin from the European Community; Community Topics.

320   UK   ISSN 0269-3852
HC240
EUROPE REVIEW. 1985. a. £40. Kogan Page Ltd., 120 Pentonville Rd., London N1 9JN, England. TEL 44-171-278-0433. FAX 44-171-837-6348. TELEX 263088 KOGAN G. Ed. Tony Axon. R&P contact: Linda Batman. adv.; illus.; stat. circ. 6,315. **Document type:** consumer publication.
—BLDSC (3829.481700).
    Description: Overview of economic and political situations in every country in Eastern and Western Europe.

338   EI
EUROPEAN ECONOMY. SERIES A: RECENT ECONOMIC TRENDS. 1979. m. $65. (Commission of the European Communities) Office for Official Publications of the European Communities, L-2985 Luxembourg, Luxembourg. (Dist. in U.S. by: Unipub, 4611-F Assembly Dr., Lanham, MD 20706-4391. TEL 800-274-4888. FAX 301-459-0056) stat. (also avail. in microfiche from CIS) **Indexed:** IIS, World Bank.Abstr.
—BLDSC (3829.697400).
    Formerly: European Economy. Supplement A: Recent Economic Trends (ISSN 0379-2056)

338   EI
EUROPEAN ECONOMY. SERIES B: BUSINESS AND CONSUMER SURVEY RESULTS. (Editions in English, French, German, Italian) m. $65. (Commission of the European Communities) Office for Official Publications of the European Communities, L-2985 Luxembourg, Luxembourg. (Dist. in U.S. by: Unipub, 4611-F Assembly Dr., Lanham, MD 20706-4391. TEL 800-274-4888. FAX 301-459-0056) stat. (also avail. in microfiche from CIS) **Indexed:** IIS.
—BLDSC (3829.697600).
    Formed by the merger of: European Economy. Supplement B: Economic Prospects - Business Survey Results (ISSN 0379-2110); European Economy. Supplement C: Economic Prospects - Consumer Survey Results (ISSN 0379-217X)

330.9 614   UK
EUROPEAN MARKET FOR THERMAL INSULATION PRODUCTS. (In five vols.: Vol.1 Germany; Vol.2 United Kingdom; Vol.3 France; Vol.4 Nordic Countries; Vol.5 European Summary) 1988. irreg., latest 1995. £1400 per vol. (all five vols. £5250). I A L Consultants, 109 Uxbridge Rd., Ealing, London W5 5TL, England. TEL 44-181-810-0919. FAX 44-181-566-4931. **Document type:** trade publication.

330.9   UK   ISSN 0961-2998
EUROPEAN REGIONAL INCENTIVES. 1980. a. £85. Bowker - Saur Ltd., A member of the Reed Elsevier plc group, Maypole House, Maypole Rd., E. Grinstead, W. Sussex RH19 1HU, England. TEL 44-1342-330100. FAX 44-1342-330191. E-mail: custserv@bowker-saur.co.uk; URL: http://www.reed-elsevier.com. Ed.Bd. circ. 500. pp./issue: 472. **Document type:** directory.
—BLDSC (3829.857000).
    Description: Provides a comprehensive review of the main regional incentives in each of the European Community countries and Sweden.

330.9   UK   ISSN 0969-4595
HC240
EUROPEAN REGIONAL PROSPECTS (ABRIDGED EDITION). (Base vol. full report also avail.) 1991. a. £80 (full report £1600). (European Economic Research Consortium (ERECO)) Cambridge Econometrics Ltd., Covent Garden, Cambridge CB1 2HS, England. TEL 01223-460760. FAX 01223-464378. (Alt. addr.: European Economic Interest Group, 48 rue de Cardinal, 1040 Brussels, Belgium. TEL 32-230-2212. FAX 32-230-6499) Ed. Richard Lewney. circ. 135 (paid). **Document type:** academic/scholarly publication.
—BLDSC (3829.890000).

330   EI   ISSN 1024-7580
EUROSTAT. KEY FIGURES; bulletin of economic trends in Europe and summaries. m. EC$100. Statistical Office of the European Communities, Eurostat, Rue Alcide de Gasperi, 2920 Luxembourg, Luxembourg. TEL 352-4301-34526. FAX 352-4301-34415. (Dist. by: Data Shop Eurostat Luxembourg, Rue J. Engling 2, L-1466 Dommeldange, Luxembourg. TEL 352-4335-2251. FAX 352-4335-22221; Dist. in the U.S. by: Unipub, 4611-F, Assembly Dr., Lanham, MD 20706-4391. TEL 800-274-4888. FAX 301-459-0056) charts; stat. **Document type:** bulletin.
—BLDSC (5091.822778).

EUROSTAT. STATISTICS IN FOCUS. ECONOMY AND FINANCE. see *BUSINESS AND ECONOMICS — Abstracting, Bibliographies, Statistics*

EUROSTAT. STATISTICS IN FOCUS. ENERGY AND INDUSTRY. see *BUSINESS AND ECONOMICS — Abstracting, Bibliographies, Statistics*

EUROSTAT. STATISTICS IN FOCUS. POPULATION AND SOCIAL CONDITIONS. see *BUSINESS AND ECONOMICS — Abstracting, Bibliographies, Statistics*

EUROSTAT. STATISTIK KURZGEFASST. BEVOELKERUNG UND SOZIALE BEDINGUNGEN. see *BUSINESS AND ECONOMICS — Abstracting, Bibliographies, Statistics*

EUROSTAT. STATISTIK KURZGEFASST. ENERGIE UND INDUSTRIE. see *BUSINESS AND ECONOMICS — Abstracting, Bibliographies, Statistics*

EUROSTAT. STATISTIK KURZGEFASST. WIRTSCHAFT UND FINANZEN. see *BUSINESS AND ECONOMICS — Abstracting, Bibliographies, Statistics*

EUROSTAT. STATISTIQUES EN BREF. ECONOMIE ET FINANCES. see *BUSINESS AND ECONOMICS — Abstracting, Bibliographies, Statistics*

EUROSTAT. STATISTIQUES EN BREF. ENERGIE ET INDUSTRIE. see *BUSINESS AND ECONOMICS — Abstracting, Bibliographies, Statistics*

EUROSTAT. STATISTIQUES EN BREF. POPULATION ET CONDITIONS SOCIALES. see *BUSINESS AND ECONOMICS — Abstracting, Bibliographies, Statistics*

330.9   US
EVALUATING AND BUYING A FRANCHISE.* 1987. irreg. $4.95. Pilot Books, Box 2102, Greenport, NY 11944-0893. TEL 516-422-2225. FAX 516-422-2227. Ed. Sam Small. R&P contact: Anne Small.

330   MX   ISSN 0014-3960
HC131
EXAMEN DE LA SITUACION ECONOMICA DE MEXICO. English edition: Review of the Economic Situation of Mexico (ISSN 0187-3407) (Text in English or Spanish) 1925. m. free. Banco Nacional de Mexico, S.A., Department of Economic Research, Madero 21, piso 2, 06000 Mexico, D.F., Mexico. FAX 525-2250025. (Subscr. to: Av. Madero 21, 2nd Fl. 06000 Mexico, D.F., Mexico) Ed. Alberto Gomez. charts; illus.; stat.; index. cum.index: 1925-1969, 1970-1979, 1980-1993. circ. 5,000. (also avail. in microfilm from OMN) **Indexed:** Int.Lab.Doc., Key to Econ.Sci., PROMT.
    Description: Examines economic conditions affecting Mexico. Includes information on all aspects of the economy, from the gold market and cattle industry, to public-sector enterprise and the commercial banking system.

330.9   CK
EXCLUSIVEDADES DE ECONOMIA. 1976. fortn. $80. Publicaciones Contextos Ltda, Calle 18 no. 7-18, Apdo. 12382, Bogota, Colombia. Ed. Jose M. Espinosa. circ. 80.
    Formerly: Colombia Economica.

330.9   KE   ISSN 0251-0332
EXECUTIVE; Kenya's premier business journal. (Text in English) 1980. m. KShs.1500 (rest of Africa $84; Europe, Middle and Near East $92; Australia, U.S. and Far East $102) (effective 1997). Space Sellers Ltd., Chepkorio Rd., P.O. Box 47186, Nairobi, Kenya. TEL 254-2-555811. FAX 254-2-557815. Ed. Ali Zaidi; Pub. Sylvia King. R&P contact: Sylvia King. TEL 254-2-530598. adv. contact: Lucy Kamau. circ. 8,000. **Document type:** trade publication.
    Description: Directed to decision makers.

330.9   UK
EXECUTIVE NORTH EAST. 1973. s-m. £12. Executive North East Magazine, 30 Queen St., Redcar, Cleveland TS10 1BD, England. TEL 0642-477155. FAX 0642-477143. Ed. John Malkin. adv.; bk.rev.; circ. 10,000 (controlled). (back issues avail.)

EXPANSION. see *BUSINESS AND ECONOMICS*

EXPANSION EN C D - R O M. see *BUSINESS AND ECONOMICS*

EXTERNAL TRADE STATISTICS OF GHANA (ANNUAL). see *BUSINESS AND ECONOMICS — Abstracting, Bibliographies, Statistics*

EXTERNAL TRADE STATISTICS OF GHANA (HALF-YEARLY). see *BUSINESS AND ECONOMICS — Abstracting, Bibliographies, Statistics*

EXTERNAL TRADE STATISTICS OF GHANA (QUARTERLY). see *BUSINESS AND ECONOMICS — Abstracting, Bibliographies, Statistics*

330.9   US   ISSN 0162-3184
EXTRAORDINARY CONTRACTUAL RELIEF REPORTER. a. $230. Federal Publications Inc., 1120 20th St., N.W., Ste. 500 S., Washington, DC 20036. TEL 202-377-7000; 800-922-4330. FAX 202-659-2233. E-mail: webmaster@fedpub.com; URL: http://www.fedpub.com.
    Description: Reports on government contracts.

F C I B COUNTRY CREDIT REPORT. (Finance, Credit and International Business - National Association of Credit Management) see *BUSINESS AND ECONOMICS — Banking And Finance*

BUSINESS AND ECONOMICS — ECONOMIC SITUATION AND CONDITIONS

FCIB-NACM. MINUTES OF ROUND TABLE CONFERENCE. (Finance, Credit and International Business - National Association of Credit Management) see BUSINESS AND ECONOMICS — Banking And Finance

330.9   US
FIDE; Argentine economic review. q. $140. Fundacion de Investigaciones para el Desarrollo, c/o Juan Ovidio Zavala, 8370 Greensboro Dr., Stes. 1007-1009, McLean, VA 22102-3523. TEL 703-356-0787.
   Description: Analysis of the main social and economic trends in Argentina and in the world.

330.9   ES
FUSADES CARTA INFORMATIVA. bi-m. Fundacion Salvadorena para el Desarrollo Economico y Social, C. Chaparrastique y Blvd. Santa Elena, Urb. Santa Elena, Antiguo Cuscatlan, Dept. de la Libertad, San Salvador, El Salvador. TEL 503-78-3366. FAX 503-78-3356.

330.9 332.6   US
FXC REPORT. 1972. s-m. $190 (effective 1997). FXC Investor Corp., 62-19 Cooper Ave., Glendale, NY 11385. TEL 718-417-1330. FAX 718-417-5950. E-mail: fxmgt@aol.com. Ed. Frank Curzio. R&P contact: Frank Curzio. adv. contact: Sabine Boehm. circ. 2,000. (looseleaf format; back issues avail.) **Document type:** newsletter.
   Formerly: FXC Newsletter.
   Description: Provides conservative and speculative recommendations, allocated to six categories: asset play, growth, hi-tech, income, special and turnaround situations.

330.9   II   ISSN 0301-7796
FACTS AND FIGURES; * monthly bulletin of basic data of economic significance. (Text in English) 1972. m. Rs.50($10) 18 Ananddham Society, Nava Vadaj, Ahmedabad 380013, India. Ed. R.C. Patel. adv.; charts; stat.

338   US   ISSN 0887-2252
FAIRFIELD COUNTY BUSINESS JOURNAL. 1967. w. $54 (effective 1997). Westfair Communications, Inc., 108 Corporate Park Dr., Ste. 105, White Plains, NY 10604-3805. TEL 914-694-3600. FAX 914-694-3699. Ed. Mills Korte; Pub. Dee DelBello. R&P contact: Bruce Spring. adv. contact: Barbara Hanlon. bk.rev.; mkt. circ. 13,000. (tabloid format) **Indexed:** Tr.& Indus.Ind. **Document type:** trade publication.
   ●Also available online. **Vendor(s):** UMI.
   —UMI.
   Former titles: Connecticut Business Journal (ISSN 0300-7529); Southern Connecticut Business Journal (ISSN 0038-3988)

FAR EAST AND AUSTRALASIA (YEAR). see POLITICAL SCIENCE

330   CC   ISSN 0014-7591
HC411   CODEN: FEERAK
FAR EASTERN ECONOMIC REVIEW. (Text in English) 1946. w. $199. Review Publishing Co. Ltd., G.P.O. Box 160, Hong Kong, People's Republic of China. TEL 852-2508-4300. FAX 852-2503-1549. TELEX 66452 REVCD HX. URL: http://www.feer.com. Ed. L. Gordon Crovitz. adv. contact: Karen Mullis. bk.rev.; stat.; q. index. circ. 80,484. (also avail. in microform from UMI; microfilm from RPI; reprint service avail. from SCH) **Indexed:** ABI Inform., Acad.Ind., AESIS, Asian-Pac.Econ.Lit., B.P.I., BPIA, Gdlns., HongKongiana, HR Rep. (1986-), Ind.Bus.Rep., Int.Lab.Doc., Key to Econ.Sci., Mgmt.& Market.Abstr., Mid.East: Abstr.& Ind., P.A.I.S., Polit.Sci.Abstr., PSI, Rural Recreat.Tour.Abstr., So.Pac.Per.Ind., Soc.Sci.Ind., World Agri.Econ. & Rural Sociol.Abstr.
   ●Also available online. **Vendor(s):** Dow Jones News Retrieval.
   —BLDSC (3865.920000); KR SourceOne; SWETS; UMI; UnCover. **CCC.**
   Description: Reports and interprets business, finance, stock market, and political and investment trends in Asia.

330.9   GW   ISSN 0343-9062
HC281
FEDERAL REPUBLIC OF GERMANY - PARTNER OF THE WORLD; documentation of economy and export. 1966. a. $12. Verlag fuer Wirtschaftliche Informationen, Malvenweg 4, 51061 Cologne, Germany. TEL 49-221-963564-0. FAX 49-221-96356427. adv. circ. 20,000. **Document type:** bulletin.

330.9   US   ISSN 0732-1813
HC107.A13   CODEN: ECRWDA
FEDERAL RESERVE BANK OF ATLANTA. ECONOMIC REVIEW. 1915. bi-m. free. Federal Reserve Bank of Atlanta, 104 Marietta N.W., Atlanta, GA 30303-2713. TEL 404-521-8020. Ed. Joycelyn Woolfolk. charts; illus.; stat.; index. circ. 23,000. (also avail. in microform from UMI,MIM; microfiche from CIS; back issues avail.; reprint service avail. from CIS) **Indexed:** ABI Inform, Amer.Stat.Ind. (1974-), Bank.Lit.Ind., BPIA, Fed Print, INSPEC, J.of Econ.Lit., P.A.I.S., PROMT, World Bank.Abstr. **Document type:** academic/scholarly publication.
   —BLDSC (3654.928000); UMI; UnCover.
   Incorporates (in Mar. 1981): Caribbean Basin Economic Survey; **Formerly** (1975-1981): Federal Reserve Bank of Atlanta. Monthly Review (ISSN 0014-9144)

330.9   US   ISSN 0899-6555
FEDERAL RESERVE BANK OF ATLANTA. ECONOMICS UPDATE. 1981. q. free. Federal Reserve Bank of Atlanta, 104 Marietta St., N.W., Atlanta, GA 30303-2713. TEL 404-521-8020. Ed. Michael Murdoch. charts. circ. 8,600. (also avail. in microfiche from CIS; back issues avail.; reprint service avail. from CIS) **Indexed:** Amer.Stat.Ind. (1988-). **Document type:** newsletter.
   Formerly (until 1987): Southeastern Economic Insight.

330.9   US   ISSN 0899-6571
FEDERAL RESERVE BANK OF ATLANTA. REGIONAL UPDATE. 1988. q. free. Federal Reserve Bank of Atlanta, 104 Marietta St., N.W., Atlanta, GA 30303-2713. TEL 404-521-8020. Ed. Michael Murdoch. circ. 6,900. (also avail. in microfiche from CIS; reprint service avail. from CIS) **Indexed:** Amer.Stat.Ind. (1988-). **Document type:** newsletter.

330.9   US   ISSN 0361-8714
FEDERAL RESERVE BANK OF BOSTON. CONFERENCE SERIES. 1969. a. Federal Reserve Bank of Boston, Research Department, 600 Atlantic Ave., Box 2076, Boston, MA 02106-2076. TEL 617-973-3397. FAX 617-973-4292. URL: http://www.bos.frb.org. Ed. J. Poskanzer. bibl.; charts; tr.lit. circ. 5,000. (also avail. in microform from UMI; reprint service avail. from SCH,UMI) **Indexed:** Fed Print, World Bank.Abstr.
   —UMI.

330.9   US   ISSN 1062-1865
HC107.A11
FEDERAL RESERVE BANK OF BOSTON. REGIONAL REVIEW. 1991. q. free. Federal Reserve Bank of Boston, Research Department, 600 Atlantic Ave., Boston, MA 02106. TEL 617-973-3397. FAX 617-973-4292. URL: http://www.bos.frb.org. Ed. Steven Sass. circ. 20,000. **Indexed:** P.A.I.S.
   Description: Contains essays on New England's economy for the general business audience.

330.9   US   ISSN 0149-5364
HC107.A165
FEDERAL RESERVE BANK OF DALLAS. ECONOMIC REVIEW. 1916. bi-m. free. Federal Reserve Bank of Dallas, Box 655906, Dallas, TX 75265-5906. TEL 214-922-5254. FAX 214-922-5268. Ed. Rhonda Harris. charts; illus.; stat. circ. 20,000. (also avail. in microform from UMI,MIM; microfiche from CIS; reprint service avail. from CIS) **Indexed:** ABI Inform, Amer.Stat.Ind. (1975-), Bank.Lit.Ind., BPIA, Chic.Per.Ind., Fed Print, Ind.Per.Art.Relat.Law, J.of Econ.Lit., P.A.I.S., World Agri.Econ.& Rural Sociol.Abstr., World Bank.Abstr.
   Former titles: Federal Reserve Bank of Dallas. Review; Federal Reserve Bank of Dallas. Business Review (ISSN 0007-702X)
   Description: Publishes analytical articles on economic and financial matters, ranging in scope from international finance to regional developments.

330.9   US   ISSN 0161-2387
HC107.A17   CODEN: ERKCDK
FEDERAL RESERVE BANK OF KANSAS CITY. ECONOMIC REVIEW. 1914. q. free. Federal Reserve Bank of Kansas City, 925 Grand Blvd., Kansas City, MO 64198-0001. TEL 816-881-2683. FAX 816-881-2569. Ed. Craig S. Hakkio. circ. 30,000. **Indexed:** Amer.Stat.Ind. (1974-), B.P.I., Bank.Lit.Ind., BPIA, C.R.E.J., Fed Print, Ind.Per.Art.Relat.Law, P.A.I.S., PROMT, World Bank.Abstr. **Document type:** academic/scholarly publication.
   —BLDSC (3654.932000); KR SourceOne; UMI; UnCover.
   Formerly (until 1978): Federal Reserve Bank of Kansas City. Monthly Review (ISSN 0014-9152)

330.9   US
HC101   CODEN: FRYMAQ
FEDERAL RESERVE BANK OF NEW YORK. ECONOMIC POLICY REVIEW. 1976. q. free. Federal Reserve Bank of New York, Public Information, 33 Liberty St., New York, NY 10045-0001. TEL 212-720-6150. charts; stat. circ. 38,000. (also avail. in microform from UMI; microfiche from CIS; reprint service avail. from CIS,SCH,UMI) **Indexed:** ABI Inform, Amer.Stat.Ind. (1974-), B.P.I, Bank.Lit.Ind., BPIA, Bus.Ind., C.R.E.J., Fed Print, Ind.Free Per., J.of Econ.Lit., Mid.East: Abstr.& Ind., P.A.I.S., PROMT, Sage Pub.Admin.Abstr., Sage Urb.Stud.Abstr., Tr.& Indus.Ind., World Bank.Abstr.
   ●Also available online. **Vendor(s):** Knight-Ridder Information, Inc., UMI.
   —KR SourceOne; UMI; UnCover.
   Formerly (until 1995): Federal Reserve Bank of New York. Quarterly Review (ISSN 0147-6580); Supersedes (with vol.58, no.10): Federal Reserve Bank of New York. Monthly Review (ISSN 0014-9160)
   Description: Describes patterns and trends in banking, investment, and capital market activities.

330 332   US   ISSN 0007-7011
HC107.A12   CODEN: FRBPBN
FEDERAL RESERVE BANK OF PHILADELPHIA. BUSINESS REVIEW. Key Title: Business Review (Philadelphia). 1918. bi-m. free. Federal Reserve Bank of Philadelphia, Research Department, Box 66, Philadelphia, PA 19105. TEL 215-574-6428. FAX 215-574-4364. URL: http://www.phil.frb.org. Ed. Sarah Burke. charts; illus.; stat.; index, cum.index. circ. 10,000. (tabloid format; also avail. in microform from UMI,MIM; microfiche from CIS; reprint service avail. from CIS,UMI) **Indexed:** ABI Inform, Amer.Stat.Ind. (1974-), B.P.I., Bank.Lit.Ind., BPIA, C.R.E.J., Fed Print, Ind.Free Per., P.A.I.S., PROMT, World Bank.Abstr.
   ●Also available online. **Vendor(s):** UMI.
   —BLDSC (2934.690000); KR SourceOne; UMI; UnCover.
   Description: Presents articles written by staff economists and dealing with economic policy, financial economics and banking, and regional economic issues.

330.9   US
FEDERAL RESERVE BANK OF PHILADELPHIA. WORKING PAPERS. irreg. Federal Reserve Bank of Philadelphia, Economic Research Division, Box 66, Philadelphia, PA 19105. TEL 215-574-6428. **Document type:** monographic series.

BUSINESS AND ECONOMICS — ECONOMIC SITUATION AND CONDITIONS

330.9   US   ISSN 1069-7225
HC107.A13
FEDERAL RESERVE BANK OF RICHMOND. ECONOMIC QUARTERLY. 1914. q. free. Federal Reserve Bank of Richmond, Research Department, 701 E. Byrd St., Richmond, VA 23219. TEL 804-697-8000. FAX 804-697-8287. E-mail: eg@rich.frb.org; URL: http://www.rich.frb.org. (Subscr. to: Public Affairs, Box 27622, Richmond, VA 23261. TEL 804-697-8111) Ed. Thomas M. Humphrey. R&P contact: Elaine Mandaleris. TEL 804-697-8144. bibl.; charts; stat. circ. 15,000. (also avail. in microform from UMI; microfiche from CIS; back issues avail.; reprint service avail. from CIS) **Indexed:** ABI Inform, Amer.Stat.Ind. (1974-), B.P.I., Bank.Lit.Ind., BPIA, Fed Print, J.of Econ.Lit., P.A.I.S, World Bank.Abstr. **Document type:** academic/scholarly publication.
●Also available online. Vendor(s): Information Access Co.
—BLDSC (3654.140000); KR SourceOne; UMI; UnCover.
Former titles (until 1992): Federal Reserve Bank of Richmond. Economic Review (ISSN 0094-6893); (until 1974): Federal Reserve Bank of Richmond. Monthly Review (ISSN 0014-9179)
Description: Articles on monetary theory and policy, banking and finance.

330.9   US
FEDERAL RESERVE BANK OF ST. LOUIS. ANNUAL REPORT. a. Federal Reserve Bank of St. Louis, Box 442, St. Louis, MO 63166. TEL 314-444-8320. **Document type:** corporate report.

330.9   US   ISSN 0430-1978
HG2563
FEDERAL RESERVE BANK OF ST. LOUIS. MONETARY TRENDS. m. free. Federal Reserve Bank of St. Louis, Box 422, St. Louis, MO 63166. TEL 314-444-8320. charts; stat.
Description: Contains charts and tables relating to monetary and reserve aggregates, selected interest rates and commercial bank loans with a brief analysis of an issue of current interest.

330.9   US   ISSN 0430-1986
HC101
FEDERAL RESERVE BANK OF ST. LOUIS. NATIONAL ECONOMIC TRENDS. m. free. Federal Reserve Bank of St. Louis, Box 244, St. Louis, MO 63166. TEL 314-444-8320. charts.
—UMI.
Description: Data on national output, employment, inflation and selected federal budget measures along with a brief analysis of an issue of current interest.

330.9   US   ISSN 0014-9187
HC107.A15   CODEN: FRBRDV
FEDERAL RESERVE BANK OF ST. LOUIS. REVIEW. 1917. bi-m. Federal Reserve Bank of St. Louis, Box 442, St. Louis, MO 63166. TEL 314-444-8320. Ed. Daniel P. Brennan. charts; stat.; index. circ. 25,000. (also avail. in microform from UMI; microfiche from CIS; reprint service avail. from CIS,UMI) **Indexed:** ABI Inform, Amer.Stat.Ind. (1974-), B.P.I, Bank.Lit.Ind., BPIA, Fed Print, IBR, J.of Econ.Lit., Mag.Ind., P.A.I.S., PROMT, Rural Recreat.Tour.Abstr., World Agri.Econ. & Rural Sociol.Abstr.
●Also available online. Vendor(s): Information Access Co., UMI.
—BLDSC (7786.125000); KR SourceOne; UMI; UnCover.
Formerly: Federal Reserve Bank of St. Louis. Monthly Review.
Description: Contains articles about national and international economic developments, particularly their monetary aspects.

330.9   US
FEDERAL RESERVE BANK OF SAN FRANCISCO. ECONOMIC LETTER. 38/yr. free (foreign $50). Federal Reserve Bank of San Francisco, Box 7702, San Francisco, CA 94120. TEL 415-974-3230. FAX 415-974-3341. URL: http://www.frbsf.org. Ed. Judith Goff. R&P contact: Erika Dyquisto. charts; stat. circ. 17,000. **Indexed:** Fed Print, PROMT, World Bank.Abstr. **Document type:** newsletter.
●Also available online.
Former titles: Federal Reserve Bank of San Francisco. Weekly Letter (ISSN 0890-927X); Federal Reserve Bank of San Francisco. Business and Financial Letter.

330.9   US   ISSN 0363-0021
HC101
FEDERAL RESERVE BANK OF SAN FRANCISCO. ECONOMIC REVIEW. 1974. 3/yr. free. Federal Reserve Bank of San Francisco, Box 7702, San Francisco, CA 94120. TEL 415-974-3230. FAX 415-974-3341. URL: http://www.frbsf.org. Ed. Judith Goff. R&P contact: Erika L. Dyquisto. charts; illus.; index. circ. 17,000. (also avail. in microfiche from CIS; reprint service avail. from CIS) **Indexed:** ABI Inform, Amer.Stat.Ind. (1974-), Bank.Lit.Ind., C.R.E.J., Fed Print, J.of Econ.Lit., P.A.I.S., PROMT, World Bank.Abstr. **Document type:** academic/scholarly publication.
●Also available online. Vendor(s): UMI.
—BLDSC (3654.940000); UMI; UnCover.
Former titles: Federal Reserve Bank of San Francisco. Business Review (ISSN 0093-8262); Federal Reserve Bank of San Francisco. Monthly Review (ISSN 0014-9195)

330.9   US
FEDERAL RESERVE BASIC INSTRUCTIONS. irreg. $50 per no. in U.S., Canada, Mexico; elsewhere $100. (Federal Reserve System, Board of Governors) U.S. National Technical Information Service, 5825 Port Royal Rd., Springfield, VA 22161. TEL 703-487-4630.
Description: Covers the following categories: insured commercial banks with domestic and foreign offices, domestic offices only and total assets of $300 million or more, domestic offices only and total assets between $100 and $300 million, domestic offices only with total assets of less than $100 million.

330.9   US
FEDERAL RESERVE FORMS. q. $170 in U.S., Canada, Mexico; elsewhere $340. (Federal Reserve System, Board of Governors) U.S. National Technical Information Service, 5825 Port Royal Rd., Springfield, VA 22161. TEL 703-487-4630.
Description: Provides the report forms used by state member banks to submit reports of condition and income to the Federal Reserve, as broken down in the basic instructions.

330.9   US
FEDERAL RESERVE INSTRUCTIONS. (Supplement to: Basic Instructions) irreg. $50 per issue in US, Canada, Mexico; elsewhere $100. (Federal Reserve System, Board of Governors) U.S. National Technical Information Service, 5825 Port Royal Rd., Springfield, VA 22161. TEL 703-487-4630.

330.9   US
HC110.P63
FEDERAL SPENDING IN THE NORTHEAST - MIDWEST. 1979. a. price varies. Northeast - Midwest Institute, Center for Regional Policy, 218 D St., S.E., Washington, DC 20003. TEL 202-544-5200. FAX 202-544-0043. URL: http://www.nemw.org. Ed. Richard Munson. R&P contact: Tim Kay. adv. contact: Tim Kay. charts, illus. **Document type:** academic/scholarly publication.
Supersedes: Guide to State and Federal Resources for Economic Development (ISSN 0894-4202)
Description: Analyzes the flow of federal funds into the states by examining per-capita federal spending and the rate of return on federal tax dollars.

660.28 330.9   BE   ISSN 0085-0489
FEDERATION DES INDUSTRIES CHIMIQUES DE BELGIQUE. RAPPORT ANNUEL. (Text in Flemish, French) 1928. a. free. Federation des Industries Chimiques de Belgique, Square Marie-Louise 49, 1000 Brussels, Belgium. TEL 32-2-2389711. FAX 32-2-2311301. Ed. Paul-F. Smets. **Document type:** corporate report.
Description: Describes the economic situation, the results, and the perspectives of the Belgian chemical industry.

330.9   US   ISSN 1045-3334
FEDGAZETTE: FEDERAL RESERVE BANK OF MINNEAPOLIS REGIONAL BUSINESS & ECONOMICS NEWSPAPER. (Includes: Agricultural Credit Conditions (ISSN 0737-948X)) 1985. q. free. Federal Reserve Bank of Minneapolis, Public Affairs Department, Box 291, Minneapolis, MN 55480-0291. TEL 612-340-2446. FAX 612-335-2855. URL: http://woodrow.mpls.frb.fed.us. Ed. David Fettig. circ. 18,000. (also avail. in microfiche from CIS; reprint service avail. from CIS) **Indexed:** Amer.Stat.Ind. (1985-1988). **Document type:** newspaper.
●Also available online. Vendor(s): UMI.
—UMI.
Incorporates (1985-1988): Federal Reserve Bank of Minneapolis. District Economic Conditions (ISSN 0882-410X)
Description: Focuses on economic issues affecting the states in the Ninth Federal Reserve District. Incorporates national and district economic data. Includes opinion poll results and business news.

330.9   LB
FINANCE BULLETIN. 1979. 3/yr. $7.50 includes Ministry of Finance Annual Report. Office of Fiscal Policy and Planning, Borad St., Monrovia, Liberia. charts; stat.

FINANCIAL MANAGEMENT SURVEY. see BUSINESS AND ECONOMICS — Management

330.9   US   ISSN 1080-9821
HG3810
FINANCIAL TIMES CURRENCY FORECASTER; consensus forecasts of the worldwide currency and economic outlook. (Supplement included: Mid-Month Global Financial Report) 1981. m. $695 (includes supplement) (foreign $731). Capitol Publications Inc., 1101 Kings St., Ste. 444, Alexandria, VA 22314. TEL 800-327-7205. FAX 800-645-4104. circ. 2,000. **Document type:** trade publication.
—CCC.
Former titles (until 1995): Currency Forecaster's Digest; (until 1987): Blue Chip Economic WorldScan (ISSN 0741-8337)
Description: Presents forecasts analysis for 40 major international currencies and key economic variables for the 20 largest industrialized countries.

330.9   US
▼**FINANCIAL TREND FORECASTER.** 1995. m. E-mail: fintrend@aol.com; URL: http://www.fintrend.com/. **Document type:** newsletter.
●Available only online.
Description: Tracks and predicts trends, inflation, and profit opportunities in gold, stocks, bonds, and mutual funds.

330   FI   ISSN 0071-5271
FINLAND. KANSANTALOUSOSASTO. TALOUDELLINEN KATSAUS. ECONOMIC SURVEY. (Supplement to the Budget) (Text in English, Finnish, Swedish) 1948. a. FIM 100. Valtion Painatuskeskus - Government Printing Centre; Ministry of Finance, Annankatu 44, 00100 Helsinki 10, Finland. **Document type:** government publication.
Formerly (until 1955): Finland. Kansantalousosasto. Taloudellinen Tilannekatsaus (ISSN 0784-7521)

330.9   US   ISSN 0015-2757
HB1
FIRST HAWAIIAN BANK. ECONOMIC INDICATORS; a bi-monthly report by the research department. 1961. bi-m. free. First Hawaiian Bank, Research Department, Box 3200, Honolulu, HI 96847. TEL 808-525-7079. FAX 808-525-6204. Ed. Leroy O. Laney. adv.; stat. circ. 7,000. **Indexed:** SRI. **Document type:** newsletter.
Formerly: First National Bank of Hawaii. Economic Indicators.

330.9   AT
FIVE YEAR FORECASTS. 1983. q. Aus.$695. Syntec Economic Services Pty.Ltd., G.P.O. Box 2455V, Melbourne, Vic. 3001, Australia. TEL 61-3-6621911. FAX 61-3-6621813. (back issues avail.)

330.9   US   ISSN 0147-7986
HC107.F6
FLORIDA OUTLOOK. q. $600. University of Florida, College of Business Administration, Bureau of Economic and Business Research, Box 117145, Matherly Hall, Gainesville, FL 32611-7145. TEL 352-392-0171. FAX 352-392-4739. Ed. Carol T. West.

BUSINESS AND ECONOMICS — ECONOMIC SITUATION AND CONDITIONS

338 US ISSN 0015-4326
HC107.F6
FLORIDA TREND; magazine of Florida business. 1958. m. $29.95 (out of state $39.95). Florida Trend Inc., (Subsidiary of: Times Publishing Co.), Box 611, St. Petersburg, FL 33731. TEL 813-821-5800. FAX 813-822-5083. Ed. John Berry. adv.: B&W page $6750; color page $8775; adv. contact: Lisa Albright. illus. circ. 50,000. (also avail. in microform from UMI; reprint service avail. from UMI) **Indexed:** P.A.I.S., Tr.& Indus.Ind. **Document type:** trade publication.
●Also available online. Vendor(s): Information Access Co., Knight-Ridder Information, Inc., Lexis-Nexis, UMI. —BLDSC (3956.172000); UMI. **CCC.**
Description: Contains articles, informational items, features, and photography on marketing, business, finance and economy in the state.

330.9 US ISSN 0364-0655
HC110.F55
FLOW OF FUNDS ACCOUNT. q. $960 in U.S., Canada, Mexico; elsewhere $1920. (Federal Reserve System) U.S. National Technical Information Service, 5285 Port Royal Rd., Springfield, VA 22161. TEL 703-487-4630. (magnetic tape; also avail. in microfiche from CIS; reprint service avail. from CIS) **Indexed:** Amer.Stat.Ind. (1973-).
Description: Contains annual data 45-51, quarterly data 52-87 in three forms: levels outstanding at end of period, unadjusted flows, and quarterly seasonally adjusted flows.

330.9 IT
FO - FIMINI E CIRCONDARIO - SAN MARINO - CESENA. w. free. G.M.P. s.r.l. Gestione Mezzi Pubblicitari, Via Marzabotto 31, 47037 Rimini, Italy. TEL 0541-777777. Ed. Alessandro Secciani. adv.: B&W page L.300000. circ. 60,000.

330.9 IT
FO - PESARO E CIRCONDARIO - URBINO E FANO. w. free. G.M.P. s.r.l. Gestione Mezzi Pubblicitari, Via Marzabotto 31III 131, 47037 Rimini, Italy. TEL 0541-777777. Ed. Alessandro Secciani. adv.: B&W page L.300000. circ. 35,000.

FOCUS. see *POLITICAL SCIENCE*

FOCUS AFRIKA; I A K Diskussionsbeitraege. see *POLITICAL SCIENCE*

330 SP
HC381
FOMENTO DEL TRABAJO. HORIZONTE EMPRESARIAL. 1889. m. 3000 ptas. Fomento del Trabajo Nacional, Via Layetana 32-34, 08003 Barcelona, Spain. adv.: B&W page 100000 ptas., color page 130000 ptas. bk.rev.; bibl.; mkt.; stat. circ. 4,500. **Indexed:** ELLIS, P.A.I.S.For.Lang.Ind. **Document type:** consumer publication.
Former titles (until 1993): Horizonte Empresarial (ISSN 0212-0607); Fomento del Trabajo Nacional. Economia Nacional, Internacional de la Empresa (ISSN 0041-0233); Trabajo Nacional.

FOODLINES. see *SOCIAL SERVICES AND WELFARE*

330.9 US ISSN 0272-0868
FORECASTS & STRATEGIES. 1980. m. $99. Phillips Publishing, Inc., Consumer Publishing, 7811 Montrose Rd., Potomac, MD 20854. TEL 301-340-2100. FAX 301-424-7034. Ed. Mark Skousen. bk.rev.
—CCC.
Formerly: Price Controls Alert.
Description: Specific recommendations on a broad range of investments, with discussion of tax, financial privacy and other issues.

330.9 UK ISSN 0305-9936
FRAMEWORK FORECAST FOR THE E E C ECONOMIES.* Variant title: Framework Forecast for the European Economic Community's Economies. 1977. q. £700. Henley Centre for Forecasting Ltd., 9 Bridewell Pl., London EC4Y 6AY, England. Ed. Stephen Radley.
Description: Review of current business climates with five-year forecasts for each EEC economy.

330.9 FR
FRANCE. DIRECTION DES AFFAIRES ECONOMIQUES ET INTERNATIONALES. S E S INFOS RAPIDES. 1980. irreg. (30-35/yr.) 800 F. (elsewhere 820 F.) (effective 1997). (Direction des Affaires Economiques et Internationales) Documentation Francaise, 29-31 quai Voltaire, 75344 Paris Cedex 07, France. TEL 33-1-40157000. FAX 33-1-40157230. TELEX 215 666 DOCFRAN. (Subscr. to: 124 rue Henri Barbusse, 93308 Aubervilliers Cedex, France. TEL 33-1-48395600. FAX 33-1-48395601) (also avail. in microfiche from DFR; back issues avail.) **Document type:** government publication.
Formerly: France. Direction des Affaires Economiques et Internationales. Informations Rapides (ISSN 0291-8897).

FRANCE. SERVICE D'ETUDE DES STRATEGIES ET DES STATISTIQUES INDUSTRIELLES. LA SITUATION DE L'INDUSTRIE: RESULTATS AGREGES. see *BUSINESS AND ECONOMICS — Abstracting, Bibliographies, Statistics*

FRANCE. SERVICE D'ETUDE DES STRATEGIES ET DES STATISTIQUES INDUSTRIELLES. LA SITUATION DE L'INDUSTRIE: RESULTATS DETAILLES. see *BUSINESS AND ECONOMICS — Abstracting, Bibliographies, Statistics*

330.9 CN ISSN 0827-7893
FRASER FORUM. 1985. m. Can.$48. Fraser Institute, 626 Bute St., Vancouver, BC V6E 3M1, Canada. TEL 604-688-0221. FAX 604-388-8539. URL: http://www.fraserinstitute.ca. Ed. Michael A. Walker. R&P contact: Kristin McCahon. circ. 6,000. (back issues avail.) **Document type:** bulletin.
●Also available on CD-ROM.
Incorporates (1988-1995): On Balance (ISSN 0840-612X).
Description: Studies market solutions for public policy problems.

330.9 CC ISSN 1000-8780
FUJIAN LUNTAN (JINGJI BAN)/FUJIAN TRIBUNE (ECONOMICS EDITION). (Text in Chinese) 1981. m. $32.20. Fujian Shehui Kexueyuan - Fujian Academy of Social Sciences, Xiao Liu Cun, Fuzhou, Fujian 350001, People's Republic of China. TEL 7550401. FAX 7550371. (Subscr. to: China International Book Trading Corp., P.O. Box 399, P.R. China) Ed. Lin Qiping. circ. 60,000. **Document type:** academic/scholarly publication.

330.9 AG ISSN 0537-3468
HC171
FUNDACION DE INVESTIGACIONES ECONOMICAS LATINOAMERICANAS. INDICADORES DE COYUNTURA. 1966. m. $340. Fundacion de Investigaciones Economicas Latinoamericanas, Esmeralda 320, 4 Piso, 1343 Buenos Aires, Argentina. TEL 541-3962387. FAX 541-3962727. Dir. Juan Luis Bour. adv.; bk.rev.; stat. circ. 2,000. **Indexed:** P.A.I.S.For.Lang.Ind.

338.9 DR
FUNDACION DOMINICANA DE DESARROLLO. INFORME ANUAL. a. Fundacion Dominicana de Desarrollo, Apdo. 857, Santo Domingo, Z.P.1, Dominican Republic. charts; illus.

338.5 UK ISSN 0016-3287
HB3730 CODEN: FUTUBD
FUTURES; the journal of forecasting, planning and policy. 1968. 10/yr. fl.1091($627) (effective 1998). Elsevier Science Ltd., Pergamon, P.O. Box 800, Kidlington, Oxford OX5 1DX, England. TEL 44-1865-843000. FAX 44-1865-843010. TELEX 83111 BHPOXF G. E-mail: nlinfo-f@elsevier.nl; usinfo-f@elsevier.com; forinfo-kyf04335@niftyserve.or.jp; URL: http://www.elsevier.nl/. (Subscr. to: Elsevier Science, Regional Sales Office, P.O. Box 211, 1000 AE Amsterdam, Netherlands. TEL 31-20-4853757. FAX 31-20-4853432; Subscr. in the Americas to: Elsevier Science, Regional Sales Office, P.O. Box 945, New York, NY 10159-0945. TEL 212-633-3730. FAX 212-633-3680; Subscr. in Australasia and the Far East to: Elsevier Science (Singapore) Pte Ltd, No.1 Temasek Ave., No.17-01 Millenia Tower, Singapore 039192, Singapore. TEL 65-434-3727. FAX 65-337-2230) Ed. Clare Degenhardt. bk.rev.; charts; illus.; index. (also avail. in microform from UMI; back issues avail.) **Indexed:** ABC, ABI Inform., Arts & Hum.Cit.Ind., BPIA, C.I.S. Abstr., CLOSS, Curr.Cont., Curr.Cont., Eng.Ind., Field Crop Abstr., Fut.Surv., Geo.Abstr.H.G., Herb.Abstr., IDA, INIS Atomind., Int.Lab.Doc., Mgmt.& Market.Abstr., Per.Islam. (1993-), Polit.Sci.Abstr., Rural Recreat.Tour.Abstr., SCIMP, Soc.Sci.Ind., SSCI, World Agri.Econ.& Rural Sociol.Abstr. **Document type:** academic/scholarly publication.
—BLDSC (4060.650000); CISTI; Genuine Article; KR SourceOne; Linda Hall; SWETS; UMI; UnCover. **CCC.**
Description: Features studies, analyses and projections of the future, for those in business, industrial R&D, academic research, defense planning, international relations, and public affairs.
Refereed Serial

330.973 US ISSN 1088-7822
FUTURESCAN. 1976. s-m. $95 (foreign $146). FutureScan, 2118 Wilshire Blvd., Ste. 826, Santa Monica, CA 90403. TEL 310-451-2990. FAX 310-828-0427. Ed. Roger Selbert; Pub. Roger Selbert. bk.rev. (looseleaf format; back issues avail.) **Document type:** newsletter.
Description: Reports on economic, social, political, technological, demographic, life-style, consumer, business, management, work force, and marketing trends.

330.9 338 UK
G K N PLC. REPORTS & ACCOUNTS (YEAR). a. G K N plc, P.O. Box 55, Redditch, Worcestershire B98 0TL, England. TEL 44-1527-517715. FAX 44-1527-517700. (Alternate addr.: 7 Cleveland Row, London SW1A 1DB, England. TEL 44-171-930-2424. FAX 44-171-930-3255) charts; illus.; stat. **Document type:** corporate report.
Description: Discusses the company's activities, strategies, financial information, and markets. Includes operations of the company's major divisions: automotive and agritechnical products, aerospace and special vehicles, and industrial services.

330.9 550 MX
GACETA INFORMATIVA I N E G I. 1978. q. free or exchange basis. Instituto Nacional de Estadistica, Geografia e Informatica, Secretaria de Programacion y Presupuesto, Prol. Heroe de Nacozari 2301 Sur, Puerta 11, Acceso, 20270 Aguascalientes Ags., Mexico. TEL 49-18-19-48. FAX 491-807-39. charts, illus. circ. 9,000.
Formerly (until 1989): Gaceta Informativa (ISSN 0185-0679).

GAZETTEER; alphabetical list of localities with statistics on population, number of houses and main source of water supply. see *BUSINESS AND ECONOMICS — Abstracting, Bibliographies, Statistics*

GAZZETTA ITALO-SVIZZERA. see *POLITICAL SCIENCE*

330.9 IT ISSN 1120-6055
GAZZETTINO DELL'ECONOMIA. 1987. w. Societa Finanziaria Editoriale San Marco, Via Torino 110, Mestre (Venice), Italy. TEL 665321. FAX 665-412. Ed. Giancarlo Campigotto.

BUSINESS AND ECONOMICS — ECONOMIC SITUATION AND CONDITIONS

330   EI   ISSN 0069-6749
HC241.2
GENERAL REPORT ON THE ACTIVITIES OF THE EUROPEAN COMMUNITIES. (Supersedes the General Report on the Activities of the Community published individually by the European Coal and Steel Community. High Authority; European Economic Community. Commission; European Atomic Energy Community. Commission) (Text in Dutch, English, French, German, and Italian) 1968. a. $50. (Commission of the European Communities) Office for Official Publications of the European Communities, L-2985 Luxembourg, Luxembourg. TEL 49-92-81. TELEX PUBOF LU 1324 B. (Dist. in U.S. by: Unipub, 4611-F Assembly Dr., Lanham, MD 20706-4391. TEL 800-274-4888. FAX 301-459-0056) **Indexed:** IIS.
—CISTI.
Description: Comprehensive source book on the history of European integration.

330.9   US   ISSN 0145-7330
HD8051
GEOGRAPHIC PROFILE OF EMPLOYMENT AND UNEMPLOYMENT. (Subseries of: B L S Bulletins Series) a. $10. U.S. Bureau of Labor Statistics, 2 Massachusetts Ave., N.E., Washington, DC 20212. TEL 202-655-4000. (Subscr. to: Superintendent of Documents, U.S. Government Printing Office, Box 371954, Pittsburgh, PA 15250-7954. TEL 202-512-1800. FAX 202-512-2250; Or: Bureau of Labor Statistics Publications Sales Center, Box 2145, Chicago, IL 60690) **Document type:** government publication.
Description: Profiles each state, 50 metropolitan areas, and 17 cities for employment and unemployment, using U.S. Census Current Population Survey data.

GHANA. STATISTICAL SERVICE. CONSUMER PRICE INDEX NUMBERS. see *BUSINESS AND ECONOMICS — Abstracting, Bibliographies, Statistics*

GHANA. STATISTICAL SERVICE. ECONOMIC SURVEY. see *BUSINESS AND ECONOMICS — Abstracting, Bibliographies, Statistics*

GHANA. STATISTICAL SERVICE. MOTOR VEHICLE REGISTRATION. see *TRANSPORTATION — Abstracting, Bibliographies, Statistics*

GHANA. STATISTICAL SERVICE. POPULATION CENSUS - DEMOGRAPHIC AND ECONOMIC CHARACTERISTICS. see *POPULATION STUDIES — Abstracting, Bibliographies, Statistics*

GHANA. STATISTICAL SERVICE. POPULATION CENSUS - SPECIAL REPORT ON LOCALITIES. see *POPULATION STUDIES — Abstracting, Bibliographies, Statistics*

GHANA. STATISTICAL SERVICE. QUARTERLY DIGEST OF STATISTICS. see *STATISTICS*

330.9   GH   ISSN 0435-9348
GHANA COMMERCIAL BANK. ANNUAL REPORT. a. free. Ghana Commercial Bank, Research Department, P.O. Box 134, Accra, Ghana. **Document type:** corporate report.

330   GH   ISSN 0855-0417
HC517.G6
GHANA COMMERCIAL BANK. QUARTERLY ECONOMIC REVIEW. 1970. q. free. Ghana Commercial Bank, Research Department, P.O. Box 134, Accra, Ghana. stat. circ. 2,000. **Document type:** corporate report.
Supersedes (in 1978): Ghana Commercial Bank. Monthly Economic Bulletin.

330.9   GH
GHANA CONFIDENTIAL. 1972. m. Ghana Interpress, Business & Education Offices, P.O. Box 4246, Accra, Ghana. Ed. Kwame Kesse-Adu. adv. circ. 10,000.

GHANA INDUSTRIAL CENSUS. DIRECTORY OF INDUSTRIAL ESTABLISHMENTS. see *BUSINESS AND ECONOMICS — Abstracting, Bibliographies, Statistics*

GHANA INDUSTRIAL CENSUS. PHASE II REPORT. see *BUSINESS AND ECONOMICS — Abstracting, Bibliographies, Statistics*

GHANA LIVING STANDARDS SURVEY. ROUND REPORT. see *BUSINESS AND ECONOMICS — Abstracting, Bibliographies, Statistics*

GHANA LIVING STANDARDS SURVEY. RURAL COMMUNITIES IN GHANA. see *BUSINESS AND ECONOMICS — Abstracting, Bibliographies, Statistics*

330.9 332.1   UK   ISSN 0968-820X
GLOBAL ECONOMIC FORECASTS.* 1993. q. (plus m. suppl.). £900($1350) (effective 1994). Henley Centre for Forecasting Ltd., 9 Bridewell Pl., London EC4Y 6AY, England. Eds. Filippo Dell'Osso, Stephen Radley. charts; stat. **Document type:** trade publication.
Description: Monitors the economic condition of nations and markets worldwide and provides currency forecasts for 23 nations.

GLOBAL INVESTOR. see *BUSINESS AND ECONOMICS — Banking And Finance*

338.91   SW   ISSN 1102-6596
GLOBALA AFFAERER. 1991. 6/yr. SEK 210 in Sweden; Nordic and Baltic countries SEK 250; elsewhere SEK 260 (effective 1996). (Styrelsen foer Internationellt Naeringslivsbistaand) Progek, P.O. Box 31003, S-400 32 Goeteborg, Sweden. TEL 46-31-24-34-40. FAX 46-31-24-38-10.

338.5   CN   ISSN 0017-1212
GLOBE AND MAIL REPORT ON BUSINESS. 1962. d. Globe and Mail Publishing, 444 Front St. W., Toronto, ON M5V 2S9, Canada. TEL 416-585-5000. Ed. Margaret Wente. adv.; bk.rev. (also avail. in microfilm) **Indexed:** Can.B.P.I., Can.Lit.Ind. **Document type:** newspaper.
●Also available online.

330.9   II
GOA, DAMAN, AND DIU. DIRECTORATE OF ECONOMICS, STATISTICS, AND EVALUATION. EVALUATION REPORT. 1969. irreg. Directorate of Economics, Statistics, and Evaluation, Panaji, Goa, India. stat. circ. 150.
Document type: government publication.

330   IT   ISSN 0017-2456
GOSPODARSTVO. (Text in Slovenian) 1947. w. L.24000($35) Zalozba (Casa Editrice) Gospodarstvo s.r.l., Via Valdirivo 40, 34122 Trieste, Italy. Ed. Elio Fornazaric. adv.; bk.rev.; mkt.; play rev.; tr.lit.; tr.mk. circ. 6,000. (tabloid format)

330.9 332.6   UK   ISSN 1361-8792
GOVERNMENT WORLD. 1976. 4/yr. £230($450) Urban Publishing Co., P.O. Box 625, Hampstead, London NW3 2TZ, England. TEL 44-181-209-1722. FAX 44-181-455-4107. Ed. Tann von Hove. bk.rev.; index. **Document type:** trade publication.
—BLDSC (3652.711000).
Former titles: Economic Development Briefing (ISSN 0268-2184); Annual Investment File.
Description: Serves as an international information service for business, finance and government. Covers legislation and policies affecting trade and investment. Examines opportunities offered and threats posed by governments to international business. Contains research analysing corporate investment intentions of interest to governments.

330   CH   ISSN 1017-9631
GRAPHICAL SURVEY OF THE ECONOMY OF TAIWAN DISTRICT, REPUBLIC OF CHINA. Key Title: Zhongua Minguo Taiwan Diqu Jingji Tongji Tubiao. (Text in Chinese and English) 1972. a. $5. Central Bank of China, 2 Roosevelt Rd., Sec. 1, Taipei, Taiwan 107, Republic of China. FAX 02-397-3768. circ. 2,000.

330.9   UK
GREAT BRITAIN. H M TREASURY. FORECASTS FOR THE UK ECONOMY; a comparison of independent forecasts. irreg., no.93, 1995 (Jan.). £75. H M Treasury, Economic Briefing Unit, Publishing Unit, Rm. 53A-4, Parliament St., London SW1P 3AG, England. TEL 44-171-270-5607. **Document type:** government publication.
Description: Summarizes published material reflecting the views of economic forecasting organizations.

GREAT BRITAIN. SEA FISH INDUSTRY AUTHORITY. FISHERIES ECONOMICS NEWSLETTER. see *FISH AND FISHERIES*

330.9   US   ISSN 0747-4652
THE GREATER BATON ROUGE BUSINESS REPORT. Variant title: Baton Rouge Business Report. 1982. bi-w. $39 (outside Louisiana $49). Louisiana Business Inc., 5757 Corporate Blvd., Ste. 402, Baton Rouge, LA 70808. TEL 504-928-1700. FAX 504-923-3448. E-mail: editors@ businessreport.com; URL: http://www. businessreport.com. (Subscr. to: Box 1949, Baton Rouge, LA 70821) Ed. Paulette W. Senior; Pub. Rolfe McCollister, Jr. R&P contact: Tracia vonDameck. adv. contact: Sara Wilensky. bk.rev. circ. 10,500. **Document type:** newspaper.
Description: Covers local, state and national business news, issues and trends, with emphasis on local Baton Rouge news.

330   BL
GUANABARA: O BALANCO ECONOMICO. 1972. a. free. Instituto de Desenvolvimento da Guanabara, Av. Calogeras, 15 - 3. andar, Rio de Janeiro, Brazil. illus.; stat. circ. 1,000.

330.9   CC
GUANGZHOU YEARBOOK (YEAR). (Text in Chinese) 1992. a. HK.$350($72) Economic Information & Agency, 342 Hennessy Rd., 10th Fl., Wanchai, Hong Kong, People's Republic of China. TEL 852-573-8217. FAX 852-838-8304. TELEX 86990 EIA HX.

GUATEMALA. BANCO NACIONAL DE DESARROLLO AGRICOLA. MEMORIA. see *AGRICULTURE — Agricultural Economics*

338   BO
GUIA BOLIVIA; industria, comercio, ganaderia. 1976. irreg. Editora Nacional, Bolivar 3235, Cochabamba, Bolivia.

330.9   CC
GUOJI JINGJI/WORLD ECONOMY. (Subseries of: Fuyin Baokan Ziliao) (Text in Chinese) m. $85.13. Zhongguo Renmin Daxue, Shubao Ziliao Zhongxin - China People's University, Book & Newspaper Information Center, 3 Zhang Zizhong Rd., P.O. Box 1122, Beijing 100007, People's Republic of China. TEL 86-10-4015080. (Dist. in US by: China Publications Service, Box 49614, Chicago, IL 60649. TEL 312-288-3291. FAX 312-288-8570) pp./issue: 112.
Description: Covers world economic situations.

GUOJI JINGMAO XIAOXI/INFORMATION - INTERNATIONAL TRADE & ECONOMICS. see *BUSINESS AND ECONOMICS — International Commerce*

GUOJI WENTI YANJIU/INTERNATIONAL STUDIES. see *POLITICAL SCIENCE — International Relations*

330.9   SZ
H P - MAGAZIN FUER HISTORISCHE PAPIERE.* (Text in English and German) 1980. q. 28 SFr. H P Verlag AG, Thunstr. 22, CH-3001 Bern, Switzerland. adv. **Document type:** academic/scholarly publication.
Formerly (until 1984): Swiss Nonvaleurs News.

HAMBURG AFRICAN STUDIES/ETUDES AFRICAINES HAMBOURGEOISES. see *POLITICAL SCIENCE*

330.9 317   US   ISSN 0082-9056
HD8051   CODEN: HLSTBW
HANDBOOK OF LABOR STATISTICS. (Subseries of: B L S Bulletins Series) 1924/26. irreg. price varies. U.S. Bureau of Labor Statistics, 441 G St., N.W., Washington, DC 20212. TEL 202-655-4000. (Subscr. to: Superintendent of Documents, U.S. Government Printing Office, Box 371954, Pittsburgh, PA 15250-7954. TEL 202-512-1800. FAX 202-512-2250; Or: Bureau of Labor Statistics Publications Sales Center, Box 2145, Chicago, IL 60690) **Document type:** government publication.
●Also available on CD-ROM.
—CASDDS.

HARRY BROWNE'S SPECIAL REPORTS. see *BUSINESS AND ECONOMICS — Investments*

BUSINESS AND ECONOMICS — ECONOMIC SITUATION AND CONDITIONS

330.9   US   ISSN 1043-6685
HC107.H3
HAWAII ANNUAL ECONOMIC REPORT. 1968. a. Bank of Hawaii, Economics Department, Box 2900, Honolulu, HI 96846. TEL 808-537-8307. FAX 808-536-9433. Ed. Paul H. Brewbaker. stat. circ. 12,000. (back issues avail.) **Indexed:** B.P.I., P.A.I.S.
—BLDSC (1085.020000).
Former titles: Hawaii Annual Economic Review (ISSN 0067-3633); Economy of Hawaii.
Description: Contains analysis and table of statistics of Hawaii's economy, including outlook and forecast for the coming year.

338   US   ISSN 0440-5056
HC687
HAWAII BUSINESS. 1955. m. $24 in Hawaii (mainland US $34; foreign $44). Hawaii Business Publishing Corp., Box 913, Honolulu, HI 96808. TEL 808-946-3978. Ed. Jeff Barrus; Pub. Kim Jacobsen. adv. contact: Kathy Rae. charts; illus.; index. circ. 10,187. **Indexed:** P.A.I.S., Tr.& Indus.Ind. **Document type:** trade publication.
●Also available online. Vendor(s): Information Access Co., Knight-Ridder Information, Inc., Lexis-Nexis, UMI.
Formerly: Hawaii Business and Industry.

330.9 658   US   ISSN 0739-8034
RA410.53
HEALTH CARE COSTS. 1981. q. D R I - McGraw-Hill, 24 Hartwell Ave., Lexington, MA 02173. TEL 617-863-5100. FAX 617-860-6332. TELEX 200 284. Ed. Sheila Smith.

330.9   UK   ISSN 0305-9928
HENLEY CENTRE FOR FORECASTING. COSTS & PRICES. 1975. q. $730. Henley Centre for Forecasting, 2 Tudor St., Blackfriars, London EC4Y OAA, England. TEL 01-353 9961. Ed. Mark Mitchell.
Description: Forecasts and analysis for five years ahead of key costs and prices movements in the UK economy.

330.9   UK   ISSN 0952-5467
HENLEY CENTRE FOR FORECASTING. DIRECTOR'S REPORT.* 1976. m. £220($330) (effective 1994). Henley Centre for Forecasting Ltd., 9 Bridewell Pl., Blackfriars, London EC4V 6AY, England. TEL 0171-353-9961. FAX 0171-353-2899. Eds. Katie Munson. charts; stat. **Document type:** trade publication.
Former titles: Henley Centre for Forecasting. Director's Guide to the U.K. Economy (ISSN 0263-2721); Henley Centre for Forecasting. Director's Guide (ISSN 0140-9719)
Description: Provides an overview of economic and social developments in the U.K. and worldwide.

HERNE IN ZAHLEN. JAHRBUCH (YEAR). see BUSINESS AND ECONOMICS — Abstracting, Bibliographies, Statistics

HERNE IN ZAHLEN. MONATSBERICHT. see BUSINESS AND ECONOMICS — Abstracting, Bibliographies, Statistics

HERNE IN ZAHLEN. VIERTELJAHRESBERICHTE. see BUSINESS AND ECONOMICS — Abstracting, Bibliographies, Statistics

HIMAL SOUTH ASIA. see POLITICAL SCIENCE

330.9 352.7   US
HD7293.A1
HOME BUILDERS' FORECAST. 1986. m. $1050 to non-members; members $950. National Association of Home Builders of the United States, 15th & M Sts., N.W., Washington, DC 20005. TEL 202-822-0245. FAX 202-822-0377. Ed. Stanley F. Duobinis. charts; stat. circ. 200. (back issues avail.)
Formerly: Forecast of Housing Activity (ISSN 1056-5159)
Description: Forecast of economic indicators with particular emphasis on housing information at the state level.

330.9   CC   ISSN 0378-4886
HONG KONG ANNUAL REPORT. a. Government Information Services, Beaconsfield House, Queen's Rd., Central, Victoria, Hong Kong, People's Republic of China. **Document type:** government publication.
Description: Information on the economic development and life of people in Hong Kong.

HONG KONG ECONOMIC TRENDS. see BUSINESS AND ECONOMICS — Abstracting, Bibliographies, Statistics

330.9   CC
HONG KONG SOCIAL AND ECONOMIC TRENDS. (Text in Chinese, English) 1968. biennial. HK.$74. Census and Statistics Department, Wanchai Tower, 12 Harbour Rd., Central, Hong Kong, People's Republic of China. TEL 852-2598-8197.
FAX 852-2598-7482. (Subscr. to: Director of Information Services, Information Services Department, 28-F Siu On Centre, 188 Lockhart Rd., Wanchai, Hong Kong; People's Republic of China)

330.9   UG
HORIZON INTERNATIONAL. 1979. m. EAs.1200. Economy Publications Ltd., P.O. Box 6787, Kampala, Uganda. Ed. Roland Mutale. film rev.; play rev.; charts; illus. circ. 25,000.

HOUSING & FINANCE - JAMAICA. see HOUSING AND URBAN PLANNING

330.9 352.7   US   ISSN 1056-5140
HD7293.A1
HOUSING ECONOMICS. vol.39, no.5, 1991. m. $175. National Association of Home Builders of the United States, Economics, Mortgage Finance and Housing Policy Division, 1201 15th St., N.W., Washington, DC 20005-2800. TEL 202-822-0245. FAX 202-822-0559. charts; stat.; index. circ. 2,000. (back issues avail.)
—UMI.
Description: Topical analysis of housing industry issues.

330.9   US
HOUSTON BUSINESS BRIEFS. 1989. every 6 weeks. free. Federal Reserve Bank of Dallas, Box 655906, Dallas, TX 75265-5906. TEL 214-922-5254. FAX 214-922-5268. Ed. Tara Barrett. circ. 1,250. (back issues avail.) **Document type:** newsletter.
Description: Concerned with the Texas Gulf Coast economy, with emphasis on Houston.

330.9 665   US   ISSN 0277-4976
HOUSTON BUSINESS JOURNAL; strictly Houston, strictly business. 1971. w. $58; newsstand price: $1. American City Business Journals, Inc. (Houston), One West Loop S., Ste. 650, Houston, TX 77027. TEL 713-688-8811. FAX 713-963-0482. E-mail: hgj@neosoft.com; URL: http://www.amcity.com. Ed. Bill Schadewald; Pub. Richard Kreuz. adv. contact: Linda Harris. bk.rev.; illus.; stat. circ. 18,000. pp./issue: 140. (tabloid format; also avail. in microform from UMI; back issues avail.; reprint service avail. from UMI) **Indexed:** Tr.& Indus.Ind. **Document type:** trade publication.
●Also available online. Vendor(s): Knight-Ridder Information, Inc., Lexis-Nexis.
—CCC.
Description: Covers marketing and other business issues in the greater Houston area. Profiles prominent businesspersons.

330.9   HU   ISSN 1215-2439
HF13   CODEN: HECRE2
HUNGARIAN ECONOMIC REVIEW. (Text in English) 1990. bi-m. 900 Ft.($42) Magyar Kereskedelmi Kamara - Hungarian Chamber of Commerce, Kossuth L. ter 6-8, 1055 Budapest, Hungary. TEL 361-153-353. FAX 361-153-1285. (Subscr. to: Forka Communications, Herman Otto u. 41, 1026 Budapest, Hungary. TEL 361-156-2812) Ed. Endre Aczel. adv. circ. 10,000. (back issues avail.)
Description: Contains analyses on financial trends, news and business offers.

HUNTER VALLEY RESEARCH FOUNDATION. WORKING PAPERS. see STATISTICS

330.9   CN   ISSN 1194-9384
HURONIA BUSINESS TIMES.* m. 24 Dunlop St. W., Barrie, Ont. L4M 1A2, Canada. TEL 705-721-1450. Ed. Wally Moran. circ. 9,750.
Formerly (until 1992): Huronia Business Journal (ISSN 1194-9376)

I A E E NEWSLETTER. (International Association for Energy Economics) see ENERGY

330.9   US   ISSN 0738-3398
HC10
I B C D: INTERNATIONAL BUSINESS CONDITIONS DIGEST. 1983. q. $120 to universities; libraries $80. International Business Resources, Inc., Economics Department, 24 Tennyson Ave., Dover, NH 03820. TEL 603-862-3363. Ed. Evangelos O. Simos.

330.9   JA
I B J MONTHLY REPORT; economic & industrial trends in Japan. (Text in English) 1969. m. free. Industrial Bank of Japan, International Department - Nippon Kogyo Ginko, 1-3-3 Marunouchi, Chiyoda-ku, Tokyo, Japan. charts; stat. **Indexed:** World Bank.Abstr. **Document type:** corporate report.
●Also available online.

I C S C RESEARCH QUARTERLY. (International Council of Shopping Centers) see REAL ESTATE

330.9   GW   ISSN 0946-7920
I F O DRESDEN STUDIEN. 1994. irreg., vol.10, 1996. price varies. I F O Institut fuer Wirtschaftsforschung, Poschingerstr. 5, 81679 Munich, Germany. TEL 49-89-9224-0. FAX 49-89-985369. **Document type:** monographic series.

330.9   GW   ISSN 0176-8689
I F O - G F K KONSUMREPORT. 1984. m. DM.150 (effective 1997). I F O Institut fuer Wirtschaftsforschung, Poschingerstr. 5, 81679 Munich, Germany. TEL 49-89-9224-0. FAX 49-89-985369. (Co-sponsor: G f K Marktforschung) **Document type:** bulletin.

330.9   GW   ISSN 0938-6955
I F O STUDIEN ZUR EUROPAEISCHEN WIRTSCHAFT. 1990. irreg., vol.9, 1996. price varies. I F O Institut fuer Wirtschaftsforschung, Poschingerstr. 5, 81679 Munich, Germany. TEL 49-89-9224-0. FAX 49-89-985369. **Document type:** monographic series.

330.9   GW   ISSN 0930-9551
I F O STUDIEN ZUR JAPANFORSCHUNG. 1986. irreg., vol.11, 1996. price varies. I F O Institut fuer Wirtschaftsforschung, Poschingerstr. 5, 81679 Munich, Germany. TEL 49-89-9224-0. FAX 49-89-985369. **Document type:** monographic series.

330.9   GW
I F O STUDIEN ZUR OSTEUROPA- UND TRANSFORMATIONSFORSCHUNG. 1988. irreg., vol.25, 1997. price varies. (I F O Institut fuer Wirtschaftsforschung) Weltforum Verlag, Marienburgerstr. 22, 50963 Cologne, Germany. TEL 49-221-93763-0. FAX 49-221-9376399. **Document type:** monographic series.
Formerly: I F O Studien zur Ostforschung.

330.9   GW
I F O STUDIEN ZUR REGIONAL- UND STADTOEKONOMIE. 1991. irreg., vol.9, 1994. price varies. I F O Institut fuer Wirtschaftsforschung, Poschingerstr. 5, 81679 Munich, Germany. TEL 49-89-9224-0. FAX 49-89-985369. **Document type:** monographic series.

330.9 331   UN   ISSN 1011-4971
I L O MULTINATIONAL ENTERPRISES PROGRAMME. WORKING PAPER. French edition: B I T Programme des Enterprises Multinationales. Documents de Travail (ISSN 1011-4963); Spanish edition: O I T Programa de Empresas Multinacionales. Documentos de Trabajo (ISSN 1011-498X); German edition: I A O Programm der Multinationale Unternehmen. Arbeitspapiere (ISSN 1011-4998) 1979. irreg., no.76, 1994. 15 SFr.($12) (International Labour Office) I L O Publications, 4 route des Morillons, CH-1211 Geneva 22, Switzerland. TEL 41-22-799-6111. FAX 41-22-799-6358. TELEX 415647-ILO-CH. (Dist. in US by: I L O Publications Center, 49 Sheridan Ave., Albany, NY 12210. TEL 518-436-9686. FAX 518-436-7433) Ed. Casimiro Miranda. **Document type:** monographic series.
—BLDSC (9349.605000).

I N S E E PICARDIE DOSSIERS. (Institut National de la Statistique et des Etudes Economiques) see BUSINESS AND ECONOMICS — Abstracting, Bibliographies, Statistics

BUSINESS AND ECONOMICS — ECONOMIC SITUATION AND CONDITIONS

I N S E E PICARDIE PREMIERE. (Institut National de la Statistique et des Etudes Economiques) see BUSINESS AND ECONOMICS — Abstracting, Bibliographies, Statistics

I N S E E PICARDIE RELAIS. (Institut National de la Statistique et des Etudes Economiques) see BUSINESS AND ECONOMICS — Abstracting, Bibliographies, Statistics

I P E A SERIE P N P E. (Programa Nacional de Pesquisa Economica) see BUSINESS AND ECONOMICS

330 II
I S E C MONOGRAPH. no.4, 1976. irreg. Rs.20($4.50) (Institute for Social and Economic Change) World Press Ltd., 37A College St., Calcutta 700073, India. Ed. F. Rao. **Document type:** monographic series.

I S E R OCCASIONAL PAPERS. (Institute of Social and Economic Research) see SOCIAL SCIENCES: COMPREHENSIVE WORKS

I S E R RESEARCH AND POLICY PAPERS. (Institute of Social and Economic Research) see SOCIOLOGY

330.9   GW   ISSN 0941-6838
I W TRENDS; Analysen, Dokumentationen, Prognosen. 1974. q. DM.74.90. Deutscher Instituts Verlag GmbH, Postfach 510670, 50942 Cologne, Germany. TEL 49-221-4981452. FAX 49-221-4981592. circ. 2,000. **Document type:** trade publication.

330.9   IQ
ICTESAD. m. National House for Publication, Distribution and Advertisement, Baghdad Sq., Baghdad, Iraq. adv.

330   US
IDAHO OCCUPATION WAGE SURVEY. 1979. a. Department of Labor, Bureau of Research and Analysis, 317 Main St., Boise, ID 83735. TEL 208-334-6168. URL: http://www.labor.state.id.us. circ. 2,000. **Document type:** government publication.

INCENTIVE TAXATION. see HOUSING AND URBAN PLANNING

INDIA INTERNATIONAL CENTRE QUARTERLY. see POLITICAL SCIENCE — International Relations

INDIA NEWS. see POLITICAL SCIENCE

330.9   US
INDIA WEEKLY FAX BULLETIN. w. $495 (foreign $595) (effective 1998). Orbis Publications, LLC, 3201 New Mexico Ave., N.W., Ste. 249, Washington, DC 20016. TEL 202-237-0155. FAX 202-237-0596. E-mail: orbis@orbispub.com; URL: http://www.earthnet.net/orbis. (only avail. by fax) **Document type:** bulletin.
   Description: Reports on political, economic, and business events in India.

330   II   ISSN 0019-4948
INDIAN INSTITUTE OF PUBLIC OPINION. QUARTERLY ECONOMIC REPORT. (Text in English) 1953. q. Rs.400($90) Indian Institute of Public Opinion Private Ltd., 2-A National Insurance Bldg., Parliament St., Box 288, New Delhi 110001, India. Ed. E.P.W. da Costa. charts. (also avail. in microform from UMI; reprint service avail. from UMI) **Indexed:** P.A.I.S.
   Description: Details results of studies on a variety of socio-economic and political subjects.

330.9   II   ISSN 0019-4999
HC435.2
INDIAN INVESTMENT CENTRE. MONTHLY NEWSLETTER. (Text in English) 1963. m. Rs.200($40) (effective 1992). Indian Investment Centre, Jeevan Vihar Bldg., Sansad Marg, New Delhi 110 001, India. TEL 11-351673. FAX 11-351205. TELEX 031-63176 ICHO IN. Ed. K.K. Trivedi. illus.; stat.; index. circ. 3,000. **Indexed:** C.R.I.Abstr., C.R.I.Curr.Cont.
   Description: Provides information on industrial licenses, letters of intent issued and foreign collaborations approved by the government. Also gives facts on current economic developments in India.

INDIAN OCEAN NEWSLETTER. see POLITICAL SCIENCE — International Relations

650   US   ISSN 1060-4154
HF107.I6
INDIANA BUSINESS MAGAZINE. (Annual supplement avail.: Indiana Corporate Directory) 1957. m. $19. Curtis Magazine Group, 1200 Waterway Blvd., Indianapolis, IN 46202-2157. TEL 317-692-1200. FAX 317-692-4250. Ed. Steve Kaelble. adv.; illus. circ. 35,000. (also avail. in microform from UMI) **Indexed:** Tr.& Indus.Ind. **Document type:** trade publication.
   ●Also available online. Vendor(s): Information Access Co., Knight-Ridder Information, Inc., Lexis-Nexis, UMI. —UMI.
   Former titles (until 1992): Indiana Business (ISSN 0273-7930); (until 1971): Indiana Business and Industry (ISSN 0019-6533)
   Description: Profiles Indiana business people, firms, and industry. Explores trends and issues affecting Indiana business, and focuses on a specific region in each issue. Annual supplement includes top 3,000 firms in the state.

338.9   PR
INDICADORES ECONOMICOS MENSUALES DE PUERTO RICO/MONTHLY ECONOMIC INDICATORS OF PUERTO RICO. (Text in English and Spanish) 1976. m. $3.50 (effective Dec. 1991). Planning Board, Area of Economic and Social Planning, Minillas Governmental Center, Box 41119, San Juan, PR 00940-9985. FAX 787-724-5598. Ed.Bd. charts; stat. circ. 400. **Document type:** government publication.

330.9   IT
INDICI MENSILI PIROLA. 1983. m. L.120000($75) Pirola Editore S.p.A., Via Parabiago 19, Casella Postale 10444, 20110 Milan, Italy. TEL 2-30-221. FAX 2-380-11-205. Ed.Bd. bk.rev. circ. 8,000.

INDIEN WIRTSCHAFTSNACHRICHTEN. see POLITICAL SCIENCE — International Relations

330   CC   ISSN 0019-7297
INDONESIA LETTER. 1969. m. $175. Asia Letter Group, G.P.O. Box 10874, Hong Kong, People's Republic of China. TEL 852-526-2950. FAX 852526-7131. TELEX HX-61166-HKNW. (US addr.: Box 88189, Los Angeles, CA 90009-8189) Ed. Charles R. Smith. bk.rev. **Indexed:** Key to Econ.Sci. **Document type:** newsletter.
   Description: Covers Indonesian affairs for business executives.

330.9   US
INDONESIA WEEKLY FAX BULLETIN. w. $495 (foreign $595) (effective 1998). Orbis Publications, LLC, 3201 New Mexico Ave., N.W., Ste. 249, Washington, DC 20016. TEL 202-237-0155. FAX 202-237-0596. E-mail: orbis@orbispub.com; URL: http://www.earthnet.net/orbis. (only avail. by fax) **Document type:** bulletin.
   Description: Reports on political, economic, and business events in Indonesia.

330   FR   ISSN 1016-5363
INDUSTRIAL POLICY IN O E C D COUNTRIES. a. $49. Organization for Economic Cooperation and Development, 2 rue Andre-Pascal, 75775 Paris Cedex 16, France. (In U.S. subscr. to: O.E.C.D. Publications and Information Center, 2001 L St., N.W., Ste. 650, Washington, DC 20036-4922. TEL 202-785-6323) **Indexed:** IIS.
   —BLDSC (4459.370000).
   Incorporates: Industrial Policy Developments in O E C D Countries (ISSN 1015-4175)

330   AU   ISSN 0019-896X
INDUSTRIE. 1896. w. S.1078 (foreign S.1500). (Vereinigung der Oesterreichischer Industrie) Signum Verlag GmbH and Co. KG, Reisnerstr. 40, A-1030 Vienna, Austria. TEL 43-1-71195-0. Ed. Milan Fruehbauer. R&P contact: Robert Grossmann. adv.: B&W page S.37000, color page S.55000; trim 210 x 280; adv. contact: Doris Dinklage. bk.rev.; index. circ. 14,500. **Indexed:** Key to Econ.Sci. **Document type:** trade publication.

330.9   IV   ISSN 0019-9230
INDUSTRIEL DE COTE D'IVOIRE. m. Syndicat des Industriels de la Cote d'Ivoire, B.P. 1340, Abidjan, Ivory Coast.

330.9   CN
INDUSTRY CANADA. DIRECTOR OF INVESTIGATION AND RESEARCH. ANNUAL REPORT. (Text in English and French) a. free. Industry Canada, Ottawa, ON K1A 0C9, Canada. TEL 613-947-7466. **Document type:** government publication.
   Formerly: Canada. Department of Consumer and Corporate Affairs. Director of Investigation and Research. Annual Report (ISSN 0837-4279)

338   US
INDUSTRY FORECAST. 1949. 16/yr. (includes q. supplements). $295. Bard College, Jerome Levy Economics Institute, Forecasting Center, 89 S. Moger Ave., Mount Kisko, NY 10549. TEL 914-238-3665. FAX 914-238-4599. Eds. S. Jay Levy, David A. Levy. R&P contact: David A. Levy. charts. (looseleaf format; back issues avail.) **Document type:** newsletter, academic/scholarly publication.
   Description: Newsletter on financial, business, and economic indicators and prospects, based on production, housing, inventory, and other key statistics.

330.9   US   ISSN 8755-2396
HF5681.R25
INDUSTRY NORMS AND KEY BUSINESS RATIOS. DESK TOP EDITION. (In 5 vols.: Vol.1: Agriculture, Mining, Construction, Transportation, Communication and Public Utilities; Vol.2: Wholesaling; Vol.3: Retailing; Vol.4: Manufacturing; Vol.5: Finance, Real Estate and Services) a. $475 per vol. ($1890 for complete set); on diskette $530 per vol. ($2115 per complete set). Dun & Bradstreet Corporation, Business Information Services, One Diamond Hill Rd., Murray Hill, NJ 07974. TEL 800-223-0141. (also avail. in diskette format)
   Formerly: Industry Norms and Key Business Ratios. Library Edition.

331.1   US   ISSN 0082-9064
INDUSTRY WAGE SURVEYS. (Subseries of: B L S Bulletins) irreg. U.S. Bureau of Labor Statistics, 441 G St., N.W., Washington, DC 20212. TEL 202-655-4000. (Subscr. to: Superintendent of Documents, U.S. Government Printing Office, Box 371954, Pittsburgh, PA 15250-7954. TEL 202-512-1800. FAX 202-512-2250; Or: Bureau of Labor Publications Sales Center, Box 2145, Chicago, IL 60690) **Document type:** bulletin, government publication.

330.9   PO   ISSN 0871-7338
INFORMACAO ECONOMICA. N.S. 1990. 3/yr. Esc.9000. Ministerio do Planeamento e Administracao Territorio, Departamento de Prospectiva e Planeamento, Avda. D. Carlos I, 126, 1200 Lisbon, Portugal. **Document type:** government publication.

330.9   SP   ISSN 0210-2633
INFORMACION COMERCIAL ESPANOLA. CUADERNOS ECONOMICOS. (Supplement to Informacion Comercial Espanola) 1977. 3/yr. 4200 ptas. (foreign 6000 ptas.) (effective 1995). Ministerio de Comercio y Turismo, P. de la Castellana 162, Planta 16, 28046 Madrid, Spain. TEL 34-1-349-36-47. FAX 34-1-349-36-34. Ed. Maria Eugenia Caumel. circ. 3,000. **Indexed:** ELLIS.
   —CINDOC; SWETS.

330.9 320   BO
INFORMACION POLITICA Y ECONOMICA. w. Calle Comercio, Casilla 2484, La Paz, Bolivia. Dir. Gonzalo Lopez Munoz.

330   TI   ISSN 0020-0050
INFORMATION ECONOMIQUE AFRICAINE. 1960. m. $50. Societe I E A, 16 rue de Rome, 1015 Tunis, Tunisia. FAX 216-1-353172. Ed. Mohamed Zerzeri. adv.: B&W page 10500 F., color page 15500 F.; bleed 205 x 270. bk.rev.; charts; illus.; stat. circ. 40,000. **Indexed:** Key to Econ.Sci.
   Description: Financial, political and economic news covering the Middle East and Africa, including new economic activity.

330.9   BL
INFORMATION ON PARANA. Portuguese edt.: Parana Informacoes. 1973. irreg. free. Banco de Desenvolvimento do Parana, S.A., Av. Vicente Machado, 445, Cx. Postal 6042, Curitiba, Parana, Brazil. Ed. Luiz Fernando Osti Magalhaes. illus.

BUSINESS AND ECONOMICS — ECONOMIC SITUATION AND CONDITIONS

330.9   GW
INFORMATIONEN AUS POLITIK UND WIRTSCHAFT. 1973. w. DM.504 (foreign DM.516) (effective 1997). Griephan Verlag GmbH und Co. KG, Nordkanalstr. 36, 20097 Hamburg, Germany. TEL 49-40-2371404. FAX 49-40-23714236. E-mail: 100135.3457@compuserve.com; URL: http://www.griephan.de. Ed. Heinz Schulte; Pub. Detlev-Karl Suchanek. adv. contact: Silke Schuback. circ. 550 (paid). (back issues avail.) **Document type:** newsletter.

330   IT   ISSN 0020-0794
INFORMAZIONE MEDITERRANEA. 1958. w. Carlo de Leva, Ed. & Pub., Via G. Campoli 49, 90145 Palermo, Italy.

330.9   SP
INFORME ANUAL INTEGRADO DE LA HACIENDA VASCA. a. (Organo de Coordinacion Tributaria de Euskadi) Eusko Jaurlaritzaren Argitalpen-Zerbitzu Nagusia - Servicio Central de Publicaciones del Gobierno Vasco, C. Duque de Wellington 2, 01010 Vitoria-Gasteiz, Spain. circ. 3,500.

330.9   SP
INFORME ECONOMICO. (Editions in English, French, German, Spanish) free. Banco de Santander, Publicidad y Estudios, Paseo de Pereda, 9-12, Santander, Spain. **Indexed:** Key to Econ.Sci.

338.9 320   UK   ISSN 0263-5372
INFORME LATINOAMERICANO. (Text in Spanish) 1982. w. £307($399) (effective 1997). Latin American Newsletters, 61 Old St., London EC1V 9HX, England. TEL 44-171-251-0012. FAX 44-171-253-8193. Ed. Eduardo Crawley. bk.rev. **Document type:** newsletter.
● Also available online. Vendor(s): Lexis-Nexis. —SWETS.
   Supersedes (in 1982): America Latina Informe de Mercados (ISSN 0263-3751); America Latina Informe Economico (ISSN 0261-3735); America Latina Informe Politico (ISSN 0261-3743)
   Description: Reports on Latin American news.

330   IT   ISSN 0020-1359
INIZIATIVA ISONTINA. (Text in Italian; summaries in German and Slovak) 1959. 3/yr. L.500 per no. Centro Studi Politici Economici e Sociali Sen. A. Rizzati, Via Seminario 7, 34170 Gorizia, Italy. Ed. Celso Macor. adv.; bibl.; charts; illus.; stat.; cum.index. circ. 2,000.

INNOVATION AND TECHNOLOGY TRANSFER. see
POLITICAL SCIENCE — International Relations

338.9   US   ISSN 1075-5349
HF1746
INSIDE N A F T A. (North American Free Trade Agreement); reporting on NAFTA implementation and trade policy in the Americas. 1994. bi-w. $625 (foreign $675) (effective 1997). Inside Washington Publishers, Box 7167, Ben Franklin Sta., Washington, DC 20044-7167. TEL 703-416-8500; 800-424-9068. FAX 703-416-8543. E-mail: service@iwpnews.com. **Document type:** newsletter.
   Description: Covers business issues, government policy and actions, and other topics relating to NAFTA.

330.9   FR   ISSN 0153-4459
HC277.F7
INSTITUT D'ECONOMIE REGIONALE BOURGOGNE-FRANCHE-COMTE. CAHIERS. irreg. no.36, 1990. 70 F. Institut d'Economie Regionale Bourgogne-Franche-Comte, 4 bd. Gabriel, 21000 Dijon, France.

INSTITUT DER DEUTSCHEN WIRTSCHAFT. FORUM. see
BUSINESS AND ECONOMICS — Management

330.9   DK   ISSN 0106-8628
INSTITUT FOR GRAENSEREGIONSFORSKNING. ARBEJDSPAPIR. no.14, 1982. irreg. price varies. Institut for Graenseregionsforskning, Persillegade 6, 6200 Aabenraa, Denmark. illus.

INSTITUT FUER AFRIKA-KUNDE. ARBEITEN. see
POLITICAL SCIENCE

330.9   GW
INSTITUT FUER WELTWIRTSCHAFT. ANNUAL REPORT. a. Institut fuer Weltwirtschaft, Duesternbrooker Weg 120, 24105 Kiel, Germany. TEL 49-431-8814305. FAX 49-431-8814527. E-mail: info@ifw.uni-kiel.de; URL: http://www.uni-kiel.de:8080/ifw/. **Document type:** corporate report.
Refereed Serial

330.9   SI
INSTITUTE OF SOUTHEAST ASIAN STUDIES. PROCEEDINGS OF INTERNATIONAL CONFERENCES. (Text in English) 1973. irreg., no.80, 1995. price varies. Institute of Southeast Asian Studies, Heng Mui Keng Terrace, Pasir Panjang, Singapore 119596, Singapore. TEL 65-7780955. FAX 65-7756259. E-mail: pubsunit@merlion.iseas. ac.sg; URL: http://www.iseas.ac.sg/pub.html. Ed. Triena Ong. **Document type:** proceedings.
   Description: Politics and economics pertaining to present day Southeast Asia.

330.9   BL
INSTITUTO DE ECONOMIA DO SETOR PUBLICO. NOTAS TECNICAS. irreg., no.5, 1994. Instituto de Economia do Setor Publico, Rua Bandeira Paulista 716, 04532 Sao Paulo, SP, Brazil. TEL 55-11-8298955. FAX 55-11-8298743. (Co-sponsor: Fundacao do Desenvolvimento Administrativo)

338.9   PE   ISSN 1019-4509
INSTITUTO DE ESTUDIOS PERUANOS. ANALISIS ECONOMICO. 1964. irreg., no.16, 1994. price varies. I E P Ediciones, Horacio Urteaga 694, Lima 11, Peru. TEL 51-14-323070. FAX 51-14-324981. E-mail: libreria@iep.org.pe. **Document type:** academic/scholarly publication.

330.9   AG
HC175
INSTITUTO DE ESTUDIOS SOBRE LA REALIDAD ARGENTINA Y LATINOAMERICANA. ESTUDIOS. 1978. q. free to qualified personnel or on exchange basis. Fundacion Mediterranea, Campillo 394, 5000 Cordoba, Argentina. FAX 54-51-724625. TELEX 51811 IERAL AR. Ed. Aldo Arnaudo. adv. contact: Olga Krajczy. circ. 1,000. **Indexed:** P.A.I.S.For.Lang.Ind. **Document type:** academic/scholarly publication.
   Formerly: Instituto de Estudios Economicos sobre la Realidad Argentina y Latinoamericana. Estudios (ISSN 0325-6928)

330.9   BL
INSTITUTO DO DESENVOLVIMENTO ECONOMICO-SOCIAL DO PARA. COMERCIO VAREJISTA. 1986. m. (donation or free). Instituto do Desenvolvimento Economico-Social do Para, Av. Nazare 871, 66035-170 Belem, Para, Brazil. TEL 55-91-2244411. FAX 55-91-2253414.

330.9   BL   ISSN 0103-5282
INSTITUTO DO DESENVOLVIMENTO ECONOMICO-SOCIAL DO PARA. INDICADORES DA SOCIO-ECONOMIA PARAENSE. 1984. irreg. $1. Instituto do Desenvolvimento Economico-Social do Para, Av. Nazare 871, 66035-170 Belem, Para, Brazil. TEL 55-91-2244411. FAX 55-91-2253414. bibl.; charts; stat. **Document type:** government publication.
   Description: Covers the economy of the Brazilian state.

330.9   BL
INSTITUTO DO DESENVOLVIMENTO ECONOMICO-SOCIAL DO PARA. INDICE DE CUSTO DE VIDA. 1976. m. donation or free. Instituto do Desenvolvimento Economico-Social do Para, Av. Nazare 871, 66035-170 Belem, Para, Brazil. TEL 55-91-2244411. FAX 55-91-2253414.

330.9 338.91   BL   ISSN 0553-1721
INSTITUTO DO DESENVOLVIMENTO ECONOMICO-SOCIAL DO PARA. PARA DESENVOLVIMENTO. 1965. s-a. $1. Instituto do Desenvolvimento Economico-Social do Para, Av. Nazare 871, 66035-170 Belem, Para, Brazil. TEL 55-91-2244411. FAX 55-91-2283414. bibl.; charts; stat.
   Description: Covers relevant areas related to the socio-economic transformation of the state of Para, contains technical, scientific and research articles. Also includes interviews, studies, depositions and other materials of interest.

INSTITUTO NACIONAL DE INVESTIGACIONES FORESTALES, AGRICOLAS Y PECUARIAS. FOLLETOS DE INVESTIGACION. see *AGRICULTURE*

330.9   CU
INTEGRACION ECONOMICA SOCIALISTA. m. $18. (Council for Mutual Economic Assistance) Prensa Latina Agencia Informativa Latinoamericana, Calle 23 No. 201, Vedado, Havana 4, Cuba.

330   CK
INTEGRACION FINANCIERA; pasado, presente y futuro de las finanzas en Colombia y el mundo. 1984. bi-m. Col.$30000($50) for 2 yrs. Medios & Medios Publicidad Cia Ltda., Calle 63 No. 11-45 Of. 802, Apdo. 036943, Bogota, Colombia. TEL 2550992. FAX 2494696. Ed. Raul Rodriguex Puerto. adv.; illus.
   Description: News on the development of the financial sector of Colombia and Latin America. Presents important information to businessmen. Includes principals of the different activities relating to banking, financing, insurance, stocks and more in the economic field.

330.968   SA   ISSN 1022-8314
INTELLIGENCE. (Text in English) 1994. m. R.66 for 10 issues. Intelligence Publishing, P.O. Box 2917, Parklands 2917, South Africa. illus.

330.9   US
INTERNATIONAL CENTER FOR ECONOMIC GROWTH. NEWSLETTER. (Editions in English, French; Spanish) 1987. q. free. International Center for Economic Growth, 720 Market St., 4th Fl., San Francisco, CA 94102-2500. TEL 415-981-5353. FAX 415-433-6841. E-mail: 71262.113@ compuserve.com. Ed. Nancy Truitt; Pub. Rachel Levine. R&P contact: Rachel Levine. adv. contact: Rachel Levine. bk.rev.; abstr.; bibl.; charts; illus.; stat.; tr.lit. circ. English ed. 12,000; French ed. 1,200; Spanish ed. 4,500. (back issues avail.) **Document type:** newsletter.
   Description: Covers new research progress and timely information on growth and developmental issues.

330   CH   ISSN 1013-9893
HC430.5.A1
INTERNATIONAL COMMERCIAL BANK OF CHINA. MONTHLY ECONOMIC SURVEY. 1973. m. free. International Commercial Bank of China, Head Office-Economic Research Department, 100 Chilin Rd., Taipei, Taiwan 10424, Republic of China. FAX 02-5611216. TELEX 11300 INCOBK. Ed. Sung-Yuen Chu. charts; stat. circ. 2,300.
   Description: Describes the economic situation and conditions of the Republic of China.

330.9   US
INTERNATIONAL COMPARISONS OF MANUFACTURING PRODUCTIVITY AND UNIT LABOR COST TRENDS (YEAR). (Subseries of: National Office News Releases) a. U.S. Bureau of Labor Statistics, 2 Massachusetts Ave., N.E., Washington, DC 20212. TEL 202-655-4000. (Subscr. to: Superintendent of Documents, U.S. Government Printing Office, Box 371954, Pittsburgh, PA 15250-7954. TEL 202-512-1800. FAX 202-512-2250; Or: Bureau of Labor Statistics Publications Sales Center, Box 2145, Chicago, IL 60690) **Document type:** government publication.

330.9   US   ISSN 0278-6680
HG3891.5
INTERNATIONAL COUNTRY RISK GUIDE. (Published in several editions: Asia & the Pacific; Europe; Statistical Section; Sub-Saharan Africa; The Americas) 1980. m. $3300 (effective 1997). The P R S Group, Box 248, East Syracuse, NY 13057-0248. TEL 315-431-0511. FAX 315-431-0200. stat.
● Also available online. Vendor(s): Data-Star, Knight-Ridder Information, Inc., Lexis-Nexis.
   Description: Provides data and analysis on events in 130 countries throughout the world. Each issue includes extended analysis of 65-80 countries, with detailed coverage of political trends, economic developments and financial risks.

330.9   US   ISSN 0738-1425
INTERNATIONAL DEVELOPMENT RESOURCE BOOKS. 1984. irreg. price varies. Greenwood Press, Inc. (Subsidiary of: Greenwood Publishing Group Inc.), 88 Post Rd. W., Box 5007, Westport, CT 06881-5007. TEL 203-226-3571. FAX 203-222-1502.

BUSINESS AND ECONOMICS — ECONOMIC SITUATION AND CONDITIONS

330.9   US   ISSN 0190-7085
HG3863
INTERNATIONAL ECONOMIC CONDITIONS. q. plus a. special ed. free. Federal Reserve Bank of St. Louis, Box 442, St. Louis, MO 63166. TEL 314-444-8320.
  Description: Contains data on US transactions and economic developments for major trading partners.

330.9   US   ISSN 1050-8481
HB1.A1
INTERNATIONAL ECONOMIC INSIGHTS. 1990. bi-m. $60. Institute for International Economics, 11 Dupont Circle N.W., Ste. 620, Washington, DC 20036-1207. TEL 202-328-9000. FAX 202-328-5432. Ed. Bailey Morris. bk.rev. circ. 5,000.
  ●Also available on CD-ROM.
  —CCC.
  Description: Presents new thinking on international economic and trade issues from all points of view and all major languages.

330.9   KO   ISSN 1016-8737
HB1.A1
INTERNATIONAL ECONOMIC JOURNAL. 1987. q. 30,000 Won($40) to non-members; institutions 40,000 Won($50). Department of International Economics, College of Social Sciences, Seoul University, Seoul 151-742, S. Korea. TEL 82-2-880-6394. FAX 82-2-876-0357. Ed. Wontack Hong. adv. **Indexed:** Asian-Pac.Econ.Lit., J.of Econ.Lit. **Document type:** academic/scholarly publication.
  —BLDSC (4539.770000); SWETS.
  Refereed Serial

330.9   US   ISSN 0270-045X
HC10   CODEN: IECSEG
INTERNATIONAL ECONOMIC SCOREBOARD. 1979. q. $295 to non-members; members $145. Conference Board, Inc., 845 Third Ave., New York, NY 10022. TEL 212-759-0900. FAX 212-980-7014. (also avail. in microfiche from CIS) **Indexed:** PROMT, SRI. **Document type:** newsletter.
  —CCC.
  Description: Forecasts of economic performance of major industrial countries.

THE INTERNATIONAL EXECUTIVE. see *BUSINESS AND ECONOMICS — International Commerce*

330.9   US   ISSN 0307-4951
INTERNATIONAL FINANCIAL BULLETIN. 1987. 8/yr. D R I - McGraw-Hill, 24 Hartwell Ave., Lexington, MA 02173. TEL 617-863-5100. FAX 617-860-6332. TELEX 200 284. Ed. N. Behravesh. **Document type:** trade publication.
  Formerly: International Business and Financial Outlook.

INTERNATIONAL JOURNAL OF ENERGY - ENVIRONMENT - ECONOMICS. see *ENERGY*

330.9   NE   ISSN 0169-2070
H61.4   CODEN: IJFOEK
INTERNATIONAL JOURNAL OF FORECASTING. (Text in English or French) 1985. q. fl.693($398) (effective 1998). (International Institute of Forecasters) North-Holland (Subsidiary of: Elsevier Science B.V.), P.O. Box 211, 1000 AE Amsterdam, Netherlands. TEL 31-20-4853911. FAX 31-20-4853598. TELEX 18582 ESPA NL. (Subscr. in the Americas to: Elsevier Science, Regional Sales Office, Box 945, New York, NY 10159-0945. TEL 212-633-3730. FAX 212-633-3680; Subscr. in Australasia and the Far East to: Elsevier Science (Singapore) Pte Ltd, No.1 Temasek Ave., No.17-01 Millenia Tower, Singapore 039192, Singapore. TEL 65-434-3727. FAX 65-337-2230; Subscr. in Japan to: Elsevier Science Japan, 9-15 Higashi-Azabu 1-chome, Minato-ku Tokyo 106, Japan. TEL 81-3-5561-5033. FAX 81-3-5561-5047) Ed. Rovert Fildes. adv.; bk.rev. (also avail. in microform from UMI; back issues avail.; reprint service avail. from SWZ) **Indexed:** ABI Inform., ASCA, C.R.E.J., Cont.Pg.Manage., Curr.Cont.(1987-), Curr.Ind.Stat., INSPEC, J.Cont.Quant.Meth., J.of Econ.Abstr., J.of Econ.Lit., Sociol.Abstr., SSCI, Stat.Theor.Meth.Abstr. (1987-). **Document type:** academic/scholarly publication.
  —BLDSC (4542.255000); AskIEEE; Genuine Article; KR SourceOne; SWETS; UMI; UnCover. **CCC.**
  Description: Publishes papers covering all aspects of forecasting.
  Refereed Serial

INTERNATIONAL MARKET REVIEW. see *BUSINESS AND ECONOMICS — Banking And Finance*

330.9 332   US   ISSN 1059-0560
HB1
INTERNATIONAL REVIEW OF ECONOMICS AND FINANCE. 1991. q. $80 to individuals (foreign $100); institutions $205 (foreign $225) (effective 1998). J A I Press Inc., 55 Old Post Rd., No. 2, Box 1678, Greenwich, CT 06830-1678. TEL 203-661-7602. FAX 203-661-0792. E-mail: jai@jaipress.com. (Addr. in Europe: J A I Press Ltd., 38 Tavistock St., Covent Garden, London WC2E 7PB, England. TEL 44-171-379-8834. FAX 44-171-379-8835) Eds. Hamid Beladi, Carl R. Chen. bk.rev. (also avail. in microform from UMI; back issues avail.) **Document type:** trade publication.
  —BLDSC (4547.095000); SWETS.
  Refereed Serial

INTERNATIONAL UNDERSTANDING. see *POLITICAL SCIENCE — International Relations*

INTERNEWSLETTER AFRIQUE; la seule revue de presse Americaine en Francais sur l'Afrique. see *POLITICAL SCIENCE — International Relations*

338   US   ISSN 1076-6456
HD72
INTLEC C D - R O M. Key Title: IntlEc CD-ROM. Variant title: Index to International Economics, Development and Finance. q. $989 (effective 1996). (Joint Bank-Fund Library) Chadwyck-Healey Inc., 1101 King St., Ste. 380, Alexandria, VA 22314-2944. TEL 703-683-4890; 800-752-0515. FAX 703-683-7589. E-mail: mktg@chadwyck.com; URL: http://www.chadwyck.com. (Outside N. America: Chadwyck-Healey Ltd., The Quorum, Barnwell Rd., Cambridge CB5 8SW, England. TEL 44-1223-215512. FAX 44-1223-215514) (Co-sponsors: International Bank for Reconstruction and Development; International Monetary Fund) adv. contact: Lara Johnson. **Document type:** abstracting/indexing.
  ●Available only on CD-ROM. Producer(s): Chadwyck-Healey Inc.
  Description: Provides bibliographic information on international development and related economic issues.

INVESTING IN KWAZULU NATAL. see *BUSINESS AND ECONOMICS — Investments*

330.9 297   TS
AL-IQTISAD AL-ISLAMI/ISLAMIC ECONOMY. (Text in Arabic) 1981. m. Bank Dubai al-Islami, P.O. Box 1080, Dubai, United Arab Emirates. TEL 285538. FAX 237243. TELEX 48772 ISLAMI EM. Ed. Muhammed Abdul Hakim Zuair. circ. 5,000.
  Description: Comprehensive treatment of Islamic economic issues.

330   UK   ISSN 0960-6475
HC471
IRAN QUARTERLY. 1990. q. £225 (£195 to subscribers to Middle East Economic Digest (ISSN 0047-7260)) (effective 1997). M E E D Publications, 21 John St., London WC1N 2BP, England. TEL 44-171-470-6406. FAX 44-171-430-0337. Ed. Vahe Petrossian. **Document type:** trade publication.
  —BLDSC (5536.142500).
  Description: Provides and in-depth analysis of political and economic trends in Iran.

330.9   IR
IRAN TRADE & INDUSTRY ANNUAL REVIEW. (Text in English) a. Echo Publications, Ave. Shiras, Kuche Khalhali No. 4, P.O. Box 2008, Teheran, Iran. adv.

ISSUES & VIEWS; an open forum on issues affecting the black community. see *ETHNIC INTERESTS*

330   IT   ISSN 0075-1995
ITALY. MINISTERO DEL BILANCIO E DELLA PROGRAMMAZIONE ECONOMICA. RELAZIONE GENERALE SULLA SITUAZIONE ECONOMICA DEL PAESE. 1951. a. free. Ministero del Bilancio, Via 20 Settembre, 97, Rome, Italy. TELEX 626432.

330.9   IT
ITALY. MINISTERO DEL BILANCIO E DELLA PROGRAMMAZIONE ECONOMICA. RELAZIONE PREVISIONALE E PROGRAMMATICA. 1965. a. free. Ministero del Bilancio e della Programmazione Economica, Via XX Settembre, 97, Rome, Italy. TELEX 626432.

330   AU
JAHRBUCH DER OESTERREICHISCHEN WIRTSCHAFT. 1969. a. free. Wirtschaftskammer Oesterreich, Wiedner Hauptstr. 63, Postfach 182, A-1045 Vienna, Austria. Ed. Werner Filek-Wittinghausen. **Document type:** government publication.

330.9   JA
JAPAN. ANNUAL REPORT ON THE NATIONAL LIFE. (Text in English) a. price varies. (Economic Planning Agency) Ministry of Finance, Printing Bureau, 2-2-4 Toranomon, Minato-ku, Tokyo 105, Japan. (Editorial addr.: 3-1-1 Kasumigaseki, Chiyoda-ku, Tokyo 100, Japan) Ed.Bd. (back issues avail.) **Document type:** government publication.

330.9   GW   ISSN 0945-1749
HC462.95
JAPAN ANALYSEN PROGNOSEN. 1986. m. DM.200 (effective 1995). I F O Institut fuer Wirtschaftsforschung, Poschingerstr. 5, 81679 Munich, Germany. TEL 49-89-9224-0. FAX 49-89-985369. **Document type:** bulletin.

JAPAN AND THE WORLD ECONOMY; international journal of theory and policy. see *BUSINESS AND ECONOMICS — Economic Systems And Theories, Economic History*

JAPAN ECONOMIC ALMANAC; an annual in-depth report on the state of the Japanese economy. see *BUSINESS AND ECONOMICS — Production Of Goods And Services*

330.9   JA   ISSN 0449-4636
JAPAN ECONOMIC REVIEW.* (Text in English) 1969. m. $7. c/o Kyodo Tsushinsha, 9-20, Asaka 1-chome, Minato-ku, Tokyo 107, Japan. illus. (also avail. in microfilm) **Indexed:** Mid.East: Abstr.& Ind.

338 952   CC   ISSN 0379-2889
JAPAN LETTER. 1973. s-m. $96. Asia Letter Group, G.P.O. Box 10874, Hong Kong, People's Republic of China. TEL 852-526-2950. FAX 852-526-7131. TELEX HX-61166-HKNW. (US addr.: Box 88189, Los Angeles, CA 90009-8189) Ed. Charles R. Smith. **Indexed:** Key to Econ.Sci. **Document type:** newsletter.
  Description: Covers business in Japan and the Japanese market.

330.9 320   US
JAPAN REPORT (ARLINGTON). 1975. 20/yr. $7 per no. (foreign $14 per no.). U.S. Joint Publications Research Service, Box 12507, Arlington, VA 22209. TEL 703-487-4630. (Orders to: NTIS, Springfield, VA 22161)

338.9   US
JAPAN TRADE CENTER INFORMATION SERVICE. MONTHLY ECONOMIC REPORT.* no.150, 1977. m. free. Ruder, Finn & Rotman, 301 E. 57th St., New York, NY 10022. charts; stat. circ. 200.

330.9   JA
JAPANESE ECONOMIC OUTLOOK; mid-term economic forecast. a. 13500 Yen. Japan Center for Economic Research, Publications Department, Nikkei Kayabacho Bldg., 6-1, Nihombashi Kayabacho 2-chome, Chuo-ku, Tokyo 103, Japan. TEL 81-3-3639-2801. FAX 81-3-3639-2839.
  Formerly: Japan's Economic Outlook.
  Description: Mid-term economic forecast analyzes and predicts the general economic trends and changes in Japan's economic structure in 5-year span. Provides guidelines for policy formation by both government and the private sector.

330.9   GW
JAPANWIRTSCHAFT. 1978. bi-m. free. Japanisches Wirtschaftsforderungsburo, Ost Str. 110, 40210 Duesseldorf, Germany. Ed.Bd. bk.rev. circ. 1,500.

JAVERIANA. see *POLITICAL SCIENCE*

JINGJI CANKAO/ECONOMIC INFORMATION. see *BUSINESS AND ECONOMICS*

BUSINESS AND ECONOMICS — ECONOMIC SITUATION AND CONDITIONS

330   CC   ISSN 0013-0265
HC59
JINGJI DAOBAO/ECONOMIC REPORTER. (Text in Chinese) 1947. w. HK.$720 in Hong Kong; China, Macao HK.$950; elsewhere $180. Economic Information & Agency, 342 Hennessy Rd., 10th Fl., Wanchai, Hong Kong, People's Republic of China. TEL 852-573-8217. FAX 852-838-8304. TELEX 86990-EIA-HX. Ed. Chan Pak Kwan. adv.; charts; illus.; stat. circ. 15,000. **Indexed:** P.A.I.S.

JINGJI DILI/ECONOMIC GEOGRAPHY. see *GEOGRAPHY*

JINGJI GAIGE/ECONOMIC REFORM. see *BUSINESS AND ECONOMICS — Economic Systems And Theories, Economic History*

330.9   CC
JINGJI RIBAO/ECONOMIC DAILY. (Text in Chinese) d. Jingji Ribao She, 277 Wangfujing Dajie, Beijing 100746, People's Republic of China. TEL 5125522. FAX 5125015. (Dist. outside China by: China International Book Trading Corp., P.O. Box 399, Beijing 100044, P.R. China. TEL 8413063; Dist. in US by: China Books & Periodicals, Inc., 2929 24th St., San Francisco, CA 94110) pp./issue: 12. **Document type:** newspaper.

JINGJI YU GUANLI YANJIU/RESEARCH ON ECONOMICS AND MANAGEMENT. see *BUSINESS AND ECONOMICS — Management*

JINRONG SHIBAO/FINANCIAL NEWS. see *BUSINESS AND ECONOMICS — Banking And Finance*

330.9   US   ISSN 0883-136X
JOHN NAISBITT'S TREND LETTER; your authoritative twice-monthly report on the forces transforming the economy, business, technology, society and the world. Variant title: Trend Letter. 1982. fortn. $195. Global Network, Inc., 1101 30th St., N.W., Ste. 130, Washington, DC 20007. TEL 202-337-5960; 800-368-0115. FAX 202-333-5198. (Subscr. to: Box 25536, Washington, DC 20007) Ed. David Franke; Pub. Daniel Levinas. circ. 20,000 (paid). **Document type:** newsletter.
—CCC.

JOURNAL OF ACCOUNTING AND ECONOMICS. see *BUSINESS AND ECONOMICS — Accounting*

330.9   UK   ISSN 0963-8024
HC800.A1
JOURNAL OF AFRICAN ECONOMIES. 1992. 3/yr. £84 (foreign $145) (effective 1998). (Centre for the Study of African Economies) Oxford University Press, Academic Division, Great Clarendon St., Oxford OX2 6DP, England. TEL 44-1865-267907. FAX 44-1865-267485. TELEX 837330-OXPRES-G. E-mail: jnl.info@oup.co.uk; URL: http://www.oup.co.uk/journals. (U.S. subscr. to: Oxford University Press Inc., 2001 Evans Rd., Cary, NC 27513. TEL 800-852-7323. FAX 919-677-1714) Ed.Bd.; Pub. Martin Green. R&P contact: Joolz Longley. adv. contact: Jane Parker. bk.rev. circ. 650. **Indexed:** Documentatieblad, Geo.Abstr.P.G., IDA. **Document type:** academic/scholarly publication.
—BLDSC (4919.989500); SWETS. CCC.

338.91 300   US   ISSN 1068-0055
HF3790.8
JOURNAL OF ASIAN BUSINESS. 1983. q. $25 to individuals; institutions $40. Association for Asian Studies, 130 Lane Hall, Ann Arbor, MI 48109-1290. TEL 313-763-4508. FAX 313-747-2083. URL: http://www.easc.indiana.edu/~aas/catalog.jas.htm. Eds. Jason Eyster, Linda Y.C. Lim. bk.rev. circ. 1,000. **Indexed:** Asian-Pac.Econ.Lit., B.P.I. **Document type:** academic/scholarly publication.
—BLDSC (4947.234000); KR SourceOne; SWETS; UMI; UnCover.
Former titles: Journal of Southeast Asia Business (ISSN 1055-2073); Southeast Asia Business (ISSN 0886-6651)
Description: Covers political, economic, business, industrial, and cultural news, analysis, and commentary about Asia for American or other business academic-oriented studies.
Refereed Serial

330.9   US   ISSN 1049-0078
HC460.5.A1
JOURNAL OF ASIAN ECONOMICS. 1990. q. $85 to individuals (foreign $105); institutions $225 (foreign $245) (effective 1998). (American Committee on Asian Economic Studies) J A I Press Inc., 55 Old Post Rd., No. 2, Box 1678, Greenwich, CT 06830-1678. TEL 203-661-7602. FAX 203-661-0792. E-mail: jai@jaipress.com. (Addr. in Europe: J A I Press Ltd., 38 Tavistock St., Covent Garden, London WC2E 7PB, England. TEL 44-171-379-8834. FAX 44-171-379-8835) Ed. M. Dutta. (also avail. in microform from UMI; back issues avail.) **Indexed:** Asian-Pac.Econ.Lit., P.A.I.S. **Document type:** academic/scholarly publication.
—BLDSC (4947.238000); SWETS; UnCover.

330   AT   ISSN 0156-5826
JOURNAL OF AUSTRALIAN POLITICAL ECONOMY. 1977. s-a. Aus.$24 for 4 issues to individuals; institutions Aus.$25 for 2 issues (effective 1997). Australian Political Economy Movement, P.O. Box 76, Wentworth Bldg., University of Sydney, N.S.W. 2006. TEL 61-2-93516617. E-mail: evanj@sue.econ.su.oz.au. Ed. Frank Stilwell. adv.; bk.rev.; circ. 500 (paid). **Indexed:** Aus.P.A.I.S. **Document type:** academic/scholarly publication.
—BLDSC (4949.470000).
Description: Presents progressive views on Australian economic, labor and social policy.
Refereed Serial

JOURNAL OF BUSINESS AND ECONOMIC STATISTICS. see *BUSINESS AND ECONOMICS — Abstracting, Bibliographies, Statistics*

330   TH   ISSN 0125-0566
JOURNAL OF COMMERCE. (Text in English and Thai) 1976. m. B.120. Department of Business Economics, Bangkok, Thailand.
Incorporates: Consumer Price Indexes for Thailand.
Description: Monthly report of consumer prices in Thailand.

JOURNAL OF EMERGING MARKETS. see *BUSINESS AND ECONOMICS — Banking And Finance*

JOURNAL OF ENVIRONMENT & DEVELOPMENT; a review of international policy. see *ENVIRONMENTAL STUDIES*

JOURNAL OF EUROPEAN INTEGRATION HISTORY/ZEITSCHRIFT FUER GESCHICHTE DER EUROPAEISCHEN INTEGRATION/REVUE D'HISTOIRE DE L'INTEGRATION EUROPEENNE. see *POLITICAL SCIENCE — International Relations*

JOURNAL OF FINANCIAL MANAGEMENT AND ANALYSIS; international review of finance. see *BUSINESS AND ECONOMICS — Banking And Finance*

030.9   JA   ISSN 0285-9556
HC462.9
JOURNAL OF JAPANESE TRADE AND INDUSTRY. (Text in English) 1982. 6/yr. £45 (effective 1992). (Japan Economic Foundation) Maruzen Co. Ltd., 3-10 Nihombashi 2-chome, Chuo-ku, Tokyo 103, Japan. TEL 03-3272-7211. FAX 03-3274-3238. TELEX 26516. Ed. Yoshimichi Hori, T. Iwasaki. adv.; bk.rev.; illus. circ. 35,000. **Indexed:** CAD CAM Abstr., Environ.Abstr., Mgmt.& Market.Abstr., P.A.I.S., Tel.Abstr., Text.Tech.Dig. **Document type:** academic/scholarly publication.
—SWETS; UnCover.

JOURNAL OF RESEARCH IN PHARMACEUTICAL ECONOMICS. see *PHARMACY AND PHARMACOLOGY*

330.9   UK   ISSN 1354-7860
▼**JOURNAL OF THE ASIA PACIFIC ECONOMY.** 1995. q. £34 (U.S. and Canada $52; rest of world £34) to individuals; institutions £98 (U.S. and Canada $135; rest of world £98) (effective 1997). Routledge, 11 New Fetter Ln., London EC4P 4EE, England. TEL 44-171-583-9855. FAX 44-171-842-2298. E-mail: info.journals@routledge.com; URL: http://www.routledge.com/routledge/journal/journals.html. (Subscr. to: ITPS Ltd., Cheriton House, North Way, Andover, Hants SP10 5BE, England. TEL 44-1264-342919. FAX 44-1264-342807; Subscr. in US & Canada to: 29 W. 35th St., New York, NY 10001-2299. TEL 212-244-3336. FAX 212-564-7854) Ed.Bd. **Document type:** academic/scholarly publication.
—BLDSC (4947.219500).
Description: Includes analyses which range from overview articles spanning the region to ones with a detailed focus on particular economic issues facing individual countries.

330.9 332.6   US
JUDGE'S RETIREMENT SYSTEM. ANNUAL FINANCIAL REPORT AND REPORT OF OPERATIONS. a. free. Judge's Retirement System, 400 P St., Rm. 3450, Sacramento, CA 95814. TEL 916-326-3688. circ. 3,000. **Document type:** government publication.

JURECO. see *LAW*

330.9   MY   ISSN 0127-1962
HC445.5.A1
JURNAL EKONOMI MALAYSIA. Short title: J E M. (Text in English, Malay) 1980. s-a. $15. Penerbit Universiti Kebangsaan Malaysia, 43600 UKM Bangi, Selangor, Malaysia. FAX 603-8256484. TELEX UNIKEB MA 31496. Ed. Osman Rani. circ. 500. **Indexed:** Asian-Pac.Econ.Lit., IDA.

K D B REPORT. (Korea Development Bank) see *BUSINESS AND ECONOMICS*

330.9   CC
KAIFA BAO/DEVELOPMENT NEWS. (Text in Chinese) w. $46.50. 287 Heping Lu, Tianjin, People's Republic of China. TEL 31-6426. (Dist. outside China by: China International Book Trading Corp., P.O. Box 399, Beijing, P.R.C.; Dist. in US by: China Books & Periodicals, Inc., 2929 24th St., San Francisco, CA 94110) **Document type:** newspaper.

330.9 338.91   JA   ISSN 0288-089X
KAIHATSU RONSHU/JOURNAL OF DEVELOPMENT POLICY STUDIES. (Text in Japanese; table of contents in English) 1965. s-a. Hokkai-Gakuen University, Institute of Development Policy Studies, Asahi-machi-4, Sapporo Toyohira 062, Japan. TEL 011-841-1161. Ed. Koichi Matsuda. index. circ. 800. (back issues avail.)
—BLDSC (4969.245000).
Description: Academic research in regional development policies.

330.9   NR
KANO (STATE). DIRECTORY OF INDUSTRIAL & COMMERCIAL ESTABLISHMENTS. 1985. quinquennial. $30 (effective 1996). Budget & Economic Planning Directorate, Ministry of Finance, Audu Bako Secretariat, P.M.B. 3291, Kano, Nigeria. **Document type:** government publication.

KANO (STATE). LOCAL GOVERNMENT SURVEY OF TOWNS, VILLAGES AND HAMLETS. see *BUSINESS AND ECONOMICS — Abstracting, Bibliographies, Statistics*

KANO (STATE). PRICES OF SELECTED COMMODITIES IN SOME TOWNS IN KANO STATE. see *BUSINESS AND ECONOMICS — Abstracting, Bibliographies, Statistics*

KANO (STATE). STATISTICAL YEAR-BOOK. see *BUSINESS AND ECONOMICS — Abstracting, Bibliographies, Statistics*

BUSINESS AND ECONOMICS — ECONOMIC SITUATION AND CONDITIONS

330.9 US ISSN 0734-2748
THE KANSAS CITY BUSINESS JOURNAL. 1982. w. $69. American City Business Journals, Inc. (Kansas City), 1101 Walnut St., Ste. 800, Kansas City, MO 64106-2122. TEL 816-421-5900. FAX 816-472-4010. Ed. Paul Wenske; Pub. Joyce Hayhow. adv. contact: Fawn Fleming. circ. 11,500 (paid). (also avail. in microform from UMI). **Indexed:** Tr.&Indus.Ind. **Document type:** newspaper.
● Also available online. Vendor(s): Information Access Co.
—UMI. **CCC.**

330 JA
KEIDANREN CLIP. (Text in Japanese) 1951. bi-w. membership. Japan Federation of Economic Organizations - Keizai Dantal Rengokai (Keidanren), 9-4 Otemachi, 1-chome, Chiyoda-ku, Tokyo 100, Japan. TEL 81-3-3279-1411. FAX 81-3-5255-6255. TELEX 0222 3188 KDRTOKJ. circ. 5,000.
Formerly: Keidanren Shuho.

330 JA
KEIDANREN SHIRYO. (Text in Japanese) 1947. irreg. $10. Japan Federation of Economic Organizations - Keizai Dantai Rengokai (KEIDANREN), 9-4 Otemachi, 1-chome, Chiyoda-ku, Tokyo 100, Japan. TEL 81-3-3279-1411. FAX 81-3-5255-6255. TELEX 0222 3188 KDRTOKJ. charts; illus.; stat.
Formerly: Keidanren Keizai Shiryo.

330.9 KE ISSN 0075-5842
HC517.K4
KENYA. CENTRAL BUREAU OF STATISTICS. ECONOMIC SURVEY. Key Title: Economic Survey. (Former name of issuing body: Kenya. Ministry of Planning and National Development) 1960. a. KShs.450. Ministry of Finance and Planning, Central Bureau of Statistics, P.O. Box 30266, Nairobi, Kenya. (Subscr. to: Government Press, Haile Selaissie Ave., Box 30266, Nairobi, Kenya. TEL 254-2-334075) stat. (back issues avail.) **Document type:** government publication.
—BLDSC (3655.985000).

330.9 KE
KENYA BUSINESS SPOTLIGHT. 1983. m. Native Publishers Ltd., P.O. Box 18379, Nairobi, Kenya. (Dist. by: Kenya Times Ltd., P.O. Box 30958, Nairobi, Kenya) Ed. Christopher Mulei.

330.9 UK
KENYA YEARBOOK. a. £10($30) New Product Newsletter Co. Ltd., 1A Chesterfield St., London W1, England. adv.; charts; illus.

330.9 II ISSN 0453-7440
KERALA; AN ECONOMIC REVIEW. (Text in English) 1959. a. price varies. Kerala State Planning Board, Trivandrum 4, India. circ. 2,000.

330.9 UK
KEY NOTE MARKET REPORT: PLANT HIRE. Variant title: Plant Hire. irreg., no.10, 1995. £205. Key Note Ltd., Field House, 72 Oldfield Rd., Hampton, Middlesex TW12 2HQ, England. TEL 44-181-783-0755. FAX 44-181-783-0049. **Document type:** trade publication.
● Also available online.
Also available on CD-ROM.
Formerly: Key Note Report: Plant Hire.

330.9 GW ISSN 0342-0787
HB5
KIELER ARBEITSPAPIERE/KIEL WORKING PAPERS. (Text in English or German) 1973. irreg. DM.10 per no. Institut fuer Weltwirtschaft, Duesternbrooker Weg 120, 24105 Kiel, Germany. TEL 49-431-8814305. FAX 49-431-8814527. TELEX 292479-WELTW-D. E-mail: info@ifw.uni-kiel.de; URL: http://www.uni-kiel.de:8080/ifw/. circ. 150. **Indexed:** Rural Recreat.Tour.Abstr., World Agri.Econ.& Rural Sociol.Abstr. **Document type:** monographic series.
—BLDSC (9349.640000).
Description: Presents preliminary results of research projects within the Kiel Institute.
Refereed Serial

330.9 GW ISSN 0455-0420
HB44
KIELER DISKUSSIONSBEITRAEGE/KIEL DISCUSSION PAPERS. (Text in English, German) 1969. irreg., no.274, 1996. DM.15 per no. Institut fuer Weltwirtschaft, Duesternbrooker Weg 120, 24105 Kiel, Germany. TEL 49-431-8814305. FAX 49-431-8814527. E-mail: info@ifw.uni-kiel.de; URL: http://www.uni-kiel.de:8080/ifw/. circ. 900. **Document type:** monographic series.
—BLDSC (5094.680000).
Description: Deals with current economic problems.
Refereed Serial

330.9 GW ISSN 0173-5241
KIELER KURZBERICHTE. irreg. Institut fuer Weltwirtschaft, Duesternbrooker Weg 120, 24105 Kiel, Germany. TEL 49-431-8814305. FAX 49-431-8814527. E-mail: info@ifw.uni-kiel.de; URL: http://www.uni-kiel.de:8080/ifw/. Ed. Dietmar Gebert. **Document type:** bulletin.
Refereed Serial

330.9 GW ISSN 0340-6970
KIELER VORTRAEGE. a. DM.10. Institut fuer Weltwirtschaft, Duesternbrooker Weg 120, 24105 Kiel, Germany. TEL 49-431-8814305. FAX 49-431-8814527. E-mail: info@ifw.uni-kiel.de; URL: http://www.uni-kiel.de:8080/ifw/. Ed. Horst Siebert. **Document type:** monographic series.
Refereed Serial

338 NE ISSN 0023-1363
HC321
KIJK OP HET NOORDEN/OUTLOOK ON THE NORTH; signaleren van de economische ontwikkeling in de provincies Groningen, Friesland en Drente. 1969. q. fl.18.50($6) N.V. Noord Nederlandse Drukkerij, Postbus 6, 7940 AA Meppel, Netherlands. TEL 05220-68600. Ed. B.P. Tammeling. adv.; bk.rev.; tr.lit. circ. 10,000.
—SWETS.

330.9 DK ISSN 0108-2612
KINA INFORMATION; en bulletin om Kinas handel og oekonomi. 1982. 6/yr. DKK 980. Aarhus University, N D R Ringgade, DK-8000 Aarhus C, Denmark. TEL 45-89-42-20-77. FAX 45-86-18-42-30. Ed. Mogens Justesen. adv.; bk.rev. circ. 150. (looseleaf format) **Document type:** bulletin.

330.9 GW
KONJUNKTUR IN BAYERN. 1981. m. free. Staatsministerium fuer Wirtschaft, Verkehr und Technologie, Prinzregentenstr. 28, 80525 Munich, Germany. FAX 49-89-2162-2614. stat. circ. 900. **Document type:** government publication.
Formerly (until 1994): Bericht zur Aktuellen Konjunkturlage im Bundesgebiet und in Bayern.
Description: Survey of the business climate of Bavarian industry, and other economic indicators.

330 KO ISSN 0017-744X
KOREA DEVELOPMENT BANK. MONTHLY ECONOMIC REVIEW. (Text in Korean) 1964. m. free. Korea Development Bank, 10-2 Kwanch'ol-dong, Chongno-gu, C.P.O. Box 28, Seoul, S. Korea. Ed. Beoung-Yun Min. charts; stat.; cum.index.
—UnCover.

330.9 KO
KOREA ECONOMIC WEEKLY. (Text in English, Korean) w. URL: http://eco.ked.co.kr/h-kew.html. **Document type:** newsletter.
● Available only online.

330.9 KO ISSN 0146-9657
DS901
KOREA NEWSREVIEW. (Text in English) 1972. w. 28600 Won (Japan, HK & China $89; Australia & US $108; elsewhere $112). Korea Herald, 1-12, 3-ga, Hoehyon-dong, Chung-gu, C.P.O. Box 6479, Seoul 100-771, S. Korea. TEL 02-756-7711. Ed. Min Dae-Ki. adv.; charts, illus. circ. 20,000. **Document type:** consumer publication.

KOREA POLICY SERIES. see *POLITICAL SCIENCE*

330.9 320.253
KOREAN AFFAIRS REPORT. 1966. 60/yr. $7 per no. (foreign $14 per no.). U.S. Joint Publications Research Service, Box 12507, Arlington, VA 22209. TEL 703-487-4630. (Orders to: NTIS, Springfield, VA 22161)
Formerly: Translations on North Korea.

330.9 KU ISSN 1016-4278
KUWAIT & GULF ECONOMIC AND FINANCIAL BULLETIN. Key Title: Kuwait & Gulf Cooperation Council. Economic & Financial Bulletin. 1982. q. free. National Bank of Kuwait S.A.K., Economic Research and Planning Division, P.O. Box 95, 13001 Safat, Kuwait. TEL 965-2422011. FAX 965-2466260. TELEX 22451. Ed.Bd. circ. 6,000. (back issues avail.) **Indexed:** World Bank.Abstr.
Former titles (until 1987): Kuwait Economic and Financial Bulletin (ISSN 1016-426X); Economics and Financial Quarterly; Kuwait Economic and Financial Quarterly.

330.9 UK ISSN 0023-5962
H1
KYKLOS; internationale Zeitschrift fuer Sozialwissenschaften. (Text in English, French, German) 1948. q. £126($202) (foreign £128) (effective 1997). Blackwell Publishers Ltd., 108 Cowley Rd., Oxford OX4 1JF, England. TEL 44-1865-791100. FAX 44-1865-791347. Ed. Rene L. Frey. adv.; bk.rev.; abstr.; bibl.; charts; index. circ. 2,600. (also avail. in microform from UMI; reprint service avail. from UMI) **Indexed:** Amer.Hist.& Life (1954-1959), (1966-1989), Arts & Hum.Cit.Ind., ASCA, C.R.E.J., Curr.Cont., Excerp.Med., Geo.Abstr.P.G., Hist.Abstr. (1954-1959), (1966-1989), IBR, IDA, Int.Lab.Doc., J.of Econ.Lit., Key to Econ.Sci., Mid.East: Abstr.& Ind., P.A.I.S., Risk Abstr., Rural Recreat.Tour.Abstr., SCIMP (1991-), Soc.Sci.Ind., SSCI, World Agri.Econ.& Rural Sociol.Abstr., World Bank.Abstr. **Document type:** academic/scholarly publication.
● Also available online. Vendor(s): UMI.
—BLDSC (5134.858000); Genuine Article; KR SourceOne; SWETS; UMI; UnCover. **CCC.**

L A R F REPORT. ANNUAL. (Latin American Reserve Fund) see *BUSINESS AND ECONOMICS*

330.9 US
LA CROSSE AREA BUSINESS AND ECONOMIC REVIEW. 1977. q. donation. University of Wisconsin at La Crosse, La Crosse, WI 54601. TEL 608-785-8782. Ed. Jan Gallagher. **Document type:** trade publication.
Former titles: La Crosse - Winona Business and Economic Review; La Crosse Economic Indicators.

330.9 US ISSN 1048-2822
LAFAYETTE BUSINESS DIGEST. 1983. w. $42.95 (effective 1997). Laurendeau Communications, Box 587, Lafayette, IN 47902. TEL 317-742-6918. FAX 317-423-8133. Ed. Gwen Rodenberger. R&P contact: Marlene Laurendeau. adv. contact: Derek Davidson. cum.index: 1983-1990. circ. 2,000. (tabloid format; also avail. in microfilm from UMI; back issues avail.) **Document type:** newspaper.
● Also available online. Vendor(s): UMI.
—UMI.
Description: Includes business news, trends, and features highlighting business and industry in Tippecanoe County and surrounding area.

LAGEBERICHT AUS AUSTRALIEN. see *POLITICAL SCIENCE — International Relations*

330.9 352 UK
LANCASHIRE COUNTY COUNCIL. PLANNING REPORT. irreg., no.5, 1995. £10. Lancashire County Council, P.O. Box 160, East Cliff County Office, Preston PR1 3EX, England. **Document type:** government publication.

330.9 GW
LANGE REIHEN DER VIERTELJAEHRLICHEN VOLKSWIRTSCHAFTLICHEN GESAMTRECHNUNG. 1973. q. free. Deutsches Institut fuer Wirtschaftsforschung, Koenigin-Luise-Str. 5, 14195 Berlin, Germany. TEL 49-30-89789-0. FAX 49-30-89789200. E-mail: bulletin@diw-berlin.de. Ed. Karin Mueller-Krumholz. circ. 150. **Document type:** academic/scholarly publication.

330.9 MY
LAPORAN KETUA ODIT NEGARA. KERAJAAN PERSEKUTUAN. a. Jabatan Percetakan Negara, Kuala Lumpur, Malaysia.

330.9 320 US
LATIN AMERICA REPORT. 1967. 120/yr. $7 per no. (foreign $14 per no.). U.S. Joint Publications Research Service, Box 12507, Arlington, VA 22209. TEL 703-487-4630. (Orders to: NTIS, Springfield, VA 22161)
Formerly: Translations on Latin America.

BUSINESS AND ECONOMICS — ECONOMIC SITUATION AND CONDITIONS

330.9   US
▼ **LATIN AMERICAN BUSINESS REVIEW.** 1997. q. $50 to individuals (Canada $65; elsewhere $70); institutions $75 (Canada $97.50; elsewhere $105); libraries $95 (Canada $123.50; elsewhere $133) (effective 1998-1999). Haworth Press, Inc., 10 Alice St., Binghamton, NY 13904. TEL 607-722-5857; 800-342-9676. FAX 607-722-6362. E-mail: getinfo@haworth.com; URL: http://www.haworth.com. Ed. Denise Dimon; Pub. Bill Cohen. R&P contact: Ruthann Heath. adv.: B&W page $300; trim 4 3/8 x 7 1/8; adv. contact: Jackie Blakeslee. (also avail. in microform from HAW,UMI; reprint service avail. from HAW) **Document type:** academic/scholarly publication.
—Haworth.
Description: Promotes the exchange of information and new ideas between the academic, business practitioner, public policymaker, and those in the international development community.

LATIN AMERICAN FINANCE & CAPITAL MARKETS. see
BUSINESS AND ECONOMICS — Investments

338.9 320   UK   ISSN 0143-5248
HC161
LATIN AMERICAN REGIONAL REPORTS - ANDEAN GROUP. 10/yr. £150($195) (subscr. to all five regional reports £492($640)) (effective 1997). Latin American Newsletters, 61 Old St., London EC1V 9HX, England. TEL 44-171-251-0012. FAX 44-171-253-8193. Ed. Colin Harding. (back issues avail.) **Document type:** trade publication.
●Also available online. Vendor(s): Lexis-Nexis.
Description: Weekly report on news from countries on the Andean mountain chain.

338.9 650   UK   ISSN 0143-5280
F1401
LATIN AMERICAN WEEKLY REPORT. 1967. w. (50/yr.). £688($895) (effective 1997). Latin American Newsletters, 61 Old St., London EC1V 9HX, England. TEL 44-171-251-0012. FAX 44-171-253-8193. Ed. Eduardo Crawley. (back issues avail.) **Indexed:** Key to Econ.Sci., Polit.Sci.Abstr. **Document type:** newsletter.
●Also available online. Vendor(s): Lexis-Nexis.
—SWETS.
Description: Weekly report on Latin American news.

330.9 658.8   CN   ISSN 0834-3586
LEADS. 1981. bi-m. price varies. Box 9333, Ottawa, Ont. K1G 3V1, Canada. TEL 800-927-1527. FAX 1-613-746-2053. Ed. Tom Kennedy. bk.rev. circ. 2,000.
Description: Follows the rebirth of free enterprise in the explosive multi-level marketing industry, provides opportunity for secondary incomes seekers, promotes barter, educates the new breed of shop-at-home consumer and advocates monetary reform.

LEBANON REPORT. see POLITICAL SCIENCE — International Relations

LECTURAS DE ECONOMIA. see BUSINESS AND ECONOMICS — Abstracting, Bibliographies, Statistics

LEGISLATIVE WATCH (WASHINGTON). see PUBLIC ADMINISTRATION

LEISURE FUTURES. see LEISURE AND RECREATION

330.9   LO
LESOTHO NATIONAL DEVELOPMENT CORPORATION. NEWSLETTER. irreg. Lesotho National Development Corporation, P.O. Box 666, Maseru, Lesotho. **Document type:** newsletter.

330.9   IS   ISSN 0334-9160
LEUMI REVIEW; Israel: macroperspectives. (Text in English) 1952. irreg. (approx. 3/yr.). free. Bank Leumi Le-Israel, P.O. Box 2, Tel Aviv 61000, Israel. TEL 972-3-5148737. FAX 972-3-5148864. Ed. Gad Shifron. charts; mkt.; stat. circ. 8,000. **Indexed:** World Bank.Abstr. **Document type:** monographic series, bulletin.
Formed by the merger of: Bank Leumi Israel Macroperspectives; Bank Leumi Economic Review (ISSN 0034-6519); **Formerly:** Review of Economic Conditions in Israel.

LEXIKON DES STEUER- UND WIRTSCHAFTSRECHTS. see
LAW

330.9   US
LIAONING JINGJI BAO/LIAONING ECONOMIC WEEKLY. (Text in Chinese) w. $143. Liaoning Jingji Baoshe, Shenyang, Liaoning, People's Republic of China. (Dist. in US by: China Books & Periodicals, Inc., 2929 24th St., San Francisco, CA 94110. TEL 415-282-2994) **Document type:** newspaper.

330.9   UK   ISSN 0267-7164
LIBERTARIAN ALLIANCE. ECONOMIC NOTES. 1985. irreg. £15($30) Libertarian Alliance, 25 Chapter Chambers, Esterbrooke St., London SW1P 4NN, England. TEL 44-171-821-5502. FAX 44-171-834-2031. E-mail: liberty@capital.demon.co.uk; URL: http://www.digiweb.com/igeldard/la. Ed. Brian Micklethwait; Pub. Chris Tame. R&P contact: Chris Tame. adv.; bk.rev.; film rev.; bibl. circ. 1,000. (back issues avail.) **Document type:** monographic series.

330.9 327   US
LIBERTY AT BAY; issues impacting on freedom in our time. (Text in English, Spanish) 1982. bi-w. $685. Aura Publishing Co., 441 Central Ave., Box 1367, Scarsdale, NY 10538. TEL 914-834-2322. FAX 914-833-0930. E-mail: rsandell@aura.com. Ed. Richard A. Sandell; Pub. Arnold P. Josevie. adv. contact: Marcel Aurevie. cum.index: 1982-1994. circ. 2,680. (looseleaf format; also avail. in microfiche) **Document type:** newsletter.
Description: Analysis of international economic and political issues affecting wealthy individuals.

LIBRI DELLE BIBLIOTECHE TRENTINE. see
ENVIRONMENTAL STUDIES

LIFELONG LEARNING MARKET REPORT. see
EDUCATION — Adult Education

LINK; Israel's international business magazine. see
BUSINESS AND ECONOMICS — International Commerce

LIST OF ITALIAN STOCKS. see BUSINESS AND ECONOMICS — Investments

330.9   JA
LONG-TERM ECONOMIC FORECAST. (Text in Japanese; summaries in English) 1970. a. 13500 Yen. Japan Center for Economic Research, Publications Department, Nikkei Kayabacho Bldg., 6-1, Nihonbashi Kayaba-cho 2-chome, Chuo-ku, Tokyo 103, Japan. TEL 81-3-3639-2801. FAX 81-3-3639-2839.
Description: Focuses on specific topics in the Japanese and world economy. Published each May.

330.9   US   ISSN 0194-2603
LOS ANGELES BUSINESS JOURNAL. 1979. w. $79.95. California Business Journals, 5700 Wilshire Blvd., Ste. 170, Los Angeles, CA 90010. Ed. Mark Lactes; Pub. Matthew Toledo. adv. contact: Maria Flannigan. circ. 40,000. (tabloid format; also avail. in microform from UMI) **Indexed:** Tr.& Indus.Ind. **Document type:** newspaper.
●Also available online. Vendor(s): Information Access Co.
—UMI.

LOTHIAN & EDINBURGH LABOUR MARKET ASSESSMENT. see BUSINESS AND ECONOMICS — Labor And Industrial Relations

330.9   US   ISSN 0193-5712
HG107.L8
LOUISIANA BUSINESS SURVEY. 1970. s-a. free. University of New Orleans, Lake Front, Division of Business and Economic Research, Lake Front, New Orleans, LA 70148. TEL 504-286-6248. FAX 504-286-6094. E-mail: pjcdb@uno.edu. Ed. Patricia J. Connor. R&P contact: Patricia J. Connor. TEL 504-280-7326. circ. 9,000 (controlled). **Indexed:** P.A.I.S.
—UMI; UnCover.

330.9   LU   ISSN 1019-6463
HC380
LUXEMBOURG. SERVICE CENTRAL DE LA STATISTIQUE ET DES ETUDES ECONOMIQUES. NOTE DE CONJONCTURE. 1972. q. 450 Fr. (effective 1997). Service Central de la Statistique et des Etudes Economiques, 6 bd. Royal, B.P. 304, 2013 Luxembourg, Luxembourg. TEL 352-478-4268. FAX 352-464289. E-mail: statec.post@statec.etat.lu; URL: http://statec.gouvernement.lu. circ. 1,000. **Document type:** government publication.
Formerly: Luxembourg. Service Central de la Statistique et des Etudes Economiques. Notes Trimestrielles de Conjoncture (ISSN 0256-1913)
Description: Analyzes the current situation and short-term perspective for the economy and the international environment.

330   UK   ISSN 0963-5572
M E E D INDEX. (Middle East Economic Digest) 1957. q. £45. M E E D Publications, 21 John St., London WC1N 2BP, England. TEL 44-171-470-6406. FAX 44-171-430-0337. **Document type:** trade publication.

330   UA   ISSN 0024-8118
AP9
M E N ECONOMIC WEEKLY. (Text in English) w. $150. Middle East News Agency, Hoda Sha'Rawi St., P.O. Box 1165, Attaba, 11511 Cairo, Egypt. Ed. Zeinab Wahby. charts; stat.
Formerly: M E N Weekly Review of World and Arab Affairs.
Description: Covers economic activities in Egypt and all Arab countries.

338   UA
M E O BULLETIN. 32/yr. Middle East Observer, 41 Sherif St., Cairo, Egypt. TEL 20-2-3939732. FAX 20-2-3606804. **Document type:** bulletin.

330   JA   ISSN 0026-6809
M E R I'S MONTHLY CIRCULAR; survey of economic conditions in Japan. (Text in English) 1923. m. $45 in Asia; N. America & Europe $47; S. America $49. Mitsubishi Economic Research Institute, 10-14, Yushima, 4-chome, Bunkyo-ku, Tokyo 113, Japan. TEL 81-3-5802-8670. TELEX J 27161 JPTCO. (Subscr. to: Japan Publications Trading Co. Ltd., P.O. Box 5030, Tokyo 100-31, Japan) Ed. Toshio Yamaguchi. adv.; charts; mkt.; stat. circ. 2,500. **Document type:** academic/scholarly publication.
Description: Attempts to provide a better understanding abroad of the Japanese economy by explaining and analyzing its principle moves.

330.9   MY
M P R C REPORT ON FINANCE, COMMERCE, INDUSTRY: INDONESIA. 1972. irreg. $30. M P R C (Asia) Sdn. Berhad, P.O. Box 10706, 50722 Kuala Lumpur, Malaysia. TEL 60-3-2217762. FAX 60-3-7564478. Ed. Paul Markandan. bk.rev.; stat.; circ. controlled.

330.9   MY
M P R C REPORT ON FINANCE, COMMERCE, INDUSTRY: INDONESIA. SUPPLEMENT. 1974. irreg. $15. M P R C (Asia) Sdn. Berhad, P.O. Box 10706, 50722 Kuala Lumpur, Malaysia. TEL 60-3-2217762. FAX 60-3-7564478. Ed. Paul Markandan. bk.rev.; stat.

330.9   MY
M P R C REPORT ON FINANCE, COMMERCE, INDUSTRY: SINGAPORE. 1972. irreg. $15. M P R C (Asia) Sdn. Berhad, P.O. Box 10706, 50722 Kuala Lumpur, Malaysia. TEL 60-3-2217762. FAX 60-3-7564478. Ed. Paul Markandan. bk.rev.; stat.; circ. controlled.

330.9   MY
M P R C REPORT ON FINANCE, COMMERCE, INDUSTRY: SOUTH EAST ASIA. 1977. irreg. $30. M P R C (Asia) Sdn. Berhad, P.O. Box 10706, 50722 Kuala Lumpur, Malaysia. TEL 60-3-2217762. FAX 60-3-7564478. Ed. Paul Markandan. bk.rev.; stat.; circ. controlled.

330.9   MY
M P R C REPORT ON FINANCE, COMMERCE, INDUSTRY: THAILAND. 1973. irreg. $30. M P R C (Asia) Sdn. Berhad, P.O. Box 10706, 50722 Kuala Lumpur, Malaysia. TEL 60-2-2217762. FAX 60-3-7564478. Ed. Paul Markandan. bk.rev.; stat.; circ. controlled.

MACHINERY: LATIN AMERICAN INDUSTRIAL REPORT. see MACHINERY

BUSINESS AND ECONOMICS — ECONOMIC SITUATION AND CONDITIONS

330   UK   ISSN 0961-9836
MAGHREB QUARTERLY. 1991. q. £225 (£195 to subscribers to Middle East Economic Digest (ISSN 0047-7260)) (effective 1997). M E E D Publications, 21 John St., London WC1N 2BP, England. TEL 44-171-470-6406. FAX 44-171-430-0337. TELEX 936564 MEEDAR G. Ed. Jon Marks. **Document type:** trade publication. —BLDSC (5334.756000).
    Description: Provides an in-depth analysis of political and economic trends in the Islamic north African nations.

330.9   II
MAHARASHTRA ECONOMIC DEVELOPMENT COUNCIL. MONTHLY ECONOMIC DIGEST FOR BUSINESS EXECUTIVES. (Text in English) 1972. m. membership. Maharashtra Economic Development Council, 106 Nagindas Master Rd., Bombay 400001, India. TEL 274660. Ed. S.B. Sakhalkar. adv.; bk.rev. circ. 2,000.

330.9   NP
MAIN ECONOMIC INDICATORS. (Text in English) m. Nepal Rastra Bank, Research Department, Baluwatar, Kathmandu, Nepal. TEL 977-1-411638. Ed. Keshav Prasad Acharya. charts; stat. **Document type:** newsletter.
    Description: Monthly notes on the economic activities of Nepal.

338.5   US   ISSN 0025-0619
HC107.M2
MAINE BUSINESS INDICATORS. 1956. q. free. University of Southern Maine, Center for Business and Economic Research, c/o Robert C. McMahon, Ed., P.O. Box 9300, Portland, ME 04104-9300. TEL 207-780-4187. FAX 207-780-4046. URL: http://www.usm.maine.edu/~cber/. charts, stat. circ. 4,600. **Document type:** newsletter.
    Description: Contains Maine-oriented articles on economic development and analysis, industry studies and economic public policy. It also maintains the Maine Business Index as a measure of changes in the level of Maine's economy.

330.9   US
MAJOR COLLECTIVE BARGAINING SETTLEMENTS IN STATE AND LOCAL GOVERNMENT. (Subseries of: National Office News Releases) s-a? U.S. Bureau of Labor Statistics, 2 Massachusetts Ave., N.E., Washington, DC 20212. TEL 202-655-4000. (Subscr. to: Superintendent of Documents, U.S. Government Printing Office, Box 371954, Pittsburgh, PA 15250-7954. TEL 202-512-1800. FAX 202-512-2250; Or: Bureau of Labor Statistics Publications Sales Center, Box 2145, Chicago, IL 60690) **Document type:** government publication.

330.9 317   US   ISSN 0160-2985
HD8051
MAJOR PROGRAMS. irreg. free. U.S. Bureau of Labor Statistics, 441 G St., Washington, DC 20212. TEL 202-655-4000. (Subscr. to: Superintendent of Documents, U.S. Government Printing Office, Box 371954, Pittsburgh, PA 15250-7954. TEL 202-512-1800. FAX 202-512-2250; Or: Bureau of Labor Statistics Publications Sales Center, Box 2145, Chicago, IL 60690) **Document type:** government publication.

330.1   MW   ISSN 0076-3101
MALAWI ECONOMIC REPORT. a. Malawi. Government Printer, P.O. Box 37, Zomba, Malawi. **Document type:** government publication.

330.9   MM
MALTA. MINISTRY OF FINANCE AND COMMERCE. ECONOMIC SURVEY. a. £1.50($6) Ministry of Finance and Commerce, Economic Planning Division, St. Calcedonius Square, Floriana CMRO2, Malta. TEL 356-250550. FAX 356-237170. (Subscr. to: Information Division, Auberge de Castille, Valletta CMRO2, Malta) **Document type:** government publication.
    Formerly: Malta. Central Office of Statistics. Economic Survey.

330.9   CN   ISSN 0226-2576
HD5729.Q4
MARCHE DU TRAVAIL. m. Can.$98 (foreign Can.$196) (effective 1996). Ministere des Communications, P.O. Box 1005, Quebec, PQ G1K 7B5, Canada. TEL 418-643-5150. (Subscr. to: Service Abonnements, CP1190, Outremont, PQ H2V 4S7, Canada. TEL 514-948-1222) **Indexed:** Pt.de Rep. (1983-). **Document type:** government publication.

MARKET: AFRICA - MID-EAST. see BUSINESS AND ECONOMICS — International Commerce

THE MARKET FOR PACKAGED FOODS IN LATIN AMERICA. see FOOD AND FOOD INDUSTRIES

THE MARKET FOR PACKAGED FOOD IN SOUTH EAST ASIA. see FOOD AND FOOD INDUSTRIES

THE MARKET FOR PERSONAL FINANCE IN CHINA. see BUSINESS AND ECONOMICS — Banking And Finance

THE MARKET FOR PERSONAL FINANCE IN LATIN AMERICA. see BUSINESS AND ECONOMICS — Banking And Finance

330.9   US
MARKET TIMING REPORT. 1978. m. $100 (effective 1997). 1539 E. Waverly St., Tucson, AZ 85719. TEL 520-795-9552. E-mail: tearle@primenet.com. (Subscr. to: Box 225, Tucson, AZ 85702) Ed. Ted C. Earle. R&P contact: Ted C. Earle. **Document type:** newsletter.

330.9   MR   ISSN 0851-0857
MAROC MAGAZINE. 1975. w. 34 rue Mohamed Smiha, Casablanca, Morocco. Ed. Ahmed Alaoui. adv. circ. 50,000.

330.9   US   ISSN 0279-960X
MARPLE'S BUSINESS NEWSLETTER; covering the Pacific Northwest. 1949. fortn. $83 (effective May 1997). Newsletter Publishing Corp., 117 W. Mercer St., Ste. 200, Seattle, WA 98119-3960. TEL 206-281-9609. FAX 206-281-8035. E-mail: marples@compuserve.com; URL: http://marples.com. Ed. Michael J. Parks; Pub. Michael J. Parks. R&P contact: Debbie Johnson. stat.; index; circ. 4,100 (paid). **Document type:** newsletter. —CCC.
    Formerly: Marple's Business Roundup (ISSN 0025-391X)
    Description: Covers business trends affecting the Pacific Northwest, with company profiles, news of recent acquisitions, demographic issues, and evaluation of international business conditions.

330.9   US
MASTER ECONOMIST. 1986. m. $39. RR 3, Box 642, Franklinville, NJ 08322-9208. TEL 609-694-3312. Ed. Kevin Debockler.

MEAT SHEET. see AGRICULTURE — Poultry And Livestock

MEDIA SELECTION; Nachrichten und Meinungen der internationalen Presse. see BUSINESS AND ECONOMICS — International Commerce

330.9   US   ISSN 1067-4926
PN4867
MEDIACRITIC; the best and worst of America's journalism. Key Title: Forbes MediaCritic. q. $29.95. Forbes, Inc., 60 Fifth Ave., New York, NY 10011. TEL 212-620-2200. E-mail: FbsMC@aol.com. (Subscr. to: Media Critic Subscriptions Dept., Box 6615, Syracuse, NY 13217-7991. TEL 800-825-0061) Ed. Terry Eastland. —UnCover.
    Formerly (until 1992): MediaGuide.
    Description: Provides in-depth coverage and critical analysis of global economics and politics.

MEDICAL BUSINESS REVIEW; medical business analysis for the doctor-executive. see BUSINESS AND ECONOMICS — Management

330.9   TH   ISSN 1014-0360
MEKONG NEWS. 1982. irreg. free. Mekong River Commission with the Mekong Secretariat, Pibulthum Villa, Kasatsuk Bridge, Bangkok 10330, Thailand. FAX 66-2-225-2796. TELEX 21 322 MEKONG TH. Ed. K.l. Matics. circ. 1,000. **Document type:** newsletter.

MELHORES E MAIORES. see BUSINESS AND ECONOMICS — Production Of Goods And Services

MEMBERSHIP DIRECTORY. see ENERGY

MEMO FROM BELGIUM. see POLITICAL SCIENCE

330.982   AG   ISSN 0325-0687
HC171
MERCADO/BUSINESS. 1969. m. $165 (effective 1994). Editorial Coyuntura S.A., Peru 263 2 piso, 1067 Buenos Aires, Argentina. TEL 541-342-3322. FAX 541-342-3475. Ed. Dolores Valle; Pub. Miguel Angel Diez. adv.: B&W page $4900, color page $6200; 175 x 250; adv. contact: Juan C. Mililllo. bk.rev.; illus.; circ. 18,350 (paid).

330.9 327   UK   ISSN 1363-9684
▼**MERCOSUR CRITIQUE.** 1996. q. £450. Urban Publishing Co., P.O. Box 625, Hampstead, London NW3 2TZ, England. TEL 44-181-209-1722. FAX 44-181-455-4107. Ed. Paulo Botas; Pub. Tann von Hove. bk.rev.; index. **Document type:** newsletter.
    Description: Examines economic, financial, political, and social conditions in Brazil, Argentina, Uruguay, Paraguay, Chile and Bolivia.

330.9   UK
MERSEYSIDE BUSINESS PROSPECT. 1986. s-a. £30 to individuals; institutions £50 (effective 1995). (University of Liverpool, Department of Economics and Accounting) Liverpool Macroeconomic Research Ltd., P.O. Box 147, Liverpool L69 3BX, England. TEL 44-151-794-3032. FAX 44-151-794-3028. TELEX 627095-UNILPL-G. E-mail: janef@liv.ac.uk. Ed. Patrick Minford. R&P contact: Patrick Minford. **Document type:** bulletin.
    Formerly (until 1995): Merseyside Economic and Business Prospect; Which was formed by the 1989 merger of: Merseyside Economic Prospect (ISSN 0952-0732); Merseyside Business Survey.

330.9   US   ISSN 1042-6825
METRO PHOENIX BLUE CHIP ECONOMIC FORECAST. (Supplement to: Arizona Blue Chip Economic Forecast (ISSN 1042-6787)) 1988. q. $39 (effective May 1995). Arizona State University, Economic Outlook Center, Box 874406, Tempe, AZ 85287-4406. TEL 602-965-5543; 800-448-0432. FAX 602-965-5458. Ed. Tracy L. Clark. **Document type:** newsletter.
    Description: Provides economic and real estate forecasts for the metropolitan Phoenix area.

977   US
METROPOLITAN MILWAUKEE ECONOMIC FACT BOOK. Title varies: Economic Fact Book on Metropolitan Milwaukee. 1965. a. $40 to members; non-members $80. Metropolitan Milwaukee Association of Commerce, Council of Small Business Executives, 756 N. Milwaukee St., Milwaukee, WI 53202. TEL 414-287-4100. circ. 300.
    Formerly: Metropolitan Milwaukee Association of Commerce. Economic Studies (ISSN 0076-7077)
    Description: Provides information on the economic characteristics of metro Milwaukee, labor force, population, U.S. Census tracts, transportation and education.

330.9   MX
MEXICAN ECONOMY. a. Mex.$85 (America $20; Europe $25; elsewhere $30) (effective Aug. 1996). Banco de Mexico, Subdireccion de Investigacion Economica y Bancaria, Av. Juarez 90, Col. Centro, Del. Cuauhtemoc, 06059 Mexico DF, Mexico. TEL 525-761-8588.

338.9 320   UK   ISSN 0968-2724
HC131
MEXICO & N A F T A REPORT. (North American Free Trade Agreement) Variant title: Latin American Regional Report - Mexico & N A F T A Report. 1979. m. £212($275) (academic institutions £104($135)) (effective 1997). Lettres (U.K.) Ltd., 61 Old St., London EC1V 9HX, England. TEL 44-171-251-0012. FAX 44-171-253-8193. Ed. Will Ollard. R&P contact: Alex McHallam. adv. contact: Alex McHallam. (back issues avail.) **Document type:** newsletter.
    ●Also available online. Vendor(s): Lexis-Nexis. —SWETS.
    Formerly (until 1993): Mexico and Central America Report (ISSN 0143-5264)
    Description: Addresses the dynamic developments of the new Mexican political and economic environment, with expanded coverage of NAFTA.

BUSINESS AND ECONOMICS — ECONOMIC SITUATION AND CONDITIONS

330.9 BL
MEXICO COMPANY HANDBOOK. (Text in English) a. $29.95. I M F Editora Ltda., Av. Almirante Barroso 63, Grupo 409, 20031 Rio de Janeiro RJ, Brazil. TEL 55-21-240-4347. FAX 55-21-262-7570. (Dist. worldwide by: The Reference Press, Inc., 6448 Hwy. 290 E., Ste. E-104, Austin, TX 78723. TEL 512-454-7778. FAX 512-454-9401) charts; stat.
Document type: trade publication.
Description: Profiles the economy, trade situation and investment climate of Mexico, along with 75 of its largest public companies and 60 mutual funds.

330.9 US ISSN 1068-8307
MEXICO CONSENSUS ECONOMIC FORECAST/CONSENSO DE PRONOSTICOS ECONOMICOS. 1993. q. $20 (effective May 1995). Arizona State University, Economic Outlook Center, Box 874406, Tempe, AZ 85287-4406. TEL 602-965-5543; 800-448-0432. FAX 602-964-5458. URL: http://www.cob.asu.edu/seid/eoc/eocmex.html. Ed. Lee R. McPheters. **Document type:** newsletter.
●Also available online.
Description: Provides forecasts and an analysis of the Mexican economy.

330.9 MX
MEXICO: INFORMACION ECONOMICA Y SOCIAL; revista internacional del Inegi. 1989. 3/yr. free or exchange basis. Instituto Nacional de Estadistica, Geografia e Informatica, Secretaria de Programacion y Presupuesto, Prol. Heroe de Nacozari 2301 Sur, Puerta 11, Acceso, 20270 Aguascalientes Ags., Mexico. TEL 49-18-19-48. FAX 491-807-39. charts; illus.; stat. circ. 3,500.

330.9 US
MEXICO WATCH. Fax edition: Mexico Weekly Fax Bulletin. m.; fax ed. w. $425 (fax ed. $465; foreign $565) (effective 1998). Orbis Publications, LLC, 3201 New Mexico Ave., N.W., Ste. 249, Washington, DC 20016. TEL 202-237-0155. FAX 202-237-0596. E-mail: orbis@orbispub.com. Ed. Richard W. Foster; Pub. Stephen M. Foster. (back issues avail.) **Document type:** newsletter, bulletin.
Description: Reports on political, economic, and business events in Mexico.

380 US ISSN 1044-1948
MICHIGAN BANKER; the news magazine of Michigan's banking industry. 1883. m. $92.50 (includes Bank Holding Company Directory). Public Relations Enterprises, Inc., Box 12236, Lansing, MI 48901-2236. TEL 517-484-0775. FAX 517-484-4676. Ed. Jerome H. O'Neil; Pub. Jerome H. O'Neil. adv. contact: Loy L. Gee. illus.; circ. 640 (paid). (also avail. in microform from UMI) **Indexed:** Mich.Mag.Ind. **Document type:** trade publication.
—UMI.
Former titles (until 1983): Michigan Banking and Business News (ISSN 0193-0257); Michigan Tradesman (ISSN 0026-248X)
Description: For executives, officers and staff members of Michigan bank and executives of companies providing services and products.

330.9 US
MICRODATA REFERENCE MANUAL FROM THE CALL AND INCOME REPORT. q. $700 in US, Canada, Mexico; elsewhere $1400. (Federal Reserve System) U.S. National Technical Information Service, 5825 Port Royal Rd., Springfield, VA 22161. TEL 703-487-4630. (magnetic tape)
Description: Data on the financial situations of banks and related corporations.

338 US ISSN 0193-2047
MID-AMERICA COMMERCE & INDUSTRY. 1973. m. $18 (effective 1997). M A C I Inc., 1824 Cheyenne Rd., Topeka, KS 66604. TEL 913-272-5280. Ed. Ray Lippe. adv.: B&W page $1070, color page $1610; trim 8 1/2 x 11. bk.rev.; circ. 9,483 (controlled). (also avail. in microform from UMI) **Document type:** trade publication.
●Also available online. Vendor(s): UMI.
—UMI.
Description: News, announcements, and advertisements on manufacturing firms in this U.S. region, targeted toward executives, purchasers, plant managers, and industrial engineers.

330 US
MID-STATE ECONOMIC INDICATORS. 1991. q. free. Middle Tennessee State University, College of Business, 1301 E. Main St., MTSU Box 102, Murfreesboro, TN 37132-0102. TEL 615-898-2387. FAX 615-898-5045. E-mail: eaeff@mtsu.edu; URL: http://www.mtsu.edu/~berc. Ed. Tony Eff. R&P contact: Reuben Kyle. adv. contact: Reuben Kyle. circ. 5,500. **Document type:** academic/scholarly publication.
Description: Provides an analysis of current economic conditions in Middle Tennessee.

MIDDLE EAST AND NORTH AFRICA (YEAR); survey and directory of lands of Middle East and North Africa. see POLITICAL SCIENCE

330.9 UK ISSN 1363-3740
▼**MIDDLE EAST BUSINESS REVIEW.** 1996. q. £34 to individuals; institutions £94 (effective 1996). University of London, School of Management, Royal Holloway, Egham, Surrey TW20 0EX, England. TEL 44-1784-443780. FAX 44-1784-439854. E-mail: a.alshamali@rhbnc.ac.uk; URL: http://sun.rhbnc.ac.uk/mgt/mbr.html. Ed.Bd. **Document type:** academic/scholarly publication.

330 UK ISSN 0047-7230
HC411 CODEN: MEEDDO
MIDDLE EAST ECONOMIC DIGEST. 1957. w. £290 in U.K., Europe & Middle East; rest of world £320 (effective 1997). M E E D Publications, 21 John St., London WC1N 2BP, England. TEL 44-171-470-6406. FAX 44-171-430-0337. Ed. Edmund O'Sullivan; Pub. Dante Mencacci. adv.; bk.rev.; stat.; index. circ. 12,340. **Indexed:** Int.Lab.Doc., Key to Econ.Sci., Mid.East: Abstr.& Ind., P.A.I.S., RICS. **Document type:** trade publication.
●Also available online. Vendor(s): Information Access Co.
—BLDSC (5536.111000); CASDDS; UnCover.
Description: Contains news articles and analysis of economic trends in the 21 Arab states and their relationship to domestic and international foreign and military policy.

330 LE ISSN 0026-3117
MIDDLE EAST EXPRESS.* 1971. m. Societe de la Presse Economique S.A.L., Box 11-0687, Beirut, Lebanon. Ed. A. Debian. stat.

330.9 UK ISSN 1351-4717
HC410.7.A1
MIDDLE EAST REVIEW. 1974. a. £40. Kogan Page Ltd., 120 Pentonville Rd., London N1 9JN, England. TEL 44-171-278-0433. FAX 44-171-837-6348. TELEX 263088 KOGAN G. Ed. Tony Axon. R&P contact: Linda Batman. adv.; illus.; stat. circ. 9,335. **Indexed:** HR Rep., P.A.I.S. **Document type:** consumer publication.
—BLDSC (5761.401300).
Formerly (until 1981): Middle East Annual Review (ISSN 0305-3210)
Description: Overview on economic and political situations in every Arabic-speaking country in the Middle East.

330.9 US
MIDDLE TENNESSEE STATE UNIVERSITY. BUSINESS AND ECONOMIC RESEARCH CENTER. CONFERENCE PAPER. 1975. irreg. price varies. Middle Tennessee State University, Business and Economic Research Center, Box 102, PH 100, Murfreesboro, TN 37132. TEL 615-898-2610. FAX 615-818-5045. Ed. Reuben Kyle. R&P contact: Reuben Kyle. **Document type:** academic/scholarly publication.

MINERALS: LATIN AMERICAN INDUSTRY REPORT. see MINES AND MINING INDUSTRY

330.9 US
MINNESOTA. DEPARTMENT OF ECONOMIC SECURITY. MINNESOTA ECONOMIC TRENDS. 1974. q. free. Department of Economic Security, Research and Statistics Office, 390 N. Robert St., St. Paul, MN 55101. TEL 612-296-3324. FAX 612-282-5429. Ed. Julia Pool. circ. 4,500. **Document type:** government publication.
Formerly: Minnesota. Department of Jobs and Training. Labor Market Trends; Incorporates (1974-1993): Minnesota. Department of Jobs and Training. Review of Labor and Economic Conditions.

330.9 US ISSN 0195-6159
HC107.M8
MISSOURI ECONOMIC INDICATORS. 1976. q. $25. University of Missouri at Columbia, Business and Public Administration Research Center, 10 Professional Bldg., Columbia, MO 65211. TEL 573-882-4805. FAX 573-882-5563. Ed. Edward Aitkens; Pub. Vickie Stokes. circ. 300. **Document type:** academic/scholarly publication.

330 SZ ISSN 0304-2162
HG35
LE MOIS; economique et financier. German edition: Monat (ISSN 0256-3533); Italian edition: Mese Economico e Finanziario (ISSN 0256-3541) (Editions in French, German, Italian) 1974. m. free. Schweizerischer Bankverein - Swiss Bank Corporation, 6 Aeschenplatz, CH-4002 Basel, Switzerland. TEL 41-61-2882020. FAX 41-61-2883708. Ed. Daniel Funk. R&P contact: Daniel Funk. charts; illus.; stat.; tr.lit. circ. 250,000. **Indexed:** Key to Econ.Sci., P.A.I.S.For.Lang.Ind., Rural Recreat.Tour.Abstr., World Agri.Econ.& Rural Sociol.Abstr. **Document type:** bulletin.
—BLDSC (5900.700000).
Former titles: Swiss Bank Corporation. Bulletin (ISSN 0039-7466); Mois.
Description: Covers the proliferation of modern technology in information retrieval applications in economics and finance.

330 IT ISSN 0026-9522
HC10
MONDO ECONOMICO; settimanale di economia, finanza, politica e cultura. 1946. w. L.160000 (foreign L.285000). (Sole 24 Ore Seme S.p.A.) Societa Editoriale Media Economici Seme S.p.A., Via P. Lomazzo, 52, 20154 Milan, Italy. TEL 39-2-331211. FAX 39-2-316905. Ed. Enrico Sassoon. adv.: B&W page L.7500000, color page L.12000000. bk.rev.; mkt.; stat.; index; circ. 25,744 (controlled). (reprint service avail. from UMI) **Indexed:** ELLIS, IBR, PROMT, Rural Recreat.Tour.Abstr., World Agri.Econ.& Rural Sociol.Abstr.
—UMI.

MONEDA. see BUSINESS AND ECONOMICS — Banking And Finance

330.9 US
MONEY WATCH BULLETIN. 1984. m. $95. International Wealth Success, Inc., 24 Canterbury Rd., Rockville Center, NY 11570. TEL 516-766-5850. FAX 516-766-5919. Ed. Tyler G. Hicks. bk.rev. **Document type:** newsletter.
Description: Information on 100 lenders for real estate, business and other income-producing activities every month.

330.9 320 US
MONGOLIA REPORT. irreg. (approx. 5/yr.) $7 per no. (foreign $14 per no.). U.S. Joint Publications Research Service, Box 12507, Arlington, VA 22209. TEL 703-487-4630. (Orders to: NTIS, Springfield, VA 22161)
Formerly: Translations on Mongolia.

MONITOR MONEY REVIEW. see BUSINESS AND ECONOMICS — Investments

330.9 US
MONTHLY BREWING INDUSTRY COMMENTARY. (Subseries of Beverage Follow-up) 1975. m. avail. to qualified personnel only. Cyrus J. Lawrence, Inc., 1290 Ave. of the Americas, New York, NY 10104. TEL 212-468-5000. circ. controlled. (looseleaf format; back issues avail.)

330 II ISSN 0027-030X
MONTHLY COMMENTARY ON INDIAN ECONOMIC CONDITIONS. (Supplement avail.) (Text in English) 1959. m. Rs.250($40) Indian Institute of Public Opinion Private Ltd., 2-A National Insurance Bldg., Parliament St., Box 288, New Delhi 110001, India. Ed. E.P.W. Da Costa. adv.; bk.rev.; charts.
—UnCover.
Formerly: Monthly Statistical Commentary on Indian Economic Conditions.
Description: Clarifies government statistics and economic indicators in the Indian economy.

MONTHLY LABOR REVIEW. see BUSINESS AND ECONOMICS — Abstracting, Bibliographies, Statistics

BUSINESS AND ECONOMICS — ECONOMIC SITUATION AND CONDITIONS

330.9   KE
MONTHLY MARKET BULLETIN. (Text in English) m. KShs.100. Ministry of Agriculture, Livestock Development and Marketing, Marketing Information Branch, P.O. Box 30028, Nairobi, Kenya. **Document type:** government publication.

MONTHLY REVIEW; a monthly review of sub-Saharan African economic, political and social affairs. see POLITICAL SCIENCE — International Relations

MOST; economic policy in transitional economies. see BUSINESS AND ECONOMICS — Economic Systems And Theories, Economic History

330.9   US
N A B E INDUSTRY SURVEY. q. $75 includes N A B E Outlook and N A B E Policy Survey. National Association of Business Economists, 1233 20th St., N.W., Ste. 505, Washington, DC 20036-2304. TEL 202-463-6223. FAX 202-462-6239. stat. (also avail. in microform from IAC)
● Also available on CD-ROM.
    Description: Survey of a special panel of NABE members on business conditions within their company and industry. Questions are asked on changes in demand, employment, inventories, and capital spending.

330.9 339   US   ISSN 0745-3205
N A B E NEWS. bi-m. $75. National Association of Business Economists, 1233 20th St., N.W., Ste. 505, Washington, DC 20036-2304. TEL 202-463-6223. FAX 202-463-6239. Ed. Anne Picker. adv. circ. 3,700. (back issues avail.) **Document type:** newsletter.
    Description: Features economic articles, reviews of seminars and annual meetings, news from local chapters and roundtables and personal notes.

330.9   US
N A B E OUTLOOK & POLICY SURVEY. q. membership (includes N A B E Industry Survey). National Association of Business Economists, 1233 20th St., N.W., Ste. 505, Washington, DC 20036-2304. TEL 202-463-6223. FAX 202-463-6239. stat. (also avail. in microform from IAC)
● Also available online. Vendor(s): Information Access Co.
Also available on CD-ROM.
    Formed by the Feb. 1994 merger of: N A B E Outlook & N A B E Policy Survey.
    Description: Survey of a special panel of NABE members on the outlook for selected macroeconomic variables including GNP, CPI, auto sales, housing starts, and unemployment.

330.9   US
N A D O NEWS. w. membership. National Association of Development Organizations, 444 N. Capitol St., N.W., Ste. 630, Washington, DC 20001. TEL 202-624-7806. FAX 202-624-8813. E-mail: nado@sso.org. Ed. Aliceann Wohlbruck; Pub. Aliceann Wohlbruck. **Document type:** newsletter.
    Description: Addresses concerns of economic development in small rural towns.

330.9   US
N A D O SPECIAL REPORT. irreg. (3-4 yr.). membership. National Association of Development Organizations, 444 N. Capitol St., N.W., Ste. 630, Washington, DC 20001. TEL 202-624-7806. FAX 202-624-8813. E-mail: nado@sso.org. Ed. Aliceann Wohlbruck. **Document type:** newsletter.
    Description: Addresses concerns of economic development in small rural towns.

N A S D A DIRECTORY OF DEVELOPMENT AGENCIES AND OFFICIALS. (National Association of State Development Agencies) see PUBLIC ADMINISTRATION

N A S D A LETTER. (National Association of State Development Agencies) see PUBLIC ADMINISTRATION

N A S D A STATE ECONOMIC DEVELOPMENT EXPENDITURES AND SALARY SURVEY. (National Association of State Development Agencies) see PUBLIC ADMINISTRATION

N A S D A STATE ENTERPRISE ZONE ROUNDUP. (National Association of State Development Agencies) see PUBLIC ADMINISTRATION

330.9   IE
N E S F FORUM OPINION. irreg., no.3, 1996. I£3. National Economic and Social Forum, Centre Block, Government Bldgs., Upper Merrion St., Dublin 2, Ireland. **Document type:** monographic series.

330.9   IE
N E S F FORUM REPORT. irreg., no.7, 1995. £4. National Economic and Social Forum, Centre Block, Government Bldgs., Upper Merion St., Dublin 2, Ireland. **Document type:** government publication.

338.6   US   ISSN 0362-3548
HD2346.U5
N F I B QUARTERLY ECONOMIC REPORT FOR SMALL BUSINESS. 1974. q. $30. National Federation of Independent Business, 53 Century Blvd., Ste. 205, Nashville, TN 37214. E-mail: comments@nfibonline.com; URL: http://www.nfibonline.com/. stat. **Indexed:** ABI Inform, BPIA, SRI.
—UMI.
    Formerly: National Federation of Independent Business. Quarterly Economic Report (ISSN 0094-7695)

330   YU   ISSN 0352-3314
NARODNA BANKA JUGOSLAVIJE. GODISNJI IZVESTAJ. English edition: National Bank of Yugoslavia. Annual Report (ISSN 0077-2798) (Text in Serbo-Croatian) 1958. a. Narodna Banka Jugoslavije, Bulevar Revolucije 15, P.O. Box 1010, 11001 Belgrade, Yugoslavia. circ. 1,200.

NATIONAL ACCOUNTS E S A - AGGREGATES (YEARS). see BUSINESS AND ECONOMICS

330.9   UA   ISSN 0304-274X
HC531
NATIONAL BANK OF EGYPT. ECONOMIC BULLETIN. (Editions in Arabic, English) 1948. q. free. National Bank of Egypt, Economic Research Department, 1187 Corniche El Nile, Cairo, Egypt. TEL 20-2-5748144. FAX 20-2-5747168. TELEX 20069 NBE UN. R&P contact: Inas El Hagrasy. charts; stat. circ. 6,000. **Indexed:** Documentatieblad, Key to Econ.Sci., P.A.I.S., PROMT, Rural Recreat.Tour.Abstr., World Agri.Econ.& Rural Sociol.Abstr., World Bank.Abstr. **Document type:** bulletin.
—BLDSC (3651.910000).
    Description: Provides coverage of domestic and international economic issues and developments, statistics of economic activities, and in-depth studies of specific topics.

NATIONAL BANK OF ETHIOPIA. QUARTERLY BULLETIN. see BUSINESS AND ECONOMICS — Banking And Finance

330.9   HU   ISSN 1216-4879
NATIONAL BANK OF HUNGARY. MONTHLY REPORT. Hungarian edition: Magyar Nemzeti Bank. Havi Jelents (ISSN 1216-4860) (Text in English) 1992. m. National Bank of Hungary, Information Department, Szabadsag ter. 8-9, 1850 Budapest V, Hungary. TEL 36-1-3023601. Pub. Janos Zadori. **Document type:** corporate report.
    Formed by the merger of (1986-1991): National Bank of Hungary. Market Letter (ISSN 0209-9268); (1983-1991): National Bank of Hungary. Quarterly Review (ISSN 0231-3456)

338   NZ   ISSN 0110-6813
NATIONAL BUSINESS REVIEW. 1970. w. NZ.$310 (foreign NZ$455); newsstand price: NZ.$6.95. Fourth Estate Holdings Ltd., P.O. Box 1734, Auckland, New Zealand. TEL 64-9-307-1629. FAX 64-9-373-3997. URL: http://www.nbr.co.nz. Ed. Nevil Gibson; Pub. Barry Colman. R&P contact: Nevil Gibson. adv.: B&W page NZ.$2795, color page NZ.$4555; adv. contact: Diane Driver. bk.rev.; illus. circ. 14,200. cols./p.: 6; pp./issue: 72. (tabloid format; back issues avail.) **Document type:** newspaper.
● Also available online. Vendor(s): Kiwinet.
Incorporates: Advertising and Marketing News (ISSN 0001-8910)
    Description: Covers business and financial news.

330.9   PK
NATIONAL DEVELOPMENT FINANCE CORPORATION. QUARTERLY REVIEW. (Text in English) 1975. q. National Development Finance Corporation, Economics Division, Finance and Trade Center, 2nd Fl., Shahrah-e Faisal, Karachi, Pakistan. FAX 525310. TELEX 23842 NDFC PK. Ed. Nader E. Morshed. illus.; circ. 1,200 (controlled).
    Formerly: National Development Finance Corporation. Monthly Economic Report.

330.9   IR   ISSN 0572-5941
NATIONAL INCOME OF IRAN. 1974. irreg., latest 1977. free. Bank Markazi Jomhouri Islami Iran, Economic Statistics Department - Central Bank of the Islamic Republic of Iran, P.O. Box 11365-8531, Tehran, Iran. FAX 98-21-390323. TELEX 216219.

330   US
NATIONAL POLICY ASSOCIATION REPORTS. 1934. irreg. latest no.284. $100. National Policy Association, 1424 16th St., N.W., Ste. 700, Washington, DC 20036. TEL 202-265-7685. FAX 202-797-5516. E-mail: npa@npa1.org; URL: http://www.npa1.org. Ed. Martha L. Benz. stat. circ. 2,000.
    Formerly (until 1997): National Planning Association Reports.

330.9 317   US   ISSN 0501-7041
HD8038.U5
NATIONAL SURVEY OF PROFESSIONAL, ADMINISTRATIVE, TECHNICAL AND CLERICAL PAY. a. price varies. U.S. Bureau of Labor Statistics, 441 G. Street, N.W., Washington, DC 20212. TEL 202-655-4000. (Subscr. to: Superintendent of Documents, U.S. Government Printing Office, Box 371954, Pittsburgh, PA 15250-7954. TEL 202-512-1800. FAX 202-512-2250; Or: Bureau of Labor Statistics Publications Sales Center, Box 2145, Chicago, IL 60690) (also avail. in microform) **Document type:** government publication.

330.9 320   US
NEAR EAST - SOUTH ASIA REPORT. 160/yr. $7 per no. (foreign $14 per no.). U.S. Joint Publications Research Service, Box 12507, Arlington, VA 22209. TEL 703-487-4630. (Orders to: NTIS, Springfield, VA 22161)
    Former titles: Near East and North Africa Report (ISSN 0145-9317) & Translations on Near East and North Africa; Translations on Near East.

330   US
NEBRASKA DEVELOPMENT NEWS. 1974. m. free. Department of Economic Development, Box 94666, Lincoln, NE 68509. TEL 402-471-3111. charts; stat. circ. 8,000. (back issues avail.)
    Former titles: Nebraska Economic Developments (ISSN 8750-9032); Nebraska Now.

330.9   SA   ISSN 1023-7097
NEDCOR GUIDE TO THE ECONOMY/NEDCOR GIDS TOT DIE EKONOMIE. (Editions in Afrikaans, English) 1966. q. free. Nedcor Economic Unit - Nedcor Ekonomiese Eenheid, P.O. Box 582, Johannesburg 2000, South Africa. TEL 27-11-4801048. FAX 27-11-4801044. Ed. Dennis M. Dykes. circ. 20,000. **Indexed:** Ind.S.A.Per. **Document type:** bulletin.
    Former titles (until 1994): Nedbank Quarterly Guide to the Economy; (until 1992): Nedbank Guide to the Economy; (until 1990): Nedcor Group. Guide to the Economy (ISSN 0258-6754); Which was formed by the 1986 merger of: Nedbank Economic Roundup & Executive Guide to the Economy; Which was formerly: U A L Executive Guide to the Economy.
    Description: Presents analytical articles on the South African economy.

330.968   SA
NEDCOR MONTHLY ECONOMIC PROFILE. Afrikaans edition: Nedcor Maandelikse Ekonomiese Profiel. (Text in English) m. Nedcor Economic Unit - Nedcor Ekonomiese Eenheid, P.O. Box 582, Johannesburg 2000, South Africa. TEL 27-11-4801048. FAX 27-11-4801044. Ed. Dennis M. Dykes. **Document type:** bulletin.
    Formerly: Monthly Economic Profile.

330.9   NP
NEPAL. RASHTRIYA PANCAYATA. ARTHIKA SAMITI. (Text in Nepali) a. Rashtriya Panchayat Sachivalaya, Rashtriya Panchayat Bhavan, Singhdarbar, Kathmandu, Nepal.

BUSINESS AND ECONOMICS — ECONOMIC SITUATION AND CONDITIONS

330.9   NP   ISSN 0028-274X
NEPAL RASTRA BANK. QUARTERLY ECONOMIC BULLETIN. (Text in English) 1966. q. free. Nepal Rastra Bank, Research Department, Baluwatar, Kathmandu, Nepal. TEL 977-1-411638. Ed. Keshav Prasad Acharya. charts; stat. Document type: bulletin.
   Description: Data on money, credit, government finance, foreign trade and payments statistics.

330.9   US   ISSN 0548-4448
HA218
NEW ENGLAND ECONOMIC INDICATORS. 1969. m. free. Federal Reserve Bank of Boston, Research Department, 600 Atlantic Ave., Boston, MA 02106. TEL 617-973-3397. FAX 617-973-4292. URL: http://www.bos.frb.org. Ed. Joshua Gleason. bk.rev.; circ. 6,000 (controlled). (also avail. in microfiche from CIS; back issues avail.; reprint service avail. from CIS) Indexed: Amer.Stat.Ind. (1974-), Fed Print.
   ●Also available online.
   —UMI.
   Description: Provides analysis of New England economy.

330   US   ISSN 0028-4726
HC107.A11   CODEN: NWEEAP
NEW ENGLAND ECONOMIC REVIEW. 1920. bi-m. free. Federal Reserve Bank of Boston, Research Department, Research Library D, Box 2076, Boston, MA 02106-2076. TEL 617-973-3397. FAX 617-973-4292. URL: http://www.bos.frb.org. Ed. J. Poskanzer. charts; illus.; stat.; index, cum.index: 1969-1984. circ. 15,000. (also avail. in microform from MIM,UMI; microfiche from CIS; reprint service avail. from CIS,UMI) Indexed: ABI Inform, Amer.Stat.Ind. (1974-), ASCA, B.P.I., BPIA, CLOA, Curr.Cont., Fed Print, J.of Econ.Lit., P.A.I.S., SSCI.
   ●Also available online. Vendor(s): Information Access Co.
   —BLDSC (6083.850000); Genuine Article; KR SourceOne; UMI; UnCover.
   Formerly: New England Business Review.
   Description: Presents articles on topics pertaining to the national economy and the regional economy, and the fields of economics and public finance.

NEW ENGLAND JOURNAL OF PUBLIC POLICY. see PUBLIC ADMINISTRATION — Municipal Government

NEW EUROPEAN SEMINAR PAPERS. see SOCIAL SCIENCES: COMPREHENSIVE WORKS

320   US   ISSN 1043-2264
NEW FEDERALIST. 1987. w. $20 for 50 issues; $35 for 100 issues. Box 889, Leesburg, VA 20175. TEL 703-777-9451. FAX 703-771-3099. Ed. Nancy Spannaus. R&P contact: Christina Huth. bk.rev.; circ. 105,000 (paid). Document type: newspaper.
   Description: Independent coverage of the national and world economy, traditional American system economics, including features on historical and scientific topics. Features work of Lyndon LaRouche, Jr. and his associates.

330.9   US
NEW JERSEY. DEPARTMENT OF LABOR. LABOR MARKET REVIEW. SOUTHERN N.J. REGION. 1981. biennial. $10. Department of Labor, Division of Labor Market and Demographic Research, CN 057, Trenton, NJ 08625-0057. TEL 609-292-2145. Ed. Jan J. DeJong. circ. 1,600. Document type: government publication.
   Description: Analyzes significant labor market and economic developments within Burlington, Camden, Cumberland, Glouster, Mercer and Salem counties.

330.9   US   ISSN 1064-5942
HC107.N5
NEW JERSEY ECONOMIC INDICATORS. 1963. m. free. Department of Labor, Division of Labor Market & Demographic Research, CN 057, Trenton, NJ 08625-0057. TEL 609-633-6434. Ed. Mary Ann R. Unger. charts; stat. circ. 2,800. (also avail. in microfiche from CIS) Indexed: SRI. Document type: government publication.
   Supersedes: Employment in Nonagricultural Establishments; Hours and Earnings of Production Workers; Production Workers in Manufacturing Establishments by Two-Digit Industry.
   Description: Disseminates the most comprehensive set of current economic statistics available in the state.

NEW MARKETS MONTHLY. see BUSINESS AND ECONOMICS — International Commerce

330.9   US   ISSN 1090-5693
NEW YORK ECONOMIC REVIEW. 1971. s-a. membership. New York State Economic Association, c/o William O'Dea, Ed., Dept. of Economics and Business, SUNY-Oneonta, Oneonta, NY 13820. TEL 607-436-2127. FAX 607-436-2107. R&P contact: William O'Dea. adv.; bk.rev. circ. 400. Document type: academic/scholarly publication.
   Formerly (until 1985): New York State Economics Association. Journal.
   Description: Publishes theoretical and empirical articles on topics in economics, with interpretative reviews of the current literature in the field.
   Refereed Serial

330.9 382   US
NEW YORK MERCANTILE EXCHANGE GUIDE. m. $286. C C H Incorporated, 2700 Lake Cook Rd., Riverwoods, IL 60015. TEL 847-267-7000; 800-835-5224. FAX 800-224-8299.

NEWS FROM GREECE. see POLITICAL SCIENCE

338.9   FR   ISSN 0258-6347
NEWS FROM O E C D. (Editions in English, French, German, Italian) 1975. m. free. Organization for Economic Cooperation and Development, 2 rue Andre-Pascal, 75775 Paris Cedex 16, France. (U.S. orders to: O.E.C.D. Publications and Information Center, 2001 L St., N.W., Ste. 650, Washington, DC 20036-4922. TEL 202-785-6323)
   Supersedes: O E C D Activities.

330   GW   ISSN 0341-1982
NIEDERSAECHSISCHE WIRTSCHAFT. 1922. m. DM.126. Schluetersche GmbH und Co. KG, Hans-Boeckler-Allee 7, 30173 Hannover, Germany. TEL 49-511-8550-0. FAX 49-511-8550402. (Subscr. to: Postfach 5440, 30054 Hannover, Germany) Ed. W. Linsenmann. adv.; bk.rev.; charts; illus.; index. circ. 30,779. Document type: trade publication.
   —CCC.

338   NR   ISSN 0048-038X
NIGERIAN BUSINESS DIGEST.* 1970. m. £N60 (Africa £NL40; Europe £NL42; elsewhere £NL50). Universal Publications Ltd., 115 Griffith St., Ebute - Metta, P.O. Box 1959, Lagos, Nigeria. Ed. Alhaji Lateef Teniola. adv.; charts; illus. circ. 40,000. (also avail. in microfilm from UMI; reprint service avail. from UMI)
   —UMI.
   Description: Reviews Nigeria's commerce, industry, finance, and economic development.

330.9   NR
NIGERIAN BUSINESSMAN'S MAGAZINE. m. Nigerian Businessman Publications, 39 Mabo St., Surulere, Lagos State, Nigeria. adv. Document type: trade publication.

338   JA   ISSN 0029-0491
NIKKEI BUSINESS. (Text in Japanese) 1969. w. 21000 Yen. Nikkei Business Publications, Inc. (Subsidiary of: Nihon Keizai Shimbun, Inc.), 2-7-6 Hirakawa-cho, Chiyoda-ku, Tokyo 102, Japan. TEL 81-3-5210-8031. FAX 81-3-5210-8119. URL: http://www.nikkeibp.co.jp/. (Subscr. to: Nikkei Business Pub. Inc., Reader Service Center, P.O. Box 20, Kasai Post Office, Tokyo 134-70, Japan) Ed. Ikuo Hirata; Pub. Fuminobu Tsuchida. adv.: B&W page 1450000 Yen, color page 2180000 Yen; adv. contact: Yoshihiko Shinmada. bk.rev. circ. 289,167. Document type: trade publication.
   —BLDSC (6113.177770).
   Description: Covers business developments in Japan and overseas, focusing on corporate strategies and management.

332.1   NO   ISSN 0029-1676
HG3166
NORGES BANK. ECONOMIC BULLETIN. 1925. q. free. Norges Bank, Information Department - Central Bank of Norway, P.O. Box 1170 Sentrum, N-0107 Oslo, Norway. TEL 47-22-316-000. FAX 47-22-316-410. TELEX 56-71-369 NBANK N. Ed. Kjell Storvik. charts; mkt.; stat.; cum.index every 3 yrs. Indexed: ABI Inform, Key to Econ.Sci., P.A.I.S., World Bank.Abstr. Document type: academic/scholarly publication.
   —UMI; UnCover. CCC.
   Formerly (until 1965): Norges Bank. Bulletin (ISSN 0802-5282).

332.1   NO   ISSN 0802-7188
NORGES BANK. SKRIFTSERIE. (Text in English or Norwegian) 1973. irreg. Norges Bank, Information Department, P.O. Box 1179 Sentrum, N-0107 Oslo, Norway. TEL 47-22-31-60-00.
   FAX 47-22-41-31-05. Document type: monographic series.

330.97 332   US   ISSN 1062-9408
HC95
THE NORTH AMERICAN JOURNAL OF ECONOMICS AND FINANCE; a journal of theory and practice. 1988. s-a. $80 to individuals (foreign $100); institutions $205 (foreign $225) (effective 1998). (North American Economics and Finance Association) J A I Press Inc., 55 Old Post Rd., No. 2, Box 1678, Greenwich, CT 06830-1678. TEL 203-661-7602. FAX 203-661-0792. E-mail: jai@jaipress.com. (Addr. in Europe: J A I Press Ltd., 38 Tavistock St., Covent Garden, London WC2E 7PB, England. TEL 44-171-379-8834. FAX 44-171-379-8835) Eds. Barry W. Poulsen, Mahmood A. Zaidi; Pub. Herbert M. Johnson. adv. contact: Miranda Garside. bk.rev. (also avail. in microform from UMI; back issues avail.) Document type: academic/scholarly publication.
   —BLDSC (6148.168800); SWETS. CCC.
   Formerly (until 1992): North American Review of Economics and Finance (ISSN 1042-752X).

NORTH AMERICAN TRADE GUIDE. see BUSINESS AND ECONOMICS — International Commerce

NORTHERN IRELAND. DEPARTMENT OF ECONOMIC DEVELOPMENT. TEXTILES INDUSTRY TRAINING BOARD. REPORT AND FINANCIAL STATEMENTS. see TEXTILE INDUSTRIES AND FABRICS

330.9   US   ISSN 1040-855X
NORTHWEST REPORT. 1986. q. free. Northwest Area Foundation, 332 Minnesota St., Ste. E-1201, St. Paul, MN 55101-1373. TEL 612-224-9635. FAX 612-225-3881. Ed. Vicki S. Itzkowitz. circ. 8,500. Document type: newsletter.
   Description: Covers public policy, economic development, health and environmental issues pertaining to the Upper Midwest and the Northwest.

338   UN   ISSN 0257-2168
HC121
NOTAS SOBRE LA ECONOMIA Y EL DESARROLLO. 1963. bi-m. free. Comision Economica para America Latina y el Caribe - Economic Commission for Latin America and the Caribbean, Casilla 179-D, Santiago, Chile. FAX 562480252. bk.rev.; charts; stat. circ. 12,000. (also avail. in microfiche from CIS) Indexed: IIS. Document type: newsletter.
   Former titles: Notas sobre la Economia y el Desarrollo de America Latina (ISSN 0251-9453); C.E.P.A.L. Noticias (ISSN 0029-3881)
   Description: Covers news and government actions on labor in the Caribbean and Latin America.

330   FR   ISSN 0029-4004
D411
NOTES ET ETUDES DOCUMENTAIRES. (Supplement avail.: Problemes d'Amerique Latine) 1949. 20/yr. 980 F. (Europe 1135 F., elsewhere 1270 F.) (effective 1997). Documentation Francaise, 29-31 quai Voltaire, 75344 Paris Cedex 07, France. TEL 33-1-40157000. FAX 33-1-40157230. TELEX 215 666 DOCFRAN. (Subscr. to: 124 rue Henri Barbusse, 93308 Aubervilliers Cedex, France. TEL 33-1-48395600. FAX 33-1-48395601) Ed. Isabelle Crucifix. adv.; charts; stat. circ. 6,000. (also avail. in microfiche from DFR) Indexed: ELLIS, Int.Lab.Doc., Int.Polit.Sci.Abstr., Key to Econ.Sci., P.A.I.S.For.Lang.Ind., Pt.de Rep. (1979-), Rural Recreat.Tour.Abstr., World Agri.Econ.& Rural Sociol.Abstr. Document type: government publication.
   —SWETS.
   Description: Stories covering political, judicial, economic, social and cultural themes. Also contains graphs, statistical tables and bibliography section.

NOTISUR; South American political and economic affairs. see POLITICAL SCIENCE

LE NOUVEL AFRIQUE ASIE. see POLITICAL SCIENCE

BUSINESS AND ECONOMICS — ECONOMIC SITUATION AND CONDITIONS

330.9   FR   ISSN 0395-6458
NOUVEL ECONOMISTE. w. 1280 F. 10 reu Juynemer, 92136 Issy les Moulineaux Cedex, France. TEL 41-09-30-00. FAX 41-09-31-00. Ed. Gilles Le Gendre. adv. contact: Nathalie Boutigny. illus. circ. 117,090. **Indexed:** Cont.Pg.Manage., Key to Econ.Sci. **Document type:** newspaper.
—SWETS.
Formed by the merger of (1945-1975): Informations Industrielles et Commerciales (ISSN 0395-644X); (1953-1975): Entreprise (ISSN 0013-9068)

330   FR   ISSN 0029-4934
NOUVELLES INDUSTRIELLES ET COMMERCIALES ET DE MIDI-PYRENEES. 1954. m. 40 F. Centre d'Etudes et d'Editions Patronales, Palais Consulaire, B.P. 1506, Toulouse, France. adv.; bk.rev.; bibl.; illus.; stat.

330.9   VE
NUEVA CIENCIA.* 1975. irreg. $10. Universidad Central de Venezuela, Facultad de Ciencias Economicas y Sociales, Ciudad Universitaria, Los Chapuaramos, ZP 104, Caracas 1051, Venezuela.

338   FR   ISSN 0474-5574
HC10   CODEN: OEEOA8
O E C D ECONOMIC OUTLOOK. French edition: Perspectives Economiques de l'O E C D (ISSN 0304-3274) 1967. s-a. Organization for Economic Cooperation and Development, 2 rue Andre-Pascal, 75775 Paris Cedex 16, France. TEL 33-1-45-24-82-00. FAX 33-1-45-24-85-00. TELEX 620-160-ODCD F. (U.S. orders to: O.E.C.D. Publications and Information Center, 2001 L St., N.W., Ste. 650, Washington, DC 20036-4922. TEL 202-785-6323) charts; stat. (also avail. in diskette format) **Indexed:** ABI Inform., BMT, BPIA, Cadscan, IIS, Intl.Polym.Sci.& Tech., Lead Abstr., PROMT, RAPRA, SCIMP, Tr.& Indus.Ind., World Bank.Abstr., Zincscan.
•Also available online. Vendor(s): Information Access Co., UMI.
—BLDSC (6235.251000); SWETS; UMI.
Description: Surveys the latest economic developments in the OECD area and, by means of an integrated set of quantitative forecasts, assesses future prospects.

338   FR   ISSN 0255-0822
HC10
O E C D ECONOMIC STUDIES. French edition: Revue Economique de l'O C D E (ISSN 0255-0830) s-a. 205 F. Organization for Economic Cooperation and Development, 2 rue Andre-Pascal, 75775 Paris Cedex 16, France. TEL 33-1-45-24-82-00. FAX 33-1-45-24-85-00. (U.S. orders to: O.E.C.D. Publication and Information Center, 2001 L St., N.W., Ste. 650, Washington, DC 20036-4922. TEL 202-785-6323) **Indexed:** Asian-Pac.Econ.Lit., C.R.E.J., ELLIS, Geo.Abstr., IDA, IIS, Int.Lab.Doc., J.of Econ.Lit., World Bank.Abstr.
•Also available online. Vendor(s): Information Access Co.
—BLDSC (6235.251280); SWETS; UnCover.
Formerly (until 1983): Organization for Economic Cooperation and Development. Occasional Studies.
Description: Focuses on the area of applied macroeconomic and statistical analyses, generally with an international or cross-country dimension.

330   FR   ISSN 0376-6438
O E C D ECONOMIC SURVEYS. (In 25 vols.) a. $220 complete series on CD-ROM $365 (effective 1994-95). Organization for Economic Cooperation and Development, 2 rue Andre-Pascal, 75775 Paris Cedex 16, France. TEL 33-1-45248200. FAX 33-1-45248500. (N. American orders to: O.E.C.D. Publications and Information Center, 2001 L St., N.W., Ste. 650, Washington, DC 20036-4922. TEL 202-785-6323)
—SWETS.
Description: Provides a detailed analysis of recent developments in demand, production, employment, prices and wages, conditions in the money and capital markets, and developments in the balance of payments, for each member country.

330.9   FR
O E C D ECONOMIC SURVEYS: AUSTRALIA. a. $20 (complete series on CD-ROM $365) (effective 1994-95). Organization for Economic Cooperation and Development, 2 rue Andre-Pascal, 75775 Paris Cedex 16, France. TEL 33-1-45248200. FAX 33-1-45248500. (N. American orders to: O.E.C.D. Publications and Information Center, 2001 L St., N.W., Ste. 650, Washington, DC 20036-4922. TEL 202-785-6323) illus.; stat.

330   FR   ISSN 0474-5124
HC261
O E C D ECONOMIC SURVEYS: AUSTRIA. 1959. a. $20 (complete series on CD-ROM $365) (effective 1994-95). Organization for Economic Cooperation and Development, 2 rue Andre Pascal, 75775 Paris 16, France. TEL 33-1-45248500. TELEX 620-160-OCDE F. (N. American orders to: O.E.C.D. Publications and Information Center, 2001 L St., N.W., Ste. 650, Washington, DC 20036-4922. TEL 202-785-6323)
•Also available online. Vendor(s): Information Access Co.
Supersedes in part: Organization for Economic Cooperation and Development. Economic Conditions in Austria and Switzerland.

330   FR   ISSN 0474-5132
HC315
O E C D ECONOMIC SURVEYS: BELGIUM - LUXEMBOURG. 1960. a. complete series on CD-ROM $365 (effective 1994-95). Organization for Economic Cooperation and Development, 2 rue Andre-Pascal, 75775 Paris Cedex 16, France. TEL 33-1-45248200. FAX 33-1-45248500. (N. American orders to: O.E.C.D. Publications and Information Center, 2001 L St., N.W., Ste. 650, Washington, DC 20036-4922. TEL 202-785-6323) **Indexed:** IIS.

330   FR   ISSN 0474-5140
HC111
O E C D ECONOMIC SURVEYS: CANADA. 1959. a. $20 (complete series on CD-ROM $365) (effective 1994-95). Organization for Economic Cooperation and Development, 2 rue Andre-Pascal, 75775 Paris Cedex 16, France. TEL 33-1-45248200. FAX 33-1-45248500. (N. American orders to: O.E.C.D. Publications and Information Center, 2001 L St., N.W., Ste. 650, Washington, DC 20036-4922. TEL 202-785-6323) **Indexed:** IIS.
•Also available online. Vendor(s): Information Access Co.
—BLDSC (3656.510000); CISTI.

330.9   FR   ISSN 0474-5159
HC351
O E C D ECONOMIC SURVEYS: DENMARK. 1960. a. complete series on CD-ROM $365 (effective 1994-95). Organization for Economic Cooperation and Development, 2 rue Andre-Pascal, 75775 Paris Cedex 16, France. TEL 33-1-45248200. FAX 33-1-45248500. (N. American orders to: O.E.C.D. Publications and Information Center, 2001 L St., N.W., Ste. 650, Washington, DC 20036-4922. TEL 202-785-6323) **Indexed:** IIS.
•Also available online. Vendor(s): Information Access Co.

330.9   FR
O E C D ECONOMIC SURVEYS: FINLAND. a. complete series on CD-ROM $365 (effective 1994-95). Organization for Economic Cooperation and Development, 2 rue Andre-Pascal, 75775 Paris Cedex 16, France. TEL 33-1-45248200. FAX 33-1-45248500. (N. American orders to: O.E.C.D. Publications and Information Center, 2001 L St., N.W., Ste. 650, Washington, DC 20036-4922. TEL 202-785-6323) **Indexed:** IIS.

330   FR   ISSN 0474-5167
O E C D ECONOMIC SURVEYS: FRANCE. 1953. a. complete series on CD-ROM $365 (effective 1994-95). Organization for Economic Cooperation and Development, 2 rue Andre-Pascal, 75775 Paris Cedex 16, France. TEL 33-1-45248200. FAX 33-1-45248500. (N. American orders to: O.E.C.D. Publications and Information Center, 2001 L St., N.W., Ste. 650, Washington, DC 20036-4922. TEL 202-785-6323)

330   FR   ISSN 0474-5175
O E C D ECONOMIC SURVEYS: GERMANY. 1953. a. complete series on CD-ROM $365 (effective 1994-95). Organization for Economic Cooperation and Development, 2 rue Andre-Pascal, 75775 Paris Cedex 16, France. TEL 33-1-45248200. FAX 33-1-45248500. (N. American orders to: O.E.C.D. Publications and Information Center, 2001 L St., N.W., Ste. 650, Washington, DC 20036-4922. TEL 202-785-6323) **Indexed:** IIS.

330   FR   ISSN 0474-5183
HC291
O E C D ECONOMIC SURVEYS: GREECE. 1954. a. complete series on CD-ROM $365 (effective 1994-95). Organization for Economic Cooperation and Development, 2 rue Andre-Pascal, 75775 Paris Cedex 16, France. TEL 33-1-45248200. FAX 33-1-45245800. (N. American orders to: O.E.C.D. Publications and Information Center, 2001 L St., N.W., Ste. 650, Washington, DC 20036-4922. TEL 202-785-6323) **Indexed:** IIS.

330   FR
O E C D ECONOMIC SURVEYS: HUNGARY. (Subseries: Partners in Transition) 1991. a. complete series on CD-ROM $365 (effective 1994-95). Organization for Economic Cooperation and Development, Center for Cooperation with European Economies in Transition, 2 rue Andre Pascal, 75775 Paris Cedex 16, France. TEL 33-1-45248200. FAX 33-1-45248500. (N. American orders to: O.E.C.D. Publications and Information Center, 2001 L St., N.W., Ste. 650, Washington, DC 20036-4922. TEL 202-785-6323)

330.9   FR   ISSN 0474-5191
HC360.5
O E C D ECONOMIC SURVEYS: ICELAND. 1960. a. complete series on CD-ROM $365 (effective 1994-95). Organization for Economic Cooperation and Development, 2 rue Andre-Pascal, 75775 Paris Cedex 16, France. TEL 33-1-45248200. FAX 33-1-45245800. (U.S. orders to: O.E.C.D. Publications and Information Center, 200a L St., N.W., Ste. 650, Washington, DC 20036-4922. TEL 202-785-6323)
•Also available online. Vendor(s): Information Access Co.

330   FR   ISSN 0474-5205
O E C D ECONOMIC SURVEYS: IRELAND. 1960. a. complete series on CD-ROM $365 (effective 1994-95). Organization for Economic Cooperation and Development, 2 rue Andre-Pascal, 75775 Paris Cedex 16, France. TEL 33-1-45248200. FAX 33-1-45248500. (N. American orders to: O.E.C.D. Publications and Information Center, 2001 L St., N.W., Ste. 650, Washington, DC 20036-4922. TEL 202-785-6323)

330   FR   ISSN 0474-5213
O E C D ECONOMIC SURVEYS: ITALY. (Not published in 1978) 1953. a. complete series on CD-ROM $365 (effective 1994-95). Organization for Economic Cooperation and Development, 2 rue Andre-Pascal, 75775 Paris Cedex 16, France. TEL 33-1-45248200. FAX 33-1-45248500. (N. American orders to: O.E.C.D. Publications and Information Center, 2001 L. St., N.W., Ste. 650, Washington, DC 20036-4922. TEL 202-785-6323) **Indexed:** IIS.

330   FR   ISSN 0474-5221
HC461.A1
O E C D ECONOMIC SURVEYS: JAPAN. 1964. a. complete series on CD-ROM $365 (effective 1994-95). Organization for Economic Cooperation and Development, 2 rue Andre-Pascal, 75775 Paris Cedex 16, France. TEL 33-1-45248200. FAX 33-1-45248500. (N. American orders to: O.E.C.D. Publications and Information Center, 2001 L St., N.W., Ste. 650, Washington, DC 20036-4922 TEL 202-785-6323)

330.9   FR
O E C D ECONOMIC SURVEYS: MEXICO. a. complete series on CD-ROM $365 (effective 1994-95). Organization for Economic Cooperation and Development, 2 rue Andre-Pascal, 75775 Paris Cedex 16, France. TEL 33-1-45248200. FAX 33-1-45248500. (N. American orders to: O.E.C.D. Publications and Information Center, 2001 L St., N.W., Ste. 650, Washington, DC 20036-4922

BUSINESS AND ECONOMICS — ECONOMIC SITUATION AND CONDITIONS

330   FR   ISSN 0474-523X
O E C D ECONOMIC SURVEYS: NETHERLANDS. 1954. a. complete series on CD-ROM $365 (effective 1994-95). Organization for Economic Cooperation and Development, 2 rue Andre-Pascal, 75775 Paris Cedex 16, France. TEL 33-1-45248200. FAX 33-1-45248500. (N. American orders to: O.E.C.D. Publications and Information Center, 2001 L St., N.W., Ste. 650, Washington, DC 20036-4922. TEL 202-785-6323) **Indexed:** IIS.

330   FR
O E C D ECONOMIC SURVEYS: NEW ZEALAND. a. complete series on CD-ROM $365 (effective 1994-95). Organization for Economic Cooperation and Development, 2 rue Andre-Pascal, 75775 Paris Cedex 16, France. TEL 33-1-45248200. FAX 33-1-45248500. (N. American orders to: O.E.C.D. Publications and Information Center, 2001 L St., N.W., Ste. 650, Washington, DC 20036-4922. TEL 202-785-6323)

330   FR   ISSN 0474-5248
O E C D ECONOMIC SURVEYS: NORWAY. 1960. a. complete series on CD-ROM $365 (effective 1994-95). Organization for Economic Cooperation and Development, 2 rue Andre-Pascal, 75775 Paris Cedex 16, France. TEL 33-1-45248200. FAX 33-1-45248500. (N. American orders to: O.E.C.D. Publications and Information Center, 2001 L St., N.W., Ste. 650, Washington, DC 20036-4922. TEL 202-785-6323) **Indexed:** IIS.

330   FR
O E C D ECONOMIC SURVEYS: POLAND. (Series title: Partners in Transition) a. complete series on CD-ROM $365 (effective 1994-95). Organization for Economic Cooperation and Development, Center for Cooperation with European Economies in Transition, 2 rue Andre Pascal, 75775 Paris Cedex 16, France. TEL 33-1-45248200. FAX 33-1-45248500. (N. American orders to: O.E.C.D. Publications and Information Centre, 2001 L St. N.W., Ste. 650, Washington, DC 20036-4922. TEL 202-785-0350)

330   FR   ISSN 0474-5256
O E C D ECONOMIC SURVEYS: PORTUGAL. 1960. a. complete series on CD-ROM $365 (effective 1994-95). Organization for Economic Cooperation and Development, 2 rue Andre-Pascal, 75775 Paris Cedex 16, France. TEL 33-1-45248200. FAX 33-1-45245800. (N. American orders to: O.E.C.D. Publications and Information Center, 2001 L St., N.W., Ste. 650, Washington, DC 20036-4922. TEL 202-785-6323) **Indexed:** IIS.

330   FR   ISSN 0474-5272
O E C D ECONOMIC SURVEYS: SPAIN. 1958. a. complete series on CD-ROM $365 (effective 1994-95). Organization for Economic Cooperation and Development, 2 rue Andre-Pascal, 75775 Paris Cedex 16, France. TEL 33-1-45248200. FAX 33-1-45248500. (N. American orders to: O.E.C.D. Publications and Information Center, 2001 L St., N.W., Ste. 650, Washington, DC 20036-4922. TEL 202-785-6323) **Indexed:** IIS.
●Also available online. Vendor(s): Information Access Co.

330   FR   ISSN 0474-5280
O E C D ECONOMIC SURVEYS: SWEDEN. 1954. a. complete series on CD-ROM $365 (effective 1994-95). Organization for Economic Cooperation and Development, 2 rue Andre-Pascal, 75775 Paris Cedex 16, France. TEL 33-1-45248200. FAX 33-1-45248500. (N. American orders to: O.E.C.D. Publications and Information Center, 2001 L St., N.W., Ste. 650, Washington, DC 20036-4922. TEL 202-785-6263)

330   FR   ISSN 0474-5299
HC395
O E C D ECONOMIC SURVEYS: SWITZERLAND. 1959. a. complete series on CD-ROM $365 (effective 1994-95). Organization for Economic Cooperation and Development, 2 rue Andre-Pascal, 75775 Paris Cedex 16, France. TEL 33-1-45248200. FAX 33-1-45248500. (N. American orders to: O.E.C.D. Publications and Information Center, 2001 L St., N.W., Ste. 650, Washington, DC 20036-4922. TEL 202-785-6323) **Indexed:** IIS.

330   FR
O E C D ECONOMIC SURVEYS: THE CZECH REPUBLIC. (Subseries of: Partners in Transition) (Editions in English, French) a. complete series in CD-ROM $365 (effective 1994-95). Organization for Economic Cooperation and Development, Center for Cooperation with European Economies in Transition, 2 rue Andre Pascal, 75775 Paris Cedex, France. TEL 33-1-45248200. FAX 33-1-45248500. (N. American orders to: O.E.C.D. Publications and Information Center, 2001 L St., Ste. 650, Washington, DC 20036-4922. TEL 202-785-0350)
●Also available on CD-ROM.
Former titles (until 1995): O E C D Economic Surveys: The Czech and Slovak Republics; O E C D Economic Surveys: Czech and Slovak Federal Republic.

330   FR   ISSN 0474-5302
O E C D ECONOMIC SURVEYS: TURKEY. (Not published in 1978) 1954. a. complete series on CD-ROM $365 (effective 1994-95). Organization for Economic Cooperation and Development, 2 rue Andre-Pascal, 75775 Paris Cedex 16, France. TEL 33-1-45248200. FAX 33-1-45248500. (N. American orders to: O.E.C.D. Publications and Information Center, 2001 L St., N.W., Ste. 650, Washington, DC 20036-4922. TEL 202-785-6323. FAX 301-459-0056) **Indexed:** IIS.

330   FR   ISSN 0474-5310
O E C D ECONOMIC SURVEYS: UNITED KINGDOM. 1953. a. complete series on CD-ROM $365 (effective 1994-95). Organization for Economic Cooperation and Development, 2 rue Andre-Pascal, 75775 Paris Cedex 16, France. TEL 33-1-45248200. FAX 33-1-45248500. (N. American orders to: O.E.C.D. Publications and Information Center, 2001 L St., N.W., Ste. 650, Washington, DC 20036-4922. TEL 202-785-6323) **Indexed:** IIS.

330   FR   ISSN 0474-5329
HC106.5
O E C D ECONOMIC SURVEYS: UNITED STATES. 1953. a. complete series on CD-ROM $365 (effective 1994-95). Organization for Economic Cooperation and Development, 2 rue Andre-Pascal, 75775 Paris Cedex 16, France. TEL 33-1-45248200. FAX 33-1-45248500. (N. American orders to: O.E.C.D. Publications and Information Center, 2001 L St., N.W., Ste. 650, Washington, DC 20036-4922. TEL 202-785-6323) **Indexed:** IIS.
●Also available online. Vendor(s): Information Access Co.

330   FR   ISSN 1013-0241
O E C D EMPLOYMENT OUTLOOK. French edition: O C D E Perspectives de l'Emploi (ISSN 0256-6192) 1983. a. price varies. Organization for Economic Cooperation and Development, 2 rue Andre-Pascal, 75775 Paris Cedex 16, France. (U.S. orders to: O.E.C.D. Publications and Information Center, 2001 L St., N.W., Ste. 650, Washington, DC 20036-4922. TEL 202-785-6323) **Indexed:** IIS.
—BLDSC (6235.251500).

330.9   FR   ISSN 0474-5523
HC10
O E C D MAIN ECONOMIC INDICATORS/O C D E PRINCIPAUX INDICATEURS ECONOMIQUES. (Text in English, French) m. $240. Organization for Economic Cooperation and Development, 2 rue Andre-Pascal, 75775 Paris Cedex 16, France. (U.S. orders to: O.E.C.D. Publications and Information Center, 2001 L St., N.W., Ste. 650, Washington, DC 20036-4922. TEL 202-785-6323) charts; stat. (magnetic tape; diskette format) **Indexed:** IIS, World Bank.Abstr.
—BLDSC (5351.800000).
Description: Designed to provide at a glance a picture of the most recent changes in the economy of the OECD countries, and a collection of international statistics on the economic developments affecting the OECD area in the past few years.

338   FR   ISSN 0029-7054
HC240.A1
O E C D OBSERVER. French edition: Observateur de l'O C D E (ISSN 0304-3398) 1962. bi-m. $25. Organization for Economic Cooperation and Development, 2 rue Andre-Pascal, 75775 Paris Cedex 16, France. TEL 33-1-45-24-82-00. FAX 33-1-45-24-85-00. (U.S. orders to: O.E.C.D. Publications and Information Center, 2001 L St., N.W., Ste. 650, Washington, DC 20036-4922. TEL 202-785-6323) Ed. Ulla Ranthall Reyners. bk.rev.; charts; illus. circ. 25,000. (reprint service avail. from UMI) **Indexed:** Acid Rain Abstr., Acid Rain Ind., B.P.I., BPIA, Bus.Ind., C.I.J.E., Cadscan, Curr.Adv.Ecol.Sci., ELLIS, Energy Info.Abstr., Environ.Abstr., Excerp.Med., Fuel & Energy Abstr., Fut.Surv., Geo.Abstr.P.G., IDA, IIS, Int.Lab.Doc., Key to Econ.Sci., Lead Abstr., Mid.East: Abstr.& Ind., Mult.Ed.Abstr., Nutr.Abstr., P.A.I.S., Pollut.Abstr., PROMT, Pt.de Rep., Pub.Admin.Abstr., Rural Recreat.Tour.Abstr., Sociol.Educ.Abstr., Stud.Wom.Abstr., Tel.Abstr., Telegen, Tr.& Indus.Ind., World Agri.Econ.& Rural Sociol.Abstr., World Text.Abstr., Zincscan.
●Also available online. Vendor(s): Information Access Co., UMI.
—BLDSC (6235.255000); KR SourceOne; SWETS; UMI; UnCover.
Description: Coverage of the most important problems dealt with by the O.E.C.D. - economic growth, employment and unemployment, social problems, agriculture, energy, financial markets, fiscal policy, multinational enterprises, environment, science and technology, aid to and trade with the developing world.

O E C S ANNUAL DIGEST OF STATISTICS. (Organisation of Eastern Caribbean States) see STATISTICS

330.9 011   AQ   ISSN 1021-7312
O E C S CURRENT AWARENESS BULLETIN. 1985. q. EC$60($24) Organisation of Eastern Caribbean States, Economic Affairs Secretariat, P.O. Box 822, St. John's, Antigua, W.I. TEL 809-462-3500. FAX 809-462-1537. circ. 75. (back issues avail.) **Document type:** abstracting/indexing, bulletin.
Description: Listing of recently acquired documents and journal articles relevant to the OECS Work Programme.

O E C S DIGEST OF EXTERNAL TRADE STATISTICS. (Organisation of Eastern Caribbean States) see BUSINESS AND ECONOMICS — Abstracting, Bibliographies, Statistics

O E C S NATIONAL ACCOUNTS DIGEST. (Organisation of Eastern Caribbean States) see STATISTICS

330.9 011   AQ   ISSN 1021-7304
O E C S SELECT BIBLIOGRAPHY. 1988. irreg. (approx. 2/yr.). EC$25($10) Organisation of Eastern Caribbean States, Economic Affairs Secretariat, P.O. Box 822, St. John's, Antigua, W.I. TEL 809-462-3500. FAX 809-462-1537. TELEX 2157 ECON SEC AK. circ. 100. **Document type:** bibliography.

O E C S STATISTICAL POCKET DIGEST. (Organisation of Eastern Caribbean States) see STATISTICS

O T C BULLETIN; the business newsletter for Europe's consumer healthcare industry. (Over the Counter) see PHARMACY AND PHARMACOLOGY

330.9   UK   ISSN 0961-7698
OCCASIONAL PAPERS IN INDUSTRIAL STRATEGY. 1991. irreg., no.36, 1996. £5. University of Birmingham, Research Centre for Industrial Strategy, Edgbaston, Birmingham B15 2TT, England. TEL 44-121-414-6690. FAX 44-121-414-6707. E-mail: v.l.nash@bham.ac.uk. **Document type:** monographic series.
—BLDSC (6224.745000).

330.9   US
OCCUPATIONAL COMPENSATION SUMMARIES. a. U.S. Bureau of Labor Statistics, 2 Massachusetts Ave., N.E., Washington, DC 20212. TEL 202-655-4000. (Subscr. to: Superintendent of Documents, U.S. Government Printing Office, Box 371954, Pittsburgh, PA 15250-7954. TEL 202-512-1800. FAX 202-512-2250; Or: Bureau of Labor Statistics Publications Sales Center, Box 2145, Chicago, IL 60690) **Document type:** government publication.
Description: Summarizes B L S findings on occupations and wages for selected regions.

BUSINESS AND ECONOMICS — ECONOMIC SITUATION AND CONDITIONS

330.9   US
OCCUPATIONAL COMPENSATION SURVEYS. (Subseries of: B L S Bulletins; avail. for each of 65 regions) a. price varies. U.S. Bureau of Labor Statistics, 2 Massachusetts Ave., N.E., Washington, DC 20212. TEL 202-655-4000. (Subscr. to: Superintendent of Documents, U.S. Government Printing Office, Box 371954, Pittsburgh, PA 15250-7954. TEL 202-512-1800. FAX 202-512-2250; Or: Bureau of Labor Statistics Publications Sales Center, Box 2145, Chicago, IL 60690) (also avail. in diskette format) **Document type:** government publication.
   Description: Analyzes regions for pay levels and occupational descriptions.

OEKONOMISK REVY. see BUSINESS AND ECONOMICS — Banking And Finance

330.948   DK   ISSN 1396-1349
▼**OEKONOMISKE UDSIGTER I NORDEN.** 1993. a. DKK 50. Nordic Council of Ministers, Store Strandstraede 18, DK-1255 Copenhagen K, Denmark. TEL 45-33-96-02-00. FAX 45-33-96-02-02. Ed.Bd. circ. 8,000.

650 330   AU   ISSN 0029-957X
DER OESTERREICHISCHE VOLKSWIRT. 1908. m. S.440. Volkswirtschaftliche Verlagsgesellschaft mbH, Schottenfeld Gasse 93-6, A-1070 Vienna, Austria. Ed. Ronald Barazon. adv.; bk.rev.; mkt.; index. **Document type:** bulletin.

330.9   AU   ISSN 0029-9898
OESTERREICHISCHES INSTITUT FUER WIRTSCHAFTSFORSCHUNG. MONATSBERICHTE. 1927. m. S.2500 (effective 1997 & 1998). Oesterreichisches Institut fuer Wirtschaftsforschung - Austrian Institute of Economic Research, Postfach 91, A-1103 Vienna, Austria. TEL 43-1-79826010. FAX 43-1-7989386. URL: http://www.wsr.ac.at/wifo.html/. Ed. Helmut Kramer. adv. contact: Christine Knoll. charts; mkt.; stat.; index, cum.index: 1927-1996. circ. 3,300. (back issues avail.) **Indexed:** ELLIS. **Document type:** academic/scholarly publication, bulletin.
   Description: Covers all aspects of the Austrian economy, featuring the economic outlook, state of markets, revenues and expenditures, unemployment, manufacturing industry, trade, statistics and more.

OIL INDUSTRY OUTLOOK FOR THE U S A. see PETROLEUM AND GAS

330.9   IT
OLTRE IL PONTE. 1983. q. L.60000 (foreign L.85000) (effective 1993). Franco Angeli Editore, Viale Monza 106, 20127 Milan, Italy. TEL 02-28-27-651.

ON PRINCIPLE. see POLITICAL SCIENCE

OOST-EUROPA VERKENNINGEN. see POLITICAL SCIENCE — International Relations

330.9   CN   ISSN 0846-5142
OPPORTUNITY. 1974. q. Can.$20 per no. Fleet Publications Inc., Box 1679, Winnipeg, MB R3C 2Z6, Canada. TEL 204-788-4884. FAX 204-786-5038. Ed. Ann Wiens; Pub. George Derksen. R&P contact: Ann Wiens. adv. contact: George Derksen. illus.
   Formerly: Opportunity in Northern Canada.

338   US   ISSN 1051-7480
ORANGE COUNTY BUSINESS JOURNAL; weekly journal of commerce & industry. 1967. w. $36. Orange County Business Journal, 4590 MacArthur Blvd., Ste. 100, Newport Beach, CA 92660. TEL 714-833-8373. FAX 714-833-8751. Ed. Rick Reiff. adv.; bk.rev.; illus.; stat. circ. 25,000. **Indexed:** Tr.& Indus.Ind.
   ●Also available online. Vendor(s): Knight-Ridder Information, Inc., UMI.
   —UMI.
   Formerly (until 1978): Orange County Business (ISSN 0030-4255)

330.9   US
ORANGE COUNTY METROPOLITAN.* 1982. s-m. $12. Churm Publishing, 1451 Quail St., Ste. 201, Newport Beach, CA 92660. TEL 714-757-1404. FAX 714-757-1996. adv.; bk.rev. circ. 36,000. (tabloid format; also avail. in microform from UMI; back issues avail.)

330.9   II
ORISSA, INDIA. FINANCE DEPARTMENT. ANNUAL FINANCIAL STATEMENT. a. Orissa Government Press, Cuttack, Orissa, India.

330.9   II
ORISSA, INDIA. FINANCE DEPARTMENT. WHITE PAPER ON THE ECONOMIC CONDITIONS AND THE DEVELOPMENTAL ACTIVITIES IN ORISSA. (Text in English) a. (Finance Department) Orissa Government Press, Cuttack, Orissa, India.
   Continues: Orissa, India. Finance Department. White Paper on Departmental Activities, Government of Orissa (ISSN 0472-0989)

330.9   IT   ISSN 1122-2980
ORIZZONTE SICILIA. 1979. q. free to qualified personnel. Banca Popolare Sant'Angelo, Via Ruggiero VII, no.78, 90141 Palermo, Italy. TEL 39-91-332922. FAX 39-91-584923. Ed. Pietro Busetta. R&P contact: Alessandro La Monica. bk.rev.; bibl.; charts; illus.; stat.; circ. controlled. (back issues avail.) **Document type:** corporate report.

339   GW   ISSN 0344-7030
OST-WIRTSCHAFTSREPORT. 1973. fortn. DM.699. Verlagsgruppe Handelsblatt GmbH, Kasernenstr. 67, 40213 Duesseldorf, Germany. TEL 49-211-8870. FAX 49-211-329954. (Subscr. to: Postfach 102717, 40018 Duesseldorf, Germany) Ed. Juliane Langenecker. circ. 1,200. (reprint service avail. from UMI) **Document type:** bulletin.
   —SWETS. CCC.

OTKRYTAYA POLITYKA; zhurnal rossiiskoi politicheskoi zhizni. see POLITICAL SCIENCE

338   CN   ISSN 0702-8210
OTTAWA LETTER. bi-w. Can.$410. C C H Canadian Ltd., 6 Garamond Ct., North York, ON M3C 1Z5, Canada. TEL 416-441-2992; 800-268-4522. FAX 416-444-9011. index. **Document type:** trade publication.
   Formerly: View from Ottawa (ISSN 0049-6383)
   Description: Reports on what is going on in Parliament and government departments, tracks progress of Bills through Parliament, highlights the economy and weekly foreign exchange rates.

330.9   US   ISSN 1064-3621
HC107.M5
OUTSTATE BUSINESS; the magazine of Michigan business & industry. 1987. q. $10. Harbor House Publishers, Inc., 221 Water St., Boyne City, MI 49712. TEL 616-582-2814. FAX 616-582-3392. Ed. David I. Knight; Pub. Michelle Cortright. adv. circ. 10,000. (also avail. in microfiche from UMI)
   ●Also available online. Vendor(s): UMI.
   —UMI.
   Formerly (until 1992): North Force (ISSN 0895-0024)
   Description: Serves the economic interests of business and commerce in Michigan. Reaches manufacturers with more than five employees, all public utilities and the Fortune 500 CEOs in the Midwest.

330.9   CN   ISSN 0700-3617
OVERVIEW. 1976. 6/yr. Can.$135 (effective 1997). National Citizens' Coalition, 907-100 Adelaide St. W., Toronto, ON M5H 1S3, Canada. TEL 416-869-3838. Ed. Jeffrey R.A. Ball. bk.rev. circ. 10,000.

330   CU   ISSN 0030-7920
P E L: PANORAMA ECONOMICO LATINOAMERICANO. 1960. 24/yr. $86 in S. America; N. America $90; elsewhere $94. Ediciones Cubanas, Obispo No. 527, Apdo. 605, Havana, Cuba. Ed. Jose Bodes Gomez. adv.; bk.rev.; illus.; stat. circ. 3,000. (also avail. in microfilm from UMI; reprint service avail. from UMI)

330.9   MG
P M E MADAGASCAR. (Text in French) 1989. m. Rue Hughes Rabesahala, B.P. 953, Antsakaviro, 101 Antananarivo, Madagascar. TEL 22536. FAX 34534. TELEX 22261. Ed. Romain Andrianarisoa. circ. 3,500.

P N B INTERNATIONAL. (Philippine National Bank) see BUSINESS AND ECONOMICS — Banking And Finance

330.9 658   US   ISSN 1040-8169
P-O-P TIMES. (Point-of-Purchase) 1988. 9/yr. $55 (free to qualified personnel) (effective 1997). Hoyt Publishing Co., 7400 Skokie Blvd., Skokie, IL 60077-3339. TEL 847-675-7400. FAX 847-675-7494. E-mail: hoytpub@interaccess.com. Ed. Rex Davenport; Pub. Peter W. Hoyt. adv. circ. 20,000. (tabloid format) **Document type:** trade publication.
   Description: Presents corporate developments, point-of-purchase campaigns, research, new technologies and personnel to consumer marketers who use point-of-purchase ads and displays.

320   US
THE P R S GROUP. COUNTRY REPORTS: WORLD SERVICE. 1979. 100/yr. (7-9 reports/m.). $6200 includes Country Forecasts, Political Risk Letter. The P R S Group, Box 248, East Syracuse, NY 13057-0248. TEL 315-431-0511. FAX 315-431-0200.
   ●Also available online. Vendor(s): Data-Star (FSRI), Lexis-Nexis (IBCRPT).
   Also available on CD-ROM.
   Formerly: World Country Report Service; World Political Risk Forecasts.
   Description: Covers political and economic risk factors for international business. Executive Reports provide up-to-date summaries and overviews of the situation in a country; Country Reports provide greater depth and detail.

330.9   US   ISSN 1054-5220
THE P R S GROUP. COUNTRY REPORTS: ALGERIA. Key Title: Algeria (Syracuse, N.Y.). 1979. a. $325 (effective 1995). The P R S Group, Box 248, East Syracuse, NY 13057-0248. TEL 315-431-0511. FAX 315-431-0200. stat. (also avail. in diskette format)
   ●Also available online. Vendor(s): Data-Star, Lexis-Nexis.
   Description: In-depth analysis and forecasts of political and economic conditions.

330.9   US   ISSN 1054-5239
THE P R S GROUP. COUNTRY REPORTS: ARGENTINA. Key Title: Argentina (Syracuse, N.Y.). 1979. a. $325 (effective 1995). The P R S Group, Box 248, East Syracuse, NY 13057-0248. TEL 315-431-0511. FAX 315-431-0200. (also avail. in diskette format)
   ●Also available online. Vendor(s): Data-Star, Lexis-Nexis.
   Description: In-depth analysis and forecasts of political and economic conditions.

330.9   US   ISSN 1054-5271
THE P R S GROUP. COUNTRY REPORTS: BOLIVIA. Key Title: Bolivia (Syracuse, N.Y.). 1979. a. $325 (effective 1995). The P R S Group, Box 248, East Syracuse, NY 13057-0248. TEL 315-431-0511. FAX 315-431-0200. (also avail. in diskette format)
   ●Also available online. Vendor(s): Data-Star, Lexis-Nexis.
   Description: In-depth analysis and forecasts of political and economic conditions.

330.9   US   ISSN 1054-528X
THE P R S GROUP. COUNTRY REPORTS: BRAZIL. Key Title: Brazil (Syracuse, N.Y.). 1979. a. $325 (effective 1995). The P R S Group, Box 248, East Syracuse, NY 13057-0248. TEL 315-431-0511. FAX 315-431-0200. (also avail. in diskette format)
   ●Also available online. Vendor(s): Data-Star, Lexis-Nexis.
   Description: In-depth analysis and forecasts of political and economic conditions.

330.9   US   ISSN 1054-5298
THE P R S GROUP. COUNTRY REPORTS: BULGARIA. Key Title: Bulgaria (Syracuse, N.Y.). 1979. a. $325 (effective 1995). The P R S Group, Box 248, East Syracuse, NY 13057-0248. TEL 315-431-0511. FAX 315-431-0200. (also avail. in diskette format)
   ●Also available online. Vendor(s): Data-Star, Lexis-Nexis.
   Description: In-depth analysis and forecasts of political and economic conditions.

BUSINESS AND ECONOMICS — ECONOMIC SITUATION AND CONDITIONS

330.9 US ISSN 1054-5301
THE P R S GROUP. COUNTRY REPORTS: CAMEROON. Key Title: Cameroon (Syracuse, N.Y.). 1979. a. $325 (effective 1995). The P R S Group, Box 248, East Syracuse, NY 13057-0248. TEL 315-431-0511. FAX 315-431-0200. (also avail. in diskette format)
●Also available online. Vendor(s): Data-Star, Lexis-Nexis.
  Description: In-depth analysis and forecasts of political and economic conditions.

330.9 US ISSN 1054-5328
THE P R S GROUP. COUNTRY REPORTS: CHILE. Key Title: Chile (Syracuse, N.Y.). 1979. a. $325 (effective 1995). The P R S Group, Box 248, East Syracuse, NY 13057-0248. TEL 315-431-0511. FAX 315-431-0200. (also avail. in diskette format)
●Also available online. Vendor(s): Data-Star, Lexis-Nexis.
  Description: In-depth analysis and forecasts of political and economic conditions.

330.9 US ISSN 1054-5336
THE P R S GROUP. COUNTRY REPORTS: CHINA. Key Title: China (Syracuse, N.Y.). 1979. a. $325 (effective 1995). The P R S Group, Box 248, East Syracuse, NY 13057-0248. TEL 315-431-0511. FAX 315-431-0200. (also avail. in diskette format)
●Also available online. Vendor(s): Data-Star, Lexis-Nexis.
  Description: In-depth analysis and forecasts of political and economic conditions.

330.9 US ISSN 1054-5344
THE P R S GROUP. COUNTRY REPORTS: COLOMBIA. Key Title: Colombia (Syracuse, N.Y.). 1979. a. $325 (effective 1995). The P R S Group, Box 248, East Syracuse, NY 13057-0248. TEL 315-431-0511. FAX 315-431-0200. (also avail. in diskette format)
●Also available online. Vendor(s): Data-Star, Lexis-Nexis.
  Description: In-depth analysis and forecasts of political and economic conditions.

330.9 US
THE P R S GROUP. COUNTRY REPORTS: CONGO (KINSHASA). 1979. a. $325 (effective 1995). The P R S Group, Box 248, East Syracuse, NY 13057-0248. TEL 315-431-0511. FAX 315-431-0200. (also avail. in diskette format)
●Also available online. Vendor(s): Data-Star, Lexis-Nexis.
  Formerly: Political Risk Services. Country Reports: Zaire (ISSN 1054-6316)
  Description: In-depth analysis and forecasts of political and economic conditions.

330.9 US ISSN 1054-5352
THE P R S GROUP. COUNTRY REPORTS: COSTA RICA. Key Title: Costa Rica (Syracuse, N.Y.). 1979. a. $325 (effective 1995). The P R S Group, Box 248, East Syracuse, NY 13057-0248. TEL 315-431-0511. FAX 315-431-0200. (also avail. in diskette format)
●Also available online. Vendor(s): Data-Star, Lexis-Nexis.
  Description: In-depth analysis and forecasts of political and economic conditions.

330.9 US ISSN 1054-5670
THE P R S GROUP. COUNTRY REPORTS: COTE D'IVOIRE. Key Title: Cote d'Ivoire (Syracuse, N.Y.). 1979. a. $325 (effective 1995). The P R S Group, Box 248, East Syracuse, NY 13057-0248. TEL 315-431-0511. FAX 315-431-0200. (also avail. in diskette format)
●Also available online. Vendor(s): Data-Star, Lexis-Nexis.
  Description: In-depth analysis and forecasts of political and economic conditions.

330.9 US ISSN 1072-8163
THE P R S GROUP. COUNTRY REPORTS: CZECH REPUBLIC. Key Title: Czech Republic (Syracuse, N.Y.). 1979. a. $325 (effective 1995). The P R S Group, Box 248, East Syracuse, NY 13057-0248. TEL 315-431-0511. FAX 315-431-0200. (also avail. in diskette format)
●Also available online. Vendor(s): Data-Star, Lexis-Nexis.
  Formerly: Political Risk Services. Country Reports: Czechoslovakia (ISSN 1054-5360)
  Description: In-depth analysis and forecasts of political and economic conditions.

330.9 US ISSN 1054-5387
THE P R S GROUP. COUNTRY REPORTS: DOMINICAN REPUBLIC. Key Title: Dominican Republic (Syracuse, N.Y.). 1979. a. $325 (effective 1995). The P R S Group, Box 248, East Syracuse, NY 13057-0248. TEL 315-431-0511. FAX 315-431-0200. (also avail. in diskette format)
●Also available online. Vendor(s): Data-Star, Lexis-Nexis.
  Description: In-depth analysis and forecasts of political and economic conditions.

330.9 US ISSN 1054-5395
THE P R S GROUP. COUNTRY REPORTS: ECUADOR. Key Title: Ecuador (Syracuse, N.Y.). 1979. a. $325 (effective 1995). The P R S Group, Box 248, East Syracuse, NY 13057-0248. TEL 315-431-0511. FAX 315-431-0200. (also avail. in diskette format)
●Also available online. Vendor(s): Data-Star, Lexis-Nexis.
  Description: In-depth analysis and forecasts of political and economic conditions.

330.9 US ISSN 1054-5484
THE P R S GROUP. COUNTRY REPORTS: EGYPT. Key Title: Egypt (Syracuse, N.Y.). 1979. a. $325 (effective 1995). The P R S Group, Box 248, East Syracuse, NY 13057-0248. TEL 315-431-0511. FAX 315-431-0200. (also avail. in diskette format)
●Also available online. Vendor(s): Data-Star, Lexis-Nexis.
  Description: In-depth analysis and forecasts of political and economic conditions.

330.9 US ISSN 1054-5492
THE P R S GROUP. COUNTRY REPORTS: EL SALVADOR. Key Title: El Salvador (Syracuse, N.Y.). 1979. a. $325 (effective 1995). The P R S Group, Box 248, East Syracuse, NY 13057-0248. TEL 315-431-0511. FAX 315-431-0200. (also avail. in diskette format)
●Also available online. Vendor(s): Data-Star, Lexis-Nexis.
  Description: In-depth analysis and forecasts of political and economic conditions.

330.9 US ISSN 1054-5522
THE P R S GROUP. COUNTRY REPORTS: GABON. Key Title: Gabon (Syracuse, N.Y.). 1979. a. $325 (effective 1995). The P R S Group, Box 248, East Syracuse, NY 13057-0248. TEL 315-431-0511. FAX 315-431-0200. (also avail. in diskette format)
●Also available online. Vendor(s): Data-Star, Lexis-Nexis.
  Description: In-depth analysis and forecasts of political and economic conditions.

330.9 US ISSN 1054-5549
THE P R S GROUP. COUNTRY REPORTS: GUATEMALA. Key Title: Guatemala (Syracuse, N.Y.). 1979. a. $325 (effective 1995). The P R S Group, Box 248, East Syracuse, NY 13057-0248. TEL 315-431-0511. FAX 315-431-0200. (also avail. in diskette format)
●Also available online. Vendor(s): Data-Star, Lexis-Nexis.
  Description: In-depth analysis and forecasts of political and economic conditions.

330.9 US ISSN 1054-5557
THE P R S GROUP. COUNTRY REPORTS: GUINEA. Key Title: Guinea (Syracuse, N.Y.). 1979. a. $325 (effective 1995). The P R S Group, Box 248, East Syracuse, NY 13057-0248. TEL 315-431-0511. FAX 315-431-0200. (also avail. in diskette format)
●Also available online. Vendor(s): Data-Star, Lexis-Nexis.
  Description: In-depth analysis and forecasts of political and economic conditions.

330.9 US ISSN 1054-5565
THE P R S GROUP. COUNTRY REPORTS: HAITI. Key Title: Haiti (Syracuse, N.Y.). 1979. a. $325 (effective 1995). The P R S Group, Box 248, East Syracuse, NY 13057-0248. TEL 315-431-0511. FAX 315-431-0200. (also avail. in diskette format)
●Also available online. Vendor(s): Data-Star, Lexis-Nexis.
  Description: In-depth analysis and forecasts of political and economic conditions.

330.9 US ISSN 1054-5573
THE P R S GROUP. COUNTRY REPORTS: HONDURAS. Key Title: Honduras (Syracuse, N.Y.). 1979. a. $325 (effective 1995). The P R S Group, Box 248, East Syracuse, NY 13057-0248. TEL 315-431-0511. FAX 315-431-0200. (also avail. in diskette format)
●Also available online. Vendor(s): Data-Star, Lexis-Nexis.
  Description: In-depth analysis and forecasts of political and economic conditions.

330.9 US ISSN 1054-5581
THE P R S GROUP. COUNTRY REPORTS: HONG KONG. Key Title: Hong Kong (Syracuse, N.Y.). 1979. a. $325 (effective 1995). The P R S Group, Box 248, East Syracuse, NY 13057-0248. TEL 315-431-0511. FAX 315-431-0200. (also avail. in diskette format)
●Also available online. Vendor(s): Data-Star, Lexis-Nexis.
  Description: In-depth analysis and forecasts of political and economic conditions.

330.9 US ISSN 1054-559X
THE P R S GROUP. COUNTRY REPORTS: HUNGARY. Key Title: Hungary (Syracuse, N.Y.). 1979. a. $325 (effective 1995). The P R S Group, Box 248, East Syracuse, NY 13057-0248. TEL 315-431-0511. FAX 315-431-0200. (also avail. in diskette format)
●Also available online. Vendor(s): Data-Star, Lexis-Nexis.
  Description: In-depth analysis and forecasts of political and economic conditions.

330.9 US ISSN 1054-5603
THE P R S GROUP. COUNTRY REPORTS: INDIA. Key Title: India (Syracuse, N.Y.). 1979. a. $325 (effective 1995). The P R S Group, Box 248, East Syracuse, NY 13057-0248. TEL 315-431-0511. FAX 315-431-0200. (also avail. in diskette format)
●Also available online. Vendor(s): Data-Star, Lexis-Nexis.

330.9 US ISSN 1054-5611
THE P R S GROUP. COUNTRY REPORTS: INDONESIA. Key Title: Indonesia (Syracuse, N.Y.). 1979. a. $325 (effective 1995). The P R S Group, Box 248, East Syracuse, NY 13057-0248. TEL 315-431-0511. FAX 315-431-0200. (also avail. in diskette format)
●Also available online. Vendor(s): Data-Star, Lexis-Nexis.
  Description: In-depth analysis and forecasts of political and economic conditions.

330.9 US ISSN 1054-562X
THE P R S GROUP. COUNTRY REPORTS: IRAN. Key Title: Iran (Syracuse, N.Y.). 1979. a. $325 (effective 1995). The P R S Group, Box 248, East Syracuse, NY 13057-0248. TEL 315-431-0511. FAX 315-431-0200. (also avail. in diskette format)
●Also available online. Vendor(s): Data-Star, Lexis-Nexis.
  Description: In-depth analysis and forecasts of political and economic conditions.

330.9 US ISSN 1054-5638
THE P R S GROUP. COUNTRY REPORTS: IRAQ. Key Title: Iraq (Syracuse, N.Y.). 1979. a. $325 (effective 1995). The P R S Group, Box 248, East Syracuse, NY 13057-0248. TEL 315-431-0511. FAX 315-431-0200. (also avail. in diskette format)
●Also available online. Vendor(s): Data-Star, Lexis-Nexis.
  Description: In-depth analysis and forecasts of political and economic conditions.

330.9 US ISSN 1054-5662
THE P R S GROUP. COUNTRY REPORTS: ISRAEL. Key Title: Israel (Syracuse, N.Y.). 1979. a. $325 (effective 1995). The P R S Group, Box 248, East Syracuse, NY 13057-0248. TEL 315-431-0511. FAX 315-431-0200. (also avail. in diskette format)
●Also available online. Vendor(s): Data-Star, Lexis-Nexis.
  Description: In-depth analysis and forecasts of political and economic conditions.

330.9 US ISSN 1054-5689
THE P R S GROUP. COUNTRY REPORTS: JAMAICA. Key Title: Jamaica (Syracuse, N.Y.). 1979. a. $325 (effective 1995). The P R S Group, Box 248, East Syracuse, NY 13057-0248. TEL 315-431-0511. FAX 315-431-0200. (also avail. in diskette format)
●Also available online. Vendor(s): Data-Star, Lexis-Nexis.
  Description: In-depth analysis and forecasts of political and economic conditions.

BUSINESS AND ECONOMICS — ECONOMIC SITUATION AND CONDITIONS

330.9   US   ISSN 1054-5700
THE P R S GROUP. COUNTRY REPORTS: KENYA. Key Title: Kenya (Syracuse, N.Y.). 1979. a. $325 (effective 1995). The P R S Group, Box 248, East Syracuse, NY 13057-0248. TEL 315-431-0511. FAX 315-431-0200. (also avail. in diskette format) ●Also available online. Vendor(s): Data-Star, Lexis-Nexis.
   Description: In-depth analysis and forecasts of political and economic conditions.

330.9   US   ISSN 1055-9434
THE P R S GROUP. COUNTRY REPORTS: KUWAIT. Key Title: Kuwait (Syracuse, N.Y.). 1979. a. $325 (effective 1995). The P R S Group, Box 248, East Syracuse, NY 13057-0248. TEL 315-431-0511. FAX 315-431-0200. (also avail. in diskette format) ●Also available online. Vendor(s): Data-Star, Lexis-Nexis.
   Description: In-depth analysis and forecasts of political and economic conditions.

330.9   US   ISSN 1054-5719
THE P R S GROUP. COUNTRY REPORTS: LIBYA. Key Title: Libya (Syracuse, N.Y.). 1979. a. $325 (effective 1995). The P R S Group, Box 248, East Syracuse, NY 13057-0248. TEL 315-431-0511. FAX 315-431-0200. (also avail. in diskette format) ●Also available online. Vendor(s): Data-Star, Lexis-Nexis.
   Description: In-depth analysis and forecasts of political and economic conditions.

330.9   US   ISSN 1054-5727
THE P R S GROUP. COUNTRY REPORTS: MALAYSIA. Key Title: Malaysia (Syracuse, N.Y.). 1979. a. $325 (effective 1995). The P R S Group, Box 248, East Syracuse, NY 13057-0248. TEL 315-431-0511. FAX 315-431-0200. (also avail. in diskette format) ●Also available online. Vendor(s): Data-Star, Lexis-Nexis.
   Description: In-depth analysis and forecasts of political and economic conditions.

330.9   US   ISSN 1054-5735
THE P R S GROUP. COUNTRY REPORTS: MEXICO. Key Title: Mexico (Syracuse, N.Y.). 1979. a. $325 (effective 1995). The P R S Group, Box 248, East Syracuse, NY 13057-0248. TEL 315-431-0511. FAX 315-431-0200. (also avail. in diskette format) ●Also available online. Vendor(s): Data-Star, Lexis-Nexis.
   Description: In-depth analysis and forecasts of political and economic conditions.

330.9   US   ISSN 1054-5743
THE P R S GROUP. COUNTRY REPORTS: MOROCCO. Key Title: Morocco (Syracuse, N.Y.). 1979. a. $325 (effective 1995). The P R S Group, Box 248, East Syracuse, NY 13057-0248. TEL 315-431-0511. FAX 315-431-0200. (also avail. in diskette format) ●Also available online. Vendor(s): Data-Star, Lexis-Nexis.
   Description: In-depth analysis and forecasts of political and economic conditions.

330.9   US   ISSN 1054-5786
THE P R S GROUP. COUNTRY REPORTS: NICARAGUA. Key Title: Nicaragua (Syracuse, N.Y.). 1979. a. $325 (effective 1995). The P R S Group, Box 248, East Syracuse, NY 13057-0248. TEL 315-431-0511. FAX 315-431-0200. (also avail. in diskette format) ●Also available online. Vendor(s): Data-Star, Lexis-Nexis.
   Description: In-depth analysis and forecasts of political and economic conditions.

330.9   US   ISSN 1054-576X
THE P R S GROUP. COUNTRY REPORTS: NIGERIA. Key Title: Nigeria (Syracuse, N.Y.). 1979. a. $325 (effective 1995). The P R S Group, Box 248, East Syracuse, NY 13057-0248. TEL 315-431-0511. FAX 315-431-0200. (also avail. in diskette format) ●Also available online. Vendor(s): Data-Star, Lexis-Nexis.
   Description: In-depth analysis and forecasts of political and economic conditions.

330.9   US   ISSN 1054-5808
THE P R S GROUP. COUNTRY REPORTS: OMAN. Key Title: Oman (Syracuse, N.Y.). 1979. a. $325 (effective 1995). The P R S Group, Box 248, East Syracuse, NY 13057-0248. TEL 315-431-0511. FAX 315-431-0200. (also avail. in diskette format) ●Also available online. Vendor(s): Data-Star, Lexis-Nexis.
   Description: In-depth analysis and forecasts of political and economic conditions.

330.9   US   ISSN 1054-6030
THE P R S GROUP. COUNTRY REPORTS: PAKISTAN. Key Title: Pakistan (Syracuse, N.Y.). 1979. a. $325 (effective 1995). The P R S Group, Box 248, East Syracuse, NY 13057-0248. TEL 315-431-0511. FAX 315-431-0200. (also avail. in diskette format) ●Also available online. Vendor(s): Data-Star, Lexis-Nexis.
   Description: In-depth analysis and forecasts of political and economic conditions.

330.9   US   ISSN 1054-6049
THE P R S GROUP. COUNTRY REPORTS: PANAMA. Key Title: Panama (Syracuse, N.Y.). 1979. a. $325 (effective 1995). The P R S Group, Box 248, East Syracuse, NY 13057-0248. TEL 315-431-0511. FAX 315-431-0200. (also avail. in diskette format) ●Also available online. Vendor(s): Data-Star, Lexis-Nexis.
   Description: In-depth analysis and forecasts of political and economic conditions.

330.9   US   ISSN 1054-6057
THE P R S GROUP. COUNTRY REPORTS: PERU. Key Title: Peru (Syracuse, N.Y.). 1979. a. $325 (effective 1995). The P R S Group, Box 248, East Syracuse, NY 13057-0248. TEL 315-431-0511. FAX 315-431-0200. (also avail. in diskette format) ●Also available online. Vendor(s): Data-Star, Lexis-Nexis.
   Description: In-depth analysis and forecasts of political and economic conditions.

330.9   US   ISSN 1054-6065
THE P R S GROUP. COUNTRY REPORTS: PHILIPPINES. Key Title: Philippines (Syracuse, N.Y.). 1979. a. $325 (effective 1995). The P R S Group, Box 248, East Syracuse, NY 13057-0248. TEL 315-431-0511. FAX 315-431-0200. (also avail. in diskette format) ●Also available online. Vendor(s): Data-Star, Lexis-Nexis.
   Description: In-depth analysis and forecasts of political and economic conditions.

330.9   US   ISSN 1054-6073
THE P R S GROUP. COUNTRY REPORTS: POLAND. Key Title: Poland (Syracuse, N.Y.). 1979. a. $325 (effective 1995). The P R S Group, Box 248, East Syracuse, NY 13057-0248. TEL 315-431-0511. FAX 315-431-0200. (also avail. in diskette format) ●Also available online. Vendor(s): Data-Star, Lexis-Nexis.
   Description: In-depth analysis and forecasts of political and economic conditions.

330.9   US   ISSN 1054-6103
THE P R S GROUP. COUNTRY REPORTS: ROMANIA. Key Title: Romania (Syracuse, N.Y.). 1979. a. $325 (effective 1995). The P R S Group, Box 248, East Syracuse, NY 13057-0248. TEL 315-431-0511. FAX 315-431-0200. (also avail. in diskette format) ●Also available online. Vendor(s): Data-Star, Lexis-Nexis.
   Description: In-depth analysis and forecasts of political and economic conditions.

330.9   US   ISSN 1060-8753
THE P R S GROUP. COUNTRY REPORTS: RUSSIA. Key Title: Russia (Syracuse, N.Y.). 1992. a. $325 (effective 1995). The P R S Group, Box 248, East Syracuse, NY 13057-0248. TEL 315-431-0511. FAX 315-431-0200. (also avail. in diskette format) ●Also available online. Vendor(s): Data-Star, Lexis-Nexis.
   Supersedes in part (1984-1991): U S S R (Syracuse, N.Y.) (ISSN 1054-6243)
   Description: In-depth analysis and forecasts of political and economic conditions.

330.9   US   ISSN 1054-6111
THE P R S GROUP. COUNTRY REPORTS: SAUDI ARABIA. Key Title: Saudi Arabia (Syracuse, N.Y.). 1979. a. $325 (effective 1995). The P R S Group, Box 248, East Syracuse, NY 13057-0248. TEL 315-431-0511. FAX 315-431-0200. (also avail. in diskette format) ●Also available online. Vendor(s): Data-Star, Lexis-Nexis.
   Description: In-depth analysis and forecasts of political and economic conditions.

330.9   US   ISSN 1054-612X
THE P R S GROUP. COUNTRY REPORTS: SINGAPORE. Key Title: Singapore (Syracuse, N.Y.). 1979. a. $325 (effective 1995). The P R S Group, Box 248, East Syracuse, NY 13057-0248. TEL 315-431-0511. FAX 315-431-0200. (also avail. in diskette format) ●Also available online. Vendor(s): Data-Star, Lexis-Nexis.
   Description: In-depth analysis and forecasts of political and economic conditions.

330.968   US   ISSN 1054-6138
THE P R S GROUP. COUNTRY REPORTS: SOUTH AFRICA. Key Title: South Africa (Syracuse, N.Y.). 1979. a. $325 (effective 1995). The P R S Group, Box 248, East Syracuse, NY 13057-0248. TEL 315-431-0511. FAX 315-431-0200. (also avail. in diskette format) ●Also available online. Vendor(s): Data-Star, Lexis-Nexis.
   Description: In-depth analysis and forecasts of political and economic conditions.

330.9   US   ISSN 1054-6146
THE P R S GROUP. COUNTRY REPORTS: SOUTH KOREA. Key Title: South Korea (Syracuse, N.Y.). 1979. a. $325 (effective 1995). The P R S Group, Box 248, East Syracuse, NY 13057-0248. TEL 315-431-0511. FAX 315-431-0200. (also avail. in diskette format) ●Also available online. Vendor(s): Data-Star, Lexis-Nexis.
   Description: In-depth analysis and forecasts of political and economic conditions.

330.9   US   ISSN 1054-6162
THE P R S GROUP. COUNTRY REPORTS: SRI LANKA. Key Title: Sri Lanka (Syracuse, N.Y.). 1979. a. $325 (effective 1995). The P R S Group, Box 248, East Syracuse, NY 13057-0248. TEL 315-431-0511. FAX 315-431-0200. (also avail. in diskette format) ●Also available online. Vendor(s): Data-Star, Lexis-Nexis.
   Description: In-depth analysis and forecasts of political and economic conditions.

330.9   US   ISSN 1054-6170
THE P R S GROUP. COUNTRY REPORTS: SUDAN. Key Title: Sudan (Syracuse, N.Y.). 1979. a. $325 (effective 1995). The P R S Group, Box 248, East Syracuse, NY 13057-0248. TEL 315-431-0511. FAX 315-431-0200. (also avail. in diskette format) ●Also available online. Vendor(s): Data-Star, Lexis-Nexis.
   Description: In-depth analysis and forecasts of political and economic conditions.

330.9   US   ISSN 1054-6197
THE P R S GROUP. COUNTRY REPORTS: SYRIA. Key Title: Syria (Syracuse, N.Y.). 1979. a. $325 (effective 1995). The P R S Group, Box 248, East Syracuse, NY 13057-0248. TEL 315-431-0511. FAX 315-431-0200. (also avail. in diskette format) ●Also available online. Vendor(s): Data-Star, Lexis-Nexis.
   Description: In-depth analysis and forecasts of political and economic conditions.

330.9   US   ISSN 1054-6200
THE P R S GROUP. COUNTRY REPORTS: TAIWAN. Key Title: Taiwan (Syracuse, N.Y.). 1979. a. $325 (effective 1995). The P R S Group, Box 248, East Syracuse, NY 13057-0248. TEL 315-431-0511. FAX 315-431-0200. (also avail. in diskette format) ●Also available online. Vendor(s): Data-Star, Lexis-Nexis.
   Description: In-depth analysis and forecasts of political and economic conditions.

BUSINESS AND ECONOMICS — ECONOMIC SITUATION AND CONDITIONS

330.9   US   ISSN 1054-6219
THE P R S GROUP. COUNTRY REPORTS: THAILAND. Key Title: Thailand (Syracuse, N.Y.). 1979. a. $325 (effective 1997). The P R S Group, Box 248, East Syracuse, NY 13057-0248. TEL 315-431-0511. FAX 315-431-0200. (also avail. in diskette format) ●Also available online. Vendor(s): Data-Star, Lexis-Nexis.
   Description: In-depth analysis and forecasts of political and economic conditions.

330.9   US   ISSN 1054-6227
THE P R S GROUP. COUNTRY REPORTS: TUNISIA. Key Title: Tunisia (Syracuse, N.Y.). 1979. a. $325 (effective 1995). The P R S Group, Box 248, East Syracuse, NY 13057-0248. TEL 315-431-0511. FAX 315-431-0200. (also avail. in diskette format) ●Also available online. Vendor(s): Data-Star, Lexis-Nexis.
   Description: In-depth analysis and forecasts of political and economic conditions.

330.9   US   ISSN 1054-6235
THE P R S GROUP. COUNTRY REPORTS: TURKEY. Key Title: Turkey (Syracuse, N.Y.). 1979. a. $325 (effective 1995). The P R S Group, Box 248, East Syracuse, NY 13057-0248. TEL 315-431-0511. FAX 315-431-0200. (also avail. in diskette format) ●Also available online. Vendor(s): Data-Star, Lexis-Nexis.
   Description: In-depth analysis and forecasts of political and economic conditions.

330.9   US   ISSN 1061-1304
THE P R S GROUP. COUNTRY REPORTS: UKRAINE. Key Title: Ukraine (Syracuse, N.Y.). 1992. a. $325 (effective 1995). The P R S Group, Box 248, East Syracuse, NY 13057-0248. TEL 315-431-0511. FAX 315-431-0200. (also avail. in diskette format) ●Also available online. Vendor(s): Data-Star, Lexis-Nexis.
   Supersedes in part (1984-1991): U S S R (Syracuse, N.Y.) (ISSN 1054-6243)
   Description: In-depth analysis and forecasts of political and economic conditions.

330.9   US   ISSN 1054-6251
THE P R S GROUP. COUNTRY REPORTS: UNITED ARAB EMIRATES. Key Title: United Arab Emirates (Syracuse, N.Y.). 1979. a. $325 (effective 1995). The P R S Group, Box 248, East Syracuse, NY 13057-0248. TEL 315-431-0511. FAX 315-431-0200. (also avail. in diskette format) ●Also available online. Vendor(s): Data-Star, Lexis-Nexis.
   Description: Provides in-depth analysis and forecasts of political and economic conditions.

330.9   US   ISSN 1054-6286
THE P R S GROUP. COUNTRY REPORTS: URUGUAY. Key Title: Uruguay (Syracuse, N.Y.). 1979. a. $325 (effective 1995). The P R S Group, Box 248, East Syracuse, NY 13057-0248. TEL 315-431-0511. FAX 315-431-0200. (also avail. in diskette format) ●Also available online. Vendor(s): Data-Star, Lexis-Nexis.
   Description: In-depth analysis and forecasts of political and economic conditions.

330.9   US   ISSN 1054-6294
THE P R S GROUP. COUNTRY REPORTS: VENEZUELA. Key Title: Venezuela (Syracuse, N.Y.). 1979. a. $325 (effective 1995). The P R S Group, Box 248, East Syracuse, NY 13057-0248. TEL 315-431-0511. FAX 315-431-0200. (also avail. in diskette format) ●Also available online. Vendor(s): Data-Star, Lexis-Nexis.
   Description: Provides in-depth analysis and forecasts of political and economic conditions.

330.9   US   ISSN 1058-3831
THE P R S GROUP. COUNTRY REPORTS: VIETNAM. Key Title: Vietnam (Syracuse, N.Y.). 1990. a. $325 (effective 1995). The P R S Group, Box 248, East Syracuse, NY 13057-0248. TEL 315-431-0511. FAX 315-431-0200. (also avail. in diskette format) ●Also available online. Vendor(s): Data-Star, Lexis-Nexis.
   Description: In-depth analysis and forecasts of political and economic conditions.

330.9   US   ISSN 1054-6324
THE P R S GROUP. COUNTRY REPORTS: ZAMBIA. Key Title: Zambia (Syracuse, N.Y.). 1979. a. $325 (effective 1995). The P R S Group, Box 248, East Syracuse, NY 13057-0248. TEL 315-431-0511. FAX 315-431-0200. (also avail. in diskette format) ●Also available online. Vendor(s): Data-Star, Lexis-Nexis.
   Description: In-depth analysis and forecasts of political and economic conditions.

330.9   US   ISSN 1054-6332
THE P R S GROUP. COUNTRY REPORTS: ZIMBABWE. Key Title: Zimbabwe (Syracuse, N.Y.). 1984? a. $325 (effective 1995). The P R S Group, Box 248, East Syracuse, NY 13057-0248. TEL 315-431-0511. FAX 315-431-0200. (also avail. in diskette format) ●Also available online. Vendor(s): Data-Star, Lexis-Nexis.
   Description: Offers in-depth analysis and forecasts of political and economic conditions.

330.9 967.3   US   ISSN 1067-7976
THE P R S GROUP. EXECUTIVE REPORTS: ANGOLA. Key Title: Angola (Syracuse, N.Y.). 1993. a. $110 (effective 1995). The P R S Group, Box 248, East Syracuse, NY 13057-0248. TEL 315-431-0511. FAX 315-431-0200.
   Description: Provides analysis and forecasts of political and economic conditions.

330.9   US   ISSN 1054-5247
THE P R S GROUP. EXECUTIVE REPORTS: AUSTRALIA. Key Title: Australia (Syracuse, N.Y.). 1979. a. $125 (effective 1997). The P R S Group, Box 248, East Syracuse, NY 13057-0248. TEL 315-431-0511. FAX 315-431-0200. (also avail. in diskette format) ●Also available online. Vendor(s): Data-Star, Lexis-Nexis.
   Formerly: Political Risk Services. Country Reports: Australia.
   Description: In-depth analysis and forecasts of political and economic conditions.

330.9   US   ISSN 1054-5255
THE P R S GROUP. EXECUTIVE REPORTS: AUSTRIA. Key Title: Austria (Syracuse, N.Y.). 1979. a. $125 (effective 1997). The P R S Group, Box 248, East Syracuse, NY 13057-0248. TEL 315-431-0511. FAX 315-431-0200. (also avail. in diskette format) ●Also available online. Vendor(s): Data-Star, Lexis-Nexis.
   Formerly: Political Risk Services. Country Reports: Austria.
   Description: In-depth analysis and forecasts of political and economic conditions.

330.9 954.92   US   ISSN 1067-7984
THE P R S GROUP. EXECUTIVE REPORTS: BANGLADESH. Key Title: Bangladesh (Syracuse, N.Y.). 1993. a. $125 (effective 1997). The P R S Group, Box 248, East Syracuse, NY 13057-0248. TEL 315-431-0511. FAX 315-431-0200.
   Description: Provides analysis and forecasts of political and economic conditions.

330.9   US   ISSN 1054-5263
THE P R S GROUP. EXECUTIVE REPORTS: BELGIUM. Key Title: Belgium (Syracuse, N.Y.). 1979. a. $125 (effective 1997). The P R S Group, Box 248, East Syracuse, NY 13057-0248. TEL 315-431-0511. FAX 315-431-0200. (also avail. in diskette format) ●Also available online. Vendor(s): Data-Star, Lexis-Nexis.
   Formerly: Political Risk Services. Country Reports: Belgium.
   Description: In-depth analysis and forecasts of political and economic conditions.

330.9 968.83   US   ISSN 1067-7992
THE P R S GROUP. EXECUTIVE REPORTS: BOTSWANA. Key Title: Botswana (Syracuse, N.Y.). 1993. a. $125 (effective 1997). The P R S Group, Box 248, East Syracuse, NY 13057-0248. TEL 315-431-0511. FAX 315-431-0200.
   Description: Provides analysis and forecasts of political and economic conditions.

330.9   US   ISSN 1054-531X
THE P R S GROUP. EXECUTIVE REPORTS: CANADA. Key Title: Canada (Syracuse, N.Y.). 1979. a. $125 (effective 1997). The P R S Group, Box 248, East Syracuse, NY 13057-0248. TEL 315-431-0511. FAX 315-431-0200. (also avail. in diskette format) ●Also available online. Vendor(s): Data-Star, Lexis-Nexis.
   Formerly: Political Risk Services. Country Reports: Canada.
   Description: In-depth analysis and forecasts of political and economic conditions.

330.9 967.24   US   ISSN 1067-8018
THE P R S GROUP. EXECUTIVE REPORTS: CONGO (BRAZZAVILLE). Key Title: Congo (Syracuse, N.Y.). 1993. a. $125 (effective 1997). The P R S Group, Box 248, East Syracuse, NY 13057-0248. TEL 315-431-0511. FAX 315-431-0200.
   Description: Provides analysis and forecasts of political and economic conditions.

330.9   US   ISSN 1067-8026
THE P R S GROUP. EXECUTIVE REPORTS: CUBA. Key Title: Cuba (Syracuse, N.Y.). 1993. a. $125 (effective 1997). The P R S Group, Box 248, East Syracuse, NY 13057-0248. TEL 315-431-0511. FAX 315-431-0200.
   Description: Provides analysis and forecasts of political and economic conditions.

330.9   US   ISSN 1054-5379
THE P R S GROUP. EXECUTIVE REPORTS: DENMARK. Key Title: Denmark (Syracuse, N.Y.). 1979. a. $125 (effective 1997). The P R S Group, Box 248, East Syracuse, NY 13057-0248. TEL 315-431-0511. FAX 315-431-0200. (also avail. in diskette format) ●Also available online. Vendor(s): Data-Star, Lexis-Nexis.
   Formerly: Political Risk Services. Country Reports: Denmark.
   Description: In-depth analysis and forecasts of political and economic conditions.

330.9   US   ISSN 1054-5506
THE P R S GROUP. EXECUTIVE REPORTS: FINLAND. Key Title: Finland (Syracuse, N.Y.). 1979. a. $125 (effective 1997). The P R S Group, Box 248, East Syracuse, NY 13057-0248. TEL 315-431-0511. FAX 315-431-0200. (also avail. in diskette format) ●Also available online. Vendor(s): Data-Star, Lexis-Nexis.
   Formerly: Political Risk Services. Country Reports: Finland.
   Description: In-depth analysis and forecasts of political and economic conditions.

330.9   US   ISSN 1054-5514
THE P R S GROUP. EXECUTIVE REPORTS: FRANCE. Key Title: France (Syracuse, N.Y.). 1979. a. $125 (effective 1997). The P R S Group, Box 248, East Syracuse, NY 13057-0248. TEL 315-431-0511. FAX 315-431-0200. (also avail. in diskette format) ●Also available online. Vendor(s): Data-Star, Lexis-Nexis.
   Formerly: Political Risk Services. Country Reports: France.
   Description: In-depth analysis and forecasts of political and economic conditions.

330.9   US   ISSN 1056-4721
THE P R S GROUP. EXECUTIVE REPORTS: GERMANY. Key Title: Germany (Syracuse, N.Y.). 1991. a. $125 (effective 1997). The P R S Group, Box 248, East Syracuse, NY 13057-0248. TEL 315-431-0511. FAX 315-431-0200. (also avail. in diskette format) ●Also available online. Vendor(s): Data-Star, Lexis-Nexis.
   Formerly: Political Risk Services. Country Reports: Germany.
   Description: In-depth analysis and forecasts of political and economic conditions.

330.9 966.7   US   ISSN 1067-8034
THE P R S GROUP. EXECUTIVE REPORTS: GHANA. Key Title: Ghana (Syracuse, N.Y.). 1993. a. $125 (effective 1997). The P R S Group, Box 248, East Syracuse, NY 13057-0248. TEL 315-431-0511. FAX 315-431-0200.
   Description: Provides analysis and forecasts of political and economic conditions.

BUSINESS AND ECONOMICS — ECONOMIC SITUATION AND CONDITIONS

330.9   US   ISSN 1054-5530
THE P R S GROUP. EXECUTIVE REPORTS: GREECE. Key Title: Greece (Syracuse, N.Y.). 1979. a. $125 (effective 1997). The P R S Group, Box 248, East Syracuse, NY 13057-0248. TEL 315-431-0511. FAX 315-431-0200. (also avail. in diskette format)
●Also available online. Vendor(s): Data-Star, Lexis-Nexis.
Formerly: Political Risk Services. Country Reports: Greece.
Description: In-depth analysis and forecasts of political and economic conditions.

330.9 988   US   ISSN 1067-8042
THE P R S GROUP. EXECUTIVE REPORTS: GUYANA. Key Title: Guyana (Syracuse, N.Y.). 1993. a. $125 (effective 1997). The P R S Group, Box 248, East Syracuse, NY 13057-0248. TEL 315-431-0511. FAX 315-431-0200.
Description: Provides analysis and forecasts of political and economic conditions.

330.9   US   ISSN 1054-5646
THE P R S GROUP. EXECUTIVE REPORTS: IRELAND. Key Title: Ireland (Syracuse, N.Y.). 1979. a. $125 (effective 1997). The P R S Group, Box 248, East Syracuse, NY 13057-0248. TEL 315-431-0511. FAX 315-431-0200. (also avail. in diskette format)
●Also available online. Vendor(s): Data-Star, Lexis-Nexis.
Formerly: Political Risk Services. Country Reports: Ireland.
Description: In-depth analysis and forecasts of political and economic conditions.

330.9   US   ISSN 1054-5654
THE P R S GROUP. EXECUTIVE REPORTS: ITALY. Key Title: Italy (Syracuse, N.Y.). 1979. a. $125 (effective 1997). The P R S Group, Box 248, East Syracuse, NY 13057-0248. TEL 315-431-0511. FAX 315-431-0200. (also avail. in diskette format)
●Also available online. Vendor(s): Data-Star, Lexis-Nexis.
Formerly: Political Risk Services. Country Reports: Italy.
Description: In-depth analysis and forecasts of political and economic conditions.

330.9   US   ISSN 1054-5697
THE P R S GROUP. EXECUTIVE REPORTS: JAPAN. Key Title: Japan (Syracuse, N.Y.). 1979. a. $125 (effective 1997). The P R S Group, Box 248, East Syracuse, NY 13057-0248. TEL 315-431-0511. FAX 315-431-0200. (also avail. in diskette format)
●Also available online. Vendor(s): Data-Star, Lexis-Nexis.
Formerly: Political Risk Services. Country Reports: Japan.
Description: In-depth analysis and forecasts of political and economic conditions.

330.9 959.1   US
THE P R S GROUP. EXECUTIVE REPORTS: MYANMAR. 1993. a. $110 (effective 1997). The P R S Group, Box 248, East Syracuse, NY 13057-0248. TEL 315-431-0511. FAX 605-431-0200.
Formerly: Political Risk Services. Executive Reports: Burma (ISSN 1067-800X)
Description: Provides analysis and forecasts of political and economic conditions.

330.9   US   ISSN 1054-5751
THE P R S GROUP. EXECUTIVE REPORTS: NETHERLANDS. Key Title: Netherlands (Syracuse, N.Y.). 1979. a. $125 (effective 1997). The P R S Group, Box 248, East Syracuse, NY 13057-0248. TEL 315-431-0511. FAX 315-431-0200. (also avail. in diskette format)
●Also available online. Vendor(s): Data-Star, Lexis-Nexis.
Formerly: Political Risk Services. Country Reports: Netherlands.
Description: In-depth analysis and forecasts of political and economic conditions.

330.9   US   ISSN 1054-5778
THE P R S GROUP. EXECUTIVE REPORTS: NEW ZEALAND. Key Title: New Zealand (Syracuse, N.Y.). 1979. a. $125 (effective 1997). The P R S Group, Box 248, East Syracuse, NY 13057-0248. TEL 315-431-0511. FAX 315-431-0200. (also avail. in diskette format)
●Also available online. Vendor(s): Data-Star, Lexis-Nexis.
Formerly: Political Risk Services. Country Reports: New Zealand.
Description: In-depth analysis and forecasts of political and economic conditions.

330.9   US   ISSN 1054-5794
THE P R S GROUP. EXECUTIVE REPORTS: NORWAY. Key Title: Norway (Syracuse, N.Y.). 1979. a. $125 (effective 1997). The P R S Group, Box 248, East Syracuse, NY 13057-0248. TEL 315-431-0511. FAX 315-431-0200. (also avail. in diskette format)
●Also available online. Vendor(s): Data-Star, Lexis-Nexis.
Formerly: Political Risk Services. Country Reports: Norway.
Description: In-depth analysis and forecasts of political and economic conditions.

330.9 995.3   US   ISSN 1067-8050
THE P R S GROUP. EXECUTIVE REPORTS: PAPUA NEW GUINEA. Key Title: Papua New Guinea (Syracuse, N.Y.). 1993. a. $125 (effective 1997). The P R S Group, Box 248, East Syracuse, NY 13057-0248. TEL 315-431-0511. FAX 315-431-0200.
Description: Provides analysis and forecasts of political and economic conditions.

330.9 989.2   US   ISSN 1067-8069
THE P R S GROUP. EXECUTIVE REPORTS: PARAGUAY. Key Title: Paraguay (Syracuse, N.Y.). 1993. a. $125 (effective 1997). The P R S Group, Box 248, East Syracuse, NY 13057-0248. TEL 315-431-0511. FAX 315-431-0200.
Description: Provides analysis and forecasts of political and economic conditions.

330.9   US   ISSN 1054-6081
THE P R S GROUP. EXECUTIVE REPORTS: PORTUGAL. Key Title: Portugal (Syracuse, N.Y.). 1979. a. $125 (effective 1997). The P R S Group, Box 248, East Syracuse, NY 13057-0248. TEL 315-431-0511. FAX 315-431-0200. (also avail. in diskette format)
●Also available online. Vendor(s): Data-Star, Lexis-Nexis.
Formerly: Political Risk Services. Country Reports: Portugal.
Description: In-depth analysis and forecasts of political and economic conditions.

330.9   US   ISSN 1054-609X
THE P R S GROUP. EXECUTIVE REPORTS: PUERTO RICO. Key Title: Puerto Rico (Syracuse, N.Y.). 1979. a. $125 (effective 1997). The P R S Group, Box 248, East Syracuse, NY 13057-0248. TEL 315-431-0511. FAX 315-431-0200. (also avail. in diskette format)
●Also available online. Vendor(s): Data-Star, Lexis-Nexis.
Formerly: Political Risk Services. Country Reports: Puerto Rico.
Description: In-depth analysis and forecasts of political and economic conditions.

330.9 953   US   ISSN 1067-8077
THE P R S GROUP. EXECUTIVE REPORTS: QATAR. Key Title: Qatar (Syracuse, N.Y.). 1993. a. $125 (effective 1997). The P R S Group, Box 248, East Syracuse, NY 13057-0248. TEL 315-431-0511. FAX 315-431-0200.
Description: Provides analysis and forecasts of political and economic conditions.

330.9   US   ISSN 1054-6154
THE P R S GROUP. EXECUTIVE REPORTS: SPAIN. Key Title: Spain (Syracuse, N.Y.). 1979. a. $125 (effective 1997). The P R S Group, Box 248, East Syracuse, NY 13057-0248. TEL 315-431-0511. FAX 315-431-0200. (also avail. in diskette format)
●Also available online. Vendor(s): Data-Star, Lexis-Nexis.
Formerly: Political Risk Services. Country Reports: Spain.
Description: In-depth analysis and forecasts of political and economic conditions.

330.9 988   US   ISSN 1067-8085
THE P R S GROUP. EXECUTIVE REPORTS: SURINAME. Key Title: Suriname (Syracuse, N.Y.). 1993. a. $125 (effective 1997). The P R S Group, Box 248, East Syracuse, NY 13057-0248. TEL 315-431-0511. FAX 315-431-0200.
Description: Provides analysis and forecasts of political and economic conditions.

330.9   US   ISSN 1054-6189
THE P R S GROUP. EXECUTIVE REPORTS: SWEDEN. Key Title: Sweden (Syracuse, N.Y.). 1979. a. $125 (effective 1997). The P R S Group, Box 248, East Syracuse, NY 13057-0248. TEL 315-431-0511. FAX 315-431-0200. (also avail. in diskette format)
●Also available online. Vendor(s): Data-Star, Lexis-Nexis.
Formerly: Political Risk Services. Country Reports: Sweden.
Description: In-depth analysis and forecasts of political and economic conditions.

330.9   US   ISSN 1067-8093
THE P R S GROUP. EXECUTIVE REPORTS: SWITZERLAND. Key Title: Switzerland (Syracuse, N.Y.). 1993. a. $125 (effective 1997). The P R S Group, Box 248, East Syracuse, NY 13057-0248. TEL 315-431-0511. FAX 315-431-0200.
Description: Provides analysis and forecasts of political and economic conditions.

330.9   US   ISSN 1067-8107
THE P R S GROUP. EXECUTIVE REPORTS: TRINIDAD & TOBAGO. Key Title: Trinidad & Tobago (Syracuse, N.Y.). 1993. a. $125 (effective 1997). The P R S Group, Box 248, East Syracuse, NY 13057-0248. TEL 315-431-0511. FAX 315-431-0200.
Description: Provides analysis and forecasts of political and economic conditions.

330.9   US   ISSN 1054-626X
THE P R S GROUP. EXECUTIVE REPORTS: UNITED KINGDOM. Key Title: United Kingdom (Syracuse, N.Y.). 1979. a. $125 (effective 1997). The P R S Group, Box 248, East Syracuse, NY 13057-0248. TEL 315-431-0511. FAX 315-431-0200. (also avail. in diskette format)
●Also available online. Vendor(s): Data-Star, Lexis-Nexis.
Formerly: Political Risk Services. Country Reports: United Kingdom.
Description: In-depth analysis and forecasts of political and economic conditions.

330.9   US   ISSN 1054-6278
THE P R S GROUP. EXECUTIVE REPORTS: UNITED STATES. Key Title: United States (Syracuse, N.Y.). 1979. a. $125 (effective 1997). The P R S Group, Box 248, East Syracuse, NY 13057-0248. TEL 315-431-0511. FAX 315-431-0200. (also avail. in diskette format)
●Also available online. Vendor(s): Data-Star, Lexis-Nexis.
Formerly: Political Risk Services. Country Reports: United States.
Description: In-depth analysis and forecasts of political and economic conditions.

330.9   US   ISSN 1067-8115
THE P R S GROUP. EXECUTIVE REPORTS: YEMEN. Key Title: Yemen (Syracuse, N.Y.). 1993. a. $125 (effective 1997). The P R S Group, Box 248, East Syracuse, NY 13057-0248. TEL 315-431-0511. FAX 315-431-0200.
Description: Provides analysis and forecasts of political and economic conditions.

330.9   UK   ISSN 1361-374X
H1
PACIFIC ECONOMIC REVIEW. 3/yr. £85($136) (effective 1997). (Hong Kong Economic Association HK) Blackwell Publishers Ltd., 108 Cowley Rd., Oxford OX4 1JF, England. TEL 44-1865-791100. FAX 44-1865-791347. E-mail: jnlinfo@blackwellpublishers.co.uk; URL: http://www.blackwellpublishers.co.uk. (N. American subscr. to: Blackwell Publishers, Journals Marketing, 238 Main St., Cambridge, MA 02142. TEL 617-547-7110. FAX 617-547-0789) Eds. Eden S.H. Yu, Kenneth S Chan. **Document type:** academic/scholarly publicatio —BLDSC (6329.187000). CCC.
Description: Analyzes economic issues in the Pacific Rim area.

BUSINESS AND ECONOMICS — ECONOMIC SITUATION AND CONDITIONS

330   PK   ISSN 0078-8082
PAKISTAN ECONOMIC SURVEY. (Text in English) 1962. a. price varies. Finance Division, Islamabad, Pakistan. (Dist. by: Manager of Publications, Government of Pakistan, 2nd Fl., Ahmad Chamber, Tariq Rd., P.E.C.H.S., Karachi 29, Pakistan) index.

330   PK   ISSN 0254-9204
HB1
PAKISTAN JOURNAL OF APPLIED ECONOMICS. (Text in English) 1982. s-a. Rs.150($40) to individuals; institutions Rs.200($60). University of Karachi, Applied Economics Research Centre, P.O. Box 8403, Karachi 75270, Pakistan. TEL 92-21-474749. FAX 92-21-4969729. Ed. Mohammad Akbar. adv.; bk.rev.; charts; illus.; stat. circ. 1,500. (reprint service avail.) **Indexed:** C.R.E.J., IDA, P.A.I.S., Per.Islam. (1988-), Rice Abstr., World Agri.Econ.& Rural Sociol.Abstr. **Document type:** academic/scholarly publication.
—BLDSC (6340.896000).
    Supersedes (1974-1982): Journal of Economic Studies; Which was formerly: Federal Economic Review (ISSN 0428-1128)
    Refereed Serial

330.9   PN
PANAMA. MINISTERIO DE PLANIFICACION Y POLITICA ECONOMICA. INFORME ECONOMICO. a. Ministerio de Planificacion y Politica Economica, Direccion de Planificacion Economica y Social, Panama. stat.

PANEUROPA DEUTSCHLAND. see *POLITICAL SCIENCE — International Relations*

330.9   MX   ISSN 0479-4346
PANORAMA ECONOMICO. English edition: Economic Panorama (ISSN 0013-0214) 1966. bi-m. free. Bancomer, Sociedad Nacional Credito, Grupo Investigaciones Economicas, Universidad Avenue 1200, C.P. 03339, Mexico 12, D.F., Mexico. TEL 534-00-34 ext. 5245. Ed. Eduardo Millan Lozano. charts; stat. circ. 5,000.
    Description: Covers the Mexican economy, with emphasis on the automotive and textile industries.

330.9   SP   ISSN 0210-9107
HC381
PAPELES DE ECONOMIA ESPANOLA. 1980. q. 7500 ptas. (foreign 9000 ptas.) (effective 1997). Fundacion de las Cajas de Ahorros Confederadas para la Investigacion Economica y Social, Padre Damian, 48, 28036 Madrid, Spain. TEL 34-1-3596158. FAX 34-1-3504959. (Subscr. to: Juan Hurtado Mendoza 19, 28036 Madrid, Spain. TEL 34-1-3504400. FAX 34-1-3508040) Ed. Fernando Gonzalez Olivares; Pub. Victorio Valle Sanchez. R&P contact: Fernando Gonzalez Olivares. circ. 10,000. (also avail. in microfiche; back issues avail.) **Indexed:** SCIMP (1989-). **Document type:** academic/scholarly publication.
—BLDSC (6358.493000); CINDOC.
    Description: Offers information on the economic problems of Spain through research done by the foundation.

338   BL   ISSN 0031-174X
PARANA EM PAGINAS.* vol.4, 1969. m. free. Rua Augusto Stellfeld, 70 Curitiba, Parana, Brazil. Ed. Candido Gomes Chagas. adv.; charts; illus.; stat.

338   UK
PARLIAMENTARY AND COMMON MARKET NEWS BULLETIN. 1947. w. £37. Parliamentary and Common Market News Services, 19 Kingsdowne Rd., Surbiton KT6 6JZ, England. **Document type:** bulletin.

PATRIKA. see *POLITICAL SCIENCE — International Relations*

330.9   PR
PENSAMIENTO CRITICO; una revista distinta de las izquierda puertorriquena. bi-m. Pensamiento Critico, P.O. Box 29918, 65 de Infanteria, Rio Piedras, PR 00928.

330.9   SP   ISSN 0212-0208
HC121
PENSAMIENTO IBEROAMERICANO; revista de economia politica. 1982. s-a. 8500 ptas. ($70 in Latin America; Europe $85; elsewhere $90) for 4 nos. to individuals; institutions 9000 ptas. ($80 in Latin America; Europe $95; elsewhere $100) for 4 nos. (effective 1993-94). (Sociedad Estatal Quinto Centenario) Instituto de Cooperacion Iberoamericana, Avda. de los Reyes Catolicos, 4, 28040 Madrid, Spain. TEL 91-583-83-91. FAX 91-583-83-10. TELEX 42134 CIBC E. (Co-sponsor: United Nations Comision Economica para America Latina y el Caribe) Dir. Osvaldo Sunkel. adv.; bk.rev. circ. 4,000. **Indexed:** Hisp.Amer.Per.Ind. (1982-), IBR, Int.Lab.Doc., Int.Polit.Sci.Abstr., J.of Econ.Lit. **Document type:** academic/scholarly publication.
—CINDOC; SWETS.
    Description: Covers articles and research papers in the field of economics, as it pertains to Spain and the rest of the world.

330.9   US   ISSN 1052-5254
HC107.T4
THE PERRYMAN TEXAS LETTER. 1990. m. $79. Texas Economic Publishers, Inc., 510 N. Valley Mills Dr., Ste. 300, Waco, TX 76710-6076. TEL 254-751-7411. FAX 254-751-7855. E-mail: perryman@acm.org; URL: http://www.acm.org/~perryman. (Subscr. to: Superior Fulfillment, Box 6256, Duluth, MN 55806-6256. TEL 800-949-9049) Ed. Nancy Cunningham. charts; stat. circ. 2,000. (looseleaf format) **Document type:** newsletter.
●Also available on CD-ROM.
    Incorporates: Texas Economic Forecast (ISSN 0748-0008); Which was formerly (1982-1984): Trends in the Texas Economy (ISSN 0737-3317)
    Description: Analyzes the political, social, and economic trends in Texas, bringing readers an insider's perspective on the latest news from job trends to legislative activity.

330.9   US
HD28
PERSPECTIVES ON BUSINESS AND GLOBAL CHANGE. 1987. q. $64. Berrett-Koehler Publishers, Inc., 450 Sansome St., Ste. 1200, San Francisco, CA 94111-3320. TEL 415-288-0260. FAX 415-362-2512. E-mail: bkpub@aol.com. Ed. Maya Porter. adv. contact: Robin Donovan. bk.rev.; circ. 400 (paid). **Document type:** academic/scholarly publication.
    Formerly: World Business Academy Perspectives (ISSN 1061-9917)
    Description: Discusses how business can be a creative, positive force for resolving the pressing issues facing global society today.

330.9   PE   ISSN 1018-0621
PERU ECONOMICO. 1979. m. $560 (effective 1997). Apoyo Comunicaciones, S.A., Juan de la Fuente 625, Lima 18, Peru. TEL 51-14-445555. FAX 51-14-445240. Ed. Augusto Alvarez-Rodrich. bk.rev. circ. 2,500. **Indexed:** Key to Econ.Sci.
    Formerly (until 1986): Peruvian Quarterly Report.

PHARMACEUTICAL COMPANIES ANALYSIS. see *PHARMACY AND PHARMACOLOGY*

330.5   US   ISSN 0744-3587
PHILADELPHIA BUSINESS JOURNAL. 1982. w. $52. American City Business Joournals, Inc., 505 Powell St., Austin, TX 78703-5121. (Subscr.to: 400 Market St., Ste. 300, Philadelphia, PA 19106. TEL 215-238-5106. FAX 215-238-1446) Ed. Jack Roberts; Pub. Lyn Kremer. adv.: B&W page $3640. circ. 13,990 (paid). (also avail. in microfilm) **Indexed:** Tr.& Indus.Ind. **Document type:** consumer publication.
●Also available online. Vendor(s): CompuServe, Inc., Data-Star, Dow Jones News Retrieval, Information Access Co., Knight-Ridder Information, Inc., Lexis-Nexis, UMI.
—UMI. **CCC.**

330.9   CC   ISSN 0379-2870
PHILIPPINE LETTER. (Text in English) 1978. s-m. $96. Asia Letter Group, G.P.O. Box 10874, Hong Kong, People's Republic of China. TEL 852-526-2950. FAX 852-526-7131. TELEX HX 61166 HKNW. (US subscr. to: Box 88189, Los Angeles, CA 90009-8189) Ed. Charles R. Smith. bk.rev. **Document type:** newsletter.

PHYLLIS SCHLAFLY REPORT. see *WOMEN'S INTERESTS*

PICENTINO. see *AGRICULTURE*

330.9   NO   ISSN 0805-083X
HD4811
PLAN; tidsskrift for regional utvikling, arbeidsmarked og samfunnsplanlegging. 1945. bi-m. NOK 505 in Nordic countries; elsewhere $100 (effective 1997). Scandinavian University Press, P.O. Box 2959 Toeyen, N-0608 Oslo, Norway. TEL 47-22-57-54-00. FAX 47-22-57-53-53. E-mail: mail@scup.no; URL: http://www.scup.no. (U.S. addr.: 875 Massachusetts Ave., Ste. 84, Cambridge, MA 02139. TEL 617-497-6515. FAX 617-354-6875) Ed. Andreas Hompland. adv.; bk.rev.; index. (tabloid format) **Indexed:** Geo.Abstr. **Document type:** academic/scholarly publication.
    Former titles (until 1995): Plan og Arbeid (ISSN 0032-0609); Arbeidsmarkedet (ISSN 0332-7043)
    Description: Focuses on community development, regional planning and employment.

330.9   UK   ISSN 0308-7751
PLANNING CONSUMER MARKETS.* 1975. q. £1100($1650) (effective 1994). Henley Centre for Forecasting Ltd., 9 Bridewell Pl., Blackfriars, London EC4V 6AY, England. TEL 0171-353-9961. FAX 0171-353-2899. Ed. Richard Woods. charts; stat. **Document type:** trade publication.
●Also available online.
    Description: Analyzes and forecasts key macroeconomic and consumer trends affecting U.K. markets.

331.11   US
PLANNING GUIDE: STATEWIDE AND NINE SERVICE DELIVERY AREAS INCLUDING BRIDGEPORT - NORWALK - STAMFORD - VALLEY. 1979. a. free. Labor Department, Employment Security Division, 200 Folly Brook Blvd., Wethersfield, CT 06109. TEL 860-566-3462. FAX 860-566-7963. Ed. John Tirinzonie. circ. 350. **Document type:** government publication.
    Former titles: Planning Guide: Bridgeport - Norwalk - Stamford - Valley Service Delivery Area; Annual Planning Information: Bridgeport - Norwalk - Stamford - Valley Service Delivery Area; Annual Planning Information for Stamford Labor Market Area; Stamford Annual Planning Information.

330.9   GW
DER PLATOW BRIEF. 1946. 3/w. DM.846. Verlag Aktuelle Information GmbH, Stuttgarterstr. 25-29, 60329 Frankfurt a.M., Germany. TEL 49-69-2426390. FAX 49-69-236909. bk.rev. **Document type:** trade publication.

330.9   GW
PLATOW PROGNOSE. 1950. a. DM.73. Verlag Aktuelle Information GmbH, Stuttgarterstr. 25-29, 60329 Frankfurt a.M., Germany. TEL 49-69-2426390. FAX 49-69-236909. **Document type:** trade publication.

330   PL   ISSN 0032-2849
HC340.3.A1
POLISH ECONOMIC SURVEY. German edition: Polnischer Wirtschaftsanzeiger. French edition: Revue de l'Economie Polonaise. Russian edition: Vestnik Pol'skoi Ekonomiki. (Text in English) 1961. fortn. $21.60. AGPOL - Polexportpress, Ul. Kerbedzia 4, 00-957 Warsaw, Poland. (Dist. by: Ars Polona, Krakowskie Przedmiescie 7, Warsaw, Poland) Ed. Danuta Gasiorowska. bk.rev.; stat. circ. 6,000.

330.9   IT   ISSN 1120-9496
HB7
POLITICA ECONOMICA. 1985. 3/yr. Lit.120000 (foreign Lit.180000) (effective 1997). Societa Editrice Il Mulino, Strada Maggiore, 37, 40125 Bologna, Italy. TEL 39-51-256011. FAX 39-51-256034. E-mail: riviste@mulino.it. Ed. Paolo Bosi. adv. contact: M. Luisa Vezzali. index. circ. 1,000. (back issues avail.) **Indexed:** J.of Econ.Lit.

BUSINESS AND ECONOMICS — ECONOMIC SITUATION AND CONDITIONS

330.9 371.2   IT   ISSN 0393-7844
POLITICA MERIDIONALISTA; rivista mensile di cultura, economia e informazione. 1972. m. L.25000 (foreign L.40000). Politica Meridionalista Editrice, Corso Umberto, 22, 80138 Naples, Italy. TEL 39-81-5527744. FAX 39-81-5536574. E-mail: pisanti@mbox.vol.it. Ed. Antonio Pisanti; Pub. Nicola Squitieri. R&P contact: Nicola Squitieri. adv. contact: Antonio Pisanti. bk.rev. circ. 5,000. (back issues avail.) **Document type:** newspaper.
    Description: Deals with Italian culture, the Italian economy and current events, specifically focused on southern Italy.

327   US   ISSN 1075-6183
POLITICAL RISK SERVICES ON C D - R O M. 12/yr. $8995 (effective 1995). The P R S Group, Box 248, East Syracuse, NY 13057-0248. TEL 315-431-0511. FAX 315-431-0200.
● Available only on CD-ROM.

330.9   EC
PONTIFICIA UNIVERSIDAD CATOLICA DEL ECUADOR. INSTITUTO DE INVESTIGACIONES ECONOMICAS. DOCUMENTOS. 1983. 3/yr. Pontificia Universidad Catolica del Ecuador, Instituto de Investigaciones Economicas, Casilla 17012184, Quito, Ecuador. FAX 593-2567117. adv.

POPULATION RESEARCH AND POLICY REVIEW. see *POPULATION STUDIES*

330.9   CG
PORTEFEUILLE; revue des entreprises. 1971. irreg. Department du Portefeuille, B.P. 3473, Kinhasa-Gombe, Democratic Republic of the Congo. Ed. Atunaku Adunagow. **Indexed:** P.A.I.S.

PORTLAND ALLIANCE. see *LABOR UNIONS*

330.9   US   ISSN 1060-586X
HC335
POST-SOVIET AFFAIRS. 1985. 4/yr. $229 in N. America; elsewhere $239 (effective 1998). V.H. Winston & Son, Inc., c/o Bellwether Publishing, Ltd., 8640 Guilford Rd., Ste. 200, Columbia, MD 21046. TEL 410-290-8726. FAX 410-290-8728. E-mail: bellpub@bellpub.com. (Co-sponsors: American Council of Learned Societies; Social Science Research Council) Ed. George Breslauer. abstr.; charts; illus.; stat.; index. circ. 500. (back issues avail.) **Indexed:** ASCA, ASSIA, Curr.Cont., Int.Polit.Sci.Abstr., J.of Econ.Lit., SSCI. **Document type:** academic/scholarly publication.
    —BLDSC (6559.600000); Genuine Article; SWETS; UnCover. CCC.
    Formerly (until 1992): Soviet Economy (ISSN 0882-6994)

330.9   YU   ISSN 0353-1163
PREGLED SVETSKE PRIVREDE/WORLD ECONOMY SURVEY. 1986. bi-m. 720 din. Institut za Medjunarodnu Politiku i Privredu - Institute of International Politics and Economics, Makedonska 25, P.O. Box 750, 11000 Belgrade, Yugoslavia. Ed. Milan Vojnovic.

330.9   AG   ISSN 0032-7433
PRENSA CONFIDENCIAL. 1966. w. Arg.$5500($25) Prensa Confidencial, Corrientes 1894, No. 1, Buenos Aires, Argentina. (Or: Carlos Pellegrini 1337, Piso 7, Buenos Aires, Argentina) Ed. Jorge Vago. circ. 6,000. (looseleaf format)

330.968   SA
PRESCON SOUTH AFRICAN NEWSLETTER. 1977. m. $100 (effective through Oct. 1997). Prescon Publishing Corporation (Pty) Ltd, P.O. Box 84004, Greenside 2034, South Africa. TEL 27-11-646-9750. FAX 27-11-646-4617. E-mail: prescon@aztec.co.za. Eds. Keith Campbell, Leon J. Kok. **Document type:** newsletter.
    Formerly: South African Newsletter.
    Description: Information, analysis and comment on political, economic and sociological issues relating to South Africa.

330.9 658   BE   ISSN 0779-8881
PRESENCES IN BUSINESS. (Text in French) 1960. q. 620 Fr. Association Royale des Ingenieurs, Commercieux, Licencies et Docteurs de Mons-Warocque (A.I.C.M.), 438 av. Louise, Box 12, B-1050 Brussels, Belgium. FAX 02-6487366. Ed. Michel Rousille. adv.; bk.rev. circ. 2,500.
    Formerly (until 1990): Presences (ISSN 0779-8873)

THE PRESIDENT. see *BUSINESS AND ECONOMICS — Management*

330.9   FR
PREVISIONS GLISSANTES DETAILLEES. (In 42 vols.) 1959. a. 7000 F. per vol.; 50000 F. per set (effective 1997). B I P E Conseil, L'Atrium - 6 Place Abel Gance, 92652 Boulogne-Billancourt Cedex, France. TEL 33-1-46944522. FAX 33-1-46944599. E-mail: 100332.644@compuserve.com. charts; stat. circ. 450.
    Supersedes: Economie Francaise en Perspectives Sectorielles (Vols. 1-5); Prevision a Un An de l'Economie Francaise; Economie Francaise consisted of 5 vols.: Vol.1: Donnees d'Encadrement; Vol.2: Filiere Agro-Alimentaire, Industrie de Consommation; Which was formerly: Industries de Biens de Consommation; Vol.3: Industries d'Equipement; Vol.4: Energie et Industries Intermediaires; Which was formerly: Industries de Biens Intermediaires; Vol.5: Filiere Batiment, Travaux Publics, Materiaux et Produits de Construction; Which was formerly: Filiere Batiment, Genie Civil, Materiaux de Construction.

330.9   FR
PREVISIONS GLISSANTES DETAILLEES EN PERSPECTIVES A MOYEN TERME. (In series of 42 vols.) 1959. s-a. 6000 F. per vol.; 50000 F. per set. Bureau d'Informations et de Previsions Economiques, Axe Seine 21, 12 rue Rouget de Lisle, 92442 Issy les Moulineaux Cedex, France. TEL 1-46-62-33-00. FAX 1-46-62-62-20. TELEX 631 586 F. charts; stat.
    Supersedes in part: Economie Francaise en Perspectives Sectorielles (Vols.1-5); Which supersedes in part: Prevision a Un An de l'Economie Francaise.

330.9   FR
PREVISIONS GLISSANTES DETAILLEES EN PERSPECTIVES MACROECONOMIQUES A COURT ET MOYEN TERME (YEAR). (In series of 42 vols.) 1959. a. 7000 F. per vol.; 50000 F. per set (effective 1997). B I P E Conseil, L'Atrium - 6 Place Abel Gance, 92652 Boulogne-Billancourt Cedex, France. TEL 33-1-46944522. FAX 33-1-46944599. E-mail: 100332.644@compuserve.com. charts; stat.
    Supersedes in part: Economie Francaise en Perspectives Sectorielles (Vols.1-5); Which supersedes in part: Prevision a Un An de l'Economie Francaise.

330.9   FR
PREVISIONS GLISSANTES DETAILLEES EN PERSPECTIVES SECTORIELLES (VOL.1): AGRICULTURE. (In series of 42 vols.) 1959. a. 7000 F. per vol.; 50000 F. per set (effective 1997). B I P E Conseil, L'Atrium - 6 Place Abel Gance, 92652 Boulogne-Billancourt Cedex, France. TEL 33-1-46944522. FAX 33-1-46944599. E-mail: 100332.644@compuserve.com. charts; stat.
    Supersedes in part: Economie Francaise en Perspectives Sectorielles (Vols.1-5); Which supersedes in part: Prevision a Un An de l'Economie Francaise.

338   FR
PREVISIONS GLISSANTES DETAILLEES EN PERSPECTIVES SECTORIELLES (VOL.2): INDUSTRIES AGRO-ALIMENTAIRES. (In series of 42 vols.) 1959. a. 7000 F. per vol.; 50000 F. per set (effective 1997). B I P E Conseil, L'Atrium - 6 Place Abel Gance, 92652 Bulogne-Billancourt Cedex, France. TEL 33-1-46944522. FAX 33-1-46944599. E-mail: 100332.644@compuserve.com. charts; stat.
    Supersedes in part: Economie Francaise en Perspectives Sectorielles (Vols.1-5); Which supersedes in part: Prevision a Un An de l'Economie Francaise.

338 685   FR
PREVISIONS GLISSANTES DETAILLEES EN PERSPECTIVES SECTORIELLES (VOL.3): TEXTILE - HABILLEMENT - CUIR. (In series of 42 vols.) 1959. a. 7000 F. per vol.; 50000 F. per set (effective 1997). B I P E Conseil, L'Atrium - 6 Place Abel Gance, 92652 Boulogne-Billancourt Cedex, France. TEL 33-1-46944522. FAX 33-1-46944599. E-mail: 100332.644@compuserve.com. charts; stat.
    Supersedes in part: Economie Francaise en Perspectives Sectorielles (Vols.1-5); Which supersedes in part: Prevision a Un An de l'Economie Francaise.

330.9 645   FR
PREVISIONS GLISSANTES DETAILLEES EN PERSPECTIVES SECTORIELLES (VOL.4): INDUSTRIES DU BOIS ET DE L'AMEUBLEMENT. (In series of 42 vols.) 1959. a. 7000 F. per vol.; 50000 F. per set (effective 1997). B I P E Conseil, L'Atrium - 6 Place Abel Gance, 92652 Boulogne-Billancourt Cedex, France. TEL 33-1-46944522. FAX 33-1-46944599. E-mail: 100332.644@compuserve.com. charts; stat.
    Supersedes in part: Economie Francaise en Perspectives Sectorielles (Vols.1-5); Which supersedes in part: Prevision a Un An de l'Economie Francaise.

338 621.9   FR
PREVISIONS GLISSANTES DETAILLEES EN PERSPECTIVES SECTORIELLES (VOL.5): CONSTRUCTION DE MACHINES. (In series of 42 vols.) 1959. a. 7000 F. per vol.; 50000 F. per set (effective 1997). B I P E Conseil, L'Atrium - 6 Place Abel Gance, 92652 Boulogne-Billancourt Cedex, France. TEL 33-1-46944522. FAX 33-1-46944599. E-mail: 100332.644@compuserve.com. charts; stat.
    Supersedes in part: Economie Francaise en Perspectives Sectorielles (Vols.1-5); Which supersedes in part: Prevision a Un An de l'Economie Francaise.

330.9 621.9   FR
PREVISIONS GLISSANTES DETAILLEES EN PERSPECTIVES SECTORIELLES (VOL.6): MACHINES - OUTILS. (In series of 42 vols.) 1959. a. 6000 F. per vol.; 50000 F. per set. B I P E Conseil, Axe Seine 21, 12 rue Rouget de Lisle, 92442 Issy les Moulineaux Cedex, France. TEL 1-46-62-33-00. FAX 1-46-62-62-20. TELEX 631 586 F. charts; stat.
    Supersedes in part: Economie Francaise en Perspectives Sectorielles (Vols.1-5); Which supersedes in part: Prevision a Un An de l'Economie Francaise.

330.9 621.9   FR
PREVISIONS GLISSANTES DETAILLEES EN PERSPECTIVES SECTORIELLES (VOL.7): EQUIPEMENT INDUSTRIEL. (In series of 42 vols.) 1959. a. 7000 F. per vol.; 50000 F. per set (effective 1997). B I P E Conseil, L'Atrium - 6 Place Abel Gance, 92652 Boulogne-Billancourt Cedex, France. TEL 33-1-46944522. FAX 33-1-46944599. E-mail: 100332.644@compuserve.com. charts; stat.
    Supersedes in part: Economie Francaise en Perspectives Sectorielles (Vols.1-5); Which supersedes in part: Prevision a Un An de l'Economie Francaise.

330.9 621.9   FR
PREVISIONS GLISSANTES DETAILLEES EN PERSPECTIVES SECTORIELLES (VOL.8): MECANIQUE DE PRECISION. (In series of 42 vols.) 1959. a. 7000 F. per vol.; 50000 F. per set (effective 1997). B I P E Conseil, L'Atrium - 6 Place Abel Gance, 92652 Boulogne-Billancourt Cedex, France. TEL 33-1-46944522. FAX 33-1-46944599. E-mail: 100332.644@compuserve.com. charts; stat.
    Supersedes in part: Economie Francaise en Perspectives Sectorielles (Vols.1-5); Which supersedes in part: Prevision a Un An de l'Economie Francaise.

330.9 669   FR
PREVISIONS GLISSANTES DETAILLEES EN PERSPECTIVES SECTORIELLES (VOL.9): FONDERIE ET TRANSFORMATION DES METAUX. (In series of 42 vols.) 1959. a. 7000 F. per vol.; 50000 F. per set (effective 1997). B I P E Conseil, L'Atrium - 6 Place Abel Gance, 92652 Boulogne-Billancourt Cedex, France. TEL 33-1-46944522. FAX 33-1-46944599. E-mail: 100332.644@compuserve.com. charts; stat.
    Supersedes in part: Economie Francaise en Perspectives Sectorielles (Vols.1-5); Which supersedes in part: Prevision a Un An de l'Economie Francaise.

BUSINESS AND ECONOMICS — ECONOMIC SITUATION AND CONDITIONS

330.9 621.3   FR
PREVISIONS GLISSANTES DETAILLEES EN PERSPECTIVES SECTORIELLES (VOL.10): CONSTRUCTION ELECTRIQUE ET ELECTRONIQUE GRAND-PUBLIC. (In series of 42 vols.) 1959. a. 7000 F. per vol.; 50000 F. per set (effective 1997). B I P E Conseil, L'Atrium - 6 Place Abel Gance, 92652 Boulogne-Billancourt Cedex, France. TEL 33-1-46944522. FAX 33-1-46944599. E-mail: 100332.644@compuserve.com. charts; stat.
Supersedes in part: Economie Francaise en Perspectives Sectorielles (Vols.1-5); Which supersedes in part: Prevision a Un An de l'Economie Francaise.

330.9 621.3   FR
PREVISIONS GLISSANTES DETAILLEES EN PERSPECTIVES SECTORIELLES (VOL.11): CONSTRUCTION ELECTRIQUE PROFESSIONNELLE. (In series of 42 vols.) 1959. a. 7000 F. per vol.; 50000 F. per set (effective 1997). B I P E Conseil, L'Atrium - 6 Place Abel Gance, 92652 Boulogne-Billancourt Cedex, France. TEL 33-1-46944522. FAX 33-1-46944599. E-mail: 100332.644@compuserve.com. charts; stat.
Supersedes in part: Economie Francaise en Perspectives Sectorielles (Vols.1-5); Which supersedes in part: Prevision a Un An de l'Economie Francaise.

330.9 621.3   FR
PREVISIONS GLISSANTES DETAILLEES EN PERSPECTIVES SECTORIELLES (VOL.12): CONSTRUCTION ELECTRONIQUE PROFESSIONNELLE. (In series of 42 vols.) 1959. a. 7000 F. per vol.; 50000 F. per set (effective 1997). B I P E Conseil, L'Atrium - 6 Place Abel Gance, 92652 Boulogne-Billancourt Cedex, France. TEL 33-1-46944522. FAX 33-1-46944599. E-mail: 100332.644@compuserve.com. charts; stat.
Supersedes in part: Economie Francaise en Perspectives Sectorielles (Vols.1-5); Which supersedes in part: Prevision a Un An de l'Economie Francaise.

330.9 001.6
631.381   FR
PREVISIONS GLISSANTES DETAILLEES EN PERSPECTIVES SECTORIELLES (VOL.13): INFORMATIQUE. (In series of 42 vols.) 1959. a. 7000 F. per vol.; 50000 F. per set (effective 1997). B I P E Conseil, L'Atrium - 6 Place Abel Gance, 92652 Boulogne-Billancourt Cedex, France. TEL 33-1-46944522. FAX 33-1-46944599. E-mail: 100332.644@compuserve.com. charts; stat.
Supersedes in part: Economie Francaise en Perspectives Sectorielles (Vols.1-5); Which supersedes in part: Prevision a Un An de l'Economie Francaise.

330.9 380   FR
PREVISIONS GLISSANTES DETAILLEES EN PERSPECTIVES SECTORIELLES (VOL.14): TELECOMMUNICATIONS. (In series of 42 vols.) 1959. a. 7000 F. per vol.; 50000 F. per set (effective 1997). B I P E Conseil, L'Atrium - 6 Place Abel Gance, 92652 Boulogne-Billancourt Cedex, France. TEL 33-1-46944522. FAX 33-1-46944599. E-mail: 100332.644@compuserve.com. charts; stat.
Supersedes in part: Economie Francaise en Perspectives Sectorielles (Vols.1-5); Which supersedes in part: Prevision a Un An de l'Economie Francaise.

330.9 629   FR
PREVISIONS GLISSANTES DETAILLEES EN PERSPECTIVES SECTORIELLES (VOL.15): CONSTRUCTION AUTOMOBILE. (In series of 42 vols.) 1959. a. 7000 F. per vol.; 50000 F. per set (effective 1997). B I P E Conseil, L'Atrium - 6 Place Abel Gance, 92652 Boulogne-Billancourt Cedex, France. TEL 33-1-46944522. FAX 33-1-46944599. E-mail: 100332.644@compuserve.com. charts; stat.
Supersedes in part: Economie Francaise en Perspectives Sectorielles (Vols.1-5); Which supersedes in part: Prevision a Un An de l'Economie Francaise.

330.9 629.13   FR
PREVISIONS GLISSANTES DETAILLEES EN PERSPECTIVES SECTORIELLES (VOL.16): CONSTRUCTION AEROSPATIALE. (In series of 42 vols.) 1959. a. 7000 F. per vol.; 50000 F. per set (effective 1997). B I P E Conseil, L'Atrium - 6 Place Abel Gance, 92652 Boulogne-Billancourt Cedex, France. TEL 33-1-46944522. FAX 33-1-46944599. E-mail: 100332.644@compuserve.com. charts; stat.
Supersedes in part: Economie Francaise en Perspectives Sectorielles (Vols.1-5); Which supersedes in part: Prevision a Un An de l'Economie Francaise.

330.9 333.79   FR
PREVISIONS GLISSANTES DETAILLEES EN PERSPECTIVES SECTORIELLES (VOL.17): ENERGIE. (In series of 42 vols.) 1959. a. 7000 F. per vol.; 50000 F. per set (effective 1997). B I P E Conseil, L'Atrium - 6 Place Abel Gance, 92652 Boulogne-Billancourt Cedex, France. TEL 33-1-46944522. FAX 33-1-46944599. E-mail: 100332.644@compuserve.com. charts; stat.
Supersedes in part: Economie Francaise en Perspectives Sectorielles (Vols.1-5); Which supersedes in part: Prevision a Un An de l'Economie Francaise.

330.9 669.1   FR
PREVISIONS GLISSANTES DETAILLEES EN PERSPECTIVES SECTORIELLES (VOL.18): SIDERURGIE ET PREMIERE TRANSFORMATION DE L'ACIER. (In series of 42 vols.) 1959. a. 7000 F. per vol.; 50000 F. per set (effective 1997). B I P E Conseil, L'Atrium - 6 Place Abel Gance, 92652 Boulogne-Billancourt Cedex, France. TEL 33-1-46944522. FAX 33-1-46944599. E-mail: 100332.644@compuserve.com. charts; stat.
Supersedes in part: Economie Francaise en Perspectives Sectorielles (Vols.1-5); Which supersedes in part: Prevision a Un An de l'Economie Francaise.

330.9 669   FR
PREVISIONS GLISSANTES DETAILLEES EN PERSPECTIVES SECTORIELLES (VOL.19): INDUSTRIE DES NON-FERREUX. (In series of 42 vols.) 1959. a. 7000 F. per vol.; 50000 F. per set (effective 1997). B I P E Conseil, L'Atrium - 6 Place Abel Gance, 92652 Boulogne-Billancourt Cedex, France. TEL 33-1-46944522. FAX 33-1-46944599. E-mail: 100332.644@compuserve.com. charts; stat.
Supersedes in part: Economie Francaise en Perspectives Sectorielles (Vols.1-5); Which supersedes in part: Prevision a Un An de l'Economie Francaise.

330.9 546   FR
PREVISIONS GLISSANTES DETAILLEES EN PERSPECTIVES SECTORIELLES (VOL.20): CHIMIE MINERALE. (In series of 42 vols.) 1959. a. 7000 F. per vol.; 50000 F. per set (effective 1997). B I P E Conseil, L'Atrium - 6 Place Abel Gance, 92652 Boulogne-Billancourt Cedex, France. TEL 33-1-46944522. FAX 33-1-46944599. E-mail: 100332.644@compuserve.com. charts; stat.
Supersedes in part: Economie Francaise en Perspectives Sectorielles (Vols.1-5); Which supersedes in part: Prevision a Un An de l'Economie Francaise.

330.9 547   FR
PREVISIONS GLISSANTES DETAILLEES EN PERSPECTIVES SECTORIELLES (VOL.21): CHIMIE ORGANIQUE. (In series of 42 vols.) 1959. a. 7000 F. per vol.; 50000 F. per set (effective 1997). B I P E Conseil, L'Atrium - 6 Place Abel Gance, 92652 Boulogne-Billancourt Cedex, France. TEL 33-1-46944522. FAX 33-1-46944599. E-mail: 100332.644@compuserve.com. charts; stat.
Supersedes in part: Economie Francaise en Perspectives Sectorielles (Vols.1-5); Which supersedes in part: Prevision a Un An de l'Economie Francaise.

330.9 615.19   FR
PREVISIONS GLISSANTES DETAILLEES EN PERSPECTIVES SECTORIELLES (VOL.22): PARACHIMIE. (In series of 42 vols.) 1959. a. 7000 F. per vol.; 50000 F. per set (effective 1997). B I P E Conseil, L'Atrium - 6 Place Abel Gance, 92652 Boulogne-Billancourt Cedex, France. TEL 33-1-46944522. FAX 33-1-46944599. E-mail: 100332.644@compuserve.com. charts; stat.
Formerly: Previsions Glissantes Detaillees en Perspectives Sectorielles (Vol.19): Parachimie et Pharmacie; Supersedes in part: Economie Francaise en Perspectives Sectorielles (Vols.1-5); Which supersedes in part: Prevision a Un An de l'Economie Francaise.

330.9 668.4 678.2   FR
PREVISIONS GLISSANTES DETAILLEES EN PERSPECTIVES SECTORIELLES (VOL.23): TRANSFORMATION DU CAOUTCHOUC ET DES MATIERES PLASTIQUES. (In series of 42 vols.) 1959. a. 7000 F. per vol.; 50000 F. per set (effective 1997). B I P E Conseil, L'Atrium - 6 Place Abel Gance, 92652 Boulogne-Billancourt Cedex, France. TEL 33-1-46944522. FAX 33-1-46944599. E-mail: 100332.644@compuserve.com. charts; stat.
Supersedes in part: Economie Francaise en Perspectives Sectorielles (Vols.1-5); Which supersedes in part: Prevision a Un An de l'Economie Francaise.

330.9 666.1   FR
PREVISIONS GLISSANTES DETAILLEES EN PERSPECTIVES SECTORIELLES (VOL.24): INDUSTRIE DU VERRE. (In series of 42 vols.) 1959. a. 7000 F. per vol.; 50000 F. per set (effective 1997). B I P E Conseil, L'Atrium - 6 Place Abel Gance, 92652 Boulogne-Billancourt Cedex, France. TEL 33-1-46944522. FAX 33-1-46944599. E-mail: 100332.644@compuserve.com. charts; stat.
Supersedes in part: Economie Francaise en Perspectives Sectorielles (Vols.1-5); Which supersedes in part: Prevision a Un An de l'Economie Francaise.

330.9 676   FR
PREVISIONS GLISSANTES DETAILLEES EN PERSPECTIVES SECTORIELLES (VOL.25): INDUSTRIE DES PATES, PAPIERS ET CARTONS. (In series of 42 vols.) 1959. a. 7000 F. per vol.; 50000 F. per set (effective 1997). B I P E Conseil, L'Atrium - 6 Place Abel Gance, 92652 Boulogne-Billancourt Cedex, France. TEL 33-1-46944522. FAX 33-1-46944599. E-mail: 100332.644@compuserve.com. charts; stat.
Supersedes in part: Economie Francaise en Perspectives Sectorielles (Vols.1-5); Which supersedes in part: Prevision a Un An de l'Economie Francaise.

330.9 676   FR
PREVISIONS GLISSANTES DETAILLEES EN PERSPECTIVES SECTORIELLES (VOL.26): EMBALLAGES. (In series of 42 vols.) 1959. a. 7000 F. per vol.; 50000 F. per set (effective 1997). B I P E Conseil, L'Atrium - 6 Place Abel Gance, 92652 Boulogne-Billancourt Cedex, France. TEL 33-1-46944522. FAX 33-1-46944599. E-mail: 100332.644@compuserve.com. charts; stat.
Supersedes in part: Economie Francaise en Perspectives Sectorielles (Vols.1-5); Which supersedes in part: Prevision a Un An de l'Economie Francaise.

330.9 352.7   FR
PREVISIONS GLISSANTES DETAILLEES EN PERSPECTIVES SECTORIELLES (VOL.27): LOGEMENT. (In series of 42 vols.) 1959. a. 7000 F. per vol.; 50000 F. per set (effective 1997). B I P E Conseil, L'Atrium - 6 Place Abel Gance, 92652 Boulogne-Billancourt Cedex, France. TEL 33-1-46944522. FAX 33-1-46944599. E-mail: 100332.644@compuserve.com. charts; stat.
Supersedes in part: Economie Francaise en Perspectives Sectorielles (Vols.1-5); Which supersedes in part: Prevision a Un An de l'Economie Francaise.

BUSINESS AND ECONOMICS — ECONOMIC SITUATION AND CONDITIONS

330.9 690   FR
PREVISIONS GLISSANTES DETAILLEES EN PERSPECTIVES SECTORIELLES (VOL.28): BATIMENTS D'ACTIVITE. (In series of 42 vols.) 1959. a. 7000 F. per vol.; 50000 F. per set (effective 1997). B I P E Conseil, L'Atrium - 6 Place Abel Gance, 92652 Boulogne-Billancourt Cedex, France. TEL 33-1-46944522. FAX 33-1-46944599. E-mail: 100332.644@compuserve.com. charts; stat.
Supersedes in part: Economie Francaise en Perspectives Sectorielles (Vols.1-5); Which supersedes in part: Prevision a Un An de l'Economie Francaise.

330.9 624   FR
PREVISIONS GLISSANTES DETAILLEES EN PERSPECTIVES SECTORIELLES (VOL.29): TRAVAUX PUBLICS. (In series of 42 vols.) 1959. a. 7000 F. per vol.; 50000 F. per set (effective 1997). B I P E Conseil, L'Atrium - 6 Place Abel Gance, 92652 Boulogne-Billancourt Cedex, France. TEL 33-1-46944522. FAX 33-1-46944599. E-mail: 100332.644@compuserve.com. charts; stat.
Supersedes in part: Economie Francaise en Perspectives Sectorielles (Vols.1-5); Which supersedes in part: Prevision a Un An de l'Economie Francaise.

330.9 691   FR
PREVISIONS GLISSANTES DETAILLEES EN PERSPECTIVES SECTORIELLES (VOL.30): MATERIAUX DE CONSTRUCTION I. (In series of 42 vols.) 1959. a. 7000 F. per vol.; 50000 F. per set (effective 1997). B I P E Conseil, L'Atrium - 6 Place Abel Gance, 92652 Boulogne-Billancourt Cedex, France. TEL 33-1-46944522. FAX 33-1-46944599. E-mail: 100332.644@compuserve.com. charts; stat.
Supersedes in part: Economie Francaise en Perspectives Sectorielles (Vols.1-5); Which supersedes in part: Prevision a Un An de l'Economie Francaise.

330.9 691   FR
PREVISIONS GLISSANTES DETAILLEES EN PERSPECTIVES SECTORIELLES (VOL.31): MATERIAUX ET COMPOSANTS DE CONSTRUCTION II. (In series of 42 vols.) 1959. a. 7000 F. per vol.; 50000 F. per set (effective 1997). B I P E Conseil, L'Atrium - 6 Place Abel Gance, 92652 Boulogne-Billancourt Cedex, France. TEL 33-1-46944522. FAX 33-1-46944599. E-mail: 100332.644@compuserve.com. charts; stat.
Supersedes in part: Economie Francaise en Perspectives Sectorielles (Vols.1-5); Which supersedes in part: Prevision a Un An de l'Economie Francaise.

330.9 300   FR
PREVISIONS GLISSANTES DETAILLEES EN PERSPECTIVES SECTORIELLES (VOL.32): INDUSTRIES DE LA COMMUNICATION. (In series of 42 vols.) 1959. a. 6000 F. per vol.; 50000 F. per set. Bureau d'Informations et de Previsions Economiques, Axe Seine 21, 12 rue Rouget de Lisle, 92442 Issy les Moulineaux Cedex, France. TEL 1-46-62-33-00. FAX 1-46-62-62-20. TELEX 631 586 F. charts; stat.
Supersedes in part: Economie Francaise en Perspectives Sectorielles (Vols.1-5); Which supersedes in part: Prevision a Un An de l'Economie Francaise.

330.9 332.1   FR
PREVISIONS GLISSANTES DETAILLEES EN PERSPECTIVES SECTORIELLES (VOL.33): BANQUES. (In series of 42 vols.) 1959. a. 7000 F. per vol.; 50000 F. per set (effective 1997). B I P E Conseil, L'Atrium - 6 Place Abel Gance, 92652 Boulogne-Billancourt Cedex, France. TEL 33-1-46944522. FAX 33-1-46944599. E-mail: 100332.644@compuserve.com. charts; stat.
Supersedes in part: Economie Francaise en Perspectives Sectorielles (Vols.1-5); Which supersedes in part: Prevision a Un An de l'Economie Francaise.

330.9 368   FR
PREVISIONS GLISSANTES DETAILLEES EN PERSPECTIVES SECTORIELLES (VOL.34): ASSURANCES. (In series of 42 vols.) 1959. a. 7000 F. per vol.; 50000 F. per set (effective 1997). B I P E Conseil, L'Atrium - 6 Place Abel Gance, 92652 Boulogne-Billancourt Cedex, France. TEL 33-1-46944522. FAX 33-1-46944599. E-mail: 100332.644@compuserve.com. charts; stat.
Supersedes in part: Economie Francaise en Perspectives Sectorielles (Vols.1-5); Which supersedes in part: Prevision a Un An de l'Economie Francaise.

330.9   FR
PREVISIONS GLISSANTES DETAILLEES EN PERSPECTIVES SECTORIELLES (VOL.35): COMMERCE. (In series of 42 vols.) 1959. a. 7000 F. per vol.; 50000 F. per set (effective 1997). B I P E Conseil, L'Atrium - 6 Place Abel Gance, 92652 Boulogne-Billancourt Cedex, France. TEL 33-1-46944522. FAX 33-1-46944599. E-mail: 100332.644@compuserve.com. charts; stat.
Supersedes in part: Economie Francaise en Perspectives Sectorielles (Vols.1-5); Which supersedes in part: Prevision a Un An de l'Economie Francaise.

330.9 380.5   FR
PREVISIONS GLISSANTES DETAILLEES EN PERSPECTIVES SECTORIELLES (VOL.36): TRANSPORTS. (In series of 42 vols.) 1959. a. 7000 F. per vol.; 50000 F. per set (effective 1997). B I P E Conseil, L'Atrium - 6 Place Abel Gance, 92652 Boulogne-Billancourt Cedex, France. TEL 33-1-46944522. FAX 33-1-46944599. E-mail: 100332.644@compuserve.com. charts; stat.
Supersedes in part: Economie Francaise en Perspectives Sectorielles (Vols.1-5); Which supersedes in part: Prevision a Un An de l'Economie Francaise.

330.9 900   FR
PREVISIONS GLISSANTES DETAILLEES EN PERSPECTIVES SECTORIELLES (VOL.37): TOURISME, HOTELLERIE, RESTAURATION, LOISIRS. (In series of 42 vols.) 1959. a. 7000 F. per vol.; 50000 F. per set (effective 1997). B I P E Conseil, L'Atrium - 6 Place Abel Gance, 92652 Boulogne-Billancourt Cedex, France. TEL 33-1-46944522. FAX 33-1-46944599. E-mail: 100332.644@compuserve.com. charts; stat.
Supersedes in part: Economie Francaise en Perspectives Sectorielles (Vols.1-5); Which supersedes in part: Prevision a Un An de l'Economie Francaise.

330.9 610   FR
PREVISIONS GLISSANTES DETAILLEES EN PERSPECTIVES SECTORIELLES (VOL.38): PHARMACIE - SANTE. (In series of 42 vols.) 1959. a. 7000 F. per vol.; 50000 F. per set (effective 1997). B I P E Conseil, L'Atrium - 6 Place Abel Gance, 92652 Boulogne-Billancourt Cedex, France. TEL 33-1-46944522. FAX 33-1-46944599. E-mail: 100332.644@compuserve.com. charts; stat.
Formerly: Previsions Glissantes Detaillees en Perspectives Sectorielles (Vol.35): Sante; Supersedes in part: Economie Francaise en Perspectives Sectorielles (Vols.1-5); Which supersedes in part: Prevision a Un An de l'Economie Francaise.

330.9 350   FR
PREVISIONS GLISSANTES DETAILLEES EN PERSPECTIVES SECTORIELLES (VOL.39): SERVICES PUBLICS. (In series of 42 vols.) 1959. a. 7000 F. per vol.; 50000 F. per set (effective 1997). B I P E Conseil, L'Atrium - 6 Place Abel Gance, 92652 Boulogne-Billancourt Cedex, France. TEL 33-1-46944522. FAX 33-1-46944599. E-mail: 100332.644@compuserve.com. charts; stat.
Supersedes in part: Economie Francaise en Perspectives Sectorielles (Vols.1-5); Which supersedes in part: Prevision a Un An de l'Economie Francaise.

330.9   FR
PREVISIONS GLISSANTES DETAILLEES EN PERSPECTIVES SECTORIELLES (VOL.40): SERVICES AUX ENTREPRISES. (In series of 42 vols.) 1959. a. 7000 F. per vol.; 50000 F. per set (effective 1997). B I P E Conseil, L'Atrium - 6 Place Abel Gance, 92652 Boulogne-Billancourt Cedex, France. TEL 33-1-46944522. FAX 33-1-46944599. E-mail: 100332.644@compuserve.com. charts; stat.
Supersedes in part: Economie Francaise en Perspectives Sectorielles (Vols.1-5); Which supersedes in part: Prevision a Un An de l'Economie Francaise.

PRICES OF AGRICULTURAL PRODUCTS AND SELECTED INPUTS IN EUROPE AND NORTH AMERICA. see AGRICULTURE — Agricultural Economics

330.9   IE
PRIVATE RESEARCH. 1991. m. I£299($300) Private Research Ltd., 7-8 Mount St. Crescent, Dublin 2, Ireland. TEL 353-1-6760774. FAX 353-1-6760773. Ed. John O'Neill. adv. contact: James Treacy. index. (also avail. in diskette format; back issues avail.) **Document type:** bulletin.

330.9   US   ISSN 0882-5270
HB235.U6
PRODUCER PRICE INDEXES. (Supplement avail.) m. plus a. supplement. $56 (foreign $70) (includes supplement). U.S. Bureau of Labor Statistics, 2 Massachusetts Ave., N.E., Washington, DC 20212. TEL 202-655-4000. (Subscr. to: Superintendent of Documents, U.S. Government Printing Office, Box 371954, Pittsburgh, PA 15254-7954. TEL 202-512-1800. FAX 202-512-2250; Or: Bureau of Labor Statistics Publications Sales Center, Box 2145, Chicago, IL 60690) stat. (also avail. in microfiche from CIS; diskette format; back issues avail.; reprint service avail. from CIS) **Indexed:** Amer.Stat.Ind. (1973-), P.A.I.S., PROMT. **Document type:** government publication.
●Also available online.
Also available on CD-ROM.
Former titles: Producer Prices and Price Indexes (ISSN 0161-7311); Wholesale Prices and Price Indexes (ISSN 0498-7667)
Description: Reports on price movements at the primary market level, arranged by stage of processing and by commodity.

330.9   US
PRODUCTIVITY AND COSTS: BUSINESS, NONFARM BUSINESS, MANUFACTURING, AND NONFINANCIAL CORPORATIONS. (Subseries of: National Office News Releases) q. U.S. Bureau of Labor Statistics, 2 Massachusetts Ave., N.E., Washington, DC 20212. TEL 202-655-4000. (Subscr. to: Superintendent of Documents, U.S. Government Printing Office, Box 371954, Pittsburgh, PA 15250-7954. TEL 202-512-1800. FAX 202-512-2250; Or: Bureau of Labor Statistics Publications Sales Center, Box 2145, Chicago, IL 60690) **Document type:** government publication.

330.9   US
PRODUCTIVITY BY INDUSTRY (YEAR). (Subseries of: National Office News Releases) a. U.S. Bureau of Labor Statistics, 2 Massachusetts Ave., N.E., Washington, DC 20212. TEL 202-655-4000. (Subscr. to: Superintendent of Documents, U.S. Government Printing Office, Box 371954, Pittsburgh, PA 15250-7954. TEL 202-512-1800. FAX 202-512-2250; Or: Bureau of Labor Statistics Publications Sales Center, Box 2145, Chicago, IL 60690) **Document type:** government publication.

330.9   US
PRODUCTIVITY MEASURES FOR SELECTED INDUSTRIES. a. price varies. U.S. Bureau of Labor Statistics, 441 G St., N.W., Washington, DC 20212. TEL 202-523-9244. (Subscr. to: Superintendent of Documents, U.S. Government Printing Office, Box 371954, Pittsburgh, PA 15250-7954. TEL 202-512-1800. FAX 202-512-2250; Or: Bureau of Labor Statistics Publications Sales Center, Box 2145, Chicago, IL 60690) (also avail. in microform) **Document type:** government publication.
●Also available on CD-ROM.
Former titles: Productivity Indexes for Selected Industries; Indexes of Output per Man-Hour: Selected Industries.

BUSINESS AND ECONOMICS — ECONOMIC SITUATION AND CONDITIONS

330.9   FR   ISSN 0247-5421
PROFILS ECONOMIQUES. 1980. q. 150 F. Edition Marketing, 32 rue Bargue, 75015 Paris, France. Ed. Jean-Pierre Benezet. adv.; bk.rev.; stat. circ. 3,000. (back issues avail.)

330.9   MX   ISSN 0033-0485
PROGRESO; comercio - industria - finanzas - desarrollo. (Supersedes an annual publication with the same title, 1965-67) 1965. m. $15. Editorial Vision, S.A., Gutenberg 143, 11590 Mexico, D.F., Mexico. FAX 212-953-1619. (Dist. in US by: Vision, 310 Madison Ave. Ste. 1412, New York, NY 10017-6000. TEL 212-953-1308) Ed. Mariano Grondona. adv.; illus. circ. 38,500. **Indexed:** Hisp.Amer.Per.Ind. (1970-1979).
    Description: Covers Latin-American developments affecting business management, including political and economic trends.

333   AT   ISSN 1035-1396
PROGRESS. 1904. bi-m. Aus.$18 (foreign Aus.$24). Tax Reform Australia, 31 Hardware St., Melbourne, Vic. 3000, Australia. TEL 61-3-96702754. FAX 61-3-96703063. Ed. Jessika Willis; Pub. Geoff Forster. bk.rev. circ. 1,000. **Document type:** newsletter.
    Description: Publication advocating public finance reform and proportional representation for all elections.

330.9 332.6 658   RU
PROMYSHLENNYI VESTNIK ROSSII. (Text in Russian) 1994. m. $100. Promyshlennyi Vestnik Rossii, Zubovskii Bul'var, 4, 119021 Moscow, Russia. TEL 7-095-2017697. FAX 7-095-2017657. Ed. Aleksander Lopukhin. adv.: page $5000. (also avail. in diskette format; back issues avail.)
    Description: Covers economics, finance and law in Russian industries.

338   NR   ISSN 0048-5608
PROSPERITY; Nigeria's business quarterly. 1971. q. People's Publishing Co. Ltd., P.O. Box 3121, Lagos, Nigeria. Ed. Olu Akinsanya. adv. circ. 5,000. (also avail. in microfilm from UMI) **Document type:** trade publication.

330   IT   ISSN 0033-1902
PROVINCIA DI FORLI IN CIFRE. 1959. irreg. L.15000. Camera di Commercio, Industria, Artigianato e Agricoltura di Forli-Cesena, Corso della Repubblica 5, 47100 Forli, Italy. Ed. Ettore Neri.

330   CN   ISSN 0827-5785
PROVINCIAL OUTLOOK. 1976. q. Can.$3000 to non-members. Conference Board of Canada, 255 Smyth Rd., Ste. 100, Ottawa, ON K1H 8M7, Canada. TEL 613-526-3280. FAX 613-526-4857. **Indexed:** CS Ind.
    ●Also available online.
    Formerly: Conference Board of Canada. Quarterly Provincial Forecast (ISSN 0381-0100)

330.9   US
PRUDENTIAL INSURANCE COMPANY OF AMERICA. ECONOMIC FORECAST. vol.31, 1982. a. Prudential Insurance Co. of America, Economic & Investment Research Dept., 5 Plaza, Newark, NJ 07101. TEL 201-877-6000. charts.

330   PL
PRZEGLAD USTAWODAWSTWA GOSPODARCZEGO/ECONOMIC LEGISLATION REVIEW. 1946. m. Panstwowe Wydawnictwo Ekonomiczne, Ul. Canaletta 4, 00-099 Warsaw, Poland. Ed. Bogdan Michalski. bk.rev.; bibl. **Indexed:** Foreign Leg.Per.

330.9   CN   ISSN 1187-8657
HJ13
PUBLIC ACCOUNTS OF BRITISH COLUMBIA. (In 3 vols.: Financial Statements; Schedule of Payments; Trust Funds, Crown Corp and Agencies.) a. Can.$46.90. Ministry of Finance and Corporate Relations, Parliament Bldgs., Victoria, BC V8V 1X4, Canada. (Subscr. to: Crown Publications, 546 Yates St., Victoria, BC V8W 1K8, Canada. TEL 604-386-4636) (back issues avail.)

330.9   US   ISSN 1066-7156
PUEBLO BUSINESS JOURNAL. 1993. s-m. $16 (effective 1994). 201 W. 8th St., Ste. 408, Box 1544, Pueblo, CO 81002. TEL 719-542-3616. FAX 719-542-4506. E-mail: thepbj@aol.com. Ed. Becky Makedon; Pub. Charles B. Shelden. R&P contact: Charles B. Shelden. adv. contact: Roger Powell. circ. 6,500 (controlled). (tabloid format; also avail. in microform from UMI; back issues avail.) **Document type:** trade publication.
    ●Also available online. Vendor(s): UMI.
    —UMI.
    Description: Provides local business news and feature articles of interest to the business and professional community.

PUERTO RICO ECONOMIC INDICATORS. see *BUSINESS AND ECONOMICS — Abstracting, Bibliographies, Statistics*

PUGET SOUND BUSINESS JOURNAL. see *BUSINESS AND ECONOMICS*

330.9   IT   ISSN 0391-3082
PUNTO; rivista di economia di Como, Lecco, Varese, Canton Ticino. 1980. bi-m. L.48000 (55 SFr.; foreign 71 SFr.) (effective 1996). Fratelli Pini Editori s.r.l., Via Vittorio Emanuele 99, 22100 Como, Italy. TEL 39-31-2654584. FAX 39-31-265414. adv.: B&W page L.1150000; adv. contact: Lilia Pini. circ. 32,000. (back issues avail.)
    Description: Provides a forum on the economy in Como, Lecce, and Varese, Italy and in Tessin Canton in Switzerland. Presents joint economical, industrial, cultural and social interests.

330.9   FR   ISSN 1015-4639
PURCHASING POWER PARITIES AND REAL EXPENDITURES/PARITES DE POUVOIR D'ACHAT ET DEPENSES REELLES. a. Organization for Economic Cooperation and Development, Statistics Directorate - Organisation de Cooperation et de Developpement Economiques, Direction des Statistiques, 2 rue Andre Pascal, 75775 Paris Cedex 16, France. (Subscr. in U.S. to: Publications Sales and Services, 2001 L St. N.W., Ste. 650, Washington, DC 20036-4922)

330   IT   ISSN 1121-9610
HC307.S3
QUADERNI DI ECONOMIA E FINANZA. (Text in English or Italian) 1971. 3/yr. free. Banco di Sardegna S.p.A., Servizio Studi, Viale Umberto I, 36, 07100 Sassari, Italy. TEL 39-79-226572. FAX 39-79-226579. Dir. Lorenzo Idda. bk.rev.; bibl.; stat.; index; circ. 2,000 (controlled). **Indexed:** P.A.I.S.For.Lang.Ind., P.A.I.S.
    —BLDSC (7166.125300).
    Former titles (until 1992): Quaderni Sardi di Economia (ISSN 0391-8394); (until 1978): Quaderni dell'Economia Sarda.

QUANTITY AND QUALITY IN ECONOMIC RESEARCH. see *STATISTICS*

338   US
QUARTERLY BUSINESS FAILURES. 1900. q. $40. Dun & Bradstreet, Economic Analysis Department, 220 E. 42nd St., 9th Fl., New York, NY 10017-4717. FAX 212-883-3400. (Subscr. to: Box 1861, New York, NY 10163-1861)
    Former titles: Quarterly Business Failures Report; Quarterly Analysis of Failures (ISSN 0033-5290)
    Description: Provides number of failures and liabilities by detailed lines of business. Includes data for all 2-digit, 3-digit and most 4-digit SIC codes.

330.9 332.6   US
QUARTERLY PERFORMANCE REPORT. 1982. q. $299 (foreign $395). Managed Account Reports Inc., 220 Fifth Ave., New York, NY 10001. TEL 212-213-6202. FAX 212-213-1870. (looseleaf format; back issues avail.)
    Description: Includes statistical reports updating performance of futures money managers and future funds.

330.9   II
QUARTERLY REVIEW OF INDIAN ECONOMY. 1990. q. $200. Economic and Scientific Research Foundation, Federation House, Tansen Marg, New Delhi 110001, India. TEL 331-9251-61. TELEX 031-2546 & 62521. Ed. Jagdish Shettigar.
    Description: An analytical report on current Indian economic situations in the fields of agriculture, infrastructure, industry, investment climate, banking and finance, price situation, foreign trade, and balance of payments positions.

330.9   CN   ISSN 1201-6195
QUEBEC INTERNATIONAL (MONTREAL). (Editions in English, French, Spanish) 1970. q. free. Ministere des Affaires Internationales - Department of International Affairs, Immigration and Cultural Communities, 380 St. Antoine St. W., 4th Fl., Montreal, Quebec H2Y 3X7, Canada. TEL 514-499-2169. FAX 514-873-7825. Ed. Celine Coulombe. adv. circ. 35,000. (back issues avail.) **Document type:** government publication.
    Former titles (until 1994): Magazine Quebec International (English Edition) (ISSN 1188-2190); (until 1992): Quebec Economique International (English Edition) (ISSN 0823-2237); (until 1983): Quebec Economique International Edition (ISSN 0705-9299); (until 1978): Quebec (Edition Anglaise) (ISSN 0705-9302).

QUINZAINE AFRICAINE. see *POLITICAL SCIENCE — International Relations*

R D P NEWS. (Reconstruction and Development Programme) see *BUSINESS AND ECONOMICS — Investments*

330.968   SA   ISSN 1022-6389
R S A REVIEW/R S A OORSIG. (Text in English, summaries in Afrikaans) 1988. m. (10/yr.) R.16. South African Communication Service - Suid-Afrikaanse Kommunikasiediens, Private Bag X745, Pretoria 0001, South Africa. illus. **Indexed:** Ind.S.A.Per. **Document type:** government publication.
    Formerly (until vol.7, no.1, 1994): R S A Policy Review (Multilingual Edition) (ISSN 1019-7427); Which was formed by the 1992 merger of: R S A Policy Review (ISSN 1012-764X) & R S A Beleidsoorsig (ISSN 1012-7658)
    Description: Provides a comprehensive picture of constitutional, economic and social development in South Africa.

330.9   US
RAPID GROWTH RATINGS. 1989. w. $77 (effective through 1988). Merrill Analysis, Elm 3325-3300 Darby Rd., Haverford, PA 19041. TEL 610-642-2011. E-mail: artam@aol.com. Ed. Arthur Merrill. (looseleaf format) **Document type:** bulletin.
    Description: Contains an analysis of approximately forty stocks selected because of their rapid growth.

330   SY   ISSN 0079-9696
HC497.S8
RAPPORT ANNUEL SUR L'ECONOMIE SYRIENNE. (Text in English, French) 1963. a. $200. Office Arabe de Presse et de Documentation, P.O. Box 3550, 67 Place Chahbandar, Damascus, Syria. Ed. Adnan Khani.

330.9   IT   ISSN 0390-010X
HC301
RASSEGNA ECONOMICA (NAPLES). 1931. q. free to qualified personnel. Banco di Napoli, Direzione Generale, Ufficio Studi, Via Roma 177-178, 80132 Naples, Italy. Ed.Bd. bk.rev.; bibl.; charts; stat.; index; circ. 5,350 (controlled). (reprint service avail.) **Indexed:** P.A.I.S.For.Lang.Ind., Rural Recreat.Tour.Abstr., World Agri.Econ.& Rural Sociol.Abstr.
    —BLDSC (7294.137000).

330.9   US
REAL EARNINGS. (Subseries of: National Office News Releases) m. U.S. Bureau of Labor Statistics, 2 Massachusetts Ave., N.E., Washington, DC 20212. TEL 202-655-4000. (Subscr. to: Superintendent of Documents, U.S. Government Printing Office, Box 371954, Pittsburgh, PA 15250-7954. TEL 202-512-1800. FAX 202-512-2250; Or: Bureau of Labor Statistics Publications Sales Center, Box 2145, Chicago, IL 60690) **Document type:** government publication.

REAL ESTATE ANALYSIS AND PLANNING SERVICE. see *REAL ESTATE*

330.9   AG   ISSN 0325-1926
HC121
REALIDAD ECONOMICA. 1970. every 45 days. A250($100) in America; elsewhere $120. Instituto Argentino para el Desarrollo Economico, Hipolito Yrigoyen 1116, Piso 4, 1086 Buenos Aires, Argentina. FAX 38-7380. Ed. Juan C. Amigo. adv.; bk.rev. **Indexed:** Hisp.Amer.Per.Ind. (1985-), P.A.I.S.For.Lang.Ind., Triticale Abstr., World Agri.Econ.& Rural Sociol.Abstr.

BUSINESS AND ECONOMICS — ECONOMIC SITUATION AND CONDITIONS

330.9   ES   ISSN 1012-5515
REALIDAD ECONOMICO-SOCIAL. 1987. bi-m. Col.40 (Central America $12; N. & S. America $15; elsewhere $25). Universidad Centroamericana Jose Simeon Canas, Departamentos de Economia, Sociologia y Ciencias Politicas, Apdo. 01-575, San Salvador, El Salvador. Ed. Francisco Javier Ibisate.

338.9   PE
REALIDAD PERUANA. no.3, 1975. irreg. price varies. Editorial Horizonte, Av. Nicolas de Pierola 995, Casilla 2118, Lima 1, Peru. charts; stat. **Document type:** monographic series.

REDAKTIONS-ARCHIV; Zahlenbilder aus Gesellschaft, Wirtschaft, Politik und Recht. see POLITICAL SCIENCE

388   US   ISSN 0080-0449
REFERENCE BOOK - ARGENTINA. (Issued in 2 vols) (Text in Spanish) a. Dun's Marketing Services (Subsidiary of: Dun & Bradstreet, Inc.), 3 Sylvan Way, Parsippany, NJ 07054-0900. TEL 201-455-0900. (And: Florida 234, Buenos Aires, Argentina)

380   US   ISSN 0080-0457
REFERENCE BOOK - REPUBLIC OF SOUTH AFRICA. (Published in 4 provincial editions: Sec. 1: Orange Free State, Sec. 2: Cape Province, Sec. 3: Natal, Sec. 4: Transvaal). a. not available to libraries. Dun's Marketing Services (Subsidiary of: Dun & Bradstreet, Inc.), 3 Sylvan Way, Parsippany, NJ 07054-3896. TEL 201-455-0900. (And: 91 Kerk St., Johannesburg, South Africa)

330.9   US   ISSN 1093-1767
REGION FOCUS. 1984. q. free. Federal Reserve Bank of Richmond, Research Department, 701 E. Byrd St., Richmond, VA 23219. TEL 804-697-8000. FAX 804-697-8287. E-mail: regionfocus@rich.frb.org; URL: http://www.rich.frb.org. (Subscr. to: Public Affairs, Box 27622, Richmond, VA 23261. TEL 804-697-8111) Ed. Cynthia Price. charts; stat. circ. 20,000. (also avail. in microfiche from CIS; back issues avail.; reprint service avail. from CIS) **Indexed:** Amer.Stat.Ind. (1984-), Fed Print.
—UMI; UnCover.
Formerly (until 1997): Cross Section (ISSN 0747-5543)
Description: Review of business conditions and economic developments in the District of Columbia.

330.9   PH   ISSN 0116-2551
REGIONAL DEVELOPMENT COMMUNICATOR. 1978. q. $6. Regional Development Council of Western Mindanao, National Economic and Development Authority, R.T. Lim Blvd., Zamboanga City, Philippines. TEL 991-6741. FAX 991-1364. Ed. Leon J. Omoso. illus. circ. 500. **Document type:** government publication, newsletter.

330   CN
REGIONAL DEVELOPMENT CORPORATION. ANNUAL REPORT/SOCIETE D'AMENAGEMENT REGIONAL. RAPPORT ANNUEL. (Text in English, French) 1967. a. free. Regional Development Corporation, P.O. Box 428, Fredericton, N.B. E3B 5R4, Canada. TEL 506-453-2277. Ed. Celine Doucet-Rousselle. circ. 1,000. (controlled).
Formerly (until Nov. 1987): Community Improvement Corporation. Annual Report (ISSN 0069-7842)

330.9 658.8   US   ISSN 0896-2537
HC101
REGIONAL ECONOMIES AND MARKETS; a quarterly analysis from the Conference Board. 1986. q. $295 to non-members; members $145. Conference Board, Inc., 845 Third Ave., New York, NY 10022. TEL 212-759-0900. FAX 212-980-7014. circ. 9,000. **Document type:** newsletter.
—CCC.
Description: Examines trends and prospects in the nine major US regions.

330.9   US
REGIONAL ECONOMIST. q. free. Federal Reserve Bank of St. Louis, Box 442, St. Louis, MO 63166. TEL 314-444-8320.
Formerly: Pieces of Eight.
Description: Addresses national and regional economic issues as they affect the Eighth Federal Reserve District.

330.9 327   SI   ISSN 0218-3056
DS520
REGIONAL OUTLOOK: SOUTHEAST ASIA. (Text in English) 1992. a. $19.90. Institute of Southeast Asian Studies, Heng Mui Keng Terrace, Pasir Panjang, Singapore 119596, Singapore. TEL 65-8702447. FAX 65-7756259. URL: http://www.iseas.ac.sg/pub.html. Ed. Triena Ong. **Document type:** academic/scholarly publication.
Description: Covers the political and economic situations in Southeast Asia.

REGIONE ABRUZZO. see SOCIAL SERVICES AND WELFARE

REGULATION (WASHINGTON, 1977); the Cato review of business & government. see POLITICAL SCIENCE

330.9   US   ISSN 1075-7848
REIMBURSEMENT UPDATE. 1984. q. $105. 355 Oak Trail Dr., Louisville, TX 75067. TEL 817-491-3593. Ed. Frederic R. Curtiss. **Document type:** newsletter.

RENKOU YU JINGJI/POPULATION & ECONOMICS. see POPULATION STUDIES

REPORT ON GUATEMALA. see POLITICAL SCIENCE — International Relations

REPORTING ON GOVERNMENTS. see BUSINESS AND ECONOMICS — Investments

323 330.9   US   ISSN 1049-2585
HC79.I5
RESEARCH ON ECONOMIC INEQUALITY. 1989. irreg., vol.7, 1997. $78.50. J A I Press Inc., 55 Old Post Rd., No. 2, Box 1678, Greenwich, CT 06830-1678. TEL 203-661-7602. FAX 203-661-0792. E-mail: jai@jaipress.com. (Subscr. in the UK and Europe to: JAI Press Ltd., 38 Tavistock St., Covent Garden, London WC2E 7PB, England. TEL 44-171-379-8834. FAX 44-171-379-8835) Ed. Daniel Slottje. **Document type:** monographic series.

RESERVE BANK BULLETIN. see BUSINESS AND ECONOMICS — Banking And Finance

RESERVE BANK OF AUSTRALIA. OCCASIONAL PAPERS. see BUSINESS AND ECONOMICS — Banking And Finance

RESERVE BANK OF AUSTRALIA. RESEARCH DISCUSSION PAPER. see BUSINESS AND ECONOMICS — Banking And Finance

330.9 332   FJ
RESERVE BANK OF FIJI. ANNUAL REPORT. 1975. a. $10 in US. Reserve Bank of Fiji, Private Mail Bag, Suva, Fiji. TEL 679-313611. FAX 679-301688. TELEX 2164. charts; stat. circ. 750. **Document type:** corporate report.
Formerly (until 1984): Fiji. Central Monetary Authority. Annual Report.
Description: Covers a comprehensive review of the domestic economy and an overview of developments in the international economy as well as operations and accounts of the bank for the calendar year. Also contains financial and economic data.

330.9 332   FJ
RESERVE BANK OF FIJI. MONTHLY ECONOMIC BULLETIN. 1994. m. $6 in US. Reserve Bank of Fiji, Private Mail Bag, Suva, Fiji. TEL 679-313611. FAX 679-301688. TELEX 2164. circ. 300. **Document type:** bulletin.
Description: Reviews Fiji economy.

330.9 332   FJ
RESERVE BANK OF FIJI. NEWS REVIEW. 1984. w. $10 in US. Reserve Bank of Fiji, Private Mail Bag, Suva, Fiji. TEL 679-313611. FAX 679-301688. TELEX 2164. circ. 350. **Document type:** newsletter.
Description: Provides edited highlights of the local and international financial as well as economic news. Also contains selected financial and economic data.

330.9 332   FJ
RESERVE BANK OF FIJI. QUARTERLY REVIEW. 1976. q. $46 in US. Reserve Bank of Fiji, Private Mail Bag, Suva, Fiji. TEL 679-313611. FAX 679-301688. TELEX 2164. stat. circ. 500. **Document type:** corporate report.
Formerly (until 1984): Fiji. Central Monetary Authority. Quarterly Review.
Description: Provides a quarterly analysis of the Fiji economy together with time series of selected economic and financial statistics.

332   MW   ISSN 0376-5725
HC517.M3
RESERVE BANK OF MALAWI. FINANCIAL AND ECONOMIC REVIEW. 1968. q. free. Reserve Bank of Malawi, Research Department, P.O. Box 30063, Lilongwe 3, Malawi. TEL 265-780600. charts; stat. **Indexed:** Key to Econ.Sci., World Bank.Abstr. **Document type:** academic/scholarly publication.
—BLDSC (3926.941000).
Formerly: Reserve Bank of Malawi. Economic and Financial Review (ISSN 0034-5520)
Description: Offers a quarterly assessment of developments in the major economic indicators. Contains sections on money and credit, public finance, balance of payments and the international economic situation, production and prices, as well as a statistical annex section.

330.9   NZ   ISSN 1170-4829
RESERVE BANK OF NEW ZEALAND. MONETARY POLICY STATEMENT. 1990. s-a. free. Reserve Bank of New Zealand, Corporate Services, 2 The Terrace, P.O. Box 2498, Wellington, New Zealand. TEL 64-4-722029. FAX 64-4-738554. (back issues avail.) **Document type:** corporate report.

330.9   NZ   ISSN 0110-523X
RESERVE BANK OF NEW ZEALAND. RESEARCH PAPERS. 1971. irreg. free. Reserve Bank of New Zealand, Corporate Services, 2 The Terrace, P.O. Box 2498, Wellington, New Zealand. TEL 64-4-472-2029. FAX 64-4-473-8554. TELEX NZ 3368. bibl.; stat. circ. 1,000.

330.9   BU   ISSN 1013-1450
LA RESTRUCTURATION/RESTRUCTURING. (Text in English, French, German, Russian, Spanish) 1987. m. $24. Sofia Press Agency, Slavyanska St., 29, 1040 Sofia, Bulgaria. TEL 359-2-885831. FAX 359-2-883455. TELEX 22622. Ed. Ekaterina Licheva. circ. 2,500. (looseleaf format; back issues avail.)
Description: Covers the process of restructuring in all spheres of life, promotes Bulgarian economy among its foreign partners.

330.9   US
RETAIL FOOD PRICE INDEX: WASHINGTON, D.C.. (Subseries of: National Office News Releases) m. U.S. Bureau of Labor Statistics, 2 Massachusetts Ave., N.E., Washington, DC 20212. TEL 202-655-4000. (Subscr. to: Superintendent of Documents, U.S. Government Printing Office, Box 371954, Pittsburgh, PA 15250-7954. TEL 202-512-1800. FAX 202-512-2250; Or: Bureau of Labor Statistics Publications Sales Center, Box 2145, Chicago, IL 60690) **Document type:** government publication.

330.9 327   UK   ISSN 0969-2290
HF1410   CODEN: RIPEFV
REVIEW OF INTERNATIONAL POLITICAL ECONOMY. 1994. q. £40 (U.S. and Canada $64; rest of world £40) to individuals; institutions £90 (U.S. and Canada $135; rest of world £92) (effective 1997). Routledge, 11 New Fetter Ln., London EC4P 4EE, England. TEL 44-171-583-9855. FAX 44-171-842-2298. E-mail: sample.journals@routledge.com; URL: http://www.routledge.com/routledge/journal/journals.html. (Subscr. to: ITPS Ltd., Cheriton House, North Way, Andover, Hants SP10 5BE, England. TEL 44-1264-342919. FAX 44-1264-342807; Subscr. in US & Canada to: 29 W. 35th St. New York, NY 10001-2299. TEL 212-244-3336. FAX 212-564-7854) Ed.Bd. adv.: page £150; trim 135 x 205. **Indexed:** ASSIA. **Document type:** academic/scholarly publication.
—BLDSC (7790.935000); SWETS; UnCover. **CCC.**

330.9   UK   ISSN 0962-2055
HB126.4
REVIEW OF ISLAMIC ECONOMICS. 1991. s-a. £12 to individuals (foreign £15); institutions £20 (foreign £24). (International Association for Islamic Economics) Islamic Foundation, Markfield Dawah Centre, Ratby Lane, Markfield, Leicester LE67 9RN, England. TEL 01530-244944. FAX 01530-244946. E-mail: islamic-foundation@islamf.demon.co.uk. Ed. Munawar Iqbal. R&P contact: Munawar Iqbal. (back issues avail.) **Document type:** academic/scholarly publication.
—BLDSC (7791.110000).
Description: Provides a forum for specialists wishing to contribute to the development of Islamic economics as a distinct branch of knowledge.
Refereed Serial

BUSINESS AND ECONOMICS — ECONOMIC SITUATION AND CONDITIONS 1287

REVIEW OF POLITICAL ECONOMY. see *POLITICAL SCIENCE*

330.9 371.42 UK ISSN 0265-9347
REVIEW OF THE ECONOMY AND EMPLOYMENT. (In two volumes) 1981. irreg. £35 (effective 1997). Institute for Employment Research, University of Warwick, Coventry CV4 7AL, England. TEL 44-203-524127. FAX 44-203-524241. Dir. R.M. Lindley. **Document type:** monographic series, academic/scholarly publication.
—BLDSC (7790.257000).
Description: Provides a medium-term assessment of the U.K. labor market. Publication form varies, but all gather information on employment prospects according to industry, occupation, gender and employment status, distinguishing employees from the self employed and splitting employees into those who are working full-time and those working part-time.

338 AG ISSN 0034-6810
REVIEW OF THE RIVER PLATE; dealing with Argentine financial, economic, agricultural and shipping affairs. (Text in English, Spanish) 1891. 2/m. $225. Bulnes 44 A, P.B."A", A1176 Buenos Aires, Argentina. Ed. Archibald B. Norman. adv.; charts; mkt. circ. 4,000. (also avail. in microfilm from KTO) **Indexed:** Key to Econ.Sci., P.A.I.S.

330.9 339 HO ISSN 0254-4210
HC141.A1
REVISTA CENTROAMERICANA DE ECONOMIA; postgrado centroamericana en economia y planificacion del desarrollo. 1979. 3/yr. $18. Universidad Nacional Autonoma de Honduras, Postgrado en Economia, Apdo. 1748, Ciudad Universitaria, Tegucigalpa D.C., Honduras. TEL 504-31-3289. (Co-sponsor: Consejo Superior Universitario Centroamericano) circ. 600. **Indexed:** IBR.

330.9 CL ISSN 0716-5927
HB1.A1
REVISTA DE ANALISIS ECONOMICO. 1987. s-a. Ch.$6000 (foreign $35) to individuals; institutions Ch.$10000 (foreign $40) (effective 1997). Instituto Latinoamericano de Doctrina y Estudios Sociales, Departamento de Publicaciones, Almirante Barroso 6, Casilla 51970, Santiago 1, Chile. TEL 56-2-6980046. FAX 56-2-6986873. (Co-sponsor: Georgetown University, Postgraduate Program in Economics) Ed. Felipe Morande. bk.rev.; abstr.
—BLDSC (7840.863000).
Description: Stimulates production and intellectual exchange of theories related to developing economies. Includes coverage of literature in this area.

REVISTA DE ECONOMIA POLITICA. see *POLITICAL SCIENCE*

330.1 SP ISSN 0212-6109
HC10
REVISTA DE HISTORIA ECONOMICA. 1943. 3/yr. 4750 ptas.($37) (Fundacion Empresa Publica) Alianza Editorial, C. Juan Ignacio Luca de Tena 15, 28027 Madrid, Spain. TEL 34-1-3938888. FAX 34-1-7414343. **Indexed:** Amer.Hist.& Life (1983-), Hist.Abstr. (1983-), IBR.
—BLDSC (7858.534000); CINDOC; SWETS.
Former titles (until 1983): Revista de Economia Politica (ISSN 0034-8058); (until 1945): Revista de Estudios Politicos. Suplemento de Informacion Economica (ISSN 1132-3159).

330 BL ISSN 0100-4956
HC186 CODEN: RENOFN
REVISTA ECONOMICA DO NORDESTE. (Text in Portuguese; summaries in English) 1969. q. $50 (effective 1997). Banco do Nordeste do Brasil, Celula da Administracao da Documentacao e Informacao, Av. Paranjana, 5700 Passare, 60740-000 Fortaleza CE, Brazil. TEL 55-85-2993137. FAX 55-85-2993524. Ed. Ademir da Silva Costa. charts; illus. circ. 1,200. **Indexed:** P.A.I.S.For.Lang.Ind. **Document type:** government publication.
Formerly (until 1973): Revista Economica.

330.9 CU ISSN 0259-8299
REVISTA ESTADISTICA. 1978. 3/yr. $24 in N. America; S. America $25; Europe $26. (Instituto de Investigaciones Estadisticas) Ediciones Cubanas, Obispo No. 527, Apdo. 605, Havana, Cuba. Dir. Ramon Sabadi Rodriguez. circ. 2,500.

330.9 338.91 FR ISSN 1245-4060
HD72
REVUE D'ECONOMIE DU DEVELOPPEMENT. 1993. q. 380 F. to individuals (foreign 450 F.); agencies 342 F. (foreign 405 F.) (effective 1998). Presses Universitaires de France, Departement des Revues, 14 av. du Bois-de-l'Epine, 91003 Evry Cedex, France. TEL 33-1-60778205. FAX 33-1-60792045. TELEX PUF 600 474 F. Ed. Patrick Guillaumont. charts; stat. **Indexed:** Geo.Abstr.P.G., IDA. **Document type:** academic/scholarly publication.

REVUE D'ECONOMIE FINANCIERE. see *BUSINESS AND ECONOMICS — Banking And Finance*

330 FR ISSN 0154-3229
HD30.22
REVUE D'ECONOMIE INDUSTRIELLE. q. 557 F. to individuals (foreign 669 F.); institutions 473.45 F. (foreign 568.65 F.) (effective June 1997). Editions Techniques et Economiques, 2 rue Soufflot, 75005 Paris, France. TEL 33-1-46341030. FAX 33-1-46345583. TELEX 260 717 F. **Indexed:** ELLIS, SCIMP (1982-).
—BLDSC (7898.745000); SWETS.
Description: Theoretical economic analyses and evaluations of different aspects of the industrial production system.

330.9 FR ISSN 0180-7307
REVUE D'ECONOMIE REGIONALE ET URBAINE. (Text in French, summary in English) 1978. 5/yr. 430 F. (Europe 500 F.; elsewhere 550 F.) Universite Montesquieu-Bordeaux IV, Institut d'Economie Regionale du Sud-Ouest, Avenue Leon Duguit, 33608 Bordeaux, France. TEL 33-56848551. FAX 33-56848647. E-mail: guesnier@zeus.univ-poitiers.fr. Ed. Claude Lacour. bk.rev.; bibl. circ. 1,000. **Indexed:** P.A.I.S.For.Lang.Ind. **Document type:** academic/scholarly publication, proceedings.
—BLDSC (7898.780000); SWETS.

330.9 CM
REVUE D'INFORMATIONS ET D'ETUDES ECONOMIQUE ET FINANCIERES. q. B.P. 1630, Yaounde, Cameroon.

REVUE D'INTEGRATION EUROPEENNE/JOURNAL OF EUROPEAN INTEGRATION. see *POLITICAL SCIENCE — International Relations*

338.9 IV ISSN 1015-2628
HC1025.A1
REVUE ECONOMIQUE ET FINANCIERE IVOIRIENNE. Short title: R E F A. 1978. q. 5000 Fr.CFA. (Ministere de l'Economie, des Finances et du Plan) Inter Afrique Presse, 01 B.P. 3901, Abidjan 01, Ivory Coast. circ. 1,500. **Indexed:** P.A.I.S.For.Lang.Ind.
Supersedes (1969-1976): Ivory Coast. Ministere de l'Economie et des Finances. Etudes Economiques et Financieres.

330.9 US ISSN 1002-7874
RIBEN XUEKAN. (Text in Chinese) bi-m. $30.60. China Books & Periodicals, Inc., 2929 24th St., San Francisco, CA 94110. TEL 415-282-2994. FAX 415-282-0994.
Formerly: Riben Wenti.

330 BL ISSN 0103-3905
HC188.R4
RIO GRANDE DO SUL, BRAZIL. FUNDACAO DE ECONOMIA E ESTATISTICA. INDICADORES ECONOMICOS F E E. 1973. q. R.70 (effective 1997). Fundacao de Economia e Estatistica, Rua Duque de Caixas, 1691, CEP 90010-283 Porto Alegre RG, Brazil. TEL 55-512-259455. FAX 55-512-25006. Ed. Carlos Octavio Augusto Conceicao. adv.; charts; illus.; stat. circ. 1,500. (processed)
Formerly (until 1988): Rio Grande so Sul, Brazil. Fundacao de Economia e Estatistica. Indicadores Economicos R S (ISSN 0102-020X)

RIVERLANDER NOTES. see *CONSERVATION*

330.9 US ISSN 0884-0199
ROCHESTER BUSINESS JOURNAL. 1987. w. $62 (effective 1997). 55 St. Paul St., Rochester, NY 14604-1309. TEL 716-546-8303. FAX 716-546-3398. E-mail: RBJournal@aol.com; URL: http://www.rbj.net. Ed. Paul Ericson; Pub. Susan R. Holliday. R&P contact: Suzanne Y. Seldes. adv. contact: Susan R. Holliday. circ. 10,000. (tabloid format; also avail. in diskette format) **Document type:** newspaper.
● Also available online.
Description: Contains local business news.

ROYAL BANK LETTER. see *BUSINESS AND ECONOMICS — Banking And Finance*

330.9 GW ISSN 0483-5654
RUND UM DIE BOERSE. 1955. a. Commerzbank AG, Neue Mainzer Str. 32-36, 60261 Frankfurt a.M., Germany. TEL 49-69-13622379. FAX 49-69-13622008. circ. 48,000. **Document type:** bulletin.

RUNDT'S WORLD BUSINESS INTELLIGENCE. see *BUSINESS AND ECONOMICS — International Commerce*

330.9 UK ISSN 0967-0793
RUSSIAN ECONOMIC TRENDS. 1992. q. £120($215) to individuals; institutions £240($430) (effective 1998). (Centre for Economic Reform, RU) Whurr Publishers Ltd., 19b Compton Terr., London N1 2UN, England. TEL 44-171-359-5979. FAX 44-171-226-5290. (Subscr. to: Turpin Distribution Services Ltd., Blackhorse Rd., Letchworth, Herts. SG6 1HN, England. TEL 44-1462-672555. FAX 44-1462-480947; Subscr. in N. America to: Whurr Publishers Ltd., Box 1897, Lawrence, KS 66044-8897. TEL 913-843-1221. FAX 913-843-1274) (Co-sponsor: London School of Economics, Centre for Economic Reform) adv.: page £200; adv. contact: Maggy Park. stat. **Document type:** academic/scholarly publication.
—BLDSC (8052.696500).
Description: Gives an authoritative and comprehensive insight into the Russian Economy and the progress of the economic liberalization and privatization reforms, together with relevant statistical tables.
Refereed Serial

330.9 RW
RWANDA. DIRECTION GENERALE DE LA STATISTIQUE. SITUATION ECONOMIQUE DE LA REPUBLIQUE RWANDAISE AU 31 DECEMBRE. 1973 (N.S.). irreg? $26 (effective Aug. 1991). Direction Generale de la Statistique, B.P. 46, Kigali, Rwanda.
Formerly: Rwanda. Direction Generale de la Documentation et de la Statistique Generale. Situation Economique de la Republique Rwandaise au 31 Decembre.

330.9 JA ISSN 0916-3158
RYUGIN KEIZAI REPORT. 1951. q. free. Bank of the Ryukyus Ltd., Research Dept., 1-7-1 Kumoji, Naha, Okinawa, Japan. FAX 098-861-5942. Ed. Hirotaka Makino. stat. circ. 1,700. **Indexed:** Amer.Hist.& Life (1960-1964), Hist.Abstr. (1960-1964).
Formerly (until Oct. 1989): Kin'yu Keizai (ISSN 0023-1711)

330 300 NE ISSN 0920-4849
S E R BULLETIN. Key Title: SER-bulletin. 1960. m. fl.45. Sociaal-Economische Raad, Postbus 90405, 2509 LK The Hague, Netherlands. TEL 31-70-3499499. FAX 31-70-3832535. (processed) **Indexed:** Key to Econ.Sci. **Document type:** bulletin.
—SWETS.
Former titles (until 1981): S E R Informatie- en Documentatiebulletin; Sociaal-Economisch Raad. Informatie- en Documentatie Bulletin (ISSN 0037-7589)
Description: News on labor and social and economic matters.

330.9 US ISSN 8755-7282
S G P B ALERT. irreg., no.38, 1994. $7.50. Southern Growth Policies Board, Box 12293, Research Triangle Park, NC 27709. TEL 919-941-5145. FAX 919-941-5145. **Document type:** bulletin.

S Z. (Sozialwirtschaftliche Korrespondenz) see *POLITICAL SCIENCE*

330.9 332.6 US ISSN 1086-251X
THE SAFE MONEY REPORT. 1971. m. $148 (effective 1997). Weiss Ratings, Inc., 4176 Burns Rd., Palm Beach Gardens, FL 33410-4606. TEL 561-627-3300. FAX 561-625-6685. E-mail: clara@weiss.com; URL: http://www.weiss.com. Ed. Martin Weiss; Pub. Martin Weiss. R&P contact: Leslie Underwood. charts. circ. 6,000. pp./issue: 8. (back issues avail.) **Document type:** newsletter.
Formerly: Money and Markets (ISSN 1047-9821)
Description: A forum for investors that deals with high returns, maximum liquidity, and speculative strategies along with bank, insurance, and brokerage safety.

BUSINESS AND ECONOMICS — ECONOMIC SITUATION AND CONDITIONS

330.9   XK
ST. LUCIA. STATISTICAL DEPARTMENT. ANNUAL BULLETIN ON C A R I C O M TRADE. (Caribbean Common Market) 1984. a. EC$6. Statistical Department, New Government Bldg., Block C, 2nd Fl., Conway, Castries, St. Lucia, W.I. TEL 758-45-22697. FAX 758-45-31648. TELEX 6394 FORAFF. Ed. Bryan Boxill. **Document type:** bulletin.

330.9   XK
ST. LUCIA. STATISTICAL DEPARTMENT. MONTHLY CONSUMER PRICE INDEX. 1960. m. free. Statistical Department, New Government Bldg., Block C, 2nd Fl., Conway, Castries, St. Lucia, W.I. TEL 758-45-22697. FAX 758-45-31648. TELEX 6394 FORAFF. Ed. Bryan Boxill.

330.9   XK
ST. LUCIA. STATISTICAL DEPARTMENT. QUARTERLY BULLETIN ON C A R I C O M TRADE. (Caribbean Common Market) 1984. q. EC$10. Statistical Department, New Government Bldg., Block C, 2nd Fl., Conway, Castries, St. Lucia, W.I. TEL 758-45-22697. FAX 758-45-31648. TELEX 6394 FORAFF. Ed. Bryan Boxill. **Document type:** bulletin.

330.9 658   US
SALARY SURVEY (WASHINGTON). 1964. biennial. $30. National Association of Business Economists, 1233 20th St., N.W., Ste. 505, Washington, DC 20046-2304. TEL 202-463-6223. FAX 202-463-6239. Ed.Bd. cum.index. (also avail. in microfiche from IAC,UMI; back issues avail.)
    Formerly: Salary Characteristics.
    Description: Covers salaries of business economists and business analysts, including median salary data by industry, geographic area, area of responsibility, size of firm, number supervised, attained education and years of experience. Also provides information on additional gross compensation from primary employment and secondary professional income.

SAMARITAN. see RELIGIONS AND THEOLOGY

330   II   ISSN 0036-3871
SAMPADA. (Text in Hindi) 1952. m. Rs.12. Ashok Prakashan Mandir, 28-11 Shaktinagar, Delhi 7, India. Ed. Sh. Krishn Chander Vidyalankar. bk.rev.; stat.; index. circ. 5,500.

330.9   CE
SAMVARDHANA. (Text in English or Sinhalese) irreg. Rs.3.75 per no. 27-3 M Housing Scheme, Kiribathgoda, Kelaniya, Sri Lanka.

SAN DIEGO BUSINESS JOURNAL. see BUSINESS AND ECONOMICS

330.968   SA
SANLAM'S ECONOMIC SURVEY. Afrikaans edition: Sanlam se Ekonomiese Oorsig. (Text in English) 1993. m. Sanlam, Economic Research Department, P.O. Box 1, Sanlamhof 7532, South Africa. **Indexed:** Ind.S.A.Per.

SASKATCHEWAN. DEPARTMENT OF INDUSTRY AND COMMERCE. INDUSTRIAL BENEFITS FROM RESOURCE DEVELOPMENT. see BUSINESS AND ECONOMICS

330.9   CN   ISSN 0558-6976
HC117.S3
SASKATCHEWAN ECONOMIC REVIEW. 1951. a. Can.$5 in Saskatchewan; elsewhere Can.$10. Bureau of Statistics, 5th Fl., 2350 Albert St., Regina, SK S4P 4A6, Canada. TEL 306-787-6327. FAX 306-787-6311. circ. 2,000. **Document type:** bulletin.

330   UK
SAUDI ARABIA QUARTERLY. 1991. q. £225. E M A P Business Information, 21 John St., London WC1N 2BP, England. TEL 071-404-5513. FAX 071-430-0337. TELEX 936564 MEEDAR G. Ed. Edmund O'Sullivan. **Document type:** trade publication.
    Description: Provides an in-depth analysis of political and economic trends in Saudi Arabia

330   UK   ISSN 0960-6483
SAUDI ARABIA QUARTERLY. 1991. q. £225 (£195 to subscribers of Middle East Economic Digest) (effective 1997). M E E D Publications, 21 John St., London WC1N 2BP, England. TEL 44-171-470-6406. FAX 44-171-470-6406. —BLDSC (8076.971450).

330.9   UK   ISSN 0952-6498
HC257.S4
SCOTTISH ECONOMIC BULLETIN. 1971. s-a. £11.50. H.M.S.O., 51 Nine Elms Ln., London SW8 5DR, England. TEL 44-171-873-0011. FAX 44-171-873-8247. (Co-sponsor: Scottish Office Industry Department) Ed. John Rigg. **Indexed:** C.R.E.J., P.A.I.S. **Document type:** government publication.
—BLDSC (8206.830000).

330.9   AU
SELBSTAENDIG IN DER WIRTSCHAFT. 1947. bi-m. S.150. Freier Wirtschaftsverband, Schottenfeldgasse 24, A-1072 Vienna, Austria. TEL 0222-938601-0. FAX 0222-938609. Ed. Wolfgang Slawik. circ. 15,000.

330.9   US
SELECTED INFORMATION ON INSURED U.S. COMMERCIAL BANKS RANKED BY ASSETS. Variant title: Siegel Report. q. $100 in US, Canada, Mexico; elsewhere $200. (Federal Reserve System, Board of Governors) U.S. National Technical Information Service, 5825 Port Royal Rd., Springfield, VA 22161. TEL 703-487-4630.
    Description: Ranks approximately 2,600 insured banks with assets totaling $100 million or more in descending order by size of consolidated assets.

330.9   SG
SENEGAL. MINISTERE DE L'ECONOMIE ET DES FINANCES. COMPTES ECONOMIQUES DU SENEGAL. a. 5000 Fr.CFA (foreign 7000 Fr.CFA). Ministere de l'Economie et des Finances, Direction de la Statistique, B.P. 116, Dakar, Senegal. TEL 221-21-03-01. **Document type:** government publication.

SENTINEL INVESTMENT LETTER. see BUSINESS AND ECONOMICS — Investments

381   UK
SERIES IN INTERNATIONAL BUSINESS AND ECONOMICS. Short title: S I B E. 1994. irreg., vol.5, 1995. price varies. Elsevier Science Ltd., Books Division, P.O. Box 800, Kidlington, Oxford OX2 1DX, England. TEL 44-1865-843000. FAX 44-1865-8430410. E-mail: nlinfo-f@elsevier.nl; usinfo-f@elsevier.com; forinfo-kyf04035@niftyserve.or.jp; URL: http://www.elsevier.nl/. (Subscr. to: Elsevier Science, Regional Sales Office, P.O. Box 211, 1000 AE Amsterdam, Netherlands. TEL 31-20-4853757. FAX 31-20-4853432; Subscr. in the Americas to: Elsevier Science, Regional Sales Office, Box 945, New York, NY 10159-0945. TEL 212-633-3730. FAX 212-633-3680; Subscr. in Australasia and the Far East to: Elsevier Science (Singapore) Pte Ltd, No.1 Temasek Ave., No.17-01 Millenia Tower, Singapore 039192, Singapore. TEL 65-434-3727. FAX 65-337-2230) (back issues avail.) **Document type:** monographic series.
    Refereed Serial

338.9   DK   ISSN 0901-800X
SETTING UP IN DENMARK; a survey of economic, legal and financial aspects of foreign investment in Denmark. 1972. biennial. free. Danske Bank Aktieselskab, Trade, Finance & Banking Relations, 2-12 Holmens Kanal, DK-1092 Copenhagen K, Denmark. TEL 45-33-44-00-00. FAX 45-33-44-57-54. URL: http://www.danskebank.dk. charts; illus.; stat.

330.9   CC
SHENZHEN TODAY. (Text in English) 1990. irreg. HK.$30($8) per no. Economic Information & Agency, 342 Hennessy Rd., 10th Fl., Wanchai, Hong Kong, People's Republic of China. TEL 852-573-8217. FAX 852-838-8304. TELEX 86990 EIA HX. Ed. Li Yang.
    Description: Introduces the investment environment of Shenzhen Economic Special Zone, a gateway to China from Hong Kong.

SHIJIE JINGJI/WORLD ECONOMY MONTHLY. see BUSINESS AND ECONOMICS — Macroeconomics

SHIJIE JINGJI YANJIU/WORLD ECONOMY RESEARCH. see BUSINESS AND ECONOMICS — Macroeconomics

330.9   FR   ISSN 1019-9829
HC244.A1
SHORT-TERM ECONOMIC INDICATORS CENTRAL AND EASTERN EUROPE. (Supplement to: O E C D Main Economic Indicators (ISSN 0474-5523)) (Text in English, French) 1993. q. Organization for Economic Cooperation and Development, 2 rue Andre-Pascal, 75775 Paris Cedex 16, France. (Subscr. in U.S. to: O.E.C.D. Publications and Information Centre, 2001 L St., N.W., Ste. 650, Washington, DC 20036-4922. TEL 202-7852-6323)

330.9   SL
SIERRA LEONE OUTLOOK. (Text in English) 6/yr. United Methodist Church, P.O. Box 523, Freetown, Sierra Leone. Ed. S.A. Warratie. adv. circ. 1,300.

380 338   SI   ISSN 0129-2951
HF41
SINGAPORE BUSINESS. 1977. m. S.$104; newsstand price: S.$4. Times Periodicals Pte. Ltd., 422 Thomson Rd., Singapore 298131, Singapore. TEL 65-255-0011. FAX 65-256-8016. URL: http://biztimes.asia1.com/. Ed. Elaine Koh. adv.: B&W page S.$1340, color page S.$2000; 275 x 205; adv. contact: Michael Phuan. bk.rev.; illus. circ. 16,000. **Indexed:** Key to Econ.Sci., P.A.I.S.
—BLDSC (8285.462000); UnCover.
    Supersedes: Singapore Trade and Industry (ISSN 0037-5705)
    Description: Covers the latest trends affecting business and the economy.

388   US   ISSN 0080-9756
SINOPSIS DUN - BRAZIL. (Text in Portuguese) a. Dun's Marketing Services (Subsidiary of: Dun & Bradstreet, Inc.), 3 Sylvan Way, Parsippany, NJ 07054-3896. TEL 201-455-0900. (And: Avenida Sao Joao 473, 1st Fl., Sao Paulo, Brazil)

332   AG   ISSN 0037-5799
HC171
SINTESIS INFORMATIVA ECONOMICA Y FINANCIERA. 1964. m. free. Banco de la Provincia de Buenos Aires, San Martin 137, Buenos Aires, Argentina. Ed. Armando V. Rey. charts; stat. circ. 3,000. (also avail. in microform)

330.1   IV   ISSN 0080-9829
SITUATION ECONOMIQUE DE COTE D'IVOIRE. 1960. irreg. Service de la Statistique, B.P. 222, Abidjan, Ivory Coast.

330   SG   ISSN 0080-9853
SITUATION ECONOMIQUE DU SENEGAL. 1962. irreg., (approx. a., latest 1986). 8000 Fr.CFA (foreign 11000 Fr.CFA). Ministere de l'Economie et des Finances, Direction de la Statistique, B.P. 116, Dakar, Senegal. TEL 221-21-03-01. (also avail. in microfiche from CHL) **Document type:** government publication.

330   FR
SITUATION ECONOMIQUE ET PERSPECTIVES D'AVENIR. 1962. irreg. Chambre de Commerce et d'Industrie de Pau, 21 rue Louis Barthou, Pau, France. Ed.Bd. circ. 6,000.

330.9   FR   ISSN 1274-3356
SOCIETAL; analyse mensuelle des realites economiques et sociales. 1996. 11/yr. 450 F. to individuals (foreign 550 F.) (effective 1997); newsstand price: 45 F. Societe d'Etudes et de Documentation Economiques Industrielles et Sociales, 1 av. Edouard Belin, 92856 Rueil-Malmaison Cedex, France. TEL 33-1-41299921. FAX 33-1-41299719. Ed. Beatrice Bazil; Pub. Albert Merlin. charts. **Indexed:** ELLIS, P.A.I.S.For.Lang.Ind.
    Formed by the merger of (1978-1996): Analyses de la S E D E I S (ISSN 0399-1245) & Chroniques Economiques (ISSN 1251-0998); Which was formerly (until 1994): Chroniques de la S.E.D.E.I.S. (ISSN 1164-8759); (until 1991): Chroniques d'Actualite de la S E D E I S (ISSN 0396-437X); (until 1975): Chroniques d'Actualites (ISSN 0009-613X); (until 1966): Bulletin Sedeis. Chroniques d'Actualite (ISSN 1140-8642); (until 1959): Sedeis. Chroniques d'Actualite (ISSN 1140-8634); (until 1955): Sedeis Notes et Informations (ISSN 1140-8626).
    Description: Covers sociopolitical issues in Europe.

BUSINESS AND ECONOMICS — ECONOMIC SITUATION AND CONDITIONS

315.4 330.9   II
SOCIO-ECONOMIC REVIEW OF PUNJAB. (Subseries of the Organisation's Publication) a. Economic and Statistical Organisation, Chandigarh, Punjab, India. stat.

330.9   US
SOUND OF THE ECONOMY. m. D R I - McGraw-Hill, 24 Hartwell Ave., Lexington, MA 02173. TEL 617-863-5100. FAX 617-860-6332. TELEX 200 284. Ed. Cynthia Latta. (audio cassette) **Document type:** trade publication.

330.9 320   US   ISSN 1054-8890
SOURCEMEX; economic and political news and analysis on Mexico. (Print edition ceased.) w. $75 to individuals; institutions $300. University of New Mexico, Latin American Institute, Latin America Data Base, 801 Yale N.E., Albuquerque, NM 87131-1016. TEL 505-277-6839. FAX 505-277-5989. E-mail: info@ladb.unm.edu; URL: http://www.ladb.unm.edu/ Ed. Carlos M. Navarro. (back issues avail.) **Document type:** academic/scholarly publication.
●Also available online. Vendor(s): Information Access Co., Knight-Ridder Information, Inc., Lexis-Nexis, NewsNet (IT99).
Also available on CD-ROM. Producer(s): NISC (Latin American Studies - Vol.2).
  Description: Focuses on Mexico's changing economic environment, including private investment, public policy, petroleum, agriculture, trade, environment and social welfare.

330.9   SA
SOUTH AFRICA (YEAR). (Text in English) 1969. a. R.6 (effective 1994). South Africa Foundation, P.O. Box 7006, Johannesburg 2000, South Africa. TEL 27-12-726-6105. FAX 27-12-726-4705. stat. circ. 40,000.
  Formerly: South Africa Foundation. Information Digest (Year).

380 320   SA   ISSN 1021-1780
SOUTH AFRICA FOUNDATION REVIEW. (Text in English) bi-m. free. South Africa Foundation, P.O. Box 7006, Johannesburg 2000, South Africa. TEL 27-12-726-6105. FAX 27-12-726-4705. Ed. G.L.M. Lewis. illus. circ. 15,000. **Indexed:** Polit.Sci.Abstr.
  Formerly: South Africa Foundation News (ISSN 1016-8486)
  Description: Attempts to foster a responsible and sophisticated reaction to the international pressures on South Africa by analyzing and then explaining the nature, sources and purposes of these pressures.

SOUTH AFRICAN INDUSTRY. see *BUSINESS AND ECONOMICS — Production Of Goods And Services*

332   SA   ISSN 0081-2528
SOUTH AFRICAN RESERVE BANK. ANNUAL ECONOMIC REPORT/SUID-AFRIKAANSE RESERWEBANK. JAARLIKSE EKONOMIESE VERSLAG. (Editions in Afrikaans and English) 1961. a. R.10 (overseas free). South African Reserve Bank, P.O. Box 427, Pretoria 0001, South Africa. TEL 27-12-3133911. FAX 27-12-3133197. E-mail: info@gwisel.resbank.co.za; URL: http://www.resbank.co.za. circ. 2,800 (English ed. 2,000; Afrikaans ed. 800). **Document type:** corporate report.
—BLDSC (1085.030000).

SOUTH AMERICA, CENTRAL AMERICA AND THE CARIBBEAN (YEAR). see *POLITICAL SCIENCE*

330   US   ISSN 0038-304X
HC107.S7
SOUTH CAROLINA ECONOMIC INDICATORS. 1968. m. free. University of South Carolina, College of Business Administration, Division of Research, The Francis M. Hipp Bldg., Columbia, SC 29208. TEL 803-777-2510. FAX 803-777-9344. E-mail: woodward@darla.badm.sc.edu. Ed. Douglas P. Woodward. R&P contact: Douglas P. Woodward. charts; stat. circ. 1,129. **Document type:** academic/scholarly publication.
  Description: Surveys economic and labor trends and indicators for South Carolina.

330.9   US   ISSN 0145-3637
HC107.S7
SOUTH CAROLINA ECONOMIC REPORT. a. $7 (effective 1997). Budget and Control Board, Board of Economic Advisors, Ste. 442, Rembert Dennis Bldg., 1000 Assembly St., Columbia, SC 29201. TEL 803-734-3805. FAX 803-734-4719. Ed. Robert W. Martin. **Indexed:** SRI. **Document type:** government publication.

SOUTH FLORIDA BUSINESS JOURNAL. see *BUSINESS AND ECONOMICS*

330.9   NL   ISSN 0377-452X
HQ1240.5.O24
SOUTH PACIFIC COMMISSION. REPORT OF MEETINGS. French edition: Commission de Pacifique Sud. Rapport de Conference (ISSN 1017-9240) (Text in English) irreg. South Pacific Commission, B.P. D5, 98848 Noumea Cedex, New Caledonia. TEL 687-262000. FAX 687-263818. E-mail: spc@spc.org.nc. **Document type:** monographic series.
—BLDSC (7610.075000).
  Formerly: South Pacific Commission. Report of S P C Fisheries Technical Meetings (ISSN 0081-2846)

330.9 320   US
SOUTHEAST ASIA REPORT. irreg. (approx. 220/yr.). $7 per no. (foreign $14 per no.). U.S. Joint Publications Research Service, Box 12507, Arlington, VA 22209. TEL 703-487-4630. (Orders to: NTIS, Springfield, VA 22161)
  Former titles: South and East Asia Report; Translations on South and East Asia.

330.9   US
SOUTHEAST ASIA WEEKLY FAX BULLETIN. w. $595 (foreign $695) (effective 1998). Orbis Publications, LLC, 3201 New Mexico Ave., N.W., Ste. 249, Washington, DC 20016. TEL 202-237-0155. FAX 202-237-0596. E-mail: orbis@orbispub.com; URL: http://www.earthnet.net/orbis. (only avail. by fax) **Document type:** bulletin.
  Description: Reports on political, economic, and business events in Cambodia, Laos, Malaysia, Myanmar, The Philippines, Singapore, Thailand, and Vietnam.

330.9   US
SOUTHEAST HOUSING & ECONOMIC TRENDS. q. free. Federal Home Loan Bank of Atlanta, 1475 Peachtree St., Atlanta, GA 30309. TEL 404-888-8000.
  Formerly: Southeast Regional Economic Report.

330.9 332   UK   ISSN 1352-2078
THE SOUTHERN AFRICA EXCLUSIVE; bulletin covering financial and political trends for southern Africa. 1993. m. £175($250) to individuals and corporations; academic institutions and charities £125 ($200). Africa Analysis Ltd., Ludgate House, 107-111 Fleet St., London EC4A 2AB, England. TEL 44-171-353-1117. FAX 44-171-353-1516. Ed. Terry Bell. circ. 500. **Document type:** newsletter.
  Description: Covers political and financial trends in the southern African nations and includes in-depth coverage of the Johannesburg Stock Exchange.

338.9 320   UK   ISSN 0143-5256
HC161
SOUTHERN CONE REPORT. Variant title: Latin American Regional Reports - Southern Cone Report. 10/yr. £150($195) (academic institutions £85 ($110)) (effective 1997). Lettres (U.K.) Ltd., 61 Old St., London EC1V 9HX, England. TEL 44-171-251-0012. FAX 44-171-253-8193. Ed. Colin Harding. R&P contact: Alex McHallam. (back issues avail.) **Document type:** newsletter.
●Also available online. Vendor(s): Lexis-Nexis.
  Description: Covers in detail political, business, economic, and financial events in Argentina, Chile, Uruguay, and Paraguay.

330.9   US
SOUTHERN GROWTH. q. Southern Growth Policies Board, Box 12293, Research Triangle Park, NC 27709. TEL 919-941-5145. FAX 919-941-5145. Ed. Robert Donnan. **Document type:** newsletter.
  Formerly: Southern Growth Problems and Promises.

330.9   UK
SOUTH WEST ECONOMY TRENDS AND PROSPECTS. 1989. a. £95. University of Plymouth, South West Economic Research Centre, Drake Circus, Plymouth, Devon PL4 8AA, England. TEL 44-1752-232827. Ed. Peter Gripaios. R&P contact: Peter Gripaios. circ. 120. **Document type:** academic/scholarly publication.

330.9   SP   ISSN 1132-0052
SPAIN. MINISTERIO DE ECONOMIA Y HACIENDA. BOLETIN DE INFORMACION TRIMESTRAL. 1986. q. 11330 ptas. (effective 1997). Ministerio de Economia y Hacienda, Direccion General de Seguros, Paseo de la Castellana 44, 28046 Madrid, Spain. TEL 34-1-3397000. FAX 34-1-3397113. circ. 550. **Document type:** government publication.

330.9   IT
SPECCHIO ECONOMICO. 1982. m. L.50000. Ciuffa Editore S.r.l., Via Rasella 139, 00187 Rome, Italy. TEL 39-6-4821150. FAX 39-6-485964. Ed. Victor Ciuffa. adv.: B&W page L.12000000, color page L.15000000; adv. contact: Anna Maria Ciuffa. circ. 30,000.

SPIEGEL DER LATEINAMERIKANISCHEN PRESSE/BOLETIN DE PRENSA LATINOAMERICANA. see *POLITICAL SCIENCE — International Relations*

330.9   CE
SRI LANKA. MINISTRY OF PLANNING AND ECONOMIC AFFAIRS. DIVISION OF EXTERNAL RESOURCES. ECONOMIC INDICATORS. a. Ministry of Planning and Economic Affairs, Division of External Resources, Box 277, Ceylingo House, 2nd Floor, Colombo 1, Sri Lanka. charts; stat.

330.9   CE
SRI LANKA ECONOMIC JOURNAL. 1986. s-a. $20. Sri Lanka Economic Association, 61, Carmel Road, Colombo 3, Sri Lanka. Ed. N.L. Sirisena. bk.rev. circ. 500. **Document type:** academic/scholarly publication.

STADT HERNE. ARBEITSMARKTBERICHT. see *BUSINESS AND ECONOMICS — Abstracting, Bibliographies, Statistics*

330.9   GW
▼**STANDORTE: JAHRBUCH RUHRGEBIET.** 1995. a. (Kommunalverband Ruhrgebiet) Klartext Verlag, Dickmannstr. 2-4, 45143 Essen, Germany. TEL 49-201-8620628. FAX 49-201-8620622. Ed.Bd. **Document type:** bulletin.

330.9   GW
STANDPUNKT (FRANKFURT). 1952. m. free. B f G Bank AG, Theaterplatz 2, 60311 Frankfurt a.M., Germany. TEL 069-258-0. FAX 069-258-7578. TELEX 412210. circ. 13,000. **Indexed:** PROMT. **Document type:** newsletter.
  Former titles: B F G: Wirtschaftsblaetter; Wirtschaftsblaetter (ISSN 0043-6208)

330.9   US
STATE AND METROPOLITAN AREA EMPLOYMENT AND UNEMPLOYMENT. (Subseries of: National Office News Releases) m. U.S. Bureau of Labor Statistics, 2 Massachusetts Ave., N.E., Washington, DC 20212. TEL 202-655-4000. (Subscr. to: Superintendent of Documents, U.S. Government Printing Office, Box 371954, Pittsburgh, PA 15250-7954. TEL 202-512-1800. FAX 202-512-2250; Or: Bureau of Labor Statistics Publications Sales Center, Box 2145, Chicago, IL 60690) **Document type:** government publication.
  Incorporates (in Feb. 1994): State Employment and Metropolitan Area Unemployment.

330.9   II
STATE BANK OF INDIA. ECONOMIC NEWSLETTER. (Text in English) w. free. State Bank of India, Economic Research Department, New Administration Bldg., Backbay Reclamation, P.O. Box 12, Bombay 400 021, India. Ed.Bd. **Document type:** newsletter.

330.9   II
STATE BANK OF INDIA. INDIAN ECONOMIC NEWSLETTER. (Text in English) bi-m. free. State Bank of India, Economic Research Department, New Administration Building, Backbay Reclamation, P.O. Box 12, Bombay 400 012, India. Ed.Bd. **Document type:** newsletter.

BUSINESS AND ECONOMICS — ECONOMIC SITUATION AND CONDITIONS

330.9 II ISSN 0039-0003
STATE BANK OF INDIA. MONTHLY REVIEW. (Text in English) 1961. m. free. State Bank of India, Economic Research Department, New Administration Bldg., Backbay Reclamation, P.O. Box 12, Bombay 400 021, India. Ed. V.R. Gundannavar. charts; stat. circ. 24,000. Indexed: Rural Devel.Abstr., Rural Recreat.Tour.Abstr., World Agri.Econ.& Rural Sociol.Abstr., World Bank.Abstr.
Formerly: State Bank of India. Economic Research Department. Studies.
Description: Covers current topics in banking and public finance in India. Includes legal decisions, parliamentary actions and empirical studies.

330.9 658 UK
THE STATE OF THE MARKET. 1991. q. membership. Chartered Institute of Marketing, Moor Hall, Cookham, Maidenhead, Berkshire SL6 9QH, England. TEL 44-1628-427500. FAX 44-1628-427499. TELEX 849462 TELFAC G. Ed. Fiona Rogers. circ. 25,000. Document type: corporate report.

330.9 US ISSN 1054-2159
HD8051
STATE OF WORKING AMERICA. 1988. biennial. $62.95. M.E. Sharpe, Inc., 80 Business Park Dr., Armonk, NY 10504. TEL 914-273-1800. FAX 914-273-2106. Ed.Bd. Indexed: SRI. Document type: academic/scholarly publication.
—BLDSC (8438.335530).

STATISTICAL INDICATORS FOR ASIA AND THE PACIFIC. see BUSINESS AND ECONOMICS — Abstracting, Bibliographies, Statistics

330.9 UN ISSN 0251-0073
STATISTICAL INDICATORS OF SHORT TERM ECONOMIC CHANGES IN E.C.E. COUNTRIES. (Text in English) m. price varies. United Nations Publications, Sales and Marketing Section, Room DC2-0853, New York, NY 10017. TEL 212-963-8302; 800-253-9646. FAX 212-963-3489. E-mail: publications@un.org; URL: http://www.un.org/publications. (Or: E.C.E. Sales Unit C115, CH-121 Geneva 10, Switzerland) circ. 1,650.
Description: Provides an up-to-date overall picture of short-term economic trends in Europe and the U.S.

STATISTICAL YEARBOOK FOR ASIA AND THE PACIFIC/ANNUAIRE STATISTIQUE POUR L'ASIE ET LE PACIFIQUE. see BUSINESS AND ECONOMICS — Abstracting, Bibliographies, Statistics

338 AU ISSN 0039-1107
STEIRISCHE WIRTSCHAFT; Mitteilungsblatt des Steirisch Wirtschaftsbundes. 1964. m. membership. Oesterreichischer Wirtschaftsbund, Landesleitung Steiermark, A-8010 Graz, Austria. Ed. Fritz Kofler. adv.; bk.rev.; stat.; index. circ. 30,000.
Formerly: Steirischer Wirtschaftsbund.

330.9 US ISSN 1051-9521
STRAIGHTTALK. 1990. 10/yr. $395 to non-members; members $195. Conference Board, Inc., 845 Third Ave., New York, NY 10022. TEL 212-759-0900. FAX 212-980-7014. Ed. Gail Fosler. circ. 8,000. Document type: newsletter.
Formerly: Chief Economist's Letter.
Description: Forecasts and commentary on the effect of domestic and international events on the economic outlook by the Conference Board's chief economist.

330.9 327 SA ISSN 1015-5309
STRATEGIC BRIEFING. (Text in English) 1989. m. Business Intelligence Consulting Group (Pty) Ltd., Private Bag 30639, Braamfontein 2017, South Africa. (looseleaf format) Document type: newsletter.

330.9 JA
STRUCTURE OF THE JAPANESE AUTO PARTS INDUSTRY. (Text in English) irreg., latest Oct. 1993. $890. Dodwell Marketing Consultants, Kowa No. 35 Bldg., 14-14, Akasaka 1-chome, Minato-ku, Tokyo 107, Japan. TEL 03-3589-0207. FAX 03-5570-7132. TELEX J22274 DODWELL. charts. Document type: directory.
Description: Covers the leading 500 Japanese auto parts and the 11 automobile manufacturers, their nearly 700 overseas subsidiaries and joint ventures, aftermarket overview and 39 major trade associations.

330.9 GW ISSN 0536-1621
STRUKTUR UND WACHSTUM. REIHE INDUSTRIE. 1964. irreg., vol.48, 1996. price varies. Duncker and Humblot GmbH, Postfach 410329, 12113 Berlin, Germany. TEL 49-30-790006-0.
FAX 49-30-79000631. Document type: monographic series.

330.9 PL
STUDIA EKONOMICZNE. (Text in Polish; summaries in English, Russian) irreg., vol.28, 1992. price varies. Polska Akademiya Nauk, Instytut Nauk Ekonomicznych - Polish Academy of Sciences, Institute of Economic Sciences, Ul. Nowy Swiat 72, 00-330 Warsaw, Poland. TEL 48-22-299146. FAX 48-22-295897. Ed. Mieczyslaw Mieszczankowski. Document type: monographic series.
Description: Papers on different items of economic systems, their reforms, legal aspects of economy and economical functions of state.

330.9 NE ISSN 0886-0416
STUDIES IN REGIONAL SCIENCE AND URBAN ECONOMICS. 1977. irreg., vol.24, 1993. price varies. Elsevier Science B.V., Books Division, P.O. Box 211, 1000 AE Amsterdam, Netherlands. TEL 31-20-4853911. FAX 31-20-4853705. TELEX 18582 ESPA NL. E-mail: nlinfo-f@elsevier.nl; usinfo-f@elsevier.com; forinfo-kyf04035@niftyserve.or.jp; URL: http://www.elsevier.nl/. (Subscr. in the Americas to: Elsevier Science, Regional Sales Office, Box 945, New York, NY 10159-0945. TEL 212-633-3730. FAX 212-633-3680; Subscr. in Australasia and the Far East to: Elsevier Science (Singapore) Pte Ltd, No.1 Temasek Ave., No.17-01 Millenia Tower, Singapore 039192, Singapore. TEL 65-434-3727. FAX 65-337-2230; Subscr. in Japan to: Elsevier Science Japan, 9-15 Higashi-Azabu 1-chome, Minato-ku, Tokyo 106, Japan. TEL 81-3-5561-5033. FAX 81-3-5561-5047) Eds. Ake Andersson, Walter Isard. Indexed: Math.R. Document type: monographic series.
—BLDSC (8491.421000); CISTI.
Refereed Serial

338.947 RU ISSN 1075-7007
HC331
STUDIES ON RUSSIAN ECONOMIC DEVELOPMENT. English translation of: Problemy Prognozirovaniya. 1990. 6/yr. $48 (effective 1998). (Russian Academy of Sciences, Institute of Economic Forecasting) Maik Nauka - Interperiodica, Mezhdunarodnyi Otdel, Ul. Profsoyuznaya, 90, 117864 Moscow, Russia. TEL 7-095-3360066. FAX 7-095-3360666. (Dist. by: Mezhdunarodnaya Kniga, B. Yakimanka 39, 117049 Moscow, Russia. TEL 7-095-2384967. FAX 7-095-2384634; Subscr. to: Maik Nauka - Interperiodica, Subscription Office, Box 1831, Birmingham, AL 35201-1831. TEL 205-995-1567. FAX 205-995-1588) Ed. Yuri V. Yaryomenko. Document type: academic/scholarly publication.
—BLDSC (8491.504800); SWETS.
Formerly (until 1993): Studies on Soviet Economic Development (ISSN 1054-6588)
Description: Provides up-to-date inside information on socioeconomic problems in Russia.

330.9 320 US
SUB-SAHARAN AFRICA REPORT. irreg. (approx. 125/yr.) $7 per no. (foreign $14 per no.). U.S. Joint Publications Research Service, Box 12507, Arlington, VA 22209. TEL 703-487-4630. (Orders to: NTIS, Springfield, VA 22161)
Former titles: Translations on Subsaharan Africa; Translations on Africa.

SUDAN. ECONOMIC AND SOCIAL RESEARCH COUNCIL. OCCASIONAL PAPER. see SOCIAL SCIENCES: COMPREHENSIVE WORKS

330 SJ
SUDAN. MINISTRY OF FINANCE AND NATIONAL ECONOMY. ECONOMIC AND FINANCIAL RESEARCH SECTION. ECONOMIC SURVEY. a. Ministry of Finance and National Economy, Economic and Financial Research Section, Box 2092, Khartoum, Sudan.
Supersedes: Sudan. National Planning Commission. Economic Survey (ISSN 0081-9050)

SUDAN. NATIONAL COUNCIL FOR RESEARCH. ECONOMIC AND SOCIAL RESEARCH COUNCIL. BULLETIN. see SOCIAL SCIENCES: COMPREHENSIVE WORKS

SUDAN. NATIONAL COUNCIL FOR RESEARCH. ECONOMIC AND SOCIAL RESEARCH COUNCIL. RESEARCH REPORT. see SOCIAL SCIENCES: COMPREHENSIVE WORKS

330.9 UK
SUDAN TRADE DIRECTORY. a. Arthur H. Thrower Ltd., 44-46 S. Ealing Rd., London W5, England. adv. Document type: directory.

330.9 331 UY ISSN 0797-0064
SUMA. (Text in Spanish; summaries in English) 1986. 2/yr. Urg.$68000($23) in Latin America; elsewhere $25. (Centro de Investigaciones Economicas (CINVE)) Ediciones Trilce, Guayabo 1729 Ap. 702, 11200 Montevideo, Uruguay. TEL 598-2-40-49-17. FAX 598-2-40-49-47. bk.rev. circ. 700. (back issues avail.) Document type: academic/scholarly publication.
Description: Publishes research done by CINVE on an academic level.

330.9 384.5 UK ISSN 1350-8148
SUMMARY OF WORLD BROADCASTS. PART 1: FORMER U S S R (DAILY). (Subseries of: S W B) 1947. d. £470 for print edition; online via Internet £550 (effective 1997). B B C Worldwide Monitoring, Caversham Park, Reading, Berks. RG4 8TZ, England. TEL 44-118-946-9289. FAX 44-118-946-3823. TELEX 848318. E-mail: marketing@mon.bbc.co.uk; URL: http://www.monitor.bbc.co.uk. Ed. Mike Elliott. R&P contact: Rosy Wolfe. (looseleaf format; back issues avail.) Document type: newspaper.
●Also available online. Vendor(s): Data-Star, Lexis-Nexis, Reuters, Ltd.
—BLDSC (8533.201000).

330.9 384.5 UK ISSN 1350-8156
SUMMARY OF WORLD BROADCASTS. PART 1: FORMER U S S R (WEEKLY ECONOMIC REPORT). (Subseries of: S W B) 1943. w. £335 for print edition; online via Internet £350 (effective 1997). B B C Worldwide Monitoring, Caversham Park, Reading, Berks. RG4 8TZ, England. TEL 44-118-946-9289. FAX 44-118-946-3823. TELEX 848318. E-mail: marketing@mon.bbc.co.uk; URL: http://www.monitor.bbc.co.uk. Ed. Mike Elliott. R&P contact: Rosy Wolfe. (looseleaf format; back issues avail.) Document type: newspaper.
●Also available online. Vendor(s): Data-Star, Lexis-Nexis, Reuters, Ltd.

330.9 384.5 UK ISSN 1352-1365
SUMMARY OF WORLD BROADCASTS. PART 2: CENTRAL EUROPE, THE BALKANS (DAILY). (Subseries of: S W B) 1947. d. £470 for print edition; online via Internet £550 (effective 1997). B B C Worldwide Monitoring, Caversham Park, Reading, Berks. RG4 8TZ, England. TEL 44-118-946-9289. FAX 44-118-946-3823. TELEX 848318. E-mail: marketing@mon.bbc.co.uk; URL: http://www.monitor.bbc.co.uk. Ed. Mike Elliott. R&P contact: Rosy Wolfe. (looseleaf format; back issues avail.) Document type: newspaper.
●Also available online. Vendor(s): Data-Star, Lexis-Nexis, Reuters, Ltd.
Supersedes (in 1993): Summary of World Broadcasts. Part 2: Eastern Europe (Daily) (ISSN 0960-0361)

330.9 384.5 UK ISSN 1352-1373
SUMMARY OF WORLD BROADCASTS. PART 2: CENTRAL EUROPE, THE BALKANS (WEEKLY ECONOMIC REPORT). (Subseries of: S W B) 1943. w. £335 for print edition; online via Internet £350 (effective 1997). B B C Worldwide Monitoring, Caversham Park, Reading, Berks. RG4 8TZ, England. TEL 44-118-946-9289. FAX 44-118-946-3823. TELEX 848318. E-mail: marketing@mon.bbc.co.ukcom; URL: http://www.monitor.bbc.co.uk. Ed. Mike Elliott. R&P contact: Rosy Wolfe. (looseleaf format; back issues avail.) Document type: newspaper.
●Also available online. Vendor(s): Data-Star, Lexis-Nexis, Reuters, Ltd.
—BLDSC (8533.206000).
Supersedes (in 1993): Summary of World Broadcasts. Part 2: Eastern Europe (Weekly Economic Report) (ISSN 0960-037X)

BUSINESS AND ECONOMICS — ECONOMIC SITUATION AND CONDITIONS

330.9 384.5   UK   ISSN 1352-139X
SUMMARY OF WORLD BROADCASTS. PART 3: ASIA - PACIFIC (DAILY). (Subseries of: S W B) 1947. d. £470 for print edition; online via Internet £550 (effective 1997). B B C Worldwide Monitoring, Caversham Park, Reading, Berks. RG4 8TZ, England. TEL 44-118-946-9289. FAX 44-118-946-3823. TELEX 848318. E-mail: marketing@mon.bbc.co.uk; URL: http://www.monitor.bbc.co.uk. Ed. Mike Elliott. R&P contact: Rosy Wolfe. (looseleaf format; back issues avail.) **Document type:** newspaper.
●Also available online. Vendor(s): Data-Star, Lexis-Nexis, Reuters, Ltd.
    Supersedes (in 1993): Summary of World Broadcasts. Part 3: Far East (Daily) (ISSN 0960-0388)

330.9 384.5   UK   ISSN 1352-1403
SUMMARY OF WORLD BROADCASTS. PART 3: ASIA - PACIFIC (WEEKLY ECONOMIC REPORT). (Subseries of: S W B) 1943. w. £335 for print edition; online via Internet £350 (effective 1997). B B C Worldwide Monitoring, Caversham Park, Reading, Berks. RG4 8TZ, England. TEL 44-118-946-9289. FAX 44-118-946-3823. TELEX 848318. E-mail: marketing@mon.bbc.co.uk; URL: http://www.monitor.bbc.co.uk. Ed. Mike Elliott. R&P contact: Rosy Wolfe. (looseleaf format; back issues avail.) **Document type:** newspaper.
●Also available online. Vendor(s): Data-Star, Lexis-Nexis, Reuters, Ltd.
—BLDSC (8533.216000).
    Supersedes (in 1993): Summary of World Broadcasts. Part 3: Far East (Weekly Economic Report) (ISSN 0960-0396)

330.9 384.5   UK   ISSN 1350-8199
SUMMARY OF WORLD BROADCASTS. PART 4: MIDDLE EAST (DAILY). (Subseries of: S W B) 1947. d. £170 for print edition; online via Internet £550 (effective 1997). B B C Worldwide Monitoring, Caversham Park, Reading, Berks. RG4 8TZ, England. TEL 44-118-946-9289. FAX 44-118-946-3823. TELEX 848318. E-mail: marketing@mon.bbc.co.uk; URL: http://www.monitor.bbc.co.uk. Ed. Mike Elliott. R&P contact: Rosy Wolfe. (looseleaf format; back issues avail.) **Document type:** newspaper.
●Also available online. Vendor(s): Data-Star, Lexis-Nexis, Reuters, Ltd.
    Supersedes in part (in 1993): Summary of World Broadcasts. Part 4: Middle East, Africa and Latin America (Daily) (ISSN 0960-040X)

330.9 384.5   UK   ISSN 1350-8202
SUMMARY OF WORLD BROADCASTS. PART 4: MIDDLE EAST (WEEKLY ECONOMIC REPORT). (Subseries of: S W B) 1943. w. £335 for print edition; online via Internet £350 (effective 1997). B B C Worldwide Monitoring, Caversham Park, Reading, Berks. RG4 8TZ, England. TEL 44-118-946-9289. FAX 44-118-946-3823. TELEX 848318. E-mail: marketing@mon.bbc.co.uk; URL: http://www.monitor.bbc.co.uk. Ed. Mike Elliott. R&P contact: Rosy Wolfe. (looseleaf format; back issues avail.) **Document type:** newspaper.
●Also available online. Vendor(s): Data-Star, Lexis-Nexis, Reuters, Ltd.
—BLDSC (8533.221000).
    Supersedes in part (in 1993): Summary of World Broadcasts. Part 4: Middle East, Africa and Latin America (Weekly Economic Report) (ISSN 0960-0418)

330.9 384.5   UK   ISSN 1350-8245
SUMMARY OF WORLD BROADCASTS. PART 5: AFRICA, LATIN AMERICA AND THE CARIBBEAN (DAILY). (Subseries of: S W B) 1993. d. £470 for print edition; online via Internet £550 (effective 1997). B B C Monitoring, Caversham Park, Reading, Berks. RG4 8TZ, England. TEL 44-118-946-9289. FAX 44-118-946-3823. TELEX 848318. E-mail: marketing@mon.bbc.co.uk; URL: http://www.monitor.bbc.co.uk. Ed. Mike Elliott. R&P contact: Rosy Wolfe. (looseleaf format; back issues avail.) **Document type:** newspaper.
●Also available online. Vendor(s): Data-Star, Lexis-Nexis, Reuters, Ltd.
    Supersedes in part (in 1993): Summary of World Broadcasts. Part 4: Middle East, Africa and Latin America (Daily) (ISSN 0960-040X)

330.9 384.5   UK   ISSN 1350-8253
SUMMARY OF WORLD BROADCASTS. PART 5: AFRICA, LATIN AMERICA AND THE CARIBBEAN (WEEKLY ECONOMIC REPORT). (Subseries of: S W B) 1993. w. £335 for print edition; online via Internet £350 (effective 1997). B B C Worldwide Monitoring, Caversham Park, Reading, Berks. RG4 8TZ, England. TEL 44-118-946-9289. FAX 44-118-946-3823. TELEX 848318. E-mail: marketing@mon.bbc.co.uk; URL: http://www.monitor.bbc.co.uk. Ed. Mike Elliott. R&P contact: Rosy Wolfe. (looseleaf format; back issues avail.) **Document type:** newspaper.
●Also available online. Vendor(s): Data-Star, Lexis-Nexis, Reuters, Ltd.
—BLDSC (8533.223000).
    Supersedes in part (in 1993): Summary of World Broadcasts. Part 4: Middle East, Africa and Latin America (Weekly Economic Report) (ISSN 0960-0418)

338   US   ISSN 0039-6222
HC101   CODEN: SVCBAK
SURVEY OF CURRENT BUSINESS. 1921. m. $41 (foreign $51.25) (effective 1995). U.S. Bureau of Economic Analysis, U.S. Department of Commerce, Washington, DC 20230. TEL 202-606-9900. URL: http://www.bea.doc.gov/scbinf.html. (Subscr. to: Superintendent of Documents, U.S. Government Printing Office, Box 371954, Pittsburgh, PA 15250-7954. TEL 202-512-1800. FAX 202-512-2250) Ed. Douglas Fox. charts; illus.; mkt.; stat.; index, s-a. index; circ. 9,400 (paid). (also avail. in microfiche from CIS; back issues avail.; reprint service avail. from CIS) **Indexed:** ABI Inform., Acad.Ind., Amer.Stat.Ind. (1974-), B.P.I., BPIA, Ind.U.S.Gov.Per., J.of Econ. Lit., Key to Econ.Sci., P.A.I.S., PROMT, Tr.& Indus.Ind. **Document type:** government publication.
●Also available online. Vendor(s): Information Access Co., Knight-Ridder Information, Inc., UMI.
—BLDSC (8549.100000); KR SourceOne; SWETS; UMI; UnCover.
    Description: Gives information on trends in industry, business, and the general economic outlook, as well as other points pertinent to the business world.

330.9   UK
SURVEY OF DUNBARTONSHIRE MANUFACTURING AND EXPORTS IN (YEAR). a. Scottish Council Development and Industry, 23 Chester St., Edinburgh EH3 7ET, Scotland. TEL 031-225-7911. FAX 031-220-2116. **Document type:** bulletin.

330.9   CE
SURVEY OF HOUSEHOLD ECONOMIC ACTIVITIES (YEAR). irreg., latest 1984-85 (2nd ed.). Rs.65. Department of Census and Statistics, P.O. Box 563, 6 Albert Crescent, Colombo 7, Sri Lanka. TEL 94-682178. (Dist. by: Superintendent, Government Publications Bureau, Colombo 1, Sri Lanka) Ed. A.G.W. Nanayakkara. circ. 1,441. **Document type:** government publication.

330.9   US   ISSN 0085-3410
HC110.S3
SURVEYS OF CONSUMERS; contributions to behavioral economics. 1947. irreg. $16. University of Michigan, Institute for Social Research, I.S.R. Administration, Box 1248, Ann Arbor, MI 48106. TEL 313-763-8363. FAX 313-747-4575. **Indexed:** SRI.
    Formerly (until 1970): Survey of Consumer Finances (ISSN 0081-9727)

330.9   FI   ISSN 1235-7405
SURVEYS OF ECONOMIES IN TRANSITION. (Text in English, Finnish) 1992. irreg. free. Bank of Finland, Unit for Eastern European Economies, FIN-00101 Helsinki, Finland. TEL 358-9183-2268.

330.9   SW   ISSN 0345-2719
SVENSKA BANKFOERENINGEN. EKONOMISKA MEDDELANDEN. 1910. w. SEK 625($60) Svenska Bankfoereningen - Swedish Bankers' Association, P.O. Box 7603, S-103 94 Stockholm, Sweden. circ. 1,350.

330.9   SQ
SWAZILAND. DEPARTMENT OF ECONOMIC PLANNING AND STATISTICS. ECONOMIC REVIEW. 1970. a. E.3. Department of Economic Planning and Statistics, P.O. Box 602, Mbabane, Swaziland. illus.
    Formerly: Swaziland. Economic Planning Office. Economic Review.

SWEDISH EXAMPLE; international newsletter. see POLITICAL SCIENCE

330.9   SZ
SWISS FINANCIAL YEAR BOOK. 1978. a. 185 SFr. (CD-ROM 995 SFr.). Elvetica Edizioni S.A., Via Vela 6, Casella Postale 134, CH-6834 Morbio, Switzerland. TEL 091-435056. FAX 091-437605. Ed. M.G. Grosso. adv. circ. 5,000. **Document type:** directory.
●Also available on CD-ROM.

330.9   SZ   ISSN 0255-9064
SWITZERLAND. KOMMISSION FUER KONJUNKTURFRAGEN. WIRTSCHAFTSLAGE. French edition: Switzerland. Commission pour les Questions Conjoncturelles. Situation Economique (ISSN 1421-3907) (Supplement to: Switzerland. Eidgenoessisches Volkswirtschaftsdepartement. Volkswirtschaft) 1932. q. Bundesamt fuer Konjunkturfragen, Kommission fuer Konjunkturfragen, Effingerstr. 27, CH-3003 Bern, Switzerland. TEL 41-31-3222138. FAX 41-31-3249615. stat. **Document type:** government publication.
    Incorporates (in 1989): Schweizerische Konjunktur und Vorausschau.

330.9   CN
T D QUARTERLY ECONOMIC REPORT; commentary, charts, tables. 1959. q. free. Toronto Dominion Bank, Toronto-Dominion Centre, P.O. Box 1, Toronto, ON M5K 1A2, Canada. TEL 416-982-8065. FAX 416-944-5536. E-mail: economic@tdbank.ca; URL: http://www.tdbank.ca. Ed. R. Getter. R&P contact: Medlinda Wong. circ. 22,000. (also avail. in microfiche from UMI; reprint service avail. from UMI) **Indexed:** Can.B.P.I., Can.Per.Ind. **Document type:** monographic series.
—UMI.
    Former titles: Canada's Business Climate (ISSN 0045-4303); Toronto-Dominion Bank Chartbook.

330.9   RE   ISSN 0994-415X
HC598.A1
TABLEAU ECONOMIQUE DE LA REUNION. 1981. a. 70 F. (France 80 F.; elsewhere 90 F.). Institut National de la Statistique et des Etudes Economiques, Direction Regionale de la Reunion, 15 rue de l'Ecole, B.P. 13, 97408 St. Denis Messag Cedex 9, Reunion. bk.rev. circ. 2,500.
    Formerly: Panorama de l'Economie de la Reunion.

330.9   FR   ISSN 0983-5733
TABLEAUX ECONOMIQUES DE L'ILE-DE-FRANCE. 1979. biennial. 65 F. Institut National de la Statistique et des Etudes Economiques (INSEE), Direction Regionale d'Ile-de-France, 7 rue Stephenson, Montigny-le-Bretonneux, 78188 Saint-Quentin-en-Yvelines Cedex, France. TEL 33-1-30969000. FAX 33-1-30969001. Ed. Annie Etienne. adv. contact: Jacqueline Riou. index. circ. 2,300. (back issues avail.)

330.9   CH   ISSN 0255-5697
TAIWAN ECONOMY. Key Title: Taiwan Jingji. (Text mainly in Chinese; occasionally in English) 1977. m. Taiwan Provincial Government, Council for Economic Planning and Mobilization, 56 Chung-Hsing Hsin-Tsun Fu W. Rd., Nantou, Taiwan, Republic of China. TEL 049-333963. (Overseas subscr. to: National Central Library, 2 Chung Shan S. Rd., Taipei, Taiwan, R.O.C.) Ed. Hsu Lai-Chun. charts; stat.

330.4   US
TAKING SIDES: CLASHING VIEWS ON CONTROVERSIAL ECONOMIC ISSUES. irreg., 5th ed., 1990. $13.95. Dushkin Publishing Group, Sluice Dock, Guilford, CT 06437-9989. TEL 203-453-4351. FAX 203-543-6000. Eds. Frank J. Bonello, Thomas R. Swartz; Pub. MiMi Egan. illus. **Document type:** academic/scholarly publication.

BUSINESS AND ECONOMICS — ECONOMIC SITUATION AND CONDITIONS

330.9   US   ISSN 0273-5830
TAMPA BAY BUSINESS JOURNAL. 1981. w. $42. American City Business Journals, Inc. (Tampa), Box 24185, Tampa, FL 33623. TEL 813-877-6627. Ed. Allen Greenberg; Pub. John Beddow. R&P contact: Allen Greenberg. TEL 813-873-8225. adv. contact: Scott McQuigg. circ. 23,500. (reprint service avail.) Indexed: Tr.& Indus.Ind. Document type: trade publication.
●Also available online. Vendor(s): Information Access Co.
—UMI. CCC.
Formerly: Tampa Bay Business Weekly.
Description: Covers business news in Hillsborough and Pinellas counties in Florida.

TENDENZE DELLA OCCUPAZIONE. see *BUSINESS AND ECONOMICS — Labor And Industrial Relations*

TENNESSEE'S BUSINESS. see *BUSINESS AND ECONOMICS — Small Business*

330.9   IT   ISSN 1121-9572
TERZIARIA. 1985. q. L.50000. Gedip s.r.l., Via Ippolito Nievo 61, 00153 Rome, Italy. TEL 39-6-5895215. FAX 39-6-5806396. Ed. Alessandro Sciorelli. adv.: B&W page L.4000000, color page L.5500000. circ. 12,000.

TEXAS LABOR MARKET REVIEW. see *BUSINESS AND ECONOMICS — Labor And Industrial Relations*

330   TH
THAILAND: ECONOMIC CONDITIONS IN AND OUTLOOK FOR. 1978. a. free. Bank of Thailand, Department of Economic Research, P.O. Box 154 BMC., Bangkok, Thailand. TEL 662-282-5617. FAX 662-282-5082. circ. 5,000.

338   TH
THAILAND INVESTMENT; a directory of companies promoted by the Board of Investment. a. $60. Cosmic Group of Companies, 4th Fl., Phyathai Bldg., 31 Phyathai Rd., Rajthevi, Bangkok 10400, Thailand. Ed.Bd. adv.: color page L1320. illus. Document type: directory.
Description: Lists about 4000 companies promoted by the Board of Investment of Thailand, and other useful contact addresses for doing business in Thailand.

330.9   TH   ISSN 0125-1074
HC445.A1
THANAKHAN HAENG PRATHET THAI RAINGAN SETTHAKIT RAIDUAN/BANK OF THAILAND. MONTHLY BULLETIN. (Text in Thai) 1961. m. B.2340($90) Bank of Thailand, Department of Economic Research, P.O. Box 154 BMC., Bangkok, Thailand. TEL 662-283-5617. FAX 662-282-5082. circ. 2,200. Document type: bulletin.

338   MW   ISSN 0563-4784
THIS IS MALAWI. (Text in English) 1964-1969; resumed 1971. m. K.5. Department of Information, P.O. Box 494, Blantyre, Malawi. TEL 265-620266. TELEX 44471. Ed. A. Livuza. adv.; bk.rev.; illus.; stat. circ. 3,000. (back issues avail.) Document type: government publication.
Formerly: Vision of Malawi.

330.9   US
THRIFT FINANCIAL REPORT. q. $960 in US, Canada, Mexico; elsewhere $1920. (Federal Home Loan Bank Board) U.S. National Technical Information Service, 5825 Port Royal Rd., Springfield, VA 22161. TEL 703-487-4630. (magnetic tape)
Description: Data are available beginning March 1987 and are reported for the institution as a whole. For geographic reports, data are reported on the basis of home office location.

TIMELY DISCLOSURE. see *BUSINESS AND ECONOMICS — Banking And Finance*

TODAY'S INTERNIST. see *MEDICAL SCIENCES — Internal Medicine*

330   JA   ISSN 0286-4827
TOKAI MONTHLY ECONOMIC LETTER. (Text in English) vol.5, 1974. m. free. Tokai Bank Ltd., 3-21-24 Nishiki, Naka-ku, Nagoya, Japan. Ed.Bd. adv. circ. 3,200. Indexed: World Bank.Abstr.

TOKYO INDUSTRY; a graphic overview. see *PUBLIC ADMINISTRATION — Municipal Government*

330.9   AT
TOOWOOMBA INDUSTRIAL PROFILE. 1984. irreg. Aus.$5. Toowoomba Regional Development Corporation Ltd., 541 Ruthven St., Toowoomba, Qld. 4350, Australia. TEL 076-385977.
Description: Presents industrial situation in Toowoomba, aimed at business immigrants.

330.9   US   ISSN 1051-7197
TRACKING EASTERN EUROPE; executive business guide. 1990. bi-w. $445 (Canada $465; Europe $475). A M F International Consultants, 812 N. Wood Ave., Ste. 204, Linden, NJ 07036. TEL 908-486-3534. FAX 908-486-4084. Ed. Fred T. Rossi; Pub. Andrew M. Findeisen. R&P contact: Andrew M. Findeisen. bk.rev. Document type: newsletter.
Description: Provides news, current trends, and listings from Eastern Europe and former Soviet marketplaces.

TRADE MONITOR. see *PUBLIC ADMINISTRATION*

330.9   US
TRANSITION NEWSLETTER. 1990. 16/yr. $20 for 4 issues (May-Dec.) (effective 1997); $30 for 16 issues (Jan.-Dec. (effective 1998); free to non-OECD countries and to Poland, Hungary , Czech Republic. c/o Jennifer Prochnow, Rm. N11-039X, 1818 H St., N.W., Washington, DC 20433. URL: http://www.worldbank.org. Ed. Richard Hirschler; Pub. Dirk Kochler. R&P contact: Audrey Heiligman. TEL 202-458-1673. adv. contact: Brett Kitchen. bk.rev. circ. 10,000. Document type: newsletter.
●Available only online.
Description: Covers transition economies, including Central and Eastern Europe, FSU, Asia, China and more.

TRAVEL BUSINESS ANALYST (ASIA PACIFIC EDITION). see *TRAVEL AND TOURISM*

TRAVEL BUSINESS ANALYST (EUROPEAN EDITION). see *TRAVEL AND TOURISM*

330   GW   ISSN 0942-1300
TRENDS. (English edition avail. (ISSN 0942-1319)) (Text in English, German) 1948. m. Dresdner Bank AG, Volkswirtschaftliche Abteilung, 60301 Frankfurt a.M., Germany. TEL 069-2633795. FAX 069-2636973. charts; stat. (reprint service avail. from SCH) Indexed: Rural Recreat.Tour.Abstr., World Agri.Econ.& Rural Sociol.Abstr. Document type: trade publication.
Former titles: Wirtschaftsberichte (ISSN 0043-6259); Dresdner Bank - Economic Quarterly (ISSN 0174-0431)

330.9   US
TRENDS IN EMPLOYMENT AND WAGES COVERED BY UNEMPLOYMENT INSURANCE. 1944. a. $10. Department of Labor, Division of Labor Market and Demographic Research, Box 934, Trenton, NJ 08625. TEL 609-984-5586. URL: http://www.state.nj.us/labor/ira. Ed. William Saley. circ. 1,100. Document type: government publication.
Former titles: Covered Employment Trends in New Jersey; Covered Employment Trends in New Jersey by Geographical Areas of the State; New Jersey Covered Employment Trends by Geographical Areas of the State (ISSN 0092-1459)

TRENTINO; rivista della provincia autonoma di Trento. see *ENVIRONMENTAL STUDIES*

330   RM   ISSN 1222-7803
TRIBUNA ECONOMICA. 1974. w. 3260 lei($125) Tribuna Economica s.r.l., Bd. Magheru 28-30, 70159 Bucharest, Rumania. TEL 59-51-58. (Subscr. to: ILEXIM, Str. 13 Decembrie Nr. 3, P.O. Box 136-137, Bucharest) Ed. Bogdan Padure. adv.; bk.rev. circ. 50,000.
Formerly (until Dec. 1989): Revista Economica.
Description: Provides information, analyses, studies, and economic and legal regulations.

TURKEY. DEVLET ISTATISTIK ENSTITUSU. YAYINLAY VE ELEKTRONIK HIZMETLER KATALOGU. see *BUSINESS AND ECONOMICS — Abstracting, Bibliographies, Statistics*

330   TU   ISSN 0034-6500
HC491
TURKIYE IS BANKASI. REVIEW OF ECONOMIC CONDITIONS. (Editions in English, Turkish) 1954. q. free. Turkiye Is Bankasi, Economic Research and Planning Department, Ataturk Bulvari 191, Kavaklidere, Ankara, Turkey.
FAX 90-312-4139090. TELEX 43388 TIBTR. Ed. Nese Demir. R&P contact: Nese Demir. abstr.; charts; stat. circ. 3,850 (1,850 English ed., 2,000 Turkish ed.). Document type: bulletin.

330.9   US   ISSN 1072-673X
TWIN CITIES BUSINESS MONTHLY. 1993. m. M S P Communications, Pillsbury Ctr., S. Tower, 220 S. Sixth St., Ste. 500, Minneapolis, MN 55402. TEL 612-339-7571. (Subscr. to: Box 697, Mt. Morris, IL 61954-7585) Document type: trade publication.

330.9 331.8   PL   ISSN 0208-8045
DK4448
TYGODNIK SOLIDARNOSC/SOLIDARITY WEEKLY. 1981(Aug.)-1981(Dec.); resumed Jun. 1989. w. $200 (effective 1998). (Niezalezny Samorzadny Zwiazek Zawodowy "Solidarnosc" - Independent Self-Governed Trade Union "Solidarity") Tygodnik Solidarnosc, Ul. Koscielna 12, 00-218 Warsaw, Poland. TEL 48-22-6376111.
FAX 48-22-3178581. (Dist. by: RSW "Prasa-Ksiazka-Ruch", Centrala Kolportazu Prasy i Wydawnictw, ul. Towarowa 28, 00-958 Warsaw, Poland; Dist. also by: Mezhdunarodnaya Kniga, B. Yakimanka 39, 117049 Moscow, Russia. TEL 7-095-2384967. FAX 7-095-2384634) Ed. Andrzej Gelberg. Indexed: AgroLibrex.
Description: Articles on the political and economic situation in Poland, with emphasis on the Solidarity labor movement.

330.9   UK
U K CHRONOLOGY. 5/yr. £150 (academic institutions and students £75). Barclays Bank plc., Economics Department, P.O. Box 12, Barclays House, 1 Wimborne Rd., Poole, Dorset BH15 2BB, England. TEL 01202-344023. FAX 01202-402303.

330.9   UK   ISSN 0968-8196
U K ECONOMIC FORECASTS.* 1974. m. £1190($1785) (effective 1994). Henley Centre for Forecasting Ltd., 9 Bridewell Pl., Blackfriars, London EC4Y 6AY, England. TEL 0171-353-9961. FAX 0171-353-2899. Eds. Stephen Radley, Krishnan Sharma. charts; stat. Document type: trade publication.
Formerly (until 1992): Framework Forecasts for the U K Economy (ISSN 0305-5620)
Description: Presents short- and medium-term views of the U.K. economy, providing detailed economic forecasts.

330.9   UK
U K ECONOMY: PRODUCER PRICE INDICES. (Part of the Business Monitor series) m. £230 (effective 1997). (Office for National Statistics) H.M.S.O., P.O. Box 276, London SW8 5DT, England.
TEL 44-171-873-9090. FAX 44-171-873-8200. charts; stat. Document type: government publication.
Formerly (until 1996): Business Monitor: Producer Price Incides.
Description: Contains indices on UK manufactured products, together with the materials and fuel purchased and the home sales at both broad and detailed industry levels.

THE U S A AND CANADA (YEAR). see *POLITICAL SCIENCE*

330.9   US
U S MARKETS REVIEW. (In 5 vols.: Regional Summary, Northeast Focus, Midwestern Focus, Southern Focus, Western Focus) q. D R I - McGraw-Hill, 24 Hartwell Ave., Lexington, MA 02173. TEL 617-863-5100. FAX 617-860-6332. TELEX 200 284. Ed. Sara Johnson. Document type: trade publication.
Formerly: Regional Information Service Review.

BUSINESS AND ECONOMICS — ECONOMIC SITUATION AND CONDITIONS

330.9   US
UNEMPLOYMENT IN STATES. (Subseries of: National Office News Releases) m. U.S. Bureau of Labor Statistics, 2 Massachusetts Ave., N.E., Washington, DC 20212. TEL 202-655-4000. (Subscr. to: Superintendent of Documents, U.S. Government Printing Office, Box 371954, Pittsburgh, PA 15250-7954. TEL 202-512-1800. FAX 202-512-2250; Or: Bureau of Labor Statistics Publications Sales Center, Box 2145, Chicago, IL 60690) **Document type:** government publication.

330   FI   ISSN 0041-7130
HC337.F5   CODEN: UNTSAK
UNITAS. (Editions in English, Finnish, German, Swedish) 1929. q. free. Union Bank of Finland, Economic Research Department, FIN-00020 UBF, Finland. FAX 358-0-6572898. TELEX 124407 UNIT FI. Ed. Juha Ahtola. charts; stat.; index every 3 yrs. circ. 125,000 (combined). **Indexed:** ABI Inform., Key to Econ.Sci., M.L.A., P.A.I.S.
• Also available online. Vendor(s): UMI.
—BLDSC (9090.791000); UMI; UnCover.

330.9 332   HT
UNITE DE PROGRAMMATION DU MINISTERE. BULLETIN DE CONJONCTURE. vol.8, 1956. q. free. Unite de Programmation du Ministere, Economie des Finances et de l'Industrie, Port-au-Prince, Haiti. FAX 509-23-12-47.
Formerly: Economie et Developpement.

330   PK
UNITED BANK LIMITED. ECONOMIC JOURNAL. (Text in English) vol.5, 1973. m. free. United Bank Limited, Research Department, State Life Bldg., I.I. Chundrigar Rd., Karachi, Pakistan. TEL 224954. Ed. Jalees Ahmed Faruqui. bk.rev.; charts; stat. circ. 4,000.
Formerly (until Dec. 1981): United Bank Limited. Monthly Economic Newsletter.

UNITED NATIONS. ECONOMIC AND SOCIAL COUNCIL. OFFICIAL RECORDS. see POLITICAL SCIENCE — International Relations

338   UN   ISSN 1014-4994
UNITED NATIONS. ECONOMIC COMMISSION FOR EUROPE. ECONOMIC STUDIES. 1949. irreg. (approx. a.). $50. Economic Commission for Europe (ECE), Palais des Nations, 1211 Geneva 10, Switzerland. TEL 022-734-6011. FAX 022-733-9879. (Or: United Nations Publications, Rm. DC2-853, New York, NY 10017. TEL 212-963-8302. FAX 212-932-3489) (also avail. in microfiche)
—BLDSC (3655.760000); SWETS; UMI. **CCC.**
Supersedes in part (in 1989): Economic Bulletin for Europe (Quarterly) (ISSN 0041-638X)

338   UN   ISSN 1014-9066
HC240.A1
UNITED NATIONS ECONOMIC COMMISSION FOR EUROPE. DISCUSSION PAPERS. 1949. 4/yr. Economic Commission for Europe (ECE), Palais des Nations, 1211 Geneva 10, Switzerland. TEL 022-917-2720. FAX 022-917-0036. (Or: United Nations Publications, Rm. DC2-853, New York, NY 10017. TEL 212-963-8302. FAX 212-963-3489) **Document type:** monographic series, government publication.
—BLDSC (3652.300000); SWETS; UMI. **CCC.**
Formerly (until 1991): United Nations Economic Commission for Europe. Occasional Studies; Supersedes in part (in 1989): Economic Bulletin for Europe (Quarterly) (ISSN 0041-638X)

330.9 317   US
U.S. BUREAU OF LABOR STATISTICS. AREA WAGE SURVEYS. (Area editions avail. separately) s-a. and a. eds. avail. U.S. Bureau of Labor Statistics, 2 Massachusetts Ave., N.W., Washington, DC 20212. TEL 202-606-6220. (Subscr. to: Superintendent of Documents, U.S. Government Printing Office, Box 371954, Pittsburgh, PA 15250-7954. TEL 202-512-1800. FAX 202-512-2250; Or: Bureau of Labor Statistics Publications Sales Center, Box 2145, Chicago, IL 60690) stat. **Document type:** government publication.

331.1   US   ISSN 0082-9021
HD8051
U.S. BUREAU OF LABOR STATISTICS. BULLETINS. Variant title: B L S Bulletins. (Comprises multiple subseries) 1913. irreg. price varies. U.S. Bureau of Labor Statistics, 2 Massachusetts Ave., Washington, DC 20212. TEL 202-655-4000. (Subscr. to: Superintendent of Documents, U.S. Government Printing Office, Box 371954, Pittsburgh, PA 15250-7954. TEL 202-512-1800. FAX 202-512-2250; Or: Bureau of Labor Statistics Publications Sales Center, Box 2145, Chicago, IL 60690) **Indexed:** P.A.I.S. **Document type:** government publication.

330.9   US   ISSN 0095-926X
HB235.U6
U.S. BUREAU OF LABOR STATISTICS. C P I DETAILED REPORT. 1919. m. $23 (foreign $28.75). U.S. Bureau of Labor Statistics, 2 Massachusetts Ave., N.E., Washington, DC 20212. TEL 202-655-4000. (Subscr. to: Superintendent of Documents, U.S. Government Printing Office, Box 371954, Pittsburgh, PA 15250-7954. TEL 202-512-1800. FAX 202-512-2250) stat. (also avail. in microfiche from CIS; back issues avail.; reprint service avail. from CIS) **Indexed:** Amer.Stat.Ind. (1973-), P.A.I.S. **Document type:** government publication.
• Also available online.
Also available on CD-ROM.
Formerly: U.S. Bureau of Labor Statistics. Consumer Price Index (ISSN 0094-8616)

330.9   US
U.S. BUREAU OF LABOR STATISTICS. NATIONAL OFFICE NEWS RELEASES. (Comprises multiple subseries) irreg. price varies. U.S. Bureau of Labor Statistics, 2 Massachusetts Ave., N.E., Washington, DC 20212. TEL 202-655-4000. (Subscr. to: Superintendent of Documents, U.S. Government Printing Office, Box 371954, Pittsburgh, PA 15250-7954. TEL 202-512-1800. FAX 202-512-2250; Or: Bureau of Labor Statistics Publications Sales Center, Box 2145, Chicago, IL 60690) **Document type:** government publication.
• Also available online.

330.9   US
U.S. BUREAU OF LABOR STATISTICS. REPORTS. Variant title: B L S Reports. (Comprises multiple subseries) irreg. price varies. U.S. Bureau of Labor Statistics, 2 Massachusetts Ave., N.E., Washington, DC 20212. TEL 202-655-4000. (Subscr. to: Superintendent of Documents, U.S. Government Printing Office, Box 371954, Pittsburgh, PA 15250-7954. TEL 202-512-1800. FAX 202-512-2250; Or: Bureau of Labor Statistics Publications Sales Center, Box 2145, Chicago, IL 60690) **Document type:** government publication.

330.9   US
U.S. BUREAU OF LABOR STATISTICS. REPRINT SERIES. irreg. U.S. Bureau of Labor Statistics, 2 Massachusetts Ave., N.E., Washington, DC 20212. TEL 202-655-4000. (Subscr. to: Superintendent of Documents, U.S. Government Printing Office, Box 371954, Pittsburgh, PA 15250-7954. TEL 202-512-1800. FAX 202-512-2250; Or: Bureau of Labor Statistics Publications Sales Center, Box 2145, Chicago, IL 60690) **Document type:** government publication.
Description: Reissues key articles from Monthly Labor Review and other B.L.S. publications.

330.9 332.6   US
U.S. IMPORT AND EXPORT PRICE INDEXES. (Subseries of: National Office News Releases) m. U.S. Bureau of Labor Statistics, 2 Massachusetts Ave., N.E., Washington, DC 20212. TEL 202-655-4000. (Subscr. to: Superintendent of Documents, U.S. Government Printing Office, Box 371954, Pittsburgh, PA 15250-7954. TEL 202-512-1800. FAX 202-512-2250; Or: Bureau of Labor Statistics Publications Sales Center, Box 2145, Chicago, IL 60690) (also avail. in diskette format) **Document type:** government publication.

330.9   EC
UNIVERSIDAD CENTRAL DEL ECUADOR. INSTITUTO DE INVESTIGACIONES ECONOMICAS. BOLETIN ECONOMIA. 4/yr. $12.50. Universidad Central del Ecuador, Instituto de Investigaciones Economicas, Ciudad Universitaria, Apdo. 17-03-0724, Quito, Ecuador. TEL 593-2-525018. FAX 593-2-229481. E-mail: secretar@iieuc.ecx.ec. Dir. Isaias Campana C.

330.9   SP
UNIVERSIDAD DE SEVILLA. INSTITUTO DE DESARROLLO REGIONAL. EDICIONES. irreg. price varies. Universidad de Sevilla, Instituto de Desarrollo Regional, Servicio de Publicaciones, Calle Porvenir 27, 041013 Seville, Spain. TEL 34-5-4231958. FAX 34-5-4232245. charts; illus.

330.9   CK   ISSN 0120-3789
UNIVERSIDAD Y COOPERATIVISMO. 1975. Col.$1500. Cooperativa I N D E S C O, Avda. Caracas 37-63, Bogota, Colombia. Ed. Armando Suescun.
Formerly: Cooperativismo y Desarrollo.

330.9   GW
UNIVERSITAET ZU KOELN. INSTITUT FUER HANDELSFORSCHUNG. BEITRAEGE ZUR DOKUMENTATION DER BETRIEBSWIRTSCHAFTLICHEN SITUATION IM GROSS- UND EINZELHANDEL. 1970. 6/yr. price varies. Verlag Otto Schwartz und Co., Annastr. 7, 37075 Goettingen, Germany. TEL 49-551-31051. FAX 49-551-372812. **Document type:** academic/scholarly publication.

330.9   US
UNIVERSITY OF COLORADO. BUSINESS RESEARCH DIVISION. ANNUAL BUSINESS - ECONOMIC OUTLOOK FORUM. 1964. a. $25 to Colorado nonresidents. University of Colorado, Business Research Division, Campus Box 420, Boulder, CO 80309-0420. TEL 303-492-8227. FAX 303-492-3620. **Document type:** proceedings.

330.9   UK
UNIVERSITY OF MANCHESTER. SCHOOL OF ECONOMIC STUDIES. DISCUSSION PAPER. irreg. University of Manchester, School of Economic Studies, Oxford Rd., Manchester M13 9PL, England. **Document type:** monographic series.
Formerly (until 1994): University of Manchester. Department of Econometrics and Social Statistics. Discussion Paper.

UNIVERSITY OF NAIROBI. INSTITUTE FOR DEVELOPMENT STUDIES. WORKING PAPER. see HISTORY — History Of Africa

330.9   SA
UNIVERSITY OF PORT ELIZABETH. INSTITUTE FOR DEVELOPMENT PLANNING AND RESEARCH. FACT PAPER SERIES. 1971. irreg., no.101, 1996. R.80. University of Port Elizabeth, Institute for Development Planning and Research, P.O. Box 1600, Port Elizabeth 6000, South Africa. TEL 27-41-5042336. FAX 27-41-531769. E-mail: piaddp@upe.ac.za. **Document type:** monographic series.
Formerly: University of Port Elizabeth. Institute for Planning Research. Fact Paper Series.
Description: Presents information compiled during the course of research projects, including spin-off investigations.

330.9   SA
UNIVERSITY OF PORT ELIZABETH. INSTITUTE FOR DEVELOPMENT PLANNING AND RESEARCH. INFORMATION BULLETIN SERIES. 1971. irreg., no.25, 1994. R.30. University of Port Elizabeth, Institute for Development Planning and Research, P.O. Box 1600, Port Elizabeth 6000, South Africa. TEL 27-41-5042336. FAX 27-41-531769. E-mail: piaddp@upe.ac.za. stat. **Document type:** monographic series.
Formerly: University of Port Elizabeth. Institute for Planning Research. Information Bulletin Series.
Description: Preliminary research results, issued upon completion of fieldwork.

330.9   SA
UNIVERSITY OF PORT ELIZABETH. INSTITUTE FOR DEVELOPMENT PLANNING AND RESEARCH. OCCASIONAL PAPERS SERIES. (Text in Afrikaans, English) 1978. irreg., no.59, 1995. R.80. University of Port Elizabeth, Institute for Development Planning and Research, P.O. Box 1600, Port Elizabeth 6000, South Africa. TEL 27-41-5042336. FAX 27-41-531769. E-mail: piaddp@upe.ac.za. **Document type:** monographic series.
Formerly: University of Port Elizabeth. Institute for Planning Research. Occasional Papers Series.

BUSINESS AND ECONOMICS — ECONOMIC SITUATION AND CONDITIONS

330.9   SA
UNIVERSITY OF PORT ELIZABETH. INSTITUTE FOR DEVELOPMENT PLANNING AND RESEARCH. RESEARCH REPORT. (Text in Afrikaans, English) 1968. irreg., no.63, 1995. R.30. University of Port Elizabeth, Institute for Development Planning and Research, P.O. Box 1600, Port Elizabeth 6000, South Africa. TEL 27-41-5042336. FAX 27-41-531769. E-mail: piaddp@upe.ac.za. **Document type:** academic/scholarly publication.
Formerly: University of Port Elizabeth. Institute for Planning Research. Research Report.

330.9   SA
UNIVERSITY OF PORT ELIZABETH. INSTITUTE FOR DEVELOPMENT PLANNING AND RESEARCH. SPECIAL PUBLICATIONS SERIES. (Text in Afrikaans, English) 1971. irreg., vol.19, 1995. R.30. University of Port Elizabeth, Institute for Development Planning and Research, P.O. Box 1600, Port Elizabeth 6000, South Africa. TEL 27-41-5042336. FAX 27-41-531769. E-mail: piaddp@upe.ac.za. **Document type:** monographic series.
Formerly: University of Port Elizabeth. Institute for Planning Research. Special Publications Series.
Description: Post graduate level research conducted at the institute.

330.968   SA   ISSN 0259-4862
UNIVERSITY OF STELLENBOSCH. BUREAU FOR ECONOMIC RESEARCH. ECONOMIC PROSPECTS. Key Title: Economic Prospects (Stellenbosch). (Supplement avail.) 1957. 2/yr. R.585 (effective 1996 & 1997). University of Stellenbosch, Bureau for Economic Research, Private Bag 5050, University, Stellenbosch 7599, South Africa. TEL 27-21-8872810. FAX 27-21-8899225. TELEX 520-383 SA. E-mail: odjs@maties.sun.ac.za. Ed. P. Laubscher. circ. 800.
Formerly (until 1986): University of Stellenbosch. Bureau for Economic Research. Survey of Contemporary Economic Conditions and Prospects (ISSN 0081-5454)
Description: Covers the entire South African economy, including consumer income considerations, the impact of political developments and international events. Reviews current economic trends and events and provides forecasts of inflation, exchange rates, interest rates and other factors.

330.968   SA
UNIVERSITY OF STELLENBOSCH. BUREAU FOR ECONOMIC RESEARCH. UPDATE. (Supplement to: University of Stellenbosch. Bureau for Economic Research. Economic Prospects (ISSN 0259-4862)) 1994. m. University of Stellenbosch, Bureau for Economic Research, Private Bag 5050, University, Stellenbosch 7599, South Africa. TEL 27-21-8872810. FAX 27-21-8839225. TELEX 520-383 SA. E-mail: nt@maties.sun.ac.za. **Indexed:** Ind.S.A.Per.
Formed by the merger of (1983-1994): South African Business Cycle Indicators; (1989-1994): Economic Update.

UNIVERZITA KOMENSKEHO. USTAV MARXIZMU-LENINIZMU. ZBORNIK: POLITICKA EKONOMIA. see BUSINESS AND ECONOMICS — Economic Systems And Theories, Economic History

330.9   PL
UNIWERSYTET OPOLSKI. ZESZYTY NAUKOWE. SERIA A. EKONOMIA. (Text in Polish; summaries in English) 1965. irreg., vol.23, 1996. price varies; avail. on exchange basis. Uniwersytet Opolski, Sienkiewicza 33, 45-037 Opole, Poland. TEL 48-77-538387. E-mail: rektorat@opole.pl. Ed. Janusz Slodczyk. **Indexed:** AgroLibrex. **Document type:** academic/scholarly publication.
Formerly (until 1994): Wyzsza Szkola Pedagogiczna, Opole. Zeszyty Naukow. Seria A. Ekonomia (ISSN 0474-2966)

330   UY   ISSN 0379-6590
HC231
URUGUAY ECONOMICO. 1978. s-a. Urg.$32. Ministerio de Economia y Finanzas, Asesoria Economico Financiera, Colonia 1013, Piso 8, Montevideo, Uruguay. circ. 2,000.

330.9   UY
URUGUAY SINTESIS ECONOMICA. s-a. Banco Central del Uruguay, Departamento de Estadisticas Economicas, Casilla 1467, Paysando y Florida, Montevideo, Uruguay.

330.9   US
USUAL WEEKLY EARNINGS OF WAGE AND SALARY WORKERS. (Subseries of: National Office News Releases) a. U.S. Bureau of Labor Statistics, 2 Massachusetts Ave., N.E., Washington, DC 20212. TEL 202-655-4000. (Subscr. to: Superintendent of Documents, U.S. Government Printing Office, Box 371954, Pittsburgh, PA 15250-7954. TEL 202-512-1800. FAX 202-512-2250; Or: Bureau of Labor Statistics Publications Sales Center, Box 2145, Chicago, IL 60690) **Document type:** government publication.

330.9   US
UTAH LABOR MARKET REPORT. 1950. m. free. Department of Employment Security, Labor Market Information Services, 140 E. Broadway, Salt Lake City, UT 84111-2333. TEL 801-536-7810. FAX 801-536-7808. Ed. W.R. Horner. circ. 3,500. (also avail. in microfiche from CIS) **Indexed:** SRI. **Document type:** government publication.
Description: Current labor market statistics and analysis for Utah.

VANTAGE POINT; developments in North Korea. see POLITICAL SCIENCE

VANUATU. STATISTICS OFFICE. STATISTICAL INDICATORS. see BUSINESS AND ECONOMICS — Abstracting, Bibliographies, Statistics

330.9   BL
VENEZUELA COMPANY HANDBOOK. (Text in English) a. $29.95. I M F Editora Ltda., Av. Almirante Barroso 63, Grupo 409, 20031 Rio de Janeiro RJ, Brazil. TEL 55-21-240-4347. FAX 55-21-262-7570. (Dist. worldwide by: The Reference Press, Inc., 6448 Hwy. 290 E., Ste. E-104, Austin, TX 78723. TEL 512-454-7778. FAX 512-454-9401) charts; stat. **Document type:** trade publication.
Formerly: Company Handbook, Venezuela.
Description: Profiles the economy, recent developments in privatization and accounting rules, as well as the Caracas Stock Exchange.

330.1   GW   ISSN 0085-7661
VERBAENDE, BEHOERDEN, ORGANISATIONEN DER WIRTSCHAFT. a. DM.365 (effective 1997). Verlag Hoppenstedt GmbH, Havelstr. 9, 64295 Darmstadt, Germany. TEL 49-6151-380-0. FAX 49-6151-380-360. circ. 30,000. **Document type:** directory.
● Also available online. Vendor(s): GBI.
Also available on CD-ROM.

330.9   VI
VIRGIN ISLANDS BUSINESS JOURNAL; serving the business community of the US Virgin Islands. 1985. s-m. $25. Media Ventures (V.I.) Inc., 40 CCC Taarenberg, P.O. Box 1208, St. Thomas, VI 00804-1208. TEL 809-776-2874. FAX 809-774-3636. Ed. Christopher B. Garrity. circ. 8,000.
Description: Covers all areas of Virgin Islands business.

330   US   ISSN 0042-6490
HC107.V8
VIRGINIA ECONOMIC INDICATORS. 1967. q. free. Employment Commission, 703 E. Main St., Box 1358, Richmond, VA 23218-1358. FAX 804-225-3923. Ed. William Mezger. charts; stat. circ. 1,200. (processed; also avail. in microfiche from CIS) **Indexed:** SRI. **Document type:** bulletin.
Description: Includes an article on a special topic of interest to Virginia's employers and workers.

330.9   TZ
VIVA AFRICA; the magazine on trade, industry and development issues in Africa. (Text in English) 1980. m. Afro-Commercial and Industrial Services, P.O. Box 6924, Dar es Salaam, Tanzania. **Document type:** trade publication.

VORTEILHAFTE GELDANLAGEN; Handbuch fuer Anleger, Berater und Vermittler. see BUSINESS AND ECONOMICS — Banking And Finance

VOTE AND SURVEY; magazine of political, social and economic issues. see POLITICAL SCIENCE

WALL STREET DIGEST. see BUSINESS AND ECONOMICS — Banking And Finance

338.9   BE   ISSN 0379-3753
WALLONIE. (Not published 1972-1974) (Text in French) 1948. bi-m. 950 BEF. Conseil Economique et Social de la Region Wallonne, 13C rue du Vertbois, B-4000 Liege, Belgium. TEL 32-41-329811. FAX 32-41-329810. Ed. Daniel Janssens. adv.; bk.rev.; abstr.; bibl.; charts; illus. circ. 2,500. **Indexed:** Econ.Abstr., Rural Recreat.Tour.Abstr., World Agri.Econ.& Rural Sociol.Abstr. **Document type:** government publication.
Former titles (1952-1972): Revue du Conseil Economique Wallon; Chronique du Conseil Economique Wallon.
Description: Covers economic developments and social issues affecting the Walloon region.

330.9   US   ISSN 1061-1622
WARFIELD'S BUSINESS RECORD. 1986. w. $30. 11 E. Saratoga St., Baltimore, MD 21202. TEL 410-752-3849. FAX 410-332-0698. Ed. Robert A. Dawson. adv.; bk.rev. circ. 10,500. (tabloid format; back issues avail.)
● Also available online. Vendor(s): Lexis-Nexis, UMI. —UMI.
Formerly (until 1992): Warfield's (ISSN 0892-7243)
Description: Features stories on companies, executives, and major trends in Maryland's business.

WASHINGTON (STATE). EMPLOYMENT SECURITY DEPARTMENT. AREA WAGE SURVEYS. see BUSINESS AND ECONOMICS — Labor And Industrial Relations

WASHINGTON (STATE). EMPLOYMENT SECURITY DEPARTMENT. COUNTY LABOR MARKET AND ECONOMIC PROFILES. see BUSINESS AND ECONOMICS — Labor And Industrial Relations

WASHINGTON (STATE). EMPLOYMENT SECURITY DEPARTMENT. STUDIES IN INDUSTRY AND EMPLOYMENT. see BUSINESS AND ECONOMICS — Labor And Industrial Relations

WASHINGTON LETTER ON PUERTO RICO; a biweekly analysis of official developments and business trends. see POLITICAL SCIENCE

WASHINGTON REPORT ON AFRICA. see POLITICAL SCIENCE

WASHINGTON REPORT ON THE HEMISPHERE. see POLITICAL SCIENCE — International Relations

WASHINGTON STATE LABOR MARKET AND ECONOMIC REPORT (YEAR). see BUSINESS AND ECONOMICS — Labor And Industrial Relations

WATER & WASTE TREATMENT: LATIN AMERICAN INDUSTRIAL REPORT. see ENGINEERING — Civil Engineering

320   EC   ISSN 0252-2659
WEEKLY ANALYSIS OF ECUADORIAN ISSUES. Spanish edition: Analisis Semanal. (Text in English) 1971. w. $440. Walter R. Spurrier, Ed. & Pub., P.O. Box 4925, Elizalde 119, 10o, Guayaquil, Ecuador. FAX 593-4326842. bk.rev.; index. circ. 1,000. **Document type:** newsletter.

330.9   US
WEEKLY BUSINESS FAILURES. w. $45. Dun & Bradstreet, Economic Analysis Department, 220 E. 42nd St., 9th Fl., New York, NY 10017-4717. FAX 212-883-3400. (Subscr. to: Box 1861, New York, NY 10163-1861)
Description: Provides number of weekly failures, the year-to-date total and changes from previous periods. Includes a 13-week moving average of failures, plus comment and analysis.

338   MW
▼**WEEKLY NEWS.** (Text in Chichewa, English) 1996. w. K.5.50. Department of Information, P.O. Box 494, Blantyre, Malawi. TEL 265-620266. circ. 3,000. **Document type:** government publication.

WEEKLY PHARMACY REPORTS: THE GREEN SHEET. see PHARMACY AND PHARMACOLOGY

330.9   UK   ISSN 0963-0864
WELSH ECONOMIC REVIEW. s-a.? Cardiff Business School, University of Wales, Aberconway Bldg., Colum Dr., Cardiff CF1 3EU, Wales. TEL 44-1222-874419. Ed. Stephen Hill.
Description: Reviews the economic and employment situation in Wales and offers forecasts.

BUSINESS AND ECONOMICS — ECONOMIC SITUATION AND CONDITIONS

330.9 320   US
WEST EUROPE REPORT. 1968. irreg. (approx. 125/yr.) $7 per no. (foreign $14 per no.). U.S. Joint Publications Research Service, Box 12507, Arlington, VA 22209. TEL 703-487-4630. (Orders to: NTIS, Springfield, VA 22161)
  Former titles: Western Europe Report; Translations on Western Europe.

338   US   ISSN 1057-686X
WESTCHESTER COUNTY BUSINESS JOURNAL. 1967. w. $54 (effective 1997). Westfair Communications, Inc., 108 Corporate Park Dr., Ste. 105, White Plains, NY 10604-3805. TEL 914-694-3600. FAX 914-694-3699. Ed. Mills Korte; Pub. Dee DelBello. R&P contact: Bruce Spring. adv. contact: Barbara Hanlon. bk.rev.; mkt. circ. 14,000. (tabloid format) **Indexed:** Tr.& Indus.Ind. **Document type:** trade publication.
  ●Also available online. Vendor(s): Lexis-Nexis, UMI.
  —UMI.
  Formerly: Westchester Business Journal (ISSN 0889-5317)

330.9   US   ISSN 1042-6795
WESTERN BLUE CHIP ECONOMIC FORECAST; what blue chip economists are saying about the Western states. 1987. 10/yr. $99 (effective May 1995). Arizona State University, Economic Outlook Center, College of Business, Box 874406, Tempe, AZ 85287-4406. TEL 602-965-5543; 800-448-0432. FAX 602-965-5458. Ed. Lee McPheters. illus. circ. 405. (back issues avail.) **Document type:** newsletter.
  Description: Provides the latest economic forecasts for 10 Western states: AZ, CA, CO, ID, NM, OR, TX, UT, and WA. Forecasts are furnished by economists in each state representing major banks, companies, universities, and state agencies.

330.9   US
WESTERN ECONOMIC DEVELOPMENTS. 8/yr. free. Federal Reserve Bank of San Francisco, Box 7702, San Francisco, CA 94120. TEL 415-974-3230. FAX 415-974-3341. URL: http://www.frbsf.org. R&P contact: Erika Dyquisto. charts; stat. **Document type:** newsletter.
  ●Also available online.

WESTERN EUROPE (YEAR); a political and economic survey. see POLITICAL SCIENCE

330   JA
WHITE PAPER ON JAPANESE ECONOMY. (Text in English) 1970. a. $67. (Ministry of Finance, Economic Planning Agency - Okura-sho Keizai Keikaku-kyoku) Business Intercommunication, Inc., C.P.O. Box 587, Tokyo 100-02, Japan. TEL 03-3486-6966. FAX 03-3486-7266.

330   TH
WHOLESALE PRICE INDEXES FOR THAILAND. (Text in English, Thai) 1976. m. B.60. Department of Business Economics, Bangkok, Thailand.

WHO'S WHO IN ECONOMIC DEVELOPMENT. see BIOGRAPHY

330.9   GW   ISSN 0433-7484
HC281
WIRTSCHAFTLICHE LAGE IN DER BUNDESREPUBLIK DEUTSCHLAND. 1947. m. Bundesministerium fuer Wirtschaft, 53107 Bonn, Germany. stat. **Document type:** government publication.

330.9   GW
WIRTSCHAFTSANALYSEN. 1974. 4/yr. free. Hamburgische Landesbank, Volkswirtschaftliche Abteilung, 20079 Hamburg, Germany. FAX 49-40-3333-3047. circ. 6,000. **Document type:** bulletin.
  Description: Economic situation of the Hamburg area.

330.9   GW
WIRTSCHAFTSBERICHT BERLIN. a. Senatsverwaltung fuer Wirtschaft und Technologie, Martin-Luther-Str. 105, 10820 Berlin, Germany. TEL 49-30-7838284. Ed. Wolf Schulgen. **Document type:** government publication.

330   GW
WIRTSCHAFTSWOCHE; das Nachrichtenmagazin fuer die Wirtschaft. 1926. w. DM.178. Verlagsgruppe Handelsblatt GmbH, Kasernenstr. 67, 40213 Duesseldorf, Germany. TEL 49-211-887-0. FAX 49-211-374955. Ed. Stefan Baron. adv. contact: Winfried Veeh. bk.rev.; abstr.; illus.; stat.; index. circ. 158,730. (also avail. in microfiche from NRP; microfilm from ALP) **Indexed:** ELLIS, Key to Econ.Sci., PROMT. **Document type:** trade publication.
  ●Also available online.
  —SWETS.
  Former titles: Wirtschaftswoche: Volkswirt (ISSN 0042-8582); Volkswirt.

330.9   US   ISSN 0740-4077
WORK AMERICA; the business voice on workforce development. m. $30. National Alliance of Business, 1201 New York Ave., N.W., Ste. 700, Washington, DC 20005. TEL 202-289-2827. FAX 202-289-1303. (Subscr. to: Box 501, Annapolis Junction, MD 20701. TEL 800-787-7788) Ed. Maureen Bozell.
  Description: Reports on and provides information about current workforce development practice, policy and legislation, with particular emphasis on education and training issues and joint initiatives between business and government in this area.

330.9 658.3 331.1
658.3   US   ISSN 0736-9166
WORK TIMES. 1982. q. $35 individual membership; institutions $75. New Ways to Work, 785 Market St., Ste. 950, San Francisco, CA 94103-2016. TEL 415-995-9860. FAX 415-995-9867. Ed. Barney Olmsted. adv.; bk.rev.; abstr.; bibl. circ. 500. (back issues avail.) **Document type:** newsletter.
  Formerly (until 1984): New Ways to Work Newsletter.
  Description: Covers national and international work time issues, and news about local San Francisco projects.

WORKING PARTY REPORTS. see POLITICAL SCIENCE — International Relations

330.9   UN   ISSN 0258-6770
HC59.69
THE WORLD BANK ECONOMIC REVIEW. 1986. 3/yr. $25 to individuals; institutions $45. World Bank, 1818 H St., N.W., Washington, DC 20433. TEL 202-477-1155. FAX 202-522-2627. E-mail: books@worldbank.org. (Subscr. to: Box 7247-7956, Philadelphia, PA 19170-7956. TEL 201-476-2192. FAX 201-476-2197) Ed. Moshe Syrquin. charts; stat. circ. 11,000. (also avail. in microform from UMI) **Indexed:** Abstr.Anthropol., ASCA, Asian-Pac.Econ.Lit., Curr.Cont., Geo.Abstr.P.G., IDA, IIS, J.of Econ.Lit., P.A.I.S., Pub.Admin.Abstr., SSCI.
  —BLDSC (9352.926200); Genuine Article; SWETS; UMI; UnCover.
  Description: For economists, social scientists in government, business, and international agencies. Focuses on policy relevance and operational aspects of economics.
  Refereed Serial

WORLD BANK LIVING STANDARDS MEASUREMENT STUDY. see BUSINESS AND ECONOMICS — International Development And Assistance

330.9   UN   ISSN 0256-7687
WORLD DATA (YEAR); World Bank indicators on CD-ROM. 1994. a. $275 (renewal $75). World Bank, 1818 H. St., N.W., Washington, DC 20433. E-mail: books@worldbank.org. (U.S. orders to: The World Bank, Box 7247-8619, Philadelphia, PA 19170-8619. TEL 202-473-1155. FAX 202-522-2629; Also avail. from: 66 av. D'Ilena, 75116 Paris, France. TEL 33-1-40-69-30-55. FAX 33-1-40-69-30-68) stat.
  ●Available only on CD-ROM.
  Description: Profiles more than 700 socioeconomic time-series indicators and surveys more than 200 economies. Contains historic data back as far as 1960.

330   UN
HC59
WORLD ECONOMIC AND SOCIAL SURVEY; current trends and policies in the world economy. (Editions in English, French, Spanish) 1945. a. $55 (effective 1997). United Nations Publications, Sales and Marketing Section, Room DC2-0853, New York, NY 10017. TEL 212-963-8302; 800-253-9646. FAX 212-963-3489. E-mail: publications@un.org; URL: http://www.un.org/publications. (Or: Distribution and Sales Section, CH-1211 Geneva 10, Switzerland) (also avail. in microfiche from CIS) **Indexed:** IIS, Int.Lab.Doc.
  —CCC.
  Formerly: World Economic Survey (ISSN 0084-1714).

330.9   US   ISSN 0256-6877
HC10
WORLD ECONOMIC OUTLOOK. (Subseries of: International Monetary Fund. World Economic and Financial Surveys) (Editions in Arabic, English, French, Spanish) 1980. s-a. $62 (effective 1995). International Monetary Fund, Publication Services, 700 19th St., N.W., Washington, DC 20431. TEL 202-623-7430. FAX 202-623-7201. TELEX RCA 248331 IMF UR. stat. circ. 8,000. (also avail. in microform from UMI,CIS) **Indexed:** IIS.
  ●Also available online. Vendor(s): Information Access Co.
  —BLDSC (9354.297000); UMI.
  Description: Discusses the problems of balance of payments adjustment by major groups of countries, the key policy options available to them, issues of inflation and interest rates, debt, and capital flows. Details scenarios for the evolution of the world economy over the medium term under various policy options.

332.6 330.9   UK   ISSN 0264-0732
HD9999.L436
WORLD LEASING YEARBOOK (YEAR). (Supplement avail.: Studies in Leasing Law and Tax) 1980. a. £115($195) (effective 1997). Euromoney Publications plc., Books, Nestor House, Playhouse Yard, London EC4V 5EX, England. TEL 0171-779-8935. FAX 0171-779-8541. TELEX 987913 HAWKIN G. (Orders to: Plymbridge Distributors Ltd., Estover, Plymouth, Devon PL6 7PZ, England. TEL 0171-779-8610. FAX 01752-695668) Ed.Bd. adv. circ. 7,000. (back issues avail.) **Document type:** directory.
  —BLDSC (9356.420000).
  Description: Lists 6,500 international leasing services companies. Includes glossary of leasing terminology.

WORLD MARKET FOR HOT DRINKS. see BEVERAGES

WORLD TODAY SERIES: AFRICA. see HISTORY — History Of Africa

WORLD TODAY SERIES: CANADA. see HISTORY — History Of North And South America

WORLD TODAY SERIES: EAST, SOUTHEAST ASIA, AND THE WESTERN PACIFIC. see HISTORY — History Of Asia

WORLD TODAY SERIES: LATIN AMERICA. see HISTORY — History Of North And South America

WORLD TODAY SERIES: MIDDLE EAST AND SOUTH ASIA. see HISTORY — History Of Asia

WORLD TODAY SERIES: RUSSIA, EURASIAN STATES, AND EASTERN EUROPE. see HISTORY — History Of Europe

WORLD TODAY SERIES: WESTERN EUROPE. see HISTORY — History Of Europe

XINCUN. see AGRICULTURE

330.9   US
YALE UNIVERSITY. ECONOMIC GROWTH CENTER. CENTER DISCUSSION PAPER. irreg., no.499, 1985. $2. Yale University, Economic Growth Center, Box 208269, New Haven, CT 06520-8269. TEL 203-432-3610. FAX 203-432-3898. **Indexed:** Geo.Abstr., Popul.Ind., Rural Devel.Abstr., World Agri.Econ.& Rural Sociol.Abstr.

330.9   KU
YAQZA. 1979. w. P.O. Box 6000, Safat, Kuwait. Ed. Ahmed Yousef Behbehani. adv. circ. 21,713.

BUSINESS AND ECONOMICS — ECONOMIC SYSTEMS AND THEORIES, ECONOMIC HISTORY

330.9   CG
ZAIRE BUSINESS. (Text in French) 1973. w. 3986, rue Ex-Belgika, Bldg. Amasco, B.P. 9839, Kinshasa, Democratic Republic of the Congo. illus.

330.9   ZA
ZAMBIA. NATIONAL COMMISSION FOR DEVELOPMENT PLANNING. ECONOMIC REPORT. a. K.450. National Commission for Development Planning, P.O. Box 50268, Lusaka, Zambia. FAX 260-1-222440. TELEX 40430. circ. 1,500. **Document type:** government publication.

330.9 320   AU
ZEITBUEHNE; Magazin fuer Wirtschaft, Politik & Kultur. 1986. 6/yr. S.200; newsstand price: S.20. Magazin-Verlag Zachl, Lederergasse 67, A-4021 Linz, Austria. TEL 49-7252-67133. FAX 49-7252-68228. Ed. Josef Zachl. adv.: B&W page S.28000; trim 180 x 257; adv. contact: Brigitte Zachl. circ. 10,000. **Document type:** bulletin.
Description: Explores topics and issues in science, politics, and culture.

ZEITSCHRIFT FUER ENERGIEWIRTSCHAFT. see ENERGY

330.9   CC   ISSN 1000-9094
             CODEN: JMCPE6
ZHONGGUO JINGJI XINWEN/CHINA ECONOMIC NEWS. (Text in Chinese) d. $139.40. P.O. Box 8025, Beijing, People's Republic of China. TEL 201-6803. (Or: 4th Fl., 97 Dewai Dajie, Beijing 100088, P.R.C.; Dist. in US by: China Books & Periodicals, Inc., 2929 24th St., San Francisco, CA 94110) **Document type:** newspaper.
—CASDDS.

ZHONGGUO NONGCUN JINGJI/CHINESE RURAL ECONOMY. see AGRICULTURE — Agricultural Economics

330.9   RH
ZIMBABWE: A FIELD FOR INVESTMENT. 1961. a. Z.$74.80 (foreign Z.$77) (effective 1997). Thomson Publications Zimbabwe (Pvt) Ltd., Thomson House, P.O. Box 1683, Harare, Zimbabwe. TEL 263-4-736835. FAX 263-4-752390. illus.; stat. **Document type:** trade publication.

330.9   RH
HC910.A01
ZIMBABWE ECONOMIC REVIEW. 1973. q. Z.$40 (in Africa $20; elsewhere $25) (effective 1994). Zimbabwe Financial Holdings Limited, P.O. Box 3198, Harare, Zimbabwe. TEL 263-4-735011. FAX 263-4-735600. TELEX 24163 ZW. Ed. I.J. Foroma. circ. 3,500. (back issues avail.)
Formerly (until 1991): Economic Review (ISSN 0256-1603)
Description: Covers the economic situation in Zimbabwe and international developments affecting Zimbabwe.

330.9   RH
ZIMBABWE IN FIGURES. (Text in English) 1982. a. Zimbabwe Financial Holdings Limited, P.O. Box 3198, Harare, Zimbabwe. TEL 263-4-735011. FAX 263-4-735600. TELEX 24163 ZW. Ed. I.J. Foroma. circ. 3,000.

330.9   FR   ISSN 0429-338X
LA ZONE FRANC EN (YEAR). Variant title: Banque de France. Comite Monetaire de la Zone Franc. Rapport Annuel. 1953. a. 90 F. Banque de France, Service de l'Information, Services des Relations avec la Zone Franc, 48, rue Croix des Petits Champs, 75001 Paris, France. TEL 1-42-92-39-08. FAX 1-42-92-39-40.

BUSINESS AND ECONOMICS —
Economic Systems And Theories, Economic History

A R E U E A MONOGRAPH SERIES. (American Real Estate and Urban Economics Association) see SOCIOLOGY

330.1   GW   ISSN 0724-9756
ABHANDLUNGEN ZU DEN WIRTSCHAFTLICHEN STAATSWISSENSCHAFTEN. 1968. irreg., vol.36, 1991. DM.92. Vandenhoeck und Ruprecht, Robert-Bosch-Breite 6, 37079 Goettingen, Germany. TEL 49-551-6959-0. FAX 49-551-695917. (Subscr. to: 37070 Goettingen, Germany) Ed. Horst C. Recktenwald. **Document type:** monographic series.

330.9   CI   ISSN 1330-0024
             CODEN: AHIUDI
ACTA HISTORICO-OECONOMICA. (Text in Serbo-Croatian; summaries in English, German) 1974. a. $5.40. (Drustvo Povjesnicara Hrvatska, Komisija za Ekonomskoj Povijest) Skolska Knjiga, Masarykova 28, 41000 Zagreb, Croatia. Ed. Ivan Erceg. bk.rev. circ. 1,000. **Indexed:** Amer.Hist.& Life (1990-), Hist.Abstr. (1990-).
Formerly (until 1991): Acta Historico-oeconomica Iugoslaviae (ISSN 0350-3631)

330.1   FI   ISSN 0355-2667
ACTA WASAENSIA. (Text and summaries in English) 1971. irreg., no.52, 1997. price varies. Vaasan Yliopisto, Library - University of Vaasa, P.O. Bpx 331, FIN-65101 Vaasa, Finland. FAX 358-61-3248200. Ed. Antero Niemikorpi. circ. 200. **Indexed:** Zent.Math.

ACTUEL MARX. see POLITICAL SCIENCE

330.1 519.5   NE
ADVANCED STUDIES IN THEORETICAL AND APPLIED ECONOMETRICS. (Text in English) 1982. irreg., vol.30, 1995. price varies. Kluwer Academic Publishers, Postbus 17, 3300 AA Dordrecht, Netherlands. TEL 31-78-6392392. FAX 31-78-6392254. TELEX 29245 KAPG NL. E-mail: services@wkap.nl; URL: http://www.wkap.nl. (Dist. by: Kluwer Academic Publishers Group, P.O. Box 322, 3300 AH Dordrecht, Netherlands. TEL 31-78-6392392. FAX 31-78-6546474; N. America dist. addr.: Box 358, Accord Sta., Hingham, MA 02018-0358. TEL 617-871-6600) (back issues avail.) **Indexed:** Zent.Math. **Document type:** monographic series.
Refereed Serial

330.1   NE   ISSN 0169-5568
ADVANCED TEXTBOOKS IN ECONOMICS. 1971. irreg., vol.32, 1992. price varies. Elsevier Science B.V., Books Division, P.O. Box 211, 1000 AE Amsterdam, Netherlands. TEL 31-20-4853911. FAX 31-20-4853705. TELEX 18582 ESPA NL. E-mail: nlinfo-f@elsevier.nl; usinfo-f@elsevier.com; forinfo-kyf04035@niftyserve.or.jp; URL: http://www.elsevier.nl/. (Subscr. in the Americas to: Elsevier Science, RegionalSales Office, Box 945, New York, NY 10159-0945. TEL 212-633-3730. FAX 212-633-3680; Subscr. in Australasia and the Far East to: Elsevier Science (Singapore) Pte Ltd, No.1 Temasek Ave., No.17-01 Millenia Tower, Singapore 039192, Singapore. TEL 65-434-3727. FAX 65-337-2230; Subscr. in Japan to: Elsevier Science Japan, 9-15 Higashi-Azabu 1-chome, Minato-ku, Tokyo 106, Japan. TEL 81-3-5561-5033. FAX 81-3-5561-5047) Eds. C.J. Bliss, M.D. Intriligator. **Indexed:** Math.R., Zent.Math. **Document type:** monographic series.
—BLDSC (0696.935500).
Refereed Serial

330.1   US   ISSN 0278-0984
HB172
ADVANCES IN APPLIED MICROECONOMICS; a research annual. 1981. irreg., vol.6, 1996. $73.25. J A I Press Inc., 55 Old Post Rd., No. 2, Box 1678, Greenwich, CT 06836-1678. TEL 203-661-7602. FAX 203-661-0792. E-mail: jai@jaipress.com. (Subscr. in UK and Europe to: J A I Press Ltd., 38 Tavistock St., Covent Garden, London WC2E 7PB, England. TEL 44-171-379-8834. FAX 44-171-379-8835) Ed. Michael Baye. **Document type:** monographic series.
—BLDSC (0699.113000). CCC.

ADVANCES IN ECONOMETRICS. see BUSINESS AND ECONOMICS — Economic Situation And Conditions

ADVANCES IN THE STUDY OF ENTREPRENEURSHIP, INNOVATION, AND ECONOMIC GROWTH. see BUSINESS AND ECONOMICS — Economic Situation And Conditions

AFRICA DEVELOPMENT. see BUSINESS AND ECONOMICS — International Development And Assistance

330.9 960   US   ISSN 0145-2258
HC501
AFRICAN ECONOMIC HISTORY. (Text in English, French) a. $16.50 to individuals; institutions $33. University of Wisconsin at Madison, African Studies Program, 1454 Van Hise Hall, Madison, WI 53706. TEL 608-262-2493. FAX 608-262-6998. Ed. David Henige. adv.: bk.rev. circ. 450. (back issues avail.; reprint service avail. from ISI) **Indexed:** Amer.Hist.& Life (1976-), Arts & Hum.Cit.Ind., ASCA, Curr.Cont.Africa, Curr.Cont., Documentatieblad, Hist.Abstr. (1976-), SSCI. **Document type:** academic/scholarly publication.
—BLDSC (0732.423000); Genuine Article; UnCover.
Formerly (until 1976): African Economic History Review (ISSN 0360-6333)

AKADEMIA ROLNICZA W SZCZECINIE. ZESZYTY NAUKOWE. NAUKI SPOLECZNE I EKONOMICZNE. see SOCIAL SCIENCES: COMPREHENSIVE WORKS

AMERICAN ECONOMIC REVIEW. see BUSINESS AND ECONOMICS — Economic Situation And Conditions

330.1   US   ISSN 0741-2150
AMERICAN UNIVERSITY STUDIES. SERIES 16. ECONOMICS. 1984. irreg. price varies. Peter Lang Publishing, Inc., 275 Seventh Ave., 28th Fl., New York, NY 10001. TEL 212-647-7700; 800-770-5264. FAX 212-647-7707. E-mail: customerservice@plang.com; URL: http://www.peterlang.com. Ed. Christopher Myers. **Document type:** academic/scholarly publication, monographic series.
Description: Explores various issues of economics and their social and political implications.

330.1   GW   ISSN 0720-8227
ANGEWANDTE STATISTIK UND OEKONOMETRIE. (Text in English, German) 1975. irreg., vol.42, 1997. Vandenhoeck und Ruprecht, Robert-Bosch-Breite 6, 37079 Goettingen, Germany. TEL 49-551-6959-0. FAX 49-551-695917. (Subscr. to: 37070 Goettingen, Germany) Ed.Bd. **Indexed:** Zent.Math. **Document type:** monographic series.

330.1   US
ANNUAL EDITIONS: MICROECONOMICS. 1991. a. $12.95. Dushkin Publishing Group, Sluice Dock, Guilford, CT 06437-9989. TEL 203-453-4351. FAX 203-453-6000. Ed. Don Cole; Pub. Ian Nielsen. illus. **Document type:** academic/scholarly publication.
Refereed Serial

330.1   CE
ARTHIKA VIDYA NIBANDHANA. (Text in Sinhala) 1977. q. Rs.30($2) Contemporary Commerce Publications Board, 50, Second Lane, Udahamulla, Nugegoda, Sri Lanka. Ed. P.M.N. Bandare. adv.; charts. circ. 3,000.

330.1   UK   ISSN 1351-3958
ASIAN ECONOMIC JOURNAL. vol.8, 1994. q. £63($100) (effective 1997). (East Asian Economic Association) Blackwell Publishers Ltd., 108 Cowley Rd., Oxford OX4 1JF, England. TEL 44-1865-791100. FAX 44-1865-791347. E-mail: jnlinfo@blackwellpublishers.co.uk; URL: http://www.blackwellpublishers.co.uk. Eds. Shinichi Ichimura, Steven N.S. Cheung. **Indexed:** Asian-Pac.Econ.Lit. **Document type:** academic/scholarly publication.
—BLDSC (1742.410000); SWETS. CCC.

330.1   II   ISSN 0970-7530
ASSAM ECONOMIC JOURNAL. (Text in English) vol.3, 1977. a. Rs.10($2) Dibrugarh University, Department of Economics, Dibrugarh 786001, India.

330   UK   ISSN 0004-8992
HC601
AUSTRALIAN ECONOMIC HISTORY REVIEW. 1962. 3/yr. £60($95) (foreign £60) (effective 1997). (Economic History Society of Australia and New Zealand) Blackwell Publishers Ltd., 108 Cowley Rd., Oxford OX4 1JF, England. TEL 44-1865-791100. FAX 44-1865-791347. E-mail: jnlinfo@blackwellpublishers.co.uk; URL: http://www.blackwellpublishers.co.uk. Eds. A.J. Whitwell, G.D. Snooks. adv.; bk.rev.; index. circ. 500. (reprint service avail.) **Indexed:** Amer.Hist.& Life (1962-), ASCA, Aus.P.A.I.S., Curr.Cont., Geo.Abstr.H.G., Hist.Abstr. (1962-), J.of Econ.Lit., P.A.I.S., SSCI. **Document type:** academic/scholarly publication.
—BLDSC (1798.650000); Genuine Article; SWETS; UMI; UnCover. CCC.
Formerly: Business Archives and History.

BUSINESS AND ECONOMICS — ECONOMIC SYSTEMS AND THEORIES, ECONOMIC HISTORY

330.1   US   ISSN 1045-3288
AUSTRIAN ECONOMICS NEWSLETTER. 1977. q. membership. Ludwig von Mises Institute, Auburn, AL 36849. TEL 334-844-2500. FAX 334-844-2583. E-mail: lvmises@mail.auburn.edu. Ed. Mark Brandly. bk.rev.; bibl.; illus.; tr.lit. circ. 5,000. (back issues avail.) **Document type:** newsletter.
  Description: Provides news and views on the Austrian school of economics as it affects the academic world, and reports on new research, conferences, and schools.

BANCA D'ITALIA. CONTRIBUTI ALLA ANALISI ECONOMICA. see BUSINESS AND ECONOMICS — Economic Situation And Conditions

BANCA SANTO PAOLO DI BRESCIA. NOTIZIARIO ECONOMICO. see BUSINESS AND ECONOMICS — Banking And Finance

330.1   SP
BANCO DE ESPANA. ESTUDIOS DE HISTORIA ECONOMIA; serie roja. irreg., no.18, 1989. 636 ptas. (foreign 1800 ptas.). Banco de Espana, Seccion de Publicaciones, Negociado de Distribucion y Gestion, Alcala 50, 28014 Madrid, Spain. TEL 521 22 59.

330.1   SZ   ISSN 0522-7216
BEITRAEGE ZUR WIRTSCHAFTSPOLITIK. 1965. irreg., no.64, 1996. price varies. Paul Haupt AG, Falkenplatz 14, CH-3001 Bern, Switzerland. TEL 41-31-3012345. FAX 41-31-3014669. **Document type:** monographic series.
—CCC.

330.1   CN
BELL CANADA PAPERS SERIES. 1993. a. Can.$25. John Deutsch Institute for the Study of Economic Policy, Policy Studies Bldg., Queen's University, Kingston, ON K7L 3N6, Canada. TEL 613-545-2294. FAX 613-545-6025. Ed. Thomas Courchene. R&P contact: Sharon Sullivan. (back issues avail.) **Document type:** monographic series.

330.1   MX   ISSN 0188-3259
HC121
BOLETIN DE FUENTES PARA LA HISTORIA ECONOMICA DE MEXICO. 1990. 3/yr. $10 to individuals; institutions $15 (effective 1993). (Centro de Estudios Historicos) Colegio de Mexico, A.C., Departamento de Publicaciones, Camino al Ajusco 20, 01000 Mexico D.F., Mexico. TEL 645-5955. FAX 645-0464. **Document type:** bulletin.

330   IT   ISSN 0006-680X
BOLLETTINO EMEROGRAFICO DI ECONOMIA INTERNAZIONALE. (Section of: Economia Internazionale) 1948. q. Istituto di Economia Internazionale, Via Garibaldi 4, 16124 Genoa, Italy. TEL 39-10-2094201. FAX 39-10-2094300. TELEX 286325 COMGEN I. abstr.; bibl. circ. 20. **Document type:** academic/scholarly publication, bulletin.
  Description: Examines the fields of economic systems, theories and history.

330.1   NE
BOSTON STUDIES IN APPLIED ECONOMICS. (Text in English) irreg. price varies. Kluwer Academic Publishers, Postbus 17, 3300 AA Dordrecht, Netherlands. FAX 31-78-6392254. TELEX 29245 KAPG NL. E-mail: services@wkap.nl; URL: http://www.wkap.nl. (Dist. by: Kluwer Academic Publishers Group, P.O. Box 322, 3300 AH Dordrecht, Netherlands. TEL 31-78-6392392. FAX 31-78-6546474; N. America dist. addr.: Box 358, Accord Sta., Hingham, MA 02018-0358. TEL 617-871-6600. FAX 617-871-6528) **Document type:** monographic series. Refereed Serial

330   US   ISSN 0007-2303
HC101
BROOKINGS PAPERS ON ECONOMIC ACTIVITY. (Supplement avail.: Brookings Papers on Economic Activity: Microeconomics (ISSN 1057-8641)) 1970. 2/yr. $25 to individuals (foreign $37); students $18. Brookings Institution, 1775 Massachusetts Ave., N.W., Washington, DC 20036-2188. TEL 202-797-6255. FAX 202-797-6195. (Subscr. to: Box 037, Washington, DC 20042-0037. TEL 202-797-6255) Ed. Debbie Styles. R&P contact: Garry Sparks. TEL 202-797-2843. (also avail. in microform from UMI; reprint service avail. from SCH,UMI) **Indexed:** ABI Inform., Acad.Ind., ASCA, Asian-Pac.Econ.Lit., B.P.I., BPIA, C.R.E.J., Cont.Pg.Manage., Curr.Cont., Int.Lab.Doc., J.of Econ.Lit., Key to Econ.Sci., P.A.I.S., PROMT, Soc.Sci.Ind., SSCI, Tr.& Indus.Ind., World Agri.Econ.& Rural Sociol.Abstr. **Document type:** academic/scholarly publication.
—BLDSC (2350.070000); Genuine Article; KR SourceOne; SWETS; UMI; UnCover. **CCC.**
  Description: Provides academic and business economists, government officials, and members of the financial and business community with analyses of current economic developments.

330.1   US   ISSN 1057-8641
HC101
BROOKINGS PAPERS ON ECONOMIC ACTIVITY: MICROECONOMICS. (Supplement to: Brookings Papers on Economic Activity (ISSN 0007-2303)) 1989. a. $14 (foreign $20). Brookings Institution, 1775 Massachusetts Ave., N.W., Washington, DC 20036-2188. TEL 202-797-6258. FAX 202-797-6195. (Subscr. to: Box 037, Washington, DC 20042-0037. TEL 202-797-6255) Ed. Debbie Styles. R&P contact: Garry Sparks. TEL 202-797-2843. (reprint service avail. from SCH) **Indexed:** Curr.Cont. **Document type:** academic/scholarly publication.
—CCC.
  Description: Focuses on research drawn from theoretical and applied microeconomics, industrial organization, labor economics, and technological change.

330.1   UK   ISSN 0260-5171
BUSINESS HISTORY NEWSLETTER. 1980. 2/yr. free. London School of Economics, Business History Unit, Houghton St., London WC2A 2AE, England. TEL 0171-955-7109. FAX 0171-955-6861. TELEX 24655-BLPES-G. adv.; bk.rev. circ. 1,500. (reprint service avail. from SCH) **Document type:** newsletter.

C E D R E S. REVUE ECONOMIQUE ET SOCIALE. (Centre d'Etudes, de Recherche Economique et Social) see AGRICULTURE — Agricultural Economics

C E M S BUSINESS REVIEW. (Community of European Management Schools) see BUSINESS AND ECONOMICS — Management

C E P S PAPERS. (Centre for European Policy Studies) see POLITICAL SCIENCE — International Relations

C E P S WORKING DOCUMENTS. (Centre for European Policy Studies) see POLITICAL SCIENCE — International Relations

330.1   HU
C E U PRIVATIZATION REPORTS. 1993. irreg, vol.4, 1995. $15 paperback; hardcover $45 (effective 1995). (Central European University, Privatization Project) Central European University Press, Nador u. 9, 1051 Budapest, Hungary. TEL 36-1-1762333. FAX 36-1-1762778. E-mail: ceupress@mail.ceu.hu. Ed. Pauline Wickham; Pub. Frances Pinter. **Document type:** monographic series, academic/scholarly publication.
  Description: Provides essential data on the privatization process in Central and Eastern Europe. Refereed Serial

330.1 331.8   FR   ISSN 0298-7899
CAHIERS D'ETUDE ET DE RECHERCHE. English edition: Notebooks for Study and Research (ISSN 0298-7902) 1986. irreg. 100 F. in Europe; elsewhere 120 F.($20) (effective 1997). (International Institute for Research and Education, NE - Institut International de Recherche et de Formation) Editions Pierre Rousset, 2 rue Richard-Lenoir, 93108 Montreuil, France. FAX 33-1-43792106. E-mail: iire@antenna.nl. (Subscr. to: c/o IIRE, Postbus 53290, 1007 RG Amsterdam, Netherlands. TEL 31-20-6717263. FAX 31-20-6732106) Ed. Peter Drucker; Pub. Pierre Rousset. R&P contact: Peter Drucker. adv.; bibl.; charts; illus.; stat. circ. 1,500. (back issues avail.) **Document type:** monographic series.
  Description: Provides an educational tool for students, trade unionists and social activists, covering Europe, both East and West, the Americas, Asia, Africa and the major issues of socialist theory.

330   BE   ISSN 0008-0195
HC311
CAHIERS ECONOMIQUES DE BRUXELLES. 1958. q. 2300 BEF (foreign 2832 BEF). (Universite Libre de Bruxelles, Department of Economics) Editions du Dulbea a.s.b.l, 50 av. F.D. Roosevelt, 1050 Brussels, Belgium. TEL 32-2-6504119. FAX 32-2-6503901. Ed. P. Kestens. adv.; bibl.; charts; illus.; index. circ. 1,000. **Indexed:** ELLIS, Int.Lab.Doc., J.of Econ.Lit., Key to Econ.Sci., P.A.I.S.For.Lang.Ind., SSCI.
  Incorporating: Series Statistiques de Bruxelles.

330.1   CN   ISSN 0705-4580
HT395.C3
CANADIAN JOURNAL OF REGIONAL SCIENCE/REVUE CANADIENNE DES SCIENCES REGIONALES. (Text in English and French) 1978. 3/yr. Can.$50. University of New Brunswick, Department of Economics, P.O. Box 4400, Fredericton, NB E3B 5A3, Canada. TEL 506-447-3206. FAX 506-453-4514. E-mail: wmilne@unb.ca. Ed. William J. Milne. bk.rev. circ. 550. (back issues avail.) **Indexed:** Can.B.P.I., CMI, Geo.Abstr., SSCI. **Document type:** academic/scholarly publication.
—BLDSC (3035.300000); SWETS; UnCover. Refereed Serial

330.1 320   UK   ISSN 0309-8168
HB97.5
CAPITAL AND CLASS. 1970. 3/yr. £18 to individuals (foreign £21 ($33)); institutions £52 (foreign £68 ($115)) (effective 1998). Conference of Socialist Economists, 25 Horsell Rd., London N5 1XL, England. TEL 44-171-607-9615. FAX 44-171-607-9615. E-mail: cseoffice@gn.apc.org. Ed.Bd. adv.; bk.rev. circ. 3,000. (back issues avail.) **Indexed:** Alt.Press Ind., Chic.Per.Ind., Left Ind. (1982-), Soc.Sci.Ind., Stud.Wom.Abstr. **Document type:** academic/scholarly publication.
—BLDSC (3050.667200); KR SourceOne; SWETS; UMI; UnCover.
  Formerly: Conference of Socialist Economists. Bulletin.

330.1   BL
CARTA DE CONJUNTURA F E E. 1991. m. free in Brazil. Fundacao de Economia e Estatistica, Rua Duque de Caxias 1691, CEP 90010-283 Porto Alegre RG, Brazil. TEL 55-51-2259455. FAX 55-21-2250006. Ed. Edison Moreira Marques. **Document type:** newsletter.
  Description: Analyzes the economic status of the country and the region. Presents recent and relevant economic events.

330.1   UK   ISSN 0265-7996
CENTRE FOR ECONOMIC POLICY RESEARCH. BULLETIN. 1983. q. Centre for Economic Policy Research, 25-28 Old Burlington St., London W1X 1LB, England. TEL 44-171-878-2900. FAX 44-171-878-2999. E-mail: cepr@cepr.org. circ. 10,000. **Document type:** bulletin.
—BLDSC (2436.790000).

330.1   UK   ISSN 0265-8003
CENTRE FOR ECONOMIC POLICY RESEARCH. DISCUSSION PAPERS. 1984. irreg. Centre for Economic Policy Research, 25-28 Old Burlington St., London W1X 1LB, England. TEL 44-171-878-2900. FAX 44-171-878-2999. E-mail: cepr@cepr.org. **Document type:** monographic series.
—BLDSC (3597.951200).

CENTRUM VOOR BEDRIJFSGESCHIEDENIS. CAHIERS. see HISTORY — History Of Europe

BUSINESS AND ECONOMICS — ECONOMIC SYSTEMS AND THEORIES, ECONOMIC HISTORY

CICLOS; en la historia, la economia y la sociedad. see HISTORY — History Of North And South America

330.1 CR ISSN 0252-9521
CIENCIAS ECONOMICAS. 1980. s-a. $25. Editorial de la Universidad de Costa Rica, Apdo. 75-2060, Ciudad Univ. R. Facio, 2050 San Pedro de Montes de Oca, San Jose, Costa Rica. TEL 506-25-3133. FAX 506-24-9367. Ed. Juan Rafael Vargas. adv. contact: Cristina Moreno Murillo. **Indexed:** IBR. **Document type:** academic/scholarly publication.

CIVILISATIONS ET SOCIETES. see HISTORY — History Of Europe

330.1 SP
COLECCION DE ECONOMIA. 1976. irreg., no.5, 1978. price varies. (Universidad de Navarra, Instituto de Estudios Superiores de la Empresa) Ediciones Universidad de Navarra, S.A., Apdo. 396, 31080 Pamplona, Spain. TEL 94 825 6850.

330.1 320.531 UK ISSN 0957-204X
COMMON SENSE. 1987. s-a. £8($18) to individuals (overseas £12); institutions £20 (overseas £30 ($45)) (effective 1997). Edinburgh Conference of Socialist Economists, c/o Werner Bonefeld, Ed., Dept. of Politics, University of York, Heslington, York YO1 4DD. adv.; bk.rev. circ. 400. **Indexed:** Alt.Press Ind. **Document type:** academic/scholarly publication.
Refereed Serial

330.1 320.532 UK ISSN 1351-4393
COMMUNIST ECONOMIES AND ECONOMIC TRANSFORMATION. 1989. q. £72($128) to individuals; institutions £216 ($416) (effective 1997). (Centre for Research into Communist Economies) Carfax Publishing Co., P.O. Box 25, Abingdon, Oxon. OX14 3UE, England. TEL 44-1235-401000. FAX 44-1235-401550. E-mail: enquiries@carfax.co.uk. (Subscr. in N. America to: Carfax Publishing Co., 875-81 Massachusetts Ave., Cambridge, MA 02139) Ed.Bd. adv.; bk.rev. (also avail. in microfiche) **Indexed:** ASCA, Asian-Pac.Econ.Lit., Curr.Cont., Geo.Abstr.H.G. **Document type:** academic/scholarly publication.
—BLDSC (3363.558375); Genuine Article; SWETS; UMI; UnCover. **CCC.**
Formerly: Communist Economies (ISSN 0954-0113)
Description: International journal concerned with the economies of communist countries, primarily, but not exclusively, the former U.S.S.R. and Eastern Europe.
Refereed Serial

330 US ISSN 0888-7233
HC701
COMPARATIVE ECONOMIC STUDIES. vol.17, 1975. 4/yr. $20 membership; institutions $40 (foreign $45 (effective 1997). Association for Comparative Economic Studies, c/o Robert Stuart, Ed., Department of Economics, Rutgers University, New Brunswick, NJ 08903-5055. TEL 908-932-7368. FAX 908-932-7416. (And: c/o Josef Brada, Exec. Sec., Dept. of Economics, Arizona State Univ., Box 873806, Tempe, AZ 85287-3806. TEL 602-965-6524. FAX 602-965-0748) R&P contact: Josef Brada. adv. contact: Robert Stuart. bk.rev.; circ. 1,000 (paid). (also avail. in microform; back issues avail.) **Indexed:** ABI Inform., Amer.Bibl.Slavic & E.Eur.Stud., C.R.E.J., J.of Econ.Lit., Mid.East: Abstr.& Ind., P.A.I.S., Tr.& Indus.Ind. **Document type:** academic/scholarly publication.
●Also available online. Vendor(s): UMI.
—SWETS; UMI.
Former titles: A C E S Bulletin; A S T E Bulletin (ISSN 0001-2645)
Description: Comparative studies of economic systems, planning and development.
Refereed Serial

330.1 US ISSN 0084-9235
CONTRIBUTIONS IN ECONOMICS AND ECONOMIC HISTORY. 1970. irreg., no.139, 1992. price varies. Greenwood Press, Inc. (Subsidiary of: Greenwood Publishing Group Inc.), 88 Post Rd. W., Box 5007, Westport, CT 06881-5007. TEL 203-226-3571. FAX 203-222-1502. Ed. Robert Sobel.
—BLDSC (3458.370000).

330 NE ISSN 0573-8555
CONTRIBUTIONS TO ECONOMIC ANALYSIS. 1952. irreg., vol.223, 1994. price varies. Elsevier Science B.V., Books Division, P.O. Box 211, 1000 AE Amsterdam, Netherlands. TEL 31-20-4853911. FAX 31-20-4853705. TELEX 18582 ESPA NL. E-mail: nlinfo-f@elsevier.nl; usinfo-f@elsevier.com; forinfo-kyf04035@niftyserve.or.jp; URL: http://www.elsevier.nl/. (Subscr. in the Americas to: Elsevier Science, Regional Sales Office, Box 945, New York, NY 10159-0945. TEL 212-633-3730. FAX 212-633-3680; Subscr. in Australasia and the Far East to: Elsevier Science (Singapore) Pte Ltd, No.1 Temasek Ave., No.17-01 Millenia Tower, Singapore 039192, Singapore. TEL 65-434-3727. FAX 65-337-2230; Subscr. in Japan to: Elsevier Science Japan, 9-15 Higashi-Azabu 1-chome, Minato-ku, Tokyo 106, Japan. TEL 81-3-5561-5033. FAX 81-3-5561-5047) Ed.Bd. **Indexed:** INSPEC, Math.R. **Document type:** monographic series.
—BLDSC (3458.320000).
Refereed Serial

COUNTRY PROFILE. ALBANIA; annual survey of political and economic background. see *POLITICAL SCIENCE*

COUNTRY PROFILE. ALGERIA; annual survey of political and economic background. see *POLITICAL SCIENCE*

COUNTRY PROFILE. ANGOLA; annual survey of political and economic background. see *POLITICAL SCIENCE*

COUNTRY PROFILE. ARGENTINA; annual survey of political and economic background. see *POLITICAL SCIENCE*

COUNTRY PROFILE. AUSTRALIA; annual survey of political and economic background. see *POLITICAL SCIENCE*

COUNTRY PROFILE. AUSTRIA; annual survey of political and economic background. see *POLITICAL SCIENCE*

COUNTRY PROFILE. AZERBAIJAN; annual survey of political and economic background. see *POLITICAL SCIENCE*

COUNTRY PROFILE. BAHRAIN, QATAR; annual survey of political and economic background. see *POLITICAL SCIENCE*

COUNTRY PROFILE. BALTIC REPUBLICS: LITHUANIA, LATVIA, ESTONIA; annual survey of political and economic background. see *POLITICAL SCIENCE*

COUNTRY PROFILE. BANGLADESH; annual survey of political and economic background. see *POLITICAL SCIENCE*

COUNTRY PROFILE. BELARUS, MOLDOVA; annual survey of political and economic background. see *POLITICAL SCIENCE*

COUNTRY PROFILE. BELGIUM, LUXEMBOURG; annual survey of political and economic background. see *POLITICAL SCIENCE*

COUNTRY PROFILE. BELIZE, BAHAMAS, BERMUDA; annual survey of political and economic background. see *POLITICAL SCIENCE*

COUNTRY PROFILE. BOLIVIA; annual survey of political and economic background. see *POLITICAL SCIENCE*

COUNTRY PROFILE. BOSNIA-HERCEGOVINA, CROATIA; annual survey of political and economic background. see *POLITICAL SCIENCE*

COUNTRY PROFILE. BOTSWANA, LESOTHO; annual survey of political and economic background. see *POLITICAL SCIENCE*

COUNTRY PROFILE. BRAZIL; annual survey of political and economic background. see *POLITICAL SCIENCE*

COUNTRY PROFILE. BULGARIA; annual survey of political and economic background. see *POLITICAL SCIENCE*

COUNTRY PROFILE. CAMBODIA, LAOS; annual survey of political and economic background. see *POLITICAL SCIENCE*

COUNTRY PROFILE. CAMEROON, CENTRAL AFRICAN REPUBLIC, CHAD; annual survey of political and economic background. see *POLITICAL SCIENCE*

COUNTRY PROFILE. CANADA; annual survey of political and economic background. see *POLITICAL SCIENCE*

COUNTRY PROFILE. CENTRAL ASIAN REPUBLICS: KYRGYZ REPUBLIC, TAJIKISTAN, TURKMENISTAN, UZBEKISTAN; annual survey of political and economic background. see *POLITICAL SCIENCE*

COUNTRY PROFILE. CHILE; annual survey of political and economic background. see *POLITICAL SCIENCE*

COUNTRY PROFILE. CHINA, MONGOLIA; annual survey of political and economic background. see *POLITICAL SCIENCE*

COUNTRY PROFILE. COLOMBIA; annual survey of political and economic background. see *POLITICAL SCIENCE*

COUNTRY PROFILE. CONGO; annual survey of political and economic background. see *POLITICAL SCIENCE*

COUNTRY PROFILE. COSTA RICA; annual survey of political and economic background. see *POLITICAL SCIENCE*

COUNTRY PROFILE. COTE D'IVOIRE, MALI; annual survey of political and economic background. see *POLITICAL SCIENCE*

COUNTRY PROFILE. CUBA; annual survey of political and economic background. see *POLITICAL SCIENCE*

COUNTRY PROFILE. CYPRUS, MALTA; annual survey of political and economic background. see *POLITICAL SCIENCE*

COUNTRY PROFILE. CZECH REPUBLIC; annual survey of political and economic background. see *POLITICAL SCIENCE*

COUNTRY PROFILE. DENMARK, ICELAND; annual survey of political and economic background. see *POLITICAL SCIENCE*

COUNTRY PROFILE. DOMINICAN REPUBLIC, HAITI, PUERTO RICO; annual survey of political and economic background. see *POLITICAL SCIENCE*

COUNTRY PROFILE. ECUADOR; annual survey of political and economic background. see *POLITICAL SCIENCE*

COUNTRY PROFILE. EGYPT; annual survey of political and economic background. see *POLITICAL SCIENCE*

COUNTRY PROFILE. ETHIOPIA, ERITREA, SOMALIA, DJIBOUTI; annual survey of political and economic background. see *POLITICAL SCIENCE*

COUNTRY PROFILE. FINLAND; annual survey of political and economic background. see *POLITICAL SCIENCE*

COUNTRY PROFILE. FRANCE; annual survey of political and economic background. see *POLITICAL SCIENCE*

COUNTRY PROFILE. GABON, EQUATORIAL GUINEA; annual survey of political and economic background. see *POLITICAL SCIENCE*

COUNTRY PROFILE. GEORGIA, ARMENIA; annual survey of political and economic background. see *POLITICAL SCIENCE*

COUNTRY PROFILE. GERMANY; annual survey of political and economic background. see *POLITICAL SCIENCE*

COUNTRY PROFILE. GHANA; annual survey of political and economic background. see *POLITICAL SCIENCE*

COUNTRY PROFILE. GREECE; annual survey of political and economic background. see *POLITICAL SCIENCE*

COUNTRY PROFILE. GUATEMALA, EL SALVADOR; annual survey of political and economic background. see *POLITICAL SCIENCE*

COUNTRY PROFILE. GUINEA, SIERRA LEONE, LIBERIA; annual survey of political and economic background. see *POLITICAL SCIENCE*

COUNTRY PROFILE. GUYANA, WINDWARD AND LEEWARD ISLANDS; annual survey of political and economic background. see *POLITICAL SCIENCE*

COUNTRY PROFILE. HONG KONG, MACAU; annual survey of political and economic background. see *POLITICAL SCIENCE*

BUSINESS AND ECONOMICS — ECONOMIC SYSTEMS AND THEORIES, ECONOMIC HISTORY

COUNTRY PROFILE. HUNGARY; annual survey of political and economic background. see POLITICAL SCIENCE

COUNTRY PROFILE. INDIA, NEPAL; annual survey of political and economic background. see POLITICAL SCIENCE

COUNTRY PROFILE. INDONESIA; annual survey of political and economic background. see POLITICAL SCIENCE

COUNTRY PROFILE. IRAN; annual survey of political and economic background. see POLITICAL SCIENCE

COUNTRY PROFILE. IRAQ; annual survey of political and economic background. see POLITICAL SCIENCE

COUNTRY PROFILE. IRELAND; annual survey of political and economic background. see POLITICAL SCIENCE

COUNTRY PROFILE. ISRAEL, THE OCCUPIED TERRITORIES; annual survey of political and economic background. see POLITICAL SCIENCE

COUNTRY PROFILE. ITALY; annual survey of political and economic background. see POLITICAL SCIENCE

COUNTRY PROFILE. JAMAICA, BARBADOS; annual survey of political and economic background. see POLITICAL SCIENCE

COUNTRY PROFILE. JAPAN; annual survey of political and economic background. see POLITICAL SCIENCE

COUNTRY PROFILE. JORDAN; annual survey of political and economic background. see POLITICAL SCIENCE

COUNTRY PROFILE. KAZAKHSTAN; annual survey of political and economic background. see POLITICAL SCIENCE

COUNTRY PROFILE. KENYA; annual survey of political and economic background. see POLITICAL SCIENCE

COUNTRY PROFILE. KUWAIT; annual survey of political and economic background. see POLITICAL SCIENCE

COUNTRY PROFILE. LEBANON; annual survey of political and economic background. see POLITICAL SCIENCE

COUNTRY PROFILE. LIBYA; annual survey of political and economic background. see POLITICAL SCIENCE

COUNTRY PROFILE. MACEDONIA, SERBIA-MONTENEGRO; annual survey of political and economic background. see POLITICAL SCIENCE

COUNTRY PROFILE. MADAGASCAR; annual survey of political and economic background. see POLITICAL SCIENCE

COUNTRY PROFILE. MALAWI; annual survey of political and economic background. see POLITICAL SCIENCE

COUNTRY PROFILE. MALAYSIA, BRUNEI; annual survey of political and economic background. see POLITICAL SCIENCE

COUNTRY PROFILE. MAURITIUS, SEYCHELLES; annual survey of political and economic background. see POLITICAL SCIENCE

COUNTRY PROFILE. MEXICO; annual survey of political and economic background. see POLITICAL SCIENCE

COUNTRY PROFILE. MOROCCO; annual survey of political and economic background. see POLITICAL SCIENCE

COUNTRY PROFILE. MOZAMBIQUE; annual survey of political and economic background. see POLITICAL SCIENCE

COUNTRY PROFILE. MYANMAR; annual survey of political and economic background. see POLITICAL SCIENCE

COUNTRY PROFILE. NAMIBIA, SWAZILAND; annual survey of political and economic background. see POLITICAL SCIENCE

COUNTRY PROFILE. NETHERLANDS; annual survey of political and economic background. see POLITICAL SCIENCE

COUNTRY PROFILE. NEW ZEALAND; annual survey of political and economic background. see POLITICAL SCIENCE

COUNTRY PROFILE. NICARAGUA, HONDURAS; annual survey of political and economic background. see POLITICAL SCIENCE

COUNTRY PROFILE. NIGER, BURKINA FASO; annual survey of political and economic background. see POLITICAL SCIENCE

COUNTRY PROFILE. NIGERIA; annual survey of political and economic background. see POLITICAL SCIENCE

COUNTRY PROFILE. NORWAY; annual survey of political and economic background. see POLITICAL SCIENCE

COUNTRY PROFILE. OMAN; annual survey of political and economic background. see POLITICAL SCIENCE

COUNTRY PROFILE. PACIFIC ISLANDS: FIJI, SOLOMON ISLANDS, WESTERN SAMOA, VANUATU, TONGA AND NEW CALEDONIA; annual survey of political and economic background. see POLITICAL SCIENCE

COUNTRY PROFILE. PAKISTAN, AFGHANISTAN; annual survey of political and economic background. see POLITICAL SCIENCE

COUNTRY PROFILE. PANAMA; annual survey of political and economic background. see POLITICAL SCIENCE

COUNTRY PROFILE. PAPUA NEW GUINEA; annual survey of political and economic background. see POLITICAL SCIENCE

COUNTRY PROFILE. PERU; annual survey of political and economic background. see POLITICAL SCIENCE

COUNTRY PROFILE. PHILIPPINES; annual survey of political and economic background. see POLITICAL SCIENCE

COUNTRY PROFILE. POLAND; annual survey of political and economic background. see POLITICAL SCIENCE

COUNTRY PROFILE. PORTUGAL; annual survey of political and economic background. see POLITICAL SCIENCE

COUNTRY PROFILE. ROMANIA; annual survey of political and economic background. see POLITICAL SCIENCE

COUNTRY PROFILE. RUSSIA; annual survey of political and economic background. see POLITICAL SCIENCE

COUNTRY PROFILE. RWANDA, BURUNDI; annual survey of political and economic background. see POLITICAL SCIENCE

COUNTRY PROFILE. SAO TOME AND PRINCIPE, GUINEA-BISSAU, CAPE VERDE; annual survey of political and economic background. see POLITICAL SCIENCE

COUNTRY PROFILE. SAUDI ARABIA; annual survey of political and economic background. see POLITICAL SCIENCE

COUNTRY PROFILE. SENEGAL; annual survey of political and economic background. see POLITICAL SCIENCE

COUNTRY PROFILE. SINGAPORE; annual survey of political and economic background. see POLITICAL SCIENCE

COUNTRY PROFILE. SLOVAKIA; annual survey of political and economic background. see POLITICAL SCIENCE

COUNTRY PROFILE. SLOVENIA; annual survey of political and economic background. see POLITICAL SCIENCE

COUNTRY PROFILE. SOUTH AFRICA; annual survey of political and economic background. see POLITICAL SCIENCE

COUNTRY PROFILE. SOUTH KOREA, NORTH KOREA; annual survey of political and economic background. see POLITICAL SCIENCE

COUNTRY PROFILE. SPAIN; annual survey of political and economic background. see POLITICAL SCIENCE

COUNTRY PROFILE. SRI LANKA; annual survey of political and economic background. see POLITICAL SCIENCE

COUNTRY PROFILE. SUDAN; annual survey of political and economic background. see POLITICAL SCIENCE

COUNTRY PROFILE. SWEDEN; annual survey of political and economic background. see POLITICAL SCIENCE

COUNTRY PROFILE. SWITZERLAND; annual survey of political and economic background. see POLITICAL SCIENCE

COUNTRY PROFILE. SYRIA; annual survey of political and economic background. see POLITICAL SCIENCE

COUNTRY PROFILE. TAIWAN; annual survey of political and economic background. see POLITICAL SCIENCE

COUNTRY PROFILE. TANZANIA, COMOROS; annual survey of political and economic background. see POLITICAL SCIENCE

COUNTRY PROFILE. THAILAND; annual survey of political and economic background. see POLITICAL SCIENCE

COUNTRY PROFILE. THE GAMBIA, MAURITANIA; annual survey of political and economic background. see POLITICAL SCIENCE

COUNTRY PROFILE. TOGO, BENIN; annual survey of political and economic background. see POLITICAL SCIENCE

COUNTRY PROFILE. TRINIDAD AND TOBAGO, SURINAME, NETHERLANDS ANTILLES, ARUBA; annual survey of political and economic background. see POLITICAL SCIENCE

COUNTRY PROFILE. TUNISIA; annual survey of political and economic background. see POLITICAL SCIENCE

COUNTRY PROFILE. TURKEY; annual survey of political and economic background. see POLITICAL SCIENCE

COUNTRY PROFILE. UGANDA; annual survey of political and economic background. see POLITICAL SCIENCE

COUNTRY PROFILE. UKRAINE; annual survey of political and economic background. see POLITICAL SCIENCE

COUNTRY PROFILE. UNITED ARAB EMIRATES; annual survey of political and economic background. see POLITICAL SCIENCE

COUNTRY PROFILE. UNITED KINGDOM; annual survey of political and economic background. see POLITICAL SCIENCE

COUNTRY PROFILE. UNITED STATES OF AMERICA; annual survey of political and economic background. see POLITICAL SCIENCE

COUNTRY PROFILE. URUGUAY, PARAGUAY; annual survey of political and economic background. see POLITICAL SCIENCE

COUNTRY PROFILE. VENEZUELA; annual survey of political and economic background. see POLITICAL SCIENCE

COUNTRY PROFILE. VIETNAM; annual survey of political and economic background. see POLITICAL SCIENCE

COUNTRY PROFILE. YEMEN; annual survey of political and economic background. see POLITICAL SCIENCE

COUNTRY PROFILE. ZAIRE; annual survey of political and economic background. see POLITICAL SCIENCE

COUNTRY PROFILE. ZAMBIA; annual survey of political and economic background. see POLITICAL SCIENCE

COUNTRY PROFILE. ZIMBABWE; annual survey of political and economic background. see POLITICAL SCIENCE

COUNTRY PROFILES; annual survey of political and economic background. see POLITICAL SCIENCE

COUNTRY REPORT. ALBANIA; analysis of economic and political trends every quarter. see BUSINESS AND ECONOMICS — Economic Situation And Conditions

COUNTRY REPORT. ALGERIA; analysis of economic and political trends every quarter. see BUSINESS AND ECONOMICS — Economic Situation And Conditions

COUNTRY REPORT. ANGOLA; analysis of economic and political trends every quarter. see BUSINESS AND ECONOMICS — Economic Situation And Conditions

BUSINESS AND ECONOMICS — ECONOMIC SYSTEMS AND THEORIES, ECONOMIC HISTORY

COUNTRY REPORT. ARGENTINA; analysis of economic and political trends every quarter. see BUSINESS AND ECONOMICS — *Economic Situation And Conditions*

COUNTRY REPORT. AUSTRALIA; analysis of economic and political trends every quarter. see BUSINESS AND ECONOMICS — *Economic Situation And Conditions*

COUNTRY REPORT. AUSTRIA; analysis of economic and political trends every quarter. see BUSINESS AND ECONOMICS — *Economic Situation And Conditions*

COUNTRY REPORT. AZERBAIJAN; analysis of economic and political trends every quarter. see BUSINESS AND ECONOMICS — *Economic Situation And Conditions*

COUNTRY REPORT. BAHRAIN, QATAR; analysis of economic and political trends every quarter. see BUSINESS AND ECONOMICS — *Economic Situation And Conditions*

COUNTRY REPORT. BALTIC REPUBLICS: LITHUANIA, LATVIA, ESTONIA; analysis of economic and political trends every quarter. see BUSINESS AND ECONOMICS — *Economic Situation And Conditions*

COUNTRY REPORT. BANGLADESH; analysis of economic and political trends every quarter. see BUSINESS AND ECONOMICS — *Economic Situation And Conditions*

COUNTRY REPORT. BELARUS, MOLDOVA; analysis of economic and political trends every quarter. see BUSINESS AND ECONOMICS — *Economic Situation And Conditions*

COUNTRY REPORT. BELGIUM, LUXEMBOURG; analysis of economic and political trends every quarter. see BUSINESS AND ECONOMICS — *Economic Situation And Conditions*

COUNTRY REPORT. BOLIVIA; analysis of economic and political trends every quarter. see BUSINESS AND ECONOMICS — *Economic Situation And Conditions*

COUNTRY REPORT. BOSNIA-HERCEGOVINA, CROATIA AND SLOVENIA; analysis of economic and political trends every quarter. see BUSINESS AND ECONOMICS — *Economic Situation And Conditions*

COUNTRY REPORT. BOTSWANA, LESOTHO; analysis of economic and political trends every quarter. see BUSINESS AND ECONOMICS — *Economic Situation And Conditions*

COUNTRY REPORT. BRAZIL; analysis of economic and political trends every quarter. see BUSINESS AND ECONOMICS — *Economic Situation And Conditions*

COUNTRY REPORT. BULGARIA; analysis of economic and political trends every quarter. see BUSINESS AND ECONOMICS — *Economic Situation And Conditions*

COUNTRY REPORT. CAMBODIA, LAOS; analysis of economic and political trends every quarter. see BUSINESS AND ECONOMICS — *Economic Situation And Conditions*

COUNTRY REPORT. CAMEROON, C.A.R., CHAD; analysis of economic and political trends every quarter. see BUSINESS AND ECONOMICS — *Economic Situation And Conditions*

COUNTRY REPORT. CANADA; analysis of economic and political trends every quarter. see BUSINESS AND ECONOMICS — *Economic Situation And Conditions*

COUNTRY REPORT. CHILE; analysis of economic and political trends every quarter. see BUSINESS AND ECONOMICS — *Economic Situation And Conditions*

COUNTRY REPORT. CHINA, MONGOLIA; analysis of economic and political trends every quarter. see BUSINESS AND ECONOMICS — *Economic Situation And Conditions*

COUNTRY REPORT. COLOMBIA; analysis of economic and political trends every quarter. see BUSINESS AND ECONOMICS — *Economic Situation And Conditions*

COUNTRY REPORT. CONGO, SAO TOME AND PRINCIPE, GUINEA-BISSAU, CAPE VERDE; analysis of economic and political trends every quarter. see BUSINESS AND ECONOMICS — *Economic Situation And Conditions*

COUNTRY REPORT. COSTA RICA; analysis of economic and political trends every quarter. see BUSINESS AND ECONOMICS — *Economic Situation And Conditions*

COUNTRY REPORT. COTE D'IVOIRE, MALI; analysis of economic and political trends every quarter. see BUSINESS AND ECONOMICS — *Economic Situation And Conditions*

COUNTRY REPORT. CUBA, DOMINICAN REPUBLIC, HAITI, PUERTO RICO; analysis of economic and political trends every quarter. see BUSINESS AND ECONOMICS — *Economic Situation And Conditions*

COUNTRY REPORT. CYPRUS, MALTA; analysis of economic and political trends every quarter. see BUSINESS AND ECONOMICS — *Economic Situation And Conditions*

COUNTRY REPORT. CZECH REPUBLIC; analysis of economic and political trends every quarter. see BUSINESS AND ECONOMICS — *Economic Situation And Conditions*

COUNTRY REPORT. DENMARK, ICELAND; analysis of economic and political trends every quarter. see BUSINESS AND ECONOMICS — *Economic Situation And Conditions*

COUNTRY REPORT. ECUADOR; analysis of economic and political trends every quarter. see BUSINESS AND ECONOMICS — *Economic Situation And Conditions*

COUNTRY REPORT. EGYPT; analysis of economic and political trends every quarter. see BUSINESS AND ECONOMICS — *Economic Situation And Conditions*

COUNTRY REPORT. ETHIOPIA, ERITREA, SOMALIA, DJIBOUTI; analysis of economic and political trends every quarter. see BUSINESS AND ECONOMICS — *Economic Situation And Conditions*

COUNTRY REPORT. FINLAND; analysis of economic and political trends every quarter. see BUSINESS AND ECONOMICS — *Economic Situation And Conditions*

COUNTRY REPORT. FRANCE; analysis of economic and political trends every quarter. see BUSINESS AND ECONOMICS — *Economic Situation And Conditions*

COUNTRY REPORT. GABON, EQUATORIAL GUINEA; analysis of economic and political trends every quarter. see BUSINESS AND ECONOMICS — *Economic Situation And Conditions*

COUNTRY REPORT. GEORGIA, ARMENIA, AZERBAIJAN; analysis of economic and political trends every quarter. see BUSINESS AND ECONOMICS — *Economic Situation And Conditions*

COUNTRY REPORT. GERMANY; analysis of economic and political trends every quarter. see BUSINESS AND ECONOMICS — *Economic Situation And Conditions*

COUNTRY REPORT. GHANA; analysis of economic and political trends every quarter. see BUSINESS AND ECONOMICS — *Economic Situation And Conditions*

COUNTRY REPORT. GREECE; analysis of economic and political trends every quarter. see BUSINESS AND ECONOMICS — *Economic Situation And Conditions*

COUNTRY REPORT. GUATEMALA, EL SALVADOR; analysis of economic and political trends every quarter. see BUSINESS AND ECONOMICS — *Economic Situation And Conditions*

COUNTRY REPORT. GUINEA, SIERRA LEONE, LIBERIA; analysis of economic and political trends every quarter. see BUSINESS AND ECONOMICS — *Economic Situation And Conditions*

COUNTRY REPORT. HONG KONG, MACAU; analysis of economic and political trends every quarter. see BUSINESS AND ECONOMICS — *Economic Situation And Conditions*

COUNTRY REPORT. HUNGARY; analysis of economic and political trends every quarter. see BUSINESS AND ECONOMICS — *Economic Situation And Conditions*

COUNTRY REPORT. INDIA, NEPAL. see BUSINESS AND ECONOMICS — *Economic Situation And Conditions*

COUNTRY REPORT. INDONESIA; analysis of economic and political trends every quarter. see BUSINESS AND ECONOMICS — *Economic Situation And Conditions*

COUNTRY REPORT. IRAN; analysis of economic and political trends every quarter. see BUSINESS AND ECONOMICS — *Economic Situation And Conditions*

COUNTRY REPORT. IRAQ; analysis of economic and political trends every quarter. see BUSINESS AND ECONOMICS — *Economic Situation And Conditions*

COUNTRY REPORT. IRELAND; analysis of economic and political trends every quarter. see BUSINESS AND ECONOMICS — *Economic Situation And Conditions*

COUNTRY REPORT. ISRAEL, THE OCCUPIED TERRITORIES; analysis of economic and political trends every quarter. see BUSINESS AND ECONOMICS — *Economic Situation And Conditions*

COUNTRY REPORT. ITALY; analysis of economic and political trends every quarter. see BUSINESS AND ECONOMICS — *Economic Situation And Conditions*

COUNTRY REPORT. JAMAICA, BELIZE, BAHAMAS, BERMUDA, BARBADOS; analysis of economic and political trends every quarter. see BUSINESS AND ECONOMICS — *Economic Situation And Conditions*

COUNTRY REPORT. JAPAN; analysis of economic and political trends every quarter. see BUSINESS AND ECONOMICS — *Economic Situation And Conditions*

COUNTRY REPORT. JORDAN; analysis of economic and political trends every quarter. see BUSINESS AND ECONOMICS — *Economic Situation And Conditions*

COUNTRY REPORT. KAZAKHSTAN. see BUSINESS AND ECONOMICS — *Economic Situation And Conditions*

COUNTRY REPORT. KENYA; analysis of economic and political trends every quarter. see BUSINESS AND ECONOMICS — *Economic Situation And Conditions*

COUNTRY REPORT. KUWAIT; analysis of economic and political trends every quarter. see BUSINESS AND ECONOMICS — *Economic Situation And Conditions*

COUNTRY REPORT. KYRGYZ REPUBLIC, TAJIKISTAN, TURKMENISTAN; analysis of economic and political trends every quarter. see BUSINESS AND ECONOMICS — *Economic Situation And Conditions*

COUNTRY REPORT. LEBANON; analysis of economic and political trends every quarter. see BUSINESS AND ECONOMICS — *Economic Situation And Conditions*

COUNTRY REPORT. LIBYA; analysis of economic and political trends every quarter. see BUSINESS AND ECONOMICS — *Economic Situation And Conditions*

COUNTRY REPORT. MACEDONIA, SERBIA-MONTENEGRO; analysis of economic and political trends every quarter. see BUSINESS AND ECONOMICS — *Economic Situation And Conditions*

COUNTRY REPORT. MALAYSIA, BRUNEI; analysis of economic and political trends every quarter. see BUSINESS AND ECONOMICS — *Economic Situation And Conditions*

COUNTRY REPORT. MAURITIUS, MADAGASCAR, SEYCHELLES; analysis of economic and political trends every quarter. see BUSINESS AND ECONOMICS — *Economic Situation And Conditions*

COUNTRY REPORT. MEXICO; analysis of economic and political trends every quarter. see BUSINESS AND ECONOMICS — *Economic Situation And Conditions*

COUNTRY REPORT. MOROCCO; analysis of economic and political trends every quarter. see BUSINESS AND ECONOMICS — *Economic Situation And Conditions*

COUNTRY REPORT. MOZAMBIQUE, MALAWI; analysis of economic and political trends every quarter. see BUSINESS AND ECONOMICS — *Economic Situation And Conditions*

BUSINESS AND ECONOMICS — ECONOMIC SYSTEMS AND THEORIES, ECONOMIC HISTORY

COUNTRY REPORT. MYANMAR (BURMA); analysis of economic and political trends every quarter. see *BUSINESS AND ECONOMICS — Economic Situation And Conditions*

COUNTRY REPORT. NAMIBIA, SWAZILAND; analysis of economic and political trends every quarter. see *BUSINESS AND ECONOMICS — Economic Situation And Conditions*

COUNTRY REPORT. NETHERLANDS; analysis of economic and political trends every quarter. see *BUSINESS AND ECONOMICS — Economic Situation And Conditions*

COUNTRY REPORT. NEW ZEALAND; analysis of economic and political trends every quarter. see *BUSINESS AND ECONOMICS — Economic Situation And Conditions*

COUNTRY REPORT. NICARAGUA, HONDURAS; analysis of economic and political trends every quarter. see *BUSINESS AND ECONOMICS — Economic Situation And Conditions*

COUNTRY REPORT. NIGER, BURKINA FASO; analysis of economic and political trends every quarter. see *BUSINESS AND ECONOMICS — Economic Situation And Conditions*

COUNTRY REPORT. NIGERIA; analysis of economic and political trends every quarter. see *BUSINESS AND ECONOMICS — Economic Situation And Conditions*

COUNTRY REPORT. NORWAY; analysis of economic and political trends every quarter. see *BUSINESS AND ECONOMICS — Economic Situation And Conditions*

COUNTRY REPORT. OMAN, YEMEN; analysis of economic and political trends every quarter. see *BUSINESS AND ECONOMICS — Economic Situation And Conditions*

COUNTRY REPORT. PACIFIC ISLANDS: PAPUA NEW GUINEA, FIJI, SOLOMON ISLANDS, WESTERN SAMOA, VANUATU, TONGA; analysis of economic and political trends every quarter. see *BUSINESS AND ECONOMICS — Economic Situation And Conditions*

COUNTRY REPORT. PAKISTAN, AFGHANISTAN; analysis of economic and political trends every quarter. see *BUSINESS AND ECONOMICS — Economic Situation And Conditions*

COUNTRY REPORT. PANAMA; analysis of economic and political trends every quarter. see *BUSINESS AND ECONOMICS — Economic Situation And Conditions*

COUNTRY REPORT. PERU; analysis of economic and political trends every quarter. see *BUSINESS AND ECONOMICS — Economic Situation And Conditions*

COUNTRY REPORT. PHILIPPINES; analysis of economic and political trends every quarter. see *BUSINESS AND ECONOMICS — Economic Situation And Conditions*

COUNTRY REPORT. POLAND; analysis of economic and political trends every quarter. see *BUSINESS AND ECONOMICS — Economic Situation And Conditions*

COUNTRY REPORT. PORTUGAL; analysis of economic and political trends every quarter. see *BUSINESS AND ECONOMICS — Economic Situation And Conditions*

COUNTRY REPORT. ROMANIA; analysis of economic and political trends every quarter. see *BUSINESS AND ECONOMICS — Economic Situation And Conditions*

COUNTRY REPORT. RUSSIA; analysis of economic and political trends every quarter. see *BUSINESS AND ECONOMICS — Economic Situation And Conditions*

COUNTRY REPORT. SAUDI ARABIA; analysis of economic and political trends every quarter. see *BUSINESS AND ECONOMICS — Economic Situation And Conditions*

COUNTRY REPORT. SENEGAL, THE GAMBIA, MAURITANIA; analysis of economic and political trends every quarter. see *BUSINESS AND ECONOMICS — Economic Situation And Conditions*

COUNTRY REPORT. SINGAPORE; analysis of economic and political trends every quarter. see *BUSINESS AND ECONOMICS — Economic Situation And Conditions*

COUNTRY REPORT. SLOVAKIA; analysis of economic and political trends every quarter. see *BUSINESS AND ECONOMICS — Economic Situation And Conditions*

COUNTRY REPORT. SOUTH AFRICA; analysis of economic and political trends every quarter. see *BUSINESS AND ECONOMICS — Economic Situation And Conditions*

COUNTRY REPORT. SOUTH KOREA, NORTH KOREA; analysis of economic and political trends every quarter. see *BUSINESS AND ECONOMICS — Economic Situation And Conditions*

COUNTRY REPORT. SPAIN; analysis of economic and political trends every quarter. see *BUSINESS AND ECONOMICS — Economic Situation And Conditions*

COUNTRY REPORT. SRI LANKA; analysis of economic and political trends every quarter. see *BUSINESS AND ECONOMICS — Economic Situation And Conditions*

COUNTRY REPORT. SUDAN; analysis of economic and political trends every quarter. see *BUSINESS AND ECONOMICS — Economic Situation And Conditions*

COUNTRY REPORT. SWEDEN; analysis of economic and political trends every quarter. see *BUSINESS AND ECONOMICS — Economic Situation And Conditions*

COUNTRY REPORT. SWITZERLAND; analysis of economic and political trends every quarter. see *BUSINESS AND ECONOMICS — Economic Situation And Conditions*

COUNTRY REPORT. SYRIA; analysis of economic and political trends every quarter. see *BUSINESS AND ECONOMICS — Economic Situation And Conditions*

COUNTRY REPORT. TAIWAN; analysis of economic and political trends every quarter. see *BUSINESS AND ECONOMICS — Economic Situation And Conditions*

COUNTRY REPORT. TANZANIA, COMOROS; analysis of economic and political trends every quarter. see *BUSINESS AND ECONOMICS — Economic Situation And Conditions*

COUNTRY REPORT. THAILAND; analysis of economic and political trends every quarter. see *BUSINESS AND ECONOMICS — Economic Situation And Conditions*

COUNTRY REPORT. TOGO, BENIN; analysis of economic and political trends every quarter. see *BUSINESS AND ECONOMICS — Economic Situation And Conditions*

COUNTRY REPORT. TRINIDAD & TOBAGO, GUYANA, WINDWARD & LEEWARD ISLANDS, SURINAME, NETHERLANDS ANTILLES, ARUBA; analysis of economic and political trends every quarter. see *BUSINESS AND ECONOMICS — Economic Situation And Conditions*

COUNTRY REPORT. TUNISIA; analysis of economic and political trends every quarter. see *BUSINESS AND ECONOMICS — Economic Situation And Conditions*

COUNTRY REPORT. TURKEY; analysis of economic and political trends every quarter. see *BUSINESS AND ECONOMICS — Economic Situation And Conditions*

COUNTRY REPORT. UGANDA, RWANDA, BURUNDI; analysis of economic and political trends every quarter. see *BUSINESS AND ECONOMICS — Economic Situation And Conditions*

COUNTRY REPORT. UKRAINE; analysis of economic and political trends every quarter. see *BUSINESS AND ECONOMICS — Economic Situation And Conditions*

COUNTRY REPORT. UNITED ARAB EMIRATES; analysis of economic and political trends every quarter. see *BUSINESS AND ECONOMICS — Economic Situation And Conditions*

COUNTRY REPORT. UNITED KINGDOM; analysis of economic and political trends every quarter. see *BUSINESS AND ECONOMICS — Economic Situation And Conditions*

COUNTRY REPORT. UNITED STATES OF AMERICA; analysis of economic and political trends every quarter. see *BUSINESS AND ECONOMICS — Economic Situation And Conditions*

COUNTRY REPORT. URUGUAY, PARAGUAY; analysis of economic and political trends every quarter. see *BUSINESS AND ECONOMICS — Economic Situation And Conditions*

COUNTRY REPORT. UZBEKISTAN; analysis of economic and political trends every quarter. see *BUSINESS AND ECONOMICS — Economic Situation And Conditions*

COUNTRY REPORT. VENEZUELA; analysis of economic and political trends every quarter. see *BUSINESS AND ECONOMICS — Economic Situation And Conditions*

COUNTRY REPORT. VIETNAM; analysis of economic and political trends every quarter. see *BUSINESS AND ECONOMICS — Economic Situation And Conditions*

COUNTRY REPORT. ZAMBIA, ZAIRE; analysis of economic and political trends every quarter. see *BUSINESS AND ECONOMICS — Economic Situation And Conditions*

COUNTRY REPORT. ZIMBABWE; analysis of economic and political trends every quarter. see *BUSINESS AND ECONOMICS — Economic Situation And Conditions*

COUNTRY REPORTS; analysis of economic and political trends every quarter. see *BUSINESS AND ECONOMICS — Economic Situation And Conditions*

330.1   PE
CRITICA. 1976. q. Universidad Nacional Mayor de San Marcos, Instituto de Investigaciones Economicas, Lima 1, Peru. Ed.Bd.

CROSSBORDER MONITOR. see *BUSINESS AND ECONOMICS — International Commerce*

330.1   CU
CUADERNOS ECONOMICOS TRIMESTRALES. 1988. 4/yr. Centro de Estudios sobre America, Ave. 3ra., No. 1805 (18 y 20), Municipio Playa, Zona 13, Havana, Cuba.

CUBA: ECONOMIA PLANIFICADA. see *BUSINESS AND ECONOMICS — Macroeconomics*

330.1   CU
CUESTIONES DE LA ECONOMIA PLANIFICADO. bi-m. $14. (Instituto de Investigaciones Economicas) Ediciones Cubanas, Obispo No. 527, Apdo. 605, Havana, Cuba. illus.

330   US   ISSN 0011-4294
Q176
CYCLES. 1950. 6/yr. $75 membership. Foundation for the Study of Cycles, 900 W. Valley Rd., Ste. 502, Wayne, PA 19087-1821. TEL 610-995-2120. FAX 610-995-2130. E-mail: cycles@cycles.org; URL: http://www.cycles.org/~cycles. Ed. Chester Joy; Pub. Richard Mogey. bk.rev.; charts; illus.; stat.; index. circ. 2,626. Indexed: P.A.I.S., Rural Recreat.Tour.Abstr., World Agri.Econ.& Rural Sociol.Abstr. **Document type**: newsletter. —BLDSC (3506.415000); UnCover.
   Description: Reports on international cyclic research, including the fields of human behavior, natural sciences, business and finance, social and cultural phenomena.

330.1   FR   ISSN 0396-8898
DOCUMENTS POUR L'ENSEIGNEMENT ECONOMIQUE ET SOCIAL. Abbreviated title: D E E S. 1970. 4/yr. 147 F. (foreign 200 F.) (effective 1997). Centre National de Documentation Pedagogique, 29 rue d'Ulm, 75230 Paris Cedex 05, France. TEL 33-1-46349000. FAX 33-1-46345544. (Subscr. to: CNDP - Abonnement, B750, 60732 Ste. Genevieve Cedex, France. FAX 33-3-44033013) Ed. Pascal Combemale. circ. 2,000.
   Description: Offers a forum for economists and social scientists.

DYNAMIC ECONOMETRIC MODELS. see *MATHEMATICS*

ECOLOGICAL ECONOMICS. see *ENVIRONMENTAL STUDIES*

BUSINESS AND ECONOMICS — ECONOMIC SYSTEMS AND THEORIES, ECONOMIC HISTORY

ECOLOGY, ECONOMY & ENVIRONMENT. see *ENVIRONMENTAL STUDIES*

330.1   UK   ISSN 0266-4666
HB139
ECONOMETRIC THEORY. 1985. bi-m. £158($242) (effective 1998). Cambridge University Press, Edinburgh Bldg., Shaftesbury Rd., Cambridge CB2 2RU, England. TEL 44-1223-312393. FAX 44-1223-315052. TELEX 851817256. E-mail: information@cup.cam.ac.uk; subscriptions@cup.cam.ac.uk; URL: http://www.cup.org/journals/CUPJNLS.html. (N. American addr.: Cambridge University Press, Journals Dept., 40 W. 20th St., New York, NY 10011. TEL 212-924-3900. FAX 212-691-3239) Ed. Peter C.B. Phillips. R&P contact: Linda Nicol. adv. contact: Rebecca Symons. bk.rev. (also avail. in microform from UMI; back issues avail.; reprint service avail. from SWZ) **Indexed:** ASCA, C.R.E.J., Compumath, Curr.Cont.(1991-), Curr.Ind.Stat., J.Cont.Quant.Meth., SSCI, Stat.Theor.Meth.Abstr. (1991-). **Document type:** academic/scholarly publication.
—BLDSC (3650.096000); Genuine Article; SWETS; UMI; UnCover. **CCC.**
Description: Contains original theoretical contributions on all areas of econometrics.

330.1   IT   ISSN 1120-7019
ECONOMIA DELLE SCELTE PUBBLICHE/JOURNAL OF PUBLIC FINANCE AND PUBLIC CHOICE. (Text and summaries in English, Italian) 1983. 3/yr. L.30000($25) to individuals; institutions and libraries L.50000($45) (effective 1994). Tibergraph Editrice s.r.l., Via G. Sorel - Zona Indle. Nord, 06011 Cerbara di Citta di Castello (PG), Italy. Ed. Domenico da Empoli. adv.; bk.rev. **Indexed:** J.of Econ.Lit., P.A.I.S.
Description: Deals with the analysis, both theoretical and empirical, of governmental action in economy, following the teachings of the Public Choice School.

330.9   UN
ECONOMIC COMMISSION FOR EUROPE. STATISTICAL YEARBOOK. a. Economic Commission for Europe (ECE), Palais des Nations, CH-1211 Geneva 10, Switzerland. TEL 41-22-9171234. FAX 41-22-9170123. **Document type:** bulletin.

330.1   NE   ISSN 0928-5040
HB1   CODEN: EDESE9
ECONOMIC DESIGN. (Text in English) 1994. q. fl.355($219) (effective 1997). North-Holland (Subsidiary of: Elsevier Science B.V.), P.O. Box 211, 1000 AE Amsterdam, Netherlands. TEL 31-20-4853911. FAX 31-20-4853598. TELEX 18582 ESPA NL. (Subscr. in the Americas to: Elsevier Science, Regional Sales Office, Box 945, New York, NY 10159-0945. TEL 212-633-3730. FAX 212-633-3680; Subscr. in Australasia and the Far East to: Elsevier Science (Singapore) Pte Ltd, No.1 Temasek Ave., No.17-01 Millenia Tower, Singapore 039192, Singapore. TEL 65-434-3727. FAX 65-337-2230; Subscr. in Japan to: Elsevier Science Japan, 9-15 Higashi-Azabu 1-chome, Minato-ku Tokyo 106, Japan. TEL 81-3-5561-5033. FAX 81-3-5561-5047) Eds. Murat Sertel, William Thompson. bk.rev.; abstr.; bibl.; stat.; index. (also avail. in microform from UMI; back issues avail.) **Document type:** academic/scholarly publication.
—BLDSC (3652.675000); SWETS. **CCC.**
Description: Provides an international forum for research in economic design, including game theory, and applications to the design and assembly of legal-economic instruments. Also includes discussions of relevant mathematical techniques and comparative assessments of the performance of economic systems.
Refereed Serial

330.1 350   US   ISSN 0891-2424
ECONOMIC DEVELOPMENT QUARTERLY; the journal of American revitalization. 1987. q. $198 to institutions (effective Sep. 1996). Sage Publications, Inc., 2455 Teller Rd., Thousand Oaks, CA 91320. TEL 805-499-0721. FAX 805-499-0871. E-mail: libraries@sagepub.com; URL: http://www.sagepub.com. (Overseas subscr. to: Sage Publications Ltd., 6 Bonhill St., London EC2A 4PU, England; Sage Publications India Pvt. Ltd., P.O. Box 4215, New Delhi 110 048, India) Ed. Edward W. Hill. adv. contact: Margaret Travers. bk.rev. circ. 1,250. (back issues avail.; reprint service avail.) **Indexed:** ASCA, Curr.Cont., Human Resour.Abstr., Sage Pub.Admin.Abstr., Sage Urb.Stud.Abstr., Sociol.Abstr. **Document type:** academic/scholarly publication.
—BLDSC (3652.727000); Genuine Article; SWETS; UMI; UnCover. **CCC.**
Description: Disseminates information on the latest research, programs, policies, and trends in the field of economic development.

330   UK   ISSN 0013-0117
HC10
ECONOMIC HISTORY REVIEW. 1927. q. £70($131) (foreign £83) (effective 1997). Blackwell Publishers Ltd., 108 Cowley Rd., Oxford OX4 1JF, England. TEL 44-1865-791100. FAX 44-1865-791347. E-mail: jnlinfo@blackwellpublishers.co.uk; URL: http://www.blackwellpublishers.co.uk. Eds. F. Capie, J. Hatcher. adv.; bk.rev.; bibl.; charts; stat.; index, cum.index: 1927-1948, 1948-1970. circ. 5,000. (also avail. in microfiche from IDC; microfilm from KTO; back issues avail.; reprint service avail. from SWZ,KTO) **Indexed:** Amer.Hist.& Life (1954-), Arts & Hum.Cit.Ind., ASCA, Br.Archaeol.Abstr., Br.Hum.Ind., Curr.Cont., Geo.Abstr.H.G., Hist.Abstr. (1954-), I.M.M.Abstr., IBR, IDA, J.of Econ.Lit., Mid.East: Abstr.& Ind., Numis.Lit., P.A.I.S., Popul.Ind., Soc.Sci.Ind., SSCI, Work Rel.Abstr. **Document type:** academic/scholarly publication.
—BLDSC (3653.500000); Genuine Article; KR SourceOne; SWETS; UMI; UnCover. **CCC.**
Refereed Serial

ECONOMIC INTELLIGENCE REVIEW. see *POLITICAL SCIENCE*

330.1 330.9   UK   ISSN 1363-7029
HB1
ECONOMIC ISSUES. 1977. 2/yr. Association of Polytechnic Teachers in Economics, Staffordshire University, Business School, Leek Rd., Stoke-on-Trent ST4 2DF, England. TEL 44-1782-294000. FAX 44-1782-747006. Ed. P.J. Reynolds. adv.; bk.rev. circ. 400. (back issues avail.) **Indexed:** Cont.Pg.Manage., J.of Econ.Lit. **Document type:** academic/scholarly publication.
—BLDSC (3653.729000).
Formerly (until 1996): British Review of Economic Issues (ISSN 0141-4739)

ECONOMIC JOURNAL OF NEPAL. see *BUSINESS AND ECONOMICS — International Development And Assistance*

330.1   NE   ISSN 0264-9993
HB141
ECONOMIC MODELLING. (Text in English) 1984. q. fl.865($497) (effective 1998). North-Holland (Subsidiary of: Elsevier Science B.V.), P.O. Box 211, 1000 AE Amsterdam, Netherlands. TEL 31-20-4853757. FAX 31-20-4853432. (Subscr. in the Americas to: Elsevier Science, Regional Sales Office, Box 945, New York, NY 10159-0945. TEL 212-633-3730. FAX 212-633-3680; Subscr. in Australasia and the Far East to: Elsevier Science (Singapore) Pte Ltd, No. 1 Temasek Ave., No.17-01 Millenia Tower, Singapore 039192, Singapore. TEL 65-434-3727. FAX 65-337-2230; Subscr. in Japan to: Elsevier Science Japan, 9-15 Higashi-Azabu 1-chome, Minato-ku, Tokyo 106, Japan. TEL 81-3-5561-5033. FAX 81-3-5561-5047) Ed. Homa Motamen. adv.; bk.rev.; abstr.; illus.; index. (also avail. in microform from UMI; back issues avail.) **Indexed:** ASCA, Asian-Pac.Econ.Lit., C.R.E.J., Curr.Cont., J.Cont.Quant.Meth., J.of Econ.Lit., SSCI. **Document type:** academic/scholarly publication.
—BLDSC (3653.913500); Genuine Article; SWETS; UMI; UnCover. **CCC.**
Description: Presents complete versions, developed for policy analysis, of large-scale models of industrially advanced economies.
Refereed Serial

ECONOMIC NOTES. see *BUSINESS AND ECONOMICS*

ECONOMIC SYSTEMS. see *BUSINESS AND ECONOMICS — International Commerce*

330.1   UK   ISSN 0953-5314
HB142
ECONOMIC SYSTEMS RESEARCH. 1989. q. £88($154) to individuals; institutions £272 ($494) (effective 1997). (Input - Output Association) Carfax Publishing Co., P.O. Box 25, Abingdon, Oxon. OX14 3UE, England. TEL 44-1235-401000. FAX 44-1235-401550. E-mail: enquiries@carfax.co.uk. (Subscr. in N. America to: Carfax Publishing Co., 875-81 Massachusetts Ave., Cambridge, MA 02139) Eds. J. Oosterhaven, E. Dietzenbacher. adv.; bk.rev. (also avail. in microfiche) **Indexed:** Geo.Abstr.H.G., IDA, J.of Econ.Lit. **Document type:** academic/scholarly publication.
—BLDSC (3656.683000); SWETS; UMI; UnCover. **CCC.**
Description: Contains practical matter-of-fact tools and data for modeling, policy analysis, planning and decision making in macroeconomic contexts.
Refereed Serial

330.1   GW   ISSN 0938-2259
HB1.A1   CODEN: ECTHEA
ECONOMIC THEORY. Online edition (GW ISSN 1432-0479) (Text in English) 1991. bi-m. DM.1202.50 (foreign DM.1217.20) (effective 1998). Springer-Verlag, Heidelberger Platz 3, 14197 Berlin, Germany. TEL 49-30-82787-0. FAX 49-30-82787448. E-mail: subscriptions@springer.de; URL: http://link.springer.de. (Subscr. in N. America to: Springer-Verlag New York, Inc., 333 Meadowlands Pkwy., Secaucus, NJ 07094. TEL 212-460-1500. FAX 212-473-6272) Ed. C.D. Aliprantis. **Indexed:** ASCA, Curr.Cont., Zent.Math. **Document type:** academic/scholarly publication.
●Also available online.
—BLDSC (3656.684200); Genuine Article; SWETS; UMI; UnCover. **CCC.**
Description: Presents research in all areas of economics based on theoretical reasoning and on specific topics in mathematics that are motivated by the analysis of economic problems.

330.1 320   UK   ISSN 0954-1985
HD72
ECONOMICS & POLITICS. 1988. 3/yr. £93($177) (foreign £114) (effective 1997). Blackwell Publishers Ltd., 108 Cowley Rd., Oxford OX4 1JF, England. TEL 44-1865-791100. FAX 44-1865-791347. E-mail: jnlinfo@blackwellpublishers.co.uk; URL: http://www.blackwellpublishers.co.uk. Ed. Jagdish Bhagwati. adv.; bk.rev.; index. circ. 300. (back issues avail.; reprint service avail. from SWZ) **Indexed:** Int.Polit.Sci.Abstr., Polit.Sci.Abstr.
—BLDSC (3656.930980); SWETS; UMI; UnCover. **CCC.**
Description: Provides a forum for the dissemination of work in political economy with emphasis on analytical political economy.
Refereed Serial

330.1   SZ   ISSN 0165-1765
HB1   CODEN: ECLEDS
ECONOMICS LETTERS. (Text in English) 1978. m. fl.2430($1397) (effective 1998). Elsevier Science S.A., P.O. Box 564, CH-1001 Lausanne 1, Switzerland. TEL 41-21-3207381. FAX 41-21-3235444. TELEX 450620-ELSA-CH. (Subscr. to: Elsevier Science, Regional Sales Office, P.O. Box 211, 1000 AE Amsterdam, Netherlands. TEL 31-20-4853757. FAX 31-20-4853432; Subscr. in the Americas to: Elsevier Science, Regional Sales Office, Box 945, New York, NY 10159-0945. TEL 212-633-3730. FAX 212-633-3680; Subscr. in Australasia to: Elsevier Science (Singapore) Pte. Ltd., No. 1 Temasek Ave., No. 17-01 Millenia Tower, Singapore 039192, Singapore. TEL 65-434-3727. FAX 65-434-3727) Ed. Jerry Green. adv.; bk.rev.; illus.; index. (also avail. in microform from UMI; back issues avail.) **Indexed:** ASCA, C.R.E.J., Curr.Cont., Fam.Ind., Math.R., Risk Abstr., SSCI, Zent.Math. **Document type:** academic/scholarly publication.
—BLDSC (3657.025000); Genuine Article; SWETS; UnCover. **CCC.**
Description: Presents new results, models and methods in all fields of economic research.
Refereed Serial

BUSINESS AND ECONOMICS — ECONOMIC SYSTEMS AND THEORIES, ECONOMIC HISTORY

330.1   UK   ISSN 0967-0750
HC244.A1
THE ECONOMICS OF TRANSITION. 1993. s-a. £185 (foreign $310) (effective 1998). (European Bank for Reconstruction and Development) Oxford University Press, Academic Division, Great Clarendon St., Oxford OX2 6DP, England. TEL 44-1865-267907. FAX 44-1865-267485. TELEX 837330-OXPRES-G. E-mail: jnl.info@oup.co.uk; URL: http://www.oup.co.uk/journals. (US subscr. to: Oxford University Press Inc., 2001 Evans Rd., Cary, NC 27513. TEL 919-677-0977. FAX 919-677-1714) Ed.Bd.; Pub. Martin Green. R&P contact: Joolz Longley. adv. contact: Jane Parker. bk.rev. circ. 1,150. **Document type:** academic/scholarly publication.
—BLDSC (3657.183000); SWETS.
    Description: Provides information on the economics of transition from centrally planned to market economies, particularly in Eastern Europe and the CIS.

330.1   BG
ECONOMICUS. (Text in English) vol.2, Apr. 1976. irreg. Tk.2. Chittagong University, Department of Economics, Chittagong, Bangladesh.

ECONOMIE ET SOCIALISME; revue marocaine de reflection et de debat. see BUSINESS AND ECONOMICS — Economic Situation And Conditions

330   FR   ISSN 0068-4864
ECONOMIES ET SOCIETES. SERIE AF. HISTOIRE QUANTITATIVE DE L'ECONOMIE FRANCAISE. 1961. irreg. 350 F. Presses Universitaires de Grenoble, B.P. 47, 38040 Grenoble Cedex 9, France. Ed. J. Marczewski. circ. 1,600.
—SWETS.

330   FR   ISSN 0013-0567
HB3
ECONOMIES ET SOCIETES. SERIE EM. ECONOMIE MATHEMATIQUE ET ECONOMETRIE. 1971. irreg. 350 F. Presses Universitaires de Grenoble, B.P. 47, 38040 Grenoble Cedex 9, France. Dir. R. Vallee. adv.; bk.rev. **Indexed:** P.A.I.S.For.Lang.Ind.
—BLDSC (3658.450000); SWETS.

330.1   FR   ISSN 0068-483X
ECONOMIES ET SOCIETES. SERIE G. ECONOMIE PLANIFIEE. 1956. irreg. 350 F. Presses Universitaires de Grenoble, B.P. 47, 38040 Grenoble Cedex 9, France. Eds. Henri Chambre, M. Lavigne.

330.1 100   FR   ISSN 0068-4880
ECONOMIES ET SOCIETES. SERIE M. PHILOSOPHIE - SCIENCES SOCIALES ECONOMIE. irreg. 350 F. Presses Universitaires de Grenoble, B.P. 47, 38040 Grenoble Cedex 9, France. Dir. Jean Lacroix. circ. 1,600.
—SWETS.

330.1 338.91   FR   ISSN 0068-4902
ECONOMIES ET SOCIETES. SERIE P. RELATIONS ECONOMIQUES INTERNATIONALES. 1944. irreg. 350 F. Presses Universitaires de Grenoble, B.P. 47, 38040 Grenoble Cedex 9, France. Dir. Jean Weiller. circ. 1,600.
—SWETS.

330.1   FR   ISSN 0068-4856
ECONOMIES ET SOCIETES. SERIE S. ETUDES DE MARXOLOGIE. 1959. irreg., latest 1987. 350 F. Presses Universitaires de Grenoble, B.P. 47, 38040 Grenoble Cedex 9, France. Dir. M. Rubel. bk.rev. circ. 1,600.
—SWETS.

THE ECONOMIST. see BUSINESS AND ECONOMICS — Economic Situation And Conditions

330.1   CC   ISSN 1011-9108
HB9
ECONOMY AND LAW. Key Title: Jingji yu Falu. (Text in Chinese, English) 1985. bi-m. HK.$180($51) Economy and Law Press, A1 5-F Lo Yong Court Commercial Bldg., 212-220 Lockhart Rd., Hong Kong, People's Republic of China. TEL 852-25197556. FAX 852-25073079. Ed. Chan Ying Liong; Pub. Chan Ying Liong. adv. contact: Chan See Wai. bk.rev.; abstr.; index. circ. 10,000. (also avail. in microfilm; back issues avail.) **Document type:** trade publication.
    Description: For the academic exchange of studies in business, investment, economics, and law.

330.1   GR
ECONOMY AND THE FOREIGN POLICY. (Supplement to: Epilogi) 1991. a. Dr.1200. Electra Press, 4 Stadiou St., 105 64 Athens, Greece. TEL 323-3203. FAX 323-5160. TELEX 210564. Ed. Christos Papaioannou. adv. circ. 11,000.

330.1   CY   ISSN 1025-5508
EKONOMIA. (Text in English) 1988. s-a. $30 to individuals; institutions $55 (effective 1997). Cyprus Economic Society, P.O. Box 8724, Nicosia, Cyprus. E-mail: eca16@keele.ac.uk. Ed. P. Demetriades. R&P contact: G.M. Georgiou. TEL 357-2-394225. adv. contact: Chris Patsalides. bk.rev.; abstr. circ. 600. (microfiche; back issues avail.) **Document type:** academic/scholarly publication.
—BLDSC (3506.726500).
    Supersedes (in 1997): Cyprus Journal of Economics (ISSN 1013-3224)
    Description: Aims to cover a wide spectrum of areas including economic theory, policy, finance, development economics, applied econometrics, history of economic thought and political economy.
Refereed Serial

330.1   KR
HC337.UU5
EKONOMIKA UKRAINY. (Editions in Russian, Ukrainian) 1958. 12/yr. $95 (effective 1998). (Akademiya Nauk Ukrainy, Institut Ekonomiki) Vidavnitstvo Presa Ukrainy, Peremogy pr., 50, 252047 Kiev 47, Ukraine. TEL 38-44-4418214. FAX 38-44-2908663. (Dist. by: Mezhdunarodnaya Kniga, B. Yakimanka 39, 117049 Moscow, Russia. TEL 7-095-2384967. FAX 7-095-2384634; Subscr. to: Smoloskyp, 52 Chkalov St., ap. 24, 252054 Kiev 54, Ukraine; Subscr. in US to: Smoloskyp, Inc., 1863 Pioneer Pkwy. E., Apt. 210, Springfield, OR 97477. TEL 503-744-0989. FAX 503-744-0989) Ed. Ivan I. Lukinov. bk.rev.; bibl.; charts; stat.; index. circ. 9,000. (tabloid format) **Indexed:** Djerelo. **Document type:** academic/scholarly publication.
    Formerly: Ekonomika Radyanskoi Ukrainy (ISSN 0131-775X)
Refereed Serial

330   TA
EKONOMIKO-MATEMATICHESKIE METODY V PLANIROVANII NARODNOGO KHOZYAISTVA. irreg. 0.97 Rub. Akademiya Nauk Tajikistana, Institut Ekonomiki, Ul. Aini 44, 734000 Dushanbe, Tajikistan. illus.

ENERGY ECONOMICS; for professionals concerned with economic analysis of energy issues. see ENERGY

ENERGY JOURNAL. see ENERGY

330.1   BL   ISSN 0101-1723
ENSAIOS F E E. 1980. s-a. R.40 (effective 1997). Fundacao de Economia e Estatistica, Rua Duque de Caxias 1691, CEP 90010-283 Porto Alegre RG, Brazil. TEL 55-512-259455. FAX 55-512-25006. Ed. Eneas Costa de Souza. **Indexed:** P.A.I.S.For.Lang.Ind.

330.1   SP
ESPECIAL DIRECTIVOS. 1985. 44/yr. 34866 ptas. Grupo Especial Directivos, C. Orense 39 2o D, 28020 Madrid, Spain. TEL 91-556-64-11. FAX 91-555-41-18. Ed. Fernando Serra. adv. contact: Francisco Romero.

330.1   US   ISSN 0896-226X
HC10
ESSAYS IN ECONOMIC AND BUSINESS HISTORY. 1979. a. $25. Ohio State University, Department of History, 106 Dulles Hall, 230 W. 17th Ave., OH 43210-1367. TEL 614-292-2674. FAX 614-292-2282. E-mail: childs.1@osu.edu. (Co-sponsor: Economic and Business Historical Society) Ed. William R. Childs. circ. 300. (back issues avail.) **Indexed:** Amer.Hist.& Life (1989-), Hist.Abstr. (1989-). **Document type:** proceedings.
—BLDSC (3811.694700).
    Description: Selected papers delivered at annual meetings of the Economic and Business Historical Society.
Refereed Serial

330.1 339   MX   ISSN 0188-6916
ESTUDIOS ECONOMICOS. (Text in English, Spanish) 1986. s-a. Mex.$38($30) to individuals (foreign $40); institutions $45 (foreign $50) (effective 1995). Colegio de Mexico, A.C., Departamento de Publicaciones, Camino al Ajusco n. 20, 01000 Mexico D.F., Mexico. TEL 525-645-6955. FAX 525-645-0464. Ed. Carlos M. Urzua. adv.; bk.rev.; abstr. circ. 1,000. (back issues avail.) **Indexed:** IBR.

ESTUDOS ECONOMICOS. see BUSINESS AND ECONOMICS

330   BE   ISSN 0071-1977
ETUDES D'HISTOIRE ECONOMIQUE ET SOCIALE. 1941. irreg., vol.10, 1993. price varies. (Institut Historique Belge de Rome - Belgische Historisch Instituut te Rome) N.V. Brepols, Steenweg op Tielen 68, 2300 Turnhout, Belgium. TEL 32-14-402500. FAX 32-14-428919. circ. controlled. **Document type:** monographic series.
    Description: Studies on social and economic history, with emphasis on the relations between Belgium and the Southern Low Countries and Italy.

330.1 914.4 944   FR   ISSN 0014-2158
ETUDES NORMANDES. 1951. q. 240 F. (foreign 220 F.) (effective 1997). Association d'Etudes Normandes, Universite de Rouen, 7 rue Thomas Becket, 76130 Mont St. Aignan, France. TEL 33-2-35743372. FAX 33-2-35146940. Ed. Francois Gay. bk.rev. circ. 1,200. **Indexed:** Geo.Abstr.H.G., Geo.Abstr. **Document type:** academic/scholarly publication.

330.1   UK   ISSN 1363-3244
EUROPA; economic policy insights for the associated countries. 1996. q. free. Centre for Economic Policy Research, 25-28 Burlington St., London W1X 1LB, England. TEL 44-171-878-2900. FAX 44-171-878-2999. E-mail: cepr@cepr.org. (Co-sponsor: Institute for EastWest Studies)

330.1   UK   ISSN 1351-7937
EUROPEAN ECONOMIC PERSPECTIVES. 1993. bi-m. free. Centre for Economic Policy Research, 25-28 Old Burlington St., London W1X 1LB, England. TEL 44-171-878-2900. FAX 44-171-878-2999. E-mail: cepr@cepr.org. Ed. Romesh Vaitilingam. circ. 14,000. **Document type:** academic/scholarly publication.
—BLDSC (3829.696500).
    Description: Presents articles on economic issues ranging from open-economy macroeconomics to trade policy, from the economic transformation of Eastern Europe to European competition, with emphasis on aspects of European integration.
Refereed Serial

330.1   UK   ISSN 0967-2567
HB1.A1
EUROPEAN JOURNAL OF THE HISTORY OF ECONOMIC THOUGHT. 1993. 3/yr. £34 (U.S. and Canada $52; rest of world £36) to individuals; institutions £112 (U.S. and Canada $168; rest of world £116) (effective 1997). Routledge, 11 New Fetter Ln., London EC4P 4EE, England. TEL 44-171-583-9855. FAX 44-171-842-2298. E-mail: sample.journals@routledge.com; URL: http://www.routledge.com/routledge/journal/journals.html. (Subscr. to: ITPS Ltd., Cheriton House, Andover, Hants SP10 5BE, England. TEL 44-1264-342919. FAX 44-1264-342807; Subscr. in US & Canada to: 29 W. 35th St., New York, NY 10001-2299. TEL 212-244-3336. FAX 212-564-7854) Ed.Bd. adv.: page £150; trim 115 x 190. **Indexed:** Amer.Hist.& Life (1993-), Hist.Abstr. (1993-). **Document type:** academic/scholarly publication.
—BLDSC (3829.729950); SWETS.
    Description: Provides a pluralistic forum for the discussion of traditions in the history of economic thought.

BUSINESS AND ECONOMICS — ECONOMIC SYSTEMS AND THEORIES, ECONOMIC HISTORY

330.1 **UK** **ISSN 1361-4916**
HC240.A1
▼**EUROPEAN REVIEW OF ECONOMIC HISTORY**. 1997. 3/yr. £59($89) (effective 1998). Cambridge University Press, Edinburgh Bldg., Shaftesbury Rd., Cambridge CB2 2RU, England. TEL 44-1223-312393. FAX 44-1223-315052. E-mail: information@cup.cam.ac.uk; URL: http://www.cup.cam.ac.uk. (N. American addr.: 40 W. 20th St., New York, NY 10011-4211. TEL 212-924-3900. FAX 212-691-3239) R&P contact: Linda Nicol. adv. contact: Rebecca Symons. **Document type:** academic/scholarly publication.
—BLDSC (3829.948000). **CCC.**
Refereed Serial

EUROSTAT. STATISTICS IN FOCUS. REGIONS. see *BUSINESS AND ECONOMICS — Abstracting, Bibliographies, Statistics*

330.1 **US** **ISSN 1386-4157**
▼**EXPERIMENTAL ECONOMICS**. Announced for publication 1998. 3/yr. fl.400 to institutions; $210 to institutions in U.S. (effective 1998). Kluwer Academic Publishers Boston, Box 358, Accord Sta., Hingham, MA 02018-0358. TEL 617-871-6600. E-mail: services@wkap.nl; URL: http://www.wkap.nl. (Dist. outside N. America by: Kluwer Academic Publishers Group, P.O. Box 322, 3300 AH Dordrecht, Netherlands. TEL 31-78-6392392. FAX 31-78-6546474)

330 **US** **ISSN 0014-4983**
HB615
EXPLORATIONS IN ECONOMIC HISTORY. 1963. q. $241 (foreign $288) (effective 1997). Academic Press, Inc., Journal Division, 525 B St., Ste. 1900, San Diego, CA 92101-4495. TEL 619-230-1840. FAX 619-699-6800. E-mail: apsubs@acad.com; URL: http://www.apnet.com/www/journal/eh/htm; http://www.idealibrary.com/. (Subscr. to: Box 861213, Orlando, FL 32886-1213. TEL 407-347-4040. FAX 407-363-9661) Ed. Larry Neal. adv.; bk.rev.; charts; index. (back issues avail.) **Indexed:** Amer.Bibl.Slavic & E.Eur.Stud., Amer.Hist.& Life (1955-), Arts & Hum.Cit.Ind., ASCA, Curr.Cont., Geo.Abstr.H.G., Hist.Abstr. (1955-), IDA, J.of Econ.Lit., Mid.East: Abstr.& Ind., P.A.I.S, Soc.Sci.Ind., SSCI. **Document type:** academic/scholarly publication.
●Also available online.
—BLDSC (3842.204000); Genuine Article; KR SourceOne; SWETS; UnCover. **CCC.**
Formerly: Explorations in Entrepreneurial History.
Description: Publishes original papers that provide broad coverage of the application of economic analysis to historical episodes.

FINANCIAL ENGINEERING AND THE JAPANESE MARKETS. see *BUSINESS AND ECONOMICS — Banking And Finance — Computer Applications*

330.1 **GW** **ISSN 0170-8252**
FINANZWISSENSCHAFTLICHE SCHRIFTEN. 1976. irreg., no.80, 1997. Peter Lang GmbH Europaeischer Verlag der Wissenschaften, Eschborner Landstr. 42-50, 60489 Frankfurt a.M., Germany. TEL 49-69-7807050. FAX 49-69-78070550. **Document type:** monographic series.

330.122 **IT**
▼**FINESECOLO**; materiali per una moderna critica del capitalismo. 1995. q. L.100000 in Europe; elsewhere L.120000 (effective 1997 & 1998). Datanews Editrice s.r.l., Via di S. Erasmo 22, 00184 Rome, Italy. TEL 39-6-70450319. FAX 39-6-70450320. Ed. Piero Di Siena. R&P contact: Corrado Perna. adv. contact: Odina Di Virgilio. **Document type:** academic/scholarly publication.

330.1 **IS**
FOERDER INSTITUTE FOR ECONOMIC RESEARCH. WORKING PAPERS. irreg. Foerder Institute for Economic Research, Tel Aviv University, Eitan Berglas School of Economics, Ramat Aviv, Tel Aviv 69978, Israel. TEL 972-3-6409255. FAX 972-3-6409908. E-mail: foerder@econ.tau.ac.il; URL: http://econ.tau.ac.il. (Co-sponsor: Sackler Institute for Economic Studies) Ed. Hal White. **Document type:** academic/scholarly publication.

330.1 **US** **ISSN 0736-0932**
HB1
FORUM FOR SOCIAL ECONOMICS. 1975. s-a. $7 (foreign $13) to non-members. Association for Social Economics, Department of Economics, Saint Louis University, 3674 Lindell Blvd., St. Louis, MO 63108. TEL 314-977-3814. FAX 314-977-3897. Ed. Patrick J. Welch. R&P contact: Patrick J. Welch. adv. contact: Patrick J. Welch. bk.rev.; circ. 500 (paid). (back issues avail.) **Indexed:** Amer.Hist.& Life (1984-1985), C.R.E.J., Cath.Ind., Hist.Abstr. (1984-1985), SSCI. **Document type:** academic/scholarly publication.
Description: Presents timely topics reflecting areas of interest to social economists.
Refereed Serial

FRAGEN DER FREIHEIT; Schriftenreihe fuer Ordnungsfragen der Wirtschaft des Staates und des kulturellen Lebens. see *POLITICAL SCIENCE*

330.1 **US** **ISSN 1051-4333**
FREEMARKET. 1983. m. donation. Ludwig von Mises Institute, Auburn, AL 36849-5301. TEL 334-844-2500. FAX 334-844-2583. (Co-sponsor: University of Nevada, Las Vegas) Ed. Jeffrey A. Tucker; Pub. Llewellyn H. Rockwell, Jr. bk.rev.; illus. circ. 15,000. (back issues avail.) **Document type:** newsletter.
Description: Features items on free-market economics.

330.1 **NE** **ISSN 0191-1708**
FUNDAMENTALS OF PURE AND APPLIED ECONOMICS SERIES. irreg., latest vol.60. price varies. Gordon and Breach - Harwood Academic, Amsteldisk 166, 1st Fl., 1079 LH Amsterdam, Netherlands. (Subscr. to: International Publishers Distributor, Box 32160, Newark, NJ 07102. TEL 800-545-8398. FAX 215-750-6343) Eds. J. Lesourne, H. Sonnenschein. (also avail. in microform) **Indexed:** Zent.Math. **Document type:** monographic series.
—BLDSC (4056.097050).
Refereed Serial

330 **US** **ISSN 0887-6290**
GEORGIST JOURNAL; an international journal serving the movement for land value taxation and free trade based on the philosophy of Henry George. 1973. q. $10. Henry George Institute, 121 E. 30th St., New York, NY 10016. TEL 212-689-0075. E-mail: lindy@henrygeorge.org. Ed. Lindrith Davies. adv. contact: Lindrith Davies. bk.rev. circ. 650. (processed) **Document type:** trade publication.
Description: Commentary, essays, articles, historical accounts, and news about this political and economic movement, which aims to distribute the outcomes of the free enterprise system more equitably among taxpayers.

330 **SW** **ISSN 0072-5080**
GOETEBORGS UNIVERSITET. EKONOMISK-HISTORISKA INSTITUTIONEN. MEDDELANDEN. (Text in Swedish; occasionally in English; occasional summaries in English or French) 1958. irreg., no.68, 1993. price varies; also available on exchange from University of Gothenburg Library. Goeteborgs Universitet, Ekonomisk-Historiska Institutionen, Skanstorget 18, S-411 22 Goeteborg, Sweden. FAX 46-31-773-47-39. Ed. Bengt Berglund. circ. 600. **Document type:** academic/scholarly publication.

330.1 **SW** **ISSN 0434-2410**
GOETEBORGS UNIVERSITET. NATIONALEKONOMISKA INSTITUTIONEN. EKONOMISKA STUDIER. 1978. irreg., no.55, 1994. SEK 500 per no. Goeteborgs Universitet, Nationalekonomiska Institutionen - University of Goeteborg, Department of Economics, Vasagatan 1, S-411 80 Goeteborg, Sweden. FAX 31-773-13-26. circ. 500. **Document type:** monographic series.

330.1 300 **AT** **ISSN 0818-2493**
GOOD GOVERNMENT; a journal of political, social & economic comment. 1905. bi-m. Aus.$18. Association for Good Government, P.O. Box 443, Enfield, N.S.W. 2136, Australia. TEL 61-2-97448815. FAX 61-2-97443804. Ed. Richard Giles. R&P contact: Richard Giles. adv.; bk.rev. circ. 650. (back issues avail.) **Document type:** academic/scholarly publication.
Description: Promotes the cause of the Henry George philosophy in Australia.

GROSS REPORT; a summary of key economic statistics. see *BUSINESS AND ECONOMICS — Abstracting, Bibliographies, Statistics*

330.1 **HT**
HAITI. SECRETAIRE D'ETAT DU PLAN. PLAN ANNUEL ET BUDGET DE DEVELOPPEMENT. a. Secretaire d'Etat du Plan, Port-au-Prince, Haiti.
Formerly: Haiti. Conseil National de Developpement et de Planification. Plan Annuel et Budget de Developpement.

330.1 **US**
HANDBOOK OF AMERICAN BUSINESS HISTORY. 1990. irreg. price varies. Praeger Publishers (Subsidiary of: Greenwood Publishing Group Inc.), 88 Post Rd. W., Box 5007, Westport, CT 06881-5007. TEL 203-226-3571. FAX 203-222-1502. **Document type:** monographic series.

330.1 **US** **ISSN 1054-7681**
HANDBOOK OF COMPARATIVE ECONOMIC POLICIES. 1991. irreg. price varies. Greenwood Press, Inc. (Subsidiary of: Greenwood Publishing Group Inc.), 88 Post Rd. W., Box 5007, Westport, CT 06881-5007. TEL 203-226-3571. FAX 203-222-1502. **Document type:** monographic series.

330.1 **NE** **ISSN 0169-7218**
HANDBOOKS IN ECONOMICS. 1981. irreg., vol.6, 1993. price varies. Elsevier Science B.V., Books Division, P.O. Box 211, 1000 AE Amsterdam, Netherlands. TEL 31-20-4853911. FAX 31-20-4853705. TELEX 18582 ESPA NL E-mail: nlinfo-f@elsevier.nl; usinfo-f@elsevier.com; forinfo-kyf04035@niftyserve.or.jp; URL: http://www.elsevier.nl/. (Subscr. in the Americas to: Elsevier Science, Regional Sales Office, Box 945, New York, NY 10159-0945. TEL 212-633-3730. FAX 212-633-3680; Subscr. in Australasia and the Far East to: Elsevier Science (Singapore) Pte Ltd, No.1 Temasek Ave., No.17-01 Millenia Tower, Singapore 039192, Singapore. TEL 65-434-3727. FAX 65-337-2230; Subscr. in Japan to: Elsevier Science Japan, 9-15 Higashi-Azabu 1-chome, Minato-ku, Tokyo 106, Japan. TEL 81-3-5561-5033. FAX 81-3-5561-5047) **Document type:** monographic series.
—BLDSC (4250.435200).
Refereed Serial

HARVARD COLLEGE ECONOMIST. see *BUSINESS AND ECONOMICS — Macroeconomics*

650 **US** **ISSN 0073-067X**
HARVARD STUDIES IN BUSINESS HISTORY. 1931. irreg., vol.41, 1989. price varies. (Harvard University Graduate School of Business Administration) Harvard University Press, 79 Garden St., Cambridge, MA 02138. TEL 617-495-2600. FAX 617-495-5898. URL: http://www.hup.harvard.edu. Ed. Alfred D. Chandler, Jr. R&P contact: Mindy Koyanis. TEL 617-495-2619. adv. contact: Denise Waddington. **Document type:** monographic series.
Refereed Serial

330 **FR** **ISSN 0752-5702**
HISTOIRE ECONOMIE ET SOCIETE. 1982. q. 580 F. Editions Sedes, Departement Nathan, 11 rue Soufflot, 75005 Paris, France. TEL 33-1-43252323. FAX 33-1-46335715. Pub. Rene Constans. bk.rev.; index. circ. 700. **Indexed:** Amer.Hist.& Life (1982-), Hist.Abstr. (1982-).
—BLDSC (4316.006850); SWETS.
Formerly: Revue d'Histoire Economique et Sociale (ISSN 0035-239X).

330.1 **FR** **ISSN 1248-6620**
HISTOIRE ECONOMIQUE ET FINANCIERE DE LA FRANCE. ANIMATION DE LA RECHERCHE. 1991. irreg. Ministere de l'Economie et des Finances, Comite pour l'Histoire Economique et Financiere de la France, 6 av. de l'Opera, 2eme Etage, 75001 Paris, France. TEL 33-1-44775264. FAX 33-1-44775298. URL: http://www.finances.gouv.fr/dicom/cheff. (Subscr. to: Imprimerie Nationa - Editions DACF, 27 rue de la Convention, 75015 Paris Cedex 15, France)

BUSINESS AND ECONOMICS — ECONOMIC SYSTEMS AND THEORIES, ECONOMIC HISTORY

330.1   FR   ISSN 1241-3496
HC271
HISTOIRE ECONOMIQUE ET FINANCIERE DE LA FRANCE. ETUDES ET DOCUMENTS. 1989. a. 199 F. (effective 1997). Ministere de l'Economie et des Finances, Comite pour l'Histoire Economique et Financiere de la France, 6 av. de l'Opera, 2eme Etage, 75001 Paris, France. TEL 33-1-44775264. FAX 33-1-44775298. URL: http://www.finances.gouv.fr/dicom/cheff. (Subscr. to: Imprimerie Nationale - Editions DACF, 27 rue de la Convention, 75015 Paris Cedex 15, France) **Document type:** academic/scholarly publication.
    Description: Compiles scientific articles and economic and financial historical documents from the Middle Ages until now.

330.1   FR   ISSN 1251-5140
HISTOIRE ECONOMIQUE ET FINANCIERE DE LA FRANCE. ETUDES GENERALES. 1990. irreg. Ministere de l'Economie et des Finances, Comite pour l'Histoire Economique et Financiere de la France, 6 av. de l'Opera, 2eme Etage, 75001 Paris, France. TEL 33-1-44775264. FAX 33-1-44775298. URL: http://www.finances.gouv.fr/dicom/cheff. (Subscr. to: Imprimerie Nationale - Editions DACF, 27 rue de la Convention, 75015 Paris Cedex 15, France)

330.1   FR
HISTOIRE ECONOMIQUE ET FINANCIERE DE LA FRANCE. RECUEILS DE DOCUMENTS. 1993. irreg. Ministere de l'Economie et des Finances, Comite pour l'Histoire Economique et Financiere de la France, 6 av. de l'Opera, 2eme Etage, 75001 Paris, France. TEL 33-1-44775264. FAX 33-1-44775298. URL: http://www.finances.gouv.fr/dicom/cheff. (Subscr. to: Imprimerie Nationale - Editions DACF, 27 rue de la Convention, 75015 Paris Cedex 15, France)

330.1   FR   ISSN 1248-6221
HISTOIRE ECONOMIQUE ET FINANCIERE DE LA FRANCE. SOURCES. 1993. irreg. Ministere de l'Economie et des Finances, Comite pour l'Histoire Economique et Financiere de la France, 6 av. de l'Opera, 2eme Etage, 75001 Paris, France. TEL 33-1-44775264. FAX 33-1-44775298. URL: http://www.finances.gouv.fr/dicom/cheff. (Subscr. to: Imprimerie Nationale - Editions DACF, 27 rue de la Convention, 75015 Paris Cedex 15, France)

330.1   IT
HISTORY OF ECONOMIC IDEAS. 1982. 3/yr. L.50000 to individuals; institutions L.75000 (foreign Fr.120) (effective 1993). Franco Angeli Editore, Viale Monza, 106, 20127 Milan, Italy. TEL 34-2-2827651. (Foreign subscr. to: Giardini Editore S.A., Piazza Monte Ceneri 13, 6900 Lugano, Switzerland) Eds. D. Cavalieri, R. Faucci. **Indexed:** Amer.Hist.& Life (1993-), Hist.Abstr. (1993-).
    Supersedes (in 1993): Quaderni di Storia dell'Economia Politica.

330   UK   ISSN 0440-9884
HB75
HISTORY OF ECONOMIC THOUGHT NEWSLETTER. 1968. s-a. £5 to individuals; institutions £7. Manchester Metropolitan University, Faculty of Humanities and Social Science, Mabel Tylecote Bldg., Cavendish St., Manchester M15 6BG, England. Ed. John Vint. adv.; bk.rev.; cum.index 1975-1979. circ. 400. (also avail. in microform from MiM,UMI; reprint service avail. from UMI) **Document type:** academic/scholarly publication.
    —SWETS; UMI.

330   US   ISSN 0018-2702
HB1
HISTORY OF POLITICAL ECONOMY. 1969. q. $65 to individuals (foreign $80); institutions $145 (foreign $160) (effective 1997). Duke University Press, Box 90660, Durham, NC 27708-0660. TEL 919-687-3600. FAX 919-688-4574. E-mail: amylee@acpub.duke.edu; URL: http://www.duke.edu/web/dupress/. Ed. Craufurd D. W. Goodwin. R&P contact: Kay Robin Alexander. adv. contact: Amy Hartzler. bk.rev.; charts. circ. 1,600. (also avail. in microform from MiM,UMI; reprint service avail. from ISI,SCH,UMI) **Indexed:** Amer.Hist.& Life (1969-), Arts & Hum.Cit.Ind., ASCA, Curr.Cont., Hist.Abstr. (1969-), J.of Econ.Lit., Key to Econ.Sci., Mid.East Abstr.& Ind., Soc.Sci.Ind., SSCI, SSCI. **Document type:** academic/scholarly publication.
    —BLDSC (4318.400000); Genuine Article; KR SourceOne; SWETS; UMI; UnCover. **CCC.**
    Refereed Serial

330   UK   ISSN 0309-1783
HC10
HOBART PAPERBACKS; studies in the translation of economic ideas into practical policy and the economics of government. 1971. irreg. $85 (combined subscription for all series). Institute of Economic Affairs, 2 Lord North St., London SW1P 3LB, England. TEL 44-171-799-3745. FAX 44-171-799-2137. E-mail: iea@iea.org.uk; URL: http://www.iea.org.uk. Ed. Colin Robinson. **Document type:** academic/scholarly publication.
    —BLDSC (4319.730000).
    Refereed Serial

HOBBES STUDIES. see PHILOSOPHY

330.1   UK   ISSN 0828-8666
                 CODEN: HUMAEB
HUMANOMICS. 1984. q. £289($429) (foreign Aus.$289) (effective 1998). Barmarick Publications, Enholmes Hall, Patrington, E. Yorks HU12 0PR, England. TEL 44-1964-630033. (Dist. by: M C B University Press Ltd., 60-62 Toller Ln., Bradford, W. Yorks BD8 9BY, England. TEL 44-1274-777700. FAX 44-1274-785200) Ed. Masudul Alam Choudhury; Pub. Barrie O. Pettman. circ. 150. **Indexed:** Per.Islam. (1991-). **Document type:** academic/scholarly publication.
    Description: Studies the theoretical foundations of etho-economics and the nature of ethics and values in economic knowledge.

I P W BERICHTE. (Internationale Politik und Wirtschaft) see POLITICAL SCIENCE

THE INDEPENDENT REVIEW; a journal of political economy. see POLITICAL SCIENCE

INDIAN ECONOMIC AND SOCIAL HISTORY REVIEW. see SOCIAL SCIENCES: COMPREHENSIVE WORKS

INDIAN JOURNAL OF MARKETING GEOGRAPHY. see GEOGRAPHY

330.1   UK   ISSN 0960-6491
HD2709
INDUSTRIAL AND CORPORATE CHANGE. 1991. q. £135 (foreign $235) (effective 1998). (Associazione I C C) Oxford University Press, Academic Division, Great Clarendon St., Oxford OX2 6DP, England. TEL 44-1865-267907. FAX 44-1865-267485. TELEX 837330-OXPRES-G. E-mail: jnl.info@oup.co.uk; URL: http://www.oup.co.uk/jnls/list/indcor. (U.S. subscr. to: Oxford University Press Inc., 2001 Evans Rd., Cary, NC 27513. TEL 800-852-7323. FAX 919-677-1714) Ed.Bd.; Pub. Martin Geen. R&P contact: Joolz Longley. adv. contact: Jane Parker. bk.rev.; index. circ. 900. **Document type:** academic/scholarly publication.
    —BLDSC (4444.973000); SWETS; UMI. **CCC.**

330.07   SW   ISSN 0283-8974
HC371
INDUSTRIAL INSTITUTE FOR ECONOMIC AND SOCIAL RESEARCH. YEARBOOK. (Text in English) 1969. a. free. Industrial Institute for Economic and Social Research - Industriens Utredningsinstitut, Box 5501, S-114 85 Stockholm, Sweden. FAX 08-6617969. Ed. Maria Hedstrom. bk.rev. circ. 10,000.
    Formerly: Industrial Institute for Economic and Social Research. Current Research Projects.

INSTITUT DER DEUTSCHEN WIRTSCHAFT. FORUM. see BUSINESS AND ECONOMICS — Management

330.1   BO
INSTITUTO DE INVESTIGACIONES ECONOMICAS. REVISTA. 1950. a. Universidad Tecnica de Oruro, Facultad de Ciencias Economicas y Financieras, Casilla 264, Oruro, Bolivia. TEL 55503. Dir. Freddy Sanjines Montan.

INTERNATIONAL ECONOMIC INSIGHTS. see BUSINESS AND ECONOMICS — Economic Situation And Conditions

INTERNATIONAL JOURNAL OF GAME THEORY. see MATHEMATICS

INTERNATIONAL JOURNAL OF INDUSTRIAL ORGANIZATION. see BUSINESS AND ECONOMICS — Management

INTERNATIONAL REVIEW OF LAW AND ECONOMICS. see LAW

INTERNATIONAL SERIES IN ECONOMIC MODELING. see BUSINESS AND ECONOMICS — Computer Applications

330.1   MX   ISSN 0185-1667
INVESTIGACION ECONOMICA. 1941. q. Mex.$110($25) (effective 1997). Universidad Nacional Autonoma de Mexico, Facultad de Economia, Departamento de Distribucion Editorial, Edificio Anexo a la Facultad, 2o. Piso, Circuito Interior, Ciudad Universitaria, 04510 Mexico, D.F., Mexico. TEL 52-5-6222137. Ed. Roberto Escalante.
    Description: Publishes articles about Latin America economic affairs from the theoretical and methodological points of view.

330.1   KR   ISSN 0320-4421
HC337
ISTORIYA NARODNOGO GOSPODARSTVA TA EKONOMICHNOI DUMKI UKRAINY; respublikanskyi mizhvidomchyi zbirnik naukovykh prac. (Text in Ukrainian; summaries in Russian) 1965. a. (Akademiya Nauk Ukrainy, Institut Ekonomiki) Vidavnitstvo Naukova Dumka, Vul. Tereshchenkivska 3, 252601 Kiev, Ukraine. TEL 044-224-4068. FAX 044-224-7060. (Dist. by: Mezhdunarodnaya Kniga, B. Yakimanka 39, 117049 Moscow, Russia) Ed. I.I. Derev'yankin.

330   US   ISSN 0021-3624
HB1   CODEN: JECIAR
J E I. (Journal of Economic Issues) 1967. q. $35 to individuals; libraries $40 (foreign $50); students $15. Association for Evolutionary Economics, 1101 McClung Tower, University of Tennessee, Knoxville, TN 37996-0411. TEL 615-974-1689. FAX 615-974-3915. E-mail: amayhew@utk.edu. Ed. Anne Mayhew. adv. contact: Roberta Niederjohn. bk.rev.; circ. 2,000 (paid). (also avail. in microform from UMI; reprint service avail. from SCH,UMI) **Indexed:** ABI Inform., Amer.Bibl.Slavic & E.Eur.Stud., ASCA, B.P.I, BPIA, Bus.Ind., C.R.E.J., CLOSS, Cont.Pg.Manage., Curr.Cont., Energy Ind., Energy Info.Abstr., Int.Lab.Doc., J.of Econ.Lit., Med.Care Rev., Mid.East: Abstr.& Ind., P.A.I.S., Polit.Sci.Abstr., Soc.Sci.Ind., SSCI, Tr.& Indus.Ind., World Agri.Econ.& Rural Sociol.Abstr. **Document type:** academic/scholarly publication.
    ●Also available online. Vendor(s): Information Access Co., UMI.
    —BLDSC (4973.052000); Genuine Article; KR SourceOne; SWETS; UMI; UnCover.
    Refereed Serial

J O I C E. (Journal of International and Comparative Economics) see BUSINESS AND ECONOMICS — International Commerce

330.1   GW   ISSN 0722-5369
HB5
JAHRBUCH FUER NEUE POLITISCHE OEKONOMIE. (Text in German; summaries in English) 1983. a. varies. Verlag Mohr Siebeck, Wilhelmstr. 18, 72074 Tuebingen, Germany. TEL 49-7071-923-0. FAX 49-7071-51104. E-mail: mohr-siebeck@t-online.de; URL: http://www.mohr.de. (Subscr. to: Postfach 2040, 72010 Tuebingen, Germany) Ed.Bd. R&P contact: Jill Sopper. **Indexed:** IBR. **Document type:** academic/scholarly publication.
    —BLDSC (4631.830000).
    Description: Current developments in the theory of "new political economy".

330   GW   ISSN 0075-2800
HC281
JAHRBUCH FUER WIRTSCHAFTSGESCHICHTE. 1960. a. (in two parts). DM.64 per part. Akademie Verlag GmbH, Muehlenstr. 33-34, 13187 Berlin, Germany. TEL 49-30-47889348. FAX 49-30-47889357. E-mail: info@akademie-verlag.de. **Indexed:** Amer.Hist.& Life (1964-), Hist.Abstr. (1964-), IBR, P.A.I.S.For.Lang.Ind. **Document type:** academic/scholarly publication.

BUSINESS AND ECONOMICS — ECONOMIC SYSTEMS AND THEORIES, ECONOMIC HISTORY

330.1　　　　　　NE　ISSN 0922-1425
HF1601
JAPAN AND THE WORLD ECONOMY; international journal of theory and policy. (Text in English) 1988. q. fl.575($330) (effective 1998). North-Holland (Subsidiary of: Elsevier Science B.V.), P.O. Box 211, 1000 AE Amsterdam, Netherlands. TEL 31-20-4853911. FAX 31-20-4853598. TELEX 18582 ESPA NL. URL: http://www.elsevier.nl:80/inca/publications/store/5/0/5/5/7/505557.pub.shtml. (Subscr. in the Americas to: Elsevier Science, Regional Sales Office, Box 945, New York, NY 10159-0945. TEL 212-633-3730. FAX 212-633-3680; Subscr. in Australasia and the Far East to: Elsevier Science (Singapore) Pte Ltd, No.1 Temasek Ave., No.17-01 Millenia Tower, Singapore 039192, Singapore. TEL 65-434-3727. FAX 65-337-2230; Subscr. in Japan to: Elsevier Science Japan, 9-15 Higashi-Azabu 1-chome, Minato-ku Tokyo 106, Japan. TEL 81-3-5561-5033. FAX 81-3-5561-5047) Ed. Ryuzo Sato. (also avail. in microform from UMI; back issues avail.) **Indexed:** ASCA, Curr.Cont., Polit.Sci.Abstr. **Document type:** academic/scholarly publication.
—BLDSC (4648.015000); Genuine Article; SWETS; UnCover. **CCC.**
　Description: Provides a forum for examining issues and problems relevant to the economic interdependence between Japan and major trading partners throughout the world.
　Refereed Serial

330.1　　　　　　CC
JIANGSU JINGJI TANTAO/JIANGSU ECONOMIC INQUIRY. (Text in Chinese) m. Jiangsu Academy of Social Sciences, Economic Research Institute, 12 Huju Beilu, Nanjing, Jiangsu 210013, People's Republic of China. TEL 635276. Ed. Gu Songnian.

338.9　　　　　　CC　ISSN 1000-7989
JINGJI GAIGE/ECONOMIC REFORM. (Text in Chinese) 1985. bi-m. $24.80. Shaanxi Sheng Shehui Kexueyuan - Shaanxi Academy of Social Sciences, No. 7, Lingyuan Nanduan, Xi'an, Shaanxi 710061, People's Republic of China. TEL 029-54006. (Dist. in US by: China Books & Periodicals, Inc., 2929 24th St., San Francisco, CA 94110. TEL 415-282-2994) Ed. Yang Peiying. adv.; bk.rev. circ. 8,000. (also avail. in microfiche)
　Description: Covers the theories and practices of the Chinese economic reform and management systems.

JINGJI LILUN YU JINGJI GUANLI/ECONOMIC THEORY & BUSINESS MANAGEMENT. see BUSINESS AND ECONOMICS — Management

JINGJI WENTI TANSUO. see BUSINESS AND ECONOMICS

330.1　　　　　　CC　ISSN 0577-9154
JINGJI YANJIU/ECONOMIC RESEARCH. (Text in Chinese; table of contents in English) 1955. m. Y18($61.20) Zhongguo Shehui Kexueyuan, Jingji Yanjiusuo - Chinese Academy of Social Sciences, Economic Research Institute, 2 Yuetan Beixiaojie, Beijing 100836, People's Republic of China. TEL 895024. (Dist. outside China by: China International Book Trading Corp., P.O. Box 399, Beijing, P.R.C.; Dist. in US by: China Books & Periodicals, Inc., 2929 24th St., San Francisco, CA 94110. TEL 415-282-2994) Ed. Zhao Renwei. charts; stat. **Indexed:** Amer.Hist.& Life (1956-1957), Hist.Abstr. (1956-1957).
—BLDSC (3654.449800).

330.1　　　　　　CN　ISSN 0840-5425
HD87
JOHN DEUTSCH INSTITUTE FOR THE STUDY OF ECONOMIC POLICY. DISCUSSION PAPER SERIES. 1989. irreg., no.17, 1994. Can.$3 per no. in Canada and U.S.; elsewhere Can.$3.50. John Deutsch Institute for the Study of Economic Policy, Policy Studies Bldg., Queen's University, Kingston, ON K7L 3N6, Canada. TEL 613-545-2294. FAX 613-545-6025. Ed. Thomas Courchene. R&P contact: Sharon Sullivan. (back issues avail.) **Document type:** monographic series.

330.1　　　　　　CN
JOHN DEUTSCH INSTITUTE FOR THE STUDY OF ECONOMIC POLICY. POLICY FORUM SERIES. 1983. irreg., no.33, 1995. Can.$15 per no. John Deutsch Institute for the Study of Economic Policy, Policy Studies Bldg., Queen's University, Kingston, ON K7L 3N6, Canada. TEL 613-545-2294. FAX 613-545-6025. Ed. Thomas Courchene. R&P contact: Sharon Sullivan. (back issues avail.) **Document type:** monographic series.

330.1　　　　　　CN
JOHN DEUTSCH INSTITUTE FOR THE STUDY OF ECONOMIC POLICY. ROUNDTABLE SERIES. 1983. a. Can.$20. John Deutsch Institute for the Study of Economic Policy, Policy Studies Bldg., Queen's University, Kingston, ON K7L 3N6, Canada. TEL 613-545-2294. FAX 613-545-6025. Ed. Thomas Courchene. R&P contact: Sharon Sullivan. circ. 500. (back issues avail.) **Document type:** monographic series.
　Formerly: John Deutsch Roundtable on Economic Policy.

330.1　　　　　　SA　ISSN 0379-6205
HB9
JOURNAL FOR STUDIES IN ECONOMICS AND ECONOMETRICS/TYDSKRIF VIR STUDIES IN EKONOMIE EN EKONOMETRIE. Short title: S E E. 1977. 3/yr. R.130 (effective 1996 & 1997). University of Stellenbosch, Bureau for Economic Research, Private Bag 5050, University, Stellenbosch 7599, South Africa. TEL 27-21-8872810. FAX 27-21-8899225. TELEX 520-383 SA. E-mail: odjs@maties.sun.ac.za. Eds. O.D.J. Stuart, E. Smit. circ. 350. **Indexed:** Ind.S.A.Per., J.of Econ.Lit. **Document type:** academic/scholarly publication.
—BLDSC (5066.897000).
　Description: Presents detailed studies of economic issues.
　Refereed Serial

JOURNAL OF APPLIED ECONOMETRICS. see MATHEMATICS

JOURNAL OF AUSTRALIAN POLITICAL ECONOMY. see BUSINESS AND ECONOMICS — Economic Situation And Conditions

JOURNAL OF BUSINESS RESEARCH. see BUSINESS AND ECONOMICS — Management

330.1　　　　　　NE　ISSN 0885-2545
NX180.S6　　　　　　CODEN: JCUEER
JOURNAL OF CULTURAL ECONOMICS. 1977. q. fl.475 to institutions; $244 to institutions in U.S. (effective 1998). (Association for Cultural Economics, US) Kluwer Academic Publishers, Postbus 17, 3300 AA Dordrecht, Netherlands. TEL 31-78-6392392. FAX 31-78-6392254. E-mail: services@wkap.nl; URL: http://www.wkap.nl. (Dist. by: Kluwer Academic Publishers Group, P.O. Box 322, 3300 AH Dordrecht, Netherlands. TEL 31-78-6392392. FAX 31-78-6546474; N. America dist. addr.: Box 358, Accord Sta., Hingham, MA 02018-02358. TEL 617-871-6600. FAX 617-871-6528) Ed. William J. Hendon. adv.; bk.rev. (reprint service avail. from SWZ) **Indexed:** Geo.Abstr.P.G., J.of Econ.Lit. **Document type:** academic/scholarly publication.
—BLDSC (4965.843000); SWETS; UnCover. **CCC.**
　Description: Publishes papers applying economic analysis to the area of all creative and performing arts, and to the heritage and cultural industries, whether publicly or privately owned.
　Refereed Serial

330.1　　　　　　NP　ISSN 0259-0956
JOURNAL OF DEVELOPMENT AND ADMINISTRATIVE STUDIES. (Text in English) 1978. s-a. Rs.30($6) Centre for Economic Development and Administration, Publications and Information Services Division, P.O. Box 797, Kirtipur Campus, Kathmandu, Nepal.

330.1　　　　　　US　ISSN 1066-9868
HF4050　　　　　　CODEN: JEBUFT
JOURNAL OF EAST - WEST BUSINESS. 1993. q. $40 to individuals (Canada $52; elsewhere $56); institutions $60 (Canada $78; elsewhere $84); libraries $125 (Canada $162.50; elsewhere $175) (effective 1997-1998). Haworth Press, Inc., 10 Alice St., Binghamton, NY 13904. TEL 607-722-5857; 800-342-9676. FAX 607-722-6362. E-mail: getinfo@haworth.com; URL: http://www.haworth.com. Ed. Erdener Kaynak; Pub. Bill Cohen. R&P contact: Ruthann Heath. adv.: B&W page $300; trim 4 3/8 x 7 1/8; adv. contact: Jackie Blakeslee. bk.rev. (also avail. in microfiche from UMI; microform from HAW; reprint service avail. from HAW) **Indexed:** G.Soc.Sci.& Rel.Per.Lit., Geo.Abstr.P.G., IDA, Mgmt.& Market.Abstr., Per.Islam. (1995-). **Document type:** academic/scholarly publication.
—BLDSC (4971.530000); EMDOCS; Haworth; KR SourceOne.
　Description: Deals with contemporary and emerging topics of business studies, strategies, development, and practice as they relate to the Russian Republic, the new Asian republics, the Eastern European republics, the Baltic republics, and other worldwide business relationships.
　Refereed Serial

330.01 519.5　　　　SZ　ISSN 0304-4076
HB139　　　　　　CODEN: JECMB6
JOURNAL OF ECONOMETRICS. 1973. m. fl.3078($1769) (effective 1998). Elsevier Science S.A., P.O. Box 564, CH-1001 Lausanne 1, Switzerland. TEL 41-21-3207381. FAX 41-21-3235444. TELEX 450620-ELSA-CH. (Subscr. to: Elsevier Science, Regional Sales Office, P.O. Box 211, 1000 AE Amsterdam, Netherlands. TEL 31-20-4853757. FAX 31-20-4853432; Subscr. in the Americas to: Elsevier Science, Regional Sales Office, Box 945, New York, NY 10159-0945. TEL 212-633-3730. FAX 212-633-3680; Subscr. in Australasia to: Elsevier Science (Singapore) Pte. Ltd., No. 1 Temasek Ave., No. 17-01 Millenia Tower, Singapore 039192, Singapore. TEL 65-434-3727. FAX 65-337-2260) Ed.Bd. adv.; bk.rev.; charts; index. (also avail. in microform from UMI) **Indexed:** ABI Inform., ASCA, BPIA, Bus.Ind., C.R.E.J., Compumath, Cont.Pg.Manage., Curr.Cont. (1973-), Curr.Ind.Stat., IBR, J.Cont.Quant.Meth., J.of Econ.Lit., Math.R., Rural Recreat.Tour.Abstr., Soc.Sci.Ind., SSCI, Stat.Theor.Meth.Abstr. (1973-), Tr.& Indus.Ind., World Agri.Econ.& Rural Sociol.Abstr., Zent.Math. **Document type:** academic/scholarly publication.
—BLDSC (4972.400000); Genuine Article; KR SourceOne; SWETS; UMI; UnCover. **CCC.**
　Description: Deals with the application of statistical inference to economic data, as well as the application of econometric techniques to substantive areas of economics. Focuses on both theoretical and applied econometrics.
　Refereed Serial

BUSINESS AND ECONOMICS — ECONOMIC SYSTEMS AND THEORIES, ECONOMIC HISTORY

330.1 NE ISSN 0165-1889
HB1 CODEN: JEDCDH
JOURNAL OF ECONOMIC DYNAMICS AND CONTROL. (Text in English) 1979. 10/yr. fl.1695($974) (effective 1998). North-Holland (Subsidiary of: Elsevier Science B.V.), P.O. Box 211, 1000 AE Amsterdam, Netherlands. TEL 31-20-4853911. FAX 31-20-4853598. TELEX 18582 ESPA NL. (Subscr. in the Americas to: Elsevier Science, Regional Sales Office, Box 945, New York, NY 10159-0945. TEL 212-633-3730. FAX 212-633-3680; Subscr. in Australasia and the Far East to: Elsevier Science (Singapore) Pte Ltd, No.1 Temasek Ave., No.17-01 Millenia Tower, Singapore 039192, Singapore. TEL 65-434-3727. FAX 65-337-2230; Subscr. in Japan to: Elsevier Science Japan, 9-15 Higashi-Azabu 1-chome, Minato-ku, Tokyo 106, Japan. TEL 81-3-5561-5033. FAX 81-3-5561-5047) Eds. Roger Crains, Berc Rustem. adv.; bk.rev.; index. (also avail. in microform from UMI; back issues avail.; reprint service avail. from SWZ) **Indexed:** ABI Inform., AIT Reports, ASCA, BPIA, Bus.Ind., C.R.E.J., Curr.Cont., Geo.Abstr.P.G., IBR, INSPEC, J.Cont.Quant.Meth., J.of Econ.Lit., Manage.Cont., Math.R., Risk Abstr., Rural Recreat.Tour.Abstr., SSCI, Tr.& Indus.Ind., World Agri.Econ.& Rural Sociol.Abstr., Zent.Math. **Document type:** academic/scholarly publication.
—BLDSC (4972.870000); AskIEEE; Genuine Article; KR SourceOne; SWETS; UMI; UnCover. **CCC.**
Description: Publishes papers on economic dynamics, computing, control and decision support in economic systems.
Refereed Serial

330.1 US ISSN 1381-4338
HD72 CODEN: JEGRFB
▼**JOURNAL OF ECONOMIC GROWTH.** 1996. q. fl.630 to institutions; $323.50 to institutions in U.S. (effective 1998). Kluwer Academic Publishers Boston, Box 358, Accord Sta., Hingham, MA 02018-0358. TEL 617-871-6600. FAX 617-871-6528. E-mail: services@wkap.nl; URL: http://www.wkap.nl. (Dist. outside N. America by: Kluwer Academic Publishers Group, P.O. Box 322, 3300 AH Dordrecht, Netherlands. TEL 31-78-6392392. FAX 31-78-6546474) Ed. Oded Galor. (back issues avail.) **Document type:** academic/scholarly publication.
—BLDSC (4973.020000); SWETS. **CCC.**
Refereed Serial

330 UK ISSN 0022-0507
HC10
JOURNAL OF ECONOMIC HISTORY. 1941. q. £66($98) (effective 1998). (Economic History Association) Cambridge University Press, Edinburgh Bldg., Shaftesbury Rd., Cambridge CB2 2RU, England. TEL 44-1223-312393. FAX 44-1223-315052. TELEX 851817256. E-mail: information@cup.cam. ac.uk; URL: http://www.cup.cam.ac.uk. (N. American addr.: Cambridge University Press, Journals Dept., 40 W. 20th St., New York, NY 10011. TEL 212-924-3900. FAX 212-691-3239) Eds. Joel Mokyr, Naomi R. Lamoreaux. R&P contact: Linda Nicol. adv. contact: Rebecca Symons. bk.rev.; bibl.; index. (also avail. in microform from MIM,UMI; back issues avail.; reprint service avail. from KTO,SWZ) **Indexed:** Acad.Ind., Amer.Bibl.Slavic & E.Eur.Stud., Amer.Hist.& Life (1954-), Arts & Hum.Cit.Ind., Arts & Hum.Cit.Ind., ASCA, Asian-Pac.Econ.Lit., Bk.Rev.Ind. (1965-), Chic.Per.Ind., Child.Bk.Rev.Ind. (1965-), Curr.Cont., Geo.Abstr.P.G., Hist.Abstr. (1954-), Hum.Ind., IBR, J.of Econ.Lit., Mid.East: Abstr.& Ind., P.A.I.S., Popul.Ind., Soc.Sci.Ind., SSCI, Tr.& Indus.Ind., Work Rel.Abstr., World Agri.Econ.& Rural Sociol.Abstr. **Document type:** academic/scholarly publication.
—BLDSC (4973.050000); Genuine Article; KR SourceOne; SWETS; UMI; UnCover. **CCC.**
Description: Examines a wide range of topics: agriculture, servitude, money and banking, trade, manufacturing, and technology.

330.1 US ISSN 0895-3309
HB1
JOURNAL OF ECONOMIC PERSPECTIVES. 1987. q. $130 (includes American Economic Review and Journal of Economic Literature). American Economic Association, 2014 Broadway, Ste. 305, Nashville, TN 37203. TEL 615-322-2595. Ed. Alan B. Krueger. R&P contact: Dana Ragan. **Indexed:** Amer.Hist.& Life (1987-), ASCA, Asian-Pac.Econ.Lit., B.P.I., Curr.Cont., Hist.Abstr. (1987-), J.of Econ.Lit., Oper.Res.Manage.Sci., Pub.Admin.Abstr., Qual.Contr.Appl.Stat., Soc.Sci.Ind. (1994-), SSCI. **Document type:** academic/scholarly publication.
—BLDSC (4973.054000); Genuine Article; KR SourceOne; SWETS; UMI; UnCover.
Description: Provides economists with accessible articles that report on and critique recent research findings, and evaluate public policy initiatives.

330 US ISSN 0022-0531
HB1 CODEN: JECTAQ
JOURNAL OF ECONOMIC THEORY. 1969. m. $1000 (foreign $1175) (effective 1997). Academic Press, Inc., Journal Division, 525 B St., Ste. 1900, San Diego, CA 92101-4495. TEL 619-230-1840. FAX 619-699-6800. E-mail: apsubs@acad.com; URL: http://www.apnet.com/www/journal/et.htm; http://www.idelibrary.com/. (Subscr. to: Box 861213, Orlando, FL 32886-1213. TEL 407-347-4040. FAX 407-363-9661) Ed. Karl Shell. adv. (back issues avail.) **Indexed:** ASCA, BPIA, Bus.Ind., C.R.E.J., Curr.Cont., J.Cont.Quant.Meth., J.of Econ.Lit., Math.R., Risk Abstr., Soc.Sci.Ind., SSCI, Tr.& Indus.Ind., Zent.Math. **Document type:** academic/scholarly publication.
●Also available online.
—BLDSC (4973.070000); Genuine Article; KR SourceOne; SWETS; UnCover. **CCC.**
Description: Publishes original research on economic theory and emphasizes the theoretical analysis of economic models, including the study of related mathematical techniques.

330.1 658 US ISSN 1058-6407
JOURNAL OF ECONOMICS & MANAGEMENT STRATEGY. 1992. q. $40 to individuals (foreign $56); institutions $102 (foreign $118); students and retired $25 (foreign $41) (effective 1997). M I T Press, 5 Cambridge Center, Cambridge, MA 02142. TEL 617-253-2889. FAX 617-577-1545. E-mail: journals-orders@mit.edu; URL: http://www.mitpress. mit.edu. Ed. Daniel F. Spulber. R&P contact: Paul Dzus. adv. (back issues avail.) **Indexed:** ASCA, Curr.Cont., Soc.Work Res.& Abstr. **Document type:** academic/scholarly publication.
—BLDSC (4973.095300); Genuine Article; SWETS; UMI. **CCC.**
Description: Provides a forum for the interaction and research on the competitive strategies of managers and the organizational structure of firms.
Refereed Serial

JOURNAL OF EMPIRICAL FINANCE. see *BUSINESS AND ECONOMICS — Banking And Finance*

330 IT ISSN 0391-5115
HC240.A1
JOURNAL OF EUROPEAN ECONOMIC HISTORY. (Text in English) 1972. 3/yr. free to qualified personnel or on exchange basis. Banca di Roma, Servizio Studi, Via del Corso 307, 00186 Rome, Italy. TEL 39-6-6705462. FAX 39-6-6705438. Ed. Luigi De Rosa. bk.rev.; abstr.; bibl.; charts; illus. circ. 3,500. (reprint service avail. from SCH) **Indexed:** Amer.Hist.& Life (1979-), Hist.Abstr. (1979-), Hum.Ind., J.of Econ.Lit., Mid.East: Abstr.& Ind., P.A.I.S. **Document type:** academic/scholarly publication.
—BLDSC (4979.603000); KR SourceOne; UnCover.

330.1 GW ISSN 0936-9937
HB1.A1 CODEN: JEECEN
JOURNAL OF EVOLUTIONARY ECONOMICS. Online edition (GW ISSN 1432-1386) (Text in English) 1991. q. DM.509.60 (foreign DM.513.20) (effective 1998). (International Joseph A. Schumpeter Society) Springer-Verlag, Heidelberger Platz 3, 14197 Berlin, Germany. TEL 49-30-82787-0. FAX 49-30-82787448. E-mail: subscriptions@springer.de; URL: http://link. springer.de. (Subscr. in N. America to: Springer-Verlag New York, Inc., 333 Meadowlands Pkwy., Secaucus, NJ 07094. TEL 212-460-1500. FAX 212-473-6272) Eds. H. Hanusch, S. Klepper. **Document type:** academic/scholarly publication.
●Also available online.
—BLDSC (4979.642500); Genuine Article; SWETS; UMI. **CCC.**
Description: Aims to provide an international forum for a new approach to economics, with an emphasis on dynamics, changing structures, and disequilibrium processes.

330.1 US ISSN 1042-9573
HG4515.2
JOURNAL OF FINANCIAL INTERMEDIATION. 1990. q. $179 (foreign $194) (effective 1997). Academic Press, Inc., Journal Division, 525 B St., Ste. 1900, San Diego, CA 92101-4495. TEL 619-230-1840. FAX 619-699-6800. E-mail: apsubs@acad.com; URL: http://www.apnet.com/www/journal/jf.htm; http://www.idealibrary.com. (Subscr. to: Box 861213, Orlando, FL 32886-1213. TEL 407-347-4040. FAX 407-363-9661) Ed. Anjan V. Thakor. (back issues avail.) **Indexed:** ASCA, Curr.Cont. **Document type:** academic/scholarly publication.
●Also available online.
—BLDSC (4984.259500); Genuine Article; SWETS. **CCC.**
Description: Collects and stimulates research in the design of financial contracts and institutions, stressing the use of contemporary analytical and empirical tools.
Refereed Serial

330.1 US ISSN 0898-5510
K10
JOURNAL OF FORENSIC ECONOMICS. 1987. every 4 mos. $100 (effective 1996). National Association of Forensic Economics, Box 30067, Kansas City, MO 64112. TEL 816-235-2833. FAX 816-235-5263. Ed. John O. Ward. adv.; bk.rev.; circ. 730 (paid). (back issues avail.) **Indexed:** IBR, J.of Econ.Lit., L.R.I. **Document type:** academic/scholarly publication.
—BLDSC (4984.587000). **CCC.**
Description: Provides a forum for applications of economics in litigation. Articles include original economic research in areas of projection of loss earnings and services, vocational rehabilitation business valuation, medical economics and antitrust.
Refereed Serial

330.1 UK ISSN 0926-6437
JOURNAL OF INCOME DISTRIBUTION; an international journal of social economics. (Text in English) 1991. s-a. $80 to individuals (outside UK $100); institutions $190 (outside UK $210) (effective 1998). (University of Utrecht, International Centre for Social Economics, NE) J A I Press Ltd., 38 Tavistock St., Covent Garden, London WC2E 7PB, England. TEL 44-171-379-8834. FAX 44-171-379-8835. E-mail: jai@cix.co.uk. Ed.Bd. adv. contact: Madeleine Johnston. abstr. (back issues avail.) **Document type:** academic/scholarly publication.
Description: Publishes original scholarly research in the field of social economics, and particularly in the sphere of the distribution of income and wealth.

JOURNAL OF INSTITUTIONAL AND THEORETICAL ECONOMICS. see *POLITICAL SCIENCE*

JOURNAL OF LAW, ECONOMICS, AND ORGANIZATION. see *LAW*

B

BUSINESS AND ECONOMICS — ECONOMIC SYSTEMS AND THEORIES, ECONOMIC HISTORY

330.1 340.6 US ISSN 1054-3023
K10 CODEN: JLECE4
JOURNAL OF LEGAL ECONOMICS. 1991. 3/yr. $60 (foreign $75) (effective 1997 & 1998). American Academy of Economic and Financial Experts, University of North Alabama, Box 5077, Florence, AL 35632. TEL 205-760-4144.
FAX 205-760-4170. E-mail: jlegecon@hiwaay.net. Ed. Michael Butler. R&P contact: Michael Butler. adv. contact: James Cox. bk.rev.; circ. 450 (paid). (also avail. in microform from UMI; reprint service avail. from WSH) **Indexed:** L.R.I. **Document type:** academic/scholarly publication.
●Also available online.
—BLDSC (5010.249000); UMI; UnCover. **CCC.**
Description: Devoted to legal economics as well as related fields of finance, sociology, and vocational rehabilitation. Addresses areas of litigation including personal injury, business valuation, antitrust, pension valuation, and divorce settlement.
Refereed Serial

JOURNAL OF MARKET - FOCUSED MANAGEMENT. see *BUSINESS AND ECONOMICS — Management*

330.01 SZ ISSN 0304-4068
HB135 CODEN: JMECDA
JOURNAL OF MATHEMATICAL ECONOMICS. 1974. 16/yr. fl.3726($2141) (effective 1998). Elsevier Science S.A., P.O. Box 564, CH-1001 Lausanne 1, Switzerland. TEL 41-21-3207381.
FAX 41-21-3235444. TELEX 450620-ELSA-CH. (Subscr. to: Elsevier Science, Regional Sales Office, P.O. Box 211, 1000 AE Amsterdam, Netherlands. TEL 31-20-4853757. FAX 31-20-4853432; Subscr. in the Americas to: Elsevier Science, Regional Sales Office, Box 945, New York, NY 10159-0945. TEL 212-633-3730. FAX 212-633-3680; Subscr. in Australasia to: Elsevier Science (Singapore) Pte. Ltd., No. 1 Temasek Ave., No. 17-01 Millenia Tower, Singapore 039192, Singapore. TEL 65-434-3727. FAX 65-434-2230) Eds. T.F. Bewley, W.J. Shafer. adv.; bk.rev.; index. (also avail. in microform from UMI; back issues avail.) **Indexed:** ABI Inform., ASCA, BPIA, Bus.Ind., C.R.E.J., Compumath., Curr.Cont., J.Cont.Quant.Meth., J.of Econ.Lit., Math.R., SSCI, Tr.& Indus.Ind., Zent.Math. **Document type:** academic/scholarly publication.
—BLDSC (5012.377000); Genuine Article; SWETS; UMI; UnCover. **CCC.**
Description: Provides a forum for work in economic theory that expresses economic ideas, using formal mathematical reasoning.
Refereed Serial

JOURNAL OF MONETARY ECONOMICS. see *BUSINESS AND ECONOMICS — Banking And Finance*

330.1 US ISSN 0160-3477
HB1
JOURNAL OF POST KEYNESIAN ECONOMICS. Key Title: J P K E Journal of Post Keynesian Economics. 1978. q. $59 to individuals (foreign $79); institutions $140 (foreign $180) (effective 1997). M.E. Sharpe, Inc., 80 Business Park Dr., Armonk, NY 10504. TEL 914-273-1800; 800-541-6563.
FAX 914-273-2106. Ed. Paul Davidson. adv.: page $300; 5 x 8. circ. 1,700. (back issues avail.; reprint service avail. from SCH) **Indexed:** ASCA, BPIA, Bus.Ind., C.R.E.J., Curr.Cont., Fut.Surv., J.of Econ.Lit., Manage.Cont., Risk Abstr., SSCI, Tr.& Indus.Ind. **Document type:** academic/scholarly publication.
●Also available online. Vendor(s): Information Access Co., UMI.
—BLDSC (5041.149000); Genuine Article; SWETS; UMI; UnCover. **CCC.**
Refereed Serial

330.01 SZ ISSN 0047-2727
HJ101 CODEN: JPBEBK
JOURNAL OF PUBLIC ECONOMICS. (Text in English) 1972. m. fl.2322($1334) (effective 1998). Elsevier Science S.A., P.O. Box 564, CH-1001 Lausanne 1, Switzerland. TEL 41-21-3207381.
FAX 41-21-3235444. TELEX 450620-ELSA-CH. (Subscr. to: Elsevier Science, Regional Sales Office, P.O. Box 211, 1000 AE Amsterdam, Netherlands. TEL 31-20-4853757. FAX 31-20-4853432; Subscr. in the Americas to: Elsevier Science, Regional Sales Office, Box 945, New York, NY 10159-0945. TEL 212-633-3730. FAX 212-633-3680; Subscr. in Australasia to: Elsevier Science (Singapore) Pte. Ltd., No. 1 Temasek Ave., No. 17-01 Millenia Tower, Singapore 039192, Singapore. TEL 65-434-3727. FAX 65-337-2230) Eds. A.B. Atkinson, N.H. Stern. adv.; bk.rev.; charts; stat.; index. (also avail. in microform from UMI) **Indexed:** ABI Inform., ASCA, Asian-Pac.Econ.Lit., ASSIA, BPIA, Bus.Ind., C.R.E.J., Curr.Cont., Excerp.Med., J.of Econ.Lit., Mid.East: Abstr.& Ind., P.A.I.S., Risk Abstr., Sage Pub.Admin.Abstr., Sage Urb.Stud.Abstr., SSCI, Tr.& Indus.Ind., World Bank.Abstr. **Document type:** academic/scholarly publication.
—BLDSC (5043.495000); Genuine Article; SWETS; UMI; UnCover. **CCC.**
Description: Covers public economics, with emphasis on the application of modern economic theory and methods of quantitative analysis.

330.1 US ISSN 0922-680X
HD3616.U45 CODEN: JRECEC
JOURNAL OF REGULATORY ECONOMICS. 1989. bi-m. fl.840 to institutions; $431 to institutions in U.S. (effective 1998). Kluwer Academic Publishers Boston, Box 358, Accord Sta., Hingham, MA 02018-0358. TEL 617-871-6600.
FAX 617-871-6528. TELEX 200190. E-mail: services@wkap.nl; URL: http://www.wkap.nl. (Dist. outside N. America by: Kluwer Academic Publishers Group, P.O. Box 322, 3300 AH Dordrecht, Netherlands. TEL 31-78-6392392. FAX 31-78-6546474) Ed. Michael A. Crew. (also avail. in microform from UMI; reprint service avail. from SWZ) **Indexed:** ASCA, Curr.Cont., J.of Econ.Lit., SSCI. **Document type:** academic/scholarly publication.
—BLDSC (5048.800000); Genuine Article; SWETS; UMI; UnCover. **CCC.**
Description: Publishes articles on the analysis of regulatory theories and institutions and on the practical aspects of regulation, including natural monopoly, deregulation, and new policy instruments.
Refereed Serial

330 US ISSN 1053-5357
HB1 CODEN: JSECFK
THE JOURNAL OF SOCIO-ECONOMICS. 1972. bi-m. $110 to individuals (foreign $140); institutions $235 (foreign $265) (effective 1998). J A I Press Inc., 55 Old Post Rd., No. 2, Greenwich, CT 06830-1678. TEL 203-661-7602.
FAX 203-661-0792. E-mail: jai@jaipress.com. (Addr. in Europe: J A I Press Ltd., 38 Tavistock St., Covent Garden, London WC2E 7PB, England. TEL 44-171-379-8834. FAX 44-171-379-8835) Ed. Richard E. Hattwick. adv.; bk.rev.; bibl.; charts; stat. circ. 360. (tabloid format; also avail. in microform from UMI; back issues avail.) **Indexed:** BPIA, Bus.Ind., Crim.Just.Abstr., J.of Econ.Lit., Manage.Cont., Psychol.Abstr. (1984-), Tr.& Indus.Ind. **Document type:** academic/scholarly publication.
●Also available online. Vendor(s): Information Access Co.
—UnCover. **CCC.**
Formerly: Journal of Behavioral Economics (ISSN 0090-5720)

JOURNAL OF THE ECONOMIC AND SOCIAL HISTORY OF THE ORIENT/JOURNAL D'HISTOIRE ECONOMIQUE ET SOCIALE DE L'ORIENT. see *HISTORY — History Of The Near East*

330 US ISSN 1042-7716
HB75
JOURNAL OF THE HISTORY OF ECONOMIC THOUGHT. 1979. s-a. $30 to individuals; institutions $50 (effective 1997). History of Economics Society, c/o John J. Bethune, Secy.-Treas., Business Administration Bldg., University of Tennessee, Martin, TN 38238. Ed. Donald Walker. R&P contact: Donald Walker. adv.; bk.rev.; illus.; index. **Indexed:** Amer.Hist.& Life (1988-), Hist.Abstr. (1988-), J.of Econ.Lit. **Document type:** academic/scholarly publication.
—SWETS.
Formerly: History of Economics Society Bulletin.

JUSTICIA SOCIAL. see *BUSINESS AND ECONOMICS — Labor And Industrial Relations*

LABOUR ECONOMICS; an international journal. see *BUSINESS AND ECONOMICS — Labor And Industrial Relations*

330.1 UK
LANCASTER WORKING PAPERS IN POLITICAL ECONOMY. POLITICAL ECONOMY OF LOCAL GOVERNANCE SERIES. 1978. irreg., no.47, 1994. Lancaster University, Department of Sociology, Lancaster LA1 4YL, England. TEL 44-1524-594178. FAX 44-1524-594256. URL: http://www.comp.lancs.ac.uk/sociology. **Document type:** monographic series.
Refereed Serial

LARRY ABRAHAM'S INSIDER REPORT. see *BUSINESS AND ECONOMICS — Investments*

LECTURAS DE ECONOMIA. see *BUSINESS AND ECONOMICS — Abstracting, Bibliographies, Statistics*

330.1 NE
LECTURES IN ECONOMICS: THEORY, INSTITUTIONS, POLICY. 1979. irreg., vol.10, 1989. price varies. Elsevier Science B.V., Books Division, P.O. Box 211, 1000 AE Amsterdam, Netherlands.
TEL 31-20-4853911. FAX 31-20-4853705. TELEX 18582 ESPA NL. E-mail: nlinfo-f@elsevier.nl; usinfo-f@elsevier.com; forinfo-kyf04035@niftyserve.or.jp; URL: http://www.elsevier.nl/. (Subscr. in the Americas to: Elsevier Science, Regional Sales Office, Box 945, New York, NY 10159-0945. TEL 212-633-3730. FAX 212-633-3680; Subscr. in Australasia and the Far East to: Elsevier Science (Singapore) Pte Ltd, No.1 Temasek Ave., No.17-01 Millenia Tower, Singapore 039192, Singapore. TEL 65-434-3727. FAX 65-337-2230 000; Subscr. in Japan to: Elsevier Science Japan, 9-15 Higashi-Azabu 1-chome, Minato-ku, Tokyo 106, Japan. TEL 81-3-5561-5033. FAX 81-3-5561-5047) **Document type:** monographic series.
Refereed Serial

LIBERTY (PORT TOWNSEND). see *LITERARY AND POLITICAL REVIEWS*

330.1 SW ISSN 1400-4860
▼**LUND STUDIES IN ECONOMIC HISTORY.** (Text in English, Swedish) 1995. a. price varies. Lund University Press, P.O. Box 141, S-221 00 Lund, Sweden. TEL 46-46-31-20-00.
FAX 46-46-30-53-38. E-mail: order@studli.se; URL: http://www.studli.se/. Ed. Christer Lundh. **Document type:** academic/scholarly publication.

330 658 SW ISSN 0284-5075
LUND STUDIES IN ECONOMICS AND MANAGEMENT. (Text in English, Swedish) 1989. irreg. price varies. Lund University Press, P.O. Box 141, S-221 00 Lund, Sweden. TEL 46-46-31-20-00.
FAX 46-46-30-53-38. E-mail: order@studli.se; URL: http://www.studli.se/. Ed. A. Malm. **Document type:** academic/scholarly publication.
—BLDSC (5304.978000).

330.1 JO
MAJALLAT AL-WAHDAH AL-IQTISADIYYAH AL-ARABIYYAH/ARAB ECONOMIC UNION JOURNAL. (Text in Arabic) q. Majlis al-Wahdah al-Iqtisadiyyah al-Arabiyyah, Al-Amanah al-Aamah - Council for Arab Economic Union, General Secretariat, P.O. Box 925100, Amman, Jordan. TEL 664329. TELEX 21900 WAHDAH JO. Ed. Hassan Ibrahim.
Refereed Serial

BUSINESS AND ECONOMICS — ECONOMIC SYSTEMS AND THEORIES, ECONOMIC HISTORY

330.1   UK   ISSN 1360-5933
MANCHESTER METROPOLITAN UNIVERSITY. DEPARTMENT OF ECONOMICS AND ECONOMIC HISTORY. DISCUSSION PAPERS. irreg. Manchester Metropolitan University, Department of Economics and Economic History, Mabel Tylecote Bldg., Cavendish St., Manchester M15 6BG, England. TEL 44-161-247-3912. FAX 44-161-247-6302. E-mail: j.tomkins@mmu.ac.uk. Ed. Judith Tomkins. **Document type:** academic/scholarly publication, monographic series.
—BLDSC (3597.940500).
Formerly (until 1995): Manchester Metropolitan University. Department of Economics and Economic History. Papers.

330 300   UK   ISSN 0025-2034
HB1
MANCHESTER SCHOOL OF ECONOMIC AND SOCIAL STUDIES. 1930. 5/yr. £98($198) (foreign £125) (effective 1997). Blackwell Publishers Ltd., 108 Cowley Rd., Oxford OX4 1JF, England. TEL 44-1865-791100. FAX 44-1865-791347. E-mail: jnlinfo@blackwellpublishers.co.uk; URL: http://www.blackwellpublishers.co.uk. Ed. R. Bladen-Hovell. adv.; bk.rev.; bibl.; charts; stat.; index. circ. 1,300. (also avail. in microform; reprint service avail. from KTO) **Indexed:** Amer.Hist.& Life (1967-1978), ASCA, ASSIA, Br.Hum.Ind., Bus.Ind., C.R.E.J., Cont.Pg.Manage., Curr.Cont., Hist.Abstr. (1967-1978), J.of Econ.Lit., Key to Econ.Sci., Mid.East: Abstr.& Ind., P.A.I.S., Rural Recreat.Tour.Abstr., Soc.Sci.Ind., SSCI, Work Rel.Abstr., World Agri.Econ.& Rural Sociol.Abstr. **Document type:** academic/scholarly publication.
—BLDSC (5359.650000); Genuine Article; KR SourceOne; SWETS; UMI; UnCover. **CCC.**
Refereed Serial

330.1   US
MICROECONOMIC STUDIES. 1986. irreg., latest 1995. price varies. Springer-Verlag, 175 Fifth Ave., New York, NY 10010. TEL 212-460-1500. FAX 212-473-6272. (Also: Berlin, Heidelberg, Tokyo and Vienna) (reprint service avail. from ISI) **Document type:** academic/scholarly publication.

330.1   FR   ISSN 0077-0434
MONNAIE, PRIX, CONJONCTURE. 1952. irreg., no.11, 1973. price varies. Editions de l' Ecole des Hautes Etudes en Sciences Sociales, 131 bd. St-Michel, 75005 Paris, France. TEL 33-1-40467080. FAX 33-1-44070889. E-mail: editions@ehess.fr; URL: http://www.ehess.fr/editions. (Dist. by: Centre Interinstitutionnel pour la Diffusion de Publications en Sciences Humaines, 131 bd. St-Michel, 75005 Paris, France. TEL 33-1-43544715. FAX 33-1-43548073)

330 300   UK
MONOGRAPHS IN ECONOMIC AND SOCIAL HISTORY. 1969. irreg. price varies. University of Hull Press, Hull HU6 7RX, England. TEL 44-1482-46311. FAX 44-1482-465936. TELEX 592592-KHMAIL-G FAO HULIB 375. **Indexed:** SSCI. **Document type:** monographic series.
Formerly: Occasional Papers in Economic and Social History (ISSN 0078-3013)

330.1   NE   ISSN 1120-7388
HC244.A1
MOST; economic policy in transitional economies. (Text in English) 1990. q. fl.460 to institutions; $236 to institutions in U.S. (effective 1998). (Nomisma, IT) Kluwer Academic Publishers, Postbus 17, 3300 AA Dordrecht, Netherlands. TEL 31-78-6392392. FAX 31-78-6392254. E-mail: services@wkap.nl; URL: http://www.wkap.nl. (Dist. by: Kluwer Academic Publishers Group, P.O. Box 322, 3300 AH Dordrecht, Netherlands. TEL 31-78-6392392. FAX 31-78-6546474; N. America dist. addr.: Box 358, Accord Sta., Hingham, MA 02018-0358. TEL 617-871-6600. FAX 617-871-6528) Ed. Roberta Benini. stat.; index. **Indexed:** Geo.Abstr.P.G. **Document type:** academic/scholarly publication.
—BLDSC (5968.140000). **CCC.**
Description: Promotes the open discussion and analysis of policy issues, present economic trends, the implementation of reform and policy choices in post-Communist economies, with particular attention to industrial policy.
Refereed Serial

330.1 600   NE
N E H A BULLETIN. 1987. s-a. fl.90 includes N E H A Jaarboek (students fl.50). Vereniging Het Nederlandsch Economisch-Historisch Archief, Cruquiusweg 31, 1019 AT Amsterdam, Netherlands. TEL 31-20-6685866. FAX 31-20-6654181. E-mail: lwi@iisg.nl. Ed. H.J.M. Winkelman. **Indexed:** Amer.Hist.& Life (1995-), Hist.Abstr. (1995-). **Document type:** academic/scholarly publication, bulletin.
Description: Covers economic history in the Netherlands and Belgium

949 330.1   NE   ISSN 1380-5517
N E H A JAARBOEK VOOR ECONOMISCHE, BEDRIJFS- EN TECHNIEKGESCHIEDENIS. 1915. a. fl.90 includes N E H A Bulletin. Vereniging Het Nederlandsch Economisch-Historisch Archief, Cruquiusweg 31, 1019 AT Amsterdam, Netherlands. TEL 31-20-6685866. FAX 31-20-6654181. Ed. J.J.M. van Gerwen. **Indexed:** Amer.Hist.& Life (1963-1984), (1986-), (1993-), Hist.Abstr. (1963-1984), (1986-), (1993-), IBR. **Document type:** academic/scholarly publication.
—KNAW.
Formed by the 1994 merger of: Jaarboek voor de Geschiedenis van Bedrijf en Techniek (ISSN 0920-7724) & Economisch- en Sociaal-historisch Jaarboek (ISSN 0167-7942); *Which supersedes* (in 1971): Economisch-Historisch Jaarboek (ISSN 0167-7845)

N W POSTHUMUS REEKS. see HISTORY — History Of Europe

NEW AMERICAN (APPLETON). see POLITICAL SCIENCE

330.1   UK   ISSN 1070-3535
HC251
NEW ECONOMY. 1994. q. £115. (Institute for Public Policy Research) Academic Press Ltd. (Subsidiary of: Harcourt Brace & Company Ltd.), 24-28 Oval Rd., London NW1 7DX, England. TEL 44-171-482-2293. FAX 44-171-482-2293. TELEX 25775 ACPRES G. E-mail: apsubs@acad.com; URL: http://www.idealibrary.com/. (Subscr. to: Harcourt Brace & Company Ltd., Journals Subscriptions Fulfillment, Foots Cray High St., Sidcup, Kent SA14 5HP, England. TEL 44-181-300-3322. FAX 44-181-309-0807) Ed. Dan Corry. R&P contact: Catherine John. adv. contact: Nik Screen. **Document type:** academic/scholarly publication.
—BLDSC (6083.670500).
Description: Publishes articles which apply the latest economic theories and research to the policy issues of the day.

NEW FEDERALIST. see BUSINESS AND ECONOMICS — Economic Situation And Conditions

330   UK   ISSN 1356-3467
▼**NEW POLITICAL ECONOMY.** 1996. 3/yr. £27($44) to individuals; institutions £94 ($144) (effective 1997). Carfax Publishing Co., P.O. Box 25, Abingdon, Oxon OX14 3UE, England. TEL 44-1235-401000. FAX 44-1235-401550. E-mail: enquiries@carfax.co.uk; URL: http://www.carfax.co.uk. (N. American subscr. to: Carfax Publishing Co., 875-81 Massachusetts Ave., Cambridge, MA 02139) Ed.Bd. **Indexed:** Alt.Press Ind. **Document type:** academic/scholarly publication.
—BLDSC (6085.740000). **CCC.**
Refereed Serial

327.111   NO   ISSN 0801-9568
H8
NORSK OEKONOMISK TIDSSKRIFT. (Text in Norwegian; summaries in English) 1887. 2/yr. NOK 175 (effective 1997). Sosialoekonomenes Forening, P.O. Box 8872 Youngstorget, N-oslo, Norway. TEL 47-22-41-32-90. FAX 47-22-41-32-93. Ed. Jon Vislie. adv.; bk.rev.; charts; index. circ. 1,600. (back issues avail.) **Indexed:** P.A.I.S.
Supersedes in part (in 1987): Statsoekonomisk Tidsskrift (ISSN 0039-0720)

NOTE ECONOMICHE. see BUSINESS AND ECONOMICS

330.1 658   TU   ISSN 1010-9927
HD85.T9
O D T U GELISME DERGISI/M E T U STUDIES IN DEVELOPMENT. (Text in English and Turkish) 1970. q. TL.1000000 (foreign $20) (effective 1997). Orta Dogu Teknik Universitesi, Iktisadi ve Idari Bilimler Fakultesi - Middle East Technical University, Faculty of Economic and Administrative Sciences, Department of Economics, Balgat 06531 Ankara, Turkey. TEL 90-312-2102006. FAX 90-312-2101244. E-mail: metusd@rorqual.cc.metu.edu.tr. (Subscr. to: METU Bookstore, Middle East Technical University, Ankara O6531, Turkey. FAX 90-312-2101230) Ed. Alper Guzel. adv. contact: Alper Guzel. bk.rev.; abstr.; index, cum.index. circ. 1,500. (back issues avail.) **Indexed:** J.of Econ.Lit., Math.R., Zent.Math. **Document type:** academic/scholarly publication.
Description: Publishes research articles in the field of economics and administrative sciences.
Refereed Serial

330   NE   ISSN 0923-7992
HB1   CODEN: OEREED
OPEN ECONOMIES REVIEW. (Text in English) 1990. q. fl.520 to institutions; $267 to institutions in U.S. (effective 1998). (Italian International Economic Center, IT) Kluwer Academic Publishers, Postbus 17, 3300 AA Dordrecht, Netherlands. TEL 31-78-6392392. FAX 31-78-6392254. TELEX 29245 KAPG NL. E-mail: services@wkap.nl; URL: http://www.wkap.nl. (Dist. by: Kluwer Academic Publishers Group, P.O. Box 322, 3300 AH Dordrecht, Netherlands. TEL 31-78-6392392. FAX 31-78-6546474; N. America dist. addr.: Box 358, Accord Sta., Hingham, MA 02018-0358. TEL 617-871-6600. FAX 617-871-6528) Eds. Paolo Savona, Michele Fratianni. (also avail. in microform from UMI; back issues avail.; reprint service avail. from SWZ) **Indexed:** ASCA, Curr.Cont., Geo.Abstr.P.G., IDA, Zent.Math. **Document type:** academic/scholarly publication.
—BLDSC (6265.953750); Genuine Article; SWETS; UMI. **CCC.**
Description: Publishes original theoretical and empirical papers dealing with international economic issues or national economic issues that have transnational relevance, such as trade flows, commercial policies, exchange rate movements, external debt, alternative monetary regimes and monetary union.
Refereed Serial

OPTOMETRIC ECONOMICS. see MEDICAL SCIENCES — Ophthalmology And Optometry

330.1   IT
PENSIERO ECONOMICO MODERNO. 1982. q. L.50000 (foreign L.88000) (effective 1997). Via di Fortezza 1, 56100 Pisa, Italy. TEL 39-50-571181. FAX 39-50-571198. Ed. Romano Molesti. R&P contact: Silvio Truceo. adv. contact: A.C. Cappuccilli. **Document type:** academic/scholarly publication.
Description: Covers topics in modern economic thought.

POLITECHNIKA KRAKOWSKA. MONOGRAFIE. SERIA: NAUKI SPOLECZNE I EKONOMICZNE. see SOCIAL SCIENCES: COMPREHENSIVE WORKS

330.1   US
POLITICAL ECONOMY AND PUBLIC POLICY; an international series of monographs in law, economics, history of economic thought and public finance. 1983. irreg., vol.9, 1995. $73.25. J A I Press Inc., 55 Old Post Rd., No. 2, Box 1678, Greenwich, CT 06830-1678. TEL 203-661-7602. FAX 203-661-0792. (Subscr. in the UK and Europe to: JAI Press Ltd., 38 Tavistock St., Covent Garden, London WC2E 7PB, England. TEL 44-171-379-8834. FAX 44-171-379-8835) Eds. William Breit, Kenneth G. Elzinga. index. **Document type:** monographic series.

330.1   II   ISSN 0971-2097
HC431
POLITICAL ECONOMY JOURNAL OF INDIA. (Text and summaries in English) 1992. 2/yr. Rs.80 to individuals; institutions Rs.120; foreign $20. Centre for Indian Development Studies, 206, Sector 9-C; Box 130, Chandigarh 160 017, India. TEL 91-172-45362. FAX 91-172-547525. Ed. V.S. Mahajan. adv.; bk.rev.; bibl. circ. 800. **Indexed:** Pub.Admin.Abstr. **Document type:** academic/scholarly publication.
Description: Covers Indian economic developments and their relations with the world economy.

BUSINESS AND ECONOMICS — ECONOMIC SYSTEMS AND THEORIES, ECONOMIC HISTORY

330.1   FR   ISSN 0079-4074
PORTS - ROUTES - TRAFICS. 1951. irreg., no.29, 1988. price varies. Editions de l' Ecole des Hautes Etudes en Sciences Sociales, 131 bd. St-Michel, 75005 Paris, France. TEL 33-1-40467080. FAX 33-1-44070889. E-mail: editions@ehess.fr; URL: http://www.ehess.fr/editions. (Dist. by: Centre Interinstitutionnel pour la Diffusion de Publications en Sciences Humaines, 131 bd. St-Michel, 75005 Paris, France. TEL 33-1-43544715. FAX 33-1-43548073)

330.1   US   ISSN 0885-6699
PRAGMATIST; a utilitarian approach. 1983. bi-m. $12 (foreign $15). Pragmatist, Box 392, Forest Grove, PA 18922. FAX 215-348-8006. Ed. Jorge E. Amador; Pub. Hans G. Schroeder. adv.; bk.rev.; charts; stat.; index; circ. 1,050 (paid). (back issues avail.; reprint service avail.) **Document type:** newsletter.
   Description: Libertarian publication proposing the abolition of all forms of taxation.

PRILOZI/CONTRIBUTIONS. see ARCHAEOLOGY

330.1   US   ISSN 0033-5533
HB1   CODEN: QJECAT
QUARTERLY JOURNAL OF ECONOMICS. 1886. q. $38 to individuals (foreign $56); institutions $110 (foreign $128); students $24 (foreign $42) (effective 1997). (Harvard University, Department of Economics) M I T Press, 5 Cambridge Center, Cambridge, MA 02142. TEL 617-253-2889. FAX 617-577-1545. E-mail: journals-orders@mit.edu; URL: http://www-mitpress.mit.edu. Ed.Bd. R&P contact: Paul Dzus. adv.; charts; index. circ. 5,000. (also avail. in microform from UMI; reprint service avail. from UMI,KTO; back issues avail.) **Indexed:** ABI Inform., Acad.Ind., Amer.Hist.& Life (1960-), ASCA, B.P.I., BPIA, Bus.Ind., C.R.E.J., Cont.Pg.Manage., Curr.Cont., Excerp.Med., Geo.Abstr.P.G., Hist.Abstr. (1960-), Human Resour.Abstr., IBR, Ind.Per.Art.Relat.Law, Int.Lab.Doc., J.of Econ.Lit., Key to Econ.Sci., Math.R., Oper.Res.Manage.Sci., Pub.Admin.Abstr., Qual.Contr.Appl.Stat., R.G., Rural Recreat.Tour.Abstr., Sage Pub.Admin.Abstr., Sage Urb.Stud.Abstr., Soc.Sci.Ind., Soc.Work Res.& Abstr., SSCI, Tr.& Indus.Ind., Work Rel.Abstr., World Agri.Econ.& Rural Sociol.Abstr., World Bank.Abstr. **Document type:** academic/scholarly publication.
●Also available online. Vendor(s): Information Access Co.
—BLDSC (7188.400000); Genuine Article; KR SourceOne; SWETS; UMI; UnCover. **CCC.**
   Description: Covers all aspects of the economics field, including theoretical and empirical macroeconomics. For professional and academic economists and students.

RAZVOJ: DEVELOPMENT - INTERNATIONAL. see BUSINESS AND ECONOMICS — International Development And Assistance

REALIZM - NOWY USTROJ SPOLECZNO-POLITYCZNY; miesiecznik IV Rzeczypospolitej. see POLITICAL SCIENCE

330.1   NE   ISSN 0924-199X
RECENT ECONOMIC THOUGHT. (Text in English) 1982. irreg., vol.36, 1994. price varies. Kluwer Academic Publishers, Postbus 17, 3300 AA Dordrecht, Netherlands. TEL 31-78-6392392. FAX 31-78-6392254. TELEX 29245 KAPG NL. E-mail: services@wkap.nl; URL: http://www.wkap.nl. (Dist. by: Kluwer Academic Publishers Group, P.O. Box 322, 3300 AH Dordrecht, Netherlands. TEL 31-78-6392392. FAX 31-78-6546474; N. American dist. addr.: Box 358, Accord Sta., Hingham, MA 02018-0358. TEL 617-871-6600. FAX 617-871-6528) (back issues avail.) **Document type:** monographic series.
   Description: Publishes scholarly articles addressing theoretical and practical issues in contemporary economic research, including policy matters, and concerns from related disciplines.
   Refereed Serial

330.1   FR   ISSN 1259-4261
RECUEIL D'ETUDES SOCIALES. (Text in French) 3/yr. 286 F. (foreign 385 F.). Institut National de la Statistique et des Etudes Economiques, 18 bd. Adolphe Pinard, 75675 Paris Cedex 14, France. TEL 41-17-50-50. FAX 41-17-66-66.

330   US   ISSN 0363-3268
HC1
RESEARCH IN ECONOMIC HISTORY. 1976. irreg., vol.16, 1996. $73.25. J A I Press Inc., 55 Old Post Rd., No. 2, Box 1678, Greenwich, CT 06830-1678. TEL 203-661-7602. FAX 203-661-0792. E-mail: jai@jaipress.com. (Subscr. in the UK and Europe to: JAI Press Ltd., 38 Tavistock St., Covent Garden, London WC2E 7PB, England. TEL 44-171-379-8834. FAX 44-171-379-8835) Ed. Alex Field. bibl.; charts; stat. **Indexed:** Amer.Hist.& Life (1976-), Hist.Abstr. (1976-), SSCI. **Document type:** monographic series.
—BLDSC (7738.920000). **CCC.**

330   US   ISSN 1054-1098
HC10
RESEARCH IN ECONOMIC HISTORY. SUPPLEMENT. 1977. irreg., no.6, 1991. $73.25. J A I Press Inc., 55 Old Post Rd., No. 2, Box 1678, Greenwich, CT 06830-1678. TEL 203-661-7602. FAX 203-661-0792. E-mail: jai@jaipress.com. (Subscr. in the UK and Europe to: JAI Press Ltd., 38 Tavistock St., Covent Garden, London WC2E 7PB, England. TEL 44-171-379-8834. FAX 44-171-379-8835) **Document type:** monographic series.

330.1   US   ISSN 0193-2306
HB1
RESEARCH IN EXPERIMENTAL ECONOMICS. (Supplement avail.: An Experiment in Non-Cooperative Oligopoly) 1979. irreg., vol.6, 1996. $73.25. J A I Press Inc., 55 Old Post Rd., No. 2, Box 1678, Greenwich, CT 06830-1678. TEL 203-661-7602. FAX 203-661-0792. E-mail: jai@jaipress.com. (Subscr. in the UK and Europe to: JAI Press Ltd., 38 Tavistock St., Covent Garden, London WC2E 7PB, England. TEL 44-171-379-8834. FAX 44-171-379-8835) Ed. R. Mark Isaac. **Document type:** monographic series.
—BLDSC (7739.970000); UnCover. **CCC.**

330.1 320   US   ISSN 0161-7230
HC10
RESEARCH IN POLITICAL ECONOMY. 1978. irreg., vol.16, 1997. $73.25. J A I Press Inc., 55 Old Post Rd., No. 2, Box 1678, Greenwich, CT 06830-1678. TEL 203-661-7602. FAX 203-661-0792. E-mail: jai@jaipress.com. (Subscr. in the UK and Europe to: JAI Press Ltd., 38 Tavistock St., Covent Garden, London WC2E 7PB, England. TEL 44-171-379-8834. FAX 44-171-379-8835) Ed. Paul Zarembka. **Document type:** monographic series.
—BLDSC (7755.077300); UnCover. **CCC.**

330.1   US   ISSN 0743-4154
HB75
RESEARCH IN THE HISTORY OF ECONOMIC THOUGHT AND METHODOLOGY. 1983. irreg., vol.14, 1996. $73.25. J A I Press Inc., 55 Old Post Rd., No. 2, Box 1678, Greenwich, CT 06830-1678. TEL 203-661-7602. FAX 203-661-0792. E-mail: jai@jaipress.com. (Subscr. in the UK and Europe to: JAI Press Ltd., 38 Tavistock St., Covent Garden, London WC2E 7PB, England. TEL 44-171-379-8834. FAX 44-171-379-8835) Ed. Warren J. Samuels. **Indexed:** Amer.Hist.& Life (1989-), Hist.Abstr. (1989-). **Document type:** monographic series.
—BLDSC (7741.308000); UnCover.

330.1   US   ISSN 1051-6751
HB75
RESEARCH IN THE HISTORY OF ECONOMIC THOUGHT AND METHODOLOGY. ARCHIVAL SUPPLEMENT. 1989. irreg., no.5, 1996. $73.25. J A I Press Inc., 55 Old Post Rd., No. 2, Box 1678, Greenwich, CT 06830-1678. TEL 203-661-7602. FAX 203-661-0792. E-mail: jai@jaipress.com. (Subscr. in the UK and Europe to: JAI Press Ltd., 38 Tavistock St., Covent Garden, London WC2E 7PB, England. TEL 44-171-379-8834. FAX 44-171-379-8835) **Document type:** monographic series.
—BLDSC (7741.308500).

330.1 320.531   US   ISSN 0893-5696
HX1
RETHINKING MARXISM. 1988. q. $30 to individuals (foreign $55); institutions $85 (foreign $107); students $20 (effective 1997). (Association for Economic and Social Analysis) Guilford Publications, Inc., 72 Spring St., 4th Fl., New York, NY 10012. TEL 212-431-9800; 800-365-7006. FAX 212-966-6708. E-mail: info@guilford.com. Ed. Jack Amariglio. R&P contact: Kathy Kuehl. adv. contact: Susan Pavliscak. bk.rev. circ. 970. (also avail. in microform from UMI; reprint service avail. from UMI) **Indexed:** Alt.Press Ind., Amer.Hist.& Life (1988-1989), Film Lit.Ind. (1990-), Hist.Abstr. (1988-1989), Human Resour.Abstr., Left Ind. (1988-), Per.Islam. (1991-), Sage Pub.Admin.Abstr., Sociol.Abstr. **Document type:** academic/scholarly publication.
—BLDSC (7785.509800); SWETS; UMI; UnCover. **CCC.**
   Description: A wide range of political and cultural perspectives are brought to the fore as developments for racial societal change are examined.

330.1 900   US   ISSN 0147-9032
D1
REVIEW (BINGHAMTON). 1977. q. $28 to individuals (foreign $36); institutions $90 (foreign $98). Fernand Braudel Center for the Study of Economies, Historical Systems, and Civilizations, Box 6000, Binghamton University, Binghamton, NY 13902-6000. TEL 607-777-4924. FAX 607-777-4315. E-mail: review@binghamton.edu. Ed. Immanuel Wallerstein. R&P contact: Donna DeVoist. adv. contact: Donna DeVoist. bk.rev.; index. circ. 1,100. (back issues avail.) **Indexed:** Alt.Press Ind., Bull.Signal., Curr.Cont., Geo.Abstr.P.G., Hist.Abstr., IDA, Left Ind. (1986-). **Document type:** academic/scholarly publication.
—SWETS; UMI; UnCover.
   Refereed Serial

330.1   US   ISSN 0889-3047
HB98
REVIEW OF AUSTRIAN ECONOMICS. 1986. s-a. fl.400 to institutions; $205.50 to institutions in U.S. (effective 1998). (Ludwig von Mises Institute) Kluwer Academic Publishers Boston, Box 358, Accord Sta., Hingham, MA 02018-0358. TEL 617-871-6600. FAX 617-871-6528. E-mail: services@wkap.nl; URL: http://www.wkap.nl. (Dist. outside N. America by: Kluwer Academic Publishers Group, P.O. Box 322, 3300 AH Dordrecht, Netherlands. TEL 31-78-6392392. FAX 31-78-6546474) Eds. Murray N. Rothbard, Walter Block. adv.; bk.rev. circ. 2,000. (also avail. in microform from UMI; back issues avail.) **Indexed:** J.of Econ.Lit. **Document type:** academic/scholarly publication.
—BLDSC (7788.170000); UnCover. **CCC.**
   Description: Covers various "heated" arguments in Austrian economics. Includes individual action, economic logic and free markets.
   Refereed Serial

330.1 658   NE   ISSN 0889-938X
HD2326   CODEN: RIOREU
REVIEW OF INDUSTRIAL ORGANIZATION. (Text in English) 1984. bi-m. fl.610 to institutions; $313 to institutions in U.S. (effective 1998). (Industrial Organization Society) Kluwer Academic Publishers, Postbus 17, 3300 AA Dordrecht, Netherlands. TEL 31-78-6392392. FAX 31-78-6392254. TELEX 29245 KAPG NL. E-mail: services@wkap.nl; URL: http://www.wkap.nl. (Dist. by: Kluwer Academic Publishers Group, P.O. Box 322, 3300 AH Dordrecht, Netherlands. TEL 31-78-6392392. FAX 31-78-6546474; N. America dist. addr.: Box 358, Accord Sta., Hingham, MA 02018-0358. TEL 617-871-6600. FAX 617-871-6528) Ed. William G. Shepard. bk.rev. (also avail. in microform from UMI; back issues avail.; reprint service avail. from SWZ) **Indexed:** ASCA, Curr.Cont., Geo.Abstr.P.G., IBR, IDA. **Document type:** academic/scholarly publication.
—BLDSC (7790.787000); Genuine Article; SWETS; UMI; UnCover. **CCC.**
   Description: Publishes research papers on all aspects of industrial organization, with particular emphasis on ideas which can be verified by econometric evidence, case studies, and analysis of real conditions.
   Refereed Serial

REVIEW OF QUANTITATIVE FINANCE AND ACCOUNTING. see BUSINESS AND ECONOMICS — Accounting

BUSINESS AND ECONOMICS — ECONOMIC SYSTEMS AND THEORIES, ECONOMIC HISTORY

330 US ISSN 0486-6134
HC101
REVIEW OF RADICAL POLITICAL ECONOMICS. 1969. q. $65 (foreign $85) to individuals; institutions $195 (foreign $215) (effective 1998). (Union for Radical Political Economics) J A I Press Inc, 55 Old Post Rd., No.2, Box 1678, Greenwich, CT 06830-1678. TEL 203-661-7602. FAX 203-661-0792. E-mail: jai@jaipress.com; URL: http://economics.csusb.edu/orgs/URPE/rrpehome.html. Ed. Sue Johnson. adv.: page $210; trim 4 1/4 x 7 1/2. bk.rev.; cum.index 1969-1979. circ. 1,800. (also avail. in microform from UMI; reprint service avail. from UMI; back issues avail.) **Indexed:** Acad.Ind., Alt.Press Ind., Amer.Bibl.Slavic & E.Eur.Stud., Amer.Hist.& Life (1971-), Geo.Abstr.P.G., Hist.Abstr. (1971-), IDA, Left Ind. (1982-), Mid.East: Abstr.& Ind., Mult.Ed.Abstr., P.A.I.S., Per.Islam. (1991-), Pub.Admin.Abstr., SSCI, Stud.Wom.Abstr. **Document type:** academic/scholarly publication.
—BLDSC (7794.185000); SWETS; UMI; UnCover. CCC.
Description: Presents articles on radical political economic theory and applied analysis from a wide source of theoretical traditions, including Marxian, institutional, feminist, and post-Keynesian.

REVISTA DE HISTORIA ECONOMICA. see BUSINESS AND ECONOMICS — Economic Situation And Conditions

REVISTA DE HISTORIA ECONOMICA E SOCIAL. see HISTORY

REVISTA DE HISTORIA ECONOMICA E SOCIAL. CADERNOS. see HISTORY

330 FR ISSN 0338-0599
HC244.A1
REVUE D'ETUDES COMPARATIVES EST-OUEST; economies et techniques de planification - droit et sciences sociales. (Text in French, summaries in English) 1970. q. 625 F. to individuals (foreign 755 F.); agencies 562.50 (foreign 679.50) (effective 1998). Presses Universitaires de France, 14 av. du Bois-de-l'Epine, 91003 Evry Cedex, France. TEL 33-1-60778205. FAX 33-1-60792045. TELEX PUF 600 474 F. Ed. M. Eugene Zaleski. bk.rev.; abstr.; bibl.; illus.; index. circ. 800. (microform) **Indexed:** A.B.C.Pol.Sci., Amer.Hist.& Life (1973-1991), Arts & Hum.Cit.Ind., ASCA, Curr.Cont., Hist.Abstr. (1973-1993), IBR, Int.Lab.Doc., Int.Polit.Sci.Abstr., Key to Econ.Sci., SSCI, World Agri.Econ.& Rural Sociol.Abstr.
—BLDSC (7900.158000); SWETS.
Formerly (until 1975): Revue de l'Est (ISSN 0035-1415)
Description: Set up to fill the gaps in the information on socialist countries.

330.1 FR ISSN 0980-1472
Q295 CODEN: RISYE3
REVUE INTERNATIONALE DE SYSTEMIQUE. (Text in English, French) 1986. 5/yr. 1050 F. (foreign 1430 F.) (effective 1997). (Association Francaise des Sciences et Technologies de l'Information et des Systemes) Dunod, 5 rue Laromiguiere, 75005 Paris, France. TEL 33-01-40-46-62-00. FAX 33-01-40-46-62-01. TELEX 634 916 F. E-mail: gauthier.villars.publisher@mail.sgip.fr; URL: http://www.gautheir-villars.fr. (Subscr. to: Societe de Periodiques Spacialises, B.P. 22-F, 41354 Vineuil Cedex, France. TEL 33-02-54-50-46-12. FAX 33-02-54-50-46-11) Ed. B. Paulre. adv. 850. **Indexed:** Curr.Cont., INSPEC (1992-), Zent.Math.
—BLDSC (7925.550000); AskIEEE; CISTI; KR SourceOne. CCC.
Description: Provides a forum for the interdisciplinary approach of scientific, philosophical and technical problems raised by systems science.

330.1 IT ISSN 0393-3415
H7
RIVISTA DI STORIA ECONOMICA. 1984. 3/yr. L.50000. Giulio Einaudi Editore s.p.a., Via U. Biancamano 1, 10121 Turin, Italy. TEL (011) 53 36 53. Ed. Gianni Toniolo. bk.rev. circ. 1,200. (back issues avail.) **Indexed:** Amer.Hist.& Life (1984-), Hist.Abstr. (1984-), J.of Econ.Lit.
—SWETS.

330.1 NE ISSN 0924-6002
ROCHESTER STUDIES IN ECONOMICS AND POLICY ISSUES. (Text in English) 1979. irreg. price varies. Kluwer Academic Publishers, Postbus 17, 3300 AA Dordrecht, Netherlands. TEL 31-78-6392392. FAX 31-78-6392254. TELEX 29245 KAPG NL. E-mail: services@wkap.nl; URL: http://www.wkap.nl. (Dist. by: Kluwer Academic Publishers Group, P.O. Box 322, 3300 AH Dordrecht, Netherlands. TEL 31-78-6392392. FAX 31-78-6546474; N. America dist. addr.: Box 358, Accord Sta., Hingham, MA 02018-0358. TEL 617-871-6600. FAX 617-871-6528) **Document type:** monographic series.
Refereed Serial

338 339.5 DK ISSN 0036-5491
SCANDINAVIAN ECONOMIC HISTORY REVIEW. 1953. 3/yr. DKK 300 to individuals; institutions DKK 400 (effective 1997). Odense University Press, 55 Campusvej, DK-5230 Odense M, Denmark. TEL 45-66-15-79-99. FAX 45-66-15-81-26. E-mail: press@forlag.ou.dk. Eds. Per Boje, Ingrid Henriksen. adv.; bk.rev.; bibl.; charts; illus.; stat.; cum.index: vols.1-20. circ. 700. (back issues avail.) **Indexed:** Amer.Hist.& Life (1954-), Geo.Abstr.P.G., Hist.Abstr. (1954-), IBR, J.of Econ.Lit., Numis.Lit. **Document type:** academic/scholarly publication.

330 GW ISSN 0036-973X
HC10
SCRIPTA MERCATURAE; half-yearly publication on the history of world economic relations. 1967. s-a. DM.23 per issue. Scripta Mercaturae Verlag, Am Roten Berg 5-9, 55595 St. Katharinen, Germany. TEL 49-6706-8800. Eds. F.R. Henning, H. Winkel. charts; illus. **Indexed:** Amer.Hist.& Life (1972-1975), Hist.Abstr. (1972-1975). **Document type:** academic/scholarly publication.
—SWETS.

SERVICE INDUSTRIES IN THE CANADIAN INPUT - OUTPUT ACCOUNTS: CURRENT PRICES, SOURCES OF DATA AND METHODS OF ESTIMATION/INDUSTRIES DE SERVICES DANS LES COMPTES D'ENTREES - SORTIES DU CANADA: EN PRIX COURANTS, SOURCES DE DONNEES ET METHODES D'ESTIMATION. see BUSINESS AND ECONOMICS — Abstracting, Bibliographies, Statistics

330.1 NE ISSN 0924-6061
SOCIAL DIMENSIONS OF ECONOMICS. (Text in English) 1981. irreg. price varies. Kluwer Academic Publishers, Postbus 17, 3300 AA Dordrecht, Netherlands. TEL 31-78-6392392. FAX 31-78-6392254. TELEX 29245 KAPG NL. E-mail: services@wkap.nl; URL: http://www.wkap.nl. (Dist. by: Kluwer Academic Publishers Group, P.O. Box 322, 3300 AH Dordrecht, Netherlands. TEL 31-78-6392392. FAX 31-78-6546474; N. America dist. addr.: Box 358, Accord Sta., Hingham, MA 02018-0358. TEL 617-871-6600. FAX 617-871-6528) **Document type:** monographic series.
Refereed Serial

330.1 UK ISSN 1366-2546
SOCIAL SCIENCE WORKING PAPER. irreg., no.19, 1996. Napier University, Department of Economics, Sighthill Ct., Edinburgh EH11 4BN, Scotland. FAX 44-131-447-3475. **Document type:** monographic series.
—BLDSC (8318.182345).

330 JA ISSN 0038-0113
HC51
SOCIO-ECONOMIC HISTORY/SHAKAI KEIZAI SHIGAKU. (Text in Japanese) 1931. bi-m. 1,390 Yen. Socio-Economic History Society, c/o Economic Department, Sophia University, Chiyodaku, Tokyo 102, Japan. TEL 03-3238-3090. Ed. Yasuo Okada. adv.; bk.rev. circ. 1,600. **Indexed:** Amer.Hist.& Life (1955-1991), (1993-), Hist.Abstr. (1955-1991), (1993-).
—BLDSC (8319.569000); UnCover.

330.1 BU ISSN 0204-9627
SOFIISKI UNIVERSITET. KATEDRA PO POLITICHESKA IKONOMIYA. GODISNIK. (Text in Bulgarian; summaries in English and Russian) irreg. price varies. (Sofiiski Universitet., Katedra po Politicheska Ikonomiya) Publishing House of the Bulgarian Academy of Sciences, Acad. G. Bonchev St., Bldg. 6, 1113 Sofia, Bulgaria. Ed.Bd. (reprint service avail. from IRC) **Indexed:** BSL Econ.
—BLDSC (0051.075000).

SOOCHOW JOURNAL OF ECONOMICS AND BUSINESS. see BUSINESS AND ECONOMICS

SOUNDVIEW EXECUTIVE BOOK SUMMARIES. see BUSINESS AND ECONOMICS — Management

320.1 SA ISSN 1011-3436
SOUTH AFRICAN JOURNAL OF ECONOMIC HISTORY. (Text in English) 1982. s-a. R.25 to individuals; institutions R.50. Economic History Society of Southern Africa, University of South Africa, Economics Department, P.O. Box 392, Pretoria 0001. TEL 27-12-4294502. FAX 27-12-4293433. TELEX 350068. E-mail: inggsej@alpha.unisa.ac.za. Ed. Andre Muller. bk.rev. circ. 250. **Indexed:** Amer.Hist.& Life (1987-), Hist.Abstr. (1987-), Ind.S.A.Per. **Document type:** academic/scholarly publication.
●Also available online.
—BLDSC (8338.858000).
Formerly (until 1986): Perspectives in Economic History (ISSN 1012-036X)
Refereed Serial

330.1 AU
SOZIAL- UND WIRTSCHAFTSHISTORISCHE STUDIEN. 1972. irreg. price varies. Verlag fuer Geschichte und Politik, Neulinggasse 26, A-1030 Vienna, Austria. TEL 43-1-7126258-0. FAX 43-1-712625819. Ed.Bd. **Indexed:** P.A.I.S.For.Lang.Ind. **Document type:** academic/scholarly publication.

STATISTICAL ABSTRACT OF LATIN AMERICA. see HISTORY — Abstracting, Bibliographies, Statistics

STATO E MERCATO. see POLITICAL SCIENCE

330.1 NE ISSN 0954-349X
HB135
STRUCTURAL CHANGE AND ECONOMIC DYNAMICS. 1989. q. fl.485($279) (effective 1998). Elsevier Science B.V., P.O. Box 211, 1000 AE Amsterdam, Netherlands. TEL 31-20-4853911. FAX 31-20-4853598. E-mail: nlinfo-f@elsevier.nl; usinfo-f@elsevier.nl; forinfo-kyf04035@niftyserve.or.jp; URL: http://www.elsevier.nl/. (Subscr. in the Americas to: Elsevier Science, Regional Sales Office, Box 945, New York, NY 10159-0945. TEL 212-633-3730. FAX 212-633-3680; Subscr. in Australasia and the Far East to: Elsevier Science (Singapore) Pte Ltd, No.1 Temasek Ave., No.17-01 Millenia Tower, Singapore 039192, Singapore. TEL 65-434-3727. FAX 65-337-2230; Subscr. in Japan to: Elsevier Science Japan, 9-15 Higashi-Azabu 1-chome, Minato-ku, Tokyo 106, Japan. TEL 81-3-5561-5033. FAX 81-3-5561-5047) Ed. M. Landesmann. adv.; bk.rev. (also avail. in microform from UMI; back issues avail.) **Indexed:** Per.Islam. (1990-). **Document type:** academic/scholarly publication.
—BLDSC (8476.350000); AskIEEE; KR SourceOne; SWETS; UMI; UnCover. CCC.
Description: Articles study theoretical, applied and methodological aspects of structural change in economic systems.
Refereed Serial

330.1 PL ISSN 0081-6485
HB9
STUDIA HISTORIAE OECONOMICAE. (Text in English, French and German) 1966. irreg., vol.22, 1997. price varies. (Uniwersytet im. Adama Mickiewicza) Adam Mickiewicz University Press, Nowowiejskiego 55, 61-734 Poznan, Poland. TEL 48-61-527380. FAX 48-61-527701. TELEX 413260 UAMPL. Ed. Jerzy Topolski; Pub. Maria Jankowska. R&P contact: Malgorzata Bis. circ. 600. **Indexed:** Amer.Hist.& Life (1979-), Hist.Abstr. (1979-). **Document type:** academic/scholarly publication, monographic series.
—BLDSC (8482.843000).
Description: Contains papers and articles in the field of economic sciences written by A. Mickiewicz University economists, and other Polish specialists.

STUDIEN ZUR RECHTS-, WIRTSCHAFTS- UND KULTURGESCHICHTE. see LAW

BUSINESS AND ECONOMICS — ECONOMIC SYSTEMS AND THEORIES, ECONOMIC HISTORY

330.1   NE   ISSN 0929-0435
STUDIES IN AUSTRIAN ECONOMICS. Key Title: Ludwig von Mises Institute's Studies in Austrian Economics. (Text in English) 1993. irreg. price varies. (Ludwig von Mises Institute) Kluwer Academic Publishers, Postbus 17, 3300 AA Dordrecht, Netherlands. TEL 31-78-6392392. FAX 31-78-6392254. E-mail: services@wkap.nl; URL: http://www.wkap.nl. (Dist. by: Kluwer Academic Publishers Group, P.O. Box 322, 3300 AH Dordrecht, Netherlands. TEL 31-78-6392392. FAX 31-78-6546474; N. America dist. addr.: Box 358, Accord Sta., Hingham, MA 02018-0358. TEL 617-871-6600. FAX 617-871-6528) **Document type:** monographic series.
Refereed Serial

330.01   NE   ISSN 0920-1793
STUDIES IN BAYESIAN ECONOMETRICS AND STATISTICS. 1980. irreg., vol.7, 1990. price varies. Elsevier Science B.V., Books Division, P.O. Box 211, 1000 AE Amsterdam, Netherlands. TEL 31-20-4853911. FAX 31-20-4853705. TELEX 18582 ESPA NL. E-mail: nlinfo-f@elsevier.nl; usinfo-f@elsevier.com; forinfo-kyf04035@niftyserve.or.jp; URL: http://www.elsevier.nl/. (Subscr. in the Americas to: Elsevier Science, Regional Sales Office, Box 945, New York, NY 10159-0945. TEL 212-633-3730. FAX 212-633-3680; Subscr. in Australasia and the Far East to: Elsevier Science (Singapore) Pte Ltd, No.1 Temasek Ave., No.17-01 Millenia Tower, Singapore 039192, Singapore. TEL 65-434-3727. FAX 65-337-2230; Subscr. in Japan to: Elsevier Science Japan, 9-15 Higashi-Azabu 1-chome, Minato-ku, Tokyo 106, Japan. TEL 81-3-5561-5033. FAX 81-3-5561-5047) Eds. Arnold Zellner, Joseph B. Kadane. **Indexed:** Zent.Math. **Document type:** monographic series.
—BLDSC (8489.595500).
Formerly: (until vol.4, 1984): Studies in Bayesian Econometrics.
Refereed Serial

330.1   BE
STUDIES IN BELGIAN ECONOMIC HISTORY. (Text in English) 1992. irreg., vol.3, 1992. price varies. Koninklijke Academie voor Wetenschappen, Letteren en Schone Kunsten van Belgie, 1 Hertogsstraat, B-1000 Brussels, Belgium. (Dist. by: N.V. Brepols, Steenweg op Tielen 68, 2300 Turnhout, Belgium. TEL 32-14-402500. FAX 32-14-428919) (back issues avail.) **Document type:** monographic series.

330   US   ISSN 0081-7643
STUDIES IN BUSINESS CYCLES. 1927. irreg., vol.30, 1997. price varies. (National Bureau of Economic Research) University of Chicago Press, 5801 S. Ellis Ave., Chicago, IL 60637. E-mail: sales@press.uchicago.edu; URL: http://www.press.uchicago.edu. (Subscr. to: 11030 S. Langley, Chicago, IL 60628. TEL 800-621-2736. FAX 800-621-8471) **Document type:** monographic series.

330.1   NE   ISSN 0927-5460
STUDIES IN COMPARATIVE ECONOMIC POLICIES. (Text in English) 1991. irreg., vol.3, 1992. price varies. Elsevier Science B.V., Books Division, P.O. Box 211, 1000 AE Amsterdam, Netherlands. TEL 31-20-4853911. FAX 31-20-4853705. E-mail: nlinfo-f@elsevier.nl; usinfo-f@elsevier.com; forinfo-kyf04035@niftyserve.or.jp; URL: http://www.elsevier.nl/. (Subscr. in the Americas to: Elsevier Science, Regional Sales Office, Box 945, New York, NY 10159-0945. TEL 212-633-3730. FAX 212-633-3680; Subscr. in Australasia and the Far East to: Elsevier Science (Singapore) Pte Ltd, No.1 Temasek Ave., No.17-01 Millenia Tower, Singapore 039192, Singapore. TEL 65-434-3727. FAX 65-337-2230; Subscr. in Japan to: Elsevier Science Japan, 9-15 Higashi-Azabu 1-chome, Minato-ku, Tokyo 106, Japan. TEL 81-3-5561-5033. FAX 81-3-5561-5047) **Document type:** monographic series.
—BLDSC (8490.235000).
Refereed Serial

330.1   NE
STUDIES IN ECONOMIC DECISION, ORGANIZATION AND BEHAVIOR. (Text in English) 1993. irreg. price varies. Elsevier Science B.V., Books Division, P.O. Box 211, 1000 AE Amsterdam, Netherlands. TEL 31-20-4853911. FAX 31-20-4853705. E-mail: nlinfo-f@elsevier.nl; usinfo-f@elsevier.com; forinfo-kyf04035@niftyserve.or.jp; URL: http://www.elsevier.nl/. (Subscr. in the Americas to: Elsevier Science, Regional Sales Office, Box 945, New York, NY 10159-0945. TEL 212-633-3730. FAX 212-633-3680; Subscr. in Australasia and the Far East to: Elsevier Science (Singapore) Pte Ltd, No.1 Temasek Ave., No.17-01 Millenia Tower, Singapore 039192, Singapore. TEL 65-434-3727. FAX 65-337-2230; Subscr. in Japan to: Elsevier Science Japan, 9-15 Higashi-Azabu 1-chome, Minato-ku, Tokyo 106, Japan. TEL 81-3-5561-5033. FAX 81-3-5561-5047) **Document type:** monographic series.

330   UK
STUDIES IN ECONOMIC HISTORY AND POLICY; the United States in 20th Century. irreg. price varies. Cambridge University Press, Edinburgh Bldg., Shaftesbury Rd., Cambridge CB2 2RU, England. TEL 44-1223-312393. FAX 44-1223-315052. TELEX 851717256. E-mail: information@cup.cam.ac.uk; URL: http://www.cup.cam.ac.uk. (N. American addr.: Cambridge University Press, Journals Dept., 40 W. 20th St., New York, NY 10011. TEL 212-924-3900. FAX 212-691-3239) Ed.Bd. R&P contact: Linda Nicol. **Document type:** monographic series.
Formerly: Cambridge Studies in Economic History.

330.1   NE
STUDIES IN ECONOMIC ORGANIZATION. (Text in English) irreg. price varies. Kluwer Academic Publishers, Postbus 17, 3300 AA Dordrecht, Netherlands. TEL 31-78-6392392. FAX 31-78-6392254. TELEX 29245 KAPG NL. E-mail: services@wkap.nl; URL: http://www.wkap.nl. (Dist. by: Kluwer Academic Publishers Group, P.O. Box 322, 3300 AH Dordrecht, Netherlands. TEL 31-78-6392392. FAX 31-78-6546474; N. America dist. addr.: Box 358, Accord Sta., Hingham, MA 02018-0358. TEL 617-871-6600. FAX 617-871-6528) **Document type:** monographic series.
Refereed Serial

330.1   US   ISSN 1086-7376
STUDIES IN ECONOMICS AND FINANCE. 1977. s-a. $10.50 to individuals (foreign $14.50); institutions $20.50 (foreign $24.50); students $7.50 (foreign $11.50) (effective 1995-1996). University of North Carolina at Charlotte, Economics Department, Charlotte, NC 28223-0001. TEL 704-547-4130. FAX 704-547-4130. Ed. Louis Amato. (also avail. in microform from UMI) **Indexed:** ABI Inform., BPIA. **Document type:** academic/scholarly publication.
—BLDSC (8490.441000); UMI.
Formerly: Studies in Economic Analysis (ISSN 0198-8263).
Description: Publishes articles from all areas of finance and economics with an emphasis on those of a more applied nature.
Refereed Serial

330.1   US
STUDIES IN HEALTH AND HUMAN VALUES. 1989. irreg. price varies. Praeger Publishers (Subsidiary of: Greenwood Publishing Group Inc.), 88 Post Rd. W., Box 5007, Westport, CT 06881-5007. TEL 203-226-3571. FAX 203-222-1502. **Document type:** monographic series.

330.1   NE   ISSN 0924-4646
STUDIES IN INDUSTRIAL ORGANIZATION. (Text in English) 1981. irreg., vol.18, 1993. price varies. Kluwer Academic Publishers, Postbus 17, 3300 AA Dordrecht, Netherlands. TEL 31-78-6392392. FAX 31-78-6392254. TELEX 29245 KAPG NL. E-mail: services@wkap.nl; URL: http://www.wkap.nl. (Dist. by: Kluwer Academic Publishers Group, P.O. Box 322, 3300 AH Dordrecht, Netherlands. TEL 31-78-6392392. FAX 31-78-6546474; N. America dist. addr.: Box 358, Accord Sta., Hingham, MA 02018-0358. TEL 617-871-6600) (back issues avail.) **Document type:** monographic series.
—BLDSC (8490.731000).
Refereed Serial

STUDIES IN NONLINEAR DYNAMICS AND ECONOMETRICS. see *MATHEMATICS*

330.1   NE   ISSN 0924-4689
STUDIES IN OPERATIONAL REGIONAL SCIENCE. (Text in English) 1986. irreg., vol.10, 1992. price varies. Kluwer Academic Publishers, Postbus 17, 3300 AA Dordrecht, Netherlands. TEL 31-78-6392392. FAX 31-78-6392254. TELEX 29245 KAPG NL. E-mail: services@wkap.nl; URL: http://www.wkap.nl. (Dist. by: Kluwer Academic Publishers Group, P.O. Box 322, 3300 AH Dordrecht, Netherlands. TEL 31-78-6392392. FAX 31-78-6546474; N. America dist. addr.: Box 358, Accord Sta., Hingham, MA 02018-0358. TEL 617-871-6600) (back issues avail.) **Document type:** monographic series.
Refereed Serial

STUDIES IN POLITICAL ECONOMY; socialist review. see *POLITICAL SCIENCE*

STUDIES IN PRODUCTIVITY ANALYSIS. see *BUSINESS AND ECONOMICS — Management*

330.1   NE   ISSN 0924-4700
STUDIES IN PUBLIC CHOICE. (Text in English) 1978. irreg. price varies. Kluwer Academic Publishers, Postbus 17, 3300 AA Dordrecht, Netherlands. TEL 31-78-6392392. FAX 31-78-6392254. TELEX 29245 KAPG NL. E-mail: services@wkap.nl; URL: http://www.wkap.nl. (Dist. by: Kluwer Academic Publishers Group, P.O. Box 322, 3300 AH Dordrecht, Netherlands. TEL 31-78-6392392. FAX 31-78-6546474; N. America dist. addr.: Box 358, Accord Sta., Hingham, MA 02018-0358. TEL 617-871-6600. FAX 617-871-6528) **Document type:** monographic series.
Refereed Serial

330.1 368   NE   ISSN 0926-972X
STUDIES IN RISK AND UNCERTAINTY. (Text in English) 1990. irreg., vol.4, 1993. price varies. Kluwer Academic Publishers, Postbus 17, 3300 AA Dordrecht, Netherlands. TEL 31-78-6392392. FAX 31-78-6392254. TELEX 29245 KAPG NL. E-mail: services@wkap.nl; URL: http://www.wkap.nl. (Dist. by: Kluwer Academic Publishers Group, P.O. Box 322, 3300 AH Dordrecht, Netherlands. TEL 31-78-6392392. FAX 31-78-6546474; N. America dist. addr.: Box 358, Accord Sta., Hingham, MA 02018-0358. TEL 617-871-6600. FAX 617-871-6528) (back issues avail.) **Document type:** monographic series.
—BLDSC (8491.444300).
Refereed Serial

330   BE
STUDIES IN SOCIAL AND ECONOMIC HISTORY. 1988. irreg., vol.31, 1996. Leuven University Press, Blijde Inkomststraat 5, 3000 Leuven, Belgium. TEL 32-16-325345. FAX 32-16-325352. E-mail: university.press@upers.kuleuven.ac.be; URL: http://www.kuleuven.ac.be/upers. (back issues avail.) **Document type:** academic/scholarly publication, monographic series.

SUMA. see *BUSINESS AND ECONOMICS — Economic Situation And Conditions*

330.1 301   IT
SVILUPPO/DEVELOPMENT. q.? Comitato Studi e Ricerche sullo Sviluppo, c/o Dipto. di Scienze Economiche, Universita la Sapienza, Via Nomentana 41, 00161 Rome, Italy. TEL 39-6-8552780. FAX 39-6-8558054. Ed.Bd. bk.rev.
Refereed Serial

330.1 658   NE   ISSN 0929-0826
T I NEWSLETTER. (Text in English) 1993. m. Tinbergen Institute, c/o Ms. Ine Driessen, Erasmus University Rotterdam, Postbus 1738, 3000 DR Rotterdam, Netherlands. TEL 31-10-4088900. FAX 31-10-4527347. Ed. Miep Oomes. **Document type:** newsletter.

TANMIAT AL-RAFIDAIN/RAFIDAIN DEVELOPMENT. see *PUBLIC ADMINISTRATION*

338.501 NE ISSN 0924-6193
TECHNOLOGY, RISK AND SOCIETY; an international series in risk analysis. (Text in English) 1986. irreg., vol.10, 1994. price varies. Kluwer Academic Publishers, Postbus 17, 3300 AA Dordrecht, Netherlands. TEL 31-78-6392392. FAX 31-78-6392254. TELEX 29245 KAPG NL. E-mail: services@wkap.nl; URL: http://www.wkap.nl. (Dist. by: Kluwer Academic Publishers Group, P.O. Box 322, 3300 AH Dordrecht, Netherlands. TEL 31-78-6392392. FAX 31-78-6546474; N. America dist. addr.: Box 358, Accord Sta., Hingham, MA 02018-0358. TEL 617-871-6600. FAX 617-871-6528) (back issues avail.) Document type: monographic series.
—BLDSC (8761.010000).
Refereed Serial

330 FR ISSN 0987-710X
TERTIAIRE. 1956. 6/yr. 215 F. (foreign 299 F.) (effective 1997). Centre National de Documentation Pedagogique, 29 rue d'Ulm, 75230 Paris Cedex 05, France. TEL 33-1-46349000. FAX 33-1-46345544. (Subscr. to: CNDP - Abonnement, B750, 60732 Ste. Genevieve Cedex, France. FAX 33-3-44033013) adv.; mkt. circ. 3,750.
Former titles: Techniques Economiques (ISSN 0040-1331); Enseignement Economique et Commercial.

330.1 658 NE ISSN 1383-2042
TINBERGEN INSTITUTE PHD RESEARCH BULLETIN. (Text in English) 1989. 3/yr. fl.30($20) Tinbergen Institute, c/o Ms Sylvia Eijsden-Noordermeer, Erasmus University Rotterdam, Burg. Oudlaanso, NL-3062 PA Rotterdam, Netherlands. TEL 31-10-4088900. FAX 31-10-4527347. Ed.Bd. adv. Document type: academic/scholarly publication, bulletin.
—BLDSC (6449.215000).
Formerly: Tinbergen Institute Research Bulletin (ISSN 0924-056X)
Description: Publishes original theoretical and applied research in progress, survey articles, reports of Institute workshops and reviews on topics covering the entire field of general and business economics.

330.1 658 NE
TINBERGEN INSTITUTE RESEARCH SERIES. (Text in English) 1991. irreg., vol.62, 1994. price varies. Thesis Publishers, P.O. Box 14791, 1001 LG Amsterdam, Netherlands. TEL 31-20-6255429. FAX 31-20-6203395. E-mail: thesis@thesis.antenna.nl. Ed. A. Leewis. (back issues avail.) Document type: monographic series.

330.1 CM
UNIVERSITE DE YAOUNDE. FACULTE DE DROIT ET DES SCIENCES ECONOMIQUES. ECONOMIE GENERALE. irreg. Universite de Yaounde, Faculte de Droit et des Sciences Economiques, B.P. 337, Yaounde, Cameroon.

330.1 UK
UNIVERSITY OF BIRMINGHAM. DEPARTMENT OF ECONOMICS. DISCUSSION PAPERS. 1991. irreg. £2 per no. University of Birmingham, Department of Economics, Edgbaston, Birmingham B15 2TT, England. FAX 0121-414-7377. Document type: academic/scholarly publication, monographic series.

UNIVERSITY OF CALIFORNIA AT BERKELEY. INTERNATIONAL AND AREA STUDIES. RESEARCH SERIES. see *POLITICAL SCIENCE*

UNIVERSITY OF NEW ENGLAND. DEPARTMENT OF ECONOMETRICS. WORKING PAPERS IN ECONOMETRICS AND APPLIED STATISTICS. see *STATISTICS*

330.1 FI ISSN 0358-870X
UNIVERSITY OF VAASA. PROCEEDINGS. DISCUSSION PAPERS. 1979. irreg., no.213, 1997. Vaasan Yliopisto, Library - University of Vaasa, P.L. 331, FIN-65101 Vaasa, Finland. FAX 358-61-3248200. Ed. Antero Niemikorpi. Indexed: Bibl.Engl.Lang.& Lit.
Formerly (until 1980): Vaasa School of Economics. Proceedings. Discussion Papers (ISSN 0357-3486)

330.1 330.9 XO ISSN 0139-5521
UNIVERZITA KOMENSKEHO. USTAV MARXIZMU-LENINIZMU. ZBORNIK: POLITICKA EKONOMIA. (Text in Slovak; summaries in German, Russian) 1972. a. exchange basis. Univerzita Komenskeho, Ustav Marxizmu-Leninizmu, c/o Study and Information Center, Safarikovo nam. 6, 818 06 Bratislava, Slovakia. Ed. Jan Kukel. circ. 400.

UNIVERZITET U ZAGREBU. PRAVNI FAKULTET. ZBORNIK. see *LAW*

330.1 SW ISSN 0346-6493
UPPSALA STUDIES IN ECONOMIC HISTORY. (Subseries of Acta Universitatis Upsaliensis) 1974. irreg. (Uppsala Universitet) A W I International AB, P.O. Box 4627, S-116 91 Stockholm, Sweden. TEL 46-8-7282500. FAX 46-8-338707. Ed. Bo Gustafsson. (back issues avail.) Document type: academic/scholarly publication.
—KNAW.
Formerly: Ekonomisk-Historiska Studier.

330.1 FI ISSN 0788-6659
VAASAN YLIOPISTO. JULKAISUJA. OPETUSMONISTEITA/UNIVERSITY OF VAASA. PROCEEDINGS. TEACHING AID SERIES. 1972. irreg., no.49, 1994. Vaasan Yliopisto, Library - University of Vaasa, P.L. 331, FIN-65101 Vaasa, Finland. FAX 358-61-3248200. Ed. Antero Niemikorpi. Indexed: Bibl.Engl.Lang.& Lit. Document type: academic/scholarly publication.
Former titles (until 1990): Vaasan Korkeakoulu. Julkaisuja. Opetusmonisteita (ISSN 0358-9110); (until 1980): Vaasan Kauppakorkeakoulu. Julkaisuja. Opetusmonisteita (ISSN 0355-2624)

330.1 FI ISSN 0788-6667
VAASAN YLIOPISTO. JULKAISUJA. TUTKIMUKSIA/UNIVERSITY OF VAASA. PROCEEDINGS. RESEARCH PAPERS. 1970. irreg., no.215, 1997. price varies. Vaasan Yliopisto, Library - University of Vaasa, P.O. Box 331, FIN-65101 Vaasa, Finland. FAX 358-61-248200. Ed. Antero Niemikorpi. Indexed: Bibl.Engl.Lang.& Lit. Document type: academic/scholarly publication.
—BLDSC (9076.172840).
Former titles (until 1990): Vaasan Korkeakoulu. Julkaisuja. Tutkimuksia (ISSN 0358-9080); (until 1980): Vaasan Kauppakorkeakoulu. Julkaisuja. Tutkimuksia (ISSN 0355-2632)

330 FI ISSN 1238-7118
▼**VAASAN YLIOPISTON JULKAISUJA. SELVITYKSIA JA RAPORTTEJA/PROCEEDINGS OF THE UNIVERSITY OF VAASA. REPORTS**. (Text in various languages) 1995. irreg. price varies. Vaasan Yliopisto - University of Vasa, Vaasa University Library, P.O. Box 331, FIN-65101 Vaasa, Finland. TEL 358-6-324-82-33. FAX 358-6-324-82-00. E-mail: vpa@uwasa.fi. Ed. Antero Niemikorpi. Document type: proceedings.

VIERTELJAHRSCHRIFT FUER SOZIAL- UND WIRTSCHAFTSGESCHICHTE. see *SOCIAL SCIENCES: COMPREHENSIVE WORKS*

VIERTELJAHRSCHRIFT FUER SOZIAL- UND WIRTSCHAFTSGESCHICHTE. BEIHEFTE. see *SOCIAL SCIENCES: COMPREHENSIVE WORKS*

VOLUME REVERSAL SURVEY; a comprehensive guide to volume trends in the major markets. see *BUSINESS AND ECONOMICS — Investments*

330.1 NE ISSN 0927-0132
VRIJE UNIVERSITEIT. FACULTEIT DER ECONOMISCHE WETENSCHAPPEN EN ECONOMETRIE. RESEARCH MEMORANDUM. (Editions in Dutch, English) irreg., no.42, 1988. free. Vrije Universiteit, Faculteit der Economische Wetenschappen en Econometrie, De Boelelaan 1105, 1081 HV Amsterdam, Netherlands. FAX 20-6462645. Ed.Bd. Document type: academic/scholarly publication.

WAKAYAMA ECONOMIC REVIEW. see *BUSINESS AND ECONOMICS — Management*

330.1 370 GW ISSN 0174-6170
WIRTSCHAFT UND ERZIEHUNG. 1949. m. DM.52. Heckner Druck und Verlag, Postfach 1559, 38285 Wolfenbuettel, Germany. FAX 05331-800858. Indexed: IBR. Document type: trade publication.
—SWETS. CCC.

330.1 US ISSN 0172-5963
WIRTSCHAFTSPOLITISCHE STUDIEN. (Text in German) 1976. irreg. price varies. Springer-Verlag, 175 Fifth Ave., New York, NY 10010. TEL 212-460-1500. FAX 212-473-6272. (Also: Berlin, Heidelberg, Tokyo and Vienna) (reprint service avail. from ISI) Document type: monographic series.

330.1 309 GW ISSN 0170-3579
WISSENSCHAFTLICHE PAPERBACKS; Sozial- und Wirtschaftsgeschichte. irreg., vol.25, 1996. price varies. Franz Steiner Verlag Wiesbaden GmbH, Birkenwaldstr. 44, 70191 Stuttgart, Germany. TEL 49-711-2582-0. FAX 49-711-2582390. (Subscr. to: Postfach 101061, 70009 Stuttgart, Germany) Ed. Hans Pohl. R&P contact: Sabine Koerner. Document type: monographic series.

XUESHU YUEKAN/ACADEMIC MONTHLY. see *SOCIAL SCIENCES: COMPREHENSIVE WORKS*

ZEITSCHRIFT FUER OSTMITTELEUROPA-FORSCHUNG. see *HISTORY — History Of Europe*

330.1 GW ISSN 0342-3956
ZEITSCHRIFT FUER UNTERNEHMENSGESCHICHTE. BEIHEFTE. irreg., vol.94, 1997. price varies. (Gesellschaft fuer Unternehmensgeschichte e.V., Koeln) Franz Steiner Verlag Wiesbaden GmbH, Birkenwaldstr. 44, 70191 Stuttgart, Germany. TEL 49-711-2582-0. FAX 49-711-2582390. (Subscr. to: Postfach 101061, 70009 Stuttgart, Germany) Ed. H. Pohl. R&P contact: Sabine Koerner. Document type: monographic series.
—BLDSC (9487.480100).

330.1 CC
ZHONGGUO JINGJISHI YANJIU/CHINESE ECONOMIC HISTORY RESEARCH. (Text in Chinese) q. $31.50. Zhongguo Shehui Kexueyuan, Jingji Yanjiusuo - Chinese Academy of Social Sciences, Institute of Economics, 2 Yuetan Beixiaojie, Beijing 100836, People's Republic of China. TEL 895191. (Dist. in US by: China Books & Periodicals, Inc., 2929, 24th St., San Francisco, CA 94110. TEL 415-282-2994) Ed. Wei Jinyu.

ZHONGGUO SHEHUI JINGJISHI YANJIU/JOURNAL OF CHINESE SOCIAL AND ECONOMIC HISTORY. see *HISTORY — History Of Asia*

330 CC ISSN 1003-5230
ZHONGNAN CAIJING DAXUE XUEBAO/CENTRAL-SOUTH UNIVERSITY OF FINANCE AND ECONOMICS. JOURNAL. (Text in Chinese) 1974. bi-m. Y18 (foreign $18). Zhongnan Caijing Daxue - Central-South University of Finance and Economics, 114 Wuluo Lu, Wuchang Qu, Wuhan, Hubei 430064, People's Republic of China. TEL 86-27-8044330. FAX 86-27-8044548. (Dist. outside China by: China National Publishing Industry Trading Corp., P.O. Box 782, Beijing, P.R. China) Ed. Qu Yanwen. adv.; bk.rev. circ. 3,500. Document type: academic/scholarly publication.
Description: Researches contemporary applications and development of Marxist economic theory, explores theoretical problems of economic development and reform in China, and introduces academic developments in the field.
Refereed Serial

BUSINESS AND ECONOMICS — International Commerce

382 GW ISSN 0343-1592
A B C EUROP PRODUCTION. (Text in English, French, German, Italian, Spanish) 1960. a. $210 (effective 1997). A B C Publishing Group, Postfach 100262, 64202 Darmstadt, Germany. TEL 49-6151-3892-0. FAX 49-6151-33164. (Dist. in US by: Western Hemisphere Publishing Corp., Box 847, Hillsboro, OR 97123. TEL 503-640-3736. FAX 503-640-2748) Pub. Margit Selka. adv. circ. 18,000. Document type: directory.
● Also available online. Vendor(s): Data-Star, FIZ Technik.
Also available on CD-ROM.
Formerly (until 1964): A B C Edition Europ Production (ISSN 0065-003X)
Description: Export-import guide covering 40 countries from Albania to the Ukraine.

BUSINESS AND ECONOMICS — INTERNATIONAL COMMERCE

382   SP   ISSN 0001-1207
A F R E. (African Trade Review) (Text and summaries in English, French) 1966. m. $45. Editorial Office, German Perez Carrasco 63, 28027 Madrid, Spain. TEL 1-267-24-03. FAX 1-408-78-37. TELEX 43782 EDOF E. Ed. Arsenio Pardo Rodriguez. adv.; illus. circ. 30,000. **Indexed:** Key to Econ.Sci.

382 332.6   PH
A F T A MONITOR. (ASEAN Free Trade Area) (Text in English) m. $415. Options Publishing Services, 10 Garcia Villa St., San Lorenzo Village, Makati City, Metro Manila, Philippines. TEL 63-2-818-3289. FAX 63-2-819-3752. E-mail: opsi@mnl.sequel.net. Pub. Melva C. Nath. **Document type:** newsletter.
  Description: Monthly guide to trade and investment news, developments and opportunities in ASEAN and the emerging economies of Asia.

382   US
A I B NEWSLETTER. 1958. q. $57 membership. Academy of International Business, c/o James R. Wills, Jr., Exec. Sec., University of Hawaii at Manoa, CBA, 2404 Maile Way, Honolulu, HI 96822-2223. TEL 313-577-4493. FAX 313-577-4641. Ed. Attila Yaprak. adv. circ. 2,300. (back issues avail.) **Document type:** newsletter.

A M L C NEWS. (Australian Meat and Livestock Corporation) see *FOOD AND FOOD INDUSTRIES*

A S A E INTERNATIONAL NEWS. (American Society of Association Executives) see *BUSINESS AND ECONOMICS — Management*

332.6   GW   ISSN 0947-3017
▼**A W - AUSSENWIRTSCHAFTLICHE PRAXIS.** 1995. m. DM.420. Bundesanzeiger Verlag, Breitestr. 78-80, 50667 Koeln, Germany. TEL 0221-2029-0. FAX 0221-2029271. Ed. Hans-Michael Wolfgang. adv.; bk.rev.; index. (back issues avail.) **Document type:** academic/scholarly publication.

382   DK
AARHUS HAVN. 1963. m. DKK 18 per no. (effective 1997). Aarhus Havn, Mindet 2, Postboks 130, DK-8100 Aarhus C, Denmark. TEL 45-86-13-32-66. FAX 45-86-12-76-62. E-mail: dkakeipd@ibmmail.com; URL: http://www.euroports.com/aarhus. adv.; B&W page DKK 3300, color page DKK 6900; trim 126 x 180; adv. contact: Mr. Bruun. circ. 4,100.

332   CN
ABSTRACT OF INTERNATIONAL ECONOMIC TREND ANALYSIS. 1990. q. Can.$60 membership; newsstand price: Can.$25. Maxiplan Financial Club, 12687 52nd Ave., Montreal, PQ H1E 2H6, Canada. Ed. Marcel Wistaff. **Document type:** newsletter.
  Description: Studies international economic activity outlooks, consolidated strategies, global confidence surveys, multinational investment strength and output, multicountry productivity growth and international trade in perspective.

380   UK   ISSN 0001-4907
HC251
ACHIEVEMENT. 1910. 4/yr. £20 (foreign £25) (effective 1997). Response Publishing Group plc, 41-45 Goswell Rd., London EC1V 7EH, England. TEL 44-171-490-0550. Ed. Clive Branson. R&P contact: Stewart McAlpine. adv. contact: James Straker. bk.rev.; illus.; circ. 10,220 (controlled). (also avail. in microfilm from UMI; reprint service avail. from UMI) **Indexed:** Met.Abstr., Rehabil.Lit. **Document type:** trade publication.
  —BLDSC (0576.300000); UMI; UnCover.

382.7   SP   ISSN 0400-5732
ADUANAS; revista de tecnicas aduaneras, comercio exterior y transportes. 1954. 4/yr. 900 ptas.($30) Promotora de Publicaciones, S.A., Evaristo San Miguel 10, 28008 Madrid, Spain. TEL 1-248-05-02. Ed. J. de la Llave de Larra. adv.; stat. circ. 36,000.
  —CINDOC.

658   US   ISSN 0747-7929
HD30.55
ADVANCES IN INTERNATIONAL COMPARATIVE MANAGEMENT. 1984. irreg., vol.11, 1996. $73.25. J A I Press Inc., 55 Old Post Rd., No. 2, Box 1678, Greenwich, CT 06830-1678. TEL 203-661-7602. FAX 203-661-0792. E-mail: jai@jaipress.com. (Subscr. in UK and Europe to: JAI Press Ltd., 38 Tavistock St., Covent Garden, London WC2E 7PB, England. TEL 44-171-379-8834. FAX 44-171-379-8835) Eds. S. Benjamin Prasad, Richard Peterson. **Document type:** monographic series.
  —BLDSC (0709.253300); UnCover. **CCC.**

382   CN
AFRICA - NORTH AMERICA BUSINESS REGISTER. (Text in English, French) 1991. a. $50. P.O. Box 264, Stn. P, Toronto, ON M5S 2S8, Canada. TEL 416-532-5427. FAX 416-532-5427. Ed. Kasekelay Francis Lufuluabo; Pub. Kasekelay Francis Lufuluabo. adv. contact: Norma E. McDonald. index. circ. 2,500. **Document type:** directory, trade publication.
  Former titles (until 1992): Africa - North America Trade Opportunities Directory (ISSN 1183-3963); (until 1992): Africa's Import - Export Trade Opportunities Directory.
  Description: Provides basic financial, trade and demography data, business associations, chambers of commerce, foreign trade representations, key ministries, ports, trade shows and exhibitions within Africa, Canada and the US. Lists trade opportunities.

382   SA   ISSN 1019-0309
AFRICA PRODUCT DIGEST. (Text in English) 1991. a. Reed Business Information South Africa (Pty.) Ltd., P.O. Box 653207, Benmore 2010, South Africa. TEL 27-11-784-1110. FAX 27-11-883-4729. adv. contact: Rosalie Solarsh. tr.lit.; circ. 10,000 (controlled). **Document type:** directory.
  Description: Information on South African products, services and technology available for export. Distributed into Africa, Indian Ocean islands, and the Gulf States.

332.6   US   ISSN 1072-0812
AFRICAN BUSINESS HANDBOOK;* a practical guide to business resources for U.S.-Africa trade and investment. 1992. biennial. (International Trade and Development Counsel) 21st Century Africa, Inc., 818 18th St., N.W., Ste. 810, Washington, DC 20006. TEL 202-429-2083. FAX 202-429-9574. Ed. Michael E.M. Sudarkasa.

382   FR   ISSN 1018-2403
AFRICAN MARKETS. m. Moreux, 190 bd. Haussmann, 75008 Paris, France. TEL 33-1-44959950. FAX 33-1-49539016. TELEX NAVIM 651131 F. E-mail: moreux@club-internet.fr.

382   FR   ISSN 0221-5772
HC800.A1
AFRIQUE ENTREPRISE. (Monthly supplement avail.: Fichier Afrique Entreprise) s-m. (22/yr.). 4000 F. (effective 1997). I C Publications, 10 rue Vineuse, 75784 Paris Cedex 16, France. TEL 33-1-44308100. FAX 33-1-44308111.

ALMANAC OF CHINA'S FOREIGN ECONOMIC RELATIONS AND TRADE. see *BUSINESS AND ECONOMICS — International Development And Assistance*

ALTERNATIVE TRADING NEWS. see *BUSINESS AND ECONOMICS — International Development And Assistance*

332.6   US   ISSN 1079-9133
AMERICAN EXPORT PRODUCTS. (Supplement to: American Export Register) 1987. 3/yr. $120 (included with American Export Register). Thomas Publishing Company, Five Penn Plaza, New York, NY 10001. FAX 212-629-1140. **Document type:** trade publication.
  Former titles (until 1994): A L R - American Literature Review (ISSN 0899-1448); (until 1988): International Literature Review (ISSN 0897-1048)
  Description: Lists brochures and catalogs available from U.S. companies seeking to export their products and services.

382.6   US   ISSN 0272-1163
HF3010
AMERICAN EXPORT REGISTER (YEAR). Abbreviated title: A E R. (Supplement avail.: American Export Products (AEP) (ISSN 1079-9133)) (Index in Arabic, Chinese, English, French, German, Italian, Japanese, Portuguese, Russian, and Spanish) 1945. a. $120 (includes American Export Review). Thomas Publishing Company, Five Penn Plaza, New York, NY 10001. TEL 212-629-1174. FAX 212-629-1140. Ed. Charles Donahue; Pub. Robert E. Ahrensdorf. illus.; index. **Document type:** directory.
  —CISTI.
  Formerly: American Register of Exporters and Importers (ISSN 0065-9967)
  Description: Lists thousands of U.S. companies that export goods and services. Includes product and service listings, as well as import-export services such as banks, cargo carriers, customs house brokers, American embassies and consulates, and chambers of commerce.

AMERICAN FOOD AND AG EXPORTER DIRECTORY. see *AGRICULTURE — Agricultural Economics*

AMERICAN FOOD AND AG EXPORTER MAGAZINE. see *AGRICULTURE — Agricultural Economics*

382   II
AMERICAN MARKET. (Text in English) m. Rs.140($25) Trade Digest Publications, S-185 Greater Kailash II, New Delhi 48, India. TEL 6414185. Ed. C.L. Khanna. circ. 7,500.
  Description: Devoted to promotion of Indo-American trade and economic relations through larger trade.

AMERICAN REVIEW OF INTERNATIONAL ARBITRATION. see *LAW — International Law*

ANALISIS ANUAL DEL MERCADO DEL AZUCAR. see *BUSINESS AND ECONOMICS — Abstracting, Bibliographies, Statistics*

382   UK   ISSN 1350-4819
ANGLO-NORDIC TIMES INTERNATIONAL. 1976. 8/yr. £24 (foreign £43). Peregrine Publishing & Trojan Graphics Co. Ltd., Yorksville, 86A Kingsley Park Terrace, Kingsley Park, Northampton, Northants NN2 7HJ, England. TEL 44-1604-713777. FAX 44-1604-717999. E-mail: nordica@wildnet.co.uk; URL: http://www2.wildnet.co.uk/nordic-times/. Ed. Geoffrey E. Hamilton. R&P contact: Geoffrey E. Hamilton. adv. contact: Anna Maria Amato. bk.rev.; illus.; circ. 5,300 (controlled). (also avail. in diskette format; back issues avail.) **Document type:** trade publication.
  Former titles: Anglo-Nordic Times (ISSN 0964-5748); (until Sep. 1990): Nordic Times International (ISSN 0951-0478); (until 1986): Anglo-Nordic Times; (until 1984): Anglo-Nordic Trade News.
  Description: Specializes in in-depth corporate and product profiles, with special emphasis on companies trading between the U.K., Nordic countries, Baltic states and northern Germany.

382   FR   ISSN 0066-2828
ANNUAIRE DES ENTREPRISES ET ORGANISMES D'OUTRE-MER. 1910. a. 715 Fr. Moreux, 190 bd. Haussmann, 75008 Paris, France. TEL 33-1-44959950. FAX 33-1-49539016. TELEX NAVIM 651131F. E-mail: moreux@club-internet.fr. **Document type:** directory.
  Formerly: Annuaire des Entreprises d'Afrique Noire, des Organismes Officiels et Professionels d'Outre-Mer, des Organismes de Cooperation Francais, Etrangers et Internationaux.
  Description: Directory of export organizations both public and private in Africa.

382   HT
ANNUAIRE DU COMMERCE EXTERIEUR D'HAITI: IMPORTATIONS, EXPORTATIONS. a. Administration Generale des Douanes, Port-au-Prince, Haiti. stat.

382   US
ANNUAL EDITIONS: INTERNATIONAL BUSINESS. 1991. a. $12.95. Dushkin Publishing Group, Sluice Dock, Guilford, CT 06437-9989. TEL 203-453-4351. FAX 203-453-6000. Ed. Fred H. Maidment; Pub. La Nielsen. illus. **Document type:** academic/scholarly publication.
  Refereed Serial

BUSINESS AND ECONOMICS — INTERNATIONAL COMMERCE

382   CC
NUAL REVIEW OF HONG KONG EXTERNAL TRADE. (Text in Chinese, English) 1964. a. HK.$46. Census and Statistics Department, Wanchai Tower, 1 Harbour Rd., Central, Hong Kong, People's Republic of China. TEL 852-25988197.
FAX 852-25987482. (Subscr. to: Director of Information Services, Information Services Department, 28-F Siu On Centre, 188 Lockhart Rd., Wanchai, Hong Kong; People's Republic of China) Ed. Raymond Tse. charts; stat. **Document type:** government publication.
   Formerly (until 1992): Hong Kong Review of Overseas Trade.

332.6   GW   ISSN 0937-2423
SCHRIFTEN FUER DIE AUSSENWIRTSCHAFT. m. DM.198. Deutscher Wirtschaftsdienst, Marienburgerstr. 22, 50968 Cologne, Germany. TEL 49-221-93763-0. FAX 49-221-9376399. (looseleaf format) **Document type:** bulletin.

382 347.7   US   ISSN 0891-8546
KF1632
TITRUST FREEDOM OF INFORMATION LOG. 1982. w. $335 (effective Oct. 1995). Washington Regulatory Reporting Associates, Box 356, Basye, VA 22810. TEL 703-856-2216. FAX 703-856-8331. Ed. William Reuter; Pub. Arthur Amolsch. (fax) **Document type:** newsletter.
●Also available online. Vendor(s): Lexis-Nexis.
—CCC.
   Description: Provides brief summaries of the Freedom of Information Act requests received at the Antitrust Division of the U.S. Department of Justice.

UARIO DE IMPORTACION - EXPORTACION DEL URUGUAY. see BUSINESS AND ECONOMICS — Abstracting, Bibliographies, Statistics

PAREL IMPORT DIGEST. see CLOTHING TRADE

382   US
AB - U S BUSINESS. bi-w. News Circle Publishing House, Box 3684, Glendale, CA 91221. TEL 818-507-0333. FAX 818-246-1936. E-mail: newscirc@pacbell.net. Ed. Joseph R. Haiek. **Document type:** newsletter.
   Description: Briefs American business executives on news, business opportunities, and trade events in the Arab world market.

BITRATION INTERNATIONAL. see LAW — International Law

GENTINA. JUNTA NACIONAL DE CARNES. EXPORTACIONES DE PRODUCTOS GANADEROS. see AGRICULTURE — Poultry And Livestock

382   US
GENTINE-AMERICAN BUSINESS REVIEW DIRECTORY.* 1978. biennial. $25. Argentina American Chamber of Commerce, 10 Rockefeller Plaza, No. 1001, New York, NY 10011-3097. TEL 212-564-3855. Ed. Barry V. Conforte. adv. circ. 15,000. **Document type:** directory.

382   II   ISSN 0066-8230
IA - AFRICA WORLD TRADE REGISTER. (Text in English; classified headings in English, French, German and Spanish) 1970. irreg. £7. Business Publications International, United India Life Building, Box 548, F-Block, Connaught Place, New Delhi 1, India. Ed. K.L. Sahgal. adv. circ. 10,000.
   Description: Contains classified business directory.

382   US   ISSN 0748-6014
IA CABLE. 1984. bi-m. $485. John Vezmar, Ed. & Pub., Box 307, Lake Oswego, OR 97034. **Document type:** newsletter.

332.6   UK
IA PACIFIC DUTY-FREE AND TRAVEL RETAIL WORLD. 1988. bi-m. £74 (overseas £98($180)) (effective 1997). Argus Business Media Ltd., International Trade Publications (Subsidiary of: D M G Exhibitions Group Ltd.), Queensway House, 2 Queensway, Redhill, Surrey RH1 1QS, England.
TEL 44-1737-768611. FAX 44-1737-761989. Ed. Kevin Rozario. adv.: B&W page £1087, color page £1600. circ. 3,000. **Document type:** trade publication.
   Former titles: Asia Pacific Duty-Free Marketing; (until 1992): Asia Pacific Duty-Free (ISSN 0957-1817)

382   US   ISSN 1089-0408
HF1642.55
ASIA PACIFIC ECONOMIC REVIEW; bridging Pacific Rim business & society. 1992. bi-m. $35; newsstand price: $5.95. Zencore, Inc., Box 14089, Seattle, WA 98119. TEL 202-860-4970. FAX 206-860-4895. URL: http://www.moshix2.net/aper/. (Dist. by: Treva Bridges, International Periodicals Distributors, 674 Via de la Valle, Ste. 200, Solana Beach, CA 92075. TEL 619-484-5928. FAX 619-259-7580) Ed. Chris Beer. adv.: B&W page $1499, color page $2499; adv. contact: Mick Matsuzawa. bk.rev.; software rev.; charts; illus.; maps; stat.; tr.lit. circ. 12,500. (back issues avail.) **Document type:** academic/scholarly publication.
●Also available online.
   Formerly (until 1994): Pacific Economic Review.
   Description: Covers U.S. business and trade policy interests in Asia Pacific; emphasis on west coast US.

ASIAN INDUSTRIAL REPORTER. see BUSINESS AND ECONOMICS

ASIAN MANUFACTURERS JOURNAL. see BUSINESS AND ECONOMICS — Production Of Goods And Services

382 338   US   ISSN 1044-8713
HF54.52.A785
ASIAN MARKETS; a guide to company and industry information sources. 1984. irreg., latest 4th ed. $335 (effective 1997). Washington Researchers, Ltd., Box 19005, 20th St. Sta., Washington, DC 20036-9005. TEL 202-333-3499.
FAX 202-625-0656. Ed. M. Newman. R&P contact: Ellen O'Kane. **Document type:** directory.
   Incorporates (in 1991): How to Find Information about Japanese Companies and Industries.
   Description: Informs executives how and where to obtain hard-to-find business information, from the U.S. and elsewhere, on the top 11 Asian nations.

ASPIS; the classified Greek commercial directory. see BUSINESS AND ECONOMICS — Trade And Industrial Directories

ASSOCIATION POUR L'ETUDE DES PROBLEMES D'OUTRE MER. DOCUMENTATION-DEVELOPPEMENT. see POLITICAL SCIENCE — International Relations

382   US
ATLANTA INTERNATIONAL MAGAZINE; the global trade resource for Georgia and the Southeast. 1992. m. $36 (effective Apr. 1995). A.I.M. Communications Inc., 119 Pharr Rd., N.W., Ste. A4, Atlanta, GA 30305-2157. TEL 404-239-9225.
FAX 404-816-9264. Ed. Ken Anderberg. adv. contact: Ken Anderberg. circ. 10,000. (tabloid format; back issues avail.) **Document type:** trade publication.
   Description: Provides how-to information about conducting business overseas. Country-specific market reports; news about international business activity in the Southeast.

382   US   ISSN 1053-2404
ATLANTIC TRADE REPORT & GLOBAL DEFENSE INDUSTRY. 1989. bi-w. $495. Bergerac International Ltd., Rt. One, Box 309, Gainesville, VA 20065. TEL 703-349-2922. FAX 703-349-2922. Ed. J.L.R. Combemale. bk.rev.; index. circ. 335. (back issues avail.) **Document type:** trade publication.
●Also available online. Vendor(s): Information Access Co.
   Formed by the 1990 merger of: Atlantic Trade Report (ISSN 1047-0824); Global Military Industrialization (ISSN 1049-4448)
   Description: Reports on the 1992 economic unification of Europe and its effect on the world economic community. Provides information on legal mechanisms utilized in the unification effort, political responses from involved countries, and opinions from US executives. Examines the relationships between Europe and the United States in the area of high technology.

AUSLAENDISCHES WIRTSCHAFTSRECHT. see LAW — International Law

382   GW
AUSSENHANDEL. 1948. m. free. Bayerische Vereinsbank AG, Zentralbereich Kommunikation und Volkswirtschaft, Kardinal-Faulhaber-Str. 1, 80333 Munich, Germany. TEL 089-2132-5530.
FAX 089-2132-5699. Ed. Manuela Fella. charts; stat. circ. 42,000. (back issues avail.) **Document type:** newsletter.
   Formerly: Vereinsbank Kundendienst.

382   GW   ISSN 0171-8126
AUSSENHANDELSBLAETTER. 1949. bi-m. free. Commerzbank AG, Neue Mainzer Str. 32-36, 60261 Frankfurt a.M., Germany.
TEL 49-69-13622379. FAX 49-69-13622008. circ. 21,000. **Document type:** bulletin.

382   SZ   ISSN 0004-8216
HF35
AUSSENWIRTSCHAFT; Swiss review of international economic relations. (Text in English, German) 1946. 4/yr. 108 SFr. (foreign 142 SFr.); students 54 SFr.(foreign 71 SFr.). Hochschule St. Gallen fuer Wirtschafts- und Sozialwissenschaften, Schweizerisches Institut fuer Aussenwirtschafts-, Struktur- und Regionalforschung, Dufourstr. 48, CH-9000 St. Gallen, Switzerland.
TEL 41-71-2242325. FAX 41-71-2242298. E-mail: hhagen@sgcl1.unisg.ch; URL: http://www.unisg.ch/~siasr; http://www.rueggerverlag.ch. (Subscr. to: Verlag Ruegger, Albisriederstr. 80A, CH-8040 Zurich, Switzerland) Ed. Heinz Hauser. adv.; bk.rev.; index. circ. 1,500. (reprint service avail. from SCH) **Indexed:** ELLIS, IBR, IDA, J. of Econ.Lit., Key to Econ.Sci., P.A.I.S., P.A.I.S.For.Lang.Ind. **Document type:** academic/scholarly publication.
—BLDSC (1792.965000); SWETS.

AUSSENWIRTSCHAFT AKTUELL. see BUSINESS AND ECONOMICS — Chamber Of Commerce Publications

382   GW   ISSN 0178-8876
AUSSENWIRTSCHAFTSBRIEF; Information fuer das Auslandsgeschaeft. 1985. bi-m. DM.198. Deutscher Wirtschaftsdienst, Marienburgerstr. 22, 50968 Cologne, Germany. TEL 49-221-93763-0.
FAX 49-221-9376399. bk.rev. circ. 11,000. (back issues avail.) **Document type:** bulletin.

332.6   GW
AUSSENWIRTSCHAFTSRECHT (REGENSBURG). 5-6/yr. DM.58. Walhalla Fachverlag, Haus an der Eisernen Bruecke, 93059 Regensburg, Germany.
TEL 49-941-5684-0. FAX 49-941-5684111. E-mail: walhalla@walhalla.de; URL: http://www.walhalla.de. adv. circ. 1,600. (looseleaf format) **Document type:** bulletin.

382   GW   ISSN 0937-3438
AUSSENWIRTSCHAFTSRECHT (YEAR); Einfuehrung - Fundstellen - Vorschriftentexte. 1970. a. DM.49.80. Deutscher Wirtschaftsdienst, Marienburgerstr. 22, 50968 Cologne, Germany. TEL 49-221-93763-0. FAX 49-221-9376399. adv.; bk.rev. **Document type:** bulletin.

AUSTRALIA. BUREAU OF STATISTICS. CONSUMER PRICE INDEX: EFFECT OF CHANGES IN PRICES OF IMPORTED ITEMS. see BUSINESS AND ECONOMICS — Abstracting, Bibliographies, Statistics

AUSTRALIA. BUREAU OF STATISTICS. EXPORT PRICE INDEX, AUSTRALIA. see BUSINESS AND ECONOMICS — Abstracting, Bibliographies, Statistics

AUSTRALIA. BUREAU OF STATISTICS. INTERNATIONAL MERCHANDISE TRADE, AUSTRALIA. see BUSINESS AND ECONOMICS — Abstracting, Bibliographies, Statistics

AUSTRALIA. BUREAU OF STATISTICS. INTERNATIONAL TRADE IN SERVICES, AUSTRALIA. see BUSINESS AND ECONOMICS — Abstracting, Bibliographies, Statistics

AUSTRALIA. BUREAU OF STATISTICS. MERCHANDISE IMPORTS, AUSTRALIA: BALANCE OF PAYMENTS BASIS. see BUSINESS AND ECONOMICS — Abstracting, Bibliographies, Statistics

AUSTRALIA. BUREAU OF STATISTICS. PRODUCER AND FOREIGN TRADE PRICE INDEXES: CONCEPTS, SOURCES AND METHODS. see BUSINESS AND ECONOMICS — Abstracting, Bibliographies, Statistics

AUSTRALIA IN BRITAIN. see BUSINESS AND ECONOMICS — Chamber Of Commerce Publications

AUSTRALIAN CUSTOMS LAW AND PRACTICE. see LAW

AUSTRALIAN EXPORTS. see BUSINESS AND ECONOMICS — Trade And Industrial Directories

AUSTRALIAN IMPORTS. see BUSINESS AND ECONOMICS — Trade And Industrial Directories

BUSINESS AND ECONOMICS — INTERNATIONAL COMMERCE

AUSTRALIAN INTERNATIONAL TAX AGREEMENTS. see *LAW*

380 AT ISSN 0045-0944
AUSTRALIAN TRADER. 1964. q. free. (Department of Overseas Trade) Exportad Pty. Ltd., 115-117 Cooper St, Surry Hills, N.S.W. 2010, Australia. Ed. Des McDonald. adv.; circ. 5,500 (controlled).

AUSTRALIAN WOOL EXPORT QUARTERLY REVIEW. see *TEXTILE INDUSTRIES AND FABRICS*

382 AU ISSN 0005-0490
AUSTRIA EXPORT. (Text in English, French and German) 1954. 4/yr. free. (Bundeskammer der Gewerblichen Wirtschaft) Internationale Werbegesellschaft m.b.H., Hoher Markt 12, A-1010 Vienna, Austria. Ed. Traute Franke. circ. 5,000.

332.6 AU
AUSTRIAN TECHNOLOGY REPORT. (Text in English and German) Iglaseegasse 21-23, A-1191 Vienna, Austria. TEL 01-549697. FAX 01-327427. TELEX 134177. Ed. Helmut Tober.

AVANCE DE INFORMACION ECONOMICA. BALANZA COMERCIAL. see *BUSINESS AND ECONOMICS — Abstracting, Bibliographies, Statistics*

AVANCE DE INFORMACION ECONOMICA. INDUSTRIA MAQUILADORA DE EXPORTACION. see *BUSINESS AND ECONOMICS — Abstracting, Bibliographies, Statistics*

THE B B I NEWSLETTER. (Biomedical Business International) see *MEDICAL SCIENCES*

382 GW ISSN 0415-7508
T12.5.G3
B D I DEUTSCHLAND LIEFERT/B D I GERMANY SUPPLIES/B D I L'ALLEMAGNE FOURNIT/B D I ALEMANIA SUMINISTRA; official export register of the Federation of German Industries. (Text in English, French, German and Spanish) 1952. a. DM.145. (Bundesverband der Deutschen Industrie) Verlag W. Sachon, Schloss Mindelburg, 87714 Mindelheim, Germany. TEL 49-8261-999-0. FAX 49-8261-999180. E-mail: sachon@t-online.de; URL: http://www.sachon.de. Ed. Werner Sachon. adv. circ. 15,122. **Document type:** trade publication.
●Also available online. Vendor(s): Data-Star, FIZ Technik.
Also available on CD-ROM.
—CISTI.

382.1 JM ISSN 0259-6776
HG3883.J2
BALANCE OF PAYMENTS OF JAMAICA. a. free. Bank of Jamaica, Balance of Payments Department, P.O. Box 621, King St., Kingston, Jamaica, W.I. TEL 809-922-0750. FAX 809-967-4265. TELEX 2165. illus.; stat.

BALANCE OF PAYMENTS OF SIERRA LEONE. see *BUSINESS AND ECONOMICS — Public Finance, Taxation*

BALANCE OF PAYMENTS OF TRINIDAD AND TOBAGO. see *BUSINESS AND ECONOMICS — Abstracting, Bibliographies, Statistics*

BALANZA DE PAGOS DE ESPANA. see *BUSINESS AND ECONOMICS — Public Finance, Taxation*

BANCO CENTRAL DE VENEZUELA. ANUARIO DE ESTADISTICAS INTERNACIONALES. see *BUSINESS AND ECONOMICS — Abstracting, Bibliographies, Statistics*

382 EC
BANCO CENTRAL DEL ECUADOR. ACUERDOS INTERNACIONALES DE COMERCIO Y PAGOS. irreg. free. Banco Central del Ecuador, Casilla 29C, Sucursal No.15, Quito, Ecuador. TEL 561-521. (Distr. by: Libreria Economia y Cultura, Av. 10 de Agosto, No. 600 y Checa, Quito, Ecuador)

BANK OF JAPAN. BALANCE OF PAYMENTS MONTHLY. see *BUSINESS AND ECONOMICS — Public Finance, Taxation*

382 JA
BANK OF JAPAN. COMMODITIES, WEIGHTS AND LINKED INDEXES OF (YEAR) BASE WHOLESALE PRICE INDEXES. (Text in English, Japanese) every 5 yrs. 1540 Yen. Bank of Japan, Research and Statistics Department - Nippon Ginko, c/o Public Relations Department, 2-1-1 Hongoku-Cho, Nihonbashi, Chuo-ku, Tokyo 103, Japan. TEL 81-3-3292-3753. FAX 81-3-3292-0410. (Dist. by: Tokiwa Sohgoh Service Co., Ltd., Kyodo Bldg., 2-4, 3-chome, Hongokucho, Nihonbashi, Chuo-ku, Tokyo 103, Japan. TEL 81-3-3270-5713. FAX 81-3-3270-5710; Overseas dist. by: Japan Publications Trading Co., Ltd., Book Export No. 2 Dept., P.O. Box 5030 Tokyo International, Tokyo 100-31, Japan. TEL 81-3-3292-3753. FAX 81-3-3290-0410) pp./issue: 230.
Formerly: Bank of Japan. Price Indexes Annual (Appendix).
Description: Contains explanation commodities surveyed and weights in wholesale price indexes, and linked indexes on the basis of 1990.

BANK OF LIBYA. BALANCE OF PAYMENTS. see *BUSINESS AND ECONOMICS — Public Finance, Taxation*

382 FR ISSN 0184-9719
BANQUE AFRIQUE. (Supplement avail.: Fichier Banque Afrique) s-m. (22/yr.). 4200 F. (effective 1997). I C Publications, 10 rue Vineuse, 75784 Paris Cedex 16, France. TEL 33-1-44308100. FAX 33-1-44308111.

BANQUE DE FRANCE. BALANCE DES PAIEMENTS ET LA POSITION EXTERIEURE DE LA FRANCE. see *BUSINESS AND ECONOMICS — Public Finance, Taxation*

382 NE ISSN 0005-5956
BARID HOLLANDA. (Text in Arabic, English and French) 1956. 3/yr. fl.25($12) Van Kouteren's Publishing Co., PO Box 4115, 3006 AC Rotterdam, Netherlands. adv.; illus. circ. 4,000. **Indexed:** Key to Econ.Sci.
Description: Promotes exports from the Netherlands to the Middle-East and Africa.

382 SP
BAYARRI INTERNACIONAL; guia nacional de la exportacion and importacion. 1973. s-a. 3000 ptas. Publicaciones Bayarri, Angel Guimera 8, Valencia 8, Spain. Ed. Vicente Bayarri. adv.; abstr.; bibl.; charts; illus.; tr.lit.

332.6 GW
BEGLEITPAPIERE FUER AUSFUHRSENDUNGEN. 1956. 10/yr. DM.168. Mendel Verlag, Robensstr. 39, 52070 Aachen, Germany. TEL 49-241-154355. FAX 49-241-154355. (looseleaf format) **Document type:** trade publication.
●Also available on CD-ROM.
Description: All necessary rules and regulations for exporting to foreign countries.

382 BE ISSN 0775-1443
TS1
BELGIUM: ECONOMIC AND COMMERCIAL INFORMATION. (Editions in Dutch, English, French, German and Spanish) q. free. Office Belge du Commerce Exterieur, 162 bd. Emile Jacqmain, 1210 Brussels, Belgium. TEL 32-2-2063511. FAX 32-2-2031812. circ. 30,000. **Document type:** government publication.
—UnCover.
Formerly: Belgium: Economic and Technical Information (ISSN 0005-8491)

380 SZ
BEST BUSINESS LOCATIONS. (Text in English) 1990. a. 100 SFr. S Q P SA, Av. de Rumine 5-7, CH-1005 Lausanne, Switzerland. TEL 021-3121701. FAX 021-3122147. Ed. Christine Pulvermacher; Pub. Ronald Cicurel. adv. contact: Pierre Blanchet. **Document type:** trade publication.

382 SW ISSN 1100-3006
BEST 'N' MOST IN D F S. (Duty Free Shopping) (Text in English) 1980. a. £150 (effective 1997). Generation AB, Storgatan 3, S-891 33 Oernskoeldsvik, Sweden. TEL 46-660-10320. FAX 46-660-84811. E-mail: best.n.most@ generation.se. Ed. Yngve Bia. adv.; charts; stat.; index. (back issues avail.) **Document type:** trade publication.
Former titles: Duty and Tax-Free Shop World Guide Series (ISSN 0349-2737); Duty and Tax-Free Shop World Review.

382 II ISSN 0006-0542
BHUSHAN'S WORLD TRADE ENQUIRIES. (Text in English) 1961. bi-m. Rs.30($4.50) B. Bhushan Lal, Ed. & Pub., 738 Mammaran St., Jagadhri, Haryana, India. adv.; tr.lit. circ. 1,000. (avail. on records)

BIBLIOEXPORT. see *PUBLISHING AND BOOK TRADE*

382 US
BOLLETTINO COMMERCIO ESTERO. s-m. free. Camera di Commercio, Industria, Artigianato e Agricoltura di Forli, Corso della Repubblica, 5, 47100 Forli, Italy. TEL 0543-713111. FAX 0543-713416.

BOTSWANA. CENTRAL STATISTICS OFFICE. EXTERNAL TRADE STATISTICS. see *BUSINESS AND ECONOMICS — Abstracting, Bibliographies, Statistics*

BOUT DE PAPIER. see *BUSINESS AND ECONOMICS — International Development And Assistance*

BOYCOTT LAW BULLETIN. see *LAW — International Law*

BRASILIANS JOURNAL. see *ETHNIC INTERESTS*

382 US ISSN 1089-6678
▼**BRAZIL PROJECT ADVISOR.** 1996. m. $595 (effective 1997). Latin American Information Services, Inc., 159 W. 53rd St., 28th Fl., New York, NY 10019. TEL 212-765-5520. FAX 212-765-2927. URL: http://www.lais.com.
Description: Identifies infrastructure investment opportunities arising from privatization and deregulation in Brazil.

BRAZILIAN AMERICAN WHO'S WHO; companies in the United States and their subsidiaries and affiliates in Brazil. see *BUSINESS AND ECONOMICS — Trade And Industrial Directories*

382 BL
BRAZILIAN EXPORT MARKET. (Text in English, Portuguese, Spanish) 1982. a. $120. (Brazilian Foreign Trade Association) Editora Pesquisa e Industria Ltda., Rua Martin Fontes, 230, 1o fl., 01050 Sao Paulo SP, Brazil. TEL 011-259-0333. FAX 011-256-8681. Ed. Hanibal Haddad. adv. circ. 30,000. (back issues avail.)
Description: General information of use to business people interested in importing from Brazil. Lists Brazilian exporters.

BREACH AND ADAPTATION OF INTERNATIONAL BUSINESS CONTRACTS; an introduction to Lex Mercatoria. see *LAW — International Law*

382 UK ISSN 0045-2866
BRITAIN AND OVERSEAS. 1971. q. £12($15) Economic Research Council, 239 Shaftsbury Ave., London WC2H 8PJ, England. TEL 0171-439-0271. Ed. James Bourlet. adv. contact: James Bourlet. bk.rev.; charts. circ. 500. (also avail. in microform from RPI) **Document type:** academic/scholarly publication.

BRITAIN'S TOP JAPANESE-OWNED COMPANIES. see *BUSINESS AND ECONOMICS — Trade And Industrial Directories*

BRITISH EXPORTS/EXPORTATIONS BRITANNIQUES/BRITISCHER EXPORT/EXPORTACIONES BRITANICAS. see *BUSINESS AND ECONOMICS — Trade And Industrial Directories*

382 CC
BRITISH INDUSTRY. (Text in Chinese, English; summaries in English) 1968. 3/yr. free. (Sino-British Trade Council, UK) China Translation and Printing Services Ltd., G.P.O. Box 4013, Hong Kong, People's Republic of China. circ. 10,000.

382 UK
BRITISH INVISIBLE EXPORTS COUNCIL. ANNUAL REPORT. 1968. a. free. British Invisible Exports Council, Windsor House, 39 King St., London EC2V 8DQ, England. TEL 071-600-1198. FAX 071-606-4248. TELEX 941-3342-BIE-G. illus. stat. circ. 3,500.
Formerly: Committee on Invisible Exports. Annual Report (ISSN 0308-4892)

BUSINESS AND ECONOMICS — INTERNATIONAL COMMERCE

382   NE   ISSN 1380-6564
BUITENLANDSE MARKTEN. 1970. fortn. fl.185 (foreign fl.320) (effective 1994). (Ministerie van Economische Zaken, Exportbevorderings- en Voorlichtendienst (EVD)) Samsom BedrijfsInformatie B.V., Postbus 4, 2400 MA Alphen aan den Rijn, Netherlands. TEL 31-172-466800. Ed. Frans van Leeuwen. adv.; bk.rev. **Document type:** government publication, trade publication.
— SWETS.
   Former titles: Export Magazine (ISSN 0168-7166); (until 1983): Wereldmarkt (ISSN 0043-2741); Economische Voorlichting; Nieuws van Buitenlandse Markten.
   Description: Provides information on export and foreign markets. Includes listings of national and international events, and relevant new publications.

382   FR   ISSN 0997-5047
BULLETIN JOLY MENSUEL D'INFORMATION DES SOCIETES. m. 1000 F. (effective 1997). Joly Editions, 1 av. Franklin D. Roosevelt, 75008 Paris, France. TEL 33-1-44951620. FAX 33-1-45638939. Dir. Daniel Lepeltier. **Document type:** bulletin.

382   FR   ISSN 0007-5264
BULLETIN QUOTIDIEN D'AFRIQUE. 1965. d. 11400 F. (foreign 14640 F.) (effective 1997). Agence France-Presse, 13 Place de la Bourse, B.P. 20, 75061 Paris Cedex 2, France. TEL 40-41-46-46. TELEX 210064 AFPA.
   Formerly: Bulletin Quotidien d'Outre Mer.

338.91   US   ISSN 0190-6275
HF1   CODEN: BUAMDM
BUSINESS AMERICA; the magazine of international trade. 1880. m. $50 (foreign $62.50) (effective 1996). U.S. Department of Commerce, 14th St. between Constitution Ave. and Pennsylvania Ave., N.W., Washington, DC 20230. TEL 202-482-3251. FAX 202-482-5819. URL: http://www.ita.doc.gov/bizam/bizam.html. Subscr. to: Superintendent of Documents, U.S. Government Printing Office, Box 371954, Pittsburgh, PA 15250-7954. TEL 202-512-1800. FAX 202-512-2250) Ed. Douglas Carroll. R&P contact: Cynthai Belechak. bk.rev.; bibl. circ. 15,000. (also avail. in microfiche from CIS; back issues avail.; reprint service avail. from CIS,UMI,WSH) **Indexed:** ABI Inform., Amer.Bibl.Slavic & E.Eur.Stud., Amer.Stat.Ind. (1974-), B.P.I., BPIA, Bus.Ind., C.L.I., Data Process.Dig., Ind.U.S.Gov.Per., Key to Econ.Sci., Leg.Per., Mag.Ind., Mid.East: Abstr.& Ind., Tr.& Indus.Ind. **Document type:** government publication, trade publication.
●Also available online. Vendor(s): Dow Jones News Retrieval, Information Access Co., Knight-Ridder Information, Inc., UMI.
—BLDSC (2933.178000); KR SourceOne; SWETS; UMI; UnCover.
   Former titles: Business Today; Commerce America (ISSN 0361-0438); Commerce Today (ISSN 0020-6385); International Commerce.
   Description: Helps US exporters penetrate overseas markets by providing them with information on opportunities for trade and methods of doing business in foreign nations.

382   US
BUSINESS AND ENVIRONMENT. irreg. $125 to non-members. United States Council for International Business, 1212 Ave. of the Americas, New York, NY 10036-1689. TEL 212-354-4480. FAX 212-575-0327. **Document type:** bulletin.

332.6   IE   ISSN 0791-9611
BUSINESS AND EXPORTING. 1979. m. £20 (foreign £35). (Irish Exporters Association) Jude Publications Ltd., Jude House, Tara St., Dublin 2, Ireland. TEL 01-6713500. FAX 01-6713074. Ed. Grace Heneghan. adv. circ. 10,000. **Document type:** bulletin.
   Formerly: Irish Exporter (ISSN 0332-0979)

332.6   US   ISSN 1041-8482
HF1
BUSINESS & THE CONTEMPORARY WORLD. 1988. 4/yr. $100 (foreign $124) (effective 1998). John Wiley & Sons, Inc., 605 Third Ave., New York, NY 10158. TEL 212-850-6645. FAX 212-850-6021. E-mail: subinfo@jwiley.com; URL: http://www.wiley.com. Ed. Herbert L. Sawyer. circ. 800. (back issues avail.) **Document type:** academic/scholarly publication.
—UnCover. CCC.
   Description: Relationships between business communities and other forces in society examined and analyzed on an international level.
   Refereed Serial

332.6 364   US   ISSN 1054-4216
HD38.7
BUSINESS ESPIONAGE REPORT; controls and countermeasures training for managers. 1987. m. $96. Business Espionage Controls & Countermeasures Association (BECCA), Box 55582, Seattle, WA 98155-0582. TEL 206-364-4672. FAX 206-367-3316. Ed. Will Johnson. bk.rev.; video rev.; software rev.; illus.; index every 3 yrs. (looseleaf format; back issues avail.) **Document type:** newsletter.
   Description: Contains training news, trends, and other information of business espionage as well as controls and countermeasures.
   Refereed Serial

338 382   US   ISSN 1351-8755
BUSINESS EUROPE. 1960. bi-w. £675($1195) Economist Intelligence Unit, 111 W. 57th St., New York, NY 10019. TEL 212-554-0600; 800-938-4685. FAX 212-586-1182. TELEX 175567. URL: http://www.eiu.com. (UK addr.: Economist Intelligence Unit Ltd., Subscriptions Dept., P.O. Box 200, Harold Hill, Romford, Essex RM3 8UX, England. TEL 44-171-830-1007. FAX 44-1708-371-850) (also avail. in microform from UMI,WMP). **Indexed:** Cont.Pg.Manage., ELLIS, Key to Econ.Sci. **Document type:** newsletter.
●Also available online. Vendor(s): Knight-Ridder Information, Inc., Lexis-Nexis.
—UnCover.
   Incorporates (1964-1992): European Trends (ISSN 0014-3162) & Management Europe.
   Description: Management advisory report for executives responsible for European operations, with latest issues, trends, policies, and corporate strategies in 16 countries, EEC developments and forecasts for each country and industrial sector. Covers finance, marketing, taxation, personnel, organization, politics and actual corporate experience.

332.6   UK
BUSINESS EYE. 1992. bi-m. free. (Department of Trade and Industry) Westoning House Ltd., 91-93 Charterhouse St., London EC1M 6HR, England. TEL 44-171-336-7212. FAX 44-171-336-7211. Ed. Steve Hurst. R&P contact: Steve Hurst. adv. contact: David Chandler. circ. 15,000. (back issues avail.) **Document type:** trade publication.
   Description: Promotes U.K. trade and investment interests in South Asia.

BUSINESS LATIN AMERICA; weekly report to managers of Latin American operations. see BUSINESS AND ECONOMICS — Economic Situation And Conditions

382   US
THE BUSINESS LINK. (Text in English, Spanish) 1985. q. 7000 ptas.($42) Spain - U.S. Chamber of Commerce Inc., Empire State Building, Ste. 3514, 350 Fifth Ave., New York, NY 10118-0110. TEL 212-967-2170. FAX 212-564-1415. Ed. Manuel A. Gonzalez. adv.; charts; illus.; stat. circ. 2,000. (also avail. in microfiche) **Indexed:** SRI.
   Formerly: Spain - U.S. Trade Bulletin (ISSN 0561-5313)
   Description: Provides a business to business forum between the United States and Spain.

382   US   ISSN 1350-7354
HF3756
BUSINESS MIDDLE EAST. bi-w. £565($925) Economist Intelligence Unit, 111 W. 57th St., New York, NY 10019. TEL 212-554-0600; 800-938-4685. FAX 212-586-1182. TELEX 175567. URL: http://www.eiu.com. (UK addr.: Economist Intelligence Unit Ltd., Subscriptions Dept., P.O. Box 200, Harold Hill, Romford, Essex RM3 8UX, England. TEL 44-171-830-1007. FAX 44-1708-371-850) Ed. David Johnson.
   Incorporates (in Jan. 1993): Iran Monitor (ISSN 0969-1626); Which was formerly: Business International Iran Service & Saudi Arabia Monitor (ISSN 0969-1634) & B I - Turkey Monitor (ISSN 0969-157X); Which was formerly: Turkey Monitor.
   Description: Identifies and tracks business issues to keep companies abreast of changes, developments and opportunities in the Middle East. For decision makers who wish to enter the market or expand their presence there.

BUSINESS MONITOR: GUIDE TO THE CLASSIFICATION OF OVERSEAS TRADE STATISTICS. see BUSINESS AND ECONOMICS — Abstracting, Bibliographies, Statistics

BUSINESS MONITOR: OVERSEAS DIRECT INVESTMENT. see BUSINESS AND ECONOMICS — Abstracting, Bibliographies, Statistics

BUSINESS MONITOR: OVERSEAS TRADE STATISTICS OF THE UNITED KINGDOM (ANNUAL REVISION). see BUSINESS AND ECONOMICS — Abstracting, Bibliographies, Statistics

BUSINESS MONITOR: OVERSEAS TRADE STATISTICS OF THE UNITED KINGDOM (QUARTERLY REVISION). see BUSINESS AND ECONOMICS — Abstracting, Bibliographies, Statistics

382   AT   ISSN 1320-0801
BUSINESS NEWS. 1983. fortn. Aus.$59 (foreign Aus.$105) (effective 1997). News Illustrated, P.O. Box 50, Northbridge, W.A. 6865, Australia. TEL 61-9-3281388. FAX 61-9-2276503. Ed. Harry Kleyn. R&P contact: Harry Kleyn. adv. contact: Wendy Keys. circ. 16,500. (tabloid format; back issues avail.) **Document type:** newspaper.
   Formerly (until 1992): W.A. Business World (ISSN 0729-8374)
   Description: Business publication aimed at small- to medium-sized business operators.

658 381   SI   ISSN 0129-4202
BUSINESS OPPORTUNITIES. 1977. m. S.$130($111) in Asia; elsewhere S.$150($129). World-Wide Import-Export Promotion Centre, Box 503, Marine Parade P.O., Singapore 9144, Singapore. FAX 65-241-3982. Ed. E. L. Tay. adv. circ. 35,000. **Document type:** trade publication.
   Description: Contains hundreds of import and export opportunities throughout the world.

332.6   CC
BUSINESS P R C; an informative bridge between China and the world. (Text in English) 1978. q. HK.$250($90) Enterprise International, 1604 Eastern Commercial Centre, 393-407 Hennessy Rd., Hong Kong, People's Republic of China. TEL 852-2573-4161. FAX 852-2838-3469. TELEX 66299-EIN-HX. Ed. C.P. Ho. adv. circ. 27,000. **Document type:** trade publication.

382 330.947   US   ISSN 1084-9246
HF3630.2
▼**BUSINESS RUSSIA (CHICAGO)**; doing business in Russia and the newly independent states. 1995. m. $29.95. Russian American Publications, Inc., 1415 N. Dayton St., Chicago, IL 60622. TEL 312-266-1716. FAX 312-266-1887. E-mail: torchy2@aol.com. Ed.Bd.; Pub. James M. Franklin. adv.; illus. circ. 10,000. **Document type:** consumer publication.
   Description: For Americans doing business in the former Soviet Union. Covers banking and finance, politics, laws and regulations, taxation, infrastructure and transportation.

BUSINESS AND ECONOMICS — INTERNATIONAL COMMERCE

382 NE ISSN 1044-498X
BUSINESS STUDIES ON THE U.S.S.R. irreg., latest vol.2. (Worldwide Information Systems, Inc.) Gordon and Breach - Harwood Academic, Amsteldisk 166, 1st Fl., 1079 LH Amsterdam, Netherlands. (Subscr. to: International Publishers Distributor, Box 32160, Newark, NJ 07102. TEL 800-545-8398. FAX 215-750-6343) Ed. Robert Starr. **Document type:** monographic series.
 Refereed Serial

BUSINESS VENEZUELA'S CORPORATE HANDBOOK. see BUSINESS AND ECONOMICS — Investments

BUSINESS WEEK - CHINA. see BUSINESS AND ECONOMICS

332.6 BG
BUSINESSMAN. m. G.P.O. Box 2355, Dhaka - 2, Bangladesh. TEL 231345. FAX 880-2-833297. TELEX 642459 COMP BJ.

382 341 UK ISSN 0142-6796
BUYER. 1979. m. £155 (foreign £180) (effective 1997). Monitor Press Ltd., Suffolk House, Church Field Rd., Sudbury, Suffolk CO10 6YA, England. TEL 44-1787-378607. FAX 44-1787-880201. (back issues avail.) **Document type:** newsletter.
 —BLDSC (2936.300000).
 Description: For specialists responsible for purchasing decisions in commerce, industry and public services. Covers new law, new regulations, statutory instruments and ministerial orders.

382 IT ISSN 0007-7380
BUYERS' GUIDE. 1962. m. Ente Italiano per lo Sviluppo dell'Esportazione, Piazzale Giotto 8, 06100 Perugia, Italy. illus.; mkt.; tr.lit. circ. 9,500.

382 RU ISSN 0320-4529
BYULLETEN' INOSTRANNOI KOMMERCHESKOI INFORMATSII. Short title: B I K I. 1948. 156/yr. $597 (effective 1998). Vsesoyuznyi Nauchno-Issledovatel'skii Kon'yunkturnyi Institut, Ul. Pudovkina 4, 119285 Moscow, Russia. TELEX 64411380. (Dist. by: Mezhdunarodnaya Kniga, B. Yakimanka 39, 117049 Moscow, Russia) (Co-sponsor: Ministerstvo Vneshnikh Ekonomicheskikh Svyazei) Ed. V. Smirnov. adv.; bk.rev.; charts; stat. circ. 5,700.

C G A - CANADA RESEARCH FOUNDATION. STUDY PAPERS. (Certified General Accountants' Association of Canada) see BUSINESS AND ECONOMICS — Accounting

C I E S FOOD BUSINESS NEWS. (Comite International des Entreprises a Succursales) see FOOD AND FOOD INDUSTRIES

382 UK ISSN 1357-2539
DK285
C I S OIL AND GAS REPORT. 1990. 8/yr. £375($750) Argument and Facts Media Ltd., P.O. Box 35, Hastings, E. Sussex TN34 2UX, England. TEL 44-1424-442741. FAX 44-1424-442913. E-mail: 100104.1406@compuserve.com. Ed. Stuart Christie; Pub. Stuart Christie. R&P contact: Stuart Christie. **Document type:** newsletter.
 Formerly: Arguments and Facts International (ISSN 0957-0020)
 Description: Provides business intelligence and assessements of oil and gas exploration and development within the Commonwealth of Independent States.

C I T B A NEWSLETTER. (Customs and International Trade Bar Association) see LAW — International Law

C I T RULES. (Court of International Trade) see LAW — International Law

C I T TEST CASE RECORD. (Court of International Trade) see LAW — International Law

382 US ISSN 0263-3701
HC244
C O M E C O N DATA. (Council for Mutual Economic Assistance) biennial; alternates with C O M E C O N Foreign Trade Data (ISSN 0891-3404). price varies. (Vienna Institute for Comparative Economic Studies) Greenwood Publishing Group Inc., (Subsidiary of: Greenwood Publishing Group Inc.), 88 Post Rd. W., Box 5007, Westport, CT 06881-5007. TEL 203-226-3571. FAX 203-222-1502.

382 US
C O M E C O N FOREIGN TRADE DATA. (Council for Mutual Economic Assistance) 1980. biennial; alternates with C O M E C O N Data (ISSN 0263-3701). price varies. (Vienna Institute for Comparative Economic Studies) Greenwood Press, Inc. (Subsidiary of: Greenwood Publishing Group Inc.), Box 5007, 88 Post Rd. W., Westport, CT 06881-5007. TEL 203-226-3571. FAX 203-222-1502. charts. (back issues avail.)

CAIMAO JINGJI/FINANCE AND TRADE ECONOMICS. see BUSINESS AND ECONOMICS — Banking And Finance

332.6 CN
CALGARY EXPORTERS DIRECTORY. 1985. q. Can.$20. Calgary Economic Development Authority, P.O. Box 2100, Sta. M, Calgary, AB T2P 2M5, Canada. TEL 403-221-7821. FAX 403-221-7837. **Document type:** directory.

CALIFORNIA INTERNATIONAL TRADE REGISTER. see BUSINESS AND ECONOMICS — Trade And Industrial Directories

382 FR ISSN 0241-0257
CAMEROUN SELECTION. (Supplement avail.: Fichier Cameroun Selection) s-m. (22/yr.). 4200 F. (effective 1997). I C Publications, 10 rue Vineuse, 75784 Paris Cedex 16, France. TEL 33-1-44308100. FAX 33-1-44308111.

382 614.7 CN ISSN 0846-5991
KE6096.A13
CANADA. CANADIAN INTERNATIONAL TRADE TRIBUNAL. ANNUAL REPORT. (Text in English and French) 1969. a. free. Canadian International Trade Tribunal, 333 Laurier Ave. W., Ottawa, ON K1A 0G7, Canada. TEL 613-993-7872. FAX 613-990-2439. E-mail: secretary@citt.gc.ca; URL: http://www.citt.gc.ca. Ed. Manon Carpentier. R&P contact: Michel Granger. **Document type:** government publication.
 Former titles (until 1989): Canada. Canadian Import Tribunal. Annual Report (ISSN 0846-6629); Canada. Anti-Dumping Tribunal. Annual Report.

382 CN ISSN 0843-6509
CANADA. CANADIAN INTERNATIONAL TRADE TRIBUNAL BULLETIN/CANADA. TRIBUNAL CANADIEN DU COMMERCE EXTERIEUR. BULLETIN. q. free. Canadian International Trade Tribunal, 333 Laurier Ave. W., Ottawa, ON K1A 0G7, Canada. TEL 613-993-7872. FAX 613-990-2439. E-mail: secretary@citt.gc.ca; URL: http://www.citt.gc.ca. Ed. Manon Carpentier. adv. contact: Michel Granger. **Document type:** government publication.

CANADA. GRAIN COMMISSION. CORPORATE SERVICES. CANADIAN GRAIN EXPORTS. see AGRICULTURE — Abstracting, Bibliographies, Statistics

382 CN ISSN 0847-0510
CANADA AND INTERNATIONAL RELATIONS. irreg., vol.9, 1994. price varies. University of British Columbia Press, 6344 Memorial Rd., Vancouver, BC V6T 1Z2, Canada. TEL 604-822-3259. FAX 800-668-0821. Ed. Jean Wilson. R&P contact: Jean Wilson. TEL 604-822-6376. adv. contact: Berit Kraus. **Document type:** monographic series.

382 CN
CANADA JAPAN BUSINESS JOURNAL. (Text in English, Japanese) 1990. 6/yr. Van Network Ltd., 220 Cambie St., Ste. 370, Vancouver, BC V6B 2M9, Canada. TEL 604-688-2468. FAX 604-688-1487. Ed. Taka Aoki. adv.: B&W page Can.$2495, color page Can.$3090; trim 11 3/8 x 17 1/2. circ. 10,858. (tabloid format)

CANADA - U S OUTLOOK. see BUSINESS AND ECONOMICS — Economic Situation And Conditions

332.6 CN ISSN 0840-5859
HD9985.C3
CANADA'S INTERNATIONAL TRANSACTIONS IN SERVICES. 1987. a. Can.$35($42) (foreign 49). Statistics Canada, Operations and Integration Division, Circulation Management, Jean Talon Bldg., 2-C12, Tunney's Pasture, Ottawa, ON K1A 0T6, Canada. TEL 613-951-7277; 800-267-6677. FAX 613-951-1584. URL: http://www.statcan.ca. adv. contact: Kathryn Bonner. **Document type:** government publication.
 Description: Contains comprehensive source on international service transactions aggregate data from 1969. Major categories include travel, freight and shipping, business services and government transactions.

382 CN ISSN 0831-4527
CANADIAN FREE TRADER. 1986. m. Can.$125 (effective 1997). Intratech (Subsidiary of: E L LittleJohn and Associates), Minto Place Postal Outlet, Box 56067, Ottawa, ON K1R 7Z1, Canada. TEL 613-235-9183. FAX 613-594-3857. Ed. B. Wrangham. adv. contact: J. Gillmore. circ. 250. (back issues avail.) **Document type:** newsletter.
 Incorporates: Canadian Free Trader International Supplement (ISSN 1183-2088)
 Description: Covers Canada, the US and Mexico.

CANADIAN INTERNATIONAL TRADE DIRECTORY. see BUSINESS AND ECONOMICS — Trade And Industrial Directories

CARGOVISION. see TRANSPORTATION — Air Transport

338 UK ISSN 0142-4742
F2155
CARIBBEAN INSIGHT. 1977. m. £90($150) West India Committee, Nelson House, 8-9 Northumberland St., London WC2N 5RA, England. TEL 44-171-976-1493. FAX 44-171-976-1541. Ed. Rod Prince. R&P contact: Rod Prince. adv. contact: Geraldine Flower. bk.rev. circ. 1,000. **Document type:** newsletter.
 Incorporates: Caribbean Chronicle; Which was formerly: West Indies Chronicle (ISSN 0043-3152); West India Committee.
 Description: Covers economic and political developments in the Caribbean.

CARIBBEAN STUDIES NEWSLETTER. see POLITICAL SCIENCE — International Relations

382 338.91 330.9 US ISSN 8756-324X
CARIBBEAN UPDATE. 1985. m. $108 to academics; institutions $216. Kal Wagenheim, Ed. & Pub., 52 Maple Ave., Maplewood, NJ 07040. TEL 201-762-1565; 800-647-9900. FAX 201-762-9585. bk.rev.; circ. controlled. (back issues avail.) **Document type:** newsletter.
 ●Also available online. Vendor(s): Information Access Co.
 —CCC.
 Description: Covers business, economic and political news in the Caribbean and Central America.

382 BL
CARTA INFORMATIVA. 1976. m. free to qualified personnel. Camara de Comercio Arabe Brasileira - Brazilian Arab Chamber of Commerce, Av. Paulista 326, 17 andar, CEP 01310-902 Sao Paulo SP, Brazil. TEL 55-11-283-4066. FAX 55-11-288-8110. TELEX 011-34379 CCAB BR. Ed. Antonio Carlos D. Greggio. adv.; bk.rev. circ. 10,000.
 Formerly (until 1992): Arabe.

382 AU
CASH. 1984. m. S.260. Manstein Zeitschriften Verlagsgesellschaft mbH, Brunner Feldstr. 45, A-2380 Perchtoldsdorf, Austria. TEL 43-1-86648-0. FAX 43-1-8664839. circ. 27,000. **Document type:** trade publication.

CASPIAN BRIEF. see BUSINESS AND ECONOMICS — Economic Situation And Conditions

382 IT
CATALOGO UNIFICATO. 1974. a. L.33000. Commercianti Italiani Filatelici, Via Priv. Maria Teres 11, Milan, Italy. TEL 39-2-877139. FAX 39-2-72022135. Ed. Igino Lottini. adv.: B&W page L.3400000, color page L.5400000; adv. contact: Paolo De Ambrosi. circ. 29,582.

CENTRAL AND EASTERN EUROPEAN LEGAL MATERIALS. see LAW — International Law

BUSINESS AND ECONOMICS — INTERNATIONAL COMMERCE

382   UK
CENTRAL - EAST EUROPE BUSINESS ANALYST. m. £89($175) Debos Oxford Publications Ltd., 31 Warnborough Rd., Oxford OX2 6JA, England.
    Formerly: East - West Business Analyst.
    Description: Analyzes economic conditions in the Commonwealth of Independent States, formerly U.S.S.R., and in central and eastern Europe. Monitors all international contracts involving the region. Provides detailed trade and production statistics.

332.6   AU
CERCLE DIPLOMATIQUE INTERNATIONAL. m. Schmidt GmbH, Elisabethstr. 13, A-1010 Vienna, Austria. TEL 01-5877707. FAX 01-5870752. TELEX 116036. circ. 20,000.

332.6   SZ
CH-D WIRTSCHAFT. 11/yr. Handelskammer Deutschland - Schweiz, Toedistr. 60, CH-8002 Zurich, Switzerland. TEL 41-1-2213702. FAX 41-1-2213766. Ed. Martin Theurer. circ. 5,200. **Document type:** bulletin.

382   FR
CHAMPAGNE - ARDENNE GUIDE DE L'EXPORTATEUR. a. 150 F. Chambre Regionale de Commerce et d'Industrie Champagne - Ardenne, Direction de la Communication, 10 rue de Chastillon, B.P. 537, 51011 Chalons-sur-Marne Cedex. TEL 33-3-26693340. FAX 33-3-26693369.

382   US
CHASE WORLD GUIDE FOR EXPORTERS. (Includes supplementary bulletins) a. $535. Global Business Communications, Box 99, Gillette, NJ 07933. TEL 908-665-2255. FAX 908-464-9363. Ed. Carol R. Cline.

382 660   II   ISSN 0009-2207
CHEMEXCIL EXPORT BULLETIN. 1967. m. Rs.200($6.06) Basic Chemicals, Pharmaceuticals & Cosmetics Export Promotion Council, Jhansi Castle, 4th Fl., 7 Cooperage Rd., Bombay 400 039, India. TEL 202-1288. FAX 202-6684. TELEX 011-4047. Ed. S. Srinivasan. adv. circ. 5,500.

382 660   II   ISSN 0531-5980
CHEMICALS AND ALLIED PRODUCTS EXPORT PROMOTION COUNCIL. EXPORTERS DIRECTORY. (Text in English) a. Chemicals and Allied Products Export Promotion Council, World Trade Centre, 14-1B Ezra St, Calcutta 700001, India.

382   US   ISSN 0884-4488
HC191
CHILE ECONOMIC REPORT. 1967. m. free. Corporacion de Fomento de la Produccion, Communications Department, 1 World Trade Center, Ste. 5151, New York, NY 10048. TEL 212-938-0555. FAX 212-938-0568. Ed. Marco A. Vallejo. circ. 8,500. (also avail. in microform from UMI.) **Indexed:** Key to Econ.Sci. **Document type:** newsletter.
—UMI.

332.6   CL   ISSN 0716-288X
CHILE, EXPORTACIONES INVERSIONES ECONOMIA. English edition: Chile, Exports Investments Economy (ISSN 0716-3304) 1982. bi-m. Ministerio de Relaciones Exteriores, Direccion de Promocion de Exportaciones, Alameda Bernardo O'Higgins 1315, 2o piso, Santiago, Chile. TEL 696-0043. Ed. Carmen Marticorena. circ. 16,250.

382   UK   ISSN 0952-9756
CHINA - BRITAIN TRADE REVIEW. 1964. m. £150 in Europe; elsewhere £180 (effective 1997 & 1998). China - Britain Trade Group, Abford House, 4th Fl., 15 Wilton Rd., London SW1V 1LT, England. TEL 44-171-828-5176. FAX 44-171-630-5780. Ed. Janet Kealey. R&P contact: Janet Kealey. adv.; bk.rev.; stat. circ. 6,000. **Document type:** trade publication.
—BLDSC (3180.117000).
    Formerly: Sino-British Trade Review (ISSN 0583-4279)
    Description: Focuses on China's economic development and opportunities for foreign companies there.

382   US   ISSN 0731-7700
CODEN: CHBTD2
CHINA BUSINESS AND TRADE. 1979. s-m. $367.20 to academic institutions (Canada and Mexico $377.20; elsewhere $397.20); others $459 (Canada and Mexico $469; elsewhere $489). Welt Publishing, LLC, 1413 K St., N.W., Ste. 1400, Washington, DC 20005. TEL 202-371-0555; 800-898-INTL. FAX 202-408-9369. Ed. John Justin Ford; Pub. Leo G.B. Welt. adv. contact: James Ford. bk.rev.; charts; stat.; tr.lit. circ. 3,500. (looseleaf format; back issues avail.) **Indexed:** Chem.Abstr. **Document type:** newsletter.
—CASDDS.
    Supersedes in part: Business and Trade (ISSN 0196-8602); Which was formerly: Soviet Business and Trade (ISSN 0092-4695)
    Description: Provides news and analysis on business and economic developments throughout China and Hong Kong.

382   US   ISSN 0163-7169
HF3128
CHINA BUSINESS REVIEW. 1974. bi-m. $99 (foreign $150). United States - China Business Council, 1818 N St., N.W., Ste. 200, Washington, DC 20036-2406. TEL 202-429-0340. FAX 202-833-9027. E-mail: akahn@uschina.org; URL: http://www.uschina.org/cbr. Ed. Kirsten Sylvester. R&P contact: Alan R. Kahn. adv. contact: Alan R. Kahn. bk.rev.; bibl.; charts; illus.; pat.; stat.; index. circ. 5,600. (also avail. in microform from UMI; back issues avail.) **Indexed:** ABI Inform., Asian-Pac.Econ.Lit., B.P.I., BPIA, Bus.Ind., Cont.Pg.Manage., Key to Econ.Sci., Manage.Cont., P.A.I.S., SRI, Tr.& Indus.Ind. **Document type:** trade publication.
●Also available online. Vendor(s): Information Access Co., Knight-Ridder Information, Inc., UMI, Wilsonline.
—BLDSC (3180.125000); KR SourceOne; SWETS; UMI; UnCover. **CCC.**
    Formerly (until 1977): U S China Business Review (ISSN 0094-0089)
    Description: US business magazine of trade and investment in China and Hong Kong, focusing on opportunities for US and other foreign companies. Trends and issues in law, economics, and politics are analyzed for both immediate and long-term business implications.
Refereed Serial

332.6   UK   ISSN 1350-6390
CHINA ECONOMIC REVIEW; the China international trade journal. 1990. m. $220. Alain Charles Publishing Ltd., Alain Charles House, 27 Wilfred St., London SW1E 6PR, England. TEL 44-171-834-7676. FAX 44-171-973-0076. TELEX 297165 ACPLTD G. circ. 9,560 (paid). **Indexed:** B.P.I. **Document type:** trade publication.
    Formerly (until 1992): Sdelano v Kitae (Made in China) (ISSN 0967-8182)
    Description: Provides business and financial news analysis for managers of organizations trading and investing in China.

382   CC
CHINA IMPORTERS & EXPORTERS. (Text in Chinese and English) 1989. biennial. $385. Han Consultants Inc., P.O. Box 71006, Wuhan, Hubei 430071, People's Republic of China. TEL 86-27-7838532. FAX 86-27-7878343. circ. 6,000. **Document type:** directory.
    Description: Provides information (names, addresses, products and services) on Chinese manufacturers and trade companies that are involved in the import and export business.

CHINA LAWS FOR FOREIGN BUSINESS - BUSINESS REGULATION. see LAW — Corporate Law

CHINA LAWS FOR FOREIGN BUSINESS - SPECIAL ZONES & CITIES. see LAW — Corporate Law

CHINA LAWS FOR FOREIGN BUSINESS - TAXATION & CUSTOMS. see LAW — Corporate Law

332.6   SI   ISSN 0218-1517
HF41
CHINA MAIL/ZHONGGUO XINXUN. (Text in English) 1988. bi-m. S.$39. T W L Publishing (Singapore) Pte. Ltd., 25 Genting Rd., No. 07-01, Soon Seng Bldg., Singapore 349482, Singapore. TEL 65-7438606. FAX 65-7436702. E-mail: cic@pacific.net.sg. Ed. Tang Kin Eng. R&P contact: Tang King Eng. adv. contact: Janet Wong. **Document type:** trade publication.

382.7   US
CHINA MARKET;* the businessman's guide to the China market. 1982. bi-m. $50. East-West Trade Publications, P.O. Box 20564, New York, NY 10025-1521. Ed. Louis F. Sharpe. adv.; charts; stat. circ. 25,000.

382   JA   ISSN 0285-7529
CHINA NEWSLETTER. 1973. bi-m. 12360 Yen($144) Japan External Trade Organization, Publications Department, 2-5 Toranomon 2-chome, Minato-ku, Tokyo 105, Japan. TEL 03-3582-3518. FAX 03-3587-2485. TELEX J 24378. (Dist. overseas by: Maruzen Co., Ltd., Export Dept., P.O. Box 5050, Tokyo International 100-31, Japan. FAX 03-3274-2270) circ. 1,000. (back issues avail.) **Indexed:** Key to Econ.Sci. **Document type:** newsletter.
    Formerly: J E T R O China Newsletter.

CHINA, REPUBLIC. MINISTRY OF FINANCE. DEPARTMENT OF STATISTICS. MONTHLY STATISTICS OF EXPORTS AND IMPORTS/CHIN CH'U K'OU MAO I T'UNG CHI YUEH PAO. see BUSINESS AND ECONOMICS — Abstracting, Bibliographies, Statistics

332.6   CC
CHINA TRADE LINK. (Text in Chinese, English) 1994. m. $345. Han Consultants Inc., P.O. Box 71006, Wuhan, Hubei 430071, People's Republic of China. TEL 86-27-783-8532. FAX 86-27-787-8343. circ. 20,000. **Document type:** newsletter.
    Description: Provides information on import and export opportunities from and into China. Lists company name, address, telephone, fax and contact person.

382   CC   ISSN 0009-448X
HF41   CODEN: CTRTAR
CHINA TRADE REPORT. 1963. m. $425. Review Publishing Co. Ltd., G.P.O. Box 160, Hong Kong, People's Republic of China. TEL 852-208-4300. FAX 852-203-1549. TELEX 66452 REVCD HX. Ed. Kari Huus. stat. **Indexed:** Key to Econ.Sci.
—BLDSC (3180.237000); CASDDS; SWETS.
    Description: Supplies trade indicators and assessments of China's trade relations.

382   CC   ISSN 0009-4498
HF41
CHINA'S FOREIGN TRADE. Chinese Edition: Zhongguo Duiwai Maoyi. (Editions in Chinese, English) 1956. m. $48. China Council for the Promotion of International Trade (CCPIT), 1 Fuxingmenwai Dajie, Beijing, People's Republic of China. TEL 86-10-851-3344. FAX 86-10-8511370. TELEX 22315-CCPIT-CN. (Dist. by: Guoji Shudian - China International Book Trading Corporation, P.O. Box 399, Beijing, People's Republic of China; Dist. in US by: China Books & Periodicals, Inc., 2929 24th St., San Francisco, CA 94110. TEL 415-282-2773) Ed. Xinyi Li; Pub. Deyu Liu. adv. contact: Jiyong Chen. circ. 70,000. **Indexed:** Key to Econ.Sci.
—UnCover.
    Description: Contains articles on Chinese economic development and specialty products, as well as information on Chinese imports and exports, and related policies and regulations.

CINA NOTIZIE; rassegna informativa di attualita cinese. see BUSINESS AND ECONOMICS

382 330.9   CU
COLABORACION INTERNACIONAL. 1979. q. $8 in N. America; S. America $10; others $12. Ministerio de Cultura, Comite Estatal de Colaboracion Economica, Calle 1 No. 201 esq. B Vedado, Havana, Cuba. (Dist. by: Ediciones Cubanas, Obispo No. 527, Apdo. 605, Havana, Cuba) Ed. Eneida L. Rodriguez Guanche. adv. circ. 4,000.

382   CK   ISSN 0120-6419
COLOMBIA. DEPARTAMENTO ADMINISTRATIVO NACIONAL DE ESTADISTICA. ANUARIO DE COMERCIO EXTERIOR. 1917. a. $80 (for 1990 ed.). Departamento Administrativo Nacional de Estadistica, Banco Nacional de Datos, Centro Administrativo Nacional, Avda. El Dorado, Apdo. Aereo 80043, Bogota D.E., Colombia. FAX 2222305. TELEX 44573. **Document type:** government publication.

382   CK   ISSN 0120-727X
COLOMBIA EXPORTA. (Text in English, Spanish) 1982. a. Proexpo Fondo de Promocion de Exportaciones, Calle 28 No. 13A-15 Piso 41, Bogota, Colombia. Ed. Amparo Jaramillo Sanin. charts; illus.; stat. circ. 10,000.
    Description: Covers Colombian trade and export industry.

650   US   ISSN 0022-5428
HF5001   CODEN: CJWBAU
COLUMBIA JOURNAL OF WORLD BUSINESS. 1965. q. $85 to individuals (foreign $105); institutions $195 (foreign $215) (effective 1998). (Columbia University, Trustees of Columbia University) J A I Press Inc., 55 Old Post Rd., No. 2, Box 1678, Greenwich, CT 06830-1678. TEL 203-661-7602. FAX 203-661-0792. E-mail: jai@jaipress.com; URL: http://www.jaipress.com/jmspub.hmt. (Addr. in Europe: J A I Press Ltd., 38 Tavistock St., Covent Garden, London WC2E 7PB, England. TEL 44-171-379-8834. FAX 44-171-379-8835) Ed. Peter B. Erchmann. adv.; bk.rev.; charts; illus.; index. circ. 3,500. (also avail. in microform from UMI; back issues avail.; reprint service avail. from ISI,SCH,UMI)
    Indexed: AAR, ABI Inform., Account.& Data Proc.Abstr., Account.Ind. (1974-), Amer.Bibl.Slavic & E.Eur.Stud., Anbar, ASCA, ASEAN Manage.Abstr., B.P.I., Bank.Lit.Ind., BPIA, Bus.Ind., Cont.Pg.Manage., Curr.Cont., Data Process.Dig., Ind.Per.Art.Relat.Law, Key to Econ.Sci., Manage.Cont., Mgmt.& Market.Abstr., Mid.East: Abstr.& Ind., P.A.I.S., Risk Abstr., Rural Recreat.Tour.Abstr., SCIMP (1978-), SSCI, Tr.& Indus.Ind., Work Rel.Abstr., World Agri.Econ.& Rural Sociol.Abstr. **Document type:** academic/scholarly publication.
    ● Also available online. Vendor(s): Information Access Co.
    —BLDSC (3323.200000); KR SourceOne; SWETS; UMI; UnCover. **CCC.**
    Formerly: Journal of World Business.

332.6   UK
COMBINED INDEPENDENTS HOLDINGS DIRECTORY. a. Argus Business Media Ltd. (Subsidiary of: D M G Exhibitions Group Ltd.), Queensway House, 2 Queensway, Redhill, Surrey RH1 1QS, England. TEL 44-1737-768611. FAX 44-1737-760510. **Document type:** directory.

382   MX
COMERCIO. 1960. m. Alberto Barrauco Chavarria, Pub., Rio Tiber 87, 70, 06500 Mexico D.F., Mexico. TEL 5-514-0873. FAX 5-514-1169. Ed. Raul Horta. adv. circ. 40,000.

382   MX   ISSN 0185-0601
HF6
COMERCIO EXTERIOR. (Text in Spanish; abstracts in English) 1951. m. $35 by air mail in N. & Central America; S. America & Europe $45; elsewhere $55; free by surface mail; CD-ROM Mex.$20000($660) (effective 1997). Banco Nacional de Comercio Exterior, S.A., Gerencia de la Revista Comercio Exterior, Camino a Santa Teresa 1679, Col. Jardines del Pedregal, 01900 Mexico D.F., Mexico. TEL 525-3276220. FAX 525-3276214. E-mail: 74173.1447@compuserve.com; URL: http://mexico.businessline.gob.mx/infotec/revista.html. (Subscr. to: Apdo. Postal 221258, 04100 Mexico DF, Mexico) Ed. Homero Urias Brambila; Pub. Sergio Hernandez Clark. bk.rev.; stat.; index. circ. 10,000.
    Indexed: Hisp.Amer.Per.Ind. (1970-), IBR, Int.Lab.Doc., P.A.I.S.For.Lang.Ind., Rural Recreat.Tour.Abstr., World Agri.Econ.& Rural Sociol.Abstr. **Document type:** trade publication.
    ● Also available online.
    Also available on CD-ROM.
    Description: Presents socio-economic matters, especially those related to Mexico and Latin America.

332.6   AG   ISSN 0326-5714
COMERCIO EXTERIOR ARGENTINO. Key Title: Comercio Exterior: Importacion. (Supplement avail.: Avance Semestral) 1916. a. Arg.$15($26) (effective 1997). Instituto Nacional de Estadistica y Censos, Av. Julio A. Roca, 609 P.B., 1067 Buenos Aires, Argentina. TEL 54-1-3499662. FAX 54-1-3499621. E-mail: CES@indec.mec.ar; URL: http://www.indec.mecon.ar. **Document type:** government publication.

COMERTUL EXTERIOR AL ROMANIEI/FOREIGN TRADE OF ROMANIA. see BUSINESS AND ECONOMICS — Abstracting, Bibliographies, Statistics

COMMERCE; English monthly. see BUSINESS AND ECONOMICS — Domestic Commerce

COMMERCE DU LEVANT. see BUSINESS AND ECONOMICS — Domestic Commerce

382   IV
COMMERCE EXTERIEUR DE LA COTE D'IVOIRE: RESULTATS ET EVOLUTION.* irreg. Direction des Affaires Economiques et des Relations Economiques Exterieures, Imprimerie Nationale, 7 av. Marchand, B.P. V 87, Abidjan, Ivory Coast. stat.

352   UK   ISSN 0962-5267
COMMERCE U S A. 1978. bi-m. free. (U.S. Embassy (London)) Mediafine Ltd., Port of Liverpool Bldg., Liverpool, Merseyside L3 1BZ, England. TEL 051-236-5757. FAX 051-227-29010. Ed. Mark Chivers. adv. circ. 7,500. (back issues avail.)
    Formerly: Commercial Newsletter.
    Description: Contains information about United States export trade relations with regard to European investment and expansion.

COMMERCIAL LAWS OF THE WORLD. see LAW — International Law

382   US   ISSN 0161-9772
HF1455
COMMERCIAL NEWS U S A. Abbreviated title: C N. 1974. 10/yr. U.S. Department of Commerce, International Trade Administration, Rm. 1310, U.S. and Foreign Commercial Services, Washington, DC 20230. TEL 202-482-4918. FAX 202-482-5362. Ed. Laura Hellstern. bk.rev.; charts; illus.; circ. (controlled). **Document type:** catalog, government publication.
    ● Also available online.
    Formerly (until Jan.-Feb. 1978): Commercial News for the Foreign Service (ISSN 0363-678X)
    Description: Contains information about U.S. goods and services for 110,000 international sales representatives, distributors, purchasing officials, licensees, and end-users in more than 33 industry categories.

332.6   IT
COMMERCIO INTERNAZIONALE. 1977. fortn. L.330000 (foreign L.660000). I P S O A s.r.l. (Subsidiary of: Wolters Kluwer N.V.), Strada 1, Palazzo F6, 20090 Assago Milanofiori (MI), Italy. TEL 39-2-824761. FAX 39-2-82476209. Ed. Massimiliano Galioni. adv.: B&W page L.3000000; adv. contact: Luciano Alcaro Menichini. circ. 10,500. **Document type:** consumer publication.

382 341   EI
COMMISSION OF THE EUROPEAN COMMUNITIES. COLLECTION OF AGREEMENTS. (Editions in Danish, Dutch, English, French, German, Italian) 1977. irreg., latest vol.12, 1982. price varies. Office for Official Publications of the European Communities; L-2985 Luxembourg, Luxembourg. (Dist. in the U.S. by: European Community Information Service, 2100 M St., N.W. Ste. 707, Washington, DC 20037)

COMMISSION OF THE EUROPEAN COMMUNITIES. REPORT ON COMPETITION POLICY. see BUSINESS AND ECONOMICS — Production Of Goods And Services

332.6   US   ISSN 1057-9966
HF1042
COMMODITY CLASSIFICATION UNDER THE HARMONIZED SYSTEM HANDBOOK. m. $100 (foreign $125). U.S. Department of the Treasury, U.S. Customs Service, 1301 Constitution Ave., N.W., Washington, DC 20229. TEL 202-566-5000. (Subscr. to: Superintendent of Documents, U.S. Government Printing Office, Box 371954, Pittsburgh, PA 15250-7954. TEL 202-512-1800. FAX 202-512-2250) (back issues avail.) **Document type:** government publication.

382   US   ISSN 0572-9780
COMMON MARKET REPORTS. 1962. bi-w. $1070. C C H Incorporated, 2700 Lake Cook Rd., Riverwoods, IL 60015. TEL 847-267-7000; 800-835-5224. FAX 800-224-8299. (looseleaf format)

382   BE
COMPAGNIE FINANCIERE EUROPEENNE ET D'OUTRE-MER. FINOUTREMER. RAPPORT ANNUEL. 1972. a. free. Compagnie Financiere Europeene et d'Outre-Mer, 30 rue Royale, 1000 Brussels, Belgium.
    Former titles: Compagnie Europeenne et d'Outre-Mer. Rapports; Compagnie du Congo pour le Commerce et l'Industrie. Assemblee Generale. Rapports.

332.6 658   US   ISSN 1059-5422
HB238   CODEN: COREFK
COMPETITIVENESS REVIEW. 1991. s-a. $40 to individuals; institutions $70 (effective 1997). American Society for Competitiveness, Box 1658, Indiana, PA 15705. TEL 412-357-5759. FAX 412-357-5743. Ed. Abbas J. Ali. R&P contact: Abbas J. Ali. adv. contact: M. Gibbs. bk.rev. circ. 750. **Document type:** academic/scholarly publication.
    —BLDSC (3363.993690).
    Description: Studies competitiveness issues around the globe. Devoted to the improvement and understanding of theory and application of issues related to competitiveness.
    Refereed Serial

382   MX
CONACEX NORESTE MAGAZINE. m. Consejo Nacional de Comercio Exterior del Noreste, Ocampo 250 Pte., Desp. 702, Apdo. 2674, 64000 Monterrey, Mexico.
    Formerly: Conacex Noreste Boletin Informativo.

CORPORATE AIR TRAVEL SURVEY. see TRANSPORTATION — Air Transport

382 341   US   ISSN 0898-9907
K3943.A13
CORPORATE COUNSEL'S INTERNATIONAL ADVISER. 1985. m. $285. Business Laws, Inc., 11630 Chillicothe Rd., Chesterland, OH 44026. TEL 216-729-7996. FAX 216-729-0645. Ed. William A. Hancock. bk.rev.; charts; cum.index: 1985-1992. (looseleaf format; back issues avail.) **Document type:** newsletter.
    —CCC.
    Description: Provides current information on international business topics.

382   FR   ISSN 0221-5780
COTE-D'IVOIRE SELECTION. (Supplement avail.: Fichier Cote-d'Ivoire Selection) s-m. (22/yr.). 5200 F. (effective 1997). I C Publications, 10 rue Vineuse, 75784 Paris Cedex 16, France. TEL 33-1-44308100. FAX 33-1-44308111.

COUNTERTRADE & OFFSET; weekly intelligence on unconventional & reciprocal international trade. see BUSINESS AND ECONOMICS — Investments

COUNTRY FORECASTS (SYRACUSE). see BUSINESS AND ECONOMICS

COW NEWS & BULL VIEWS. see AGRICULTURE — Poultry And Livestock

CRAIGHEAD'S COUNTRY REPORTS. see TRAVEL AND TOURISM

382   US
CRICKET LETTER. 1972. m. $275. Cricket Communications, Inc., Box 527, Ardmore, PA 19003. TEL 215-789-2480. Ed. Mark E. Battersby bk.rev. circ. 3,150.
    Description: Aimed at multinationals interested in US taxation, financing strategies and regional site development.

382   US
CRICKET TRADE; trade without borders. m. Cricket Communications, Inc., Box 527, Ardmore, PA 19003. TEL 215-747-6684. FAX 215-747-7082. Ed. Mark E. Battensby. stat.; index; circ. 2,615 (paid). (back issues avail.) **Document type:** newslette

332.6   UK
CRONER'S EUROPE. 1988. base vol. (plus m. updates) £200. Croner Publications Ltd. (Subsidiary of: Wolters Kluwer N.V.), Croner House, 100 London Rd., Kingston-upon-Thames, Surrey KT2 6SR, England. TEL 44-181-547-3333. FAX 44-181-547-2637. Ed. Jane Bradbury. (also avail. in diskette format) **Document type:** trade publication.

BUSINESS AND ECONOMICS — INTERNATIONAL COMMERCE

382   UK   ISSN 0070-1599
CRONER'S REFERENCE BOOK FOR EXPORTERS. 1942. base vol. (plus m. updates). £198.30 (updates £138.60) (effective 1995). Croner Publications Ltd. (Subsidiary of: Wolters Kluwer N.V.), Croner House, 100 London Rd., Kingston-upon-Thames, Surrey KT2 6SR, England. TEL 44-181-547-3333. FAX 44-181-547-2637. TELEX 267778. Ed. David Wright. (looseleaf format) **Document type:** trade publication.
  Description: Provides comprehensive, current information for exporters.

382   UK   ISSN 0070-1602
CRONER'S REFERENCE BOOK FOR IMPORTERS. 1959. m. £87.45 (subscr. includes m. newsletter) (effective 1993). Croner Publications Ltd. (Subsidiary of: Wolters Kluwer N.V.), Croner House, London Rd., Kingston, Surrey KT2 6SR, England. TEL 081-547-3333. FAX 081-547-2637. TELEX 267778. Ed. V. Ganley. (looseleaf format)
  Description: Provides comprehensive information on regulations governing imports to the United Kingdom.

332.6   US
HD2755.5
CROSSBORDER MONITOR. 1993. w. £525($795) Economist Intelligence Unit, 111 W. 57th St., New York, NY 10019. TEL 212-554-0600; 800-938-4685. FAX 212-586-1182. TELEX 175567. URL: http://www.eiu.com. (UK addr.: Economist Intelligence Unit Ltd., Subscriptions Dept., P.O. Box 200, Harold Hill, Romford, Essex RM3 8UX, England. TEL 44-1708-381-444. FAX 44-1708-371-850) Ed. Nico Cilchester; Pub. Debra Langley. adv. contact: Leslie Magee.
  Formerly: Crossborder (ISSN 1070-5953)

382   CU
CUBA. MINISTERIO DEL COMERCIO EXTERIOR. BOLETIN DE INFORMACION COMERCIAL. 1969. s-w. C.$60. Ministerio del Comercio Exterior (MINCEX), Instituto de Coyuntura, Infanta No. 16, Vedado, Havana, Cuba. TEL 537-7421853. FAX 537-786234. TELEX 51-1174. **Document type:** government publication, bulletin.
  Description: Provides information on international markets, commerce, products and countries' economies.

382   CU
CUBA. MINISTERIO DEL COMERCIO EXTERIOR. BOLETIN SEMANAL DE PRECIOS DE LOS ALIMENTOS. 1984. w. C.$14. (Ministerio del Comercio Exterior (MINCEX)) Empresa Alimport, Calle 23 No. 55, Vedado, Havana, Cuba. TEL 7-4971. TELEX 51-1454. **Document type:** government publication, bulletin.
  Description: Covers markets and prices information on food.

382   CU
CUBA. MINISTERIO DEL COMERCIO EXTERIOR. REPORTE SEMANAL DEL AZUCAR. 1981. w. C.$14. (Ministerio del Comercio Exterior (MINCEX)) Empresa Cubazucar, Calle 23 No. 55, Vedado, Havana, Cuba. TEL 70-9742. TELEX 51-1147.
  Description: Provides markets and prices information on sugar.

CUBA FOREIGN TRADE. see *BUSINESS AND ECONOMICS — Chamber Of Commerce Publications*

382   PK   ISSN 0011-4154
CUSTOMS IMPORTS AND EXPORTS JOURNAL. (Text in English) vol.5, 1967. m. Rs.55. Taxation Publishers, 6 Liaqat Rd., Lahore 8, Pakistan. Ed. S.M. Raza Naqvi. charts; stat.

382   AT
CUSTOMS OFFICER'S ASSOCIATION OF AUSTRALIA. FOURTH DIVISION. FOURTH DIVISION CUSTOMS OFFICER. 1968. irreg. Aus.$0.05 per no. Percival Publishing Co. Pty. Ltd., 862-870 Elizabeth St., Sydney, N.S.W. 2000, Australia.

CYPRUS. DEPARTMENT OF STATISTICS AND RESEARCH. STATISTICS OF IMPORTS AND EXPORTS. see *BUSINESS AND ECONOMICS — Abstracting, Bibliographies, Statistics*

CYPRUS. TOURISM ORGANISATION. ANNUAL REPORT. see *TRAVEL AND TOURISM*

382   XR
HF37.C9
CZECH BUSINESS AND TRADE. German edition: Wirtschaft und Handel in det Tschechischen Republik. French edition: Industrie et Commerce Tcheque. (Text in English) m. $89 (foreign $95). (Ministry of Industry and Trade) P.P. Agency, V. Jircharich 8, 110 00 Prague 1, Czech Republic. TEL 42-2-24912185. FAX 42-2-290329. Ed. Pavla Podskalska. adv.: page $600; adv. contact: Alena Kobercova. abstr.; illus.; stat.; index. circ. 15,000 (3 eds. combined). (back issues avail.) Indexed: Key to Econ.Sci., Mid.East: Abstr.& Ind., PROMT. **Document type:** trade publication.
  Former titles (until Feb. 1994): Czech Foreign Trade (ISSN 1210-5546); (until 1993): Czechoslovak Foreign Trade (ISSN 0011-460X)
  Description: Covers economic policy, international cooperation, Czech trading and manufacturing organizations, exhibitions and fairs, finance, joint ventures, legislation.

332.6   KO
DAILY TRADE NEWS. (Text in Korean) 1949. 2/d. 24000 Won per mo. Korea Foreign Trade Association, 159-1 Samsung-dong, Dang-nam-ku, Seoul 135-729, S. Korea. TEL 02-551-5441. FAX 02-551-5400. Ed. Choi Jung Keun; Pub. Koo Pyong Hwoi. adv.: B&W page $1840, color page $3060; trim 35 x 24; adv. contact: Yong Soo Chang. bk.rev.; circ. 80,000 (paid); 20,000 (controlled). (back issues avail.) **Document type:** newspaper.

382 388.025   II
▼**DALIL AL-MUSADDIRIN/DIRECTORY OF EXPORTERS.** (Text in Arabic and English) 1996. a. $20. Pharos Media & Publishing (P) Ltd., P.O. Box 9701, D-84 Abul Fazl Enclave, Jamia Nagar, New Delhi 110025, India. TEL 91-11-692-7483. FAX 91-11-683-5825. E-mail: zik.pharos@axcess.net.in. Ed. Zafarul-Islam Khan. adv. contact: Asghar Ali. circ. 20,000. **Document type:** directory.
  Description: Carries classified listings and advertisements of exporters of goods and services to the Arab world.

382   DK   ISSN 0109-2669
DANSK-FRANSK HANDELSUNION. BULLETIN/CHAMBRE DE COMMERCE FRANCO-DANOISE. BULLETIN. (Text in Danish and French) 1983. q. free to members. Dansk-Fransk Handelsunion, c/o P.R. Meurs-Gerken, Advokaterne, Amaliegade 42, 1256 Copenhagen K, Denmark. TEL 33-113399. FAX 33-32-46-25. TELEX 27223 AMALEX DK. adv.; illus. circ. 10,000. **Document type:** bulletin.

332.6   US
DEALER - DISTRIBUTOR MAGAZINE; the international business magazine. 1975. q. $6. Interstate Publications, Drawer 19689, Houston, TX 77224. TEL 281-578-6993. FAX 281-578-6993. E-mail: intpub@aol.com. Ed. Linda Graham. adv. circ. 10,000.
  Description: Covers income opportunities, wholesale sources, dealerships, franchises, distributorships, businesses for sale, businesses wanted, real estate, advertising services, import and export, MLM.

382   RU   ISSN 0235-7607
HF25
DELOVYE SVYAZI. English edition: Business Contact (ISSN 0235-764X) (Text in Russian) 1957. m. $194 (effective 1997). Ul. Kahovka 31, Korp. 2, 113461 Moscow, Russia. TEL 7-095-3319577. FAX 7-095-3107005. TELEX 411265. Ed. V.L. Novikov. adv.; charts; illus. circ. 80,000 (Rus.ed.); 50,000 (Eng.ed.). Indexed: Key to Econ.Sci., PROMT. **Document type:** trade publication.
  —UMI.
  Description: Aims to help Russian enterprises access foreign markets. Provides information on the export of goods and services, proposals to cooperate, the establishment of joint ventures, and the development of new forms of foreign economic activity.

382   UK   ISSN 1351-9786
DERBY TRADER. 1966. w. free. Trader Group of Newspapers, Abbotshill Chambers, Gower St., Derby, England. Ed. T. Mather. adv.; bk.rev. circ. 130,300.

382   UN
DEVELOPMENT BUSINESS. 1985. w. $295. United Nations, Sales and Marketing Section, Room DC2-0853, New York, NY 10017. TEL 212-963-1516. E-mail: publications@un.org; URL: http://www.un.org/publications. (looseleaf format)
  Formerly: International Business Opportunities Service.
  Description: Geared towards civil works, contractors, subcontractors, suppliers, and consultants around the world by providing comprehensive information about the Bank's procurement opportunities and upcoming projects.

332.6   UK   ISSN 1354-7895
DEVELOPMENT OF LATIN AMERICA. 1994. a. £55. Sterling Publications Ltd., 86-88 Edgware Rd., London W2 2YW, England. TEL 44-171-915-9600. FAX 44-171-915-9619. R&P contact: Sandy Tucker. circ. 10,000. **Document type:** trade publication.

DIAMOND INSIGHT; penetrating the multi-faceted world of diamonds. see *JEWELRY, CLOCKS AND WATCHES*

382 341   FR
DICTIONNAIRE JOLY PRATIQUE DES CONTRATS INTERNATIONAUX. 7 base vols. plus s-a. updates. 3500 F. (effective 1997). Joly Editions, 1 av. Franklin D. Roosevelt, 75008 Paris, France. TEL 33-1-44951620. FAX 33-1-45638939. Ed. Vincent Heuze. (looseleaf format) **Document type:** trade publication.

DIGEST OF COMMERCIAL LAWS OF THE WORLD. see *LAW — International Law*

DIRECTION OF TRADE STATISTICS. see *BUSINESS AND ECONOMICS — Abstracting, Bibliographies, Statistics*

382   SI   ISSN 0217-8141
DIRECTIONS. (Text in English) 1986. bi-m. S.$35($53); newsstand price: S.$3.50. Integrated Information (Pte) Ltd., 585 N. Bridge Rd. 07-01, Blanco Ct., 188770, Singapore. TEL 65-2968080. FAX 65-2914561. E-mail: info@iipl.com.sg. Ed. Neil Riley; Pub. Emmanuel Joseph. adv.: page S.$2200; trim 289 x 210. bk.rev.; software rev. circ. 18,000. **Document type:** trade publication.
  Description: Includes information on business opportunities, management and marketing tips, and lifestyle stories for businessmen.

382   UK   ISSN 0958-2347
DIRECTORY IN RUSSIAN OF BRITISH FIRMS INTERESTED IN TRADE WITH THE F S U. (Former Soviet Union) (Text in Russian) 1903. a. Exact Communications Ltd., 90 Moorsom St., Birmingham B6 4NT, England. TEL 44-121-333-4644. FAX 44-121-333-5823. circ. controlled. **Document type:** directory.
  Former titles (until 1990): Directory in Russian of British Firms Interested in Trade with the U S S R; (until 1946): Russian Buyers' Guide.
  Description: Promotes British and other products and services through the former U.S.S.R.

DIRECTORY OF ARIZONA EXPORTERS. see *BUSINESS AND ECONOMICS — Trade And Industrial Directories*

DIRECTORY OF BRITISH IMPORTERS. see *BUSINESS AND ECONOMICS — Trade And Industrial Directories*

382 332.6   US
DIRECTORY OF COUNTERTRADE & OFFSET SERVICES. irreg., latest 1996/97. $160 (foreign $180). C T O Data Services, Box 7130, Fairfax Station, VA 22039. TEL 703-425-1323. FAX 703-425-0399. TELEX (RCA) 263 128 CTO UR. (back issues avail.)
  Former titles: Directory of Countertrade Services; Index to Countertrade (Year).

DIRECTORY OF EXPORT BUYERS IN THE U K. see *BUSINESS AND ECONOMICS — Trade And Industrial Directories*

BUSINESS AND ECONOMICS — INTERNATIONAL COMMERCE

382   PK
DIRECTORY OF EXPORTERS (YEAR).* (Text in English) 1966. a. Rs.200($20) Export Promotion Bureau, Export Information & Advisory Centre, Press Trust Bldg., Chundrigrar Rd., Karachi, Pakistan. FAX 21-213415. TELEX 23663-EXPOM-PK. Ed. G. Naseeruddin. adv. circ. 2,000. **Document type:** directory.
    Former titles: Directory of Pakistan Exporters; Pakistan Export Directory (ISSN 0078-8090)
    Description: Contains profiles of Pakistani exporters with well-established businesses.

382   II
DIRECTORY OF INDIAN EXPORTERS. (Text in English) 1919. triennial, latest 23rd ed. $129.60 (or £41.98). (Ministry of Commerce, Directorate General of Commercial Intelligence and Statistics) Controller of Publications, Department of Publications, Ministry of Urban Development, Civil Lines, Delhi 110 054, India. (Subscr. to: Controller of Publications, Civil Lines, New Delhi 110054, India) adv. circ. 2,500. **Document type:** directory.
    Formerly: Indian Export Directory.

382   US   ISSN 1057-6878
HF3011
DIRECTORY OF UNITED STATES EXPORTERS. 1988. a. $450 (effective 1997). Journal of Commerce, Inc. (Subsidiary of: Economist Group), 2 World Trade Center, 27th fl., New York, NY 10048-0203. TEL 212-837-7000. FAX 212-837-7035. (Subscr. to: 445 Marshall St., Phillipsburg, NJ 08865. TEL 908-859-1300. FAX 908-454-6507) Ed. Richard Paige. adv. contact: Mitzi McCullough. circ. 2,500. (also avail. in diskette format) **Document type:** directory.
    ●Also available on CD-ROM.
    —CISTI. **CCC.**
    Supersedes in part (in 1990): United States Importers and Exporters Directory (ISSN 1057-512X); Which was formed by the merger of (1967-1988): Directory of United States Importers (ISSN 0070-6531); (1978-1988): Exporters Directory - U S Buying Guide (ISSN 0149-8479)
    Description: Lists U.S. export companies, including S.I.C. codes, air, land or sea indicator, executive names, phone and fax numbers.

382   US   ISSN 1057-5111
HF3012
DIRECTORY OF UNITED STATES IMPORTERS. 1988. a. $450 (effective 1997). Journal of Commerce, Inc. (Subsidiary of: Economist Group), 2 World Trade Center, 27th fl., New York, NY 10048. TEL 212-837-7000. (Subscr. to: 445 Marshall St., Phillipsburg, NJ 08865. TEL 908-859-1300) Ed. Richard Paige. adv.; index.
    —CISTI. **CCC.**
    Supersedes in part (in 1990): United States Importers and Exporters Directory (ISSN 1057-512X); Which was formed by the merger of (1967-1988): Directory of United States Importers (ISSN 0070-6531); (1978-1988): Exporters Directory - U S Buying Guide (ISSN 0149-8479)

382   IT   ISSN 0391-6111
DIRITTO COMUNITARIO E DEGLI SCAMBI INTERNAZIONALI. 1962. s-a. Editoriale Scientifica s.r.l., Via Generale Orsini 42, 80132 Naples, Italy. TEL 39-81-7646084. **Indexed:** ELLIS.
    —BLDSC (3595.406000); SWETS.
    Formerly (until 1975): Diritto negli Scambi Internazionali (ISSN 0419-3938)

382 341   IT
DIRITTO DEL COMMERCIO INTERNAZIONALE; practica internazionale e diritto interno. 1987. q. Lit.120000 (foreign Lit.180000) (effective 1997). Casa Editrice Dott. A. Giuffre, Via Busto Arsizio 40, 20151 Milan, Italy. TEL 39-2-38089200. FAX 39-2-38009582. Ed. F. Bonelli. **Indexed:** ELLIS, IBR.

382   US   ISSN 1057-641X
KKF78.B86 b D65
DOING BUSINESS IN HUNGARY. 1990. irreg. Price Waterhouse, 1251 Ave. of the Americas, New York, NY 10020. TEL 212-819-5000.

382   US   ISSN 1057-3925
KNX1040.A13
DOING BUSINESS IN JAPAN. 1975. irreg. Price Waterhouse, 1251 Ave. of the Americas, New York, NY 10020. TEL 212-819-5000.

382   US   ISSN 1057-3801
KTL1051.A13
DOING BUSINESS IN SOUTH AFRICA. 1977. irreg. Price Waterhouse, 1251 Ave. of the Americas, New York, NY 10020. TEL 212-819-5000.

382   US   ISSN 1057-381X
KTZ107.5.A13
DOING BUSINESS IN ZIMBABWE. 1984. irreg. Price Waterhouse, 1251 Ave. of the Americas, New York, NY 10020. TEL 212-819-5000.

DOMINICA. MINISTRY OF FINANCE. CENTRAL STATISTICAL OFFICE. ANNUAL OVERSEAS TRADE REPORT. see *BUSINESS AND ECONOMICS — Abstracting, Bibliographies, Statistics*

382   DR
DOMINICAN REPUBLIC. CENTRO DOMINICANO DE PROMOCION DE EXPORTACIONES. BOLETIN ESTADISTICO. 1972. a. RD.$35($10) Centro Dominicano de Promocion de Exportaciones, Apdo. 199-2, Plaza de la Independencia, Santo Domingo, Dominican Republic. illus. **Document type:** government publication, bulletin.

382   CC
DUIWAI JINGJI MAOYI/JOURNAL OF FOREIGN ECONOMICS AND TRADE. (Text in Chinese) q. Tianjin Shehui Kexueyuan, Duiwai Jingji Yanjiusuo - Tianjin Academy of Social Sciences, Institute of Foreign Economics, 34 Youyi Lu, Heping Qu, Tianjin 300061, People's Republic of China. TEL 344032. Ed. Hou Yigang.

382   CC
DUIWAI JINGJI MAOYI DAXUE XUEBAO/UNIVERSITY OF INTERNATIONAL BUSINESS AND ECONOMICS. JOURNAL. (Text in Chinese) bi-m. Duiwai Jingji Maoyi Daxue, Yinghua Dongjie Beikou, Andingmenwai, Beijing 100029, People's Republic of China. TEL 86-10-4225522. FAX 96-10-4212022. Ed. Wang Linsheng.

382   CC
DUIWAI JINGMAO/INTERNATIONAL ECONOMICS AND TRADE. (Text in Chinese) bi-m. Heilongjiang Sheng Duiwai Maoyi Jingji Yanjiusuo - Heilongjiang Institute of International Trade and Economics, 55, Heping Lu, Dongli-qu, Harbin, Heilongjiang 150001, People's Republic of China. TEL 226987. Ed. Wang Cheng.

382   CC   ISSN 1003-5559
DUIWAI JINGMAO SHIWU/PRACTICE IN FOREIGN ECONOMIC RELATIONS AND TRADE. (Text in Chinese) 1983. m. Y42. Duiwai Jingji Maoyi Bu, Jiaoyu Ju - Ministry of Foreign Economics and Trade, Education Bureau, No. 38, Zhuodaoquan Lu, Wuchang-qu, Wuhan, Hubei 430073, People's Republic of China. TEL 86-27-7800575. Ed. Yongyou Yuan. R&P contact: Wangsheng Bai. adv.: page Y3800; adv. contact: Zheng Zhang. circ. 20,000. **Document type:** trade publication.

382.63060489   DK   ISSN 0902-2236
E F R - AARSBERETNING. 1982. a. free. E F R - Erhvervsfremme Styrelsen, Tagensvej 137, DK-2200 Copenhagen N, Denmark. TEL 45-35-86-86-87. FAX 45-35-86-86-87. illus. **Document type:** government publication.
    Supersedes in part (in 1985): Eksportkredit, Eksportfremme. Aarsberetninger (ISSN 0108-7509); Which was formed by the merger of: Eksportkreditraadet. Beretning (ISSN 0108-755X); Eksportfremmeraadet. Beretning (ISSN 0107-1890)

332.66   GW   ISSN 0937-2369
E G WIRTSCHAFTSRECHT AUSSENWIRTSCHAFT. 12/yr. DM.298. Deutscher Wirtschaftsdienst, Marienburgerstr. 22, 50968 Cologne, Germany. TEL 49-221-93763-0. FAX 49-221-9376399. Ed.Bd. (looseleaf format) **Document type:** bulletin.

    PH
E P Z A NEWS. 12/yr. Export Processing Zone Authority, Legaspi Towers 300 4F, Roxas Blvd., Makati MM, Philippines.

    GW   ISSN 0014-3871
E W G - WARENHANDEL. 1966. q. DM.48($20) Zeitungs- und Zeitschriftenverlag Heinrichs, Brueggekamp 1, 30890 Barsinghausen, Germany. TEL 49-5105-2289. Ed. G. Heinrichs. adv.; bk.rev.; charts; stat.; tr.lit. circ. 12,800. (tabloid format) **Document type:** trade publication.

EAST AFRICAN FREIGHT FORWARDING. see *TRANSPORTATION*

382   US   ISSN 0888-580X
EAST ASIAN BUSINESS INTELLIGENCE. 1986. 22/yr. $345 (foreign $355) (effective 1997). International Executive Reports, Ltd., 717 D St., N.W., Ste. 300, Washington, DC 20004-2807. TEL 202-628-6900. FAX 202-628-6618. Ed. Anne Phelan; Pub. William C. Hearn. R&P contact: William C. Hearn. adv. contact: Lloyd Gibson. circ. 300. **Document type:** newsletter.
    ●Also available online. Vendor(s): Lexis-Nexis.
    —**CCC.**
    Description: For business executives looking for sales and contracting opportunities in East Asia. Provides more than 1700 new business leads each year with a brief description of the business opportunity, the person to contact, and full address, phone and fax number.

382   II   ISSN 0012-8457
EAST EUROPEAN TRADE. (Text in English) 1963. m. Rs.50($10) Gurdip Singh, Ed. & Pub., B-3-69 Safdarjang Enclave, New Delhi 110 029, India. adv.; bk.rev.; pat.; stat. circ. 5,000.

EAST-WEST INVESTMENT NEWS. see *BUSINESS AND ECONOMICS — Investments*

ECHO DES M.I.N.; mensuel de la filiere fruits et legumes. see *AGRICULTURE*

382   FR   ISSN 1148-1757
ECHOS DE L'EXPORTATION. 1984. 48/yr. 46 rue la Boetie, 75381 Paris Cedex 08, France. TEL 49-53-65-65. FAX 45-62-43-44. TELEX 640 331 F. Ed. Roselyne de Clapiers. circ. 25,000.
    Formerly (until 1991): Exportation Magazine (ISSN 0761-2818)

382 330.1   GW
HF1351
ECONOMIC SYSTEMS. 1992. q. DM.409.60 (foreign DM.413.20) (effective 1998). Physica-Verlag GmbH und Co. (Subsidiary of: Springer-Verlag), Postfach 105280, 69042 Heidelberg, Germany. TEL 49-6221-487492. FAX 49-6221-487177. E-mail: physica@springer.de. (Subscr. to: Springer Verlag GmbH, Postfach 311340, 10643 Berlin, Germany. TEL 49-30-82787-0. FAX 49-30-82787448; Dist. in N. America by: Springer-Verlag New York Inc., Box 2485, Secaucus, NJ 07096-2485. TEL 212-460-1500. FAX 212-473-6272) Ed.Bd. (also avail. in microform from UMI; reprint service avail. from SWZ) **Document type:** academic/scholarly publication.
    —BLDSC (3656.682500); SWETS; UMI. **CCC.**
    Supersedes in part (in 1997): Economic Systems - J O I C E; Which was formed by the merger of (1992-1996): J O I C E (ISSN 0940-4821); (1992-1996): Economic Systems (ISSN 0939-3625)
    Description: Analysis of market and non-market solutions to allocation and distribution problems. *Refereed Serial*

382   FR   ISSN 1240-8093
HC10
ECONOMIE INTERNATIONALE. (Text in French; summaries in English) 1979. q. 420 F. (Europe 440 F., elsewhere 465 F.) (effective 1997). (Centre d'Etudes Prospectives et d'Informations Internationales) Documentation Francaise, 29-31 quai Voltaire, 75344 Paris Cedex 07, France. TEL 33-1-40157000. FAX 33-1-40157230. TELEX 215 666 DOCFRAN. (Subscr. to: 124 rue Henri Barbusse, 93308 Aubervilliers Cedex, France. TEL 33-1-48395600. FAX 33-1-48395601) circ. 1,800. (also avail. in microfiche from DFR) **Indexed:** ELLIS, Int.Lab.Doc., SCIMP (1985-). **Document type:** government publication.
    —BLDSC (3658.050000).
    Formerly (until 1993): Economie Prospective Internationale (ISSN 0242-7818)

382   GO
ECONOMISTE GABONAIS. q. Centre Gabonais du Commerce Exterieur, B.P. 3906, Libreville, Gabon.

EGYPT. SUEZ CANAL AUTHORITY. MONTHLY REPORT. see *TRANSPORTATION — Ships And Shipping*

BUSINESS AND ECONOMICS — INTERNATIONAL COMMERCE

382   NO   ISSN 0800-6733
HF29
EKSPORT AKTUELT. 1922. s-m. NOK 350. Norges Eksportraad - Export Council of Norway, Drammensvn. 40, Oslo 2, Norway. FAX 47-22-926400. TELEX 78532. Ed. Joern Inge Doerum. adv.; bk.rev. circ. 3,500. **Indexed:** Key to Econ.Sci.
   Formerly: Norges Utenrikshandel (ISSN 0029-1722)

382   ES
EL SALVADOR. MINISTERIO DE COMERCIO EXTERIOR. DIRECTORIO DE OFERTA EXPORTABLE (YEAR)/EL SALVADOR. MINISTRY OF FOREIGN COMMERCE. EXPORTABLE OFFER DIRECTORY. (Text in English, Spanish) a. Ministerio de Comercio Exterior - Ministry of Foreign Trade of El Salvador, San Salvador, El Salvador. **Document type:** government publication, directory.

EL SALVADOR. MINISTERIO DE COMERCIO EXTERIOR. ESTADISTICAS. see BUSINESS AND ECONOMICS — Abstracting, Bibliographies, Statistics

332.6   UK   ISSN 0968-302X
ENCYCLOPAEDIA OF POLISH INDUSTRY. 1993. a. £55. Sterling Publications Ltd., 86-88 Edgware Rd., London W2 2YW, England. TEL 44-171-915-9600. FAX 44-171-915-9619. R&P contact: Sandy Tucker. circ. 10,000. **Document type:** trade publication.

ENFORCEMENT OF FOREIGN JUDGEMENTS. see LAW — International Law

ENVIRONMENT WATCH: LATIN AMERICA; news and analysis for business and policy professionals. see ENVIRONMENTAL STUDIES

ENVIRONMENT WATCH: WEST EUROPE. see ENVIRONMENTAL STUDIES

662.6   GR
ERMIS. (Text in Greek, Russian) 1990? s-a.? Exodos Publicitas (Subsidiary of: Publishing Property Unitrade Ltd.), 5 Vironos St., 546 22 Thessaloniki, Greece. TEL 30-31-261393. FAX 30-31-261636. Ed. Erofili Pantelidou. adv. **Document type:** trade publication.
   Description: Discusses all aspects of trade between Greece and Russia, including tourism.

382   IT   ISSN 0014-0740
ESPORTAZIONE; mensile per gli esportatori. 1961. 11/yr. Ente Italiano per lo Sviluppo dell'Esportazione, Piazzale Giotto 8, 06100 Perugia, Italy. adv.; bk.rev.; bibl.; tr.lit. circ. 9,500.

382   FR   ISSN 1152-6963
ESSOR; French companies database. (Text in French) 1971. a. 9000 F. Union Francaise d'Annuaires Professionnels, 130 av des Bouleaux, B.P.36, 78192 Trappes Cedex, France. TEL 01-30-13-82-00. FAX 01-30-13-82-11. adv. circ. 50,000. **Document type:** directory.
●Also available online.

382   FR
ESSOR FRANCAIS DU COMMERCE INTERNATIONAL/FRENCH FOREIGN TRADE DIRECTORY. 1950. a. 950 F. Union Francaise d'Annuaires Professionnels, 13 av. Hennequin, B.P. 36, 78192 Trappes Cedex, France. TEL 01-30-13-82-00. FAX 01-30-13-82-11. TELEX 698284 F. adv. circ. 6,000. **Document type:** directory.
   Former titles: Essor Francais du Commerce Exterieur; Repertoire Francais du Commerce Exterieur (ISSN 1242-3262)
   Description: Contains a list of main goods that France produces and exports, and a list of companies and products with their representatives abroad.

ESTADISTICA DE LA INDUSTRIA MAQUILADORA DE EXPORTACION. see BUSINESS AND ECONOMICS — Abstracting, Bibliographies, Statistics

ESTADISTICA PANAMENA. SITUACION ECONOMICA. SECCION 341. BALANZA DE PAGOS. see BUSINESS AND ECONOMICS — Public Finance, Taxation

382   CU
ESTIMADO DE PRODUCCION Y CONSUMO DE AZUCAR. 1981. q. C.$13. (Ministerio del Comercio Exterior (MINCEX)) Empresa Cubazucar, Calle 23 No. 55, Vedado, Havana, Cuba. TEL 70-9742. TELEX 51-1147.
   Description: Lists production and consumption estimates by countries and geographical areas.

382   CU
ESTIMADOS SOBRE REQUERIMIENTOS DE IMPORTACION DE AZUCAR. 1981. q. C.$10. (Ministerio del Comercio Exterior (MINCEX)) Empresa Cubazucar, Calle 23 No. 55, Vedado, Havana, Cuba. TEL 70-9742. TELEX 51-1147.
   Description: Covers import requirements of principal sugar importing countries.

ETAGE; Chef-Informationen. see BUSINESS AND ECONOMICS

382   UK   ISSN 1355-2759
EURO-JAPANESE JOURNAL. 1987. s-a. £50 in Europe; elsewhere £60. Anglo-Japanese Economic Institute, Morley House, Rm. 1-6, 2nd Fl., 314-322 Regent St., London W1R 5AD, England. TEL 44-171-637-7872. FAX 44-171-636-3614. Ed. George Bull; Pub. George Bull. R&P contact: David Morris. bk.rev.; charts; stat.; circ. 1,000 (controlled). **Indexed:** Met.Abstr., World Alum.Abstr., World Bank.Abstr. **Document type:** academic/scholarly publication.
—BLDSC (3829.233500).
   Incorporates (in 1994): Anglo-Japanese Journal (ISSN 0955-5129); **Former titles** (until 1989): Anglo-Japanese Economic Journal (ISSN 0951-5860); Which was formed by the 1987 merger of: Japan (London, 1961) (ISSN 0143-7216); Japan (London, 1962) (ISSN 0143-7224)
   Description: Presents analysis and comment on current issues in Anglo-Japanese relations and on significant developments in Japanese economic policy.

EUROMONEY; the monthly journal of international money and capital markets. see BUSINESS AND ECONOMICS — Banking And Finance

337.1 327   NO   ISSN 0803-8767
EUROPABREVET. NYHETSBREV; informasjon for norske ledere om utviklingen av EFs indre marked. (Supplement avail.: Temahefte (ISSN 0803-8783)) 1988. 30/yr. NOK 2460 in Nordic countries; elsewhere $468 (effective 1996). Alpha Beta Media, Boks 1663 Vika, N-0120 Oslo, Norway. TEL 47-22-831381. FAX 47-22-831319. E-mail: hans.chr.erlandsen@login.eunet.no. Ed. Hans Chr. Erlandsen. **Document type:** newsletter.
   Formerly (until 1992): 1992 - Nyhetsbrev (ISSN 0802-2607)
   Description: Focuses on the development of the internal market of the European Community, aimed at Norwegian public leaders and leaders of private companies.

EUROPE. see BUSINESS AND ECONOMICS — Economic Situation And Conditions

382   EI   ISSN 0379-3133
HC241.2
EUROPEAN FILE. Danish edition: Europa Noter (ISSN 0379-315X); Dutch edition: Notities over Europa (ISSN 0379-3117); French edition: Dossier de l'Europe (ISSN 0379-3109); German edition: Stichwort Europa (ISSN 0379-3141); Greek edition: Eropaika Themata. Italian edition: Schede Europee (EI ISSN 0379-3125) Portuguese edition: Dossier da Europa (EI ISSN 0258-8277) Spanish edition: Documentos Europeos (EI ISSN 0258-8269) (Text in English) 1979. s-m. free. Commission of the European Communities, Directorate General for Information, Rue de la Loi, 200, B-1049 Brussels, Belgium. (Subscr. to: Office for Official Publications, 2 rue Mercier, L-3985 Luxembourg, Luxembourg; Dist. in U.S. by: European Community Information Service, 2100 M St. N.W., Ste. 707, Washington, DC 20037) adv. contact: Rebecca Zahn. **Indexed:** Br.Ceram.Abstr., Build.Manage.Abstr., World Bank.Abstr., World Surf.Coat., World Text.Abstr. **Document type:** corporate report.
—BLDSC (3829.710600).

382   SZ   ISSN 0531-4127
HF1531
EUROPEAN FREE TRADE ASSOCIATION. ANNUAL REPORT. French edition: Association Europeenne de Libre-echange. Rapport Annuel (ISSN 0258-0756); German edition: Europaeische Freihandelsassoziation. Jahresbericht (ISSN 0258-3852) (Text in English) 1960. a. free. European Free Trade Association, 9-11 rue de Varembe, CH-1211 Geneva 20, Switzerland. TEL 41-22-7491111. FAX 41-22-7339291. URL: http://www.efta.be. Ed. Nikulas Hannigan. **Indexed:** IIS. **Document type:** corporate report.

332.6   UK   ISSN 0964-6299
EUROPEAN GOVERNMENT. q. The Publishing House, Highbury Station Rd., Islington, London N1 1SE, England. TEL 071-226-2222. FAX 071-226-1255. Ed. Alan Spence.

332.6   UK   ISSN 1351-6620
JN15
THE EUROPEAN JOURNAL. 1993. q. $20 or higher donation (rest of Europe £24; elsewhere £28 or more). European Foundation, 61 Pall Mall, London SW1Y 5HZ, England. TEL 0171-930-7319. FAX 0171-930-9706. Ed. David Matthews. **Document type:** academic/scholarly publication.
—BLDSC (3829.721950).
   Description: Addresses the economic and political concerns of the European Community debate among politicians and other policy-makers, journalists, academics, trade unionists, and businessmen.

EUROPEAN JOURNAL OF INTERNATIONAL AFFAIRS. see POLITICAL SCIENCE — International Relations

330 338   US   ISSN 1044-9280
HF3493
EUROPEAN MARKETS: A GUIDE TO COMPANY AND INDUSTRY INFORMATION SOURCES. 1983. irreg., latest 6th ed. $335 (effective 1997). Washington Researchers, Ltd., Box 19005, 20th St. Sta., Washington, DC 20036-9005. TEL 202-333-3499. FAX 202-625-0656. Ed. M. Newman. R&P contact: Ellen O'Kane. **Document type:** directory.
   Description: Informs executives of the best sources of business information for each European nation.

337.142   DK   ISSN 0900-5323
EUROPEISK NYHEDSBREV. 1984. s-m. DKK 50. Europa - Kommissionen, Repraesentation i Danmark, Hoejbrohus, Oestergade 61, P.O. Box 144, DK-1004 Copenhagen K, Denmark. TEL 45-33-14-41-40. FAX 45-33-11-12-03. Ed. Thomas A. Christensen. bk.rev. circ. 8,000. **Document type:** newsletter.

EUROSTAT. E U EXTERNAL TRADE INDICES/INDICES DU COMMERCE EXTERIEUR DE L'U E. see BUSINESS AND ECONOMICS — Abstracting, Bibliographies, Statistics

EUROSTAT. STATISTICS IN FOCUS. EXTERNAL TRADE. see BUSINESS AND ECONOMICS — Abstracting, Bibliographies, Statistics

382   II
EX-IMP TIMES. 1979. fortn. Rs.500($50) Anupam Publishers, R-98, Model Town III, Delhi-110009, India. TEL 7127784. Ed. Anil Kumar. adv.; bk.rev. circ. 2,000.

382.7   II
EXCISE AND CUSTOMS REPORTER. Short title: E C R. (Text in English) 1973. fortn. Rs.1200($120) (effective 1995). Cencus Publications, C-7 Main Market, Vasant Vihar, New Delhi 110 057, India. TEL 673313. FAX 011-6883942. Ed. S.K. Kohli. adv.; charts; stat.; index. circ. 3,400. **Document type:** trade publication.
   Formerly: C E N C U S: Central Excise and Customs Journal (ISSN 0376-7809)
   Description: Covers the technical fields of customs and excise. Provides information on import and export duties, policy and procedures, connected trade restrictions, government notifications, tariff advices and interpretation of international classification and valuation of goods in the import and export trade.

EXHIBIT REVIEW. see BUSINESS AND ECONOMICS — Trade And Industrial Directories

BUSINESS AND ECONOMICS — INTERNATIONAL COMMERCE

382   SP   ISSN 1133-8075
EXPANSION INTERNACIONAL. 1984. 11/yr. 4000 ptas.($50) (effective June 1994). Instituto Espanol de Comercio Exterior, Paseo de la Castellana 14, 28046 Madrid, Spain. TEL 34-1-3496237. FAX 34-1-4358876. TELEX 44838 IECE. Ed. Jose Antonio Garcia Rubio. adv.: color page 120000 ptas.; 185 x 250. bk.rev.; index. circ. 7,000. **Document type:** government publication, trade publication.
—CINDOC.
    Formerly (until 1994): Expansion Comercial (ISSN 0212-7350)
    Description: Aimed at export companies or companies related to foreign trade. Contains information on economic conditions, buying trends, investment opportunities, and international issues.

382   FR   ISSN 1145-8836
EXPO-NEWS. (Monthly edition avail.) 1978. w. 1200 F. (effective 1997 & 1998). Groupe Expo News, 5 rue de Chazelles, 75017 Paris, France. TEL 33-1-44299740. FAX 33-1-47664164. Ed. Pierre Gougeon; Pub. Jean Dominique. R&P contact: Jean Dominique. adv. contact: Jean Dominique. bk.rev. circ. 20,000. (tabloid format) **Document type:** newsletter, directory, trade publication.
    Formerly (until 1983): Infos-Expos.
    Description: Contains professional and confidential information about trade shows, conventions, congresses and business travel.

382 330.9   DK   ISSN 0900-3177
EXPORT; udenrigsministeriets tidsskrift. 1920. w. DKK 732 (effective 1996 & 1997). Udenrigsministeriet, Secretariat for Foreign Trade, Asiatisk Plads 2, DK-1448 Copenhagen K, Denmark. TEL 45-33920825. FAX 45-33920819. Ed. Ulrik Helweg-Larsen. R&P contact: Mogens Lange. adv.; index. circ. 2,600. **Document type:** trade publication.
    Former titles (until 1985): U T (ISSN 0106-3952); Udenrigsministeriets Tidsskrift (ISSN 0041-5685)

382   US   ISSN 0014-519X
EXPORT. Spanish edition: Export en Espanol (ISSN 1065-6677) (Editions in English, Spanish) 1877. 6/yr. $60 (free to qualified personnel) (effective 1997). Hunter Publishing Limited Partnership, 2101 S. Arlington Heights Rd., Ste 150, Arlington Heights, IL 60005. TEL 847-427-9512. FAX 847-427-2097. Ed. Ted P. Eugenis. adv.; bk.rev.; charts; illus.; tr.lit. circ. 39,843 (29,489 English ed.; 9,816 Spanish ed.). (back issues avail.) **Indexed:** Key to Econ.Sci.
    Formerly: Exportador Americano - American Exporter.
    Description: Serving importing distributors and retailers of consumer, commercial and light industrial goods in 183 countries and territories worldwide.

332.6   UK
EXPORT & FREIGHT; Ireland's transport journal. m. Main Stream Publications, 139 Thomas St., Portadown, Co. Armagh BT62 3BE, N. Ireland. TEL 44-1762-334272. FAX 44-1762-351046. adv.: B&W page £850, color page £950; trim 297 x 210; adv. contact: Karen Neill. **Document type:** trade publication.
    Description: Examines market trends and the key players in the Northern Ireland export and freight industries.

382   UK   ISSN 0014-5122
EXPORT COURIER; product information for international buyers. (Text in Arabic, English, French, German and Spanish) 1967. 4/yr. Stokes & Lindley-Jones Ltd., 36 Stonehills House, Welwyn Garden City, Herts AL8 6NA, England. TEL 44-1707-326688. FAX 44-1707-323447. E-mail: exporters@exportcourier.co.uk; URL: http://www.exportcourier.co.uk. Ed. I. Warren; Pub. L.G. Warren. adv. contact: L.G. Warren. illus.; circ. 9,500 (controlled). **Document type:** trade publication.
    Description: Details of British consumer products and manufacturers seeking trading partners and importers worldwide.

382   UK
EXPORT DIGEST. 1947. m. £29 (effective 1995). Croner Publications Ltd. (Subsidiary of: Wolters Kluwer N.V.), Croner House, 100 London Rd., Kingston-upon-Thames, Surrey TW2 6SR, England. TEL 44-181-547-3333. FAX 44-181-547-2637. TELEX 267778. Ed. D. Wright. adv. contact: Jane Hamilton. **Document type:** trade publication.

EXPORT DIRECTORY; members and buyers guide. see BUSINESS AND ECONOMICS — Trade And Industrial Directories

EXPORT DIRECTORY, ISLAMIC REPUBLIC OF IRAN. see BUSINESS AND ECONOMICS — Trade And Industrial Directories

382   US
EXPORT FINANCE WEEKLY. 1992. w. $475. Trade Reports International Group, 2104 National Press Bldg., Washington, DC 20045. TEL 301-946-0817. FAX 301-946-2631. Ed. Jim Berger. R&P contact: Jim Berger. (looseleaf format; back issues avail.) **Document type:** newsletter.
    Description: Offers detailed reporting on the activities of the U.S. Export-Import Bank, the Overseas Private Investment Corporation, the Trade and Development Agency, and the U.S. Small Business Administration.

382   II   ISSN 0970-6186
HF41
EXPORT GAZETTE. (Text in English) 1956. m. Rs.280($40) Amalgamated Press, Narang House, 41 Ambalal Doshi Marg, Fort, Mumbai 400001, India. TEL 91-22-2650268. FAX 91-22-2641275. Ed. Norman Da Silva. adv.: B&W page Rs.4500($350); trim 250 x 197. illus.; mkt.; stat. circ. 8,000. **Document type:** trade publication.
    Incorporates: Afrasian Markets (ISSN 0001-9712)
    Description: Import-export trade journal for the promotion of Indian products worldwide.

382 332.1   JA   ISSN 0071-3503
EXPORT - IMPORT BANK OF JAPAN. ANNUAL REPORT. (Text in English) 1951. a. free. Export - Import Bank of Japan, 1-4-1 Ohtemachi, Chiyoda-ku, Tokyo, Japan. TEL 3287-9101. FAX 3287-9539. TELEX 222-3728 YUGIN J. Ed. Seiichiro Shimamoto. circ. 7,000. **Document type:** corporate report.

332.1   KO
EXPORT - IMPORT BANK OF KOREA. ANNUAL REPORT. (Text in English) a. Export - Import Bank of Korea, Box 4009, Seoul 100, S. Korea. charts; illus.; stat. **Document type:** corporate report.

382   II   ISSN 0014-5149
EXPORT - IMPORT NEWS; a fortnightly journal about export-import trade. (Text in English) 1969. fortn. Rs.500($100) (Exporters - Importers Club) India - International News Service, 12 India Exchange Place, Calcutta 700 001, India. Ed. H. Kothari. circ. controlled.

382   MW
EXPORT INFORMATION. (Text in English) q. Malawi Export Promotion Council, P.O. Box 1299, Blantyre, Malawi. Ed. Chatonda S. Mhone.

332.6   US   ISSN 1064-1513
EXPORT LEADS; worldwide export marketing opportunities monthly. 1989. m. $95 (foreign $135). Export Leads, Circulation Dept., 1741 Kekamek N.W., Poulsbo, WA 98370. TEL 360-779-1511. FAX 360-697-4696. adv. contact: Barbara MacIntyre. circ. 2,500. **Document type:** newspaper.
    Description: Contains specific listings of products wanted by world importers.

EXPORT LEVELS OF NEW ZEALAND WOOL PRODUCTS AND THEIR CURRENT MARKETS. see TEXTILE INDUSTRIES AND FABRICS

332.6   US   ISSN 0896-0216
HD9030.1
EXPORT MARKETS FOR U.S. GRAIN AND PRODUCTS. 1987. m. U.S. Department of Agriculture, Foreign Agricultural Service, Information Division, Rm. 4644-S, Washington, DC 20250-1000. **Document type:** government publication.

382   CN   ISSN 0713-0341
EXPORT NEWS. bi-m. Can.$125. Canadian Exporters' Association, Ste. 250, 99 Bank St., Ottawa, ON K1P 6B9, Canada. TEL 613-238-8888. FAX 613-563-9218. Ed. Katherine Carne. adv.; bk.rev. circ. 1,200. **Document type:** trade publication.
    Formerly (until 1981): Export News Bulletin (ISSN 0316-7631); **Incorporates:** Export U.S.A. (ISSN 0712-2349); Export Digest (ISSN 0713-0376)

332.6   US   ISSN 1054-8327
HF1416.5
EXPORT SALES AND MARKETING MANUAL (YEAR). 1988. a. (plus q. updates). $295 for annual; updates $175 (effective through 1998). Export USA Publications, 6901 W. 84th St., Ste. 157, Minneapolis, MN 55438. TEL 800-876-0624. FAX 612-943-1535. E-mail: info@exportusa.com; URL: http://www.exportusa.com. Pub. John Jagoa. bk.rev.; charts; illus.; circ. 12,000 (paid). (looseleaf format; back issues avail.) **Document type:** trade publication.
● Also available on CD-ROM.
    Description: Contains comprehensive plans for exporting U.S. products, including locating foreign markets and agents, pricing, payment, shipping, budgeting and how to start your own export business.

382   JA
EXPORT STATISTICAL SCHEDULE OF JAPAN (YEAR). (Text in English, Japanese) 1965. a. 9515 Yen($36) Japan Tariff Association, c/o Jibiki Daini Bldg., 4-7-8 Kojimachi, Chiyoda-ku, Tokyo, Japan. **Document type:** government publication.
    Supersedes in part: Commodity Classification for Foreign Trade Statistics: Japan (ISSN 0546-0786)

382   UK
EXPORT TIMES; newspaper for international business & travel. 1969. m. £45($75) Nexus Media Ltd., Nexus House, Swanley, Kent BR8 8HY, England. TEL 44-1322-660070. FAX 44-1322-666408. Ed. Laura McCaffrey. adv. contact: Gordon Russell. circ. 11,972. **Indexed:** Int.Packag.Abstr.; Mgmt.& Market.Abstr. **Document type:** trade publication.

382   UK
EXPORT TODAY. 1937. bi-m. £22.50. (Institute of Export) Nexus Media Ltd., Nexus House, Azalea Dr., Swanley, Kent BR8 8HY, England. TEL 44-1322-660070. FAX 44-1322-666408. Ed. Laura McCaffrey. adv. contact: Gordon Russell. bk.rev.; illus. circ. 10,000. **Indexed:** Key to Econ.Sci. **Document type:** trade publication.
    Incorporates: Export (ISSN 0014-5084)

382   US   ISSN 0882-4711
HF1455
EXPORT TODAY. 1985. m. $49. Trade Communications Inc., 733 15th St. N.W., Ste. 1100, Washington, DC 20005. TEL 202-737-1060. FAX 202-783-5966. E-mail: Mjohn@interserv.com. Ed. Barry Lynn; Pub. John Mooney. R&P contact: Julie Wallace. adv. contact: Patricia Steele. index. circ. 68,656. (back issues avail.) **Document type:** trade publication.
—CCC.

382   TU
EXPORT TURKEY; ticaret. 1981. q. Nesriyat ve Matbaacilik Ltd. Sti., Gazi Bulvari 18, Izmir, Turkey. TEL 51-25-93-50. Ed. Ahmet S. Tukel. circ. 6,800.
    Description: Promotes Turkish exports in order to increase trade relations with foreign countries.

332.6   UK
EXPORT WALES. m. Welsh Office, Export Branch, New Crown Bldg., Cathays Park, Cardiff CF31 3NQ, Wales. TEL 0222-825414. FAX 0222-825350. Ed. Roy Chappell. **Document type:** government publication.

332.6   US   ISSN 1055-8365
EXPORT YELLOW PAGES. 1990. a. free. (U.S. Department of Commerce) U S West, 1101 30th St., N.W., Ste. 200, Washington, DC 20007. TEL 202-337-0336. FAX 202-944-4680. Ed. Patricia Lingeman. circ. 100,000. **Document type:** directory.
    Description: Source book of US companies exporting products and services covering all industries.

382   DR
EXPORTADOR DOMINICANO/EXPORT NEWS. 1973. bi-m. RD.$18($10) Centro Dominicano de Promocion de Exportaciones, Apdo. 199-2, Plaza de la Independencia, Santo Domingo, Dominican Republic. stat.
    Formerly: Dominican Republic. Centro Dominicano de Promocion de Exportaciones. Informes.

382   CO
EXPORTADOR LATINOAMERICANO. 1973. 6/yr. Transversal 6, no. 51A-43, Apdo. Aereo 54520 & 91391, Bogota, Colombia. TEL 240-2053. Ed. Alfonso Martinez T. circ. 55,000.

BUSINESS AND ECONOMICS — INTERNATIONAL COMMERCE 1325

382 PO ISSN 0870-9173
EXPORTAR. 1988. 6/yr. Esc.3150. ICEP, Av. 5 de Outubro 101, 1016 Lisbon Codex, Portugal. TEL 351-1-7930103. FAX 351-1-7935028. TELEX 16498 ICEP P. Ed. Eurico Roseta. adv. contact: Joaquim Santos. bk.rev. circ. 6,000. **Document type:** government publication.

382 US ISSN 0736-9239
THE EXPORTER; the magazine for the business of exporting. 1980. m. $198 (effective 1998). Trade Data Reports, Inc., 90 John St., 5th Fl., New York, NY 10038-3202. Ed. L. Stroh; Pub. L. Stroh. R&P contact: Kathleen Bingham. adv. contact: Bruce Milles. bk.rev. circ. 8,000. **Document type:** trade publication.
●Also available online. Vendor(s): NewsNet (IT04).
—CCC.
  Formerly: Export Shipper.
  Description: Provides a guide to exporting services and resources for people involved in the business who need to understand and meet foreign import or U.S. export requirements.

332.6 UK ISSN 1366-2406
EXPORTER. Variant title: East Midlands Exporter. 1991. q. T D A Marketing Communications, Apex House, Bank St., Lutterworth, Leicestershire LE17 4AG, England. TEL 44-1455-558377. FAX 44-1455-559845. Ed. Brian Drescher. adv. contact: Susan Darrall. **Document type:** trade publication.
—BLDSC (3842.944476).
  Formerly (until 1994): D T I East Midlands Exporter (ISSN 0969-3750)

382.6 US ISSN 0732-0159
HF3011
EXPORTERS' ENCYCLOPAEDIA. 1904. a. (with s-m. updates). $495 to commercial institutions; libraries $450. Dun and Bradstreet (Subsidiary of: Dun & Bradstreet Corporation), 3 Sylvan Way, Parsippany, NJ 07054-3896. TEL 201-605-6000. Ed. Joseph Douress. adv.; index. circ. 5,100.
  Former titles: Dun and Bradstreet Exporters' Encyclopaedia - World Marketing Guide (ISSN 0149-8118); Exporters' Encyclopaedia-World Marketing Guide (ISSN 0071-3546)
  Description: Essential exporting, travel, communications and research information for over 170 world markets

382 EI
EXTERNAL TRADE: NOMENCLATURE OF GOODS/COMMERCE EXTERIEUR: NOMENCLATURE DES PAYS. (In 5 vols.) (Multilingual text) irreg. price varies. Office for Official Publications of the European Communities, L-2985 Luxembourg, Luxembourg. (Dist. in the U.S. by: Unipub, 4611-F Assembly Dr., Lanham, MD 20706-4391. TEL 800-274-4888. FAX 301-459-0056)

382.5 LB
EXTERNAL TRADE OF LIBERIA: IMPORT AND EXPORT.* (Text in English) a. $5. Ministry of Planning and Economic Affairs, PO Box 9016, Monrovia, Liberia.

EXTERNAL TRADE STATISTICS OF GAMBIA. see BUSINESS AND ECONOMICS — Abstracting, Bibliographies, Statistics

EXTERNAL TRADE STATISTICS OF GHANA (ANNUAL). see BUSINESS AND ECONOMICS — Abstracting, Bibliographies, Statistics

EXTERNAL TRADE STATISTICS OF GHANA (HALF-YEARLY). see BUSINESS AND ECONOMICS — Abstracting, Bibliographies, Statistics

EXTERNAL TRADE STATISTICS OF GHANA (QUARTERLY). see BUSINESS AND ECONOMICS — Abstracting, Bibliographies, Statistics

F A O YEARBOOK, TRADE. see AGRICULTURE — Agricultural Economics

338.025 332.6 UK ISSN 1358-5754
▼**THE F I S DIRECTORY OF U K EXPORTERS**. 1995. a. £125 (overseas £135). F I S Publications Ltd., 32 Vauxhall Bridge Rd., London SW1V 2SS, England. TEL 44-171-973-6402. FAX 44-171-233-5056. Ed. David Ricketts. adv. contact: Adrian Clarke. **Document type:** directory.

338.025 332.6 UK ISSN 1358-5762
▼**THE F I S DIRECTORY OF U K IMPORTERS**. 1995. a. £115 (foreign £125). F I S Publications Ltd., 32 Vauxhall Bridge Rd., London SW1V 2SS, England. TEL 44-171-973-6402. FAX 44-171-233-5056. Ed. David Ricketts. adv. contact: Adrian Clarke. **Document type:** directory.

382 PN
F O B COLON FREE ZONE. (Text in English and Spanish) 1979. a. $10. (Colon Free Zone Users Association) Focus Publications (Int.) S.A., Apdo. 6-3287, El Dorado, Panama, Panama. TEL 507-225-6638. FAX 507-225-0466. E-mail: focusint@sinfo.net; URL: http://znalibre.by.net. Ed. Kenneth J. Jones. adv. circ. 35,000. **Document type:** directory.
  Formerly: Colon Free Zone Directory.
  Description: Directory of companies, products and trademarks incorporating full color product catalogue and information for potential investors.

382 340 US ISSN 0161-7036
F T C FREEDOM OF INFORMATION LOG. (Federal Trade Commission) 1980. w. $345 (effective Oct. 1995). Washington Regulatory Reporting Associates, Box 356, Basye, VA 22810. TEL 703-856-2216. FAX 703-856-8331. Ed. Arthur Amolsch; Pub. Arthur Amolsch. (fax) **Document type:** newsletter.
●Also available online. Vendor(s): Lexis-Nexis.
—CCC.
  Description: Provides summaries of the Freedom of Information Act requests received at the U.S. Federal Trade Commission.

382 JA
F T C - JAPAN VIEW: INFORMATION & OPINION FROM THE FAIR TRADE COMMISSION OF JAPAN. 1988. a. free. Fair Trade Commission, International Affairs Division, 1-1-1 Kasumigaseki, Chiyoda-ku, Tokyo 100, Japan. TEL 81-3-3581-4968. FAX 81-3-3581-1944. Ed. Kazuyuki Funhashi; Pub. Masaya Sakuma. R&P contact: Masaya Sakuma. **Document type:** government publication.

382 US ISSN 0196-0016
KF1602
F T C WATCH. (Federal Trade Commission) 1976. fortn. $690 (effective Oct. 1997). Washington Regulatory Reporting Associates, Box 356, Basye, VA 22810. TEL 703-856-2216. Ed. Arthur Amolsch; Pub. Arthur Amolsch. bk.rev. (looseleaf format) **Document type:** newsletter.
●Also available online. Vendor(s): Lexis-Nexis, NewsNet (GT17).
—CCC.
  Description: Provides information on the policies, personnel and law enforcement programs of the U.S. Federal Trade Commission, the Antitrust Division of the U.S. Department of Justice, and the multistate task force of the National Association of Attorneys General, including merger enforcement.

382 US ISSN 1050-0782
F X WEEK. (Foreign Exchange) 1990. w. $1495. Waters Information Services, Inc., Box 2248, Binghamton, NY 13902-2248. TEL 607-770-9242; 800-947-7947. FAX 607-770-9435. URL: http://www.watersinfo.com. (European and Asian subscr. to: Waters Information Services Ltd., 57-59 Neal St., London EC2H 9PJ, England. TEL 44-171-240-2090. FAX 44-171-240-2076) Ed. John Whelan. **Document type:** newsletter.

FEDERAL REPUBLIC OF GERMANY - PARTNER OF THE WORLD; documentation of economy and export. see BUSINESS AND ECONOMICS — Economic Situation And Conditions

382 FR ISSN 0992-7425
FEDERATION FRANCAISE DE LA FRANCHISE. LETTRE. Key Title: Lettre de la F F F. 10/yr. 500 F. Federation Francaise de la Franchise, 60 rue la Boetie, 75008 Paris, France. TEL 33-1-53752225. FAX 33-1-53752220. E-mail: fff@club-internet.fr; URL: http://www.club-internet.fr/perso/fff/. Ed. Chantal Zimmer. bk.rev. **Document type:** newsletter.
  Formerly: Franchise Actualites.

382 NE ISSN 1381-7647
FENENDEXPRESS. 1980. m. Federatie voor de Nederlandse Export, Postbus 90409, 2509 LK The Hague, Netherlands. TEL 31-70-3305600. FAX 31-70-3305656.

FERTILIZER TRADE INFORMATION MONTHLY BULLETIN. see AGRICULTURE — Crop Production And Soil

FINANCE & TREASURY. see BUSINESS AND ECONOMICS — Banking And Finance

382 US
FINANCIAL EXCHANGE. 1982. q. free. Chicago Board of Trade, Communications Department, 141 W. Jackson Blvd., Chicago, IL 60604. TEL 312-435-3651. FAX 312-341-3306. E-mail: gpod46@cbot.com; URL: http://www.cbot.com. Ed. Gene Podrazik. R&P contact: Gene Podrazik. adv. contact: Gene Podrazik. circ. 20,000. **Document type:** trade publication.

382 US
FINANCIAL EXECUTIVE'S COUNTRY RISK ALERT. 3/yr. $475. S.J. Rundt & Associates, Inc., 130 E. 63rd. St., New York, NY 10021-7334. TEL 212-838-0141. Ed. Hans P. Belcsak. stat. (also avail. in diskette format)
  Description: Provides surveys and forecast information on international trade and currency matters, with specific risk evaluations for all countries.

FINANCING OPERATIONS. AFRICA. see BUSINESS AND ECONOMICS — Banking And Finance

FINANCING OPERATIONS. ARGENTINA. see BUSINESS AND ECONOMICS — Banking And Finance

FINANCING OPERATIONS. AUSTRALIA. see BUSINESS AND ECONOMICS — Banking And Finance

FINANCING OPERATIONS. BELGIUM. see BUSINESS AND ECONOMICS — Banking And Finance

FINANCING OPERATIONS. BRAZIL. see BUSINESS AND ECONOMICS — Banking And Finance

FINANCING OPERATIONS. CANADA. see BUSINESS AND ECONOMICS — Banking And Finance

FINANCING OPERATIONS. CHILE. see BUSINESS AND ECONOMICS — Banking And Finance

FINANCING OPERATIONS. CHINA. see BUSINESS AND ECONOMICS — Banking And Finance

FINANCING OPERATIONS. COLOMBIA. see BUSINESS AND ECONOMICS — Banking And Finance

FINANCING OPERATIONS. COSTA RICA. see BUSINESS AND ECONOMICS — Banking And Finance

FINANCING OPERATIONS. CZECH REPUBLIC. see BUSINESS AND ECONOMICS — Banking And Finance

FINANCING OPERATIONS. EL SALVADOR. see BUSINESS AND ECONOMICS — Banking And Finance

FINANCING OPERATIONS. FRANCE. see BUSINESS AND ECONOMICS — Banking And Finance

FINANCING OPERATIONS. GERMANY. see BUSINESS AND ECONOMICS — Banking And Finance

FINANCING OPERATIONS. GREECE. see BUSINESS AND ECONOMICS — Banking And Finance

FINANCING OPERATIONS. GUATEMALA. see BUSINESS AND ECONOMICS — Banking And Finance

FINANCING OPERATIONS. HONDURAS. see BUSINESS AND ECONOMICS — Banking And Finance

FINANCING OPERATIONS. HONG KONG. see BUSINESS AND ECONOMICS — Banking And Finance

FINANCING OPERATIONS. HUNGARY. see BUSINESS AND ECONOMICS — Banking And Finance

FINANCING OPERATIONS. INDIA. see BUSINESS AND ECONOMICS — Banking And Finance

FINANCING OPERATIONS. INDONESIA. see BUSINESS AND ECONOMICS — Banking And Finance

FINANCING OPERATIONS. ITALY. see BUSINESS AND ECONOMICS — Banking And Finance

FINANCING OPERATIONS. JAPAN. see BUSINESS AND ECONOMICS — Banking And Finance

FINANCING OPERATIONS. MALAYSIA. see BUSINESS AND ECONOMICS — Banking And Finance

BUSINESS AND ECONOMICS — INTERNATIONAL COMMERCE

FINANCING OPERATIONS. MEXICO. see *BUSINESS AND ECONOMICS — Banking And Finance*

FINANCING OPERATIONS. NETHERLANDS. see *BUSINESS AND ECONOMICS — Banking And Finance*

FINANCING OPERATIONS. NEW ZEALAND. see *BUSINESS AND ECONOMICS — Banking And Finance*

FINANCING OPERATIONS. NICARAGUA. see *BUSINESS AND ECONOMICS — Banking And Finance*

FINANCING OPERATIONS. NIGERIA. see *BUSINESS AND ECONOMICS — Banking And Finance*

FINANCING OPERATIONS. NORWAY. see *BUSINESS AND ECONOMICS — Banking And Finance*

FINANCING OPERATIONS. PANAMA. see *BUSINESS AND ECONOMICS — Banking And Finance*

FINANCING OPERATIONS. PHILIPPINES. see *BUSINESS AND ECONOMICS — Banking And Finance*

FINANCING OPERATIONS. POLAND. see *BUSINESS AND ECONOMICS — Banking And Finance*

FINANCING OPERATIONS. PORTUGAL. see *BUSINESS AND ECONOMICS — Banking And Finance*

FINANCING OPERATIONS. RUSSIA. see *BUSINESS AND ECONOMICS — Banking And Finance*

FINANCING OPERATIONS. SAUDI ARABIA. see *BUSINESS AND ECONOMICS — Banking And Finance*

FINANCING OPERATIONS. SINGAPORE. see *BUSINESS AND ECONOMICS — Banking And Finance*

FINANCING OPERATIONS. SOUTH AFRICA. see *BUSINESS AND ECONOMICS — Banking And Finance*

FINANCING OPERATIONS. SOUTH KOREA. see *BUSINESS AND ECONOMICS — Banking And Finance*

FINANCING OPERATIONS. SPAIN. see *BUSINESS AND ECONOMICS — Banking And Finance*

FINANCING OPERATIONS. SWEDEN. see *BUSINESS AND ECONOMICS — Banking And Finance*

FINANCING OPERATIONS. SWITZERLAND. see *BUSINESS AND ECONOMICS — Banking And Finance*

FINANCING OPERATIONS. TAIWAN. see *BUSINESS AND ECONOMICS — Banking And Finance*

FINANCING OPERATIONS. THAILAND. see *BUSINESS AND ECONOMICS — Banking And Finance*

FINANCING OPERATIONS. TURKEY. see *BUSINESS AND ECONOMICS — Banking And Finance*

FINANCING OPERATIONS. UNITED KINGDOM. see *BUSINESS AND ECONOMICS — Banking And Finance*

FINANCING OPERATIONS. UNITED STATES OF AMERICA. see *BUSINESS AND ECONOMICS — Banking And Finance*

FINANCING OPERATIONS. VENEZUELA. see *BUSINESS AND ECONOMICS — Banking And Finance*

FINDING EXPORT MARKETS. see *BUSINESS AND ECONOMICS — Trade And Industrial Directories*

382   FI   ISSN 0015-251X
FINSKIJ TORGOVYJ ZHURNAL. (Text in Russian) 1932-1993. irreg. FIM 55. Finnish Foreign Trade Association - Suomen Ulkomaankauppaliite, P.O. Box 908, FIN-00101 Helsinki, Finland. TEL 308-0-69591. TELEX 121969. circ. 18,000. **Document type:** trade publication.

382 338   US   ISSN 0146-1958
HF1
FLAGSTAFF INSTITUTE. JOURNAL. 1976. s-a. $50 to individuals and non-profits; government and industry $150. Flagstaff Institute, Box 986, Flagstaff, AZ 86002. TEL 520-779-0052. FAX 520-774-8589. E-mail: instflag@aol.com. Ed. Richard L. Bolin. R&P contact: Judy Babbitt. index. circ. 100. (back issues avail.) **Document type:** academic/scholarly publication.
  Description: Covers world trade in production-sharing goods made cooperatively in two or more countries, especially Third World manufacturing for advanced markets.

382   JA   ISSN 0388-0311
HF41
FOCUS JAPAN. 1974. m. 4944 Yen (Europe $32; elsewhere $31). Japan External Trade Organization, International Communication Department, 2-5 Toranomon 2-chome, Minato-ku, Tokyo 105, Japan. TEL 03-3582-5521. FAX 03-3582-0504. TELEX J 24378. Ed. Akira Moromi. **Indexed:** Int.Packag.Abstr., JTA, Key to Econ.Sci., Mgmt.& Market.Abstr. **Document type:** newspaper.
● Also available online.
  Former titles: Trade and Industry of Japan (ISSN 0041-0381); Japan Trade Bulletin (ISSN 0021-4760)

382   NE
FOCUS ON HOLLAND; tijdschrift t.b.v. de Nederlandse industrie, handel, landbouwen verkeer, ter bevordering van de Nederlandse export naar diverse landen. q. Nederlands Centrum voor Handelsbevordering, Postbus 10, 2501 CA The Hague, Netherlands. adv. circ. 5,000. **Indexed:** Key to Econ.Sci.

382   CK
FONDO DE PROMOCION DE EXPORTACIONES. DIRECTORIO DE EXPORTADORES/EXPORT DIRECTORY. (Text in English, Spanish) 1969. a. free. Proexpo Fondo de Promocion de Exportaciones, Calle 28 No. 13A-15 Piso 41, Bogota, Colombia. FAX 2825071. TELEX 45690-44452. adv.; charts; illus.; stat. circ. 15,000. **Document type:** directory.

FOOD AND AGRICULTURAL EXPORT DIRECTORY. see *AGRICULTURE — Agricultural Economics*

FOREIGN AGRICULTURAL TRADE OF THE UNITED STATES. see *AGRICULTURE — Agricultural Economics*

382   US   ISSN 0732-0418
HG4501
FOREIGN DIRECT INVESTMENT IN THE UNITED STATES; operations of U.S. affiliates of foreign companies. 1977. a. U.S. Department of Commerce, Bureau of Economic Analysis, International Investment Division, Washington, DC 20230. TEL 202-523-0640. FAX 202-523-7538. **Document type:** government publication.
  Description: Covers the financial structure and operations of the non-bank U.S. affiliates of foreign direct investors.

FOREIGN INVESTMENT IN CENTRAL AND EASTERN EUROPE. see *LAW — International Law*

382 346   BL
FOREIGN INVESTMENTS IN BRAZIL. LEGISLATION. 1967. irreg. R.2227($132.22) (effective 1997). Banco Central do Brasil - Central Bank of Brazil, Departamento de Capitais Estrangeiros - FIRCE, SBS, Ed. Sede Banco Central, 2 SS, 70074-900 Brasilia, DF, Brazil. TEL 55-61-4142227. (Subscr to: DEBRA-RESUP, SIG, Quadra 8, Lote 2025, 70610-400 Brasilia DF, Brazil. TEL 55-61-3441554. FAX 55-61-4142982) Ed. Marcio Cartier Marques. circ. 1,500. **Document type:** directory.
  Formerly: Foreign Investments in Brazil.
  Description: Set of current laws and other normatives concerning foreign capital in Brazil.

382   US   ISSN 1055-1468
HF1371
FOREIGN TRADE.* 1991. 10/yr. $45 (effective 1993). Defense & Diplomacy, Inc., 7010 Churchill Rd., McLean, VA 22101-2608. TEL 703-448-1338. FAX 703-448-1841. Ed. Russell Goodman. circ. 11,600. **Document type:** trade publication.
  Description: Covers innovations in world trade, with each issue focusing on a specific country.

382   II   ISSN 0015-7317
HF41
FOREIGN TRADE BULLETIN. (Text in English) 1970. m. Rs.100 (foreign $25). Indian Institute of Foreign Trade, B-21, Mehrauli Institutional Area, New Delhi 110016, India. Ed.Bd. adv.; charts; stat. **Document type:** bulletin.
  Description: Provides commercial information and market intelligence on export opportunities and sales prospects of Indian products in foreign markets.

382 658   US   ISSN 0883-4687
FOREIGN TRADE FAIRS NEW PRODUCTS NEWSLETTER. 1980. m. $45 (effective 1998). International Intertrade Index, Box 636, Federal Sq., Newark, NJ 07101. TEL 908-686-2382. FAX 201-622-1740. Ed. John E. Felber. (looseleaf format; back issues avail.) **Document type:** newsletter.
  Description: New products displayed at foreign trade fairs seeking U.S. importers and distributors.

382   US
FOREIGN TRADE MARKETPLACE. 1977. irreg. $130. Gale Research, 835 Penobscot Bldg., 645 Griswold St., Detroit, MI 48226-4094. TEL 313-961-2242; 800-877-4253. FAX 800-414-5043. E-mail: daniel__snyder@gale.com. Ed. George J. Schultz.

382   KN
FOREIGN TRADE OF THE DEMOCRATIC PEOPLE'S REPUBLIC OF KOREA. (Editions in Arabic, Chinese, English, French, Japanese, Russian and Spanish) bi-m. $18.90. Foreign Trade Publishing House, Potongang District, Pyongyang, N. Korea. TELEX 37018 EPB KP. (Dist. by: Korean Publications Exchange Association, Export Section, P.O. Box 222, Pyongyang, N. Korea. FAX 850-2-814632) Ed. Mun Sun Hui. adv.; illus.

382   US
HF105
FOREIGN TRADE REPORTS. U.S. EXPORT AND IMPORT MERCHANDISE TRADE AND SUPPLEMENT. (Series FT-900) 1945. m. $120. U.S. Bureau of the Census, Foreign Trade Division, Washington, DC 20233. TEL 301-763-5140. (Subscr. to: Supt. of Documents, Washington, DC 20402) (also avail. in microfiche from CIS; reprint service avail. from CIS) **Indexed:** Amer.Stat.Ind. (1973-).
● Also available online. Vendor(s): CompuServe, Inc., Knight-Ridder Information, Inc.
  Former titles: Foreign Trade Reports. Summary of U.S. Export and Import Merchandise Trade (ISSN 0361-0047); (until 1988): Foreign Trade Reports. Highlights of U.S. Export and Import Trade (ISSN 0565-0941)

382   US   ISSN 0565-1204
HF3060
FOREIGN TRADE REPORTS. U.S. TRADE WITH PUERTO RICO AND U.S. POSSESSIONS. (Series FT-895) 1943. a. price varies. U.S. Bureau of the Census, Foreign Trade Division, Washington, DC 20233. TEL 301-763-5140. (Dist. by: Supt. of Documents, Washington, DC 20402) (also avail. in microfiche from CIS; reprint service avail. from CIS) **Indexed:** Amer.Stat.Ind. (1973-).

382   US   ISSN 0095-0890
HF105
FOREIGN TRADE REPORTS. U.S. WATERBORNE EXPORTS AND GENERAL IMPORTS; trade area, district, port, type service and U.S. flag. (Series TM 985) 1952. m. and a. $120. U.S. Bureau of the Census, Foreign Trade Division, Washington, DC 20233. TEL 301-763-5140. (Subscr. to: Supt. of Documents, Washington, DC 20402) (also avail. in microfiche from CIS; reprint service avail. from CIS) **Indexed:** Amer.Stat.Ind. (1973-).

382   II   ISSN 0015-7325
HF41
FOREIGN TRADE REVIEW. (Text in English) 1966. q. Rs.275 (foreign $30). Indian Institute of Foreign Trade, B-21, Mehrauli Institutional Area, New Delhi 110016, India. TEL 91-11-6965124. FAX 91-11-6853956. Ed. R. Jaikumar. adv. **Indexed:** BPIA, C.R.E.J., Key to Econ.Sci. **Document type:** trade publication.
—BLDSC (3987.320000).
  Description: Publishes papers and articles on foreign trade for trade and industry, government departments, research and academic institutions.

BUSINESS AND ECONOMICS — INTERNATIONAL COMMERCE

382 II
FOREIGN TRADE - TRENDS & TIDINGS. (Text in English) m. Rs.215($50) Indian Institute of Foreign Trade, B-21, Mehrauli Institutional Area, New Delhi 110016, India. TEL 91-11-6965124. FAX 91-116853956.

FORWARD MARKETS BULLETIN. see *BUSINESS AND ECONOMICS — Domestic Commerce*

FRANCE. DIRECTION DES AFFAIRES ECONOMIQUES ET INTERNATIONALES. S E S INFOS RAPIDES. see *BUSINESS AND ECONOMICS — Economic Situation And Conditions*

382 FR ISSN 0071-8645
FRANCE. DIRECTION GENERALE DES DOUANES ET DROITS INDIRECTS. RESULTATS ANNUELS DES STATISTIQUES DU COMMERCE EXTERIEUR. a. 250 F. Imprimerie Nationale, B.P. 514, 59505 Douai Cedex, France. TEL 27-93-70-70. FAX 27-93-70-96. TELEX 120 389 F.
Formerly: France. Direction Generale des Douanes et Droits Indirects. Commentaires Annuels des Statistiques du Commerce Exterieur (ISSN 0532-4416).

382 FR ISSN 0071-8726
FRANCE. DIRECTION NATIONALE DES DOUANES ET DROITS INDIRECTS. TABLEAU GENERAL DES TRANSPORTS. 1964. a. price varies. Imprimerie Nationale, B.P. 514, 59505 Douai Cedex, France. TEL 27-93-70-90. FAX 27-93-70-96. TELEX 120 389 F.

382 FR ISSN 0071-8718
FRANCE. DIRECTION NATIONALE DES DOUANES ET DROITS INDIRECTS. TRANSPORT DU COMMERCE EXTERIEUR. a. 390 F. Imprimerie Nationale, B.P. 514, 59505 Douai Cedex, France. TEL 27-93-70-90. FAX 27-93-70-96. TELEX 120 389 F.

338.1 382 FR
FRANCE. MINISTERE DE L'AGRICULTURE, DE LA PECHE ET DE L'ALIMENTATION. CONJONCTURE EXTERIEUR AGRO-ALIMENTAIRE. 1976. m. 178 F. (foreign 200 F.) (effective 1997). Ministere de l'Agriculture, de la Peche et de l'Alimentation, Service Central des Enquetes et Etudes Statistiques, 4 av. Saint Mande, 75570 Paris Cedex 12, France. TEL 33-1-49558585. FAX 33-1-49558503. (Subscr. to: B.P. 88, 31326 Castanet Tolosan Cedex, France) **Document type:** government publication.
Former titles: France. Ministere de l'Agriculture et de la Foret. Conjoncture Exterieure Agro-Alimentaire; France. Ministere de l'Agriculture. Informations Rapides Commerce Exterieur Agro-Alimentaire (ISSN 0153-1999).

FRANCE TELEXPORT. see *BUSINESS AND ECONOMICS — Trade And Industrial Directories*

FRANCHISE INTERNATIONAL. see *BUSINESS AND ECONOMICS — Marketing And Purchasing*

FRANCO-BRITISH TRADE DIRECTORY. see *BUSINESS AND ECONOMICS — Trade And Industrial Directories*

382 PO
▼**FROM PORTUGAL.** (Text in English) 1975. m. free. Interfil - Centro de Promocao de Informacao Tecnica Lda, Rua Heliodoro Salgado 44-r-c, 1100 Lisbon, Portugal. Ed. Fernando Bravo. adv.; illus.; stat. circ. 7,500.

382 CN ISSN 1194-630X
▼**FROM THE CENTRE.** 1989. s-a. free. Centre for International Business Studies, Dalhousie University, 6152 Coburg Rd., Halifax, NS B3H 1Z5, Canada. TEL 902-494-6553. FAX 902-494-1483. Ed. Mary Brooks. circ. 1,200. (back issues avail.) **Document type:** newsletter.
Description: Reports student and faculty activities at the Centre.

332.6 341 EI ISSN 1021-2353
HC241.2.A1
FRONTIER-FREE EUROPE. French edition: Europe sans Frontieres (ISSN 1021-237X); German edition: Europa ohne Grenzen (ISSN 1021-2345); Spanish edition: Europa sin Fronteras (ISSN 1021-2361); Danish edition: Graenseloese Europa (ISSN 1021-2337); Dutch edition: Europa zonder Grenzen (ISSN 1021-240X) Italian edition: Europa senza Frontiere (EI ISSN 1021-2396) Greek edition: Europe horis Sunora (EI ISSN 1021-2388) Portuguese edition: Europa sem Fronteiras (EI ISSN 1021-2418) (Text in English) 1988. m. free. (Commission of the European Communities, Directorate-General for Audiovisual Media, Information, Communication and Culture) Office for Official Publications of the European Communities, DG XXIII, Rue de la Loi 200, 1049 Brussels, Belgium. **Document type:** newsletter.
Formerly (until 1993): Target 92 (ISSN 0776-8508)
Description: Reports on the progress of internal market legislation.

382 UK
FRONTIERS; planning for consumer change in Europe. (Text in English, French) 1991. a. Henley Centre for Forcasting Ltd., 9 Bridewell Pl., London EC4Y 6AY, England. TEL 44-171-353-9961. FAX 44-171-353-2899. E-mail: jmurphy@hancent.co.uk. Ed. James Murphy. **Document type:** trade publication.
Description: Presents a pan-European forecast of consumer trends in the E.U. for companies with ambitions or operations in Europe.

382 CC
FUJIAN DUIWAI JINGMAO/FUJIAN FOREIGN TRADE. (Text in Chinese) m. Fujian Sheng Duiwai Jingji Maoyi Yanjiusuo - Fujian Institute of Foreign Trade, No.17, Hualin Lu, 15th Fl., Fuzhou, Fujian 350003, People's Republic of China. TEL 572614. Ed. Gu Ming.

382 UN ISSN 0072-0615
G A T T ACTIVITIES; an annual review of the work of GATT. Spanish edition: G A T T Actividades (ISSN 0251-0618); French edition (ISSN 0251-060X) 1959. a. 20 SFr. General Agreement on Tariffs and Trade, Centre William Rappard, 154 rue de Lausanne, 1211 Geneva 21, Switzerland. TEL 022-739-5208. FAX 022-739-5458. (Dist. in U.S. by: Unipub, 4611-F Assembly Dr., Lanham, MD 20706-4391. TEL 800-274-4447. FAX 301-459-0056) circ. 7,700 (combined). (also avail. in microfiche from CIS) **Indexed:** IIS. **Document type:** corporate report.

330 UN ISSN 0256-0119
HF1701
G A T T FOCUS. French edition (ISSN 0256-0127); Spanish edition (ISSN 0256-0135) (Text in English) 1981. 10/yr. free. General Agreement on Tariffs and Trade, Information and Media Relations Division - Accord General sur les Tarifs Douaniers et le Commerce, Centre William Rappard, 154 rue de Lausanne, 1211 Geneva 21, Switzerland. TEL 022-7395111. FAX 022-7395458. TELEX 4122324-GATT-CH. Ed. Luis Ople. bk.rev. circ. 5,000. **Document type:** newsletter.
Description: Covers current events and issues in international trade, member countries' efforts to resolve trade problems, and the Uruguay Round multilateral trade negotiations.

G A T T LEGAL SYSTEM AND WORLD TRADE DIPLOMACY. see *LAW — International Law*

G S R. (Gakki Shoho Review) see *MUSIC*

382 FR ISSN 0247-8315
GABON SELECTION. s-m. (2/yr.). 4200 F. (effective 1997). I C Publications, 10 rue Vineuse, 75784 Paris Cedex 16, France. TEL 33-1-44308100. FAX 33-1-44308111.

GAMBIA. CENTRAL STATISTICS DEPARTMENT. MONTHLY SUMMARY OF EXTERNAL TRADE STATISTICS. see *BUSINESS AND ECONOMICS — Abstracting, Bibliographies, Statistics*

382 IT
GAZZETTA VALUTARIA E DEL COMMERCIO INTERNAZIONALE.* 1977. s-m. L.200000. I P S O A s.r.l. (Subsidiary of: Wolters Kluwer N.V.), Strada 1, Palazzo F6, 20090 Assago (Milan), Italy. TEL 2-824-761. Ed. Francesco Zuzic. adv.

382 UN ISSN 0072-0623
K4602
GENERAL AGREEMENT ON TARIFFS AND TRADE. BASIC INSTRUMENTS AND SELECTED DOCUMENTS SERIES. SUPPLEMENT. (Editions in English, French and Spanish) 1952. a. price varies. General Agreement on Tariffs and Trade, Centre William Rappard, 154 rue de Lausanne, 1211 Geneva 21, Switzerland. TEL 022-739-5208. FAX 022-739-5458. (Dist. in U.S. by: Unipub, 4611-F, Assembly Dr., Lanham, MD 20706-4391) cum.index. circ. 4,700 (combined). (also avail. in microfiche from CIS) **Indexed:** IIS. **Document type:** trade publication.
Description: Presents the decisions, recommendations and reports adopted by the GATT Contracting Parties each year.

382 UN ISSN 0072-064X
GENERAL AGREEMENT ON TARIFFS AND TRADE. INTERNATIONAL TRADE. (In two volumes) (Editions in English, French and Spanish) 1953. a. 30 SFr. General Agreement on Tariffs and Trade, Centre William Rappard, 154 rue de Lausanne, 1211 Geneva 21, Switzerland. TEL 022-739-5208. FAX 022-739-5458. (Dist. in U.S. by: Unipub, 4611-F Assembly Dr., Lanham, MD 20706-4391) stat. circ. 7,200. (also avail. in microfiche from CIS) **Indexed:** IIS.
Description: Analyzes main trends and developments in international trade. Contains comprehensive statistical information.

382.0973 CN ISSN 1182-803X
HF3099
GERMAN AMERICAN TRADE. (Text in English, German) 1949. 10/yr. DM.100($50) (German American Chamber of Commerce, US) Ruland Communications Inc., 12 Lawton Blvd., Toronto, ON M4V 1Z4, Canada. TEL 416-927-9129. FAX 416-927-9118. (Subscr. in U.S. to: GACC Publication Services, 40 W. 57th St., 31st Fl., New York, NY 10019. TEL 212-874-8830. FAX 212-974-8867) Ed. Daniel Mahler; Pubs. Joseph Ruland, Ulli Ruland. adv.; bk.rev.; illus.; tr.lit. circ. 4,000. (also avail. in microform from UMI; reprint service avail. from UMI) **Indexed:** PROMT. **Document type:** trade publication.
—UMI.
Supersedes (in 1990): German American Commerce; Which was formerly: German Business Weekly (ISSN 0433-6305); G A T N (ISSN 0192-0103); German American Trade News (ISSN 0016-8718); (until 1952): United States German Chamber of Commerce. Monthly Bulletin (ISSN 0733-3854).

GLOBAL ASSET ALLOCATION. see *BUSINESS AND ECONOMICS — Investments*

332.6 332 658 US ISSN 1088-6931
HG3879 CODEN: GBFRFK
▼**GLOBAL BUSINESS AND FINANCE REVIEW.** 1996. s-a. $30 to individuals; institutions $80 (effective 1997); newsstand price: $30. Indiana State University, School of Business, Terre Haute, IN 47809. TEL 912-237-2117. FAX 812-237-8563. E-mail: mfkim@befac.indstate.edu. Ed. David J. Kim. R&P contact: David J. Kim. adv.: page $150; adv. contact: David J. Kim. bk.rev.; index. circ. 750. (also avail. in microfiche; back issues avail.) **Document type:** academic/scholarly publication.
—BLDSC (4195.354400).
Description: Provides a forum for the exchange of ideas, information, and analysis in this era of globalization. Applied research on domestic issues will also be included.
Refereed Serial

332.6 US ISSN 1062-1261
HF1351 CODEN: GBWBEM
GLOBAL BUSINESS WHITE PAPERS. 1991. irreg. $60 to non-members; members $15. Conference Board, Inc., 845 Third Ave., New York, NY 10022. TEL 212-759-0900. FAX 212-980-7014. (back issues avail.)
Description: Each issue deals with a specific topic. Analyzes key trends in the external environment and their impact on the management of multinational corporations.

BUSINESS AND ECONOMICS — INTERNATIONAL COMMERCE

382　　　　　　　　US
▼**GLOBAL COMMERCE.** 1995. q. free. Middle Tennessee State University, College of Business, 1301 E. Main St., MTSU Box 102, Murgreesboro, TN 37132. TEL 615-898-5627. FAX 615-898-5045. E-mail: slivings@mtsu.edu; URL: http://www.mtsu.~berc/inter.html. (Co-sponsors: Project International; World Trade Council of Middle Tennessee, Inc.) Ed. Steven G. Livingston. R&P contact: Reuben Kyle. adv. contact: Reuben Kyle. circ. 3,800. **Document type:** academic/scholarly publication.
  Description: Provides an analysis of current international trade relations in Middle Tennessee.

332.6 322　　　　US　　ISSN 1060-8710
HG4009
GLOBAL COMPANY HANDBOOK. 1992. a. $495. C I F A R Publications, Inc., 3490 US Hwy 1, BL012, Princeton, NJ 08540-5920. TEL 609-520-9333. FAX 609-520-0905. Ed. Vinod B. Bavishi. (also avail. in magnetic tape)
  ●Also available online. Vendor(s): Lexis-Nexis. Also available on CD-ROM.
  Description: Analysis of the financial performance of the world's leading 10,000 companies.

GLOBAL FINANCE JOURNAL. see BUSINESS AND ECONOMICS — Banking And Finance

382　　　　　　　　US
GLOBAL GLIMPSES. 1991. bi-w. $60. Assist International, 60 Madison Ave., 2nd Fl., New York, NY 10010. TEL 212-725-3311. FAX 212-725-3312. circ. 1,000 (paid). (back issues avail.) **Document type:** newsletter.
  Description: Provides information on resources, events and tools available to the international business and education communities.

GLOBAL INVESTOR. see BUSINESS AND ECONOMICS — Banking And Finance

382 327　　　　US　　ISSN 0739-4640
HG4538
GLOBAL RISK ASSESSMENTS; issues, concepts and applications. 1983. irreg., vol.4, 1997. $42.50. Global Risk Assessments, Inc., 3638 University Ave., Ste. 215, Riverside, CA 92501. TEL 909-788-0672. FAX 909-788-0672. E-mail: jrogers@grai.com; URL: http://www.grai.com. Ed. Jerry Rogers. bk.rev. circ. 1,000. **Indexed:** Curr.Cont., Manage.Cont., P.A.I.S., Polit.Sci.Abstr., Sociol.Abstr. **Document type:** trade publication, academic/scholarly publication.
  Description: Contains manuscripts on international business environment assessment; country, investment and trade risk analysis; political risk assessment and management.
  Refereed Serial

382　　　　　　　US　　ISSN 1056-3857
HJ6622
GLOBAL TRADE TALK. 1991. bi-m. $11 (foreign $13.75). U.S. Customs Service, National Support Staff, Rm. B338, 1301 Constitution Ave., N.W., Washington, DC 20229. (Subscr. to: Superintendent of Documents, Box 371954, Pittsburgh, PA 15250-7954. TEL 202-512-1800. FAX 202-512-2250) (back issues avail.) **Document type:** government publication.
  —UnCover.
  Description: Focuses on pertinent and timely issues concerning international trade and the role of the U.S. Customs Service in facilitating it while enforcing U.S. trade law.

GOVERNMENT WORLD. see BUSINESS AND ECONOMICS — Economic Situation And Conditions

332.6　　　　　　　　UK
GREAT BRITAIN. OFFICE OF FAIR TRADING. REPORT. 1975. a. £12. H.M.S.O., 51 Nine Elms Ln., London SW8 5DR, England. TEL 44-171-873-0011. FAX 44-171-873-8247. (reprint service avail. from UMI) **Document type:** government publication.

GREY BOOK. see AGRICULTURE — Abstracting, Bibliographies, Statistics

382　　　　　　　　CC
GUANGDONG DUIWAI JINGMAO/GUANGDONG FOREIGN ECONOMICS AND TRADE. (Text in Chinese) m. Guangdong Sheng Duiwai Jingji Maoyi Weiyuanhui, No. 774, Dongfeng Donglu, Building No. 11, Guangzhou, Guangdong 510087, People's Republic of China. TEL 775090. Ed. Ren Lao.

382　　　　　　　　DR
GUIA; del exportador de la Republica Dominicana. (Text in Spanish; contents page in English) 1982. bi-m. Editora Corripio, C. Por A., Box 20374, Santo Domingo, Dominican Republic. TEL 682-7092. Ed. Andres Gomez Solis.

GUIA DE COMERCIO EXTERIOR EXPORTADORES/GUIDE TO FOREIGN TRADE EXPORTERS. see BUSINESS AND ECONOMICS — Trade And Industrial Directories

GUIDE - DANISH CLOTHING AND TEXTILE INDUSTRIES. see TEXTILE INDUSTRIES AND FABRICS

GUIDE TO AMERICAN STATE AND LOCAL LAWS ON SOUTH AFRICA. see LAW — International Law

382　　　　　　　　UK
THE GUIDE TO EXPORT FINANCE. a. Euromoney Publications plc., Nestor House, Playhouse Yard, London EC4V 5EX, England. TEL 071-779-8888. FAX 071-779-8617. Eds. James Ball, Martin Knight. **Document type:** trade publication.

GUIDE TO FOREIGN TRADE STATISTICS. see BUSINESS AND ECONOMICS — Abstracting, Bibliographies, Statistics

GUIDE TO INTERNATIONAL ARBITRATION AND ARBITRATORS (YEAR). see LAW — International Law

382　　　　　　　　CC
GUOJI CHANYE JINGJI JISHU. (Text in Chinese) bi-m. Guangxi Kexue Jishu Weiyuanhui, 17 Xinghu Lu, Nanning, Guangxi 530022, People's Republic of China. TEL 43817. Ed. Zhang Zhengyou.

GUOJI JINGJI HEZUO/INTERNATIONAL ECONOMIC COOPERATION. see BUSINESS AND ECONOMICS — International Development And Assistance

382　　　　　　　CC　　ISSN 1002-0594
GUOJI JINGMAO TANSUO/INTERNATIONAL ECONOMICS AND TRADE RESEARCH. (Text in Chinese; abstracts in English) 1993. q.? newsstand price: Y1.40. Guangzhou Duiwai Maoyi Xueyuan, Darang, Baiyun-qu, Guangzhou, Guangdong 510450, People's Republic of China. TEL 6621819. FAX 6622212. (Dist. overseas by: China International Book Trading Corp., Box 399, Beijing, P.R. China)
  —BLDSC (4539.814000).

382 330.9　　　　US
GUOJI JINGMAO XIAOXI/INFORMATION - INTERNATIONAL TRADE & ECONOMICS. (Text in Chinese) 3/w. $152. China Books & Periodicals, Inc., 2929 24th St., San Francisco, CA 94110. TEL 415-282-2994. FAX 415-282-0994. **Document type:** newspaper.

382　　　　　　　　CC
GUOJI JINGMAO XIAOXI BAO/INTERNATIONAL TRADE NEWS. (Supplement avail.) (Text in Chinese; summaries in English) 1958. 3/w. (150/yr.). $250. Ministry of Foreign Economic Relations & Trade, International Trade Research Institute - Duiwai Jingji Maoyi Bu, Guoji Maoyi Yanjiusuo, Donghouxiang 28, Andingmenwai, Beijing 100710, People's Republic of China. TEL 421-4124. FAX 422-2661. TELEX 22168-MFTPK-CN. adv.; stat. circ. 960,000.
  Description: Aims to bridge China with the world and promote trade development. Uses a world-wide network to monitor global economic activities, world economy, international trade, financial and commodities markets, and economic cooperation.

382　　　　　　　　CC
GUOJI JINGMAO XIAOXI BAO. SHUANGBIAN JINGMAO ZHUANKAN/INTERNATIONAL TRADE NEWS SUPPLEMENT. (Supplement to: Guoji Jingmao Xiaoxi Bao) (Text in Chinese; summaries in English) 1980. 30/yr. Ministry of Foreign Economic Relations & Trade, International Trade Research Institute - Duiwai Jingji Maoyi Bu, Guoji Maoyi Yanjiusuo, Donghouxiang 28, Andingmenwai, Beijing 100710, People's Republic of China. TEL 421-4124. FAX 422-2661. TELEX 22168-MFTPK-CN. adv. circ. 960,000.
  Description: Each supplement covers a specific country or region. Focuses mainly on bilateral trade and mutual economic cooperation.

382　　　　　　　CC　　ISSN 1002-4999
GUOJI MAOYI/INTERNATIONAL TRADE. (Text in Chinese) 1982. m. $49.50. Duiwai Jingji Maoyi Bu, Guoji Maoyi Yanjiusuo - Ministry of Foreign Economics and Trade, International Trade Research Institute, No. 28, Andingmenwai Donghouxiang, Beijing 100710, People's Republic of China. TEL 4212149. (Dist. in US by: China Books & Periodicals, Inc., 2929 24th St., San Francisco, CA 94110. TEL 415-282-2994) Ed. Qin Xuanren.

382　　　　　　　CC　　ISSN 1002-4670
GUOJI MAOYI WENTI/INTERNATIONAL TRADE JOURNAL. (Text in Chinese) 1975. m. $17.76 (foreign $41.30). Duiwai Jingji Maoyi Daxue - University of International Business and Economics, Yinghua Dongjie Beikou, Andingmenwai, Beijing 100029, People's Republic of China. TEL 4225522. FAX 86-1-4212022. (Dist. overseas by: Guoji Shudian - China International Book Trading Corp., P.O. Box 399, Beijing, P.R.C.; Dist. in US by: China Books & Periodicals, Inc., 2929 24th St., San Francisco, CA 94110. TEL 415-282-2994) Ed. Li Kanghua.

382　　　　　　　　CC
GUOJI SHANGBAO/INTERNATIONAL BUSINESS. (Text in Chinese) d. Y96 (foreign $300). Guoji Shangbao She, P.O. Box 6115, Bldg. 14, Part 3, Fangxing Yuan, Fangzhuang Lu, Beijing 100061, People's Republic of China. TEL 7628822. FAX 7629153. (Dist. in US by: China Books & Periodicals, Inc., 2929 24th St., San Francisco, CA 94110. TEL 415-282-2994) **Document type:** newspaper.
  Description: Contains trade and economic information, and development trends in domestic and foreign trade.

382　　　　　　　　CC
GUOJI SHANGBAO YUEKAN/INTERNATIONAL BUSINESS MONTHLY. (English edition avail.) (Text in Chinese) b-m. Guoji Shangbao She, P.O. Box 6115, Bldg. 14, Part 3, Fangxing Yuan, Fangzhuang Lu, Beijing 100061, People's Republic of China. TEL 7019921. Ed. Cao Shonjiang. adv. contact: Yao Tingli. **Document type:** trade publication.

382　　　　　　　CC　　ISSN 1001-5450
GUOJI SHICHANG/INTERNATIONAL MARKET. (Text in Chinese) m. Shanghai Guoji Jingji Maoyi Yanjiusuo - Shanghai International Economics and Trade Institute, 33 Zhongshan Dongyi Lu, Shanghai 200002, People's Republic of China. TEL 3212659. Ed. Xu Pengyuan.

GUYANA. STATISTICAL BUREAU. ANNUAL ACCOUNT RELATING TO EXTERNAL TRADE. see BUSINESS AND ECONOMICS — Abstracting, Bibliographies, Statistics

382　　　　　　　GW　　ISSN 0017-6931
HAMBURGER EXPORT-WOCHE. 1951. w. DM.92.40. Verlag Holger Stuenings, Inselstr. 34, 22297 Hamburg, Germany. Ed. H. Stuenings. adv.; bk.rev.; abstr. circ. 1,500.

HANDBOOK OF INTERNATIONAL TRADE AND DEVELOPMENT STATISTICS - UNITED NATIONS/MANUEL DE STATISTIQUES DU COMMERCE INTERNATIONAL ET DU DEVELOPMENT - NATIONS UNIES. see BUSINESS AND ECONOMICS — Abstracting, Bibliographies, Statistics

HANDBOOK OF STATE TRADING ORGANIZATIONS OF DEVELOPING COUNTRIES/REPERTOIRE DES ORGANISMES DE COMMERCE D'ETAT DES PAYS EN DEVELOPPEMENT/REPERTORIO DE LAS ORGANIZACIONES COMERCIALES ESTATALES DE PAISES EN DESARROLLO/DALIL AL-HAY'AT AL-TIGANIYYA AL-HUKUMIYYA FI AL-BULDAN AN-NAMIYA. see BUSINESS AND ECONOMICS — Abstracting, Bibliographies, Statistics

HANDBOOK OF W T O - G A T T DISPUTE SETTLEMENT. see LAW — International Law

332.6 336　　　　　GW
HANDBUCH DER AUSLANDSZOELLE. 1956. bi-m. DM.575. Mendel Verlag, Robensstr. 39, 52070 Aachen, Germany. TEL 49-241-154355. FAX 49-241-154355. **Document type:** trade publication.
  ●Available only on CD-ROM.
  Description: Provides complete information about all custom-tariffs in the world.

BUSINESS AND ECONOMICS — INTERNATIONAL COMMERCE

332.6   GW
HANDBUCH DER EINFUHR NEBENABGABEN. 1956. bi-m. DM.160. Mendel Verlag, Robensstr. 39, 52070 Aachen, Germany. TEL 49-241-154355. FAX 49-241-154355. Ed. Peter Kuessner. **Document type:** trade publication.
  Description: Complete survey about VAT, import taxes, and consumption taxes for countries throughout the world.

332.6   GW   ISSN 0947-5931
HANDBUCH FUER DAS ERFOLGREICHE OSTGESCHAEFT. irreg. (6-8/yr.). DM.168. Deutscher Wirtschaftsdienst, Marienburgerstr. 22, 50968 Cologne, Germany. TEL 49-221-93763-0. FAX 49-221-9376399. Ed. Wolfgang von Lingelsheim-Seibicke. (looseleaf format) **Document type:** directory.
  Formerly: Handbuch fuer den Osthandel (ISSN 0937-2784)

382   PL   ISSN 0017-7245
HANDEL ZAGRANICZNY/FOREIGN TRADE. 1955. m. (plus special numbers). $84. Krajowa Izba Gospodarcza, Ul. Trebacka 4, 00-074 Warsaw, Poland. (Dist. by: Ars Polona-Ruch, Krakowskie Przedmiescie 7, Warsaw, Poland) Ed. Maciej Deniszczuk. adv.; bk.rev.; abstr.; bibl.; charts; illus.; stat.; index. circ. 3,000. (also avail. in microform from UMI; reprint service avail. from UMI) **Indexed:** AESIS.
  —UMI.

HARVARD INTERNATIONAL REVIEW. see *POLITICAL SCIENCE — International Relations*

HARVESTING, MARKETING AND DISTRIBUTION COSTS FOR AUSTRALIAN WOOL - SHEEP'S BACK TO OVERSEAS MILL. see *TEXTILE INDUSTRIES AND FABRICS*

382   NE   ISSN 1380-846X
HF3613
HOLLAND EXPORTS. (Consists of five sections: Industrial Products; Consumer Goods--Non Food; Consumer Goods--Food; Commercial Gardening and Farming; Services) (Text in English, French, German and Spanish) 1993. a. $110 (CD-ROM $175). A B C voor Handel en Industrie C.V., P.O. Box 190, 2000 AD Haarlem, Netherlands. TEL 31-23-5319031. FAX 31-23-5327033. E-mail: info@abs-d.nl; URL: http://www.hollandexports.com. adv. circ. 14,000. **Document type:** directory.
  ●Also available online. Vendor(s): Data-Star. Also available on CD-ROM.
  —BLDSC (4322.304000).
  Formed by the 1993 merger of: Industrial Products (ISSN 0923-8077); Consumer Goods - Non Food (ISSN 0923-8069); Consumer Goods - Food (ISSN 0923-8050); Commercial Gardening and Farming (ISSN 0923-8042); Services (ISSN 0923-8085).
  Description: Provides information on more than 8000 exporting firms in the Netherlands.

HONG KONG. CENSUS AND STATISTICS DEPARTMENT. TRADE INDEX NUMBERS. see *BUSINESS AND ECONOMICS — Abstracting, Bibliographies, Statistics*

HONG KONG EXTERNAL TRADE. see *BUSINESS AND ECONOMICS — Abstracting, Bibliographies, Statistics*

HONG KONG IMPORTERS' DIRECTORY (YEAR). see *BUSINESS AND ECONOMICS — Trade And Industrial Directories*

HONG KONG TRADE STATISTICS. see *BUSINESS AND ECONOMICS — Abstracting, Bibliographies, Statistics*

332.6   CC
HONG KONG TRADER. (Text in English) 1976. m. free to qualified personnel. Hong Kong Trade Development Council, 36-39th Fl., Office Tower, Convention Plaza, 1 Harbour Rd., Wanchai, Hong Kong, People's Republic of China. TEL 25844333. FAX 28240249. Ed. Cheung Poling. adv.; illus.; stat. circ. 52,000. **Indexed:** HongKongiana, Text.Tech.Dig. **Document type:** trade publication.

HOUSTON JOURNAL OF INTERNATIONAL LAW. see *LAW*

382   HU   ISSN 0230-4139
HUNGARIAN PANORAMA. (Text in English and German) 1969. 6/yr. Magyar Tavirati Iroda, Kiadvanyszerkesztoseg - Hungarian News Agency, Editorial Office, Pl. Naphegy ter. 8, 1016 Budapest, Hungary. Ed. Tibor Kohut. adv. circ. 6,000.

382   SW   ISSN 0347-3899
I C A - NYHETER. 1968. 43/yr. SEK 810 (effective 1997). I C A Foerlaget AB, Storagatan 41, S-721 85 Vaesteraas, Sweden. TEL 46-21-19-40-00. FAX 46-8-756-83-28. Ed. Aake Bergholm; Pub. Aake Bergholm. adv.; B&W page SEK 42000, color page SEK 64700; trim 280 x 410; adv. contact: Roger Zetterlund. circ. 28,500. cols./p.: 5. **Document type:** trade publication.

382   US
I G O REPORT. (Intergovernmental Organizations) bi-m. United States Council for International Business, 1212 Ave. of the Americas, New York, NY 10036. TEL 212-354-4480. FAX 212-575-0327. Ed. William J. Stibravy. **Document type:** newsletter.
  Description: Reports on developments in the major intergovernmental organizations of interest to the business community.

382   II   ISSN 0019-4980
I I T C BULLETIN. (Text in English) 1967. s-m. Rs.50($16) Indian International Trade Center, 59 Jolly Maker Chambers I, Nariman Point, Bombay 400020, India. Ed. S.K. Urval. circ. 500. (avail. on records) **Document type:** bulletin.

382   II   ISSN 0073-6546
I I T C DIRECTORY. (Text in English) 1969. a. free to qualified personnel. Indian International Trade Center, 59 Jolly Maker Chambers I, Nariman Point, Bombay 400020, India.

I N F. (Information Nederland France) see *BUSINESS AND ECONOMICS — Chamber Of Commerce Publications*

382   CC   ISSN 0129-0789
I T SINGAPORE. (International Trade) 12/yr. Newsources Investments Ltd., 1501 Shiu Lam Bldg., 23 Luard Rd., Wanchai, Hong Kong, People's Republic of China. TEL 852-2528-4808. FAX 852-2865-6832. Ed. Mira Kashinath; Pub. Austin Morais. adv. contact: Kelly Ang.

382   IC   ISSN 1022-7024
HF3651
▼**ICELAND BUSINESS.** (Text in English) 1995. q. $19.95; newsstand price: ISK 399 (foreign $6). (Trade Council of Iceland) Kynning ehf (Subsidiary of: Iceland Review), Noatun 17, IS-105 Reykjavik, Iceland. TEL 354-511-5700. FAX 354-511-5701. E-mail: business@icenews.is; URL: http://www.centrum.is/icerev/daily1.html. Ed. Gary Gunning; Pub. Haraldur J. Hamar. **Document type:** trade publication, consumer publication.

382   NE
IDEELE IMPORT INFORMATIE. (Text in Dutch) 1980. w. $10. Stichting Ideele Import, Herengracht 142, 1015 BW Amsterdam, Netherlands. TEL 020-272566. FAX 020-277034. Ed.Bd. adv.; bk.rev. circ. 3,000.
  Formerly: Stichting Ideele Import. Informatiekrant.

382   US
IMPORT - EXPORT CLUBLETTER.* m. $36. Keith Kittrell Associates, Inc., 33831 Oldbridge Rd., Dana Point, CA 92629-2029. TEL 913-628-9466. FAX 714-859-9131.
  Formerly: Import - Export Newsletter.

382   II   ISSN 0536-9983
IMPORT TRADE CONTROL: HANDBOOK OF RULES AND PROCEDURES. (Text in English) a. Ministry of Commerce, New Delhi, India. (Order from: Controller of Publications, Government of India, Civil Lines, Delhi 110054, India)

382   II   ISSN 0536-9061
IMPORT TRADE CONTROL POLICY. (Issued in 2 vols.) (Text in English) a. price varies. Ministry of Commerce, New Delhi, India. (Order from: Controller of Publications, Government of India, Civil Lines, Delhi 110054, India)

332.6   UK
IMPORTING TODAY. 6/yr. £21. Seltform Ltd., Europa House, 13-17 Ironmonger Row, London EC1V 3QN, England. TEL 071-253-2545. FAX 071-608-1600. TELEX 8813271. Ed. Carol Debell. circ. 12,000. **Indexed:** Mgmt.& Market.Abstr.
  Description: Offers news and features on finance, legal matters, transportation, customs, and other aspects of overseas markets.

382   CH
IMPORTS - EXPORTS OF THE REPUBLIC OF CHINA. 1970. a. $150. China External Trade Development Council, 8th Fl., 333 Keelung Rd., Sec. 1, Taipei, Taiwan, Republic of China. TEL 02-725-5200. circ. 4,500. **Document type:** directory.
  Formed by the merger of (1973-1992): Imports of the Republic of China; (1970-1992): Exports of the Republic of China (ISSN 0301-9217)
  Description: Directory of select Taiwan import and export commodities and leading importers and exporters. Selection of entries is based on a set level of import - export value supplied by the ROC's customs office.

382   CN   ISSN 0045-494X
IMPORTWEEK. 1936. w. Can.$695 membership. Canadian Importers Association, Inc. - Association des Importateurs Canadiens Inc., 210 Dundas St., W., Ste. 700, Toronto, ON M5G 2E8, Canada. TEL 416-595-5333. FAX 416-595-8226. TELEX 065-24115. Ed. Catherine McPherson. adv.; bk.rev.; s-a. index. circ. 1,800. **Document type:** bulletin.
  Formerly: Canadian Importers Association. Importers' Bulletin.
  Description: Provides brief authoritative news and analysis of issues in Canada's international trade as well as statistical information and Customs notices of concern to all importers.

332.6   CN   ISSN 1189-6728
IMPORTWORLD MAGAZINE. 1991. a. free. Canadian Importers Association Inc. - Association des Importateurs Canadiens Inc., 210 Dundas St., W., Ste. 700, Toronto, ON M5G 2E8, Canada. TEL 416-585-5333. FAX 416-585-8226. TELEX 065-24115. R&P contact: Catherine McPherson. circ. 4,000. **Document type:** trade publication.
  Description: Provides in-depth analyses of topical trade issues.

382   NE   ISSN 0019-3178
IN- EN UITVOER NIEUWS. (Includes bi-m. supplement: U T C (ISSN 0167-4064)) 30/yr. fl.558 (effective 1996). Uitgeverij Kluwer B.V., Postbus 23, 7400 GA Deventer, Netherlands. TEL 31-570-633155. FAX 31-570-633834. bk.rev.; index. circ. 1,300. **Document type:** trade publication.
  —SWETS.

387   UK   ISSN 0308-7212
IN TOUCH (LONDON). (Text in Dutch, English) m. Netherlands-British Chamber of Commerce, Dutch House, 307-308 High Holborn, London WC1V 7LS, England. Eds. Wim Kootstra, Koenraad van Hasselt.
  —BLDSC (4372.470000).

382   CK   ISSN 0121-604X
HF3421
INCOMEX SIN FRONTERAS. 1992. bi-m. exchange basis. Instituto Colombiano de Comercio Exterior (Incomex), Calle 28 no. 13A-15, Apdo. Aereo 240423, Santafe de Bogota, Colombia. TEL 2812200. FAX 2849592. circ. 5,000.
  Description: Covers foreign commerce and related themes.

INDEX TO BUSINESS REPORTS. see *BUSINESS AND ECONOMICS — Abstracting, Bibliographies, Statistics*

332.6   US
INDIA BUSINESS & INVESTMENT REPORT. 1990. m. $385 (outside N. America $410). P S I, Inc., 75 Maiden Ln., New York, NY 10038. TEL 212-806-8840. FAX 212-514-9766. Ed. I. Ghosh. **Document type:** newsletter.
  Formerly: India Business News.
  Description: Covers international trade and investment in India, including regulation, infrastructure and political risk issues.

BUSINESS AND ECONOMICS — INTERNATIONAL COMMERCE

382   II   ISSN 0019-4239
INDIA TODAY AND TOMORROW. (Text in English) 1968. q. Rs.450($25) V.J. Joseph, Ed. & Pub., 41, Hamam St., 2nd Fl., Orange House, Mumbai 400 001, India. TEL 91-22-265-3187. FAX 91-22-265-5691. adv.; bk.rev.; illus. circ. 11,000. (reprint service avail.)
    Description: Devoted to the country's economic development, industrial and agricultural growth and social progress.

382   II
INDIAN EXPORT BULLETIN. (Text in English) 1965. w. Rs.25 per no. (free to qualified personnel). India Trade Promotion Organisation, Pragati Maidan, New Delhi 110 001, India. TEL 91-11-332-8239. FAX 91-11-331-8142. TELEX 031-61022-COMX-IN. adv. circ. 5,000. **Document type:** bulletin.
    Incorporates (1978-1992): Trade Intelligence Bulletin; **Formerly:** Indian Export Service Bulletin.

382   II
INDIAN EXPORT YEAR BOOK. (Text in Arabic, English) 1975. a. $100. Sales Overseas, D-20 Green Park, New Delhi 110 016, India. TEL 91-11-651-6279. FAX 91-11-686-2206. Ed. H.R. Suri. adv.; page $800; 210 x 160. circ. 10,000. **Document type:** directory.
    Description: Reference annual on foreign trade of India. Contains product indices in Arabic and English.

382   II   ISSN 0073-6473
INDIAN INSTITUTE OF FOREIGN TRADE. REPORT. (Text in English) a. price varies. Indian Institute of Foreign Trade, B-21, Mehrauli Institutional Area, New Delhi 110016, India.

382 633   II   ISSN 0019-6401
INDIAN SPICES. (Text in English) 1964. q. Rs.100($20) Ministry of Commerce, Spices Board, K.C. Ave., St. Vincent Cross Rd., P.B. No. 1909, Ernakulam, Kochi 682 018, India. TEL 91-484-333610. FAX 91-484-331429. TELEX 0885-6534 SEPC IN. E-mail: sbhochn@giasmd01.vsnl.net.in. Ed. P.S. Sreekantan Thampi. adv.; abstr.; bibl.; charts; illus.; mkt.; stat. circ. 1,500. **Indexed:** Food Sci.& Tech.Abstr. **Document type:** government publication.
    —BLDSC (4429.757000).

382   US
INDIANA DIRECTORY OF INTERNATIONAL BUSINESS SERVICES. a. free. Department of Commerce, International Trade Division, One N. Capitol, Ste. 700, Indianapolis, IN 46204-2288. TEL 317-232-8845. FAX 317-232-4146. Ed. Kristin Jones. **Document type:** directory.
    Formerly: Indiana International Trade Directory.

382   II
INDIA'S PRODUCTION, EXPORTS, AND INTERNAL CONSUMPTION OF COIR. (Text and summaries in English) 1967. a. Rs.50. Coir Board, Cochin 682016, Kerala, India. stat. circ. 300.
    Formerly: India's Exports and Internal Consumption of Coir and Coir Goods.

382   CL   ISSN 0716-2405
HF3411
INDICADORES DE COMERCIO EXTERIOR. 1978. m. Ch.$69000($300) Banco Central de Chile, Casilla 967, Santiago, Chile. TEL 56-2-6702000. FAX 56-2-6984847. TELEX 40569 CENBC CL. index. circ. 700. (back issues avail.) **Indexed:** P.A.I.S.For.Lang.Ind. **Document type:** government publication.
    Description: Statistics of Chilean foreign trade.

382   IO   ISSN 0126-3714
INDONESIA. EXPORT BY COMMODITY, COUNTRY OF DESTINATION AND PORT OF EXPORT. 1967. a. Rps.150000($65.21) Central Bureau of Statistics - Biro Pusat Statistik, Jalan Dr. Sutomo No. 8, Box 3, Jakarta Pusat, Indonesia. TEL 62-21-372808. circ. 300. **Document type:** government publication.

382   IO   ISSN 0126-4419
HF247
INDONESIA. IMPORT BY COMMODITY AND COUNTRY OF ORIGIN. (Text in English) 1963. a. Rps.150000($65.21) Central Bureau of Statistics - Biro Pusat Statistik, Jalan Dr. Sutomo No. 8, Box 3, Jakarta Pusat, Indonesia. TEL 62-21-372808. circ. 300. **Document type:** government publication.

INDONESIAN IMPORTERS DIRECTORY. see *BUSINESS AND ECONOMICS — Trade And Industrial Directories*

382   BE   ISSN 0772-4942
INDUSTRIE MAGAZINE; magazine voor produktie, inkoop en techniek. French edition: Industrie (ISSN 0772-4950) (Editions in Dutch, French) 1984. m. 1650 BEF in Belgium; Europe 1690 BEF; airmail 2340 BEF. Publindus N.V., Brasschaatsteenweg 30B, B-2920 Kalmthout, Belgium. Ed. Wim Heirbaut. circ. 27,000. (also avail. in microfiche; back issues avail.)

382   GW
INDUSTRY AND DEVELOPMENT. Chinese edition (ISSN 0940-5326) (Editions Arabic, Chinese, Farsi) 1974. q. (Arabic and Chinese eds. s-a.). DM.50 (foreign $30) (effective 1998). Dr. Harnisch Verlagsgesellschaft mbH, Blumenstr. 15, 90402 Nuernberg, Germany. TEL 49-911-2018-0. FAX 49-911-2018100. E-mail: uepost@aol.com. Ed. Hans Riedel. adv.; B&W page DM.5950, color page DM.8200; trim 190 x 270. bk.rev.; illus. circ. 10,500. **Indexed:** J.of Econ.Lit. **Document type:** trade publication.

350.827   US
INDUSTRY, TRADE, AND TECHNOLOGY REVIEW. Abbreviated title: I T T R. 1992. q. free. U.S. International Trade Commission, Office of Industries, 500 E St., S.W., Washington, DC 20436. TEL 202-205-2104. FAX 202-205-3161. URL: http://www.usitc.gov. Eds. Larry Brookhart, Robert Hughes. R&P contact: Larry Brookhart. **Document type:** government publication.
    Description: Analyzes important issues and provides insight into the global position of U.S. industries, the technological competitiveness of the U.S., and implications of trade and policy developments.

INFORMACION COMERCIAL ESPANOLA. SECTOR EXTERIOR (YEAR). see *BUSINESS AND ECONOMICS — Abstracting, Bibliographies, Statistics*

382   IT   ISSN 1136-9159
▼**INFORMACION SEMANAL DE COMERCIO EXTERIOR.** Short title: Incoex. 1995. 46/yr. 38950 ptas. (foreign $355) (effective 1998). Canalejas 30, entlo. 2o, 08028 Barcelona, Spain. TEL 34-3-4226199. FAX 34-3-4211858. E-mail: revista.econo@redestb.es. Ed. Ricardo Rabella; Pub. Susana Torre. R&P contact: Ricardo Rabella. circ. 460,000. **Document type:** bulletin.
    Description: Contains information about foreign trade, international fairs and competitive biddings. *Refereed Serial*

382   US   ISSN 0196-3643
F548.18
INFORMATION CHICAGO. 1979. a. $25. Information Consultants, 222 W. Ontario St., Ste. 502, Chicago, IL 60610. TEL 312-787-2677. FAX 312-787-2680. Ed. Arnie Matanky. R&P contact: Arnie Matanky. adv. contact: Arnie Matanky. circ. 5,000. **Document type:** directory.
    Description: Presents a comprehensive listing of individual names, addresses and direct phone numbers of governmental, including foreign, transportation, business and professional organizations, news media, sports and religious officials in Chicago area.

382 016   BE   ISSN 0770-3058
HF3601
INFORMATIONS DU COMMERCE EXTERIEUR. (Includes supplements) (Text in Dutch, French) 1963. s-m. 4000 BEF. Office Belge du Commerce Exterieur, 162 bd. Emile Jacqmain, 1210 Brussels, Belgium. TEL 32-2-2063511. FAX 32-2-2031812. adv.; bk.rev.; abstr.; bibl.; index. circ. 7,000. **Document type:** government publication.
    Formerly: Belgium. Office Belge du Commerce Exterieur. Informations du Commerce Exterieur (ISSN 0037-1416)

382   GW
INFORMATIONSDIENST GROSS- UND AUSSENHANDEL. 1947. s-m. DM.890 membership. Wirtschaftsvereinigung Gross- und Aussenhandel Hamburg e.V., Gotenstr. 21, 20097 Hamburg, Germany. TEL 49-40-236016-0. FAX 49-40-23601610. adv.; bk.rev. circ. 1,200. **Document type:** trade publication.
    Description: Promotion of wholesale and international trade.

382   SP
INFORME S E A T; boletin economico financiero destinado a accionistas de la empresa. s-a. free. Subdireccion de Estudios Economicos y Marketing, Avda. del Generalisimo, 146, 28016 Madrid, Spain. **Document type:** bulletin.

382   UK
INITIATIVE. 1972. bi-m. £20 (DM 60). German British Chamber of Industry and Commerce, 16 Buckingham Gate, London SW1E 6LB, England. TEL 071-233-5656. FAX 071-233-7835. E-mail: 100634.3032@compuserve.com. Ed. Ian Wivell. R&P contact: Ian Wivell. adv.: B&W page £900, color page £1000; adv. contact: Ian Wivell. bk.rev.; circ. 4,000. (controlled). **Document type:** trade publication.
    Formerly (until 1993): British German Trade.

INSIDE EXPORT; a guide to growing international markets for the U.S. publishing industry. see *PUBLISHING AND BOOK TRADE*

INSIDE N A F T A; reporting on NAFTA implementation and trade policy in the Americas. see *BUSINESS AND ECONOMICS — Economic Situation And Conditions*

382   US   ISSN 0897-1676
HF3000
INSIDE U S TRADE. 1983. w. $940 (foreign $990) (online ed. $1440) (effective 1997). Inside Washington Publishers, Box 7167, Ben Franklin Sta., Washington, DC 20044-7167. TEL 703-416-8500. FAX 703-416-8543. E-mail: service@iwpnews.com; URL: http://www.insidetrade.com. **Document type:** newsletter.
    ●Also available online.

382 341.57   UK   ISSN 0141-7584
INTELLECTUAL PROPERTY DECISIONS. 1978. m. £325 (foreign £350) (effective 1997). Monitor Press Ltd., Suffolk House, Church Field Rd., Sudbury, Suffolk CO10 6YA, England. TEL 44-1787-378607. FAX 44-1787-880201. Ed. Barry Stonelake. (back issues avail.) **Document type:** abstracting/indexing.
    Description: Abstracts of significant UK and EU decisions in the field of industrial property.

382 341.57   UK   ISSN 0141-9749
INTELLECTUAL PROPERTY NEWSLETTER. m. £200 (foreign £225) (effective 1997). Monitor Press Ltd., Suffolk House, Church Field Rd., Sudbury, Suffolk CO10 6YA, England. TEL 44-1787-378607. FAX 44-1787-880201. (back issues avail.) **Indexed:** LJI. **Document type:** newsletter.
    Description: Reports on patents, trademarks, commercial secrets and the increasing trend toward legislation about all forms of unfair competition.

332.6   UK   ISSN 0967-3466
INTELPROP NEWS. 1992. m. £260 (effective 1996). Interforum Services Ltd., 565 Fulham Rd., London SW6 1ES, England. TEL 44-171-386-9322. FAX 44-171-381-8914. **Document type:** trade publication.
    Description: Information about intellectual property and investment in Russia, Ukraine, Eastern Europe and Central Asia.

382   MX
INTERCAMBIO INTERNACIONAL. 1975. s-a. $12. Grupo Internacional Editores, S.A., Nicolas San Juan No. 1154, Mexico 12, D.F., Mexico. Dir. Arq. Dolores Norma. adv.; bk.rev. circ. 50,000.

BUSINESS AND ECONOMICS — INTERNATIONAL COMMERCE

330 382   GW   ISSN 0020-5346
HF1410
INTERECONOMICS; review of international trade and development. (Text in English) 1966. bi-m. DM.93 (foreign DM.101) (effective 1996). (H W W A - Institut fuer Wirtschaftsforschung, Hamburg) Nomos Verlagsgesellschaft mbH und Co. KG, Waldseestr. 3-5, 76530 Baden-Baden, Germany. TEL 49-7221-2104-0. FAX 49-7221-210427. Ed. Otto G. Mayer. adv.; index. (reprint service avail. from ISI) **Indexed**: Asian-Pac.Econ.Lit., C.R.E.J., ELLIS, Int.Lab.Doc., Key to Econ.Sci., P.A.I.S., PROMT, Rural Recreat.Tour.Abstr., World Agri.Econ.& Rural Sociol.Abstr. **Document type**: trade publication.
—BLDSC (4533.400000); SWETS; UMI; UnCover. CCC.
Description: Provides a European perspective on major issues in international trade and development. Examines the European Economic Community, monetary policy, resource trade, and overall economic trends as they affect the relationship between Europe, America, and the Third World.

382   US   ISSN 0748-4631
HF1371
INTERFLO; trade monitor of the former Soviet republics. 1981. m. $172 (foreign $192). Box 42, Maplewood, NJ 07040. TEL 201-763-9493. Ed. Paul R. Surovell; Pub. Paul R. Surovell. R&P contact: Paul R. Surovell. adv. contact: Paul R. Surovell. abstr.; index. circ. 400. (back issues avail.) **Document type**: abstracting/indexing.
Description: Covers comprehensive information on trade, investment, and joint ventures in the former Soviet republics, as well as information about technology and management.

383   US   ISSN 1060-4073
HD2755.5
INTERNATIONAL BUSINESS. 1988. m. $48 (foreign $120) (effective 1997). New Media Productions, 9 E. 40th St., 10 Fl., New York, NY 10016. TEL 212-683-2426. Ed. Linda Lynton; Pub. Lloyd Sembler. R&P contact: Linda Lynton. adv. contact: Michael Henry. circ. 50,000. (also avail. in microform from UMI; reprint service avail.) **Indexed**: B.P.I. **Document type**: trade publication.
●Also available online. Vendor(s): UMI.
—KR SourceOne; UMI.
Former titles (until Nov. 1991): North American International Business; (until Mar. 1990): Northeast International Business (ISSN 1040-9041)
Description: Provides information to international top management in mid-sized corporations and owners and entrepreneurs in small U.S. businesses involved or interested in the world markets.

INTERNATIONAL BUSINESS SERIES. VOLUME 1: LEGAL ASPECTS OF DOING BUSINESS IN EUROPE. see *LAW — International Law*

INTERNATIONAL BUSINESS SERIES. VOLUME 2: LEGAL ASPECTS OF DOING BUSINESS IN LATIN AMERICA. see *LAW — International Law*

INTERNATIONAL BUSINESS SERIES. VOLUME 3: LEGAL ASPECTS OF DOING BUSINESS IN ASIA AND THE PACIFIC. see *LAW — International Law*

INTERNATIONAL BUSINESS SERIES. VOLUME 4: LEGAL ASPECTS OF DOING BUSINESS IN AFRICA. see *LAW — International Law*

INTERNATIONAL BUSINESS SERIES. VOLUME 5: LEGAL ASPECTS OF DOING BUSINESS IN THE MIDDLE EAST. see *LAW — International Law*

INTERNATIONAL BUSINESS SERIES. VOLUME 6-7: LEGAL ASPECTS OF DOING BUSINESS IN NORTH AMERICA. see *LAW — International Law*

INTERNATIONAL BUSINESS TRANSACTIONS; commercial forms and documents including wordprocessing software. see *LAW — International Law*

INTERNATIONAL COAL. see *MINES AND MINING INDUSTRY*

INTERNATIONAL CONTRACT ADVISER; the newsletter for global business. see *LAW — International Law*

INTERNATIONAL CONTRACT MANUAL. see *LAW — International Law*

382   US   ISSN 0738-8888
INTERNATIONAL CURRENCY REPORT. 1978. s-m. $797. International Business Information, Inc., Box 8312, Cincinnati, OH 45208-0312. TEL 513-871-5501. FAX 513-871-5458. Pub. Walter Lynch. (back issues avail.) **Document type**: newsletter.

INTERNATIONAL CUSTOMS JOURNAL/BULLETIN INTERNATIONAL DES DOUANES. see *BUSINESS AND ECONOMICS — Public Finance, Taxation*

332.6   UK
THE INTERNATIONAL DIRECTORY OF BUSINESS INFORMATION SOURCES & SERVICES. irreg., 2nd ed., 1996. $185. Europa Publications, 18 Bedford Sq., London WC1B 3JN, England. TEL 44-171-580-8236. FAX 44-171-636-1664. (Orders to: Sales and Publicity, 43 Gower St., London WC1E 6HH, England. TEL 44-171-631-3361. FAX 44-171-637-0922) **Document type**: directory.
Description: Lists government and private-industry organizations that produce information on international commerce, along with business libraries, chambers of commerce, and research institutions.

INTERNATIONAL DIRECTORY OF IMPORTERS. see *BUSINESS AND ECONOMICS — Trade And Industrial Directories*

INTERNATIONAL DIRECTORY OF IMPORTERS: AFRICA. see *BUSINESS AND ECONOMICS — Trade And Industrial Directories*

INTERNATIONAL DIRECTORY OF IMPORTERS: ASIA - PACIFIC. see *BUSINESS AND ECONOMICS — Trade And Industrial Directories*

INTERNATIONAL DIRECTORY OF IMPORTERS: EUROPE. see *BUSINESS AND ECONOMICS — Trade And Industrial Directories*

INTERNATIONAL DIRECTORY OF IMPORTERS: MIDDLE EAST. see *BUSINESS AND ECONOMICS — Trade And Industrial Directories*

INTERNATIONAL DIRECTORY OF IMPORTERS: NORTH AMERICA. see *BUSINESS AND ECONOMICS — Trade And Industrial Directories*

INTERNATIONAL DIRECTORY OF IMPORTERS: SOUTH - CENTRAL AMERICA. see *BUSINESS AND ECONOMICS — Trade And Industrial Directories*

330   US   ISSN 0898-4336
HG3879
INTERNATIONAL ECONOMY; the magazine of the G7 Council. 1987. bi-m. $72. International Economy Publications, 1133 Connecticut Ave., N.W., Ste. 901, Washington, DC 20036. TEL 202-861-0791. FAX 202-861-0790. Ed. David M. Smick. adv. contact: Noelle McGlynn. bk.rev. circ. 10,000. (back issues avail.) **Indexed**: B.P.I. **Document type**: trade publication.
—BLDSC (4539.827000); KR SourceOne; SWETS; UnCover.
Description: Provides a forum for the emerging international financial and trade debate at the highest level; serves the world's top strategic decision makers.

658   US   ISSN 0020-6652
HF1
THE INTERNATIONAL EXECUTIVE. 1959. bi-m. $250 (foreign $343) (effective 1998). (Thunderbird American Graduate School of International Management) John Wiley & Sons, Inc., Journals, 605 Third Ave., New York, NY 10158. TEL 212-850-6645. FAX 212-850-6021. TELEX 12-7063. E-mail: subinfo@jwiley.com; URL: http://www.wiley.co.uk. Ed. Beverly Springer. adv.: B&W page £640, color page £1515. abstr.; bibl. circ. 2,500. (also avail. in microform from UMI; back issues avail.; reprint service avail. from UMI) **Indexed**: B.P.I., Mid.East: Abstr.& Ind. **Document type**: academic/scholarly publication.
—BLDSC (4540.050000); KR SourceOne; SWETS; UMI; UnCover. CCC.
Description: Reports on international business and commerce, including international marketing, finance, and international human resources issues. Addresses related political, economic, legal, and cultural issues affecting international business.
Refereed Serial

INTERNATIONAL GRAINS COUNCIL. WHEAT AND COARSE GRAIN SHIPMENTS. see *AGRICULTURE — Feed, Flour And Grain*

INTERNATIONAL JOURNAL OF COMMERCE AND MANAGEMENT. see *BUSINESS AND ECONOMICS — Management*

INTERNATIONAL MARKET INDEXES. see *BUSINESS AND ECONOMICS — Investments*

INTERNATIONAL MARKET REVIEW. see *BUSINESS AND ECONOMICS — Banking And Finance*

INTERNATIONAL MONETARY FUND. BALANCE OF PAYMENTS STATISTICS YEARBOOK. see *BUSINESS AND ECONOMICS — Abstracting, Bibliographies, Statistics*

382 665.5   AT
INTERNATIONAL OFFSHORE FINANCIAL CENTRES. (Complements: International Tax Planning - Expatriates & Migrants; International Tax Planning Manual - Corporations) 1988. q. C C H Australia Ltd., P.O. Box 230, N. Ryde, N.S.W. 2113, Australia. TEL 61-1-300300224. FAX 61-1-300306224. (looseleaf format)
Description: Discusses the practical use of tax havens to reduce the overall tax liability of a corporate group.

382   II   ISSN 0047-0953
INTERNATIONAL PRESS CUTTING SERVICE: IMPORT - EXPORT - LICENSES; customs notifications. 1967. w. Rs.635($75) International Press Cutting Service, P.O. Box 121, Allahabad 211001, India. Ed. N. Khanna. bk.rev.; index. circ. 1,200. (processed) **Document type**: newsletter.

382   II   ISSN 0047-1127
INTERNATIONAL PRESS CUTTING SERVICE: TENDER NOTIFICATIONS (INDIAN & GLOBAL). 1967. fortn. Rs.650($75) International Press Cutting Service, P.O. Box 121, Allahabad 211001, India. Ed. N. Khanna. bk.rev.; index. circ. 1,200. (processed) **Document type**: newsletter.

332.6   UK   ISSN 1356-2703
▼**INTERNATIONAL REVIEW OF WORLD TRADE**. 1995. a. £55. Sterling Publications Ltd., 86-88 Edgware Rd., London W2 2YW, England. TEL 44-171-915-9600. FAX 44-171-915-9619. R&P contact: Sandy Tucker. circ. 20,000. **Document type**: trade publication.

382   UK   ISSN 0263-5488
INTERNATIONAL TAX-FREE TRADE BUYERS GUIDE & DIRECTORY. a. £48($75) (overseas £53) (effective Sep. 1995). International Trade Publications Ltd. (Subsidiary of: Argus Press Group), Queensway House, 2 Queensway, Redhill, Surrey RH1 1QS, England. TEL 01737-768611. FAX 01737-761989. TELEX 948669 TOPJNL G. Ed. Peter Topthorpe; Pub. Roy Greenslade. adv. contact: Martin Neale. **Document type**: trade publication.

INTERNATIONAL TAX PLANNING MANUAL - CORPORATIONS. see *BUSINESS AND ECONOMICS — Public Finance, Taxation*

382.7 336   UK   ISSN 0896-7903
K4456.2
INTERNATIONAL TAX REVIEW. 1989. 10/yr. £335 (foreign $595) (effective 1997). Euromoney Publications plc, Nestor House, Playhouse Yard, London EC4V 5EX, England. TEL 44-171-779-8935. FAX 44-171-779-8541. (Dist. in Us by: American Educational Systems, 173 W. 81st St., New York, NY 10024. TEL 800-717-2669. FAX 212-501-8926) Ed. Adrian Preston. **Indexed**: Euro.LJI, LJI. **Document type**: trade publication.
●Also available online. Vendor(s): UMI.
—UMI.
Description: Covers the most recent developments in cross-border taxation. Analyzes all tax issues including new case law, opinions, treaties and statutes affecting corporations and financial institutions.

BUSINESS AND ECONOMICS — INTERNATIONAL COMMERCE

382   US   ISSN 0744-5660
INTERNATIONAL TRADE ALERT. w. membership. American Association of Exporters and Importers, 11 W. 42nd St., New York, NY 10036. TEL 212-944-2606. FAX 212-382-2606. Ed. Elizabeth Stern Bayer. R&P contact: Elizabeth Stern Bayer. (looseleaf format; back issues avail.) **Document type:** newsletter.
   Formerly: Import Alert (ISSN 0195-4458)
   Description: Covers international trade and US Customs and other government regulations affecting imports and exports.

382   US   ISSN 0890-4251
INTERNATIONAL TRADE AND INVESTMENT LETTER; trends in US policies, trade finance, and trading operations. 1979. m. $240. International Business Affairs Corporation, 4938 Hampden Ln., Bethesda, MD 20814-2914. TEL 301-907-8647. Ed. Richard L. Barovich. **Document type:** newsletter.

INTERNATIONAL TRADE FINANCE. see *BUSINESS AND ECONOMICS — Banking And Finance*

382   UN   ISSN 0020-8957
HF1410   CODEN: ITFREV
INTERNATIONAL TRADE FORUM. Spanish edition: Forum de Comercio Internacional (ISSN 0251-009X); French edition: Forum du Commerce International (ISSN 0591-2512) 1964. q. $20 (free to qualified personnel). International Trade Centre, Palais des Nations, CH-1211 Geneva 10, Switzerland. FAX 41-22-733-4439. TELEX 414119 ITC. Ed. Janice Goertz. bk.rev.; bibl.; charts; illus.; index. circ. 29,600. (also avail. in microform from UMI; reprint service avail. from UMI) **Indexed:** ABI Inform., Account.& Data Proc.Abstr., Anbar, B.P.I., BPIA, Bus.Ind., Food Sci.& Tech.Abstr., Key to Econ.Sci., Manage.Cont., Mgmt.& Market.Abstr., P.A.I.S., P.I.R.A., Rural Recreat.Tour.Abstr., Tr.& Indus.Ind., World Agri.Econ.& Rural Sociol.Abstr. **Document type:** bulletin.
   ●Also available online. Vendor(s): Information Access Co., UMI.
   —BLDSC (4551.280000); KR SourceOne; SWETS; UMI; UnCover.

382   US   ISSN 0885-3908
    CODEN: ITRJEX
THE INTERNATIONAL TRADE JOURNAL. 1986. q. £103($170) to institutions (effective 1998). Taylor & Francis Inc., 1900 Frost Rd., Bristol, PA 19007-1598. TEL 215-785-5800; 800-821-8312. FAX 215-785-5515. E-mail: info@tandf.co.uk; URL: http://www.tandf.co.uk/. (Subscr. in Europe to: Taylor & Francis Ltd., Rankine Rd., Basingstoke, Hants. RG24 8PR, England. TEL 44-1256-840366. FAX 44-1256-479438) Ed. Khosrow Fatemi. adv.; bk.rev. **Indexed:** Geo.Abstr.H.G., IDA, World Agri.Econ.& Rural Sociol.Abstr. **Document type:** academic/scholarly publication.
   —BLDSC (4551.301000); SWETS; UnCover. **CCC.**
   Description: Provides a forum for ideas among academicians, government officials, and both macro- and microeconomic practitioners; covers both practical and theoretical contributions to the field of international trade.
   Refereed Serial

382.7   US   ISSN 1075-833X
HF3000
INTERNATIONAL TRADE REPORTER. 1947. w. $1056. The Bureau of National Affairs, Inc., 1231 25th St., N.W., Washington, DC 20037. TEL 202-452-4200. FAX 202-822-8092. TELEX 285656 BNAI WSH. URL: http://www.bna.com/. (Subscr. to: 9435 Key West Ave., Rockville, MD 20850. TEL 800-372-1033) Ed. Linda G. Botsford. s-a. index. (back issues avail.)
   ●Also available online. Vendor(s): Lexis-Nexis (INTRAD), West Group (BNA-ITR).
   —CCC.
   Formerly (until 1995): International Trade Reporter Current Reporter (ISSN 0748-0172); Incorporates (1979-1984): US Import Weekly (ISSN 0195-7589)
   Description: Reports and analyzes legislative and regulatory developments as well as private sector activities affecting international trade (both export and import).

382   US   ISSN 1043-5662
INTERNATIONAL TRADE REPORTER. IMPORT REFERENCE MANUAL. (Subseries of: International Trade Reporter) 1980. bi-m. $1079. The Bureau of National Affairs, Inc., 1231 25th St., N.W., Washington, DC 20037. TEL 202-452-4200. FAX 202-822-8092. TELEX 285656 BNAI WSH. URL: http://www.bna.com/. (Subscr. to: 9435 Key West Ave., Rockville, MD 20850. TEL 800-372-1033) Ed. Linda G. Bosford. index. (looseleaf format; back issues avail.)
   —CCC.
   Former titles (until 1989): International Trade Reporter's Reference File (ISSN 0748-0695); (until 1984): International Trade Reporter's U S Import Weekly Reference File (ISSN 1040-4058)
   Description: Guide to the entire import process with analysis and full text of statutes, regulations, and executive orders on subjects such as custom house brokers, dumping, countervailing duties, escape clauses, and presidential retaliation.

382 341.57   US   ISSN 0748-0709
INTERNATIONAL TRADE REPORTER DECISIONS. (Subseries of: International Trade Reporter) 1980. bi-w. $1079. The Bureau of National Affairs, Inc., 1231 25th St., N.W., Washington, DC 20037. TEL 202-452-4200. FAX 202-822-8092. TELEX 285656 BNAI WSH. URL: http://www.bna.com/. (Subscr. to: 9435 Key West Ave., Rockville, MD 20850. TEL 800-372-1033) Ed. Linda G. Botsford. (also avail. in looseleaf format; back issues avail.)
   —CCC.
   Formerly (until 1984): International Trade Reporter's U S Import Weekly. Decisions.
   Description: Digested, classified, and indexed judicial and administrative decisions dealing with legal issues arising from US trade law (mostly import cases).

382   US   ISSN 1043-5670
    CODEN: ITRME8
INTERNATIONAL TRADE REPORTER EXPORT REFERENCE MANUAL. (Subseries of: International Trade Reporter) 1947. w. $675. The Bureau of National Affairs, Inc., 1231 25th St., N.W., Washington, DC 20037. TEL 202-452-4200. FAX 202-822-8092. TELEX 285656 BNAI WSH. URL: http://www.bna.com/. (Subscr. to: 9453 Key West Ave., Rockville, MD 20850. TEL 800-327-1033) Ed. Deanne E. Neuman. (looseleaf format; back issues avail.)
   —CCC.
   Formerly (until 1989): Export Shipping Manual (ISSN 0014-5181)
   Description: Comprehensive source for foreign import regulations, US export controls, and related requirements for preparing US exports for shipment abroad.

382   II   ISSN 0020-8981
INTERNATIONAL TRADE REVIEW. (Text in English) 1969. m. Rs.20($5) (Indian Council of Foreign Trade) United Asia Publications Pvt. Ltd., 12 Rampart Row, Bombay 1, India. Ed. G.S. Pohekar. adv.; bk.rev.; stat.; tr.lit.

382 011   US
INTERNATIONAL UPDATE. bi-m. membership. International Real Estate Section, 700 11th St., N.W., Washington, DC 20001-4507. TEL 202-383-1032. FAX 202-383-7528. Ed. Scott Sherwood; Pub. Miriam Meyer-Lowe. adv.; circ. 2,000 (paid). (back issues avail.) **Document type:** newsletter.
   Formerly: F I A B C I - U S A News.
   Description: Aimed at international real estate practitioners in more than twenty five nations.

382   US   ISSN 1091-3637
INTERNATIONAL WEALTH SUCCESS NEWSLETTER; the monthly newsletter of worldwide wealth opportunities. 1967. m. $24 (foreign $42). International Wealth Success, Inc., Box 186, Merrick, NY 11566. TEL 516-766-5850. FAX 516-766-5919. Ed. Tyler G. Hicks. adv.; bk.rev.; tr.lit. (also avail. in microform from UMI; reprint service avail. from UMI) **Document type:** newsletter.
   —UMI.
   Description: Covers a variety of small-business topics including borrowing money, raising capital, mail order, real estate, and import-export.

382   AU   ISSN 0020-935X
INTERNATIONALE WIRTSCHAFT; Aussenhandel. 1946. w. S.980 q. Oesterreichischer Wirtschaftsverlag, Nikolsdorfergasse 7-11, A-1051 Vienna, Austria. TEL 0222-555585. TELEX 1-11669. Ed. Nikolaus Gerstmayer. adv.; mkt.; tr.lit.; index. circ. 13,000. **Document type:** newspaper.

382   US
INTERNATIONALIST; the journal of international activity. 1993. 3/yr. $15. Assist International, 60 Madison Ave., 2nd Fl., New York, NY 10010-1600. TEL 212-725-3311. FAX 212-725-3312. Eds. Juan C. Heredia, Brooks Shumway. **Document type:** trade publication.

INTERNET INFOSCAVENGER; sites and insights for growing businesses. see *COMPUTERS — Computer Networks*

338.5   NE   ISSN 0165-2826
INTERTAX; international tax review. (Includes q. supplement: E C Tax Review) (Text in English) m. fl.890 to institutions; $456.50 to institutions in U.S. (effective 1998). Kluwer Law International (Subsidiary of: Wolters Kluwer N.V.), Postbus 85889, 2508 CN The Hague, Netherlands. TEL 31-70-3081500. FAX 31-70-3081515. E-mail: services@wkap.nl. (Dist. by: Kluwer Academic Publishers Group, P.O. Box 322, 3300 AH Dordrecht, Netherlands. TEL 31-78-6392392. FAX 31-78-6546474; In N. America: Kluwer Law International, 675 Massachusetts Ave., Cambridge, MA 02139. TEL 617-354-0140. FAX 617-354-8595) Ed. Fred de Hosson. adv. **Indexed:** ELLIS, Key to Econ.Sci., LJI, P.A.I.S.
   —BLDSC (4557.455000); SWETS. **CCC.**
   Formerly: Fiscalite du Marche Commun (ISSN 0015-282X)
   Description: Provides practical, up-to-date and high level international tax information, including coverage of transnational tax issues.

382 336   US
INVESTING, LICENSING AND TRADING. AMERICAS. (Includes: Argentina, Brazil, Canada, Central America, Chile, Colombia, Ecuador, Mexico, Panama, Peru, Puerto Rico, United States, Uruguay, and Venezuela) base vol. (plus s-a. updates). Economist Intelligence Unit, 111 W. 57th St., New York, NY 10019. TEL 212-554-0600; 800-938-4685. FAX 212-586-1181. TELEX 1755677. URL: http://www.eiu.com. (UK addr.: Economist Intelligence Unit Ltd., Subscriptions Dept., P.O. Box 200, Harold Hill, Romford, Essex RM3 8UX, England. TEL 44-1708-381-444. FAX 44-1708-371-850)
   ●Also available online. Vendor(s): Knight-Ridder Information, Inc., Lexis-Nexis.
   Former titles (until 1997): Investing, Licensing and Trading Conditions Abroad. Americas & Investing, Licensing and Trading Conditions Abroad. Latin America.
   Description: Offers information on corporate tax rules, exchange and price controls, trade and licensing restrictions, labor conditions and investment rules.

332.6 336   US
INVESTING, LICENSING AND TRADING. ARGENTINA. a. £185($275) Economist Intelligence Unit, 111 W. 57th St., New York, NY 10019. TEL 212-554-0600; 800-938-4685. FAX 212-586-1181. TELEX 175567. URL: http://www.eiu.com. (UK addr.: Economist Intelligence Unit Ltd., Subscriptions Dept., P.O. Box 200, Harold Hill, Romford, Essex RM3 8UX, England. TEL 44-1708-381-444. FAX 44-1708-371-850) **Document type:** trade publication.
   ●Also available online. Vendor(s): Knight-Ridder Information, Inc., Lexis-Nexis.
   Formerly (until 1997): Investing, Licensing and Trading Conditions Abroad. Argentina (ISSN 1352-9838)
   Description: Provides information on corporate tax rules, exchange and price controls, trade and licensing restrictions, labor conditions and investment rules for Argentina.

BUSINESS AND ECONOMICS — INTERNATIONAL COMMERCE

332.6 336 US
INVESTING, LICENSING AND TRADING. ASIA. (Includes: Australia, China, Hong Kong, India, Indonesia, Japan, Malaysia, New Zealand, Pakistan, Philippines, Singapore, South Korea, Taiwan, Thailand and Vietnam.) base vol. (plus s-a. updates). Economist Intelligence Unit, 111 W. 57th St., New York, NY 10019. TEL 212-554-0600; 800-938-4685. FAX 212-586-1181. TELEX 1755677. URL: http://www.eiu.com. (UK addr.: Economist Intelligence Unit Ltd., Subscriptions Dept., P.O. Box 200, Harold Hill, Romford, Essex RM3 8UX, England. TEL 44-1708-381-444. FAX 44-1708-371-850)
●Also available online. Vendor(s): Knight-Ridder Information, Inc., Lexis-Nexis.
 Former titles (until 1997): Investing, Licensing and Trading Conditions Abroad. Asia & Investing, Licensing and Trading Conditions Abroad. Asia - Pacific.
 Description: Offers information on corporate tax rules, exchange and price controls, trade and licensing restrictions, labor conditions and investment rules.

332.6 336 US
INVESTING, LICENSING AND TRADING. AUSTRALIA. a. £185($275) Economist Intelligence Unit, 111 W. 57th St., New York, NY 10019. TEL 212-554-0600; 800-938-4685. FAX 212-596-1181. TELEX 175567. URL: http://www.eiu.com. (UK addr.: Economist Intelligence Unit Ltd., Subscriptions Dept., P.O. Box 200, Harold Hill, Romford, Essex RM3 8UX, England. TEL 44-1708-381-444. FAX 44-1708-371-850)
Document type: trade publication.
●Also available online. Vendor(s): Knight-Ridder Information, Inc., Lexis-Nexis.
 Formerly (until 1997): Investing, Licensing and Trading Conditions Abroad. Australia (ISSN 1353-5889)
 Description: Provides information on corporate tax rules, exchange and price controls, trade and licensing restrictions, labor conditions and investment rules.

332.6 336 US
INVESTING, LICENSING AND TRADING. AUSTRIA. a. £185($275) Economist Intelligence Unit, 111 W. 57th St., New York, NY 10019. TEL 212-554-0600; 800-938-4685. FAX 212-586-1181. TELEX 175567. URL: http://www.eiu.com. (UK addr.: Economist Intelligence Unit Ltd., Subscriptions Dept., P.O. Box 200, Harold Hill, Romford, Essex RM3 8UX, England. TEL 44-1708-381-444. FAX 44-1708-371-850)
Document type: trade publication.
●Also available online. Vendor(s): Knight-Ridder Information, Inc., Lexis-Nexis.
 Formerly (until 1997): Investing, Licensing and Trading Conditions Abroad. Austria (ISSN 1352-9943)
 Description: Provides information on corporate tax rules, exchange and price controls, trade and licensing restrictions, labor conditions and investment rules.

332.6 336 US
INVESTING, LICENSING AND TRADING. BELGIUM. a. £185($275) Economist Intelligence Unit, 111 W. 57th St., New York, NY 10019. TEL 212-554-0600; 800-938-4685. FAX 212-586-1181. TELEX 175567. URL: http://www.eiu.com. (UK addr.: Economist Intelligence Unit Ltd., Subscriptions Dept., P.O. Box 200, Harold Hill, Romford, Essex RM3 8UX, England. TEL 44-1708-381-444. FAX 44-1708-371-850)
Document type: trade publication.
●Also available online. Vendor(s): Knight-Ridder Information, Inc., Lexis-Nexis.
 Formerly (until 1997): Investing, Licensing and Trading Conditions Abroad. Belgium (ISSN 1352-5913)
 Description: Provides information on corporate tax rules, exchange and price controls, trade and licensing restrictions, labor conditions and investment rules.

332.6 336 US
INVESTING, LICENSING AND TRADING. BRAZIL. a. £185($275) Economist Intelligence Unit, 111 W. 57th St., New York, NY 10019. TEL 212-554-0600; 800-938-4685. FAX 212-586-1181. TELEX 175567. URL: http://www.eiu.com. (UK addr.: Economist Intelligence Unit Ltd., Subscriptions Dept., P.O. Box 200, Harold Hill, Romford, Essex RM3 8UX, England. TEL 44-1708-381-444. FAX 44-1708-371-850)
Document type: trade publication.
●Also available online. Vendor(s): Knight-Ridder Information, Inc., Lexis-Nexis.
 Formerly (until 1997): Investing, Licensing and Trading Conditions Abroad. Brazil (ISSN 1352-5921)
 Description: Provides information on corporate tax rules, exchange and price controls, trade and licensing restrictions, labor conditions and investment rules.

332.6 336 US
INVESTING, LICENSING AND TRADING. BRITAIN. a. £185($275) Economist Intelligence Unit, 111 W. 57th St., New York, NY 10019. TEL 212-554-0600; 800-938-4685. FAX 212-586-1181. TELEX 175567. URL: http://www.eiu.com. (UK addr.: Economist Intelligence Unit Ltd., Subscriptions Dept., P.O. Box 200, Harold Hill, Romford, Essex RM3 8UX, England. TEL 44-1708-381-444. FAX 44-1708-371-850)
Document type: trade publication.
●Also available online. Vendor(s): Knight-Ridder Information, Inc., Lexis-Nexis.
 Former titles (until 1997): Investing, Licensing and Trading Conditions Abroad. Britain; Investing, Licensing and Trading Conditions Abroad. United Kingdom (ISSN 1352-9765)
 Description: Provides information on corporate tax rules, exchange and price controls, trade and licensing restrictions, labor conditions and investment rules.

332.6 336 US
INVESTING, LICENSING AND TRADING. CANADA. a. £185($275) Economist Intelligence Unit, 111 W. 57th St., New York, NY 10019. TEL 212-554-0600; 800-938-4685. FAX 212-586-1181. TELEX 175567. URL: http://www.eiu.com. (UK addr.: Economist Intelligence Unit Ltd., Subscriptions Dept., P.O. Box 200, Harold Hill, Romford, Essex RM3 8UX, England. TEL 44-1708-381-444. FAX 44-1708-371-850)
Document type: trade publication.
●Also available online. Vendor(s): Knight-Ridder Information, Inc., Lexis-Nexis.
 Formerly (until 1997): Investing, Licensing and Trading Conditions Abroad. Canada (ISSN 1352-9811)
 Description: Provides information on corporate tax rules, exchange and price controls, trade and licensing restrictions, labor conditions and investment rules.

322.6 336 US
INVESTING, LICENSING AND TRADING. CENTRAL AMERICA; including El Salvador, Guatemala, Honduras and Costa Rica. a. £185($275) Economist Intelligence Unit, 111 W. 57th St., New York, NY 10019. TEL 212-554-0600; 800-938-4685. FAX 212-586-1181. TELEX 175567. URL: http://www.eiu.com. (UK addr.: Economist Intelligence Unit Ltd., Subscriptions Dept., P.O. Box 200, Harold Hill, Romford, Essex RM3 8UX, England. TEL 44-1708-381-444. FAX 44-1708-371-850) **Document type:** trade publication.
●Also available online. Vendor(s): Knight-Ridder Information, Inc., Lexis-Nexis.
 Formerly (until 1997): Investing, Licensing and Trading Conditions Abroad. Central America (ISSN 1353-6273); Which was formed by the merger of: Investing, Licensing and Trade Conditions Abroad. Honduras; Investing, Licensing and Trade Conditions Abroad. Guatemala; Investing, Licensing and Trade Conditions Abroad. El Salvador; Investing, Licensing and Trading Conditions Abroad. Costa Rica.
 Description: Provides information on corporate tax rules, exchange and price controls, trade and licensing restrictions, labor conditions and investment rules.

322.6 336 US
INVESTING, LICENSING AND TRADING. CHILE. a. £185($275) Economist Intelligence Unit, 111 W. 57th St., New York, NY 10019. TEL 212-554-0600; 800-938-4685. FAX 212-586-1181. TELEX 175567. URL: http://www.eiu.com. (UK addr.: Economist Intelligence Unit Ltd., Subscriptions Dept., P.O. Box 200, Harold Hill, Romford, Essex RM3 8UX, England. TEL 44-1708-381-444. FAX 44-1708-371-850)
Document type: trade publication.
●Also available online. Vendor(s): Knight-Ridder Information, Inc., Lexis-Nexis.
 Formerly (until 1997): Investing, Licensing and Trading Conditions Abroad. Chile (ISSN 1352-593X)
 Description: Provides information on corporate tax rules, exchange and price controls, trade and licensing restrictions, labor conditions and investment rules.

332.6 336 US
INVESTING, LICENSING AND TRADING. CHINA. a. £185($275) Economist Intelligence Unit, 111 W. 57th St., New York, NY 10019. TEL 212-554-0600; 800-938-4685. FAX 212-586-1181. TELEX 175567. URL: http://www.eiu.com. (UK addr.: Economist Intelligence Unit Ltd., Subscriptions Dept., P.O. Box 200, Harold Hill, Romford, Essex RM3 8UX, England. TEL 44-1708-381-444. FAX 44-1708-371-850)
Document type: trade publication.
●Also available online. Vendor(s): Knight-Ridder Information, Inc., Lexis-Nexis.
 Formerly (until 1997): Investing, Licensing and Trading Conditions Abroad. China (ISSN 1353-6265)
 Description: Provides information on corporate tax rules, exchange and price controls, trade and licensing restrictions, labor conditions and investment rules.

332.6 336 US
INVESTING, LICENSING AND TRADING. COLOMBIA. a. £185($275) Economist Intelligence Unit, 111 W. 57th St., New York, NY 10019. TEL 212-554-0600; 800-938-4685. FAX 212-586-1181. TELEX 175567. URL: http://www.eiu.com. (UK addr.: Economist Intelligence Unit Ltd., Subscriptions Dept., P.O. Box 200, Harold Hill, Romford, Essex RM3 8UX, England. TEL 44-1708-381-444. FAX 44-1708-371-850)
Document type: trade publication.
●Also available online. Vendor(s): Knight-Ridder Information, Inc., Lexis-Nexis.
 Formerly (until 1997): Investing, Licensing and Trading Conditions Abroad. Colombia (ISSN 1352-5948)
 Description: Provides information on corporate tax rules, exchange and price controls, trade and licensing restrictions, labor conditions and investment rules.

332.6 336 US
INVESTING, LICENSING AND TRADING. CZECH REPUBLIC. a. £185($275) Economist Intelligence Unit, 111 W. 57th St., New York, NY 10019. TEL 212-554-0600; 800-938-4685. FAX 212-586-1181. TELEX 175567. URL: http://www.eiu.com. (UK addr.: Economist Intelligence Unit Ltd., Subscriptions Dept., P.O. Box 200, Harold Hill, Romford, Essex RM3 8UX, England. TEL 44-1708-381-444. FAX 44-1708-371-850)
●Also available online. Vendor(s): Knight-Ridder Information, Inc., Lexis-Nexis.
 Formerly (until 1997): Investing, Licensing and Trading Conditions Abroad. Czech Republic (ISSN 1353-629X); Which superseded in part: Investing, Licensing and Trading Conditions. Czech Republic and Slovakia; Which was formerly (until 1993): Investing, Licensing and Trading Conditions Abroad. Czechoslovakia (ISSN 1352-9951)
 Description: Provides information on corporate tax rules, exchange and price controls, trade and licensing restrictions, labor conditions and investment rules.

BUSINESS AND ECONOMICS — INTERNATIONAL COMMERCE

332.6 336   US
INVESTING, LICENSING AND TRADING. DENMARK. a. £185($275) Economist Intelligence Unit, 111 W. 57th St., New York, NY 10019. TEL 212-554-0600; 800-938-4685. FAX 212-586-1181. TELEX 175567. URL: http://www.eiu.com. (UK addr.: Economist Intelligence Unit Ltd., Subscriptions Dept., P.O. Box 200, Harold Hill, Romford, Essex RM3 8UX, England. TEL 44-1708-381-444. FAX 44-1708-371-850)
Document type: trade publication.
●Also available online. Vendor(s): Knight-Ridder Information, Inc., Lexis-Nexis.
   Formerly (until 1997): Investing, Licensing and Trading Conditions Abroad. Denmark (ISSN 1352-5956)
   Description: Provides information on corporate tax rules, exchange and price controls, trade and licensing restrictions, labor conditions and investment rules.

332.6 336   US
INVESTING, LICENSING AND TRADING. FINLAND. a. £185($275) Economist Intelligence Unit, 111 W. 57th St., New York, NY 10019. TEL 212-554-0600; 800-938-4685. FAX 212-586-1181. TELEX 175567. URL: http://www.eiu.com. (UK addr.: Economist Intelligence Unit Ltd., Subscriptions Dept., P.O. Box 200, Harold Hill, Romford, Essex RM3 8UX, England. TEL 44-1708-381-444. FAX 44-1708-371-850)
●Also available online. Vendor(s): Knight-Ridder Information, Inc., Lexis-Nexis.
   Formerly (until 1997): Investing, Licensing and Trading Conditions Abroad. Finland.
   Description: Provides information on corporate tax rules, exchange and price controls, trade and licensing restrictions, labor conditions and investment rules.

332.6 336   US
INVESTING, LICENSING AND TRADING. GREECE. a. £185($275) Economist Intelligence Unit, 111 W. 57th St., New York, NY 10019. TEL 212-554-0600; 800-938-4685. FAX 212-586-1181. TELEX 175567. URL: http://www.eiu.com. (UK addr.: Economist Intelligence Unit Ltd., Subscriptions Dept., P.O. Box 200, Harold Hill, Romford, Essex RM3 8UX, England. TEL 44-1708-381-444. FAX 44-1708-371-850)
Document type: trade publication.
●Also available online. Vendor(s): Knight-Ridder Information, Inc., Lexis-Nexis.
   Formerly (until 1997): Investing, Licensing and Trading Conditions Abroad. Greece (ISSN 1352-9919)
   Description: Provides information on corporate tax rules, exchange and price controls, trade and licensing restrictions, labor conditions and investment rules.

332.6 336   US
INVESTING, LICENSING AND TRADING. ECUADOR. a. £185($275) Economist Intelligence Unit, 111 W. 57th St., New York, NY 10019. TEL 212-554-0600; 800-938-4685. FAX 212-586-1181. TELEX 175567. URL: http://www.eiu.com. (UK addr.: Economist Intelligence Unit Ltd., Subscriptions Dept., P.O. Box 200, Harold Hill, Romford, Essex RM3 8UX, England. TEL 44-1708-381-444. FAX 44-1708-371-850)
Document type: trade publication.
●Also available online. Vendor(s): Knight-Ridder Information, Inc., Lexis-Nexis.
   Formerly (until 1997): Investing, Licensing and Trading Conditions Abroad. Ecuador (ISSN 1352-9846)
   Description: Provides information on corporate tax rules, exchange and price controls, trade and licensing restrictions, labor conditions and investment rules.

332.6 336   US
INVESTING, LICENSING AND TRADING. FRANCE. a. £185($275) Economist Intelligence Unit, 111 W. 57th St., New York, NY 10019. TEL 212-554-0600; 800-938-4685. FAX 212-586-1181. TELEX 175567. URL: http://www.eiu.com. (UK addr.: Economist Intelligence Unit Ltd., Subscriptions Dept., P.O. Box 200, Harold Hill, Romford, Essex RM3 8UX, England. TEL 44-1708-381-444. FAX 44-1708-371-850)
Document type: trade publication.
●Also available online. Vendor(s): Knight-Ridder Information, Inc., Lexis-Nexis.
   Formerly (until 1997): Investing, Licensing and Trading Conditions Abroad. France (ISSN 1352-9897)
   Description: Provides information on corporate tax rules, exchange and price controls, trade and licensing restrictions, labor conditions and investment rules.

332.6 336   US
INVESTING, LICENSING AND TRADING. HONG KONG. a. £185($275) Economist Intelligence Unit, 111 W. 57th St., New York, NY 10019. TEL 212-554-0600; 800-938-4685. FAX 212-586-1181. TELEX 175567. URL: http://www.eiu.com. (UK addr.: Economist Intelligence Unit Ltd., Subscriptions Dept., P.O. Box 200, Harold Hill, Romford, Essex RM3 8UX, England. TEL 44-1708-381-444. FAX 44-1708-371-850)
●Also available online. Vendor(s): Knight-Ridder Information, Inc., Lexis-Nexis.
   Formerly (until 1997): Investing, Licensing and Trading Conditions Abroad. Hong Kong.
   Description: Provides information on corporate tax rules, exchange and price controls, trade and licensing restrictions, labor conditions and investment rules.

332.6 336   US
INVESTING, LICENSING AND TRADING. EGYPT. a. £185($275) Economist Intelligence Unit, 111 W. 57th St., New York, NY 10019. TEL 212-554-0600; 800-938-4685. FAX 212-586-1181. TELEX 175567. URL: http://www.eiu.com. (UK addr.: Economist Intelligence Unit Ltd., Subscriptions Dept., P.O. Box 200, Harold Hill, Romford, Essex RM3 8UX, England. TEL 44-1708-381-444. FAX 44-1708-371-850)
Document type: trade publication.
●Also available online. Vendor(s): Knight-Ridder Information, Inc., Lexis-Nexis.
   Formerly (until 1997): Investing, Licensing and Trading Conditions Abroad. Egypt (ISSN 1352-9781)
   Description: Provides information on corporate tax rules, exchange and price controls, trade and licensing restrictions, labor conditions and investment rules.

332.6 336   US
INVESTING, LICENSING AND TRADING. GERMANY. a. £185($275) Economist Intelligence Unit, 111 W. 57th St., New York, NY 10019. TEL 212-554-0600; 800-938-4685. FAX 212-586-1181. TELEX 175567. URL: http://www.eiu.com. (UK addr.: Economist Intelligence Unit Ltd., Subscriptions Dept., P.O. Box 200, Harold Hill, Romford, Essex RM3 8UX, England. TEL 44-1708-381-444. FAX 44-1708-371-850)
Document type: trade publication.
●Also available online. Vendor(s): Knight-Ridder Information, Inc., Lexis-Nexis.
   Formerly (until 1997): Investing, Licensing and Trading Conditions Abroad. Germany (ISSN 1352-9900)
   Description: Provides information on corporate tax rules, exchange and price controls, trade and licensing restrictions, labor conditions and investment rules.

332.6 336   US
INVESTING, LICENSING AND TRADING. HUNGARY. a. £185($275) Economist Intelligence Unit, 215 Park Ave. S., New York, NY 10003-1658. TEL 212-554-0600; 800-938-1181. FAX 212-586-1182. TELEX 175567. URL: http://www.eiu.com. (UK addr.: Economist Intelligence Unit Ltd., Subscriptions Dept., P.O. Box 200, Harold Hill, Romford, Essex RM3 8UX, England. TEL 44-1708-381-444. FAX 44-1708-371-850)
Document type: trade publication.
●Also available online. Vendor(s): Knight-Ridder Information, Inc., Lexis-Nexis.
   Formerly (until 1997): Investing, Licensing and Trading Conditions Abroad. Hungary (ISSN 1353-6281)
   Description: Provides information on corporate tax rules, exchange and price controls, trade and licensing restrictions, labor conditions and investment rules.

332.6 336   US
INVESTING, LICENSING AND TRADING. EUROPEAN UNION. a. £185($275) Economist Intelligence Unit, 111 W. 57th St., New York, NY 10019. TEL 212-554-0600; 800-938-4685. FAX 212-586-1181. TELEX 175567. URL: http://www.eiu.com. (UK addr.: Economist Intelligence Unit Ltd., Subscriptions Dept., P.O. Box 200, Harold Hill, Romford, Essex RM3 8UX, England. TEL 44-1708-381444. FAX 44-1708-371850)
   Formerly (until 1997): Investing, Licensing and Trading Conditions Abroad. European Union.
   Description: Provides information on corporate tax rules, exchange and price controls, trade and licensing restrictions, labor conditions and investment rules.

332.6 336   US
INVESTING, LICENSING AND TRADING. GLOBAL EDITION. (Avail. in global, regional and individual country eds.) 1965. base vol. (plus bi-m. updates). $2445. Economist Intelligence Unit, 111 W. 57th St., New York, NY 10019. TEL 212-554-0600; 800-938-4685. FAX 212-586-1181. TELEX 175567. URL: http://www.eiu.com. (UK addr.: Economist Intelligence Unit Ltd., Subscriptions Dept., P.O. Box 200, Harold Hill, Romford, Essex RM3 8UX, England. TEL 44-1708-381-444. FAX 44-1708-371-850) Ed. Bob Harris.
●Also available online. Vendor(s): Knight-Ridder Information, Inc., Lexis-Nexis.
   Former titles (until 1997): Investing, Licensing and Trading Conditions Abroad. Global Edition (ISSN 0021-003X); Investing, Licensing and Trading Conditions in 5 Countries.
   Description: Reference service that advises on how to operate profitably in 60 countries.

332.6 336   US
INVESTING, LICENSING AND TRADING. INDIA. a. £185($275) Economist Intelligence Unit, 111 W. 57th St., New York, NY 10019. TEL 212-554-0600; 800-938-4685. FAX 212-586-1181. TELEX 175567. URL: http://www.eiu.com. (UK addr.: Economist Intelligence Unit Ltd., Subscriptions Dept., P.O. Box 200, Harold Hill, Romford, Essex RM3 8UX, England. TEL 44-1708-381-444. FAX 44-1708-371-850)
●Also available online. Vendor(s): Knight-Ridder Information, Inc., Lexis-Nexis.
   Formerly (until 1997): Investing, Licensing and Trading Conditions Abroad. India.
   Description: Provides information on corporate tax rules, exchange and price controls, trade and licensing restrictions, labor conditions and investment rules.

BUSINESS AND ECONOMICS — INTERNATIONAL COMMERCE

322.6 336 US
INVESTING, LICENSING AND TRADING. INDONESIA. a. £185($275) Economist Intelligence Unit, 111 W. 57th St., New York, NY 10019. TEL 212-554-0600; 800-936-4685. FAX 212-586-1181. TELEX 175567. URL: http://www.eiu.com. (UK addr.: Economist Intelligence Unit Ltd., Subscriptions Dept., P.O. Box 200, Harold Hill, Romford, Essex RM3 8UX, England. TEL 44-1708-381-444. FAX 44-1708-371-850) **Document type:** trade publication. ●Also available online. Vendor(s): Knight-Ridder Information, Inc., Lexis-Nexis.
Formerly (until 1997): Investing, Licensing and Trading Conditions Abroad. Indonesia (ISSN 1353-5749)
Description: Provides information on corporate tax rules, exchange and price controls, trade and licensing restrictions, labor conditions and investment rules.

322.6 336 US
INVESTING, LICENSING AND TRADING. JAPAN. a. £185($275) Economist Intelligence Unit, 111 W. 57th St., New York, NY 10019. TEL 212-554-0600; 800-938-4685. FAX 212-586-1181. TELEX 175567. URL: http://www.eiu.com. (UK addr.: Economist Intelligence Unit Ltd., Subscriptions Dept., P.O. Box 200, Harold Hill, Romford, Essex RM3 8UX, England. TEL 44-1708-381-444. FAX 44-1708-371-850) **Document type:** trade publication. ●Also available online. Vendor(s): Knight-Ridder Information, Inc., Lexis-Nexis.
Formerly (until 1997): Investing, Licensing and Trading Conditions Abroad. Japan (ISSN 1353-579X)
Description: Provides information on corporate tax rules, exchange and price controls, trade and licensing restrictions, labor conditions and investment rules.

322.6 336 US
INVESTING, LICENSING AND TRADING. MEXICO. a. £185($275) Economist Intelligence Unit, 111 W. 57th St., New York, NY 10019. TEL 212-554-0600; 800-938-4685. FAX 212-586-1181. TELEX 175567. URL: http://www.eiu.com. (UK addr.: Economist Intelligence Unit Ltd., Subscriptions Dept., P.O. Box 200, Harold Hill, Romford, Essex RM3 8UX, England. TEL 44-1708-381-444. FAX 44-1708-371-850) **Document type:** trade publication. ●Also available online. Vendor(s): Knight-Ridder Information, Inc., Lexis-Nexis.
Formerly (until 1997): Investing, Licensing and Trading Conditions Abroad. Mexico (ISSN 1352-9854)
Description: Provides information on corporate tax rules, exchange and price controls, trade and licensing restrictions, labor conditions and investment rules.

332.6 336 US
INVESTING, LICENSING AND TRADING. IRELAND. a. £185($275) Economist Intelligence Unit, 111 W. 57th St., New York, NY 10019. TEL 212-554-0600; 800-938-4685. FAX 212-586-1181. TELEX 175567. URL: http://www.eiu.com. (UK addr.: Economist Intelligence Unit Ltd., Subscriptions Dept., P.O. Box 200, Harold Hill, Romford, Essex RM 8UX, England. TEL 44-1708-381-444. FAX 44-1708-371-850) **Document type:** trade publication. ●Also available online. Vendor(s): Knight-Ridder Information, Inc., Lexis-Nexis.
Formerly (until 1997): Investing, Licensing and Trading Conditions Abroad. Ireland (ISSN 1352-9927)
Description: Provides information on corporate tax rules, exchange and price controls, trade and licensing restrictions, labor conditions and investment rules.

332.6 336 US
INVESTING, LICENSING AND TRADING. KENYA. a. £185($275) Economist Intelligence Unit, 111 W. 57th St., New York, NY 10019. TEL 212-554-0600; 800-938-4685. FAX 212-586-1181. TELEX 175567. URL: http://www.eiu.com. (UK addr.: Economist Intelligence Unit Ltd., Subscriptions Dept., P.O. Box 200, Harold Hill, Romford, Essex RM3 8UX, England. TEL 44-1708-381-444. FAX 44-1708-371-850) **Document type:** trade publication. ●Also available online. Vendor(s): Knight-Ridder Information, Inc., Lexis-Nexis.
Formerly (until 1997): Investing, Licensing and Trading Conditions Abroad. Kenya (ISSN 1352-5964)
Description: Provides information on corporate tax rules, exchange and price controls, trade and licensing restrictions, labor conditions and investment rules.

332.6 336 US
INVESTING, LICENSING AND TRADING. MIDDLE EAST - AFRICA. (Includes: Egypt, Israel, Kenya, Nigeria, Saudi Arabia, South Africa, and Turkey) base vol. (plus bi-m. updates). $790. Economist Intelligence Unit, 111 W. 57th St., New York, NY 10019. TEL 212-554-0600; 800-938-4685. FAX 212-586-1181. TELEX 175567. URL: http://www.eiu.com. (UK addr.: Economist Intelligence Unit Ltd., Subscriptions Dept., P.O. Box 200, Harold Hill, Romford, Essex RM3 8UX, England. TEL 44-1708-381-444. FAX 44-1708-371-850) ●Also available online. Vendor(s): Knight-Ridder Information, Inc., Lexis-Nexis.
Former titles (until 1997): Investing, Licensing and Trading Conditions Abroad. Middle East - Africa & Investing, Licensing and Trading Conditions Abroad. Europe - Middle East - Africa.
Description: Offers information on corporate tax rules, exchange and price controls, trade and licensing restrictions, labor conditions and investment rules.

332.6 336 US
INVESTING, LICENSING AND TRADING. ISRAEL. a. £185($275) Economist Intelligence Unit, 111 W. 57th St., New York, NY 10019. TEL 212-554-0600; 800-938-4685. FAX 212-586-1181. TELEX 175567. URL: http://www.eiu.com. (UK addr.: Economist Intelligence Unit Ltd., Subscriptions Dept., P.O. Box 200, Harold Hill, Romford, RM3 8UX, England. TEL 44-1708-381-444. FAX 44-1708-371-850) **Document type:** trade publication. ●Also available online. Vendor(s): Knight-Ridder Information, Inc., Lexis-Nexis.
Formerly (until 1997): Investing, Licensing and Trading Conditions Abroad. Israel (ISSN 1352-979X)
Description: Provides information on corporate tax rules, exchange and price controls, trade and licensing restrictions, labor conditions and investment rules.

322.6 336 US
INVESTING, LICENSING AND TRADING. LUXEMBOURG. a. £185($275) Economist Intelligence Unit, 111 W. 57th St., New York, NY 10019. TEL 212-554-0600; 800-938-4685. FAX 212-586-1181. TELEX 175567. URL: http://www.eiu.com. (UK addr.: Economist Intelligence Unit Ltd., Subscriptions Dept., P.O. Box 200, Harold Hill, Romford, Essex RM3 8UX, England. TEL 44-1708-381-444. FAX 44-1708-371-850) **Document type:** trade publication. ●Also available online. Vendor(s): Knight-Ridder Information, Inc., Lexis-Nexis.
Formerly (until 1997): Investing, Licensing and Trading Conditions Abroad. Luxembourg (ISSN 1353-5781)
Description: Provides information on corporate tax rules, exchange and price controls, trade and licensing restrictions, labor conditions and investment rules.

332.6 336 US
INVESTING, LICENSING AND TRADING. NETHERLANDS. a. £185($275) Economist Intelligence Unit, 111 W. 57th St., New York, NY 10019. TEL 212-554-0600; 800-938-4685. FAX 212-586-1181. TELEX 175567. URL: http://www.eiu.com. (UK addr.: Economist Intelligence Unit Ltd., Subscriptions Dept., P.O. Box 200, Harold Hill, Romford, Essex RM3 8UX, England. TEL 44-1708-381-444. FAX 44-1708-371-850) ●Also available online. Vendor(s): Knight-Ridder Information, Inc., Lexis-Nexis.
Formerly (until 1997): Investing, Licensing and Trading Conditions Abroad. Netherlands.
Description: Provides information on corporate tax rules, exchange and price controls, trade and licensing restrictions, labor conditions and investment rules.

332.6 336 US
INVESTING, LICENSING AND TRADING. ITALY. a. £185($275) Economist Intelligence Unit, 111 W. 57th St., New York, NY 10019. TEL 212-554-0600; 800-938-4685. FAX 212-586-1181. TELEX 175567. URL: http://www.eiu.com. (UK addr.: Economist Intelligence Unit Ltd., Subscriptions Dept., P.O. Box 200, Harold Hill, Romford, Essex RM3 8UX, England. TEL 44-1708-381-444. FAX 44-1708-371-850) **Document type:** trade publication. ●Also available online. Vendor(s): Knight-Ridder Information, Inc., Lexis-Nexis.
Formerly (until 1997): Investing, Licensing and Trading Conditions. Italy (ISSN 1353-5803)
Description: Provides information on corporate tax rules, exchange and price controls, trade and licensing restriction, labor conditions and investment rules.

322.6 336 US
INVESTING, LICENSING AND TRADING. MALAYSIA. a. £185($275) Economist Intelligence Unit, 111 W. 57th St., New York, NY 10019. TEL 212-554-0600; 800-938-4685. FAX 212-586-1181. TELEX 175567. URL: http://www.eiu.com. (UK addr.: Economist Intelligence Unit Ltd., Subscriptions Dept., P.O. Box 200, Harold Hill, Romford, Essex RM3 8UX, England. TEL 44-1708-381-444. FAX 44-1708-371-850) **Document type:** trade publication. ●Also available online. Vendor(s): Knight-Ridder Information, Inc., Lexis-Nexis.
Formerly (until 1997): Investing, Licensing and Trading Conditions Abroad (ISSN 1353-5765)
Description: Provides information on corporate tax rules, exchange and price controls, trade and licensing restrictions, labor conditions and investment rules.

332.6 336 US
INVESTING, LICENSING AND TRADING. NEW ZEALAND. a. £185($275) Economist Intelligence Unit, 111 W. 57th St., New York, NY 10019. TEL 212-554-0600; 800-938-4685. FAX 212-586-1181. TELEX 175567. URL: http://www.eiu.com. (UK addr.: Economist Intelligence Unit Ltd., Subscriptions Dept., P.O. Box 200, Harold Hill, Romford, Essex RM3 8UX, England. TEL 44-1708-381-444. FAX 44-1708-371-850) **Document type:** trade publication. ●Also available online. Vendor(s): Knight-Ridder Information, Inc., Lexis-Nexis.
Formerly (until 1997): Investing, Licensing and Trading. New Zealand (ISSN 1353-5919)
Description: Provides information on corporate tax rules, exchange and price controls, trade and licensing restrictions, labor conditions and investment rules.

BUSINESS AND ECONOMICS — INTERNATIONAL COMMERCE

332.6 336   US
INVESTING, LICENSING AND TRADING. NIGERIA. a.
£185($275) Economist Intelligence Unit, 111 W. 57th St., New York, NY 10019. TEL 212-554-0600; 800-938-4685. FAX 212-586-1181. TELEX 175567. URL: http://www.eiu.com. (UK addr.: Economist Intelligence Unit Ltd., Subscriptions Dept., P.O. Box 200, Harold Hill, Romford, Essex RM3 8UX, England. TEL 44-1708-381-444. FAX 44-1708-371-850)
Document type: trade publication.
●Also available online. Vendor(s): Knight-Ridder Information, Inc., Lexis-Nexis.
Formerly (until 1997): Investing, Licensing and Trading Conditions Abroad. Nigeria (ISSN 1352-5972)
Description: Provides information on corporate tax rules, exchange and price controls, trade and licensing restrictions, labor conditions and investment rules.

332.6 336   US
INVESTING, LICENSING AND TRADING. PERU. a.
£185($275) Economist Intelligence Unit, 111 W. 57th St., New York, NY 10019. TEL 212-554-0600; 800-938-4685. FAX 212-586-1181. TELEX 175567. URL: http://www.eiu.com. (UK addr.: Economist Intelligence Unit Ltd., Subscriptions Dept., P.O. Box 200, Harold Hill, Romford, Essex RM3 8UX, England. TEL 44-1708-381-444. FAX 44-1708-371-850)
Document type: trade publication.
●Also available online. Vendor(s): Knight-Ridder Information, Inc., Lexis-Nexis.
Formerly (until 1997): Investing, Licensing and Trading Conditions Abroad. Peru (ISSN 1352-9870)
Description: Provides information on corporate tax rules, exchange and price controls, trade and licensing restrictions, labor conditions and investment rules.

332.6 336   US
INVESTING, LICENSING AND TRADING. PUERTO RICO. a.
£185($275) Economist Intelligence Unit, 111 W. 57th St., New York, NY 10019. TEL 212-554-0600; 800-938-4685. FAX 212-586-1181. TELEX 175567. URL: http://www.eiu.com. (UK addr.: Economist Intelligence Unit Ltd., Subscriptions Dept., P.O. Box 200, Harold Hill, Romford, Essex RM3 8UX, England. TEL 44-1708-381-444. FAX 44-1708-371-850)
Document type: trade publication.
●Also available online. Vendor(s): Knight-Ridder Information, Inc., Lexis-Nexis.
Formerly (until 1997): Investing, Licensing and Trading Conditions Abroad. Puerto Rico (ISSN 1352-6057)
Description: Provides information on corporate tax rules, exchange and price controls, trade and licensing restrictions, labor conditions and investment rules.

332.6 336   US
INVESTING, LICENSING AND TRADING. NORWAY. a.
£185($275) Economist Intelligence Unit, 111 W. 57th St., New York, NY 10019. TEL 212-554-0600; 800-938-4685. FAX 212-586-1181. TELEX 175567. URL: http://www.eiu.com. (UK addr.: Economist Intelligence Unit Ltd., Subscriptions Dept., P.O. Box 200, Harold Hill, Romford, Essex RM3 8UX, England. TEL 44-1708-381-444. FAX 44-1708-371-850)
Document type: trade publication.
●Also available online. Vendor(s): Knight-Ridder Information, Inc., Lexis-Nexis.
Formerly (until 1997): Investing, Licensing and Trading Conditions Abroad. Norway (ISSN 1352-996X)
Description: Provides information on corporate tax rules, exchange and price controls, trade and licensing restrictions, labor conditions and investment rules.

332.6 336   US
INVESTING, LICENSING AND TRADING. PHILIPPINES. a.
£185($275) Economist Intelligence Unit, 111 W. 57th St., New York, NY 10019. TEL 212-554-0600; 800-938-4685. FAX 212-586-1181. TELEX 175567. URL: http://www.eiu.com. (UK addr.: Economist Intelligence Unit Ltd., Subscriptions Dept., P.O. Box 200, Harold Hill, Romford, Essex RM3 8UX, England. TEL 44-1708-381-444. FAX 44-1708-371-850)
Document type: trade publication.
●Also available online. Vendor(s): Knight-Ridder Information, Inc., Lexis-Nexis.
Formerly (until 1997): Investing, Licensing and Trading Conditions Abroad. Philippines (ISSN 1352-5980)
Description: Provides information on corporate tax rules, exchange and price controls, trade and licensing restrictions, labor conditions and investment rules.

332.6 336   US
INVESTING, LICENSING AND TRADING. RUSSIA. a.
£185($275) Economist Intelligence Unit, 111 W. 57th St., New York, NY 10019. TEL 212-554-0600; 800-938-4685. FAX 212-586-1181. TELEX 175567. URL: http://www.eiu.com. (UK addr.: Economist Intelligence Unit Ltd., Subscriptions Dept., P.O. Box 200, Harold Hill, Romford, Essex RM3 8UX, England. TEL 44-1708-381-444. FAX 44-1708-371-850)
Document type: trade publication.
●Also available online. Vendor(s): Knight-Ridder Information, Inc., Lexis-Nexis.
Formerly (until 1997): Investing, Licensing and Trading Conditions Abroad. Russia (ISSN 1352-9773)
Description: Provides information on corporate tax rules, exchange and price controls, trade and licensing restrictions, labor conditions and investment rules.

332.6 336   US
INVESTING, LICENSING AND TRADING. PAKISTAN. a.
£185($275) Economist Intelligence Unit, 111 W. 57th St., New York, NY 10019. TEL 212-554-0600; 800-938-4685. FAX 212-586-1181. TELEX 175567. URL: http://www.eiu.com. (UK addr.: Economist Intelligence Unit Ltd., Subscriptions Dept., P.O. Box 200, Harold Hill, Romford, Essex RM3 8UX, England. TEL 44-1708-381-444. FAX 44-1708-371-850)
Document type: trade publication.
●Also available online. Vendor(s): Knight-Ridder Information, Inc., Lexis-Nexis.
Formerly (until 1997): Investing, Licensing and Trading Conditions Abroad. Pakistan (ISSN 1353-5927)
Description: Provides information on corporate tax rules, exchange and price controls, trade and licensing restrictions, labor conditions and investment rules.

332.6 336   US
INVESTING, LICENSING AND TRADING. POLAND. a.
£185($275) Economist Intelligence Unit, 111 W. 57th St., New York, NY 10019. TEL 212-554-0600; 800-938-4685. FAX 212-586-1181. TELEX 175567. URL: http://www.eiu.com. (UK addr.: Economist Intelligence Unit Ltd., Subscriptions Dept., P.O. Box 200, Harold Hill, Romford, Essex RM3 8UX, England. TEL 44-1708-381-444. FAX 44-1708-371-850)
Document type: trade publication.
●Also available online. Vendor(s): Knight-Ridder Information, Inc., Lexis-Nexis.
Formerly (until 1997): Investing, Licensing and Trading Conditions Abroad. Poland (ISSN 1352-5999)
Description: Provides information on corporate tax rules, exchange and price controls, trade and licensing restrictions, labor conditions and investment rules.

332.6 336   US
INVESTING, LICENSING AND TRADING. SAUDI ARABIA. a.
£185($275) Economist Intelligence Unit, 111 W. 57th St., New York, NY 10019. TEL 212-554-0600; 800-938-4685. FAX 212-586-1181. TELEX 175567. URL: http://www.eiu.com. (UK addr.: Economist Intelligence Unit Ltd., Subscriptions Dept., P.O. Box 200, Harold Hill, Romford, Essex RM3 8UX, England. TEL 44-1708-381-444. FAX 44-1708-371-850)
Document type: trade publication.
●Also available online. Vendor(s): Knight-Ridder Information, Inc., Lexis-Nexis.
Formerly (until 1997): Investing, Licensing and Trading Conditions Abroad. Saudi Arabia (ISSN 1352-6065)
Description: Provides information on corporate tax rules, exchange and price controls, trade and licensing restrictions, labor conditions and investment rules.

332.6 336   US
INVESTING, LICENSING AND TRADING. PANAMA. a.
£185($275) Economist Intelligence Unit, 111 W. 57th St., New York, NY 10019. TEL 212-554-0600; 800-938-4685. FAX 212-586-1181. TELEX 175567. URL: http://www.eiu.com. (UK addr.: Economist Intelligence Unit Ltd., Subscriptions Dept., P.O. Box 200, Harold Hill, Romford, Essex RM3 8UX, England. TEL 44-1708-381-444. FAX 44-1708-371-850)
Document type: trade publication.
●Also available online. Vendor(s): Knight-Ridder Information, Inc., Lexis-Nexis.
Formerly (until 1997): Investing, Licensing and Trading Conditions Abroad. Panama (ISSN 1352-9862)
Description: Provides information on corporate tax rules, exchange and price controls, trade and licensing restrictions, labor conditions and investment rules.

332.6 336   US
INVESTING, LICENSING AND TRADING. PORTUGAL. a.
£185($275) Economist Intelligence Unit, 111 W. 57th St., New York, NY 10019. TEL 212-554-0600; 800-938-4685. FAX 212-586-1181. TELEX 175567. URL: http://www.eiu.com. (UK addr.: Economist Intelligence Unit Ltd., Subscriptions Dept., P.O. Box 200, Harold Hill, Romford, Essex RM3 8UX, England. TEL 44-1708-381-444. FAX 44-1708-371-850)
Document type: trade publication.
●Also available online. Vendor(s): Knight-Ridder Information, Inc., Lexis-Nexis.
Formerly (until 1997): Investing, Licensing and Trading Conditions Abroad. Portugal (ISSN 1352-9935)
Description: Provides information on corporate tax rules, exchange and price controls, trade and licensing restrictions, labor conditions and investment rules.

332.6 336   US
INVESTING, LICENSING AND TRADING. SINGAPORE. a.
£185($275) Economist Intelligence Unit, 111 W. 57th St., New York, NY 10019. TEL 212-554-0600; 800-938-4685. FAX 212-586-1181. TELEX 175567. URL: http://www.eiu.com. (UK addr.: Economist Intelligence Unit Ltd., Subscriptions Dept., P.O. Box 200, Harold Hill, Romford, Essex RM3 8UX, England. TEL 44-1708-381-444. FAX 44-1708-371-850)
Document type: trade publication.
●Also available online. Vendor(s): Knight-Ridder Information, Inc., Lexis-Nexis.
Formerly (until 1997): Investing, Licensing and Trading Conditions Abroad. Singapore (ISSN 1353-5994)
Description: Provides information on corporate tax rules, exchange and price controls, trade and licensing restrictions, labor conditions and investment rules.

BUSINESS AND ECONOMICS — INTERNATIONAL COMMERCE

332.6 336   US
INVESTING, LICENSING AND TRADING. SLOVAKIA. a. £185($275) Economist Intelligence Unit, 111 W. 57th St., New York, NY 10019. TEL 212-554-0600; 800-938-4685. FAX 212-586-1181. TELEX 175567. URL: http://www.eiu.com. (UK addr.: Economist Intelligence Unit Ltd., Subscriptions Dept., P.O. Box 200, Romford, Essex RM3 8UX, England. TEL 44-1708-381444. FAX 44-1708-371850)
●Also available online. Vendor(s): Knight-Ridder Information, Inc., Lexis-Nexis.
Formerly (until 1997): Investing, Licensing and Trading Conditions Abroad. Slovakia; Which superseded in part: Investing, Licensing and Trading Conditions. Czech Republic and Slovakia; Which was formerly (until 1993): Investing, Licensing and Trading Conditions Abroad. Czechoslovakia (ISSN 1352-9951)
Description: Provides information on corporate tax rules, exchange and price controls, trade and licensing restrictions, labor conditions and investment rules.

332.6 336   US
INVESTING, LICENSING AND TRADING. SOUTH AFRICA. a. £185($275) Economist Intelligence Unit, 111 W. 57th St., New York, NY 10019. TEL 212-554-0600; 800-938-4685. FAX 212-586-1181. TELEX 175567. URL: http://www.eiu.com. (UK addr.: Economist Intelligence Unit Ltd., Subscriptions Dept., P.O. Box 200, Harold Hill, Romford, Essex RM3 8UX, England. TEL 44-1708-381-444. FAX 44-1708-371-850)
Document type: trade publication.
●Also available online. Vendor(s): Knight-Ridder Information, Inc., Lexis-Nexis.
Formerly (until 1997): Investing, Licensing and Trading Conditions Abroad. South Africa (ISSN 1352-6073)
Description: Provides information on corporate tax rules, exchange and price controls, trade and licensing restrictions, labor conditions and investment rules.

332.6 336   US
INVESTING, LICENSING AND TRADING. SOUTH KOREA. a. £185($275) Economist Intelligence Unit, 111 W. 57th St., New York, NY 10019. TEL 212-554-0600; 800-938-4685. FAX 212-586-1181. TELEX 175567. URL: http://www.eiu.com. (UK addr.: Economist Intelligence Unit Ltd., Subscriptions Dept., P.O. Box 200, Harold Hill, Romford, Essex RM3 8UX, England. TEL 44-1708-381-444. FAX 44-1708-371-850)
Document type: trade publication.
●Also available online. Vendor(s): Knight-Ridder Information, Inc., Lexis-Nexis.
Formerly (until 1997): Investing, Licensing and Trading Conditions Abroad. South Korea (ISSN 1353-6257)
Description: Provides information on corporate tax rules, exchange and price controls, trade and licensing restrictions, labor conditions and investment rules.

443.6 336   US
INVESTING, LICENSING AND TRADING. SPAIN. a. £185($275) Economist Intelligence Unit, 111 W. 57th St., New York, NY 10019. TEL 212-554-0600; 800-938-4685. FAX 212-586-1181. TELEX 175567. URL: http:///www.eiu.com. (UK addr.: Economist Intelligence Unit Ltd., Subscriptions Dept., P.O. Box 200, Harold Hill, Romford, Essex RM3 8UX, England. TEL 44-1708-381-444. FAX 44-1708-371-850)
Document type: trade publication.
●Also available online. Vendor(s): Knight-Ridder Information, Inc., Lexis-Nexis.
Formerly (until 1997): Investing, Licensing and Trading Conditions Abroad. Spain (ISSN 1352-6081)
Description: Provides information on corporate tax rules, exchange and price controls, trade and licensing restrictions, labor conditions and investment rules.

332.6 336   US
INVESTING, LICENSING AND TRADING. SWEDEN. a. £185($275) Economist Intelligence Unit, 111 W. 57th St., New York, NY 10019. TEL 212-544-0600; 800-938-4685. FAX 212-586-1181. TELEX 175567. URL: http://www.eiu.com. (UK addr.: Economist Intelligence Unit Ltd., Subscriptions Dept., P.O. Box 200, Harold Hill, Romford, Essex RM3 8UX, England. TEL 44-1708-381-444. FAX 44-1708-371-850)
Document type: trade publication.
●Also available online. Vendor(s): Knight-Ridder Information, Inc., Lexis-Nexis.
Formerly (until 1997): Investing, Licensing and Trading Conditions Abroad. Sweden (ISSN 1352-609X)
Description: Provides information on corporate tax rules, exchange and price controls, trade and licensing restrictions, labor conditions and investment rules.

332.6 336   US
INVESTING, LICENSING AND TRADING. SWITZERLAND. a. £185($275) Economist Intelligence Unit, 111 W. 57th St., New York, NY 10019. TEL 212-554-0600. FAX 212-586-1181. TELEX 175567. URL: http://www.eiu.com. (UK addr.: Economist Intelligence Unit Ltd., Subscriptions Dept., P.O. Box 200, Harold Hill, Romford, Essex RM3 8UX, England. TEL 44-1708-381-444. FAX 44-1708-371-850) **Document type:** trade publication.
●Also available online. Vendor(s): Knight-Ridder Information, Inc., Lexis-Nexis.
Formerly (until 1997): Investing, Licensing and Trading Conditions Abroad. Switzerland (ISSN 1352-9757)
Description: Provides information on corporate tax rules, exchange and price controls, trade and licensing restrictions, labor conditions and investment rules.

332.6 336   US
INVESTING, LICENSING AND TRADING. TAIWAN. a. £185($275) Economist Intelligence Unit, 111 W. 57th St., New York, NY 10019. TEL 212-554-0600; 800-938-4685. FAX 212-586-1181. TELEX 175567. URL: http://www.eiu.com. (UK addr.: Economist Intelligence Unit Ltd., Subscriptions Dept., P.O. Box 200, Harold Hill, Romford, Essex RM3 8UX, England. TEL 44-1708-381-444. FAX 44-1708-371-850)
●Also available online. Vendor(s): Knight-Ridder Information, Inc., Lexis-Nexis.
Formerly (until 1997): Investing, Licensing and Trading Conditions Abroad. Taiwan.
Description: Provides information on corporate tax rules, exchange and price controls, trade and licensing restrictions, labor conditions and investment rules.

332.6 336   US
INVESTING, LICENSING AND TRADING. THAILAND. a. £185($275) Economist Intelligence Unit, 111 W. 57th St., New York, NY 10019. TEL 212-554-0600; 800-938-4685. FAX 212-586-1181. TELEX 175567. URL: http://www.eiu.com. (UK addr.: Economist Intelligence Unit Ltd., Subscriptions Dept., P.O. Box 200, Harold Hill, Romford, Essex RM3 8UX, England. TEL 44-1708-381-444. FAX 44-1708-371-850)
●Also available online. Vendor(s): Knight-Ridder Information, Inc., Lexis-Nexis.
Formerly (until 1997): Investing, Licensing and Trading Conditions Abroad. Thailand.
Description: Provides information on corporate tax rules, exchange and price controls, trade and licensing restrictions, labor conditions and investment rules.

332.6 336   US
INVESTING, LICENSING AND TRADING. TURKEY. a. £185($275) Economist Intelligence Unit, 111 W. 57th St., New York, NY 10019. TEL 212-554-0600; 800-938-4685. FAX 212-586-1181. TELEX 175567. URL: http://www.eiu.com. (UK addr.: Economist Intelligence Unit Ltd., Subscriptions Dept., P.O. Box 200, Harold Hill, Romford, Essex RM3 8UX, England. TEL 44-1708-381-444. FAX 44-1708-371-850)
Document type: trade publication.
●Also available online. Vendor(s): Knight-Ridder Information, Inc., Lexis-Nexis.
Formerly (until 1997): Investing, Licensing and Trading Conditions Abroad. Turkey (ISSN 1352-9803)
Description: Provides information on corporate tax rules, exchange and price controls, trade and licensing restrictions, labor conditions and investment rules.

332.6 336   US
INVESTING, LICENSING AND TRADING. UNITED STATES OF AMERICA. a. £185($275) Economist Intelligence Unit, 111 W. 57th St., New York, NY 10019. TEL 212-554-0600; 800-938-4685. FAX 212-586-1181. TELEX 175567. URL: http://www.eiu.com. (UK addr.: Economist Intelligence Unit Ltd., Subscriptions Dept., P.O. Box 200, Harold Hill, Romford, Essex RM3 8UX, England. TEL 44-1708-381-444. FAX 44-1708-371-850)
Document type: trade publication.
●Also available online. Vendor(s): Knight-Ridder Information, Inc., Lexis-Nexis.
Formerly (until 1997): Investing, Licensing and Trading Conditions Abroad. United States of America (ISSN 1352-982X)
Description: Provides information on corporate tax rules, exchange and price controls, trade and licensing restrictions, labor conditions and investment rules.

332.6 336   US
INVESTING, LICENSING AND TRADING. URUGUAY. a. £185($275) Economist Intelligence Unit, 111 W. 57th St., New York, NY 10019. TEL 212-554-0600; 800-938-4685. FAX 212-586-1181. TELEX 175567. URL: http://www.eiu.com. (UK addr.: Economist Intelligence Unit Ltd., Subscriptions Dept., P.O. Box 200, Harold Hill, Romford, Essex RM3 8UX, England. TEL 44-1708-381-444. FAX 44-1708-371-850)
Document type: trade publication.
●Also available online. Vendor(s): Knight-Ridder Information, Inc., Lexis-Nexis.
Formerly (until 1997): Investing, Licensing and Trading Conditions Abroad. Uruguay (ISSN 1352-6103)
Description: Provides information on corporate tax rules, exchange and price controls, trade and licensing restrictions, labor conditions and investment rules.

322.6 336   US
INVESTING, LICENSING AND TRADING. VENEZUELA. a. £185($275) Economist Intelligence Unit, 111 W. 57th St., New York, NY 10019. TEL 212-554-0600; 800-938-4685. FAX 212-586-1181. TELEX 175567. URL: http://www.eiu.com. (UK addr.: Economist Intelligence Unit Ltd., Subscriptions Dept., P.O. Box 200, Harold Hill, Romford, Essex RM3 8UX, England. TEL 44-1708-381-444. FAX 44-1708-371-850)
Document type: trade publication.
●Also available online. Vendor(s): Knight-Ridder Information, Inc., Lexis-Nexis.
Formerly (until 1997): Investing, Licensing and Trading Conditions Abroad. Venezuela (ISSN 1352-9889)
Description: Provides information on corporate tax rules, exchange and price controls, trade and licensing restrictions, labor conditions and investment rules.

BUSINESS AND ECONOMICS — INTERNATIONAL COMMERCE

322.6 336 US
INVESTING, LICENSING AND TRADING. VIETNAM. a. £185($275) Economist Intelligence Unit, 111 W. 57th St., New York, NY 10019. TEL 212-554-0600; 800-938-4685. FAX 212-586-1181. TELEX 175567. URL: http://www.eiu.com. (UK addr.: Economist Intelligence Unit Ltd., Subscriptions Dept., P.O. Box 200, Harold Hill, Romford, Essex RM3 8UX, England. TEL 44-1708-381-444. FAX 44-1708-371-850)
●Also available online. Vendor(s): Knight-Ridder Information, Inc., Lexis-Nexis.
Formerly (until 1997): Investing, Licensing and Trading Conditions Abroad. Vietnam.
Description: Provides information on corporate tax rules, exchange and price controls, trade and licensing restrictions, labor conditions and investment rules.

332 TS
AL-IQTISAD WAL-TIJARAH/ECONOMY AND COMMERCE. (Text in Arabic) 1972. s-m. free. Ministry of Economy and Commerce, P.O. Box 433, Abu Dhabi, United Arab Emirates. TEL 726000.
Description: Covers the local economy of Abu Dhabi, the U.A.E., and economic relations with the Arab world and the international community.

332.6 IR
IRAN EXPORTS & IMPORTS MAGAZINE. (Text in English) 1987. bi-m. IRI.34000 (Asia & Middle East $39; Europe $39; elsewhere $42). Iran Exports Publication Co. Ltd., P.O. Box 15815-3373, Tehran 15956, Iran. TEL 4401800. FAX 890547. Ed. Hussein Sanai. illus. circ. 5,000. (also avail. in diskette format; back issues avail.) **Document type:** trade publication.
Formerly: Iran Exports (ISSN 1016-8885)
Description: Covers the production of goods and services, exports and imports, and Iranian economic issues, with the intent of promoting trade between Iran and other countries.

382 IE
IRISH CUSTOMS JOURNAL. 4/yr. 2-6 Tara St., Dublin 2, Ireland. TEL 713500. FAX 731074. Ed. Seamus McGowen. circ. 2,000.

ISRAEL CONVENTIONS, TRADE SHOWS, FESTIVALS & SPECIAL EVENTS. see MEETINGS AND CONGRESSES

382 IS ISSN 0793-4939
ISRAEL EXPORT (YEAR). (Supplement to: Link (ISSN 0792-9765)) (Text in English) 1993. a. (Ministry of Industry and Trade) Pick Communications Ltd., P.O. Box 57500, Tel Aviv 61574, Israel. TEL 972-3-5759790. FAX 972-3-5759791. Ed. Nicky Blackburn; Pub. Amos Pick. R&P contact: Amos Pick. adv. contact: Anna Schein. charts; illus.; stat.; tr.lit. (back issues avail.) **Document type:** trade publication.
Description: Profiles the leading companies, including high technology projects. Reports on prize-winning companies.

332.6 296.7 US
ISRAEL QUALITY.* 1976. q. Government of Israel Trade Center, 800 Second Ave., 16th Fl., New York, NY 10017-4709. TEL 212-971-0310. (Co-sponsor: American-Israel Chamber of Commerce and Industry) Ed. Beth Belkin. **Document type:** trade publication.

382 SA
ISRAEL SOUTH AFRICA BUSINESS OPPORTUNITIES NEWSLETTER. (Text in English) 1994. q. Israel Trade Centre, P.O. Box 542541, Saxonwold 2132, South Africa. illus. **Document type:** newsletter.

382 338.95694 IS ISSN 0793-4955
ISRAELI FORUM. (Text in English) 1993. a. free. Pick Communications Ltd., P.O. Box 57500, Tel Aviv 61574, Israel. TEL 972-3-5759790. FAX 972-3-5759791. R&P contact: Amos Pick. **Document type:** trade publication.
Description: Covers issues relating to business investment in Israel, including technological, scientific and banking developments.

382 US ISSN 1056-3024
HD2755.5
ISSUES IN INTERNATIONAL BUSINESS. 1984. 2/yr. $9. Montclair State College, School of Business Administration, Upper Montclair, NJ 07043. Ed.Bd. abstr.; bibl.; charts. circ. 2,000.

382 IT
ISTITUTO DI COMMERCIO ESTERO. GIORNALE; settimanale di commercio estero. 52/yr. L.260000. (Istituto di Commercio Estero - National Institute for Foreign Trade) Edizioni Sistema Italia S.p.A., Via Liszt, 21, 00144 Rome, Italy. TEL 06-5992-1. FAX 06-59926702. Ed. Stefano Sassi. circ. 50,000. **Document type:** newspaper.

ITALY. ISTITUTO NAZIONALE DI STATISTICA. STATISTICA ANNUALE DEL COMMERCIO CON L'ESTERO. TOMO 2: MERCI PER PAESI. see BUSINESS AND ECONOMICS — Abstracting, Bibliographies, Statistics

ITALY. ISTITUTO NAZIONALE DI STATISTICA. STATISTICA TRIMESTRALE DEL COMMERCIO CON L'ESTERO. see BUSINESS AND ECONOMICS — Abstracting, Bibliographies, Statistics

ITALY. ISTITUTO NAZIONALE DI STATISTICA. STATISTICA TRIMESTRALE DEL COMMERCIO CON L'ESTERO. DATI GENERALI E RIASSUNTIVI. see BUSINESS AND ECONOMICS — Abstracting, Bibliographies, Statistics

382 JA ISSN 0386-3042
J C A JOURNAL. Key Title: J C A Janaru. (Text in Japanese) 1953. m. 14000 Yen. Japan Commercial Arbitration Association - Kokusai Shoji Chusai Kyokai, 9-1, Yurakucho 1-chome, Chiyoda-ku, Tokyo 100, Japan. TEL 81-3-3287-3061. FAX 81-3-3287-3064. Ed. Yoshitoshi Munakata. circ. 1,700.
Formerly (until 1972): Boeki Kuremu to Chusai (ISSN 0523-8153)

382.7 US ISSN 0744-6489
HF1602.15.U6
J E I REPORT. (In two parts: A & B) w. $80 (foreign $140) (effective 1997). Japan Economic Institute, 1000 Connecticut Ave., N.W., Washington, DC 20036. TEL 202-296-5633. FAX 202-296-8333. E-mail: subscription@jei.org. Ed. Susan MacKnight. R&P contact: Arthur Alexander. index. (looseleaf format; also avail. in microfiche from CIS; back issues avail.; reprint service avail. from SCH) **Indexed:** SRI. **Document type:** newsletter.
●Also available online. Vendor(s): NewsNet.
Formerly: J E I Council Report.
Description: In-depth analysis of economic, political and financial issues that affect U.S.-Japan economic relations.

382 330.1 GW
J O I C E. (Journal of International and Comparative Economics) 1992. q. DM.348. Physica-Verlag GmbH und Co., Postfach 105280, 69042 Heidelberg, Germany. TEL 49-6221-487492. E-mail: physica@springer.de; URL: http://www.springer.de. (Subscr. to: Springer-Verlag, Postfach 311340, 10643 Berlin, Germany. TEL 49-30-82787-0. FAX 49-30-82787448; Subscr. in N. America to: Springer-Verlag New York, Inc., 333 Meadowlands Pkwy., Secaucus, NJ 07094, USA. TEL 212-460-1500. FAX 212-473-6272) Ed.Bd. **Document type:** academic/scholarly publication.
—BLDSC (3656.682500); SWETS. CCC.
Supersedes in part (in 1997): Economic Systems - J O I C E; Which was formed by the merger of (1992-1996): J O I C E (ISSN 0940-4821); (1992-1996): Economic Systems (ISSN 0939-3625)
Description: Comparative view of the development of the integration and enlargement of international competition.

332.6 GW
JAHRBUCH ZUR AUSSENWIRTSCHAFTSPOLITIK. 1992. a. DM.78.80. Lit Verlag, Dieckstr. 56, 48145 Muenster, Germany. TEL 0251-235091. FAX 0251-231972. Ed.Bd. index. (back issues avail.) **Document type:** academic/scholarly publication.

382 JM
JAMAICAN EXPORTER. 1972. a. free. Jamaica Exporters' Association, 13 Dominica Dr., Kingston 5, Jamaica, W.I. TEL 92-91292. Dir. Puline Gray. adv.

JAPAN AND THE WORLD ECONOMY; international journal of theory and policy. see BUSINESS AND ECONOMICS — Economic Systems And Theories, Economic History

322.6 341 AT
JAPAN BUSINESS LAW GUIDE. 1988. q. C C H Australia Ltd., P.O. Box 230, North Ryde, N.S.W. 2113, Australia. TEL 61-1-300300224. FAX 61-1-300306224. (looseleaf format)
Description: Explaining Japan's business laws for foreigners investing in Japan.

382 JA ISSN 0452-3385
JAPAN COMMERCIAL ARBITRATION ASSOCIATION. QUARTERLY. (Text in English) q. Japan Commercial Arbitration Association - Kokusai Shoji Chusai Kyokai, 9-1, Yurakucho 1-chome, Chiyoda-ku, Tokyo 100, Japan. TEL 81-3-3287-3061. FAX 81-3-3287-3064. Ed. Yoshitoshi Munakata. circ. 300.

332.6 UK ISSN 0957-1426
JAPAN CONTACT. (Text in English, Japanese) 1989. 6/yr. £12 to individuals (foreign £18); institutions £18 (foreign £24). Brennan Publications, 148 Birchover Way, Allestree, Derby DE22 2RW, England. TEL 0332-551884. Ed. James Brennan.

JAPAN ELECTRONICS ALMANAC. see ELECTRONICS

JAPAN EXPORTS & IMPORTS: COMMODITY BY COUNTRY. see BUSINESS AND ECONOMICS — Abstracting, Bibliographies, Statistics

382.7 US ISSN 0888-5702
HF1602.15.U6
JAPAN - U S BUSINESS REPORT. m. $160 (foreign $170) (effective 1997). Japan Economic Institute, 1000 Connecticut Ave., N.W., Washington, DC 20036. TEL 202-296-5633. FAX 202-296-8333. R&P contact: Arthur Alexander. **Document type:** newsletter.
●Also available online. Vendor(s): NewsNet.
Formerly: Japan Report.
Description: Detailed look at what American companies are doing in Japan and vice versa.

382 GW ISSN 0931-3230
JAPANINFO; Fernost Berichte: Deutscher Dienst fuer Wirtschaft, Politik, Technologie und Gesellschaft. 1980. every 3 weeks. DM.448. Japaninfo Verlag, Bismarckring 40, 89077 Ulm, Germany. TEL 0731-68093. FAX 0731-68095. Ed. I. Botskor. adv.; bk.rev. circ. 550. (back issues avail.) **Document type:** newsletter.

382 600 CC ISSN 1002-1221
JINZHAN: GUOJI MAOYI YU KEJI JIAOLIU/PROGRESS: INTERNATIONAL EXCHANGE IN TRADE, SCIENCE AND TECHNOLOGY. (Text in Chinese) 1988. bi-m. $20. Zhongguo Keji Xinxisuo, Chongqing Fensuo - China Science and Technology Information Institute, Consultation Center, 132 Shengli Lu, Shizhong Qu, Chongqing, Sichuan, People's Republic of China. TEL 0811-3852750. FAX 0811-3852473. TELEX 62128 CBIST CN. Eds. Wangzihe, Fred H. Laughter. circ. 10,000.

JOINT VENTURES IN THE SOVIET UNION; a legal treatise with forms and commentary. see LAW — International Law

JOINT VENTURES WITH INTERNATIONAL PARTNERS. see LAW — International Law

382 346.066 FR
JOLY COMMUNAUTAIRE. 4 base vols. plus a. updates. 2400 Fr. (effective 1997). Joly Editions, 1 av. Franklin D. Roosevelt, 75008 Paris, France. TEL 33-1-44951620. FAX 33-1-45638939. Ed.Bd. (looseleaf format) **Document type:** trade publication.
Formerly: Dictionnaire du Marche Commun.

382 SP
JOMAR; boletin de informacion de comercio exterior. 1951. w. 33500 ptas. (foreign 43200 ptas.). Tecnipublicaciones, S.A., C. Albacete 5, 28027 Madrid, Spain. TEL 34-1-3261440. FAX 34-1-3262407. stat. circ. 3,000. (processed) **Description:** Covers the subject of imports.

382 YU ISSN 0021-8227
JOURNAL EXPORT; export-import, international, forwarding agencies, industry, mining, agriculture, finance, films, tourism, hunting, information. (Text in English) 1957. m. $16.80. Export Press, Francuska 27, Belgrade, Yugoslavia. Ed. Dragoljub Ivanovic. circ. 10,000.

BUSINESS AND ECONOMICS — INTERNATIONAL COMMERCE

332.6 US ISSN 1059-9231
HD70.A7
JOURNAL OF ASIA - PACIFIC BUSINESS. 1993. q. $40 to individuals (Canada $52; elsewhere $56); institutions $75 (Canada $97.50; elsewhere $105); libraries $125 (Canada $162.50; elsewhere $175) (effective 1998-1999). Haworth Press, Inc., 10 Alice St., Binghamton, NY 13904. TEL 607-722-5857; 800-342-9676. FAX 607-722-6362. E-mail: getinfo@haworth.com; URL: http://www.haworth.com. Ed. Zahir A. Quraeshi; Pub. Bill Cohen. R&P contact: Ruthann Heath. adv.: B&W page $300; trim 4 3/8 x 7 1/8; adv. contact: Jackie Blakeslee. bk.rev. (also avail. in microfiche from UMI; microform from HAW; reprint service avail. from HAW) **Indexed:** Asian-Pac.Econ.Lit., Cont.Pg.Manage., Geo.Abstr.P.G., IDA, Mgmt.& Market.Abstr. **Document type:** academic/scholarly publication.
—BLDSC (4947.219000); Haworth.
  Description: Covers the gamut of marketing, management, finance, accounting, business law, manufacturing, service and other areas of business in Asia-Pacific region.
  Refereed Serial

JOURNAL OF BORDERLAND STUDIES. see *POLITICAL SCIENCE — International Relations*

JOURNAL OF COMMERCE AND COMMERCIAL. see *BUSINESS AND ECONOMICS — Domestic Commerce*

382 US ISSN 0162-2854
JOURNAL OF COMMERCE EXPORT BULLETIN. 1976. w. Journal of Commerce (Subsidiary of: Economist Group), 2 World Trade Center, 27th Fl., New York, NY 10048. TEL 212-837-7000. FAX 212-837-7035.
—CCC.

JOURNAL OF EUROMARKETING. see *BUSINESS AND ECONOMICS — Marketing And Purchasing*

JOURNAL OF GLOBAL MARKETING. see *BUSINESS AND ECONOMICS — Marketing And Purchasing*

JOURNAL OF INTERNATIONAL COMPENSATION AND BENEFITS. see *BUSINESS AND ECONOMICS — Personnel Management*

JOURNAL OF INTERNATIONAL CONSUMER MARKETING. see *BUSINESS AND ECONOMICS — Marketing And Purchasing*

JOURNAL OF INTERNATIONAL MARKETING. see *BUSINESS AND ECONOMICS — Marketing And Purchasing*

JOURNAL OF LANGUAGE FOR INTERNATIONAL BUSINESS. see *LINGUISTICS*

JOURNAL OF LAW & COMMERCE. see *LAW — Corporate Law*

JOURNAL OF MULTINATIONAL FINANCIAL MANAGEMENT. see *BUSINESS AND ECONOMICS — Management*

JOURNAL OF TEACHING IN INTERNATIONAL BUSINESS. see *EDUCATION*

382 US ISSN 0889-1583
HF1601
JOURNAL OF THE JAPANESE AND INTERNATIONAL ECONOMIES; an international Journal. 1987. q. $239 (foreign $270) (effective 1997). (Tokyo Center for Economic Research) Academic Press, Inc., Journal Division, 525 B St., Ste. 1900, San Diego, CA 92101-4495. TEL 619-230-1840. FAX 619-699-6800. E-mail: apsubs@acad.com; URL: http://www.apnet.com/www/journal/jj.htm; http://www.idealibrary.com/. (Subscr. to: Box 861213, Orlando, FL 32886-1213. TEL 407-347-4040. FAX 407-363-9661) Ed. Masahiko Aoki. (back issues avail.) **Indexed:** ASCA, Asian-Pac.Econ.Lit., J.of Econ.Lit., SSCI. **Document type:** academic/scholarly publication.
●Also available online.
—BLDSC (5008.650000); Genuine Article; SWETS; UnCover. **CCC.**
  Description: Publishes original reports of research devoted to academic analyses of the Japanese economy and its interdependence with other national economies.

332.6 US ISSN 1068-6061
HD62.4 CODEN: JTMDEZ
JOURNAL OF TRANSNATIONAL MANAGEMENT DEVELOPMENT. 1994. q. $45 to individuals (Canada $58.50; elsewhere $63); institutions $80 (Canada $104; elsewhere $112); libraries $175 (Canada $227.50; elsewhere $245) (effective 1997-1998). (International Management Development Association) Haworth Press, Inc., 10 Alice St., Binghamton, NY 13904. TEL 607-722-5857; 800-342-9676. FAX 607-722-6362. E-mail: getinfo@haworth.com; URL: http://www.haworth.com. Ed. Kip Becker; Pub. Bill Cohen. R&P contact: Ruthann Heath. adv.: B&W page $300; trim 4 3/8 x 7 1/8; adv. contact: Jackie Blakeslee. (also avail. in microform from HAW,UMI; reprint service avail. from HAW) **Indexed:** Geo.Abstr.P.G., Mgmt.& Market.Abstr., Oper.Res.Manage.Sci., Per.Islam. (1994-), Ref.Zh., Work Rel.Abstr. **Document type:** academic/scholarly publication.
—BLDSC (5069.866000); Haworth.
  Description: Offers transnational research across business and related disciplines and across geographies and levels of economic development.
  Refereed Serial

JOURNAL OF WORLD TRADE. see *LAW — International Law*

382 YU ISSN 0022-5452
HF37.Y8
JOURNAL OF YUGOSLAV FOREIGN TRADE. (Editions in English and Russian) 1954. q. $8. Export Press, Francuska 27, Belgrade, Yugoslavia. Ed. D. Kostic. adv.; illus. circ. 10,000. **Indexed:** P.A.I.S.

382 PK
KARACHI. CHAMBER OF COMMERCE AND INDUSTRY. PATTERN OF FOREIGN TRADE OF PAKISTAN. (Text in English) irreg. Rs.250. Karachi Chamber of Commerce and Industry, Aiwan-e-Tijarat, P.O. Box 4158, Nicol Rd., Karachi 2, Pakistan.

382 KE
KENYA. COMMISSIONER OF CUSTOMS AND EXCISE. ANNUAL TRADE REPORT. a. KShs.300. Customs and Excise Department, Statistical Branch, P.O. Box 40160, Nairobi, Kenya. TEL 254-2-715540. Ed. V. Da. Costa. circ. 1,000. (also avail. in magnetic tape) **Document type:** government publication.
  Supersedes in part: Annual Trade Report of Tanzania, Uganda and Kenya.

382 052 KE
KENYA EXPORT DIRECTORY. 1977? irreg., latest 1985. K.100. (Ministry of Commerce and Industry, Department of External Trade) News Publisher, P.O. Box 43137, Nairobi, Kenya. Ed. Joe Rodrigues. adv.; stat. circ. 4,000. **Document type:** directory, government publication.
  Description: Covers general information about Kenya, special articles on the economy and management of the economy, and names of all exporters registered with the Central Bank of Kenya. It also contains useful names and addresses for the prospective investor who may be interested in setting up business in Kenya.

382 GW ISSN 0340-6989
KIELER STUDIEN. (Text in English, German) 1949. irreg., vol.283, 1997. price varies. (Universitaet Kiel, Institut fuer Weltwirtschaft) Verlag Mohr Siebeck, Wilhelmstr. 18, 72074 Tuebingen, Germany. TEL 49-7071-923-0. FAX 49-7071-51104. E-mail: mohr-siebeck@t-online.de; URL: http://www.uni-kiel.de:8080/ifw/pub/studien/. (Subscr. to: Postfach 2040, 72010 Tuebingen, Germany) Ed. Horst Siebert. R&P contact: Jill Sopper. circ. 700. **Indexed:** M.L.A., World Agri.Econ.& Rural Sociol.Abstr. **Document type:** monographic series.
—BLDSC (5095.100000).
  Description: Studies in international economics.

382 UK ISSN 0968-1701
THE KIEV LETTER. 1993. m. £220 (effective 1996). Interforum Services Ltd., 565 Fulham Rd., London SW6 1ES, England. TEL 44-171-386-9322. FAX 44-171-381-8914. Ed. Oliver Campbell. R&P contact: Sue Wake. adv. contact: Sophie Rezzonico. **Document type:** newsletter.

382 SW ISSN 1100-4959
KINA-NYTT. 1987. 8/yr. Sweden-China Trade Council (SCTC), P.O. Box 5513, S-114 85 Stockholm, Sweden.

380.025489 DK ISSN 0106-1100
KOMPASS SELECT EXPORT. BUSINESS SERVICES. Cover title: Euro Kompass Denmark. Services. (Text in Danish, English, French, German and Spanish) 1980. a. DKK 300 (listed companies DKK 100). Forlaget Kompass-Danmark, Oeveroedvej 5, DK-2840 Holte, Denmark. TEL 45-45-41-21-00. FAX 45-45-41-21-00. illus. **Document type:** directory.
●Also available on CD-ROM.
  Formerly: Kompass Select Denmark. Business Services.

354.489 382 DK ISSN 0108-4291
KONTAKTKALENDER; danske repraesentanter i udlandet. 1973. a. Udenrigsministeriet, Sekretariatet for Udenrigshandel, Copenhagen, Denmark. adv. circ. 6,000. **Document type:** government publication, directory.

382 KO ISSN 0023-3943
KOREA TRADE. (Editions in Arabic, English, French, Japanese and Spanish) 1962. irreg. (8/yr.). free. Korea Trade Promotion Corp., 159 Samsung-dong, Kangnam-ku, Seoul, S. Korea. TEL 753-4181-9. Ed. Kwang Ho Ahn. adv.; illus.; tr.lit. **Indexed:** P.A.I.S.

382 KO ISSN 1012-0742
KOREA TRADE & BUSINESS. (Text in English, French and Spanish) 1962. m. free. Korea Trade Promotion Corp., 159 Samsung-dong, Kangnam-ku, Seoul, S. Korea. TEL 551-4181. Ed. Lee Sun-Ki. circ. 12,000.

380.102 DK ISSN 1395-4067
HF3643
KRAKS EXPORT DIRECTORY OF DENMARK. (Text in English, French, German and Spanish; summaries in English) 1927. a. DKK 600. Kraks Forlag AS, Virumgaardsvej 21, DK-2830 Virum, Denmark. TEL 45-45-83-45-83. FAX 45-45-83-10-11. Ed. Per Engel Moeller. adv. contact: Elizabeth Wuertzen. circ. 25,000. **Document type:** directory.
  Formerly: Export Directory of Denmark (ISSN 0905-9652)

L A - LATINAMERIKA. see *HISTORY — History Of North And South America*

332 US ISSN 1040-3175
LAGNIAPPE LETTER; bi-weekly report of issues affecting business in Latin America. fortn. $675 includes Lagniappe Quarterly Monitor (effective through 1998). Latin American Information Services, Inc., 159 W. 53rd St., 28th fl., New York, NY 10019. TEL 212-765-5520. FAX 212-765-2927. URL: http://www.lais.com. Ed. Rosemary H. Werrett.
●Also available online. Vendor(s): Information Access Co., Knight-Ridder Information, Inc., Lexis-Nexis.
  Description: Business and financial report covering the markets of Latin America.

381 US ISSN 1084-5526
LAGNIAPPE MONTHLY ON LATIN AMERICAN PROJECTS & FINANCE; monthly report on project and infrastructure development opportunities in Latin America. 1992. m. $495 (effective through 1998). Latin American Information Services, Inc., 159 W. 53rd St., 28th fl., New York, NY 10019. TEL 212-765-5520. FAX 212-765-2927. URL: http://www.lais.com. Ed. Rosemary H. Werrett. stat.; index. (back issues avail.) **Document type:** newsletter.
  Formerly: Americas Trade and Finance (ISSN 1062-8118)
  Description: Provides information and analysis executives need to invest in large projects in Latin America.

382 341 FR
LAMY CONTRATS INTERNATIONAUX. (Supplements avail.) a. 3950 F. (with supplements 5420 F.) (effective 1993). Lamy S.A., 187-189 quai de Valmy, 75490 Paris Cedex 10, France. TEL 33-1-44721343. FAX 33-1-444721395. TELEX 214 398.
  Description: Covers international contracts, construction and industrial contracts, the public sector market, sales, distribution, banking, and litigation.

382 DK ISSN 0106-3812
HD9015.D4
LANDBRUGSEKSPORTEN. 1960. irreg. free. Landbrugets Afsaetningsudvalg, Afdeling for Markedsanalyse, Axelborg, Axeltorn 3, 1609 Copenhagen V, Denmark. circ. 1,100.

BUSINESS AND ECONOMICS — INTERNATIONAL COMMERCE

332.6   UK   ISSN 0961-7647
LANGUAGE EXPORT LEXEL ABROAD. 1991-199? bi-m. J.D. Gravell, Ed. & Pub., 28 Barclay Rd., London SW6 1EH, England. TEL 44-171-736-7604. adv. contact: W. Yeates. bk.rev. **Document type:** newsletter.

382   UK   ISSN 0960-8702
HC121   CODEN: LAEBFF
LATIN AMERICAN ECONOMY AND BUSINESS. 1989. 16/yr. £535($695) (subscr. includes q. statistical bulletin) (effective 1997). Latin American Newsletters, 61 Old St., London EC1V 9HX, England. TEL 44-171-251-0012. FAX 44-171-253-8193. Ed. Will Ollard. (back issues avail.) **Document type:** newsletter.
●Also available online. Vendor(s): Lexis-Nexis. —CASDDS; SWETS; UnCover.
Incorporates (in 1990): Latin America Commodities Report (ISSN 0309-300X); Latin American Economic Report.
Description: Monthly coverage of every economy in the region and the impact of world and local events on them.

332.6   US
LATIN AMERICAN MARKET PLANNING HANDBOOK; population - demography - household buying power - comparative market data. a. $295. Strategy Research Corporation, 100 N.W. 37th Ave., Miami, FL 33125. TEL 305-649-5400. FAX 305-649-6312. **Document type:** trade publication.

332.6 020   US   ISSN 1067-0408
HF3230.5.A48
LATIN AMERICAN MARKETS: A GUIDE TO COMPANY AND INDUSTRY INFORMATION SOURCES. 1994. irreg., latest 2nd ed. $335 (effective 1997). Washington Researchers, Ltd., Box 19005, 20th St. Sta., Washington, DC 20036-9005. TEL 202-333-3499. FAX 202-625-0656. E-mail: research@researchers.com; URL: http://www.researchers.com/pub/busintel/researchers.html. R&P contact: Ellen O'Kane. **Document type:** directory.
Description: Lists domestic and foreign information sources on each nation, including Mexico and the rest of Central America, South America, and the Caribbean.

382 327   UK   ISSN 0265-0886
F1401
LATIN AMERICAN TIMES. 1979. 10/yr. £200($350) (effective 1996). World Reports Ltd., 108 Horseferry Rd., Westminster, London SW1P 2EF, England. TEL 44-171-222-3836. FAX 44-171-233-0185. (U.S. subscr. to: 280 Madison Ave., Ste. 1209, New York, NY 10016-0802. TEL 212-679-0095. FAX 212-679-1094) Ed. Christopher Story. (back issues avail.) Indexed: P.A.I.S. **Document type:** trade publication.
—BLDSC (5160.180000).
Description: Covers financial, economic, political and social developments in Central and South America, and the Caribbean.

382   US   ISSN 1087-0857
HF3230.5
LATIN TRADE; your business source for Latin America. Spanish edition: Revista Latin Trade: su fuente de negocios para America Latina. 1993. m. $36 (foreign $48) (effective 1998); newsstand price: $3.95. Freedom Publications, Inc. (Miami), 200 S. Biscayne Blvd., Ste. 1150, Miami, FL 33131. TEL 305-358-8373; 800-783-4903. FAX 305-358-9166. E-mail: lattrade@aol.com; URL: http://www.latintrade.com. (Subscr. to: Box 3000, Denville, NJ 07834-3000. TEL 973-627-2997. FAX 201-627-5872) Ed. Joachim Bamrud; Pub. Lynn H. Roberts. adv.: B&W page $6695, color page $8700; trim 7 x 10; adv. contact: Rose Claytor. bk.rev.; software rev.; charts; illus.; mkt.; maps; stat.; tr.lit. circ. 74,000. (back issues avail.) **Document type:** consumer publication.
●Also available online.
Formerly (until 1996): U S - Latin Trade (ISSN 1086-198X)
Description: Business reporting and analysis on Latin American commerce for corporate decision makers and government leaders.

382 341   US
LAW REPRINTS: TRADE REGULATION SERIES. 1967. irreg. $312 (effective 1997). Law Reprints, c/o Bartlett Sigerson, Ed., 5442 30th St., N.W., Washington, DC 20015. TEL 800-356-0671. Ed. Bartlett Sigerson. index. circ. 150. **Document type:** monographic series.
—CCC.
Former titles: B N A's Law Reprints: Trade Regulation Series (ISSN 0275-6978); Law Reprints. Trade Regulation Series (ISSN 0075-8256)
Description: Presents all antitrust and trade regulation briefs filed with the U.S. Supreme Court.

327 382   US   ISSN 0194-3510
LEADERS. 1978. q. Leaders Magazine, Inc., 59 E. 54th St., New York, NY 10022. TEL 212-758-0740. FAX 212-593-5194. TELEX 649333. E-mail: leadersmag@aol.com; URL: http://www.enews.com/magazines/leaders. Ed. Henry O. Dormann. adv.; circ. 33,000 (controlled).

332.6 346   GW
LEITFADEN DES AUSSENHANDELS. 1956. m. DM.598. Mendel Verlag, Robensstr. 39, 52070 Aachen, Germany. TEL 49-241-154355. FAX 49-241-154355. **Document type:** trade publication.
Description: Complete information about all laws and rules for exporting and importing throughout the world.

LETTRES INTERNATIONALES DU MARKETING BANCAIRE. see BUSINESS AND ECONOMICS — Banking And Finance

LICENSING LAW HANDBOOK. see LAW

382 338.95694   IS   ISSN 0792-9765
LINK; Israel's international business magazine. (Text in English) 1991. m. IS.109 ($54 in US; elsewhere $79). Pick Communications Ltd., P.O. Box 57500, Tel Aviv 61574, Israel. TEL 972-3-5628511. FAX 972-3-5628512. E-mail: linkmrkt@link2link.co.il; URL: http://link2link.co.il. (Subscr. in US to: Link Magazine, Box 3000, Denville, NJ 07834) Ed. Michael Eilan; Pub. Tamara Genosar. R&P contact: Michael Eilan. adv. contact: Alan Klein. bk.rev.; software rev.; charts; illus.; stat.; tr.lit. (back issues avail.) **Document type:** consumer publication.
Description: Promotes investment in Israel, and covers technological and political developments affecting Israeli businesses and their activities inside Israel and in the global market.

LLOYD'S LOADING LIST. see TRANSPORTATION — Ships And Shipping

LLOYD'S PORTS OF THE WORLD (YEAR). see TRANSPORTATION — Ships And Shipping

332.6   UK
LLOYD'S REGISTER. ANNUAL REVIEW OF THE L R GROUP. a. Lloyd's Register Ltd., 71 Fenchurch St., London EC3M 4BS, England. TEL 44-171-709-9166. FAX 44-171-488-4796. **Document type:** corporate report.
Formerly: Lloyd's Register. Annual Report.

LUXEMBOURG. SERVICE CENTRAL DE LA STATISTIQUE ET DES ETUDES ECONOMIQUES. INDICATEURS RAPIDES. SERIE H: COMMERCE EXTERIEUR DU LUXEMBOURG. see BUSINESS AND ECONOMICS — Abstracting, Bibliographies, Statistics

332.6   UK   ISSN 1358-6874
M E E D MONEY; the Middle East Money Weekly. w. E M A P Media, 33-39 Bowling Green Ln., London WC1R 0DA, England. TEL 44-171-837-1212. FAX 44-171-833-4519. Ed. Edmund O'Sullivan. adv.; bk.rev. **Document type:** trade publication.
Description: Covers the markets of the Middle East countries.

382   FR   ISSN 0026-9719
HF15
M O C I. (Moniteur du Commerce International) (Includes special issues; annual supplement avail.: Leaders of French Export) 1883. w. 1940 F. (foreign 2280 F.) (effective 1997). Societe d'Edition de Documentation Economique et Commerciale (SEDEC), 24 Bd. de l'Hopital, 75005 Paris, France. TEL 33-1-40733925. FAX 33-1-43364798. TELEX 206 811 F. Ed. Jean Marchand; Pub. Paul Rechter. R&P contact: Anton Keil. adv.: B&W page 23000 F., color page 34000 F.; trim 210 x 295; adv. contact: Anton Keil. bk.rev.; bibl.; illus.; stat.; index. circ. 15,000. Indexed: ELLIS, PROMT. **Document type:** newspaper.
—BLDSC (5879.965000); SWETS.
Former titles (until 1966): Moniteur Officiel du Commerce International (ISSN 0991-7977); (until 1961): Moniteur Officiel du Commerce et de l'Industrie (ISSN 0991-7993)
Description: Provides a selection of technical and strategic informations to develop sales abroad.

M T I A'S ENGINEERING EXPORTER. (Metal Trades Industry Association) see ENGINEERING

MACAO. DIRECCAO DOS SERVICOS DE ESTATISTICA E CENSOS. ANUARIO ESTATISTICO DO COMERCIO EXTERNO/MACAO. CENSUS AND STATISTICS DEPARTMENT. YEARBOOK OF EXTERNAL TRADE STATISTICS. see BUSINESS AND ECONOMICS — Abstracting, Bibliographies, Statistics

MACAO. DIRECCAO DOS SERVICOS DE ESTATISTICA E CENSOS. ESTATISTICAS DO COMERCIO EXTERNO/MACAO. CENSUS AND STATISTICS DEPARTMENT. STATISTICS ON EXTERNAL TRADE. see BUSINESS AND ECONOMICS — Abstracting, Bibliographies, Statistics

MACAO. DIRECCAO DOS SERVICOS DE ESTATISTICA E CENSOS. INDICADORES DO COMERCIO EXTERNO/MACAO. CENSUS AND STATISTICS DEPARTMENT. EXTERNAL TRADE INDICATORS. see BUSINESS AND ECONOMICS — Abstracting, Bibliographies, Statistics

382   MH
MACAU IMAGE; the trade and investment magazine of the Government of Macau. (Text in English) 1982. s-a. free. Macau Trade and Investment Promotion Institute, Luso Intl. Bldg. 8F, 1-3 Rua Pedro Jose Lobo, Macao, Macau. TEL 853-710528. FAX 853-590309. adv.: page P.7500. circ. 35,000. **Document type:** government publication.
Description: Includes a directory of the main producers and exporters by product.

382 336   CN   ISSN 1183-3246
MCGOLDRICK'S CANADIAN CUSTOMS GUIDE "HARMONIZED SYSTEM". 1921. a. $225 (effective 1996). McMullin Publishers Ltd., 417 St. Pierre, Montreal, PQ H2Y 2M4, Canada. TEL 514-849-1424. FAX 514-849-9809. adv.; bk.rev. circ. 10,000. **Document type:** trade publication.
●Also available on CD-ROM.
Former titles: McGoldrick's Canadian Customs Tariff "Harmonized System; McGoldrick's Handbook of Canadian Customs Tariff and Excise Duties (ISSN 0076-1990)
Refereed Serial

382 332.6   MG
MADAGASCAR. DIRECTION GENERALE DE L'INSTITUT NATIONAL DE LA STATISTIQUE. SITUATION ECONOMIQUE AU 1 JANVIER (YEAR). 1960. a. FMG.9200. Direction Generale de l'Institut National de la Statistique, Ministere de l'Economie et du Plan, B.P. 485, Antananarivo 101, Madagascar. TEL 261-2-200-70. FAX 261-2-332-50. **Document type:** government publication.
Formerly: Malagasy Republic. Direction Generale de la Banque des Donnees de l'Etat. Situation Economique au 1 Janvier (Year).
Description: Covers industrial production, transportation, foreign commerce, prices, investments.

382   BL
MADE IN BRAZIL; Brazilian export market. no.6, 1977. a. Assessoria de Promocao e Cultura Editora Ltda., Avda Brigadeiro Luis Antonio 402, P.O. Box 5390, 01318 Sao Paulo, Brazil. (Co-sponsors: Ministerio da Industria; Banco do Brasil) Ed. Jose L. Ribeiro Leite. adv.; charts; illus.; stat.

BUSINESS AND ECONOMICS — INTERNATIONAL COMMERCE

382   GW   ISSN 0172-2182
MADE IN EUROPE. GENERAL MERCHANDISE. (Text in English) 1954. m. $120 (effective 1997). Made in Europe Marketing Organisation GmbH, Hahnstr. 70, 60528 Frankfurt a.M., Germany. TEL 49-69-668038. FAX 49-69-66803838. E-mail: 100734.3642@compuserve.com; URL: http://www.miesys.com. Ed. Martin Romer; Pub. Martin Romer. R&P contact: Martin Romer. adv. contact: Franziska Bastanier. bk.rev.; illus.; mkt. circ. 18,000. **Document type:** catalog, directory.
●Also available on CD-ROM.
Supersedes in part: Made in Europe (ISSN 0024-9378)
Description: International purchasing handbook for importers, distributors, agents and traders in over 180 countries.

382   GW   ISSN 0946-5170
MADE IN EUROPE. INDUSTRIAL SUPPLY GUIDE. (Text in English) 1966. q. $60 (effective 1997). Made in Europe Marketing Organisation GmbH, Hahnstr. 70, 60528 Frankfurt a.M., Germany. TEL 49-69-668038. FAX 49-69-66803838. E-mail: 100734.3642@compuserve.com; URL: http://www.miesys.com. Ed. Martin Romer; Pub. Martin Romer. R&P contact: Martin Romer. adv. contact: Franziska Bastanier. bk.rev. circ. 18,000. **Document type:** catalog.
—UMI.
Former titles: Made in Europe. Technical and Industrial Supply Guide; Made in Europe. Technical Equipment Catalog (ISSN 0047-5424)

382   HU
MADE IN HUNGARY MONTHLY. (Text mainly in English and German; occasionally in French, Italian, Russian) 1990. m. (10/yr.) free. Magyar Tavirati Iroda, Kiadvanyszerkesztoseg - Hungarian News Agency, Editorial Office, Pl. Naphegy ter. 8, 1016 Budapest, Hungary. TEL 156-9363. Ed. Tibor Kohut. circ. 6,000.

382   HU   ISSN 0133-9680
MADE IN HUNGARY SPECIAL. (Text mainly in English; occasionally in French, German, Italian, Russian) 1971. irreg. (6-8/yr.) free. Magyar Tavirati Iroda, Publications Office - Hungarian News Agency, Publications Office, Pl. Naphegy ter. 8, 1016 Budapest, Hungary. TEL 156-9363. Ed. Tibor Kohut. adv.
Description: Aimed at countries or regions of importance to Hungary's foreign trade activity.

382   HU   ISSN 0209-4401
MADE IN HUNGARY YEARBOOK. (Text in English and German) 1974. a. $27.50. Magyar Tavirati Iroda, Kiadvanyszerkesztoseg - Hungarian News Agency, Editorial Office, Pl. Naphegy ter. 8, 1016 Budapest, Hungary. Ed. Tibor Kohut. adv. circ. 6,000.

382   FR   ISSN 0153-4157
MAGHREB SELECTION. 1975. w.(45/yr). 5800 F. (effective 1997). I C Publications, 10 rue Vineuse, 75784 Paris Cedex 16, France. TEL 33-1-44308100. FAX 33-1-44308111.

MAGYAR KIADAS - BUSINESS WEEK. see *BUSINESS AND ECONOMICS*

MAJOR BUSINESS ORGANISATIONS OF EASTERN EUROPE AND THE COMMONWEALTH OF INDEPENDENT STATES. see *BUSINESS AND ECONOMICS — Trade And Industrial Directories*

MALAWI. NATIONAL STATISTICAL OFFICE. BALANCE OF PAYMENTS. see *BUSINESS AND ECONOMICS — Abstracting, Bibliographies, Statistics*

382   MW
MALAWI BUYERS' GUIDE. 1982. biennial. $20. Malawi Export Promotion Council, P.O. Box 1299, Blantyre, Malawi. adv.; bk.rev. circ. 6,000.
Supersedes (1976-1981): Malawi Export.

MALAYSIA. DEPARTMENT OF STATISTICS. EXTERNAL TRADE SUMMARY MALAYSIA. see *BUSINESS AND ECONOMICS — Abstracting, Bibliographies, Statistics*

382   MM
MALTA. CENTRAL OFFICE OF STATISTICS. TRADE STATISTICS. 1866. a. L.5 per no. Central Office of Statistics, Merchants' St., Valletta, Malta. FAX 356-248483. (Subscr. to: Publications Bookshop, Auberge de Castille, Valletta, Malta) **Document type:** government publication.
Former titles: Malta Trade Statistics; Trade of the Maltese Islands (ISSN 0041-0462)

MANUAL FOR THE PRACTICE OF UNITED STATES IMPORT LAW. see *LAW — International Law*

382   FR   ISSN 0984-9521
MARCHES AFRICAINS. w.(45/yr). 5900 F. (effective 1997). I C Publications, 10 rue Vineuse, 75784 Paris Cedex 16, France. TEL 33-1-44308100. FAX 33-1-44308111.
Formerly (until 1988): Afrique Informations (ISSN 0753-0145)

382   FR   ISSN 1147-7717
MARCHES ARABES. s-m. (22/yr.). 5800 F. (effective 1997). I C Publications, 10 rue Vineuse, 75784 Paris Cedex 16, France. TEL 33-1-44308100. FAX 33-1-44308111.
Formerly (until 1988): Marches Arabes, Moyen-Orient Selection (ISSN 0986-6868); Which was formed by the 1987 merger of: Marches Arabes (ISSN 0756-0486); Moyen-Orient Selection (ISSN 0182-0176)

382   FR   ISSN 0767-9491
MARCHES ASIATIQUES. 1988. s-m. (22/yr.) 5400 F. (effective 1997). I C Publications, 10 rue Vineuse, 75784 Paris, France. TEL 33-1-44308100. FAX 33-1-44308111.
Formed by the merger of (1973-1988): Eurasie Echanges (ISSN 0769-0576); (1984-1988): Export (ISSN 0766-1584)
Description: Covers economic information in the Asian-Pacific zone, with priority given to China, Japan and India.

382   FR   ISSN 0998-2906
MARCHES EST-EUROPEENS. 1989. 22/yr. 5900 F. (effective 1997). I C Publications, 10 rue Vineuse, 75784 Paris, France. TEL 33-1-44308100. FAX 33-1-44308111.
Description: Economic information for eastern Europe and the countries of the Commonwealth of Independent States.

382   FR   ISSN 0989-8131
MARCHES LATINO-AMERICAINS. 1977. s-m. (22/yr.). 5400 F. (effective 1997). I C Publications, 10 rue Vineuse, 75784 Paris, France. TEL 33-1-44308100. FAX 33-1-44308111.
Formerly (until 1988): Amerique Latine (ISSN 0151-9530)
Description: Presents financial, industrial and commercial information and analyzes current events.

382   FR   ISSN 0025-2859
HC10
MARCHES TROPICAUX ET MEDITERRANEENS. 1945. w. 3590 F. (Africa 3890 F.; elsewhere $3800) (effective 1997-1998); newsstand price: 67 F. Moreux, 190 bd. Haussmann, 75008 Paris, France. TEL 33-1-44959950. FAX 33-1-49539016. TELEX NAVIM 651131F. E-mail: moreux@club-internet.fr. Ed. Serge Marpaud. adv./ bk.rev.; charts; illus.; stat.; index. circ. 18,000. **Indexed:** Agri.Eng.Abstr., Cott.& Trop.Fibr.Abstr., Documentatieblad, ELLIS, HR Rep., Int.Lab.Doc., Irr.& Drain.Abstr., Key to Econ.Sci., P.A.I.S.For.Lang.Ind., Poult.Abstr., Rural Devel.Abstr., Soils & Fert.
—SWETS.
Description: African trade review.

MARITIME RESEARCH CHARTER NEWSLETTER. see *TRANSPORTATION — Ships And Shipping*

382.9142   SP
▼**MARKET**; vademecum union europea. 1996. 46/yr. 49900 ptas. (foreign $360) (effective 1998). Canalejas 30, entlo. 2o, 08028 Barcelona, Spain. TEL 34-3-4226289. FAX 34-3-4211858. E-mail: revista.econo@redestb.es. Ed. Susana Torre. circ. 460,000. **Document type:** bulletin.
Description: Contains economic news about the European Union.
Refereed Serial

332.6 312 330.9   US   ISSN 1083-5512
HC800.A1
▼**MARKET: AFRICA - MID-EAST.** 1995. m. $295. The P R S Group, Market: newsletters (Subsidiary of: International Business Communications), Box 248, East Syracuse, NY 13057-0248. TEL 315-431-0511. FAX 315-431-0200. E-mail: custserv@polrisk.com; URL: http://www.prsgroup.com.
●Also available online. Vendor(s): CompuServe, Inc., Data-Star, Information Access Co., Knight-Ridder Information, Inc.
Description: Covers demographic and marketing trends in Africa and the Middle East.

382   US   ISSN 1059-275X
MARKET: ASIA PACIFIC. 1992. m. $325 (effective 1996). The P R S Group, Market: newsletters (Subsidiary of: International Business Communications), Box 248, East Syracuse, NY 13057-0248. TEL 315-431-0511. FAX 315-431-0200. E-mail: custserv@polrisk.com; URL: http://www.prsgroup.com. Ed. Doris Walsh; Pub. Doris Walsh. **Document type:** newsletter.
●Also available online. Vendor(s): Data-Star, Information Access Co., Knight-Ridder Information, Inc., NewsNet.
Description: Covers a wide variety of topics, including the demographics and life-styles of the Asia-Pacific consumers.

382   US   ISSN 1050-9410
MARKET: EUROPE.* 1990. m. $395. Market: Newsletters, Box 248, East Syracuse, NY 13057-0248. TEL 607-277-0934. FAX 607-277-0935. Ed. Doris Walsh; Pub. Doris Walsh. bk.rev.; index. (back issues avail.) **Document type:** newsletter.
●Also available online. Vendor(s): CompuServe, Inc., Data-Star, Information Access Co., Knight-Ridder Information, Inc., NewsNet.
Description: Covers a wide variety of subjects, including the demographics and life-styles of European consumers.

332.6   US   ISSN 1066-7024
MARKET: LATIN AMERICA. 1993. m. $325. The P R S Group, Market: newsletters (Subsidiary of: International Business Communications), Box 248, East Syracuse, NY 13057-0248. TEL 315-431-0511. FAX 315-431-0200. E-mail: custserv@polrisk.com; URL: http://www.prsgroup.com. Ed. Paula Kephart; Pub. Doris Walsh. bk.rev. **Document type:** newsletter.
●Also available online. Vendor(s): CompuServe, Inc., Data-Star, Information Access Co., Knight-Ridder Information, Inc., NewsNet.
Description: Covers a variety of marketing-related topics, including demographic and life-style trends among Latin American consumers.

332.6   UK   ISSN 0959-2482
MARKET SOUTH EAST. m. The Lodge, 37 Fairhazel Gardens, London NW6 3QN, England. TEL 071-624-8675. FAX 081-341-2750. Ed. Michael Griffin.

382   NE
MARKTGILDE GIDS; vakblad voor de ambulante handel. 5/yr. fl.45. R. Barbieri, Pub., Postbus 427, 2280 AK Rijswijk, Netherlands. adv.
Formerly: Attent.

MARYLAND JOURNAL OF INTERNATIONAL LAW AND TRADE. see *LAW — International Law*

MAURITIUS. CENTRAL STATISTICAL OFFICE. EXTERNAL TRADE STATISTICS. see *BUSINESS AND ECONOMICS — Abstracting, Bibliographies, Statistics*

MEALEY'S INTERNATIONAL ARBITRATION REPORT. see *LAW — International Law*

382   GW   ISSN 0934-4217
MEDIA SELECTION; Nachrichten und Meinungen der internationalen Presse. 1988. 26/yr. DM.234. Dr. Horst Kerlikowsky Verlag, Haimhauserstr. 5a, 80802 Munich, Germany. TEL 49-89-344012. FAX 49-89-390662. Ed. Horst Kerlikowsky. R&P contact: Horst Kerlikowsky. circ. 1,000. **Document type:** abstracting/indexing, newsletter.
Description: Contains news and opinions of the International Press for executives.

BUSINESS AND ECONOMICS — INTERNATIONAL COMMERCE

382   GW   ISSN 0076-6208
MEIER-DUDY/MEIER'S DIRECTORY OF EXPORTERS AND IMPORTERS; Meier's Addressbuch der Exporteure und Importeure. (Text in English, French, Italian, Spanish) 1903. a. DM.80. Verlag von Meier's Adressbuch der Exporteure Rudolf Dudy KG, Neue Kirchgasse 10-12, 61279 Graevenwiesbach, Germany. FAX 069-731330. TELEX 411249-ATLAS-D. (Dist. by: Intl. Publications Service, 114 E. 32nd St., New York, N.Y. 10016) Ed. Christa Reichel. adv.; bk.rev. circ. 5,000.

382   SP   ISSN 0539-3728
MERCADO MUNDIAL/WORLD MARKET. (Text in English and Spanish) 1962. m. $45. Editorial Oifce, German Perez Carrasco, 63, 28027 Madrid, Spain. TEL 1-267-24-03. FAX 1-408-78-37. Ed. Pilar Pardo. circ. 30,000. (back issues avail.) **Document type:** newspaper.
—CINDOC.

332.6   CN
MERCHANDISE IMPORTS AMERICA DIRECTORY. 1994. a. $110. Global Traders Association, P.O. Box 797, Sta. A, Scarborough, ON M1K 5C8, Canada. TEL 416-650-9309. FAX 416-650-9280. Ed. K. Bhattacharyya. bk.rev.; charts; illus.; stat. **Document type:** directory.

MEXICAN PRODUCT GUIDE. see BUSINESS AND ECONOMICS — Trade And Industrial Directories

382   US   ISSN 1054-2663
HF3066
MEXICO BUSINESS MONTHLY. 1991. m. $108 to academics; institutions $216. Kal Wagenheim, Ed. & Pub., 52 Maple Ave., Maplewood, NJ 07040. TEL 201-762-1565; 800-647-9900. FAX 201-762-9585. adv.; circ. controlled. (back issues avail.) **Document type:** newsletter.
●Also available online. Vendor(s): Information Access Co.
—CCC.
Description: Covers business, economic, and political news.

382   FR
MICROTABLES IMPORTS - EXPORTS OF O E C D COUNTRIES. (Supplements avail.) a. 2000 F.($360) Organization for Economic Cooperation and Development, 2 rue Andre-Pascal, 75775 Paris Cedex 16, France. (U.S. orders to: O.E.C.D. Publications Center, 2001 L St., N.W., Ste. 650, Washington, DC 20036-4922. TEL 202-785-6323)

382   US   ISSN 0731-6305
MIDDLE EAST BUSINESS INTELLIGENCE. 1982. 22/yr. $345 (foreign $355) (effective 1997). International Executive Reports Ltd., 717 D. St., N.W., Ste. 300, Washington, DC 20004-2807. TEL 202-628-6900. FAX 202-628-6618. TELEX 440462 MEER UI. Ed. Mimi Mann; Pub. William Hearn. circ. 400. (back issues avail.; reprint service avail. from SCH)
●Also available online. Vendor(s): Lexis-Nexis.
—CCC.
Description: For business executives looking for sales and contracting opportunities in the Middle East or North Africa. Provides more than 1700 new business leads each year, with a brief description of the business opportunity, the person to contact, address, phone and fax number.

330.9   US   ISSN 0271-0498
MIDDLE EAST EXECUTIVE REPORTS. 1978. m. $455 (effective 1997). International Executive Reports, Ltd., 717 D St., N.W., Ste. 300, Washington, DC 20004-2807. TEL 202-628-6900. FAX 202-628-6618. Ed. Mimi Mann; Pub. William Hearn. **Indexed:** L.R.I.
●Also available online. Vendor(s): Lexis-Nexis, UMI, West Group.
—BLDSC (5761.373950); SWETS. **CCC.**
Description: Provides legal and practical information on the requirements for doing business in the Middle East and North Africa. Provides in-depth analysis of trade, contracting, marketing and investment.

MIDDLE EAST FORUM. see POLITICAL SCIENCE — International Relations

MIDDLE EAST POLICY. see POLITICAL SCIENCE — International Relations

382   UK   ISSN 0026-3192
MIDDLE EAST TRADE/TIJJARAT AL SHARQ AL AUSSAT. (Text in Arabic; summaries in English) 1961. 10/yr. Middle East Trade Publications Ltd., 21 Newman St., London W1P 3HB, England. TEL 44-171-636-2911. FAX 44-171-637-5733. Ed. Armea I. Bekheit. adv.; illus.; tr.lit.; circ. 15,320 (controlled). **Document type:** trade publication.

MILANO FINANZA. see BUSINESS AND ECONOMICS — Investments

382   BE
MONITEUR DU COMMERCE INTERNATIONAL. 1991. w. 15750 BEF (effective 1998). Editions De Boeck, Fond Jean-Paques 4, 1348 Louvain-la-Neuve, Belgium. TEL 32-10-482511. FAX 32-10-482519. index. **Document type:** trade publication.

382   JA
MONITOR. (Text in English) 1987. m. free to qualified personnel. Mitsubishi Public Affairs Committee, Mitsubishi Shoji Bldg. Annex (DK-M), 2-3-1 Marunouchi, Chiyoda-ku, Tokyo 100, Japan. TEL 03-3210-2524. FAX 03-3210-2527. Ed. Hisashi Akazome. circ. 10,000. **Document type:** newsletter.
Description: Newsletter of Mitsubishi companies for overseas employees.

MONTHLY EXPORT TRENDS; monitor of Pakistan's export trade. see BUSINESS AND ECONOMICS — Chamber Of Commerce Publications

382   US
MONTHLY IMPORT DETENTION LIST. m. $350 in the U.S., Canada, Mexico; elsewhere $700. U.S. Food and Drug Administration, Office of Public Affairs, 5600 Fisher's Ln., Rockville, MD 20857. TEL 301-443-3220. (Subscr. to: National Technical Information Service, 5285 Port Royal Rd., Springfield, VA 22161. TEL 703-487-4630. FAX 703-321-8547) (also avail. in microfiche from CIS; reprint service avail. from CIS) **Indexed:** Amer.Stat.Ind. (1976-). **Document type:** government publication.
Description: Detentions are arranged by: product code, sample number, the product, district and port of entry, manufacturer's and shipper's names, city and country of origin, the primary and secondary reasons for detention, unit type and quantity, and value.

MONTSERRAT. STATISTICS OFFICE. DIGEST OF STATISTICS. see BUSINESS AND ECONOMICS — Abstracting, Bibliographies, Statistics

332.6   UK   ISSN 0966-4394
THE MOSCOW LETTER. 1992. m. £220 (effective 1996). Interforum Services Ltd., 565 Fulham Rd., London SW6 1ES, England. TEL 44-171-386-9322. FAX 44-171-381-8914. **Document type:** trade publication.

332.6   US
MULTINATIONAL BUSINESS REVIEW. 1993. s-a. $30 to individuals (outside N. America $40); institutions $60 (outside N. America $70); students $15 (outside N. America $25) (effective 1997). University of Detroit Mercy, College of Business Administration, Box 19900, Detroit, MI 48219-0900. TEL 313-993-1264. FAX 313-993-1052. Ed. Suk H. Kim. circ. 375 (paid). (also avail. in microform from UMI) **Indexed:** P.A.I.S., Polit.Sci.Abstr. **Document type:** academic/scholarly publication.
●Also available online. Vendor(s): UMI.
Also available on CD-ROM. Producer(s): UMI.
Description: Publishes application-oriented articles dealing with international aspects of accounting, management and information systems, finance, management, and marketing.
Refereed Serial

382   US   ISSN 0149-0818
MULTINATIONAL INDUSTRIAL RELATIONS SERIES. 1977. irreg. University of Pennsylvania, Wharton School, Industrial Research Unit, 3733 Vance Hall, Philadelphia, PA 19104-6358. TEL 215-898-5605. **Document type:** academic/scholarly publication.

MULTINATIONAL MANAGERS AND DEVELOPING COUNTRIES. see BUSINESS AND ECONOMICS — Management

382   US   ISSN 0197-4637
HD2755.5
MULTINATIONAL MONITOR. 1980. m. $25 to individuals; non-profit institutions $30; businesses $40. Essential Information, Box 19405, Washington, DC 20036. TEL 202-387-8034. FAX 202-234-5176. E-mail: monitor@essential.org; URL: http://www.essential.org/monitor/monitor.html. Ed. Robert Weissman. R&P contact: Donna Calvin. adv. contact: Donna Calvin. bk.rev.; film rev.; bibl.; charts; illus.; index. circ. 10,000. (also avail. in microfiche from UMI; talking book) **Indexed:** Alt.Press Ind., HR Rep. (1986-), Left Ind. (1982-), P.A.I.S. **Document type:** academic/scholarly publication.
●Also available online. Vendor(s): Information Access Co.
—BLDSC (5983.162000); UMI; UnCover.
Supersedes: Elements.
Description: Provides current news and analysis on Third World development, the environment and the politics of business.

N A C L A REPORT ON THE AMERICAS. (North American Congress on Latin America, Inc.) see POLITICAL SCIENCE — International Relations

332.6   US
N A F T A FASTSEARCH. (North American Free Trade Agreement) 1994. a. (plus irreg. updates). $299. FastSearch Corporation, Box 421057, Plymouth, MN 55442-0057. TEL 800-232-4590. FAX 612-595-0229. Ed. Alan Rosenauer. circ. 6,000.
Description: Contains the entire North American Free Trade Agreement.

N A F T A: LAW & BUSINESS REVIEW OF THE AMERICAS. (North American Free Trade Agreement) see LAW — International Law

N A F T A LAW AND POLICY SERIES. (North American Free Trade Agreement) see LAW — International Law

382   BE
N A T O ANNUAL ECONOMIC COLLOQUIA. PROCEEDINGS. 1975. a. free. North Atlantic Treaty Organization, Office of Information and Press, 1110 Brussels, Belgium. TEL 32-2-7074567. FAX 32-2-7074579. E-mail: natodocs@hq.nato.int; URL: http://www.nato.int/. circ. 2,500. (also avail. in microfiche from CIS) **Indexed:** IIS. **Document type:** proceedings.
Formerly: North Atlantic Treaty Organization. Directorate of Economic Affairs. Colloquium. Series.

NATIONAL ASSOCIATION OF BEVERAGE IMPORTERS. BULLETIN. see BEVERAGES

NATIONAL ASSOCIATION OF BEVERAGE IMPORTERS. IMPORT REPORT. see BEVERAGES

NATIONAL ASSOCIATION OF BEVERAGE IMPORTERS. STATISTICAL REPORT. see BEVERAGES — Abstracting, Bibliographies, Statistics

332.6 336   US
NATIONAL CUSTOMS TARIFF GUIDEBOOK - AUSTRIA. a. $340 (diskette $272) (effective 1997). Worldtariff, 220 Montgomery St., Ste. 432, San Francisco, CA 94104-3410. TEL 415-391-7501. FAX 415-391-7537. (looseleaf format; also avail. in diskette format) **Document type:** directory.
Description: Reference guidebook to import duties, other charges and domestic taxes assessed on foreign goods.

332.6 336   US
NATIONAL CUSTOMS TARIFF GUIDEBOOK - BRAZIL. 1994. a. $465 (diskette $372) (effective 1997). Worldtariff, 220 Montgomery St., Ste. 432, San Francisco, CA 94104-3410. TEL 415-391-7501. FAX 415-391-7537. (looseleaf format; also avail. in diskette format) **Document type:** directory.

332.6   US
NATIONAL CUSTOMS TARIFF GUIDEBOOK - BULGARIA. 1994. a. $465 (diskette $372) (effective 1997). Worldtariff, 220 Montgomery St., Ste. 432, San Francisco, CA 94104-3410. TEL 415-391-7501. FAX 415-391-7537. (looseleaf format; also avail. in diskette format) **Document type:** directory.

BUSINESS AND ECONOMICS — INTERNATIONAL COMMERCE   1343

332.6 336 US
NATIONAL CUSTOMS TARIFF GUIDEBOOK - CANADA. a. $340 (diskette $272) (effective 1997). Worldtariff, 220 Montgomery St., Ste. 432, San Francisco, CA 94104-3410. TEL 415-391-7501. FAX 415-391-7537. (looseleaf format; also avail. in diskette format) **Document type:** directory.

332.6 336 US
NATIONAL CUSTOMS TARIFF GUIDEBOOK - CZECH AND SLOVAK REPUBLICS. 1994. a. $340 (diskette $272) (effective 1997). Worldtariff, 220 Montgomery St., Ste. 432, San Francisco, CA 94104-3410. TEL 415-391-7501. FAX 415-291-7537. (looseleaf format; also avail. in diskette format) **Document type:** directory.

332.6 336 US
NATIONAL CUSTOMS TARIFF GUIDEBOOK - EUROPEAN UNION. a. $340 (diskette $272) (effective 1997). Worldtariff, 220 Montgomery St., Ste. 432, San Francisco, CA 94104-3410. TEL 415-391-7501. FAX 415-391-7537. (looseleaf format; also avail. in diskette format) **Document type:** directory.
   Formerly: National Customs Tariff Guidebook - European Community.

332.6 336 US
NATIONAL CUSTOMS TARIFF GUIDEBOOK - FINLAND. a. $340 (diskette $272) (effective 1997). Worldtariff, 220 Montgomery St., Ste. 432, San Francisco, CA 94104-3410. TEL 415-391-7501. FAX 415-391-7537. (looseleaf format; also avail. in diskette format) **Document type:** directory.

332.6 336 US
NATIONAL CUSTOMS TARIFF GUIDEBOOK - HUNGARY. 1994. a. $340 (diskette $272) (effective 1997). Worldtariff, 220 Montgomery St., Ste. 432, San Francisco, CA 94104-3410. TEL 415-391-7501. FAX 415-391-7537. (looseleaf format; also avail. in diskette format) **Document type:** directory.

332.6 336 US
NATIONAL CUSTOMS TARIFF GUIDEBOOK - INDIA. 1994. a. $465 (diskette $372) (effective 1997). Worldtariff, 220 Montgomery St., Ste. 432, San Francisco, CA 94104-3410. TEL 415-391-7501. FAX 415-391-7537. **Document type:** directory.

332.6 336 US
NATIONAL CUSTOMS TARIFF GUIDEBOOK - ISRAEL. 1994. a. $465 (diskette $372) (effective 1997). Worldtariff, 220 Montgomery St., Ste. 432, San Francisco, CA 94104-3410. TEL 415-391-7501. FAX 415-391-7537. (looseleaf format; also avail. in diskette format) **Document type:** directory.

332.6 336 US
NATIONAL CUSTOMS TARIFF GUIDEBOOK - JAPAN. a. $340 (diskette $272) (effective 1997). Worldtariff, 220 Montgomery St., Ste. 432, San Francisco, CA 94104-3410. TEL 415-391-7501. FAX 415-391-7537. (looseleaf format; also avail. in diskette format) **Document type:** directory.

332.6 336. US
NATIONAL CUSTOMS TARIFF GUIDEBOOK - MEXICO. a. $465 (diskette $372) (effective 1997). Worldtariff, 220 Montgomery St., Ste. 432, San Francisco, CA 94104-3410. TEL 415-391-7501. FAX 415-391-7537. (looseleaf format; also avail. in diskette format) **Document type:** directory.

332.6 336 US
NATIONAL CUSTOMS TARIFF GUIDEBOOK - NORWAY. a. $340 (diskette $272) (effective 1997). Worldtariff, 220 Montgomery St., Ste. 432, San Francisco, CA 94104-3410. TEL 415-391-7501. FAX 415-391-7537. (looseleaf format; also avail. in diskette format) **Document type:** directory.

332.6 336 US
NATIONAL CUSTOMS TARIFF GUIDEBOOK - PEOPLE'S REPUBLIC OF CHINA. 1994. a. $465 (diskette $372) (effective 1997). Worldtariff, 220 Montgomery St., Ste. 432, San Francisco, CA 94104-3410. TEL 415-391-7501. FAX 415-391-7537. (looseleaf format; also avail. in looseleaf format) **Document type:** directory.

332.6 336 US
NATIONAL CUSTOMS TARIFF GUIDEBOOK - POLAND. 1994. a. $340 (diskette $272) (effective 1997). Worldtariff, 220 Montgomery St., Ste. 432, San Francisco, CA 94104-3410. TEL 415-391-7501. FAX 415-391-7537. (looseleaf format; also avail. in diskette format) **Document type:** directory.

332.6 336 US
NATIONAL CUSTOMS TARIFF GUIDEBOOK - REPUBLIC OF KOREA. 1994. a. $465 (diskette $372) (effective 1997). Worldtariff, 220 Montgomery St., Ste. 432, San Francisco, CA 74104-3410. TEL 415-291-7501. FAX 415-391-7501. (looseleaf format; also avail. in diskette format) **Document type:** directory.

332.6 336 US
NATIONAL CUSTOMS TARIFF GUIDEBOOK - ROMANIA. 1994. a. $465 (diskette £372) (effective 1997). Worldtariff, 220 Montgomery St., Ste. 432, San Francisco, CA 74104-3410. TEL 415-391-7501. FAX 415-391-7537. (looseleaf format; also avail. in diskette format) **Document type:** directory.

332.6 336 US
NATIONAL CUSTOMS TARIFF GUIDEBOOK - SWEDEN. a. $340 (diskette $272) (effective 1997). Worldtariff, 220 Montgomery St., Ste. 432, San Francisco, CA 94104-3410. TEL 415-391-7501. FAX 415-391-7537. (looseleaf format; also avail. in diskette format) **Document type:** directory.

332.6 336 US
NATIONAL CUSTOMS TARIFF GUIDEBOOK - SWITZERLAND. a. $340 (diskette $272) (effective 1997). Worldtariff, 220 Montgomery St., Ste. 432, San Francisco, CA 94104-3410. TEL 415-391-7501. FAX 415-391-7537. (looseleaf format; also avail. in diskette format) **Document type:** directory.

332.6 336 US
NATIONAL CUSTOMS TARIFF GUIDEBOOK - TURKEY. 1994. a. $465 (diskette $371) (effective 1997). Worldtariff, 220 Montgomery St., Ste. 432, San Francisco, CA 94104-3410. TEL 415-391-7501. FAX 415-391-7537. (looseleaf format; also avail. in diskette format) **Document type:** directory.

332.6 336 US
NATIONAL CUSTOMS TARIFF GUIDEBOOK - UNITED STATES OF AMERICA. a. $340 (diskette $272) (effective 1997). Worldtariff, 220 Montgomery St., Ste. 432, San Francisco, CA 94104-3410. TEL 415-391-7501. FAX 415-391-7537. (looseleaf format; also avail. in diskette format) **Document type:** directory.

382 AT ISSN 0159-4702
NATIONAL REPORTER. w. Aus.$295. Australian Press Services Pty. Ltd., P.O. Box E 160, Queen Victoria Terrace, A.C.T. 2006, Australia. Ed. Rob Chalmers. **Document type:** newsletter.

382 UK ISSN 0960-8710
NEGOCIOS AL DIA. (Text in Spanish) 1990. 12/yr. £153($199) (effective 1997). Latin American Newsletters, 61 Old St., London EC1V 9HX, England. TEL 44-171-251-0012. FAX 44-171-253-8193. Ed. Miguel Angel Diez. (back issues avail.) **Document type:** newsletter.

NELSON'S DIRECTORY OF INVESTMENT RESEARCH. see BUSINESS AND ECONOMICS — Trade And Industrial Directories

382 NP
NEPAL FOREIGN TRADE ASSOCIATION. BULLETIN. irreg., (2-5/w.). Nepal Foreign Trade Association, Meera Home, Khichapokhari, P.O. Box 541, Kathmandu, Nepal. TEL 223784. TELEX 2542 JTREDS NP.

382 SZ ISSN 0028-3339
NEUE PRODUKTE;* Weltmarkt-Umschau fuer Industrie und Handel. (Text in German) 1964. fortn. 137 Fr. G. Buechi Verlag, Schaffhauserstr. 439, Postfach 236, CH-8052 Zurich, Switzerland. Ed. Heinrich Roth. adv.; pat. circ. 5,000. (tabloid format)

382 336 UK
NEW IN DUTY FREE. 1983. s-a. Argus Business Media Ltd. (Subsidiary of: D M G Exhibitions Group Ltd.), Queensway House, 2 Queensway, Redhill, Surrey RH1 1QS, England. TEL 44-1737-768611. FAX 44-1737-760510. adv. contact: Michael Lewis. **Document type:** trade publication.

332.6 UK ISSN 0967-781X
NEW MARKETS MONTHLY. 1992. m. £55($160) B S B Publishing, Paper Mews Pl., 290 High St., Dorking, Surrey RH4 1QT, England. TEL 44-1306-877111. FAX 44-1306-889191. E-mail: 100434,1125@compuserve.com. Ed. Paul Colston; Pub. Alan Baker. adv.: B&W page £2120; color page £2800; bleed 346 x 238; adv. contact: Alan Baker. circ. 5,000. (back issues avail.)
   Description: For traders and investors entering the emerging markets of Eastern Europe, the former Soviet Union, and Southeast Asia.

NEW YORK MERCANTILE EXCHANGE GUIDE. see BUSINESS AND ECONOMICS — Economic Situation And Conditions

NEW ZEALAND. DEPARTMENT OF STATISTICS. OVERSEAS TRADE. see BUSINESS AND ECONOMICS — Abstracting, Bibliographies, Statistics

382.7 NZ
NEW ZEALAND. MINISTRY OF COMMERCE. IMPORT LICENSING SCHEDULE. 1938. irreg. price varies. Government Printing Office, Private Bag, Wellington, New Zealand. TEL 04-737-320. FAX 04-734-943. circ. 2,000.
   Formerly: New Zealand. Department of Trade and Industry. Import Licensing Schedule.

NEW ZEALAND EXPORT YEARBOOK. see BUSINESS AND ECONOMICS — Trade And Industrial Directories

NEW ZEALAND FOREIGN AFFAIRS AND TRADE RECORD. see POLITICAL SCIENCE — International Relations

382.7 BE
NIEUWSBRIEF DOUANE. (Text in Flemish) s-m. 5247 BEF. C E D Samsom (Subsidiary of: Wolters Samsom Belgie n.v.), Kouterveld 14, B-1831 Diegem, Belgium. TEL 32-2-7231111.
   Description: Customs information.

382 BE
NIEUWSBRIEF TRANSPORT. (Text in Flemish) s-m. 4929 BEF. C E D Samsom (Subsidiary of: Wolters Samsom Belgie n.v.), Kouterveld 14, B-1831 Diegem, Belgium. TEL 32-2-7231111.
   Description: Transportation information.

382 NR ISSN 0029-0041
NIGERIA TRADE JOURNAL. 1953. q. $3. Department of Information, 15 Awolowo Rd., Ikoyi, Lagos State, Nigeria. Philip Ideh. adv.; charts; illus.; mkt.; stat.; index. circ. 20,000. **Document type:** trade publication, government publication.

382 NR ISSN 0078-0650
NIGERIA TRADE SUMMARY. 1964. a. $10. National Integrated Survey of Households, P.M.B. 12528, Lagos, Nigeria. TEL 234-1-630264. bk.rev. circ. 3,000. **Document type:** trade publication, government publication.

382 NR ISSN 0189-0840
NIGERIAN INSTITUTE OF INTERNATIONAL AFFAIRS. DIALOGUES. 1978. irreg., latest 1985. £N60($6) (Nigerian Institute of International Affairs, Research Department) N I I A Press, Kofo Abayomi Rd., G.P.O. Box 1727, Lagos, Nigeria. TEL 234-1-615606. FAX 234-1-611360. TELEX 22638. Dir. George A. Obiozor. R&P contact: George A. Obiozor. adv. contact: E.A. Ude. **Document type:** monographic series.
   Description: Establishes contact with other organizations with similar objectives.

B

BUSINESS AND ECONOMICS — INTERNATIONAL COMMERCE

382 US
NORTH AMERICAN FREE TRADE & INVESTMENT REPORT; biweekly news on trade, investment, and related trans-border issues. 22/yr. $660 (foreign $710) (effective 1997). WorldTrade Executive Inc., Box 761, Concord, MA 01742. TEL 508-287-0301. FAX 508-287-0302. URL: http://pages.map.com/~wtel/. Ed. Kathryn Rosenblum; Pub. Gary Brown. R&P contact: Gary Brown. adv.: page $975; 7 1/2 x 9 1/2; adv. contact: Ken Parker. **Document type:** newsletter.
  Formerly: U S - Mexico Free Trade Reporter; Incorporates (in Nov. 1995): Direct Investment in North America (ISSN 1352-6367); Which had former titles (until Jan. 1994): Foreign Investment in the U S (ISSN 0958-3076); (until 1989): Investment - U S A (ISSN 0142-6354)
  Description: Covers important North American Free Trade Agreement developments, plus the latest information on trade, investment and related trans-border issues in Mexico, the United States, and Canada.

380 US ISSN 1071-958X
HF1746
NORTH AMERICAN TRADE GUIDE. 1994. biennial. $399 (effective 1996). K-III Directory Corp., 10 Lake Dr., Hightstown, NJ 08520. TEL 609-371-7700. (Subscr. to: 1735 Technology Dr., Ste. 410, San Jose, CA 95110. TEL 800-547-8753)

382 GR
NORTHERN GREECE - THESSALONIKI INTERNATIONAL TRADE FAIR (YEAR). (Supplement to: Epilogi) 1990. a. Dr.1000. Electra Press, 4 Stadiou St., 105 64 Athens, Greece. TEL 323-3203. FAX 323-5160. TELEX 210564. Ed. Christos Papaioannou. adv. circ. 9,000.

NORTHWESTERN JOURNAL OF INTERNATIONAL LAW & BUSINESS. see *LAW — International Law*

382 SP ISSN 1133-6447
NOTICIARI DE COMERC EXTERIOR. 1960. 4/yr. 6500 ptas. Cambra Oficial de Comerc, Industria i Navegacio de Barcelona, Avda. Diagonal, 452-454, 08006 Barcelona, Spain. TEL 34-3-4169300. FAX 34-3-4169301. Ed. Carles Castells i Oliveres. circ. 6,000.
  Formerly (until 1993): Noticiario de Comercio Exterior (ISSN 0210-8267)

382 IT
NOTIZIARIO COMMERCIALE QUINDICINALE DI COMMERCIO ESTERO. 26/yr. Via Meravigli 9B, 20123 Milan, Italy.

NOTIZIARIO MOTORISTICO/MOTOR NEWS/MOTOR - NACHRICHTEN/NOUVELLES DE L'AUTOMOBILE; autoattrezzature-impiantistica. see *TRANSPORTATION — Automobiles*

O E C D CODE OF LIBERALIZATION OF CAPITAL MOVEMENTS/O C D E CODE DE LA LIBERATION DES MOUVEMENTS DE CAPITAUX. see *BUSINESS AND ECONOMICS — Banking And Finance*

O E C D ECONOMIC OUTLOOK. see *BUSINESS AND ECONOMICS — Economic Situation And Conditions*

382 US ISSN 0278-6389
KF1987.A15
OFFICIAL EXPORT GUIDE. (Supplement avail.) a. $425 (international $499)(effective 1996). K-III Directory Corp., 10 Lake Dr., Hightstown, NJ 08520. TEL 609-371-7700. (Subscr. to: 1735 Technology Dr., Ste. 410, San Jose, CA 95110. TEL 800-547-8753) **Document type:** trade publication, directory.
  Description: The export handbook for freight forwarders and all exporters who do documentation. Includes the current Schedule B plus the listing of world ports, documentary requirements for 180 nations and the computer hardware and software directory.

382 665.5 UK ISSN 0952-7125
OFFSHORE CENTRES REPORT. 1989. 10/yr. £125 (U.S. $200) (effective 1996). World Reports Ltd., 108 Horseferry Rd., Westminster, London SW1P 2EF, England. TEL 44-171-222-3836. (Subscr. in US to: World Reports Ltd., 280 Madison Ave., Ste. 1209, New York, NY 10016-0802. TEL 212-679-0095. FAX 212-679-1094) **Document type:** trade publication.

OPEN ECONOMIES REVIEW. see *BUSINESS AND ECONOMICS — Economic Systems And Theories, Economic History*

382 US ISSN 0731-9096
HF3161.07
OREGON INTERNATIONAL TRADE DIRECTORY. biennial. $30. Economic Development Department (Portland), 1 World Trade Center, 121 S.W. Salmon St., Ste. 300, Portland, OR 97204. TEL 503-229-5625. FAX 503-222-5050. TELEX 821481.

382 US
OUTLOOK (SAN JOSE); the American business journal on emerging markets in Eastern Europe, Soviet Union, China, unified Europe and other areas of the world. m. $144 (foreign $200). 1782 Wyrick, San Jose, CA 95124.

332.6 II
OVERSEAS BUSINESS CONTACTS. (Text in English) fortn. Rs.800. Associated Chambers of Commerce and Industry of India, Allahabad Bank Bldg., 2nd Fl., 17 Parliament St., New Delhi 110 001, India. TEL 91-11-3360704. FAX 91-11-3342193. E-mail: assocham@ibis.delhi.nic.in. circ. 1,000.

382 CN
OVERSEAS EXPORTERS. 1994. m. $75. Global Traders Association, P.O. Box 797, Sta. A, Scarborough, ON M1K 5C8, Canada. TEL 416-650-9309. FAX 416-650-9280. adv.; bk.rev.; charts; illus.; stat. circ. 370. **Document type:** newsletter.

382 GW ISSN 0942-6337
OVERSEAS POST. CONSUMER GOODS. bi-m. DM.60 (foreign $35) (effective 1998). Dr. Harnisch Verlagsgesellschaft mbH, Blumenstr. 15, 90402 Nuernberg, Germany. TEL 49-911-2018-0. FAX 49-911-2018100. E-mail: uepost@aol.com. **Document type:** trade publication.
  Former titles (until 1991): Overseas Post. Product and Design (ISSN 0940-5356); (until 1983): Uebersee-Post. Product and Design (ISSN 0943-9803)

382 GW ISSN 0942-6345
OVERSEAS POST. TECHNOLOGY EDITION. (Text in English) 1919. bi-m. DM.60 (foreign $35) (effective 1998). Dr. Harnisch Verlagsgesellschaft mbH, Blumenstr. 15, 90402 Nuernberg, Germany. TEL 49-911-2018-0. FAX 49-911-2018100. E-mail: uepost@aol.com. Ed. H. Riedel; Pub. Benno Keller. adv.: B&W page DM.5950, color page DM.8200; trim 190 x 270. bk.rev.; illus. circ. 24,000 (combined edts.). **Document type:** trade publication.
  Former titles (until 1991): Overseas Post. Innovation and Technology (ISSN 0940-5348); (until 1983): Uebersee-Post. Innovation and Technology (ISSN 0943-979X)
  Description: Trade magazines for all industries issued in two parts: a technology edition and consumer goods edition.

332.6 UK ISSN 0268-1684
OVERSEAS TRADE. 1984. 10/yr. free. Brass Tacks Publishing, 143 Charing Cross Rd., London WC2E OEE, England. TEL 44-171-478-4700. FAX 44-171-478-4701. E-mail: london_new_business_sales@brasstacks.co.uk. Ed. Richard Braggins; Pub. Kim Conchie. R&P contact: Richard Braggins. adv. contact: Simon Whiten. bk.rev.; circ. 30,762. **Document type:** bulletin.
  Description: Provides news updates on all British export-related activity including initiatives launched by the export arm of Britain's Department of Trade and Industry; a diary of forthcoming export seminar events; European country market updates, international country market updates; sector reports; how-to-export features.

382 II
OVERSEAS TRADE ENQUIRIES MONTHLY BULLETIN. (Text in English) m. Rs.500 (foreign $40). Amalgamated Press, Narang House, 41 Ambalal Doshi Marg, Fort, Mumbai 400 001, India. TEL 91-22-265-0268. FAX 91-22-264-1275. adv.: B&W page Rs.3000; 240 x 187.
  Description: Each issue contains over 800 foreign buyers enquiries, sourced from all kinds of commercial reports.

THE P R S GROUP. COUNTRY REPORTS: WORLD SERVICE. see *BUSINESS AND ECONOMICS — Economic Situation And Conditions*

919.6 US ISSN 0744-1754
PACIFIC MAGAZINE. 1976. bi-m. $15 to US Pacific islands (mainland US $27; foreign $39). Pacific Magazine Corporation, Box 25488, Honolulu, HI 96825. TEL 808-377-5335. FAX 808-373-3953. URL: http://www.pacificmagazine.com. Ed. Bud Benedix; Pub. Bruce Jensen. adv.; bk.rev. circ. 10,000. Indexed: So.Pac.Per.Ind. **Document type:** consumer publication.
  Former titles: New Pacific (ISSN 0192-2408); American Pacific.

332.6 UK ISSN 1362-2072
▼**PACIFIC RIM MANAGEMENT.** 1996. a. £55. Sterling Publications Ltd., 86-88 Edgware Rd., London W2 2YW, England. TEL 44-171-915-9600. FAX 44-171-915-9619. R&P contact: Sandy Tucker. circ. 10,000. **Document type:** trade publication.

332.6 SP ISSN 1134-2145
PAISES DEL I C E. (Informacion Comercial Espanola) 15/yr. 800 ptas. per no. Ministerio de Comercio y Turismo, P. de la Castellana 162, Pl. 16, 28046 Madrid, Spain. TEL 34-1-349-36-47. FAX 34-1-349-36-34.
  Description: Each issue pertains to a country which has business dealings with Spain.

332 382 PK ISSN 0078-8058
PAKISTAN CUSTOMS TARIFF. (Text in English) 1960. irreg. price varies. Central Board of Revenue, Islamabad, Pakistan. (Dist. by: Manager of Publications, Government of Pakistan, 2nd Fl., Ahmad Chamber, Tariq Rd., P.E.C.H.S., Karachi 29, Pakistan) Ed. M.I. Said. bk.rev. circ. 6,000. **Document type:** government publication.

382 PK ISSN 0030-977X
HF41
PAKISTAN EXPORTS. (Text in English) vol.19, 1968. m. $45. (Export Promotion Bureau) Publishers (Private) Ltd., Shafi Court Merewether Rd., P.O. Box 10449, Karachi-4, Pakistan. TEL 522032. TELEX 25737-PAGE-PK. Ed. Tahir Shaikh. charts; stat.; tr.lit.

PAKISTAN'S BALANCE OF PAYMENTS. see *BUSINESS AND ECONOMICS — Public Finance, Taxation*

PAKISTAN'S BALANCE OF PAYMENTS (QUARTERLY). see *BUSINESS AND ECONOMICS — Public Finance, Taxation*

332.6 EI ISSN 1021-349X
HC241.2
PANORAMA OF E U INDUSTRY; an extensive review of the situation and outlook of the manufacturing and service industries in the European Union. a., plus bi-m. supplement. $195. Office for Official Publications of the European Communities, L-2985 Luxembourg, Luxembourg. TEL 352-49-92-81. FAX 352-48-85-73. (Dist. in the U.S. by: Unipub, 4611-F, Assembly Dr., Lanham, MD 2070604391. TEL 800-274-4888. FAX 301-459-0056)
  Formerly (until 1994): Panorama of E C Industry (ISSN 1017-592X)

PAPUA NEW GUINEA. NATIONAL STATISTICAL OFFICE. EXPORT PRICE INDEXES. see *BUSINESS AND ECONOMICS — Abstracting, Bibliographies, Statistics*

PAPUA NEW GUINEA. NATIONAL STATISTICAL OFFICE. IMPORT PRICE INDEXES. see *BUSINESS AND ECONOMICS — Abstracting, Bibliographies, Statistics*

PAPUA NEW GUINEA. NATIONAL STATISTICAL OFFICE. INTERNATIONAL TRADE - EXPORTS. see *BUSINESS AND ECONOMICS — Abstracting, Bibliographies, Statistics*

PAPUA NEW GUINEA. NATIONAL STATISTICAL OFFICE. INTERNATIONAL TRADE - IMPORTS. see *BUSINESS AND ECONOMICS — Abstracting, Bibliographies, Statistics*

382 PY
PARAGUAY. CENTRO DE PROMOCION DE LAS EXPORTACIONES. DIRECTORIO DE EXPORTADORES - EXPORT DIRECTORY. a. $12. Ministerio de Industria y Comercio, Centro de Promocion de las Exportaciones, Avda. Espana 374, C.C. 1772, Asuncion, Paraguay. TEL 204-880-44 231.

BUSINESS AND ECONOMICS — INTERNATIONAL COMMERCE

382 381 PH
PHILIPPINES. DEPARTMENT OF TRADE AND INDUSTRY. ANNUAL REPORT. (Text in English) 1948. a. free. Department of Trade and Industry, Trade & Industry Information Center, 4th Fl., Industry & Investment Bldg., 385 Sen. Gil J. Puyat Ave., Makati, Metro Manila 3117, Philippines. TEL 02-895-3611. FAX 02-895-6487. TELEX 14830 MTI PS. Ed. Minerva R. Fajardo. R&P contact: Alfonso M. Valenzuela. Document type: government publication.
Former titles (until 1981): Philippines. Ministry of Trade. Annual Report; Philippines. Department of Commerce and Industry. Annual Report (ISSN 0079-1539)

PHILIPPINES. NATIONAL STATISTICS OFFICE. COMMODITY FLOW IN THE PHILIPPINES. see BUSINESS AND ECONOMICS — Domestic Commerce

382 US
PLATT'S EXPORT - IMPORT REPORT. m. $400 (foreign $485). McGraw-Hill Companies, Commodity Services Group, 1221 Ave. of the Americas, 42nd Fl., New York, NY 10020. TEL 212-512-2000. Ed. Joseph Link. Document type: trade publication.

POLISH ENGINEERING. see ENGINEERING

382 PL ISSN 0032-2881
POLISH FOREIGN TRADE. French edition (ISSN 0208-6565); German edition: Polnischer Aussenhandel (ISSN 0477-4477); Russian edition: Pol'skaya Vneshnyaya Torgovlya. (Editions in English, French, German, Russian and Spanish) 1949. 6/yr. $78. AGPOL - Polexportpress, Ul. Kierbedzia 4, 00-957 Warsaw, Poland. (Dist. by: Ars Polona, Krakowskie Przedmiescie 7, Warsaw, Poland) Ed. Danuta Gasiorowska. adv.; bk.rev.; charts; illus.; mkt.; pat.; tr.mk. circ. 20,000. Indexed: Mid.East. Abstr.& Ind.
—BLDSC (6543.650000).
Incorporates (1959-1975): Polish Export-Import (ISSN 0238-969X)

382 PL ISSN 0239-989X
POLISH TRADE MAGAZINE. German edition: Polnisches Handelsmagazin. Russian edition: Polskii Torgovyi Zhurnal. French edition: Magazine Commercial Polonais. 1952. q. $40. AGPOL - Polexportpress, Ul. Kierbedzia 4, 00-957 Warsaw, Poland. (Dist. by: Ars Polona, Krakowskie Przedmiescie 7, Warsaw, Poland) Ed.Bd. adv.; illus. circ. 20,000.
Supersedes (in 1982): Polish Fair Magazine.
Description: Presents the offer of Poland's foreign trade in the line of consumer goods and services.

332 382 US ISSN 0887-7629
POLITICAL RISK LETTER. 1979. m. $395 (foreign $435) (effective 1997). The P R S Group, Box 248, East Syracuse, NY 13057-0248. TEL 315-431-0511. FAX 315-431-0200. Eds. William D. Coplin, Michael K. O'Leary. (looseleaf format; also available online. Vendor(s): Information Access Co., NewsNet (IT29).
●Also available online. Vendor(s): Information Access Co., NewsNet (IT29).
Description: Provides the latest evaluations in table format for 100 countries and territories, with expanded analysis for 20 countries each month; assessments cover categories including turmoil risk, transfer risk, direct investment risk, export risk, and regime stability for 18-month and 5-year forecast periods.

POLITICAL RISK YEARBOOK. see BUSINESS AND ECONOMICS — Banking And Finance

POLITICAL RISK YEARBOOK. VOLUME 1: NORTH & CENTRAL AMERICA. see BUSINESS AND ECONOMICS — Banking And Finance

POLITICAL RISK YEARBOOK. VOLUME 2: MIDDLE EAST & NORTH AFRICA. see BUSINESS AND ECONOMICS — Banking And Finance

POLITICAL RISK YEARBOOK. VOLUME 3: SOUTH AMERICA. see BUSINESS AND ECONOMICS — Banking And Finance

POLITICAL RISK YEARBOOK. VOLUME 4: SUB-SAHARAN AFRICA. see BUSINESS AND ECONOMICS — Banking And Finance

POLITICAL RISK YEARBOOK. VOLUME 5: ASIA & THE PACIFIC. see BUSINESS AND ECONOMICS — Banking And Finance

POLITICAL RISK YEARBOOK. VOLUME 6: EUROPE. see BUSINESS AND ECONOMICS — Banking And Finance

382.021 PO ISSN 0871-9144
PORTUGAL. INSTITUTO NACIONAL DE ESTATISTICA. INDICE DO COMERCIO EXTERNO. 1991. irreg. Esc.2700. Instituto Nacional de Estatistica, Ave. Antonio Jose de Almeida, 1078 Lisbon, Portugal. TEL 351-8470050. FAX 351-8478578. TELEX 351-63738 PCDINE P.

382 PO
PORTUGUESE EXPORTER. 4/yr. Rua Cedofeita 678-2o, Lisbon, Portugal.

382 PL ISSN 0860-0023
POZNAN FAIR MAGAZINE. German edition: Poznan Messemagazin (ISSN 0860-0031) (Text in English) 1982. 4/yr. $11. (Poznan International Fair) AGPOL - Polexportpress, Ul. Kierbedzia 4, 00-957 Warsaw, Poland. (Dist. by: Ars Polona, Krakowskie Przedmiescie 7, Warsaw, Poland) Ed. Lidia Neuman-Gisnka. circ. 4,000.

382.7 EI
PRACTICAL GUIDE TO THE USE OF THE EUROPEAN COMMUNITIES' SCHEME OF GENERALIZED TARIFF PREFERENCES. (Text in English) irreg. $12. (Commission of the European Communities, Directorate-General for External Relations) Office for Official Publications of the European Communities, L-2985 Luxembourg, Luxembourg. (Dist. in U.S. by: Unipub, 4611-F Assembly Dr., Lanham, MD 20706-4391. TEL 800-274-4888. FAX 301-459-0056) charts; stat.

332.6 UK
THE PRINCIPLES OF EXPORT GUIDEBOOKS. 1994. irreg. $34.95 in N. America. (Institute of Export) Blackwell Publishers Ltd., 108 Cowley Rd., Oxford OX4 1JF, England. TEL 44-1865-791100. FAX 44-1865-791347. E-mail: jnlinfo@blackwellpublishers.co.uk; URL: http://www.blackwellpublishers.co.uk. Ed. Michael Z. Brooke. Document type: monographic series.

382 338.91 PH
PRIVATE DEVELOPMENT CORPORATION OF THE PHILIPPINES. EXECUTIVE UPDATE; international markets report. (Text in English) 1986. bi-m. $50. Private Development Corporation of the Philippines - Pribadong Korporasyon sa Pagpapaunlad ng Pilipinas, P.O. Box 757 Makati, Metro Manila 3117, Philippines. TEL 02-8100231. FAX 02-8195376. TELEX RCA-22080.

332.6 US
PRODUCT CUSTOMS TARIFF GUIDEBOOKS. ceased. a. Worldtariff, 220 Montgomery St., Ste. 432, San Francisco, CA 94104-3410. TEL 415-391-7501. FAX 415-391-7537. Document type: directory.
Description: Focuses more precisely on the range of tariff and nontariff measures that affect trade of a particular product both at the border of the customs district and within it.

PROJECT & TRADE FINANCE. see BUSINESS AND ECONOMICS — Banking And Finance

382 SP
▼**PROMOCION COMERCIAL EUROPEA.** Short title: Procoe. 1996. 46/yr. 48940 ptas. (foreign $357) (effective 1998). Canalejas 30, entlo. 2o, 08028 Barcelona, Spain. TEL 34-3-4226289. FAX 34-3-4211858. E-mail: revista.econo@redestb.es. Ed. Ricardo Rabella. circ. 460,000. Document type: bulletin.
Description: Contains brief economic news from the European Union.
Refereed Serial

382 CG
PROMOTEUR ZAIROIS. (Text in French) 1979. bi-m. 120 Fr.CFA. Centre de Commerce International du Zaire, 119 av. Colonel Tshatshi, B.P. 13.396 Kin 1, Kinshasa, Democratic Republic of the Congo.

382 MX
PUERTOS: TOWARD WORLD COMMERCE. 1946. m. $30. Balderas no. 44 Desp. 402-403, Apdo. Postal 1281, 06000 Mexico DF, Mexico. TELEX 5128280. Ed. Alejandro Hernandez Romo. adv. circ. 18,000. Document type: newspaper.

382 JA
PURCHASE GUIDE OF JAPAN. (Text in English, Japanese) 1952. 8/yr. (plus 4 intl. nos.). 1200 Yen($35) P.G.J. Press, Inc., 20-3 Shonainishi-machi 4-chome, Toyonakai-shi, Osaka 561, Japan. Ed. Eiji Shibayama. adv. circ. 15,000.

382 US ISSN 0270-5435
HF3092
QUARTERLY REPORT TO THE CONGRESS AND THE TRADE POLICY COMMITTEE ON TRADE BETWEEN THE UNITED STATES AND CHINA, THE SUCCESSOR STATES TO THE FORMER SOVIET UNION, AND OTHER TITLE IV COUNTRIES. (Subseries of: U S I T C Publication (ISSN 0196-9153)) 1975. q. U.S. International Trade Commission, Office of Information Services, Trade Reports Division, 500 E St., S.W., Washington, DC 20436. TEL 202-205-2000. (Orders to: Superintendent of Documents, U.S. Government Printing Office, Box 371954, Pittsburgh, PA 15250-7954. TEL 202-512-1800. FAX 202-512-2250) stat. (also avail. in microfiche from CIS; reprint service avail. from CIS) Indexed: Amer.Stat.Ind. (1979-). Document type: government publication.
Formerly (until 1980): Quarterly Report to the Congress and the East-West Foreign Trade Board on Trade between the United States and the Nonmarket Economy Countries During (Year) (ISSN 0098-910X)
Description: Contains information and analysis on U.S. trade with nonmarket economy countries.

382 UK ISSN 0141-1780
QUEEN'S AWARDS MAGAZINE. 1966. a. £9.95. Nexus Media Ltd., Nexus House, Azalea Dr., Swanley, Kent BR8 8HY, England. TEL 44-1322-660070. FAX 44-1322-666408. Ed. Laura McCaffrey; Pub. Tony Salter. adv. contact: Gordon Russell. circ. 10,000. (back issues avail.) Document type: trade publication.
Description: Provides a platform for the success stories of each year's award winners in British export, technology and environmental achievement.

RANDOM LENGTHS EXPORT; a bi-weekly report on international markets for forest products. see FORESTS AND FORESTRY — Lumber And Wood

382 IT ISSN 0483-9722
RASSEGNA DI DIRITTO E TECNICA DOGANALE E DELLE IMPOSTE DI FABBRICAZIONE. 1952. m. L.12000. Via Conca d'Oro 348, 00141 Rome, Italy. TEL 6-810-33-51. Ed. Efisio Serra. adv. circ. 2,800.

RECHT UND SCHADEN; Monatliche Informationsschrift fuer Schadensversicherung und Schadenersatz. see LAW — International Law

RECHT-WIRTSCHAFT-AUSSENHANDEL SCHRIFTENREIHE. see LAW

382 FR ISSN 0080-1070
REPERTOIRE DES SOCIETES DE COMMERCE EXTERIEUR FRANCAISES. 1969. biennial. 435 F. (Federation Francaise des Societes de Commerce International) Editions Techniques Professionnelles (E.T.P.), 31 Ave. Pierre I de Serbie, 75784 Paris Cedex 16, France. TEL 40-69-44-43. FAX 47-23-47-32. circ. 3,000. Document type: directory.

330 US ISSN 0275-5319
HD2755.5
RESEARCH IN INTERNATIONAL BUSINESS AND FINANCE; an annual compilation of research. 1979. irreg., vol.13, 1996. $73.25. J A I Press Inc., 55 Old Post Rd., No. 2, Box 1678, Greenwich, CT 06830-1678. TEL 203-661-7602. FAX 203-661-0792. E-mail: jai@jaipress.com. (Subscr. in the UK and Europe to: JAI Press Ltd., 38 Tavistock St., Covent Garden, London WC2E 7PB, England. TEL 44-171-379-8834. FAX 44-171-379-8835) Eds. Lawrence Lang, John Doukas. Document type: monographic series.
—BLDSC (7741.554900).

RESUMENES ESTADISTICOS DE IMPORTACION. see BUSINESS AND ECONOMICS — Abstracting, Bibliographies, Statistics

382 BL ISSN 0014-5203
REVISTA MENSAL DE EXPORTACAO/EXPORTATION MONTHLY REVIEW. 1914. m. $280. Revista Mensal de Exportacao Ltda., Rua General Camara 77, 5 Andar, Santos, SP, Brazil. Ed. G.S. Fernandes. adv. circ. 7,800.
Formerly (until 1968): Fernandes Bulletin.

BUSINESS AND ECONOMICS — INTERNATIONAL COMMERCE

382 338.91   RM   ISSN 1220-2908
REVISTA ROMANA DE STUDII INTERNATIONALE/ROMANIAN JOURNAL OF INTERNATIONAL STUDIES. 6/yr. 150 lei($50) Academia Romana, Asociatia de Drept International si Relatii Internationale N. Titulescu, Kiseleff 47, 71268 Bucharest, Rumania. TEL 40-1-227462. Ed. A. Pop.

REVUE DE DROIT DES AFFAIRES INTERNATIONALES/INTERNATIONAL BUSINESS LAW JOURNAL. see *LAW — International Law*

338   FR   ISSN 0035-2616
HF1531
REVUE DU MARCHE COMMUN; et de l'Union Europeenne. 1958. m. 960 F. to individuals (foreign 1133 F.); institutions 816 F. (foreign 963 F.) (effective June 1997). Editions Techniques et Economiques, 3 rue Soufflot, 75005 Paris, France. TEL 33-1-46341030. FAX 33-1-46345583. TELEX 260 717 F. adv.; bk.rev.; charts. (reprint service avail. from SCH) Indexed: ELLIS, Geo.Abstr.P.G., IDA, Int.Polit.Sci.Abstr., Mar.Aff.Bibl., P.A.I.S.For.Lang.Ind., Rice Abstr., Rural Recreat.Tour.Abstr., World Agri.Econ.& Rural Sociol.Abstr.
— BLDSC (7880.365000); SWETS.
   Description: For those who wish to understand the goals, difficulties, set-backs and achievements of European construction.

382 327   FR   ISSN 1155-4274
HC241.A1
REVUE DU MARCHE UNIQUE EUROPEEN. 1991. q. 840 F. (effective 1994). Clement Juglar, 62 av. de Suffren, 75015 Paris, France. TEL 45-67-58-06. FAX 45-66-50-70. Ed.Bd. bk.rev.
— BLDSC (7926.855000); SWETS.

327 300   US
RISK MANAGEMENT REVIEW. 1981. q. $120 includes membership. Council for International Business Risk Management, 61 Broadway, Ste. 310, New York, NY 10006-2704. TEL 212-510-0404. FAX 212-797-2502. Ed. Stephen Blank. bk.rev. circ. 200. **Document type:** newsletter.
   Formerly: Political Risk Review.
   Description: Focuses on business implications of country, cross-border, and government policy issues.

332.6   GW
RISTER ZOLLGESETZE; Sammlung von Vorschriften der Bundes Zollverwaltung. 6/yr. DM.138. Walhalla Fachverlag, Haus an der Eisernen Bruecke, 93059 Regensburg, Germany. TEL 49-941-5684-0. FAX 49-941-5684111. E-mail: walhalla@walhalla.de; URL: http://www.walhalla.de. adv. circ. 7,100. (looseleaf format) **Document type:** bulletin.

RIVISTA DI DIRITTO VALUTARIO E DI ECONOMIA INTERNAZIONALE/REVIEW OF CURRENCY LAW AND INTERNATIONAL ECONOMICS; legislazione internazionale - ricerche - giurisprudenza - documenti. see *LAW - International Law*

RIVISTA DI MERCEOLOGIA. see *BUSINESS AND ECONOMICS — Domestic Commerce*

382 387   GW   ISSN 0170-5253
ROLL ON ROLL OFF IN EUROPE; international guide for roll-on-roll-off shipping. 1972. a. DM.268. Walter Stork-Edition, Hamburg, Postfach 106011, 20041 Hamburg, Germany. Ed. Walter W. Stork. circ. 5,000.

382   UK   ISSN 1359-7930
▼**ROUTLEDGE STUDIES IN INTERNATIONAL BUSINESS AND THE WORLD ECONOMY.** 1995. irreg., vol.6, 1997. Routledge, 11 New Fetter Ln., London EC4P 4EE, England. TEL 44-171-583-9855. FAX 44-171-842-2298. E-mail: info.journals@routledge.com; URL: http://www.routledge.com/routledge/journal/journals.html. Eds. Dilip Ghosh, Edgar Ortiz. **Document type:** academic/scholarly publication, monographic series.

RUMANIA. COMISIA NATIONALA PENTRU STATISTICA. BULETIN STATISTIC DE COMERT EXTERIOR/RUMANIA. NATIONAL COMMISSION FOR STATISTICS. FOREIGN TRADE STATISTICS. see *BUSINESS AND ECONOMICS — Abstracting, Bibliographies, Statistics*

330.9   US
RUNDT'S WORLD BUSINESS INTELLIGENCE. Variant title: Rundt's New York Intelligence Briefs. 1952. w. $695. S.J. Rundt & Associates, Inc., 130 E. 63rd St., New York, NY 10021-7334. TEL 212-838-0141. FAX 201-744-3073. Ed. Hans Belcsak. (also avail. in diskette format)
   Formerly: Rundt's Weekly Intelligence.
   Description: Covers international trade, security risk evaluations, political, financial, export and currency exchange forecasting for all countries.

RUSSIA AND THE REPUBLICS LEGAL MATERIALS. see *LAW — International Law*

THE RUSSIA DESK; business opportunities and financing for civil aviation, aerospace, and defense conversion. see *TRANSPORTATION — Air Transport*

382   US   ISSN 1061-2009
HF25
RUSSIAN AND EAST EUROPEAN FINANCE AND TRADE; a journal of translations. 1965. bi-m. $110 to individuals (foreign $176); institutions $630 (foreign $710) (effective 1997). M.E. Sharpe, Inc., 80 Business Park Dr., Armonk, NY 10504. TEL 914-273-1800; 800-541-6563. FAX 914-273-2106. Ed. Ben Slay. adv.: page $300; trim 5 x 8; adv. contact: Barbara Ladd. charts; pat.; stat.; index. (back issues avail.) Indexed: ASCA, C.R.E.J., Curr.Cont., J.of Econ.Lit., Mid.East: Abstr.& Ind., P.A.I.S., SSCI. **Document type:** academic/scholarly publication.
●Also available online. Vendor(s): UMI.
— BLDSC (8052.673000); Genuine Article; SWETS; UMI; UnCover. CCC.
   Former titles: Soviet and Eastern European Foreign Trade (ISSN 0038-5263); American Review of Soviet and Eastern European Foreign Trade.
   Refereed Serial

332.6   UK   ISSN 0969-1693
RUSSIAN BUSINESS INTERNATIONAL. Key Title: R B I. Russian Business International. (Text in English, Russian) 1990. q. £72. B S B Publishing, Paper Mews Pl., 290 High St., Dorking, Surrey RH4 1QT, England. TEL 44-1306-877111. FAX 44-1306-889191. E-mail: 100434,1125@compuserve.com. Ed. Paul Coulston; Pub. Alan Baker. adv. contact: Alan Baker. bk.rev.
   Formerly: British Soviet Business (ISSN 0965-5336).

382   UK
RUSSIAN JOURNAL OF BRITISH INDUSTRY AND COMMERCE. 1903. a. Exact Communications Ltd., 90 Moorsom St., Birmingham B6 4NT, England. TEL 44-121-333-4644. FAX 44-121-333-5823. adv. contact: Michael Burgess. **Document type:** directory.
   Formerly: Russian Journal of British Machinery and Trade.
   Description: Promotes British and other products and services throughout the former Soviet Union.

382   PL   ISSN 0036-052X
RYNKI ZAGRANICZNE/FOREIGN MARKETS. (Text in Polish) 1957. 156/yr. $234. Krajowa Izba Gospodarcza, Ul. Trebacka 4, 00-074 Warsaw, Poland. (Dist. by: Ars Polona-Ruch, Krakowskie Przedmiescie 7, Warsaw, Poland) Ed. Andrzej Zielinski. adv.; bk.rev.; index. circ. 5,000.
   Description: Covers world economy, international business, Polish export-import.

382   SA   ISSN 0081-2552
S A F T O ANNUAL REPORT/SUID-AFRIKAANSE BUITELANDSE HANDELSORGANISASIE JAARVERSLAG. (Text in Afrikaans, English) a. free. (South African Foreign Trade Organisation) S A F T O, P.O. Box 782706, Sandton 2146, South Africa. TEL 27-11-883-3737. FAX 27-11-883-6569. **Document type:** corporate report.

S A I S REVIEW; a journal of international affairs. (Paul H. Nitze School of Advanced International Studies) see *POLITICAL SCIENCE — International Relations*

382   US
THE S GUIDE: INTERNATIONALIST'S GUIDE TO SERVICE PROVIDERS. 1994. a. $59.95. Assist International, 60 Madison Ave., 2nd Fl., New York, NY 10010. TEL 212-725-3311. FAX 212-725-3312. Ed. Peter J. Robinson, Jr. adv. contact: Brooks Shumway. **Document type:** directory.

ST. LUCIA. STATISTICAL DEPARTMENT. ANNUAL OVERSEAS TRADE REPORT: PART 2. see *BUSINESS AND ECONOMICS — Abstracting, Bibliographies, Statistics*

ST. LUCIA. STATISTICAL DEPARTMENT. QUARTERLY OVERSEAS TRADE REPORTS. see *BUSINESS AND ECONOMICS — Abstracting, Bibliographies, Statistics*

SAUDI ARABIA. CENTRAL DEPARTMENT OF STATISTICS. QUARTERLY DIGEST OF FOREIGN TRADE STATISTICS. see *BUSINESS AND ECONOMICS — Abstracting, Bibliographies, Statistics*

SEATRADE REVIEW. see *TRANSPORTATION — Ships And Shipping*

SEATRADE WEEK NEWSFRONT. see *TRANSPORTATION — Ships And Shipping*

382   GT
SECRETARIA PERMANENTE DEL TRATADO GENERAL DE INTEGRACION ECONOMICA CENTROAMERICANA. CUADERNOS. s-a. $8 per no. Secretaria Permanente del Tratado General de Integracion Economica Centroamericana - Permanent Secretariat of the General Treaty on Central American Economic Integration, 4a Avda. 10-25, Zona 14, Apdo. 1237, 01901 Guatemala, Guatemala. TEL 2-682151. FAX 2-681071. TELEX 5676.

332.6   US
SECTOR CUSTOMS TARIFF GUIDEBOOKS. ceased. a. Worldtariff, 220 Montgomery St., Ste. 432, San Francisco, CA 94104-3410. TEL 415-391-7501. FAX 415-391-7537. **Document type:** directory.

382   SG
SENEGAL. MINISTERE DE L'ECONOMIE ET DES FINANCES. ANALYSE DU COMMERCE EXTERIEUR. 1975. a. 6000 Fr.CFA. Ministere de l'Economie et des Finances, Direction de la Statistique, B.P. 116, Dakar, Senegal. TEL 221-21-03-01. **Document type:** government publication.
   Formerly (until 1982): Commerce Exterieur du Senegal.

SERIES IN INTERNATIONAL BUSINESS AND ECONOMICS. see *BUSINESS AND ECONOMICS — Economic Situation And Conditions*

382   SP   ISSN 0488-3721
SERVEX; el semanario del comercio exterior. w. free. Banco de Bilbao, Servicio de Estudios, Apdo. 29, Bilbao, Spain. charts; stat.

382   SE
SEYCHELLES TRADE REPORT. a., latest 1983. 60 Fr.CFA. President's Office, Department of Finance, Statistics Division, Box 206, Mahe, Seychelles.

332.6   CC
SHENZHEN SHANGBAO/SHENZHEN TRADE NEWS. (Text in Chinese) d. Shenzhen Shangbao She, Shangbao Lu, Jingtian Shenghuo-qu, 3 Xiao-qu, Futian Qu, Shenzhen 518034, People's Republic of China. TEL 3344736. FAX 3209410. (Dist. overseas by: China International Book Trading Corp., P.O. Box 399, Bejing 100044, P.R. China) pp./issue: 16. **Document type:** newspaper.
   Description: Focuses on economic and trade news.

SHIPPING AND TRADE NEWS. see *TRANSPORTATION — Ships And Shipping*

SILK EXPORT BULLETIN. see *TEXTILE INDUSTRIES AND FABRICS*

SINGAPORE EXPORTERS. see *BUSINESS AND ECONOMICS — Trade And Industrial Directories*

332.6   SI
SINGAPORE TRADE CONNECTION; a powerful single source of statistical and company data. m. $300. Singapore Trade Development Board, 1 Maritime Square No. 10-40, World Trade Centre, Telok Blangah Rd., Singapore 0409, Singapore. TEL 279-0426. FAX 278-7073. TELEX RS 28617 TRADEV. stat.
●Available only on CD-ROM.
   Description: Analyses Singapore's trade performance, market trends and competition. Provides source for products and services.

BUSINESS AND ECONOMICS — INTERNATIONAL COMMERCE 1347

SINGLE EUROPEAN MARKET REPORTER. see *LAW — International Law*

382   SP   ISSN 0213-2273
HC381
SITUACION; review of the Spanish economy. International edition (ISSN 0213-2303) (Editions in English, Spanish) 1973. q. free. Banco de Bilbao - Vizcaya, Servicio de Estudios, Gran Via 1, 48001 Bilbao, Spain. TEL 447-6100. Dir. Roberto Alvarez Llano. charts; stat. **Indexed:** Ind.SST.
—CINDOC.

382   SP   ISSN 0213-229X
HC381
SITUACION. SUPLEMENTO DE COYUNTURA. 1980. m. Banco de Bilbao - Vizcaya, Servicio de Estudios, Gran Via 1, 48001 Bilbao, Spain. Ed.Bd. charts; stat.

382   CU
SITUACION DE LOS EDULCORANTES. 1981. a. C.$10. (Ministerio del Comercio Exterior (MINCEX)) Empresa Cubazucar, Calle 23 No. 55, Vedado, Havana, Cuba. TEL 70-9742. TELEX 51-1147.
Description: Covers the market development of sugar substitutes.

SITUATION & OUTLOOK REPORT. AGRICULTURAL EXPORTS. see *AGRICULTURE — Agricultural Economics*

330.94   UK
Z7185.E8S87
SOURCES OF EUROPEAN ECONOMIC AND BUSINESS INFORMATION. irreg., latest 6th ed. (British Library Business Information Service) Ashgate Publishing Ltd. (Subsidiary of: Gower Publishing Co. Ltd.), Gower House, Croft Rd., Aldershot, Hants. GU11 3HR, England. TEL 44-1252-331551. FAX 44-1252-344405. (Addr. in US: Gower, Old Post Rd., Brookfield, VT 05036)

SOUTH AFRICA. COMMISSIONER FOR CUSTOMS AND EXCISE. MONTHLY ABSTRACT OF TRADE STATISTICS. see *BUSINESS AND ECONOMICS — Abstracting, Bibliographies, Statistics*

382   332.67   US
HG5851.A2
SOUTH AFRICA INVESTOR. 1983. q. $395. Investor Responsibility Research Center, Inc., 1350 Connecticut Ave., N.W., Ste. 700, Washington, DC 20036. TEL 202-833-0700. FAX 202-833-3555. Ed. Meg Voorhes. bk.rev. circ. 1,500. (looseleaf format)
Formerly: South Africa Reporter (ISSN 1053-5497).
Description: In-depth news and analysis on developments that will affect multinational businesses in South Africa.

381   SA   ISSN 0259-1855
SOUTH AFRICAN EXPORTERS/EXPORTATEURS SUD-AFRICAINS/SUEDAFRIKANISCHE EXPORTEURE/EXPORTADORES SUL-AFRICANOS/EXPORTADORES DE SUD AFRICA. Alternate title: South African Exporters Directory. (Text in English) 1978. a. Reed Business Information South Africa (Pty.) Ltd., P.O. Box 653207, Benmore 2010, South Africa. TEL 27-11-784-1110. FAX 27-11-883-4729. stat.; circ. 14,000 (controlled). **Document type:** directory.
Description: Provides information on products and services available for export from South Africa, including detailed company listings, bankers and contact names. Provides an overview of South Africa, its infrastructure and economy.

382   US
SOUTH AFRICAN MARKET NEWS. 1989. 7/yr. free. South African Embassy, 3201 New Mexico Ave., N.W., Ste. 300, Washington, DC 20016. E-mail: saedc@ix.netcom.com; URL: http://www.southafrica.net. Ed. Jennifer Cheong. illus. circ. 9,000. **Document type:** newsletter.
Description: Provides information and news on South African trade, business, investment, products and services, trade exhibitions and conferences, and the economy.

382   659.1   SA   ISSN 1019-0317
SOUTH AFRICAN PRODUCT DIGEST; export news from South Africa. Cover title: S A Product Digest. (Text in English) m. R.132 (free outside RSA). Reed Business Information South Africa (Pty.) Ltd., P.O. Box 653207, Benmore 2010, South Africa. TEL 27-11-784-1110. FAX 27-11-883-4729. adv. contact: Rosalie Solarsh. illus.; tr.lit. circ. 25,000. **Document type:** trade publication.
Description: Promotes the export of South African goods abroad.

SOUTH CAROLINA PORT NEWS. see *TRANSPORTATION — Ships And Shipping*

SOVEREIGN ASSESSMENT MONTHLY. see *BUSINESS AND ECONOMICS — Investments*

SPACE NEWS (SPRINGFIELD). see *AERONAUTICS AND SPACE FLIGHT*

382.7   SP   ISSN 0584-6544
SPAIN. DIRECCION GENERAL DE ADUANAS. INFORME MENSUAL SOBRE EL COMERCIO EXTERIOR. 1965. m. Direccion General de Aduanas, Madrid, Spain. (Dist. by: Promotora de Publicaciones, Velazquez 92, Madrid 6, Spain) **Document type:** government publication.

SPORT PARTNER. see *SPORTS AND GAMES*

382   CE   ISSN 0069-2360
SRI LANKA EXPORT DIRECTORY. a. free. Export Development Board, Trade Information Service, 115, Sir Chittampalam A Gardiner, Mawatha, Colombo 2, Sri Lanka. TEL 438523. FAX 438404. TELEX 21245-TRADINF-CE. adv.; illus. circ. 5,000. **Document type:** government publication, directory.
Description: Contains alphabetical listing of exports from Sri Lanka, exporting companies, products, and CCCN numbers. Includes cross-references and general information on Sri Lanka relevant to overseas customers.

STAT (BLAINE). see *AGRICULTURE*

382   PK   ISSN 0585-1009
STATE BANK OF PAKISTAN. EXPORT RECEIPTS. (Text in English) 1966. m. Rs.264($60) State Bank of Pakistan, Central Directorate, Public Relations Department, I.I. Chundrigar Rd., P.O. Box 4456, Karachi, Pakistan. TEL 92-2414141. FAX 92-2417865. TELEX 2754 SBPK PK. **Document type:** government publication.
Description: Discusses exports covered under the Barter Agreement.

382   US   ISSN 0887-364X
HC59   CODEN: STWOED
STATE OF THE WORLD; a Worldwatch Institute report on progress toward a sustainable society. 1984. a. $13.95 for softcover ed.; hardcover ed. $25. (Worldwatch Institute) W.W. Norton & Co., Inc., 500 5th Ave., New York, NY 10110. TEL 800-555-2028. E-mail: wwpub@igc.worldwatch.org; URL: http://www.worldwatch.org. (Orders to: Worldwatch Institute, 1776 Massachusetts Ave., N.W., Washington, DC 20036. TEL 202-452-1999. FAX 202-296-7365; Published in the U.K. by: Earthscan Publications Ltd., Kogan Page Ltd., 120 Pentonville Rd., London N1 9JN, England. TEL 44-171-278-0435. FAX 44-171-278-1142) (also avail. in diskette format) **Document type:** monographic series.
—BLDSC (8438.335550); UnCover.
Description: Presents papers covering a wide variety of topics, including air and water pollution, urban planning, public health, social justice, women's health, energy consumption, and mineral resources, all of which pertain to environmental degradation and conservation.

STATISTICS OF MARINE PRODUCTS EXPORTS. see *BUSINESS AND ECONOMICS — Abstracting, Bibliographies, Statistics*

382   FR
STRATEGIC EUROPE. w. 3650 F. (effective 1991). Lamy S.A., 187-189 quai de Valmy, 75490 Paris Cedex 10, France. TEL 33-1-44721343. FAX 33-1-44721395.

382   IT
STUDI RICERCHE DOCUMENTAZIONE. 1975. 3/yr. L.50000. Unione Regionale Camere di Commercio dell'Emilia-Romagna (C.E.R.E.S.), Via Montegrappa 4-D, 40121 Bologna, Italy. TEL 39-51-223030. FAX 39-51-234945. TELEX 512807 UCAMER. Dir. Claudio Pasini. bk.rev. circ. 1,000. **Document type:** trade publication.

332.6   NE   ISSN 1023-6147
▼**STUDIES IN GLOBAL COMPETITION.** 1995. irreg. £42. Gordon and Breach - Harwood Academic, Amsteldisk 166, 1st Fl., 1079 LH Amsterdam, Netherlands. (Subscr. to: International Publishers Distributor, Box 32160, Newark, NJ 07102. TEL 800-545-8398. FAX 215-750-6343) Ed. John Cantwell. **Document type:** monographic series.

382   US
▼**SUCCESSFUL FRANCHISING.** 1996. m. $34.95. H I S Publishing, 1224 Westwind Trail, Berne, IN 46711. TEL 219-589-3997; 219-589-2507. E-mail: sfmag@aol.com; URL: http://www.entremkt.com/sf. (Subscr. to: 1105 Leighton Ave., Anniston, AL 36207. TEL 205-236-3788) Ed. John P. Hayes; Pub. Brad Bentley. adv.: page $3995; trim 8 x 10 3/4; adv. contact: Kevin Miller. bk.rev.; software rev, video rev, bibl, charts, illus, stat, tr.lit. circ. 75,000. (back issues avail.) **Document type:** consumer publication.
●Also available online.
Description: Designed to help people who are looking to buy a franchise make wise investment decisions.

382   JA
SUMITOMO CORPORATION. ANNUAL REPORT. 1980. a. free. Sumitomo Corporation, Corporate Communications Department, 2-2, Hitotsubashi 1-chome, Chiyoda-ku, Tokyo 100, Japan. TEL 81-3-3217-5114. FAX 81-3-3217-5128. TELEX 22202 SUMIT A J22202. E-mail: info@sumitomocorp.co.jp. charts; stat. **Document type:** corporate report.
Description: Reviews financial highlights of the Sumitomo Corporation, and its activities in the industrial, commercial, and consumer sectors worldwide.

382   FI   ISSN 0355-7820
SUOMEN TUKKUKAUPPA. 10/yr. Suomen Tukkukauppiaiden Liitto, Mannerheimintie 76, FIN-00250 Helsinki 25, Finland.

382   AG
SUPERAVIT. (Editions in English and Spanish) m. Edigar S.A., 15 de Noviembre 2547, 1261 Buenos Aires, Argentina. TEL 941-2344. TELEX 24788. Ed. Luis Mori. circ. 25,000.

SURVEY OF EAST EUROPEAN LAW. see *LAW — International Law*

382   SW   ISSN 0039-6508
SVENSK EXPORT; svensk utenriksshandel. 1895. 6/yr. SEK 260. (Svensk Export) Affaerspress, Kungsgatan 35, S-111 56 Stockholm, Sweden. TEL 46-08-454-64-01. FAX 46-08-108-408. Ed. Lars Torekull. adv.: B&W page SEK 12900, color page SEK 18900; trim 185 x 260. bk.rev.; charts; illus.; stat. circ. 103,847.
Incorporates (in 1987): Sverige paa Vaerldsmarknaden; Former titles (until 1956): Svensk Utenriksshandel; (until 1941): Svensk Export.
Description: Covers the Swedish export industry, foreign trade, foreign markets and trade politics.

SWEDEN. STATENS INDUSTRIVERK. CURRENT RESEARCH PROJECTS. see *BUSINESS AND ECONOMICS — Domestic Commerce*

382   SZ
SWISSEXPORT. q. (Swissexport Association) Exim Index AG, Hintere Hauptgasse 9, CH-4800 Zofingen, Switzerland. TEL 41-62-7468888. FAX 41-62-7518553. Ed. Jakon Geisiger. adv.: B&W page 2700 SFr., color page 3500 SFr.; adv. contact: Hans Fasnacht. circ. 13,500. **Document type:** bulletin.

382   SZ
SWISSEXPORT EXTERN. q. (Swissexport Association) Exim Index AG, Hintere Hauptgasse 9, CH-4800 Zofingen, Switzerland. TEL 41-62-7468888. FAX 41-62-7518553. **Document type:** bulletin.

BUSINESS AND ECONOMICS — INTERNATIONAL COMMERCE

382   SZ
SWISSTRADE;* current business opportunities with Switzerland. 1979. m. (10/yr.). 25 SFr. (Swissexport Cooperation Alliance) EXIM-INDEX, Postfach, CH-4800 Zofingen, Switzerland.

382 658   SZ
SWITZERLAND. CENTER FOR TRADE FAIRS. a. Swiss Office for Trade Promotion, Stampfenbachstr. 85, CH-8035 Zurich, Switzerland. TEL 41-1-3655151. FAX 41-1-3655221. **Document type:** directory.
    Formerly: Swiss Fairs.

SYNDICAT DES EXPORTATEURS ET NEGOCIANTS EN BOIS DE COTE D'IVOIRE. BULLETIN DE LIAISON ET D'INFORMATION. see *FORESTS AND FORESTRY*

SYRACUSE JOURNAL OF INTERNATIONAL LAW & COMMERCE. see *LAW — International Law*

382   SP
T E T. (The East Trade) (Text in English) 1968. m. $45. German Perez Editore, Carrasco, 63, Edif. Ofice, Apdo. 14013, 28027 Madrid, Spain. TEL 1-267-24-03. FAX 1-406-78-37. TELEX 43782 EDOF E. Ed. Arsenio Pardo Rodriquez. (back issues avail.) **Document type:** newspaper.

382.7   SZ   ISSN 1421-2773
▼**T V A - M W S T - V A T JOURNAL.** (Text in English, French, German) 1996. q. 102 SFr. (Institut fuer Abgabe- und Wirtschaftsrecht) Staempfli AG, Hallerstr. 7-9, CH-3012 Bern, Switzerland. TEL 41-31-3006666. FAX 41-31-3006699. circ. 500 (paid). **Document type:** bulletin.

TAIPAN. see *BUSINESS AND ECONOMICS — Investments*

382   CH
TAIWAN EXPORTERS. no.92, 1980. s-m. $12. Nancy Yu Huang, 8 Fu Shun St., Taipei, Taiwan 104, Republic of China.

382.6   CH   ISSN 0494-5336
TAIWAN EXPORTS. (Text mainly in English) 1957. irreg. Board of Foreign Trade, 1 Hu Kou St., Taipei, Taiwan, Republic of China. illus.

382.0951   CH   ISSN 0257-8158
TAIWAN INTERNATIONAL TRADE. 1971. m. $60 in Asia, Oceania, Middle East; elsewhere $70. United Pacific International Inc., P.O. Box 81-417, Taipei, Taiwan, Republic of China. TEL 02-7150751. FAX 886-2-7125591. TELEX 28784-UNIPAINC. **Document type:** catalog.
    Formerly: Trade Monthly.
    Description: A detailed guide to general merchandise from Taiwan, including footwear, houseware, D.I.Y. products, hardware, and sporting goods.

382   CH
TAIWAN TRADE OPPORTUNITIES. 1973. m. NT.$900($50) China External Trade Development Council, 8th Fl., 333 Keelung Rd., Sec. 1, Taipei, Taiwan, Republic of China. TEL 02-725-5200. FAX 02-7576444. TELEX 21676-CETRA. adv. circ. 4,000. Indexed: Key to Econ.Sci.
    Formerly (until 1993): Trade Opportunities in Taiwan.
    Description: Provides information on sources of supply and demand in Taiwan. Also covers industry reports, company profiles and trade statistics.

382   TZ
TANZANIA IMPORT AND EXPORT DIRECTORY. 1975. irreg. 1800 F. National Bank of Commerce, Directorate of International Operations, P.O. Box 6826, Dar es Salaam, Tanzania. adv.; illus. circ. 3,000. **Document type:** directory.

332.6   TZ   ISSN 0856-2105
HF1612.9
TANZANIA TRADE CURRENTS. 1983. bi-m. $25. Board of External Trade, P.O. Box 5402, Dar es Salaam, Tanzania. TEL 255-51-36303. FAX 255-51-46240. TELEX 41408 EXTRADE. Ed. R.L. Mkenda. circ. 2,000. **Document type:** newsletter.
    Formed by the 1987 merger of: Market Newsletter. Trade Brief (ISSN 0856-0668) & Market Newsletter. World Market Prices and Trends for Agricultural Commodities (ISSN 0856-0544)
    Description: Publishes information on trade fairs, marketing research, trade and investment opportunities.

382   FR
TARGET INTERNATIONAL MAGAZINE; your best source of money making opportunities. Variant title: T I M. 1975. q. $36. Rendement - Plus, 32 rue de la Favorite, 69246 Lyon Cedex 05, France. TEL 78-36-36-38. FAX 78-25-55-00. Ed. Annabel DuBois; Pub. Thierry C. Pradat. adv.: B&W page $1260; 195 x 130; adv. contact: Thierry C. Pradat. circ. 15,000. **Document type:** trade publication.
    Formerly (until 1995): Globe - Contact International (ISSN 1018-1830)
    Description: Contains information on new products, ideas, services and inventions from around the world. Gives tips on import - export and international trade.

332.6 336   GW   ISSN 0944-1824
TARIF AKTUELL. s-m. DM.180. Luchterhand Verlag, Heddesdorferstr. 31, 56564 Neuwied, Germany. TEL 49-2631-801-0. FAX 49-2631-801210. **Document type:** newsletter.

382   UK   ISSN 1361-9519
TAX-FREE TRADER & TRAVEL RETAIL WORLD. 1972. 10/yr. £98 (overseas £123) (effective 1997). Argus Business Media Ltd. (Subsidiary of: D M G Exhibitions Group Ltd.), Queensway House, 2 Queensway, Redhill, Surrey RH1 1QS, England. TEL 44-1737-768611. FAX 44-1737-761989. Ed. Peter Tipthorpe. adv. contact: Michael Lewis. circ. 4,971. **Document type:** trade publication.
    Former titles (until 1995): International Tax-Free Trader (ISSN 1354-0548); (until 1994): International Tax-Free Trader & Duty-Free World (ISSN 0306-6045)

TAX MANAGEMENT COUNTRY PORTFOLIOS. see *BUSINESS AND ECONOMICS — Public Finance, Taxation*

TAXATION AND ECONOMY. see *BUSINESS AND ECONOMICS — Banking And Finance*

382 600   US   ISSN 0886-103X
TECHNOLOGY MANAGEMENT ACTION. 1973. m. $160 (Canada and Mexico $181; overseas $217) (effective 1996-1997). Technology News Center, 6810 Butler Valley Rd., Korbel, CA 95550. TEL 707-668-4027. FAX 707-668-4055. E-mail: western@razorlogic.com. Ed. Norman Lynn; Pub. Norman Lynn. R&P contact: Shirley Annis. bk.rev.; charts; stat.; index; circ. 3,650 (paid). (back issues avail.) **Document type:** newsletter.
    ●Also available online.
    Former titles: Technology Transfer Action; Overseas Business Action.
    Description: Shows how technology managers and executives worldwide improve competitiveness, productivity, and innovation through the wise use of technology tools and enlightened policies. Covers topics in engineering, research, finance, trade, technology transfer, and productivity.

TECHNOLOGY TRANSFER SOCIETY. INTERNATIONAL SYMPOSIUM PROCEEDINGS. see *BUSINESS AND ECONOMICS — Management*

TELECOMEUROPA'S INTERNATIONAL REGULATORY UPDATE; your guide to telecoms liberalisation worldwide. see *COMMUNICATIONS*

TELECOMEUROPA'S TELECOMS TARIFFS INNOVATION; your guide to telecoms service pricing for profit. see *COMMUNICATIONS*

TELEMARKETER. see *BUSINESS AND ECONOMICS — Marketing And Purchasing*

332.6   TH   ISSN 0857-6548
THAILAND EXIMPORT REVIEW. (Text in English) 1987. m. Eximport Publishing Co., Ltd., P.O. Box 11 - 1165, Nana Post Office, Bangkok 10110, Thailand. TEL 662-234-7768. FAX 662-234-2567. circ. 50,000. **Document type:** academic/scholarly publication.

332.6   TH
THAILAND SHOWCASE; a buyers' guide. 1992. a. $40. (Thai Chamber of Commerce) Cosmic Group of Companies, 4th Fl., Phyathai Bldg., 31 Phyathai Rd., Rajthevi, Bangkok 10400, Thailand. TEL 245-3850. FAX 246-4737. Ed. Gordon E. Fairclough. adv.: color page $1320; adv. contact: Porntip Petchsingh. circ. 10,000 (controlled). **Document type:** directory, trade publication.
    Description: Lists over 3,000 selected exporters broken down into 19 industrial sectors. Also provides an overview of the Thai economy.

382   TH
THAILAND TRADE INDEX. (Text in English, Thai) 1976. a. Interstate Publications, P.O. Box 5-85, Pathumwan, Bangkok 5, Thailand. adv.; illus.; stat.

332.6 665.5   VN   ISSN 0866-7500
THUONGMAI/COMMERCIAL REVIEW. bi-m. Vietnam National Petroleum Export - Import Corporation, No. 1 Kham Thien, Hanoi, Vietnam. TEL 42-52603. FAX 84-42-59203. TELEX 411241 TCTXD VT.

332.6   SI
TODAY WORLD TRADE OPPORTUNITIES DIGEST. 1987. m. S.$60 (Asia $50; America $66; elsewhere $60). Rightway Marketing & Trade Promotions, Toa Payoh Central, P.O. Box 221, Singapore 9131, Singapore. TEL 065-4670083. FAX 065-4677372. adv. **Document type:** trade publication.
    Description: Covers world trade opportunities for importers, exporters, manufacturers, agents, trade associations, and chambers of commerce & industry worldwide.

332.6   AT   ISSN 0157-3764
TOMODACHI. 1968. bi-m. free to members. Australia - Japan Society of N.S.W., Inc., G.P.O. Box 3802, Sydney, N.S.W. 2001, Australia. TEL 61-2-2992242. FAX 61-2-2992708. Ed. Michael March. adv. contact: Richard Eskell. bk.rev. circ. 6,000.
    Formerly: A J S Newsletter.
    Description: Established to promote better business and social relations between Australia and Japan.

332.6   CC
TOP 500 FOREIGN TRADE COMPANIES IN CHINA. (Text in Chinese, English) 1991. a. $79.50. Han Consultants Inc., P.O. Box 71006, Wuhan, Hubei 430071, People's Republic of China. TEL 86-27-787-8532. FAX 86-27-787-8343. circ. 6,000. **Document type:** directory.
    Description: Provides information on the top 500 import and export companies ranked by their annual turnover, company name, address, phone, fax, contact person and business activity.

TOTAL RATE-OF-RETURN INDEXES. see *BUSINESS AND ECONOMICS — Investments*

332.6   US
TOWARD SEAMLESS BORDERS. 1993. irreg., no.3, 1994. National Law Center for Inter-American Free Trade, 111 Church Ave., Ste. 200, Tucson, AZ 85701-1629. TEL 602-622-1200. FAX 602-622-0957. **Document type:** monographic series.
    Description: Deals with the major aspects of free trade in the Americas.

TOYS AND GAMES IMPORTS AMERICA DIRECTORY. see *GIFTWARE AND TOYS*

TRADE ACTION MONITORING SYSTEM. see *BUSINESS AND ECONOMICS — Domestic Commerce*

382   US   ISSN 1068-0411
HF1371
TRADE & CULTURE.* 1992. q. $29.95. Key Communications Corp., 3500 Bank St., Baltimore, MD 21224-2303. TEL 301-426-2906. FAX 301-444-7837. Ed. Thomas D. Boettcher. adv. circ. 10,000. **Document type:** trade publication.
    Description: For executives of small to mid-size firms that produce competitive products or services. Feature columns on trade zones and trade functions.

BUSINESS AND ECONOMICS — INTERNATIONAL COMMERCE

332.6 338.91 US
TRADE & DEVELOPMENT; news and trade opportunities. 1992. bi-w. $120 (foreign $270). Congressional Information Bureau, Inc., 3030 Clarendon Blvd., Ste. 202, Arlington, VA 22201. TEL 703-516-4801. FAX 703-516-4804. Ed. R. Cazalas. circ. 500. (looseleaf format; back issues avail.)
  Description: International trade and development clearinghouse.

382 338.91 US
TRADE AND DEVELOPMENT AGENCY. bi-w. $160 (foreign $306) (effective 1997). Congressional Information Bureau, Inc., 3030 Clarendon Blvd., Ste. 202, Arlington, VA 22201. TEL 703-516-4804. FAX 703-516-4804. E-mail: cibaech@erols.com; URL: http://www.cibpub.scom.

382 338.91 UN
TRADE AND DEVELOPMENT REPORT AND OVERVIEW. (Editions in English, French, Spanish) 1981. a. $48 (effective 1997). (United Nations Conference on Trade and Development (UNCTAD)) United Nations Publications, Sales and Marketing Section, Room DC2-0853, New York, NY 10017. TEL 212-963-8302; 800-253-9646. FAX 212-963-3489. E-mail: publications@un.org; URL: http://www.un.org/publications. (also avail. in microfiche from CIS) **Indexed:** IIS.
—BLDSC (8879.247000). **CCC.**
  Formerly: Trade and Development Report (ISSN 0255-4607)

382 NE
TRADE CHANNEL (CONSUMER PRODUCTS EDITION). 1946. m. $88. Trade Channel Organisation B.V., Stolbergstraat 14, 2012 EP Haarlem, Netherlands. TEL 31-23-5319022. FAX 31-23-5317974. E-mail: 100673.1364@compuserve.com; URL: http://www.tradechannel.com. Ed. Henk van Capelle; Pub. Paul Vroom. R&P contact: Paul Vroom. adv. contact: Fred van der Heydan. bk.rev. circ. 40,000. **Indexed:** Key to Econ.Sci. **Document type:** trade publication.
  Former titles (until 1996): Export Channel (Consumer Products Edition) & Export Channel (Consumer Edition).
  Description: Gives product offerings and business opportunities in housewares, hobbies, textiles and fashion, food, cosmetics and health, gifts and toys, luxuries, and office equipment.

382 NE
TRADE CHANNEL (TECHNICAL PRODUCTS EDITION). 1946. m. $88. Trade Channel Organisation B.V., Stolbergstraat 14, 2012 EP Haarlem, Netherlands. TEL 31-23-5319022. FAX 31-23-5317974. E-mail: 100673.1364@compuserve.com; URL: http://www.tradechannel.com. Ed. Henk van Capelle; Pub. Paul Vroom. R&P contact: Paul Vroom. adv. contact: Fred van der Heydan. bk.rev. circ. 55,000. **Indexed:** Key to Econ.Sci. **Document type:** trade publication.
  Former titles (until 1996): Export Channel (Technical Products Edition) & Export Channel (Technical Edition); Trade Channel (ISSN 0041-0403).
  Description: Gives product offerings and business opportunities in metalworking, machinery, construction, electronics, transportation and industrial supplies.

332.6 US
TRADE CONNECTIONS. s-a. free to qualified personnel. Federation of International Trade Associations, 1851 Alexander Bell Ave., Reston, VA 20191. TEL 703-620-1588. FAX 703-391-0159. E-mail: fita@mcimail.com; URL: http://www.fita.org. Ed. N.T. Joyner. circ. 5,000. **Document type:** directory.

382 US
TRADE DIRECTORY OF MEXICO. a. $90 (magnetic tape $295). Mexican Foreign Trade Bank, c/o Walker's Western Research, 1650 Borel Pl., Ste. 130, San Mateo, CA 94402-3507. TEL 800-258-5737. (also avail. in magnetic tape) **Document type:** directory.

332.6 US
TRADE LINES. 1984. q. free to members. (National Association of Export Companies) Assist International, 60 Madison Ave., 2nd Fl., New York, NY 10010. TEL 212-725-3311. FAX 212-725-3312. Ed. Peter Robinson, Jr. circ. 1,000. **Document type:** newsletter.
  Description: Designed for the international trade community. Provides advice on exporting, export news and information on incoming trade missions, conferences, and seminars.

382 IE
TRADE-LINKS JOURNAL. 1979. 6/yr. $25. Libra House Ltd., 4 St. Kevin's Terrace, Dublin 8, Ireland. TEL 353-1-4542717. Ed. C.G. Tyrrell. bk.rev.; abstr.; charts; illus.; mkt.; pat.; stat. circ. 3,240. **Document type:** trade publication.
  Formerly: Dublin Chamber of Commerce Journal (ISSN 0009-1138)

382 CH
TRADE PAGES. (Text in English) 4/yr. $40. Taiwan Trade Pages Corp., P.O. Box 72-50, Taipei, Taiwan, Republic of China. TEL 02-3050759. FAX 886-2-3071000. TELEX 24838TRADEPAG.
  Description: Emphasizes gifts, premiums, novelties, houseware, toys and games, electronic and electric appliances, personal care items, sporting goods.

382 UN ISSN 1014-7411
HF1455
TRADE POLICY REVIEW. (Editions in English, French, Spanish) 1990. a. price varies. General Agreement on Tariffs and Trade, Centre William Rappard, Rue. de Lausanne 154, 1211 Geneva 21, Switzerland. TEL 022-739-5208. FAX 022-739-5458. TELEX 412 234 GATT CH. **Document type:** trade publication.
  Description: Contains comprehensive trade policy analysis prepared by the country under review and the GATT secretariat.

382 CC
TRADE WATCH. m. Hong Kong Trade Development Council, Research Department, 38-F, Office Tower, Convention Plaza, 1 Harbour Rd., Wanchai, Hong Kong, People's Republic of China. TEL 852-2584-4333. FAX 852-2824-0249. Ed. Edward Leung.

382 KE
TRADE WAYS. 1982. m. $21. Mecka Publicity, P.O. Box 70287, Nairobi, Kenya. TELEX 22953 DAAD KE. Ed. Henry Omware. adv.; bk.rev. circ. 15,000. (also avail. in microfiche) **Document type:** academic/scholarly publication.
  Description: Carries interesting and well-researched features on land, air, sea and rail transport.

382 CH
TRADE WEEKLY. (Text in Chinese) w. $120 for Hong Kong; elsewhere $140. Importers & Exporters Association of Taipei, 5th Fl., 350 Sungkiang Rd., Taipei, Taiwan 104, Republic of China. TEL 02-581-3521. FAX 02-536-3328.

382 US
TRADE-WEIGHTED VALUE OF THE DOLLAR. 1987. m. $48. Federal Reserve Bank of Dallas, Sta. K, Dallas, TX 75222. TEL 214-651-6289. circ. 500. (also avail. in microfiche from CIS; reprint service avail. from CIS) **Indexed:** Amer.Stat.Ind. (1987-).
  Description: Presents a measure of the trade-weighted value of the U.S. dollar against 101 U.S. trading partners.

382 380 CH ISSN 1024-9028
TRADE WINDS' INDUSTRY WEEKLY. (Text in English) 1975. w. $90 in Asia-Pacific; elsewhere $110. Trade Winds, Inc., No. 7, Lane 75, Yungkang St., P.O. Box 7-179, Taipei, Taiwan 10602, Republic of China. TEL 02-393-2718. FAX 02-396-4022. E-mail: tradwind@ms2.hinet.net; URL: http://www.tradewinds.com.tw. (Subscr. in U.S. to: Trade Wind Inc., Box 820519, Dallas, TX 75382. TEL 972-699-1188. FAX 972-699-1189) Ed. Donald Shapiro; Pub. Henry Ou. R&P contact: Donald Shapiro. adv. contact: Janice Hsieh. illus.; tr.lit. circ. 12,000. (tabloid format) **Document type:** trade publication.
  Formerly: Trade Winds.
  Description: Covers Taiwan's export industries and products, especially hardware, auto parts, machinery and industrial supplies.

382 CH ISSN 0259-9880
TRADE WINDS MONTHLY. 1980. m. $90 in Asia-Pacific; elsewhere $110. Trade Winds, Inc., No. 7, Lane 75, Yungkang St., P.O. Box 7-179, Taipei, Taiwan 10602, Republic of China. TEL 02-393-2718. FAX 02-396-4022. E-mail: tradwind@ms2.hinet.net; URL: http://www.tradewinds.com.tw. (Subscr. in U.S. to: Trade Winds Inc., Box 820519, Dallas, TX 75382. TEL 972-699-1188. FAX 972-699-1189) Ed. Donald Shapiro; Pub. Henry Ou. R&P contact: Donald Shapiro. adv.; tr.lit. circ. 10,000.
  Description: Covers Taiwan's economy and export industries, and explores economic situations in other Asian countries.

TRADELINK - CHINESE. see BUSINESS AND ECONOMICS — Trade And Industrial Directories

TRADELINK - ENGLISH. see BUSINESS AND ECONOMICS — Trade And Industrial Directories

332.6 UK
TRADEWINDS. 1980. 4/yr. membership. Portuguese UK Chamber of Commerce, 22-25a Sackville St., 4th Fl., London W1X 1DE, England. TEL 44-171-494-1844. FAX 44-171-494-1822. E-mail: price@pukc.demon.co.uk. Ed. Ronald Price. R&P contact: Ronald Price. adv.; bk.rev.; circ. 2,000. **Document type:** newsletter, trade publication.
  Formerly: Tradewinds Newsletter (ISSN 1352-1152)

382 GW
TRANSIT COURIER. 1926. s-w. DM.538. Transit Courier Verlag, Postfach 750779, 81337 Munich, Germany. TEL 49-89-774499. FAX 49-89-775410. Ed. Volker Robl. adv. circ. 2,400. **Document type:** trade publication.

382 UN ISSN 1014-9562
HD2755.5
TRANSNATIONAL CORPORATIONS. Short title: T N Cs. 1976. 3/yr. $35. (Centre on Transnational Corporations) United Nations Publications, Sales and Marketing Section, Room DC2-0874, New York, NY 10017. TEL 212-963-8302; 800-253-9646. FAX 212-963-3489. E-mail: publications@un.org; URL: http://www.un.org/publications. (Or: Distribution and Sales Section, Palais des Nations, 1211 Geneva 10, Switzerland) (also avail. in microfiche from CIS) **Indexed:** C.R.E.J., IIS, Int.Polit.Sci.Abstr., P.A.I.S.
—BLDSC (9024.975220); SWETS; UMI; UnCover. **CCC.**
  Formerly: C T C Reporter (ISSN 0255-4216)
  Description: Contains reports on matters related to transnational corporations in all governmental and non-governmental organizations.

382 AT ISSN 0810-025X
TRAVELTRADE VISA GUIDE. 1977. a. Aus.$32 (effective 1996). Reed Business Publishing Pty. Ltd. (Subsidiary of: Reed International PLC), P.O. Box 5487, W. Chatswood, N.S.W. 2057, Australia. TEL 61-2-372-5222. FAX 61-2-419-7064. Ed. Kaye Tanner. circ. 1,912.
  Former titles (until 1982): Traveltrade Travel Guide (ISSN 0159-7752); (until 1980): Traveltrade Visa Handbook (ISSN 0156-1545)
  Description: Contains the names, addresses and telephone numbers of embassies, consulates, and high commissions in Australia and New Zealand.

382 YU ISSN 0041-2457
TRGOVINSKI GLASNIK; informativni list za trgovinu. 1891. m. 100 din.($10.45) Export Press, Francuska 27, Belgrade, Yugoslavia. Ed. Dragoljub Ivanovic.

338 382 FR ISSN 0041-2872
TRIBUNE LIBRE. 1906. m. 600 F. Chambre Syndicale Nationale des Forces de Vente, 2 rue d'Hauteville, 75480 Paris Cedex 10, France. Ed. Jean de Santis. adv.; bk.rev.; charts; illus.; stat.; index. circ. 30,000.

382 UK ISSN 0082-657X
TRINIDAD AND TOBAGO TRADE DIRECTORY. 1963. a. Arthur H. Thrower Ltd., 44-46 S. Ealing Rd., London W5, England. Ed. Arthur H. Thrower. index.

BUSINESS AND ECONOMICS — INTERNATIONAL COMMERCE

382 US ISSN 1046-9427
HD9734.M43
TWIN PLANT NEWS; the magazine of the maquiladora industry. 1985. m. $65. Nibbe, Hernandez & Associates, Inc., 4110 Rio Bravo Dr., No. 108, El Paso, TX 79902. TEL 915-532-1567. FAX 915-544-7556. Ed. Don Nibbe. R&P contact: Don Nibbe. adv.; bk.rev. circ. 10,000. **Document type:** trade publication.
—UnCover.
Description: Provides information on doing business in Mexico.

382 UN ISSN 0259-3181
U N C T A D BULLETIN. French edition: C N U C E D Bulletin (ISSN 1011-1131) 1966. m. (United Nations Conference on Trade and Development) United Nations Publications, Sales and Marketing Section, Room DC2-0853, New York, NY 10017. TEL 212-963-8302; 800-253-9646. FAX 212-963-3489. E-mail: publications@un.org; URL: http://www.un.org/publications. (Or: United Nations Sales Section, Palais des Nations, CH-1211 Geneva 10, Switzerland) bibl. (processed) **Indexed:** Environ.Abstr.
—KR SourceOne.
Formerly (until 1983): U N C T A D Monthly Bulletin (ISSN 0252-5232)

382 338.91 UN
HF1410
U N C T A D REVIEW. 1979. 2/yr. $30. (United Nations Conference on Trade and Development) United Nations Publications, Sales and Marketing Section, Room DC2-0853, New York, NY 10017. TEL 212-963-8302; 800-253-9646. FAX 212-963-3489. E-mail: publications@un.org; URL: http://www.un.org/publications. (Or: Palais des Nations, 1211-Geneva 10, Switzerland) (also avail. in microfiche from CIS) **Indexed:** C.R.E.J., IIS, P.A.I.S.
Formerly: Trade and Development: An U N C T A D Review (ISSN 0252-5216)
Description: International journal on trade, finance and development issues.

332.6 UK ISSN 1351-1637
U S A AND EUROPE IN BUSINESS. a. £55. Sterling Publications Ltd., 86-88 Edgware Rd., London W2 2YW, England. TEL 44-171-915-9600. FAX 44-171-915-9619. R&P contact: Sandy Tucker. circ. 17,500. **Document type:** trade publication.

382 GW
U S A HANDEL. 1963. bi-m. $18.75. American Embassy, Foreign Commercial Service, Deichmanns Ave. 29, 53179 Bonn, Germany. TEL 0228-339-2944. FAX 0228-334649. adv.: B&W page $620, color page $1675; trim 185 x 265. circ. 4,500. **Document type:** trade publication.
Description: Covers import-export topics, new products and services, investment opportunities, trade policy issues and US Dept. of Commerce export promotion programs.

382 US ISSN 0070-2250
HE953.N5
U S CUSTOM HOUSE GUIDE. (Supplement avail.) 1862. a. $425 (effective 1996). K-III Directory Corp., 10 Lake Dr., Hightstown, NJ 08520. TEL 609-371-7700. (Subscr. to: 1735 Technology Dr., Ste. 410, San Jose, CA 95110. TEL 800-547-8753) circ. 5,600. **Document type:** trade publication.
Description: Provides current customs regulations, U.S. tariff schedules, and U.S. customs ports.

382 380.1 US
U S EXPORT DIRECTORY. 1990. a. Reed Information Services, Division of Reed Elsevier Inc., 1350 E. Touhy Ave., Box 5080, Des Plaines, IL 60017. TEL 800-347-8743. FAX 708-390-2850. (Subscr. to: 44 Cook St., Boulder, CO 80206. TEL 800-662-7776) Ed. Anne Brickley. circ. 40,000. **Document type:** directory.
Formerly: U S Industrial Export Directory.
Description: Serves as an international buyer's guide for industrial products.

350.827 US ISSN 0196-9153
CODEN: USPUDA
U S I T C PUBLICATION. (Has subseries: Harmonized Tariff Schedule of the United States (ISSN 1066-0925); Year in Trade: Operation of the Trade Agreements Program; Trade Between the United States and China, the Successor States to the Former Soviet Union, and other Title Countries (ISSN 0270-5435)) irreg. U.S. International Trade Commission, Office of Information Services, 500 E St., S.W., Washington, DC 20436. TEL 202-205-2000. **Document type:** monographic series, government publication.
—BLDSC (9099.800000); CASDDS.
Former titles: I T C Publication (ISSN 0196-9277); U.S. Tariff Commission. T C Publication (ISSN 0502-5338)

332.6 US
THE U S OFFSHORE FUNDS DIRECTORY. a. 405 Park Ave., Ste. 500, New York, NY 10022. TEL 212-371-5935. FAX 212-758-9032. Pub. Antoine Bernheim. **Document type:** directory.

U T C. (Uitspraken van de Tariefcommissie) see BUSINESS AND ECONOMICS — Public Finance, Taxation

332.6 346.04 US
UNFAIR COMPETITION AND THE I T C. a. $165. Clark - Boardman - Callaghan, 375 Hudson St., New York, NY 10014. TEL 212-929-7500; 800-422-2101. FAX 212-924-0460. Ed. Donald Knox Duvall.
Formerly: Federal Unfair Competition Actions.
Description: Offers complete procedural guidance to prosecuting and defending unfair import trade practice cases.

382 US
UNIFIED LIST OF UNITED STATES COMPANIES DOING BUSINESS IN SOUTH AFRICA AND NAMIBIA.* irreg., 2nd ed., 1988. $8. American Committee on Africa, 17 John St., Fl. 12, New York, NY 10038-4010. Eds. Richard Knight, Roger Walke.

332.6 US ISSN 1075-7627
UNITED IMPORT EXPORT. 1992. m. $78 (foreign $98). Tiborone International, 2614 Briar Ridge., Ste. V-98, Houston, TX 77057. FAX 713-493-0823. (Overseas dist.: C.V. Abadi Sukses, Jolan Diponigoto 77A, P.O. Box 126, Salatiga 50715, Indonesia. FAX 62-298-22-895) Pub. Julius E. Polonyi. circ. 25,000. **Document type:** trade publication.
Description: Lists international sellers and buyers, business opportunities, agency offers, and licensing offers. Also reports world trade news, business news, and finder's fee opportunities.

UNITED KINGDOM TRADE BULLETIN IMPORTS AND EXPORTS OF FISH & FISH PRODUCTS. see FISH AND FISHERIES

UNITED NATIONS COMMISSION ON INTERNATIONAL TRADE LAW. YEARBOOK. see LAW — International Law

382 338.91 UN
UNITED NATIONS CONFERENCE ON TRADE AND DEVELOPMENT: PROCEEDINGS.* irreg., 6th, 1983, Belgrade. price varies. United Nations Conference on Trade and Development (UNCTAD), Reference Unit, 1211 Geneva 10, Switzerland. TEL 022-346011. FAX 022-339879. **Document type:** proceedings.

UNITED NATIONS WEEKLY REPORT. see POLITICAL SCIENCE — International Relations

353.1 382 US ISSN 0083-002X
HF1455
U.S. DEPARTMENT OF STATE. COMMERCIAL POLICY SERIES. (Subseries of: U.S. Department of State. Departmental Series) 1934. irreg. price varies. U.S. Department of State, Bureau of Public Affairs, 2201 C St., N.W., Washington, DC 20520. TEL 202-632-1394. (Orders to: Superintendent of Documents, U.S. Government Printing Office, Box 371954, Pittsburgh, PA 15250-7954. TEL 202-512-1800. FAX 202-512-2250) **Document type:** government publication.

382 US ISSN 0094-8411
KF1987.A329 CODEN: EARGDG
U.S. EXPORT ADMINISTRATION REGULATIONS. 1941-1987; resumed 199? base vol. plus irreg. updates. $88 (foreign $110) (includes updating Export Administration Bulletins). U.S. International Trade Administration, Office of Export Administration, Department of Commerce, Herberg C. Hoover Bldg., Rm. 3850, 14th St. and Constitution Ave, DC 20230. TEL 202-377-2000. (Subscr. to: Superintendent of Documents, U.S. Government Printing Office, Box 371954, Pittsburgh, PA 15250-7954. TEL 202-512-1800. FAX 202-512-2250) (looseleaf format) **Document type:** government publication.
—CASDDS.
Formerly: Export Control Regulations (ISSN 0082-8947)
Description: Compiles official regulations and policies governing the export licensing of commodities and technical data.

U.S. IMPORT AND EXPORT PRICE INDEXES. see BUSINESS AND ECONOMICS — Economic Situation And Conditions

382 US
U.S. INTERNATIONAL TRADE COMMISSION. ANNUAL REPORT. 1917. a. $6. U.S. International Trade Commission, Office of Information Services, 500 E St., S.W., Washington, DC 20436. TEL 202-205-2000. (Orders to: Superintendent of Documents, U.S. Government Printing Office, Box 371954, Pittsburgh, PA 15250-7954. TEL 202-512-1800. FAX 202-512-2250; Or: Bernan, 4611-F Assembly Dr., Lanham, MD 20706. TEL 301-459-7666. FAX 301-459-0056) Ed. Peg O'Laughlin. circ. 3,000. **Document type:** government publication.
Formerly: U.S. Tariff Commission. Annual Report (ISSN 0083-3428)
Description: Describes the Commission's activities during the fiscal year with lists of investigations and studies conducted.

382 US ISSN 1057-9680
HF3001
U.S. MERCHANDISE TRADE: EXPORTS, GENERAL IMPORTS, AND IMPORTS FOR CONSUMPTION - STANDARD INTERNATIONAL TRADE CLASSIFICATION REVISION 3 - COMMODITY BY COUNTRY. (Series FT-925) 1943. m. $136. U.S. Bureau of the Census, Foreign Trade Division, Washington, DC 20233. TEL 301-763-5140. (Subscr. to: Superintendent of Documents, U.S. Government Printing Office, Box 371954, Pittsburgh, PA 15250-7954. TEL 202-783-3238. FAX 202-512-2233) (also avail. in microfiche from CIS; reprint service avail. from CIS) **Indexed:** Amer.Stat.Ind. (1973-). **Document type:** government publication.
Formed by the 1988 merger of: Foreign Trade Reports. U.S. Exports - Schedule E - Commodity by Country (ISSN 0198-6759); Which was formerly: Foreign Trade Reports. U.S. Exports - Schedule E - Commodity Groupings Commodity by Country (ISSN 0190-499X) & Foreign Trade Reports. U.S. General Imports and Imports for Consumption. Schedule A - Commodity by Country (ISSN 0736-234X); Which was formerly: Foreign Trade Reports. U.S. Exports - Schedule A - Commodity by Country (ISSN 0095-5493)

UNITED STATES - GERMAN ECONOMIC YEARBOOK (YEAR). see BUSINESS AND ECONOMICS — Chamber Of Commerce Publications

UNITED STATES IMPORT TRADE LAW. see LAW — International Law

UNITED STATES IMPORTERS PRODUCT GUIDE. see BUSINESS AND ECONOMICS — Trade And Industrial Directories

BUSINESS AND ECONOMICS — INTERNATIONAL COMMERCE

382   **PL**   **ISSN 1230-6444**
HF37.P6
UNIWERSYTET GDANSKI. WYDZIAL EKONOMIKI TRANSPORTU. ZESZYTY NAUKOWE. HANDEL ZAGRANICZNEGO. PRACE I MATERIALY. (Text in Polish; summaries in English, Russian) 1971. irreg., latest no.13. price varies. Uniwersytet Gdanski, Wydzial Ekonomiki Transportu, c/o Biblioteka Glowna, Ul. Armii Krajowej 110, 81-824 Sopot, Poland. TEL 51-0061. TELEX 051 2247 BMOR PL. (Dist. by: Ars Polona-Ruch, Krakowskie Przedmiescie 7, 00-680 Warsaw, Poland) circ. 300. **Document type:** academic/scholarly publication.
    Former titles (until 1991): Uniwersytet Gdanski. Wydzial Ekonomiki Transportu. Zeszyty Naukowe. Instytut Ekonomiki Handlu Zagranicznego. Prace i Materialy (ISSN 0239-9377); (until 1982): Uniwersytet Gdanski. Wydzial Ekonomiki Transportu. Zeszyty Naukowe. Ekonomika Handlu Zagranicznego. Prace i Materialy (ISSN 0208-4864); Uniwersytet Gdanski. Wydzial Ekonomiki Transportu. Zeszyty Naukowe. Instytut Handlu Zagranicznego. Prace i Materialy (ISSN 0208-4848)
    Description: Covers international economic and financial relations, international transport and forwarding, economics and organization of foreign trade.

UNIWERSYTET SLASKI W KATOWICACH. PRACE NAUKOWE. PROBLEMY PRAWNE HANDLU ZAGRANICZNEGO. see *LAW — International Law*

382   **UY**
URUGUAY. DIRECCION GENERAL DE COMERCIO EXTERIOR. ESTADISTICAS DE COMERCIO EXTERIOR. 1977. a. Direccion General de Comercio Exterior, Montevideo, Uruguay. circ. 1,000. **Document type:** government publication.

382   **SZ**
V S I G - MITTEILUNGEN/INFORMATIONS V S I G. 1942. m. membership. Vereinigung der Schweizerischen Import- und Grosshandels, Gueterstr. 78, CH-4010 Basel, Switzerland. TEL 41-61-2713385. FAX 41-61-2723039. Pub. J.R. Zeller. **Document type:** bulletin.

382   **GW**
V W D AUSSENHANDELSDIENST. Variant title: Vereinigte Wirschaftsdienste Aussenhandelsdienst. 1951. w. DM.86.30 per month. V W D - Vereinigte Wirtschaftsdienste GmbH, Niederurseler Allee 8-10, 65760 Eschborn, Germany. FAX 49-6196-405240. Ed. Armin Kalbfleisch. bk.rev.; index. circ. 1,700. Indexed: Key to Econ.Sci. **Document type:** bulletin.
    Formerly: Aussenhandelsdienst der Industrie- und Handelskammern und Wirtschaftsverbaende (ISSN 0001-1401); Which was formed by the merger of (1950-1956): Aussenhandelsdienst der Industrie- und Handelskammern und Wirtschaftsverbaende. Ausgabe A (ISSN 0343-8031); (1950-1956): Aussenhandelsdienst der Industrie- und Handelskammern und Wirtschaftsverbaende. Ausgabe B (ISSN 0343-804X)

V W D - EUROPA. see *BUSINESS AND ECONOMICS — Investments*

VANUATU. STATISTICS OFFICE. ANNUAL SUMMARY OF OVERSEAS TRADE. see *BUSINESS AND ECONOMICS — Abstracting, Bibliographies, Statistics*

382   **GW**
VEREIN HAMBURGER EXPORTEURE. RUNDSCHREIBENDIENST FUER MITGLIEDSUNTERNEHMEN. bi-m. DM.1100. Verein Hamburger Exporteure e.V., Gotenstr. 21, 20097 Hamburg, Germany. TEL 49-40-23601625. FAX 49-40-23601610. adv.; bk.rev. circ. 300. **Document type:** newsletter.

382 332.6   **VN**
VIETNAM BUSINESS. (Text in Chinese, English, Vietnamese) 1991. bi-w. Vietnam Trade Information Center, 46 Ngo Nguyen St., Hanoi, Socialist Republic of Vietnam. TEL 262319. FAX 263177. Ed. Ho Hai Long. adv.: B&W page $200, color page $500. circ. 10,000.
    Description: For foreign traders and investors.

332.6   **VN**
VIETNAM TRADE REVIEW. (Text mainly in Vietnamese, sometimes in Chinese, English) 1961. s-m. D.4000. (Ministry of Trade) Vietnam Trade Review, 46 Ngo Quyen, Hanoi, Vietnam. TEL 84-4-8252046. FAX 84-4-8262311. Ed. Truong Duc Ngai. adv.: color page $300. circ. 10,000. **Document type:** trade publication.
    Formerly (until 1990): Vietnam Trade and Tourism Review.
    Description: Covers Vietnamese policies on foreign economic relations, foreign trade, economic situations and international economic ties.

382   **RU**   **ISSN 0321-057X**
VNESHNAYA TORGOVLYA. English edition: Foreign Trade (ISSN 0134-8469); French edition: Commerce Exterieur (ISSN 0134-8272); German edition: Aussenhandel (ISSN 0134-8280); Spanish edition: Comercio Exterior (ISSN 0134-8299) (Supplements avail.) (Text in Russian) 1931. m. $103 (effective 1997). (Ministerstvo Vneshnei Torgovli) Vneshnaya Torgovlya, Minskaya ul., 11, 121108 Moscow, Russia. TEL 7-095-1456894. (Dist. by: Mezhdunarodnaya Kniga, B. Yakimanka 39, 117049 Moscow, Russia) Ed. V.B. Spandaryan. adv.; bk.rev.; bibl.; illus.; mkt.; stat.; index. circ. 30,000. Indexed: Key to Econ.Sci., Mid.East: Abstr.& Ind.

382   **US**   **ISSN 0047-5068**
W C N COMMERCIAL NEWS. Running title: L.A. Commercial News. (Monthly supplement avail.: Cargo) 1912. w. $25. C.A. Page Publishing Co., Box 530, Redondo Beach, CA 90277-0530. TEL 213-608-3350. Ed. Shay Ramos. adv. contact: Mark Wagner. circ. 5,500. **Document type:** newspaper, trade publication.
—UMI.

382 338   **US**   **ISSN 0887-9990**
W E P Z A NEWSLETTER. (World Export Processing Zones Association) 1978. q. membership only. Flagstaff Institute, Box 986, Flagstaff, AZ 86002. TEL 520-779-0052. FAX 520-774-8589. Ed. Richard L. Bolin. circ. 100. **Document type:** newsletter.
    Description: Stimulates industrial development in export processing zones through exchange of information, research, and management training.

382   **GW**   **ISSN 0042-966X**
W G A GESCHAEFTSBERICHT. 1947. a. free. Wirtschaftsvereinigung Gross- und Aussenhandel Hamburg e.V., Gotenstr. 21, 20097 Hamburg, Germany. TEL 49-40-23601610. Ed. Hans-Juergen Mueller. adv.; bk.rev.; illus. circ. 2,000. **Document type:** bulletin.

W S S A GRAPEVINE. (Wine and Spirits Shippers Association) see *BEVERAGES*

382   **CC**   **ISSN 1001-3407**
WAIMAO JINGJI, GUOJI MAOYI. (Subseries of: Fuyin Baokan Ziliao) (Text in Chinese) 1980. m. $65.19. Zhongguo Renmin Daxue, Shubao Ziliao Zhongxin - China People's University, Book & Newspaper Information Center, 3 Zhang Zizhong Rd., P.O. Box 1122, Beijing 100007, People's Republic of China. TEL 86-10-4015080. (Dist. in US by: China Publications Service, Box 49614, Chicago, IL 60649. TEL 312-288-3291. FAX 312-288-8570) pp./issue: 96.
    Description: Covers issues related to international commerce and international market management.

382   **US**   **ISSN 0049-691X**
WASHINGTON INTERNATIONAL BUSINESS REPORT. 1972. m. $288. International Business-Government Counsellors Inc., 818 Connecticut Ave. N.W., 12th Fl., Washington, DC 20006-2702. TEL 202-872-8181. FAX 202-872-8696. TELEX 440511 IBGC UI. Ed. Solveig B. Spielmann. circ. 800. (processed; reprint service avail.)
● Also available online.

332.6   **US**   **ISSN 0893-1232**
WASHINGTON REPORT ON LATIN AMERICA AND THE CARIBBEAN. 1986. bi-w. (24/yr.). $365 (foreign $395) (effective 1996 & 1997). Gilston Communications Group, Box 467, Washington, DC 20044. TEL 301-570-4544. FAX 301-570-4545. Ed. Samuel M. Gilston. **Document type:** newsletter.
    Description: Reports on the policies and actions of the US government, Congress and multilateral banks and their impact on business trade and investment in Latin America, the Caribbean and Mexico.

WASHINGTON TARIFF & TRADE LETTER; a weekly report for business executives on U.S. international trade policies, legislation, opportunities and restrictions. see *LAW — International Law*

382   **US**
WASHINGTON TRADE DAILY. 1988. d. $550. Trade Reports International Group, 2104 National Press Bldg., Washington, DC 20045. TEL 301-946-0817. FAX 301-946-2631. Ed. Jim Berger. (only avail. by fax) **Document type:** newsletter.
● Also available online. Vendor(s): NewsNet.
Formerly (until 1988): Washington Trade Week.
    Description: Covers international trade policy developments from Washington.

380.1   **IS**   **ISSN 0302-5489**
WE REPRESENT IN ISRAEL AND ABROAD. (Text in English) 1969. irreg. $33. Tanne Advertising Ltd., 68 Shlomo Hamelech St., P.O.B. 29322, Tel Aviv, Israel. Ed. Milo Ewas. adv. circ. 8,000.

332.6   **GW**
WEINRECHT; der Europaeischen Gemeinschaft, der Bundesrepublik Deutschland und der Bundeslaender. irreg. (approx. 6/yr.) DM.198. Walhalla Fachverlag, Haus an der Eisernen Bruecke, 93059 Regensburg, Germany. TEL 49-941-5684-0. FAX 49-941-5684111. E-mail: walhalla@walhalla.de; URL: http://www.walhalla.de. adv. circ. 4,200. (looseleaf format) **Document type:** bulletin.

382   **GW**   **ISSN 0720-3683**
WELTHANDEL/WORLD TRADE. 1981. m. DM.75($40) H P B Welthandel Verlag GmbH, Postfach 650909, 22369 Hamburg, Germany. TEL 49-40-6004670. FAX 49-40-6013114. Ed. Hiltrud Boeckmann. adv.: B&W page DM.6450, color page DM.11287; trim 175 x 258; adv. contact: Viktoria Stelter. bk.rev. circ. 36,600. **Document type:** trade publication.
    Description: Economic news about world markets.

382   **GW**   **ISSN 0935-1582**
WELTMARKT. 1981. bi-m. DM.90($50) H P B Welthandel Verlag GmbH, Postfach 650909, 22369 Hamburg, Germany. TEL 49-40-6004670. FAX 49-40-6013114. Ed. Hiltrud Boeckmann. adv. contact: Viktoria Stelter. circ. 25,000. **Document type:** trade publication.

330   **GW**   **ISSN 0043-2652**
HC59.A15
DIE WELTWIRTSCHAFT. 1950. q. DM.96 (effective 1998). (Institut fuer Weltwirtschaft, Kiel) Verlag Mohr Siebeck, Wilhelmstr. 18, 72074 Tuebingen, Germany. TEL 49-7071-923-0. FAX 49-7071-51104. E-mail: mohr-siebeck@t-online.de; URL: http://www.uni-kiel.de:8080/ifw/pub/ww.htm. (Subscr. to: Postfach 2040, 72010 Tuebingen, Germany) Ed. Horst Siebert. R&P contact: Jill Sopper. adv. contact: Tilman Gaebler. charts. circ. 1,250. Indexed: ELLIS, IBR, Key to Econ.Sci., P.A.I.S.For.Lang.Ind., SCIMP (1991-), World Agri.Econ.& Rural Sociol.Abstr. **Document type:** academic/scholarly publication.
—BLDSC (9295.040000); SWETS. CCC.
    Description: Current facts about the world economy.

382   **AU**   **ISSN 0043-2954**
WEST-OST-JOURNAL; unabhaengige wirtschaftspolitische Zeitschrift. 1968. 6/yr. S.590. (Donaueuropaeisches Institut) Jupiter Verlag GmbH, Robertgasse 2, A-1020 Vienna, Austria. Ed. Dr. Hans-Georg Zeiner. Indexed: Key to Econ.Sci. **Document type:** newsletter.

382   **JA**   **ISSN 0921-8475**
WHITE PAPER ON INTERNATIONAL TRADE, JAPAN (YEAR). (Text in English) a. $143. Japan External Trade Organization, Publications Department, 2-5 Toranomon 2-chome, Minato-ku, Tokyo 105, Japan. TEL 03-3582-3518. FAX 03-3587-2485. TELEX J 24378. circ. 1,000.
    Description: Analyzes the trend of world trade and economy in the past year, the development of international activity and a sophisticated system of international work sharing and the conditions of long-term world economic growth.

382.782   **UK**   **ISSN 0953-6957**
WHO'S WHO IN DUTY FREE. (Supplement to: Frontier (ISSN 0266-5883)) 1986. a. Reed Business Information (Subsidiary of: Reed Elsevier group), Quadrant House, The Quadrant, Sutton, Surrey SM2 5AS, England. TEL 44-181-652-4942. FAX 44-181-652-8991.

BUSINESS AND ECONOMICS — INTERNATIONAL COMMERCE

332.6   GW   ISSN 0937-2415
WIRTSCHAFTSVERKEHR MIT DEM AUSLAND. m. DM.298. Deutscher Wirtschaftsdienst, Marienburgerstr. 22, 50968 Cologne, Germany. TEL 49-221-93763-0. FAX 49-221-9376399. (looseleaf format) **Document type:** bulletin.

382   CN
WISH TO IMPORT. 1993. m. $100. Global Traders Association, P.O. Box 797, Sta. A, Scarborough, ON M1K 5C8, Canada. TEL 416-650-9309. FAX 416-650-9280. Ed. K. Bhattacharyya. bk.rev.; charts; illus.; stat.; circ. 300 (paid). **Document type:** newsletter.
   Description: Lists consumer and commercial ventures wishing to import goods.

WOOD PRODUCTS: INTERNATIONAL TRADE AND FOREIGN MARKETS. see AGRICULTURE — *Agricultural Economics*

382   TS
WORLD ARAB TRADE. 1947. q. Mussad Bader Al Sayer Establishment, c/o Zabeel Printing Press, P.O. Box 5143, Dubai, United Arab Emirates. FAX 229504. adv. circ. 12,580.

382 614.7   UN   ISSN 1014-8132
HC79.E5
THE WORLD BANK AND THE ENVIRONMENT. 1990. a. World Bank, International Bank for Reconstruction and Development, 1818 H St., N.W., Washington, DC 20433. TEL 202-473-1155. FAX 202-522-2627. E-mail: books@worldbank.org. (U.S. orders to: Box 7247-8619, Philadelphia, PA 19170-8619; And: 66 av. D'lena, 75116 Paris, France. TEL 1-40-69-30-55. FAX 33-1-40-69-30-68)

332.6   US   ISSN 1081-3284
WORLD BUSINESS REVIEW. (Text in English; summaries in Chinese) 1991. bi-m. $20.95 (foreign $39.95). World Business Research Center, Box 11437, Baltimore, MD 21239. TEL 410-685-0032. FAX 410-661-0032. Ed. Patrick Ngwolo. R&P contact: Patrick Ngwolo. adv. contact: William Dadson. circ. 10,000. **Document type:** trade publication.
   Description: Analyzes national and global business, along with political events affecting business for manufacturers, importers and exporters, bankers, and investors.

WORLD COFFEE & TEA. see *BEVERAGES*

382   II   ISSN 0084-1501
WORLD COMMERCE ANNUAL. (Text in English) 1967. a. £9. Business Publications International, United India Life Building, Box 548, F-Block, Connaught Place, New Delhi 1, India. Ed. K.L. Saghal. adv. circ. 10,000. (back issues avail.)

WORLD DIRECTORY OF LINER SHIPPING AGENTS. see BUSINESS AND ECONOMICS — *Trade And Industrial Directories*

WORLD DIRECTORY OF NON-OFFICIAL STATISTICS SOURCES. see BUSINESS AND ECONOMICS — *Abstracting, Bibliographies, Statistics*

THE WORLD ECONOMY. see BUSINESS AND ECONOMICS

382 332   US
WORLD GUIDE FOR EXPORTERS. m. $535. Global Business Communications, Box 99, Gillette, NJ 07933. TEL 908-665-2255.
   Incorporates: Export Credit Reports.

WORLD OIL TRADE. see *PETROLEUM AND GAS*

382   US
WORLD RISK ANALYSIS REPORTS. a. $2000 (includes 3 supplements). S.J. Rundt & Associates, Inc., 130 E. 63rd St., New York, NY 10021-7334. TEL 212-838-0141. Ed. Hans P. Belcsak. stat. (also avail. in diskette format)
   Description: Covers international trade and currency concerns, providing specific country risk analyses for 56 countries.

WORLD STAINLESS STEEL STATISTICS. see METALLURGY — *Abstracting, Bibliographies, Statistics*

382   II   ISSN 0043-9142
WORLD TRADE. (Text in English) 1964. s-a. Rs.3($2.) Onlooker Publications Pvt. Ltd., 20-G Sleater Rd., Bombay 7, India. Ed. N.K. Kanga. circ. 5,000.

382   US   ISSN 1054-8637
HF1371
WORLD TRADE. (Former name of issuing body: Taipan Press, Inc.) 1987. m. $24 (foreign $50). Freedom Magazines, Inc., 17700 Cowan, Ste. 100, Irvine, CA 92714-6035. TEL 714-798-3500. Ed. J.L. Sullivan; Pub. Christopher O. Schulz. adv.; bk.rev. circ. 62,000. (also avail. in microform from UMI) **Document type:** trade publication.
   ●Also available online. Vendor(s): UMI.
   —BLDSC (9360.151500); UMI. **CCC.**
   Description: Directed to senior executives of U.S.-based international companies focusing on banking, finance, computers and communications, insurance, and other business topics.

382 341.522   NE   ISSN 1022-6583
K27
WORLD TRADE AND ARBITRATION MATERIALS. bi-m. fl.550 to institutions; $282.50 to institutions in U.S. (effective 1998). Kluwer Law International (Subsidiary of: Wolters Kluwer N.V.), Postbus 85889, 2508 CN The Hague, Netherlands. TEL 31-70-3081500. FAX 31-70-3081515. E-mail: services@wkap.nl; URL: http://www.wkap.nl. (Dist. by: Kluwer Academic Publishers Group, P.O. Box 322, 3300 AH Dordrecht, Netherlands. TEL 31-78-6392392. FAX 31-78-6546474; In N. America: Kluwer Law International, 675 Massachusetts Ave., Cambridge, MA 02139. TEL 617-354-0140. FAX 617-354-8595) Ed. Jacques Werner. (back issues avail.) **Document type:** bulletin.
   —SWETS; UnCover.
   Formed by the 1994 merger of: Arbitration Materials (ISSN 1013-7432) & World Trade Materials (ISSN 1013-4514)
   Description: Reports on the texts of current documents relating to international trade and arbitration.

WORLD TRADE ANNUAL. see BUSINESS AND ECONOMICS — *Abstracting, Bibliographies, Statistics*

WORLD TRADE ANNUAL SUPPLEMENT. see BUSINESS AND ECONOMICS — *Abstracting, Bibliographies, Statistics*

382   II
WORLDWIDE BUSINESS COLLABORATIONS - CONSULTANTS NEWS AND BUSINESS OPPORTUNITIES. 1977. w. Rs.615($75) International Press Cutting Service, P.O. Box 121, Allahabad 211001, India. Ed. Nandi Khanna. (looseleaf format) **Document type:** newsletter.
   Formerly: World Business Opportunities - Consultants News.

382   II   ISSN 1069-4447
WORLDWIDE BUSINESS PRACTICES REPORT. m. $195. International Cultural Enterprises, Inc., Box 514, Deerfield, IL 60015. TEL 800-626-2772. FAX 708-945-9614. Pub. Yuri Kovalenko. **Document type:** newsletter.
   Description: Dedicated to helping busy international executives conduct successful business abroad. Offers practical recommendations and tips on how to successfully cope with a variety of situations abroad.

382   US   ISSN 0192-5512
TA1
WORLDWIDE PROJECTS. 1967-1987; N.S. 1993. 4/yr. $68 (foreign $78). (American Society of Civil Engineers) Intercontinental Media, Box 3410, Milford, CT 06460. TEL 203-874-1401. (Subscr. to: ASCE, 345 E. 47th St., New York, NY 10017-2398. TEL 800-548-ASCE. FAX 212-705-7179) Ed. Maria D'Aniello; Pub. James R. Coffey. R&P contact: Maria D'Aniello. adv. contact: James R. Coffey. circ. 16,000. **Document type:** trade publication.
   Formerly: Worldwide Projects and Installation Planning (ISSN 0091-4800)
   Description: Market news for international design engineers and construction companies.

350.827   US
HF1731.A32
THE YEAR IN TRADE: OPERATION OF THE TRADE AGREEMENTS PROGRAM. (Subseries of: U S I T C Publication (ISSN 0196-9153)) 1934. a. U.S. International Trade Commission, Office of Information Services, 500 E St., S.W., Washington, DC 20436. TEL 202-205-2000. (Orders to: Superintendent of Documents, U.S. Government Printing Office, Box 371954, Pittsburgh, PA 15250-7954. TEL 202-512-1800. FAX 202-512-2250) (also avail. in microfiche) **Document type:** government publication.
   Formerly (until 1990): Operation of the Trade Agreements Program (ISSN 0083-3444)
   Description: Highlights major American trade policy developments.

YEAR BOOK OF INTERNATIONAL EXHIBITIONS. see *PACKAGING*

YEARBOOK OF ISRAEL PORTS STATISTICS/SHENATON STATISTI: LE NEMLEI ISRAEL. see BUSINESS AND ECONOMICS — *Abstracting, Bibliographies, Statistics*

YINJIN YU ZIXUN/IMPORTING AND CONSULTING. see BUSINESS AND ECONOMICS — *Investments*

YUGOSLAV EXPORT - IMPORT DIRECTORY. see BUSINESS AND ECONOMICS — *Trade And Industrial Directories*

382   XV   ISSN 0352-6828
YUGOSLAVIA ECHO; economy - finance - trade. (Text in English) 1961. q. $10. Gospodarski Vestnik - Economic Courier, Miklosiceva 38, 61000 Ljubljana, Slovenia. FAX 3861-311-871. TELEX 31255. Ed. Dusan Snoj. adv.; charts; illus.; stat. circ. 6,000.
   Formerly: Economic Echo from Yugoslavia (ISSN 0012-916X)

050   GW   ISSN 0938-7870
ZENTRALMARKT. 1946. w. DM.129 (foreign DM.169). Max Schimmel Verlag GmbH, Im Kreuz 9, 97076 Wuerzburg, Germany. TEL 0931-2791400. FAX 0931-2791444. Ed. Martina Schimmel-Schloo; Pub. Annemarie Schimmel. adv. contact: Gudrun Schimmel-Wanner. **Document type:** trade publication.

382.7   CC   ISSN 1001-0637
ZHONGGUO HAIGUAN/CHINA CUSTOMS. (Text in Chinese) m. $41.30. (Haiguan Zongshu - General Office of China Customs) Zhongguo Haiguan Bianjibu, 4 Taipingqiao Dajie, Beijing 100810, People's Republic of China. TEL 6011155. (Dist. in US by: China Books & Periodicals, Inc., 2929 24th St., San Francisco, CA 94110. TEL 415-282-2994) Ed. Yang Bingyue.

382   CC
ZHONGGUO MAOYI BAO/CHINA TRADE NEWS. (Text in Chinese) 1988. 3/w. (Zhongguo Guoji Maoyi Cujin Weiyuanhui) Zhongguo Maoyi Bao Bianjibu, No.2 Building, Jing'an Xijie, Beisanhuan Donglu, Chaoyang Qu, Beijing 100028, People's Republic of China. TEL 86-10-4667277. (Dist. overseas by: China International Book Trading Corp., P.O. Box 399, Beijing 100044, P.R. China) (Co-sponsor: Zhongguo Guoji Shanghui) **Document type:** newspaper.
   Description: Covers Chinese import and export as well as international market situation and trends.

382   CC
ZHONGGUO YINJIN BAO/CHINA IMPORT NEWS. (Text in English) 2/w. (Guojia Waiguo Zhuanjia Ju) Zhongguo Yinjin Bao Bianjibu, 1 Dingfu Jie, Xicheng, Beijing 100009, People's Republic of China. TEL 86-10-6030106. FAX 86-10-6011677. (Dist. overseas by: China International Book Trading Corp., P.O. Box 399, Beijing 100044, P.R. China) Ed. Wang Zuoli. **Document type:** newspaper.
   Description: Provides up-to-date information on Chinese import of technology, equipment, capital and management experiences as well as related policies and regulations.

ZIMBABWE EXPORT DIRECTORY. see BUSINESS AND ECONOMICS — *Trade And Industrial Directories*

ZISE; told- og skattehistorisk tidsskrift. see BUSINESS AND ECONOMICS — *Public Finance, Taxation*

BUSINESS AND ECONOMICS — INTERNATIONAL DEVELOPMENT AND ASSISTANCE

332.6   GW
DAS ZOLL- UND VERBRAUCHSSTEUERSTRAFRECHT. irreg. (1-2/yr.). DM.58. Walhalla Fachverlag, Haus an der Eisernen Bruecke, 93059 Regensburg, Germany. TEL 49-941-5684-0.
FAX 49-941-5684111. E-mail: walhalla@walhalla.de; URL: http://www.walhalla.de. adv. circ. 600. (looseleaf format) **Document type:** bulletin.

332.6   AU
ZOLLWACHT. bi-m. Flossgasse 6, Postfach 6, A-1025 Vienna, Austria. TEL 01-332383. Ed. Herwig Jordan.

332.6   SZ
ZUELLNER. 26/yr. Postes, Telephones et Telegraphes Suisses, Monbijoustr. 130, CH-3000 Bern 23, Switzerland. TEL 031-452886. FAX 031-460592. Ed. Jean-Marc Eggenberger. circ. 4,000. **Document type:** bulletin.

382   US   ISSN 1063-0503
HF3833
3 W REGISTER OF CHINESE BUSINESS.* 1992. a. 3 W International Digital Publishing Corporation, 42-10 82nd St., Apt. 6N, Elmhurst, NY 11373-3508. Ed.Bd.

BUSINESS AND ECONOMICS — International Development And Assistance

338.9   LY
A C A R T S O D MONOGRAPH SERIES. Variant series title: African Social Challenges. 1990. irreg., vol.4, 1991. African Centre for Applied Research and Training in Social Development, P.O. Box 80606, Tripoli, Libya. TEL 218-21-833640. (Dist. by: Hans Zell Publishers (Subsidiary of: Bowker - Saur Ltd.), P.O. Box 56, Oxford OX1 2SJ, England. TEL 44-856-511428; N. American subscr. to: K.G. Saur, A Reed Reference Publishing Company, 121 Chanlon Rd., New Providence, NJ 07974. TEL 908-665-3576) **Document type:** monographic series, proceedings.
Description: Scholarly research into social, labor, development issues and policies affecting Africa.

360   LY
A C A R T S O D NEWSLETTER. (Text in Arabic, English, French) 1980. q. free. African Centre for Applied Research and Training in Social Development, P.O. Box 80606, Tripoli, Libya. TEL 218-21-833640. TELEX 20803. Ed. Oscar Gasana. circ. 1,500. (back issues avail.) **Document type:** newsletter.

338.91   CN   ISSN 1192-1846
A C C C INTERNATIONAL. (Text in English, French) 1990. q. Association of Canadian Community Colleges, 1223 Michael St. N., Ste. 200, Ottawa, ON K1J 7T2, Canada. TEL 613-746-2222.
FAX 613-746-6721. E-mail: lmalcolmson@cccc.ca; URL: http://www.accc.ca. Ed. Lorna Malcomson. circ. 1,700. **Document type:** newsletter.
Description: Provides a forum for the discussion of issues pertinent to international development. Features the perspective and experience of the college and institute personnel.

338.91   370.196   AT   ISSN 0811-4692
A C F O A NEWS. 1982. irreg., approx. 6/yr. Aus.$10 (foreign Aus.$15) (effective 1997 & 1998). Australian Council for Overseas Aid, Pravate Bag 3, Deakin, A.C.T. 2600, Australia. TEL 61-6-2851816. FAX 61-2-2851720. Ed. Janet Hunt. circ. 1,500. **Document type:** newsletter.

338.91   EI
HC241.25.A3
A C P - E C COUNCIL OF MINISTERS. ANNUAL REPORT (YEAR). (Text in Danish, Dutch, English, French, German, Greek, Italian, Portuguese, Spanish) a., latest 1995. $10. Office for Official Publications of the European Communities, L-2985 Luxembourg, Luxembourg. URL: http://europa.eu.int. (Subscr. to: Bernan Associates, 4611-F Assembly Dr., Lanham, MD 20706-4391. TEL 800-274-4888. FAX 301-459-0056) Indexed: IIS.
—BLDSC (1095.814000).
Formerly (until 1995): A C P - E E C Council of Ministers. Annual Report (Year) (ISSN 1010-1446)
Description: Covers civil services, international organizations, trade and professional bodies, research foundations. Also of concern to individuals interested in the problems of development and co-operation.

338   PH
A D B REVIEW. (Text in English, French, German, Japanese) 1969. q. free. Asian Development Bank, Information Office, P.O. Box 789, 1099 Manila, Philippines. TEL 63-2-711-3851.
FAX 63-2-741-7961. TELEX 29066 ADB PH. E-mail: adpub@mail.asiandevbank.org. charts; illus.; stat. (also avail. in microfiche from CIS) Indexed: IIS, Rural Recreat.Tour.Abstr., World Agri.Econ.& Rural Sociol.Abstr., World Bank.Abstr. **Document type:** bulletin.
Former titles: A D B Quarterly Review (ISSN 0194-9985); (until 1976): A D B Quarterly Newsletter; Asian Development Bank. Newsletter (ISSN 0044-9199)
Description: Reports on social, education, economic, and political issues in the bank's member nations. Reviews A.D.B. symposia and meetings, and offers economic statistics.

338.91   327   US   ISSN 0743-5436
A I D HIGHLIGHTS. 1984. q. free. U.S. Agency for International Development, Bureau for External Affairs, Washington, DC 20523-0056.
TEL 202-647-4330. FAX 202-647-3945. Ed. Jane Sanchez. circ. 100,000. **Document type:** government publication.

A P O ANNUAL REPORT. (Asian Productivity Organization) see BUSINESS AND ECONOMICS — Production Of Goods And Services

A P O NEWS. (Asian Productivity Organization) see BUSINESS AND ECONOMICS — Production Of Goods And Services

338.91   IO   ISSN 0854-543X
A S E A N ECONOMIC INFO VIEW. (Text in English) 1993. q. Association of South East Asian Nations, Bureau of Economic Cooperation, ASEAN Secretariat, 70A Jl. Sisingamangaraja, Jakarta 12110, Indonesia. TEL 021-716451. FAX 021-7398134. Ed.Bd. **Document type:** bulletin.

ACTION AFRICA. see RELIGIONS AND THEOLOGY

338.9   FR   ISSN 0395-9481
HC59.7
ACTUEL DEVELOPPEMENT. 1974. bi-m. 85 F.($19) Groupement d'Edition et d'Information Technique, Economique et Culturelle, 18 rue de Varenne, 75007 Paris, France. Ed. Robert Ginesy. adv.; bk.rev.; bibl. circ. 16,000. Indexed: Geo.Abstr., Rural Recreat.Tour.Abstr., World Agri.Econ.& Rural Sociol.Abstr.
Formed by the merger of: Cahiers d'Agriculture Pratique des Pays Chauds (ISSN 0007-9677) & Cooperation Technique (ISSN 0010-8383) & Cooperation et Developpement (ISSN 0010-8375) & Techniques et Developpement.

338.91   BD
ADMINISTRATION, GESTION, FORMATION. 1982. q. (Ministere de la Fonction Publique) Centre de Perfectionnement et de Formation en Cours d'Emploi, B.P. 732, Bujumbura, Burundi. Indexed: P.L.E.S.A. **Document type:** government publication.

338   SG   ISSN 0850-3907
HC501
AFRICA DEVELOPMENT. (Text in English, French) 1976. q. $30 to individuals; institutions $45 (effective 1997). Council for the Development of Social Science Research in Africa, B.P. 3304, Dakar, Senegal. FAX 24-12-89. TELEX 61339 CODES SG. URL: http://wsi.cso.uiuc.edu/CAS/Codesria/afdev.htm. Ed. Tade Akin Aina. adv.; index. (back issues avail.) Indexed: Abstr.Anthropol., Curr.Cont.Africa, Documentatieblad, Geo.Abstr., IBR, Int.Lab.Doc., Per.Islam. (1992-), Rural Recreat.Tour.Abstr., World Agri.Econ.& Rural Sociol.Abstr.
—BLDSC (0732.154800).

338   UK   ISSN 0141-3929
HC800.A1
AFRICAN BUSINESS. 1978. m. £36($90) (overseas £50) (effective 1997). I.C. Publications Ltd., 7 Coldbath Sq., London EC1R 4LQ, England. TEL 44-171-713-7711. FAX 44-171-713-7898. E-mail: icpubs@dial.pipex.com. Ed. Anver Versi; Pub. Afif Ben Tedder. R&P contact: Carole Jones. adv.; bk.rev.; illus.; stat. circ. 16,433. (also avail. in microfilm from UMI; back issues avail.) Indexed: B.P.I., Key to Econ.Sci., P.A.I.S., PROMT. **Document type:** trade publication.
● Also available online.
—BLDSC (0732.370000); KR SourceOne; SWETS; UMI. CCC.
Description: Provides pan-African coverage of business: economics, industry, marketing and commodities for executives living in and trading with Africa.

AFRICAN DEVELOPMENT BANK. COMPENDIUM OF STATISTICS/BANQUE AFRICAINE DE DEVELOPPEMENT. COMPENDIUM DE STATISTIQUES. see BUSINESS AND ECONOMICS — Abstracting, Bibliographies, Statistics

AFRICAN DEVELOPMENT BANK. ECONOMIC RESEARCH PAPERS. see BUSINESS AND ECONOMICS — Economic Situation And Conditions

338.9   IV   ISSN 0568-1308
AFRICAN DEVELOPMENT BANK. REPORT BY THE BOARD OF DIRECTORS/BANQUE AFRICAINE DE DEVELOPPEMENT. RAPPORT DU CONSEIL D'ADMINISTRATION. Cover title: African Development Bank. Annual Report. French cover title: Banque Africaine de Developpement. Rapport Annuel. 1966. a. African Development Bank, B.P. 1387, Abidjan 01, Ivory Coast. TEL 20-44-44. FAX 22-78-39. TELEX 23717. (also avail. in microfiche from CIS) Indexed: IIS. **Document type:** corporate report.

AFRICAN DEVELOPMENT BANK. SELECTED STATISTICS ON REGIONAL MEMBER COUNTRIES/BANQUE AFRICAINE DE DEVELOPPEMENT. STATISTIQUES CHOISIES SUR LES PAYS-MEMBRES REGIONAUX. see BUSINESS AND ECONOMICS — Abstracting, Bibliographies, Statistics

338.91   IV
AFRICAN DEVELOPMENT FUND. ANNUAL REPORT/FONDS AFRICAIN DE DEVELOPPEMENT. RAPPORT ANNUEL. 1974. a. free. (African Development Fund) African Development Bank, B.P. 1387, Abidjan 01, Ivory Coast. TEL 20-44-44. FAX 22-78-39. TELEX 23717. circ. 5,000. **Document type:** corporate report.

338.96   IV
AFRICAN DEVELOPMENT REPORT/RAPPORT SUR LE DEVELOPPEMENT EN AFRIQUE. a. $5 to individuals (outside Africa $20); institutions $15 (outside Africa $25). African Development Bank, Development Research and Policy Department - Banque Africaine de Developpement, Departement de la Recherche et Politique de Developpement, B.P. 1387, Abidjan 01, Ivory Coast. TEL 225-20-44-44. FAX 225-20-49-48.
Description: Covers recent economic developments in Africa, provides in-depth analysis of a development policy issues of major importance to Africa and updated statistical information on the African economies.

338.91   IV   ISSN 1017-6772
HC800.A1
AFRICAN DEVELOPMENT REVIEW/REVUE AFRICAINE DE DEVELOPPEMENT. 1989. s-a. $5 to individuals in Africa (elsewhere $15); institutions $10 (elsewhere $20). African Development Bank - Banque Africaine de Developpement, B.P. 1387, Abidjan 01, Ivory Coast. URL: http://www.dfait-maeci.gc.ca/ifinet/afdb-e.html. charts; stat. Indexed: Documentatieblad, Geo.Abstr.H.G., Geo.Abstr.
—BLDSC (0732.412000).
Description: Offers study and analysis of development issues in Africa.
Refereed Serial

B

BUSINESS AND ECONOMICS — INTERNATIONAL DEVELOPMENT AND ASSISTANCE

338.9 SG
AFRICAN INSTITUTE FOR ECONOMIC DEVELOPMENT AND PLANNING. PROSPECTUS. (Text in English, French) 1972. a. free. African Institute for Economic Development and Planning, B.P. 3186, Dakar, Senegal. FAX 221-22-29-64. TELEX 51579 IDEP SG.
Formerly: African Institute for Economic Development and Planning. Programme.

AFRICAN URBAN QUARTERLY. see *HOUSING AND URBAN PLANNING*

338.91 327 GW ISSN 0947-8353
AFRIKA SUED. 1971. 6/yr. DM.50 to individuals; institutions DM.70. Informationsstelle Suedliches Afrika (I.S.S.A.), Koenigswintererstr. 116, 53227 Bonn, Germany. TEL 49-228-464369. FAX 49-228-468177. Ed. Hein Moellers. adv.; bk.rev. circ. 2,500. (back issues avail.) Document type: bulletin.
Formerly (until 1994): Informationsdienst Suedliches Afrika (ISSN 0721-5088)
Description: Covers political, social and economic development in southern Africa.

330 FR ISSN 0002-0540
AFRIQUE SERVICE. 1960. bi-m. 500 F. 23 rue de Cheroy, 75017 Paris, France. Ed. Jacques Neme. bk.rev. (processed)

338 UA ISSN 0002-0613
AFRO ASIAN ECONOMIC REVIEW.* (Text in English) 1959. bi-m. $7. Afro-Asian Organization for Economic Co-Operation, Cairo Chamber of Commerce Bldg., Midan el Falaky, 4, Cairo, Egypt. Ed. Emad el Rashidi. adv.; charts; illus.; stat. Indexed: Amer.Hist.& Life (1973-), Hist.Abstr. (1973-).

338.91 CC
ALMANAC OF CHINA'S FOREIGN ECONOMIC RELATIONS AND TRADE. Chinese edition: Zhongguo Duiwai Jingji Maoyi Nianjian. (Editions in Chinese, English) 1984. a. HK.$700($90) for English edition; Chinese edition HK.$540($70). (Ministry of Foreign Economic Relations and Trade - Duiwai Jingji Maoyi Bu) China Resources Advertising Co. Ltd., 40-F, High Block, China Resources Bldg., 26 Harbour Rd., Wanchai, Hong Kong, People's Republic of China. TEL 2593-8831. FAX 2827-5453. TELEX 76757-CRACL-HX. Ed. Mudefu. adv.; stat. circ. 10,000. (back issues avail.) Document type: trade publication.
Description: Contains statistics and information on the PRC's imports and exports, utilization of foreign capital, contracted projects and labor service cooperation, foreign economic aid, and bilateral or multilateral economic and technical cooperation.

ALPHA (YEAR): CURRENT RESEARCH IN LITERACY. see *EDUCATION*

338.91 334 327 US ISSN 0892-2950
ALTERNATIVE TRADING NEWS. 1975. q. $10 (effective 1995). Friends of Third World, Inc., 611 W. Wayne St., Ft. Wayne, IN 46802-2167. TEL 219-422-6821. FAX 219-422-1650. E-mail: fotw@igc.apc.org. Ed. Jim Goetsch; Pub. Marian Waltz. R&P contact: Jim Goetsch. adv. contact: Marian Waltz. bk.rev.; bibl. circ. 12,000. (looseleaf format) Document type: newsletter.
Formerly: Friends in Action.
Description: News and informational items pertaining to the projects, educational resources, activities, and members of the Friends of the Third World, which promotes building the product exportation capabilities of poverty-prone countries to raise their standard of living.

AMERICAS UPDATE. see *POLITICAL SCIENCE — International Relations*

ANNUAL EDITIONS: DEVELOPING THIRD WORLD. see *GEOGRAPHY*

338.91 UN
ANNUAL REPORT ON DEVELOPMENT ASSISTANCE TO MAURITIUS. (Text in English) a. free. United Nations Development Programme, Office of the Resident Representative for Mauritius and the Seychelles, Box 253, Port Louis, Mauritius. Ed. Robert J. Utz. circ. 175. Document type: government publication.

ANNUAL THIRD WORLD CONFERENCE PROCEEDINGS. see *HISTORY*

ARAB BANK FOR ECONOMIC DEVELOPMENT IN AFRICA. ANNUAL REPORT. see *BUSINESS AND ECONOMICS — Banking And Finance*

338.9 KU ISSN 0304-6729
HC498.A1
ARAB FUND FOR ECONOMIC AND SOCIAL DEVELOPMENT. ANNUAL REPORT. (Text in Arabic, English) 1973. a. free. Arab Fund for Economic and Social Development, P.O. Box 21923, Safat, Kuwait. illus. (also avail. in microfiche from CIS) Indexed: IIS. Document type: corporate report.

ARISE; a women's developmental magazine. see *WOMEN'S INTERESTS*

338.91 UK ISSN 1360-7456
AS741
ASIA-PACIFIC VIEWPOINT; specialises in the study of development, change and underdevelopment. 1960. 3/yr. £43($68) (effective 1997). (Victoria University of Wellington, Department of Geography, NZ) Blackwell Publishers Ltd., 108 Cowley Rd., Oxford OX4 1JF, England. TEL 44-1865-791100. FAX 44-1865-791347. E-mail: jnlinfo@blackwellpublishers.co.uk; URL: http://www.blackwellpublishers.co.uk. Eds. R.T. Lawrence, P. Morrison. adv.; bk.rev.; charts; illus.; maps. circ. 850. (also avail. in microfilm from UMI; back issues avail.) Indexed: Amer.Hist.& Life (1974-), Anthropol.Lit., Asian-Pac.Econ.Lit., Geo.Abstr.P.G., Hist.Abstr. (1974-), IBR, IDA, Int.Polit.Sci.Abstr., Key to Econ.Sci., So.Pac.Per.Ind. Document type: academic/scholarly publication.
—KR SourceOne. CCC.
Formerly (until 1996): Pacific Viewpoint (ISSN 0030-8978)
Refereed Serial

ASIAN DEVELOPMENT BANK. ANNUAL REPORT. see *BUSINESS AND ECONOMICS — Banking And Finance*

332.1 PH ISSN 0066-8389
ASIAN DEVELOPMENT BANK. BOARD OF GOVERNORS. SUMMARY OF PROCEEDINGS.. 1968. a. Asian Development Bank, P.O. Box 789, 1099 Manila, Philippines. TEL 632-711-3851. FAX 632-741-7961. TELEX 29066-ADB-PH.
Description: Records the bank's annual meeting.

ASIAN DEVELOPMENT BANK. KEY INDICATORS OF DEVELOPING ASIAN AND PACIFIC COUNTRIES. see *BUSINESS AND ECONOMICS — Banking And Finance*

338.91 PH ISSN 0116-1105
HC411
ASIAN DEVELOPMENT REVIEW; studies of Asian and Pacific economic issues. (Text in English) 1983. s-a. $8. Asian Development Bank, Information Office, P.O. Box 789, 1099 Manila, Philippines. TEL 63-2-711-3851. FAX 63-2-741-7961. TELEX 63587 ADB PN. URL: http://www.asiandeubank.org/ready/pubs.html. Ed. Satish C. Jha. (also avail. in microfiche from CIS; back issues avail.; reprint service avail.) Indexed: Abstr.Rural Dev.Trop., Asian-Pac.Econ.Lit., Geo.Abstr.H.G., IDA, IIS, J.of Ferroc., P.A.I.S., Pub.Admin.Abstr., Rural Devel.Abstr., World Agri.Econ.& Rural Sociol.Abstr., World Bank.Abstr.
—BLDSC (1742.407750); SWETS; UnCover.
Description: Covers economic issues in the Asia-Pacific region. Focuses on questions of development.

ASIAN ECONOMIC AND SOCIAL REVIEW; techno-economic quarterly of Asian co-operation. see *SOCIAL SCIENCES: COMPREHENSIVE WORKS*

ASIAN ECONOMIES/AJIA KEIZAI. see *BUSINESS AND ECONOMICS*

ASIAN-PACIFIC ECONOMIC LITERATURE. see *BUSINESS AND ECONOMICS — Abstracting, Bibliographies, Statistics*

338.91 AT ISSN 0818-0512
AUSTRALIAN NATIONAL UNIVERSITY. NATIONAL CENTRE FOR DEVELOPMENT STUDIES. ANNUAL REPORT (YEAR). Key Title: Annual Report - National Centre for Development Studies. 1985. a. Australian National University, National Centre for Development Studies, Canberra, A.C.T. 0200, Australia. TEL 61-6-249-4705. FAX 61-6-257-2886. Ed. Maree Tait. Document type: corporate report.
Description: Summarizes the Centre's past year's activities, including programs sponsored, research results, graduate studies and scholarships.

338.91 AT ISSN 0815-6301
AUSTRALIAN NATIONAL UNIVERSITY. NATIONAL CENTRE FOR DEVELOPMENT STUDIES. HISTORY OF DEVELOPMENT STUDIES. 1985. irreg. price varies. Australian National University, National Centre for Development Studies, Canberra, A.C.T. 0200, Australia. TEL 61-6-2494705. FAX 61-6-2572886. Ed. Maree Tait. Document type: monographic series.
—BLDSC (4317.972000).
Description: A monograph series that details the life and work of prominent development economists.

338.91 AT ISSN 1030-1976
AUSTRALIAN NATIONAL UNIVERSITY. NATIONAL CENTRE FOR DEVELOPMENT STUDIES. INDIAN OCEAN POLICY PAPERS. 1988. irreg., no.3, 1994. price varies. Australian National University, National Centre for Development Studies, Canberra, A.C.T. 0200, Australia. TEL 616-249-4705. FAX 616-257-2886. Ed. Maree Tait. Indexed: Geo.Abstr.H.G. Document type: monographic series.
—BLDSC (4425.180000).
Description: Policy-oriented research monographs on the Indian Ocean island economies and their economic performance.

338.91 AT
AUSTRALIAN NATIONAL UNIVERSITY. NATIONAL CENTRE FOR DEVELOPMENT STUDIES. PROCEEDINGS. irreg. price varies. Australian National University, National Centre for Development Studies, Canberra, A.C.T. 0200, Australia. TEL 61-6-2494705. FAX 61-6-2572886. Ed. Maree Tait. Document type: proceedings.

AUSTRALIAN NATIONAL UNIVERSITY. NATIONAL CENTRE FOR DEVELOPMENT STUDIES. PACIFIC ECONOMIC BULLETIN. see *BUSINESS AND ECONOMICS — Economic Situation And Conditions*

338.91 AT ISSN 0817-0444
AUSTRALIAN NATIONAL UNIVERSITY. NATIONAL CENTRE FOR DEVELOPMENT STUDIES. PACIFIC POLICY PAPERS. 1987. irreg. price varies. Australian National University, National Centre for Development Studies, Canberra, A.C.T. 0200, Australia. TEL 61-6-2494705. FAX 61-6-2572886. Ed. Maree Tait. Indexed: Geo.Abstr.P.G., IDA. Document type: monographic series.
—BLDSC (6330.807000).
Description: Covers economics, trade, development and policy issues.

338.91 AT ISSN 1034-1471
AUSTRALIAN NATIONAL UNIVERSITY. NATIONAL CENTRE FOR DEVELOPMENT STUDIES. REPRINT SERIES. 1989. irreg. free. Australian National University, National Centre for Development Studies, Canberra, A.C.T. 0200, Australia. TEL 61-6-249-4705. FAX 61-6-257-2886. Ed. Maree Tait. (looseleaf format; back issues avail.)
Description: Reprints of selected articles published in academic journals by staff members of the National Centre for Development Studies.

B I D S MONOGRAPH. see *SOCIOLOGY*

338.91 301 BG
B I D S NEWSLETTER. (Text in English) 1985. m. Bangladesh Unnayan Gobeshona Protishthan - Bangladesh Institute of Development Studies, G.P.O. Box 3854, E-17 Agargaon, Sher-e-Banglanagar, Dhaka 1207, Bangladesh. TEL 325041. Eds. Atiq Rahman, Trina Haque. abstr.; bibl.; stat. Document type: newsletter.
Description: Presents research on development problems of Bangladesh and promotes dissemination of knowledge regarding these issues.

B I D S RESEARCH REPORTS. see *SOCIOLOGY*

B I D S WORKING PAPER. see *SOCIOLOGY*

BUSINESS AND ECONOMICS — INTERNATIONAL DEVELOPMENT AND ASSISTANCE

338.9   GW
B M Z - MATERIALIEN. 1970. bi-m. free. Bundesministerium fuer Wirtschaftliche Zusammenarbeit und Entwicklung, Friedrich-Ebert-Allee 114-116, 53113 Bonn, Germany. **Document type:** government publication.

338.91   SG   ISSN 0966-9035
DT800.A1
BAOBAB. 1990. 3/yr. $30 (effective 1998). Alin - Arid Lands Information Network, Casier Postal 3, Dakar-Fann, Senegal. TEL 221-251808. FAX 221-254521. E-mail: ritaalin@sonatel.sonet.net. Ed. Robert C. Wagner. bk.rev.; circ. 200 (controlled). (back issues avail.) **Document type:** bulletin, newsletter.
    Description: Offers community development news.

338.91   BH
BELIZE EXTERNAL TRADE BULLETIN. q. $25 (effective 1997). Ministry of Finance, Central Statistical Office, Belmopan, Belize. TEL 501-8-22352. FAX 501-8-23206. URL: csogob@btl.net. charts; stat. **Document type:** government publication, bulletin.
    Description: Records trade activity in Belize. Focuses on the country's gross imports, retained imports, re-exports, domestic exports, transhipment, and visible balance of trade. Includes brief commentaries and analysis.

BIJEEN; mensen mondiaal. see *RELIGIONS AND THEOLOGY*

BOSTON THIRD WORLD LAW JOURNAL. see *LAW — International Law*

338.91   CN   ISSN 0833-9864
BOUT DE PAPIER. 1973. q. Can.$16($20) (foreign Can.$26) (effective 1997). Professional Association of Foreign Service Officers, 45 Rideau St., Ste 600, Ottawa, ON K1N 5W8, Canada. TEL 613-241-1391. FAX 613-241-5911. Ed. Kevin O'Shea. adv.: page Can.$475; trim 8 1/2 x 11; adv. contact: Debra Hulley. (back issues avail.)
    Description: Examines all aspects of Canadian foreign policy and life in the foreign service.

BRATISLAVA. see *HOUSING AND URBAN PLANNING*

BRITISH AID STATISTICS; statistics of U.K. economic aid to developing countries and countries of Central and Eastern Europe, and the former Soviet Union. see *BUSINESS AND ECONOMICS — Abstracting, Bibliographies, Statistics*

BRITISH COUNCIL ANNUAL REPORT AND ACCOUNTS (YEAR). see *EDUCATION — Higher Education*

338.91   UK   ISSN 0950-9607
BRITISH OVERSEAS AID ANNUAL REVIEW. a. free. Overseas Development Administration, Publications Section, Abercrombie House, Eaglesham Rd., East Kilbride, Glasgow G75 8EA, Scotland. TEL 44-1355-843599. FAX 44-1355-844099. **Document type:** government publication.
—BLDSC (2332.660000).

338.9   UK
BRITISH OVERSEAS DEVELOPMENT. 1966. 6/yr. free. Overseas Development Administration, Information Department, 94 Victoria St., London SW1E 5JL, England. URL: http://www.oneworld.org/oda. Ed. Carolyn Oxlee. R&P contact: Carolyn Oxlee. bk.rev. circ. 25,000. **Indexed:** Agri.Eng.Abstr., Apic.Abstr., IDA. **Document type:** government publication, newspaper.
—CCC.
    Formerly (until Apr. 1988): Overseas Development (ISSN 0030-7440)

BULLETIN DE L'AFRIQUE NOIRE. see *POLITICAL SCIENCE*

BUSINESS COUNCIL FOR THE U N BRIEFING. see *POLITICAL SCIENCE — International Relations*

BUSINESS P R C; an informative bridge between China and the world. see *BUSINESS AND ECONOMICS — International Commerce*

338.91 226   UK
C A F O D MAGAZINE. 1993. 3/yr. free. Catholic Fund for Overseas Development, Romero Close, Stockwell Rd., London SW9 9TY, England. TEL 0171-733-7900. FAX 0171-274-9630. TELEX 893347 CAFOD G. Ed. Christina Holt. bk.rev. circ. 20,000.

338.91 266   UK
C A F O D REPORT. 1966. s-a. free. Catholic Fund for Overseas Development, Romero Close, Stockwell Rd., London SW9 9TY, England. TEL 0171-733-7900. FAX 0171-274-9630. TELEX 893347 CAFOD G. circ. 220,000.
    Formerly (until 1992): C A F O D Journal.

338.91   FR
C C E INTERNATIONAL. 1911. m. (10/yr.). 490 F. Comite National des Conseillers du Commerce Exterieur, 22 av. Franklin Roosevelt, 75008 Paris, France. TEL 42508060. Ed. Madeleine Barbier Decrozes; Pub. Luc Lehericy. adv. contact: Luc Lehericy. bk.rev. circ. 2,900. **Indexed:** Key to Econ.Sci. **Document type:** trade publication, consumer publication.
    Formerly: Conseiller du Commerce Exterieur (ISSN 0294-8494)

330   DK   ISSN 0904-4701
HD72
C D R WORKING PAPER. (Text in English) 1969. irreg. Centre for Development Research - Center for Udviklingsforskning, Gammel Kongevej 5, DK-1610 Copenhagen V, Denmark. TEL 45-33-25-12-00. FAX 45-33-25-81-10. E-mail: cdr@cdr.dk. **Indexed:** Geo.Abstr.P.G., IDA. **Document type:** monographic series, academic/scholarly publication.
—EMDOCS; KR SourceOne.
    Description: Explores Third World socio-economic development issues.

C E D P A NETWORK. (Centre for Development and Population Activities) see *WOMEN'S INTERESTS*

338.9   CN   ISSN 0826-4228
C - F A R NEWSLETTER. 1976. m. Can.$16. Citizens for Foreign Aid Reform Inc., Box 332, Stn. B, Etobicoke, Ont. M9W 5L3, Canada. TEL 905-897-7221. FAX 905-277-3914. Ed. Paul Fromm. bk.rev.; circ. 1,500 (controlled). **Document type:** newsletter.
    Formerly (until 1983): C - F A R (ISSN 0711-5725)

C H F NEWSBRIEFS. (Cooperative Housing Foundation) see *HOUSING AND URBAN PLANNING*

338.91   US
C H R I A NEWS. 1983. q. $20 includes membership. Committee for Health Rights in the Americas, 474 Valencia St., Ste. 120, San Francisco, CA 94103-3415. TEL 415-431-7760. FAX 415-431-7768. Ed. Lazaro Cuevas. R&P contact: Lazaro Cuevas. bk.rev. **Document type:** newsletter.
    Formerly: C H R I C A News.
    Refereed Serial

C O D E S R I A BULLETIN. (Council for the Development of Social Science Research in Africa) see *HISTORY — History Of Africa*

338.91   CN   ISSN 0823-5740
C U S O FORUM. 1969. 2/yr. free. C U S O, 2255 Carling Ave., Ottawa, ON K2B 1A6, Canada. TEL 613-829-7445. FAX 613-829-7996. TELEX 053-4706. circ. 5,000. **Document type:** newsletter.

CANADIAN JOURNAL OF REGIONAL SCIENCE/REVUE CANADIENNE DES SCIENCES REGIONALES. see *BUSINESS AND ECONOMICS — Economic Systems And Theories, Economic History*

CARIBBEAN UPDATE. see *BUSINESS AND ECONOMICS — International Commerce*

338.91   BD
CENTRE UNIVERSITAIRE DE RECHERCHE POUR LE DEVELOPPEMENT ECONOMIQUE ET SOCIAL. CAHIERS. Cover title: Cahiers du C U R D E S. (Text in French) 1982. irreg., no.7, 1989. Universite de Burundi, Centre Universitaire de Recherche pour le Developpement Economique et Social, B.P. 1049, Bujumbura, Burundi. **Indexed:** P.L.E.S.A.

338.91   AT
CHINESE ECONOMIC ASSOCIATION PROCEEDINGS. 1989. irreg. price varies. Australian National University, National Centre for Development Studies, Canberra, A.C.T. 0200, Australia. TEL 61-6-2494705. FAX 61-6-2572886. (Subscr. to: Bibliotech, Canberra, A.C.T. 0200, Australia) Ed. Maree Tait. **Document type:** proceedings.
    Formerly: Chinese Students' Conference Proceedings.
    Description: Papers presented at annual seminars held amongst Chinese doctoral students studying in Australia and New Zealand. Covers topics related to reform, trade and development.

338.91   JA   ISSN 0910-8882
JX1395
CHUBU UNIVERSITY. COLLEGE OF INTERNATIONAL STUDIES. JOURNAL. Japanese edition: Kokusai Kankei Gakubu. Kiyo. 1985. approx.1/yr. exchange basis to libraries. Chubu University, College of International Studies, Kasugai, Aichi 487, Japan.

338.91   US   ISSN 1066-9531
HT101
CITIES INTERNATIONAL NEWSLETTER. (Text in English, French, Russian, Spanish) 1990. q. free. International City - County Management Association, 777 North Capitol St., N.E., Ste. 500, Washington, DC 20002-4201. TEL 202-962-3516. FAX 202-962-3681. E-mail: crothblum@icma.org. Ed. Corinne Rothblum. R&P contact: Corinne Rothblum. **Document type:** newsletter.
    Description: Reports on innovative municipal and urban programs worldwide.

338   CE
COLOMBO PLAN BUREAU. THE COLOMBO PLAN COUNCIL REPORT. (Text in English) 1951. a. free. (Colombo Plan for Co-Operative Economic and Social Development in Asia and the Pacific) Colombo Plan Bureau, 12 Melbourne Ave., P.O. Box 596, Colombo 4, Sri Lanka. TEL 94-1-581813. FAX 94-1-581754. TELEX 21537-METALIX-CE. Ed. J.P. Pathirana. circ. 1,500. **Document type:** newsletter, proceedings.
    Formerly: Colombo Plan Bureau. Technical Cooperation under the Colombo Plan. Report (ISSN 0069-5947)

338.9   CE
COLOMBO PLAN FOR CO-OPERATIVE ECONOMIC AND SOCIAL DEVELOPMENT IN ASIA AND THE PACIFIC. CONSULTATIVE COMMITTEE. PROCEEDINGS AND CONCLUSIONS. (Text in English) 1952. biennial. free. (Colombo Plan for Co-Operative Economic and Social Development in Asia and the Pacific) Colombo Plan Bureau, 12 Melbourne Ave., P.O. Box 596, Colombo 4, Sri Lanka. TEL 94-1-581813. FAX 94-1-581754. TELEX 21537-METALIX-CE. Ed. J.P. Pathirana. index, cum.index: 1952-1972. circ. 1,500. **Document type:** proceedings.
    Former titles: Colombo Plan for Co-operative Economic and Social Development in Asia and the Pacific. Consultative Committee. Report; Colombo Plan for Co-operative Economic Development in South and South-East Asia. Report of the Consultative Committee (ISSN 0069-5963)

338.9   CE
COLOMBO PLAN FOR CO-OPERATIVE ECONOMIC AND SOCIAL DEVELOPMENT IN ASIA AND THE PACIFIC. DEVELOPMENT PERSPECTIVES. COUNTRY ISSUES PAPERS BY MEMBER GOVERNMENTS TO THE CONSULTATIVE COMMITTEE. (Text in English) 1980. biennial. free. (Colombo Plan for Co-operative Economic and Social Development in Asia and the Pacific) Colombo Plan Bureau, 12 Melbourne Ave., P.O. Box 596, Colombo 4, Sri Lanka. TEL 94-1-581813. FAX 94-1-581754. TELEX 21537-METALIX-CE. Ed. J.P. Pathirana. cum.index. circ. 1,500. **Document type:** proceedings.
    Formerly: Colombo Plan for Co-operative Economic Development in South and South East Asia. Country Issues Papers.

338.9   CE   ISSN 0010-1419
HC411
COLOMBO PLAN NEWSLETTER. (Text in English) 1970. m. free. (Colombo Plan for Co-Operative Economic and Social Development in Asia and the Pacific) Colombo Plan Bureau, 12 Melbourne Ave., P.O. Box 596, Colombo 4, Sri Lanka. TEL 94-1-581813. FAX 94-1-581754. TELEX 21537-METALIX-CE. Ed. J.P. Pathirana. illus.; stat.; circ. 2,500 (controlled). **Document type:** newsletter.

BUSINESS AND ECONOMICS — INTERNATIONAL DEVELOPMENT AND ASSISTANCE

338.9   AU
COMECON DATA (YEAR). (Published in alternate years with: Comecon Foreign Trade Data (Year)) (Text in German; key and index in English) 1968. a. £40. Wiener Institut fuer Internationale Wirtschaftsvergleiche - Vienna Institute for Comparative Economic Studies, Oppolzergasse 6, A-1010 Vienna, Austria. circ. 1,200. **Document type:** trade publication.
Formerly (until 1979): R G W in Zahlen.

338.91   UN
COMISION ECONOMICA PARA AMERICA LATINA Y EL CARIBE. DESARROLLO PRODUCTIVO. irreg. Comision Economica para America Latina y el Caribe, Edificio Naciones Unidas, Av. Dag Hammarskjold, Casilla 179-D, Santiago, Chile.

338.911   UN
COMISION ECONOMICA PARA AMERICA LATINA Y EL CARIBE. SERIE FINANCIAMIENTO DEL DESARROLLO. irreg. Comision Economica para America Latina y el Caribe, Edificio Naciones Unidas, Av. Dag Hammarskjold, Casilla 179-D, Santiago, Chile.

338.91   UN   ISSN 0259-0107
COMISION ECONOMICA PARA AMERICA LATINA Y EL CARIBE. SERIE INFOPLAN; temas especiales del desarrollo. 1986. irreg. $10 per no. Comision Economica para America Latina y el Caribe - Economic Commission for Latin America and the Caribbean, Casilla 179-D, Santiago, Chile. FAX 562480252.

338.91   UY
COMISION SECTORIAL PARA EL MERCOSUR. BOLETIN. q.? Comision Sectorial para el Mercosur, Paysandu 919, Montevideo, Uruguay. TEL 91-55-56. FAX 92-36-55.

COMMODITY MARKETS AND THE DEVELOPING COUNTRIES. see BUSINESS AND ECONOMICS — Investments

338.9   UK   ISSN 0967-0130
COMMON CAUSE; open the window on the developing world. 1989. s-a. free to supporters. ACTIONAID, Hamlyn House, Macdonald Rd., Archway, London N19 5PG, England. TEL 44-171-281-4101. FAX 44-171-272-0899. TELEX 266272 ACTAID G. E-mail: mail@actionaid.org.uk; URL: http://www.actionaid.org. Ed. Kay Parris. R&P contact: Kay Parris. adv. contact: Vermira Nelson-Okrapor. bk.rev.; charts; stat.; index. circ. 120,000. (also avail. in Braille) **Document type:** consumer publication.
Description: Serves as ACTIONAID's supporter magazine.

338.91   US
COMMUNIQUE (TALLAHASSEE); the newsletter of Florida's unique development partnership with the Caribbean and Central America. 1982. q. $35 donation. Florida Association of Voluntary Agencies for Caribbean Action, 1311 Executive Center Dr., No. 202, Tallahassee, FL 32301-5029. TEL 904-877-4705. Ed. David A. Pasquarelli. R&P contact: David Pasquarelli. adv. circ. 2,300. (back issues avail.) **Document type:** newsletter.
Description: Covers the work of the Florida International Volunteer Corps, which conducts training and provides technical assistance by request to Caribbean and Central American nations.

COMMUNIQUE (WASHINGTON, 1971). see BUSINESS AND ECONOMICS

338.6   FR   ISSN 1013-0020
COMPETITION POLICY IN O E C D COUNTRIES. Title varies. (Text in English) 1972. a. price varies. Organization for Economic Cooperation and Development, 2 rue Andre-Pascal, 75775 Paris Cedex 16, France. (U.S. orders to: O.E.C.D. Publications and Information Center, 2001 L St., N.W., Suite 650, Washington, DC 20036-4922. TEL 202-785-6323) **Indexed:** IIS.
—BLDSC (3363.993200).
Formerly: Annual Reports on Competition in O E C D Member Countries (ISSN 0300-1547)

338.91   UY
CONEXION; revista latinoamericana de integracion. 1991. q. Fundacion Banco de Boston, Bulevar Artigas 934-902, Montevideo, Uruguay. TEL 986342. Ed. Claudio Trobo.

CONSULTING ENGINEER INTERNATIONAL. see ENGINEERING

CONSUMER - ECONOMIST. see BUSINESS AND ECONOMICS

338.91   GW
CONTACTS. (Text in German) 1965. q. DM.8. Arbeitsgemeinschaft fuer Entwicklungshilfe e.V., Postfach 210128, 50527 Cologne, Germany. TEL 49-221-8896-0. FAX 49-221-8896100. E-mail: ageh-contacts@geod.geonet.de. Ed. Martin Fuchs. bk.rev. circ. 7,000. **Document type:** bulletin.

338.91   AG   ISSN 0326-4068
HC121
CONTRIBUCIONES; estudios interdisciplinarios sobre desarrollo y cooperacion internacional. 1984. q. $40. (Konrad Adenauer Stiftung Asociacion Civil) Centro Interdisciplinario de Estudios sobre el Desarrollo Latinoamericano, Av. L.N. Alem 690, piso 20o, 1001 Buenos Aires, Argentina. TEL 541-313-3522. FAX 541-311-2902. E-mail: konrad@datamarkets.com.ar. Dir. Horst Schonbohm. bk.rev. circ. 3,900. **Indexed:** IBR. **Document type:** academic/scholarly publication.

338.9   GT   ISSN 0553-6863
CONVENIOS CENTROAMERICANOS DE INTEGRATION ECONOMICA. 1963. irreg., latest, vol.11. $5. Secretaria Permanente del Tratado General de Integracion Economica Centroamericana, 4a Avda. 10-25, Zona 14, Apdo. 1237, 01901 Guatemala, Guatemala.

338.91   MX
COOPERACION. 1966. bi-m. free. Camara Mexicano-Alemana de Comercio e Industria, A.C., Apdo. Postal 41-740, 11000 Mexico, D.F., Mexico. TEL 251-40-22. FAX 5967695. TELEX 01771226 DEHAME. Ed. Peter Klees. adv.; bk.rev. circ. 2,000.

338.91   SP
COOPERACION PUBLICA VASCA PARA EL DESARROLLO. MEMORIA (YEARS); ayudas al tercer mundo. 1991. irreg., latest 1988-94 ed. (Secretaria de la Presidencia, Secretaria General de Accion Exterior) Eusko Jaurlaritzaren Argitalpen-Zerbitzu Nagusia - Servicio Central de Publicaciones del Gobierno Vasco, C. Duque de Wellington 2, 01010 Vitoria-Gasteiz, Spain. circ. 1,000. **Document type:** government publication.

338.91   SJ
COOPERATION FOR DEVELOPMENT. (Text in Arabic, English, French) 1979. 3/yr. free. Arab Bank for Economic Development in Africa, P.O. Box 2640, Khartoum, Sudan. FAX 22248. TELEX 22739 BADEA SD. circ. 750.
Description: Reflects bank's development activities and Arab assistance to non-Arab African countries.

338.91 630   US
COOPERATIVE NEWS INTERNATIONAL. 1963. q. $10. Agricultural Cooperative Development International, 50 F St., N.W., Ste. 1100, Washington, DC 20001. TEL 202-638-4661. FAX 202-626-8726. TELEX 160-923. E-mail: acdi-hq@mcimail.com. Ed. Perry Letson. circ. 2,050. **Document type:** newsletter.

338.91   UK   ISSN 1352-3163
CORPORATE LOCATION. (Supplement avail.: Mergers & Acquisitions (ISSN 1355-1787)) 1988. bi-m. £150 (foreign $255) (effective 1997). Euromoney Publications plc., Nestor House, Playhouse Yard, London EC4 5EX, England. TEL 44-171-779-8368. FAX 44-171-779-8369. Ed. Fiona Jebb. adv. circ. 30,000. (also avail. in microform from UMI; back issues avail.) **Document type:** trade publication.
●Also available online. Vendor(s): UMI.
—UMI.
Formed by the 1991 merger of: Corporate Location Europe (ISSN 0953-1505); Corporate Location International (ISSN 0962-2578)
Description: Examines the economic conditions and trends in various countries for senior decision makers at companies considering expanding overseas.

338.91   US
COUNCIL ON HEMISPHERIC AFFAIRS NEWS AND ANALYSIS. s-w. $125. Council on Hemispheric Affairs, 724 9th St., N.W., Ste. 401, Washington, DC 20001. TEL 202-393-3322. FAX 202-393-3423. Ed. Laurence Birns; Pub. Laurence Birns. circ. 1,500. (back issues avail.)

338.91 341   EI   ISSN 1013-7335
COURIER. AFRICA - CARIBBEAN - PACIFIC - EUROPEAN UNION. French edition: Courrier. Afrique - Caraibes - Pacifique - Communaute Europeenne (ISSN 1013-7343) 1975. bi-m. free. Commission of the European Communities, Rue de la Loi, 200, B-1049 Brussels, Belgium. TEL 32-2-299-11-11. FAX 32-2-299-30-02. TELEX COMEURBRU 21877. Ed. Dominique David; Pub. Peter Pooley. adv. contact: Rebecca Zahn. **Indexed:** So.Pac.Per.Ind. **Document type:** newsletter.
Description: Profiles a country and analyzes social, economic, and political issues in Africa, the Caribbean, Oceania, and the European Union.

COW NEWS & BULL VIEWS. see AGRICULTURE — Poultry And Livestock

338.91   GW   ISSN 0723-7006
D & C - DESARROLLO Y COOPERACION. (Text in Spanish, Portuguese) 1974. bi-m. DM.19. Deutsche Stiftung fuer Internationale Entwicklung - German Foundation for International Development, Postfach 300462, 53184 Bonn, Germany. (Subscr. to: Frankfurter Societaets Druckerei, Postfach 100801, 60008 Frankfurt a.M., Germany. TEL 49-69-75014366. FAX 49-69-75014855) Ed. J. Pablo Kummetz. circ. 11,000. **Document type:** bulletin.

338.91   GW   ISSN 0723-6980
D & C - DEVELOPMENT AND COOPERATION. (Text in English) 1974. bi-m. DM.19. Deutsche Stiftung fuer internationale Entwicklung - German Foundation for International Development, Postfach 300462, 53184 Bonn, Germany. (Subscr. to: Frankfurter Societaets Druckerei, Postfach 100801, 60008 Frankfurt a.M., Germany. TEL 49-69-75014366. FAX 49-69-75014855) Ed. Dieter Brauer. circ. 23,000. **Indexed:** Excerp.Med., Mid.East: Abstr.& Ind., Rice Abstr., Rural Devel.Abstr. **Document type:** bulletin.
—BLDSC (3578.760000).

338.91   GW   ISSN 0723-6999
D & C - DEVELOPPEMENT ET COOPERATION. (Text in French) 1974. bi-m. DM.19. Deutsche Stiftung fuer Internationale Entwicklung, Postfach 300462, 53184 Bonn, Germany. (Subscr. to: Frankfurter Societaets Druckerei, Postfach 100801, 60008 Frankfurt a.M., Germany. TEL 49-69-75014366. FAX 49-69-75014855) Ed. Reinhold Meyer. circ. 7,000. **Document type:** bulletin.

338.91   GW
D E A B - RUNDBRIEF. 1975. 2/yr. DM.20. Dachverband Entwicklungspolitischer Aktionsgruppen in Baden-Wuerttemberg, Blumenstr. 15, 70182 Stuttgart, Germany. TEL 49-711-243235. FAX 49-711-2366123. bk.rev. circ. 350. (back issues avail.) **Document type:** newsletter.

338.91   GW
D E D BRIEF. 1964. q. free. Deutscher Entwicklungsdienst, Kladower Damm 299, 14089 Berlin, Germany. TEL 49-30-36881-0. FAX 49-30-36881271. circ. 20,000. **Document type:** newsletter.
Description: Experiences of DED development workers in different aspects of personal aid in Third World countries.

338.91   GW   ISSN 0935-1809
D E S W O S - BRIEF. 1974. bi-m. DM.6. Deutsche Entwicklungshilfe fuer Soziales Wohnungs- und Siedlungswesen e.V., Bismarckstr. 7, 50672 Cologne, Germany. TEL 49-221-5798972. FAX 49-221-5798999. Ed. Andrea Geiger-Blau. bk.rev.; bibl.; illus.; stat. circ. 10,000. **Document type:** bulletin.
Description: Project information on housing and development in Third World countries.

338.91   DK   ISSN 0106-0090
HC60
DANMARKS DELTAGELSE I DET INTERNATIONALE UDVIKLINGSSAMARBEJDE. AARSRAPPORT. a. free. Danida, Ministry of Foreign Affairs - Danish International Development Assistance, Asiatisk Plads 2, DK-1448 Copenhagen K, Denmark. TEL 45-33-92-00-00. FAX 45-33-92-07-10. TELEX 31292-ETR-DK. E-mail: um@um.dk. illus.; stat. **Document type:** government publication.

BUSINESS AND ECONOMICS — INTERNATIONAL DEVELOPMENT AND ASSISTANCE

338.91   DK   ISSN 0905-3336
DENMARK'S DEVELOPMENT ASSISTANCE. ANNUAL REPORT. 1974. a. free. Danida, Ministry of Foreign Affairs - Danish International Development Assistance, Asiatisk Plads 2, DK-1448 Copenhagen K, Denmark. TEL 45-33-92-00-00. FAX 33-92-07-10. TELEX 31292-ETR-DK. E-mail: um@um.dk. stat. **Document type:** government publication.

338.91 301   US   ISSN 0733-6594
HC121
DESARROLLO DE BASE. English edition: Grassroots Development (ISSN 0733-6608); Portuguese edition: Desenvolvimento de Base. (Text in Spanish) 1977. 2/yr. free. Inter-American Foundation, 901 N. Stuart St., 10th Fl., Arlington, VA 22203-1821. TEL 202-841-3800. FAX 703-841-0973. bk.rev. circ. 10,200. (also avail. in microfilm; back issues avail.) **Document type:** newsletter.
   Description: Reports on how the poor in Latin America and the Caribbean organize and work to improve their lives.

DESARROLLO Y ENERGIA. see *ENERGY*

338.91   UG
THE DEVELOPER. 1990. q. Sh.24000 (effective 1993). Foundation for African Development, P.O. Box 16206, Kampala, Uganda. TEL 256-41-231824. FAX 256-41-251243. (Co-sponsor: Konrad Adenauer) Ed. Syed A. Abidi. bk.rev.; bibl.; illus.; circ. 2,000 (controlled). **Indexed:** P.L.E.S.A. **Document type:** academic/scholarly publication.
   Description: Sensitizes readers on development.

338   JA   ISSN 0012-1533
HC59.7
DEVELOPING ECONOMIES. (Text in English) 1962. q. 6300 Yen($98) Institute of Developing Economies - Ajia Keizai Kenkyusho, 42 Ichigaya-Hommura-cho, Shinjuku-ku, Tokyo 162, Japan. TEL 3353-4231. FAX 3226-8475. (Subscr. to: Maruzen Co. Ltd., Box 5050, Tokyo International 100-31, Japan) adv.; bk.rev.; abstr.; bibl.; stat.; index. circ. 1,600. (also avail. in microform) **Indexed:** ASCA, Asian-Pac.Econ.Lit., C.R.E.J., Curr.Cont., E.I., Excerp.Med., Geo.Abstr.H.G., IDA, Int.Lab.Doc., J.of Econ.Lit., Key to Econ.Sci., Lang.& Lang.Behav.Abstr., Maize Abstr., Mid.East: Abstr.& Ind., Pub.Admin.Abstr., Rural Devel.Abstr., Rural Recreat.Tour.Abstr., So.Pac.Per.Ind., Soyabean Abstr., SSCI, Triticale Abstr., World Agri.Econ. & Rural Sociol.Abstr. **Document type:** academic/scholarly publication.
—BLDSC (3578.545000); SWETS; UnCover.
   Description: An international and interdisciplinary forum for social studies of the developing countries.

338 327   UK   ISSN 1011-6370
HC60
DEVELOPMENT (LONDON). Spanish edition: Desarrollo. Italian ed.: Sviluppo. 1959. q. £25($40) to individuals; institutions £99($158) (effective 1998). (Society for International Development, IT) Sage Publications Ltd., 6 Bonhill St., London EC2A 4PU, England. TEL 44-171-374-0645. FAX 44-171-374-8741. E-mail: market@sagepub.co.uk; URL: http://www.sagepub.co.uk/. (Edit. addr.: Palazzo Civilta del Lavoro, 00144 Rome, Italy. TEL 39-6-5925506) Ed. Wendy Harcourt. adv. contact: Bernie Folan. bk.rev. circ. 7,000. (also avail. in microform then current; reprint service avail. from UMI) **Indexed:** A.B.C.Pol.Sci., Amer.Hist.& Life, Bus.Ind., Commun.Abstr., Curr.Cont., Fut.Surv., Hist.Abstr., HR Rep., IDA, Int.Lab.Doc., Media Rev.Dig., P.A.I.S., Per.Islam. (1991-), Pub.Admin.Abstr., Rural Recreat.Tour.Abstr., Soc.Sci.Ind., SSCI, World Agri.Econ.& Rural Sociol.Abstr. **Document type:** academic/scholarly publication.
—BLDSC (3578.680000); SWETS; UMI; UnCover. CCC.
   Former titles: Development: Seeds of Change; Development - Developpement - Desarrollo; (1963-1977): International Development Review (ISSN 0020-6555)
   Description: Keeps readers abreast of the cutting edge issues of sustainable human development, from views on development alternatives to strategies at the local level and reports on the inside debates at the UN.

338.91   UK   ISSN 0012-155X
HD82
DEVELOPMENT AND CHANGE. 1969. q. £129($204) (foreign £129) (effective 1997). (Institute of Social Studies, The Hague, NE) Blackwell Publishers Ltd., 108 Cowley Rd., Oxford OX4 1JF, England. TEL 44-1865-791100. FAX 44-1865-791347. E-mail: jnlinfo@blackwellpublishers.co.uk; URL: http://www.blackwellpublishers.co.uk. Ed.Bd. bk.rev.; charts. (also avail. in microform from UMI) **Indexed:** A.B.C.Pol.Sci., Abstr.Rural Dev.Trop., Amer.Hist.& Life (1975-), Arts & Hum.Cit.Ind., ASCA, Asian-Pac.Econ.Lit., ASSIA, Commun.Abstr., Curr.Cont., Documentatieblad, E.I., Energy Ind., Energy Info.Abstr., Geo.Abstr.H.G., Hist.Abstr. (1975-), HR Rep., IBR, IDA, Int.Lab.Doc., Int.Polit.Sci.Abstr., J.of Econ.Lit., Key to Econ.Sci., Mid.East: Abstr.& Ind., Per.Islam. (1992-), Pub.Admin.Abstr., Rice Abstr., Rural Devel.Abstr., Rural Ext.Educ.& Tr.Abstr., Rural Recreat.Tour.Abstr., Sage Fam.Stud.Abstr., Sage Urb.Stud.Abstr., SSCI. **Document type:** academic/scholarly publication.
—BLDSC (3578.750000); Genuine Article; SWETS; UMI; UnCover. CCC.
   Description: Contributes to the understanding of Third World problems. Publishes critical analysis and articles from all disciplines of the social sciences discussing current development issues.
   Refereed Serial

338.91 330.9   XV
DEVELOPMENT AND INTERNATIONAL COOPERATION. (Text in English; summaries in English and Slovenian) 1985. s-a. $25 to individuals; institutions $35. Centre for International Relations, Faculty of Social Sciences, University of Ljubljana, P.O. Box 2547, 1001 Ljubljana, Slovenia. TEL 386-61-1682174. FAX 386-61-1682339. Eds. Miran Mejak, Maja Bucar. adv.; bk.rev. circ. 750. (back issues avail.) **Indexed:** Per.Islam. (1991-), World Agri.Econ.& Rural Sociol.Abstr. **Document type:** academic/scholarly publication.
   Formerly (until June 1991): Development and South-South Cooperation (ISSN 0352-7670)
   Description: Devoted to international economic relations, various development issues, especially to the issues of economic and technological cooperation among developing countries, their strategies and policies.

338.0968   SA
DEVELOPMENT BANK OF SOUTHERN AFRICA. DEVELOPMENT PAPERS. (Includes subseries: Construction & Development Series; Provincial Education Series) (Text in English) 1993. irreg., no.68, 1995. price varies. Development Bank of Southern Africa, P.O. Box 1234, Halfway House 1685, South Africa. TEL 27-11-3133911. FAX 27-11-3133086. TELEX 4-25546. Ed. Mrs. Anne E. Wille. (back issues avail.) **Document type:** monographic series.
   Formerly: Development Bank of Southern Africa. Centre for Policy Analysis. Policy Working Paper (ISSN 1022-0127)
   Description: Makes available the bank's work on policy, information, evaluation and related development issues.

338.9 327   UN   ISSN 0259-5893
DEVELOPMENT BUSINESS. (Text in English) 1978. fortn. $495 (effective 1998). United Nations, Division of Public Information, United Nations Plaza, DC1-574, New York, NY 10017. TEL 212-963-1517. FAX 212-963-1381. TELEX 422311 UNUI. E-mail: dbusiness@un.org. (Subscr. addr: Box 5850, G.C. P.O. New York, NY 10163) Ed. Evelyn Samore. R&P contact: Evelyn Samore. TEL 212-963-8065. adv. contact: Sherifa Kahn. illus. circ. 4,500. **Indexed:** C.R.I.Abstr., C.R.I.Curr.Cont., Key to Econ.Sci. **Document type:** newspaper.
●Also available online. Vendor(s): Data-Star, Knight-Ridder Information, Inc.
—BLDSC (3579.016400).
   Formerly (until 1984): Development Forum. Business Edition; Incorporates: U N D P Business Bulletin; Which superseded in part: Pre-Investment News (ISSN 0032-7093)
   Description: Lists procurement notices and bid invitations that alert readers to consulting, contracting, and supply opportunities as soon as projects are proposed.

338.91   NZ   ISSN 1171-4859
DEVELOPMENT BUSINESS. 1992. irreg. Ministry of Foreign Affairs and Trade, Development Cooperation Division, Private Bag 18-901, Wellington, New Zealand. TEL 64-4-4948500. FAX 64-4-4948514. **Document type:** government publication.
   Description: Explores avenues for the private sector to become involved with aid programmes.

327 338.91   US
DEVELOPMENT CONNECTIONS. 1957. bi-m. $75 to regular members; student members $35; institutions $500. (Society for International Development - Washington Chapter) Society for International Development, 1875 Connecticut Ave., N.W., Ste. 720, Washington, DC 20009. TEL 202-884-8590. FAX 202-884-8499. E-mail: sid@aed.org. Ed. Andy Karas. adv.; bk.rev.; index. circ. 1,000. (back issues avail.) **Document type:** newsletter.
   Former titles (until 1987): Society for International Development. Newsletter; International Society for Community Development. Newsletter.

338.91   NZ   ISSN 1171-9575
DEVELOPMENT COOPERATION. 1992. irreg. Ministry of Foreign Affairs and Trade, Development Cooperation Division, Private Bag 18-901, Wellington, New Zealand. TEL 64-4-4948500. FAX 64-4-4948514. **Document type:** government publication.
   Description: Items of interest surrounding NZ's aid to developing countries.

DEVELOPMENT DIALOGUE; a journal of international development cooperation. see *POLITICAL SCIENCE — International Relations*

338.9   AT   ISSN 0815-9424
DEVELOPMENT DOSSIER. 1972. q. Australian Council for Overseas Aid, Private Bag 3, Deakin, A.C.T. 2600, Australia. TEL 61-2-2851816. FAX 61-2-2851720. Ed. Kerrie Griffin. bk.rev.; illus. circ. 2,000. **Indexed:** HR Rep., So.Pac.Per.Ind.
   Incorporates (in 1980): Development News Digest (ISSN 0155-0489)

338.91   UN   ISSN 0251-6632
HC59
DEVELOPMENT FORUM. French edition: Forum du Developpement (ISSN 0251-6640); German edition: Forum (ISSN 0251-6659); Spanish edition: Foro del Desarrollo (ISSN 0251-6667) 1978. irreg. free. Division for Economic and Social Information (DESI), Room S-0556, New York, NY 10017. TEL 212-963-8070. Ed. Paul Hoeffel. **Indexed:** Environ.Abstr., Ind.Per.Art.Relat.Law.

338.91   UK   ISSN 0961-4524
                                 CODEN: DEPRFO
DEVELOPMENT IN PRACTICE. 1991. 4/yr. £50($85) to individuals; institutions £125 ($218) (effective 1997). Oxfam, 274 Banbury Rd., Oxford OX2 7DZ, England. TEL 44-1865-311311. FAX 44-1865-313925. (Subscr. to: Carfax Publishing Co., P.O. Box 25, Abingdon, Oxon. OX14 3UE, England. TEL 44-1235-521154. FAX 44-1235-401550) Ed. Deborah Eade. adv.; bk.rev. circ. 150. (back issues avail.) **Indexed:** Documentatieblad, Geo.Abstr.H.G., IDA. **Document type:** bulletin.
—BLDSC (3579.039930); UnCover. CCC.
   Refereed Serial

338.91   UK   ISSN 0957-4115
HC59.8
DEVELOPMENT JOURNAL. 1990. q. £60 (foreign $115) (effective 1994). Development Journal Ltd., 150 Regent St., Ste. 500, London W1R 5FA, England. TEL 071-242-1280. Ed. Irvine Cohen. adv.; bk.rev. circ. 3,447. **Document type:** academic/scholarly publication.
—BLDSC (3579.037300). CCC.
   Description: International journal dealing with investment and privatization in Eastern Europe and the Third World for investors, investment institutions, banks, consultancies, and business leaders.

DEVELOPMENT ORIENTED RESEARCH IN AGRICULTURE. see *AGRICULTURE*

BUSINESS AND ECONOMICS — INTERNATIONAL DEVELOPMENT AND ASSISTANCE

338.9   UK   ISSN 0950-6764
HC59.7   CODEN: DPORER
DEVELOPMENT POLICY REVIEW. 1974. q. £116($183) (foreign £116) (effective 1997). Blackwell Publishers Ltd., 108 Cowley Rd., Oxford OX4 1JF, England. TEL 44-1865-791100. FAX 44-1865-791347. E-mail: jnlinfo@blackwellpublishers.co.uk; URL: http://www.blackwellpublishers.co.uk. Ed. Sheila Page. adv.; bk.rev. **Indexed:** Asian-Pac.Econ.Lit., C.R.E.J., Documentatieblad, Geo.Abstr.H.G., IDA, Int.Polit.Sci.Abstr., Key to Econ.Sci., Mid.East: Abstr.& Ind., P.A.I.S., Polit.Sci.Abstr., Rice Abstr., Rural Devel.Abstr., Rural Recreat.Tour.Abstr., World Agri.Econ.& Rural Sociol.Abstr. **Document type:** academic/scholarly publication.
—BLDSC (3579.039850); SWETS; UMI; UnCover. **CCC.**
   Formerly: O D I Review (ISSN 0078-7116)
   Description: Provides a forum for new research and information on social and economic issues in development among persons directly concerned with development in business, government, and other organizations.
Refereed Serial

338.91   PH   ISSN 0115-9097
DEVELOPMENT RESEARCH NEWS. Short title: D R N. (Text in English) 1983. bi-m. $20 (effective 1996). Philippine Institute for Development Studies, NEDA sa Makati Bldg., 3rd Fl., Rm. 304, 106 Amorsolo St., Legaspi Village, Makati 1229, Metro Manila, Philippines. TEL 632-8935705. FAX 632-8161091. Ed. Jennifer P.T. Liguton. circ. 1,500. (back issues avail.) **Indexed:** J.of Ferroc. **Document type:** newsletter.
   Description: Covers questions of development, with an emphasis on the Asian Pacific perspective.

338.91 282   IE   ISSN 0790-9403
DEVELOPMENT REVIEW. 1985. a. Trocaire, 169 Booterstown Ave., Blackrock, Co. Dublin, Ireland. TEL 353-1-2885385. FAX 353-1-2883577. E-mail: e-mail@trocaire.ie. **Document type:** newsletter.
—BLDSC (9050.782490).

338.91   SA   ISSN 0376-835X
HC900.A1
DEVELOPMENT SOUTHERN AFRICA. (Text in English) 1974. bi-m. R.75 (overseas $50). Development Bank of Southern Africa, P.O. Box 1234, Halfway House 1685, South Africa. TEL 27-11-3133911. FAX 27-11-3133086. TELEX 4-25546. adv. B&W page R.500; adv. contact: C.A. Jobe. bk.rev.; bibl.; illus. circ. 2,000. **Indexed:** Geo.Abstr.H.G., IDA, Ind.S.A.Per. **Document type:** academic/scholarly publication.
—BLDSC (3579.042780).
   Description: Promotes research and discussion on development issues relating to southern Africa.

370.91   SG
DIRECTORY OF DEVELOPMENT AND TRAINING INSTITUTES IN AFRICA. (Text in English, French) 1983. a. $35 (effective 1997). Council for the Development of Social Science Research in Africa, B.P. 3304, Dakar, Senegal. TEL 23-02-11. FAX 24-12-89. TELEX 3339 CODES SG24. circ. 1,000. **Document type:** directory.

DIRECTORY OF THE NATIONAL PRODUCTIVITY ORGANIZATIONS IN A P O MEMBER COUNTRIES. see BUSINESS AND ECONOMICS — Production Of Goods And Services

338.91   UK   ISSN 0361-3666
HV553
DISASTERS; the journal of disaster relief and management. 1977. q. £116($183) (foreign £116) (effective 1997). (Overseas Development Institute) Blackwell Publishers Ltd., 108 Cowley Rd., Oxford OX4 1JF, England. TEL 44-1865-791100. FAX 44-1865-791347. E-mail: jnlinfo@blackwellpublishers.co.uk. Eds. Joanne MacRae, Charlotte Benson. adv.; bk.rev.; charts; illus.; stat.; index. circ. 2,000. (also avail. in microform from UMI; reprint service avail. from SWZ,UMI) **Indexed:** Abstr.Hyg., Abstr.J.Earthq.Eng., Abstr.Rural Dev.Trop., Archit.Per.Ind., ASCA, Asian-Pac.Econ.Lit., Curr.Cont., Environ.Abstr., Excerp.Med, Geo.Abstr.H.G., GeoRef., HR Rep (1984-1985), Ind.Med. (1994-), Int.Lab.Doc., Nutr.Abstr., Refug.Abstr., Repindex, Risk Abstr., Rural Devel.Abstr., Rural Recreat.Tour.Abstr., SSCI, Trop.Dis.Bull. **Document type:** academic/scholarly publication.
—BLDSC (3595.510000); Genuine Article; SWETS; UMI; UnCover. **CCC.**
Refereed Serial

DRITTE-WELT-KALENDER. see POLITICAL SCIENCE — International Relations

338.91 360   EI
E C H O NEWS. (Editions in English, French) q. free. (European Community Humanitarian Office) Commission of the European Communities, Rue de la Loi 200, B-1049 Brussels, Belgium. TEL 32-2-295-44-00. FAX 32-2-295-45-72. adv. contact: Rebecca Zahn. **Document type:** newsletter.
   Description: Discusses the organizations humanitarian and relief efforts in countries worldwide ravaged by war or natural disaster.

EAST ASIAN BUSINESS INTELLIGENCE. see BUSINESS AND ECONOMICS — International Commerce

338 320 330.9   US
ECOCENTRAL; Central America & Caribbean Sustainable Development. w. $75 to individuals; institutions $300. University of New Mexico, Latin American Institute, Latin American Database, 801 Yale N.E., Albuquerque, NM 87131-1016. TEL 505-277-6839. FAX 505-277-5989. URL: http://www.ladb.unm.edu/. Ed. Kevin Robinson. **Document type:** academic/scholarly publication, bulletin.
●Also available online. Vendor(s): Knight-Ridder Information, Inc., Lexis-Nexis, NewsNet.
Also available on CD-ROM. Producer(s): NISC.
   Description: Covers news relating to sustainable development, politics and economic issues in Central America and the Caribbean.

338.91   UN   ISSN 0252-2284
ECONOMIC AND SOCIAL COMMISSION FOR ASIA AND THE PACIFIC. ANNUAL REPORT. French edition: Commission Economique et Sociale pour l'Asie et le Pacifique. Rapport Annuel (ISSN 0252-2276); Chinese edition: Yazhou ji Taipingyang Jingji Shehui Weiyuanhui. Niandu Baogao (ISSN 0257-0343); Russian edition: Ekonomicheskaya i Social'naya Komissiya Dlya Azii i Tikhogo Okeana. Godovoi Doklad (ISSN 0257-0335) (Supplement avail.) (Text in English) 1947. a. $17. United Nations Economic and Social Commission for Asia and the Pacific, United Nations Bldg., Rajdamnern Ave., Bangkok 10200, Thailand. (Orders to: United Nations Publications, Rm. DC2-0853, New York, NY 10017; Distribution and Sales Section, Palais des Nations, CH-1211 Geneva, Switzerland) (back issues avail.)
   Formerly (until 1974): Economic Commission for Asia and the Far East. Report (ISSN 1011-2731)

338.91   UN
ECONOMIC AND SOCIAL COMMISSION FOR ASIA AND THE PACIFIC. ANNUAL REPORT. SUPPLEMENT. (Supplement to: Annual Report (ISSN 0252-2284)) (Text in English) irreg. price varies. United Nations Economic and Social Commission for Asia and the Pacific (ESCAP), Rajdamnerm Ave., Bangkok 10200, Thailand. (Orders to: United Nations Publications, Rm. DC2-0853, New York, NY 10017; Distribution and Sales Section, Palais des Nations, CH-1211 Geneva, Switzerland) (back issues avail.)

338.91 300   US   ISSN 0013-0079
HC10   CODEN: EDCCAF
ECONOMIC DEVELOPMENT AND CULTURAL CHANGE. 1952. q. $42 to individuals (Canada $51.94; elsewhere $49); institutions $113 (Canada $127.91; elsewhere $120) (effective 1998). University of Chicago Press, Journals Division, Box 37005, Chicago, IL 60637. TEL 773-753-3347. FAX 773-753-0811. TELEX 25-4603. E-mail: subscriptions@journals.uchicago.edu; URL: http://www.journals.uchicago.edu/EDCC/. Ed. D. Gale Johnson. adv.: page $355; trim 6 x 9. bk.rev.; index, cum.index: vols. 1-25. circ. 3,100. (also avail. in microform from UMI,PMC; reprint service avail. from ISI,SCH,UMI) **Indexed:** A.B.C.Pol.Sci., A.I.C.P., ABI Inform., Abstr.Anthropol., Abstr.Rural Dev.Trop., Acad.Ind., Amer.Bibl.Slavic & E.Eur.Stud., Amer.Hist.& Life (1963-), ASCA, Asian-Pac.Econ.Lit., ASSIA, B.P.I., BPIA, Bus.Ind., C.R.E.J., Cott.& Trop.Fibr.Abstr., Curr.Cont., Deep Sea Res.& Oceanogr.Abstr., E.I., Energy Ind., Energy Info.Abstr., Fam.Ind., Forest.Abstr., Geo.Abstr.H.G., Hisp.Amer.Per.Ind. (1970-), Hist.Abstr. (1963-), HRIS, IBR, IDA, IMFL, Int.Polit.Sci.Abstr., J.of Econ.Lit., Key to Econ.Sci., Lang.& Lang.Behav.Abstr., Mid.East: Abstr.& Ind., P.A.I.S., Polit.Sci.Abstr., Popul.Ind., Pub.Admin.Abstr., Rural Devel.Abstr., Rural Ext.Educ.& Tr.Abstr., Rural Recreat.Tour.Abstr., Sage Fam.Stud.Abstr., Sage Urb.Stud.Abstr., So.Pac.Per.Ind., Soc.Sci.Ind., Sociol.Abstr., SSCI, Tr.& Indus.Ind., World Agri.Econ.& Rural Sociol.Abstr., World Bank.Abstr. **Document type:** academic/scholarly publication.
—BLDSC (3652.700000); Genuine Article; KR SourceOne; SWETS; UMI; UnCover. **CCC.**
   Description: Searches for new theoretical approaches that integrate the concepts of social change with economic theories. Examines the social and economic forces that affect development and its effect on culture.
Refereed Serial

338.91 330.1   NP   ISSN 1018-631X
ECONOMIC JOURNAL OF NEPAL. (Text in English) 1977. q. Rs.280($88) Tribhuvan University, Central Department of Economics, P.O. Box 3821, Kirtipur, Kathmandu, Nepal. TEL 977-1-213277. Ed. V.P. Sharma. bk.rev.; bibl.; charts; stat. circ. 500. **Indexed:** IDA, Rural Devel.Abstr., Rural Ext.Educ.& Tr.Abstr., Soils & Fert., Triticale Abstr., World Agri.Econ.& Rural Sociol.Abstr. **Document type:** academic/scholarly publication.
   Formerly (until 1978): Economic Monthly.
   Description: Contains research papers on the economic and social problems facing Nepal and other developing countries.

338.91   AT   ISSN 1038-412X
HC59.69
ECONOMICS DIVISION WORKING PAPERS. DEVELOPMENT ISSUES. 1992. irreg. Aus.$10. Australian National University, Economics Division, Canberra, A.C.T. 0200, Australia. (Subscr. to: Bibliotech, Canberra, A.C.T. 0200, Australia) Ed. Maree Tait. **Indexed:** Geo.Abstr.H.G., IDA.
   Incorporates: National Centre for Development Studies. Working Papers in Trade and Development (ISSN 0816-5181); Incorporates in part: Australian National University. National Centre for Development Studies. Working Papers. Series: N C D S Working Papers (ISSN 0815-7596)
   Description: Covers economics, trade, development and policy issues.

338.91   AT   ISSN 1038-412X
ECONOMICS DIVISION WORKING PAPERS. EAST ASIA. (Text in English) 1992. irreg. Aus.$10 per no. Australian National University, Economics Division, Canberra, A.C.T. 0200, Australia. TEL 61-6-2494705. FAX 61-6-2572886. (Subscr. to: Bibliotech, Australian National University, Canberra, A.C.T. 0200, Australia) Ed. Maree Tait. **Indexed:** Geo.Abstr.H.G., IDA.
   Incorporates: Australian National University. National Centre for Development Studies. Working Papers. Series: China Working Papers (ISSN 1030-360X)
   Description: Covers economics, trade, development and policy issues.

338.91 AT ISSN 1038-412X
ECONOMICS DIVISION WORKING PAPERS. SOUTH ASIA. irreg. Aus.$10 per no. Australian National University, Economics Division, Canberra, A.C.T. 0200, Australia. TEL 61-6-2494705. FAX 61-6-2572886. (Subscr. to: Bibliotech, Australian National University, Canberra, A.C.T. 0200, Australia) Ed. Maree Tait.
   Description: Covers economics, trade, development and policy issues.

338.91 AT ISSN 1038-412X
ECONOMICS DIVISION WORKING PAPERS. SOUTH PACIFIC. irreg. Aus.$10 per no. Australian National University, Economics Division, Canberra, A.C.T. 0200, Australia. TEL 61-6-2494705. FAX 61-6-2572886. (Subscr. to: Bibliotech, Australian National University, Canberra, A.C.T. 0200, Australia) Ed. Maree Tait. **Indexed:** Geo.Abstr.H.G., IDA.
—BLDSC (4583.131700).
   Incorporates: Australian National University. National Centre for Development Studies. Working Papers. Series: Islands - Australia Working Papers (ISSN 0816-5165)
   Description: Covers economics, trade, development and policy issues.

338.91 AT ISSN 1038-412X
ECONOMICS DIVISION WORKING PAPERS. SOUTHEAST ASIA. irreg. Aus.$10 per no. Australian National University, Economics Division, Canberra, A.C.T. 0200, Australia. TEL 61-6-2494705. FAX 61-6-2572886. (Subscr. to: Bibliotech, Australian National University, Canberra, A.C.T. 0200, Australia) Ed. Maree Tait. **Indexed:** Geo.Abstr.H.G., IDA, Rural Devel.Abstr., Rural Recreat.Tour.Abstr., Triticale Abstr., World Agri.Econ.& Rural Sociol.Abstr.
   Incorporates in part: Australian National University. National Centre for Development Studies. Working Papers. Series: N C D S Working Papers (ISSN 0815-7596)
   Description: Economics, trade, development and policy issues.

338.9 FR ISSN 0068-4813
ECONOMIES ET SOCIETES. SERIE F. DEVELOPPEMENT, CROISSANCE, PROGRES DES PAYS EN VOIE DE DEVELOPPEMENT. 1955. irreg. 350 F. Presses Universitaires de Grenoble, B.P. 47, 38040 Grenoble Cedex 9, France. Ed. Pierre Pascallon. circ. 1,600.
—SWETS.

ECONOMIES ET SOCIETES. SERIE P. RELATIONS ECONOMIQUES INTERNATIONALES. see *BUSINESS AND ECONOMICS — Economic Systems And Theories, Economic History*

ENTWICKLUNGSLAENDER-STUDIEN; Bibliographie entwicklungslaenderbezogener Forschungsarbeiten. see *BUSINESS AND ECONOMICS — Abstracting, Bibliographies, Statistics*

ENVIRONMENT AND URBANIZATION. see *ENVIRONMENTAL STUDIES*

338.91 628 UN
ENVIRONMENTALLY SUSTAINABLE DEVELOPMENT PROCEEDINGS SERIES. (Editions in English, French) 1994. irreg. $47.95. World Bank, 1818 H St., N.W., Washington, DC 20433. TEL 202-473-1155. FAX 202-522-2627. E-mail: books@worldbank.org. (U.S. orders to: Box 7247-8619, Philadelphia, PA 19170-8619; Also avail. from: 66 av. D'Iena, 75116 Paris, France. TEL 33-1-40693055. FAX 33-1-40693068) **Document type:** monographic series.
   Description: Discusses how World Bank policies can effect and affect ecologically sustainable development worldwide.

338.91 SZ
ERITREA-INFO.* (Text in German) 1977. 3/yr. 10 SFr. Schweizerisches Unterstuetzungskomitee fuer Eritrea, Schwyzerstr. 12, CH-5430 Wettingen, Switzerland. Ed. Toni Locher.

338.91 UN ISSN 0256-9795
ESTUDIOS E INFORMES DE LA C E P A L/C E P A L STUDIES AND REPORTS. (Text mainly in Spanish; English edition also avail.) 1980. irreg., no.80, 1991. price varies. Comision Economica para America Latina y el Caribe, Casilla 179-D, Santiago, Chile. (Subscr. to: United Nations Publications, Room DC2-0853, New York, NY 10017; or Distribution and Sales Section, Palais des Nations, 1211 Geneva 10, Switzerland) (back issues avail.) **Document type:** proceedings.

ETHIOPIAN JOURNAL OF DEVELOPMENT RESEARCH. see *BUSINESS AND ECONOMICS — Production Of Goods And Services*

338.91 EI ISSN 1012-2184
EUROPE INFORMATION DEVELOPMENT. French edition: Europe Information Developpement (ISSN 1012-2192) m. free. (Commission of European Communities) Office for Official Publications of the European Communities, DG VIII, Rue de la Loi 200, 1040 Brussels, Belgium. **Document type:** newsletter.
—BLDSC (3829.619430).

338.91 UK ISSN 0969-8906
EUROPEAN BANK FOR RECONSTRUCTION AND DEVELOPMENT. WORKING PAPER. 1993. irreg., no.4. free. European Bank for Reconstruction and Development, Publications Unit, One Exchange Sq., London EC2A 2EH, England. TEL 44-171-338-6541. FAX 44-171-338-7544. Ed.Bd. (back issues avail.) **Document type:** monographic series.
   Description: Discusses the finances and governance of international development programs.

338.9 EI ISSN 0423-6831
EUROPEAN COAL AND STEEL COMMUNITY. CONSULTATIVE COMMITTEE. YEARBOOK. French edition: Communaute Europeenne du Charbon et de l'Acier. Comite Consultatif. Annuaire. German edition: Europaeische Gemeinschaft fuer Kohle und Stahl. Beratender Ausschuss. Jahrbuch. 1954. a. free. European Coal and Steel Community, Consultative Committee, Secretariat, B.P. 1907, L-2920 Luxembourg, Luxembourg. FAX 430134455. TELEX 3423 COMEUR LU. Ed. G. Wachter. circ. 1,170 (controlled). **Document type:** bulletin.

338.91 EI
EUROPEAN COMMISSION. TACIS PROGRAMME. CONTRACT INFORMATION UPDATE. 1994. irreg., latest May 1995. European Commission, Tacis Information Office, Directorate General for External Economic Relations, AN 88 1-26, Rue Montoyer 34, 1049 Brussels, Belgium. TEL 33-2-2952585. FAX 33-2-2310441.
   Description: Outlines projects funded by the Tacis Programme to support initiatives among the nations of the former Soviet Union to foster the transition to market economies and to forge harmonious links between these countries.

338.91 360 EI
EUROPEAN COMMUNITY HUMANITARIAN OFFICE. ANNUAL REPORT. a. free. (European Community Humanitarian Office) Commission of the European Communities, Rue de Geneve 3, 1140 Brussels, Belgium. TEL 32-2-295-44-00.
FAX 32-2-295-45-72. adv. contact: Rebecca Zahn. **Document type:** corporate report.
   Description: Shows the work of ECHO in terms of how and why humanitarian aid was distributed in the past year.

338.91 UK
EUROPEAN DEVELOPMENT DIRECTORY. irreg., latest 1993. £160($335) (effective 1996). Euromonitor, 60-61 Britton St., London EC1M 5NA, England. TEL 44-171-251-8024. FAX 44-171-608-3149. E-mail: info@euromonitor.com; URL: http://www.euromonitor.com. (Addr. in N. America: Euromonitor International, 122 S. Michigan Ave., Ste. 1200, Chicago, IL 60603. TEL 800-577-3876. FAX 312-922-1157) **Document type:** directory.
   Description: Provides a guide to financial aid and business grants available in 27 European nations.

338.91 320 UK ISSN 0957-8811
HC59.69 CODEN: EJDRE9
THE EUROPEAN JOURNAL OF DEVELOPMENT RESEARCH. 1989. s-a. £35($55) to individuals; institutions £85($125) (effective 1998). Frank Cass, Newbury House, 890-900 Eastern Ave., Newbury Park, Ilford, Essex 1G2 7HH, England. TEL 44-181-599-8666. FAX 44-181-599-0984. E-mail: jnlsubs@frankcass.com; URL: http://www.frankcass.com. (Dist. in US by: ISBS, 5084 N.E. Hassalo St., Portland, OR 97213-3644. TEL 800-944-6190. FAX 503-280-8832) Ed. Cristobal Kay. adv.: B&W page £195($275); adv. contact: Anne Kidson. bk.rev.; index. (back issues avail.) **Indexed:** Br.Hum.Ind., Geo.Abstr.H.G., IDA, Int.Polit.Sci.Abstr., Intl.Bibl.S.S.Pol.Sci. **Document type:** academic/scholarly publication.
—BLDSC (3829.728280); SWETS.
   Description: Covers research articles on matters of policy, theory, and practice in all aspects of development studies.
   Refereed Serial

338.9 BE ISSN 0071-2884
EUROPEAN LEAGUE FOR ECONOMIC COOPERATION. PUBLICATIONS. (Text in English or French) 1949. irreg. free. European League for Economic Cooperation, Rue de Namur 2, 1000 Brussels, Belgium.

336 BE ISSN 0531-7436
EUROPEAN LEAGUE FOR ECONOMIC COOPERATION. REPORT OF THE SECRETARY GENERAL ON THE ACTIVITIES OF E.L.E.C.. (Text in English, French) a. free. European League for Economic Cooperation, Rue de Namur 2, 1000 Brussels, Belgium.

338.9 BE ISSN 0071-2892
EUROPEAN LEAGUE FOR ECONOMIC COOPERATION. REPORTS OF THE INTERNATIONAL CONGRESS. (Issued in the League's Publications) irreg. free. European League for Economic Cooperation, Rue de Namur 2, B-1000 Brussels, Belgium.

EUROPEAN PERSPECTIVES ON RURAL DEVELOPMENT. see *AGRICULTURE*

EUROWATCH. see *POLITICAL SCIENCE — International Relations*

EXECUTIVE INTELLIGENCE REVIEW. see *POLITICAL SCIENCE*

F A O INVESTMENT CENTRE TECHNICAL PAPER. (Food and Agriculture Organization of the United Nations (Rome)) see *AGRICULTURE — Agricultural Economics*

338.91 US ISSN 0325-5476
HC171
F I D E COYUNTURA Y DESARROLLO. m. $170. Fundacion de Investigaciones para el Desarrollo, c/o Juan Zavalo, 8370 Greensboro Dr., Stes. 1007-1009, McLean, VA 22102-3523. **Indexed:** P.A.I.S.For.Lang.Ind.
   Description: Analysis of the main social and economic trends in Argentina and the world.

FACTS & FIGURES; a graphical analysis of world energy. see *ENERGY*

FINANCE AND DEVELOPMENT. see *BUSINESS AND ECONOMICS — Banking And Finance*

338.9 UN ISSN 1020-0975
HG3891
FINANCIAL FLOWS AND THE DEVELOPING COUNTRIES. 1993. q. $150. World Bank, 1818 H St., N.W., Washington, DC 20433. TEL 202-473-1155. FAX 202-522-2627. E-mail: books@worldbank.org. (Subscr. to: Box 7247-7956, Philadelphia, PA 19170-7956. TEL 201-476-2192. FAX 201-476-2197) **Document type:** newsletter.
—BLDSC (3926.955150).
   Description: Examines the latest events and trends affecting developing-country access to international capital and looks at capital markets, emerging stock markets, foreign direct investment, debt flows.

BUSINESS AND ECONOMICS — INTERNATIONAL DEVELOPMENT AND ASSISTANCE

338.91   FR   ISSN 1013-042X
FINANCING AND EXTERNAL DEBT OF DEVELOPING COUNTRIES. a. $38. Organization for Economic Cooperation and Development, 2 rue Andre-Pascal, 75775 Paris Cedex 16, France. (U.S. orders to: O.E.C.D. Publications and Information Center, 2001 L St., N.W., Ste. 650, Washington, DC 20036-4922. TEL 202-785-6323) **Indexed:** IIS.
   Formerly (until 1986): External Debt of Developing Countries (ISSN 1010-1489)

FOI ET DEVELOPPEMENT. see *SOCIAL SCIENCES: COMPREHENSIVE WORKS*

338.91   US
FOOD AID NEEDS ASSESSMENT REPORT. a. U.S. Department of Agriculture, Economic Research Service, 1301 New York Ave., N.W., Washington, DC 20005-4789. TEL 202-219-0512; 800-999-6779. (Dist. by: ERS-NASS, 341 Victory Dr., Herndon, VA 22070. TEL 202-512-1800) **Document type:** government publication.
   Description: Assesses the cereal food aid needs of developing nations.

338.91   GW   ISSN 0932-285X
FORUM (BREMEN); entwicklungspolitischer Aktionsgruppen. 1979. 7/yr. DM.50 (foreign DM.120); newsstand price: DM.6. Verein zur Foerderung Entwicklungspaedagogischer Zusammenarbeit e.V., Buchtstr. 14-15, 28195 Bremen, Germany. TEL 0421-325156. FAX 0421-3378177. Ed. Juergen Floeter. adv.: page DM.675. bk.rev.; film rev.; music rev. circ. 1,000. (back issues avail.) **Document type:** bulletin.

338.91   IT   ISSN 1121-2616
FORUM VALUTAZIONE. 1991. s-a. L.48000 (foreign L.65000) (effective 1993). (Comitato Internazionale per lo Sviluppo dei Popoli) Franco Angeli Editore, Viale Monza, 106, Casella Postale 17175, 20100 Milan, Italy. TEL 02-2895762.

338.9   FR
FRANCE. SECRETARIAT D'ETAT AUX AFFAIRES ETRANGERES CHARGE DE LA COOPERATION. DIRECTION DE L'AIDE AU DEVELOPPEMENT. COTE D'IVOIRE. DOSSIER D'INFORMATION ECONOMIQUE. 1969. irreg. free. Secretariat d'Etat aux Affaires Etrangeres Charge de la Cooperation, Direction de l'Aide au Developpement, 37 Quai d'Orsay, 75007 Paris, France. circ. 500. (processed) **Document type:** government publication.

338.9   FR
FRANCE. SECRETARIAT D'ETAT AUX AFFAIRES ETRANGERES CHARGE DE LA COOPERATION. DIRECTION DE L'AIDE AU DEVELOPPEMENT. MALI. DOSSIER D'INFORMATION ECONOMIQUE. 1971. irreg. free. Secretariat d'Etat aux Affaires Etrangeres Charge de la Cooperation, Direction de l'Aide au Developpement, 37 Quai d'Orsay, 75007 Paris, France. circ. 500. (processed) **Document type:** government publication.

338.9   FR
FRANCE. SECRETARIAT D'ETAT AUX AFFAIRES ETRANGERES CHARGE DE LA COOPERATION. DIRECTION DE L'AIDE AU DEVELOPPEMENT. NIGER. DOSSIER D'INFORMATION ECONOMIQUE. 1970. irreg. free. Secretariat d'Etat aux Affaires Etrangeres Charge de la Cooperation, Direction de l'Aide au Developpement, 37 Quai d'Orsay, 75007 Paris, France. abstr.; charts; stat. circ. 500. (processed) **Document type:** government publication.

338.91   US
FRONT LINES (WASHINGTON). 1961. m. free. U.S. Agency for International Development, Publications, 320 21st St., N.W., Rm. 4889, Washington, DC 20523-0056. TEL 202-647-4330. Ed. Nancy Long. circ. 27,700. **Document type:** government publication, newsletter.
   Description: Discusses agency projects and policy, and broader issues in international development.

GENDER AND DEVELOPMENT. see *WOMEN'S STUDIES*

GENDER AND DEVELOPMENT DIRECTORY. AUSTRALIA. see *WOMEN'S STUDIES*

338.9   GT   ISSN 0553-6898
GENERAL TREATY FOR CENTRAL AMERICAN ECONOMIC INTEGRATION. PERMANENT SECRETARIAT. NEWSLETTER. 1963. irreg. Secretaria Permanente del Tratado General de Integracion Economica Centroamericana, 4a Avda. 10-25, Zona 14, Apdo. 1237, 01901 Guatemala, Guatemala.

338.9   FR   ISSN 1026-1869
HC60
GEOGRAPHICAL DISTRIBUTION OF FINANCIAL FLOWS TO AID RECIPIENTS. DISBURSEMENTS - COMMITMENTS - COUNTRY INDICATORS/REPARTITION GEOGRAPHIQUE DES RESSOURCES FINANCIERES ALLOUEES AUX PAYS BENEFICIAIRES DE L'AIDE. VERSEMENTS - ENGAGEMENTS - INDICATEURS PAR PAYS. (Text in English, French) 1966. a. $69. Organization for Economic Cooperation and Development, 2 rue Andre-Pascal, 75775 Paris Cedex 16, France. (U.S. orders to: O.E.C.D. Publications and Information Center, 2001 L St., N.W., Suite 650, Washington, DC 20036-4922. TEL 202-785-6323) charts; stat. **Indexed:** IIS.
   —BLDSC (4125.790000).
   Former titles (until 1994): Geographical Distribution of Financial Flows to Developing Countries. Disbursements - Commitments - Economic Indicators (ISSN 1015-3934); (until 1977): Geographical Distribution of Financial Flows to Less Developed Countries. (Disbursements) (ISSN 0474-5434); Which superseded: Organization for Economic Cooperation and Development. Flow of Financial Resources to Less Developed Countries.
   Description: Provides comprehensive data on the volume, origin, and types of aid and other resource flows to more than 180 recipient nations, including new ones in Eastern Europe.

338.91 327   US
GLOBAL LINKS. 1986. q. $25 membership; students $15. Overseas Development Network (San Francisco), 333 Valencia St., Ste. 330, San Francisco, CA 94103. TEL 415-431-4204. FAX 415-431-5953. Ed. Estee Neuwirth. R&P contact: Stefano DeZerega. adv.; bk.rev. circ. 600. **Document type:** newspaper.
   Description: Provides network updates, grassroots development news, resource and calendar listings and more.

338.9   CN   ISSN 0383-6711
GLOBAL VILLAGE VOICE. 1967. q. Can.$10 (effective 1997). Canadian Catholic Organization for Development and Peace, 420 - 10 St. Mary St., Toronto, ON M4Y 1P9, Canada. TEL 416-922-1592; 800-494-1401. FAX 416-922-0957. E-mail: ccodp@web.net. Ed. Jack Panozzo. bk.rev.; circ. 45,000 (controlled). **Document type:** newsletter.
   Description: Focuses on international development, social justice, human rights, socio-economic development issues in Third World countries.

338.91   US   ISSN 1056-649X
HC59.8
GRANTS FOR FOREIGN AND INTERNATIONAL PROGRAMS. (Subseries of: Grant Guides) 1991. a. $75 (effective Oct. 1997). Foundation Center, 79 Fifth Ave., New York, NY 10003. TEL 212-807-3690; 800-424-9836. FAX 212-807-3677. E-mail: http://www.fdncenter.org.
   Description: Lists grants for broad purposes to institutions and organizations in foreign countries, to domestic recipients for international activities, development and relief, peace and security, arms control, policy research, human rights, and conferences and research.

338.91 301 572   US   ISSN 0733-6608
HC121
GRASSROOTS DEVELOPMENT. Spanish edition: Desarrollo de Base (ISSN 0733-6594); Portuguese edition: Desenvolvimento de Base. 1977. 2/yr. free. Inter-American Foundation, 901 N. Stuart St., 10th Fl., Arlington, VA 22203-1821. TEL 703-841-3800. FAX 703-527-3529. bk.rev.; bibl.; illus. circ. 11,700. (also avail. in microfilm from UMI) **Indexed:** C.I.J.E., Geo.Abstr.H.G., Hisp.Amer.Per.Ind. (1982-1996), IDA, Int.Lab.Doc., J.of Ferroc., P.A.I.S., Rural Devel.Abstr, Rural Ext.Educ.& Tr.Abstr., Rural Recreat.Tour.Abstr., World Agri.Econ.& Rural Sociol.Abstr. **Document type:** newsletter.
   —BLDSC (4213.580000); UMI; UnCover.
   Formerly: Inter-American Foundation. Journal.
   Description: Reports on how the poor in Latin America and the Caribbean organize and work to improve their lives.

GREAT BRITAIN. NATURAL RESOURCES INSTITUTE. BULLETIN. see *AGRICULTURE*

338.9   UK   ISSN 0950-9593
GREAT BRITAIN. OVERSEAS DEVELOPMENT ADMINISTRATION. REPORT ON RESEARCH AND DEVELOPMENT.* 1983. a. free. Overseas Development Administration, Abercrombie House, Library, Eaglesham Rd., E. Kilbride, Glasgow G75 8EA, Scotland. (Subscr. to: Publications and Publicity Section, N R I, Chatham Maritime, Kent ME4 4TB, England. TEL 0634-880088) circ. controlled. (also avail. in microfiche) **Document type:** government publication.
   —CCC.

338.41 351   UK   ISSN 0952-1518
GUIDE TO EUROPEAN COMMUNITY GRANTS AND LOANS. 1980. a. £160 (effective Sept. 1996). Eurofi Ltd., 44 Melville St., Edinburgh EH3 7HF, Scotland. TEL 44-131-225-8451. FAX 44-131-220-1972. Ed. Verna Ingram. circ. 600 (paid). **Document type:** directory.
   —BLDSC (4226.387000).
   Description: Provides a guide to EC funding, indicating scheme objectives, legislative basis, eligibility, levels of award, deadlines, and contact points in the EC. Aimed at libraries, academic institutions, government bodies, business persons, and lawyers.

338.91   CC   ISSN 1002-1515
GUOJI JINGJI HEZUO/INTERNATIONAL ECONOMIC COOPERATION. (Text in Chinese) 1986. m. $36.80. Duiwai Jingji Maoyi Bu, Guoji Jingji Hezuo Yanjiusuo - Ministry of Foreign Economics and Trade, International Economic Cooperation Research Institute, No. 28, Andingmenwai Donghouxiang, Beijing 100710, People's Republic of China. TEL 4211078. FAX 01-4212149. (Dist. in US by: China Books & Periodicals, Inc., 2929 24th St., San Francisco, CA 94110. TEL 415-282-0994) **Document type:** government publication.

338.91   NE
H I V O S MAGAZINE. 1983. q. free. Humanistisch Instituut voor Ontwikkelingssamenwerking - Humanist Institute for Development Cooperation, Raamweg 16, 2596 HL The Hague, Netherlands. TEL 31-701-3636907. FAX 31-70-3617447. TELEX 34472 HIVOS NL. Ed. Steven Spaargaren. adv.; circ. 9,000 (controlled). **Document type:** bulletin.
   Former titles: H I V O S - Projectbericht (ISSN 0169-0337); H I V O S - Informatie Bulletin.

338.91 327   US   ISSN 1062-578X
HAITI NEWS. 1985. 3/yr. $16 (effective 1995-1996). Haiti News, Box 2120, Brewster, MA 02631. TEL 508-896-5647. FAX 508-896-9790. E-mail: tortora@meol.mass.edu. (Subscr. to: 131 N. Main St., Sharon, MA 02067. TEL 617-784-8067) Ed. Patrick Tortora; Pub. Peter Kinney. bk.rev.; film rev. circ. 632. **Document type:** newsletter, directory.
   Description: Contains articles on development programs in Haiti, resources, classifieds and a directory with indices for geographical location and type of program.

HANDBOOK OF INTERNATIONAL TRADE AND DEVELOPMENT STATISTICS - UNITED NATIONS/MANUEL DE STATISTIQUES DU COMMERCE INTERNATIONAL ET DU DEVELOPMENT - NATIONS UNIES. see *BUSINESS AND ECONOMICS — Abstracting, Bibliographies, Statistics*

BUSINESS AND ECONOMICS — INTERNATIONAL DEVELOPMENT AND ASSISTANCE

338.91   NE
HANDBOOK OF NATIONAL DEVELOPMENT PLANS. a. (plus s-a. supplements). £93.50($174) for basic work; supplement service £93.50 ($174). Kluwer Law International (Subsidiary of: Wolters Kluwer N.V.), Postbus 85889, 2508 CN The Hague, Netherlands. TEL 31-70-3081500. FAX 31-70-3081515. E-mail: services@wkap.nl; URL: http://www.wkap.nl. (Dist. by: Libresso Distribution Centre, P.O. Box 23, 7400 GA Deventer, Netherlands. TEL 31-5700-33155. FAX 31-5700-33834; In N. America: Kluwer Law International, 675 Massachusetts Ave., Cambridge, MA 02139. TEL 617-354-0140. FAX 617-354-8595) **Document type:** trade publication.

HANDBOOK OF STATE TRADING ORGANIZATIONS OF DEVELOPING COUNTRIES/REPERTOIRE DES ORGANISMES DE COMMERCE D'ETAT DES PAYS EN DEVELOPPEMENT/REPERTORIO DE LAS ORGANIZACIONES COMERCIALES ESTATALES DE PAISES EN DESARROLLO/DALIL AL-HAY'AT AL-TIGANIYYA AL-HUKUMIYYA FI AL-BULDAN AN-NAMIYA. see BUSINESS AND ECONOMICS — Abstracting, Bibliographies, Statistics

338.91   NE   ISSN 0168-2229
HANDELSKRANT; nieuws over de andere handel. (Supplement avail.: Koffrekrant (ISSN 1382-1172)) q. fl.21. Fair Trade Organisation, Postbus 115, 4100 AC Culemborg, Netherlands. TEL 31-345-513744. FAX 31-345-521423. TELEX 40876 SOSTR NL. E-mail: FairTrade@antenna.nl. Ed. Hester Staflen. circ. 3,000. (also avail. in Braille) **Document type:** newspaper.
Supersedes in part: S O S Wereldhandel (ISSN 0166-249X); Which was formerly (until 1977): 3e Wereldhandel (ISSN 0922-0348)

HARAMATA - BULLETIN OF THE DRYLANDS. see ENVIRONMENTAL STUDIES

THE I D B. (Inter-American Development Bank) see BUSINESS AND ECONOMICS — Banking And Finance

338.91   BB
I D C IMPACT. (Industrial Development Corporation) q. Pelican Industrial Pk., Bridgetown, Barbados, W.I. (U.S. Addr.: 800 Second Ave., 17th Fl., New York, NY 10017, U.S.A.)

338.91   JA
I D E SYMPOSIUM PROCEEDINGS. (Text in English) 1974. irreg., no.17, 1997. Institute of Developing Economies - Ajia Keizai Kenkyusho, 42 Ichigaya-Hommura-cho, Shinjuku-ku, Tokyo 162, Japan. TEL 81-3-3353-4231. FAX 81-3-3226-8475. (Subscr. to: Maruzen Co., Ltd., Box 5050, Tokyo International 100-31, Japan) circ. 700. **Document type:** proceedings.

338.9   CN   ISSN 0315-9981
HC59.69   CODEN: IDRIDJ
I D R C REPORTS. French edition: C R D I Explore (ISSN 0380-1438); Spanish edition: C I I D Informa (ISSN 0304-5544) 1972. w. International Development Research Centre - Centre de Recherches pour le developpement international, Box 8500, Ottawa, ON K1G 3H9, Canada. TEL 613-236-6163. FAX 613-563-2476. E-mail: order@idrc.ca; URL: http://www.idrc.ca. Ed. Neale MacMillan. circ. 34,300. (back issues avail.) **Indexed:** Can.B.P.I., Can.Per.Ind., CMI, Energy Info.Abstr., Environ.Abstr., Environ.Per.Bibl. (1991-), Food Sci.& Tech.Abstr., J.of Ferroc., Med.Care Rev., Repindex, Sage Fam.Stud.Abstr., Trop.Oil Seeds Abstr., W.R.C.Inf. **Document type:** academic/scholarly publication.
● Available only online.
—CASDDS; CISTI.
Description: For researchers and educators interested in development issues and who can help spread the knowledge of research results in their community; members of government bodies that formulate policies or help in the dissemination of technologies; libraries and information networks in Third World countries.

338   UK   ISSN 0265-5012
HC59.7
I D S BULLETIN. 1969. q. £40 (effective 1995). Institute of Development Studies, University of Sussex, Brighton, Sussex BN1 9RE, England. TEL 44-1273-606261. FAX 44-1273-621202. TELEX 877997 IDS BTN G. E-mail: ids.subs@sussex.ac.uk. Ed. Katherine Henry. adv.; bk.rev.; bibl.; charts; stat. circ. 2,500. (back issues avail.) **Indexed:** ASCA, Asian-Pac.Econ.Lit., ASSIA, Cott.& Trop.Fibr.Abstr., Curr.Adv.Ecol.Sci., Curr.Cont., E.I., Geo.Abstr.H.G., IDA, Int.Lab.Doc., J.of Ferroc., Mult.Ed.Abstr., Rural Devel.Abstr., Rural Ext.Educ.& Tr.Abstr., Rural Recreat.Tour.Abstr., SSCI, Stud.Wom.Abstr., Tech.Educ.Abstr., World Agri.Econ.& Rural Sociol.Abstr. **Document type:** academic/scholarly publication, bulletin.
—BLDSC (4362.585000); EMDOCS; Genuine Article; KR SourceOne; SWETS; UnCover.
Former titles (until 1984): Institute of Development Studies. Bulletin (ISSN 0960-734X); (until 1980): I D S Bulletin (1975) (ISSN 0308-5872); (until 1975): Institute of Development Studies Bulletin (ISSN 0020-2835)
Description: Covers themes of topical importance to all working on development. Combines scholarly research with clear explanation.

338   UK   ISSN 0308-5864
HD72
I D S DISCUSSION PAPER. 1972. irreg. (8-12/yr.). Institute of Development Studies, University of Sussex, Brighton, Sussex BN1 9RE, England. TEL 44-1273-606261. FAX 44-1273-621202. TELEX 877997 IDS BTN G. E-mail: ids.subs@sussex.ac.uk. Ed. Katherine Henry. circ. 600. **Indexed:** Forest.Abstr., Geo.Abstr.H.G., IDA, Rural Devel.Abstr., Rural Recreat.Tour.Abstr., World Agri.Econ.& Rural Sociol.Abstr. **Document type:** academic/scholarly publication.
Description: Contains preliminary field and theoretical research findings circulated to stimulate feedback.

338   UK   ISSN 0141-1314
I D S RESEARCH REPORTS. 1978. irreg. (1-3/yr). Institute of Development Studies, University of Sussex, Brighton, Sussex BN1 9RE, England. TEL 44-1273-606261. FAX 44-1273-6210202. TELEX 877997 IDS BTN G. Ed. Katherine Henry. circ. 500. **Indexed:** Rural Recreat.Tour.Abstr., World Agri.Econ.& Rural Sociol.Abstr. **Document type:** academic/scholarly publication, monographic series.
—BLDSC (7762.352700).
Description: Contains the final results of major research projects regarding a range of development themes.

338.91 630   UN
I F A D UPDATE. (Editions in Arabic, English, French, Spanish) q. free. International Fund for Agricultural Development, Information and Communications Division - Fonds International de Developpement Agricole, Via del Serafico, 107, 00142 Rome, Italy. TEL 39-6-54591. FAX 39-6-5043463. TELEX 620330 IFAD. Dir. Allegra Morelli. circ. 14,000. **Document type:** newsletter.
Description: Studies the fight to combat hunger and rural poverty in the low-income food deficit regions of the world.

338.91 332.6   UN   ISSN 1012-8069
I F C DISCUSSION PAPER. (Subseries avail.: Trends in Private Investment in Developing Countries (ISSN 1018-208X)) (Text in English) 1989. a. International Finance Corporation, 1818 H St., N.W., Washington, DC 20433. TEL 202-473-1155. FAX 202-676-0581. (Subscr. to: Box 7247-8619, Philadelphia, PA 19170-8619) **Indexed:** Geo.Abstr.H.G., IDA. **Document type:** monographic series.
—BLDSC (3597.364500).
Description: Reports on private-sector economic and finance issues worldwide.

339   GW
I F O MITTEILUNGEN DER ABTEILUNG ENTWICKLUNGSLAENDER. 1965. a. free. I F O Institut fuer Wirtschaftsforschung, Poschingerstr. 5, 81679 Munich, Germany. TEL 49-89-9224-0. FAX 49-89-985369. Ed. Axel J. Halbach. adv.; bk.rev.; abstr.; charts; illus. circ. 400.
Former titles: I F O Mitteilungen: Entwicklungslaender - Afrika Studienstelle; Informationen der Afrika-Studienstelle (ISSN 0046-9394)
Description: Compilation of research in developing countries.

338.91   GW   ISSN 0170-5709
I F O STUDIEN ZUR ENTWICKLUNGSFORSCHUNG. (Supplement avail.: I F O Studien zur Entwicklungsforschung. Sonderreihe Information und Dokumentation (ISSN 0723-8975)) 1976. irreg., vol.28, 1995. price varies. I F O Institut fuer Wirtschaftsforschung, Poschingerstr. 5, 81679 Munich, Germany. TEL 49-89-9224-0. FAX 49-89-985369. circ. 400. **Document type:** monographic series.

338.91   GW   ISSN 0723-8975
I F O STUDIEN ZUR ENTWICKLUNGSFORSCHUNG. SONDERREIHE INFORMATION UND DOKUMENTATION. (Supplement to: I F O Studien zur Entwicklungsforschung (ISSN 0170-5709)) 1980. irreg., no.8, 1996. price varies. (I F O Institut fuer Wirtschaftsforschung) Weltforum Verlag, Marienburgerstr. 22, 50963 Cologne, Germany. TEL 49-221-93763-0. FAX 49-221-9376399. **Document type:** monographic series.

338.91489   DK   ISSN 0901-6171
HC59.7
I F U ANNUAL REPORT. 1978. a. free. Industrialiseringsfonden for Udviklingslandene - Industrialization Fund for Developing Countries, Bremerholm 4, P.O. Box 2155, DK-1016 Copenhagen K, Denmark. TEL 45-33-63-75-00. FAX 45-33-3225-24. TELEX 15493 IFU DK. circ. 13,000. **Document type:** corporate report.
Formerly: I F U's Participation in Joint Ventures (ISSN 0108-1969)
Description: Focuses on all aspects of economic activity in developing countries in order to promote investments in these countries in collaboration with Danish trades and industries.

I I E P SEMINAR PAPERS. (International Institute for Educational Planning) see EDUCATION — International Education Programs

338.9   US   ISSN 1011-8721
I I R R REPORT. 1960. s-a. free. International Institute of Rural Reconstruction, 475 Riverside Dr., New York, NY 10115. TEL 212-870-2992. Ed. Eric Blitz. circ. 2,500.
Description: Carries out research and training in rural development in the Third World.

338.91   SW   ISSN 0345-5165
I M. 1944. 10/yr. SEK 100 (effective 1997). Individuell Maenniskohjaelp, P.O. Box 45, S-221 00 Lund, Sweden. TEL 46-46-211-79-80. FAX 46-46-15-83-09. (also avail. in audio cassette)

338.91   UN   ISSN 1022-5412
HD58.8
I O D A JOURNAL. 1993. s-a. International Organization Development Association, Box 33376, Washington, DC 20033.

332.673489   DK   ISSN 0906-3560
I OE ANNUAL REPORT. 1991. a. I OE, Investment Fund for Central and Eastern Europe - Denmark, 4 Bremerholm, P.O. Box 2155, DK-1016 Copenhagen K, Denmark. TEL 45-33-63-75-00. FAX 45-33-322524. TELEX 15493 IFU DK.

338.91   CM   ISSN 0256-4912
I P D CAHIER/P A I D REPORTS. (Text in English, French) 1981. s-a. 9000 Fr.CFA($45) Institut Panafricain pour le Developpement - Panafrican Institute for Development, P.O. Box 4056, Douala, Cameroon. TEL 42-10-61. FAX 237-42-43-35. TELEX 6048 KN. Ed. Alfred Comlan Mondjanagni. circ. 2,000. (back issues avail.)
Description: Reflections and information concerning training, research and support-consultancy activities for rural development in sub-Saharan Africa.

BUSINESS AND ECONOMICS — INTERNATIONAL DEVELOPMENT AND ASSISTANCE

338.91   IT   ISSN 0390-6272
HC301
I R I GRUPPO YEARBOOK. a. Istituto per la Ricostruzione Industriale, Via Vittorio Veneteo 89, 00187 Rome, Italy. TEL 06-47271. FAX 06-47272308.

338.91 330.904   FR
▼**I S T E D LETTRE**. 1996. m. Institut des Sciences et des Techniques de L'Equipement et de l'Environnement pour le Developpement, La Grande Arche, Paroi Sud, 92055 Paris la Defense, Cedex 04, France. TEL 33-1-40812406. FAX 33-1-40812331. Ed. Xavier Crepin; Pub. Jean Baudon. **Document type:** newsletter.
    Description: Provides a forum for ideas, information, and action at the service of members in the private and public sectors of public works, development, and the environment. Promotes French expertise at the international level and disseminates scientific and technical information.

338.91   II   ISSN 0970-1532
HB1
INDIAN JOURNAL OF QUANTITATIVE ECONOMICS; an international journal of development economics. 1985. s-a. Rs.60 to individuals (foreign $10); institutions Rs.80 (foreign $15). Guru Nanak Dev University, Punjab School of Economics, Amritsar 143 005, India. TEL 258841. Ed. P.S. Raikhy. adv.; bk.rev. circ. 200. **Indexed:** J.of Econ.Lit., Rural Devel.Abstr., Soc.Sci.Ind. **Document type:** academic/scholarly publication.

INDIAN JOURNAL OF RURAL TECHNOLOGY. see TECHNOLOGY: COMPREHENSIVE WORKS

333.7 600   NE   ISSN 0928-1460
INDIGENOUS KNOWLEDGE AND DEVELOPMENT MONITOR. (Text in English) 1993. 3/yr. fl.40 in Europe, Japan, Australia & New Zealand; $27 in U.S. and Canada; free to persons in developing countries. Centre for International Research and Advisory Networks (CIRAN), P.O. Box 29777, 2502 LT The Hague, Netherlands. TEL 31-70-4260324. FAX 31-70-4260329. E-mail: ikdm@nufficcs.nl; URL: http://www.nuffics.nl/ciran. Ed. Anna van Marrewijk. R&P contact: Akke W. Tick. bk.rev. circ. 3,200. **Document type:** academic/scholarly publication, bulletin.
    —BLDSC (4437.084000).
    Description: Disseminates research and information relating to the study and application of indigenous knowledge. Encourages international cooperation in matters relating to sustainable development in policy and practice.
    Refereed Serial

338   UN
HC411
INDUSTRIAL DEVELOPMENT NEWS FOR ASIA AND THE PACIFIC. 1962. irreg., no.22, 1994. $15. United Nations Economic and Social Commission for Asia and the Pacific (ESCAP), Division of Industry, Housing and Technology, United Nations Bldg., Rajadamnern Ave., Bangkok 10200, Thailand. (Dist. by: United Nations Publications, Rm. DC2-0853, New York, NY 10017; or Distribution and Sales Section, Palais des Nations, CH-1211 Geneva 10, Switzerland; or Conference Services Unit, E.S.C.A.P., Bangkok) (back issues avail.)
    Former titles: Industry and Technology Development News - Asia and the Pacific (ISSN 1010-514X); Former titles (until 1983): Industrial Development News - Asia and the Pacific (ISSN 0252-4481); (until 1977): Asian Industrial Development News (ISSN 0572-4171)

338.91 600   UN   ISSN 0259-2398
INDUSTRIALIZACION Y DESARROLLO TECNOLOGICO. 1985. s-a. Comision Economica para America Latina y el Caribe - Economic Commission for Latin America and the Caribbean, Casilla 179-D, Santiago, Chile. FAX 562480252.

INDUSTRIE EUROPEENNE. see BUSINESS AND ECONOMICS — Production Of Goods And Services

338.91   EI
INFO PHARE. 1994. bi-m. free. Commission of European Communities, Phare Information Office, Directorate General for External Economic Relations, DG I, MO 34 3-80, Rue de la Loi, 200, 1049 Brussels, Belgium. TEL 32-2-299-14-44. FAX 32-2-299-17-77. URL: http://www.cec.lu. Eds. P. Vinther, G. Burghardt; Pub. G. Burghardt. illus. circ. 20,000. **Document type:** newsletter.
    Description: Provides information on developments of Phare to provide financial aid for the social and economic conversion of Central and Eastern Europe's economies.

338.91 004   NE   ISSN 0268-1102
HC59.72.I55
INFORMATION TECHNOLOGY FOR DEVELOPMENT. 1986-1990; resumed with vol.6, 1995. q. fl.310($184) (effective 1997). I O S Press, Van Diemenstraat 94, 1013 CN Amsterdam, Netherlands. TEL 31-20-6382189. FAX 31-20-6203419. E-mail: market@iospress.nl; URL: http://www.iospress.nl/iospress. (Subscr. in N. America to: Box 10558, Burke, VA 22009-0558. TEL 703-250-4705) Ed. S. Ramani. adv. circ. 1,000. **Indexed:** INSPEC (1986-1990, 1995-). **Document type:** academic/scholarly publication.
    —BLDSC (4496.368810); AskIEEE; KR SourceOne. CCC.
    Description: Encourages a critical debate on the role of information technology in the development process.
    Refereed Serial

338.91   FR   ISSN 0252-2683
INFORMATIONS RECENTES SUR LES COMPTES NATIONAUX DES PAYS EN DEVELOPPEMENT/LATEST INFORMATION ON NATIONAL ACCOUNTS OF DEVELOPING COUNTRIES. (Text in English, French) 1967. a. free. Organization for Economic Cooperation and Development, 2 rue Andre-Pascal, 75775 Paris Cedex 16, France. (U.S. orders to: O.E.C.D. Publications and Information Center, 2001 L St., N.W., Ste. 650, Washington, DC 20036-4922. TEL 202-785-6323) adv. (back issues avail.) **Indexed:** IIS.
    ●Also available online.

INFOTERRA PROGRAMME ACTIVITY CENTRE. EXCHANGE OF ENVIRONMENTAL EXPERIENCE SERIES. see ENVIRONMENTAL STUDIES

338.91   US   ISSN 1063-0260
HC79.C3
INFRASTRUCTURE FINANCE; the magazine for global development. 1992. q. free to qualified personnel. Institutional Investor, Inc., 488 Madison Ave., New York, NY 10022. TEL 212-224-3570. FAX 212-224-3592. Ed. Elizabeth Bailey. adv. contact: Sabrina Clarke. illus.; circ. 16,000 (controlled). **Indexed:** HRIS. **Document type:** trade publication.
    —CCC.
    Description: Covers international issues pertaining to infrastructure investment and maintenance.

INGENIEURS SANS FRONTIERES. see ENGINEERING

INSIDE INDONESIA. see POLITICAL SCIENCE — International Relations

330   FR   ISSN 0073-8247
INSTITUT D'EMISSION D'OUTRE MER, PARIS. RAPPORT D'ACTIVITE. 1967. a. 300 F. Institut d'Emission d'Outre Mer, Paris, 1 Cite du Retiro, 75008 Paris, France. TEL 40-06-41-41. FAX 47-42-75-53. TELEX 281-286.

338.9   SZ
INSTITUT D'ETUDES DU DEVELOPPEMENT. CAHIERS. 1975. irreg. price varies. Institut d'Etudes du Developpement, 24, rue Rothschild, CH-1211 Geneva 21, Switzerland. TEL 022-7319408. FAX 022-7385797. (reprint service avail. from KTO) **Document type:** monographic series.

338.91 658   CM
INSTITUT PANAFRICAIN POUR LE DEVELOPPEMENT. CENTRE D'ETUDES ET DE RECHERCHES APPLIQUEES. EVALUATION DU SEMINAIRE SUR LA METHODOLOGIE DU MANAGEMENT DES PROJETS. a. $25. Institut Panafricain pour le Developpement, Centre de Documentation, B.P. 4078, Douala, Cameroon. Ed. Adovi John-Bosco. bk.rev. circ. 1,500.

338.91 658   CM
INSTITUT PANAFRICAIN POUR LE DEVELOPPEMENT. CENTRE DE FORMATION AU MANAGEMENT DES PROJETS. BILAN DES ACTIVITES. irreg.? Institut Panafricain pour le Developpement, Centre de Documentation, B.P. 4078, Douala, Cameroon.

338   CM
INSTITUT PANAFRICAIN POUR LE DEVELOPPEMENT. TRAVAUX D'ETUDIANTS. BULLETIN ANALYTIQUE. 1967. q. Institut Panafricain pour le Developpement, Centre de Documentation, B.P. 4078, Douala, Cameroon. bk.rev. **Document type:** bulletin.
    Formerly: Institut Panafricain pour le Developpement. Annuaire des Anciens Etudiants (ISSN 0046-9734)

INSTITUT PANAFRICAIN POUR LE DEVELOPPEMENT. TRAVAUX MANUSCRITS. see AGRICULTURE — Agricultural Economics

338.91   GW   ISSN 0341-616X
HB5
INSTITUTE FOR SCIENTIFIC CO-OPERATION WITH DEVELOPING COUNTRIES. ECONOMICS; a biannual collection of recent German contributions to the field of economic science. (Text in English) 1968. s-a. DM.40 per no. Institute for Scientific Co-operation with Developing Countries, Vogtshaldenstr. 24, 72074 Tuebingen, Germany. TEL 49-7071-5066. FAX 49-7071-26753. Ed. Hans-Bernard Pfannenberg. circ. 3,000. (back issues avail.) **Document type:** academic/scholarly publication.

330.06   JA
INSTITUTE OF DEVELOPING ECONOMIES. ANNUAL REPORT. (Text in English) a. Institute of Developing Economies, 42 Ichigaya-Hommura-cho, Shinjuku-ku, Tokyo 162, Japan. TEL 81-3-3353-4231. FAX 81-3-3226-8475. **Document type:** corporate report.

338.9   UK
INSTITUTE OF DEVELOPMENT STUDIES. ANNUAL REPORT. a. Institute of Development Studies, University of Sussex, Brighton, Sussex BN1 9RE, England. TEL 44-1273-606261. FAX 44-1273-691647. E-mail: ids.subs@sussex.ac.uk; URL: http://www.ids.ac.uk/ids/publicat/. Ed. Katherine Henry. **Document type:** corporate report.
    Description: Provides a full account of the year's activities and a listing of current staff and research interests. Includes a teaching schedule.

INSTITUTO DO DESENVOLVIMENTO ECONOMICO-SOCIAL DO PARA. PARA DESENVOLVIMENTO. see BUSINESS AND ECONOMICS — Economic Situation And Conditions

338.91   AG   ISSN 1026-0463
HC121
▼**INTEGRACION Y COMERCIO**. English edition: Integration & Trade (ISSN 1027-5703) (Text English, Spanish) 1996. 3/yr. Arg.$60($60) (C. and S. America $70; N. America $70; elsewhere $95) (effective 1997). Banco Interamericano de Desarrollo, Instituto para la Integracion de America Latina - Inter-American Development Bank, Esmeralda 130, Piso 16, 17, 1035 Buenos Aires, Argentina. TEL 54-1-3201871. FAX 54-1-3201872. E-mail: int/inl@iabd.org. Ed.Bd. abstr. **Indexed:** Hisp.Amer.Per.Ind. (1996-).
    Description: Covers trade relations within Latin American and Caribbean countries.

INTEGRATED RURAL DEVELOPMENT. PUBLICATIONS. see POPULATION STUDIES

380 338   UY   ISSN 0538-3048
INTER-AMERICAN COUNCIL OF COMMERCE AND PRODUCTION. URUGUAYAN SECTION. PUBLICACIONES. 1951. irreg. Inter-American Council of Commerce and Production, Misiones 1400, Montevideo, Uruguay.

INTER-AMERICAN DEVELOPMENT BANK. ANNUAL REPORT. see BUSINESS AND ECONOMICS — Banking And Finance

INTER-AMERICAN DEVELOPMENT BANK. BOARD OF GOVERNORS. PROCEEDINGS OF THE MEETING. see BUSINESS AND ECONOMICS — Banking And Finance

BUSINESS AND ECONOMICS — INTERNATIONAL DEVELOPMENT AND ASSISTANCE

330   US
INTER-AMERICAN FOUNDATION. YEAR IN REVIEW. Spanish edition: Fundacion Interamericana. Anuario. (Editions in English, Spanish, Portuguese) a. free. Inter-American Foundation, 901 N. Stuart St., 10th Fl., Arlington, VA 22203-1821. TEL 703-841-3800. FAX 703-527-3529. circ. 23,700 (English ed. 11,700; Portuguese ed. 1,800; Spanish ed. 10,200). (back issues avail.) **Document type:** corporate report.
Formerly: Inter-American Foundation. Annual Report.

338.91   GW
INTERMEDICA POST. 1973. s-a. free. Intermedica e.V., Im Kalten Tale 33, 38304 Wolfenbuettel, Germany. TEL 49-5331-46880. FAX 49-5331-46880. circ. 2,000. **Document type:** bulletin.

INTERNATIONAL AWARD FOR LITERACY RESEARCH/PRIX INTERNATIONAL DE RECHERCHE EN ALPHABETISATION/PREMIO INTERNACIONAL A LA INVESTIGACION EN ALFABETIZACION. see EDUCATION

338.91   UK   ISSN 0964-699X
INTERNATIONAL DEVELOPMENT POLICIES; review of the activities of international organisations. q. £40. Commonwealth Secretariat, Marlborough House, Pall Mall, London SW1Y 5HX, England. TEL 44-171-839-3411. FAX 44-171-747-6235. Ed. Ian Thomas. adv. 350. (back issues avail.) **Document type:** bulletin.
Description: Reviews the main developments in the evolution of international development policies and related economic topics at various international organizations.

INTERNATIONAL DIRECTORY OF SOURCES. INFOTERRA. see ENVIRONMENTAL STUDIES

INTERNATIONAL ECONOMIC DEVELOPMENT LAW. see LAW — International Law

INTERNATIONAL EMPLOYMENT HOTLINE. see OCCUPATIONS AND CAREERS

INTERNATIONAL INSTITUTE FOR ENVIRONMENT AND DEVELOPMENT. DRYLANDS PAPER. see ENVIRONMENTAL STUDIES

INTERNATIONAL INSTITUTE FOR ENVIRONMENT AND DEVELOPMENT. PASTORAL LAND TENURE SERIES. see ENVIRONMENTAL STUDIES

INTERNATIONAL INSTITUTE FOR ENVIRONMENT AND DEVELOPMENT. SUSTAINABLE AGRICULTURE PROGRAMME. GATEKEEPER SERIES. see AGRICULTURE

INTERNATIONAL INSTITUTE FOR ENVIRONMENT AND DEVELOPMENT. SUSTAINABLE AGRICULTURE PROGRAMME. RESEARCH SERIES. see AGRICULTURE

338.91   II   ISSN 0970-1044
HG1505
▼**INTERNATIONAL JOURNAL OF DEVELOPMENT BANKING.** Short title: I J D B. 1983. s-a. Rs.100($40) Industrial Credit and Investment Corporation of India Limited, 163 Backbay Reclamation, Bombay 400 020, India. TEL 22-2022535. FAX 22-2046582. TELEX 11-83062 ICIC IN. Ed. N.J. Jhaveri. bk.rev.; bibl. circ. 500. (back issues avail.)
Description: Studies the role of finance and related areas in the development of Third World countries from an international perspective.

338.91   UK   ISSN 1358-8257
▼**THE INTERNATIONAL JOURNAL OF TECHNICAL COOPERATION.** 1995. s-a. £30($45) to individuals; institutions £85($125) (effective 1997). Frank Cass, Newbury House, 890-900 Eastern Ave., Newbury Park, Ilford, Essex IG2 7HH, England. TEL 44-181-559-8866. FAX 44-181-599-0984. E-mail: jnlsubs@frankcass.com; URL: http://www.frankcass.com. (Dist. in US by: ISBS, 5804 N.E. Hassalo St., Portland, OR 97213-3644. TEL 800-944-6190. FAX 503-280-8832) Ed. Gerald E. Caiden. adv.: B&W page £195($275); adv. contact: Anne Kidson. bk.rev.; index. **Indexed:** Geo.Abstr., IDA. **Document type:** academic/scholarly publication.
—BLDSC (4542.693150); EMDOCS; KR SourceOne.
Description: Addresses the professional needs of practitioners and researchers in the field of international technical cooperation.
Refereed Serial

INTERNATIONAL MONETARY FUND. WORLD ECONOMIC AND FINANCIAL SURVEYS. see BUSINESS AND ECONOMICS — Banking And Finance

INTERNATIONAL POLITICAL ECONOMY YEARBOOK. see POLITICAL SCIENCE

INTERNATIONAL RESEARCH CENTER FOR ENERGY AND ECONOMIC DEVELOPMENT. ANNUAL CONFERENCE. PROCEEDINGS. see ENERGY

INTERNATIONAL RESEARCH CENTER FOR ENERGY AND ECONOMIC DEVELOPMENT. OCCASIONAL PAPERS. see ENERGY

338.91   US   ISSN 1011-8713
INTERNATIONAL SHARING. 1986. 3/yr. International Institute of Rural Reconstruction, 475 Riverside Dr., New York, NY 10115. TEL 212-870-2992. circ. 1,000.
Description: Covers issues, resources and practical methods for implementing rural development programs in the Third World.

338.91   US
INTERNATIONAL SURVEY OF BUSINESS EXPECTATIONS. q. $40. Dun & Bradstreet, Economic Analysis Department, 220 E. 42nd St., 9th Fl., New York, NY 10017-4717. FAX 212-883-3400. (Subscr. to: Box 1861, New York, NY 10163-1861)
Description: International survey of business executives worldwide, regarding their expectations for sales, profits, prices, inventories, employment and new orders in the upcoming quarter. Results are provided by country.

338.91 361   US
INTERNATIONAL WORKCAMP LISTING (YEAR). 1982. a. $5. Service Civil International, 5474 Walnut Level Rd., Crozet, VA 22932. TEL 804-823-1826. E-mail: sciivsusa@igc.apc.org; URL: http:wworks-com-sciivs. Eds. Claire ANdrews, Dave Axtell. circ. 1,000. **Document type:** directory.
Description: Provides description of voluntary, community-based, service workcamps available in the U.S. and throughout Europe.

INTERNATIONALE POLITIK UND GESELLSCHAFT. see POLITICAL SCIENCE — International Relations

INTERNATIONALE SPECTATOR; maandblad voor internationale politiek. see LAW — International Law

INTLEC C D - R O M. see BUSINESS AND ECONOMICS — Economic Situation And Conditions

IRISH STUDIES IN INTERNATIONAL AFFAIRS. see POLITICAL SCIENCE — International Relations

338.91   JA
JAPAN INTERNATIONAL COOPERATION AGENCY. ORGANIZATION AND FUNCTIONS. (Text in English, French, Japanese and Spanish) 1975. a. free. Japan International Cooperation Agency, P.O. Box 216, Mitsui Bldg., Shinjuku-ku, Tokyo 163, Japan. TEL 81-3-3346-5051. FAX 81-3-3346-5032. E-mail: matuyama@ific.or.jp. circ. 2,000.

JEUNE AFRIQUE; le devoir d'informer - la liberte d'ecrire. see POLITICAL SCIENCE — International Relations

JOINT VENTURES WITH THE SOVIET REPUBLICS; law and practice. see LAW — International Law

338.91 327   GW   ISSN 0258-2384
JOURNAL FUER ENTWICKLUNGSPOLITIK. (Text and summaries in English, German) 1984. q. DM.79. (Mattersburger Kreis fuer Entwicklungspolitik) Brandes und Apsel Verlag GmbH, Zeilweg 20, 60439 Frankfurt a.M., Germany. TEL 49-69-588613. FAX 49-69-5870359. bk.rev. **Indexed:** IBR. **Document type:** academic/scholarly publication.

338.91   US
▼**JOURNAL OF BUSINESS IN DEVELOPING NATIONS.** 1997. q. free. North Carolina Central University, School of Business, JBND, Durham, NC 27707. E-mail: jparnell@nccu.campus.mci.net; URL: http://www.nccu.edu/business/journal.htm. Ed. John A. Parnell. R&P contact: John A. Parnell. **Document type:** academic/scholarly publication.
●Available only online.
Description: Contains reports on research concerning business advances as they relate to the developing world.
Refereed Serial

338   US   ISSN 0022-037X
HC59.7   CODEN: JDARB4
JOURNAL OF DEVELOPING AREAS. 1966. q. $29 to individuals; institutions $39 (foreign $39) (effective 1996). Western Illinois University, Morgan Hall 232, Macomb, IL 61455. TEL 309-298-1108. FAX 309-298-2865. E-mail: se-schisler@wiu.edu. Ed. Nicholas C. Pano. R&P contact: Joan Pano. TEL 309-298-1108. adv. contact: Joan Pano. bk.rev.; bibl.; charts; illus.; index. circ. 1,264. (back issues avail.; reprint service avail. from SCH) **Indexed:** A.B.C.Pol.Sci., ABI Inform., Abstr.Anthropol., Abstr.Rural Dev.Trop., Agri.Eng.Abstr., Amer.Hist.& Life (1966-), ASCA, Asian-Pac.Econ.Lit., ASSIA, B.P.I, BPIA, Bull.Signal., Bus.Ind., Curr.Cont., Documentatieblad, Econ.Abstr., Geo.Abstr.P.G., Hisp.Amer.Per.Ind. (1977-), Hist.Abstr. (1966-), IBR, IDA, Int.Lab.Doc., Int.Polit.Sci.Abstr., J.of Econ.Lit., Key to Econ.Sci., Mar.Aff.Bibl., Mid.East: Abstr.& Ind., P.A.I.S., Per.Islam. (1990-), Polit.Sci.Abstr., Pub.Admin.Abstr., Ref.Zh, Rural Devel.Abstr., Rural Ext.Educ.& Tr.Abstr., Rural Recreat.Tour.Abstr., Sage Urb.Stud.Abstr., So.Pac.Per.Ind., Sociol.Abstr., Soils & Fert., SSCI, Tr.& Indus.Ind. **Document type:** academic/scholarly publication.
—BLDSC (4969.200000); Genuine Article; KR SourceOne; SWETS; UMI; UnCover.
Description: Focuses on development issues affecting Third World countries and less-developed regions of other nations.
Refereed Serial

338.9   JA   ISSN 1341-3953
▼**JOURNAL OF DEVELOPMENT ASSISTANCE.** Japanese edition: Kaihatsu Enjo Kenkyu (ISSN 1340-7198) (Text in English) 1995. s-a. free. Overseas Economic Cooperation Fund - Kaigai Keizai Kyoryoku Kikin, Takebashi Godo Bldg., 4-1, Ohtemachi 1-chome, Chiyoda-ku, Tokyo 100, Japan. FAX 81-3-3215-2897. TELEX J28430 COOPFUND.
Description: Discusses major development issues and the results of recent research.

338.9   NE   ISSN 0304-3878
HC59.7   CODEN: JDECDF
JOURNAL OF DEVELOPMENT ECONOMICS. (Text in English) 1974. bi-m. fl.1710($983) (effective 1998). North-Holland (Subsidiary of: Elsevier Science B.V.), P.O. Box 211, 1000 AE Amsterdam, Netherlands. TEL 31-20-4853911. FAX 31-20-4853598. TELEX 18582 ESPA NL. (Subscr. in the Americas to: Elsevier Science, Regional Sales Office, Box 945, New York, NY 10159-0945. TEL 212-633-3730. FAX 212-633-3680; Subscr. in Australasia and the Far East to: Elsevier Science (Singapore) Pte Ltd, No.1 Temasek Ave., No.17-01 Millenia Tower, Singapore 039192, Singapore. TEL 65-434-3727. FAX 65-337-2230; Subscr. in Japan to: Elsevier Science Japan, 9-15 Higashi-Azabu 1-chome, Minato-ku, Tokyo 106, Japan. TEL 81-3-5561-5033. FAX 81-3-5561-5047) Ed. Pranab Bardhan. adv.; bk.rev.; index. (also avail. in microform from UMI; back issues avail.; reprint service avail. from SWZ) **Indexed:** ABI Inform., Abstr.Rural Dev.Trop., ASCA, Asian-Pac.Econ.Lit., BPIA, Bus.Ind., C.R.E.J., CLOSS, Curr.Cont., Geo.Abstr.P.G., IBR, IDA, Int.Lab.Doc., J.of Econ.Lit., Mid.East: Abstr.& Ind., P.A.I.S., Popul.Ind., Rural Devel.Abstr., Rural Recreat.Tour.Abstr., Soc.Sci.Ind., SSCI, World Agri.Econ.& Rural Sociol.Abstr. **Document type:** academic/scholarly publication.
—BLDSC (4969.220000); Genuine Article; KR SourceOne; SWETS; UMI; UnCover. **CCC.**
Description: Publishes papers relating to all aspects of economic development - from immediate policy concerns to structural problems of underdevelopment.
Refereed Serial

BUSINESS AND ECONOMICS — INTERNATIONAL DEVELOPMENT AND ASSISTANCE

338.9   UN   ISSN 0085-2392
HC59
JOURNAL OF DEVELOPMENT PLANNING. French edition: Journal de la Planification et du Developpement (ISSN 0251-3684); Spanish edition: Revista de la Planificacion del Desarrollo (ISSN 0255-5050) 1969. irreg., latest vol.24, 1994. price varies. (Department of International Economic and Social Affairs (DIESA)) United Nations Publications, Sales and Marketing Section, Room DC2-0853, New York, NY 10017. TEL 212-963-8302; 800-253-9646. FAX 212-963-3489. E-mail: publications@un.org; URL: http://www.un.org/publications. (Or: United Nations Sales Section, Palais des Nations, CH-1211 Geneva 10, Switzerland) (also avail. in microfiche from CIS; back issues avail.) **Indexed:** E.I., IIS, P.A.I.S. **Document type:** monographic series.
—BLDSC (4969.230000); SWETS; UnCover.

320 338 300   UK   ISSN 0022-0388
HC10
THE JOURNAL OF DEVELOPMENT STUDIES. 1964. bi-m. £48($70) to individuals; institutions £195($260) (effective 1998). Frank Cass, Newbury House, 890-900 Eastern Ave., Newbury Park, Ilford, Essex IG2 7HH, England. TEL 44-181-599-8866. FAX 44-181-599-0984. E-mail: jnlsubs@frankcass.com; URL: http://www.frankcass.com. (Dist. in US by: ISBS, 5804 N.E. Hassalo St., Portland, OR 97213-3644. TEL 800-944-6190. FAX 503-280-8832) Ed.Bd. adv.: B&W page £195 ($275); adv. contact: Anne Kidson. bk.rev.; index. (also avail. in microfilm from UMI; back issues avail.) **Indexed:** A.B.C.Pol.Sci., Abstr.Rural Dev.Trop., Amer.Hist.& Life (1968-), ASCA, Asian-Pac.Econ.Lit., ASSIA, BPIA, Br.Hum.Ind., Bus.Ind., C.R.E.J., Curr.Cont., Documentatieblad, E.I., Geo.Abstr.P.G., Hist.Abstr. (1968-), IBR, IDA, Int.Lab.Doc., Int.Polit.Sci.Abstr., Intl.Bibl.S.S.Soc.Cult.Anthro., Irr.& Drain.Abstr., J.of Econ.Lit., J.of Econ.Lit., Key to Econ.Sci., Mid.East Abstr.& Ind., P.A.I.S., Rice Abstr., Risk Abstr., Rural Devel.Abstr., Rural Recreat.Tour.Abstr., Sage Pub.Admin.Abstr., Sage Urb.Stud.Abstr., Soc.Sci.Ind., Sociol.Abstr., SSCI, Stud.Wom.Abstr., Tr.& Indus.Ind., Work Rel.Abstr., World Agri.Econ.& Rural Sociol.Abstr., World Bank.Abstr. **Document type:** academic/scholarly publication.
●Also available online. Vendor(s): Information Access Co., UMI.
Also available on CD-ROM.
—BLDSC (4969.250000); Genuine Article; KR SourceOne; SWETS; UMI; UnCover. CCC.
Description: Covers development studies and the concept of development: economic, political, and social.
Refereed Serial

JOURNAL OF EASTERN AFRICAN RESEARCH & DEVELOPMENT. see HISTORY — History Of Africa

JOURNAL OF ENERGY AND DEVELOPMENT. see ENERGY

JOURNAL OF HIMALAYAN STUDIES AND REGIONAL DEVELOPMENT. see ENVIRONMENTAL STUDIES

338.91   UK   ISSN 0963-8199
HF1371
THE JOURNAL OF INTERNATIONAL TRADE AND ECONOMIC DEVELOPMENT. 1992. 3/yr. £36 (U.S. and Canada $56; rest of world £38) to individuals; institutions £130 (U.S. and Canada $195; rest of world £135) (effective 1997). Routledge, 11 New Fetter Ln., London EC4P 4EE, England. TEL 44-171-583-9855. FAX 44-171-842-2298. E-mail: sample.journals@routledge.com; URL: http://www.routledge.com/routledge/journal/journals.html. (Subscr. to: ITPS Ltd., Dept. J, Cheriton House, North Way, Andover, Hants SP10 5BE, England. TEL 44-1264-342919. FAX 44-1264-342807; Subscr. in US & Canada to: 29 W. 35th St., New York, NY 10001-2299. TEL 212-244-3336. FAX 212-564-7854) Ed.Bd. adv.: page £150; trim 115 x 190. circ. 500. **Indexed:** Geo.Abstr.P.G., IDA. **Document type:** academic/scholarly publication.
—BLDSC (5007.686900); SWETS.
Description: Covers international economics, economic development, and the interface between trade and development.

338.2   SW
HF1051
JOURNAL OF MINERAL POLICY, BUSINESS AND ENVIRONMENT - RAW MATERIALS REPORT. (Text in English) 1981. q. SEK 500 to individuals (foreign $75); institutions SEK 1100 (foreign 150) (effective 1997). Raavarugruppen Ekonomisk Foerening - Raw Materials Group, Sweden, P.O. Box 44062, S-100 73 Stockholm, Sweden. TEL 46-8-744-00-65. FAX 46-8-7440066. E-mail: Raw.Materials.Group@RMG.se. (Co-sponsor: University of Dundee, Centre for Mineral and Petroleum Law and Policy) Eds. Magnus Ericsson, Chris Rogers. adv.; bk.rev.; illus.; bibl.; charts; stat.; index. circ. 500. (also avail. in microfilm from UMI; back issues avail.; reprint service avail. from UMI) **Indexed:** Alloys Ind., Alt.Press Ind., Eng.Mat.Abstr., Geo.Abstr.P.G., I.M.M.Abstr., IDA, Met.Abstr.Ind., Met.Abstr., Nonfer.Met.Alert, P.A.I.S., PCC Alert, Per.Islam. (1993-), Steels Alert, World Alum.Abstr. **Document type:** academic/scholarly publication.
●Also available on CD-ROM.
—BLDSC (7296.559000); EMDOCS; KR SourceOne; UMI.
Formerly: Raw Materials Report (ISSN 0349-6287)
Refereed Serial

338.91   GW
JOURNALISTENHANDBUCH ENTWICKLUNGSPOLITIK. 1974. a. Bundesministerium fuer Wirtschaftliche Zusammenarbeit und Entwicklung, Friedrich-Ebert-Allee 114-116, 53113 Bonn, Germany. **Document type:** government publication.

338.91   NE   ISSN 1380-1643
G905
K I T NEWSLETTER. 1991. 2/yr. Koninklijk Instituut voor de Tropen - Royal Tropical Institute, Mauritskade 63, 1092 AD Amsterdam, Netherlands. TEL 31-20-5688711. FAX 31-20-5688286. **Document type:** newsletter.

338.9   JA   ISSN 1340-7198
KAIHATSU ENJO KENKYU. English edition: Journal of Development Assistance (ISSN 1341-3953) 1968. q. free. Overseas Economic Cooperation Fund - Kaigai Keizai Kyoryoku Kinkin, 4-1, Ohtemachi 1-chome, Chiyoda-ku, Tokyo 100, Japan. FAX 81-3-3215-2897. TELEX J28430 COOPFUND.
Formerly (until 1994): Kikin Chosa Kiho - Overseas Economic Cooperation Fund Research Quarterly (ISSN 0910-9668)

KAIHATSU RONSHU/JOURNAL OF DEVELOPMENT POLICY STUDIES. see BUSINESS AND ECONOMICS — Economic Situation And Conditions

KONINKLIJK INSTITUUT VOR DE TROPEN. ANNOTATED BIBLIOGRAPHIES SERIES. see AGRICULTURE — Abstracting, Bibliographies, Statistics

338.91   II
KRISHI SAMEEKSHA. (Text in Hindi) m. Rs.100($36) Ministry of Agriculture, Directorate of Economics and Statistics, A-2E-3 Kasturba Gandhi Marg Barracks, New Delhi 110 001, India. **Document type:** government publication.

L A W G LETTER. (Latin American Working Group) see POLITICAL SCIENCE — International Relations

338.91 918   US   ISSN 1040-3183
HC121
LAGNIAPPE QUARTERLY MONITOR; trend analysis for business operations in Latin America. 1984. q. $675 includes Lagniappe Letter (effective 1998). Latin American Information Services, Inc., 159 W. 53rd St., 28th fl., New York, NY 10019. TEL 212-765-5520. FAX 212-765-2927. URL: http://www.lais.com. Ed. Rosemary H. Werrett. **Document type:** newsletter.
●Also available online. Vendor(s): Information Access Co.
Formerly: Lagniappe Quarterly Report.
Description: Statistics of financial indicators, short-term forecasts and production trends of Latin America's nine key markets.

338.91 327   GW   ISSN 0174-6324
LATEINAMERIKA NACHRICHTEN. 1973. m. DM.70 to individuals; institutions DM.85 (effective 1996). Lateinamerika Nachrichten GbR, Gneisenaustr. 2, 10961 Berlin, Germany. TEL 49-30-6946100. FAX 49-30-6926590. adv.; bk.rev.; index. circ. 2,500. (back issues avail.) **Indexed:** Hisp.Amer.Per.Ind. (1986-1995), IBR, Irr.& Drain.Abstr., Rural Devel.Abstr. **Document type:** academic/scholarly publication.

338.9   PK
LECTURES IN DEVELOPMENT ECONOMICS. 1982. irreg., no.8, 1990. price varies. Pakistan Institute of Development Economics, P.O. Box 1091, Islamabad 44000, Pakistan. TEL 92-51-9206610. FAX 92-51-9210886. Ed. Sarfraz Khan Qureshi. bibl.; charts; stat. circ. 1,000. (back issues avail.) **Document type:** academic/scholarly publication.
Supersedes (1970-1982): Readings in Development Economics (ISSN 0557-8280)

LETTRE DE LA FRANCOPHONIE. see BUSINESS AND ECONOMICS — Cooperatives

LIFELONG EDUCATION NETWORK. see EDUCATION

338.91   UN   ISSN 0255-5182
LIST OF E C A DOCUMENTS ISSUED/LISTE DES DOCUMENTS PUBLIES PAR LA C E A. q. United Nations Economic Commission for Africa, P.O. Box 3001, Addis Ababa, Ethiopia.

338.91   JA   ISSN 0456-5339
HC461
LOOK JAPAN. Spanish edition (ISSN 0915-8308) (Text in English) 1953. m. 9000 Yen (Spanish ed. 10000Yen; Chinese ed. 10000Yen). Look Japan, Ltd., 2-2, Kanda Ogawamachi, Chiyoda-ku, Tokyo 101, Japan. TEL 81-3-3291-8951. FAX 81-3-3291-8955. E-mail: look@gol.com; URL: http://www.lookjapan.com. (Singapore Office: Look Japan Publishing Pte. Ltd., 24Raffles Place, 25-02 Clifford Centre, Singapore 048621. TEL 533-0333. FAX 534-6166; H.K. Office: Look Japan International Ltd., P.O. Box 47544, Morrison Hill Post Office, Wanchai, Hong Kong. TEL 5980113) Ed. Kunio Nishimura; Pub. Takenori Kimura. adv. contact: Akira Watanabe. bk.rev. circ. 75,000. (back issues avail.) **Document type:** consumer publication.
—UnCover.
Description: Covers Japanese business and economic trends, politics and culture.

338.91 361   LU
LUXEMBOURG INCOME STUDY; working paper series. q? Centres d'Etudes de Populations, de Pauvrete et de Politiques Socio-Economiques - International Networks for Studies in Technology, Environment, Alternatives, Development, B.P. 65, L-7201 Walferdange, Luxembourg. TEL 352-33-32-33-518. FAX 352-33-27-05. E-mail: CAROLINE@POST.CEPS.LU. Ed. Timothy M. Smeeding.

M A P NEWS. (Medical Aid for Palestine) see SOCIAL SERVICES AND WELFARE

338.91   GW   ISSN 0942-2269
MISEREOR AKTUELL. 1968. q. DM.15 (foreign DM.18). (Bischoefliches Hilfswerk Misereor e.V.) Misereor Vertriebsgesellschaft mbH, Mozartstr. 9, 52064 Aachen, Germany. TEL 49-241-4420. FAX 49-241-442524. E-mail: postmaster@misereor.de; URL: http://www.misereor.de. Ed. Walter Schaefer. bk.rev. circ. 11,000.

MONDAY DEVELOPMENTS. see SOCIAL SERVICES AND WELFARE

338.9   BE   ISSN 0302-3052
HD83
MONDES EN DEVELOPPEMENT. (Text in English, French, Spanish) 1973. q. 5300 BEF($200) (880 F.) (effective 1997). (Institut des Sciences Mathematiques et Economiques Appliquees, Paris, FR) I.S.M.E.A. - CECOEDUC, Av. des Naiades 11, B-1170 Brussels, Belgium. TEL 32-2-6758563. FAX 32-2-6758563. Eds. Andre Philippart, Rene Gendarme. adv.; bk.rev.; index. circ. 800. (back issues avail.; reprint service avail. from SCH) **Indexed:** Abstr.Rural Dev.Trop., Curr.Cont., Geo.Abstr.P.G., IDA, P.A.I.S.For.Lang.Ind., Rural Recreat.Tour.Abstr., World Agri.Econ.& Rural Sociol.Abstr. **Document type:** academic/scholarly publication.
—BLDSC (5908.055000); EMDOCS; KR SourceOne; SWETS.

BUSINESS AND ECONOMICS — INTERNATIONAL DEVELOPMENT AND ASSISTANCE

338.91 622   SX   ISSN 1012-2818
NAMIBIA BRIEF. (Text in English) no.13, 1991. m. R.6 per no. Namibia Foundation, P.O. Box 2123, Windhoek, Namibia. TEL 061-37250. FAX 061-37251. Ed. Cathy Blatt. adv.; charts; illus.
    Description: Covers economic, social, and political issues relating to development in independent Namibia, including government policy, education and training projects, mining, and famine relief.

338.91   SX   ISSN 0963-8229
NAMIBIA DEVELOPMENT BRIEFING; the voice of the Namibian non-governmental forum. (Text in English) 1991. bi-m. Bricks Community Project, 4 Katatura Community Centre, P.O. Box 20642, Windhoek 9000, Namibia. TEL 264-61-62726. FAX 264-61-63510. film rev. circ. 1,000. (back issues avail.)
    Description: Informs the international community of development issues facing Namibia.

338.91 327   US
NEAR EAST FOUNDATION. ANNUAL REPORT. 1930. a. Near East Foundation, 342 Madison Ave., Ste. 1030, New York, NY 10173. TEL 212-867-0064. FAX 212-867-0169. TELEX 226000 ETLX-UR-NEF. circ. 5,000. **Document type:** corporate report.

NETHERLANDS INVESTMENT BANK FOR DEVELOPING COUNTRIES. REPORT/NEDERLANDSE INVESTERINGSBANK VOOR ONTWIKKELINGSLANDEN. VERSLAG. see *BUSINESS AND ECONOMICS — Banking And Finance*

NETZ. see *SOCIAL SERVICES AND WELFARE*

338   UK   ISSN 0142-9345
HC511
NEW AFRICAN. (Supplement avail.: New African Life) 1966. m. (11/yr.) £36($90) (overseas £50) (effective 1996-97) (includes q. supplement). I.C. Publications Ltd., 7 Coldbath Sq., London EC1R 4LQ, England. TEL 44-171-713-7711. FAX 44-171-713-7898. E-mail: icpubs@dial.pipex.com. Ed. Alan Rake. adv.; bk.rev.; charts; illus. circ. 27,103. (also avail. in microfilm from UMI; back issues avail.; reprint service avail. from UMI) **Indexed:** Key to Econ.Sci., Mid.East: Abstr.& Ind., Polit.Sci.Abstr., PROMT, Rural Recreat.Tour.Abstr., World Agri.Econ.& Rural Sociol.Abstr. **Document type:** consumer publication.
    ●Also available online.
    —BLDSC (6081.750500); SWETS; UMI; UnCover. CCC.
    Former titles (until 1978): New African Development (ISSN 0140-833X); (until 1977): African Development (ISSN 0001-9984)
    Description: Contains a balanced mix of political reporting and commentary, economic and financial analysis, and features on social and cultural affairs.

338.91 333.8   SA   ISSN 1016-9075
NEW GROUND; the journal of development and environment. (Text in English) 1990. q. R.45($27) (£16). Environmental and Development Agency, P.O. Box 322, Newtown 2113, South Africa. TEL 27-11-8341905. FAX 27-11-8360188. Ed. Dick Cloete. adv.; illus. circ. 4,500. **Indexed:** C.I.J.E., Ind.S.A.Per.
    Description: Covers environmental aspects of development issues in South Africa from legal, social and political perspectives.

338.91   NZ   ISSN 1172-1901
NEW ZEALAND OFFICIAL DEVELOPMENT ASSISTANCE PROGRAMME. ANNUAL REVIEW. 1991. a. Ministry of Foreign Affairs and Trade, Development Cooperation Division, Private Bag 18-901, Wellington, New Zealand. TEL 64-4-4948500. FAX 64-4-4948514.

NEWS FROM APROVECHO. see *EDUCATION — International Education Programs*

338.91   GW   ISSN 0943-2019
NEWSLETTER - THE INTERNATIONAL COMMUNICATION PROJECT. English edition (ISSN 0943-2027) 1990. bi-m. DM.40. AStA Universitaet Hannover, Foundation for International Communication, Welfengarten 1, 30167 Hannover, Germany. TEL 49-511-7625063. FAX 49-511-717441. E-mail: asta.unih@oln.comlink.apc.org; URL: http://www.comlink.apc.org/fic/newslett/. Ed. Bernd Schneider; Pub. Paul Schneider Riggert. adv.: page DM.800; adv. contact: Andreas Paul. bk.rev. (back issues avail.) **Document type:** newsletter.
    ●Also available online.

338.91 323.4   US
NICARAGUA MONITOR. (Text mainly in English; occasionally in Spanish) 1986. m. $15. Nicaragua Network, 1247 E St., N.E., Washington, DC 20003-2221. TEL 202-544-9355. Ed. Katherine Hoyt. R&P contact: Katherin Hoyt. adv.; bk.rev.; film rev. circ. 5,000. (back issues avail.) **Document type:** newsletter.
    Formerly: Nicaragua Network News.
    Description: News and analysis of the effects of U.S. policy on the people of Nicaragua. Seeks to establish ties of peace and friendship between the people of the U.S. and Nicaragua.

NIGERIA FORUM. see *POLITICAL SCIENCE — International Relations*

NOEDVAENDIGA NYHETER. see *POLITICAL SCIENCE — International Relations*

338.91   SW   ISSN 1100-2131
NORDISKA AFRIKAINSTITUTET. DISCUSSION PAPERS. (Text in English) 1988. irreg. SEK 60 (effective 1997). Nordiska Afrikainstitutet, P.O. Box 1703, S-751 47 Uppsala, Sweden. TEL 018-562200. FAX 018-695629. circ. 1,500.

338.91   DK   ISSN 0902-9206
NOTAT C U F. Variant title: C U F Notat. 1987. irreg. Centre for Development Research, Gammel Kongevej 5, DK-1610 Copenhagen V, Denmark. TEL 45-33-25-12-00. FAX 45-33-25-81-10. E-mail: cdr@cdr.dk. circ. 500. **Document type:** monographic series.
    Description: Explores Third World socio-economic development issues.

330.91724   DK   ISSN 0029-6775
AP42
DEN NY VERDEN. (Text in Danish) 1964. q. DKK 195 (effective 1997). Centre for Development Research - Center for Udviklingsforskning, Gammel Kongevej 5, DK-1610 Copenhagen V, Denmark. TEL 45-33-25-12-00. FAX 45-33-25-81-10. E-mail: cdr@cdr.dk. circ. 1,000.
    Description: Explores social science development in the Third World.

338.91 630   UK   ISSN 0952-2468
O D I AGRICULTURAL RESEARCH AND EXTENSION NETWORK PAPERS. s-a. £15. Overseas Development Institute, Regent's College, Inner Circle, Regent's Park, London NW1 4NS, England. TEL 0171-487-7413. FAX 0171-487-7590. E-mail: odi@odi.org.uk. **Document type:** bulletin.
    —BLDSC (6077.203645).

338.91 333.7   UK   ISSN 1356-9228
O D I NATURAL RESOURCE PERSPECTIVES. 1994. 5/yr. Overseas Development Institute, Regent's College, Inner Circle, Regent's Park, London NW1 4NS, England. TEL 0171-487-7413. FAX 0171-487-7590. E-mail: odi@odi.org.uk. circ. 6,000. **Document type:** bulletin.
    Description: Presents accessible information on development issues.

338.91   UK   ISSN 0951-1911
GN387
O D I PASTORAL DEVELOPMENT NETWORK PAPERS. s-a. £15. Overseas Development Institute, Regent's College, Inner Circle, Regent's Park, London NW1 4NS, England. TEL 0171-487-7413. FAX 0171-487-7590. E-mail: odi@odi.org.uk. **Document type:** bulletin.
    Description: Aims to promote development policy research and the dissemination of research findings by facilitating exchanges between field practitioners, funding agencies and academics.

338.91   UK   ISSN 1353-8691
O D I RELIEF AND REHABILITATION NETWORK PAPERS. (Text in English, French) s-a. £15. Overseas Development Institute, Regent's College, Inner Circle, Regent's Park, London NW1 4NS, England. TEL 0171-487-7413. FAX 0171-487-7590. E-mail: odi@odi.org.uk. **Document type:** bulletin.

338.91 634.9   UK   ISSN 0968-2627
O D I RURAL DEVELOPMENT FORESTRY NETWORK PAPERS. (Text in English, French, Spanish) s-a. £15. Overseas Development Institute, Regent's College, Inner Circle, Regent's Park, London NW1 4NS, England. TEL 0171-487-7413. FAX 0171-487-7590. E-mail: odi@odi.org.uk. **Document type:** bulletin.
    —BLDSC (6077.203658).

O D T U GELISME DERGISI/M E T U STUDIES IN DEVELOPMENT. (Orta Dogu Teknik Universitesi) see *BUSINESS AND ECONOMICS — Economic Systems And Theories, Economic History*

O E C D CATALOGUE OF PUBLICATIONS. (Organization for Economic Cooperation and Development) see *BIBLIOGRAPHIES*

O E C D CODE OF LIBERALIZATION OF CAPITAL MOVEMENTS/O C D E CODE DE LA LIBERATION DES MOUVEMENTS DE CAPITAUX. see *BUSINESS AND ECONOMICS — Banking And Finance*

338.91   FR
O E C D DEVELOPMENT CENTRE SEMINARS. irreg. price varies. Organization for Economic Cooperation and Development, 2 rue Andre-Pascal, 75775 Paris Cedex 16, France. (U.S. orders to: O.E.C.D. Publications and Information Center, 2001 L St., N.W., Ste. 650, Washington, DC 20036-4922. TEL 202-785-6323)

338.91   FR
O E C D DEVELOPMENT CENTRE STUDIES. irreg. price varies. Organization for Economic Cooperation and Development, 2 rue Andre-Pascal, 75775 Paris Cedex 16, France. (U.S. subscr. to: O.E.C.D. Publications and Information Center, 2001 L St., N.W., Ste. 650, Washington, DC 20036-4922. TEL 202-785-6323) **Indexed:** Abstr.Rural Dev.Trop.

338.9   FR   ISSN 0474-5663
O E C D DEVELOPMENT COOPERATION; efforts and policies of the members of the Development Assistance Committee. (Editions in English, French) a. price varies. Organization for Economic Cooperation and Development, 2 rue Andre-Pascal, 75775 Paris Cedex 16, France. (U.S. orders to: O.E.C.D. Publications and Information Center, 2001 L St., N.W., Ste. 650, Washington, DC 20036-4922. TEL 202-785-6323) **Indexed:** IIS.

338.91   UK   ISSN 1351-8569
OASIS (LONDON, 1986). 1986. s-a. free. WaterAid, Prince Consort House, 17-29 Albert Embankment, London SE1 7UB, England. TEL 44-171-793-4500. FAX 44-171-793-4545. E-mail: wateraid@compuserve.com; URL: http://www.oneworld.org/wateraid/. Ed. Michelle Bell. R&P contact: Michelle Bell. circ. 85,000. **Document type:** newsletter.
    Description: Reports on technology for drinking water supply and sanitation projects funded by WaterAid throughout Africa and Asia.

338.9   AU   ISSN 0078-3536
OESTERREICHISCHE SCHRIFTEN ZUR ENTWICKLUNGSHILFE. 1963. irreg., vol.12, 1985. price varies. Verlag Ferdinand Berger und Soehne GmbH, Wienerstr. 21-23, A-3580 Horn, Austria. TEL 43-2982-4161232. FAX 43-2982-2317235. Ed. Leopold Scheidl. **Document type:** monographic series.

338.91   SW
HC60
OMVAERLDEN. 1970. 8/yr. SEK 195 in Sweden; Nordic and Baltic countries SEK 235; elsewhere SEK 260 (effective 1997). Swedish International Development Cooperation Agency (Sida), S-105 25 Stockholm, Sweden. TEL 46-8-698-55-52. (Subscr. to: PROGEK, P.O. Box 31003, S-400 32 Goeteborg, Sweden. TEL 46-31-24-34-25. FAX 46-31-24-38-10) Ed. Mats Sundgren.
    Former titles: S I D A Rapport (ISSN 0282-6011); (until 1985): Rapport fraan S I D A (ISSN 0345-9705)

OPEN ECONOMIES REVIEW. see *BUSINESS AND ECONOMICS — Economic Systems And Theories, Economic History*

330   FR
ORGANIZATION FOR ECONOMIC COOPERATION AND DEVELOPMENT. ACTIVITIES: REPORT BY THE SECRETARY GENERAL. 1971. a. free. Organization for Economic Cooperation and Development, 2 rue Andre-Pascal, 75775 Paris Cedex 16, France. (U.S. orders to: O.E.C.D Publication and Information Center, 2001 L St., N.W., Ste. 650, Washington, D.C. 20036-4922. TEL 202-785-6323)

BUSINESS AND ECONOMICS — INTERNATIONAL DEVELOPMENT AND ASSISTANCE

338.91   US   ISSN 0092-7643
HD82
OVERSEAS DEVELOPMENT COUNCIL. ANNUAL REPORT. Key Title: Annual Report - Overseas Development Council. 1971. a. free. Overseas Development Council, 1875 Connecticut Ave., N.W., Ste. 1012, Washington, DC 20009. TEL 202-234-8701. FAX 202-745-0067. URL: http://www.odc.org. Ed. Jacqueline Edlund-Braun. R&P contact: Jacqueline Edlund-Brown. illus. **Document type:** corporate report.
—CCC.

338.91   UK   ISSN 0140-8682
OVERSEAS DEVELOPMENT INSTITUTE. BRIEFING PAPER. 1976. 6/yr. Overseas Development Institute, Regent's College, Inner Circle, Regent's Park, London NW1 4NS, England. TEL 0171-487-7413. FAX 0171-487-7590. E-mail: odi@odi.org.uk. circ. 6,500. **Document type:** monographic series.
●Also available online.
—BLDSC (2283.958270).

338.9   JA
OVERSEAS ECONOMIC COOPERATION FUND. ANNUAL REPORT/KAIGAI KEIZAI KYORYOKU KIKIN NENPO. (Text in English, French, Japanese, Spanish) 1982. a. free. Overseas Economic Cooperation Fund - Kaigai Keizai Kyoryoku Kikin, Takebashi Godo Bldg., 4-1, Ohtemachi 1-chome, Chiyoda-ku, Tokyo 100, Japan. FAX 81-3-3215-2897. TELEX J28430 COOPFUND.

338.1   UK   ISSN 1360-0818
HD1401
OXFORD DEVELOPMENT STUDIES. 1933. 3/yr. £39($98) to individuals; institutions £242 ($428) (effective 1997). (Agricultural Economics Unit) Carfax Publishing Co., P.O. Box 25, Abingdon, Oxon. OX14 3UE, England. TEL 44-1235-401000. FAX 44-1235-401550. E-mail: enquiries@carfax.co.uk. (Subscr. in N. America to: Carfax Publishing Co., 875-81 Massachusetts Ave., Cambridge, MA 02139) Ed. G.H. Peters. bibl.; charts; stat.; index. **Indexed:** Agri.Eng.Abstr., Asian-Pac.Econ.Lit., C.R.E.J., Curr.Cont., Dairy Sci.Abstr., Food Sci.& Tech.Abstr., Forest.Abstr., Forest Prod.Abstr., Geo.Abstr.P.G., Hort.Abstr., IDA, Int.Abstr.Oper.Res., Nutr.Abstr., Rural Ext.Educ.& Tr.Abstr., Rural Recreat.Tour.Abstr., Sociol.Abstr., World Agri.Econ.& Rural Sociol.Abstr. **Document type:** academic/scholarly publication.
—BLDSC (6320.696300); EMDOCS; KR SourceOne; UnCover. **CCC.**
Former titles (until vol.24): Oxford Agrarian Studies (ISSN 0264-5491); Farm Economist (ISSN 0014-7931)
Description: Presents articles in agricultural economics and development issues worldwide.
Refereed Serial

338.9   US   ISSN 8755-3848
P A D F NEWS. 2/yr. Pan American Development Foundation, 1889 F St., N.W., Washington, DC 20006. TEL 202-458-3969. Ed. Jeanine Hess. circ. 9,000.
Formerly: Action (Washington).
Description: News of the foundation's activities, including environmental programs and corporate in-kind donations.

338.91   PH
P I D S RESEARCH PAPER SERIES. (Text in English) 1979. irreg., latest 1994. price varies. Philippine Institute for Development Studies, NEDA sa Makati Bldg., 3rd Fl., Rm. 304, 106 Amorsolo St., Legaspi Village, Makati 1229, Metro Manila, Philippines. TEL 632-8935705. FAX 632-8161091. Ed. Jennifer P.T. Liguton.
Formerly (until 1994): P I D S Working Paper Series; Which superseded (in 1987): P I D S Staff Paper Series.
Refereed Serial

338.91   PH
P I D S SPECIAL PUBLICATIONS. (Text in English) 1979. irreg., latest 1995. price varies. Philippine Institute for Development Studies, NEDA sa Makati Bldg., 3rd Fl., Rm. 304, 106 Amorsolo St., Legaspi Village, Makati 1229, Metro Manila, Philippines. TEL 632-8935705. FAX 632-8161091.
Description: Contains research papers on various development issues in the Philippines.

P L A NOTES. (Participatory Learning and Action) see AGRICULTURE

PACIFIC MAGAZINE. see BUSINESS AND ECONOMICS — International Commerce

PAKISTAN DEVELOPMENT REVIEW; international journal of development economics. see BUSINESS AND ECONOMICS

338.91   PK   ISSN 1011-002X
HC440.5.A1
PAKISTAN ECONOMIC AND SOCIAL REVIEW. (Text in English) 1952. 2/yr. Rs.70($30) University of the Punjab, Department of Economics, New Campus, Lahore 54590, Pakistan. Ed. Refique Ahmad. adv.; bk.rev.; index, cum.index: 1952-1983. circ. 2,500. **Indexed:** IDA, Int.Lab.Doc., J.of Econ.Lit., Mid.East: Abstr.& Ind., P.A.I.S., Per.Islam. (1991-), Rural Recreat.Tour.Abstr., World Agri.Econ.& Rural Sociol.Abstr. **Document type:** academic/scholarly publication.
—BLDSC (6340.683000).
Formerly (until 1971): Punjab University Economist (ISSN 0031-0794)
Description: Publishes articles concerned with the economic and social problems facing Pakistan and other emerging nations.

PAKISTAN INSTITUTE OF DEVELOPMENT ECONOMICS. REPORT. see BUSINESS AND ECONOMICS

PAKISTAN INSTITUTE OF DEVELOPMENT ECONOMICS. RESEARCH REPORTS. see BUSINESS AND ECONOMICS

980   US   ISSN 0552-9913
PAN AMERICAN DEVELOPMENT FOUNDATION. ANNUAL REPORT. 1964. a. free. Pan-American Development Foundation, 1889 F St., N.W., Washington, DC 20006. TEL 202-458-3969. Ed. Jeanine Hess. circ. 3,000.

338.91   UK   ISSN 0268-4020
PAPERS IN THE ADMINISTRATION OF DEVELOPMENT. irreg. (2-3/yr.). price varies. University of Birmingham, Institute of Local and Government Studeis, Development and Administration Group, Univ. of Birmingham, Birmingham, B15 2TT, England. (back issues avail.) **Indexed:** Geo.Abstr. **Document type:** monographic series.
—BLDSC (2072.173000).

PARTNERSCHAFT MIT DER ARABISCHEN WELT; Berichte und Meinungen ueber die Deutsch-Arabische Zusammenarbeit. see POLITICAL SCIENCE — International Relations

338.91 327   US   ISSN 0884-9196
HC60.5
PEACE CORPS TIMES. 1978. q. free to qualified personnel. U.S. Peace Corps, 1990 K St., N.W., Washington, DC 20526. TEL 202-254-3371. FAX 202-606-3110. Ed. James C. Flanigan. circ. 19,000 (controlled). **Document type:** government publication.
●Also available on CD-ROM.

338.91 572   GW   ISSN 0173-184X
PERIPHERIE; Zeitschrift fuer Politik und Oekonomie in der dritten Welt. (Text in German; summaries in English) 1980. q. DM.45 to individuals, institutions DM.80. Wissenschaftliche Vereinigung fuer Entwicklungstheorie und Entwicklungspolitik e.V., c/o LN-Vertrieb, Im Mehringhof, Gneisenaustr. 2, 10961 Berlin, Germany. TEL 49-30-6946100. FAX 49-30-6926590. Ed.Bd. adv.; bk.rev. circ. 1,500. (back issues avail.) **Indexed:** Abstr.Rural Dev.Trop., Geo.Abstr.H.G., Geo.Abstr.P.G., IBR, IDA. **Document type:** academic/scholarly publication.
—CCC.
Description: Interdisciplinary studies of the problems of underdevelopment and development, and liberation movements in the Third World.

338.91   UN
PERSONNEL DES NATIONS UNIES ET DES AGENCES SPECIALISEES EN REPUBLIQUE DE RWANDA. (Text in French) a. United Nations Development Programme, Rwanda, B.P. 445, Kigali, Rwanda.

PERSPECTIVES (MADISON). see BUSINESS AND ECONOMICS — Banking And Finance

PLAN AND ACTION. see SOCIAL SERVICES AND WELFARE

338.1 613   US
PLENTY BULLETIN. 1974. q. $10 donation. Plenty, Box 394, Summertown, TN 38483-0394. TEL 615-964-4864. E-mail: plenty1@usit.net; URL: http://www.public.usit.net/plenty1. Dir. Peter Schweitzer. bk.rev. circ. 4,500. **Document type:** bulletin.
Formerly: Plenty News.
Description: Covers agricultural relief and development activities of Plenty.

PORTUGAL - MAGAZIN. see POLITICAL SCIENCE

PRIVATE DEVELOPMENT CORPORATION OF THE PHILIPPINES. EXECUTIVE UPDATE; international markets report. see BUSINESS AND ECONOMICS — International Commerce

338.91   PH
PRIVATE DEVELOPMENT CORPORATION OF THE PHILIPPINES. POLICY ANALYSIS. (Text in English) 1986. bi-m. $35. Private Development Corporation of the Philippines - Pribadong Korporasyon sa Pagpapaunlad ng Pilipinas, P.O. Box 757 Makati, Metro Manila 3117, Philippines. TEL 02-8100231. FAX 02-8195376. TELEX RCA-22080.

338.91   SA
PRODDER NEWSLETTER. q. free. Human Sciences Research Council, Environmental Management Division, Programme for Development Research, Private Bag X41, Pretoria 0001, South Africa. (Co-sponsor: Sasol) Ed. David Bernard. circ. 4,000. **Document type:** newsletter.
Description: Publishes articles on development trends, current and completed research, and reports on conferences of interest to the development community.

338.91 320   UK   ISSN 0271-2075
JF60   CODEN: PADEDR
PUBLIC ADMINISTRATION AND DEVELOPMENT; an international journal of training, research and practice. 1981. 5/yr. £625 (foreign £625) (effective 1998). (Royal Institute of Public Administration) John Wiley & Sons Ltd., Journals, Baffins Ln., Chichester, W. Sussex PO19 1UD, England. TEL 44-1243-779777. FAX 44-1243-775878. E-mail: info-assets@wiley.co.uk; URL: http://www.wiley.co.uk. (Subscr. in the Americas to: John Wiley & Sons, Inc., 605 Third Ave., New York, NY 10158. TEL 212-850-6645. FAX 212-850-6021) Ed. Paul Collins; Pub. Richard Baggeley. adv.; B&W page £595, color page £1495; trim 248 x 165; adv. contact: Bob Kern. bk.rev. circ. 1,800. (also avail. in microform from UMI; back issues avail.; reprint service avail. from SWZ,UMI) **Indexed:** A.B.C.Pol.Sci., A.I.C.P., ASCA, ASSIA, BPIA, Curr.Cont.Africa, Curr.Cont., Documentatieblad, E.I., Geo.Abstr.P.G., IDA, IDA, Int.Lab.Doc., Int.Polit.Sci.Abstr., Irr.& Drain.Abstr., Mar.Aff.Bibl., Mid.East: Abstr.& Ind., Mult.Ed.Abstr., P.A.I.S., Polit.Sci.Abstr., Pub.Admin.Abstr., Rural Devel.Abstr., Rural Recreat.Tour.Abstr., Sage Pub.Admin.Abstr., Sage Urb.Stud.Abstr., So.Pac.Per.Ind., SSCI, Stud.Wom.Abstr., Tech.Educ.Abstr., World Agri.Econ.& Rural Sociol.Abstr. **Document type:** academic/scholarly publication.
—BLDSC (6962.560800); Genuine Article; SWETS; UMI; UnCover. **CCC.**
Supersedes: Journal of Administration Overseas (ISSN 0021-8472)
Description: Focuses on administrative practice at the local, regional and national levels.
Refereed Serial

R P C V WRITERS & READERS; returned Peace Corps volunteers write about their world. see LITERARY AND POLITICAL REVIEWS

338.91   UN
RAPPORT ANNUEL SUR L'ASSISTANCE AU DEVELOPPEMENT: RWANDA. (Text in French) a. United Nations Development Programme, Rwanda, B.P. 445, Kigali, Rwanda.

338.91   UN
RAPPORT ANNUEL SUR LA COOPERATION AU DEVELOPPEMENT: BURUNDI. (Text in French) a. United Nations Development Program, Programme des Nations Unies pour le Developpement au Burundi, c/o Ms. Linda Schrieber, Chief, Documentation and Statistics Office, BPPE, UNDP, New York, NY 10017. circ. controlled.
Formerly (until 1984): Rapport Annuel sur l'Assistance au Developpement: Burundi.

BUSINESS AND ECONOMICS — INTERNATIONAL DEVELOPMENT AND ASSISTANCE

338.91 327   CI   ISSN 0352-4728
HD72
RAZVOJ/DEVELOPMENT; casopis za probleme drustveno-ekonomskog razvoja, zemalja u razvoju i medunarodnih odnosa. (Text in Croatian or Serbian) q. $20 to individuals; institutions 3000 din. Institut za Razvoj i Medunarodne Odnose (IRMO) - Institute for Development and International Relations, Ul. 8 Maja 1945, Br. 82, P.O. Box 303, 41000 Zagreb, Croatia. TEL 41-444-522. FAX 41-444-059. TELEX 222273.
    Description: A forum for scientific thought on social, economic, political, cultural, technological, environmental and other developmental problems.

338.91   CI   ISSN 0352-8553
HD72
RAZVOJ: DEVELOPMENT - INTERNATIONAL. (Text in English, French, Spanish) 1986. s-a. $35 to individuals; institutions $65. Institut za Razvoj i Medunarodne Odnose (IRMO) - Institute for Development and International Relations, Ul. 8 Maja 1945, Br. 82, P.O. Box 303, 41001 Zagreb, Croatia. TEL 41-444-522. FAX 41-444-069. TELEX 222273. Ed. Rikard Stajner. adv.; bk.rev. circ. 500. **Indexed:** Rural Devel.Abstr., World Agri.Econ.& Rural Sociol.Abstr.
    —BLDSC (7298.979000).
    Description: A forum for scientific thought on social, economic, political, cultural, technological, environmental and other developmental problems.

338.91   UK
THE REALITY OF AID (YEAR). 1993. irreg., latest vol.2, 1997-98. £14.95. Earthscan Publications Ltd., 120 Pentonville Rd., London N1 9JN, England. TEL 44-171-278-0433. FAX 44-171-278-1142. TELEX 266272 ACTAID G. E-mail: earthinfo@earthscan.co.uk; earthsales@earthscan.co.uk; URL: http:www.earthscan.co.uk. **Document type:** bulletin.
    Description: Provides an independent evaluation of the aid policies of major donors and their effectiveness in fulfilling their official purpose of relieving poverty and assisting development.

060   IR   ISSN 0034-3358
REGIONAL CULTURAL INSTITUTE. JOURNAL. (Text in English) 1967. q. free to qualified personnel. Regional Cultural Institute, 5 Los Angeles Ave., North of Elizabeth II Blvd., Teheran, Iran. Ed. Dr. Salim Neysari. charts; illus. circ. 2,000. **Indexed:** Amer.Hist.& Life (1971-1977), Hist.Abstr. (1971-1977).

338.91 352.7   UN   ISSN 0250-6505
HT390
REGIONAL DEVELOPMENT DIALOGUE; an international journal focusing on Third World development problems. (Text in English) 1980. s-a. $40 (developing nations $15). United Nations Centre for Regional Development, Nagono 1-47-1, Nakamura-ku, Nagoya 450, Japan. TEL 81-52-561-9377. FAX 81-52-561-9375. TELEX J59620 UNCENTRE. Ed. Hideki Kaji. adv.; bk.rev.; charts. circ. 1,000. (also avail. in microfiche from CIS) **Indexed:** Asian-Pac.Econ.Lit., Geo.Abstr.P.G., IDA, IIS, Int.Lab.Doc., P.A.I.S., Pub.Admin.Abstr., Rural Devel.Abstr., Sage Pub.Admin.Abstr., Sage Urb.Stud.Abstr., World Agri.Econ.& Rural Sociol.Abstr. **Document type:** academic/scholarly publication.
    —BLDSC (7336.595400); EMDOCS; KR SourceOne; SWETS; UnCover.
    Description: Provides a forum for critical discussion of regional development problems, policies, and perspectives among academicians and practitioners.

338.9 352.7   UN   ISSN 1020-3060
HT390
REGIONAL DEVELOPMENT STUDIES. (Text in English) 1995. a. $20 (developing nations $15). United Nations Centre for Regional Development, Nagono 1-47-1, Nakamura-ku, Nagoya 450, Japan. TEL 052-561-9377. FAX 052-561-9375. TELEX J59620 UNCENTRE. Ed.Bd. charts; illus. circ. 500. **Document type:** academic/scholarly publication.
    Description: Covers various issues in international development assistance for regional development.
    Refereed Serial

338.9   SG   ISSN 0850-4008
REGISTER DEVELOPMENT RESEARCH PROJECTS AFRICA. (Text in English, French) 1973. a. $35. Council for the Development of Social Science Research in Africa, B.P. 3304, Dakar, Senegal. Ed. Tade Akin Aina. bibl.
    Formerly (until 1983): Africa Development Research Annual-Annuaire des Recherches Africaines sur les Problemes de Developpement.

338.9   UN
REPORT ON DEVELOPMENT ASSISTANCE TO ETHIOPIA. (Text in English) a. United Nations Development Programme, Office of the Resident Representative in Ethiopia, Box 5580, Addis Ababa, Ethiopia.

338.91   UN
REPORT ON DEVELOPMENT COOPERATION TO THE DEMOCRATIC REPUBLIC OF THE SUDAN. (Text in English) a. United Nations Development Programme, Sudan, Box 913, Khartoum, Sudan.
    Formerly: Development Assistance to the Democratic Republic of the Sudan.

338.91   UK   ISSN 1363-6669
REVIEW OF DEVELOPMENT ECONOMICS. 3/yr. £118($161) (effective 1997). Blackwell Publishers Ltd., 108 Cowley Rd., Oxford OX4 1JF, England. TEL 44-1865-791100. FAX 44-1865-791347. E-mail: jnlinfo@blackwellpublishers.co.uk; URL: http://www.blackwellpublishers.co.uk. **Document type:** academic/scholarly publication.
    —CCC.

338.91   BL   ISSN 0100-977X
REVISTA AMAZONENSE DE DESENVOLVIMENTO. Cover title: R A D. 1973. q. Cr.$20000. Centro de Desenvolvimento, Pesquisa e Tecnologia do Estado do Amazonas, Rua Emilio Moreira, 1308, 69020-240 Manaus, AM, Brazil. Ed. Jose Augusto de Almeida. stat. **Document type:** government publication.
    Description: Covers planning and development in the Amazonian province.

338   HO   ISSN 0252-8762
HC141.A1
REVISTA DE LA INTEGRACION Y EL DESARROLLO DE CENTROAMERICA. 1976. s-a. Banco Centroamericano de Integracion Economica, Apdo. Postal 772, Tegucigalpa D.C., Honduras. TEL 504-222230. Dir. Carlos Guillermo Herrera; Pub. Alejandro Arpenal. adv. contact: Carlos Imendia. **Indexed:** P.A.I.S.For.Lang.Ind. **Document type:** academic/scholarly publication.
    Formerly: Revista de la Integracion Centroamericana.

338.91   EC
REVISTA INTERAMERICANA DE PLANIFICACION. CORREO INFORMATIVO. 1967. q. $30 in America; Europe $40; elsewhere $42 (effective 1995). Sociedad Interamericana de Planificacion, Casilla 01-05-1978, Cuenca, Ecuador. TEL 593-7-823860. FAX 593-7-823949. E-mail: siap1@siap.org.ec. Ed. Luis E. Camacho. adv.; bk.rev.; stat.; cum.index every 2 yrs.; circ. 2,000 (paid). **Document type:** academic/scholarly publication.
    —SWETS.
    Formerly: Sociedad Interamericana de Planificacion. Correo Informativo (ISSN 0579-3718)

REVISTA ROMANA DE STUDII INTERNATIONALE/ROMANIAN JOURNAL OF INTERNATIONAL STUDIES. see BUSINESS AND ECONOMICS — International Commerce

REVUE D'ECONOMIE DU DEVELOPPEMENT. see BUSINESS AND ECONOMICS — Economic Situation And Conditions

338   FR   ISSN 0040-7356
HC59.7
REVUE TIERS MONDE. 1960. q. 480 F. to individuals (foreign 530 F.); agencies 432 F. (foreign 477 F.) (effective 1998). (Institut d'Etude du Developpement Economique et Social) Presses Universitaires de France, Departement des Revues, 14 av. du Bois-de-l'Epine, 91003 Evry Cedex, France. TEL 33-1-60778205. FAX 33-1-60792045. TELEX PUF 600 474 F. Dir. Maxine Haubert. bk.rev.; abstr.; index. (reprint service avail. from KTO/SCH) **Indexed:** E.I., Hisp.Amer.Per.Ind. (1977-), IBR, Int.Lab.Doc., Int.Polit.Sci.Abstr., P.A.I.S.For.Lang.Ind.
    —BLDSC (8833.400000); SWETS. **CCC.**
    Description: Studies the economic and social problems of Third World countries.

338.91 360   SG
ROSTER OF AFRICA SOCIAL SCIENTISTS. (Text in English, French) 1981. a. $35. Council for the Development of Social Science Research in Africa, B.P. 3304, Dakar, Senegal. Ed. Tade Akin Aina.

ROYAL TROPICAL INSTITUTE. BULLETIN. see ANTHROPOLOGY

338.1   UN   ISSN 0252-5038
RURAL PROGRESS. (Text in English) 1977. s-a. United Nations Economic Commission for Africa - Commission Economique pour l'Afrique, P.O. Box 3001, Addis Ababa, Ethiopia. bk.rev. circ. 2,000. **Indexed:** Documentatieblad, Rural Devel.Abstr., World Agri.Econ.& Rural Sociol.Abstr. **Document type:** bulletin.
    Supersedes: African Women; Rural Development Newsletter.

338.91   US   ISSN 1011-873X
HN981.C6
RURAL RECONSTRUCTION REVIEW. 1979. a. International Institute of Rural Reconstruction, 475 Riverside Dr., New York, NY 10115. TEL 212-870-2992. Ed. Jaime P. Ronquillo. adv.; bk.rev. circ. 2,000. **Indexed:** Int.Lab.Doc., Rural Devel.Abstr., Rural Ext.Educ.& Tr.Abstr.
    —BLDSC (8052.497900).
    Description: Action research on rural development in the Third World.

338.91   US
RUSSIAN DEFENSE BUSINESS DIRECTORY (YEAR). 1992. a. U.S. Department of Commerce, U.S.-Russia Defense Conversion Subcommittee, 14th St. between Constitution & E Sts., N.W., Washington, DC 20230. TEL 202-482-4695. Ed. Daniel C. Hurley, Jr. **Document type:** government publication, directory.
    ●Also available online.
    Description: Discusses the U.S. government's program to encourage American private investment in Russian companies that are converting from military to commercial goods or services.

338.91   SW   ISSN 1401-0402
S I D A EVALUATION. Key Title: Sida Evaluation. (Text in English) 1986. irreg. Swedish International Development Cooperation Agency, Styrelsen foer Internationell Utveckling, S-105 25 Stockholm, Sweden. TEL 46-8-698-50-00. FAX 46-8-698-56-10.
    —BLDSC (8271.710300).
    Formerly (until 1995): S I D A Evaluation Report (ISSN 0283-0736)

338.91   SW
▼**S I D A EVALUATIONS NEWSLETTER.** Variant title: Sida Evaluation Newsletter. (Text in English) 1996. irreg. free. Swedish International Development Cooperation Agency, Department of Evaluation and Internal Audit (UTV), S-105 25 Stockholm, Sweden. TEL 46-8-698-50-00. FAX 46-8-698-56-10. E-mail: claes.bennedich@sida.se. Ed. Claes Bennedich. **Document type:** newsletter.
    Description: Contains summaries of evaluation reports.

BUSINESS AND ECONOMICS — INTERNATIONAL DEVELOPMENT AND ASSISTANCE

338.91   TS
SANDUQ ABU DHABI LIL-INMA' AL-IQTISADI AL-ARABI. AL-TAQRIR AL-SANAWI/ABU DHABI FUND FOR ARAB ECONOMIC DEVELOPMENT. ANNUAL REPORT. (Text in Arabic) 1984. a. Abu Dhabi Fund for Arab Economic Development - Sanduq Abu Dhabi lil-Inma' al-Iqtisadi al-Arabi, P.O. Box 814, Abu Dhabi, United Arab Emirates. TEL 725800. stat.; circ. 1,000 (controlled). **Document type:** corporate report.
   Description: Provides an overview of domestic and international development projects under the administration of the fund, including loans and technical assistance.

338.91 500 600   UK   ISSN 0950-0707
Q127.2
SCIENCE, TECHNOLOGY & DEVELOPMENT; journal of the Third World Science, Technology & Development Forum. 1983. 3/yr. £28($45) to individuals; institutions £95 ($135) (effective 1997). Frank Cass, Newbury House, 890-900 Eastern Ave., Newbury Park, Ilford, Essex IG2 7HH, England. TEL 44-181-599-8866. FAX 44-181-599-0984. E-mail: jnlsubs@frankcass.com; URL: http://www.frankcass.com. (Dist. in US by: ISBS, 5804 N.E. Hassalo St., Portland, OR 97213-3644. TEL 800-944-6190. FAX 503-280-8832) Ed. Girma Zawdie. adv.: B&W page £195 ($275); adv. contact: Anne Kidson. bk.rev.; index. (back issues avail.) **Indexed:** Geo.Abstr.P.G., IDA, Per.Islam. (1989-). **Document type:** academic/scholarly publication. —BLDSC (8164.832000); EMDOCS; KR SourceOne.
   Description: Discusses issues related to science, technology, and development in Third World countries.
   Refereed Serial

338.91   CD
SECOURS CATHOLIQUE ET DEVELOPPEMENT. RAPPORT D'ACTIVITES ET COMPTE-RENDU FINANCIER (YEAR). a. Secours Catholique et Developpement, B.P. 1166, N'Djamena, Chad. TEL 54-44-53. FAX 51-40-60.

338.9   GT
SECRETARIA PERMANENTE DEL TRATADO GENERAL DE INTEGRACION ECONOMICA CENTROAMERICANA. BOLETIN INFORMATIVO. 1961. m. $25. Secretaria Permanente del Tratado General de Integracion Economica Centroamericana - Permanent Secretariat of the General Treaty on Central American Economic Integration, 4a Avda. 10-25, Zona 14, Apdo. 1237, 01901 Guatemala, Guatemala. Ed. Eduardo Bolanos. bk.rev. circ. 6,000.
   Formerly: Secretaria Permanente del Tratado General de Integracion Economica Centroamericana. Carta Informativa (ISSN 0553-6855)

SEEDS; hope for the healing and hunger of poverty. see *SOCIAL SERVICES AND WELFARE*

338.91   BL
SELECOES ECONOMICAS/JITSUGYO NO BURAJIRU. (Text in Japanese) m. Cr.$1200. Selecoes Economicas, Av. Paulista 807, Sao Paulo, Brazil. illus.

338.91   CN
SERVICE CONTRACTS AND LINES OF CREDIT. s-a. Canadian International Development Agency, Communications Branch, 200 Promenade du Portage, Hull, Que K1A 0G4, Canada. TEL 819-997-6100. FAX 819-953-6088. URL: http://www.acdi.cida.gc.ca. Ed. Jim Holmes.
   Former titles: Business of Development. Service Contracts Bilateral Program (ISSN 1187-693X); (until 1991): Business of Development. Active Contracts (ISSN 0835-1651)

338.91   IS   ISSN 0792-8262
SHALOM; magazine for alumni of Israel training courses. (Text in English, French and Spanish) 1962. 3/yr. free. Society for Transfer of Technology, P.O. Box 13006, Jerusalem 91130, Israel. TEL 972-2-6524383. FAX 972-2-6512636. URL: http://www.israel-mfa.gov.il. Ed. Joan Hooper. adv.; illus. circ. 50,000. **Document type:** government publication, newsletter.
   ●Also available online.

SHARE INTERNATIONAL. see *NEW AGE PUBLICATIONS*

338.91   US   ISSN 1055-3584
HG4538
SITEWORLD. 1991. a. $95. Conway Data, Inc., 35 Technology Pkwy., Ste. 150, Norcross, GA 30092-9934. TEL 770-446-6996; 800-554-5686. FAX 770-263-8825. TELEX 80-4468ATL. Ed. McKinley Conway. illus.
   Description: Reference guide to international industrial and economic development of super projects.

338.91   UN   ISSN 1012-8026
HC59.69
SOCIAL INDICATORS OF DEVELOPMENT (YEAR). a. $26.95 (diskette $45). World Bank, 1818 H St., N.W., Washington, DC 20433. TEL 202-473-1155. FAX 202-522-2627. E-mail: books@worldbank.org. (U.S. orders to: Box 7247-8619, Philadelphia, PA 19170-8619; Also avail. from: 66 av. D'lena, 75116 Paris, France. TEL 33-1-40-69-30-55. FAX 33-1-40-69-30-68) (also avail. in diskette format) **Document type:** academic/scholarly publication.
   Description: Discusses the economic condition of developing nations.

338.91   NL   ISSN 0081-2811
CODEN: SPHAD3
SOUTH PACIFIC COMMISSION. HANDBOOK. French edition: Commission de Pacifique Sud. Manuel (ISSN 0377-9955) (Text in English) 1968. irreg., no.32, 1993. South Pacific Commission, B.P. D5, 98848 Noumea Cedex, New Caledonia. TEL 687-262000. FAX 687-263818. E-mail: spc@spc.org.nc.

338.9   MY
SOUTHEAST ASIA DEVELOPMENT CORPORATION BERHAD. REPORTS AND ACCOUNTS. a. Southeast Asia Development Corporation Berhad, G.P.O. Box 2171, Kuala Lumpur 01-20, Malaysia. charts; stat.

SPIEGEL DER LATEINAMERIKANISCHEN PRESSE/BOLETIN DE PRENSA LATINOAMERICANA. see *POLITICAL SCIENCE — International Relations*

338.91   UK   ISSN 0306-5367
SPUR. 1972. bi-m. £16 to individuals; institutions £30. World Development Movement, 25 Beehive Pl., London SW9 7QR, England. TEL 44-171-737-6215. FAX 44-171-274-8232. Ed. Kay Parris. R&P contact: Kay Parris. adv. contact: Anna-Zohra Tikly. bk.rev.; charts; illus.; index; circ. 7,000 (paid). (tabloid format; back issues avail.) **Document type:** newsletter.
   Refereed Serial

338.9   NE   ISSN 0924-607X
STUDIES IN DEVELOPMENT AND PLANNING. (Text in English) 1973. irreg. price varies. (Erasmus University, Centre for Development and Planning) Kluwer Academic Publishers, Postbus 17, 3300 AA Dordrecht, Netherlands. TEL 31-78-6392392. FAX 31-78-6392254. TELEX 29245 KAPG NL. E-mail: services@wkap.nl; URL: http://www.wkap.nl. (Dist. by: Kluwer Academic Publishers Group, P.O. Box 322, 3300 AH Dordrecht, Netherlands. TEL 31-78-6392392. FAX 31-78-6546474) **Document type:** monographic series.
   Refereed Serial

SUARA SAM; Malaysia's leading environmental newspaper. see *CONSERVATION*

SUDAN. NATIONAL COUNCIL FOR RESEARCH. ECONOMIC AND SOCIAL RESEARCH COUNCIL. RESEARCH METHODS. see *SOCIAL SCIENCES: COMPREHENSIVE WORKS*

338.91   SJ
SUDAN DEVELOPMENT STUDIES REVIEW. s-a. University of Khartoum, Development Studies and Research Centre, Box 321, Khartoum, Sudan.

338.91   UN   ISSN 0252-5712
SURVEY OF ECONOMIC AND SOCIAL CONDITIONS IN AFRICA. French edition: Etude des Conditions Economiques et Sociales en Afrique. a. United Nations Economic Commission for Africa, P.O. Box 3001, Addis Ababa, Ethiopia.
   Continues: Survey of Economic Conditions in Africa.

338.91   XO
SZOVJETBARAT. (Text in Hungarian) m. $28. (Svaz Ceskoslovensko-Sovetskeho Pratelstvi - Czechoslovak-Soviet Friendship) Obzor, Spitalska ul. 35, 815 85 Bratislava, Slovakia.

T R A C ANNUAL REPORT. (Transvaal Rural Action Committee) see *AGRICULTURE*

T R A C NEWLLETTER. (Transvaal Rural Action Committee) see *AGRICULTURE*

338   SI   ISSN 0217-247X
TECHNONET ASIA. NEWSLETTER; Asian network for industrial technology information and extension. 1974. q. $15 for 3 yrs. Technonet Asia, Owen Road P.O. Box 0165, Singapore 9121, Singapore. TEL 65-291-2372. FAX 65-292-2372. TELEX RS 55002 TECNET. E-mail: ansmed@signet.com.sg. Ed. C. Anton Balasuriya. bk.rev. circ. 2,000. **Indexed:** C.R.I.Abstr., C.R.I.Curr.Cont. **Document type:** newsletter.

338.91   BL   ISSN 0103-2704
TEMAS RURAIS. 1988? 3/yr. Rede Nacional de Informacoes sobre o Campo do Nordeste, Rua Dom Bosco 779, Boa Vista, 50070 Recife PE, Brazil. TEL 55-81-2221906.

THIRD WORLD LEGAL STUDIES (YEAR). see *LAW — International Law*

THIRD WORLD PLANNING REVIEW. see *HOUSING AND URBAN PLANNING*

338.9   UK   ISSN 0143-6597
HC59.7
THIRD WORLD QUARTERLY. Online edition (UK ISSN 1360-2241) 1979. 5/yr. £46($82) to individuals; institutions £198 (outside EU £198 ($334)) (effective 1997). Carfax Publishing Co., P.O. Box 25, Abingdon, Oxon. OX14 3UE, England. TEL 44-1235-401000. FAX 44-1235-401550. E-mail: enquiries@carfax.co.uk. (Subscr. in N. America to: Carfax Publishing Co., 875-81 Massachusetts Ave., Cambridge, MA 02139) Ed. Shahid Qadir. adv.; bk.rev. circ. 6,000. (also avail. in microform; microfiche; reprint service avail.) **Indexed:** ABC, Amer.Hist.& Life (1990-), ASCA, Asian-Pac.Econ.Lit., Br.Hum.Ind., Curr.Cont., Deep Sea Res.& Oceanogr.Abstr., E.I., Geo.Abstr.P.G., Hist.Abstr. (1990-), HR Rep., IDA, Int.Lab.Doc., Int.Polit.Sci.Abstr., Key to Econ.Sci., Mar.Aff.Bibl., P.A.I.S., Per.Islam. (1993-), Polit.Sci.Abstr., Pub.Admin.Abstr., Refug.Abstr., Rural Devel.Abstr., Rural Recreat.Tour.Abstr., Sage Pub.Admin.Abstr., So.Pac.Per.Ind., Sociol.Abstr., SSCI, World Agri.Econ.& Rural Sociol.Abstr. **Document type:** academic/scholarly publication.
   ●Also available online.
—BLDSC (8820.145300); EMDOCS; Genuine Article; KR SourceOne; SWETS; UMI; UnCover. CCC.
   Description: Covers social, economic and political studies relating to the Third World.
   Refereed Serial

382   PK   ISSN 1018-8991
HC59.7
THIRDWORLD. (Text in English) 1977. m. $45. Corporate & Marketing Communications (Pvt) Ltd., 47-A-2, Block 6, Pechs, Karachi 75400, Pakistan. TEL 92-21-448569. FAX 92-21-437656. TELEX 23531-INDMN-PK. Ed. Syed Jawaid Iqbal. adv.; bk.rev.; illus. circ. 45,000. **Document type:** academic/scholarly publication.
   Former titles (until 1988): Third World International (ISSN 0253-9527); Third World Quarterly.
   Description: Covers all aspects of developing countries' affairs, including political and economic analysis, international assistance programs, human rights issues, the environment, education, law, with business surveys, interviews, and more.

TRADE & DEVELOPMENT; news and trade opportunities see *BUSINESS AND ECONOMICS — International Commerce*

TRADE AND DEVELOPMENT AGENCY. see *BUSINESS AND ECONOMICS — International Commerce*

TRADE AND DEVELOPMENT REPORT AND OVERVIEW. see *BUSINESS AND ECONOMICS — International Commerce*

BUSINESS AND ECONOMICS — INTERNATIONAL DEVELOPMENT AND ASSISTANCE

338.91   UN   ISSN 1014-7004
HC59.69
TRENDS IN DEVELOPING ECONOMIES (YEAR). 1990. a. World Bank, 1818 H. St., N.W., Washington, DC 20433. TEL 202-473-1155. FAX 202-522-2627. E-mail: books@worldbank.org. (U.S. orders to: Box 7247-8619, Philadelphia, PA 19170-8619; Also avail. from: 66 av. D'Iena, 75116 Paris, France. TEL 33-1-40-69-30-55. FAX 33-1-40-69-30-68) (Co-sponsor: International Bank for Reconstruction & Development) (also avail. in microfiche from CIS) **Indexed:** IIS.

338.91 327   US   ISSN 1055-3630
HC59.69   CODEN: CPOREG
TWENTY-FIRST CENTURY POLICY REVIEW; an American, Caribbean and African forum. s-a. $35 to individuals; institutions $65; students $25. International Development Options, Box 4871, Largo, MD 20775. TEL 301-350-3910. adv.

TYGODNIK SOLIDARNOSC/SOLIDARITY WEEKLY. see BUSINESS AND ECONOMICS — Economic Situation And Conditions

U I E HANDBOOKS. (Unesco Institute for Education) see EDUCATION

U I E STUDIES IN EDUCATION. (Unesco Institute for Education) see EDUCATION

U I E STUDIES SERIES. (Unesco Institute for Education) see EDUCATION

U I P - BERICHTE/U I E REPORTS/DOSSIERS I U E. (UNESCO Institut fuer Paedagogik) see EDUCATION

338.91 352.7   UN
U N C R D ANNUAL REPORT. (Text in English) 1993. a. free. United Nations Centre for Regional Development, Nagono 1-47-1, Nakamura-ku, Nagoya 450, Japan. TEL 052-561-9377. FAX 052-561-9375. TELEX UNCENTRE NAGOYA. Ed.Bd. charts; illus. circ. 1,000. **Document type:** corporate report.

338.91 352.7   UN   ISSN 0379-0347
U N C R D NEWSLETTER. (Text in English) 1975. s-a. free. United Nations Centre for Regional Development, Nagono 1-47-1, Nakamura-ku, Nagoya 450, Japan. TEL 052-561-9377. FAX 052-561-9375. TELEX J59620 UNCENTRE. Ed.Bd. illus. circ. 3,500. **Document type:** newsletter.

U N C T A D BULLETIN. (United Nations Conference on Trade and Development) see BUSINESS AND ECONOMICS — International Commerce

U N C T A D REVIEW. (United Nations Conference on Trade and Development) see BUSINESS AND ECONOMICS — International Commerce

338   UN   ISSN 1020-2781
HD72   CODEN: UNINAI
U N I D O LINKS. (Print edition ceased 1997) (Editions in Arabic, Chinese, English, French, Russian, Spanish) 1967. m. free. United Nations Industrial Development Organization, Box 300, A-1400 Vienna, Austria. TEL 43-1-211-31-5538. FAX 43-1-209-2669. URL: http://www.unido.org. Ed. Peter Ellwood. circ. 12,000 (controlled). **Indexed:** Abstr.Bull.Inst.Pap.Chem., C.R.I.Abstr., C.R.I.Curr.Cont., Fluidex, Intl.Polym.Sci.& Tech., Key to Econ.Sci., RAPRA, World Surf.Coat. **Document type:** newsletter.
●Available only online.
Formerly (until 1994): U N I D O Newsletter (ISSN 0049-5387)
Description: Features expertise and other resources sought by developing countries' firms, resources available to them, recent publications and information products from UNIDO and forthcoming UNIDO events.

338.91   UN   ISSN 1016-0531
N V NEWS. (Text in English, French, Spanish) 1975. q. United Nations Volunteers, Martin-Luther-King-Str. 8, 53153 Bonn, Germany. E-mail: enquiry@unv.org; URL: http://www.unv.org. Ed. Bill Jackson. circ. 10,000. (also avail. in microfiche from CIS) **Indexed:** IIS. **Document type:** newsletter.
—BLDSC (9121.327620).
Formerly: U N V Newsletter (ISSN 0251-5334)
Description: Concerns contributions of UN Volunteer specialists to international assistance for development, humanitarian relief and peace-building.

338.91 327.1   DK   ISSN 0106-3014
U-VEJVISER (YEAR); U-landsaktiviteter i Danmark. 1979. a. DKK 118 (effective 1997). Mellemfolkeligt Samvirke - Danish Association for International Co-operation, Borgergade 14, DK-1300 Copenhagen K, Denmark. TEL 45-33-32-62-44. FAX 45-33-15-62-43. Ed. Lene Nielsen. circ. 1,700.
Description: Registers and describes 280 Danish organizations and groups concerned with developing countries.

338.90 370.196   UN   ISSN 1033-1891
AS4.U825
UNESCO AUSTRALIA. 1991. s-a. free to approved institutions. Australian National Commission for UNESCO, International Organisations Branch, Department of Foreign Affairs Trade, Parkes, A.C.T. 2600, Australia. TEL 06-261-2289. FAX 06-261-3424. circ. 3,000. **Indexed:** GdIns, So.Pac.Per.Ind. **Document type:** government publication, newsletter.
Formed by the merger of (1985-1991): Australian National Commission for UNESCO Newsletter (ISSN 0725-5756); (1979-1991): UNESCO Review (ISSN 0158-779X)
Description: Thematic issues on subjects related to education, science and culture in UNESCO, and Australian National Commission activities.

338.9   UN   ISSN 0503-4108
UNITED NATIONS. CONFERENCE ON TRADE AND DEVELOPMENT. TRADE AND DEVELOPMENT BOARD. OFFICIAL RECORDS. (Supplements avail.) 1965. irreg. price varies. United Nations Publications, Room DC2-853, New York, NY 10017. TEL 212-963-8302; 800-253-9646. FAX 212-963-3489. (Or: Palais des Nations, 1211 Geneva 10, Switzerland.)
Formerly: United Nations. Trade and Development Board. Official Records (ISSN 0082-8475)

338.91   UN   ISSN 0379-8119
JX1977
UNITED NATIONS. DEVELOPMENT PROGRAMME. COMPENDIUM OF APPROVED PROJECTS. a. $20. United Publications, One U.N. Plaza, Rm. DC2-0853, New York, NY 10017.

UNITED NATIONS. ECONOMIC COMMISSION FOR AFRICA. PROPOSALS FOR PROGRAMME BUDGET. see BUSINESS AND ECONOMICS

UNITED NATIONS CONFERENCE ON TRADE AND DEVELOPMENT: PROCEEDINGS. see BUSINESS AND ECONOMICS — International Commerce

338.91   UN
UNITED NATIONS ECONOMIC COMMISSION FOR AFRICA. ANNUAL REPORT. (Text in English) a. United Nations Economic Commission for Africa, P.O. Box 3001, Addis Ababa, Ethiopia.

338.91   UN   ISSN 0252-2128
UNITED NATIONS ECONOMIC COMMISSION FOR AFRICA. BIENNIAL REPORT OF THE EXECUTIVE SECRETARY. (Text in English) biennial. United Nations Economic Commission for Africa, Office of the Executive Secretary, P.O. Box 3001, Addis Ababa, Ethiopia. (also avail. in microfiche from CIS) **Indexed:** IIS.

338.91 614.7   UN   ISSN 0259-4285
UNITED NATIONS UNIVERSITY. WORK IN PROGRESS. (Editions in English, French, Japanese, Spanish) 1976. 3/yr. free. United Nations University, Public Affairs Section, 53-70, Jingumae 5-chome, Shibuya-ku, Tokyo 150, Japan. TEL 03-3499-2811. FAX 03-3499-2828. TELEX J25442 UNATUNIV. bk.rev.; charts; illus. circ. 35,000. **Document type:** newsletter.
—BLDSC (9348.205000).

UNITED NATIONS WEEKLY REPORT. see POLITICAL SCIENCE — International Relations

338.91   US
U.S. AGENCY FOR INTERNATIONAL DEVELOPMENT. ANNUAL REPORT. a. free. U.S. Agency for International Development, Office of Housing and Urban Developments, Bureau for Global Programs, Field Support and Research, Rm. 401, State Annex 2, Washington, DC 20523-0214. TEL 202-663-2530. **Document type:** government publication.
Description: Summarizes the programs supported by U.S.A.I.D.

338.91   US   ISSN 0276-6469
HC60
U.S. AGENCY FOR INTERNATIONAL DEVELOPMENT. CONGRESSIONAL PRESENTATION, FISCAL YEAR. 1961. a. free to qualified personnel. U.S. Agency for International Development, Office of Public Affairs, Washington, DC 20523. TEL 202-647-4330. **Document type:** government publication.

338.91   US
U.S. DEPARTMENT OF COMMERCE. LATIN AMERICAN - CARIBBEAN BUSINESS DEPARTMENT CENTER. BULLETIN. m. free. U.S. Department of Commerce, Latin American - Caribbean Business Department Center, Rm. H-3203, Washington, DC 20230. TEL 202-482-0841. FAX 202-482-2218. circ. 10,500. **Document type:** government publication.
Description: Offers trade and investment leads and news for businesses interested in opportunities in Latin America and the Caribbean (excluding Mexico). Also features a calendar of events.

338.9   US   ISSN 0083-0062
HC101
U.S. DEPARTMENT OF STATE. ECONOMIC COOPERATION SERIES. 1948. irreg. price varies. U.S. Department of State, Bureau of Public Affairs, 2201 C St., N.W., Washington, DC 20520. TEL 202-632-1394. (Subscr. to: Superintendent of Documents, U.S. Government Printing Office, box 371954, Pittsburgh, PA 15250-7954. TEL 202-512-1800. FAX 202-512-2250) **Document type:** government publication, monographic series.

338.91   UK
UNIVERSITY OF BRADFORD. DEVELOPMENT AND PROJECT PLANNING CENTRE. BRADFORD DEVELOPMENT PAPERS. N.S. 1989. irreg. University of Bradford, Development and Project Planning Centre, The Library, Bradford, W. Yorks BD1 1DP, England. E-mail: n.matthews@bradford.ac.uk; URL: http://www.brad.ac.uk/acad/dppc/dppclib/publist.html. Ed. John Weiss. R&P contact: John Weiss. adv. contact: Lesley Knight. **Document type:** monographic series.
—BLDSC (6088.080000).
Former titles (until 1997): University of Bradford. Development and Project Planning Centre. New Series Discussion Papers (ISSN 0957-6479); University of Bradford. Development and Project Centre. Occasional Paper Series.
Description: Discusses practical aspects of international development planning and management.
Refereed Serial

338.91 300   SJ
UNIVERSITY OF KHARTOUM. DEVELOPMENT STUDIES AND RESEARCH CENTRE. DISCUSSION PAPERS. irreg. University of Khartoum, Development Studies and Research Centre, Faculty of Economic & Social Studies, Khartoum, Sudan.

338.91   SJ
UNIVERSITY OF KHARTOUM. DEVELOPMENT STUDIES AND RESEARCH CENTRE. MONOGRAPH SERIES. irreg. University of Khartoum, Development Studies and Research Centre, Box 321, Khartoum, Sudan. Ed. Sadig Rasheed. **Indexed:** Geo.Abstr. **Document type:** monographic series.

338.91   SJ
UNIVERSITY OF KHARTOUM. DEVELOPMENT STUDIES AND RESEARCH CENTRE. OCCASIONAL PAPERS. 1979. irreg. University of Khartoum, Development Studies and Research Centre, Box 321, Khartoum, Sudan. Ed. Sadig Rasheed.

338.91   KE
UNIVERSITY OF NAIROBI. INSTITUTE FOR DEVELOPMENT STUDIES. CONSULTANCY REPORTS. irreg., latest no.16. University of Nairobi, Institute for Development Studies, P.O. Box 30197, Nairobi, Kenya. TEL 254-2-332986. FAX 254-2-222036. TELEX 22095. E-mail: ids.uon@elci.sasq.unon.org. **Document type:** monographic series, academic/scholarly publication.

BUSINESS AND ECONOMICS — INTERNATIONAL DEVELOPMENT AND ASSISTANCE

960 338.91   KE   ISSN 0547-1788
UNIVERSITY OF NAIROBI. INSTITUTE FOR DEVELOPMENT STUDIES. DISCUSSION PAPER. 1965. irreg., no. 294, 1993. price varies. University of Nairobi, Institute for Development Studies, P.O. Box 30197, Nairobi, Kenya. TEL 254-2-332986. FAX 254-2-222036. TELEX 22095. E-mail: ids.uon@elci.sasa.unon.org. Ed. Mr. Kibisu-Kabatesi. **Indexed:** Abstr.Rural Dev.Trop., Rural Recreat.Tour.Abstr., World Agri.Econ.& Rural Sociol.Abstr. **Document type:** monographic series.

338.41   KE
UNIVERSITY OF NAIROBI. INSTITUTE FOR DEVELOPMENT STUDIES. OCCASIONAL PAPER. 1967. irreg., no.63, 1996. price varies. University of Nairobi, Institute for Development Studies, P.O. Box 30197, Nairobi, Kenya. TEL 254-2-332986. FAX 254-2-222036. TELEX 22095. E-mail: ids.uon@elci.sasa.unon.org. Ed. Mr. Kibisu-Kabatesi. bibl.; illus.; stat. **Document type:** monographic series, academic/scholarly publication.
Formerly: University College, Nairobi. Institute for Development Studies. Occasional Papers.

338.91   SA
UNIVERSITY OF PORT ELIZABETH. INSTITUTE FOR DEVELOPMENT PLANNING AND RESEARCH. ANNUAL REPORT. (Text in Afrikaans, English) 1970. a. free. University of Port Elizabeth, Institute for Development Planning and Research, P.O. Box 1600, Port Elizabeth 6000, South Africa. TEL 27-41-5042336. FAX 27-41-531769. E-mail: piaddp@upe.ac.za. circ. 400 (controlled). (back issues avail.)
Formerly: University of Port Elizabeth. Institute for Planning Research. Annual Report.
Description: Features studies in demographical, sociological, and economic findings related to the Port of Elizabeth region.

338.91   UK   ISSN 0956-0742
UPFRONT. 1989. q. $15. War on Want, Fenner Brockway House, 37-39 Great Guildford St., London SE1 0ES, England. TEL 0171-620-1111. FAX 0171-261-9291. E-mail: wew@gn.apc.org. Ed. Ken Hulme. adv. contact: Avan Wadia. bk.rev. circ. 10,000. **Document type:** newsletter.
Description: Provides information on matters and issues causing poverty in Third World countries.

338.91   UN
URBAN AGE. (Text in Arabic, English, French, Spanish) 10/yr. $20 to developed countries; free elsewhere. World Bank, 1818 H St., N.W., Rm. S6-147, Washington, DC 20433. TEL 202-458-5071. FAX 202-522-2627. E-mail: books@worldbank.org. **Indexed:** J.of Ferroc., Pub.Admin.Abstr. **Document type:** newsletter.
Formerly: Urban Edge.
Description: Focuses on timely and relevant urban issues, such as violence in the cities, transportation, immigration, and infrastructure.

URBAN ANTHROPOLOGY AND STUDIES OF CULTURAL SYSTEMS AND WORLD ECONOMIC DEVELOPMENT. see ANTHROPOLOGY

338.91   US   ISSN 1062-2292
HT101
URBAN REPORT. 1992. q. free. U.S. Agency for International Development, Office of Housing and Urban Programs, Bureau for Global Programs, Field Support and Research, Attn.: Communications, Rm. 401, State Annex 2, Washington, DC 20523-0214. TEL 202-663-2530. abstr. **Document type:** newsletter, government publication.

W I D BULLETIN. (Women and International Development Program) see POLITICAL SCIENCE — Civil Rights

W I D FORUM. (Women and International Development Program) see POLITICAL SCIENCE — Civil Rights

338.9   AU
W I I W CURRENT ANALYSES. (Text in English) 1991. irreg., vol.9, 1994. S.250. Wiener Institut fuer Internationale Wirtschaftsvergleiche - Vienna Institute for Comparative Economic Studies, Oppolzergasse 6, A-1010 Vienna, Austria. TEL 43-1-5336610. FAX 43-1-533661050. E-mail: wiiw@wsr.ac.at; URL: http://www.wsr.ac.at/wiiw-html/. **Document type:** academic/scholarly publication, monographic series.

338.9   AU
W I I W FORSCHUNGSBERICHTE/W I I W RESEARCH REPORTS. 1972. irreg., no.227, 1996. S.2500 (foreign S.2650) (includes Reprint Series). Wiener Institut fuer Internationale Wirtschaftsvergleiche - Vienna Institute for Comparative Economic Studies, Oppolzergasse 6, A-1010 Vienna, Austria. TEL 43-1-5336610. FAX 43-1-533661050. E-mail: wiiw@wsr.ac.at; URL: http://www.wsr.ac.at/wiiw-html/. Ed. Michael Landesmann. R&P contact: Ingrid Gazzari. circ. 700. **Document type:** academic/scholarly publication, monographic series.
Description: Studies on the economies of the countries of Eastern Europe and the Commonwealth of Independent States and China, major issues of East-West trade, and Eastern enlargement for the European Union.

338.9   AU
W I I W MONOGRAPHS/W I I W MONOGRAPHIEN. (Text in English, German) irreg. Wiener Institut fuer Internationale Wirtschaftsvergleiche - Vienna Institute for Comparative Economic Studies, Oppolzergasse 6, A-1010 Vienna, Austria. TEL 43-1-5336610. FAX 43-1-533661050. E-mail: wiiw@wsr.ac.at; URL: http://www.wsr.ac.at/wiiw-html/. **Document type:** academic/scholarly publication, monographic series.

338.9   AU
W I I W REPRINT SERIES. 1972. irreg., no.163, 1996. S.2500 (foreign S.2650) (includes Forschungsberichte). Wiener Institut fuer Internationale Wirtschaftsvergleiche - Vienna Institute for Comparative Economic Studies, Oppolzergasse 6, A-1010 Vienna, Austria. TEL 43-1-5336610. FAX 43-1-533661050. E-mail: wiiw@wsr.ac.at; URL: http://www.wsr.ac.at/wiiw-html/. Ed. Michael Landesmann. R&P contact: Ingrid Gazzari. circ. 700. **Document type:** academic/scholarly publication, monographic series.
Description: Brief studies on the economies of Eastern European countries (including Commonwealth of Independent States) and China, major issues of East-West trade, and Eastern enlargement of the European Union.

338.9   AU
W I I W WORKING PAPERS. (Text in English) irreg., vol.6, 1995. Wiener Institut fuer Internationale Wirtschaftsvergleiche - Vienna Institute for Comparative Economic Studies, Oppolzergasse 6, A-1010 Vienna, Austria. TEL 43-1-5336610. FAX 43-1-533661050. E-mail: wiiw@wsr.ac.at; URL: http://www.wsr.ac.at/wiiw-html/. **Document type:** monographic series.

THE WASHINGTON PACIFIC REPORT; the insider's newsletter highlighting the latest developments of interest involving the insular Pacific. see POLITICAL SCIENCE

338.91   US   ISSN 1069-5958
WASHINGTON WEEKLY REPORT (WASHINGTON); a review of Congressional action affecting multilateral issues and institutions. 1974. w. $60 to individuals; institutions $100. United Nations Association of the United States of America, 1010 Vermont Ave., N.W., Ste. 904, Washington, DC 20005. TEL 202-347-5004. FAX 202-628-5945. Ed. Steven A. Dimoff. circ. 400.

338.91   US   ISSN 1045-893X
HQ1240
WOMEN AND INTERNATIONAL DEVELOPMENT ANNUAL. 1989. a. $47.50. (Michigan State University, Office of Women in International Development) Westview Press, 5500 Central Ave., Boulder, CO 80301. TEL 303-444-3541. FAX 303-449-3356. Eds. Rita Gallin, Anne Ferguson. bibl.; charts; index. circ. 650. **Document type:** academic/scholarly publication.

WOMEN'S ENVIRONMENT AND DEVELOPMENT ORGANIZATION NEWS & VIEWS. see WOMEN'S INTERESTS

338.91 301.412   US   ISSN 0888-5354
WORKING PAPERS ON WOMEN IN INTERNATIONAL DEVELOPMENT. 1981. irreg., no.253, 1995. price varies. Michigan State University, Women and International Development Program, 202 International Center for International Programs, East Lansing, MI 48824-1035. TEL 517-353-5040. FAX 517-353-7254. Ed. Rita S. Gallin. adv.; bk.rev. circ. 1,000. **Indexed:** Geo.Abstr., IDA, P.A.I.S., Popul.Ind., Rural Devel.Abstr., Vert.File.Ind. **Document type:** monographic series.
Formerly: W I D Working Papers.
Description: Features journal-length articles based on original research or analytical summaries of relevant research, theoretical analyses, and evaluations of development programming and policy.
Refereed Serial

338.9   UN   ISSN 0252-2942
HG3881
WORLD BANK. ANNUAL REPORT. (Text in Arabic, Chinese, English, French, German, Japanese, Spanish) 1947. a. free. World Bank, 1818 H St., N.W., Washington, DC 20433. TEL 202-473-1155. FAX 202-522-2627. E-mail: books@worldbank.org. (U.S. orders to: Box 7247-8619, Philadelphia, PA 19170-8619; Also avail. from: 66 av. D'lena, 75116 Paris, France. TEL 33-1-40-69-30-55. FAX 33-1-40-69-30-68) charts; stat. **Indexed:** IIS, World Bank.Abstr. **Document type:** corporate report.
—BLDSC (1497.370000); SWETS.

338.91 332   UN   ISSN 1020-105X
WORLD BANK. E D I DEVELOPMENT STUDY. 1991. irreg. price varies. World Bank, Economic Development Institute, 1818 H St., N.W., Washington, DC 20433. TEL 202-522-2627. E-mail: books@worldbank.org. (U.S. orders to: Box 7247-8619, Philadelphia, PA 19170-8619; Also avail. from: 66 av. D'lena, 75116 Paris, France. TEL 33-1-40-69-30-55. FAX 33-1-40-69-30-68) (back issues avail.) **Document type:** monographic series.
Description: Discusses worldwide economic issues affecting and affected by E.D.I.

338.91 628   UN   ISSN 1020-0894
WORLD BANK. GLOBAL ENVIRONMENT FACILITY PAPER. 1993. irreg., no.12, 1994. price varies. World Bank, Global Environment Facility, 1818 H St., N.W., Washington, DC 20433. TEL 202-473-1155. FAX 202-522-2627. E-mail: books@worldbank.org. (U.S. orders to: Box 7247-8619, Philadelphia, PA 19170-8619; Also avail. from: 66 av. D'lena, 75116 Paris, France. TEL 33-1-40-69-30-55. FAX 33-1-40-69-30-68) (back issues avail.)
Description: Discusses global issues affecting and affected by the World Bank Global Environment Facility.

332.1 016   UN
Z7164.F5
WORLD BANK. PUBLICATIONS UPDATE. 1973. bi-m. free. World Bank, 1818 H St., N.W., Washington, DC 20433. TEL 202-473-1155. FAX 202-522-2627. E-mail: books@worldbank.org. (U.S. orders to: Box 7247-8619, Philadelphia, PA 19170-8619; Also avail. from: 66 av. D'lena, 75116 Paris, France. TEL 33-1-40-69-30-55. FAX 33-1-40-69-30-68) Ed. Brett Kitchen. index.
Former titles: World Bank Publications. Index (ISSN 0095-5434); Catalog of World Bank Publications; (1973-1974): World Bank Catalog. Accession List.
Description: Lists of new World Bank titles with brief descriptions and ordering information.

332.1 912   UN   ISSN 0512-2457
WORLD BANK ATLAS. 1967. a. World Bank, 1818 H St., N.W., Washington, DC 20433. TEL 202-473-1155. FAX 202-522-2627. E-mail: books@worldbank.org. (U.S. orders to: Box 7247-8619, Philadelphia, PA 19170-8619; Also avail. from: 66 av. D'lena, 75116 Paris, France. TEL 33-14-0-69-30-55. FAX 33-1-40-69-30-68) (also avail. in microfiche from CIS) **Indexed:** IIS.

BUSINESS AND ECONOMICS — INTERNATIONAL DEVELOPMENT AND ASSISTANCE

338.91 320 UN
WORLD BANK COUNTRY STUDY. (Text in English; translations sometimes avail. in language of country covered) irreg. price varies. World Bank, 1818 H St., N.W., Washington, DC 20433. TEL 202-473-1155. FAX 202-522-2627. E-mail: books@worldbank.org. (U.S. orders to: Box 7247-8619, Philadelphia, PA 19170-8619; Also avail. from: 66 av. D'Iena, 75116 Paris, France. TEL 33-1-40-69-30-55. FAX 33-1-40-69-30-68) (back issues avail.) **Indexed:** Geo.Abstr. **Document type:** monographic series.
  Description: Covers, in detail, a sociopolitical issue of a nation in the context of World Bank international development assistance.

338.91 UN ISSN 0259-210X
WORLD BANK DISCUSSION PAPER. 1986. irreg. price varies. World Bank, 1818 H St., N.W., Washington, DC 20433. TEL 202-473-1155. FAX 202-522-2627. E-mail: books@worldbank.org. (U.S. orders to: Box 7247-8619, Philadelphia, PA 19170-8619; Also avail. from: 66 av. D'Iena, 75116 Paris, France. TEL 33-1-40-69-30-55. FAX 33-1-40-69-30-68) (back issues avail.) **Indexed:** Abstr.Anthropol., Geo.Abstr.P.G., IDA. **Document type:** monographic series.
  —BLDSC (9352.926100).
  Description: Discusses topics of regional and global importance affected by World Bank loans.

338.91 628 UN
WORLD BANK ENVIRONMENT PAPER. irreg. price varies. World Bank, 1818 H St., N.W., Washington, DC 20433. TEL 202-473-1155. FAX 202-522-2631. E-mail: books@worldbank.org. (U.S. orders to: Box 7247-8619, Philadelphia, PA 19170-8619; Also avail. from: 66 av. d'Iena, 75116 Paris, France. TEL 33-1-40-69-30-55. FAX 33-1-40-69-30-68) (back issues avail.) **Indexed:** Geo.Abstr.P.G., IDA. **Document type:** monographic series.
  Description: Treats, within the context of World Bank assistance, various environmental issues worldwide.

304.6 UN
WORLD BANK LIVING STANDARDS MEASUREMENT STUDY. Variant title: Living Standards Measurement Study. Abbreviated title: L S M S. irreg. price varies. World Bank, 1818 H St., N.W., Washington, DC 20433. TEL 202-473-1155. FAX 202-522-2627. E-mail: books@worldbank.org. (U.S. orders to: Box 7247-8619, Philadelphia, PA 19170-8619; Also avail. from: 66 av. d'Iena, 75116 Paris, France. TEL 33-1-40-69-30-55. FAX 33-1-40-69-30-68) (back issues avail.) **Indexed:** Geo.Abstr.P.G., IDA. **Document type:** monographic series.
  Description: Covers demographic and socioeconomic issues in the context of World Bank international monetary aid.

338.91 UN ISSN 0258-2120
WORLD BANK POLICY PAPER. (Text mainly in English; other language editions avail.) 1986. irreg. price varies. World Bank, International Bank for Reconstruction and Development, 1818 H St., N.W., Washington, DC 20433. TEL 202-473-1155. FAX 202-522-2627. E-mail: books@worldbank.org. (U.S. orders to: Box 7247-8619, Philadelphia, PA 19170-8619; Also avail. from: 66 av. D'Iena, 75116 Paris, France. TEL 33-1-40-69-30-55. FAX 33-1-40-69-30-68) (back issues avail.)
  Description: Discusses worldwide issues of importance affecting World Bank loans.

338.9 UN ISSN 1014-8590
HC60
WORLD BANK POLICY RESEARCH BULLETIN. 1980. bi-m. free. World Bank, 1818 H St., N.W., Washington, DC 20433. TEL 202-473-3984. FAX 202-522-2627. E-mail: books@worldbank.org. **Indexed:** Geo.Abstr.H.G., IDA, Mid.East: Abstr.& Ind., Rural Recreat.Tour.Abstr., World Agri.Econ. & Rural Sociol.Abstr., World Bank.Abstr. **Document type:** bulletin.
  Formerly (until 1989): World Bank Research News (ISSN 0253-3928)

338.91 320 UN
WORLD BANK REGIONAL AND SECTORAL STUDIES. irreg., latest Feb. 1994. price varies. World Bank, 1818 H St., N.W., Washington, DC 20433. TEL 202-473-1155. FAX 202-522-2627. E-mail: books@worldbank.org. (U.S. orders to: Box 7247-8619, Philadelphia, PA 19170-8619; Also avail. from: 66 av. D'Iena, 75116 Paris, France. TEL 33-1-40-69-30-55. FAX 33-1-40-69-30-68) (back issues avail.) **Document type:** monographic series.
  Description: Discusses various social and political issues in the context of World Bank aid.

338.91 628 UN ISSN 0253-7494
CODEN: WBTPEL
WORLD BANK TECHNICAL PAPER. (Text mainly in English; occasionally in other languages) 1982. irreg. price varies. World Bank, 1818 H St., N.W., Washington, DC 20433. TEL 202-473-1155. FAX 202-676-2627. (Subscr. to: Box 7247-8619, Philadelphia, PA 19170-8619) (back issues avail.) **Indexed:** Geo.Abstr.H.G., Geo.Abstr.P.G., IDA. **Document type:** monographic series.
  —BLDSC (9352.934500).
  Description: Covers environmental, energy, or sociopolitical topics worldwide.

338.91 UN ISSN 0253-2859
HJ8899
WORLD DEBT TABLES. a. $200 (diskette or CD-ROM $125). World Bank, 1818 H St., N.W., Washington, DC 20433. TEL 202-473-1155. FAX 202-522-2627. E-mail: books@worldbank.org. (U.S. orders to: Box 7247-8619, Philadelphia, PA 19170-8619; Also avail. from: 66 av. D'Iena, 75116 Paris, France. TEL 33-1-40-69-30-55. FAX 33-1-40-69-30-68) (diskette format) **Indexed:** IIS.
  ●Also available online. Vendor(s): GSI-ECO. Also available on CD-ROM.
  —BLDSC (9354.115000).
  Description: Covers data on the external debt of 109 developing countries. Includes periodic updates.

942 UK ISSN 0305-750X
HC4 CODEN: WODEDW
WORLD DEVELOPMENT. 1973. m. fl.2215($1273) to institutions (effective 1998). Elsevier Science Ltd., Pergamon, P.O. Box 800, Kidlington, Oxford OX5 1DX, England. TEL 44-1865-843010. E-mail: nlinfo-f@elsevier.nl; usinfo-f@elsevier.com; forinfo-kyf04035@niftyserve.or.jp; URL: http://www.elsevier.nl/. (Subscr. to: Elsevier Science, Regional Sales Office, P.O. Box 211, 1000 AE Amsterdam, Netherlands. TEL 31-20-4853757. FAX 31-20-4853432; Subscr. in the Americas to: Elsevier Science, Regional Sales Office, Box 945, New York, NY 10159-0945. TEL 212-633-3730. FAX 212-633-3680; Subscr. in Australasia and the Far East to: Elsevier Science (Singapore) Pte Ltd, No.1 Temasek Ave., No.17-01 Millenia Tower, Singapore 039192, Singapore. TEL 65-434-3727. FAX 65-337-2230) Eds. Paul Streeten, Janet L. Craswell. adv.: B&W page $550, color page $1350. bk.rev.; charts; illus. circ. 1,600. (also avail. in microfilm from UMI; back issues avail.) **Indexed:** A.B.C.Pol.Sci., Abstr.Rural Dev.Trop., ASCA, Asian-Pac.Econ.Lit., BPIA, Br.Hum.Ind., Bus.Ind., C.R.E.J., Curr.Cont., Documentatieblad, E.I., Food Sci.& Tech.Abstr., Fut.Surv., Geo.Abstr.P.G., Int.Lab.Doc., Int.Polit.Sci.Abstr., J.of Econ.Lit., J.of Ferroc., Key to Econ.Sci., Lang.& Lang.Behav.Abstr., Maize Abstr., P.A.I.S., Polit.Sci.Abstr., Rural Devel.Abstr., Rural Recreat.Tour.Abstr., So.Pac.Per.Ind., Soc.Sci.Ind., SSCI, Tr.& Indus.Ind., World Agri.Econ.& Rural Sociol.Abstr. **Document type:** academic/scholarly publication.
  —BLDSC (9354.150000); Genuine Article; KR SourceOne; SWETS; UMI; UnCover. **CCC.**
  Incorporates: New Commonwealth (ISSN 0028-4475)
  Description: Multidisciplinary journal publishing research and review articles on the social, economic and political consequences of development, focusing on reforms and cooperative efforts to eliminate disease, poverty, and illiteracy.
  Refereed Serial

338.91 UN ISSN 0163-5085
HC59.7
WORLD DEVELOPMENT REPORT. (Translations avail. in: Arabic, Chinese, French, German, Japanese, Portuguese, Russian, Spanish) 1978. a. $22.95 (hardcover edition $45.95). World Bank, 1818 H St., N.W., Washington, DC 20433. TEL 202-473-1155. FAX 202-522-2627. E-mail: books@worldbank.org. (Orders to: Box 7247-8619, Philadelphia, PA 19170-8619; Also avail. from: 66 av. D'Iena, 75116 Paris, France. TEL 33-1-40-69-30-55. FAX 33-1-40-69-30-68) stat. (also avail. in microfiche from CIS; diskette format) **Indexed:** IIS, Rice Abstr.
  —BLDSC (9354.170000); CISTI; SWETS.
  Description: Summary of the state of economic development in developing countries. Includes a current overview of the world economy, statistics on social and economic development, and a special theme of current importance.

338.91 UN
WORLD FOOD PROGRAMME. ANNUAL REPORT. 1987. a. World Food Programme, Via Cristoforo Colombo 426, 00145 Rome, Italy. TEL 396-522821. FAX 396-5228240. TELEX 626675 WFP 1. Ed. Sylvana Foa. circ. 24,000.
  Formerly (until 1994): Food Aid Review (ISSN 1014-8574); Supersedes (in 1990): World Food Programme. Annual Report (ISSN 1014-8515); Which was formerly (until 1988): World Food Programme ... in Review (ISSN 1014-1596)

WORLD LIBRARIES; an international journal focusing on libraries and socio-economic development in Africa, Asia, and Latin America. see LIBRARY AND INFORMATION SCIENCES

WORLD TODAY SERIES: LATIN AMERICA. see HISTORY — History Of North And South America

338.91 370.196 US ISSN 1047-5338
HC60.5
WORLDVIEW MAGAZINE. 1980. q. $25 to non-members. National Peace Corps Association, 1900 L St., N.W., Ste. 205, Washington, DC 20036. TEL 202-293-7728. FAX 202-293-7554. E-mail: david__arnold@csgi.com; URL: http://www.vita.org/npca. Ed. David Arnold. R&P contact: David Arnold. adv.; bk.rev.; illus.; circ. 16,000 (paid). (back issues avail.) **Document type:** consumer publication.
  Formerly (until 1988): R P C Voice (ISSN 0892-1008)
  Description: Publishes news and opinion about the changing communities of the developing world.

330.9 338.91 US ISSN 1085-7559
Z7164.U5
WORLDVIEWS; a quarterly review of resources for education and action. 1985. q. $25 to individuals (outside N. America $45); institutions $50 (outside N. America $65) (effective 1998). (Third World Resources) DataCenter, 464 19th St., Oakland, CA 94612-2297. TEL 510-835-4692. FAX 510-835-3017. E-mail: worldviews@igc.apc.org; URL: http://www.igc.apc.org/worldviews/. Eds. Thomas P. Fenton, Mary J. Heffron. adv.: B&W page $600; 8 1/2 x 11. bk.rev.; film rev.; bibl.; index. circ. 2,000. (also avail. in microfiche; back issues avail.) **Indexed:** Bk.Rev.Ind. (1989-), Child.Bk.Rev.Ind. (1989-), Media Rev.Dig., Per.Islam. (1992-), Refug.Abstr. **Document type:** abstracting/indexing.
  ●Also available online. Vendor(s): Knight-Ridder Information, Inc.
  Formerly (until 1996): Third World Resources (ISSN 8755-8831)
  Description: Lists organizations and newly released print, audiovisual, on-line, and other educational resources on Third World regions and issues.

ZAMBIA NIEUWSBRIEF. see HISTORY — History Of Africa

BUSINESS AND ECONOMICS — Investments

332.6   UK
A A A INVESTMENT GUIDE. 1982. a. £12.99. Wisebuy Publications, 25 West Cottages, London NW6 1RJ, England. TEL 44-171-433-1121. URL: http://www.wisebuy.co.uk. Ed. David Lewis. circ. 10,000. (diskette format; back issues avail.) **Document type:** consumer publication.
    Former titles: Savers and Investors Guide; (until 1986): Money Mail Savers Guide (ISSN 0265-2579)
    Refereed Serial

332.6   US   ISSN 0192-3315
HG4501
A A I I JOURNAL. 1979. 10/yr. $49 (foreign $59). American Association of Individual Investors, 625 N. Michigan Ave., Ste. 1920, Chicago, IL 60611. TEL 312-280-0170. FAX 312-280-1625. E-mail: aaiigenl@aol.com; URL: http://www.aaii.org. Ed. Maria Crawford Scott. R&P contact: Maria Crawford Scott. bk.rev. circ. 170,000. **Indexed:** B.P.I. **Document type:** trade publication.
    —KR SourceOne.
    Description: Provides investment information and research to enable individual investors to become more effective managers of their own assets.

A F T A MONITOR. (ASEAN Free Trade Area) see BUSINESS AND ECONOMICS — International Commerce

332.6   US
A I C INVESTMENT BULLETIN.* 1934. s-m. $48. A I C Investment Advisors, Inc., 440 South St., Pittsfield, MA 01201-8217. TEL 413-499-1111. Ed. Richard F. Maloney. bk.rev.; charts; stat.; index. (looseleaf format)
    Formerly: Investment Bulletin (ISSN 0021-0072)

332.6   SP
A I F REVISTA. 6/yr. Association of Professional Financial and Investment Consultants, Gran Via 594, 4o, 108007 Barcelona, Spain.

332.6   UK
A I T C INVESTMENT TRUST DIRECTORY. a. (Association of Investment Trust Companies) Professional and Business Information plc, Munro House, 14 St. Cross St., London EC1N 8YY, England. TEL 0171-430-2020. FAX 0171-430-1773. **Document type:** directory.

332   US
A P P A DIGEST. 1963. q. membership. American Professional Practice Association, 292 Madison Ave., New York, NY 10017. TEL 212-949-5900. Ed. William Driscoll. adv.; bk.rev.; charts; illus. circ. 20,000. **Document type:** newsletter.

ABSTRACT OF AMERICAN ECONOMIC TREND ANALYSIS. see BUSINESS AND ECONOMICS — Banking And Finance

ACCESS TO CANADIAN COMMODITY TAXES. see BUSINESS AND ECONOMICS — Public Finance, Taxation

ACCOUNTANTS S E C PRACTICE MANUAL. see BUSINESS AND ECONOMICS — Accounting

ACCOUNTING RESEARCH JOURNAL. see BUSINESS AND ECONOMICS — Accounting

332   US   ISSN 8755-5735
HG4028.M4
ACQUISITION MART.* 1982. m. $445. Business Publications, Inc. (San Diego), 5060 Shoreham Pl., Ste. 200, San Diego, CA 92122-5904. TEL 619-457-7577. FAX 619-453-1091. Ed. Ronald Goetz. adv.; bk.rev. **Document type:** newsletter.
    Description: Profiles of 50-100 middle market companies for sale. Lists names, addresses, and telephone numbers of target company representatives.

332.6   UK   ISSN 0952-3618
ACQUISITIONS MONTHLY. 1984. m. $397. Tudor House Publications, Ltd., Tudor House, 78 Mount Ephraim, Tunbridge Wells, Kent TN4 8BS, England. TEL 44-1892-515454. FAX 44-1892-511547. (U.S. addr.: Tudor House Publications, Ltd., Box 48429, Washington, DC 20002-0429. TEL 202-396-1052. FAX 202-396-1053) Ed. Philip Healey. R&P contact: Philip Healey. adv. contact: Lucy Greenfield. index. circ. 7,000. (back issues avail.) **Document type:** trade publication.
    —BLDSC (0578.882300); SWETS.

ACTUALIDAD EN SEGUROS Y FIANZAS. see INSURANCE

332.6   CU
ACTUALIZACION DE LAS INVERSIONES AZUCARERAS. 1981. a. C.$10. (Ministerio del Comercio Exterior (MINCEX)) Empresa Cubazucar, Calle 23 No. 55, Vedado, Havana, Cuba. TEL 70-9742. TELEX 51-1147.
    Description: Provides information on the relations of new plants and modernizations for the world sugar industry.

332.6   US
ADDISON REPORT. 1980. every 3 wks. $250 for 18 nos. (includes telephone hotline service). Addison Investment Management Co., Box 402, Franklin, MA 02038-0402. TEL 508-528-8678. Ed. Andrew L. Addison; Pub. Andrew L. Addison. charts. circ. 1,000. (back issues avail.) **Document type:** newsletter.
    Description: Advisory service utilizing "market integration." Analyzes the interaction of stocks, bonds and commodities. Provides specific mutual fund switch advice for gold, stock and Fidelity Select investors.

332.6   US   ISSN 1063-2808
ADRIAN DAY'S INVESTMENT ANALYST. 1987. m. $87. Investment Consultants International, P.O. Box 6644, Annapolis, MD 21401. TEL 410-224-8885. Ed. Adrian Day. bk.rev. circ. 41,000. **Document type:** newsletter.
    Description: Covers analysis, forecasts, recommendations, techniques on all major markets.

332   NE
▼**ADVANCES IN FINANCE, INVESTMENT AND BANKING.** (Text in English) 1995. irreg. Elsevier Science B.V., Books Division, P.O. Box 211, 1000 AE Amsterdam, Netherlands. TEL 31-20-4853911. FAX 31-20-4853705. E-mail: nl-info@elsevier.nl; usinfo-f@elsevier.com; forinfo-kyf04035@niftyserve.or.jp; URL: http://www.elsevier.nl/. (Subscr. in the Americas to: Elsevier Science, Regional Sales Office, Box 945, New York, NY 10159-0945. TEL 212-633-3730. FAX 212-633-3680; Subscr. in Australasia and the Far East to: Elsevier Science (Singapore) Pte Ltd, No.1 Temasek Ave., No.17-01 Millenia Tower, Singapore 039192, Singapore. TEL 65-434-3727. FAX 65-337-2230; Subscr. in Japan to: Elsevier Science Japan, 9-15 Higashi-Azabu 1-chome, Minato-ku, Tokyo 106, Japan. TEL 81-3-5561-5033. FAX 81-3-5561-5047) bibl. **Document type:** monographic series.
    Refereed Serial

332.6   SW   ISSN 0345-3766
HC371
AFFAERSVAERLDEN. 1901. w. (42/yr.). SEK 1460 in Sweden; Europe SEK 2132; elsewhere SEK 2008 (effective 1997). Affaersvaerlden Foerlag AB, S-106 12 Stockholm, Sweden. TEL 46-8-796-65-00. FAX 46-8-20-21-57. URL: http://www.afv.se. Ed. Carl Rosen. adv.: B&W page SEK 26500, color page SEK 29800; trim 188 x 274; adv. contact: Kerstin Pettersson. bk.rev.; charts; stat.; index; circ. 23,500 (paid). (also avail. in microform from UMI)
    Formerly: Affaersvaerlden - Finanstidningen (ISSN 0001-9658)
    Description: In-depth coverage, analyses and commentary of important developments and trends of Swedish companies and the international economy.

332.6   SW   ISSN 0281-7586
AFFAERSVAERLDENS AARSBOK. 1978. a. SEK 250. Affaersvaerlden, S-106 12 Stockholm, Sweden. TEL 46-8-796-65-40. FAX 46-8-20-21-57. adv. circ. 22,000.

332.6   FR   ISSN 0001-9615
HC271
AFFAIRES. 1963. m. 100 F.($25) Express-Documents, 61 rue de Malte, 75541 Paris Cedex 11, France. Ed. Robert Monteux. adv.; bk.rev.; bibl.; charts; illus.; stat.; index, cum.index. circ. 40,000. **Indexed:** INSPEC.

AFRICAN BUSINESS HANDBOOK; a practical guide to business resources for U.S.-Africa trade and investment. see BUSINESS AND ECONOMICS — International Commerce

332.6   IT
AGENDA DEL RENDITO FISSO. (Text in Italian; glossary in English) 1990. a. $90. Databank S.p.A., SASIP Division, Via Spartaco 19, 20135 Milan, Italy. FAX 392-55183152. Ed. Carlo Colombi. index. circ. 2,000.
    Description: Contains information on all fixed interest securities listed on the Italian stock exchanges having circulating amounts in excess of 10 billion lire.

332.6   GW   ISSN 0944-7598
AKTIEN ANALYZE. 1993. m. DM.1176. Verlag Norman Rentrop, Theodor-Heuss-Str. 4, 53177 Bonn, Germany. TEL 49-228-82050. FAX 49-228-364411. TELEX 17228309. Ed. Hans Joachim Oberhettinger. (looseleaf format) **Document type:** bulletin.
    Description: Information on stocks and the stock market.

332.6   US   ISSN 0736-007X
AL HANSON'S ECONOMIC NEWSLETTER; the professional trader. 1972. m. $120. Al Hanson, Ed. & Pub., Box 9, Ottertail, MN 56571. TEL 218-367-2404. R&P contact: Al Hanson. circ. 100,000. **Document type:** newsletter.

332.6   US   ISSN 0095-2931
ALAN SHAWN FEINSTEIN INSIDERS REPORT. Variant Title--Alan Shawn Feinstein's International Insiders Report. 1973. m. $45. Alan Shawn Feinstein & Associates, 41 Alhambra Circle, Cranston, RI 02905. TEL 401-467-5155. Ed. Alan Shawn Feinstein. bk.rev.; charts; stat. circ. 10,000.
    Formerly: Insiders Report.

332.6 350   US   ISSN 0092-6736
HJ3835.A4
ALASKA. DEPARTMENT OF REVENUE. STATE INVESTMENT PORTFOLIO. Key Title: State Investment Portfolio. (Juneau). (Report year ends Jun. 30) a. Department of Revenue, Box SB, Juneau, AK 99811 TEL 907-465-2173. stat. **Document type:** government publication.

332.6   UK
ALLIED DUNBAR INVESTMENT AND SAVINGS HANDBOOK. a. Longman Group Ltd., Law, Tax and Finance Division, 21-27 Lamb's Conduit St., London WC1N 3NJ, England. TEL 44-171-242-2548. FAX 44-171-831-8119. **Document type:** corporate report.
    Former titles (until 1994): Allied Dunbar Investment and Savings Guide; (until 1990): Allied Dunbar Investment Guide.

ALMANAC OF BUSINESS AND INDUSTRIAL FINANCIAL RATIOS. see BUSINESS AND ECONOMICS — Banking And Finance

AMERICAN GUIDANCE FOR SENIORS. see GERONTOLOGY AND GERIATRICS

332.6   US   ISSN 1075-1637
HG4575.1
AMERICAN STOCK EXCHANGE. AMEX FACT BOOK. 1968. a. $20. American Stock Exchange, Inc, 86 Trinity Pl., New York, NY 10006-1881. TEL 212-306-1386. Dir. John Lum. circ. 9,000.
    Former titles (until 1983): American Stock Exchange. AMEX Databook (ISSN 0066-0760); American Stock Exchange. AMEX Statistical Review

332.6   US   ISSN 0066-0779
AMERICAN STOCK EXCHANGE. ANNUAL REPORT. a. American Stock Exchange Inc., 86 Trinity Pl., New York, NY 10006-1881. TEL 212-306-1386. **Document type:** corporate report.

BUSINESS AND ECONOMICS — INVESTMENTS

332.6 US
AMERICAN STOCK EXCHANGE WEEKLY BULLETIN. 1927. w. $20. American Stock Exchange, Inc., 86 Trinity Pl., New York, NY 10006-1881. TEL 212-306-1441. (looseleaf format) Document type: bulletin.

332.6 US ISSN 0883-7953
AMERICA'S FASTEST GROWING COMPANIES.* 1959. m. $245. Financial Data Systems, Inc., 333 Seventh Ave., 5th Fl., New York, NY 10001-5004. TEL 212-689-2777. Ed. Jonathan Steinberg.
Formerly: Johnson Survey (ISSN 0732-9466)
Description: Provides statistics on the development of America's fastest growing companies.

332.6 US ISSN 1088-0194
▼**AMERNICK MARKET REPORT.** 1995. w. $249 e-mail subscr. Amernick Publishing Co., Box 10065, Berkeley, CA 94709-1065. TEL 510-525-3055. FAX 510-525-6586. E-mail: amernick@ix.netcom.com. Ed. Larry Amernick. (back issues avail.) Document type: newsletter.
Description: International stock market news for the general public, academicians, and new and experienced investors.

332.6 341 NE
▼**AMSTERDAM FINANCIAL SERIES. STOCK EXCHANGE AND E E C LAW: COMMENTARY.** (Text in English) 1995. base vol. (plus irreg. updates). Kluwer Law International (Subsidiary of: Wolters Kluwer N.V.), Postbus 85889, 2508 CN The Hague, Netherlands. TEL 31-70-3081500. FAX 31-70-3081515. (Dist. by: Libresso Distribution Center, P.O. Box 23, 7400 GA Deventer, Netherlands. TEL 31-570-633155. FAX 31-570-633834; In N. America: Kluwer Law International, 675 Massachusetts Ave., Cambridge, MA 02139. TEL 617-354-0140. FAX 617-354-8595) Ed. Martijn van Empel. (looseleaf format)
Description: Discusses the impact of EC directives and legislation on the securities industry and stock exchanges in Europe.

332.6 NE
AMSTERDAM STOCK EXCHANGE. (Text in English) 1969. a. Amsterdam Stock Exchange, Beursplein 5, Amsterdam 1001, Netherlands. charts; illus.; stat. circ. 5,000.
Description: Covers issues, stocks, indices, trading activity, and bond market. Includes general information, statistics, and list of members.

332.6 340 US ISSN 0887-1337
KF1439
ANALYSIS OF KEY S E C NO-ACTION LETTERS. 1985. a. $140. Clark - Boardman - Callaghan, 375 Hudson St., New York, NY 10014. TEL 212-929-7500; 800-422-2101. FAX 212-924-0460. Ed. Robert J. Haft.
Description: Focuses on what currently constitutes the "common law" of the SEC, and its implications for today's securities practice.

332.6 US ISSN 0884-6936
HG4905
ANALYST'S HANDBOOK. 1964. a. (plus m. updates). $795. Standard & Poor's Corporation (Subsidiary of: McGraw-Hill, Inc.), 65 Broadway, New York, NY 10004. TEL 212-208-8000. Ed. C. Levine. stat. Document type: trade publication.
Description: Enables anyone concerned with company or industry performance to compare the most important financial and per-share data for the S&P Industrial and the Index's 88 industry groups.

ANNUAL DIVIDEND RECORD - TEN YEAR PRICE RANGE. see BUSINESS AND ECONOMICS — Banking And Finance

332.6 UK ISSN 1361-7842
ANNUAL REGISTRARS SERVICE. (Supplement avail.: Annual Registrars Service Supplement (ISSN 1366-4611)) 1953. a. £90 for print version; with s-a. supplement £135. Financial Times Information Ltd., Extel, Fitzroy Hosue, 13-17 Epworth St., London EC2A 4DL, England.
TEL 44-171-825-8000. FAX 44-171-608-2032. TELEX 884319. E-mail: eic@ft.com; URL: http://www.info.ft.com/.
●Also available on CD-ROM.
Former titles (until 1995): Extel Financial Annual Registrars Service (ISSN 1351-444X); (until 1993): Register of Registrars (ISSN 0482-1319)
Description: Provides information on registrars for UK quoted companies. Provides details on types of stocks and shares issues and the nominal value on each entry. Includes registration amendments occuring during the previous year including name changes, liquidations, new companies, etc.

332.96 IT
ANNUARIO DELL'INVESTITORE; tutti i numeri dell'anno finanziario. 1994. a. Sole 24 Ore, S.p.A., Via Lomazzo 52, 20154 Milan, Italy. TEL 39-2-31031. Ed. Adamo Gentile. Document type: directory.

ANNUITY & LIFE INSURANCE SHOPPER. see INSURANCE

333.33 US ISSN 8755-4348
APPRAISERS' INFORMATION EXCHANGE.* 1980. bi-m. membership. International Society of Appraisers, 16040 Christensen RD 320, Seattle, WA 98188-2929. TEL 708-882-0706.
FAX 708-885-2116. Ed. Janis L. Walters. adv.; bk.rev. circ. 3,000.

332.6 US
ARGUS WEEKLY STAFF REPORT. w. Argus Research, 17 Battery Pl., New York, NY 10004.
TEL 212-425-7500. Ed. Jim Kelleher. adv. contact: Karena Bernard.

ART - ANTIQUES INVESTMENT REPORT. see ART

332.6 330.9 CN
AS A MATTER OF FACT. a. Can.$5. Toronto Stock Exchange, Exchange Tower, 2 First Canadian Pl., Toronto, ON M5X 1J2, Canada.
TEL 416-947-4222. index.
Former titles: Everything You Ever Wanted to Know about the Toronto Stock Exchange; Toronto Stock Exchange Fact Book.
Description: Information on the structure and services of the Toronto Stock Exchange.

332.6 UK ISSN 0966-0453
ASIA PACIFIC HANDBOOK. 1991. s-a. Exeter Financial Ltd., Research Products Sales and Marketing Department, 13-17 Epworth St., London EC2A 4DL, England. TEL 44-171-825-8000.
FAX 44-171-608-3514. Ed.Bd.
Description: Covers up to three years' of financial data on the 1,300 leading companies in Southeast Asia and Australia.

ASIA TODAY; Australia's regional business magazine. see BUSINESS AND ECONOMICS

332.6 IE ISSN 0332-4567
ASPECT. 1982. 11/yr. P.O. Box 15, New Road, Greystones, Dublin, Ireland. TEL 875514.
FAX 875118. Ed. John O'Neill. circ. 10,512.
Description: An investors' business magazine.

332.6 330.9 UK
ASSET FINANCE AND LEASING DIGEST. 1976. m. £195 (foreign $315) (effective 1997). Euromoney Publications plc., Nestor House, Playhouse Yard, London EC4V 5EX, England.
TEL 44-171-779-8935. FAX 44-171-779-8541. TELEX 2907001 EUROMON G; 226511 EURO UR. (Dist. in US by: American Educational Systems, 173 W. 81st St., New York, NY 10024. TEL 800-717-2669. FAX 212-501-8926) Ed. Louise Bowman. adv. circ. 7,500. (back issues avail.) Document type: trade publication.
●Also available online. Vendor(s): UMI.
—UMI.
Formerly: Leasing Digest (ISSN 0309-5258)
Description: Information on asset-based finance and leasing, domestic and international.

332.6 US ISSN 0894-6175
ASSET SALES REPORT. 1987. 48/yr. $1125 (foreign $1175). American Banker - Bond Buyer, Newsletter Division (Subsidiary of: Thomson Financial Services Company), 1 State St. Plaza, New York, NY 10004-1549. TEL 800-733-4371.
FAX 212-943-2224. (Subscr. to: Box 28315, Washington, DC 20038-8315. TEL 202-347-2665) Ed. Bruce Dorskind. adv. Document type: newsletter.
●Also available online. Vendor(s): Data-Star, Information Access Co., Knight-Ridder Information, Inc., Lexis-Nexis, NewsNet (FI33).
—CCC.
Description: Covers the field of loan sales and asset securitization, including reports on industry developments and trends, the volume of commercial loans sold by 10 of North America's largest banks, closing prices, and yield on activity traded asset-backed securities, and interviews with market leaders.

332.6 FR ISSN 0066-9008
ASSOCIATION DES SOCIETES ET FONDS FRANCAIS D'INVESTISSEMENT. ANNUAIRE. 1963. a. 600 F. Association des Societes et Fonds Francais d'Investissement, 31 rue de Miromesnil, 75008 Paris, France. TEL 42-65-75-26. FAX 42-65-16-31. Ed. Pierre Boeglin. abstr.; stat.; cum.index. circ. 2,500. Document type: directory.

332.6 658 US ISSN 1056-6074
HG4928.5
ASSOCIATION FOR INVESTMENT MANAGEMENT AND RESEARCH. MEMBERSHIP DIRECTORY. a. $150. Association for Investment Management and Research, Box 3668, Charlottesville, VA 22903. TEL 804-980-3668. FAX 804-980-9755. circ. 25,000. Document type: directory.
Formerly (until 1990): Institute of Chartered Financial Analysts. Joint Membership Directory (ISSN 0897-3040); Which incorporates (in 1987): Financial Analysts Federation. Membership Directory (ISSN 0430-4756)
Description: Lists financial analysts and other investment professionals worldwide.

133.5 332.6 US
THE ASTRO-INVESTOR; a newsletter for investors. 1986. m. $45 (effective 1997). Mull Publications, Box 11133, Indianapolis, IN 46201-0133.
TEL 317-357-6855. FAX 317-353-6246. Ed. Carol S. Mull. adv.; bk.rev.; charts. circ. 250. (looseleaf format; back issues avail.) Document type: newsletter.
Former titles (until 1991): Carol Mull's Market Forecast; (until 1990): Wall Street Astrologer.
Description: Predicts the Dow Jones Industrial Average via Gann and Elliott Wave theories, Fibonacci ratios and astrology. One industry is reviewed each month.

332.6 US ISSN 0736-7643
ASTUTE INVESTOR (KINGSTON). 1982. m. $30 (foreign $38). Charles E. Cardwell, Ed. & Pub., 135 Beechwood Ln., Kingston, TN 37763.
TEL 423-376-2732. E-mail: ASTUTE__INVESTOR@compuserve.com. bk.rev.; stat. circ. 1,000. (back issues avail.) Document type: newsletter.
Description: Benjamin-Graham stock screens service for value-oriented investors. Reviews investment strategies.

332.66 658.91 793 US
ATLANTIC CITY ACTION. 1978. m. $125 (foreign $150) (effective 1996). Glasco Associates, Inc., 33 S. Presbyterian Ave., Atlantic City, NJ 08404. TEL 609-347-1225. FAX 609-345-4168. (Subscr. to: 33 Gordon Alley, Box 5059, Atlantic City, NJ 08404) Ed. Al Glasgow. bk.rev. circ. 2,000. (back issues avail.) Document type: trade publication.
Description: Provides news and statistics for the gaming industry.

AURA WEALTH NEWSLETTER; economic survival in perilous times. see BUSINESS AND ECONOMICS — Economic Situation And Conditions

AUSTRALIA. BUREAU OF STATISTICS. ASSETS OF SUPERANNUATION FUNDS AND APPROVED DEPOSIT FUNDS. see BUSINESS AND ECONOMICS — Abstracting, Bibliographies, Statistics

AUSTRALIA. BUREAU OF STATISTICS. INTERNATIONAL INVESTMENT POSITION, AUSTRALIA (ANNUAL). see BUSINESS AND ECONOMICS — Abstracting, Bibliographies, Statistics

BUSINESS AND ECONOMICS — INVESTMENTS

AUSTRALIA. BUREAU OF STATISTICS. INTERNATIONAL INVESTMENT POSITION, AUSTRALIA: AUSTRALIAN SECURITIES HELD BY NOMINEES ON BEHALF OF NON-RESIDENTS. see BUSINESS AND ECONOMICS — *Abstracting, Bibliographies, Statistics*

AUSTRALIA. BUREAU OF STATISTICS. INTERNATIONAL INVESTMENT POSITION, AUSTRALIA: PURCHASES AND SALES OF PORTFOLIO CORPORATE EQUITIES BY NON-RESIDENTS. see BUSINESS AND ECONOMICS — *Abstracting, Bibliographies, Statistics*

AUSTRALIA. BUREAU OF STATISTICS. INTERNATIONAL INVESTMENT POSITION, AUSTRALIA (QUARTERLY). see BUSINESS AND ECONOMICS — *Abstracting, Bibliographies, Statistics*

AUSTRALIA. BUREAU OF STATISTICS. INTERNATIONAL INVESTMENT POSITION, AUSTRALIA: SUPPLEMENTARY COUNTRY STATISTICS. see BUSINESS AND ECONOMICS — *Abstracting, Bibliographies, Statistics*

332.6 AT ISSN 0815-9076
AUSTRALIA INVESTMENT QUARTERLY. 1984. q. free. Westpac Banking Corporation, Investment Division, G.P.O. Box 3874, Sydney, N.S.W. 2000, Australia. circ. 15,000.

338.01 US ISSN 0067-1959
AUSTRALIAN MARKET GUIDE. biennial. Dun's Marketing Services (Subsidiary of: Dun & Bradstreet, Inc.), 3 Sylvan Way, Parsippany, NJ 07054-3896. TEL 201-455-0900. (And: 24 Albert Rd., Melbourne South 3205, Australia)

AUSTRALIAN NUGGET JOURNAL. see MINES AND MINING INDUSTRY

AUTOMOTIVE INVESTOR. see TRANSPORTATION — *Automobiles*

332.6 CN ISSN 0849-1364
HG226 CODEN: BIRFE3
B C A INTEREST RATE FORECAST; a monthly analysis and forecast of U.S. bond and money market trends. 1979. m. $695. B C A Publications Ltd., 1002 Sherbrooke St. W., 16th Fl., Montreal, PQ H3A 3L6, Canada. TEL 514-499-9706. FAX 514-499-9709. Ed. J. Anthony Boeckh.
 Formerly: (until 1990): Bank Credit Analyst. Interest Rate Forecast (ISSN 0821-7858)
 Description: Analyzes bond and money market trends in the US based on a continuous appraisal of money and credit flows, economic developments, currency movements, budget and monetary policy.

332.6 US
B I RESEARCH. 1980. every 6 wks. $110 (foreign $125). B I Research, Inc., Box 133, Redding, CT 06875. TEL 203-438-9924. URL: http://www.biresearch.com. Ed. Thomas C. Bishop. circ. 5,000 (paid). (back issues avail.) **Document type**: newsletter.
 Description: Features one new recommended stock, a market commentary, and updates on every stock recommended.

332.6 GW
BADEN-WUERTTEMBERGISCHE WERTPAPIERBOERSE ZU STUTTGART. AMTLICHES KURSBLATT. 1861. 5/wk. DM.1600. Postfach 100441, 70003 Stuttgart, Germany. TEL 49-711-290183. FAX 49-711-2268119. circ. 200. **Document type**: bulletin.
 Formerly: Wertpapierboerse in Stuttgart. Amtliches Kursblatt (ISSN 0003-2158)
 Description: Lists stocks and their prices from the local stock exchange.

332.6 910.202 US ISSN 0749-5714
BAHAMAS DATELINE. 1976. m. $46 (effective 1998). Caribbean Dateline Publications, Box 23276, Washington, DC 20026. Ed. N. Poteat Day; Pub. N. Poteat Day. adv. contact: Kathy Richards. circ. 1,250. (back issues avail.) **Document type**: newsletter.
 Description: Reports on real estate, economic and political news and conditions, business, investment, banking laws and regulations, vacation living and other pertinent information for the foreign investor.

332.6 BF
BAHAMAS FINANCIAL DIGEST & BUSINESS TODAY. 1973. q. $60 (foreign $75). Symonette's Communication of the Bahamas Ltd., P.O. Box N-4824, Nassau, Bahamas. TEL 242-393-5545. FAX 242-324-2359. (Subscr. to: P.O. Box N-4271, Nassau, Bahamas. TEL 242-356-2981. FAX 242-356-5050; Alt. addr.: P.O. Box N-4846, Nassau, Bahamas) Ed. Michael A.J. Symonette. adv.: B&W page $495, color page $1864; adv. contact: Rhonda Lighthouse. bk.rev. circ. 17,500. (back issues avail.) **Document type**: trade publication.
 Description: Contains business and financial information.

332.66 BL ISSN 0100-767X
BALANCO FINANCEIRO. 1978. m. Gazetta Mercantil, Rua da Consolacao 247, 5 andar, Sao Paulo CEP 01301, Brazil. TELEX 391-113-2871. Ed. Klaus Kleber. circ. 32,000.

332.6 SP ISSN 0213-2648
BANCO DE BILBAO. INFORMACION SEMANAL DE VALORES. no.2227, 1985. w. Banco de Bilbao, Servicio de Estudios, Gran Via 12, Bilbao, Spain. stat.
 Description: Lists the latest financial news concerned with the stock market.

332.6 SP ISSN 0005-4992
BANIF'S INVESTMENT BULLETIN. 1969. m. 5000 ptas. Publibanif S.A., Juan Bravo 2, Madrid 6, Spain. Ed. Jose Luis Sanchez Fernandez Valderrama. charts; stat. circ. 5,000.

BANK AND LENDER LIABILITY LITIGATION REPORTER. see LAW

332.6 CN ISSN 0821-7866
BANK CREDIT ANALYST. 1949. m. $695. B C A Publications Ltd., 1002 Sherbrooke St. W. 16th Fl., Montreal, PQ H3A 3L6, Canada. TEL 514-499-9706. FAX 514-499-9709. Ed. J. Anthony Boeckh. charts; stat.; circ. controlled. (tabloid format)
 Description: Provides a forecast of trends in major US investment markets, with particular emphasis on equities, business conditions, inflationary trends, interest rates, gold and the dollar.

332.6 US ISSN 1074-2220
BANK INVESTMENT MARKETING; insights and analysis for bank securities and insurance professionals. Variant title: Financial Planning's Bank Investment Marketing. m. (Securities Data Company, Inc.) Securities Data Publishing, 40 W. 47th St., 11th Fl., New York, NY 10019. TEL 212-765-5311. FAX 212-765-6123. Ed. Pat Durner; Pub. Wendy Winshall. adv. contact: Merry Wells. (reprint service avail.) **Document type**: trade publication.
 —CCC.

332.6 US
BANK INVESTMENT PRODUCT NEWS. w. $1195 (Canada $1225; elsewhere $1270). Institutional Investor Newsletters, 477 Madison Ave., New York, NY 10022. TEL 212-224-3233. FAX 212-224-3353. **Document type**: newsletter.
 Description: Provides information on mutual fund, brokerage and insurance product sales through bank channels.

332.6 US ISSN 1064-9484
HG1723
BANK STOCK ANALYST. (Supplement to: Growth Stock Outlook) 1990. a. $5 per issue. Growth Stock Outlook, Inc., 4405 East-West Hwy., Ste. 305, Bethesda, MD 20814. TEL 301-654-5205. Ed. Charles Allmon. **Document type**: newsletter.
 Description: Provides comparative data on over 100 regional banks and multibank holding companies. Explores timely topics in the banking industry.

BANKERS/BUNUK. see BUSINESS AND ECONOMICS — *Banking And Finance*

332.6 BE ISSN 0771-6273
BANQUE BRUXELLES LAMBERT. BULLETIN FINANCIER. (Editions in Dutch, French) 1928. m. free. Banque Bruxelles Lambert s.a., Ave. Marnix 24, B-1050 Brussels, Belgium. TEL 32-2-5472111. FAX 32-2-5473844. charts; stat.; illus. circ. 33,000. Indexed: ELLIS. **Document type**: bulletin.

332.6 US ISSN 1060-3158
BARCLAY MANAGED FUTURES REPORT. 1990. q. $150 (foreign $165) (effective 1997). Barclay Trading Group, Ltd., 508 N, Second St., Ste. 201, Fairfield, IA 52556. TEL 515-472-3456. FAX 515-472-9514. E-mail: barclay@lisco.com; URL: http://www.fairfield.com/barclay/index.html. Ed. Sol Waksman; Pub. Sol Waksman. R&P contact: Sol Waksman. adv. contact: Sol Waksman. circ. 6,000. **Document type**: newsletter.
 Description: Overview of performance of money managers specializing in futures markets. Includes interviews with money managers on current issues facing investors.

332.63 UK ISSN 0260-261X
BARCLAYS COMMODITIES SURVEY. (Part of Industry Reports series) 1979-198?; resumed. q. £60 (academic institutions and students £30). Barclays Bank plc., Economics Department, P.O. Box 12, Barclays House, 1 Wimborne Rd., Poole, Dorset BH15 2BB, England. illus. circ. 8,000.

332.6 US ISSN 1077-8039
HG1
BARRON'S; the Dow Jones business and financial weekly. 1921. w. $140 (effective 1996). Dow Jones & Co., Inc., 200 Liberty St., New York, NY 10281. TEL 212-416-2700. FAX 212-416-2829. URL: http://www.barrons.com. (Subscr. to: Box 300, Princeton, NJ 08543-0300. TEL 800-628-9320) Ed. Edward A. Finn, Jr. adv.: page $18311; adv. contact: Jeff Meyer. bk.rev. circ. 235,600. (also avail. in microform from UMI; microfilm from BHP,KTO; reprint service avail. from UMI) **Indexed**: B.P.I., Bk.Rev.Ind. (1989-), BPIA, Bus.Ind., Energy Info.Abstr., Mag.Ind., PMR, Tr.& Indus.Ind. **Document type**: newspaper.
 ●Also available online. Vendor(s): Dow Jones News Retrieval.
 —BLDSC (1863.825000); KR SourceOne; SWETS; UMI. **CCC**.
 Former titles (until vol.74, no.13, 1994): Barron's National Business and Financial Weekly (ISSN 0005-6073); (until 1942): Barron's.

332.6 US
BARTLETT LETTERS. 1953. m. $25. Bartlett Letters, 151 S. Evanslawn, Box 465, Aurora, IL 60507. TEL 708-896-3143. Ed. John W. Bartlett. (looseleaf format; back issues avail.) **Document type**: newsletter.
 Description: Investment advisory service recommending conservative stocks.

332.6 SZ
BASLER BOERSE. JAHRESBERICHT/BASEL STOCK EXCHANGE. ANNUAL REPORT. (Text in English, German) 1961. a. Basler Effektenboerse - Basel Stock Exchange, Aeschenplatz 7, Postfach, CH-4002 Basel, Switzerland. TEL 061-2720555. FAX 061-2720626. TELEX 962524-BIA-CH. charts. circ. 12,000. **Document type**: corporate report.
 Formerly: Basler Effektenboerse. Jahresbericht.
 Description: Covers the trading, share and bond market. Includes association news, list of members of the Basel Stock Exchange, comparative statistics and share quotations.

BAXTER; a world economic and investment service. see BUSINESS AND ECONOMICS — *Production Of Goods And Services*

332.6 GW ISSN 0005-7029
BAYERISCHE BOERSE IN MUENCHEN. AMTLICHES KURSBLATT. 1869. 5/w. DM.90 per month. Muenchner Handelsverein e.V., Lenbachplatz 2a, 80333 Munich, Germany. TEL 49-89-549045-0. FAX 49-89-54904532. URL: http://www.bayerischeboerse.de. circ. 500. **Document type**: trad publication.

332.6 NE
BELEGGEN MET VAN LANSCHOT. 1980. fortn. free. F. van Lanschot Bankiers, Box 1021, 5200 HC's Hertogenbosch, Netherlands. TEL 073-153911. FAX 070-153151. Ed. R. Verdam. adv.; charts. circ. 15,000.

BENEFITS CANADA. see BUSINESS AND ECONOMICS — *Labor And Industrial Relations*

BEOGRAD (ZEMUN); list. see SHOES AND BOOTS

BERLINER BANK. BOERSENBRIEF. see BUSINESS AND ECONOMICS — *Banking And Finance*

BUSINESS AND ECONOMICS — INVESTMENTS

332.6   GW   ISSN 0003-214X
BERLINER WERTPAPIERBOERSE. AMTLICHES KURSBLATT. 5/w. DM.6.65 per no. Berliner Wertpapierboerse, Fasanenstr. 3, 10623 Berlin, Germany. TEL 49-30-3110910. FAX 49-30-31109179. Ed. Ursula Wiegand. mkt. circ. 500. **Document type:** newspaper.

332.6   GW
BERLINER WERTPAPIERBOERSE AKTUELL. 1994. q. Berliner Wertpapierboerse, Fasanenstr. 3, 10623 Berlin, Germany. TEL 49-30-3110910. FAX 49-30-31109179. Ed. Ursula Wiegand. **Document type:** newsletter.

332.6   SZ
BERNER BOERSENVEREIN. JAHRESBERICHT. (Text in German) a. membership. Berner Boersenverein - Berne Stock Exchange, Aarbergergasse 36, CH-3011 Bern, Switzerland. TEL 031-3114042. FAX 031-3115309. **Document type:** corporate report.

332.96   US
BERT DOHMEN'S MUTUAL FUND STRATEGY. m. $149. Phillips Publishing, Inc., 1201 Seven Locks Rd., Potomac, MD 20854. TEL 301-340-1520; 800-777-5005. FAX 301-424-4297. Ed. Bert Dohmen.

332.6   US
BERT DOHMEN'S WELLINGTON LETTER. 1977. m. $350 (includes irreg. supplement). Dohmen Capital Research Institute, Inc., 66 Queen St., Ste. 3801, Honolulu, HI 96813-4419. TEL 808-545-2243; 800-992-9989. FAX 808-545-2243. E-mail: dohmcap@aol.com. Ed. Bert Dohmen. circ. 8,000. **Document type:** newsletter.
    Description: Provides analysis and forecasts of the economy, Federal Reserve policy, and the global scene.

332.6   YU   ISSN 0354-1975
BERZA (BELGRADE). 1991. m. Trziste Novca i Kratkorocnih Hartija od Vrednosti, Terazije 23, Belgrade, Yugoslavia. Ed. Nikola Arandelovic.

332.6   US
▼**THE BEST OF YOUR MONEY MATTERS.** 1995. m. $29.95. Edelman Communications, Inc., 12450 Fair Lakes Circle, Ste. 200, Fairfax, VA 22033. Ed. Ric Edelman. circ. 2,100.

332.6   US   ISSN 0006-016X
BETTER INVESTING. 1951. m. $20. National Association of Investors Corp., Box 220, Royal Oak, MI 48067. TEL 313-543-0612. FAX 313-543-8442. Ed. Donald E. Danko. adv.; bk.rev.; circ. 125,000 (paid). (also avail. in microform from UMI; reprint service avail. from UMI) **Indexed:** Abr.R.G., R.G.
    —UMI.

332.6   NE   ISSN 0168-2636
BEURSPLEIN 5. 1961. w. fl.132. Beursdata B.V., Beursplein 5, 1012 JW Amsterdam, Netherlands. TEL 31-20-5234477. FAX 31-20-6836215. Ed. T. Nillissen. adv. circ. 9,500. **Document type:** trade publication.
    —SWETS.

BIDNET LINK; communication between buyer and seller. see BUSINESS AND ECONOMICS — Marketing And Purchasing

332.6   US
BILLINGTON'S STOCK FOCUS II. (Editions in Chinese, English) 1987. q. free. Billington Publications Inc., 1660 Benson Rd., Pt. Roberts, WA 98281. TEL 360-945-1491; 800-828-1866. FAX 800-721-5726. E-mail: info@ipos.com; URL: http://www.billingtons.com/. (And: 1095 Jervis St., No. 3, Vancouver, BC V6E 5C2, Canada) Ed. Lance Fortt. adv. contact: Michael Hansen. bk.rev.; charts; stat.; tr.lit.; circ. 200,000. (back issues avail.) **Document type:** newsletter.

IONICS. see MEDICAL SCIENCES — Experimental Medicine, Laboratory Technique

332   US   ISSN 1063-2123
BLOOMBERG. 1992. m. free to qualified personnel only. Bloomberg Financial Markets, Box 888, Princeton, NJ 08542-0888. TEL 609-279-3000. E-mail: magazine@bloomberg.com; URL: http://www.bloomberg.com. Ed. William Inman; Pub. Michael Bloomberg.
    Description: Provides news and information of interest to clients and investors.

332.6   US
BLOOMBERG PERSONAL. bi-m. $22.95. Bloomberg Financial Markets, 100 Business Park Dr., Box 888, Princeton, NJ 08542-0888. TEL 609-279-3000. FAX 609-683-7523. (Subscr. to: Box 5463, Harlan, IA 51593) Ed. William Inman; Pub. Michael Bloomberg. illus. **Document type:** trade publication.
    Description: Provides first-tier investors with practical, in-depth investment advice.

332.6   CN
BLUE BOOK OF STOCK REPORTS. fortn. Can.$279. M P L Communications Inc., 700-133 Richmond St. W., Toronto, ON M5H 3M8, Canada. TEL 416-869-1177. FAX 416-869-0456. Ed. Marc Johnson; Pubs. Barrie Martland, Steven Pepper. adv. contact: Mindy Tenenbaum. charts; stat. (looseleaf format; back issues avail.) **Document type:** newsletter.
    Formerly: Blue Book of C B S Stock Reports (ISSN 0384-7802)
    Description: Information about over 250 Canadian companies.

332.6   US   ISSN 0741-8345
BLUE CHIP FINANCIAL FORECASTS. 1982. m. $545 (foreign $557) (effective 1998). Capitol Publications Inc., 1101 King St., Ste. 444, Alexandria, VA 22314. TEL 703-683-4100. FAX 703-739-6517. Ed. Randell Moore. **Document type:** newsletter.
    —CCC.
    Description: Addresses what top analysts are saying about interest rates and monetary policy.

332.6   US   ISSN 0896-4904
BLUE CHIP STOCKS. 1974. a. $45. Elton Stephens Investments, 4016 S. Michigan St., South Bend, IN 46614-2544. TEL 219-291-3823. (Subscr. to: Box 476, South Bend, IN 46624-0746) Ed. Elton Stephens. R&P contact: Elton Stephens. index. circ. 3,000. (looseleaf format; back issues avail.) **Document type:** newsletter.

332.6   US
BLUE LIST OF CURRENT MUNICIPAL AND CORPORATE OFFERINGS. 1935. d. (5/w.). $940. Standard & Poors Corporation (Subsidiary of: McGraw-Hill, Inc.), 25 Broadway, New York, NY 10004. TEL 212-208-8000. Ed. Marjorie Schmidt. adv. contact: Dominick DiDiorgio. circ. 4,700 (paid). (back issues avail.) **Document type:** trade publication.
    ●Also available online.
    Description: Gives municipal bond listings for municipal bond dealers.

332.6   US
BLUE SKY PRACTICE; for public and private limited offerings. a. $140. Clark - Boardman - Callaghan, 375 Hudson St., New York, NY 10014. TEL 212-929-7500; 800-422-0101. FAX 212-924-0460. Eds. Peter M. Fass, Derek A. Wittner.
    Description: Offers an overview and update of state regulation covering public and private offerings of securities of direct participation programs.

332.6   US
BOB BRINKER'S MARKETIMER. 1986. m. $185. 2023 N. Atlantic Ave., Ste. 301, Cocoa Beach, FL 32931. Ed. Bob Brinker; Pub. Bob Brinker. **Document type:** newsletter.
    Description: An investment advisory newsletter providing stock market and interest rate timing forecasts, no-load mutual fund recommendations, model portfolios, and discussions on the factors leading to conclusions.

332.6   US   ISSN 1050-9011
HG4501
BOB NUROCK'S ADVISORY. 1979. s-w. $247. Investor's Analysis, Inc., Box 460, Santa Fe, NM 87504-0460. TEL 505-820-2737. Ed. Robert J. Nurock. charts; illus.; stat. (back issues avail.) **Document type:** newsletter.
    Formerly: Astute Investor (Paoli).
    Description: Provides investment strategy for stock market, mutual and sector funds. Includes E-mail or fax reports, and data for technical market index formerly shown on Wall $treet Week.

332.6 332   AU
BOERSE. a. Girozentrale Vienna, Schubertring 5, 1010 Vienna, Austria. Ed. Michael Briem. circ. 2,000.

332.6   GW   ISSN 0934-8441
BOERSE ONLINE; Wochenzeitung fuer moderne Kapitalanlage. 1987. w. DM.249 (foreign DM.296). Markt und Technik Verlag AG, Hans-Pinsel-Str. 2, 85540 Haar, Germany. TEL 089-4613-0. FAX 089-4613775. TELEX 5218484. (Subscr. to: Boerse Online Leserservice, Postfach 1173, 7107 Neckarsulm) Eds. Frank B. Werner, Michael Koelmel. adv.; bk.rev. circ. 45,000. (back issues avail.) **Document type:** consumer publication.
    Description: Stock exchange magazine for investors.

BOERSEN JAHRBUCH. see BUSINESS AND ECONOMICS — Economic Situation And Conditions

332.6   AU
BOERSEN-KURIER. 1922. w. S.1100 (foreign S.1400); newsstand price: S.28. Observer GmbH, Lessinggasse 21, A-1020 Vienna, Austria. TEL 01-21322-0. FAX 01-2160683. TELEX 131742-OBSER-A. Ed. Herbert Laszlo. adv.: B&W page S.50000, color page S.67400; trim 266 x 390; adv. contact: Anatol Eschelmueller. bk.rev. circ. 12,900. **Document type:** newspaper.
    Formerly: Wiener Boersen-Kurier.
    Description: Reports on all areas of investment, including stock markets, options and futures, antiques, investor relations, related software, etc.

332.6   SW   ISSN 0281-3149
BOERSGUIDE. 1966. s-a. SEK 195 (effective 1993). Oehman, P.O. Box 7415, S-103 91 Stockholm, Sweden. (Dist. by: Sveriges Aktiespararers Riksfoerbund, P.O. Box 21194, S-100 31 Stockholm, Sweden)
    Formerly (until 1975): Investment Guide (ISSN 0579-4013)

332.6   SW   ISSN 0284-0162
BOERSINSIKT. 1982. 30/yr. SEK 1795 (effective 1993). Boersinsikt, P.O. Box 6044, S-191 06 Sollentuna, Sweden. TEL 46-8-754-92-00. FAX 46-8-754-89-40. Ed. Mab Jonnerhag.
    Former titles (until 1985): Insikt - Placeringsraadgivning; (until 1983): Insikt i Aktier, Raavaror, Valutor, Obligationer, Skatter, Privatekonomi.

332.6   SW   ISSN 1100-1275
BOERSVECKAN. 1986. 40/yr. SEK 2190. Boersveckan, P.O. Box 7465, S-103 92 Stockholm, Sweden. TEL 46-8-103-350. FAX 46-8-201-400. Ed. Bjoern Davegaardh. circ. 3,500. **Document type:** newsletter.

332.6   PE
BOLETIN BURSATIL. 1978. m. free. Bolsa de Valores de Lima, Miro Quesada 265, Lima, Peru. **Document type:** bulletin.

332.6   SP   ISSN 0214-2368
BOLETIN DE BOLSA EN DISKETTE. 1988. 52/yr. 5800 ptas. San Niceforo S.L., C. Xavier Cabello 10, 28200 S.L. Escorial, Spain. TEL 34-1-8903998. E-mail: sesamo@nodo50.gn.apc.org. (diskette format)

332.6 070.5   US
BOLITHO - CRIBB REPORT; a broker's report on the free newspaper, shopper, and specialty paper industry. m. Bolitho - Cribb & Associates, 1 Annette Park Dr., Bozeman, MT 59715. TEL 406-586-6621. FAX 406-586-6774. E-mail: jcribb@imt.net; URL: http://www.cribb.com/jcribb/bcreport.html. **Document type:** newsletter.
    Formerly: Cribb Report.

BUSINESS AND ECONOMICS — INVESTMENTS

332.64   SP   ISSN 1132-3337
BOLSA DE BARCELONA. INFORME ANUAL. 1978. a. 3000 ptas. (effective 1993). Sociedad Rectora de la Bolsa de Valores de Barcelona, S.A., Paseo Isabel II s-n, 08003 Barcelona, Spain. TEL 34-3-401-35-55. FAX 34-3-401-37-57. TELEX 54-131. circ. 2,000.
Former titles (until 1990): Bolsa de Barcelona. Memoria (ISSN 1132-1377); Bolsa de Barcelona. Estadistica.

332.64   AG
BOLSA DE COMERCIO DE ROSARIO. INFORMATIVO SEMANAL. vol.13, 1995. w. Arg.$66 (foreign $140) to non-members for 6 mos. Bolsa de Comercio de Rosario, Direccion de Informaciones y Estudios Economicos, Cordoba 1402, 2000 Rosario, Santa Fe, Argentina. TEL 54-41-213471. FAX 54-41-241019. TELEX 41894 BOROS AR. adv.; charts; stat.
Formerly: Bolsa de Comercio de Rosario. Boletin Informativo.

332.6   VE
BOLSA DE VALORES DE CARACAS. ANUARIO BURSATIL/CARACAS STOCK EXCHANGE. ANNUAL REPORT.* 1979. a. $65. Bolsa de Valores de Caracas, C.A., Ed. Atrium, Nivel P, C. Sorocaima e Avdas. Tamanazo y Venezuela, Caracas 1061, Venezuela. TEL 81 51 11. TELEX BOLVA 26536. Ed. Ariel Viale. Document type: corporate report.

332.6   VE
BOLSA DE VALORES DE CARACAS. MONTHLY BULLETIN.* 1976. m. $25. Bolsa de Valores de Caracas, C.A., Ed. Atrium, Nivel P, C. Sorocaima e Avdas. Tamanaco y Venezuela, Caracas 1061, Venezuela. TEL 81 51 11. TELEX BOLVA 26536. Ed. Ariel Viale. Document type: bulletin.

332.6   VE
BOLSA DE VALORES DE CARACAS. REVISTA TRIMESTRAL/CARACAS STOCK EXCHANGE. QUARTERLY BULLETIN.* 1947. 2. $60. Bolsa de Valores de Caracas, C.A., Ed. Atrium, Nivel P, C. Sorocaima e Avdas. Tamanaco y Venezuela, Caracas 1061, Venezuela. TEL 81-51-11. TELEX BOLVA 26536. Ed. Ariel Viale. Document type: bulletin.

332.6   VE
BOLSA DE VALORES DE CARACAS. WEEKLY BULLETIN.* 1988. w. $50. Bolsa de Valores de Caracas, C.A., Ed. Atrium, Nivel P, C. Sorocaima e Avdas. Tamanaco y Venezuela, Caracas 1061, Venezuela. TEL 81 51 41. TELEX BOLVA 26536. Ed. Ariel Viale. Document type: bulletin.

332.64   PE
BOLSA DE VALORES DE LIMA. MEMORIA. 1975. a. free. Bolsa de Valores de Lima, Miro Quesada 265, Lima, Peru.

332.6   PO
BOLSA DE VALORES DE LISBOA. BOLETIM DE COTACOES. 250/yr. Bolsa de Valores de Lisboa, Editora da Bolsa, Rua Soeiro Pereira Gomes, 1600 Lisbon, Portugal. TEL 351-1-7909904. FAX 351-1-7952021. TELEX 44751 BVLISB P. circ. 1,000. Document type: bulletin.

332.64   UY   ISSN 0797-5198
BOLSA DE VALORES DE MONTEVIDEO. BOLETIN MENSUAL. 1981. m. $7. Bolsa de Valores de Montevideo, Misiones 1400, Montevideo, Uruguay.

332.6   UY
BOLSA DE VALORES DE MONTEVIDEO. ESTUDIO ESTADISTICOS. BOLETIN TRIMESTRAL. q. Bolsa de Valores de Montevideo, Misiones 1400, Montevideo, Uruguay.

332.64   EC
BOLSA DE VALORES DE QUITO. INFORMES Y MEMORIA ANUAL. a. Bolsa de Valores de Quito, Av. 6 de Diciembre y Pazmino 245, Apartado 3272, Quito, Ecuador.

332.6   BL   ISSN 0557-0506
BOLSA DE VALORES DO RIO DE JANEIRO. RESUMO ANUAL. 1964. a. Cr.$1500($20) Bolsa de Valores do Rio de Janeiro - Rio de Janeiro Stock Exchange, Praca 15 de Novembro, 20, Rio de Janeiro, Brazil. FAX 5521-221-2151. circ. 500.

332.64   MX
BOLSA MEXICANA DE VALORES. BOLETIN BURSATIL CAPITALES/MEXICAN STOCK EXCHANGE. CAPITAL MARKET BULLETIN. d. $230 (effective May 1996). Bolsa Mexicana de Valores, S.A. de C.V. - Mexican Stock Exchange, Paseo de la Reforma 255, 06500 Mexico D.F., Mexico. TEL 525-726-67-91. FAX 525-591-05-34. Document type: bulletin.
Description: Provides daily market operation in this market. Includes an analysis and capital market instruments valuation section, news and methodological notes.

332.64   MX
HG5710.M48
BOLSA MEXICANA DE VALORES. BOLETIN BURSATIL DINERO Y METALES/MEXICAN STOCK EXCHANGE. MONEY & METAL MARKET BULLETIN. d. $305 (effective May 1996). Bolsa Mexicana de Valores, S.A. de C.V. - Mexican Stock Exchange, Paseo de la Reforma 255, 06500 Mexico D.F., Mexico. TEL 525-726-67-91. FAX 525-591-06-34. Document type: bulletin.
Formerly: Bolsa Mexicana de Valores. Boletin Bursatil Dinero (ISSN 0188-3887)
Description: Provides information related to rates, news of interest and Banco de Mexico information.

332   MX
BOLSA MEXICANA DE VALORES. INFORMACION FINANCIERA ANUAL SOBRE ASAMBLEAS/MEXICAN STOCK EXCHANGE. GENERAL STOCKHOLDERS' MEETINGS INFORMATION. a. $505 (effective May 1996). Bolsa Mexicana de Valores, S.A. de C.V. - Mexican Stock Exchange, Paseo de la Reforma 255, 06500 Mexico D.F., Mexico. TEL 525-726-67-91. FAX 525-591-05-94.
Description: Contains information on the main financial data of companies registered on the stock exchange.

332.6   MX
BOLSA MEXICANA DE VALORES. INFORMACION FINANCIERA MENSUAL/MEXICAN STOCK EXCHANGE. MONTHLY FINANCIAL INFORMATION. m. $385 (effective May 1996). Bolsa Mexicana de Valores, S.A. de C.V. - Mexican Stock Exchange, Paseo de la Reforma 255, 06500 Mexico DF, Mexico. TEL 525-7266791. FAX 525-5910534.
Description: Publishes financial reports on the mutual funds listed on the stock exchange.

332.6   MX
BOLSA MEXICANA DE VALORES. PROGRAMA EXTRAORDINARIO DE DIVULGACION DE INFORMACION FINANCIERA. irreg. $30 (effective May 1996). Bolsa Mexicana de Valores, S.A. de C.V., Paseo de la Reforma 255, 06500 Mexico DF, Mexico. TEL 525-7266791. FAX 525-591-0534.
Description: Contains preliminary information on the foreign currency position trade balance and cash flow information for companies registered on the exchange.

BOLSA MEXICANA DE VALORES. RESUMEN BURSATIL/MEXICAN STOCK EXCHANGE. STATISTICS SUMMARY. see BUSINESS AND ECONOMICS — Abstracting, Bibliographies, Statistics

332.6   US   ISSN 0732-0469
HG4501
THE BOND BUYER. 1891. d. (5/wk.) & w. $1897 for daily ed. American Banker - Bond Buyer, Newsletter Division (Subsidiary of: Thomson Financial Services Company), One State St. Plaza, New York, NY 10004-1549. TEL 800-733-4371. FAX 212-943-2224. (Subscr. to: Box 28315, Washington, DC 20038-8315. TEL 202-347-2665) Ed. Joseph Mysak. adv. (also avail. in microfilm from PMC) Indexed: Tr.& Indus.Ind. Document type: newspaper.
●Also available online. Vendor(s): Information Access Co., Knight-Ridder Information, Inc. (File no.626), Lexis-Nexis, NewsNet (FI08).
—CCC.
Formerly: Daily Bond Buyer (ISSN 0884-3937)

BOND BUYER'S MUNICIPAL MARKETPLACE. see BUSINESS AND ECONOMICS — Trade And Industrial Directories

332.6   US
BOND FUND REPORT. 1993. w. $1095. IBC - Donoghue, Inc., Box 9104, Ashland, MA 01721-9104. TEL 800-343-5413. FAX 508-881-0982. URL: www.ibcdonoghue.com. Ed. Tracy Burke. charts. Document type: trade publication.
Description: Provides 30 day SEC yields, distribution rate, average duration, average maturity and cash position for more than 1000 bond funds. Features commentary, charts and summary data.

332.6   US   ISSN 0738-5579
BOND FUND SURVEY.* 1983. m. $450. Survey Publications Co., Box 20429, New York, NY 10028-0053. TEL 212-988-2498. Ed. Judith C. Lack. charts; stat. (looseleaf format; back issues avail.)
Description: Performance and descriptive reports on over 300 corporate, municipal, government, closed-end funds and unit trusts.

BOND INFORMATION DATABASE SERVICE. see COMPUTERS — Electronic Data Processing

332.63   US
BOND MARKET: ANALYSIS AND OUTLOOK. a. Salomon Brothers, Inc., Marketing Department, 7 World Trade Center, New York, NY 10048. TEL 212-783-7000.

332.6   GW   ISSN 0931-119X
BOND UND SHARE; der Wertpapiersammler. 1985. q. DM.32 (foreign DM.85). Aktien Galerie GmbH, Spetzgarter Weg 1, 88662 Ueberlingen, Germany. TEL 49-7551-1335. FAX 49-7551-65680. Ed. Wilhelm Kuhlmann. adv.; bk.rev. circ. 3,300. (back issues avail.) Document type: bulletin.
Description: Reports on bonds and sharecertificates for collecting, as gift items and investment.

332.6   UK   ISSN 0961-8171
HG4502
THE BONDHOLDER; with Euro shares coverage. (Supplement avail.) 1872. w. (plus d. online updates). £2750 (index £100) (effective 1997). Valorinform, Aldgate House, 33 Aldgate High St., 2nd. Fl., London EC3N 1DL. TEL 44-171-369-7059. FAX 44-171-369-7065. E-mail: bassfeldr@tfseur.co.uk. Ed. Ralph Bassfeld. adv.: page £990; 261 x 175; adv. contact: Ralph Bassfeld. stat.; q. index. Document type: newsletter.
Formerly: Bondholder's Register (ISSN 0006-7075)
Description: Covers corporate action on worldwide bonds, warrants, and European equities and funds.

332   US   ISSN 0278-8896
HG1
BONDWEEK (NEW YORK, 1981); the newsweekly of fixed income and credit markets. 1981. w. $1495 (Canada $1525; elsewhere $1570). Institutional Investor Newsletters, 477 Madison Ave., New York, NY 10022. TEL 212-224-3233. FAX 212-224-3353. Ed. Tom Lamont. adv. (reprint service avail. from UMI) Document type: newsletter. —UMI. CCC.
Description: Covers the major taxable debt markets - treasuries and foreign sovereigns, mortgage and asset-backed, and investment-grade and high-yield corporates.

332.6   US
BOSTON STOCK EXCHANGE GUIDE. 1970. bi-m. $378. C C H Incorporated, 2700 Lake Cook Rd., Riverwoods, IL 60015. TEL 847-267-7000; 800-835-5224. FAX 800-224-8299.

338.7   BS
BOTSWANA DEVELOPMENT CORPORATION. ANNUAL REPORT. 1971. a. free. Botswana Development Corporation, Private Bag 160, Gaborone, Botswana. TEL 267-351151. FAX 267-373539. TELEX 2251-BD. Ed.Bd. circ. 2,500.
Description: Reports on BDC's role in identifying investment opportunities in Botswana for exploitation by both local and foreign investors.

332.6   BS
BOTSWANA DEVELOPMENT CORPORATION NEWSLETTER. 1971. q. free. Botswana Development Corporation, Public Relations Unit, Private Bag 160, Gaborone, Botswana. TEL 267-351151. FAX 267-0373539. TELEX 2251 BD. illus. circ. 1,500.
Description: Informs the public of ongoing activities within BDC.

BUSINESS AND ECONOMICS — INVESTMENTS

332.6   FR   ISSN 1168-3155
BOURSE DE PARIS. ACTIONS STATISTIQUES MENSUELLES. 1967. m. 1900 F. Bourse de Paris, 39 rue Cambon, 75001 Paris, France. TEL 49-27-10-00. FAX 49-27-14-33. TELEX 215 561 F. charts; mkt.; stat. circ. 900.
Former titles (until 1992): Bourse de France. Revue Mensuelle de Statistiques (ISSN 0995-1164); (until 1988): Bourse de Paris. Statistiques Mensuelles (ISSN 0039-0623)
Description: Studies the French stock market evolution.

332.6   FR
BOURSE DE PARIS. DECISIONS & AVIS. d. 15000 F. (outside EC 30000 F.). Bourse de Paris, 39 rue Cambon, 75001 Paris, France. TEL 49-27-10-00. FAX 49-27-14-33. TELEX 215 561 F. (only avail. by fax)
Description: Looks at the lives of quoted companies in terms of voting rights, new stock issues, halts of trading, stock listings.

332.6   BE
BOURSE REVUE. (Text in French) 1916. w. 1500 BEF. 107 rue de Brabant, Bte 2, B-1210 Brussels, Belgium. TEL 2-217-98-05. FAX 2-218-33-08. Ed. Albert Perlot. adv.; bk.rev. circ. 5,000. **Document type:** trade publication, newspaper.

BOWNE DIGEST FOR CORPORATE & SECURITIES LAWYERS; abstracts of current articles from more than 280 legal periodicals. *see LAW — Abstracting, Bibliographies, Statistics*

332.6   US   ISSN 1053-0908
BOWSER DIRECTORY OF SMALL STOCKS. 1991. m. $89 (foreign $107). Bowser Report, Box 6278, Newport News, VA 23606. TEL 757-877-5979. Ed. Cindy Bowser. **Document type:** directory.
Description: Covers 14 fields of information on over 700 low-priced stocks for the do-it-yourself researchers.

332.6   US   ISSN 0738-7288
BOWSER REPORT; a newsletter for minipriced stocks. 1976. m. $48. Bowser Report, Box 6278, Newport News, VA 23606. TEL 804-877-5979. FAX 804-595-0622. Ed. R. Max Bowser. circ. 10,000. (back issues avail.) **Document type:** newsletter.
Description: Up-to-date information on stocks selling for $3 a share or less.

332.6   US   ISSN 1086-0436
▼**BOWSER WARRANT REGISTER.** 1995. m. $57 (foreign $68). Bowser Report, Box 6278, Newport News, VA 23606. TEL 804-877-5979. FAX 804-595-0622. Ed. R. Max Bowser.
Description: Lists over 100 warrants $3 a share or less. Two line entry with everything readers want to know about that warrant.

332.6   US
BRAUN'S SYSTEMS.* 1969. m. $695 (for either stock or gold indexes). Braun's Systems, 127 Linder Dr., Homosassa, FL 34446-4038. Ed. Robert F. Braun. R&P contact: Robert F. Braun. **Document type:** newsletter.
Description: Features advice on buying and selling mutual funds, including gold fund.

332.6   UK
BRIEFING ON BRITAIN. 1985. 3/yr. free. Invest in Britain Bureau, 1 Victoria St., London SW1H 0ET, England. TEL 44-171-215-5638. FAX 44-171-215-5651. URL: http://www.dti.gov.uk/ibb. (Dist. in U.S. by: British Trade & Investment Office, British Consulate-General, 11th Fl., 845 Third Ave., New York, NY 10022) Ed. Lynnette Falk. adv.: B&W page £1350. circ. 13,750 (controlled). **Document type:** government publication.
Description: Designed to meet the needs of the U.S. corporate investor and executive thinking of locating their business in the U.K.

332.6   UK
BRITAIN THE PREFERRED LOCATION. (Editions in Chinese-Mandarin, Japanese, Korean) 1987. a. free. Invest in Britain Bureau, 1 Victoria St., London SW1H 0ET, England. TEL 44-171-215-5638. FAX 44-171-215-5651. URL: http://www.dti.gov.uk/ibb. Ed. Michael White. charts; illus.; stat.; circ. 11,500 (controlled). **Document type:** government publication.
Description: Informs corporate executives on the advantages of investing in the U.K. rather than other European nations.

BRITAIN'S SECURITY INDUSTRY. *see BUSINESS AND ECONOMICS — Trade And Industrial Directories*

332.6   CN   ISSN 0068-161X
HJ8514.B72
BRITISH COLUMBIA MUNICIPAL YEARBOOK (REDBOOK). *Variant title:* RedBook. 1940. a. Can.$94. Journal of Commerce Ltd. (Subsidiary of: Southam Information and Technology Group), 4285 Canada Way, Burnaby, BC V5G 1H2, Canada. TEL 604-433-8164. FAX 604-433-9549. Ed. Anne Crittenden; Pub. Judy Sirett. adv.: B&W page Can.$1340, color page Can.$2042; trim 8 1/2 x 11. circ. 1,517. **Document type:** directory.
Formerly (until 1949): Red Book of British Columbia Municipal Information (ISSN 0317-4557)

332.6 384.55   US   ISSN 0146-0110
BROADCAST INVESTOR; newsletter on radio-TV station finance. 1975. m. $795 (effective 1997). Paul Kagan Associates, Inc., 126 Clock Tower Pl., Carmel, CA 93923. TEL 408-624-1536. TELEX 408-625-3225. Eds. Paul Kagan, Sharon Armbrust. charts; index. **Document type:** newsletter.
Description: Covers investments in private radio and TV stations plus public broadcast companies. Gives analysis of cash flow multiples, valuations of stations and companies.

BROADCAST INVESTOR CHARTS; monthly service showing price movements of broadcast stocks over two-year spans. *see COMMUNICATIONS — Television And Cable*

BROADCAST STATS. *see COMMUNICATIONS — Abstracting, Bibliographies, Statistics*

332.6   UK
THE (YEAR) BROKERS 1000. a. £170($295) Euromoney Publications plc., Books, Nestor House, Playhouse Yard, London EC4V 5EX, England. TEL 0171-779-8935. FAX 0171-779-8541. (Orders to: Plymbridge Distributors Ltd., Estover, Plymouth, Devon PL6 7PZ, England. TEL 0171-779-8610. FAX 01752-695668) **Document type:** directory.
Description: Profiles more than 54 markets worldwide, giving an economic overview of each country, including the structure, operation, and performance of the equity and debt markets, along with trading, settlement, and clearing details.

BROWNING NEWSLETTER. *see METEOROLOGY*

332.6
BRUCE GOULD ON COMMODITIES. 1976. bi-w. $285. Bruce Gould Publications, Box 16, Seattle, WA 98111. FAX 509-422-5109. Ed. Bruce Gould. (looseleaf format; back issues avail.) **Document type:** newsletter.

BUILDING & CONSTRUCTION MARKET FORECAST. *see BUILDING AND CONSTRUCTION*

332.6   US   ISSN 0319-1362
BULL & BEAR FINANCIAL NEWSPAPER. 1974. m. $29. Box 917179, Longwood, FL 32791. TEL 407-682-6170. Ed. David J. Robinson. adv.; bk.rev.; circ. 45,000 (paid); 10,000 (controlled). (tabloid format; back issues avail.) **Document type:** newspaper.
Description: Presents articles on precious metals, stocks, mutual funds, coins, real estate, and economic trends.

332.6   FR   ISSN 1166-5785
BULLETIN BOURSE ET PRODUITS FINANCIERS. bi-m. 1000 F. (effective 1997). Joly Editions, 1 av. Franklin D. Roosevelt, 75008 Paris, France. TEL 33-1-44951620. FAX 33-1-45638939. **Document type:** bulletin.

332.645   US
BULLION ADVISORY.* m. $36. Moneypower, 1304 Edgewood Ave., Ann Arbor, MI 48103-5522. TEL 612-537-8096. Ed. James H. Moore.
Description: Specializes in gold, silver and platinum.

332.6   GW
BUNDESVERBAND DEUTSCHER VERMOEGENSBERATER. INFODIENST. irreg. (5-6/yr.). Bundesverband Deutscher Vermoegensberater, Goethepl. 11, 60313 Frankfurt, Germany. TEL 069-287347.

332.6   US   ISSN 1082-2054
HG4501
BUSINESS AND INVESTMENT CYCLES. m. $295. Foundation for the Study of Cycles, 900 W. Valley Rd., Ste. 502, Wayne, PA 19087-1821. TEL 610-995-2120. FAX 610-995-2130. E-mail: cycles@cycles.org; URL: http://www.cycles.org-cycles. Ed. Chester Joy. **Document type:** newsletter.
Formerly (until 1995): Investment Cycles (ISSN 1080-1073)
Description: Presents an analysis of major investment opportunities. Demonstrates the practical application of cycles to investment strategies.

BUSINESS AND THE ENVIRONMENT; twice-monthly global news and analysis. *see ENVIRONMENTAL STUDIES*

332.6 338   CN
BUSINESS EXCHANGE. 1994. m. Can.$25($25) (effective 1995). WordStock Publications, 673 Caron Ave., Ste 4, Windsor, ON N9A 5B8, Canada. TEL 519-977-5022. FAX 519-977-5023. Ed. Deborah Jones. adv. contact: Greg Saunders. **Document type:** trade publication.

BUSINESS MONEY. *see BUSINESS AND ECONOMICS — Banking And Finance*

332.6   US   ISSN 0193-3221
BUSINESS OPPORTUNITIES JOURNAL. 1969. m. $50. Business Service Corporation, Box 60762, San Diego, CA 92166. TEL 619-223-5661. FAX 619-223-1705. E-mail: BussOppJrnl@AOL.COM. Ed. Gina Petrone; Pub. Wayne Wakefield. R&P contact: Wayne Wakefield. adv. contact: Maria Constantine. bk.rev.; circ. 25,000 (controlled). **Document type:** newspaper.
Incorporates (1989-199?): Business Ventures.
Description: Specializes in franchising and business opportunities in the US.

332.6 658.8   UK   ISSN 0954-2167
BUSINESS RATIO REPORT: INVESTMENT TRUSTS; an industry sector analysis. 1988. a. I C C Business Ratios Ltd., Freepost, Field House, Hampton, Mddx. TW12 1BR, England. TEL 081-783-0977. FAX 081-783-1940. charts; stat. **Document type:** trade publication.

BUSINESS SALES AND ACQUISITIONS DIGEST. *see BUSINESS AND ECONOMICS — Economic Situation And Conditions*

336.74   NE   ISSN 0927-8370
BUSINESS SUPPORTER. Key Title: A B N Amro Business Supporter. (Text in Dutch) 1991. s-m. A B N Amro Bank N.V., P.O. Box 283, 1000 EA Amsterdam, Netherlands.

332.6   VE
BUSINESS VENEZUELA'S CORPORATE HANDBOOK. a. $30. Venezuelan - American Chamber of Commerce and Industry - Camara Venezolano-Americano de Comercio e Industria, Apdo. 5181, Caracas 1010A, Venezuela. TEL 58-2-2630833. FAX 58-2-2631829. **Document type:** directory.
Formerly: Investing in Venezuela.
Description: Guide to Venezuela's political, economic and legal environment for foreign investors.

BUSINESS AND ECONOMICS — INVESTMENTS

332.6 US ISSN 1074-0139
HG1
C D A INVESTNET INSIDERS' CHRONICLE. 1896. w. $445. C D A Investment Technologies, Inc., 1355 Piccard Dr., Rockville, MD 20850. TEL 800-232-6362. FAX 301-590-1329. Ed. Bob Gabele. adv. (also avail. in microform from UMI; reprint service avail. from UMI) Indexed: Bus.Ind., Tr.& Indus.Ind. Document type: newsletter.
● Also available online. Vendor(s): Information Access Co.
— UMI. **CCC.**
Supersedes in part (in 1993): Insiders' Chronicle (ISSN 0162-5152); Which was formerly (until 1976): Commercial and Financial Chronicle (ISSN 0010-2903)
Description: Reports on the buy-sell stock transactions of corporate officers, directors and beneficial owners, providing a gauge of corporate confidence levels and expectations.

C D RATE WATCH. (Certificate of Deposit) see BUSINESS AND ECONOMICS — Banking And Finance

332.6 CN ISSN 0834-1508
C H W LETTER. 1940. 50/yr. Can.$250. Pente Investment Management Ltd., 330 Bay St., Ste. 1204, Toronto, ON M5H 2S8, Canada. TEL 416-861-9555. Ed. R.J.V. Fielding.
Description: Provides specific stock market investment recommendations.

332.6 US
C R B COMMODITY INDEX REPORT. w. $295 (effective 1997). (Commodity Research Bureau) Bridge Publishing, 30 S. Wacker Dr., Ste. 1810, Chicago, IL 60606. TEL 312-454-1801; 800-621-5271. FAX 312-454-0239. E-mail: crbino@ais.net; URL: http://www.krf.com/crb/. Ed. Bob Hafer. R&P contact: Carlene Camera. adv. contact: Bob Hafer. Document type: trade publication.
Description: Provides CRB price index data including technical analysis, and a daily recorded statistical hotline that provides closing prices on all CRB indices.

332.6 US ISSN 1057-4883
HD9001
C R B FUTURES MARKET SERVICE. 1934. w. $150 (effective 1997). (Commodities Research Bureau) Bridge Publishing, 30 S. Wacker Dr., Ste. 1810, Chicago, IL 60606. TEL 312-454-1801; 800-621-5271. FAX 312-454-0239. E-mail: crbinfo@ais.net. Ed. Bob Hafer. R&P contact: Carlene Camera. mkt. circ. 8,000. (processed) Document type: trade publication.
● Also available online.
Description: Provides a synopsis update about 36 major markets. Analyzes the week's most active commodity or futures-related conditions.

332.63 US
C R B FUTURES PERSPECTIVE - AGRICULTURAL EDITION. 1972. w., bi-w., and m. versions avail. $230 for w. version (Europe & Asia $490); $155 for bi-w. version (Europe & Asia $285); $95 for m. version (Europe & Asia $155). (Commodity Research Bureau) Bridge Publishing, 30 S. Wacker Dr., Ste. 1810, Chicago, IL 60606. TEL 312-454-1801. FAX 312-454-0239. Ed. Robert Hafer; Pub. Robert Hafer. R&P contact: Carlene Camera. Document type: trade publication.

332.63 US
C R B FUTURES PERSPECTIVE - FINANCIAL EDITION. 1972. w., bi-w., and m. versions avail. $275 for w. version (Europe & Asia $535); $175 for bi-w. version (Europe & Asia $305); $105 for m. version (Europe & Asia $165). (Commodity Research Bureau) Bridge Publishing, 30 S. Wacker Dr., Ste. 1810, Chicago, IL 60606. TEL 312-454-1801. FAX 312-454-0239. Ed. Robert Hafer; Pub. Robert Hafer. R&P contact: Carlene Camera. Document type: trade publication.

332.63 US
HG6046
C R B FUTURES PERSPECTIVE - FULL EDITION. w., bi-w., and m. versions avail. $425 for w. version (Europe and Asia $685); $265 for bi-w. version (Europe and Asia $395); $175 for m. version (Europe & Asia $235). (Commodity Research Bureau) Bridge Publishing, 30 S. Wacker Dr., Ste. 1810, Chicago, IL 60606. TEL 312-454-1801; 800-621-5271. FAX 312-454-0239. E-mail: crbinfo@ais.net. Ed. Robert Hafer; Pub. Robert Hafer. R&P contact: Carlene Camera. charts; mkt.; stat. (tabloid format) Document type: trade publication.
Former titles (until 1996): Commodity Perspective (ISSN 0730-7217) & K R - C R B Futures Perspective; C R B Futures Chart Service; Commodity Chart Service (ISSN 0010-3225)
Description: Charting service on 87 major international (US, Canadian, European, Asian) futures markets displaying over 425 daily price charts for futures, cash, spreads, moving averages, momentum oscillators, RSI, and CFTC commitment of Traders Report.

332.6 US
C T A OUTPUT. 1976. m. Corporate Transfer Agents Association, c/o Mobil Corporation, 3225 Gallows Rd., Fairfax, VA 22037-0001. Document type: newsletter.
Description: Contains articles of interest to securities transfer industry.

332.6 US
HG4907
C U S I P CORPORATE DIRECTORY. (Committee on Uniform Security Identification Procedures) a. $1375. Standard & Poor's (Subsidiary of: McGraw-Hill Companies, Inc.), 25 Broadway, New York, NY 10004. TEL 212-208-8347.
Formerly: American Bankers Association. Committee on Uniform Security Identification Procedures. C U S I P Directory: Corporate Directory (ISSN 0091-3804)

332.6 US ISSN 0569-2954
C U S I P MASTER DIRECTORY. (Committee on Uniform Security Identification Procedures) 1969. a. $2225. Standard & Poor's (Subsidiary of: McGraw-Hill Companies, Inc.), 25 Broadway, New York, NY 10004. TEL 212-208-8000. R&P contact: Harry Lopez. Document type: directory.
● Also available on CD-ROM.
Formerly: American Bankers Association. Committee on Uniform Security Identification Procedures. C U S I P Directory (ISSN 0091-2212)

CABLE NETWORK INVESTOR. see BUSINESS AND ECONOMICS — Banking And Finance

CABLE T V INVESTOR; newsletter on investments in cable T V systems and publicly held cable T V stocks. see COMMUNICATIONS — Television And Cable

332.6 US ISSN 0733-8554
CABOT MARKET LETTER. 1970. 24/yr. $250. Cabot Heritage Corporation, Box 3044, Salem, MA 01970-6344. TEL 508-745-5532; 800-777-2658. FAX 508-745-1283. Ed. Carlton G. Lutts.

332.6 US
CADENCE INVESTMENT ADVISORS PERFORMANCE SURVEY. q. $650. C D A - Cadence, 1355 Piccard Dr., Rockville, MD 20850. TEL 301-975-9600. FAX 301-590-1350. circ. 700. (magnetic tape; also avail. on IBM PC software)
Description: Performance statistics for equity, fixed income and balanced accounts. Over 850 investment advisors disclosed by name.

332.6 US
CADENCE UNIVERSE PERFORMANCE REPORT. q. $850. C D A - Cadence, 1355 Piccard Dr., Rockville, MD 20850. TEL 301-975-9600. FAX 301-590-1350. circ. 300. (also avail. in magnetic tape; also avail. on PC software)
● Also available online.
Description: Provides return, comparative performance and risk statistics of individual bank pooled funds, mutual funds, insurance company funds and investment advisors, as well as market and specialized indices.

332.6 US ISSN 0749-2375
CALIFORNIA MUNICIPAL BOND ADVISOR. 1984. m. $125. 1037 S. Palm Canyon Dr., Palm Springs, CA 92264-8378. TEL 619-320-7997. Ed. Zane B. Mann. Document type: newsletter.
Description: Monetary, economic, investment analysis for tax-exempt bond investors.

CALIFORNIA PUBLIC FINANCE. see BUSINESS AND ECONOMICS — Public Finance, Taxation

332.6 US ISSN 8756-2154
CALIFORNIA TECHNOLOGY STOCK LETTER; authoritative, independent advice for high-technology investing. 1982. bi-w. $295. C T S L Publishing Partners, Box 308, Half Moon Bay, CA 94019. TEL 415-726-8495. Ed. Michael Murphy. R&P contact: Pamela Floquet. circ. 6,000. (back issues avail.) Document type: newsletter.
Description: Covers computers, electronics, biotechnology and medical stocks.

CALLAHAN'S CREDIT UNION REPORT. see BUSINESS AND ECONOMICS — Banking And Finance

332.6 US
CALLAHAN'S FUND ADVISOR.* 1986. m. $135. Asset Control Services, Inc., 9101 E. Kenyon Ave. Ste. 3000, Denver, CO 80237-1855. TEL 303-751-6661. Ed. Craig Callahan. circ. 400.
Formerly: Sectorfund Advisor.
Description: Provides model portfolios, investment timing signals, and market analysis for sector funds, single premium variable life funds, and closed-end international funds.

332.6 US
CALLED BOND SERVICE. w. $5,000. Moody's Investors Service (Subsidiary of: Dun & Bradstreet Corporation), 99 Church St., New York, NY 10007-0300. TEL 212-553-0300. FAX 212-553-4700.
Description: Provides current information on US corporate and municipal bonds called for redemption. Covers issue description, series, maturity date, and list of serial numbers called.

332.6 CN
CANADA STOCKWATCH. EASTERN EDITION. 1987. d. $395. Canjex Publishing, 700 W. Georgia St., Box 10371, Vancouver, BC V7Y 1J6, Canada. TEL 604-687-1500. FAX 604-687-2304. Ed. John Woods. Document type: trade publication.
● Also available online.
Formerly: Toronto Stockwatch.
Description: Covers daily-issued news by every company listed on the Toronto and Montreal Stock Exchanges.

332.6 CN
CANADA STOCKWATCH. WESTERN EDITION. 1984. d. $395. Canjex Publishing, 700 W. Georgia St., Box 10371, Vancouver, BC V7Y 1J6, Canada. TEL 604-687-1500. FAX 604-687-2304. Ed. John Woods. Document type: trade publication.
● Also available online.
Formerly: Vancouver Stockwatch.
Description: Covers news issued that day or week by every company listed on the Vancouver and Alberta stock exchanges.

CANADIAN CAPITAL PROJECTS. see BUSINESS AND ECONOMICS — Domestic Commerce

332.6 CN
THE CANADIAN CREDIT AND COLLECTION MANUAL. 1989. 1-2/yr. Can.$172. Carswell, One Corporate Plaza, 2075 Kennedy Rd., Scarborough, ON M1T 3V4, Canada. TEL 416-609-8000. FAX 416-298-5094. Ed. Jacques Bendavid. charts; illus.; cum.index. circ. 900. (looseleaf format)

332.6 CN ISSN 0713-3286
CANADIAN MONEYSAVER; your personal finance guide. 1981. m. (11/yr.). Can.$21.35 (foreign $33) (effective 1997). Canadian Money Saver Inc., Box 370, Bath, ON K0H 1G0, Canada. TEL 613-352-7448. FAX 613-352-7700. Ed. Dale Ennis; Pub. Dale Ennis. R&P contact: Dale Ennis. bk.rev. circ. 30,100. (also avail. in microfiche from MML) Indexed: Can.B.P.I., Can.Per.Ind., CMI. Document type: consumer publication.
Description: Details investment advice for Canadian and global investments. Advisors include portfolio managers, financial planners, lawyers, money managers, accountants, and related professionals.

BUSINESS AND ECONOMICS — INVESTMENTS

332.6   CN   ISSN 1182-1590
CANADIAN RESOURCES AND PENNYMINES ANALYST. 1986. m. Can.$157. M P L Communications Inc., 133 Richmond St., W., Ste. 700, Toronto, ON M5H 3M8, Canada. TEL 416-869-1177. FAX 416-869-0456. Document type: trade publication.
Formerly (until 1990): Canadian PennyMines Analyst (ISSN 0836-6357)
Description: Covers resource, penny and junior mining stocks from a geological point of view, with emphasis on minimizing risk.

CANADIAN SECURITIES LAW REPORTER. see *LAW*

332.6   CN   ISSN 0836-0960
CANADIAN SHAREOWNER. 1987. bi-m. Can.$54 (foreign Can.$86) (effective 1997). 1090 University Ave. W., Ste. 204, P.O. Box 7337, Windsor, ON N9C 5S4, Canada. TEL 519-252-1555. FAX 519-252-9570. Ed. John T. Bart. adv. contact: Dawn M. Paupst. bk.rev.; charts. circ. 6,000. (back issues avail.) Indexed: Can.B.P.I.
● Also available online. Vendor(s): UMI. —BLDSC (3044.705000); UMI.
Description: Education about stock-market investment.

332.6   CN
CANADIAN STOCK EXCHANGES MANUAL. m. Can.$325. C C H Canadian Ltd., 6 Garamond Ct., North York, ON M3C 1Z5, Canada. TEL 416-441-0086; 800-268-4522. FAX 416-444-9011. Document type: trade publication.
Description: Contains policies, charters, by-laws and regulations of Investment Dealers Association, Investment Funds Institute, Toronto Futures Exchange, Winnipeg Commodity Exchanges and all stock exchanges in Canada.

CANADIAN TREASURY MANAGEMENT REVIEW. see *BUSINESS AND ECONOMICS — Banking And Finance*

CAPITAL CHANGES REPORTS. see *BUSINESS AND ECONOMICS — Public Finance, Taxation*

332.65   US   ISSN 0577-571X
HD9560.1
CAPITAL INVESTMENTS OF THE WORLD PETROLEUM INDUSTRY. 1946. a. free. Chase Manhattan Bank, Energy Economics Division, One Chase Manhattan Plaza, New York, NY 10015. TEL 212-552-5586. Ed. Monica S. Tabb. circ. 30,000.

332.6   CC
CAPITAL MAGAZINE. (Text in Chinese) m. Capital Communications Corp. Ltd., 7-F, Paramount Bldg., 12 Ka Yip St., Chaiwan, Hong Kong, People's Republic of China. TEL 852-2557-9332. FAX 852-2556-1627. adv.: B&W page HK.$245000, color page HK.$28000; trim 210 x 286. circ. 25,112.

332.6 910.202   US
CARIBBEAN DATELINE. 1980. m. $95 (effective 1998). Caribbean Dateline Publications, Box 23276, Washington, DC 20026. Ed. N. Poteat Day; Pub. N. Poteat Day. adv. contact: Kathy Richards. circ. 1,100. (back issues avail.) Document type: newsletter.
Description: Reports on tax haven activities, real estate, banking, incorporation, trust formation, tax free businesses, vacation living, retirement, direct investments, stocks and other securities. Covers news, trends, opinions and opportunities in the Caribbean and Central America.

332.6   US
CAROLAN'S SPIRAL CALENDAR RESEARCH. 1993. m. $279 (overseas $299). (Calendar Research, Inc.) Elliott Wave International, Box 1618, Gainesville, GA 30503. TEL 770-536-0309. Ed. Christopher Carolan. Document type: newsletter.
Description: Covers the U.S. stock market, bonds, precious metals, major foreign stock markets and currencies. Forecasts market movements that are related to exact time relationships.

CASH; die Wirtschaftszeitung der Schweiz. see *BUSINESS AND ECONOMICS — Banking And Finance*

332.6   US   ISSN 1054-9994
CASH RICH COMPANIES. Cover title: Cash Rich Cos. 1991. m. $24 (foreign $32). Charles E. Cardwell, Ed. & Pub., 135 Beechwood Ln., Kingston, TN 37763. TEL 423-376-2732. E-mail: ASTUTE__INVESTOR@compuserve.com. R&P contact: Charles E. Cardwell. circ. 500. Document type: newsletter.
Description: Identifies (as potential investments) companies which have the greatest amount of unencumbered quick assets in relation to share price. Intended for value-oriented investors.

CASPIAN BRIEF. see *BUSINESS AND ECONOMICS — Economic Situation And Conditions*

332.6   US   ISSN 0742-6534
HG4528
CATALYST (MONTPELIER);* economics for the living earth. 1984. q. $25. Catalyst Press, Box 734, Montpelier, VT 05601-0734. TEL 802-223-7943. Ed. Susan Meeker-Lowry. bk.rev.; bibl.; illus.; stat. circ. 1,000. (back issues avail.) Document type: newsletter.
Description: Profiles of and articles on social investing: small businesses, revolving loan funds, co-ops, land trusts, and other organizations to support positive economic change for disadvantaged populations and to save and regenerate existing farm and forestland. Focuses on small-scale, grass roots enterprises seeking some form of capital: loans, partnerships, equity, and grants.

332.6   PL   ISSN 1231-9511
CEDULA GIELDY WARSAWSKIEJ; oficjalny biuletyn. (Text in English, Polish) 1991. 5/wk. 172 Zl.($128) Gielda Papierow Wartosciowych w Warszawie S.A., Nowy Swiat 6-12, 00-400 Warsaw, Poland. TEL 48-22-6617484. FAX 48-22-6617484. (back issues avail.) Document type: bulletin.
Description: Provides results of the Warsaw Stock Exchange daily sessions.

332.6   UK
▼**CHARITY FINANCE YEARBOOK.** 1996. a. £25. Plaza Publishing Ltd., 1A Tradescant Rd., London SW8 1XD, England. TEL 44-171-793-0001. FAX 44-171-735-2009. Ed. Daniel Phelan. adv.: page £795; adv. contact: Alice Frackelton. Document type: academic/scholarly publication.
Description: Provides full coverage of all aspects of managing the finances of a charity.

332.6   US
CHARTCRAFT COMMODITY SERVICE. 1958. w. $256. Chartcraft, Inc., 30 Church St., Box 2046, New Rochelle, NY 10801. TEL 914-632-0422. FAX 914-632-0335. Ed. John E. Gray.

332.6   US
CHARTCRAFT MONTHLY N Y S E AND A S E CHARTBOOK. m. $402. Chartcraft, Inc., 30 Church St., Box 2046, New Rochelle, NY 10801. TEL 914-632-0422. FAX 914-632-0335. Ed. Mike Burke.

332.6   US
CHARTCRAFT OVER-THE-COUNTER CHARTBOOK. q. $114. Chartcraft, Inc., 30 Church St., Box 2046, New Rochelle, NY 10801. TEL 914-632-0422. FAX 914-632-0335. Ed. Michael Burke.

332.6   US
CHARTCRAFT QUARTERLY OPTION CHARTBOOK. q. $160. Chartcraft, Inc., 30 Church St., Box 2046, New Rochelle, NY 10801. TEL 914-632-0422. FAX 914-632-0335. Ed. Michael Burke.

332.6   US
CHARTCRAFT WEEKLY FUTURES SERVICE. w. $256. Chartcraft, Inc., 30 Church St., Box 2046, New Rochelle, NY 10801. TEL 914-632-0422. FAX 914-632-0335. Ed. John E. Gray.
Formerly: Chartcraft Weekly Commodity Service.
Description: Illustrates more than 40 different futures through point and figure charts.

332.6   US
CHARTCRAFT WEEKLY N Y S E. w. $256. Chartcraft, Inc., 30 Church St., Box 2046, New Rochelle, NY 10801. TEL 914-632-0422. FAX 914-632-0335. Ed. Michael Burke.

332.6   US
CHARTCRAFT WEEKLY OPTIONS SERVICE. w. $186. Chartcraft, Inc., 30 Church St., Box 2046, New Rochelle, NY 10801. TEL 914-632-0422. FAX 914-632-0335. Ed. Michael Burke.
Description: Covers the technical needs of options traders.

332.6   US
CHARTIST. 18/yr. $150. Box 758, Seal Beach, CA 90740. TEL 310-596-2385. Ed. Dan Sullivan; Pub. Dan Sullivan. Document type: newsletter.

332.96   US   ISSN 1048-2717
HG4501
CHASE INVESTMENT PERFORMANCE DIGEST. 1988. a. $23.95 (effective 1996). Chase Global Data & Research, Inc., 73 Junction Square, Concord, MA 01742. TEL 508-371-9100. FAX 508-371-9105. Ed. C. David Chase. adv. contact: Herb Benjamin. illus. Document type: trade publication.
Formerly (until 1990): Chase Global Investment Almanac (ISSN 1041-8636)
Description: Includes performance, returns and rankings on the world's major investments.

332.6   US   ISSN 0747-7236
CHEAP INVESTOR. 1981. m. $98 (foreign $128) (effective 1997). Mathews and Associates, Inc., 2549 W. Golf Rd., Ste. 350, Hoffman Estates, IL 60194. TEL 630-830-5666. Ed. Bill Mathews. circ. 6,000.
Description: Investor's guide to quality stocks and new issues under $5 a share.

332.6   US
CHICAGO BOARD OPTIONS EXCHANGE. 1973. m. $497. C C H Incorporated, 2700 Lake Cook Rd., Riverwoods, IL 60015. TEL 847-267-7000; 800-835-5224. FAX 800-224-8299. (looseleaf format)

332.6   US
CHICAGO STOCK EXCHANGE GUIDE. 1967. m. $475. C C H Incorporated, 2700 Lake Cook Rd., Riverwoods, IL 60015. TEL 847-267-7000; 800-835-5224. FAX 800-224-8299. (looseleaf format)
Formerly (until 1993): Midwest Stock Exchange Guide.

332.96   CC
CHINA INVESTMENT GUIDE. (Text in English) irreg., latest 5th ed. HK.$1500. (Ministry of Foreign Trade and Economic Co-operation, Department of Foreign Investment) Pearson Professional (Hong Kong) Limited, Ste. 1808, Asian House, 1 Hennessy Rd., Wanchai, Hong Kong, People's Republic of China. TEL 852-2863-2659. FAX 852-2520-6954. E-mail: pphkg@hk.super.net. (Co-publisher: CITIC Publishing House)
Description: Covers joint-venture negotiations, rules and regulations, and the investment environment.

CHINESE BUSINESS JOURNAL. see *BUSINESS AND ECONOMICS — Economic Situation And Conditions*

332.6   MX
CIRCULARES DE FIANZAS. a. Comision Nacional de Seguros y Fianzas, Av. de los Insurgentes Sur 1971, Plaza Inn, Torre 2 N., 2o piso, 01020 Mexico DF, Mexico. TEL 525-724-7519. FAX 525-661-6800. Document type: government publication.
Description: Official communications on surety bond law reforms.

332.6   US   ISSN 0882-3820
HG4528
CLEAN YIELD. 1985. bi-m. $80 to individuals; businesses $100. Clean Yield Publications, Box 117, Greensboro, VT 05841. TEL 802-533-7178. FAX 802-533-2907. Ed. Rick Hausman. R&P contact: Rick Hausman. adv. contact: Doug Fleer. bk.rev. circ. 1,200. Document type: newsletter.
Description: Stock market newsletter for investors concerned with the social responsibilities of publicly held companies.

332.6   UK   ISSN 0964-671X
CLEARING & SETTLEMENT. 1991. bi-m. £250. Metal Bulletin plc, Park House, Park Terrace, Worcester Park, Surrey KT4 7HY, England. TEL 44-171-827-9977. FAX 44-181-337-8943. Pub. David Setters. Document type: trade publication.
Description: Looks at the financial operations sector of the cash and derivatives markets.

BUSINESS AND ECONOMICS — INVESTMENTS

332.6 US
CLOSED-END FUND DIGEST. 1987. m. $200. Madent Publishing, Inc., 1224 Coast Village Circle, Ste. 11, Santa Barbara, CA 93108. TEL 805-565-5651. Ed. Patrick L. Winton. circ. 4,800. **Document type:** newsletter.
Refereed Serial

332.63 US ISSN 1067-6279
CLOSED-END FUND SOURCEBOOK. 1992. a. $195 in U.S.; Canada $105; elsewhere $125. Morningstar, Inc., 225 W. Walker Dr., Ste. 400, Chicago, IL 60606. TEL 312-696-6000. FAX 312-696-6001. Ed. Catherine Gillis. circ. 400.
Description: Provides performance data, star ratings, and portfolio information for 500 closed-end funds.

332.6 US
COASTLINES (SAN FRANCISCO); quarterly newsletter published by the Pacific Stock Exchange. 1990. q. free. Pacific Stock Exchange, Inc., 301 Pine St., San Francisco, CA 94104. TEL 415-393-4253. FAX 415-393-4108. TELEX 203025 PSE UR (RCA). Ed. Genie W. Williams. circ. 4,000. (back issues avail.) **Document type:** newsletter.
Formed by the 1990 merger of: Final Quotes & Pacific Stock Exchange Highlights.
Description: Presents news and activities of the Pacific Stock Exchange, the securities industry, trading highlights, and related topics.

332.6 US
COGENT COMMENTS. w. Market Vane Corporation, Box 90490, Pasadena, CA 91109-0490. TEL 818-395-7436. FAX 818-795-7654. Ed. Richard Ishida. **Document type:** newsletter.
Description: Contains pertinent selections from more than 120 market letters surveyed weekly by the Bullish Consensus.

COIN PREVIEWER; numismatic investment newsletter. see *NUMISMATICS*

COIN WORLD ANNUAL PRICE GUIDE. see *NUMISMATICS*

COINFIDENTIAL REPORT. see *NUMISMATICS*

332.6 US
COMEX WEEKLY MARKET REPORT. 1976. w. $35. Commodity Exchange, Inc., c/o Fabian Joseph, Statistics Dept., Room 9108, 4 World Trade Center, New York, NY 10048. TEL 212-938-2937. FAX 212-938-2660.

COMICS VALUES MONTHLY. see *ART*

COMMERCIAL INVESTMENT REAL ESTATE JOURNAL. see *REAL ESTATE*

332.6 UK ISSN 0951-9556
COMMERCIAL LEASES. 1987. m. £170 (foreign £195) (effective 1997). Monitor Press Ltd., Suffolk House, Church Field Rd., Sudbury, Suffolk CO10 6YA, England. TEL 44-1787-378607. FAX 44-1787-880201. Ed. J.E. Adams. (back issues avail.) **Indexed:** Euro.LJI, LJI. **Document type:** newsletter.
Description: For professional property and investment managers, solicitors and chartered surveyors.

332.6 US ISSN 0279-0939
COMMODEX SYSTEM. 1959. d. $575. Equidex, 7000 Boulevard E., Ste. 1787, Guttenberg, NJ 07093-4808. TEL 201-868-2600. circ. 5,000. (back issues avail.) **Document type:** newsletter.

332.6 630 US ISSN 0279-0947
COMMODITY FUTURES FORECAST SERVICE. 1956. w. $350. Equidex, 7000 Boulevard E., Guttenberg, NJ 07093-4808. TEL 201-868-2600. Ed. Philip Gotthelf. (back issues avail.) **Document type:** newsletter.

COMMODITY FUTURES LAW REPORTS. see *LAW*

332.6 338.9 UN ISSN 1020-0967
HG6051.D44
COMMODITY MARKETS AND THE DEVELOPING COUNTRIES. 1993. q. $150. World Bank, 1818 H St., N.W., Washington, DC 20433. TEL 202-473-1155. FAX 202-522-2627. (Subscr. to: Box 7247-7956, Philadelphia, PA 19170-7956. TEL 201-476-2192. FAX 201-476-2197) **Document type:** newsletter.
—SWETS.
Description: Looks at production, consumption and trade patterns to pinpoint why commodities thrive or falter. Checks current market climate for such items as food, agricultural raw materials, energy and fertilizers.

332.6 US
COMMODITY PRICE CHARTS. 1976. w. $435. Oster Communications, Inc., 219 Parkade, Cedar Falls, IA 50613. TEL 319-277-1271. FAX 319-277-7982. Ed. Karla Kelley.

332.6 US
COMMODITY PRICES. 1974. irreg., 2nd ed., 1990. $69.50. Gale Research, 835 Penobscot Bldg., 645 Griswold St., Detroit, MI 48226-4094. TEL 313-961-2242; 800-877-4253. FAX 800-414-5043. URL: daniel__snyder@gale.com. Ed. Paul Wasserman.

COMMONWEALTH LETTERS; for investors in single family homes. see *REAL ESTATE*

COMMUNICATIONS BUSINESS & FINANCE. see *COMMUNICATIONS*

COMMUNITY ECONOMICS. see *BUSINESS AND ECONOMICS — Cooperatives*

332.6 352.7 US
COMMUNITY INVESTMENT AND AFFORDABLE HOUSING. 1990. q. free. Federal Home Loan Bank of Des Moines, 907 Walnut St., Des Moines, IA 50309. TEL 515-281-1101. FAX 515-281-1022.

COMPANY R E F S. see *BUSINESS AND ECONOMICS — Banking And Finance*

COMPLETE COMMODITY FUTURES DIRECTORY. see *BUSINESS AND ECONOMICS — Trade And Industrial Directories*

332.6 MX
COMPORTAMIENTO DEL SISTEMA ASEGURADOR Y AFIANZADOR MEXICANO. a. Comision Nacional de Seguros y Fianzas, Avda. de los Insurgentes Sur 1971, Plaza Inn, Torre 2 N., 2o piso, 01020 Mexico DF, Mexico. TEL 525-724-7519. FAX 525-661-6800. **Document type:** government publication.
Formed by the merger of: Comportamiento del Sistema Asegurador Mexicano & Comportamiento del Sistema Afianzador Mexicano.
Description: Contains information on the historical development of the insurance and surety bond market during the previous five years.

332.6 CN
CONFERENCE BOARD OF CANADA. INDEX OF BUSINESS CONFIDENCE. q. membership. Conference Board of Canada, 255 Smyth Rd., Ste 100, Ottawa, ON K1H 8M7, Canada. TEL 613-526-3280. FAX 613-526-4857. charts. **Indexed:** CS Ind. **Document type:** trade publication.
Former titles: Conference Board of Canada. Business Attitudes and Investment Spending Intentions (ISSN 0827-6277); (until 1986): Conference Board of Canada. Survey of Business Attitudes and Investment Spending Intentions (ISSN 0703-1920).

332.6 US ISSN 1056-9766
CONSENSUS (KANSAS CITY); national futures and financial weekly. 1971. w. $365. Consensus, Inc. (Kansas City), 1737 McGee St., Ste. 401, Kansas City, MO 64108. TEL 816-471-3862. FAX 816-221-2045. Ed. Robert E. Salva; Pub. Robert E. Salva. R&P contact: Robert E. Salva. adv. contact: Sharon Buchko. charts; stat. (tabloid format) **Document type:** newspaper, trade publication.
Description: Investment newspaper for the futures industry used by most brokers and traders. Market letters, special reports, and buy/sell advise from over 100 top national and international sources. Covers all stock and financial markets, metals, agricultural markets, livestock, grains and oilseeds.

332.645 US
CONSERVATIVE SPECULATOR. 1988. m. $198 (foreign $222) (effective 1997 & 1998). Guidera Publishing Corp., 3 Myrtle Bank Rd., Hilton Head Island, SC 29926. TEL 803-681-3399. URL: http://www.richfamous.com. (Subscr. to: P.O. Drawer 22509, Hilton Head Island, SC 29925) Ed. Lawrence C. Oakley; Pub. Rosanne C. Oakley. bk.rev.; software rev.; circ. 13,000 (paid). (back issues avail.) **Document type:** newsletter.
Description: Helps readers make more with the 10 percent they put into special situations than they make with the 90 percent put into everything else. Includes 2-3 special situations, inflation - interest rate forecasts, bond advice, and Dow 30 timing.

332.6 US
THE CONTRARIAN'S VIEW. 1986. m. $39 (foreign $54). 132 Moreland St., Worcester, MA 01609. TEL 508-757-2881. URL: http://www.assumption.edu. Ed. Nick Chase. circ. 50 (paid). **Document type:** newsletter.
●Also available online.
Description: Stock market advisory service.

332.6 US ISSN 0010-793X
CONTRARY INVESTOR. 1963. fortn. $125. Fraser Management Associates, Inc., 309 S. Willard St., Box 494, Burlington, VT 05402. TEL 802-658-0322. FAX 802-658-0260. Ed. James L. Fraser. charts; illus. (processed) **Document type:** newsletter.
Description: Ponders the fields of investment and financial speculation. Lists specific securities, with contrarian speculative possibilities most likely to succeed.

332.6 US ISSN 0015-6019
CONTRARY INVESTOR FOLLOW-UP SERVICE. 1965. fortn. $75. Fraser Management Associates, Inc., 309 S. Willard St., Box 494, Burlington, VT 05402. TEL 802-658-0322. FAX 802-658-0260. Ed. James L. Fraser. mkt. (processed) **Document type:** newsletter.
Description: Analyses and regular reports on all Contrary Investor selections until closed out with a definite selling price.

332.6 US
CONTRARY OPINION LIBRARY. 1969. a. free. Fraser Publishing Co., Inc., 309 S. Willard St., Box 494, Burlington, VT 05402. TEL 802-658-0324; 800-253-0900. FAX 802-658-0260. E-mail: fraserbk@togethe.net; URL: http://www.ambook.org/bookstore/fraser. Ed. Karla Ferrelli. circ. 30,000. **Document type:** catalog.

332.6 US ISSN 0897-6740
KF1477
CORPORATE ANTI-TAKEOVER DEFENSES: THE POISON PILL DEVICE. 1987. a. $164. Clark - Boardman - Callaghan, 375 Hudson St., New York, NY 10014. TEL 212-929-7500; 800-422-2101. FAX 212-924-0460. Ed. Joy Marlene Bryan.
Description: Summarizes the various features of poison pill plans, analyzes their potential benefits and risks, and provides counsel with the necessary guidance to the procedures and drafting language required for the adoption or recission of shareholder rights plans.

332.6 US
CORPORATE BOND MARKET MONTHLY. (Included in: United States Corporate Bond Research) m. Salomon Brothers, Inc., 7 World Trade Center, New York, NY 10048. TEL 212-783-7000. stat.

332.6 US ISSN 1059-7964
HG4057
CORPORATE DIRECTORY OF US PUBLIC COMPANIES. 1988. a. $360 hardcover; CD-ROM $595. Walker's Western Research, 1650 Borel Pl., Ste. 130, San Mateo, CA 94402. TEL 415-341-1110. FAX 415-341-2351. (Dist. in the U.K. by: Globe Book Services Ltd., Brunel Rd., Houndmills, Basingstoke, Hants. RG21 2XS, England. TEL 0256-817245) Ed. Elizabeth Walsh. **Document type:** directory.
●Also available on CD-ROM.
Formerly (until 1991): Corporate Directory (ISSN 1044-3525)
Description: Profiles the business activities and finances of more than 10,000 publicly traded companies. Includes officers' and directors' names, subsidiaries and ownership information, as well as stock data and financial information.

BUSINESS AND ECONOMICS — INVESTMENTS

CORPORATE FINANCING WEEK; the newsweekly of corporate finance, investment banking and M & A. see *BUSINESS AND ECONOMICS — Banking And Finance*

346 US ISSN 1050-320X
HG4028.M4
CORPORATE GROWTH REPORT. 1981. w. $795. Quality Services Company, 5290 Overpass Rd., Ste. 126, Santa Barbara, CA 93111-9950. TEL 805-964-7841. FAX 805-964-1073. Pub. Walter Jurek. R&P contact: Walter Jurek. adv.; circ. 600 (paid). (also avail. in microform from UMI)
Indexed: BPIA, P.A.I.S. **Document type:** newsletter.
●Also available online. Vendor(s): UMI.
—BLDSC (3472.066300); UMI.
Formed by the 1992 merger of: Acquisition - Divestiture Weekly Report (ISSN 0279-4160) & Corporate Growth Magazine (ISSN 0898-8390); Which was formerly: Buyouts and Acquisitions Magazine; Journal of Buyouts and Acquisitions (ISSN 0736-5527)
Description: Provides legal and financial details on current mergers and acquisitions, as well as joint ventures, restructurings and methods of increasing shareholder value.

332.67 US
CORPORATE SHAREHOLDER; first in financial-investor-shareholder relations. 1974. s-m. $225. Market Value, Inc., 300 W. 108th St., New York, NY 10025. TEL 212-662-0877. Ed. Edward Kulkosky. bk.rev. circ. 1,000.

CORPORATION AND SECURITIES. see *LAW — Corporate Law*

332.6 CR
COSTA RICAN BEACON. 1982. m. $48. Consorcio de Comunicaciones Interamericanas, S.A., P.O. Box 196, San Jose 2120, Costa Rica. TEL 506-2236833. Ed. Edwin L. Lowery. R&P contact: Jaime Vargas. bk.rev. circ. 5,400. **Document type:** newsletter.
Description: Offers information on international finance, living and investing in Costa Rica. Covers tourism and news analysis.

332.6 FR ISSN 0220-6358
HG4503
COTE OFFICIELLE. d. 390 F. Bourse de Paris, 39 rue Cambon, 75001 Paris, France. TEL 49-27-10-00. FAX 49-27-14-33. TELEX 215 561 F. **Document type:** newspaper.
Description: Daily stock exchange price list.

332.6 US
HF1414.3.C68
COUNTERTRADE & OFFSET; weekly intelligence on unconventional & reciprocal international trade. 1983. 24/yr. $588 (foreign $648); includes Directory of Countertrade Services. C T O Data Services, Box 7130, Fairfax Station, VA 22039. TEL 703-425-1323. FAX 703-425-0399. TELEX (RCA) 263 128 CTO UR. Ed. James Thomas; Pub. Judith Fischer. **Document type:** newsletter.
Formerly: Countertrade Outlook (ISSN 0743-0396)

COUNTRY FORECASTS (SYRACUSE). see *BUSINESS AND ECONOMICS*

332.6 US
COURAGEOUS CONTRARIAN.* 1985. m. $75. Mann Consultants, 3065 Branch Dr., Clearwater, FL 34620-1741. Ed. David Cheesman.
Formerly (until 1987): Bond Market Manager.
Description: Features stock selection reports complete with five years of financial data.

332.6 US
CRAWFORD PERSPECTIVES. 1977. 12/yr. $250 (foreign $275). Arch Crawford, Ed. & Pub., 1382 Third Ave., Ste. 403, New York, NY 10021-0403. TEL 212-744-6973. FAX 212-535-6202. bk.rev. circ. 1,000. **Document type:** newsletter.
Description: Presents stock market forecasting methods which focus on astronomic cycles and technical analysis.

332.6 US ISSN 0731-1974
HG4501
CREDITWEEK. 1973. w. $1695. Standard & Poor's Corporation (Subsidiary of: McGraw-Hill, Inc.), 25 Broadway, New York, NY 10004. TEL 212-208-8000. Ed. Matthew Korten. **Document type:** trade publication.
Former titles (until 1981): Standard & Poor's Fixed Income Investor (ISSN 0193-9335); Fixed Income Investor (ISSN 0091-8415); Standard & Poor's Bond Outlook (ISSN 0006-7067)

332.6 US ISSN 1058-6679
CREDITWEEK (MUNICIPAL EDITION). 1991. w. Standard & Poor's Corporation (Subsidiary of: McGraw-Hill, Inc.), 25 Broadway, New York, NY 10004. TEL 212-208-8000. **Document type:** trade publication.

332.6 US ISSN 1084-8053
CRIMINAL POLITICS. 1975. m. $187.50. Patterson Strategy Organization, Box 37812, Cincinnati, OH 45222. TEL 513-475-0100. FAX 513-475-6014. TELEX 466053 LT PATSN SLCI. E-mail: crimpol@eos.net. Ed. Lawrence T. Patterson; Pub. Lawrence T. Patterson. R&P contact: Judy Pieper. adv. contact: Nita Kennedy. bk.rev.; index. circ. 30,000. (also avail. in microform from UMI; back issues avail.) **Document type:** newsletter.
Former titles (until 1989): Monthly Lesson in Criminal Politics; Patterson Strategy Letter.
Description: Covers offshore investment news, current and pending legislation relevant to financial management, with conservative analysis of political news and issues.

332.678 US
CRISIS INVESTING. 1979. m. $145. Agora, Inc., 105 W. Monument St., Baltimore, MD 21201. TEL 410-223-2611. FAX 410-223-2696. Ed. Douglas R. Casey.
Formerly: Investing in Crisis (ISSN 0740-3666)
Description: Information on precious metals, gold mining, commodities, start-up companies and technologically innovative firms.

CROSS-SHAREHOLDINGS IN EUROPE. see *BUSINESS AND ECONOMICS — Banking And Finance*

332.6 US ISSN 0011-3026
CUMULATIVE STOCK PROFITS. 1969. fortn. $160. Cumulative Stock Profits Advisor, Box 246, Forest Hills, NY 11375. Ed. S.J. Rifkin. charts; mkt.; stat. circ. 150 (controlled). (processed)

332.6 US
CURRENT DEVELOPMENTS.* 1972. m. $10,000. Callard, Madden & Associates, Inc., 11 S. La Salle St., Ste. 820, Chicago, IL 60603-1205. TEL 312-263-0027. Ed. Charles G. Callard. circ. 200.
Formerly: Expectations Monitor.
Description: Investment policy report describing capital markets, asset allocation, industry ratings and buy and sell decisions.

332.6 US
CYRUS J. LAWRENCE PORTFOLIO STRATEGY SERVICE. WEEKLY ECONOMIC DATA. 1975. w. avail. to qualified personnel only. Cyrus J. Lawrence, Inc., 1290 Ave. of the Americas, New York, NY 10104. TEL 212-468-5000. (back issues avail.)

CZERWENSKY INTERN. see *BUSINESS AND ECONOMICS — Banking And Finance*

332.6 340 US
D & O LIABILITY HANDBOOK: LAW, SAMPLE DOCUMENTS, FORMS. a. $140. Clark - Boardman - Callaghan, 375 Hudson St., New York, NY 10014. TEL 212-929-7500; 800-422-2101. FAX 212-924-0460. Ed. Mark A. Sargent.
Description: Provides a concise guide to the director and officer liability landscape through a collection of legal commentary, statutory provisions, and sample documents and forms.

332.6 KO
DAE WOO SECURITIES MONTHLY. (Text in Korean) m. 34-3 Yoido-dong, Yongdeungpo-ku, Seoul, S. Korea. TEL 784-8851. Ed. Kim Chang-Hee.

332.64 CN ISSN 0838-9365
THE DAILIES. w. Can.$738.60 (U.S. Can.$829.60; overseas Can.$894.60) (effective 1997). Canadian Analyst Ltd., 30 Duncan St., Toronto, ON M5V 2C3, Canada. TEL 416-971-6543; 800-348-6661. FAX 416-598-0049.
Formerly (until 1988): Canadian Daily Stock Charts (ISSN 0045-4656)
Description: For the short-term trader who needs a closer view of what is currently happening in the market.

332.6 US
DAILY GRAPHS. LONG TERM VALUES. 1981. 48/yr. $269. Daily Graphs Inc., Box 66919, Los Angeles, CA 90066-0919. TEL 310-448-6843; 800-472-7479.

332.6 US
HG4916
DAILY GRAPHS. N A S D A Q O.T.C. - AMERICAN STOCK EXCHANGE - O.T.C. w. $519. Daily Graphs Inc., Box 66919, Los Angeles, CA 90066-0919. TEL 310-448-6843; 800-472-7479. charts.
Formerly: Daily Graphs. American Stock Exchange - O.T.C. (ISSN 1055-0658)

332.6 US
DAILY GRAPHS. N.Y.S.E.. 1972. w. $519. Daily Graphs Inc., Box 66919, Los Angeles, CA 90066-0919. TEL 310-448-6843; 800-472-7479. charts. circ. 5,000.
Formerly: Daily Graphs. N.Y.S.E.-O.T.C.

332.6 US
DAILY GRAPHS. OPTION GUIDE. w. $300. Daily Graph Inc., Box 66919, Los Angeles, CA 90066-0919. TEL 310-448-6843; 800-472-7479.
Formerly: Daily Graphs. Stock Option Guide (ISSN 0195-2021)

332.6 US
DAILY MARKET REPORT. d. $110. Coffee, Sugar & Cocoa Exchange, Inc., Four World Trade Center, New York, NY 10048. TEL 212-938-2800. FAX 212-524-9863.
Description: Discusses trading and spot prices, open interest, volume and warehouse stocks.

DAILY TENDER BULLETIN. see *BUSINESS AND ECONOMICS — Banking And Finance*

DAVID HALL'S INSIDE VIEW. see *NUMISMATICS*

332.6 US ISSN 1057-7521
DEFAULTED BONDS NEWSLETTER. 1987. m. $365. Bond Investors Association, Inc., 6175 N.W. 153rd St., Ste. 221, Miami Lakes, FL 33014-2435. TEL 305-557-1832. Ed. C. Richard Lehmann. **Document type:** newsletter.
●Also available online.

332.6 US
DEFINED CONTRIBUTION NEWS. 1993. bi-w. $1595 (Canada $1625; elsewhere $1670). Institutional Investor Newsletters, 477 Madison Ave., New York, NY 10022. TEL 212-224-3233. FAX 212-224-3353. **Document type:** newsletter.
Description: Provides information on who's hiring managers, recordkeepers or consultants and why. Includes news on new educational products, alliances and plan sponsor profiles.

332.6 US
DELIBERATIONS ON WORLD MARKETS. 1972. 18/yr. $225. P.O. Box 40097, Tucson, AZ 85717-0097. TEL 416-964-1359. Ed. Ian McAvity. **Document type:** newsletter.
Formerly (until 1991): Deliberations.

DELUXE; ideas for the business of living. see *BUSINESS AND ECONOMICS — Banking And Finance*

332.6 DK ISSN 0907-3752
HG5594.5
DENMARK. FINANSTILSYNET. STATISTISK MATERIALE: INVESTERINGSFORENINGER. 1989. a. DKK 40. Finanstilsynet, Gl. Kongevej 74A, DK-1850 Frederiksberg C, Denmark. TEL 45-31-23-11-88. FAX 45-31-23-04-41. (Dist. by: D B K Bogdistribution, Siljangade 2-8, DK-2300 Copenhagen S, Denmark) **Document type:** government publication.
Formerly (until 1991): Denmark. Finanstilsynet. Beretning. Bilag 5: Investeringsforeninger.

BUSINESS AND ECONOMICS — INVESTMENTS

332.6 DK ISSN 0907-3701
DENMARK. FINANSTILSYNET. STATISTISK MATERIALE. LIVSFORSIKRINGSSELSKABER M.V. 1989. a. DKK 75. Finanstilsynet, Gl. Kongevej 74 A, DK-1850 Frederiksberg C, Denmark. TEL 45-33-55-82-82. FAX 45-33-55-82-00. (Dist. by: D B K Bogdistribution, Siljangade 2-8, DK-2300 Copenhagen S, Denmark) **Document type:** government publication.
    Formerly (until 1991): Denmark. Finanstilsynet. Beretning. Bilag 2: Livsforsikringsselskaber m.v.

DERIVATIVES QUARTERLY. see *BUSINESS AND ECONOMICS — Banking And Finance*

332.6 US
DERIVATIVES: TAX, REGULATION, FINANCE. bi-m. $183.75. Warren, Gorham & Lamont, One Penn Plaza, New York, NY 10119. TEL 212-971-5000. FAX 212-971-5113.
    Description: Aims to provide comprehensive coverage of developments in the derivative industry.

332.6 UK ISSN 1357-0927
DERIVATIVES USE, TRADING & REGULATION. 1994. q. £205 to Europe (N. America $310; elsewhere £220). Henry Stewart Publications, Russell House, 28-30 Little Russell St., London WC1A 2HN, England. TEL 44-171-404-3040. FAX 44-171-404-2081. E-mail: 100622.3264@compuserve.com. (Subscr. in. N. America to: 810 E. 10th St., Box 1897, Lawrence, KS 66044. TEL 913-843-1221. FAX 913-843-1274) Ed. Daryn Moody. adv. contact: Fraser Tant. **Document type:** trade publication.
—BLDSC (3554.967300).
    Description: Publishes papers which educate in the use, trading and regulation of all forms of derivatives.
    Refereed Serial

332.6 US
DERIVATIVES WEEK; the newsweekly on derivatives worldwide. 1992. w. $1595 (Canada $1625; elsewhere $1670). Institutional Investor Newsletters, 477 Madison Ave., New York, NY 10022. TEL 212-224-3233. FAX 212-224-3353. Ed. Tom Lamont. adv. **Document type:** newsletter.
    Description: Tells who's using derivatives and how. Includes coverage of instruments linked to equities, interest rates, commodities and currencies worldwide.

DIAMOND INSIGHT; penetrating the multi-faceted world of diamonds. see *JEWELRY, CLOCKS AND WATCHES*

332.6 JA
DIAMOND REPORT. (Text in Japanese) 1916. w. 60000 Yen. Diamond Inc., 4-2, 1-chome, Kasumigaseki, Chiyoda-ku, Tokyo 100, Japan. Ed. Kiichi Sakai.

332.6 JA
DIAMOND, STOCK INVESTMENT EDITION/DAIYAMONDO KABUSHIKI-TOSHI-BAN. (Text in Japanese) 1977. bi-m. 5700 Yen. Diamond Inc., 4-2, 1-chome, Kasumigaseki, Chiyoda-ku, Tokyo 100, Japan. Ed. Toshikazu Yatsu.

332.6 US ISSN 0890-0957
DICK DAVIS DIGEST. 1982. s-m. $165. Dick Davis Publishing Inc., 1080 S.E. Third Ave., Ft. Lauderdale, FL 33316. TEL 954-467-8500. (Subscr. to: Box 350630, Fort Lauderdale, FL 33335-0630) Ed. Steven Halpern. R&P contact: Lorianne Kiesl. s-a. index. circ. 33,000. (back issues avail.) **Document type:** newsletter.
    Description: Features the latest opinions of the nation's top-performing market letter writers, as well as specific stock recommendations.

332.6 FR
DICTIONNAIRE JOLY BOURSE ET PRODUITS FINANCIERS. 5 base vols. plus updates. 3400 F. (effective 1997). Joly Editions, 1 av. Franklin D. Roosevelt, 75008 Paris, France. TEL 33-1-44951620. FAX 33-1-45638939. Ed. Thierry Bonneau. (looseleaf format) **Document type:** trade publication.

332.6 US ISSN 0012-2971
DINES LETTER; advice and information for traders and investors. 1960. 20/yr. $195 (foreign $249). James Dines & Co., Inc., Box 22, Belvedere, CA 94920. TEL 800-845-8259. Ed. James Dines. bk.rev.; charts; mkt.; stat.; index. (looseleaf format) **Document type:** newsletter.
    Description: Contains buy and sell advice based on mass psychology, technical analysis, and fundamental considerations for stocks, options and the economy.

DIRECTORY OF BUYOUT FINANCING SOURCES. see *BUSINESS AND ECONOMICS — Trade And Industrial Directories*

DIRECTORY OF COMPANIES OFFERING DIVIDEND REINVESTMENT PLANS. see *BUSINESS AND ECONOMICS — Trade And Industrial Directories*

DIRECTORY OF COUNTERTRADE & OFFSET SERVICES. see *BUSINESS AND ECONOMICS — International Commerce*

DIRECTORY OF INSTITUTIONAL INVESTMENT FUNDS. see *BUSINESS AND ECONOMICS — Trade And Industrial Directories*

332.63 US ISSN 1062-1857
HG4930
DIRECTORY OF MUTUAL FUNDS. 1991. a. Investment Company Institute, 1401 H St. N.W., Ste. 1200, Washington, DC 20005. TEL 202-293-7700. FAX 202-293-7016. **Document type:** directory.
    Description: Contains general information on mutual funds.

332.6 UK ISSN 0967-9626
DIRECTORY OF NOMINEES. 1974. a. £75. Tertiary Publications, Brook House, Eriswell Crescent, Walton-on-Thames, Surrey, England. TEL 01932-248358. FAX 01932-245569. **Document type:** directory.

332.6 US ISSN 0085-0551
HG4961
DIRECTORY OF OBSOLETE SECURITIES. 1927. a. $595 to qualified personnel (effective 1997). Financial Information Incorporated, 30 Montgomery St., Jersey City, NJ 07302. TEL 800-367-3441. FAX 800-344-3292. Ed. Don Hardie. R&P contact: Gil Michalsky. **Document type:** directory.
●Also available online.

DIRECTORY OF PREMIUM, INCENTIVE & TRAVEL BUYERS. see *BUSINESS AND ECONOMICS — Trade And Industrial Directories*

DIRECTORY OF PROPERTY INVESTORS AND DEVELOPERS. see *BUSINESS AND ECONOMICS — Trade And Industrial Directories*

DIRECTORY OF THE WORLD'S LARGEST SERVICE COMPANIES. see *BUSINESS AND ECONOMICS — Trade And Industrial Directories*

332.6 US ISSN 0094-2561
HG4905
DISCLOSURE RECORD. 1973. w. $50. Newsfeatures, Inc., 8511 249th St., Jamaica, NY 11426-2105. Ed. Lori Link. adv.; tr.lit. circ. 10,000. (tabloid format)
    Description: Full text of corporate news releases.

DISTRESSED PROPERTY INVESTOR'S MONTHLY. see *REAL ESTATE*

332.6 US ISSN 1052-5092
DIVIDEND REINVESTMENT PLANS; guide almanac. 1989. a. $69. Evergreen Enterprises, Box 763, Laurel, MD 20725-0763. **Document type:** academic/scholarly publication.

332.67 US
DOLLAR-WISE INVESTOR. vol.6, 1991. q? Gentsch Financial, 1700 Commerce St., Ste. 1630, Dallas, TX 75201-5320. TEL 214-480-8237.

DOLLARSENSE; your money management magazine. see *BUSINESS AND ECONOMICS — Banking And Finance*

332.3 GW ISSN 0932-7142
DOMUS MAGAZIN. 1950. 4/yr. DM.14. Domus-Verlag GmbH, Servatiusstr. 8, 53129 Bonn, Germany. TEL 49-228-230041. FAX 49-228-230044. Ed. W. Duerpisch. adv.; bk.rev.; illus. circ. 1,700,000. **Document type:** consumer publication.
    Formerly (until 1987): Zeitschrift fuer Eigenheimfreunde (ISSN 0049-8629)

332.6 US ISSN 0300-7324
DOW THEORY FORECASTS; business and stock market. 1946. w. $233. Dow Theory Forecasts, Inc., 7412 Calumet Ave., Hammond, IN 46324-2692. TEL 219-931-6480. FAX 219-931-6487. Ed. Richard J. Moroney. circ. 20,000.

332.6 US
DOW THEORY LETTERS. 1958. 26/yr. $250. Dow Theory Letters, Inc., Box 1759, La Jolla, CA 92038. TEL 619-454-0481. Ed. Richard Russell. bk.rev. circ. 7,500. (also avail. in microfiche) **Document type:** newsletter.

332.6 US
DOWBEATERS. 1977. m. $100. Dow Beaters Inc., Box 284, Ironia, NJ 07845. TEL 201-273-0120. Ed. P. DeAngelis.

332.6 US
DRIP INVESTOR. 1992. m. $79. NorthStar Financial, Inc., 7412 Calumet Ave., Ste. 200, Hammond, IN 46324-2692. TEL 219-852-3220. FAX 219-931-6487. Ed. Charles B. Carlson. R&P contact: Charles B. Carlson. TEL 219-852-3200. circ. 34,000. **Document type:** trade publication.

332.6 US
DRISCOLL INSIDER. s-m. $95. Driscoll Industrial, Box AV, Carmel, CA 93921. TEL 408-625-9026. Ed. Joseph L. Driscoll, Jr.
    Description: Provides a complete listing of all initial public stock offerings.

332.6 US ISSN 0098-2466
HG4905
DUN & BRADSTREET'S GUIDE TO YOUR INVESTMENTS (YEAR). 1973. a. $17.95 paperback; hardcover $35 (effective 1996). HarperCollins Publishers, Inc., 10 E. 53rd St., New York, NY 10022. TEL 800-242-7737.
    Formerly: Your Investments: How to Increase Your Capital and Income.

332.66 EI ISSN 0250-3891
E I B - INFORMATION. Danish edition: Europaeiske Investeringsbank - Information (ISSN 0250-3875); German edition: Europaeische Investitionsbank - Informationen (ISSN 0250-3883); Italian edition: Banca Europea per gli Investimenti - Informazioni (ISSN 0250-3905); Dutch edition: Europese Investeringsbank - Mededelingen (ISSN 0250-3913); Greek edition: Europaike Trapeza Ependuseon - Plerofories (ISSN 0251-0677); Spanish edition: B E I - Informaciones (EI ISSN 0258-2139); Portuguese edition: B E I - Informacoes (EI ISSN 0258-2147); French edition: Banque Europeenne d'Investissement - Informations (EI ISSN 0250-3867); Swedish edition: Europeiska Investeringsbanken. Information. Finnish edition: Euroopan Investointipankki. Tiedote. (Text in English) 1975. 4/yr. free. European Investment Bank - Banque Europeenne d'Investissement, 100 Bd. Konrad Adenauer, L-2950 Luxembourg, Luxembourg. TEL 43791. FAX 437704. TELEX 3530 BNKEU LU. URL: http://www.eib.org. (Dist. in U.S. by: European Community Information Service, 2100 M St. NW, Ste. 707, Washington, DC 20037) charts. **Indexed:** IIS, World Bank.Abstr.
—BLDSC (3664.770000).
    Formerly: European Investment Bank - Information.
    Description: Articles on European Investment Bank's activities and its specific role within the European Union.

332.6 PK
E I P INVESTORS SERVICE. (Text in English) 1968. w. Rs.4000($400) Economic and Industrial Publications, Al-Masiha, 47 Abdullah Haroon Rd., P.O. Box 7843, Karachi 74400, Pakistan. Ed.Bd; Pub. Iqbal Haidari. charts; stat. circ. 1,000. (looseleaf format) **Document type:** trade publication.

E S O P REPORT. (Employee Stock Ownership Plan) see *BUSINESS AND ECONOMICS — Management*

BUSINESS AND ECONOMICS — INVESTMENTS

332.6 US ISSN 1064-7678
EARNINGS GUIDE. 1991. m. $147. Standard & Poor's (Subsidiary of: McGraw-Hill Companies, Inc.), 25 Broadway, New York, NY 10004. TEL 212-208-8275. FAX 212-208-0040. Ed. Frank LoVaglio. stat. circ. 4,000. (back issues avail.) **Document type:** trade publication.
  Description: Provides quarterly and yearly estimates of corporate stock earnings.

332.6 US ISSN 1063-5262
HG5430.7.A2
EAST EUROPEAN INVESTMENT MONTHLY.* m. $290. Dixon & Co., 146 E. 49th St., Apt. 2B, New York, NY 10017-1247. TEL 212-388-1500. FAX 212-254-3386. Ed. Mark Dixon.

332.6 UN ISSN 1014-6911
EAST-WEST INVESTMENT NEWS. q. $80. Economic Commission for Europe (ECE), Palais des Nations, CH-1211 Geneva 10, Switzerland. TEL 022-917-1234. FAX 022-917-0123. TELEX 412962. (Or: United Nations Publications, Rm. DC2-853, New York, NY 10017. TEL 212-963-8302. FAX 212-932-3489) **Document type:** government publication.

332.6 US
ECONOMIC LOGIC. 1981. bi-m. $12 (effective 1996 & 1997). 23031 Britner Ct., Bingham Farms, MI 48025. TEL 313-642-6373. Ed. Richard K. Greene. R&P contact: Richard K. Greene. circ. 500. **Document type:** newsletter.
  Description: Presents concise, logical analyses of current economic issues and a stock market forecast.

332.6 US
▼**EFFICIENT FRONTIER.** 1996. q. free. William J. Bernstein, 3333 East Bay Dr., North Bend, OR 97459. E-mail: wbern@mail.coos.or.us; URL: http://www.coos.or.us/~wbern.
  Description: Investing-portfolio theory for sophisticated investors.

ELECTRONICS INDUSTRY OUTLOOK. see *ELECTRONICS*

332.6 US
ELIOT SHARP'S FINANCING NEWS. 1950. 5/w. $4600 (effective 1997). Investment Dealers' Digest, 2 World Trade Ctr., 18th Fl., New York, NY 10048. TEL 212-432-0045. E-mail: subscribe@iddis.com. Ed. David Kwateng. R&P contact: Denise Robbins. adv. contact: Todd Miller. charts; stat. (looseleaf format) **Document type:** newsletter.
  Former titles: Eliot Sharp's Municipal Newsletter; Eliot Sharp's Tax Exempt Newsletter (ISSN 0013-6204)

332.6 US ISSN 0742-5252
◀**ELLIOTT WAVE THEORIST.** 1979. m. $233 (foreign $250). Elliott Wave International, Box 1618, Gainesville, GA 30503. TEL 770-536-0309. Ed. Robert Prechter. **Document type:** newsletter.
  Description: Each issue thoroughly analyzes Elliott waves, Fibonacci relationships, fixed time cycles, momentum, sentiment and supply-demand factors in a comprehensive approach covering stocks, precious metals, interest rates, and the economy.

332.6 US ISSN 0882-5440
◀**EMERGING & SPECIAL SITUATIONS.** 1982. m. $210. Standard & Poor's Corporation (Subsidiary of: McGraw-Hill, Inc.), 25 Broadway, New York, NY 10004. TEL 212-208-8000. Ed. Robert Natale. **Document type:** trade publication.
  ●Also available online. Vendor(s): Knight-Ridder Information, Inc. (ESS), Dow Jones News Retrieval (ESS), NewsNet (FI16).
  Formerly (until 1984): New Issue Investor (ISSN 0737-4089)

332.6 UK ISSN 1354-8549
◀**EMERGING MARKETS INVESTOR.** 1994. m. £249($429) (effective 1997). Financial Engineering Ltd., Risk Publications, 104-112 Marylebone Ln., London W1M 5FU, England. TEL 44-171-487-5326. FAX 44-171-486-0879. Ed. Graham Cooper; Pub. Tony Gibson. adv.: B&W page £5350, color page £6590; trim 230 x 297. **Document type:** bulletin.
  Description: Coverage includes debt and equity markets in all emerging economies.

332.6 US
EMERGING MARKETS WEEK. 1993. w. $1695 (Canada $1725, elsewhere $1770). Institutional Investor Newsletters, 447 Madison Ave., New York, NY 10022. TEL 212-224-3233. FAX 212-224-3353. **Document type:** newsletter.
  Description: Provides the latest financing plans and investment strategies from Latin America, Southeast Asia, Africa and Eastern Europe.

332.6 340 US ISSN 1049-3808
KF1439
EMERGING TRENDS IN SECURITIES LAW. a. $125. Clark - Boardman - Callaghan, 375 Hudson St., New York, NY 10014. TEL 212-929-7500; 800-221-9428. FAX 212-924-0460. Eds. Harold S. Bloomenthal, Samuel Wolff.
  Description: Features detailed coverage of the latest developments in securities regulation.

332.6 US
ENCYCLOPEDIA OF STOCK MARKET TECHNIQUES. base vol. (plus irreg. updates). $65. Investors Intelligence, 30 Church St., Box 2046, New Rochelle, NY 10801. TEL 914-632-0422. FAX 914-632-0335. (looseleaf format)

ENTREPRENEUR'S FRANCHISE SPECIAL. see *BUSINESS AND ECONOMICS — Small Business*

332.6 US
ENVEST;* the business and investment newsletter for energy and the environment. bi-w. $225. Energy Investment Research, Box 73, Glenville Sta., Greenwich, CT 06830. TEL 914-937-6939.

332.6 US ISSN 1053-2544
HG4501
EQUITIES; investment news of promising public companies. 1951. m. $36. Equities Magazine, Inc., 160 Madison Ave., 3rd Fl., New York, NY 10016-5412. TEL 212-213-1300; 800-237-8400. FAX 212-832-7823. Ed. Robert J. Flaherty. R&P contact: Dorean Flaherty. adv.: B&W page $2400, color page $3300; adv. contact: Lawrence Dameron. bk.rev. circ. 17,000. **Indexed:** PROMT. **Document type:** consumer publication.
  —CCC.
  Former titles (until Sep. 1990): O T C Review (ISSN 0161-0694); (until Feb. 1977): Over-the-Counter Securities Review (ISSN 0030-736X)
  Description: Covers investment news and developments relating to middle market companies publicly listed on stock exchanges.

332.6 US
EQUITY ANALYST.* m. $110. 1163 Perrot St., Green Bay, WI 54302-1623. TEL 414-437-9474. Ed. Louie Nejedlo.

332.6 US
EQUITY INVESTMENT STRATEGY REPORT. w? Salomon Brothers, Inc., Marketing Department, 7 World Trade Center, New York, NY 10048.

332.6 336 US
ERNST & YOUNG FINANCIAL PLANNING REPORTER. 1975. m. $96. Ernst & Young (Washington), Box 33337, Washington, DC 20033-0337. TEL 202-663-9756. (back issues avail.)
  Formerly (until 1988): Brennan Reports on Sophisticated Tax and Investment Planning.
  Description: For the professional entrepreneur, investor, CPA, attorney or high, net-worth individual.

ESTATE PLANNER'S ALERT. see *LAW — Estate Planning*

332.6 UK
EUROPE BUYOUT MONITOR. bi-m. £455. Initiative Europe, 69 Bondway, London SW8 1SQ, England. TEL 44-171-735-9838. FAX 44-171-820-0802. **Document type:** trade publication.
  Description: Provides information for the specialist provider of buyout finance in the European markets.

332.6 UK ISSN 0965-2698
EUROPE BUYOUT REVIEW. 1990. a. £255. Initiative Europe, 69 Bondway, London SW8 1SQ, England. TEL 44-171-735-9838. FAX 44-171-820-0802. **Document type:** trade publication.

EUROPEAN CABLE - PAY T V. see *COMMUNICATIONS — Television And Cable*

332.6 UK ISSN 0966-4858
EUROPEAN HANDBOOK. 1991. s.a. Extel Financial Ltd., Research Products Sales and Marketing Department, 13-17 Epworth St., London EC2A 4DL, England. TEL 44-171-825-8000. FAX 44-171-608-3514. Ed.Bd.
  Description: Provides detailed financial information on 2,000 leading European companies.

332.6 333.33 UK ISSN 0961-9712
EUROPROPERTY (LONDON, 1991). 1991. m. £225 (Europe £235; U.S. £245; elsewhere £255). I F R Publishing (Subsidiary of: Thomson Financial Services Ltd.), Aldgate House, 33 Aldgate High St., London EC3N 1DL, England. TEL 0171-396-7000. FAX 0171-396-7525. Ed. Adrienne Margolis. adv. contact: Jonathan Holmes. **Document type:** trade publication.
  —BLDSC (3830.427760).

EVALUATING AND BUYING A FRANCHISE. see *BUSINESS AND ECONOMICS — Economic Situation And Conditions*

332.6 US ISSN 0195-0746
CODEN: EWADE9
EXECUTIVE WEALTH ADVISORY.* 1978. m. $96. National Institute of Business Management, Box 9070, McLean, VA 22102-9660. TEL 703-905-8000. (Subscr. to: Box 25288, Alexandria, VA 22313) Ed. Phillip Springer. circ. 23,200.
  —CCC.
  Description: Provides analysis and advice on how to make and keep money.

EXEMPT ORGANIZATIONS REPORTS. see *BUSINESS AND ECONOMICS — Public Finance, Taxation*

332.6 US
F I I ANNUAL GUIDE TO BONDS. 1972. a. (plus m. supplements). $1695 (effective 1997). Financial Information Incorporated, 30 Montgomery St., Jersey City, NJ 07302. TEL 800-367-3441. FAX 800-344-3292. Ed. Don Hardie. R&P contact: Gil Michalsky. **Document type:** directory.
  ●Also available online.
  Former titles: Financial Corporate - Municipal Bond Transfer Service; Financial Corporate Bond Transfer Service (ISSN 0360-5825)

332.678 US
HG4512
F I I ANNUAL GUIDE TO STOCKS. a. (plus m. supplements). $2250 (effective 1997). Financial Information Incorporated, 30 Montgomery St., Jersey City, NJ 07302. TEL 800-367-3441. FAX 800-344-3292. Ed. Don Hardie. R&P contact: Gil Michalsky. **Document type:** directory.
  ●Also available online.
  Formerly: Financial Stock Guide Service. Directory of Active Stocks (ISSN 0364-0752)

332.6 340 US
F P WEEK. (Fairchild Publications) 1987. s-m. Fairchild Fashion & Merchandising Group, 7 W. 34th St., New York, NY 10001. TEL 212-630-4000. Ed. Gail Brown. circ. 50,000. (tabloid format)

F X C REPORT. see *BUSINESS AND ECONOMICS — Economic Situation And Conditions*

332.63 US
FAMENT STOCK SERVICE ADVISORY. 1980. bi-m. $168. Fament Stock Advisory Service, 9157 Trujillo Way, Sacramento, CA 95826. TEL 916-363-2138. FAX 916-366-7326. Ed. Gordon D. Mors; Pub. Gordon D. Mors. circ. 10,000. (looseleaf format) **Document type:** newsletter.
  Description: Uses methods developed by Ted Warren to recommend buy, sell, and hold positions on various stocks.

332.63 US
FANNIE MAE INVESTOR ANALYST REPORT. q. (Fannie Mae, Office of Investor Relations) Federal National Mortgage Association, 3900 Wisconsin Ave., N.W., Washington, DC 20016. TEL 202-752-4422. FAX 202-752-4933.

FAST COMPANY. see *BUSINESS AND ECONOMICS — Management*

BUSINESS AND ECONOMICS — INVESTMENTS

332.6　　　　US　　ISSN 8756-4769
FAVORABLY POSITIONED STOCKS.* 1984. m. $117 (free to qualified personnel). Barrow Investment Management, Inc., 3800 W. Bay To Bay Blvd., Ste. 21, Tampa, FL 33629-6826. (Subscr. to: Box 1260, Tampa, FL 33601. TEL 813-254-7779) Ed. Alston M. (Mac) Barrow. circ. 5,000.
Description: Provides data on growth stocks currently undervalued according to fundamental and technical criteria.

FEDERAL SECURITIES LAW REPORTS. see *LAW*

FELL'S U S COINS QUARTERLY INVESTMENT GUIDE. see *NUMISMATICS*

332.6　　　　US
FIDELITY FOCUS; the magazine for Fidelity investors. q. free to shareholders. Fidelity Investments, 82 Devonshire St., R20E, Boston, MA 02109. Ed. Leslie Schultz. R&P contact: Tanya Lawe. circ. controlled. **Document type:** newsletter.
Description: Offers views on trends in the stock and bond markets in the U.S. and overseas; profiles key portfolio managers.

332.632　　　US
FIDELITY MONITOR; the independent newsletter for Fidelity Investors. 1986. m. $96. Independent Fidelity Investors, Inc., Box 1294, Rocklin, CA 95677. TEL 800-397-3094. Ed. Jack Bowers. **Document type:** newsletter.
Description: Covers buy, sell, and hold recommendations for most Fidelity funds.

332.6　　　　UK
FINANCIAL ADVISER (LONDON). w. (50/yr.). free to qualified personnel. Financial Times Business Information, Magazines (Subsidiary of: Financial Times Group), 2 Greystoke Pl., Fetter Ln., London EC4A 1ND, England. TEL 0171-405-6969. FAX 0171-405-5276. TELEX 296926 BUSINF G. URL: http://www.iii.co.uk/ftmags/fa/. stat.; circ. controlled. **Document type:** newspaper, trade publication.
Description: Covers the financial intermediary market, from new products to new legislation.

332　　　US　　ISSN 0015-198X
HG4501　　　　CODEN: FIAJA4
FINANCIAL ANALYSTS JOURNAL. 1945. bi-m. $150. Association for Investment Management and Research, Box 3668, Charlottesville, VA 22903. TEL 804-980-3668. FAX 804-980-9755. Ed. W. Van Harlow. adv.; bk.rev.; charts; stat.; cum.index: vols. 1-51 (1945-1995). circ. 30,000. (also avail. in microform from UMI; back issues avail.; reprint service avail. from UMI) **Indexed:** Account.Ind. (1974-), B.P.I., BPIA, Bus.Ind., Comput.Lit.Ind., Cont.Pg.Manage., INSPEC, Manage.Cont., Mid.East: Abstr.& Ind., PROMT, SCIMP, World Bank.Abstr.
●Also available online. Vendor(s): UMI. —BLDSC (3926.938000); AskIEEE; KR SourceOne; SWETS; UMI; UnCover. CCC.

332.6　　　　CH
FINANCIAL & INVESTMENT YEARBOOK R O C. a. NT.$500($25) in Asia, Middle East, Oceania; elsewhere $30. China Economic News Service, 561 Chunghsiao E. Rd. Sec. 4, Taipei, Taiwan 10516, Republic of China. TEL 02-642-2629. FAX 02-642-7422. TELEX 27710-CENSPC.

FINANCIAL CYCLES; wealth creation & investment success through person-centered financial astrology. see *ASTROLOGY*

330　　　　US
FINANCIAL EDGE. 1993. bi-m. $15 (effective 1994). Institute for Financial Integrity, Inc., 4150 123rd Trl. N., Royal Palm Beach, FL 33411. TEL 407-845-2867. Ed. Frank A. Provenzano. adv.; bk.rev. circ. 50,000. **Document type:** consumer publication.
Description: Publishes articles on financial planning, investing and money management.

332.6　　　US　　ISSN 0816-6897
FINANCIAL MONITOR. bi-m. American Society of C L U & Ch F C, 270 Bryn Mawr Ave., Bryn Mawr, PA 19010. TEL 215-526-2500. Ed. Roslyn Myers. **Document type:** trade publication.
Description: For consumers interested in money management and financial and retirement planning.

FINANCIAL POST MAGAZINE. see *BUSINESS AND ECONOMICS — Banking And Finance*

332.6　　　CN　　ISSN 0071-5050
FINANCIAL POST SURVEY OF INDUSTRIALS. 1927. a. Can.$59.75. Financial Post Co., Ltd., 333 King St. E., Toronto, ON M5A 4N2, Canada. TEL 416-350-6477. FAX 416-350-6501. Ed. Steven Pattison. adv. circ. 11,000.
Description: Gives investment and statistical data on public Canadian securities.

332.6　　　CN　　ISSN 0829-1640
HG4090
FINANCIAL POST 500. (Supplement to: Financial Post) a. Financial Post Co., Ltd., 333 King St. E., Toronto, ON M5A 4N2, Canada. TEL 416-350-6176. FAX 416-350-6171. Ed. Wayne Gooding. adv. contact: Bill Neill. circ. 242,000. **Indexed:** Can.B.P.I. —CISTI.
Formerly (until 1978): Financial Post 300 (ISSN 0829-1632)

FINANCIAL SURVEY. METAL STOCKHOLDERS. see *BUSINESS AND ECONOMICS — Trade And Industrial Directories*

332.6　　　US　　ISSN 1071-3646
HG173
FINANCIAL TECHNOLOGY REVIEW.* 1993. m. $8 per no. Rand Publishing (Stamford), 263 Tresser Blvd., 6th Fl., Stamford, CT 06901-3200. Ed. Teri Robinson. adv.: B&W page $4860. circ. 30,000. (also avail. in microform from UMI) **Document type:** trade publication.
—KR SourceOne.

330.9　　　US　　ISSN 1080-9813
HG4521
FINANCIAL TIMES GLOBAL INVESTORS' DIGEST. (Supplement included: Mid-Month Global Financial Report) m. $695 (includes supplement) (foreign $731). Capitol Publications, Inc., 1101 King St., Ste. 444, Alexandria, VA 22314. TEL 800-327-7205. FAX 800-645-4104. **Document type:** trade publication.
Formerly: Global Investor's Digest.
Description: Provides forecasts and analyses for interest rates, bond prices and equity prices in 23 nations, including all major, minor and emerging markets.

332.6　　　DK　　ISSN 0106-1798
FINANS - INVEST. 10/yr. Fabtidskriftet Finans - Invest, Holmstrupaardvej 140, DK-8210 Aarhus V, Denmark. TEL 38-33-80-00. FAX 38-33-82-80. adv. circ. 3,300.

332.6　　　SZ　　ISSN 0015-220X
FINANZ UND WIRTSCHAFT. 1928. s-w. 235 SFr. (foreign 301 SFr.). Verlag Finanz und Wirtschaft AG, Hallwylstr. 71, Postfach, CH-8021 Zurich, Switzerland. TEL 41-1-2983535. FAX 41-1-2983500. Ed. Peter Bohnenblust; Pub. Gerhart Isler. adv.; bk.rev. circ. 38,441. **Document type:** newspaper.
Description: Covers the national and international markets, stock markets, banking, art and automobile markets.

332.65　　　GW
FINANZWOCHE KAPITALBRIEF FUER ANLEGER IN DEUTSCHLAND UND DER SCHWEIZ. 1978. w. DM.540. Finanzwoche GmbH, Georg-Kalb-Str. 9, 82049 Pullach, Germany. TEL 089-7911076. FAX 089-7911653. (back issues avail.) **Document type:** newspaper.

332.6　　　US
FINVESTOR REPORT - STOCKS AROUND FIVE DOLLARS. 1985. m. $50. Nils G. Peterson, Ed. & Pub., 7322 Pinewood St., Falls Church, VA 22046.
Description: Provides information on inexpensive stocks that are typically not followed by Wall Street brokerage houses.

332.6　　　US
FIVE PERCENT OWNERSHIP PORTFOLIOS. m. $495. C D A Investment Technologies, Inc., 1355 Piccard Dr., Rockville, MD 20850. TEL 800-232-6362. FAX 301-590-1350. circ. 200. (also avail. in magnetic tape; back issues avail.)
●Also available online.
Former titles: Spectrum 5: Five Percent Ownership Based on 13D, 13G, and 14D-1 Filings; (until 1980): Spectrum Five: Five per Cent Beneficial Ownership.

332.632　　　US　　ISSN 1065-3414
HG4501
FIVE STAR INVESTOR. 1992. m. $65 in U.S.; Canada and Mexico $80; elsewhere $105. Morningstar, Inc., 225 W. Walker Dr., Ste. 400, Chicago, IL 60606. TEL 312-696-6000. FAX 312-696-6001. Ed. Kylelane Purcell. circ. 45,000.
Description: Provides performance data and ratings on 500 select open- and closed-end funds, in a format geared towards the individual investor. Features commentaries on various fund-related subjects.

332.6　　　US　　ISSN 1073-6727
HG4650
THE FIXED INCOME ALMANAC.* 1993. a. Probus Publishing Co., 1333 Burr Ridge Pkwy., Burr Ridge, IL 60521-6489. TEL 312-868-1100. FAX 312-868-6250. Ed. Livingston Douglas. **Document type:** directory.

FLORIDA SECURITIES LAW. see *LAW — Corporate Law*

332.6 664　　　US
FOOD & BEVERAGE MONITOR. w. free to qualified personnel. Donaldson, Lufkin & Jenrette, 140 Broadway, New York, NY 10005. TEL 212-504-4209. Ed. Bill Leach. circ. controlled.
Description: Provides updates on industry performance for investment research purposes.

332.6 664　　　US
FOOD & BEVERAGE SPOTLIGHT. m. free to qualified personnel. Donaldson, Lufkin & Jenrette, 140 Broadway, New York, NY 10005. TEL 212-504-4209. Ed. Bill Leach. stat.; circ. controlled.
Description: Provides comprehensive information on industry performance for investment research purposes.

332.6　　　　US
FORD DATA BASE REPORT. 1982. w. $1,800. Ford Investor Services, 11722 Sorrento Valley Rd., Ste. 1, San Diego, CA 92121. TEL 619-755-1327. Ed. David C. Morse.
Description: Contains all the information from the Ford Data Base, a computerized database covering 2,680 common stocks, with 93 data items per stock.

332.6　　　　US
FORD INVESTMENT MANAGEMENT REPORT. 1974. m. $240. Ford Investor Services, 11722 Sorrento Valley Rd., Ste. 1, San Diego, CA 92121. TEL 619-755-1327. Ed. David C. Morse. (also avail. in magnetic tape; diskette format; back issues avail.)
●Also available online.
Description: Financial data on common stocks plus proprietary inputs.

332.6　　　　US
FORD VALUE REPORT. 1970. m. $120. Ford Investor Services, 11722 Sorrento Valley Rd., Ste. 1, San Diego, CA 92121. TEL 619-755-1327. Ed. David C. Morse. (also avail. in magnetic tape; diskette format; back issues avail.)
●Also available online.
Description: Financial data on common stocks.

332.6　　　　US
FOREIGN ACTIVITY REPORT. q. $75 to non-members; members $50. Securities Industry Association, 120 Broadway, 35th Fl., New York, NY 10271. TEL 212-608-1500. Ed. David G. Strongin. (back issues avail.) **Indexed:** SRI. **Document type:** trade publication.
Description: Tracks purchases and sales of U.S. securities by foreign investors.

332.6　　　　US
FOREIGN EXCHANGE LETTER. w. $1595 (Canada $1625; elsewhere $1670). Institutional Investor Newsletter, 477 Madison Ave., New York, NY 10022. TEL 212-224-3233. FAX 212-224-3353. **Document type:** newsletter.
Description: Covers foreign investment and currency plans of funds and corporations worldwide.

332.6　　　　AT
FOREIGN INVESTMENT IN AUSTRALIA. 1994. irreg. (3-4/yr.). Aus.$495. L B C Information Services, 50 Waterloo Rd., N. Ryde, N.S.W. 2113, Australia. TEL 61-2-99366444. FAX 61-2-98889706. TELEX ASBOOK 27995. Ed. A. Millhouse. (looseleaf format)
Description: Covers regulation of foreign investment in Australia.

332.6   PK   ISSN 0071-7339
FOREIGN LIABILITIES, ASSETS AND FOREIGN INVESTMENTS IN PAKISTAN. (Text in English) a. Rs.17($3.50) State Bank of Pakistan, Central Directorate, Public Relations Department, I.I. Chundrigar Rd., P.O. Box 4456, Karachi, Pakistan. TEL 92-2414141. FAX 92-2417865. TELEX 2754 SBPK PK. **Document type:** government publication.

FOREIGN TRADE AND INVESTMENT. see *LAW — International Law*

332.6   II
FORTUNE INDIA;* premier investment magazine. (Text in English) 1982. fortn. newsstand price: Rs.10. Fortune Publications Pvt. Ltd., 98 Mody St., Karachiwala Bldg., Bombay 400 001, India. TEL 22-2049870. Ed. Deven Malkan. adv.: B&W page Rs.12000, color page Rs.24000; trim 240 x 180; adv. contact: Semira Hajare. circ. 21,000.
    Description: Covers economic business affairs and investment.

FORUM (NEW YORK, 1986). see *BUSINESS AND ECONOMICS*

332.6   FR   ISSN 0533-0742
FRANCE. COMMISSION DES OPERATIONS DE BOURSE. RAPPORT AU PRESIDENT DE LA REPUBLIQUE. irreg. Imprimerie Nationale, B.P. 514, 59505 Douai Cedex, France. FAX 27-93-70-96.

332.67   US
FRANKLIN RESEARCH'S INSIGHT; the advisory letter for concerned investors. 1983. m. $225. Franklin Research and Development Corporation, 711 Atlantic Ave., Boston, MA 02111. TEL 800-548-5684. Ed. Eric Becker. adv. contact: A. Brosco. bk.rev.; charts; stat.; index. circ. 800. (looseleaf format; back issues avail.) Indexed: High.Educ.Curr.Aware.Bull. **Document type:** newsletter.
    Former titles: Franklin's Insight; Insight (ISSN 0742-5244)
    Description: News and research pertaining to capital investment, with analyses of the social and financial performance of selected companies and quarterly profiles on specific industries.

332.6   US   ISSN 0740-0276
FRASER OPINION LETTER. 1949. fortn. $100. Fraser Management Associates, Inc., 309 S. Willard St., Box 494, Burlington, VT 05402. TEL 802-658-0322. FAX 802-658-0260. Ed. James L. Fraser. bk.rev.; charts. (processed) **Document type:** newsletter.
    Formerly: Neill Letter of Contrary Opinion (ISSN 0028-2553)
    Description: Contrary comments in a survey of current economic events and trends in business, finance and public thinking.

332.6   US   ISSN 1073-0796
FREEMARKET GOLD & MONEY REPORT. 1987. 20/yr. $220. Box 4634, Greenwich, CT 06830. TEL 203-661-5474. Ed. James Turk; Pub. James Turk. **Document type:** newsletter.
    Description: Provides specific advice on monetary and investment matters.

FREQUENTLY ASKED QUESTIONS ABOUT R E I TS. see *REAL ESTATE*

332.6   US
FUND DECODER. w. $1295 (Canada $1325; elsewhere $1370). Institutional Investor Newsletters, 477 Madison Ave., New York, NY 10022. TEL 212-224-3233. FAX 212-224-3353. **Document type:** newsletter.
    Description: Covers trends in mutual fund marketing and analysis of new fund filings.

332.6   US   ISSN 1076-4135
FUND DIRECTIONS. m. Institutional Investor Newsletters, 477 Madison Ave., New York, NY 10022. TEL 212-224-3233. FAX 212-224-3353. **Document type:** newsletter.
    —CCC.
    Description: Identifies trends in the rapidly-changing fund environment and presents analyses of issues in fund governance for fund trustee.

332.6   US
FUND EXCHANGE. 1983. m. $125 free online. Paul A. Merriman & Associates, Inc., 1200 Westlake Ave., N., Ste. 700, Seattle, WA 98109. TEL 206-285-8877. URL: http://www.paulmerriman.com. Ed. Paul A. Merriman. R&P contact: Paul A. Merriman.
    •Also available online.
    Formerly: Fund Exchange Report.
    Description: Mutual fund market timing service.

332.6   US
FUND PROFIT ALERT. 1991. 12/yr. $200. Investment Research Institute Inc., 1259 Kemper Meadow Dr., Ste. 100, Cincinnati, OH 45240. TEL 513-589-3800; 800-448-2080. FAX 513-589-3810. E-mail: bernielRI@aol.com; URL: http://www.options-iri.com. Ed. Bernard G. Schaeffer; Pub. Robert D. Bergen. **Document type:** newsletter.
    Description: Utilizes a contrarian approach to provide strategic, carefully researched recommendations, sector analysis, market timing indicators and specific advice aimed to generate high profits in short time periods.

332.6   US   ISSN 1057-6703
FUND WATCH; the official guide to high-performance mutual funds. 1991. m. $80. Institute for Econometric Research, 2200 S.W. 10th St., Deerfield Beach, FL 33442-8799. TEL 954-421-1000; 800-442-9000. FAX 954-570-8200. Ed. Norman G. Fosback. charts; stat.; circ. 30,000 (paid). (back issues avail.) **Document type:** newsletter.
    Description: Charts of the price performance of leading equity mutual funds.

332.6   CN
THE FUNDLETTER. 1994. m. Can.$89. Hume Publishing Company Ltd., 604-2200 Yonge St., Toronto, ON M4S 2C6, Canada. TEL 800-733-4863. FAX 416-440-8268. Ed. A. Michael Keerma. **Document type:** newsletter.
    Description: Investment advice and recommendations on investing in mutual funds.

332.6   US   ISSN 1049-4332
HG4530
FUNDLINE. 1968. 12/yr. $127 (effective 1997). David H. Menashe & Co., Box 663, Woodland Hills, CA 91365. TEL 818-346-5637. Ed. David H. Menashe. charts; stat. circ. 2,000. (looseleaf format) **Document type:** newsletter.
    Formerly (until 1971): Menashe Timing Service.
    Description: Graphs and indexes depicting long-term indicators, trading oscillators, selling signals, boundaries, and composites for U.S., international, and gold funds.

332.6   US
FUNDS FOCUS. q. free to shareholders. Neuberger & Bermann Management Co., 605 Third Ave., New York, NY 10158. **Document type:** newsletter.
    Description: Offers views on the stock and bond markets, reports on how Neuberger & Bermann is responding, and profiles fund managers.

332.63   US   ISSN 0746-2468
HG6046   CODEN: FUTSEA
FUTURES (CEDAR FALLS); news, analysis and strategies for futures, options and derivatives traders. 1972. m. $39 in N. America; elsewhere $92. Oster Communications, Inc., 219 Parkade, Cedar Falls, IA 50613. TEL 319-277-1271. FAX 319-277-5803. E-mail: futuresm@aol.com. (Or: 250 S. Wacker Dr., Ste. 1150, Chicago, IL 60606. TEL 312-977-0999) Ed. Ginger Szala. adv.; bk.rev.; charts; illus.; stat.; circ. 62,000 (controlled). (also avail. in microform from UMI; reprint service avail.) Indexed: ABI Inform., B.P.I, BPIA, CLOSS, Educ.Admin.Abstr., Tr.& Indus.Ind.
    •Also available online. Vendor(s): Information Access Co.
    —BLDSC (4060.642000); KR SourceOne; UMI; UnCover.
    Formerly: Commodities (ISSN 0219-5550)

333.6   UK   ISSN 1352-1039
Kb
THE FUTURES & DERIVATIVES LAW REVIEW. 1994. q. £150 (effective 1996). Cavendish Publishing Ltd., The Glass House, Wharton St., London WC1X 9PX, England. TEL 44-171-278-8000. FAX 44-171-278-8080. Ed. Edward J. Swan. adv. contact: Annabel Jackson. bk.rev. circ. 1,000. **Document type:** academic/scholarly publication.
    —BLDSC (4060.651100).
    Description: Discusses legal issues worldwide concerning futures and derivatives.

332.64   CN   ISSN 1183-4242
FUTURES AND OPTIONS. (Text in French and English) 1985. q. free. Montreal Exchange, Derivative Products Department, Stock Exchange Tower, P.O. Box 61, 800 Victoria Sq., Montreal, PQ H4Z 1A9, Canada. TEL 514-871-3585. FAX 514-871-3531. Ed. Jose Slobodrian; Pub. Jean Laflamme. charts; stat.; circ. 2,400 (paid). (looseleaf format) **Document type:** newsletter.
    Formerly: Montreal Options Monthly Strategies.
    Description: Covers new products' development in the derivatives market, trading and hedging strategies using interest rates, derivative products targeted towards institutional and corporate end-users.

332.6   US   ISSN 0892-0869
FUTURES & OPTIONS FACTORS; the futures portfolio advisor. Variant title: Russel R. Wasendorf's Futures & Options Factors. (Text in English and Spanish) 1980. w. $239 (effective 1997). Russell R. Wasendorf, Ed. & Pub., P.O. Box 849, Cedar Falls, IA 50613. TEL 319-268-0441. FAX 319-277-0880. E-mail: Russ-Wasendorf@msn.com; URL: http://www.flight2quality.com. bk.rev.; circ. 2,000 (paid). (looseleaf format; back issues avail.) **Document type:** newsletter.
    Formerly: Futures Portfolio Advisor.

332.6   UK   ISSN 0953-6620
FUTURES & OPTIONS WORLD. 1982. m. $330. Metal Bulletin plc, Park House, Park Terrace, Worcester Park, Surrey KT4 7HY, England. TEL 44-171-827-9977. FAX 44-181-337-8943. Ed. Emma Davey. adv. circ. 11,000. **Document type:** trade publication.
    —SWETS.
    Formerly: Futures World (ISSN 0262-8376)
    Description: Contains articles and analysis of the investment and trade activities of the risk management market, with survey research findings, announcements of conferences and seminars, industry profiles, and news briefs.

332.6   US
FUTURES WORLD NEWS. Abbreviated title: F W N. 1981. d. Oster Communications, Inc., 219 Parkade, Cedar Falls, IA 50613. TEL 319-277-1271. FAX 319-277-5803. (Or: 250 S. Wacker Dr., Ste. 1150, Chicago, IL 60606. TEL 312-977-0999) Ed. Terry Wooten.
    •Available only online.
    Formerly: Commodity World News.
    Description: News service available via computer terminal.

332.6   US
FUTURESCOPE. 1983. m. $1500. Decision Resources, Inc., 1100 Winter St., Waltham, MA 02154-1238. TEL 617-487-3737. FAX 617-487-5750. Dir. Jean Carbone.
    •Also available online. Vendor(s): Knight-Ridder Information, Inc. (File no. 192).
    Description: Executive portfolio that focuses on tomorrow's technologies, products and markets, as well as trends and emerging ideas.

332.6   US
GARSIDE FORECAST. 1972. bi-w. $145. Garside & Co., 5200 Irvine Blvd., Ste. 370, Irvine, CA 92720. TEL 714-259-1670. Ed. Ben C. Garside. **Document type:** newsletter.

332.6   GW   ISSN 0939-4966
GELDANLAGE BERATER. 1991. bi-m. DM.298. Verlag Norman Rentrop, Theodor-Heuss-Str. 4, 53177 Bonn, Germany. TEL 49-228-8205-0. FAX 49-228-364411. Ed. Hans Joachim Oberhettinger. (looseleaf format) **Document type:** bulletin.

GELDANLAGE UND STEUERN. see *BUSINESS AND ECONOMICS — Banking And Finance*

BUSINESS AND ECONOMICS — INVESTMENTS

GENERIC LINE. see *PHARMACY AND PHARMACOLOGY*

332.6 658   US   ISSN 1044-7121
GEORGESON REPORT. 1952. q. free. Georgeson & Company Inc., 88 Pine St., New York, NY 10005. FAX 212-440-9014. Ed. Ernest Sando. bk.rev.; circ. 8,000 (controlled). **Document type:** newsletter.
  Formerly: Trends in Management - Stockholder Relations (ISSN 0041-2406)

GET RICH NEWS. see *BUSINESS AND ECONOMICS — Small Business*

332.6   NE   ISSN 0922-7822
GIDS BIJ DE PRIJSCOURANT. 1894. a. fl.209. Uitgeverij Kluwer B.V., Postbus 23, 7400 GA Deventer, Netherlands. TEL 31-570-633155. FAX 31-570-633834. Ed. O. Blikslager. circ. 1,600. **Document type:** trade publication.
  Description: Covers stocks and bonds at the Amsterdam Stock Exchange.

GILBERT LAW SUMMARIES. SECURITIES REGULATION. see *LAW*

332   US
GLOBAL ASSET ALLOCATION. (Included in: International Index Research) m. Salomon Brothers, Inc., 7 World Trade Center, New York, NY 10048. TEL 212-783-7000. charts; stat.
  Description: Covers both equity and bond markets including the impact of fiscal conditions on these markets.

332.6   US   ISSN 1047-8736
HG3810
GLOBAL CUSTODIAN. 1989. q. $80. Asset International, Inc., 125 Greenwich Ave., Greenwich, CT 06830. TEL 203-629-5014. FAX 203-629-5024. TELEX 262356 ASIN UR. Ed. Charles Ruffel. adv. circ. 17,000. **Document type:** trade publication.
  —BLDSC (4195.385000); UnCover. **CCC.**
  Description: For investors, custodial and operational decision-makers in the international investment industry.

GLOBAL INVESTMENT TECHNOLOGY. see *BUSINESS AND ECONOMICS — Banking And Finance*

GLOBAL INVESTOR. see *BUSINESS AND ECONOMICS — Banking And Finance*

332.6   US   ISSN 1055-9671
HG1
GLOBAL MARKET PERSPECTIVE. 1991. m. $599 ($645 in Europe; elsewhere $899). Elliott Wave International, Box 1618, Gainesville, GA 30503. TEL 770-536-0309. Ed. Robert R. Prechter, Jr. **Document type:** newsletter.
  Description: Provides the intermediate to long-term technical outlook for all major world stock, bond and currency markets, as well as the outlook for precious metals, and economic and social trends.

332.6   US
GLOBAL MONEY MANAGEMENT. 1990. bi-w. $1595. Institutional Investor Newsletters, 477 Madison Ave., New York, NY 10022. TEL 212-224-3233. FAX 212-224-3353. Ed. Tom Lomont. adv. (back issues avail.) **Document type:** newsletter.
  Description: Covers the international fund management industry.

332.6   UK
GLOBAL TRENDS. 1980. m. £445. Investment Research of Cambridge Ltd., 28 Panton St., Cambridge CB2 1DH, England. FAX 0223-329806. circ. 200.
  Former titles (until 1990): World Markets Service (ISSN 0961-0472) & International Investment Guide (ISSN 0144-5324)

332.645   US   ISSN 0743-8508
GOLD MINING STOCK REPORT. 1983. m. $159. Gold Mining Stock Report, Box 1217, Lafayette, CA 94549. TEL 510-283-4848. FAX 510-283-8901. Ed. Robert Bishop. stat. circ. 5,000. (looseleaf format)
  Formerly (until Mar. 1989): Penny Mining Stock Report.
  Description: Specializes in gold and precious metals mining shares. Includes specific recommendations and follow-ups.

332.6   US   ISSN 0891-2351
GOLD STOCKS ADVISORY. 1987. m. $150 (effective 1997); newsstand price: $15. (Agora Inc.) Marketing and Publishing Associates, Ltd., 23-00 Rte. 208, Fairlawn, NJ 07410. TEL 201-794-8886. FAX 201-794-1221. Ed. Paul Sarnoff. Pub. N.S. Hayden. (back issues avail.) **Document type:** newsletter.
  Description: Carries analysis and recommendation of gold mining stocks on a global basis.

332.6   US   ISSN 0742-4515
HG4528
GOOD MONEY; the newsletter for socially concerned investors. 1982. bi-m. $75 subscr. includes Netback. Good Money Publications, Inc., Box 363 UIP, Worcester, VT 05682-0363. TEL 802-223-3911; 800-535-3551. FAX 802-223-8949. Ed. Ritchie P. Lowry. abstr.; bibl.; charts; stat. (back issues avail.)

332.632   US
GOOD MONEY'S SOCIAL FUNDS GUIDE. a. $30. Good Money Publications, Inc., Box 363 UPI, Worcester, VT 05682. TEL 802-223-3911; 800-535-3551. FAX 802-223-8949. Ed.Bd.
  Description: Guide to socially screened mutual funds. Includes an analysis of the holdings of social and environmental funds.

332.6   US   ISSN 0743-5185
GOURGUES REPORT. 1984. m. $125. Harold W. Gourgues Co., Inc., Box 81668, Atlanta, GA 30366-1668. TEL 770-772-0110. Ed. Ron Davis. circ. 600. **Document type:** newsletter.

GOVERNMENT WORLD. see *BUSINESS AND ECONOMICS — Economic Situation And Conditions*

332.6   US
GRANVILLE MARKET LETTER.* 46/yr. $250. Box 413006, Kansas City, MO 64141. TEL 800-876-5388. Ed. Joseph E. Granville.

332.6327   US
GRAPHIC FUND FORECASTER. 1984. w., m. versions avail. $129 for m. letter, $229 for weekly. Time Your Switch Management Services, 6 Pioneer Circle, Andover, MA 01810. TEL 508-470-3511; 800-532-2322. E-mail: 76772,477@compuserve.com. Ed. Fred W. Hohn; Pub. Fred W. Hohn. R&P contact: Fred W. Hohn. adv. contact: Fred W. Hohn. **Document type:** newsletter.
  Formerly (until Dec. 1988): T Y S Fund Letter.
  Description: Uses the market-timing approach for Fidelity and Invesco funds. Offers hotline and exchange management service.

332.6   CN   ISSN 0046-631X
GRAPHOSCOPE. bi-m. Can.$262.70 (U.S. Can.$282.20; overseas Can.$288.20) (effective 1997); newsstand price: Can.$47. Canadian Analyst Ltd., 30 Duncan St., Toronto, ON M5V 2C3, Canada. TEL 416-971-6543; 800-348-6661. FAX 416-598-0049. E-mail: call@grapscope.com; URL: http://www.graphoscope.com. **Document type:** trade publication.
  Description: Compilation of vital statistics to aid decision-making in the stock market.

332.6   US
▼ **GREEN (NEW YORK);** personal finance for the unashamed. 1995. q. $10 (foreign $20). 245 Eighth Ave., Ste. 286, New York, NY 10011. TEL 201-746-0395. FAX 201-746-0972. E-mail: greenzine@aol.com; URL: http://members.aol.com/greenzine. Ed. Ken Kurson; Pub. John Packel. R&P contact: Ken Kurson. adv. contact: John Packel. circ. 15,000 (paid). **Document type:** newsletter.
  Description: Features jargon-free, no-hype investment and money management advice on topics including first time home-buying, mutual funds, and how to follow stocks.

GREEN MONEY JOURNAL. see *BUSINESS AND ECONOMICS — Banking And Finance*

332.6   US
GROUND FLOOR.* 1981. m. $144. Hirsch Organization Inc., Box 2069, River Vale, NJ 07675-9001. TEL 201-767-4100. FAX 201-767-7337. Ed. Yale Hirsch. circ. 5,000.
  Description: Focuses on dynamic companies with fast growth potential, but still young enough to have most of their growth ahead of them. Each issue includes our performance records as well as current advice, stock recommendations and follow-ups.

332.6   BE
GROUPE BRUXELLES LAMBERT. ANNUAL REPORTS. 1979. a. Groupe Bruxelles Lambert, S.A., 24 Ave. Marnix, 1000 Brussels, Belgium. TEL 32-2-5472352. FAX 32-2-5472285. **Document type:** corporate report.

332.6   BE
GROUPE BRUXELLES LAMBERT. INTERIM REPORTS. 1988. a. Groupe Bruxelles Lambert, S.A., 24 Ave. Marnix, 1000 Brussels, Belgium. TEL 32-2-5472352. FAX 32-2-5472285. **Document type:** corporate report.

332.678   US   ISSN 0017-4831
GROWTH FUND GUIDE; the investors guide to dynamic growth funds. 1968. m. $99. Growth Fund Research, Inc., Box 6600, Rapid City, SD 57709. TEL 605-341-1971. Ed. Walter J. Rouleau. charts; stat. **Document type:** newsletter.
  Description: Includes value-ratio programs and telephone hotline.

332.6   US   ISSN 1073-7626
HG4501
GROWTH STOCK OUTLOOK. 1965. s-m. $195 subscr. includes Junior Growth Stocks, New Issue Digest, Bank Stock Analyst. Growth Stock Outlook, Inc., 4405 East-West Hwy., Ste. 305, Bethesda, MD 20814. TEL 301-654-5205. Ed. Charles Allmon. charts; stat. **Document type:** newsletter.
  Description: Provides data on stock earnings, sales, price-earnings ratios, dividends, book values, return on shareholder equity, and institutional holdings. Recommends specific companies for long-term investment.

GRUNDLAGEN UND PRAXIS DES BANK- UND BOERSENWESENS. see *BUSINESS AND ECONOMICS — Banking And Finance*

332.6   IT
GUIDA DEL MERCATO RISTRETTO; the unlisted market guide. 1962. a. $130. Databank S.p.A., SASIP Division, Via Spartaco 19, 20135 Milan, Italy. FAX 392-55183152. TELEX 24217 DTBK I.
  Description: Lists 80 companies quoted on the official Italian second market and traded over-the-counter.

GUIDE TO AMERICAN STATE AND LOCAL LAWS ON SOUTH AFRICA. see *LAW — International Law*

332.6   US   ISSN 1080-4188
GUIDE TO DIVIDEND REINVESTMENT PLANS. 1986. q. $142. Evergreen Enterprises, Box 763, Laurel, MD 20725-0763. **Document type:** directory.

332.6 345   US
GUIDE TO S E C CRIMINAL CASES. a. Clark - Boardman - Callaghan, 375 Hudson St., New York, NY 10014. TEL 212-929-7500; 800-422-2101. FAX 212-924-0460. Ed. Marvin G. Pickholz.
  Description: Focuses on criminal cases involving issues regulated by the Securities Exchanges Commission.

HAMBROS DEALERS DIRECTORY (YEAR); foreign exchange treasury and bullion. see *BUSINESS AND ECONOMICS — Trade And Industrial Directories*

332.6   US   ISSN 0736-6264
HG4501
HANDBOOK FOR NO-LOAD FUND INVESTORS. 1981. a. $48 (with No-Load Fund Investor $139). No-Load Fund Investor, Inc., Box 318, Irvington-on-Hudson, NY 10533. TEL 914-693-7420; 800-252-2042. Ed. Sheldon Jacobs. charts; stat.
  Description: Covers no-load and low-load funds.

332.6   US   ISSN 1061-7094
HG4936
HANDBOOK OF U S GOVERNMENT AND FEDERAL AGENCY & RELATED MONEY MARKET INSTRUMENTS.* 1922. biennial. $29.95. Probus Publishing Co., 1333 Burr Ridge Pkwy., Burr Ridge, IL 60521-6489. TEL 312-868-1100. FAX 312-868-6250. Ed. Zwen A. Goy. circ. 60,000
  Formerly: Handbook of Securities of the United States Government and Federal Agencies and Related Money Market Instruments (ISSN 0072-9892)

BUSINESS AND ECONOMICS — INVESTMENTS

332.6   US   ISSN 0888-8574
HARMONIC RESEARCH. 1984. m. $240. 650 Fifth Ave., New York, NY 10019. TEL 212-484-2065. FAX 212-333-5741. Ed. Mason S. Sexton. **Document type:** newsletter.
  Description: Tracks stocks and bonds.

332.6 330.9   US
HARRY BROWNE'S SPECIAL REPORTS. 1974. 10/yr. $225. Harry Browne's Special Reports, Inc., Box 5586, Austin, TX 78763. TEL 800-531-5142. FAX 512-453-2015. Ed. Harry Browne. bk.rev.; charts; stat.; index. circ. 2,000. (looseleaf format; back issues avail.) **Document type:** newsletter.
  Description: Investment advice for short-term and long-term investors; covers stocks, bonds, precious metals, and foreign currencies.

332.6   US   ISSN 0745-7073
HAWAII INVESTOR. m. $15 (Continental U.S. $21). Honolulu Publishing Company, Ltd., 36 Merchant St., Honolulu, HI 96813. TEL 808-524-7400. FAX 808-531-2306. Ed. Lucy Jokiel.
  Formerly: Hawaii Real Estate Investor (ISSN 0273-5806)

332.6   NZ   ISSN 0110-9790
HEADLINER; investment newsletter. 1979. fortn. NZ.$81($50) Headliner Publishing Company Ltd., 2nd Fl., 64 Cashel St., P.O. Box 3762, Christchurch, New Zealand. TEL 64-3-3650301. FAX 64-3-3654255. Ed. W.P. Head. adv. circ. 10,000. (back issues avail.)
  Description: Covers domestic and international areas of investment, including New Zealand, Australian, Asian, US, and European stockmarkets, managed funds and bonds.

332.64   GR
HELLENIC INDUSTRIAL DEVELOPMENT BANK. INVESTMENT GUIDE. Spine title: E T B A Investment Guide. (Supplements avail.) (Text in English and Greek) 1961. irreg. Dr.500($5) Hellenic Industrial Development Bank S.A., 18 Panepistimiou Str., 106 72 Athens, Greece. TEL 3237-981. FAX 3621023. TELEX 215203 ETVA GR. circ. 3,000.
  Description: Provides information on the Greek economy and the country's infrastructure. Presents a concise picture of the legal and economic framework of business activity in Greece.

332.6   US
HERZFELD'S GUIDE TO CLOSED-END FUNDS. biennial. $25.95 (effective 1997). Thomas J. Herzfeld Advisors, Inc., Box 161465, Miami, FL 33116. TEL 305-271-1900; 800-854-3863. FAX 305-270-7040. Ed. Cecilia L. Gondor. adv. contact: Thomas Herzfeld. stat. **Document type:** newsletter.
  Description: Provides a complete guide from the basics of every risk level, including chapters on takeovers, hedging, and arbitrage. Also offers a complete statistical section comparing each fund by performance, expense ratio, income ratio, size, and management.

332.6   US
HIGH RETURN, LOW RISK INVESTMENTS; using stock selection and market timing. 1993. biennial. $25.95 (effective 1997). Thomas J. Herzfeld Advisors Inc., Box 161465, Miami, FL 33116. TEL 305-271-1900; 800-854-3863. FAX 305-270-1040. Eds. Thomas J. Herzfeld, Robert F. Drach.
  Description: Insider's perspective on playing the stock market.

332.6   US
HIGH TECH GROWTH FORECASTER. 1985. m. $195. 10467 Waterbird Way, Bradenton, FL 34209-3000. Ed. Robert S. Morrow; Pub. Robert S. Morrow. circ. 400. **Document type:** newsletter.
  Description: Advisory report featuring high tech and growth stock selections.

332.6   US   ISSN 0736-427X
HIGH TECH INVESTOR.* 1983. m. $180. (Barrington Research Associates) H M R Publishing Co., 161 N Clark St., Ste. 2950, Chicago, IL 60601-3221. Ed. James B. Powell.

332.6 330   US
HIGH TECHNOLOGY AND OTHER GROWTH STOCKS. 1981. m. $175. High Technology Growth Stocks, 402 Border Rd., Concord, MA 01742. TEL 508-371-0096. Ed. Bud Anderson.
  Description: Covers investments in fast growing companies.

332.6   US   ISSN 1055-9337
KF1477.Z9
HIGH-YIELD BONDS. a.? Practising Law Institute, 810 Seventh Ave., New York, NY 10019.

332.6   US
HIGHER RETURNS.* m. $89. Hirsch Organization Inc., Box 2069, River Vale, NJ 07675-9001. TEL 201-767-4100. FAX 201-767-7337. Ed. Yale Hirsch.
  Description: Covers the investment universe, discovering stocks and investment situations that offer high yields or rapid growth with lower risk. We also handpick the best investment ideas published elsewhere, and combine them with our own analysis.

332.6   US
HONE REPORT. 1980. m. $95. Money School, Box 473, Williamsburg, VA 23187. TEL 804-725-2234. Ed. Harry Hone. circ. 7,000. **Document type:** newsletter.
  Formerly: Money School Monitor.

HOOVER'S HANDBOOK OF EMERGING COMPANIES. see BUSINESS AND ECONOMICS — Trade And Industrial Directories

332.6   GW
HOPPENSTEDT AKTIENFUEHRER. 1868. a. DM.225 (effective 1997). Verlag Hoppenstedt GmbH, Havelstr. 9, 64295 Darmstadt, Germany. TEL 49-6151-380-0. FAX 49-6151-380-360. adv. **Document type:** trade publication.
  Formerly: Saling Aktienfuehrer (ISSN 0080-5572)

HOPPENSTEDT CHARTS. see BUSINESS AND ECONOMICS — Banking And Finance

332.6   GW   ISSN 0174-1284
HOPPENSTEDT KURSTABELLEN - KURSANALYSEN. 1947. m. DM.270 (effective 1997). Verlag Hoppenstedt GmbH, Havelstr. 9, 64295 Darmstadt, Germany. TEL 49-6151-380-0. FAX 49-6151-380-360. stat. **Document type:** trade publication.
  Formerly: Hoppenstedt-Monatskurstabellen (ISSN 0018-4896)

332.6   GW   ISSN 0933-3169
HOPPENSTEDT STOCK GUIDE GERMANY. (Text in English, German) 1987. a. DM.379 (effective 1997). Verlag Hoppenstedt GmbH, Havelstr. 9, 64295 Darmstadt, Germany. TEL 49-6151-380-0. FAX 49-6151-380-360. **Document type:** trade publication.
  Description: Current and historical characteristics in terms of financial analysis for the purpose of stock evaluation of the most important listed German stock corporations.

332.6   GW   ISSN 0073-3342
HOPPENSTEDT VADEMECUM DER INVESTMENTFONDS. 1961. a. DM.330 (CD-ROM DM.379) (effective 1997). Verlag Hoppenstedt GmbH, Havelstr. 9, 64295 Darmstadt, Germany. TEL 49-6151-380-0. FAX 49-6151-380-360. adv.; bk.rev. **Document type:** directory.
  ●Also available on CD-ROM.

HORSE OWNERS AND BREEDERS TAX MANUAL. see SPORTS AND GAMES — Horses And Horsemanship

332.6 300   US   ISSN 1048-1443
HD60.5.U5
HOW INSTITUTIONS VOTED ON SOCIAL RESPONSIBILITY SHAREHOLDER RESOLUTIONS. 1985. a. Investor Responsibility Research Center Inc., 1350 Connecticut Ave., N.W. Ste. 700, Washington, DC 20036. TEL 202-833-0700. FAX 202-833-3555. Ed. Ken Bertsch. R&P contact: Ken Bertsch.
  Formerly: How Institutions Voted on Shareholder Resolutions (ISSN 8755-2264)

332.6   BL
HOW TO INVEST IN BRAZIL. (Text in English) a., with q. supplements. $100. E S T E P E, Publishing Department, Rua Senador Dantas 19 Grupo 707, ZC-06 20000 Rio de Janeiro, Brazil.

332.6   US   ISSN 1042-4261
HG4515.9
HULBERT FINANCIAL DIGEST. 1980. m. $135. Agora, Inc., 105 W. Monumnet St., Baltimore, MD 21201. TEL 410-223-2611; 800-851-7100. FAX 410-223-2696. circ. 5,000. (back issues avail.)

332.6
HG201
I B C'S MONEY FUND REPORT. 1975. w. $1595 (effective 1997). I B C Financial Data, Inc., 290 Eliot St., Ashland, MA 01721. TEL 508-881-2800. FAX 508-881-0982. URL: http://www.ibcdata.com. (In U.K.: Eurostudy Publishing Co. Ltd., 9-13 St. Andrews St., London EC4A 3AE, England. TEL 44-71-936-2016) Ed. Tracy Burk; Pub. Kenneth B. Bohlin. R&P contact: Mike Krasner. charts. circ. 600. (looseleaf format; back issues avail.) **Document type:** newsletter.
  ●Also available online.
  —CCC.
  Former titles: Money Fund Report & I B C - Donoghue's Money Fund Report; Donoghue's Money Fund Report (ISSN 0197-7091); Butler's Money Fund Report (ISSN 0363-5716)
  Description: For investment professionals and bankers who compete with money funds. Reports on money fund portfolio holdings, 7-day and 30-day yields, and average maturities. Covers 1200-plus taxable and tax-free money funds registered in the U.S. and digests summary data for distinct groups of funds, from no-risk U.S. Treasury funds to more aggressive funds that buy second-tier paper.

332.6   US   ISSN 1082-2569
▼**I B C'S RATED MONEY FUND REPORT.** 1995. m. $995 (effective 1997). I B C Financial Data, Inc., 290 Eliot St., Ashland, MA 01721. TEL 508-881-2800. FAX 508-881-0982. URL: http://www.ibcdata.com. Ed. Tracy Burk; Pub. Kenneth B. Bohlin. R&P contact: Mike Krasner. circ. 130. (looseleaf format) **Document type:** newsletter.
  Description: Dedicated to improving cash management decision by focusing on the performance, trends and composition of rated money market mutual funds.

332.63   UK   ISSN 1355-8455
I C B SETTLEMENTS REPORT. (International Correspondent Banker) q. £260 (foreign £485) (effective 1996). Euromoney Publications plc., Nestor House, Playhouse Yard, London EC4V 5EX, England. TEL 44-171-779-8935. FAX 44-171-779-8541. (Dist. in US by: American Educational Systems, 173 W. 81st St., New York, NY 10024. TEL 800-717-2669. FAX 212-501-8926) **Document type:** newsletter.
  Description: Monitor of worldwide transaction standards devoted to international securities clearing and settlement.

332.6 340   US   ISSN 0258-3690
K9
I C S I D REVIEW: FOREIGN INVESTMENT LAW JOURNAL. 1986. s-a. $57 to institutions (effective 1997). (International Center for Settlement of Investment Disputes) Johns Hopkins University Press, Journals Publishing Division, 2715 N. Charles St., Baltimore, MD 21218. TEL 410-516-6987. FAX 410-516-6968. Ed. Ibrahim F.I. Shihata. adv. contact: Stasia Macsherry. bk.rev.; bibl. circ. 410. (reprint service avail. from WSH) **Indexed:** IBR. **Document type:** academic/scholarly publication.
  —BLDSC (4362.091525); SWETS; UMI; UnCover. CCC.
  Description: Consists of articles, comments, cases, and documents pertinent to investment law and international business transactions.

332.6   UK
I D E A S BULLETIN.* (Investment Diversification & Economic Analysis) 1986. 3/yr. £45. Headline Promotions, Osborn House, 21-25 Lower Stone St., Maidstone, Kent ME15 6YT, England. TEL 01-248-1404. FAX 01-353-0612. Ed. R. Hill. **Document type:** bulletin.

I F C DISCUSSION PAPER. (International Finance Corporation) see BUSINESS AND ECONOMICS — International Development And Assistance

BUSINESS AND ECONOMICS — INVESTMENTS

332.6   UK   ISSN 1362-1157
▼**I F R C - LLOYDS BANK PLC FRANCHISING IN BRITAIN REPORT.** Variant title: Franchising in Britain Report. 1995. q. £20. University of Westminster, International Franchise Research Centre, 35 Marylebone Rd., London NW1 5LS, England. TEL 44-171-911-5000. FAX 44-171-911-5059. URL: http://www.wmin.ac.uk/~purdyd. (Co-sponsor: Lloyds Bank Plc) Ed.Bd. **Document type:** trade publication.

332.6   US   ISSN 0892-6018
I R A - INDIVIDUAL RETIREMENT ACCOUNT STOCKS. 1972. a. $45. Elton Stephens Investments, 4016 S. Michigan St., South Bend, IN 46614-2544. TEL 219-291-3823. (Subscr. to: Box 476, South Bend, IN 46624-0476) Ed. Elton Stephens. index. circ. 3,000. (looseleaf format; back issues avail.) **Document type:** newsletter.
   Description: Lists IRA stocks, arranged by category.

332.6   US   ISSN 0739-2168
I R A REPORTER. (Individual Retirement Account) m. $115. Universal Pensions, Inc., Box 979, Brainerd, MN 56401-9965. TEL 218-829-4781; 800-346-3860. FAX 218-829-2106. Ed. Jennifer Norquist. **Document type:** newsletter.

332.6   HU
IDEAS FOR JOINT VENTURES. (Text in English) 1988. irreg. (2-3/yr.) $10 per no. (effective 1992). Magyar Kereskedelmi Kamara - Hungarian Chamber of Commerce, Kossuth L. ter 6-8, 1055 Budapest, Hungary. TEL 361-153-1225. FAX 361-153-1285. circ. 2,500.
   Description: Covers investments in 4 areas: Agricultural & Food industries; Travel & Trade, Service; Industry; and, Real Estate for rent or sale.

332.6   US
IN THE VANGUARD; investment views from the Vanguard Group. q. free to shareholders. Vanguard Group, Box 2600, Valley Forge, PA 19482. Ed. Brian S. Mattes. bk.rev.; charts; illus. **Document type:** newsletter.
   Description: Informs Vanguard shareholders of investment opportunities and offers general advice.

332.6   US
INCOME FUND OUTLOOK. 1981. m. $100. Institute for Econometric Research, 2200 S.W. 10th St., Deerfield Beach, FL 33442-8799. TEL 954-421-1000; 800-442-9000. FAX 954-570-8200. Ed. Norman G. Fosback. charts; stat.; circ. 30,000 (paid) **Document type:** newsletter.
—CCC.
   Former titles (until 1994): Income and Safety (ISSN 0891-1215); Money Fund Safety Ratings (ISSN 0730-2894)
   Description: Offers advice and recommendations on income-oriented mutual funds, money market mutual funds, bank certificates of deposit and other fixed-income investments.

332.6   US   ISSN 0890-0515
INCOME INVESTOR PERSPECTIVES.* 1985. fortn. $119. Uniplan, Inc., 839 Jefferson St., Ste. 200, Milwaukee, WI 53202-3733. TEL 414-529-0675. Ed. Richard Imperiale.
   Description: Overview of events and trends that have an impact on credit and stock markets.

INCOME OPPORTUNITIES; America's best money-making ideas. see *BUSINESS AND ECONOMICS — Small Business*

332.6   US
INCOME SECURITIES ADVISOR. 1984. m. $145. Bond Investors Association, Inc., 617 N.W. 153rd St., Ste. 221, Miami Lakes, FL 33014-2435. TEL 305-557-1832. Ed. C. Richard Lehmann.
●Also available online.
   Incorporates (1984-1994): Bond Investors Newsletter; Which was formerly: B I A Newsletter (ISSN 1057-7513); **Former titles:** High Yield Securities Journal (ISSN 1065-089X); Preferred Stock Journal.

332.6   US   ISSN 0895-2183
INCOME STOCKS. 1972. a. $45. Elton Stephens Investments, 4016 S. Michigan St., South Bend, IN 46614-2544. TEL 219-291-3823. (Subscr. to: Box 476, South Bend, IN 46624-0476) Ed. Elton Stephens. index. circ. 3,000. (looseleaf format; back issues avail.) **Document type:** newsletter.

332.6   US
INDEPENDENT THINKER. 1985. m. $65. Box 40325, Rochester, NY 14604. TEL 716-427-0350. Ed. Rama S. Marda.
   Description: Covers portfolios of common stocks for long-term gains.

332.6   II
INDIA INVESTMENT OPPORTUNITIES. (Text in English) 1987. w. newsstand price: Rs.4. Regent Publishers Pvt. Ltd., 1st Fl., Bank Bldg., 17-B Horniman Circle, Fort, Bombay 400 023, India. TEL 2664075. Pub. Rusi J. Daruwala. circ. 55,000.

332.6   US   ISSN 1049-4596
HG4751
INDIVIDUAL INVESTOR.* 1981. m. $29.95. Financial Data Systems, Inc., 333 Seventh Ave., 5th Fl., New York, NY 10001-5004. TEL 212-689-2777. FAX 212-689-6663. adv. circ. 75,000.
   Formerly (until 1990): Penny Stock Journal (ISSN 0745-4457)
   Description: Investor's guide to value and growth among America's small companies. Features in-depth stories on dynamic and undervalued stocks. Reviews the best performing mutual funds.

332.6 621.381   US
INDIVIDUAL INVESTOR'S GUIDE TO COMPUTERIZED INVESTING. 1900. a. $24.95. American Association of Individual Investors, 625 N. Michigan Ave., Ste. 1920, Chicago, IL 60611. TEL 312-280-0170. FAX 312-280-1625. E-mail: aaiigenl@aol.com; URL: http://www.aaii.org. Ed. John Bajkowski. R&P contact: Anna Chan. circ. 51,000 (paid). **Document type:** consumer publication.
   Formerly: Individual Investor's Microcomputer Resource Guide.

332.6327   US
INDIVIDUAL INVESTOR'S GUIDE TO LOW-LOAD MUTUAL FUNDS. 1900. a. $24.95. American Association of Individual Investors, 625 N. Michigan Ave., Ste. 1920, Chicago, IL 60611. TEL 312-280-0170. FAX 312-280-1625. E-mail: aaiigenl@aol.com; URL: http://www.aaii.com. R&P contact: Anna Chan. circ. 175,000 (paid). **Document type:** consumer publication.
   Formerly: Individual Investor's Guide to No-Load Mutual Funds.
   Description: Provides ten-year fund data on over 850 mutual funds.

332.6   CC
INDUSTRIAL INVESTMENT HONG KONG. (Editions in English, French, German, Japanese) 1978. biennial. free to qualified personnel. Hong Kong Government Industry Department, 14-Fl., Ocean Centre, 5, Canton Rd., Tsimshatsui, Kowloon, Hong Kong, People's Republic of China. TEL 852-737-2434. FAX 852-730-4633. TELEX 50151-INDHK-HX. illus.; stat. circ. 15,000. **Document type:** government publication.
   Description: Promotes industrial investment in Hong Kong.

INDUSTRIES IN TRANSITION. see *BUSINESS AND ECONOMICS — Production Of Goods And Services*

332.6   CN   ISSN 1188-0996
INDUSTRY CANADA RESEARCH SERIES. (Text in English, French) 1991. irreg. price varies. (Industry Canada) University of Calgary Press, 2500 University Dr. N.W., Calgary, AB T2N 1N4, Canada. TEL 403-220-7578. FAX 403-282-0085. URL: http://www.ucalgary.ca/ucpress. (Subscr. to: UBC Press, 6344 Memorial Rd., Vancouver, BC V6T 1Z2, Canada. TEL 604-822-5959. FAX 604-822-6083) Dir. Shirley A. Onn. R&P contact: Sharon Boyle. TEL 403-220-5284. adv. contact: Sharon Boyle. **Document type:** academic/scholarly publication, trade publication.
   Formerly: Investment Canada Research Series (ISSN 1188-0988)
   Description: Provides a forum for the analysis of key microeconomic challenges facing the Canadian economy, with the intent of aiding constructive public policy determination in the area.

332.6   US
INDUSTRY GROUP MARKET VALUES. w. $1175. Standard & Poor's (Subsidiary of: McGraw-Hill Companies, Inc.), 25 Broadway, New York, NY 10004. TEL 212-208-8000. Ed. Carol Levine; Pub. Thomas Nugent. **Document type:** trade publication.
●Also available online.
Also available on CD-ROM.
   Formerly: Industry Group Market Values and Shares Outstanding.
   Description: Supplies market values for each industry included in the Standard & Poor's 500 Index.

INDUSTRY REVIEW. see *BUSINESS AND ECONOMICS — Abstracting, Bibliographies, Statistics*

332.6   CN
THE INFORMED INVESTOR. m. Can.$89 (effective 1997). Canadian Analyst Ltd., 30 Duncan St., Toronto, ON M5V 2C3, Canada. TEL 416-971-6543; 800-348-6661. FAX 416-598-0049. **Document type:** trade publication.
   Description: Provides timely, concise and unbiased opinions on Canadian mutual funds.

INFRASTRUCTURE FINANCE; the magazine for global development. see *BUSINESS AND ECONOMICS — International Development And Assistance*

332.6   UK   ISSN 0955-1697
INITIATIVE EUROPE MONITOR. 1988. bi-m. £475. Initiative Europe, 69 Bondway, London SW8 1SQ, England. TEL 44-171-735-9838. FAX 44-171-80-0802. **Document type:** trade publication.

332.6   SZ
INKASSO-PRAXIS. q. Verband Schweizerischer Inkasso- und Treuhandinstitut, Seeburgstr. 20, CH-6002 Lucerne, Switzerland. TEL 041-311055.

INSIDE M B S & A B S. see *BUSINESS AND ECONOMICS — Banking And Finance*

332.6   US   ISSN 8756-0003
INSIDE MORTGAGE FINANCE. 1984. 48/yr. $645 (effective 1997). Inside Mortgage Finance Publications, Box 42387, Washington, DC 20015. TEL 301-951-1240. FAX 301-656-1709. URL: http://users.aol.com/imfpubs. Ed. Guy D. Cecala; Pub. Guy D. Cecala. R&P contact: Didi Parks. stat.
   Description: Contains complete coverage and analysis of trends and developments affecting residential mortgage finance. Studies regulatory, legislative and market developments impacting lending, servicing and securitization.

332.67   US
INSIDER HOLDINGS. s-a. $250. C D A Investment Technologies, Inc., 1355 Piccard Dr., Rockville, MD 20850. TEL 800-232-6362. FAX 301-590-1329. circ. 200. (also avail. in magnetic tape)
●Also available online.
   Formerly: Spectrum 6: Insider Ownership.

332.678   US   ISSN 0730-2908
INSIDERS; America's most knowledgeable investors. 1980. s-m. $100. Institute for Econometric Research, 2200 S.W. 10th St., Deerfield Beach, FL 33442-8799. TEL 954-421-1000; 800-442-9000. FAX 954-570-8200. Ed. Norman G. Fosback. charts; stat. circ. 7,000. **Document type:** newsletter.
—CCC.
   Description: Summary of insider trading activity over the past 12 months for more than 1000 listed and over-the-counter stocks, with specific buy and sell recommendations.

INSOLVENCY BULLETIN. see *BUSINESS AND ECONOMICS*

332.6   US
INSTITUTIONAL HOLDINGS OF OIL STOCKS. 1984. m. (Argus Research Group) Vickers Stock Research Corp., 226 New York Ave., Huntington, NY 11743.

BUSINESS AND ECONOMICS — INVESTMENTS

332.6 US ISSN 0020-3580
HG4501 CODEN: ITIVAK
INSTITUTIONAL INVESTOR; the magazine for finance and investment. (International edition avail. (ISSN 0192-5660)) m. $380 (effective July 1996). Institutional Investor, Inc., 488 Madison Ave., New York, NY 10022. TEL 212-224-3570. FAX 212-224-3592. Ed. David Wachtel. adv.: B&W page $22425, color page $31628. charts; illus. circ. 136,952. (also avail. in microform from UMI; reprint service avail. from UMI) Indexed: ABI Inform., Account.Ind. (1974-), B.P.I., BPIA, Bus.Ind., CAD CAM Abstr., Environ.Abstr., Key to Econ.Sci., Manage.Cont., P.A.I.S., Risk Abstr., SSCI, Tr.& Indus.Ind., World Bank.Abstr. **Document type**: trade publication.
●Also available online. Vendor(s): Information Access Co.
Also available on CD-ROM.
—BLDSC (4523.345000); KR SourceOne; SWETS; UMI; UnCover. **CCC.**
 Incorporates (1970-19??): Corporate Financing (ISSN 0010-8960).

332.6 US ISSN 0192-5660
HG4501
INSTITUTIONAL INVESTOR INTERNATIONAL EDITION; the magazine for international finance and investment. 1976. m. $415. Institutional Investor, Inc., 488 Madison Ave., New York, NY 10022. TEL 212-224-3570. FAX 212-224-3592. Ed. David Cudaback. (also avail. in microform from UMI; reprint service avail. from UMI) Indexed: BPIA, Bus.Ind., Tr.& Indus.Ind.
●Also available on CD-ROM.
—BLDSC (4523.345100); KR SourceOne; SWETS; UMI; UnCover. **CCC.**

332.6 384 US ISSN 1068-9834
INTERACTIVE MULTIMEDIA INVESTOR. 1993. s-m. $695 (effective 1997). Paul Kagan Associates, Inc., 126 Clock Tower Place, Carmel, CA 93923. TEL 408-624-1536. FAX 408-625-3225. Ed. Paul Kagan.
 Description: Tracks and analyzes publicly held interactive and multimedia companies, tracks key industry subgroups through seven Kagan stock averages, growth projections, economic models of new corporate ventures, and exclusive reporting on industry developments.

INTER-AMERICAN TRADE AND INVESTMENT LAW. see *LAW — International Law*

THE INTER-CITY EXPRESS. see *REAL ESTATE*

332.6 FR ISSN 0153-9884
INTERETS PRIVES. m. 210 F. (foreign 280 F.) (effective Jan. 1997). Publications Fiduciaires, 100 rue LaFayette, 75485 Paris Cedex 10, France. TEL 33-1-41835252. FAX 33-1-41835253. URL: http://www.revuefiduciaire.fr. Ed. Christian Micheaud. **Document type**: consumer publication.
 Description: Gives its readers practical information to make better decisions in real estate, finance, and other personal interests.

332.6 US
INTERINVEST REVIEW AND OUTLOOK. 1976. m. $125. Interinvest Corporation, 84 State St., 7th Fl., Boston, MA 02109-2200. TEL 617-723-7870. FAX 617-723-1966. Ed. Hans Black. circ. 1,100. **Document type**: newsletter.
 Description: Discusses international markets, provides a U.S. stock market analysis, a bond market commentary, a discussion concerning precious metals markets, a currency comment, portfolio review, and an international political overview.

332.6 UK
THE INTERNATIONAL (LONDON, 1988). 1988. m. free to qualified personnel. Financial Times Business Information, Magazines (Subsidiary of: Financial Times Group), 2 Greystoke Pl., Fetter Ln., London EC4A 1ND, England. TEL 0171-405-6969. FAX 0171-405-5276. TELEX 296926 BUSINF G. Ed. Bruce Wraight. adv. contact: Ian Prickett. circ. 35,000 (controlled). (also avail. in microform from UMI) **Document type**: trade publication.
 Description: Offers investors outside the U.K. and U.S. tips and information on currency-exchange markets, U.K. domestic equities, offshore deposits, bonds, mutual funds, unit trusts, and international equities.

332.65 UK ISSN 1352-0431
INTERNATIONAL BOND INVESTOR. q. £100 (foreign $180) (effective 1996). Euromoney Publications plc., Nestor House, Playhouse Yard, London EC4V 5EX, England. TEL 44-171-779-8935. FAX 44-171-779-8541. (Dist. in US by: American Educational Systems, 173 W. 81st St., New York, NY 10024. TEL 800-717-2669. FAX 212-501-8926) **Document type**: trade publication.

332.6 341 US ISSN 0074-2163
INTERNATIONAL CENTRE FOR SETTLEMENT OF INVESTMENT DISPUTES. ANNUAL REPORT. (Editions also in French, Spanish) 1966. a. free. International Centre for Settlement of Investment Disputes, 1818 H St., N.W., Washington, DC 20433. TEL 202-458-1533. FAX 202-522-2615. TELEX ITT 440098 WORLDBANK. Ed. Antonio R. Parra. circ. 5,000. **Document type**: corporate report.

INTERNATIONAL FINANCIER. see *BUSINESS AND ECONOMICS — Banking And Finance*

THE INTERNATIONAL GUIDE TO TAXATION OF LIFE ASSURANCE AND MUTUAL FUNDS. see *BUSINESS AND ECONOMICS — Public Finance, Taxation*

INTERNATIONAL INVESTOR'S DIRECTORY; sourcebook for international investor. see *BUSINESS AND ECONOMICS — Trade And Industrial Directories*

332.6 US
▼**INTERNATIONAL JOINT VENTURES**. 1996. 2 base vols. (plus a. update). $350 for base vols.; update $140. (Center for International Legal Studies) Matthew Bender & Co., Inc., 2 Park Ave., New York, NY 10016. TEL 212-448-2000. E-mail: international@bender.com; URL: http://www.bender.com. Ed. Dennis Campbell.
 Description: Covers legal aspects of joint ventures in 37 countries plus the European Union, including alternate business structures, financing, restrictions, drafting of agreements and protections from foreign investors.

332.6 US ISSN 1051-8061
INTERNATIONAL MARKET ALERT.* d. price varies. International Reports, Inc. (Subsidiary of: I B C U.S.A.), 11300 Rockville Pike, Ste. 1100, Rockville, MD 20852-3035. TELEX 233139 RPTUR.
●Also available online. Vendor(s): Lexis-Nexis, NewsNet (FI58).
—**CCC.**
 Description: Provides in-depth coverage of developments in the world economy as well as forecasts for foreign exchange and U.S. interest rates.

332.6 US
INTERNATIONAL MARKET INDEXES. (Included in: Global Index Group) m. Salomon Brothers, Inc., 7 World Trade Center, New York, NY 10048. TEL 212-783-7000. charts; stat.

332.6 327 US
INTERNATIONAL MONEY & POLITICS. 1990. bi-m. $39. Sound Money Investors Inc., 531 Versailles Dr., Ste. 110, Maitland, FL 32751-4591. TEL 407-629-9229. Ed. Carl Surran. R&P contact: Carl Surran. adv. contact: Paul Zuromski. **Document type**: consumer publication.
 Description: Contrarian view of political developments and their impact on individual finance and investing.

332.6 US ISSN 0896-3010
K1114.A13
INTERNATIONAL SECURITIES REGULATION REPORT. 1987. bi-w. $795 (foreign $817) (effective 1997). L R P Publications, 747 Dresher Rd., Box 980, Horsham, PA 19044-0980. TEL 215-784-0941; 800-341-7874. FAX 215-784-9639. URL: http://www.lrp.com. Ed. Stephen Ackerman. (back issues avail.) **Document type**: newsletter.
●Also available online. Vendor(s): Lexis-Nexis.
—**CCC.**
 Description: Timely and in-depth reports from regulators in today's key financial centers and emerging markets. Monitors proposals and rule changes in every world market.

INTERNATIONAL TRADE AND INVESTMENT LETTER; trends in US policies, trade finance, and trading operations. see *BUSINESS AND ECONOMICS — International Commerce*

332.6 US
THE INTERNATIONAL WHO'S WHO OF INSTITUTIONS & MUTUAL FUNDS. a. $499. Carson Publications, 1790 Broadway, New York, NY 10019. **Document type**: directory.

332.6 IO ISSN 0535-4900
AP95.I5
INTISARI/DIGEST. 1962. m. Jalan Palmerah Selatan 22-26, Jakarta 10270, Indonesia. TEL 62-21-5490666. FAX 62-21-5494035. Ed. Rudy Badil; Pub. Yayasan Intisari. adv. contact: Panji Indra. circ. 141,000.

332 KO
INTRODUCTION TO THE KOREAN SECURITIES MARKET. (Text in English) irreg. free. Korea Stock Exchange, 33, Yoido-dong, Youngdeungpo-gu, Seoul 150-010, S. Korea. TEL 783-2271. FAX 786-0263. TELEX K28384 KOSTEX. illus. circ. 1,500.
 Formerly: Securities Market in Korea.

332.6 MX ISSN 1405-0595
INVERSION Y FINANZAS/FINANCE AND INVESTMENT. s-a. $20 (effective May 1996). Bolsa Mexicana de Valores, S.A. de C.V. - Mexican Stock Exchange, Paseo de la Reforma 255, 06500 Mexico DF, Mexico. TEL 525-7266791. FAX 525-5910534.
 Description: Covers issues about the securities industry.

332.6 VE
INVERSIONES, VENEZUELA. 1988. m. Bs.3648($150) (effective Jan. 1992). Edipress, C.A., Parque Cristal, Of. Local 5, Mezz.2, Ave. Francisco de Miranda, Los Palos Grandes, Caracas 1050A, Venezuela. TEL 582-285-4833. FAX 582-285-2513. (Subscr. to: Jet Cargo Int'l, Casella M-675, Box 020010, Miami, FL 33102) Ed. Arlene Shapiro. adv.: B&W page $2500, color page $3300; trim 218 x 288. circ. 25,000. (back issues avail.)
 Description: Informs the investment community, both private and institutional, on trends, opportunities and dangers. Gives rates and information on all capital market instruments, national and international.

332.6 MX ISSN 1405-0811
INVERSIONISTA MEXICANO. 1969. s-m. (22/yr.) $310 in US & Canada; elsewhere $350 (effective 1997). Inversionista Mexicano, S.A. de C.V., Felix Cuevas 301-204, Col. del Valle, Deleg. Benito Juarez, 03100 Mexico, D.F., Mexico. TEL 905-524-3131. FAX 905-524-3794. Ed. Hugo Ortiz Dietz; Pub. Ruben Sanchez Crespo. R&P contact: Baron Levin. adv. contact: Baron F. Levin. bk.rev. circ. 3,000. **Document type**: newsletter.
 Description: Investment business newsletter for company policy makers and money managers.

332.6 US ISSN 0896-4157
INVESTECH MARKET ANALYST. 1981. every 3 wks. $175. InvesTech Research, 2472 Birch Glen, Whitefish, MT 59937. TEL 406-862-7777; 800-955-8500. FAX 406-862-7707. Ed. James B. Stack. adv. contact: Stacy Tandy. **Document type**: newsletter.
 Description: Technical and monetary analysis focusing on mutual funds.

332.6 US ISSN 0896-4165
INVESTECH MUTUAL FUND ADVISOR; professional switching and timing analysis. 1987. every 3 wks. $175. InvesTech Research, 2472 Birch Glen, Whitefish, MT 59937. TEL 406-862-7777; 800-955-8500. FAX 406-862-7707. Ed. James B. Stack. adv. contact: Stacy Tandy. **Document type**: newsletter.

332.67 US
INVESTING FOR A BETTER WORLD. m. $29.95. Franklin Research & Development Corporation, 711 Atlantic Ave., 4th Fl., Boston, MA 02111. TEL 617-423-6655. Ed. Eric Becker; Pub. Elliott Sclar. **Document type**: newsletter.
 Description: Explores how social and environmental concerns can impact investment choices.

332 700 US ISSN 1053-4857
N8670
INVESTING IN ART.* 1990. a. Beacon Publishing, P.O. Box 273, Brimfield, MA 01010.

BUSINESS AND ECONOMICS — INVESTMENTS

332.6 330.968 SA
INVESTING IN KWAZULU NATAL. 1994. a. free. KwaNatal Marketing Initiative, P.O. Box 1105, Durban 4000, South Africa. TEL 27-31-9078700. FAX 27-31-9075685. E-mail: kmi@neptune.infolink.co.za; URL: http://www.lia.ca.za/users/kmi. Ed. J.A. Griesel. R&P contact: C.W. Rudman. maps. circ. 25,000.
  Description: Covers aspects of investment in the KwaZulu-Natal province, with the foreign investor in mind.
  Refereed Serial

332.6 GW ISSN 0935-1744
INVESTMENT. 1970. irreg. DM.168. Erich Schmidt Verlag GmbH & Co. (Berlin), Genthiner Str. 30G, 10785 Berlin, Germany. TEL 49-30-250085-0. FAX 49-30-25008521. (looseleaf format) **Document type:** bulletin.

332.6 JA
INVESTMENT ADVICE/TOSHI SODAN. (Text in Japanese) 1953. m. 7300 Yen. Jitsugyo no Nihon Sha, Ltd., 3-9 Ginza, 1-chome, Chuo-ku, Tokyo 104, Japan. TEL 81-3-3562-1967. FAX 81-3-3562-3200. E-mail: lebo2234@niftyserve.or.jp. Ed. Shinichi Nemoto.
  Formerly: Investment Consultation.

332.6 333.33 AT ISSN 0158-7021
INVESTMENT ADVISER. 1979. fortn. Aus.$185. Information Australia, 45 Flinders Lane, Melbourne, Vic. 3000, Australia. Ed. Kevin Forde. circ. 3,000.

332.67 US
INVESTMENT ADVISORS EQUITY CHARACTERISTICS. q. $525. C D A - Cadence, 1355 Piccard Dr., Rockville, MD 20850. TEL 301-975-9600. FAX 301-590-1350. (also avail. in magnetic tape)
●Also available online.
  Formerly: Investment Advisors Equity Performance.
  Description: Portrays the management style of over 500 investment advisors. Portfolios are evaluated in terms of P-E ratio, dividend yield, volatility, market capital of the underlying stockholdings, and commitment to major economic sectors.

332.6 SA
INVESTMENT ANALYSTS JOURNAL/BELEGGINGSONTLEDERS TYDSKRIF. (Text in Afrikaans, English) 1972. s-a. R.30. Investment Analysts Society of S.A., P.O. Box 4229, Honeydew 2040, South Africa. TEL 27-11-9573009. FAX 27-11-9572576. Ed. R.W. Bethlehem. adv. circ. 1,000. **Indexed:** Ind.S.A.Per.

INVESTMENT & MARKETING. see *BUSINESS AND ECONOMICS — Marketing And Purchasing*

332.6 PH
INVESTMENT AND OPERATING COST IN THE PHILIPPINES. (Text in English) 1990. a. Board of Investments, Industry & Investment Bldg., 385 Sen. Gil J. Puyat Ave., MCC P.O. Box 676, Makati, Metro Manila 3117, Philippines. TEL 818-1831. FAX 815-0702.

332.6 US
INVESTMENT BLUE BOOK. 1983. s-a. $145 per no. Securities Investigations, Inc., Box 888, 2626 Rte. 212, Woodstock, NY 12498. TEL 914-679-2300. FAX 914-679-2301. Ed. Stuart A. Ober; Pub. Stuart A. Ober. adv. circ. 10,000. (back issues avail.) **Document type:** directory.
  Former titles: Investment and Tax Shelter Blue Book; Tax Shelter Blue Book.
  Description: Professional directory for investment, mutual fund, money market, tax shelter and financial planning industries.

INVESTMENT BULLETIN; survey of mortgage commitments on commercial properties. see *INSURANCE*

332.6 UK ISSN 0951-3736
THE INVESTMENT CALENDAR. 1980. a. £12.50. Square Mile Publications Ltd., Park House, Park Terrace, Worcester Park, Surrey KT4 7HY, England. TEL 44-171-827-9977. FAX 44-181-337-8943. adv. contact: Phil Owen. bk.rev.; circ. 35,000 (paid). **Document type:** bulletin.

332.6 US ISSN 0739-6449
INVESTMENT COLUMN QUARTERLY. 1983. q. $125. N A R Publications, Box 233, Barryville, NY 12719. TEL 914-557-8713. FAX 914-557-6770. Ed. Nicholas A. Roes. R&P contact: Nicholas A. Roes. bk.rev.; charts. **Document type:** newsletter.
  Description: Provides investment guidance for long-term investors (not traders).

332.6 US ISSN 1068-9958
HG4530
INVESTMENT COMPANIES YEARBOOK. Variant title: C D A - Wiesenberger Investment Companies Service Yearbook: Management Results - Mutual Funds & Closed-End Companies. a. $295 (effective 1996). (Wiesenberger Services, Inc.) C D A - Wiesenberger (Subsidiary of: Thomson Financial Services), 1355 Piccard Dr., Rockville, MD 20850. TEL 800-232-2285. FAX 301-548-5105. E-mail: wies@cda.com. Ed. Daniel L. Phelps. charts; stat. **Document type:** trade publication.
  Former titles (until 1993): Investment Companies (C D A - Wiesenberger Firm) (ISSN 1070-2334); (until 1992): Investment Companies (ISSN 0075-0271).
  Description: Reports on the long-term performance of more than 8,300 mutual funds, 3,200 variable annuity subaccounts, and 500 closed-end investment companies.

332.6 US
INVESTMENT COMPANY PORTFOLIOS. 1973. q. $275. C D A Investment Technologies, Inc., 1355 Piccard Dr., Rockville, MD 20850. TEL 800-232-6362. FAX 301-590-1329. circ. 200. (also avail. in magnetic tape)
●Also available online.
  Former titles: Spectrum 2: U S and European Investment Company Portfolios; Spectrum Two: Investment Company Portfolios (ISSN 0091-6862)

332.6 US
INVESTMENT COMPANY STOCK HOLDINGS. 1973. q. $250. C D A Investment Technologies, Inc., 1355 Piccard Dr., Rockville, MD 20850. TEL 800-232-6362. FAX 301-590-1329. circ. 275. (also avail. in magnetic tape)
●Also available online.
  Former titles: Spectrum 1: U S and European Investment Company Stock Holdings Survey; Spectrum One: Stock Holdings Survey (ISSN 0091-6854)

332.6 US ISSN 0021-0080
HG4501
INVESTMENT DEALERS' DIGEST; news magazine of the financial community. 1935. w. $625 (Canada $700; elsewhere $900) (effective 1997). Investment Dealers' Digest, 2 World Trade Ctr., 18th Fl., New York, NY 10048. TEL 212-432-0045. E-mail: pmaher@iddis.com; subscribe@iddis.com. Ed. Philip Maher. R&P contact: Denise Robbins. adv. contact: Todd Miller. **Indexed:** P.A.I.S., PROMT. **Document type:** trade publication.
●Also available online. Vendor(s): Information Access Co., UMI.
—UMI; UnCover. **CCC**
  Formerly (until 1997): I D D.

332.6 JA
INVESTMENT ECONOMICS/TOSHI KEIZAI. 1933. fortn. Toshi-Keizai-Sha, Nihonbashi 2-14-9, Chuo-ku, Tokyo, Japan. Ed. Koichi Takei. adv. circ. 35,000.

332.6 CN ISSN 0840-9137
INVESTMENT EXECUTIVE. 1989. m. Can.$48 (foreign $60) (effective 1997). 90 Richmond St. E., Ste. 400, Toronto, ON M5C 1P1, Canada. TEL 416-366-4200. FAX 416-366-7846. E-mail: adsales@iemoney.com. Ed. Tessa Wilmott; Pub. Barbara Hyland. R&P contact: Ozy Camacho. adv. contact: Ozy Camacho. bk.rev. circ. 30,373. (tabloid format)
  Description: For stockbrokers, mutual fund salespeople, financial advisors and investment industry executives.

332.6 UK ISSN 0954-2485
HG5436
INVESTMENT FUND INDEX - INVESTMENT TRUSTS. 1988. s-a. £15. (Association of Investment Trust Companies) Centaur Communications Ltd., St. Giles House, 50 Poland St., London W1V 4AX, England. TEL 44-171-287-9800. FAX 44-171-439-1480. circ. 10,000. **Document type:** trade publication.

332.6 US ISSN 0736-2919
INVESTMENT HORIZONS.* 1983. s-m. $250. Investment Information Services, Inc., 120 S. Riverside Plz., Rm. 1745, Chicago, IL 60606-3911. TEL 312-649-6940; 800-326-6941. Ed. Gerald W. Perritt. adv. contact: Michael Corbett. circ. 2,000. **Document type:** newsletter.
  Description: Provides information for investing in small emerging growth stocks.

332 UK ISSN 0950-6195
INVESTMENT INTERNATIONAL.* 1986. m. £20. Charterhouse Communications Ltd., 4-8 Tabernacle St., 3rd Fl., London EC2A 4LU, England. Ed. Iain Yule. circ. 20,000.
  Description: Provides investment information for people living outside the U.K. and seeks to make them aware of the services available to them.

332.6 382 JA
INVESTMENT JAPAN (YEAR). irreg., latest 1995. 3000 Yen($60) Japan External Trade Organization, Publications Department, 2-5, Toranomon 2-chome, Minato-ku, Tokyo 105, Japan. TEL 03-3582-3518. FAX 03-3587-2485. **Document type:** directory.
  Description: Provides the latest information on institutions and firms offering assistance required during the several stages of setting up a business in Japan.

336 340 US ISSN 0893-3944
KF6415.A152
INVESTMENT LIMITED PARTNERSHIPS HANDBOOK. a. $140. Clark - Boardman - Callaghan, 375 Hudson St., New York, NY 10014. TEL 212-929-7500; 800-422-2101. FAX 212-924-0460.
  Formerly: Tax Sheltered Investments Handbook (ISSN 0731-5821)

INVESTMENT MANAGEMENT. see *BUSINESS AND ECONOMICS — Banking And Finance*

INVESTMENT MANAGEMENT TECHNOLOGY. see *BUSINESS AND ECONOMICS — Banking And Finance — Computer Applications*

332.6 US ISSN 0896-8500
INVESTMENT MANAGEMENT WEEKLY. 1988. w. $1195. Investment Management Publications, Inc., One Liberty Sq., 12th Fl., Boston, MA 02109. TEL 617-426-5450. FAX 617-422-0162. E-mail: impubscaol.com. Ed. Richard Chimberg. adv. **Document type:** newsletter.
  Description: Reports on the activities of institutional investors, primarily U.S. and Canadian plan sponsors, and the investment management business worldwide.

332.6 330 KE
INVESTMENT NEWS. (Text in English) 1985. w. $460. New Press Publications, P.O. Box 8454, Nairobi, Kenya. Ed. Muli wa Kyendo. adv.; bk.rev. circ. 18,580.

332.6 UK ISSN 0262-4257
INVESTMENT OPPORTUNITIES;* an independent monthly guide to investment alternatives. 1980. m. £40. Leasing Report Ltd., 73 Mill Lane, London NW6, England.

INVESTMENT PLANNING AND PROJECT EVALUATION BIBLIOGRAPHY. see *BIBLIOGRAPHIES*

332.6 AT ISSN 0725-3850
INVESTMENT PROJECTS IN THE HUNTER REGION. 1980. q. Hunter Valley Research Foundation, P.O. Box 3023, Hamilton DC, N.S.W. 2303, Australia. TEL 61-49-69-4566. FAX 61-49-614981. E-mail: oukhvrf@cc.newcastle.edu.au. stat. circ. 750. (back issues avail.)

332.6 US ISSN 0021-0110
INVESTMENT QUALITY TRENDS; for the enlightened investor. 1966. bi-m. $275 (foreign $325). Value Trend Analysis, 7440 Girard Ave., Ste. 4, La Jolla, CA 92037. TEL 619-459-3818. FAX 619-459-3819. E-mail: IQTrends@aol.com; URL: http://www.IQTrends.com. Ed. Geraldine Weiss; Pub. Geraldine Weiss. bk.rev.; charts; stat. circ. 5,000. pp./issue: 12. (looseleaf format; back issues avail.) **Document type:** newsletter.
●Also available online.

BUSINESS AND ECONOMICS — INVESTMENTS

332.6 — CN — ISSN 0700-5539
INVESTMENT REPORTER. (Monthly supplement avail.: Investment Planning Guide) 1941. w. Can.$279. M P L Communications Inc., 133 Richmond St. W., Ste. 700, Toronto, ON M5H 3M8, Canada. TEL 416-869-1177. FAX 416-869-0456. Ed. David Driscoll. charts; stat.; index. (looseleaf format) Indexed: PROMT.
  Incorporates (in 1990): Personal Wealth Reporter; (in 1989): Low-Priced Stock Analyst.
  Description: Stock market news and recommendations.

332.6 — US — ISSN 1062-4678
THE INVESTMENT REPORTER. 1989. m. $38. Share Holder Communication Systems, 4600 Campus Dr., Ste. 205, Newport Beach, CA 92660-1801. TEL 714-724-0444. Ed. Peggy Powel; Pub. Joh Robbins. R&P contact: John Robbins. adv. contact: John Robbins. bk.rev.; circ. 11,235 (paid); 36,204 (controlled). **Document type:** newspaper.
  Description: For stockbrokers, analysts, fund managers, corporate executives and individual investors.
  Refereed Serial

332.6 — US
INVESTMENT STRATEGY. 1970. m. free to qualified personnel. Crosby-Ware Trusts, 201 Squire Row, San Antonio, TX 78213. TEL 512-344-7211. Ed. Stephen H. Crosby, Jr. circ. 300.

332.64
INVESTMENT STRATEGY QUARTERLY. q. Green Mountain Asset Management Corp., E-mail: bobbose@stockresearch.com; URL: http://www.stockresearch.com/. Ed. Bob Bose. **Document type:** newsletter.
  ●Available only online.
  Description: Contains timely and educational investment information.

332.6 — UK
INVESTMENT TRUSTS. 1986. q. £14 (foreign £30). Flaxdale Printers Ltd., 5 Malvern Dr., Woodford Green, Essex IG8 0JR, England. TEL 44-181-504-6862. (Dist. by: United Magazine Distribution, 16-18 Tabernacle St., London EC2A 4BN, England. TEL 44-171-638-4666. FAX 44-171-638-4665; Subscr. to: Freepost SCE 1925, Woking, Surrey, QU21 1BR. TEL 44-1858-410510. FAX 44-1858-434190) Ed. John Davis; Pub. John Davis. adv.: B&W page £1250, color page £1500; trim 297 x 210; adv. contact: Rupert Simmons. index. circ. 25,000. (back issues avail.) **Document type:** consumer publication.
  Description: Provides comprehensive information about UK investment, or closed-end, trusts.

INVESTMENTS IN EMERGING MARKETS. see FOOD AND FOOD INDUSTRIES

332.6 — TH — ISSN 0021-0153
INVESTOR. (Text in English; summaries in Thai) 1968. m. B.95($6.50) Pansak Bldg., 4th Fl., 138-1 Petchburi Rd., Bangkok 10400, Thailand. Ed. Tos Patumsen. adv.; bk.rev.; bibl.; charts; illus.; stat.; index.
  Supersedes: Investment Newsletter.

332.96 — II
THE INVESTOR. (Text in English) a.? Rs.25 per no. (Securities Analysis Pvt. Ltd.) Mid-Day Publications Ltd., 156 D.J. Dadajee Rd., Tardeo, Bombay - 400 034, India. TEL 4942586. FAX 3054536. Ed. Rajasjekar Iyer.

659.2 332.6 — US
INVESTOR RELATIONS NEWSLETTER. 1964. m. $195. Remy Publishing Co., 350 W. Hubbard St., No. 440, Chicago, IL 60610-4011. TEL 312-464-0300. Ed. Gerald Murray. index. (looseleaf format) **Document type:** newsletter.

332.6 — US
INVESTOR RELATIONS UPDATE. m. $125. National Investor Relations Institute, 8045 Leesburg Pike, Ste. 600, Vienna, VA 22182-2737. TEL 703-506-3570. Ed. William F. Mahoney. circ. 3,000.
  Description: For investor relations practitioners who maintain contact with the financial community on behalf of their companies or clients.

332.67 — US
INVESTOR RESPONSIBILITY RESEARCH CENTER. ANNUAL REPORT. 1973. a. Investor Responsibility Research Center, Inc., 1350 Connecticut Ave., N.W. Ste. 700, Washington, DC 20036. TEL 202-833-0700. FAX 202-833-3555. Ed. Scott Fenn.

332.6 — US — ISSN 1061-2890
HF5001
INVESTOR'S BUSINESS DAILY. 1984. d. (5/w.). $169 (effective 1994). Investor's Business Daily, Inc., 12655 Beatrice St., Los Angeles, CA 90066. TEL 310-448-6000. Ed. Wesley Mann. adv. circ. 120,000.
  —CCC.
  Formerly (until 1991): Investor's Daily (ISSN 0743-9423)
  Description: For the upper echelon of corporate America. Covers business and finance and provides decision-making information.

332.6 — JM
THE INVESTOR'S CHOICE. 1989. m. J.$100($2.50) per issue. Financial & Economic Resources Ltd., 12 Merrick Ave., Kingston 10, Jamaica, W.I. TEL 809-929-2993. FAX 809-968-1188. Ed. John Jackson. adv. contact: Paul Anderson. circ. 10,000.

332.6 — UK — ISSN 0261-3115
HG4502
INVESTORS CHRONICLE (LONDON, 1860). 1860. w. £80 (Europe £96; elsewhere £115). Financial Times Business Information, Magazines (Subsidiary of: Financial Times Group), 2 Greystoke Pl., Fetter Ln., London EC4A 1ND, England. TEL 0171-405-6969. FAX 0171-405-5276. TELEX 296926 BUSINF G. (Subscr. to: 126 Jermyn St., London SW1Y 4UJ, England) Ed. Gillian O'Connor. adv.; bk.rev.; charts; illus.; stat.; index. circ. 44,770. (also avail. in microfilm from RPI; microform from UMI; reprint service avail. from RPI) Indexed: Build.Manage.Abstr., Ind.Bus.Rep., P.A.I.S., RICS, World Bank.Abstr. **Document type:** trade publication.
  —BLDSC (4562.520000); SWETS; UMI.
  Formerly: Investors Chronicle and Stock Exchange Gazette (ISSN 0021-0161); *Incorporates:* Stock Exchange Gazette; Financial World.
  Description: Provides private and professional investors with analysis and comment on the U.K. investment scene.

332.6 — US
INVESTOR'S DAILY.* America's business newspaper. 1984. d. $94. Box 66370, Los Angeles, CA 90066-0370. Ed. Stephen P. Fox. adv.; index. circ. 110,000. (also avail. in microfiche) Indexed: Tel.Abstr., Telegen. **Document type:** newspaper.
  ●Also available online. Vendor(s): Lexis-Nexis.

332.6 — US — ISSN 1057-6711
INVESTOR'S DIGEST. 1989. m. $60. Institute for Econometric Research, 2200 S.W. 10th St., Deerfield Beach, FL 33442-8799. TEL 954-421-1000; 800-442-9000. FAX 954-570-8200. Ed. Norman G. Fosback. charts; stat.; circ. 80,000 (paid). (back issues avail.) **Document type:** newsletter.
  —CCC.
  Description: A digest of stock market advice and recommendations condensed from hundreds of Wall Street analysts.

332.6 — CN — ISSN 0047-1356
INVESTOR'S DIGEST OF CANADA. 1969. s-m. Can.$137. M P L Communications Inc., 133 Richmond St. W., Ste. 700, Toronto, ON M5H 3M8, Canada. TEL 416-869-1177. FAX 416-869-0456. Ed. Richard Morrison. adv. circ. 20,000. Indexed: Can.B.P.I., Can.Per.Ind., CMI. **Document type:** trade publication.
  Description: Covers current digests and news on the stock market.

332.6 — SA — ISSN 0250-1732
HG5851.A2
THE INVESTORS' GUIDE. 1971. 4/yr. R.70. The Investors' Group (Pty) Ltd., P.O. Box 62000, Marshalltown 2107, South Africa. TEL 27-11-836-9321. FAX 27-11-836-9328. Ed. Adele Ribnick. adv.: B&W page R.1840, color page R.2620; trim 270 x 205; adv. contact: T. Kuiper. circ. 4,300.
  Former titles: Facts Investors Guide; Investor's Guide.
  Description: Provides investors and business people with relevant, current data on every company listed on the Johannesburg stock exchange.

332.6 — CN
INVESTOR'S GUIDE. 1990. a. Financial Post Co., Ltd., 333 King St. E., Toronto, ON M5A 4N2, Canada. TEL 416-350-6176. FAX 416-350-6171. Ed. Wayne Gooding. adv.

332.6 — US
THE INVESTOR'S GUIDE TO CLOSED-END FUNDS. m. $365 (effective 1997). Thomas J. Herzfeld Advisors, Inc., Box 161465, Miami, FL 33116. TEL 305-271-1900. FAX 305-270-7040. Ed. Thomas J. Herzfeld. charts. (looseleaf format)
  Description: Offers comprehensive timely information on closed-end funds, including editor's recommendations.

332.6 — HU — ISSN 0865-6746
INVESTORS' GUIDE TO HUNGARY. (Text in English, German) 1989. a. $30 (effective 1992). Magyar Kereskedelmi Kamara - Hungarian Chamber of Commerce, Kossuth L. ter 6-8, 1055 Budapest, Hungary. TEL 361-153-333. FAX 361-153-1285.

332.6 — US
INVESTOR'S GUIDE TO LOW-COST MUTUAL FUNDS. 1976. a. $15 per issue. Mutual Fund Education Alliance, Dept. 0148, Box 419263, Kansas City, MO 64193-0148. TEL 816-464-2213. FAX 816-454-9322. E-mail: mfeamail@mfea.com; URL: http://www.mfea.com. Dir. Michelle Smith. R&P contact: Michelle Smith. **Document type:** directory.
  Description: Provides educational information on the use of mutual funds to achieve financial goals, and performance listings of low and no-load funds.

332.6 — NP
INVESTORS' GUIDE TO NEPAL. (Text in English) 1975. irreg. Industrial Services Centre, Documentation & Publication Branch, Balaju Industrial Districts, Balaju, Kathmandu, Nepal. adv. circ. 3,000.

332.6 — SI — ISSN 0129-5276
HG5750.6.S5
INVESTOR'S GUIDE TO SINGAPORE. (Text in English) 1973. a. S.$15 per no. Singapore International Chamber of Commerce, 6 Raffles Quay, No. 10-01, John Hancock Tower, Singapore 048580, Singapore. TEL 65-2241255. FAX 65-2242785. E-mail: singicc@asianconnect.com; URL: http://www.sicc.com.sg. circ. 4,500.
  Formerly: Investor's Guide to the Economic Climate of Singapore.
  Description: Explains in detail the investment requirements and opportunities in Singapore.

INVESTOR'S GUIDE TO THE PHILIPPINES. see BUSINESS AND ECONOMICS — Trade And Industrial Directories

332.6 — US
INVESTOR'S HOTLINE. 1976. m. $225. Audio Alert Inc., 10616 Beaver Dam Rd., Hunt Valley, MD 21030. TEL 410-771-0064. FAX 410-584-1043. Ed. Joanne Schenk. adv. contact: F. Joseph Bradley. bk.rev. (audio cassette) **Document type:** newsletter.
  Formerly: Audio Alert.
  Description: Features current investment interviews with world authorities.

332.63 — US
INVESTORS INTELLIGENCE. 1957. fortn. $184. Chartcraft, Inc., 30 Church St., Box 2046, New Rochelle, NY 10801. TEL 914-632-0422. FAX 914-632-0335. Ed. Michael Burke.

BUSINESS AND ECONOMICS — INVESTMENTS

332.6 — **US**
INVESTORS UPDATE; real news report. 1956. q. $25. (California Numismatic Investments, Inc.) C N I Newsletter, 525 W. Manchester Blvd., Inglewood, CA 90301. TEL 213-674-3330. FAX 213-330-3766. Ed. Richard Schwary. circ. 12,000. **Document type:** newsletter.
Description: Reviews of precious metals and economic - financial - political commentary.

332.6 — **EC**
INVIERTA EN EL ECUADOR. English edition: Invest in Ecuador. (Editions in French, German) a. free. Banco Central del Ecuador, Casilla 29C, Sucursal No.15, Quito, Ecuador. TEL 561-521. (Distr. by: Libreria Economia y Cultural, Av. 10 de Agosto, No. 600 y Checa, Quito, Ecuador) circ. 5,000.

332.6 — **IE**
IRISH STOCK MARKET ANNUAL. 1987. a. I£15.95($30) Private Research Ltd., 7-8 Mount St. Crescent, Dublin 2, Ireland. TEL 353-1-6760774. FAX 353-1-6760773. Ed. John O'Neill. adv.: B&W page I£995, color page I£1575; adv. contact: James Treacy. circ. 5,000. (also avail. in diskette format; back issues avail.) **Document type:** corporate report.

332.6 — **US** — **ISSN 1080-3912**
HG4921
THE IRWIN INVESTOR'S HANDBOOK. 1982. a. $25. Irwin Professional Publishing, 1333 Burr Ridge Pkwy., Burr Ridge, IL 60521-6489. Ed. Phyllis Pierce.
Former titles (until 1994): Business One Investor's Handbook (ISSN 1062-0028); (until 1991): Dow Jones Investor's Handbook (ISSN 0748-2140)

ISRAEL HIGH-TECH & INVESTMENT REPORT. see *TECHNOLOGY: COMPREHENSIVE WORKS*

332.6 332 — **AT** — **ISSN 0313-5934**
J A S S A. 1966. q. Aus.$40 (effective 1996). Securities Institute of Australia, P.O. Box H99, Australia Square, N.S.W. 2000, Australia. TEL 61-2-251-6799. FAX 61-2-251-6287. Ed. John Hoffmann. bk.rev. circ. 7,500. **Document type:** academic/scholarly publication.
—UnCover.
Description: Contains articles on topics of current interest to the professional investment community.

332.6 — **US**
J. MICHAEL PINSON'S INVESTMENT DIGEST.* 1983. m. $69. Tower Financial Group, c/o Pinson and Associates, 2653 McCormick Dr., Clearwater, FL 34619-1041. TEL 813-538-4111. Ed. J. Michael Pinson. circ. 8,000.
Formerly: Investment Digest.
Description: Contains reviews of mutual funds, individual stocks as well as market predictions.

332.6 — **SA** — **ISSN 1018-3329**
THE J S E HANDBOOK. (Text in English) 1934. s-a. R.60($18) (effective 1996). Flesch Financial Publications (Pty) Ltd., P.O. Box 3473, Cape Town 8000, South Africa. TEL 27-21-4617472. FAX 27-21-4613758. E-mail: 100077.260@COMPUSERVE.COM. Ed. M. Maher; Pub. S. Flesch. adv. circ. 19,645. **Document type:** consumer publication.
Formerly (until 1991): Johannesburg Stock Exchange. Handbook (ISSN 0075-3793); (until 1967): Investors' Financial Directory of Southern Africa.
Description: Provides personnel and five year abstracts of financial accounts of all companies listed on the Johannesburg Stock Exchange.

332.6 — **US**
J TAYLOR'S GOLD & GOLD STOCKS. 1981. m. $99. Taylor Hard Money Advisors, Inc., 33-42 61st St., Woodside, NY 11377. TEL 718-457-1426. Ed. Jay L. Taylor. circ. 400 (paid). **Document type:** newsletter.
Formerly: North American Gold Mining Stocks.
Description: Develops gold mining stocks.

332.6327
JACKSON FINANCIAL LETTER. 1984. m. $95. Jackson Financial Company, Box 1028, Mt. Pleasant, SC 29465. TEL 803-881-3434. FAX 803-881-1180. Ed. James B. Jackson. circ. 2,000.
Formerly: Jackson Letter.
Description: Covers all aspects of investing.

332.6 — **US**
JAKE BERNSTEIN'S LETTER OF LONG TERM TRENDS. m. $400. M B H Commodity Advisors, Inc., 2 Northbrook Pl., 60 Revere Dr., Ste. 888, Northbrook, IL 60062. TEL 708-291-1870. FAX 708-291-9435. E-mail: jbtrend@mcs.com. (Subscr. to: Box 353, Winnetka, IL 60093) Ed. Jacob Bernstein. **Document type:** newsletter.

332.6327 — **US**
JAY SCHABACKER'S MUTUAL FUND BUYING GUIDE. q. $88.85. Phillips Publishing, Inc., Consumer Publishing, 7811 Montrose Rd., Potomac, MD 20854. TEL 301-340-2100. FAX 301-309-3847. Ed. Jay Schabacker.
Formerly: Mutual Fund Quarterly Performance Review.

332.6327 — **US** — **ISSN 8756-5161**
JAY SCHABACKER'S MUTUAL FUND INVESTING; your key to knowledge, action, and profits. 1985. m. $99. Phillips Publishing, Inc., Consumer Publishing, 7811 Montrose Rd., Potomac, MD 20854. TEL 301-340-2100. FAX 301-424-7034. Ed. Jay Schabacker.
—CCC.
Incorporates: Schabacker's Switch Fund Advisory.
Description: Interprets mutual funds and their performance for the investor.

332.6327 — **US**
JIM HIGHLAND'S FUND SWITCH.* 1985. m. $140. Highland Associates, Inc., 24001 W. Rockwood Creek Ln., Rhododendron, OR 97049-9750. TEL 503-622-4990. Ed. Jim Highland.
Description: Provides commentary on stocks, bonds, metals, and international markets, with recommendations on the strongest markets. Examines specific funds within those markets.

332.63 — **AT** — **ISSN 1038-2194**
HG5891
JOBSON'S YEAR BOOK OF AUSTRALIAN COMPANIES. 1920. a. Aus.$295. Dun & Bradstreet Marketing Pty. Ltd., 19 Havilan St., Chatswood, N.S.W. 2065, Australia. TEL 61-2-9352700. FAX 61-2-9352777. URL: http://www.dbmarketing.com.au. adv.; illus. circ. 5,000. **Document type:** directory.
Formerly: Jobson's Year Book of Public Companies (ISSN 0075-3785)
Description: Covers the industrial and second board listed companies on Australian and New Zealand stock exchanges.

332.6 — **SA** — **ISSN 0021-7182**
JOHANNESBURG STOCK EXCHANGE MONTHLY BULLETIN. 1969. m. R.221 (rest of Africa R.296; Australasia R.296; N. America R.437; Europe R.445; Far East R.516) (effective 1996). Johannesburg Stock Exchange, P.O. Box 1174, Johannesburg, South Africa. TEL 27-11-377-2206. FAX 27-11-834-7402. adv.; charts; stat. circ. 3,400. **Document type:** bulletin.
Description: Publishes information on markets, JSE Actuaries Index movement, securities, and notes on companies, including rights and capitalization issues, changes in capital, and special situations.

332.6 — **US**
JOHN BOLLINGER'S CAPITAL GROWTH LETTER. 1987. m. $225. Bollinger Capital Management, Box 3358, Manhattan Beach, CA 90266. TEL 310-798-8855. Ed. John Bollinger; Pub. Dorit Kehr. R&P contact: Dorit Kehr. (back issues avail.) **Document type:** newsletter.
Description: Provides investors with specific investment advice on stocks, bonds, precious metals, energy, the dollar and the international markets.

JOHN LINER REVIEW. see *INSURANCE*

JOHN T. REED'S REAL ESTATE INVESTOR'S MONTHLY. see *REAL ESTATE*

332.67 — **US** — **ISSN 0735-7672**
HG4530
JOHNSON'S INVESTMENT COMPANY CHARTS. 1949. a. $469 includes 4 performance reports (effective 1996 & 1997). Johnson's Charts, Inc., 175 Bridle Path, Buffalo, NY 14221-4537. TEL 716-626-0845. FAX 716-626-4899. Ed. Fred C. Cohn. R&P contact: Fred C. Cohn. film rev.; charts; illus.; stat. circ. 1,000. **Document type:** trade publication.
Description: Chartbook on mutual funds, interest rates, inflation, market indexes, stocks, bonds, and financial planning.

JOURNAL OF DERIVATIVES. see *BUSINESS AND ECONOMICS — Banking And Finance*

JOURNAL OF EMERGING MARKETS. see *BUSINESS AND ECONOMICS — Banking And Finance*

JOURNAL OF ENTERTAINMENT FINANCE. see *BUSINESS AND ECONOMICS — Banking And Finance*

JOURNAL OF FINANCIAL INTERMEDIATION. see *BUSINESS AND ECONOMICS — Economic Systems And Theories, Economic History*

332.6 336 657 — **US** — **ISSN 1040-3981**
HG179
JOURNAL OF FINANCIAL PLANNING. 1979. bi-m. $60 to non-members (Canada $70; elsewhere $80) (effective 1997). Institute of Certified Financial Planners, 3801 E. Florida Ave., No. 708, Denver, CO 80210-2571. TEL 303-759-4900. FAX 303-759-0749. E-mail: journal@icfp.org; URL: http://www.icfp.org/member/journal. Ed. Marvin W. Tuttle; Pub. Marvin W. Tuttle. index. circ. 25,000. (back issues avail.) **Indexed:** Account.Ind. (1979-), B.P.I. **Document type:** trade publication.
—BLDSC (4984.260500); KR SourceOne; UMI; UnCover.
Formerly (until 1988): Institute of Certified Financial Planners. Journal (ISSN 0746-1984)
Description: Acts as a forum for the free exchange of ideas, facts, and information relevant to the financial planning profession.
Refereed Serial

JOURNAL OF FINANCIAL SERVICES RESEARCH. see *BUSINESS AND ECONOMICS — Banking And Finance*

332.6 — **US** — **ISSN 1059-8596**
HG4961
JOURNAL OF FIXED INCOME. 1991. q. $280 (foreign $355) (effective 1996). Institutional Investor Journals, 488 Madison Ave., New York, NY 10022. TEL 212-224-3185. FAX 212-224-3527. Ed. Douglas T. Breeden; Pub. Gauri Goyal. adv.: B&W page $4500, color page $7700; adv. contact: Lisa C. Aadal.
—BLDSC (4984.380000); SWETS; UMI. **CCC.**
Description: Offers original works of applied research in the field of fixed income, covering topics such as mortgage-backed securities, corporate bonds, asset-backed securities, international bond markets, and more.

332.63 — **US** — **ISSN 0270-7314**
HG6001 — **CODEN: JFMADT**
THE JOURNAL OF FUTURES MARKETS. 1981. 8/yr. $885 (foreign $1025) (effective 1998). John Wiley & Sons, Inc., Journals, 605 Third Ave., New York, NY 10158. TEL 212-850-6645. FAX 212-850-6021. TELEX 12-7063. E-mail: SUBINFO@JWILEY.COM; URL: http://www.wiley.co.uk. (Subscr. outside the Americas to: John Wiley & Sons Ltd., Baffins Ln., Chichester, W. Sussex PO19 1UD, England. TEL 44-1243-779777. FAX 44-1243-776128) Ed. Mark J. Powers. adv.: B&W page £640, color page £1515; trim 254 x 172. circ. 1,100. (also avail. in microform from UMI; back issues avail.) **Indexed:** ABI Inform., Account.Ind. (1983-), ASCA, B.P.I., Bank.Lit.Ind., BPIA, Bus.Ind., Cont.Pg.Manage., Curr.Cont., J.of Econ.Lit., Manage.Cont., P.A.I.S., PSI, Risk Abstr., SSCI, Tr.& Indus.Ind. **Document type:** trade publication.
—BLDSC (4986.910000); Genuine Article; KR SourceOne; SWETS; UMI; UnCover. **CCC.**
Description: Topics include financial futures, commodity forecasting techniques, corporate hedging strategies, tax and accounting implications of hedging, analysis of commodity trading systems.

332.6 — **US** — **ISSN 1068-0896**
HG4501
JOURNAL OF INVESTING. 1992. q. $250 (foreign $325) (effective 1996). Institutional Investor Journals, 488 Madison Ave., New York, NY 10022. TEL 212-224-3185. FAX 212-224-3527. Ed. Brian Bruce; Pub. Gauri Goyal. adv.: B&W page $4500, color page $7700; adv. contact: Robin DuCharme. circ. 2,500 (paid).
—BLDSC (5008.050000).
Description: Provides articles on the latest developments affecting financial and investment decisions.

BUSINESS AND ECONOMICS — INVESTMENTS

332.6 US ISSN 0095-4918
HG4501
JOURNAL OF PORTFOLIO MANAGEMENT; the journal for investment professionals. 1975. q. $305 (foreign $380) (effective 1996). Institutional Investor Journals, 488 Madison Ave., New York, NY 10022. TEL 212-224-3185. FAX 212-224-3527. Ed. Frank Fabozzi; Pub. Gauri Goyal. adv.: B&W page $4500, color page $7700. bk.rev.; bibl.; charts; illus. (also avail. in microform from UMI; back issues avail. from UMI,KTO) **Indexed:** ABI Inform., ASCA, B.P.I., Bank.Lit.Ind., BPIA, Bus.Ind., Curr.Cont., J.of Econ.Lit., Manage.Cont., P.A.I.S., Risk Abstr., SSCI, Tr.& Indus.Ind.
●Also available online. Vendor(s): Information Access Co., Lexis-Nexis.
Also available on CD-ROM.
—BLDSC (5041.147000); Genuine Article; KR SourceOne; SWETS; UMI; UnCover. **CCC.**
Description: Reports and explores the development and application of theoretical concepts dominating the investment scene.

JOURNAL OF TAXATION OF INVESTMENTS. see BUSINESS AND ECONOMICS — Public Finance, Taxation

JOURNAL OF TAXATION OF S CORPORATIONS. see BUSINESS AND ECONOMICS — Public Finance, Taxation

JUDGE'S RETIREMENT SYSTEM. ANNUAL FINANCIAL REPORT AND REPORT OF OPERATIONS. see BUSINESS AND ECONOMICS — Economic Situation And Conditions

332.6 US
JUMBO FLASH REPORT. w. $245. Advertising News Service, Inc., 11811 Federal Hwy. One, Box 088888, N. Palm Beach, FL 33408-8888. TEL 407-627-7330. FAX 407-627-7335. URL: www.bankrate.com. Ed. Linda Green.
Description: Covers high yielding jumbo CD's and money markets offered by federally-insured institutions nationwide.

JUMBO RATE NEWS. see BUSINESS AND ECONOMICS — Banking And Finance

332.6 US
JUNCTURE RECOGNITION. 1977. s-m. $135. Box 1209, Pompano Beach, FL 33061. TEL 305-564-0643. Ed. W.G. Brentz.
Description: Deals with market timing based on monetary and technical factors.

332.6 US ISSN 1073-7634
JUNIOR GROWTH STOCKS. (Supplement to: Growth Stock Outlook) 1971. q. $50 per issue. Growth Stock Outlook, Inc., 4405 East-West Hwy., Ste. 305, Bethesda, MD 20814. TEL 301-654-5205. Ed. Charles Allmon. **Document type:** newsletter.
Description: Provides investors with data on more than 300 growth companies, most of which are "emerging growth" companies. Includes data on earnings, sales, shares outstanding, compound growth rates, book values, and price-earnings ratio.

332.63 JA
KABUSHIKI NIPPON. (Text in Japanese) 3/mo. Shijo Shimbun Sha, 5-6 Shinkawa 2-chome, Chuo-ku, Tokyo 104, Japan. TEL 81-3-5566-1805. FAX 81-3-5566-1811. adv. contact: Hiroshi Yasuzawa. circ. 30,800.
Description: For businessmen interested in the securities market.

KAGAN MEDIA INDEX. see BUSINESS AND ECONOMICS — Abstracting, Bibliographies, Statistics

332.678 PK
KARACHI. CHAMBER OF COMMERCE AND INDUSTRY. GUIDE FOR INDUSTRIAL INVESTMENT IN PAKISTAN. (Text in English) irreg. Rs.100. Karachi Chamber of Commerce and Industry, Aiwan-e-Tijarat, Box 4158, Nicol Rd., Karachi 2, Pakistan.

380 332.6 KE
KENYA: THE GATEWAY TO AFRICA; guidelines to investors. irreg. free. Ministry of Industry, Industrial Promotion Department, P.O. Box 30418, Nairobi, Kenya. **Document type:** government publication.
Formerly: Guidelines for Industrial Investors in Kenya.

332.6 NE ISSN 0927-4340
KERNGETALLEN NEDERLANDSE BEURSFONDSEN. English edition: Dutch Company Profiles (ISSN 0927-4790) 1962. 3/yr. fl.100. A B N Amro Bank N.V., P.O. Box 283, 1000 EA Amsterdam, Netherlands. (Subscr. to: Amro Effecten Centrum, Postbus 3200, 4800 DE Breda, Netherlands) Ed. Wim Sprey. stat. circ. 14,000. **Indexed:** Key to Econ.Sci.
Formerly (until 1991): Kerngetallen van Nederlandse Effecten (ISSN 0023-0669)

332.6 UK
KEY NOTE MARKET REPORT: STEEL STOCKHOLDING. Variant title: Steel Stockholding. irreg., no.11, 1995. £185. Key Note Ltd., Field House, 72 Oldfield Rd., Hampton, Middlesex TW12 2HQ, England. TEL 44-181-783-0755. FAX 44-181-783-1940. **Document type:** trade publication.
●Also available online.
Also available on CD-ROM.
Formerly: Key Note Report: Steel Stockholding (ISSN 0954-5123)

332.64 UK
KEY NOTE MARKET REPORT: STOCKBROKING. Variant title: Stockbroking. irreg., no.4, 1996. £205. Key Note Ltd., Field House, 72 Oldfield Rd., Hampton, Middlesex TW12 2HQ, England. TEL 44-181-783-0755. FAX 44-181-783-0049. **Document type:** trade publication.

332.6 UK
KEY NOTE MARKET REPORTS: PENSIONS. Variant title: Pensions. irreg. £205. Key Note Ltd., Field House, 72 Oldfield Rd., Hampton, Middlesex TW12 2HQ, England. TEL 44-181-783-0755. FAX 44-181-783-0049. **Document type:** trade publication.

332.6 US ISSN 0453-9249
KIPLINGER CALIFORNIA LETTER. 1965. fortn. $73. Kiplinger Washington Editors, Inc., 1729 H St., N.W., Washington, DC 20006. TEL 202-887-6400. FAX 202-778-8976. URL: http://www.kiplinger.com/. Ed. John Fogarty. charts; stat. **Document type:** trade publication.
●Also available online.
—CCC.

330 US ISSN 1073-5593
KIPLINGER FLORIDA BUSINESS LETTER. 1956. m. $48. Kiplinger Washington Editors, Inc., 1729 H St., N.W., Washington, DC 20006. TEL 202-887-6400. FAX 202-778-8976. Ed. Ken Dalecki. **Document type:** trade publication.
Formerly (until 1993): Kiplinger Florida Letter (ISSN 0023-1754)
Description: Newsletter focusing on items of interest to those with business interests or investments in the state.

332.6 US ISSN 0023-1770
HC101 CODEN: KIWNAB
KIPLINGER WASHINGTON LETTER. 1923. w. $73. Kiplinger Washington Editors, Inc., 1729 H St., N.W., Washington, DC 20006. TEL 202-887-6400. FAX 202-778-8976. URL: http://www.kiplinger.com/newsletter/wash.html. Ed. Austin H. Kiplinger. **Document type:** trade publication.
●Also available online.
—CASDDS. **CCC.**
Description: Weekly news, information, analyses, and forecasts, affecting personal lives and finances.

338 US ISSN 1074-1933
HF1041
KNIGHT-RIDDER C R B COMMODITY YEAR BOOK. 1939. a. $95 (effective 1997). (Commodity Research Bureau) Bridge Publishing, 30 S. Wacker Dr., Ste. 1810, Chicago, IL 60606. TEL 312-454-1801; 800-621-5271. FAX 312-454-0239. E-mail: crbinfo@ais.net; URL: http://www.krf.com/crb/. Eds. Bob Hafer, Ann Ingles. R&P contact: Carlene Camera. charts; index. **Indexed:** SRI. **Document type:** trade publication.
Former titles (until 1993): C R B Commodity Yearbook (ISSN 1046-8226); (until 1985): Commodity Year Book (ISSN 0069-6862)
Description: Covers previous year's activity for over 100 commodities. Includes approximately 1,000 charts, tables, supply and demand data, and background information on each market.

332.642 DK ISSN 0907-1016
KOEBENHAVNS FONDSBOERS. AARSRAPPORT/COPENHAGEN STOCK EXCHANGE. ANNUAL REPORT. 1963. a. DKK 50. Koebenhavns Fondsbers - Copenhagen Stock Exchange, Nikolaj Plads 6, 1067 Copenhagen K, Denmark. TEL 01-933366. FAX 45-33-128613. TELEX stat. circ. 2,000.

332.6 US
THE KON-LIN LETTER. m. $95 (effective 1997). Kon-Lin Research & Analysis Corp., 5 Water Rd., Rocky Point, NY 11778. TEL 516-744-8536. FAX 516-744-3096. Ed. Konrad J. Kuhn. **Document type:** newsletter, trade publication.
Description: Covers low-priced stocks under $10, with emphasis on emerging growth and special situations for price appreciation potential.

332.64 KO
KOREA STOCK EXCHANGE. FACT BOOK. (Text in English) 1979. a. free. Korea Stock Exchange, 33, Yoido-dong, Youngdeungpo-gu, Seoul 150-010, S. Korea. TEL 783-2271. FAX 786-0263. TELEX K28384 KOSTEX. Ed. Se-Yeal Yang; Pub. Byung-Woo Koh. circ. 1,000.

KOTHARI'S INDUSTRIAL DIRECTORY OF INDIA. see BUSINESS AND ECONOMICS — Trade And Industrial Directories

332.6 MY ISSN 0126-7558
KUALA LUMPUR STOCK EXCHANGE. COMPANIES HANDBOOK. (Text in English) 1974. s-a. price varies. Kuala Lumpur Stock Exchange, 3rd, 4th & 5th Fls., Exchange Square, Off Jalan Semantan, Damansara Heights, 50490 Kuala Lumpur, Malaysia. TEL 03-2546433. FAX 03-2557463. TELEX KLSE-MA-30241-28009. Ed. Qua Gek Kim. adv.; stat. circ. 5,500. (also avail. in diskette format)
Description: Covers history, significant activities, directors, capital structure, subsidiaries, top 10 shareholders, balance sheet, and profit and loss account figures for the past five years.

332.6 AU
KURSBLATT DER WIENER WERTPAPIERBOERSE. 1948. d. (5/w.). S.8650 (effective 1996). Boersedruck GmbH, Boersegasse 11, A-1010 Vienna, Austria. TEL 43-1-5332106. FAX 43-1-5332106-49. **Document type:** bulletin.
Former titles: Kursblatt der Wiener Wertpapierboerse - Geregelter Freiverkehr; Kursblatt der Amtlich Nicht Notierten Wertpapiere - Geregelter Freiverkehr an der Wiener Boerse (ISSN 0003-2093)

332.6 US ISSN 0890-8079
LALOGGIA'S SPECIAL SITUATION REPORT AND STOCK MARKET FORECAST. 1974. every 3 wks. $230. C M L Market Letter, Inc., Box 167, Rochester, NY 14601. TEL 800-836-4330. Ed. Charles M. LaLoggia. charts; illus. circ. 3,000. **Document type:** newsletter.

332.678 US
LAMBDA FINANCIAL ADVISOR. 1984. m. $36. Lambda Publishing Co., Box 3569, Jersey City, NJ 07303-3569. TEL 201-963-1357. Ed. Julius J. Spohn. charts; stat. (back issues avail.) **Document type:** newsletter.

332.67 US
LANCZ LETTER. 1981. irreg. (every 3-4 wks.). $250. Alan B. Lancz & Associates, Inc., 2400 N. Reynolds Rd., Toledo, OH 43615-2818. TEL 419-536-5200. FAX 419-536-5401. Ed. Alan B. Lancz. R&P contact: Jody Stoner. circ. 1,200. (back issues avail.) **Document type:** newsletter.
Description: Analysis of contemporary issues in stock market investment, including specific recommendations on additions to general straegies and investment tips.

332.6 330.1 US
LARRY ABRAHAM'S INSIDER REPORT. 1983. m. $199. Soundview Communications, Box 467939, Atlanta, GA 30346. TEL 800-728-2288. Ed. Larry Abraham. bk.rev. circ. 10,000. (back issues avail.) **Document type:** newsletter.

LATIN AMERICAN CABLE & PAY T V. see COMMUNICATIONS — Television And Cable

BUSINESS AND ECONOMICS — INVESTMENTS

332.6 330.9 332   US
LATIN AMERICAN FINANCE & CAPITAL MARKETS. 22/yr. $595 (foreign $645). WorldTrade Executive, Inc., Box 761, Concord, MA 01742. TEL 508-287-0301. FAX 508-287-0302. adv.: page $975; 7 1/2 x 9 1/2.
   Description: Covers opportunities, hazards, and important developments for the treasury manager or investor involved in Latin American markets. Includes risk-management techniques, economic performance, and financial sector developments in the area.

332.6 332   UK   ISSN 0266-2914
LATIN AMERICAN INFORMES ESPECIALES. Variant title: Informes Especiales. (Text in Spanish) 1983. bi-m. £188($245) (effective 1997). Lettres (U.K.) Ltd., 61 Old St., London EC1V 9HX, England. TEL 44-171-251-0012. FAX 44-171-253-8193. Ed. Eduardo Crawley. R&P contact: Alex McHallam. (back issues avail.)
   •Also available online. Vendor(s): Lexis-Nexis.
   Description: Covers six areas of topical interest in Latin America.

332.6 332   UK   ISSN 0264-2867
LATIN AMERICAN SPECIAL REPORTS. 1983. bi-m. £219($285) (effective 1997). Latin American Newsletters, 61 Old St., London EC1V 9HX, England. TEL 44-171-251-0012. FAX 44-171-253-8193. Ed. Eduardo Crawley. (back issues avail.) **Document type:** newsletter.
   •Also available online. Vendor(s): Lexis-Nexis.
   Description: Covers in detail six areas of topical interest in Latin America.

332 350.08   US
LENDERLINK. (Supplement to: Keynotes (Trenton)) 1993. q. free to qualified personnel. New Jersey Housing and Mortgage Finance Agency, Division of Planning and Intergovernmental Relations, 3625 Quakerbridge Rd., CN 18550, Trenton, NJ 08650-2085. TEL 609-890-8900. FAX 609-890-6128. circ. 2,000. **Document type:** newsletter.
   Description: Provides timely, in-depth information on the agency's mortgage financing to participating mortgage bankers.

332.6 340   US   ISSN 1069-2312
KF313.A15
LIABILITY OF ATTORNEYS AND ACCOUNTANTS FOR SECURITIES TRANSACTIONS. a. $140. Clark-Boardman - Callaghan, 375 Hudson St., New York, NY 10014. TEL 212-929-7500; 800-422-2101. FAX 212-924-0460. Ed. Robert J. Haft.
   Description: Explores potential attorney liability for disclosure advise to clients, preparation of disclosure documents, agreements, and closing documents, and creation of formal legal opinions.

LIFESTYLE AND LONDON LIVING. see *REAL ESTATE*

332.6   US
LINDQUIST - LEPIC MARKET LETTER. 1979. m. $120. Lindquist - Frank Capital Management, Inc., 1115 Elkton Dr., Ste. 101, Colorado Springs, CO 80907-3535. TEL 303-759-8471. Ed. Larry E. Lindquist. circ. 300. **Document type:** newsletter.
   Description: Reviews stocks and commodity markets.

332.63 330.9   IT
LIST OF ITALIAN BANKS. 1950. m. free. Banca Commerciale Italiana, Piazza della Scala 6, Milan, Italy. Ed. Franco Pedriali. stat. circ. 2,000.

332   US   ISSN 0196-0628
LIST OF O T C MARGIN STOCKS. q. free. U.S. Federal Reserve System, Board of Governors, Publications Services, Rm. MS-138, Washington, DC 20551. TEL 202-452-3244. FAX 202-728-5886. **Document type:** government publication.

332.6   UK   ISSN 0966-4343
HG4576
LONDON STOCK EXCHANGE. QUALITY OF MARKETS QUARTERLY REVIEW. (Former name of issuing body: International Stock Exchange) 1972. q. £79. London Stock Exchange, Old Broad St., London EC2N 1HP, England. circ. 2,000. **Document type:** bulletin.
   Former titles (until 1991): International Stock Exchange. Quality of Markets Quarterly (ISSN 0953-3133); London. Stock Exchange. Stock Exchange Quarterly (ISSN 0267-1530); London. Stock Exchange. Stock Exchange Fact Book (ISSN 0143-229X); Supersedes in part: London. Stock Exchange. Stock Exchange Fact Service.

332.6   UK
LONDON STOCK EXCHANGE FACT SHEET MONTHLY. (Former name of issuing body: International Stock Exchange) 1980. m. £53. London Stock Exchange, Old Broad St., London EC2N 1HP, England. Ed. R.Q. Rangecroft. charts; stat. circ. 2,500. **Document type:** bulletin.
   Former titles: International Stock Exchange Fact Sheet Monthly; Stock Exchange Fact Sheet Monthly (ISSN 0265-1513); Supersedes in part: London. Stock Exchange. Stock Exchange Fact Service.

332.6   UK   ISSN 0965-4356
LONDON STOCK EXCHANGE MEMBER FIRMS. Cover title: Member Firms. (Former name of issuing body: International Stock Exchange) 1802. a. £25. London Stock Exchange, Old Broad St., London EC2N 1HP, England. TEL 0171-797-1000. FAX 0171-410-6861. circ. 6,000. **Document type:** directory.
   Former titles: I S E Firms and Members; Stock Exchange, London. Members and Firms of the Stock Exchange (ISSN 0305-1129)

332.645   US
LONG TERM INVESTING. 1967. m. $98. Concept Publishing, Box 500, York, NY 14592. TEL 716-243-3148. FAX 716-243-3148. Ed. David Coleman. charts; index. circ. 200. (tabloid format)
   Description: General information on investing, estate planning, and tax planning for sophisticated investors.

332.6   US
LONG-TERM SCORE. 1987. m. $900. Financial Market Models, Box 308, Williamsport, PA 17703-0663. TEL 717-433-4236. Eds. Gregory P. Breon, David Chessman.
   Description: Provides signals (buy, short, hedge, neutral) on market momentum based on a proprietary model that uses internal market data and economic analysis.

332.6   US   ISSN 1060-9903
HG4501
LOUIS RUKEYSER'S WALL STREET. 1992. m. $79. Louis Rukeyser's Wall Street, 1750 Old Meadow Rd., Ste. 300, McLean, VA 22102-4304. TEL 800-892-9702. (Subscr. to: Box 25527, Alexandria, VA 22313-5527) Ed. Louis Rukeyser. circ. 400,000. **Document type:** newsletter.
   Description: Provides tips on how the personal investor can make money on Wall Street.

332.64   US   ISSN 0273-7752
LOW PRICED STOCK SURVEY. 1980. fortn. $82. NorthStar Financial, Inc., 7412 Calumet Ave., Ste. 200, Hammond, IN 46324-2692. TEL 219-852-3210. Ed. Randall Roeing. circ. 8,000. (looseleaf format; back issues avail.)

332.6   US   ISSN 0892-984X
LOW PRICED STOCKS. 1972. a. $45. Elton Stephens Investments, 4016 S. Michigan St., South Bend, IN 46614-2544. TEL 219-291-3823. (Subscr. to: Box 476, South Bend, IN 46624-0476) Ed. Elton Stephens. index. circ. 3,000. (looseleaf format; back issues avail.) **Document type:** newsletter.

LUNDBERG LETTER. see *PETROLEUM AND GAS*

332.6   US
LYNCH INTERNATIONAL INVESTMENT SURVEY.* 1971. w. $175. Lynch-Bowes, Inc., 431 Beach 136th St., Far Rockaway, NY 11694-1325. TEL 516-883-7094. FAX 516-883-4338. Ed. Walter A. Lynch. charts; stat. circ. 3,000. **Document type:** newsletter.

332.6   US
LYNCH MUNICIPAL BOND ADVISORY. 1986. m. $250. Lynch Municipal Bond Advisory, Inc., 2840 Broadway, No. 201, New York, NY 10025. TEL 212-663-5552. Ed. James F. Lynch. **Document type:** newspaper.

M & A JAPAN; international journal of Japanese mergers and acquisitions. (Mergers & Acquisitions) see *BUSINESS AND ECONOMICS — Banking And Finance*

M & A REVIEW. (Mergers & Acquisitions) see *BUSINESS AND ECONOMICS — Banking And Finance*

332.6   US
M B A CATALOG.* m. Business Publications, Inc. (San Diego), 5060 Shoreham Pl., Ste. 200, San Diego, CA 92122-5904. TEL 619-457-7577. FAX 619-453-1091. **Document type:** catalog.
   Description: Presents books, software and cassettes in the area of mergers and acquisitions.

332.6   US
M B H WEEKLY FUTURES TRADING LETTER. w. $895. M B H Commodity Advisors, Inc., 2 Northbrook Pl., 60 Revere Dr., Ste. 888, Northbrook, IL 60062. TEL 708-291-1870. FAX 708-291-9435. E-mail: jbtrend@ms.com. (Subscr. to: Box 353, Winnetka, IL 60094) Ed. Jacob Bernstein. **Document type:** newsletter.
   Formerly: M B H Weekly Commodity Letter.

332.63   TH
M F C INVESTMENT HANDBOOK (YEAR). (Text in English) a. Mutual Fund Public Co., Ltd., Research and Planning Department, 30th-32nd Fl., Lake Rajada Bldg., 193-195 Ratchadaphisek Rd., Khlong-Toey, Bangkok 10110, Thailand. TEL 662-661-9000. FAX 662-661-9106. TELEX 72603 MFCTHAI-TH.

332.6   US
M J F GROWTH STOCK ADVISORY.* 1986. m. $78. Kephart Communications, Inc., 1750 Old Meadow Rd., 3rd Fl., McLean, VA 22102-4304. TEL 703-548-2400. FAX 703-683-6974. TELEX 901806 KEPCOM. Ed. Michael J. Funke. circ. 15,000.

332.678   US
M P T REVIEW; specializing in modern portfolio theory. 1980. m. $225. Navellier and Associates, Inc., 1 E. Liberty St., Reno, NV 89501-2110. TEL 800-454-1395. FAX 702-785-2323. Ed. Louis G. Navellier; Pub. Louis G. Navellier. R&P contact: Jerry Rushing. TEL 702-785-9426. adv. contact: Jan Rushing. charts; illus.; stat.; index. circ. 15,000. (looseleaf format; back issues avail.) **Document type:** newsletter.
   •Also available online. Vendor(s): NewsNet (IV48).
   Formerly (until 1987): O T C Insight.
   Description: Provides quantitative analysis of stocks.

332.6   US
MCALVANY INTELLIGENCE ADVISOR.* 1975. m. $97. International Collectors Associates, Box 84904, Phoenix, AZ 85071. TEL 800-528-0559. Ed. Donald McAlvany. circ. 5,000.
   Description: Provides current analysis of market trends and geopolitical developments.

MCGREGOR'S WHO OWNS WHOM (SOUTHERN AFRICAN EDITION). see *BUSINESS AND ECONOMICS — Trade And Industrial Directories*

332.6   UK
MACMILLAN STOCK EXCHANGE YEARBOOK. 1875. a. £225. (Stock Exchange Council, London) Macmillan Reference, 25 Eccleston Pl., London SW1W 9NF, England. TEL 44-171-881-8000. FAX 44-171-881-8001. (Dist. in the U.S. by: Stockton Press, 345 Park Ave. S., 10th Fl., New York, NY 10010. TEL 212-689-9200. FAX 212-689-9711) Eds. Gavin Harrap Fryer, David Martin Michael Davies. adv. circ. 6,750. **Document type:** trade publication.
   Formerly: Stock Exchange Official Year Book (ISSN 0076-0684)
   Description: Gives comprehensive information on companies traded on the London Stock Exchange, including senior managers, major shareholders, trading histories, and professional advisers.

MADAGASCAR. DIRECTION GENERALE DE L'INSTITUT NATIONAL DE LA STATISTIQUE. SITUATION ECONOMIQUE AU 1 JANVIER (YEAR). see BUSINESS AND ECONOMICS — International Commerce

332.6 IS ISSN 0333-8037
MADRICH LEGROTE CHOVE. 1973. q. $12. Tel Aviv Stock Exchange, 54 Ahad Ha'am St., Tel Aviv 65202, Israel. TEL 972-3-5677411. FAX 972-3-5105379. TELEX 341762.

332.6 CN ISSN 1187-0176
MAGAZINE AFFAIRES PLUS. (Text in French) 1978. m. (10/yr.). Can.$12.84. Publications Transcontinental Inc., 1100 Boul. Rene Levesque W., 24th Fl., Montreal, PQ H3B 4X9, Canada. TEL 514-392-9000. FAX 514-392-1586. TELEX 055-61971. Dir. Pierre Duhamel. adv. circ. 94,587. (back issues avail.) **Indexed:** Can.B.P.I., Pt.de Rep. (1991-).
Former titles (until 1991): A Plus, Le Magazine Affaires Plus (ISSN 0836-6942); (until 1986): Magazine Affaires (ISSN 0229-9992)
Description: Personal business magazine for professionals, entrepreneurs and other business people.

332 HU ISSN 1216-0229
MAGYAR ELEKTRONIKUS TOZSDE/HUNGARIAN ELECTRONIC EXCHANGE. (Text in English, Hungarian) 1990. w. free. Pf. 311, Budapest 1536, Hungary. TEL 361-252-6697. E-mail: orcznz@mars.iif.hu; URL: http://www.metpress.hu. Ed. Csaba Orczan; Pub. Zsolt Orczan. adv.; bk.rev. (back issues avail.) **Document type:** newsletter.
•Available only online.
Description: News of the stock exchange and House of Parliament.

332.6 AT ISSN 0728-4438
MAJOR DEVELOPMENT PROJECTS AND PROPOSALS IN QUEENSLAND. a. Department of Tourism, Small Business and Industry, Library, G.P.O. Box 1141, Brisbane, Qld. 4001, Australia. TEL 61-7-2248568. FAX 61-7-2295289. circ. 10,000. **Document type:** government publication.
Description: Major manufacturing, minerals processing, mining, infrastructure and energy project proposals in Queensland.

332.64 UK ISSN 1355-7939
MAJOR U K COMPANIES HANDBOOK. 1976. s-a. £185 (foreign £210). Financial Times Information Ltd., Extel, Fitzroy House, 13-17 Epworth St., London EC2A 4DL, England. TEL 44-171-825-8000. FAX 44-171-608-2032. TELEX 884319. E-mail: eic@ft.com; URL: http://www.info.ft.com/. stat. (back issues avail.)
Supersedes: Extel Handbook of Market Leaders (ISSN 0308-9673)
Description: Provides background and financial information on all UK quoted companies contained in the FTSE All Share Index. Includes market capitalisation, share price, business summary, performance ratios, dividend details, and more.

332.6 US ISSN 0197-5382
MANAGED ACCOUNTS REPORTS; the clearing house for commodity money management. 1979. m. $299 (foreign $370). Managed Account Reports Inc., 220 Fifth Ave., 19th Fl., New York, NY 10001. TEL 212-213-6202. FAX 212-213-1870. Ed. Lois Peltz. charts; stat. (back issues avail.)
Incorporates: Futures Industry (ISSN 0197-5390)
Description: Features, analysis, and indexes on money management, and performance data for individual accounts, private pools, and publicly offered futures funds.

MANAGING RISK FOR LOSS PREVENTION AND COST CONTROL. see INSURANCE

332 SA
▼**MANAGING YOUR FINANCES AFTER RETIREMENT.** 1995. a. R.31.95. (A B S A Bank) Southern Book Publishers, P.O. Box 3103, Halfway House 1685, South Africa. TEL 27-11-3153633. FAX 27-11-3153810. Eds. C.W. Luus, R. Obelholzer.

332.6
MANSFIELD STOCK CHART SERVICE. 1938. w. $733. R.W. Mansfield Co., Inc., 2973 Kennedy Blvd., Jersey City, NJ 07306. TEL 201-795-0630. FAX 201-795-5476. Ed. R.W. Mansfield. stat.
Description: Provides charts with technical indicators and market commentary to assist investors and market professionals with stock selections.

LE MARCHE DES EMPRUNTS OBLIGATAIRES EN E C U/BOND MARKET IN E C U. see BUSINESS AND ECONOMICS — Abstracting, Bibliographies, Statistics

LE MARCHE DES EMPRUNTS OBLIGATAIRES EN FRANCS LUXEMBOURGEOIS/BOND MARKET IN LUXEMBOURG FRANCS. see BUSINESS AND ECONOMICS — Abstracting, Bibliographies, Statistics

332.6 US
MARGO'S MARKET MONITOR. 1980. s-m. $125. Minuteman Publishing Co., P.O. Box 642, Lexington, MA 02173. TEL 617-861-0302. FAX 617-861-1489. Ed. Margo Parrish. bk.rev.; circ. 4,000 (paid). **Document type:** newsletter.
Description: Discusses the stock market, small stocks and Fidelity Select mutual funds.

332.642 US ISSN 1071-1740
MARKET CHARTS. 1962. m, bi-w. $335 m; bi-w $555 (foreign $355 m, bi-w $595) (effective 1997). Market Charts, Inc., 350 Hudson St., New York, NY 10014. TEL 212-243-0829. E-mail: MKTCHTS@aol.com. (Subscr. to: Market Charts, Box 824-Village Sta., NY.,NY10014-0824. TEL 800-431-6082) Ed. Dirk J. vandenHeuvel. (back issues avail.) **Document type:** consumer publication.
•Also available online.
Description: Publishes 1 pt. reversal point & figure charts on all stocks on ASE & NYSE and 60 NASDAQ.

332.6 US ISSN 0892-3272
MARKET CYCLE INVESTING;* my bucks report. 1974. 12/yr. $98.50. Andrews Publications (Templeton), 156 Shadow Creek Ln., Paso Robles, CA 93446-1922. TEL 408-778-2925. Ed. R. Earl Andrews. (looseleaf format; back issues avail.) **Document type:** newsletter.
Formerly (until 1983): Andrews Market Cycle Investing.
Description: Growth stocks for long-term investors.

332.6 US
MARKET EXPRESS. 1984. irreg. $49. Gulf Atlantic Publishing, Inc., 1801 Lee Rd., No. 301, Winter Park, FL 32789-2165. TEL 407-628-5700. FAX 407-628-0807. Ed. Roberto Veitia. circ. 25,000.
Description: Provides information and analysis concerning the financial and investment markets.

332.6 640.73 US ISSN 1046-2171
THE MARKET GUIDE. 1983. q. $345. Market Guide Inc., 2001 Marcus Ave., Lake Success, NY 11042. TEL 516-327-2400. FAX 516-327-2425. circ. 500. **Document type:** directory.
Formerly (until 1989): Unlisted Market Guide (ISSN 0882-0775)
Description: Covers 800 research reports on NASDAQ companies demonstrating high growth, financial strength and underlying value.

332.63 US
MARKET LETTER. m. E-mail: jwalker@qadas.com; URL: http://www.qadas.com/~jwalker/newslett.html.
•Available only online.
Description: Provides useful information and tips on stock investment.

332.6 US ISSN 0162-6817
MARKET LOGIC. 1975. s-m. $200. Institute for Econometric Research, 2200 S.W. 10th St., Deerfield Beach, FL 33442-8799. TEL 954-421-1000; 800-442-9000. FAX 954-570-8200. Ed. Norman G. Fosback. charts; stat. circ. 13,000. (looseleaf format) **Document type:** newsletter.
—CCC.
Description: Forecasts of average market price levels in 3, 6, and 12 months of the major market trend.

332.6 US ISSN 0890-023X
MARKET MONTH; Standard & Poor's investment review and forecast. m. $59. Standard & Poor's (Subsidiary of: McGraw-Hill Companies, Inc.), 25 Broadway, New York, NY 10004. TEL 212-281-8000. Ed. Jean Kozlowski. adv. **Document type:** newsletter.
Description: Offers discount brokerage customers third-party investment advice and recommendations.

332.6 US
MARKET NEWS.* bi-w. $125. Danforth Investor Services, Box 340075, Milwaukee, WI 53234-0075.
Description: Provides market and economic statistics and analysis. Includes market reviews.

332.6 CN ISSN 1194-2339
MARKET PROGRESS EXECUTIVE REPORT. m. Can.$133.75 (U.S. Can.$132.10; elsewhere Can.$137.45). Toronto Stock Exchange, Exchange Tower, 2 First Canadian Pl., Toronto, ON M5X 1J2, Canada. TEL 416-947-4655. FAX 416-947-4585.
Description: Regional and international analysis including equities, options, futures, interlisted stocks, 5 Canadian exchanges and market quality analysis.

332.6 US
MARKET SCREEN. 1985. w. price varies. Market Guide Inc., 49 Glen Head Rd., Glen Head, NY 11545. TEL 516-759-1253. FAX 516-676-9240. circ. 1,000.
•Also available online.
Description: An investment analysis program that allows the user to screen all 6,600 publicly traded companies in the Market Guide electronic database, or a selected subset of the user's choice.

MARKET SURVEY CUM DETAILED TECHNO ECONOMIC FEASIBILITY REPORTS. see BUSINESS AND ECONOMICS — Marketing And Purchasing

332.6 US
MARKET SYSTEMS. 1987. m. (plus special reports). $366 (effective 1997). Market Systems Newsletter, 2761 Mansfield Dr., Burbank, CA 91504. TEL 818-247-1133. FAX 818-247-6310. E-mail: meadors@ix.netcom.com; URL: http://ison.com/mktsys/. Ed. Greg Meadors. R&P contact: Greg Meadors. adv. contact: Greg Meadors. **Document type:** newsletter.
Formerly: Market Watch.
Description: Stockmarket timing newsletter with short-term and long-term recommendations on the Dow Jones average and SEP 500.

332.6 US ISSN 0889-7840
MARKET VANE'S BULLISH CONSENSUS. 1964. w. $395. Market Vane Corporation, Box 90490, Pasadena, CA 91109-0490. TEL 818-395-7436. FAX 818-795-7654. Ed. R. Earl Hadady. abstr.; charts; illus.; stat. (looseleaf format)
Former titles: Bullish Consensus; Market Vane.
Description: Futures market advisory service for traders and professionals.

332.6 US ISSN 0898-0799
MARKETBRIEF. 1982. m. $195 (effective 1997). Lovejoy Corporation, Box 1442, Palmer Square, Princeton, NJ 08542. TEL 609-989-9484. FAX 609-989-8455. Ed. David P. Luciano. (back issues avail.) **Document type:** newsletter.
Description: Provides buy, sell, hold, avoid ratings on optionable stocks and client stocks.

332.6 US ISSN 0047-6188
MASTER INDICATOR OF THE STOCK MARKET. 1966. 24/yr. $100. Box 3024, West Palm Beach, FL 33402. Ed. John T. Goddess. charts. circ. 3,700.

332.6 US ISSN 1065-996X
MEDICAL TECHNOLOGY STOCK LETTER. 1983. 24/yr. $320. Piedmont Venture Group, Box 40460, Berkeley, CA 94704. TEL 510-843-1857. FAX 510-843-0901. Ed. Jim McCamant.
Description: Investment advisory providing specific buy and sell recommendations on medical and biotechnology stocks.

BUSINESS AND ECONOMICS — INVESTMENTS

332.6   MX   ISSN 0185-1268
HG4503
MERCADO DE VALORES. 1940. m. free (cum. CD-ROM ed. Mex.$920) (effective Jan. 1997). Nacional Financiera, S.N.C., Subdireccion de Informacion Tecnica y Publicaciones, Insurgentes Sur 1971, Nivel Fuente, Col. Guadalupe Inn, 01020 Mexico, D.F., Mexico. TEL 52-5-3256047. Ed. Dauno Totoro Nieto. bk.rev.; bibl.; charts; mkt.; index, cum.index: 1946-1995. circ. 10,000. **Document type:** government publication.
● Also available on CD-ROM.

332.6   MX
MERCADO DE VALORES (ENGLISH EDITION); an update on Mexico's economy and finance. 1994. bi-m. free. Nacional Financiera, S.N.C., Subdireccion de Informacion Tecnica y Publicaciones, Insurgentes Sur 1971, Nivel Fuente, Col. Guadalupe Inn, 01020 Mexico DF, Mexico. TEL 52-5-3256047. Ed. Dauno Totoro Nieto. bk.rev.; bibl.; charts; mkt.; index. circ. 2,000. **Document type:** government publication.

332.6   AU   ISSN 0025-9926
MERCUR; authentischer Verlosungsanzeiger mit Anzeiger aufgebotener Wertpapiere. m. S.330 (foreign S.400). Oesterreichischer Kontrollbank, Am Hof 4, A-1010 Vienna, Austria. adv.; index. circ. 2,000. (tabloid format) **Document type:** bulletin.

MERGERS AND RESTRUCTURINGS. see *BUSINESS AND ECONOMICS*

332.6   US
MERRILL LYNCH MARKET LETTER. s-m. $49. Merrill Lynch, Pierce, Fenner & Smith, Inc., 1 Liberty Plaza, New York, NY 10006. (Subscr. to: Subscription Processing Center, New Brunswick, NJ 08988-0009)

332.6   US
▼**THE MESSENGER.** 1996. irreg. E-mail: sdelsol@netcom.com; URL: http://members.tripod.com/~dowjones/home.htm. **Document type:** newsletter.
● Available only online.
   Description: Provides the independent investor with key information and a mature vision of the market.

332.6   MX
MEXICAN STOCK EXCHANGE. QUARTERLY FINANCIAL INFORMATION. q. $895 (effective May 1996). Bolsa Mexicana de Valores, S.A. de C.V., Paseo de la Reforma, 255, 06500 Mexico DF, Mexico. TEL 525-7266791. FAX 525-5910534.
   Description: Focuses on the main financial data of all the companies listed on the stock exchange. Includes notes on each company's operational performance and significant issues.

332.6   US   ISSN 1044-6303
HC131
MEXICO SERVICE. fortn. $695. International Reports, Inc., 11300 Rockville Pike, Ste. 1100, Rockville, MD 20852-3035. TEL 301-816-8950. FAX 301-816-8945. Ed. Robert G. Taylor. **Document type:** bulletin.
● Also available online.
—CCC.
   Description: Reports on economic, financial and political developments in Mexico.

332.6 382   IT
MILANO FINANZA.* 1986. w. L.135000. Milano Finanza Editori S.p.A., Via Burigozzo 5, 20122 Milan, Italy. TEL 02-809161. Ed. Paolo Panerai. circ. 90,000.

332.6   UK
MITSUBISHI FINANCE RISK DIRECTORY (YEAR); a guide to risk management products and services worldwide. 1991. a. £65($110) (effective 1996). (Mitsubishi Finance International plc) Risk Magazine, 104-112 Marylebone Ln., London W1M 5FU, England. TEL 44-171-487-5326. FAX 44-171-486-0879. Ed. Robert Jameson. R&P contact: Robert Jameson. adv. contact: Noreen Sultan. **Document type:** directory.
   Description: Lists banks, brokerages, and exchanges worldwide offering financial risk management and derivatives.

332.6   US   ISSN 0734-3957
MODERN SECURITIES TRANSFERS (SUPPLEMENT). Key Title: Israels and Guttman's Modern Securities Transfers. Cumulative Supplement. base vol. (plus irreg. updates). $115 (foreign $166.95) (effective 1994). Warren, Gorham & Lamont, One Penn Plaza, New York, NY 10119. TEL 212-971-5000. FAX 212-971-5113. (Subscr. to: The Park Square Bldg., 31 St. James Ave., Boston, MA 02116-4112. TEL 800-950-1207) **Document type:** trade publication.

332.6   US
MONETARY DIGEST. 1974. q. $36. Certified Mint, Inc., 3550 N. Central Ave., Ste. 705, Phoenix, AZ 85012. bk.rev. circ. 3,000. (reprint service avail.)
   Description: Covers political, economic and social issues affecting the price of precious metals.

332.6   US
MONEY - FORECAST LETTER.* 1980. m. $150. Financial Research Center, 1750 Washington St., Holliston, MA 01746-2234. TEL 508-429-1920. Ed. Adrian Van Eck. circ. 5,000.
   Formerly: Financial Forecast Letter.

332.6 332   US
MONEY MANAGEMENT LETTER; bi-weekly newsletter covering the pensions & money management industry. 1980. bi-w. $1595 (Canada $1625; elsewhere $1670). Institutional Investor Newsletters, 477 Madison Ave., New York, NY 10022. TEL 212-224-3233. FAX 212-224-3353. Ed. Tom Lamont. adv. (also avail. in microfiche; reprint service avail. from UMI) **Document type:** newsletter.
● Also available on CD-ROM.
   Incorporates: Trust News.
   Description: Covers the business of U.S. pension fund investment managers. Reports on which funds are hiring new money managers and why, what new strategies and products are being used, personnel changes that shift market power, and trends in master trust and custodial services.

332.6   US
MONEY MANAGER PORTFOLIOS.* 1980. q. $1500. H.F. Pearson & Co., 1355 Piccard Dr., Rockville, MD 20850-4315. Ed. Jean Baner. (also avail. in magnetic tape; back issues avail.)

332.6   US   ISSN 0271-7751
MONEY MARKET FUND SURVEY.* 1980. m. $450. Survey Publications Co., Box 20429, New York, NY 10028-0053. TEL 212-988-2498. Ed. Judith C. Lack. charts; stat. (looseleaf format; back issues avail.)

332.6   US
MONEY MARKET INSIGHT. 1989. m. $675. IBC - Donoghue, Inc., 290 Eliot St., Ashland, MA 01721. TEL 508-881-2800. FAX 508-881-0982. (In U.K.: Eurostudy Publishing Co. Ltd., 9-13 St.Andrews St., London EC4A 3AE, England. TEL 44-171-936-2016) Ed. Tracy Burke. charts. circ. 1,000. (looseleaf format) **Document type:** trade publication.
● Also available online.
   Formerly: I B C's Money Market Insight (ISSN 1043-285X)
   Description: Provides the investment professional with statistical summary on over 1100 taxable and tax-free money funds and reports on trends in short term investing with in-depth analysis of the fixed income market.

332.6   AT   ISSN 0729-3836
MONEY MATTERS. 1949. w. Aus.$295. Australian Press Services Pty. Ltd., P.O. Box E 160, Queen Victoria Terr., A.C.T. 2600, Australia. TEL 61-6-2731600. FAX 61-6-2734071. Ed. R.D. Chalmers. **Document type:** newsletter.

332.6   UK   ISSN 0263-7669
MONEY OBSERVER. 1979. m. £27. Guardian Magazines, 75 Farringdon Rd., London EC1M 3JY, England. TEL 071-713-4199. FAX 071-713-4217. Ed. John Davis. circ. 40,000 (paid). **Document type:** consumer publication.
   Description: Covers investment subjects.

332.6   CN   ISSN 0709-0579
MONEY REPORTER; the insider's letter for investors whose interest is more interest. (Supplement avail.: Monthly Key Investment) 1978. bi-w. Can.$197. M P L Communications Inc., 133 Richmond St. W., Ste. 700, Toronto, ON M5H 3M8, Canada. TEL 416-869-1177. FAX 416-869-0456. **Document type:** newsletter.
   Description: Financial news about interest.

332.6   US   ISSN 0899-1391
THE MONEYCHANGER. 1981. m. $95 (foreign $107) (effective 1996). Box 341753, Memphis, TN 38184-1753. TEL 901-853-6136. FAX 901-854-5138. E-mail: 76473.2425@compuserve.com. Ed. Franklin Sanders. R&P contact: Franklin Sanders. bk.rev. (tabloid format; back issues avail.) **Document type:** bulletin.

332.6   CN   ISSN 0703-7163
THE MONEYLETTER. 1976. s-m. Can.$97. Hume Publishing Company Ltd., 604-2200 Yonge St., Toronto, ON M4S 2C6, Canada. TEL 800-733-4863. FAX 416-440-8268. Ed. A. Micheal Keerma. adv. contact: Barbara Ritchie. **Document type:** newsletter.
   Description: Stock market advice with how-to tips on personal investment planning and strategy.

332.6   US
MONEYLETTER (ASHLAND). 1980. s-m. $109. IBC - Donoghue, Inc., Box 9104, Ashland, MA 01721-9104. TEL 508-881-2800; 800-343-5413. FAX 508-881-0982. Ed. Peter Crane. charts; stat. circ. 30,000. (looseleaf format) **Document type:** newsletter.
● Also available online.
   Formerly: Donoghue's Moneyletter (ISSN 0197-7083); Butler's Moneyletter.
   Description: Information on no- and low-load mutual funds.

332.6   US   ISSN 0745-9858
MONEYPAPER. 1982. m. $81. Temper of the Times Communications, Inc., 1010 Mamaroneck Ave., Mamaroneck, NY 10543. TEL 914-381-5400. FAX 914-381-7206. Ed. Vita Nelson; Pub. Vita Nelson. R&P contact: Maria Blasi. **Document type:** newsletter.
   Description: Publishes the comments of the most credible and responsible people in every area where investments are feasible.

332.6   US
MONEYWORLD. 1987. m. $29. Gulf Atlantic Publishing, Inc., 1801 Lee Rd., No. 301, Winter Park, FL 32789-2165. TEL 407-628-5700. FAX 407-628-0807. Ed. Roberto Veitia. adv.; bk.rev. circ. 150,000.
   Description: Offers new information, insights and specific recommendations for investors and professional financial planners.

332.6 330.9   AT
MONITOR MONEY REVIEW. 1961. s-m. Aus.$85 (effective Jan. 1990). Monitor Money Corporation, 845 Pacific Hwy., Chatswood, N.S.W. 2067, Australia. TEL 61-2-419 8199. FAX 61-2-413-1181. circ. 8,000.
   Former titles: Monitor Money Marketwatch; Midas Newsletter.

353.9 332.6   US   ISSN 0090-9912
HJ3835.M9
MONTANA. OFFICE OF THE LEGISLATIVE AUDITOR. STATE OF MONTANA BOARD OF INVESTMENTS. REPORT ON EXAMINATION OF FINANCIAL STATEMENTS. Key Title: State of Montana Investment Program. Report on Audit. (Report year ends June 30) a. free. Office of the Legislative Auditor, Box 201705, Helena, MT 59620-1705. TEL 406-444-3122. stat. **Document type:** government publication.

332.6   CN   ISSN 0828-8178
MONTHLY STOCK CHARTS - CANADIAN COMPANIES. 1984. q. Can.$98.44. Independent Survey Co., P.O. Box 6000, Vancouver, BC V6B 4B9, Canada. TEL 604-731-5777; 800-665-3389. E-mail: isc@mail.isccharts.com. Ed. Michael den Hertog. **Document type:** bulletin.
   Description: Charts 12 years of monthly share price and volume for 1300 Canadian resource and industrial companies.

BUSINESS AND ECONOMICS — INVESTMENTS

332   US   ISSN 0027-0814
MOODY'S BANK AND FINANCE NEWS REPORTS. 1928. s-w. included in subscr. to Moody's Bank and Finance Manual. Moody's Investors Service (Subsidiary of: Dun & Bradstreet Corporation), 99 Church St., New York, NY 10007. TEL 212-553-0300. FAX 212-553-4700. Ed. Robert Hanson. stat.; index, cum.index. (also avail. in microform from MIS)
—CCC.
Description: Informs readers of any new mergers, developments, and interim earnings.

332.6   US   ISSN 0148-1878
HG4905
MOODY'S BOND RECORD AND ANNUAL BOND RECORD SERVICE. m. $280. Moody's Investors Service (Subsidiary of: Dun & Bradstreet Corporation), 99 Church St., New York, NY 10007. TEL 212-553-0300. FAX 212-553-4700. (also avail. in microform from MIS)
—CCC.
Formerly: Moody's Bond Record.
Description: Comprehensive, fact-filled guide to 56,000 fixed-income issues.

332.6   US   ISSN 0027-0822
HG4905
MOODY'S BOND SURVEY. (Includes annual number) w. $1350. Moody's Investors Service (Subsidiary of: Dun & Bradstreet Corporation), 99 Church St., New York, NY 10007. TEL 212-553-0300. FAX 212-553-4700. (also avail. in microform from MIS)
—CCC.
Description: Highlights new and prospective fixed-income offerings and includes commentaries on economic and market conditions.

332.6   US
MOODY'S DIVIDEND RECORD AND ANNUAL DIVIDEND RECORD. (Includes a. & cum. supplement) s-w. $620. Moody's Investors Service (Subsidiary of: Dun & Bradstreet Corporation), 99 Church St., New York, NY 10007-0300. TEL 212-553-0300. FAX 212-553-4700. (also avail. in microform from MIS)
Formerly: Moody's Dividend Record.
Description: Reports on current dividend data of 17,000 securities.

332.6   US   ISSN 0027-0830
HG4501
MOODY'S HANDBOOK OF COMMON STOCKS. 1955. q. $225. Moody's Investors Service (Subsidiary of: Dun & Bradstreet Corporation), 99 Church St., New York, NY 10007-0300. TEL 212-553-0300. FAX 212-553-4700. Ed. John J. Esposito. adv.; charts; stat. (also avail. in microform from MIS)
—CCC.
Description: Covers performing trends and financial summaries of 950 NYSE and AMEX companies, and financial listings of 750 additional companies.

332.6   US   ISSN 1059-8057
HG4501
MOODY'S HANDBOOK OF N A S D A Q STOCKS. (National Association of Securities Dealers Automated Quotations) 1981. q. $65. Moody's Investors Service (Subsidiary of: Dun & Bradstreet Corporation), 99 Church St., New York, NY 10007-0300. TEL 212-553-0300. FAX 212-553-4700. Ed. John J. Esposito. (also avail. in microform from MIS)
—CCC.
Formerly: Moody's Handbook of O T C Stocks (ISSN 0276-3516)
Description: Reference for fast facts, performance trends and financial summaries of over 600 NASDAQ companies.

332.6   US   ISSN 0545-0217
HG4961
MOODY'S INDUSTRIAL MANUAL. (Includes: News Reports) 1900. a. $1395. Moody's Investors Service (Subsidiary of: Dun & Bradstreet Corporation), 99 Church St., New York, NY 10007-0300. TEL 212-553-0300. FAX 212-553-4700. Ed. Robert Hanson. stat.; index. (also avail. in microfiche from MIS)
—CCC.
Description: Provides business and financial information on nearly 2,000 top industrial corporations.

332.6   US   ISSN 0027-0849
HG4961
MOODY'S INDUSTRIAL NEWS REPORTS. 1900. 2/wk. (included in subscr. to Moody's Industrial Manual). Moody's Investors Service (Subsidiary of: Dun & Bradstreet Corporation), 99 Church St., New York, NY 10007-0300. TEL 212-553-0300. FAX 212-553-4200. Ed. Robert Hanson. stat.; index, cum.index. (also avail. in microform from MIS)
—CISTI. CCC.
Formerly: (until 1970): Moody's Industrials.
Description: Informs readers of mergers and acquisitions, interim earnings, new products and any other financial developments.

332.6   US
MOODY'S INTERNATIONAL COMPANY DATA. q. (plus m. updates). $7000. Moody's Investors Service (Subsidiary of: Dun & Bradstreet Corporation), 99 Church St., New York, NY 10007. TEL 212-553-0300. FAX 212-553-4700. (also avail. in microform from MIS)
● Available only on CD-ROM.
Formerly: Moody's International Plus.
Description: Provides business and financial information on over 7,000 non-US based companies operating in more than 90 countries.

332.678   US   ISSN 0278-3509
HG4009
MOODY'S INTERNATIONAL MANUAL. 1981. a. $2495 (includes w. News Reports). Moody's Investors Service (Subsidiary of: Dun & Bradstreet Corporation), 99 Church St., New York, NY 10007-0300. TEL 212-553-0300. FAX 212-553-4700. Ed. Robert Hanson. (also avail. in microfiche from MIS)
—CCC.
Description: Financial and business data on over 7,500 companies in nearly 90 countries.

332.678   US   ISSN 0278-3517
MOODY'S INTERNATIONAL NEWS REPORTS. 1981. w. (included in subscr. to Moody's International Manual). Moody's Investors Service (Subsidiary of: Dun & Bradstreet Corporation), 99 Church St., New York, NY 10007-0300. TEL 212-553-0300. FAX 212-553-4700. Ed. Robert Hanson. (also avail. in microform from MIS)
—CCC.
Description: Keeps readers on top of mergers and acquisitions, new companies, joint ventures, interim earnings, revised Moody's ratings and any news and developments affecting companies in this manual.

332.6   US   ISSN 0545-0233
HG4931
MOODY'S MUNICIPAL AND GOVERNMENT MANUAL. 1988. a. $1995 (includes s-w. news report). Moody's Investors Service (Subsidiary of: Dun & Bradstreet Corporation), 99 Church St., New York, NY 10007-0300. TEL 212-553-0300. FAX 212-553-4700. Ed. Robert Hanson. stat.; index. (also avail. in microfiche from MIS)
—CCC.
Description: Covers over 15,000 bond-issuing municipalities and government agencies.

332.6   US   ISSN 0027-0857
MOODY'S MUNICIPAL AND GOVERNMENT NEWS REPORTS. 1928. s-w. (incl. in subscr. to Moody's Municipal and Government Manual). Moody's Investors Service (Subsidiary of: Dun & Bradstreet Corporation), 99 Church St., New York, NY 10007-0300. TEL 212-553-0300. FAX 212-553-4700. Ed. Robert Hanson. stat.; index, cum.index. (also avail. in microform from MIS)
—CCC.
Formerly: Moody's Municipals and Government.
Description: Updates changes in Moody's ratings and new bond descriptions, financial statistics and audit reports, plus news affecting issues rated and covered in the manual.

332.6   US   ISSN 0192-7167
HG4961
MOODY'S O T C INDUSTRIAL MANUAL. (Over-the-Counter) a. $1275 (includes bi-w. Moody's O T C Industroal News Report). Moody's Investors Service (Subsidiary of: Dun & Bradstreet Corporation), 99 Church St., New York, NY 10007-0300. TEL 212-553-0300. FAX 212-553-4700. Ed. Robert Hanson. (also avail. in microfiche from MIS)
—CCC.
Description: Covers more than 2,000 industrial companies traded on NASDAQ over-the-counter and regional exchanges.

332.6   US   ISSN 0027-0865
HG4965
MOODY'S O T C INDUSTRIAL NEWS REPORTS. (Over-the-Counter) 1970. s-w. (included in subscr. to Moody's OTC Industrial Manual). Moody's Investors Service (Subsidiary of: Dun & Bradstreet Corporation), 99 Church St., New York, NY 10007-0300. TEL 212-553-0300. FAX 212-553-4700. Ed. Robert Hanson. stat.; index, cum.index. (also avail. in microform from MIS)
—CCC.
Formerly: Moody's O T C Industrials.

332.6   US   ISSN 0890-5282
HG4907
MOODY'S O T C UNLISTED MANUAL. (Over-the-Counter) (Supplement avail.: Moody's O T C Unlisted News Reports (ISSN 0895-3252)) 1986. a. $1150 (includes w. supplement). Moody's Investors Service (Subsidiary of: Dun & Bradstreet Corporation), 99 Church St., New York, NY 10007-0300. TEL 212-553-0300. FAX 212-553-4700. Ed. Robert Hanson. stat.; index. (also avail. in microform from MIS)
—CCC.
Description: Covers financial facts and corporate data on more than 2,000 companies not listed on the national or regional exchange systems.

332.6   US   ISSN 0545-0241
HG4961
MOODY'S PUBLIC UTILITY MANUAL. a. $1250 (includes bi-w. Moody's Public Utility News Reports). Moody's Investors Service (Subsidiary of: Dun & Bradstreet Corporation), 99 Church St., New York, NY 10007-0300. TEL 212-553-0300. FAX 212-553-4700. Ed. Robert Hanson. (also avail. in microfiche from MIS)
—CCC.
Description: Covers financial and operating data on all U.S. public and privately-held utilities.

332.6   US   ISSN 0027-0873
MOODY'S PUBLIC UTILITY NEWS REPORTS. 1928. s-w. included in subscr. to Moody's Public Utility Manual. Moody's Investors Service (Subsidiary of: Dun & Bradstreet Corporation), 99 Church St., New York, NY 10007-0300. TEL 212-553-0300. FAX 212-553-4700. Ed. Robert Hanson. stat.; index, cum.index. (also avail. in microform from MIS)
—CCC.
Description: Informs readers of news affecting companies listed in the Public Utility Manual.

332.6   US   ISSN 0545-025X
HG4971
MOODY'S TRANSPORTATION MANUAL. a. $1150 includes w. Moody's Transportation News Reports. Moody's Investors Service (Subsidiary of: Dun & Bradstreet Corporation), 99 Church St., New York, NY 10007-0300. TEL 212-553-0300. FAX 212-553-4700. Ed. Robert Hanson. (also avail. in microfiche from MIS)
—CCC.
Description: Covers financial and operating data on all major public and private air, rail, bus, trucking, vehicle leasing and rental, and shipping companies.

332.6   US   ISSN 0027-089X
MOODY'S TRANSPORTATION NEWS REPORTS; railroads, airlines, shipping, bus, pipe and truck lines. 1928. w. included in subscr. to Moody's Transportation Manual. Moody's Investors Service (Subsidiary of: Dun & Bradstreet Corporation), 99 Church St., New York, NY 10007-0300. TEL 212-553-0300. FAX 212-553-4700. Ed. Robert Hanson. stat.; index, cum.index. (also avail. in microform from MIS)
—CCC.
Formerly: Moody's Transportation.
Description: Informs readers of news affecting companies listed in the manual.

BUSINESS AND ECONOMICS — INVESTMENTS

332.6 US ISSN 1081-2598
MORE THAN MONEY; exploring the personal, political, and spritual impact of wealth in our lives. 1993. q. $35 (Canada & Mexico $40; elsewhere $45). Impact Project, 2244 Alder St., Eugene, OR 97405-8900. TEL 541-343-2420. E-mail: impact@epn.orgm; URL: http://www.efn.org/~impact. Ed. Anne Slepian; Pub. Allen Hancock. R&P contact: Allen Hancock. adv. contact: Allen Hancock. bk.rev.; illus.; circ. 1,000. Document type: monographic series.
  Description: Explores various ethical issues concerning possessing and creating monetary wealth and offers practical advice.

332.6 US ISSN 1059-1419
HG4530
MORNINGSTAR CLOSED-END FUNDS. 1991. bi-w. $195 in U.S; Canada $225; elsewhere $275. Morningstar, Inc., 225 W. Wacker Dr., 400, Chicago, IL 60606. TEL 312-696-6000. FAX 312-696-6001. Ed. Catherine Gillis. charts; stat. circ. 7,000. (back issues avail.) Document type: newsletter.
  Description: Provides performance data, rankings, portfolio information and written analysis for over 280 closed-ends funds.

332.632 US ISSN 1059-1443
HG4530
MORNINGSTAR MUTUAL FUNDS. 1986. bi-w. $395 in U.S; Canada and Mexico $465; elsewhere $525. Morningstar, Inc., 225 W. Wacker Dr., Ste. 400, Chicago, IL 60606. TEL 312-696-6000. FAX 312-696-6001. Ed. John Rekenthaler. charts; stat. circ. 45,000. (looseleaf format; back issues avail.) Document type: newsletter.
  Formerly: Mutual Fund Values (ISSN 0890-7153)
  Description: Provides comprehensive information, including performance data, ratings, portfolio listings, and written analyses on 1240 mutual funds. Features commentaries on various fund-related subjects.

332.6 US ISSN 1059-1427
HG4530
MORNINGSTAR MUTUAL FUNDS ONDISC. 1991. m. (plus q. and a. updates). price varies. Morningstar, Inc., 225 W. Wacker Dr., Chicago, IL 60606. TEL 312-696-6000. FAX 312-696-6001. Ed. Michael Van Dam. circ. 2,000.
  ●Available only on CD-ROM.
  Description: Compares, analyzes and tracks over 3,200 mutual funds and produces customized reports and graphs.

332.6 US ISSN 1059-1435
HG8790
MORNINGSTAR VARIABLE ANNUITY PERFORMANCE REPORT. 1991. m. $125 in U.S.; Canada and Mexico $130; elsewhere $175. Morningstar, Inc., 225 W. Wacker Dr., Ste. 400, Chicago, IL 60606. TEL 312-696-6000. FAX 312-696-6001. Ed. Jennifer Strickland. circ. 2,500. (back issues avail.)
  Description: Contains performance data, rankings and statistics for over 1500 variable-annuity and variable-life subaccounts.

332.6 US ISSN 1062-3361
HG8790
MORNINGSTAR VARIABLE ANNUITY SOURCEBOOK. 1992. a. $195 in U.S. and Canada and Mexico $215; elsewhere $235. Morningstar, Inc., 225 W. Wacker Dr., Ste. 400, Chicago, IL 60606. TEL 312-696-6000. FAX 312-696-6001. Ed. Jennifer Strickland. circ. 1,150.
  Description: Provides performance data, star ratings, and underlying mutual fund information for over 1500 variable-annuity and variable-life subaccounts.

MORTGAGE AND REAL ESTATE EXECUTIVES REPORT.
  see REAL ESTATE

MORTGAGE-BACKED SECURITIES; developments and trends in the secondary mortgage market. see BUSINESS AND ECONOMICS — Banking And Finance

332.64 US
MORTGAGE-BACKED SECURITIES LETTER. w. $1595 (effective 1997). Investment Dealers' Digest, 2 World Trade Center, 18th Fl., New York, NY 10048-0638. TEL 212-432-0045. FAX 212-321-2336. Ed. Mark Kollar. R&P contact: Denise Robbins. adv. contact: Todd Miller.
  ●Also available online. Vendor(s): Information Access Co., UMI.

332.6 US ISSN 0744-3927
THE MORTGAGE MARKETPLACE. 1970. 48/yr. $675 for new subscr. (foreign $725); renewal $750 (foreign $809). American Banker - Bond Buyer, Newsletter Division (Subsidiary of: Thomson Financial Services Company), One State St. Plaza, New York, NY 10004-1549. TEL 800-733-4371. FAX 212-943-2224. (Subscr. to: Box 28315, Washington, DC 20038-8315. TEL 202-347-2665) Ed. James Byrne. Document type: newsletter.
  ●Also available online. Vendor(s): Information Access Co.
  —CCC.
  Incorporates: Mortgage Securities Watch; Mortgage Accountants; Mortgage Commentary; Mortgage Backed Securities Reports; Secondary Market Reporter.
  Description: Covers political developments, regulatory changes, and accounting issues affecting the market for mortgages, and mortgage-backed securities traded by banks and other financial institutions in the US.

332.6 US ISSN 1076-8491
▼**MUNICIPAL ISSUERS REGISTRY.** m. $1994. Thomson Financial Publishing, 4709 West Golf Rd., Skokie, IL 60076-1253. TEL 847-676-9600; 800-321-3373. FAX 847-933-8101. Ed. Rene Reynaldo. adv. Document type: trade publication.

332.63 US ISSN 1050-656X
HG4930
MUTUAL FUND ADVISOR. 1989. m. Mutual Fund Advisor, Inc., One Sarasota Tower, 2N Tamiami Trail, Sarasota, FL 34236. TEL 813-954-5500. FAX 813-364-8447. Ed. Donald H. Rowe. circ. 19,000 (paid). (back issues avail.) Document type: newsletter.

332.6 US ISSN 1067-1358
MUTUAL FUND BUYER'S GUIDE. 1992. m. $80. Institute for Econometric Research, 2200 S.W. 10th St., Deerfield Beach, FL 33442-8799. TEL 954-421-1000; 800-442-9000. FAX 954-570-8200. Ed. Norman G. Fosback. charts; stat.; circ. 45,000 (paid). (back issues avail.) Document type: newsletter.
  Description: Comprehensive array of ratings, statisitcs, past performance data and basic information on more than 1,500 mutual funds, covering all major stock funds, bond funds and tax-free funds.

332.63 US
MUTUAL FUND DIRECTORY. s-a. $325 (foreign $385) (effective 1997). Investment Dealers' Digest, 2 World Trade Center, 18th Fl., New York, NY 10048-0638. TEL 212-432-0045. FAX 212-321-2336. E-mail: subscribe@iddis.com. Ed. Michele Stibgen. R&P contact: Denise Robbins. adv. contact: Todd Miller. Document type: directory.

332.6327 US ISSN 8755-9889
MUTUAL FUND FORECASTER; profit and projections and risk ratings for traders and investors. 1985. m. $100. Institute for Econometric Research, 2200 S.W. 10th St., Deerfield Beach, FL 33442-8799. TEL 954-421-1000; 800-442-9000. FAX 954-570-8200. Ed. Norman G. Fosback. charts; circ. 250,000 (paid). (looseleaf format) Document type: newsletter.
  —CCC.
  Description: One-year profit projections and risk ratings for common stock mutual funds in every issue.

332.6327 US ISSN 0742-9657
MUTUAL FUND LETTER.* 1984. m. $125. Investment Information Services, Inc., 120 S. Riverside Plz., Rm. 1745, Chicago, IL 60606-3911. TEL 312-649-6940; 800-326-6941. Ed. Gerald W. Perritt. adv. contact: Michael Corbett. circ. 4,000. Document type: newsletter.

332.6 US ISSN 1070-3373
HG4530
MUTUAL FUND MARKET NEWS. w. $1250. Dalbar Inc., 600 Atlantic Ave., T-30, Boston, MA 02210-2226. TEL 617-723-6400. FAX 617-624-7200. E-mail: mfmn@dalbar.com. Ed. Susan Weiner. adv. contact: Margaret M. Misdom. (back issues avail.) Document type: newsletter, trade publication.
  Formerly (until 1993): F A C S of the Week (ISSN 1056-2540)

332.6327 US ISSN 0897-5108
HG4930
MUTUAL FUND PROFILES. Key Title: Standard & Poor's - Lipper Mutual Fund Profiles. 1987. q. $158. Standard & Poor's (Subsidiary of: McGraw-Hill Companies, Inc.), 25 Broadway, New York, NY 10004. TEL 212-208-8000. Ed. Joseph Spiers. R&P contact: James Branscome. Document type: trade publication.
  Description: Profiles more than 3,500 mutual funds, categorized by investment objective, offering year-to-date and 5-year performance data.

332.6 US ISSN 0741-1278
MUTUAL FUND SPECIALIST.* 1978. m. $95. Royal R. Lemier & Co., S7720 State Rd. 37, Eau Claire, WI 54701-9075. TEL 715-834-7425. Ed. Royal R. Lemier. (looseleaf format; back issues avail) Document type: newsletter.
  Description: Provides analyses of equity markets and mutual fund trends. Focus on family of funds concept to mutual funds investing.

332.6327 US
MUTUAL FUND STRATEGIES. 1982. m. $127. Progressive Investing, Inc., Box 446, Burlington, VT 05402. TEL 802-658-3515. Ed. Charlie Hooper.
  Description: Focuses on the top-performing Fidelity, Vanguard, and Charles Schwab mutual funds.

332.632 US ISSN 0889-0064
MUTUAL FUND TRENDS. 1985. m. $139. Growth Fund Research, Inc., Box 6600, Rapid City, SD 57709. TEL 607-341-1971. Ed. Cheryl R. Johnson. charts.
  Formerly: Mutual Fund Chartist; Incorporates: Strongest Funds (ISSN 0889-0870)
  Description: Provides charts and database for top-performing mutual funds. Includes weekly telephone hotline.

332.63 US ISSN 1067-6228
HG4530
MUTUAL FUND 500. 1993. a. $35. Morningstar, Inc., 225 W. Walker Dr., Ste. 400, Chicago, IL 60606. TEL 312-696-6000. FAX 312-696-6001. Ed. Hrach Alexanian. circ. 5,000.
  Description: Provides performance data, star ratings, and portfolio information for 500 select open- and closed-end funds.

332.6 US ISSN 1060-8524
HG4930
MUTUAL FUNDS ALMANAC. 1969. a. $39.95 soft cover. IBC - Donoghue, Inc., Box 9104, Ashland, MA 01721-9104. TEL 508-881-2800; 800-343-5413. FAX 508-881-0982. Ed. Peter Crane. adv. contact: Randy Wood. circ. 10,000. Indexed: SRI.
  Formerly: Manual of Mutual Funds (ISSN 0076-4175)
  Description: Provides names, addresses, telephone numbers and past ten year performance history.

332.6 US ISSN 0027-5182
MUTUAL FUNDS GUIDE. 1969. bi-w. $767. C C H Incorporated, 2700 Lake Cook Rd., Riverwoods, IL 60015. TEL 847-267-7000; 800-835-5224. FAX 80-224-8299. cum.index. (looseleaf format)
  —CCC.

332.6 US
MUTUAL FUNDS MAGAZINE; your monthly guide to America's best investments. 1994. m. $9.97. Institute for Econometric Research, 2200 S.W. 10th St., Deerfield Beach, FL 33442-8799. TEL 954-421-1000; 800-442-9000. FAX 954-570-8200. Ed. Norman G. Fosback. adv. contact: Ned Frey. bk.rev. circ. 350,000. Document type: consumer publication.

BUSINESS AND ECONOMICS — INVESTMENTS

332.6327 US
MUTUAL FUNDS REPORT. Variant title: C D A - Wiesenberger Mutual Funds Report. m. $275 (effective 1996). (Wiesenberger Services, Inc.) C D A - Wiesenberger (Subsidiary of: Thomson Financial Services), 1355 Piccard Dr., Rockville, MD 20850. TEL 800-232-2285. FAX 301-548-5105. E-mail: wies@cda.com. Ed. Daniel L. Phelps. circ. 1,300. **Document type:** trade publication.
  Description: Analyzes the performance, risk posture, and percentile rankings of more than 8,300 funds.

332.6 US ISSN 1066-9264
HG4930
MUTUAL FUNDS UPDATE. Variant title: C D A - Wiesenberger Mutual Funds Update. m. $295 (effective 1996). (Wiesenberger Services, Inc.) C D A - Wiesenberger (Subsidiary of: Thomson Financial Services), 1355 Piccard Dr., Rockville, MD 20850. TEL 800-232-2285. FAX 301-548-5105. E-mail: wies@cda.com. Ed. Daniel L. Phelps. circ. 2,500. **Document type:** trade publication.
  Formerly (until 1991): Wiesenberger Mutual Funds Investment Report (ISSN 0894-5977)
  Description: Provides performance review and analysis on 8,300 open-end mutual funds. Includes the top-performing funds each month, as well as top-yielding funds.

332.6 US
MYERS' FINANCE REVIEW. 1967. m. $129. Myers Finance and Energy, Inc., 104 S. Freya St., Ste. 214A, Spokane, WA 99202-4814. TEL 509-534-7132. FAX 509-534-8054. Ed. John Myers. circ. 3,000.
  Former titles (until Feb. 1993): Myers' Finance and Energy (ISSN 0376-6454); (until 1972): Myers' Finance and Petroleum (ISSN 0384-5435); Myers' Finance Review (ISSN 0376-6446); Myers' Finance Weekly (ISSN 0384-5427)
  Description: Covers the world political and economic situation with emphasis on its effect upon international monetary conditions, precious metals, stocks, bonds and interest rates.

332 US
N A R I STETHOSCOPE. 1961. q. membership. National Association of Residents and Interns, 292 Madison Ave., New York, NY 10017. TEL 212-949-5900. Ed. William Driscoll. charts; illus. circ. 15,000. **Document type:** newsletter.

332.6 338 US ISSN 0469-323X
N A S B I C NEWS. 1959. m. $125. National Association of Small Business Investment Companies, 666 11th St., N.W., Ste. 750, Washington, DC 20001. E-mail: nasbic@nasbic.org; URL: http://www.nasbic.org. Ed. Jeanette D. Paschal. circ. 1,500. **Document type:** newsletter.

332.6 332 US ISSN 0741-0921
HG4905
N A S D A Q FACT BOOK. (National Association of Securities Dealers Automated Quotations) a. $20. National Association of Securities Dealers, Inc., 1735 K St., N.W., Washington, DC 20006. TEL 202-728-6900. FAX 202-728-8882. (Dist. by: Reference Press, Inc., 6448 Hwy. 290 E., Ste. E-104, Austin, TX 78723. TEL 512-454-7778. FAX 512-454-9401) Ed. Jean Robinson. Indexed: SRI. **Document type:** directory.
  Incorporates: N A S D A Q Company Directory.
  Description: Provides extensive data on the performance of Nasdaq securities in the preceding year, and on an historical basis.

332.6 US
N A S D A Q FINANCIAL EXECUTIVE JOURNAL. (National Association of Securities Dealers Automated Quotations) 1991. bi-m. $50. National Association of Securities Dealers, Inc., 1735 K St., N.W., Washington, DC 20006. TEL 202-728-6900. FAX 202-728-8882. Ed. William Skaff. **Document type:** newsletter.
  Formerly: N A S D A Q Chief Financial Officer Newsletter.
  Description: Covers topics of interest to chief financial officers of Nasdaq companies, including investor relations, securities valuation issues, capital raising options, and other updates.

332.6 US
N A S D A Q SUBSCRIBER BULLETIN. (National Association of Securities Dealers Automated Quotations) bi-m. $80. National Association of Securities Dealers, Inc., 1735 K St., N.W., Washington, DC 20006. TEL 202-728-8474. FAX 202-728-8882. Ed. Jean Robinson. **Document type:** newsletter.
  Description: Provides information on developments in the Nasdaq market and enhancements of the Nasdaq system.

332.6 332 US
N A S D ANNUAL REPORT. a. National Association of Securities Dealers, Inc., 1735 K St., N.W., Washington, DC 20006. TEL 202-728-6900. FAX 202-728-8882. **Document type:** corporate report.

332.6 US ISSN 0274-7340
N A S D MANUAL. 1967. q. $381. (National Association of Securities Dealers, Inc.) C C H Incorporated, 2700 Lake Cook Rd., Riverwoods, IL 60015. TEL 847-267-7000; 800-835-5224. FAX 800-224-8299.

332.6 US
N A S D NOTICES TO MEMBERS. m. $225 (effective 1992). National Association of Securities Dealers, Inc., 1735 K St., N.W., Washington, DC 20006. TEL 202-728-6900. FAX 202-728-8882. Ed. Thomas P. Mathers. **Document type:** newsletter.
  Supersedes in part: N A S D Executive Digest.
  Description: Provides updates on NASD - Nasdaq regulations and legal topics, and summaries of actions taken at bi-monthly NASD Board meetings.

332.6 US
N A S D REGULATORY AND COMPLIANCE ALERT. q. $80. National Association of Securities Dealers, Inc., 1735 K St., N.W., Washington, DC 20006. TEL 202-728-6000. FAX 202-728-8882. Ed. Dick DeLouise. **Document type:** newsletter.
  Description: Provides updates on regulatory developments and disciplinary actions affecting securities trading firms.

332.6 UK ISSN 0963-0295
N G O FINANCE. (Non-Governmental Organization); professional information for non-governmental organisations. 1991. bi-m. £55 to charities; others £89 (effective 1997). Plaza Publishing Ltd., 1A Tradescant Rd., London SW8 1XD, England. TEL 44-171-793-0001. FAX 44-171-735-2009. Ed. Daniel Phelan; Pub. Daniel Phelan. adv.: B&W page £1495, color page £1695; adv. contact: Alice Frackelton. circ. 5,500. **Document type:** trade publication.
  —BLDSC (6109.401550).
  Description: Essential information and analysis on all matters relating to the financial and legal management of charitable NGOs.

N I M A - NELSON DIRECTORY OF MINORITY & WOMAN-OWNED INVESTMENT MANAGERS. (National Investment Managers Association) see BUSINESS AND ECONOMICS — Trade And Industrial Directories

332.6 US ISSN 1060-6629
N Y S E WEEKLY STOCK BUYS. 1991. w. $45. Elton Stephens Investments, 4016 S. Michigan St., South Bend, IN 46614-2544. TEL 219-291-3823. (Subscr. to: Box 476, South Bend, IN 46624-0476) Ed. Elton Stephens. index. circ. 8,000. (looseleaf format; back issues avail.) **Document type:** newsletter.

332.63 GW ISSN 0027-741X
NACHRICHTEN FUER AUSSENHANDEL. Short title: N F A. 1947. d. (5/w.). DM.150.10. Vereinigte Wirtschaftsdienste GmbH, Niederurseler Allee 8-10, 65760 Eschborn, Germany. TEL 06196-4050. FAX 06196-482007. (Subscr. to: Postfach 6105, 65735 Eschborn, Germany) **Document type:** trade publication.
  Former titles: V W D - Nachrichten fuer Aussenhandel; V W D - Informationen.

NATIONAL AGENCY OF INDUSTRY AND TRADE. ANNUAL REPORTS (YEAR)/AARSBERETNINGER. see BUSINESS AND ECONOMICS — Production Of Goods And Services

332.62 US ISSN 0277-5018
NATIONAL ASSOCIATION OF SMALL BUSINESS INVESTMENT COMPANIES. MEMBERSHIP DIRECTORY. a. $20. National Association of Small Business Investment Companies, 666 11th St., N.W., Ste. 750, Washington, DC 20001. E-mail: nasbic@masbic.org; URL: http://www.nasbic.org. **Document type:** directory.

332.6 346.066 US ISSN 0737-4062
NATIONAL FUTURES ASSOCIATION MANUAL. 1983. q. National Futures Association, 200 W. Madison St., Ste. 1600, Chicago, IL 60606. TEL 312-781-1300. FAX 312-781-1467. E-mail: publicaffairs@nfa.futures.org; URL: http://www.nfa.futures.org. (looseleaf format)

332.6 US
NATIONAL INVESTOR RELATIONS INSTITUTE. ANNUAL REPORT. a. National Investor Relations Institute, 8045 Leesburg Pike, Ste. 600, Vienna, VA 22182-2737. TEL 703-506-3570.

NELSON'S DIRECTORY OF INSTITUTIONAL REAL ESTATE. see BUSINESS AND ECONOMICS — Trade And Industrial Directories

NELSON'S DIRECTORY OF INVESTMENT MANAGERS. see BUSINESS AND ECONOMICS — Trade And Industrial Directories

NELSON'S DIRECTORY OF INVESTMENT RESEARCH. see BUSINESS AND ECONOMICS — Trade And Industrial Directories

NELSON'S DIRECTORY OF PLAN SPONSORS. see BUSINESS AND ECONOMICS — Trade And Industrial Directories

332.6 US ISSN 1049-3344
HG4915
NELSON'S EARNINGS OUTLOOK. 1990. m. $240 (effective 1993). Nelson Publications, 1 Gateway Plaza, Box 591, Port Chester, NY 10573. TEL 914-937-8400. FAX 914-937-8908. **Document type:** trade publication.
  Description: Reports on consensus earnings per share estimates for over 3000 stocks based on forecasts by analysts from approximately 200 investment firms worldwide; includes quarterly industry profiles.

332.6 US ISSN 1059-9290
Z7164.F5
NELSON'S GUIDE TO INSTITUTIONAL RESEARCH. (Supplement to: Nelson's Directory of Investment Research) 1985. 10/yr. $125 (effective 1993). Nelson Publications, 1 Gateway Plaza, Box 591, Port Chester, NY 10573. TEL 914-937-8400. FAX 914-937-8908. adv. circ. 4,000. (looseleaf format)
  Former titles (until 1992): Nelson's Global Research (ISSN 1044-0267); (until 1990): Nelson's Research Monthly (ISSN 0886-0521); Nelson's Official Research Guide (ISSN 0883-7287)
  Description: Lists job changes in the investment world, and catalogues securities research reports on general industries and specific companies.

NELSON'S GUIDE TO PENSION FUND CONSULTANTS. see BUSINESS AND ECONOMICS — Trade And Industrial Directories

332.6 US
NEST EGG. 1993. m. Investment Dealers' Digest, Inc., Two World Trade Center, New York, NY 10048-0638. TEL 212-227-1200. Ed. Paul Lengemann. adv.: B&W page $29750. **Document type:** trade publication.

332.6 US ISSN 0742-4507
HG4528
NETBACK. 1982. bi-m. $75 included in subscr. to Good Money. Good Money Publications, Inc., Box 363 UIP, Worcester, VT 05682. TEL 802-223-3911; 800-535-3551. FAX 802-223-8949. Ed. Lisa M. Syverson. bk.rev.; abstr.; stat.; tr.lit. (back issues avail.)
  Formerly (until 1985): Netbacking.

NETHERLANDS INSTITUTE OF BANKERS AND STOCK BROKERS. PUBLICATIONS. see BUSINESS AND ECONOMICS — Banking And Finance

NEW & EMERGING TECHNOLOGY; executive newsreport and forecast on industrial innovation. see TECHNOLOGY: COMPREHENSIVE WORKS

BUSINESS AND ECONOMICS — INVESTMENTS

332.6   US   ISSN 1073-7642
NEW ISSUE DIGEST. (Supplement to: Growth Stock Outlook) 1971. q. $50 per issue. Growth Stock Outlook, Inc., 4405 East-West Hwy., Ste. 305, Bethesda, MD 20814. TEL 301-654-5205. Ed. Charles Allmon. charts. **Document type:** newsletter.
    Description: Monitors the new issue market; refers to the more attractive new issues before the public offering.

332.678   US   ISSN 0162-9050
HG4501
NEW ISSUES; the investor's guide to initial public offerings. 1978. m. $200. Institute for Econometric Research, 2200 S.W. 10th St., Deerfield Beach, FL 33442-8799. TEL 954-421-1000; 800-442-9000. FAX 954-570-8200. Ed. Norman G. Fosback. charts; stat. (back issues avail.) **Document type:** newsletter.
—CCC.
    Description: In-depth analyses of attractive forthcoming initial public offerings, including fundamental and earnings data and details on the offerings and their underwriters.

332.6   US   ISSN 0271-0714
NEW YORK STOCK EXCHANGE GUIDE. 1957. m. $489. C C H Incorporated, 2700 Lake Cook Rd., Riverwoods, IL 60015. TEL 847-267-7000; 800-835-5224. FAX 800-224-8299.

382   US
NEWS, FACTS, ACTIONS. 1983. bi-m. free. National Futures Association, 200 W. Madison St., Ste. 1600, Chicago, IL 60606. TEL 312-781-1373. FAX 312-781-1467. E-mail: publicaffairs@nfa.futures.org; URL: www.nfa.futures.org. Ed. Larry Dyekman. circ. 4,500. **Document type:** newsletter.
    Formerly: N F A News, Facts, Actions.
    Description: Covers the activities of the self-regulatory organization of the commodity futures industry.

332.6   US   ISSN 1015-0188
NEWS FROM I C S I D. 1984. 2/yr. free. International Centre for Settlement of Investment Disputes, 1818 H St., N.W., Washington, DC 20433. TEL 202-458-1533. FAX 202-522-2615. TELEX ITT 440098 WORLDBANK. circ. 3,000. **Document type:** newsletter.

NEWSLETTER DIGEST. see BUSINESS AND ECONOMICS — Abstracting, Bibliographies, Statistics

332   US   ISSN 0736-6256
NO-LOAD FUND INVESTOR. 1979. m. $129 (with Handbook [$149). No-Load Fund Investor, Inc., Box 318, Irvington-on-Hudson, NY 10533. TEL 914-693-7420; 800-252-2042. Ed. Sheldon Jacobs.
    Description: Provides coverage of no-load funds available to the public, as well as direct-marketed low-loads. Includes specific fund recommendations, market timing advice, and fund news.

332.64   US
▼**NO-LOAD STOCK INSIDER**. 1996. bi-m. $33. NorthStar Financial, Inc., 7412 Calumet Ave., Ste. 200, Hammond, IN 46324-2692. TEL 219-852-3270. Ed. Charles B. Carlson. circ. 4,500.

332.6   US   ISSN 0194-0104
NOLOAD FUND X. 1976. m. $129 ($178 with Mid-Month supplement). Dal Investment Co., Russ Bldg., Ste. 662, 235 Montgomery St., San Francisco, CA 94104. TEL 415-986-7979; 800-763-8639. FAX 415-986-1595. E-mail: noloadfx@aol.com. Eds. Burton Berry, Janet Brown; Pub. Burton Berry. R&P contact: Donald Patrick. stat. circ. 6,500. (back issues avail.) **Document type:** newsletter.
    Description: Investment system and performance data covering all no-load and low-load funds.

332.6   US   ISSN 0549-8333
NORTH DAKOTA SECURITIES BULLETIN. a. free. Commissioner of Securities, 601 East Boulevard, Bismarck, ND 58505. Ed. Cal Hoovestol. circ. 225. **Document type:** bulletin.

NORTHERN NEW ENGLAND REAL ESTATE JOURNAL. see REAL ESTATE

332.6   CN   ISSN 0226-9325
O S C BULLETIN. 1981. w. price varies. Micromedia Ltd., 20 Victoria St., Toronto, ON M5C 2N8, Canada. TEL 416-362-5211. FAX 416-362-6161. TELEX 065-24668. E-mail: info@micromedia.on.ca; URL: http://www.mmltd.com. Ed.Bd. R&P contact: Gail Dykstra. adv.; cum.index. circ. 1,500. **Document type:** bulletin.
● Also available on CD-ROM.
    Formed by the merger of: Ontario Securities Commission. Monthly Bulletin (ISSN 0030-3097); Ontario Securities Commission. Weekly Summary (ISSN 0030-3100)
    Description: Summarizes corporate changes and filings, insider trading, and Commission rulings.

332.6   US   ISSN 0892-2632
O T C GROWTH STOCK WATCH. (Over the Counter) 1979. m. $299. O T C Research Corporation, 1040 Great Plain Ave., Needham, MA 02192-2517. TEL 617-444-6100. Ed. John McElligotten; Pub. Geoffrey J. Eiten. circ. 1,000. (back issues avail.) **Document type:** newsletter.
—CCC.

332.643   US   ISSN 0733-026X
HG4009
O T C HANDBOOK. (Over the Counter) 1981. s-a. $74. Standard & Poor's Corporation (Subsidiary of: McGraw-Hill, Inc.), 25 Broadway, New York, NY 10004. TEL 212-208-8000. Ed. Ronald Oliver.

332.6   UK   ISSN 1352-030X
OFFSHORE FINANCIAL REVIEW. m. free to qualified personnel. Financial Times Business Information, Magazines (Subsidiary of: Financial Times Group), 2 Greystoke Pl., Fetter Ln., London EC4A 1ND, England. TEL 0171-405-6969. FAX 0171-405-5726. TELEX 296926 BUSINF G. stat.; circ. controlled. (also avail. in microform from UMI) **Document type:** trade publication.
    Description: Covers industry changes and fund performance for financial advisors whose clients have offshore businesses.

OFFSHORE INVESTMENT. see BUSINESS AND ECONOMICS — Banking And Finance

332.6   US
ON WALL STREET. 1991. bi-m. $48. Securities Data Publishing, 40 W. 57th St., 11th Fl., New York, NY 10019. TEL 212-765-5311. FAX 212-765-6123. Ed. Greg Bresiger; Pub. Wendi Winshall. adv.: B&W page $4850. circ. 90,000. **Document type:** trade publication.
—CCC.
    Formerly (until Apr. 1996): Financial Planning on Wall Street (ISSN 1074-4282)
    Description: Features articles on competition from new financial services firms, tax and regulatory developments affecting clients, mutual funds, new products and investments, and long-term investment strategies.

332.6   US
OPERATIONS MANAGEMENT. bi-w. $1395 (Canada $1425; elsewhere $1470). Institutional Investor Newsletters, 477 Madison Ave., New York, NY 10022. TEL 212-224-3233. FAX 212-224-3353. **Document type:** newsletter.
    Description: Provides information on securities clearance, settlement and processing for money managers, brokers-dealers and custodians.

332.6   US
OPPORTUNIST; tomorrow's opportunity today. 1993. q. $10; newsstand price: $3.99. Grant Douglas Publishing, 455 Douglas Ave., Ste. 2155-10, Altamonte Springs, FL 32714-3315. TEL 407-786-3701. FAX 407-786-3712. E-mail: Opp-Mag@magicnet.com. Ed. Phil Robertson; Pub. Roy Meadows. adv.: color page $6000; trim 7 7/8 x 10 1/2; adv. contact: Phil Robertson. mkt. circ. 250,000. **Document type:** consumer publication.
● Also available online.
    Description: Provides profiles of small companies and emerging markets for independent investors and brokers.

332.6   US
OPPORTUNITIES IN OPTIONS. 1984. m. $119 includes hotline service (effective 1996). Box 2126, Malibu, CA 90265. TEL 800-456-9699. FAX 310-456-3840. URL: http://www.oio.com. Ed. David L. Caplan; David L. Caplan. R&P contact: Wayne Gordon. adv. contact: Wayne Gordon. bk.rev./ circ. 5,000 (paid); 5,000 (controlled). **Document type:** newsletter.
    Description: Specializes in using option strategies on all financial markets worldwide for investment, trading, and hedging. Shows how to recognize and use option-premium disparity (under- and over-valued options). Includes professional option traders' manual, notebook, and personal strategy service.

332.6   US
OPTION ADVISOR. 1981. 12/yr. $200. Investment Research Institute Inc., 1259 Kemper Meadow Dr., Ste. 100, Cincinnati, OH 45240. TEL 513-589-3800; 800-448-2080. FAX 513-589-3810. E-mail: bernielRI@aol.com; URL: http://www.options-iri.com. Ed. Bernard G. Schaeffer; Pub. Robert D. Bergen. **Document type:** newsletter.
    Description: Provides both aggressive and conservative recommendations on listed stock options.

332.6   US
OPTION STRATEGIST. 1990. s-m. $250 (foreign $280) (effective 1997). McMillan Analysis Corp, 39 Meadowbrook Rd., Randolph, NJ 07869. TEL 201-328-1674; 800-724-1817. FAX 201-328-1303. E-mail: mac19@ix.netcom.com; URL: http://www.spidertelcom/mcmillan. Ed. Lawrence G. McMillan. circ. 500 (paid). **Document type:** newsletter.
    Description: Publishes news and information on equity, index and futures option strategies.

332.6   US
OPTIONS ALERT. 1977. w. $175. Merrill Lynch, Pierce, Fenner & Smith, Inc., 1 Liberty Plaza, New York, NY 10006. Ed. Anthony H. Scholl.

THE ORIENTALIA JOURNAL. see ANTIQUES

332.6   NO   ISSN 0085-4565
HG5620.075
OSLO BOERS. BERETNING/OSLO STOCK EXCHANGE. ANNUAL REPORT. 1896. a. free. Oslo Boers - Oslo Stock Exchange, Tollbugt. 2, Oslo, Norway. FAX 47-22-416-590. Ed. Bernt Bangstad. circ. 5,000. **Document type:** corporate report.
    Former titles (until 1970): Oekonomisk Beretning - Oslo Boers, Oslo Handelskammer (ISSN 0800-4528); (until 1948): Beretning om Oslo Handel, Industri og Skibsfart (ISSN 0800-451X)

332.6   US   ISSN 0030-7246
THE OUTLOOK (NEW YORK). 1937. w. $268. Standard & Poor's Corporation (Subsidiary of: McGraw-Hill, Inc.), 25 Broadway, New York, NY 10004. TEL 212-208-8000. Ed. Arnold Kaufman. charts; illus.; mkt.; stat. **Document type:** newsletter.
    Description: Identifies developments that affect stock performance, and makes recommendations on when to buy, hold, and sell.

332.678   US
OVERPRICED STOCK SERVICE; authoritative independent advice for short selling. 1983. m. $495. C T S L Publishing Partners, Box 308, Half Moon Bay, CA 94019-0308. TEL 415-726-8495. Ed. Michael Murphy. R&P contact: Pamela Floquet. circ. 1,000. (back issues avail.) **Document type:** newsletter.
    Description: Contains recommendations of stocks to sell short.

332.6   US   ISSN 0196-1276
HG4538
OVERSEAS PRIVATE INVESTMENT CORPORATION. ANNUAL REPORT. Key Title: Annual Report - Overseas Private Investment Corporation. 1971. a. free. Overseas Private Investment Corporation, c/o Daven Oswalt, Dir. of Public Affairs, 1100 New York Ave., N.W., Washington, DC 20527. circ. 30,000. **Document type:** corporate report.

BUSINESS AND ECONOMICS — INVESTMENTS

332.6   PK   ISSN 0078-8198
P I C I C ANNUAL REPORT. (Text in English) 1962. a. Pakistan Industrial Credit and Investment Corporation Ltd., Economic and Research Department, State Life Bldg., No. 1, P.O. Box 5080, I.I. Chundrigar Rd., Karachi 2, Pakistan. TELEX 2710 PICIC PK. Ed. Abdul Hafeez Khan. charts; stat.

332.6   PK   ISSN 0030-8005
P I C I C NEWS. (Text in English) 1962. q. free. Pakistan Industrial Credit and Investment Corporation Ltd., Economic and Research Department, State Life Bldg., No. 1, P.O. Box 5080, I.I. Chundrigar Rd., Karachi 2, Pakistan. TELEX 2710 PICIC PK. charts; illus. circ. 2,000.

332.6   US   ISSN 0164-176X
HG4905
P I P E R. (Pensions & Investments Performance Evaluation Reports) 1977. q. $879. Crain Communications, Inc. (New York), Pensions & Investments, c/o Joel Hauer, 220 E. 42nd St., New York, NY 10017. TEL 212-210-0199. Ed. Michael Clowes; Pub. William Bisson, Jr. R&P contact: Joel A. Hauer. adv. contact: Laura Hashagen. charts; illus.; stat. circ. 300.
—CCC.

332.6327   US
P I P S' - INVESTMENT ADVISORY MONTHLY NEWSLETTER. 1983. m. $60. Personal Investment Portfolio Service, 374 Venus Dr., Prescott, AZ 86301. TEL 602-776-0660. circ. 1,000. **Document type:** newsletter.
    Formerly: P I P S' - Monthly Newsletter.
    Description: Recommends four diversified investment portfolios comprised of no-load and low load mutual and money market funds for long-term growth of investment savings. Provides non-technical investment advice.

332.6   US
THE P Q WALL FORECAST. 1980. m. $198 (effective 1997 & 1998). P Q Wall Forecast, Inc., Box 15558, New Orleans, LA 70175. TEL 504-895-4901; 800-259-0088. FAX 504-895-4852. (Alt. addr.: 3307 Prytania St., New Orleans, LA 70115) Eds. P.Q. Wall, Ellen C. Wall; Pub. P.Q. Wall. R&P contact: Ellen Wall. TEL 504-895-4891. circ. 4,000 (paid). (looseleaf format; back issues avail.) **Document type:** newsletter.
    Description: Covers market timing of the stock, bond, financial, and commodity markets. Aimed at cycle analysts, stock brokers, private investors, and students of the financial markets.

332.6   US
PACIFIC STOCK EXCHANGE. ANNUAL REPORT. a. free. Pacific Stock Exchange, Inc., 301 Pine St., San Francisco, CA 94104. TEL 415-393-4000. FAX 415-393-4202. TELEX 203025 PSE UR (RCA). Ed. Genie W. Williams. **Document type:** corporate report.

332.6   US
PACIFIC STOCK EXCHANGE GUIDE. 1967. m. $437. C C H Incorporated, 2700 Lake Cook Rd., Riverwoods, IL 60015. TEL 847-267-7000; 800-835-5224. FAX 800-224-8299.

332.6327   PY
PARAGUAY. MINISTRY OF INDUSTRY AND TRADE. INVESTMENT GUIDE. 1986. irreg. free. Ministerio de Industria y Comercio, Avda. Espana 374, C.C. 1772, Asuncion, Paraguay. TEL 204-795. FAX 21-210-570. TELEX 259 PY MIC. **Document type:** government publication.
    Description: Contains information useful to those who are considering investing in the country.

332.6   UK   ISSN 1353-6907
PARIBAS DERIVATIVES HANDBOOK (YEAR). 1993. a. £140($250) Euromoney Publications plc., Books, Nestor House, Playhouse Yard, London EC4V 5EX, England. TEL 44-171-779-8935. FAX 44-171-779-8541. (Orders to: Plymbridge Distributors Ltd., Estover, Plymouth, Devon PL6 7PZ, England. TEL 44-1752-695668) **Document type:** trade publication, directory.
    Description: Combines a detailed analysis of derivative products and practices with a worldwide directory of derivative instruments and intermediaries. Lists more than 2,000 institutions active in the world derivatives markets, along with key personnel.

PARKER'S (YEAR) TEXAS BUSINESS STATUTES AND SECURITIES RULES. see *LAW — Corporate Law*

336   US
PARTNERSHIP AND S CORPORATION COORDINATOR. 1987. m. $250. Research Institute of America, Inc., 90 Fifth Ave., New York, NY 10011. TEL 212-645-4800. FAX 212-337-4279. (Subscr. to: 117 E. Stevens Ave., Valhalla, NY 10595) (looseleaf format)
    Description: Provides tax analysis, planning guidance and practice aids for partnerships and S corporations.

332.6   US
PAST, PRESENT, FUTURES. 1990. m. $269 (foreign $289). National Institute of Investment Research, 1821 Wilshire Blvd., Ste. 415, Santa Monica, CA 60403-5679. TEL 310-829-4146; 800-545-9331. Ed. James Flanagan. R&P contact: Forrest James. **Document type:** newsletter.
    Formerly: Investor's Edge.
    Description: Analyzes stock market trends and tracks time cycles and their relation to stock prices, using W.D. Gann's master time factor.

332.6   US
PAX CONNECTION. q. free to shareholders. Pax World Fund, 224 State St., Portsmouth, NH 03801. Eds. Randy Bernard, Rian Fried.
    Description: Discusses the fund's investments to promote social reforms.

332.6   US
PEARSON INVESTMENT LETTER. 1982. m. $175. 1628 White Arrow Dr., Dover, FL 33527. TEL 813-659-2560. Eds. Walter D. Pearson, L. Scott Pearson. circ. 450 (paid). **Document type:** newsletter.
    Description: Includes outlines of several stocks each month which seem ready for growth and advancement at that particular time, plus items of financial, political and economic interest. Also includes stocks recommended previous year and their present status as well as past 12 month featured stocks and progress and lists special changes (dividend increases, splits, etc.) of recommended stocks.

332.6   US
PENNY STOCKS NEWSLETTER. 1978. irreg. (1-3/yr.). $750. 31731 Outer Hwy. 10, Redlands, CA 92373. Ed. Vello Kulbin; Pub. Vello Kulbin. (looseleaf format; back issues avail.) **Document type:** newsletter.
    Description: Specifically pinpoints one to three stocks per year that are poised to go from pennies per share to dollars per share.

332.6   NE   ISSN 0925-496X
PENSIOEN ADVIES; onafhankelijk vakblad voor de adviespratijk. 1990. 10/yr. fl.184 (effective 1996). Kluwer Bedrijfswetenschappen B.V. (Subsidiary of: Wolters Kluwer N.V.), Postbus 23, 7400 GA Deventer, Netherlands. TEL 31-5700-48999. FAX 31-5700-11504. (Subscr. to: Intermedia bv, Postbus 4, 2400 MA Alphen aan den Rijn, Netherlands. TEL 31-172-466321. FAX 31-172-435527) adv. **Document type:** trade publication.

332.67   JA
PENSIONS & INVESTMENT. w. Japan Bond Research Institute, 2-6-1 Nihonbashi Kayabacho, Chuo-ku, Tokyo 103, Japan. TEL 03-3639-2840. FAX 03-3639-2848. **Indexed:** B.P.I. **Document type:** newsletter.
    Description: Contains news on pension management.

332.67   US   ISSN 1050-4974
PENSIONS & INVESTMENTS; the newspaper of corporate and institutional investing. 1973. fortn. $205. Crain Communications, Inc. (New York), 220 E. 42nd St., New York, NY 10017-5806. TEL 212-210-0100. FAX 212-210-0799. (Subscr. to: 965 E. Jefferson Ave., Detroit, MI 48207-9966. TEL 800-678-9595) circ. 60,000. (also avail. in microform from UMI; microfiche from CIS; reprint service avail. from UMI) **Indexed:** ABI Inform., B.P.I., Bank.Lit.Ind., BPIA, PROMT, SRI, Tr.& Indus.Ind. **Document type:** newspaper.
    ●Also available online. Vendor(s): Information Access Co., Lexis-Nexis (PENINV).
    —BLDSC (6422.720100); KR SourceOne; SWETS; UMI. **CCC.**
    Former titles: Pensions and Investment Age (ISSN 0273-5466); Pensions and Investments (ISSN 0095-4772)

PENSIONS WORLD. see *INSURANCE*

332.6   US
PERSONAL FINANCE.* 1974. 24/yr. $118. Kephart Communications, Inc., 1750 Old Meadow Rd., 3rd Fl., McLean, VA 22102-4304. TEL 703-548-2400. FAX 703-683-6974. TELEX 901806 KEPCOM. (Subscr. to: Box 1462, Alexandria, VA 22313) Ed. Richard E. Band. adv.; bk.rev.; charts; stat.; index. circ. 100,000. (back issues avail.)
    Former titles: Personal Finance: The Inflation Survival Letter (ISSN 0164-7768) & Inflation Survival Letter.
    Description: Stock market investment advice.

332.6   US   ISSN 1044-4343
HG179
PERSONAL FINANCIAL PLANNING. 1988. bi-m. $120 (overseas $155) (effective 1997). Warren, Gorham & Lamont, 395 Hudson St., New York, NY 10014. TEL 212-367-6300. FAX 212-367-6314. (Subscr. to: The Park Square Bldg., 31 St. James Ave., Boston, MA 02116-4112. TEL 800-950-1205) Ed. Jack Robinson; Pub. Larry Selby. R&P contact: Sarah Rutledge. TEL 212-367-6536. adv. contact: Meg Chornicz. (also avail. in microform from UMI) **Indexed:** Account.Ind. (1989-). **Document type:** trade publication.
    —UMI. **CCC.**
    Description: Provides investment advisors, CPAs, and financial planners with articles, case studies, and interviews about investment strategies and portfolio management, insurance planning, tax strategies and tax shelters, and regulatory and legal issues.

332.6   US   ISSN 1042-3087
                              CODEN: PLINEL
PERSONAL INVESTING NEWS. 1988. m. $29. Sound Money Investors Inc., 531 Versailles Dr., Ste. 110, Maitland, FL 32751-4591. TEL 407-629-9229. Ed. Carl Surran. R&P contact: Carl Surran. adv. contact: Paul Zuromski. **Document type:** consumer publication.
    Description: For the personal investor; covers the entire range of investment vehicles: stocks, bonds, mutual funds, real estate, commodities, and precious metals.

332.6   AT   ISSN 0813-2992
HG4503
PERSONAL INVESTMENT. (Supplement avail.: S X J (Stock Exchange Journal) (ISSN 1036-840X)) 1983. m. Aus.$60. B R W Media, Level 2, 469 La Trobe St., Melbourne, Vic. 3000, Australia. TEL 61-3-96033888. FAX 61-3-96704328. Ed. Ross Greenwood. adv.: B&W page $3460, color page $4945; bleed 282 x 213. index. circ. 60,072. (back issues avail.)
    —UnCover.
    Description: How-to magazine about investing money, spending money and making money. Directed to the average person.

332.6   SA
PERSONAL WEALTH & FINANCIAL INDEPENDENCE. (Text in English) 1994. a. R.31.95. (A B S A Bank) Southern Book Publishers, P.O. Box 3103, Halfway House 1685, South Africa. TEL 27-11-3153633. FAX 27-11-3153810. Eds. H.B. Falkena, C.W. Luus. **Document type:** consumer publication.

332.6   SA
PERSPECTIVE/PERSPEKTIEF; economic, investment & portfolio review for employee benefit funds. (Text in Afrikaans, English) 1993. q. Southern Life Association, Investments Division, Great Westerford, Rondebosch 7700, South Africa.

BUSINESS AND ECONOMICS — INVESTMENTS

332.6 615.1   US   ISSN 1076-9382
PHARMACEUTICAL VENTURES. 1991. 48/yr. $360. Scitec Services, 5324 Sinclair Rd., Columbus, OH 43229. TEL 614-433-0648. FAX 614-433-0432. Ed. David C. Carlson. (looseleaf format; back issues avail.) **Indexed:** ABC. **Document type:** newsletter.
   Description: For sophisticated investors. Covers the financial markets of the pharmaceutical manufacturers and researchers.

332.6   PH
PHILIPPINE COMMERCIAL AND INDUSTRIAL BANK. INVESTMENT INFORMATION FOLIO.* 1973. m. $100. Philippine Commercial and Industrial Bank., Antonio Bldg., T. M. Kalaw St., Manila, Philippines. charts; illus.; stat.

332.63   PH
PHILIPPINE STANDARD COMMODITY CLASSIFICATION. irreg., latest 1993. $205 in Asia (Australia & New Zealand $211; US & Canada $227; Europe $230; Latin America $265; elsewhere $285). National Statistical Coordination Board, c/o National Statistical Information Center, Midland-Buendia Bldg., 403 Sen. Gil Puyat Ave., Makati City, Philippines. TEL 63-2-890-9405. FAX 63-2-890-9408. E-mail: nscb_nsic@mozcom.com. **Document type:** government publication.
   Description: Represents the latest reclassification of commodities, particularly those that enter Philippine trade.

332.6   PH   ISSN 0079-1504
PHILIPPINES. BOARD OF INVESTMENTS. ANNUAL REPORT. 1968. a. free. Board of Investments, Industry & Investment Bldg., 385 Sen. Gil J. Puyat Ave., MCC P.O. Box 676, Makati, Metro Manila 3117, Philippines. circ. 3,000.

332.6   PH
PHILIPPINES. BOARD OF INVESTMENTS. INDIVIDUAL SUMMARY OF WEEKLY APPROVED PROJECTS. (Text in English) 1983. w. Board of Investments, Industry & Investment Bldg., 385 Sen. Gil J. Puyat Ave., MCC P.O. Box 676, Makati, Metro Manila 3117, Philippines. TEL 818-1831. FAX 815-0702.

PHOTOGRAPH COLLECTOR; for collectors, curators and dealers. see PHOTOGRAPHY

331.6   US
PICKY PROFITS. 1984. irreg. (6-12/yr.). $19 per no. Financial Guidance, Inc., Box 3831, Albany, GA 31706. TEL 912-883-7774. Ed. Price Howard.

PLANNING TAX-DEFERRED PROPERTY TRANSACTIONS. see LAW — Estate Planning

PLATT'S OIL PRICE HANDBOOK. see PETROLEUM AND GAS

332.6   US
PLATT'S PRICE REPORT. d. $1,347. McGraw-Hill Companies, Commodity Services Group, 1221 Ave. of the Americas, 42nd Fl., New York, NY 10020. TEL 212-512-2000. Ed. Joseph Link. **Document type:** trade publication.

POLITICAL RISK LETTER. see BUSINESS AND ECONOMICS — International Commerce

POLITICAL RISK YEARBOOK. see BUSINESS AND ECONOMICS — Banking And Finance

POLITICAL RISK YEARBOOK. VOLUME 1: NORTH & CENTRAL AMERICA. see BUSINESS AND ECONOMICS — Banking And Finance

POLITICAL RISK YEARBOOK. VOLUME 2: MIDDLE EAST & NORTH AFRICA. see BUSINESS AND ECONOMICS — Banking And Finance

POLITICAL RISK YEARBOOK. VOLUME 3: SOUTH AMERICA. see BUSINESS AND ECONOMICS — Banking And Finance

POLITICAL RISK YEARBOOK. VOLUME 4: SUB-SAHARAN AFRICA. see BUSINESS AND ECONOMICS — Banking And Finance

POLITICAL RISK YEARBOOK. VOLUME 5: ASIA & THE PACIFIC. see BUSINESS AND ECONOMICS — Banking And Finance

POLITICAL RISK YEARBOOK. VOLUME 6: EUROPE. see BUSINESS AND ECONOMICS — Banking And Finance

332.6   CN   ISSN 0822-6970
POLYMETRIC REPORT. CANADIAN EDITION. 1968. m. Can.$210.28 (effective 1997). Canadian Analyst Ltd., 30 Duncan St., Toronto, ON M5V 2C3, Canada. TEL 416-971-6543; 800-348-6661. FAX 416-598-0049. **Document type:** trade publication.
   Formerly (until 1981): Polymetric Report. Canadian Stocks (ISSN 0229-222X)
   Description: Fundamental and technical rating service covering Canadian securities.

332.6   CN   ISSN 0711-7965
POLYMETRIC REPORT. N Y S E EDITION. m. Can.$210.28 (effective 1997). Canadian Analyst Ltd., 30 Duncan St., Toronto, ON M5V 2C3, Canada. TEL 416-971-6543; 800-348-6661. FAX 416-598-0049. **Document type:** trade publication.
   Formerly (until 1981): Polymetric Report. N Y S E Stocks (ISSN 0822-6989)
   Description: Fundamental and technical rating service covering American securities.

PONDICHERRY INDUSTRIAL PROMOTION, DEVELOPMENT AND INVESTMENT CORPORATION. ANNUAL REPORTS AND ACCOUNTS. see BUSINESS AND ECONOMICS — Domestic Commerce

332.67   US
PORTFOLIO LETTER; newsweekly covering the US equity markets. 1979. w. $1595 (Canada $1625; elsewhere $1670). Institutional Investor Newsletters, 477 Madison Ave., New York, NY 10022. TEL 212-224-3233. FAX 212-224-3353. Ed. Tom Lamont. adv. (also avail. in microfiche; reprint service avail. from UMI) **Document type:** newsletter.
   ●Also available on CD-ROM.
   Description: Focuses on the equity markets worldwide by breaking news on issues that affect both the broad market and its industry groups, and by covering developments in specific stocks.

332.66021   PO   ISSN 0870-4376
PORTUGAL. INSTITUTO NACIONAL DE ESTATISTICA. INQUERITO DE CONJUNTURA AO INVESTIMENTO. 1987. 6/m. Esc.1550. Instituto Nacional de Estatistica, Ave. Antonio Jose de Almeida, 1078 Lisbon, Portugal. TEL 351-1-8470050. FAX 351-1-8478578. TELEX 351-1-63738 PCDINE P.
   Description: Provides estimates and variations about investments made by companies in the financial sector.

332.6   II
PRACTICAL PROJECT EXECUTION KNOW HOW REPORTS. (Text in English) irreg. Rs.5000($500) per no. Small Industry Research Institute, 4-43, Roop Nagar, P.O. Box 2106, New Delhi 110 007, India. TEL 91-11-2910805. FAX 91-11-2923955. TELEX 031-61028 SIRI IN. charts.
   Description: Provides information on how to implement a practical project, including market survey, process of manufacture, raw materials, plant and machinery, land and building, and project economics.

332.678   US
PRACTICAL STOCK PICKER. 1983. m. $95 (effective 1993). 8 W. Parish Ct., Havenhill, MA 01832-1166. Ed. William J. Fallon. **Document type:** newsletter.

PRACTICE UNDER THE CALIFORNIA CORPORATION SECURITIES LAWS. see LAW — Corporate Law

332.6   US   ISSN 0884-1616
HG65
PRATT'S GUIDE TO VENTURE CAPITAL SOURCES. 1970. a. $325. (Securities Data Co., Inc.) Securities Data Publishing, 40 W. 57th St., 11th Fl., New York, NY 10019. TEL 212-765-5311. FAX 212-765-6123. Ed. Daniel Bokser. bibl. **Document type:** directory. —BLDSC (6603.023530).
   Formerly: Guide to Venture Capital Sources.
   Description: Provides detailed profiles of more than 950 active U.S. and Canadian venture capital firms, with addresses, telephone and fax numbers, contact names, investment amounts, industry and project preferences, and capital under management.

332.6   US
PRECIOUS METALS DATA BASE.* 1985. m. $36. Moneypower, 1304 Edgewood Ave., Ann Arbor, MI 48103-5522. TEL 612-537-8096. Ed. James H. Moore.
   Description: Features decision-data for precious metals investors.

332.6   FR
PREVISIONS.* 1972. w. 340 F. Sepreco S.A.R.L, 15 rue Cassette, 75006 Paris, France. TEL 45-49-54-42. FAX 45-49-92-70. Ed. Nicole Jeunet. adv.; charts; index. circ. 20,000. (tabloid format)
   Formerly: Opinion Graphique (ISSN 0030-3828)

332.6 338.1   US
PRICE PERCEPTIONS. 1970. s-m. $360. Commodity Information Systems, 210 Park Ave., Ste. 2970, Oklahoma City, OK 73102-5604. TEL 405-810-8894. FAX 405-232-4354. E-mail: cis@ionet.net. Ed. William K. Gary. charts; illus.; stat. (back issues avail.) **Document type:** newsletter.
   Incorporates (in Jan. 1997): Timing; **Formerly:** Commodity Investment Analyst.
   Description: Commodity market research and analysis.

332.6   US
PRIMARY TREND. 1979. s-m. $180 (foreign $200). Arnold Investment Counsel, Inc., First Financial Center, 700 N. Water St., Milwaukee, WI 53202. TEL 414-271-2726. Ed. James R. Arnold, Sr. circ. 3,000. (back issues avail.)

332.6   US
PRIVATE ASSET MANAGEMENT. bi-w. $1595 (Canada $1625; elsewhere $1670). Institutional Investor Newsletters, 477 Madison Ave., New York, NY 10022. TEL 212-224-3233. FAX 212-224-3353. **Document type:** newsletter.
   Description: Covers how to find, service and retain high-net-worth clients. Includes new investment products, services and fee structures.

332.6   PH
PRIVATE DEVELOPMENT CORPORATION OF THE PHILIPPINES. ANNUAL P D C P SURVEY ON BUSINESS PERFORMANCE. (Text in English) 1977. a. $40. Private Development Corporation of the Philippines - Pribadong Korporasyon sa Pagpapaunlad ng Pilipinas, P.O. Box 757 Makati, Metro Manila 3117, Philippines. TEL 02-8100231. FAX 02-8195376. TELEX RCA-22080. Ed. Lucia C. Laquindanum.

332.62   US   ISSN 1057-526X
PRIVATE EQUITY ANALYST. 1991. m. $395 (foreign $455) (effective 1997). Asset Alternatives, Inc., 180 Linden St., Ste. 3, Wellesley, MA 02181-7922. TEL 617-431-7353. FAX 617-431-7451. URL: http://www.assetalt.com. Ed. Steven P. Galante; Pub. Steven P. Galante. adv.: page $11375 trim 7 1/2 x 10 1/4; adv. contact: Barbara Bissonette. charts; stat.; tr.lit.; circ. 1,500 (paid). (back issues avail.) **Document type:** newsletter.
   ●Also available online.
   Description: Covers the private equity market and its investment specialties, such as venture capital, buyouts, mezzanine and turnaround funds. Also tracks the fund-raising activities of private limited partnerships and institutional investors' participation in the market.

332.67 341   US   ISSN 0090-9742
K3829.6
PRIVATE INVESTMENTS ABROAD; problems and solutions in international business. 1967. a. $75. (Southwestern Legal Foundation, International and Comparative Law Center) Matthew Bender & Co., Inc., 2 Park Ave., New York, NY 10016. TEL 212-448-2000. E-mail: international@bender.com; URL: http://www.bender.com. (also avail. in microfilm from RRI) **Indexed:** C.L.I., L.R.I., Leg.Per. —KR SourceOne.

332.6   US   ISSN 1053-6434
KF1428.A15
PRIVATE PLACEMENT ALERT. 1990. m. $345. Faulkner & Gray, Inc. (New York), 11 Penn Plaza, 17th Fl., New York, NY 10001. TEL 212-967-7000. FAX 212-967-7155. Ed. Howard Wolosky.
   Description: Provides investment guidance on turnarounds, LBO's, bailouts, and licensing agreements.

PROBE DIRECTORY OF FOREIGN DIRECT INVESTMENT IN THE UNITED STATES. see BUSINESS AND ECONOMICS — Trade And Industrial Directories

BUSINESS AND ECONOMICS — INVESTMENTS

332.6 US
PROFESSIONAL TAPE READER. 1972. s-m. $395 (foreign $420) (includes investor hotline service). Radcap, Inc., Box 2407, Hollywood, FL 33022. TEL 800-868-7857. Ed. Stan Weinstein; Pub. Stan Weinstein. R&P contact: Rita Berg. charts; stat. circ. 12,000. **Document type:** newsletter.
  Description: Stock market advisory service with charts, advice, information, and forecasts for long and short-term trends, analysis of promising and vulnerable stocks, and fund performance data.

332.678 US
PROFESSIONAL TIMING SERVICE. 3/w. $185. Curtis J. Hesler, Pub., Box 7483, Missoula, MT 59807. TEL 406-543-4131.

332.6 331 US ISSN 0033-0280
PROFIT SHARING. vol.18, 1970. bi-m. membership. Profit Sharing - 401(K) Council of America, 10 S. Riverside Plaza, Ste. 1610, Chicago, IL 60606-3802. TEL 312-441-8550. FAX 312-441-8559. Ed. Debra Schloesslin; Pub. David L. Wray. R&P contact: Charlie Seten. adv. circ. 3,000. **Document type:** trade publication.
—UnCover.
  Description: Covers legislative and regulatory activity affecting defined contribution plans and provides information on profit-sharing and 401(k) plan design, compliance, administration, investment and communication. Geared toward plan administrators, benefits managers and benefits communicators.

332.6 US
PROFIT STRATEGY LETTER.* 1981. q. free. Box 514, Banner Elk, NC 28604-0514. TEL 919-452-1788. Ed. John V. Holmes. circ. 150,000.
  Description: Features companies believed to have a very high potential for growth and revenues.

332.64 600 UK ISSN 0268-8867
CODEN: PRAPET
PROJECT APPRAISAL. 1986. q. £36($64) to individuals; institutions £99($175) (in developing nations £72($132)) (effective 1998). Beech Tree Publishing, 10 Watford Close, Guildford, Surrey GU1 2EP, England. TEL 44-1483-567497. FAX 44-1483-567497. (Subscr. to: Turpin Distribution Services Ltd., Blackhorse Rd., Letchworth, Herts. SG6 1HN, England. TEL 44-1462-672555. FAX 44-1462-480947) Eds. Vary Coates, John Weiss. bk.rev. (back issues avail.) Indexed: Asian-Pac.Econ.Lit., C.R.E.J., CLOSS, Cont.Pg.Manage., Dairy Sci.Abstr., Environ.Abstr., Geo.Abstr.H.G., Geo.Abstr.P.G., IDA, Rice Abstr., Rural Devel.Abstr., Weed Abstr., World Agri.Econ.& Rural Sociol.Abstr. **Document type:** academic/scholarly publication.
—BLDSC (6924.841000); SWETS. **CCC.**
  Description: Covers cost-benefit analysis, technology assessment, environmental impact assessment, and risk analysis.
  Refereed Serial

332.6 II
PROJECT FEASIBILITY CUM MARKET SURVEY REPORT. (Text in English) irreg. Rs.500($75) per no. Small Industry Research Institute, 4-43, Roop Nagar, P.O. Box 2106, New Delhi 110 007, India. TEL 91-11-2910805. FAX 91-11-2923955. TELEX 031-61028 SIRI IN.
  Description: Contains all information necessary for entrepreneurs looking for new investment opportunities.

PROMYSHLENNYI VESTNIK ROSSII. see BUSINESS AND ECONOMICS — Economic Situation And Conditions

332.6 SA
PROPERTY UNIT TRUSTS. (Text in English) 1994. 3/yr. (Association of Property Unit Trust Management Companies) Diagonal Street Communications, P.O. Box 264, Johannesburg 2000, South Africa. **Document type:** newsletter.

332.6 US
PROXY RULES HANDBOOK. a. $145. Clark - Boardman - Callaghan, 375 Hudson St., New York, NY 10014. TEL 212-929-7500; 800-422-2101. FAX 212-924-0460. Ed. Mark A. Sargent.
  Formerly: Proxy Contests Handbook.
  Description: Focuses on the issues involved in electing and proposing a proxy contest.

332.6 US ISSN 0743-0809
THE PRUDENT SPECULATOR. 1977. m. $175 (foreign $199) (effective 1997). Al Frank Asset Management, Inc., Box 1438, Laguna Beach, CA 92652. TEL 714-497-7657. FAX 714-797-7658. Ed. Al Frank. R&P contact: Vitoria Baldwin. TEL 505-983-1579. bk.rev.; circ. 700 (paid). (also avail. in looseleaf format; back issues avail.) **Document type:** newsletter.
  Description: Stock advisory letter showing investors what to consider in buying and selling stocks, managing a portfolio and adjusting to significant market-wide changes.

332.6 US
PUBLIC INVESTOR. 1982. m. $85 to non-members; members $55. Government Finance Officers Association, 180 N. Michigan Ave., Ste. 800, Chicago, IL 60601. TEL 312-977-9700. FAX 312-977-4806. Ed. M. Corinne Larson. bk.rev.; charts; cum.index. circ. 1,700. **Document type:** newsletter.
  Description: Reports and analyzes major economic, political and market events affecting public-sector investment officers.

332.63 UK ISSN 0966-467X
PUBLIC LEDGER'S WORLD COMMODITY REPORT. 1979. fortn. £500 (foreign £545) (effective 1996). U K Publications, 10 Little College St., London SW1P 3SH, England. TEL 44-171-976-7772. FAX 44-171-976-0861. Ed. Chris Lewis; Pub. Keith Young. **Document type:** newsletter.
  Formerly: Financial Times World Commodity Report.

PUBLIC TREASURER. see BUSINESS AND ECONOMICS — Public Finance, Taxation

332.6 SP
PULSO BURSATIL. m. free. Banco Hispano Americano, Division de Banca Corporativa y Mercado de Capitales, Plaza de Canalejas, 1, 28014 Madrid, Spain. TEL 531-18-36. charts; stat.

332.6 US ISSN 1066-0631
HG6024.U6
PUT BOND HANDBOOK. 1992. q. $435. Standard & Poor's Corporation, Ratings Group (Subsidiary of: McGraw-Hill, Inc.), 25 Broadway, New York, NY 10004. TEL 212-208-1146. Ed.Bd. charts; stat. **Document type:** trade publication.

QUARTERLY BANK DIGEST. see BUSINESS AND ECONOMICS — Banking And Finance

332.6 II ISSN 0033-5312
QUARTERLY BLUE BOOK ON JOINT STOCK COMPANIES IN INDIA.* (Text in English) 1966. q. Rs.14($5.04) Department of Company Affairs, Research and Statistics Division, Shastri Bhawan, Dr. Rajendraprasad Rd., New Delhi, India. (Subscr. to: Controller of Publications, Civil Lines, Delhi 110006, India) circ. 220.

332.6 US ISSN 0889-4396
QUARTERLY PENSION INVESTMENT REPORT. 1986. q. $1500 (includes Issue Briefs). Employee Benefit Research Institute, 2121 K St., N.W., Ste. 600, Washington, DC 20037-1896. TEL 202-659-0670. FAX 202-775-6312. R&P contact: Stephanie Robinson. charts; stat. circ. 350. (looseleaf format) **Document type:** academic/scholarly publication.
—CCC.
  Description: Data on assets in the private and public pension system and the performance of pension investments.

QUARTERLY PERFORMANCE REPORT. see BUSINESS AND ECONOMICS — Economic Situation And Conditions

332.6 US
QUARTERLY REPORT ON MONEY FUND PERFORMANCE. 1988. q. $525. IBC - Donoghue, Inc., 290 Eliot St., Ashland, MA 01721. TEL 508-881-2800. FAX 508-881-0982. (In U.K.: Eurostudy Publishing Co. Ltd., 9-13 St. Andrews St., London EC41 3AE, England. TEL 44-171-930-2016) Ed. Tracy Burke. circ. 1,000.
—CCC.
  Former titles: I B C's Quarterly Report on Money Fund Performance; Quarterly Report on Money Fund Expense Ratios (ISSN 0897-2044)
  Description: Provides expense ratios and other information for a comparative analysis of money fund performance.

332.6 CN
QUEBEC (PROVINCE). COMMISSION DES VALEURS MOBILIERES DU QUEBEC. BULLETIN HEBDOMADAIRE. (Text in French) w. Can.$395 (foreign Can.$790). (Commission des Valeurs Mobilieres du Quebec) Ministere des Communications, P.O. Box 1005, Quebec, PQ G1K 7B5, Canada. TEL 514-948-1222; 800-465-9266. (Subscr. to: Service Abonnements, CP 1190, Outrement, PQ H2V 4S7, Canada)
  Description: Report activities in the real estate sector of the province of Quebec.

332.6 US
QUOTE AMERICAN.* 1962. w. $279. Lankford-Quote Digest, 7 Rock Rd., Marion, KS 66861-9305. TEL 316-262-2111. Ed. Theresa Hogan. circ. 200.
  Description: Shows weekly price range, close, and volume on a semi-log scale.

332.6 US
QUOTE NEW YORK.* 1961. w. $338. Lankford-Quote Digest, 7 Rock Rd., Marion, KS 66861-9305. TEL 316-262-2111. Ed. Theresa Hogan. circ. 460.

332.6 US
QUOTE O-T-C.* (Over-the-Counter) 1968. w. $293. Lankford-Quote Digest, 7 Rock Rd., Marion, KS 66861-9305. TEL 316-262-2111. Ed. Theresa Hogan. circ. 260.

332.6 SA ISSN 1023-9286
R D P MONITOR. (Reconstruction and Development Programme) (Text in English) 1994. m. R.550($199) Stock Information Service, P.O. Box 938, Pinegowrie 2123, South Africa. E-mail: stock@iahica.com. Ed. Gavin Lewis. circ. 400 (paid).
  Description: Reports on national and international media coverage of the RDP.

332.6 330.968 SA
▼**R D P NEWS.** (Reconstruction and Development Programme) 1995. m. South African Communication Service, Private Bag X745, Pretoria 0001, South Africa. Ed. Elise Keyter. illus. **Document type:** government publication.

R E I T REPORT. (National Association of Real Estate Investment Trusts, Inc.) see REAL ESTATE

332.6 TZ ISSN 0856-0382
RASILIMALI; Tanzania investment outlook. (Text in English) 1972. irreg., no.10, 1983. Tanzania Investment Bank, P.O. Box 9373, Dar es Salaam, Tanzania.

RATEGRAM. see BUSINESS AND ECONOMICS — Banking And Finance

REAL ESTATE INVESTING LETTER. see REAL ESTATE

REAL ESTATE INVESTMENT TRUSTS HANDBOOK; a pass-through entity to make mortgage loans and operate real estate. see REAL ESTATE

332.6 US
REALTY STOCK DIGEST; news summary of public REITs and real estate companies. 1987. m. $265. M J H Research Associates, 92 Kennedy Rd., Box 7, Tranquility, NJ 07879-0007. TEL 908-850-1155. Ed. Michael J. Houston. index. circ. 200. (looseleaf format; back issues avail.)

332.6 US ISSN 1075-7554
REALTY STOCK REVIEW; market analysis of securities of reits and real estate companies. 1970. s-m. $325. 92 Kennedy Rd., Box 7, Tranquility, NJ 07879-0007. TEL 908-850-1155. Ed. Michael J. Houston. index. circ. 400. (looseleaf format; back issues avail.)
  Formerly: Realty Trust Review.

332.6 US
RECOMMENDED LENDING STANCE. 1987. m. $300. Quantum Group, Ltd., 1501 Oakes, Williamsport, PA 17701. TEL 717-433-4236. Eds. Gregory P. Breon, David Cheesman.
  Description: Review of the mortgage market with emphasis on a propriety FHLMC forecast model.

BUSINESS AND ECONOMICS — INVESTMENTS

332.6 US ISSN 0193-1865
HG4621
REGISTERED REPRESENTATIVE. 1976. m. $48 (foreign $57). Plaza Communications, Inc., 18818 Teller Ave., No. 280, Irvine, CA 92612-1680. TEL 714-851-2220. FAX 714-851-1636. E-mail: webmaster@rrmag.com; URL: http://www.rrmag. com. Ed. Dan Jamison; Pub. Tolman F. Geffs. adv. contact: Myrna Shinbaum. bk.rev.; circ. 90,000 (controlled). **Document type:** trade publication.
   Description: Information of interest to registered representatives.

332.6 340 US ISSN 1076-2337
KF1072
REGULATION OF INVESTMENT ADVISERS. a. $155. Clark - Boardman - Callaghan, 375 Hudson St., New York, NY 10014. TEL 212-929-7500; 800-422-2101. FAX 212-924-0460. Eds. Thomas P. Lemke, Gerald T. Lins.
   Description: Provides detailed explanations of SEC regulation requirements and procedures to help investment advisers avoid SEC violations.

332.6 SP ISSN 0486-3518
RELACIONES FINANCIERAS. 12/yr. Madonado 55, 1o, Ofc. 116, 28001 Madrid, Spain. TEL 1-411-0653. FAX 1-411-07-52. Ed. Miriam Dias Aroca.

332.6 US
RELEASE TO THE MEMBERSHIP. d. $60. Coffee, Sugar & Cocoa Exchange, Inc., Four World Trade Center, New York, NY 10048. TEL 212-938-2800. FAX 212-524-9863.
   Description: Covers all coffee, sugar and cocoa exchange releases. Also discusses rule and margin changes, warehouse information and notice days.

332.6 LU
RELEVE DES SOCIETES DONT LES ACTIONS, PARTS ET CERTIFICATS SONT COTES EN BOURSE DE LUXEMBOURG/LIST OF COMPANIES OF WHICH SHARES, PARTS AND FOREIGN SHARE CERTIFICATES ARE LISTED ON THE LUXEMBOURG STOCK EXCHANGE. (Text in English, French) 1988. q. free. Societe de la Bourse de Luxembourg - Luxembourg Stock Exchange, P.O. Box 165, 11 av. de la Porte-Neuve, L-2011 Luxembourg, Luxembourg. TEL 352-4779361. FAX 352-473298. TELEX 2559-STOEX-LU. circ. 120.

332.6 CN ISSN 0847-2831
REPORT ON BUSINESS CANADA COMPANY HANDBOOK. 1989. a. Can.$49.95. Globe Information Services, 444 Front St. W., Toronto, ON M5V 2S9, Canada. TEL 416-585-5250. FAX 416-585-5249. (Dist. in the U.S. by: Reference Press, Inc., 6448 Hwy. 290 E., Ste. E-104, Austin, TX 78723. TEL 512-454-7778. FAX 512-454-9401) Ed. Alan Husdal; Pub. Michael J. Ryan. adv.; charts. **Document type:** directory.
   —CISTI. **CCC**.
   Description: Fundamental financial data on all TSE 300 and former TSE 300 companies, with current news summaries and stock price performance charts. Includes company officer names and addresses.

332.6 628.1 UK
REPORT ON CAPITAL INVESTMENT AND FINANCIAL PERFORMANCE OF THE WATER COMPANIES IN ENGLAND AND WALES. 1991. a. free. Office of Water Services, Centre City Tower, 7 Hill St., Birmingham B5 4UA, England. TEL 44-121-625-1373. FAX 44-121-625-1362. URL: http://www.open.gov.uk/ofwat. circ. 2,000. **Document type:** monographic series.
   Formerly: Report on Capital Investment by the Water Companies in England and Wales.

332.6 US ISSN 0034-4834
REPORTING ON GOVERNMENTS.* 1944. w. $250. Reporting on Governments, Inc., 650 Park Ave., No. 6C, New York, NY 10021-6115. Ed. Ben Weberman. (processed)
   Description: Analysis of highest-grade bond and money markets, monetary and fiscal policies, the economic outlook and interest-rate trends.

332.6 US ISSN 1049-7110
KF1439.A1
RESALES OF RESTRICTED SECURITIES. a. $155. Clark - Boardman, 375 Hudson St., New York, NY 10014. TEL 212-929-7500; 800-422-2101. FAX 212-924-0460. Ed. J. William Hicks.
   Description: Contains analysis of the latest case law, SEC no-action letters, and regulatory changes.

332.6 US
RESEARCH (SAN FRANCISCO); stockmarketing ideas for brokers. m. $35. Research Holdings Ltd., 2201 Third St., San Francisco, CA 94107. TEL 415-621-0220. FAX 415-621-0735. Ed. Rebecca McReynolds; Pub. Bob Tyndall. circ. 61,500 (controlled). **Document type:** trade publication.

332.024 646.79 US
RETIREMENT PLANNING ADVISOR. 1958. q. sold in bulk only. Hearst Business Communications, Inc., R A I division, 645 Stewart Ave., Garden City, NY 11530. TEL 516-227-1300. FAX 516-229-3636. Ed. Jacqueline Coleman Fried; Pub. W. Boyd Griffin. **Document type:** newsletter.
   Description: Information on retirement planning issues for persons approaching retirement.

332.6 US
RETIREMENT PLANS BULLETIN. 1994. m. $89. Universal Pensions, Inc., Box 979, Brainerd, MN 56401-9965. TEL 218-829-4781; 800-346-3860. FAX 218-829-2106. Ed. Jennifer Norquist. **Document type:** newsletter.
   Formed by the 1994 merger of: I R A Bulletin (ISSN 1062-7499) & Qualified Plan Update (ISSN 1062-7480)

332 US ISSN 1077-9493
HG226
RETURN ON INVESTMENT. Variant title: R O I. 1994. bi-m. $150. Investment Management Publications, Inc., One Liberty Sq., 12th Fl., Boston, MA 02109. TEL 617-422-5450. FAX 617--422-0162. E-mail: impubs@aol.com. Ed. Richard Chimberg; Pub. Melanie DeCarolis. circ. 30,000. cols./p.: 2; pp./issue: 60. (back issues avail.; reprint service avail.) **Document type:** trade publication, newsletter.
   Description: Reports exclusively on the business of investment management worldwide for money management professionals and others involved in this rapidly growing global business.

332.6 FR ISSN 0180-8389
REVENU FRANCAIS. w. (45/yr.). 399 F. (foreign 610 F.). Groupe Revenu Francais, 1 bis av. de la Republique, 75011 Paris, France. TEL 43-55-39-99. FAX 43-55-82-82. (Subscr. to: B.P. 520, 60732 Ste. Genevieve Cedex, France. TEL 44-07-45-56. FAX 44-07-43-36) Ed. Robert Monteux. adv.; illus. circ. 210,163.

REVIEW OF DERIVATIVES RESEARCH. see *BUSINESS AND ECONOMICS — Banking And Finance*

332.6 340 US ISSN 0884-2426
KF1432
THE REVIEW OF SECURITIES & COMMODITIES REGULATION; an analysis of current laws, regulations affecting the securities and futures industries. 1967. s-m. (22/yr.). $630. Standard & Poor's (Subsidiary of: McGraw-Hill Companies, Inc.), 25 Broadway, New York, NY 10004. TEL 212-208-8650. FAX 212-412-0240. Ed. Michael Finkelstein. R&P contact: Joseph Tigue. index. (looseleaf format; back issues avail.) **Indexed:** C.L.I., L.R.I. **Document type:** newsletter.
   ●Also available online. Vendor(s): Dow Jones News Retrieval (RSCR), Knight-Ridder Information, Inc. (SCR), Lexis-Nexis (RSCR), NewsNet (FI20).
   Formerly (until 1985): Standard and Poor's Review of Securities Regulation (ISSN 0034-6756)
   Description: Emphasizes coverage of new rulings and case decisions as they affect an attorney's clients and practice.

REVISTA BRASILEIRA DE MERCADO DE CAPITAIS. see *BUSINESS AND ECONOMICS*

332.6 FR ISSN 0223-4718
LA REVUE FIDUCIAIRE. (Supplement avail.: Legi - Social) w. 690 F. (foreign 1040 F.) (effective 1997). Publications Fiduciaires, 100 rue LaFayette, 75485 Paris Cedex 10, France. TEL 33-1-41835252. FAX 33-1-41835253. URL: http://www. revuefiduciaire.fr.
   Description: Explores the different fields of management with comments and analyses.

332.6 FR ISSN 0396-3640
REVUE FIDUCIAIRE - COMPTABLE. m. 340 F. (foreign 410 F.) (effective 1997). Publications Fiduciaires, 100 rue LaFayette, 75485 Paris Cedex 10, France. TEL 33-1-41835252. FAX 33-1-41835253. URL: http://www.revuefiduciaire.fr. Ed. Monique Henrard. index. (back issues avail.)
   —CCC.
   Description: Covers the management of business in terms of law, finance, computers and accounting.

332.6 GW ISSN 0035-4457
RHEINISCH-WESTFAELISCHE BOERSE ZU DUESSELDORF. AMTLICHES KURSBLATT. 1935. d. (Mon.-Fri.). DM.98 per mo. (effective 1997). Rheinisch-Westfaelische Boerse zu Duesseldorf, Ernst-Schneider-Platz 1, 40212 Duesseldorf, Germany. TEL 49-211-13890. FAX 49-211-133287. adv. contact: Wolfgang Peterhoff. circ. 250. **Document type:** bulletin.

332.6 US ISSN 0884-3031
RICHARD C. YOUNG'S INTELLIGENCE REPORT. 1986. m. $99. Phillips Publishing, Inc., Consumer Publishing, 7811 Montrose Rd., Potomac, MD 20854. TEL 301-340-2100. FAX 301-424-7034. Ed. Richard C. Young.
   —CCC.
   Description: Provides investment strategies for all types of securities and mutual funds.

332.6 US ISSN 0895-1306
RICHARD C. YOUNG'S INTERNATIONAL GOLD REPORT. 1978. m. $99. Phillips Publishing, Inc., Consumer Publishing, 7811 Montrose Rd., Potomac, MD 20854. TEL 301-340-2100. FAX 301-424-7034.
   —CCC.
   Description: Looks at a variety of investment strategies within the gold market.

332 US ISSN 1048-3667
RICHARD E. BAND'S PROFITABLE INVESTING. 1990. m. $99. Phillips Publishing, Inc., Consumer Publishing, 7811 Montrose Rd., Potomac, MD 20854. TEL 301-340-2100; 800-722-9000. FAX 301-424-7034. Ed. Richard E. Band.
   —CCC.
   Description: Covers ways to ensure the safety of investment strategies.

332.6 US
RICHLAND REPORT. 1976. 24/yr. $197. Richland Company, Box 222, La Jolla, CA 92038. TEL 619-459-2611. FAX 619-459-2612. Ed. Kennedy Gammage; Pub. Kennedy Grammage. **Document type:** newsletter.

332.6 US
RIPPLES IN THE WAVE. 1991. 17/yr. $157 (effective 1997). The Hood Co., 5200 N.W. 43rd St., Ste. 102376, Gainesville, FL 32606. TEL 352-378-8008. Ed. Leo F. Hood. R&P contact: Leo F. Hood. **Document type:** trade publication.

332.6 US
RISK FACTOR METHOD OF INVESTING. 1977. w. service $300; s-m. $175; m. $100. INVEST-O-Registered Investment Advisors, Box 5996, Bend, OR 97708-5996. TEL 541-389-3676. Ed. William Kuhn. charts. circ. 150. (back issues avail.) **Document type:** newsletter.

RISK MANAGEMENT. see *INSURANCE*

332.6 IT ISSN 1120-5318
RIVISTA DELLA BORSA. 1989. q. L.39900 (foreign L.70000). Arnoldo Mondadori Editore S.p.A., Centro Direzionale, Palazzo Canova, 20090 Milan - Segrate Italy. TEL 02-75421. FAX 041-5238307. Ed. Paolo Costa.

332.6 US
ROBBINS REPORT.* 1966. s-m. $125 (new subscribers $30 for 10 issues). William Spencer Educational Foundation, 6701 Blanco Rd., Apt. 1010, San Antonio, TX 78216-6112. TEL 512-733-0051. Ed. Richard S. Robbins. circ. 1,600.

332.6 US
ROESCH MARKET MEMO.* 1981. m. $42. 6511 W. 80th St., Overland Park, KS 66204-3811. TEL 913-381-0857. Ed. Larry E. Roesch. **Document type:** newsletter.
   Description: Covers all technical and fundamental data pertinent to the market, with buy and sell recommendations.

BUSINESS AND ECONOMICS — INVESTMENTS

338 332.6 US ISSN 0891-5547
RUFF TIMES. 1975. m. every 3 wks. $149. Phoenix Ink, Box 31, Springville, UT 84663-0031. TEL 801-489-8681. FAX 801-489-9290. Ed. Howard J. Ruff. adv.; bk.rev.; charts; stat. circ. 150,000.
    Former titles (until 1986): Howard Ruff's Financial Success Report (ISSN 0747-0541); Howard Ruff's Financial Survival Report (ISSN 0745-0672); (until 1984): Ruff Times (ISSN 0279-2303)

332.6 US
RUSS REPORTS. 1981. m. $130 (diskette $180). 321 Hillcove Pt., Wellford, SC 29385-9041. TEL 803-281-1561. Ed. Russ Klein. circ. 3,750. (also avail. in diskette format) **Document type:** newsletter.
    Description: Provides investment advice, with buy and sell recommendations for selected stocks.

RUSSIAN TELECOMMUNICATIONS INVESTOR'S GUIDE. see COMMUNICATIONS

332 RU ISSN 0869-6608
RYNOK TSENNYKH BUMAG/SECURITIES MARKET; analiticheskii zhurnal. (Text in Russian; summaries in English) 1992. s-m. $276 (effective 1998). Rynok Tsennykh Bumag, Raspletina ul., 3, 123060 Moscow, Russia. TEL 7-094-9469820. FAX 7-095-9469822. E-mail: root@smmag.msk.su. (Dist. by: Mezhdunarodnaya Kniga, B. Yakimanka 39, 117049 Moscow, Russia. TEL 7-095-2384967. FAX 7-095-2384634) Ed. Valery Kolankov. adv.: page $3900; 205 x 282; adv. contact: Vladimir Kadysev. abstr.; charts; illus. circ. 25,000. (also avail. in diskette format; back issues avail.) **Document type:** trade publication.
    Description: Provides analytical information on the state and prospects of Russia's financial and stock market.

332.6 US
S.A. ADVISORY. 1983. m. $100 (with phone service $280). 2274 Arbor Ln., Ste. 3, Salt Lake City, UT 84117. TEL 801-272-4761. Ed. William Velmer. circ. 1,000. **Document type:** newsletter.
    Description: Deals with low- and high-priced stock investments, between $0.25 and $100.

332 340 US
S A C AWARD REVIEW. (Securities Arbitration Commentator) 1990. q. $98 ($200 with subscr. to Award Database Service). Richard P. Ryder, Ed. & Pub., Box 112, Maplewood, NJ 07040. TEL 201-761-5880. FAX 201-761-1504. R&P contact: Richard P. Ryder. (back issues avail.) **Document type:** newsletter.
    Formerly (until 1994): S A C Reporter.
    Description: Tracks, records, and reports on arbitration awards in the securities and commodities industry.

332.9 US ISSN 1088-8861
HG4907
S & P MIDCAP 400 DIRECTORY. a. Standard & Poor's (Subsidiary of: McGraw-Hill Companies, Inc.), 25 Broadway, New York, NY 10004. TEL 212-208-8000. charts; stat. **Document type:** directory.
    Description: Lists and profiles companies in the Standard and Poor's MidCap 400 Index.

332.6 US ISSN 1088-8381
S & P 100 INFORMATION BULLETIN. m. $220. Standard & Poor's (Subsidiary of: McGraw-Hill Companies, Inc.), 25 Broadway, New York, NY 10004. TEL 212-208-8275. FAX 212-208-8624. Ed. Cynthia Giglio. stat. (back issues avail.) **Document type:** bulletin.
    Description: Provides a monthly statistical summary of stock prices of the Standard and Poor's 100 index component companies.

332.6 US ISSN 1088-8926
HG4907
S & P 500 DIRECTORY. a. Standard & Poor's (Subsidiary of: McGraw-Hill Companies, Inc.), 25 Broadway, New York, NY 10004. TEL 212-208-8000. charts; stat. **Document type:** directory.
    Description: Lists and profiles all companies included in the Standard and Poor's 500 Index.

332.6 657 US ISSN 0277-3953
S E C ACCOUNTING RULES. (Securities and Exchange Commission) 1968. base vol. plus updates. $378. C C H Incorporated, 2700 Lake Cook Rd., Riverwoods, IL 60015. TEL 847-267-7000; 800-835-5224. FAX 800-224-8299. (looseleaf format)
—CCC.

332.6 340 US
S E C COMPLIANCE: FINANCIAL REPORTING AND FORMS. (Securities Exchange Commission) 5 base vols. (plus m. updates). $895 (effective 1995). Warren, Gorham & Lamont, One Penn Plaza, New York, NY 10119. TEL 212-971-5000. FAX 212-971-5113. (Orders to: The Park Square Bldg., 31 St. James Ave., Boston, MA 02116-4112. TEL 800-950-1207) Eds. Daniel Schechtman, Michael A. Walker. (looseleaf format) **Document type:** trade publication.
    Description: Contains the official text of the rules and forms required by the Securities and Exchange Commission along with explanations of periodic reporting forms, and coverage of other related developments.

332.6 US ISSN 0091-4061
KF1436.A2
S E C DOCKET. 1973. w. $79. U.S. Securities and Exchange Commission, 450 Fifth St., N.W., MISC-11, Washington, DC 20549. TEL 202-272-7460. FAX 202-272-7050. (Orders to: The Commerce Clearing House, Inc., 4025 W. Peterson Ave., Chicago, IL 60646) circ. 12,500 (controlled). (looseleaf format; reprint service avail. from UMI)
● Also available online. Vendor(s): West Group.
—UMI.

332.6 657 US
S E C FINANCIAL REPORTING: ANNUAL REPORTS TO SHAREHOLDERS, FORM 10-K, QUARTERLY FINANCIAL REPORTING. (Issued as base vol. with supplements) 1977. irreg. $185. Matthew Bender & Co., Inc., 2 Park Ave., New York, NY 10016. TEL 212-448-2000. E-mail: international@bender.com; URL: http://www.bender.com. Ed.Bd. (looseleaf format)
    Description: Comprehensive coverage of every aspect of financial reporting and disclosure under regulations S-X and S-K, with emphasis on common problem areas. Attempts to keep readers abreast of current developments in the field.

332.6 346.066 US
S E C GUIDELINES: RULES AND REGULATIONS. a. $60 (foreign $113). Warren, Gorham & Lamont, One Penn Plaza, New York, NY 10119. TEL 212-971-5000. FAX 212-971-5113. (Orders to: The Park Square Bldg., 31 St. James Ave., Boston, MA 02116-4112. TEL 800-950-1207) **Document type:** trade publication.

332.6 US ISSN 0364-6718
S E C NEWS DIGEST. d. $100. U.S. Securities and Exchange Commission, 450 Fifth St., N.W., MISC-11, Washington, DC 20549. TEL 202-272-7460. FAX 202-272-7050. (Dist. by: Washington Service Bureau, 1225 Connecticut Ave., N.W., Washington, DC 20036) circ. controlled. (reprint service avail. from UMI)
● Also available online. Vendor(s): Bureau of National Affairs, NewsNet (EV96), West Group.

S I A DIRECTORY & GUIDE. (Securities Industry Association) see BUSINESS AND ECONOMICS — Trade And Industrial Directories

332.6 US
S I A WASHINGTON REPORT.* irreg. Securities Industry Association (Washington), 1401 I St. N.W., Ste. 1000, Washington, DC 20005. TEL 202-296-9410.
    Description: Informs members of pertinent legislative and regulatory developments in Washington.

332.678 US
S I E (YEAR) GUIDE TO INVESTMENT SERVICES. 1966. a. $1. Select Information Exchange, 244 W. 54th St., 6th Fl., New York, NY 10024. TEL 212-247-7123. FAX 212-247-7326. Ed. George Wein; Pub. George Wein. adv. contact: Alex Wein. bk.rev.; bibl. circ. 135,000. **Document type:** directory.
    Former titles: S I E Sophisticated Investor; Investment Sources and Ideas (ISSN 0085-6355); Sources and Ideas; Which incorporates: Sophisticated Investor.
    Description: Describes, analyzes, prices and categorizes investment publications indexed by subject.

332.6 US
S M R COMMODITY CHARTS. 1967. w. $575 (d. fax update service $250; d. fax comments and recommendations $1500; free via web site). Security Market Research, Box 7476, Boulder, CO 80306-7476. TEL 303-494-8035. FAX 303-494-5474. URL: http://www.smr.com. Ed. Brad Crotzer; Pub. Brad Crotzer. R&P contact: Brad Crotzer. adv. contact: Brad Crotzer. circ. 150. **Document type:** newsletter.
● Also available online.
    Formerly: S M R Commodity Service.
    Description: Provides a technical charting service wherein short-term signals are used as indicators to direct market investments.

332.6 US
S M R STOCK CHARTS. 1964. w. $575 (d. fax update service $150; d. fax comments and recommendations $1500; free via web site). Security Market Research, Box 7476, Boulder, CO 80306-7476. TEL 303-494-8035. FAX 303-494-5474. URL: http://www.smr.com. Ed. Brad Crotzer; Pub. Brad Crotzer. R&P contact: Brad Crotzer. adv. contact: Brad Crotzer. circ. 300. **Document type:** newsletter.
● Also available online.
    Formerly: Wall Street's Top 50.
    Description: Provides a technical charting service wherein short-term signals are used as indicators to direct market investments.

332.6 US ISSN 1074-6609
THE S N L FINANCIAL SERVICES DAILY. 1993? d. S N L Securities LP, 410 E. Main St., Box 2124, Charlottesville, VA 22902. TEL 804-977-1600. FAX 804-977-4466. Pub. Reid Nagle.

332.6 US ISSN 1074-5912
THE S N L FINANCIAL SERVICES QUARTERLY. 1992? q. $696. S N L Securities, LP, 410 E. Main St., Box 2124, Charlottesville, VA 22902. TEL 804-977-4466. FAX 804-277-4466. Ed. Jenn Nagaj; Pub. Reid Nagle.
    Description: Provides financial analysts, executives, investors and other members of the investment community with detailed, financial and investment information.

332.6 US ISSN 8750-2356
HG4501
S R C BLUE BOOK OF 5-TREND CYCLI-GRAPHS; 12 years of prices, earnings, dividends, relative performance, volume. q. $119 (effective 1997). Securities Research Company (Subsidiary of: Babson-United Investment Advisors, Inc.), 101 Prescott St., Wellesley Hills, MA 02181-7528. TEL 617-235-0900. Ed. Donald S. Jones; Pub. Donald S. Jones. **Document type:** directory.
    Description: Explores price ranges, relative performance, volume, quarterly earnings and dividends.

332.678 US ISSN 1042-1610
S R C BROWN BOOK OF 5-TREND O T C CHARTS; 20 months of prices, earnings, dividends, relative performance, volume. m. $164 (effective 1997). Securities Research Company (Subsidiary of: Babson-United Investment Advisors, Inc.), 101 Prescott St., Wellesley Hills, MA 02181-7528. TEL 617-235-0900. Ed. Donald S. Jones; Pub. Donald S. Jones. charts. (back issues avail.)
    Description: Compares prices, earnings, dividends, relative performance, volume.

332.6 US ISSN 0884-8475
HG4916
S R C GREEN BOOK OF 5-TREND 35-YEAR CHARTS. 1981. a. $109 (effective 1997). Securities Research Company (Subsidiary of: Babson-United Investment Advisors, Inc.), 101 Prescott St., Wellesley Hills, MA 02181-7528. TEL 617-235-0900. Ed. Donald S. Jones; Pub. Donald S. Jones. circ. 2,000.
Description: Covers 400 stocks, 39 industry groups, and 11 stock market averages.

332.6 US ISSN 1063-5173
HG4916
S R C ORANGE BOOK OF 5-TREND LONG-TERM O T C CHARTS; 12 years of prices, earnings, dividends, relative performance, volume. 1992. q. $124 (effective 1997). Securities Research Company (Subsidiary of: Babson-United Investment Advisors, Inc.), 101 Prescott St., Wellesley Hills, MA 02181-7528. TEL 617-235-0900. Ed. Donald S. Jones; Pub. Donald S. Jones.
Description: Provides 1,012 stock charts that include 12-year monthly price ranges, relative market action, moving average and volume, as well as capitalization data, earnings on a 12-month basis and dividends on an annual rate basis.

332.6 US ISSN 8750-2461
HG4501
S R C RED BOOK OF 5-TREND SECURITY CHARTS; 21 months of prices, earnings, dividends, relative performance, volume. 1934. m. $139 (effective 1997). Securities Research Company (Subsidiary of: Babson-United Investment Advisors, Inc.), 101 Prescott St., Wellesley Hills, MA 02181-7528. TEL 617-235-0900. Ed. Donald S. Jones; Pub. Donald S. Jones.
Description: Shows weekly price ranges, relative performances, moving averages, volume and quality, earnings and dividends.

THE SAFE MONEY REPORT. see *BUSINESS AND ECONOMICS — Economic Situation And Conditions*

SCOTTISH BUSINESS INSIDER. see *BUSINESS AND ECONOMICS — Banking And Finance*

332.6 333.33 CJ
SEALES CAYMAN LETTER; an investment, economic and real estate review of the tax-free Cayman Islands. bi-m. C.$60($180) Seales & Company Ltd., Cayman Falls W. Bay Rd., P.O. Box 1103, Grand Cayman, British W.I. TEL 809-94-74325. FAX 809-94-74230.

332.6 US
SEASONAL TRADER. 48/yr. $349. Steiner & Co., Box 38388, Germantown, TN 38138.

332.6327 US
SECTOR FUND NEWSLETTER. 1985. bi-w. $157. Box 270048, San Diego, CA 92198-2048. TEL 619-748-0805. Ed. Cato B. Ohrn. bk.rev. **Document type:** newsletter.

332.6 US
SECURE MAGAZINE. q. Security Service Federal Credit Union, 7323 Hwy. 90 W., San Antonio, TX 78227. TEL 512-670-4490. Ed. Mary Glenewinkel.

332.6 US
SECURED TRANSACTION GUIDE. 1969. fortn. $1053. C C H Incorporated, 2700 Lake Cook Rd., Riverwoods, IL 60015. TEL 847-267-7000; 800-835-5224. FAX 800-224-8299.

332.6 US ISSN 0739-8689
SECURITIES & SYNDICATION REVIEW. 1983. bi-m. $75. Securities Sources, Inc., Box 85600, University Sta., Seattle, WA 98145-1600. TEL 206-284-5249. Ed. Robert E. Frey. circ. 500. (back issues avail.)
Description: Covers the securities industry and financial planning.

332.6 340 US ISSN 1041-3057
KF9085.A59
SECURITIES ARBITRATION COMMENTATOR; covering significant issues & events in securities-commodities arbitration. 1988. m. $348 (foreign $382.80) (effective Feb. 1996). Richard P. Ryder, Ed. & Pub., Box 112, Maplewood, NJ 07040. TEL 201-761-5880. FAX 201-761-1504. R&P contact: Richard P. Ryder. index. (back issues avail.) **Document type:** newsletter.

332.6 US ISSN 0896-7954
SECURITIES CLASS ACTION ALERT. 1988. m. $545 (foreign $620) (effective 1997). Investors Research Bureau, Inc., 10 Mountainview Rd., N. Lobby, 2nd Fl., Upper Saddle River, NJ 07458-1933. TEL 201-236-9777. FAX 201-236-9738. Ed. James Newman. (looseleaf format; back issues avail.) **Document type:** newsletter.
Formerly (until 1989): Investors Class Action Monitor.

332.6 TH
SECURITIES EXCHANGE OF THAILAND. HANDBOOK. (Print version ceased in 1995.) 1975. irreg. Securities Exchange of Thailand, Sinthom Bldg., 2nd Fl., 132 Wireless Rd., Bangkok 10500, Thailand. (diskette format)
●Also available online.

SECURITIES FRAUD: LITIGATING UNDER RULE 10B-5. see *LAW*

332.6 US
SECURITIES INDUSTRY FACT BOOK. a. Securities Industry Association, 120 Broadway, 35th Fl., New York, NY 10271. TEL 212-608-1500. Eds. Grace Toto, George Monahan. **Document type:** trade publication.

332.6 US
SECURITIES INDUSTRY TRENDS. irreg. $125 to non-members; members $75. Securities Industry Association, 120 Broadway, 35th Fl., New York, NY 10271. TEL 212-608-1500. Eds. Jeffrey M. Schaeffer, George Monahan. (back issues avail.) **Indexed:** SRI. **Document type:** trade publication.
Description: Provides information on economic developments affecting securities firms. Includes profitability and financial statements of the securities industry.

332.6 US
SECURITIES INDUSTRY YEARBOOK. 1980. a. $125 to non-members; members $85. Securities Industry Association, 120 Broadway, 35th Fl., New York, NY 10271. TEL 212-608-1500. Ed. Rosalie Pepe. adv.; stat. circ. 3,500. (also avail. in microfiche from CIS) **Indexed:** SRI. **Document type:** trade publication.
Formerly: Security Industry Yearbook (ISSN 0730-5796)
Description: Lists association members and capital statistics.

332.6 340 US ISSN 0731-5805
KF1439
SECURITIES LAW HANDBOOK. 1978. a. $140. Clark - Boardman - Callaghan, 375 Hudson St., New York, NY 10014. TEL 212-929-7500; 800-422-2101. FAX 212-924-0460. Ed. Harold S. Bloomenthal. **Document type:** trade publication.
—CCC.

332.6 JA
SECURITIES MARKET IN JAPAN. (Text in English) 1973. biennial, latest Jan. 1996. price varies. Japan Securities Research Institute, Shokenkaikan, 1-5-8 Nihonbashi Kayaba-cho, Chuo-ku, Tokyo 103, Japan. TEL 81-3-3669-0737. FAX 81-3-3662-8294. Ed. Shozo Koyama. illus.; stat.

332.6 340 US
SECURITIES REGULATION. 6 base vols. (plus fortn. updates). $895 (effective 1995). Warren, Gorham & Lamont, One Penn Plaza, New York, NY 10019-4098. TEL 212-971-5000. FAX 212-971-5113. (Orders to: The Park Square Bldg., 31 St. James Ave., Boston, MA 02116-4112. TEL 800-950-1207) (looseleaf format)
Description: Covers U.S. legislation and other topics affecting the securities trading industries.

332.6 340 US ISSN 0097-9554
K23
SECURITIES REGULATION LAW JOURNAL. 1973. q. $183 (overseas $271.45) (effective 1995). Warren, Gorham & Lamont, One Penn Plaza, New York, NY 10119. TEL 212-971-5000. FAX 212-971-5113. (Subscr. to: The Park Square Bldg., 31 St. James Ave., Boston, MA 02116-4112. TEL 800-950-1207) Ed. Marc I. Steinberg. bk.rev. circ. 1,659. (also avail. in microform from UMI; reprint service avail. from RRI,UMI,WSH) **Indexed:** ABI Inform., Abstr.Bk.Rev.Curr.Leg.Per., Account.Ind. (1974-), ASCA, Bank.Lit.Ind., BPIA, Bus.Ind., C.L.I., Curr.Cont., L.R.I., Leg.Cont., Leg.Per., Manage.Cont., SSCI, Tr.& Indus.Ind. **Document type:** academic/scholarly publication, trade publication.
—BLDSC (8217.140000); Genuine Article; KR SourceOne; SWETS; UMI; UnCover. **CCC.**
Description: Offers analysis and advice through articles and features by noted practitioners and scholars to help readers keep up with the constant changes in the law, rules, and regulations.
Refereed Serial

332.6 US ISSN 0149-3582
SECURITIES WEEK. 1973. w. $1310 (foreign $1325). McGraw-Hill Companies, 1221 Ave. of the Americas, New York, NY 10020. TEL 212-512-4214. Ed. Michael Ocrant. (back issues avail.; reprint service avail. from UMI) **Document type:** newsletter, trade publication.
●Also available online. Vendor(s): Dow Jones News Retrieval (SW), Knight-Ridder Information, Inc. (File no.624/McGRAW-HILL PUBLICATIONS ONLINE), Lexis-Nexis (SECWK), NewsNet (FI27).
—CCC.
Description: Contains news and analysis of the securities industry, futures and options industries.

332 US
SECURITY DEALERS OF NORTH AMERICA. 1923. s-a., plus cum. supplement every 6 wks. $565. Standard & Poor's (Subsidiary of: McGraw-Hill Companies, Inc.), 25 Broadway, New York, NY 10004. TEL 212-208-8275. FAX 212-208-8624. Ed. Lily DeAngelis; Pub. Tom Lupo. R&P contact: Peggy Smith. adv. contact: Rose Tanzi. (also avail. in magnetic tape; diskette format) **Document type:** directory.
Description: Lists more than 5,000 main offices and more than 8,500 branch offices of security dealers in North America; includes the names and addresses of more than 45,000 key executives, trade organizations, stock exchanges, and state securities administrators.

332 US ISSN 1059-1389
SELLER - SERVICER UPDATE. Key Title: Inside Mortgage Finance's Seller - Servicer Update. 1988. m. $395. Inside Mortgage Finance Publications, Box 42387, Washington, DC 20015. TEL 301-951-1240. FAX 301-656-1709. URL: http://users.aol.com/imfpubs. Ed. Guy D. Cecala; Pub. Guy D. Cecala. R&P contact: Didi Parks. **Document type:** trade publication.
Description: Reports on all seller and servicer notices issued.

332.6 381 US
SENTINEL INVESTMENT LETTER. 1978. m. $150 (effective 1997). Hanover Investment Management Corp., 853 Second St. Pike, No.A-2, Richboro, PA 18954-1082. TEL 215-853-6960. (tabloid format) **Document type:** newsletter.

332.6 CC
SHANGHAI TOUZI/SHANGHAI INVESTMENT. (Text in Chinese) bi-m. Zhongguo Renmin Jianshe Yinhang, Shanghai Fenhang, Guding Zichan Touzi Yanjiusuo China People's Construction Bank, Shanghai Branch Institute of Fixed Assets Investment, 14544 Yan'an Donglu, Room 508, Shanghai 200003, People's Republic of China. TEL 3273187. Ed. Zhang Yimin

332.6 340 CN
SHAREHOLDER REMEDIES IN CANADA. 1989. q. Can.$240. Butterworths Canada Ltd., Part of the Reed Elsevier group, 75 Clegg Rd., Markham, ON L6G 1A1, Canada. TEL 905-479-2665. FAX 905-479-2826. Ed. Dennis H. Peterson. (looseleaf format) **Document type:** trade publication.
Description: For practitioners. Provides a comprehensive and detailed examination of statutory provisions and common-law principles governing the remedies of shareholders.

BUSINESS AND ECONOMICS — INVESTMENTS

332.6 US
SHELBURNE SECURITIES FORECAST. 1976. bi-w. $49. 1017 N. Quintana St., Box 5566, Arlington, VA 22205. Ed. Robert W. Shelburne. (tabloid format; back issues avail.)
  Description: Specializes in the stocks of companies involved in natural resources and electric utilities.

SHICHANG ZHOUBAO/MARKET WEEKLY. see BUSINESS AND ECONOMICS — Domestic Commerce

332.6 US
SHORT ALERT. 1987. irreg. $69. Gulf Atlantic Publishing, Inc., 1801 Lee Rd., No. 301, Winter Park, FL 32789-2165. TEL 407-628-5700. FAX 407-628-0807. Ed. Roberto Veitia. circ. 2,600.

332.6 US ISSN 1073-1733
HG4907
SHORT ON VALUE. 1992. m. $288 (effective 1995). 2480 Briarcliff Rd., Ste. 336, Atlanta, GA 30329. TEL 404-233-0120. Ed. William D. Lyons. **Document type:** newsletter.
  Description: Covers overvalued U.S. equities and short selling.

332.6 US ISSN 1083-6721
SID CATO'S NEWSLETTER ON ANNUAL REPORTS. 1983. m. $197 (effective 1995). Cato Communications, Inc., Box 19850, Kalamazoo, MI 49019-0850. TEL 616-344-2286. FAX 616-344-4145. E-mail: sidcato@sidcato.com. Ed. Sid Cato; Pub. Sid Cato. R&P contact: Sid Cato. **Document type:** newsletter.
  Description: Provides analysis and commentary on annual reports to shareholders for publicly held companies.

332.6 US ISSN 0195-8054
SILVER AND GOLD REPORT. 1976. m. $195. Weiss Ratings, Inc., 4176 Burns Rd., Palm Beach Gardens, FL 33410. TEL 407-627-3300. FAX 407-625-6685. E-mail: tom-r@weiss.com; URL: http://www.weissinc.com. Ed. James DiGeorgia; Pub. Martin Weiss. R&P contact: Steve H. Ackerman. pp./issue: 8. **Document type:** newsletter.
  Description: Specializes in showing investors how to avoid the traps, pitfalls, scams and frauds that abound in the silver and gold industry.

332.6 US
SILVER BARON'S MONEY FEVER. 1984. m. $120. S B Stocks U S A, 1 E. Camelback Rd., Ste. 680, Phoenix, AZ 85012-1051. TEL 602-265-4245. FAX 602-265-2806. Ed. Elliott R. Pearson; Pub. Elliott R. Pearson. R&P contact: Elliott R. Pearson. adv. contact: Elliott R. Pearson. circ. 1,900 (controlled). **Document type:** newsletter.
  Former titles: Silver Baron - Stocks U S A; Silver Baron.
  Description: Picks huge winners with as little risk as possible under the circumstances.

332.67 621.385 CN ISSN 0846-3131
SILVER SCREEN. 1988. q. Can.$53.50. Malcolm Silver & Co. Ltd., 194 Merton St., Ste. 210, Toronto, ON M4S 3B5, Canada. TEL 416-488-3393. FAX 416-488-5217. E-mail: msilver@davisville.ca; URL: http://www.davisville.ca/msilver. Ed. Jill Battson. R&P contact: Jill Battson. adv. contact: Keith Cole. bk.rev.; circ. 1,300 (paid). **Document type:** newsletter.
  Description: Targeted towards multimedia and entertainment finance and investment, specifically video, television and film. For readers in Canada, the US, Europe and the Pacific Rim.

332.6 SI ISSN 0217-3476
SINGAPORE STOCK EXCHANGE JOURNAL.* m. S.$39 in Singapore; S.E. Asia S.$99; elsewhere S.$111. Stock Exchange of Singapore Ltd., Robinson Rd., P.O. Box 2306, Singapore 9043, Singapore. TEL 535-3788. FAX 532-4476. TELEX RS-21853. adv. circ. 18,000.
  Description: Summarizes trading in all listed stocks. Provides stock market data, information on half-yearly reports, annual accounts, and chairmen's statements. Includes financial articles and reviews of activities in listed companies.

332.6 US
THE SLANKER REPORT. 1992. m. $195. Ted E. Slanker, Jr., Ed. & Pub., R.R.2, Box 175, Powderly, TX 75473-9740. TEL 903-732-4653. FAX 903-732-4151. E-mail: 72722,51@compuserve.com; slanker@koyote.com. **Document type:** newsletter.
  Description: Hard money letter for conservative and aggressive investors.

SMALL BUSINESS WORLD MAGAZINE. see BUSINESS AND ECONOMICS — Small Business

332.6 UK ISSN 1356-2894
SMALLER COMPANIES HANDBOOK. 1994. a. (in 2 vols.). £165 (single vol. £110). Exeter Financial Ltd., Research Products Sales and Marketing Department, 13-17 Epworth St., London EC2A 4DL, England. TEL 44-171-825-8000. FAX 44-171-608-3514. Ed.Bd. charts; stat.
  Description: Covers 1,400 smaller companies quoted on the Main and Unlisted securities markets. Provides background and financial data for each company.

332.64 UK
SMALLER UK MARKETS HANDBOOK. 1980. a. £180 for vols. 1 & 2. Financial Times Information Ltd., Extel, Fitzroy House, 13-17 Epworth St., London EC2A 4DL, England. TEL 44-171-825-8000. FAX 44-171-608-2032. TELEX 884319. E-mail: eic@ft.com; URL: http://www.info.ft.com/.
  Supersedes: Secondary Markets Handbook; Which was formerly: Extel Unlisted Securities Market Service.
  Description: Covers 1500 smaller companies (with a market capitalisation of under 250 million) quoted on the London Stock Exchange. Includes a ranking of all companies by market capitalisation as well as indexes by industry sector and registrars.

332.6 US
SMART MONEY.* 1973. m. $120. Hirsch Organization Inc., Box 2069, River Vale, NJ 07675-9001. TEL 201-767-4100. FAX 201-767-7337. Ed. Yale Hirsch. circ. 10,000. **Indexed:** Access (1992-).
  Description: Provides both market advice and stock recommendations. A regular features is "America's Most Undiscovered Companies".

332.67 US
HD60.5.U5
SOCIAL ISSUES REPORTER. 1974. 11/yr. $275 (effective 1996). Investor Responsibility Research Center, Inc., 1350 Connecticut Ave., N.W., Ste. 700, Washington, DC 20036. TEL 202-833-0700. FAX 202-833-3555. Ed. Ken Bertsch. R&P contact: Ken Bertsch. bk.rev. circ. 1,200. **Document type:** newsletter.
  Formerly: News for Investors (ISSN 1053-5470)
  Description: Updates readers on developments affecting corporate social responsibility in such areas as investment in South Africa, Northern Ireland, military production, tobacco, labor laws and practices, energy, the environment and equal employment opportunity.

332.6 SP
SOCIEDADES COTIZADAS EN BOLSA. no.152, 1991. w. free. Banco Hispano Americano, Division de Banca Corporativa y Mercado de Capitales, Plaza de Canalejas, 1, 28014 Madrid, Spain. TEL 531-18-36. FAX 522-18-23. charts; stat.

332.6 LU
SOCIETE DE LA BOURSE DE LUXEMBOURG. COTE OFFICIELLE DE LA BOURSE DE LUXEMBOURG (BI-MONTHLY)/LUXEMBOURG STOCK EXCHANGE. OFFICIAL PRICE LIST. 1929. bi-m. 7402 Fr. (outside Europe 11400 Fr.) (effective 1997). Societe de la Bourse de Luxembourg - Luxembourg Stock Exchange, P.O. Box 165, 11 av. de la Porte-Neuve, L-2011 Luxembourg, Luxembourg. TEL 352-4779361. FAX 352-473298. TELEX 2559-STOEX-LU. circ. 550.
  Description: Contains latest updates for active securities.

332.6 LU
SOCIETE DE LA BOURSE DE LUXEMBOURG. COTE OFFICIELLE DE LA BOURSE DE LUXEMBOURG (DAILY)/LUXEMBOURG STOCK EXCHANGE. OFFICIAL PRICE LIST. 1929. d. 34.550 Fr. (outside Europe 62.200 Fr.). Societe de la Bourse de Luxembourg - Luxembourg Stock Exchange, P.O. Box 165, 11 av. de la Porte-Neuve, L-2011 Luxembourg, Luxembourg. TEL 352-4779361. FAX 352-473298. TELEX 2559-STOEX-LU. circ. 550.
  Description: Contains latest updates for active securities.

332.6 LU
SOCIETE DE LA BOURSE DE LUXEMBOURG. COTE OFFICIELLE DE LA BOURSE DE LUXEMBOURG (MONTHLY)/LUXEMBOURG STOCK EXCHANGE. OFFICIAL PRICE LIST. 1929. m. 4775 Fr. (outside 6100 Fr.) (effective 1997). Societe de la Bourse de Luxembourg - Luxembourg Stock Exchange, P.O. Box 165, 11 av. de la Porte-Neuve, L-2011 Luxembourg, Luxembourg. TEL 352-4779361. FAX 352-473298. TELEX 2559-STOEX-LU. circ. 1,100.
  Description: Contains all 13,000 listed securities, gives information about prices, yields of debt securities, and highest and lowest prices of listed securities.

332.6 LU
SOCIETE DE LA BOURSE DE LUXEMBOURG. COTE OFFICIELLE DE LA BOURSE DE LUXEMBOURG (WEEKLY)/LUXEMBOURG STOCK EXCHANGE. OFFICIAL PRICE LIST. 1929. w. 10950 Fr. (outside Europe 18000 Fr.) (effective 1997). Societe de la Bourse de Luxembourg - Luxembourg Stock Exchange, P.O. Box 165, 11 av. de la Porte-Neuve, L-2011 Luxembourg, Luxembourg. TEL 352-4779361. FAX 352-473298. TELEX 2559-STOEX-LU. circ. 700.
  Description: Contains latest updates for active securities.

332.6 LU
SOCIETE DE LA BOURSE DE LUXEMBOURG. FACT BOOK. (Text in English) 1997. a. free. Societe de la Bourse de Luxembourg - Luxembourg Stock Exchange, P.O. Box 165, 11 av. de la Porte-Neuve, L-2011 Luxembourg, Luxembourg. TEL 352-4779361. FAX 352-473298. TELEX 2559-STOEX-LU. circ. 4,500.
  Description: Gives information on the activities of the Luxembourg Stock Exchange.

SOCIETE DE LA BOURSE DE LUXEMBOURG. FAITS ET CHIFFRES/LUXEMBOURG STOCK EXCHANGE. FACTS AND FIGURES. see BUSINESS AND ECONOMICS — Abstracting, Bibliographies, Statistics

332.6 LU
SOCIETE DE LA BOURSE DE LUXEMBOURG. RAPPORT ANNUEL/LUXEMBOURG STOCK EXCHANGE. ANNUAL REPORT. (Text in English, French) 1929. a. free. Societe de la Bourse de Luxembourg - Luxembourg Stock Exchange, P.O. Box 165, 11 av. de la Porte-Neuve, L-2011 Luxembourg, Luxembourg. TEL 352-4779361. FAX 352-473298. TELEX 2559-STOEX-LU. circ. 3,500.

332.6 BE
SOCIETE DE LA BOURSE DE VALEURS MOBILIERES DE BRUXELLES. BULLETIN MENSUEL. (Text in Dutch, French) 1943. m. 2500 BEF. Societe de la Bourse de Valeurs Mobilieres de Bruxelles S.C., Departement de Statistiques, Palais de la Bourse, B-1000 Brussels, Belgium. FAX 32-2-5091375. TELEX 21186. Ed. D. Valschaerts. charts; stat. circ. 200. **Document type:** bulletin.
  Formerly: Commission de la Bourse de Bruxelles. Indices et Statistiques. Bulletin Mensuel.

332.64 MR
SOCIETE DE LA BOURSE DES VALEURS DE CASABLANCA. STATISTIQUES MENSUELLES. 1976. m. DH.330. Societe de la Bourse des Valeurs de Casablanca, Avenue de l'Armee Royale, Casablanca, Morocco. TEL 212-2-452626. FAX 212-2-452612. **Document type:** bulletin.
  Formerly: Bourse des Valeurs de Casablanca. Bulletin Mensuel d'Information.

SOFTWARE ECONOMICS LETTER; maximizing your return on corporate software. see COMPUTERS — Software

BUSINESS AND ECONOMICS — INVESTMENTS

332.6 US ISSN 1053-5845
SOLID VALUE; financially sound bargain-priced stocks. 1986. s-m. $276 (effective 1997). Happy Man Corporation, 4410 S.W. Pt. Robinson Rd., Vashon Island, WA 98070-7399. TEL 206-463-9399. FAX 206-463-9255. Ed. Irving Scott Wolfe; Pub. Leona V. Troese. adv.; bk.rev. (looseleaf format; back issues avail.) **Document type:** newsletter.
  Description: Lists the market's most under-priced stocks; includes commentaries and updates on recommendations and market analysis.

332.67 US
▼**SOUND INVESTING BASICS**. 1995. q. $100 (effective 1997). Alan B. Lancz & Associates, Inc., 2400 N. Reynolds Rd., Toledo, OH 43615-2818. TEL 419-536-5200. FAX 419-536-5401. Ed. Alan B. Lancz. R&P contact: Jody Stoner. circ. 55. **Document type:** newsletter.

332.6 US ISSN 1056-8654
HF5429.235.U5
SOURCE BOOK OF FRANCHISE OPPORTUNITIES. 1985. a. $35 softcover. Irwin Professional Publishing, 1333 Burr Ridge Pkwy., Burr Ridge, IL 60521-6489. Eds. Christopher E. Bond, Robert E. Bond.

SOUTH AFRICA INVESTOR. see BUSINESS AND ECONOMICS — International Commerce

SOUTHERN ILLINOIS UNIVERSITY AT EDWARDSVILLE. REGIONAL RESEARCH AND DEVELOPMENT SERVICES. REPORT: PRIVATE SECTOR INVESTMENTS. see HOUSING AND URBAN PLANNING

332 US
SOVEREIGN ASSESSMENT MONTHLY. (Included in: Global Corporate Bond Research) m. Salomon Brothers, Inc., 7 World Trade Center, New York, NY 10048. TEL 212-783-7000. **Document type:** trade publication.
  Description: Includes assessments of foreign bonds, fiscal policies, and credit outlook.

332.6 US ISSN 0038-6499
SPARE TIME. 1955. 11/yr. $16.95 (foreign $34). Kipen Publishing Corporation, 5810 W. Oklahoma Ave., Milwaukee, WI 53219. TEL 414-543-8110. FAX 414-543-9767. E-mail: ads@spare-time.com; publisher@spare-time.com; editor@spare-time.com. Ed. Peter Abbott; Pub. Dennis Wilk. R&P contact: Dennis Wilk. adv.; bk.rev.; illus.; circ. 301,000 (controlled). **Document type:** consumer publication.

332.6 US
SPECIAL INVESTMENT SITUATIONS. 1979. m. $120. Box 4254, Chattanooga, TN 37405. TEL 615-886-1628. Ed. George W. Southerland. circ. 800.
  Description: Recommends stocks under $20 possessing 100-300 per cent upside potential.

332.6 US ISSN 1081-129X
SPECIAL SITUATIONS NEWSLETTER; in-depth survey of under-valued stocks. 1977. 12/yr. $75 (effective 1997). C.H. Kaplan, Ed. & Pub., 26 Broadway, Ste. 200, New York, NY 10004-1703. TEL 201-418-4411; 800-756-1811. FAX 201-418-5085. (back issues avail.) **Document type:** newsletter.
  Description: Researches undervalued asset plays, neglected stocks, takeover candidates and turnaround situations. Emphasis is on small-cap stocks traded on NASDAQ and the NYSE.

332.67 US
SPECTRUM CONVERTIBLES; 13(F) institutional convertible holdings survey. q. $450. C D A Investment Technologies, Inc., 1355 Piccard Dr., Rockville, MD 20850. TEL 800-232-6362. FAX 301-590-1329. circ. 100. (also avail. in magnetic tape)
●Also available online.

332.6 US
SPECTRUM INTERNATIONAL. 1990. s-a. (in 2 vols.). $1000. C D A Investment Technologies, Inc., 1355 Piccard Dr., Rockville, MD 20850. TEL 800-232-6362. FAX 301-590-1329. (magnetic tape)
●Also available online.
  Description: Institutional holdings and ownership information on worldwide securities. Covers over 9,200 equities domiciled in 51 countries outside the US, and over 2,200 institutional trusts and funds in 14 countries worldwide.

332.6 US
SPECULATOR; investment advisory service specializing in listed stocks under $20. 1966. s-m. $175. Growth-in-Funds, 77 So. Palm Ave., Sarasota, FL 34236. TEL 201-792-0801. FAX 813-954-0647. Ed. Byron Sanders. charts. circ. 2,500. (looseleaf format)
  Formerly: Penny Speculator.

332.6 US ISSN 1072-3846
HG4915
STANDARD & POOR'S. DAILY STOCK PRICE RECORD. NASDAQ. Key Title: Daily Stock Price Record: NASDAQ. 1968. q. $505. Standard & Poor's (Subsidiary of: McGraw-Hill Companies, Inc.), 25 Broadway, New York, NY 10004. TEL 212-208-8000. mkt.stat. (also avail. in microfiche; back issues avail.) **Document type:** trade publication.
  Formerly (until 1992): Daily Stock Price Record. Over the Counter (ISSN 0737-4100); Supersedes: Standard and Poor's Over-the-Counter (ISSN 0030-7351)
  Description: Gives the daily prices for all stocks traded on the NASDAQ and compiles their averages.

332.6 US
HG4905
STANDARD & POOR'S BOND GUIDE. Cover title: Bond Guide. 1938. m. $230. Standard & Poor's (Subsidiary of: McGraw-Hill Companies, Inc.), 25 Broadway, New York, NY 10004. TEL 212-208-8000. Ed. Frank LoVaglio. stat. (also avail. in microfiche) **Document type:** trade publication.
  Description: Covers domestic and international corporate bonds and their issuing companies.

332.6 US
STANDARD & POOR'S CORPORATE REGISTERED BOND INTEREST RECORD. 1967. a. (with w. updates). $2600. Standard & Poor's Corporation (Subsidiary of: McGraw-Hill, Inc.), 25 Broadway, New York, NY 10004. TEL 212-208-8000. Ed. V. Calbi. (looseleaf format; also avail. in magnetic tape)
●Also available on CD-ROM.

332.6 US ISSN 0277-500X
STANDARD & POOR'S CORPORATION RECORDS; with daily news. Key Title: Standard Corporation Descriptions. (Daily update edition avail. (ISSN 0196-4674)) 1915. s-m. (in 6 vols.), plus 5/wk. Daily News Section. $3400. Standard & Poor's (Subsidiary of: McGraw-Hill Companies, Inc.), 25 Broadway, New York, NY 10004. TEL 212-208-8000. FAX 212-412-0459. Pub. Michael Antinoro. stat.; circ. controlled. (looseleaf format; also avail. in microfiche) **Document type:** trade publication.
●Also available online. Vendor(s): Knight-Ridder Information, Inc. (File no.133/Corporate Descriptions), Lexis-Nexis, NewsNet.
Also available on CD-ROM.
  Description: Provides financial and descriptive information on more than 12,000 publicly held U.S. companies.

332.6 US ISSN 0737-4127
HG4915
STANDARD & POOR'S. DAILY STOCK PRICE RECORD. AMERICAN STOCK EXCHANGE. Key Title: Daily Stock Price Record. American Stock Exchange. 1962. q. $395. Standard & Poor's (Subsidiary of: McGraw-Hill Companies, Inc.), 25 Broadway, New York, NY 10004. TEL 212-208-8000. Ed. Carol Levine. mkt.stat. (looseleaf format; also avail. in microfiche) **Document type:** trade publication.
  Supersedes: Standard and Poor's I S L Daily Stock Price Index. American Stock Exchange (ISSN 0019-0640)
  Description: Reports on the high, low, and close of stocks traded on the American Stock Exchange, along with bid and asked prices for nontraded securities, daily and weekly volumes, shares outstanding, dividend information, and earnings reported most recently for the past four quarters.

332.6 US ISSN 0737-4119
STANDARD & POOR'S DAILY STOCK PRICE RECORD. NEW YORK STOCK EXCHANGE. Key Title: Daily Stock Price Record. New York Stock Exchange. 1962. q. $420. Standard & Poor's (Subsidiary of: McGraw-Hill Companies, Inc.), 25 Broadway, New York, NY 10004. TEL 212-208-8000. Ed. Teresa Kowalski. mkt.; stat. (also avail. in microfiche) **Document type:** trade publication.
  Supersedes: Standard and Poor's I S L Daily Stock Price Index. New York Stock Exchange (ISSN 0019-0659)
  Description: Covers the high, low, and close of stocks traded on the New York Stock Exchange, along with bid and asking prices for nontraded securities, daily and weekly volumes, number of shares outstanding, dividends distributed, and earnings most recently reported for the past four quarters.

332.6 US
STANDARD & POOR'S DIRECTORY OF BOND AGENTS. Short title: Directory of Bond Agents. (Includes bi-m. cum. supplement) 1975. bi-m. $1075. Standard & Poor's Corporation (Subsidiary of: McGraw-Hill, Inc.), 25 Broadway, New York, NY 10004. TEL 212-208-8000. Ed. Vito Calbi. **Document type:** directory.

332.6 US ISSN 1062-5607
HG4028.D5
STANDARD & POOR'S DIRECTORY OF DIVIDEND REINVESTMENT PLANS. 1991. a. $39.95. Standard & Poor's (Subsidiary of: McGraw-Hill Companies, Inc.), 25 Broadway, New York, NY 10004. TEL 212-208-8000; 800-852-1641. FAX 212-412-0240. Ed. Joseph Tigue. charts. **Document type:** directory.
  Description: Helps investors locate more than 700 stocks of companies that feature asset-building dividend reinvestment plans and shows what $1,000 invested 10 years ago would be worth today.

332.6 US ISSN 0196-4658
HG4908
STANDARD & POOR'S DIVIDEND RECORD (DAILY). d. $825. Standard & Poor's Corporation (Subsidiary of: McGraw-Hill, Inc.), 25 Broadway, New York, NY 10004. TEL 212-208-8000. Ed. Anthony Onofrio. stat. (looseleaf format; also avail. in magnetic tape) **Document type:** trade publication.
●Also available online.

332.6 US
STANDARD & POOR'S DIVIDEND RECORD (QUARTERLY). 1925. q. $160. Standard & Poor's Corporation (Subsidiary of: McGraw-Hill, Inc.), 25 Broadway, New York, NY 10004. TEL 212-208-8000. Ed. Anthony Onofrio. stat. (looseleaf format) **Document type:** trade publication.

332.6 US
STANDARD & POOR'S DIVIDEND RECORD (WEEKLY). w. $420. Standard & Poor's Corporation (Subsidiary of: McGraw-Hill, Inc.), 25 Broadway, New York, NY 10004. TEL 212-208-8000. Ed. Anthony Onofrio. stat. (looseleaf format; also avail. in magnetic tape) **Document type:** trade publication.

332.1 US ISSN 1055-0070
HG1501
STANDARD & POOR'S FINANCIAL INSTITUTIONS RATINGS. EUROPE, ASIA, OCEANIA. a. Standard & Poor's Corporation (Subsidiary of: McGraw-Hill, Inc.), 25 Broadway, New York, NY 10004. TEL 212-280-8000. charts; stat. **Document type:** trade publication.
  Supersedes in part (in 1990): S and P's Bank Book, C D Ratings (ISSN 0899-5931)

332.1 US ISSN 1060-3468
HG1660.U5
STANDARD & POOR'S FINANCIAL INSTITUTIONS RATINGS. NORTH AMERICA. 1988. a. Standard & Poor's Corporation (Subsidiary of: McGraw-Hill, Inc.), 25 Broadway, New York, NY 10004. TEL 212-208-8000. charts; stat. **Document type:** trade publication.
  Supersedes in part (in 1990): S and P's Bank Book, C D Ratings (ISSN 0899-5931)

332.6 US
STANDARD & POOR'S INDUSTRY REPORTS. m. Standard & Poor's Corporation (Subsidiary of: McGraw-Hill, Inc.), 25 Broadway, New York, NY 10004. TEL 212-208-8000. charts; stat. (looseleaf format) **Document type:** trade publication.
Description: Provides timely and topical economic, market, and industry reviews and forecasts.

332.6 US ISSN 0196-4666
HC106.6
STANDARD & POOR'S INDUSTRY SURVEYS. 1973. s-a., plus m. supplements. $1800. Standard & Poor's (Subsidiary of: McGraw-Hill Companies, Inc.), 25 Broadway, New York, NY 10004. TEL 212-208-8000. Ed. Eileen Martines. charts; illus.; stat. (also avail. in looseleaf format; diskette format) **Document type:** trade publication.
Description: Provides a broad picture of major U.S. industries, including financial data on more than 1,000 companies. Report on 52 industry segments semi-annually and provides monthly investment outlooks on 120 industries.

332.6 US
STANDARD & POOR'S INSTITUTIONAL EQUITY RESEARCH. m. (plus q. updates). Standard & Poor's Corporation (Subsidiary of: McGraw-Hill, Inc.), 25 Broadway, New York, NY 10004. TEL 212-208-8000. charts; stat. **Document type:** trade publication.
Description: Thoroughly researches often undervalued and overlooked small- and mid-cap companies and initial public offerings that show promising investment potential.

332.6 US
STANDARD & POOR'S NEW ISSUES RESEARCH. irreg. (120-150/yr.). Standard & Poor's (Subsidiary of: McGraw-Hill Companies, Inc.), 25 Broadway, New York, NY 10004. TEL 212-208-8000. Ed. Robert S. Natale. (only avail. by fax) **Document type:** trade publication.
Description: Offers asset managers descriptions of promising initial public offerings, supplying investment appraisals, covering first-day investment factors, and providing buy-flip-avoid opinions.

332.6 US ISSN 1061-0855
HG4501
STANDARD & POOR'S RATINGS HANDBOOK. 1986. m. $275. Standard & Poor's Corporation, 25 Broadway, New York, NY 10004. TEL 212-208-8000. Ed.Bd. R&P contact: Linda Merizalde. **Document type:** trade publication.
Formerly (until 1992): CreditWeek International Ratings (ISSN 0895-2639)
Description: Rates international money market and mutual bond funds and their ability to pay claims. Lists key contacts.

332.6 US ISSN 0737-299X
STANDARD & POOR'S SEMI-WEEKLY CALLED BOND RECORD. 1941. s-w. $1173. Standard & Poor's Corporation (Subsidiary of: McGraw-Hill, Inc.), 25 Broadway, New York, NY 10004. TEL 212-208-8000. Ed. V. Calbi. stat. (looseleaf format) **Document type:** trade publication.

332.6 US ISSN 0147-636X
HC101
STANDARD & POOR'S STATISTICAL SERVICE. CURRENT STATISTICS. (Supplement avail.: Standard & Poor's Statistical Service. Security Price Index) m. $655. Standard & Poor's (Subsidiary of: McGraw-Hill Companies, Inc.), 25 Broadway, New York, NY 10004. TEL 212-208-8000. Ed. Karen Each. **Document type:** trade publication.
Description: Provides the performance history of particular stock groups during economic ups and downs, stock and bond prices during periods of inflation, and more.

332.63 US ISSN 0272-0914
HG4915
STANDARD & POOR'S STATISTICAL SERVICE. SECURITY PRICE INDEX. (Supplement to: Standard & Poor's Statistical Service. Current Statistics) 1978. biennial. $220. Standard & Poor's (Subsidiary of: McGraw-Hill Companies, Inc.), 25 Broadway, New York, NY 10004. TEL 212-208-8000. charts; stat. (looseleaf format) **Document type:** trade publication.
Description: Provides the performance history of particular stock groups during economic ups and downs, along with data on stock and bond prices during inflationary periods.

332.6 US ISSN 0737-4135
STANDARD & POOR'S STOCK GUIDE. 1943. m. $145. Standard & Poor's Corporation (Subsidiary of: McGraw-Hill, Inc.), 25 Broadway, New York, NY 10004. TEL 212-208-8000. Ed. Frank Lovaglio. charts; stat. circ. 400,000. (also avail. in microfiche) **Document type:** trade publication.
Formerly: Standard and Poor's Security Owner's Stock Guide (ISSN 0038-9412)

332.6 US ISSN 0191-1112
STANDARD & POOR'S STOCK REPORTS. AMERICAN STOCK EXCHANGE. Variant title: American Stock Exchange Reports. irreg. (approx. 4/yr.). $1035. Standard & Poor's (Subsidiary of: McGraw-Hill Companies, Inc.), 25 Broadway, New York, NY 10004. TEL 212-208-8000. Ed. (looseleaf format) **Document type:** trade publication.
●Also available on CD-ROM.
Description: Provides current and 10-year historical data on the stocks publicly traded on the American Stock Exchange.

332.6 US
STANDARD & POOR'S STOCK REPORTS. N A S D A Q AND REGIONAL EXCHANGES. 1934. irreg. (approx. 4/yr.). $1100. Standard & Poor's (Subsidiary of: McGraw-Hill Companies, Inc.), 25 Broadway, New York, NY 10004. TEL 212-208-8000. Ed. Stephen Vallance. stat.; index. (looseleaf format) **Document type:** trade publication.
●Also available on CD-ROM.
Formerly (until 1994): Standard and Poor's Stock Reports: Over the Counter (ISSN 0163-1993)
Description: Reports on more than 1,500 of the most active companies whose securities are traded over the counter.

332.6 US ISSN 0160-4899
STANDARD & POOR'S STOCK REPORTS. NEW YORK STOCK EXCHANGE. 1933. irreg. (approx. 4/yr.). $1295. Standard & Poor's (Subsidiary of: McGraw-Hill Companies, Inc.), 25 Broadway, New York, NY 10004. TEL 212-208-8000. Ed. Joseph Spiers. stat.; charts; index. (looseleaf format) **Document type:** trade publication.
●Also available on CD-ROM.
Description: Provides current and 10-year historical profiles on the stocks of companies actively traded on the New York Stock Exchange.

332.6 US ISSN 0038-9420
HG4921
STANDARD & POOR'S STOCK SUMMARY. m. $56. Standard & Poor's Corporation (Subsidiary of: McGraw-Hill, Inc.), 25 Broadway, New York, NY 10004. TEL 212-208-8000. Ed. William Coughlin. charts; stat. **Document type:** trade publication.

332.6 US ISSN 1088-890X
HG4916
STANDARD & POOR'S TRENDLINE CURRENT MARKET PERSPECTIVES. 1962. m. $275. Standard & Poor's (Subsidiary of: McGraw-Hill Companies Inc.), 25 Broadway, New York, NY 10004. TEL 212-208-8000. FAX 212-412-0288. Ed. Frank LoVaglio. R&P contact: James G. Branscome. charts; stat. **Document type:** trade publication.
Former titles: Trendline Current Market Perspectives; Standard & Poor's Trendline Current Market Perspectives (ISSN 0041-2333)
Description: Presents almost 4 years of weekly price-volume data on over 2350 stocks from the NYSE, ASE and NASDAQ.

332.6 US ISSN 1088-8373
STANDARD & POOR'S 500 INDEXES OF THE SECURITIES MARKETS - FLASH REPORT. w. $585. Standard & Poor's (Subsidiary of: McGraw-Hill Companies, Inc.), 25 Broadway, New York, NY 10004. TEL 212-208-8000. charts. **Document type:** trade publication.
Description: Contains the current week's reading of more than 100 industry group stock price indexes.

332.6 US ISSN 1088-839X
HG4915
STANDARD & POOR'S 500 INFORMATION BULLETIN. m. $220. Standard & Poor's (Subsidiary of: McGraw-Hill Companies, Inc.), 25 Broadway, New York, NY 10004. TEL 212-208-8725. FAX 212-208-8624. Ed. Cynthia Giglio. stat. (back issues avail.) **Document type:** bulletin.
Description: Provides a monthly statistical suummary of stock prices of the Standard & Poor's 500 companies.

332.6 US ISSN 0195-6620
STANGER REPORT; a guide to partnership investing. 1979. m. $447. Robert A. Stanger & Co., Inc., 1129 Broad St., 2nd Fl., Shrewsbury, NJ 07702-4314. TEL 908-389-3600. FAX 908-544-0779. Ed. Nancy Schabel Mahon. adv. contact: Tara Collins. **Document type:** newsletter. —UnCover.

332.63 US
THE STARK REPORT; quarterly trading advisor performance report. 1989. $495. International Traders Research, 1020 Prospect St., Ste. 405, La Jolla, CA 92037. TEL 619-459-0818. FAX 619-459-0819. E-mail: cta@ManagedFutures. com; URL: http://www.ManagedMoney.com. Ed. David Sworder. circ. 250 (controlled). **Document type:** trade publication.

STATE BANK OF PAKISTAN. EQUITY YIELDS ON ORDINARY SHARES. see BUSINESS AND ECONOMICS — Abstracting, Bibliographies, Statistics

STATE BANK OF PAKISTAN. INDEX NUMBERS OF STOCK EXCHANGE SECURITIES. see BUSINESS AND ECONOMICS — Abstracting, Bibliographies, Statistics

332.6 US
STATON INSTITUTE ADVISORY. 1986. m. $137. Staton Institute Inc., 300 East Blvd., Ste. B-4, Charlotte, NC 28203-4784. TEL 704-332-7514. FAX 704-332-0427. URL: http://www.statoninstitute.com. Ed. Bill Staton. circ. 105,000. (back issues avail.) **Document type:** newsletter.
Former titles: Bill Staton's Money Advisory; (until June 1990): Staton's Stock Market Advisory (ISSN 0886-5078)
Description: Helps people cut risk and taxes to virtually zero, and double their money in 5 years.

332.6 AT ISSN 1036-840X
HG4503
STOCK EXCHANGE JOURNAL. Short title: S X J. (Supplement to: Personal Investment (ISSN 0813-2992)) 1972. m. Aus.$3.66. B R W Media, Level 2, 469 La Trobe St., Melbourne, Vic. 3000, Australia. TEL 61-3-96033888. FAX 61-3-96704328. Ed. Dimon Kaye. adv.; bk.rev.; charts; illus.; stat. **Indexed:** P.A.I.S. —UnCover.
Former titles (until 1990): Australian Stock Exchange Journal (ISSN 1033-288X); Sydney Stock Exchange Limited Gazette (ISSN 0039-7598)

332.6 CC
STOCK EXCHANGE OF HONG KONG. ALL SALES RECORD. d. HK.$360 (Asia HK.$880; elsewhere HK.$1120). Stock Exchange of Hong Kong, Distribution Centre, 1-F One & Two Exchange Sq., Central, Hong Kong, People's Republic of China. TEL 852-2522-1122. FAX 852-2845-3554. TELEX 86839 STOEX HX.

332.6 CC
STOCK EXCHANGE OF HONG KONG. SECURITIES (DISCLOSURE OF INTERESTS) NOTIFICATION HISTORY REPORTS. (Text in English) m. Stock Exchange of Hong Kong, Distribution Centre, 1-F One & Two Exchange Sq., Central, Hong Kong, People's Republic of China. TEL 852-2522-1122. FAX 852-2845-3554. TELEX 86839 STOEX HX.

332.6 CC
STOCK EXCHANGE OF HONG KONG. SECURITIES (DISCLOSURE OF INTERESTS) NOTIFICATION SUMMARIES. (Text in English) m. Stock Exchange of Hong Kong, Distribution Centre, 1-F One & Two Exchange Sq., Central, Hong Kong, People's Republic of China. TEL 852-2522-1122. FAX 852-2845-3554. TELEX 86839 STOEX HX.

332.6 SI
STOCK EXCHANGE OF SINGAPORE. HANDBOOK.* (Text in English) 1966. q. S.$99 (Southeast Asia S.$185; elsewhere S.$255). Stock Exchange of Singapore Ltd., Robinson Rd., P.O. Box 2306, Singapore 9043, Singapore. TEL 535-3788. FAX 532-4476. TELEX RS-21853. adv. circ. 2,500.

STOCK EXCHANGE OFFICIAL DIRECTORY. see BUSINESS AND ECONOMICS — Trade And Industrial Directories

BUSINESS AND ECONOMICS — INVESTMENTS

332.6   US   ISSN 0882-5467
HG4057
STOCK MARKET ENCYCLOPEDIA. 1962. q. $124. Standard & Poor's Corporation (Subsidiary of: McGraw-Hill, Inc.), 25 Broadway, New York, NY 10004. TEL 212-208-8000. Ed. Ronald Oliver. **Document type:** trade publication.
   Former titles (until 1985): S and P Stock Market Encyclopedia (ISSN 0737-5026); (until 1983): Standard and Poor's Stock Market Encyclopedia of the S and P "500." Annual Report Edition (ISSN 0730-9740)
   Description: Researches 750 of the most actively traded stocks. Includes net quarterly sales for four years, dividends paid, price per share, and 10-year balance sheet data for each company covered.

332.6   US
STOCK SELECTOR. 1986. m. $120. High Technology Growth Stocks, 402 Border Rd., Concord, MA 01742. TEL 617-371-0096. Ed. Bud Anderson.
   Description: Identifies the most attractive stocks each month based on momentum, relative strength, and valuations (PEs).

332.6   US   ISSN 1080-3157
HG4905
STOCK SUMMARY (MONTHLY EDITION). Semi-annual edition (ISSN 1080-3165) (Quarterly edition also avail.) 1913. m. $528 for m.; q. $330; s-a. $220. National Quotation Bureau, LLC, 11 Penn Plaza, 15th Fl., New York, NY 10001. TEL 212-868-7100. FAX 212-868-3848. Ed. Allen C. Swartz. R&P contact: Evelyn Walsh. adv. contact: John Condon. **Document type:** directory.
   Formerly: National Monthly Stock Summary (ISSN 0275-8326)

332.6   US
STOCK TRADER'S ALMANAC.* 1967. a. $34.95. Hirsch Organization Inc., Box 2069, River Vale, NJ 07675-9001. TEL 201-767-4100. FAX 201-767-7337. Ed. Yale Hirsch. circ. 30,000.
   Description: Summarizes years of research into patterns that help both traders and investors.

336.2 332.6   US   ISSN 0081-5624
HG4915
STOCK VALUES AND DIVIDENDS FOR TAX PURPOSES. 1969. a. $29. C C H Incorporated, 2700 Lake Cook Rd., Riverwoods, IL 60015. TEL 847-267-7000; 800-835-5224. FAX 800-224-8299.

332.6   SW
STOCKHOLM STOCK EXCHANGE. ANNUAL REPORT. 1864. a. Stockholm Stock Exchange, P.O. Box 1256, S-111 82 Stockholm, Sweden. FAX 8-108110. TELEX 13551-BOURSE-S.
   Formerly: Stockholm Stock Exchange and the Stock Market. (Year).

332.6   US
STOCKMARKET CYCLES. 1975. 3/w. $252 with periodic mutual fund telephone updates; with daily updates $480. Box 6873, Santa Rosa, CA 95406-0873. TEL 707-579-8444; 800-888-4351. FAX 707-579-0274. (Alt. addr.: 3806 Skyfarm Dr., Santa Rosa, CA 95403) Ed. Peter G. Eliades. circ. 3,200. **Document type:** newsletter.
   Description: Aids investors and traders in identifying market tops and bottoms.

332.6   US   ISSN 1047-2436
HG4501
STOCKS, BONDS, BILLS AND INFLATION (YEAR) YEARBOOK. 1984. a. $92. Ibbotson Associates, 225 N. Michigan Ave., Ste. 700, Chicago, IL 60601. TEL 312-616-1620. FAX 312-616-0404. adv. contact: Rita B. Brief. charts, stat.; index. circ. 5,000. (back issues avail.) **Document type:** corporate report.
   ●Also available online.
   Description: Covers the history of U.S. capital markets. Contains monthly returns from 1926 to the present.

332.6   US   ISSN 0163-6235
HG4501
STOCKS IN THE S & P 500. OFFICIAL SERIES. m. $835. Standard & Poor's (Subsidiary of: McGraw-Hill Companies, Inc.), 25 Broadway, New York, NY 10004. TEL 212-208-8000. **Document type:** trade publication.
   ●Also available online.
   Also available on CD-ROM.
   Description: Details price performance and the precise composition of the Standard & Poor's 500 Index.

332.6   US   ISSN 0277-2450
HG1
SUMMARY OF INSIDER TRANSACTIONS.* 1980. q. $250. Thomson Financial Services, One State St. Plaza, New York, NY 10004. TEL 301-654-5580. FAX 301-654-1678. (reprint service avail. from UMI)
   Formerly: Encyclopedia of Insider Trading.

332.6   FI   ISSN 0781-4437
SUOMEN JOUKKOVELKAKIRJALAINAT/FINNISH BOND ISSUES/FINLANDSKA MASSKULDEBREVSLAAN; statistical bulletin. (Text in English, Finnish and Swedish) 1945. a. free. Suomen Pankki - Bank of Finland, Financial Markets Department, P.O. Box 160, FIN-00101 Helsinki, Finland. TEL 358-0-1832566. FAX 358-0-174872. Ed. Arja Saaksmaki. circ. 700.
   Formerly (until 1983): Suomen Obligaatiokirja (ISSN 0585-9581)

332.6   US
SUPERINVESTOR HOTSHEET. 1987. w. $398. (Hume and Associates) Hume Group Inc., 2839 Paces Furry Rd., Ste. 1170, Atlanta, GA 30339. TEL 404-426-1920. FAX 404-423-7349. (Subscr. addr.: P.O. Box 740110, Atlanta, GA 30374) Ed. Larry D. Spears. circ. 2,800.
   Description: Analysis and tracking of specific futures market trades, with recommendations.

SUPERMARKEDSHAANDBOGEN (YEAR)/SUPERMARKETS AND OTHER LARGE GROCERY STORES. see *BUSINESS AND ECONOMICS — Small Business*

332.6   GW   ISSN 0178-9945
SWINGTREND. 1968. w. DM.980($650) Gamma Verlag GmbH, Postfach 400720, 80707 Munich, Germany. TEL 49-89-3009011. FAX 49-89-3009211. Ed. Albrecht Pfeiffer. circ. 5,000. **Document type:** newsletter.

332.6   BE   ISSN 0772-4799
SWINGTREND; beleggersbrief. French edition: Swingtrend (ISSN 0772-4780) (Text in Dutch) 1970. s-w. 8680 BEF (in Europe 9316 BEF; elsewhere 9979 BEF). Biblo N.V., Brasschaatsteenweg 308, 2920 Kalmthout, Belgium. Ed. L. van den Borre. circ. 15,000. (also avail. in microfiche) **Document type:** newsletter.

332.6   SZ
SWISS BUSINESS. (Text in English) bi-m. 52 SFr. (foreign 65 SFr.). S H Z Fachverlag AG, Seestr. 37, CH-8027 Zurich, Switzerland. TEL 41-1-2022046. FAX 41-1-2811970. Ed. John Wicks. circ. 50,000. **Indexed:** Art.Hosp.& Tour. **Document type:** trade publication.
   ●Also available online. **Vendor(s):** Information Access Co.

332.6   SZ
SWISS ECONOMIC VIEWPOINT. 1969. 4/yr. free. Overland Bank, P.O. Box 5022, CH-8022 Zurich, Switzerland. TEL 01-4826688. FAX 01-4822884. TELEX 815201. Ed.Bd. bk.rev. circ. 20,000. **Document type:** newsletter.
   Description: Evaluation of current events in Switzerland and in world markets.

SYMPOSIUM ON PRIVATE INVESTMENTS ABROAD. see *LAW — International Law*

332.6   US
SYSTEMS AND FORECASTS. 1973. fortn. $225. Signalert Corporation, 150 Great Neck Rd., Rm. 301, Great Neck, NY 11021-3309. TEL 516-829-6444. FAX 516-829-9366. Ed. Gerald Appel. bk.rev.; charts; stat. circ. 2,500. **Document type:** newsletter.

T V PROGRAM INVESTOR. see *COMMUNICATIONS — Television And Cable*

332.6   IT   ISSN 0082-1446
TACCUINO DELL'AZIONISTA. 1935. a. $300. Databank S.p.A., SASIP Division, Via Spartaco 19, 20135 Milan, Italy. FAX 392-55183152. Ed. Carlo Colombi. index. circ. 5,000.
   Description: Detailed profiles for each of the 240 companies listed on the Italian stock exchange.

332.6   UK
TAIEI TOSHI NEWS. (Text in Japanese) 1987. 3/yr. free. Invest in Britain Bureau, 1 Victoria St., London SW1H OET, England. TEL 44-171-215-5638. FAX 44-171-215-5651. URL: http://www.dti.gov.uk/ibb. (Dist. by: Burrups Japan Ltd., Ishinara Bldg., 3-3-12 Iidabashi, Chiyoda-ku, Tokyo 102, Japan) Ed. Stefano Hoyland. adv.: B&W page £1350. charts; illus.; stat.; circ. 11,300 (controlled). (back issues avail.) **Document type:** government publication.
   Formerly: Eikoku Toshi News.
   Description: Serves Japanese corporate investors and executives planning to locate in the U.K.

332.6 332.6   US   ISSN 1062-1016
TAIPAN. 1988. m. $129. Agora Inc., 105 W. Monument St., Baltimore, MD 21201. TEL 410-223-2611; 800-851-7100. FAX 410-223-2696. Ed. J. Christoph Amberger. adv. contact: Doug Cooke. circ. 70,000. (back issues avail.) **Document type:** newsletter.
   Description: Covers international investment and business opportunity for open-minded, globally thinking investors.

332.6   US
TAURUS TOP 16. 1976. w. $595 includes nightly hotline service. Taurus Corporation, 133 W. Boscawen St., Winchester, VA 22601. TEL 703-667-4827. FAX 703-667-7484. Ed. Michael P. Chisholm. adv. contact: Rachel Chisholm. bk.rev. circ. 1,000.
   Former titles: Taurus (Winchester); Taurus and Optimum Trades.
   Description: Offers specific recommendations covering 16 commodity futures markets.

TAX-ADVANTAGED SECURITIES LAW REPORT. see *LAW — Corporate Law*

332.6   US   ISSN 0739-6619
KF6415.A15
TAX FACTS 2; taxation on investments. a. $22. National Underwriter Co., 505 Gest St., Cincinnati, OH 45203. TEL 513-721-2140. FAX 513-721-0126.
   Description: Provides answers to tax questions about investments in stocks, bonds and mutual funds, commodities futures, and more.

TAX HAVEN REPORTER NEWSLETTER. see *BUSINESS AND ECONOMICS — Public Finance, Taxation*

TAX HAVENS OF THE WORLD. see *BUSINESS AND ECONOMICS — Public Finance, Taxation*

332.6   US   ISSN 0886-3547
KF6571.A15
TAX MANAGEMENT ESTATES, GIFTS AND TRUSTS JOURNAL. (Subseries of: Tax Management Estates, Gifts and Trusts Series) 1976. bi-m. $238. Tax Management, Inc. (Subsidiary of: The Bureau of National Affairs, Inc.), 1250 23rd St., N.W., Washington, DC 20037-1166. TEL 202-452-4200. FAX 202-822-8092. TELEX 285656 BNAI WSH. (Subscr. to: 9435 Key West Ave., Rockville, MD 20850. TEL 800-372-1033) Ed. Glenn Davis. bk.rev.; index. (back issues avail.) **Indexed:** ABI Inform, Account.Ind. (1976-), BPIA, Bus.Ind., C.L.I., L.I.I., L.R.I. **Document type:** trade publication.
   ●Also available online. **Vendor(s):** Knight-Ridder Information, Inc. (Files 15, 485), UMI, West Group (File TM-EGTJ).
   —UMI. **CCC.**
   Formerly: Estates, Gifts and Trusts Journal (ISSN 0364-9253)
   Description: Practical guidance and current review of developments in estates, gifts and trusts.

TAXATION & INVESTMENT IN CANADA. see *BUSINESS AND ECONOMICS — Public Finance, Taxation*

TAXATION & INVESTMENT IN THE CARIBBEAN. see *BUSINESS AND ECONOMICS — Public Finance, Taxation*

TAXATION & INVESTMENT IN THE PEOPLE'S REPUBLIC OF CHINA. see *BUSINESS AND ECONOMICS — Public Finance, Taxation*

BUSINESS AND ECONOMICS — INVESTMENTS

332.6 US ISSN 0738-3355
TECHNICAL ANALYSIS OF STOCKS & COMMODITIES; the traders magazine. 1982. 13/yr. $64.95. Technical Analysis, Inc., 4757 California Ave., S.W., Seattle, WA 98116-4499. TEL 206-938-0570; 800-832-4642. FAX 206-938-1307. TELEX 4993678-TECHANALYSIS. E-mail: mail@Traders.com; URL: http://www.Traders.com. Ed. Jack K. Hutson; Pub. Jack K. Hutson. R&P contact: Jack K. Hutson. adv.: B&W page $3675, color page $5210; trim 8 3/8 x 10 7/8; adv. contact: Ed Schramm. bk.rev.; charts; illus.; stat.; index; circ. 53,000 (paid). (also avail. in microform from UMI) **Document type:** trade publication.
● Also available online.
Also available on CD-ROM.
—BLDSC (8615.362500); UMI. **CCC.**
 Description: Covers computerized investing and charting techniques. Explains methods of trading publicly held stocks, bonds, mutual funds, options, commodities (futures), cash and hard money.
 Refereed Serial

332.6 US
TECHNICAL STOCK ADVISORY SERVICE. 1967. w. $960 (effective 1997). John Magee Inc., 118 Clinton St., Ste. 306, Chicago, IL 60661. TEL 312-627-1521. FAX 312-627-1523. E-mail: johnm@chicagopublishing.com; URL: http://www.chicagopublishing.com. Ed. Jonathan McDermott. circ. 300.
 Description: Features articles of general interest to investors.

332.6 US ISSN 0889-9525
TECHNICAL TRENDS; the indicator accuracy service. 1960. 40/yr.). $147 (foreign)$180). Technical Trends, Inc., Box 792, Wilton, CT 06897. TEL 203-762-0229; 800-736-0229. FAX 203-761-1504. URL: http://www.capecod.net/techtrends. Ed. John R. McGinley; Pub. John/McGinley. R&P contact: John McGinley. adv. contact: John McGinley. charts; stat. **Document type:** newsletter.
 Description: Provides data and charts on the most accurate, publicly available stock market indicators.

332.6 US
TED SLANKER'S MARKET UPDATE. 1985. bi-m. free to investors of gold resource stocks. Ted E. Slanker, Jr., Ed. & Pub., R.R. 2, Box 175, Powderly, TX 75473-9740. TEL 903-732-4653. FAX 903-732-4151. E-mail: 72722,51@compuserve.com; slanker@koyote.com. circ. 10,650 (controlled). **Document type:** newsletter.
 Formerly: Saturn Five's Market Update.
 Description: Gold stock letter for aggressive investors.

332.6
THAILAND UPDATE. (Text in English) m. Office of the Board of Investment, 555 Vipavadee Rangsit Rd., Jatuchuck, Bangkok 10900, Thailand. TEL 537-8111. FAX 537-8177. circ. 10,000.

332.6 TH ISSN 0857-8702
HG5750.55.A2
THAILAND'S INVESTMENT PROMOTION JOURNAL. (Text in Thai) m. Office of the Board of Investment, 555 Vipavadee Rangsit Rd., Jatuchuck, Bangkok 10900, Thailand. TEL 537-8111. FAX 537-8177. circ. 6,000.

332.6 US ISSN 1055-9035
HG4530
THOMAS J. HERZFELD ENCYCLOPEDIA OF CLOSED-END FUNDS. 1990. biennial. $50 (foreign $160) (effective 1997). Thomas J. Herzfeld Advisors, Inc., Box 161465, Miami, FL 33116. TEL 305-271-1900; 800-854-3863. FAX 305-270-1040. Ed. Thomas J. Hezfeld. adv. contact: Thomas Herzfeld.
 Description: Analyzes approximately 300 closed-end funds.

332.6 US
TICKER (NEW YORK, 1996). 1996. bi-m. Investment Investor Group, 1633 Broadway, 38th Fl., New York, NY 10019. TEL 212-843-2740. Pub. Jay Burzon. adv. **Document type:** trade publication.

TIMELY DISCLOSURE. see *BUSINESS AND ECONOMICS — Banking And Finance*

332.6 US
▼**TIMELY INVESTMENT INFORMATION.** 1996. w. Green Mountain Asset Management Corp., 139 Bank St., Burlington, VT 05401. TEL 802-658-7806; 800-385-2673. E-mail: bobbose@stockresearch.com; URL: http://www.stockresearch.com. Ed. Bob Bose. **Document type:** newsletter.
● Available only online.
 Description: Provides timely investment information for serious do-it-yourself investors.

332.6 UN
TISNET TRADE AND INVESTMENT INFORMATION BULLETIN. 1996. fortn. $75 (effective 1997). United Nations Economic and Social Commission for Asia and the Pacific (UN ESCAP), International Trade and Economic Cooperation Division, United Nations Bldg., Rajadamnern Ave., Bangkok 10200, Thailand.
 Former titles (1994-1995): Tisnet Trade Information Bulletin; (1985-1993): Tisnet Trade Information Sheet; (1982-1984): Trade Information Sheet.

332.6 US ISSN 1068-090X
TODAY'S PAWNBROKER. 1988. q. $25. B K B Publications Inc., 98 Grenwich Ave., No. 1 FL, New York, NY 10011-7743. TEL 212-807-6558. FAX 212-807-1821. Ed. Charlene Komar Storey; Pub. Brian K. Burkart. R&P contact: Brian K. Burkart. adv.: B&W page $1450, color page $2115; trim 8 1/4 x 10 7/8. circ. 15,000. **Document type:** trade publication.
 Description: Helps executives in the pawnbroking industry manage their business for continued growth. Includes general news, feature articles, legislative updates, reports on trends, marketing tips, product information and news of state and national association activities.

332.6 CN
TORONTO STOCK EXCHANGE. NOTICE TO MEMBERS. 1957. irreg. Can.$187.25($175) Toronto Stock Exchange, Exchange Tower, 2 First Canadian Pl., Toronto, ON M5X 1J2, Canada. TEL 416-947-4223. FAX 416-947-4662. circ. 500.
 Description: Relates changes in by-laws, listings, members, committees, events, holidays.

332.6 CN ISSN 0705-2170
TORONTO STOCK EXCHANGE DAILY RECORD. 1934. d. Can.$731.78($744.54) (foreign $1046.28). T.S.E. Publications, 2 First Canadian Place, Toronto, Ont. M5X 1J2, Canada. TEL 416-947-4681. FAX 416-814-8811. Ed. Peter Traynor. R&P contact: Peter Traynor. adv. contact: Terry Snider. circ. 2,500. (also avail. in microfiche)
 Description: Complete record of each day's trading in all listed stocks, stock options and futures.

332.64 CN ISSN 0049-4216
HG5160.T6
TORONTO STOCK EXCHANGE REVIEW. 1949. m. Can.$156.22($155) (US Can.$154.24; elsewhere Can.$225.93). Toronto Stock Exchange, 2 First Canadian Place, Toronto, ON M5X 1J2, Canada. TEL 416-947-4222. FAX 416-947-4585. Ed. Peter Traynor. circ. 2,200 (paid); 1,150 (controlled).
 Indexed: Can.B.P.I., Can.Per.Ind.
 Description: Summary of all equity trading on the Toronto Stock Exchange for each month.

232 US
TOTAL RATE-OF-RETURN INDEXES. (Included in: Global Index Group) m. Salomon Brothers, Inc., 7 World Trade Center, New York, NY 10048. TEL 212-783-7000. charts; stat.

332.6 CC
TOUZI GUANLI YU YANJIU/INVESTMENT MANAGEMENT AND STUDY. (Text in Chinese) bi-m. Zhongguo Renmin Yinhang, Guangxi Fenhang - China People's Bank, Guangxi Branch, Taoyuan Lu, Nanning, Guangxi 530021, People's Republic of China. TEL 26731.

332.6 US ISSN 1003-7624
TOUZI YANJIU/INVESTMENT RESEARCH. (Text in Chinese) m. $48.50. China Books & Periodicals, Inc., 2929 24th St., San Francisco, CA 94110. TEL 415-282-2994. FAX 415-282-0994.

332.6 CC
TOUZI YU JIANSHE/INVESTMENT AND CONSTRUCTION. (Text in Chinese) m. Hubei Sheng Touzi Xuehui - Hubei Investment Society, No. 171, Zhongshan Lu, Wuchang-qu, Wuhan, Hubei 430061, People's Republic of China. TEL 877121. Ed. Wang Chengdiao.

TRADERS MAGAZINE; the magazine for the professional securities trader. see *BUSINESS AND ECONOMICS — Banking And Finance*

332.6 US
TRADER'S OPTION. 1985. m. $217. Box 727, Quincy, IL 62306. TEL 217-222-4827. Ed. Thomas J. Lavery. (back issues avail.)

332.6 US ISSN 1045-7690
TRADER'S WORLD MAGAZINE. 1989. q. $15 (effective 1997). Halliker's Inc., 2508 Grayrock, Springfield, MO 65810-2114. TEL 417-882-9697. FAX 417-886-5180. Ed. Larry Jacobs. R&P contact: Larry Jacobs. adv. contact: Larry Jacobs. bk.rev.; software rev. circ. 9,000. **Document type:** trade publication.
 Description: Covers both classical and modern methods of technical analysis. Subjects covered are cycles, trend analysis, studies of oscillators and more.

332.6 US ISSN 0892-3280
TRADING CYCLES.* 1974. 12/yr. $97.99. Andrews Publications (Templeton), 156 Shadow Creek Ln., Paso Robles, CA 93446-1922. TEL 408-778-2925. Ed. R. Earl Andrews. (looseleaf format; back issues avail.) **Document type:** newsletter.
 Formerly: Andrews Trading Cycles.
 Description: Market timing service for stocks, bonds, precious metals; currencies, options, computer generated decisions.

332.6 658 US ISSN 1067-0432
HG4028.C45   CODEN: TRMAFL
TREASURY & RISK MANAGEMENT. 1991. 10/yr. $64 (foreign $80). C F O Publishing Corporation (Subsidiary of: Economist Group), 253 Summer St., Boston, MA 02210. TEL 617-345-9700. FAX 617-951-4090. E-mail: mrs@cfo.ccmail.compuserve.com; URL: http://www.cfonet.com. Ed. Maile Hulihan; Pub. Maile Hulihan. adv.: B&W page $10562, color page $13354; trim 8 1/8 x 10 3/4; adv. contact: Lissa Short. circ. 46,000 (controlled). (back issues avail.; reprint service avail.) **Document type:** trade publication.
● Also available online.
—UnCover. **CCC.**
 Formerly (until no.2, 1992): Treasury; *Incorporates* (1989-1992): Corporate Risk Management (ISSN 1046-5626)
 Description: Provides specific solutions to day-to-day problems faced by corporate risk managers.

332.6 IT
TREND & MARKET. 11/yr. Trend & Market Editrice s.r.l., Via Nino Bixio 30, 20129 Milan, Italy. TEL 2-204-66-87. FAX 2-204-65-07. Ed. Anna Righini. circ. 16,000.

332.6 AT
TRENDEX. 1975. fortn. Aus.$200. B R W Media, Level 2, 469 La Trobe St., Melbourne, Vic. 3000, Australia. TEL 61-3-96033888. FAX 61-3-96704328. Ed. Merril Armstrong. adv. contact: John Briggs. circ. 3,050. (back issues avail.) **Document type:** newsletter.
 Incorporates (1977-1990): Investment Action Newsletter (ISSN 0819-3320)
 Description: In-depth analysis of and comment on stockmarket trents. Advice given on what stock to hold, sell or buy now and in the future.

332.6 US ISSN 1061-7477
HG4916
TRENDLINE CHART GUIDE. 1991. m. $175. Standard & Poor's (Subsidiary of: McGraw-Hill Companies Inc.), 25 Broadway, New York, NY 10004. TEL 212-208-8000. FAX 212-412-0288. Ed. Frank LoVaglio. R&P contact: James G. Branscome. charts; stat. **Document type:** trade publication.
 Description: Offers one-year price data, detailing weekly high, low, and closing prices and volume, along with 30-week moving averages, for each of more than 4,400 stocks.

BUSINESS AND ECONOMICS — INVESTMENTS

332.6 US ISSN 0277-4968
TRENDLINE DAILY ACTION STOCK CHARTS (WEEKLY). 1959. w. $630. Standard & Poor's (Subsidiary of: McGraw-Hill Companies Inc.), 25 Broadway, New York, NY 10004. TEL 212-208-8000. FAX 212-412-0288. Ed. Frank LoVaglio. R&P contact: James G. Branscome. charts; stat. (looseleaf format) **Document type:** trade publication.
Formerly (until 1980): Trendline Daily Basis Stock Charts (ISSN 0564-1896)
Description: Covers 52 weeks of daily price-volume performance on more than 720 stocks, and compares past performance against the Standard and Poor's 500 index.

332.6 US
TRENDS IN FUTURES. 1974. w. $199. Oster Communications, Inc., 219 Main St., Box 6, Cedar Falls, IA 50613. TEL 319-277-1271. FAX 319-277-7982. Ed. Glen Ring.
Formerly: Commodity Closeup.
Description: Provides insight and perspective on 27 key futures markets.

332.6 US ISSN 0041-3682
HG4341 CODEN: TRUSB9
TRUSTS AND ESTATES (ATLANTA). 1904. m. (plus a. Directory). $82 (foreign $142). Intertec Publishing Corp. (Atlanta), 6151 Powers Ferry Rd., N.W., Atlanta, GA 30339-2941. TEL 770-955-2500. FAX 770-955-0400. Ed. Michael S. Klim. adv.; bk.rev.; charts; illus.; index, cum.index: 1945-1964. circ. 12,583. (also avail. in microform from UMI; microfiche from CIS; reprint service avail. from UMI,WSH) **Indexed:** ABI Inform., Account.Ind. (1974-), B.P.I., BPIA, Bus.Ind., C.L.I., Data Process.Dig., L.I.I., L.R.I., Leg.Cont., Leg.Per., Manage.Cont., P.A.I.S., PSI, SRI, Tr.& Indus.Ind. **Document type:** trade publication.
●Also available online. Vendor(s): Information Access Co., UMI.
—BLDSC (9066.600000); KR SourceOne; UMI; UnCover. **CCC.**
Description: Serves the field of estate planning, trust administration and related areas of investment in the U.S. Covers investments, law, taxes, life insurance, accounting, property appraisal and liquidation, and employee benefits.

332.6 US ISSN 1056-0173
TURNAROUND LETTER. 1986. m. $195. New Generation Research, Inc., 225 Friend St., Ste. 801, Boston, MA 02114. TEL 617-573-9550. Ed. George Putnam, III; Pub. George Putnam, III. R&P contact: Stacey Vivieros. circ. 2,000. (looseleaf format; back issues avail.) **Document type:** newsletter.
Description: Covers turnaround investing opportunities.

332.63 US ISSN 0274-8894
TURNING POINTS. 1979. s-m. $200. Concept Publishing, Box 500, York, NY 14592. TEL 716-243-3148. FAX 716-243-3148. Ed. David Coleman. circ. 200. **Indexed:** Rehabil.Lit.
Description: Specific timing service for the stock market short term, stock market long term and bonds.

332.6 332 UG
U C B INVESTOR'S HANDBOOK. 1983. biennial. Uganda Commercial Bank, PO Box 973, Kampala, Uganda. circ. 1,500.
Description: Investment opportunities and addresses of exporters and importers from commercial and industrial sectors in Uganda.

332.6 UK ISSN 0265-8364
HG5431
U K VENTURE CAPITAL JOURNAL. 1983. bi-m. $750. Venture Capital (Subsidiary of: S D C Publishing, Inc.), The Quadrangle, 180 Wardour, London W1A 4YG, England. TEL 44-171-434-0411. FAX 44-171-434-3918. Ed. Maurice Anslow. adv.: B&W page £500; trim 8 3/8 x 11 3/4. charts; s-a. index. circ. 140.
●Also available online. Vendor(s): Information Access Co.
—BLDSC (9082.669180). **CCC.**
Description: Contains news, analysis and insights about the UK venture capital industry.

332.6 UK
U K VENTURE INDUSTRY REVIEW. a. £450. Initiative Europe, 69 Bondway, London SW8 1SQ, England. TEL 44-171-735-9838. FAX 44-171-820-0802. **Document type:** trade publication.

332.6 US
U S A FINANCIAL NEWS. m. $69. 5160 S. Valley View, Ste. 106, Las Vegas, NV 89118. Ed. James Bartel; Pub. Mitchell Milgaten. R&P contact: Mitchel Milgaten. TEL 702-739-6552. circ. 11,000. **Document type:** newsletter.
Formerly: Bonanza (ISSN 0888-4889)

332 US
HG1 CODEN: USBAEH
U S BANKER. 1891. m. $59 (foreign $99) (effective 1995). Faulkner & Gray, Inc. (New York), 11 Penn Plaza, 17th Fl., New York, NY 10001. TEL 212-967-7000; 800-535-8403. FAX 212-967-7155. Ed. Robert A. Bennett. adv.; illus.; index. circ. 39,000. (also avail. in microform from UMI; reprint service avail. from UMI) **Indexed:** ABI Inform., B.P.I., Bank.Lit.Ind., BPIA, Bus.Ind., P.A.I.S., PSI, Tr.& Indus.Ind.
●Also available online. Vendor(s): Information Access Co., Lexis-Nexis, UMI.
—BLDSC (9124.741800); AskIEEE; KR SourceOne; UMI; UnCover. **CCC.**
Former titles (until 1994): United States Banker (ISSN 0148-8848); (until 1977): United States Investor - Eastern Banker (ISSN 0362-6741); (until 1971): United States Investor (ISSN 0041-7718)

332.6 NE ISSN 0041-5936
UITLOTINGS-ARCHIEF. 1912. 3/w. price on request. Internationale Uitlotingsdienst - International Service of Drawings of Bonds, Postbus 1071, 1000 BB Amsterdam, Netherlands. stat. circ. controlled. (looseleaf format)

332.6 US ISSN 1088-0208
UNDISCOVERED STOCKS. m. $179. Weiss Ratings, Inc., 4176 Burns Rd., Palm Beach Garden, FL 33410. TEL 407-627-3311. FAX 407-625-6685. E-mail: tom-r@weiss.com; URL: http://www.weissinc.com. Ed. Nancy Zambell; Pub. Martin Weiss. R&P contact: Steve H. Ackerman. pp./issue: 8. **Document type:** newsletter.
Description: Provides tips on how to invest in quality, undiscovered stocks that are ignored by Wall Street.

332.6 US
UNIT INVESTMENT TRUSTS SERVICE MANUALS. a. $975. Moody's Investors Service (Subsidiary of: Dun & Bradstreet Corporation), 99 Church St., New York, NY 10007-0300. TEL 212-553-0300. FAX 212-553-4700. (also avail. in microform from MIS)
Description: Provides information on over 10,000 unit investment trusts, including multi-state series.

332.6 US
UNIT INVESTMENT TRUSTS WEEKLY REPORTS. w. $450. Moody's Investors Service (Subsidiary of: Dun & Bradstreet Corporation), 99 Church St., New York, NY 10007-0300. TEL 212-553-0300. FAX 212-553-4700.
Description: Provides current interest-principal payment data on over 13,000 series.

332.6 SA ISSN 1025-0506
UNIT TRUSTS HANDBOOK. (Text in English) 1994. a. R.48.95 (foreign R.84.90) (effective 1997). Profile Media, 26 11th Ave., Houghton Estate, Johannesburg 2198, South Africa. TEL 27-11-728-5510. FAX 27-11-728-5845. Ed. Hugo Lambrechts. adv. contact: Ernie Alexander. circ. 14,000.
Description: Complete reference to unit trusts and unit trust management companies operating in South Africa.
Refereed Serial

332.6 US
UNITED & BABSON GRAPHIC GUIDE. Abbreviated title: U & B Graphic Guide. 1965. a. $24. Babson - United Investment Advisors, Inc., 101 Prescott St., Wellesley Hills, MA 02181-3319. TEL 617-235-0900. FAX 617-235-9450. Ed. Donald Jones. charts.
Formerly: United Graphic Guide (ISSN 0082-7916)

332.6 US ISSN 0895-5689
HC101
UNITED & BABSON INVESTMENT REPORT. 1919. w. $268 (foreign air mail $303). Babson - United Investment Advisors, Inc., 101 Prescott St., Wellesley Hills, MA 02181-3319. TEL 617-235-0900. Ed. Donald D. Fox. **Indexed:** PROMT. **Document type:** newsletter.
Former titles: United Business and Investment Report (ISSN 0360-8662); United Business Service (ISSN 0041-7203)
Description: Business and investment advisory service.

332.63 US ISSN 0083-3215
HG4556.U5
U.S. SECURITIES AND EXCHANGE COMMISSION. ANNUAL REPORT. 1935. a. price varies. U.S. Securities and Exchange Commission, 500 N. Capitol St., Washington, DC 20549. TEL 202-655-4000. (Orders to: Supt. of Documents, Washington, DC 20402) (reprint service avail. from RRI,UMI)
Description: Based on a company's annual report on Form 10-K. All reports are different.

332.63 US ISSN 0083-3223
HG4556.U5
U.S. SECURITIES AND EXCHANGE COMMISSION. DECISIONS AND REPORTS. 1934. irreg. price varies. U.S. Securities and Exchange Commission, 450 Fifth St., N.W., MISC-11, Washington, DC 20549. TEL 202-655-4000. (Orders to: Supt. of Documents, Washington, DC 20402) (also avail. in microform from UMI,BHP; microfilm from BHP; reprint service avail. from UMI)
—UMI.

332.63 US ISSN 0083-3231
HG4556.U5
U.S. SECURITIES AND EXCHANGE COMMISSION. JUDICIAL DECISIONS. 1934. irreg. price varies. U.S. Securities and Exchange Commission, 450 Fifth St., N.W., MISC-11, Washington, DC 20549. TEL 202-655-4000. (Orders to: Supt. of Documents, Washington, DC 20402) (reprint service avail. from UMI)

332.6 US ISSN 0364-2267
HG4556.U5
U.S. SECURITIES AND EXCHANGE COMMISSION. OFFICIAL SUMMARY OF SECURITY TRANSACTIONS AND HOLDINGS. 1935. m. $61.05. U.S. Securities and Exchange Commission, 450 Fifth St., N.W., MISC-11, Washington, DC 20549. TEL 202-655-4000. (Orders to: Supt. of Documents, Washington, DC 20402) circ. 7,000. (also avail. in microfiche from CIS; reprint service avail. from CIS,UMI) **Indexed:** Amer.Stat.Ind. (1973-).

332.6 UK ISSN 0967-4616
UNQUOTE. 1992. fortn. £275. Initiative Europe, 69 Bondway, London SW8 1SQ, England. TEL 44-171-735-9838. FAX 44-171-820-0802. **Document type:** trade publication.
Description: Provides news on the UK venture capital industry.

332.6 US ISSN 1052-0341
HC110.H53
UPSIDE; the business magazine for the technology elite. 1989. m. $48; newsstand price: $4.95. Upside Publishing Company, 2015 Pioneer Ct., San Mateo, CA 94403-1736. TEL 415-377-0950. FAX 415-377-1961. E-mail: feedback@upside.com; URL: http://www.upside.com. (Subscr. to: Box 3804 Escondido, CA 92033) Ed. Eric Nee; Pub. Susan Scott. adv. contact: Cheryl Lucanegro. circ. 60,000. (also avail. in microform from UMI; back issues avail.) **Document type:** trade publication.
●Also available online. Vendor(s): UMI.
—BLDSC (9122.802000); KR SourceOne; UMI.
Description: Covers the business of high-technology for executives and investors; includes company profiles, interviews, and coverage of business trends.

330 CN
UPTREND; Canadian penny market newsletter. 1979. every 3 wks. Can.$149. Yorkton Continental Securities Inc., 1055 Dunsmuir St., 10th Fl., P.O. Box 49333, Bentall Four, Vancouver, B.C. V7X 1L4 Canada. TEL 604-640-0360. FAX 604-640-0300. Ed. Henry P.M. Huber. bk.rev. circ. 2,000. (looseleaf format) **Document type:** newsletter.

BUSINESS AND ECONOMICS — INVESTMENTS

332.63 US
UTAH UNIFORM SECURITIES ACT AND RULES. a., latest 1995 ed. $8. Michie, A Division of Reed Elsevier Inc., Box 7587, Charlottesville, VA 22906-7587. TEL 804-972-7566; 800-562-1197. FAX 800-643-1280. E-mail: custserv@michie.com; URL: http://www.michie.com. Ed. George Harley.

332.6 US ISSN 1064-5373
UTILITY FORECASTER.* 1992. m. $109. Kephart Communications, Inc., 1750 Old Meadow Rd., 3rd Fl., McLean, VA 22102-4304. TEL 800-832-2330. Ed. Roger S. Conrad.

332.63 333.79 UK ISSN 1352-7983
UTILITY PRIVATISATIONS IN DEVELOPING COUNTRIES. 1994. a. £265. O X E R A Press, Blue Boar Ct., Alfred St., Oxford OX1 4EH, England. TEL 44-1865-251142. FAX 44-1865-201080. **Document type:** bulletin.
   Description: Provides a record of the privatization experience in Latin America and East Asia, highlighting the investment opportunities in those countries embarking on major privatization programs.

V A R D S REPORT. (Variable Annuity Research & Data Service) see *INSURANCE*

332.63 690 GW ISSN 0723-564X
V W D - BAUWIRTSCHAFT. d. (5/w.). DM.208.50. Vereinigte Wirtschaftsdienste GmbH, Niederurseler Allee 8-10, 65760 Eschborn, Germany. TEL 06196-4050. FAX 06196-482007. (Subscr. to: Postfach 6105, 65735 Eschborn, Germany) **Document type:** trade publication.

332.63 540 GW
V W D - CHEMIE: KAUTSCHUK. d. (5/w.). DM.230.80. Vereinigte Wirtschaftsdienste GmbH, Allee 8-10, 65760 Eschborn, Germany. TEL 06196-4050. FAX 06196-482007. (Subscr. to: Postfach 6105, 65735 Eschborn, Germany). **Document type:** trade publication.
   Formerly: V W D - Chemie.

332.63 621.3 GW ISSN 0722-222X
V W D - ELEKTRO. d. (5/w.). DM.222.80. Vereinigte Wirtschaftsdienste GmbH, Niederurseler Allee 8-10, 65760 Eschborn, Germany. TEL 06196-4050. FAX 06196-482007. (Subscr. to: Postfach 6105, 65735 Eschborn, Germany) **Document type:** trade publication.
   Formerly (until 1981): Elektro (ISSN 0344-7383)

332.63 333.79 GW
V W D - ENERGIE. d. (5/w.). DM.258.80. Vereinigte Wirtschaftsdienste GmbH, Niederurseler Allee 8-10, 65760 Eschborn, Germany. TEL 06196-4050. FAX 06196-482007. (Subscr. to: Postfach 6105, 65735 Eschborn, Germany) **Document type:** trade publication.

332.63 382 GW ISSN 0344-7391
V W D - EUROPA. d. (5/w.). DM.293.60. Vereinigte Wirtschaftsdienste GmbH, Niederurseler Allee 8-10, 65760 Eschborn, Germany. TEL 06196-4050. FAX 06196-482007. (Subscr. to: Postfach 6105, 65735 Eschborn, Germany) **Document type:** trade publication.

332.63 GW ISSN 0723-2993
V W D - FINANZ- UND WIRTSCHAFTSSPIEGEL. d. (5/w.). DM.448.80. Vereinigte Wirtschaftsdienste GmbH, Niederurseler Allee 8-10, 65760 Eschborn, Germany. TEL 06196-4050. FAX 06196-482007. (Subscr. to: Postfach 6105, 65735 Eschborn, Germany) **Document type:** trade publication.
   Formerly: V W D - Finanz.

332.63 663.1 GW
V W D - GETRAENKE. d. (5/w.). DM.217.80. Vereinigte Wirtschaftsdienste GmbH, Niederurseler Allee 8-10, 65760 Eschborn, Germany. TEL 06196-4050. FAX 06196-482007. (Subscr. to: Postfach 6105, 65735 Eschborn, Germany) **Document type:** trade publication.

332.63 633.1 GW ISSN 0944-5447
V W D - GETREIDE, FUTTERMITTEL, OELE. d. (5/w.). DM.232.80. Vereinigte Wirtschaftsdienste GmbH, Niederurseler Allee 8-10, 65760 Eschborn, Germany. TEL 06196-4050. FAX 06196-482007. (Subscr. to: Postfach 6105, 65735 Eschborn, Germany) **Document type:** trade publication.
   Formerly: V W D - Getreide und Futtermittel (ISSN 0723-6344)

332.63 663.94 GW ISSN 0175-1662
V W D - KAFFEE, KAKAO, TEE, SUESSWAREN. d. (5/w.). DM.240.80. Vereinigte Wirtschaftsdienste GmbH, Niederurseler Allee 8-10, 65760 Eschborn, Germany. TEL 06196-4050. FAX 06196-482007. (Subscr. to: Postfach 6105, 65735 Eschborn, Germany) **Document type:** trade publication.
   Formerly: V W D - Kaffee, Kakao, Tee, Gewuerze.

332.63 677 GW ISSN 0723-628X
V W D - LANDWIRTSCHAFT UND ERNAEHRUNG. d. (5/w.). DM.306.80. Vereinigte Wirtschaftsdienste GmbH, Niederurseler Allee 8-10, 65760 Eschborn, Germany. TEL 06196-4050. FAX 06196-482007. (Subscr. to: Postfach 6105, 65735 Eschborn, Germany) **Document type:** trade publication.
   Formerly: V W D - Hart- und Bastfasern.

332.63 681 GW
V W D - MASCHINEN. d. (5/w.). DM.258.80. Vereinigte Wirtschaftsdienste GmbH, Niederurseler Allee 8-10, 65760 Eschborn, Germany. TEL 06196-4050. FAX 06196-482007. (Subscr. to: Postfach 6105, 65735 Eschborn, Germany) **Document type:** trade publication.
   Formerly: V W D - Maschinenbau.

332.63 622 GW ISSN 0723-4937
V W D - MONTAN. d. (5/w.). DM.331.80. Vereinigte Wirtschaftsdienste GmbH, Niederurseler Allee 8-10, 65760 Eschborn, Germany. TEL 06196-4050. FAX 06196-482007. (Subscr. to: Postfach 6105, 65735 Eschborn, Germany) **Document type:** newspaper.

332.63 669 GW ISSN 0723-5755
V W D - N E - METALLE. d. (5/w.). DM.302.80. Vereinigte Wirtschaftsdienste GmbH, Niederurseler Allee 8-10, 65760 Eschborn, Germany. TEL 06196-4050. FAX 06196-482007. (Subscr. to: Postfach 6105, 65735 Eschborn, Germany) **Document type:** newspaper.

332.63 669.142 GW
V W D - STAHL. d. (5/w.). DM.252.80. Vereinigte Wirtschaftsdienste GmbH, Niederurseler Allee 8-10, 65760 Eschborn, Germany. TEL 06196-4050. FAX 06196-482007. (Subscr. to: Postfach 6105, 65735 Eschborn, Germany) **Document type:** trade publication.

332.63 685 GW ISSN 0944-2839
V W D - TEXTIL, BEKLEIDUNG, LEDER. d. (5/w.). DM.222.80. Vereinigte Wirtschaftsdienste GmbH, Niederurseler Allee 8-10, 65760 Eschborn, Germany. TEL 06196-4050. FAX 06196-482007. (Subscr. to: Postfach 6105, 65735 Eschborn, Germany) **Document type:** trade publication.
   Formed by the 1991 merger of: V W D - Textil (ISSN 0175-1719) & V W D - Haeute und Leder (ISSN 0722-7957); Which was formerly (until 1982): V W D - Haeute, Leder, Rauchwaren (ISSN 0344-760X)

332.63 636 GW ISSN 0723-8037
V W D - VIEH UND FLEISCH. d. (5/w.). DM.243.80. Vereinigte Wirtschaftsdienste GmbH, Niederurseler Allee 8-10, 65760 Eschborn, Germany. TEL 06196-4050. FAX 06196-482007. (Subscr. to: Postfach 6105, 65735 Eschborn, Germany) **Document type:** trade publication.

332.63 664.1 GW ISSN 0723-6301
V W D - ZUCKER. d. (5/w.). DM.163.80. Vereinigte Wirtschaftsdienste GmbH, Niederurseler Allee 8-10, 65760 Eschborn, Germany. TEL 06196-4050. FAX 06196-482007. (Subscr. to: Postfach 6105, 65735 Eschborn, Germany) **Document type:** trade publication.

332.6 PE
VADEMECUM BURSATIL. 1979. a. Bolsa de Valores de Lima, Miro Quesada 265, Lima, Peru. (Co-sponsor: Banco Continental) circ. 1,000.

VALUATION. see *BUSINESS AND ECONOMICS — Banking And Finance*

332.6 US ISSN 1051-5380
VALUE FORECASTER; professional econometric research for your important investment decisions. 1988. m. $195 (effective 1997 & 1998). Robert A. Freitas, Jr., Ed. & Pub., Post Office Box 50, Pilot Hill, CA 95664. TEL 916-939-9140. bk.rev.; charts; illus.; stat. circ. 500. (looseleaf format; back issues avail.) **Document type:** newsletter.
   Description: Provides an investment-research service, using nonlinear econometrics to forecast investments.

332.6 US ISSN 0737-0717
HG4501
THE VALUE LINE CONVERTIBLES SURVEY. (Issued in 2 vols.: Part 1. The Convertible Strategist; Part 2. The Convertible Evaluation Section) 1970. w. (48/yr.). $625. Value Line Publishing, Inc., 220 E. 42nd St., New York, NY 10017. TEL 212-907-1500. FAX 212-818-9474. Ed. Stephen Sanborn. **Document type:** newsletter.
   Description: Contains general articles about convertible securities, lists purchase recommendations, and provides current information about those securities evaluated. Evaluates 585 convertible securities, along with 100 warrants and SCOREs.

332.6 US ISSN 0042-2401
HG4501
THE VALUE LINE INVESTMENT SURVEY. 1931. w. $570. Value Line Publishing, Inc., 220 E. 42nd St., New York, NY 10017. TEL 212-907-1500. FAX 212-818-9474. Ed. Jean Bernhard. (looseleaf format) Indexed: PROMT. **Document type:** newsletter.
   Description: Comprehensive reference source, including investment advice, on the 1,700 most widely traded stocks.

332.6 US ISSN 0361-2589
HG4050
VALUE LINE O-T-C SPECIAL SITUATIONS SERVICE. 1951. bi-m. $429. Value Line Publishing, Inc., 220 E. 42nd St., New York, NY 10017. TEL 212-907-1500. FAX 212-818-9747. Ed. Peter Shraga. **Document type:** newsletter.
   Description: Focuses on fast-growing, smaller companies.

332.6 US ISSN 0737-0709
HG4501
VALUE LINE OPTIONS;* the all in one service for listed options. 1970. 4/mo. $445. Value Line, Inc., 220 E. 42nd St., New York, NY 10017-5891. TEL 212-907-1500. Ed. Jean Bernhard Butler. charts; stat. (back issues avail.) **Document type:** newsletter.
   Former titles: Value Line Option and Convertible Survey (ISSN 0146-7581); Value Line Convertible Survey (ISSN 0042-2398); Formed by the merger of: Value Line Convertible Bond Service & Value Line Convertible Preferred Stock Service; Formerly: Value Line Merger Evaluation Service; Value Line Warrant Service.
   Description: Divided in two parts: Part A - The Strategist contains feature articles, news briefs, option statistics and specific options recommendations; Part B - The Evaluation Section lists "Value Line's" evaluation and rank for future performance on over 15,000 options, along with deltas, volatilities, theoretical prices, and tickers.

332.6 US
VALUTRAC. 1990. m. $225. Audio Alert Inc., 10616 Beaver Dam Rd., Hunt Valley, MD 21030. TEL 410-771-0064. FAX 410-584-1043. Ed. Joanne Schenk. adv. contact: F. Joseph Bradley. bk.rev. (audio cassette) **Document type:** newsletter.
   Description: Provides information on long-term investments to double or triple in value in 3-5 years.

332.6 CN ISSN 0083-520X
VANCOUVER STOCK EXCHANGE. ANNUAL REPORT. 1908. a. Can.$12.84. Vancouver Stock Exchange, Stock Exchange Tower, P.O. Box 10333, 609 Granville St., Vancouver, BC V7Y 1H1, Canada. TEL 604-689-3334. FAX 604-688-6051. Ed. David Morton. circ. 7,500. **Document type:** corporate report.
   Description: Contains comparative financial details, market summary and operational highlights for the preceding fiscal year as well as consolidated financial statements.

BUSINESS AND ECONOMICS — INVESTMENTS

332.64   CN   ISSN 0049-5832
VANCOUVER STOCK EXCHANGE REVIEW. 1960. m. Can.$122.46. Vancouver Stock Exchange, Stock Exchange Tower, P.O. Box 10333, 609 Granville St., Vancouver, BC V7Y 1H1, Canada. TEL 604-689-3334. FAX 604-688-6051. Ed. Wade Murray. circ. 2,000. **Indexed:** Can.B.P.I., Can.Per.Ind.
    Description: Provides a summary of trading in equities and options. Includes trading statistics and cumulative figures, listing changes, financings and related topics.

332.6   US   ISSN 1077-9922
VARIABLE ANNUITY MARKET NEWS. 1994. m. $550 (effective 1997). Dalbar Inc., 600 Atlantic Ave., T-30, Boston, MA 02210-2226. TEL 617-723-6400. FAX 617-624-7200. E-mail: vamn@dalbar.com. Ed. David Oliveri. adv. contact: John Harrington.

332.6   US   ISSN 0883-2773
HG4961
VENTURE CAPITAL JOURNAL; the only financial analyst of small business investment companies and venture capital companies. 1961. m. $960. (Securities Data Company, Inc.) Securities Data Publishing, 40 W. 57th St., 11th Fl., New York, NY 10019. TEL 212-765-5311. FAX 212-765-6123. Ed. Kathleen Devlin; Pub. Ted Weissberg. adv. contact: Deborah Chieglis. charts; stat.; s-a. index. **Document type:** trade publication.
    ●Also available online. Vendor(s): Information Access Co.
    Former titles: Venture Capital; S B I C - Venture Capital (ISSN 0036-1046); S B I C-Venture Capital Service.

VENTURE CAPITAL REPORT. see *BUSINESS AND ECONOMICS — Small Business*

332.6   US   ISSN 1046-5340
HG4509
VICKERS DIRECTORY OF INSTITUTIONAL INVESTORS. 1982. s-a. $195. Vickers Stock Research, 226 New York Ave., Huntington, NY 11743. **Document type:** directory.
    Formerly: Directory of Institutional Investors (ISSN 8755-0318).

VIETNAM BUSINESS. see *BUSINESS AND ECONOMICS — International Commerce*

332.6   US
VIEWPOINTS (HOUSTON). q. free to VALIC customers. Variable Life Insurance Co., 2919 Allen Pkwy., Ste. L3-01, Houston, TX 77019. Ed. Cheryl Gochenour. charts; stat. circ. 500,000. **Document type:** newsletter.
    Description: Contains financial information on annuity investments of interest to VALIC customers.

VIRGINIA AGRICULTURE COMMODITY NEWSLETTER. see *AGRICULTURE*

332.6   AU
VOLKSWIRT. 1954. m. S.135. Oesterreichischer Schutzverband der Wertpapierbesitzer, Schellinggasse 6, A-1010 Vienna, Austria. Ed.Bd. adv.; charts. circ. 3,000(approx.).
    Formerly (until 1984): Wertpapierbesitzer.

332.6 330.1   US   ISSN 8755-3406
VOLUME REVERSAL SURVEY; a comprehensive guide to volume trends in the major markets. 1979. m. $195. Almarco L C C, Box 1451, Sedona, AZ 86339. TEL 602-282-1275. FAX 602-282-6364. Ed. Mark Leibovit. R&P contact: Mark Leibovit. charts; illus.; circ. 500 (paid). (also avail. by fax) **Document type:** newsletter.
    —CCC
    Refereed Serial

VORTEILHAFTE GELDANLAGEN; Handbuch fuer Anleger, Berater und Vermittler. see *BUSINESS AND ECONOMICS — Banking And Finance*

332.63   US
▼**THE WALKER MARKET LETTER.** 1996. 2/m. TEL 303-980-1168. E-mail: jwalker@lowrisk.com; URL: http://www.lowrisk.com. Ed. Jeff Walker. **Document type:** bulletin.
    ●Available only online.
    Description: Focuses on the stock market and investing in mutual funds.

WALL STREET DIGEST. see *BUSINESS AND ECONOMICS — Banking And Finance*

332.6   US
WALL STREET GENERALIST.* 1983. every 3 weeks. $160. Market Metrics, P.O. Box 716, Boca Grande, FL 34921-0716. TEL 813-366-5642. FAX 813-365-1471. Ed. Raymond L. Hines. circ. 200. **Document type:** newsletter.
    Description: Reviews our stock market timing models and how they are calling the market moves.

THE WALL STREET JOURNAL INDEX. see *BUSINESS AND ECONOMICS — Banking And Finance*

332   US   ISSN 0277-4992
WALL STREET LETTER; newsweekly for investment banking and brokerage community. 1969. w. $1695 (Canada $1725; elsewhere $1770). Institutional Investor Newsletters, 477 Madison Ave., New York, NY 10022. TEL 212-224-3233. FAX 212-224-3353. Ed. Tom Lamont. adv. (processed; also avail. in microfiche; reprint service avail. from UMI) **Document type:** newsletter.
    ●Also available on CD-ROM.
    —UMI.
    Description: Coverage includes the big firms as well as a number of smaller regional brokerage, mutual fund companies and firms providing services to the brokerage industry.

332.6   US
WALL STREET RESEARCH REPORTS.* irreg. Frost & Sullivan, Inc., 90 West St., No. 1301, New York, NY 10005-1039. TEL 212-233-1080.

332 330   US   ISSN 0043-0102
WALL STREET TRANSCRIPT; a professional publication for the business and financial community. 1963. w. $1890 (Europe and S. America $2190; Africa and Asia $2,290). Wall Street Transcript Corp., 100 Wall St., New York, NY 10005. TEL 212-747-9500. Ed.Bd. (also avail. in microform from UMI) **Indexed:** PROMT, Tr.& Indus.Ind. **Document type:** trade publication.
    ●Also available online. Vendor(s): Information Access Co., MediaStream.
    —BLDSC (9261.487000).
    Description: Contains securities reports and analyses of stock market trends from brokerage houses, interviews with CEO's and money managers; also covers the art market.

332.6   US   ISSN 1059-017X
WASHINGTON BOND & MONEY MARKET REPORT; federal monetary and economic policies, interest rates and the fixed income markets. 1936. bi-w. $405 (foreign $447) (effective 1997). Newsletter Services, Inc., 9700 Philadelphia Ct., Lanham, MD 20706-4405. TEL 301-731-5200; 800-345-2611. FAX 301-731-5201. Ed. Joseph R. Slevin; Pub. Lisa Anthony. R&P contact: Lisa Anthony. **Document type:** newsletter.
    Former titles (until 1990): R O G - Bond and Money Market Letter; Reporting on Governments - Bond and Money Market Letter; (until May 1986): Goldsmith-Nagan Bond and Money Market Letter (ISSN 0017-1697)
    Description: Provides reporting, analysis and judgements on Federal Reserve policy, interest rates and market trends to professional money managers.

332.6 333.91   US   ISSN 1049-443X
WATER INVESTMENT NEWSLETTER. 1987. m. $140. U S Water News, Inc., 230 Main St., Halstead, KS 67056-1913. TEL 316-835-2222. FAX 316-835-2223. Ed. Mary H. DeSena; Pub. Thomas C. Bell. (looseleaf format; back issues avail.) **Document type:** newsletter.
    Description: Covers water stocks and investments.

WEEKLY COTTON TRADE REPORT. see *AGRICULTURE — Agricultural Economics*

332.64   US
WEEKLY ECONOMIC UPDATE. w. Green Mountain Asset Management Corp., E-mail: bobbose@stockresearch.com; URL: http://www.stockresearch.com/. Ed. Bob Bose.
    ●Available only online.
    Description: Contains timely investment information.

332.6   US
WEEKLY INSIDER REPORT. 1971. w. $137. (Argus Research Group) Vickers Stock Research Corp., 226 New York Ave., Huntington, NY 11743. Ed. Edwin A. Buck Jr. bk.rev. circ. 2,000. (tabloid format)
    Description: Contains all open market trades of corporate insiders, rates all stocks, commentary suggested portfolio, indicative ratios.

332.6   US
WEEKLY REVIEW OF THE MARKET. w. $20 (foreign $55). Coffee, Sugar & Cocoa Exchange, Inc., Four World Trade Center, New York, NY 10048. TEL 212-938-2800. FAX 212-524-9863.
    Description: Synopsis of market activity in each commodity trade on the Coffee, Sugar & Cocoa Exchange.

332.6   CN   ISSN 1196-4685
WEEKLY STOCK CHARTS - CANADIAN INDUSTRIAL COMPANIES. 1965. m. Can.$261.08. Independent Survey Co., P.O. Box 6000, Vancouver, BC V6B 4B9, Canada. TEL 604-731-5777; 800-665-3389. E-mail: isc@mail.isccharts.com. **Document type:** bulletin.
    Former titles: Weekly Stock Charts - Canadian and U S Industrial Companies (ISSN 0830-1972); (until 1985): Weekly Stock Charts - Canadian Industrial Companies (ISSN 0829-3120); Canadian Weekly Stock Charts: Industrials (ISSN 0383-2945); Industrials: Four Hundred and Twenty Five Canadian Weekly Stock Charts (ISSN 0019-8935)
    Description: Charts a two year record of weekly share price and volume for 1500 Canadian industrial companies.

332.6   CN   ISSN 0829-3139
WEEKLY STOCK CHARTS - CANADIAN RESOURCE COMPANIES. 1965. m. Can.$261.08. Independent Survey Co., P.O. Box 6000, Vancouver, BC V6B 4B9, Canada. TEL 604-731-5777; 800-665-3389. E-mail: isc@mail.isccharts.com. **Document type:** bulletin.
    Former titles: Canadian Weekly Stock Charts: Mines and Oils (ISSN 0383-2953); Mines and Oils; Four Hundred and Fifty Canadian Weekly Stock Charts (ISSN 0026-5039)
    Description: Charts a year record of weekly share price and volume for 1500 Canadian resource companies.

332.6   US
WEISS BROKERAGE FIRM SAFETY DIRECTORY. 1992. a. $219 (effective 1997). Weiss Ratings, Inc., 4176 Burns Rd., Palm Beach Gardens, FL 33410. TEL 407-627-3300. FAX 407-625-6685. E-mail: tom-r@weiss.com; URL: http://www.weissinc.com. Pub. Martin Weiss. R&P contact: Steve H. Ackerman. pp./issue: 150. **Document type:** directory.
    Former titles: Weiss Research's Brokerage Firm Safety Directory (ISSN 1074-2123); Brokerage Firm Safety Directory (ISSN 1067-8794)
    Description: Guide to determining the safety of brokerage firms and brokers.

332.6   SZ
WELT KONJUNKTUR. 24/yr. Postfach, CH-8123 Ebmatingen, Switzerland. TEL 01-9803622. Ed. Ue? Vonau. circ. 4,000.

332.6   GW   ISSN 0049-7169
WERTPAPIER; Zeitschrift fuer Kapitalanlage. 1953. s-m. DM.92. Deutsche Schutzvereinigung fuer Wertpapierbesitz e.V., Humboldtstr. 9, 40237 Dusseldorf, Germany. Ed. Hans Peter Schreib. adv.; charts; circ. 34,000 (controlled). (looseleaf format)

332.6   CN
WESTCOAST SPECULATOR. w. Gert Investment Corporation, Box 23, Kelowna, B.C. V1Y 7N3, Canada. TEL 604-763-8773. Ed. George Simone.

BUSINESS AND ECONOMICS — INVESTMENTS

332.6   AT   ISSN 1037-4590
WESTERN AUSTRALIAN PROSPECT. 1978. q. Aus.$12. Department of Resources Development, S.G.I.O. Atrium, 168 St. George's Terr., Perth, W.A. 6000, Australia. TEL 61-09-3275555. FAX 61-09-3275500. URL: http://www.drd.wa.gov.au. Ed. Matthew Coomber. adv.: B&W page Aus.$1375, color page Aus.$1955; adv. contact: Alizabeth Petrich. circ. 8,500. **Indexed:** AESIS, Alloys Ind., Eng.Mat.Abstr., Met.Abstr.Ind., Met.Abstr., Nonfer.Met.Alert, PCC Alert, Soils & Fert., Steels Alert, World Alum.Abstr. **Document type:** government publication.
     Former titles: Prospect (Perth) (ISSN 1033-5196); (until 1988): Prospect Western Australia (ISSN 1033-5188)
     Description: Showcases the diverse range of economic activity and investment opportunities in Western Australia - from a huge resources mining sector to manufacturing.

332.6   US   ISSN 0300-662X
WESTERN MINING NEWS.* 1968. bi-w. $55. Western Mining News, Inc., 2716 N. Center Rd., Spokane, WA 99212-2226. TEL 509-922-4184. Ed. Roger Rutcosky. charts; stat. circ. 9,000.
     Description: Provides quotes on North American penny mining stocks.

WESTERN REAL ESTATE NEWS. see *REAL ESTATE*

332.6   UK   ISSN 0263-953X
WHAT INVESTMENT.* 1982. m. £22.60. Charterhouse Communications Ltd., 4 Tabernacle St., London ECXA 4LU, England. Ed. Michael Beacher. adv.; bk.rev. circ. 30,000.

332.6
WHISPER ON WALL STREET. 1982. irreg. (3-5/yr.). $128. G.H. Brooks Associates, Inc., 221 West Ave., Darien, CT 06820. TEL 203-656-0261. Ed. George H. Brooks. **Document type:** newsletter.
     Description: Analysis of stock market, stock selection; focuses on smaller issues.

332.6
WHITE'S TAX EXEMPT BOND MARKET RATINGS.* 1954. a. $300. Delta Press, 250 Hudson St. 8Fl., New York, NY 10013. TEL 212-285-6400. Ed. Wilson White, Jr.

332.6   UK   ISSN 0961-9763
WHO'S WHO IN RISK CAPITAL. VOL. 1: UNITED KINGDOM. 1991. a. Initiative Europe, 69 Bondway, London SW8 1SQ, England. TEL 44-171-735-9838. FAX 44-171-820-0802. **Document type:** directory.

332.6   UK   ISSN 0961-9771
WHO'S WHO IN RISK CAPITAL. VOL. 2: CONTINENTAL EUROPE. 1991. a. Initiative Europe, 69 Bondway, London SW8 1SQ, England. TEL 44-171-735-9838. FAX 44-171-820-0802. **Document type:** directory.

332.6   US   ISSN 0090-418X
HG4907
WHO'S WHO IN THE SECURITIES INDUSTRY. (Published for the annual convention of the Securities Industry Association as a part of the Economist SIA convention editions. Issued formerly as part of Economist I.B.A. convention editions) 1912. a. $18. (Securities Industry Association) Economist Publishing Co., 11 E. Hubbard St., Ste. 300, Chicago, IL 60611-3536. TEL 312-467-1888; 800-843-3266. FAX 312-467-0225. Ed. John C. Cutler. adv.; illus. circ. 6,000. **Document type:** academic/scholarly publication, directory.

332.6   AU   ISSN 0003-2166
WIENER WARENBOERSE. AMTLICHES KURSBLATT. HOLZ. 1949. m. S.100. Wiener Boerse, Wipplingerstr. 34, A-1013 Vienna, Austria. TEL 43-1-53499-0. FAX 43-1-5356857. R&P contact: Gerhard Reidlinger. (looseleaf format) **Document type:** bulletin.

332.6   AU   ISSN 0003-2174
WIENER WARENBOERSE. AMTLICHES KURSBLATT. ROHHAEUTE UND FELLE, LEDER TREIBRIEMEN UND TECHNISCHE LEDERARTIKEL. 1951. m. S.300. Wiener Boerse, Wipplingerstr. 34, A-1011 Vienna, Austria. TEL 43-1-53499-0. FAX 43-1-5356857. R&P contact: Gerhard Reidlinger. **Document type:** bulletin.

WIRELESS TELECOM INVESTOR. see *COMMUNICATIONS — Telephone And Telegraph*

332.6
WISCONSIN. COMMISSIONER OF SECURITIES. BIENNIAL REPORT. 1924. biennial. free. Commissioner of Securities, Box 1768, Madison, WI 53701. TEL 608-266-3431. circ. 2,000.
     Formerly: Wisconsin. Commissioner of Securities. Annual Report (ISSN 0084-0548)

332.6   US
WISCONSIN SECURITIES BULLETIN. 1939. bi-m. $15. Commissioner of Securities, Box 1768, Madison, WI 53701. TEL 608-266-3431. index. circ. 1,650. **Document type:** bulletin.

332.6   UK
WORLD AFFAIRS REVIEW. 1980. m. $175. Centre for International Studies Ltd., Bramley House, Woolstone, Cheltenham, Glos. GL52 4RG, England. TEL 44-1242-679100. FAX 44-1242-679101. Ed. Allen Keyte; Pub. Allen Keyte. R&P contact: Allen Keyte. **Document type:** newsletter.
     Description: Publishes up-to-date guidelines on international stock, currency, and precious metals markets with the aim of guiding internationally-oriented investors into the right areas; includes timely and relevant political updates.

332.6   US
WORLD COMMODITY PERSPECTIVE. 1983. m. $225 (foreign $255). Elliott Wave International, Box 1618, Gainesville, GA 30503. TEL 770-536-0309. Ed. Jim Martens. **Document type:** newsletter.
     Former titles (until 1996): Elliott Wave Currency and Commodity Forecast & Elliott Wave Commodity Forecast; Elliott Wave Commodity Letter.
     Description: Designed for professionals and institutions. Analyzes agricultural and industrial commodities, using the wave principle, Fibonacci calculations and supporting technical methods.

332.6   UK   ISSN 1181-8573
HG4551
WORLD DIRECTORY OF STOCK EXCHANGES. irreg., 2nd ed., 1992. £225. Bowker - Saur Ltd., A member of the Reed Elsevier plc group, Maypole House, Maypole Rd., E. Grinstead, W. Sussex RH19 1HU, England. TEL 44-1342-330100. FAX 44-1342-330191. E-mail: custserv@bowker-saur.co.uk; URL: http://www.reed-elsevier.com. Ed. Maurice Garneau. **Document type:** directory.
     Description: Details 117 stock exchanges in 63 countries.

WORLD FINE ART. see *ART*

332.6   UK
THE WORLD GUIDE TO WORLD EQUITY MARKETS. a. £140 (foreign $255) (effective 1997). (G T Management plc.) Euromoney Publications plc., Nestor House, Playhouse Yard, London EC4V 5EX, England. TEL 0171-779-8935. FAX 0171-779-8541. Eds. Stuart Allen, Selina O'Connor. **Document type:** trade publication.
     Formerly (until 1992): G T Guide to World Equity Markets (ISSN 0957-2503)

332.6   UN   ISSN 1020-2218
WORLD INVESTMENT REPORT. 1991. a. $45. United Nations, Department of Economic and Social Development, Transnational Corporations and Management Division, New York, NY 10017. (Subscr. to: UN Publications, Room DC-0853, Dept. 162A, New York, NY 10017. TEL 800-253-9646. FAX 212-963-3489)

332.6   US
WORLD INVESTOR. 1987. m. $94. Agora Inc., 105 W. Monument St., Baltimore, MD 21201. TEL 410-223-2611; 800-851-7100. FAX 410-223-2696. Ed. Eric Roseman; Pub. Ruth Lyons. adv. contact: Ruth Zeller. circ. 11,500. **Document type:** newsletter.
     Former titles: Czeschin's World Investor; (until 1994): Czescin's Mutual Fund Outlook and Recommendations.
     Description: Includes commentary on US and foreign financial markets, outlook, and specific recommendations for two model portfolios: the income, and the long-term growth.

WORLD RISK ANALYSIS REPORTS. see *BUSINESS AND ECONOMICS — International Commerce*

332.63 346   UK   ISSN 1357-0889
K1114.A13
▼**WORLD SECURITIES LAW REPORT.** 1995. m. £420($660) B N A International, Inc. (Subsidiary of: The Bureau of National Affairs, Inc.), Heron House, 10 Dean Farrar St., London SW1H 0DX, England. TEL 44-171-222-8831. FAX 44-171-222-0294. E-mail: bnai@bna.com; URL: http://www.bna.com. (US addr.: 1250 23rd St., N.W., Washington, DC 20037-1166. TEL 800-727-3116. FAX 800-473-9284) Ed. S. Joel Kolko.
●Also available online.
—CCC.
     Description: Comprehensive coverage of the international regulation of securities. Provides news from around the world on moves made by national stock exchanges; analysis of issues such as the regulation of derivatives trading, and full-text of important documents.

338.91   US
WORLD STOCK MARKET ROUNDUP. m. Salomon Brothers, Inc., Marketing Department, 7 World Trade Center, New York, NY 10048. TEL 212-783-7000. charts; stat. **Document type:** trade publication.

332.6   US
WORLDSCOPE COMPANY DATABASE. 1986. base vol. (plus w. updates). Worldscope-Disclosure Partners, 1000 Lafayette Blvd., Bridgeport, CT 06604. TEL 203-330-5000. FAX 203-330-5001. (also avail. in magnetic tape) **Document type:** trade publication.
●Also available online. Vendor(s): Dow Jones News Retrieval, Lexis-Nexis, OCLC.
     Former titles: Disclosure - Worldscope Company Database; Worldscope Industrial Company Profiles.
     Description: Provides a complete financial profile on more than 13,500 of the world's leading industrial and service companies.

332.6   US   ISSN 1060-5967
HG4501
WORTH. 1986. 10/yr. $18 (foreign $50) (effective 1996). (Fidelity Capital Publishing) Worth Magazine, 575 Lexington Ave., New York, NY 10022. TEL 212-223-3100. URL: http://www.worth.com. (Subscr. to: Box 55420, Boulder, CO 80322-5420. TEL 800-777-1851) Ed. John Koten. adv.; illus. circ. 500,000. **Indexed:** Access (1992-). **Document type:** consumer publication.
     Formerly (until Jan. 1992): Investment Vision (ISSN 1055-2375); Which incorporated (1985-1991): Personal Investor (ISSN 0747-3044)
     Description: For personal investors, discusses new investment opportunities, finance strategies and tax updates, emphasizing diversification of assets.

332.6   US
YAMAMOTO FORECAST. 1983. m. $350. Box 573, Kahului, HI 96732. TEL 808-877-2690. Ed. Irwin T. Yamamoto. R&P contact: Irwin T. Yamamoto. adv. contact: Irwin T. Yamamoto. **Document type:** newsletter.
     Description: Analyzes and reports on undervalued, low-priced stocks, selling at bargain prices and ready to emerge.

332.6   LE   ISSN 0075-8361
YEAR-BOOK OF THE LEBANESE JOINT-STOCK COMPANIES/ANNUAIRE DES SOCIETES LIBANAISES PAR ACTION. (Text in French; index in Arabic, English and French) 1964. biennial. $45. Middle East Commercial Information Center, P.O. Box 6466, Beirut, Lebanon. (Dist. by Bernan Associates-Unipub, 4611-F Assembly Dr., Lanham, MD 20706-4391) Ed. Charles G. Gedeon. adv. circ. 2,000. **Document type:** trade publication.

332.6   LE
YEAR-BOOK OF THE LEBANESE LIMITED LIABILITY COMPANIES/ANNUAIRE DES SOCIETES LIBANAISES A RESPONSABILITE LIMITEE. (Text in French) 1973. a. $45. Middle East Commercial Information Center, Box 6466, Beirut, Lebanon. (Dist. by: Bernan Associates-Unipub, 4611-F Assembly Dr., Lanham, MD 20706-4391) Ed. Charles C. Gadeon. adv.; index. circ. 2,000.

BUSINESS AND ECONOMICS — LABOR AND INDUSTRIAL RELATIONS

332.6 382 CC
YINJIN YU ZIXUN/IMPORTING AND CONSULTING. (Text in Chinese) q. Y4. Fujian Sheng Keji Zixun Zhongxin - Fujian Science and Technology Consultation Center, Gaoqiao Dasha, 7th Floor, Wuyi Zhonglu, Fuzhou, Fujian 350005, People's Republic of China. TEL 537795. (Dist. overseas by: Jiangsu Publications Import & Export Corp., 56 Gao Yun Ling, Nanjing, Jiangsu, P.R.C.) Ed. Fang Yue.
 Description: Provides consulting services to such issues as technology importing, financial loaning and international cooperation in technology and economics.

332.6 US
YOUR FINANCIAL FUTURE; Standard & Poor's guide to retirement planning. q. Standard & Poor's (Subsidiary of: McGraw-Hill Companies, Inc.), 25 Broadway, New York, NY 10004. TEL 212-208-8000. E-mail: pneal@penn.com; URL: http://users.penn.com/~pneal/index.html. charts; stat. **Document type:** newsletter.
 ●Also available online.
 Description: Enables corporations to help their employees make financially sound investment decisions regarding their retirement plans.

YOUR MONEY. see CONSUMER EDUCATION AND PROTECTION

332.6 AT ISSN 0158-2836
YOUR MONEY WEEKLY. 1979. w. Aus.$387. Ian Huntley Pty. Ltd., P.O. Box 90, Cremorne, N.S.W. 2090, Australia. TEL 61-2-9953-5788. FAX 61-2-9953-2280. Ed. Ian Huntley. (back issues avail.)

332.6 UK ISSN 1357-437X
YOUR PENSION. 1994. q. newsstand price: £2.50. Brass Tacks Publishing Company Ltd., 62-68 Roseberry Ave., London EC1R 4RR, England. TEL 44-171-833-5566. FAX 44-171-833-8050. Ed. Andrew Stuart; Pub. Andrew Stuart. adv. contact: Bharat Sagar. circ. 50,000 (paid). **Document type:** consumer publication.
 Formerly (until 1995): Which Pension (ISSN 1352-4011).
 Description: Provides consumers with the information they need to select a pension.

332.6 610 UK ISSN 1357-4388
YOUR PRIVATE HEALTH OPTION. 1994. q. newsstand price: £1.50. Brass Tacks Publishing Company Ltd., 62-68 Roseberry Ave., London EC1R 4RR, England. TEL 44-171-833-5566. FAX 44-171-833-8050. Ed. Andrew Stuart; Pub. Andrew Stuart. adv. contact: Bharat Sagar. circ. 50,000 (paid). **Document type:** consumer publication.
 Formerly (until 1995): Which Private Health Option (ISSN 1354-9936).
 Description: Provides consumers with the information they need to select the private health care plan that best meets their needs.

332.6 UK ISSN 1357-4361
YOUR SAVINGS AND INVESTMENT. 1993. q. newsstand price: £1.95. Brass Tacks Publishing Company Ltd., 62-68 Rosebery Ave., London EC1R 4RR, England. TEL 44-171-833-5566. FAX 44-171-833-8050. Ed. Andrew Stuart; Pub. Andrew Stuart. adv. contact: Daniel Frohwein. circ. 50,000 (paid). **Document type:** consumer publication.
 Formerly (until 1995): Which Savings (ISSN 0969-9597).
 Description: Provides consumers with the information they need to choose an investment and savings package.

332.6327 US
YOUR WINDOW INTO THE FUTURE.* 1982. m. $99. Moneypower, 1304 Edgewood Ave., Ann Arbor, MI 48103-5522. TEL 612-537-8096. Ed. James H. Moore.
 Description: Specializes in accurate prediction of future interest and inflation rates. Analyzes mutual fund bonds, utility and goldfund portfolios.

332.6 SZ
ZUERCHER BOERSE. JAHRESBERICHT. 1877. a. free. (Zuercher Boerse - Zurich Stock Exchange) Effektenboersenverein Zuerich, Selnaustr. 32, CH-8021 Zurich, Switzerland. FAX 01-2292233. charts; illus.; stat. circ. 12,000. **Document type:** trade publication.

332.6 SZ
ZUERCHER EFFEKTENBOERSE. KURSBLATT. d. 958.80 SFr. (Europe 1063 SFr.). Zuerichsee Medien AG, Seestr. 86, CH-8712 Staefa, Switzerland. TEL 01-9285611. FAX 01-9285600. **Document type:** newspaper.

332.6 US
ZWEIG FORECAST. 1971. every 3 weeks. $265. Zweig Securities Advisory Service, Box 360, Bellmore, NY 11710. TEL 516-223-3800. Ed. Martin E. Zweig. R&P contact: Susan Diskin. circ. 13,000. **Document type:** newsletter.

332.6 US ISSN 1090-5103
ZWEIG PERFORMANCE RATINGS REPORT. s-m. $225. Zweig Securities Advisory Service, Box 360, Bellmore, NY 11710. TEL 516-223-3800. Ed. Michael Schaus. R&P contact: Michael Schaus. circ. 6,000. **Document type:** newsletter.
 Description: Ratings of more than 3,000 stocks with model portfolio and 3 individual stock picks each issue.

332.66 US
13(F) INSTITUTIONAL PORTFOLIOS. 1978. q. $725. C D A Investment Technologies, Inc., 1355 Piccard Dr., Rockville, MD 20850. TEL 800-232-6362. FAX 301-590-1329. circ. 230. (also avail. in magnetic tape)
 ●Also available online.
 Formerly: Spectrum 4: 13(F) Institutional Portfolios.

332.66 US
13(F) INSTITUTIONAL STOCK HOLDINGS. 1975. q. $725. C D A Investment Technologies, Inc., 1355 Piccard Dr., Rockville, MD 20850. TEL 800-232-6362. FAX 301-590-1329. circ. 400. (also avail. in magnetic tape)
 ●Also available online.
 Former titles: Spectrum 3: 13(F) Institutional Stock Holdings Survey; (until 1978): Spectrum Three: Institutional Stock Holdings Survey.

332.6 US
▼**20-20 INSIGHT.** 1995. m. $98 (e-mail $55). Mercury Capital Management, 2010 Corporate Ridge, Ste. 700, McLean, VA 22102. E-mail: mercury@2020insight.com; URL: http://www.2020insight/cp. Ed. Robert Black.
 ●Also available online.
 Description: Contains articles, commentary and fundamentals related to the stock market.

BUSINESS AND ECONOMICS — Labor And Industrial Relations

see also Labor Unions

A C A JOURNAL; Perspectives in Compensation and Benefits. (American Compensation Association) see BUSINESS AND ECONOMICS — Personnel Management

A C A NEWS. (American Compensation Association) see BUSINESS AND ECONOMICS — Personnel Management

331.86 US
A D A COMPLIANCE MANUAL FOR EMPLOYERS. (Americans with Disabilities Act) 1992. base vol. (plus s-a. updates). $79.50. Butterworth Legal Publishers (Salem) (Subsidiary of: Reed Elsevier plc), 8 Industrial Way, Bldg. C, Salem, NH 03079. TEL 800-548-4001. FAX 603-898-9858. Eds. Jonathan L. Adler, Maureen F. Moore. (looseleaf format)

A F C O M'S ANNUAL SURVEY OF DATA PROCESSING OPERATIONS SALARIES. (Association for Computer Operations Management) see COMPUTERS — Data Base Management

331 658 GW
A G P MITTEILUNGEN; Zeitschrift fuer Partnerschaft in der Wirtschaft. 1953. q. DM.30. Arbeitsgemeinschaft zur Foerderung der Partnerschaft in der Wirtschaft e.V., Wilhelmshoeher Allee 283A, 34131 Kassel, Germany. TEL 0561-36044. FAX 0561-33850. Ed. Ina Rudolph-Loesel. adv.: B&W page DM.940; trim 186 x 258. bk.rev.; charts; illus.; stat.; index, cum.index. circ. 4,000. (looseleaf format) **Document type:** bulletin.
 Former titles (until 1995): Neue Unternehmen (ISSN 0723-2500); A G P Mitteilungen (ISSN 0001-1347).

A I D - AUSLAENDER IN DEUTSCHLAND. see POPULATION STUDIES

331 II ISSN 0001-1630
A I O E LABOUR NEWS. (Text in English) 1966. m. $30. All India Organisation of Employers, Federation House, Tansen Marg, New Delhi 110001, India. TEL 11-3319251. FAX 11-3320714. TELEX 031-61768. Ed. R.C. Pande. adv.; bk.rev. circ. 1,000. (processed)

331 340 US
A K O O EMPLOYMENT LAW INSIDER. q. free. Anderson Kill Olick & Oshinsky, P C, 2000 Pennsylvania Ave., N.W., Ste. 7500, Washington, DC 20006. TEL 202-728-3108. **Document type:** newsletter.
 Description: Informs clients, friends and fellow professionals of developments in labor and employment law.

331 DK ISSN 0109-9167
A - KASSE INFORMATION. 1985. q. membership. Kristelig Arbejdsloeshedskasse, P.O. Box 239, DK-8900 Randers, Denmark. FAX 45-86-11-22-01. Ed. Carsten Jensen. bk.rev.; illus. circ. 83,000.

331 DK ISSN 0903-8876
A M I - RAPPORT. 1978. irreg. DKK 25. Arbejdstilsynet, Tryksagsafdelningen, Landskronagade 33-35, 2100 Copenhagen OE, Denmark. (Co-sponsor: Arbejdsmiljoeinstituttet) illus.
 Formerly (until 1987): Denmark. Arbejdstilsynet. Rapport (ISSN 0106-6838).

A Q P REPORT. (Association for Quality and Participation) see BUSINESS AND ECONOMICS — Management

A S T D BUYERS GUIDE AND CONSULTANTS DIRECTORY (American Society for Training and Development) see BUSINESS AND ECONOMICS — Trade And Industrial Directories

331 DK ISSN 0908-8962
AARHUS SCHOOL OF BUSINESS. CENTRE FOR LABOUR MARKET AND SOCIAL RESEARCH. WORKING PAPERS
 1981. irreg. price varies. Aarhus School of Business. Centre for Labour Market and Social Research, Science Park Aarhus, Gustav Wieds Vej 10, DK-8000 Aarhus C, Denmark. TEL 45-89-42-23-66. FAX 45-89-42-23-66. E-mail hbunzel@cls.dk; URL: http://www.cls.dk/~hbunzel. Ed. Henning Bunzel. illus. circ. 400.
 Former titles (until 1994): Aarhus School of Business. Centre for Labour Economics. Working Papers (ISSN 0905-6955); (until 1989): Studies in Labor Market Dynamics (ISSN 0108-2469).

331 CN
ABORDAGE. 1974. irreg. Syndicat Canadien de la Fonction Publique, Local 1575, Universite du Quebec a Rimouski, 300 Allee des Ursulines, Rimouski, Que. G5L 3A1, Canada. TEL 418-724-1582. bk.rev. circ. 290. (looseleaf format; back issues avail.)

331 CN
ABSTRACT OF AMERICAN INDUSTRIAL TREND ANALYSIS 1990. q. Can.$60 membership; newsstand price: Can.$25. Maxiplan Financial Club, 12687 52nd Ave., Montreal, PQ H1E 2H6, Canada. Ed. Marcel Wistaff. **Document type:** newsletter.
 Description: Contains winning strategies in business opportunities, financial outlook, productive growth, marketing surveys, technology developments, management perspective, global operations.

352 US ISSN 0362-8493
KFN5562.P8
ACROSS THE TABLE. 1974. m. $40. New York Conference of Mayors and Municipal Officials, 119 Washington Ave., Albany, NY 12210. Ed. John H. Galligan. bk.rev.; bibl.; index. circ. 1,300.

613.62 FR ISSN 0335-136X
ACTION SOCIALE ET SANTE. 1974. bi-m. (with 2 special nos.). 50 F. Association Paritaire d'Action Sociale du Batiment, 113-115 Av. de Choisy, 75013 Paris, France. TEL 40-77-51-23. Ed. J. Brillouet. adv.

331 JA
ADAPT JAPAN: EMPLOYMENT OPPORTUNITIES FOR YOU. q. Selnate Publishing Co. Ltd., Fujibo Bldg. 2F, 10-28 Fujimi 2-chome, Chiyoda-ku, Tokyo 102, Japan. TEL 03-2347717. FAX 03-2347716. Ed. Judith Yarrow.
Description: Ads and articles aimed at those who would like to work in Japan.

331 US
ADMINISTRATIVE AND OFFICE SUPPORT SURVEY. a. $450. MidAtlantic Employers' Association, Box 770, Valley Forge, PA 19482. TEL 215-666-7330. FAX 215-666-7866.
Description: Provides comparative salary information and compensation practices for 86 administrative and office support positions, representing 6,350 employees among 264 businesses throughout PA, NJ, MD, and DE.

331.2 378 US
ADMINISTRATIVE COMPENSATION SURVEY. a. $300 to non-members; non-member participants $180; member participants $80. College and University Personnel Association, 1233 20th St., N.W., Washington, DC 20036. TEL 202-429-0311. FAX 202-429-0149. Ed.Bd. R&P contact: Audrey Rothstein. Indexed: SRI.
Description: Offers salary data on 167 positions at 1,390 public and private institutions.

331.1 US ISSN 0742-6186
HD6958.5
ADVANCES IN INDUSTRIAL AND LABOR RELATIONS. 1983. irreg., vol.7, 1996. $73.25. J A I Press Inc., 55 Old Post Rd., No. 2, Box 1678, Greenwich, CT 06830-1678. TEL 203-661-6702. FAX 203-661-0792. E-mail: jai@jaipress.com. (Subscr. in UK and Europe to: JAI Press Ltd., 38 Tavistock St., Covent Garden, London WC2E 7PB, England. TEL 44-171-379-8834. FAX 44-171-379-8835) Ed.Bd. Document type: monographic series.
—CCC.

331 IC
AF VETTVANGI. 1988. bi-m. free. Vinnuveitendasamband Islands - Confederation of Icelandic Employers, Gardastraeti 41, P.O. Box 520, IS-121 Reykjavik, Iceland. TEL 354-511-5000. FAX 354-511-5050. Ed. Gudni N. Adalsteinsson. circ. 5,400. Document type: newsletter.
Description: Deals with business and economics, labor and industrial relations from the view of Icelandic employers.

331 US ISSN 0148-8147
AFFIRMATIVE ACTION COMPLIANCE MANUAL FOR FEDERAL CONTRACTORS. 1975. m. $355 (effective July 1995). The Bureau of National Affairs, Inc., 1231 25th St., N.W., Washington, DC 20037. TEL 202-452-4200. FAX 202-822-8092. TELEX 285656 BNAI WSH. URL: http://www.bna.com/. (Subscr. to: 9435 Key West Ave., Rockville, MD 20850. TEL 800-372-1033) Ed. Jeff Day. index. (looseleaf format; back issues avail.)
—CCC.
Description: Contains the official text of the Office of Federal Contract Compliance Programs Manual and reports on related developments.

AFFIRMATIVE ACTION REGISTER; the E E O recruitment publication. see *OCCUPATIONS AND CAREERS*

AFFIRMATIVE EMPLOYMENT STATISTICS. see *BUSINESS AND ECONOMICS — Abstracting, Bibliographies, Statistics*

AGRICULTURAL WAGES IN INDIA. see *AGRICULTURE — Agricultural Economics*

AKADEMIX; nyhetsbrev fraan SACO studentraad. see *EDUCATION — Higher Education*

AL DIA. see *POLITICAL SCIENCE — International Relations*

ALABAMA EMPLOYMENT LAW LETTER. see *LAW*

ALASKA EMPLOYMENT LAW LETTER. see *LAW*

331.1 US ISSN 1063-3758
ALASKA WAGE RATES (YEAR). a. free. Department of Labor, Research & Analysis Section, Box 22201, Juneau, AK 99802-5501. TEL 907-465-4508. FAX 907-465-2101. Document type: government publication.
Description: Presents the results of a wage survey of nearly 1,500 employers for 160 occupations. Data are provided for Alaska statewide and by economic region.

331 371.42 US
ALMANAC OF AMERICAN EMPLOYERS. (Supplement to: Corporate Jobs Outlook! (ISSN 0892-5232)) 1985. a. $131.50 (effective 1996). Plunkett Research, Ltd., P.O. Drawer 8270, Galveston, TX 77553-8270. TEL 409-765-8530. FAX 409-765-8571. Ed. Jack W. Plunkett. Document type: newsletter.
Description: Complete reference guide to America's 500 largest, fastest-growing employers.

AMERICAN ASSOCIATION OF ENGINEERING SOCIETIES. ENGINEERING WORKFORCE COMMISSION. ENGINEERING AND TECHNOLOGY ENROLLMENTS (YEAR). see *ENGINEERING*

AMERICAN ASSOCIATION OF ENGINEERING SOCIETIES. ENGINEERING WORKFORCE COMMISSION. ENGINEERS' SALARIES: SPECIAL INDUSTRY REPORT (YEAR). see *ENGINEERING*

AMERICAN ASSOCIATION OF ENGINEERING SOCIETIES. ENGINEERING WORKFORCE COMMISSION. PROFESSIONAL INCOME OF ENGINEERS (YEAR). see *ENGINEERING*

331 US
AMERICAN DIRECTORY OF ORGANIZED LABOR; unions, locals, agreements and employers. 1992. irreg. $275. Gale Research, 835 Penobscot Bldg., 645 Griswold St., Detroit, MI 48226-4094. TEL 313-961-2242; 800-877-4253. FAX 800-414-5043. E-mail: daniel__snyder@gale.com. Ed. Cynthia Russell Spomer. Document type: directory.

331 US ISSN 0889-0609
AMERICAN LABOR. 1979. irreg. $9.95 (foreign $15). American Labor Education Center, 2000 P St., N.W., Ste. 300, Washington, DC 20036-5915. TEL 202-828-5170. Eds. Matt Witt, Debi Duke. adv.; bk.rev. circ. 5,000.

331 US
AMERICAN WORKPLACE. 1986. bi-m. free. U.S. Department of Labor, Office of the American Workplace, 200 Constitution Ave., No. N-5402, Washington, DC 20210. TEL 202-219-6098. FAX 202-219-8762. Ed. Barbara Schrader. bk.rev. circ. 25,000. (back issues avail.) Document type: trade publication, government publication.
Formerly (until 1993): Labor Relations Today.

AMERICANS WITH DISABILITIES ACT: EMPLOYEE RIGHTS AND EMPLOYER OBLIGATIONS. see *HANDICAPPED*

AMERICANS WITH DISABILITIES NEWSLETTER. see *HANDICAPPED*

331 GW
AMTLICHE BEKANNTMACHUNG ZUM ARBEITSSCHUTZ. (Supplement to: Bundesarbeitsblatt (ISSN 0007-5868)) m. DM.112 (effective 1997). (Bundesminister fuer Arbeit und Sozialordnung) W. Kohlhammer GmbH, Hessbruehlstr. 69, 70565 Stuttgart, Germany. TEL 49-711-7863290. FAX 49-711-7863430. Document type: government publication.

331 PE
ANALISIS LABORAL. 1977. m. $75. Asesoramiento y Analisis Laborales S.A., Mariano Odicio 334, Miraflores, Lima 18, Peru. TEL 469477.

331 GW ISSN 0341-0900
ANGEWANDTE ARBEITSWISSENSCHAFT. 1975. q. DM.26. (Institut fuer Angewandte Arbeitswissenschaft e.V.) Wirtschaftsverlag Bachem GmbH, Ursulaplatz 1, 50668 Cologne, Germany. TEL 49-221-1619-0. FAX 49-221-1619231. Ed. Wilfried Brokmann. index. circ. 4,000. Document type: academic/scholarly publication.
—CCC.

ANNOTATED BRITISH COLUMBIA LABOUR RELATIONS CODE. see *LAW*

344.73 331 US ISSN 0743-4146
ANNUAL INSTITUTE ON EMPLOYMENT LAW. 1972. a. $99 (effective 1996). Practising Law Institute, 810 Seventh Ave., New York, NY 10019. TEL 212-824-5700; 800-260-4754. FAX 800-321-0093. E-mail: info@pli.edu; URL: http://www.pli.edu.
Formerly (until 1983): Annual Institute on Equal Employment Opportunity Compliance (ISSN 0198-9022)

331.2 CN ISSN 1184-9525
ANNUAL SALARY SURVEYS. ADMINISTRATIVE & FINANCE REPORT. a. Can.$425. K P M G, Box 10427, Pacific Centre, 500 - 777 Dunsmuir St., Vancouver, BC V7Y 1K5, Canada. TEL 604-691-3407. FAX 604-691-3456.
Supersedes in part: Salary Survey. Administrative, Finance and Information Systems Report (ISSN 1184-9509); Which was formerly: Salary Survey. Administrative, Finance and Data Processing Report (ISSN 0711-3196); Which supersedes in part: Salary Survey (ISSN 0711-3153); Which was formerly: Stevenson and Kellogg Salary Survey. An Annual Study of Compensation Across Canada (ISSN 0706-6945).
Description: Covers clerical, office management, personnel, purchasing, finance and accounting; union and non-union comparison, hours of work, bonus data, pay indices.

331.2 CN ISSN 1185-3581
ANNUAL SALARY SURVEYS. ENGINEERING & TECHNICAL REPORT. a. Can.$240. K P M G, Box 10427, Pacific Centre, 500 - 777 Dunsmuir St., Vancouver, BC V7Y 1K5, Canada. TEL 604-691-3407. FAX 604-691-3456.
Formerly (until 1990): Salary Survey. Engineering and Technical Report (ISSN 0711-317X); Which supersedes in part: Salary Survey (ISSN 0711-3153); Which was formerly: Stevenson and Kellogg Salary Survey. An Annual Study of Compensation Across Canada (ISSN 0706-6945).
Description: Covers draftspersons, engineering assistants, technologists-technicians and chief engineers; union and non-union comparison, bonus data, pay indices.

331.2 CN ISSN 1185-3565
ANNUAL SALARY SURVEYS. EXECUTIVE COMPENSATION REPORT. a. Can.$695. K P M G, Box 10427, Pacific Centre, 500 - 777 Dunsmuir St., Vancouver, BC V7Y 1K5, Canada. TEL 604-691-3407. FAX 604-691-3456.
Former titles (until 1990): Salary Survey. Executive Compensation Report (ISSN 0842-5280); (until 1987): Executive Salary Survey (ISSN 0830-9876); (until 1985): Salary Survey. Executive Report (ISSN 0711-3161)
Description: Covers general management, corporate staff, finance, administration, sales, marketing, manufacturing, distribution, engineering and human resources, and board of directors.

331.2 CN ISSN 1184-9517
ANNUAL SALARY SURVEYS. INFORMATION SYSTEMS REPORT. a. Can.$425. K P M G, Box 10427, Pacific Centre, 500 - 777 Dunsmuir St., Vancouver, BC V7Y 1K5, Canada. TEL 604-691-3407. FAX 604-691-3456.
Supersedes in part: Salary Survey. Administrative, Finance and Information Systems Report (ISSN 1184-9509); Which was formerly: Salary Survey. Administrative, Finance and Data Processing Report (ISSN 0711-3196); Which supersedes in part: Salary Survey (ISSN 0711-3153); Which was formerly: Stevenson and Kellogg Salary Survey. An Annual Study of Compensation Across Canada (ISSN 0706-6945).
Description: Compares union to non-union, hours of work, bonus data, pay indices; from entry level to corporate director.

BUSINESS AND ECONOMICS — LABOR AND INDUSTRIAL RELATIONS

331.2   CN   ISSN 1185-3573
ANNUAL SALARY SURVEYS. PRODUCTION & DISTRIBUTION REPORT. a. Can.$350. K P M G, Box 10427, Pacific Centre, 500 - 777 Dunsmuir St., Vancouver, BC V7Y 1K5, Canada. TEL 604-691-3407. FAX 604-691-3456.
Former titles (until 1990): Salary Survey. Production and Distribution Report (ISSN 0830-9868); (until 1982): Salary Survey. Production Report (ISSN 0711-3188)
Description: Covers lead hand, foreman, superintendents, maintenance, shipping, warehouse, production and distribution management.

331.2   CN   ISSN 1185-3557
ANNUAL SALARY SURVEYS. SALES & MARKETING REPORT. a. Can.$425. K P M G, Box 10427, Pacific Centre, 500 - 777 Dunsmuir St., Vancouver, BC V7Y 1K5, Canada. TEL 604-691-3407. FAX 604-691-3456.
Former titles (until 1990): Salary Survey. Sales and Marketing Report (ISSN 0830-985X); (until 1985): Salary Survey. Sales Report (ISSN 0826-0362); (until 1981): Salary Survey. Marketing Report (ISSN 0711-320X)
Description: Covers junior and senior sales representatives, supervisor, and sales and marketing management.

331 340   NE   ISSN 0929-9289
ARBEIDSRECHT; maandblad voor de praktijk. 1994. 11/yr. fl.175 (effective 1996). Uitgeverij Kluwer B.V., Postbus 23, 7400 GA Deventer, Netherlands. TEL 31-570-633155. FAX 31-570-633834. Ed. P.F. van der Heijden. adv. (back issues avail.) **Document type:** trade publication.
—SWETS.

331 340   GW   ISSN 0323-4568
K1
ARBEIT UND ARBEITSRECHT; Zeitschrift fuer betriebliche Praxis. 1946. m. DM.156. (foreign DM.192) (effective 1997). Verlag Die Wirtschaft GmbH, Am Friedrichshain 22, 10407 Berlin, Germany. TEL 49-30-42151421. FAX 49-30-42151123. (Co-publisher: Verlag C.H. Beck) Ed. Brigitte Udke. adv.: B&W page DM.2900, color page DM.5800; trim 260 x 186. bk.rev.; index. **Indexed:** Acoust.Abstr., C.I.S. Abstr. **Document type:** trade publication.
Description: Articles cover labor relations, production, safety, health protection, automation, unemployment, rationalization, education and training, labor law, and court decisions. Includes questions and answers.

331   GW   ISSN 0343-1886
ARBEIT UND BERUF; Fachzeitschrift fuer die Aufgaben der Bundesanstalt fuer Arbeit. 1950. m. DM.108 (foreign DM.126). Verlag Arbeit und Beruf, Bingstr. 30, 90480 Nuernberg, Germany. TEL 49-911-4030355. Ed. Dr. Walter Lutz. R&P contact: Dr. Walter Lutz. adv.; bk.rev.; bibl. circ. 5,000. **Indexed:** World Bibl.Soc.Sec. **Document type:** bulletin.
Formerly (until 1975): Arbeit, Beruf, und Arbeitslosenhilfe (ISSN 0003-7621)

ARBEIT UND RECHT; Zeitschrift fuer Arbeitsrechtspraxis. see *LAW*

331   GW   ISSN 0171-8819
ARBEIT UND SOZIALES; statistische Mitteilungen. 1945. q. free. Staatsministerium fuer Arbeit und Sozialordnung, Familie, Frauen und Gesundheit, Winzererstr. 9, 80792 Munich, Germany. TEL 49-89-12611407. FAX 49-89-12611508. Ed. Hugo Walzel. charts; stat. **Document type:** government publication.
Formerly: Arbeit und Wirtschaft in Bayern.

331   GW   ISSN 0340-8434
ARBEIT UND SOZIALPOLITIK. 1946. bi-m. DM.154 (foreign DM.166) (effective 1996). Nomos Verlagsgesellschaft mbH und Co. KG, Waldseestr. 3-5, 76530 Baden-Baden, Germany. TEL 49-7721-21040. FAX 49-7721-210427. (Subscr. to: Postfach 610, 76484 Baden-Baden, Germany) **Indexed:** SCIMP (1991-), World Bibl.Soc.Sec. **Document type:** academic/scholarly publication.
—SWETS. CCC.

331.2   AU
ARBEITSKOSTEN IN DER INDUSTRIE OESTERREICHS. 1960. triennial. free. Wirtschaftskammer Oesterreich, Wiedner Hauptstr. 63, Postfach 182, A-1045 Vienna, Austria. TEL 43-1-50105-4120. FAX 43-1-50206-246. TELEX 111871-BUKA. Ed. Guenther Herget. equ. math. stat. circ. 2,000. **Document type:** government publication, monographic series.

331.2   GW   ISSN 0172-2751
ARBEITSMARKT IN HESSEN; Monatsbericht zur Arbeitsmarktlage. 1952. m. Landesarbeitsamt Hessen, Referat Statistik, Saonestr. 2-4, 60528 Frankfurt a.M., Germany. TEL 069-66701. FAX 069-6670459. **Document type:** government publication.

331.15 340   GW   ISSN 0066-586X
ARBEITSRECHT DER GEGENWART. 1963. a. price varies. Erich Schmidt Verlag GmbH & Co. (Bielefeld), Viktoriastr. 44A, 33602 Bielefeld, Germany. TEL 49-521-583080. (Subscr. to: Postfach 102451, 33524 Bielefeld, Germany) Ed. Otto R. Kissel. adv.; bk.rev. **Indexed:** IBR. **Document type:** academic/scholarly publication.

331 340   GW   ISSN 0003-7761
ARBEITSRECHT IN STICHWORTEN; Arbeitsrechtliche Entscheidungssammlung. 1946. m. DM.180 (foreign DM.192) (effective 1997). Forkel Verlag GmbH, Im Weiher 10, 69121 Heidelberg, Germany. TEL 49-6221-489-250. FAX 49-6221-489476. URL: http://www.huethig.de. bk.rev.; index. circ. 1,400. (reprint service avail. from SCH) **Document type:** bulletin.
—CCC.

331   SZ   ISSN 0003-777X
ARBEITSRECHT UND ARBEITSLOSENVERSICHERUNG. (Text in French, German, Italian) 1953. irreg. (3-4/yr.) 36 SFr. (foreign DM.45) (effective 1997). (Bundesamt fuer Industrie, Gewerbe und Arbeit) Schulthess Polygraphischer Verlag AG, Zwingliplatz 2, CH-8022 Zurich, Switzerland. TEL 41-1-2519336. FAX 41-1-2616394. E-mail: schulthess@access.ch. adv.; index. circ. 1,677. **Document type:** government publication.

331 340   GW   ISSN 0938-5800
ARBEITSRECHTLICHE PRAXIS C D - R O M. Abbreviated title: A P C D - R O M. a. (with s-a. updates). DM.3498 (effective 1997). Verlag C.H. Beck, 80791 Munich, Germany. TEL 49-89-38189338. FAX 49-89-38189398. **Document type:** abstracting/indexing.
●Available only on CD-ROM.
Description: Covers the practice of labor law. Contains full text of important cases.

331   GW   ISSN 0863-3924
ARBEITSSCHUTZ AKTUELL. 1990. bi-m. DM.54 (effective 1997). Erich Schmidt Verlag GmbH & Co. (Berlin), Genthiner Str. 30G, 10785 Berlin, Germany. TEL 49-30-2500850. FAX 49-30-25008521. **Document type:** trade publication.

331   GW
ARBEITSSCHUTZ UND ARBEITSSICHERHEIT. 1989. irreg. DM.96 (effective 1997). Erich Schmidt Verlag GmbH & Co. (Berlin), Genthiner Str. 30G, 10785 Berlin, Germany. TEL 49-30-250085-0. FAX 49-30-25008521. (looseleaf format) **Document type:** bulletin.
Formerly: Arbeitssicherheitsgesetz (ISSN 0936-8574)

331   GW   ISSN 0933-2448
ARBEITSSTAETTEN. 1984. irreg. DM.128. Erich Schmidt Verlag GmbH & Co. (Berlin), Genthiner Str. 30G, 10785 Berlin, Germany. TEL 49-30-250085-0. FAX 49-30-25008521. (looseleaf format) **Document type:** bulletin.

ARBEJDERBEVAEGELSENS BIBLIOTEK OG ARKIV. AARSSKRIFT. see *POLITICAL SCIENCE*

331   DK   ISSN 0108-9625
ARBEJDERBEVAEGELSENS ERHVERVSRAAD. BERETNING. 1982. a. free. Arbejderbevaegelsens Erhvervsraad, Faellessekretariat, Kooperationens Hus, Reventlowsgade 14-2, 1651 Copenhagen V, Denmark. TEL 31-31-22-62. FAX 31-31-30-41. illus. circ. 2,500.

322.2   DK   ISSN 0107-8461
HD4811
ARBEJDERHISTORIE; tidskrift for historie, kultur og politik. 1973. q. DKK 325 (foreign DKK 375) (effective 1997). Selskabet til Forskning i Arbejderbevaegelsens Historie, Noerrebrogade 66 D, Ed.Bd., Denmark. TEL 45-35-361522. FAX 45-35-363222. E-mail: SFAH@aba.DK. bk.rev.; bibl. circ. 750. **Indexed:** Amer.Hist.& Life (1978-1994), Hist.Abstr. (1978-1994), (1995-). **Document type:** academic/scholarly publication.
Formerly (until 1982): Meddelelser om Forskning i Arbejderbevaegelsens Historie (ISSN 0106-5904)
Description: Presents articles on labor and trade union history.
Refereed Serial

658 331   DK   ISSN 0909-9077
ARBEJDSMARKEDSPOLITISK AGENDA. 1994. s-m. Dansk Arbejdsgiverforening - Danish Employers Confederation, 113 Vester Voldgade, DK-1790 Copenhagen V, Denmark. TEL 45-33-93-40-00. FAX 45-33-12-29-76. circ. 4,500. **Document type:** trade publication.

344.489   DK   ISSN 0108-7150
ARBEJDSRETLIGT TIDSSKRIFT; arbejdsrettens domme, arbejdsretlige kendelser. 1980. a. DKK 425 (effective 1997). Jurist- og Oekonomforbundets Forlag, Gothersgade 133, D-1123 Copenhagen K, Denmark. TEL 45-33-95-97-00. FAX 45-33-95-99-97. Ed. Niels Waage. circ. 800.
Formed by the merger of: Arbejdsretlige Domme & Arbejdsretlige Kendelser.
Description: Reports on decisions by the Danish Labor Court and other collective labor law awards.

371.2   US   ISSN 0003-7885
ARBITRATION IN THE SCHOOLS. 1970. m. $120. American Arbitration Association, 140 W. 51st St., New York, NY 10020-1203. TEL 212-484-4011. FAX 212-541-4841. (Co-sponsor: Labor Relations Press) s-a. cum.index. circ. 3,500. (looseleaf format; also avail. in microfiche; reprint service avail. from KTO)
Description: Summarizes decisions on disputes between teachers and their employers.

331.1   CN   ISSN 0702-9381
ARBITRATION SERVICES REPORTER/REVUE DES SERVICES D'ARBITRAGE. 1973. m. free. Labour Canada, Publications Distribution, Ottawa, ON K1A 0J2, Canada. TEL 819-994-0543. FAX 819-997-1664. circ. 1,800.
Formerly (until 1977): Labour Case Reporter (ISSN 0702-9373)
Description: Indexes and lists arbitration awards under the industrial relations and unjust dismissal provisions of the Code.

331.09   AU   ISSN 0003-8849
ARCHIV; Jahrbuch des Vereins fuer Geschichte der Arbeiterbewegung. 1961. a. S.250 or membership. Verein fuer Geschichte der Arbeiterbewegung, Rechte Wienzeile 97, A-1050 Vienna, Austria. TEL 43-1-5457870, FAX 43-1-5440734. Ed. Wolfgang Maderthaner. bk.rev.; bibl.; illus.; index. circ. 1,000. **Document type:** academic/scholarly publication.

331   US
ARCHIVES OF LABOR AND URBAN AFFAIRS NEWSLETTER. 1971. irreg. free. Wayne State University, Archives of Labor and Urban Affairs, Walter Reuther Library, 5401 Cass Ave., Detroit, M 48202. TEL 313-577-4024. FAX 313-577-4300. E-mail: mosmith@cms.cc.wayne.edu; URL: http://www.reuther.wayne.edu. Ed. Mike Smith. bibl. circ. 3,000. (back issues avail.) **Document type:** newsletter.
Formerly: Archives of Labor History and Urban Affairs Newsletter (ISSN 0044-8729)

BUSINESS AND ECONOMICS — LABOR AND INDUSTRIAL RELATIONS

331.13   US   ISSN 0004-0916
HD5723
AREA TRENDS IN EMPLOYMENT AND UNEMPLOYMENT. m. $41 (foreign 51.25). Employment and Training Administration, Frances Perkins Bldg., Rm. S2307, 200 Constitution Ave., N.W., Washington, DC 20210. TEL 202-219-5185. (Subscr. to: Superintendent of Documents, U.S. Government Printing Office, Box 371954, Pittsburgh, PA 15250-7954. TEL 202-512-1800. FAX 202-512-2250) stat. circ. 3,000. (also avail. in microfiche from CIS; back issues avail.; reprint service avail. from CIS) **Indexed:** Amer.Stat.Ind. (1984-), Ind.U.S.Gov.Per. **Document type:** government publication.
—UMI.
   Description: Lists eligible labor surplus areas in which employers are given preference in bidding on federal procurement contracts. Also lists civil jurisdictions in each area.

ARIZONA EMPLOYMENT LAW LETTER. see *LAW*

331   US
ARIZONA'S WORKFORCE. 1977. m. free. Department of Economic Security, 1789 W. Jefferson, Box 6123, SC-733A, Phoenix, AZ 85005. TEL 602-542-3871. FAX 602-542-6474. charts; stat. circ. 5,000. (also avail. in microfiche from CIS) **Indexed:** SRI. **Document type:** newsletter.
   Former titles: Arizona Labor Market Information Newsletter; Arizona Labor Market Newsletter (ISSN 0743-5657)

331.1   US
ARKANSAS COVERED EMPLOYMENT AND EARNINGS. 1948. irreg. free. Employment Security Department, U I Research Section, Box 2981, Little Rock, AR 72203-2981. TEL 501-682-3197. circ. 300.
   Formerly: Arkansas Average Covered Employment and Earnings by County and Industry (ISSN 0092-2889)

ARKANSAS EMPLOYMENT LAW LETTER. see *LAW*

331 948   SW   ISSN 0345-0333
ARKIV FOR STUDIER I ARBETARROERELSENS HISTORIA. 1971. 3/yr. SEK 120 to individuals; institutions SEK 160 (effective 1997). Saellskapet for Studier i Arbetarroerelsens Historia, P.O. Box 1559, S-221 01 Lund, Sweden. TEL 46-46-13-39-20. FAX 46-46-13-39-29. bk.rev. **Indexed:** Amer.Hist.& Life (1989-), Hist.Abstr. (1989-).

331.1   US   ISSN 0270-8388
ART OF NEGOTIATING NEWSLETTER. 8/yr. $150. Negotiation Institute, Inc., 14 E. 48th St., 5th Fl., New York, NY 10017-1008. TEL 212-715-0176. URL: http://negotiation.com. Ed. Gerard Nirenberg. **Document type:** newsletter.

331.88   CC
ASIA LABOUR UPDATE. q. $20 to individuals and institutions worldwide. Asia Monitor Research Center, 444 Nathan Rd., 8-B, Kowloon, Hong Kong, People's Republic of China. TEL 852-2232-1346. FAX 852-2385-5319. E-mail: AMRC@HK.Super.Net. Ed. Jennifer L. Porges. **Indexed:** Alt.Press Ind.

331   JA
ASIAN REGIONAL CONFERENCE ON INDUSTRIAL RELATIONS. PROCEEDINGS. (Text in English) 1965. biennial. free. Japan Institute of Labour - Nihon Rodo Kenkyu Kiko, Shinjuku Monolith, P.O. Box 7040, Tokyo 163-09, Japan. TEL 03-5991-5165. FAX 03-3594-1112. circ. 500. **Document type:** proceedings.
   Formerly: Japan Institute of Labour. Proceedings.
   Description: Contains papers presented at the Asian Regional Conference on Industrial Relations.

ASSOCIATION FOR QUALITY AND PARTICIPATION. ANNUAL CONFERENCE AND RESOURCE MART TRANSACTIONS. see *BUSINESS AND ECONOMICS — Management*

331   US   ISSN 1061-9925
HD5650
AT WORK; stories of tomorrow's workplace. 1992. 6/yr. $75. Berrett-Koehler Publishers, Inc., 450 Sansome St., Ste. 1200, San Francisco, CA 94111-3320. TEL 415-288-0260. FAX 415-362-2512. E-mail: bkpub@aol.com. (Co-publisher: Designed Learning Inc.) Ed. Alis Valencia. bk.rev.; circ. 1,200 (paid). **Document type:** newsletter.
   Description: Focuses on innovative practices that are being implemented in organizations around the world.

331.1 341.57   IO
ATMA JAYA RESEARCH CENTRE. INTERNATIONAL CONTRACT LABOUR. 1983. irreg. Atma Jaya Research Centre - Pusat Penelitian Atma Jaya, Jalan Jenderal Sudirman 51, P.O. Box 2639, Jakarta 10001, Indonesia.

AUSTRALIA. BUREAU OF STATISTICS. AUSTRALIAN LABOUR MARKET. see *BUSINESS AND ECONOMICS — Abstracting, Bibliographies, Statistics*

AUSTRALIA. BUREAU OF STATISTICS. AVERAGE WEEKLY EARNING, AUSTRALIA, PRELIMINARY. see *BUSINESS AND ECONOMICS — Abstracting, Bibliographies, Statistics*

AUSTRALIA. BUREAU OF STATISTICS. AVERAGE WEEKLY EARNINGS, STATE AND AUSTRALIA. see *BUSINESS AND ECONOMICS — Abstracting, Bibliographies, Statistics*

AUSTRALIA. BUREAU OF STATISTICS. DIRECTORY OF INDUSTRIAL RELATIONS STATISTICS. see *BUSINESS AND ECONOMICS — Abstracting, Bibliographies, Statistics*

AUSTRALIA. BUREAU OF STATISTICS. DIRECTORY OF LABOUR MARKET AND SOCIAL SURVEY DATA. see *BUSINESS AND ECONOMICS — Abstracting, Bibliographies, Statistics*

AUSTRALIA. BUREAU OF STATISTICS. DISTRIBUTION AND COMPOSITION OF EMPLOYEE EARNINGS AND HOURS, STATES AND AUSTRALIA - DATA SERVICE. see *BUSINESS AND ECONOMICS — Abstracting, Bibliographies, Statistics*

AUSTRALIA. BUREAU OF STATISTICS. EMPLOYER TRAINING EXPENDITURE, AUSTRALIA. see *BUSINESS AND ECONOMICS — Abstracting, Bibliographies, Statistics*

AUSTRALIA. BUREAU OF STATISTICS. INDUSTRIAL DISPUTES, AUSTRALIA (MONTHLY). see *BUSINESS AND ECONOMICS — Abstracting, Bibliographies, Statistics*

AUSTRALIA. BUREAU OF STATISTICS. INFORMATION PAPER: MEASURING EMPLOYMENT AND UNEMPLOYMENT. see *BUSINESS AND ECONOMICS — Abstracting, Bibliographies, Statistics*

AUSTRALIA. BUREAU OF STATISTICS. LABOUR COSTS, AUSTRALIA. see *BUSINESS AND ECONOMICS — Abstracting, Bibliographies, Statistics*

AUSTRALIA. BUREAU OF STATISTICS. LABOUR FORCE, AUSTRALIA. see *BUSINESS AND ECONOMICS — Abstracting, Bibliographies, Statistics*

AUSTRALIA. BUREAU OF STATISTICS. LABOUR FORCE, AUSTRALIA, PRELIMINARY. see *BUSINESS AND ECONOMICS — Abstracting, Bibliographies, Statistics*

AUSTRALIA. BUREAU OF STATISTICS. LABOUR STATISTICS IN BRIEF, AUSTRALIA. see *BUSINESS AND ECONOMICS — Abstracting, Bibliographies, Statistics*

AUSTRALIA. BUREAU OF STATISTICS. NEW SOUTH WALES OFFICE. THE LABOUR FORCE, NEW SOUTH WALES AND AUSTRALIAN CAPITAL TERRITORY. see *BUSINESS AND ECONOMICS — Abstracting, Bibliographies, Statistics*

AUSTRALIA. BUREAU OF STATISTICS. QUEENSLAND OFFICE. LABOUR FORCE, QUEENSLAND. see *BUSINESS AND ECONOMICS — Abstracting, Bibliographies, Statistics*

AUSTRALIA. BUREAU OF STATISTICS. TRAINING AND EDUCATION EXPERIENCE, AUSTRALIA. see *BUSINESS AND ECONOMICS — Abstracting, Bibliographies, Statistics*

354.940   AT   ISSN 1032-7266
HD5850
AUSTRALIA. DEPARTMENT OF INDUSTRIAL RELATIONS. ANNUAL REPORT. 1988. a. Australian Government Publishing Service, P.O. Box 84, Canberra A.C.T. 2601, Australia. TEL 61-6-295-4411. FAX 61-6-295-4455. TELEX AA62013.
   Supersedes in part (1983-1987): Australia. Department of the Special Minister of State. Annual Report (ISSN 0812-2113)

331   AT   ISSN 0311-6336
AUSTRALIAN BULLETIN OF LABOUR. 1974. q. Aus.$48 (foreign Aus.$53) for new subcsr.; renewal Aus.$60 (foreign Aus.$65) (effective 1997 & 1998). National Institute of Labour Studies, Inc., c/o Flinders University of South Australia, G.P.O. Box 2100, Adelaide, S.A. 5001, Australia. TEL 61-8-201-2642. FAX 61-8-276-9060. TELEX AA 89624 FLINDU. E-mail: lesley.johnson@flinders.edu.au. Ed. Leslie Johnson. adv.; bibl.; charts; stat. circ. 960. (back issues avail.) **Indexed:** Aus.P.AIS., C.I.J.E., Int.Lab.Doc., J.of Econ.Lit. **Document type:** bulletin.
—BLDSC (1798.093500); UnCover.
   Description: Provides a forum for the discussion of issues, policies and developments as they affect the Australian labour market.

AUSTRALIAN EMPLOYMENT LAW GUIDE. see *LAW — Corporate Law*

AUSTRALIAN EMPLOYMENT LEGISLATION. see *LAW — Corporate Law*

331   AT
AUSTRALIAN ENTERPRISE BARGAINING MANUAL. 1992. q. C C H Australia Ltd., P.O. Box 230, North Ryde, N.S.W. 2113, Australia. TEL 61-1-300300224. FAX 61-1-300306224. (looseleaf format)
   Description: Provides an overview of enterprise bargaining in Australia and the steps involved in the bargaining process. Includes documents for registration, a model agreement, sample clauses and case studies.

331   AT   ISSN 1328-1143
AUSTRALIAN JOURNAL OF LABOUR ECONOMICS. 1989. s-a. Aus.$30 (foreign Aus.$35) (effective 1997). Centre for Labour Market Research, Curtin University of Technology, Bentley West, W.A. 6102, Australia. TEL 61-9-3512871. FAX 61-9-3512872. E-mail: maddenp@cbs.curtin.edu.au. Eds. Keith Norris, Charles Mulvey. bk.rev. (back issues avail.) **Document type:** consumer publication.
—UnCover.
   Formerly: Labour Economics and Productivity (ISSN 1033-4882)
   Refereed Serial

AUSTRALIAN JOURNAL OF LABOUR LAW. see *LAW — Corporate Law*

AUSTRALIAN LABOUR LAW REPORTER. see *LAW — Corporate Law*

331   AT
AUSTRALIAN WORKERS COMPENSATION GUIDE. (In 3 vols.) 1984. 10/yr. C C H Australia Ltd., P.O. Box 230, North Ryde, N.S.W. 2113, Australia. TEL 61-1-300300224. FAX 61-1-300306224. (looseleaf format)
   Description: Discusses employer and employee rights and obligations. Each jurisdiction is covered with full text legislation.

AVANCE DE INFORMACION ECONOMICA. EMPLEO. see *BUSINESS AND ECONOMICS — Abstracting, Bibliographies, Statistics*

AVERAGE ANNUAL PAY BY STATE AND INDUSTRY. see *BUSINESS AND ECONOMICS — Economic Situation And Conditions*

BUSINESS AND ECONOMICS — LABOR AND INDUSTRIAL RELATIONS

331   CN   ISSN 0715-2574
HD6523
B C LABOUR DIRECTORY. 1973; N.S. 1983. a. Can.$9.25. Ministry of Skills, Training & Labour, Parliament Bldgs., Victoria, BC V8V 1X4, Canada. TEL 604-387-1776. (Subscr. to: Crown Publications, 546 Yates St., Victoria, BC V8W 1K8, Canada. TEL 604-386-4636) Ed. Patrick Stanton. circ. 600. **Document type:** directory, government publication.
  Formerly: Labour Directory (Victoria) (ISSN 0702-0759)
  Description: Compiles information on membership and officials of collective bargaining organizations in British Columbia.

B L S REPORTS ON EMPLOYEE BENEFITS IN THE UNITED STATES. (U.S. Bureau of Labor Statistics) see BUSINESS AND ECONOMICS — Economic Situation And Conditions

B L S UPDATE. (U.S. Bureau of Labor Statistics) see BUSINESS AND ECONOMICS — Economic Situation And Conditions

331   US   ISSN 1067-7356
HD6500
B N A (YEAR) SOURCEBOOK ON COLLECTIVE BARGAINING AND EMPLOYEE RELATIONS. a. $95. The Bureau of National Affairs, Inc., 1231 25th St., N.W., Washington, DC 20037. TEL 202-452-4200. FAX 202-822-8092. TELEX 285656 BNAI WSH. E-mail: http://www.bna.com/ (Subscr. to: 9435 Key West Ave., Rockville MD 20850. TEL 800-372-1033)
  —CCC.
  Formerly: Briefing Sessions on Collective Bargaining and Employee Relations.
  Description: Provides labor relations and human resources practitioners with up-to-date information on where workforce and workplace issues are headed.

331.2   US   ISSN 1069-5117
HD7106.U5
B N A PENSION & BENEFITS REPORTER. 1974. w. $868. The Bureau of National Affairs, Inc., 1231 25th St., N.W., Washington, DC 20037. TEL 202-452-4200. FAX 202-822-8092. TELEX 285656 BANI WSH. URL: http://www.bna.com/. (Subscr. to: 9435 Key West Ave., Rockville, MD 20850. TEL 800-372-1033) Ed. David A. Sayer. (looseleaf format; also avail. in microform from UMI; back issues avail.) **Indexed:** L.I.I., P.I.I.I.
  ●Also available online. Vendor(s): Human Resources Information Network (CDD, HDD), Lexis-Nexis (PENSN), West Group (BNA-PEN).
  —CCC.
  Formerly (until vol.20, no.20, 1993): B N A Pension Reporter (ISSN 0095-7100)
  Description: Covers latest pension developments stemming from the passage of ERISA and its amendments, plus pension and welfare benefit regulations, standards, enforcement actions, court decisions, legislative and administrative actions, agency options, and employee benefit trust fund requirements.

331.2 658.3   US   ISSN 0279-5418
KF3315
B N A POLICY AND PRACTICE SERIES. COMPENSATION. (Subseries of: B N A Policy and Practice Series (ISSN 0005-3228)) 1952. w. $683. The Bureau of National Affairs, Inc., 1231 25th St., N.W., Washington, DC 20037. TEL 202-452-4200. FAX 202-822-8092. TELEX 285656 BNAI WSH. URL: http://www.bna.com/. (Subscr. to: 9435 Key West Ave., Rockville, MD 20850. TEL 800-372-1033) Ed. Bill L. Manville. (looseleaf format; back issues avail.) **Document type:** newsletter.
  ●Also available online. Vendor(s): Human Resources Information Network.
  —CCC.
  Formerly (until 1981): Payroll Compensation (ISSN 0149-2705)
  Description: Covers the compensation field, including guidelines on setting up and maintaining a balanced compensation program. Offers many examples of compensation policies, benefit plans, and special pay practices.

440   US   ISSN 0149-2683
KF3315
B N A POLICY AND PRACTICE SERIES. FAIR EMPLOYMENT PRACTICES. (Subseries of: B N A Policy and Practice Series (ISSN 0005-3228)) 1965. w. $1280 (effective July 1995). The Bureau of National Affairs, Inc., 1231 25th St., N.W., Washington, DC 20037. TEL 202-452-4200. FAX 202-822-8092. TELEX 285656 BNAI WSH. URL: http://www.bna.com/. (Subscr. to: 9435 Key West Ave., Rockville, MD 20850. TEL 800-372-1033) Ed. Bill L. Manville. (looseleaf format; back issues avail.) **Document type:** newsletter.
  ●Also available online. Vendor(s): Human Resources Information Network, Knight-Ridder Information, Inc.
  —CCC.
  Description: Provides a notification and reference covering developments affecting fair employment practices. Includes federal laws, orders and regulations; policy guides and discussions of federal court decisions; and state and local fair employment practice laws.

331   US   ISSN 0149-2713
KF3315
B N A POLICY AND PRACTICE SERIES. LABOR RELATIONS. (Subseries of: B N A Policy and Practice Series (ISSN 0005-3228)) bi-w. $683. The Bureau of National Affairs, Inc., 1231 25th St., N.W., Washington, DC 20037. TEL 202-452-4200. FAX 202-822-8092. TELEX 285656 BNAI WSH. URL: http://www.bna.com/. (Subscr. to: 9435 Key West Ave., Rockville, MD 20850. TEL 800-372-1033) Ed. Bill L. Manville. (looseleaf format; back issues avail.) **Document type:** newsletter.
  ●Also available online. Vendor(s): Human Resources Information Network.
  —CCC.
  Description: Covers federal and state labor laws, including explanations of arbitration, NLRB and court decisions, and state board rulings. Reference materials cover many labor relations concerns: layoffs, strikes, grievances, and collective bargaining.

331.2   US   ISSN 0149-2691
KF3315
B N A POLICY AND PRACTICE SERIES. WAGES AND HOURS. (Subseries of: B N A Policy and Practice Series (ISSN 0005-3228)) 1938. bi-w. $432. The Bureau of National Affairs, Inc., 1231 25th St., N.W., Washington, DC 20037. TEL 202-452-4200. FAX 202-822-8092. TELEX 285656 BNAI WSH. E-mail: http://www.bna.com/ (Subscr. to: 9435 Key West Ave., Rockville, MD 20850) Ed. Bill L. Manville. (looseleaf format; back issues avail.)
  —CCC.

331.88   US   ISSN 1084-8584
HD6971.5
B N A'S COLLECTIVE BARGAINING BULLETIN; a biweekly review of contract negotiation and administration. 1945-1995 (Dec.); resumed 1996. bi-w. $225. The Bureau of National Affairs, Inc., 1231 25th St., N.W., Washington, DC 20037. TEL 202-452-4200. FAX 202-822-8092. TELEX 285656 BNAI WSH. URL: http://www.bna.com/. (Subscr. to: 9435 Key West Ave., Rockville, MD 20850. TEL 800-372-1033) Ed. Leslie Goldman. (back issues avail.) **Document type:** newsletter.
  ●Also available online. Vendor(s): Human Resources Information Network (File DD).
  —CCC.
  Formerly (until Jan. 1996): What's New in Collective Bargaining Negotiations and Contracts (ISSN 0190-5244)
  Description: Presents current developments in collective bargaining, including contract settlements, bargaining techniques and trends, and contract interpretations by the courts, administrative agencies, and arbitrators.

331   US
▼**B N A'S EMPLOYEE BENEFITS LIBRARY ON C D.** 1995. m. $2450. The Bureau of National Affairs, Inc., 1231 25th St., N.W., Washington, DC 20037. TEL 202-452-4200. FAX 202-822-8092. TELEX 285656 BNAI WSH. URL: http://www.bna.com/. (Subscr. to: 9435 Key West Ave., Rockville, MD 20850. TEL 800-372-1033) Ed. Chris Cosby.
  ●Available only on CD-ROM.
  Description: Contains tax management's compensation planning portfolios, BNA's employee benefits cases, the ABA-BNA employee benefits law treatise, BNA's compensation and benefits guide, IRS and treasury regulations, federal statutes, IRS documents, federal agency opinion letters, and more than 150 IRS, DOL, SEC, SSA and PBGC interactive forms and instructions.

331.1   US   ISSN 0739-3016
HD8051
B N A'S EMPLOYEE RELATIONS WEEKLY. (Supplement avail.: Workforce Strategies (ISSN 1062-8991)) 1983. w. $796 includes suppl. The Bureau of National Affairs, Inc., 1231 25th St., N.W., Washington, DC 20037. TEL 202-452-4200. FAX 202-822-8092. TELEX 285656 BNAI WSH. URL: http://www.bna.com/. (Subscr. to: 9435 Key West Ave., Rockville, MD 20850. TEL 800-372-1033) Ed. Jeff Day. (looseleaf format; back issues avail.)
  ●Also available online. Vendor(s): Human Resources Information Network (Files CDD, HDD).
  —CCC.
  Description: Gives an overview of the developments influencing employee relations in both private and public sectors, with information on EEO policy, federal and state legislative and regulatory actions, NLRB actions, federal and state court decisions, and the impact of foreign competition.

331   US   ISSN 1051-4775
B N A'S WORKERS' COMPENSATION REPORT. 1990. bi-w. $490. The Bureau of National Affairs, Inc., 1231 25th St., N.W., Washington, DC 20037. TEL 202-452-4200. FAX 202-822-8092. TELEX 285656 BNAI WSH. URL: http://www.bna.com/. (Subscr. to: 9435 Key West Ave., Rockville, MD 20850. TEL 800-372-1033) Ed. Jeff Day. index. (back issues avail.)
  ●Also available online. Vendor(s): Human Resources Information Network (File DD).
  —CCC.
  Description: Provides comprehensive coverage of national and state workers' compensation developments. Includes information on legal, legislative, and industry developments, actions, and trends related to workers' compensation.

B W C NEWS. see INSURANCE

331   UK   ISSN 0143-2680
BARGAINING REPORT. 1979. 11/yr. £35. (Labour Research Department) L R D Publications Ltd., 78 Blackfriars Rd., London SE1 8HF, England. TEL 071-928-3649. FAX 071-928-0621. Ed. S. Peck. circ. 2,500. (back issues avail.) **Indexed:** C.I.S. Abstr.
  —BLDSC (1863.627000).
  Incorporates (in 1983): L R D Book of Wage Rates, Hours and Holidays (ISSN 0262-3447)

331   GW   ISSN 0342-3875
BEIHEFTE ZUR INTERNATIONALEN WISSENSCHAFTLICHEN KORRESPONDENZ ZUR GESCHICHTE DER DEUTSCHEN ARBEITERBEWEGUNG. 1973. irreg. price varies. (Historische Kommission zu Berlin) Colloquium Verlag, Luetzowstr. 105, 10785 Berlin, Germany. Ed. Peter Loesche. circ. 1,000.

BELGIUM. HOGE RAAD VOOR DE MIDDENSTAND. JAARVERSLAG VAN DE SECRETARIS GENERAAL. see PUBLIC ADMINISTRATION

331.11   BE
BELGIUM. OFFICE NATIONAL DE L'EMPLOI. BULLETIN MENSUEL. 1970. m. 3500 BEF (effective 1997). Office National de l'Emploi, Direction Statistiques-Etudes-Information, Bd. de l'Empereur 1000 Brussels, Belgium. TEL 32-2-5154860. FAX 32-2-5141106. Ed. Karel Baeck. R&P contact: Dirk De Bie. charts; stat. circ. 2,000. **Indexed:** P.A.I.S.For.Lang.Ind. **Document type:** government publication.

BUSINESS AND ECONOMICS — LABOR AND INDUSTRIAL RELATIONS

331   BE
BELGIUM. OFFICE NATIONAL DE L'EMPLOI. COMMUNIQUE MENSUEL. m. 310 BEF (effective 1996). Office National de l'Emploi, Bd. de l'Empereur 7, 1000 Brussels, Belgium. TEL 32-2-5154860. FAX 32-2-5141106. Ed. Karel Baeck. R&P contact: Dirk De Bie. **Document type:** government publication.
    Formerly: Belgium. Office National de l'Emploi. Communique Bimensuel.

331   BE
BELGIUM. OFFICE NATIONAL DE L'EMPLOI. ETUDES ECONOMIQUES ET SOCIALES. 1935. a. 600 BEF (effective 1995). Office National de l'Emploi, Bd. de l'Empereur 7, 1000 Brussels, Belgium. TEL 32-2-5154860. FAX 32-2-5141106. Ed. Karel Baeck. R&P contact: Dirk De Bie. circ. 3,000. **Document type:** government publication.
    Incorporates: Belgium. Office National de l'Emploi. Rapport Annuel (ISSN 0067-5644)

BENEFITS & COMPENSATION INTERNATIONAL. see INSURANCE

BENEFITS & COMPENSATION UPDATE. see BUSINESS AND ECONOMICS — Personnel Management

331.2 368   CN   ISSN 0703-7732
BENEFITS CANADA. 1977. 11/yr. Can.$75 (foreign Can.$150) (effective 1997). Maclean-Hunter Publishing Ltd., Business Publication Division, 777 Bay St., Toronto, ON M5W 1A7, Canada. TEL 416-596-5000. FAX 416-596-5071. Ed. Lori Bak; Pub. Paul Williams. adv. contact: Alison Webb. circ. 139,536. (also avail. in microform from MML) **Indexed:** Can.B.P.I.
    —BLDSC (1891.469000). **CCC.**
    Description: News and trends in Canada's pension fund investment and employee benefits industry.

344.730189   US   ISSN 1067-7666
K9
BERKELEY JOURNAL OF EMPLOYMENT AND LABOR LAW. 1976. s-a. $34 to individuals (foreign $38); institutions $40 (foreign $44) (effective July 1997). (University of California at Berkeley, Boalt Hall School of Law) University of California Press, Journals Division, 2120 Berkeley Way, No. 5812, Berkeley, CA 94720-5812. TEL 510-643-7154. FAX 510-642-9917. E-mail: journal@ucop.edu; URL: http://library.berkeley.edu:8080/ucalpress/journals. adv.: B&W page $275; adv. contact: Marge Dean. bk.rev.; index; circ. 700 (paid). (also avail. in microform from UMI; microfilm from RRI; microfilm from WSH; back issues avail.; reprint service avail. from UMI,WSH) **Indexed:** ABI Inform., Abstr.Bk.Rev.Curr.Leg.Per., ASSIA, BPIA, Bus.Ind., C.L.I., Crim.Just.Abstr., Curr.Cont., L.R.I., Leg.Cont., Leg.Per., P.A.I.S., SSCI. **Document type:** academic/scholarly publication.
    ●Also available online. Vendor(s): Information Access Co.
    —BLDSC (1940.348000); KR SourceOne; UMI; UnCover. **CCC.**
    Formerly (until 1993): Industrial Relations Law Journal (ISSN 0145-188X)
    Description: Covers the full range of employment and labor law.
    Refereed Serial

BIBLIOGRAFIA DE POLITICA INDUSTRIAL. see BUSINESS AND ECONOMICS — Abstracting, Bibliographies, Statistics

BIBLIOGRAPHIE ZUR GESCHICHTE DER DEUTSCHEN ARBEITERBEWEGUNG. see HISTORY — History Of Europe

331.1   US   ISSN 0045-2238
BLACK NEWS DIGEST. 1971. w. free. U.S. Department of Labor, Office of Information and Public Affairs, Third & Constitution Ave., N.W., Rm. S-1032, Washington, DC 20210. TEL 202-523-7323. Ed. S. Blumenthal. circ. 2,000. (also avail. in microform from UMI; reprint service avail. from UMI) **Indexed:** Ind.U.S.Gov.Per.
    —UMI.

BOLCHEVIQUE. see POLITICAL SCIENCE

331   II   ISSN 0067-9917
BOMBAY LABOUR JOURNAL.* (Text in English) 1960. a. free. Bombay Labour Institute, Dadabhai Chamarbaugwala Rd., Parel, Bombay 12, India. Ed. S.A. Vaidya.

BOTSWANA. CENTRAL STATISTICS OFFICE. LABOUR STATISTICS. see BUSINESS AND ECONOMICS — Abstracting, Bibliographies, Statistics

331   GW
BRENNPUNKTE DES ARBEITSRECHTS (YEAR). a. DM.78. (Deutscher Anwaltsverein eV.) Verlag fuer die Rechts- und Anwaltspraxis, Eschstr. 22, 44629 Herne, Germany. TEL 49-2323-141-0. FAX 49-2323-141123. **Document type:** bulletin.

331   CN
BRITISH COLUMBIA. LABOUR RELATIONS BOARD. ANNUAL REPORT. 1974. a. Can.$6. Labour Relations Board, 900-360 W. Georgia St., Vancouver, BC V6B 6B2, Canada. TEL 604-660-1300. FAX 604-660-1892. Ed. C. Lyte. stat. circ. 500. **Document type:** government publication.
    Former titles: British Columbia. Industrial Relations Council. Annual Report (ISSN 0838-0899); British Columbia. Labour Relations Board. Annual Report (ISSN 0319-0404)
    Description: Covers the structure of the Board, biographies of O.I.C.'s, statistics of all applications received.

331.2   CN   ISSN 0703-0665
HD8101.5.B74
BRITISH COLUMBIA. MINISTRY OF SKILLS, TRAINING AND LABOUR. NEGOTIATED WORKING CONDITIONS. Key Title: Negociated Working Conditions. (Ministry name varies) a. Can.$35.85. Ministry of Skills, Training and Labour, Victoria, BC V8V 1X4, Canada. TEL 604-387-1776. (Subscr. to: Crown Publications, 546 Yates St., Victoria, BC V8W 1K8, Canada. TEL 604-386-4636) illus.
    Former titles (until 1973): Analysis of Collective Agreements in British Columbia (ISSN 0703-0673); (until 1971): Survey of Collective Bargaining Agreements in British Columbia (ISSN 0701-791X); (until 1968): Survey of Collective Agreements in British Columbia (ISSN 0703-0681)
    Description: Information on the content of major collective agreements covering workers in the province.

331.1 347.9   CN   ISSN 0824-7218
BRITISH COLUMBIA DECISIONS - LABOUR ARBITRATION. 1982. m. Can.$350. Western Legal Publications, 301 One Alexander St., Vancouver, BC V6A 1B2, Canada. TEL 604-687-5671; 800-663-0422. FAX 604-687-2796. E-mail: wlp@mindlink.bc.ca. index. (looseleaf format)
    ●Also available online.
    Description: Digest of labour arbitrations filed with the Ministry of Labour.

346 331   CN
BRITISH COLUMBIA DECISIONS - LABOUR RELATIONS BOARD DIGESTS. m. Can.$299.50. Western Legal Publications, 301-1 Alexander St., Vancouver, BC V6A 1B2, Canada. TEL 604-687-5671; 800-663-0422. FAX 604-687-2796. E-mail: wlp@mindlink.bc.ca. Ed. John Chesko. R&P contact: Nancy Nesbitt. index. (looseleaf format)
    ●Also available online.
    Former titles: British Columbia Decisions - Industrial Relations Council; British Columbia Decisions - Labour Relations Board Decisions (ISSN 0715-5808)
    Description: Provides full summaries of all written and letter decisions of the Industrial Relations Council of British Columbia.

331.1   UK   ISSN 0007-1080
HD6951   CODEN: BJIRAV
BRITISH JOURNAL OF INDUSTRIAL RELATIONS. 1963. q. £92($175) (foreign £111) (effective 1997). (London School of Economics and Political Science) Blackwell Publishers Ltd., 108 Cowley Rd., Oxford OX4 1JF, England. TEL 44-1865-791100. FAX 44-1865-791347. E-mail: jnlinfo@blackwellpublishers.co.uk; URL: http://www.blackwellpublishers.co.uk. Ed. John Kelly. adv.; bk.rev.; bibl.; charts; stat.; index. circ. 2,000. (repint service avail. from SWZ,UMI) **Indexed:** ABI Inform, Arts & Hum.Cit.Ind., ASCA, ASCA, ASSIA, B.P.I., BPIA, Br.Hum.Ind., Bus.Ind., C.R.E.J., Cont.Pg.Manage., Curr.Cont., E.I., IBR, Int.Lab.Doc., Int.Polit.Sci.Abstr., J.of Econ.Lit., Manage.Cont., Mgmt.& Market.Abstr., Mid.East: Abstr.& Ind., P.A.I.S., SCIMP (1978-), SSCI, Work Rel.Abstr., World Bank.Abstr. **Document type:** academic/scholarly publication.
    —BLDSC (2310.500000); Genuine Article; KR SourceOne; SWETS; UMI; UnCover. **CCC.**
    Refereed Serial

BUILDING COST INFORMATION SERVICE. LABOUR, HOURS & WAGES. see BUILDING AND CONSTRUCTION

331   NE   ISSN 0770-3724
K2
BULLETIN OF COMPARATIVE LABOUR RELATIONS. (Text in English) 1975. irreg. (1-2/yr.), no.26, 1993. price varies. (Rijksuniversiteit Te Leuven, Institute for Labour Relations, BE) Kluwer Law International (Subsidiary of: Wolters Kluwer N.V.), Postbus 85889, 2508 CN The Hague, Netherlands. TEL 31-70-3081500. FAX 31-70-3081515. (Dist. by: Libresso Distribution Centre, P.O. Box 23, 7400 GA Deventer, Netherlands. TEL 31-570-633155. FAX 31-570-633834; In N. America: Kluwer Law International, 675 Massachusetts Ave., Cambridge, MA 02139. TEL 617-354-0140. FAX 617-354-8595) Ed. R. Blanpain. **Indexed:** BPIA, Int.Lab.Doc. **Document type:** bulletin.
    —BLDSC (2839.080000).
    Description: Discusses labor relations in various countries at an international level, as well as specific topical issues in labor law and labor relations.

331   FR   ISSN 0242-5874
BULLETIN SOCIAL. vol.9, 1977. m. 382 F. (effective 1997). Editions Francis Lefebvre, 42 rue de Villiers, 92300 Levallois, France. TEL 41-05-22-00. FAX 41-05-22-30.
    Formerly: Bulletin de Documentation Pratique de Securite Sociale et de Legislation du Travail.

331   CN   ISSN 0704-0865
BULLETIN SUR LES RELATIONS DU TRAVAIL. English edition (ISSN 0704-0873) (Editions in English, French) 1969. m. Can.$30 to non-members. Conseil du Patronat du Quebec, 2075 rue University, Ste. 606, Montreal, PQ H3A 2L1, Canada. TEL 514-288-5161. FAX 514-288-5165. Ed.Bd. circ. 1,500. **Document type:** bulletin.

331   GW
BUNDESARBEITSBLATT. 1949. m. DM.210 (effective 1997). (Bundesministerium fuer Arbeit und Sozialordnung) W. Kohlhammer GmbH, Hessbruehlstr. 69, 70565 Stuttgart, Germany. TEL 49-711-7863-1. FAX 49-711-7863263. Ed. Claus J. Schmidt. adv.; bk.rev.; bibl.; charts; stat.; index. circ. 7,500. (reprint service avail.) **Indexed:** C.I.S. Abstr., INIS Atomind., Int.Lab.Doc., P.A.I.S.For.Lang.Ind., World Bibl.Soc.Sec. **Document type:** government publication.
    —BLDSC (2930.105000); SWETS. **CCC.**
    Incorporates (in Jan. 1979): Arbeitsschutz (ISSN 0003-7788); Germany (Federal Republic, 1949-). Bundesministerium Fuer Arbeit und Sozialordnung. Arbeits- und Sozialstatistik; Bundesversorgungsblatt (ISSN 0007-5868)

331   GW   ISSN 0407-9132
BUNDESVERSORGUNGSBLATT. (Supplement to: Bundesarbeitsblatt (ISSN 0007-5868)) 1951. 5/yr. DM.64 (effective 1997). (Bundesministerium fuer Arbeit und Sozialordnung) W. Kohlhammer GmbH, Hessbruehlstr. 69, 70565 Stuttgart, Germany. TEL 49-711-7863290. FAX 49-711-7863430. **Document type:** government publication.

BUSINESS ORGANIZATIONS: PENSION AND PROFIT-SHARING PLANS. see LAW — Corporate Law

BUTTERWORTHS EMPLOYMENT LAW BULLETIN. see LAW — Corporate Law

C B I A NEWS. (Connecticut Business and Industry Association) see BUSINESS AND ECONOMICS — Economic Situation And Conditions

C I R NEWS. (Committee of Interns and Residents) see MEDICAL SCIENCES

331.8   NE   ISSN 0925-8787
C N V - OPINIE. 1947. 8/yr. fl.30 to non-members; members fl.15 (effective 1998). Christelijk Nationaal Vakverbond (C.N.V.), Postbus 2475, 3500 GL Utrecht, Netherlands. TEL 31-30-2913646. FAX 31-30-2913774. Ed. Mariche v. Dommele; Pub. Willem Tlooglugrt. adv. contact: Casoline v. Amerongen. bk.rev.; charts; stat. circ. 15,000. **Indexed:** Key to Econ.Sci.
    —SWETS.
    Formerly (until 1991): Evangelie en Maatschappij (ISSN 0014-3383)
    Description: Covers social and economic topics of interest to labor union members.

BUSINESS AND ECONOMICS — LABOR AND INDUSTRIAL RELATIONS

331.1   US   ISSN 0194-3073
JK8755
C P E R. (California Public Employee Relations) 1969. bi-m. $250 (effective 1995). University of California at Berkeley, Institute of Industrial Relations, Berkeley, CA 94720. TEL 510-643-7092. FAX 510-642-6432. Ed. Carol Vendrillo. bk.rev.; index, cum.index; circ. 1,000 (paid). **Document type:** trade publication.

331.1   US
CALIFORNIA. DEPARTMENT OF INDUSTRIAL RELATIONS. BIENNIAL REPORT. Key Title: Biennial Report for the Department of Industrial Relations. 1883. biennial. Department of Industrial Relations, Box 420603, San Francisco, CA 94142. TEL 415-703-4981. Ed. Richard Stephens. illus. **Document type:** government publication.
    Formerly: California. Department of Industrial Relations. Annual Report (ISSN 0362-4129)

331.1   US   ISSN 0362-4110
HD6274.C3
CALIFORNIA. DEPARTMENT OF THE YOUTH AUTHORITY. AFFIRMATIVE ACTION STATISTICS; report. Key Title: Affirmative Action Statistics. 1974. s-a, latest July, 1983. free. Department of the Youth Authority, 4241 Williamsbourgh Dr., Sacramento, CA 95823. TEL 916-445-9962. illus.

CALIFORNIA COMPENSATION CASES. see *LAW*

331.86   US   ISSN 0098-1435
HD5725.C2
CALIFORNIA EMPLOYER. 1937. q. free. Employment Development Department, 800 Capitol Mall, MIC 84, Sacramento, CA 95814. TEL 916-654-7079. FAX 916-654-5843. Ed. Kevin Callori. illus. circ. 800,000. **Indexed:** Br.Ceram.Abstr., Build.Manage.Abstr., Cal.Per.Ind. (1986-), Mgmt.& Market.Abstr. **Document type:** newsletter, government publication.
    Former titles (until 1974): Employment News; (until 1969): H R D Newsletter to Employers; H R D News (ISSN 0017-6214)

331   US   ISSN 1058-4293
CALIFORNIA EMPLOYER ADVISOR. 1991. m. $167. Employer Resource Institute, Inc., 98 Main St., Ste. 700, Tiburon, CA 94920. TEL 415-435-9360. Ed. Larry J. Shapiro. index. (back issues avail.) **Document type:** newsletter.
    Description: Award-winning guide to employment law and employee relations.

331   US
CALIFORNIA EMPLOYERS' GUIDE TO EMPLOYEE HANDBOOKS AND PERSONNEL POLICY MANUALS. 1989. base vol. with a. supplements. $100. (Morrison & Foerster) Matthew Bender & Co., Inc., 2 Park Ave., New York, NY 10016. TEL 212-448-2000. E-mail: international@bender.com; URL: http://www.bender.com. (looseleaf format)
    Description: Complete guide to writing, revising and updating employee handbooks and personnel policy manuals. Includes checklists, sample clauses, authority and cross references to California Employment Law.

331   US   ISSN 1062-5054
CALIFORNIA EMPLOYMENT LAW. (Issued in 4 vols. with supplements) 1989. m. $495. Matthew Bender & Co., Inc., 2 Park Ave., New York, NY 10016. TEL 212-448-2000. E-mail: international@bender.com; URL: http://www.bender.com. Ed. Judy Freeman. (looseleaf format)
    Description: Provides a comprehensive treatment of California law governing employer-employee relations in the private sector. Includes in-depth discussion of the law, practice tips from experienced employment law practitioners, factual illustrations, sample employment documents, and litigation forms.

CALIFORNIA EMPLOYMENT LAW MONITOR. see *LAW*

331   US
KFC557.A15C3
CALIFORNIA LABOR AND EMPLOYMENT ALERT NEWSLETTER. 1982. bi-m. $75 (with binder $88). Castle Publications Ltd., Box 580, Van Nuys, CA 91408. TEL 818-708-3208. Ed. Richard Simmons. adv. contact: Elliot Berk. index. (looseleaf format) **Document type:** newsletter.
    Formerly: California Labor and Employment Alert for All California Employers.
    Description: Provides summaries of significant developments in labor and personal laws.

CALIFORNIA LABOR MARKET BULLETIN. see *BUSINESS AND ECONOMICS — Economic Situation And Conditions*

CALIFORNIA LAW OF EMPLOYEE INJURIES AND WORKMEN'S COMPENSATION. see *LAW*

306.38   US
CALIFORNIA PUBLIC EMPLOYEES' RETIREMENT LAW. a. $25. Michie, A Division of Reed Elsevier Inc., Box 7587, Charlottesville, VA 22906-7587. TEL 804-972-7566; 800-562-1197. FAX 800-643-1280. E-mail: custserv@michie.com; URL: http://www.michie.com. Ed. George Harley. pp./issue: 570.

CALIFORNIA WORKERS' COMPENSATION REPORTER. see *LAW*

CAMARA PANAMENA DE LA CONSTRUCCION. PRESTACIONES LABORALES EN LA CONSTRUCCION. see *BUILDING AND CONSTRUCTION*

331 301   UK
CAMBRIDGE STUDIES IN WORK AND SOCIAL INEQUALITY. irreg. U C L Press Ltd., 1 Gunpowder Sq., London EC4A 3DE, England. TEL 44-171-380-7707. FAX 44-171-413-8392. Ed.Bd. adv. contact: Tina Jeavons. **Document type:** monographic series.

330   UK
CAMBRIDGE UNIVERSITY. DEPARTMENT OF APPLIED ECONOMICS. PAPERS IN INDUSTRIAL RELATIONS AND LABOUR. 1975. irreg., no.6, 1981. price varies. Cambridge University Press, Edinburgh Bldg., Shaftesbury Rd., Cambridge CB2 2RU, England. TEL 44-1223-312393. FAX 44-1223-315052. TELEX 851817256. E-mail: information@cup.cam.ac.uk; URL: http://www.cup.cam.ac.uk. (N. American addr.: Cambridge University Press, Journals Dept., 40 W. 20th St., New York, NY 10011. TEL 212-924-3900. FAX 212-691-3239) R&P contact: Linda Nicol. **Document type:** monographic series.

331.11   CN
CANADA. LABOUR CANADA. ANNUAL REPORT ON PROCEEDINGS UNDER THE CANADA LABOUR CODE, PART 3 (LABOUR STANDARDS)/CANADA. LABOUR CANADA. RAPPORT ANNUEL SUR LES MESURES PRISES EN VERTU DU CODE CANADIEN DU TRAVAIL, PARTIE 3 (LES NORMES DU TRAVAIL). 1972. a. free. Labour Canada, Publications Distribution, Ottawa, ON K1A 0J2, Canada. TEL 819-994-0543. FAX 819-997-1664. circ. 700.

331   CN
CANADA. LABOUR CANADA. FEDERAL MEDIATION AND CONCILIATION SERVICE. ANNUAL REPORT ON PROCEEDINGS UNDER THE CANADA LABOUR CODE. PART 1/CANADA. LABOUR CANADA. SERVICE FEDERAL DE MEDIATION ET DE CONCILIATION. RAPPORT DES ACTIVITES ENTREPRISES EN VERTU DU CODE CANADIEN DU TRAVAIL. PARTIE 1. (Text in English, French) a. free. Labour Canada, Publications Distribution, Ottawa, ON K1A 0J2, Canada. TEL 819-994-0543. FAX 819-997-1664. TELEX 819-997-3453. circ. 1,000. **Document type:** government publication.
    Description: Review of activities under the dispute resolution provisions of the code.

331.2   CN   ISSN 0848-6433
HD4977
CANADA. LABOUR CANADA. MAJOR WAGE SETTLEMENTS - GRANDS REGLEMENTS SALARIAUX. (Catalog no. L12-19) 1976. q. Can.$60 (foreign $72). Supply and Services Canada, Publishing Center, Ottawa, ON K1A 0S9, Canada. TEL 819-956-4802.
    Formerly (until 1984): Canada. Labour Canada. Labour Data (ISSN 0228-1678)
    Description: News on base rate increases from major collective bargaining settlements during the quarter, includes the construction industry.

331.4 340   CN
CANADA. LABOUR CANADA. WOMEN'S BUREAU. WOMEN IN THE LABOUR FORCE. French edition: Canada. Bureau de la Main-d'Oeuvre Feminine. Les Femmes dans la Population Active. 1964. irreg. Can.$40($48) (foreign $56) (effective 1998). Statistics Canada, Operations and Integration Division, Circulation Management, Jean Talon Bldg., 2-C12, Tunney's Pasture, Ottawa, ON K1A 0T6, Canada. TEL 613-951-7277; 800-267-6677. FAX 613-951-1584. URL: http://www.statcan.ca. (also avail. in microform from MML)
    Former titles: Canada. Women's Bureau. Women in the Labour Force. Facts and Figures (ISSN 0382-2192); (until 1979): Canada. Women's Bureau. Facts and Figures. Women in the Labour Force (ISSN 0068-7448)
    Description: Describes trends related to women's participation in the labour force.

CANADA. STATISTICS CANADA. PUBLIC SECTOR EMPLOYMENT AND WAGES AND SALARIES/CANADA. STATISTIQUE CANADA. EMPLOI ET SALAIRES ET TRAITEMENTS DANS LE SECTEUR PUBLIQUE. see *BUSINESS AND ECONOMICS — Abstracting, Bibliographies, Statistics*

340   CN
CANADA LABOUR ARBITRATION. base vol. (plus s-a. updates). Can.$240 (effective 1997). Canada Law Book Inc., 240 Edward St., Aurora, ON L4G 3S9, Canada. TEL 905-841-6472; 800-263-2037. FAX 905-841-5085. Eds. Donald J.M. Brown, David M. Beatty. adv. contact: Mary Powell. **Document type:** trade publication.

331 340   CN
CANADA LABOUR RELATIONS BOARD; an annotated guide. base vol. (plus irreg. updates). Can.$173 (includes binder) (effective 1997). Canada Law Book Inc., 240 Edward St., Aurora, ON L4G 3S9, Canada. TEL 905-841-6472; 800-263-2037. FAX 905-841-5085. Ed. Graham J. Clarke. adv. contact: Mary Powell. (looseleaf format) **Document type:** trade publication.

CANADIAN CONSTRUCTION LABOUR AND EMPLOYMENT LAW. see *LAW — Civil Law*

CANADIAN EMPLOYMENT LAW FOR U.S. COMPANIES. see *LAW*

331.1   CN   ISSN 0045-4966
CANADIAN INDUSTRIAL RELATIONS AND PERSONNEL DEVELOPMENTS. 1969. s-m. Can.$475. C C H Canadian Ltd., 6 Garamond Ct., North York, ON M3C 1Z5, Canada. TEL 416-441-2992; 800-268-4522. FAX 416-444-9011. bk.rev.; abstr.; bibl.; charts; stat.; index. (looseleaf format) **Document type:** trade publication.
    Description: Reports major developments in industrial relations and personnel management. Presents Canadian economic indicators of the labor market.

340 331   CN   ISSN 0831-7348
CANADIAN LABOUR ARBITRATION SUMMARIES. 1986. w. Can.$450 (includes binder) (effective 1997). Canada Law Book Inc., 240 Edward St., Aurora, ON L4G 3S9, Canada. TEL 905-841-6472; 800-263-2037. FAX 905-841-5085. Eds. P.J. Barnacle, E.B. Willis. (looseleaf format; back issues avail.) **Document type:** trade publication.

BUSINESS AND ECONOMICS — LABOR AND INDUSTRIAL RELATIONS

340 331   CN   ISSN 0008-4328
CANADIAN LABOUR LAW REPORTER. 1946. s-m. Can.$775. C C H Canadian Ltd., 6 Garamond Ct., North York, ON M3C 1Z5, Canada. TEL 416-441-2992; 800-268-4522. FAX 416-444-9011. (looseleaf format; back issues avail.) Document type: trade publication.
—CCC.
Description: Federal and provincial laws on employer-employee relations, fair wages, vacations, statutory holidays, hours of work, industrial standards, fair employment practices. Outlines unemployment insurance and worker's compensation law.

347.9 331   CN   ISSN 0317-0535
KE3146.4
CANADIAN LABOUR RELATIONS BOARD REPORTS. (Second series) a. (in 8 parts and 4 vols.). Can.$648. Butterworths Canada Ltd., Part of the Reed Elsevier group, 75 Clegg Rd., Markham, ON L6G 1A1, Canada. TEL 905-479-2665. FAX 905-479-2826. Document type: trade publication.
Description: Presents the decisions of the federal and various provincial labour relations boards.

331   UK
CENTRAL LONDON SALARY SURVEY. 2/yr. £250 (effective 1997). The Reward Group Ltd., Reward House, Diamond Way, Stone Business Park, Stone, Staffordshire ST15 0SD, England. TEL 44-1785-813566. FAX 44-1785-817007. E-mail: 101364.661@compuserve.com. Document type: bulletin.
Description: Pay and benefit salary survey for Central London.

331   UK
CENTRAL SCOTLAND SALARY SURVEY. 2/yr. £250 (effective 1997). The Reward Group Ltd., Reward House, Diamond Way, Stone Business Park, Stone, Staffordshire ST15 0SD, England. TEL 44-1785-813566. FAX 44-1785-817007. E-mail: 101364.661@compuserve.com. Document type: bulletin.
Description: Pay and benefit survey for Central Scotland covering the Tayside, Central Fife, Lothian and Strathclyde areas.

331.11   PY   ISSN 1017-6055
CENTRO DE DOCUMENTACION Y ESTUDIOS. INFORMATIVO LABORAL. 1987. m. $60. Centro de Documentacion y Estudios, Pai Perez 737, Asuncion, Paraguay. (Dist. by: D.I.P.P., Box 2507, Asuncion, Paraguay) Ed. Roberto Villalba. circ. 1,000.

331   AT   ISSN 1038-0515
CHAMBER OF COMMERCE & INDUSTRY OF WESTERN AUSTRALIA BUSINESS REPORT. Short title: C C I Business Report. 1979. m. Aus.$30. Chamber of Commerce & Industry of Western Australia, P.O. Box 6892, Hay St. East, Perth, W. A. 6000, Australia. TEL 61-9-4217555. Ed. R. Pride. adv.; bk.rev. circ. 7,000. Document type: trade publication.
Former titles (until 1992): Confederation of Western Australian Industry. Confederation Report (ISSN 0810-1442); (until 1978): Industrial News.
Description: Information on latest developments in Western Australian business and industry.

331 360   UK   ISSN 1357-7921
CHARITIES REWARDS. 1990. a. £250 (effective 1997). The Reward Group Ltd., Reward House, Diamond Way, Stone Business Park, Stone, Staffordshire ST15 0SD, England. TEL 44-1785-813566. FAX 44-1785-817007. E-mail: 101364.661@compuserve.com. Document type: bulletin.
Formerly (until 1994): Charity Salary Survey (ISSN 0962-6158)
Description: Provides pay and benefits information for the voluntary sector.

331   US
CHECKOFF (TALLAHASSEE). irreg. (3-4/yr.). membership. Florida Bar, Labor and Employment Law Section, 650 Apalachee Pkwy., Tallahassee, FL 32399-3200. TEL 904-561-5631. circ. 1,000. Document type: newsletter.

331   AU
CHEMIEARBEITER. m. Gewerkschaft der Chemiearbeiter, Stumpergasse 60, 1060 Vienna, Austria. TEL 571501.

331.2 378   US
CHIEF EXECUTIVE COMPENSATION AND BENEFITS SURVEY. biennial. $485 to non-members; non-participating members $345; members $225. College and University Personnel Association, 1233 20th St., N.W., Washington, DC 20036. TEL 202-429-0311. FAX 202-429-0149. Indexed: SRI.
Former titles: Compensation, Benefits and Conditions of Employment for College and University Chief Executive Officers; Compensation and Benefits Survey of College and University Chief Executive Officers.
Description: Provides data on chief executive officers, their institutions, salary and other cash compensation, employment policies and practices, and executive benefits and other perquisites.

331.2   UK   ISSN 1353-6729
CITIZENS INCOME BULLETIN. 1984. biennial. £25 (overseas £27) (effective 1995-1997). Citizens Income Trust, Citizens Income Study Centre, St. Philips Bldg., Sheffield St., London WC2A 3EX, England. TEL 44-171-955-7453. FAX 44-171-955-7534. E-mail: citizens-income@rse.ac-uk. Hermione Parker. R&P contact: Carolyn Armstrong. adv. contact: Carolyn Armstrong. bk.rev. circ. 1,000. Document type: bulletin.
—BLDSC (3267.793200).
Formerly (until 1993): B I R G Citizens Income (ISSN 0954-8246)
Description: Presents research and viewpoints on alternatives to the current welfare state that would guarantee everyone at least a small income.

331.1 368   US   ISSN 0364-3603
KF2258.A15
THE CLAIMS FORUM. q. free. American Arbitration Association, 140 W. 51st St., New York, NY 10020-1203. TEL 212-484-4010. FAX 212-541-4841. Ed. Ted Pons. circ. 7,000. Document type: newsletter.
Description: Offers insurance professionals informative articles and advice on alternative dispute resolution.

CLASSIFIED INDEX OF N.L.R.B. AND RELATED COURT DECISIONS. see BUSINESS AND ECONOMICS — Abstracting, Bibliographies, Statistics

331   UK
CLERICAL AND OPERATIVE REWARDS. 2/yr. £210 (effective 1997). The Reward Group Ltd., Reward House, Diamond Way, Stone Business Park, Stone, Staffordshire ST15 0SD, England. TEL 44-1785-813566. FAX 44-1785-817007. E-mail: 101364.661@compuserve.com. Document type: bulletin.
Description: Provides salary data on a wide range of clerical and operative positions.

690 331   US   ISSN 0094-0372
COCKSHAW'S CONSTRUCTION LABOR NEWS & OPINION. 1971. m. $239 (effective 1997). Communications Counselors, Inc., Box 427, Newtown Square, PA 19073. TEL 610-353-0123. FAX 610-353-0111. Ed. Peter A. Cockshaw. R&P contact: Peter A. Cockshaw. bk.rev.; circ. 15,000. (paid). (looseleaf format; back issues avail.) Document type: newsletter.
Former titles: Cockshaw's Construction Capsules; Cockshaw's Open Shop News and Trends; Open Shop News and Trends; Dual Shop News and Trends.
Description: News, trends and analysis of labor-management developments in the construction industry.

331.88   US   ISSN 0010-079X
HD6500
COLLECTIVE BARGAINING NEGOTIATIONS & CONTRACTS. 1945. bi-w. $908. The Bureau of National Affairs, Inc., 1231 25th St., N.W., Washington, DC 20037. TEL 202-452-4200. FAX 202-822-8092. TELEX 285656 BNAI WSH. URL: http://www.bna.com/. (Subscr. to: 9435 Key West Ave., Rockville, MD 20850. TEL 800-372-1033) Ed. Mary P. Dunn. charts; stat.; index. (looseleaf format; back issues avail.) Document type: newsletter.
●Also available online. Vendor(s): Human Resources Information Network, West Group.
—CCC.
Description: Notification and reference service containing information designed to help unions and management prepare, negotiate, and administer contracts.

331.88   CN   ISSN 0010-0803
HD6521
COLLECTIVE BARGAINING REVIEW. French edition: Revue de la Negotiation Collective (ISSN 0705-5072) (Catalog no. L12-13E) 1966. m. Can.$100 (foreign $120). Canada Communication Group, Publishing Division, Ottawa, ON K1A 0S9, Canada. TEL 819-956-4802. Ed. H. Beaufort. circ. 4,200. Indexed: Can.Per.Ind., CS Ind.
Description: Provides details on major collective bargaining developments and summaries of major negotiations in progress.

331.116   US   ISSN 0045-7345
COLLECTIVE BARGAINING SETTLEMENTS IN NEW YORK STATE. 1947. q. $75. Department of Labor, Division of Research and Statistics, 1 Main St., 9th Fl., Brooklyn, NY 11201. TEL 718-797-7722. Ed. Larry Viger. Document type: government publication.

COLLEGE INSTITUTE EDUCATORS' ASSOCIATION. PROFILE. see EDUCATION — Higher Education

331 368.4   CK
COLOMBIA. MINISTERIO DE TRABAJO Y SEGURIDAD SOCIAL. CARTA INFORMATIVA. m. Ministerio de Trabajo y Seguridad Social, Seccion de Biblioteca & Publicaciones, Av. 19, No. 6-68, Of. 806 y 809, Santafe de Bogota, Colombia. TEL 2829769. FAX 2829709. illus. Document type: government publication, newsletter.

331 368.4   CK
COLOMBIA. MINISTERIO DE TRABAJO Y SEGURIDAD SOCIAL. MEMORIA AL CONGRESO NACIONAL. 1967. a. Ministerio de Trabajo y Seguridad Social, Seccion de Biblioteca & Publicaciones, Av. 19, No. 6-68, Of. 806 y 809, Santafe de Bogota, Colombia. Ed. Maria Teresa Forero de Saade.
Supersedes: Colombia. Ministerio de Trabajo, Higiene y Prevision Social. Memoria.

COLORADO EMPLOYMENT LAW LETTER. see LAW

331.1   US
COLORADO LABOR FORCE REVIEW. 1964. m. free. Department of Labor and Employment, 251 E. 12th Ave., Denver, CO 80203. TEL 303-620-4856. Ed. David L. Larson. charts; stat. circ. 2,600. (also avail. in microfiche from CIS) Indexed: SRI. Document type: government publication.
Former titles: Colorado Manpower Review (ISSN 0010-1656); Labor Area Highlights.

331   US   ISSN 0745-6514
THE COMMUNICATOR (ALBANY). 1978. m. membership. New York State Public Employees Federation, 1168-70 Troy-Schenectady Rd., Box 12414, Albany, NY 12212-2414. TEL 518-785-1900. FAX 518-785-1814. Ed. Denyce Duncan Lacy; Pub. James J. Sheedy. R&P contact: Sherry Halbrook. adv. contact: Martha Ekstrom. circ. 60,000. (tabloid format; back issues avail.) Document type: newspaper.
Description: Publishes news and commentary of interest to employees in NY state service.
Refereed Serial

331.1   CN   ISSN 1198-6131
COMPARATIVE INDUSTRIAL RELATIONS NEWSLETTER. 1991. s-a. Can.$25($20) to individuals; institutions Can.$43($35) (effective 1997 & 1998). c/o DeGroote School of Business, McMaster University, Hamilton, ON L8S 4M4, Canada. TEL 905-525-9140. FAX 905-521-8995. E-mail: adamsr@mcmail.cis.mcmaster.ca. Ed. Roy Adams; Pub. Roy Adams. R&P contact: Roy Adams. bk.rev.; circ. 600 (paid). Document type: newsletter.
Description: Intended to foster cross-disciplinary communication among those interested in comparative and international labor issues.

BUSINESS AND ECONOMICS — LABOR AND INDUSTRIAL RELATIONS

347.9   US   ISSN 1043-5255
K3
COMPARATIVE LABOR LAW JOURNAL. 1976. q. $30 (foreign $40). International Society for Labor and Social Security, U.S. National Branch, University of Pennsylvania, Wharton School of Business, 2203 Steinberg-Dietrich Hall, Philadelphia, PA 19104-6369. TEL 215-898-6851. FAX 215-898-2400. Ed. Benjamin Aaron. bk.rev.; abstr.; index. circ. 700. (also avail. in microform from WSH; reprint service avail. from WSH) **Indexed:** Abstr.Bk.Rev.Curr.Leg.Per., BPIA, C.L.I., Int.Lab.Doc., L.R.I., Leg.Per., World Bibl.Soc.Sec. **Document type:** academic/scholarly publication.
—BLDSC (3363.784200); KR SourceOne; SWETS; UnCover.
    Former titles (until 1986): Comparative Labor Law (ISSN 0147-9202); (until 1975): U.S. National Committee. International Society for Labor Law and Social Legislation. Bulletin (ISSN 0146-0234)
    Description: Comparative studies of various aspects of labor, employment, and labor-related matters.

COMPARISON OF STATE UNEMPLOYMENT INSURANCE LAWS. see *INSURANCE*

COMPENSATION (WASHINGTON, 1982); an annual report on local government executive salaries and fringe benefits. see *BUSINESS AND ECONOMICS — Personnel Management*

331 620   US
▼**COMPENSATION & BENEFITS IN CONSULTING ENGINEERING FIRMS.** 1995. a. $495. (National Society of Professional Engineers) Abbott, Langer & Associates, 548 First St., Crete, IL 60417. TEL 708-672-4200. FAX 708-672-4674. Ed. Steven Langer.

331 620   US
COMPENSATION AND BENEFITS IN ENGINEERING FIRMS IN THE GEOTECHNICAL FIELD. 1989. a. $395. (Association of Engineering Firms Practicing in the Geosciences) Abbott, Langer & Associates, 548 First St., Crete, IL 60417. TEL 708-672-4200. Ed. Steven Langer.

331   US
COMPENSATION & BENEFITS MANAGER'S MONTHLY. 1989. m. $131.40. ProPub Inc., Box 102, Wyckoff, NJ 07481-0102. TEL 201-447-6485. FAX 201-447-9356. Ed. James A. Seidel; Pub. Randy Cochran. (looseleaf format; back issues avail.) **Document type:** newsletter.
    Formerly: Employee Benefits Consultant.

331.2   US   ISSN 0886-3687
HD4973   CODEN: CBRVED
COMPENSATION AND BENEFITS REVIEW. 1969. bi-m. $179 to non-members (foreign $214); members $161.10 (foreign $196.10). American Management Association, 1601 Broadway, New York, NY 10019. TEL 212-903-8069. FAX 212-903-8168. E-mail: amapubs@aol.com. (Subscr. to: Trudeau Rd., Box 319, Saranac Lake, NY 12983-0319) Ed. Linda Bennett. bk.rev.; abstr.; charts; index. circ. 3,500. (also avail. in microform from UMI; back issues avail.; reprint service avail. from UMI,SCH) **Indexed:** ABI Inform., Account.& Data Proc.Abstr., Anbar, ASEAN Manage.Abstr., B.P.I., BPIA, Bus.Ind., Curr.Cont., Hlth.Ind., Manage.Cont., Pers.Lit., Pers.Manage.Abstr., SSCI, Tr.& Indus.Ind., Work Rel.Abstr. **Document type:** trade publication.
●Also available online. Vendor(s): Information Access Co., Knight-Ridder Information, Inc., UMI.
—BLDSC (3363.985000); CASDDS; KR SourceOne; SWETS; UMI; UnCover. **CCC.**
    Formerly (until 1985): Compensation Review (ISSN 0010-4248)
    Description: Provides information on the strategic use of compensation and benefits, plus reports from other business and professional publications.

COMPENSATION AND WORKING CONDITIONS. see *BUSINESS AND ECONOMICS — Economic Situation And Conditions*

331 664 663   US
▼**COMPENSATION IN FOOD & BEVERAGE PROCESSING.** 1995. biennial. $450. Abbott, Langer & Associates, 548 First St., Crete, IL 60417. TEL 708-672-4200. FAX 708-672-4674. Ed. Steven Langer.

331   US   ISSN 1047-0344
T56.3
COMPENSATION IN MANUFACTURING. 1976. a. $495. Abbott, Langer & Associates, 548 First St., Crete, IL 60417. TEL 708-672-4200. Ed. Steven Langer.
    Formerly (until 1988): Compensation in Manufacturing - Engineers and Managers (ISSN 0278-0992)

331   US
COMPENSATION IN NONPROFIT ORGANIZATIONS. 1988. a. $225. Abbott, Langer & Associates, 548 First St., Crete, IL 60417. TEL 708-672-4200. Ed. Steven Langer.

331   US
COMPENSATION IN RESEARCH & DEVELOPMENT. 1986. a. $650. Abbott, Langer & Associates, 548 First St., Crete, IL 60417. TEL 708-672-4200. Ed. Steven Langer.

331 657   US
COMPENSATION IN THE ACCOUNTING - FINANCIAL FIELD. 1980. a. $495. Abbott, Langer & Associates, 548 First St., Crete, IL 60417. TEL 708-672-4200. Ed. Steven Langer.
    Formerly: Accounting - Financial Report.

331   US   ISSN 1044-0879
HD4965.5.U6
COMPENSATION IN THE HUMAN RESOURCES FIELD. 1979. a. $595. Abbott, Langer & Associates, 548 First St., Crete, IL 60417. TEL 708-672-4200. Ed. Steven Langer.
    Former titles: Salaries and Bonuses in Personnel - Industrial Relations Functions; Personnel - Industrial Relations Report, Parts 1 and 2; Incorporates (1981-1983 (vol.3): Compensation in Training and Development.

331   US   ISSN 1069-7063
HD4966.D372
COMPENSATION IN THE M I S - D P FIELD. (Management Information Systems - Data Processing) 1984. a. $750. (Data Processing Management Association) Abbott, Langer & Associates, 548 First St., Crete, IL 60417. TEL 708-672-4200. (Co-sponsor: Association for Systems Management) Ed. Steven Langer.

331   US
COMPENSATION IN THE SECURITY - LOSS PREVENTION FIELD. 1978. biennial. $435. (American Society for Industrial Security) Abbott, Langer & Associates, 548 First St., Crete, IL 60417. TEL 708-672-4200. Ed. Steven Langer.
    Formerly: Security Report.

331 658.5   US
COMPENSATION OF INDUSTRIAL ENGINEERS. 1972. biennial. $180. (Institute of Industrial Engineers) Abbott, Langer & Associates, 548 First St., Crete, IL 60417. TEL 708-672-4200. FAX 708-672-4674. Ed. Steven Langer.

331   US
COMPENSATION OF LEGAL AND RELATED JOBS (NON-LAW FIRMS). 1979. a. $575. Abbott, Langer & Associates, 548 First St., Crete, IL 60417. TEL 708-672-4200. Ed. Steven Langer.
    Formerly: Compensation of Attorneys (Non-Law Firms).

331 658   US
COMPENSATION OF PLANT - FACILITIES MANAGERS & ENGINEERS. 1993. biennial. $150. (American Institute of Plant Engineers Foundation and Plant Engineering) Abbott, Langer & Associates, 548 First St., Crete, IL 60417. TEL 708-672-4200. FAX 708-672-4674. Ed. Steven Langer.

331 550   US
COMPENSATION OF PROFESSIONAL GEOLOGISTS. 1994. biennial. $150. (American Institute of Professional Geologists) Abbott, Langer & Associates, 548 First St., Crete, IL 60417. TEL 708-672-4200. FAX 708-672-4674. Ed. Steve Langer.

CONCEPTS AND TRANSFORMATION; international journal of action research and organizational renewal. see *BUSINESS AND ECONOMICS — Personnel Management*

CONNECTICUT EMPLOYMENT LAW LETTER. see *LAW*

346.066   US   ISSN 0732-0833
KFC3942
CONNECTICUT WORKERS' COMPENSATION REVIEW OPINIONS. (In 7 vols.) 1983. q. $65. Butterworth Legal Publishers (Salem) (Subsidiary of: Reed Elsevier plc), 8 Industrial Way, Bldg. C, Salem, NH 03079. TEL 800-548-4001. FAX 603-898-9858. Ed. Clifford Davis. index. (looseleaf format) **Document type:** newsletter.

331 690   US   ISSN 0161-990X
CONSTRUCTION LABOR NEWS. 1978. s-m. $48. Construction Labor News, Inc., 2102 Almaden Rd., Ste. 303, San Jose, CA 95125. TEL 408-265-6280. FAX 408-265-7371. Ed. Mindy Dravis-Gonzales. adv.; tr.lit. circ. 17,000. (tabloid format; back issues avail.) **Document type:** newspaper.

331.1 690   US   ISSN 0010-6836
HD8039.B892
CONSTRUCTION LABOR REPORT. 1955. w. $893. The Bureau of National Affairs, Inc., 1231 25th St., N.W., Washington, DC 20037. TEL 202-452-4200. FAX 202-822-8092. TELEX 285656 BNAI WSH. URL: http://www.bna.com/. (Subscr. to: 9435 Kew West Ave., Rockville, MD 20850. TEL 800-372-1033) Ed. Anthony A. Harris. bk.rev.; charts; stat.; cum.index. (looseleaf format; back issues avail.) **Document type:** newsletter.
●Also available online. Vendor(s): Human Resources Information Network (File DD).
—**CCC.**
    Description: Covers union-management relations in the construction industry, reporting on significant legislative, judicial, economic, management and union developments.

CONSUMER EXPENDITURE SURVEY. see *BUSINESS AND ECONOMICS — Economic Situation And Conditions*

331.4   US   ISSN 0886-8239
CONTRIBUTIONS IN LABOR STUDIES. 1977. irreg., no.41, 1992. price varies. Greenwood Press, Inc. (Subsidiary of: Greenwood Publishing Group Inc.), 88 Post Rd. W., Box 5007, Westport, CT 06881-5007. TEL 203-226-3571. FAX 203-222-1502. Eds. Milton Cantor, Bruce Laurie.
—BLDSC (3458.825000).
    Formerly: Contributions in Labor History (ISSN 0146-3608)

331   RW
COOPERATIVE TRAFIPRO UMUNYAMALYANGO. (Text in French) m. B.P. 302, Kigali, Rwanda.

331.1   US   ISSN 0070-0029
CORNELL INTERNATIONAL INDUSTRIAL AND LABOR RELATIONS REPORTS. 1954. irreg., no.29, 1996. price varies. (New York State School of Industrial and Labor Relations) I L R Press, Cornell University Press, 512 E. State St., Ithaca, NY 14850. TEL 607-277-2338; 800-666-2211. Ed. Frances Benson. R&P contact: Clare Wellnitz. adv. contact: Heidi Marschner. **Document type:** monographic series.

331.1   US   ISSN 0070-0053
CORNELL STUDIES IN INDUSTRIAL AND LABOR RELATIONS. 1951. irreg., no.30, 1994. price varies. (New York State School of Industrial and Labor Relations) I L R Press, Cornell University Press, 512 E. State St., Ithaca, NY 14850. TEL 607-277-2338; 800-666-2211. Ed. Frances Benson. R&P contact: Clare Wellnitz. adv. contact: Heidi Marschner. **Document type:** monographic series.

CRITIQUE REGIONALE; cahiers de sociologie et d'economie regionales. see *SOCIOLOGY*

CRONER'S REFERENCE BOOK FOR EMPLOYERS. see *BUSINESS AND ECONOMICS — Personnel Management*

331   AG
CUADERNOS DE INVESTIGACION - ACCION. 1992. s-a. $20; newsstand price: Arg.$5. Centro de Estudios Laborales y Sociales, San Mauro 444, 1878 Quilmes, BA, Argentina. (Ed. Addr.: Casilla de Correo 3147, 1000 Buenos Aires, Argentina) Ed. Daniel Cieza.

BUSINESS AND ECONOMICS — LABOR AND INDUSTRIAL RELATIONS

331   SP   ISSN 1131-8635
CUADERNOS DE RELACIONES LABORALES. 1992. s-a. 2500 ptas.($27) (effective 1997). Universidad Complutense, Escuela de Relaciones Laborales, Servicio de Publicaciones, Calle Isaac Peral s-n, Ciudad Universitaria, 28040 Madrid, Spain. TEL 34-1-3946934. FAX 34-1-3946954. (back issues avail.)
—CINDOC.
Description: Presents studies on working conditions in Spanish institutions.

CURRENT GOVERNMENTS REPORTS: COUNTY GOVERNMENT EMPLOYMENT. see *PUBLIC ADMINISTRATION*

CURRENT GOVERNMENTS REPORTS: FINANCES OF EMPLOYEE RETIREMENT SYSTEMS OF STATE AND LOCAL GOVERNMENTS. see *BUSINESS AND ECONOMICS — Public Finance, Taxation*

331   US   ISSN 0196-4437
HD8011.A1
CURRENT GOVERNMENTS REPORTS: PUBLIC EMPLOYMENT. (Series GE-1) 1940. a. price varies. U.S. Bureau of the Census, Governments Division, Washington, DC 20233. TEL 301-457-1523. FAX 301-457-4714. (Subscr. to: Superintendent of Documents, U.S. Government Printing Office, Box 371954, Pittsburgh, PA 15250-7954. TEL 202-783-3238. FAX 202-512-2233) (also avail. in microfiche) **Document type:** government publication.
● Also available online. Vendor(s): CompuServe, Inc., Knight-Ridder Information, Inc.

331 340   SA
CURRENT LABOUR LAW; a review of recent developments in key areas of labour law. 1990. a. R.78. Juta & Co. Ltd., P.O. Box 14373, Kenwyn 7790, South Africa. TEL 27-21-7975101. FAX 27-21-7970121. Ed.Bd. **Document type:** proceedings.

368.4 331   CY   ISSN 0070-2390
CYPRUS. MINISTRY OF LABOUR AND SOCIAL INSURANCE. ANNUAL REPORT. (Text in Greek; summaries in English) 1943. a. free. Ministry of Labour and Social Insurance, Nicosia, Cyprus. TEL 357-2-303481. FAX 357-2-450993. **Document type:** government publication.

331   US   ISSN 0418-2693
HD4802
DAILY LABOR REPORT. 1941. d. (Mon.-Fri.). $5561. The Bureau of National Affairs, Inc., 1231 25th St., N.W., Washington, DC 20037. TEL 202-452-4200. FAX 202-822-8092. TELEX 285656 BNAI WSH. URL: http://www.bna.com/. (Subscr. to: 9435 Key West Ave., Rockville, MD 20850. TEL 800-372-1033) Ed. Susan J. Sala. m. index. (looseleaf format; also avail. in microform; back issues avail.)
● Also available online. Vendor(s): Bureau of National Affairs, Human Resources Information Network (CDD, HDD), Lexis-Nexis (DLABRT), West Group (BNA-DLR).
—CCC.
Former titles: Daily Economic Reports on Current Trends Affecting Management and Labor; Washington Daily Reporter: Labor Section; Washington Daily Reporter System: Daily Labor Report.
Description: Notification service that comprehensively covers labor developments in Congress, the courts, federal agencies, unions, management, and the NLRB.

331   US
DATA PROCESSING SURVEY. a. $450. MidAtlantic Employers' Association, Box 770, Valley Forge, PA 19482. TEL 215-666-7330.
Description: Offers comparative information on compensation practices for 81 data processing positions among 136 businesses, representing 835 employees, in PA, NJ, MD, and DE.

331.1   CR   ISSN 1121-6573
DEBATE LABORAL; revista americana e italiana de derecho del trabajo. 1988. 3/yr. I S C O S, c/o Daniel Lara S., P.O. Box 1119-1002, San Jose, Costa Rica.

DELAWARE EMPLOYMENT LAW LETTER. see *LAW*

731   US
DELAWARE VALLEY EXECUTIVE COMPENSATION SURVEY. a. $450. MidAtlantic Employers' Association, Box 770, Valley Forge, PA 19482. TEL 215-666-7330. FAX 215-666-7866.
Description: Provides comparative information regarding 29 executive position compensation practices among companies in PA, NJ, MD, and DE.

614.8   XV   ISSN 0011-7943
DELO IN VARNOST; revija za varstvo pri delu. (Text in Slovenian) 1956. bi-m. 650 SLT. Zavod Republiki Slovenije za Varstvo Pri Delu, Bohoriceva 22a, 61000 Ljubljana, Slovenia. FAX 061-312-562. Ed. Tatjana Srol. adv.; bk.rev. circ. 1,400. **Indexed:** C.I.S. Abstr.

331   DK   ISSN 0900-6885
DENMARK. DIREKTORATET FOR ARBEJDSTILSYNET. ARBEJDSTILSYNETS AARSBERETNING. (Text in Danish; summaries in English) a. Arbejdstilsynet Trybsagsafdelingen, Landskronagade 33-35, DK-2100 Copenhagen Oe, Denmark. TEL 01-180088. **Document type:** catalog.

331 340   AG   ISSN 0325-3627
DERECHO DEL TRABAJO; revista critica mensual de jurisprudencia, doctrina y legislacion. (Includes a. compilation) 1941. m. $600 (effective 1996). Ediciones la Ley S.A., Tucuman 1471, 1050 Buenos Aires, Argentina. TEL 541-495481. FAX 541-4760953. Ed. Juan J. Etala. bk.rev.; abstr.; bibl. **Indexed:** World Bibl.Soc.Sec.
Description: Critical review of labor jurisprudence and legislation.

331 340   US
DESKBOOK ENCYCLOPEDIA OF EMPLOYMENT LAW. 1993. a. $95.75 for 5th ed. Data Research, Inc., 4635 Nicols Rd., Ste. 100, Eagan, MN 55122-3337. TEL 612-452-8267. FAX 612-452-8694. (Subscr. to: Box 490, Rosemount, MN 55068-9987. TEL 800-365-4900) **Document type:** trade publication.
Description: An up-to-date compilation of summarized federal and state appellate court decisions that affect employment.

DESKBOOK ENCYCLOPEDIA OF PUBLIC EMPLOYMENT LAW. see *PUBLIC ADMINISTRATION — Municipal Government*

331   US
DETROIT LABOR MARKET REVIEW. 1946. m. free. Employment Security Commission, Bureau of Research and Statistics, 7310 Woodward Ave., Detroit, MI 48202. TEL 313-876-5000. Ed. James Astalos, Jr. charts; stat. circ. 1,800.
Formerly (until 1975): Detroit Manpower Review.

331   GW
DEUTSCHE HANDWERKS ZEITUNG. 1947. fortn. DM.38 (foreign DM.67.46) (effective 1997). Hans Holzmann Verlag GmbH, Gewerbestr. 2, 86825 Bad Woerishofen, Germany. TEL 49-8247-35401. FAX 49-8247-354170. circ. 429,350 (paid). **Document type:** newspaper.
Supersedes (1950-1978): Wirtschaftszeitung fuer Handwerk und Gewerbe.

DIALOGUES ON WORK AND INNOVATION. see *BUSINESS AND ECONOMICS — Personnel Management*

331   FR   ISSN 0767-2187
DICTIONNAIRE PERMANENT: SECURITE ET CONDITIONS DE TRAVAIL. 2 base vols. plus m. updates. 1510 F. for base vols. (updates 380 F.). Editions Legislatives et Administratives, 80 ave. de la Marne, 92546 Montrouge Cedex, France. TEL 40-92-68-68. FAX 46-56-00-15. TELEX 632 855 F. (looseleaf format)
Description: Focuses on working conditions, on-site safety and hygiene.

DIGEST OF CURRENT INDUSTRIAL AND LABOUR LAW. see *LAW*

331 658   UK   ISSN 0954-8165
DIRECTORS REWARDS. 1980. a. £450 (effective 1997). The Reward Group Ltd., Reward House, Diamond Way, Stone Business Park, Stone, Staffordshire ST15 OSD, England. TEL 44-1785-813566. FAX 44-1785-817007. E-mail: 101364.661@compuserve.com. **Document type:** bulletin.
—BLDSC (3591.100000).
Description: Details the pay and benefits for Chairman, Managing Director, Director and other management positions.

331   US
DIRECTORY OF CAREER RESOURCES FOR MINORITIES; a guide to career resources and opportunities for minorities. 1980. a? $37.50. Ready Reference Press, Box 5169, Santa Monica, CA 90405. Ed. Alvin Renetzky.

331   UK   ISSN 0965-9633
DIRECTORY OF EMPLOYERS ASSOCIATIONS, TRADE UNIONS, JOINT ORGANIZATIONS ETC.. irreg. H.M.S.O., 51 Nine Elms Ln., London SW8 5DR, England. TEL 44-171-873-0011. FAX 44-171-873-8247. circ. 1,325. **Document type:** directory, government publication.

331   US   ISSN 0735-3707
HF5549.5.D55
DIRECTORY OF OUTPLACEMENT FIRMS. 1980. a. $89.95 (effective 1997). Kennedy Publications, Templeton Rd., Fitzwilliam, NH 03447. TEL 603-585-6544. FAX 603-585-9555. Ed. Giles Goodhead. adv. contact: Carolyn D. Edwards. **Document type:** directory.

331.1 340   IT   ISSN 1121-8762
DIRITTO DELLE RELAZIONI INDUSTRIALI. 1991. 3/yr. Lit.100000 (foreign Lit.150000) (effective 1997). (Associazione Lavoro e Ricerche) Casa Editrice Dott. A. Giuffre, Via Busto Arsizio 40, 20151 Milan, Italy. TEL 39-2-38089200. FAX 39-2-38009582. Eds. L. Spagnuolo Vigonta, M. Biagi.

331   US
▼**DISABILITY LEAVE & ABSENCE REPORTER.** 1997. m. $295. Bureau of Business Practice, 24 Rope Ferry Rd., Waterford, CT 06386. TEL 860-442-4365. FAX 860-437-3555. URL: http://www.bbpnews.com. Ed. Mary Lou Devine; Pub. Peter Garabedian. R&P contact: Debra Ferraro. **Document type:** newsletter.
Description: Focuses on the laws and policies that govern employee leave, absence, workers' compensation, and disabilities.

323.4   AT   ISSN 1324-9681
DISCRIMINATION ALERT; the national independent newsletter on equal opportunity & workforce diversity. w. Newsletter Information Services, P.O. Box 693, Manly, N.S.W. 2095, Australia. TEL 61-2-99777500. FAX 61-2-9773310. E-mail: hww@hww.com.au; URL: http://www.hww.com.au. Ed. Peter Schwab. **Document type:** newsletter.

331 658.3   UK
DISCRIMINATION CASE LAW DIGEST. q. £60 (foreign £67) (effective 1997). Eclipse Group Ltd., Industrial Relations Services, 18-20 Highbury Pl., London N5 1QP, England. TEL 44-171-354-5858. FAX 44-171-226-8618. **Document type:** bulletin.
Description: Reports on every significant development in case law involving discrimination in the workplace.

331   US
▼**DISGRUNTLED;** the business magazine for people who work for a living. 1995. m. free. Counterpoint Press, Inc., 61 Arlington Court, Kensington, CA 94707. E-mail: dslevine@disgruntled.com; URL: http://www.disgruntled.com. Ed. Daniel IS. Levine.
● Available only online.
Description: Commentary and satire on the darker side of the world of work, written from the employee's perspective.

340   CN   ISSN 0831-2516
DISMISSAL AND EMPLOYMENT LAW DIGEST. 1986. 9/yr. Can.$152 (effective 1997). Canada Law Book Inc., 240 Edward St., Aurora, ON L4G 3S9, Canada. TEL 905-841-6472; 800-263-2037. FAX 905-841-5085. Ed. Howard A. Levitt. **Document type:** trade publication.

BUSINESS AND ECONOMICS — LABOR AND INDUSTRIAL RELATIONS

DISPLACED WORKERS. see *BUSINESS AND ECONOMICS — Abstracting, Bibliographies, Statistics*

340 300   US   ISSN 1074-8105
K1
DISPUTE RESOLUTION JOURNAL. 1937. q. $55. American Arbitration Association, 140 W. 51st St., New York, NY 10020-1203. TEL 212-484-4011. FAX 212-541-4841. Ed. Jack Smith. bk.rev.; bibl.; index. circ. 10,000. (also avail. in microform from UMI; reprint service avail. from WSH) **Indexed:** ABI Inform., Abstr.Bk.Rev.Curr.Leg.Per., Amer.Hist.& Life (1969-1974), B.P.I., BPIA, Bus.Ind., C.L.I., Curr.Cont., Hist.Abstr. (1969-1974), L.R.I., Leg.Cont., Leg.Per., Pers.Lit., SSCI, Tr.& Indus.Ind. —BLDSC (3598.785000); Genuine Article; KR SourceOne; SWETS; UMI; UnCover.
   Formerly (until 1993): Arbitration Journal (ISSN 0003-7893)
   Description: Covers the spectrum of the dispute resolution field. Articles by practitioners and scholars analyze current trends in commercial dispute settlement, construction, accident claims, international arbitration, and labor relations.

331   US
HD5503
DISPUTE RESOLUTION TIMES. 1951. q. American Arbitration Association, 140 W. 51st St., New York, NY 10020-1203. TEL 212-484-4005. FAX 212-541-4841. Ed. Jack Smith. charts. circ. 65,000. (tabloid format; back issues avail.)
   Former titles (until 1993): Arbitration Times (ISSN 8756-5455); (until 1982): American Arbitration Association. News and Views (ISSN 0093-6979); (until 1974): Arbitration News (ISSN 0518-262X).
   Description: Reports on AAA activities and other matters of interest to resolution professionals. Includes current developments in many areas, from the passage of new arbitration laws to announcements of new publications and videotapes.

331   UK
DISTRIBUTION REWARDS. 2/yr. £250 (effective 1997). The Reward Group Ltd., Reward House, Diamond Way, Stone Business Park, Stone, Staffordshire ST15 OSD, England. TEL 44-1785-813566. FAX 44-1785-817007. E-mail: 101364.661@compuserve.com. **Document type:** bulletin.
   Description: Information on pay and benefits in distribution jobs from director to warehouse laborer.

DRUG DETECTION REPORT. see *BUSINESS AND ECONOMICS — Personnel Management*

331   US   ISSN 0012-6918
DUBUQUE LEADER.* 1906. w. $3.50. 1527 Central Ave., Dubuque, IA 52001. Ed. William J. Ryder. circ. 5,100.

331.1   US
E E O C COMPLIANCE MANUAL. (Equal Employment Opportunity Commission) 1975. irreg. $238. The Bureau of National Affairs, Inc., 1231 25th St., N.W., Washington, DC 20037. TEL 202-452-4200. FAX 202-822-8092. TELEX 285656 BNAI WSH. URL: http://www.bna.com/. (Subscr. to: 9435 Key West Ave., Rockville, MD 20850. TEL 800-372-1033) Ed. Jeff Day. (looseleaf format; back issues avail.)
   Description: Contains the complete text of the EEOC Compliance Manual, as issued by the EEOC, with monthly notification of related developments.

THE E E O REVIEW; a supervisor's guide to managing lawfully in the workplace. (Equal Employment Opportunity) see *BUSINESS AND ECONOMICS — Personnel Management*

E I R E C KENKYU HOKOKUSHU. (Rehabilitation Engineering Center for Employment Injuries) see *MEDICAL SCIENCES — Physical Medicine And Rehabilitation*

E L F. (European Labour Forum) see *POLITICAL SCIENCE — International Relations*

331 658.3   US
E M A REPORTER. 1969. 24/yr. membership only. Employment Management Association, 4101 Lake Boone Trail, Ste. 201, Raleigh, NC 27607. TEL 919-787-6010. FAX 919-787-4916. URL: http://www.cweb.com/ema/welcome.html. Ed. Carol Crane. R&P contact: Carol Crane. adv. contact: Tracy Williams. bk.rev.; cum.index: 1979-1988. circ. 1,900.
   Description: Forum for the exchange of ideas and information on employment issues.

331.2   US   ISSN 8755-5379
E R I S A NEWSLETTER. (Employee Retirement Income Security Act) m. $89. Two Crows, 11 Pleasant St., Berlin, MA 01503. Ed. Joanne Bergen. circ. 2,000. (back issues avail.) **Document type:** newsletter.

331 340   US
E R I S A: THE LAW AND THE CODE. (Employee Retirement Income Security Act) a., latest 1996 ed. $65. B N A Books (Subsidiary of: The Bureau of National Affairs, Inc.), 1231 25th St., N.W., Washington, DC 20037. TEL 202-833-7470. FAX 202-833-7490. E-mail: books@bna.com. (Subscr. to: BNA Books Distribution Center, 130 Campus Dr., Box 7816, Edison, NJ 08818-7816. TEL 800-960-1220. FAX 908-417-0482) Eds. Anthony A. Harris, David A. Sayre.

331   UK
EAST ANGLIA SALARY SURVEY. 2/yr. £250 (effective 1997). The Reward Group Ltd., Reward House, Diamond Way, Stone Business Park, Stone, Staffordshire ST15 OSD, England. TEL 44-1785-813566. FAX 44-1785-817007. E-mail: 101364.661@compuserve.com. **Document type:** bulletin.
   Description: Pay and benefit survey for East Anglia covering the Norfolk, Suffolk and Cambridgeshire areas.

331   PK   ISSN 0012-8953
EASTERN WORKER; bi-monthly journal on labour laws, labour-management relations & socio-economic affairs. (Text in English) 1950. bi-m. $70. Bureau of Labour Publications, 8, Business Centre, Mumtaz Hasan Rd., P.O. Box 5833, Karachi 74000, Pakistan. TEL 92-21-2414975. Ed. P. Shafi. adv.; bk.rev.; charts; illus.; stat.; index. circ. 1,000. **Document type:** academic/scholarly publication.

331   IT   ISSN 0012-978X
ECONOMIA E LAVORO. 1967. q. L.120000 (foreign L.140000) (effective 1995). Marsilio Editori S.p.A., Marittima - Fabbricato 205, 30135 Venice, Italy. TEL 39-41-5227822. FAX 39-41-5238352. (Edit. addr.: Via Torino 122, 00184 Rome, Italy. TEL 39-6-4746552) Ed. Renato Brunetta. adv.: page L.1200000. bk.rev.; illus. circ. 4,000. **Indexed:** Int.Lab.Doc., J.of Econ.Lit.
—BLDSC (3650.450000).

330.1   AT
ECONOMIC AND LABOUR RELATIONS REVIEW. 1977. s-a. Aus.$30 to individuals; institutions Aus.$55. Centre for Applied Economic Research, University of New South Wales, Sydney, N.S.W. 2052, Australia. TEL 61-2-3853343. Ed. John W. Nevile. R&P contact: John W. Nevile. circ. 1,000. (back issues avail.) **Document type:** academic/scholarly publication.
—BLDSC (2947.361350).
   Formerly: University of New South Wales. Centre for Applied Economic Research. Paper (ISSN 0314-853X)

ECONOMIES ET SOCIETES. SERIE AB. ECONOMIE DU TRAVAIL. see *BUSINESS AND ECONOMICS*

EFFECTIVE TELEPHONE TECHNIQUES. see *BUSINESS AND ECONOMICS — Management*

EKSPRESS - ZAKON. see *BUSINESS AND ECONOMICS — Public Finance, Taxation*

331 643   UK
ELECTRONICS INDUSTRY REWARDS. a. £250 (effective 1997). The Reward Group Ltd., Reward House, Diamond Way, Stone Business Park, Stone, Staffordshire ST15 OSD, England. TEL 44-1785-813566. FAX 44-1785-817007. E-mail: 101364.661@compuserve.com. **Document type:** bulletin.
   Description: Provides detailed pay information on the electronics industry, from large international to small specialized companies.

331   IT
ELENCO UFFICIALE PROTESTI. 24/yr. L.50000. Camera di Commercio, Industria, Artigianato e Agricoltura di Forlì-Cesena, Corso della Repubblica 5, 47100 Forli, Italy. TEL 0543-713111. FAX 0543-713416.

331.1   PR   ISSN 0555-6635
EMPLEO Y DESEMPLEO EN PUERTO RICO/EMPLOYMENT AND UNEMPLOYMENT IN PUERTO RICO. (Text in English and Spanish) 1967. a. free. Department of Labor & Human Resources, 505 Munoz Rivera Ave., Hato Rey, PR 00918. **Document type:** government publication.

331 658   US   ISSN 0896-0941
EMPLOYEE ASSISTANCE PROGRAM MANAGEMENT LETTER. 1987. 12/yr. $227 (effective 1997). Health Resources Publishing, Brinley Professional Plaza, 3100 Hwy. 138, Box 1442, Wall Township, NJ 07719-1442. TEL 908-681-1133. FAX 908-681-0490. E-mail: 75673.624@compuserve.com. Ed. Beth Kerber; Pub. Robert K. Jenkins. R&P contact: Jillian Philipp. adv. contact: Judith Granholm. index. (tabloid format; back issues avail.) **Document type:** newsletter.
—CCC.
   Description: Contains information on what EAP's across the country are doing.

331   US   ISSN 0273-236X
KF3509
EMPLOYEE BENEFIT CASES. 1981. w. (50/yr.). $976. The Bureau of National Affairs, Inc., 1231 25th St., N.W., Washington, DC 20037. TEL 202-452-4200. FAX 202-822-8092. TELEX 285656 BNAI WSH. URL: http://www.bna.com/. (Subscr. to: 9435 Key West Ave., Rockville, MD 20850. TEL 800-372-1033) Ed. David A. Sayre. index. (looseleaf format; back issues avail.)
   ●Also available online.
—CCC.
   Description: Decisional service that reports the full text of federal and state court decisions and selected decisions of arbitrators and the NLRB employee benefits issues.

331   US   ISSN 1044-6265
HD4928.N62
EMPLOYEE BENEFIT NEWS. 1987. 14/yr. $84 (N. America $90; elsewhere $140). Enterprise Communications Inc., 1483 Chain Bridge Rd., Ste. 202, McLean, VA 22101. TEL 703-448-0336. FAX 703-448-0270. (Subscr. to: 1165 Northchase Pkwy., N.E., Ste. 350, Marietta, GA 30067. TEL 770-988-9558) Ed. Richard Stolz; Pub. James Snyder. R&P contact: Richard Stolz. adv. contact: Murray Kasmenn. charts; illus.; stat.; tr.lit. circ. 63,000. (tabloid format; back issues avail.) **Document type:** trade publication.
—CCC.
   Incorporates (1988-1990): Pension Fund News.
   Description: Covers news and trends, healthcare, retirement plans, insurance, legislation, and day care for employee benefits managers.

331   US   ISSN 0887-1388
HD4928.N62
EMPLOYEE BENEFIT NOTES. 1982. m. $25 per no. Employee Benefit Research Institute, 2121 K St., N.W., Ste. 600, Washington, DC 20037-1896. TEL 202-659-0670. FAX 202-775-6312. R&P contact: Stephanie Robinson. circ. 3,500. (also avail. in microform from UMI) **Document type:** newsletter.
—UMI. CCC.
   Description: Covers employee benefits, with emphasis on legislative and regulatory actions, statistical findings, and research studies and publications.

331.25   US   ISSN 0013-6808
HD7106.U5   CODEN: EBPVAL
EMPLOYEE BENEFIT PLAN REVIEW. 1946. m. $65. Charles D. Spencer & Associates, Inc., 250 S. Wacker Dr., Ste. 600, Chicago, IL 60606-5834. TEL 312-993-7900. Ed. Bruce F. Spencer. R&P contact: Art Cohen. adv.; stat.; index. circ. 15,300. (also avail. in microform from UMI; reprint service avail. from UMI) **Indexed:** ABI Inform., B.P.I., BPIA, Bus.Ind., CINAHL, Hlth.Ind., L.I.I., Manage.Cont., Pers.Lit., Tr.& Indus.Ind., World Bibl.Soc.Sec. **Document type:** trade publication.
   ●Also available online. Vendor(s): UMI.
—BLDSC (3737.032500); KR SourceOne; SWETS; UMI; UnCover.

BUSINESS AND ECONOMICS — LABOR AND INDUSTRIAL RELATIONS

331   US
KFI1534.5.P4A134
EMPLOYEE BENEFITS. 1982. 4/yr. $14 to members; non-members $68. Illinois State Bar Association, Section on Employee Benefits, Illinois Bar Center, Springfield, IL 62701. TEL 217-525-1760. FAX 217-525-0712. Eds. John Brophy, Gregory Brownaley. circ. 550. (looseleaf format; back issues avail.) **Document type:** newsletter.

331   US   ISSN 1068-4204
KF3509.A15
EMPLOYEE BENEFITS COUNSELOR. 1993. m. $245. Business Law, Inc., 11630 Chillicothe Rd., Chesterland, OH 44026. TEL 216-729-7996. FAX 216-729-0645. Ed. William A. Hancock. bk.rev.; index, cum.index. (looseleaf format; back issues avail.) **Document type:** newsletter.
—CCC.
   Description: Discusses current ERISA and employee benefit issues.

368.4 331   US
EMPLOYEE BENEFITS DIGEST. 1963. m. International Foundation of Employee Benefit Plans, 18700 W. Bluemound Rd., Box 69, Brookfield, WI 53008-0069. TEL 414-786-6700. Ed. Mary Jo Brzezinski. bk.rev.; charts; illus.; index. circ. 34,000. (looseleaf format) **Indexed:** Bus.Ind.
—CCC.
   Former titles: International Foundation of Employee Benefit Plans. Digest (ISSN 0146-1141); N F Digest (National Foundation of Health, Welfare and Pension Plans).
   Description: News of foundation's activities, abstracts of current literature and articles on benefit topics.

EMPLOYEE BENEFITS IN MEDIUM AND LARGE FIRMS. see BUSINESS AND ECONOMICS — Economic Situation And Conditions

331   US   ISSN 1048-2814
HD7106.U5
EMPLOYEE BENEFITS ISSUES: THE MULTIEMPLOYER PERSPECTIVE; proceedings of the annual employee benefits conference with papers from other multi-employer conferences. 1957. a. price varies. International Foundation of Employee Benefit Plans, 18700 W. Bluemound Rd., Box 69, Brookfield, WI 53008-0069. TEL 414-786-6700. Ed. Judy Sankey. **Document type:** proceedings.
—CCC.
   Formerly: Employee Benefits Annual (Year).

331.2   US   ISSN 0361-4050
HD4932.N6
EMPLOYEE BENEFITS JOURNAL. 1975. q. $60 to non-members. International Foundation of Employee Benefit Plans, 18700 W. Bluemound Rd., Box 69, Brookfield, WI 53008-0069. TEL 414-786-6700. FAX 414-786-2990. Ed. Mary Brennan. bk.rev. circ. 40,000. (also avail. in microform from UMI) **Indexed:** ABI Inform., B.P.I., BPIA, Bus.Ind., L.I.I., Manage.Cont., PROMT.
—BLDSC (3737.036300); KR SourceOne; UMI; UnCover. **CCC.**
   Description: Articles on benefits-related topics, with abstracts of current literature and summaries of research in the field.

331   UK
EMPLOYEE BENEFITS 1. a. £250 (effective 1997). The Reward Group Ltd., Reward House, Diamond Way, Stone Business Park, Stone, Staffordshire ST15 0SD, England. TEL 44-1785-813566. FAX 44-1785-817007. E-mail: 101364.661@compuserve.com. **Document type:** bulletin.
   Description: Overview of the current practices and trends in employee benefits.

331   UK
EMPLOYEE BENEFITS 2. a. £250 (effective 1997). The Reward Group Ltd., Reward House, Diamond Way, Stone Business Park, Stone, Staffordshire ST15 0SD, England. TEL 44-1785-813566. FAX 44-1785-817007. E-mail: 101364.661@compuserve.com. **Document type:** bulletin.
   Description: Analysis of recent trends in pensions and related benefits.

331   US
EMPLOYEE DISCIPLINE LAW BULLETIN. m. $51.82. Quinlan Publishing Co., Inc., 23 Drydock Ave., 2nd Fl., Boston, MA 02110. TEL 617-542-0048. FAX 617-345-9646. index. (looseleaf format; back issues avail.) **Document type:** bulletin, newsletter.

EMPLOYEE FRINGE AND WELFARE BENEFIT PLANS. see BUSINESS AND ECONOMICS — Personnel Management

331   UK   ISSN 0142-5455
CODEN: EMREDQ
EMPLOYEE RELATIONS. 1979. bi-m. £3959($6139) (foreign Aus.$7699) (effective 1998). M C B University Press Ltd., 60-62 Toller Ln., Bradford, W. Yorks BD8 9BY, England. TEL 44-1274-777700. FAX 44-1274-785200. TELEX 51317 MCBUNI G. URL: http://www.mcb.co.uk. Ed. John Berridge. bk.rev.; charts; illus.; stat. (reprint service avail. from SWZ) **Indexed:** ABI Inform., Account.& Data Proc.Abstr., Anbar, ASEAN Manage.Abstr., ASSIA, BPIA, Bus.Ind., C.I.J.E., Cont.Pg.Manage., Curr.Cont., Int.Lab.Doc., Key to Econ.Sci., Manage.Cont., Mgmt.& Market.Abstr., Tech.Educ.Abstr. **Document type:** academic/scholarly publication.
●Also available online. Vendor(s): Information Access Co.
—BLDSC (3737.040000); SWETS; UMI; UnCover. **CCC.**
   Description: Aims to help all those involved in the management of organizations to find and compare alternative strategies for improving employment conditions. Covers developments in collective bargaining, management of industrial relations, and more.

331.25   US   ISSN 1080-1871
EMPLOYEE RELATIONS BULLETIN. 1963. s-m. $176.88. Bureau of Business Practice, 24 Rope Ferry Rd., Waterford, CT 06386. TEL 860-442-4365. FAX 860-437-3555. Ed. Joyce Ann Grabel; Pub. Peter Garabedian. R&P contact: Debra Ferraro. bk.rev.; charts; s-a. index. **Document type:** newsletter.
   Former titles (until 1990): Employee Relations and Human Resources Bulletin (ISSN 0744-7779); (until 1982): Employee Relations Bulletin (ISSN 0013-6816).
   Description: Deals primarily with the latest trends in employee relations management and new strategies for organizational development.

331   AT
EMPLOYEE RELATIONS COMMISSION OF VICTORIA. MONTHLY NEWSLETTER. m. Aus.$80. Law Press (Victoria), 52-58 Chetwynd St., W. Melbourne, Vic. 3003, Australia. TEL 61-3-93208686. FAX 61-3-93208699. (Subscr. addr.: P.O. Box 334, N. Melbourne, Vic. 3051, Australia. TEL 61-3-93208623) (looseleaf format) **Document type:** newsletter.

331 340.5   US
EMPLOYEE RELATIONS GUIDE TO FEDERAL LAWS AND REGULATIONS. a. $150. MidAtlantic Employers' Association, Box 770, Valley Forge, PA 19482. TEL 215-666-7330. FAX 215-666-7866.
   Description: Offers employers a reference source to assure compliance with all federal or state laws and regulations regarding employee relations.

EMPLOYEE RELATIONS LAW JOURNAL. see LAW

331.1   US   ISSN 0892-7545
HD6958.5   CODEN: ERRJE9
EMPLOYEE RESPONSIBILITIES AND RIGHTS JOURNAL. 1988. q. $215 (foreign $250) (effective 1998). (Council on Employee Responsibilities and Rights) Plenum Publishing Corp., 233 Spring St., New York, NY 10013-1578. TEL 212-620-8000. FAX 212-463-0742. TELEX 23-421139. URL: http://ns1.infor.com:6800/cgi/getarec?ple20000059. Ed. C.A.B. Osigweh. adv.; bk.rev. (also avail. in microfilm from UMI; back issues avail.; reprint service avail. from WSH) **Indexed:** IMFL, Int.Polit.Sci.Abstr., Psychol.Abstr. (1988-). **Document type:** academic/scholarly publication.
—BLDSC (3737.053500); UMI; UnCover. **CCC.**
   Description: Focuses on the shifting rights and responsibilities between employer and employee. Refereed Serial

331.011 344.010   US
EMPLOYEE RIGHTS LITIGATION: PLEADING AND PRACTICE. 3 base vols. (plus a. update). $405 for base vols.; update $170. (National Employment Lawyers Association) Matthew Bender & Co., Inc., 2 Park Ave., New York, NY 10016. TEL 212-448-2000. E-mail: international@bender.com; URL: http://www.bender.com. (looseleaf format)
   Description: Advocates for employee rights. Covers legal standards for statutory and common law claims raised on behalf of employees.

331   US   ISSN 1063-097X
KF3471.A59
EMPLOYEE TERMINATIONS LAW BULLETIN. 1982. m. $62. Quinlan Publishing Co., Inc., 23 Drydock Ave., Boston, MA 02210-2307. TEL 617-542-0048; 800-229-2084. FAX 617-345-9646. index. (looseleaf format; back issues avail.) **Document type:** newsletter.
—UMI. **CCC.**
   Former titles (until 1991): Employee Terminations Bulletin (ISSN 1049-0914); National Report on Employee Terminations (ISSN 1042-4407); Employee Terminations Law Bulletin (1986) (ISSN 0898-5057); (until 1986): Discharged Worker (ISSN 8755-822X)
   Description: Publishes case law summaries and prevention ideas om harassment, whistle blowing, discrimination, constructive discharge, employment contacts and more.

EMPLOYER. see BUSINESS AND ECONOMICS — Management

EMPLOYER COSTS FOR EMPLOYEE COMPENSATION. see BUSINESS AND ECONOMICS — Economic Situation And Conditions

EMPLOYER RESOURCES NEWSLETTER. see PRINTING

613   CN
EMPLOYER'S HEALTH & SAFETY MANUAL - ONTARIO. 1989. 6/yr. Can.$215. Carswell, One Corporate Plaza, 2075 Kennedy Rd., Scarborough, ON M1T 3V4, Canada. TEL 416-609-8000. FAX 416-298-5094. Ed. Jacques Bendavid. circ. 2,800. (looseleaf format; back issues avail.)
   Description: Provides a complete text of the Occupational Health and Safety Act and amendments, as well as vital information on how to meet its responsibilities and obligations. Includes checklists and sample forms for supervisors and front-line managers.

331.1   UK   ISSN 0267-5374
EMPLOYMENT AFFAIRS REPORT. 1985. bi-m. £135 to non-members. Confederation of British Industry, Centre Point, 103 New Oxford St., London WC1A 1DU, England. TEL 44-171-379-7400. FAX 44-171-240-1578. TELEX 21332. **Document type:** bulletin.

EMPLOYMENT AND EARNINGS. see BUSINESS AND ECONOMICS — Economic Situation And Conditions

EMPLOYMENT AND EARNINGS: STATES AND AREAS. see BUSINESS AND ECONOMICS — Economic Situation And Conditions

EMPLOYMENT AND EARNINGS: UNITED STATES. see BUSINESS AND ECONOMICS — Economic Situation And Conditions

331 340   CN   ISSN 1183-7152
EMPLOYMENT AND LABOUR LAW REPORTER. 1989. m. Can.$255. Butterworths Canada Ltd., Part of the Reed Elsevier group, 75 Clegg Rd., Markham, ON L6G 1A1, Canada. TEL 905-479-2665. FAX 905-479-2826. (back issues avail.) **Document type:** newsletter.
   Formerly: British Columbia Employment and Labour Law Reporter.
   Description: Covers employment and other labor issues in Canada. For labor, management and legal practitioners.

EMPLOYMENT AND THE ECONOMY. ATLANTIC COASTAL REGION. see BUSINESS AND ECONOMICS — Economic Situation And Conditions

BUSINESS AND ECONOMICS — LABOR AND INDUSTRIAL RELATIONS

331.11 US ISSN 0146-9673
HD5724
EMPLOYMENT AND TRAINING REPORTER. 1969. w. $698. M I I Publications Inc., 1211 Connecticut Ave., N.W., Washington, DC 20036. TEL 202-293-1740. FAX 202-524-8960. Ed. Mildred Charley-Greene; Pub. Cecilio Morales. bk.rev.; q. index. (looseleaf format; back issues avail.) **Document type:** trade publication.
—CCC.
  Formerly (until 1979): Manpower Information Service (ISSN 0542-5794)
  Description: Provides coverage of government-sponsored employment and training programs for the unemployed, including youth, laid-off workers, and the economically disadvantaged.

EMPLOYMENT AND WAGES ANNUAL AVERAGES. see BUSINESS AND ECONOMICS — Abstracting, Bibliographies, Statistics

344 US
EMPLOYMENT AT WILL REPORTER. vol.11, 1993. m. $510. New England Legal Publishers, Box 425, Weston, MA 02193. TEL 617-891-6200.
  Description: Digests of decisions from all federal and state jurisdictions concerning non-unionized employment law, including wrongful discharge, non-competition, invasion of privacy, and related issues.

EMPLOYMENT BULLETIN; legal issues in the workplace. see LAW

EMPLOYMENT CASE DIGEST. see BUSINESS AND ECONOMICS — Personnel Management

331 UK ISSN 0969-255X
EMPLOYMENT CASE LAW BULLETIN. (Variant title: Croner's Employment Case Law Bulletin) 1993. base vol. (plus m. updates). £193 (updates £138) (effective 1995). Croner Publications Ltd. (Subsidiary of: Wolters Kluwer N.V.), Croner House, 100 London Rd., Kingston-upon-Thames, Surrey TW2 6SR, England. TEL 44-181-547-3333. FAX 44-181-247-1300. TELEX 267778. (looseleaf format) **Document type:** trade publication.

EMPLOYMENT COST INDEXES AND LEVELS. see BUSINESS AND ECONOMICS — Economic Situation And Conditions

658.3 UK ISSN 0309-4995
EMPLOYMENT DIGEST. 1977. fortn. £97.50 (effective 1992). Croner Publications Ltd. (Subsidiary of: Wolters Kluwer N.V.), Croner House, 100 London Rd., Kingston-upon-Thames, Surrey TW2 6SR, England. TEL 44-181-547-3333. FAX 44-181-547-2637. TELEX 267778. Ed. Susan Mison. **Indexed:** Mgmt.& Market.Abstr. **Document type:** trade publication.
  Description: Provides current information on employment legislation, with analysis of prospective changes.

340 US
EMPLOYMENT DISPUTES; law and strategies for representing the employer. 1991. base vol. (plus a. supplement). $95. Butterworth Legal Publishers (Salem) (Subsidiary of: Reed Elsevier plc), 8 Industrial Way, Bldg. C, Salem, NH 03079. TEL 800-548-4001. Ed. Carter K. Combe. (looseleaf format) **Document type:** trade publication.

EMPLOYMENT GUIDE. see BUSINESS AND ECONOMICS — Personnel Management

EMPLOYMENT, HOURS, AND EARNINGS: UNITED STATES. see BUSINESS AND ECONOMICS — Economic Situation And Conditions

EMPLOYMENT IN ALBERTA; a guide to conditions of work and employee benefits. see LAW

EMPLOYMENT IN BRITISH COLUMBIA; a guide to conditions of work and employee benefits. see LAW

331.11 US
EMPLOYMENT IN CONNECTICUT. 1985. base vol. (plus a. supplement). $45. Butterworth Legal Publishers (Salem) (Subsidiary of: Reed Elsevier plc), 8 Industrial Way, Bldg. C, Salem, NH 03079. TEL 800-548-4001. FAX 603-898-9858. (looseleaf format)

331 330 EI ISSN 1016-5444
EMPLOYMENT IN EUROPE. irreg. $16. (Commission of the European Communities, Directorate-General Employment, Industrial Relations and Social Affairs) Office for Official Publications of the European Communities, B.P. 1003, 2 rue Mercier, L-2985 Luxembourg, Luxembourg. TEL 352-49-92-81. FAX 352-48-85-73. stat.

331.11 US
EMPLOYMENT IN ILLINOIS. 1983. base vol. (plus supplement). $55. Butterworth Legal Publishers (Salem) (Subsidiary of: Reed Elsevier plc), 8 Industrial Way, Bldg. C, Salem, NH 03079. TEL 800-548-4001. FAX 603-898-9858. Ed. M.G. Sautter. (looseleaf format)

331.11 US
EMPLOYMENT IN IOWA. 1984. base vol. (plus supplement). $55. Butterworth Legal Publishers (Salem) (Subsidiary of: Reed Elsevier plc), 8 Industrial Way, Bldg. C, Salem, NH 03079. TEL 800-548-4001. FAX 603-898-9858. Ed. M.G. Sautter. (looseleaf format)

331.11 US
EMPLOYMENT IN MINNESOTA. 1982. base vol. (plus supplement). $55. Butterworth Legal Publishers (Salem) (Subsidiary of: Reed Elsevier plc), 8 Industrial Way, Bldg. C, Salem, NH 03079. TEL 800-548-4001. FAX 603-898-9858. Ed. M.G. Sautter. (looseleaf format)

331 340 US
EMPLOYMENT IN MISSOURI; a guide to employment practice and regulations. Second ed., 1990. base vol. (plus a. supplement). $60. Butterworth Legal Publishers (Salem) (Subsidiary of: Reed Elsevier plc), 8 Industrial Way, Bldg. C, Salem, NH 03079. TEL 800-548-4001. FAX 603-898-9858. Eds. William R. Barr, Mark S. Summers. (looseleaf format)
  Description: Covers all aspects of employer-employee relations from interviewing to termination.

331 US
EMPLOYMENT IN NEW YORK STATE. 1991. m. free. Department of Labor, W. Averell Harriman Office Bldg., Rm.401, Albany, NY 12240. **Document type:** government publication.

331.11 US
EMPLOYMENT IN OHIO. 1984. base vol. (plus supplement). $55. Butterworth Legal Publishers (Salem) (Subsidiary of: Reed Elsevier plc), 8 Industrial Way, Bldg. C, Salem, NH 03079. TEL 800-548-4001. FAX 603-898-9858. Ed. M.G. Sautter. (looseleaf format)

EMPLOYMENT IN ONTARIO; a guide to conditions of work and employee benefits. see LAW

331.11 US
EMPLOYMENT IN OREGON. (Revised ed.) 1982. base vol. (plus supplement). $55. Butterworth Legal Publishers (Salem) (Subsidiary of: Reed Elsevier plc), 8 Industrial Way, Bldg. C, Salem, NH 03079. TEL 800-541-4001. FAX 603-898-9858. (looseleaf format)

EMPLOYMENT IN PERSPECTIVE: MINORITY WORKERS. see BUSINESS AND ECONOMICS — Abstracting, Bibliographies, Statistics

EMPLOYMENT IN PERSPECTIVE: WOMEN IN THE LABOR FORCE. see BUSINESS AND ECONOMICS — Economic Situation And Conditions

331.11 US
EMPLOYMENT IN TEXAS. (3rd Edition) 1984. base vol. (plus supplement). $70. Butterworth Legal Publishers (Salem) (Subsidiary of: Reed Elsevier plc), 8 Industrial Way, Bldg. C, Salem, NH 03079. TEL 800-548-4001. FAX 603-898-9858.

331.11 US
EMPLOYMENT IN WASHINGTON STATE. 1987. base vol. (plus supplement). $55. Butterworth Legal Publishers (Salem) (Subsidiary of: Reed Elsevier plc), 8 Industrial Way, Bldg. C, Salem, NH 03079. TEL 800-548-4001. FAX 603-898-9858. Ed. Michael Killeen. (looseleaf format)

331.11 US
EMPLOYMENT IN WISCONSIN. 1983. base vol. (plus supplement). $55. Butterworth Legal Publishers (Salem) (Subsidiary of: Reed Elsevier plc), 8 Industrial Way, Bldg. C, Salem, NH 03079. TEL 800-548-4001. FAX 603-898-9858. Ed. M.G. Sautter. (looseleaf format)

EMPLOYMENT JOURNAL. see OCCUPATIONS AND CAREERS

EMPLOYMENT LAW. see LAW — Corporate Law

331 346 US
EMPLOYMENT LAW BRIEFING. 1986. q. free. Sachnoff & Weaver, Ltd., 30 S. Wacker Dr., Ste. 2900, Chicago, IL 60606. TEL 312-207-1000. FAX 312-207-6400. (looseleaf format) **Document type:** newsletter.

331 UK
EMPLOYMENT LAW CASES; a comprehensive case-law reference service. Variant title: I D S Employment Law Cases. 10 base vols. (plus 6/yr. updates). £310 (effective 1997). Incomes Data Services Ltd., 77 Bastwick St., London EC1V 3TT, England. TEL 0171-250-3434. FAX 0171-608-0949. (looseleaf format)
  ●Also available on CD-ROM.
  Description: Compiles reported and unreported labor-law cases, along with summaries and indices.

331 346 US ISSN 1052-2964
KF3302
EMPLOYMENT LAW COUNSELOR. 1990. m. $285. Business Laws, Inc., 11630 Chillicothe Rd., Chesterland, OH 44026. TEL 216-729-7996. FAX 216-729-0645. Ed. William A. Hancock. bk.rev.; index, cum.index. (looseleaf format; back issues avail.) **Document type:** newsletter.
—CCC.
  Description: Covers developments in all areas of employment relations law.

EMPLOYMENT LAW DESK BOOK FOR TENNESSEE EMPLOYERS. see LAW

344.01 US
EMPLOYMENT LAW DESKBOOK. base vol. (plus a. update). $125 for base vol.; update $76. Matthew Bender & Co., Inc., 2 Park Ave., New York, NY 10016. TEL 212-448-2000. E-mail: international@bender.com; URL: http://www.bender.com. (looseleaf format)
  Description: Covers issues arising in employer-employee relationship and provides federal and state employment law analysis for human resources professionals, employers and attorneys.

EMPLOYMENT LAW GUIDE (YEAR). see LAW

331 346 US
KF3457.A15E45
EMPLOYMENT LAW NEWS.* 1979. 6/yr. $30. National Employment Law Project, 55 John St., 7th Fl., New York, NY 10038-3712. TEL 212-870-2121. FAX 212-870-2197. bk.rev. circ. 1,400. (back issues avail.) **Document type:** newsletter.

331 346 US ISSN 1058-1308
KF3457
EMPLOYMENT LAW REPORT. 1991. m. $133 (foreign $153). Data Research, Inc., 4635 Nicols Rd., Ste. 100, Eagan, MN 55122-3337. TEL 612-452-8267. FAX 612-452-8694. (Subscr. to: Box 490, Rosemount, MN 55068-9987. TEL 800-365-4900) Ed. Warren Cody. cum.index. (looseleaf format; back issues avail.) **Document type:** newsletter.
  Description: Covers the latest court cases and late-breaking legislation along with the most recent law review articles affecting employment.

346 331 US
EMPLOYMENT LAW STRATEGIST. 1993. m. $185. New York Law Publishing Co., 345 Park Ave. S., New York, NY 10010. TEL 212-545-6170. FAX 212-696-1848. URL: http://www.ljx.com. Ed. Stephen L. Tenfold. (looseleaf format; back issues avail.) **Document type:** newsletter.

EMPLOYMENT LAW UPDATE. see LAW

EMPLOYMENT LITIGATION REPORTER; the national journal of record for termination lawsuits alleging tort and contract claims against employers. see LAW

BUSINESS AND ECONOMICS — LABOR AND INDUSTRIAL RELATIONS

EMPLOYMENT MANAGEMENT TODAY. see *BUSINESS AND ECONOMICS — Personnel Management*

330.9   US   ISSN 0737-9633
EMPLOYMENT OUTLOOK SURVEY. 1976. q. free to qualified personnel. Manpower Temporary Services, International Headquarters, 5301 N. Ironwood Rd., Milwaukee, WI 53217. TEL 414-961-1000. FAX 414-961-2124. URL: http://www.manpower.com. Ed. Mary B. Stewart. circ. 40,000 (controlled). Indexed: SRI.
Description: Measurement of hiring intentions of more than 16,000 employers in 487 cities on whether to increase, decrease or maintain the size of their present workforce for the upcoming 3-month period.

331 371.42   US
THE EMPLOYMENT PAPER (PITTSBURGH). 1994. w. free. American City Business Journals, Inc. (Austin), 505 Powell St., Austin, TX 78703-5121. (Subscr. to: Pittsburgh Business Times, 2313 E. Carson St., Ste. 200, Pittsburgh, PA 15203-2109. TEL 412-481-5627. FAX 412-481-9956) adv.: B&W page $850. circ. 31,000.

331   UK   ISSN 1351-2145
EMPLOYMENT POLICY INSTITUTE ECONOMIC REPORT. (Former name of issuing body: Employment Institute) 1985. 10/yr. £35 (overseas £40) (effective 1997). Employment Policy Institute, Southbank House, Black Prince Road, London SE1 7SJ, England. TEL 44-171-735-0777. FAX 44-171-793-8192. E-mail: 100130.2374@compuserve.com. Ed. John Philpott; Pub. John Philpott. R&P contact: Nick Isles. TEL 44-171-735-0777. adv. contact: Nick Isles. circ. 1,200 (paid). (back issues avail.) **Document type:** bulletin.
—BLDSC (3654.390000).
Formerly (until 1994): Employment Institute Economic Report.
Description: Provides a regular review of key topical labor market issues along with analysis.

331   US   ISSN 0746-9683
EMPLOYMENT RELATIONS BULLETIN. 10/yr. Florida State University, College of Law, Center for Employment Relations and Law, Tallahassee, FL 32306-1034. TEL 904-644-4287.

EMPLOYMENT RELATIONS LAW VICTORIA. see *LAW*

331.1   US   ISSN 0745-7790
HD4903.5.U58   CODEN: EEOTDY
EMPLOYMENT RELATIONS TODAY. 1974. q. $195 (foreign $219) (effective 1998). John Wiley & Sons, Inc., Journals, 605 Third Ave., New York, NY 10158. TEL 212-850-6645. FAX 212-850-6021. E-mail: subinfo@jwiley.com; URL: http://www.wiley.co.uk. Ed. Carol Di Paola. adv.: B&W page £640, color page £1515; trim 279 x 210. (also avail. in microform from UMI; reprint service avail. from UMI) Indexed: B.P.I., BPIA, Bus.Ind., Manage.Cont., Tr.& Dev.Alert. **Document type:** trade publication.
—BLDSC (3737.510000); KR SourceOne; SWETS; UMI; UnCover. **CCC**.
Formerly (1976-1983): E E O Today (ISSN 0362-5818).
Description: For senior human resources specialists. Covers the significance of changes in the workplace.

331.1 658.3   CC   ISSN 1022-4238
THE EMPLOYMENT REPORT. (Text in English) 1993. 10/yr. HK.$1595. Pearson Professional (Hong Kong) Limited, Ste. 1808, Asian House, 1 Hennessy Rd., Wanchai, Hong Kong, People's Republic of China. TEL 852-2863-2659. FAX 852-2520-6954. E-mail: pphkg@hk.super.net.
Description: Provides up-to-date coverage of human resources issues in Hong Kong.

331.1   US   ISSN 0013-6883
HD8053.N7
EMPLOYMENT REVIEW. 1947? m. free. Department of Labor, Division of Research and Statistics, 1 Main St., 9th Fl., Brooklyn, NY 11201. TEL 718-797-7703. (Subscr. to: Division of Research and Statistics, State Campus, Albany, NY 12240) Ed. Sanford Fialkoff. charts; stat. Indexed: BPIA, Bus.Ind., SRI. **Document type:** government publication.

THE EMPLOYMENT SITUATION. see *BUSINESS AND ECONOMICS — Economic Situation And Conditions*

EMPLOYMENT STANDARDS HANDBOOK AND DIGEST SERVICE. see *LAW*

331   CN   ISSN 1185-2429
KE3244.A72
EMPLOYMENT STANDARDS LEGISLATION IN CANADA. French edition: Legislation en Matiere d'Emploi. 1951. a. free. Canada Communication Group, Publishing Division, Ottawa, ON K1A 0S9, Canada. circ. 2,150. (reprint service avail. from MML) **Document type:** government publication.
Formerly: Labour Standards in Canada - Normes du Travail au Canada (ISSN 0075-7586)
Description: Reports on minimum labor standards, such as hours of work, overtime pay, minimum wage and leave provisions in federal, provincial and territorial jurisdictions.

EMPLOYMENT TESTING; law and policy reporter. see *LAW*

ENCUESTA NACIONAL DEL EMPLEO TOTAL PAIS. see *BUSINESS AND ECONOMICS — Economic Situation And Conditions*

731   US
ENGINEERING, SCIENTIFIC AND TECHNICAL SURVEY. a. $450. MidAtlantic Employers' Association, Box 770, Valley Forge, PA 19482. TEL 215-666-7330. FAX 215-666-7866.
Description: Provides comparative information for 78 engineering, scientific and technical position compensation practices among 160 companies, representing 4,100 employees in PA, NJ, MD, and DE.

331   IR
EQTESAD-E-MELLI. 1979. m. Rs.150($5) Eqtesade of Iran, 47 Gaffary St., 2nd floor, Miadan Haft Tir, Tehran 15, Iran. Ed. Bejan Yazamadhie. adv.; bk.rev. circ. 280.

331.1   US   ISSN 0160-435X
KF3464.A15
EQUAL EMPLOYMENT COMPLIANCE UPDATE. m. $195. Clark - Boardman - Callaghan, 375 Hudson St., New York, NY 10014. TEL 212-929-7500; 800-422-2101. FAX 212-924-0460. Eds. Andrew J. Ruzicho, Louis A. Jacobs. (looseleaf format) **Document type:** newsletter.
—**CCC**.
Formerly (until 1977): Equal Employment Compliance Special Report (ISSN 0160-4368)
Description: Contains current interpretations of E.E.O. laws and regulations, including recent court cases.

331   NZ   ISSN 1170-3784
EQUAL EMPLOYMENT OPPORTUNITIES PLAN. 1989. a. Ministry of Foreign Affairs and Trade, Private Bag 18-901, Wellington, New Zealand. TEL 64-4-472-8877. **Document type:** government publication.

EQUAL MEANS; women organizing economic solutions. see *WOMEN'S INTERESTS*

331 658.3   UK   ISSN 0268-7143
EQUAL OPPORTUNITIES REVIEW. 1985. bi-m. £185 (foreign £205) (includes q. supplements and a. Digest) (effective 1997). Eclipse Group Ltd., Industrial Relations Services, 18-20 Highbury Pl., London N5 1QP, England. TEL 44-171-354-5858. FAX 44-171-226-8618. Eds. Michael Rubenstein, Gary Bowker. index. (also avail. in microform from UMI; back issues avail.) Indexed: Euro.LJI, LJI, Mgmt.& Market.Abstr., Stud.Wom.Abstr. **Document type:** trade publication.
●Also available online. Vendor(s): UMI.
—BLDSC (3794.504800); UMI.
Description: Covers equal-opportunity law and employment practice: sex, race, disability, religion, and age.

331   CY
ERGATIKI PHONI/WORKER'S VOICE. (Text in Greek) 1946. w. S E K, SEK Bldg., 23 Alkeon St., P.O. Box 5018, Egnomi, Nicosia, Cyprus. TEL 357-2-441142. FAX 357-2-476360. TELEX 6180. Ed. Gregoris Gregoriades. circ. 8,850.

231   CY
ERGATIKO VIMA/WORKER'S HERALD. (Text in Greek) 1956. w. Pan-Cyprian Federation of Labor, 31-35 Archemos St., P.O. Box 1885, Nicosia, Cyprus. TEL 357-2-472192. Ed. Pantlis Varnavas. circ. 15,850.

331   GW   ISSN 0170-2793
ERSATZKASSEN-REPORT. 1978. q. free. Verband der Angestellten-Krankenkassen e.V., Frankfurter Str. 84, 53721 Siegburg, Germany. Ed. Rainer Josten. **Document type:** bulletin.

ESSEX COUNTY COUNCIL. PLANNING. SUBJECT MONITORING REPORTS. EMPLOYMENT. see *PUBLIC ADMINISTRATION — Municipal Government*

331   AG   ISSN 0327-5744
ESTUDIOS DEL TRABAJO. 1991. s-a. $58 (N. and C. America $64; Europe $66; elsewhere $70) (effective 1997). Asociacion Argentina de Especialistas en Estudios del Trabajo, Araoz 2838, 1425 Buenos Aires, Argentina. TEL 54-1-8044949. FAX 54-1-8045856. Ed. Silvio Feldman. R&P contact: Silvio Feldman. bk.rev. circ. 500. **Document type:** academic/scholarly publication.
Description: Devoted to social sciences related to labor: labor economics, labor sociology and industrial relations. Publishes theoretical and empirical articles.
Refereed Serial

331.1   UK   ISSN 0309-7234
HD8380.5.A5
EUROPEAN INDUSTRIAL RELATIONS REVIEW. Abbreviated title: E I R R. 1974. m. £270 (foreign £305) (effective 1997). Eclipse Group Ltd., Industrial Relations Services, 18-20 Highbury Pl., London N5 1QP, England. TEL 44-171-354-5858. FAX 44-171-226-8618. Ed. Andrea Broughton. (also avail. in microform from UMI; reprint service avail. from SCH,UMI) Indexed: BPIA, ELLIS, Euro.LJI, Int.Lab.Doc., Key to Econ.Sci., Mgmt.& Market.Abstr., World Bibl.Soc.Sec. **Document type:** trade publication.
●Also available online. Vendor(s): UMI.
—BLDSC (3829.720500); SWETS; UMI.
Description: Reviews developments in all major European nations and relevant EC institutions.

331   UK
EUROPEAN INFORMATION BULLETIN; a quarterly publication for European Trade Unionists. q. c/o Alan Burnett, Ed., 36 Sackville Rd., Crookes, Sheffield S10 1GT, England.

331   UK   ISSN 0959-6801
HD8371   CODEN: EJIRFZ
▼**EUROPEAN JOURNAL OF INDUSTRIAL RELATIONS.** 1995. 3/yr. £34($54) to individuals; institutions £112($179) (effective 1998). Sage Publications Ltd., 6 Bonhill St., London EC2A 4PU, England. TEL 44-171-374-0645. FAX 44-171-374-8741. E-mail: market@sagepub.co.uk; URL: http://www.sagepub.co.uk/. Ed. Richard Hyman. adv. contact: Bernie Folan. bk.rev. Indexed: Anbar, ASSIA, Curr.Cont., Sociol.Abstr., SSCI. **Document type:** academic/scholarly publication.
—BLDSC (3829.730300); Genuine Article; SWETS.
Description: Provides a forum for advancing understanding of the key developments, and their theoretical and practical implications, in industrial relations in Europe.

331   BE   ISSN 1024-7947
▼**EUROPEAN TRADE UNION INSTITUTE. ANNUAL REPORT.** (Text in English, French, German) 1995. a. Institut Syndical Europeen, Bd. Emile Jacqmain 155, 1210 Brussels, Belgium. TEL 32-2-2240470. FAX 32-2-2240502.
Description: Reports on issues affecting trade unions and activities of the institute.

331   BE   ISSN 1025-2533
▼**EUROPEAN TRADE UNION INSTITUTE. DISCUSSION & WORKING PAPERS.** (Text in English or French) 1995. irreg. 100 BEF. Institut Syndical Europeen, Bd. Emile Jacqmain 155, 1210 Brussels, Belgium. TEL 32-2-2240470. FAX 32-2-2240502. **Document type:** monographic series.
Description: Reports on issues affecting European trade unions and labor and industrial relations.

331   BE   ISSN 0775-597X
EUROPEAN TRADE UNION INSTITUTE. DOCUMENTATION CENTRE. BULLETIN. 1987. q. Institut Syndical Europeen, Bd. Emile Jacqmain 155, 1210 Brussels, Belgium. TEL 32-2-2240470. FAX 32-2-2240502. **Document type:** bulletin.

BUSINESS AND ECONOMICS — LABOR AND INDUSTRIAL RELATIONS

331.1   UK
▼**EUROPEAN WORKS COUNCILS BULLETIN.** 1995. q. £165 (foreign £175) (effective 1997). (University of Warwick. Business School. Industrial Relations Research Unit) Eclipse Group Ltd., Industrial Relations Services, 18-20 Highbury Pl., London N5 1QP, England. TEL 44-171-354-5858. FAX 44-171-226-8618. Eds. Mark Carley, Mark Hall. **Document type:** newsletter.
  Description: Reports on European Works Council developments, negotiations, and agreements and contains the full text of important documents.

EVALUATING YOUR FIRM'S INJURY & ILLNESS RECORD. CONSTRUCTION INDUSTRIES. see *OCCUPATIONAL HEALTH AND SAFETY*

EVALUATING YOUR FIRM'S INJURY & ILLNESS RECORD. SERVICE INDUSTRIES. see *OCCUPATIONAL HEALTH AND SAFETY*

EVALUATING YOUR FIRM'S INJURY & ILLNESS RECORD. TRANSPORTATION & PUBLIC UTILITIES INDUSTRIES. see *OCCUPATIONAL HEALTH AND SAFETY*

EVALUATING YOUR FIRM'S INJURY & ILLNESS RECORD. WHOLESALE & RETAIL TRADE INDUSTRIES. see *OCCUPATIONAL HEALTH AND SAFETY*

331   TG
EVEIL DU TRAVAILLEUR TOGOLAIS. (Text in Elrato) q. Confederation Nationale des Travailleurs du Togo, B.P. 163, Lome, Togo. TEL 21-57-39. Ed. M.K. Agbeka. circ. 5,000.

331.2   US   ISSN 0738-6982
EXECUTIVE COMPENSATION REPORTS; an executive service covering corporate compensation programs. 1980. s-m. $475 (foreign $535). Harcourt Brace Professional Publishing, 525 B St., Ste. 1900, San Diego, CA 92101-4495. TEL 619-699-6716. FAX 619-699-6593. Ed. Carol M. Bowie. (looseleaf format)
  Description: Provides a reference on executive compensation payments, plans, policies and procedures.

731   US
EXECUTIVE COMPENSATION SURVEY REPORT. a. $400. MidAtlantic Employers' Association, Box 770, Valley Forge, PA 19482. TEL 215-666-7330. FAX 215-666-7866.
  Description: Provides comparative information about executive compensation practices among businesses in the Mid-Atlantic states.

331 368.4   UK   ISSN 0268-6910
EXPATRIATE. 1977. m. £75 (foreign £85.60). (Centre for Legal & Business Information) First Market Intelligence Ltd., 175 Vauxhall Bridge Rd., Westminster, London SW1V 1ER, England. TEL 071-834-9192. FAX 071-630-0194. TELEX 917071-FMILDN-G. Ed. Vera Madan. adv.; bk.rev.; index. circ. 400. **Document type:** newsletter.

331.1   US   ISSN 0732-0345
F L R A REPORTS OF CASE DECISIONS, F S I P RELEASES AND ADMINISTRATIVE LAW JUDGE DECISIONS. 1979. base vol. plus irreg. updates. $92 (foreign $115) (effective 1997). U.S. Federal Labor Relations Authority, 607 Fourteenth St., N.W., Washington, DC 20424-0001. TEL 202-382-0751. (Subscr. to: Superintendent of Documents, U.S. Government Printing Office, Box 371954, Pittsburgh, PA 15250-7954. TEL 202-512-1800. FAX 202-512-2250) **Document type:** government publication.
  Description: Includes the full text of all published Authority decisions, FSIP releases, digest summaries of the Authority's decisions, news releases, citators and certain indexes.

331 651   US   ISSN 0885-7172
FAIR EMPLOYMENT COMPLIANCE;* a confidential letter to management. 1975. s-m. $245. Management Resources, Inc., Box 105, Hampton, NH 03843-0105. Ed. Kenneth Swann. bk.rev. circ. 2,000. **Document type:** newsletter.

331   US
FAIR EMPLOYMENT PRACTICES SUMMARY OF LATEST DEVELOPMENTS. (Subseries of: B N A Policy and Practice Series (ISSN 0005-3228)) 1965. bi-w. $123. The Bureau of National Affairs, Inc., 1231 25th St., N.W., Washington, DC 20037. TEL 202-452-4200. FAX 202-822-8092. TELEX 285656 BNAI WSH. URL: http://www.bna.com/. (Subscr. to: 9435 Key West Ave., Rockville, MD 20850. TEL 800-372-1033) Ed. Bill L. Manville. (back issues avail.)
  ●Also available online. Vendor(s): Human Resources Information Network (CDD, HDD).
  Description: Covers developments affecting equal employment opportunities, fair employment practice policies, and affirmative action programs, from trends to relevant regulations, rules and guidelines to federal and state court decisions.

331.113   US   ISSN 0014-6919
FAIR EMPLOYMENT REPORT. 1963. bi-w. $286. Business Publishers, Inc., 951 Pershing Dr., Silver Spring, MD 20910-4464. TEL 301-587-6300. FAX 301-585-9075. Ed. Steve Lash. bk.rev.; stat. (looseleaf format; back issues avail.) **Document type:** newsletter.
  ●Also available online. Vendor(s): NewsNet.
  —CCC.
  Formerly: Civil Rights Employment Reporter.
  Description: Studies developments in federal programs aimed at eliminating employment discrimination.

331.2   SW
FAKTA OM LOENER. 1989. a. SEK 100 (effective 1997). Svenska Arbetsgivarefoereningen (SAF), S-103 30 Stockholm, Sweden.
  Former titles (until 1997): Loen foer Tjaenstemaen (ISSN 1100-6722); (until 1989): Salaries of Salaried Employees.

FEDERAL CIVILIAN WORK FORCE STATISTICS. AFFIRMATIVE EMPLOYMENT STATISTICS. see *BUSINESS AND ECONOMICS — Abstracting, Bibliographies, Statistics*

FEDERAL CIVILIAN WORK FORCE STATISTICS. PAY STRUCTURE OF THE FEDERAL CIVIL SERVICE. see *BUSINESS AND ECONOMICS — Abstracting, Bibliographies, Statistics*

FEDERAL CIVILIAN WORK FORCE STATISTICS. WORK YEARS AND PERSONNEL COSTS. EXECUTIVE BRANCH, UNITED STATES GOVERNMENT. see *BUSINESS AND ECONOMICS — Abstracting, Bibliographies, Statistics*

FEDERAL CIVILIAN WORKFORCE STATISTICS. OCCUPATIONS OF FEDERAL WHITE-COLLAR AND BLUE-COLLAR WORKERS. see *BUSINESS AND ECONOMICS — Abstracting, Bibliographies, Statistics*

344.73   US   ISSN 1066-8764
FEDERAL EQUAL OPPORTUNITY (YEAR) DESK BOOK. 1992. a. $59 (effective 1997). L R P Publications, 747 Dresher Rd., Box 980, Horsham, PA 19044-0980. TEL 215-784-0941; 800-341-7874. FAX 215-784-9639. URL: http://www.lrp.com. Ed.Bd.

344.73 347.304   US   ISSN 1043-7274
KF3464
FEDERAL EQUAL OPPORTUNITY REPORTER. 1982. bi-w. $890 (effective 1997). L R P Publications, 747 Dresher Rd., Box 980, Horsham, PA 19044-0980. TEL 215-784-0941; 800-341-7874. FAX 215-784-9639. URL: http://www.lrp.com. Ed.Bd. index. (looseleaf format; back issues avail.)
  —CCC.

331 344.73   US
FEDERAL HUMAN RESOURCES WEEK. 1994. 48/yr. $295 (effective 1997). L R P Publications, 747 Dresher Rd., Box 980, Horsham, PA 19044-0980. TEL 215-784-0941; 800-341-7874. FAX 215-784-9639. URL: http://www.lrp.com. Ed. Ken Hughes. index. (back issues avail.) **Document type:** newsletter.
  Description: Focuses on the latest trends and news in the federal sector.

FEDERAL LABOR LAWS. see *LAW*

331.1   US   ISSN 0885-3061
KF5365.A59
THE FEDERAL LABOR - MANAGEMENT AND EMPLOYEE RELATIONS CONSULTANT. 1971. 24/yr. $39 (foreign $48.75). U.S. Office of Personnel Management, Office of Labor Relations and Workforce Performance, Rm. 7429, Washington, DC 20415. TEL 202-606-2930. (Subscr. to: Superintendent of Documents, U.S. Government Printing Office, Box 37194, Pittsburgh, PA 15250-7954. TEL 202-512-1800. FAX 202-512-2250) Ed. Mary L. Hennessy. bk.rev. circ. 10,000. (tabloid format) **Indexed:** Pers.Lit. **Document type:** government publication.
  Formerly: Federal Labor - Management Consultant (ISSN 0046-3418)
  Description: Reports on developments in Federal sector labor-management and employee relations.

344.73   US   ISSN 1065-8238
FEDERAL LABOR RELATIONS (YEAR) DESK BOOK. 1992. a. $57.50 (effective 1997). L R P Publications, 747 Dresher Rd., Box 980, Horsham, PA 19044-0980. TEL 215-784-0941; 800-341-7874. FAX 215-784-9639. URL: http://www.lrp.com. Ed. Richard B. Grant, Jr.

344.73 347.304   US   ISSN 0199-4883
KF5365.A57
FEDERAL LABOR RELATIONS REPORTER. 1978. w. $795 (effective 1997). L R P Publications, 747 Dresher Rd., Box 980, Horsham, PA 19044-0980. TEL 215-784-0941; 800-341-7874. FAX 215-784-9639. URL: http://www.lrp.com. Eds. Susan Dixon, Richard Grant. q. index. (looseleaf format; back issues avail.)
  —CCC.

351.6 344.73   US   ISSN 1075-6590
FEDERAL MERIT SYSTEMS (YEAR) DESK BOOK. a. $58 (effective 1997). L R P Publications, 747 Dresher Rd., Box 980, Horsham, PA 19044-0980. TEL 215-784-0941; 800-341-7874. FAX 215-784-9639. URL: http://www.lrp.com. Ed. Joseph V. Kaplan.
  Description: Presents an overview of Merit Systems Protection Board (MSPB) decisions that have shaped the year in review.

344.73 347.304   US   ISSN 0746-035X
KF5336
FEDERAL MERIT SYSTEMS REPORTER. 1979. w. $795 (effective 1997). L R P Publications, 747 Dresher Rd., Box 980, Horsham, PA 19044-0980. TEL 215-784-0941; 800-341-7874. FAX 215-784-9639. URL: http://www.lrp.com. Ed. Susan Dixon. q. index. (looseleaf format; back issues avail.)
  —CCC.

331.2 344.73   US   ISSN 0888-269X
KF5370
FEDERAL PAY AND BENEFITS REPORTER. m. $550 (effective 1997). L R P Publications, 747 Dresher Rd., Box 980, Horsham, PA 19044-0980. TEL 215-784-0941; 800-341-7874. FAX 215-784-9639. URL: http://www.lrp.com. Ed. Richard Grant. q. index. (looseleaf format; back issues avail.)
  —CCC.

331.88   KE
FEDERATION OF KENYA EMPLOYERS. NEWSLETTER. q. free to qualified personnel. Federation of Kenya Employers, P.O. Box 48311, Nairobi, Kenya. TEL 254-2-721929. FAX 254-2-721990. TELEX 22642 FKE KE. circ. 3,000 (controlled). **Document type:** newsletter.
  Formerly: Kenya Employer (ISSN 0428-1845)

331   FR   ISSN 0753-5732
FEUILLET RAPIDE SOCIAL. 1983. 3/m. 335 F. (effective 1997). Editions Francis Lefebvre, 42 reu de Villiers, 92300 Levallois, France. TEL 41-05-22-00. FAX 41-05-22-30.

FIJI. BUREAU OF STATISTICS. EMPLOYMENT SURVEY OF FIJI. see *BUSINESS AND ECONOMICS — Abstracting, Bibliographies, Statistics*

FIJI. BUREAU OF STATISTICS. NATIONWIDE UNEMPLOYMENT SURVEY. see *BUSINESS AND ECONOMICS — Abstracting, Bibliographies, Statistics*

BUSINESS AND ECONOMICS — LABOR AND INDUSTRIAL RELATIONS

331.11 — FJ
FIJI CLASSIFICATION & DICTIONARY OF OCCUPATIONS. 1975. irreg. $5 per no. (effective 1997). Bureau of Statistics, P.O. Box 2221, Suva, Fiji. **Document type:** government publication.

FLASH. see *LABOR UNIONS*

FLORIDA EMPLOYMENT LAW LETTER. see *LAW*

FLORIDA EMPLOYMENT LAW MANUAL. see *LAW*

331 340 — US
FLORIDA WORKERS' COMPENSATION MANUAL. 1979. 3 base vols. (plus suppl. 2-3/yr.) $160. Butterworth Legal Publishers (Salem) (Subsidiary of Reed Elsevier plc), 8 Industrial Way, Bldg. C, Salem, NH 03079. TEL 800-548-4001. FAX 603-898-9858. (looseleaf format)

FLORIDA WORKERS' COMPENSATION REPORTER. see *INSURANCE*

FOCUS ON CANADIAN EMPLOYMENT AND EQUALITY RIGHTS. see *BUSINESS AND ECONOMICS — Personnel Management*

331 — SW — ISSN 0015-5306
FOERSVARSTJAENSTEMANNEN/CIVIL SERVANT IN THE DEFENCE FORCES. Variant title: Nya Foersvarstjaenstemannen. (Text in Swedish) 1938. 9/yr. membership only. Foersvarets Civila Tjanstemannafoerbund - Union of Civilian Employees in the Defence Forces, Sturegatan 15, P.O.Box 5328, 102 46 Stockholm, Sweden. TEL 46-8-790-52-00. FAX -46-8-20-56-92. Ed. Olle Forsberg. adv.; bk.rev.; illus.; index. circ. 12,500. **Document type:** newspaper.
   Formerly (until 1959): Civila Foersvarstjaenstemannen.

FOOD SHOP. see *FOOD AND FOOD INDUSTRIES*

338.1 388.3 — US — ISSN 0046-4538
FORD WORLD. 1964. 11/yr. free. Ford Motor Co. (Dearborn), The American Rd., Rm. 956, Dearborn, MI 48121. TEL 313-322-2738. Ed. Nancy Carollo. adv. contact: Bev Boyer. charts; illus. circ. 250,000. (tabloid format) **Indexed:** HRIS. **Document type:** newspaper.
   Description: For Ford employees and retirees, keeping them informed of company news.

331 374 — GW — ISSN 0340-8973
FORSCHUNGSDOKUMENTATION ZUR ARBEITSMARKT- UND BERUFSFORSCHUNG. 1970. 3/yr. DM.80. Bundesanstalt fuer Arbeit, Institut fuer Arbeitsmarkt- und Berufsforschung, Regensburgerstr. 104, 90327 Nuernberg, Germany. TEL 49-911-1793011. FAX 49-911-1793258. E-mail: iab.ba@t-online.de. circ. 3,000. (back issues avail.) **Document type:** government publication.
   Description: Lists ongoing and completed research projects on labor market and occupations.

331.11 — FR — ISSN 0249-5562
FRANCE. CENTRE D'ETUDES DE L'EMPLOI. CAHIERS. 1972. irreg., no. 35, 1996. price varies. Centre d'Etudes de l'Emploi, Le Descartes I, 29 promenade Michel-Simon, 93166 Noisy-le-Grand Cedex, France. TEL 33-1-45926800. FAX 33-1-49310244. E-mail: cee@msh-paris.fr. Ed. Mrs. A. Fouquet. R&P contact: A. Azouvi. **Document type:** monographic series.
   —BLDSC (2947.875000).

331 — FR
FRANCE. CENTRE D'ETUDES DE L'EMPLOI. DOSSIERS. 1980. irreg., N.S. no.8, 1996. 450 F. for 6 nos. (effective 1997). Centre d'Etudes de l'Emploi, Le Descartes I, 29 promenade Michel-Simon, 93166 Noisy-le-Grand Cedex, France. TEL 33-1-45926817. FAX 33-1-49310244. E-mail: cee@msh-paris.fr. Ed. Francoise Laroche. **Document type:** monographic series.
   —BLDSC (3619.746048).
   Formerly: France. Centre d'Etudes de l'Emploi. Dossiers de Recherche (ISSN 0291-9249)

331.11 — FR — ISSN 1257-001X
FRANCE. CENTRE D'ETUDES DE L'EMPLOI. LETTRE. 1971. 5/yr. 150 F. (effective 1997). Centre d'Etudes de l'Emploi, Le Descartes I, 29 promenade Michel-Simon, 93166 Noisy-le-Grand Cedex, France. TEL 33-1-45926848. FAX 33-1-49310244. E-mail: cee@msh-paris.fr. Ed. Marie-Madeleine Vennat. **Document type:** monographic series.
   Former titles: France. Centre d'Etudes de l'Emploi. Lettre d'Information (ISSN 0982-460X); (until 1986): France. Centre d'Etudes de l'Emploi. Bulletin d'Information (ISSN 0294-8400)

331 — FR — ISSN 1251-8107
FRANCE. CENTRE D'ETUDES DE L'EMPLOI. QUATRE PAGES. Key Title: 4 Pages. 1994. 6/yr. free. Centre d'Etudes de l'Emploi, Le Descartes I, 29 promenade Michel Simon, 93166 Noisy-Le-Grand Cedex, France. TEL 33-1-45926854. FAX 33-1-49310244. E-mail: cee@msh-paris.fr. Ed. Jean-Claude Barbier. R&P contact: A. Azouvi. **Document type:** bulletin.

FRANCE. MINISTERE DES AFFAIRES SOCIALES ET DE LA SOLIDARITE NATIONALE. MINISTERE CHARGE DE L'EMPLOI. CONVENTIONS COLLECTIVES. see *PUBLIC ADMINISTRATION*

331 — HO
FRENTE. 1981. q. Universidad Nacional Autonoma de Honduras, Sindicato de Trabajadores, Tegucigalpa D.C., Honduras. circ. 1,000.

331 — US
FRINGE BENEFITS AND WORKING CONDITIONS IN NONPROFIT ORGANIZATIONS. 1992. biennial. $125. Abbott, Langer & Associates, 548 First St., Crete, IL 60417. TEL 708-672-4200. Ed. Steven Langer.

331 — GW
G D E D INFORM. 1897. m. membership. Gewerkschaft der Eisenbahner Deutschlands, Postfach 170331, 60077 Frankfurt a.M., Germany. TEL 49-69-7078575. FAX 49-69-7078657. adv.; bk.rev. circ. 450,000. **Document type:** trade publication.
   Formerly (until 1995): Deutsche Eisenbahner (ISSN 0343-7108)

GAMBIA. CENTRAL STATISTICS DEPARTMENT. QUARTERLY SURVEY OF EMPLOYMENT AND EARNINGS. see *BUSINESS AND ECONOMICS — Abstracting, Bibliographies, Statistics*

331.8 — PL — ISSN 1231-8345
GAZETA PRACY. 1994. m. 9.60 Zl. (effective June 1996). Fundacja na Rzecz Restrukturyzacji Regionu Lodzkiego, Ul. Tuwima 22-26, 90-002 Lodz, Poland. TEL 48-42-322651. FAX 48-42-301741. adv. (back issues avail.)
   Description: Describes labor law regulations, unemployment and labor problems. Contains labor offers.

GEOGRAPHIC PROFILE OF EMPLOYMENT AND UNEMPLOYMENT. see *BUSINESS AND ECONOMICS — Economic Situation And Conditions*

GEORGIA EMPLOYMENT LAW LETTER. see *LAW*

331.1 — US — ISSN 0147-9865
HD5725.G4
GEORGIA LABOR MARKET TRENDS. 1975. m. free. Department of Labor, Labor Information System, Sussex Pl., 148 International Blvd., N.E., Atlanta, GA 30303. TEL 404-656-3177. stat. circ. 4,000. **Indexed:** SRI. **Document type:** government publication. **Incorporates** (in 1978): Georgia Labor Force Newsletter; **Formerly:** Georgia Manpower Trends (ISSN 0091-3464)

344.012 — US
GEORGIA WORKERS' COMPENSATION LAWS, RULES AND REGULATIONS ANNOTATED. a. $22.50 (diskette $49.95). Michie, A Division of Reed Elsevier Inc., Box 7587, Charlottesville, VA 22906-7587. TEL 804-972-7566; 800-562-1197. FAX 800-643-1280. E-mail: custserv@michie.com; URL: http://www.michie.com. Ed. George Harley. (also avail. in diskette format)
   Description: Contains case notes and annotations.

331.1 368.4 — GW — ISSN 0007-585X
GERMANY. BUNDESANSTALT FUER ARBEIT. AMTLICHE NACHRICHTEN. 1953. m. DM.195. Bundesanstalt fuer Arbeit, Regensburgerstr. 104, 90478 Nuernberg, Germany. TEL 49-911-1795034. FAX 49-911-1792123. charts; illus.; stat.; index. circ. 5,000. **Document type:** government publication.
   —SWETS.

331 — GW — ISSN 0943-8289
GESAMTE OEFFENTLICHE DIENSTRECHT. 1972. irreg. DM.168. Erich Schmidt Verlag GmbH & Co. (Berlin), Genthiner Str. 30G, 10785 Berlin, Germany. TEL 49-30-250085-0. FAX 49-30-25008521. (looseleaf format) **Document type:** bulletin.

GIDS VOOR SOCIALE REGLEMENTERING IN ONDERNEMINGEN. see *LAW — Civil Law*

331 — IT
GIORNALE DI DIRITTO DEL LAVORO E RELAZIONI INDUSTRIALI. 1979. q. L.100000 (foreign L.130000) (effective 1993). Franco Angeli Editore, Viale Monza 106, 20127 Milan, Italy. TEL 02-28-27-651. Ed. Gino Giugni. **Indexed:** ELLIS.

331 — US
GOLDEN LODGE NEWS. 1954. m. Golden Lodge, 1234 Harrison Ave., S.W., Canton, OH 44706. TEL 216-454-6137. FAX 216-454-3461. Ed. Tom Spauhour. circ. 7,000. **Document type:** newspaper.

331 — CC — ISSN 1001-3237
GONGREN ZUZHI YU HUODONG. (Subseries of: Fuyin Baokan Ziliao) (Text in Chinese) q. $14.45. Zhongguo Renmin Daxue, Shubao Ziliao Zhongxin - China People's University, Book & Newspaper Information Center, 3 Zhang Zizhong Rd., P.O. Box 1122, Beijing 100007, People's Republic of China. TEL 86-10-4015080. (Dist. in US by: China Publications Service, Box 49614, Chicago, IL 60649. TEL 312-288-3291. FAX 312-288-8570) Ed. Xie Zili. index.
   Description: Reprints articles and papers on workers' organizations and activities.

331 — RU — ISSN 0007-7666
GOSUDARSTVENNYI KOMITET SOVETA MINISTROV S.S.S.R. PO VOPROSAM TRUDA I ZARABOTNOI PLATY. BYULLETEN'. (Text in Russian) 1966. m. $5.40. Gosudarstvennyi Komitet Soveta Ministrov po Voprosam Truda i Zarabotnoi Platy, Moscow, Russia.

350 — US — ISSN 0017-260X
HD8008.A1
GOVERNMENT EMPLOYEE RELATIONS REPORT. 1963. w. $903. The Bureau of National Affairs, Inc., 1231 25th St., N.W., Washington, DC 20037. TEL 202-452-4200. FAX 202-822-8092. TELEX 285656 BNAI WSH. URL: http://www.bna.com/. (Subscr. to: 9435 Key West Ave., Rockville, MD 20850. TEL 800-372-1033) Ed. Anthony A. Harris. bk.rev.; charts; stat.; cum.index. (looseleaf format; also avail. in microfilm; back issues avail.)
   ●Also available online. Vendor(s): Human Resources Information Network (CDD, HDD), Lexis-Nexis (GOVEMP), West Group.
   —BLDSC (4204.100000). **CCC**.
   Description: Notification and reference service covering federal, state and municipal government employee relations.

331.1 — US — ISSN 0270-2487
HD8008.A1
GOVERNMENT UNION REVIEW. 1980. q. $20. Public Service Research Foundation, 527 Maple Ave. E., 3rd Fl., Vienna, VA 22180. TEL 703-242-3575. FAX 703-242-3579. E-mail: info@psrf.org; URL: http://www.psrf.org. Ed. David Y. Denholm. circ. 5,000. (also avail. in microform from UMI; back issues avail.; reprint service avail. from UMI,WSH) **Indexed:** ABI Inform., BPIA, C.I.J.E., C.L.I., Ind.Per.Art.Relat.Law, L.R.I., P.A.I.S., Pers.Lit., Sage Pub.Admin.Abstr. **Document type:** academic/scholarly publication.
   —BLDSC (4206.078000); UMI; UnCover.
   Description: Academic journal covering the labor relations field.

331 — UK
GRAMPIAN SALARY SURVEY. 2/yr. £250 (effective 1997). The Reward Group Ltd., Reward House, Diamond Way, Stone Business Park, Stone, Staffordshire ST15 OSD, England. TEL 44-1785-813566. FAX 44-1785-817007. E-mail: 101364.661@compuserve.com. **Document type:** bulletin.

BUSINESS AND ECONOMICS — LABOR AND INDUSTRIAL RELATIONS

331.1   UK
GREAT BRITAIN. DEPARTMENT OF EMPLOYMENT. RESEARCH. 1972. a. free. Employment Department, Research Management, Moorfoot, Sheffield S1 4PQ, London, England. TEL 071-273-4875. FAX 071-273-5364. (Avail. from: H.M.S.O., 49 High Holborn, London WC1V 6HB, England) circ. 2,000.
Document type: government publication.
Description: Provides details of research projects carried out for the department by external researchers and contractors.

GUDOK. see TRANSPORTATION — Railroads

331   IT
GUIDA PRATICA DEL LAVORO. s-a. L.110000 (effective 1996). Sole 24 Ore, S.p.A., Via Lomazzo 52, 20154 Milan, Italy. TEL 39-2-3022323. FAX 39-6-3022004. (Subscr. to: Via Parabiago 19, 20151 Milan, Italy) Eds. Gabriele Bonati, Pietro Gremigni.

331 344.73   US   ISSN 1089-456X
KF3464.Z9
GUIDE TO FAIR EMPLOYMENT PRACTICES. (Supplement to: Labor Law Reports) 1973. irreg., latest 1996. included with Labor Law Reports. C C H Incorporated, 2700 Lake Cook Rd., Riverwoods, IL 60015. TEL 847-267-7000; 800-835-5224. FAX 800-224-8299.
Formerly: Guidebook to Fair Employment Practices (ISSN 0196-7975)

331   II   ISSN 0017-5501
GUJARAT LABOUR GAZETTE. (Text in English) vol.7, 1967. m. Rs.10. Office of the Commissioner of Labour, Ahmedabad, India. charts; stat.; index.

331   CC   ISSN 1002-7823
GUOJI LAOGONG TONGXUN/INTERNATIONAL LABOR BULLETIN. (Text in Chinese) 1990. 5/yr. Laodong Renshi Chubanshe, 12 Hepingli Zhongjie, Beijing 100009, People's Republic of China. TEL 4665588. Ed. Wang Jianxin.

H C E P. see LAW — Corporate Law

331.86 371.42   US   ISSN 1067-2702
H R D I ADVISORY. 1972. bi-m. free. Human Resources Development Institute, 815 16th St., N.W., Washington, DC 20006. TEL 202-638-3912. Ed. Jim Templeton. circ. 2,700 (controlled). (tabloid format) **Document type:** newsletter.
Description: Provides information on labor-involved employment, training, and workplace literacy activities for dislocated and disabled workers, and skill upgrading of employed workers.

H R REPORTER. (Human Resources) see BUSINESS AND ECONOMICS — Personnel Management

HADASHOT KUPOT HOLIM. see INSURANCE

331   US
HANDBOOK OF LABOR FORCE DATA FOR SELECTED AREAS OF OKLAHOMA. 1966. a. free. Employment Security Commission, Research Department, Will Rogers Bldg., 2401 N. Lincoln Blvd., Oklahoma City, OK 73105. Ed. Brenda Beed. stat. circ. 300.
Document type: government publication.

HANDBOOK OF LABOR STATISTICS. see BUSINESS AND ECONOMICS — Economic Situation And Conditions

331 341   NE
HANDBOOK ON EUROPEAN EMPLOYEE CO-MANAGEMENT. (Text in English) 1987. 2 base vols. (pus a. update). $247 (effective 1996). Kluwer Law International (Subsidiary of: Wolters Kluwer N.V.), Postbus 85889, 2508 CN The Hague, Netherlands. TEL 31-70-3081500. FAX 31-70-3081515. (Dist. by: Libresso Distribution Centre, P.O. Box 23, 7400 GA Deventer, Netherlands. TEL 31-570-633155. FAX 31-570-633834; In N. America: Kluwer Law International, 675 Massachusetts Ave., Cambridge, MA 02139. TEL 617-354-0140. FAX 617-354-8595) Eds. Walter Kolvenbach, Peter Hanau. (looseleaf format)
Description: Covers contractual and other regulations governing employee participation in management at the shop floor and boardroom level for countries in Europe (including non-EC countries). Includes regulations drawn up by international organizations such as the ILO and OECD, and comparisons with relevant US law and practice.

331.4   US
(YEAR) HANDBOOK ON WOMEN WORKERS: TRENDS & ISSUES. (Subseries of: Women's Bureau Bulletin) 1948. irreg. price varies. U.S. Department of Labor, Women's Bureau, 200 Constitution Ave., N.W., Washington, DC 20210. TEL 202-219-6652. FAX 202-219-5529. (Orders to: Supt. of Documents, Washington, DC 20402) Ed. Bernia Friedlander.
Former titles: Trends and Issues: Handbook on Women Workers (Year); Time of Change: Handbook on Women Workers; Handbook of Women Workers (ISSN 0083-3622); Time of Change.
Description: Offers a comprehensive view of the labor force activity of women and describes a range of legal and socioeconomic developments that have impacted upon women's participation and progress in the work force.

331   DK   ISSN 0107-4458
HANDELSHOEJSKOLEN I KOEBENHAVN. INSTITUT FOR ORGANISATION OG ARBEJDSSOCIOLOGI. H D STUDIET I ORGANISATION; haandbog for studerende. vol.15, 1981. a. DKK 48. Handelshoejskolen i Koebenhavn, Institut for Organisation og Arbejdssociologi, Copenhagen, Denmark. TEL 01-370-555. (Dist. by: Danske Boghandleres Kommissionsanstalt, Siljangade 6, 2300 Copenhagen-S, Denmark) circ. 700.
Formerly: Haandbog for Studerende ved H D Studiet i Organisation.

HANDICAPPED REQUIREMENTS HANDBOOK. see HANDICAPPED

331 346   UK
HARVEY ON INDUSTRIAL RELATIONS & EMPLOYMENT LAW. 3 base vols. (plus bi-m. updates). £275($520) Butterworth & Co. (Publishers) Ltd., Part of the Reed Elsevier group, Halsbury House, 35 Chancery Ln., London WC2A 1EL, England. TEL 071-400-2500. FAX 071-400-2842. (U.S. addr.: Butterworth Legal Publishers, 90 Stiles Rd., Salem, NH 03079-9981. TEL 603-898-9664) Ed. Bryn Perrins. (looseleaf format) **Document type:** trade publication.
Description: Provides a complete compendium of industrial relations and employment law and practice. Gives narrative guidance, analyzing the law, clarifying obscure passages and filling in the practical background.

331   II   ISSN 0046-6921
HARYANA LABOUR JOURNAL. (Text in English, Hindi) 1970. q. Rs.20. Department of Labour, Haryana, Chandigarh, India. Ed.Bd. adv.; charts; illus.

331   AU
HAUSNACHRICHTEN. 6/yr. free. Shell Austria AG, Rennweg 12, A-1030 Vienna, Austria. TEL 43-1-797972206. FAX 43-1-797972201. TELEX 133241-SHEL-A. Ed. H. Bieber. abstr.; illus. circ. 1,500. **Document type:** bulletin.
Formerly: Shell Hausnachrichten (ISSN 0037-3540)

HEALTH CARE LABOR MANUAL. see HOSPITALS

340   US   ISSN 0890-9245
KF3580.H4
HEALTH EMPLOYMENT LAW UPDATE. 1985. 12/yr. $97.50. Rutkowski & Associates Inc., Box 15250, Evansville, IN 47716-0250. TEL 812-476-4520. Eds. Arthur D. Rutkowski, Barbara Lang Rutkowski. R&P contact: Barbara Lang Rutkowski. index. (looseleaf format; back issues avail.) **Document type:** newsletter.
Description: Pragmatic advice for human resources executives, covering current legislation and legal decisions, issues and trends, policy concerns, and authoritative legal analysis.

HEALTH LABOR RELATIONS REPORTS. see HOSPITALS

HEALTH PROFESSIONS REPORT; the independent bi-weekly newsletter on the education & training of medical, nursing and health professionals. see EDUCATION

331   UK
HERTFORDSHIRE - ESSEX SALARY SURVEY. 2/yr. £250 (effective 1997). The Reward Group Ltd., Reward House, Diamond Way, Stone Business Park, Stone, Staffordshire ST15 0SD, England. TEL 44-1785-813566. FAX 44-1785-817007. E-mail: 101364.661@compuserve.com. **Document type:** bulletin.
Description: Pay and benefit salary survey for the Hertfordshire and Essex areas.

331 900   UK   ISSN 1362-1572
▼**HISTORICAL STUDIES IN INDUSTRIAL RELATIONS.** 1996. s-a. Keele University Press, Keele University, Keele, Staffordshire ST5 5BG, England. TEL 44-1782-583099. FAX 44-1782-584120. **Document type:** academic/scholarly publication.
—BLDSC (4317.057000).

HOFSTRA LABOR LAW JOURNAL. see LAW

331   CU
HOMBRE Y TRABAJO; informacion especializada. 1979. q. $2. Comite Estatal de Trabajo y Seguridad Social, 23 Calle O y P, Vedado Plaza, Havana, Cuba. circ. 2,000.
Formerly: Economia del Trabajo (ISSN 0864-0130)

331   IT   ISSN 0439-4291
HOMO FABER; rassegna internazionale de lavoro e dell'istruzione. 1950. m. Mario Pantaleo, Ed. & Pub., Via dei Gracchi 181-185, Rome, Italy. bk.rev.

HONOLULU EMPLOYEE JOURNAL. see PUBLIC ADMINISTRATION — Municipal Government

HORECA INFO; vakblad voor werknemers. see HOTELS AND RESTAURANTS

HOSPITAL EMPLOYEE HEALTH. see HOSPITALS

331   US   ISSN 0885-0275
HOTEL - BAR - RESTAURANT REVIEW. 1935. q. 18600 W. Ten Mile Rd., Southfield, MI 48075. TEL 313-569-7090. FAX 810-569-0871. Ed. Candace Landers. R&P contact: Candace Landers. bk.rev. circ. 8,000. (tabloid format) **Document type:** newsletter.

731   US
HOURLY EARNINGS SURVEY. a. $225. MidAtlantic Employers' Association, Box 770, Valley Forge, PA 19482. TEL 215-666-7330. FAX 215-666-7866.
Description: Summarizes data on employment, hours worked and earnings of hourly paid production workers from 148 companies, representing 9,800 employees in PA, NJ, MD, and DE.

HUMAN RESOURCE MANAGEMENT NEWS; the weekly newsletter for the human resource management field. see BUSINESS AND ECONOMICS — Personnel Management

658.3   US
HUMAN RESOURCES MANAGEMENT. (Consists of: Ideas and Trends; Employment Relations; Compensation; Equal Employment Opportunity; Personnel Practices - Communications; O S A H Compliance) 9 base vols. (plus m. updates). $1572. C C H Incorporated, 2700 Lake Cook Rd., Riverwoods, IL 60015. TEL 847-267-7000; 800-835-5224. FAX 800-224-8299. (looseleaf format) **Indexed:** Bus.Ind., Manage.Cont., Mgmt.& Market.Abstr.
●Also available on CD-ROM.

HUMAN RESOURCES MANAGEMENT - COMPENSATION. see BUSINESS AND ECONOMICS — Personnel Management

HUMAN RESOURCES MANAGEMENT - EMPLOYEE RELATIONS. see BUSINESS AND ECONOMICS — Personnel Management

331 658   US   ISSN 1077-4335
HUMAN SIDE. no.855, Feb.1971. s-m. $61.92. Bureau of Business Practice, 24 Rope Ferry Rd., Waterford, CT 06386. TEL 860-442-4365. FAX 860-437-3555. URL: http://www.bbpnews.com. Ed. Kathleen Cipriani; Pub. Peter Garabedian. R&P contact: Debra Ferraro. illus. (looseleaf format)
Formerly (until 1992): Human Side of Supervisior (ISSN 0018-7135)
Description: Teaches front-line supervisors the right way to motivate workers, solve people problems, manage effectively, and promote teamwork.

BUSINESS AND ECONOMICS — LABOR AND INDUSTRIAL RELATIONS 1433

50 300   FR   ISSN 0018-7372
...MANISME ET ENTREPRISE; revue informant des problemes humains, sociaux et economiques dans entreprise. 1959. bi-m. 1000 F. (foreign 1050 F.) (effective 1997). Association des Anciens Eleves de lettres et Sciences Humaines des Universites de Paris, 140 rue Jules Guesde, 92593 Levallois Perret Cedex, France. TEL 33-1-41407863. FAX 33-1-41407862. Ed. Charles-Pierre Guillebeau. adv.; bk.rev.; mkt.; stat.; tr.lit.; tr.mk. **Indexed:** ELLIS.
—BLDSC (4336.499000).

...NGARY. KOZPONTI STATISZTIKAI HIVATAL. ...OGLALKOZTATOTTSAG ES KERESETI ARANYOK. see *BUSINESS AND ECONOMICS — Abstracting, Bibliographies, Statistics*

331   II
...M R REPORT. (Text in English) irreg. Institute of Applied Manpower Research, Indraprastha Estate, Mahatma Gandhi Marg, New Delhi 110002, India. TEL 91-11-3267996. FAX 91-11-3267437.

331   II
...M R WORKING PAPER. (Text in English) 1963. irreg. price varies. Institute of Applied Manpower Research, Indraprastha Estate, Mahatma Gandhi Marg, New Delhi 110002, India. TEL 91-11-3317849. FAX 91-11-3319909. Ed.Bd.

331.25   US   ISSN 0018-8611
I S BRIEFING SERVICE. (International Benefits Information Service) 1969. m. $825. Charles D. Spencer & Associates, Inc., 250 S. Wacker Dr., Ste. 500, Chicago, IL 60606-5834. TEL 312-993-7900. (looseleaf format) **Indexed:** Geo.Abstr., Sci.Cit.Ind., World Bibl.Soc.Sec.

331.2   UK   ISSN 0308-9312
...S BRIEF; the legal side of employee relations. (Includes special section: Employment Law Problems) 1972. fortn. £234 (effective 1997). Incomes Data Services Ltd., 77 Bastwick St., London EC1V 3TT, England. TEL 44-171-250 3434. FAX 44-171-608-0949. **Indexed:** Euro.LJI, LJI. **Document type:** trade publication.
—BLDSC (4362.571500).
Description: Keeps subscribers up-to-date on the legal side of industrial relations.

331.2   UK   ISSN 0959-2199
...S EMPLOYMENT EUROPE; employment practices in Western Europe. Variant title: I D S European Service. (Includes: Pay and Conditions Documents; Recruitment and Dismissal Documents) 1975. m. £225 (outside Europe £261) (effective 1997). Incomes Data Services Ltd., 77 Bastwick St., London EC1V 3TT, England. TEL 0171-250-3434. FAX 0171-608-0949. **Document type:** trade publication.
Former titles (until 1995): I D S European Report (ISSN 0952-6374); (until 1988): I D S International Report.
Description: Provides information for the international employee relation specialist with news of trends and developments in Europe.

331.2   UK   ISSN 0144-0209
...S FOCUS. Variant title: Focus (London, 1976). 1976. q. £54 (effective 1997). Incomes Data Services Ltd., 77 Bastwick, London EC1V 3TT, England. TEL 0171-250 3434. FAX 0171-608-0949. **Document type:** trade publication.
—BLDSC (4362.598500).
Description: Presents news, commentary, and analysis concerning pay, conditions of employment, employee relations, collective bargaining, employment law, and developments across Europe.

331.2   UK   ISSN 1351-4954
...D S MANAGEMENT PAY REVIEW; monitoring executive and professional pay. Variant title: Management Pay Review. (Supplements avail.: Research File; Personnel Tax Guide; Directory of Salary Surveys) m. £224 (effective 1997) (includes 4 Research Files). Incomes Data Services Ltd., 77 Bastwick St., London EC1V 3TT, England. TEL 0171-250-3434. FAX 0171-608-0949. **Document type:** trade publication.
—BLDSC (4362.607800).
Former titles (until 1993): I D S Monthly Review of Salaries and Benefits (ISSN 0262-7361); (until 1981): Incomes Data Top Pay Unit Review.
Description: Reports on a wide range of salary surveys and research reports with commentary.

331.2   UK   ISSN 0265-6019
I D S PAY DIRECTORY. Variant title: Pay Directory. 1982. 3/yr. £60 (effective 1997). Incomes Data Services Ltd., 77 Bastwick St., London EC1V 3TT, England. TEL 44-171-250-3434. FAX 44-171-608-0949. **Document type:** directory.
—BLDSC (4362.610000).
Description: Compiles salary data by profession; also includes data on benefits and work conditions.

I D S PENSIONS SERVICE; guidance through the law and company practice. see *BUSINESS AND ECONOMICS — Personnel Management*

331.2   UK   ISSN 0019-3461
I D S REPORT; authority on pay and the labour market. Key Title: Incomes Data Report. 1966. s-m. £268 (effective 1997). Incomes Data Services Ltd., 77 Bastwick St., London EC1V 3TT, England. TEL 44-171-250-3434. FAX 44-171-608-0949. **Indexed:** Cont.Pg.Manage. **Document type:** trade publication.
Description: Provides a factual record of all the latest news on pay bargaining and developments in pay.

331.2   UK   ISSN 0308-9339
I D S STUDIES; benchmarking personnel policies and practice. 1971. bi-m. £186 (effective 1997). Incomes Data Services Ltd., 77 Bastwick St., London EC1V 3TT, England. TEL 44-171-250 3434. FAX 44-171-608-0949. **Document type:** trade publication.
—BLDSC (4362.616500).
Description: Covers pay, terms, and conditions; working patterns and practices; and topical personnel issues for the personnel manager.

331   GW   ISSN 0175-2944
I F O STUDIEN ZUR ARBEITSMARKTFORSCHUNG. 1983. irreg., vol.9, 1992. price varies. I F O Institut fuer Wirtschaftsforschung, Poschingerstr. 5, 81679 Munich, Germany. TEL 49-89-9224-0. FAX 49-89-985369. **Document type:** monographic series.

331 620   US   ISSN 0745-2098
I F P T E OUTLOOK.* 1943. bi-m. International Federation of Professional and Technical Engineers, 8630 Fenton St., Ste. 400, Silver Spring, MD 20910-3803. FAX 301-565-0018. Ed.Bd. illus. (tabloid format)
Formerly (until 1976?): Engineer's Outlook.

331   SZ
I I R A BULLETIN. French edition: Bulletin de l'A I R P. Spanish edition: Boletin de la A I R T. (Text in English) 1975. 3/yr. $25. International Industrial Relations Association, CH-1211 Geneva 22, Switzerland. TEL 41-22-7996841. FAX 41-22-7998541. TELEX 415647-ILO-CH. E-mail: mennie@ilo.org. Ed. Kate Mennie-Cecconi. circ. 1,450. (back issues avail.) **Document type:** bulletin.

331   UN   ISSN 0251-3803
HD4964
I L O COMMITTEE ON SALARIED EMPLOYEES AND PROFESSIONAL WORKERS. REPORT. French edition: B I T Commission des Employes et des Travailleurs Intellectuels. Rapport (ISSN 0251-379X); Spanish edition: O I T Comision de Empleados y de Trabajadores Intelectuales. Informe (ISSN 1014-6784) 1949. irreg. 20 SFr. (International Labour Office) I L O Publications, 4 route des Morillons, CH-1211 Geneva 22, Switzerland. TEL 41-22-799-6111. FAX 41-22-799-6358. TELEX 415647-ILO-CH. (Dist. in US by: I L O Publications Center, 49 Sheridan Ave., Albany, NY 12210. TEL 518-436-9686. FAX 518-436-7433) **Document type:** monographic series.

331 350   UN   ISSN 0253-7834
I L O JOINT COMMITTEE ON THE PUBLIC SERVICE. REPORT. French edition: B I T Commission Paritaire de la Fonction Publique. Rapport (ISSN 0253-7826); Spanish edition: O I T Comision Paritaria del Servicio Publico. Informe (ISSN 0253-7818) irreg. 20 SFr.($16) (International Labour Office) I L O Publications, 4 route des Morillons, CH-1211 Geneva 22, Switzerland. TEL 41-22-799-6111. FAX 41-22-799-6358. TELEX 415647-ILO-CH. (Dist. in US by: I L O Publications Center, 49 Sheridan Ave., Albany, NY 12210. TEL 518-436-9686. FAX 518-436-7433) **Document type:** monographic series.

331 669   UN   ISSN 1010-2388
I L O METAL TRADES COMMITTEE. REPORT. French edition: B I T Commission des Industries Mecaniques. Rapport (ISSN 0259-3300); Spanish edition: O I T Comision de Industrias Mecanicas. Informe (ISSN 1011-8543) irreg. 25 SFr.($20) (International Labour Office) I L O Publications, CH-1211 Geneva 22, Switzerland, Switzerland. TEL 41-22-799-6111. FAX 41-22-799-6358. TELEX 415647-ILO-CH. (Dist. in US by: I L O Publications Center, 49 Sheridan Ave., Albany, NY 12210. TEL 518-436-9686. FAX 518-436-7433) **Document type:** monographic series.

I L O MULTINATIONAL ENTERPRISES PROGRAMME. WORKING PAPER. (International Labour Office) see *BUSINESS AND ECONOMICS — Economic Situation And Conditions*

331   UN   ISSN 1014-9287
I L O TRAINING PAPERS IN POPULATION AND FAMILY WELFARE EDUCATION IN THE WORKSETTING. 1993. irreg., no.2, 1994. 15 SFr.($12) (International Labour Office) I L O Publications, 4 route des Morillons, CH-1211 Geneva 22, Switzerland. TEL 41-22-799-6111. FAX 41-22-799-6358. TELEX 415647-ILO-CH. (Dist. in US by: I L O Publications Center, 49 Sheridan Ave., Albany, NY 11210. TEL 518-436-9686. FAX 518-436-7433) Ed. Judi Aubel. **Document type:** monographic series.

331.1   US   ISSN 0070-0177
I L R PAPERBACKS. 1967. irreg., no.21, 1994. price varies. (New York State School of Industrial and Labor Relations) I L R Press, Cornell University Press, 512 E. State St., Ithaca, NY 14850. TEL 607-277-2338; 800-666-2211. Ed. Frances Benson. R&P contact: Clare Wellnitz. adv. contact: Heidi Marschner. **Document type:** monographic series.

331   PH
I L S NEWS DIGEST. (Text in English) bi-m. Department of Labor and Employment, Institute for Labor Studies, 5th Fl., Dole Bldg., Muralla & Gen. Luna Sts., Intramuros, Manila, Philippines. TEL 63-2-47-52-96. Ed.Bd. charts; illus.; stat. **Indexed:** Ind.Phil.Per. **Document type:** newsletter.
Description: Covers labor issues, including workers' rights and unions. Also covers social issues as they relate to labor relations.

331   UK
I M I MONITOR. 1962. q. free. I M I plc., P.O. Box 216, Witton, Birmingham B6 7BA, England. TEL 0121-356 4848. FAX 0121-356-3526. Ed. Alan Deeley. circ. 10,200. (tabloid format; back issues avail.)
Formerly (until no.233, 1992): Metals Monitor.

I M P A C T NEWS. (Irish Municipal Public and Civil Trade Union) see *PUBLIC ADMINISTRATION*

I O M A'S REPORT ON SALARY SURVEYS. (Institute of Management & Administration, Inc.) see *BUSINESS AND ECONOMICS — Personnel Management*

331   GW
I-PUNKT. a. Echter Wuerzburg, Fraenkische Gesellschaftsdruckerei und Verlag GmbH, Postfach 5560, 97005 Wuerzburg, Germany. TEL 49-931-6671-171. circ. controlled. **Document type:** newsletter.

331   US
I R R A MEMBERSHIP DIRECTORY. 1949. irreg, latest 1994. $25. Industrial Relations Research Association, 4233 Social Science Bldg., University of Wisconsin, Madison, WI 53706. TEL 608-262-2762. FAX 608-265-4591. **Document type:** directory.

331.1   US   ISSN 0019-0500
I R R A NEWSLETTER. 1958. q. $56 (foreign $66) membership. Industrial Relations Research Association, 4233 Social Science Bldg., University of Wisconsin, Madison, WI 53706. TEL 608-262-2762. FAX 608-265-4591. **Document type:** newsletter.
—BLDSC (4580.600000).

BUSINESS AND ECONOMICS — LABOR AND INDUSTRIAL RELATIONS

331.1 UK ISSN 1358-2216
I R S EMPLOYMENT REVIEW. 1971. fortn. £475 (foreign £515) (effective 1997) includes Employee Development Bulletin, Industrial Relations Law Bulletin, Pay and Benefits Bulletin. Eclipse Group Ltd., Industrial Relations Services, 18-20 Highbury Pl., London N5 1QP, England. TEL 44-171-354-5858. FAX 44-171-226-8618. stat. (also avail. in microform from UMI; reprint service avail. from UMI) **Indexed:** Cont.Pg.Manage., L.R.I., Mgmt.& Market.Abstr. **Document type:** trade publication.
—BLDSC (4581.695800); SWETS.
Formerly (until Jan. 1995): Industrial Relations Review and Report (ISSN 0309-7269); Incorporates (in 1995): I R S Employment Trends (ISSN 1358-2194); Incorporates in part (in 1995): Health and Safety Bulletin (ISSN 1358-2208); Which was formerly (until 1994): Health and Safety Information Bulletin (ISSN 0142-9086)
Description: Discusses topics in labor relations, labor law, personnel management, and occupational health and safety.

331 SZ
I U F NEWS BULLETIN. (Text in English, French, German, Spanish, Swedish) 1920. q. 60 SFr. International Union of Food, Agricultural, Hotel, Restaurant, Catering, Tobacco and Allied Workers, Rampe du Pont-Rouge 8, CH-1213 Petit-Lancy 2, Switzerland. TEL 41-22-7932233. FAX 41-22-7932238. bk.rev.; index. circ. 4,000. **Document type:** bulletin.
Description: Trade workers union publication featuring reports of events and activities, and union news of various countries.

331.12 US
IDAHO. DEPARTMENT OF LABOR. IDAHO DEMOGRAPHIC PROFILE. 1972. a. free. Department of Labor, Bureau of Research and Analysis, 317 Main St., Boise, ID 83735. TEL 208-334-6168. Ed. Katie Lamm. circ. 1,200. (also avail. in microfiche from CIS) **Indexed:** SRI. **Document type:** government publication.
Former titles: Idaho. Department of Employment. Idaho Demographic Profile; Idoho. Department of Employment. Annual Planning Report.

331 US ISSN 0536-2733
IDAHO EMPLOYMENT. m. Department of Labor, Bureau of Research and Analysis, 317 Main St., Boise, ID 83735. TEL 208-334-6168. URL: http://www.labor.state.id.us. Ed. Katie Lamm. stat. **Document type:** government publication.

IDAHO EMPLOYMENT LAW LETTER. see LAW

IDAHO OCCUPATION WAGE SURVEY. see BUSINESS AND ECONOMICS — Economic Situation And Conditions

331.8 301 US ISSN 0894-024X
IDEAS & ACTION.* 1982. 3/yr. $7.50 for 4 issues; libraries $12. Workers Solidarity Alliance, Box 339 Lafayette St., Rm. 202, New York, NY 10012-2725. bk.rev. circ. 1,400. (tabloid format; back issues avail.) **Indexed:** Rural Devel.Abstr., Rural Ext.Educ.& Tr.Abstr.
Description: Analyzes worker struggles, U.S. and international. Also covers issues such as sexism and ecology from a working class standpoint.

ILLINOIS EMPLOYMENT LAW LETTER. see LAW

331.11 US ISSN 0085-1728
ILLINOIS LABOR HISTORY SOCIETY REPORTER. 1970. irreg. (approx. 3/yr.) $10. Illinois Labor History Society, 28 E. Jackson Blvd., Chicago, IL 60604. TEL 312-663-4107. Ed. Leslie F. Orear. bk.rev. circ. 500. **Document type:** newsletter.
Description: Labor force studies.

331 341 NE
ILOLEX C D - R O M. (Text in English, French, Spanish) 1992. a. fl.465 (effective 1996). (International Labour Office) Kluwer Law International, Postbus 85889, 2508 CN The Hague, Netherlands. TEL 31-70-3081500. FAX 31-70-3081515. E-mail: services@wkap.nl; URL: http://www.wkap.nl. (Dist. by: Kluwer Academic Publishers Group, P.O. Box 322, 3300 AH Dordrecht, Netherlands. TEL 31-78-6392392. FAX 31-78-6546474; N. America dist. addr.: Box 358, Accord Sta., Hingham, MA 02018-0358. TEL 617-871-6600. FAX 617-871-6528)
●Available only on CD-ROM.
Description: Contains the ILO database relating to international labor standards.

IMMIGRATION EMPLOYMENT COMPLIANCE HANDBOOK. see LAW

340 331 CN
IMPACT; labour law and management. 10/yr. Can.$154 (includes binders) (effective 1997). Canada Law Book Inc., 240 Edward St., Aurora, ON L4G 3S9, Canada. TEL 905-841-6472; 800-263-2037. FAX 905-841-5085. Eds. Simon P. Ovellet, Lynn H. Harnden. **Document type:** newsletter.
Description: Links managers at all levels to the law which relates to the labor force.

331 690 UN ISSN 1020-0584
IMPROVE YOUR CONSTRUCTION BUSINESS SERIES. 1994. irreg. 27.50 SFr.($22) (International Labour Office) I L O Publications, 4 route des Morillons, CH-1211 Geneva 22, Switzerland. TEL 41-22-799-6111. FAX 41-22-799-6358. TELEX 415647-ILO-CH. (Dist. in US by: I L O Publications Center, 49 Sheridan Ave., Albany, NY 12210. TEL 518-436-9686. FAX 518-436-7433) Ed.Bd. **Document type:** monographic series.

331 651 US ISSN 0885-7229
IN DEPTH (NEW YORK);* report to management. (Supplement to: Fair Employment Compliance) 1975. s-m. $195. Management Resources, Inc., Box 105, Hampton, NH 03843-0105. Ed. Ken Swann. bk.rev. (looseleaf format; back issues avail.)

331 US ISSN 1050-7329
HD4965.5.U6
INCOME IN SALES - MARKETING MANAGEMENT. 1978. a. $395. (Sales & Marketing Executives International) Abbott, Langer & Associates, 548 First St., Crete, IL 60417. TEL 708-672-4200. Ed. Steven Langer.

331 II
INDIA. MINISTRY OF LABOUR. ANNUAL REPORT. (Text in English) a. Ministry of Labour, New Delhi, India.
Supersedes (in 1974): India. Department of Labour and Employment. Annual Report (ISSN 0579-3238)

331.1 II ISSN 0019-5286
HD8682
INDIAN JOURNAL OF INDUSTRIAL RELATIONS. (Text in English) 1964. q. Rs.250 (foreign $65). Shri Ram Centre for Industrial Relations & Human Resources, 4E-16 Jhandewalan Extention, New Delhi 110 055, India. TEL 91-11-7519064. FAX 91-11-7526036. TELEX 031-62310 CCS IN. Ed. Rama J. Joshi. adv.; bk.rev.; charts; stat.; index. circ. 825. **Indexed:** ASSIA, Ind.India, Ind.Per.Lit., Indian Psychol.Abstr., Int.Lab.Doc., Psychol.Abstr., Pub.Admin.Abstr., Rural Recreat.Tour.Abstr., SSCI, World Agri.Econ.& Rural Sociol.Abstr. **Document type:** academic/scholarly publication.
—BLDSC (4415.400000); UnCover.
Description: Covers various aspects of industrial relations and human resources in India and abroad.
Refereed Serial

331 II ISSN 0019-5308
HD4811
INDIAN JOURNAL OF LABOUR ECONOMICS. (Text in English) 1958. q. Rs.30($10.50) University of Lucknow, Indian Society of Labour Economics, Badshaw Bagh, Lucknow, Uttar Pradesh, India. Ed. Dr. R.S. Mathur. bk.rev.; charts; index. circ. 481. **Indexed:** C.R.E.J., Int.Lab.Doc.
—UnCover.

331 II ISSN 0019-5723
HD8681
INDIAN LABOUR JOURNAL. 1960. m. Rs.1320($475.20) Government of India, Department of Publications, Civil Lines, Delhi 110 054, India. TEL 11-2512527. adv.; bk.rev.; charts; stat.; index. circ. 1,250. **Indexed:** Int.Lab.Doc. **Document type:** government publication.

331 US
INDIANA. DEPARTMENT OF EMPLOYMENT AND TRAINING SERVICES. COUNTY EMPLOYMENT PATTERNS. a. free. Department of Employment and Training Services, Labor Market Information, 10 Senate Ave., Rm. 101, Indianapolis, IN 46204. TEL 317-232-7716. **Document type:** government publication.
Description: Covers employment monthly and annual averages by county and selected industry divisions by county.

331 US
INDIANA. DEPARTMENT OF EMPLOYMENT AND TRAINING SERVICES. COVERED EMPLOYMENT AND PAYROLLS. q. free. Department of Employment and Training Services, Labor Market Statistics, 10 Senate Ave., Rm. 101, Indianapolis, IN 46204. TEL 317-232-7716. FAX 317-232-6950. URL: http://www.dwd.state.in.us.
Description: Based on employment and payroll reports from establishments covered by the Indiana Employment and Training Services Act.

331 US
INDIANA. DEPARTMENT OF EMPLOYMENT AND TRAINING SERVICES. LABOR FORCE ESTIMATES. m. (plus a. suppl.). free. Department of Employment and Training Services, Labor Market Information, 10 Senate Ave., Rm. 101, Indianapolis, IN 46204. TEL 317-232-8546. FAX 317-232-6950.
Description: Provides labor force, employment, and unemployment rates prepared under the Local Area Unemployment Statistics Program (LAUS).

331 US
INDIANA. DEPARTMENT OF EMPLOYMENT AND TRAINING SERVICES. NON - M S A ESTABLISHMENT EMPLOYMENT. (Metropolitan Statistical Area) a. free. Department of Employment and Training Services, Labor Market Information, 10 Senate Ave., Rm. 101 Indianapolis, IN 46204. TEL 317-232-8546. FAX 317-232-6950.
Description: Covers individual counties that are not part of an area. Provides annual average wages and salaried employment in county establishments.

INDIANA EMPLOYMENT LAW. see LAW — Corporate Law

INDIANA EMPLOYMENT LAW LETTER. see LAW

331 US
INDIANA EMPLOYMENT REVIEW. m. free. Department of Employment and Training Services, Labor Market Statistics, 10 Senate Ave., Rm. 101, Indianapolis, IN 46204. TEL 317-232-7716. FAX 317-232-6950. URL: http://www.dwd.state.in.us.
Description: Provides current establishment employment by industry for Indiana and its MSAs; includes hours and gross earnings for manufacturing.

344.012 US
INDIANA WORKERS' COMPENSATION LAWS AND RULES ANNOTATED. a. $35. Michie, A Division of Reed Elsevier Inc., Box 7587, Charlottesville, VA 22906-7587. TEL 804-972-7566; 800-562-1197. FAX 800-643-1280. E-mail: custserv@michie.com; URL: http://www.michie.com. Ed. George Harley.

331   US
INDIVIDUAL EMPLOYMENT RIGHTS. (Subseries of: Labor Relations Reporter (ISSN 0148-7981)) 1986. bi-w. $663 (effective July 1995). The Bureau of National Affairs, Inc., 1231 25th St., N.W., Washington, DC 20037. TEL 202-452-4200. FAX 202-822-8092. TELEX 285656 BNAI WSH. URL: http://www.bna. com/. (Subscr. to: 9435 Key West Ave., Rockville, MD 20850. TEL 800-372-1033) Ed. Nancy J. Sedmak. (looseleaf format; back issues avail.) **Document type:** newsletter.
● Also available online. Vendor(s): Human Resources Information Network (CDD, HDD), Lexis-Nexis (File LRRIER, IERNEW), West Group (File FLB-CS, LRR-IERN).
Description: Presents case reference and notification on individual employment rights issues, including employment at will, privacy, polygraph testing, and other issues outside the traditional labor-management relations context.

331.1   US   ISSN 0019-7939
CODEN: ILREA
INDUSTRIAL AND LABOR RELATIONS REVIEW. Short title: I L R Review. 1947. q. $26 to individuals (foreign $34); institutions $43 (foreign $50); students $13 (foreign $20). Cornell University, New York State School of Industrial and Labor Relations, Ithaca, NY 14853-3901. TEL 607-255-2732. FAX 607-255-8016. E-mail: blk5@cornell.edu; URL: http://www.ILR.cornell.edu/depts/ILRrev/. Ed. Tove Hammer. R&P contact: Brian Keeling. adv. contact: Brian Keeling. bk.rev.; bibl.; charts; index, cum.index: vols.1-50 (1947-1997); circ. 3,100. circ. 2,900 (paid); 400 (controlled). (also avail. in microfilm from UMI,WSH; reprint service avail. from SCH,UMI,KTO,WSH) **Indexed:** A.B.C.Pol.Sci., ABI Inform., Abstr.Bk.Rev.Curr.Leg.Per., Amer.Hist.& Life (1969-), Arts & Hum.Cit.Ind., ASCA, Asian-Pac.Econ.Lit., ASSIA, B.P.I., Bk.Rev.Ind. (1965-), BPIA, Bus.Ind., C.I.J.E., C.L.I., C.R.E.J., Chic.Per.Ind., Child.Bk.Rev.Ind. (1965-), CLOA, Cont.Pg.Manage., Curr.Cont., Hist.Abstr. (1969-), Human Resour.Abstr., IBR, Ind.Per.Art.Relat.Law, Int.Bibl.Soc.Sci., Int.Lab.Doc., Int.Polit.Sci.Abstr., J.of Econ.Lit., Key to Econ.Sci., L.R.I., Leg.Per., Manage.Abstr., Manage.Cont., Mid.East: Abstr.& Ind., P.A.I.S., Pers.Manage.Abstr., PHRA., Psychol.Abstr., Sage Urb.Stud.Abstr., SCIMP, Soc.Sci.Ind., Sociol.Abstr., SSCI, Tr.& Indus.Ind., Wom.Stud.Abstr., Work Rel.Abstr., World Bibl.Soc.Sec. **Document type:** academic/scholarly publication.
● Also available online. Vendor(s): Information Access Co., Knight-Ridder Information, Inc., Lexis-Nexis, West Group, Wilsonline.
—BLDSC (4445.225000); Genuine Article; KR SourceOne; SWETS; UMI; UnCover. **CCC.**
Description: Inter-disciplinary journal with articles on all aspects of the employment relationship.
Refereed Serial

331   AT   ISSN 0155-2589
HD5630.N4
INDUSTRIAL ARBITRATION REPORTS, NEW SOUTH WALES. 1900. irreg. Aus.$50. Department of Industrial Relations, 50 Phillip St., Sydney, N.S.W. 2000, Australia. (Subscr. addr.: 1 Oxford St., Darlinghurst, N.S.W. 2010, Australia) Ed. G.K. Robertson.

INDUSTRIAL CASES REPORTS. see *LAW — Corporate Law*

331 346   II   ISSN 0019-8102
INDUSTRIAL COURT REPORTER. (Text in English) 1948. m. Rs.50. Commissioner of Labour, Commerce Centre, Tardeo, Bombay 400 034, India. Ed. Shri R.R. Karosiya. adv.; index. circ. 750.

344   UK   ISSN 0305-9332
K9
INDUSTRIAL LAW JOURNAL. 1972. q. £44 (foreign $81) (effective 1998). (Industrial Law Society) Oxford University Press, Academic Division, Great Clarendon St., Oxford OX2 6DP, England. TEL 44-1865-267907. FAX 44-1865-267485. TELEX 837330-OXPRES-G. E-mail: jnl.info@oup.co.uk; URL: http://www.oup.co.uk/journals. (U.S. subscr. to: Oxford University Press Inc., 2001 Evans Rd., Cary, NC 27513. TEL 800-852-7323. FAX 919-677-1714) Ed. Paul Davies; Pub. Philip Joseph. R&P contact: Joolz Longley. adv. contact: Jane Parker. bk.rev.; bibl. circ. 6,250. (reprint service avail. from WSH) **Indexed:** ASSIA, C.L.I., Cont.Pg.Manage., Euro.LJI, IBR, Ind.S.A.Per., Int.Lab.Doc., L.R.I., Leg.Per., LJI, Stud.Wom.Abstr. **Document type:** academic/scholarly publication.
—BLDSC (4457.535000); KR SourceOne; SWETS; UMI. **CCC.**
Description: Comment, in-depth analysis and information for academics, practicing lawyers and lay industrial relations experts on all aspects of UK labor law and unemployment law in USA.

INDUSTRIAL LAW - NEW SOUTH WALES. see *LAW*

331.1   US   ISSN 0019-8676
HD6951   CODEN: IDRLAP
INDUSTRIAL RELATIONS; a journal of economy and society. 1961. 4/yr. $38 to individuals (foreign $68); institutions $75 (foreign $102.50) (effective 1997). (University of California at Berkeley, Institute of Industrial Relations) Blackwell Publishers, 238 Main St., Cambridge, MA 02142. TEL 617-547-7110. FAX 617-547-0789. E-mail: subscript@blackwellpub.com. Eds. David I. Levine, Jeffrey Perloff. charts; index. circ. 2,300. (also avail. in microform from UMI; back issues avail.; reprint service avail. from SCH,UMI) **Indexed:** ABI Inform., Acad.Ind., Account.& Data Proc.Abstr., Anbar, B.P.I., BPIA, Bus.Ind., C.L.I., Cont.Pg.Manage., Curr.Cont., E.I., IBR, Int.Lab.Doc., Int.Polit.Sci.Abstr., J.of Econ.Abstr., J.of Econ.Lit., L.R.I., Manage.Cont., Mid.East: Abstr.& Ind., P.A.I.S., Pers.Manage.Abstr., Soc.Work Res.& Abstr., SSCI, Tr.& Indus.Ind., Work Rel.Abstr. **Document type:** academic/scholarly publication.
—BLDSC (4461.080000); Genuine Article; KR SourceOne; SWETS; UMI; UnCover. **CCC.**
Description: Offers a valuable international perspective on current topics in labor and employment.

331 658.3   AT
INDUSTRIAL RELATIONS AND MANAGEMENT LETTER. m. Aus.$287. Ian Huntley Pty. Ltd., P.O. Box 99, Cremorne, N.S.W. 2090, Australia. TEL 61-2-9953-5788. FAX 61-2-9953-2280. Ed. Pat Huntley. (back issues avail.) **Document type:** trade publication.
Description: Reports on trends and current actions of labor unions and on labor-management relations.

331   UK   ISSN 0770-0148
INDUSTRIAL RELATIONS EUROPE. 1973. m. 10950 BEF. Wyatt Co., c/o Mike Groushko, Ed., 49 Bushey Grove Rd., Bushey, Herts., England. TEL 0293-252440. FAX 0923-818271. bk.rev. circ. 1,000. **Document type:** newsletter.
—SWETS.

331.1   UK   ISSN 0019-8692
HD4805
INDUSTRIAL RELATIONS JOURNAL. 1970. q. £132($264) (foreign $167) (effective 1997). Blackwell Publishers Ltd., 108 Cowley Rd., Oxford OX4 1JF, England. TEL 44-1865-791100. FAX 44-1865-791347. E-mail: jnlinfo@ blackwellpublishers.co.uk; URL: http://www.blackwellpublishers.co.uk. Ed. Brian Towers. adv.; bk.rev.; abstr.; charts; stat. circ. 1,100. (also avail. in microform from UMI; reprint service avail. from SWZ,UMI) **Indexed:** Account.& Data Proc.Abstr., Anbar, ASSIA, BMT, BPIA, Bus.Ind., C.R.E.J., Cont.Pg.Manage., ELLIS, IBR, Int.Lab.Doc., Mgmt.& Market.Abstr., Oper.Res.Manage.Sci., Qual.Contr.Appl.Stat., SCIMP (1978-), Stud.Wom.Abstr., Tech.Educ.Abstr., Tr.& Indus.Ind., Work Rel.Abstr. **Document type:** academic/scholarly publication.
● Also available online. Vendor(s): Information Access Co.
—BLDSC (4461.140000); SWETS; UMI; UnCover. **CCC.**
Refereed Serial

331.1 340   UK   ISSN 0969-3637
INDUSTRIAL RELATIONS LAW BULLETIN. Abbreviated title: I R L B. (Section of: I R S Employment Review (ISSN 1358-2216)) 1974. fortn. £215 (overseas £260) (effective 1997). Eclipse Group Ltd., Industrial Relations Services, 18-20 Highbury Pl., London N5 1QP, England. TEL 44-171-354-5858. FAX 44-171-226-8618. Ed. Marian Bell. (reprint service avail. from UMI) **Indexed:** Br.Ceram.Abstr., L.R.I. **Document type:** trade publication, bulletin.
—BLDSC (4461.144000).
Formerly (until 1994): Industrial Relations Legal Information Bulletin (ISSN 0307-5540)
Description: Presents labor law news and case notes covering unfair dismissal, discrimination, layoffs, strikes, employment contracts, and business transfers.

331.1 340   UK   ISSN 0307-5591
INDUSTRIAL RELATIONS LAW REPORTS. Abbreviated title: I R L R. 1972. m. £365 (foreign £410) (effective 1997). Eclipse Group Ltd., Industrial Relations Services, 18-20 Highbury Pl., London N5 1QP, England. TEL 44-171-354-5858. FAX 44-171-226-8618. Ed. Michael Rubenstein. (also avail. in microform from UMI; reprint service avail. from UMI) **Document type:** trade publication.
● Also available online. Vendor(s): Lexis-Nexis.
—BLDSC (4461.147000); UMI.
Description: Keeps readers informed of developments in employment case law, analyzing the implications of key decisions.

331   CN   ISSN 1192-7283
KE3142
INDUSTRIAL RELATIONS LEGISLATION IN CANADA. French edition: Relations Industrielles au Canada. (Catalog no. L31-79-1991E) (Text in English) 1989. a. Can.$24.95 (foreign $29.95). Supply and Services Canada, Publishing Centre, Ottawa, ON K1A 0S9, Canada. TEL 819-965-4802. circ. 2,000. **Indexed:** Amer.Hist.& Life, Hist.Abstr. **Document type:** government publication.
Description: Reports on collective bargaining and related legislation in federal, provincial and territorial jurisdictions.

331.1   US
INDUSTRIAL RELATIONS RESEARCH ASSOCIATION. ANNUAL RESEARCH VOLUME. 1947. a. price varies. Industrial Relations Research Association, 4233 Social Science Bldg., University of Wisconsin, Madison, WI 53706. TEL 608-262-2762. FAX 608-265-4591. Ed.Bd. **Document type:** academic/scholarly publication.

331   US
INDUSTRIAL RELATIONS RESEARCH ASSOCIATION. PROCEEDINGS OF THE ANNUAL MEETING. a. price varies. Industrial Relations Research Association, 4233 Social Science Bldg., University of Wisconsin, Madison, WI 53706. TEL 608-262-2762. FAX 608-265-4591. **Indexed:** BPIA, Bus.Ind. **Document type:** proceedings.
—BLDSC (6841.483000).
Former titles: Industrial Relations Research Association. Proceedings of the Annual Winter Meeting (ISSN 0277-7347); Industrial Relations Research Association. Proceedings of Annual Winter Meeting (ISSN 0275-3081)

331   US
INDUSTRIAL RELATIONS RESEARCH ASSOCIATION. PROCEEDINGS OF THE ANNUAL SPRING MEETING. a. newsstand price: $5. Industrial Relations Research Association, 4233 Social Science Bldg., University of Wisconsin, Madison, WI 53706. TEL 608-262-2762. FAX 608-265-4591. Ed. Paula B. Voos. **Indexed:** BPIA. **Document type:** proceedings.

331.7   US   ISSN 0019-8870
HD8055.I4
INDUSTRIAL WORKER. 1909. m. $15 to individuals; institutions $20. Industrial Workers of the World, 103 W. Michigan Ave., Ypsilanti, MI 48197. TEL 313-483-3548. E-mail: iww@igc.apc.org; URL: http://iww.org/~iw/. Ed. Jon Bekken. bk.rev.; film rev.; illus.; circ. 4,000 (paid). (tabloid format; also avail. in microfilm from UMI,BHP,KTO; reprint service avail. from UMI) **Indexed:** Alt.Press Ind. **Document type:** newspaper.
—UMI.
Description: Provides rank and file labor news from the leading edge of the North American and world labor movement.

BUSINESS AND ECONOMICS — LABOR AND INDUSTRIAL RELATIONS

331.1 GW ISSN 0943-2779
INDUSTRIELLE BEZIEHUNGEN; Zeitschrift fuer Arbeit, Organisation und Management. (Text in German; occasionally in English) 1994. q. DM.84 (students DM.39). Rainer Hampp Verlag, Meringerzellerstr. 16, 86415 Mering, Germany. TEL 49-8233-4783. FAX 49-8233-30755. E-mail: rainer_hampp_verlag@t-online.de. Ed.Bd. **Document type:** trade publication.
—BLDSC (4474.809000).
Description: Forum for up-to-date analysis and discussion for those with an interest in industrial relations.
Refereed Serial

INDUSTRY WAGE SURVEYS. see *BUSINESS AND ECONOMICS — Economic Situation And Conditions*

331 CU
INFORMACION LABORAL. q. $22. (Comite Estatal de Trabajo y Seguridad Social) Ediciones Cubanas, Obispo No. 527, Apdo. 605, Havana, Cuba. TEL 32-5556/60.

344.0101 US ISSN 1088-9922
▼**INSIDE EMPLOYEE RIGHTS LITIGATION.** 1996. m. $149 (foreign $221) (effective 1998). John Wiley & Sons, Inc., 605 Third Ave., New York, NY 10158. TEL 212-850-6645. FAX 212-850-6021. E-mail: subinfo@jwiley.com. (Subscr. outside the Americas to: John Wiley & Sons Ltd., Baffins Ln., Chichester, W. Sussex PO19 1UD, England. TEL 44-1243-779777. FAX 44-1243-775878) Ed. Sarah Magee. **Document type:** trade publication.
Description: Contains articles and information on the changing field of employee rights litigation.

331 AT
INSIDE ENTERPRISE BARGAINING. m. Aus.$195 (effective May 1995). Newsletter Information Services, P.O. Box 693, Manly, N.S.W. 2095, Australia. TEL 61-2-9777500. FAX 61-2-9773310. E-mail: hww@hww.com.au; URL: http://www.hww.com.au. Ed. Bernadette McBride. **Document type:** newsletter.
Description: Covers issues such as penalty rates, performance pay, productivity targets, demarcations, work teams, dispute resolution. Analyzes how selected organizations negotiated specific enterprise bargaining matters.

331 US
INSIDE NEGOTIATIONS.* 1965. m. $98. E F R Corp., Box 15236, Colorado Spring, FL 80935-5236. Ed. Eric Rhodes. bk.rev. circ. 1,200.
Formerly: Negotiations Management (ISSN 0047-9292)

380 GW ISSN 0943-5670
INSIGHT KOMMUNIKATION. 1976. m. DM.40. (B D W Deutscher Kommunikationsverband, Bonn) B D W Service- und Verlagsgesellschaft Kommunikation mbH, Koenigswintererstr. 552, 53227 Bonn, Germany. TEL 0228-444560. FAX 0228-444503. Ed. Lutz E. Weidner. adv.; bk.rev. circ. 4,600.
Former titles (until 1993): Kommunikation (ISSN 0178-7365); (until 1985): Werbeforum (ISSN 0178-7357)

331 340.5 NE ISSN 1381-401X
▼**INSPRAAK;** maandblad voor medezeggenschap bij de overheid. 1995. 10/yr. fl.150 (effective 1996). Uitgeverij Kluwer B.V., Postbus 23, 7400 GA Deventer, Netherlands. TEL 31-570-633155. FAX 31-570-633834. (back issues avail.)

331 SZ ISSN 1022-5625
INSTITUT FUER SCHWEIZERISCHES ARBEITSRECHT. MITTEILUNGEN. 1982. a. 34 SFr. Staempfli AG, Hallerstr. 7-9, CH-3012 Bern, Switzerland. TEL 41-31-3006666. FAX 41-31-3006699. Ed. Manfred Rehbinder. circ. 400. **Document type:** bulletin.

331.2 ZR
INSTITUT NATIONAL DE PREPARATION PROFESSIONNELLE. CAHIER.* irreg. Institut National de Preparation Professionnelle, B.P. 7248, Kinshasa 1, Zaire. illus.

331 BE ISSN 0772-5353
INSTITUT SYNDICAL EUROPEEN. NOUVELLES. English edition: European Trade Union Institute. Newsletter (ISSN 0772-537X); German edition: Europaeische Gewerkschaftsinstitut. Nachrichten (ISSN 0772-5361); Norwegian edition: Europaeiske Fagforeningsinstituttet. Nyhetsbulletin (ISSN 0772-6317) (Text in French) 1984. q. Institut Syndical Europeen - European Trade Union Institute, Bd. Emile Jacqmain 155, 1210 Brussels, Belgium. TEL 32-2-2240470. FAX 32-2-2240502. **Document type:** newsletter.

331 BE ISSN 0771-4610
INSTITUT SYNDICAL EUROPEEN. RAPPORT D'ACTIVITES. English edition: Report on E T U I Activities (ISSN 0771-4564); German edition: Europaeische Gewerkschaftsinstitut. Taetigkeitsbericht (ISSN 0771-4513) (Text in French) 1978. a. Institut Syndical Europeen - European Trade Union Institute, Bd. Emile Jacqmain 155, 1210 Brussels, Belgium. TEL 32-2-2240470. FAX 32-2-2240502. **Document type:** corporate report.
Description: Reports on issues affecting European trade unions, and activities of the institute.

INSTITUT ZUR ERFORSCHUNG DER EUROPAEISCHEN ARBEITERBEWEGUNG. MITTEILUNGSBLATT. see *LABOR UNIONS*

331.11 BL
INSTITUTO DO DESENVOLVIMENTO ECONOMICO-SOCIAL DO PARA. BOLETIM DE PESQUISA EMPREGO E DESEMPREGO NA REGIAO METROPOLITANA DE BELEM. 1989. m. donation or free. Instituto do Desenvolvimento Economico-Social do Para, Av. Nazare 871, 66035-170 Belem, Para, Brazil. TEL 55-91-2244411. FAX 55-91-2253414. **Document type:** government publication.
Description: Covers the employment situation in the regional area of Belem.

331 NG ISSN 0538-2807
INTER-AFRICAN LABOUR CONFERENCE REPORTS, RECOMMENDATIONS AND CONCLUSIONS.* Title varies slightly. irreg. (Commission for Technical Co-Operation in Africa South of the Sahara) Maison de l'Afrique, B.P. 878, Niamey, Niger.

331 US ISSN 0196-3457
HD4975
INTER-CITY WAGE & SALARY DIFFERENTIALS. 1978. a. $250. Abbott, Langer & Associates, 548 First St., Crete, IL 60417. TEL 708-672-4200. Ed. Steven Langer.

331.8 US ISSN 0020-6008
INTERNATIONAL ASSOCIATION OF PERSONNEL IN EMPLOYMENT SECURITY. NEWS. 1941. 6/yr. $25. International Association of Personnel in Employment Security, 1801 Louisville Rd., Frankfort, KY 40601. TEL 502-223-4459. FAX 502-223-4127. Ed. Michael R. Stone. charts; illus. circ. 25,000. (tabloid format) **Document type:** newsletter.
Description: Provides news, updates and policies of employment programs.

INTERNATIONAL COMPARISONS OF MANUFACTURING PRODUCTIVITY AND UNIT LABOR COST TRENDS (YEAR). see *BUSINESS AND ECONOMICS — Economic Situation And Conditions*

331 690 UN ISSN 1020-0142
INTERNATIONAL CONSTRUCTION MANAGEMENT SERIES. 1994. irreg., no.6, 1995. 15 SFr.($12) (International Labour Office) I L O Publications, 4 route des Morillons, CH-1211 Geneva 22, Switzerland. TEL 41-22-799-6111. FAX 41-22-799-6358. TELEX 415647-ILO-CH. (Dist. in US by: I L O Publications Center, 49 Sheridan Ave., Albany, NY 12210. TEL 518-436-9686. FAX 518-436-7433) Ed. Derek Miles. **Document type:** monographic series.

331.1 US ISSN 1058-0506
INTERNATIONAL EMPLOYMENT GAZETTE. 1990. fortn. $95 (foreign $135). International Employment Gazette (Subsidiary of: Global Resources Organization Ltd.), 200 N. Main St., Ste. 100, Greenville, SC 29601. TEL 803-235-4444; 800-882-9188. FAX 803-235-3369. E-mail: intljobs@aol.com. Ed. Leslie Stultz; Pub. Patricia C. Stultz. adv. contact: Denise Snydam.
Description: Lists current employment openings worldwide, along with organizations under various geographic areas, and under various occupations within each area.

INTERNATIONAL EMPLOYMENT LAW. see *LAW — International Law*

331 341 NE
INTERNATIONAL ENCYCLOPAEDIA OF LAWS. LABOUR LAW AND INDUSTRIAL RELATIONS. Variant title: International Encyclopaedia for Labour Law and Industrial Relations. (Text in English) 1977. 23 base vols. (plus m. updates). $2908 (effective 1996). Kluwer Law International (Subsidiary of: Wolters Kluwer N.V.), Postbus 85889, 2508 CN The Hague, Netherlands. TEL 31-70-3081500. FAX 31-70-3081515. (Dist. by: Libresso Distribution Centre, P.O. Box 23, 7400 GA Deventer, Netherlands. TEL 31-570-633155. FAX 31-570-633834; In N. America: Kluwer Law International, 675 Massachusetts Ave., Cambridge, MA 02139. TEL 617-354-0140. FAX 617-354-8595) Ed. Roger Blanpain. (looseleaf format) **Document type:** monographic series.
Description: Presents comparative studies of the principles and practice of labor law and industrial relations in 60 countries throughout the world, with discussion of case law, EC labor regulations and the International Trade Union Movement.

331 341 NE
INTERNATIONAL HANDBOOK ON CONTRACTS OF EMPLOYMENT. (Text in English) 1988. 2 base vols. (plus s-a. updates). $250 (effective 1996). Kluwer Law International (Subsidiary of: Wolters Kluwer N.V.), Postbus 85889, 2508 CN The Hague, Netherlands. TEL 31-70-3081500. FAX 31-70-3081515. (Dist. by: Libresso Distribution Centre, P.O. Box 23, 7400 GA Deventer, Netherlands. TEL 31-570-633155. FAX 31-570-633834; In N. America: Kluwer Law International, 675 Massachusetts Ave., Cambridge, MA 02139. TEL 617-354-0140. FAX 617-354-8595) Ed. A. Williamson. (looseleaf format)
Description: Comprehensive coverage of labor laws in force in individual countries throughout the world.

327.17 DK ISSN 0109-2650
INTERNATIONAL HORISONT. 1982. q. DKK 100. Arbejderbevaegelsens Internationale Forum, Teglvaerksgade 27, DK-2100 Copenhagen OE, Denmark. TEL 45-39-29-60-66. FAX 45-39-29-05-38. Ed. Hans Stavnsager; Pub. Ib Wistisen. adv. contact: Bent Christensen. bk.rev. circ. 2,500. **Document type:** bulletin.
Formerly (until 1984): Horisont (ISSN 0108-8440)

INTERNATIONAL INSTITUTE FOR LABOUR STUDIES. BIBLIOGRAPHY SERIES. see *BUSINESS AND ECONOMICS — Abstracting, Bibliographies, Statistics*

331 UN
INTERNATIONAL INSTITUTE FOR LABOUR STUDIES. RESEARCH SERIES. 1976. irreg., no.109, 1996. price varies. International Institute for Labour Studies, P.O. Box 6, CH-1211 Geneva 22, Switzerland. TEL 41-22-799-6128. FAX 41-22-788-0950. (back issues avail.) **Document type:** monographic series.
Description: Monographs reflecting the results and findings of research projects carried out by the institute.

THE INTERNATIONAL JOURNAL OF COMPARATIVE LABOUR LAW AND INDUSTRIAL RELATIONS. see *LAW*

331   UK   ISSN 0143-7720
HD4805
INTERNATIONAL JOURNAL OF MANPOWER. 1980. 8/yr. £3699($5729) (foreign Aus.$7229) (effective 1998). M C B University Press Ltd., 60-62 Toller Ln., Bradford, W. Yorks BD8 9BY, England. TEL 44-1274-777700. FAX 44-1274-785200. TELEX 51317-MCBUNI-G. URL: http://www.mcb.co.uk. Ed. David Sapsford. bk.rev.; charts; illus.; index. (back issues avail.; reprint service avail. from SWZ) **Indexed:** ABI Inform., Account.& Data Proc.Abstr., ASCA, ASSIA, BPIA, Bus.Ind., C.I.J.E., Curr.Cont., Geo.Abstr.H.G., IDA, Int.Lab.Doc., Key to Econ.Sci., Manage.Cont., Mgmt.& Market.Abstr., Mult.Ed.Abstr., Stud.Wom.Abstr., Tech.Educ.Abstr. **Document type:** academic/scholarly publication.
●Also available online. Vendor(s): Information Access Co.
—BLDSC (4542.329000); Genuine Article; SWETS; UMI. **CCC.**
Description: Aims to cover all key issues in the development of manpower planning and economics and their practical applications.

331   UK   ISSN 0147-5479
HD4802
INTERNATIONAL LABOR AND WORKING CLASS HISTORY. 1972. s-a. £33($46) (effective 1998). Cambridge University Press, Edinburgh Bldg., Shaftesbury Rd., Cambridge CB2 2RU, England. TEL 44-1223-312393. FAX 44-1223-315052. TELEX 851817256. E-mail: information@cup.cam.ac.uk; URL: http://www.cup.cam.ac.uk. (N. American addr.: Cambridge University Press, Journals Dept., 40 W. 20th St., New York, NY 10011. TEL 212-924-3900. FAX 212-691-3239) Eds. Helmut Gruber, Louise Tilly. R&P contact: Linda Nicol. adv. contact: Rebecca Symons. bk.rev.; bibl. circ. 1,000. (back issues avail.) **Indexed:** Amer.Bibl.Slavic & E.Eur.Stud., Amer.Hist.& Life, Arts & Hum.Cit.Ind., ASCA, Curr.Cont., Hist.Abstr., Left Ind. (1985-), Mid.East: Abstr.& Ind. **Document type:** academic/scholarly publication.
—BLDSC (4542.702900); Genuine Article; SWETS; UMI; UnCover. **CCC.**
Former titles: Labor and Working Class History Newsletter & European Labor and Working Class History Newsletter (ISSN 0097-8523)
Description: Links historians throughout the world and presents new scholarship on important issues and controversies in the field.
Refereed Serial

331   UN   ISSN 0074-6681
HD4813
INTERNATIONAL LABOUR CONFERENCE. REPORTS TO THE CONFERENCE AND RECORD OF PROCEEDINGS. French edition: Conference Internationale du Travail. Compte Rendu des Travaux (ISSN 0251-3218); Spanish edition: Conferencia Internacional del Trabajo. Actas (ISSN 0251-3226); German edition: I A O Internationale Arbeitskonferenz. Bericht (ISSN 0251-4095) (Text in English; Arabic, Chinese, Russian editions also avail.) 1919. a. 395 SFr.($316) covering 14 to 18 vols. per conference. (International Labour Office) I L O Publications, CH-1211 Geneva 22, Switzerland. TEL 41-22-799-6111. FAX 41-22-798-6358. TELEX 415647-ILO-CH. (Dist. in US by: I L O Publications, 49 Sheridan Ave., Albany, NY 12210. TEL 518-436-9686. FAX 518-436-7433) (also avail. in microform from ILO,CIS; back vols. avail. in microform from WMP) **Indexed:** IIS. **Document type:** proceedings.

INTERNATIONAL LABOUR LAW REPORTS. see *LAW*

331   UN   ISSN 0378-5882
INTERNATIONAL LABOUR OFFICE. OFFICIAL BULLETIN. SERIES A. (Editions in English, French and Spanish) 1920. 3/yr. 140 SFr.($112) both series. I L O Publications, CH-1211 Geneva 22, Switzerland. TEL 41-22-799-6111. FAX 41-22-798-6358. TELEX 415647-ILO-CH. (Dist. in US by: ILO Publications Center, 49 Sheridan Ave., Albany, NY 12210. TEL 518-436-9686. FAX 518-436-7433) bibl.; index. circ. 2,300. (also avail. in microfiche from ILO) **Indexed:** C.I.S. Abstr. **Document type:** bulletin.
—CCC.
Superseded in part: International Labour Office. Official Bulletin (ISSN 0020-7772)

331   UN   ISSN 0378-5890
HD4811
INTERNATIONAL LABOUR OFFICE. OFFICIAL BULLETIN. SERIES B. (Editions in English, French and Spanish) 1920. 3/yr. 140 SFr.($112) for both series. I L O Publications, CH-1211 Geneva 22, Switzerland. TEL 41-22-799-6111. FAX 41-22-798-6358. TELEX 415647-ILO-CH. (Dist. in US by: ILO Publications Center, 49 Sheridan Ave., Albany, NY 12210. TEL 518-436-9686. FAX 518-436-7433) bibl.; index. circ. 2,300. (also avail. in microform; microfiche from ILO) **Document type:** bulletin.
Superseded in part: International Labour Office. Official Bulletin (ISSN 0020-7772)

331   UN   ISSN 0020-7780
HD4811   CODEN: ILREDT
INTERNATIONAL LABOUR REVIEW. (Editions in English, French, Spanish) 1921. bi-m. 80 SFr.($64) (International Labour Office) I L O Publications, CH-1211 Geneva 22, Switzerland. TEL 41-22-799-6111. FAX 41-22-798-6358. TELEX 415647-ILO-CH. (Dist. in US by: I L O Publications Center, 49 Sheridan Ave., Albany, NY 12210. TEL 518-436-9686. FAX 518-436-7433) Ed. T. Lines. adv.; bk.rev.; bibl.; stat.; s-a. index. circ. 5,300. (also avail. in microform from UMI,PMC; microfiche from ILO,CIS; reprint service avail. from SCH) **Indexed:** ABI Inform., Abstr.Hyg., ASCA, Asian-Pac.Econ.Lit., B.P.I., Bk.Rev.Ind. (1965-), BPIA, Bus.Ind., C.I.J.E., C.I.S. Abstr., C.R.E.J., Child.Bk.Rev.Ind. (1965-), CLOA, CLOSS, Cont.Pg.Manage., Curr.Cont., ELLIS, Fut.Surv., Geo.Abstr.H.G., HR Rep., Hum.Ind., IBR, IDA, IIS, Int.Lab.Doc., J.of Econ.Lit., Key to Econ.Sci., Manage.Cont., Med.Care Rev., Mgmt.& Market.Abstr., Mid.East: Abstr.& Ind., P.A.I.S., Pers.Lit., Pers.Manage.Abstr., Popul.Ind., Rehabil.Lit., Rice Abstr., Rural Devel.Abstr., Rural Ext.Educ.& Tr.Abstr., Rural Recreat.Tour.Abstr., SCIMP (1978-), Soc.Sci.Ind., Sp.Ed.Needs Abstr., SSCI, SSCI, Stud.Wom.Abstr., Tech.Educ.Abstr., Trop.Dis.Bull., Work Rel.Abstr., World Agri.Econ.& Rural Sociol.Abstr., World Bank.Abstr. **Document type:** bulletin.
●Also available online. Vendor(s): Information Access Co., UMI.
—BLDSC (4542.780000); Genuine Article; KR SourceOne; SWETS; UMI; UnCover. **CCC.**
Description: Contains articles based on present I.L.O. and other research into economic and social topics of international interest affecting labor.

331 658.3   II   ISSN 0047-097X
INTERNATIONAL PRESS CUTTING SERVICE: LABOUR WELFARE - INDUSTRIAL LEGISLATION AND PERSONNEL MANAGEMENT. 1967. w. Rs.635($75) International Press Cutting Service, P.O. Box 121, Allahabad 211001, India. Ed. N. Khanna. bk.rev.; index. circ. 1,200. (processed) **Document type:** newsletter.

331 368 346.066   TH
INTERNATIONAL SOCIETY FOR LABOR LAW AND SOCIAL SECURITY. BULLETIN. (Text in English) 1976. irreg. membership. International Society for Labor Law and Social Security - Societe Internationale de Droit du Travail et de la Securite Sociale, c/o Jean-Michel Servais, Sec.-Gen., ILO Office for Asia & the Pacific, P.O. Box 1759, Bangkok 10501, Thailand. FAX 66-2-2801735. **Document type:** bulletin.

INTERNATIONAL WORKERS BULLETIN. see *POLITICAL SCIENCE*

342.73 347.3   US
INTERPRETATIONS OF THE FEDERAL TRAVEL REGULATIONS. 1992. a. $92 (effective 1997). L R P Publications, 747 Dresher Rd., Box 980, Horsham, PA 19044. TEL 215-784-0941; 800-341-7874. FAX 215-784-9639. URL: http://www.lrp.com. Ed. Al Celmer.
Description: Examines, interprets and illustrates the Federal Travel Regulations (FTR).

INVESTING, LICENSING AND TRADING. AMERICAS. see *BUSINESS AND ECONOMICS — International Commerce*

INVESTING, LICENSING AND TRADING. ARGENTINA. see *BUSINESS AND ECONOMICS — International Commerce*

INVESTING, LICENSING AND TRADING. ASIA. see *BUSINESS AND ECONOMICS — International Commerce*

INVESTING, LICENSING AND TRADING. AUSTRALIA. see *BUSINESS AND ECONOMICS — International Commerce*

INVESTING, LICENSING AND TRADING. AUSTRIA. see *BUSINESS AND ECONOMICS — International Commerce*

INVESTING, LICENSING AND TRADING. BELGIUM. see *BUSINESS AND ECONOMICS — International Commerce*

INVESTING, LICENSING AND TRADING. BRAZIL. see *BUSINESS AND ECONOMICS — International Commerce*

INVESTING, LICENSING AND TRADING. BRITAIN. see *BUSINESS AND ECONOMICS — International Commerce*

INVESTING, LICENSING AND TRADING. CANADA. see *BUSINESS AND ECONOMICS — International Commerce*

INVESTING, LICENSING AND TRADING. CENTRAL AMERICA; including El Salvador, Guatemala, Honduras and Costa Rica. see *BUSINESS AND ECONOMICS — International Commerce*

INVESTING, LICENSING AND TRADING. CHILE. see *BUSINESS AND ECONOMICS — International Commerce*

INVESTING, LICENSING AND TRADING. CHINA. see *BUSINESS AND ECONOMICS — International Commerce*

INVESTING, LICENSING AND TRADING. COLOMBIA. see *BUSINESS AND ECONOMICS — International Commerce*

INVESTING, LICENSING AND TRADING. CZECH REPUBLIC. see *BUSINESS AND ECONOMICS — International Commerce*

INVESTING, LICENSING AND TRADING. DENMARK. see *BUSINESS AND ECONOMICS — International Commerce*

INVESTING, LICENSING AND TRADING. ECUADOR. see *BUSINESS AND ECONOMICS — International Commerce*

INVESTING, LICENSING AND TRADING. EGYPT. see *BUSINESS AND ECONOMICS — International Commerce*

INVESTING, LICENSING AND TRADING. EUROPEAN UNION. see *BUSINESS AND ECONOMICS — International Commerce*

INVESTING, LICENSING AND TRADING. FINLAND. see *BUSINESS AND ECONOMICS — International Commerce*

INVESTING, LICENSING AND TRADING. FRANCE. see *BUSINESS AND ECONOMICS — International Commerce*

INVESTING, LICENSING AND TRADING. GERMANY. see *BUSINESS AND ECONOMICS — International Commerce*

INVESTING, LICENSING AND TRADING. GLOBAL EDITION. see *BUSINESS AND ECONOMICS — International Commerce*

INVESTING, LICENSING AND TRADING. GREECE. see *BUSINESS AND ECONOMICS — International Commerce*

INVESTING, LICENSING AND TRADING. HONG KONG. see *BUSINESS AND ECONOMICS — International Commerce*

INVESTING, LICENSING AND TRADING. HUNGARY. see *BUSINESS AND ECONOMICS — International Commerce*

INVESTING, LICENSING AND TRADING. INDIA. see *BUSINESS AND ECONOMICS — International Commerce*

INVESTING, LICENSING AND TRADING. INDONESIA. see *BUSINESS AND ECONOMICS — International Commerce*

BUSINESS AND ECONOMICS — LABOR AND INDUSTRIAL RELATIONS

INVESTING, LICENSING AND TRADING. IRELAND. see BUSINESS AND ECONOMICS — International Commerce

INVESTING, LICENSING AND TRADING. ISRAEL. see BUSINESS AND ECONOMICS — International Commerce

INVESTING, LICENSING AND TRADING. ITALY. see BUSINESS AND ECONOMICS — International Commerce

INVESTING, LICENSING AND TRADING. JAPAN. see BUSINESS AND ECONOMICS — International Commerce

INVESTING, LICENSING AND TRADING. KENYA. see BUSINESS AND ECONOMICS — International Commerce

INVESTING, LICENSING AND TRADING. LUXEMBOURG. see BUSINESS AND ECONOMICS — International Commerce

INVESTING, LICENSING AND TRADING. MALAYSIA. see BUSINESS AND ECONOMICS — International Commerce

INVESTING, LICENSING AND TRADING. MEXICO. see BUSINESS AND ECONOMICS — International Commerce

INVESTING, LICENSING AND TRADING. MIDDLE EAST - AFRICA. see BUSINESS AND ECONOMICS — International Commerce

INVESTING, LICENSING AND TRADING. NETHERLANDS. see BUSINESS AND ECONOMICS — International Commerce

INVESTING, LICENSING AND TRADING. NEW ZEALAND. see BUSINESS AND ECONOMICS — International Commerce

INVESTING, LICENSING AND TRADING. NIGERIA. see BUSINESS AND ECONOMICS — International Commerce

INVESTING, LICENSING AND TRADING. NORWAY. see BUSINESS AND ECONOMICS — International Commerce

INVESTING, LICENSING AND TRADING. PAKISTAN. see BUSINESS AND ECONOMICS — International Commerce

INVESTING, LICENSING AND TRADING. PANAMA. see BUSINESS AND ECONOMICS — International Commerce

INVESTING, LICENSING AND TRADING. PERU. see BUSINESS AND ECONOMICS — International Commerce

INVESTING, LICENSING AND TRADING. PHILIPPINES. see BUSINESS AND ECONOMICS — International Commerce

INVESTING, LICENSING AND TRADING. POLAND. see BUSINESS AND ECONOMICS — International Commerce

INVESTING, LICENSING AND TRADING. PORTUGAL. see BUSINESS AND ECONOMICS — International Commerce

INVESTING, LICENSING AND TRADING. PUERTO RICO. see BUSINESS AND ECONOMICS — International Commerce

INVESTING, LICENSING AND TRADING. RUSSIA. see BUSINESS AND ECONOMICS — International Commerce

INVESTING, LICENSING AND TRADING. SAUDI ARABIA. see BUSINESS AND ECONOMICS — International Commerce

INVESTING, LICENSING AND TRADING. SINGAPORE. see BUSINESS AND ECONOMICS — International Commerce

INVESTING, LICENSING AND TRADING. SLOVAKIA. see BUSINESS AND ECONOMICS — International Commerce

INVESTING, LICENSING AND TRADING. SOUTH AFRICA. see BUSINESS AND ECONOMICS — International Commerce

INVESTING, LICENSING AND TRADING. SOUTH KOREA. see BUSINESS AND ECONOMICS — International Commerce

INVESTING, LICENSING AND TRADING. SPAIN. see BUSINESS AND ECONOMICS — International Commerce

INVESTING, LICENSING AND TRADING. SWEDEN. see BUSINESS AND ECONOMICS — International Commerce

INVESTING, LICENSING AND TRADING. SWITZERLAND. see BUSINESS AND ECONOMICS — International Commerce

INVESTING, LICENSING AND TRADING. TAIWAN. see BUSINESS AND ECONOMICS — International Commerce

INVESTING, LICENSING AND TRADING. THAILAND. see BUSINESS AND ECONOMICS — International Commerce

INVESTING, LICENSING AND TRADING. TURKEY. see BUSINESS AND ECONOMICS — International Commerce

INVESTING, LICENSING AND TRADING. UNITED STATES OF AMERICA. see BUSINESS AND ECONOMICS — International Commerce

INVESTING, LICENSING AND TRADING. URUGUAY. see BUSINESS AND ECONOMICS — International Commerce

INVESTING, LICENSING AND TRADING. VENEZUELA. see BUSINESS AND ECONOMICS — International Commerce

INVESTING, LICENSING AND TRADING. VIETNAM. see BUSINESS AND ECONOMICS — International Commerce

331.88   UK
INVOLVEMENT OF PARTICIPATION.* 1894. q. £38. Involvement of Participation Association, 42 Colebrook Row, London N1 8AF, England. FAX 0171-407-9083. Ed. Anthony Barry. adv.; bk.rev.; abstr. circ. 1,500. (also avail. in microfilm from UMI; reprint service avail. from UMI) **Indexed:** Account.& Data Proc.Abstr., Anbar, Br.Hum.Ind., Int.Lab.Doc., Mgmt.& Market.Abstr.
 Former titles: Industrial Participation; Co-Partnership (ISSN 0009-9864)

331.1   US
HD7096.U6
IOWA. DEPARTMENT OF EMPLOYMENT SERVICES. ANNUAL REPORT. 1938. a. free. Department of Employment Services, 1000 E. Grand Ave., Des Moines, IA 50319. TEL 515-281-3201. circ. 2,000 (controlled). **Document type:** government publication.
 Formerly: Iowa. Department of Job Service. Annual Report (ISSN 0149-449X); Iowa. Employment Security Commission. Annual Report.

IOWA EMPLOYMENT LAW LETTER. see LAW

IRELAND. CENTRAL STATISTICS OFFICE. INDUSTRIAL DISPUTES. see BUSINESS AND ECONOMICS — Abstracting, Bibliographies, Statistics

IRELAND. CENTRAL STATISTICS OFFICE. LIVE REGISTER AGE BY DURATION ANALYSIS. see BUSINESS AND ECONOMICS — Abstracting, Bibliographies, Statistics

IRELAND. CENTRAL STATISTICS OFFICE. LIVE REGISTER AREA ANALYSIS. see BUSINESS AND ECONOMICS — Abstracting, Bibliographies, Statistics

IRELAND. CENTRAL STATISTICS OFFICE. LIVE REGISTER STATEMENT. see BUSINESS AND ECONOMICS — Abstracting, Bibliographies, Statistics

331.88   IC   ISSN 1022-7741
ISLENSKUR IDNADUR; frettabref Landssambands Idnadarmanna. 1977. m. membership. Samtoek Idnadarins - Federation of Icelandic Crafts and Industries, Hallveigarstig 1, IC-121 Reykjavik, Iceland. TEL 354-551-6010. FAX 354-552-5380. Ed. Ingi Bogi Bogason. adv.; illus.; stat.; tr.lit. circ. 4,500. **Document type:** newsletter.
 Former titles (until 1993): Idnadurinn (ISSN 1019-8245); (until 1985): Landsamband Idnadarmanna - Frettabref.

331   JA   ISSN 0916-3816
J I L RISACHI. Variant title: Nihon Rodo Kenkyu Kiko Kenkyu Kohoshi. (Text in Japanese) 1970. q. Japan Institute of Labour - Nihon Rodo Kenkyu Kiko, Shinjuku Monolith, P.O. Box 7040, Tokyo 163-09, Japan. TEL 03-5321-3074. FAX 03-5321-3015.
 (until 1981): Shokken (ISSN 0285-6476)

331 360   EI   ISSN 1018-3183
JANUS. French edition (ISSN 1018-3140); German edition (ISSN 1018-3124); Italian edition (ISSN 1018-3159); Danish edition (ISSN 1017-7647); Spanish edition (ISSN 1018-3132) Greek edition (EI ISSN 1018-3175) Portuguese edition (EI ISSN 1018-3167) Dutch edition (EI ISSN 1018-3191) (Text in English) 1989. q. (Commission of European Communities) Office for Official Publications of the European Communities, Rue de la Loi 200, 1049 Brussels, Belgium. **Indexed:** Intl.Polym.Sci.& Tech., RAPRA.
 —BLDSC (4647.507500).

331   JA   ISSN 0021-4469
HD8721
JAPAN LABOUR BULLETIN. (Text in English) 1962. m. 4200 Yen. Japan Institute of Labour - Nihon Rodo Kenkyu Kiko, Shinjuku Monolith, P.O. Box 7040, Tokyo 163-09, Japan. Dir. M. Matsumiya. stat.; index, cum.index. circ. 3,100. pp./issue: 8. **Indexed:** Int.Lab.Doc., World Bibl.Soc.Sec. **Document type:** bulletin.
 —BLDSC (4648.345000).
 Description: Introduces and analyzes current developments in Japanese industrial relations to overseas readers.

JAPAN STATISTICAL ASSOCIATION. ANNUAL REPORT ON THE LABOUR FORCE SURVEY. see BUSINESS AND ECONOMICS — Abstracting, Bibliographies, Statistics

JAPAN STATISTICAL ASSOCIATION. MONTHLY REPORT ON THE LABOUR FORCE SURVEY. see BUSINESS AND ECONOMICS — Abstracting, Bibliographies, Statistics

331   JA
JAPANESE INDUSTRIAL RELATIONS SERIES. (Text in English) 1988. irreg., no.17, 1990. Japan Institute of Labour - Nihon Rodo Kenkyu Kiko, Shinjuku Monolith, P.O. Box 7040, Tokyo 163-09, Japan. TEL 03-5991-5165. FAX 03-3594-1112.
 Description: Book series on Japanese industrial relations.

JEWISH LABOR COMMITTEE REVIEW. see ETHNIC INTERESTS

JINGJIFAXUE, LAODONGFAXUE. see LAW — Corporate Law

JINRUI DOTAI GAKKAI KAIHO/HUMAN ERGOLOGY SOCIETY. NEWSLETTER. see PHYSICS

JOB PRATIQUE MAGAZINE. see OCCUPATIONS AND CAREERS

331.11   US
JOB SERVICE NORTH DAKOTA. ANNUAL REPORT. 1937 a. free. Job Service North Dakota, 1000 E. Divide Ave., Box 5507, Bismarck, ND 58506. TEL 701-328-2825. Ed. Tom Pederson. circ. 200. **Document type:** government publication.
 Formerly: North Dakota. Employment Security Bureau. Annual Report (ISSN 0078-155X)

BUSINESS AND ECONOMICS — LABOR AND INDUSTRIAL RELATIONS

331.11   US
JOB SERVICE NORTH DAKOTA. BIENNIAL REPORT TO THE GOVERNOR. 1964. biennial. free. Job Service North Dakota, 1000 E. Divide Ave., Box 5507, Bismarck, ND 58506. TEL 701-328-2825. Ed. Gayle Schuck. circ. 75. **Document type:** government publication.
    Formerly: North Dakota. Employment Security Bureau. Biennial Report to the Governor (ISSN 0078-1568)

JOBS IN HIGHER EDUCATION. see *EDUCATION — Higher Education*

JOHN BURTON'S WORKERS' COMPENSATION MONITOR. see *INSURANCE*

JOHN LINER LETTER. see *INSURANCE*

JOINT GOVERNMENTAL SALARY AND BENEFITS SURVEY: ARIZONA. see *BUSINESS AND ECONOMICS — Abstracting, Bibliographies, Statistics*

JORDAN. DEPARTMENT OF STATISTICS. EMPLOYMENT SURVEY FOR ESTABLISHMENTS ENGAGING FIVE PERSONS OR MORE. see *BUSINESS AND ECONOMICS — Abstracting, Bibliographies, Statistics*

JOURNAL DES TRIBUNAUX DU TRAVAIL. see *LAW*

350 331   US   ISSN 0047-2301
LB2842.2
JOURNAL OF COLLECTIVE NEGOTIATIONS IN THE PUBLIC SECTOR. 1971. q. $136 (effective 1997). Baywood Publishing Co., Inc., 26 Austin Ave., Box 337, Amityville, NY 11701. TEL 516-691-1270. FAX 516-691-1770. E-mail: baywood@baywood.com; URL: http://baywood.com. Ed. Harry Kershen. R&P contact: Julie Krempa. abstr.; charts; illus.; index. (back issues avail.) **Indexed:** ABI Inform., ASCA, B.P.I., BPIA, Bus.Ind., C.I.J.E., C.L.I., Curr.Cont., Educ.Admin.Abstr., Ind.Per.Art.Relat.Law, L.R.I., Manage.Cont., P.A.I.S., Pers.Lit., SSCI, Work Rel.Abstr. **Document type:** academic/scholarly publication.
    —BLDSC (4958.799500); KR SourceOne; SWETS; UnCover. **CCC.**
    Description: Serves as a forum for the interchange of ideas and information for those in the international community concerned with the negotiation process.

612.042   JA   ISSN 0300-8134
QP301   **CODEN: JHEGAI**
JOURNAL OF HUMAN ERGOLOGY. (Text in English) 1972. s-a. $74. (Human Ergology Society) Center for Academic Publications, 2-4-16 Yayoi, Bunkyo-ku, Tokyo 113, Japan. TEL 03-3817-5821. FAX 03-3817-5820. (Dist. by: Business Center for Academic Societies Japan, 5-16-9 Honkomagome, Bunkyo-ku, Tokyo 113, Japan) adv.; illus. circ. 500. **Indexed:** Abstr.Anthropol., Abstr.Hyg., Agri.Eng.Abstr., Biol.Abstr., C.I.S.Abstr., Curr.Adv.Ecol.Sci., Ergon.Abstr., Excerp.Med., Ind.Med., Indian Psychol.Abstr., Psychol.Abstr. (1972-), Psycscan. **Document type:** academic/scholarly publication.
    —BLDSC (5003.414000); CISTI; KNAW; Linda Hall; SWETS.

JOURNAL OF HUMAN RESOURCES; education, manpower and welfare economics. see *BUSINESS AND ECONOMICS — Personnel Management*

331   US   ISSN 1055-7512
K10
JOURNAL OF INDIVIDUAL EMPLOYMENT RIGHTS. 1991. q. $118 (effective 1997). Baywood Publishing Co., Inc., 26 Austin Ave., Box 337, Amityville, NY 11701. TEL 516-691-1270. FAX 516-691-1770. E-mail: baywood@baywood.com; URL: http://baywood.com. Eds. Kurt H. Decker, Harry Kershen. R&P contact: Julie Krempa. **Document type:** academic/scholarly publication.
    —UnCover. **CCC.**
    Description: Researches and addresses the areas of individual employee rights as they are debated and developed by courts, academicians, legal practitioners, and personnel managers.
    Refereed Serial

331.1   AT   ISSN 0022-1856
HD4811
JOURNAL OF INDUSTRIAL RELATIONS. 1959. q. Aus.$55. Industrial Relations Society of Australia, c/o Braham Dabscheck, Ed., School of Industrial Relations and Organisational Behaviour, Univ.of N.S.W., Sydney, N.S.W. 2052, Australia. TEL 61-2-93852148. FAX 61-2-96628531. (Subscr. addr.: P.O. Box 74, Oatlands, N.S.W. 2117, Australia) R&P contact: Braham Dabscheck. adv.; bk.rev.; charts; stat.; index; circ. 4,200 (paid). **Indexed:** Asian-Pac.Econ.Lit., ASSIA, Aus.P.A.I.S., C.R.E.J., Int.Lab.Doc., Lang.& Lang.Behav.Abstr., Work Rel.Abstr. **Document type:** academic/scholarly publication.
    —BLDSC (5006.380000); SWETS; UnCover. **CCC.**
    Description: Publishes articles on Australian and international industrial relations.
    Refereed Serial

331.1   CN   ISSN 1198-3310
JOURNAL OF INDUSTRIAL RELATIONS. Abbreviated title: J I R. a. Can.$50. (Strategic Training Consultants) Universal Publications, P.O. Box 7305, Ottawa, ON K1L 8E4, Canada. TEL 613-831-1052; 888-659-4845. FAX 613-831-8452. E-mail: title@upinfo.com; URL: http://www.upinfo.com/-up. Ed. Amarjit S. Sethi. R&P contact: Bob Smith. adv. contact: Bob Smith. bk.rev.
    Description: Promotes interdisciplinary dialogue among management, union, and government leaders, policymakers, negotiators, conciliation officers, mediators, and arbitrators in the field of cooperative industrial relations.
    Refereed Serial

JOURNAL OF INTERNATIONAL ARBITRATION. see *LAW — International Law*

331   US   ISSN 0734-306X
HD4802
JOURNAL OF LABOR ECONOMICS. 1983. q. $46 to individuals (Canada $54.12; elsewhere $51); institutions $130 (Canada $144.10; elsewhere $135) (effective 1998). (National Opinion Research Center, Economics Research Center) University of Chicago Press, Journals Division, Box 37005, Chicago, IL 60637. TEL 773-753-3347. FAX 773-753-0811. E-mail: subscriptions@journals.uchicago.edu; URL: http://www.journals.uchicago.edu/JOLE/. Ed. Edward P. Lazear. adv.; page $355; trim 6 x 9. bk.rev.; stat. circ. 1,500. (also avail. in microform from UMI) **Indexed:** ABI Inform., ASCA, BPIA, C.R.E.J., Curr.Cont., Fam.Ind., J.of Econ.Lit., Soc.Sci.Ind., SSCI. **Document type:** academic/scholarly publication.
    —BLDSC (5009.940000); Genuine Article; KR SourceOne; SWETS; UMI; UnCover. **CCC.**
    Description: Presents theoretical and empirical articles pertaining to labor economics, very broadly defined.
    Refereed Serial

331.1   US   ISSN 0195-3613
HD4802
JOURNAL OF LABOR RESEARCH. 1980. q. $35 to individuals; institutions $110. George Mason University, Department of Economics, MSN 3G4, 4400 University Dr., Fairfax, VA 22030-4444. TEL 703-993-1155. FAX 703-993-1133. Ed. James T. Bennett. adv.; bk.rev.; circ. 1,200 (paid). **Indexed:** ABI Inform., Abstr.Bk.Rev.Curr.Leg.Per., ASCA, BPIA, Bus.Ind., Curr.Cont., J.of Econ.Lit., Manage.Cont., P.A.I.S., Soc.Sci.Ind., SSCI, Tr.& Indus.Ind. **Document type:** academic/scholarly publication.
    —BLDSC (5009.960000); Genuine Article; KR SourceOne; SWETS; UMI; UnCover. **CCC.**
    Description: Focuses on policy issues in the workplace, including unions and their political and economic activities.
    Refereed Serial

JOURNAL OF PENSION PLANNING AND COMPLIANCE. see *BUSINESS AND ECONOMICS — Public Finance, Taxation*

JOURNAL OF WORKERS COMPENSATION. see *INSURANCE*

331   YU   ISSN 0022-6068
T55.A1
JUGOSLOVENSKA I INOSTRANA DOKUMENTACIJA ZASTITE NA RADU. (Text in Serbocroatian) 1964. m. Institut za Dokumentaciju Zastite na Radu, Nis, Stanka Paunovica 17, Nis, Serbia, Yugoslavia. Ed. Zdravkovic Moma. **Indexed:** C.I.S. Abstr.

331 330.1   AG   ISSN 0327-1404
JUSTICIA SOCIAL. 1985. 3/yr. $15. Centro de Estudios Laborales, San Mauro 444, 1878 Quilmes, B.A., Argentina. TEL 311-4886. Ed. Hector Roberto Roudil. bk.rev. circ. 1,250.

K A B A M. (Krant voor Aktieve Baanlozen in Amsterdam) see *SOCIAL SERVICES AND WELFARE*

331   JA   ISSN 0285-3094
KAIGAI RODO JIHO/INTERNATIONAL LABOR INFORMATION. (Text in Japanese) 1977. m. 6000 Yen. Japan Institute of Labour - Nihon Rodo Kenkyu Kiko, Shinjuku Monolith, P.O. Box 7040, Tokyo 163-09, Japan. TEL 03-5321-3074. FAX 03-5321-3015.

KANO (STATE) MANPOWER STATISTICS. see *BUSINESS AND ECONOMICS — Abstracting, Bibliographies, Statistics*

KANSAS EMPLOYMENT LAW LETTER. see *LAW*

KARMAKSHETRA. see *OCCUPATIONS AND CAREERS*

KENTUCKY EMPLOYMENT LAW LETTER. see *LAW*

344.012   US
KENTUCKY UNEMPLOYMENT COMPENSATION LAWS AND REGULATIONS. a. $15. Michie, A Division of Reed Elsevier Inc., Box 7587, Charlottesville, VA 22906-7587. TEL 804-972-7566; 800-562-1197. FAX 800-643-1280. E-mail: custserv@michie.com; URL: http://www.michie.com. Ed. George Harley. pp./issue: 110.

KIBBUTZ STUDIEN. see *BUSINESS AND ECONOMICS — Cooperatives*

KIRCHLICHER DIENST IN DER ARBEITSWELT; Zeitschrift fuer evangelische Arbeitnehmer und evangelische Industrie- und Sozialarbeit. see *RELIGIONS AND THEOLOGY — Protestant*

059.89   CY
KIRYKAS/HERALD. (Text in Greek) 1981. w. Centre Union Party, 12 Diagorou St., Nicosia, Cyprus. Ed. George Eliades. circ. 3,000.
    Description: Right-of-center political review.

331   SW   ISSN 0345-6307
KOMMUNALARBETAREN. 1911. 22/yr. SEK 200. Svenska Kommunalarbetarefoerbundet - Union of Municipal Workers, P.O. Box 19034, 104 32 Stockholm, Sweden. TEL 46-8-728-28-00. FAX 46-8-30-61-42. E-mail: redaktionen@tidningerkom.se. adv. circ. 700,000. (also avail. in audio cassette)

331 301.16   GW   ISSN 0176-246X
KONTAKT. 1955. q. free. Richard Hirschmann GmbH, Stuttgarterstr. 45-51, 72654 Neckartenzlingen, Germany. TEL 49-7127-141289. FAX 49-7127-141835. E-mail: wdommers@nt.hirschmann.de; URL: http://www.hirschmann.de. Ed. Wolfgang Dommershausen. bk.rev.; charts; stat. circ. 4,200. (back issues avail.) **Document type:** newspaper.

KOREA (REPUBLIC). NATIONAL STATISTICAL OFFICE. ANNUAL REPORT ON THE ECONOMICALLY ACTIVE POPULATION SURVEY. see *BUSINESS AND ECONOMICS — Abstracting, Bibliographies, Statistics*

KWARTALNIK HISTORII I TEORII RUCHU ZAWODOWEGO. see *HISTORY — History Of Europe*

331.11   US
L M I REVIEW. (Labor Market Information); a quarterly review of Washington State labor market information. 1984. q. free. Employment Security Department, Labor Market and Economic Analysis Branch, Box 9046, Olympia, WA 98507-9046. TEL 360-438-3155. FAX 360-438-4846. Ed. Robert Baker. charts; stat. circ. 2,400. **Document type:** government publication.
    Description: Examines the labor market and economic conditions of the state of Washington and contains articles on the labor market, occupations, the economy, and demographics.

BUSINESS AND ECONOMICS — LABOR AND INDUSTRIAL RELATIONS

331   US   ISSN 0895-5220
HC101
L R A'S ECONOMIC NOTES. 1933. m. (except Aug.). $30 to individuals; institutions $50 (effective 1997). Labor Research Association, 145 W. 28th St., 6th Fl., New York, NY 10001-6191. TEL 212-714-1677. FAX 212-714-1674. Ed. Gregory Tarpinian. adv.; bk.rev.; index. circ. 3,000. (back issues avail.) **Indexed:** Alt.Press Ind., C.R.E.J. **Document type:** newsletter.
   Formerly: Economic Notes (ISSN 0013-0184)
   Description: Explains the how and why of labor-capital relations.

331   US
L S A - ZIP. (Labor Surplus Areas); the purchasing agent's guide to labor surplus areas. 1990. 3/yr. $145 (effective 1996); $160 (effective 1997). Business Research Services, Inc., 4201 Connecticut Ave., N.W., Ste. 610, Washington, DC 20008. TEL 202-864-6473. FAX 202-686-3228. Pub. Thomas D. Johnson. (also avail. in diskette format) **Document type:** directory.
   Description: Lists all federally designated areas of high employment. Organized by zip code, city, county, and state.

331   IT   ISSN 0023-6489
DG401
LABOR. 1960. q. L.30000 (foreign L.50000). Via Tunisi 4, 98138 Palermo, Italy. TEL 39-91-580091. Ed. Cosmo Crifo. adv.: B&W page L.900000. bk.rev.; abstr.; index. circ. 700.

331.795   BE
LABOR (YEAR). (Supplements avail.: Events) (Text in Dutch, English, French, German, Spanish) 1980. bi-m. 650 BEF($16) (effective 1992). World Confederation of Labour, 33 rue de Treves, B-1040 Brussels, Belgium. TEL 32-2-2306295. FAX 32-2-2308722. TELEX 26-966. Ed. Carlos Luis Custer. bk.rev. circ. 500.
   Former titles: Labor Trade Action; Labor Professional Action; Which incorporated: Labor I N F E D O P - W C T (World Confederation of Teachers); Which was formerly (1923-1979): Labor I N F E D O P (International Federation of Employees in Public Service).
   Description: Review of trade union information and training.

331   TG
LABOR AND DEVELOPMENT; a monthly review of African socio-economic events of interest to trade union leaders. m. Regional Economic Research and Documentation Center, PO Box 7138, Lome, Togo. **Indexed:** HR Rep.
   Supersedes in part: Labor in Perspective (ISSN 0377-0737)

331 340   US
LABOR AND EMPLOYMENT IN CONNECTICUT. 1991. base vol. (plus a. suppl.) $65. Butterworth Legal Publishers (Salem) (Subsidiary of: Reed Elsevier plc), 8 Industrial Way, Bldg. C, Salem, NH 03079. TEL 800-548-4001. FAX 603-898-9858. Ed. Jeffrey L. Hirsch. (looseleaf format)
   Description: Provides a comprehensive analysis and explanation of state and federal laws and regulations governing all aspects of employer-employee relationships.

331   US
LABOR & EMPLOYMENT IN MASSACHUSETTS; a guide to employment laws, regulations and practices. 1990. base vol. (plus a. suppl.). $65. Butterworth Legal Publishers (Salem) (Subsidiary of: Reed Elsevier plc), 8 Industrial Way, Bldg. C, Salem, NH 03079. TEL 800-548-4001. FAX 603-898-9858. (looseleaf format)
   Description: Provides private employers with information on state and federal laws and regulations governing employer-employee relationships.

331 340   US
LABOR AND EMPLOYMENT IN NEW YORK. 1988. base vol. (plus a. suppl.). $79.50. Butterworth Legal Publishers (Salem) (Subsidiary of: Reed Elsevier plc), 8 Industrial Way, Bldg. C, Salem, NH 03079. TEL 800-548-4001. FAX 603-898-9858. Eds. Jeffrey L. Liddle, Michael F. Marino, III. (looseleaf format)

331   US   ISSN 0193-5739
KF325.15
LABOR & EMPLOYMENT LAW. 4/yr. membership only. American Bar Association, Labor and Employment Law Section, 750 N. Lake Shore Dr., Chicago, IL 60611. TEL 312-988-6076. (reprint service avail. from WSH) **Indexed:** C.L.I., L.R.I.
   Former titles: Labor Relations and Employment (ISSN 0163-5077); Labor Relations Law Letter.
   Description: News items and developments in the field of labor law.

331 340   US
LABOR AND EMPLOYMENT UPDATE. 1994. 4/yr. free. Reed McClure, 3600 Columbia Center, 701 Fifth Ave., Seattle, WA 98104-7081. TEL 206-292-4900. FAX 206-223-0152. E-mail: info@rmlaw.com. Ed. Denise Dee Behrens. circ. 4,400 (controlled). **Document type:** newsletter.

331.155 340   US   ISSN 0023-6500
LABOR ARBITRATION AWARDS. 1961. w. $1044. C C H Incorporated, 2700 Lake Cook Rd., Riverwoods, IL 60015. TEL 847-267-7000; 800-835-5224. FAX 800-224-8299. (looseleaf format)
—CCC.

331   US   ISSN 0047-3839
KF3409.P77
LABOR ARBITRATION IN GOVERNMENT. 1971. m. $120. American Arbitration Association, 140 W. 51st St., New York, NY 10020-1203. TEL 212-484-4011. FAX 212-541-4841. (Co-sponsor: Labor Relations Press) s-a. index. (looseleaf format; also avail. in microfiche; reprint service avail. from KTO) **Indexed:** Pers.Lit.
   Description: Covers selected awards involving city, county, state, and federal employees (other than those employed by schools).

340   US   ISSN 8755-7886
KF3407.A75
LABOR CONTRACT LAW BULLETIN. 1977. m. $62. Quinlan Publishing Co., Inc., 23 Drydock Ave., Boston, MA 02110. TEL 617-542-0048; 800-229-2084. FAX 617-345-9646. index. (back issues avail.) **Document type:** newsletter.
—UMI. CCC.
   Description: Covers legal decisions concerning labor contract disputes. Covers decisions from the National Labor Relations Board and the Federal Labor Relations Association.

LABOR FORCE AND NONAGRICULTURAL EMPLOYMENT ESTIMATES. see BUSINESS AND ECONOMICS — Abstracting, Bibliographies, Statistics

331   US
LABOR FORCE IN IDAHO. a. free. Department of Labor, Bureau of Research and Analysis, 317 Main St., Boise, ID 83735. TEL 208-334-6168. URL: http://www.labor.state.id.us. stat. (also avail. in microfiche from CIS) **Indexed:** SRI. **Document type:** government publication.
   Supersedes in part: Labor Force in Idaho and Basic Economic Data for Idaho; **Formerly:** Labor Force in Idaho.

331   US
LABOR HERALD. 1936. bi-w. $10 (effective 1997). Labor Herald Press, 4005 Seven Mile Lane, Baltimore, MD 21208-6116. TEL 410-484-3832. Ed. Daniel Bernstein. adv. contact: Edward Burns. bk.rev. circ. 39,850. **Document type:** newspaper.

331 900   US   ISSN 0023-656X
HD4802
LABOR HISTORY. 1960. q. $40 to individuals; institutions $60. Tamiment Institute, Ben Josephson Library, New York University, Bobst Library, 10th Fl., 70 Washington Sq. S., New York, NY 10012. TEL 212-737-2715. FAX 212-741-6790. (Subscr. to: B P Ink, Box 1236, Washington, CT 06493) Ed. Daniel J. Leab. R&P contact: Dan Leab. TEL 212-741-6790. adv. contact: Dan Leab. bk.rev.; charts; pat.; tr.mk.; index; circ. 1,800 (paid). (also avail. in microform; reprint service avail. from SCH) **Indexed:** Acad.Ind., Alt.Press Ind., Amer.Bibl.Slavic & E.Eur.Stud., Amer.Hist.& Life (1960-), Arts & Hum.Cit.Ind., ASCA, B.P.I., CERDIC, Chic.Per.Ind., Curr.Cont., Hist.Abstr. (1960-), Hum.Ind., IBR, J.of Econ.Lit., SSCI, Work Rel.Abstr. **Document type:** academic/scholarly publication.
—BLDSC (5137.907000); Genuine Article; KR SourceOne; SWETS; UMI; UnCover. CCC.
   Formerly: Labor Historian's Bulletin.
   Refereed Serial

LABOR LAW INSTITUTE. see LAW

LABOR LAW JOURNAL; to promote sound thinking on labor law problems. see LAW

331   US
LABOR LAW REPORTS: SUMMARY. w. $98. C C H Incorporated, 2700 Lake Cook Rd., Riverwoods, IL 60015. TEL 847-267-7000; 800-835-5224. FAX 800-224-8299.

344.012   US
LABOR LAWS OF VIRGINIA. a. $15. Michie, A Division of Reed Elsevier Inc., Box 7587, Charlottesville, VA 22906-7587. TEL 804-972-7566; 800-562-1197. FAX 800-643-1280. E-mail: custserv@michie.com; URL: http://www.michie.com. Ed. George Harley. pp./issue: 151.

331 340   US
LABOR LETTER.* m. $145 to non-members; members $95. Pennsylvania Chamber of Business and Industry, 417 Walnut St., Harrisburg, PA 17101. TEL 800-326-3252. FAX 717-255-3298.
   Description: Covers recent developments affecting employee relations, including reports of Pennsylvania legislative and judicial activity.

331.2   US
LABOR - MANAGEMENT RELATIONS ANALYSIS - NEWS AND BACKGROUND INFORMATION. (Subseries of: Labor Relations Reporter (ISSN 0148-7981)) w. $295. The Bureau of National Affairs, Inc., 1231 25th St., N.W., Washington, DC 20037. TEL 202-452-4200. FAX 202-822-8092. TELEX 285656 BANI WSH. URL: http://www.bna.com/. (Subscr. to: 9435 Key West Ave., Rockville, MD 20850. TEL 800-372-1033) Ed. Nancy J. Sedmak. (looseleaf format; back issues avail.)
   ●Also available online. Vendor(s): Human Resources Information Network (File DD), West Group (File LLR-NEWS).

331   US
LABOR NEWS (INDIANAPOLIS). 1965. m. $24 to non-members; members $12. 2620 E. Tenth St., Indianapolis, IN 46201. TEL 317-264-4288. FAX 317-264-4280. Ed. Sandra L. Morris; Pub. Fred W. Levin. adv. contact: Marsha L. Watson. (tabloid format) **Document type:** newspaper.

331   US   ISSN 1053-7023
LABOR NEWS (NEW YORK). 1986. m. free. New York City Central Labor Council, A F L - C I O, 386 Park Ave. S., New York, NY 10016. TEL 212-685-9552. FAX 212-685-9557. Ed. Ted H. Jacobsen. circ. 5,000.
   Formerly: Labor Chronicle.
   Description: Covers the New York City Trade Union Movement and labor scene.

614.85   US
LABOR NEWSLETTER. 1957. bi-m. $19 to non-members; members $15. National Safety Council, Periodicals Department, 1121 Spring Lake Dr., Itasca, IL 60143. TEL 708-775-2281. Ed. Kathy Henderson; Pub. Kevin H. Axe. circ. 1,200. (processed) **Document type:** newsletter.
   Former titles: Labor Organization Newsletter; Labor Safety Newsletter (ISSN 0023-6632)

331   US   ISSN 0275-4452
LABOR NOTES. 1979. m. $20 to individuals; institutions $30 (effective 1997 & 1998). Labor Education & Research Project, 7435 Michigan Ave., Detroit, MI 48210. TEL 313-842-6262. FAX 313-842-0227. E-mail: labornotes@igc.apc.org. Ed. Jim West. bk.rev. circ. 11,000. (reprint service avail. from UMI) **Indexed:** Alt.Press Ind. **Document type:** newsletter.
—UMI.
   Description: Newsletter covering union issues and activities.

331   US   ISSN 8750-2313
LABOR PAPER (PEORIA). 1936. s-m. $15. West Central Illinois Building & Construction Trades Council, 400 N.E. Jefferson St., Rm. 400, Peoria, IL 61603. TEL 309-674-3148. FAX 309-674-9714. adv.; bk.rev.; illus.; tr.mk. circ. 10,000. (tabloid format)
   Formerly (until 1981): Peoria Labor News (ISSN 0031-5052)

LABOR PARTY PRESS. see POLITICAL SCIENCE

BUSINESS AND ECONOMICS — LABOR AND INDUSTRIAL RELATIONS

331.89 658.3 US ISSN 1080-3211
LABOR RELATIONS BULLETIN. 1950. m. $99.84. Bureau of Business Practice, 24 Rope Ferry Rd., Waterford, CT 06386. TEL 860-442-4365. FAX 860-437-3555. URL: http://www.bbpnews.com. Ed. Emily Mitchell; Pub. Peter Garabedian. R&P contact: Debra Ferraro. s-a. index. **Document type:** newsletter.
Former titles (until 1994): Discipline and Grievances. White Collar Edition (ISSN 0271-3462); (until 1993): Discipline and Grievances (ISSN 0012-351X)
Description: Reports on the most current and relevant developments in labor law and labor relations; includes discipline and grievance cases and discusses the implications of the ruling.

340 US
LABOR RELATIONS CIRCULAR. bi-m. $150. R.C. Simpson Co., 5950 Fairview Rd., No. 604, Charlotte, NC 28210. TEL 704-553-0716. FAX 704-553-0734. (back issues avail.) **Document type:** abstracting/indexing.
Description: Contains arbitration awards and decisions of the courts and government agencies.

331.1 US
LABOR RELATIONS EXPEDITER. (Subseries of: Labor Relations Reporter (ISSN 0148-7981)) 1937. w. $560 (effective July 1995). The Bureau of National Affairs, Inc., 1231 25th St., N.W., Washington, DC 20037. TEL 202-452-4200. FAX 202-822-8092. TELEX 285656 BNAI WSH. URL: http://www.bna.com/. (Subscr. to: 9435 Key West Ave., Rockville, MD 20850. TEL 800-372-1033)
Formerly: Labor Relations Reporter. Analysis and Expediter.

340 US ISSN 1046-3682
KF3352.L3
LABOR RELATIONS LAW. 1964. q. $18 to members; non-members $68. Illinois State Bar Association, Section on Labor Law, Illinois Bar Center, Springfield, IL 62701. TEL 217-525-1760; 800-252-8908. FAX 217-525-0712. Eds. Michael R. Lied, Alisa Arnoff. circ. 1,200. (back issues avail.) **Document type:** newsletter.

331 US ISSN 1043-5506
KF3315
LABOR RELATIONS REFERENCE MANUAL. (Subseries of: Labor Relations Reporter (ISSN 0148-7981)) 1937. 3/yr. price varies. The Bureau of National Affairs, Inc., 1231 25th St., N.W., Washington, DC 20037. TEL 202-452-4200. FAX 202-822-8092. TELEX 285656 BNAI WSH. URL: http://www.bna.com/. (Subscr. to: 9435 Key West Ave., Rockville, MD 20850. TEL 800-372-1033) Ed. Nancy J. Sedmak. (back issues avail.)
●Also available online. Vendor(s): Human Resources Information Network (Files BOARDS, COURTS), Lexis-Nexis (File LRRM), West Group (File FLB-CS, MLR-CS).
—CCC.
Description: Contains a table of cases, summaries of all published NLRB decisions, and full-text of opinions of the U S Supreme Court, U S Courts of Appeals, and other courts.

331.1 US ISSN 0148-7981
KF3315
LABOR RELATIONS REPORTER. Variant title: B N A Labor Relations Reporter. (Avail. in separate parts or combinations: State Labor Laws; Wages and Hours; Fair Employment Practices; Labor Arbitration and Dispute Settlements; Labor Relations Expediter) 1937. bi-w. $3479. The Bureau of National Affairs, Inc., 1231 25th St., N.W., Washington, DC 20037. TEL 202-452-4200. FAX 202-822-8092. TELEX 285656 BNAI WSH. URL: http://www.bna.com/. (Subscr. to: 9435 Key West Ave., Rockville, MD 20850. TEL 800-372-1033) Ed. Nancy J. Sedmak. (looseleaf format; back issues avail.) **Document type:** newsletter.
●Also available online. Vendor(s): Knight-Ridder Information, Inc. (File no. 244, Laborlaw); Lexis-Nexis, West Group.
—CCC.
Description: Multi-part notification and reference service covering labor-management relations, wages and hours, labor arbitration, fair employment practices, and individual employment rights.

440 US
LABOR RELATIONS REPORTER. FAIR EMPLOYMENT PRACTICES. (Subseries of: Labor Relations Reporter (ISSN 0148-7981)) 1965. w. $1280 (effective July 1995). The Bureau of National Affairs, Inc., 1231 25th St., N.W., Washington, DC 20037. TEL 202-452-4200. FAX 202-822-8092. TELEX 285656 BNAI WSH. URL: http://www.bna.com/. (Subscr. to: 9435 Key West Ave., Rockville, MD 20850. TEL 800-372-1033) Ed. Nancy J. Sedmak. (looseleaf format; also avail. in microfiche; back issues avail.)
●Also available online. Vendor(s): Knight-Ridder Information, Inc., West Group.
Description: Guide to the regulation of fair employment practices. Includes federal laws, orders, and regulations, policy guides and ground rules, and state and local fair employment practice laws.

331.1 US
LABOR RELATIONS REPORTER. LABOR ARBITRATION AND DISPUTE SETTLEMENTS. (Subseries of: Labor Relations Reporter (ISSN 0148-7981)) 1937. w. $936 (effective July 1995). The Bureau of National Affairs, Inc., 1231 25th St., N.W., Washington, DC 20037. TEL 202-452-4200. FAX 202-822-8092. TELEX 285656 BNAI WSH. URL: http://www.bna.com/. (Subscr. to: 9435 Key West Ave., Rockville, MD 20850) Ed. Nancy J. Sedmak. (looseleaf format; back issues avail.)
●Also available online. Vendor(s): Human Resources Information Network (File LAR), Knight-Ridder Information, Inc. (Files 243, 244), Lexis-Nexis, West Group (File LRR-LA).
Former titles: Labor Relations Reporter. Labor Arbitration; War Labor Reports.
Description: Contains full-text arbitration cases and digests of court decisions involving arbitration.

331 340 US
LABOR RELATIONS REPORTER. STATE LABOR LAWS. (Subseries of: Labor Relations Reporter (ISSN 0148-7981)) w. $959 (effective July 1995). The Bureau of National Affairs, Inc., 1231 25th St., N.W., Washington, DC 20037. TEL 202-452-4200. FAX 202-822-8092. TELEX 285656 BNAI WSH. URL: http://www.bna.com/. (Subscr. to: 9435 Key West Ave., Rockville, MD 20850. TEL 800-372-1033) Ed. Roberto Federigan. (looseleaf format; back issues avail.)
Description: Provides text and digest of state labor laws, covering their scope, jurisdiction, administration, and enforcement. Also discusses how state labor law relates to federal laws affecting labor relations and employment regulation, and provides directories of state agencies that administer and enforce these laws.

331.2 US
LABOR RELATIONS REPORTER. WAGES AND HOURS. (Subseries of: Labor Relations Reporter (ISSN 0148-7981)) 1938. bi-w. $611 (effective July 1995). The Bureau of National Affairs, Inc., 1231 25th St., N.W., Washington, DC 20037. TEL 202-452-4200. FAX 202-822-8092. TELEX 285656 BNAI WSH. URL: http://www.bna.com/. (Subscr. to: 9435 Key West Ave., Rockville, MD 20850. TEL 800-372-1033) Ed. Nancy J. Sedmak. (looseleaf format; back issues avail.)
●Also available online. Vendor(s): Knight-Ridder Information, Inc., West Group.
Description: Full text, summaries, and explanations of federal laws and regulations in such areas as reporting, exemptions, wage-hour division inspection, minimum wages, equal pay, overtime, and child labor. Includes enforcement policies, procedures, and precedent-setting decisions.

331.7 US ISSN 0891-4141
KF3352
LABOR RELATIONS WEEK. 1957. w. $891. The Bureau of National Affairs, Inc., 1231 25th St., N.W., Washington, DC 20037. TEL 202-452-4200. FAX 202-822-8092. TELEX 285656 BNAI WSH. URL: http://www.bna.com/. (Subscr. to: 9435 Key West Ave., Rockville, MD 20850. TEL 800-372-1033) Ed. Greg McCaffery. charts; stat.; cum.index. (looseleaf format; back issues avail.)
●Also available online. Vendor(s): Human Resources Information Network (CDD, HDD).
—CCC.
Formerly: White Collar Report (ISSN 0043-4892); Incorporates: Retail - Services Labor Report (ISSN 0148-7930); Which was formerly titled: Retail Labor Report (ISSN 0034-6071)
Description: Reporting service providing an overview of developments influencing labor relations in the private sector.

331 US
LABOR STUDIES FORUM. 1988. q. $60 membership (individuals $36; institutions $72 with subscr. to Labor Studies Journal). University and College Labor Education Association, Center for Labor Research and Studies, Florida International University, University Park Campus, Miami, FL 33199. TEL 305-348-2371. FAX 305-348-2241. Ed. Margaret Gibbons Wilson. circ. 2,000. (back issues avail.) **Document type:** newsletter.
Description: Discusses topics in labor education and labor studies.

331 US ISSN 0160-449X
HD4802
LABOR STUDIES JOURNAL. 1976. q. $36 to individuals (foreign $68); institutions $80 (foreign $112) (includes Labor Studies Forum) (effective 1997). (University and College Labor Education Association) Transaction Publishers, Transaction Periodicals Consortium, Department 3092, Rutgers University, New Brunswick, NJ 08903. TEL 908-445-2280. FAX 908-445-3138. Ed. John Remington. adv.: page $200; 4 3/8 x 7 1/2. bk.rev. circ. 800. (also avail. in microfilm from UMI; reprint service avail. from UMI) **Indexed:** Amer.Bibl.Slavic & E.Eur.Stud., Amer.Hist.& Life (1983-), B.P.I., BPIA, C.I.S. Abstr., Hist.Abstr.(1983-), IBR, Ind.Per.Art.Relat.Law, Int.Polit.Sci.Abstr., Tr.& Indus.Ind. **Document type:** academic/scholarly publication.
●Also available online. Vendor(s): Information Access Co.
—BLDSC (5137.934000); KR SourceOne; SWETS; UMI; UnCover. **CCC.**
Description: Explores the role of the trade union movement in forging U.S. economic and social policy.

331 US ISSN 1041-5904
HD8051
LABOR'S HERITAGE. 1989. q. $19.95 (Canada $24.95; elsewhere $29.95). (George Meany Memorial Archives) George Meany Center for Labor Studies, 10000 New Hampshire Ave., Silver Spring, MD 20903. TEL 301-431-5457. FAX 301-431-0385. R&P contact: Bob Reynolds. TEL 301-431-5443. circ. 8,000 (paid). **Indexed:** Amer.Hist.& Life (1989-), Hist.Abstr. (1989-). **Document type:** academic/scholarly publication.
—UnCover.
Description: Scholarly-based articles written by historians, archivists, museum curators, folklorists and other writers for the general reader interested in the history of the American workplace.
Refereed Serial

340 US ISSN 1084-2160
LABORWATCH. 1984. m. $198. Berens-Tate Consulting Group, 10050 Regency Circle, Ste. 403, Omaha, NE 68114. TEL 402-391-6188; 800-729-1441. FAX 402-391-7363. Ed. Deborah L. Peck. R&P contact: Deborah L. Peck. index. circ. 3,000. (back issues avail.) **Document type:** newsletter.
Description: Contains practical analysis of recent developments in labor law and updates in human resources management.

331 UA
LABOUR.* (Text in English) no.10, 1974. s-a. Alamal Magazine, 42 Elgomhoriah St., P.O. 1862, Cairo, Egypt. Ed. Abdel M. Said. bibl.; illus. **Indexed:** Arts & Hum.Cit.Ind.

BUSINESS AND ECONOMICS — LABOR AND INDUSTRIAL RELATIONS

331 971   CN   ISSN 0700-3862
HD8101   CODEN: LATREZ
LABOUR/TRAVAIL; journal of Canadian labour studies - revue d'etudes ouvrieres canadiennes. (Text in English and French) 1976. s-a. Can.$25 (foreign $30) to individuals; institutions Can.$35 (foreign $50); students Can.$15 (foreign $25) (effective 1997). Canadian Committee on Labour History, Department of History, Memorial University of Newfoundland, St. John's, NF A1C 5S7, Canada. TEL 709-737-2144. FAX 709-737-4342. TELEX 016-4101. E-mail: joanb@plato.ucs.mun.ca; URL: http://www.mun.ca/cclh/labour.html. Ed. Gregory S. Kealey. R&P contact: Irene Whitfield. adv. contact: Irene Whitfield. bk.rev.; bibl. circ. 1,200. (back issues avail.) **Indexed:** Alt.Press Ind., Amer.Hist.& Life (1976-), Arts & Hum.Cit.Ind., ASCA, Can.B.P.I., Can.Per.Ind., Curr.Cont., Hist.Abstr. (1976-), Human Resour.Abstr., P.A.I.S.For.Lang.Ind., P.A.I.S., Sage Pub.Admin.Abstr., SSCI. **Document type:** academic/scholarly publication.
—Genuine Article; KR SourceOne; UMI; UnCover. **CCC.**
    Description: An interdisciplinary journal of Canadian labor history. Aims to foster imaginative approaches to both teaching and research in labor studies through an open exchange of viewpoints.
    Refereed Serial

331   UK   ISSN 1121-7081
LABOUR. 1987. 3/yr. £65($100) (foreign £65) (effective 1997). Blackwell Publishers Ltd., 108 Cowley Rd., Oxford OX4 1JF, England. TEL 44-1865-791100. FAX 44-1865-791347. E-mail: jnlinfo@blackwellpublishers.co.uk; URL: http://www.blackwellpublishers.co.uk. **Document type:** academic/scholarly publication.
—BLDSC (5141.950530). **CCC.**
    Refereed Serial

331 340   II
LABOUR AND INDUSTRIAL CASES. (Text in English) 1968. m. Rs.203($96) All India Reporter Ltd., P.O. Box 209, Nagpur 440012, India. Ed. V.R. Manohar. adv.; bk.rev.; bibl.; charts; index. circ. 4,000.

331 340   II
LABOUR AND INDUSTRIAL LAW REPORTER. 1975. m. $100 (effective 1998). International Law Book Co., Nijhawan Bldg., 1562 Church Rd., Kashmere Gate, New Delhi 110 006, India. TEL 91-11-296-7810. E-mail: lakshmin@giasdla.vsnl.net.in.
    Description: Reports all judgments of the Supreme Court and important judgments of high courts under the Industrial Disputes Act, Minimum Wages Act, Provident Fund Act, and more.

331 301   AT   ISSN 1030-1763
LABOUR & INDUSTRY; a journal of the social and economic relations of work. 1987. 3/yr. Aus.$65 to individuals (foreign Aus.$75); institutions Aus.$80 (foreign Aus.$90). Centre for Workplace Culture Change, Faculty of Arts, P.O. Box 581, Market St., Melbourne, Vic. 8007, Australia. TEL 61-3-96421269. FAX 61-3-96421326. (Co-sponsors: Association of Industrial Relations Academics of Australia and New Zealand; Australian Sociological Association) Eds. Ray Jureidini, Belinda Probert. adv. contact: Ray Jureidini. bk.rev. (back issues avail.) **Document type:** academic/scholarly publication.
—BLDSC (5141.955300).
    Description: Covers industrial relations, industrial sociology, labor economics, labor law, labor history, organization studies, labor process studies, political economy, management, public policy, and administration.
    Refereed Serial

331 368.4   IS   ISSN 0005-2299
HD8761.P3
LABOUR AND NATIONAL INSURANCE/AVODA UBITUACH LEUMI. (Text in English) 1949. m. Ministry of Labour and Social Affairs, 10 Yad Harutzim St., Box 1260, Talpiod, Jerusalem, Israel. Ed. Zalman Heyn. charts; stat.; cum.index every 2 yrs. circ. 2,500.

331.155 340   CN   ISSN 0023-690X
LABOUR ARBITRATION CASES. 1948. bi-w. Can.$134 (effective 1997). Canada Law Book Inc., 240 Edward St., Aurora, ON L4G 3S9, Canada. TEL 905-841-6472; 800-263-2037. FAX 905-841-5085. Ed. C.G. Simmons. adv. contact: Mary Powell. index, cum.index. (looseleaf format) **Document type:** trade publication.
●Also available online.

331.1
LABOUR BULLETIN. (Text in English) 1940. m. Rs.24. Labour Department, Office of the Labour Commissioner, P.O. Box 220, Kanpur 208002, Uttar Pradesh, India. Eds. C.S. Saxena, Hemant K. Pant. adv.; bk.rev. circ. 500.

331   II
LABOUR CHRONICLE. (Text in English) 1968. m. Rs.15. Institute of Workers Education, A-30-37, Chittaranjan, Bombay 400077, India. Ed. R. Muthuswamy. adv.; bk.rev.; bibl. circ. 26,000. (also avail. in microfilm from KTO)

331   PK
LABOUR CODE OF PAKISTAN. (Text in English) 1953. irreg., latest 1993. $250. Bureau of Labour Publications, 8, Business Centre, Mumtaz Hasan Rd., P.O. Box 5833, Karachi 74000, Pakistan. TEL 92-21-2414975. Ed. P. Shafi.

331 347   SA   ISSN 1019-9268
LABOUR COURT DIGEST. (Text in English) 1992. 6/yr. R.179.95. Juta & Co. Ltd., P.O. Box 14373, Kenwyn 7790, South Africa. TEL 27-21-7975101. FAX 27-21-7970121.

331   NE   ISSN 0927-5371
HD5701   CODEN: LECOE3
LABOUR ECONOMICS; an international journal. (Text in English) 1993. q. fl.500($287) (effective 1998). North-Holland (Subsidiary of: Elsevier Science B.V.), P.O. Box 211, 1000 AE Amsterdam, Netherlands. TEL 31-20-4853911. FAX 31-20-4853598. TELEX 18582 ESPA NL. (Subscr. in the Americas to: Elsevier Science, Regional Sales Office, Box 945, New York, NY 10159-0945. TEL 212-633-3730. FAX 212-633-3680; Subscr. in Australasia and the Far East to: Elsevier Science (Singapore) Pte Ltd, No.1 Temasek Ave., No.17-01 Millenia Tower, Singapore 039192, Singapore. TEL 65-434-3727. FAX 65-337-2230; Subscr. in Japan to: Elsevier Science Japan, 9-15 Higashi-Azabu 1-chome, Minato-ku Tokyo 106, Japan. TEL 81-3-5561-5033. FAX 81-3-5561-5047) Eds. K. Burditt, T. MaCurdy. bk.rev. (also avail. in microform from UMI; back issues avail.) **Document type:** academic/scholarly publication.
—BLDSC (5142.086000); SWETS; UnCover. **CCC.**
    Description: Publishes research in the field of labor economics both on the microeconomic and macroeconomic level, covering theory, empirical testing and policy applications and analysis.
    Refereed Serial

331.8 374   UN   ISSN 0378-5467
LC5001
LABOUR EDUCATION. (Editions in English, French and Spanish) 1964. q. 50 SFr.($40) (International Labour Office) I L O Publications, CH-1211 Geneva 22, Switzerland. TEL 41-22-799-6111. FAX 41-22-798-6350. TELEX 425647-ILO-CH. (Dist. in US by: I L O Publications Center, 49 Sheridan Ave., Albany, NY 12210. TEL 518-436-9686. FAX 518-436-7433) Ed. Clara Foucault-Mohammed. bk.rev.; bibl.; illus. circ. 2,500. (also avail. in microform from ILO; reprint service avail. from UMI) **Indexed:** C.I.J.E., Cont.Pg.Educ., Int.Lab.Doc. **Document type:** bulletin.
—BLDSC (5142.090000); UMI. **CCC.**
    Description: Articles of interest to trade union organizations, public authorities and individuals concerned with labor education. Includes activities of the ILO, methods and techniques, and history.

331   UK   ISSN 0141-7746
DJK1
LABOUR FOCUS ON EASTERN EUROPE. 1977. 3/yr. £12 to individuals (overseas £18($30)); institutions £30 (overseas £35($60)) (effective 1998). Labor Focus on Eastern Europe, 30 Bridge St., Oxford OX2 OBA, England. TEL 44-1865-723207. E-mail: labfocus@gn.apc.org. Ed. Gus Fagan. bk.rev. circ. 2,600. (back issues avail.) **Indexed:** Left Ind. **Document type:** academic/scholarly publication.
—BLDSC (5142.115000).
    Description: Deals with the broader issues of European politics, with special emphasis on the process of social and political transformation in Central and Eastern Europe.
    Refereed Serial

331   II   ISSN 0023-6934
LABOUR GAZETTE. (Text in English) 1921. m. Rs.100. Commissioner of Labour, Commerce Center, Tardeo, Maharashtra State, Bombay 400 034, India. Ed. Shri R.R. Korosiya. adv.; bk.rev.; bibl.; charts; stat.; index. circ. 700. (also avail. in microfiche from BHP)

331 900   AT   ISSN 0023-6942
HD6891.A13
LABOUR HISTORY; a journal of labour and social history. 1962. s-a. Aus.$38 to individuals; institutions Aus.$60 (effective July 1996). Australian Society for the Study of Labour History, Institute Bldg. H03, Faculty of Economics, University of Sydney, N.S.W. 2006, Australia. TEL 61-2-93513786. FAX 61-2-93514729. TELEX AA26169 UNISYD. Ed. Terry Irving. R&P contact: Mark Hearn. TEL 61-2-97166710. bk.rev.; charts; illus. circ. 1,000. (back issues avail.) **Indexed:** Amer.Hist.& Life (1975-), Aus.P.A.I.S., Hist.Abstr. (1975-), Work Rel.Abstr. **Document type:** academic/scholarly publication.
—BLDSC (5142.160000); UnCover.
    Refereed Serial

331   UK   ISSN 0961-5652
HD4805
LABOUR HISTORY REVIEW. 1960. 3/yr. £15 (foreign £17) to individuals; institutions £25 (foreign £29.50) (effective 1997). (Society for the Study of Labour History) Edinburgh University Press, 22 George Sq., Edinburgh EH8 9LF, Scotland. TEL 44-131-650-6207. FAX 44-131-662-0053. Ed.Bd. R&P contact: Malcolm Chase. adv. contact: Pam O'Connor. bk.rev.; bibl.; cum.index. circ. 1,000. (also avail. in microfiche) **Indexed:** Amer.Hist.& Life (1965-), Hist.Abstr. (1965-), Mid.East: Abstr.& Ind. **Document type:** academic/scholarly publication.
—UnCover.
    Formerly: Society for the Study of Labour History. Bulletin (ISSN 0049-1179)
    Refereed Serial

331   II   ISSN 0377-077X
HD8013.I41
LABOUR IN THE PUBLIC SECTOR UNDERTAKINGS: BASIC INFORMATION. 1968. irreg. price varies. Ministry of Labour, Implementation and Evaluation Division, New Delhi, India. (Subscr. to: Controller of Publications, Government of India, Civil Lines, Delhi 110054, India) stat.

331   JA   ISSN 0917-7086
LABOUR ISSUES QUARTERLY. (Text in English) 1988. q. 4200 Yen. Japan Institute of Labour - Nihon Rodo Kenkyu Kiko, Shinjuku Monolith, P.O. Box 7040, Tokyo 163-09, Japan. TEL 03-5991-5165. FAX 03-3594-1112. pp./issue: 21.

LABOUR LAW JOURNAL. see LAW

331 340
LABOUR LAW REPORTER; a magazine of decision makers. m. H.L. Kumar, Ed. & Pub., 5B-45 Mall Rd., Delhi 110007, India.
    Description: Helps readers to find out their required points for drafting of pleadings, advice and arguments.

331 340   SA   ISSN 1023-3806
LABOUR LAW REPORTS. (Text in English) m. Butterworth Publishers (Pty.) Ltd., Part of the Reed Elsevier group, P.O. Box 792, Durban 3000, South Africa. TEL 27-31-294247. FAX 27-31-283255. (back issues avail.)
    Formerly (until 1994): Labour Law Compendium.

331 340   CN   ISSN 0383-3372
KEN7799.A72
LABOUR LEGISLATION IN NOVA SCOTIA. irreg. Department of Labour, Research Division, P.O. Box 697, Halifax, NS B3J 2T8, Canada. TEL 902-424-8474. URL: http://www.gov.ns.ca//labr/. **Document type:** government publication.
    Description: Summary of legislative provisions applicable to labor in Nova Scotia.

331   UN   ISSN 0538-8325
HD6961.A1
LABOUR-MANAGEMENT RELATIONS SERIES. irreg. price varies. (International Labour Office) I L O Publications, CH-1211 Geneva 22, Switzerland. TEL 41-22-799-6111. FAX 41-22-798-6358. TELEX 415647-ILO-CH. (Dist. in US by: I L O Publications Center, 49 Sheridan Ave., Albany, NY 11210. TEL 518-436-9686. FAX 518-436-7433) (also avail. in microform from ILO) **Document type:** monographic series.

BUSINESS AND ECONOMICS — LABOR AND INDUSTRIAL RELATIONS

331 301 FR
LABOUR MARKET AND SOCIAL POLICY OCCASIONAL PAPERS. 1990. irreg., no.9, 1992. free. Organization for Economic Cooperation and Development, Directorate for Education, Employment, Labour and Social Affairs, 2 rue Andre Pascal, 75775 Paris Cedex 16, France.

331.1 UK
HD8381
LABOUR MARKET TRENDS. 1893. m. £63.50 (foreign £89.50); newsstand price: £6. Office for National Statistics, 1 Drummond Gate, Rm. B3-05, London SW1V 2QQ, England. TEL 44-171-533-6155. FAX 44-171-533-6185. (Subscr. to: Stationery Office Publications Center, P.O. Box 276, London, SW8 5DT) Ed. David Bradbury. charts; stat.; index. circ. 5,000. (also avail. in microform from UMI; reprint service avail. from UMI) **Indexed:** Art.Hosp.& Tour., Mgmt.& Market.Abstr., P.A.I.S., World Text.Abstr. **Document type:** government publication.
—BLDSC (5142.264740); UMI. **CCC.**
Former titles (until 1995): Employment Gazette (ISSN 0264-7052); (until 1980): Great Britain. Department of Employment. Employment Gazette (ISSN 0013-6859)
Description: Covers manpower planning, industrial relations, earnings, prices, labor and training costs. Includes detailed labor market statistics.

331 UK ISSN 0023-7000
HD4805
LABOUR RESEARCH. 1917. m. £26.75 to non-members. Labour Research Department, 78 Blackfriars Rd., London SE1 8HF, England. Ed. Clare Ruhemann. adv. contact: Ali Brown. bk.rev.; stat.; index. circ. 6,000. (also avail. in microform from WMP) **Indexed:** ASSIA, P.A.I.S. **Document type:** trade publication.
—BLDSC (5142.500000); SWETS; UnCover.
Description: Covers political and industrial issues from a trade union perspective.

331.11 UK ISSN 0047-388X
LABOUR RESEARCH DEPARTMENT. FACT SERVICE. 1939. w. £48.25 to non-members. Labour Research Department, 78 Blackfriars Rd., London SE1 8HF, England. Ed. Roger Simon. stat.; index. circ. 2,000. **Document type:** trade publication.
Description: Concise summaries of useful information on pay, prices, production, employment, profits and all significant economic and social developments.

331 II ISSN 0023-7035
HD4811
LABOUR WORLD.* (Text in English) 1969. m. Labour World Publications, 36-4 Ganya Ram Hospital, New Delhi 5, India. Ed. E.X. Joseph. adv.; charts; illus.; stat.

331 340 SW ISSN 0349-7143
LAG & AVTAL; tidningen om arbetsraett i praktiken. (Supplement available) 1978. 9/yr. SEK 561 (effective 1996). Stiftelsen Arbetsraettslig Tidskrift, PO Box 7572, S-103 93 Stockholm, Sweden. TEL 46-8-243520. FAX 46-8-242438. Ed. Annika Berg. adv.; bk.rev.; index. circ. 9,000. (also avail. in audio cassette; back issues avail.)
Description: News and features on Swedish labor law and industrial relations and legal questions that affect labor.

331 VN ISSN 0866-7950
LAO DONG/LABOR. 1929. 4/w. newsstand price: D.2000. General Confederation of Labour, 51 Hang Bo, Hanoi, Socialist Republic of Vietnam. TEL 84-4-8252441. FAX 84-4-8254441. (Dist. overseas by: Xunhasaba, 32 Hai Ba Trung St., Honoi, S.R. Vietnam. TEL 84-4-8260382) Ed. Pham Huy Hoan. adv.; B&W page B.D.17000, color page D.26000; adv. contact: Truong Loc. circ. 90,000. **Document type:** newspaper.
Description: Covers domestic and foreign politics, external relations, economics, culture, as well as issues relating to Vietnamese working class.

331.11 CC ISSN 1005-4324
LAODONG JINGJI YU RENLI ZIYUAN GUANLI. (Subseries of: Fuyin Baokan Ziliao) (Text in Chinese) m. $65.19. Zhongguo Renmin Daxue, Shubao Ziliao Zhongxin - China People's University, Book & Newspaper Information Center, 3 Zhang Zizhong Rd., P.O. Box 1122, Beijing 100007, People's Republic of China. TEL 86-10-4015080. (Dist. in US by: China Publications Service, Box 49614, Chicago, IL 60649. TEL 312-288-3291. FAX 312-288-8570) pp./issue: 96.
Description: Contains labor force studies.

331 US ISSN 1059-8782
LATIN AMERICAN LABOR NEWS. 1989. s-a. $15 to individuals; institutions $30; newsstand price: $7.50. (Center for Labor Research and Studies) Latin American Labor Studies Publications, Florida International University, University Park Campus-LC 304, Miami, FL 33199. TEL 305-348-1415. FAX 305-348-2241. E-mail: jdfrench@acpub.duke-edu. Ed. John D. French. adv.; B&W page $200; trim 13 x9; adv. contact: Carmen S. Figueredo. bk.rev. circ. 600. (back issues avail.) **Document type:** newsletter.
Description: Dedicated to news on Latin American trade unions, inter-American labor solidarity, research on labor, workers, and women. Covers news about labor-studies organizations and projects.

158.7 152.4 US ISSN 1061-0367
LAUGHTER WORKS. 1987. q. $18 (effective 1997). Laughter Works, Box 1076, Fair Oaks, CA 95628. TEL 916-863-1592. FAX 916-863-5072. E-mail: laftrworks@aol.com. Ed. Jim Pelley. bk.rev. (looseleaf format; back issues avail.) **Document type:** newsletter.
Description: Seeks to provide the tools and skill to use humor in the workplace.

331 IT
LAVORO E SICUREZZA SOCIALE. 1985; N.S. q. L.95000 (foreign L.130000) (effective 1993). (Confederazione Italiana Dirigenti d'Azienda) Franco Angeli Editore, Viale Monza, 106, Casella Postale 17175, 20100 Milan, Italy. TEL 02-2895762.
Indexed: ELLIS.

331 IT ISSN 0390-0991
Z7164.T7
LAVORO E SINDACATO; bollettino emerografico internazionale. 1975; N.S. 1989. bi-m. L.62000 (foreign L.85000) (effective 1993). (Fondazione Giulio Pastore) Franco Angeli Editore, Viale Monza 106, 20127 Milan, Italy. TEL 02-2827651. Dir. Vincenzo Saba. bk.rev.

331 IT
LAVORO INFORMAZIONE. 1982. s-m. L.580000 (foreign L.650000) (effective 1993). Franco Angeli Editore, Viale Monza 106, 20127 Milan, Italy. TEL 02-2827651. Ed.Bd.

331.881 DK ISSN 0909-6418
LEDERNE. 1908. m. membership. Ledernes Hovedorganisation - Organization of Managerial and Executive Staff in Denmark, Vermlandsgade 65, DK-2300 Copenhagen S, Denmark. Ed. Finn Poulsen. adv.; bk.rev.; stat.; index. circ. 78,532. **Document type:** newsletter.
Formerly (until 1994): Arbejdslederen (ISSN 0003-7826); Which incorporates (1910-1948): Staalet (ISSN 0038-8831)

331 US ISSN 0458-9599
KF3512.A16
LEGAL - LEGISLATIVE REPORTER. NEWS BULLETIN. 1966. m. membership. International Foundation of Employee Benefit Plans, 18700 W. Bluemound Rd., Box 69, Brookfield, WI 53008-0069. TEL 414-786-6700. Ed. William J. Curtin. circ. 34,000. (also avail. in microform from UMI) **Indexed:** L.l.I. **Document type:** bulletin.
—CCC.
Former titles: N F Legal Legislative Reporter News Bulletin (National Foundation of Health, Welfare and Pension Plans) (ISSN 0027-6510); Legal Legislative Reports. News Bulletin.
Description: Summaries of legal, legislative and regulatory developments related to employee benefits.

331 GW
DER LETRONER. 1985. s-a. Letron GmbH, Dorfstr. 2, 63741 Aschaffenburg, Germany. TEL 06021-406350. Ed. Jochen E. Kamenik.
Description: News for employees of the Letron company and neighbors of its plant.

331 658 FR ISSN 0024-1725
LIAISONS SOCIALES. 1946. d. 2395 F. Groupe Liaisons S.A., 1 av. Edouard Belin, 92856 Rueil Malmaison, France. TEL 1-41299999. FAX 33-1-41299838. adv.; bk.rev.; stat.; index. circ. 35,000. **Indexed:** C.I.S. Abstr., Int.Lab.Doc., World Bibl.Soc.Sec.

335.82 320.57 331 US ISSN 1069-1995
LIBERTARIAN LABOR REVIEW; anarchosyndicalist ideas and discussion. 1986. s-a. $6 (foreign $7); newsstand price: $3.50. Box 2824, Champaign, IL 61825-2824. E-mail: jbekken@igc.apc.org. Ed.Bd. adv. contact: Jon Bekken. bk.rev.; film rev.; video rev.; illus.; tr.lit.; cum.index 1986-96; circ. 1,000 (paid). (also avail. in microfilm; back issues avail.) **Indexed:** Alt.Press Ind. **Document type:** consumer publication.
Description: Features news of syndicalist unions around the world, documents, articles on anarchist economics and labor history and analysis.

331 531.64 US ISSN 0456-0434
LIGHT (WASHINGTON). 1945. m. $1 (effective 1993). A F L - C I O, Utility Workers Union of America, 815 Sixteenth St., N.W., Washington, DC 20006. TEL 202-347-8105. FAX 202-347-4872. Ed. Marshall M. Hicks. circ. 65,000 (controlled). (tabloid format; back issues avail.)
Description: Contains information for people who are associated with the Utility Workers Union.

331 UK ISSN 0262-1452
LINCOLNSHIRE INFORMATION. EMPLOYMENT. 1981. a. Lincolnshire County Council, County Planning Office, Lincoln NL1 1YL, England. charts; illus.

331 US
LITERATURE OF AMERICAN LABOR SERIES. 1989. irreg. price varies. (New York State School of Industrial and Labor Relations) I L R Press, Cornell University Press, 512 E. State St., Ithaca, NY 14850. TEL 607-277-2338; 800-666-2211. Ed. Frances Benson. R&P contact: Clare Wellnitz. adv. contact: Heidi Marschner. **Document type:** academic/scholarly publication.

331 UK ISSN 0306-0837
LLAFUR. 1972. a. membership. Welsh Labour History Society, c/o Dr. P.B. O'Leary, Department of History, University College, Aberystwyth SY23 3DY, Wales. adv.; bk.rev. circ. 1,200. (back issues avail.) **Indexed:** Amer.Hist.& Life, Hist.Abstr. (1972-). **Document type:** academic/scholarly publication.
—BLDSC (5285.560000).

331.2 SW ISSN 1103-3878
HD5051
LOENNER I SVERIGE/WAGES AND SALARIES IN SWEDEN; en redovisning av loener och loeneutveckling for olika loentagargrupper. 1991. biennial. SEK 230 (effective 1993). (Statiska Centralbyraan) S C B Foerlag, S-701 89 Oerebro, Sweden.

331 UK
LONDON EXCLUDING CENTRAL SALARY SURVEY. 2/yr. £250 (effective 1997). The Reward Group Ltd., Reward House, Diamond Way, Stone Business Park, Stone, Staffordshire ST15 0SD, England. TEL 44-1785-813566. FAX 44-1785-817007. E-mail: 101364.661@compuserve.com. **Document type:** bulletin.
Description: Pay and benefit salary survey for the outer circle of London.

331 US ISSN 0024-6484
LORAIN LABOR LEADER. m. membership. 2501 Broadway, Lorain, OH 44052. TEL 216-244-1358. FAX 216-244-3795. Ed. John Koscho. circ. 3,000. **Document type:** newspaper.

BUSINESS AND ECONOMICS — LABOR AND INDUSTRIAL RELATIONS

331.11 330.9   UK
LOTHIAN & EDINBURGH LABOUR MARKET ASSESSMENT. a. free. City of Edinburgh Council, City Development Department, 1 Cockburn St., Edinburgh EH1 1BJ, Scotland. TEL 44-131-5294849. FAX 44-131-5293215. Ed. Martin Wight. **Document type:** government publication.
    Description: Provides an insight into industrial, employment, occupational, skill, and travel-to-work trends in the Lothian labor market.

LOUISIANA EMPLOYMENT LAW LETTER. see *LAW*

331.1   US
LOUISIANA LABOR MARKET INFORMATION. m. Department of Labor, Box 44094, Baton Rouge, LA 70804-9094. TEL 504-342-3141. illus. circ. 2,500. (also avail. in microfiche from CIS) **Indexed:** SRI. **Document type:** government publication.
    Formerly: Louisiana Labor Market (ISSN 0091-4711)
    Description: Articles and statistics of employment and payroll trends and other labor information.

331 669   AT   ISSN 0085-3321
M T I A ANNUAL REPORT. a. Metal Trades Industry Association of Australia, 51 Walker St., N. Sydney, N.S.W. 2060, Australia. TEL 61-2-99295566. FAX 61-2-99565044.
    Description: Covers summary of the association's activities over the previous year, includes financial statements.

331 669   AT   ISSN 0815-3590
M T I A INPUT. 1969. m. Aus.$100. Metal Trades Industry Association of Australia, 51 Walker St., North Sydney, N.S.W. 2060, Australia. TEL 61-2-99295566. FAX 61-2-99565044. Ed. D.M. Wishart. adv.; bk.rev.; stat. circ. 8,000. (processed)
    Formerly: M T I A News Bulletin (ISSN 0047-6854)
    Description: Covers issues of current concern, both commercial and industrial, to association members.

MACAO. DIRECCAO DOS SERVICOS DE ESTATISTICA E CENSOS. INDICES E SALARIOS DA CONSTRUCAO CIVIL/MACAO. CENSUS AND STATISTICS DEPARTMENT. INDEXES AND WAGES IN CIVIL CONTRUCTION. see *BUSINESS AND ECONOMICS — Abstracting, Bibliographies, Statistics*

331   US
MAINE. DEPARTMENT OF LABOR. BUREAU OF LABOR STANDARDS. CHARACTERISTICS OF WORK-RELATED INJURIES & ILLNESSES. (Subseries of: Maine Bureau of Labor Standards. B L S Bulletin) a. free. Department of Labor, Bureau of Labor Standards, Technical Services Division, 45 State House Station, Augusta, ME 04333-0045. TEL 207-624-6440. FAX 207-624-6449. E-mail: webmaster__bls@state.me.us. Ed. Janet Austin. circ. 400. **Document type:** government publication.
    Description: Summary of data collected from workers' compensation reports of injury or illness.

331.2   US
MAINE CONSTRUCTION WAGE RATES. (Subseries of: Maine. Bureau of Labor Standards. B L S Bulletin) a. free. Department of Labor, Bureau of Labor Standards, Technical Services Division, 45 State House Station, Augusta, ME 04333-0045. TEL 207-624-6440. FAX 207-624-6449. E-mail: webmaster__bls@state.me.us. Ed. Ruth A. Ladd. circ. 1,100. **Document type:** government publication.
    Description: Contains results of the annual construction wage rate survey.

MAINE EMPLOYMENT LAW LETTER. see *LAW*

331.1   US
MAINE LABOR MARKET DIGEST. 1962. m. free. Department of Labor, Division of Economic Analysis and Research, 20 Union St., Augusta, ME 04330-6826. TEL 207-287-2271. Ed. Ray A. Fongemie. charts. circ. 3,600. (also avail. in microfiche from CIS) **Indexed:** SRI. **Document type:** government publication.
    Formerly: Maine Manpower (ISSN 0025-0686)
    Description: Updates on labor force, employment, unemployment and other related economic data.

340   US
MAINE WORKERS' COMPENSATION. (2nd ed., 1992) 1988. 2 base vols. (plus a supplement). $135. Butterworth Legal Publishers (Salem) (Subsidiary of: Reed Elsevier plc), 8 Industrial Way, Bldg. C, Salem, NH 03079. TEL 800-548-4001. FAX 603-898-9858. Ed. Charles D. Devoe. (looseleaf format)
    Formerly (until 1992): Maine Workers' Compensation Act.

340   US
MAINE WORKERS COMPENSATION COMMISSION: APPELLATE DIVISION DECISIONS. (In 5 vols.) 1983. a. $55 per vol. Butterworth Legal Publishers (Salem) (Subsidiary of: Reed Elsevier plc), 8 Industrial Way, Bldg. C, Salem, NH 03079. TEL 800-548-4001. FAX 603-898-9858. Ed. Charles D. Devoe. (looseleaf format)

MAJOR COLLECTIVE BARGAINING SETTLEMENTS IN PRIVATE INDUSTRY. see *BUSINESS AND ECONOMICS — Abstracting, Bibliographies, Statistics*

MAJOR COLLECTIVE BARGAINING SETTLEMENTS IN STATE AND LOCAL GOVERNMENT. see *BUSINESS AND ECONOMICS — Economic Situation And Conditions*

MAJOR PROGRAMS. see *BUSINESS AND ECONOMICS — Economic Situation And Conditions*

331   MY
MALAYSIAN EMPLOYERS FEDERATION ANNUAL REPORT. (Text in English) 1962. a. membership only. Malaysian Employers Federation - Persekutuan Majikan Malaysia, P.O. Box 11026, 50732 Kuala Lumpur, Malaysia. FAX 03-2550830. TELEX MEF MA 31862. Ed. M. Zain Majid. circ. 2,000. **Document type:** corporate report.

331   II   ISSN 0258-042X
HD28
MANAGEMENT AND LABOUR STUDIES. (Text in English) 1975. q. Rs.100($25) Xavier Labour Relations Institute, Jamshedpur 831 001, India. FAX 91-657-7814. TELEX 626 240 XLRI IN. Ed. T.A. Mathias. R&P contact: T.A. Mathias. adv.; bk.rev. circ. 1,500. (reprint service avail.) **Indexed:** Human Resour.Abstr., Manage.Abstr., Psychol.Abstr., Pub.Admin.Abstr., Sage Pub.Admin.Abstr., Sage Urb.Stud.Abstr. **Document type:** academic/scholarly publication.
    —BLDSC (5359.008500); UnCover.

331   US   ISSN 0745-4880
MANAGEMENT REPORT; for non-union organizations. 1978. m. $375 (foreign $447) (effective 1998). John Wiley & Sons, Inc., Journals, 605 Third Ave., New York, NY 10158. TEL 212-850-6645. FAX 212-850-6021. E-mail: subinfo@jwiley.com; URL: http://www.wiley.co.uk. Eds. Alfred T. DeMaria, Sarah Magee. adv.: B&W page £640, color page £1515; trim 279 x 210. **Document type:** newsletter.
—CCC.
    Formerly: Hughes Report (ISSN 0732-7919)
    Description: Discusses non-union alternatives for organization management.

650 975   UK   ISSN 0309-0558
KD3006.A2
MANAGERIAL LAW. 1966. bi-m. £1270($1939) (foreign Aus.$1919) (effective 1998). Barmarick Publications, Enholmes Hall, Patrington, E. Yorks HU12 0PR, England. TEL 44-1964-630033. (Dist. by: M C B University Press Ltd., 60-62 Toller Ln., Bradford, W. Yorks BD8 9BY, England. TEL 44-1274-777700. FAX 44-1274-785200) Ed. Barrie O. Pettman; Pub. Barrie O. Pettman. circ. 150. (back issues avail.; reprint service avail. from SWZ) **Indexed:** ABI Inform. **Document type:** academic/scholarly publication.
    ●Also available online. Vendor(s): Lexis-Nexis.
    —BLDSC (5359.245000); UMI.
    Incorporates: Knight's Industrial Reports (ISSN 0023-2270)
    Description: Provides details on the latest legislation, tribunal hearings, government orders and consultative documents. Focuses on labor relations, employment conditions, training, marketing, consumer sales, and credit transactions.

331 340.5   US
MANAGERS GUIDE TO THE AMERICANS WITH DISABILITIES ACT. irreg. $195. MidAtlantic Employers' Association, Box 770, Valley Forge, PA 19482. TEL 215-666-7330. FAX 215-666-7866.
    Description: Features a detailed and easily understandable explanation of the provisions of the law and offers practical tips and a checklist of steps employers should take to assure compliance.

331 658.3   US   ISSN 1067-5361
MANAGING FLEXIBLE BENEFITS PLANS. Abbreviated title: M F B P. 1993. m. $279 (outside N. America $303). Institute of Management & Administration, Inc., 29 W. 35th St., 5th Fl., New York, NY 10001-2299. TEL 212-244-0360. FAX 212-564-0465. URL: http://www.ioma.com. Ed. Rebecca M. Morrow; Pub. Lee Rath. R&P contact: Sofie Kourkoutakis. index. (looseleaf format; back issues avail.) **Document type:** newsletter.
—CCC.
    Description: Information on managing cafeteria-type benefits plans. Covers plan design and communication, administration, enrollment, plan structure, rules and regulations. Helps control costs and ensure that employees use the plan effectively.

350.1   CN   ISSN 0706-3792
JS1721.M3
MANITOBA. MUNICIPAL EMPLOYEES BENEFITS BOARD. ANNUAL REPORT. 1977. a. Municipal Employees Benefits Board, 308-131 Provencher Blvd., Winnipeg, MB R2H 0G2, Canada. TEL 204-237-6574. FAX 204-945-8181. circ. 4,500. **Document type:** government publication.

331.1   CN   ISSN 0076-3853
HD8109.M3
MANITOBA LABOUR - MANAGEMENT REVIEW COMMITTEE. ANNUAL REPORT. 1965. a. free. Department of Labour, Room 606, Norquay Bldg., Winnipeg, Man. R3C 0V8, Canada. TEL 204-944-3411.

MANNESMANN ILLUSTRIERTE. see *BUSINESS AND ECONOMICS — Domestic Commerce*

331   US   ISSN 0149-080X
MANPOWER AND HUMAN RESOURCES STUDIES. 1962. irreg. University of Pennsylvania, Wharton School, Industrial Research Unit, 3733 Vance Hall, Philadelphia, PA 19104-6358. TEL 215-898-5605. **Document type:** academic/scholarly publication.

331   US
MANPOWER DEMONSTRATION RESEARCH CORPORATION. ANNUAL REPORT. a. Manpower Demonstration Research Corp., 3 Park Ave., New York, NY 10016. TEL 212-532-3200.

331   II   ISSN 0542-5808
HD5701
MANPOWER JOURNAL. (Text in English) 1965. q. Rs.400($60) Institute of Applied Manpower Research, Indraprastha Estate, Mahatma Gandhi Marg, New Delhi 110 002, India. (Dist. by: New Age International Pvt. Ltd., Publishers (Journals Division), 4835-24, Ansari Rd., Daryaganj, New Delhi 110 002, India. TEL 91-11-3267996. FAX 91-11-3267437) Ed. M.L. Nakhasi. bk.rev.; bibl. circ. 500. **Indexed:** Account.& Data Proc.Abstr., Ind.India, Manage.Abstr., Pub.Admin.Abstr., Rural Recreat.Tour.Abstr., World Agri.Econ.& Rural Sociol.Abstr.

331   PK
MANPOWER REVIEW. (Text in English) 1975. q. Rs.5 per no. Manpower Division, Islamabad, Pakistan. bk.rev. circ. 500.

MARYLAND EMPLOYMENT LAW LETTER. see *LAW*

331.1   US
MARYLAND MONTHLY LABOR REVIEW. vol.16, 1970. m. free. Department of Labor, Licensing and Regulation, Office of Labor Market Analysis and Information, 1100 N. Eutaw St., Rm. 601, Baltimore, MD 21201. TEL 410-767-2250. charts; stat. circ. 1,000. **Indexed:** SRI. **Document type:** government publication, newsletter.
    Former titles: Maryland Labor Market Dimensions; Employment Report for Maryland and Metropolitan Baltimore; Manpower Trends (ISSN 0025-2433)

MASHABEI EINOSH. see *BUSINESS AND ECONOMICS — Personnel Management*

BUSINESS AND ECONOMICS — LABOR AND INDUSTRIAL RELATIONS 1445

331.2 US
MASS RETAILERS' EXECUTIVE PERQUISITE REPORT.* biennial. $85 to non-members; members $40; institutions $20. International Mass Retail Association, 1700 N. Moore St., Ste. 2250, Arlington, VA 22209-1903. TEL 202-861-0774. FAX 202-785-4588. Indexed: SRI. **Document type:** bulletin.

MASSACHUSETTS. DEPARTMENT OF EMPLOYMENT AND TRAINING. EMPLOYMENT AND WAGES STATE SUMMARY. see *BUSINESS AND ECONOMICS — Abstracting, Bibliographies, Statistics*

MASSACHUSETTS EMPLOYMENT LAW LETTER. see *LAW*

344 US ISSN 1051-6123
MASSACHUSETTS LABOR CASES. 1975. m. $355. New England Legal Publishers, Box 425, Weston, MA 02193. TEL 617-891-6200.
Description: Full text of all decisions issued by the Massachusetts Labor Relations Commission.

344 US
MASSACHUSETTS LABOR RELATIONS REPORTER. vol.20, 1993. m. $355. New England Legal Publishers, Box 425, Weston, MA 02193. TEL 617-891-6200.
Description: Digest of all decisions of the Massachusetts Labor Relations Commission and relevant court decisions.

MASSACHUSETTS WORKERS' COMPENSATION PRACTICE MANUAL. see *LAW — Corporate Law*

MASSACHUSETTS WORKERS' COMPENSATION REPORTS. see *LAW — Corporate Law*

331 US
MATCHING GIFT NOTES NEWSLETTER. q. $49. Council for Advancement and Support of Education, 11 Dupont Circle, Ste. 400, Washington, DC 20036. TEL 202-328-5900. FAX 202-387-4973. circ. 1,200. (back issues avail.) **Document type:** newsletter.
Description: Contains articles about corporate matching gift trends and issues, and matching gift program changes.

331 658.3 GW ISSN 0177-1426
MATERIALIEN AUS DER ARBEITSMARKT- UND BERUFSFORSCHUNG. 1970. irreg. (6-8/yr.) DM.15. Bundesanstalt fuer Arbeit, Institut fuer Arbeitsmarkt- und Berufsforschung, Regensburgstr. 104, 90327 Nuernberg, Germany. TEL 49-911-1793041. FAX 49-911-1793258. E-mail: iab.ba@t-online.de. charts; stat.; index. (back issues avail.) **Document type:** government publication.
Description: Discusses topics of employment research.

MAURITIUS. CENTRAL STATISTICAL OFFICE. DIGEST OF LABOUR STATISTICS. see *BUSINESS AND ECONOMICS — Abstracting, Bibliographies, Statistics*

331 MF
MAURITIUS. MINISTRY OF LABOUR AND INDUSTRIAL RELATIONS. ANNUAL REPORT. (Text in English) a. Government Printing Office, Elizabeth II Ave., Port Louis, Mauritius.
Formerly (until 1976): Mauritius. Ministry of Labour. Annual Report.

MAZENGARB'S EMPLOYMENT LAW SERVICE. see *LAW*

MEANS LABOR RATES FOR THE CONSTRUCTION INDUSTRY. see *BUILDING AND CONSTRUCTION*

ME'ASEF; studies in the history and problems of the Israeli labor movement. see *HISTORY — History Of The Near East*

331.86 AU
MENSCH UND ARBEIT; internationale Zeitschrift fuer Arbeitspaedagogik, Arbeitspsychologie, Arbeitstechnik und Betriebswirtschaft. 1947. irreg. S.95. (Arbeitsgemeinschaft fuer Psychotechnik in Oesterreich) Psychotechnisches Institut, Vegagasse 4, A-1190 Vienna, Austria. Ed. Dr. Guido Hackl. bk.rev. circ. 2,000. Indexed: C.I.S. Abstr. **Document type:** bulletin.

331 CN
MERCER PENSION MANUAL. 1988. 6/yr. Can.$439. Carswell, One Corporate Plaza, 2075 Kennedy Rd., Scarborough, ON M1T 3V4, Canada. TEL 416-609-8000. FAX 416-298-5094. Ed. William M. Mercer. charts; illus. circ. 1,500. (also avail. in looseleaf format; back issues avail.)
Description: Provides solutions to the problems of meeting payroll reporting requirements, plan costs, surplus withdrawls, employee termination, corporate restructuring or winding up a plan.

THE MERCHANT. see *BUSINESS AND ECONOMICS — Marketing And Purchasing*

371.42 331.8 US
MERIT SYSTEMS PROTECTION BOARD SERVICE. Variant title: M S P B Digest Service. 1984. m. $340. Hawkins Publishing Co., Inc., Box 480, Mayo, MD 21106-0480. TEL 301-798-1677. Ed. Carl R. Eyler. circ. 100. (looseleaf format; back issues avail.) **Document type:** abstracting/indexing.

331 US
METROPOLITAN WASHINGTON D.C. AREA LABOR SUMMARY. 1969. m. free. Department of Employment Services, 500 C St., N.W., Ste. 201, Washington, DC 20001-2187. TEL 202-724-7213. FAX 202-724-7216. Ed. Eileen Dent. charts; stat. circ. 1,500. (also avail. in microfiche from CIS) Indexed: SRI. **Document type:** government publication.
Formerly: Greater Washington Area Labor Summary.

MEXICO. INSTITUTO NACIONAL DE ESTADISTICA, GEOGRAFIA E INFORMATICA. ENCUESTA NACIONAL DE EDUCACION CAPACITACION Y EMPLEO. see *EDUCATION — Abstracting, Bibliographies, Statistics*

331 MX ISSN 0302-5004
MEXICO. SECRETARIA DEL TRABAJO Y PREVISION SOCIAL. SUBDIRECCION DE DOCUMENTACION. RESENA LABORAL.* 2/yr. Mex.$70. Secretaria del Trabajo y Prevision Social, Periferico Sur 4271, Ed. A, 4o, Col. Fuentes de Pedregal, 14140 Mexico DF, Mexico. Ed. Javier Patino. illus. circ. 5,000.

331.11 US
MICHIGAN. CIVIL SERVICE DEPARTMENT. ANNUAL WORK FORCE REPORT. 1980. a. free. Civil Service Department, Capitol Commons Center, 400 S. Pine St., Box 30002, Lansing, MI 48909. TEL 517-335-0318. FAX 517-335-4510. URL: http://www.mdcs.state.mi.us/index.html. Ed. Linda S. Coe. **Document type:** government publication.

331.1 US
MICHIGAN. EMPLOYMENT SECURITY COMMISSION. ANNUAL PLANNING REPORT. Variant title: Annual Planning Information Report. 1972. a. free. Employment Security Commission, 7310 Woodward Ave., Detroit, MI 48202. TEL 313-876-5427. illus.; stat. circ. 1,000.
Formerly: Michigan. Employment Security Commission. Labor Market Analysis Section. Annual Manpower Planning Report: Detroit Labor Market Area (ISSN 0090-8401)

MICHIGAN EMPLOYMENT LAW LETTER. see *LAW*

331.1 US
HD5725.M5
MICHIGAN LABOR MARKET NEWS. 1946. m. free. Employment Security Commission, Bureau of Research and Statistics, 7310 Woodward, Detroit, MI 48202. TEL 313-876-5000. Ed. James Astalos, Jr. charts; stat. circ. 2,800. (also avail. in microfiche from CIS) Indexed: SRI. **Document type:** government publication.
Former titles (until 1992): Michigan Labor Market Review (ISSN 0098-0307); Michigan Manpower Review; Michigan's Labor Market.

353.9 US ISSN 0092-9212
JK5860.P4
MICHIGAN STATE EMPLOYEES' RETIREMENT SYSTEM FINANCIAL AND STATISTICAL REPORT. Key Title: Michigan State Employees' Retirement System. 1953. a. free. State Employees Retirement System, 3rd Fl., General Office Bldg., P.O. Box 30171, Lansing, MI 48909. TEL 517-322-6275. stat. circ. 1,100.

331 US ISSN 0036-6706
MICHIGAN STATE UNIVERSITY. SCHOOL OF LABOR AND INDUSTRIAL RELATIONS. NEWSLETTER. 1962. 2/yr. free. Michigan State University, School of Labor and Industrial Relations, South Kedzie Hall, East Lansing, MI 48824. TEL 517-355-1801. FAX 517-355-7656. Ed. Michael L. Moore. bk.rev. circ. 1,800. (processed) **Document type:** newsletter.
Description: Contains information on school activities, its faculty, students and alumni.

331.11 US
MICRO O L M. (Occupations in the Labor Market) irreg. (updated periodically). $8. Employment Security Department, Labor Market and Economic Analysis Branch, Box 9046, Olympia, WA 98507-9046. TEL 360-438-4813. charts; stat. (diskette format) **Document type:** government publication.
Description: Comprises the most recent information on occupations, including supply and demand, characteristics, and wages.

331 323.42 US
MILWAUKEE 9 TO 5. 1973. 5/yr. $25 to individuals; institutions $40. 9 to 5 National Association of Working Women, 231 W. Wisconsin Ave., Ste. 900, Milwaukee, WI 53203-2306. Ed. Linda Garcia. adv.; bk.rev. circ. 13,000. (back issues avail.) **Document type:** newsletter.
Formerly: 9 to 5 Newsletter.

331 US
MINNESOTA. DEPARTMENT OF JOBS AND TRAINING. ANNUAL REPORT.* 1936. a. free. Department of Jobs and Training, Communications Team (CommTeam) Office, 390 N. Robert St., St. Paul, MN 55101. TEL 612-297-2979. Ed. Clifford Miller. circ. 1,500.
Former titles (until 1979): Minnesota. Department of Employment Services. Annual Report (ISSN 0364-717X); (until 1974): Minnesota. Department of Manpower Services. Annual Report (ISSN 0076-9126); (until 1969): Minnesota. Department of Employment Security. Annual Report.

MINNESOTA EMPLOYMENT LAW LETTER. see *LAW*

331.11 US
MINNESOTA LABOR MARKET REVIEW. m. free. Minnesota Department of Economic Security, Research and Statistics Office, 390 N. Robert St., St. Paul, MN 55101. TEL 612-296-6545. FAX 612-282-5429. E-mail: http://www.peter./tsc.md.US/MN/ Ed. Julia Pool. circ. 4,500. Indexed: SRI. **Document type:** government publication.
Incorporates (1974-1993): Current Minnesota Labor Conditions.

MISSISSIPPI EMPLOYMENT LAW LETTER. see *LAW*

331.1 US ISSN 0148-4214
HD5725.M8
MISSOURI AREA LABOR TRENDS. 1977. m. free. Department of Labor and Industry, Division of Employment Security, Box 59, Jefferson City, MO 65101. TEL 314-751-3602. Ed. Linda J. Rackers. illus. circ. 1,700. Indexed: SRI. **Document type:** newsletter.
Formerly: Missouri State and Area Labor Trends.

MISSOURI EMPLOYMENT LAW LETTER. see *LAW*

331 AU
MITBESTIMMUNG; Zeitschrift fuer demokratisierung der arbeitswelt. 1972. bi-m. S.250. Arbeitsgemeinschaft zur Demokratisierung Arbeitswelt, Postfach 371, A-1171 Vienna, Austria. TEL 43-1-4807793. Ed. Peter Lehner. adv.: page S.10000; adv. contact: Paul Habr. bk.rev.; index. (back issues avail.) **Document type:** bulletin.
Description: Contains and deals with questions concerning working life, relations between work and capital, trade unions, marxism and socialism.

331 GW ISSN 0340-3254
HD4824
MITTEILUNGEN AUS DER ARBEITSMARKT- UND BERUFSFORSCHUNG. (Text in German; summaries in English, German) 1909. q. DM.98 (effective 1997). (Bundesanstalt fuer Arbeit, Institut fuer Arbeitsmarkt- und Berufsforschung (Stuttgart)) W. Kohlhammer GmbH, Hessbruehlstr. 69, 70565 Stuttgart, Germany. TEL 49-711-7863-1. FAX 49-711-7863263. Ed.Bd. adv.; bk.rev. circ. 5,000. (back issues avail.) Indexed: IBR, Int.Lab.Doc. **Document type:** government publication.
—BLDSC (5876.388000); SWETS. CCC.

BUSINESS AND ECONOMICS — LABOR AND INDUSTRIAL RELATIONS

331   CM
MONDE DU TRAVAIL/WORLD OF LABOUR; revue trimestrielle d'informations/quarterly information review. 1979. q. 2800 Fr.CFA. Ministere du Travail et de la Prevoyance Sociale - Ministry of Labour and Social Insurance, Yaounde, Cameroon. TELEX 8415 KN. (Co-sponsor: Societe de Presse et d'Editions du Cameroun) Ed.Bd. circ. 3,000.

MONOGRAFIEEN SOCIAAL RECHT. see *LAW — Civil Law*

MONOGRAPHS IN ORGANIZATIONAL BEHAVIOUR AND INDUSTRIAL RELATIONS. see *SOCIAL SCIENCES: COMPREHENSIVE WORKS*

MONTANA EMPLOYMENT LAW LETTER. see *LAW*

MONTHLY LABOR REVIEW. see *BUSINESS AND ECONOMICS — Abstracting, Bibliographies, Statistics*

331   SZ
MOTZART. 6/yr. 12 SFr. Schweizerischer Gewerkschaftsbund - Swiss Federation of Trade Unions, Monbijoustr. 61, CH-3000 Bern 23, Switzerland. TEL 41-31-3715666. FAX 41-31-3710837. Ed. Simon Ackermann. circ. 22,000. Document type: bulletin.
  Formerly: Gewerkschaftsjugend.

331   CU
MOVIMIENTO SINDICAL DE AMERICA LATINA Y EL CARIBE. q. Central de Trabajadores de Cuba, Palacio de los Trabajadores, San Carlos y Penalver, Havana, Cuba.

N C A NEWSLETTER. (National Constructors Association) see *BUILDING AND CONSTRUCTION*

N T E U ADVOCATE. (National Tertiary Education Union) see *EDUCATION — Higher Education*

331   US
N T S A REPORTER. 1966. m. membership. National Technical Services Association, 325 S. Patrick St., Ste. 104, Alexandria, VA 22314-3501. TEL 703-684-4722. FAX 703-684-7627. Ed. Laura Mackail. adv.; bk.rev.; index. circ. 800. (back issues avail.)

344.73 331   GW   ISSN 0949-7137
▼**N Z A RECHTSPRECHUNGS REPORT ARBEITSRECHT.** (Neue Zeitschrift fuer Arbeitsrecht) Abbreviated title: N Z A - R R. 1996. m. DM.248 (effective 1997). Verlag C.H. Beck, 80791 Munich, Germany. TEL 49-89-38189338. FAX 49-89-38189398. Ed.Bd. Document type: abstracting/indexing.

331 340   GW   ISSN 0469-4333
NACHSCHLAGEWERK DES BUNDESARBEITSGERICHTS - ARBEITSRECHTLICHE PRAXIS. 1954. m. DM.780 (effective 1997). Verlag C.H. Beck, 80791 Munich, Germany. TEL 49-89-38189340. FAX 49-89-38189398. Ed.Bd. Document type: academic/scholarly publication.

331.1   US   ISSN 0148-4176
HD5481
NATIONAL ACADEMY OF ARBITRATORS. ANNUAL MEETING. PROCEEDINGS. 1948. a. $40. B N A Books (Subsidiary of: The Bureau of National Affairs, Inc.), 1250 23rd St., N.W., Washington, DC 20037. TEL 202-833-7470. FAX 202-833-7490. E-mail: books@bna.com. (Subscr. to: BNA Books Distribution Center, 130 Campus Dr., , Box 7816, Edison, NJ 08818-7816. TEL 800-960-1220. FAX 908-417-0482) Ed. Walter Gershenfeld. Indexed: L.R.I., Leg.Per. Document type: proceedings.
  —BLDSC (6841.538000); KR SourceOne. CCC.

NATIONAL CENTER FOR THE STUDY OF COLLECTIVE BARGAINING IN HIGHER EDUCATION AND THE PROFESSIONS. NEWSLETTER. see *EDUCATION — Higher Education*

331 350   US
NATIONAL CONFERENCE ON PUBLIC RETIREMENT SYSTEMS. PROCEEDINGS RECORD. a. National Conference on Public Retirement Systems, c/o Carlos Resendez, Exec. Admin., 4414 Centerview Dr., Ste. 226, San Antonio, TX 78228. TEL 210-732-8600. FAX 210-732-8684. E-mail: resendez@ncpers.org. circ. 1,000.
  Description: Concerned with promoting and safeguarding the rights and benefits of government employees participating in retirement plans.

731   US
NATIONAL EXECUTIVE COMPENSATION SURVEY. a. $450. MidAtlantic Employers' Association, Box 770, Valley Forge, PA 19482. TEL 215-666-7330. FAX 215-666-7866.
  Description: Provides comparative information about 29 executive position compensation practices among 1,800 businesses, representing 16,500 executives throughout the country. All information is broken down by geographic region.

331.2 378   US
NATIONAL FACULTY SALARY SURVEY BY DISCIPLINE AND RANK IN PRIVATE COLLEGES AND UNIVERSITIES. a. $80 to non-members; non-participating member $55; members $33. College and University Personnel Association, 1233 20th St., N.W., Washington, DC 20036. TEL 202-429-0311. FAX 202-429-0149. Indexed: SRI.
  Description: Provides salary data on faculty members at nearly 500 private institutions.

344.01   US
NATIONAL LABOR RELATIONS ACT: LAW AND PRACTICE. 3 base vols. (plus updates 2/yr.). $285 for base vols.; updates $119. Matthew Bender & Co., Inc., 2 Park Ave., New York, NY 10016. TEL 212-448-2000. E-mail: international@bender.com; URL: http://www.bender.com.
  Description: Covers all aspects of the law and practice under the NLRA.

658.3 340   US   ISSN 0194-889X
KF3580.G6
NATIONAL PUBLIC EMPLOYMENT REPORTER. Short title: N P E R. 1979. q. $475 (effective 1997). L R P Publications (Subsidiary of: Axon Group), 747 Dresher Rd., Box 980, Horsham, PA 19044-0980. TEL 215-784-0941; 800-341-7874. FAX 215-784-9639. index. circ. 300. (also avail. in microfiche; back issues avail.) Document type: trade publication.
  —CCC.
  Description: Provides state-by-state reporting of the indexed summaries of all public-sector labor decisions issued by every state and local labor board.

331   US   ISSN 0197-7032
NATIONAL RIGHT TO WORK NEWSLETTER. 1955. m. $15 (effective 1993). National Right to Work Committee, 8001 Braddock Rd., Ste. 500, Springfield, VA 22160. TEL 703-321-9820. FAX 703-321-7342. Ed. Stanley Greer. circ. 150,000. (tabloid format; back issues avail.) Document type: newsletter.

NATIONAL SURVEY OF PROFESSIONAL, ADMINISTRATIVE, TECHNICAL AND CLERICAL PAY. see *BUSINESS AND ECONOMICS — Economic Situation And Conditions*

331 614.7 352.7
360   GW   ISSN 0172-276X
NEBELHORN; Regionalmagazin fuer Politik und Kultur. 1980. m. DM.40. S & N Verlags GmbH, Schottenstr. 3, 78462 Konstanz, Germany. Ed.Bd. adv.; bk.rev. circ. 2,500.

NEBRASKA EMPLOYMENT LAW LETTER. see *LAW*

NEUE B S. see *OCCUPATIONAL HEALTH AND SAFETY*

NEVADA EMPLOYMENT LAW LETTER. see *LAW*

331.2   US
NEVADA WAGE SURVEY. Variant title: Nevada Statewide Wage Survey. 1973. a. Employment, Training and Rehabilitation Department, Employment Security Division, 500 E. Third St., Carson City, NV 89713. TEL 702-687-4550. circ. 2,500. Document type: government publication.
  ●Also available online.
  Formerly: State of Nevada Wage Report (ISSN 0081-4563)

331   CN
NEW BRUNSWICK. DEPARTMENT OF ADVANCED EDUCATION AND LABOUR. ANNUAL REPORT. (Text in English, French) 1944. a. free. Department of Advanced Education and Labour, P.O. Box 6000, Fredericton, NB E3B 5H1, Canada. TEL 506-453-2568. FAX 506-453-3806. URL: http://www.gov.nb.ca/ael/index.htm. Ed. Margot Brewer. circ. 700 (controlled). Document type: government publication.
  Former titles: New Brunswick. Department of Labour. Annual Report; New Brunswick. Department of Labour and Human Resources. Annual Report; New Brunswick. Department of Labour and Manpower. Annual Report; New Brunswick. Department of Labour. Annual Report (ISSN 0077-8052)

NEW DEVELOPMENTS IN EMPLOYMENT DISCRIMINATION. see *LAW*

331.2   UK   ISSN 0262-0502
NEW EARNINGS SURVEY. PART A: REPORT AND KEY RESULTS. 1970. a. Office for National Statistics, Government Offices, Rm. 65c-3, Great George St., London SW1P 3AQ, England. TEL 44-171-270-6081. FAX 44-171-270-6019. (Dist. by: HMSO Publications Centre, P.O. Box 276, London SW8 5DT, England. TEL 44-171-873-9090. FAX 44-171-873-8200) Document type: government publication.
  —CCC.
  Supersedes in part (1970-1975): Great Britain. Department of Employment. New Earnings Survey (ISSN 0308-1419)
  Description: Reports on earnings and work hours in Great Britain.

331.2   UK   ISSN 0262-0510
NEW EARNINGS SURVEY. PART B: ANALYSES BY AGREEMENT. a. Office for National Statistics, Government Offices, Rm. 65c-3, Great George St., London SW1P 3AQ, England. TEL 44-171-270-6081. FAX 44-171-270-6019. (Dist. by: HMSO Publications Centre, P.O. Box 276, London SW8 5DT, England. TEL 44-171-873-9090. FAX 44-171-873-8200) Document type: government publication.
  —CCC.
  Supersedes in part (1970-1975): Great Britain. Department of Employment. New Earnings Survey (ISSN 0308-1419)

331.2   UK   ISSN 0262-0529
NEW EARNINGS SURVEY. PART C: ANALYSES BY INDUSTRY. a. Office for National Statistics, Government Offices, Rm. 65c-3, Great George St., London SW1P 3AQ, England. TEL 44-171-270-6081. FAX 44-171-270-6019. (Dist. by: HMSO Publications Centre, P.O. Box 276, London SW8 5DT, England. TEL 44-171-873-9090. FAX 44-171-873-8200) Document type: government publication.
  —CCC.
  Supersedes in part (1970-1975): Great Britain. Department of Employment. New Earning Survey (ISSN 0308-1419)

331.2   UK   ISSN 0262-0537
NEW EARNINGS SURVEY. PART D: ANALYSES BY OCCUPATION. a. Office for National Statistics, Government Offices, Rm. 65c-3, Great George St., London SW1P 3AQ, England. TEL 44-171-270-6081. FAX 44-171-270-6019. (Dist. by: HMSO Publications Centre, P.O. Box 276, London SW8 5DT, England. TEL 44-171-873-9090. FAX 44-171-873-8200) Document type: government publication.
  —CCC.
  Supersedes in part (1970-1975): Great Britain. Department of Employment. New Earnings Survey (ISSN 0308-1419)

331.2   UK   ISSN 0262-0545
NEW EARNINGS SURVEY. PART E: ANALYSES BY REGION AND AGE GROUP. a. Office for National Statistics, Government Offices, Rm. 65c-3, Great George St., London SW1P 3AQ, England. TEL 44-171-270-6081. FAX 44-171-270-6019. (Dist. by: HMSO Publications Centre, P.O. Box 276, London SW8 5DT, England. TEL 44-171-873-9090. FAX 44-171-873-8200) Document type: government publication.
  —CCC.
  Supersedes in part (1970-1975): Great Britain. Department of Employment. New Earnings Survey (ISSN 0308-1419)

BUSINESS AND ECONOMICS — LABOR AND INDUSTRIAL RELATIONS

331.2   UK   ISSN 0262-0553
NEW EARNINGS SURVEY. PART F: HOURS, EARNINGS AND HOURS OF PART-TIME WOMEN WORKERS. a. Office for National Statistics, Government Offices, Rm. 65c-3, Great George St., London SW1P 3AQ, England. TEL 44-171-270-6081. FAX 44-171-270-6019. (Dist. by: HMSO Publications Centre, P.O. Box 276, London SW8 5DT, England. TEL 44-171-873-9090. FAX 44-171-873-8200) **Document type:** government publication.
—BLDSC (6083.642000). **CCC.**
   Supersedes in part (1970-1975): Great Britain. Department of Employment. New Earnings Survey (ISSN 0308-1419)

NEW GROUND. see *POLITICAL SCIENCE*

NEW HAMPSHIRE EMPLOYMENT LAW LETTER. see *LAW*

NEW JERSEY ECONOMIC INDICATORS. see *BUSINESS AND ECONOMICS — Economic Situation And Conditions*

NEW JERSEY EMPLOYMENT LAW LETTER. see *LAW*

NEW JERSEY LABOR AND EMPLOYMENT LAW QUARTERLY. see *LAW*

331   US
NEW LABOR REVIEW. 1978. irreg., no.4, 1981. free. San Francisco State University, Labor Studies Forum, Division of Cross Disciplinary Programs in the Behavioral and Social Sciences, 1600 Holloway Ave., San Francisco, CA 94132. TEL 415-469-2055. Ed.Bd. adv.; bk.rev. circ. 1,000. (also avail. in microform from UMI)

331.11   US
NEW MEXICO. DEPARTMENT OF LABOR. COVERED EMPLOYMENT AND WAGES. QUARTERLY REPORT. 1948. q. free. Department of Labor, Box 1928, Albuquerque, NM 87103. TEL 505-841-8697. Ed. Vincent Brunacini. circ. 250.
   Formerly: New Mexico. Employment Security Department. Covered Employment and Wages. Quarterly Report.

NEW MEXICO EMPLOYMENT LAW LETTER. see *LAW*

331.11   US
NEW MEXICO LABOR MARKET REVIEW. vol.2, 1974. m. free. Department of Labor, Bureau of Economic Research & Analysis, Box 1928, Albuquerque, NM 87103. TEL 505-841-8645. Ed. Gerard P. Bradley. stat. circ. 4,000. (also avail. in microfiche from CIS) **Indexed:** SRI. **Document type:** government publication.
   Former titles: New Mexico Manpower Review; New Mexico Labor Market Trends (ISSN 0550-9483)

614.85   AT
NEW SOUTH WALES. DEPARTMENT OF INDUSTRIAL RELATIONS. SAFETY. 1956. s-a. free. Department of Industrial Relations and Technology, 50 Phillip St., Sydney, N.S.W. 2000, Australia. (Subscr. addr.: 1 Oxford St., Darlinghurst, N.S.W. 2010, Australia)
   Former titles: New South Wales. Department of Industrial Relations and Technology. Safety; New South Wales. Department of Labour and Industry. Safety.

331.1   AT   ISSN 0028-677X
HD8849.N48
NEW SOUTH WALES INDUSTRIAL GAZETTE. 1912. w. Aus.$584. Department of Industrial Relations, 50 Phillip St., Sydney, N.S.W. 2000, Australia. (Subscr. addr.: 1 Oxford St., Darlinghurst, N.S.W. 2010, Australia) charts; stat.; index. circ. 630.

331   UK   ISSN 0268-1072
HD6331   CODEN: NWEMEJ
NEW TECHNOLOGY, WORK & EMPLOYMENT. 1986. s-a. £52($106) (foreign £67) (effective 1997). Blackwell Publishers Ltd., 108 Cowley Rd., Oxford OX4 1JF, England. TEL 44-1865-791100. FAX 44-1865-791347. E-mail: jnlinfo@blackwellpublishers.co.uk; URL: http://www.blackwellpublishers.co.uk. Ed. Colin Gill. adv.; bk.rev. (also avail. in microform) **Indexed:** ASCA, ASSIA, Compumath, Cont.Pg.Manage., Curr.Cont., Geo.Abstr.P.G., IBR, IDA, INSPEC (1994-), Sp.Ed.Needs Abstr., Tech.Educ.Abstr. **Document type:** academic/scholarly publication.
—BLDSC (6088.840800); AskIEEE; Genuine Article; KR SourceOne; SWETS; UMI; UnCover. **CCC.**
   Refereed Serial

NEW UNIONIST. see *POLITICAL SCIENCE*

331   US
NEW YORK (CITY). HUMAN RESOURCES ADMINISTRATION. EQUAL EMPLOYMENT OPPORTUNITY QUARTERLY REPORT. q. Human Resources Administration, Office of Equal Employment Opportunity, 250 Church St., New York, NY 10013. TEL 212-553-5883.

NEW YORK (STATE). DEPARTMENT OF LABOR. DIVISION OF RESEARCH AND STATISTICS. LABOR RESEARCH REPORT. see *BUSINESS AND ECONOMICS — Abstracting, Bibliographies, Statistics*

331.11   US
NEW YORK (STATE). DEPARTMENT OF LABOR. OPERATIONS - EMPLOYMENT SERVICE AND UNEMPLOYMENT INSURANCE. m. free. Department of Labor, Division of Research and Statistics, 1 Main St., 9th Fl., Brooklyn, NY 11201. TEL 718-797-7703. Ed. Eileen DeVeau. circ. controlled. **Document type:** government publication.

331 340   US
NEW YORK EMPLOYER'S ALERT. (Suppl. to: New York Employer's Guide) q. Butterworth Legal Publishers (Salem) (Subsidiary of: Reed Elsevier plc), 8 Industrial Way, Bldg. C, Salem, NH 03079. TEL 800-548-4001. FAX 603-898-9858. (looseleaf format)

331 350   US
NEW YORK EMPLOYER'S GUIDE. (Supplement avail.: New York Employer's Alert) 1988. irreg. (plus q. supplement) $79.50. Butterworth Legal Publishers (Salem) (Subsidiary of: Reed Elsevier plc), 8 Industrial Way, Bldg. C, Salem, NH 03079. TEL 603-898-9664. FAX 603-898-9859. Ed. Jeffrey L. Liddle. (looseleaf format)
   Description: Covers city, state, and federal regulations and statutes concerning the entire employment process.

NEW YORK EMPLOYMENT LAW LETTER. see *LAW*

331 340   US
NEW YORK STATE BAR ASSOCIATION. LABOR AND EMPLOYMENT LAW SECTION. NEWSLETTER. Key Title: Labor and Employment Law Section Newsletter. 1975. 4/yr. $30 to libraries (effective 1996). New York State Bar Association, Labor and Employment Law Section, 1 Elk St., Albany, NY 12207-1096. TEL 518-463-3200. FAX 518-463-8844. Ed. Judith LaManna. R&P contact: Daniel J. McMahon. bk.rev.; circ. 2,000 (controlled). (back issues avail.) **Document type:** newsletter.
   Formerly (until 1980): New York State Bar Association. Labor Law Section Newsletter (ISSN 0160-5186)

331   US   ISSN 0070-0134
NEW YORK STATE SCHOOL OF INDUSTRIAL AND LABOR RELATIONS. BULLETIN. 1951. irreg., no.70, 1995. price varies. (New York State School of Industrial and Labor Relations) I L R Press, Cornell University Press, 512 E. State St., Ithaca, NY 14850. TEL 607-277-2338; 800-666-2211. Ed. Frances Benson. R&P contact: Clare Wellnitz. adv. contact: Heidi Marschner. **Document type:** monographic series.
   Supersedes in part: Extension Bulletin & Research Bulletin.

331   US
NEW YORK STATE SCHOOL OF INDUSTRIAL AND LABOR RELATIONS. INSTITUTE OF PUBLIC EMPLOYMENT. MONOGRAPH. 1973. irreg., no.10, 1982. price varies. I L R Press, Cornell University Press, 512 E. State St., Ithaca, NY 14850. TEL 607-277-2338; 800-666-2211. Ed. Frances Benson. R&P contact: Clare Wellnitz. adv. contact: Heidi Marschner. **Document type:** monographic series.

331   US   ISSN 0070-0185
NEW YORK STATE SCHOOL OF INDUSTRIAL AND LABOR RELATIONS. KEY ISSUES SERIES. 1967. irreg., no.30, 2nd ed., 1990. price varies. I L R Press, Cornell University Press, 512 E. State St., Ithaca, NY 14850. TEL 607-277-2338; 800-666-2211. Ed. Frances Benson. R&P contact: Clare Wellnitz. adv. contact: Heidi Marschner. **Document type:** monographic series.

331   NZ   ISSN 0110-0637
HD8930.5
NEW ZEALAND JOURNAL OF INDUSTRIAL RELATIONS. 1976. 3/yr. NZ.$50 to individuals; institutions NZ.$80. Foundation for Industrial Relations Research and Education (New Zealand), P.O. Box 6088, Dunedin, New Zealand. FAX 64-3-479-8173. Ed. Alan Geare. adv.; bk.rev. circ. 350. (back issues avail.) **Indexed:** Aus.P.A.I.S. **Document type:** academic/scholarly publication.
—BLDSC (6094.540000); UMI; UnCover.
   Description: Publishes articles on industrial relations and labor law with an emphasis on New Zealand and the Asia-Pacific region.

331.11   NZ   ISSN 0113-1222
NEW ZEALAND LABOUR FORCE. 1986. q. $75. Department of Statistics, P.O. Box 2922, Wellington, New Zealand.
—CCC.

NEWSMONTH. see *LABOR UNIONS*

331 340.5   NE   ISSN 0169-6971
NIEUWSBRIEF P Z; actuele en praktische informatie over personeelszaken. Variant title: Nieuwsbrief Personeelszaken. 1985. 16/yr. fl.183 (effective 1996). Uitgeverij Kluwer B.V., Postbus 23, 7400 GA Deventer, Netherlands. TEL 31-570-633155. FAX 31-570-633834. Ed. V.J. de Haan. (back issues avail.) **Document type:** newsletter.

331 340   NE   ISSN 0923-8646
NIEUWSBRIEF WERK. 1989. bi-w. Samsom H.D. Tjeenk Willink B.V. (Subsidiary of: Wolters Kluwer N.V.), Postbus 316, 2400 AH Alphen aan den Rijn, Netherlands. TEL 31-1720-66822. FAX 31-1720-66639. **Document type:** newsletter.

331   NR
NIGERIA. FEDERAL MINISTRY OF LABOUR AND PRODUCTIVITY. ANNUAL REPORT. 1958. a. free. Federal Ministry of Labour and Productivity, Planning, Research and Statistics Department, Federal Secretariat, Phase I, Ikoyi, P.M.B. 12576, Lagos, Nigeria. stat. circ. 1,000. (processed) **Document type:** government publication.
   Formerly: Nigeria. Federal Ministry of Labour. Quarterly Review (ISSN 0549-2351)

NIGERIA. FEDERAL MINISTRY OF LABOUR AND PRODUCTIVITY. QUARTERLY BULLETIN OF LABOUR STATISTICS. see *BUILDING AND CONSTRUCTION — Abstracting, Bibliographies, Statistics*

331.11   NR
NIGERIA. NATIONAL MANPOWER BOARD. MANPOWER STUDIES. 1963. irreg. (1-2/yr.). price varies. National Manpower Board, P.M.B. 12558, Ikoyi, Lagos State, Nigeria. Ed. C.C. Mmereole. stat. circ. 1,000. **Document type:** government publication.

331   JA   ISSN 0917-1843
NIHON RODO KENKYU KIKO KENKYU KIYO/JAPAN INSTITUTE OF LABOUR. STUDIES. (Text in English, Japanese) 1991. s-a. Japan Institute of Labour - Nihon Rodo Kenkyu Kiko, Shinjuku Monolith, P.O. Box 7040, Tokyo 163-09, Japan. TEL 03-5321-3074. FAX 03-5321-3015.

331   JA   ISSN 0916-3808
HD4811
NIHON RODO KENKYU ZASSHI/JAPAN INSTITUTE OF LABOUR. JOURNAL. (Text in Japanese) 1959. m. 9600 Yen. Japan Institute of Labour - Nihon Rodo Kenkyu Kiko, Shinjuku Monolith, P.O. Box 7040, Tokyo 163-09, Japan. TEL 03-5321-3074. FAX 03-5321-3015. Ed. Akira Takanashi. bk.rev.; bibl.; charts; stat.; s-a. cum.index. circ. 4,000. **Indexed:** Amer.Hist.& Life (1966-), Hist.Abstr. (1966-). **Document type:** academic/scholarly publication.
—UnCover.
   Formerly (until 1990): Nihon Rodo Kyokai Zasshi (ISSN 0029-0378)
   Description: Information on industrial relations in Japan.

NORTH CAROLINA EMPLOYMENT LAW LETTER. see *LAW*

BUSINESS AND ECONOMICS — LABOR AND INDUSTRIAL RELATIONS

344.012   US
NORTH CAROLINA WORKERS' COMPENSATION LAW ANNOTATED. a., latest 1994 ed. $35. Michie, A Division of Reed Elsevier Inc., Box 7587, Charlottesville, VA 22906-7587. TEL 804-972-7566; 800-562-1197. FAX 800-643-1280. E-mail: custserv@michie.com; URL: http://www.michie.com. Ed. George Harley.
  Description: A compendium of relevant laws and cases in use by the North Carolina Industrial Commission.

331.11   US
NORTH COAST LABOR TRENDS. 1982. m. free. Oregon Employment Division, 875 Union St., N.E., Salem, OR 97311. TEL 503-378-8657. circ. 365.
  Document type: newsletter, government publication.
  Formerly: North Coast Labor Force Trends.
  Description: Describes and analyzes labor force and economic trends for the north coastal region of Oregon.

NORTH DAKOTA EMPLOYMENT LAW LETTER. see *LAW*

344.012   US
NORTH DAKOTA WORKERS' COMPENSATION LAW. a., latest 1995 ed. $11. Michie, A Division of Reed Elsevier Inc., Box 7587, Charlottesville, VA 22906-7587. TEL 804-972-7566; 800-562-1197. FAX 800-643-1280. E-mail: custserv@michie.com; URL: http://www.michie.com. Ed. George Harley.

331   UK
NORTH EAST LABOUR HISTORY BULLETIN. 1967. a. £5 to individuals; institutions £6. North East Labour History Society, University of Northumbria, Dept. of English and History, Lipman Bldg., Newcastle Upon Tyne NE1 8ST, England. TEL 44-191-227-3738. FAX 44-191-227-4572. Ed. Bill Lancaster. R&P contact: Bill Lancaster. adv. contact: Bill Lancaster. bk.rev.; bibl.; charts; stat.; circ. 250 (paid). **Document type:** academic/scholarly publication, bulletin.
  Formerly: North East Group for the Study of Labour History Bulletin (ISSN 0029-2818)
  Refereed Serial

331   UK
NORTH EAST MIDLANDS SALARY SURVEY. 2/yr. £250 (effective 1997). The Reward Group Ltd., Reward House, Diamond Way, Stone Business Park, Stone, Staffordshire ST15 0SD, England. TEL 44-1785-813566. FAX 44-1785-817007. E-mail: 101364.661@compuserve.com. **Document type:** bulletin.
  Description: Salary survey covering the Derbyshire, Burton-upon-Trent, Nottinghamshire, Leicestershire and Lincolnshire areas.

331   UK
NORTHERN IRELAND SALARY SURVEY. 2/yr. £450 (effective 1997). The Reward Group Ltd., Reward House, Diamond Way, Stone Business Park, Stone, Staffordshire ST15 0SD, England. TEL 44-1785-813566. FAX 44-1785-817007. E-mail: 101364.661@compuserve.com. **Document type:** bulletin.
  Description: Pay and benefit salary survey covering Northern Ireland.

NORTHWEST LABOR PRESS. see *LABOR UNIONS*

NORTH WEST LABOUR HISTORY. see *HISTORY — History Of Europe*

331   UK
NORTH WEST SALARY SURVEY. 2/yr. £250 (effective 1997). The Reward Group Ltd., Reward House, Diamond Way, Stone Business Park, Stone, Staffordshire ST15 0SD, England. TEL 44-1785-813566. FAX 44-1785-817007. E-mail: 101364.661@compuserve.com. **Document type:** bulletin.
  Description: Salary survey for the North West covering the Lancashire, Greater Manchester, Merseyside, Cheshire and Clwyd areas.

331   NO   ISSN 0801-1621
NORWAY. ARBEIDSDIREKTORATET. AARSMELDING. (Editions in English, Norwegian) a. free. Arbeidsdirektoratet, P.O. Box 8127, N-0032 Oslo, Norway. TEL 22-94-24-00. FAX 02-364959.

NOTEBOOKS FOR STUDY AND RESEARCH. see *POLITICAL SCIENCE*

331   US
NOTICIAS DE LA SEMANA. w. free. U.S. Department of Labor, Office of Information and Public Affairs, Third & Constitution Ave., N.W., Rm. S-1032, Washington, DC 20210. TEL 202-523-7323. Ed. Dolores Martinez Board. circ. 2,000.

331.2   CN   ISSN 0380-5689
HD8101.N6
NOVA SCOTIA. DEPARTMENT OF LABOUR. ANNUAL REPORT. 1935. a. Department of Labour, Research Division, P.O. Box 697, Halifax, NS B3J 2T8, Canada. TEL 902-424-4313. URL: http://www.gov.ns.ca//labr/. **Document type:** government publication.
  Description: Summary report of the year's activities of the Nova Scotia Department of Labour.

331   CN
NOVA SCOTIA. DEPARTMENT OF LABOUR. COMPENDIUM OF GRIEVANCE ARBITRATION DECISIONS. 1978. q. Can.$30. Department of Labour, Research Division, P.O. Box 697, Halifax, NS B3J 2T8, Canada. TEL 902-424-8474. URL: http://www.gov.ns.ca//labr/. circ. 300. **Document type:** government publication.
  Formerly: Nova Scotia. Department of Labour and Manpower. Compendium of Grievance Arbitration Decisions (ISSN 0226-3890)
  Description: Summaries of grievance arbitration awards filed under Nova Scotia Trade Union Act.

331.11021 310   FR   ISSN 0474-5515
HD5764.A6
O E C D LABOUR FORCE STATISTICS/O C D E STATISTIQUES DE LA POPULATION ACTIVE. (Text in English, French) 1968. a. price varies. Organization for Economic Cooperation and Development, 2 rue Andre-Pascal, 75775 Paris Cedex 16, France. (U.S. orders to: O.E.C.D. Publications and Information Center, 2001 L St., N.W., Ste. 650, Washington, DC 20036-4922. TEL 202-785-6323) (magnetic tape) **Indexed:** IIS.
  —BLDSC (5142.130000).

331.2   FR   ISSN 0255-3627
HD5701
O E C D QUARTERLY LABOUR FORCE STATISTICS/O C D E STATISTIQUES TRIMESTRIELLES DE LA POPULATION ACTIVE. q. 185 F.($46) Organization for Economic Cooperation and Development, 2 rue Andre-Pascal, 75775 Paris Cedex 16, France. (U.S. orders to: O.E.C.D. Publications and Information Center, 2001 L St., N.W., Ste. 650, Washington, D.C. 20036-4922. TEL 202-785-6323) (magnetic tape; diskette format) **Indexed:** IIS.
  Formerly: Organization for Economic Cooperation and Development. Labour Statistics (ISSN 0304-3312)
  Description: Provides data for the short-term evolution of the major labor force components and employment by sector.

331   CN   ISSN 0229-8104
O P S E U NEWS. (Text in English, occasionally in French) 1966. 15/yr. free. Ontario Public Service Employees Union, 100 Lesmill Rd., North York, ON M3B 3P8, Canada. TEL 416-443-8888. FAX 416-443-1762. Ed.Bd. bk.rev.; circ. 20,000 (controlled). **Document type:** newspaper.
  Former titles (until Feb. 1993): Voices (ISSN 0838-7176); (until June 1987): O P S E U News.
  Description: News, feature articles, columns and letters by and about public sector workers in Ontario and the problems they face in a labour relations context.

331   NE   ISSN 0165-0823
O R INFORMATIE. (Ondernemingsraad) 1975. 16/yr. fl.185. Samsom Bedrijfsinformatie B.V. (Subsidiary of: Wolters Kluwer N.V.), Postbus 4, 2400 MA Alphen aan den Rijn, Netherlands. TEL 31-172-466775. FAX 31-172-440681. circ. 12,100. **Document type:** trade publication.
  —KNAW; SWETS.

331 346   US
O S H A FASTSEARCH; Occupational Safety and Health Administration regulations. 1992. q. (plus m. updates). $299. FastSearch Corporation, Box 421057 Corporation, Plymouth, MN 55442-0057. TEL 800-232-4590. FAX 612-595-0229. Ed. Alan Rosenauer. circ. 1,600.

OCCUPATIONAL COMPENSATION SUMMARIES. see *BUSINESS AND ECONOMICS — Economic Situation And Conditions*

OCCUPATIONAL COMPENSATION SURVEYS. see *BUSINESS AND ECONOMICS — Economic Situation And Conditions*

OCCUPATIONAL ERGONOMICS. see *OCCUPATIONAL HEALTH AND SAFETY*

331   US   ISSN 0198-7771
HD7262.5.U62
OCCUPATIONAL INJURIES & ILLNESSES IN MAINE. (Subseries of: Maine. Bureau of Labor Standards. B L S Bulletins) a. free. Department of Labor, Bureau of Labor Standards, Division of Research & Statistics, 45 State House Station, Augusta, ME 04333-0045. TEL 207-624-6440. FAX 207-624-6449. E-mail: webmaster_bls@state.me.us. Ed. Robert W. Leighton, Jr. circ. 550. **Document type:** government publication.
  Description: Data collected from the survey of occupational injuries and illnesses.

OCCUPATIONAL PENSIONS. see *INSURANCE*

OCCUPATIONAL PENSIONS LAW REPORTS. see *INSURANCE*

331.1   PL   ISSN 0029-8220
OCHRONA PRACY. (Text in Polish; summaries in English and Russian) 1947. m. $20.50. (Naczelna Organizacja Techniczna) Wydawnictwo Czasopism i Ksiazek Technicznych SIGMA - NOT, Ul. Ratuszowa 11, P.O. Box 1004, 00-950 Warsaw, Poland. TEL 48-22-180918. FAX 48-22-192187. TELEX 814550 SIGMA PL. (Dist. by: SIGMA NOT Ltd., Ul. Bartycka 20, 00-716 Warsaw, Poland) (Co-sponsor: Panstwowa Inspekcja Pracy) adv.; bk.rev.; bibl.; illus.; pat.; index. circ. 7,550. **Indexed:** AgroLibrex, C.I.S. Abstr., Chem.Abstr.
  Description: Covers work safety and hygiene, labor medicine.

331.11   CL   ISSN 0716-4521
OCUPACION Y DESOCUPACION EN EL GRAN SANTIAGO. q. Universidad de Chile, Facultad de Ciencias Economicas y Administrativas, Av. Ranacagua 257, Santiago, Chile. TEL 2228521. charts; stat.

OFFICIAL DISABILITY GUIDELINES. see *INSURANCE*

OHIO EMPLOYMENT LAW LETTER. see *LAW*

331.11   US
OHIO LABOR MARKET INFORMATION: LABOR MARKET REVIEW. 1983. m. free. Ohio Bureau of Employment Services, Labor Market Information Division, Box 1618, Columbus, OH 43216. TEL 614-752-9494. FAX 614-752-9621. Dir. Keith Ewald. circ. 3,000. **Indexed:** SRI. **Document type:** government publication.

OKHRANA TRUDA I SOTSIAL'NOE STRAKHOVANIE. see *INSURANCE*

331   US
OKLAHOMA. EMPLOYMENT SECURITY COMMISSION. RESEARCH DIVISION. ANNUAL REPORT TO THE GOVERNOR. 1939. a. free. Employment Security Commission, Research Department, Will Rogers Bldg., 2401 N. Lincoln Blvd., Oklahoma City, OK 73105. Ed. Arthur Jordan. charts; stat. circ. 1,200. **Document type:** government publication.
  Formerly: Oklahoma. Employment Security Commission. Research and Planning Division. Annual Report to the Governor.

OKLAHOMA EMPLOYMENT LAW LETTER. see *LAW*

331.8 322.4   US
ON THE LINE (NEW YORK). 1978. 6/yr. $5 to individuals (foreign $10); libraries and institutions $15. Workers Solidarity Alliance, New York Area Group, 339 Lafayette St., Rm. 202, New York, NY 10012. TEL 212-979-8353. Ed. Mike Harris. bk.rev. circ. 200. (back issues avail.) **Document type:** newsletter.
  Former titles (until 1994): East European News; (until 1989): On the Line (New York).
  Description: Covers labor and anarchist issues.

ONDERNEMERS-SIGNAAL SOCIALE ZEKERHEID; nieuwsmagazine over de gevolgen van privatisering voor het MKB. see *INSURANCE*

BUSINESS AND ECONOMICS — LABOR AND INDUSTRIAL RELATIONS

331 CN ISSN 0711-849X
KEO641.A72
ONTARIO. LABOUR RELATIONS BOARD. ANNUAL REPORT. 1980. a. free. Labour Relations Board, 400 University Ave., Toronto, ON M7A 1V4, Canada. TEL 416-965-4151. FAX 416-326-7531. TELEX 06218387. circ. 1,150. **Document type:** government publication.

331 CN ISSN 0383-4778
KEO636.4
ONTARIO. LABOUR RELATIONS BOARD. REPORTS. A MONTHLY SERIES OF DECISIONS. 1944. m. Can.$67.50. Labour Relations Board, 400 University Ave., Toronto, ON M7A 1V4, Canada. TEL 416-965-4151. FAX 416-326-7531. Ed. Ron Lebi. circ. 1,200. (also avail. in microfiche) **Document type:** government publication.
● Also available online. Vendor(s): QL Systems Ltd.
Formerly: Ontario. Labour Relations Board. Decisions (ISSN 0472-9986)

ONTARIO EDUCATION RELATIONS COMMISSION. ANNUAL REPORT. see EARTH SCIENCES

331 CN
ONTARIO LABOUR RELATIONS BOARD LAW AND PRACTICE. 2nd ed., 1985. base vol. (plus s-a. updates). $395 (effective 1997). Butterworths Canada Ltd., 75 Clegg Rd., Markham, ON L6G 1A1, Canada. TEL 905-479-2665. FAX 905-479-2826. (Editorial addr.: 20 Dundas St. W., Ste. 1130, Box 180, Toronto, ON M5G 2G8, Canada. TEL 416-977-6070) Ed. Kim Brewster. circ. 400 (paid). (looseleaf format)
Description: Directed mainly at lawyers. Contains legislation and jurisprudence concerning labor relations in Ontario insofar as that law is administered by the Labour Relations Board.

ONTARIO PAY & EMPLOYMENT EQUITY GUIDE. see LAW — Corporate Law

ONTSLAGZAKBOEKJE. see LAW — Civil Law

331.4 BE ISSN 0078-5164
OPEN DOOR INTERNATIONAL FOR THE EMANCIPATION OF THE WOMAN WORKER. REPORT OF CONGRESS. 1929. irreg., 1966, 13th, London. free. Open Door International, 16 rue Americain, B-1050 Brussels, Belgium. Ed. Adele Hauwel. (also avail. in microfilm from AMP)

OREGON EMPLOYMENT LAW LETTER. see LAW

331 YU ISSN 0471-9506
ORGANIZACIJA RADA. (Issued also as part of Tehnika) (Text in Serbo-Croatian; summaries in English, Russian) m. $50. Savez Inzenjera i Tehnicara Jugoslavije, Kneza Milosa 9, Box 187, 11000 Belgrade, Yugoslavia. Ed. Vuksan Bulat. **Indexed:** Ergon.Abstr.

331 US
OUTLOOK (WASHINGTON). 1963. q. free. American Institute for Free Labor Development, 1925 K. St., N.W., Washington, DC 20006. TEL 202-659-6300. FAX 202-778-6352. URL: http://www.aifld.org. Ed. David Jessup. illus. circ. 3,500. **Document type:** newsletter.
Formerly (until 1992): A I F L D Report (ISSN 0001-1576)

P E I T F NEWSLETTER. (Prince Edward Island Teachers Federation) see EDUCATION

P E R B NEWS. (Public Employment Relations Board) see PUBLIC ADMINISTRATION

PAKISTAN LABOUR CASES; a monthly law journal containing cases on service laws and labour laws. see LAW

334.01
PARKER'S CALIFORNIA LABOR CODE. a. $32 (diskette $45). Michie, A Division of Reed Elsevier Inc., Box 7587, Charlottesville, VA 22906-7587. TEL 804-972-7566; 800-562-1197. FAX 800-643-1280. E-mail: custserv@michie.com; URL: http://www.michie.com. Ed. George Harley. (also avail. in diskette format)

331 FR
PARTICIPATION. (Supplement to: France. Ministere des Affaires Sociales et de la Solidarite Nationale. Bulletin Mensuel des Statistiques du Travail) irreg. (Ministere des Affaires Sociales et de la Solidarite Nationale, Service des Etudes et de la Statistique Travail-Emploi) Documentation Francaise, 124 rue Henri Barbusse, 93308 Aubervilliers, France.
Description: Statistical information relevant to employment, finances and shareholding.

PAY AND BENEFITS BULLETIN. see BUSINESS AND ECONOMICS — Personnel Management

331 614 UK
PAY FOR SENIOR MANAGERS IN THE N H S. a. £250 (effective 1997). (Institute of Health Service Managers) The Reward Group Ltd., Reward House, Diamond Way, Stone Business Park, Stone, Staffordshire ST15 OSD, England. TEL 44-1785-813566. FAX 44-1785-817007. E-mail: 101364.661@compuserve.com. **Document type:** bulletin.

331 US
PAYROLL ADMINISTRATION GUIDE. 1990. bi-w. $495. The Bureau of National Affairs, Inc., 1231 25th St., N.W., Washington, DC 20037. TEL 202-452-4200. FAX 202-822-8092. TELEX 285656 BNAI WSH. URL: http://www.bna.com/. (Subscr. to: 9435 Key West Ave., Rockville, MD 20850. TEL 800-372-1033) Ed. Roslyn Rosenberg. **Document type:** newsletter.
● Also available online. Vendor(s): Human Resources Information Network (File DD).
Description: Notification and reference service for payroll managers. Covers federal and state employment tax, wage-hour, and wage-payment laws.

331 US
PAYROLL ADMINISTRATION GUIDE NEWSLETTER. 1990. bi-w. $98. The Bureau of National Affairs, Inc., 1231 25th St., N.W., Washington, DC 20037. TEL 202-452-4200. FAX 202-822-8092. TELEX 285656 BNAI WSH. URL: http://www.bna.com/. (Subscr. to: 0435 Key West Ave., Rockville, MD 20850. TEL 800-372-1033) Ed. Roslyn Rosenberg. (back issues avail.) **Document type:** newsletter.
● Also available online. Vendor(s): Human Resources Information Network (File DD).
Description: For payroll professionals. Covers federal and state employment tax, wage-hour, and wage-payment laws.

331.2 US ISSN 1063-9047
PAYTECH. 1978. bi-m. $125 includes membership. American Payroll Association, 30 E. 33rd St., 5th fl., New York, NY 10016. TEL 212-686-2030. FAX 212-686-2789. Ed. Eileen Anderson. adv. circ. 9,000.
— KR SourceOne.
Formerly (until 1992): Payroll Exchange (ISSN 0194-6196)
Description: Serves professionals within the payroll and human resource industries by providing current information on tax legislation and innovations in payroll systems and processing procedures.

331 US
PENNSYLVANIA. LABOR RELATIONS BOARD. ANNUAL REPORT. 1937. a. free. Department of Labor and Industry, 1601 Labor & Industry Bldg., Seventh & Forster Sts., Harrisburg, PA 17120. TEL 717-787-1091. Ed. Patricia A. Crawford. charts; stat. circ. 1,000. **Document type:** government publication.
Formerly: Pennsylvania. Labor Relations Board. Report.
Description: Provides statistical information on the Board's case load and case processing activities, a summary of Board final orders and court decisions.

PENNSYLVANIA EMPLOYMENT LAW LETTER. see LAW

331.2 NE ISSN 0031-4854
PENSIOEN BULLETIN. 1961. bi-m. fl.85. Consultas N.V., Dr. van Deenweg 34, P.O. Box 70, 8000 AB Zwolle, Netherlands. TEL 31-38-4550400. FAX 31-38-4550200. E-mail: consultas@compuserve.com. (Co-sponsor: A B N Amro Bank) Ed. J. Bosman. bk.rev.; index. circ. 1,200. (looseleaf format) **Document type:** bulletin.

344.01 331.252 NE ISSN 1382-4015
▼**PENSIOEN JURISPRUDENTIE.** 1995. 10/yr. fl.300 (effective 1996). Uitgeverij Fed bv (Subsidiary of: Wolters Kluwer N.V.), Postbus 23, 7400 GA Deventer, Netherlands. TEL 31-570-633155. FAX 31-570-633834. Eds. E. Lutjens, J.Th.L. Brouwer. (back issues avail.) **Document type:** trade publication.
Description: Covers developments affecting pension management and administration, including recent jurisprudence, civil, social and tax law issues.

331.252 NE
▼**PENSIOEN MONOGRAFIEEN.** 1995. irreg., no.3, 1995. price varies. Uitgeverij Fed bv (Subsidiary of: Wolters Kluwer N.V.), Postbus 23, 7400 GA Deventer, Netherlands. TEL 31-570-633155. FAX 31-570-633834. (back issues avail.) **Document type:** monographic series.

331.252 NE ISSN 1383-3693
▼**PENSIOEN PASPOORT.** 1995. a. fl.14.95 (effective 1996). Uitgeverij Fed bv (Subsidiary of: Wolters Kluwer N.V.), Postbus 23, 7400 GA Deventer, Netherlands. TEL 31-570-633155. FAX 31-570-633834. Eds. E. Frans, W. de Haan. **Document type:** trade publication.

331.252 NE ISSN 0929-8681
PENSIOENBRIEF. 1993. every 3 wks. fl.204 (effective 1996). Uitgeverij Fed bv (Subsidiary of: Wolters Kluwer N.V.), Postbus 23, 7400 GA Deventer, Netherlands. TEL 31-570-633155. FAX 31-570-633834. Ed. P. Kavelaars. (back issues avail.) **Document type:** newsletter.

331.252 NE ISSN 1383-617X
▼**PENSIOENGIDS.** 1995. a. fl.80 (effective 1996). Uitgeverij Fed bv (Subsidiary of: Wolters Kluwer N.V.), Postbus 23, 7400 GA Deventer, Netherlands. TEL 31-570-633155. FAX 31-570-633834. Eds. L.G.M. Stevens, G.J.B. Dietvorst. **Document type:** trade publication.

PENSION PLAN GUIDE. see INSURANCE

PENSIONS LAW REPORTS; the key pensions cases without delay. see BUSINESS AND ECONOMICS — Personnel Management

331 UK ISSN 0965-5409
PENSIONS POCKET BOOK. 1989. a. £17.50. (Bacon & Woodrow) N T C Publications Ltd., Farm Rd., Henley-on-Thames, Oxfordshire RG9 1EJ, England. TEL 01491-411000. FAX 01491-571188. **Document type:** bulletin.

PERIODIEK VOOR SOCIALE VERZEKERING, SOCIALE VOORZIENING EN ARBEIDSRECHT. see INSURANCE

331.1 658.3 GW ISSN 0031-5605
HD28
PERSONAL; Zeitschrift fuer Human Resource Management. 1948. m. DM.330 (effective 1996). Wirtschaftsverlag Bachem GmbH, Ursulaplatz 1, 50668 Cologne, Germany. TEL 49-221-1619224. FAX 49-221-1619231. Ed. Hans-J. Schneider. adv.: B&W page DM.2400, color page DM.4800; trim 166 x 271. bk.rev.; bibl.; charts; illus.; mkt.; index, cum.index. circ. 4,500. (reprint service avail. from SCH) **Indexed:** C.I.S. Abstr., Key to Econ.Sci., Manage.Abstr. **Document type:** trade publication.
— BLDSC (6427.800000); SWETS. **CCC.**
Formerly: Mensch und Arbeit.

PERSONAL INJURY DAMAGE ASSESSMENTS IN ALBERTA. see LAW

PERSONAL INJURY DAMAGE ASSESSMENTS IN BRITISH COLUMBIA. see LAW

THE PERSONNEL ALERT (RAMSEY). see BUSINESS AND ECONOMICS — Personnel Management

PERSONNEL IN PRACTICE. see BUSINESS AND ECONOMICS — Personnel Management

331 658.3 UK ISSN 0964-2668
PERSONNEL REWARDS. 1991. a. £250 (effective 1997). The Reward Group Ltd., Reward House, Diamond Way, Stone Business Park, Stone, Staffordshire ST15 OSD, England. TEL 44-1785-813566. FAX 44-1785-817007. E-mail: 101364.661@compuserve.com. **Document type:** bulletin.
Description: Salary survey for personnel departments based on over 8,500 job recordings.

BUSINESS AND ECONOMICS — LABOR AND INDUSTRIAL RELATIONS

PERSONNEL TODAY. see *BUSINESS AND ECONOMICS — Personnel Management*

PETROLEO Y SOCIEDAD. see *PETROLEUM AND GAS*

331.86   PH
HD6958.5
PHILIPPINE JOURNAL OF LABOR AND INDUSTRIAL RELATIONS. 1978. s-a. P.200 (foreign $24). University of the Philippines, School of Labor and Industrial Relations, Diliman, Quezon City 1101, Philippines. TEL 99-63-96. FAX 632-98-83-40. Ed. Marie E. Aganon. adv.; bk.rev.; index. circ. 200. Indexed: Ind.Phil.Per.
   Supersedes: Philippine Journal of Industrial Relations (ISSN 0115-6373); A L E C Report (ISSN 0001-1762); Asian Labor Education Center. Labor Review.
   Description: Promotes discussion and research on labor and industrial relations using a multidisciplinary approach.

331   US
PHILIPPINE LABOR ALERT. 1984. q. $10 to individuals; institutions $15. Philippine Workers Support Committee, 2252 Puna St., Honolulu, HI 96817. TEL 808-595-7362. Ed. John Witeck. R&P contact: John Witeck. adv.; bk.rev. circ. 1,000. (back issues avail.) **Document type:** newsletter.
   Description: News and analysis of the Philippine workers' movement. Seeks to foster solidarity between North American workers and unions and their counterparts in the Philippines.

331   PH   ISSN 0115-2629
HD8712
PHILIPPINE LABOR REVIEW. 1976. s-a. $25. Department of Labor and Employment, Institute for Labor Studies, 5th Fl., Dole Bldg., Muralla & Gen. Luna Sts., Intramuros, Manila, Philippines. TEL 47-52-96. FAX 5301014. Ed. Ronald S. Abrigo. bk.rev. circ. 1,000. Indexed: Ind.Phil.Per.
   Description: Contains papers on labor and employment, the economy, industry, and other labor-related topics.

PHILIPPINES. BUREAU OF LABOR AND EMPLOYMENT STATISTICS. CURRENT LABOR STATISTICS. see *BUSINESS AND ECONOMICS — Abstracting, Bibliographies, Statistics*

PHILIPPINES. BUREAU OF LABOR AND EMPLOYMENT STATISTICS. LABOR AND EMPLOYMENT STATISTICAL REPORT. see *BUSINESS AND ECONOMICS — Abstracting, Bibliographies, Statistics*

PHILIPPINES. BUREAU OF LABOR AND EMPLOYMENT STATISTICS. OCCUPATIONAL WAGES SURVEY. see *BUSINESS AND ECONOMICS — Abstracting, Bibliographies, Statistics*

331.1   PH   ISSN 0031-787X
PHILIPPINES LABOR RELATIONS JOURNAL.* vol.3, 1970. m. P.36($36) 40 Gasan St., Quezon City D-502, Philippines. Ed. Samson S. Alcantara.

331   US
PIERCE MEMORIAL LECTURESHIP AND CONFERENCE SERIES. 1963. irreg. price varies. (New York State School of Industrial and Labor Relations) I L R Press, Cornell University Press, 512 E. State St., Ithaca, NY 14850. TEL 607-277-2338; 800-666-2211. Ed. Frances Benson. R&P contact: Clare Wellnitz. adv. contact: Heidi Marschner. **Document type:** academic/scholarly publication.

PLAN; tidsskrift for regional utvikling, arbeidsmarked og samfunnsplanlegging. see *BUSINESS AND ECONOMICS — Economic Situation And Conditions*

331   US   ISSN 1077-1816
HD7105.45.U6
PLAN SPONSOR. 1993. m. Asset International, Inc., 125 Greenwich Ave., Greenwich, CT 06830. TEL 203-629-5014. FAX 203-629-5024. adv.: B&W page $7810, color page $10580; trim 8 1/4 x 10 7/8; adv. contact: Charles Ruffel. circ. 30,000. **Document type:** trade publication.
—KR SourceOne. **CCC.**
   Description: Edited for institutional investors focusing on the role of public and corporate pension funds, insurance companies, bank trust departments, and other large institutions.

PLANNING GUIDE: STATEWIDE AND NINE SERVICE DELIVERY AREAS INCLUDING BRIDGEPORT - NORWALK - STAMFORD - VALLEY. see *BUSINESS AND ECONOMICS — Economic Situation And Conditions*

PLANT SHUTDOWNS DIRECTORY. see *BUSINESS AND ECONOMICS — Management*

POLICE DEPARTMENT DISCIPLINARY LAW BULLETIN. see *CRIMINOLOGY AND LAW ENFORCEMENT*

POLICE OFFICER GRIEVANCES BULLETIN. see *CRIMINOLOGY AND LAW ENFORCEMENT*

731   US
POLICIES, PRACTICES, AND EMPLOYEE BENEFITS SURVEY. a. $550. MidAtlantic Employers' Association, Box 770, Valley Forge, PA 19482. FAX 215-666-7866.
   Description: Provides information regarding more than 400 personnel practices and benefits policies of 350 companies in PA, NJ, MD, and DE.

331 320   IT   ISSN 0394-7475
POLITICHE DEL LAVORO. 1986. 3/yr. L.75000 (foreign L.90000) (effective 1993). Franco Angeli Editore, Viale Monza, 106, Casella Postale 17175, 20100 Milan, Italy. TEL 02-2895762.

331   US
PORTLAND LABOR TRENDS. m. free. Oregon Employment Division, 875 Union St., N.E., Salem, OR 97311. TEL 503-378-8657. FAX 503-373-7515. stat. circ. 2,600. (back issues avail.) **Document type:** newsletter, government publication.
   Formerly: Portland Metropolitan Labor Trends.
   Description: Describes and analyzes labor force and economic trends in the greater Portland area.

331   PO
PORTUGAL. MINISTERIO DO TRABALHO. BOLETIM. 26/yr. Ministerio do Trabalho, Praca de Londres 2 r-c, 1000 Lisbon, Portugal. TEL 847-00-10.

331.11   PO
PORTUGAL. MINISTERIO DO TRABALHO. SERVICO DE INFORMACAO CIENTIFICA E TECNICA. BOLETIM DO TRABALHO E EMPREGO. irreg. Esc.600. Ministerio do Trabalho, Servico de Informacao Cientifica e Tecnica, Praca de Londres 2 r-c, 1000 Lisbon, Portugal.

331   XR   ISSN 0032-6208
PRACE A MZDA.* 1953. 13/yr. $27.90. Vydavatelstvi a Nakladatelstvi Prace, s r.o., Vaclavske nam. 17, 112 58 Prague 1, Czech Republic. Ed. Sandze Stepanov. bk.rev.; charts; stat.; index.

PRAKTIJK SOCIAAL RECHT. see *LAW — Civil Law*

331.2 614.85   CN
PREVENTION AT WORK. 6/yr. free. Workers' Compensation Board, Communications Department, P.O. Box 5350, Stn. Terminal, Vancouver, BC V6B 5L5, Canada. TEL 604-279-7572. FAX 604-279-7406. URL: http://www.wcb.bc.ca. Ed. Kathy Eccles. R&P contact: Dawn Knoll. circ. 25,000. (back issues avail.) **Document type:** newspaper, government publication.
●Also available online.
   Formerly: W C B News (ISSN 0825-2580)
   Description: Provides information on workplace health and safety in BC, as well as information on policies and operations of the WCB.

331 340   US   ISSN 0272-0574
KF3408.Z9
PRIMER OF LABOR RELATIONS. irreg., 25th ed., 1994. $45. B N A Books (Subsidiary of: The Bureau of National Affairs, Inc.), 1231 25th St., N.W., Washington, DC 20037. TEL 202-833-7470. FAX 202-833-7490. E-mail: books@bna.com. (Subscr. to: BNA Books Distribution Center, 130 Campus Dr., Box 7816, Edison, NJ 08818-7816. TEL 800-960-1220. FAX 908-417-0482) Eds. John J. Kenny, Linda G. Kahn.
   Description: Explores basic federal labor legislation and policies, as interpreted by the courts and the National Labor Relations Board.

331 340   US
PRIMER ON EMPLOYEE RETIREMENT INCOME SECURITY ACT. (Subseries of: Legal Primer Series) irreg., 4th ed., 1993. $45. B N A Books (Subsidiary of: The Bureau of National Affairs, Inc.), 1231 25th St., N.W., Washington, DC 20037. TEL 202-833-7470. FAX 202-833-7490. E-mail: books@bna.com. (Subscr. to: BNA Books Distribution Center, 130 Campus Dr., Box 7816, Edison, NJ 08818-7816. TEL 800-960-1220. FAX 908-417-0482) Ed. Barbara J. Coleman.
   Description: Reviews ERISA's provisions on pension, health care, disability, and accident plans; examines parts of the Internal Revenue Code; and clarifies exemptions, plan funding, protection, and termination.

331   CN
HD8101.5.P75
PRINCE EDWARD ISLAND. DEPARTMENT OF PROVINCIAL AFFAIRS. ANNUAL REPORT. 1967. a. free. Department of Provincial Affairs, Box 2000, Charlottetown, PE C1A 7N8, Canada. Ed. Douglas Carr. circ. 250. **Document type:** government publication.
   Supersedes in part (in 1985): Prince Edward Island. Department of Fisheries and Labor. Annual Report (ISSN 0833-5869); Which was formed by the 1984 merger of: Prince Edward Island. Department of Fisheries. Annual Report (ISSN 0079-5143); Prince Edward Island. Labour Division. Annual Report (ISSN 0833-5850); Formerly (until 1982): Prince Edward Island. Department of Labor. Annual Report (ISSN 0085-512X); Supersedes in part (in 1971): Prince Edward Island. Department of Labour, Industry and Commerce. Annual Report (ISSN 0380-3007); Which was formerly (until 1970): Prince Edward Island. Department of Labour and Manpower Resources. Annual Report.
   Description: Provides annual reporting of the activities of the department; includes list of employees, organization chart, acts administered.

331.1   ISSN 0079-5305
PRINCETON UNIVERSITY. INDUSTRIAL RELATIONS SECTION. RESEARCH REPORT. 1926. irreg., no.124, 1984. price varies. Princeton University, Industrial Relations Section, Firestone Library, Princeton, NJ 08544. TEL 609-258-4040. circ. 1,000. **Document type:** academic/scholarly publication.
   Formerly: Princeton University. Industrial Relations Section. Research Series.

331 368   US
PRIVATE PENSION PLAN BULLETIN. irreg., no.4, 1995. U.S. Department of Labor, Pension and Welfare Benefits Administration, 200 Constitution Ave., N.W., Washington, DC 20216. TEL 202-523-8921. **Document type:** government publication, bulletin.
   Description: Abstract of Form 5500 annual reports.

PRODUCER PRICE INDEXES. see *BUSINESS AND ECONOMICS — Economic Situation And Conditions*

331   US
PRODUCTION, MAINTENANCE AND SERVICE SURVEY. a. $405. MidAtlantic Employers' Association, Box 770, Valley Forge, PA 19482. TEL 215-666-7330. FAX 215-666-7866.
   Description: Offers comparative information about 86 production, maintenance and service position compensation practices, including salary information among 205 companies, representing 10,100 employees throughout PA, NJ, MD, and DE.

PRODUCTIVITY BY INDUSTRY (YEAR). see *BUSINESS AND ECONOMICS — Economic Situation And Conditions*

PRODUCTIVITY MEASURES FOR SELECTED INDUSTRIES. see *BUSINESS AND ECONOMICS — Economic Situation And Conditions*

PROFESSIONAL AND OCCUPATIONAL LICENSING DIRECTORY. see *OCCUPATIONS AND CAREERS*

331.2   US   ISSN 1042-4482
HD4965.C2
PROFESSIONAL, SALES & TECHNICAL REMUNERATION, CANADA. 1986. a. (Executive Compensation Service (ECS)) Wyatt Data Services, 218 Rte. 17, N., Roselle Park, NJ 07662-9832. TEL 201-843-1177. FAX 201-843-0101. **Document type:** trade publication.

BUSINESS AND ECONOMICS — LABOR AND INDUSTRIAL RELATIONS

331   CN   ISSN 0709-5597
HD4965.C2
PROFESSIONAL, SCIENTIFIC, TECHNICAL REMUNERATION, CANADA.* 1978. a. Can.$225. Canadian Management Centre, 150 York St., Toronto, ON M5H 3S5, Canada.
TEL 416-593-4600.

PROFIT SHARING. see BUSINESS AND ECONOMICS — Investments

PSICOLOGIA E LAVORO. see PSYCHOLOGY

331   US
PUBLIC EMPLOYEE DISCIPLINE & TERMINATIONS LAW BULLETIN. m. $60. Quinlan Publishing Co., Inc., 23 Drydock Ave., 2nd Fl., Boston, MA 02210-2387. TEL 617-542-0048; 800-229-2084.
FAX 617-345-9646. index. (back issues avail.) **Document type:** newsletter.
—UMI. **CCC.**
  Formed by the 1992 merger of: Public Employee Terminations Law Bulletin & Municipal Worker Law Bulletin (ISSN 0893-8172); Which was formerly (until 1987): Public Employee Law Bulletin (ISSN 0739-9294)
  Description: Covers case summaries on employee's rights during termination, discrimination, employee classification, union disputes and more.

331   US   ISSN 1071-1732
PUBLIC EMPLOYMENT LAW NOTES. m. $295. Nyper Publications, Box 662, Latham, NY 12110.
TEL 518-786-1654. FAX 518-456-8582. URL: http://www.nyper.com.
  Description: Summarizes court and administrative decisions concerning public employment.

331 346   US   ISSN 1043-8211
KF5336.A15
PUBLIC EMPLOYMENT LAW REPORT. 1989. m. $135 (foreign $155). Data Research, Inc., 4635 Nicols Rd., Ste. 100, Eagan, MN 55122-3337.
TEL 612-452-8267. FAX 612-452-8694. (Subscr. to: Box 490, Rosemount, MN 55068-9987. TEL 800-452-8267) cum.index. (looseleaf format; back issues avail.) **Document type:** newsletter.
  Description: Reports the latest court cases and late-breaking legislation along with the most recent law review articles affecting public employment.

331   US
PUBLIC EMPLOYMENT REPORTER. m. $95. Nyper Publications, Box 662, Latham, NY 12110.
TEL 518-786-1654. FAX 518-456-8582. URL: http://www.nyper.com.

331   AT
PUBLIC RELATIONS HANDBOOK FOR MANAGERS AND EXECUTIVES.* 1984. biennial. Aus.$19.50. Information Australia, 384 Flinders Lane, Melbourne, Vic. 3000, Australia. Ed. Jim Macnamara.

331.1 340   US
THE PUNCH LIST. q. $300. American Arbitration Association, 140 W. 51st St., New York, NY 10020-1203. TEL 212-484-4010.
FAX 212-541-4841. Ed. Ted Pons. circ. 14,000.
  Description: Addresses the concerns of the construction industry, and features insightful, practical articles for those involved in resolving disputes.

331.11   US
PURDUE UNIVERSITY. OFFICE OF MANPOWER STUDIES. MANPOWER & TECHNICAL EDUCATION REQUIREMENTS REPORTS. 1965. irreg. $3.50. Purdue University, Office of Manpower Studies, Knoy Hall, W. Lafayette, IN 47907. TEL 317-494-2559. FAX 317-494-0486. Ed. Kevin D. Shell. circ. controlled. **Indexed:** ERIC.
  Formerly: Purdue University. Office of Manpower Studies. Manpower Report (ISSN 0079-8134)

331 658   IT   ISSN 0390-105X
QUADERNI DI ECONOMIA DEL LAVORO. 1974? 3/yr. L.75000 (foreign L.90000) (effective 1993). Franco Angeli Editore, Viale Monza, 106, Casella Postale 17175, 20100 Milan, Italy.
TEL 02-2895762. Ed. Luigi Frey.

331.1   IT
QUADERNI ISRIL. 1970. q. L.56000 (foreign L.70000) (effective 1993). Franco Angeli Editore, Viale Monza 106, 20127 Milan, Italy. TEL 02-2827651. (Subscr. to: Via Piemonte 101, 00187 Rome, Italy) Ed. Giuseppe Bianchi. circ. 3,000.

331.11   US   ISSN 1049-8699
HD66   **CODEN:** QUDIFM
QUALITY DIGEST. 1981. m. $59. Q C I International, Box 1769, Chico, CA 95927-1769.
TEL 916-893-4095. FAX 916-893-0395. E-mail: qualitydigest@qualitydigest.com; URL: http://www.qualitydigest.com. Ed. Scott Paton. adv. contact: Joyce McClelland. bk.rev.; index. circ. 50,000. (back issues avail.) **Indexed:** BPIA, Oper.Res.Manage.Sci., Q.Abstr., Qual.Contr.Appl.Stat.
—BLDSC (7168.151800); SWETS. **CCC.**
  Formerly: Quality Circle Digest (ISSN 0278-2642)

331   CN   ISSN 0838-6609
HD8101
QUEEN'S UNIVERSITY. INDUSTRIAL RELATIONS CENTRE. QUEEN'S PAPERS IN INDUSTRIAL RELATIONS SERIES. 1987. irreg., no.95-2, 1995. Can.$10. Queen's University, Industrial Relations Centre, Kingston, ON K7L 3N6, Canada. TEL 613-545-6709.
FAX 613-545-6812. **Document type:** monographic series, academic/scholarly publication.

331   FR   ISSN 0984-1725
R C E: REVUE DES COMITES D'ENTREPRISE ET EQUIVALENTS.* (Supplement avail.: Lettre R C E - C G T (ISSN 1168-996X)) 1960. 5/yr. 110 F. Vie Ouvriere, 263 rue de Paris, case 600, 93516 Montreuil cedex, France. TEL 48-51-81-26. Ed. F. Marest. adv.; charts; illus.
  Former titles (until 1986): Revue des Comites d'Enterprise (ISSN 0249-9142); (until 1980): V C O (ISSN 0249-9134); (until 1966): Vie des Collectivites Ouvrieres (ISSN 0399-1156)

331   GW   ISSN 0033-6874
HD28   **CODEN:** REFNA9
R E F A NACHRICHTEN. 1948. bi-m. DM.72. R E F A - Verband fuer Arbeitsstudien und Betriebsorganisation e.V., Wittichstr. 2, 64295 Darmstadt, Germany. TEL 06151-8801-0. (Dist. by: Beuth Verlag GmbH, Burggrafenstr. 6, 10787 Berlin, Germany. TEL 030-2601-0. FAX 030-26011260) adv.; bk.rev.; charts. circ. 50,000. **Indexed:** C.I.S. Abstr., Excerp.Med. **Document type:** trade publication.
—UMI. **CCC.**
  Description: Technical articles and reports on the REFA organization for the study of work.

RAGGED EDGE. see HANDICAPPED

331   US
RATE RANGE SURVEY. a. $225. MidAtlantic Employers' Association, Box 770, Valley Forge, PA 19482.
TEL 215-666-7330. FAX 215-666-7866.
  Description: Summarizes rate range information of companies in PA, NJ, MD, and DE.

331 355.115   US
REGULAR.* 1934. q. $15. Regular Veterans Association, 5200 Wilkinson Blvd., Charlotte, NC 28208-5450. adv. circ. 20,000.
  Description: Provides information on pay compensation and medical benefits to veterans and military.

331.1 918.7   VE
RELACIONES DE TRABAJO. 1982. irreg., latest no.13. price varies. Asociacion de Relaciones de Trabajo (ART), Apdo. 5110, Naguanagua, Carabobo 2005, Venezuela. TEL 58-41-234780.
FAX 58-41-670676. Ed. Hector Lucena. circ. 1,000. **Document type:** monographic series.
  Supersedes: Revista Relaciones de Trabajo.

331.1   CN   ISSN 0034-379X
  CODEN: RLINE9
RELATIONS INDUSTRIELLES/INDUSTRIAL RELATIONS. (Text in English, French) 1945. 4/yr. Can.$28 (foreign $24) to individuals; institutions Can.$55 (foreign $48) (effective 1997). Laval University, Department of Industrial Relations, Cite Universitaire, Quebec, PQ G1K 7P4, Canada. TEL 418-656-2468. FAX 418-656-3175. Ed. Jean Sexton. adv.; bk.rev.; bibl.; charts; index, cum.index. circ. 2,800. (also avail. in microform from BNQ,MIM,UMI; reprint service avail. from UMI) **Indexed:** Amer.Hist.& Life (1963-1978), ASCA, BPIA, C.L.I., Can.B.P.I., Can.Per.Ind., Can.Wom.Per.Ind., Curr.Cont., Hist.Abstr. (1963-1978), Ind.Can.L.P.L., Int.Lab.Doc., L.R.I., Manage.Cont., Mar.Aff.Bibl., P.A.I.S.For.Lang.Ind., P.A.I.S., Pt.de Rep. (1983-), Sage Fam.Stud.Abstr., Sage Pub.Admin.Abstr., Sage Urb.Stud.Abstr., SSCI, Tr.& Indus.Ind., World Bibl.Soc.Sec. **Document type:** academic/scholarly publication.
—BLDSC (4461.120000); Genuine Article; KR SourceOne; SWETS; UMI.

331.2   CN   ISSN 0828-4547
HD7096.C2
REPORT ON THE ADMINISTRATION OF THE LABOUR ADJUSTMENT BENEFITS ACT/RAPPORT SUR L'APPLICATION DE LA LOI SUR LES PRESTATIONS D'ADAPTATION POUR LES TRAVAILLEURS. 1983. q. free. Labour Canada, Publications Distribution, Ottawa, ON K1A 0J2, Canada. TEL 819-994-0543. FAX 819-997-1664. circ. 1,000. **Document type:** government publication.
  Description: Reports on disbursement of income support payments to eligible workers in designated industries and regions.

331   UK
RESEARCH AND DEVELOPMENT REWARDS. 1982. a. £250 (effective 1997). The Reward Group Ltd., Reward House, Diamond Way, Stone Business Park, Stone, Staffordshire ST15 0SD, England.
TEL 44-1785-813566. FAX 44-1785-817007. **Document type:** bulletin.
  Formerly (until 1993): Research and Development Survey (ISSN 0954-8173)
  Description: Provides information on over 100 research, development and scientific jobs from research associations and research and development departments in the UK.

331   US   ISSN 0194-3057
HD4802
RESEARCH IN LABOR ECONOMICS. 1977. irreg., vol.15, 1996. $78.50. J A I Press Inc., 55 Old Post Rd., No. 2, Box 1678, Greenwich, CT 06830-1678. TEL 203-661-7602. FAX 203-661-0792. E-mail: jai@jaipress.com. (Subscr. in the UK and Europe to: JAI Press Ltd., 38 Tavistock St., Covent Garden, London WC2E 7PB, England. TEL 44-171-379-8834. FAX 44-171-379-8835) Ed. Solomon Polachek. **Document type:** monographic series.
—**CCC.**

RESEARCH IN THE SOCIOLOGY OF WORK. see SOCIOLOGY

331   UK
RETAIL REWARDS. a. £250 (effective 1997). The Reward Group Ltd., Reward House, Diamond Way, Stone Business Park, Stone, Staffordshire ST15 0SD, England. TEL 44-1785-813566.
FAX 44-1785-817007. E-mail: 101364.661@compuserve.com. **Document type:** bulletin.
  Description: Covers pay levels for all professional, management and technical jobs in the retail sector.

331.1   II
REVIEW OF EMPLOYMENT IN TAMIL NADU. (Text in English) q. Director of Employment and Training, Madras, India.
  Formerly: Review of Employment in Madras State.

BUSINESS AND ECONOMICS — LABOR AND INDUSTRIAL RELATIONS

331 UK ISSN 0969-4080
REVIEW OF EMPLOYMENT TOPICS. 1993. a. £15. Labour Relations Agency, Windsor House, 9-15 Bedford St., Belfast BT2 7NU, N. Ireland. TEL 44-1232-321442. FAX 44-1232-330827. Ed. Mary O'Brien. **Document type:** bulletin.
—BLDSC (7790.367000).
Description: Covers all issues relating to employment, with special interest in regional influences on industrial relations systems and comparative studies of Northern Ireland with other regions of Europe.
Refereed Serial

331.11 FR ISSN 0473-6788
REVIEWS OF MANPOWER AND SOCIAL POLICIES. 1963. irreg. Organization for Economic Cooperation and Development, 2 rue Andre-Pascal, 75775 Paris Cedex 16, France. (U.S. orders to: O.E.C.D. Publications and Information Center, 2001 L St., N.W., Ste. 650, Washington, D.C. 20036-4922. TEL 202-785-6323).

REVISTA DE DERECHO LABORAL. see *LAW*

REVISTA DE DIREITO DO TRABALHO (SAO PAULO). see *LAW*

331 VE ISSN 0034-8988
REVISTA DE TRABAJO. 1950-1963; resumed 1965. q. Ministerio del Trabajo, Servicio de Publicaciones, Torre Sur, Centro S. Bolivar, Caracas 1010, Venezuela. FAX 582-4838914. stat.

331.1 614.8 309 UN ISSN 0378-5548
REVISTA INTERNACIONAL DEL TRABAJO. (Editions in English, French, Spanish) 1930. q. 80 SFr.($64) (International Labour Organisation) I L O Publications, CH-1211 Geneva 22, Switzerland. TEL 41-22-799-6111. FAX 41-22-798-6358. TELEX 415647-ILO-CH. (Dist. in US by: I L O Publications Center, 49 Sheridan Ave., Albany, NY 12210. TEL 518-436-9686. FAX 518-436-7433) Ed. T. Lines. bk.rev.; bibl.; charts; index. circ. 1,200. (back issues avail.) **Indexed:** ELLIS, IBR, J.of Econ.Lit., P.A.I.S., Pers.Manage.Abstr. **Document type:** bulletin.
—CINDOC; SWETS.
Description: Covers aspects of labor, social policy, and administration. Directed to government, employer, and union circles.

REVISTA JURIDICA DEL TRABAJO. see *LAW*

331 MQ ISSN 0755-2742
REVOLUTION SOCIALISTE ANTILLES. (Text in Creole, French) 1973. w. 120 Fr. Groupe Revolution Socialiste, B.P. 1031, 97200 Fort-de-France, Martinique. TEL 703649. circ. 2,500.
Formerly (until 1976): Revolution Socialiste (ISSN 0755-2734)

331 344 FR ISSN 0997-7422
REVUE DE JURISPRUDENCE SOCIALE. 1989. m. 870 F. (effective 1997). Editions Francis Lefebvre, 42 rue de Villiers, 92300 Levallois, France. TEL 41-05-22-00. FAX 41-05-22-30.

331 BE ISSN 0035-2705
HD8501
REVUE DU TRAVAIL. Dutch edition: Arbeidsblad. 1896. q. 3000 BEF (effective Jan. 1991). Ministere de l'Emploi et du Travail, 53 rue Belliard, 1040 Brussels, Belgium. bk.rev.; bibl.; charts; stat.; index. circ. 1,250. (also avail. in microfiche from BHP) **Indexed:** C.I.S. Abstr., Int.Lab.Doc., P.A.I.S.For.Lang.Ind.
—BLDSC (7956.450000).
Description: Examines labour situation, laws and regulations.

331 361.3 HT ISSN 0482-8062
REVUE DU TRAVAIL. 1951. a. Departement du Travail et du Bien-Etre Social, Port-au-Prince, Haiti. stat. **Indexed:** P.A.I.S.For.Lang.Ind.

REVUE FRANCAISE DES AFFAIRES SOCIALES. see *SOCIOLOGY*

331.1 614.8 309 UN ISSN 0378-5599
REVUE INTERNATIONALE DU TRAVAIL. (Editions in English, French, Spanish) 1921. bi-m. 80 SFr.($64) (Bureau International du Travail - International Labour Organisation) I L O Publications, 4 route des Morillons, CH-1211 Geneva 22, Switzerland. TEL 41-22-799-6111. FAX 41-22-798-6358. TELEX 415647-ILO-CH. (Dist. in US by: I L O Publications Center, 49 Sheridan Ave., Albany, NY 12210. TEL 518-436-9686. FAX 518-436-7433) Ed. T. Lines. bk.rev.; bibl.; charts; index. circ. 2,400. (back issues avail.) **Indexed:** Bull.Signal., ELLIS, Int.Polit.Sci.Abstr., J.of Econ.Abstr., Pt.de Rep. (1979-). **Document type:** bulletin.
—SWETS.
Description: Covers aspects of labor, social policy, and administration. Directed to government, employer and labor circles.

331 658 UK
REWARD: THE MANAGEMENT SURVEY. 2/yr. £250 (effective 1997). The Reward Group Ltd., Reward House, Diamond Way, Stone Business Park, Stone, Staffordshire ST15 OSD, England. TEL 44-1785-813566. FAX 44-1785-817007. E-mail: 101364.661@compuserve.com. **Document type:** bulletin.
Description: Comprehensive salary survey containing data on over 180 management, administrative and technical jobs within the private and public sectors.

331.1 US
RHODE ISLAND. DEPARTMENT OF LABOR AND TRAINING. EMPLOYMENT BULLETIN. 1954. m. free. Department of Labor and Training, 101 Friendship St., Providence, RI 02903-3740. TEL 401-277-3706. FAX 401-277-2731. E-mail: rfitzgerald@dlt.state.ri.us; URL: http://www.dlt.state.ri.us. charts; stat. circ. 4,000. **Indexed:** SRI. **Document type:** government publication, academic/scholarly publication.
Former titles: Rhode Island. Department of Employment Security. Employment Bulletin; Rhode Island. Department of Labor and Employment Security. Employment Bulletin (ISSN 0035-4600)

RHODE ISLAND EMPLOYMENT LAW LETTER. see *LAW*

344.012 US
RHODE ISLAND WORKERS' COMPENSATION LAW. a. $25. Michie, A Division of Reed Elsevier Inc., Box 7587, Charlottesville, VA 22906-7587. TEL 804-972-7566; 800-562-1197. FAX 800-643-1280. E-mail: custserv@michie.com; URL: http://www.michie.com. Ed. George Harley.
Description: A reference for selected laws in the workers' compensation arena.

331 IS
RIVACHA VEAVADA. q. Havaad Hapoal, Hagaf Le'eigud Miktzoei, 93 Arlozov St., Tel Aviv 61 002, Israel. TEL 03-210322.

331 IT ISSN 0483-142X
RIVISTA DEL LAVORO. 1951. m. (Istituto de Studi Sul Lavoro) Edizioni del Lavoro s.r.l., Via G.B. Martini 6, 00198 Rome, Italy.

331.15 IT ISSN 1122-0147
RIVISTA DELL'ARBITRATO. 1961. q. Lit.110000 (foreign Lit.165000) (effective 1997). (Associazione Italiana per l'Arbitrato) Casa Editrice Dott. A. Giuffre, Via Busto Arsizio, 40, 20151 Milan, Italy. TEL 39-2-38089200. FAX 39-2-38009582. Ed. Elio Fazzalari. bk.rev.; index; circ. 1,500 (controlled).
Formerly (until 1990): Rassegna dell'Arbitrato (ISSN 0033-9415)

RIVISTA ITALIANA DI DIRITTO DEL LAVORO. see *LAW*

340 331 JA ISSN 0386-0639
RODO HO/JOURNAL OF LABOR LAW. (Text in Japanese) 1951. s-a. Japan Labour Law Association - Nihon Rodoho Gakkai, Tokyo University, Hongo, Bunkyo-ku, Tokyo 113, Japan.

331 UK ISSN 0261-5649
RUSKIN COLLEGE, OXFORD. LIBRARY. OCCASIONAL PUBLICATION. 1979. irreg. price varies. Ruskin College, Library, Oxford OX1 2HE, England. TEL 44-1865-554331. Ed. D. Horsfield. **Document type:** monographic series.
—BLDSC (8052.647700).

331.11 US
RUSSIAN LABOR REVIEW. q. $30 to individuals; institutions $50. Box 8461, Berkeley, CA 94707. TEL 510-489-8554. FAX 510-471-4454. Ed.Bd. **Indexed:** Left Ind.

331 340 GW ISSN 0048-9069
K2
S A E. (Sammlung Arbeitsrechtlicher Entscheidungen) 1948. 8/yr. DM.126.26. (Bundesvereinigung der Deutschen Arbeitgeberverbaende e.V.) Wirtschaftsverlag Bachem GmbH, Ursulaplatz 1, 50668 Cologne, Germany. TEL 49-221-1619224. FAX 49-221-1619231. Eds. Ernst-Guenther Mager, Christel Finke-Hollweg. bk.rev.; index. circ. 2,500. **Document type:** trade publication.
—CCC.

331.86 GW
S A L Z. 1986. bi-m. DM.70. Koordination Saarlaendischer Arbeitsloseninitiativen e.V., Gatterstr. 13, 66333 Voelklingen, Germany. TEL 06898-16590. circ. 2,000.

S K T F! TIDNINGEN. (Sveriges Kommunaltjaenstemannafoerbund) see *PUBLIC ADMINISTRATION — Municipal Government*

S P E E A SPOTLITE. (Seattle Professional Engineering Employees Association) see *LABOR UNIONS*

331 NE ISSN 0165-8131
S W JOURNAAL. (Sociale Werkvoorziening) 1971. 10/yr. fl.39. Nationaal Overlegorgaan Sociale Werkvoorziening, Karel Doormanlaan 155, 2283 AL Rijswijk, Netherlands. TEL 31-70-3360062. FAX 31-70-3360584. Ed. A. van Eijnsbergen. R&P contact: A. van Eijnsbergen. adv. (also avail. in Braille; audio cassette)
—SWETS.

331 US
SALARIES & BONUSES IN THE SERVICE DEPARTMENT. 1973. a. $310. (National Association of Service Managers) Abbott, Langer & Associates, 548 First St., Crete, IL 60417. TEL 708-672-2400. Ed. Steven Langer.
Formerly: Salaries and Related Matters in the Service Department.

SALARY BUDGET SURVEY. see *BUSINESS AND ECONOMICS — Personnel Management*

SALARY INCREASE SURVEY REPORT. see *OCCUPATIONS AND CAREERS*

331.2 378 US
SALARY SURVEY (YEARS) (ST. LOUIS). a. $25 (foreign $30) (effective 1995). American Assembly of Collegiate Schools of Business, 600 Emerson Rd., Ste. 300, St. Louis, MO 63141-6762. TEL 314-872-8481. FAX 314-872-8495. URL: http://www.aacsb.edu. R&P contact: Sharon Barber. circ. 1,000. **Indexed:** SRI.
Description: Lists aggregate salary data of business school administrators and faculty by rank within discipline, with further breakdowns by school status, such as accredited and non-accredited, public and private.

331 658 UK
SALES AND MARKETING SALARY SURVEY. a. £250 (effective 1997). (Chartered Institute of Marketing) The Reward Group Ltd., Reward House, Diamond Way, Stone Business Park, Stone, Staffordshire ST15 OSD, England. TEL 44-1785-813566. FAX 44-1785-817007. E-mail: 101364.661@compuserve.com. **Document type:** bulletin.
Description: Salary survey for sales and marketing departments covering jobs from director level to telesales jobs.

331 SZ
SCHWEIZER ARBEITGEBER/EMPLOYEUR SUISSE/IMPRENDITORE SVIZZERO. (Text in French, German, Italian) 1906. 2/m. 105 SFr. (effective 1997). Union Patronale Suisse - Confederation of Swiss Employers, Florastr. 44, CH-8034 Zurich, Switzerland. FAX 41-1-3833980. Eds. Alexandre Plassard, Hans Reis. adv.; bk.rev.; abstr.; charts; illus.; stat.; index. circ. 6,000. **Indexed:** C.I.S. Abstr., Key to Econ.Sci. **Document type:** newspaper.
Formerly (until 1994): Schweizerische Arbeitgeber-Zeitung (ISSN 0036-7516)
Description: Reports on the various positions taken by Swiss employers on various major social, economic and political matters.

BUSINESS AND ECONOMICS — LABOR AND INDUSTRIAL RELATIONS

331 943 UK ISSN 0586-7762
HD8399.S3
SCOTTISH LABOUR HISTORY SOCIETY. JOURNAL. 1969. a. Aberdeen Scottish Labour History Society, c/o Department of History, University of Strathclyde, McCance Bldg., 16 Richmond St., Glasgow G1 1XQ, Scotland. Ed. Ian S. Wood. **Indexed:** Amer.Hist.& Life (1978-), Hist.Abstr. (1978-).
—BLDSC (4874,100000).

331 UK
SECRETARIAL STAFF IN LONDON. 2/yr. £250 (effective 1997). The Reward Group Ltd., Reward House, Diamond Way, Stone Business Park, Stone, Staffordshire ST15 OSD, England. TEL 44-1785-813566. FAX 44-1785-817007. E-mail: 101364.661@compuserve.com. **Document type:** bulletin.
Description: Salary survey providing information on secretarial jobs based in London.

331 TH ISSN 0857-1163
SECRETARIES YEAR BOOK. (Text in English) 1976. a. Advertising and Media Consultants Ltd., Silom Condominium, 12th Fl., 52-38 Soi Saladaeng 2, Bangkok, Thailand. TEL 235-6186. FAX 236-6764. TELEX 82463 LOOKEAS TH. circ. 8,000.

331 BE
SECURITE AU TRAVAIL. 1982. 24/yr. 3735 BEF. C E D Samsom (Subsidiary of: Wolters Samsom Belgie n.v.), Kouterveld 14, B-1831 Diegem, Belgium. TEL 32-2-7231111.

331 CU
SERIE LEGISLACION LABORAL. m. Comite Estatal de Trabajo y Seguridad Social, 23 Calle O y P, Vedado Plaza, Havana, Cuba.

331 UK
SEVERNSIDE - SOUTH WALES SALARY SURVEY. 2/yr. £250 (effective 1997). The Reward Group Ltd., Reward House, Diamond Way, Stone Business Park, Stone, Staffordshire ST15 OSD, England. TEL 44-1785-813566. FAX 44-1785-817007. E-mail: 101364.661@compuserve.com. **Document type:** bulletin.
Description: Salary survey covering the mid Glamorgan, Gwent, South Glamorgan, Avon, Gloucestershire and North Wiltshire areas.

331 II
SHRAM PATRIKA. (Text in English) vol.4, 1974. q. Rs.8. Labour Commissioner, 15 Rajpur Rd., Delhi, India. charts; stat.

331.1 II
SHRAMJIVI. (Text in Hindi) m. Rs.18. Labour Department, Office of the Labour Commissioner, Box 220, Kanpur 208002, Uttar Pradesh, India. Eds. C.S. Saxena, Hemant K. Pant.

331 613 GW ISSN 0300-3337
SICHERHEITSBEAUFTRAGTER; Zeitschrift fuer Unfallverhuetung und Arbeitssicherheit. 1966. m. DM.56.40 (foreign DM.82.20) (effective 1996). Dr. Curt Haefner Verlag, Bachstr. 14-16, 69121 Heidelberg, Germany. TEL 49-6221-6446-0. FAX 49-6221-644640. (Subscr. to: Postfach 106060, 69050 Heidelberg, Germany) adv.; bk.rev.; abstr.; illus. circ. 40,000. **Document type:** bulletin.
—SWETS. **CCC.**

331 613 GW ISSN 0300-3329
SICHERHEITSINGENIEUR; Zeitschrift fuer Arbeitssicherheit. 1970. m. DM.136.80 (foreign DM.164.40) (effective 1996). Dr. Curt Haefner Verlag, Bachstr. 14-16, 69121 Heidelberg, Germany. TEL 49-6221-6446-0. FAX 49-6221-644640. (Subscr. to: Postfach 106060, 69050 Heidelberg, Germany) adv.; bk.rev.; abstr.; illus. circ. 6,000. **Indexed:** C.I.S. Abstr., Ergon.Abstr. **Document type:** bulletin.
—SWETS. **CCC.**

331 SI ISSN 0129-6310
SINGAPORE. MINISTRY OF LABOUR. ANNUAL REPORT. (Text in English) 1946. a. price varies. Ministry of Labour, Havelock Rd., Singapore 0105, Singapore. FAX 5344840. TELEX RS34364-LABOUR. Ed.Bd. charts; stat. circ. 1,100. **Document type:** government publication.

331.2 US ISSN 1059-1702
SMALL CORPORATION UPDATE; maximizing benefits for the small business owner. m. $96 (effective 1997). Harcourt Brace Professional Publishing, 525 B St., Ste. 1900, San Diego, CA 92101-4495. TEL 619-699-6716. FAX 619-699-6593. Ed. Dorinda DeScherer.
Description: Offers solutions to day-to-day business issues and focuses on the constantly changing laws affecting small businesses and introduces alternative, money-saving procedures.

331 340.5 BE
SOCIAAL COMPENDIUM ARBEIDSRECHT; arbeidsrecht met fiscale notities. (In 2 vols.) (Text in Dutch) 1991. biennial. 5670 BEF includes s-a. updates. Kluwer Rechtswetenschappen Belgie (Subsidiary of: Wolters Kluwer N.V.), Santvoortbeeklaan 21-25, 2100 Antwerp, Belgium. FAX 32-3-3600467. Ed. Willy van Eeckhoutte. **Document type:** trade publication.
Supersedes in part: Sociaal Compendium (ISSN 0778-5763)

331.1 NE ISSN 0037-7600
SOCIAAL MAANDBLAD ARBEID; tijdschrift voor sociaal recht en sociaal beleid. 1946. m. fl.164.50 (students fl.125). Samsom H.D. Tjeenk Willink B.V. (Subsidiary of: Wolters Kluwer N.V.), Postbus 316, 2400 AH Alphen aan den Rijn, Netherlands. TEL 31-1720-66822. FAX 31-1720-66639. Ed.Bd. adv.; bk.rev.; charts; stat.; index. circ. 930. **Indexed:** ELLIS, Key to Econ.Sci.
—BLDSC (8318.025000); SWETS.

SOCIAAL ZAKBOEKJE. see LAW — Civil Law

SOCIAALRECHTELIJKE KRONIEKEN/CHRONIQUE DE DROIT SOCIAL. see LAW — Civil Law

331 301 FR ISSN 0038-0296
HD4807
SOCIOLOGIE DU TRAVAIL. 1959. 4/yr. 345 F. to individuals (foreign 505 F.); institutions 550 F. (foreign 750 F.) (effective 1997). Dunod, 5 rue Laromiguiere, 75005 Paris, France. TEL 33-01-40-46-62-00. FAX 33-01-40-46-62-01. TELEX 634 916 F. (Subscr. to: Societe de Periodiques Specialises, B.P. 22-F, 41354 Vineuil Cedex, France. TEL 33-02-54-50-46-12. FAX 33-02-54-50-46-11) Ed. Annie Borzeix. charts; stat. (also avail. in microform from UMI; reprint service avail. from SCH,UMI) **Indexed:** Arts & Hum.Cit.Ind., ASCA, Curr.Cont., Excerp.Med., Int.Lab.Doc., Int.Polit.Sci.Abstr., Lang.& Lang.Behav.Abstr., P.A.I.S.For.Lang.Ind., SCIMP (1979-), Sociol.Abstr. (1961-), SSCI.
—BLDSC (8319.651000); Genuine Article; SWETS. **CCC.**
Description: Addresses all major problems of our industrial societies: growth, urbanization, health, justice, education, and new social moves. Includes papers that present the actual results of empirical research as well as theoretical studies, debates, notes and bibliographical analysis.

331 AU
SOLIDARITAET; die Illustrierte des Oe G B. 11/yr. membership. Oesterreichischer Gewerkschaftsbund, Hohenstaufengasse 10-12, A-1010 Vienna, Austria. TEL 43-1-534440. FAX 43-1-5335293. E-mail: presse@ugb.or.at. Ed. Anne-Marie Kramser. circ. 1,538,365. **Document type:** bulletin.

331 RU ISSN 0037-8216
HD4811
SOTSIALISTICHESKII TRUD. 1956. m. 12 Rub. Gosudarstvennyi Komitet Soveta Ministrov po Voprosam Truda i Zarabotnoi Platy, Pl. Kuibysheva 1, Moscow K-12, Russia. Ed. P.M. Loznevoi. bk.rev.; charts; illus.; index. circ. 65,000. **Indexed:** Int.Lab.Doc.

SOUTH AFRICA. UNEMPLOYMENT INSURANCE FUND. REPORT/SOUTH AFRICA. WERKLOOSHEIDVERSEKERINGSFONDS. VERSLAG. see INSURANCE

331 331.8 SA ISSN 0379-8410
HD8801.A5
SOUTH AFRICAN JOURNAL OF LABOUR RELATIONS. (Text in English) 1977. q. R.125.40 (foreign R.165). University of South Africa, Graduate School of Business Leadership, P.O. Box 392, Pretoria 0001, South Africa. TEL 27-11-6520343. FAX 27-11-6520299. Ed. B. Swanepoel. circ. 400. (back issues avail.) **Indexed:** Ind.S.A.Per. **Document type:** academic/scholarly publication.
Description: Features labor - industrial relations and related issues of interest to academics and practitioners.
Refereed Serial

331.096 SA ISSN 0377-5429
HD8799.S72
SOUTH AFRICAN LABOUR BULLETIN. 1974. 6/yr. R.95($70) to individuals; institutions R.220($120); companies R.540 (effective 1997). Umanyano Publications c.c., P.O. Box 3851, Johannesburg 2000, South Africa. TEL 27-11-4871603. FAX 27-11-4871508. Ed. Deanne Collins. adv.; bk.rev.; circ. 6,000 (paid). (also avail. in microfiche; reprint service avail.) **Indexed:** Documentatieblad, HR Rep. (1985-), Ind.S.A.Per. **Document type:** bulletin.
—BLDSC (8340.400000).
Description: Analyzes current developments in the South African labor movement. Attempts to reflect the constantly changing face of industrial relations in South Africa. Includes workplace issues, the political interface with unions, and international unionism.
Refereed Serial

331 340 SA ISSN 1022-8349
SOUTH AFRICAN LABOUR LIBRARY; cases, legislation and reference works. 1994. q. R.660. Juta & Co. Ltd., P.O. Box 14373, Kenwyn 7790, South Africa. TEL 27-21-7975101. FAX 27-21-7970121.
●Available only on CD-ROM.

310 331 US
SOUTH CAROLINA. DEPARTMENT OF LABOR. ANNUAL REPORT. 1936. a. free. Department of Labor, Box 11329, 3600 Forest Dr., Columbia, SC 29211. TEL 803-734-9600. Ed. James Knight. **Document type:** government publication.

SOUTH CAROLINA EMPLOYMENT LAW LETTER. see LAW

331 UK
SOUTH COAST SALARY SURVEY. 2/yr. £250 (effective 1997). The Reward Group Ltd., Reward House, Diamond Way, Stone Business Park, Stone, Staffordshire ST15 OSD, England. TEL 44-1785-813566. FAX 44-1785-817007. E-mail: 101364.661@compuserve.com. **Document type:** bulletin.
Description: Salary survey covering the West Sussex, East Sussex, Hampshire and East Kent areas.

331 US
SOUTH DAKOTA. DEPARTMENT OF LABOR. LABOR BULLETIN. 1949. m. free. Department of Labor, Labor Market Information Center, 420 S. Roosevelt, Box 4730, Aberdeen, SD 57402-4730. TEL 605-626-2314. Ed. Melodee Lane. R&P contact: Philip charts; stat. circ. 1,200. (back issues avail.) **Indexed:** SRI. **Document type:** government publication, bulletin.
Formerly: South Dakota. Department of Labor. Manpower Bulletin; Which superseded (in 1975): South Dakota Labor Bulletin.

SOUTH DAKOTA EMPLOYMENT LAW LETTER. see LAW

331 UK
SOUTH EAST MIDLANDS SALARY SURVEY. 2/yr. £250 (effective 1997). The Reward Group Ltd., Reward House, Diamond Way, Stone Business Park, Stone, Staffordshire ST15 OSD, England. TEL 44-1785-813566. FAX 44-1785-817007. E-mail: 101364.661@compuserve.com. **Document type:** bulletin.
Description: Salary survey covering the Bedfordshire, North Oxfordshire and North Buckinghamshire areas.

SOUTHERN COMMUNITIES. see HOUSING AND URBAN PLANNING

BUSINESS AND ECONOMICS — LABOR AND INDUSTRIAL RELATIONS

331 UK
SOUTH WEST SALARY SURVEY. 2/yr. £250 (effective 1997). The Reward Group Ltd., Reward House, Diamond Way, Stone Business Park, Stone, Staffordshire ST15 0SD, England. TEL 44-1785-813566. FAX 44-1785-817007. E-mail: 101364.661@compuserve.com. **Document type:** bulletin.
Description: Salary survey covering the Cornwall, Devon, Somerset, Dorset and South Wiltshire areas.

SOZIALES SEMINAR INFORMATIONEN; politisch-soziale Bildung in katholischer Traegerschaft. see *RELIGIONS AND THEOLOGY — Roman Catholic*

331 AU ISSN 0038-6197
SOZIALPOLITIK UND ARBEITSRECHT. 1950. bi-m. S.110 (foreign S.300). (Vereinigung der Oesterreichischen Industrie) Signum Verlag GmbH und Co. KG, Reisnerstr. 40, A-1030 Vienna, Austria. TEL 43-1-71195-0. Ed. Dr. Franz Dungl. R&P contact: Robert Grossmann. adv. contact: Doris Dinklage. bk.rev.; index. circ. 5,000. **Document type:** bulletin.
—BLDSC (8361.146500).

331 301 SP
SPAIN. MINISTERIO DE TRABAJO Y ASUNTOS SOCIALES. REVISTA. (In 5 series: Derecho del Trabajo, Seguridad Social, Legislacion Internal y U.E., Economia y Sociologia del Trabajo, Asuntos Sociales) m. (10/yr.). 17000 ptas. for all 5 series (effective 1997). Ministerio de Trabajo y Seguridad Social, Centro de Publicaciones, Agustin de Bethencourt, 11, 28003 Madrid, Spain. TEL 34-1-5543400. FAX 34-1-5540813. (Subscr. to: Mundi-Prensa Libros, S.A., Castello 37, 28001 Madrid, Spain. TEL 34-1-4313222. FAX 34-1-5753998) **Document type:** government publication.
—CINDOC.
Formerly (until 1997): Economia y Sociologia del Trabajo (ISSN 0214-6029)

SPARTACIST CANADA. see *POLITICAL SCIENCE — International Relations*

SPARTACO. see *POLITICAL SCIENCE*

331 US
SPENCER'S RESEARCH REPORTS ON EMPLOYEE BENEFITS. 1953. w. $585. Charles D. Spencer & Associates, Inc., 250 S. Wacker Dr., Ste. 600, Chicago, IL 60606-5834. TEL 312-993-7900. Ed. Seymour LaRock. bk.rev. (looseleaf format)
Formerly: E B P R Research Reports.

331 790.1 US
SPORTING GOODS MANUFACTURERS ASSOCIATION. EXECUTIVE COMPENSATION STUDY. a. Sporting Goods Manufacturers Association, 200 Castlewood Dr., N. Palm Beach, FL 33408. TEL 407-842-4100. Ed. Sebastian DiCasoli. **Document type:** trade publication.

331 790.1 US
SPORTING GOODS MANUFACTURERS ASSOCIATION. FINANCIAL PERFORMANCE STUDY. a. membership. Sporting Goods Manufacturers Association, 200 Castlewood Dr., N. Palm Beach, FL 33408. TEL 561-842-4100. Ed. Sebastian DiCasoli. **Document type:** trade publication.

SPROG OG ERHVERV. see *LABOR UNIONS*

331 CE ISSN 0379-3737
HD8670.8.A5
SRI LANKA LABOUR GAZETTE. (Editions in English, Sinhala) 1950. q. Rs.200($4) Ministry of Labour and Vocational Training, Labour Secretariat, Colombo 5, Sri Lanka. Ed. Sumanasiri Hulugalle. adv.; bk.rev.; stat.; index. circ. 1,500. **Indexed:** P.A.I.S., Sri Lanka Sci.Ind.
Formerly: Ceylon Labour Gazette (ISSN 0009-0859)

331.7 361 UK ISSN 0262-5172
STAFF OF SOCIAL SERVICES DEPARTMENTS. 1980. a. £5. Welsh Office, Statistical Directorate, Publication Unit, Cathays Park, Cardiff CF1 3NQ, Wales. TEL 44-1222-825054. FAX 44-1222-825350. E-mail: statswales@gtnet.gov.uk. **Document type:** government publication.
—BLDSC (8426.369700).

350.1 SW ISSN 0346-1815
STATSTJAENSTEMANNEN. 1907. 14/yr. SEK 250. Statstjaenstemannafoerbundet, P.O. Box 5044, 102 41 Stockholm, Sweden. FAX 46-8-790-52-86. Ed. Jan-Aake Porseryd. adv. circ. 120,500. (also avail. in audio cassette)
Former titles (until 1945): Tidskrift foer den Centrala Statsforvaltningens Tjaenstemaen; (until 1933): Medlemsblad foer Statsfoervaltningens Tjaenstemannafoerening; (until 1930): Fraan Svenska Statsfoervaltningen.

331 340 US
STATUTES, REGULATIONS AND CASE LAW PROTECTING INDIVIDUALS WITH DISABILITIES. 1994. a. $102.25 for 2nd ed. Data Research, Inc., 4635 Nicols Rd., Eagan, MN 55122-3337. TEL 612-452-8694. FAX 612-452-8694. (Subscr. to: Box 490, Rosemount, MN 55068-9987. TEL 800-365-4900)
Description: Compilation of federal statutes and regulations that affect the rights of disabled Americans.

331 GW
STICHWORT: BAYER; fuer mehr Umweltschutz und sichere Arbeitsplaetze. 1983. bi-m. DM.48. Coordination gegen Bayer Gefahren e.V., Jaegerstr. 78, 40231 Duesseldorf, Germany. TEL 0211-2292601. Ed. Hubert Ostendorf. bk.rev. circ. 3,000. (back issues avail.)

331.1 US
STUDY TIME. q. free to qualified personnel. American Arbitration Association, 140 W. 51st St., New York, NY 10020-1203. TEL 212-484-4012. FAX 212-541-4841. (Co-sponsor: Labor Relations Press) Ed. Earl Braderschneider.
Description: Provides labor arbitrators with commentary and opinion on substantive and procedural matters. Includes announcements of conferences, seminars, and new publications.

SUMA. see *BUSINESS AND ECONOMICS — Economic Situation And Conditions*

331.155 340 US ISSN 0039-5005
SUMMARY OF LABOR ARBITRATION AWARDS. 1959. m. $120. American Arbitration Association, 140 W. 51st St., New York, NY 10020-1203. TEL 212-484-4011. FAX 212-541-4841. Ed. Margaret S. Leibowitz. s.a. index. circ. 4,500. (also avail. in microfiche)
Description: Summarizes decisions in disputes between private businesses and unions.

331.1 658.3 US ISSN 0039-5854
TS155.A1 CODEN: SUPRAO
SUPERVISION; the magazine of industrial relations and operating management. 1939. m. $46.95 (foreign $58.25). National Research Bureau, 320 Valley St., Burlington, IA 52601-5513. TEL 319-752-5415. FAX 319-752-3421. Ed. Barbara Boeding; Pub. Michael Darnall. circ. 3,091. (also avail. in microform from UMI; reprint service avail. from UMI) **Indexed:** ABI Inform., B.P.I., BPIA, Bus.Ind., Excerp.Med., Pers.Lit., Tr.& Indus.Ind., Work Rel.Abstr. **Document type:** trade publication.
—BLDSC (8547.130000); Ei; Genuine Article; KR SourceOne; SWETS; UMI; UnCover. **CCC.**
Supersedes: Foreman.

731 US
SUPERVISORY AND MANAGEMENT SURVEY. a. $450. MidAtlantic Employers' Association, Box 770, Valley Forge, PA 19482. TEL 215-666-7330. FAX 215-666-7866.
Description: Offers salary information for 90 supervisory and management positions among 220 companies, representing 2,950 employees in PA, NJ, MD, and DE.

331 UK
SURREY - WEST KENT SALARY SURVEY. 2/yr. £250 (effective 1997). The Reward Group Ltd., Reward House, Diamond Way, Stone Business Park, Stone, Staffordshire ST15 0SD, England. TEL 44-1785-813566. FAX 44-1785-817007. E-mail: 101364.661@compuserve.com. **Document type:** bulletin.
Description: Pay and benefits salary survey for the Surrey, West Kent, Maidstone, Gillingham, Dartford, Severnoaks and Turnbridge areas.

331 350 US
SURVEY OF STATE RETIREMENT SYSTEMS. biennial. National Association of State Retirement Administrators, 540 E. 2005, Salt Lake City, UT 84102. TEL 801-355-3884. stat.
Description: Reviews pension and retirement programs of state government employees.

SVENSKA JAERNVAEGSTIDNINGEN. see *TRANSPORTATION — Railroads*

331.2 SQ ISSN 0303-3953
SWAZILAND. CENTRAL STATISTICAL OFFICE. EMPLOYMENT AND WAGES. 1969. a. free. Central Statistical Office, P.O. Box 456, Mbabane, Swaziland. TEL 268-43765. circ. 500. **Document type:** government publication.

331 SW
T C O STYRELSE- OCH REVISIONS; berettelse. 1944. a. Tjaenstemaennens Central Organisation - Swedish Confederation of Salaried Employees, Linnegatan 14, 102 45 Stockholm, Sweden. FAX 46-8-663-75-20. TELEX 19104 TCO S. circ. 15,000.
Former titles: Aaret som Gaatt.

331 SW ISSN 0346-2935
T C O - TIDNINGEN. 1946. 33/yr. SEK 300. Tjaenstemaennens Centralorganisation, S-114 94 Stockholm, Sweden. TEL 46-8-782-91-00. FAX 46-8-662-48-22. Ed. Anna-Britt Benjour. adv.: B&W page SEK 35000, color page SEK 43500; trim 252 x 360. circ. 80,300. cols./p.: 5; pp./issue: 16. (tabloid format) **Document type:** newspaper.

331 370 US
T.I.C. NEWSLETTER. 1969. m. $20. Teacher Information Center, 61 Surrey Ln., Sudbury, MA 01776. TEL 617-443-0424. Eds. Len Solo, Deanna Solo. charts. **Document type:** newsletter.
Formerly: T.D.O.C. Newsletter.

331 PH
TALA INDUSTRIAL RELATIONS BULLETIN. (Text in English) 1976. m. P.240($60) Tala Publishing Corporation, Box 95, University of the Philippines, Quezon City, Philippines. Ed. Perfecto V. Fernandez. bk.rev.; illus.; index. circ. 1,000. (back issues avail.) **Document type:** bulletin.

331 II
TAMIL NADU LABOUR JOURNAL. (Text in English, Tamil) vol.15, no.12, 1972. m. Rs.16. Commissioner of Labour, Chepauk, Madras 5, India. bk.rev.; bibl.; charts; stat.
Formerly: Madras Labour Gazette. (ISSN 0024-9610)

TANZANIA. BUREAU OF STATISTICS. SURVEY OF EMPLOYMENT. see *BUSINESS AND ECONOMICS — Abstracting, Bibliographies, Statistics*

331 GW ISSN 0937-0951
TASCHENLEXIKON ARBEITSRECHTLICHER ENTSCHEIDUNGEN. 1961. irreg. DM.128 (effective 1997). Erich Schmidt Verlag GmbH & Co. (Berlin), Genthiner Str. 30G, 10785 Berlin, Germany. TEL 49-30-250085-0. FAX 49-30-25008521. (looseleaf format) **Document type:** bulletin.

331.2 US ISSN 0746-0384
TAX UPDATE FOR BUSINESS OWNERS; tax saving strategies for savvy business owners. m. $96 (effective 1997). Harcourt Brace Professional Publishing, 525 B St., Ste. 1900, San Diego, CA 92101-4495. TEL 619-699-6716. FAX 619-699-6593. Ed. Terence Myers. **Document type:** newsletter.
Description: Delivers information on the latest laws, trends, and loopholes, as well as summaries of the latest IRS rulings that effect your business.

306.38 US
THE TEACHER RETIREMENT LAWS OF THE STATE OF ARKANSAS. a., latest 1995 ed. $18. Michie, A Division of Reed Elsevier Inc., Box 7587, Charlottesville, VA 22906-7587. TEL 804-972-7566; 800-562-1197. FAX 800-643-1280. E-mail: custserv@michie.com; URL: http://www.michie.com. Ed. George Harley.

TECHNICAL & SKILLED TRADE PERSONNEL REPORT. see *BUSINESS AND ECONOMICS — Management*

BUSINESS AND ECONOMICS — LABOR AND INDUSTRIAL RELATIONS

331   SP   ISSN 0213-0750
TEMAS LABORALES; revista andaluza de trabajo y bienestar social. 1984. q. 8000 ptas. (effective 1997). Junta de Andalucia, Consejeria de Trabajo e Industria, Secretaria General Tecnica, Av. Heroes de Toledo s-n, Edificio Junta de Andalucia, 41071 Seville, Spain. (Dist. by: Mailing Andalucia, Almirante Topete s-n, Seville, Spain. TEL 34-54-236863. FAX 34-54-239749)
—CINDOC.
    Description: Covers social welfare, employee-employer relationships and all work related issues.

TEMPORARY DISABILITY INSURANCE AND UNEMPLOYMENT INSURANCE LAWS OF RHODE ISLAND. see *INSURANCE*

331 330.9   IT   ISSN 0391-7940
TENDENZE DELLA OCCUPAZIONE. 1976. m. L50000. (foreign L.60000). Centro di Ricerche Economiche e Sociali (CERES), Via Nomentana 201, 00161 Rome, Italy. TEL 06-8541016. Ed. Luigi Frey. circ. 1,100. **Document type**: bulletin.

331   US   ISSN 0749-9930
HD5701.85
TENNESSEE. LABOR MARKET INFORMATION DIRECTORY. a. Department of Employment Security, Research and Statistics Division, 500 James Robertson Pkwy., 11th Fl., Nashville, TN 37245-1040. TEL 615-741-1729. **Document type**: directory, government publication.

331   US
TENNESSEE. THE LABOR MARKET REPORT. m. free. Department of Employment Security, Research and Statistics Division, 500 James Robertson Pkwy., 11th Fl., Nashville, TN 37245-1040. TEL 615-741-1729. charts; stat. (also avail. in microfiche from CIS) **Indexed**: SRI. **Document type**: government publication, newsletter.

TENNESSEE EMPLOYMENT LAW UPDATE. see *LAW*

344.012   US
TENNESSEE WORKERS' COMPENSATION LAWS. a. $15. Michie, A Division of Reed Elsevier Inc., Box 7587, Charlottesville, VA 22906-7587. TEL 804-972-7566; 800-562-1197. FAX 800-643-1280. E-mail: custserv@michie.com; URL: http://www.michie.com. Ed. George Harley.

331.1   IT
TEOREMA ITALIA. 1984. bi-m. L.18000 (foreign L.35000). Editrice Teorema, Via XXIII Settembre 31, 47037 Rimini, Italy. TEL 39-541-738111. Ed. Umberto Grassi. adv.: B&W page L.2200000.

TEXAS EMPLOYMENT LAW LETTER. see *LAW*

331.1   US
TEXAS LABOR MARKET REVIEW. 1945. m. free. Texas Workforce Commission, Labor Market Information Department, 101 E. 15th St., Rm. 252T, Austin, TX 78778. TEL 512-463-2843. FAX 512-475-1701. E-mail: cgriffis@twc.state.tx.us; URL: http://www.twc.state.tx.us. Ed. Clayton Griffis. charts; stat. circ. 5,500. (also avail. in microfiche from CIS) **Indexed**: SRI. **Document type**: government publication, newsletter.
●Also available online.
    Formerly: Texas Manpower Trends (ISSN 0040-4462)

TEXTILE LABOUR COST COMPARISON - INTERNATIONAL. see *TEXTILE INDUSTRIES AND FABRICS*

331   TH
THAILAND STANDARD INDUSTRIAL CLASSIFICATION. (Text in English, Thai) 1972. irreg. Department of Labour, Bangkok, Thailand.

331   UK
THAMES VALLEY SALARY SURVEY. 2/yr. £250 (effective 1997). The Reward Group Ltd., Reward House, Diamond Way, Stone Business Park, Stone, Staffordshire ST15 0SD, England. TEL 44-1785-813566. FAX 44-1785-817007. E-mail: 101364.661@compuserve.com. **Document type**: bulletin.
    Description: Pay and benefit salary survey covering the Berkshire, Swindon, South Oxfordshire and South Buckinghamshire areas.

796.3 331   US
TIME OUT. 1983. q. membership only. National Basketball Players Association, 1775 Broadway, Ste. 2401, New York, NY 10019. TEL 212-333-7510. FAX 212-956-5687. Ed. Carolyn Parello. circ. 2,000. **Document type**: newsletter.
    Description: Educates NBA players, retired players and agents on union issues, and discusses educational programs designed to enhance the lives of players and their families.

TOKYO INDUSTRY; a graphic overview. see *PUBLIC ADMINISTRATION — Municipal Government*

331 658.3   UK   ISSN 0262-2548
TOPICS (CAMBRIDGE). (Former name of issuing body: Employment Relations) 1979. q. £50 (foreign £60) (effective 1997). E R Consultants, Compass House, 80 Newmarket Rd., Cambridge CB5 8DZ, England. TEL 01223-315944. FAX 01223-322565. Ed. Bronwen Rees. R&P contact: Mark Goodridge. bk.rev.; circ. 2,500 (paid). **Indexed**: Mgmt.& Market.Abstr. **Document type**: academic/scholarly publication.
—BLDSC (8867.415500).
    Description: Covers all aspects of human resource issues; aimed at senior and middle managers as well as personnel managers.
    Refereed Serial

331   CU
TRABAJADORES. 1970. w. $40. Central de Trabajadores de Cuba, Palacio de los Trabajadores, San Carlos y Penalver, Havana, Cuba. (Dist. by: Ediciones Cubanas, Obispo No. 461, Apdo. 605, Havana, Cuba) Ed. Jorge Luis Canela Ciurana. circ. 250,000.

331   DR   ISSN 0564-0334
TRABAJO. 1966. q. Secretaria de Estado de Trabajo, Departamento de Relaciones Publicas y Prensa, Santo Domingo, Dominican Republic. Ed. Rafael A. Grullon.

331   CK
TRABAJO. 1950. irreg. Ministerio del Trabajo y Seguridad Social, Av. 19, No. 6-68, Of. 806-809, Santafe de Bogota, Colombia. Ed. I. Reyes Rosada.

331   AO   ISSN 0564-0342
TRABALHO. (Text in Portuguese; summaries in English, French, Portuguese) 1963. q. Instituto do Trabalho, Previdencia e Accao Social de Angola, Avenida Alvaro Ferreira 5, Luanda, Angola. charts.

TRADESWOMEN; for women in blue-collar work. see *WOMEN'S INTERESTS*

TRAINING & DEVELOPMENT. see *BUSINESS AND ECONOMICS — Personnel Management*

374   AT   ISSN 0310-4664
TRAINING AND DEVELOPMENT IN AUSTRALIA. 1972. bi-m. Aus.$54 (foreign Aus.$60) (effective 1998). Australian Institute of Training and Development, P.O. Box 1011, Lalor, Vic. 3075, Australia. TEL 61-3-94651107. FAX 61-3-94658054. E-mail: aitdjrnl@ozemail.com.au. Ed. Les Pickett. adv. contact: Christine Felle. bk.rev. circ. 4,500. **Document type**: trade publication.
—UnCover.

331   SZ
TRAIT D'UNION. 6/yr. 7 Chemin des Feuillus, CH-1217 Meyrin, Switzerland. TEL 022-208811. Ed. Andre Conte. circ. 900.

331   BE   ISSN 1024-2589
▼**TRANSFER**; European review of labour and research. (Text in English; abstracts in English, French, German) 1995. q. 1200 BEF. Institut Syndical Europeen - European Trade Union Institute, Bd. Emile Jacqmain 155, 1210 Brussels, Belgium. TEL 32-2-2240470. FAX 32-2-2240502.
—BLDSC (9020.583280).
    Description: Contains information on European trade union policy, labor, and industrial relations.

331   UK   ISSN 0041-1531
TRANSPORT SALARIED STAFF JOURNAL. 1904. m. £6 (foreign £8.50). Transport Salaried Staffs' Association, Walkden House, 10 Melton St., Euston, London NW1 2EJ, England. FAX 0171-383-0656. Ed. Jim Cobley. adv.; bk.rev.; illus. circ. 40,000. (tabloid format) **Document type**: newsletter.

331   FR   ISSN 0224-4365
HD8421
TRAVAIL ET EMPLOI. 4/yr. 320 F. (Europe 345 F., elsewhere 365 F.) (effective 1997). (Ministere du Travail, de l'Emploi et de la Formation Professionnelle, Direction de l'Animation, de la Recherche, des Etudes et des Statistiques) Documentation Francaise, 29-31 quai Voltaire, 75344 Paris Cedex 07, France. TEL 33-1-40157000. FAX 33-1-40157230. TELEX 215 666 DOCFRAN. (Subscr. to: 124 rue Henri Barbusse, 93308 Aubervilliers Cedex, France. TEL 33-1-48395600. FAX 33-1-48395601) abstr. (also avail. in microfiche) **Indexed**: SCIMP (1981-). **Document type**: government publication.
●Also available online. Vendor(s): Telesystemes - Questel.
—BLDSC (9026.859500); SWETS.
    Former titles (until 1979): Formation-Emploi; Emploi et Formation.

LE TRAVAIL HUMAIN. see *PSYCHOLOGY*

TRENDS IN EMPLOYMENT AND WAGES COVERED BY UNEMPLOYMENT INSURANCE. see *BUSINESS AND ECONOMICS — Economic Situation And Conditions*

331 371.42   US
TWIN CITIES EMPLOYMENT WEEKLY. 1993. w. American City Business Journals, Inc. (Austin), 505 Powell St., Austin, TX 78703-5121. adv.: B&W page $1250. circ. 25,500.

U C GUIDE (YEAR). (Unemployment Compensation) see *LAW — Corporate Law*

370 796   FR
U F C V. 1910. m. (9/yr.). 170 F. Union Francaise des Centres de Vacances, 19 rue Dareau, 75014 Paris, France. TEL 47-07-11-22. FAX 43-36-80-93. TELEX 202 400. Ed. D. Mascolo. adv.; bk.rev. circ. 7,500.

U K ECONOMY: PRODUCER PRICE INDICES. see *BUSINESS AND ECONOMICS — Economic Situation And Conditions*

368   US   ISSN 1063-3812
HD7096.U6
UNEMPLOYMENT INSURANCE ACTUARIAL STUDY & FINANCIAL HANDBOOK (YEAR). a. free. Department of Labor, Research & Analysis Section, Box 25501, Juneau, AK 99802-5501. TEL 907-465-4507. FAX 907-465-2101. **Document type**: government publication.
    Description: Report of Alaska's unemployment insurance (UI) system focusing on the benefit and tax structures. Includes an overview of the current UI system and an analysis of fund adequacy with respect to potential future benefit obligations.

UNEMPLOYMENT INSURANCE REPORTS WITH SOCIAL SECURITY. see *INSURANCE*

331 340   US
UNFAIR LABOR PRACTICES BULLETIN. 1987. m. $60 (effective 1993). Quinlan Publishing Co., Inc., 23 Drydock Ave., Boston, MA 02210-2387. TEL 617-542-0048; 800-229-2084. FAX 617-345-9646. index. (looseleaf format; back issues avail.) **Document type**: newsletter.
—UMI. CCC.
    Formerly: Unfair Labor Practices Law Bulletin (ISSN 0895-8904)
    Description: Covers the latest decisions in lawsuits brought against employers and unions for unfair labor practices, including anti-union activities by employers, unfair union representation, unsafe workplaces, election pressure tactics, strikes and wage disputes.

UNION DEMOCRACY REVIEW. see *LABOR UNIONS*

BUSINESS AND ECONOMICS — LABOR AND INDUSTRIAL RELATIONS

344.73 US ISSN 0091-5459
KF3365
UNION LABOR REPORT. 1947. fortn. $733. The Bureau of National Affairs, Inc., 1231 25th St., N.W., Washington, DC 20037. TEL 202-452-4200. FAX 202-822-8092. TELEX 285656 BNAI WSH. URL: http://www.bna.com/. (Subscr. to: 9435 Key West Ave., Rockville, MD 20850. TEL 800-372-1033) Ed. Bill L. Manville. bk.rev.; index. (looseleaf format; back issues avail.) **Document type:** newsletter.
●Also available online. Vendor(s): Human Resources Information Network.
—CCC.
Description: Notification and reference service that provides practical guidance on day-to-day labor relations questions. Includes current reports on employee relations and union developments.

331 US ISSN 0190-5260
UNION LABOR REPORT WEEKLY NEWSLETTER. (Supplement avail.: Union Labor Report's On the Line (ISSN 0731-0307)) 1947. w. $156. The Bureau of National Affairs, Inc., 1231 25th St., N.W., Washington, DC 20037. TEL 202-452-4200. FAX 202-822-8092. TELEX 285656 BNAI WSH. URL: http://www.bna.com/. (Subscr. to: 9435 Key West Ave., Rockville, MD 20850. TEL 800-372-1033) Ed. Bill L. Manville. (back issues avail.) **Document type:** newsletter.
●Also available online. Vendor(s): Human Resources Information Network (CDD, HDD).
—CCC.
Description: Presents a roundup of developments in the labor field, including summaries of significant arbitration awards, labor facts, and special reports.

331 US ISSN 0731-0307
UNION LABOR REPORT'S ON THE LINE; a guide for union stewards. (Supplement to: Union Labor Report Weekly Newsletter (ISSN 0190-5260)) 1978. q. $2. The Bureau of National Affairs, Inc., 1231 25th St., N.W., Washington, DC 20037. TEL 202-452-4200. FAX 202-822-8092. TELEX 285656 BNAI WSH. URL: http://www.bna.com/. (Subscr. to: 9435 Key West Ave., Rockville, MD 20850. TEL 800-372-1033) Ed. Bill L. Manville. (back issues avail.) **Document type:** newsletter.
—CCC.
Description: Designed for union shop stewards. Includes articles that deal with the real-life problems and situations they face, and summaries of arbitration awards involving shop stewards.

U.S. BUREAU OF LABOR STATISTICS. AREA WAGE SURVEYS. see *BUSINESS AND ECONOMICS — Economic Situation And Conditions*

U.S. BUREAU OF LABOR STATISTICS. BULLETINS. see *BUSINESS AND ECONOMICS — Economic Situation And Conditions*

U.S. BUREAU OF LABOR STATISTICS. NATIONAL OFFICE NEWS RELEASES. see *BUSINESS AND ECONOMICS — Economic Situation And Conditions*

U.S. BUREAU OF LABOR STATISTICS. REPORTS. see *BUSINESS AND ECONOMICS — Economic Situation And Conditions*

U.S. BUREAU OF LABOR STATISTICS. REPRINT SERIES. see *BUSINESS AND ECONOMICS — Economic Situation And Conditions*

344 368.4 US ISSN 0191-118X
KF3612.5
U.S. CHAMBER OF COMMERCE. ANALYSIS OF WORKERS' COMPENSATION LAWS. Key Title: Analysis of Workers' Compensation Laws. 1954. a. $25. U.S. Chamber of Commerce, 1615 H St., N.W., Washington, DC 20062. TEL 202-463-5650. FAX 202-887-3437. Indexed: SRI.
Formerly (until 1976): U.S. Chamber of Commerce. Analysis of Workmen's Compensation Laws (ISSN 0577-5183)
Description: Summarizes laws of the United States and its territories, the District of Columbia, and various Canadian provinces. Compares benefits, details coverage, insurance and state requirements of the various jurisdictions.

344.73 US ISSN 0271-1567
KF3512
U.S. DEPARTMENT OF LABOR. EMPLOYEE RETIREMENT INCOME SECURITY ACT. REPORT TO CONGRESS. Key Title: Employee Retirement Income Security Act. Report to Congress. 1975. a. free. U.S. Department of Labor, Pension and Welfare Benefits Administration, 200 Constitution Ave., N.W., Washington, DC 20216. TEL 202-523-8921. Ed. William C. Russell. circ. 3,000. **Document type:** government publication.
Formerly: Administration of the Employee Retirement Income Security Act (ISSN 0146-7352)

331 US ISSN 0083-0526
HD4903.5.U58
U.S. EQUAL EMPLOYMENT OPPORTUNITY COMMISSION. ANNUAL REPORT. Title varies: Equal Employment Opportunity Report. 1968. a. free. U.S. Equal Employment Opportunity Commission, 1801 L St., N.W., Washington, DC 20507. TEL 800-669-3362. **Document type:** government publication.

331.15 US ISSN 0083-0771
U.S. FEDERAL MEDIATION AND CONCILIATION SERVICE. ANNUAL REPORT. 1948. a. free. U.S. Federal Mediation and Conciliation Service., 2100 K St., N.W., Washington, DC 20427. TEL 202-606-8100. FAX 202-606-4251. R&P contact: Eileen Hoffman. **Document type:** government publication.

331.155 US ISSN 0083-2200
HD5503
U.S. NATIONAL LABOR RELATIONS BOARD. ANNUAL REPORT. 1936. a. price varies. U.S. National Labor Relations Board, 1099 14th St., N.W., Washington, DC 20570-0001. TEL 202-273-1991. FAX 202-273-1789. (Subscr. to: Superintendent of Documents, U.S. Government Printing Office, Washington DC 20402. TEL 202-512-1800) (reprint service avail. from RRI) **Document type:** government publication.

331.156 US ISSN 0083-2219
KF3360.A2
U.S. NATIONAL LABOR RELATIONS BOARD. COURT DECISIONS RELATING TO THE NATIONAL LABOR RELATIONS ACT. 1939. irreg., latest vol.38. $38. U.S. National Labor Relations Board, 1099 14th St., N.W., Washington, DC 20570-0001. TEL 202-273-1991. FAX 202-273-1789. (Subscr. to: Superintendent of Documents, U.S. Government Printing Office, Washington DC 20402. TEL 202-512-1800. FAX 202-512-2250) (also avail. in microfiche from WSH) **Document type:** government publication.

331.11 US
U.S. NATIONAL LABOR RELATIONS BOARD. OFFICE OF THE GENERAL COUNSEL. QUARTERLY REPORT. q. U.S. National Labor Relations Board, Office of the General Counsel, 1717 Pennsylvania Ave., N.W., Washington, DC 20570. TEL 202-275-2091. (Subscr. to: Superintendent of Documents, U.S. Government Printing Office. Box 371954, Pittsburgh, PA 15250-7954. TEL 202-783-3238. FAX 202-512-2233) **Document type:** government publication.

331.1 US
U.S. NATIONAL LABOR RELATIONS BOARD. WEEKLY SUMMARY OF THE NATIONAL LABOR RELATIONS BOARD CASES. no.W-1869, 1983. w. $135 (foreign $168.75). U.S. National Labor Relations Board, 1099 14th St., N.W., Washington, DC 20570-0001. TEL 202-273-1991. FAX 202-273-1789. (Subscr. to: Superintendent of Documents, U.S. Government Printing Office, Washington, DC 20402. TEL 202-512-1800. FAX 202-512-2250) (also avail. in microfiche from WSH; back issues avail.) **Document type:** government publication.
Description: Contains a synopsis of each published decision of the N.R.L.B. in unfair labor practices and representative election cases; lists decisions of N.L.R.B. administrative law judges and directions of elections by regional directors; carries guideline memoranda of the N.L.R.B. general counsel to field offices on important case-handling subjects; and carries notices of publication of volumes of N.L.R.B. decisions and orders, the Annual Report, and other agency informational literature.

331.154 US ISSN 0083-2286
HD5503
U.S. NATIONAL MEDIATION BOARD. ANNUAL REPORT. 1935. a. price varies. U.S. National Mediation Board, 1301 K St., N.W., Ste. 250E, Washington, DC 20572. TEL 202-523-5920. FAX 202-523-1494. (Orders to: Superintendent of Documents, U.S. Government Printing Office, Box 371954, Pittsburgh, PA 15250-7954. TEL 202-512-1800. FAX 202-512-2250; Or: Bernan, 4611-F Assembly Dr., Lanham, MD 20706. TEL 800-274-4447. FAX 301-459-0056) **Document type:** government publication.

331.154 US
U.S. NATIONAL MEDIATION BOARD. DETERMINATIONS. a. $18.75. U.S. National Mediation Board, 1301 K St., N.W., Ste. 250E, Washington, DC 20572. (Orders to: Superintendent of Documents, U.S. Government Printing Office, Box 371954, Pittsburgh, PA 15250-1954. TEL 202-512-1800. FAX 202-512-2250; Or: Bernan, 4611-F Assembly Dr., Lanham, MD 20706. TEL 800-274-4447. FAX 301-459-0056) **Document type:** government publication.

331 US ISSN 0083-2278
U.S. NATIONAL MEDIATION BOARD. (REPORTS OF EMERGENCY BOARDS). irreg. (3-4/yr.). $175 includes Annual Reports, Emergency Board Reports, Certifications and Dismissals, Determinations of Craft or Class, Findings upon Investigation, other N.M.B. information releases. U.S. National Mediation Board, 1301 K St., N.W., Ste. 250E, Washington, DC 20572. TEL 202-523-5335. (Orders to: Superintendent of Documents, U.S. Government Printing Office, Box 371954, Pittsburgh, PA 15250-7954. TEL 202-512-1800. FAX 202-512-2250) **Document type:** government publication.

331 US
U.S. OFFICE OF PERSONNEL MANAGEMENT. NEGOTIABILITY DETERMINATIONS BY THE FEDERAL LABOR RELATIONS AUTHORITY (FLRA). biennial? U.S. Office of Personnel Management, Office of Labor Relations and Workforce Performance, Labor-Management Relations Division, Personnel Systems and Oversight Group, Theodore Roosevelt Bldg., 1900 E St., N.W., Washington, DC 20415. TEL 202-606-2930. (Dist by: Superintendent of Documents, U.S. Government Printing Office, Box 317954, Pittsburgh, PA 15250-7954. TEL 202-512-1800. FAX 202-512-2250) **Document type:** government publication.
Description: Summarizes negotiability determinations issued by F.L.R.A. over the previous two years.

332.6 US ISSN 0891-8066
HD7116.R12
U.S. RAILROAD RETIREMENT BOARD. ANNUAL REPORT. 1936. a. U.S. Railroad Retirement Board, 844 N. Rush St., Chicago, IL 60611-2092. TEL 312-751-4776. (Subscr. to: Superintendent of Documents, U.S. Government Printing Office, Box 371954, Pittsburgh, PA 15250-7954. TEL 202-512-1800. FAX 202-512-2250; Or: Bernan, 4611-F Assembly Dr., Lanham, MD 20706. TEL 301-459-7666. FAX 301-459-0056) Ed. William Poulos. R&P contact: William Poulos. TEL 312-751-4777. circ. 1,700. **Document type:** government publication.

U.S. RAILROAD RETIREMENT BOARD. QUARTERLY BENEFIT STATISTICS. see *BUSINESS AND ECONOMICS — Abstracting, Bibliographies, Statistics*

331 US
U.S. SUPREME COURT EMPLOYMENT CASES. 1993. a. $74.70 for 3rd ed. Data Research, Inc., 4635 Nicols Rd., Eagan, MN 55122-3337. TEL 612-452-8267. FAX 612-452-8694. (Subscr. to: Box 490, Rosemount, MN 55068-9987. TEL 800-365-4900)
Description: Compilation of summarized U.S. Supreme Court decisions which affect employment.

BUSINESS AND ECONOMICS — LABOR AND INDUSTRIAL RELATIONS

331   US   ISSN 0739-439X
UNIVERSITY OF CALIFORNIA AT LOS ANGELES. INSTITUTE OF INDUSTRIAL RELATIONS. MONOGRAPH AND RESEARCH SERIES. 1953. irreg., no.58, 1994. price varies. University of California at Los Angeles, Institute of Industrial Relations, Los Angeles, CA 90095. TEL 310-794-0393. FAX 310-794-8017. (Orders to: Book Masters, Box 2039, Mansfield, OH 44905. TEL 800-247-6553) Ed. Jeannine Schummer. R&P contact: Carli Rogers. TEL 310-825-0759. circ. 500 (paid). (back issues avail.) **Document type:** monographic series.
  Formerly: University of California at Los Angeles. Institute of Industrial Relations. Monograph Series (ISSN 0068-6255)

331   US   ISSN 0073-1226
UNIVERSITY OF HAWAII. INDUSTRIAL RELATIONS CENTER. OCCASIONAL PUBLICATIONS. 1948. irreg., no.173, 1994. price varies. University of Hawaii, Industrial Relations Center, 2425 Campus Rd., Honolulu, HI 96822. TEL 808-956-8132. FAX 808-956-3609. **Document type:** monographic series.

331   TR
UNIVERSITY OF THE WEST INDIES, TRINIDAD. INSTITUTE OF SOCIAL & ECONOMIC RESEARCH. OCCASIONAL PAPERS: HUMAN RESOURCES SERIES. 1977. irreg. price varies. University of the West Indies, Institute of Social & Economic Research, St. Augustine, Trinidad & Tobago, W.I. Ed. Jack Harewood. charts; stat. circ. 220. (back issues avail.)

UTAH EMPLOYMENT LAW LETTER. see *LAW*

UTTAR PRADESH ROZGAR DIGEST; an employment oriented & consultative Hindi fortnightly. see *OCCUPATIONS AND CAREERS*

331 338.31   GW
V W-AUTOGRAMM. 1971. m. free. Volkswagen AG, 3180 Wolfsburg, Germany. Ed. Hansjuergen Meisert. bk.rev. circ. 100,000. (back issues avail.) **Document type:** newsletter.

VANUATU. STATISTICS OFFICE. MANPOWER AND EMPLOYMENT SURVEYS. see *BUSINESS AND ECONOMICS — Abstracting, Bibliographies, Statistics*

331   GW   ISSN 0936-224X
VERGUETUNG DER ARBEITNEHMER BEI KRANKHEIT UND MUTTERSCHAFT. 1970. irreg. DM.128. Erich Schmidt Verlag GmbH & Co. (Berlin), Genthiner Str. 30G, 10785 Berlin, Germany. TEL 49-30-250085-0. FAX 49-30-25008521. (looseleaf format) **Document type:** bulletin.

VERMONT EMPLOYMENT LAW LETTER. see *LAW*

331   US
VERMONT LABOR MARKET. 1964. m. free. Department of Employment & Training, Box 488, Montpelier, VT 05601-0488. TEL 802-828-4321. FAX 802-828-4022. charts; stat. circ. 2,500. **Document type:** government publication.
  Formerly: Vermont Labor Force (ISSN 0506-7472)
  Description: Contains information on the labor market, economic conditions, and the department's programs.

VICTORIAN ACCIDENT COMPENSATION PRACTICE GUIDE. see *LAW*

VINNUMARKADUR/LABOR MARKET STATISTICS. see *BUSINESS AND ECONOMICS — Abstracting, Bibliographies, Statistics*

331.11   VI
VIRGIN ISLANDS (U.S.). DEPARTMENT OF LABOR. ANNUAL REPORT. FISCAL YEAR. a. Department of Labor, Bureau of Labor Statistics, P.O. Box 3359, Charlotte Amalie, St. Thomas, VI 00803. **Document type:** government publication.

331   VI   ISSN 8756-1638
HD5744.3
VIRGIN ISLANDS (U.S.). DEPARTMENT OF LABOR. BUREAU OF LABOR STATISTICS. LABOR MARKET REVIEW. Key Title: Virgin Islands Labor Market Review. 1978. m. Department of Labor, Bureau of Labor Statistics, P.O. Box 3359, Charlotte Amalie, St. Thomas, VI 00803. TEL 809-776-3700. FAX 809-774-5908. circ. 900. **Document type:** government publication.
  Description: Provides an update on labor market changes, on nonagricultural wage and slary employment and average hours and earnings for production workers in selected industries.

VIRGINIA EMPLOYMENT LAW LETTER. see *LAW*

344.012   US
VIRGINIA WORKERS' COMPENSATION ACT ANNOTATED. a. $35. Michie, A Division of Reed Elsevier Inc., Box 7587, Charlottesville, VA 22906-7587. TEL 804-972-7566; 800-562-1197. FAX 800-643-1280. E-mail: custserv@michie.com; URL: http://www.michie.com. Ed. George Harley.

331.2   CN   ISSN 1183-7780
VISION. 1991. q. free. Labour Canada, Publications Distribution, Ottawa, ON K1A 0J2, Canada. TEL 819-994-0543. FAX 819-997-1664. circ. 3,000.
  Description: Reports on pay equity for employers in the federal jurisdiction.

331   CI   ISSN 0042-7632
VJESNIK RADA; casopis za pitanja rada, radnih odnosa, zaposljavanja i socijalnog osiguranja. (Text in Serbo-Croatian) vol.13, 1970. m. 60 din. Narodne Novine, Zagreb, Ratkajev Prolaz 4, Zagreb, Croatia. Ed. Ivica Kranzelic.

331 320.531   UK
VOICE OF THE UNIONS. 1925. m. $21.50. Voice Newspapers, 30 Adolphus Rd., London N4 2AY, England. adv.; bk.rev. (tabloid format)
  Description: Coverage of trade unions and political events, sex and race equality, armaments conversion, socialism and grass root control, specialists' opinions and interviews.

331 323.4   US
W D L NEWS. 1972. 3/yr. $10 or membership. Workers Defense League, Inc., 275 Seventh Ave., 15th fl., New York, NY 10001. TEL 212-627-1931. FAX 212-627-4628. Ed. Jon Bloom. bk.rev.; bibl. circ. 5,000.
  Supersedes: Workers Defense Bulletin.

331.2   CN   ISSN 1186-6640
WAGE SETTLEMENTS BULLETIN. French edition: Bulletin des Reglements Salariaux (ISSN 1186-6632) (Text in English, French) 1990. m. Can.$214. Labour Canada, Bureau of Labour Information, Ottawa, ON K1A 0J2, Canada. TEL 819-997-3117. FAX 819-953-9582. **Document type:** bulletin.
  Description: Information and analysis of major wage developments.

344.012   US
WAGES AND HOURS: LAW & PRACTICE. base vol. (plus a. update). $115 for base vol.; update $68. Matthew Bender & Co., Inc., 2 Park Ave., New York, NY 10016. TEL 212-448-2000. E-mail: international@bender.com; URL: http://www.bender.com. (looseleaf format)
  Description: Describes federal and state laws governing minimum wage, overtime and child labor standards. Includes both state and federal wage-hour provisions.

331   SW   ISSN 0280-4743
WAGES AND TOTAL LABOUR COSTS FOR WORKERS: INTERNATIONAL SURVEY. 1966. a. SEK 250 (effective 1997). Svenska Arbetsgivarefoereningen (SAF) - Swedish Employers' Confederation, S-103 30 Stockholm, Sweden. TEL 46-8-762-6000. FAX 46-8-762-6290. (Dist. by: S A Fs Foerlagsservice, S-811 88 Sandviken, Sweden) Ed. Marianne Lindahl. circ. 1,000.

331.11 323.4   US
WASHINGTON (STATE). EMPLOYMENT SECURITY DEPARTMENT. AFFIRMATIVE ACTION INFORMATION. Regional edition: Affirmative Action Information. Pasco and Franklin Counties (ISSN 0742-2970); Regional edition: Affirmative Action Information. Yakima County (ISSN 0742-2962) biennial. $1 per region. Employment Security Department, Box 9046, Olympia, WA 98507-9046. charts; stat. **Document type:** government publication.
  Description: Provides statistics and other information regarding the hiring of minority applicants to implement affirmative action programs.

331.11   US
WASHINGTON (STATE). EMPLOYMENT SECURITY DEPARTMENT. AREA WAGE SURVEYS. (Published in 15 regional vols.) biennial (issued in 15 vols.). $1 per vol. Employment Security Department, Labor Market and Economic Analysis Branch, Box 9046, Olympia, WA 98507-9046. charts; stat. **Document type:** government publication.
  Description: Supplies data on occupational salaries and wages for selected managerial, technical, clerical, and general professions in each of 15 urban or rural areas of Washington State.

331.11 330.9   US
WASHINGTON (STATE). EMPLOYMENT SECURITY DEPARTMENT. COUNTY LABOR MARKET AND ECONOMIC PROFILES. (Issued in 39 separate editions for each county.) a. Employment Security Department, Labor Market and Economic Analysis Branch, Box 9046, Olympia, WA 98507-9046. TEL 360-438-4818. charts; stat. **Document type:** government publication.
  Description: Highlights labor market and economic conditions in each county.

WASHINGTON (STATE). EMPLOYMENT SECURITY DEPARTMENT. OCCUPATIONAL PROJECTIONS. see *OCCUPATIONS AND CAREERS*

331.11   US
WASHINGTON (STATE). EMPLOYMENT SECURITY DEPARTMENT. STUDIES IN INDUSTRY AND EMPLOYMENT. 1994. irreg. latest no.2. price varies. Employment Security Department, Labor Market and Economic Analysis Branch, Box 9046, Olympia, WA 98507-9046. charts; stat. **Document type:** government publication.
  Description: Profiles and analyzes a specific industry, along with employment trends and prospects.

WASHINGTON EMPLOYMENT LAW LETTER. see *LAW*

331.1 350.9   US
WASHINGTON STATE LABOR MARKET AND ECONOMIC REPORT (YEAR). a. $7.50. Employment Security Department, Labor Market and Economic Analysis Branch, Box 9046, Olympia, WA 98507-9046. charts; stat. **Document type:** government publication.
  Description: Supplies the Governor and state legislators with Washington state labor market data and information.

331.1 387.7   US
WEEKLY REVIEW OF COLLECTIVE BARGAINING. w. Airline Industrial Relations Conference, 1920 N St., N.W., Ste. 250, Washington, DC 20036. TEL 202-861-7550.

360   US
WELFARE BENEFITS GUIDE. a. $150. Clark - Boardman - Callaghan, 375 Hudson St., New York, NY 10014. TEL 212-929-7500; 800-422-2101. FAX 212-924-0460. Eds. Ronald A. Kladder, Paul J. Routh.
  Description: Provides step-by-step guidance for properly structuring and managing non-pension benefit plans, while detailing federal tax law and the methods that ensure compliance.

WELFARE TO WORK; a review of developments in the welfare job training and placement field. see *SOCIAL SERVICES AND WELFARE*

331.1   NZ
WELLINGTON REGIONAL EMPLOYERS ASSOCIATION NEWSLETTER. 1966. m. membership. Wellington Regional Employers Association (Inc.), Federation House, 6th Floor, Box 1087, 95-99 Molesworth St., Wellington, New Zealand. TEL 64-4-737224. FAX 374501. TELEX NZ 30270. Ed.Bd. circ. controlled. **Document type:** newsletter.

BUSINESS AND ECONOMICS — LABOR AND INDUSTRIAL RELATIONS

WERKGELEGENHEID IN DE NEDERLANDSE ZEEHAVENS. see *TRANSPORTATION* — *Abstracting, Bibliographies, Statistics*

331   US
WERTHEIM PUBLICATIONS IN INDUSTRIAL RELATIONS. irreg. Harvard University, J.F.K. School of Government, Cambridge, MA 02138. TEL 617-495-4157. FAX 617-495-5898. **Document type:** monographic series.
Refereed Serial

331   II   ISSN 0043-3071
WEST BENGAL LABOUR GAZETTE. (Text in English) 1957. irreg. (Department of Labour) West Bengal Government Press, Publication Branch, 38 Gopal Nagar Rd., Alipore, Calcutta 27, India. stat.

331   UK
WEST MIDLANDS SALARY SURVEY. 2/yr. £250 (effective 1997). The Reward Group Ltd., Reward House, Diamond Way, Stone Business Park, Stone, Staffordshire ST15 0SD, England. TEL 44-1785-813566. FAX 44-1785-817007. E-mail: 101364.661@compuserve.com. **Document type:** bulletin.
   Description: Salary survey covering the Shropshire, Staffordshire, West Midlands, Warwickshire, Hereford and Worcester areas.

331   US
WEST VIRGINIA ECONOMIC SUMMARY. vol.3, 1977. m. free. Bureau of Employment Programs, Labor and Economic Research, 112 California Ave., Charleston, WV 25305-0112. TEL 304-558-2660. charts; stat. circ. 3,000. **Indexed:** SRI. **Document type:** government publication, newsletter.
   Former titles: West Virginia. Department of Employment Security. Labor Market Trends; West Virginia. Department of Employment Security. Area Manpower Summary.

331.11   US
WEST VIRGINIA EMPLOYMENT AND EARNINGS TRENDS: ANNUAL SUMMARY. 1968. a. free. Bureau of Employment Programs, Labor and Economic Research, 112 California Ave., Charleston, WV 25305-0112. TEL 304-558-2660. circ. 400. **Document type:** government publication.

WEST VIRGINIA EMPLOYMENT LAW LETTER. see *LAW*

331   AT   ISSN 0706-2176
WESTERN AUSTRALIAN ECONOMIC REVIEW. 1981. 2/yr. Aus.$80. Chamber of Commerce & Industry of Western Australia, P.O. Box 6209, Hay St., E., Perth, W.A. 6892, Australia. TEL 61-9-4217555. Ed. Nikki Cusworth. **Document type:** academic/scholarly publication.
   Description: Survey of current trends and prospects for the Western Australian and Australian economies.

331   344.02   BE
WETBOEK ARBEIDSRECHT. (Text in Dutch) 6 base vols. (plus updates 3/yr.). 9100 BEF. Kluwer Rechtswetenschappen Belgie, Editions Story-Scientia (Subsidiary of: Wolters Kluwer N.V.), Santvoortbeeklaan 21-25, 2100 Antwerp, Belgium. FAX 32-3-3600467. Eds. Roger Blanpain, Othmar Vanachter. (looseleaf format) **Document type:** trade publication.
   Description: Covers individual, collective, international and European labor law.

WILEY EMPLOYMENT LAW UPDATE ON C D - R O M. see *LAW*

WISCONSIN EMPLOYMENT LAW LETTER. see *LAW*

331.11   US   ISSN 0882-0910
HD6046
WOMEN AND WORK (NEWBURY PARK). 1985. irreg., vol.4, Mar. 1993. $22.95 (hardcover edition $48) (effective 1996). Sage Publications, Inc., 2455 Teller Rd., Thousand Oaks, CA 91320. TEL 805-499-0721. FAX 805-499-0871. E-mail: libraries@sagepub.com; URL: http://www.sagepub.com. (Overseas orders to: Sage Publications Ltd., 6 Bonhill St., London EC2A 4PU, England; Sage Publications India Pvt. Ltd., P.O. Box 4215, New Delhi 110 048, India) Ed.Bd. (back issues avail.) **Document type:** monographic series.

331.11   US   ISSN 0196-8394
WOMEN AND WORK (WASHINGTON); news from the Department of Labor. 1972. m. free. U.S. Department of Labor, Office of Information and Public Affairs, Third St. & Constitution Ave., N.W., Rm. S-1032, Washington, DC 20210. TEL 202-523-7323. Ed. Sue Blumenthal. circ. 13,000. (also avail. in microform) **Indexed:** Ind.U.S.Gov.Per., Pers.Lit.
   —UMI.

331   350   US
WORD FROM WASHINGTON (SAN ANTONIO). m. National Conference on Public Employee Retirement Systems, Attn: Carlos Resendez, 4414 Centerview Dr., Ste. 226, San Antonio, TX 78228. TEL 210-732-8600. FAX 210-732-8684.
   Description: Concerned with promoting and safeguarding the rights and benefits of government employees in retirement plans.

331   AT
▼**WORK ALERT;** briefings on employment matters. 1995. s-m. C C H Australia Ltd., P.O. Box 230, North Ryde, N.S.W. 2113, Australia. TEL 61-1-300300224. FAX 61-1-300306224. **Document type:** newsletter.
   ●Also available online.
   Description: Reports on employment-related matters. Covers current news, recent cases and developments in legislation and standards.

WORK TIMES. see *BUSINESS AND ECONOMICS* — *Economic Situation And Conditions*

331   282   ZA
WORKERS' CHALLENGE; from the workers to the workers. 1982. bi-m. Z2 per no. Workers' Pastoral Centre, P.O. Box 270035, Kitwe, Zambia. Eds. Fr. Elias Afwenye, Clement Katongo. circ. 18,000.

WORKERS' COMP. ADVISOR (NEW YORK). see *INSURANCE*

331.8   340   US   ISSN 1054-7819
WORKERS' COMP ADVISOR;* helping doctors, lawyers, and employers cope with the workers' comp system. 1987. m. $197. Genesis Publishing, 550 Torrey Point Rd., Del Mar, CA 92014-3630. TEL 619-453-0858. Ed. Donna Buys Hawkins. adv.; bk.rev. (back issues avail.) **Document type:** newsletter.
   —CCC.
   Description: Covers the workers compensation industry.

WORKERS' COMP MANAGED CARE. see *INSURANCE*

WORKERS COMPENSATION; exposures, coverage, claims. see *INSURANCE*

WORKERS' COMPENSATION COST CONTROL. see *INSURANCE*

331   US   ISSN 0748-7878
KF3613.36
WORKERS' COMPENSATION LAW BULLETIN. 1978. m. $63 (s-m. ed. $92) (effective 1993). Quinlan Publishing Co., Inc., 23 Drydock Ave., 2nd Fl., Boston, MA 02210-2307. TEL 800-229-2084. FAX 617-345-9646. index. (back issues avail.) **Document type:** newsletter.
   —UMI. CCC.
   Formerly: Worker's Compensation.
   Description: Covers court decisions on when and how compensation is awarded in workers' compensation cases, including stress-related injuries, equipment malfunctions, travel-related injuries, employee negligence, toxic exposure and more.

344.012   US
WORKERS' COMPENSATION LAW OF MARYLAND ANNOTATED. base vol. (plus a. update). $30. Michie, A Division of Reed Elsevier Inc., Box 7587, Charlottesville, VA 22906-7587. TEL 804-972-7566; 800-562-1197. FAX 800-643-1280. E-mail: custserv@michie.com; URL: http://www.michie.com. Ed. George Harley.

WORKERS' COMPENSATION LAWS OF CALIFORNIA. see *LAW*

340   AT
WORKERS COMPENSATION N S W. base vol. (plus 6/yr. updates). Aus.$550 (effective 1997). Butterworths, Division of Reed International Books Australia Pty. Ltd. (Subsidiary of: Reed Elsevier Australia Pty. Ltd.), 271-273 Lane Cove Rd., North Ryde, N.S.W. 2113, Australia. TEL 61-2-93354444. FAX 61-2-93354655. Ed. C.P. Mills. R&P contact: Deanne Castellino. adv. contact: Rebecca Browning. (looseleaf format)

331   US
WORKERS' COMPENSATION NEWS AND FOUR-FORTY REPORT. q. $27.50 to non-members. Florida Bar, Workers' Compensation Section, 650 Apalachee Pkwy., Tallahassee, FL 32399-2300. TEL 904-561-5621. circ. 1,430. **Document type:** newsletter.

WORKERS' COMPENSATION OUTLOOK. see *INSURANCE*

331   AT   ISSN 0816-2107
WORKERS COMPENSATION REPORT. 1984. fortn. Aus.$325 (effective 1996). Newsletter Information Services, P.O. Box 693, Manly, N.S.W. 2095, Australia. TEL 61-2-9777500. FAX 61-2-9773310. E-mail: hww@hww.com.au; URL: http://www.hww.com.au. Ed. Mathew Cark.
   Description: Provides information for people involved in the field of workers compensation. Analysis of judgments from tribunals in all states. Explains implications of legal and government developments and changing requirements on employers and unions.

WORKERS EDUCATION JOURNAL. see *EDUCATION* — *Adult Education*

331   UK
WORKERS PRESS. 1986. w. £27.50 (foreign £63.50). P.O. Box 735, London SW8 1YB, England. TEL 44-171-387-0564. FAX 44-171-387-0569. E-mail: s0gp@exnet.co.uk. Ed. M. Cooke. **Document type:** newspaper.

WORKFORCE; the business magazine for leaders in human resources. see *BUSINESS AND ECONOMICS* — *Personnel Management*

331   AT   ISSN 0811-9023
WORKFORCE. (Supplements avail.: Workforce N.S.W. Reports; Workforce Victoria Reports) 1974. w. Aus.$455 (effective 1996). Newsletter Information Services, P.O. Box 693, Manly, N.S.W. 2095, Australia. TEL 61-2-9777500. FAX 61-2-9773310. E-mail: hww@hww.com.au; URL: http://www.hww.com.au. Ed. David Vincent. **Document type:** newsletter.
   Description: Provides coverage of all industrial relations issues: dispute outcomes, tribunal judgements, settlements, latest enterprise agreements, award changes, interpretations and predictions and industrial trends.

331   US
WORKFORCE DIVERSITY; the monthly report on managing a changing workforce. m. $170 (foreign $190). Remy Publishing Co., 350 W. Hubbard St., No. 440, Chicago, IL 60610-4011. TEL 312-464-0300. Ed. Catherine Davis. index. **Document type:** newsletter.
   Description: Helps with managing the changing demographics of today's workforce and of the global workplace by reporting on innovative diversity programs, surveys, and resources.

331.1   US   ISSN 1062-8991
HD8051
WORKFORCE STRATEGIES. (Supplement to: B N A's Employee Relations Weekly (ISSN 0739-3016)) 1990. m. $148. The Bureau of National Affairs, Inc. 1231 25th St., N.W., Washington, DC 20037. TEL 202-452-4200. FAX 202-822-8092. TELEX 285656 BNAI WSH. URL: http://www.bna.com/. (Subscr. to: 9435 Key West Ave., Rockville, MD 20850. TEL 800-372-1033) Ed. Jeff Day. (back issues avail.) **Document type:** newsletter.
   —CCC.
   Description: Provides analysis and case studies of developments in training, recruiting, and employee development.

BUSINESS AND ECONOMICS — MACROECONOMICS

331 910.202 UK
WORKING ABROAD (LONDON). a. £9.99. Kogan Page Ltd., 120 Pentonville Rd., London N1 9JN, England. TEL 44-171-278-0433. FAX 44-171-837-6348. TELEX 263088 KOGAN G. Ed. Godfrey Golzen. R&P contact: Linda Batman. adv. **Document type:** trade publication.

331 UK
WORKING FOR YOURSELF. a. £9.99. Kogan Page Ltd., 120 Pentonville Rd., London N1 9JN, England. TEL 44-171-278-0433. FAX 44-171-837-6348. TELEX 263088 KOGAN G. Ed. Godfrey Golzen. R&P contact: Linda Batman. adv. **Document type:** bulletin, trade publication.
 Description: Provides tried and tested guidance for anyone thinking of becoming self-employed.

WORKING U S A. see *LABOR UNIONS*

331 CN ISSN 0834-292X
WORKLIFE REPORT. 1981. bi-m. Can.$35 (foreign Can.$39). I R Research Services, P.O. Box 1092, Kingston, ON K7L 4Y5, Canada. TEL 613-542-5596. Ed. L.A. Kelly. bk.rev. circ. 1,500. (reprint service avail. from UMI) **Indexed:** ABI Inform.
 ●Also available online. Vendor(s): UMI.
 —BLDSC (9351.222000); UMI. **CCC.**
 Description: Aims to promote awareness of research, issues and trends in labor relations, personnel, and other work-related areas.

331 340 CN
WORKPLACE NEWS. 1991. m. Can.$120 (effective 1997). Canada Law Book Inc., 240 Edward St., Aurora, ON L4G 3S9, Canada. TEL 905-841-6472; 800-263-2037. FAX 905-841-5085. (tabloid format) **Document type:** newspaper.
 Formerly: Labour Times (ISSN 1183-2878)
 Description: Covers the most recent developments in the areas of arbitration, industrial relations, pay equity, occupational health and safety and employment law.

331 SZ ISSN 1020-3079
HD5701
▼**WORLD EMPLOYMENT (YEAR).** 1995. a. 25 SFr. (International Labour Office) I L O Publications, CH-1211 Geneva 22, Switzerland. TEL 022-799-6111. FAX 022-798-6358. TELEX 415647-ILO-CH. **Document type:** bulletin.
 Description: Provides a comprehensive review of the worldwide employment crisis.

331 UN ISSN 0255-5514
HD4802
WORLD LABOUR REPORT. Spanish edition: Trabajo en el Mundo (ISSN 0255-5522); French edition: Travail dans le Monde (ISSN 0255-5506) (Text in English) 1984. irreg., vol.8, 1995. price varies. (International Labour Office) I L O Publications, CH-1211 Geneva 22, Switzerland. TEL 41-22-799-6111. FAX 41-22-798-6358. TELEX 415647-ILO-CH. (Dist. in US by: I L O Publications Center, 49 Sheridan Ave., Albany, NY 12210. TEL 518-436-9686. FAX 518-436-7433) (also avail. in microfiche from CIS) **Indexed:** IIS. **Document type:** monographic series.
 —BLDSC (9356.120000). **CCC.**
 Description: A round-up of developments, trends and major indicators in areas of interest to the ILO.

WRONGFUL DISMISSAL PRACTICE MANUAL. see *LAW*

331 GW
WUESTENROT - JOURNAL; Zeitschrift fuer Mitarbeiter der Wuestenrot-Gruppe. 1973. q. membership. Wuestenrot Holding GmbH, Hohenzollernstr. 46, 71630 Ludwigsburg, Germany. FAX 49-7141-163867. Ed. Katja Baecker-Wittke. circ. 10,000. **Document type:** corporate report.

331 US
WYOMING. EMPLOYMENT SECURITY COMMISSION. ANNUAL REPORT. 1973. a. Employment Security Commission, Box 2760, Casper, WY 82602. TEL 307-335-3200. Ed. Philip J. McAulay. circ. 150. **Document type:** government publication.

WYOMING EMPLOYMENT LAW LETTER. see *LAW*

331 US ISSN 0512-4409
WYOMING LABOR FORCE TRENDS. 1963. m. free. Wyoming Department of Employment, Research & Planning Division, Box 2760, Casper, WY 82602. TEL 307-438-3808. FAX 307-473-3834. E-mail: edlin.gayle@keberos.state.wy.us; URL: http://wyjobs.state.wy.us/mi/rphome.htm. Ed. Gayle C. Edlin. R&P contact: Gayle Edlin. TEL 307-473-3801. circ. 900. (also avail. in microfiche from CIS) **Indexed:** SRI. **Document type:** government publication.
 ●Also available online.
 Formerly: Wyoming. Employment Security Commission. Research and Analysis Section. Labor Force Trends.
 Description: Features articles on issues relating to Wyoming's labor force including wages, occupational and industrial projections, unemployment insurance, nonagricultural employment, and civilian labor force and employment statistics.

BELIZE LABOUR FORCE INDICATORS. see *BUSINESS AND ECONOMICS — Abstracting, Bibliographies, Statistics*

331 UK
YORKSHIRE AND NORTH EAST SALARY SURVEY. 2/yr. £250 (effective 1997). The Reward Group Ltd., Reward House, Diamond Way, Stone Business Park, Stone, Staffordshire ST15 0SD, England. TEL 44-1785-813566. FAX 44-1785-817007. E-mail: 101364.661@compuserve.com. **Document type:** bulletin.
 Description: Pay and benefit salary survey for Yorkshire and the North East.

344.73 331 GW ISSN 0342-328X
Z F A. (Zeitschrift fuer Arbeitsrecht) q. DM.148 (effective 1996). Carl Heymanns Verlag KG, Luxemburgerstr. 449, 50939 Cologne, Germany. TEL 49-221-94373-0. FAX 49-221-94373901. Ed. E.-G. Mager. circ. 1,050. **Indexed:** ELLIS, IBR. **Document type:** bulletin.
 —SWETS.

331 ZA ISSN 0084-4632
ZAMBIA. DEPARTMENT OF LABOUR. REPORT. a. K.200. Zambia Government Printing Department, P.O. Box 30136, Lusaka, Zambia. **Document type:** government publication.
 Description: Paper covering all aspects of labor matters.

331.1 XV
ZAPOSLENI PO OBCINAH. irreg. 20 din. Zavod SR Slovenije za Statistiko, Vozarski Pot 12, Ljubljana, Slovenia. Ed. Mlinar Branko.

ZEITSCHRIFT: BEHINDERTE IM BERUF. see *SOCIAL SERVICES AND WELFARE*

ZEITSCHRIFT FUER ARBEITSRECHT UND SOZIALRECHT. see *LAW*

331 658 GW ISSN 0340-2444
HD4809
ZEITSCHRIFT FUER ARBEITSWISSENSCHAFT; Zentralblatt fuer Arbeitswissenschaft und soziale Betriebspraxis. 1946. q. DM.135 (effective 1997). (Gesellschaft fuer Arbeitswissenschaft e.V.) Verlag Dr. Otto Schmidt KG, Unter den Ulmen 96-98, 50968 Cologne, Germany. TEL 49-221-9373801. FAX 49-221-93738943. E-mail: dr.otto.schmidt@t-online.de. Ed. Th. Hettinger. adv.; bk.rev.; charts; illus.; index. circ. 1,400. (reprint service avail. from SCH) **Indexed:** Agri.Eng.Abstr., C.I.S. Abstr., Ergon.Abstr., Excerp.Med., Ger.J.Psych., Key to Econ.Sci., P.A.I.S.For.Lang.Ind. **Document type:** trade publication.
 —BLDSC (9452.040000); SWETS. **CCC.**
 Formerly: Arbeit und Leistung (ISSN 0003-763X)

ZEITSCHRIFT FUER AUSLAENDISCHES UND INTERNATIONALES ARBEITS- UND SOZIALRECHT. see *LAW*

331 CC ISSN 1000-6230
ZHONGGUO LAODONG KEXUE/LABOR SCIENCE OF CHINA. (Text in Chinese) 1986. m. Y14.40. (Laodong Renshibu, Laodong Kexue Yanjiusuo) Laodong Renshi Chubanshe, 12 Hepingli Zhongjie, Beijing 100013, People's Republic of China. TEL 4214015. (Co-sponsor: Zhongguo Laodong Xuehui) Ed. Sun Zhen. (back issues avail.)

BUSINESS AND ECONOMICS — Macroeconomics

339 330.9 SW ISSN 0345-0236
AKTUELL EKONOMI. 1973. 10/yr. SEK 350 (effective 1997). Svenska Handelsbanken, Markets Research, S-106 70 Stockholm, Sweden. FAX 46-8-0110869. Ed. Christofer Halldin. **Document type:** newsletter.

AMERICAECONOMIA. see *BUSINESS AND ECONOMICS — Economic Situation And Conditions*

337 US
ANNUAL EDITIONS: MACROECONOMICS. 1975. a. $12.95. Dushkin Publishing Group, Sluice Dock, Guilford, CT 06437-9989. TEL 203-453-4351. FAX 203-453-6000. Ed. Don Cole; Pub. Ian Nielsen. illus. **Document type:** academic/scholarly publication. Refereed Serial

AUSTRALIA. BUREAU OF STATISTICS. A GUIDE TO THE CONSUMER INDEX. see *BUSINESS AND ECONOMICS — Abstracting, Bibliographies, Statistics*

AUSTRALIA. BUREAU OF STATISTICS. N I F - 10S MODEL DATA BASE MANUAL. see *BUSINESS AND ECONOMICS — Abstracting, Bibliographies, Statistics*

339 UY
BANCO CENTRAL DEL URUGUAY. DEPARTAMENTO DE ESTADISTICAS ECONOMICAS. PRODUCTO E INGRESO NACIONALES. irreg. Banco Central del Uruguay, Departamento de Estadisticas Economicas, Casilla 1467, Paysando y Florida, Montevideo, Uruguay. FAX 598-2-921782. TELEX 26939 BACENUR UY. charts.
 Formerly: Banco Central del Uruguay. Division Asesoria Economica y Estudios. Producto e Ingreso Nacionales. Actualizacion de las Principales Variables.

339 330.9 CN ISSN 0849-3049
HC111
CANADIAN MARKET OUTLOOK. q. D R I Canada, 2 First Canadian Place, The Exchange Tower, Ste. 1100, P.O. Box 193, Toronto, ON M5X 1A6, Canada. TEL 416-360-8885. FAX 416-360-0088. (back issues avail.)
 Formerly: Canadian Review (ISSN 0381-1085)

CHINA MONTHLY STATISTICS. see *BUSINESS AND ECONOMICS — Abstracting, Bibliographies, Statistics*

339 CH
CHINA, REPUBLIC. EXECUTIVE YUAN. DIRECTORATE-GENERAL OF BUDGET, ACCOUNTING & STATISTICS. REPORT ON THE SURVEY OF FAMILY INCOME & EXPENDITURE IN TAIWAN AREA. Key Title: Report on the Survey of Family Income & Expenditure in Taiwan Area. (Text in English, Chinese) 1966. a. NT.$400. Executive Yuan, Directorate-General of Budget, Accounting & Statistics, 2 Kwangchow St., Taipei, Taiwan, Republic of China. TEL 886-2-381-4910. (Subscr. to: Chen Chung Book Co., 3F, 20 Heng-Yang Rd., Taipei, Taiwan, R.O.C.. TEL 886-2-381-3980) charts; illus.; stat.
 Formerly: China, Republic. Executive Yuan. Directorate-General of Budget, Accounting and Statistics. Report on the Survey of Personal Income Distribution in Taiwan Area (ISSN 0257-5752)

339 CK
COLOMBIAN ECONOMY. (Text in English) 1978. m. $65. Camara de Comercio Colombo-Americana, Apdo. Aereo 8008, Bogota, Colombia. TEL 285-7800. FAX 288-6434. Ed. Alexandra Obolensky. adv.; charts. circ. 1,000. **Document type:** trade publication.

CONSUMER POLICY REVIEW. see *CONSUMER EDUCATION AND PROTECTION*

339 IR
CONSUMER PRICE INDEX IN URBAN AREAS OF IRAN. m. Bank Markazi Jomhouri Islami Iran, Economic Statistics Department - Central Bank of the Islamic Republic of Iran, P.O. Box 11365-8532, Tehran, Iran. FAX 98-21-390323. TELEX 216219.

BUSINESS AND ECONOMICS — MACROECONOMICS

330.9   CU   ISSN 0864-1420
HC152.5.A1
CUBA: ECONOMIA PLANIFICADA. 1986. q. $14 in N. and S. America; Europe $16; elsewhere $18. Junta Central de Planificacion (JUCEPLAN), 11 y C, Vedado, Havana, Cuba. TEL 809 79-8661. TELEX 1158 Y 1170. (Dist. by: Ediciones Cubanas, Obispo No. 527, Apdo. 605, Havana 1, Cuba) Ed. Fernando Jimenez Gomez. charts; illus.; stat. circ. 2,000.

D R I - MCGRAW-HILL COUNTRY REPORTS. see BUSINESS AND ECONOMICS — Economic Situation And Conditions

D R I - MCGRAW-HILL GLOBAL RISK REPORT. see BUSINESS AND ECONOMICS — Economic Situation And Conditions

D R I - MCGRAW-HILL REVIEW OF THE U S ECONOMY. see BUSINESS AND ECONOMICS — Economic Situation And Conditions

D R I - MCGRAW-HILL REVIEW OF THE U S ECONOMY: LONG RANGE FOCUS. see BUSINESS AND ECONOMICS — Economic Situation And Conditions

D R I - MCGRAW-HILL U S FORECAST SUMMARY. see BUSINESS AND ECONOMICS — Economic Situation And Conditions

ECONOMIC INDICATORS. see BUSINESS AND ECONOMICS — Abstracting, Bibliographies, Statistics

339   TU   ISSN 1300-9265
ECONOMIC INDICATORS OF TURKEY. (Editions in English, Turkish) a. free. Turkiye Is Bankasi, Economic Research and Planning Department, Ataturk Bulvari 191, Kavaklidere, Ankara, Turkey. FAX 90-312-413-9090. TELEX 42082 TAB TR. Ed. Nese Demir. R&P contact: Nese Demir. stat. circ. 4,350 (2,000 English ed., 2,300 Turkish ed.). **Document type:** bulletin.

339   SW   ISSN 0349-7860
EKONOMISK INFORMATION. 1981. 8/yr. SEK 400 (effective 1997). Nordbanken (NB), Ekonomiska Sekretariatet, S-105 71 Stockholm, Sweden. Ed. Olle Djerf; Pub. Nils Lundgren. **Document type:** newsletter.

339   UY   ISSN 0797-6291
ENCUESTA DE HOGARES: OCUPACION Y DESOCUPACION. 1968. s-a. Direccion General de Estadistica y Censos, Montevideo, Uruguay. stat.

ESTADISTICAS MACROECONOMICAS DE CENTROAMERICA. see BUSINESS AND ECONOMICS — Abstracting, Bibliographies, Statistics

339   NE   ISSN 0176-2680
HB1
EUROPEAN JOURNAL OF POLITICAL ECONOMY. (Text in English) 1985. q. fl.785($451) (effective 1998). North-Holland (Subsidiary of: Elsevier Science B.V.), P.O. Box 211, 1000 AE Amsterdam, Netherlands. TEL 31-20-4853911. FAX 31-20-4853598. TELEX 18582 ESPA NL. (Subscr. in the Americas to: Elsevier Science, Regional Sales Office, Box 945, New York, NY 10159-0945. TEL 212-633-3730. FAX 212-633-3680; Subscr. in Australasia and the Far East to: Elsevier Science (Singapore) Pte Ltd, No.1 Temasek Ave., No.17-01 Millenia Tower, Singapore 039192, Singapore. TEL 65-434-3727. FAX 65-337-2230; Subscr. in Japan to: Elsevier Science Japan, 9-15 Higashi-Azabu 1-chome, Minato-ku Tokyo 106, Japan. TEL 81-3-5561-5033. FAX 81-3-5561-5047) Ed. M.J. Holler. adv.; bk.rev.; index. (also avail. in microform from UMI; back issues avail.) **Indexed:** Curr.Cont., IBR, Int.Polit.Sci.Abstr., Sociol.Abstr. **Document type:** academic/scholarly publication.
—BLDSC (3829.736500); SWETS; UnCover. **CCC.**
Description: Devoted to the study of classical and neoclassical political economy, public choice and collective decision making, law and economics, and economic history.
Refereed Serial

339   SW   ISSN 0280-3364
FAKTA OM SVERIGES EKONOMI. 1978. a. SEK 160 (effective 1997). Svenska Arbetsgivarefoereningen (SAF), S-103 30 Stockholm, Sweden. URL: http://www.saf.se.

339   CI   ISSN 0350-5669
FINANCIJSKA PRAKSA. (Text in Serbo-Croatian; summaries in English) 1977. bi-m. $90. Institut za Javne Financije - Institute of Public Finance, Katanciceva 5, 41000 Zagreb, Croatia. FAX 38-41-433-006. Ed. Guste Santini. circ. 3,000.
—BLDSC (3927.230000).
Description: Covers theory and practice of public finance, macro and micro finance, fiscal and monetary policy, local finance.

339   GM
GAMBIA. CENTRAL STATISTICS DEPARTMENT. MONTHLY BULLETIN OF PRICES. (Formerly issued by Central Statistics Division) m. D.12. Central Statistics Department, Wellington St., Banjul, Gambia.

GREAT BRITAIN. BOARD OF INLAND REVENUE. SURVEY OF PERSONAL INCOMES. see BUSINESS AND ECONOMICS — Public Finance, Taxation

339   UK   ISSN 0072-5927
HD7023
GREAT BRITAIN. CENTRAL STATISTICAL OFFICE. FAMILY EXPENDITURE SURVEY. 1957. a. £20.50 (Nov. 1992 edition). Office for National Statistics, Government Bldgs., 155 Cardiff Rd., Newport, Gwent NP9 1XG, Wales. TEL 44-1633-812973. FAX 44-1633-812599. TELEX 497121 BSO NPT G. (Orders to: Stationery Office Publications Centre, P.O. Box 276, London SW8 5DT, England. TEL 44-171-873-9090. FAX 44-171-873-8200) stat. (also avail. in microfiche from CHL) **Document type:** government publication.
—**CCC.**
Description: Contains macroeconomics research focusing on private households and how they spend their money, following a representative sampling of U.K. families.

339 332   US   ISSN 0197-7636
HARVARD COLLEGE ECONOMIST. 1976. s-a. $10 to individuals (foreign $15); institutions $15 (foreign $20) (effective 1998). Harvard Economics Association, 200 Littauer Center, Dept. of Economics, Harvard University, Cambridge, MA 02138. TEL 617-495-2145. FAX 617-495-7730. E-mail: econ@hcs.harvard.edu; URL: http://hcs.harvard.edu/~econ. Ed. Carlo N. Forcione. R&P contact: Carlo N. Forcione. adv. contact: Jared Beck. bk.rev. circ. 2,000. (back issues avail.) **Document type:** academic/scholarly publication.
Formerly: Harvard Undergraduate Journal of Economics.
Description: Presents interviews with economists, articles on economic policy and theory, papers in economics by Harvard undergraduates.

339   CC
HONG KONG. GOVERNMENT PUBLICATION CENTRE. ECONOMIC BACKGROUND. (Editions in Chinese, English) a. HK.$28. Government Publication Centre, G.P.O. Bldg., Ground Fl., Connaught Place, Hong Kong, People's Republic of China. TEL 5-8428801. (Subscr. to: Director of Information Services, Information Services Dept., 1 Battery Path, G-F, Central, Hong Kong; People's Republic of China) Ed.Bd.

339   CC
HONG KONG. GOVERNMENT PUBLICATION CENTRE. ECONOMIC PROSPECTS. (Editions in Chinese, English) a. HK.$10. Government Publication Centre, G.P.O. Bldg., Ground Fl., Connaught Pl., Hong Kong, People's Republic of China. TEL 5-8428801. (Subscr. to: Director of Information Services, Information Services Dept., 1 Battery Path, G-F, Central, Hong Kong; People's Republic of China) Ed.Bd.

339   CC
HONG KONG. GOVERNMENT PUBLICATION CENTRE. ECONOMIC REPORT. (Editions in Chinese, English) q. HK.$60. Government Publication Centre, G.P.O. Bldg., Ground Fl., Connaught Pl., Hong Kong, People's Republic of China. TEL 5-8428801. (Subscr. to: Director of Information Services, Information Services Dept., 1 Battery Path, G-f, Central, Hong Kong; People's Republic of China) Ed.Bd.

338   UN   ISSN 0020-4080
HC121
I L P E S CUADERNOS. (In 3 sections) (Text in Spanish) 1967. irreg., no.38, 1993. price varies. Instituto Latinoamericano y del Caribe de Planificacion Economica y Social - Latin American and Caribbean Institute for Economic and Social Planning, Casilla 179-D, Santiago, Chile. FAX 562480252. (Dist. in U.S. by: Economic Commission for Latin America, 1801 K St. N.W., Suite 1261, Washington, DC 20006)

INDIA. CENTRAL STATISTICAL ORGANIZATION. NATIONAL ACCOUNTS STATISTICS: SOURCES AND METHODS. see BUSINESS AND ECONOMICS — Abstracting, Bibliographies, Statistics

INDONESIA. CENTRAL BUREAU OF STATISTICS. ECONOMIC INDICATOR BULLETIN. see BUSINESS AND ECONOMICS — Abstracting, Bibliographies, Statistics

INTERNATIONAL MONETARY FUND. BALANCE OF PAYMENTS STATISTICS YEARBOOK. see BUSINESS AND ECONOMICS — Abstracting, Bibliographies, Statistics

IRELAND. CENTRAL STATISTICS OFFICE. NATIONAL INCOME AND EXPENDITURE. see BUSINESS AND ECONOMICS — Abstracting, Bibliographies, Statistics

JAPAN AND THE WORLD ECONOMY; international journal of theory and policy. see BUSINESS AND ECONOMICS — Economic Systems And Theories, Economic History

JAPAN STATISTICAL ASSOCIATION. MONTHLY REPORT ON THE FAMILY INCOME AND EXPENDITURE SURVEY. see BUSINESS AND ECONOMICS — Abstracting, Bibliographies, Statistics

339   CC
JINGJI TIZHI GAIGE/REFORMATION OF ECONOMIC SYSTEM. (Text in Chinese; summaries in Chinese and English) bi-m. Y12. Sichuan Sheng Shehui Kexueyuan - Sichuan Academy of Social Science, Qingyang Gong, Chengdu, Sichuan 610072, People's Republic of China. TEL 669347. (Dist. outside China by: China Publications Foreign Trade Corp., P.O. Box 782, Beijing, P.R.C.) Ed. Lin Ling.

JOURNAL OF CONSUMER POLICY; consumer issues in law, economics and behavioral sciences. see CONSUMER EDUCATION AND PROTECTION

339   US   ISSN 0164-0704
HB1
JOURNAL OF MACROECONOMICS. 1979. q. $35 to individuals (foreign $41); institutions $75 (foreign $81) (effective 1997). Louisiana State University Press, Box 25053, Baton Rouge, LA 70894-5053. TEL 504-388-8271. FAX 504-388-6461. Eds. David J. Smyth, Douglas McMillin. R&P contact: Mary Holt. adv. contact: Margaret Hart. index. circ. 950. (also avail. in microform from UMI; reprint service avail. from UMI) **Indexed:** ABI Inform., ASCA, C.R.E.J., Curr.Cont., J.of Econ.Lit., Sage Pub.Admin.Abstr., SSCI. **Document type:** academic/scholarly publication.
—BLDSC (5010.730000); Genuine Article; SWETS; UMI; UnCover. **CCC.**

K D B REPORT. (Korea Development Bank) see BUSINESS AND ECONOMICS

KUWAIT. CENTRAL STATISTICAL OFFICE. MONTHLY CONSUMER PRICE INDEX NUMBERS. see BUSINESS AND ECONOMICS — Abstracting, Bibliographies, Statistics

338   US   ISSN 0747-525X
HC101
LOOKING AHEAD (WASHINGTON). 1952. q. $35. National Policy Association, 1424 16th St., N.W., Ste. 700, Washington, DC 20036. TEL 202-265-7685. FAX 202-797-5516. Ed. M.L. Benz. charts; stat. circ. 1,000. **Indexed:** Fut.Surv.
—BLDSC (5294.515000); UnCover.
Former titles: Looking Ahead and Projection Highlights; Looking Ahead (ISSN 0024-6409)

BUSINESS AND ECONOMICS — MACROECONOMICS

339   UK   ISSN 1365-1005
MACROECONOMIC DYNAMICS. q. £99($149) (effective 1998). Cambridge University Press, Edinburgh Bldg., Shaftesbury Rd., Cambridge CB2 2RU, England. TEL 44-1223-312393. FAX 44-1223-315052. E-mail: information@cup.cam.ac.uk; URL: http://www.cup.org/journals/CUPJNLS.html. (N. America addr.: 40 W. 20th St., New York, NY 10011-4211. TEL 212-924-3900. FAX 212-691-3239)

339   CN   ISSN 0712-4791
MONTHLY ECONOMIC REVIEW. 1974. m. Can.$375 (effective 1997). Informetrica Limited, P.O. Box 828, Stn. B, Ottawa, ON K1P 5P9, Canada. TEL 613-238-4831. FAX 613-238-7698. Ed. Martha Justus. index. circ. 500. (back issues avail.) —CISTI.
Description: Provides economic forecasts and analysis for the professional advisor or executive, and objective appraisal of economic conditions and policy for senior officials in government and business.

N A B E INDUSTRY SURVEY. (National Association of Business Economists) see BUSINESS AND ECONOMICS — Economic Situation And Conditions

N A B E NEWS. (National Association of Business Economists) see BUSINESS AND ECONOMICS — Economic Situation And Conditions

N A B E OUTLOOK & POLICY SURVEY. (National Association of Business Economists) see BUSINESS AND ECONOMICS — Economic Situation And Conditions

339   US   ISSN 0889-3365
HB172.5
N B E R MACROECONOMICS ANNUAL. 1986. a. $40 hardcover (foreign $50); paperback $20 (foreign $30) (effective 1996). (National Bureau of Economic Research) M I T Press, 5 Cambridge Center, Cambridge, MA 02142. TEL 617-253-2889. FAX 617-577-1545. E-mail: journals-orders@mit.edu; URL: http://www-mitpress.mit.edu. (Editorial addr.: 1050 Massachusetts Ave., 3rd Fl., Cambridge, MA 02138) Eds. Ben S. Bernanke, Julio Rotenberg. R&P contact: Paul Dzus. (back issues avail.; reprint service avail. from UMI) Indexed: ASCA, J.of Econ.Lit. **Document type:** academic/scholarly publication.
—BLDSC (6067.717700). **CCC.**
Description: Links theoretical and empirical developments in economics with real-world examples and problems.

339.368   BS   ISSN 0302-2056
HC517.B63
NATIONAL ACCOUNTS OF BOTSWANA. a. P.10. Central Statistics Office, Ministry of Finance and Development Planning, Private Bag 0024, Gaborone, Botswana. TEL 267-352200. (Orders to: Government Printer, P.O. Box 87, Gaborone, Botswana) Ed. G.M. Charumbira; Pub. J.G. Segwe. stat. **Document type:** government publication.
Description: Contains data on Botswana from a macroeconomic perspective.

339   PH
NATIONAL INCOME ACCOUNTS OF THE PHILIPPINES. (Text in English) q. $163 in Asia (Australia & New Zealand $187; US & Canada $203; Europe $243; elsewhere $255). National Statistical Coordination Board, c/o National Statistical Information Center, Midland-Buendia Bldg., 403 Sen. Gil Puyat Ave., Makati City, Philippines. TEL 63-2-890-9405. FAX 63-2-890-9408. E-mail: nscb__nsic@mozcom.com. illus. (processed) **Document type:** government publication.
Formerly: Philippines. National Economic and Development Authority. National Income Series.
Description: Presents measures of the aggregate or sum of factor incomes-payments arising from the production activities of the country. Valuates total final goods and services produced in a given period, and records flows from production to consumption, accumulation, and foreign trade.

339   AG   ISSN 0326-5730
HC171
NUEVA ECONOMIA. 1984. bi-m. Arg.$20($24) Zarco S.C.A. (Schwartzman y Asociados), Av. Pueyrredon 480, Piso 11-Of. 71, Caixa Postal 1032, Buenos Aires, Argentina. Eds. Leon S. Schwartzman, Daniel M. Schwartzman. adv.; bk.rev.; film rev.; bibl.; tr.lit. circ. 7,500. (back issues avail.)

339   SW   ISSN 0349-5671
OUTLOOK ON THE SWEDISH ECONOMY. (Text in English) 1976. 4/yr. $45 (effective 1997). Nordbanken (NB), Ekonomiska Sekretariatet, S-105 71 Stockholm, Sweden. Ed. Thomas Pousette; Pub. Nils Lundgren. **Document type:** newsletter.

OUZHOU/EUROPE. see SOCIAL SCIENCES: COMPREHENSIVE WORKS

339   CK   ISSN 0121-9782
PANORAMA MACROECONOMICO Y FINANCIERO. m. $70 (effective 1998). Asociacion Bancaria y de Entidades Financieras, Apdo. Aereo 13994, Bogota D.C., Colombia. TEL 57-1-2114811. FAX 57-1-2119915. E-mail: info@asobancaria.com; URL: http://ww.asobancaria.com.
Description: Provides analyses on current national and international macroeconomic subjects.

339.2   US
PERSONAL INCOME IN AREAS AND COUNTIES OF NEW YORK STATE. 1961. a. free. Department of Economic Development, 1 Commerce Plaza, Albany, NY 12245. Ed. William Grainger. circ. 1,500. **Document type:** government publication.
Formerly: Personal Income in Counties of New York State (ISSN 0079-0907)
Description: Detailed estimates of income by type and source.

PERU. INSTITUTO NACIONAL DE ESTADISTICA. BOLETIN ANUAL. see BUSINESS AND ECONOMICS — Abstracting, Bibliographies, Statistics

339.021   PO   ISSN 0870-2659
PORTUGAL. INSTITUTO NACIONAL DE ESTADISTICA. CONTAS NACIONAIS. (Supplement to: Portugal. Instituto Nacional de Estatistica. Anuario Estatistico (ISSN 0079-4112)) 1972. a. Esc.4000 (effective 1997). Instituto Nacional de Estatistica, Ave. Antonio Jose de Almeida, 1078 Lisbon, Portugal. TEL 351-1-8470050. FAX 351-1-8478578. TELEX 351-1-63738 PCDINE P. **Document type:** government publication.
Description: Includes the Portuguese macroeconomic aggregates for the year under review.

339.021   PO   ISSN 0872-1602
PORTUGAL. INSTITUTO NACIONAL DE ESTADISTICA. CONTAS NACIONAIS TRIMESTRAIS. 1992. q. Esc.3050. Instituto Nacional de Estatistica, Ave. Antonio Jose de Almeida, 1078 Lisbon, Portugal. TEL 351-1-8470050. FAX 351-1-8478578. TELEX 351-1-63738 PCDINE P.

339   SZ
PRICES AND EARNINGS AROUND THE GLOBE. (Editions in English, French, German, and Italian) 1970. triennial, 9th ed., 1994. free. Union Bank of Switzerland, Bahnhofstr. 45, CH-8021 Zurich, Switzerland. TEL 41-1-2341111. FAX 41-1-2343245. TELEX 813811. circ. 36,000 (English ed.); 140,000 (combined). **Document type:** bulletin.
Description: Survey of prices and earnings in 53 cities. Includes a comparison of purchasing power.

PRIVATE DEVELOPMENT CORPORATION OF THE PHILIPPINES. POLICY ANALYSIS. see BUSINESS AND ECONOMICS — International Development And Assistance

339   NZ   ISSN 0033-5711
HC670.I5
QUARTERLY PREDICTIONS OF NATIONAL INCOME AND EXPENDITURE. 1964. q. NZ.$300. New Zealand Institute of Economic Research, P.O. Box 3479, Wellington 1, New Zealand. TEL 64-4-4721880. FAX 64-4-4721211. E-mail: econ@nzier.org.nz. Ed. D. Cook. charts; stat. Indexed: Key to Econ.Sci., P.A.I.S. **Document type:** academic/scholarly publication.
—CCC.
Incorporates (in 1987): New Zealand Institute of Economic Research. Medium Term Review (ISSN 0112-1170)
Description: Forecast of the New Zealand economy up to 2 years ahead.

RENKOU YU JINGJI/POPULATION & ECONOMICS. see POPULATION STUDIES

339   US   ISSN 0194-3960
HD82
RESEARCH IN HUMAN CAPITAL AND DEVELOPMENT. 1979. irreg., vol.9, 1996. $73.25. J A I Press Inc., 55 Old Post Rd., No. 2, Box 1678, Greenwich, CT 06830-1678. TEL 203-661-7602. FAX 203-661-0792. E-mail: jai@jaipress.com. (Subscr. in the UK and Europe to: JAI Press Ltd., 38 Tavistock St., Covent Garden, London WC2E 7PB, England. TEL 44-171-379-8834. FAX 44-171-379-8835) Ed. Alan Sorkin. **Document type:** monographic series.
—BLDSC (7741.314000); UnCover.

RESERVE BANK OF AUSTRALIA. RESEARCH DISCUSSION PAPER. see BUSINESS AND ECONOMICS — Banking And Finance

339   ET
RETAIL PRICE INDEX FOR ADDIS ABABA (EXCLUDING RENT). 1963. m. free. Central Statistical Authority, P.O. Box 1143, Addis Ababa, Ethiopia. TELEX 2167 STAT ET. **Document type:** government publication.

339   US   ISSN 0034-6586
HC79.I5
REVIEW OF INCOME AND WEALTH. 1966. q. $110 (effective 1997). International Association for Research in Income and Wealth, New York University, Dept. of Economics, 269 Mercer St., Rm. 700, New York, NY 10003. TEL 212-998-8917. FAX 212-366-5067. E-mail: wolffe@fasecon.econ.nyu.edu; URL: http://www.econ.nyu.edu/dept/iariw. Ed. Edward Wolff. bk.rev.; charts; stat. circ. 2,000. (reprint service avail. from SCH) Indexed: ASCA, Asian-Pac.Econ.Lit., BPIA, C.R.E.J., Curr.Cont., IBR, Int.Lab.Doc., J.of Econ.Lit., Mid.East: Abstr.& Ind., P.A.I.S., SSCI, World Bank.Abstr., World Bibl.Soc.Sec. **Document type:** academic/scholarly publication.
—BLDSC (7790.770000); SWETS; UnCover.
Supersedes: Income and Wealth Series.
Description: Covers national and social accounting; microdata analysis of issues related to income and wealth; development and integration of micro and macro systems of economic, financial and social statistics; international comparisons of productivity, income and wealth; and related problems of measurement and statistical methodology.
Refereed Serial

REVISTA CENTROAMERICANA DE ECONOMIA; postgrado centroamericana en economia y planificacion del desarrollo. see BUSINESS AND ECONOMICS — Economic Situation And Conditions

RYNOK TSENNYKH BUMAG/SECURITIES MARKET; analiticheskii zhurnal. see BUSINESS AND ECONOMICS — Investments

339   CC   ISSN 1003-9589
SHANDONG JINGJI ZHANLUE YANJIU/STRATEGIC STUDY OF SHANDONG ECONOMICS. (Text in Chinese) 1984. bi-m. $5. Shandong Sheng Jingji Yanjiu Zhongxin - Shandong Economic Research Center, No. 1, Shengfu Qianjie, Jinan, Shandong 250011, People's Republic of China. TEL 0531-612828. Ed. Guan Shenglan. adv.; bk.rev. circ. 5,000.

339 330.9   CC   ISSN 1001-3377
SHIJIE JINGJI/WORLD ECONOMY MONTHLY. (Text in Chinese) m. $44. Zhongguo Shehui Kexueyuan, Shijie Jingji yu Zhengzhi Yanjiusuo - Chinese Academy of Social Sciences, Institute of World Economics and Politics, 5 Jianguomennei Dajie, Beijing 100732, People's Republic of China. TEL 5137744. (Dist. outside China by: Guoji Shudian - China International Book Trading Corp., P.O. Box 399, Beijing, P.R.C.. TEL 8413063; Dist. in US by: China Books & Periodicals, Inc., 2929 24th St., San Francisco, CA 94110. TEL 415-282-2994) Ed. Li Zong.

339 330.1   US
SHIJIE JINGJI YANJIU/WORLD ECONOMY RESEARCH. (Text in Chinese) bi-m. $30.50. China Books & Periodicals, Inc., 2929 24th St., San Francisco, CA 94110. TEL 415-282-2994. FAX 415-282-0994.

SOOCHOW JOURNAL OF ECONOMICS AND BUSINESS. see BUSINESS AND ECONOMICS

BUSINESS AND ECONOMICS — MANAGEMENT

339.2 US
STUDIES IN INCOME AND WEALTH. 1937. irreg., no.57, 1993. price varies. University of Chicago Press, Journals Division, Box 37005, Chicago, IL 60637. TEL 775-753-3347. FAX 775-753-0811. E-mail: subscriptions@journals.uchicago.edu.
—BLDSC (8490.716000).
  Formerly: Conference on Research in Income and Wealth (ISSN 0069-8652)

339 UK ISSN 0081-864X
STUDIES IN THE NATIONAL INCOME AND EXPENDITURE OF THE UNITED KINGDOM. 1966. irreg., no.6, 1977. price varies. (National Institute of Economic and Social Research) Cambridge University Press, Edinburgh Bldg., Shaftesbury Rd., Cambridge CB2 2RU, England. TEL 44-1223-312393. FAX 44-1223-315052. TELEX 851817256. E-mail: information@cup.cam.ac.uk; URL: http://www.cup.cam.ac.uk. (N. American addr.: Cambridge University Press, Journals Dept., 40 W. 20th St., New York, NY 10011. TEL 212-924-3900. FAX 212-691-3239) (Co-sponsor: University of Cambridge, Department of Applied Economics) Ed. Richard Stone. R&P contact: Linda Nicol. **Document type:** academic/scholarly publication.

339.2 SJ ISSN 0377-1652
HC591.S83
SUDAN. DEPARTMENT OF STATISTICS. NATIONAL INCOME ACCOUNTS AND SUPPORTING TABLES. (Text in Arabic, English) a. Department of Statistics, National Income Division, Box 700, Khartoum, Sudan. illus.; stat. **Document type:** government publication.

339 SW ISSN 0284-4974
SWEDEN'S ECONOMY. (Text in English) 1986. s-a. SEK 190 (effective 1990). Ministry of Finance, Roedbodg. 6, S-103 33 Stockholm, Sweden. (Dist. by: Almaenna Foerlaget AB, S-106 47 Stockholm, Sweden) **Document type:** government publication.

339 CC
TIGAI XINXI/ECONOMIC REFORM NEWS. (Text in Chinese) 1985. s-m. Y24. Chongqing Jingji Tizhi Gaige Weiyuanhui - Chongqing Economic System Reform Commission, 72-7 Zhongshan Silu, Chongqing, Sichuan 630015, People's Republic of China. TEL 352240. Ed. Chen Yuanhu. adv.

339.5 US ISSN 0361-6665
HC101
WAGE-PRICE LAW & ECONOMICS REVIEW. q. $108. Antitrust Law & Economics Review, Inc., Beach P.O. Box 3532, Vero Beach, FL 32964-3532. FAX 407-461-6007. URL: http://www.metrolink.net/~cmueller/.
—UnCover.

WASHINGTON C E O. see BUSINESS AND ECONOMICS — Management

WHOLESALE PRICE INDEX IN IRAN. see BUSINESS AND ECONOMICS — Abstracting, Bibliographies, Statistics

339 327 UK ISSN 1016-359X
HD82
WORLD LINK. 1988. bi-m. £145 (foreign $215) (effective 1996). (World Economic Forum) World Link Publications Ltd., Nestor House, Playhouse Yard, London EC4V 5EX, England. TEL 44-171-779-8726. FAX 44-171-779-8727. E-mail: 100432.773@compuserve.com. (Dist. in US by: American Educational Systems, 173 W. 81st St., New York, NY 10024. TEL 800-717-2669. FAX 212-501-8926) Ed. Susan Greenberg; Pub. David Derrick. adv.: B&W page £12800, color page £16000; trim 229 x 300. bk.rev. circ. 27,047. Indexed: Per.Islam. (1991-). **Document type:** trade publication.
—BLDSC (9356.510000).

XI'OU YANJIU/WESTERN EUROPEAN STUDIES. see SOCIAL SCIENCES: COMPREHENSIVE WORKS

339 CC ISSN 1002-5928
ZHONGGUO GONGYE JINGJI YANJIU/CHINA INDUSTRIAL ECONOMICS RESEARCH. (Text in Chinese) 1984. m. Y18. (Zhongguo Shehui Kexueyuan, Gongye Jingji Yanjiusuo - Chinese Academy of Social Sciences, Institute of Industrial Economics) Jingji Guanli Chubanshe - Economic Management Publishing House, 8, Hongyuan Hutong, 6 Tiao, Xinjiekou, Beijing 100035, People's Republic of China. TEL 8312679. (Dist. outside China by: Guoji Shudian - China International Book Trading Corp., P.O. Box 399, Beijing, P.R.C.. TEL 8413063; Dist. in US by: China Books & Periodicals, Inc., 2929 24th St., San Francisco, CA 94110. TEL 415-282-2994) Ed. Zhou Shulian. bk.rev. circ. 10,000. **Document type:** academic/scholarly publication.
  Description: Covers theories and policies of Chinese industrial economics.

339 CC ISSN 1002-865X
HC427.92
ZHONGGUO JINGJI TIZHI GAIGE/CHINA'S ECONOMIC STRUCTURE REFORM. (Text in Chinese) m. Y22.20($45.80) (Guojia Jingji Tizhi Gaige Weiyuanhui - State Commission for Restructuring Economic Systems) Zhongguo Jingji Tizhi Gaige Zazhishe - China's Economic Structure Reform Magazine House, 22, Xi'anmen Dajie, Beijing 100017, People's Republic of China. TEL 3097726. (Dist. outside China by: Guoji Shudian - China International Book Trading Corp., P.O. Box 399, Beijing, P.R.C.; Dist. in US by: China Books & Periodicals, Inc., 2929 24th St., San Francisco, CA 94110. TEL 415-282-2994) Ed. Xiao Yingzhi. adv.
—UnCover.

339 CC ISSN 1000-4181
HC427.92
ZHONGGUO JINGJI WENTI. (Text in Chinese) 1959. bi-m. Y15($21.58) Xiamen Daxue, Jingji Yanjiusuo - Xiamen University, Institute of Economics, c/o Xiamen Daxue Tushuguan, Xiamen, Fujian 361005, People's Republic of China. TEL 86-592-218-6144. FAX 86-592-218-6227. E-mail: xiaodh@xmu.edu.cn; URL: http://www.xmu.edu.cn/library.html. (Dist. outside China by: China International Book Trading Corp., P.O. Box 399, Beijing, P.R.C.; Dist. in US by: China Books & Periodicals, Inc., 2929 24th St., San Francisco, CA 94110. TEL 415-282-2994) Ed. Hu Peizhao. bk.rev. circ. 10,000. **Document type:** academic/scholarly publication.
  Description: Examines Chinese economic problems.

ZHONGGUO JINGJI XINWEN/CHINA ECONOMIC NEWS. see BUSINESS AND ECONOMICS — Economic Situation And Conditions

BUSINESS AND ECONOMICS — Management

A B A MANAGEMENT UPDATE OF PERSONAL TRUST & PRIVATE BANKING. see BUSINESS AND ECONOMICS — Banking And Finance

658 011 US
A C O M MODATE QUARTERLY. q. Association for Convention Operations Management, c/o William H. Just & Assoc., Inc., 1819 Peachtree St., N.E., Ste. 560, Atlanta, GA 30309. TEL 404-351-3220. FAX 404-351-3348. **Document type:** newsletter.

A F M EXPLANATORY SERIES (NO.). (Department of Accounting and Financial Management) see BUSINESS AND ECONOMICS — Accounting

A G P MITTEILUNGEN; Zeitschrift fuer Partnerschaft in der Wirtschaft. (Arbeitsgemeinschaft zur Foerderung der Partnerschaft in der Wirtschaft e.V.) see BUSINESS AND ECONOMICS — Labor And Industrial Relations

658 US
A I M C FORUM. 1983. s-a. free. Association of Internal Management Consultants, 7960 Soquel Dr., Ste. B296, Aptos, CA 95003-3945. TEL 408-662-9890. FAX 408-662-9855. E-mail: aimc@benchnet.com; URL: http://www.benchnet.com/aimc. Ed. Michael J. Burtha. R&P contact: Michael J. Burtha. TEL 908-524-6931. bk.rev.; circ. 500 (controlled). **Document type:** trade publication.

A I M - R NEWS. (Association of Industry Manufacturers Representatives) see BUSINESS AND ECONOMICS — Production Of Goods And Services

650 US
A M A MANAGEMENT BRIEFINGS. 1971. irreg. (approx. 2/yr.). price varies. American Management Association, 1601 Broadway, New York, NY 10019. TEL 212-586-8100. (Subscr. to: Box 319, Saranac Lake, NY 12983) charts; illus.; circ. controlled.

650 US
A M A SURVEY REPORTS. 1973. irreg. price varies. American Management Association, 1610 Broadway, New York, NY 10019. TEL 212-586-8100. (Subscr. to: Box 319, Saranac Lake, NY 12983) charts; illus.; stat.

658
TS157.A1 US
A P I C S CONFERENCE PROCEEDINGS. 1960. a. $35 to non-members. A P I C S - The Educational Society for Resource Management, 500 W. Annandale Rd., Falls Church, VA 22046-4274. TEL 703-237-8344; 800-444-2742. FAX 703-237-1087. URL: http://www.apics.org. circ. 72,000. **Document type:** proceedings.
—BLDSC (4538.847100).
  Former titles: American Production and Inventory Control Society. International Conference Proceedings (ISSN 1064-1939); (until 1989): American Producation and Inventory Control Society. Annual International Conference Proceedings (ISSN 0895-6367); American Production and Inventory Control Society. Annual Conference Proceedings (ISSN 0191-1783); A P I C S Annual Conference Proceedings (ISSN 0065-9819); A P I C S International Technical Conference Proceedings (ISSN 0190-8340)

658.5 338 US ISSN 1056-0017
TS155.A1
A P I C S THE PERFORMANCE ADVANTAGE. 1991. m. $47 (Canada and Mexico $59; elsewhere $75) (effective 1997). (American Production and Inventory Control Society - The Educational Society for Resource Management) Lionheart Publishing, Inc., 2555 Cumberland Pkwy., Ste. 299, Atlanta, GA 30339. TEL 770-431-0867. FAX 770-432-6969. E-mail: lpi@lionhrtpub.com; URL: http://lionhrtpub.com. Ed. David Greenfield; Pub. John Llewellyn. R&P contact: David Greenfield. adv. contact: Marvin Diamond. bk.rev. circ. 72,153. **Document type:** trade publication.
—BLDSC (1568.356000); UnCover. **CCC.**
  Description: For professionals in all phases of resource management, manufacturing, production and inventory control.

A P P A NEWSLETTER. (Association of Physical Plant Administrators) see EDUCATION — School Organization And Administration

A P P A: THE ASSOCIATION OF HIGHER EDUCATION FACILITIES OFFICERS. PROCEEDINGS OF THE ANNUAL MEETING. see EDUCATION — School Organization And Administration

658 US ISSN 1050-8813
A Q P REPORT. 1983. bi-m. $45. Association for Quality and Participation, 801-B W. 8th St., Ste. 501, Cincinnati, OH 45203. TEL 513-381-1959. FAX 513-381-0070. Ed. Ned Hamson. bk.rev. circ. 9,500. (back issues avail.) **Document type:** newsletter.
—CCC.
  Formerly: I A Q C Circle Report.
  Description: Quality and productivity improvement through team problem solving.

658 US
A S A E ASSOCIATE MEMBER UPDATE. Variant title: A S A E Update. q. membership. American Society of Association Executives, 1575 Eye St., N.W., Washington, DC 20005-1168. TEL 202-626-2739. FAX 202-408-9635. circ. 3,500.
  Description: Includes association news, marketing strategies, and new services available to those who exhibit or market products or services to associations.

658 US
A S A E ASSOCIATION LAW AND POLICY. 1987. fortn. $295. American Society of Association Executives, Legal Section, 1575 Eye St., N.W., Washington, DC 20005-1168. TEL 202-626-2739. FAX 202-408-9635. circ. 1,950.
  Description: Includes relevant case reviews of non-profit organizations.

BUSINESS AND ECONOMICS — MANAGEMENT

658   US
A S A E INTERNATIONAL NEWS. bi-m. membership. American Society of Association Executives, International Section, 1575 Eye St., N.W., Washington, DC 20005-1168. TEL 202-626-2739. FAX 202-408-9635. Ed. Joseph S. Cavarretta. circ. 1,000. Document type: newsletter.
   Description: Includes trade and tourism statistics; association management, meetings and marketing information; resources; and calendar of events.

658   II   ISSN 0257-8069
HD20.15.I4
A S C I JOURNAL OF MANAGEMENT. 1971. s-a. Rs.20($5) Administrative Staff College of India, Bella Vista, Box 4, Hyderabad 500 049, India. Ed. K.K. Singh. Indexed: ABI Inform, BPIA, Bus.Ind., Curr.Cont., Manage.Cont., Pub.Admin.Abstr., Tr.& Indus.Ind. Document type: academic/scholarly publication.
   —BLDSC (1739.220000); UMI.

003   AT   ISSN 0812-860X
A S O R BULLETIN. 1981. q. Aus.$24. Australian Society for Operations Research Inc., University of New South Wales, School of Computer Science, Northcott Dr., Canberra, A.C.T. 2600, Australia. TEL 61-6-2688177. FAX 61-6-2688581. Ed. David Hoffman. adv.: page Aus.$200; adv. contact: David Hoffman. bk.rev. circ. 400. (back issues avail.) Document type: academic/scholarly publication, bulletin.
   —BLDSC (1745.680000).
   Description: Covers the area of operations research, dissemination of information from other (governing) OR organizations. Aimed for persons in the business community, and academics.

658 378   US
A U P H A EXCHANGE. bi-m. Association of University Programs in Health Administration, 1911 N. Fort Myer Dr., Ste. 503, Arlington, VA 22209. TEL 703-524-5500. FAX 703-525-4791. Ed. Mary-Louise Giunta. Document type: newsletter.

658   UK
A - Z OF BUSINESS INFORMATION SOURCES. Variant title: Croner's A - Z of Business Information Sources. a. £99.95 (effective 1995). Croner Publications Ltd. (Subsidiary of: Wolters Kluwer N.V.), Croner House, 100 London Rd., Kingston-upon-Thames, Surrey TW2 6SR, England. TEL 44-181-547-3333. FAX 44-181-247-1300. TELEX 267778. (looseleaf format) Document type: trade publication.

658   UK
A - Z OF EUROPEAN BUSINESS INFORMATION SOURCES. Variant title: Croner's A - Z of European Business Information Sources. a. £112.30. Croner Publications Ltd. (Subsidiary of: Wolters Kluwer N.V.), Croner House, 100 London Rd., Kingston-upon-Thames, Surrey TW2 6SR, England. TEL 44-181-547-3333. FAX 44-181-247-1300. TELEX 267778. (looseleaf format) Document type: trade publication.

658   CN
ABSTRACT OF MANAGEMENT SERVICES ANALYSIS. 1990. q. Can.$60 membership; newsstand price: Can.$25. Maxiplan Financial Club, 12687 52nd Ave., Montreal, PQ H1E 2H6, Canada. Ed. Marcel Wistaff. Document type: newsletter.
   Description: Contains specific executive diagnosis, operations analysis, financial perspectives, productivity coordinations, technological orientations, business opportunities and marketing surveys.

658   US   ISSN 0001-4273
HD28
ACADEMY OF MANAGEMENT. JOURNAL. 1958. bi-m. $95 in US, Canada, Mexico; elsewhere $105. Academy of Management, Box 3020, Briarcliff Manor, NY 10510-8020. TEL 914-923-2607. FAX 914-923-2615. Ed. Amme Tsui. R&P contact: Hope Tinsley. adv. contact: Terese Vivenzo. bk.rev.; charts; tr.lit.; index. circ. 11,500. (also avail. in microform from UMI; reprint service avail. from UMI,SCH) Indexed: ABI Inform., Abstr.Health Care Manage.Stud., Anbar, ASCA, B.P.I., BPIA, Bus.Ind., CINAHL, CLOSS, Commun.Abstr., Cont.Pg.Manage., Curr.Cont., High.Educ.Curr.Aware.Bull., Manage.Cont., Mgmt.& Market.Abstr., Mid.East: Abstr.& Ind., Oper.Res.Manage.Sci., Pers.Lit., Psychol.Abstr. (1968-), Psycscan, Q.Abstr., SCIMP (1978-), SSCI, Tr.& Dev.Alert, Work Rel.Abstr. Document type: academic/scholarly publication.
   ●Also available online. Vendor(s): Information Access Co., UMI.
   —BLDSC (0570.587000); KR SourceOne; SWETS; UMI; UnCover.
   Description: Articles and research notes of an empirical nature from original research.

658   US   ISSN 0065-0668
HD29
ACADEMY OF MANAGEMENT. PROCEEDINGS. 1938. a. $30. Academy of Management, Box 3020, Briarcliff Manor, NY 10510. TEL 914-923-2607. FAX 914-923-2615. Ed.Bd. R&P contact: Hope Tinsley. adv. contact: Terese Vivenzo. illus.; index. circ. 4,000. (also avail. in microform from UMI; back issues avail; reprint service avail. from SCH,UMI) Indexed: BPIA, Bus.Ind. Document type: proceedings.
   —UMI.
   Description: Summary of research findings presented at the academy's annual meeting.

658   US   ISSN 0896-3789
ACADEMY OF MANAGEMENT EXECUTIVE. 1987. q. $75 in US, Canada, Mexico; elsewhere $85. Academy of Management, Box 3020, Briarcliff Manor, NY 10510-8020. TEL 914-923-2607. FAX 914-923-2615. URL: http://aom.pace.edu/publications/. bk.rev. circ. 10,200. (reprint service avail. from UMI) Indexed: ABI Inform., B.P.I., Q.Abstr., Tr.& Dev.Alert. Document type: trade publication.
   ●Also available online. Vendor(s): Information Access Co., UMI.
   —KR SourceOne; SWETS; UMI; UnCover.
   Description: Provides information in both theory and practice of management.

658 658.3   US   ISSN 0161-5998
ACADEMY OF MANAGEMENT NEWSLETTER. 1971. q. membership. Academy of Management (Monroe), c/o Lawrence R. Jauch, Ed., Northeast Louisiana Univ., ADMN-3-17, Monroe, LA 71209-8813. TEL 318-342-1210. FAX 318-342-1209. E-mail: mmjauch@alpha.nlu.edu. adv.; bibl.; circ. 10,000 (controlled). (looseleaf format; reprint service avail. from UMI) Document type: newsletter.
   Description: Announcements, special features, and informed coverage of individual members and organizational elements of the Academy.

658   US   ISSN 0363-7425
HD28
ACADEMY OF MANAGEMENT REVIEW. 1976. q. $80 in US, Canada, Mexico (elsewhere $90). Academy of Management, Box 3020, Briarcliff Manor, NY 10510. TEL 914-923-2607. FAX 914-923-2615. Ed. Richard J. Klimoski. R&P contact: Hope Tinsley. adv. contact: Terese Vivenzo. bk.rev. circ. 11,500. (also avail. in microform from UMI; reprint service avail. from SCH,UMI) Indexed: ABI Inform., Abstr.Health Care Manage.Stud., Account.& Data Proc.Abstr., ASEAN Manage.Abstr., B.P.I., BPIA, Cont.Pg.Manage., Curr.Cont., Manage.Cont., Mid.East: Abstr.& Ind., Pers.Lit., Psychol.Abstr. (1981-), Psycscan, Q.Abstr., Risk Abstr., SCIMP (1978-), SSCI, Tr.& Dev.Alert. Document type: academic/scholarly publication.
   ●Also available online. Vendor(s): Information Access Co., UMI.
   —BLDSC (0570.587600); KR SourceOne; SWETS; UMI; UnCover.
   Description: Presents conceptual and theoretical manuscripts.

658   SP   ISSN 0044-5894
ACCION EMPRESARIAL; la revista del directivo. 1971. 4/yr. Accion Social Empresarial Comision Nacional, Jose Maranon 3, 28010 Madrid, Spain. TEL 593-27-58. FAX 5593-28-21. Ed. Alfonso Sanchez. adv.; bk.rev.; bibl.; charts; illus.; stat. circ. 3,000.
   —SWETS.

ACCOUNTING OFFICE MANAGEMENT & ADMINISTRATION REPORT. see BUSINESS AND ECONOMICS — Accounting

658   US   ISSN 0147-1554
HC101   CODEN: ACBODW
ACROSS THE BOARD; reporting to management on business affairs. 1939. 10/yr. $40 to non-members; members $20. Conference Board, Inc., 845 Third Ave., New York, NY 10022. TEL 212-759-0900. FAX 212-980-7014. E-mail: atb@conference-board.com. Ed. A.J. Vogl. adv.; charts; illus.; index. circ. 35,000. (back issues avail.) Indexed: ABI Inform., Account.& Data Proc.Abstr., Account.Ind. (1974-), ASEAN Manage.Abstr., B.P.I., Bank.Lit.Ind., BPIA, Bus.Ind., CAD CAM Abstr., Cont.Pg.Manage., Cont.Pg.Manage., Data Process.Dig., Fut.Surv., INIS Atomind., Key to Econ.Sci., Manage.Cont., Mgmt.& Market.Abstr., Mid.East: Abstr.& Ind., P.A.I.S., Pers.Lit., PROMT, PSI, Q.Abstr., SSCI, Tr.& Dev.Alert, Tr.& Indus.Ind. Document type: trade publication.
   ●Also available online. Vendor(s): Information Access Co., UMI.
   —BLDSC (0578.887000); CASDDS; KR SourceOne; UMI; UnCover. CCC.
   Formerly (until 1976): Conference Board Record (ISSN 0010-5546); Supersedes: Conference Board Business-Management Record.
   Description: Offers information and insights on matters of interest to managers in business and industry.

ADAM VEAVODA/MAN AND WORK; journal in labor studies. see OCCUPATIONS AND CAREERS

658   AG   ISSN 0325-0814
ADMINISTRACION. Variant title: C G C E Administracion. Cover title: Revista de Ciencias Economicas. Temas de Administracion. 1913. q. Colegio de Graduados en Ciencias Economicas, Viamonte 1582, Buenos Aires, Argentina. adv.; bk.rev. circ. 15,000.
   Formerly (until 1972): Revista de Ciencias Economicas. Temas de Administracion (ISSN 0325-0806); Supersedes in part (in 1970): Revista de Ciencias Economicas (ISSN 0034-7779)

658.4   CN
ADMINISTRATIVE SCIENCES ASSOCIATION OF CANADA. PROCEEDINGS, ANNUAL CONFERENCE. 1973. a. Can.$350 (foreign $350). (Administrative Sciences Association of Canada) A S A C Publications, c/o Irene Lepine, Dept. of Administrative Sciences, Universite du Quebec a Montreal, P.O. Box 6192, Sta. Centreville, Montreal, PQ H3C 4RZ, Canada. TEL 514-987-3697. FAX 514-987-3343. adv. contact: Alain Gosselin. illus. circ. 900. Document type: proceedings, academic/scholarly publication.
   Former titles: Canadian Association of Administrative Sciences. Proceedings, Annual Conference (ISSN 0318-5036); Association of Canadian Schools of Business. Proceedings of the Annual Conference (ISSN 0066-9490)
   Refereed Serial

658 346   UK   ISSN 0263-3868
ADMINISTRATOR. 1891. m. £37 to non-members (overseas £49). Institute of Chartered Secretaries and Administrators, 16 Park Cresc., London W1N 4AH, England. TEL 44-171-580-4741. FAX 44-171-323-1132. E-mail: 10530.1426@compuserve.com. Ed. Andrew Caley. adv. contact: Ashley Smith. bk.rev.; charts; illus.; index. circ. 41,000. Indexed: Intl.Mgmt.Info., World Bank.Abstr. Document type: trade publication.
   Formerly: Professional Administration.
   Description: Contains practical articles on law, finance, and personnel-oriented problems and developments affecting senior managers in public and private businesses.

ADULT DAY CARE LETTER. see GERONTOLOGY AND GERIATRICS

BUSINESS AND ECONOMICS — MANAGEMENT

658 US ISSN 0036-0805
HD28 CODEN: SAMMBP
ADVANCED MANAGEMENT JOURNAL. Variant title: S A M Advanced Management Journal. 1935. q. $39 (foreign $49). Society for Advancement of Management, Texas A&M University - Corpus Christi, College of Business, 6300 Ocean Dr., FC 111, Corpus Christi, TX 78412. TEL 512-994-6045. FAX 512-994-2725. Ed. M.H. Abdelsamad. adv.; bk.rev.; charts; illus.; stat.; tr.lit.; index. circ. 5,000. (also avail. in microform from UMI; back issues avail.; reprint service avail. from UMI) **Indexed:** ABI Inform, Account.& Data Proc.Abstr., Account.Ind. (1974-), Anbar., B.P.I., BPIA, Bus.Ind., Comput.Lit.Ind., Cont.Pg.Manage., Data Process.Dig., Manage.Cont., Mgmt.& Market.Abstr., Mid.East: Abstr.& Ind., Pers.Manage.Abstr., PROMT, SCIMP (1978-). ●Also available online. Vendor(s): Information Access Co., UMI.
—BLDSC (8071.870000); UnCover. **CCC.**

658 NE
ADVANCED SERIES IN MANAGEMENT. 1983. irreg., vol.19, 1993. price varies. Elsevier Science B.V., Books Division, P.O. Box 211, 1000 AE Amsterdam, Netherlands. TEL 31-20-4853911. FAX 31-20-4853705. TELEX 18582 ESPA NL. E-mail: nlinfo-f@elsevier.nl; usinfo-f@elsevier.com; forinfo-kyf04035@niftyserve.or.jp; URL: http://www.elsevier.nl/. (Subscr. in the Americas to: Elsevier Science, Regional Sales Office, Box 945, New York, NY 10159-0945. TEL 212-633-3730. FAX 212-633-3680; Subscr. in Australasia and the Far East to: Elsevier Science (Singapore) Pte Ltd, No.1 Temasek Ave., No.17-01 Millenia Tower, Singapore 039192, Singapore. TEL 65-434-3727. FAX 65-337-2230; Subscr. in Japan to: Elsevier Science Japan, 9-15 Higashi-Azabu 1-chome, Minato-ku, Tokyo 106, Japan. TEL 81-3-5561-5033. FAX 81-3-5561-5047) **Indexed:** INSPEC, Zent.Math. **Document type:** monographic series.
Refereed Serial

658 US ISSN 0749-6826
HD30.28
ADVANCES IN APPLIED BUSINESS STRATEGY. 1984. irreg., vol.5, 1996. $73.25. J A I Press Inc., 55 Old Post Rd., No. 2, Box 1678, Greenwich, CT 06836-1678. TEL 203-661-7602. FAX 203-661-0792. E-mail: jai@jaipress.com. (Addr. in the U.K. and the rest of Europe: J A I Press Ltd., 38 Tavistock St., Covent Garden, London WC2E 7PB, England. TEL 44-171-379-8834. FAX 44-171-379-8835) Ed. Lawrence Foster. **Document type:** monographic series.
—**CCC.**

659 US
▼**ADVANCES IN COLLECTION DEVELOPMENT AND RESOURCE MANAGEMENT.** 1995. irreg. $73.25. J A I Press Inc., 55 Old Post Rd., No.2, Box 1678, Greenwich, CT 06830-1678. TEL 203-661-7602. FAX 203-661-0792. E-mail: jai@jaipress.com. (In Europe: JAI Press Ltd., 38 Tavistock St., Covent Garden, London WC2E 7PB, England. TEL 44-171-379-8834. FAX 44-171-379-8835) Ed. Thomas Leonhardt. **Document type:** monographic series.

ADVANCES IN EXPERT SYSTEMS FOR MANAGEMENT. see *COMPUTERS — Artificial Intelligence*

658.15 332 US ISSN 1046-5847
HG4001
ADVANCES IN FINANCIAL PLANNING AND FORECASTING. SUPPLEMENT. 1989. irreg. $90.25. J A I Press Inc., 55 Old Post Rd., No. 2, Box 1678, Greenwich, CT 06830-1678. TEL 203-661-7602. FAX 203-661-0792. E-mail: jai@jaipress.com. (Subscr. in UK and Europe to: JAI Press Ltd., 38 Tavistock St., Covent Garden, London WC2E 7PB, England. TEL 44-171-379-8834. FAX 44-171-379-8835) **Document type:** monographic series.
—BLDSC (0706.580000).

ADVANCES IN INTERNATIONAL COMPARATIVE MANAGEMENT. see *BUSINESS AND ECONOMICS — International Commerce*

658 US
ADVANCES IN ORGANIZATION DEVELOPMENT. 1990. irreg., vol.3, 1995. price varies. Ablex Publishing Corporation, Box 5297, Greenwich, CT 06831-0504. TEL 203-661-7602. FAX 203-661-0792. Ed. Fred Massarik. **Document type:** academic/scholarly publication.

658 US ISSN 0742-3322
HD30.28
ADVANCES IN STRATEGIC MANAGEMENT. 1983. irreg., vol.13, 1996. $73.25. J A I Press Inc., 55 Old Post Rd., No. 2, Box 1678, Greenwich, CT 06830-1678. TEL 203-661-7602. FAX 203-661-0792. E-mail: jai@jaipress.com. (Addr. in the U.K. and rest of Europe: J A I Press Ltd., 38 Tavistock St., Covent Garden, London WC2E 7PB, England. TEL 44-171-379-8834. FAX 44-171-379-8835) Ed.Bd. **Document type:** monographic series.
—BLDSC (0711.584000); UnCover. **CCC.**

658 US
▼**ADVANCES IN THE MANAGEMENT OF ORGANIZATIONAL QUALITY.** 1996. irreg. J A I Press Inc., 55 Old Post Rd., No. 2, Box 1678, Greenwich, CT 06836-1678. TEL 203-661-7602. FAX 203-661-0792. (Subscr. in UK to: J A I Press Ltd., The Courtyard, 28 High St., Hampton Hill, Middlesex TW12 1PD, England. TEL 44-181-943-9296. FAX 44-181-943-9317) Eds. Donald Fedor, Soumen Ghosh. **Document type:** monographic series.

ADVISOR (NEW YORK). see *BUSINESS AND ECONOMICS — Marketing And Purchasing*

658 SW ISSN 0282-2768
AFFAERSIDEER. 1984. q. SEK 450 (effective 1991). Svenska Handels-Institutet, P.O. Box 49418, S-100 28 Stockholm, Sweden.

658 UK ISSN 0963-8296
AFTERSALES MANAGEMENT. 1989. m. £105. Sewells International Emap Automotive Ltd., Wentworth House, Wentworth St., Peterborough PE1 1DS, England. TEL 44-1733-467191. FAX 44-1733-467199. Ed. Jerry Conolly. **Document type:** trade publication.
Formerly (until 1991): Sewells Training on Aftersales Management (ISSN 0963-2549)

658 IT ISSN 1122-8490
AGENDA MONACI. 1970. a. L.138000 (effective 1996). Guida Monaci S.p.A., Via Vitorchiano 107, 00189 Rome, Italy. TEL 39-6-3331333. FAX 39-6-3335555. TELEX 623234 MONACI.
Former titles: Agenda Nazionale; Agenda Edizione Guida Monaci.
Description: Contains information on the first 1000 top ranking Italian companies.

658 US
▼**AGILE ENTERPRISE.** 1996. q. $150 (foreign $174) (effective 1997). (Agility Forum) John Wiley & Sons, Inc., Journals, 605 Third Ave., New York, NY 10158-0012. TEL 212-850-6645. FAX 212-850-6021. E-mail: subinfo@jwiley.com; URL: http://www.wiley.co.uk. (Subscr. outside the Americas to: John Wiley & Sons Ltd., Baffins Ln., Chichester, W. Sussex PO19 1UD, England. TEL 44-1243-779777. FAX 44-1243-843232) Ed. Kenneth Preiss. adv.: B&W page £640, color page £1515; trim 279 x 210. **Document type:** academic/scholarly publication.
Formerly (until 1997): Agility and Virtual Organization (ISSN 1083-1339)
Description: Covers the new "agile" organizations which provide goods and information in an information-rich environment by coordinating intercompany processes. Includes articles on the following areas: enbling subsystems, organizational infrastructure, human resources, international aspects, legal, accounting and organizational issues, performance measures, and technology.

AIRLINE BUSINESS. see *TRANSPORTATION — Air Transport*

330 GW ISSN 0065-5384
AKADEMIE FUER FUEHRUNGSKRAEFTE DER WIRTSCHAFT. TASCHENBUECHER ZUR BETRIEBSPRAXIS.* irreg. price varies. Verlag fuer Wissenschaft, Wirtschaft und Technik GmbH und Co. KG, Postfach 1116, 38653 Bad Harzburg, Germany. TEL 0532-73333. TELEX 957623.

658 SW ISSN 0282-7336
AKTUELL SAEKERHET; Scandinavian security & safety news. 1982. bi-m. SEK 300 (effective 1995). Saekerhetsfoerlaget, Kaknaes, S-115 27 Stockholm, Sweden. TEL 46-8-663-25-63. FAX 46-8-6611-42-00. Ed. Lars Dahlloef. adv. contact: L. Roennquist. circ. 25,000. **Document type:** trade publication.
Incorporates (in 1985): Det Handlar om Saekerhet; *Formerly* (until vol.3, 1985): Aktuellt Foeretagsskydd.

658 651 SW ISSN 0283-4391
AKTUELLT FOER KONTOR. 1966. 8/yr. SEK 300($50) Nya Mediaplan AB, P.O. Box 6903, S-102 39 Stockholm, Sweden. TEL 46-8-669-08-20. FAX 46-8-31-00-11. Ed. Alexander Scarlat. adv.; bk.rev. circ. 130,000.
Description: Focuses on office management, facilities, equipment.

658 SP ISSN 0002-6549
HD28
ALTA DIRECCION. 1965. bi-m. 9360 ptas. Alta Direccion, S.A., Infanta Carlota, 123, 08029 Barcelona, Spain. Ed. Rafael Badet Vilanova. adv.; bk.rev.; charts; illus.; stat.; index, cum.index. circ. 9,360. **Indexed:** Mgmt.& Market.Abstr., P.A.I.S.For.Lang.Ind., SCIMP (1989-).
—BLDSC (0802.500000); CINDOC; SWETS. **CCC.**

658 SP
ALTA DIRECCION. MONOGRAFIAS. irreg. 2500 ptas. Alta Direccion, S.A, Infanta Carlota, 123, 08029 Barcelona, Spain. **Document type:** monographic series.

658 340 US ISSN 0191-863X
KF318.A1
ALTMAN WEIL PENSA REPORT TO LEGAL MANAGEMENT. 1974. m. Can.$245($195) (foreign $220). Altman Weil Pensa Publications, Inc., Box 625, Newtown Sq PA 19073. TEL 610-359-9900. FAX 610-359-0467. URL: http://www.altmanweil.com. (Editorial addr.: 1100 Commerce Dr., Ste. 107, Racine, WI 53406. TEL 414-886-1304. FAX 414-886-1139) Ed. James Wilber. R&P contact: Charles Huxsan. TEL 610-359-9900. bk.rev.; bibl.; charts; illus.; stat.; index. circ. 1,000. (back issues avail.) **Document type:** trade publication.
—**CCC.**
Description: Geared to the legal profession.

658 CK
ALTO GERENCIA. m. Carrera 18, no. 93A, 60 Bogota, Colombia. TEL 256-3530. Ed. Sonia Gomez Sanchez. circ. 28,000.

AMAX NEWS. see *MINES AND MINING INDUSTRY*

658 US ISSN 0360-7100
HD30.23
AMERICAN INSTITUTE FOR DECISION SCIENCES. SOUTHEAST SECTION. PROCEEDINGS. 1971. a. $10 American Institute for Decision Sciences, Southeast Section, Dept. of Business Administration, Virginia Polytechnic Institute and State University, Blacksburg, VA 24061. TEL 203-961-6601. Ed. Bernard W. Taylor, III. abstr.; charts; pat.; index. circ. 400. **Document type:** proceedings.

658 UK ISSN 1354-5787
HD28
▼**AMERICAN JOURNAL OF MANAGEMENT DEVELOPMENT.** 1995. q. £89($129) (effective 1996). M C B University Press Ltd., 60-62 Toller Ln., Bradford, W. Yorks BD8 9BY, England. TEL 44-1274-777700. FAX 44-1274-785200. URL: http://www.mcb.co.uk. **Document type:** trade publication.

BUSINESS AND ECONOMICS — MANAGEMENT

658 368 US ISSN 1062-8606
RA399.A3
AMERICAN JOURNAL OF MEDICAL QUALITY. 1986. q. $143 to individuals (foreign $170); institutions $166 (foreign $193) (effective 1998). (American College of Medical Quality) Williams & Wilkins (Subsidiary of: Waverly International), 351 W. Camden St., Baltimore, MD 21201-2436. TEL 410-528-4068; 800-222-3790. FAX 410-528-4452. E-mail: sisaacson@wwilkins.com; URL: http://www.wwilkins.com. Ed. Dr. David J. Jones. adv. contact: Sharlene Isaacson. index. circ. 2,165. (also avail. in microfilm from WWS) **Indexed:** Ind.Med. (1992-). **Document type:** academic/scholarly publication.
—BLDSC (0827.990000); Genuine Article; KNAW; UnCover. **CCC.**
Formerly: Quality Assurance and Utilization Review (ISSN 0885-713X)
Description: Covers case studies, literature reviews and original papers regarding quality assurance, utilization review, cost containment, and risk management.
Refereed Serial

658 US ISSN 0065-9185
AMERICAN MANAGEMENT ASSOCIATION. RESEARCH REPORTS. irreg. price varies. American Management Association, 1601 Broadway, New York, NY 10019. TEL 212-586-8100. (Subscr. to: Box 319, Saranac Lake, NY 12983)
—CCC.
Formerly: American Management Association. Research Studies.

658 US ISSN 0065-9193
AMERICAN MANAGEMENT ASSOCIATION. SEMINAR PROGRAM. 1963. irreg. American Management Association, 1601 Broadway, New York, NY 10019. TEL 212-586-8100. (Subscr. to: Box 319, Saranac Lake, NY 12983)

658 346.066 US ISSN 0894-0622
AMERICAN SOCIETY OF CORPORATE SECRETARIES. LOS ANGELES CHAPTER. NEWSLETTER. 1981. 3/yr. membership. American Society of Corporate Secretaries, Los Angeles Chapter, c/o American Society of Corporate Secretaries, 521 5th Ave., New York, NY 10175-0003. Ed. James K. Baer. circ. 300. (looseleaf format) **Document type:** newsletter.
Description: Business and legal information for elected corporate secretaries in southwestern states.

658 UK ISSN 1360-709X
HD28
ANBAR MANAGEMENT MAGAZINE. 1996. q. (Anbar Management Intelligence) M C B University Press Ltd., Anbar Electronic Intelligence, 60-62 Toller Ln., Bradford, W. Yorks BD8 9BY, England. TEL 44-1274-785277. FAX 44-1274-785202. E-mail: spuesey@anbar.co.uk; URL: http://www.mcb.co.uk/anbar/nethome.htm. (Japan subscr. to: Anbar Electronic Intelligence, M C B University Press Ltd., Kaneichi Bldg. No. 2, 3-32-13 Hongo, Bunkyo-ku, Tokyo 113, Japan; Australia & N.Z. to Anbar Electronic Intelligence, The Australian Institute of Management, Queensland Division, P.O. Box 200, Spring Hill Queensland 4004, Australia) Ed. Sarah Powell. **Document type:** trade publication.
—BLDSC (0900.140000).

ANNALS OF OPERATIONS RESEARCH. see *COMPUTERS*

658 US
ANNUAL EDITIONS: MANAGEMENT. 1991. a. $12.95. Dushkin Publishing Group, Sluice Dock, Guilford, CT 06437-9989. TEL 203-453-4351. FAX 203-453-6000. Ed. Fred H. Maidment; Pub. Ian Nielsen. illus. **Document type:** academic/scholarly publication.
Refereed Serial

658 US ISSN 0276-8976
HD30.23
APPLICATIONS OF MANAGEMENT SCIENCE. (Supplement avail.) 1981. irreg., vol.9, 1996. $73.25 to institutions. J A I Press Inc., 55 Old Post Rd., No. 2, Box 1678, Greenwich, CT 06830-1678. TEL 203-661-7602. FAX 203-661-0792. E-mail: jai@jaipress.com. (Subscr. in UK and Europe to: JAI Press Ltd., 38 Tavistock St., Covent Garden, London WC2E 7PB, England. TEL 44-171-379-8834. FAX 44-171-379-8835) Eds. Kenneth Lawrence, Gary Reeves. **Document type:** monographic series.
—BLDSC (1571.150000).

AQUATICS INTERNATIONAL; the source for facility products, services and management. see *SPORTS AND GAMES*

658 792 UK ISSN 0961-9313
ARTS MANAGEMENT WEEKLY. 1989. w. £80. Rhinegold Publishing Ltd., 241 Shaftesbury Ave., London WC2H 8EH, England. TEL 44-171-333-1721. FAX 44-171-333-1769. Ed. Alex Bannock. **Document type:** newsletter.

658 SI ISSN 0217-4561
HD28
ASIA - PACIFIC JOURNAL OF MANAGEMENT. 1983. s-a. $95 (foreign $95) (effective 1998). National University of Singapore, Faculty of Business Administration, 10 Kent Ridge Crescent, Singapore 119260, Singapore. TEL 65-7723161. FAX 65-7765641. TELEX UNISPO RS 33943. (Subscr. to: John Wiley & Sons (Asia) Pte. Ltd., 2 Clementi Loop 02-01, Jin Xing Distripark, Singapore 129809, Singapore. TEL 65-4632400. FAX 65-4634605) Ed. Lim Kian Guan. adv.; bk.rev. circ. 400. **Indexed:** Asian-Pac.Econ.Lit., B.P.I. **Document type:** academic/scholarly publication.
●Also available online. Vendor(s): UMI.
—BLDSC (1742.260700); KR SourceOne; SWETS; UMI; UnCover.
Description: Contains articles on economic analysis, environment and development of the Asia-Pacific Region.

ASIA - PACIFIC JOURNAL OF OPERATIONAL RESEARCH. see *COMPUTERS*

658.07 NE
▼**ASIA PACIFIC MANAGEMENT EDUCATION DIRECTORY**. (Text in English) 1995. a. fl.335. E M D Centre, Naarderstraat 296, 1272 NT Huizen, Netherlands. TEL 31-35-6951111. FAX 31-35-6951900. Ed. Rino Schreuder. adv. **Document type:** directory.
Formerly: Asian Management Education Directory (ISSN 1383-6226)
Description: Lists executive training programs at Asia Pacific business schools and management training centers.

658 PH
ASIAN MANAGER. (Text in English) 1988. bi-m. $27. Asian Institute of Management, Joseph McMicking Campus, 123 Paseo de Roxas, Makati, Metro Manila, Philippines. TEL 63-2-892-4011. FAX 63-2-817-9240. E-mail: tam@aim.edu.ph; URL: http://www.aim.edu.ph. Ed. Patricia L. Lontoc; Pub. Felipe Alfonso. adv.: B&W page $1659, color page $2371; trim 8 1/4 x 10 7/8. bk.rev.; circ. 2,150 (paid); 22,850 (controlled). **Document type:** academic/scholarly publication.
Description: Covers management trends and analysis, realistic management issues and the opinions of key Asian decision-makers.

658 US ISSN 0731-2350
ASK!. 1982. m. $95. Accurate Information Service, 9711 MacArthur Blvd., Bethesda, MD 20817. TEL 301-365-0412. Ed. Louis V. Lombardo. bk.rev.

658 US ISSN 0098-9169
HV8290
ASSETS PROTECTION; for senior managers responsible for internal controls and safeguards for financial, physical and intellectual assets. 1975. bi-m. $72 (Canada & Mexico $84; elsewhere $104) (effective 1997 & 1998). Assets Protection Publishing, Box 5323, Madison, WI 53705-0323. TEL 608-231-6730. Ed. Paul Shaw. R&P contact: Paul Shaw. **Document type:** trade publication.
—UMI.
Description: Provides management with ideas and tools to create and maintain a practical, cost-effective compliance program.

658 US
ASSOCIATION EDUCATOR. m. membership. American Society of Association Executives, Education Section, 1575 Eye St., N.W., Washington, DC 20005-1168. TEL 202-626-2821. FAX 202-289-4049. circ. 1,400.
Former titles: Association Education Directory; Education Director.
Description: For managers of educational programs of associations.

ASSOCIATION FOR COMMUNICATION ADMINISTRATION. JOURNAL. see *COMMUNICATIONS*

658 011 US
ASSOCIATION FOR CONVENTION OPERATIONS MANAGEMENT. CONVENTION PROCEEDINGS. a. Association for Convention Operations Management, c/o William H. Just & Assoc., Inc., 1819 Peachtree St., N.E., Ste. 560, Atlanta, GA 30309. TEL 404-351-3220. FAX 404-351-3348. **Document type:** proceedings.

ASSOCIATION FOR INVESTMENT MANAGEMENT AND RESEARCH. MEMBERSHIP DIRECTORY. see *BUSINESS AND ECONOMICS — Investments*

658 US
ASSOCIATION FOR QUALITY AND PARTICIPATION. ANNUAL CONFERENCE AND RESOURCE MART TRANSACTIONS. 1979. a. $27.50. Association for Quality and Participation, 801-B W. 8th St., Ste. 501, Cincinnati, OH 45203. TEL 513-381-1959. FAX 513-381-0070. circ. 3,000. (back issues avail.) **Document type:** proceedings.
Formerly: International Association of Quality Circles. Annual Conference and Resource Mart Transactions.
Description: Quality and productivity improvements through team problem solving.

658 US ISSN 0004-5578
HF5001
ASSOCIATION MANAGEMENT. 1949. m. $30. American Society of Association Executives, 1575 Eye St., N.W., Washington, DC 20005-1168. TEL 202-626-2735. FAX 202-408-9635. Ed. Ann Mahoney. adv.; bk.rev.; bibl.; index, cum.index: 1970-1988. circ. 24,000. (also avail. in microform from UMI; back issues avail.) **Indexed:** ABI Inform., Account.Ind. (1974-), B.P.I., BPIA, Build.Manage.Abstr., Bus.Ind., Manage.Cont., P.A.I.S., Pers.Manage.Abstr., PSI, Tr.& Indus.Ind., Work Rel.Abstr. **Document type:** trade publication.
●Also available online. Vendor(s): Information Access Co., UMI.
—BLDSC (1746.703000); KR SourceOne; UMI; UnCover.
Formerly: American Society of Association Executives. Journal.
Description: Covers the management of an association.

658 UK ISSN 1368-4213
▼**ASSOCIATION MANAGER**. 1997. bi-m. £42 (effective 1998). Plaza Publishing Ltd., 1A Tradescant Rd., London SW8 1XD, England. TEL 44-171-793-0001. FAX 44-171-735-2009. Ed. Daniel Phelan; Pub. Andrew Maiden. adv.: B&W page £1195, color page £1395; adv. contact: Alice Frackelton. **Document type:** trade publication.
Description: Provides full coverage of all aspects of running and managing a modern and effective membership organization.

658 UK
ASSOCIATION OF M B A ADDRESS BOOK. 1969. a. £65 to non-members. (Association of M B As Ltd.) A P Information Services, Roman House, 296 Golders Green Rd., London NW11 9PZ, England. TEL 44-181-455-4550. FAX 44-181-455-6381. Ed. Alan Philipp. adv.: page £600; 210 x 150. circ. 8,500. (also avail. in diskette format) **Indexed:** Anbar. **Document type:** directory.
Formerly: Business Graduates Association Address Book (ISSN 0308-0455)
Description: Lists all members of the association in alphabetical and geographical order, by business school and by business sector and company.

ASSOCIATION OF TALENT AGENTS. NEWSLETTER. see *THEATER*

658 US ISSN 0744-1088
ASSOCIATIONS REPORT.* 1979. m. $64. R.G. Bischof Enterprises, 158 Pinedale Ave., Sacramento, CA 95838-4802. TEL 206-256-0300. Ed. R.G. Bischof. adv.; bk.rev.; illus.; index. circ. 700. (looseleaf format; back issues avail.)
Description: Provides practical management aids for executives of membership organizations.

AUDITOPICS. see *BUSINESS AND ECONOMICS*

658 GW ISSN 0945-4470
AUSSENDIENST 1. 1983. bi-m. DM.98. Verlag Wirtschaft Recht und Steuern, Fraunhoferstr. 5, 82152 Planegg, Germany. TEL 49-89-89517-0. FAX 49-89-89517250. (Subscr. to: Postfach 1363, 82142 Planegg, Germany) (looseleaf format) **Document type:** trade publication.

BUSINESS AND ECONOMICS — MANAGEMENT

658   GW   ISSN 0945-4462
AUSSENDIENST 2. 1983. bi-m. DM.78. Verlag Wirtschaft Recht und Steuern, Fraunhoferstr. 5, 82152 Planegg, Germany. TEL 49-89-89517-0. FAX 49-89-89517250. (Subscr. to: Postfach 1363, 82142 Planegg, Germany) (looseleaf format) **Document type:** trade publication.

AUSTRALASIAN TRANSPORT NEWS. see *TRANSPORTATION — Trucks And Trucking*

658   AT   ISSN 1323-9406
AUSTRALIAN COMPANY SECRETARY. 1948. m. (except Jan.). Aus.$56 (foreign Aus.$85). Chartered Institute of Company Secretaries in Australia Ltd., G.P.O. Box 1594, Sydney, N.S.W. 2001, Australia. TEL 61-2-223-5744. FAX 61-2-232-7174. Ed. P.W. Walford. R&P contact: Gina Berger. adv: B&W page Aus.$1235, color page Aus.$2150; trim 297 x 210; adv. contact: Gina Berger. bk.rev.; index. circ. 9,330. **Indexed:** AESIS, Aus.P.A.I.S., Intl.Mgmt.Info. **Document type:** newsletter.
Former titles (until 1995): Journal of Corporate Management (ISSN 1038-2410); until 1992: Corporate Management (ISSN 1034-0408); (until 1989): Professional Administrator (ISSN 0159-4672); (until 1980): Chartered Secretary (ISSN 0009-1928)
Description: Presents articles on corporate management, finance, economics, taxation, human resources and administration, principally in Australia and New Zealand.
Refereed Serial

AUSTRALIAN DENTAL PRACTICE MAGAZINE. see *MEDICAL SCIENCES — Dentistry*

658   AT   ISSN 0313-7112
AUSTRALIAN GRADUATE SCHOOL OF MANAGEMENT. HANDBOOK. 1976. a. Aus.$4. University of New South Wales, Sydney, N.S.W. 2052, Australia. TEL 61-2-385-2840. FAX 61-2-662-2163.

658   AT   ISSN 0312-8962
AUSTRALIAN JOURNAL OF MANAGEMENT. 1976. s-a. Aus.$35 to individuals (foreign $30); institutions Aus.$60 (foreign $50) (effective 1998). Australian Graduate School of Management, University of New South Wales, Sydney, N.S.W. 2052, Australia. TEL 61-2-99319259. FAX 61-2-96627621. E-mail: sandra@agsm.unsw.edu.au; URL: http://www.agsm.unsw.edu.au/~eajm/. Ed. John Roberts. bk.rev. (also avail. in microfiche; back issues avail.) **Indexed:** BPIA, Manage.Cont. **Document type:** academic/scholarly publication.
●Also available online.
—BLDSC (1809.200000); SWETS; UMI; UnCover.
Description: Research in the field of management.

658   AT   ISSN 1325-8591
AUSTRALIAN PROJECT MANAGER. 1974. q. Aus.$25. Australian Institute of Project Management, Attn: B. Hovey, 28 Bond St., Mosman, N.S.W. 2088, Australia. TEL 61-2-99601834. FAX 61-2-99681846.
Description: For project managers working in all types of organizations and industries.

658   GW   ISSN 0177-6932
B B E CHEF-TELEGRAMM; aktueller Beratungsbrief fuer die Unternehmensfuehrung im Einzelhandel. 1966. s-m. DM.354. Betriebswirtschaftliche Beratungsstelle fuer den Einzelhandel) B B E Unternehmensberatung GmbH, Postfach 250425, 50520 Cologne, Germany. **Indexed:** Biol.Dig. **Document type:** trade publication.
Formerly (until 1982): Chef-Telegramm (ISSN 0171-841X)

658   US   ISSN 0886-0475
KF1397
B N A'S CORPORATE COUNSEL WEEKLY. (Subseries of: Corporate Practice Series) 1978. w. $617. The Bureau of National Affairs, Inc., 1231 25th St., N.W., Washington, DC 20037. TEL 202-452-4200. FAX 202-822-8092. TELEX 285656 BNAI WSH. URL: http://www.bna.com/. (Subscr. to: 9435 Key West Ave., Rockville, MD 20850. TEL 800-372-1033) Ed. Larry Lampert. index. (looseleaf format; back issues avail.) **Document type:** newsletter.
●Also available online.
—CCC.
Formerly (until 1981): B N A's Washington Memorandum (ISSN 0162-5683)
Description: Covers current developments in law that affect business, including the courts, federal regulatory agencies, the executive branch, states and professional associations.

B O M A EXPERIENCE EXCHANGE REPORT; income - expense analysis for office buildings. (Building Owners and Managers Association International) see *REAL ESTATE*

658 797.21   AU
BAEDER JOURNAL. 1968. q. S.150. Oesterreichischer Baederverband, Rosenhuegelstr. 198, A-1238 Vienna, Austria. TEL 43-3339-7346. FAX 43-3339-7346. Ed. Kurt Bruk. R&P contact: Kurt Bruk. adv. contact: Monika Barwick. bk.rev.; circ. 200. **Document type:** newsletter.

BANK ASSET - LIABILITY MANAGEMENT. see *BUSINESS AND ECONOMICS — Banking And Finance*

BANK UND MARKT UND TECHNIK; Zeitschrift fuer Management, Marketing und Organisation. see *BUSINESS AND ECONOMICS — Banking And Finance*

650   NO   ISSN 0803-642X
BEDRE OEKONOMI OG PERSONAL. 1991. 8/yr. NOK 380. Vanebo Forlag AS, P.O. Box 130, N-2260 Kirkenaer, Norway. TEL 47-62-94-75-88. FAX 47-62-94-81-95. Ed. Odd H. Vanebo. adv.: B&W page NOK 11200, color page NOK 15700. circ. 7,000.

658   NE   ISSN 0165-0971
BEDRIJFSKUNDE; tijdschrift voor modern management. q. fl.210 (effective 1996). Kluwer Bedrijfswetenschappen B.V. (Subsidiary of: Wolters Kluwer N.V.), Postbus 23, 7400 GA Deventer, Netherlands. TEL 31-5700-48999. FAX 31-5700-11504. (Subscr. to: Intermedia bv, Postbus 4, 2400 MA Alphen aan den Rijn, Netherlands. TEL 31-172-466321. FAX 31-172-435527) Ed. C. van Dam. adv. circ. 2,100. **Indexed:** Key to Econ.Sci., SCIMP (1982-). **Document type:** trade publication.
—SWETS.
Formerly (until 1974): Maandblad Bedrijfskunde.

658   CC   ISSN 1002-3135
BEIJING GONGSHANG GUANLI/BEIJING INDUSTRIAL AND COMMERCIAL MANAGEMENT. (Text in Chinese) 1987. bi-m. Beijing Gongshang Xingzheng Guangli-ju, 18, Enjizhuang, Haidian-qu, Beijing 100036, People's Republic of China. TEL 8311924. Ed. Chai Su'er.

BELGIAN JOURNAL OF OPERATIONS RESEARCH, STATISTICS AND COMPUTER SCIENCE. see *COMPUTERS*

658.3   UK   ISSN 1354-8107
▼**THE BENCHMARK (KEMPSTON).** 1995. q. £145 (overseas £160($250)) (effective 1996). I F S International Ltd., Wolseley Business Park, Kempston, Bedford MK42 7PW, England. TEL 44-1234-853605. FAX 44-1234-854499. Ed. Rory L. Chase. R&P contact: David Watts. adv. contact: David Watts. bk.rev.; charts; stat. **Document type:** trade publication.
—CCC.
Description: Provides managers with proven strategies, tools, and techniques for introducing competitive benchmarking within their organizations. Features case studies.

658   UK   ISSN 1351-3036
HD62.15   CODEN: BQMTF9
BENCHMARKING FOR QUALITY MANAGEMENT AND TECHNOLOGY. 1994. q. £399($639) (foreign Aus.$839) (effective 1998). M C B University Press Ltd., 60-62 Toller Ln., Bradford, W. Yorks BD8 9BY, England. TEL 44-1274-777700. FAX 44-1274-785200. TELEX 51317-MCBUNI-G. URL: http://www.mcb.co.uk. (N. American subscr. to: M C B University Press Limited, Box 1943, Birmingham, AL 35201. TEL 205-995-1567. FAX 205-995-1588) Ed. Mohamed Youssef. **Document type:** academic/scholarly publication.
—BLDSC (1891.290700); AskIEEE; KR SourceOne; SWETS. CCC.

BENEFITS & COMPENSATION UPDATE. see *BUSINESS AND ECONOMICS — Personnel Management*

BENEFITS REPORT - ASIA. see *BUSINESS AND ECONOMICS — Personnel Management*

338   UK   ISSN 0889-3136
BEST OF LONG RANGE PLANNING. 1989. irreg., vol.9, 1995. price varies. Elsevier Science Ltd., Books Division, P.O. Box 800, Kidlington, Oxford OX5 1DK. TEL 44-1865-843000. FAX 44-1865-843010. E-mail: nlinfo-f@elsevier.nl; usinfo-f@elsevier.com; forinfo-kyf04035@niftyserve.or.jp; URL: http://www.elsevier.nl/. (Subscr. to: Elsevier Science, Regional Sales Office, P.O. Box 211, 1000 AE Amsterdam, Netherlands. TEL 31-20-4853757. FAX 31-20-4853432; Subscr. in the Americas to: Elsevier Science, Regional Sales Office, Box 945, New York, NY 10159-0945. TEL 212-633-3730. FAX 212-633-3680; Subscr. in Australasia and the Far East to: Elsevier Science (Singapore) Pte Ltd, No.1 Temasek Ave., No.17-01 Millenia Tower, Singapore 039192, Singapore. TEL 65-434-3727. FAX 65-337-2230) Ed. Bernard Taylor. (back issues avail.) **Document type:** monographic series.
Description: Collects outstanding articles on specific topics in strategic planning from the journal.
Refereed Serial

658   SA   ISSN 1019-567X
BESTUURSDINAMIKA/MANAGEMENT DYNAMICS. (Text in Afrikaans, English) 1992. q. R.120 (effective 1997). Suider-Afrika Instituut vir Bestuurswetenskaplikes - Southern African Institute for Management Scientists, c/o Dept. Ondernemingsbestuur, Privaatsak X1, Matieland 7602, South Africa. TEL 27-21-8082222. FAX 27-21-8082226. E-mail: PGDP@maties.sun.ac.za. Ed. P.G. du Plessis. circ. 350. **Indexed:** Ind.S.A.Per. **Document type:** academic/scholarly publication.
Description: Publishes contributions of a scientific nature on the theory and practice of economic and management sciences.
Refereed Serial

658   NO   ISSN 0801-3322
BETA. (Text in English, Norwegian) 1987. s-a. NOK 510 in Nordic countries; elsewhere $95 (effective 1997). Scandinavian University Press, P.O. Box 2959 Toeyen, N-0608 Oslo, Norway. TEL 47-22-57-00. FAX 47-22-57-53-53. E-mail: mail@scup.no; URL: http://www.scup.no. (U.S. addr. 875 Massachusetts Ave., te. 84, Cambridge, MA 02139. TEL 617-497-6515. FAX 617-354-6875) Ed. Odd Nordhaug. **Document type:** academic/scholarly publication.

BETRIEBS-BERATER; Zeitschrift fuer Recht und Wirtschaft. see *LAW*

658   GW   ISSN 0344-5941
DER BETRIEBSLEITER. 1958. 11/yr. DM.114 (foreign DM.130) (effective 1996). Verlag fuer Technik und Wirtschaft GmbH & Co., Lise-Meitner-Str. 2, 55129 Mainz, Germany. TEL 49-6131-992-0. FAX 49-6131-992100. (Subscr. to: Postfach 4029 55030 Mainz, Germany) Ed. Hans Hauck. adv.: B&W page DM.6800, color page DM.9200; trim 265 x 185; adv. contact: Michael Spahn. circ. 17,000 (controlled). **Document type:** trade publication.
Formerly (until 1977): Betriebs-Management Service.

BUSINESS AND ECONOMICS — MANAGEMENT

658   GW   ISSN 0342-7064
DIE BETRIEBSWIRTSCHAFT. Variant title: D B W. 1908-1943; N.S. 1977. bi-m. DM.174 to individuals; students DM.132 (effective 1997). Schaeffer - Poeschel Verlag, Postfach 103241, 70028 Stuttgart, Germany. TEL 49-711-2194102. FAX 49-711-2194119. Ed. Marita Rollnik-Mollenhauer. adv. contact: Susanne Schroeder. bk.rev. circ. 1,500. (also avail. in microform from UMI; reprint service avail. from UMI) Indexed: Excerp.Med., IBR, SCIMP (1978-). **Document type:** trade publication.
—BLDSC (1946.881950); SWETS. **CCC.**
    Description: Deals with the problems and solutions of private and public enterprises in all fields and areas of activity.

658 332   GW   ISSN 0723-9629
BETRIEBSWIRTSCHAFTLICHE BLAETTER. 1950. m. DM.210 (effective 1996). (Deutscher Sparkassen- und Giroverband e.V.) Deutscher Sparkassenverlag GmbH, Am Wallgraben 115, 70565 Stuttgart, Germany. Ed. Arnulf Sauter. adv.; bk.rev.; index. circ. 7,000. (reprint service avail. from SCH) **Document type:** bulletin.
—**CCC.**
    Former titles (until 1981): Betriebswirtschaftliche Blaetter fuer die Praxis der Sparkassen und Landesbanken, Girozentralen (ISSN 0172-0260); (Until 1975): Betriebswirtschaftliche Blaetter fuer die Praxis der Sparkassen und Girozentralen (ISSN 0006-0011)

658   GW   ISSN 0340-5370
BETRIEBSWIRTSCHAFTLICHE FORSCHUNG UND PRAXIS. 1949. 6/yr. DM.150 (effective 1996). Verlag Neue Wirtschafts-Briefe GmbH, Eschstr. 22, 44629 Herne, Germany. Ed. Guenter Sieben. bk.rev.; charts; index. circ. 1,500. Indexed: ASCA, Excerp.Med., INIS Atomind., Key to Econ.Sci., SSCI. **Document type:** bulletin.
—BLDSC (1946.895000); Genuine Article; SWETS. **CCC.**

384.6 658   US
BETTER BUSINESS BY TELEPHONE.* 1964. s-m. $5.95 per month; includes Fone Talk. Kirkley Press Inc., Box 20175, Baltimore, MD 21284-0175. Ed. Julie Fraunholz. adv.; illus.; tr.lit.

BIBLIOGRAPHY OF ECONOMIC AND SOCIAL DEVELOPMENT SRI LANKA. see *BUSINESS AND ECONOMICS — Abstracting, Bibliographies, Statistics*

658   US
BOARD AND ADMINISTRATOR.* m. Center for Management Systems, 11 Twin Oaks E., Sioux Falls, SD 57105-7015. TEL 712-568-2418.
    Description: For managers of non-profit organizations.

658.4   US   ISSN 1061-4249
BOARD LEADERSHIP; a bimonthly workshop with John Carver. 1992. bi-m. $105 (effective 1997). Jossey-Bass Inc., Publishers, 350 Sansome St., 5th Fl., San Francisco, CA 94104. TEL 800-956-7739. FAX 800-605-2665. URL: http://www.josseybass.com. Ed. John Carver. circ. 4,400 (paid). (back issues avail.) **Document type:** newsletter.
    Description: an approach to improve the way boards conduct business.

658 360   US   ISSN 1058-5419
BOARD MEMBER. 1992. 10/yr. $58 membership. National Center for Nonprofit Boards, 2000 L St., N.W., Ste. 510, Washington, DC 20036-4907. TEL 202-452-6262. FAX 202-452-6299. URL: http://www.ncnb.org. Ed. Richard Moyers. bk.rev.; circ. 6,800 (paid). **Document type:** newsletter.
    Description: Covers board leadership issues and trends in the nonprofit sector, including case studies, interviews, current news.

658   US
BOARD OF DIRECTORS REPORT. a. $640. (Executive Compensation Service (ECS)) Wyatt Data Services, 218 Rte. 17, N., Roselle Park, NJ 07662-9832. TEL 201-843-1177. FAX 201-843-0101. charts. **Document type:** corporate report.
    Description: Provides data, reported by industry and company size, on board compensation and organization.

BOARDROOM. see *BUSINESS AND ECONOMICS*

BODYSHOP MANAGEMENT BRIEFINGS. see *TRANSPORTATION — Automobiles*

BOERSENS NYHEDSMAGASIN. see *BUSINESS AND ECONOMICS*

BOLETIM QUALIDADE E PRODUTIVIDADE: EVENTOS E CURSOS. see *BUSINESS AND ECONOMICS — Production Of Goods And Services*

658   US   CODEN: BREPDU
BOTTOM LINE - BUSINESS. 1972. s-m. $49. Boardroom, Inc., Box 2614, 55 Railroad Ave., Greenwich, CT 06936-2614. TEL 212-239-9000; 800-234-3834. FAX 212-695-7492. (Subscr. to: Box 58415, Boulder, CO 80322) Ed. Peter Goldmann. bk.rev. circ. 200,000. (also avail. in microform from UMI)
—CASDDS.
    Formerly (until 1995): Boardroom Reports (ISSN 0045-2300)

BOTTOMLINE (AUSTIN). see *BUSINESS AND ECONOMICS — Accounting*

BOWMAN'S ACCOUNTING REPORT. see *BUSINESS AND ECONOMICS — Accounting*

658   UK   ISSN 1393-0869
BREAKING THE MOULD. 1992. fortn. £58 (foreign £80). Richbell Publishing, Richbell House, 77 St. John St., London EC1M 4AN, England. TEL 44-171-490-7444. FAX 44-171-490-3107. Ed. Emma Gilpin. bk.rev.; index. (back issues avail.) **Document type:** trade publication.

658 378   US   ISSN 1078-2257
HD30.4
BRICKER'S INTERNATIONAL DIRECTORY. 1969. a. $325. Peterson's, 202 Carnegie Center, Box 2123, Princeton, NJ 08543-2123. TEL 609-243-9111. FAX 609-243-9150. URL: http://www.petersons.com. Ed. Barbara Lawrence. **Document type:** directory.
    Formed by the 1995 merger of: Bricker's International Directory, Volume 1: Long-Term University-Based Executive Programs (Year) (ISSN 1054-7835); Bricker's International Directory, Volume 2: Short-Term University-Based Executive Programs (Year) (ISSN 1054-7843); Which supersedes in part (in 1989) Bricker's International Directory (ISSN 0277-7312); Which was formerly (until 1980): Bricker's International Directory of University-Sponsored Executive Development Programs (ISSN 0191-2682); (until 1977): Bricker's International Directory of University-Sponsored Executive Development Programs Including Marketing and Management Programs (ISSN 0191-2992); (until 1976): Bricker's International Directory of University Executive Development Programs Including Marketing and Management Programs (ISSN 0361-1108).
    Description: Covers programs offered by university-based executive education programs worldwide specifically for middle-level and senior managers and executives.

BRIEFINGS ON PRACTICE MANAGEMENT. see *MEDICAL SCIENCES*

658   UK
BRITISH ACADEMY OF MANAGEMENT. CONFERENCE PROCEEDINGS. a. M C B University Press Ltd., 60-62 Toller Ln., Bradford, W. Yorks BD8 9BY, England. TEL 44-1274-777700. FAX 44-1274-785200. URL: http://www.mcb.co.uk. **Document type:** proceedings.

658   UK   ISSN 1045-3172
HD28   CODEN: BJMAE4
BRITISH JOURNAL OF MANAGEMENT. 1990. q. £157/($248) (foreign £157) (effective 1997). (British Academy of Management) Blackwell Publishers Ltd., 108 Cowley Rd., Oxford OX4 1JF, England. TEL 44-1865-791100. FAX 44-1865-791347. E-mail: jnlinfo@blackwellpublishers.co.uk; URL: http://www.blackwellpublishers.co.uk. Ed. D. Otley. circ. 1,072. (also avail. in microform from UMI; back issues avail.) Indexed: Cont.Pg.Manage., Mgmt.& Market.Abstr., SCIMP (1991-), Tech.Educ.Abstr. **Document type:** academic/scholarly publication.
—BLDSC (2311.180000); SWETS; UMI. **CCC.**
    Description: Aims to provide an outlet for research and scholarship on managerial oriented themes and topics.
    Refereed Serial

BUILDINGS; the facilities construction and management magazine. see *BUILDING AND CONSTRUCTION*

BULLETIN DES ELUS LOCAUX. see *PUBLIC ADMINISTRATION*

658 341   FR   ISSN 1264-9120
▼**BULLETIN EUROPEEN ET INTERNATIONAL.** 1995. bi-m. 395 F. (effective 1997). Editions Francis Lefebvre, 42 rue de Villiers, 92300 Levallois, France. TEL 41-05-22-00. FAX 41-05-22-30.

370   FR
BULLETIN OFFICIEL DU TRAVAIL ET DE L'EMPLOI. 1975. 23/yr. 550 F. (foreign 680 F.). 26 rue Desaix, 75727 Paris Cedex 15, France. TEL 40-58-77-17. bk.rev.
    Incorporates: Centre I N F F O. Bulletin de Liason (ISSN 0758-0266)

658 340   FR   ISSN 0395-451X
BULLETIN RAPIDE DE DROIT DES AFFAIRES. 1959. bi-m. 325 F. (effective 1997). Editions Francis Lefebvre, 42 rue de Villiers, 92300 Levallois, France. TEL 41-05-22-00. FAX 41-05-22-30. pat.stat.
    Formerly: Documentation Rapide du Chef d'Entreprise (ISSN 0012-4680)

658   UK   ISSN 1352-5549
BUSINESS BASICS: GUIDE TO BUSINESS RECORDS. Key Title: Croner's Business Basics Bulletin. Records. 1994. base vol. (plus m. update). £80.50 (update service £56.50) (effective 1995). Croner Publications Ltd. (Subsidiary of: Wolters Kluwer N.V.), Croner House, 100 London Rd., Kingston-upon-Thames, TW2 6SR, England. TEL 44-181-547-3333. FAX 44-181-247-1300. TELEX 237778. (looseleaf format) **Document type:** trade publication.

658 336   UK   ISSN 1357-146X
BUSINESS BASICS: TAX A - Z. Key Title: Croner's Business Basics Bulletin. Tax. 1994. base vol. (plus m. updates). £80.60 (update service £56.60) (effective 1995). Croner Publications Ltd. (Subsidiary of: Wolters Kluwer N.V.), Croner House, 100 London Rd., Kingston-upon-Thames, Surrey TW2 6SR, England. TEL 44-181-547-3333. FAX 44-181-247-1300. TELEX 267778. (looseleaf format) **Document type:** trade publication.

358   US
BUSINESS BREAKTHROUGHS. Variant title: Jay Abraham's Business Breakthroughs. m. $99.95. Phillips Publishing, Inc., 7811 Montrose Rd., Potomac, MD 20854. TEL 800-777-5005. FAX 301-340-2647. Ed. Jay Abraham.
    Description: Provides management and marketing tips.

1468   BUSINESS AND ECONOMICS — MANAGEMENT

B

651.7   US   ISSN 1080-5699
HF5717   CODEN: ABCACL
BUSINESS COMMUNICATION QUARTERLY. 1935. q. $40 membership (includes Journal of Business Communication). Association for Business Communication, c/o Dr. Robert J. Myers, Dept. of Speech Communication, Baruch College, 17 Lexington Ave., New York, NY 10010. TEL 817-565-4423. E-mail: 70511.753@ compuserve.com; URL: http://www.cohums.ohio-state.edu/english/facstf/kol/abc/bcq.htm. Ed. John D. Pettit. adv.; bk.rev.; index. circ. 2,475. (processed; also avail. in microform from UMI; reprint service avail. from UMI) Indexed: BPIA, Bus.Educ.Ind., Bus.Ind., C.I.J.E., Tr.& Indus.Ind. **Document type:** academic/scholarly publication.
●Also available online. Vendor(s): Information Access Co.
—BLDSC (2933.345000); SWETS; UMI; UnCover.
   Former titles (until 1994): Association for Business Communication. Bulletin (ISSN 8756-1972); (until 1985): A B C A Bulletin (American Business Communication Association) (ISSN 0001-0383); A B W A Bulletin (American Business Writing Association).
   Description: Practice-oriented publication covering teaching and organizational applications. Includes course outlines, descriptions of training programs, problems and solutions and more.

658   US   ISSN 1064-0223
HF5387
BUSINESS ETHIC RESOURCE; a resource on ethics management for the CEO. 1987. q. $36 (foreign $40). Business Ethics Foundation, 28 Marshal St., Ste. 3, Brookline, MA 02146. TEL 617-232-1820. FAX 617-232-2775. Ed. William H.P. Smith; Pub. Verne E. Henderson. bk.rev. circ. 1,000. **Document type:** newsletter.
   Description: Covers news of ethics related issues for the business community.

658   UK   ISSN 0951-1792
   CODEN: BUEXE8
BUSINESS EXECUTIVE. 1987. bi-m. £20. (Association of Business Executives) Business Executive Ltd., William House, 3rd Fl., 14 Worple Rd., Wimbledon, London SW19 4DD, England. TEL 44-181-879-1973. FAX 44-181-946-7153. Ed. Gillian Frank. R&P contact: J.S. Sewter. adv.: B&W page £350; color page £450; 297 x 210; adv. contact: J.S. Sewter. bk.rev.; index. circ. 22,000. Indexed: INSPEC (1987-), Mgmt.& Market.Abstr., SOMA. **Document type:** academic/scholarly publication.
—BLDSC (2933.643000); AskIEEE; KR SourceOne.
   Incorporates (in 1993): Business Education International; Which was formerly: Institute of Commerce, London. Magazine (ISSN 0046-9781)
   Description: Covers innovations in business management and administration.

658 338   UK
BUSINESS GAZETTE. 1986. m. free. Datateam Publishing Ltd., Attn: Rob Foreman, Fairmeadow, Maidstone, Kent ME14 IN9, England. TEL 01622-687031. FAX 01622-757646. Ed. William Campbell. adv. contact: Chris Lethbridge. bk.rev.; software rev.; video rev.; circ. 15,000 (controlled). cols./p.: 6; pp./issue: 28. (tabloid format; back issues avail.) **Document type:** newspaper, trade publication.
   Description: Covers financial, accounting, management, legal, TQM, technology, and training topics for owners and managers of small businesses in southern England.

658   II   ISSN 0007-6783
BUSINESS HERALD; management magazine. (Text in English) 1965. m. Rs.32.50($10) K.G.P. Nayar, Herald House, Box 133, Trivandrum, Kerala, India. Ed. T.A.A. Latif. adv.; bk.rev.; abstr.; charts; index. circ. 3,000. (tabloid format; also avail. in microform from UMI)

658   NE   ISSN 0925-0913
BUSINESS MAGAZINE. (Published in 22 regional editions) (Text in Dutch) 1989. 6/yr. fl.100. Business Publishers Nederland, Postbus 155, 6500 AD Nijmegen, Netherlands. TEL 31-24-3779447. FAX 31-24-3779441. Ed. P.P.W. Oostdam; Pub. M. de Kok. adv. **Document type:** trade publication.

658   UK   ISSN 0968-2015
BUSINESS MATTERS. 1990. bi-a. £6. Associated Examining Board, Stag Hill House, Guildford, Surrey GU2 5XJ, England. TEL 44-1483-506506. FAX 44-1483-300152. Ed. George Turnbull. illus. circ. 13,000. Indexed: INSPEC (1980-1982), RICS. **Document type:** newsletter.

658   US   ISSN 0190-4914
HF5001
THE BUSINESS OWNER; the key reference source for owners and managers of growing businesses and the professionals who advise them. 1977. bi-m. $96 (effective 1996). Business Owner, Inc., 16 Fox LN, Locust Valley, NY 11560-1119. Ed. Thomas J. Martin; Pub. Thomas J. Martin. R&P contact: Tricia Wasih. Indexed: ABI Inform., BPIA, Bus.Ind., Tr.& Indus.Ind. **Document type:** newsletter.

BUSINESS PEOPLE MAGAZINE. see BUSINESS AND ECONOMICS — Domestic Commerce

658   UK   ISSN 1355-2503
HD28
▼**BUSINESS PROCESS RE-ENGINEERING AND MANAGEMENT JOURNAL.** 1995. q. £329($499) (foreign Aus.$639) (effective 1998). M C B University Press Ltd., 60-62 Toller Ln., Bradford, W. Yorks BD8 9BY, England. TEL 44-1274-777700. FAX 44-1274-785200. URL: http://www.mcb.co.uk. Ed. Mohamed Zairi. **Document type:** trade publication.
—BLDSC (2934.637000). **CCC.**

658   CN   ISSN 0007-6996
HF1   CODEN: BUQUAL
BUSINESS QUARTERLY. 1933. q. Can.$49($45) (effective 1997). University of Western Ontario, Western Business School, c/o Angela Smith, London, ON N6A 3K7, Canada. TEL 519-661-3309. FAX 519-661-3838. E-mail: bg@uwo.ca. Ed. Angela Smith. adv. contact: Agnes Bellegris. bk.rev.; illus.; index. circ. 8,000. (also avail. in microform from MIM,UMI; reprint service avail. from SCH,UMI) Indexed: ABI Inform., Account.& Data Proc.Abstr., Anbar, ASEAN Manage.Abstr., B.P.I., BPIA, Bus.Ind., Can.B.P.I., Can.Per.Ind., Can.Wom.Per.Ind., Cont.Pg.Manage., Curr.Cont., Ind.Can.L.P.L., INSPEC (1982-), Manage.Cont., Mgmt.& Market.Abstr., Mid.East: Abstr.& Ind., P.A.I.S., Pers.Lit., SCIMP, SSCI, Tr.& Dev.Alert, Tr.& Indus.Ind. **Document type:** trade publication, academic/scholarly publication.
●Also available online. Vendor(s): Information Access Co., Knight-Ridder Information, Inc., UMI.
—BLDSC (2934.641000); AskIEEE; CISTI; KR SourceOne; SWETS; UMI; UnCover.
   Formerly (until 1950): Quarterly Review of Commerce.
   Description: For senior managers looking for ways to improve their management practices.

658   UK   ISSN 0950-9666
BUSINESS RATIO REPORT: FRANCHISES; an industry sector analysis. 1987. a. I C C Business Ratios Ltd., Freepost, Field House, Hampton, Mddx. TW12 1BR, England. TEL 081-783-0977. FAX 081-783-1940. charts; stat. **Document type:** trade publication.

658   UK   ISSN 0952-8539
BUSINESS RATIO REPORT: MANAGEMENT CONSULTANTS; an industry sector analysis. 1987. a. I C C Business Ratios Ltd., Freepost, Field House, Hampton, Mddx. TW12 1BR, England. TEL 081-783-0977. FAX 081-783-1940. charts; stat. **Document type:** trade publication.

650   AT   ISSN 0727-758X
BUSINESS REVIEW WEEKLY. w. Aus.$135. B R W Media, Level 2, 469 La Trobe St., Melbourne, Vic. 3000, Australia. TEL 61-3-96033888. FAX 61-3-96704328. Ed. David Uren. adv. contact: John Briggs. bk.rev.; charts; illus.; mkt.; index. circ. 72,758. (back issues avail.; reprint service avail.) Indexed: AESIS, Anbar, Aus.P.A.I.S., INSPEC, Intl.Mgmt.Info., P.A.I.S. **Document type:** trade publication.
—BLDSC (2934.714400); UMI; UnCover.
   Incorporates (1928-1987): Rydge's (ISSN 0036-0511).
   Description: Gives an overall view of Australian business. Deals with current events, industrial relations, accounting, law, management, special events issues, personnel, agriculture and leisure.

BUSINESS SALES AND ACQUISITIONS DIGEST. see BUSINESS AND ECONOMICS — Economic Situation And Conditions

BUSINESS SOLUTIONS. see COMPUTERS — Electronic Data Processing

BUSINESS STRATEGY AND THE ENVIRONMENT. see ENVIRONMENTAL STUDIES

658   UK   ISSN 0955-6419
HD28
BUSINESS STRATEGY REVIEW. 1990. q. £85($134) (effective 1997). (Centre for Business Strategy) Blackwell Publishers Ltd., 108 Cowley Rd., Oxford OX4 1JF, England. TEL 44-1865-791100. FAX 44-1865-791347. E-mail: jnlinfo@ blackwellpublishers.co.uk; URL: http://www. blackwellpublishers.co.uk. Eds. David Stout, Patrick Barwise. index. circ. 1,200. Indexed: Cont.Pg.Manage., Mgmt.& Market.Abstr., SCIMP (1991-). **Document type:** academic/scholarly publication.
—BLDSC (2934.802000); SWETS; UMI. **CCC.**

658   NE   ISSN 1380-698X
BUSINESS TOPICS. (Supplement to: Management Team (ISSN 0166-1256)) 1994. q. fl.110. Benelux Periodieken B.V., Postbus 397, 3900 AJ Veenendaal, Netherlands. TEL 31-8385-21422. FAX 31-8385-23136. adv. circ. 10,000. **Document type:** trade publication.

658 028.5 375   AT   ISSN 1320-971X
BUSINESSDATE. 1993. q. Aus.$45. Warringal Publications, 114 Argyle St., Fitzroy, Vic. 3065, Australia. TEL 61-3-94160200. FAX 61-3-94160402. Ed. Anthony Drinan; Pub. Jane Arter. circ. 1,000. (back issues avail.)
   Description: Presents various aspects of business for 12 grade students.

658   PL   ISSN 0867-1389
BUSINESSMAN. 1990. m. Conecta Ltd., Ul. Kosciuszki 61, 81-703 Sopot, Poland. TEL 48-58-517254. Ed. Marek Michalski. adv. circ. 10,000.

658   UK   ISSN 0965-9455
BUSINESSMATTERS. 1992. bi-m. £14.95. (Guild of Master Craftsmen) G M C Publications Ltd., 166 High St., Lewes, E. Sussex BN7 1XU, England. TEL 01273-477374. FAX 01273-486300. Ed. David Bridle; Pub. A.E. Phillips. adv. contact: Linda Grace. bk.rev.; circ. 30,000 (controlled). **Document type:** trade publication.
   Description: Promotes excellence among small business by providing advice on management and purchasing, sharing experiences, and providing new and entertainment.

BUTLER AVIATION'S ECHELON; the magazine for corporate executives. see TRANSPORTATION — Air Transport

C C A NEWS. (Consumer Credit Association) see BUSINESS AND ECONOMICS — Banking And Finance

658   AT
C C H MANAGEMENT MANUAL. (Commerce Clearing House) 1992. q. NZ.$463. C C H Australia Ltd., P.O. Box 230, North Ryde, N.S.W. 2113, Australia. TEL 61-1-300300224. FAX 61-1-300306224. (looseleaf format)
   Description: Provides easily accessible, up-to-date information on current management practice.

658 336   AT
C C H MANAGEMENT MANUAL. 1992. q. C C H Australia Ltd., P.O. Box 230, North Ryde, N.S.W. 2113, Australia. TEL 61-1-300300224. FAX 61-1-300306224. (looseleaf format)
   Description: Provides managers with information on finance, marketing, leadership, human resource operations, quality and performance, legal issues, taxation, insurance and trade.

BUSINESS AND ECONOMICS — MANAGEMENT

658 330.1 US ISSN 1381-4346
▼**C E M S BUSINESS REVIEW**. 1995. q. fl.575 to institutions; $295 to institutions in U.S. (effective 1998). (Community of European Management Schools) Kluwer Academic Publishers Boston, Box 358, Accord Sta., Hingham, MA 02018-0358. TEL 617-871-6600. FAX 617-871-6528. E-mail: services@wkap.nl; URL: http://www.wkap.nl. (Dist. outside N. America by: Kluwer Academic Publishers Group, P.O. Box 322, 3300 AH Dordrecht, Netherlands. TEL 31-78-6392392. FAX 31-78-6546474) Ed. Eric Briys. (back issues avail.) **Document type**: academic/scholarly publication. —BLDSC (3102.240000). **CCC**.
Description: Provides an integrative forum for management research in Europe, and stimulates cross-fertilization with management research on a global basis.
Refereed Serial

C M A MAGAZINE; for better management decisions. (Certified Management Accountant) see *BUSINESS AND ECONOMICS — Accounting*

C P A CLIENT BULLETIN. (American Institute of Certified Public Accountants) see *BUSINESS AND ECONOMICS — Accounting*

C P A MANAGING PARTNER REPORT; management news for accounting executives. see *BUSINESS AND ECONOMICS — Accounting*

658 UK
C R O M T E C WORKING PAPER SERIES. 1989. irreg. price varies. Centre for Research on Organisations, Management and Technical Change, University of Manchester, Institute of Science and Technology, School of Management, P.O. Box 88, Manchester M60 1QD, England. TEL 0161-200-3401. FAX 0161-200-3505. TELEX 666094. **Document type**: academic/scholarly publication, monographic series.

658 II ISSN 0068-5356
CALCUTTA MANAGEMENT ASSOCIATION. ANNUAL REPORT. (Text in English) 1959. a. membership. Calcutta Management Association, 1 Shakespeare Sarani, Calcutta 700071, India.

658 II
CALCUTTA MANAGEMENT ASSOCIATION. NEWSLETTER. 1959. m. membership. Calcutta Management Association, 1 Shakespeare Sarani, Calcutta 700071, India. Ed. N.K. Sharan. adv.; bk.rev. circ. 1,500. **Document type**: newsletter.

658 US ISSN 0008-1256
HD28
CALIFORNIA MANAGEMENT REVIEW. 1958. q. $50 to individuals; institutions $65; overseas $80. University of California at Berkeley, S549 Haas School of Business, Ste. 1900, Berkeley, CA 94720-1900. TEL 510-642-7159. FAX 510-642-1318. E-mail: cmr@haas.berkeley.edu; URL: http://haas.berkeley.edu/news/cmr.html. Ed. David Vogel. R&P contact: Walda Thompson. TEL 510-642-7159. adv. contact: Gundars Strads. illus.; index. circ. 6,500. (also avail. in microform from UMI; back issues avail.; reprints avail.) Indexed: A.B.C.Pol.Sci., AAR, ABI Inform., Account.& Data Proc.Abstr., Account.Ind. (1974-), Anbar, ASCA, ASEAN Manage.Abstr., B.P.I., Bank.Lit.Ind., BPIA, Bus.Ind., Comput.Lit.Ind., Cont.Pg.Manage., Curr.Cont., Data Process.Dig., Educ.Admin.Abstr., Excerp.Med., Fam.Ind., Fut.Surv., IBR, Key to Econ.Sci., Manage.Cont., Mgmt.& Market.Abstr., Mid.East: Abstr.& Ind., Oper.Res.Manage.Sci., Oper.Res.Manage.Sci., P.A.I.S., Pers.Lit., Pers.Manage.Abstr., Qual.Contr.Appl.Stat., SCIMP (1978-), SSCI, World Bank.Abstr. **Document type**: academic/scholarly publication.
●Also available online. Vendor(s): Information Access Co., UMI.
—BLDSC (3015.060000); Genuine Article; KR SourceOne; SWETS; UMI; UnCover. **CCC**.
Description: Serves as a bridge of communication between those who study management and those who practice it.
Refereed Serial

ANADIAN ASSOCIATION OF UNIVERSITY RESEARCH ADMINISTRATORS. BULLETIN. see *EDUCATION — Higher Education*

651.37 346.066 CN
CANADIAN CORPORATE SECRETARY'S GUIDE. 1978. m. Can.$405. (Institute of Chartered Secretaries and Administrators) C C H Canadian Ltd., 6 Garamond Ct., North York, ON M3C 1Z5, Canada. TEL 416-441-2992; 800-268-4522. FAX 416-444-9011. **Document type**: trade publication.
Supersedes: Canadian Corporate Secretary and Administrator.
Description: Reference manual for corporate secretaries and administrators.

CANADIAN JOURNAL OF ADMINISTRATIVE SCIENCES. see *BUSINESS AND ECONOMICS*

658 CN ISSN 0045-5156
HD28
CANADIAN MANAGER. 1942. q. Can.$12($18) (Canadian Institute of Management) Taylor Enterprises Ltd., 2175 Sheppard Ave. E., Ste. 310, Willowdale, ON M2J 1W8, Canada. TEL 416-493-0155. FAX 416-491-1670. Ed. Ruth Max. adv.; bk.rev. circ. 10,200. Indexed: ABI Inform., BPIA, Bus.Ind., Can.B.P.I., Can.Per.Ind., Manage.Cont., Tr.& Indus.Ind. **Document type**: trade publication.
●Also available online. Vendor(s): Information Access Co., UMI.
—BLDSC (3037.820000); UMI; UnCover. **CCC**.
Supersedes: Industrial Manager (ISSN 0319-4027)
Description: Management techniques for middle to upper management.

658 CN ISSN 0008-4611
CANADIAN OCCUPATIONAL SAFETY. 6/yr. Clifford Elliot & Associates Ltd., 3228 South Service Rd., Burlington, ON L7N 3H8, Canada. TEL 905-634-2100. FAX 905-634-2238. Ed. Jackie Roth; Pub. George Clifford. R&P contact: Vent Milfarl. adv. contact: Vent Milfarl. circ. 12,000 (controlled). **Document type**: trade publication.
—BLDSC (3043.140000).
Description: Informs and educates Canadian safety professionals on a wide variety of safety topics, practices and concerns in today's workplace.

658 US
▼**CAREER CONFIDENTIAL**. 1997. s-m. $84. Bureau of Business Practice, 24 Rope Ferry Rd., Waterford, CT 06386. TEL 860-442-4365. FAX 860-437-3555. Ed. Elaine Stattler; Pub. Peter Garabedian. R&P contact: Debra Ferraro. s-a. index. **Document type**: newsletter.

CAREER DEVELOPMENT INTERNATIONAL. see *OCCUPATIONS AND CAREERS*

CAREER SECRETARY. see *BUSINESS AND ECONOMICS — Office Equipment And Services*

658 333.33 US ISSN 0889-2288
CARLSONREPORT FOR SHOPPING CENTER MANAGEMENT. 1982. m. $125 (foreign $145). Raven Communications, Inc., Box 502830, Indianapolis, IN 46250-7830. TEL 800-546-9889. E-mail: ravencom@prodigy.net. Ed. William R. Wilburn; Pub. William R. Wilburn. adv.; bk.rev. circ. 1,700. (back issues avail.) **Document type**: newsletter.
—**CCC**.
Description: Industry newsletter for shopping center management professionals at the mall and corporate level.

658 340 338 CK
CARTA DE GERENCIA. 1964. fortn. $64. Legis S.A., Av. Eldorado 81-10, Apdo. Aereo 98888, Bogota, Colombia. FAX 4100628. TELEX 43300. Ed. Roberto Escobar. bibl. circ. 10,000.

CATALYST DIRECTORY NEWSLETTER. see *NEW AGE PUBLICATIONS*

CATERING SERVICE IDEA NEWSLETTER. see *FOOD AND FOOD INDUSTRIES*

658.5 US ISSN 1072-5296
CENTER FOR QUALITY MANAGEMENT JOURNAL. 1992. q. Center for Quality Management, 150 Cambridge Park Dr., Cambridge, MA 02140.
—BLDSC (3113.152292).

658 UK
CENTINEL. 1992. m. £35; newsstand price: £2.95. (Central England Tec) Belou Group PLC, Russell House, Ely St., Stratford-upon-Avon, Warwickshire CU37 6LW, England. TEL 44-1789-297437. FAX 44-1789-266418. Ed. Andrew Partridge; Pub. Steven Matthews. adv.: color page £1375; trim 297 x 210. bk.rev. circ. 17,000. (back issues avail.) **Document type**: trade publication.

658 US
CERTIFIED LETTER. 1979. q. free to members. Institute of Certified Professional Managers, James Madison University, Harrisonburg, VA 22807. TEL 703-568-3247. FAX 703-568-3587. E-mail: ADM-ICPM@VAX1.ACS.Jmu.EDU. bk.rev.; circ. 5,300 (controlled). (tabloid format; back issues avail.) **Document type**: newsletter.
Formerly: I C P M Newsletter.
Description: Newsletter about assessment, benchmaking and competency for general managers who have earned certification.

CESTE I MOSTOVI/ROADS AND BRIDGES. see *ENGINEERING — Civil Engineering*

658 US ISSN 0164-9914
CHAIN DRUG REVIEW; the reporter for the chain drug store industry. 1978. fortn. (except m. in May & Dec.) $119. Racher Press, Inc., 220 Fifth Ave., 18th Fl., New York, NY 10001. TEL 212-213-6000. FAX 212-213-6106. Ed. David Pinto. adv. circ. 44,000. (tabloid format) **Document type**: trade publication.
—BLDSC (3128.734150).

658 MP
CHANAR STANDART/QUALITY AND STANDARDS. (Text in Mongolian) 1982. bi-m. Ulan Bator, Mongolia. TEL 32965. circ. 1,500.

CHANGING MEDICAL MARKETS; the international monthly newsletter for executives in the healthcare and biotechnology industries. see *MEDICAL SCIENCES*

658 US
CHAPTER RELATIONS. bi-m. membership. American Society of Association Executives, Chapter Relations Section, 1575 Eye St., N.W., Washington, DC 20005-1168. TEL 202-626-2775. FAX 202-842-1109. circ. 350.
Description: Provides information on operating federations and associations composed of chapters (national and international); management techniques; activities calendar.

CHARTER INDUSTRY; management magazine for the marine charter industry. see *SPORTS AND GAMES — Boats And Boating*

CHARTERED SECRETARY. see *BUSINESS AND ECONOMICS — Small Business*

CHICAGO ARTISTS' NEWS. see *ART*

658 US ISSN 0160-4724
HC10 CODEN: CHIEER
CHIEF EXECUTIVE MAGAZINE. 1977. 10/yr. $95 (foreign $135). Chief Executive Group, Inc., 733 Third Ave., 21st Fl., New York, NY 10017. TEL 212-687-8288. FAX 212-687-8456. Ed. J.P. Donlon. R&P contact: Michael Winkleman. adv.; bk.rev. circ. 40,000. (also avail. in microform from UMI) Indexed: BPIA, PROMT. **Document type**: trade publication.
●Also available online. Vendor(s): Information Access Co.
—BLDSC (3172.824200); UMI.
Description: Offers opinion written by and for CEOs in the US and elsewhere. Covers management, financial or business strategy, marketing, economic and public policy issues.

658 US
CHIEF EXECUTIVE OFFICERS NEWSLETTER; for the entrepreneurial manager and the professionals who advise him. 1979. m. $96. Center for Entrepreneurial Management, Inc., 180 Varick St., Penthouse, New York, NY 10014. TEL 212-633-0060. FAX 212-633-0063. Ed. Joseph R. Mancuso. bk.rev. circ. 3,000. (looseleaf format) **Document type**: newsletter.
●Also available online. Vendor(s): NewsNet.
Formerly: Entrepreneurial Manager's Newsletter (ISSN 0272-0396)

BUSINESS AND ECONOMICS — MANAGEMENT

CHIEF EXECUTIVES COMPENSATION IN CANADA. see BUSINESS AND ECONOMICS — Personnel Management

658.2   US   ISSN 8755-2523
CHILTON'S INDUSTRIAL MAINTENANCE & PLANT OPERATION. Short title: I M P O. 1940. m. $70 (foreign $80). Chilton Co., One Chilton Way, Radnor, PA 19089. TEL 610-964-4041. FAX 610-964-4947. URL: http://www.impomag.com. Ed. Jerry Steinbrink; Pub. Scott Sward. R&P contact: Jerry Steinbrink. TEL 610-964-4041. adv.: B&W page $8440; 7 x 10; adv. contact: Hank Pendrak. charts; illus.; tr.lit.; index. circ. 127,000. (tabloid format; also avail. in microfilm from UMI; reprint service avail. from UMI) **Indexed:** Key to Econ.Sci. **Document type:** trade publication.
—Ei; UMI. **CCC.**
Formerly: Industrial Maintenance and Plant Operation (ISSN 0192-8201)

350 650   CH   ISSN 0009-4579
CHINESE JOURNAL OF ADMINISTRATION. (Text in Chinese, English) 1963. s-a. NT.$400($20) to individuals (foreign $20); libraries NT.$800 (foreign $40). National Chengchi University, Center for Public and Business Administration Education, 187 Chin Hua St., Taipei, Taiwan, Republic of China. TEL 886-2-3940690. FAX 886-2-3975219. Ed. Yung-Chien Lou; Pub. Paul Shian Su. adv. contact: Der Chyuan Su. bk.rev.; charts; illus. circ. 1,500.
Description: Provides a forum for exchanging ideas and information among administrators, scholars, and others interested in public and business administration and related fields.
Refereed Serial

658.3 200   US
CHRISTIAN MANAGEMENT REPORT. 1979. bi-m. $29.95 to non-members. Christian Management Association, 22632 E. Golden Springs Dr., Ste. 390, Diamond Bar, CA 91765-4181. TEL 909-861-8861. FAX 909-860-8247. Ed. Sandy Scruggs; Pub. John Pearson. adv. contact: Jim McDonald. bk.rev. circ. 7,000. (back issues avail.) **Document type:** trade publication.
Description: Covers management areas of fund raising, computers, tax and legal, accounting and finance, communications, personnel and others for Christian ministries.

CHURCH BUSINESS. PRODUCTS & TECHNOLOGY. see RELIGIONS AND THEOLOGY

331 658.1   SW   ISSN 1400-0997
CIVILEKONOMEN. 1924. 8/yr. SEK 250 (effective 1997). Civilekonomernas Riksfoerbund (CR), P.O. Box 7667, S-103 94 Stockholm, Sweden. TEL 08-613-81-30. FAX 08-796-06-35. Ed. Jane Anden. adv.; bk.rev.; illus.; index. circ. 18,800. (also avail. in audio cassette) **Document type:** trade publication.
Former titles (until vol.4, 1994): Civilekonomnytt (ISSN 0280-915X); (until 1983): Ekonomen (ISSN 0013-2977)

658   US   ISSN 0009-8434
JK468.S4
CLASSIFICATION MANAGEMENT. 1965. a. $30. National Classification Management Society, 994 Old Eagle School Rd., Ste. 1019, Wayne, PA 19087-1802. TEL 610-971-4856. FAX 610-971-4859. E-mail: classmgmt@aol.com. Ed. Sharon K. Tannahill. circ. 1,800. **Document type:** bulletin.

CLEANING BUSINESS; published monthly for the self-employed cleaning & maintenance professional. see BUSINESS AND ECONOMICS — Small Business

CLINICAL LABORATORY MANAGEMENT REVIEW. see MEDICAL SCIENCES — Experimental Medicine, Laboratory Technique

367 658   AT   ISSN 0045-7205
CLUB MANAGEMENT IN AUSTRALIA. 1960. m. Aus.$40. Club Managers' Association Australia, 2A Lord St., Botany, N.S.W. 2019, Australia. TEL 02-316-6788. FAX 02-316-6244. Ed.Bd. adv. contact: Judy Rayner. charts; stat.; circ. controlled. **Document type:** trade publication.
Former titles: Secretaries and Managers Journal of Australia; Club Managers Journal (ISSN 0009-9597)

658   FR
CODE DES SOCIETES. base vol. plus updates. 270 F. (effective 1997). Joly Editions, 1 av. Franklin D. Roosevelt, 75008 Paris, France. TEL 33-1-44951620. FAX 33-1-45638939. Ed. Daniel Lepeltier. (looseleaf format) **Document type:** trade publication.

658   SP
COLECCION DIRECCION DE EMPRESAS Y ORGANIZACIONES. 1976. irreg., no.7, 1979. price varies. (Universidad de Navarra, Instituto de Estudios Superiores de la Empresa) Ediciones Universidad de Navarra, S.A., Apdo. 396, 31080 Pamplona, Spain. TEL 94 825 6850.

658   SP
COLECCION LA EMPRESA Y SU ENTORNO. SERIE A C. 1967. irreg., no.7, 1975. price varies. Ediciones Universidad de Navarra, S.A., Apdo. 396, 31080 Pamplona, Spain. TEL 94 825 6850.
Formerly: Universidad de Navarra. Instituto de Estudios Superiores de la Empresas. Coleccion I E S E. Serie A C (ISSN 0078-8716)

658   SP   ISSN 0212-0763
COLECCION LA EMPRESA Y SU ENTORNO. SERIE L. 1970. irreg., no.14, 1981. price varies. Ediciones Universidad de Navarra, S.A., Apdo. 396, 31080 Pamplona, Spain. TEL 94 825 6850.
Formerly: Universidad de Navarra. Instituto de Estudios Superiores de la Empresa. Coleccion I E S E. Serie L (ISSN 0078-8708)

658.4   US   ISSN 1085-911X
COLUMBUS C.E.O. 1992. m. $20.05; newsstand price: $2.25. Metropolitan C.E.O., 911 E. 86th St., Ste. 100, Indianapolis, IN 46240-1840. TEL 317-257-8000. FAX 317-257-1482. Ed. Cindy Ludlow. circ. 25,000 (controlled). (back issues avail.)

COMMUNICATION BRIEFINGS; a monthly idea source for decision-makers. see COMMUNICATIONS

658   US
COMMUNICATION NEWS. m. membership. American Society of Association Executives, Communication Section, 1575 Eye St., N.W., Washington, DC 20005-1168. TEL 202-626-2739. FAX 202-408-9635. circ. 2,050.
Description: Features common public and employee relations problems faced by association executives who manage the communication of their association.

658.45   US   ISSN 0744-7612
CODEN: COMWEE
COMMUNICATION WORLD. 1970. m. (10/yr.). $95 to libraries (effective 1997). International Association of Business Communicators, One Hallidie Plaza, Ste. 600, San Francisco, CA 94102. TEL 415-433-3400. FAX 415-362-8762. Ed. Gloria Gordon. adv. contact: Thomas Gradie. bk.rev.; illus. circ. 13,400. **Indexed:** ABI Inform., BPIA, Manage.Cont., Tr.& Indus.Ind. **Document type:** trade publication.
●Also available online. Vendor(s): Information Access Co., Knight-Ridder Information, Inc., Lexis-Nexis, UMI. —BLDSC (3363.469500); UMI; UnCover. **CCC.**
Former titles: I A B C News; I A B C Journal (ISSN 0092-7384)
Description: For members of IABC whose business is communication, public relations and related disciplines.

658   UK   ISSN 0264-4576
COMMUNICATIONS MANAGEMENT. 1983. m. E M A P Business & Computer Publications Ltd., 33-39 Bowling Green Ln., London EC1R ODA, England. TEL 44-171-837-1212. FAX 44-171-278-4008. TELEX 936566. adv. circ. 15,000. **Indexed:** Mgmt.& Market.Abstr. **Document type:** trade publication.
Formerly: C S and M (ISSN 0264-455X)

658   US   ISSN 1071-5967
COMMUNITY MANAGEMENT. 1993. bi-m. Community Associations Institute, 1630 Duke St., Alexandria, VA 22314. TEL 703-548-8600. FAX 703-684-1581. URL: http://www.caionline.com. adv.: B&W page $950. circ. 2,100 (paid). **Document type:** trade publication.
Description: Presents strategies, trends and news for managers of condominiums and planned communities.

COMPANY CAR REPORT - EUROPE. see BUSINESS AND ECONOMICS — Personnel Management

658 340   AT   ISSN 0816-5521
COMPANY DIRECTOR. 1983. m. Aus.$295. Australian Institute of Company Directors, Level 3,, 71 York St., Sydney, N.S.W. 2000, Australia. TEL 02-299-8788. FAX 02-299-1006. Ed. Mark Phillips. adv. contact: Sarah Coles. bk.rev. circ. 12,000.
Formed by the 1983 merger of: Director's Law Reporter (ISSN 0311-0389); (1979-1983): Directors Early Warner; (1975-1983): Directors Economic Review.

658   CC   ISSN 1023-4128
COMPANY SECRETARY. (Text in English) 1990. m. HK.$1635. (Hong Kong Institute of Company Secretaries) Pearson Professional (Hong Kong) Limited, Ste. 1808, Asian House, 1 Hennessy Rd., Wanchai, Hong Kong, People's Republic of China. TEL 852-2863-2659. FAX 852-2520-6954. E-mail: pphkg@hk.super.net.
Description: Contains commentary on developments in legal, accounting and company secretarial practices as they affect the Hong Kong and PRC business environment.

658   UK
COMPARATIVE MANAGEMENT. q. £45($85) Debos Oxford Publications Ltd., 31 Warnborough Rd., Oxford OX2 6JA, England. Ed. Oscar Werdmuller.
Description: Academic and management journal that focuses on the institutional, legal and cultural environment in which businesses operate. Has a heavy emphasis on Europe.

658   US
COMPENSATION & BENEFITS REPORT. 1986. s-m. $210.36. Bureau of Business Practice, 24 Rope Ferry Rd., Waterford, CT 06386. TEL 860-442-4365. FAX 860-437-3555. URL: http://www.bbpnews.com. Ed. Joanne Mitchell-George; Pub. Peter Garabedian. R&P contact: Debra Ferraro. **Document type:** newsletter.
Formerly: Compensation and Benefits Manager's Report (ISSN 1062-0796)
Description: Shows compensation and benefits managers how to get the most out of their companies' salary and benefits dollars.

COMPENSATION OF PLANT - FACILITIES MANAGERS & ENGINEERS. see BUSINESS AND ECONOMICS — Labor And Industrial Relations

658   US   ISSN 1058-0247
CODEN: CINREU
COMPETITIVE INTELLIGENCE REVIEW. q. $175 (foreign $245) (effective 1998). (Society of Competitive Intelligence Professionals) John Wiley & Sons, Inc., Journals, 605 Third Ave., New York, NY 10158. TEL 212-850-6645. FAX 212-850-6021. TELEX 12-7063. E-mail: SUBINFO@JWILEY.COM; URL: http://www.wiley.co.uk. (Subscr. outside the Americas to: John Wiley & Sons Ltd., Baffins Ln., Chichester, W. Sussex PO19 1UD, England. TEL 44-1243-779777. FAX 44-1243-776128) Ed. John Prescott. adv.: B&W page £640, color page £1515; trim 279 x 210. circ. 3,250. (also avail. in microform from UMI; back issues avail.; reprint service avail.) **Document type:** academic/scholarly publication.
—**CCC.**
Formerly (until 1990): Competitive Intelligencer (ISSN 1040-9645)
Refereed Serial

COMPETITIVENESS REVIEW. see BUSINESS AND ECONOMICS — International Commerce

COMPLEAT ANBAR. see BUSINESS AND ECONOMICS — Abstracting, Bibliographies, Statistics

658.32   US   ISSN 0274-8304
HD7106.U5
COMPLIANCE GUIDE FOR PLAN ADMINISTRATORS. 1976. m. $747 (CD-ROM ed. $802). C C H Incorporated, 2700 Lake Cook Rd., Riverwoods, IL 60015. TEL 847-267-7000; 800-835-5224. FAX 800-224-8299. (looseleaf format)
—**CCC.**
Formerly: C C H Compliance Guide for Plan Administrators (ISSN 0363-7476)

COMPUTATIONAL & MATHEMATICAL ORGANIZATION THEORY. see MATHEMATICS — Computer Applications

COMPUTATIONAL ECONOMICS. see BUSINESS AND ECONOMICS — Computer Applications

COMPUTER LAW & SECURITY REPORT. see COMPUTERS — Computer Security

COMPUTERS & OPERATIONS RESEARCH; and their application to problems of world concern. see COMPUTERS

658   FR
CONSEIL NATIONAL DU PATRONAT FRANCAIS. ANNUAIRE. a. 132 F. 31 av. Pierre 1er de Serbie, 75784 Paris, France. index.

658   UK   ISSN 1363-6804
CONSPECTUS. 1992. m. £95 (foreign £190) (effective 1997). Prime Marketing Publications Ltd., Witton House, Lower Rd., Chorleywood, Hertfordshire WD3 5LB, England. TEL 44-1923-285323. FAX 44-1923-285819. E-mail: conspectus@pmp.co.uk; URL: http://www.pmp.co.uk. Ed. Tim Ring. circ. 25,000. **Document type:** consumer publication. —AskIEEE; KR SourceOne.
   Formerly (until 1996): Consultants' Conspectus (ISSN 1351-0908)
   Description: Publication for decision makers and management consultants who are interested in current developments in information technology.

658 690   US   ISSN 1089-733X
CONSTRUCTION COMPANY STRATEGIST. m. $255. Brownstone Publishers, Inc., 149 Fifth Ave., New York, NY 10010-6801. TEL 212-473-8200. FAX 212-473-8786. Ed. George Schaeffer; Pub. John M. Striker. **Document type:** newsletter.
   Description: Strategies, legal tips, and how-to advice for successfully managing a construction company. Features model contract language, forms, guidelines, and more.

CONSTRUCTION MANAGEMENT. see BUILDING AND CONSTRUCTION

658   US   ISSN 0196-1292
HD69.C6
CONSULTANTS AND CONSULTING ORGANIZATIONS DIRECTORY; a reference guide to concerns and individuals engaged in consultation for business, industry and government. (Supplement avail.: New Consultants) a. $445 (supplement $375). Gale Research, 835 Penobscot Bldg., 645 Griswold St., Detroit, MI 48226-4094. TEL 313-961-2242; 800-877-4253. FAX 800-414-5043. E-mail: daniel__snyder@gale.com. Ed. Janice McLean. **Document type:** directory.
●Also available online. Vendor(s): Human Resources Information Network (CCOD).
—CISTI.
   Formerly: Consultants and Consulting Organizations (ISSN 0589-4859)
   Description: Details on firms, individuals and organizations active in consulting fields.

658   US   ISSN 0045-8201
CONSULTANTS NEWS. 1970. m. $188 (effective 1997). Kennedy Publications, Templeton Rd., Fitzwilliam, NH 03447. TEL 603-585-6544. FAX 603-585-9555. Ed. James H. Kennedy. adv. contact: Carolyn D. Edwards. bk.rev.; index. **Document type:** newsletter.
●Also available online. Vendor(s): UMI.
—UMI.
   Description: Covers trends and developments in management consulting.

658   US   ISSN 0273-4613
CONSULTING OPPORTUNITIES JOURNAL. 1981. bi-m. $69. Consultants National Resource Center, Box 430, Clear Spring, MD 21722. TEL 301-791-9332. Ed. J. Stephen Lanning. adv.; bk.rev. circ. 3,000. **Document type:** newsletter.
   Incorporates: Consultant's Digest.

658   US
▼**CONSULTING - TOOLS.** 1995. s-w. National Consultant Referrals, Inc., 4918 N. Harbor Dr., Ste. 103, San Diego, CA 92106. TEL 619-523-2188. E-mail: ncri@referrals.com; URL: http://referrals.com. Ed. Carl G. Kline. R&P contact: Leona Kline. **Document type:** newsletter.
●Available only online.

658 338.4   BE
CONTACT TRANSPORT & LOGISTICS; le trait d'union industrie - prestataires de services - bindeteken tussen industrie en dienstverlenende sektor. (Editions in Dutch, French) bi-m. 2100 BEF. Multi Media Management, Rue des Pres 2-001, 4802 Verviers Heusy, Belgium. TEL 32-87-292929. FAX 32-87-225600. adv.; illus. **Document type:** trade publication.

658   UK
CONTROL. 1964. bi-m. £125. Institute of Operations Management, University of Warwick Science Park, Sir William Lyons Rd., Coventry, Warks. CV4 7EZ, England. TEL 44-1203-692266. FAX 44-1203-692305. E-mail: iom@iomnet.demon.co.uk; URL: http://www.iomnet.demon.co.uk. Ed. D. Angove. adv. contact: R.G. Turner. bk.rev.; circ. 5,000 (paid). **Document type:** academic/scholarly publication.
   Former titles: B P I C S Control (ISSN 0266-1713); (until 1983): B P I C S News.
   Description: Supplies the UK manufacturing industry with information on software, hardware, consultants, and training services. Seeks to enhance professional production and inventory-management skills.
Refereed Serial

658   GW   ISSN 0343-267X
CONTROLLER MAGAZIN. 1976. 6/yr. DM.124. (Controller Verein e.V., Muenchen) Management Service Verlag, Postfach 1168, 82116 Gauting, Germany. TEL 49-8153-8041. FAX 49-8153-8043. Ed. Albrecht Deyhle. adv. contact: Christa Kiessling. bk.rev.; charts; illus.; stat.; index. circ. 6,000. (back issues avail.) Indexed: INSPEC. **Document type:** trade publication.
   Description: Publication of interest to controllers and managers. Covers new ideas and developments, new systems, new regulations, organization, planning and international news. Includes bibliographies and positions available.

658 011   US   ISSN 1065-0938
CONVENE. 1986. 10/yr. $50 (foreign $75). Professional Convention Management Association, 100 Vestavia Parkway, Ste. 220, Birmingham, AL 35216. TEL 205-823-7262. FAX 205-822-3891. E-mail: joliver@pcma.org. Ed. Peter Shure; Pub. Roy B. Evans, Jr. R&P contact: Carla Krause. TEL 205-978-4917. adv. contact: John Oliver. circ. 30,000.

658   US   ISSN 0746-8652
HD2745
CORPORATE BOARD; the journal of corporate governance. 1980. bi-m. $420 to individuals; corporations $2695. Vanguard Publications, Inc., 4440 Hagadorn Rd., Okemos, MI 48864-2414. E-mail: info@corporateboard.com; URL: http://www.corporateboard.com. Ed. Ralph D. Ward; Pub. Irving A. Lesher, III. R&P contact: Judith Scheidt. bk.rev.; index. (back issues avail.) Indexed: BPIA, Bus.Ind., Manage.Cont., Tr.& Indus.Ind. **Document type:** newsletter.
●Also available online. Vendor(s): Information Access Co.
—BLDSC (3472.060500). CCC.
   Formerly (until 1983): Corporate Director (ISSN 0196-2116)

CORPORATE COMMUNICATIONS. see COMMUNICATIONS

658   US   ISSN 1083-7930
CORPORATE COMMUNITY RELATIONS LETTER; the newsletter for the community relations professional. m. (except combined May-Jun., Jul.-Aug.) $115. Boston College, Center for Corporate Community Relations, 36 College Rd., Chestnut Hill, MA 02167-3835. TEL 617-552-4545. FAX 617-552-8499. E-mail: labanca@bc.edu; URL: http://www.bc.edu/cccr. Ed. Lisa LaBanca. R&P contact: Susan Thomas. bk.rev.; cum.index: 1989-1994; 1994-1996. circ. 2,200. (back issues avail.) **Document type:** newsletter.
   Description: Trends and issues affecting corporations and their involvement in the community, corporate citizenship, and corporate social responsibility.

658   SW   ISSN 1103-0011
CORPORATE COMPUTING. 1928. 6/yr. SEK 300 in Scandinavia; elsewhere SEK 400. C W - Communications AB, Soedra Hamnvaagen 22, S-115 41 Stockholm, Sweden. TEL 46-8-667-91-80. FAX 46-8-665-31-32. Ed. Mikael Lagerwall. adv.; bk.rev.; charts; illus. circ. 12,000. (reprint service avail. from UMI) Indexed: C.I.S. Abstr.
   Formed by the 1992 merger of: Digitalvaerlden (ISSN 0284-4508) & Unix (ISSN 1102-2361) & Affaersekonomi - Management (ISSN 0346-5381); Which was formerly (until 1975): Affaersekonomi (ISSN 0001-9607)

CORPORATE COUNSEL. see LAW — Corporate Law

CORPORATE ENVIRONMENTAL STRATEGY; the journal of environmental leadership. see ENVIRONMENTAL STUDIES

658.7 388   CN
CORPORATE FLEET MANAGEMENT. 1991. 4/yr. Maclean Hunter Ltd., 777 Bay St., Toronto, ON M5W 1A7, Canada. TEL 416-596-5624. FAX 416-596-5866. Ed. Joe Terrett. adv.: B&W & color, B&W page Can.$3200; trim 8 x 10 3/4. circ. 20,530.

658.4 346.066   US
▼**CORPORATE GOVERNANCE.** 1995. d. free. James McRichtie, Ed. & Pub., 2461 Second Ave., Sacramento, CA 95818. E-mail: jm@corpgov.net; URL: http://www.corpgov.net/.
●Available only online.
   Description: Provides news, discussions and links to consultants, sites policies and organizations with a focus on corporate governance.

CORPORATE LEGAL TIMES; the national monthly on managing in-house corporate legal departments. see LAW — Corporate Law

338 332   US   ISSN 0279-5299
HC107.M6   CODEN: CRPMEK
CORPORATE REPORT MINNESOTA. (Supplements avail.: Corporate Report Ventures (q.); Corporate Report Fact Book) 1969. m. $29. American City Business Journals, Inc. (Austin), 505 Powell St., Austin, TX 78703-5121. (Subscr. to: 105 S. Fifth St., Ste. 100, Minneapolis, MN 55402. TEL 612-338-4288. FAX 612-373-0195) Ed. Eric Wieffering; Pub. J. Craig Wessel. adv.: B&W page $3885; adv. contact: Lori Freeman. bk.rev.; circ. 11,397 (paid); 1,491 (controlled). (back issues avail.) Indexed: P.A.I.S., Tr.& Indus.Ind. **Document type:** consumer publication.
●Also available online. Vendor(s): CompuServe, Inc., Data-Star, Dow Jones News Retrieval, Information Access Co., Knight-Ridder Information, Inc., Lexis-Nexis, UMI.
Also available on CD-ROM. Producer(s): UMI.
—UMI. CCC.
   Formerly (until 1981): Corporate Report (ISSN 0190-9517)

658   UK   ISSN 1363-3589
▼**CORPORATE REPUTATION REVIEW.** 1996. q. £50 (U.S. & Canada $75; rest of world £60) to individuals; institutions £125 (U.S. & Canada $190; rest of world £135). (International Corporate Identity Group) Henry Stewart Publications, Russell House, 28-30 Little Russell St., London WC1A 2HN, England. TEL 44-171-404-3040. FAX 44-171-404-3041. E-mail: 100622.3264@compuserve.com. (Subscr. in US and Canada to: 810 E. 10th St., Box 1897, Lawrence, KS 66044. TEL 913-843-1221. FAX 913-843-1274) Ed. Daryn Moody. adv. contact: Fraser Tant. **Document type:** trade publication.
   Description: Provides an international forum for original research on corporate identity, corporate image, and corporate brand management.
Refereed Serial

BUSINESS AND ECONOMICS — MANAGEMENT

658   US   ISSN 1058-2908
HG4057
CORPORATE YELLOW BOOK; who's who at the leading U.S. companies. (Companion volume to: Financial Yellow Book) 1985. q. $265 (effective 1997). Leadership Directories, Inc., 104 Fifth Ave., 2nd Fl., New York, NY 10011. TEL 212-629-4140. FAX 212-645-0931. Ed. Catherine Shih. **Document type:** directory.
●Also available on CD-ROM. Producer(s): Chadwyck-Healey Inc.
—CISTI. **CCC.**
    Former titles: Corporate 1000 Yellow Book (ISSN 1049-7943); (until 1990): Corporate 1000 (ISSN 0882-3227)
    Description: Lists names, titles, addresses, and telephone numbers of corporate leaders. Provides business descriptions, information on product lines and annual revenues. Includes indexes by state, industry, individual's name, and company name.

CORPUS OCCUPATIONAL HEALTH AND SAFETY MANAGEMENT HANDBOOK. see *OCCUPATIONAL HEALTH AND SAFETY*

CORRECTIONAL INDUSTRIES ASSOCIATION NEWSLETTER. see *PUBLIC ADMINISTRATION*

COSMETIC MANAGEMENT INTERNATIONAL. see *BEAUTY CULTURE — Perfumes And Cosmetics*

COURAGEOUS CONTRARIAN. see *BUSINESS AND ECONOMICS — Investments*

LE COURIER DU MAIRE. see *PUBLIC ADMINISTRATION — Municipal Government*

658   SW   ISSN 1101-2765
CRAFOORD LECTURES. (Text in English) 1989. irreg. price varies. Lund University Press, P.O. Box 141, S-221 00 Lund, Sweden. TEL 46-46-31-20-00. FAX 46-46-30-53-38. E-mail: order@studli.se. Ed. A. Malm. **Document type:** academic/scholarly publication.

CREATIVE TRAINING TECHNIQUES; a newsletter of tips, tactics and how-tos for delivering effective training. see *EDUCATION*

658 370 100   US   ISSN 0093-5263
CREATIVITY IN ACTION. 1972. m. $50 (Canada and Mexico $55; elsewhere $60). Creative Education Foundation, Inc., 1050 Union Rd., Buffalo, NY 14224. TEL 716-675-3181. FAX 716-675-3209. E-mail: cefhq@aol.com. Ed. Arthur Van Gundy. R&P contact: Grace Guzzotta. bk.rev. circ. 500. (looseleaf format; back issues avail.) **Document type:** newsletter, academic/scholarly publication.
    Description: Helps readers learn more about and practice more of many important ideas and techniques that enhance creative thinking and action.

CREDIT & COLLECTION MANAGER'S LETTER. see *BUSINESS AND ECONOMICS — Banking And Finance*

CREDIT-CURIER. see *BUSINESS AND ECONOMICS — Economic Situation And Conditions*

CREDIT MANAGEMENT. see *BUSINESS AND ECONOMICS — Marketing And Purchasing*

CRITICAL ISSUES IN FACILITIES MANAGEMENT. see *EDUCATION — School Organization And Administration*

658   UK   ISSN 0965-2841
CRONER'S COMPANY ADMINISTRATION BRIEFING. Key Title: Company Administration Briefing. 1992? base vol. (plus bi-w. updates). £224.55 (updated £169.55) (effective 1995). Croner Publications Ltd. (Subsidiary of: Wolters Kluwer N.V.), Croner House, 100 London Rd., Kingston-upon-Thames, Surrey TW2 6SR, England. TEL 44-181-547-3333. FAX 44-181-247-1300. TELEX 267778. (looseleaf format) **Document type:** trade publication.

658   UK   ISSN 0969-7144
CRONER'S EXECUTIVE COMPANION. 1978. base vol. (plus bi-m. updates). £152.15 (updates £99.50) (effective 1995). Croner Publications Ltd. (Subsidiary of: Wolters Kluwer N.V.), Croner House, 100 London Rd., Kingston-upon-Thames, Surrey TW2 6SR, England. TEL 44-181-547-3333. FAX 44-181-547-2637. TELEX 267778. Ed. Paula Quinn. (looseleaf format)
    Formerly: Management Information Manual.
    Description: Discusses a broad range of business questions ranging from finance, taxation, communications, and export to government and economic issues in the U.K.

658   UK   ISSN 1352-7606
CROSS CULTURAL MANAGEMENT. 1994. q. £179($279) (foreign Aus.$349) (effective 1998). Patrington Press Ltd., Enholmes Hall, Patrington, Hull HU12 0PR, England. TEL 44-1964-630033. (Dist. by: M C B University Press Ltd., 60-62 Toller Ln., Bradford, W. Yorks BD8 9BY, England. TEL 44-1274-777700. FAX 44-1274-785200) Ed. Samuel Natale; Pub. Marjorie Brown. R&P contact: B.O. Pettman. **Document type:** academic/scholarly publication.
—BLDSC (3488.807000).

658   CK   ISSN 0120-3592
CUADERNOS DE ADMINISTRACION. 1981. s-a. Col.$7000($8) (effective 1997). Pontificia Universidad Javeriana, Facultad de Ciencias Economicas y Administrativas, Calle 40 No. 6-23, Piso 7, Santafe de Bogota, Colombia. TEL 57-1-2870388. FAX 57-1-2857289. E-mail: jrey@javercol.javeriana.edu.co.

658   UK
CUMBRIAN EXECUTIVE. 1986. bi-m. £15. Cumbrian Press, 3 Chatsworth Sq., Carlisle, Cumbria CA11 1HB, England. TEL 44-1228-471444. FAX 44-1228-514747. Ed. Tony Thornton. adv. contact: Alan Taylor. circ. 5,000. **Document type:** bulletin.

658   US
▼**CUSTOMER SERVICE MANAGEMENT REPORT.** 1997. 17/yr. $199. Dartnell Corporation, 4660 N. Ravenswood Ave., Chicago, IL 60640. TEL 773-561-4000; 800-621-5463. FAX 773-561-3801. URL: http://www.dartnellcorp.com. Ed. Romy Schafer. **Document type:** newsletter.
    Description: Provides customer service managers with information to better train, motivate and communicate with employees, to improve their departments' profitability and performance, and to further their career and personal development.

658 640.73   US   ISSN 1068-154X
CUSTOMER SERVICE MANAGER'S LETTER. 1987. s-m. $176.88. Bureau of Business Practice, 24 Rope Ferry Rd., Waterford, CT 06386. TEL 860-442-4365. FAX 860-437-3555. URL: http://www.bbpnews.com. Ed. Anna Trusky; Pub. Peter Garabedian. R&P contact: Debra Ferraro. s-a. index. **Indexed:** Mgmt.& Market.Abstr. **Document type:** newsletter.
    Formerly: Customer Service Management Bulletin.
    Description: Shows managers how to reduce costs, increase customer base and maximize employee capability.

658 659.1   US   ISSN 0145-8442
CUSTOMER SERVICE NEWSLETTER. 1973. m. $127. Alexander Research & Communications, Inc., 215 Park Ave. S., Ste. 1301, New York, NY 10003. TEL 212-228-0246. FAX 212-228-0376. Ed. Susan Hash; Pub. Margaret DeWitt. R&P contact: Mary Dalessandro. **Document type:** newsletter.
    Description: Reports on practical techniques for improving customer service operations including: training, measurement, benchmarking, using new technology and more.

658   US
CUSTOMERS FIRST. 1987. bi-w. $68.90. Dartnell Corporation, 4660 N. Ravenswood Ave., Chicago, IL 60640. TEL 773-561-4000; 800-621-5463. FAX 773-561-3801. URL: http://www.dartnellcorp.com. Ed. Romy Schafer. **Document type:** newsletter.
    Description: Motivates and instructs employees on how to improve customer relations.

D B M S; client - server computing. (Database Management Systems) see *COMPUTERS — Software*

D E C A DIMENSIONS. (Distributive Education Clubs of America) see *BUSINESS AND ECONOMICS — Marketing And Purchasing*

658   UK
D W P S. 1988, no.1; N.S. Feb. 1992. irreg. Aston Business School, 11th Fl., S. Wing, Aston University, Aston Triangle, Birmingham B4 7ET, England. E-mail: dwps@aston.ac.uk. Eds. P. Seltsikas, P. Boynton. **Document type:** monographic series.
    Formerly (until 1992): Doctoral Working Papers Series (ISSN 0952-2247)
    Refereed Serial

658   NE
DAGELIJKS BELEID; tips & adviezen voor uw werk. 1982. m. fl.103 (effective 1995). V N U Business Publications B.V., Postbus 9194, 1006 CC Amsterdam, Netherlands. TEL 31-20-5102911. FAX 31-20-6173346. Ed. A.P. van de Bovenkamp. circ. 5,100. (back issues avail.) **Document type:** trade publication.
    Description: Publication for managers in business and industry, covering managerial skills and management-employee relations.

658   US   ISSN 0148-8155
DAILY REPORT FOR EXECUTIVES. 1943. 5/w. $5985. The Bureau of National Affairs, Inc., 1231 25th St., N.W., Washington, DC 20037. TEL 202-452-4200. FAX 202-822-8092. TELEX 285656 BNAI WSH. URL: http://www.bna.com/. (Subscr. to: 9435 Key West Ave., Rockville, MD 20850. TEL 800-372-1033) Ed. Nancee L. Simonson. m. index. (looseleaf format; back issues avail.)
●Also available online. Vendor(s): Human Resources Information Network (CDD, HDD), Lexis-Nexis (DREXEC), NewsNet, West Group (BNA-DER).
—**CCC.**
    Description: Covers legislative, regulatory, legal, tax, and economic developments which affect both national and international businesses.

658   DK   ISSN 1397-3266
▼**DANSK MANAGEMENT FORUM.** 1995. 3/yr. DKK 275 (effective 1997). Dansk Management Forum, Folke Bernadottes Alle 45, DK-2100 Copenhagen Oe, Denmark. TEL 45-33-48-88-88. FAX 45-33-48-88-89. E-mail: dmforum@dmforum.dk. Ed. Ruth Znaider. circ. 2,600.

658 388   UK   ISSN 0963-2522
DEALER PRINCIPAL. 1986. m. £150. Sewells International Emap Automotive Ltd., Wentworth House, Wentworth St., Peterborough PE1 1DS, England. TEL 44-1733-467191. FAX 44-1733-467199. **Document type:** trade publication.

658.4   II   ISSN 0304-0941
HD28
DECISION. (Text in English) 1974. q. Rs.200($30) Indian Institute of Management, P.B. No. 16757, Alipore P.O., Calcutta 700 027, India. TEL 77-2429 TELEX 021-2501. Ed. Rahul Mukherjee. adv.; bk.rev.; abstr. circ. 300. **Document type:** academic/scholarly publication.

658   US   ISSN 0732-6823
HD30.23
DECISION LINE. 1970. bi-m. (5/yr.). $6 to non-members. Decision Sciences Institute, University Plaza, Atlanta, GA 30303. TEL 404-651-4000. Ed. Terry R. Rakes. bibl. circ. 5,000. **Document type:** newsletter.
—SWETS; UnCover.

658   US   ISSN 1044-5641
DECISION RESEARCH; a series of monographs. 1984. irreg., vol.3, 1988. $73.25. J A I Press Inc., 55 Old Post Rd., No. 2, Box 1678, Greenwich, CT 06830-1678. TEL 203-661-7602. FAX 203-661-0792. E-mail: jai@jaipress.com. (Subscr. in UK and Europe to: JAI Press Ltd., 38 Tavistock St., Covent Garden, London WC2E 7PB, England. TEL 44-171-379-8834. FAX 44-171-379-8835) Ed. Howard Thomas. **Document type:** monographic series.

BUSINESS AND ECONOMICS — MANAGEMENT

658   HD30.23   US   ISSN 0011-7315   CODEN: DESCDQ
DECISION SCIENCES. 1970. bi-m. $59 (effective 1995). Decision Sciences Institute, University Plaza, Atlanta, GA 30303. TEL 404-651-4000. URL: gopher.gsu.edu/11/DecSciInst. Ed. Lee J. Krajewski. adv. circ. 4,000. (also avail. in microform from UMI) **Indexed:** AAR, ABI Inform., Account.Ind. (1974-), ASCA, B.P.I., BPIA, Bus.Ind., Compumath, Cont.Pg.Manage., Curr.Cont., Excerp.Med., INSPEC, Int.Abstr.Oper.Res., J.Cont.Quant.Meth., Manage.Cont., Oper.Res.Manage.Sci., Qual.Contr.Appl.Stat., SCIMP (1978-), Sport Fish.Abstr., SSCI, Tr.& Indus.Ind., Wild.Rev. **Document type:** academic/scholarly publication.
—BLDSC (3537.150000); AskIEEE; Genuine Article; KR SourceOne; SWETS; UMI; UnCover.

658   T57.95   US   ISSN 0360-375X
DECISION SCIENCES INSTITUTE. ANNUAL MEETING PROCEEDINGS. 1970. a. $25 (effective 1995). Decision Sciences Institute, University Plaza, Atlanta, GA 30303. TEL 404-651-4000. circ. 2,500. (also avail. in microfiche) **Indexed:** BPIA. **Document type:** proceedings.
Formerly: American Institute for Decision Sciences. National Conference Proceedings.

658 330   NE   ISSN 0167-9236   CODEN: DSSYDK
DECISION SUPPORT SYSTEMS; an international journal. (Text in English) 1985. m. fl.1455($836) (effective 1998). North-Holland (Subsidiary of: Elsevier Science B.V.), P.O. Box 211, 1000 AE Amsterdam, Netherlands. TEL 31-20-4853911. FAX 31-20-4853598. TELEX 18582 ESPA NL. E-mail: usinfo@elsevier.nl; URL: http://www.elsevier. nl:80/inca/publications/store/5/0/5/5/4/0/ 505540.pub.shtml. (Subscr. in the Americas to: Elsevier Science, Regional Sales Office, Box 945, New York, NY 10159-0945. TEL 212-633-3730. FAX 212-633-3680; Subscr. in Australasia and the Far East to: Elsevier Science (Singapore) Pte Ltd, No.1 Temasek Ave., No.17-01 Millenia Tower, Singapore 039192, Singapore. TEL 65-434-3727. FAX 65-337-2230; Subscr. in Japan to: Elsevier Science Japan, 9-15 Higashi-Azabu 1-chome, Minato-ku Tokyo 106, Japan. TEL 81-3-5561-5033. FAX 81-3-5561-5047) Eds. H.J. Schneider, A.B. Winston. (back issues avail.; reprint service avail. from SWZ) **Indexed:** A.I.Abstr., ABI Inform., ASCA, CAD CAM Abstr., Compumath, Comput.Abstr., Comput.Lit.Ind., Cont.Pg.Manage., Curr.Cont., Cyb.Abstr., INSPEC (1986-), SSCI. **Document type:** academic/scholarly publication.
—BLDSC (3537.160000); AskIEEE; Ei; Genuine Article; KR SourceOne; Linda Hall; SWETS; UMI; UnCover. CCC.
Description: Covers the concept of using computers for supporting the decision process in managerial settings. Articles discuss operations research, management science, cognitive psychology and organizational behavior.
Refereed Serial

658   GR   ISSN 0011-8087
DELTION DIIKISEOS EPICHIRISEON/BUSINESS ADMINISTRATION BULLETIN. 1962. m. Dr.1000 per no. John Papamichalakis, Ed. & Pub., 26 Odos Rigillis, 106-75 Athens, Greece. FAX 30-71-7240000. TELEX 219006 OLKI GR. (And: 1 sq. Marguerite, 1040 Brussels, Belgium) adv. contact: Ecaterini Papamihalaki. bk.rev.; bibl.; charts; illus.; stat.; index. circ. 25,000. (tabloid format) **Document type:** bulletin.

ENTAL PRACTICE MANAGEMENT. see *MEDICAL SCIENCES — Dentistry*

658   US   ISSN 1057-2864
DESIGN FIRM MANAGEMENT & ADMINISTRATION REPORT. Abbreviated title: D F M A R. 1991. m. $249 (outside N. America $273). Institute of Management & Administration, Inc., 29 W. 35th St., 5th Fl., New York, NY 10001-2299. TEL 212-244-0360. FAX 212-564-0465. URL: http://www.ioma.com. Ed. Kneeland Godfrey; Pub. Lee Rath. R&P contact: Sofie Kourkoutakis. index. circ. 2,000. (looseleaf format; back issues avail.) **Document type:** newsletter.
—CCC.
Incorporates (1986-1991): Architect's Office Management and Administration Report (ISSN 0890-9814); **Formerly** (until 1991): Engineering Office Management and Administration Report (ISSN 0749-1557)
Description: Offers actionable strategies for improving design firm efficiency and profitability. Practical guidance on fees and billing rates, compensation levels and benefits for architects and engineers, staff, office equipment.

658   T342   US   ISSN 1045-7194
DESIGN MANAGEMENT JOURNAL. 1989. q. $96 (foreign $126). Design Management Institute, 29 Temple Place, 2nd Fl., Boston, MA 02111-1350. TEL 617-338-6380. FAX 617-338-6570. E-mail: dmistaff@dmi.org; URL: http://www.dmi.org. Ed. Thomas Walton; Pub. Earl N. Powell. R&P contact: John Tobin. adv. contact: John Tobin. bk.rev. **Indexed:** DAAI. **Document type:** academic/scholarly publication.
—BLDSC (3559.978350); SWETS.
Description: Devoted to exploring "how design" in products, communication, and environments.

658   GW   ISSN 0343-9496
DEUTSCHE VERWALTUNGSPRAXIS. 1949. m. DM.148.80. Maximilian-Verlag, Striepenweg 31, 21147 Hamburg, Germany. TEL 49-40-79713302. Ed.Bd. adv.: B&W page DM.2900, color page DM.4400; trim 176 x 260; adv. contact: Rainer Metzner. bk.rev.; abstr.; charts; illus.; stat.; index. circ. 7,850. (reprint service avail. from SCH) **Document type:** trade publication.

658   JA   ISSN 0385-4272
DIAMOND HARVARD BUSINESS. Japanese translation of: Harvard Business Review (US ISSN 0017-8012) 1976. bi-m. Diamond, Inc., 4-2 Kasumigaseki, 1-chome, Chiyoda-ku, Tokyo 100-60, Japan. TEL 81-3-3504-6558. FAX 81-3-3591-3895. Ed. Yoshihiro Kamimuro; Pub. Mineo Iwamochi. adv.: B&W page 400000 Yen, color page 470000 Yen; trim 208 x 280; adv. contact: Katsutoshi Hirose. circ. 12,500.
Description: Covers commercial, chemical, fishing, electrical and machinery industries.

658   JA
DIAMOND WEEKLY. (Text in Japanese) 1913. w. Diamond, Inc., 4-2, 1-chome, Kasumigaseki, Chiyoda-ku, Tokyo 100, Japan. TEL 81-3-3504-6548. Ed. Yutaka Iwasa; Pub. Hiromichi Sone. adv.: B&W page $8917, color page $11562; trim 182 x 257; adv. contact: Katsutoshi Hirose. circ. 100,287.
Formerly: Bessatsu Daiyamondo (ISSN 0385-3802)

658   FR
DICTIONNAIRE JOLY SOCIETES. 12 base vols. plus q. updates. 5500 F. (effective 1997). Joly Editions, 1 av. Franklin D. Roosevelt, 75008 Paris, France. TEL 33-1-44951620. FAX 33-1-45638939. Ed. Daniel Lepeltier. (looseleaf format; also avail. in diskette format) **Document type:** trade publication.
●Also available on CD-ROM.
Formed by the merger of: Dictionnaire Joly Societes Anonymes & Dictionnaire Joly Societes a Responsabilite Limitee.

658   FR   ISSN 0767-1555
DICTIONNAIRE PERMANENT: DIFFICULTES DES ENTREPRISES. base vol. plus m. updates. 1150 F. for base vol. (updates 320 F.) (effective 1995). Editions Legislatives et Administratives, 80 ave. de la Marne, 92546 Montrouge Cedex, France. TEL 40-92-68-68. FAX 46-56-00-15. TELEX 632 855 F. (looseleaf format)
Description: Analyzes the performance of businesses at various levels from the most to least successful.

658 333.33   FR   ISSN 0758-7309
DICTIONNAIRE PERMANENT: GESTION IMMOBILIERE. 1977. 2 vols. plus m. updates. 1180 F. for base vols. (updates 320 F.) (effective 1995). Editions Legislatives et Administratives, 80 ave. de la Marne, 92546 Montrouge Cedex, France. TEL 40-92-68-68. FAX 46-56-00-15. TELEX 632 855 F. (looseleaf format)
Description: Discusses legal and fiscal problems linked with the management of urban real estate.

658   JO   ISSN 1026-373X   CODEN: DUJOES
DIRASAT. ADMINISTRATIVE SCIENCES. (Text in Arabic, English) 2/yr. $30 (effective 1998). University of Jordan, Deanship of Academic Research, Amman, Jordan. TEL 962-6-843555. FAX 962-6-840263. E-mail: research@amra.noc.gov.jo. Ed.Bd.
—BLDSC (3589.613000); CASDDS; CISTI.
Supersedes in part (in 1996): Dirasat. Series A: Humanities (ISSN 0255-8033)
Refereed Serial

DIRECT (STAMFORD); the magazine for direct marketing management. see *BUSINESS AND ECONOMICS — Marketing And Purchasing*

658.3   BE   ISSN 0779-7672
LE DIRECTEUR. Dutch edition: Directeur. (Text in French) 1977. s-m. 7110 BEF (in Europe 7296 BEF; elsewhere 7500 BEF). Biblo N.V., Brasschaatsteenweg 308, 2920 Kalmthout, Belgium. Ed. Jan Van Dyck. index. (also avail. in microfiche; back issues avail.) **Document type:** newsletter.
Supersedes (in 1993): Personeel - L'Employeur; Social Trends (French Edition) (ISSN 0772-4802)

658   FR   ISSN 0012-320X
DIRECTION ET GESTION DES ENTREPRISES. 1965. 5/yr. (includes one double issue). 970 F. (Europe 1190 F.; elsewhere 1410 F.) (effective 1997). Direction et Gestion S.A.R.L., 5 rue de la Gatinelle, B.P. 49, 91360 Epinay-sur-Orge, France. TEL 33-1-69099339. FAX 33-1-69093897. Ed. Jean-Pierre Gravier; Pub. Philippe Naszalyi. adv.: B&W page 3000 F., color page 5000 F.; trim 210 x 270; adv. contact: Philippe Naszalyi. bk.rev.; abstr.; bibl.; charts; stat. circ. 3,500. **Indexed:** Pt.de Rep., SCIMP. **Document type:** academic/scholarly publication, bulletin.
—BLDSC (3590.300000).
Description: Offers observations on management and business methods to put into practive. Published for managers, executives and directors in the public and private sectors.

DIRECTIONS. see *INSURANCE*

658 350   AT   ISSN 1030-391X
DIRECTIONS IN GOVERNMENT. 1987. 11/yr. Aus.$75. Direction Publishing Pty. Ltd., Box 551, Artarmon, N.S.W. 2064, Australia. TEL 61-2-411-2388. FAX 61-2-411-6102. Ed. Len Hall; Pub. Chris Chasoling. adv. contact: Chris Chaseling. index.
—UnCover.
Description: Source of information about new policies, programs, regulations and issues in the management of the public sector.

658   HC251   UK   ISSN 0012-3242
DIRECTOR. (Supplement avail.) 1947. m. £36 (foreign £63) (effective 1997). (Institute of Directors) Director Publications Ltd., Mountbarrow House, Elizabeth St., London SW1, England. TEL 0171-730-8320. FAX 0171-235-5627. TELEX 918802 DP G. Ed. Tim Hindle; Pub. Andrew Main Wilson. adv. contact: Edwards Hicks. bk.rev.; illus. circ. 40,616. (also avail. in microform from UMI; reprint service avail. from UMI) **Indexed:** Account.& Data Proc.Abstr., Anbar., B.P.I., BPIA, Bus.Ind., Ind.Bus.Rep., Intl.Mgmt.Info., Key to Econ.Sci., Manage.Cont., Mgmt.& Market.Abstr., P.A.I.S., PSI, Work Rel.Abstr. **Document type:** newsletter.
—BLDSC (3590.400000); SWETS; UMI; UnCover.

658   II   ISSN 0012-3250
DIRECTOR; India's top management journal. 1964. q. Rs.100($25) (Institute of Directors, 12 India India-International News Service, 12 India Exchange Place, Calcutta 700 001, India. Ed. H. Kothari. adv.; bk.rev.

BUSINESS AND ECONOMICS — MANAGEMENT

658 US ISSN 0364-9156
HD2709
DIRECTORS & BOARDS. 1976. q. $195 (foreign $220) (effective 1995). 229 S. 18th St., 3rd Fl., Philadelphia, PA 19103. TEL 215-790-7000. FAX 215-790-7005. Ed. James Kristie; Pub. James Kristie. R&P contact: James Kristie. adv. contact: Martin Porter. bk.rev.; index. circ. 3,000. (also avail. in microform from UMI; back issues avail.; reprint service avail. from UMI) **Indexed:** ABI Inform., Account.& Data Proc.Abstr., Account.Ind. (1976-), Anbar., ASEAN Manage.Abstr., BPIA, Bus.Ind., C.L.I., Hosp.Lit.Ind., L.R.I., Manage.Cont., Mgmt.& Market.Abstr., P.A.I.S., PROMT, Tr.& Indus.Ind. **Document type:** trade publication.
●Also available online. Vendor(s): Information Access Co., UMI.
—BLDSC (3590.570000); UMI; UnCover.
Description: A forum for discussion and analysis of topics such as corporate governance, the role and responsibilities of the board, corporate strategy, CEO succession and human resource development, global business and management trends, and executive and director compensation.

658 US
DIRECTOR'S MONTHLY. 1977. m. $350. National Association of Corporate Directors, 1707 L St., N.W., Ste. 560, Washington, DC 20036. TEL 202-775-0509. FAX 202-775-4857. Ed. Alexandra Reed Lajoux. bk.rev. circ. 7,000. **Document type:** newsletter.
Description: Includes feature articles on current topics of concern to corporate and not-for-profit directors; news updates and analysis; and legal, financial, and accounting briefs.

DIRECTORS REWARDS. see *BUSINESS AND ECONOMICS — Labor And Industrial Relations*

658 US ISSN 0193-4279
DIRECTORSHIP; information service for the corporate director. 1976. m. $495. Directorship Inc., 8 Sound Shore Dr., Ste. 250, Greenwich, CT 06830-7242. TEL 203-861-7000. FAX 203-861-7007. Ed. B.J. Dunn; Pub. Peter C. Garrett. bk.rev.; index. (back issues avail.) **Document type:** newsletter.

658 II ISSN 0070-5322
DIRECTORY OF COMPANY SECRETARIES. (Text in English) 1969. irreg. Rs.30($9) Kothari Publications, 12 India Exchange Pl., Calcutta 700 001, India. TEL 91-33-220-9563. Ed. H. Kothari. adv. **Document type:** directory.
Description: Lists names, addresses, education of company secretaries. Includes information about their professional organizations.

DIRECTORY OF DIRECTORS. see *BIOGRAPHY*

658 UK ISSN 0070-5438
DIRECTORY OF DIRECTORS. 1878. a. £189($290) Reed Information Services (Subsidiary of: Reed Elsevier group), Windsor Court, E. Grinstead House, E. Grinstead, W. Sussex RH19 1XA, England. TEL 01342-335832. FAX 01342-335948. TELEX 95127-INFSER-G. adv. circ. 4,000. **Document type:** directory.
●Also available online. Vendor(s): Reed Information Services Ltd.
Description: Provides essential information on over 54,000 directors, who control the top 15,000 British companies.

658.31 US ISSN 1059-163X
HD38.25.U6
DIRECTORY OF EXECUTIVE RECRUITERS. 1971. a. $44.95 (effective 1997). Kennedy Publications, Templeton Rd., Fitzwilliam, NH 03447. TEL 603-585-6544. FAX 603-585-9555. Ed. James H. Kennedy. adv. contact: Carolyn D. Edwards. **Document type:** directory.
Description: Lists over 2,800 executive recruiting offices in the United States, Canada and Mexico. Five indexes: functions, industries, geographic, recruiter specialties and key principals.

658.3 US ISSN 0743-6890
HD69.C6
DIRECTORY OF MANAGEMENT CONSULTANTS. 1976. a. $149 (effective 1997). Kennedy Publications, Templeton Rd., Fitzwilliam, NH 03447. TEL 603-585-6544. FAX 603-585-9555. Ed. Giles Goodhead. adv. contact: Carolyn D. Edwards. **Document type:** directory.
Description: Lists 2,000 management consulting firms with paragraph descriptions, billings, staff sizes, and five indexes: services, industries, geographic, consultant specialties and key principals.

658 UK ISSN 0268-375X
DIRECTORY OF MANAGEMENT CONSULTANTS IN THE UK. 1983. a. £89.75. A P Information Services, Roman House, 296 Golders Green Rd., London NW11 9PZ, England. TEL 44-181-455-4550. FAX 44-181-455-6381. Ed. Helen Irwin. adv.: B&W page £700, color page £1,100; trim 270 x 190. circ. 2,200. (also avail. in diskette format) **Document type:** directory.
—BLDSC (3594.485900).
Description: Lists more than 3,000 consultancy firms in the U.K. Includes statistical information on firms and articles addressing topical issues.

DIRECTORY OF TRAINING. see *COMPUTERS*

658 YU ISSN 0419-3903
DIREKTOR; casopis za teoriju i praksu rukovodjenja i upravljanja. 1969. m. 1300 din.($126.30) Privredni Pregled, Marsala Birjuzova 3-5, 11000 Belgrade, Yugoslavia. Ed. Slobodan Sindovic. adv.; bk.rev.; charts; illus.

658 IT
DIRIGENTE D'AZIENDA. 1979. m. Unione Regionale Piemontese della Federazione Nazionale Dirigenti di Azienda Industriali, Via San Francesco da Paola, 20, 10123 Turin, Italy. TEL 011-547650. Ed. Antonio Coletti. adv.: B&W page L.1815000.

658.5 BL ISSN 0012-3366
DIRIGENTE INDUSTRIAL. 1959. m. $70. Editora Visao Ltda., Rua Alvaro de Carvalho, 350, 2o andar, C.P. 3082, 01050 Sao Paulo, Brazil. TEL 256-5011. FAX 258-1919. TELEX 1121436. Ed. Hamilton Lucas de Oliveira. adv.; bk.rev.; abstr.; bibl.; charts; illus. circ. 25,750.

658 IT
DIRIGENTI INDUSTRIA. 1946. m. L.7500. Associazione Lombarda Dirigenti Aziende Industriali, Via Larga 31, 20122 Milan, Italy. TEL 02-583761. FAX 02-58307557. Ed. Bruno Losito. adv.: B&W page L.3500000, color page L.5000000. bk.rev. circ. 33,000.

658 UK ISSN 0953-7147
DISTRIBUTION BUSINESS. 1989. 8/yr. £32 (overseas £42) (effective 1995). Landor Industrial Services Publications Ltd. (Subsidiary of: Landor Publishing Ltd.), Quadrant House, 250 Kennington Ln., London SE11 5RD, England. TEL 44-171-735-4502. FAX 44-171-587-0497. E-mail: 100570,73@ compuserve.com. Ed. Peter Rowlands. adv. contact: Chris Propert-Lewis. circ. 11,500 (controlled). (back issues avail.) **Document type:** trade publication.
Description: Probes issues of current interest to retail business and industrial users of distribution services.

DISTRIBUTION CENTER MANAGEMENT. see *BUSINESS AND ECONOMICS — Marketing And Purchasing*

DISTRIBUTION MANAGEMENT DIGEST. see *BUSINESS AND ECONOMICS — Marketing And Purchasing*

THE DISTRIBUTOR'S & WHOLESALER'S ADVISOR; reports for management in a competitive era. see *BUSINESS AND ECONOMICS — Marketing And Purchasing*

658 551 CC ISSN 1003-6369
DIZHI KEJI GUANLI/SCIENTIFIC AND TECHNOLOGICAL MANAGEMENT IN GEOLOGICAL EXPLORATION. (Text in Chinese) 1986. bi-m. $1.50 per no. Chengdu Ligong Xueyuan - Chengdu Institute of Technology, Shilidian, Chengdu, Sichuan 610059, People's Republic of China. TEL 86-28-333-4712. FAX 86-28-334-1299. (Co-sponsor: Chinese Geological Society) Ed. Xingjian Li. circ. 2,000. **Document type:** academic/scholarly publication.

658 NE ISSN 0923-9154
DOELMATIGE BEDRIJFSVOERING; vakblad voor bedrijfskunde, produktie en onderhoud. 1951. m. fl.147.50 (foreign fl.195). (Nederlandse Vereniging voor Doelmatig Onderhoud) Kommunikatie Service Nederland BV, Postbus 146, 5430 AC Cuijk, Netherlands. adv.; bk.rev.; bibl.; charts; illus.; index. circ. 5,000. **Indexed:** Excerp.Med., Key to Econ.Sci. **Document type:** trade publication.
Former titles (until 1989): Technische Bedrijfsvoering (ISSN 0169-3018); (until 1983): Bedrijfsvoering (ISSN 0165-6333); Formed by the 1974 merger of: Produktie en Onderhoud (ISSN 0920-9883); Arbeidskundig Tijdschrift (ISSN 0003-7591); Incorporates: Inkoop (ISSN 0020-1413)

658 US
DOLLARS & CENTS. m. membership. American Society of Association Executives, Finance and Administration Section, 1575 Eye St., N.W., Washington, DC 20005. TEL 202-626-2781. FAX 202-842-1145. circ. 3,600.
Description: For finance directors, chief executive officers, and personnel managers of associations. Legislative, financial, human resources, technology issues.

380 658 AT ISSN 0818-5093
DUN'S GAZETTE. (In 5 state editions: N.S.W., Vic., S.A., W.A., Qld.) 1887. w. Aus.$425. Dun & Bradstreet Marketing Pty. Ltd., 19 Havilah St., Chatswood, N.S.W. 2065, Australia. TEL 61-2-6352700. FAX 61-2-9352777. URL: http://www.dbmarketing.com.au. adv.; stat. circ. 10,000. (looseleaf format; also avail. in microfiche)
Formerly: Bradstreet Gazette.

DYNAMIK IM HANDEL. see *FOOD AND FOOD INDUSTRIES — Grocery Trade*

E B; Handbuch fuer Selbstaendige und Unternehmer. see *BUSINESS AND ECONOMICS*

E M M S. (Electronic Mail & Micro Systems) see *COMMUNICATIONS*

658 332.6 US
E S O P REPORT. (Employee Stock Ownership Plan) 1979. m. E S O P Association, 1726 M St., N.W., Ste. 501, Washington, DC 20036. TEL 202-293-2971. FAX 202-293-7568. URL: http://www.the-esop-emplowner.org. Ed. Susan Diliddo. R&P contact: Susan Diliddo. bk.rev. circ. 2,200. **Document type:** newsletter.
Incorporates: Profile.

658 KE ISSN 0012-8341
EAST AFRICAN MANAGEMENT JOURNAL. 1966. q. (East African Management Foundation) English Press Ltd., Accra Rd., P.O. Box 30127, Nairobi, Kenya. Ed. R.A. West. adv. circ. 5,000.

658 LU
ECHO DE L'INDUSTRIE. 1920. m. 750 Fr. (foreign 950 F.) (effective 1996). Federation des Industriels Luxembourgeois, 7 rue Gasperi, B.P. 1304, L-1013 Luxembourg, Luxembourg. TEL 43-53-66-1. FAX 43-23-28. TELEX 60174. adv. circ. 1,900. **Indexed:** Key to Econ.Sci.

658 333.7 UK ISSN 0968-9427
ECO-MANAGEMENT AND AUDITING. 1993. 3/yr. £325 (foreign $325) (effective 1998). (E R P Environment) John Wiley & Sons Ltd., Journals, Baffins Ln., Chichester, W. Sussex PO19 1UD, England. TEL 44-1243-779777. FAX 44-1243-775878. E-mail: info-assets@wiley.co.uk; URL: http://www.wiley.co.uk. (Subscr. in the Americas to: John Wiley & Sons, Inc., 605 Third Ave., New York, NY 10158. TEL 212-850-6645. FAX 212-850-6021) Ed. Richard Welford. adv.: B&W page £595, color page £1495; trim 297 x 210; adv. contact: Bob Kern. **Indexed:** Environ.Per.Bibl. **Document type:** trade publication.
—BLDSC (3650.049520). **CCC.**

658 IT ISSN 1120-5032
ECONOMIA & MANAGEMENT. 1988. bi-m. L.172000 (effective 1997). R C S Libri S.p.A., Via Mecenate 91, 20138 Milan, Italy. TEL 39-2-50952333. FAX 39-2-50952309. Ed. Luisa Finocchi; Pub. Gian Maria Fiameni. R&P contact: Pia Barbieri. adv.: B&W page L.6070000; adv. contact: Alfio Patane. circ. 10,000. **Indexed:** SCIMP (1989-). **Document type:** academic/scholarly publication.

BUSINESS AND ECONOMICS — MANAGEMENT

658   FR
ECONOMIES ET SOCIETES. SERIE SG. SCIENCE DE GESTION. 2/yr. 350 F. Presses Universitaires de Grenoble, B.P. 47, 38040 Grenoble Cedex 9, France. Ed. Henri Savall. **Indexed:** SCIMP (1986-).

658   UK
EFFECTIVE MANAGEMENT SERIES; a skills and activity based approach. 1994. irreg. $24.95 per no. Blackwell Publishers Ltd., 108 Cowley Rd., Oxford OX4 1JF, England. TEL 44-1865-791100. FAX 44-1865-791347. E-mail: jnlinfo@blackwellpublishers.co.uk; URL: http://www.blackwellpublishers.co.uk. Ed. Alan Anderson. **Document type:** monographic series, trade publication.
Refereed Serial

658 331.86   US
EFFECTIVE TELEPHONE TECHNIQUES. 1991. bi-w. $68.90. Dartnell Corporation, 4660 N. Ravenswood Ave., Chicago, IL 60640. TEL 773-561-4000; 800-621-5463. FAX 773-561-3801. URL: http://www.dartnellcorp.com. Ed. Romy Schafer. **Document type:** newsletter.
Description: Helps employees build profitable customer relations with every phone call.

EINKAEUFER IM MARKT. see *BUSINESS AND ECONOMICS — Marketing And Purchasing*

658   GW
EINZELHANDELS BERATER. 1958. m. DM.145. (Betriebswirtschaftliche Beratungsstelle fuer den Einzelhandel) B B E Unternehmensberatung GmbH, Postfach 250425, 50520 Cologne, Germany. **Indexed:** Key to Econ.Sci. **Document type:** trade publication.

658   MX
EJECUTIVOS DE FINANZAS. (Text mainly in Spanish; occasionally in Spanish) 1972. m. Mex.$220 (foreign $50) (effective 1996). Instituto Mexicano de Ejecutivos de Finanzas, A.C., Patricio Sanz 1516, Col. del Valle, 03100 Mexico, D.F., Mexico. TEL 52-5-5598366. FAX 52-5-5754410. E-mail: mexfin@ibm.net; URL: http://www.mexfin.com. Ed. Jose Antonio Castillo. adv.: B&W page Mex.$17515, color page Mex.$21490; adv. contact: Leticia Laso. bk.rev. circ. 15,000. **Document type:** trade publication.
Description: Covers finance and economics for top executives.

EKONOMI & STYRNING. see *BUSINESS AND ECONOMICS — Production Of Goods And Services*

658   PL   ISSN 0860-6846
HC337.P7
EKONOMIKA I ORGANIZACJA PRZEDSIEBIORSTWA. 1950. m. 108 Zl. (foreign $63) (effective 1997). Instytut Organizacji i Zarzadzania w Przemysle, Ul. Zelazna 87, 00-879 Warsaw, Poland. TEL 48-22-6546061. FAX 48-22-6204360. Ed. Wieslaw Grudzewski. adv.; bk.rev. circ. 3,200. **Document type:** newspaper.
Formerly (until 1988): Ekonomika i Organizacja Pracy (ISSN 0013-3043)
Description: Covers economy and financial management.
Refereed Serial

658   NE   ISSN 0921-5220
ELAN (DEVENTER); magazine voor directeuren en commissarissen. 1986. 11/yr. fl.210 (effective 1996). (Nederlands Centrum van Directeuren en Commissarissen) Kluwer Bedrijfswetenschappen B.V. (Subsidiary of: Wolters Kluwer N.V.), Postbus 23, 7400 GA Deventer, Netherlands. TEL 31-570-648940. FAX 31-570-645261. (Subscr. to: Intermedia bv, Postbus 4, 2400 MA Alphen aan den Rijn, Netherlands. TEL 31-172-466321. FAX 31-172-435527) Ed. Reint Gaastra. adv.: B&W page fl.4600, color page fl.7550; trim 297 x 210; adv. contact: Ad Nuesink. bk.rev.; illus. circ. 11,000. **Indexed:** Account.& Data Proc.Abstr., Excerp.Med., Key to Econ.Sci., Mgmt.& Market.Abstr. **Document type:** trade publication.
—BLDSC (3670.150000); SWETS.
Formed by the merger of (1981-1986): Management Monitor (ISSN 0167-5664); Elan (Deurne) (ISSN 0167-3939); Which was formerly: Management Totaal (ISSN 0770-3716)
Description: Discusses corporate stratgey, leadership, organization and other management issues.

ELECTRONIC TRADER. see *BUSINESS AND ECONOMICS — Computer Applications*

ELECTRONIC WORLD NEWS. see *ELECTRONICS*

658   SP
ELITES; de los negocios. 1976. 6/yr. 2000 ptas. P. de la Castellana 210, 28046 Madrid, Spain. TEL 3594779. FAX 3452782. Ed. Fernando Ruiz-Ogarrio. adv.: B&W page 270000 ptas.; color page 380000 ptas.; trim 190 x 260. bk.rev. circ. 15,000.

EMPLOYEE ASSISTANCE PROGRAM MANAGEMENT LETTER. see *BUSINESS AND ECONOMICS — Labor And Industrial Relations*

EMPLOYEE BENEFIT NEWS. see *BUSINESS AND ECONOMICS — Labor And Industrial Relations*

658   US
EMPLOYEE BENEFITS MANAGEMENT. 1990. s-m. $714 (CD-ROM ed. $791). C C H Incorporated, 2700 Lake Cook Rd., Riverwoods, IL 60015. TEL 847-267-7000; 800-835-5224. FAX 800-224-8299. (looseleaf format)
●Also available on CD-ROM.

658 790 658.8   US   ISSN 0744-3676
GV1
EMPLOYEE SERVICES MANAGEMENT; the journal of employee services, recreation, health and education. 1958. 10/yr. $44 (foreign $59) (effective 1998). National Employee Services and Recreation Association, 2211 York Rd., Ste. 207, Oak Brook, IL 60523-2371. TEL 630-368-1280. FAX 630-360-1286. E-mail: nesrahq@aol.com; URL: http://www.nesra.org. Ed. Cynthia M. Helson. adv.; charts; illus.; tr.lit.; index. circ. 5,000. (also avail. in microform from UMI; reprint service avail. from UMI) **Indexed:** Sportsearch (1981-).
—UMI; UnCover.
Formerly (until 1982): Recreation Management (ISSN 0034-1770)
Description: Employee services management's editorial program administration, wellness programs, management, athletic teams and leagues, travel and discount services, eldercare, and childcare.

658   NZ   ISSN 0046-1903
EMPLOYER. 1971. 5/yr. membership or on exchange. New Zealand Employers Federation, P.O. Box 1786, Wellington, New Zealand. TEL 64-4-4994111. FAX 64-4-4994112. E-mail: nzef@nzef.org.nz. Ed. John McCaskey. adv. contact: John McCaskey. bk.rev.; charts; illus.; stat. circ. 11,000. **Document type:** newsletter.
—CCC.
Description: Deals with all current issues affecting the employing community, with emphasis on public policy, particularly but not exclusively labor issues and economy as it affects business.

EMPLOYERS' HEALTH BENEFITS BULLETIN; news and analysis on cost containment and compliance issues. see *INSURANCE*

EMPLOYERS' MANAGED HEALTHCARE BENEFITS ADVISOR. see *INSURANCE*

EMPLOYMENT MANAGEMENT TODAY. see *BUSINESS AND ECONOMICS — Personnel Management*

EMPLOYMENT TERMS AND CONDITIONS REPORT REPORT - ASIA. see *BUSINESS AND ECONOMICS — Personnel Management*

658   MX   ISSN 0187-7828
EMPRENDEDORES. 1987. bi-m. Mex.$55 (effective 1997). Universidad Nacional Autonoma de Mexico, Facultad de Contaduria y Administracion, Apartado Postal 70-287, Edificio de la Direccion, 2o. Piso, Cub. 21, Circuito Exterior, Ciudad Universitaria, 04510 Mexico, D.F., Mexico. TEL 52-5-6228396. FAX 52-5-6161355. Ed. Adrian Mendez Salvatorio.
Description: Designed for top-managers, CEOs and VIPs in small and medium organizations.

658   SP
EMPRESAS Y EMPRESARIOS. 11/yr. Conde de Romanones 9, 3o izda., 28012 Madrid, Spain. TEL 1-369-28-60. FAX 1-369-35-86. Ed. Lilian Aguirre. circ. 10,000.

650   US   ISSN 0071-0210
Z7164.C81
ENCYCLOPEDIA OF BUSINESS INFORMATION SOURCES. irreg., 8th ed., 1990. $235. Gale Research, 835 Penobscot Bldg., 645 Griswold St., Detroit, MI 48226-4094. TEL 313-961-2242; 800-877-4253. FAX 800-414-5043. E-mail: daniel__snyder@gale.com. Ed. James Woy.
—CISTI.
Formerly: Executives Guide to Information Sources.
Description: On-line and other business information sources.

658   US
ENCYCLOPEDIC DICTIONARY OF ECONOMICS. 1973. irreg., 3rd ed., 1985. $14.95. Dushkin Publishing Group, Sluice Dock, Guilford, CT 06437-9989. TEL 203-453-4351. FAX 203-453-6000. Ed. Don Cole; Pub. Rick Connelly. illus.
Formerly: Economics: Encyclopedia (ISSN 0090-4422)

ENGINEERING MANAGEMENT JOURNAL. see *ENGINEERING*

ENJINIASU/ENGINEERS. see *ENGINEERING*

658   SA   ISSN 1024-154X
ENTERPRISE 200; the business magazine for black entrepreneurs and decision makers. (Text in English) 1994. a. R.40. Mafube Publishing (Pty) Ltd., P.O. Box 2185, Houghton 2041, South Africa. TEL 27-11-4833863. FAX 27-11-4833194. Ed. Thami Mazwai; Pub. Thami Mazwai. R&P contact: Thami Mazwai. adv.: B&W page R.10450, color page R.13500; trim 297 x 210; adv. contact: Cheryl Pheiffer. illus. **Document type:** trade publication.

ENTERTAINMENT LAW & FINANCE. see *LAW*

338 658   US   ISSN 1059-0137
HB615   CODEN: EICHEZ
ENTREPRENEURSHIP, INNOVATION AND CHANGE. 1992. q. $155 (foreign $180) (effective 1997). Plenum Publishing Corp., 233 Spring St., New York, NY 10013-1578. TEL 212-620-8000. FAX 212-463-0742. TELEX 23-421139. (Editorial addr.: 20 Oakfield Ct., Cottingham Rd., Hull HU6 8QF, England) Ed. John C. Oliga. adv.; bk.rev. **Indexed:** B.P.I. **Document type:** academic/scholarly publication.
—BLDSC (3790.547700); KR SourceOne; SWETS; UMI. CCC.
Description: International coverage of entrepreneurship in a broad and holistic theoretical framework, with an interdisciplinary approach to relevant social science literature.
Refereed Serial

658   FR
L'ENTREPRISE - A POUR AFFAIRES. (Text in French) 1985. m. 386 F. Societe des Publications de l'Entreprise, 25, rue Leblanc, 75510 Paris Cedex 15, France. TEL 40-60-40-60. FAX 40-60-41-20. TELEX EXPANSN 205581 F. Eds. Jacques Barraux, Claude Villeneuve. adv.; bk.rev.
—BLDSC (3790.552000); SWETS.
Formed by the 1991 merger of: Entreprise (ISSN 0769-6248) & A pour Affaires.

658   BE   ISSN 0046-2160
HD83
L'ENTREPRISE ET L'HOMME. 1923. bi-m. 1600 BEF($130) (effective 1996). Association Chretienne des Dirigeants et Cadres, 8, Avenue Konrad Adenauer, 1200 Brussels, Belgium. TEL 32-2-771-47-31. FAX 32-2-772-46-33. Ed. Krystyna Delahaye; Pub. Michel Dussenne. R&P contact: Krystyna Delahaye. adv. contact: B. Janssens de Bisthoven. bk.rev.; bibl.; charts; illus. circ. 6,500. **Document type:** academic/scholarly publication, trade publication.

ENVIRONMENT & MANAGEMENT. see *ENVIRONMENTAL STUDIES*

ENVIRONMENTAL EXCELLENCE. see *ENVIRONMENTAL STUDIES*

ENVIRONMENTAL MANAGEMENT & AUDIT MANUAL. see *ENVIRONMENTAL STUDIES*

ENVIRONMENTAL MANAGER; environmental solutions that make good business sense. see *ENVIRONMENTAL STUDIES*

BUSINESS AND ECONOMICS — MANAGEMENT

ENVIRONMENTAL MANAGER; the independent, weekly newsletter on industry and the environment. see *ENVIRONMENTAL STUDIES*

ENVIRONMENTAL QUALITY MANAGEMENT. see *ENVIRONMENTAL STUDIES*

ESSENTIALS OF MANAGED HEALTH CARE. see *INSURANCE*

ESSOR FRANCAIS DE L'INDUSTRIE. see *BUSINESS AND ECONOMICS — Production Of Goods And Services*

658 SP ISSN 0425-3698
HD28
ESTUDIOS EMPRESARIALES. 1965. 3/yr. 3000 ptas. (Europe $50) (effective 1997 & 1998). Universidad de Deusto, Facultad de Ciencias Economicas y Empresariales, Mundaiz, 50, 20012 San Sebastian, Spain. TEL 34-43-273100. FAX 34-43-273932. Ed. Antonio Masse; Pub. Francisco Olarte. R&P contact: Antonio Masse. adv. contact: Paloma Gonzalez. bk.rev.; bibl.; abstr.; charts; illus. circ. 2,000. **Indexed:** P.A.I.S.For.Lang.Ind. **Document type:** academic/scholarly publication.
—CINDOC; SWETS.

ETHICS TODAY. see *PHILOSOPHY*

ETHIKOS; examining ethical issues in business. see *PHILOSOPHY*

ETHIQUE DES AFFAIRES. see *PHILOSOPHY*

EUROPEAN CONSULTANTS DIRECTORY. see *BUSINESS AND ECONOMICS — Trade And Industrial Directories*

658 UK ISSN 1355-0292
THE EUROPEAN DIRECTORY OF MANAGEMENT CONSULTANTS. 1990. biennial. £130. A P Information Services, Roman House, 296 Golders Green Rd., London NW11 9PZ, England. TEL 44-181-455-4550. FAX 44-181-455-6381. Ed. Helen Irwin. adv.: B&W page £600, color page £900; trim 297 x 210. circ. 2,000. (also avail. in diskette format) **Document type:** directory.
—BLDSC (3829.689540).
Description: Provides details on more than 3,250 consultancy firms in Western and Eastern Europe on national and international levels. Indexed by country.

EUROPEAN JOURNAL OF INFORMATION SYSTEMS. see *COMPUTERS — Information Science And Information Theory*

003 658 NE ISSN 0377-2217
T57.6 CODEN: EJORDT
EUROPEAN JOURNAL OF OPERATIONAL RESEARCH. 1977. 24/yr. fl.6160($3540) (effective 1998). (Association of European Operational Research Societies) North-Holland (Subsidiary of: Elsevier Science B.V.), P.O. Box 211, 1000 AE Amsterdam, Netherlands. TEL 31-20-4853911. FAX 31-20-4853598. TELEX 18582 ESPA NL. E-mail: usinfo@elsevier.nl; URL: http://www.elsevier.nl:80/homepage/saw/about/. (Subscr. in the Americas to: Elsevier Science, Regional Sales Office, Box 945, New York, NY 10159-0945. TEL 212-633-3730. FAX 212-633-3680; Subscr. in Australasia and the Far East to: Elsevier Science (Singapore) Pte Ltd, No.1 Temasek Ave., No.17-01 Millenia Tower, Singapore 039192, Singapore. TEL 65-434-3727. FAX 65-337-2230; Subscr. in Japan to: Elsevier Science Japan, 9-15 Higashi-Azabu 1-chome, Minato-ku, Tokyo 106, Japan. TEL 81-3-5561-5033. FAX 81-3-5561-5047) Ed.Bd. (also avail. in microform from UMI; reprint service avail. from SWZ) **Indexed:** ABI Inform., Abstr.Health Care Manage.Stud., ASCA, Biostat., BPIA, Bus.Ind., Compumath, Comput.Abstr., Cont.Pg.Manage., Curr.Cont.(1988-), Energy Ind., Energy Info.Abstr., Excerp.Med., INSPEC, Int.Abstr.Oper.Res., J.Cont.Quant.Meth., Manage.Cont., Math.R., Oper.Res.Manage.Sci., Qual.Contr.Appl.Stat., Risk Abstr., SCIMP (1979-), SSCI, Stat.Theor.Meth.Abstr. (1988-), Tr.& Indus.Ind., Zent.Math. **Document type:** academic/scholarly publication.
—BLDSC (3829.733200); AskIEEE; Ei; Genuine Article; KR SourceOne; Linda Hall; SWETS; UMI; UnCover. **CCC.**
Description: Publishes papers on the theory and practice of decision making.
Refereed Serial

658 370 NE ISSN 1383-6218
EUROPEAN MANAGEMENT EDUCATION DIRECTORY. (Text in English) 1987. a. fl.335. E M D Centre, Naarderstraat 296, 1272 NT Huizen, Netherlands. TEL 31-35-6951111. FAX 31-35-6951900. Eds. Rino Schreuder, Leo Steverink. adv. **Document type:** directory.
Former titles: World Management Education Guide - Europe; European Management Education Guide.
Description: Lists executive training programs at European business schools and management training centers.

658 UK ISSN 0263-2373
HD28
EUROPEAN MANAGEMENT JOURNAL. 1983. bi-m. fl.753($433) (effective 1998). Elsevier Science Ltd., Pergamon, P.O. Box 800, Kidlington, Oxford OX5 1DX, England. TEL 44-1865-843000. FAX 44-1865-843010. E-mail: nlinfo-f@elsevier.nl; usinfo-f@elsevier.com; forinfo-kyf04035@niftyserve.or.jp; URL: http://www.elsevier.nl/. (Subscr. to: Elsevier Science, Regional Sales Office, P.O. Box 211, 1000 AE Amsterdam, Netherlands. TEL 31-20-4853757. FAX 31-20-4853432; Subscr. in the Americas to: Elsevier Science, Regional Sales Office, Box 945, New York, NY 10159-0945. TEL 212-633-3730. FAX 212-633-3680; Subscr. in Australasia and the Far East to: Elsevier Science (Singapore) Pte Ltd, No.1 Temasek Ave., No.17-01 Millenia Tower, Singapore 039192, Singapore. TEL 65-434-3727. FAX 65-337-2230) Ed. Paul Stonham. adv. circ. 1,000. (also avail. in microfilm from UMI; reprint service avail. from SWZ,UMI) **Indexed:** B.P.I., Cont.Pg.Manage., Mgmt.& Market.Abstr., Oper.Res.Manage.Sci., Qual.Contr.Appl.Stat., SCIMP (1984-). **Document type:** academic/scholarly publication.
—BLDSC (3829.750430); KR SourceOne; SWETS; UMI. **CCC.**
Description: Publishes articles based on experience or research of immediate relevance to European business affairs, for both practicing managers and management academics.
Refereed Serial

658 PK
EXECUTIVE. (Text in English) 1975. a. free. Institute of Business Administration, University of Karachi, University Campus, Karachi 32, Pakistan. Ed. Noman Afzal Tariq. adv.; illus. circ. 1,500.

EXECUTIVE EMPLOYMENT LAW. see *LAW — Corporate Law*

658 371.42 UK
EXECUTIVE GRAPEVINE, VOLUME 1: DIRECTORY OF EXECUTIVE RECRUITMENT CONSULTANTS - UK EDITION (YEAR); recruitment library. 1979. a. £75. Executive Grapevine International Ltd., 2nd Fl., New Barnes Mill, Cottonmill Ln., St. Albans, Herts. AL1 2HA, England. TEL 44-1727-844335. FAX 44-1727-844779. E-mail: executive.grapevine@dial.pipex.com; URL: http://www.d-net.com/executive.grapevine. Ed. Helen Barrett. adv. **Document type:** directory.
Description: Provides up-to-date profiles and information on more than 750 executive recruitment consultancies based in the UK.

658 371.2 UK
EXECUTIVE GRAPEVINE, VOLUME 2: INTERNATIONAL DIRECTORY OF EXECUTIVE RECRUITMENT CONSULTANTS; Grapevine recruitment library. 1993. a. £90. Executive Grapevine International Ltd., 2nd Fl., New Barnes Mill, Cottonmill Ln., St. Albans, Herts. AL5 2HA, England. TEL 44-1727-844335. FAX 44-1727-844779. E-mail: executive.grapevine@dial.pipex.com; URL: http://www.d-net.com/executive.grapevine. Ed. Helen Barrett. **Document type:** directory.
Description: Lists and profiles executive recruiters in more than 65 non-UK nations. Lists functional specializations, remuneration levels, fees, and other data.

658 371.2 UK
EXECUTIVE GRAPEVINE, VOLUME 3: EUROPEAN DIRECTORY OF CAREER MANAGEMENT, OUTPLACEMENT AND ASSESSMENT; Grapevine recruitment library. 1988. a. £40 (rest of Europe £35). Executive Grapevine International Ltd., 2nd Fl., New Barnes Mill, Cottonmill Ln., St. Albans, Herts. AL1 2HA, England. TEL 44-1727-844338. FAX 44-1727-844779. E-mail: executive.grapevine@dial.pipex.com. Ed. Helen Barrett. **Document type:** directory.
Description: Lists consultancies that provide services to both individual and corporate clients, including career counselling, psychological assessments, and job search seminars.

658 371.2 UK
EXECUTIVE GRAPEVINE, VOLUME 4: DIRECTORY OF NON EXECUTIVE DIRECTORS, INTERIM MANAGEMENT AND CONSULTANTS; Grapevine recruitment library. 1992. a. £30. Executive Grapevine International Ltd., 2nd Fl., New Barnes Mill, Cottonmill Ln., St. Albans, Herts. AL1 2HA, England. TEL 44-1727-844335. FAX 44-1727-844779. E-mail: executive.grapevine@dial.pipex.com. Ed. Helen Barrett. **Document type:** directory.
Formerly: Executive Grapevine, Volume 4: Directory of Interim Management and Non Executive Directors.
Description: Profiles consultants active in carrying out assignments for temporary executive positions and non-executive directorship appointments.

658 371.42 UK
EXECUTIVE GRAPEVINE, VOLUME 5: GRAPEVINE INDEX OF CHIEF EXECUTIVE & MANAGING DIRECTORS. 1993. a. £40 (rest of Europe £42). Executive Grapevine International Ltd., 2nd Fl., New Barnes Mill, Cottonmill Ln., St. Albans, Herts. AL1 2HA, England. TEL 44-1727-844335. FAX 44-1727-844779. E-mail: executive.grapevine@dial.pipex.com. Ed. Helen Barrett. **Document type:** directory.
Former titles: Executive Grapevine, Volume 5: Directory of Assessment and Development Consultants; Executive Grapevine, Volume 5: Directory of Executive and Management Development Consultants.
Description: Aims to give visibility to over 2,000 of the UK's most prominent chief executives and managing directors and the role they play within both public and private companies in the UK

658.3 371.42 UK
▼**EXECUTIVE GRAPEVINE, VOLUME 6: THE GRAPEVINE INDEX OF H R DIRECTORS, U K EDITION;** recruitment library. 1995. a. £75 (rest of Europe £77). Executive Grapevine International Ltd., 2nd Fl., New Barnes Mill, Cottonmill Ln., St. Albans, Herts. AL5 2HA, England. TEL 44-1727-844335. FAX 44-1727-844779. E-mail: executive.grapevine@dial.pipex.com. Ed. Helen Barrett. **Document type:** directory.
Formerly: Executive Grapevine, Volume 6: List of Human Resource Professionals.
Description: Lists human resource directors and managers at the largest UK companies.

658 371.2 UK
▼**EXECUTIVE GRAPEVINE, VOLUME 7: THE GRAPEVINE INDEX OF I T DIRECTORS.;** Grapevine recruitment library. 1996. a. £70. Executive Grapevine International Ltd., 2nd Fl., New Barnes Mill, Cottonmill Ln., St. Albans, Herts. AL1 2HA, England. TEL 44-1727-844335. FAX 44-1727-844779. E-mail: executive.grapevine@dial.pipex.com. Ed. Helen Barrett. **Document type:** directory.
Formerly: Executive Grapevine, Volume 7: The Directory of I T Directors and Consultants.
Description: Aims to provide a focus and greater awareness of Information Technology positions and their function. Lists some of the UK's most influential IT directors and professional consultants.

658 CC
EXECUTIVE HONG KONG. 1980. m. HK.$210. Executive Media, Ltd., 3rd Fl., Hollywood Centre, 223 Hollywood Rd., Hong Kong, People's Republic of China. TEL 8155221. FAX 8542794. TELEX 83013 AFNOC HX. Ed. Gerry Delilikhan. adv. circ. 23,078.
Former titles: Yong Executive Hong Kong; Asean Executive.

BUSINESS AND ECONOMICS — MANAGEMENT 1477

658 US
EXECUTIVE ISSUES. q. University of Pennsylvania, Wharton School, Wharton Executive Education Division, 255 S. 38th St., Philadelphia, PA 19130. TEL 215-898-4560. Ed. Pamela J. Whitman.
Description: Forum for the discussion of topical business issues.

658 US
EXECUTIVE PERQUISITES REPORT. a. $640. (Executive Compensation Service (ECS)) Wyatt Data Services, 218 Rte. 17, N., Roselle Park, NJ 07662-9832. TEL 201-843-1177. FAX 201-843-0101. charts. **Document type:** trade publication.
Description: Provides information specific to company size and industry, on current US perquisite practices.

658 US ISSN 0271-0781
EXECUTIVE RECRUITER NEWS. 1980. m. $187 (effective 1997). Kennedy Publications, Templeton Rd., Fitzwilliam, NH 03447. TEL 603-585-6544. FAX 603-585-9555. Ed. James H. Kennedy. adv. contact: Carolyn D. Edwards. bk.rev.; index. **Document type:** newsletter.
Description: Covers trends and developments, key personnel changes, fees, mergers, defections, legal questions, ethics and association news.

658 US ISSN 1064-8623
EXECUTIVE REPORT ON CUSTOMER SATISFACTION. 1988. s-m. $199. Alexander Research & Communications, Inc., 215 Park Ave. S., Ste. 1301, New York, NY 10003. TEL 212-228-0246. FAX 212-228-0376. Ed. Susan Hash; Pub. Margaret DeWitt. R&P contact: Mary Dalessandro. **Document type:** newsletter.
Description: For senior managers concerned with corporate-level customer service policy. Covers how successful companies of all sizes are using innovative strategies to retain their best customers and attract new ones. Plus trends, statistics, timely news and information.

658 US ISSN 1050-9003
EXECUTIVE SEARCH REVIEW. 1989. m. $185. Hunt - Scanlon Publishing Co., Inc., 1 East Putnam Ave., Greenwich, CT 06830. TEL 203-629-3629. FAX 203-629-3701. Eds. Scott Scanlon, Christopher Hunt. adv.; bk.rev. (back issues avail.)

658 UK ISSN 0955-6230
EXECUTIVE SECRETARY. 1989. q. £75 (Europe £85; U.S. $150) (effective 1996). Salisbury House Publishing Ltd., 182 Hill Top Rd., Thornton, Bradford BD13 3QL, England. TEL 44-1274-832099. FAX 44-1274-831832. E-mail: 100555,2456@compuserve.com. Ed. Jo Denby. bk.rev. circ. 400. **Document type:** trade publication.
Description: Provides a wide range of articles on important and often controversial topics within the executive secretary profession.

658 US
▼**EXECUTIVE SOLUTIONS.** 1995. m. $89. Dartnell Corporation, 4660 N. Ravenswood Ave., Chicago, IL 60640. TEL 773-561-4000; 800-621-5463. FAX 773-561-3801. URL: http://www.dartnellcorp.com. Ed. Linda Segall. **Document type:** newsletter.
Description: Helps executives solve practical problems in all areas of management.

658 US ISSN 1042-0657
EXECUTIVE STRATEGIES;* business, personal. 1986. m. $59. National Institute of Business Management, Box 9266, McLean, VA 22102-9662. TEL 703-905-8000. (Subscr. to: Box 25337, Alexandria, VA 22313) Ed. Tom Weyr. circ. 55,000.
Formerly: Career Letter for Managers.

658 UK
EXECUTIVE STRATEGY. q. 29 Tivoli Rd., Brighton BN1 5BG, England. TEL 0273-565505. FAX 0273-550072. Ed. Peter Bartram. circ. 4,116.

658 UK
EXECUTIVE WOMAN. 1987. bi-m. £15 (foreign £35) (effective 1997). Saleworld Ltd., 2 Chantry Pl., Harrow, Middlesex HA3 6NY, England. TEL 44-181-420-1210. FAX 44-181-420-1691. Ed. Angela Giveon. adv.: B&W page £2200, color page £3200; adv. contact: Angie Greene. bk.rev.; circ. 70,000 (paid). **Document type:** consumer publication.

658 US ISSN 1073-8355
CODEN: EXPMEG
EXPANSION MANAGEMENT; growth strategies for companies on the move. 1986. bi-m. $40 (free to qualified personnel) New Hope Communications, Inc., 1301 Spruce St., Boulder, CO 80302-4832. TEL 303-939-8440. FAX 303-939-8640. Ed. Jack Wimer; Pub. Fred Hernandez. adv.; circ. 40,000 (controlled). (back issues avail.) **Document type:** trade publication.
—KR SourceOne.
Description: Directed to executives responsible for site selection. Covers relocation topics, including real estate and industry trends, state profiles, family and employee issues.

658 US ISSN 1046-3925
T396
EXPO (KANSAS CITY); the magazine for exposition management. 1989. 10/yr. $48 (Canada & Mexico $59; elsewhere $80) (effective 1997). (International Association for Exposition Management) Atwood Convention Publishing, 11600 College Blvd., Overland Park, KS 66210. TEL 913-469-1185. FAX 913-469-0806. E-mail: drorer@expoweb.com. Ed. Cathy Chatfield-Taylor; Pub. Donna Sanford. adv. contact: Kathy Hungerford. circ. 7,500 (controlled). (back issues avail.) **Document type:** trade publication.
●Also available online.
Description: For managers of trade shows and public expositions. Offers information on the administration and operation of trade shows, and current news on the industry.

F & W - FUEHREN UND WIRTSCHAFTEN IM KRANKENHAUS. see HOSPITALS

658.5 628.5 GW
HD28
F B - I E; Zeitschrift fuer Unternehmensentwicklung und Industrial Engineering. 1952. bi-m. DM.86.40. R E F A - Verband fuer Arbeitsgestaltung, Betriebsorganisation und Unternehmensentwicklung e.V., Wittichstr. 2, 64295 Darmstadt, Germany. TEL 49-6151-8801-181. FAX 49-6151-8801177. Ed. Manfred Stroh. adv. contact: Willy Wassmuth. bk.rev. circ. 6,500. **Indexed:** Account.& Data Proc.Abstr., C.I.S. Abstr., Dok.Arbeitsmed., Key to Econ.Sci., SCIMP (1982-). **Document type:** trade publication.
—BLDSC (3901.004900); SWETS; UMI. CCC.
Formerly (until 1995): Fortschrittliche Betriebsfuehrung und Industrial Engineering (ISSN 0340-8302); Which was formed by the 1975 merger of: Fortschrittliche Betriebsfuehrung (ISSN 0015-8216); Industrial Engineering (ISSN 0340-8272); Which (until 1971): Zeitschrift fuer Fuehrungskraefte im Arbeitsstudium und Industrial Engineering (ISSN 0514-6410)
Description: Covers all aspects of industrial organization: market surveys, CA-systems, announcements of conferences and trade fairs.

658.4
F M A BULLETIN.* 1948. 9/yr. $45. Fulfillment Management Association, 60 E. 42nd St., Ste. 1146, New York, NY 10165. TEL 212-725-6140. Ed. Tracy Purcell. tr.lit. rate. 600. (processed)
Formerly: S F M A Bulletin (ISSN 0049-2434)

F M R A NEWS. (American Society of Farm Managers and Rural Appraisers) see AGRICULTURE — Agricultural Economics

FACILITIES; monthly digest for the building administration manager. see BUILDING AND CONSTRUCTION

658 US ISSN 1084-3922
FACILITIES; the bible for convention, exposition and event management. 1991. m. $36 (Canada $66; elsewhere $96). Bedrock Communications, Inc., 650 First Ave., 7th Fl., New York, NY 10016-3240. TEL 212-532-4150. FAX 212-213-6382. E-mail: ber3@inch.com. Ed. Michael Caffin. R&P contact: Michael Caffin. adv.: B&W page $3495, color page $4470; trim 10 7/8 x 13 1/2; adv. contact: Mark Gold. circ. 30,000 (controlled). (tabloid format) **Document type:** trade publication.
Formerly: Agent and Manager (ISSN 1065-5921)
Description: On convention, exposition, and event management from the facilities' viewpoints. Features include state and regional spotlights, special sections on entertainment, convention facility markets, and products and services.

338 720 US ISSN 0279-4438
HF5547.2
FACILITIES DESIGN AND MANAGEMENT. 1982. 12/yr. $65 (foreign $67) (effective 1996). Miller Freeman Inc. (New York) (Subsidiary of: United News & Media), One Penn Plaza, New York, NY 10119. TEL 212-714-1300. FAX 212-714-1313. (Subscr. to: Box 1057, Skokie, IL 60076-8057. TEL 800-255-2824) Ed. Eileen McMorrow. adv. circ. 35,000. (also avail. in microform from UMI)
●Also available online. Vendor(s): UMI.
—BLDSC (3863.453000); KR SourceOne; UMI. CCC.
Description: For corporate executives interested in the efficiency of office design.

FACILITIES MANAGER. see EDUCATION — School Organization And Administration

658.2 721 US ISSN 1059-3667
TS177
FACILITY MANAGEMENT JOURNAL. 1988. bi-m. $75 (foreign $100). International Facility Management Association, 1 E. Greenway Plaza, Ste. 1100, Houston, TX 77062-0194. TEL 713-623-4362. FAX 713-623-6124. Ed. Heather McLean Wiederhoefr. adv.: page $1750; adv. contact: Heather McLean Wiederhoefr. circ. 14,200. (back issues avail.) **Document type:** trade publication.
—CCC.
Description: Covers facility management and real estate issues, the environment, the bottom line, security, technology, innovation.

658 US ISSN 0888-0085
FACILITY MANAGER.* 1985. q. $45 to non-members. International Association of Auditorium Managers, 4425 W. Airport Fwy., Ste. 590, Irving, TX 75062. TEL 214-255-8020. FAX 214-255-9582. Ed. Lawrence R. Quinn. adv.; charts; illus. circ. 2,300.
Formerly (until 1985): Auditorium News.

FACT; feiten, cijfers, trends voor financieel en administratief management. see BUSINESS AND ECONOMICS — Banking And Finance

FAILURE & LESSONS LEARNED IN INFORMATION TECHNOLOGY MANAGEMENT. see COMPUTERS — Information Science And Information Theory

FAIR CATALOGUE K I LIVE. see BEAUTY CULTURE — Perfumes And Cosmetics

FARMING BUSINESS. see AGRICULTURE — Dairying And Dairy Products

658 332.6 US
CODEN: FACOFC
FAST COMPANY. 1993. bi-m. $14.95 (Canada $20; elsewhere $30). Fast Company, Inc., 77 N. Washington St., Boston, MA 02114. TEL 617-973-0300; 800-688-1545. FAX 617-973-0373. E-mail: content@fastcompany.com; URL: http://www.fastcompany.com. Pub. Thomas Evans. R&P contact: Kimberly Smith Jensen. adv.: B&W page $5225; adv. contact: Linda Sepp. circ. 300,000. **Document type:** trade publication.
Description: Presents path-breaking businesses to find out what makes them tick, who they are, how they work, what they know and what they can teach.

FEDERAL GRANTS MANAGEMENT HANDBOOK. see BUSINESS AND ECONOMICS

658 US
JK404
FEDERAL MANAGER. 1983. q. $24 (effective 1997 & 1998). Federal Managers' Association, 1641 Prince St., Alexandria, VA 22314-2818. TEL 703-683-8700. FAX 703-683-8707. E-mail: fma@ix.netcom.com; URL: http://www.fpmi.com. Ed. Michael B. Styles. R&P contact: Frances Webb. adv. contact: Katherine DiBitetto. circ. 25,000. **Indexed:** Pers.Lit. **Document type:** trade publication.
Formerly (until 1997): Federal Managers Quarterly (ISSN 0893-8415)

FILM AUSTRALIA BUSINESS & MANAGEMENT CATALOGUE. see MOTION PICTURES

BUSINESS AND ECONOMICS — MANAGEMENT

658 US ISSN 0895-4186
HF5001 CODEN: FIEXAW
FINANCIAL EXECUTIVE. 1932. bi-m. $45 (foreign $50) (effective July 1995). Financial Executives Institute, 10 Madison Ave., Box 1938, Morristown, NJ 07962-1938. TEL 201-898-4621; 800-336-0773. FAX 201-267-4031. E-mail: rcc@fei.org. Ed. Catherine Coult. R&P contact: Amanda Lewicki. adv. contact: Carol Kelton. bk.rev.; charts; illus.; index. circ. 17,000. (also avail. in microfilm from UMI; reprint service avail. from UMI) Indexed: ABI Inform., Account.& Data Proc.Abstr., Account.Ind. (1974-), Anbar, ASEAN Manage.Abstr., B.P.I., BPIA, Comput.Lit.Ind., Cont.Pg.Manage., INSPEC, Intl.Mgmt.Info., Key to Econ.Sci., Manage.Cont., Mgmt.& Market.Abstr., Oper.Res.Manage.Sci., P.A.I.S., PROMT, SCIMP, Tr.& Indus.Ind. **Document type:** trade publication.
●Also available online. Vendor(s): Information Access Co., Knight-Ridder Information, Inc., UMI.
—BLDSC (3926.954000); AskIEEE; KR SourceOne; SWETS; UMI; UnCover. **CCC.**
Former titles (until 1987): F E: The Magazine for Financial Executives (ISSN 0883-7481); (until Jan. 1985): Financial Executive (ISSN 0015-1998); Controller.
Description: Examines professional and technical developments that affect financial executives' day-to-day responsibilities, as well as long-range issues that reflect financial executives' increasing involvement in the general management of their companies.
Refereed Serial

FINANCIAL INFORMATION SYSTEMS MANUAL. see *BUSINESS AND ECONOMICS — Accounting*

658 US ISSN 0046-3892
HG4001 CODEN: FINMEE
FINANCIAL MANAGEMENT. 1972. q. $80 membership; libraries $100. Financial Management Association, University of South Florida, College of Business, Tampa, FL 33620. TEL 813-974-2084. FAX 813-974-3318. E-mail: fma@bsn01.bsn.usf.edu; URL: http://www.webspace.com/-fma/. Ed. Doug Emery, John Finnerty. adv.; charts; index. circ. 12,000. (also avail. in microform from UMI; reprint service avail. from UMI) Indexed: ABI Inform., Account.& Data Proc.Abstr., Account.Ind. (1974-), ASCA, B.P.I., BPIA, Bus.Ind., Cont.Pg.Manage., Curr.Cont., Mgmt.& Market.Abstr., Mid.East: Abstr.& Ind., Oper.Res.Manage.Sci., P.A.I.S., PROMT, Qual.Contr.Appl.Stat., Risk Abstr., SCIMP (1978-), SSCI, Tr.& Indus.Ind. **Document type:** academic/scholarly publication, trade publication.
●Also available online. Vendor(s): Information Access Co., UMI.
—BLDSC (3926.961000); CASDDS; Genuine Article; KR SourceOne; SWETS; UMI; UnCover. **CCC.**
Description: Presents research papers and analysis on the economic aspects of operating a corporation, focusing on markets, stocks, financial leverage, pricing, trading, purchase-lease options, and cash flow, with news briefs on the latest developments in the field.
Refereed Serial

658 330.9 US
FINANCIAL MANAGEMENT SURVEY. a. $300. A C I L: The American Council of Independent Laboratories, 1629 K. St., N.W., Washington, DC 20006. TEL 202-887-5872. FAX 202-887-0021.

FINANCIAL MONITOR. see *BUSINESS AND ECONOMICS — Investments*

FINANCIAL PARTICIPATION - EUROPE. see *BUSINESS AND ECONOMICS — Personnel Management*

658 332 US
FINANCIAL PLANNING (NEW YORK). 1974. m. $79. (Securities Data Company, Inc.) Securities Data Publishing, 40 W. 57th St., 11th Fl., New York, NY 10019. TEL 212-765-5311. FAX 212-765-6123. Ed. Evan Simonoff. adv.; bk.rev. circ. 60,696. **Document type:** trade publication.
●Also available online. Vendor(s): Information Access Co.

658 CN ISSN 0071-5042
FINANCIAL POST DIRECTORY OF DIRECTORS. 1931. a. Can.$82.50. Financial Post Co., Ltd., 333 King St. E., Toronto, ON M5A 4N2, Canada. TEL 416-350-6116. FAX 416-350-6501. Ed. Jean Graham. adv. circ. 6,000. **Document type:** directory.
●Also available online. Vendor(s): Southam Electronic Publishing.
—CISTI.

658 US ISSN 1058-2878
HG65
FINANCIAL YELLOW BOOK; who's who at the leading U.S. financial institutions. s-a. $200 (effective 1997). Leadership Directories, Inc., 104 Fifth Ave., 2nd Fl., New York, NY 10011. TEL 212-627-4140. FAX 212-645-0931. Ed. Rob Zangara. **Document type:** directory.
●Also available on CD-ROM. Producer(s): Chadwyck-Healey Inc.
—CCC.
Former titles: Financial 1000 Yellow Book (ISSN 1049-7935); (until 1990): Financial 1000 (ISSN 0894-7627)
Description: Provides over 35,000 specific names and titles, direct-dial phone numbers of key executives, alphabetical listings of boards of directors. Also lists major subsidiaries and divisions, business descriptions, and information on assets.

FINANCIEEL MANAGEMENT SECLECT; het beste uit de international vakpers. see *BUSINESS AND ECONOMICS — Banking And Finance*

658 IT
FINANZA MARKETING E PRODUZIONE; rivista di economia d'impresa. (Special biennial English issue avail.) 1983. q. L.150000 (effective 1997). (Universita Commerciale Luigi Bocconi) E G E A s.p.a., Via Sarfatti 25, 20136 Milan, Italy. TEL 39-2-58363726. FAX 39-2-58363793. (Subscr. to: Casa Editrice Dott. A. Giuffre, Via Busto Arsizio 40, 20151 Milan, Italy. TEL 39-2-38089200. FAX 39-2-38009582) Ed. Giovanna Dossena. adv.; page L.800000; adv. contact: Luca Bubbi. bk.rev.; circ. 3,000 (controlled). **Document type:** academic/scholarly publication.
Refereed Serial

658 US
FIRST LINE SUPERVISOR. 1967. bi-w. $68.90. Dartnell Corporation, 4660 N. Ravenswood Ave., Chicago, IL 60640. TEL 773-561-4000; 800-621-5463. FAX 773-561-3801. URL: http://www.dartnellcorp.com. Ed. Linda Segall. **Document type:** newsletter.
Description: Provides manufacturing, construction, and warehouse supervisors with instructional information to help them manage their work and workers better.

658 UK ISSN 0954-8653
FIRST MAGAZINE; forum for decision makers. 1986. q. £145. First Magazine Ltd., 77 Oxford St., London W1R 1RB, England. TEL 44-171-287-0561. FAX 44-171-287-1437. TELEX 269886 TYPO G. Pub. Rupert Goodman. R&P contact: Eamonn Daly. adv.: B&W page $9460, color page $11352; trim 297 x 440; adv. contact: Rupert Goodman. charts; illus.; stat.; circ. 21,000 (paid). (back issues avail.) **Document type:** trade publication.
Description: Covers long-term business and political strategy.
Refereed Serial

658 332 NE ISSN 0928-8457
FISC; fiscale nieuwsbrief voor de onderneming. 1992. 10/yr. fl.420 (effective 1996). Kluwer Bedrijfswetenschappen B.V. (Subsidiary of: Wolters Kluwer N.V.), Postbus 23, 7400 GA Deventer, Netherlands. TEL 31-5700-48999. FAX 31-5700-11504. (Subscr. to: Intermedia bv, Postbus 4, 2400 MA Alphen aan den Rijn, Netherlands. TEL 31-172-466321. FAX 31-172-435527) **Document type:** newsletter.

FITNESS MANAGEMENT. see *PHYSICAL FITNESS AND HYGIENE*

658 388 UK ISSN 1358-8591
▼**FLEET DEALER.** 1995. 10/yr. £125. Sewells International Emap Automotive Ltd., Wentworth House, Wentworth St., Peterborough PE1 1DS, England. TEL 44-1733-467191. FAX 44-1733-467199. **Document type:** trade publication.

658 UK ISSN 1360-9505
FLEXIBLE WORKING. 1996. q. £175 (foreign £185) (effective Sept. 1996). Eclipse Group Ltd., 18-20 Highbury Pl., London N5 1QP, England. TEL 44-171-354-5858. FAX 44-171-226-8618. Ed. Julia Gosling; Pub. Andrew Brode. bk.rev. **Document type:** trade publication.
—BLDSC (3950.672000).
Description: Presents articles and case studies in strategic planning, human resource management, facilities management, finance, and information technology.

658 UK ISSN 1352-9501
FOCUS ON CHANGE MANAGEMENT. 1994. 10/yr. £295($450) (effective Jan. 1997). Armstrong International Ltd., The Courtyard, 12 Hill St., St. Helier, Jersey JE2 4UB, Channel Islands. TEL 44-1534-613650. FAX 44-1534-613651. E-mail: 106001.446@compuserve.com. Ed. Joanna Reeves; Pub. Richard Armstrong. adv. contact: Sarah Witts. (back issues avail.) **Document type:** trade publication.
—BLDSC (3964.203930).

FOOD SHOP. see *FOOD AND FOOD INDUSTRIES*

658 US ISSN 0015-6914
HF5001 CODEN: FORBA5
FORBES. (Includes supplements: Forbes A S A P; Forbes F Y I) 1917. bi-w. $57 (Canada Can.$98; elsewhere $128). Forbes, Inc., 60 Fifth Ave., New York, NY 10011. TEL 212-620-2200. URL: http://www.forbes.com/forbes. (Subscr. to: Box 10048, Des Moines, IA 50340-0048. TEL 800-888-9896) Ed. James W. Michaels. adv.; charts; illus.; mkt.; s-a. index. circ. 765,000. (also avail. in microform from UMI; microfiche from NBI; reprint service avail.) Indexed: A.I.Abstr., ABI Inform., Abstr.Bull.Inst.Pap.Chem., Acad.Ind., Account.Ind. (1975-), B.P.I., Bank.Lit.Ind., BPIA, Bus.Ind., CAD CAM Abstr., Chem.Abstr., Comput.Bus., Comput.Lit.Ind., Data Process.Dig., Energy Ind., Energy Info.Abstr., Environ.Abstr., Hlth.Ind., Ind.Per.Art.Relat.Law, Key to Econ.Sci., Mag.Ind., Manage.Cont., Mid.East: Abstr.& Ind., Oper.Res.Manage.Sci., PROMT, PSI, Qual.Contr.Appl.Stat., R.G., R.G.Abstr., Rehabil.Lit., Robomat., SRI, Tel.Abstr., Tel.Alert, Telegen, TOM, Tr.& Indus.Ind.
●Also available online. Vendor(s): Dow Jones News Retrieval, Information Access Co., Knight-Ridder Information, Inc., Lexis-Nexis.
—BLDSC (3985.525000); CASDDS; Genuine Article; KR SourceOne; SWETS; UMI; UnCover. **CCC.**
Description: Covers U.S. and international business issues for executives, managers, and investors in U.S. corporations.

FORBES F Y I. see *GENERAL INTEREST PERIODICALS — United States*

FOREMAN'S PRODUCTION PLANNER; a monthly production guide to better leadership and supervision. see *BUSINESS AND ECONOMICS — Production Of Goods And Services*

FORMATION EMPLOI. see *BUSINESS AND ECONOMICS — Personnel Management*

658 US ISSN 0015-7805
FORMS OF BUSINESS AGREEMENTS. q. $264. Macmillan Information Company Inc., 90 Fifth Ave., New York, NY 10011-7629. TEL 800-562-0245. FAX 201-816-3569. adv.; bk.rev. (looseleaf format)

BUSINESS AND ECONOMICS — MANAGEMENT

650 — US — ISSN 0015-8259
HF5001 — CODEN: FORTAP
FORTUNE MAGAZINE. 1930. bi-w. $57 (Canada $65). Time Inc. (Subsidiary of: Time Warner, Inc.), Time & Life Bldg., Rockefeller Center, New York, NY 10020-1393. TEL 212-522-1212. URL: http://wwww.fortune.com. (Subscr. to: Fortune, Box 60001, Tampa, FL 33660-0001. TEL 800-621-8000) Ed. John Huey; Pub. Jolene Sykes. R&P contact: Jo Maitern. TEL 212-522-2582. adv. contact: Michael Federle. bk.rev.; illus.; circ. 860,000 (paid). (also avail. in microform from UMI; reprint service avail. from UMI) **Indexed:** A.I.Abstr., ABI Inform., Abstr.Bull.Inst.Pap.Chem., Acad.Ind., Account.Ind. (1974-), Amer.Bibl.Slavic & E.Eur.Stud., B.P.I, Bk.Rev.Ind. (1989-), BMT, BPIA, Bus.Ind., CAD CAM Abstr., Child.Bk.Rev.Ind. (1989-), Comput.Bus., Comput.Indus.Up., Comput.Lit.Ind., Cont.Pg.Manage., ELLIS, Energy Info.Abstr., Environ.Abstr., Excerp.Med., Fuel & Energy Abstr., Hlth.Ind., Ind.Bus.Rep., INIS Atomind., INSPEC, Int.Lab.Doc., Intl.Mgmt.Info., Intl.Polym.Sci.& Tech., Key to Econ.Sci., Mag.Ind., Manage.Cont., Mgmt.& Market.Abstr., Ocean.Abstr., Oper.Res.Manage.Sci., P.A.I.S., PCR2, PMR, Pollut.Abstr., PROMT, Qual.Contr.Appl.Stat., R.G., RAPRA, Ref.Pt.Food Indus.Abstr., Resour.Ctr.Ind., Robomat., Sel.Water Res.Abstr., SRI, Tel.Abstr., Tel.Alert, Telegen, Text.Tech.Dig., TOM, Tr.& Indus.Ind., Work Rel.Abstr., World Bank.Abstr. **Document type:** consumer publication.
● Also available online.
Also available on CD-ROM.
—CASDDS; CISTI; Genuine Article; KR SourceOne; Linda Hall; SWETS; UMI; UnCover.

658 — NE — ISSN 1384-2102
FORUM (HAGUE). 1968. s-w. fl.80. Confederation of Dutch Employers and Industry, V N O - N C W, Bezwidenhoutseweg 12, P.O. Box 93002, 2509 AA The Hague, Netherlands. TEL 31-70-3490166. FAX 31-70-3490181. Ed. R.G. Smit. adv.; bk.rev.; illus.; index. circ. 25,200. **Indexed:** C.I.S. Abstr., Key to Econ.Sci.
—SWETS.
Former titles (until 1995): Onderneming (ISSN 0165-6643); Nederlandse Onderneming (ISSN 0028-2294)

658 — GW — ISSN 0176-232X
FORUM BUERO WIRTSCHAFT. 1946. s-m. DM.70. Verlag Dragon, Markeneck 3, 46286 Dorsten, Germany. TEL 02369-4210. FAX 02369-4209. Ed. Harald Neumann; Pub. Alfred Dragon. adv. contact: Wolfgang Dragon. bk.rev. **Document type:** bulletin.

FRACHT UND MATERIALFLUSS. see *TRANSPORTATION*

658 — GW — ISSN 0940-8762
G V MANAGER. (Gross Verbraucher) 1950. 10/yr. DM.80 (foreign DM.100). Verlag Neuer Merkur GmbH, Ingolstaedter Str. 63a, 80939 Munich, Germany. TEL 089-318905-0. FAX 089-31890553. **Document type:** trade publication.

658 — GW — ISSN 0932-3961
GABLERS - MAGAZIN; Zeitschrift fuer innovative Fuehrungskraefte. 10/yr. DM.175 (students DM.98) (foreign DM.195) (effective 1997). Betriebswirtschaftlicher Verlag Dr. Th. Gabler GmbH, Abraham-Lincoln-Str. 46, 65189 Wiesbaden, Germany. TEL 49-611-7878129. FAX 49-611-7878423. Ed.Bd. adv.; bk.rev.; abstr.; charts; illus. **Document type:** consumer publication.
—SWETS. CCC.
Formerly: Betriebswirtschafts-Magazin (ISSN 0005-9986)

658 — FR — ISSN 0769-3508
HC271
GAZETTE DES COMMUNES, DES DEPARTEMENTS, DES REGIONS. 1980. w. 595 F. (foreign 1040 F.). Groupe Moniteur, 17 rue d'Uzes, 75002 Paris, France. FAX 33-1-42333819. TELEX 220 528F. Ed. Jean Dumonteil. adv.; circ. 20,079 (controlled).
Formerly (until 1985): Gazette des Communes (ISSN 0242-570X); Which was formed by the merger of (1934-1980): Gazette des Communes et du Personnel Communal (ISSN 0242-5718); (1949-1980): L'Action Municipale (ISSN 0001-7450)

658 690 — NE — ISSN 0927-0140
GEBOUWBEHEER. 1990. 10/yr. fl.110. Misset (Subsidiary of: Reed Elsevier plc), Postbus 4, 7000 BA Doetinchem, Netherlands. TEL 31-314-349371. FAX 31-314-363638. adv. rates: B&W page fl.3154, color page fl.5047; trim 215 x 285; adv. contact: Cor van Nek. illus. circ. 5,010. **Document type:** trade publication.
—SWETS.
Description: Covers building management and maintenance, for public and private sector managers.

658 — JA
GEKKAN GENDAI. (Text in Japanese) 1967. m. Kodansha Ltd., 12-21 Otowa 2-chome, Bunkyo-ku, Tokyo 112, Japan. TEL 03-3945-1111. FAX 03-3943-7815. TELEX J34509 KODANSHA. Ed. Ryosuke Sasaki. circ. 250,000.
Formerly: Monthly Gendai.
Description: Covers general topics for businessmen.

658 305.4 — UK — ISSN 0968-6673
CODEN: GWORF8
GENDER, WORK AND ORGANIZATION. 1994. q. £125($173) (foreign £125) (effective 1997). Blackwell Publishers Ltd., 108 Cowley Rd., Oxford OX4 1JF, England. TEL 44-1865-791100. FAX 44-1865-791347. E-mail: jnlinfo@blackwellpublishers.co.uk; URL: http://www.blackwellpublishers.co.uk. Eds. David Knights, Jill Rubery. **Indexed:** Stud.Wom.Abstr. **Document type:** academic/scholarly publication.
—BLDSC (4096.401680); UMI. CCC.
Description: Dedicated to advancing theory, research, and applications of gender studies at work. Investigates various gender issues in the workplace.
Refereed Serial

GEORGESON REPORT. see *BUSINESS AND ECONOMICS — Investments*

GERER ET COMPRENDRE/TO MANAGE AND TO UNDERSTAND. see *MINES AND MINING INDUSTRY*

658 — FR — ISSN 0766-9755
GESTION SOCIALE. 1984. w. 4250 F. Groupe Liaisons S.A., 1 av. Edouard Belin, 92856 Rueil Malmaison, France. TEL 33-1-41299879. FAX 33-1-41299880.

658 — US
HF5549.A2 — CODEN: SPMNAU
GETTING RESULTS...FOR THE HANDS-ON MANAGER. (Avail. in two editions: Office & Plant) 1955. m. $75 to non-members. American Management Association, 1601 Broadway, New York, NY 10019. TEL 212-586-8100. FAX 212-903-8083. (Subscr. addr.: Box 58155, Boulder, CO 80322-8155) Ed. Florence Stone; Pub. Rosemary Kang/Carlough. R&P contact: Theresa New. adv. contact: Margaret Joseph. bk.rev.; illus.; index; circ. 15,000 (paid). (also avail. in microform from ISI,UMI,KTO,SCH) **Indexed:** ABI Inform., B.P.I., Bank.Lit.Ind., Bibl.Agri., BPIA, Manage.Cont., Pers.Lit., Pers.Manage.Abstr., Work Rel.Abstr. **Document type:** newsletter.
● Also available online. Vendor(s): Information Access Co., UMI.
—BLDSC (8547.150000); Genuine Article; KR SourceOne; UMI; UnCover. CCC.
Former titles: Supervisory Management (New York) (ISSN 1045-263X); (until 1989): Management Solutions (ISSN 0889-0226); (until 1986): Supervisory Management (New York) (ISSN 0039-5919)
Description: For first and second-line managers. Includes how-to articles to help with supervisory problems and management situations.

GIFT BASKET IDEA NEWSLETTER. see *GIFTWARE AND TOYS*

658 — IT
GIORNALE DEL DIRIGENTE. 1974. m. (10/yr.). L.30000 (effective Jan. 1997). Federazione Nazionale Dirigenti di Aziende Commerciali (FENDAC Servizi), Via Stoppani 6, 20129 Milan, Italy. TEL 39-2-29516028. FAX 39-2-29516093. E-mail: fsgior@mbox.vol.it. Ed. Guido Gay. adv.: B&W page L.5000000, color page L.6500000. bk.rev. circ. 21,240.

GLOBAL BUSINESS AND FINANCE REVIEW. see *BUSINESS AND ECONOMICS — International Commerce*

658 — UK — ISSN 0961-4001
GLOBAL MANAGEMENT. 1985. a. £55. Sterling Publications Ltd., 86-88 Edgware Rd., London W2 2YW, England. TEL 44-171-915-9600. FAX 44-171-915-9619. R&P contact: Sandy Tucker. circ. 15,000. **Document type:** trade publication.
—BLDSC (4195.460000).

GLOBAL MONEY MANAGEMENT. see *BUSINESS AND ECONOMICS — Investments*

GLOBAL REINSURANCE. see *INSURANCE*

GLOBAL RISK MANAGER (YEAR). see *INSURANCE*

GOLF CLUB MANAGEMENT & EQUIPMENT NEWS. see *SPORTS AND GAMES — Ball Games*

658 — CC — ISSN 1001-2516
GONGYE QIYE GUANLI/INDUSTRIAL ENTERPRISE MANAGEMENT. (Subseries of: Fuyin Baokan Ziliao) (Text in Chinese) 1978. m. $121.13. Zhongguo Renmin Daxue, Shubao Ziliao Zhongxin - China People's University, Book & Newspaper Information Center, 3 Zhang Zizhong Rd., P.O. Box 1122, Beijing 100007, People's Republic of China. TEL 86-10-4015080. (Dist. in US by: China Publications Service, Box 49614, Chicago, IL 60649. TEL 312-288-3291. FAX 312-288-8570) pp./issue: 176.

658 — US — ISSN 0145-6598
KF846.5
GOVERNMENT CONTRACTS SERVICE. 1962. bi-m. $595 (renewals $495). Procurement Associates, Inc., 733 N. Dodsworth Ave., Covina, CA 91724. TEL 818-966-4576. Ed. Paul R. McDonald, Sr. index. circ. 2,000. (looseleaf format; back issues avail.)
Description: Information for managers interested in government contracts.

658 — US
GOVERNMENT RELATIONS. m. membership. American Society of Association Executives, Government Relations Section, 1575 Eye St., N.W., Washington, DC 20005-1168. TEL 202-626-2703. FAX 202-371-1673. circ. 1,400.
Description: For government affairs managers of associations.

GRAFISCH NEDERLAND; informatie voor en over grafisch management. see *PRINTING*

GREEN PRODUCTIVITY. see *ENVIRONMENTAL STUDIES*

GREENER MANAGEMENT INTERNATIONAL; the journal of corporate environmental strategy and practice. see *ENVIRONMENTAL STUDIES*

658 — NE — ISSN 0926-2644
HD30.23 — CODEN: GDNEEY
GROUP DECISION AND NEGOTIATION. (Text in English) 1992. bi-m. fl.670 to institutions; $344 to institutions in U.S. (effective 1998). (The Institute of Management Sciences, College on Group Decision and Negotiation, US) Kluwer Academic Publishers, Postbus 17, 3300 AA Dordrecht, Netherlands. TEL 31-78-6392392. FAX 31-78-6392254. TELEX 29245 KAPG NL. E-mail: services@wkap.nl; URL: http://www.wkap.nl. (Dist. by: Kluwer Academic Publishers Group, P.O. Box 322, 3300 AH Dordrecht, Netherlands. TEL 31-78-6392392. FAX 31-78-6546474; N. America dist. addr.: Box 358, Accord Sta., Hingham, MA 02018-0358. TEL 617-871-6600. FAX 617-871-6528) Ed. Melvin F. Shakun. (also avail. in microform from UMI; back issues avail.; reprint service avail. from SWZ) **Indexed:** ASCA, Curr.Cont., Psychol.Abstr. (1991-). **Document type:** academic/scholarly publication.
● Also available online.
—BLDSC (4220.174200); Genuine Article; UMI; UnCover. CCC.
Description: Publishes papers discussing all aspects of the process of group decision-making and negotiation, including descriptive, normative and design viewpoints.
Refereed Serial

BUSINESS AND ECONOMICS — MANAGEMENT

658   CC
GUANLI KEXUE/MANAGEMENT SCIENCE. (Subseries of: Fuyin Baokan Ziliao) (Text in Chinese) $21.67. Zhongguo Renmin Daxue, Shubao Ziliao Zhongxin - China People's University, Book & Newspaper Information Center, 3 Zhang Zizhong Rd., P.O. Box 1122, Beijing 100007, People's Republic of China. TEL 86-10-4015080. (Dist. in US by: China Publications Service, Box 49614, Chicago, IL 60649. TEL 312-288-3291. FAX 312-288-8570) pp./issue: 64.
Description: Contains reprints of articles on management theories as well as related Chinese policies.

658   CC   ISSN 1002-5502
GUANLI SHIJIE/JOURNAL OF MANAGEMENT WORLD. (Text in Chinese) 1985. bi-m. $64.60. (Guowuyuan, Fazhan Yanjiu Zhongxin - State Council, Research Center for Economic Development) Guanli Shijie Bianjibu, 6 Beisanhuan Zhonglu, Beijing 100010, People's Republic of China. TEL 86-10-2029312. (Dist. in US by: China Books & Periodicals, Inc., 2929 24th St., San Francisco, CA 94110. TEL 415-282-2994) Ed. Li Kemu. pp./issue: 224.
Description: Analyzes China's economic situations, policies and regulations as well as problems facing both managers and regulators.

658   CC   ISSN 1004-5414
GUANLI YU XIAOYI/MANAGEMENT AND BENEFIT. (Text in Chinese) 1987. q-m. Y1.50 per no. (effective 1993). (Chinese Mechanical Engineering Society, Management Association) Zhongguo Tequ Jidian Zazhishe, No.1, Shenhu Lu, Fuzhou, Fujian 350001, People's Republic of China. TEL 554120. (Dist. overseas by: Jiangsu Publications Import & Export Corp., 56 Gao Yun Ling, Nanjing, Jiangsu, P.R.C.) Ed. Chen Peijing. adv.; bk.rev. circ. 30,000.
Description: Exchanges methods and experiences of management.

658   350   360   US
GUIDE TO ARKANSAS FUNDING SOURCES. 1981. biennial. $75. Independent Community Consultants, Inc., P.O. Box 141, Hampton, AR 71744. TEL 501-798-4510. FAX 501-798-4513. Ed. Jerry Cronin. adv. contact: Monica Gilmore. circ. 1,000. **Document type:** bulletin.
Description: Financial and program information on all Arkansas-based private foundations, out-of-state foundations making grants in Arkansas, corporate donors to Arkansas charities.

658   US   ISSN 0899-9791
H V A C PROFITMAKER. 1988. 10/yr. $285. Tom Davies and Associates, 674 Western Dr., Mobile, AL 36607. TEL 205-471-2001. Ed. Tom Davies. index. circ. 87. (back issues avail.)

658   GW
HAMBURG NACHRICHTEN. m. Wirtschaftsvereinigung Handelsvertreter und Handelsmakler Hamburg - Schleswig Holstein, Raboisen 16, 20095 Hamburg, Germany. TEL 040-331025.

658   US   ISSN 1077-5730
HD30.28
HANDBOOK OF BUSINESS STRATEGY. 1986. a. Faulkner & Gray, Inc. (New York), 11 Penn Plaza, 17th Fl., New York, NY 10001. TEL 212-967-7000; 800-535-8403. FAX 212-967-7155.
—CISTI.
Formerly (until 1994): Handbook of Business Strategy. Yearbook (ISSN 0894-4318)

HANDBOOK OF COST MANAGEMENT. see BUSINESS AND ECONOMICS — Accounting

658   330   US
T58.6
HANDBOOK OF I S MANAGEMENT. (Information Systems) 1984. triennial (plus a. update). $142. Auerbach Publishers (Subsidiary of: Warren, Gorham & Lamont), One Penn Plaza, New York, NY 10119. TEL 212-971-5000. FAX 212-971-5024. (Subscr. to: 31 St. James Ave., Boston, MA 02116-4122. TEL 800-950-1218. FAX 617-423-1914) Ed. Robert E. Umbaugh. **Document type:** trade publication.
—CISTI.
Formerly: Handbook of M I S Management (ISSN 1055-5870)
Description: Covers current MIS technologies and applications and shows how to manage an organization's information systems more effectively.

HANDBOOK OF SYSTEMS MANAGEMENT; development and support. see BUSINESS AND ECONOMICS — Computer Applications

HANDBOOKS IN OPERATIONS RESEARCH AND MANAGEMENT SCIENCE. see COMPUTERS

658   GW   ISSN 0942-2609
HANDBUCH KULTURMANAGEMENT. 1992. q. DM.188. Dr. Josef Raabe Verlags GmbH, Postfach 103922, 70034 Stuttgart, Germany. TEL 49-711-62900-0. FAX 49-711-6290010. E-mail: info@raabe.de; URL: http://www.raabe.de. Ed. Peter Bendixen. bk.rev.; software rev.; bibl.; illus.; circ. 2,500. (looseleaf format) **Document type:** academic/scholarly publication.

DER HANDEL; das Wirtschaftsmagazin fuer Handelsmanagement. see BUSINESS AND ECONOMICS — Domestic Commerce

658   331.1   NO   ISSN 0332-8066
HANDELSBESTYREREN. 1920. m. (11/yr.). NOK 90. Handelsbestyrerforbundet, Arbeidersamfundets Plass 1, 0181 Oslo, Norway. TEL 02-20-52-40. FAX 47-2-113194. Ed. Arne Randen. adv.; circ. 1,450. (controlled).

658.01   GW
HARVARD BUSINESS MANAGER. 1979. q. DM.104. Manager Magazin Verlagsgesellschaft mbH, Brandstwiete 19, 20457 Hamburg, Germany. TEL 040-30072557. FAX 040-30072247. adv.: B&W page DM.3150, color page DM.5355; trim 178 x 252. circ. 10,000. **Document type:** consumer publication.
—SWETS.
Formerly: Harvard - Manager (ISSN 0174-335X)

HARVARD BUSINESS SCHOOL CAREER GUIDE. MANAGEMENT CONSULTING. see OCCUPATIONS AND CAREERS

650   658.01   US   ISSN 0073-0785
HARVARD UNIVERSITY. GRADUATE SCHOOL OF BUSINESS ADMINISTRATION. PROGRAM FOR MANAGEMENT DEVELOPMENT. PUBLICATION. 1960. a. price varies. Harvard University, Graduate School of Business Administration, Boston, MA 02163. TEL 617-495-6000.

658   UK   ISSN 0967-6813
HEADS OF SCIENCE BRIEFING. Variant title: Croner's Heads of Science Briefing. 1992. base vol. (plus bi-m. updates). £91.70 (updates £60.80) (effective 1995). Croner Publications Ltd. (Subsidiary of: Wolters Kluwer N.V.), Croner House, 100 London Rd., Kingston-upon-Thames, Surrey TW2 6SR, England. TEL 44-181-547-3333. FAX 44-181-247-1300. TELEX 26778. (looseleaf format) **Document type:** trade publication.

HEALTH & SAFETY MANAGER. see OCCUPATIONAL HEALTH AND SAFETY

HEALTH CARE INFORMATION MANAGEMENT WEEK. see MEDICAL SCIENCES

HEALTH CARE MANAGEMENT REVIEW. see HOSPITALS

HEALTH CARE MANAGEMENT SCIENCE. see HOSPITALS

HEALTH CARE MANAGEMENT: STATE OF THE ART REVIEWS. see HOSPITALS

HEALTH CLUB MANAGEMENT. see LEISURE AND RECREATION

HEALTH LABOR RELATIONS ALERT. see MEDICAL SCIENCES

658   UK   ISSN 0955-2065
HEALTH MANPOWER MANAGEMENT. 1975. bi-m. £1199($1859) (foreign Aus.$2339) (effective 1998). M C B University Press Ltd., 60-62 Toller Ln., Bradford, W. Yorks BD8 9BY, England. TEL 44-1274-777700. FAX 44-1274-785200. TELEX 51317-MCBUNI-G. URL: http://www.mcb.co.uk. Ed. A. Hyde. bk.rev. **Indexed:** Abstr.Hyg., ASSIA, Trop.Dis.Bull. **Document type:** academic/scholarly publication.
●Also available on CD-ROM.
—BLDSC (4275.052150); UMI. **CCC.**
Supersedes (as of 1988): Health Services Manpower Review (ISSN 0306-0233)

HEALTH PRACTICE MANAGEMENT HANDBOOK (YEAR). see MEDICAL SCIENCES

HEALTHCARE INFORMATION MANAGEMENT. see HOSPITALS

HEALTHCARE LEADERSHIP REVIEW. see HOSPITALS

658   613.7   US   ISSN 0891-9267
HEALTHCARE MANAGEMENT TEAM LETTER. 1985. 12/yr. $187 (effective 1997). Health Resources Publishing, Brinley Professional Plaza, 3100 Hwy. 138, Box 1442, Wall Township, NJ 07719-1442. TEL 908-681-1133. FAX 908-681-0490. E-mail: 75673.624@compuserve.com. Ed. Robert K. Jenkins; Pub. Robert K. Jenkins. adv. contact: Marcia Balkin. index. (tabloid format; back issues avail.) **Document type:** newsletter.
—CCC.
Description: Includes the latest in grants, fund raising techniques, marketing, capital, reimbursement, hospice, capital equipment, hospital restructuring, financing, and hospital energy issues.

HILDEBRANDT REPORT; a management and marketing newsletter for law firms. see LAW

658.2   389   JA   ISSN 0018-1951
HINSHITSU KANRI/TOTAL QUALITY CONTROL. (Text in Japanese) 1950. m. 18100 Yen. Union of Japanese Scientists and Engineers - Nihon Kagaku Gijutsu Renmei, 5-10-11 Sendagaya, Shibuya-ku, Tokyo 151, Japan. TEL 03-5379-1227. FAX 03-3225-1813. Ed. Kohei Suzue. adv.; abstr.; charts; illus.; index. circ. 15,000. **Indexed:** JTA.
—CISTI.

658.3   JA   ISSN 0439-2795
HITACHI ZOSEN NEWS. (Text in English) vol.19, 1976. s-a. free. Hitachi Zosen Corporation, 1-1, Hitotsubashi 1-chome, Chiyoda-ku, Tokyo 100, Japan. FAX 03-3217-8545. TELEX 24490 SHIPYARD J. Ed. T. Nishijima. illus. circ. 2,800. **Indexed:** BMT.
—CISTI.

380   658   JA   ISSN 0018-2796
HF53
HITOTSUBASHI JOURNAL OF COMMERCE AND MANAGEMENT. 1961. a. 2500 Yen (effective 1997). Hitotsubashi Daigaku, Hitotsubashi Gakkai - Hitotsubashi University, Hitotsubashi Academy, 2-1 Naka, Kunitachi-shi, Tokyo 186, Japan. (Subscr. to: Japan Publications Trading Co. Ltd., P.O. Box 5030, Tokyo International, Tokyo, Japan. TEL 81-3-3292-3751. FAX 81-3-3292-0410) Ed. S. Yonekura. charts; illus.; stat.; cum.index. circ. 700. **Indexed:** Excerp.Med., P.A.I.S. **Document type:** academic/scholarly publication.

658   378   UK
HOBSONS MANAGEMENT CASEBOOK. a. £9.99 (includes Logistics Casebook) (complete set £119.88). (Careers Research and Advisory Centre) Hobsons Publishing plc., Bateman St., Cambridge CB2 1LZ, England. TEL 44-1223-460366. FAX 44-1223-301506. TELEX 81546 HOBCAM G. (Dist. by: Biblios Publishers' Distribution Services Ltd., Star Rd., Partridge Green, W. Sussex RH13 8LD, England. TEL 44-1403-710851. FAX 44-1403-711143)
Description: Recent graduates discuss their management careers.

HOBSONS MARKETING, RETAILING AND SALES CASEBOOK. see OCCUPATIONS AND CAREERS

658   US   ISSN 0738-7490
HOME BUSINESS IDEA POSSIBILITY NEWSLETTER. 1991. a. $7.50. Sought After Publications, c/o Prosperity & Profits Unlimited, Box 416, Denver, CO 80201-0416. TEL 303-575-5676. Ed. A. Doyle. R&P contact: A. Doyle. (looseleaf format) **Document type:** newsletter.
Description: Offers ideas and suggestions on starting and operating a home-based business.

BUSINESS AND ECONOMICS — MANAGEMENT

658 338.476   US   ISSN 1073-9572
HOME HEALTH BUSINESS REPORT; news trends & strategies for the home healthcare executive. 1994. s-m. $307. American Health Consultants Inc., 3525 Piedmont Rd., N.E., Bldg. 6, Ste. 400, Atlanta, GA 30305. TEL 800-668-2421. Ed. Carolyn Davis; Pub. David Wilson. R&P contact: Lauren Dryfuss. TEL 404-262-5476. bk.rev.; circ. 1,300 (paid). (back issues avail.) **Document type:** newsletter.
    Description: Contains home care business news regarding company and industry trends, including public company financial data, stock indexes, and company and payor profiles.

658   CC   ISSN 0018-4594
HONG KONG MANAGER. (Text in Chinese and English) 1965. bi-m. HK.$300. Hong Kong Management Association, 14-F Fairmont House, 8 Cotton Tree Dr., Central, Hong Kong, People's Republic of China. FAX 852-2868-4387. TELEX 81903 HKMGR HX. Ed. P.L. Ng. adv.: B&W page HK.$6800, color page HK.$9500; trim 220 x 292; adv. contact: P.L. Ng. bk.rev.; abstr.; charts; illus.; stat.; tr.lit.; index. circ. 6,000. **Indexed:** HongKongiana. **Document type:** trade publication.
   —BLDSC (4326.390000).
    Description: Covers the latest developments in management theories and skills.

HOSPITAL MANAGEMENT INTERNATIONAL. see *HOSPITALS*

HOSPITAL MATERIALS MANAGEMENT; the newsletter for materials management and group purchasing. see *HOSPITALS*

HOSPITAL RISK CONTROL; an information and consultation system. see *HOSPITALS*

HOSPITAL RISK MANAGEMENT. see *HOSPITALS*

330.1   US
HG179
HOW TO AVOID FINANCIAL TANGLES. 1938. irreg., latest 1997. $8 per no. American Institute for Economic Research, Box 1000, Great Barrington, MA 01230. TEL 413-528-1216.
    Incorporates: How to Avoid Financial Tangles: Section B. Wills and Trusts, Taxes, and Help for the Widow; How to Avoid Financial Tangles: Section A. Elementary Property Problems and Financial Relationships.

HUMAN RESOURCE MANAGEMENT. see *BUSINESS AND ECONOMICS — Personnel Management*

658   CC
HUMAN RESOURCES JOURNAL. (Text in English) 1985-1992; resumed 199? s-a. $18 (outside Asia $25). Asian Research Service, G.P.O. Box 2232, Hong Kong, People's Republic of China. TEL 852-2570-7227. FAX 852-2512-8050. (Canadian addr.: 140-5671 Minoru Blvd., Richmond, B.C. V6X 2B1, Canada. TEL 604-276-8115. FAX 604-276-0813) adv. contact: Winnie Leung. circ. 3,000.

658   US
HUMAN RESOURCES MANAGEMENT - IDEAS AND TRENDS. (Part of: Human Resources Management) 1981. bi-w. $197. C C H Incorporated, 2700 Lake Cook Rd., Riverwoods, IL 60015. TEL 847-267-7000; 800-835-5224. FAX 800-224-8299. **Document type:** newsletter.
   —CCC.
    Formerly: Human Resources Management - Ideas and Trends in Personnel (ISSN 0745-0613)
    Description: Covers human resources developments in business and government.

658   NE   ISSN 0167-2533
CODEN: HSMADU
HUMAN SYSTEMS MANAGEMENT. (Text in English) 1980. q. fl.440($244) (effective 1997). I O S Press, Van Diemenstraat 94, 1013 CN Amsterdam, Netherlands. TEL 31-20-6382189. FAX 31-20-6203419. E-mail: market@iospress.nl; zeleny@mary.fordham.edu; URL: http://www.iospress.nl/iospress. (In N. America: Box 10558, Burke, VA 22009-0558. TEL 703-323-5554. FAX 703-250-4705) Ed. M. Zeleny. adv.; bk.rev. (also avail. in microform; back issues avail.) **Indexed:** ABI Inform., ASSIA, BPIA, Bus.Ind., CLOSS, Cont.Pg.Manage., Curr.Cont., INSPEC (1980-), Int.Polit.Sci.Abstr., Manage.Cont., Mgmt.& Market.Abstr., Mult.Ed.Abstr., SCIMP, SSCI, Tech.Educ.Abstr. **Document type:** academic/scholarly publication.
   ●Also available online. Vendor(s): UMI.
   —BLDSC (4336.468000); AskIEEE; Ei; KR SourceOne; SWETS; UMI; UnCover. **CCC.**
    Description: For managers and social scientists. Provides information on the science, technology and art of management. Articles cover productivity, performance and competence improvement.

658   US
I A A M NEWS. m. $75 to non-members. International Association of Auditorium Managers, 4425 W. Airport Fwy., Ste. 590, Irving, TX 75062. TEL 214-255-8020. FAX 214-255-9582. adv. circ. 2,200. **Document type:** newsletter.

658   IE
I B E C - E S R I MONTHLY INDUSTRIAL SURVEY. m. Irish Business and Employers Confederation, Confederation House, 84-86 Lower Baggot St., Dublin 2, Ireland. TEL 353-1-6601011. FAX 353-1-6601717. URL: http://www.iol.ie/ibec. (Co-sponsor: Social Research Institute) Ed. David Croughan. stat. **Document type:** bulletin.
    Formerly: Monthly Industrial Survey - Business Forecast.

658   SZ
I B SUISSE. (Text in French) 1979. m. 95 SFr. (Europe 107 SFr.; overseas 129 SFr.) (effective 1997). (Schweizerischen Gesellschaft fuer Organisation) Fachpresse Goldach, Sulzstr. 12, CH-9403 Goldach, Switzerland. TEL 41-71-8449111. FAX 41-71-8449511. E-mail: 100442.1657@compuserve.com; URL: http://www.fachpresse.ch. Ed. Jean-Pascal Baechler. adv.: B&W page 4771 SFr., color page 7157 SFr.; trim 185 x 267. illus. circ. 10,000. **Indexed:** Cyb.Abstr. **Document type:** bulletin.
    Formerly: Bureaux et Systemes (ISSN 0257-8328)

658   US   ISSN 1058-5036
I C 2 MANAGEMENT AND MANAGEMENT SCIENCE SERIES. 1991. irreg. price varies. Greenwood Press, Inc. (Subsidiary of: Greenwood Publishing Group Inc.), 88 Post Rd. W., Box 5007, Westport, CT 06881-5007. TEL 203-226-3571. FAX 203-222-1502. **Document type:** monographic series.

658   GW   ISSN 0173-0665
I D - INFORMATIONSDIENST FUER DIE PERSONALABTEILUNG. 1979. m. DM.177.60. Verlag Recht und Wirtschaft GmbH, Haeusserstr. 14, 69115 Heidelberg, Germany. TEL 06221-906-1. (Subscr. to: Postfach 105960, 69049 Heidelberg, Germany) adv.; bk.rev. circ. 900.

I E E E ENGINEERING MANAGEMENT REVIEW. see *ENGINEERING*

658 004   NE   ISSN 0167-9740
I & I. (Informatie en Informatiebeleid) 1983. q. fl.140. Otto Cramwinckel Uitgever, Herengracht 416, 1017 BZ Amsterdam, Netherlands. TEL 31-20-6276609. FAX 31-20-6383817. Ed. B. Tisselaar; Pub. Otto Cramwinckel. adv. circ. 3,000. **Indexed:** ELLIS. **Document type:** academic/scholarly publication.
   —SWETS.

658   US   ISSN 0747-6221
I F M A NEWS. 1982. m. $75 to non-members (foreign $100). International Facility Management Association, 1 E. Greenway Plaza, Ste. 1100, Houston, TX 77046-0194. TEL 713-623-4362. FAX 713-623-6124. Ed. Allison Tilly. R&P contact: Allison Tilly. adv.; bk.rev. circ. 14,500. **Document type:** newsletter.
   —CCC.
    Description: Association news, industry codes, regulations and standards, research updates.

658   II
I F M R PUBLICATIONS. no. 12, 1975. irreg. Institute for Financial Management and Research, Madras 600034, India. (Dist. by: Vora & Co., Publishers, 3 Round Bldg., Kalbadevi, Bombay 400 002, India)

370   FR   ISSN 0397-3301
I N F F O - FLASH. 22/yr. 604 F. (foreign 809 F.) (effective 1997). Centre I N F F O, Tour Europe, 92049 Paris - La Defense Cedex, France. TEL 33-1-41252222. FAX 33-1-47737420. TELEX 615 383. bk.rev.

I O M A'S REPORT ON CONTROLLING LAW FIRMS COSTS. (Institute of Management & Administration, Inc.) see *LAW — Corporate Law*

658.5   SZ
HD45.A1   CODEN: IIOODN
I O MANAGEMENT. (Industrielle Organisation) (Text in German; summaries in German, French and English) 1932. m. 149 SFr. (Betriebswissenschaftliches Institut der Eidgenoessischen Technischen Hochschule Zuerich, Stiftung fuer Forschung und Beratung) Verlag Industrielle Organisation, Seestr. 37, CH-8027 Zurich, Switzerland. TEL 41-1-2883500. FAX 41-1-2883565. Ed. Dr. Roland Mueller. adv.; bk.rev.; illus.; stat.; index. circ. 12,000. (also avail. in microfilm from UMI) **Indexed:** Account.& Data Proc.Abstr., C.I.S. Abstr., Ergon.Abstr., Excerpt.Med., Key to Econ.Sci., SCIMP (1982-). **Document type:** trade publication.
   —CISTI; Linda Hall; SWETS; UMI.
    Formerly: I O Management Zeitschrift (ISSN 0019-9281)
    Description: Features research in automation, manufacturing, production, technology, organization, personnel and marketing. Includes events, courses, new products, software news, and positions available.

658   LE
AL-IDARI. (Text in Arabic) 1976. m. $125. Dar Assayad S.A.L., P.O. Box 1038, Hazmieh, Beirut, Lebanon. FAX 961-1-456373. (UK addr.: c/o Contact PR & Mgt (UK) Ltd., 3 Park Pl., 12 Lawn Ln., London SW8, England. TEL 071-582-2220) Ed. H. El Khoury. adv. contact: Salim Zreik. circ. 25,350. (back issues avail.)

658   MX   ISSN 0188-7181
HC131
IDEA ECONOMICA. 1982. q. $50 (effective 1997). Universidad Iberoamericana, Division Economico Administrativa, Prol. Paseo de la Reforma 880, Col. Lomas de Santa Fe, 01210 Mexico DF, Mexico. TEL 52-5-2923883. FAX 52-5-7231104. Ed. Gabriela Romero. bk.rev.; index. circ. 10,000. **Document type:** academic/scholarly publication.
    Description: Contains economic, administrative and accounting information and analysis.

658   GW   ISSN 0940-7693
DER IDEENBRIEF FUER DEN CHEF. 1991. m. DM.234. Verlag Norbert Mueller AG und Co. KG, Ingolstaedterstr. 20, 80807 Munich, Germany. TEL 49-89-3509302. FAX 49-89-35093218. Ed. Ralf Koschut. index. circ. 2,500. (back issues avail.) **Document type:** newsletter.

ILLINOIS LEGAL TIMES. see *LAW*

658   AT   ISSN 0310-0316
IMPACT (DUNDAS).* 1972. q. Aus.$5. Association of Foremen and Supervisors, 50 Moffats Dr., Dundas, N.S.W. 2117, Australia. Ed. Ted Young. adv.; bk.rev. circ. 1,500. **Indexed:** World Bibl.Soc.Sec.

658   FR
IMPACT MEDECIN. 45/yr. 600 F. 20 bd. du Parc, 92521 Neuilly-sur-Seine Cedex, France. TEL 46-41-33-00. FAX 46-41-02-00. TELEX 613 715. Ed. J. de Charon. circ. 90,000. **Document type:** newspaper.

BUSINESS AND ECONOMICS — MANAGEMENT

658 — **UK**
IMPERIAL COLLEGE MANAGEMENT REPORTS. 1992. irreg. (Imperial College, Management School) Whurr Publishers Ltd., 19B Compton Terrace, London N1 2UN, England. TEL 44-171-359-5979. FAX 44-171-226-5290. E-mail: 101325.1205@compuserve.com. (Subscr. to: Turpin Distribution Services, Blackhorse Rd., Letchworth, Herts SG6 1HN, England. TEL 44-1462-672555. FAX 44-1462-480947) Ed.Bd. **Document type:** academic/scholarly publication, monographic series.

658.8 — **IT** — **ISSN 0035-6816**
HF5387
IMPRESA; rivista italiana di management. (Text in Italian; summaries in English) 1959. 10/yr. L.128000 (foreign L.230000). L' Impresa Edizioni s.r.l., Via Paolo Lomazzo 52, 20154 Milan, Italy. TEL 39-2-31-031. FAX 39-2-310-37-18. Ed. Enrico Sassoon. adv.: color page L.5000000. bk.rev.; charts; index. circ. 10,121. **Indexed:** ELLIS, J.of Econ.Lit., SCIMP (1989-).
—BLDSC (4371.467000).
Formerly: Rivista Italiana di Amministrazione Industriale; Which incorporated: Ratio (ISSN 0034-0014)

658.2 — **GW** — **ISSN 0344-4546**
IMPULS; Zeitung fuer Sicherheit im Betrieb. 1968. m. membership. Berufsgenossenschaft der Feinmechanik und Elektrotechnik, Postfach 510580, 50941 Cologne, Germany. (Co-sponsor: Berufsgenossenschaft der Chemischen Industrie) Ed. Walter Mertzig. **Indexed:** Fluidex.

IN BUSINESS (MADISON); Dane county's business magazine. see *BUSINESS AND ECONOMICS — Domestic Commerce*

INDEPENDENT BUSINESS. see *BUSINESS AND ECONOMICS*

658 — **II** — **ISSN 0019-5812**
HD70.I4
INDIAN MANAGEMENT; business and management. (Text and summaries in English) 1963. m. Rs.112($30) All Indian Management Association, Management House, 14 Institutional Area, Lodi Rd., New Delhi 110 003, India. TEL 617354. FAX 91-11-4626689. TELEX 031-74066 AIMA IN. Ed. Utpal K. Banerjee; Pub. Vinod Shanbhag. adv.: B&W page Rs.4000, color page Rs.8000; trim 210 x 280; adv. contact: Laila Ramanathan. bk.rev.; charts; illus.; stat.; index. circ. 10,000. (back issues avail.; reprint service avail. from KTO) **Indexed:** Manage.Abstr.
—BLDSC (4422.580000); UMI.
Incorporates (1972-1989): Management Abstracts.

658 — **II** — **ISSN 0046-9025**
INDIAN MANAGER. (Text in English) 1970. q. Rs.100($28) Cochin University of Science and Technology, School of Management Studies, Cochin 682 022, Kerala, India. TEL 91-484-555310. FAX 91-484-532495. Eds. K.C. Sankaranarayanan, Jose T. Payyappilly. adv.; bk.rev.; bibl.; charts. circ. 1,000.

658.4 — **US** — **ISSN 1078-8476**
HD38.25.I6
INDIANAPOLIS C.E.O. 1988. m. $19.95; newsstand price: $2.25. Metropolitan C.E.O., 911 E. 86th St., Ste. 100, Indianapolis, IN 46240-1840. TEL 317-257-8000. FAX 317-257-1482. Ed. Julie Sturgeon; Pub. Joe Cole. adv.: B&W page $3830; trim 8 3/8 x 10 7/8; adv. contact: Joe Cole. circ. 30,000 (controlled). (back issues avail.) **Document type:** trade publication.
●Also available online.

INDUSTRIAL AND COMMERCIAL TRAINING; management of human resources. see *BUSINESS AND ECONOMICS — Personnel Management*

INDUSTRIAL ENGINEERING AND MANAGEMENT. see *ENGINEERING — Industrial Engineering*

658.5 — **US** — **ISSN 0019-8471**
HD28 CODEN: IMNGDM
INDUSTRIAL MANAGEMENT. 1952. bi-m. $39 (foreign $50). Institute of Industrial Engineers, 25 Technology Park-Atlanta, Norcross, GA 30092. TEL 770-449-0460; 800-494-0460. FAX 770-263-8532. bk.rev.; abstr.; charts; illus.; index. circ. 8,000. (reprint service avail. from UMI) **Indexed:** ABI Inform., B.P.I., BPIA, Bus.Ind., Intl.Mgmt.Info., Manage.Cont., Oper.Res.Manage.Sci., Qual.Contr.Appl.Stat., Text.Tech.Dig., Work Rel.Abstr. **Document type:** trade publication.
●Also available online. Vendor(s): Information Access Co., UMI.
—BLDSC (4457.700000); AskIEEE; Ei; KR SourceOne; Linda Hall; SWETS; UMI; UnCover. **CCC.**
Description: Offers management advice for professionals in various industries. Articles cover productivity improvement, management technologies, automation applications, and management techniques.

658.3 — **JA** — **ISSN 0036-438X**
INDUSTRIAL TRAINING/SANGYO KUNREN. (Text in Japanese) 1955. m. 9600 Yen to non-members; members 7200 Yen. Japan Industrial Training Association - Nihon Sangyo Kunren Kyokai, 6th Floor, Minamizuka Bldg., 2-17-3 Shibuya, Shibuya-ku, Tokyo 150, Japan. TEL 03-3409-3551. FAX 03-3409-7334. Ed. Fukuda Hiroshi. adv.; bk.rev.; abstr.; stat. circ. 5,000. **Indexed:** JTA.

658 — **SW** — **ISSN 1101-5578**
INDUSTRIELL FOERNYELSE; regional utveckling i Sverige och Europa - kompetens, infrastruktur, internationalisering, omstrukturering, teknikspridning, allianser. (Includes Naetverket) 1990. 20/yr. SEK 1600 membership (effective 1991). Industriell Information, Nygraend 10, S-111 30 Stockholm, Sweden.

INDUSTRY REPORT ON PROFESSIONAL AND SCIENTIFIC PERSONNEL COMPENSATION. see *BUSINESS AND ECONOMICS — Personnel Management*

658 — **US** — **ISSN 1041-908X**
HD4965.5.U6
INDUSTRY REPORT ON SUPERVISORY MANAGEMENT COMPENSATION. (Supplement to: Supervisory Management Report - Geographic Edition) a. $490. (Executive Compensation Service (ECS)) Wyatt Data Services, 218 Rte. 17, N., Roselle Park, NJ 07662-9832. TEL 201-843-1177. FAX 201-843-0101. charts. **Document type:** trade publication.
Description: Supervisory pay data examined from an industry-by-industry perspective.

INDUSTRY REPORT ON TECHNICIAN AND SKILLED TRADES PERSONNEL COMPENSATION. see *BUSINESS AND ECONOMICS — Personnel Management*

658 — **US** — **ISSN 0039-0895**
TS300 CODEN: IWEEA4
INDUSTRY WEEK; the industry management magazine. 1882. 23/yr. $60 (free to qualified personnel). Penton Publishing Co. (Subsidiary of: Pittway Company), 1100 Superior Ave., Cleveland, OH 44114-2543. TEL 216-696-7000. FAX 216-969-7670. URL: http://www.industryweek.com. (Subscr. to: Box 95759, Cleveland, OH 44101) Ed. John Brandt. adv.: page $15930. illus.; charts; mkt.; stat.; s-a. index; circ. 233,000 (controlled). (also avail. in microform from UMI; reprint service avail. from UMI) **Indexed:** A.I.Abstr., A.S.& T.Ind., ABI Inform., B.P.I., BPIA, Bus.Ind., CAD CAM Abstr., Comput.Indus.Up., Comput.Lit.Ind., Eng.Ind., Environ.Abstr., Hlth.Ind., Intl.Mgmt.Info., Mag.Ind., Manage.Cont., Met.Abstr., Pers.Lit., PROMT, PSI, Q.Abstr., Resour.Ctr.Ind., Robomat., SRI, Tel.Abstr., Telegen, Tr.& Dev.Alert, Tr.& Indus.Ind., Work Rel.Abstr., World Alum.Abstr. **Document type:** trade publication.
●Also available online. Vendor(s): Information Access Co., Knight-Ridder Information, Inc., Lexis-Nexis, UMI.
—BLDSC (4478.235000); AskIEEE; CISTI; Ei; Genuine Article; KR SourceOne; Linda Hall; SWETS; UMI; UnCover. **CCC.**
Incorporates (1930-1995): Electronics (ISSN 0883-4989); Formerly (1930-1969): Steel.
Description: Covers general management techniques for the purposes of improving industrial productivity, motivating employees and increasing profitability.

INFO BURO MAG. see *FOOD AND FOOD INDUSTRIES*

658 — **CN** — **ISSN 0828-525X**
INFO OUTLOOK (YEAR); a guide to trends and sources for the information community. 1985. irreg. free. Information Plus, Inc., 2 Bloor St., W. Ste. 404, Toronto, ON M4W 3E2, Canada. TEL 416-968-1062. FAX 416-968-2591. Ed. D.C. Sawyer. circ. 1,000. (back issues avail.) **Document type:** newsletter.
—**CCC.**

INFORM (SILVER SPRING); the magazine of information and image management. see *COMPUTERS — Information Science And Information Theory*

658 — **GR** — **ISSN 1105-5502**
INFORMATION. 1986. m. Dr.12500 in Europe; Dr.13500 in U.S. (effective 1996). Compupress S.A., 44 Syngrou, 117 42 Athens, Greece. TEL 30-1-9238-672. FAX 30-1-9216-847. Ed. M. Daskalakis; Pub. N.O. Manousos. adv. contact: V. Giakamozis. bk.rev. circ. 15,000. (back issues avail.)
Description: Concerned with management marketing and economics on an international and national level in Greece.

658 — **FR** — **ISSN 0153-9868**
INFORMATION FISCALE ET SOCIALE.* 1964. m. (Union des Fonctionnaires des Finances en Europe) Centre de Documentation et Informations, 19 ave. Pierre, B.P. 130, Brossolette, 9254 Montrouge Cedex, France. Ed. Jacques Michelot.

658 — **US** — **ISSN 1080-286X**
CODEN: INMAF8
INFORMATION MANAGEMENT.* 1988. s-a. $40 to individuals; institutions $60. (Information Resources Management Association) Idea Group Publishing, 1331 E. Chocolate Ave., Hershey, PA 17033-1117. TEL 717-541-9150. FAX 717-541-9159. E-mail: 75364,3150@compuserve.com. Ed. Mehdi Khosrowpour. bk.rev.; tr.lit. circ. 800. **Indexed:** INSPEC (1993-). **Document type:** newsletter, bulletin.
—BLDSC (4493.686300); AskIEEE; KR SourceOne.
Formerly: Information Management Bulletin (ISSN 1046-9303)
Description: Digest of information advancements in the information resources management field. Enumerates current and future issues and trends in the field of information technology.

658 020 — **UK** — **ISSN 0968-5227**
T58.64 CODEN: IMCSE4
INFORMATION MANAGEMENT & COMPUTER SECURITY. 1992. 5/yr. L£1289($1979) (foreign Aus.$2499) (effective 1998). M C B University Press Ltd., 60-62 Toller Ln., Bradford, W. Yorks BD8 9BY, England. TEL 44-1274-777700. FAX 44-1274-785200. TELEX 51317-MCBUNI-G. URL: http://www.mcb.co.uk. Eds. John Beaumont, Kevin Fitzgerald. (reprint service avail. from SWZ) **Indexed:** INSPEC (1993-), LISA. **Document type:** academic/scholarly publication.
—BLDSC (4493.687056); AskIEEE; KR SourceOne; UMI. **CCC.**
Formed by merger of (1990-1992): International Journal of Information Resource Management (ISSN 0956-4225); (1982-1992): Computer Control Quarterly (ISSN 0813-7099)

658 — **US**
INFORMATION MANAGEMENT FOR REHABILITATION ADMINISTRATORS.* m. Center for Management Systems, 11 Twin Oaks E., Sioux Falls, SD 57105-7015. TEL 712-568-2418.

658 020 — **US** — **ISSN 1040-1628**
CODEN: IRMAEZ
INFORMATION RESOURCES MANAGEMENT JOURNAL.* 1988. q. $65 to individuals; institutions $110. (Information Resource Management Association) Idea Group Publishing, 1331 E. Chocolate Ave., Hershey, PA 17033-1117. TEL 717-541-9150. FAX 717-541-9159. E-mail: 75364,3150@compuserve.com. Ed. Mehdi Khosrowpour. adv.; bk.rev.; circ. 500 (controlled). (also avail. in microform from UMI) **Indexed:** Anbar, Bus.Educ.Ind., Comput.Lit.Ind., Inform.Sci.Abstr., INSPEC (1988-). **Document type:** academic/scholarly publication.
—BLDSC (4494.145000); AskIEEE; KR SourceOne; SWETS; UMI; UnCover.
Description: Provides a forum on information resources management technology among academicians, practitioners and public officials. Includes interviews with leading experts in the field. *Refereed Serial*

BUSINESS AND ECONOMICS — MANAGEMENT

658 US ISSN 0824-3514
INFORMATION SOLUTIONS; a newsletter of ideas and techniques about how to profit from information. 1984. bi-m. $65 to individuals; institutions $115; students $35. Information Plus Inc., 14 Lafayette Square, Ste. 2000, Buffalo, NY 14203-1920. TEL 716-852-2220. FAX 716-852-1653. (In Canada: 2 Bloor St. W., Ste. 404, Toronto, ON M4W 3E2, Canada. TEL 416-968-1062. FAX 416-968-2591) Ed. D.C. Sawyer. (back issues avail.) **Document type:** newsletter.
Description: Discusses the use of competitive market, supplier and customer intelligence in business. Each issue is devoted to an intelligence theme.

001.64 US ISSN 0743-8613
INFORMATION STRATEGY: THE EXECUTIVE'S JOURNAL. 1984. q. $172.25 (overseas $258.45) (effective 1995). Warren, Gorham & Lamont, One Penn Plaza, New York, NY 10119. TEL 212-367-6300. FAX 212-367-6718. (Subscr. to: The Park Square Bldg., 31 St. James Ave., Boston, MA 02116-4112. TEL 800-950-1207) Ed. L.R. DeJarnett. bk.rev. circ. 3,055. (reprint service avail. from SCH) **Indexed:** ABI Inform., B.P.I., Comput.Lit.Ind., INSPEC (1986-). **Document type:** trade publication.
—BLDSC (4496.352000); AskIEEE; CISTI; KR SourceOne; SWETS; UMI; UnCover. **CCC**.
Description: Helps senior executives without DP backgrounds make policy and strategy decisions about business and information management, gain a competitive advantage through the use of information systems, assess IS departments, and manage IS applications.

658 US ISSN 1057-7939
Z678.9.A1
INFORMATION TECHNOLOGY NEWSLETTER; * international newsletter of information technology and libraries. 1990. s-a. $20 to individuals; institutions $35. Idea Group Publishing, 1331 E. Chocolate Ave., Hershey, PA 17033-1117. TEL 717-541-9150. FAX 717-541-5195. E-mail: 75364,3150@compuserve.com. Ed. Karen Cullings. circ. 750. **Document type:** newsletter.
—BLDSC (4496.368879).
Description: Designed to help librarians strategically plan aspects of implementing information technology resources.

658 IT ISSN 0390-2447
INFORMAZIONI AZIENDALI E PROFESSIONALI. 1974. 36/yr. De Lillo Editore s.r.l., Via Mecenate 76,3, 20138 Milan, Italy. TEL 39-2-58043112. FAX 39-2-58012450. Ed. Pietro de Lillo. circ. 14,000.

INFRASTRUCTURE (NEW YORK). see *ENGINEERING — Civil Engineering*

658 MX
INGENIERIA DE COSTOS. 1970. 4/yr. Mex.$25 per no. (Sociedad Mexicana de Ingenieria de Costos, A.C.) D'Pastrana Editores, S.A., Kepler 147-A, Mexico 5, D.F., Mexico. Ed. Jorge L. Castillo Tufino. adv.; circ. 5,000 (controlled).

INLINE RETAILER & INDUSTRY NEWS. see *SPORTS AND GAMES*

371.3 360 US ISSN 1053-2587
HC79.T4
INNOVATING. 1990. q. $24 (Canada $42) (effective 1993). Rensselaerville Institute, Pond Hill Rd., Rensselaerville, NY 12147. TEL 518-797-3783. FAX 518-797-5270. E-mail: thetute@aol.com. Ed. Harold S. Williams. R&P contact: Anna Y. Dickerson. bk.rev. circ. 1,500. (back issues avail.) **Indexed:** Soc.Work Res.& Abstr. **Document type:** academic/scholarly publication.
Description: Discusses innovative assumptions, paradigms, and examples of leadership, for individuals and organizations.

658 NE
INNOVATIONS IN FINANCIAL MARKETS AND INSTITUTIONS. (Text in English) irreg., latest 1992. price varies. Kluwer Academic Publishers, Postbus 17, 3300 AA Dordrecht, Netherlands. TEL 31-78-6392392. FAX 31-78-6392254. TELEX 29245 KAPG NL. E-mail: services@wkap.nl; URL: http://www.wkap.nl. (Dist. by: Kluwer Academic Publishers Group, P.O. Box 322, 3300 AH Dordrecht, Netherlands. TEL 31-78-6392392. FAX 31-78-6546474; N. America dist. addr.: Box 358, Accord Sta., Hingham, MA 02018-0358. TEL 617-871-6600. FAX 617-871-6528) **Document type:** monographic series.

658 UK ISSN 0304-4270
INSEAD ALUMNI ASSOCIATION ADDRESS BOOK. 1968. a. £95. (I N S E A D Alumni Association) A P Information Services, Roman House, 296 Golders Green Rd., London NW11 9PZ, England. TEL 0181-455-1607. FAX 0181-455-6381. Ed. Alan Philipp. adv.: B&W & color, B&W page £4,200; trim 210 x 148. circ. 9,200. (also avail. in diskette format) **Document type:** directory.

INSIDE P P M CS. see *MEDICAL SCIENCES*

INSIDE RADIO; the latest news, trends and management information. see *COMMUNICATIONS — Radio*

658 330.9 GW
INSTITUT DER DEUTSCHEN WIRTSCHAFT. FORUM. 1951. w. DM.82.82. Deutscher Instituts Verlag GmbH, Postfach 510670, 50942 Cologne, Germany. TEL 49-221-4981452. FAX 49-221-4981592. index. circ. 1,300. (back issues avail.) **Document type:** bulletin.
Formerly (until 1988): Institut der Deutschen Wirtschaft. Vortragsreihe.

INSTITUT PANAFRICAIN POUR LE DEVELOPPEMENT. CENTRE D'ETUDES ET DE RECHERCHES APPLIQUEES. EVALUATION DU SEMINAIRE SUR LA METHODOLOGIE DU MANAGEMENT DES PROJETS. see *BUSINESS AND ECONOMICS — International Development And Assistance*

INSTITUT PANAFRICAIN POUR LE DEVELOPPEMENT. CENTRE DE FORMATION AU MANAGEMENT DES PROJETS. BILAN DES ACTIVITES. see *BUSINESS AND ECONOMICS — International Development And Assistance*

658.007 IO
INSTITUTE FOR MANAGEMENT EDUCATION AND DEVELOPMENT. REPORT. (Text in English) 1980. a. $20. Institute for Management Education and Development - Lembaga Pendidikan dan Pembinaan Management, Jalan Mentang Raya 9, Jakarta, Indonesia. circ. 10,000.

INSTITUTE NEWS. see *PHARMACY AND PHARMACOLOGY*

658 SA
INSTITUTE OF ADMINISTRATION AND COMMERCE OF SOUTH AFRICA. JOURNAL. (Text in Afrikaans and English) 1967. 4/yr. membership. Institute of Administration & Commerce of South Africa, Plein St., Box 2907, Cape Town 8000, South Africa. Ed.Bd. adv.; illus. circ. 7,200. (back issues avail.)
Formerly: Business and Administration (ISSN 0007-6449)

658 TZ
INSTITUTE OF DEVELOPMENT MANAGEMENT. REPORT OF THE ACTIVITIES OF THE INSTITUTE. 1973. a. Institute of Development Management, P.O. Box 5, Mzumbe-Morogoro, Tanzania. circ. 500. **Document type:** corporate report.

658 UK ISSN 0967-652X
INSTITUTE OF MANAGEMENT INTERNATIONAL DATABASES PLUS. 1992. q. £799($1395) (effective 1997). (Institute of Management) Bowker - Saur Ltd., A member of the Reed Elsevier plc group, Maypole House, Maypole Rd., E. Grinstead, W. Sussex RH19 1HU, England. TEL 44-1342-330100. FAX 44-1342-330191. E-mail: custserv@bowker-saur.co.uk; URL: http://www.reed-elsevier.com. **Document type:** trade publication.
● Available only on CD-ROM. Producer(s): Bowker - Saur Ltd.
Former titles: British Institute of Management International Databases Plus; British Institute of Management Databases on C D - R O M.

658 II ISSN 0971-1864
INSTITUTE OF PUBLIC ENTERPRISE. JOURNAL. (Text in English) 1978. q. Rs.50($20) Institute of Public Enterprise, Osmania University Campus, Hyderabad 500 007, India. TEL 868937. TELEX 0425-7064 IPE IN. Ed. T.L. Sankar. adv.; bk.rev. circ. 800.
Former titles (until 1990, vol.13, no.1): I P E Journal; I.P.E. News Letter.
Description: Devoted to professional and academic research in the economics and management aspects of public enterprises.

658 AG ISSN 0325-9064
INSTITUTO PARA EL DESARROLLO DE EJECUTIVOS EN LA ARGENTINA. REVISTA. no.8, 1977. m. $25. Instituto para el Desarrollo de Ejecutivos en la Argentina, Sistema de Actualizacion Empresaria, Moreno 1850, Buenos Aires, Argentina. adv.; bk.rev.
Formerly: Instituto para el Desarrollo de Ejecutivos en la Argentina. Noticias.

658 005 US ISSN 0092-2102
HD28 CODEN: INFAC
INTERFACES (LINTHICUM). 1971. bi-m. $75 to individuals (foreign $87); institutions $114 (foreign $126) (effective 1997). Institute for Operations Research and the Management Sciences, 901 Elkridge Landing Rd., Ste. 400, Linthicum, MD 21090-2909. TEL 410-850-0300; 800-343-0062. Ed. Michael Rothkopf. R&P contact: Fran Silverman. adv. contact: Kathye Long. bk.rev. circ. 5,849. (also avail. in microform from UMI; reprint service avail. from UMI) **Indexed:** ABI Inform., Abstr.Hum.Comp.Inter., B.P.I, BMT, BPIA, Bus.Ind., Compumath, Comput.Abstr., Comput.Cont., Comput.Rev., Cont.Pg.Manage., Curr.Cont., Data Process.Dig., Ergon.Abstr., Excerp.Med., INSPEC, Int.Abstr.Oper.Res., Intl.Mgmt.Info., J.Cont.Quant.Meth., Lang.& Lang.Behav.Abstr., Lang.Teach.& Ling.Abstr., Manage.Cont., Oper.Res.Manage.Sci., Pers.Manage.Abstr., Psychol.Abstr., Qual.Contr.Appl.Stat., SSCI, Tr.& Indus.Ind., Work Rel.Abstr. **Document type:** academic/scholarly publication.
—BLDSC (4533.461000); AskIEEE; CISTI; Genuine Article; KR SourceOne; Linda Hall; SWETS; UMI; UnCover. **CCC**.
Formerly: Institute of Management Sciences Bulletin (ISSN 0020-2916)

THE INTERMOUNTAIN RETAILER. see *FOOD AND FOOD INDUSTRIES — Grocery Trade*

658 UK ISSN 0965-5999
INTERNAL COMMUNICATION FOCUS. 10/yr. $395 (effective Jan. 1997). Armstrong International Ltd., The Courtyard, 12 Hill St., St. Helier, Jersey JE2 4UB, Channel Islands. TEL 44-1534-613650. FAX 44-1534-613651. E-mail: 106001.446@compuserve.com. Ed. Joanna Reeves; Pub. Richard Armstrong. (back issues avail.) **Document type:** trade publication.

INTERNATIONAL ARTS MANAGER. see *ART*

INTERNATIONAL FASHION GROUP. ANNUAL REPORT. see *CLOTHING TRADE — Fashions*

INTERNATIONAL FASHION GROUP. BULLETIN. see *CLOTHING TRADE — Fashions*

INTERNATIONAL FASHION GROUP. NEWSLETTER. see *CLOTHING TRADE — Fashions*

658 332.6 US ISSN 1056-9219
CODEN: ICMAFX
INTERNATIONAL JOURNAL OF COMMERCE AND MANAGEMENT. 1991. q. $40 to individuals; institutions $70 (effective 1997). Indiana University of Pennsylvania, International Academy of Business Disciplines, Indiana, PA 15705. TEL 412-357-5759. FAX 412-357-5743. E-mail: aaali@grove.iup.edu. (Subscr. to: Box 1659, Indiana, PA 15705) Ed. Abbas J. Ali. R&P contact: Abbas J. Ali. adv. contact: Ramesh Soni. bk.rev. **Document type:** academic/scholarly publication.
—BLDSC (4542.172450).
Description: Promotes the understanding of managers and organizations within and across nations. Directed toward academicians, policy makers and practitioners in business and non-profit organizations.
Refereed Serial

BUSINESS AND ECONOMICS — MANAGEMENT

658 320   US   ISSN 1044-4068
HD42   CODEN: IOCMEY
INTERNATIONAL JOURNAL OF CONFLICT MANAGEMENT. 1990. q. $52 to individuals (foreign $62); institutions $129 (foreign $139); students $45 (foreign $55) (effective 1996). Center for Advanced Studies in Management, 1574 Mallory Ct., Bowling Green, KY 42103-1300. TEL 502-782-2601. Ed. M. Afzalur Rahim. adv.; bk.rev. **Indexed:** ASCA, Curr.Cont., Fam.Ind., Per.Islam. (1990-). **Document type:** academic/scholarly publication.
—BLDSC (4542.175700); Genuine Article; UnCover. **CCC.**
   Description: Publishes original empirical and conceptual articles, case studies, simulations, and teaching notes on various aspects of conflict management.

658   UK   ISSN 0951-354X
INTERNATIONAL JOURNAL OF EDUCATIONAL MANAGEMENT. bi-m. £1329($1999) (foreign Aus.$2599) (effective 1998). M C B University Press Ltd., 60-62 Toller Ln., Bradford, W. Yorks BD8 9BY, England. TEL 44-1274-777700. FAX 44-1274-785200. TELEX 51317-MCBUNI-G. URL: http://www.mcb.co.uk. Ed. B. E. Roberts. (reprint service avail. from SWZ) **Indexed:** Br.Educ.Ind., Cont.Pg.Educ., Educ.Tech.Abstr., SOMA, Tech.Educ.Abstr. **Document type:** academic/scholarly publication.
—BLDSC (4542.199700); UMI. **CCC.**
   Description: Seeks to widen the horizons of education and management by focusing on a whole range of related issues. The Journal crosses the conventional boundaries which separate the two fields.

INTERNATIONAL JOURNAL OF HOSPITALITY MANAGEMENT. see HOTELS AND RESTAURANTS

658   NE   ISSN 0167-7187
HD28   CODEN: IJIODY
INTERNATIONAL JOURNAL OF INDUSTRIAL ORGANIZATION. (Text in English) 1983. bi-m. fl.930($534) (effective 1998). North-Holland (Subsidiary of: Elsevier Science B.V.), P.O. Box 211, 1000 AE Amsterdam, Netherlands. TEL 31-20-4853911. FAX 31-20-4853598. TELEX 18582 ESPA NL. (Subscr. in the Americas to: Elsevier Science, Regional Sales Office, Box 945, New York, NY 10159-0945. TEL 212-633-3730. FAX 212-633-3680; Subscr. in Australasia and the Far East to: Elsevier Science (Singapore) Pte Ltd, No.1 Temasek Ave., No.17-01 Millenia Tower, Singapore 039192, Singapore. TEL 65-434-3727. FAX 65-337-2230; Subscr. in Japan to: Elsevier Science Japan, 9-15 Higashi-Azabu 1-chome, Minato-ku Tokyo 106, Japan. TEL 81-3-5561-5033. FAX 81-3-5561-5047) Eds. Paul Geroski, Norman Ireland. bk.rev.; stat.; index. (also avail. in microfiche; back issues avail.; reprint service avail. from SWZ) **Indexed:** ABI Inform., ASCA, C.R.E.J., Cont.Pg.Manage., Curr.Cont., J.of Econ.Abstr., J.of Econ.Lit., Sage Pub.Admin.Abstr., SCIMP (1985-), SSCI. **Document type:** academic/scholarly publication.
—BLDSC (4542.304500); Genuine Article; SWETS; UMI; UnCover. **CCC.**
   Description: Provides a full coverage of both theoretical and empirical work within the field of industrial organization, as well as covering traditional issues of market structure and performance.
Refereed Serial

658   CH   ISSN 1017-1819
T58.6   CODEN: IIMSEQ
INTERNATIONAL JOURNAL OF INFORMATION AND MANAGEMENT SCIENCES. (Text in English) q. NT.$800($60) Tamkang University, Graduate Institute of Management Sciences, King Hwa St., Taipei, Taiwan 10606, Republic of China. Ed. C.L. Sheng. abstr.; bibl.; charts; stat. circ. 400. **Indexed:** Curr.Cont., INSPEC (1990-), Math.R., Zent.Math. **Document type:** academic/scholarly publication.
—BLDSC (4542.304850); AskIEEE; Ei; KR SourceOne.
   Formed by the 1990 merger of: Tamkang Journal of Management Sciences (ISSN 0255-6863) & International Journal on Policy and Information.
   Description: Publishes original contributions on information systems, general systems, stochastic systems, transportation systems, industrial management, industrial engineering, management sciences, regional science, decision science, operations research, and applied statistics.

658   SI   ISSN 1363-9196
▼**INTERNATIONAL JOURNAL OF INNOVATION MANAGEMENT.** Abbreviated title: I J I M. (Text in English) 1997. 4/yr. $100 to individuals; institutions $200. World Scientific Publishing Co. Pte. Ltd., Farrer Rd., P.O. Box 128, Singapore 9128, Singapore. TEL 65-3825663. FAX 65-3825919. E-mail: wspcsl@singnet.com.sg; sales@wspc2.demon.co.uk; wspc@wspc.com; URL: http://www.singnet.com.sg/-wspclib/. (UK addr.: 57 Shelton St., Covent Garden, London WC2H 9HE, England. TEL 44-171-836-0888. FAX 44-171-836-2020; US addr.: 1060 Main St., Ste. 1B, River Edge, NJ 07661. TEL 800-227-7562. FAX 201-487-9656) Ed. Joe Tidd. **Document type:** academic/scholarly publication.
   Description: Dedicated to the advancement of academic research and management practice in the field of innovation management.

658   US
INTERNATIONAL JOURNAL OF LOGISTICS MANAGEMENT. 1990. 2/yr. $75 (foreign $85). International Logistics Research Institute, Inc., Box 2166, Pt. Vedra Beach, FL 32004-2166. TEL 904-880-8653. FAX 904-880-8654. Eds. Douglas Lambert, Martin Christopher. adv. contact: Marian C. Kuhn. bk.rev.; circ. 2,000 (paid). (back issues avail.) **Document type:** academic/scholarly publication.
   Description: Aims to provide executives and teachers with reports of current developments in the fields of logistics management and supply chain management. Facilitates the interchange of information about logistics management among business planners and researchers on a worldwide basis.
Refereed Serial

658 657   UK   ISSN 0813-0183
INTERNATIONAL JOURNAL OF MANAGEMENT. 1984. q. £60($120) (effective 1997 & 1998). P.O. Box 982, Poole, Dorset BH12 5YF, England. Ed. Christopher Orpen. R&P contact: Anna Orpen. adv. contact: Anna Orpen. circ. 1,000 (paid). **Indexed:** Anbar, Bus.Ind., Cont.Pg.Manage., Curr.Cont.(1993-), Pers.Manage.Abstr., Stat.Theor.Meth.Abstr. (1993-), Work Rel.Abstr. **Document type:** academic/scholarly publication.
—BLDSC (4542.325700); SWETS.
Refereed Serial

658   II   ISSN 0970-7328
INTERNATIONAL JOURNAL OF MANAGEMENT AND SYSTEMS. (Text in English) 1985. 3/yr. $48. (Technocrat Publications Centre) Hindustan Publishing Corp., 4805-24, 1st Fl., Bharat Ram Rd., Darya Ganj, New Delhi 110 002, India. TEL 91-11-3254401. FAX 91-11-6863511. E-mail: hpcpd@giasdl01.vsnl.net.in.
—BLDSC (4542.325720).
   Formerly (until 1988): Indian Journal of Management and Systems (ISSN 0970-0439)

658   UK   ISSN 0144-3577
TS155.A1   CODEN: IOPMDU
INTERNATIONAL JOURNAL OF OPERATIONS AND PRODUCTION MANAGEMENT. 1980. m. £2379($3689) (foreign Aus.$4629) (effective 1998). M C B University Press Ltd., 60-62 Toller Ln., Bradford, W. Yorks BD8 9BY, England. TEL 44-1274-777700. FAX 44-1274-785200. TELEX 51317-MCBUNI-G. URL: http://www.mcb.co.uk/cgi-bin/mcb_serve/table1.txt&ijopm&journal1.htm. Ed.Bd. cum.index. (reprint service avail. from SWZ) **Indexed:** ABI Inform., Account.& Data Proc.Abstr., ASCA, BPIA, Bus.Ind., Cont.Pg.Manage., Curr.Cont., INSPEC, Int.Abstr.Oper.Res. **Document type:** academic/scholarly publication.
●Also available online. Vendor(s): Information Access Co.
Also available on CD-ROM.
—BLDSC (4542.425000); AskIEEE; Ei; Genuine Article; KR SourceOne; SWETS; UMI; UnCover. **CCC.**
   Description: Examines the managerial, rather than the technical manufacturing problems of operating systems.

658.8   US   ISSN 1082-1910
INTERNATIONAL JOURNAL OF OPERATIONS AND QUANTITATIVE MANAGEMENT. Abbreviated title: I J O Q M. 1995. 3/yr. Indiana University Northwest, Division of Business and Economics, 3400 Broadway, Gary, IN 46408-1197. TEL 219-980-6500. URL: http://www.iun.indiana.edu/busad.htm. Ed. Omprakash K. Gupta. adv.; bk.rev.; abstr. **Document type:** academic/scholarly publication.
—BLDSC (4542.427000).
   Description: Provides an international forum to discuss advancements in operations management, operations research, quantitative management, and management science.
Refereed Serial

658   US   ISSN 1055-3185
HD28   CODEN: IJOAEN
THE INTERNATIONAL JOURNAL OF ORGANIZATIONAL ANALYSIS. 1993. q. $52 to individuals (foreign $62); institutions $129 (foreign $139); students $45 (foreign $55). Center for Advanced Studies in Management, 1574 Mallory Ct., Bowling Green, KY 42103-1300. TEL 502-782-2601. URL: http://irc.mcmaster.ca/irc/journals/ijoa.htm. Ed. M. Afzalur Rahim. R&P contact: Masuda Rahim. adv.; bk.rev. **Indexed:** Cont.Pg.Manage., Per.Islam. (1993-). **Document type:** academic/scholarly publication.
—BLDSC (4542.435200). **CCC.**
   Description: Publishes original empirical and conceptual articles, case studies, teaching notes in the following areas: business and society, organization theory, organizational behavior, strategic management, and human resource management.

INTERNATIONAL JOURNAL OF PRODUCTION ECONOMICS; an international journal for industry. see ENGINEERING — Industrial Engineering

INTERNATIONAL JOURNAL OF PROJECT MANAGEMENT. see BUSINESS AND ECONOMICS — Computer Applications

658   UK   ISSN 0951-3558
HD3840
INTERNATIONAL JOURNAL OF PUBLIC SECTOR MANAGEMENT. 7/yr. £879($1299) (foreign Aus.$1599) (effective 1998). M C B University Press Ltd., 60-62 Toller Ln., Bradford, W. Yorks BD8 9BY, England. TEL 44-1274-777700. FAX 44-1274-785200. TELEX 51317-MCBUNI-G. URL: http://www.mcb.co.uk. Ed. Colin Talbot. (reprint service avail. from SWZ) **Indexed:** Anbar, ASSIA, Geo.Abstr.H.G., Geo.Abstr.P.G., IDA. **Document type:** academic/scholarly publication.
—BLDSC (4542.509200); SWETS; UMI. **CCC.**
   Description: Includes contributions from a wide diversity of interests within public sector management: the civil service, health and education services, local government and state organizations in developed and developing countries.

658   UK   ISSN 0265-671X
TS156   CODEN: IJQMEZ
INTERNATIONAL JOURNAL OF QUALITY & RELIABILITY MANAGEMENT. 1985. 9/yr. £2129($3289) (foreign Aus.$4149) (effective 1998). M C B University Press Ltd., 60-62 Toller Ln., Bradford, W. Yorks BD8 9BY, England. TEL 44-1274-777700. FAX 44-1274-785200. TELEX 51317-MCBUNI-G. URL: http://www.mcb.co.uk. Eds. Alf Keller, Barrie Dale. (reprint service avail. from SWZ) **Indexed:** ABI Inform., Anbar, Cont.Pg.Manage., Tech.Educ.Abstr. **Document type:** academic/scholarly publication.
●Also available online. Vendor(s): Information Access Co.
—BLDSC (4542.510000); CISTI; Ei; SWETS; UMI. **CCC.**
   Description: Aims to provide the essential information needed to achieve competitive standards in an easily assimilated form. Describes new techniques and systems - focusing particularly on their application.

658   UK   ISSN 1359-8538
TS156.A1
▼INTERNATIONAL JOURNAL OF QUALITY SCIENCE.
1996. q. £159($249) (effective 1997). M C B
University Press Ltd., 60-62 Toller Ln., Bradford, W.
Yorks BD8 9BY, England. TEL 44-1274-777700.
FAX 44-1274-785200. URL: http://www.mcb.co.uk.
Document type: academic/scholarly publication.
●Also available online.
—BLDSC (4542.511000). CCC.
   Description: Provides and outlet for academic
research and scientific studies in the quality field.

658   338   UK   ISSN 0956-4233
HD9980.1
INTERNATIONAL JOURNAL OF SERVICE INDUSTRY
MANAGEMENT. 1990. 5/yr. £919($1429) (foreign
Aus.$1799) (effective 1998). M C B University
Press Ltd., 60-62 Toller Ln., Bradford, W. Yorks BD8
9BY, England. TEL 44-1274-777700.
TELEX 51317-MCBUNI-G.
URL: http://www.mcb.co.uk. Ed. Robert Johnston.
(reprint service avail. from SWZ) Indexed: ASCA,
Cont.Pg.Manage., Curr.Cont., Mgmt.& Market.Abstr.
Document type: academic/scholarly publication.
—BLDSC (4542.544680); Genuine Article; SWETS;
UMI. CCC.
   Description: Provides current information on
research and developments worldwide in
management within the service sector.

INTERNATIONAL JOURNAL OF TECHNOLOGY
MANAGEMENT. see TECHNOLOGY:
COMPREHENSIVE WORKS

658   US   ISSN 0895-8815
HD60   CODEN: IVBMEA
INTERNATIONAL JOURNAL OF VALUE-BASED
MANAGEMENT. 1988. 3/yr. fl.270 to institutions;
$138.50 to institutions in U.S. (effective 1998).
(Iona College, Hagan School of Business) Kluwer
Academic Publishers Boston, Box 358, Accord Sta.,
Hingham, MA 02018-0358. TEL 617-871-6600.
FAX 617-871-6528. E-mail: services@wkap.nl; URL:
http://www.wkap.nl. (Dist. outside N. America by:
Kluwer Academic Publishers Group, P.O. Box 322,
3300 AH Dordrecht, Netherlands. TEL
31-78-6392392. FAX 31-78-6546474) Ed.
Samuel M. Natale. bk.rev. circ. 500. Indexed: Work
Rel.Abstr. Document type: academic/scholarly
publication.
—BLDSC (4542.697300); UnCover. CCC.
   Description: Publishes case studies, empirical
studies, comparative studies and review papers
clarifying the roles of values in organizational
behavior and decision making.
   Refereed Serial

INTERNATIONAL REVIEW OF ADMINISTRATIVE
SCIENCES. see PUBLIC ADMINISTRATION

658   UK   ISSN 1067-9987
INTERNATIONAL REVIEW OF PROFESSIONAL ISSUES IN
SELECTION AND ASSESSMENT. 1993. a. John Wiley
& Sons Ltd., Journals, Baffins Ln., Chichester, W.
Sussex PO19 1UD, England.
TEL 44-1243-779777. FAX 44-1243-843232.
E-mail: cs-journals@wiley.co.uk; URL: http://www.
wiley.co.uk. Document type: academic/scholarly
publication.
—BLDSC (4547.512000).
   Refereed Serial

658   NE   ISSN 1055-7180
INTERNATIONAL STUDIES IN GLOBAL CHANGE. irreg.,
vol.7, 1995. Gordon and Breach - Harwood
Academic, Amsteldisk 166, 1st Fl., 1079 LH
Amsterdam, Netherlands. (Subscr. to: International
Publishers Distributor, Box 32160, Newark, NJ
07102. TEL 800-545-8398. FAX 215-750-6343)
Eds. Tom Burns, Thomas Dietz. (also avail. in
microform; back issues avail.) Document type:
monographic series.
—BLDSC (4549.786000).
   Description: Publishes investigations of human
ecology, technology and management and their
interrelations.
   Refereed Serial

650   US   ISSN 0020-8825
HD28
INTERNATIONAL STUDIES OF MANAGEMENT AND
ORGANIZATION. 1971. q. $110 to individuals
(foreign $160); institutions $540 (foreign $620)
(effective 1997). M.E. Sharpe, Inc., 80 Business
Park Dr., Armonk, NY 10504. TEL 914-273-1800;
800-541-6563. FAX 914-273-2106. Ed. J.
Boddewyn. adv.: page $300; 5 x 8; adv. contact:
Barbara Ladd. (back issues avail.) Indexed: ABI
Inform., Asian-Pac.Econ.Lit., BPIA, Bus.Ind., IBR,
Manage.Cont., Mid.East: Abstr.& Ind. Document type:
academic/scholarly publication.
●Also available online. Vendor(s): Information Access
Co., UMI.
—BLDSC (4549.790000); SWETS; UMI; UnCover.
CCC.
   Formerly: International Journal of Management
and Organization.
   Description: Publishes English translations of
international articles on business administration.
   Refereed Serial

INTERNATIONAL TRANSACTIONS IN OPERATIONAL
RESEARCH. see COMPUTERS

INTERNET BUSINESS ADVANTAGE; online solutions for
business success. see COMPUTERS — Data
Communications And Data Transmission Systems

658   IR
IQTISAD VA MUDIRIYAT/ECONOMIC AND MANAGEMENT
QUARTERLY JOURNAL OF THE ISLAMIC AZAD
UNIVERSITY. (Text in English, Persian) no.7, 1991.
q. IRl.500 per no. Danishgah-i Azad-i Islami - Islamic
Azad University, P.O. Box 19395-1775, Tehran,
Iran.
   Description: Scholarly papers on topics in
economics and management with an Islamic
perspective.

658   US   ISSN 0730-9368
J. CROSS EXECUTIVE ALERT.* m. $60. J. Cross
Consulting Service, Box 846, San Diego, CA 92112.
TEL 619-584-7727.

658   JA   ISSN 0287-5802
J M A JANARU/JAPAN MANAGEMENT ASSOCIATION.
JOURNAL. 1942. m. Nippon Noritsu Kyokai, 1-22,
Shiba Koen 3-chome, Minato-ku, Tokyo 105, Japan.
adv. circ. 27,805.
   Formed by the merger of (1951-1982):
Manejimento (ISSN 0287-5799); I E: Industrial
Engineering (ISSN 0445-0612)

658   NE   ISSN 1381-4109
JAARBOEK OVERHEIDSCOMMUNICATIE. 1993. a.
(Vereniging voor Overheidscommunicatie) Vuga
Uitgeverij B.V., Postbus 16400, 2500 BK The
Hague, Netherlands. TEL 31-70-3614011.
FAX 31-70-3632338. adv.: B&W page fl.2235;
color page fl.4335; trim 155 x 240. circ. 1,500.
Document type: trade publication.

658   UK   ISSN 0968-7130
HD70.J3
JAPAN MANAGEMENT REVIEW. 1993. q. £459($699)
(effective 1997). M C B University Press Ltd., 60-62
Toller Ln., Bradford, W. Yorks BD8 9BY, England.
TEL 44-1274-777700. FAX 44-1274-785200.
URL: http://www.mcb.co.uk. Ed. Alan Margerison.
(reprint service avail. from SWZ) Indexed:
Text.Tech.Dig. Document type: academic/scholarly
publication.
—CCC.

JIANZHU GUANLI XIANDAIHUA/CONSTRUCTION
MANAGEMENT MODERNIZATION. see BUILDING AND
CONSTRUCTION

658   CC   ISSN 1002-5766
JINGJI GUANLI/ECONOMIC MANAGEMENT. (Text in
Chinese) 1979. m. Y18($48.50) (Zhongguo Shehui
Kexueyuan, Gongye Jingji Yanjiusuo - Chinese
Academy of Social Sciences, Institute of Industrial
Economics) Jingji Guanli Chubanshe - Economic
Management Publishing House, 8, Hongyuan
Hutong, 6 Tiao, Xinjiekou, Beijing 100035, People's
Republic of China. TEL 2253756. (Dist. outside
China by: China International Book Trading Corp.,
P.O. Box 399, Beijing, P.R.C. TEL 8413063; Dist. in
US by: China Books & Periodicals, Inc., 2929 24th
St., San Francisco, CA 94110. TEL 415-282-2994)
Ed. Zhang Zuoyuan. adv. contact: Li Li. bk.rev. circ.
110,000.
   Description: Covers theories, experiences and
policies of Chinese and foreign economic
management.

658   CC   ISSN 1002-8668
JINGJI GUANLI WENZHAI/ECONOMIC MANAGEMENT
DIGEST. (Text in Chinese) 1987. s-m. Y120 (foreign
$120). (Guojia Jingji Tizhi Gaige Weiyuanhui - State
Commission for Restructuring the Economics) Jingji
Guanli Wenzhai Bianjibu, No. 11, Rendinghu
Beixiang, Huangshi Dajie, Beijing 100011, People's
Republic of China. TEL 86-10-6201-5945.
FAX 86-10-6204-9117. E-mail: cmie@public3.bta.
net.cn. (Dist. overseas by: China International Book
Trading Corp., P.O. Box 399, Beijing 100044, P.R.
China) Ed. Haichun Chen; Pub. Jingrao Zhang. R&P
contact: Xinying Lin. adv. contact: Jingrao Zhang.
bk.rev. pp./issue: 32. Document type:
abstracting/indexing.
   Description: Abstracts of articles and researches
on economic policies, trends, investment
environment, market conditions and economic
management.
   Refereed Serial

658   330.1   US   ISSN 1000-596X
JINGJI LILUN YU JINGJI GUANLI/ECONOMIC THEORY &
BUSINESS MANAGEMENT. (Text in Chinese) bi-m.
$35.10. China Books & Periodicals, Inc., 2929 24th
St., San Francisco, CA 94110. TEL 415-282-2994.
FAX 415-282-0994.

658   CC   ISSN 1003-3890
JINGJI YU GUANLI/ECONOMICS AND MANAGEMENT.
(Text in Chinese) 1986. bi-m. newsstand price:
Y1.50. Hebei Jingji Guanli Ganbu Xueyuan, Wu Qi
Lu, Beijiao (North Suburb), Shijiazhuang, Hebei
050061, People's Republic of China.
TEL 0311-639306. Ed. Liu Chunzhong. adv.; bk.rev.
circ. 5,000. Document type: academic/scholarly
publication.
   Formerly (until 1988): Hebei Jingji Guanli Ganbu
Xueyuan Xuebao.

658   330   CC   ISSN 1000-7636
JINGJI YU GUANLI YANJIU/RESEARCH ON ECONOMICS
AND MANAGEMENT. (Text in Chinese) 1980. bi-m.
$22.10. Beijing Jingji Xueyuan - Beijing Institute of
Economics, Hongmiao, Chaoyangmen, Beijing
100026, People's Republic of China.
TEL 86-1-5061188. (Dist. outside China by: China
International Book Trading Corp., P.O. Box 2820,
Beijing, P.R.C.; Dist. in US by: China Books &
Periodicals, Inc., 2929 24th St., San Francisco, CA
94110. TEL 415-282-2994) Ed. Ningwu Qu.
bk.rev. Document type: academic/scholarly
publication.
—UnCover.

658   CC   ISSN 1003-3475
JINGYING YU GUANLI. (Text in Chinese) m. Tianjin Qiye
Guanli Xiehui, 16, Shuishang Gongyuan Lu,
Nankai-qu, Tianjin 300191, People's Republic of
China. TEL 348615. Ed. Song Fucheng.

658   CC   ISSN 1004-292X
JISHU JINGJI YU GUANLI YANJIU/TECHNOECONOMICS
AND MANAGEMENT RESEARCH. (Text in Chinese,
English) 1980. bi-m. $4. Shanxi Sheng Jishu Jingji
Yanjiu Zhongxin, 18 Wenyuanxiang, Rm. 233,
Xinjian Nan Lu, Taiyuan, Shanxi 030001, People's
Republic of China. TEL 86-351-2021450.
FAX 86-351-4040802. Ed. Zhu Guanxin. adv.: page
$1800; adv. contact: Dai Ziwei. circ. 280,000.

BUSINESS AND ECONOMICS — MANAGEMENT

658 US ISSN 1041-1488
JOB TRAINING AND PLACEMENT REPORT. 1978. m. $117 (effective 1997). (Center for Management Systems) Jones Publishing Inc., Box 5000, N. 7450 Aanstad Rd., Iola, WI 54945. TEL 715-445-5000. FAX 415-445-4053. Ed. Diane Nordell. adv.; bk.rev. circ. 3,000. **Indexed:** PROMT, Rehabil.Lit.
Formerly (until 1988): Information Management (ISSN 0197-6524)
Description: For professionals and organizations who train and place people with disabilities into employment. Includes practical marketing tips, funding program opportunities and technologies available.

658 II
JODHPUR MANAGEMENT JOURNAL. 1971. a. Rs.15($5) University of Jodhpur, Department of Management Studies, Jodhpur 342 001, Rajasthan, India. Ed. Raj K. Agarwala. adv.; bk.rev. circ. 1,000.

JOHN LINER LETTER. see INSURANCE

JOHN LINER REVIEW. see INSURANCE

JOURNAL CONTENTS IN QUANTITATIVE METHODS. see BUSINESS AND ECONOMICS — Abstracting, Bibliographies, Statistics

658 GW ISSN 0949-6181
JOURNAL FOR EAST EUROPEAN MANAGEMENT STUDIES. 1982. q. DM.84. Rainer Hampp Verlag, Meringerzellerstr. 16, 86415 Mering, Germany. TEL 49-8233-4783. FAX 49-8233-30755. E-mail: rainer__hampp__verlag@t-online.de. Ed. R. Lang. **Document type:** academic/scholarly publication.
—BLDSC (4971.510000).
Description: Designed to promote a dialogue between East and West over issues emerging from management practice, theory and related research in the transforming societies of Central and Eastern Europe.
Refereed Serial

658 AU ISSN 0344-9327
JOURNAL FUER BETRIEBSWIRTSCHAFT. 1950. 6/yr. S.896. Linde Verlag Wien GmbH, Scheydgasse 24, A-1210 Vienna, Austria. TEL 43-1-313364692. FAX 43-1-31336712. E-mail: michael.nitsche@wu-wien.ac.at. Ed. Michael Nitsche. R&P contact: Heidelinde Langmayr. bk.rev. circ. 1,000. (reprint service avail. from SCH) **Indexed:** Key to Econ.Sci., SCIMP (1982-). **Document type:** academic/scholarly publication.
—BLDSC (4951.520000); SWETS.
Description: Promotion of academic research in business administration and management.
Refereed Serial

658 387.7 UK ISSN 0969-6997
HE9781
JOURNAL OF AIR TRANSPORT MANAGEMENT. 1994. q. fl.477($274) (effective 1998). Elsevier Science Ltd., Pergamon, P.O. Box 800, Kidlington, Oxford OX5 1DX, England. TEL 44-1865-843000. FAX 44-1865-843010. E-mail: nlinfo-f@elsevier.nl; usinfo-f@elsevier.com; forinfo-kyf04035@niftyserve.or.jp; URL: http://www.elsevier.nl/. (Subscr. to: Elsevier Science, Regional Sales Office, P.O. Box 211, 1000 AE Amsterdam, Netherlands. TEL 31-20-4853757. FAX 31-20-4853432; Subscr. in the Americas to: Elsevier Science, Regional Sales Office, Box 945, New York, NY 10159-0945. TEL 212-633-3730. FAX 212-633-3730; Subscr. in Australasia and the Far East to: Elsevier Science (Singapore) Pte Ltd, No.1 Temasek Ave., No.17-01 Millenia Tower, Singapore 039192, Singapore. TEL 65-434-3727. FAX 65-337-2230) Ed. Rigas Doganis. bk.rev. (also avail. in microform from UMI; back issues avail.) **Document type:** academic/scholarly publication.
—BLDSC (4926.550000); SWETS; UMI; UnCover.
Description: Provides an international forum among practioners and academics for important issues affecting the air transport industry. Focuses on analyzing developments and trends while encouraging speculative and creative thought about new operational or managerial concepts or challenges.
Refereed Serial

658 UK ISSN 1360-0796
JOURNAL OF APPLIED MANAGEMENT STUDIES. 1973-1980; resumed N.S. 1992. s-a. £36($52) to individuals; institutions £112 ($148) (effective 1997). (University of Wolverhampton) Carfax Publishing Co., P.O. Box 25, Abingdon, Oxon. OX14 3UE, England. TEL 44-1235-401000. FAX 44-1235-401550. E-mail: enquiries@carfax.co.uk. (Subscr. in N. America to: Carfax Publishing Co., 875-81 Massachusetts Ave., Cambridge, MA 02139) Ed. Sue Williams. adv.; bk.rev.; index. circ. 300. (also avail. in microfiche; back issues avail.) **Indexed:** B.P.I., Br.Hum.Ind., C.R.E.J., Manage.Abstr., World Bank.Abstr. **Document type:** academic/scholarly publication.
—BLDSC (4942.660000). **CCC.**
Formerly (until vol.5): Journal of Industrial Affairs (ISSN 0143-084X)
Description: Provides a forum for debate on issues facing managers in different functional, sectoral, national and cultural settings. Aims to improve and enhance anagement practice through the transfer of recent advances in management theory and research into such practice.
Refereed Serial

658 US
▼**JOURNAL OF APPLIED QUALITY MANAGEMENT.** Announced for publication in 1998. q. $50 (foreign $70) to individuals; institutions $175 (foreign $195) (effective 1998). J A I Press Inc., 55 Old Post Rd., No. 2, Box 1678, Greenwich, CT 06830-1678. TEL 203-661-7602. FAX 203-661-0792. E-mail: jai@jaipress.com. (Subscr. in the UK and Europe to: JAI Press Ltd., 38 Tavistock St., Covent Garden, London WC2E 7PB, England. TEL 44-171-379-8834. FAX 44-171-379-8835) **Document type:** academic/scholarly publication.

658 UK ISSN 0894-3257
CODEN: BDMAEU
JOURNAL OF BEHAVIORAL DECISION MAKING. 1988. q. $345 (foreign $345) (effective 1998). John Wiley & Sons Ltd., Journals, Baffins Ln., Chichester, W. Sussex PO19 1UD, England. TEL 44-1243-779777. FAX 44-1243-775878. E-mail: info-assets@wiley.co.uk; URL: http://www.wiley.co.uk. (Subscr. in N. America to: John Wiley & Sons, Inc., 605 Third Ave., New York, NY 10158. TEL 212-850-6645. FAX 212-850-6021) Ed. George Wright. adv.: B&W page £595, color page £1495; trim 260 x 200; adv. contact: Bob Kern. circ. 417. (also avail. in microform from UMI; back issues avail.; reprint service avail. from SWZ) **Indexed:** ASCA, Comput.Abstr., Curr.Cont.(1992-), INSPEC (1990-), Psychol.Abstr. (1988-), SSCI, Stat.Theor.Meth.Abstr. (1992-). **Document type:** academic/scholarly publication.
—BLDSC (4951.256600); AskIEEE; Genuine Article; KR SourceOne; SWETS; UMI; UnCover. **CCC.**
Description: Covers research in psychology, management science, sociology, political science and economics.

658 CN ISSN 0021-941X
JOURNAL OF BUSINESS ADMINISTRATION. 1969. s-a. Can.$20($16) University of British Columbia, Faculty of Commerce and Business Administration, Vancouver, BC V6T 1Z2, Canada. TEL 604-822-9434. FAX 604-822-8489. Ed. Peter N. Nemetz. adv.; bk.rev.; bibl.; illus. circ. 400. (also avail. in microform from UMI; reprint service avail. from MML, UMI, SCH) **Indexed:** ABI Inform., BPIA, Bus.Ind., Can.B.P.I., Cont.Pg.Manage., Manage.Cont.
●Also available online. Vendor(s): Information Access Co.
—BLDSC (4954.658000); SWETS; UMI; UnCover. **CCC.**

651.7 US ISSN 0021-9436
HF5718 CODEN: JBCOAO
JOURNAL OF BUSINESS COMMUNICATION.* 1963. q. $40 includes Association for Business Communication Bulletin. Association for Business Communication, c/o Dr. Rovert J. Myers, Dept. of Speech Communication, Baruch College, 17 Lexington Ave., New York, NY 10010. TEL 817-565-4423. E-mail: 70511.753@compuserve.com; URL: http://www.cohums.ohio-state.edu/english/facstf/kol/abc/jbc.html. Ed. Lamar Reinsch. adv.; bk.rev.; charts; index. circ. 2,475. (also avail. in microform from UMI; reprint service avail. from SCH,UMI) **Indexed:** ABI Inform., Abstr.Anthropol., B.P.I, BPIA, Bus.Educ.Ind., Bus.Ind., C.I.J.E., Commun.Abstr., Manage.Cont. **Document type:** academic/scholarly publication.
●Also available online. Vendor(s): Information Access Co., UMI.
—BLDSC (4954.665000); KR SourceOne; SWETS; UMI; UnCover.
Description: Contains major papers dealing with important areas and aspects of business communication.

JOURNAL OF BUSINESS LOGISTICS. see BUSINESS AND ECONOMICS — Marketing And Purchasing

658 330.01 US ISSN 0148-2963
HF5001 CODEN: JBRED4
JOURNAL OF BUSINESS RESEARCH. 1973. 9/yr. fl.1221($702) (effective 1998). Elsevier Science Inc., Box 945, New York, NY 10159-0945. TEL 212-633-3730. FAX 212-633-3680. TELEX 420643 AEP UI. E-mail: usinfo-f@elsevier.com; URL: http://www.elsevier.nl:80/inca/publications/store/5/0/5/7/2/2/505722.pub.shtml. (Subscr. outside the Americas to: Elsevier Science, Regional Sales Office, P.O. Box 211, 1000 AE Amsterdam, Netherlands. TEL 31-20-4853757. FAX 31-20-4853432; Subscr. in Australasia and the Far East to: Elsevier Science (Singapore) Pte Ltd, No.1 Temasek Ave., No.17-01 Millenia Tower, Singapore 039192, Singapore. TEL 65-434-3727. FAX 65-337-2230; Subscr. in Japan to: Elsevier Science Japan, 9-15 Higashi-Azabu 1-chome, Minato-ku, Tokyo 106, Japan. TEL 81-3-5561-5033. FAX 81-3-5561-5047) Ed. Arch G. Woodside. adv.; bk.rev.; bibl. (also avail. in microform from UMI; reprint service avail. from SWZ,UMI) **Indexed:** ABI Inform., Anbar, ASCA, B.P.I, BPIA, Bus.Ind., Commun.Abstr., Cont.Pg.Manage., Curr.Cont., Manage.Cont., Mid.East: Abstr.& Ind., Oper.Res.Manage.Sci., P.A.I.S., Pers.Manage.Abstr., Psychol.Abstr. (1983-), Qual.Contr.Appl.Stat., Risk Abstr., SSCI, Tr.& Indus.Ind., Work Rel.Abstr. **Document type:** academic/scholarly publication.
—BLDSC (4954.715000); Genuine Article; KR SourceOne; SWETS; UMI; UnCover. **CCC.**
Formerly (until 1979): Southern Journal of Business (ISSN 0038-4259)
Description: Applies theory developed from business research to actual business situations.
Refereed Serial

658.4012 US ISSN 0887-2058
JOURNAL OF BUSINESS STRATEGIES. 1984. s-a. Gibson D. Lewis Center for Business and Economic Development, Sam Houston State University, Huntsville, TX 77341. Ed. Jo Ann Duffy.
—BLDSC (4954.716500); UnCover.

658   US   ISSN 0275-6668
HD28   CODEN: JBSTDK
JOURNAL OF BUSINESS STRATEGY. 1980. bi-m. $98 (foreign [$128) (effective 1995). Faulkner & Gray, Inc. (New York), 11 Penn Plaza, 17th Fl., New York, NY 10001. TEL 212-967-7000; 800-535-8403. FAX 212-967-7155. URL: http://www.faulknergray.com/business/business.html. Ed. Bristol Lane Voss; Pub. Michael Winkleman. adv. contact: Xavier Jenkins. illus. circ. 9,051. (also avail. in microform from UMI; reprint service avail. from SCH,UMI) **Indexed:** ABI Inform., Account.& Data Proc.Abstr., ASEAN Manage.Abstr., B.P.I, BPIA, Bus.Ind., Cont.Pg.Manage., Manage.Cont., Mgmt.& Market.Abstr., P.A.I.S., PROMT, Q.Abstr., Sage Urb.Stud.Abstr., SCIMP, Tr.& Dev.Alert, Tr.& Indus.Ind.
• Also available online. **Vendor(s):** Information Access Co., UMI.
— BLDSC (4954.717000); CASDDS; KR SourceOne; SWETS; UMI; UnCover.
Incorporates (1975-1995): Small Business Reports (ISSN 0164-5382)
Description: Covers theory and practice of strategy, planning, implementation and competitive analysis.

JOURNAL OF CLINICAL EFFECTIVENESS. see *MEDICAL SCIENCES*

658 380   UK   ISSN 1363-254X
▼ **JOURNAL OF COMMUNICATION MANAGEMENT.** 1996. q. £120 to Europe; U.S. & Canada $180; rest of world £135. Henry Stewart Publications, Russell House, 28-30 Little Russell St., London WC1A 2HN, England. TEL 44-171-404-3040. FAX 44-171-404-2081. E-mail: 100622.3264@compuserve.com. (Subscr. in US and Canada to: 810 E. 10th St., Box 1897, Lawrence, KS 66044. TEL 913-843-1221. FAX 913-843-1274) Ed. Daryn Moody. adv. contact: Fraser Tant. **Document type:** trade publication.
— BLDSC (4961.634900).
Description: Concerned with the latest developments and thinking in the management of internal and external communications.
Refereed Serial

658   UK   ISSN 0966-0879
HD49
JOURNAL OF CONTINGENCIES AND CRISIS MANAGEMENT. 1993. q. £130($178) (foreign £130) (effective 1997). Blackwell Publishers Ltd., 108 Cowley Rd., Oxford OX4 1JF, England. TEL 44-1865-791100. FAX 44-1865-791347. E-mail: jnlinfo@blackwellpublishers.co.uk; URL: http://www.blackwellpublishers.co.uk. Eds. Uriel Rosenthal, Alexander Kouzmin. (reprint service avail. from SWZ) **Indexed:** Geo.Abstr.P.G., IDA, Int.Polit.Sci.Abstr. **Document type:** academic/scholarly publication.
— BLDSC (4965.244000); SWETS; UMI. **CCC.**
Description: Discusses all aspects of contingency planning, scenario management, and crisis management for executives and researchers in corporate, agency, and government.
Refereed Serial

JOURNAL OF CUSTOMER SERVICE IN MARKETING & MANAGEMENT; innovations for service, quality & value. see *BUSINESS AND ECONOMICS*

JOURNAL OF ECONOMICS & MANAGEMENT STRATEGY. see *BUSINESS AND ECONOMICS — Economic Systems And Theories, Economic History*

658 338   NE   ISSN 0923-4748
TA190   CODEN: JETMEQ
JOURNAL OF ENGINEERING AND TECHNOLOGY MANAGEMENT. (Text in English) 1981. q. fl.470($270) (effective 1998). Elsevier Science B.V., P.O. Box 211, 1000 AE Amsterdam, Netherlands. TEL 31-20-4853911. FAX 31-20-4853598. TELEX 18582 ESPA NL. E-mail: nlinfo-f@elsevier.nl; usinfo-f@elsevier.com; forinfo-kyf04035@niftyserve.or.jp; URL: http://www.elsevier.nl/. (Subscr. in the Americas to: Elsevier Science, Regional Sales Office, Box 945, New York, NY 10159-0945. TEL 212-633-3730. FAX 212-633-3680; Subscr. in Australasia and the Far East to: Elsevier Science (Singapore) Pte Ltd, No.1 Temasek Ave., No.17-01 Millenia Tower, Singapore 039192, Singapore. TEL 65-434-3727. FAX 65-337-2230; Subscr. in Japan to: Elsevier Science Japan, 9-15 Higashi-Azabu 1-chome, Minato-ku, Tokyo 106, Japan. TEL 81-3-5561-5033. FAX 81-3-5561-5047) Ed. M.K. Badawy. (also avail. in microform from UMI; reprint service avail. from SWZ) **Indexed:** ABI Inform., ASCA, BPIA, Curr.Cont., Energy Info.Abstr., Eng.Ind., Environ.Abstr., INSPEC (1981-), J.of Ferroc., Manage.Cont., Soc.Sci.Ind., Tech.Educ.Abstr. **Document type:** academic/scholarly publication.
— BLDSC (4978.550000); AskIEEE; CISTI; Ei; Genuine Article; KR SourceOne; Linda Hall; SWETS; UMI; UnCover. **CCC.**
Formerly (until 1989): Engineering Management International (ISSN 0167-5419)
Description: Links engineering and management disciplines to address issues involved in planning, development, and implementation of technological capabilities that shape and accomplish the strategic and operational objectives of an organization. Includes research and development, the managing of process technology and product technology.
Refereed Serial

658   II   ISSN 0971-3557
JOURNAL OF ENTREPRENEURSHIP. 1992. s-a. $75 to institutions (effective Sep. 1996). (Entrepreneurship Development Institute of India) Sage Publications India Pvt. Ltd., P.O. Box 4215, New Delhi 110 048, India. TEL 91-11-644-4958. FAX 91-11-647-2426. (Overseas subscr. to: Sage Publications, Ltd., 6 Bonhill St., London EC2A 4PU, England. TEL 44-171-374-0645. FAX 44-171-374-8741; Subscr. in N. America to: Sage Publications, Inc., 2455 Teller Rd., Thousand Oaks, CA 91320. TEL 805-499-0721. FAX 805-477-0871) Ed. Dwijendra Tripathi; Pub. Tejeshwar Singh. adv.: page Rs.1500. bk.rev.; abstr.; index. circ. 500. (back issues avail.; reprint service avail.) **Document type:** academic/scholarly publication.
— BLDSC (4979.354500).
Description: Publishes original contributions, both conceptual and empirical. Useful to researchers, policymakers, practicing entrepreneurs, as well as students and teachers of management and development processes.
Refereed Serial

658.3   UK   ISSN 0309-0590
HF5549.5.T7   CODEN: JEITDP
JOURNAL OF EUROPEAN INDUSTRIAL TRAINING. 1977. 9/yr. £3799($5899) (foreign Aus.$5849) (effective 1998). M C B University Press Ltd., 60-62 Toller Ln., Bradford, W. Yorks BD8 9BY, England. TEL 44-1274-777700. FAX 44-1274-785200. TELEX 51317-MCBUNI-G. URL: http://www.mcb.co.uk. Ed. Thomas Garavan. adv.; charts; illus. (reprint service avail. from SWZ) **Indexed:** ABI Inform., Account.& Data Proc.Abstr., Anbar, ASEAN Manage.Abstr., BPIA, Br.Educ.Ind., Bus.Ind., C.I.J.E., Cont.Pg.Educ., Cont.Pg.Manage., Curr.Cont., Educ.Tech.Abstr., High.Educ.Curr.Aware.Bull., Manage.Cont., Mgmt.& Market.Abstr., Mult.Ed.Abstr., Res.High.Educ.Abstr., Sage Pub.Admin.Abstr., SCIMP (1978-), SOMA, Stud.Wom.Abstr., Tech.Educ.Abstr., Tr.& Dev.Alert. **Document type:** academic/scholarly publication.
• Also available online. **Vendor(s):** Information Access Co.
— BLDSC (4979.605000); CISTI; SWETS; UMI. **CCC.**
Formerly: H R D: Human Resource Development.
Description: Covers training techniques and effectiveness, new developments and their application, self-development, new research, sales and marketing training, company-based experience, and management education.

658 301   UK   ISSN 0277-6693
H61.4   CODEN: JOFODV
JOURNAL OF FORECASTING. 1981. 7/yr. $575 (foreign $575) (effective 1998). John Wiley & Sons Ltd., Journals, Baffins Ln., Chichester, W. Sussex PO19 1UD, England. TEL 44-1243-779777. FAX 44-1243-775878. E-mail: info-assets@wiley.co.uk; URL: http://www.wiley.com/wilcat-bin/ops/ID1/0277-6693/prod. (Subscr. in the Americas to: John Wiley & Sons, Inc., 605 Third Ave., New York, NY 10158. TEL 44-243-779777. FAX 44-243-776128) Ed. Derek Bunn. adv.: B&W page £595, color page £1495; trim 260 x 200; adv. contact: Bob Kern. (also avail. in microform from UMI; back issues avail.; reprint service avail. from SWZ,UMI) **Indexed:** ABI Inform., Account.& Data Proc.Abstr., ASCA, BPIA, C.R.E.J., CLOSS, Comput.Abstr., Cont.Pg.Manage., Curr.Cont. (1988-), Curr.Ind.Stat., Int.Abstr.Oper.Res., J.Cont.Quant.Meth., Met.Abstr., Oper.Res.Manage.Sci., P.A.I.S., Qual.Contr.Appl.Stat., SCIMP, SSCI, Stat.Theor.Meth.Abstr. (1988-), Tr.& Indus.Ind., W.R.C.Inf., World Alum.Abstr. **Document type:** academic/scholarly publication.
— BLDSC (4984.577000); CASDDS; Genuine Article; SWETS; UMI; UnCover. **CCC.**
Description: Designed to provide a centralized focus on recent developments in the art and science of forecasting.
Refereed Serial

658   UK   ISSN 0306-3070
HD28   CODEN: JGMAAX
JOURNAL OF GENERAL MANAGEMENT. 1973. q. £105($250) (foreign £140) (effective Sep. 1995). Braybrooke Press Ltd., The Coach House, Remenham House, Remenham Hill, Henley-on-Thames, Oxon. RG9 3EP, England. TEL 01491-412061. FAX 01491-411428. Ed. Keith MacMillan. adv.; bk.rev.; illus. circ. 1,000. (reprint service avail. from SWZ) **Indexed:** ABI Inform., Account.& Data Proc.Abstr., Anbar, ASEAN Manage.Abstr., Asian-Pac.Econ.Lit., BPIA, Bus.Ind., Cont.Pg.Manage., Curr.Cont., Excerp.Med., Key to Econ.Sci., Manage.Cont., Mgmt.& Market.Abstr., P.A.I.S., SCIMP (1978-), SSCI, Work Rel.Abstr., World Bank.Abstr. **Document type:** academic/scholarly publication.
— BLDSC (4987.900000); SWETS; UMI; UnCover.
Description: Aims to help top managers understand the main economic, social, political and technological issues that affect the success of their organization. Keeps the readers up-to-date with new developments in theory and practice of general management.

658   US   ISSN 1062-7375
T58.64   CODEN: JGLMEY
JOURNAL OF GLOBAL INFORMATION MANAGEMENT. 1993. q. $65 to individuals; institutions $125. (Information Resources Management Association) Idea Group Publishing, 1331 E. Chocolate Ave., Hershey, PA 17033-1117. TEL 717-541-9150. FAX 717-541-9159. E-mail: 75364,3150@compuserve.com. Ed. Prashant Palvia. **Indexed:** Bus.Educ.Ind., INSPEC (1993-). **Document type:** academic/scholarly publication.
— BLDSC (4996.270000); AskIEEE; KR SourceOne; UMI.
Description: Publishes research and practical articles related to a broad range of topics in global information technology management, including managerial, technological, and behavioral aspects of international information systems.

JOURNAL OF HEURISTICS. see *PHILOSOPHY*

JOURNAL OF HIGH TECHNOLOGY MANAGEMENT RESEARCH. see *BUSINESS AND ECONOMICS — Computer Applications*

JOURNAL OF HUMAN VALUES. see *PHILOSOPHY*

658   UK   ISSN 1364-3142
JOURNAL OF INTERIM MANAGEMENT AND CONSULTANCY; research into quality flexible resources. q. £139($219) (effective 1997). M C B University Press Ltd., 60-62 Toller Ln., Bradford, W. Yorks BD8 9BY, England. TEL 44-1274-777700. FAX 44-1274-785200. **Document type:** academic/scholarly publication.

JOURNAL OF INTERNATIONAL FINANCIAL MARKETS, INSTITUTIONS & MONEY. see *BUSINESS AND ECONOMICS — Banking And Finance*

BUSINESS AND ECONOMICS — MANAGEMENT

JOURNAL OF INTERNATIONAL HOSPITALITY, LEISURE AND TOURISM MANAGEMENT; a multinational and cross-cultural journal of applied research. see HOTELS AND RESTAURANTS

658.4 US ISSN 1063-519X
T58.64
JOURNAL OF INTERNATIONAL INFORMATION MANAGEMENT. 1992. s-a. $65 to non-members (effective 1996 & 1997). International Information Management Association, Department of Information and Decision Sciences, California State University, San Bernardino, CA 92407. TEL 909-880-5786. FAX 909-880-5994. E-mail: trohm@gallium.csusb.edu. Ed. C.E. Tarif Rohm Jr. R&P contact: Walter T. Stewart. adv. contact: Diana Catalano. bk.rev.; software rev.; circ. 1,000 (paid). **Document type:** academic/scholarly publication.
—BLDSC (5007.664000); AskIEEE; KR SourceOne.
Description: Reports the findings of scholars and practitioners who are concerned with information management.
Refereed Serial

658 US ISSN 1075-4253
HD62.4 CODEN: JIMAFI
▼**JOURNAL OF INTERNATIONAL MANAGEMENT.** 1995. q. $160 (Canada & Mexico $200; elsewhere $226) (effective 1997). (Thunderbird American Graduate School of International Management) John Wiley & Sons, Inc., Journals, 605 Third Ave., New York, NY 10158. TEL 212-850-6645. FAX 212-820-6021. TELEX 12-7063. E-mail: SUBINFO@JWILEY.COM; URL: http://www.wiley.co.uk. (Subscr. outside N. America to: John Wiley & Sons Ltd., Baffins Ln., Chichester, W. Sussex PO19 1UD, England. TEL 44-1243-779777. FAX 44-1243-776128) Ed. David A. Ricks. adv.; B&W page £640, color page ££1515; trim 254 x 178. circ. 850. (also avail. in microform from UMI; back issues avail.) **Document type:** academic/scholarly publication.
—BLDSC (5007.673200). CCC.
Description: Reports on the latest theoretical and empirical research into all major international management issues.
Refereed Serial

658 US ISSN 1071-7919
HD57.7
JOURNAL OF LEADERSHIP STUDIES. 1993. q. $59.95 (effective 1995 & 1996). Baker College, Center for Graduate Studies, 1050 W. Bristol Rd., Flint, MI 48507. TEL 810-766-4105. FAX 810-766-4399. Ed. Stephen L. Williams. R&P contact: Dawn Prueter. TEL 810-766-4024. adv. contact: Dawn Prueter. bk.rev.; index; circ. 3,000 (paid). (back issues avail.) **Document type:** academic/scholarly publication.
Description: Provides materials, thoughts, sources and networking opportunities in leadership education in business and college settings.
Refereed Serial

JOURNAL OF LOSS PREVENTION IN THE PROCESS INDUSTRIES. see ENGINEERING — Chemical Engineering

658 US ISSN 0149-2063
HD28 CODEN: JOMADO
JOURNAL OF MANAGEMENT. 1975. bi-m. $110 to individuals (foreign $140); institutions $245 (foreign $275) (effective 1998). (Southern Management Association) J A I Press Inc., 55 Old Post Rd., No. 2, Box 1678, Greenwich, CT 06830-1678. TEL 203-661-7602. FAX 203-661-0792. E-mail: jai@jaipress.com. (Addr. in the U.K. and Europe: J A I Press Ltd., 38 Tavistock St., Covent Garden, London WC2E 7PB, England. TEL 44-171-379-8834. FAX 44-171-379-8835) (Co-sponsor: Indiana University Graduate School of Business) Ed. Ricky W. Griffin. adv.; bk.rev.; index. circ. 2,000. (also avail. in microfilm from UMI; back issues avail.) **Indexed:** ABI Inform., ASCA, B.P.I, BPIA, Bus.Ind., C.I.J.E., Cont.Pg.Manage., Curr.Cont., Lang.& Lang.Behav.Abstr., Manage.Cont., Mgmt.& Market.Abstr., Oper.Res.Manage.Sci., P.A.I.S., Pers.Manage.Abstr., Psychol.Abstr. (1978-), Psyscan, Qual.Contr.Appl.Stat., Sage Pub.Admin.Abstr., Sociol.Abstr., SSCI, Work Rel.Abstr. **Document type:** academic/scholarly publication.
●Also available online. Vendor(s): Information Access Co.
—BLDSC (5011.100000); Genuine Article; KR SourceOne; SWETS; UMI; UnCover. CCC.

JOURNAL OF MANAGEMENT ACCOUNTING RESEARCH. see BUSINESS AND ECONOMICS — Accounting

658 US ISSN 1385-3457
▼**JOURNAL OF MANAGEMENT & GOVERNANCE.** Announced for publication in 1997. q. fl.500 to institutions; $256.50 to institutions in U.S. (effective 1998). Kluwer Academic Publishers Boston, Box 358, Accord Sta., Hingham, MA 02018-0358. TEL 617-871-6600. FAX 617-871-6528. URL: http://www.wkap.nl. (Dist. outside N. America by: Kluwer Academic Publishers Group, P.O. Box 322, 3300 AH Dordrecht, Netherlands. TEL 31-78-6392392. FAX 31-78-6546474) adv. **Document type:** academic/scholarly publication.
Refereed Serial

658.46 US ISSN 0168-7778
HD69.C6
JOURNAL OF MANAGEMENT CONSULTING; the forum for management consultants worldwide. 1982. s-a. (4 nos./vol.). $60 per vol. (Canada & Mexico $68; elsewhere $84) (effective through 1998); newsstand price: $20 (Canada & Mexico $22; elsewhere $26). 858 Longview Rd., Burlingame, CA 94010-6974. TEL 415-342-1954. FAX 415-344-5005. E-mail: JMC@jmcforum.com; URL: http://www.jmcforum.com/jmc/. Ed. Gerald A. Simon. adv. contact: E. Michael Shays. bk.rev.; charts; illus. circ. 7,000. (also avail. in microform from UMI; back issues avail.; reprint service avail. from UMI) **Indexed:** ABI Inform., Account.& Data Proc.Abstr., Account.Ind. (1982-), B.P.I., BPIA, Cont.Pg.Manage. **Document type:** academic/scholarly publication.
●Also available online. Vendor(s): UMI.
Also available on CD-ROM.
—BLDSC (5011.250000); KR SourceOne; SWETS; UMI; UnCover. CCC.
Description: Covers all aspects of management consulting, including issues and trends, the consulting process, practice development and management, professional ethics, computer applications, and more.
Refereed Serial

658 UK ISSN 0262-1711
HF5549.5.T7
JOURNAL OF MANAGEMENT DEVELOPMENT. 1982. 9/yr. £3189($4949) (foreign Aus.$6239) (effective 1998). M C B University Press Ltd., 60-62 Toller Ln., Bradford, W. Yorks BD8 9BY, England. TEL 44-1274-777700. FAX 44-1274-785200. TELEX 51317-MCBUNI-G. URL: http://www.mcb.co.uk. Ed. Andrew Kakabadse. charts; illus. (reprint service avail. from SWZ) **Indexed:** ABI Inform., Account.& Data Proc.Abstr., Anbar, ASEAN Manage.Abstr., BPIA, Br.Educ.Ind., C.I.J.E., Curr.Cont., Mgmt.& Market.Abstr., Mult.Ed.Abstr., Psychol.Abstr., SOMA, Tech.Educ.Abstr., Tr.& Dev.Alert, Tr.& Indus.Ind. **Document type:** trade publication.
—BLDSC (5011.300000); SWETS; UMI. CCC.
Description: Covers evaluating assessment centers, experimental learning methods, new technology of management development, use of appraisal systems, value of a management training survey, team building, self-appraisal and self-development, management knowledge and more.

658 371 US ISSN 1052-5629
JOURNAL OF MANAGEMENT EDUCATION. 1975. q. $152 to institutions (effective Sep. 1996). (Organizational Behavior Teaching Society) Sage Publications, Inc., 2455 Teller Rd., Thousand Oaks, CA 91320. TEL 805-499-0721. FAX 805-499-0871. E-mail: libraries@sagepub.com; URL: http://www.sagepub.co.uk/journals/usdetails/j0130.htm. (Overseas subscr. to: Sage Publications Ltd., 6 Bonhill Rd., London EC2A 4PU, England; Sage Publications India Pvt. Ltd., P.O. Box 4125, New Delhi 110 048, India) Ed. Joan V. Gallos. adv. contact: Margaret Travers. bk.rev. circ. 1,750. (back issues avail.; reprint service avail.) **Indexed:** Cont.Pg.Educ., Curr.Cont., Human Resour.Abstr., Pers.Manage.Abstr., Sociol.Educ.Abstr. **Document type:** academic/scholarly publication.
—BLDSC (5011.305000); SWETS; UMI; UnCover. CCC.
Former titles (until 1977): Organizational Behavior Teaching Review; Exchange - The Organizational Behavior Teaching Journal (ISSN 0162-1858); Teaching Organization Behavior; Teaching of Organization Behavior.
Description: Provides an international forum for the analysis and improvement of teaching and training business students and managers.

658 UK ISSN 1355-252X
HD30.5
▼**JOURNAL OF MANAGEMENT HISTORY.** 1995. m. £199($299) (foreign Aus.$419) (effective 1998). M C B University Press Ltd., 60-62 Toller Ln., Bradford, W. Yorks BD8 9BY, England. TEL 44-1274-777700. FAX 44-1274-785200. URL: http://www.mcb.co.uk. (Dist. in N. America by: MCB University Press Ltd., Box 10812, Birmingham, AL 35201-0812. TEL 800-633-4931. FAX 205-995-1588) **Document type:** academic/scholarly publication.
●Also available on CD-ROM.
—CCC.

658 US ISSN 1056-4926
HD28 CODEN: JMNIE6
JOURNAL OF MANAGEMENT INQUIRY. 1992. q. $150 to institutions (effective Sep. 1996). (Western Academy of Management) Sage Publications, Inc., 2455 Teller Rd., Thousand Oaks, CA 91320. TEL 805-499-9821. FAX 805-499-0871. E-mail: libraries@sagepub.com; URL: http://www.sagepub.com. (Overseas subscr. to: Sage Publications Ltd., 6 Bonhill St., London EC2A 4PU, England; Sage Publications India Pvt. Ltd., P.O. Box 4215, New Delhi 110 048,India) Ed. Thomas G. Cummings. adv. contact: Margaret Travers. circ. 1,500. (back issues avail.; reprint service avail.) **Indexed:** ASCA, Curr.Cont., Fam.Ind. **Document type:** academic/scholarly publication.
—BLDSC (5011.360000); Genuine Article; SWETS; UnCover. CCC.
Description: Provides a forum for nontraditional research and practice in the fields of management and organization.

JOURNAL OF MANAGEMENT SCIENCE & POLICY ANALYSIS. see PUBLIC ADMINISTRATION

658 GH ISSN 0022-2399
HD28
JOURNAL OF MANAGEMENT STUDIES. (Text in English) 1961. a. $15 (effective Jan. 1997). University of Ghana, School of Administration, P.O. Box 78, Legon, Ghana. TEL 233-21-500592. FAX 233-21-500024. E-mail: soa@ug.gnapc.org. Ed. Kwabena Adu Poku. adv.: page $250. bk.rev.; illus. circ. 4,000. (also avail. in microfiche) **Indexed:** ASCA, Curr.Cont., Mgmt.& Market.Abstr., P.A.I.S., Sage Pub.Admin.Abstr., SSCI, World Bank.Abstr. **Document type:** academic/scholarly publication.
Refereed Serial

658 UK ISSN 0022-2380
HD28 CODEN: JMASB2
JOURNAL OF MANAGEMENT STUDIES. 1964. bi-m. £180($356) (foreign £225) (effective 1997). Blackwell Publishers Ltd., 108 Cowley Rd., Oxford OX4 1JF, England. TEL 44-1865-791100. FAX 44-1865-791347. E-mail: jnlinfo@blackwellpublishers.co.uk; URL: http://www.blackwellpublishers.co.uk. Eds. Geoff Lockett, Karen Legge. adv.; bk.rev. circ. 1,600. (reprint service avail. from SWZ,UMI) **Indexed:** ABI Inform., Abstr.Health Care Manage.Stud., Account.& Data Proc.Abstr., Anbar, ASEAN Manage.Abstr., Asian-Pac.Econ.Lit., B.P.I, BPIA, Bus.Ind., Cont.Pg.Manage., Curr.Cont., Educ.Admin.Abstr., IBR, INSPEC, Int.Abstr.Oper.Res., Int.Lab.Doc., Key to Econ.Sci., Manage.Cont., Oper.Res.Manage.Sci., Pers.Lit., Pub.Admin.Abstr., Qual.Contr.Appl.Stat., SCIMP (1978-), SOMA, SSCI, Work Rel.Abstr. **Document type:** academic/scholarly publication.
●Also available online. Vendor(s): Information Access Co.
—BLDSC (5011.500000); Genuine Article; KR SourceOne; SWETS; UMI; UnCover. CCC.
Description: Publishes articles on organization theory, strategic management, and human resource management.
Refereed Serial

BUSINESS AND ECONOMICS — MANAGEMENT

658 US ISSN 1041-2808
HD31
JOURNAL OF MANAGEMENT SYSTEMS.* 1989. q. $125. (Association of Management) Maximillian Press, Box 64841, Virginia Beach, VA 23467-4841. TEL 804-479-5363. FAX 804-479-0656. Ed. Willem A. Hamel. circ. 2,000. **Document type:** academic/scholarly publication.
—BLDSC (5011.512000). **CCC.**
Incorporates (in 1991): Journal of Management in Practice (ISSN 1042-1300)
Description: Publishes articles by academics and practitioners on current organization and management issues.

658 US ISSN 1045-3695
HD28 CODEN: JMAIE9
JOURNAL OF MANAGERIAL ISSUES. Short title: J M I. 1989. q. $25 to individuals; institutions $35 (foreign $55) (effective 1996 & 1997). Pittsburg State University, Department of Economics, Finance & Banking, 1701 S. Broadway, Pittsburg, KS 66762-7533. TEL 316-235-4547. FAX 316-235-4578. E-mail: chuck@pittstate.edu; URL: http://www.pittstate.edu/econ/jmi.html. (Subscr. to: Kathy Benard, Customer Services Executive, Pittsburg State University, Pittsburg, KS 66762) Ed. Charles C. Fischer. R&P contact: Charles C. Fischer. TEL 316-235-4546. index; circ. 1,000 (paid). (also avail. in microform from UMI; back issues avail.) **Indexed:** Bus.Ind., C.I.J.E., Curr.Cont., Human Resour.Abstr., Inform.Sci.Abstr., Int.Polit.Sci.Abstr., Oper.Res.Manage.Sci., P.A.I.S., Psychol.Abstr. (1989-), Pub.Admin.Abstr., Qual.Contr.Appl.Stat., Sociol.Abstr. **Document type:** academic/scholarly publication.
●Also available online. Vendor(s): Information Access Co.
—BLDSC (5011.525000); UMI. **CCC.**
Description: Serves as a bridge of communication between those who study management and those who practice it. Seeks to contribute to the practice of management and the theory of organizations.
Refereed Serial

658 158 UK ISSN 0268-3946
JOURNAL OF MANAGERIAL PSYCHOLOGY. 1986. 8/yr. £1599($2479) (foreign Aus.$3119) (effective 1998). M C B University Press Ltd., 60-62 Toller Ln., Bradford, W. Yorks BD8 9BY, England. TEL 44-1274-777700. FAX 44-1274-785200. TELEX 51317-MCBUNI-G. URL: http://www.mcb.co.uk. Ed. Yochanan Altman. (back issues avail. from SWZ) **Indexed:** ABI Inform., Anbar, Br.Educ.Ind., Mgmt.& Market.Abstr., SOMA, Tech.Educ.Abstr., Tr.& Dev.Alert. **Document type:** academic/scholarly publication.
●Also available online. Vendor(s): Information Access Co.
—BLDSC (5011.530000); SWETS; UMI. **CCC.**
Description: Offers practical guidance for personnel and training managers. Provides personnel managers with an essential digest of the latest legislation, research and publications affecting their profession.

658 330.1 US ISSN 1382-3019
CODEN: JMFMFD
▼**JOURNAL OF MARKET - FOCUSED MANAGEMENT.** 1996. q. fl.510 to institutions; $262 to institutions in U.S. (effective 1998). Kluwer Academic Publishers Boston, Box 358, Accord Sta., Hingham, MA 02018-0358. TEL 617-871-6600. FAX 617-871-6528. E-mail: services@wkap.nl; URL: http://www.wkap.nl. (Dist. outside N. America by: Kluwer Academic Publishers Group, P.O. Box 322, 3300 AH Dordrecht, Netherlands. TEL 31-78-6392392. FAX 31-78-6546474) Ed. Rajiv Grover. (back issues avail.) **Document type:** academic/scholarly publication.
—BLDSC (5012.080000). **CCC.**
Refereed Serial

658 UK ISSN 1057-9214
T57.95 CODEN: JMDAEY
JOURNAL OF MULTI-CRITERIA DECISION ANALYSIS. 1992. bi-m. $305 (foreign $305) (effective 1998). John Wiley & Sons Ltd., Journals, Baffins Ln., Chichester, W. Sussex PO19 1UD, England. TEL 44-1243-779777. FAX 44-1243-775878. E-mail: info-assets@wiley.co.uk; URL: http://www.wiley.co.uk. (Subscr. in the Americas to: John Wiley & Sons, Inc., 605 Third Ave., New York, NY 10158. TEL 212-850-6645. FAX 212-850-6021) Ed. Simon French. adv.: B&W page £595, color page £1495; trim 260 x 200; adv. contact: Bob Kern. circ. 450. (also avail. in microform from UMI; back issues avail.; reprint service avail. from SWZ) **Indexed:** Curr.Cont. (1992-), Stat.Theor.Meth.Abstr. (1992-), Zent.Math. **Document type:** academic/scholarly publication.
—BLDSC (5021.054000); UMI; UnCover. **CCC.**
Description: Provides an international forum for the presentation and discussion of all aspects of research, application and evaluation of multicriteria decision analysis.

658.15 NE ISSN 1042-444X
HG4027.5
JOURNAL OF MULTINATIONAL FINANCIAL MANAGEMENT. 1990. q. fl.350($201) (effective 1998). North-Holland (Subsidiary of: Elsevier Science B.V.), P.O. Box 211, 1000 AE Amsterdam, Netherlands. TEL 31-20-4853757. FAX 31-20-4853432. E-mail: nlinfo-f@elsevier.nl; usinfo-f@elsevier.com; kyf04035@niftyserve.or.jp. (Subscr. in the Americas to: Elsevier Science, Regional Sales Office, Box 945, New York, NY 10159-0945. TEL 212-633-3730. FAX 212-633-3680; Subscr. in Australasia and the Far East to: Elsevier Science (Singapore) Pte Ltd, No.1 Temasek Ave., No.17-01 Millenia Tower, Singapore 039192, Singapore. TEL 65-434-3727. FAX 65-337-2230; Subscr. in Japan to: Elsevier Science Japan, 9-15 Higashi-Azabu 1-chome, Minato-ku, Tokyo 106, Japan. TEL 81-3-5561-5033. FAX 81-3-5561-5047) (also avail. in microform from UMI; reprint service avail.) **Indexed:** Cont.Pg.Manage. **Document type:** academic/scholarly publication.
—BLDSC (5021.065000); SWETS. **CCC.**
Description: Focuses on the management of multinational enterprises.
Refereed Serial

JOURNAL OF NURSING MANAGEMENT. see *MEDICAL SCIENCES — Nurses And Nursing*

JOURNAL OF OPERATIONS MANAGEMENT. see *ENGINEERING — Industrial Engineering*

658 UK ISSN 0953-4814
HD58.8
JOURNAL OF ORGANIZATIONAL CHANGE MANAGEMENT. 1988. bi-m. £1489($2299) (foreign Aus.$2899) (effective 1998). M C B University Press Ltd., 60-62 Toller Ln., Bradford, W. Yorks BD8 9BY, England. TEL 44-1274-777700. FAX 44-1274-785200. TELEX 51317-MCBUNI-G. URL: http://www.mcb.co.uk. (In U.S.: Box 1943, Birmingham, AL 35201) Ed. David Boje. (reprint service avail. from SWZ) **Indexed:** Anbar, ASCA, Curr.Cont., Mgmt.& Market.Abstr. **Document type:** academic/scholarly publication.
●Also available on CD-ROM.
—BLDSC (5027.069000); Genuine Article; SWETS; UMI; UnCover. **CCC.**
Description: Focuses on organizational development, quality of work life, organizational behavior modification, and consultation.

JOURNAL OF PARK AND RECREATION ADMINISTRATION. see *SPORTS AND GAMES — Outdoor Life*

JOURNAL OF PHARMACEUTICAL MARKETING AND MANAGEMENT. see *PHARMACY AND PHARMACOLOGY*

658 NE ISSN 1384-1289
▼**JOURNAL OF POLICY REFORM.** 1997. q. $46 (effective 1998). Gordon and Breach - Harwood Academic, Amsteldisk 166, 1st Fl., 1079 LH Amsterdam, Netherlands. (Subscr. to: International Publishers Distributor, Box 32160, Newark, NJ 07102. TEL 800-545-8398. FAX 215-750-6343)

JOURNAL OF PRODUCT INNOVATION MANAGEMENT. see *BUSINESS AND ECONOMICS — Production Of Goods And Services*

658 338 US ISSN 0895-562X
HD56
JOURNAL OF PRODUCTIVITY ANALYSIS. 1989. bi-m. fl.730 to institutions; $375 to institutions in U.S. (effective 1998). Kluwer Academic Publishers Boston, Box 358, Accord Sta., Hingham, MA 02018-0358. TEL 617-871-6600. FAX 617-871-6528. TELEX 200190. E-mail: services@wkap.nl; URL: http://www.wkap.nl/kapis/CGI-BIN/WORLD/journalhome.html?0895-562X. (Dist. outside N. America by: Kluwer Academic Publishers Group, P.O. Box 322, 3300 AH Dordrecht, Netherlands. TEL 31-78-6392392. FAX 31-78-6546474) Ed. C.A. Knox Lovell. adv. (also avail. in microform; reprint service avail. from SWZ,UMI) **Indexed:** ASCA, Curr.Cont., J.of Econ.Lit., Oper.Res.Manage.Sci., Qual.Contr.Appl.Stat. **Document type:** academic/scholarly publication.
—BLDSC (5042.660000); Genuine Article; SWETS; UMI. **CCC.**
Description: Publishes theoretical and applied research that addresses issues involving the measurement, explanation and improvement of productivity.
Refereed Serial

JOURNAL OF PROJECT & CONSTRUCTION MANAGEMENT. see *ENGINEERING*

JOURNAL OF PROMOTION MANAGEMENT; innovations in planning & applied research for advertising, sales promotion, personal selling, public relations, re-seller support. see *ADVERTISING AND PUBLIC RELATIONS*

JOURNAL OF PUBLIC HEALTH MANAGEMENT AND PRACTICE. see *PUBLIC HEALTH AND SAFETY*

658 US
▼**JOURNAL OF QUALITY MANAGEMENT.** 1996. s-a. $70 to individuals (foreign $90); institutions $145 (foreign $165) (effective 1998). J A I Press Inc., 55 Old Post Rd., No. 2, Box 1678, Greenwich, CT 06830-1678. TEL 203-661-7602. FAX 203-661-0792. E-mail: jai@jaipress.com. (In Europe: J A I Press Ltd., 38 Tavistock St., Covent Garden, London WC2E 7PB, England. TEL 44-171-379-8834. FAX 44-171-379-8835) Ed. Robert Cardy. **Document type:** academic/scholarly publication.
Refereed Serial

JOURNAL OF QUALITY TECHNOLOGY. see *ENGINEERING — Engineering Mechanics And Materials*

658 615.82 US ISSN 0148-3846
HD7255.A2
JOURNAL OF REHABILITATION ADMINISTRATION. 1977. q. $24 to individuals; institutions $48 (effective 1995). Journal of Rehabilitation Administration, Inc., c/o Fred McFarlane, Man.Ed., Box 19891, San Diego, CA 92159. TEL 619-594-6115. FAX 619-594-4208. Ed. Dennis Gay. adv.; bk.rev.; cum.index: 1977-1984. circ. 1,850. (back issues avail.) **Indexed:** Psychol.Abstr. **Document type:** academic/scholarly publication.
—BLDSC (5048.870000).
Description: Theoretical papers, applied research studies, and practice reports designed to improve administration, management, and supervision in human service fields.
Refereed Serial

JOURNAL OF RISK AND UNCERTAINTY. see *PSYCHOLOGY*

JOURNAL OF SPORT MANAGEMENT. see *SPORTS AND GAMES*

BUSINESS AND ECONOMICS — MANAGEMENT

658 US ISSN 0022-4839
HD28 CODEN: JSYMA9
JOURNAL OF SYSTEMS MANAGEMENT. 1950. 12/yr. $60. Association for Systems Management, Box 38370, Cleveland, OH 44138. TEL 216-243-6900. adv.; bk.rev.; abstr.; charts; illus.; index, cum.index every 10 yrs. circ. 14,000. (also avail. in microform from UMI,MIM; reprint service avail. from UMI)
Indexed: ABI Inform., Account.& Data Proc.Abstr., Account.Ind. (1974-), Anbar, B.P.I, BMT, BPIA, Bus.Ind., Compumath, Comput.Cont., Comput.Dtbs., Comput.Lit.Ind., Cont.Pg.Manage., Curr.Cont., Cyb.Abstr., Data Process.Dig., INSPEC, Intl.Civil Eng.Abstr., Law Ofc.Info.Svc., Manage.Cont., Mgmt.& Market.Abstr., Pers.Lit., Q.Abstr., Resour.Ctr.Ind., Risk Abstr., SCIMP, Soft.Abstr.Eng., SSCI, Tr.& Dev.Alert, Tr.& Indus.Ind., Work Rel.Abstr.
● Also available online. Vendor(s): Information Access Co., Knight-Ridder Information, Inc., UMI.
—AskIEEE; Genuine Article; KR SourceOne; SWETS; UMI; UnCover. **CCC**.
Formerly: Systems and Procedures.

JOURNAL OF WORKERS COMPENSATION. see *INSURANCE*

658 MY ISSN 0127-2713
JURNAL PENGURUSAN. (Text in English and Malay) 1977. a. $15. Penerbit Universiti Kebangsaan Malaysia, 43600 UKM Bangi, Selangor, Malaysia.
Indexed: Asian-Pac.Econ.Lit.
—UnCover.

658 GW ISSN 0931-9077
K R P. (Kostenrechnungspraxis); Zeitschrift fuer Controlling. 1957. bi-m. DM.164 (student DM.115) (foreign DM.175) (effective 1997). Betriebswirtschaftlicher Verlag Dr. Th. Gabler GmbH, Abraham-Lincoln-Str. 46, 65189 Wiesbaden, Germany. TEL 49-611-7878129. FAX 49-611-7878423. adv.; bk.rev. (reprint service avail. from SCH) Indexed: SCIMP (1991-). **Document type:** trade publication.
—BLDSC (5115.020000); SWETS. **CCC**.
Formerly: Kostenrechnungspraxis (ISSN 0023-4265)

658 CE
KALAMANAKARANAYA; management. (Text in Sinhalese) 1977. irreg.? Rs.1.50. University of Sri Lanka, Vidyodaya Campus, Management Studies Society, Gangodawila, Nugegoda, Sri Lanka.

658 NO ISSN 0332-5423
KAPITAL. 1971. fortn. (22/yr.). NOK 750. Periscopus A-S, P.O. Box 188, 1324 Lysaker, Norway. TEL 67-58 28 50. FAX 67-58-28-70. Ed. Trygve Hegnar. adv. circ. 45,000.

658 600 CC ISSN 1001-313X
KEJI GUANLI YU CHENGJIU/SCIENCE AND TECHNOLOGY MANAGEMENT AND ACHIEVEMENTS. (Subseries of: Fuyin Baokan Ziliao) (Text in Chinese) 1986. m. $65.19. Zhongguo Renmin Daxue, Shubao Ziliao Zhongxin - China People's University, Book & Newspaper Information Center, 3 Zhang Zizhong Rd., P.O. Box 1122, Beijing 100007, People's Republic of China. TEL 86-10-4015080. (Dist. in US by: China Publications Service, Box 49614, Chicago, IL 60649. TEL 312-288-3291. FAX 312-288-8570) pp./issue: 96.

658 600 JA ISSN 0914-7020
KENKYU GIJUTSU KEIKAKU/JOURNAL OF SCIENCE POLICY AND RESEARCH MANAGEMENT. (Text in English and Japanese) 1986. 2/yr. $60. Kenkyu Gijutsu Keikaku Gakkai - Japan Society for Science Policy and Research Management, c/o Prof. Ryo Hirasawa, Tokyo Daigaku Kyoyogakubu, Kiso Kagaku Dai-2, 3-8-1 Komaba, Meguro-ku, Tokyo 153, Japan. bk.rev.; abstr. circ. 900.
Description: Contains reviews, commentary, and news of the society.

658 UK
KEY NOTE MARKET REPORT: MANAGEMENT CONSULTANTS. Variant title: Management Consultants. irreg., no.3, 1995. £205. Key Note Ltd., Field House, 72 Oldfield Rd., Hampton, Middlesex TW12 2HQ, England. TEL 44-181-783-0755. FAX 44-181-783-0049.
Document type: trade publication.
● Also available online.
Also available on CD-ROM.
Formerly: Key Note Report: Management Consultants.

KEYAN GUANLI/SCIENCE RESEARCH MANAGEMENT. see *SCIENCES: COMPREHENSIVE WORKS*

658 790 US
KEYNOTES (OAK BROOK). m. membership. National Employee Services and Recreation Association, 2211 York Rd., Ste. 207, Oak Brook, IL 60521. TEL 630-368-1280. FAX 630-368-1286. E-mail: nesrahq@aol.com. Ed. Karen G. Beagley. circ. 4,000. **Document type:** newsletter.
Description: Information on effective implementation of employee recreation, sports and wellness education programs.

658 KO
KIYUP KYUNGYUNG/BUSINESS MANAGEMENT. (Text in Korean) 1958. m. 44000 Won (effective 1991). Korea Productivity Center, 122-1 Sangsansung Blvd., Jeokseon-dong, Jongro-ku, Seoul 110-052, S. Korea. TEL 02-739-5868. FAX 02-736-0322. TELEX KPCENTR-K27672. Ed. Hiwhoa Moon. adv. circ. 30,000.
Description: Aims to impart concepts and techniques of enterprise management to help domestic industries develop competitive power in the world economy. Contains articles, comments, diary for top and middle managers, overseas economic information, field reports on productivity improvement, and case studies on industrial relations.

658 UK ISSN 1092-4604
HD58.8 CODEN: BCAREE
KNOWLEDGE AND PROCESS MANAGEMENT. 1993. q. $345 (foreign $345) (effective 1998). John Wiley & Sons Ltd., Journals, Baffins Ln., Chichester, W. Sussex PO19 1UD, England. TEL 44-1243-779777. FAX 44-1243-843232. E-mail: cs-journals@wiley.co.uk; URL: http://www.wiley.co.uk. (Subscr. in N. America to: John Wiley & Sons, Inc., 605 Third Ave., New York, NY 10158. TEL 212-850-6645. FAX 212-850-6021) adv.; B&W page £475, color page £1325; trim 297 x 210; adv. contact: Caroline Melling. (also avail. in microform from UMI; back issues avail.) **Document type:** academic/scholarly publication.
—BLDSC (5100.439500). **CCC**.
Formerly: Business Change and Re-engineering (ISSN 0969-3866)
Refereed Serial

658 JA ISSN 0085-2570
HF5001
KOBE UNIVERSITY. SCHOOL OF BUSINESS ADMINISTRATION. ANNALS. (Text in English) 1957. a. exchange basis. Kobe Daigaku, School of Business Administration - Kobe University, Rokkodai-cho, Nada-ku, Kobe-shi, Hyogo-ken 657, Japan. FAX 81-78-881-8100. Ed. Koji Okubayashi. bibl.; charts; circ. controlled. (back issues avail.) Indexed: Account.Ind. (1974-).
—BLDSC (1031.630000).
Description: Covers issues in business and economics in Japan.

KOBIETA I BIZNES/WOMEN & BUSINESS; akademicko-gospodarcze forum. see *BUSINESS AND ECONOMICS — Small Business*

658.5 JA ISSN 0023-2777
KOJO KANRI/FACTORY MANAGEMENT. (Text in Japanese) 1955. m. 980 Yen. Industrial Daily News Ltd. - Nikkan Kogyo Shinbunsha, 1-8-10 Kudan Kita, Chiyoda-ku, Tokyo 102, Japan. Ed. Tomio Wada. adv.; bk.rev.; abstr.; bibl.; charts; illus.; stat.; tr.lit.; index. circ. 36,500. Indexed: JTA.
Description: Covers the business environment regarding management strategy, development of human ability, reorganization of production systems, measures taken by developed enterprises.

KOMPASS PROFESSIONNEL. DISTRIBUTION, COMMERCE DE GROS. see *BUSINESS AND ECONOMICS — Trade And Industrial Directories*

KOMPASS U.K. REGIONAL SALES GUIDE (YEAR). see *BUSINESS AND ECONOMICS — Trade And Industrial Directories*

650 KO ISSN 0023-396X
KOREAN BUSINESS JOURNAL. (Text in English, Korean) 1967. q. free or on exchange basis. Institute of Management Research, School of Management, Seoul National University, 56-1 Shinrim-Dong, Kwanak-Ku, Seoul 151, S. Korea. Ed. Chung-Nyun Kim. adv.; bk.rev.; bibl.; charts; mkt.; index. circ. 2,000.

658 KO
KYUNG-YOUNG SHINMUN/MANAGEMENT NEWS. (Text in Korean) 1955. bi-m. 50000 Won($62.50) (Korea University, Graduate School of Business Administration) Korea University Press, 1 Anam-dong, Sungbuk-ku, Seoul 136-70, S. Korea. TEL 82-2-926-1926. FAX 82-2-923-4661. Ed. Il Kweon Dong. adv.; bk.rev. circ. 12,000.

L A M A MANAGER. (Legal Assistant Management Association) see *LAW*

658 332 US
▼**L I M R A'S VISION**; effective strategy for tomorrow's leaders. 1996. bi-m. $59.97 (foreign $74.97) (effective 1996). LIMRA International, Inc., 300 Day Hill Rd., Windsor, CT 06095. TEL 800-235-4672. Ed. Brad M. Ragaglia.
Description: Dedicated to leadership and business management issues affecting managers in the financial services industry.

658 US
L R I GUIDES TO MANAGEMENT. MONOGRAPHS.* 1965. irreg., latest no.7. price varies. Leadership Resources Inc., Box 629, Luray, VA 22835-0629. Ed. Ronald E. Kieloch. **Document type:** monographic series.
Formerly: Management Monographs (ISSN 0076-3640)

LABORATORY INDUSTRY REPORT; the bi-monthly on lab management and marketing intelligence. see *SCIENCES: COMPREHENSIVE WORKS*

658 US
LAKEWOOD REPORT ON POSITIVE EMPLOYEE PRACTICES. 1995. 12/yr. $128 (Canada $138; elsewhere $148). Lakewood Publications, Inc., 50 S. Ninth St., Minneapolis, MN 55402. TEL 612-333-0471. FAX 612-333-6526. Ed. Brian McDermott. (also avail. in microform from UMI) **Document type:** newsletter.
● Also available online. Vendor(s): UMI.
—UMI. **CCC**.
Formed by the merger of (1990-1995): Total Quality (ISSN 1053-1718); (1988-1995): Service Edge (ISSN 1053-1734); Which incorporates: Front-Line Service (ISSN 1053-1726)
Description: Provides case studies from innovative companies and how-to information on the best business practices in business today.

658 FR
LAMY SOCIETES COMMERCIALES - FORMULAIRE. S.A. CONSEIL D'ADMINISTRATION. (Supplement to: Lamy Societes Commerciales; also s-a. updates avail.) a. 620 F. (effective 1991). Lamy S.A., 187-189 quai de Valmy, 75490 Paris Cedex 10, France. TEL 33-1-44721343. FAX 33-1-44721395. (looseleaf format)

658 FR
LAMY SOCIETES COMMERCIALES - FORMULAIRE. S.A. DIRECTOIRE. (Supplement to: Lamy Societes Commerciales; also s-a. updates avail.) a. 620 F. (effective 1991). Lamy S.A., 187-189 quai de Valmy, 75490 Paris Cedex 10, France. TEL 33-1-44721343. FAX 33-1-44721395. (looseleaf format)

658 FR
LAMY SOCIETES COMMERCIALES - FORMULAIRE. S.A.R.L. (Supplement to: Lamy Societes Commerciales; also s-a. updates avail.) a. 620 F. (effective 1991). Lamy S.A., 187-189 quai de Valmy, 75490 Paris Cedex 10, France. TEL 33-1-44721343. FAX 33-1-44721395. (looseleaf format)

658 FR
LAMY SOCIETES COMMERCIALES - FORMULAIRE. SOCIETES AUTRES QUE S.A.R.L. ET S.A. REGROUPEMENTS DE SOCIETES. (Supplement to: Lamy Societes Commerciales; also s-a. updates avail.) a. 700 F. (effective 1991). Lamy S.A., 187-189 quai de Valmy, 75490 Paris Cedex 10, France. TEL 33-1-44721343. FAX 33-1-44721395. (looseleaf format)

658 CN ISSN 0023-9038
LAVAL ADMINISTRATION. 1969. q. free. Universite Laval, Faculte des Sciences de l'Administration, Cite Universitaire, Ste-Foy, PQ G1K 7P4, Canada. adv.; bk.rev.; bibl.; charts; illus.; stat. circ. 1,000.
Supersedes: Economie et Commerce.

BUSINESS AND ECONOMICS — MANAGEMENT

648 340   US   ISSN 1071-7242
LAW OFFICE ADMINISTRATOR. 1992. m. $137 (effective 1997); $147 (effectie 1998). Ardmore Publishing Company, Box 11670, Atlanta, GA 30355. TEL 404-367-1991. FAX 404-367-1995. Ed. Bill Kimbro; Pub. Susan Crawford. R&P contact: Susan Crawford. bk.rev.; index. circ. 1,800. (looseleaf format; back issues avail.) **Document type:** newsletter.
   Description: Covers issues and regulations affecting the administration of law firms.

LAW PRACTICE MANAGEMENT; the magazine of law office management. see *LAW*

658.4092   US   ISSN 1087-8149
▼**LEADER TO LEADER.** 1996. q. $199 sample issue free to librarians (effective 1997). (Peter F. Drucker Foundation for Nonprofit Management) Jossey-Bass Inc., Publishers, 350 Sansome St., 5th Fl., San Francisco, CA 94104. TEL 800-956-7739. FAX 800-605-2665. URL: http://www.josseybass.com; http://www.pfdf.org. Eds. Frances Hesselbein, Paul Cohen. R&P contact: Lorri Wimer. circ. 6,000 (paid). (back issues avail.) **Document type:** academic/scholarly publication.
   Description: Reports on management, leadership and strategy written by world-class executives, best-selling management authors, top consultants and respected social thinkers.

658   US
LEADERSHIP (FAIRFIELD). 1985. m. $1.35 per no. Economics Press, Inc., 12 Daniel Rd., Fairfield, NJ 07006. TEL 800-526-2554. FAX 201-227-9742. Ed. Arthur F. Lenehan. circ. 60,000.
   Formerly: Soundings (Fairfield).
   Description: Contains wit, wisdom and common sense about the art of managing people.

658   US   ISSN 0195-9204
HF5001
LEADERSHIP (WASHINGTON, 1980). 1980. a. $4.50. American Society of Association Executives, 1575 Eye St., N.W., Washington, DC 20005-1168. TEL 202-626-2735. FAX 202-408-9635. Ed. Ann Mahoney. adv. circ. 50,000. (reprint service avail. from UMI) **Indexed:** Chr.Per.Ind., Rel.Ind.One.

658   UK   ISSN 0143-7739
HD58.8
LEADERSHIP AND ORGANIZATION DEVELOPMENT JOURNAL. 1980. 7/yr. £3329($4999) (foreign Aus.$6479) (effective 1998). M C B University Press Ltd., 60-62 Toller Ln., Bradford, W. Yorks BD8 9BY, England. TEL 44-1274-777700. FAX 44-1274-785200. TELEX 51317-MCBUNI-G. URL: http://www.mcb.co.uk. Eds. Tony Berry, Charles Cox. (reprint service avail. from SWZ) **Indexed:** ABI Inform., Account.& Data Proc.Abstr., Anbar, ASEAN Manage.Abstr., BPIA, Br.Educ.Ind., Bus.Ind., Cont.Pg.Manage., Curr.Cont., Educ.Tech.Abstr., Mgmt.& Market.Abstr., Mult.Ed.Abstr., Psychol.Abstr., SOMA, Stud.Wom.Abstr., Tech.Educ.Abstr., Tr.& Dev.Alert, Tr.& Indus.Ind. **Document type:** academic/scholarly publication.
—BLDSC (5162.866600); SWETS; UMI; UnCover.CCC.
   Description: Covers leadership style, team building, conflict management, politics in organizations, OD technology, communication, business policy and OD consultation practice, and managing planned change.

658   US   ISSN 1080-1863
LEADERSHIP FOR THE FRONT LINES. 1988. s-m. $83.88. Bureau of Business Practice, 24 Rope Ferry Rd., Waterford, CT 06386. TEL 860-442-4365. FAX 860-437-3555. URL: http://www.bbpnews.com. Ed. Emily Mitchell; Pub. Peter Garabedian. R&P contact: Debra Ferraro. s-a. index. **Document type:** newsletter.
   Former titles (until 1994): Front Line Leadership (ISSN 1077-5498) & Front Line Supervisor's Bulletin (ISSN 1067-8956)
   Description: Focuses on how supervisors and team leaders can become more effective in their current positions by following detailed guidelines and specific steps to success.

658.071 303.34   US   ISSN 1093-6092
LEADERSHIP IN ACTION. 1980. q. $99 to individuals; institutions $124; sample issue free to librarians (effective 1997). (Center for Creative Leadership) Jossey-Bass Inc., Publishers, 350 Sansome St., 5th Fl., San Francisco, CA 94104. TEL 800-956-7739. FAX 800-605-2665. URL: http://www.josseybass.com. Ed. Martin J. Wilcox. R&P contact: Lorri Wimer. circ. 60,000. **Indexed:** Tr.& Dev.Alert. **Document type:** academic/scholarly publication, newsletter.
   Formerly: Issues and Observations (ISSN 1065-464X)
   Description: Covers management education, executive development, and leadership development.

658   US   ISSN 1048-9843
HD57.7   CODEN: LEQUEN
THE LEADERSHIP QUARTERLY; an international journal of political, social and behavioral science. 1990. q. $85 to individuals (foreign $105); institutions $205 (foreign $225) (effective 1998). J A I Press Inc., 55 Old Post Rd., No. 2, Box 1678, Greenwich, CT 06830-1678. TEL 203-661-7602. FAX 203-661-0792. E-mail: jai@jaipress.com. (Addr. in Europe: J A I Press Ltd., 38 Tavistock St., Covent Garden, London WC2E 7PB, England. TEL 44-171-379-8834. FAX 44-171-379-8835) Ed. Bernard M. Bass. bk.rev. (also avail. in microform from UMI; back issues avail.) **Indexed:** ASCA, Curr.Cont., Psychol.Abstr. (1990-), Sociol.Abstr. **Document type:** academic/scholarly publication.
—BLDSC (5162.866600); Genuine Article; SWETS.CCC.

658   SW   ISSN 1101-2277
LEDARSKAP/MANAGEMENT FOR PROFITABILITY. 1959. m. SEK 350. Institutet foer Lederskap och Loensamhet, P.O. Box 704970, 107 26 Stockholm, Sweden. Ed. Palle Hansen. adv.; illus.; stat.; index. circ. 6,623.
   Formerly (until 1990): Ledarskap, Ekonomen (ISSN 0280-7823); Which was formed by the 1982 merger of: Ekonomen; Ledarskap och Loensamhet (ISSN 0024-0168)

658   DK   ISSN 0905-8966
HD28
LEDELSE I DAG. 1990. q. DKK 752 (effective 1996). Ledernes Hovedorganisation, Vermlandsgade 63, DK-2300 Copenhagen S, Denmark. TEL 45-31-57-26-44. FAX 45-31-57-90-22. E-mail: lideo.inet.uni-c.dk. Ed. Paul Hegedahl. adv. circ. 2,000. **Document type:** trade publication.
   Description: Directed to leaders and decision makers in business, industry and the public sector. Focuses on what is happening in management in Denmark, Scandinavia and internationally.
   Refereed Serial

LEGAL ASSISTANT MANAGEMENT ASSOCIATION. DIRECTORY. see *LAW*

LEGAL BULLETIN. see *LAW*

LEGAL MANAGEMENT. see *LAW*

658   FR
LEGI - SOCIAL. (Supplement to: La Revue Fiduciaire (ISSN 0223-4718)) Publications Fiduciaires, 100 rue LaFayette, 75485 Paris Cedex 10, France. TEL 33-1-41835252. FAX 33-1-41835253. URL: http://www.revuefiduciaire.fr.

658.5   NE   ISSN 0169-281X
LEIDINGGEVEN & ORGANISEREN. 1973. 6/yr. fl.132 to non-members; members fl.110. N I V E - Nederlandse Vereniging voor Management, Postbus 266, 2270 AG Voorburg, Netherlands. TEL 31-70-3001500. FAX 31-70-3001599. E-mail: nive@euronet.nl. bibl.; charts; illus.; index. circ. 4,000. **Indexed:** Key to Econ.Sci. **Document type:** trade publication.
—SWETS.
   Former titles (until 1985): M F. Management Facetten (ISSN 0165-6937); Groei (ISSN 0017-4467)

920 650   GW   ISSN 0935-4859
LEITENDE MAENNER UND FRAUEN DER WIRTSCHAFT. 1952. a. DM.530 (effective 1997). Verlag Hoppenstedt GmbH, Havelstr. 9, 64295 Darmstadt, Germany. TEL 49-6151-380-0. FAX 49-6151-380-360. adv. circ. 56,000. **Document type:** trade publication.
   Formerly (until 1979): Leitende Maenner der Wirtschaft (ISSN 0075-871X)

LETTRE DES ASSOCIATIONS. see *LAW — Corporate Law*

658   FR
LETTRES DES ELUS LOCAUX. 1985. w. 1900 F. (foreign 1960 F.) Groupe Moniteur, 17 rue d'Uzes, 75002 Paris, France. FAX 33-1-42333819. TELEX 220 528F. Ed. Franck Bouaziz. circ. 700.

LEWIS LETTER ON ENERGY COMMUNICATION. see *ENERGY*

LIBERIAN ECONOMIC AND MANAGEMENT REVIEW. see *BUSINESS AND ECONOMICS*

LITERATUURINFORMATIE PERSONEELSBELEID EN ORGANISATIE. see *BUSINESS AND ECONOMICS — Personnel Management*

LOGISTIC. see *TRANSPORTATION*

658.5   BE
LOGISTIC DIGEST. (Supplement to: Logistic) (Text in Dutch, French) 1986. q. Techniparess nv, Stationsstraat 30 bus 1, 1702 Groot-Bijgaarden, Belgium. TEL 32-2-4818100. FAX 32-2-4818182. adv.; illus. **Document type:** trade publication.
   Former titles: Professional Direct & Handleiding en Digest Industrial (ISSN 0778-9173); (until 1992): Handling Digest (ISSN 0775-2059)

658   IT   ISSN 1120-3587
LOGISTICA MANAGEMENT. 1990. 11/yr. L.130000 (Europe L.190000; elsewhere L.225000) (effective 1997). Edizioni Ritman s.r.l., Via Varesina 76, 20156 Milan, Italy. TEL 39-2-38008859. FAX 39-2-38008828. E-mail: comunica@progres.it. Ed. Massimo Merlino. R&P contact: Alessandro Delfino. adv. B&W page L.2900000, color page L.3900000; trim 170 x 245; adv. contact: Fabrizio Marioli. bk.rev.; circ. 5,269 (controlled). **Document type:** trade publication.
   Description: Covers logistic topics: supply, materials handling, warehousing, distribution, packaging, transport.
   Refereed Serial

658.324 388.324   AT
LOGISTICS AND MATERIALS HANDLING; the magazine for managers. 1991. 6/yr. Publishing Services (Australia) Pty. Ltd., 244 St. Paul's Terrace, Spring Hill, Brisbane, QLD 4000, Australia. TEL 61-7-38541286. FAX 61-7-32524829. E-mail: lmh@pubserv.com.au. Ed. Andrew Stewart. adv.: B&W page Aus.$1645, color page Aus.$2695; trim 275 x 205; adv. contact: Dave Rigby. circ. 7,803. **Document type:** trade publication.
   Description: Covers materials handling, distribution and customer service for decision-making managers.

658   UK   ISSN 1353-5595
LOGISTICS MANAGER. 1994. bi-m. £27.50 (foreign £60). Seven Kings Publications Ltd., 1a Sutton Court Rd., Sutton, Surrey SM1 1HW, England. TEL 44-181-661-1160. FAX 44-181-661-1173. Ed. Neil Asten. R&P contact: Neil Asten. adv. contact: Richard Milbourn. bk.rev.; abstr. circ. 5,000. (back issues avail.) **Indexed:** Account.& Data Proc.Abstr., INSPEC. **Document type:** trade publication.
   Description: Provides comprehensive information on logistics applications in manufacturing and service industries and on materials storage and handling. Articles concentrate on improving productivity, systems analysis, cost reduction and management techniques.

LOGISTICS NEWS. see *TRANSPORTATION*

658 380.5   NE   ISSN 0922-8675
LOGISTIEKKRANT. 1988. bi-w. fl.119 (2350 BEF). Misset (Subsidiary of: Reed Elsevier plc), Postbus 4, 7000 BA Doetinchem, Netherlands. TEL 31-314-349371. FAX 31-314-363638. Ed. P.C. Wieman. adv.: B&W page fl.8775, color page fl.11578; trim 307 x 465; adv. contact: Cor van Nek. illus. circ. 26,130. (tabloid format) **Document type:** trade publication, newspaper.
   Description: Management-oriented publication covering all aspects of logistics within a business operation, including internal transport and storage, packaging, computerization and distribution.

BUSINESS AND ECONOMICS — MANAGEMENT

658 GW ISSN 0930-7834
LOGISTIK IM UNTERNEHMEN; materialfluss, organisation, transport. 1986. 8/yr. DM.255($52) (Verein Deutscher Ingenieure - Society of German Engineers) Springer V D I Verlag, Heinrichstr. 24, 40239 Duesseldorf, Germany. TEL 49-211-6103-0. FAX 49-211-6103414. (Subscr. to: Postfach 101022, 40001 Duesseldorf, Germany) Ed. Eckard Muckelberg. adv.; bk.rev.; abstr.; bibl. circ. 12,300. **Document type:** trade publication.
—Ei; SWETS.

338 UK ISSN 0024-6301
HD1 CODEN: LRPJA4
LONG RANGE PLANNING. 1968. bi-m. fl.1590($914) (effective 1998). (Strategic Planning Society) Elsevier Science Ltd., Pergamon, P.O. Box 800, Kidlington, Oxford OX5 1DX, England. TEL 44-1865-843000. FAX 44-1865-843010. E-mail: nlinfo-f@elsevier.nl; usinfo-f@elsevier.com; forinfo-kyf04035@niftyserve.or.jp; URL: http://www.elsevier.nl/. (Subscr. to: Elsevier Science, Regional Sales Office, P.O. Box 211, 1000 AE Amsterdam, Netherlands. TEL 31-20-4853757. FAX 31-20-4853432; Subscr. in the Americas to: Elsevier Science, Regional Sales Office, Box 945, New York, NY 10159-0945. TEL 212-633-3730. FAX 212-633-3680; Subscr. in Australasia and the Far East to: Elsevier Science (Singapore) Pte Ltd, No.1 Temasek Ave., No.17-01 Millenia Tower, Singapore 039192, Singapore. TEL 65-434-3727. FAX 65-337-2230) (Co-sponsor: European Strategic Planning Federation) Ed. Bernard Taylor. adv.; bk.rev.; charts; stat. circ. 4,700. (also avail. in microfiche from MIM; microfilm from UMI; back issues avail.) **Indexed:** ABI Inform., Account.& Data Proc.Abstr., Anbar., ASCA, ASEAN Manage.Abstr., Asian-Pac.Econ.Lit., B.P.I, BPIA, Br.Rail.Bd.Bus., Bus.Ind., CLOSS, Cont.Pg.Manage., Curr.Cont., Environ.Abstr., Excerp.Med., Fuel & Energy Abstr., Fut.Surv., Geo.Abstr., Key to Econ.Sci., Manage.Cont., Mgmt.& Market.Abstr., Mid.East: Abstr.& Ind., Oper.Res.Manage.Sci., P.A.I.S., PROMT, Q.Abstr., Risk Abstr., Sage Urb.Stud.Abstr., SCIMP (1978-), SSCI, Tr.& Indus.Ind. **Document type:** academic/scholarly publication.
—BLDSC (5294.220000); Ei; Genuine Article; KR SourceOne; SWETS; UMI; UnCover. **CCC.**
Description: Provides authoritative information on developments and new thinking about problems and techniques of forward planning in business and government.
Refereed Serial

658 665 US ISSN 1080-9449
▼**LUBES 'N' GREASES;** the magazine of industry in motion. 1995. m. (free to qualified personnel in U.S.; Canada and Mexico $50; elsewhere $80 (effective 1997); newsstand price: $10. L N G Publishing Company, Inc., 6105-G Arlington Blvd., Falls Church, VA 22044. TEL 703-536-0800. FAX 703-536-0803. Ed. Lisa Tocci; Pub. Nancy J. DeMarco. adv.; B&W page $2950; trim 8 1/2 x 11; adv. contact: Gloria Steinberg Briskin. charts, illus. circ. 15,000. (back issues avail.) **Document type:** trade publication.
—BLDSC (5300.940000).

LUND STUDIES IN ECONOMICS AND MANAGEMENT. see *BUSINESS AND ECONOMICS — Economic Systems And Theories, Economic History*

658 US
M A C NEWS. 1986. q. (Mid-Atlantic Council of Shopping Center Managers) John Bachner Communications, Inc., 8811 Colesville Rd., Ste. G106, Silver Spring, MD 20910. TEL 301-589-9121. FAX 301-589-2017. Ed. Diane B. Perlman. circ. 175. (looseleaf format; back issues avail.)
Description: Covers shopping centers management and marketing.

658 NE ISSN 0165-1722
HD28
M & O; tijdschrift voor organisatiekunde en sociaal beleid. (Text in Dutch; summaries in English) 1947. bi-m. fl.245 includes M & O Quarterly. Samsom BedrijfsInformatie B.V. (Subsidiary of: Wolters Kluwer N.V.), Postbus 4, 2400 MA Alphen aan den Rijn, Netherlands. TEL 31-172-466775. FAX 31-172-440681. TELEX 39682. Ed. J. A. Buijs; Pub. Fridtjof Gorter. adv.; bk.rev.; bibl.; charts; illus.; stat.; index. circ. 4,400. **Indexed:** Abstr.Hyg., C.I.S. Abstr., Psychol.Abstr., Trop.Dis.Bull. **Document type:** trade publication.
—SWETS.
Former titles: Mens en Organisatie; Mens en Onderneming (ISSN 0025-9470)

658 004 US ISSN 0276-7783
T58.6 CODEN: MISQDP
M I S QUARTERLY. (Management Information Systems) 1977. q. $70 (foreign $80) (effective through 1998). (University of Minnesota, School of Management) M I S Research Center, University of Minnesota, Carlson School of Management, 271 19th Ave. S, Minneapolis, MN 55455. TEL 612-624-2035. FAX 612-624-2056. E-mail: misq@csom.umn.edu; URL: http://www.misq.org/. (Co-sponsor: Society for Information Management) Ed. Robert Zmud. R&P contact: Susan Scanlon. adv. contact: Susan Scanlan. circ. 4,500. (also avail. in microfiche; back issues avail.; reprint service avail. from SCH) **Indexed:** ABI Inform., ASCA, B.P.I., BPIA, Compumath, Comput.Cont., Comput.Dtbs., Comput.Lit.Ind., Cont.Pg.Manage., Curr.Cont., INSPEC (1982-), SSCI. **Document type:** academic/scholarly publication.
●Also available online. Vendor(s): Information Access Co., UMI.
—BLDSC (5359.039000); AskIEEE; CISTI; Genuine Article; KR SourceOne; SWETS; UMI; UnCover. **CCC.**

658 US
M M R; reporter for supermarket, drug and discount chains. 1983. fortn. (except m. in May & Dec.) $91. Racher Press, Inc., 220 Fifth Ave., New York, NY 10001. TEL 212-213-6000. FAX 212-213-6106. Ed. David Pinto. adv. circ. 26,200. **Document type:** trade publication.
Former titles: Mass Market Retailers (ISSN 0743-5258); ChainSigns (ISSN 0739-3776)
Description: Reports events and trends pertinent to the growth and development of the supermarket and the drug and discount chain industry.

658 SW
MAALARDALEN - BERGSLAGENS AFFAERER; med Gaevle-Dala. 1988. 6/yr. SEK 295 (effective 1996). Affaersinfo, P.O. Box 2041, S-700 02 Oerebro, Sweden. TEL 46-19-170-760. FAX 46-19-125-642. Ed. Claes-Goeran Hanberg. adv. contact: Ronny Stenbergh. circ. 20,000.
Formerly: Begslagens Affaerer (ISSN 0284-8732)

658 DK ISSN 0900-6028
MAANEDSMAGASINET ERHVERV - NORDJYLLAND. 1984. m. (11/yr.) DKK 200. Sct. Thoegersvej 8, P.O. Box 30, 7770 Vestervig, Denmark. FAX 97-94-14-10. Ed. Ole Gudmundsen. adv.; circ. 16,600. (controlled). (reprint service avail.)

338.5 US ISSN 0047-5394
HD28
THE McKINSEY QUARTERLY. 1964. q. free to qualified personnel. McKinsey & Co. Inc., 55 E. 52nd St., New York, NY 10022. TEL 212-446-7000. charts; illus.; cum.index every 2 yrs.; circ. controlled. **Indexed:** Account.& Data Proc.Abstr., Anbar, ASEAN Manage.Abstr., B.P.I., Cont.Pg.Manage., Mgmt.& Market.Abstr., Tr.& Indus.Ind.
●Also available online. Vendor(s): Information Access Co., UMI.
—BLDSC (5413.497000); KR SourceOne; UMI; UnCover.

658.2 FR ISSN 0025-0880
MAINTENANCE. 1970. 11/yr. 240 F. Edipresse, 16 rue Guillaume Tell, 75017 Paris, France. TEL 47-66-00-05. FAX 47-66-46-94. Ed. G. Baudesson. adv.; bibl.; tr.lit. circ. 7,500.

658 US ISSN 1080-188X
MAINTENANCE MANAGEMENT. s-m. $137.88. Bureau of Business Practice, 24 Rope Ferry Rd., Waterford, CT 06386. TEL 860-442-4365. FAX 860-437-3555. URL: http://www.bbpnews.com. Ed. Peter Hawkins; Pub. Peter Garabedian. R&P contact: Debra Ferraro. s-a.index. **Document type:** newsletter.
Formerly: Maintenance Supervisor's Bulletin (ISSN 0194-5912)
Description: Features interviews with experienced supervisors and other experts in the maintenance or supervisory field, sharing field-tested ways to upgrade maintenance machinery or procedures, and providing solutions to any of the myriad problems or tasks supervisors face daily.

658 US ISSN 0025-1623
HD28
MANAGE. 1948. q. $5. National Management Association, 2210 Arbor Blvd., Dayton, OH 45439. TEL 513-294-0421. Ed. Douglas E. Shaw. adv.; bk.rev.; charts; illus. circ. 60,000. (also avail. in microform from UMI; reprint service avail. from UMI) **Indexed:** ABI Inform., BPIA, Bus.Ind., Pers.Lit., Work Rel.Abstr. **Document type:** trade publication.
●Also available online. Vendor(s): Information Access Co., UMI.
—BLDSC (5358.400000); UMI; UnCover.

658 IE ISSN 0025-164X
MANAGEMENT. 1953. m. £24. (Irish Management Institute) Jemma Publications Ltd., Marino House, 53 Glasthule Rd., Sandycove, Co. Dublin, Ireland. TEL 01-800000. FAX 01-844041. (Subscr. to: P.O. Box 1973, Rathmines, Dublin 6, Ireland) Ed. Frank Dillon. adv.; bk.rev.; abstr.; charts; illus.; index; circ. 8,000 (controlled). (also avail. in microform from UMI) **Indexed:** Account.& Data Proc.Abstr., Anbar.

658 NZ ISSN 0025-1658
MANAGEMENT; for business and professional executives. 1955. m. NZ.$65 (foreign NZ.$125). Profile Publishing Ltd., P.O. Box 5544, Wellesley St., Auckland, New Zealand. TEL 64-9-6308940. FAX 64-9-6301046. E-mail: sprofile@iconz.co.nz. Ed. Carroll du Chateau. adv.; bk.rev.; illus. circ. 12,000. (also avail. in microfilm from UMI; reprint service avail. from UMI) **Indexed:** Work Rel.Abstr. **Document type:** trade publication.
—BLDSC (5358.800000); UMI. **CCC.**
Description: Trade publication for business and professional executives in New Zealand.

650 AT ISSN 1039-4729
HD28
MANAGEMENT; executive ideas, advice and information. 1993. 10/yr. Aus.$95 (foreign Aus.$100) (effective 1998). Australian Institute of Management, N.S.W. Ltd., 215 Pacific Highway, North Sydney, N.S.W. 2060, Australia. TEL 61-29-9563030. FAX 61-29-9565613. Ed. Cathy Gordon. adv.; B&W page Aus.$2000, color page Aus.$3000; 245 x 180; adv. contact: Joan Rideout. bk.rev. circ. 33,201. **Indexed:** Anbar. **Document type:** academic/scholarly publication.
—BLDSC (5358.875000); UnCover.
Incorporates (in 1994): A I M (Queensland) & A I M (South Australia) & A I M (Western Australia); In 1993 the Management was formed by the merger of: A I M (Victoria); A I M (Tasmania); A I M (Australian Capital Territory); A I M (New South Wales) (ISSN 0817-5713); Which was formerly (1970-1989): A I M News (ISSN 0813-6785).
Description: Keeps managers up to date with the latest in management thought, and equips them with an understanding of current issues that affect business life.

MANAGEMENT (BALTIMORE); a bibliography for N A S A managers. see *BUSINESS AND ECONOMICS — Abstracting, Bibliographies, Statistics*

658 US ISSN 0198-8557
JK671
MANAGEMENT (WASHINGTON); a magazine for government supervisors, managers, private contractors. 1979. q. $5.50. U.S. Office of Personnel Management, Office of Public Affairs, Washington, DC 20415. TEL 202-655-4000. (Dist. by: Supt. of Documents, Washington, DC 20402) Ed. David A. Turner. adv.; bk.rev. circ. 45,000. **Indexed:** BPIA, Ind.U.S.Gov.Per., Pers.Lit.
—UMI.
Formerly: Civil Service Journal (ISSN 0009-7985)

BUSINESS AND ECONOMICS — MANAGEMENT

658   UK
MANAGEMENT AND INDUSTRIAL RELATIONS SERIES. 1982. irreg., no.9, 1985. price varies. Cambridge University Press, Edinburgh Bldg., Shaftesbury Rd., Cambridge CB2 2RU, England. TEL 44-1223-312393. FAX 44-1223-315052. TELEX 851817256. E-mail: information@cup.cam.ac.uk; URL: http://www.cup.cam.ac.uk. (N. American addr.: Cambridge University Press, Journals Dept., 40 W. 20th St., New York, NY 10011. TEL 212-924-3900. FAX 212-691-3239) Ed.Bd. R&P contact: Linda Nicol. **Document type:** monographic series.

658 600   UK   ISSN 1356-3769
MANAGEMENT & TECHNOLOGY. 1994. q. Pira International, Randalls Rd., Leatherhead, Surrey KT22 7RU, England. TEL 44-1372-802080. FAX 44-1372-802079. E-mail: publications@pira.co.uk; URL: http://www.pira.co.uk. Ed. Michael Barnard; Pub. Marie Rushton. **Document type:** trade publication.
—BLDSC (5359.009010); AskIEEE; KR SourceOne.

658.16   UK   ISSN 1353-8950
MANAGEMENT BUY-OUTS. 1988. q. £100 (effective 1997). University of Nottingham, School of Management and Finance, Centre for Management Buy-Out Research, University Park, Nottingham NG7 2RD, England. TEL 44-115-951-5494. FAX 44-115-951-5204. E-mail: kenneth.robbie@nottingham.ac.uk; URL: http://www.ccc.nottingham.ac.uk/~lizsmf/cmbor/html. Ed. Ren Robbie. adv. contact: Margaret Burdeed. circ. 500. **Document type:** academic/scholarly publication.
—BLDSC (5359.013130).
Formerly (until 1994): U K Management Buy-Outs (ISSN 0961-0197)

658   UK   ISSN 1351-0924
MANAGEMENT CONSULTANCY. 1989. m. £45 (foreign £55) (effective 1996). V N U Business Publications BV, VNU House, 32-34 Broadwick St., London W1A 2HG, England. TEL 44-171-439-4242. FAX 44-171-437-4841. Ed. Mick James. adv.; bk.rev. circ. 15,000. **Indexed:** Mgmt.& Market.Abstr. **Document type:** trade publication.
—BLDSC (5359.014630); SWETS.

MANAGEMENT CONSULTANCY - FINANCIAL SURVEY (YEAR). see BUSINESS AND ECONOMICS — Trade And Industrial Directories

658   IE   ISSN 0956-3253
MANAGEMENT CONSULTANT INTERNATIONAL. 10/yr. I£649. Lafferty Publications Ltd., The Tower, IDA Enterprise Centre, Pearse St., Dublin 2, Ireland. TEL 353-1-6718022. FAX 353-1-6718520. E-mail: cvserv@lafferty.ie; URL: http://www.unm.lafferty.co.uk. (US subscr. to: 420 Lexington Ave., Ste. 1745, New York, NY 10170. TEL 212-557-6726) Ed. Sandra Burke. R&P contact: David Barry. **Document type:** newsletter.
Description: Gives worldwide news and trends in the management consultancy industry.

658   UK   ISSN 1351-0894
MANAGEMENT CONSULTANTS NEWS. 1989. 24/yr. £48 (Europe & rest of world £120) (effective 1997). Prime Marketing Publications Ltd., Witton House, Lower Rd., Chorleywood, Hertfordshire WD3 5LB, England. TEL 44-1923-285323. FAX 44-1923-285819. E-mail: mcn@pmp.co.uk; URL: http://www.pmp.co.uk. Ed. Tim Ring; Pub. Steve Markwell. adv. contact: Steve Markwell. circ. 11,000. **Document type:** newsletter.
Description: Provides information for management consultancy professionals in Europe and the UK.

MANAGEMENT CONSULTING; annotated bibliography of selected references. see BUSINESS AND ECONOMICS — Abstracting, Bibliographies, Statistics

658   IO   ISSN 0302-9859
HD70.I5
MANAGEMENT DAN USAHAWAN INDONESIA. bi-m. Rps.5500. University of Indonesia, Institute of Management Studies, Jalan Salemba Raya 4, Box 404, Jakarta 10430, Indonesia.

658   UK   ISSN 0025-1747
HD28   CODEN: MANDA4
MANAGEMENT DECISION. 1963. 10/yr. £3429($5299) (foreign Aus.$6699) (effective 1998). M C B University Press Ltd., 60-62 Toller Ln., Bradford, W. Yorks BD8 9BY, England. TEL 44-1274-777700. FAX 44-1274-785200. TELEX 51317-MCBUNI-G. URL: http://www.mcb.co.uk. Ed. J. Peters. bk.rev.; charts; illus. (reprint service avail. from SWZ) **Indexed:** ABI Inform., Account.& Data Proc.Abstr., Anbar, ASEAN Manage.Abstr., B.P.I., BPIA, Br.Educ.Ind., Br.Hum.Ind., Bus.Ind., Cont.Pg.Manage., Curr.Cont., INSPEC, Intl.Mgmt.Info., Key to Econ.Sci., Manage.Cont., Mark.Res.Abstr. (1967-), Mgmt.& Market.Abstr., P.A.I.S., SCIMP (1978-), Work Rel.Abstr. **Document type:** academic/scholarly publication.
●Also available online. Vendor(s): Information Access Co.
—BLDSC (5359.019000); AskIEEE; KR SourceOne; SWETS; UMI; UnCover. CCC.
Incorporates: Management in Action (ISSN 0030-0217); Scientific Business.
Description: Presents important issues and topics in a style appropriate for a general managerial audience. Covers corporate planning, management training and development, personnel, industrial relations and more.

658   BG   ISSN 0378-7532
MANAGEMENT DEVELOPMENT. 1972. q. Tk.200($50) Bangladesh Management Development Centre, Mirpur Rd., Dhaka 7, Bangladesh. TEL 802-817405-7. FAX 802-814304. Ed. Akm Shaheedul Hoq Mollah. adv.: page $130. bk.rev.; bibl.; charts; stat.; index. circ. 350. **Indexed:** Int.Lab.Doc.
Formerly: Management Development Centre, Dacca. Quarterly Bulletin (ISSN 0047-567X)
Refereed Serial

658   UN   ISSN 0074-6703
MANAGEMENT DEVELOPMENT SERIES. irreg. price varies. (International Labour Office) I L O Publications, CH-1211 Geneva 22, Switzerland. TEL 41-22-799-6111. FAX 41-22-798-6358. TELEX 415647-ILO-CH. (Dist. in US by: I L O Publications Center, 49 Sheridan Ave., Albany, NY 12210. TEL 518-436-9686. FAX 518-436-7433) (also avail. in microform from ILO) **Document type:** monographic series.

658   FR   ISSN 0997-3729
MANAGEMENT ET QUALITE. q. 800 F. Communication et Developpement, 63 ave. de Villiers, 75017 Paris, France. TEL 47-66-84-22. FAX 42-27-11-63. Ed. Bernard Monteil. charts. circ. 10,000.
Formerly (until 1988): Cercles de Qualite (ISSN 0758-8828)

658   UK
MANAGEMENT EXPRESS. w. Anbar Electronic Intelligence, 60-62 Toller Lane, Bradford, West Yorkshire, England. TEL 44-1274-777700. FAX 44-1274-785200. E-mail: mwills@anbar.co.uk; URL: http://www.anbar.co.uk/anbar.htm. Ed. Mathew Wills.
●Available only online.
Description: Reviews the most significant new ideas and practice from over 400 of the world's top management journals.

658   US
MANAGEMENT FORUM. 1989. q. membership. International Management Council, 430 S. 20th St., No. 3, Omaha, NE 68102. TEL 402-345-1904. FAX 402-345-4480. Ed. Jodeen M. Sterba. bk.rev.; circ. 6,000 (controlled). (looseleaf format; back issues avail.) **Document type:** newsletter.

658   II   ISSN 0025-1771
MANAGEMENT IDEAS. (Text in English) 1963. m. $25. M.M.C. School of Management, 3 E-1 Court Chambers, 3rd Fl., New Marine Lines, Mumbai 400 020, India. Ed. N.H. Atthreya. bk.rev. circ. 1,000. **Document type:** trade publication.
Description: Reports practical solutions to difficulties arising at work for business managers.

658 370   UK   ISSN 0892-0206
MANAGEMENT IN EDUCATION. 5/yr. £49 (Europe £50; elsewhere £55). (British Educational Management & Administration Society) Pitman Publishing, 128 Long Acre, London WC2E 9AN, England. TEL 44-171-447-2000. FAX 44-171-240-5771. (Subscr. to: Galleon Ltd., Fulham House, Goldsworth Rd., Woking, Surrey GU21 1LY, England. TEL 44-1483-747008. FAX 44-1483-776573) Ed. A. Thody. adv.; bk.rev.; charts; illus.; stat. (back issues avail.) **Indexed:** Cont.Pg.Educ., SOMA. **Document type:** trade publication.
—BLDSC (5359.024200).
Description: Provides a forum for the exchange of trends and innovations, where contributors and readers may evaluate development, share management ideas and techniques, and otherwise deal with any aspect of the broad spectrum of education management at all levels.
Refereed Serial

MANAGEMENT IN GOVERNMENT. see PUBLIC ADMINISTRATION

658   NR   ISSN 0025-178X
HD28
MANAGEMENT IN NIGERIA. 1965. q. £N100. Nigerian Institute of Management, 22 Idowu Taylor St., Victoria Island, P.O. Box 2557, Lagos, Nigeria. TEL 234-1-616203. Ed. Dele Osundahunsi. R&P contact: Dele Osundahunsi. adv. contact: Dele Osundahunsi. bk.rev.; charts; illus. circ. 100,000. **Document type:** academic/scholarly publication.
—UnCover.

658   II   ISSN 0300-2667
HD28
MANAGEMENT INFORMATION SERVICE. (Text in English) vol.3, 1971. 10/yr. University of Cochin, Foundation for Management Education, School of Management, Cochin 22, Kerala, India. Ed.Bd. bk.rev.; bibl.; stat.

658   GW   ISSN 0025-181X
HD28   CODEN: MINRAY
MANAGEMENT INTERNATIONAL REVIEW; journal of International Business. 1961. q. DM.294 (foreign DM.310) (effective 1997). Betriebswirtschaftlicher Verlag Dr. Th. Gabler GmbH, Abraham-Lincoln-Str. 46, 65189 Wiesbaden, Germany. TEL 49-611-7878129. FAX 49-611-7878423. Ed. L. Perridon. illus.; stat.; index. circ. 3,000. (reprint service avail. from SWZ) **Indexed:** ABI Inform., Account.& Data Proc.Abstr., B.P.I., BPIA, Bus.Ind., Cont.Pg.Manage., Curr.Cont., Excerpt.Med., Key to Econ.Sci., Manage.Cont., Mgmt.& Market.Abstr., Mid.East: Abstr.& Ind., P.A.I.S., Risk Abstr., SCIMP (1978-), SSCI. **Document type:** trade publication.
●Also available online. Vendor(s): Information Access Co., UMI.
—BLDSC (5359.041000); KR SourceOne; UMI; UnCover. CCC.

658   JA   ISSN 0025-1828
MANAGEMENT JAPAN; IMAJ management review. (Text in English) 1967. s-a. $22 (effective 1997). International Management Association of Japan, Mori 10 Bldg., 1-18-1 Toranomon, Minato-ku, Tokyo 105, Japan. (Subscr. to: Japan Publications Trading Co. Ltd., P.O.Box 5030, Tokyo International, 2-1 Sarugaku-cho 1-chome, Chiyoda-ku, Tokyo, Japan. FAX 81-292-0410) adv.; bk.rev.; charts; illus.; stat. circ. 10,000. **Indexed:** ABI Inform., Account.& Data Proc.Abstr., ASEAN Manage.Abstr., BPIA, JCT, JTA, Key to Econ.Sci., Mgmt.& Market.Abstr., Tr.& Indus.Ind. **Document type:** academic/scholarly publication.
—BLDSC (5359.042000); UMI; UnCover.
Formerly: Quarterly Review of Management.

658.4   UG   ISSN 0300-2144
HD70.U35
MANAGEMENT JOURNAL. Short title: Management. 1968. a. Sh.2. Management Training and Advisory Centre, P.O. Box 4655, Kampala, Uganda. adv.; illus. circ. 2,500.
Formerly: M T A C Journal.

BUSINESS AND ECONOMICS — MANAGEMENT

658
HD20.15.G7   UK   ISSN 1350-5076
MANAGEMENT LEARNING. 1994. q. £42($67) to individuals; institutions £150($240) (effective 1998). Sage Publications Ltd., 6 Bonhill St., London EC2A 4PU, England. TEL 44-171-374-0645. FAX 44-171-374-8741. E-mail: market@sagepub.co.uk; URL: http://www.sagepub.co.uk/. Ed. David Sims, Yiannis Gabriel. adv. contact: Bernie Folan. bk.rev.; **Indexed:** Anbar, ASCA, Br.Educ.Ind., C.I.J.E., Cont.Pg.Educ., Cont.Pg.Manage., Curr.Cont., Educ.Tech.Abstr., Mgmt.& Market.Abstr., Psychol.Abstr. (1981-), SCIMP, Sociol.Educ.Abstr., SOMA, Tech.Educ.Abstr., Top Manage.Abstr., Tr.& Dev.Alert, Work Rel.Abstr. **Document type:** bulletin.
—BLDSC (5359.042300); Genuine Article; SWETS; UMI; UnCover.
Incorporates (in 1994): Management Education and Development (ISSN 0047-5688)
Description: For those concerned with issues of learning, change and development in organizations, including educators and practitioners in organizational behaviour, organizational change and development, organizational psychology, and human resource management.

658   CH   ISSN 1011-7792
MANAGEMENT MAGAZINE. (Text in Chinese) 1973. m. NT.$2100 (Asia $148; elsewhere $161). Frank L. Hung, Ed. & Pub., 9th Fl., 118 Nanking E. Rd., Sec. 5, Taipei, Taiwan, Republic of China. TEL 886-2-7150471. FAX 886-2-7135701. R&P contact: Tony Hung. adv. contact: Kathy Kuo. circ. 54,000. **Document type:** trade publication.

658   US   ISSN 1054-4275
MANAGEMENT MATTERS. m. $289 (Canada $329; elsewhere $359) (effective 1997). Marton Allen Associates, InfoTeam Inc., Box 15640, Plantation, FL 33318-5640. TEL 954-473-9560. FAX 954-473-0544. Ed. Dr. David R. Allen. **Document type:** newsletter.
●Also available online. Vendor(s): Data-Star, Human Resources Information Network, Information Access Co., NewsNet (MT11).
—CCC.
Description: Covers all facts, topics, and issues of effective management.

658.5   SW   ISSN 1102-5581
MANAGEMENT OF TECHNOLOGY. 1982. q. Institute for Management of Innovation and Technology (IMIT), P.O. Box 6501, S-113 83 Stockholm, Sweden.
Formerly (until 1992): I M I T - Nytt (ISSN 0280-6592)

MANAGEMENT OF VOLUNTARY ORGANISATIONS. see SOCIAL SERVICES AND WELFARE

658   US   ISSN 1050-2114
MANAGEMENT PORTFOLIO. 1989. m. (except July-Aug. combined). membership only. Printing Industries of America, Inc., 100 Daingerfield Rd., Alexandria, VA 22314. TEL 703-519-8100. Ed. Cliff Weiss. tr.lit. circ. 10,000. (back issues avail.) **Indexed:** Abstr.Bull.Inst.Pap.Chem. **Document type:** trade publication.
Description: Covers news and instructive information for management of graphic arts businesses.

658   II
MANAGEMENT PROFESSIONALS ASSOCIATION. EVENTS DIARY. (Text in English) 1981. m. free. Management Professionals Association, 25 Krishna St., T Nagar, Madras 600 017, India. FAX 91-44-441514. TELEX 041 23189 MPA IN. Ed. J. Sudershan. circ. 30,000.

658   II   ISSN 0970-0447
MANAGEMENT PROFESSIONALS ASSOCIATION. JOURNAL. (Text in English) 1981. m. free. Management Professionals Association, 25 Krishna St., T Nagar, Madras 600 017, India. FAX 91-44-441514. TELEX 041 23189 MPA IN. Ed. J. Sudershan. circ. 30,000.

658   US   ISSN 0025-1860
HD28   CODEN: MQMQAE
MANAGEMENT QUARTERLY; a guide to better management. 1960. q. National Rural Electric Cooperative Association, Management Services Department, 4301 Wilson Blvd., Arlington, VA 22203-1860. TEL 703-907-5500. Ed. June B. Lane. bk.rev.; index, cum.index: 1960-1967. circ. 7,000. (also avail. in microform from UMI) **Indexed:** ABI Inform., BPIA, Bus.Ind., Ind.U.S.Gov.Per., Manage.Cont., Work Rel.Abstr. **Document type:** trade publication.
●Also available online. Vendor(s): Information Access Co., UMI.
—BLDSC (5359.053000); SWETS; UMI; UnCover.

658   UK   ISSN 0140-9174
MANAGEMENT RESEARCH NEWS. m. £1079($1639) (foreign Aus.$1439) (effective 1998). Barmarick Publications, Enholmes Hall, Patrington, E. Yorks HU12 OPR, England. TEL 44-1964-630033. (Dist. by: M C B University Press Ltd., 60-62 Toller Ln., Bradford, W. Yorks BD8 9BY, England. TEL 44-1274-777700. FAX 44-1274-785200) Ed. Richard Dobbins; Pub. Barrie O. Pettman. bk.rev.; bibl.; charts; stat. circ. 400. (back issues avail.; reprint service avail. from SWZ) **Document type:** academic/scholarly publication.
—BLDSC (5359.058500); UMI.
Description: Provides precise, informative and readable accounts of management research.

658   US   ISSN 0025-1895
T58.A2
MANAGEMENT REVIEW. 1923. m. $45 to non-members (foreign $80). American Management Association, 1601 Broadway, New York, NY 10019. TEL 212-586-8100. FAX 212-903-8168. E-mail: amapubs@aol.com. (Subscr. to: Box 57938, Boulder, CO 80322-7938) Ed. Martha H. Peak. bk.rev.; charts; illus.; index. circ. 85,000. (also avail. in microform from UMI; reprint service avail. from SCH) **Indexed:** ABI Inform., B.P.I., Bk.Rev.Ind. (1990-), BPIA, Child.Bk.Rev.Ind. (1990-), Comput.Lit.Ind., Intl.Mgmt.Info., Mgmt.& Market.Abstr., Oper.Res.Manage.Sci., P.A.I.S., Pers.Lit., Pers.Manage.Abstr., Psychol.Abstr., Pub.Admin.Abstr., Q.Abstr., Qual.Contr.Appl.Stat., Tr.& Dev.Alert, Tr.& Indus.Ind., Work Rel.Abstr. **Document type:** trade publication.
●Also available online. Vendor(s): Information Access Co., UMI.
—BLDSC (5359.060000); Genuine Article; KR SourceOne; SWETS; UMI; UnCover. CCC.
Incorporates (1987-1990): A M A Council Reports; Management in Practice.
Description: Describes management trends, techniques and issues for middle and upper-level managers in the corporate and public sector.

658   US   ISSN 0025-1909
HD28   CODEN: MSCIAM
MANAGEMENT SCIENCE. 1954. m. $109 to individuals (foreign $129); institutions $248 (foreign $268) (effective 1997). Institute for Operations Research and the Management Sciences, 901 Elkridge Landing Rd., Ste. 400, Linthicum, MD 21090-2909. TEL 410-850-0300; 800-343-0062. Ed. Hau L. Lee. R&P contact: Fran Silverman. adv. contact: Kathye Long. bibl.; charts; illus.; stat. (also avail. in microform from UMI) **Indexed:** ABI Inform., Account.Ind. (1974-), Arts & Hum.Cit.Ind., ASCA, B.P.I., BMT, BPIA, Bus.Ind., CLOSS, Compumath, Comput.Abstr., Comput.Cont., Cont.Pg.Manage., Crim.Just.Abstr., Curr.Cont., Cyb.Abstr., Educ.Admin.Abstr., Energy Ind., Energy Info.Abstr., Eng.Ind., HRIS, INSPEC, Int.Abstr.Oper.Res., Int.Aerosp.Abstr., Intl.Mgmt.Info., J.Cont.Quant.Meth., Key to Econ.Sci., Manage.Cont., Mark.Res.Abstr. (1968-), Math.R., Med.East: Abstr.& Ind., Oper.Res.Manage.Sci., Risk Abstr., SCIMP (1978-), SSCI. **Document type:** academic/scholarly publication.
—BLDSC (5359.080000); AskIEEE; CISTI; Ei; Genuine Article; KR SourceOne; Linda Hall; SWETS; UMI; UnCover. CCC.

658   NE   ISSN 0923-8735
MANAGEMENT SELECTUUR. 1990. 6/yr. fl.525 (effective 1996). Kluwer Bedrijfswetenschappen B.V. (Subsidiary of: Wolters Kluwer N.V.), Postbus 23, 7400 GA Deventer, Netherlands. TEL 31-5700-48999. FAX 31-5700-11504. (Subscr. to: Intermedia bv, Postbus 4, 2400 MA Alphen aan den Rijn, Netherlands. TEL 31-172-466321. FAX 31-172-435527) **Document type:** trade publication.

658.5   UK   ISSN 0307-6768
                CODEN: MASEDZ
MANAGEMENT SERVICES. 1965. m. £43 (rest of Europe £54; elsewhere £70.50-£73) (effective 1996). Institute of Management Services, 1 Cecil Ct., London Rd., Enfield, Mddx., England. TEL 44-181-366-1260. FAX 44-181-367-8149. Ed. D.M. Charlton. R&P contact: D.M. Charlton. adv. contact: Richard Langrish. bk.rev.; charts; illus.; stat. circ. 8,500. (also avail. in microform from UMI; reprint service avail. from UMI) **Indexed:** ABI Inform., Account.& Data Proc.Abstr., Anbar, ASEAN Manage.Abstr., BMT, BPIA, Bus.Ind., Br.Tech.Ind., C.I.S. Abstr., Cont.Pg.Manage., INSPEC, Int.Lab.Doc., Intl.Mgmt.Info., Mgmt.& Market.Abstr., Oper.Res.Manage.Sci., Pub.Admin.Abstr., SCIMP, Tech.Educ.Abstr., Work Rel.Abstr. **Document type:** trade publication.
●Also available online. Vendor(s): UMI.
—BLDSC (5359.084000); AskIEEE; CISTI; KR SourceOne; SWETS; UMI; UnCover.
Formerly (until 1976): Work Study and Management Services (ISSN 0043-8030)

658   US   ISSN 0889-9444
MANAGEMENT STRATEGY. Short title: M S. 1977. q. $22 (foreign $30). Sagamore Publishing Inc., 804 Neil St., Ste. 100, Champaign, IL 61820. Ed. Joseph J. Bannon; Pub. Joseph J. Bannon. R&P contact: Brad Wesner. circ. 6,000. **Document type:** newsletter.
Description: Provides discussions about how to enhance career potentials, staff harmony, and personal growth.

658   NE   ISSN 0166-1256
MANAGEMENT TEAM. 1979. 21/yr. fl.127.50. Benelux Periodieken B.V., Postbus 397, 3900 AJ Veenendaal, Netherlands. TEL 31-8385-21422. FAX 31-8385-23136. Ed. T. Lucas. adv.; circ. 120,000 (paid). **Document type:** trade publication.
—SWETS.

658   UK   ISSN 0025-1925
HD70.G7   CODEN: MANTAI
MANAGEMENT TODAY. 1966. m. £70 (rest of Europe £80; elsewhere £130) (includes Professional Manager (ISSN 0969-6695)). Institute of Management Foundation, 2 Savoy Ct., 3rd. Fl., Strand, London, England. TEL 44-171-497-0580. FAX 44-171-497-0463. E-mail: institute@easynet.co.uk. (Subscr. to: Publications Subscription, Registrars Dept., The Institute of Management Foundation, Cottingham Rd., Corby, Northants. NN17 1TT, England) adv. contact: Peter Welland. bk.rev.; bibl.; charts; illus.; stat.; index. circ. 98,000. **Indexed:** ABI Inform., Anbar, Art.Hosp.& Tour., ASEAN Manage.Abstr., B.P.I., BMT, BPIA, Br.Ceram.Abstr., Br.Educ.Ind., Br.Hum.Ind., Build.Manage.Abstr., Bus.Ind., DAAI, Excerp.Med., Ind.Bus.Rep., INIS Atomind., Intl.Mgmt.Info., Key to Econ.Sci., Mag.Ind., Manage.Cont., Mgmt.& Market.Abstr., Mid.East: Abstr.& Ind., Res.High.Educ.Abstr., SCIMP (1978-), SOMA, Tr.& Indus.Ind., Work Rel.Abstr., World Text.Abstr. **Document type:** trade publication.
●Also available online. Vendor(s): UMI.
—BLDSC (5359.150000); KR SourceOne; SWETS; UMI; UnCover. CCC.
Supersedes: Manager.

658   MX   ISSN 0186-5609
MANAGEMENT TODAY; en espanol. (Text in Spanish) 1973. every 45 days. $160. Comunicacion Profesional Impresa, S.A., Baja California 275-601, 06170 Mexico D.F., Mexico. TEL 52-5-286-9421. FAX 52-5-286-9612. E-mail: cpi@spin.com.mx. Ed. Laura Serralde Diaz. adv. contact: Jose Maria Serralde Diaz. circ. 10,000 (paid). **Indexed:** Account.& Data Proc.Abstr., B.P.I., Br.Educ.Ind., Br.Rail.Bd., High.Educ.Curr.Aware.Bull., Tr.& Indus.Ind. **Document type:** trade publication.
Description: Publishes current information about theories, new trends, and new tools. Includes articles on management, quality, productivity, leadership, training, marketing, and human resources development.

658   II
MANAGEMENT TRAINING AND RESEARCH CENTRES IN INDIA. DIRECTORY. 1982. irreg. Rs.150($20) Information Research Academy, 37 Amir Ali Ave., Flat 9, Calcutta 700019, India. Ed. Partha Subir Guhe.

658   UK   ISSN 0267-8802
THE MANAGEMENT TRAINING DIRECTORY. 1980. a. £59.75. A P Information Services, Roman House, 296 Golders Green Rd., London NW11 9PZ, England. TEL 0181-455-4550. FAX 0181-455-6381. Ed. Alex Kamusky. adv.: B&W page £600, color page £900; trim 297 x 210. circ. 3,000. (also avail. in diskette format) **Document type:** directory.
—BLDSC (5359.156000).
Description: Information on over 10,000 public and in-company management training sources, lists information on organisations providing these courses.

658 330   GW
MANAGEMENT UND COMPUTER. 1993. 4/yr. DM.185 (foreign DM.195) (effective 1996). Betriebswirtschaftlicher Verlag Dr. Th. Gabler GmbH, Abraham-Lincoln-Str. 46, 65189 Wiesbaden, Germany. TEL 49-611-7878129. FAX 49-611-7878423. **Document type:** trade publication.

MANAGEMENT UND KRANKENHAUS; Informationsdienst fuer alle Fuehrungskraefte im Krankenhaus. see *HOSPITALS*

658   US   ISSN 1088-8578
▼**MANAGEMENT UPDATE (BOSTON).** Cover title: Harvard Management Update. 1996. m. $97 (Canada and Mexico $99; elsewhere $139). Harvard Business School Publishing, 60 Harvard Way, Boston, MA 02163. TEL 800-988-0866. E-mail: MUOpinion@hbsp.harvard.edu; URL: http://www.hbsp.harvard.edu. Ed. Walter Kiechel. R&P contact: Randi Krout. **Document type:** newsletter.
Description: Aims to help managers and their organizations be more effective. Includes a short list of "web sites for managers," summaries of articles found in other business journals, and sources for further reading.

MANAGEMENT UPDATE (DENVER). see *MEDICAL SCIENCES*

658 621.381   US
MANAGEMENT UPDATE (GREENCASTLE). 1978. bi-m. $12. Electronics Technicians Association International, 602 N. Jackson St., Greencastle, IN 46135. index. circ. 2,000. (back issues avail.) **Document type:** monographic series.

MANAGEMENTBLAD RIJKSDIENST. see *PUBLIC ADMINISTRATION*

658   SJ
MANAGER. (Text in English) 1975. irreg. (1-2/yr.). Management Development Centre, Box 2308, Khartoum, Sudan. Ed. Sowar El Dabab Ahmed.

658   UK
HD28   CODEN: OMINEH
MANAGER - THE BRITISH JOURNAL OF ADMINISTRATIVE MANAGEMENT. 1964. bi-m. £34 to non-members (overseas £44); institutions £74; students £26 (overseas £38). Institute of Administrative Management, 40 Chatsworth Parade, Petts Wood, Orpington, Kent BR5 1RW, England. TEL 44-1689-875555. FAX 44-1689-870891. E-mail: iadmin@cix.compulink.co.uk; URL: http://www.electranet.com.iam. Ed. Mark Rosselli. adv. contact: Raye Hallett. bk.rev.; index. circ. 15,000. **Indexed:** Account.& Data Proc.Abstr., ASEAN Manage.Abstr., BPIA, Build.Manage.Abstr., INSPEC (1990-), Law Ofc.Info.Svc. **Document type:** trade publication.
—BLDSC (2303.886000); AskIEEE; Ei; KR SourceOne.
Former titles: British Journal of Administrative Management (ISSN 1353-5188); (until 1990): Office and Information Management International (ISSN 1351-6019); Office Management International (ISSN 0951-5062); (until 1987): British Journal of Administrative Management (ISSN 0260-9096); (until 1981): Administrative Management (London) (ISSN 0144-9079); Administrative Management Bulletin.
Description: Aims to promote and develop, for the public benefit, the science of administrative management in all branches. Provides information to enable institute members to keep up to date with the latest techniques and developments in the field of administrative management.

658   GW   ISSN 0047-5726
MANAGER MAGAZIN. 1971. m. DM.108. Manager Magazin Verlagsgesellschaft mbH, Brandstwiete 19, 20457 Hamburg, Germany. TEL 040-30072557. FAX 040-30072247. adv.: B&W page DM.16600, color page DM.27440; trim 178 x 252. bk.rev.; abstr.; bibl.; charts; illus.; stat. circ. 95,000. **Indexed:** Key to Econ.Sci., Mgmt.& Market.Abstr., SCIMP (1991-). **Document type:** trade publication.
—SWETS. CCC.

658   UK   ISSN 0957-4212
HD28
MANAGER UPDATE. 1973. q. £85($185) (foreign £115) (effective Sep. 1995). Braybrooke Press Ltd., The Coach House, Remenham House, Remenham Hill, Henley-on-Thames, Oxon. RG2 3AU, England. TEL 01491-412061. FAX 01491-411928. Ed. Keith MacMillan. circ. 1,000. (back issues avail.) **Document type:** academic/scholarly publication.
—BLDSC (5359.231000); SWETS; UnCover.
Formerly (until 1988): Journal of General Management. Supplement.
Description: Aims to help the general manager keep abreast of the latest articles in specialist management journals.

658   UK   ISSN 0143-6570
HD30.22   CODEN: MDECDE
MANAGERIAL AND DECISION ECONOMICS; the international journal of research and progress in management economics. Abbreviated title: M D E. 1980. 8/yr. £695 (foreign £695) (effective 1998). John Wiley & Sons Ltd., Journals, Baffins Ln., Chichester, W. Sussex PO19 1UD, England. TEL 44-1243-779777. FAX 44-1243-775878. E-mail: info-assets@wiley.co.uk; URL: http://www.wiley.co.uk. (Subscr. in the Americas to: John Wiley & Sons, Inc., 605 Third Ave., New York, NY 10158. TEL 212-850-6645. FAX 212-850-6021) Ed. Paul Rubin. adv.: B&W page £595, color page £1495; trim 260 x 200; adv. contact: Bob Kern. bk.rev.; charts; illus.; stat.; index. circ. 429. (also avail. in microform from UMI; back issues avail.; reprint service avail. from SWZ) **Indexed:** ABI Inform., Cont.Pg.Manage., Curr.Cont., J.of Econ.Lit., Oper.Res.Manage.Sci., Qual.Contr.Appl.Stat. **Document type:** academic/scholarly publication.
—BLDSC (5359.232000); SWETS; UMI; UnCover. CCC.
Description: Deals with economic problems in the field of managerial and decision economics. *Refereed Serial*

658   UK   ISSN 0268-6902
MANAGERIAL AUDITING JOURNAL. 1986. 9/yr. £1329($1999) (foreign Aus.$2599) (effective 1998). M C B University Press Ltd., 60-62 Toller Ln., Bradford, W. Yorks BD8 9BY, England. TEL 44-1274-777700. FAX 44-1274-785200. TELEX 51317-MCBUNI-G. URL: http://www.mcb.co.uk. Ed. Gerald Vinten. (reprint service avail. from SWZ) **Indexed:** SCIMP (1991-). **Document type:** academic/scholarly publication.
●Also available on CD-ROM.
—BLDSC (5359.233000); SWETS; UMI. CCC.
Description: Covers a broad range of issues including management implications of auditing, planning and implementing the auditing process, operations auditing, psychological aspects of the auditor's work, and the organizational structure of auditing.

658   UK   ISSN 0307-4358
HG4001
MANAGERIAL FINANCE. 1975. m. £1729($2629) (foreign Aus.$2399) (effective 1998). Barmarick Publications, Enholmes Hall, Patrington, E. Yorks HU12 0PR, England. TEL 44-1964-630033. (Dist. by: M C B University Press Ltd., 60-62 Toller Ln., Bradford, W. Yorks BD8 9BY, England. TEL 44-1274-777700. FAX 44-1274-785200) Ed. Richard Dobbins; Pub. Barrie O. Pettman. index. circ. 400. (back issues avail.; reprint service avail. from SWZ) **Indexed:** ABI Inform., Account.& Data Proc.Abstr., Anbar, BPIA, Bus.Ind., Cont.Pg.Manage., Curr.Cont., Manage.Cont., Mgmt.& Market.Abstr., SCIMP (1978-), Tr.& Indus.Ind. **Document type:** academic/scholarly publication.
—BLDSC (5359.240000); UMI; UnCover.
Description: Disseminates information about the practice of financial management, including financial objectives, security valuation, diversification, assessment of new projects, borrowing requirements, and dividends.

658   II
MANAGER'S DIGEST. (Text in English) 1971. s-a. $20 to individuals; institutions $40. Management Development Centre, 1 Shakespeare Sarani, Calcutta 700 071, India. Ed. M.A. Mabud. bk.rev. circ. 500.

658   US
MANAGER'S INTELLIGENCE REPORT. 1994. m. $129. Ragan Communications, 212 W. Superior St., Ste. 200, Chicago, IL 60610. TEL 800-878-5331. FAX 312-335-9583. Ed. Brian Ragan. **Document type:** newsletter.
Description: For managers at all levels of organizations.

658 346   US   ISSN 0889-4493
KF3455.A15
MANAGER'S LEGAL BULLETIN. 1986. s-m. $44.64. Alexander Hamilton Institute, 70 Hilltop Rd., Ramsey, NJ 07446-1119. TEL 201-825-3377. FAX 201-825-8695. Ed. Brian L.P. Zevnik. index. (back issues avail.) **Document type:** newsletter.
Description: Sets scenarios of potential legal problems in the workplace based on cases.

MANAGER'S REPORT; journal for community association management. see *REAL ESTATE*

658 374   GW   ISSN 0938-6211
MANAGERSEMINARE; das Weiterbildungsmagazin. 1990. q. DM.48; newsstand price: DM.14.80. ManagerSeminare Gerhard May Verlags GmbH, Endenicherstr. 282, 53121 Bonn, Germany. TEL 49-228-97791-0. FAX 49-228-616164. (Dist. by: Omnia Vertrieb GmbH, Breslauerstr. 17, 65307 Bad Schwalbach, Germany) Ed. Juergen Graf. adv. contact: Juergen Koch. bk.rev.; software rev.; charts; illus.; tr.lit.; circ. 48,000. (back issues avail.) **Document type:** consumer publication. *Refereed Serial*

658.5   UK   ISSN 0961-4036
MANAGING. 1982. a. £55. (Institute of Management Consultants) Sterling Publications Ltd., 86-88 Edgware Rd., London W2 2YW, England. TEL 44-171-915-9600. FAX 44-171-915-9619. adv.; circ. 10,000. **Document type:** trade publication.
—BLDSC (5359.281000).
Former titles (until 1990): Management (ISSN 0953-055X); (until 1988): Institute of Management Consultants. Yearbook (ISSN 0260-373X)

MANAGING AUTOMATION. see *COMPUTERS — Automation*

MANAGING CLINICAL NURSING. see *MEDICAL SCIENCES — Nurses And Nursing*

MANAGING INTELLECTUAL PROPERTY. see *PATENTS, TRADEMARKS AND COPYRIGHTS*

MANAGING L A N COSTS. see *COMPUTERS — Computer Networks*

658   UK   ISSN 0960-4529
MANAGING SERVICE QUALITY. bi-m. £459($699) (foreign Aus.$899) (effective 1998). M C B University Press Ltd., 60-62 Toller Ln., Bradford, W. Yorks BD8 9BY, England. TEL 44-1274-777700. FAX 44-1274-785200. TELEX 51317-MCBUNI-G. URL: http://www.mcb.co.uk. Ed. Chris Taylor. bk.rev. (also avail. in microform from UMI; reprint service avail. from SWZ) **Indexed:** Br.Educ.Ind., Mgmt.& Market.Abstr. **Document type:** academic/scholarly publication.
●Also available on CD-ROM.
—BLDSC (5359.305000); SWETS; UMI. CCC.
Description: Provides managers in the service sector with the information needed to create the Total Quality organisation. Emphasis is placed on providing practitioners with the concepts, strategies, implementation methods, and continuous quality improvement techniques.

658 600   US   ISSN 1062-3310
MANAGING TECHNOLOGY TODAY. 1992. bi-m. $69 to libraries. Quality Observer Corp., Box 1111, Fairfax, VA 22030. TEL 703-691-9496. Ed. Johnson A. Edosomwan.
—BLDSC (5359.314000).

MANAGING YOUR ACCOUNTING AND CONSULTING PRACTICE. see *BUSINESS AND ECONOMICS — Accounting*

BUSINESS AND ECONOMICS — MANAGEMENT

658 378　　　UK　　ISSN 0260-4388
MANCHESTER TRAINING HANDBOOKS. 1981. irreg. £4.50 (foreign £7.50($15)). University of Manchester, Institute for Development Policy and Management, Crawford House, Precinct Centre, Oxford Rd., Manchester M13 9GH, England. TEL 4-161-275-2804. FAX 44-161-273-8829. E-mail: idpm@email.ac.uk; URL: http://www.man.ac.uk/ikpm/. Ed. Ron Clarke. **Document type:** bulletin.
—BLDSC (5359.663000).
　Description: Training handbooks designed to assist those involved in development administration and public sector management in the Third World.

658　　　CN　　ISSN 0709-2423
MANITOBA BUSINESS MAGAZINE. 1979. 10/yr. Can.$16.95. 470 River Ave., 3rd Fl., Winnipeg, MB R3L 0C8, Canada. TEL 204-477-4620. Ed. Ritchie Gage. adv. contact: Louise Ayre. circ. 10,000. (back issues avail.) **Indexed:** Can.B.P.I., Tr.& Indus.Ind. **Document type:** trade publication.
●Also available online. Vendor(s): Information Access Co., Lexis-Nexis.
　Description: Presents prominent business leaders and key developments in the local area. Provides data on business trends and opportunities.

338　　　BE
LE MARCHE; hebdomadaire du dirigeant. 1963. w. 1950 Fr. J.J. Gaudisart, 140 Bd. Lambermont, 1030 Brussels, Belgium. adv.; bk.rev.; charts; illus.; stat.; tr.lit. circ. 15,300. **Indexed:** Key to Econ.Sci.

MARKETING MANAGEMENT. see *BUSINESS AND ECONOMICS — Marketing And Purchasing*

THE MARKETING MANAGER'S YEARBOOK. see *BUSINESS AND ECONOMICS — Marketing And Purchasing*

MARKETING SCIENCE. see *BUSINESS AND ECONOMICS — Marketing And Purchasing*

658　　　II　　ISSN 0970-8219
MARKETOLOGY QUARTERLY. Short title: Marketology. (Text in English) 1969. q. $25. Institute of Marketing & Management, 62-F Sujan Singh Park, New Delhi 110 003, India. TELEX 31-74043 IMM IN. Ed. Jagjit Singh. adv.; bk.rev.; illus. circ. 30,000.
　Former titles (until 1982): Marketing Digest; Marketing and Management Monthly; Marketing and Management Digest; Management Digest.
　Description: Contains articles on agricultural, industrial, services, and international marketing by professionals in the fields.

658　　　GW　　ISSN 0343-043X
MASCHINEN ANLAGEN VERFAHREN. Abbreviated title: M A V. 1958. 10/yr. Konradin Verlag Robert Kohlhammer GmbH, Ernst-Mey-Str. 8, 70771 Leinfelden-Echterdingen, Germany. TEL 49-711-7594-0. FAX 49-711-7594-390. Ed. Rudolf Beyer. adv.: B&W page DM.7320; trim 190 x 270; adv. contact: Walter Schwager. circ. 18,134 (controlled). (back issues avail.) **Indexed:** Excerp.Med. **Document type:** trade publication.
—CCC.
　Description: Discusses production engineering, automation and plant equipment.

658　　　AT　　ISSN 0814-916X
MATERIALS HANDLING & DISTRIBUTION. 1970. bi-m. Aus.$48 (includes annual directory). (Australian Institute of Materials Management) Intermedia Group Pty. Ltd., P.O. Box 606, Rozelle, N.S.W. 2039, Australia. TEL 61-2-818-4738. FAX 61-2-818-4738. Ed. Martin Coleman. adv.: B&W page Aus.$1280, color page Aus.$2300; trim 297 x 210. bk.rev. circ. 7,000. **Document type:** trade publication.
　Formerly (until Feb. 1984): Materials Handling and Storage (ISSN 0047-6234).
　Description: Provides comprehensive coverage of automation in the materials handling, storage and distribution industry. Offers articles on the latest technology, systems in use and product developments in process.

658 658　　　GW　　ISSN 0937-4183
MATERIALWIRTSCHAFT UND LOGISTIK IM UNTERNEHMEN; Materialwirtschaft fuer Manager. 1979. m. DM.168 (foreign DM.184). Verlag Praxiswissen, Hauert 20, 44227 Dortmund, Germany. Ed. A. Juenemann. **Document type:** trade publication.
—CCC.
　Formerly: Materialwirtschaft im Unternehmen (ISSN 0179-499X)

MATHEMATICAL METHODS OF OPERATIONS RESEARCH. see *MATHEMATICS — Computer Applications*

658 330.9 610　　　US
MEDICAL BUSINESS REVIEW;* medical business analysis for the doctor-executive. 1981. m. $144. Cast, Hursh & Associates, 4401 Taylor Rd., Fort Wayne, IN 46804-1913. TEL 219-436-3036. Ed. William Cast. bk.rev. circ. 2,000. (looseleaf format; back issues avail.)

MEDICAL GROUP MANAGEMENT ASSOCIATION. DIRECTORY. see *MEDICAL SCIENCES*

658　　　US　　ISSN 1052-4894
MEDICAL OFFICE MANAGER; the newsletter for physician office administrators. 1987. m. $182 (effective 1997); $192 (effective 1998). Ardmore Publishing Company, Box 52843, Atlanta, GA 30355. TEL 404-367-1991. FAX 404-367-1995. Ed. Susan Crawford; Pub. Susan Crawford. R&P contact: Susan Crawford. bk.rev.; index; circ. 3,700 (paid). (looseleaf format; back issues avail.) **Document type:** newsletter.
　Description: Covers issues and regulations affecting the management of medical practices.

658　　　GW
MEDIENREPORT. 1974. m. DM.162. Medienreport Verlags GmbH, Hegnacherstr. 30, 71336 Waiblingen, Germany. TEL 49-7151-23331. FAX 49-7151-23338. Ed. Rolf G. Lehmann. circ. 1,500. (back issues avail.) **Document type:** newsletter.

658　　　US
MEETINGS & EXPOSITIONS. m. membership. American Society of Association Executives, Meetings & Exhibitions Section, 1575 Eye St., N.W., Washington, DC 20005-1168. TEL 202-626-2789. FAX 202-289-4049. circ. 3,500.
　Formerly: Conventions and Expositions.
　Description: Features information for association meeting planning.

658　　　GW　　ISSN 0941-8342
DER MEISTERBRIEF FUER DEN BETRIEBSLEITER; Arbeitstechnik, Betriebspraxis, Menschenfuehrung. 1963. m. DM.132. Verlag Norbert Mueller AG und Co. KG, Ingolstaedterstr. 20, 80807 Munich, Germany. TEL 49-89-3509302. FAX 49-89-35093218. Ed. Stefan Uhlig. index. circ. 1,600. (back issues avail.) **Document type:** newsletter.

658　　　CC　　ISSN 1002-8315
MEITAN QIYE GUANLI/COAL INDUSTRY MANAGEMENT. (Text in Chinese) 1985. m. Beijing Meitan Guanli Ganbu Xueyuan, 2 Dingfu Zhuang, Chaoyang-qu, Beijing 199924, People's Republic of China. TEL 571031. Ed. Zhou Peiyu.

658　　　US
MEMBERSHIP DEVELOPMENTS. m. membership. American Society of Association Executives, Membership Section, 1575 Eye St., N.W., Washington, DC 20005-1168. TEL 202-626-2829. FAX 202-408-9635. circ. 2,650.
　Formerly: Membership Marketer.
　Description: Provides membership recruitment and retention techniques, job listings, and a calendar of events for membership professionals of associations.

658　　　UK　　ISSN 0963-6404
THE MENTOR MANAGEMENT DIGEST. 1991. 10/yr. £80 for 6 nos. 33 Kingsley Place, Newcastle-upon-Tyne NE6 5AN, England. TEL 0191-265-0838. FAX 0191-224-2868. Ed. Chris Ashton. bk.rev. circ. 1,000. **Document type:** bulletin.
　Description: Provides information on the realities and practice of management, human resources, training and staff development.

658 332　　　US
MERGERS & ACQUISITIONS CONSULTANT;* the management report and information resource. 1968. m. $297 (foreign $333). Princeton Research Institute, Management Centers, Box 2702, Scottsdale, AZ 85252-2702. TEL 609-396-0305. adv.; bk.rev.; charts; illus.; stat.
　Description: Covers all aspects of mergers, acquisitions, divestitures, leveraged buyouts, corporate restructurings, and joint ventures world-wide. Profiles acquirers, sellers, intermediaries and professional M and A service forms.

658 669.1　　　US　　ISSN 0894-0843
METALCASTER. (Former name of issuing body: Iron Casting Society) 1947. q. $14.50. American Cast Metals Association, 455 State St., Des Plaines, IL 60016. TEL 708-299-9160. FAX 708-299-3105. Ed. Nancy Brinkman. adv.; index. circ. 1,000. (processed) **Indexed:** B.C.I.R.A., Met.Abstr., World Alum.Abstr.
—CISTI.
　Former titles (until Winter 1987): Ironcaster (ISSN 0362-0425); Gray and Ductile Iron News (ISSN 0017-3584); Gray Iron News.

658　　　US
MIDDLE MANAGEMENT AND CLERICAL COMPENSATION REPORT - MEXICO. a. $860. (Executive Compensation Service (ECS)) Wyatt Data Services, 218 Rte. 17, N., Roselle Park, NJ 07662-9832. TEL 201-843-1177. FAX 201-843-0101. charts. **Document type:** trade publication.
　Description: Comprehensive information on what companies in Mexico are paying their middle management and clerical personnel.

658　　　US
MIDDLE MANAGEMENT COMPENSATION - REGRESSION ANALYSIS REPORT. (Supplement to: Regional Report on Middle Management Compensation) a. $690. (Executive Compensation Service (ECS)) Wyatt Data Services, 218 Rte. 17, N., Roselle Park, NJ 07662-9832. TEL 201-843-1177. FAX 201-843-0101. charts. **Document type:** trade publication.
　Description: Presents salary and total compensation equations for each position which are presented separately for ten industry categories.

658　　　US
MIDDLE MANAGEMENT HI - COMP REPORT. a. $490. (Executive Compensation Service (ECS)) Wyatt Data Services, 218 Rte. 17, N., Roselle Park, NJ 07662-9832. TEL 201-843-1177. FAX 201-843-0101. **Document type:** trade publication.
　Description: Presents data on the highest paid one-third of the sample.

658　　　US　　ISSN 0270-9023
HD4965.5.U6
MIDDLE MANAGEMENT REPORT. (In 2 vols.) a. $690. (Executive Compensation Service (ECS)) Wyatt Data Services, 218 Rte. 17, N., Roselle Park, NJ 07662-9832. TEL 201-843-1177. FAX 201-843-0101. **Document type:** trade publication.
　Description: Allows you to compare your rates and policies with other companies in your industry and of your size.

658 381　　　FR　　ISSN 0076-8812
MILLESIME. 1953. a. 25 F.($5) Association des Anciens Eleves de l'Ecole Superieur de Commerce de Paris, 79 Avenue de la Republique, 75011 Paris, France. adv.; bk.rev. circ. 8,000.

658　　　US
MINDPLAY; creativity & innovation in today's business environment. 1989. 4/yr. $135 membership. Innovation Network, 34 E. Sola St., Santa Barbara, CA 93101-1302. TEL 805-965-8477. FAX 805-963-8220. Ed. Joyce Wycoff. bk.rev. **Document type:** newsletter.
　Description: Presents ideas and information related to building 21st century thinking skills. For business managers, trainers, team leaders, new-product developers, and consultants.

MINI-STORAGE MESSENGER. see *BUSINESS AND ECONOMICS — Domestic Commerce*

MODERN BAKING. see *FOOD AND FOOD INDUSTRIES — Bakers And Confectioners*

BUSINESS AND ECONOMICS — MANAGEMENT

658   SW   ISSN 1101-492X
MODERN INDUSTRI. 1989. q. SEK 150 (effective 1990). (Modern Industri) Wall Street Media Inc., P.O. Box 19069, S-104 32 Stockholm, Sweden. TEL 46-8-32-09-06. Ed. Erkki Karjalainen.

658   UK   ISSN 0951-6522
MODERN MANAGEMENT. (Former name of issuing body: Institute of Supervisory Management) 1949. bi-m. £24 (overseas £39) (effective 1994-1995). Institute for Supervision and Management, 22 Bore St., Lichfield, Staffs. WS13 6LP, England. TEL 44-1543-251346. FAX 44-1543-415804. Ed. R.G. Hewitt. R&P contact: R.G. Hewitt. adv.; bk.rev.; film rev.; charts; illus. circ. 25,000. (reprint service avail. from SCH) **Indexed:** Account.& Data Proc.Abstr., ASEAN Manage.Abstr., Bus.Ind., PROMT, Stud.Wom.Abstr. **Document type:** newsletter.
—BLDSC (5889.048000).
Former titles: Supervisory Management (Lichfield) (ISSN 0950-9895); Supervisor (ISSN 0039-5862)

658   UK
MODERN QUALITY MANAGEMENT JOURNAL. 1991. a. Longman Group UK Ltd., Longman House, Burnt Mill, Harlow, Essex CM20 2JE, England. TEL 44-1279-426721. FAX 44-1279-431059. E-mail: longhe@cityscape.co.uk. (Subscr. to: Pearson Professional, P.O. Box 77, Fourth Ave., Harlow, Essex CM19 5BQ, England. TEL 44-1279-623924. FAX 44-1279-639609) cum.index. (looseleaf format)

658   XR   ISSN 1210-4094
MODERNI OBCHOD. bi-m. Ceske a Slovenske Odborne Nakladatelstvi (Subsidiary of: Deutscher Fachverlag GmbH), Na Prikope 27, 11349 Prague 1, Czech Republic. TEL 02-2688964. FAX 02-262893. circ. 13,000. **Document type:** trade publication.
Description: Provides information on management in the wholesale and retail trade in the Czech Republic and Slovak Republic.

658   XR   ISSN 0026-8720
MODERNI RIZENI. 1966. m. (Ceska Tiskova Kancelar - Czech News Agency) Economia, a.s., Na Florenci 3, 115 43 Prague 1, Czech Republic. Ed. E. Motejzikova. bk.rev.; abstr.; charts; illus.; cum.index: 1966-1970. circ. 8,200.

658   AT
MONASH MT. ELIZA BUSINESS REVIEW. 1980. s-a. Aus.$40 (effective 1997). (Monash Mt. Eliza Business School) Niche Media Pty. Ltd., Level 3, 165 Fitzroy St., St. Kilda, Vic. 3182, Australia. TEL 61-3-95255566. FAX 61-3-95255628. URL: http://www.mteliza.edu.au. Ed. Clarence D.G. Pinto; Pub. Steven Metter. R&P contact: Terri Hosking. TEL 61-3-92151173. adv.: B&W page Aus.$2700, color page Aus.$3200; trim 275 x 210; adv. contact: Steven Metter. bk.rev. circ. 6,000. **Indexed:** ABI Inform., Aus.P.A.I.S. **Document type:** academic/scholarly publication.
—BLDSC (6597.810000); UMI; UnCover.
Formerly (until 1997): Practising Manager (ISSN 0159-1193)
Description: For top management in the Asia-Pacific region. Presents thoughtful articles on innovations in global leadership and management thinking.

658   GW   ISSN 0936-3041
MOTIVATION; Magazin fuer Feuhrungskraefte. 1990. bi-m. DM.78. Huss-Verlag GmbH, Joseph-Dollinger-Bogen 5, 80807 Munich, Germany. TEL 49-89-32391-0. FAX 49-89-32391416. (Subscr. to: Postfach 460480, 80912 Munich, Germany) **Document type:** trade publication.

MOTIVATIONAL MANAGER. see COMMUNICATIONS

MOTOR FLEET SUPERVISION; principles and practices. see BUSINESS AND ECONOMICS — Personnel Management

658   GW   ISSN 0721-6823
MUENZAUTOMAT; Fachzeitschrift fuer der Automatenbranche. 1952. m. DM.138 (foreign DM.168) (effective 1997). Universitaet-Druckerei und Verlag H. Schmidt GmbH, Robert-Koch-Str. 8, 55129 Mainz, Germany. TEL 49-6131-958350-0. FAX 49-6131-958366. Ed. Manfred Schloesser. adv. contact: Ingrid Goetz. bk.rev. circ. 4,800. **Document type:** trade publication.

658 332.6   US
MULTINATIONAL MANAGERS AND DEVELOPING COUNTRIES. 1987. irreg., vol.5, 1996. price varies. University of Notre Dame Press, Notre Dame, IN 46556. TEL 219-631-6346. FAX 219-631-8148. (Subscr. in US to: 11030 S. Langley Ave., Chicago, IL 60628. TEL 800-621-2736; Overseas subscr. to: Eurospan University Press Group, 3 Henrietta St., London WC2E 8LU, England) R&P contact: Ann Bromley. TEL 219-631-6346. **Document type:** monographic series.
Description: Discussions of the social, economic, and ethical issues faced by managers of multinational corporations in the context of today's global community.

MUSIC MANAGEMENT & INTERNATIONAL PROMOTION; the magazine behind the business news. see MUSIC

658 370   US
N A I E C NEWSLETTER. 1964. bi-m. $25. National Association for Industry - Education Cooperation, 235 Hendricks Blvd., Buffalo, NY 14226-3304. TEL 716-837-7047. FAX 716-834-7047. Ed. Vito Pace. adv. contact: Donald M. Clark. bk.rev.; cum.index. circ. 728. (back issues avail.) **Document type:** newsletter.
Description: Provides information on industry involvement in education, including summaries of studies and research projects, news of events, conferences, legislation and resources.
Refereed Serial

N A P A M A NEWS. (National Association of Performing Arts Managers and Agents) see THEATER

658   US   ISSN 0047-8717
HD9697.U4
N A R D A NEWS. 1943. m. $65. North American Retail Dealers Association, 10 E. 22nd St., Ste. 310, Lombard, IL 60148-6191. TEL 630-953-8950. FAX 630-953-8957. E-mail: nardanews@aol.com. Ed. Russ Gager. R&P contact: Russ Gager. adv. contact: Russ Gager. charts; illus.; index. circ. 5,000. **Document type:** trade publication.

658   US
N A W REPORT. 1972. 6/yr. membership. National Association of Wholesaler - Distributors, 1725 K St., N.W., Washington, DC 20006. TEL 202-872-0885. bk.rev. circ. 10,000. **Document type:** newsletter.
Former titles: Channels; N A W Newsletter.
Description: Covers business issues affecting wholesaling.

658   NE   ISSN 1380-7374
N I V E MANAGEMENT MAGAZINE. 1976. 6/yr. fl.125 to non-members. N I V E, Nederlandse Vereniging voor Management, Postbus 266, 2270 AG Voorburg, Netherlands. TEL 31-70-3001500. FAX 31-70-3001599. E-mail: nive@euronet.nl. Ed. W. Pisa; Pub. Th. Wiersma. adv. contact: A.H.C. Thijssen. illus. circ. 19,000. **Document type:** trade publication.
Former titles (until 1994): N M2 (N I V E Management Magazine) (ISSN 0926-4221); (until 1992): N2 (N I V E Nieuws) (ISSN 0926-423X); (until 1991): N I V E Nieuws (ISSN 0926-4000)

N M A BULLETIN BOARD. (Nonprofit Management Association) see CLUBS

658 331.88   XR
N O S. (Noviny Odboroveho Svazu Statnich Organu a Organizaci) Variant title: Odvorovy Svaz Statnich Organu a Organizaci. Noviny. vol.10, 1965. s-m. $16.70. Kveta Dedovska, Ed. & Pub., Konevova 134, 130 00 Prague 3, Czech Republic. (Subscr. to: Artia, Ve Smeckach 30, 111 27 Prague 1, Czech Republic) **Document type:** trade publication.
Formerly (until 1990): Sluzba Lidu (ISSN 0037-7082)

DE NAAMLOOZE VENNOOTSCHAP; voorlichting op juridisch, economisch, bedrijfseconomisch en fiscaal gebied. see LAW

658   JA   ISSN 0912-6147
NANZAN KEIEI KENKYU/NANZAN MANAGEMENT REVIEW. (Text in Japanese) 1968. 3/yr. free. Nanzan University, 18 Yamazato-cho, Showa-ku, Nagoya 466, Japan. TEL 052-832-3111. FAX 052-832-6157. **Document type:** academic/scholarly publication.
—BLDSC (6015.343910).
Supersedes in part (in 1986): Akademia. Keizai Keieigaku Hen (ISSN 0389-844X); Which superseded in part (in 1975): Akademia (ISSN 0515-8680)

NATIONAL ADVERTISING AGENCY NETWORK. MANAGEMENT REPORT. see ADVERTISING AND PUBLIC RELATIONS

658 615   US   ISSN 1079-1116
NATIONAL ASSOCIATION OF CHAIN DRUG STORES. EXECUTIVE NEWSLETTER. Variant title: N A C D S Executive Newsletter. bi-w. $100. National Association of Chain Drug Stores, Box 1417-D49, Alexandria, VA 22313-1417. TEL 703-549-3001. FAX 703-836-4869. Ed. John Covert. circ. 3,000. **Document type:** newsletter.
Description: Summaries of government and pharmacy activity on issues of concern to top level chain drug store executives. Includes member news, as well as activities of the Association.

NATIONAL BUSINESS WOMAN. see WOMEN'S INTERESTS

658   US   ISSN 1045-1668
K14   CODEN: NCMJB9
NATIONAL CONTRACT MANAGEMENT JOURNAL. 1966. s-a. $35. National Contract Management Association, 1912 Woodford Rd., Vienna, VA 22182-3728. bk.rev.; bibl.; charts; illus. **Indexed:** ABI Inform., Air Un.Lib.Ind., BPIA, Bus.Ind., INSPEC, Tr.& Indus.Ind. **Document type:** academic/scholarly publication.
●Also available online. Vendor(s): UMI.
—BLDSC (6021.854000); UMI; UnCover.
Former titles: National Contract Management Quarterly Journal (ISSN 0163-2124); National Contract Management Journal (ISSN 0027-9064)
Description: Publishes research and in-depth studies of issues in contract management.
Refereed Serial

NATIONAL CREDITOR-DEBTOR REVIEW; a journal of creditor-debtor relations. see BUSINESS AND ECONOMICS — Banking And Finance

NATIONAL FORUM OF EDUCATION ADMINISTRATION AND SUPERVISION JOURNAL. see EDUCATION — School Organization And Administration

NATIONAL FUND RAISER. see SOCIAL SERVICES AND WELFARE

658.4   MY
NATIONAL PRODUCTIVITY CORPORATION, MALAYSIA. ANNUAL REPORT/PERBADANAN PRODUKTIVITI NEGARA. LAPURAN TAHUNAN. (Text in English and Malay) 1962. a. free. National Productivity Centre - Pusat Daya Pengeluaran Negara, Sultan St., Box 64, 46904 Petaling Jaya, Malaysia. TEL 03-7557266. FAX 03-7578068. TELEX MA-36312. circ. 2,000.
Formerly: National Productivity Centre, Malaysia. Annual Report (ISSN 0126-8392)

658   US   ISSN 0277-8556
HD56
NATIONAL PRODUCTIVITY REVIEW; the journal of productivity management. 1981. q. $240 (foreign $264) (effective 1998). John Wiley & Sons, Inc., Journals, 605 Third Ave., New York, NY 10158. TEL 212-850-6645. FAX 212-850-6021. E-mail: subinfo@jwiley.com; URL: http://www.wiley.co.uk. Ed. Mary Ann Castronovo Fusco. adv.: B&W page £640, color page £1515; trim 279 x 210. (also avail. in microform from UMI; reprint service avail. from UMI) **Indexed:** ABI Inform., Account.& Data Proc.Abstr., B.P.I., BPIA, Bus.Ind., Manage.Cont., Oper.Res.Manage.Sci., P.A.I.S., Pers.Lit., Q.Abstr., Qual.Contr.Appl.Stat., Tr.& Dev.Alert, Tr.& Indus.Ind. **Document type:** trade publication.
●Also available online. Vendor(s): Information Access Co.
—BLDSC (6029.735000); KR SourceOne; SWETS; UMI; UnCover. **CCC.**
Description: Focuses on productivity management, practical productivity programs, work innovation and design, human services, quality of work life, robotics, and systems improvement.

BUSINESS AND ECONOMICS — MANAGEMENT

658   US   ISSN 0749-9884
NATIONAL REPORT FOR TRAINING AND DEVELOPMENT. Running title: A S T D National Report. 1975. 6/yr. $25 to non-members. American Society for Training and Development, 1640 King St., Box 1443, Alexandria, VA 22313. TEL 703-683-8129. FAX 703-683-8103. Ed. Craig Steinburg. circ. 28,000. (reprint service avail. from UMI)

658   UK
NATWEST S B R T QUARTERLY SURVEY OF SMALL BUSINESS IN BRITAIN. 1985. q. £55. Open University, Small Business Research Trust, Business School, Walton Hall, Milton Keynes, Bucks. MK7 6AA, England. TEL 44-1908-655831. FAX 44-1908-655898. E-mail: oubs-sbrt@open.ac.uk; URL: http://www.iet.open.ac.uk/iet/sbrt/sbrt.htm. R&P contact: Colin Gray. **Document type:** trade publication.
    Former titles: NatWest S B R T Quarterly Survey of Small Business in the UK (ISSN 0961-4222); NatWest Quarterly Survey of Small Business in Britain (ISSN 0952-1534)

NEIL MUSCOTT'S SUCCESS NEWSLETTER; strategies and stories for successful people. see PSYCHOLOGY

DIE NEUE VERWALTUNG. see PUBLIC ADMINISTRATION

658   US
NEW APPROACHES TO EMPLOYEE MANAGEMENT. 1992. irreg., vol.4, 1996. $73.25. J A I Press Inc., 55 Old Post Rd., No. 2, Box 1678, Greenwich, CT 06830-1678. TEL 203-661-7602. FAX 203-661-0792. E-mail: jai@jaipress.com. (Subscr. in UK and Europe to: JAI Press Ltd., 38 Tavistock St., Covent Garden, London WC2E 7PB, England. TEL 44-171-379-8834. FAX 44-171-379-8835) Ed. David Saunders. **Document type:** monographic series.

658   US   ISSN 0192-091X
HD69.C6
NEW CONSULTANTS. (Supplement to: Consultants and Consulting Organizations Directory) 1973. s-a. $360. Gale Research, 835 Penobscot Bldg., 645 Griswold St., Detroit, MI 48226-4094. TEL 313-961-2242; 800-877-4253. FAX 800-414-5043. TELEX 810-221-7086. E-mail: daniel_snyder@gale.com. Ed. Janice McLean.
—CISTI.

NEW DIRECTIONS FOR PHILANTHROPIC FUND RAISING. see SOCIAL SERVICES AND WELFARE

NEW ENGLAND ACCOUNTING RESEARCH STUDIES (NO.). see BUSINESS AND ECONOMICS — Accounting

NEW JERSEY STATE BAR ASSOCIATION. CREDITOR AND DEBTOR RELATIONS SECTION NEWSLETTER. see BUSINESS AND ECONOMICS — Banking And Finance

NEW MANAGEMENT. see COMMUNICATIONS — Postal Affairs

NEWSINC. see PUBLISHING AND BOOK TRADE

NEWSINC.'S STATE OF THE INDUSTRY REPORT. see JOURNALISM

658 070   US   ISSN 0889-4590
PN4734
NEWSPAPER FINANCIAL EXECUTIVES JOURNAL.* 1949. 10/yr. $100. International Newspaper Financial Executives, 21525 Ridgetop Circle, Ste. 200, Sterling, VA 20166-6510. TEL 703-648-1160. FAX 703-476-5961. Ed. Jeanie E. Ingram. adv.; bk.rev.; index, cum.index. circ. 1,200. (reprints avail. from UMI) Indexed: Account.Ind. (1974-).
—UMI; UnCover.
    Formerly: Newspaper Controller (ISSN 0028-9558)
    Description: Contains original articles contributed by members and others about accounting, information processing, profit planning, cost control, systems and procedures, and related problems in the newspaper field.

658   NE   ISSN 0929-7774
NIEUWSBRIEF ABSENT! Cover title: Absent! 1994. bi-m. Samsom H.D. Tjeenk Willink B.V. (Subsidiary of: Wolters Kluwer N.V.), Postbus 316, 2400 AH Alphen aan den Rijn, Netherlands. TEL 31-1720-66822. FAX 31-1720-66639. **Document type:** newsletter.

658   NR   ISSN 0331-0612
NIGERIAN JOURNAL OF BUSINESS MANAGEMENT. 1977. bi-m. $115.20. Fred Atoki Publishing Co. Ltd., Plot 25 Kekere-Ekun St., Orile-Iganmu, Box 7313, Lagos, Nigeria. Ed. F.O.A. Atoki. adv.; illus. circ. 20,600.

658   NR   ISSN 0189-2568
NIGERIAN MANAGEMENT REVIEW. (In 1 vol.) (Text in English) 1985. q. $38.03 to individuals; institutions $40. Centere for Management Development, Management Village, P.M.B. 21578, Ikeja, Lagos State, Nigeria. TEL 234-64-901120-2. Ed. Udo Udo-Aka. adv.; bk.rev. circ. 25,000. **Document type:** trade publication.

658   JA   ISSN 0386-4812
NIHON KEIKEI KOGAKKAISHI/JAPAN INDUSTRIAL MANAGEMENT ASSOCIATION. JOURNAL. (Text in Japanese; summaries in English) 1950. bi-m. Nihon Keikei Kogakkai, Nihon Gakkai Jimu Senta, 16-9, Honkomagome 5-chome, Bunkyo-ku, Tokyo 113, Japan. Indexed: JCT.
    Formerly (until 1974): J I M A News (ISSN 0386-4804)

658   IS   ISSN 0333-5658
HD28
NIHUL; Israel managers magazine. q. Israel Management Center, P.O. Box 33033, Tel Aviv, Israel. TEL 03-257202. Ed. Avraham Tal.

658   JA   ISSN 0913-3429
NIKKEI DESIGN. (Text in Japanese) 1987. m. 18500 Yen. Nikkei Business Publications, Inc. (Subsidiary of: Nihon Keizai Shimbun, Inc.), 2-7-6 Hirakawa-cho, Chiyoda-ku, Tokyo 102, Japan. TEL 81-3-5210-8321. FAX 81-3-5210-8119. URL: http://www.nikkeibp.co.jp/. Ed. Akiko Moriyama; Pub. Tomoe Nishmura. adv.: B&W page 291000 Yen, color page 497000 Yen; trim 210 x 280; adv. contact: Tatsuya Saito. circ. 16,672. **Document type:** trade publication.
    Description: Provides information on all aspects of corporate design activities, from the perspective of business and management.

658.048   US   ISSN 1048-6682
HD62.6   CODEN: NMLEES
NONPROFIT MANAGEMENT AND LEADERSHIP. 1990. q. $54 to individuals; institutions $105; sample issue free to librarians (effective 1997). Jossey-Bass Inc., Publishers, 350 Sansome St., 5th Fl., San Francisco, CA 94104. TEL 800-956-7739. FAX 800-605-2665. URL: http://www.josseybass.com. (Editorial sponsoring bodies: Mandel Center for Nonprofit Organizations of Case Western Reserve University; London School of Economics Centre for Voluntary Organisation) Eds. Dennis R. Young, David Billis. R&P contact: Lorri Wimer. bk.rev. circ. 1,300. (Back issues avail.) Indexed: B.P.I. **Document type:** academic/scholarly publication.
—BLDSC (6117.340150); KR SourceOne; UMI.
    Description: Offers authoritative insights of top executives and researchers on the common concerns of all nonprofit managers.
    Refereed Serial

658   US   ISSN 0896-5048
NONPROFIT TIMES; the leading publication for nonprofit news and management. 1987. m. $59 (Canada $89; elsewhere $129); newsstand price: $6. Davis Information Group, 240 Cedar Knolls Rd., Ste. 318, Cedar Knolls, NJ 07927-1621. TEL 201-734-1700. FAX 201-734-1777. E-mail: nptimes@haven.ios.com. Pub. Kevin Landers. R&P contact: Paul Clolery. adv.; bk.rev.; bibl.; charts; illus.; stat.; tr.lit.; index. circ. 34,000. (tabloid format; also avail. in microfiche; back issues avail.) **Document type:** trade publication.
    Description: News and "how to" information on funding, management for any nonprofit organization.

658   IT   ISSN 0393-8212
NUOVO GOVERNO LOCALE. 1983. 3/yr. L.66000 (foreign L.80000); with supplements L.80000 (foreign L.95000) (effective 1993). (Provincia di Milano) Franco Angeli Editore, Via Monza, 106, 20127 Milan, Italy. TEL 02 28-27-651. Ed. A. Martinelli. adv.; bk.rev. circ. 6,400. (tabloid format; back issues avail.)

650   DK
NYHEDSBREV (COPENHAGEN). 1987. 6/yr. free. Danish Management Forum, Folke Bernadottes Alle 45, DK-2100 Copenhagen OE, Denmark. TEL 45-35-27-77-77. FAX 4535-27-77-99. Ed. Ruth Znaider. R&P contact: Inger Skytte. bk.rev.; illus. circ. 3,000. **Document type:** newsletter.
    Former titles: NetNyt (ISSN 0902-4468); Netvaerk; Netvaerkstedet; D.M.C. Information (ISSN 0107-8216)

O B G MANAGEMENT. (Obstetrics and Gynecology) see MEDICAL SCIENCES — Obstetrics And Gynecology

658   SA
O D DEBATE; reflecting on organisations and development. 1994. bi-m. R.95 in South Africa; other African countries R.125; elsewhere R.185. Olive Subscription Service, 21 Sycamore Rd., Glenwood, Durban 4001, South Africa. TEL 27-31-253947. FAX 27-31-252114. E-mail: oliveodt@iafrica.com; URL: http://www.epages.net/olive. Indexed: Ind.S.A.Per.
    Description: Aimed at development workers, OD practitioners, managers, and all other people who are grappling with organizational change and development.

O D T U GELISME DERGISI/M E T U STUDIES IN DEVELOPMENT. (Orta Dogu Teknik Universitesi) see BUSINESS AND ECONOMICS — Economic Systems And Theories, Economic History

O R - M S TODAY. (Operations Research - Management Science) see SCIENCES: COMPREHENSIVE WORKS

O R - M S TOMORROW. (Operations Research - Management Science) see COMPUTERS

OEKONOMETRIE UND UNTERNEHMENSFORSCHUNG/ECONOMETRICS AND OPERATIONS RESEARCH. see BUSINESS AND ECONOMICS

658.4   DK   ISSN 0900-8322
OEKONOMISTYRING OG INFORMATIK. 1986. 6/yr. DKK 1200 (effective 1997). Jurist- og Oekonomforbundets Forlag, Gothersgade 133, DK-1123 Copenhagen K, Denmark. TEL 45-33-95-97-00. FAX 45-33-95-99-97. Ed. Preben Melander. circ. 700. **Document type:** academic/scholarly publication.
    Description: Theoretical and practical information for professionals in the fields of management accounting, management information systems and leadership.

OF COUNSEL; the monthly legal practice report. see LAW

658   UK   ISSN 1352-5573
OFFICE COMPANION BULLETIN. Variant title: Croner's Office Companion Bulletin. 1994. base vol. (plus q. updates). £145 (updates £92.20) (effective 1995). Croner Publications Ltd. (Subsidiary of: Wolters Kluwer N.V.), Croner House, 100 Kingston Rd., Kingston-upon-Thames, Surrey TW2 6SR, England. TEL 44-181-547-3333. FAX 44-181-247-1300. TELEX 267778. (looseleaf format) **Document type:** trade publication.

OFFICE PERSONNEL REPORT. see BUSINESS AND ECONOMICS — Personnel Management

BUSINESS AND ECONOMICS — MANAGEMENT

658　　　　　　UK　　ISSN 0305-0483
HD28　　　　　　　CODEN: OMEGA6
OMEGA; international journal of management science. 1973. bi-m. fl.1221($702) (effective 1998). Elsevier Science Ltd., Pergamon, P.O. Box 800, Kidlington, Oxford OX5 1DX, England. TEL 44-1865-843000. FAX 44-1865-843010. E-mail: nlinfo-f@elsevier.nl; usinfo-f@elsevier.com; forinfo-kyf04035@niftyserve.or.jp; URL: http://www.elsevier.nl/. (Subscr. to: Elsevier Science, Regional Sales Office, P.O. Box 211, 1000 AE Amsterdam, Netherlands. TEL 31-20-4853757. FAX 31-20-4853432; Subscr. in the Americas to: Elsevier Science, Regional Sales Office, Box 945, New York, NY 10159-0945. TEL 212-633-3730. FAX 212-633-3680; Subscr. in Australasia and the Far East to: Elsevier Science (Singapore) Pte Ltd, No.1 Temasek Ave., No.17-01 Millenia Tower, Singapore 039192, Singapore. TEL 65-434-3727. FAX 65-337-2230) Ed. Samuel Eilon. adv.; bk.rev.; abstr.; bibl.; illus. circ. 1,400. (also avail. in microfilm from UMI; back issues avail.) **Indexed:** Account.& Data Proc.Abstr., Appl.Mech.Rev., BPIA, Bus.Ind., C.I.J.E., Compumath, Cont.Pg.Manage., Crim.Just.Abstr., Curr.Cont., Data Process.Dig., Excerp.Med., Geo.Abstr.P.G., High.Educ.Curr.Aware.Bull., IMFL, INPEC, Manage.Cont., Mid.East: Abstr.& Ind., Oper.Res.Manage.Sci., Qual.Contr.Appl.Stat., Risk Abstr., SCIMP, Tr.& Indus.Ind. **Document type:** academic/scholarly publication.
—BLDSC (6256.426000); AskIEEE; Genuine Article; KR SourceOne; Linda Hall; SWETS; UMI. **CCC.**
Description: Reports on the latest developments in management, including research results and applications, as well as assessments of specific management techniques.
Refereed Serial

658 352.84　　US　　ISSN 1087-6391
▼**ON THE MARK**. 1995. q. Underwriters Laboratories Inc., Corporate Communications, 333 Pfingsten Rd., Northbrook, IL 60062-2096. TEL 847-272-8800. FAX 847-272-8129. TELEX 6502543343. E-mail: nissenm@ul.com; URL: http://www.ul.com. Ed. Michael Nissen. R&P contact: Carole Feil. circ. 80,000(controlled). (back issues avail.) **Document type:** newsletter.
Description: Provides news and insight into conformity assessment issues to help companies manage global certification problems.

ONLINE AND C D - R O M MANAGEMENT AND MARKETING DATABASES. see *LIBRARY AND INFORMATION SCIENCES — Computer Applications*

OPERATING RESULTS OF INDEPENDENT SUPERMARKETS. see *BUSINESS AND ECONOMICS — Small Business*

658　　　　　　US
OPERATION ENTERPRISE NEWS. 1970. s-a. free. American Management Association, 1601 Broadway, New York, NY 10019. Ed. Andrew Mason. circ. 6,500. (looseleaf format; back issues avail.)
Description: Provides news about Operation Enterprise programs, alumni, and sponsors.

OPERATIONAL RESEARCH SOCIETY. JOURNAL. see *COMPUTERS*

658　　　　　　US　　ISSN 1069-6083
OPERATIONS & FULFILLMENT; practical solutions for catalog and direct response operations management. 1993. bi-m. $36. Target, 535 Connecticut Ave., Norwalk, CT 06854. TEL 203-857-5656. FAX 203-857-5654. Ed. Bristol Voss. adv. contact: Lisa Blumenschine. software rev.; charts; illus. circ. 10,500. (back issues avail.) **Document type:** trade publication.
Description: Covers call centers, warehouses distribution, shipping, systems, and software for executives involved with direct response and direct mail fulfillment.

OPERATIONS RESEARCH. see *COMPUTERS*

OPERATIONS RESEARCH COMPUTER SCIENCE INTERFACE. see *COMPUTERS*

658.4　　　　　　JA　　ISSN 0453-4514
T57.6.A1　　　　　　CODEN: JORJA5
OPERATIONS RESEARCH SOCIETY OF JAPAN. JOURNAL/NIHON OPERESHONZU RISACHI GAKKAI RONBUNSHI. (Text in English, French, German, Japanese) 1957. q. 13200 Yen($90) Operations Research Society of Japan - Nihon Opereshonzu Risachi Gakkai, Gakkai-Center Building, 2-4-16, Yayoi 2-chome, Bunkyo-ku, Tokyo 113, Japan. TEL 81-3-3815-3351. FAX 81-3-3815-3352. Ed. Takashi Kobayashi. index. circ. 3,000. **Indexed:** ASCA, Compumath, INSPEC, Int.Abstr.Oper.Res., J.Cont.Quant.Meth., JTA, Sci.Cit.Ind., SSCI, Zent.Math.
—BLDSC (4836.010000); AskIEEE; CISTI; Genuine Article; KR SourceOne; Linda Hall; SWETS. **CCC.**

OPERATIONS UPDATE (NEW YORK). see *BUSINESS AND ECONOMICS*

003　　　　　　JA　　ISSN 0030-3674
OPERESHONZU RISACHI/OPERATIONS RESEARCH SOCIETY OF JAPAN. COMMUNICATIONS. 1956. m. 12160 Yen. Operations Research Society of Japan - Nihon Opereshonzu Risachi Gakkai, Gakkai-Center Building, 2-4-16 Yayoi, Bunkyo-ku, Tokyo 113, Japan. TEL 81-3-3815-3351. FAX 81-3-3815-3352. Ed. Hiroshi Takamori. bk.rev.; abstr.; index. circ. 4,200. **Indexed:** Compumath, Int.Abstr.Oper.Res.
—CISTI.
Formerly: Keiei Kagaku - Management Science (ISSN 0451-5978)

658　　　　　　II　　ISSN 0030-3887
HD20.5　　　　　　CODEN: OPSEAN
OPSEARCH. (Text in English) 1964. q. $32. Operational Research Society of India, Care Institute for Systems Studies and Analyses, T-44, Metcalfe House, Delhi 110 054, India. Ed. N.K. Jaiswal. adv.; bk.rev.; charts; illus.; index. circ. 2,000. **Indexed:** Biostat., Curr.Cont. (1993)-, INSPEC, Int.Abstr.Oper.Res., J.Cont.Quant.Meth., Math.R., Oper.Res.Manage.Sci., Qual.Contr.Appl.Stat., Stat.Theor.Meth.Abstr. (1993-), Zent.Math. **Document type:** academic/scholarly publication.
—BLDSC (6272.700000); AskIEEE; KR SourceOne; SWETS. **CCC.**

658　　　　　　CN　　ISSN 0475-1906
HD28
OPTIMUM. (Catalog no. P73-1) (Text in English or French) 1970. q. Can.$20 (foreign $24). Canada Communication Group, Publishing Division, Ottawa, ON K1A 0S9, Canada. TEL 819-956-4802. Ed. Mrs. J. Howes. bk.rev.; adv.; index; circ. 1,200 (controlled). **Indexed:** ABI Inform., Account.& Data Proc.Abstr., Anbar, BPIA, Can.B.P.I., Can.Per.Ind., Data Process.Dig., INSPEC, Int.Polit.Sci.Abstr., Int.Polit.Sci.Abstr., Manage.Cont., P.A.I.S., P.A.I.S.For.Lang.Ind., Pers.Lit., Pers.Manage.Abstr., Work Rel.Abstr. **Document type:** trade publication.
●Also available online. Vendor(s): Information Access Co.
—BLDSC (6275.200000); AskIEEE; KR SourceOne; UMI; UnCover. **CCC.**
Description: A forum for management.

658　　　　　　FR　　ISSN 0030-4964
ORGANISATION GESTION DES ENTERPRISES. m. Editions Jean Deit, 14 rue de la Somme, Cachan (Seine), France. adv.; bk.rev.; charts; stat.

658　　　　　　UK　　ISSN 1350-6269
ORGANISATIONS & PEOPLE. 1994. q. £85 (N. and S. America $160) (effective 1997). (Association for Management Education and Development) Kogan Page Ltd., 120 Pentonville Rd., London N1 9JN, England. TEL 44-171-278-0433. FAX 44-171-837-6348. TELEX 263088 KOGAN G. (Subscr. to: Turpin Distribution Services Ltd., Blackhorse Rd., Letchworth, Herts. SG6 1HN, England. TEL 44-1462-672555. FAX 44-1462-480947) Ed. Prabhu Guptara. R&P contact: Linda Batman. **Indexed:** Mgmt.& Market.Abstr. **Document type:** trade publication.
—BLDSC (6289.370000). **CCC.**

658　　　　　　SZ　　ISSN 0473-2839
DER ORGANISATOR. 10/yr. Verlag Organisator AG, Flueelastr. 47, CH-8047 Zurich, Switzerland. TEL 01-4011212. FAX 01-4010815. Ed. Franz Schnyder. circ. 15,000. **Document type:** trade publication.

658　　　　　　YU　　ISSN 0351-3432
ORGANIZACIJA SAMOUPRAVLJANJA OUR; casopis za pitanja stimulativne raspodele i obracuna po ekonomskim jedinicama. (Text in Serbo-Croatian) 1962. m. 500 din. Zavod za Ekonomske Ekspertize, Palmira Toljatija 3, Belgrade, Yugoslavia. Ed. Dr. Bogdan Orlovic. circ. 2,000.
Former titles: Radna Jedinica (ISSN 0013-3221); Ekonomska Jedinica.

658 330　　　PL　　ISSN 0137-5466
ORGANIZACJA I KIEROWANIE/ORGANIZATION AND MANAGEMENT. (Text in Polish; summaries in English) 1975. q. $15. (Polskia Akademia Nauk, Komitet Nauk Organizacji i Zarzadzania) Centrum Informacji Naukowo Technicznej, Ul. Zelazna 87, 00-879 Warsaw, Poland. FAX 48-22-246061. (Dist. by: Ars Polona, Krakowskie Przedmiescie 7, 00-068 Warsaw, Poland) Ed. Leszek J. Krzyzanowski.
Description: Covers cybernetics, computer science, sociology of organization, economics of organization and related fields.

658　　　　　　UK　　ISSN 1350-5084
HM131　　　　　　CODEN: OGANF4
ORGANIZATION; the interdisciplinary journal of organization, theory and society. 1994. q. £42($67) to individuals; institutions £140($224) (effective 1998). Sage Publications Ltd., 6 Bonhill St., London EC2A 4PU, England. TEL 44-171-374-0645. FAX 44-171-374-8741. E-mail: market@sagepub.co.uk; URL: http://www.sagepub.co.uk/. (Addr. in the U.S.: Sage Publications Inc., Box 5096, Thousand Oaks, CA 91359) Ed.Bd. adv. contact: Bernie Folan. bk.rev. **Indexed:** Anbar, ASCA, Cont.Pg.Manage., Curr.Cont., Int.Polit.Sci.Abstr., Pub.Admin.Abstr., Stud.Wom.Abstr., Urb.Aff.Abstr. **Document type:** academic/scholarly publication.
—BLDSC (6290.630000); Genuine Article; SWETS.
Description: Provides an interdisciplinary forum to address a broad spectrum of issues and to establish a "neo-disciplinary" organization studies framework relevant to the 1990s and beyond.

ORGANIZATION & ENVIRONMENT. see *OCCUPATIONAL HEALTH AND SAFETY*

658　　　　　　US　　ISSN 0889-6402
ORGANIZATION DEVELOPMENT JOURNAL; guiding the future of people working together. 1983. q. $60 to libraries & institutions (effective 1997 & 1998). Organization Development Institute (Cleveland), 781 Beta Dr., Ste. K, Cleveland, OH 44143. TEL 216-461-4333. FAX 216-729-9319. E-mail: donwcole@aol.com; URL: http://members.aol.com/odinst. (Subscr. to: 11234 Walnut Ridge Rd., Chesterland, OH 44021) Ed. Donald W. Cole. R&P contact: Donald W. Cole. adv.; bk.rev. circ. 800. (also avail. in microform from UMI; back issues avail; reprint service avail. from UMI) **Indexed:** Psychol.Abstr. (1984-), Q.Abstr., Tr.& Dev.Alert.
—BLDSC (6290.716000); KR SourceOne; UMI; UnCover.
Description: Practical journal for those interested in organization development and management development.
Refereed Serial

658　　　　　　US　　ISSN 1047-7039
HD28　　　　　　CODEN: ORSCEZ
ORGANIZATION SCIENCE. 1990. q. $65 to individuals (foreign $77); institutions $118 (foreign $130) (effective 1997). Institute for Operations Research and the Management Sciences, 901 Elkridge Landing Rd., Ste. 400, Linthicum, MD 21090-2909. TEL 410-850-0300; 800-343-0062. Ed. Arie Lewin. R&P contact: Fran Silverman. adv. contact: Kathye Long. **Indexed:** ASCA, Compumath, Curr.Cont., Oper.Res.Manage.Sci., Psychol.Abstr. (1990-), Qual.Contr.Appl.Stat., SSCI. **Document type:** academic/scholarly publication.
—BLDSC (6290.728000); Genuine Article; SWETS; UnCover. **CCC.**
Description: Interdisciplinary forum for research on organizations from diverse fields such as management, sociology, economics, political science, and psychology.

BUSINESS AND ECONOMICS — MANAGEMENT

658 US ISSN 0749-5978
BF636.A1 CODEN: OBDPFO
ORGANIZATIONAL BEHAVIOR AND HUMAN DECISION PROCESSES; a journal of fundamental research and theory in applied psychology. 1966. m. $775 (foreign $852) (effective 1997). Academic Press, Inc., Journal Division, 525 B St., Ste. 900, San Diego, CA 92101-4495. TEL 619-230-1840. FAX 619-699-6800. E-mail: apsubs@acad.com; URL: http://www.apnet.com/www/journal/ob.htm; http://www.idealibrary.com/. (Subscr. to: Box 861213, Orlando, FL 32886 12130. TEL 407-347-4040. FAX 407-363-9661) Ed. James C. Naylor. adv.; bibl.; charts; stat. (back issues avail.) **Indexed:** ASCA, ASSIA, B.P.I, BPIA, Bus.Ind., CINAHL, Commun.Abstr., Cont.Pg.Manage., Curr.Cont., Fam.Ind., Int.Lab.Doc., Mid.East: Abstr.& Ind., Psychol.Abstr. (1966-), Psycscan, Risk Abstr., SCIMP, SSCI, Tr.& Indus.Ind. **Document type:** academic/scholarly publication.
●Also available online.
—BLDSC (6290.749000); Genuine Article; KR SourceOne; SWETS; UMI. **CCC.**
   Formerly (until 1985): Organizational Behavior and Human Performance (ISSN 0030-5073)
   Description: Features articles that describe original empirical research and theoretical developments in all areas of human decision processes and organizational psychology.

658 US ISSN 0090-2616
HD28 CODEN: ORDYA
ORGANIZATIONAL DYNAMICS. 1972. q. $63 to non-members (foreign $98); members $56.70 (foreign $91.70). American Management Association, 1601 Broadway, New York, NY 10019. TEL 212-586-8100; 800-262-9699. E-mail: amapubs@aol.com. (Subscr. to: Box 319, Saranac Lake, NY 12983-0319) Ed. Don Bohl. index. circ. 5,500. (also avail. in microform from UMI; reprint service avail. from ISI,SCH,UMI) **Indexed:** ABI Inform., Account.& Data Proc.Abstr., Anbar, ASCA, ASEAN Manage.Abstr., B.P.I, BPIA, Bus.Ind., Cont.Pg.Manage., Curr.Cont., Manage.Cont., Pers.Lit., Pers.Manage.Abstr., Psychol.Abstr. (1973-), Psycscan, Pub.Admin.Abstr., Q.Abstr., SCIMP (1978-), SSCI, Tr.& Dev.Alert, Tr.& Indus.Ind., Work Rel.Abstr. **Document type:** trade publication.
●Also available online. Vendor(s): Information Access Co., UMI.
—BLDSC (6290.770000); CISTI; Genuine Article; KR SourceOne; SWETS; UMI; UnCover. **CCC.**
   Description: Features articles and interviews with leading managers and behavioral scientists on the application of the behavioral sciences to organizations.

ORGANIZATIONS AND CHANGE. see BUSINESS AND ECONOMICS — Personnel Management

658 RU
ORGANIZATSIYA UPRAVLENIYA. 1971. irreg. 0.81 Rub. Izdatel'stvo Ekonomika, Berezhkovskaya nab., 6, 121864 Moscow, Russia.

658 IT ISSN 0474-635X
ORGANIZZARSI. 1962. q. L.5000. Edizioni O.R.G.A, Via Amadeo d'Aosta 3, 20129 Milan, Italy. Ed. Pierluigi Malinverni. adv.

ORION. see COMPUTERS

658 US
OTO'S SCOPE. 1983. 3/yr. membership. Association of Otolaryngology Administrators, Box 3150, Iowa City, IA 52244-3150. TEL 319-356-2371. Ed. Richard M. Harding. circ. 600. **Document type:** newsletter.

658 UK
OXFORD INSTITUTE OF RETAIL MANAGEMENT. RESEARCH PAPERS. MEADOWHALL CENTRE STUDY. 1989. irreg., no.9, 1992. £25. Oxford Institute of Retail Management, Templeton College, Kennington, Oxford OX1 5NY, England. TEL 01865-735422. FAX 01865-736374. Ed. Elizabeth Howard. **Document type:** monographic series.

658 UK
OXFORD INSTITUTE OF RETAIL MANAGEMENT. RESEARCH PAPERS. NEW TECHNOLOGY AND RETAILING. 1986. irreg., no.11, 1993. £10. Oxford Institute of Retail Management, Templeton College, Kennington, Oxford OX1 5NY, England. TEL 01865-735422. FAX 01865-736374. **Document type:** monographic series.

658 UK
OXFORD INSTITUTE OF RETAIL MANAGEMENT. RESEARCH PAPERS. RETAIL DEVELOPMENT, PLANNING AND POLICY. 1986? irreg., no.31, 1994. £25. Oxford Institute of Retail Management, Templeton College, Kennington, Oxford OX1 5NY, England. TEL 01865-735422. FAX 01865-736374. **Document type:** monographic series.

658 UK
OXFORD INSTITUTE OF RETAIL MANAGEMENT. RESEARCH PAPERS. RETAIL MARKETING. 1990. irreg., no.2, 1990. £10. Oxford Institute of Retail Management, Templeton College, Kennington, Oxford OX1 5NY, England. TEL 01865-735422. FAX 01865-736374. Ed. Gary Davies. **Document type:** monographic series.

P B L BUSINESS LEADER. (Phi Beta Lambda) see OCCUPATIONS AND CAREERS

658 CN ISSN 0710-362X
P E M: PLANT ENGINEERING & MAINTENANCE. (Supplement avail.: P E M: Plant Engineering and Maintenance Sourcebook (ISSN 1187-1547)) 1978. 5/yr. Can.$42($96) Clifford Elliot & Associates Ltd., 3228 South Service Rd., Burlington, ON L7N 3H8, Canada. TEL 905-634-2100. FAX 905-634-2238. Ed. Todd Phillips. adv. circ. 21,500. **Indexed:** ABI Inform. **Document type:** trade publication.
—BLDSC (6516.095000); CISTI; UMI. **CCC.**
   Former titles: Industrial Products and Services; Maintenance Management (ISSN 0707-1965)
   Description: Provides coverage of Canada's plant and maintenance engineers and operating managers by reporting on the processes, methods and products that are essential to operating, equipping and maintaining Canada's industrial facilities.

658 CN ISSN 1187-1547
P E M: PLANT ENGINEERING AND MAINTENANCE SOURCEBOOK. (Supplement to: P E M: Plant Engineering and Maintenance (ISSN 0710-362X)) 2/yr. Can.$12. Clifford Elliot & Associates Ltd., 3228 South Service Rd., Burlington, ON L7N 3H8, Canada. TEL 905-634-2100. FAX 905-634-2238. Ed. Todd Phillips. circ. 21,000. **Document type:** directory.
   Description: Committed to helping Canada's industrial managers meet the challenges of running and operating a competitive industrial facility.

658 NE ISSN 0929-1660
P E M SELECT. (Permanente Educatie Managers); het beste uit de internationale vakpers. 1985. 4/yr. fl.215 (effective 1996). Kluwer Bedrijfswetenschappen B.V. (Subsidiary of: Wolters Kluwer N.V.), Postbus 23, 7400 GA Deventer, Netherlands. TEL 31-5700-48999. FAX 31-5700-11504. (Subscr. to: Intermedia bv, Postbus 4, 2400 MA Alphen aan den Rijn, Netherlands. TEL 31-172-466321. FAX 31-172-435527) **Document type:** trade publication.
—SWETS.
   Formerly (until 1993): P E M (ISSN 0169-5061)

P M A DIRECTORY. (Property Management Association) see BUSINESS AND ECONOMICS — Trade And Industrial Directories

658 SZ
P M E MAGAZINE. 10/yr. 75 SFr. (foreign 108 SFr.). S H Z Fachverlag AG, Alte Landstr. 43, CH-8700 Kuesnacht, Switzerland. TEL 01-9108022. FAX 01-9105155. Ed. Francis Kahn. circ. 20,000.

658 US ISSN 1040-8754
HD69.P75
P M NETWORK. (Project Management) 1987. 12/yr. $100. (Project Management Institute) Project Management Institute, Publications Division, Attn: Shirley Parker, 40 Colonial Sq., Sylva, NC 28779. TEL 704-586-3715. FAX 704-586-4020. E-mail: pmieo@pmi.org; URL: http://www.pmi.org. (Subscr. to: 130 S. State Rd., Upper Darby, PA 19082. TEL 610-734-3330. FAX 610-734-3266) Ed. James Pennypacker; Pub. James Pennypacker. R&P contact: Shirley Parker. adv. contact: Richard Barwis. bk.rev.; software rev.; circ. 28,500 (paid). (back issues avail.) **Document type:** trade publication.
—SWETS. **CCC.**
   Description: Cover project management in various industries, practical issues, news of projects, case studies, management tutorials, new products, legal and organizational news of interest to project managers.

658 GW ISSN 0930-8490
P P S REPORT. (Produktion-Plannung-Steuerung) 1986. m. DM.175.80 (foreign DM.192). Wirtschaftsverlag GmbH, Im Weiher 10, 69121 Heidelberg, Germany. TEL 06221-489440. Ed. Klaus Bichler. **Document type:** trade publication.

PAINT DEALER. see PAINTS AND PROTECTIVE COATINGS

658 PK ISSN 0969-8027
PAKISTAN MANAGEMENT REVIEW. (Text in English) 1960. q. Rs.180($55) Pakistan Institute of Management, Shahrah-Iran, Clifton, Karachi 6, Pakistan. TEL 537123. Ed. Zarrar R. Zubair. adv.; bk.rev.; charts; illus.; stat.; index, cum.index: 1960-1969, 1970-1979. circ. 1,600.

PARCEL SHIPPING & DISTRIBUTION; managing the package and document shipment process. see TRANSPORTATION

658 332 UK
PARTNERS IN BUSINESS. 1994. irreg., 2nd ed., 1995. Bank of Scotland, Business Banking, c/o UK Banking, Uberior House, 61 Grassmarket, Edinburgh EH1 2JF, Scotland. TEL 44-131-243-5944. FAX 44-131-243-5738. (Co-sponsor: Insider Group) Ed. Chris Baur. **Document type:** trade publication.
   Description: Contains articles on how to help a business grow with sections on finances, management, customer service, and human resource issues.

PEOPLE DYNAMICS. see BUSINESS AND ECONOMICS — Personnel Management

658 US ISSN 0734-029X
PERFORMANCE MANAGEMENT MAGAZINE. 1983. s-m. $24. Aubrey Daniels & Associates, 3531 Habersham at Northlake, Tucker, GA 30084. TEL 404-493-5080. FAX 404-493-5095. Ed. Gail Snyder. adv.; bk.rev.; charts; illus.; tr.lit. circ. 3,000.
   Description: Covers use of applied behavioral analysis concepts to business, education, family and government, with emphasis on business.

267 US ISSN 0745-3027
BV1000
PERSPECTIVES (BLOOMINGTON). 1919. 8/yr. $20 (effective 1996). Association of Professional Directors of Y M C A's, 8200 Humboldt Ave., Ste. 111, Bloomington, MN 55431. TEL 612-885-0273. FAX 612-885-0227. Ed. Steve Kendall; Pub. James G. Stooke. adv.: page $1046; trim 8 5/8 x 11 1/4; adv. contact: Carol Steinfeld. bk.rev. circ. 5,500. (back isuues avail.) **Indexed:** Sportsearch (1986-). **Document type:** trade publication.
—UnCover.
   Incorporated (in 1985): Journal of Physical Education and Program; Which was formerly (until 1981): Journal of Physical Education (ISSN 0022-3662); (until 1975): Forum.

BUSINESS AND ECONOMICS — MANAGEMENT

658 686.2 US ISSN 1073-0737
PERSPECTIVES (LIBERTY). 1986. m. $50 to non-members (foreign $72); free to members; newsstand price: $5. International Publishing Management Association, 1205 W. College St., Liberty, MO 64068-3733. TEL 816-781-1111. FAX 816-781-2790. URL: http://www.ipma.org. Ed. Susan Murphy. R&P contact: Susan Murphy. adv. contact: Susan Murphy. bk.rev. circ. 2,300. (back issues avail.) **Document type:** trade publication, newsletter.
  Description: Covers in-house printing, the copying and mailing management industry, managerial and technical advances, and association news.

PETERSON'S JOB OPPORTUNITIES IN BUSINESS (YEAR). see *OCCUPATIONS AND CAREERS*

658 US
HM134
PFEIFFER. ANNUAL; developing human resources. 1972. a. $39.95 paperbound; $89.95 looseleaf. Pfeiffer, 350 Sansome St., San Francisco, CA 94104-1304. Ed. J. William Pfeiffer. circ. 9,000. **Document type:** academic/scholarly publication, trade publication.
—BLDSC (1073.611700).
  Former titles: Pfeiffer and Company. Annual (ISSN 1046-333X); (until 1984): University Associates. Annual; Facilitators, Trainers, and Consultants. Annual and Handbook.
  Description: Contains activities, instruments, and articles for use in human resource development.

PHOTO LAB MANAGEMENT. see *PHOTOGRAPHY*

PHYSICIAN EXECUTIVE REVIEW; quarterly abstracts from medical management literature. see *MEDICAL SCIENCES — Abstracting, Bibliographies, Statistics*

PHYSICIAN'S MANAGEMENT MANUALS. see *MEDICAL SCIENCES*

658 US
PLANNING FORUM NETWORK.* 1988. m. membership only. Planning Forum, 435 N. Michigan Ave., Ste. 1700, Chicago, IL 60611-4008. TEL 513-523-4185. FAX 513-523-7539. Ed. Marthann Heard. bk.rev. circ. 6,000. **Document type:** newsletter.
  Description: Executive briefing on strategic planning and management.

658.2 620 CN
PLANT - CANADA'S INDUSTRIAL NEWSPAPER. (Supplements avail.: Plant Maintenance; Plant Controls & Instrumentation; Plant Automation; Plant Brochure Guide; Plant Action Pac) 1941. 18/yr. Can.$48 (foreign Can.$90). Maclean Hunter Ltd., 777 Bay St., Toronto, ON M5W 1A7, Canada. TEL 416-596-5000. FAX 416-596-5553. Ed. Ron Richardson. adv.; bk.rev.; illus.; tr.lit. circ. 42,000. (tabloid format; also avail. in microform from UMI; reprint service avail. from UMI) **Indexed:** BPIA, Can.B.P.I.
—CISTI.
  Former titles: Plant - Canada's Industrial Newsletter (ISSN 0845-4213); (until 1988): Plant Management and Engineering (ISSN 0315-9183); Plant Administration and Engineering (ISSN 0032-0773)
  Description: Provides news and technical information of interest to Canada's manufacturing and processing industries, from raw material resourcing through to finished products.

658 690 UK ISSN 1352-8637
PLANT MANAGERS JOURNAL. 1973. m. £46 (foreign £55.20). Reed Business Publishing Group (Subsidiary of: Reed Elsevier group), Quadrant House, The Quadrant, Sutton, Surrey SM2 5AS, England. TEL 44-181-652-4890. FAX 44-181-652-4804. (Subscr. to: Stuart House, 35 Perrymount Rd., Haywards Heath, W. Sussex RH16 3DH, England) circ. 10,084. **Document type:** trade publication.
  Description: Provides business information for plant managers.

658 US
PLANT SHUTDOWNS DIRECTORY. 1982. m. $340 to non-profit and educational institutions; corporations $450. DataCenter, 464 19th St., Oakland, CA 94612-1197. TEL 510-835-4692. FAX 510-835-3017. E-mail: datacenter@datacenter.org. Ed. Andy Kivel. circ. 60. (looseleaf format; back issues avail.) **Document type:** directory.
  Formerly: Plant Shutdowns Monitor (ISSN 0742-5422)
  Description: Provides company name, S.I.C. codes, location, number of workers affected and explanatory notes.

658 PL ISSN 0324-9484
POLITECHNIKA WROCLAWSKA. INSTYTUT ORGANIZACJI I ZARZADZANIA. PRACE NAUKOWE. KONFERENCJE. (Text in Polish; summaries in English and Russian) 1973. irreg., no.21, 1995. price varies. Oficyna Wydawnicza Politechniki Wroclawskiej, Wybrzeze Wyspianskiego 27, 50-370 Wroclaw, Poland. TEL 48-71-222940. FAX 48-71-223664. TELEX 712559 PWRPL. (Dist. by: Ars Polona, Krakowskie Przedmiescie 7, Warsaw, Poland) Ed. Zofia Licznerska. R&P contact: Halina Dudek. adv. **Document type:** proceedings.

658 PL ISSN 0324-9492
POLITECHNIKA WROCLAWSKA. INSTYTUT ORGANIZACJI I ZARZADZANIA. PRACE NAUKOWE. MONOGRAFIE. (Text in Polish; summaries in English and Russian) 1970. irreg., no.28, 1994. price varies. Oficyna Wydawnicza Politechniki Wroclawskiej, Wybrzeze Wyspianskiego 27, 50-370 Wroclaw, Poland. TEL 48-71-222940. FAX 48-71-223664. TELEX 712559 PWRPL. (Dist. by: Ars Polona, Krakowskie Przedmiescie 7, Warsaw, Poland) Ed. Zofia Licznerska. R&P contact: Halina Dudek. adv. **Document type:** monographic series.
—Ei.

658 PL ISSN 0324-9468
POLITECHNIKA WROCLAWSKA. INSTYTUT ORGANIZACJI I ZARZADZANIA. PRACE NAUKOWE. STUDIA I MATERIALY. (Text in Polish; summaries in English and Russian) 1970. irreg., no.15, 1990. price varies. Oficyna Wydawnicza Politechniki Wroclawskiej, Wybrzeze Wyspianskiego 27, 50-370 Wroclaw, Poland. TEL 48-71-222940. FAX 48-71-223664. TELEX 712550 PWRPL. (Dist. by: Ars Polona, Krakowskie Przedmiescie 7, Warsaw, Poland) Ed. Zofia Licznerska. R&P contact: Halina Dudek. adv. **Document type:** academic/scholarly publication.

POLITICAL RISK YEARBOOK. see *BUSINESS AND ECONOMICS — Banking And Finance*

POLITICAL RISK YEARBOOK. VOLUME 1: NORTH & CENTRAL AMERICA. see *BUSINESS AND ECONOMICS — Banking And Finance*

POLITICAL RISK YEARBOOK. VOLUME 2: MIDDLE EAST & NORTH AFRICA. see *BUSINESS AND ECONOMICS — Banking And Finance*

POLITICAL RISK YEARBOOK. VOLUME 3: SOUTH AMERICA. see *BUSINESS AND ECONOMICS — Banking And Finance*

POLITICAL RISK YEARBOOK. VOLUME 4: SUB-SAHARAN AFRICA. see *BUSINESS AND ECONOMICS — Banking And Finance*

POLITICAL RISK YEARBOOK. VOLUME 5: ASIA & THE PACIFIC. see *BUSINESS AND ECONOMICS — Banking And Finance*

POLITICAL RISK YEARBOOK. VOLUME 6: EUROPE. see *BUSINESS AND ECONOMICS — Banking And Finance*

PRAJNAN (PUNE); journal of social and management sciences. see *BUSINESS AND ECONOMICS — Banking And Finance*

PRATICA AZIENDALE. see *BUSINESS AND ECONOMICS — Accounting*

658 GW ISSN 0937-6828
PRAXIS-HANDBUCH UNTERNEHMENSFUEHRUNG. 1990. bi-m. DM.98. Verlag Wirtschaft Recht und Steuern, Fraunhoferstr. 5, 82152 Planegg, Germany. TEL 49-89-89517-0. FAX 49-89-89517250. (looseleaf format) **Document type:** trade publication.

PRESENCES IN BUSINESS. see *BUSINESS AND ECONOMICS — Economic Situation And Conditions*

658 JA ISSN 0032-7751
PRESIDENT; business in-sight magazine. (Text in Japanese) 1963. m. 10800 Yen. President, Inc. (Subsidiary of: Time Inc.), Bridgestone Hirakawa-cho Bldg., 1st Fl., 2-13-12 Hirakawa-cho, Chiyoda-ku, Tokyo 102, Japan. TEL 81-3-3237-3711. FAX 81-3-3237-3745. TELEX J24914 PREMAG. (Or: Time Inc., Time-Life Bldg., Rockefeller Center, New York, NY 10020) Eds. Hirofumi Kobashima, Norihisa Yamamoto. adv.: B&W page 1260000 Yen, color page 1900000 Yen; trim 210 x 275; adv. contact: Takashi Kikuchi. bk.rev.; charts; illus.; index. circ. 273,323. **Document type:** trade publication.
  Description: General business interest magazine whose core readers are corporate owners and executive managers. Highlights successful people and their strategies and important business trends.

658 330.9 346 US ISSN 0552-007X
THE PRESIDENT. q. American Management Association, 1601 Broadway, New York, NY 10019. TEL 212-903-7990; 800-262-9699. FAX 212-903-8168. E-mail: amapubs@aol.com. Ed. Barbara Parker. (reprint service avail.) **Document type:** newsletter.
—CCC.
  Description: Aims to help CEOs and presidents manage their businesses more effectively.

330 US ISSN 1044-4998
PRINCIPAL'S REPORT. 1988. m. $249 (outside N. America $273). Institute of Management & Administration, Inc., 29 W. 35th St., 5th Fl., New York, NY 10001-2299. TEL 212-244-0360. FAX 212-564-0465. URL: http://www.ioma.com. Ed. Kneeland Godfrey; Pub. Lee Rath. R&P contact: Sofie Kourkoutakis. index. (looseleaf format; back issues avail.) **Document type:** newsletter.
—CCC.
  Description: Management publication for owners and partners in design firms dealing with market placement, transitions and successions, liability insurance, and principal compensation.

658 657 US ISSN 1072-5318
KF6436
PRINCIPLES OF PAYROLL ADMINISTRATION; the complete learning and reference guide. 1988. a. $125.95 (overseas $188.45) (effective 1995). Warren, Gorham & Lamont, One Penn Plaza, New York, NY 10119. TEL 212-971-5000. FAX 212-971-5113. (Subscr. to: The Park Square Bldg., 31 St. James Ave., Boston, MA 02116-4112. TEL 800-950-1207) Eds. Debera J. Salam, Lucy Key Price. (looseleaf format) **Document type:** trade publication.
  Description: Outlines laws and procedures that apply to payroll administration, covers complex items relating to benefits, and provides professional training.

PRINTING MANAGER. see *PRINTING*

658 US ISSN 0895-3228
PRIVATE PRACTICE NEWS.* 1987. m. $69. Private Practice Institute, Box 1485, Shawnee, OK 74802-1485. Ed. Katherine O'Halloran. bk.rev.; index. circ. 700. (looseleaf format; back issues avail.)

658 YU ISSN 0350-9435
PRIVREDA I RUKOVODJENJE. (Text in Serbo-Croatian) 1967. m. 1200 din.($130) Tanjug Economic Service - Tanjug Redakcija Ekonomskih Informacija, Oblicev venac 2, Belgrade, Yugoslavia. Ed. Dragoslav Pavlovic. adv.; bk.rev.; charts; illus.; stat.; index. circ. 1,700.
  Formerly: Menadzer u Privredi (ISSN 0025-9225)

658 IT ISSN 0032-9363
PROBLEMI DI GESTIONE; selezione da riviste straniere. 1968. 6/yr. free. Centro di Formazione e Studi (Formez), Via Campi Flegrei 34, Comprensorio Olivetti, 80072 Arco Felice (NA), Italy. TEL 39-81-5250111. FAX 39-81-8041348. Ed. Roberto Stampacchia. R&P contact: Ezio Esposito. bk.rev.; charts; index; circ. 7,000 (controlled). **Document type:** monographic series.
  Formerly: Studi di Economia della Produzione Industriale.

BUSINESS AND ECONOMICS — MANAGEMENT

658　　　　　　　　RU　　ISSN 0257-9928
PROBLEMY TEORII I PRAKTIKI. (Text in Russian; summaries in English) 1983. s-m. 108000 Rub. (Mezhdunarodnyi Naucho-issledovatel'skii Institut Problem Upravleniya) Editorial Board Problemy Teorii i Praktiki, Medvedeva ul., 13, stproen. 1, 103006 Moscow, Russia. TEL 7-095-9730660. FAX 7-095-9730543. Ed. V. Silin. adv. circ. 5,000.
　　Document type: monographic series.
　　Description: Presents theoretical and practical aspects of management.

658　　　　　　　　UK　　ISSN 0143-1587
K16
PRODUCT LIABILITY INTERNATIONAL. 1979. m. $495. L L P Limited, Sheepen Pl., Colchester, Essex CO3 3LP, England. TEL 44-1206-772277. FAX 44-1206-46273. TELEX 987321 LLOYDS G. (U.S. subscr. to: L L P Inc., 611 Broadway, Ste. 308, New York, NY 10012. TEL 212-529-9500) Ed. J.S. Ashworth. **Indexed:** Euro.LJI, LJI.
　　—BLDSC (6853.016000); SWETS.
　　Incorporates (as of vol.3, no.8, 1981): Product Liability Bulletin (ISSN 0142-050X)
　　Description: Provides update on international product liability and product safety for manufacturers, insurers and lawyers.

658　　　　　　　　US　　ISSN 0897-8336
TS155.A1　　　　　　　　CODEN: PIMJE8
PRODUCTION AND INVENTORY MANAGEMENT JOURNAL. 1959. q. $80 to non-members (foreign $96). A P I C S - The Educational Society for Resource Management, 500 W. Annandale Rd., Falls Church, VA 22046-4274. TEL 703-237-8344; 800-444-2742. FAX 703-237-1087. URL: http://www.apics.org. Ed. R.E.D. Woolsey. bk.rev.; charts; illus.; stat.; index. circ. 72,000. (back issues avail.; reprint service avail. from UMI) **Indexed:** A.S.& T.Ind., ABI Inform., Account.& Data Proc.Abstr., Account.Ind. (1974-), Comput.Cont., Eng.Ind., INSPEC (1981-), J.Cont.Quant.Meth., Oper.Res.Manage.Sci., Qual.Contr.Appl.Stat.
　　●Also available online. Vendor(s): UMI.
　　—BLDSC (6853.075500); SWETS; AskIEEE; Ei; KR SourceOne; Linda Hall; SWETS; UMI; UnCover.
　　Former titles (until 1987): Production and Inventory Management (ISSN 0032-9843); A P I C S Quarterly Bulletin.
　　Description: Offers news on the research and development of production and inventory management techniques. Evaluates new and existing systems.

658 338　　　　　　　US　　ISSN 1059-1478
TS155.A1　　　　　　　　CODEN: POMAEN
PRODUCTION AND OPERATIONS MANAGEMENT. 1992. q. $55 to individuals; libraries $90. Production and Operations Management Society, c/o Dr. Sushil K. Gupta, PC-543, Florida International University, Miami, FL 33199. TEL 410-837-4976. FAX 410-837-5675. Ed. Kalyan Singhal; Pub. Sushil K. Gupta. R&P contact: Sushil J. Gupta. adv. contact: Sushil K. Gupta. circ. 1,200 (paid). **Indexed:** INSPEC (1992-). **Document type:** academic/scholarly publication.
　　—BLDSC (6853.076600); AskIEEE; KR SourceOne; SWETS; UnCover.
　　Refereed Serial

658 338　　　　　　　US　　ISSN 0275-8040
HD57
PRODUCTIVITY; techniques and technologies supporting lean manufacturing. 1979. 10/yr. $167 (foreign $197) (effective 1997). Productivity, Inc., 101 Merritt 7, Norwalk, CT 06851. TEL 203-846-3777; 800-966-5423. FAX 203-846-6883. E-mail: cmarchwi@prodinc.com; URL: http://www.mfgnet.com. Ed. Chet Marchwinski; Pub. Norman Bodek. R&P contact: Chet Marchwinski. bk.rev.; abstr.; charts; illus.; stat.; circ. 2,400 (paid). (back issues avail.) **Indexed:** Pers.Lit., Text.Tech.Dig. **Document type:** newsletter.
　　—CCC.
　　Description: Helps heighten managers' awareness of the best practices in production.

658　　　　　　　　TR
PRODUCTIVITY NEWS. (Text in English) 1974. q. free. Management Development Centre, Library, Salvatori Bldg., P.O. Box 1301, Port-of-Spain, Trinidad & Tobago, W.I. TEL 809-623-1961. FAX 809-623-2111. Ed. Heather Baldwin-MacDowell. bibl. circ. 1,000.
　　Former titles: M D C News; (until 1976): Trinidad and Tobago Management Development Centre. Quarterly Newsletter.
　　Description: Focuses on management and productivity issues related to Trinidad and Tobago.

658　　　　　　　　SA　　ISSN 1018-7227
PRODUCTIVITY S A; for excellence in management. (Text in English) vol.16, 1990. bi-m. National Productivity Institute (NPI), P.O. Box 3971, Pretoria 0001, South Africa. TEL 012-341-1470. FAX 012-44-1866. TELEX 3-20485-SA. Ed. Len Ashton. adv. **Indexed:** Ind.S.A.Per.

PROFESSIONAL ADVISOR. see *ADVERTISING AND PUBLIC RELATIONS*

PROFESSIONAL AND SCIENTIFIC PERSONNEL REPORT - GEOGRAPHIC EDITION. see *BUSINESS AND ECONOMICS — Personnel Management*

PROFESSIONAL MANAGEMENT REVIEW. see *BUSINESS AND ECONOMICS — Marketing And Purchasing*

658　　　　　　　　UK　　ISSN 0969-6695
THE PROFESSIONAL MANAGER. 1974. bi-m. £16 to non-members (rest of Europe £19; elsewhere £22). Institute of Management Foundation, 2 Savoy Ct., 3rd. Fl., Strand, London WC2R OEZ, England. TEL 44-171-497-0580. FAX 44-171-497-0463. E-mail: savoy@inst_mgl.org.uk. (Subscr. to: Publications Subscription, Registrars Dept., Institute of Management Foundation, Cottingham Rd., Corby, Northants. NN17 1TT, England) Ed. Sue Mann. R&P contact: Sue Mann. adv.: B&W page £2600, color page £2950; trim 280 x 205. bk.rev.; abstr.; index, cum.index. circ. 80,000. (back issues avail.) **Indexed:** BMT, Build.Manage.Abstr., INSPEC, Mgmt.& Market.Abstr., SOMA, World Text.Abstr. **Document type:** trade publication.
　　—BLDSC (6859.555000); SWETS.
　　Formed by the Nov. 1992 merger of: Industrial Management (ISSN 0962-4732) & Management News; Which was previously: Management Review and Digest (ISSN 0307-3580); Management Abstracts (ISSN 0025-1666)
　　Description: Covers employment and management issues in the private and public sectors.
　　Refereed Serial

658 720 620　　　　US　　ISSN 0732-2119
PROFESSIONAL SERVICES MANAGEMENT JOURNAL. m. $195. P S M J Resources, Inc., 10 Midland Ave., Newton, MA 02158. TEL 617-965-0055. FAX 617-965-5152. E-mail: psmj@tiac.com. Ed. Susan Yoder; Pub. Frank Stasiowski. R&P contact: Christa Matukaitis. index. (back issues avail.) **Document type:** newsletter.
　　—BLDSC (6864.220310).
　　Description: Strategies for design firms worldwide.

658 300　　　　　　　FR　　ISSN 0033-0213
PROFESSIONS ET ENTREPRISES. 1894. 10/yr. 130 F. Centre Chretien des Patrons et Dirigeants d'Entreprise, 24 rue Hamelin, 75016 Paris, France. TEL 45-53-31-59. Ed. Max Chalus. bk.rev.; abstr.; bibl.; index. circ. 2,500.

658　　　　　　　　US
PROGRESO. (Text in Spanish) 1964. m. Vision, Inc., 305 Madison Ave., Ste. 1531, New York, NY 10165. TEL 212-953-1308. FAX 212-953-1619. Ed. Luis Vidal Rucabado. adv. circ. 38,500. **Document type:** trade publication.
　　Description: Covers Latin-American developments affecting business management, including political and economic trends.

658 747　　　　　　　US　　ISSN 8750-6106
PROGRESSIVE RENTALS; the magazine of the home entertainment, appliance, and furniture rental industry. 1981. bi-m. $30. Association of Progressive Rental Organizations, 9171 N. Capital of Texas Hwy., Ste. 220, Austin, TX 78759-7252. TEL 512-794-0095. FAX 512-794-0097. URL: http://www.apro-rto.com. Ed. Julie Sherrier. R&P contact: Julie Sherrier. adv. contact: Cindy Ganther. bk.rev.; index; circ. 2,862 (paid). (back issues avail.) **Document type:** trade publication.
　　Formerly: A P R Oach (ISSN 0736-1874)
　　Description: Trade magazine for the "rental-purchase" industry.

658　　　　　　　　US　　ISSN 8756-9728
HD69.P75
PROJECT MANAGEMENT JOURNAL. Short title: P M J. 1969. 4/yr. $100. (Project Management Institute) Project Management Institute, Publications Division, Attn: Shirley Parker, 40 Colonial Sq., Sylva, NC 28779. TEL 704-586-3715. FAX 704-586-4020. E-mail: pmipub@dnet.net; URL: http://www.pmi.org. (Subscr. to: 130 S. State Rd., Upper Darby, PA 19082. TEL 610-734-3330. FAX 610-734-3266) Ed. William G. Wells; Pub. James Pennypacker. R&P contact: Shirley Parker. adv. contact: Richard Barwis. bk.rev.; software rev.; charts; illus. circ. 18,000. (back issues avail.) **Indexed:** ABI Inform., Comput.Lit.Ind., Pub.Admin.Abstr. **Document type:** academic/scholarly publication.
　　—BLDSC (6924.847810); SWETS; UnCover. **CCC.**
　　Formerly (until 1984): Project Management Quarterly (ISSN 1047-5363)
　　Description: Contains technical articles dealing with the field of project management.
　　Refereed Serial

658　　　　　　　　GW　　ISSN 0942-1017
PROJEKTMANAGEMENT. 4/yr. DM.142 (foreign DM.166). Verlag T Ue V Rheinland GmbH, Viktoriastr. 26, 51149 Cologne, Germany. TEL 49-2203-9118073. FAX 49-2203-15411. adv. contact: Gudrun Karafiol. **Document type:** trade publication.

PROMYSHLENNYI VESTNIK ROSSII. see *BUSINESS AND ECONOMICS — Economic Situation And Conditions*

PROPERTY MANAGEMENT ASSOCIATION. BULLETIN. see *REAL ESTATE*

PRYOR REPORT. see *OCCUPATIONS AND CAREERS*

658　　　　　　　　PL　　ISSN 0137-7221
PRZEGLAD ORGANIZACJI. 1926. m. Towarzystwo Naukowe Organizacji i Kierownictwa, Ul. Sienkiewicza 12, p.337, 00-010 Warsaw, Poland. TEL 48-22-274606. Ed. Marek Dziduszko. circ. 6,000. **Indexed:** AgroLibrex.
　　Formerly (until 1962): Towarzystwo Naukowe Organizacji i Kierownictwa. Biuletyn.
　　Description: Covers management and organization issues.

PUBLIC PRODUCTIVITY AND MANAGEMENT REVIEW. see *PUBLIC ADMINISTRATION*

621.3　　　　　　　　US
K16
PUBLIC UTILITIES FORTNIGHTLY. 1929. 22/yr. $119 (foreign $178). Public Utilities Reports, Inc., 8229 Boone Blvd., Ste. 401, Vienna, VA 22182. TEL 703-847-7720; 800-368-5001. FAX 703-917-6964. E-mail: pur_info@pur.com; URL: http://www.pur.com. Ed. Bruce W. Radford. adv.: B&W page $3630, color page $5445. circ. 7,177. (also avail. in microform from UMI) **Indexed:** ABI Inform., Account.Ind. (1974-), Acid Pre.Dig., Acid Rain Abstr., Acid Rain Ind., B.P.I., BPIA, C.L.I., CAD CAM Abstr., Energy Info.Abstr., Environ.Abstr., Fuel & Energy Abstr., Gas Abstr., INSPEC (1993-), L.R.I., P.A.I.S., Tel.Abstr., Tr.& Indus.Ind. **Document type:** trade publication.
　　●Also available online. Vendor(s): Information Access Co., Lexis-Nexis, UMI, West Group.
　　—BLDSC (6969.650000); AskIEEE; KR SourceOne; SWETS; UMI; UnCover. **CCC.**
　　Former titles (until Sep. 1994): Fortnightly (ISSN 1074-6099); (until Oct. 1993): Public Utilities Fortnightly (ISSN 0033-3808)

PURCHASING MANAGEMENT BULLETIN. see *BUSINESS AND ECONOMICS — Marketing And Purchasing*

BUSINESS AND ECONOMICS — MANAGEMENT

658 UK ISSN 1354-8638
PUTTERIDGE BURY MANAGEMENT REVIEW. 1993. s-a. £25. University of Luton, Putteridge Bury, Hitchin Rd., Luton, Beds. LU2 8LE, England. TEL 01582-482555. FAX 01582-482689. Ed. Tom Connor. adv. contact: Christine Matthews. circ. 300. Document type: academic/scholarly publication. —BLDSC (7161.624600).
  Formerly: Putteridge Papers (ISSN 1352-2736)
  Description: Provides informed comment, either conceptual or research based, on matters of interest in the field of management.
  Refereed Serial

658 BR
PYINNYA LAWKA JOURNAL. (Text in Burmese) q. Sarpay Beikman Management Board, 529 Merchant St., Yangon, Union of Myanmar. circ. 18,000.

658 JA ISSN 0914-5001
Q C CIRCLE. (Quality Control) 1962. m. 10000 Yen. Union of Japanese Scientists and Engineers - Nihon Kagaku Gijutsu Renmei, 5-10-11 Sendagaya, Shibuya-ku, Tokyo 151, Japan. TEL 03-5379-1227. FAX 03-3225-1813. TELEX 02322485 JUSE J. Ed. Kohei Suzue. charts. circ. 182,000. **Indexed:** JTA.
  Formerly (until 1988): Quality Control for the Foreman (ISSN 0914-3831)

658 338 CC ISSN 1003-2320
QIYE GUANLI/ENTERPRISE MANAGEMENT. (Text in Chinese) 1980. m. $34.10 (effective 1995). Qiye Guanli Zazhishe, 17 Zizhuyuan Nanlu, Beijing 100044, People's Republic of China. TEL 86-10-8414646. (Dist. in US by: China Books & Periodicals, Inc., 2929 24th St., San Francisco, CA 94110. TEL 415-282-2994) Ed. Zhu Tao. circ. 200,000.

QUADERNI DI ECONOMIA DEL LAVORO. see BUSINESS AND ECONOMICS — Labor And Industrial Relations

658 US ISSN 0360-9936
TS156.A1 CODEN: QULTDP
QUALITY; the magazine of product assurance. 1962. m. $65. Hitchcock Publishing (Subsidiary of: Capital Cities - A B C, Inc.), 191 S. Gary Ave., Carol Stream, IL 60188. TEL 708-665-1000. FAX 708-462-2225. TELEX 72-0404. (Subscr. to: Box 830409, Birmingham, AL 35283-0409) Ed. Chester Placek. adv.; charts; illus.; stat.; tr.lit.; index. circ. 84,300. (also avail. in microform from UMI; reprint service avail. from UMI) **Indexed:** A.I.Abstr. (until 1992), ABI Inform., Alloys Ind., BPIA, CAD CAM Abstr. (until 1992), Eng.Mat.Abstr., Met.Abstr.Ind., Met.Abstr., Nonfer.Met.Alert, Oper.Res.Manage.Sci., PCC Alert, Q.Abstr., Qual.Contr.Appl.Stat., Robomat. (until 1992), Steels Alert, World Alum.Abstr.
 —BLDSC (7168.127000); CISTI; Ei; Linda Hall; SWETS; UMI. **CCC.**
  Former titles: Quality Management and Engineering; Quality Assurance.

346.066 UK ISSN 1052-9411
TS156.6 CODEN: QUASE2
QUALITY ASSURANCE; good practice, regulation, and law. 1991. q. £151($250) to institutions (effective 1998). Taylor & Francis Ltd., 1 Gunpowder Sq., London EC4A 3DE, England. TEL 44-171-5830490. FAX 44-171-5830585. E-mail: info@tandf.co.uk; URL: http://www.tandf.co.uk/. (Subscr. in N. America to: Taylor & Francis Inc., 1900 Frost Rd., Ste. 101, Bristol, PA 19007-1598. TEL 800-821-8312. FAX 215-785-5515) Ed. Frederick Coulston. **Indexed:** Ind.Med. (1994-). Document type: academic/scholarly publication.
 —CASDDS; KNAW; SWETS. **CCC.**
  Description: Examines issues of quality assurance and quality control as they relate to biological, physical, and engineering science, and technology.

658 US
QUALITY - EUROPE. 1992. q. Hitchcock Publishing (Subsidiary of: Capital Cities - A B C, Inc.), 191 S. Gary Ave., Carol Stream, IL 60188. TEL 708-665-1000. FAX 708-462-2225. adv.: B&W page $3000; trim 8 x 10 3/4. circ. 20,000. **Indexed:** World Surf.Coat.
  Description: Covers quality management, quality philosophy and quality technology.

658 US
QUALITY FIRST. 1990. bi-w. $68.90. Dartnell Corporation, 4660 N. Ravenswood Ave., Chicago, IL 60640. TEL 773-561-4000; 800-621-5463. FAX 773-561-3801. URL: http://www.dartnellcorp.com. Ed. David Dee.
  Description: Helps employees commit to quality products and services.

658 350.821 AT ISSN 1039-558X
THE QUALITY MAGAZINE. 1992. bi-m. Aus.$60 (foreign Aus.$100) (effective 1997). Quality Society of Australasia, P.O. Box 742, Crows Nest, N.S.W. 2065, Australia. TEL 61-2-99019938. FAX 61-2-99014677. E-mail: qsa@qualitysociety.org.au/; URL: http://www.qualitysociety.org.au/~qsa. Ed. David Scarfe. R&P contact: David Scarfe. adv.: B&W page Aus.$1925, color page Aus.$2585; trim 275 x 210; adv. contact: Ken Lane. bk.rev.; software rev.; video rev, tr.lit. circ. 10,580. (back issues avail.) Document type: consumer publication.
 —UnCover.
  Formerly (until 1984): Quality Australia (ISSN 0813-0272)
  Description: Discusses quality issues and practices.
  Refereed Serial

658 US ISSN 1080-0883
QUALITY MANAGEMENT. s-m. $148.92. Bureau of Business Practice, 24 Rope Ferry Rd., Waterford, CT 06386. TEL 860-442-4365. FAX 860-437-3555. URL: http://www.bbpnews.com. Ed. Peter Hawkins; Pub. Peter Ferraro. R&P contact: Debra Ferraro. Document type: newsletter.
  Former titles: Quality Assurance Bulletin (ISSN 1040-0664); Quality Control Supervisor's Bulletin (ISSN 0199-6223)
  Description: Covers a vast range of quality topics pertaining to quality in manufacturing, including TQM, benchmarking, customer relationships, manufacturing and supplier quality, cycle time reduction, controlling quality costs, innovative quality techniques and technologies, and more.

658 US ISSN 1068-6967
HD62.15
QUALITY MANAGEMENT JOURNAL. 1993. q. $60 to non-members; members $50. American Society for Quality Control, 611 E. Wisconsin Ave., Box 3005, Milwaukee, WI 53201-3005. TEL 414-272-8575. FAX 414-272-1734. URL: http://www.asqc.org/about/divtech.html. Ed. William Golomski. circ. 8,500. Document type: newsletter.
 —BLDSC (7168.152630); SWETS. **CCC.**

658 338 620 NZ ISSN 1170-6775
QUALITY NEW ZEALAND. 1981. s-a. NZ.$20 (effective 1996 & 1997). New Zealand Organisation for Quality Inc., P.O. Box 622, Palmerston North, New Zealand. TEL 64-6-3505825. FAX 64-6-3505820. Ed. Ian Carden. adv.; bk.rev.; charts; illus.; tr.lit. circ. 1,200. (back issues avail.)
 —CISTI. **CCC.**
  Formerly: Quality Assurance New Zealand (ISSN 0111-7416)
  Description: Features articles of a practical and theoretical nature about all aspects of quality management.

QUALITY PROGRESS. see ENGINEERING

658 US ISSN 1058-0417
QUALITY QUIPS NEWSLETTER. 1991. q. $30. Q P Publishing, Box 237, Finleyville, PA 15332-0237. TEL 412-348-8949. Ed. Nancy Sue Swoger; Pub. Nancy Sue Swoger. adv. contact: Nancy Sue Mitchell. bk.rev. circ. 2,000. (back issues avail.) Document type: newsletter.
  Description: Provides information, instruction, examples of quality performance, and improvement to the business world.

QUICK FREEZE FRANCE. see FOOD AND FOOD INDUSTRIES

658 UK ISSN 0033-6807
T175.5 CODEN: RDMAAW
R & D MANAGEMENT. 1970. q. £187($362) (foreign £229) (effective 1997). Blackwell Publishers Ltd., 108 Cowley Rd., Oxford OX4 1JF, England. TEL 44-1865-791100. FAX 44-1865-791347. E-mail: jnlinfo@blackwellpublishers.co.uk; URL: http://www.blackwellpub.com/scripts/webjrn1.idc?issn00336807. Eds. A.W. Pearson, J. Butler. adv.; bk.rev. circ. 1,150. (reprint service avail. from SWZ) **Indexed:** ABI Inform., Account.& Data Proc.Abstr., Anbar, ASCA, BMT, BPIA, Br.Ceram.Abstr., Br.Rail.Bd., Bus.Ind., CLOSS, Cont.Pg.Manage., Curr.Cont., High.Educ.Curr.Aware.Bull., INSPEC, Int.Abstr.Oper.Res., Mgmt.& Market.Abstr., Oper.Res.Manage.Sci., P.A.I.S., Qual.Contr.Appl.Stat., SCIMP (1978-), SSCI, Tech.Educ.Abstr., Tr.& Indus.Ind., World Text.Abstr. Document type: academic/scholarly publication.
 ●Also available online. Vendor(s): Information Access Co.
 —BLDSC (7218.400000); AskIEEE; CISTI; Ei; Genuine Article; KR SourceOne; Linda Hall; SWETS; UMI. **CCC.**
  Description: Aims to improve the efficiency of research and development management by providing a forum for applying theoretical aspects to the practical needs of industry and government.
  Refereed Serial

658 US
▼**R T.** (Retail Technology) 1996. m. newsstand price: $10. Progressive Grocer Associates, 263 Tresser Blvd., Stamford, CT 06901. TEL 203-325-3500. FAX 203-325-4377. Ed. Bruce Fox. Document type: trade publication.

658 GW
RADAR FUER TRENDS. 1983. s-m. DM.690($336) (Institut fuer Trend-Forschung) Muditax GmbH, Postfach 1230, 27723 Worpswede, Germany. TEL 04792-2656. FAX 04792-2686. Ed. Gerd Gerken. circ. 1,500. (back issues avail.) Document type: newsletter.

RADIO ONLY MAGAZINE; the monthly management tool. see COMMUNICATIONS — Radio

RANGE MANAGEMENT NEWSLETTER. see AGRICULTURE

REALITES INDUSTRIELLES. see MINES AND MINING INDUSTRY

658 UK ISSN 0956-5698
HF5735 CODEN: RMJOFP
RECORDS MANAGEMENT JOURNAL. 3/yr. £60($102) to non-members; members $48($82). Aslib, Association for Information Management, Publications Department, Information House, 20-24 Old St., London EC1V 9AP, England. TEL 44-171-253-4488. FAX 44-171-430-0514. E-mail: pubs@aslib.co.uk; URL: http://www.aslib.co.uk/. Eds. Catherine Hare, Julie McLeod. R&P contact: Oliver Bond. adv. contact: Brian Thackray. bk.rev. circ. 200. **Indexed:** LISA. Document type: trade publication.
 —BLDSC (7325.792500); AskIEEE; KR SourceOne.

RECYCLAGE RECUPERATION. see ENVIRONMENTAL STUDIES — Waste Management

658 US ISSN 0735-6498
HD2745
REFERENCE BOOK OF CORPORATE MANAGEMENTS. 1967. a. Dun's Marketing Services (Subsidiary of: Dun & Bradstreet, Inc.), 3 Sylvan Way, Parsippany, NJ 07054-3896. TEL 201-455-0900. circ. 3,500.
 ●Also available online. Vendor(s): Questel Orbit Inc. (RBCM).
  Former titles (until 1981): Dun and Bradstreet Reference Book of Corporate Managements (ISSN 0070-7627); Moody's Handbook of Corporate Managements (ISSN 0545-0209)

658 US
REGIONAL REPORT ON MIDDLE MANAGEMENT COMPENSATION. (Supplement to: Middle Management Compensation - Regression Analysis Report) a. $690. (Executive Compensation Service (ECS)) Wyatt Data Services, 218 Rte. 17, N., Roselle Park, NJ 07662-9832. TEL 201-843-1177. FAX 201-843-0101. charts. Document type: trade publication.
  Description: Analyzes the geographic influences affecting middle management pay.

BUSINESS AND ECONOMICS — MANAGEMENT

658 US ISSN 1056-9561
HD4965.5.U5
REGIONAL REPORT ON TOP MANAGEMENT COMPENSATION. (Supplement to: Top Management Compensation - Regression Analysis Report) a. $690. (Executive Compensation Service (ECS)) Wyatt Data Services, 218 Rte. 17, N., Roselle Park, NJ 07662-9832. TEL 201-843-1177. FAX 201-843-0101. charts.
  Description: Aimed at managers of companies who wish to consider the role of geography on executive compensation.

REGISTRY NEWS. see SPORTS AND GAMES — Horses And Horsemanship

RELIGIOUS CONFERENCE MANAGER. see RELIGIONS AND THEOLOGY

REMUNERATION REPORT - AUSTRIA. see BUSINESS AND ECONOMICS — Personnel Management

REMUNERATION REPORT - BELGIUM. see BUSINESS AND ECONOMICS — Personnel Management

REMUNERATION REPORT - DENMARK. see BUSINESS AND ECONOMICS — Personnel Management

REMUNERATION REPORT - FINLAND. see BUSINESS AND ECONOMICS — Personnel Management

REMUNERATION REPORT - FRANCE. see BUSINESS AND ECONOMICS — Personnel Management

REMUNERATION REPORT - GERMANY. see BUSINESS AND ECONOMICS — Personnel Management

REMUNERATION REPORT - GREECE. see BUSINESS AND ECONOMICS — Personnel Management

REMUNERATION REPORT - IRELAND. see BUSINESS AND ECONOMICS — Personnel Management

REMUNERATION REPORT - ITALY. see BUSINESS AND ECONOMICS — Personnel Management

REMUNERATION REPORT - LUXEMBOURG. see BUSINESS AND ECONOMICS — Personnel Management

REMUNERATION REPORT - NETHERLANDS. see BUSINESS AND ECONOMICS — Personnel Management

REMUNERATION REPORT - NORWAY. see BUSINESS AND ECONOMICS — Personnel Management

REMUNERATION REPORT - PORTUGAL. see BUSINESS AND ECONOMICS — Personnel Management

REMUNERATION REPORT - SPAIN. see BUSINESS AND ECONOMICS — Personnel Management

REMUNERATION REPORT - SWEDEN. see BUSINESS AND ECONOMICS — Personnel Management

REMUNERATION REPORT - SWITZERLAND. see BUSINESS AND ECONOMICS — Personnel Management

REMUNERATION REPORT - TURKEY. see BUSINESS AND ECONOMICS — Personnel Management

REMUNERATION REPORT - UNITED KINGDOM. see BUSINESS AND ECONOMICS — Personnel Management

658 NE ISSN 0926-3314
RENDEMENT; tijdschrift voor winstverbetering. 1991. 10/yr. fl.192.50. Benelux Periodieken B.V., Postbus 397, 3900 AJ Veenendaal, Netherlands. TEL 31-8385-21422. FAX 31-8385-23136. Ed. M. Dijkstra. circ. 10,500. **Document type:** trade publication.
—SWETS.
  Description: For senior managers, directors, financial executives and others with corporate financial responsibilities.

628 614 DK ISSN 0906-270X
RENT I DANMARK. 1974. 8/yr. DKK 208.20. Forlaget Thorsgaard ApS, Holmensvej 5, P.O. Box 5, 3600 Frederikssund, Denmark. TEL 42-31-21-05. FAX 47-38-36-33. Ed.Bd. adv.: B&W page DKK 10850, color page DKK 13850; trim 175 x 270; adv. contact: Erik Hvalsoe. bk.rev.; circ. 7,000 (controlled).
  Formerly: Renhold Vedligehold.

658 338 US ISSN 0272-7323
REP TALK.* 1978. m. $117. Berman Publications, 11785 Barrington Ct., Ste. 341, Los Angeles, CA 90049-2930. TEL 408-246-4582. Ed. Norma Zonay. circ. 300.
  Description: Features business management for the independent representative.

658 US ISSN 1066-8063
HD4965.5.C3
REPORT ON CANADIAN EXECUTIVE AND MIDDLE MANAGEMENT REMUNERATION. a. $930. (Executive Compensation Service (ECS)) Wyatt Data Services, 218 Rte. 17, N., Roselle Park, NJ 07662-9832. TEL 201-843-1177. FAX 201-843-0101. **Document type:** trade publication.
  Formerly: Report on Canadian Executive Remuneration (ISSN 1050-0766)

REPORT ON EXECUTIVE REMUNERATION. see BUSINESS AND ECONOMICS — Personnel Management

REPORT ON HUMAN RESOURCES COMPENSATION. see BUSINESS AND ECONOMICS — Personnel Management

REPORT ON OFFICE PERSONNEL REMUNERATION. see BUSINESS AND ECONOMICS — Personnel Management

REPORTS ON FLEET MANAGEMENT. see TRANSPORTATION — Automobiles

RESEARCH IN DOMESTIC AND INTERNATIONAL AGRIBUSINESS MANAGEMENT. see AGRICULTURE — Agricultural Economics

RESEARCH IN PUBLIC POLICY ANALYSIS AND MANAGEMENT. see SOCIOLOGY

658 US ISSN 0279-8050
HC101
RESEARCH INSTITUTE REPORT. w. Research Institute of America, Inc., 90 Fifth Ave., New York, NY 10011. TEL 212-645-4800. FAX 212-337-4279. (Subscr. to: 117 E. Stevens Ave., Valhalla, NY 10595) **Document type:** trade publication.
—CCC.

658 US ISSN 1040-9556
HD42
RESEARCH ON NEGOTIATION IN ORGANIZATIONS. 1986. irreg., vol.6, 1996. $73.25. J A I Press Inc., 55 Old Post Rd., No.2, Box 1678, Greenwich, CT 06830-1678. TEL 203-661-7602. FAX 203-661-0792. E-mail: jai@jaipress.com. (Subscr. in the UK and Europe to: JAI Press Ltd., 38 Tavistock St., Covent Garden, London WC2E 7PB, England. TEL 44-171-379-8834. FAX 44-171-379-8835) Ed.Bd. **Document type:** monographic series.
—BLDSC (7743.708000); UnCover. **CCC.**

RESEARCH POLICY; a journal devoted to research policy, research management and planning. see SCIENCES: COMPREHENSIVE WORKS

658 US ISSN 0895-6308
T175.5 CODEN: RTMAEC
RESEARCH TECHNOLOGY MANAGEMENT; international journal of research management. 1958. bi-m. $55 to individuals (foreign $75); institutions $120 (foreign $119). Industrial Research Institute, 1550 M St., N.W., Washington, DC 20005. TEL 202-296-8811. FAX 202-776-0756. (Subscr. to: Sheridan Press, 450 Fame Ave., Box 465, Hanover, PA 17331. TEL 800-352-2210) Ed. Michael Wolff. R&P contact: Lodita Vallarta. bk.rev.; charts; illus.; index; circ. 4,400 (paid). (also avail. in microfilm from UMI; back issues avail.; reprint service avail. from SCH) **Indexed:** ABI Inform, Abstr.Bull.Inst.Pap.Chem., Account.& Data Proc.Abstr., ASCA, ASEAN Manage.Abstr., B.P.I., BPIA, Bus.Ind., CAD CAM Abstr., Compumath, Cont.Pg.Manage., Curr.Cont., Energy Info.Abstr., Eng.Ind., High.Educ.Curr.Aware.Bull., Ind.U.S.Gov.Per., Key to Econ.Sci., Mgmt.& Market.Abstr., Oper.Res.Manage.Sci., P.A.I.S., PROMT, Risk Abstr., SCIMP, SSCI, Tel.Abstr., Work Rel.Abstr. **Document type:** academic/scholarly publication.
—BLDSC (7773.714500); CASDDS; CISTI; Ei; Genuine Article; KR SourceOne; Linda Hall; SWETS; UMI; UnCover. **CCC.**
  Formerly: Research Management (ISSN 0034-5334)

658 II
▼**RESEARCHES IN MANAGEMENT IN ASIA SERIES.** (Text in English) 1997. irreg. price varies. Hindustan Publishing Corp., 4805-24, 1st Fl., Bharat Ram Rd., Darya Ganj, New Delhi 110 002, India. TEL 91-11-3254401. FAX 91-11-6863511.
Document type: monographic series, academic/scholarly publication.

658 NZ ISSN 1170-344X
RESERVE BANK OF NEW ZEALAND. CORPORATE PLAN. 1990. a. free. Reserve Bank of New Zealand, Corporate Services, 2 The Terrace, P.O. Box 2498, Wellington, New Zealand. TEL 64-4-722029. FAX 64-4-738554. TELEX NZ 3368. circ. 150. (back issues avail.) **Document type:** corporate report.

RESISTANT PEST MANAGEMENT. see AGRICULTURE

RETAIL BANKER INTERNATIONAL. see BUSINESS AND ECONOMICS — Banking And Finance

658 US
RETAIL OPPORTUNITY LETTER. 1975. m. $77. Management Facts Co., Inc., 6223 E. Lake Dr., Haslett, MI 48840-8737. TEL 517-339-8025. Ed. John Moon. (back issues avail.)
  Former titles: Productive Management & Executive Management.

658.8 US ISSN 0360-506X
RETAILING TODAY. 1966. m. $60 (foreign $72) (effective 1997). Robert Kahn and Associates, Box 249, Lafayette, CA 94549. TEL 510-254-4434. FAX 510-284-5612. Ed. Robert Kahn. circ. 1,200. **Document type:** newsletter.
  Description: For CEO's in retailing. Commentary on current trends, with emphasis on ethical business practices.

REVIEW OF INDUSTRIAL ORGANIZATION. see BUSINESS AND ECONOMICS — Economic Systems And Theories, Economic History

658 BL ISSN 0080-2107
JA5
REVISTA DE ADMINISTRACAO. vol.12, 1977. q. $28 (foreign $45) (effective 1997). Universidade de Sao Paulo, Instituto de Administracao, c/o Sonia Maria Eira-Velha, Pub., Caixa Postal 11498, 05422-970 Sao Paulo, Brazil. TEL 55-11-818-5922. FAX 55-11-8143814. TELEX 11-838299. Ed. Jacques Marcovitch. R&P contact: Sonia Maria Eira-Velha. adv. contact: Daniela Maria Siaulys. bk.rev.; bibl.; illus. circ. 4,000. (back issues avail.) **Document type:** academic/scholarly publication.
  Description: Publishes original articles and research papers in the field of business administration and related topics.

BUSINESS AND ECONOMICS — MANAGEMENT

658 BL ISSN 0034-7590
HD28
REVISTA DE ADMINISTRACAO DE EMPRESAS. 1961. q. $170 (effective 1997). (Escola de Administracao de Empresas de Sao Paulo, Centro de Pesquisas e Publicacoes) Fundacao Getulio Vargas, Caixa Postal 62591, 2257-970 Rio de Janeiro, RJ, Brazil. TEL 55-21-5369196. FAX 55-21-5369155. Ed. Roberto Venosa. adv. contact: Milton Gondim. bk.rev.; bibl.; stat. circ. 5,000. **Indexed:** Hisp.Amer.Per.Ind. **Document type:** academic/scholarly publication.
   Description: Provides original articles by both Brazilian and foreign authors, including notes, commentaries and information on topics of interest to the administrator. Covers practical administrative aspects as well as research linked to administration.

658 AG
REVISTA IDEA. 1977. m. Moreno 1850-5, Buenos Aires 1094, Argentina. Ed. Graciela Zeberio. adv.

658 BL ISSN 0104-088X
TS156.A1
REVISTA INDICADORES DA QUALIDADE E PRODUTIVIDADE. 1993. s-a. Instituto de Pesquisa Economica Aplicada, Av. Presidente Antonio Carlos, 51, 13 andar, 20020-010 Rio de Janeiro RJ, Brazil. TEL 021-220-5533. FAX 021-240-1920.

658 CK ISSN 0120-341X
HD28
REVISTA UNIVERSIDAD E A F I T. 1965. q. Col.$25000($30) (effective 1997). (Escuela de Administracion y Finanzas y Tecnologias) Editorial E A F I T, Apdo. Aereo 3300, Medellin, Colombia. TEL 57-4-2660500. FAX 57-4-2664284. E-mail: anrestre@sigma.eafit.edu.co. Ed. Jorge Enrique Devia. adv.; bk.rev.; bibl.; charts; illus.; stat.; index, cum.index. circ. 2,000. **Indexed:** IBR. **Document type:** academic/scholarly publication.
   Former titles: Revista E A F I T - Temas Administrativos (ISSN 0120-033X); Temas Administrativos (ISSN 0040-2877)

658 VE ISSN 1315-9984
▼**REVISTA VENEZOLANA DE GERENCIA.** 1996. s-a. exchange basis. Universidad del Zulia, Vicerrectorado Academico, Edificio del Rectorado, Apdo. Postal 15401, Ave. Guajira con Calle 66, Maracaibo, Estado Zulia, Venezuela. TEL 58-61-528397. FAX 58-61-528397. E-mail: revista_venezolana_gerencia@luz.ve; URL: http://www.luz.ve/vice_academico/rvg.html. Dir. Haydee Ochoa Henriquez.
   Description: Covers all aspects of management. *Refereed Serial*

REVUE ADMINISTRATIVE. see *PUBLIC ADMINISTRATION*

658 346 FR ISSN 1156-2935
REVUE DE JURISPRUDENCE DE DROIT DES AFFAIRES. 1991. m. 890 F. (effective 1997). Editions Francis Lefebvre, 42 rue de Villiers, 92300 Levallois, France. TEL 41-05-22-00. FAX 41-05-22-30.

658 FR ISSN 1167-7848
REVUE FIDUCIAIRE - CONSEIL. 1990. m. 290 F. (foreign 345 F.) (effective 1997). Publications Fiduciaires, 100 rue LaFayette, 75485 Paris Cedex 10, France. TEL 33-1-41835252. FAX 33-1-41835253. URL: http://www.revuefiduciaire.fr. Ed. J.J. Veron. index. (back issues avail.)
   Formerly (until 1992): Fidu-Conseil (ISSN 1150-1790)
   Description: Covers all the elements of managing a business.

658 FR ISSN 1240-4640
REVUE FIDUCIAIRE - PAYE. Key Title: RF Paye. m. 285 F. (foreign 340 F.) (effective 1997). Publications Fiduciaires, 100 rue Lafayette, 75485 Paris Cedex 10, France. TEL 33-1-41835252. FAX 33-1-41835253. URL: http://www.revuefiduciaire.fr. Ed. J.J. Veron. index. (back issues avail.)
   Description: Covers the latest news and laws on wages.

658 FR ISSN 0338-4551
REVUE FRANCAISE DE GESTION. 1975. 5/yr. 590 F. (Fondation Nationale pour l'Enseignement de la Gestion des Entreprises) Groupe Liaisons S.A., 1 av. Edouard Belin, 92856 Rueil Malmaison, France. TEL 33-1-49299879. FAX 33-1-41299880. Ed. Jean-Marie Doublet. adv.; bk.rev. **Indexed:** Cont.Pg.Manage., Key to Econ.Sci., Mgmt.& Market.Abstr., P.A.I.S.For.Lang.Ind., SCIMP (1978-). —BLDSC (7904.160000); SWETS.
   Incorporates (1945-1975): Hommes et Techniques (ISSN 0018-4381); (1975-1976): Direction (ISSN 0338-4543); (1986-1987): Formation et Gestion (ISSN 0765-7587); Which was formerly: Enseignement et Gestion (ISSN 0765-7579); Supersedes in part (in 1975): Management France (ISSN 0542-4801); Which was previously (until 1969): C N O F: Comite National de l'Organisation Francaise (ISSN 0998-5476); (1927-1934): Comite National de l'Organisation Francaise. Bulletin (ISSN 0998-5484).
   Description: Bibliographic guide offering critical analyses of recent publications that give managerial advice as it applies to all industries.

REWARD: THE MANAGEMENT SURVEY. see *BUSINESS AND ECONOMICS — Labor And Industrial Relations*

658 IT ISSN 0391-6960
RIFORMA AMMINISTRATIVA. 1961. m. L.25000. Federazione Nazionale Dirigenti Stato, Via Ezio, 12, 00192 Rome, Italy. TEL 06-32-11-535. Ed. Dr. Arcangelo D'Ambrosio. adv.; B&W page L.1200000. bk.rev. circ. 10,000. (reprint service avail.)

658 690.1 US
RINKSIDER; independent voice of the industry! 1956. bi-m. $20 effective 1995. Target Publishing Co., Inc. (Columbus), 2470 E. Main St., Columbus, OH 43209. TEL 614-235-1022. FAX 614-235-3584. Ed. Susie Young; Pub. Linda Katz. adv. contact: Linda Katz. circ. 3,000 (controlled). cols./p.: 4; pp./issue: 56. (tabloid format) **Document type:** newspaper, trade publication.
   Description: Provides rink operators with promotional ideas and legislative, insurance, operational and supplier news.

658 US ISSN 1053-556X
HG9395
RISK & BENEFITS JOURNAL (MARINA DEL REY). 1991. bi-m. Allied Health Care Publications, 4676 Admiralty Way, Ste. 202, Marina del Rey, CA 90292.

658 368 UK ISSN 1357-5309
▼**RISK, DECISION AND POLICY.** 1996. 3/yr. £65 (foreign $110) to individuals; institutions £135 (foreign $225); print & online eds. combined £160 (foreign $270) (effective 1998). Thomson Professional (Subsidiary of: International Thomson Publishing Group), 2-6 Boundary Row, London SE1 8HN, England. TEL 44-171-8650066. FAX 44-171-5229623. TELEX 290164 CHAPMA G. URL: http://rdp.thomsonprofessional.com. (Subscr. to: International Thomson Publishing Services Ltd., Cheriton House, North Way, Andover, Hants. SP10 5BE, England. TEL 44-1264-342713. FAX 44-1264-342807; Subscr. in US & Canada to: 400 Market St., Philadelphia, PA 19106. TEL 800-552-5866) Ed. Paul Anand. bk.rev. (back issues avail.; reprint service avail.) **Document type:** academic/scholarly publication.
   ●Also available online.
   —BLDSC (7972.585800).
   Description: Disseminates research articles that apply decision and game theory, both broadly defined, to policy problems in the public and private sectors.
   Refereed Serial

S A DIRECTORY OF BLACK MANAGERS. see *BUSINESS AND ECONOMICS — Trade And Industrial Directories*

658.3 SW ISSN 0349-6740
S A F - TIDNINGEN. 1953. 40/yr. SEK 385 (effective 1994). Svenska Arbetsgivarefoereningen - Swedish Employers' Confederation, S-103 30 Stockholm, Sweden. TEL 08-762-6000. FAX 08-762-6885. (Dist. by: S A Fs Foerlagsservice, S-811 Vandriken, Sweden) Ed. Marianne Kronberg. bk.rev.; charts; illus. circ. 62,000. (tabloid format) **Document type:** trade publication.
   Formerly (until vol.16, 1980): Arbetsgivaren (ISSN 0044-8567)

658 SA ISSN 1026-6550
S A I M A S NEWS. q. R.80 to non-members (foreign R.180). South African Institute of Management Services - Suidelike Afrika Instituut vir Bestuursdienste, P.O. Box 693, Pretoria 0001, South Africa. TEL 27-12-3185797. FAX 27-12-3185797. E-mail: saimas@global.co.za; URL: http://www.global.co.za/saimas. Ed. Hercules A. du Plessis. adv.; page R.600. bk.rev. circ. 1,200. **Document type:** newsletter.
   Formerly: South African Institute of Organization and Methods. Newsletter.
   Description: Concerned with the enhancement, practice and development of management services methodologies and techniques.

658 US
S A M ADVANCED MANAGEMENT JOURNAL. 1935. q. $44 (effective 1998). Society for Advancement of Management, Texas A&M University - Corpus Christi, College of Business, 6300 Ocean Dr., FC 111, Corpus Christi, TX 78412. TEL 512-994-6045. FAX 512-994-2725. Ed. Moustafa Abdelsamad. charts; illus.; index. (also avail. in microform from UMI; reprint service avail. from UMI)
   Former titles: S A M Management Journal; What's Happening; S A M News International (ISSN 0049-1144)

658 US
S R A NEWSLETTER. bi-m. $50. Society of Research Administrators, Inc., 1200 19th St., N.W., Ste. 300, Washington, DC 20036-2401. TEL 202-857-1141. FAX 202-223-4579. E-mail: llindow-plus-adcp2%sbadc@mcimail.com. Ed. Bruce Steinert. adv. contact: Amy McNamara. circ. 2,800. (tabloid format; back issues avail.) **Document type:** newsletter.
   Description: Covers SRA news and issues affecting members.

SAFETY MANAGEMENT. see *OCCUPATIONAL HEALTH AND SAFETY*

SALARY SURVEY (WASHINGTON). see *BUSINESS AND ECONOMICS — Economic Situation And Conditions*

SALES AND MARKETING EXECUTIVE REPORT. see *BUSINESS AND ECONOMICS — Marketing And Purchasing*

658 US
▼**SALES AUTOMATION REPORT.** 1996. 10/yr. $175. Dartnell Corporation, 4660 N. Ravenswood Ave., Chicago, IL 60640. TEL 773-561-4000; 800-621-5463. FAX 773-561-3801. URL: http://www.dartnellcorp.com. Ed. Tim McMahon. pp./issue: 12. **Document type:** newsletter.
   Description: Provides advice, information, and ideas about sales automation.

658.8 NE ISSN 1381-0553
SALES MANAGEMENT. 1987. 10/yr. fl.199 (effective 1996). Kluwer Bedrijfswetenschappen B.V. (Subsidiary of: Wolters Kluwer N.V.), Postbus 23, 7400 GA Deventer, Netherlands. TEL 31-570-648995. FAX 31-570-611504. (Subscr. to: Intermedia bv, Postbus 4, 2400 MA Alphen aan den Rijn, Netherlands. TEL 31-172-466321. FAX 31-172-435527) Ed. M. Berghuis; Pub. Ph. van Borselen. adv.; circ. 8,000 (paid). **Document type:** trade publication.
   Formerly (until 1994): Verkopen (Deurne) (ISSN 0774-9082)

658 UK ISSN 1356-1952
SALES MANAGEMENT. m. £105. Sewells International Emap Automotive Ltd., Wentworth House, Wentworth St., Peterborough PE1 1DS, England. TEL 44-1733-467191. FAX 44-1733-467199. **Document type:** trade publication.
   Former titles (until 1994): Sales Manager (ISSN 0963-2530); (until 1991): Sales Management.

658 US
SALES MEMOS. m. $28.32. Dartnell Corporation, 4660 N. Ravenswood Ave., Chicago, IL 60640. TEL 773-561-4000; 800-621-5463. FAX 773-561-3801. URL: http://www.dartnellcorp.com. Ed. Terry Breen.
   Description: Helps salespeople schedule appointments to save time and maximize their efficiency.

BUSINESS AND ECONOMICS — MANAGEMENT

658　　　　　FI　　ISSN 0786-2113
SAMPOVISIO. bi-m. Erikoislehdet Oy Business Publications, P.O. Box 16, FIN-00381 Helsinki, Finland. Ed. Eero Sauri. circ. 60,000.
　Formerly: Riskienhallinta (ISSN 0782-0496)

SAMSOM SUBSIDIE-INFO. see *BUSINESS AND ECONOMICS — Production Of Goods And Services*

SATELLITE NEWS. see *COMMUNICATIONS*

658　　　　　UK　　ISSN 0956-5221
HD28
SCANDINAVIAN JOURNAL OF MANAGEMENT. 1984. q. fl.795($457) (effective 1998). Elsevier Science Ltd., Pergamon, P.O. Box 800, Kidlington, Oxford OX5 1DX, England. TEL 44-1865-843000. FAX 44-1865-843010. E-mail: nlinfo-f@elsevier.nl; usinfo-f@elsevier.com; forinfo-kyf04035@niftyserve.or.jp; URL: http://www.elsevier.nl/. (Subscr. to: Elsevier Science, Regional Sales Office, P.O. Box 211, 1000 AE Amsterdam, Netherlands. TEL 31-20-4853757. FAX 31-20-4853432; Subscr. in the Americas to: Elsevier Science, Regional Sales Office, Box 945, New York, NY 10159-0945. TEL 212-633-3730. FAX 212-633-3680; Subscr. in Australasia and the Far East to: Elsevier Science (Singapore) Pte Ltd, No.1 Temasek Ave., No.17-01 Millenia Tower, Singapore 039192, Singapore. TEL 65-434-3727. FAX 65-337-2230) Ed. Sten Jonsson. (also avail. in microfilm from UMI) **Indexed:** Psychol.Abstr. (1989-). **Document type:** academic/scholarly publication.
　—BLDSC (8087.517240); SWETS; UMI. **CCC.**
　Formerly (until 1988): Scandinavian Journal of Management Studies (ISSN 0281-7527)
　Description: Dedicated to the advancement of understanding of management in private and public organizations through empirical investigation and theoretical analysis.
　Refereed Serial

SCOTTISH BUSINESS INSIDER. see *BUSINESS AND ECONOMICS — Banking And Finance*

SECURITY JOURNAL. see *CRIMINOLOGY AND LAW ENFORCEMENT — Security*

658 658.3　　US　　ISSN 0145-9406
HD38　　　　　　　CODEN: SECME6
SECURITY MANAGEMENT. 1957. m. $48. American Society for Industrial Security, 1655 N. Fort Myer Dr., Ste. 1200, Arlington, VA 22209-3198. TEL 703-522-5800. FAX 703-522-5226. TELEX 901892 ASIS AGTN. Ed. Sherry Harowitz; Pub. Mary Alice Crawford. R&P contact: Nello Caramat. adv. contact: Sandra Wade. bk.rev.; charts; illus.; stat.; cum.index. circ. 25,000. (also avail. in microform from UMI; reprint service avail. from UMI) **Indexed:** ABI Inform., Abstr.Crim.& Pen., B.P.I, BPIA, Bus.Ind., CJPI, Comput.Lit.Ind., Crim.Just.Abstr., INSPEC (1988-), Manage.Cont., PSI, Tr.& Indus.Ind. **Document type:** trade publication.
　●Also available online. Vendor(s): Information Access Co., UMI.
　—BLDSC (8217.210000); AskIEEE; KR SourceOne; SWETS; UMI; UnCover. **CCC.**
　Formerly: Industrial Security (ISSN 0019-8773)

658.5　　　　　MX
SEGURINOTAS. 1955. m. $4. Instituto Tecnologico y de Estudios Superiores de Monterrey, Departamento de Seguridad Industrial, Sucursal de Correos "J", Monterrey N.L., Mexico. Ed. Marco Antonio Ledesma. circ. 2,400. (tabloid format)

658　　　　　UK　　ISSN 0963-2638
SELECTION AND DEVELOPMENT REVIEW. 1984. bi-m. £37($50) (free to qualified personnel) (effective 1997). British Psychological Society, St Andrew's House, 48 Princess Rd. E., Leicester LE1 7DR, England. TEL 44-166-254-9568. FAX 44-166-247-0787. E-mail: bps-journals@mailbox.ulcc.ac.uk; URL: http://www.journals.eecs.qub.ac.uk. (Subscr. to: Turpin Distribution Services Ltd., Blackhorse Rd., Letchworth, Herts. SB6 1HN, England. TEL 44-1462-672555. FAX 44-1462-480947) Eds. Roderic Vincent, Sean Boyle. adv. contact: H. Daeuker. bk.rev. (back issues avail.) **Document type:** academic/scholarly publication.
　—BLDSC (8235.144870).
　Formerly: Guidance and Assessment Review (ISSN 0265-1610)
　Description: Focuses on selection and development issues for professional people whose job it is to assess other people.
　Refereed Serial

SELF-STORAGE ALMANAC. see *BUSINESS AND ECONOMICS — Domestic Commerce*

SELF-STORAGE NOW. see *BUSINESS AND ECONOMICS — Domestic Commerce*

SELLING POWER; advisory for sales and marketing executives. see *BUSINESS AND ECONOMICS — Marketing And Purchasing*

658　　　　　NE
SERIES ON APPLIED BUSINESS LOGISTICS. (Text in English) irreg. price varies. Kluwer Academic Publishers, Postbus 17, 3300 AA Dordrecht, Netherlands. TEL 31-78-6392392. FAX 31-78-6392254. TELEX 29245 KAPG NL. E-mail: services@wkap.nl; URL: http://www.wkap.nl. (Dist. by: Kluwer Academic Publishers Group, P.O. Box 322, 3300 AH Dordrecht, Netherlands. TEL 31-78-6392392. FAX 31-78-6546474; N. America dist. addr.: Box 358, Accord Sta., Hingham, MA 02018-0358. TEL 617-871-6600. FAX 617-871-6528) **Document type:** monographic series.

SERVICE & SUPPORT MANAGEMENT. see *COMPUTERS*

658　　　　　US　　ISSN 0739-6236
SERVICE DEALER'S NEWSLETTER; business and personal insights for service dealers and managers. 1984. m. $87 (effective 1997 & 1998). Whitaker Newsletters Inc., 313 South Ave., Box 192, Fanwood, NJ 07023. TEL 908-889-6336. FAX 908-889-6339. Ed. Fred Rossi. bk.rev. circ. 6,000.
　Description: How-to tips on improving sales and profits for owners and managers of service-repair businesses.

648 658　　　NE　　ISSN 0928-3021
SERVICE MANAGEMENT; vakblad voor facilitaire dienstverlening. (Text in Dutch) 1974. 11/yr. fl.139. Samsom BedrijfsInformatie B.V. (Subsidiary of: Wolters Kluwer B.V.), Postbus 4, 2400 MA Alphen aan den Rijn, Netherlands. TEL 31-172-466533. FAX 31-172-422886. adv.; illus.; circ. 14,838 (paid). **Document type:** trade publication.
　Former titles (until 1992): Bedrijfshuishouding (ISSN 0165-1323); (until 1978): Schoonmaak en Hygiene (ISSN 0928-3471)

658　　　　　CC　　ISSN 1000-2154
HB9
SHANGYE JINGJI YU GUANLI/ECONOMICS AND BUSINESS ADMINISTRATION. (Text in Chinese) bi-m. Y28.80 (effective 1997). Hangzhou Shangxueyuan - Hangzhou Institute of Commerce, 29 Jiaogong Rd., Hangzhou, Zhejiang 310035, People's Republic of China. TEL 86-571-8081002. FAX 86-571-8053079. (Dist. in US by: China Books & Periodicals, Inc., 2929 24th St., San Francisco, CA 94110. TEL 415-282-2994) Eds. Guangming Wang, Junyang Li. adv. contact: Huaizheng Li. bk.rev. **Document type:** academic/scholarly publication.

658　　　　　CC　　ISSN 1005-4367
SHANGYE QIYE GUANLI. (Subseries of: Fuyin Baokan Ziliao) (Text in Chinese) m. $85.13. Zhongguo Renmin Daxue, Shubao Ziliao Zhongxin, 3 Zhang Zizhong Rd., P.O. Box 1122, Beijing 100007, People's Republic China. TEL 86-10-4015080. (Dist. in US by: China Publications Service, Box 49614, Chicago, IL 60649. TEL 312-288-3291. FAX 312-288-8570) pp./issue: 112.
　Description: Cover the management of commercial enterprises.

658　　　　　US
SHARING OF EXPERTISE AND EXPERIENCE. Variant title: A S A E. Management Conference. Proceedings. a. $50 to non-members; members $35. American Society of Association Executives, 1575 Eye St., N.W., Washington, DC 20005-1168. TEL 202-626-2723. FAX 202-408-9635. circ. 1,750.

658 333.33　　US　　ISSN 1089-7364
SHOPPING CENTER MANAGEMENT INSIDER. 1995. m. $255 (effective 1997). Brownstone Publishers, Inc., 149 Fifth Ave., New York, NY 10010-6801. TEL 212-473-8200. FAX 212-473-8786. Ed. Steven Gordon; Pub. John M. Striker. **Document type:** newsletter.
　Description: Tested management techniques, legal insights, and how-to guidelines for running a shopping center or mall. Includes model notices to tenants, letters, agreements and rules.

SHUIYUN GUANLI/WATER TRANSPORTATION MANAGEMENT. see *TRANSPORTATION — Ships And Shipping*

658　　　　　JA
SHUKAN GENDAI. (Text in Japanese) 1954. w. 26900 Yen. Kodansha Ltd., 12-21 Otawa 2-chome, Bunkyo-ku, Tokyo 112-02, Japan. TEL 81-3-5322-3438. FAX 81-3-3945-8403. TELEX J34509 KODANSHA. URL: http://www.kodansha.co.jp. Ed. Masahiko Motoki. circ. 940,000 (paid).
　Description: Covers general topics for businessmen.

658　　　　　GW　　ISSN 0344-8746
SICHERHEITS-BERATER; Informationsdienst zu Problemen der Sicherheit in Betrieb, Unternehmen und Verwaltung. 1974. s-m. DM.492. Verlagsgruppe Handelsblatt GmbH, Kasernenstr. 67, 40213 Duesseldorf, Germany. TEL 49-211-8870. FAX 49-211-374955. (Subscr. to: Postfach 102717, 40018 Duesseldorf, Germany) Ed. Rainer A.H. von zur Muehlen. circ. 1,900. **Document type:** bulletin.
　—SWETS. **CCC.**

658　　　　　NE　　ISSN 0166-6967
SIGMA. 1955. 6/yr. fl.128. Kluwer Bedryfsinformatie B.V., P.O. Box 23, 7400 GA Deventer, Netherlands. Ed. B.H. van Lochem. adv.: B&W page fl.1585; adv. contact: Sylvia Kodde. circ. 4,000. **Document type:** trade publication.
　—KNAW.
　Description: Professional journal for quality professionals.

658　　　　　US　　ISSN 0193-4201
HD2745
SIGNIFICANT ISSUES FACING DIRECTORS. 1977. a. $50. Directorship Inc., 8 Sound Shore Dr., Ste. 250, Greenwich, CT 06830-7242. TEL 203-861-7000. FAX 203-861-7007. Ed. B.J. Dunn. (back issues avail.) **Document type:** trade publication.

658 338　　　IT　　ISSN 0393-5108
SINERGIE; rivista di studi e ricerche. (Text in Italian; summaries in English and Italian) 1983. 3/yr. L.60000. Consorzio Universitario Economia Industriale e Manageriale, Via S. Cristoforo 4, 37129 Verona, Italy. TEL 39-45-597655. FAX 39-45-597550. Ed. Gaetano M. Golinelli. adv.: page L.850000; trim 235 x 17; adv. contact: Federico Brunetti. bibl.; illus.; stat.; index. circ. 700. **Document type:** academic/scholarly publication.
　Refereed Serial

SIR FREDERIC HOOPER AWARD ESSAY. see *BUSINESS AND ECONOMICS*

SKYLINES (WASHINGTON); news of the commercial real estate industry. see *BUILDING AND CONSTRUCTION*

BUSINESS AND ECONOMICS — MANAGEMENT 1507

658.5 US ISSN 0019-848X
HD28 CODEN: SMRVAO
SLOAN MANAGEMENT REVIEW. 1960. q. $69 in U.S.; Canada and Mexico $89; elsewhere $99 (effective 1997). (Sloan Management Review Association) Massachusetts Institute of Technology, Sloan School of Management, 77 Massachussetts Ave., E53-416, Cambridge, MA 02139. TEL 617-253-7170. FAX 617-258-9739. E-mail: smr@mit.edu; URL: http://web.mit.edu/smr-online/. Ed. Sarah Cliffe. R&P contact: Joan Carr. adv. contact: Susan Petrie. bk.rev.; bibl.; charts; illus.; stat.; index. circ. 20,000. (also avail. in microform from UMI; reprint service avail. from UMI,KTO) **Indexed:** ABI Inform., Anbar, ASCA, ASEAN Manage.Abstr., B.P.I., Bank.Lit.Ind., BMT, BPIA, Bus.Ind., CAD CAM Abstr., Compumath, Comput.Lit.Ind., Cont.?g.Manage., Curr.Cont., Data Process.Dig., Educ.Admin.Abstr., Eng.Ind., Environ.Abstr., INSPEC, Key to Econ.Sci., Manage.Cont., Mgmt.& Market.Abstr., Oper.Res.Manage.Sci., P.A.I.S., Pers.Lit., Pers.Manage.Abstr., PROMT, Qual.Contr.Appl.Stat., Risk Abstr., SCIMP (1978-), SSCI, Tel.Abstr., Work Rel.Abstr. **Document type:** academic/scholarly publication, trade publication.
●Also available online. Vendor(s): UMI.
—BLDSC (8309.530000); AskIEEE; CISTI; Genuine Article; KR SourceOne; SWETS; UMI; UnCover. **CCC.**
Formerly: Industrial Management Review.
Description: Articles on key issues that affect national and international senior management professionals, focusing on entrepreneurial technologies and business intelligence systems.
Refereed Serial

SMALL BUSINESS AND ENTERPRISE DEVELOPMENT. see BUSINESS AND ECONOMICS — Small Business

SMALL BUSINESS CHRONICLE. see BUSINESS AND ECONOMICS — Small Business

658 UN ISSN 0252-3426
HD2346.A744
SMALL INDUSTRY BULLETIN FOR ASIA AND THE PACIFIC. 1965. a. $15. United Nations Economic and Social Commission for Asia and the Pacific (ESCAP), United Nations Bldg., Rajadamnern Ave., Bangkok 10200, Thailand. (Dist. by: United Nations Publications, Rm. DC2-0853, New York, NY 10017; or Distribution and Sales, Palais des Nations, CH-1211 Geneva 10, Switzerland; or Conference Services Unit, E.S.C.A.P., Bangkok) (also avail. in microfiche from CIS; back issues avail.) **Indexed:** IIS. **Document type:** bulletin.
Formerly: Small Industry Bulletin for Asia and the Far East.

SMETKOVODSTVENO FINANSISKA REVIJA; spisanie za smetkovodstveno-finansiska i organizaciona problematika na rabotnite organizacii. see BUSINESS AND ECONOMICS — Accounting

SOCIAL POLICY AND ADMINISTRATION. see SOCIOLOGY

SOCIETY OF MANAGEMENT ACCOUNTANTS OF CANADA. ANNUAL REPORT. see BUSINESS AND ECONOMICS — Accounting

SOCIETY OF PHOTOGRAPHER AND ARTIST REPRESENTATIVES. NEWSLETTER. see PHOTOGRAPHY

658 US ISSN 0038-0024
Q180.55.M3
SOCIETY OF RESEARCH ADMINISTRATORS. JOURNAL. Abbrev. title: S R A Journal. 1969. q. $45 in N. America (foreign $50); members in N. America $35 (foreign $40) (effective 1997). Society of Research Administrators, Inc., 1200 19th St., N.W., Ste. 300, Washington, DC 20036-2401. TEL 202-857-1141. FAX 202-223-4579. Ed. Pamela Miller. adv.; bk.rev.; index. circ. 3,100. (also avail. in microfilm from UMI; back issues avail.; reprint service avail. from SCH) **Indexed:** ABI Inform, ASCA, BPIA, Bus.Ind., C.I.J.E., Curr.Cont., INSPEC, P.A.I.S., SSCI. **Document type:** academic/scholarly publication.
●Also available online. Vendor(s): Information Access Co., UMI.
—BLDSC (4896.800000); CISTI; UMI; UnCover.
Description: For researchers and administrators in universities, industry, non-profit organizations and medical facilities.

658 658 JA ISSN 0913-1620
HD70.J3
SOPHIA UNIVERSITY. INSTITUTE OF COMPARATIVE CULTURE. BUSINESS SERIES. (Text in English) 1960. irreg. (3-5/yr.), latest no.145, 1995. 1200 Yen per copy. Sophia University, Institute of Comparative Culture, IMDS Office, 4 Yonban-cho, Chiyoda-ku, Tokyo 102, Japan. TEL 81-3-3238-4080. FAX 81-3-3238-4081. Ed. Robert J. Ballon. circ. 600. **Document type:** monographic series.
Description: Covers specific problems faced by foreign firms operating in Japan, particularly business strategy and personnel administration.

658 US ISSN 0195-1718
SOUNDVIEW EXECUTIVE BOOK SUMMARIES. 1979. m. $89.50 in US & Canada; Mexico $95; elsewhere $139. Concentrated Knowledge, Inc., 3 Pond Lane, Middleburg, VT 05753. TEL 802-388-8910. FAX 802-388-8939. E-mail: sales@summary.ccm; URL: http://www.summary.com/. Ed. Roger Griffith; Pub. Cynthia Folino. adv. contact: Robert Carter. bk.rev.; circ. 49,500 (paid). **Document type:** newsletter.
Formerly: Soundview Summaries.
Description: Concise, 8-page distillations of new business books.

658 SA ISSN 0378-9098
CODEN: SAJMDC
SOUTH AFRICAN JOURNAL OF BUSINESS MANAGEMENT/SUID-AFRIKAANSE TYDSKRIF VIR BEDRYFSLEIDING. (Text and summaries in English) 1970. q. R.118 to individuals; institutions R.138 (foreign $45) (effective 1997). (South African Association of Business Management) Foundation for Education, Science & Technology, P.O. Box 1758, Pretoria 0001, South Africa. TEL 27-12-3226404. FAX 27-12-3207803. E-mail: buro@shuttle.up.ac.za. Ed. Linda Human. adv. contact: Linda Human. bk.rev.; charts; illus.; stat. circ. 1,150. **Indexed:** Account.& Data Proc.Abstr., Biol.Abstr., Curr.Cont., Ind.S.A.Per. **Document type:** academic/scholarly publication.
—BLDSC (8338.750000). **CCC.**
Formerly (until 1979): Bedryfsleiding - Business Management (ISSN 0045-1614)
Description: Publishes articles of real significance for business practice.
Refereed Serial

658 II ISSN 0971-5428
HD70.S62
SOUTH ASIAN JOURNAL OF MANAGEMENT. 1994. q. Rs.450($60) New Age International Pvt. Ltd., Journals Division, 4835-24 Ansari Rd., Daryaganj, New Delhi 110 002, India. TEL 91-11-3261487. FAX 91-11-3267437. Pub. N.K. Muraleedharan. **Indexed:** Pub.Admin.Abstr. **Document type:** academic/scholarly publication.
—BLDSC (8348.628500).

658 GW ISSN 0936-9198
SOZIALVERISCHERUNGS-BERATER; Unternehmer-Handbuch fuer zeit- und kostensparenden Umgang mit den Sozialversicherungsvorschriften. 1989. 7/yr. DM.198. Verlag Norman Rentrop, Theodor-Heuss-Str. 4, 53177 Bonn, Germany. TEL 49-228-8205-0. FAX 49-228-364411. Eds. H. Max, H.G. Kalinowski. (looseleaf format) **Document type:** bulletin.
Description: How-to information for social security.

658 NE ISSN 0166-7068
SPECIFIEK. 1977. 10/yr. fl.37.50. K D I, Stichting Kwaliteitsdienst, Postbus 84031, 3009 CA Rotterdam, Netherlands. TEL 31-10-4554700. FAX 31-10-4558857. adv.: B&W page fl.1870. circ. 6,000. **Document type:** newsletter.
—KNAW; SWETS.
Description: Covers quality issues.

658 790.1 GW
SPORTMANAGEMENT. 1966. a. DM.44. Philippka-Verlag, Postfach 6540, 48034 Muenster, Germany. TEL 49-251-23005-0. FAX 49-251-23005-99. Ed. Konrad Honig.

SPRINGER SERIES IN OPERATIONS RESEARCH. see COMPUTERS

658 US
STAFF.* m. Center for Management Systems, 11 Twin Oaks E., Sioux Falls, SD 57105-7015. TEL 712-568-2418.

THE STANDARD (BOSTON); New England's insurance weekly. see INSURANCE

658 338 US ISSN 0361-3623
HG4057
STANDARD & POOR'S REGISTER OF CORPORATIONS, DIRECTORS AND EXECUTIVES. 1928. a. with q. supplements. $650. Standard & Poor's (Subsidiary of: McGraw-Hill Companies, Inc.), 25 Broadway, New York, NY 10004. TEL 212-208-8000. Ed. Lily DeAngelis; Pub. Tom Lupo. R&P contact: Peggy Smith. (also avail. in magnetic tape) **Document type:** directory.
●Also available online.
Also available on CD-ROM.
—CISTI.
Formerly (until 1973): Poor's Register of Corporations, Directors and Executives (ISSN 0079-3825)
Description: Lists some 55,000 companies, giving such information as addresses and telephone numbers, key officers and directors, numbers of employees, S.I.C. codes, their principal products, and annual sales.

658 US
▼**STANDARDS WATCH;** a briefing on standards for business information management professionals. 1997. q. $25 via fax to members (foreign $100); non-members $75 (foreign $120). A I I M International, 1100 Wayne Ave., Ste. 1100, Silver Spring, MD 20910. TEL 301-587-8202. FAX 301-587-2711. E-mail: aiim@aiim.org. Ed. Marilyn Wright. **Document type:** newsletter.
Description: Covers major developments in standardization within information and document management technologies that could affect business information management professionals in the future.

658 NO ISSN 0803-0103
JN7461
STAT OG STYRING. (Text in Norwegian) 1991. bi-m. NOK 510 in the Nordic countries; elsewhere $96 (effective 1997). (Directorate of Organization and Management) Scandinavian University Press, P.O. Box 2959 Toeyen, N-0608 Oslo, Norway. TEL 47-22-57-54-00. FAX 47-22-57-53-53. E-mail: mail@scup.no; URL: http://www.scup.no. (US addr.: 875 Massachusetts Ave., Ste. 84, Cambridge, MA 02139. TEL 617-497-6515. FAX 617-354-6875) Ed. Bjoern Talen. **Document type:** academic/scholarly publication.
Description: Focuses on government and leadership issues.

658 336.2 GW ISSN 0945-5558
STEUER-BRIEF FUER DEN GMBH-GESCHAEFTSFUEHRER. m. DM.9.85 per no. (effective 1997). Verlag Peter Deubner GmbH, Wolfgang-Mueller-Str. 14, 50968 Cologne, Germany. TEL 49-221-9370180. FAX 49-221-93701890. **Document type:** bulletin.

658.87 US ISSN 0039-1867
HD9951
STORES. 1912. m. $49 to individuals (foreign $79); institutions $120 (effective 1997). (National Retail Federation) N R F Enterprises, Inc., 325 7th St., N.W., Ste. 1000, Washington, DC 20004-2802. TEL 202-626-8101. FAX 202-626-8191. URL: http://www.stores.com/. Ed. Harrison Donnelly; Pub. Rick Gallagher. R&P contact: Amy B. Clotworthy. adv. contact: Michael R. Gribbin. bk.rev.; illus.; tr.lit. circ. 33,577. (back issues avail.) **Indexed:** B.P.I., Data Process.Dig., Tr.& Indus.Ind. **Document type:** trade publication.
●Also available online. Vendor(s): Information Access Co., Lexis-Nexis.
—BLDSC (8466.380000); KR SourceOne; SWETS; UMI; UnCover.
Description: Reports on the full spectrum of retail operations and merchandising. For senior retail headquarters executives in chain store retailing, including specialty stores, general merchandise chains, department stores, home furnishings stores, drug stores, wholesale clubs, hardware stores, grocery chains and convenience stores; restaurants; and direct mail and marketing firms.

BUSINESS AND ECONOMICS — MANAGEMENT

658　　　　　UK　ISSN 1086-1718
HD58.8　　　　　CODEN: JSCHEO
STRATEGIC CHANGE. 1992. 8/yr. $350 (foreign $350) (effective 1998). John Wiley & Sons Ltd., Journals, Baffins Ln., Chichester, W. Sussex PO19 1UD, England. TEL 44-1243-779777. FAX 44-1243-775878. E-mail: info-assets@wiley.co.uk; URL: http://www.wiley.co.uk. (Subscr. in N. America to: John Wiley & Sons, Inc., 605 Third Ave., New York, NY 10158. TEL 212-850-6645. FAX 212-850-6021) Ed. David E. Hussey. adv.: B&W page £595, color page £1495; trim 297 x 210; adv. contact: Bob Kern. circ. 240. (also avail. in microform from UMI; back issues avail.; reprint service avail. from SWZ) **Indexed:** Cont.Pg.Manage., SOMA. **Document type:** academic/scholarly publication.
—BLDSC (8474.031423); UMI. **CCC.**
Formerly (until 1996): Journal of Strategic Change (ISSN 1057-9265)
Description: Provides information on the planning and implementation of organizational change to meet the demands of changing business, economic and social environments.
Refereed Serial

658　　　　　UK　ISSN 0968-0829
HD62.15
STRATEGIC INSIGHTS INTO QUALITY. 1993. 5/yr. £649($999) (effective 1997). M C B University Press Ltd., 60-62 Toller Ln., Bradford, W. Yorks BD8 9BY, England. TEL 44-1274-777700. FAX 44-1274-785200. TELEX 51317-MCBUNI-G. URL: http://www.mcb.co.uk. (N. American subscr. to: M C B University Press Limited, Box 1943, Birmingham, AL 35201) Ed. Martin Fojt. **Document type:** academic/scholarly publication.
—**CCC.**

658　　　　　UK　ISSN 0143-2095
HD30.28　　　　CODEN: SMAJD8
STRATEGIC MANAGEMENT JOURNAL. 1979. m. $795 (foreign $795) (effective 1998). John Wiley & Sons Ltd., Journals, Baffins Ln., Chichester, W. Sussex PO19 1UD, England. TEL 44-1243-779777. FAX 44-1243-775878. E-mail: info-assets@wiley.co.uk; URL: http://www.wiley.co.uk. (Subscr. in the Americas to: John Wiley & Sons, Inc., 605 Third Ave., New York, NY 10158. TEL 212-850-6645. FAX 212-820-6021) Ed. Dan Schendel. adv.: B&W page £595, color page £1495; trim 260 x 200; adv. contact: Bob Kern. circ. 3,456. (also avail. in microform from UMI; back issues avail.; reprint service avail. from ISI,SWZ,UMI) **Indexed:** ABI Inform., Account.& Data Proc.Abstr., Arts & Hum.Cit.Ind., ASCA, ASEAN Manage.Abstr., B.P.I, BPIA, Bus.Ind., Cont.Pg.Manage., Curr.Cont., Manage.Cont., Mgmt.& Market.Abstr., Oper.Res.Manage.Sci., PROMT, Qual.Contr.Appl.Stat., Risk Abstr., SCIMP (1981-), SSCI, SSCI. **Document type:** academic/scholarly publication.
—BLDSC (8474.031460); Ei; Genuine Article; KR SourceOne; SWETS; UMI; UnCover. **CCC.**
Description: Concerned with all aspects of strategic management and improving both theory and practice.
Refereed Serial

658　　　　　US　ISSN 1087-8572
HD28　　　　　CODEN: STLEFV
STRATEGY & LEADERSHIP. 1972. bi-m. $95 (foreign $115). Strategic Leadership Forum, 435 N. Michigan Ave., Ste. 1700, Chicago, OH 60611-4008. TEL 312-644-0829. FAX 312-644-8557. E-mail: 76105.1024@compuserve.com. Ed. Liam Fahey; Pub. Robert E. Becker. adv. contact: Marthann Heard. bk.rev.; charts; illus. circ. 10,000. (also avail. in microform from UMI; reprint service avail. from UMI) **Indexed:** ABI Inform., Account.& Data Proc.Abstr., Account.Ind. (1980-), Anbar, ASEAN Manage.Abstr., B.P.I., Bus.Ind., Comput.Lit.Ind., Cont.Pg.Manage., Fut.Abstr., Manage.Cont., Mgmt.& Market.Abstr., P.A.I.S., PROMT, SCIMP. **Document type:** academic/scholarly publication.
●Also available online. Vendor(s): Information Access Co.
—BLDSC (8474.037950); CASDDS; KR SourceOne; SWETS; UMI; UnCover. **CCC.**
Formerly (until Mar. 1996): Planning Review (ISSN 0094-064X); Which superseded (in 1985): Managerial Planning (ISSN 0025-1941); Which was formerly: Budgeting.
Description: Offers practical information on issues and topics encountered daily in strategic management and planning.

658　　　　　IE　ISSN 0790-6536
STUBBS GAZETTE. 1828. 50/yr. I£131 (England and Wales I£326). Dun & Bradstreet Ltd., Holbrook House, Holles St., Dublin 2, Ireland. TEL 01-6764239. FAX 01-6789301. Ed. Carmel Conroy. adv.: B&W page I£400, color page I£900. stat. circ. 3,000. **Document type:** bulletin.
Description: Provides vital public record information.

658　　　　　IT　ISSN 0391-8769
STUDI ORGANIZZATIVI. 1969. q. L.98000 (foreign L.130000) (effective 1993). Franco Angeli Editore, Viale Monza 106, 20127 Milan, Italy. TEL 02-28-27-651. Ed. Piero Bontadini.

658　　　　　NE　ISSN 0921-3163
STUDIES IN MANAGEMENT SCIENCE AND SYSTEMS. 1975. irreg., vol.20, 1992. price varies. Elsevier Science B.V., Books Division, P.O. Box 211, 1000 AE Amsterdam, Netherlands. TEL 31-20-4853911. FAX 31-20-4853705. TELEX 18582 ESPA NL. E-mail: nlinfo-f@elsevier.nl; usinfo-f@elsevier.com; forinfo-kyf04035@niftyserve.or.jp; URL: http://www.elsevier.nl/. (Subscr. in the Americas to: Elsevier Science, Regional Sales Office, Box 945, New York, NY 10159-0945. TEL 212-633-3730. FAX 212-633-3680; Subscr. in Australasia and the Far East to: Elsevier Science (Singapore) Pte Ltd, No.1 Temasek Ave., No.17-01 Millenia Tower, Singapore 039192, Singapore. TEL 65-434-3727. FAX 65-337-2230; Subscr. in Japan to: Elsevier Science Japan, 9-15 Higashi-Azabu 1-chome, Minato-ku, Tokyo 106, Japan. TEL 81-3-5561-5033. FAX 81-3-5561-5047) Ed. B. V. Dean. **Indexed:** INSPEC, Math.R. **Document type:** monographic series.
—BLDSC (8491.045200).
Refereed Serial

658　　　　　NE　ISSN 0081-8194
STUDIES IN MATHEMATICAL AND MANAGERIAL ECONOMICS. 1964. irreg., vol.37, 1994. price varies. Elsevier Science B.V., Books Division, P.O. Box 211, 1000 AE Amsterdam, Netherlands. TEL 31-20-4853911. FAX 31-20-4853705. TELEX 18582 ESPA NL. E-mail: nlinfo-f@elsevier.nl; usinfo-f@elsevier.com; forinfo-kyf04035@niftyserve.or.jp; URL: http://www.elsevier.nl/. (Subscr. in the Americas to: Elsevier Science, Regional Sales Office, Box 945, New York, NY 10159-0945. TEL 212-633-3730. FAX 212-633-3680; Subscr. in Australasia and the Far East to: Elsevier Science (Singapore) Pte Ltd, No.1 Temasek Ave., No.17-01 Millenia Tower, Singapore 039192, Singapore. TEL 65-434-3727. FAX 65-337-2230; Subscr. in Japan to: Elsevier Science Japan, 9-15 Higashi-Azabu 1-chome, Minato-ku, Tokyo 106, Japan. TEL 81-3-5561-5033. FAX 81-3-5561-5047) Eds. H. Theil, H. Glejser. **Indexed:** Int.Abstr.Oper.Res., Math.R., Zent.Math. **Document type:** monographic series.
Refereed Serial

658.311 338.09　　NE
STUDIES IN PRODUCTIVITY ANALYSIS. (Text in English) irreg. price varies. Kluwer Academic Publishers, Postbus 17, 3300 AA Dordrecht, Netherlands. TEL 31-78-6392392. FAX 31-78-6392254. TELEX 29245 KAPG NL. E-mail: services@wkap.nl; URL: http://www.wkap.nl. (Dist. by: Kluwer Academic Publishers Group, P.O. Box 322, 3300 AH Dordrecht, Netherlands. TEL 31-78-6392392. FAX 31-78-6546474; N. America dist. addr.: Box 358, Accord Sta., Hingham, MA 02018-0358. TEL 617-871-6600. FAX 617-871-6528) **Document type:** monographic series.
Refereed Serial

658　　　　　US
SUCCESS ORIENTATION; the management newsletter for executives, for supervisors, for salesmen, and for personal development. 1969. m. $59.95 (effective July 1997). (Jordan International Enterprises) Success Publications, Inc., Box 487, Roswell, GA 30077. TEL 770-992-6060; 800-672-8677. FAX 770-992-7722. Ed. DuPree Jordan, Jr. R&P contact: Margaret Jordan. bk.rev. circ. 2,800. **Document type:** newsletter.

658　　　　　US
SUCCESSFUL NONPROFITS. * 1987. q. $18. Development and Technical Assistance (D.A.T.A.), 426 State St., New Haven, CT 06510-2018. TEL 203-772-1345; 800-788-5598. FAX 203-772-1614. Ed. Laura Margolin. adv.; bk.rev. (looseleaf format) **Document type:** newsletter.
Description: Carries articles on governing practices of nonprofit boards, and information for staff and volunteers.

658　　　　　US　ISSN 0193-5763
SUCCESSFUL SELF-MANAGEMENT. 1979. q. $45. Stahlka Associates, 60 Westchester Rd., Williamsville, NY 14221-5021. TEL 716-634-5032. FAX 716-626-4188. Ed. Clayton Stahlka. circ. 1,800 (paid). **Document type:** newsletter.
Description: Covers self-directed learning to enable individuals to become better-performing team players in today's complex employment market.

658　　　　　US
SUCCESSFUL SUPERVISOR; a bulletin of ideas and inspiration for those who manage people. 1973. bi-w. $68.90. Dartnell Corporation, 4660 N. Ravenswood Ave., Chicago, IL 60640. TEL 773-561-4000; 800-621-5463. FAX 773-561-3801. URL: http://www.dartnellcorp.com. Ed. Linda Segall. **Document type:** newsletter.
Description: Provides supervisors with valuable information and innovative ideas on people management, decision making, problem solving, and time management.

658　　　　　UK
SUCCESSFUL SUPERVISOR. 1990. 24/yr. £120. Fulcrum Publishing Ltd., 77-83 Walnut Tree Close, Guildford GU1 4UH, England. TEL 44-1483-35753. FAX 44-1483-37086. Ed. Jenny Hayes. bk.rev. **Document type:** newsletter.

SUPERVISION; the magazine of industrial relations and operating management. see BUSINESS AND ECONOMICS — Labor And Industrial Relations

658　　　　　US　ISSN 1077-9337
SUPERVISOR'S MEMORY JOGGER. 1956. m. $16.20. Bureau of Business Practice, 24 Rope Ferry Rd., Waterford, CT 06386. TEL 860-442-4365. FAX 860-437-3555. URL: http://www.bbpnews.com. Ed. Emily Mitchell; Pub. Peter Garabedian. R&P contact: Debra Ferraro.

658　　　　　US
SUPERVISORY MANAGEMENT REPORT - GEOGRAPHIC EDITION. (Supplement to: Industry Report on Supervisory Management Compensation) a. $490. (Executive Compensation Service (ECS)) Wyatt Data Services, 218 Rte. 17, N., Roselle Park, NJ 07662-9832. TEL 201-843-1177. FAX 201-843-0101. charts. (reprint service avail. SCH) **Document type:** trade publication.
Description: Features a wide variety of data cuts ranging from broad regional scans to city-by-city analyses.

658　　　　　UK　ISSN 1359-8546
HF5415.7
▼**SUPPLY CHAIN MANAGEMENT.** 1996. q. £199($329) (foreign Aus.$399) (effective 1998). M C B University Press Ltd., 60-62 Toller Ln., Bradford, W. Yorks BD8 9BY, England. TEL 44-1274-777700. FAX 44-1274-785200. URL: http://www.mcb.co.uk. (Subscr. in N. America to: Box 10812, Birmingham, AL 35201-0812. TEL 800-633-4931. FAX 205-995-1588) Ed. Andrew Fearne. **Document type:** academic/scholarly publication.
—BLDSC (8547.630600). **CCC.**
Description: Focuses on risk management and the logistics of multiple sourcing that brings additional costs for multi-product enterprises.

658　　　　　US
▼**SUPPLY CHAIN MANAGEMENT REVIEW.** 1997. 4/yr. $179. Cahners Publishing Company (Newton), Division of Reed Elsevier Inc., 275 Washington St., Newton, MA 02158-1630. TEL 617-558-4473. FAX 617-558-4327. Ed. Francis J. Quinn; Pub. Mitchell E. MacDonald. circ. 8,000.
Description: Aimed at high-level corporate and supply chain executives. Provides in-depth information on managing the supply chain, which encompasses all of the activities involved in moving goods from the raw materials stage to the end user

BUSINESS AND ECONOMICS — MANAGEMENT

658 360 II ISSN 0586-0008
HD28
SURVEY; a quarterly journal. (Text in English) vol.13, 1973. q. $10. Indian Institute of Social Welfare and Business Management, College Square West, Calcutta 700 073, India. Ed. A.C. Ray. adv.; bk.rev. circ. 800. **Document type:** academic/scholarly publication.
Description: Covers the study of management and welfare in India and abroad including labor economics, human relations, personnel management, sociology, psychology, economics, and public systems management.

SURVEY REPORT ON VARIABLE PAY PROGRAMS. see BUSINESS AND ECONOMICS — Personnel Management

658.2 IT ISSN 0391-7045
SVILUPPO E ORGANIZZAZIONE. 1970. s-m. L.140000 (foreign L.170000). Edizioni Scientifiche Tecniche Europee s.r.l., Via Giorgio Vasari 15, 20135 Milan, Italy. TEL 39-2-55018039. FAX 39-2-5455644. E-mail: edizioni.este@iol.it. Ed. Raoul C.D. Macamulli. R&P contact: Gianni Ceriani. adv. contact: Emma Samaretti. bk.rev.; charts. circ. 8,500. (also avail. in microform from UMI; reprint service avail. from UMI)

658 300 UK ISSN 0883-7066
QA402 CODEN: SDREEG
SYSTEM DYNAMICS REVIEW. 1975. q. $325 (foreign $325) (effective 1998). (System Dynamics Society) John Wiley & Sons Ltd., Journals, Baffins Ln., Chichester, W. Sussex PO19 1UD, England. TEL 44-1243-779777. FAX 44-1243-775878. E-mail: info-assets@wiley.co.uk; URL: http://www.wiley.co.uk. (Subscr. in the Americas to: John Wiley & Sons, Inc., 605 Third Ave., New York, NY 10158. TEL 212-850-6645. FAX 212-850-6021) Ed. Graham W. Winch. adv.: B&W page £595, color page £1495; trim 260 x 200; adv. contact: Bob Kern. bk.rev. circ. 900. (also avail. in microform from UMI; back issues avail.; reprint service avail. from SWZ) **Indexed:** ASCA, Curr.Cont., Geo.Abstr.H.G., Geo.Abstr.P.G., IDA, INSPEC (1993-), Psychol.Abstr. (1985-), SSCI. **Document type:** academic/scholarly publication.
—BLDSC (8589.151000); AskIEEE; Ei; Genuine Article; KR SourceOne; SWETS; UMI; UnCover. **CCC.**
Supersedes: Dynamica (ISSN 0306-7564)
Description: Provides information and advances in the application of the perspective and methods of system dynamics to societal, technical, managerial, and environmental problems.
Refereed Serial

658 US
Q295 CODEN: SYPREM
SYSTEMIC PRACTICE AND ACTION RESEARCH. 1988. bi-m. $325 (foreign $380) (effective 1998). Plenum Publishing Corp., 233 Spring St., New York, NY 10013-1578. TEL 212-620-8000. FAX 212-463-0742. TELEX 23-421139. Ed. Robert L. Flood. adv.; bk.rev. (also avail. in microfilm from UMI; back issues avail.) **Indexed:** ASCA, Compumath, Curr.Cont., IMFL, Oper.Res.Manage.Sci., Qual.Contr.Appl.Stat., SSCI. **Document type:** academic/scholarly publication.
—BLDSC (8589.422000); Ei; Genuine Article; SWETS; UMI; UnCover. **CCC.**
Formerly: Systems Practice (ISSN 0894-9859)
Description: Provides an interdisciplinary approach to the study of systems. Attempts to find ways to utilize and apply the concepts of system science.
Refereed Serial

SYSTEMS RESEARCH. see COMPUTERS — Computer Systems

658 003 US ISSN 1050-2726
THE SYSTEMS THINKER; building shared understanding. 1990. 10/yr. $117 (foreign $138). Pegasus Communications, Inc., Box 120, Kendal Sq., Cambridge, MA 02142. TEL 617-576-1231. FAX 617-576-3114. E-mail: query@pegasuscom.com; URL: http://www.pegasuscom.com. Ed. Colleen Lannon. R&P contact: Coleen Lannon. bk.rev.; circ. 5,000 (paid). (looseleaf format; back issues avail.) **Document type:** newsletter.
—BLDSC (8589.472000).
Description: Presents a systems perspective on current issues and challenges facing managers in the business world.
Refereed Serial

T H & M A. (Tijdschrift voor Hoger Onderwijs en Management) see EDUCATION — School Organization And Administration

T I NEWSLETTER. (Tinbergen Institute) see BUSINESS AND ECONOMICS — Economic Systems And Theories, Economic History

658 UK ISSN 0954-478X
HD62.15 CODEN: TQMMEF
THE T Q M MAGAZINE. (Total Quality Management) bi-m. £529($819) (foreign Aus.$989) (effective 1998). M C B University Press Ltd., 60-62 Toller Ln., Bradford, W. Yorks BD8 9BY, England. TEL 44-1274-777700. FAX 44-1274-785200. TELEX 51317-MCBUNI-G. URL: http://www.mcb.co.uk. Ed. John Peters. (also avail. in microform from UMI) **Indexed:** Br.Educ.Ind., Curr.Cont., Mgmt.& Market.Abstr., Q.Abstr., Tech.Educ.Abstr. **Document type:** academic/scholarly publication.
—BLDSC (8873.783000); Ei; SWETS; UMI. **CCC.**
Incorporates (1991-1996): Asia Pacific Journal of Quality Management (ISSN 0954-3570)

TABAK PLUS BENELUX; vakblad voor de tabaksdetailhandel. see TOBACCO

658 US
THE TAKE - CHARGE ASSISTANT. m. $75 (foreign $110). American Management Association, 1601 Broadway, New York, NY 10019. TEL 212-586-8100. FAX 212-903-8083. E-mail: amapubs@aol.com. (Subscr. to: Dept. 95L, Box 408, Saranac Lake, NY 12983. TEL 800-262-9699) **Document type:** newsletter.
Description: Helps office professionals manage stress; develop a strong verbal professional image; build verbal, written, and mathematics skills; hone their management and interpersonal skills; and balance their professional and personal lives.

TAX & BUSINESS ADVISER. see BUSINESS AND ECONOMICS — Accounting

658.153 US ISSN 0747-8607
KF6289.8.E9
TAX MANAGEMENT COMPENSATION PLANNING JOURNAL. (Subseries of: Tax Management Compensation Planning Series) 1973. m. $389. Tax Management, Inc. (Subsidiary of: The Bureau of National Affairs, Inc.), 1250 23rd St., N.W., Washington, DC 20037-1166. TEL 202-833-7240. FAX 202-833-7297. TELEX 285656 BNAI WSH. (Subscr. to: 9435 Key West Ave., Rockville, MD 20850. TEL 800-372-1033) Ed. Glenn B. Davis. s-a. index, cum.index. (also avail. in microform from UMI; back issues avail.) **Indexed:** Account.Ind. (1989-), BPIA, Bus.Ind., C.L.I., L.I.I., L.R.I. **Document type:** trade publication.
●Also available online. Vendor(s): UMI, West Group (File TM-CPJ).
—UMI. **CCC.**
Former titles (until 1983): Compensation Planning Journal (ISSN 0148-690X); (until 1977): Executive Compensation Journal (ISSN 0094-789X); (until 1974): Tax Management Ecexutive Compensation Journal (ISSN 0093-6995)
Description: Reviews major employee benefit plans in use as well as developments in retirement, profit sharing, welfare plans, stock options, and other employee compensation arrangements.

658 US
TEAM LEADER. 1992. bi-w. $68.90. Dartnell Corporation, 4660 N. Ravenswood Ave., Chicago, IL 60640. TEL 773-561-4000; 800-621-5463. FAX 773-561-3801. URL: http://www.dartnellcorp.com. Ed. Linda Segall. **Document type:** newsletter.
Description: Provides managers, supervisors, foremen, and other team leaders with information on how to develop teams with a positive effect.

658.402 UK ISSN 0969-7136
TEAM LEADER'S BRIEFING. Variant title: Croner's Team Leader's Briefing. 1993. q. Croner Publications Ltd. (Subsidiary of: Wolters Kluwer N.V.), Croner Hosue, 100 London Rd., Kingston-upon-Thames, Surrey TW2 6SR, England. TEL 44-181-547-3333. FAX 44-181-547-2637. TELEX 267778. **Document type:** newsletter.

658 UK ISSN 1352-7592
▼**TEAM PERFORMANCE MANAGEMENT;** an international journal. 1995. m. £199($299) (foreign Aus.$419) (effective 1998). M C B University Press Ltd., 60-62 Toller Ln., Bradford, W. Yorks BD8 9BY, England. TEL 44-1274-777700. FAX 44-1274-785200. URL: http://www.mcb.co.uk. Ed. Malcolm Higgs; Pub. Marjorie Brown. **Document type:** trade publication.
—BLDSC (8614.560200). **CCC.**

658 US ISSN 1359-8066
▼**TEAMS.** 1995. q. £125 (overseas £155($245)) (effective 1996). I F S International Ltd., Wolseley Business Park, Kempston, Bedford MK42 7PW, England. TEL 44-1234-853605. FAX 44-1234-854499. E-mail: IFSIntl@eWorld.com. Ed. Chris Ashton; Pub. Rory L. Chase. R&P contact: David Watts. adv. contact: David Watts. **Document type:** trade publication.
—BLDSC (8614.560600).
Description: Reports on the issues, trends and activities leading to superior team-based organizations and team-working performance.

658 US
TECHCOMP REVIEW. 1988. q. $10. Central Michigan University, School of Business Administration, Smith Hall, Mt. Pleasant, MI 48859. TEL 517-774-3450. Ed. S. Benjamin Prasad. circ. 500. (back issues avail.)
Description: Examines the interface between technology and competition within the context of various industries.

330 US
TA158
TECHNICAL & SKILLED TRADE PERSONNEL REPORT. 1973. a. $470. (Executive Compensation Service (ECS)) Wyatt Data Services, 218 Rte. 17, N., Roselle Park, NJ 07662-9832. TEL 201-843-1177. FAX 201-843-0101. Ed. Michael D. Marvin. **Document type:** trade publication.
Formerly (until 1980): Executive Compensation Service. Technician Report (ISSN 0093-8750)

TECHNICIAN AND SKILLED TRADES PERSONNEL REPORT - GEOGRAPHIC EDITION. see BUSINESS AND ECONOMICS — Personnel Management

658 600 GW ISSN 0344-9696
TECHNOLOGIE-NACHRICHTEN - MANAGEMENT-INFORMATIONEN. 1968. s-m. DM.485. T N V GmbH, An den Eichen, 53773 Hennef, Germany. TEL 02248-1881. FAX 02248-1796. Ed. Nicola Gasterstaedt. circ. 500.
—SWETS. **CCC.**

TECHNOLOGIE UND MANAGEMENT. see TECHNOLOGY: COMPREHENSIVE WORKS

TECHNOLOGY ANALYSIS & STRATEGIC MANAGEMENT. see TECHNOLOGY: COMPREHENSIVE WORKS

TECHNOLOGY MANAGEMENT; strategies & applications for practitioners. see TECHNOLOGY: COMPREHENSIVE WORKS

658 UK ISSN 0258-0551
TECHNOLOGY STRATEGIES. 1984. 10/yr. £769($1269) (foreign Aus.$1599) (effective 1998). M C B University Press Ltd., 60-62 Toller Ln., Bradford, W. Yorks BD8 9BY, England. TEL 44-1274-777700. FAX 44-1274-785200. URL: http://www.mcb.co.uk. (N. American subscr. to: M C B University Press Limited, Box 1943, Birmingham, AL 35201) Ed. Martin Fojt. **Document type:** academic/scholarly publication.
—BLDSC (8761.023500); AskIEEE; KR SourceOne; SWETS. **CCC.**

658 382 600 US ISSN 1072-0782
TECHNOLOGY TRANSFER SOCIETY. INTERNATIONAL SYMPOSIUM PROCEEDINGS.* 1980. a. $50 (effective 1996). Technology Transfer Society, 435 N. Michigan Ave., Chicago, IL 60611-4001. TEL 317-738-3908. FAX 317-738-3908. E-mail: tls@iquest.net; URL: www://157.185.5.3/defaultts/html. bk.rev.; cum.index. circ. 500. (back issues avail.) **Document type:** proceedings.
Description: Full text papers presented at the symposium on methods, models and case studies of technology transfer.
Refereed Serial

TELEMARKETER. see BUSINESS AND ECONOMICS — Marketing And Purchasing

BUSINESS AND ECONOMICS — MANAGEMENT

658   SW   ISSN 1102-3597
TEMAARKIV;* med Arkivforum. 1991. q. SEK 175 (effective 1996). Svensk Arkivtidskrift, P.O. Box 390, S-101 27 Stockholm, Sweden. TEL 46-8-24-17-60. Ed. Owe Norberg. bk.rev. circ. 10,000.
    Formed by the merger of (1983-1991): Arkivforum (ISSN 0281-2371); (1951-1991): Arkivinformation (ISSN 0571-0731)

658   IT   ISSN 0040-3040
TEMPO ECONOMICO; rivista mensile d'informazione manageriale. 1963. m. (10/yr.) L.58000 (foreign L.85000). Editoriale Syncro, Via L.B. Alberti 10, 20149 Milan, Italy. TEL 39-2-33103707. FAX 39-2-3310468. Dir. Giordano Pini. adv.: B&W page L.8320000, color page L.12480000; adv. contact: Lilia Pini. bk.rev.; bibl.; charts; illus.; mkt.; pat.; stat.; index. circ. 33,000. **Document type**: trade publication.
    Description: Covers management theory and practice.

TEORIE VEDY/THEORY OF SCIENCE. see *SCIENCES: COMPREHENSIVE WORKS*

658   UK
THAMESMAN PUBLICATIONS. OCCASIONAL PAPERS. 1978. irreg. Oxford Brookes University, School of Business, Wheatley, Oxford OX33 1HX, England. FAX 0865-485830. Ed. B. Axford. bk.rev. **Document type**: monographic series.

658   US
THOUGHT STARTERS FOR MANAGEMENT. 1971. m. $100. Ascot Publishing Enterprises, Inc., 22 Ascot Ridge, Great Neck, NY 11021. TEL 516-466-7999. Ed. Lawrence Bernard. bk.rev. circ. 10,000. (processed)

658   NE   ISSN 0928-8627
HD28
TIJDSCHRIFT VOOR BEDRIJFSADMINISTRATIE. 1894. 10/yr. fl.82. Delwel Uitgeverij B.V., Postbus 19110, 2500 CC The Hague, Netherlands. TEL 31-70-3624800. FAX 31-70-3605606. Ed.Bd. adv.; bk.rev.; charts; illus. circ. 9,000. **Indexed**: Excerp.Med. (until 19??), Key to Econ.Sci.
—SWETS.
    Former titles (until 1993): Maandblad voor Bedrijfsadministratie en Bedrijfsorganisatie; Maandblad voor Bedrijfsadministratie en Organisatie (ISSN 0024-8630)
    Description: Publishes studies on all aspects of business administration, industrial organization, management economics, and relevant issues in law, computerization, accounting and statistics.

658   NE   ISSN 0169-5304
TIJDSCHRIFT VOOR INKOOP & LOGISTIEK. Cover title--I & L. 1985. 10/yr. fl.199 (effective 1996). (Nederlandse Vereniging voor Inkoopmanagement) Kluwer Bedrijfswetenschappen B.V. (Subsidiary of: Wolters Kluwer N.V.), Postbus 23, 7400 GA Deventer, Netherlands. TEL 31-570-648905. FAX 31-570-611504. (Subscr. to: Intermedia bv, Postbus 4, 2400 MA Alphen aan den Rijn, Netherlands. TEL 31-172-466321. FAX 31-172-435527) (Co-sponsor: Vereniging voor Logistiek Management) Ed. Erik Wiegerinck; Pub. Philip van Borselen. adv.: B&W page fl.2625, color page fl.4775; trim 297 x 210; adv. contact: Ad Nuesink. circ. 7,900. **Document type**: trade publication.
—SWETS.
    Description: Covers news and issues of importance to purchasing managers and logistics managers, with particular emphasis on the integral business approach.

TINBERGEN INSTITUTE PHD RESEARCH BULLETIN. see *BUSINESS AND ECONOMICS — Economic Systems And Theories, Economic History*

TINBERGEN INSTITUTE RESEARCH SERIES. see *BUSINESS AND ECONOMICS — Economic Systems And Theories, Economic History*

658   US   ISSN 1089-5949
CODEN: TPAEEQ
TOM PETERS FAST FORWARD. 1986. m. $150 (foreign $200). T P G Communications, 555 Hamilton Ave., Palo Alto, CA 94301. TEL 415-326-4496; 800-827-3095. FAX 415-326-7065. E-mail: oaex@aol.com. (Subscr. to: Box 652, Mt. Morris, IL 61054-0652) Ed. Liz Mitchell; Pub. Tom Peters. bk.rev. **Document type**: newsletter.
—CASDDS. **CCC**.
    Formerly: Tom Peters on Achieving Excellence (ISSN 0887-5332)
    Description: Presents management case studies and commentary on organizational change and innovation.

658   US
▼**TOMORROW'S BUSINESS.*** 1996. m. 493 Santa Barbara Dr., Los Altos, CA 94022-3810. TEL 703-759-7947. FAX 703-759-7655. E-mail: sarahengel@aol.com. Ed. Sarah Engel. **Document type**: newsletter.
    Description: Examines future business trends for middle- to upper-middle management.

658.5   GW   ISSN 0942-5497
TOP BUSINESS; Management international. 1966. m. DM.96. Verlag Moderne Industrie, Justus-von-Liebig-Str. 1, 86899 Landsberg, Germany. TEL 49-8191-125-0. FAX 49-89-8191-125312. TELEX 5215777. Ed. Peter Carl. adv.; bk.rev.; charts; illus.; stat.; circ. controlled. (tabloid format) **Indexed**: Key to Econ.Sci., Packag.Sci.Tech. **Document type**: trade publication.
    Formerly (until 1991): Industriemagazin (ISSN 0019-929X)

658   US
TOP EXECUTIVE COMPENSATION. (Subseries of: Conference Board. Report) 1960. a. $120 to non-members; members $30. Conference Board, Inc., 845 Third Ave., New York, NY 10022. TEL 212-759-0900. FAX 212-980-7014. illus.; stat. (also avail. in microfiche from CIS) **Indexed**: SRI. **Document type**: monographic series.
    Description: Analyzes compensation of the five highest-paid executives in approximately 900 companies representing seven major types of business.

658 920   BE
TOP MANAGEMENT BELGIUM - LUXEMBURG. (Text in Dutch, English, French) 1984. a. 8900 BEF. Alain Renier & Co. S.P.R.L., Ave. des Casernes 41A, 1040 Brussels, Belgium. TEL 32-2-6462740. FAX 32-2-6462017. URL: http://www.guideline.be/arenier. Ed. Alain Renier. R&P contact: Alain Renier. adv. contact: Thierry Roberti-Lintermans. circ. 5,000. **Document type**: directory.
●Also available on CD-ROM.
    Formerly: Top Management Belgium (ISSN 0779-5920)

658   US
TOP MANAGEMENT COMPENSATION - REGRESSION ANALYSIS REPORT. (Supplement to: Regional Report on Top Management Compensation) a. $690. (Executive Compensation Service (ECS)) Wyatt Data Services, 218 Rte. 17, N., Roselle Park, NJ 07662-9832. TEL 201-843-1177. FAX 201-843-0101. charts. **Document type**: trade publication.
    Description: Calculates salary and total compensation levels for companies in different industries.

658   US
TOP MANAGEMENT HI-COMP REPORT. a. $490. (Executive Compensation Service (ECS)) Wyatt Data Services, 218 Rte. 17, N., Roselle Park, NJ 07662-9832. TEL 201-843-1177. FAX 201-843-0101. (also avail. in diskette format) **Document type**: trade publication.
    Description: Presents data on the highest paid one-third of the sample.

658   US
TOP MANAGEMENT REMUNERATION REPORT - EUROPE. a. $940. (Executive Compensation Service (ECS)) Wyatt Data Services, 218 Rte. 17, N., Rochelle Park, NJ 07662-9832. TEL 201-843-1177. FAX 201-843-0101. charts. **Document type**: trade publication.
    Description: Provides a comprehensive guide to total compensation practices for executives in 17 Western European countries and Turkey.

658   US
TOP MANAGEMENT REPORT. (In 2 vols.) a. $690. (Executive Compensation Service (ECS)) Wyatt Data Services, 218 Rte. 17, N., Roselle Park, NJ 07662-9832. TEL 201-843-1177. FAX 201-843-0101. **Document type**: trade publication.
    Description: Features analyses of executive pay reported by company size for over 50 industry categories.

658   AU
TOP SERVICE. bi-m. Nikolsdorfergasse 7-11, A-1051 Vienna, Austria. TEL 01-555585. FAX 01-555585215. TELEX 0111669. Ed. Michael Stenzel. circ. 105,200.

658   UK   ISSN 0954-4127
CODEN: TQMAED
TOTAL QUALITY MANAGEMENT. Online edition (UK ISSN 1360-0613) 1990. bi-m. £116($198) to individuals; institutions £280 ($528) (effective 1997). Carfax Publishing Co., P.O. Box 25, Abingdon, Oxon. OX14 3UE, England. TEL 44-1235-401000. FAX 44-1235-401550. E-mail: enquiries@carfax.co.uk. (Subscr. in N. America to: Carfax Publishing Co., 875-81 Massachusetts Ave., Cambridge, MA 02139) Ed. Gopal K. Kanji. adv.; bk.rev.; index. (back issues avail.) **Indexed**: ASCA, Cont.Pg.Manage., Curr.Cont. (1991-), Stat.Theor.Meth.Abstr. (1991-). **Document type**: academic/scholarly publication.
●Also available online.
—BLDSC (8870.274000); CISTI; Genuine Article; SWETS; UMI. **CCC**.
    Refereed Serial

TOURISM MANAGEMENT. see *TRAVEL AND TOURISM*

TOURIST ATTRACTIONS AND PARKS. see *LEISURE AND RECREATION*

658   US   ISSN 0095-5892
HF5549.5.T7   CODEN: TRNGB6
TRAINING; the magazine covering the human side of business. 1964. m. $78 (Canada $88; elsewhere $99). Lakewood Publications, Inc., 50 S. Ninth St., Minneapolis, MN 55402. TEL 612-333-0471. FAX 612-333-6526. Ed. Jack Gordon. adv.; bk.rev.; charts; illus.; stat.; tr.lit. circ. 50,000. (also avail. in microform from UMI; back issues avail.; reprint service avail. from UMI) **Indexed**: ABI Inform., B.P.I., Bibl.Agri., BPIA, Bus.Ind., C.I.J.E., Manage.Cont., Pers.Lit., Q.Abstr., Sage Fam.Stud.Abstr., Work Rel.Abstr. **Document type**: trade publication.
●Also available online. Vendor(s): Human Resources Information Network, Information Access Co., UMI.
—BLDSC (8883.480000); CASDDS; KR SourceOne; SWETS; UMI; UnCover. **CCC**.
    Formerly: Training in Business and Industry (ISSN 0041-0896)
    Description: Covers all aspects of training, management and organizational development, motivation and performance improvement

658   GW   ISSN 0939-2688
TRAINING AKTUELL; Spezial-Informationsdienst fuer die gesamte Weiterbildungsbranche. 1990. m. DM.181.90 (includes ManagerSeminare). ManagerSeminare Gerhard May Verlags GmbH, Endenicherstr. 282, 53121 Bonn, Germany. TEL 49-228-97791-0. FAX 49-228-616164. Ed. Elke Abels. adv. contact: Juergen Koch. bk.rev.; software rev.; charts; illus.; tr.lit.; circ. 1,300. (back issues avail.) **Document type**: newsletter.

TRAINING & DEVELOPMENT ORGANISATIONS DIRECTORY. see *EDUCATION*

658   US   ISSN 0278-5749
HD30.42.U5
TRAINING AND DEVELOPMENT ORGANIZATIONS DIRECTORY; a reference work describing firms, institutes, and other agencies offering training programs for business, industry and government. 1978. irreg., 5th ed., 1991. $310. Gale Research, 835 Penobscot Bldg., 645 Griswold St., Detroit, MI 48226-4094. TEL 313-961-2242; 800-877-4253. FAX 800-414-5043. E-mail: daniel_snyder@gale.com. Eds. Paul Wasserman, Janice McLean.
●Also available online. Vendor(s): Human Resources Information Network (TDOD).
—CISTI.
    Description: Describes U.S. organizations providing vocational and brush-up training.

BUSINESS AND ECONOMICS — MANAGEMENT

658 UK ISSN 0951-3507
TRAINING AND MANAGEMENT DEVELOPMENT METHODS. 5/yr. £1729($2679) (foreign Aus.$3359) (effective 1998). M C B University Press Ltd., 60-62 Toller Ln., Bradford, W. Yorks BD8 9BY, England. TEL 44-1274-777700. FAX 44-1274-785200. TELEX 51317-MCBUNI-G. URL: http://www.mcb.co.uk. Ed. Margaret Reid. Indexed: Mgmt.& Market.Abstr., Tr.& Dev.Alert. Document type: academic/scholarly publication. —BLDSC (8883.501180); SWETS; UMI. CCC.
  Description: Concentrates on presenting usable, up-to-date learning methods. Includes practical examples of exercises and case studies.

TRAINING DIRECTORS' FORUM NEWSLETTER. see EDUCATION

TRANSPORT LOGISTICS. see TRANSPORTATION

TRANSPORTATION EXECUTIVE UPDATE. see TRANSPORTATION — Trucks And Trucking

658.5 FR ISSN 0041-185X
HD28
TRAVAIL ET METHODES; revue des techniques nouvelles au service de l'entreprise. 1947. m. 650 F. Editions Entreprises et Techniques, 5 bis, rue Fontaine au Roi, Paris 75011, France. TEL 48-05-25-70. Ed. G. Fuchs. adv.; bk.rev.; charts; illus.; cum.index. circ. 10,000. Indexed: C.I.S. Abstr., Excerp.Med., Key to Econ.Sci. Document type: academic/scholarly publication, bibliography, proceedings.

TREASURY & RISK MANAGEMENT. see BUSINESS AND ECONOMICS — Investments

658 336 AT
TRENDS, TIPS AND TAX. 1992. 4/yr. Aus.$1300. Cullen Egan Dell, Level 8, 50 Bridge St., Sydney, N.S.W. 2000, Australia. TEL 61-2-93756800. FAX 61-2-92336800. Ed. Michelle Seddon. circ. 140. (looseleaf format)
  Description: Comprehensive practical guide to current employment reward issues in Australia, including taxation review.

658 PH ISSN 0042-0158
U E BUSINESS REVIEW; a magazine for business leaders. 1958. 3/yr. University of the East, College of Business Administration, Sampaloc, Manila, Philippines. abstr.; charts; stat.; index.

658 US ISSN 0740-2678
HD2425
U S ASSOCIATION EXECUTIVE. 1982. w. $95. Custom News, Inc., 4341 Montgomery Ave., Bethesda, MD 20814-4401. TEL 301-951-1881. FAX 301-656-2845. Ed. Diane Kirsh. adv. circ. 18,500. Document type: newspaper.
  Description: Publishes news about the association management profession and association suppliers.

658 SW ISSN 0280-8072
UNDERHAALL OCH DRIFTSAEKERHET. 1982. 11/yr. SEK 690 (foreign SEK 769) (effective 1998). Mentor Communications ab, Box 27817, S-115 93 Stockholm, Sweden. TEL 46-8-670-41-28. FAX 46-8--661-64-55.

U.S. DEPARTMENT OF AGRICULTURE. RURAL BUSINESS - COOPERATIVE DEVELOPMENT SERVICE. SERVICE REPORT. see AGRICULTURE

UNIVERSAL DIRECTORY - CONFERENCES - EXHIBITIONS - FUNCTIONS. see MEETINGS AND CONGRESSES

658 EC
UNIVERSIDAD CENTRAL DEL ECUADOR. INSTITUTO DE ESTUDIOS ADMINISTRATIVOS. BOLETIN. bi-m. Universidad Central del Ecuador, Instituto de Estudios Administrativos, Avda. America 1396, Casilla 3474, Quito, Ecuador. Document type: bulletin.

658 650 UY
UNIVERSIDAD DE LA REPUBLICA. INSTITUTO DE ADMINISTRACION. BOLETIN. 1976. irreg. no.4, 1979. Universidad de la Republica, Instituto de Administracion, 18 de Julio 1953 4p, Montevideo, Uruguay. Document type: bulletin.

658 UY ISSN 0077-1287
UNIVERSIDAD DE LA REPUBLICA. INSTITUTO DE ADMINISTRACION. CUADERNO. 1956. irreg. no.80, 1979. price varies. Universidad de la Republica, Instituto de Administracion, 18 de Julio 1953 4p, Montevideo, Uruguay.

UNIVERSIDAD DE MEDELLIN. FACULTAD DE CIENCIAS ADMINISTRATIVAS. REVISTA. see PUBLIC ADMINISTRATION

UNIVERSIDAD DE SEVILLA. INSTITUTO GARCIA OVIEDO. PUBLICACIONES. see LAW

658 SZ
UNIVERSITAET ZUERICH. INSTITUT FUER BETRIEBSWIRTSCHAFTLICHE FORSCHUNG. SCHRIFTENREIHE. 1970. irreg., no.84, 1997. price varies. Paul Haupt AG, Falkenplatz 14, CH-3001 Bern, Switzerland. TEL 41-31-3012345. FAX 41-31-3014669. Document type: monographic series.

UNIVERSITY MANAGER. see EDUCATION — Higher Education

658 UK
UNIVERSITY OF BRADFORD. MANAGEMENT CENTRE. WORKING PAPER SERIES. irreg. University of Bradford, Management Centre, Emm Ln., Bradford, W. Yorks BD9 4JL, England. TEL 44-1274-384387. FAX 44-1274-546866. Ed. N. Wilson. Document type: academic/scholarly publication, monographic series.

UNIVERSITY OF NEW ENGLAND. DEPARTMENT OF ACCOUNTING & FINANCIAL MANAGEMENT. WORKING PAPERS. see BUSINESS AND ECONOMICS — Accounting

658 PL ISSN 0867-6569
HD36
UNIWERSYTET GDANSKI. WYDZIAL EKONOMIKI PRODUKCJI. ZESZYTY NAUKOWE. ORGANIZACJA I ZARZADZANIE. (Text in Polish; summaries in English and Russian) 1974. irreg., latest no.11. price varies. Uniwersytet Gdanski, Wydzial Ekonomiki Produkcji, c/o Biblioteka Glowna, Ul. Armii Krajowej 110, 81-824 Sopot, Poland. TEL 51-0061. TELEX 051 2247 BMOR PL. Ed. Alfred Czerminski. Document type: academic/scholarly publication.
  Formerly (until 1987): Uniwersytet Gdanski. Wydzial Ekonomiki Produkcji. Zeszyty Naukowe. Organizacja Pracy i Zarzadzanie (ISSN 0208-4791)
  Description: Covers basic elements and functions of managing organizations, work study, ergonomics, and the practice of managerial psychology.

658 GW ISSN 0173-3664
UNTERNEHMER MAGAZIN. 1953. m. DM.42. (Arbeitsgemeinschaft Selbst. Unternehmer) Unternehmerwirtschaft Verlags-GmbH, Postfach 201328, 53143 Bonn, Germany. TEL 0228-9545980. FAX 0228-9545990. TELEX 885498. (Co-sponsor: Bundesverband Junger Unternehmer) Ed. Erwin Bidder. adv.; bk.rev.; index. circ. 11,500. Document type: consumer publication.
  Formerly: Junge Wirtschaft (ISSN 0022-6416)
  Description: Covers news and practical information for those owning a business. Features automation, finance, economics, and international trade.

658 SZ ISSN 0042-059X
DIE UNTERNEHMUNG; Schweizerische Zeitschrift fuer Betriebswirtschaft Organisation und modernes Foerderwesen. 1947. 6/yr. 110 SFr. Paul Haupt AG, Falkenplatz 14, CH-3001 Bern, Switzerland. TEL 41-31-3012345. FAX 41-31-3014669. Eds. Jan Krulis-Rauda, Bruno Staffelbach. adv.; bk.rev.; charts; illus.; index. circ. 2,000. Indexed: IBR, Int.Abstr.Oper.Res., Key to Econ.Sci., P.A.I.S.For.Lang.Ind., SCIMP (1978-), SSCI. Document type: trade publication.
—SWETS. CCC.

658 658.8 IT
UOMO MANAGER. 10/yr. Renoma Editrice S.p.A., Via Pierre e Marie Curie 3, 20019 Seguro de Settimo (MI), Italy. TEL 2-31-23-03. FAX 2-33-500-521. Ed. Giampiero Muggiani. circ. 35,000.

658 TZ ISSN 0856-1435
UONGOZI: JOURNAL OF MANAGEMENT DEVELOPMENT. (Text in English) 1976. 3/yr. Sh.2000 (rest of Africa $23; elsewhere $30). Institute of Development Management, P.O. Box 5, Mzumbe-Morogoro, Tanzania. TEL 255-56-4380-4. Ed. P.C. Ndunguru. adv.: page $30; adv. contact: S.K. Fimnbo. bk.rev. circ. 3,000. (also avail. in diskette format) Document type: academic/scholarly publication.
  Formerly: Tanzania Management Journal.

658.2 620 CN
USINE. (Text in French) 1993. 4/yr. Maclean Hunter Ltd., Maclean Hunter Bldg., 777 Bay St., Toronto, ON M5W 1A7, Canada. TEL 416-586-5777. FAX 416-596-5552. Ed. Pierre Deschamps. adv.: B&W page Can.$3455, color page Can.$4250; trim 11 x 16. circ. 15,132. (tabloid format) Document type: trade publication.

USING ENVIRONMENTAL MANAGEMENT SYSTEMS TO IMPROVE PROFITS. see ENVIRONMENTAL STUDIES

658 II ISSN 0083-5102
VAIKUNTH MEHTA NATIONAL INSTITUTE OF COOPERATIVE MANAGEMENT. PUBLICATIONS. irreg. (effective Apr. 1990). Vaikunth Mehta National Institute of Cooperative Management, University Road, Poona 411 007, India.

658 US ISSN 0275-4371
VALUE ENGINEERING AND MANAGEMENT DIGEST - DEFENSE CONTRACT GUIDE. 1960. m. $180. Tufty Communications Co., 2107 National Press Bldg., Washington, DC 20045. TEL 202-347-8998. E-mail: htufty@capaccess.org; URL: http://www.valuedigest.com. Ed. Harold G. Tufty. bk.rev. circ. 5,000. Document type: newsletter.
  Former titles: Cost Reduction Digest; Value Engineering Digest - Defense Contract Guide (ISSN 0010-9622)
  Description: Provides the only English-language commercial publication devoted primarily to value-engineering and analysis. Covers management news and related disciplines.

658 SZ
VERBANDS MANAGEMENT. (Text in English, French, German) 1976. q. 90 SFr. Forschungsinstitut fuer Verbands- und Genossenschafts-Management, Universitaet Freiburg, Postfach 284, CH-1701 Freiburg, Switzerland. TEL 41-26-3008400. FAX 41-26-3009755. Ed. Guido Kaufmann. R&P contact: Michel Mueller. adv. contact: Michel Mueller. circ. 900. Document type: bulletin.

DER VEREIN. see CLUBS

658 GW ISSN 0178-5893
VERKAUFSLEITER SERVICE; Beratungsbrief zur Aussendienstfuehrung. (Text in Dutch, English, Finnish, French, German, Italian, Spanish and Swedish) 1972. bi-w. DM.537.60. Verlag Norbert Mueller AG und Co. KG, Ingolstaedterstr. 20, 80807 Munich, Germany. TEL 49-89-3509302. FAX 49-89-35093218. Ed. Andrea Krukow. bk.rev.; tr.lit.; index. circ. 2,900. (back issues avail.) Document type: newsletter.

330 658 FR ISSN 0083-6095
VIE DES AFFAIRES;* bulletin consacre a l'analyse des avis emis par les dirigeants d'entreprise a l'egard du droit economique et des politiques gouvernementales. 1970. irreg. price varies. Agence Legislative, 22 rue de Chateaudun, Paris 11e, France.

658 NE ISSN 1382-7936
▼**VIEW.** (Supplement to: Management Team (ISSN 0166-1256)) 1995. q. Benelux Periodieken B.V., Postbus 397, 3900 AJ Veenendaal, Netherlands. TEL 31-8385-21422. FAX 31-8385-23136. adv. Document type: trade publication.

658 II ISSN 0256-0909
HD28
VIKALPA; journal for decision makers. (Text in English) 1976. q. Rs.110($25) to institutions; individuals Rs.60($20). Indian Institute of Management Ahmedabad, Publications Department, Vastrapur, Ahmedabad 380 015, India. Ed. K.R.S. Murthy. adv.; bk.rev. circ. 1,600. Indexed: Psychol.Abstr. (1976-), Pub.Admin.Abstr. Document type: academic/scholarly publication.
—BLDSC (9236.373000); UnCover.

BUSINESS AND ECONOMICS — MANAGEMENT

658 **II**
HD28
VISION; a journal of business perspective. (Text in English) 1987. s-a. Rs.400($25) (effective 1997). Management Development Institute, P.O. Box 60, Mehrauli Road, Gurgaon 122 001, Haryana, India. TEL 91-124-340173. FAX 91-124-341189. E-mail: mandev.mdi@axcess.net.in. Ed. Devi Singh. bk.rev. circ. 500. **Indexed:** Pub.Admin.Abstr. **Document type:** academic/scholarly publication.
 Formerly: (until Jan. 1997): M D I Management Journal (ISSN 0970-6623)
 Description: Provides a forum for research and practical results of interest and relevance to business managers. Includes behavioral science, development banking, quantitative techniques, modern trends and developments in management.
 Refereed Serial

658 330.1 **JA**
WAKAYAMA ECONOMIC REVIEW. (Text in Japanese) 1950. 6/yr. 300 Yen. Wakayama Daigaku, Keizai Gakkai - Wakayama University, Economic Society, 930 Sakaedani, Wakayama-shi, Japan. bk.rev. circ. 1,800. **Indexed:** Hum.Ind., Jap.Per.Ind., Soc.Sci.Ind.
 Formerly: Keizai Riron - Economic Theory (ISSN 0451-6222)

658 **US** **ISSN 1079-0101**
WAREHOUSE MANAGEMENT & CONTROL SYSTEMS. base vol. (plus m. updates). $270. Alexander Research & Communications, Inc., 215 Park Ave. S., Ste. 1301, New York, NY 10003. TEL 212-228-0246. FAX 212-228-0376. Ed. Jim Tompkins. R&P contact: Mary Dalessandro. **Document type:** newsletter.
 Description: This regularly updated service shows managers how to use warehouse management systems to get control of their warehouses.

658 339 **US** **ISSN 1048-4981**
HD38.25.U6
WASHINGTON C E O. (Chief Executive Officer) (Former name of issuing body: Washington CEO, Inc.) 1989. m. $29.95 (effective Jul. 1995). Fivash Publishing Group, 2505 Second Ave., Ste. 602, Seattle, WA 98121. TEL 206-441-8415. FAX 206-441-8325. E-mail: fivash@fine.com; URL: http://fivash.com. Ed. Jack Mayne; Pub. Scott Fivash. R&P contact: Helene Adler. adv.: B&W page $3280, color page $4270; trim 8 3/8 x 10 7/8; adv. contact: June Ford. circ. 24,000. **Document type:** consumer publication.
 ●Also available online.
 Description: For top corporate executives. Provides state-wide business news on the personalities, events, trends and ideas which shape the character, dynamics and direction of the state's economy.

WASHINGTON STATE BAR ASSOCIATION. CREDITOR - DEBTOR LAW SECTION NEWSLETTER. see *BUSINESS AND ECONOMICS — Banking And Finance*

658 **GW**
WER LEITET - DIE FUEHRUNGSKRAEFTE DER OESTERREICHISCHEN WIRTSCHAFT. 1986. a. DM.255 (effective 1997). Verlag Hoppenstedt GmbH, Havelstr. 9, 64295 Darmstadt, Germany. TEL 49-6151-380-0. FAX 49-6151-380-360. circ. 32,000. **Document type:** directory.

658.562 **US** **ISSN 0083-8217**
WEST COAST RELIABILITY SYMPOSIUM. 5th, 1964. irreg., latest 1991. American Society for Quality Control, Los Angeles Section, 611 E. Wisconsin Ave., Box 3005, Milwaukee, WI 53201-3005. TEL 213-331-6204.

658 **US** **ISSN 1062-5771**
WESTERN ASSOCIATION NEWS. 1976. m. free to qualified personnel. Schneider Publishing Company, Box 5657, Santa Monica, CA 90409-5657. TEL 213-458-3777. FAX 213-458-3770. Ed. Timothy Schneider. R&P contact: Timothy Schneider. adv.: B&W page $2300, color page $3285; 7 x 10; adv. contact: Sandi Kaczmarek. bk.rev.; circ. controlled. (back issues avail.) **Document type:** trade publication.
 Description: Contains information of interest to association executives and meeting planners.

WESTERN TECHNOLOGY & MANAGEMENT. see *TECHNOLOGY: COMPREHENSIVE WORKS*

658 **US**
WHAT IT COSTS TO RUN AN AGENCY. 1955. a. $39.75. Rough Notes Co., Inc., Box 1990, Carmel, IN 46032-4990. TEL 317-582-1600; 800-428-4384. FAX 317-816-1003. E-mail: rnc@in.net; URL: http://www.roughnotes.com.

WHICH M B A?; a critical guide to the world's best programmes. see *EDUCATION — Guides To Schools And Colleges*

658 338 **UK** **ISSN 0140-6582**
HG4132.Z5 **CODEN: WOWCEK**
WHO OWNS WHOM. CONTINENTAL EUROPE. (In 2 vols.) (Text in English, French and German) 1961. a. £275. Dun & Bradstreet Ltd., Holmers Farm Way, High Wycombe, Bucks. HP12 4UL, England. TEL 44-1494-422000. FAX 44-1494-422260. index. **Document type:** directory.
 ●Also available online.
 —BLDSC (9311.922000).
 Formerly: (until 1977): Who Owns Whom. Continental Edition (ISSN 0083-9302)

658.31 920 **US** **ISSN 0092-4598**
HF5549.5.T7
WHO'S WHO IN TRAINING AND DEVELOPMENT. 1970. a. $40 to members; public libraries $50. American Society for Training and Development, 1640 King St., Box 1443, Alexandria, VA 22313. TEL 703-683-8129. FAX 703-683-8103. adv.; illus. circ. 28,000. **Document type:** directory.
 —CCC.
 Formerly: American Society for Training and Development. Membership Directory (ISSN 0569-776X)

658 **JA** **ISSN 0286-7877**
WILL. (Text in Japanese) 1962. m. 8450 Yen. Chuokoron-Sha, Inc., 2-8-7 Kyobashi, Chuo-ku, Tokyo 104, Japan. TEL 03-3563-1866. FAX 03-3561-5920. adv.; bk.rev.
 Former titles (until 1982): Chuokoron Keieimondai - Chuokoron Management Affairs (ISSN 0385-7379); (until 1972): Bessatsu Chuokoron. Keieimondai (ISSN 0409-2465)

658 **US**
WOMEN DIRECTORS OF THE TOP 1000 CORPORATIONS. 1986. a. $50 to individuals; institutions $100. National Women's Economic Alliance Foundation, 808 17th St., N.W., Ste. 600, Washington, DC 20006-3910. TEL 202-393-5257. Ed. Elise Garfinkel. index. (back issues avail.) **Document type:** directory.

658 301.412 **UK** **ISSN 0955-8357**
HD6054.3
WOMEN IN MANAGEMENT REVIEW & ABSTRACTS. 1985. 8/yr. £1699($2799) (effective 1997). M C B University Press Ltd., 60-62 Toller Ln., Bradford, W. Yorks BD8 9BY, England. TEL 44-1274-777700. FAX 44-1274-785200. TELEX 51317-MCBUNI-G. URL: http://www.mcb.co.uk. Ed. M. Davidson. bk.rev. (reprint service avail. from SWZ) **Indexed:** ABI Inform., Cont.Pg.Manage., Mult.Ed.Abstr., Stud.Wom.Abstr., Tech.Educ.Abstr., Tr.& Dev.Alert. **Document type:** academic/scholarly publication.
 ●Also available on CD-ROM.
 —UMI. **CCC.**
 Formerly (until 1989): Women in Management Review (ISSN 0267-4602)
 Description: Covers a diverse range of topics about women in management.

658.54 **UK** **ISSN 0043-8022**
T60.T5
WORK STUDY. 1952. 7/yr. £899($1399) (foreign Aus.$1759) (effective 1998). M C B University Press Ltd., 60-62 Toller Ln., Bradford, W. Yorks BD8 9BY, England. TEL 44-1274-777700. FAX 44-1274-785200. TELEX 51317-MCBUNI-G. URL: http://www.mcb.co.uk. Ed. John Heap. adv.; bk.rev.; charts; illus.; index. (reprint service avail. from SWZ) **Indexed:** Account.& Data Proc.Abstr., Anbar, ASEAN Manage.Abstr., C.I.S. Abstr., Intl.Mgmt.Info., Mgmt.& Market.Abstr., Oper.Res.Manage.Sci., Work Rel.Abstr. **Document type:** academic/scholarly publication.
 ●Also available on CD-ROM.
 —BLDSC (9348.290000); Genuine Article; SWETS; UMI; UnCover. **CCC.**
 Formerly: Time and Motion Study.

WORKERS' COMPENSATION OUTLOOK. see *INSURANCE*

WORKFLOW MAGAZINE. see *COMPUTERS — Automation*

658 **US** **ISSN 0749-6532**
WORKING SMART;* human relations - management advisory letter. 1972. m. $59. National Institute of Business Management, Box 9186, McLean, VA 22102-9668. TEL 703-905-8000. (Subscr. to: Box 25338, Alexandria, VA 22313) Ed. Donna Brodsky. circ. 52,500. **Document type:** newsletter.

WORKPLACE. see *INTERIOR DESIGN AND DECORATION*

658.5 **UK** **ISSN 0374-4795**
TS155.A1
WORKS MANAGEMENT. 1947. m. £67 (foreign £100; airmail £130). Findlay Publications Ltd., Hadlow House, 9 High St., Green St. Green, Orpington, Kent BR6 6BG, England. TEL 44-1689-862562. FAX 44-1689-857735. Ed. Adam Lawrence; Pub. Chris Wyles. adv. contact: Julian Taylor. bk.rev. circ. 25,000. **Indexed:** Account.& Data Proc.Abstr., Anbar, ASEAN Manage.Abstr., Br.Tech.Ind., C.I.S. Abstr., Mgmt.& Market.Abstr. **Document type:** trade publication.
 —BLDSC (9352.200000). **CCC.**
 Formerly: Istitution of Works Managers. Journal.

658 **CC** **ISSN 0115-4842**
HD28
WORLD EXECUTIVE'S DIGEST. (Text in English) 1980. m. $35. Asian Sources Media Group, 22-F Vita Tower, 29 Wong Chuk Hang Rd., Aberdeen, Hong Kong, People's Republic of China. TEL 852-2555-4777. FAX 852-2873-0488. E-mail: asmgroup@singnet.com.sg. (Subscr. to: Raffles City, P.O. Box 0199, Singapore 9117. TEL 65-8401-800. FAX 65-8401-402) Ed. Barrie Goodridge. adv.; bk.rev.; charts; illus.; index. circ. 72,000. **Document type:** trade publication.

658 **CC** **ISSN 1022-7784**
WORLD EXECUTIVE'S DIGEST - CHINA EDITION. (Text in Chinese) m. $35. Asian Sources Media Group, G.P.O. Box 12367, Hong Kong, People's Republic of China. TEL 852-2555-4777. FAX 852-2834-5201. E-mail: asmgroup@singnet.com.sg. Ed. Jeff Zhou; Pub. Barrie C. Goodridge. adv.: B&W page $4210, color page $5610; trim 206 x 273. circ. 46,350. **Document type:** trade publication.

WORLD MEETINGS: SOCIAL & BEHAVIORAL SCIENCES, HUMAN SERVICES AND MANAGEMENT. see *MEETINGS AND CONGRESSES*

658 **CC** **ISSN 1002-5499**
XIANDAI QIYE DAOKAN/MODERN ENTERPRISE HERALD. (Text in Chinese) m. Guowuyuan, Fazhan Yanjiu Zhongxin - State Council, Development Research Center, 6 Beisanhuan Zhonglu, Beijing 100010, People's Republic of China. TEL 2016699. Ed. Chen Dongsheng.

YELLOW SHEET (BALLWIN); the practical newsletter on agency management. see *ADVERTISING AND PUBLIC RELATIONS*

658 **FI** **ISSN 0358-4208**
YRITYSTALOUS. 1942. m. FIM 1250 (effective 1997). Oy Rastor AB, Wavulinintie 3, FIN-00210 Helsinki, Finland. TEL 353-9-615181. FAX 353-9-692-266. E-mail: rastor@co.inet.fi. Ed. Anneli Puukari. adv.: B&W page FIM 10500; trim 210 x 280. bk.rev.; charts; illus.; index. circ. 2,500. **Document type:** trade publication.
 —BLDSC (9421.605000).
 Former titles (until 1981): Tehokas Yritys (ISSN 0356-5327); Yritystalous (ISSN 0044-1309); Which was formed by the merger of: Liiketalous; Tehostaja.

YUGOSLAV JOURNAL OF OPERATIONS RESEARCH; an international journal dealing with theoretical and computational aspects of operations research, systems science, and management science. see *COMPUTERS*

BUSINESS AND ECONOMICS — MARKETING AND PURCHASING

658   GW   ISSN 0044-2372
HD28
Z F B. (Zeitschrift fuer Betriebswirtschaft) 1931. m. DM.285 (foreign DM.305) (effective 1997). Betriebswirtschaftlicher Verlag Dr. Th. Gabler GmbH, Abraham-Lincoln-Str. 46, 65189 Wiesbaden, Germany. TEL 49-611-7878419. FAX 49-611-7878423. Ed. Erich Gutenberg. adv.; bk.rev.; illus. (reprint service avail. from SCH) **Indexed:** Excerp.Med., IBR, Key to Econ.Sci., P.A.I.S.For.Lang.Ind., SCIMP, SSCI. **Document type:** trade publication.
—BLDSC (9453.890000); SWETS. **CCC**.

658   GW   ISSN 0341-2687
HF17
Z F B F. (Zeitschrift fuer Betriebswirtschaftliche Forschung) 1949. m. DM.198. (Schmalenbach-Gesellschaft) Verlagsgruppe Handelsblatt GmbH, Kasernenstr. 67, 40213 Duesseldorf, Germany. TEL 49-211-8870. FAX 49-211-374955. (Subscr. to: Postfach 102717, 40018 Duesseldorf, Germany) Ed. H. Hax. adv.; bk.rev.; charts; stat.; index, cum.index. circ. 3,900. (reprint service avail. from SCH) **Indexed:** ELLIS, Excerp.Med., IBR, Key to Econ.Sci., SCIMP (1980-). **Document type:** academic/scholarly publication.
—SWETS. **CCC**.
   Formerly: Schmalenbachs Zeitschrift fuer Betriebswirtschaftliche Forschung (ISSN 0036-6196)

658   PL   ISSN 1230-3747
ZARZADZANIE NA SWIECIE. 1985. m. Polska Agencja Prasowa (P.A.P.), Redakcja Zagraniczna, P.O. Box 898, 00-950 Warsaw, Poland. Ed. Marek Fijalkowski.

658   GW   ISSN 0722-7485
HF5001   CODEN: ZFORET
ZEITSCHRIFT FUEHRUNG UND ORGANISATION. Short title: Z F O. (Text in German; summaries in English) 1926. bi-m. DM.132. (Gesellschaft fuer Organisation) F B O - Fachverlag fuer Buero- und Organisationstechnik GmbH, Hermannstr. 2, 76530 Baden-Baden, Germany. TEL 07221-271066. FAX 07221-33228. circ. 5,500. **Indexed:** IBR, SCIMP (1978-). **Document type:** bulletin.
—BLDSC (9462.205000); SWETS; UMI.

658   GW   ISSN 0945-5892
ZEITSCHRIFT FUER VORSCHLAGSWESEN. 1975. q. DM.64. (Deutsches Institut fuer Betriebswirtschaft) Erich Schmidt Verlag GmbH & Co. (Bielefeld), Viktoriastr. 44A, 33602 Bielefeld, Germany. TEL 49-521-583080. (Subscr. to: Postfach 102451, 33524 Bielefeld, Germany) Ed.Bd. **Document type:** trade publication.
—SWETS. **CCC**.
   Formerly: (until 1994): Betriebliches Vorschlagswesen (ISSN 0340-9279)

658   CC
HC427.92.A1
ZHONGGUO JINGJI NIANJIAN/ALMANAC OF CHINA'S ECONOMY. (Text in Chinese) 1981. a. Y70. (Chinese Academy of Social Sciences, Institute of Industrial Economics) Jingji Guanli Chubanshe, 8, Hongyuan Hutong, 6 Tiao, Xinjiekou, Beijing 100035, People's Republic of China. TEL 2253956. FAX 8312679. (Dist. outside China by: Guoji Shudian - China International Book Trading Corp., P.O. Box 399, Beijing, P.R.C.. TEL 8413063; Dist. in US by: China Books & Periodicals, Inc., 2929 24th St., San Francisco, CA 94110. TEL 415-282-2994) Ed. Wang Haibo. adv. contact: Li Li. circ. 15,000. **Document type:** academic/scholarly publication.
   Description: Covers Chinese economic policies, development in economic construction, and economic statistics.

658   CC   ISSN 1001-5876
ZHONGGUO SHEBEI GUANLI/CHINESE EQUIPMENT MANAGEMENT. (Text in Chinese) bi-m. Zhongguo Shebei Guanli Zazhishe, Xizhimenwai, Beijing 100081, People's Republic of China. TEL 892531. Ed. Ding Deli.

BUSINESS AND ECONOMICS — Marketing And Purchasing

see also Advertising and Public Relations

A A D A NEWS. (Associated Antique Dealers of America) see *ANTIQUES*

658.8   720 620   US   ISSN 0732-7943
A - E MARKETING JOURNAL; marketing tactics for project success. Variant title: A E M J. m. $249 in N. America; elsewhere $295 (effective Dec. 1996). P S M J Resources, Inc., 10 Midland Ave., Newton, MA 02158. TEL 617-965-0055. FAX 617-965-5152. E-mail: psmj@tiac.com. Ed. Winslow Pettingill; Pub. Frank Stasiowski. R&P contact: Christa Marukaitis. index. (back issues avail.) **Document type:** newsletter.
   Description: Marketing for architects and engineers.

658   US
A F & P A STATISTICAL ROUNDUP. 1984. m. $157 to non-members; members $57. American Forest and Paper Association, 1111 19th St., N.W., Washington, DC 20036. TEL 202-463-2700. FAX 202-463-2785. Ed. Alberto Goetzl. circ. 100. (back issues avail.) **Indexed:** SRI.
   Former titles: N F P A Statistical Roundup; National Forest Products Association. Economics Monthly.
   Description: Covers topics of interest to forest products companies, focusing on industry statistics.

658   US   ISSN 1059-7425
A I M.* (Age of Information Marketing) (Editions in English, French, German, Italian, Portuguese and Spanish) 1979. q. Nielsen Marketing Research, 150 N. Martingale Rd., Schaumburg, IL 60173-2408. circ. 30,000. (back issues avail.)
   Formerly (until 1989): Marketing Trends (ISSN 0882-4754)

658   US
A I M NEWSLETTER. (Former name of sponsoring body: National Premium Sales Executives, Inc.) 1956. m. membership. Association of Incentive Marketing, 1620 Rte. 22, Ste. 300, Union, NJ 07083. TEL 908-687-3090. Ed. Marie Beyer. R&P contact: Marie Beyer. circ. 400. **Document type:** newsletter, trade publication.
   Former titles: A I M Newsletter and Incentive Report; (until Oct. 1990): N P S E Newsletter - Incentive Report.

A L A WORLDWIDE DIRECTORY AND FACT BOOK. (American Logistics Association) see *MILITARY*

658.8   US   ISSN 1054-0806
HF5411
A M A ANNUAL MARKETING EDUCATORS' CONFERENCE. PROCEEDINGS. (Winter Edition) 1944. a. $50 to non-members; members $40. American Marketing Association, 250 S. Wacker Dr., Ste. 200, Chicago, IL 60606. TEL 312-648-0536. FAX 312-993-7542. URL: http://www.ama.org. Ed. Francesca Van Gorp. R&P contact: Una Moon. adv. contact: Kathy Harp. index. **Indexed:** BPIA, Bus.Ind. **Document type:** proceedings.
   Supersedes: American Marketing Association. Proceedings (ISSN 0065-9231); Incorporates: A M A Combined Proceedings Series; A M A Papers of the Conferences; A M A Abstracts of Papers of the Conferences (ISSN 0065-9215)

658.8   US   ISSN 0888-1839
HF5410
A M A EDUCATORS' PROCEEDINGS. (Summer Edition) a. $50 to non-members; members $40. American Marketing Association, 250 S. Wacker Dr., Ste. 200, Chicago, IL 60606. TEL 312-648-0536. FAX 312-993-7542. URL: http://www.ama.org. Ed. Francesca Van Gorp. R&P contact: Una Moon. adv. contact: Kathy Harp. **Document type:** proceedings.

658.8
A M R NEWSLETTER.* m. Association Marketing Roundtable, 3770 Parkview Way, Naples, FL 33940-2737. TEL 202-244-7256. **Document type:** newsletter.
   Description: Includes case studies and industry developments.

A S A E ASSOCIATE MEMBER UPDATE. (American Society of Association Executives) see *BUSINESS AND ECONOMICS — Management*

A S A EXPO GUIDE AND MEMBERSHIP DIRECTORY (YEARS). (American Sportfishing Association) see *FISH AND FISHERIES*

658   011   GW   ISSN 0934-9790
A U M A HANDBOOK INTERNATIONAL. s-a. free. Ausstellungs- und Messe-Ausschuss der Deutschen Wirtschaft e.V. - Confederation of German Trade Fair and Exhibition Industries, Lindenstr. 8, 50674 Cologne, Germany. TEL 49-221-20907-0. FAX 49-221-2090712. TELEX 8881507. Ed. Kornelia Gelhausen. circ. 8,000. **Document type:** directory.
   Formerly: A U M A Kalender Ausland (ISSN 0721-2720)
   Description: Trade fairs and exhibitions outside of Germany which are of importance to the German economy.

658   011   GW   ISSN 0939-7078
A U M A HANDBOOK REGIONAL. 1973. a. free. Ausstellungs- und Messe-Ausschuss der Deutschen Wirtschaft e.V. - Confederation of German Trade Fair and Exhibition Industries, Lindenstr. 8, 50674 Cologne, Germany. TEL 49-221-20907-0. FAX 49-221-2090712. TELEX 8881507. Eds. Manuela Goerzen, Harald Koetter. circ. 8,000. (back issues avail.) **Document type:** directory.
   Formed by the merger of: A U M A Zahlenspiegel Regional (ISSN 0724-0457); A U M A Kalender Regional (ISSN 0721-2747)
   Description: Lists dates, groups of offers, visitor, exhibitor and space figures, including information on visitor structures of the regional exhibitions in Germany.

658   GW
HF5474.G3
A U M A HANDBOOK TRADE FAIR CENTER GERMANY. (Text in English, German) s-a. free. Ausstellungs- und Messe-Ausschuss der Deutschen Wirtschaft e.V. - Confederation of German Trade Fair and Exhibition Industries, Lindenstr. 8, 50674 Cologne, Germany. TEL 49-221-20907-0. FAX 49-221-2090712. TELEX 8881507. Eds. Mathias Wuestefeld, Harald Koetter. circ. 12,000. **Document type:** directory.
   Formerly: A U M A Handbook Germany - Trade Fair Country (ISSN 0933-6206); Which was formed by the merger of: A U M A Kalender Messeplatz Deutschland (ISSN 0930-8768); A U M A Zahlenspiegel Messeplatz Deutschland (ISSN 0724-0554); Deutsche Messen und Ausstellungen - Ein Zahlenspiegel (ISSN 0084-9766)
   Description: Lists dates, groups of offers, visitor, exhibitor and space figures, including information on visitor structures of the international trade fairs in Germany.

A U M A INFOBLAETTER; Daten und Fakten ueber Messen und Ausstellungen im In- und Ausland. (Ausstellungs- und Messe-Ausschuss der Deutschen Wirtschaft e.V.) see *ADVERTISING AND PUBLIC RELATIONS*

A U M A - MITTEILUNGEN. (Ausstellungs- und Messe-Ausschuss der Deutschen Wirtschaft e.V.) see *ADVERTISING AND PUBLIC RELATIONS*

ABERDEEN'S CONSTRUCTION MARKETING TODAY. see *BUILDING AND CONSTRUCTION*

658.84   US
ABOUT MARKETING TO WOMEN; lifestyle studies about women in America. 1987. m. $289 (foreign $335) (effective 1996). About Women, Inc., 33 Broad St., Boston, MA 02109. TEL 617-723-4337. FAX 617-723-7107. Ed. E. Janice Leeming. bk.rev. **Document type:** newsletter.
   ●Also available online. Vendor(s): Information Access Co.
   Former titles: Marketing to Women (ISSN 1047-1677); (until 1989): Women Scope: Surveys of Women (ISSN 1040-5240); Marketing to Women (ISSN 0894-5861)
   Description: Covers psychographics, demographics and the purchasing behavior of women.

BUSINESS AND ECONOMICS — MARKETING AND PURCHASING

658.8   GW   ISSN 0001-3374
ABSATZWIRTSCHAFT; Zeitschrift fuer Marketing. 1958. m. DM.192. Verlagsgruppe Handelsblatt GmbH, Kasernenstr. 67, 40213 Duesseldorf, Germany. TEL 49-211-8870. FAX 49-211-329954. (Subscr. to: Postfach 102717, 40018 Duesseldorf, Germany) Ed. F. Paelike. adv.; bk.rev.; abstr.; charts; illus.; stat.; index. circ. 21,163. (reprint service avail. from SCH,UMI) **Indexed:** Account.& Data Proc.Abstr., Excerp.Med., Key to Econ.Sci., Mgmt.& Market.Abstr., P.A.I.S.For.Lang.Ind., SCIMP (1991-). **Document type:** trade publication.
●Also available online.
—BLDSC (0551.450000); SWETS. **CCC.**

ABSTRACT OF MANAGEMENT SERVICES ANALYSIS. see *BUSINESS AND ECONOMICS — Management*

658.8   US   ISSN 0092-0703
HF5415
ACADEMY OF MARKETING SCIENCE. JOURNAL. 1973. q. $170 to institutions (effective Sep. 1996). Sage Publications, Inc., 2455 Teller Rd., Thousand Oaks, CA 91320. TEL 805-499-0721. FAX 805-499-0871. E-mail: libraries@sagepub.com; URL: http://www.sagepub.com/journals/usdetails/j0140.html. (Overseas subscr. to: Sage Publications Ltd., 6 Bonhill St., London EC2A 4PU, England; Sage Publications India Pvt. Ltd., P.O. Box 4125, New Delhi 110 048, India; Membership inquiries to: Academy of Marketing Science, University of Miami, Box 248012, Coral Gables, FL 33124. TEL 305-284-6673) Ed. David W. Cravens. adv. contact: Margaret Travers. bk.rev.; bibl.; charts. circ. 3,000. (also avail. in microform; back issues avail.; reprint service avail. from SCH,UMI) **Indexed:** ABI Inform., Account.Ind. (1974-), BPIA, Bus.Ind., J.Cont.Quant.Meth., Manage.Cont., Mgmt.& Market.Abstr., P.A.I.S., PSI, Psychol.Abstr. (1990-). **Document type:** academic/scholarly publication.
●Also available online. Vendor(s): Knight-Ridder Information, Inc.
—BLDSC (4674.967000); SWETS; UMI; UnCover. **CCC.**
Description: Furthers the science of marketing as an economic, ethical, and social force worldwide by conducting research and disseminating the results.
Refereed Serial

ACCOUNT LIST FILE. see *ADVERTISING AND PUBLIC RELATIONS*

658.7   FR   ISSN 0001-4893
ACHETEURS; documentation technique sur les problemes d'approvisionnement dans l'industrie. 1951. m. 240 F. Edipresse, 16 rue Guillaume Tell, 75017 Paris, France. TEL 1-47 66 00 05. FAX 47-66-46-94. Ed. Guy Baudesson. adv.; bibl.; illus.; tr.lit.; circ. 2,143 (paid); 4,478 (controlled).

AD MEDIA. see *ADVERTISING AND PUBLIC RELATIONS*

658.8   NE   ISSN 0926-7689
ADFODIRECT MAGAZINE. 22/yr. Samsom Bedrijfsinformatie B.V. (Subsidiary of: Wolters Kluwer N.V.), Postbus 4, 2400 MA Alphen aan den Rijn, Netherlands. TEL 31-172-466775. FAX 31-172-440681. adv. circ. 10,000. **Indexed:** Bus.Ind. **Document type:** trade publication.
Former titles (until 1991): D M Magazine (Direct Marketing) (ISSN 0923-8670); (until 1989): Direct Effect (ISSN 0169-0183)

659   NE   ISSN 0926-7670
ADFOMEDIANIEUWS. 1991. s-m. Samsom Bedrijfsinformatie B.V. (Subsidiary of: Wolters Kluwer N.V.), Postbus 4, 2400 MA Alphen aan den Rijn, Netherlands. TEL 31-172-466775. FAX 31-172-440681. adv. **Document type:** newsletter.

ADLINE; the marketing magazine for the regions. see *ADVERTISING AND PUBLIC RELATIONS*

ADVANCE; editorial features directory. see *ADVERTISING AND PUBLIC RELATIONS*

ADVANCE NEWS FOR SUPERMARKETERS. see *FOOD AND FOOD INDUSTRIES — Grocery Trade*

658.8   US   ISSN 1069-0964
HF5410
ADVANCES IN BUSINESS MARKETING AND PURCHASING. 1986. a. $73.25. J A I Press Inc., 55 Old Post Rd., No. 2, Box 1678, Greenwich, CT 06830-1678. TEL 203-661-7602. FAX 203-661-0792. E-mail: jai@jaipress.com. (Europe addr.: J A I Press Ltd., 38 Tavistock St., Covent Garden, London WC2E 7PB, England. TEL 44-171-379-8834. FAX 44-171-379-8835) Ed. Paul Bloom. **Document type:** monographic series.
—CCC.
Formerly (until 1992): Advances in Business Marketing (ISSN 0894-5969)

658   US   ISSN 0098-9258
HF5415.3
ADVANCES IN CONSUMER RESEARCH. 1974. a. $59. Association for Consumer Research, Brigham Young University, Graduate School of Management, 632 TNRB, Provo, UT 84602. TEL 801-378-2080. FAX 801-226-7650. E-mail: hkhunt@acd1.byu.edu. Ed. H. Keith Hunt. circ. 1,500 (paid). **Indexed:** BPIA, Chic.Per.Ind., Manage.Cont., SSCI. **Document type:** proceedings.
—BLDSC (0704.136000).
Description: Proceedings of the annual conference of the Association for Consumer Research. Contains papers on all aspects of consumer behavior, including the mental and emotional processes and physical actions that people engage in when selecting, purchasing, using, and discarding products and services so as to satisfy needs and desires.
Refereed Serial

658.8   US   ISSN 1071-9679
HF5415.129
ADVANCES IN DISTRIBUTION CHANNEL RESEARCH. 1992. biennial. $73.25. J A I Press Inc., 55 Old Post Road, No. 2, Greenwich, CT 06830. Ed. Gary L. Frazier.
—BLDSC (0704.248000).

658 350   US   ISSN 1048-1540
HF5410
ADVANCES IN MARKETING AND PUBLIC POLICY. 1987. irreg., latest 1991. $73.25. J A I Press Inc., 36 Sherwood Pl., Greenwich, CT 06836-1678. TEL 203-661-7602.

658   US   ISSN 0892-9556
HF5410
ADVANCES IN NONPROFIT MARKETING. 1985. a. $73.25 to institutions. J A I Press Inc., 55 Old Post Rd., No. 2, Box 1678, Greenwich, CT 06836-1678. TEL 203-661-7602. FAX 203-661-0792. (Addr. in the U.K. and rest of Europe: J A I Press Ltd., The Courtyard, 28 High St., Hampton Hill, Mddx. TW12 1PD, England. TEL 44-81-943-9296. FAX 44-81-843-9317)
—BLDSC (0709.484000); UnCover.

ADVERTISING AGE; the international newspaper of marketing. see *ADVERTISING AND PUBLIC RELATIONS*

ADVERTISING, P R, MARKETING CURRENTS. see *ADVERTISING AND PUBLIC RELATIONS*

ADVERTLINK; a newspaper on advertising and marketing. see *ADVERTISING AND PUBLIC RELATIONS*

658 330.9   US
ADVISOR (NEW YORK). q. Vos, Gruppo, & Capell, Inc., 60 E. 42nd St., Ste. 3810, New York, NY 10165. TEL 212-697-5753.
Description: Contains business news and feature articles relevant to the direct marketing industry. Covers recent acquisitions, strategies, and other topics.

AFTERSALES MANAGEMENT. see *BUSINESS AND ECONOMICS — Management*

658.8   US   ISSN 0749-2332
HF5419
AGENCY SALES; the marketing magazine for manufacturers' agencies and their principals. 1949. m. $49 (effective 1997). Manufacturers' Agents National Association, 23016 Mill Creek Rd., Box 3467, Laguna Hills, CA 92654-3467. TEL 714-859-4040. Ed. Bert Holtje. adv.; bk.rev.; charts; bibl.; tr.ind. circ. 18,000. **Indexed:** ABI Inform, BPIA, Tr.& Indus.Ind. **Document type:** trade publication.
●Also available online. Vendor(s): Information Access Co., UMI.
—BLDSC (0736.228990); UMI.
Incorporates: Manufacturers' Agents National Association. Rep Letter; **Former titles:** Agency Sales Magazine (ISSN 0162-3656); Agency Sales - With Agent and Representative (ISSN 0044-6718)
Description: Articles, news updates and announcements on marketing issues that affect manufacturers' agents and their principals.

AIR FRESHENERS AND INSECTICIDES: THE INTERNATIONAL MARKET. see *CLEANING AND DYEING*

658   US   ISSN 0191-9113
ALABAMA & GULF COAST RETAILING NEWS. 1970. m. free. Retailing Newspapers Inc., 3851 Wake Forest Rd., Decatur, GA 30034. adv. (tabloid format) **Document type:** newspaper.

658.7   US   ISSN 0002-4325
ALABAMA PURCHASOR. 1945. m. $24. Purchasing Management Association of Alabama, c/o Sid Donaldson, Ed., Box 11506, Birmingham, AL 35202. TEL 205-879-3515. circ. 9,310.

658   US
ALERT (ROCKY HILL). m. $35 to non-members (effective 1997). Marketing Research Association, Inc., 2189 Silas Deane Hwy., Ste. 5, Box 230, Rocky Hill, CT 06067. TEL 860-257-4008. FAX 860-257-3990. adv. contact: Maureen Peruta. circ. 2,500. (also avail. in microform from UMI) **Document type:** newsletter.

ALFORJA; revista mensual de la produccion y distribucion moderna. see *FOOD AND FOOD INDUSTRIES*

658   GW
ALLENSBACHER MARKT-ANALYSE - WERBETRAEGER-ANALYSE. (Text in English and German) 1959. a. DM.1200. Institut fuer Demoskopie, Allensbach, Radolfzellerstr. 8, 78476 Allensbach, Germany. TEL 49-7533-8050. FAX 49-7533-3048. R&P contact: Johannes Schneller. stat.; index. circ. 1,250. (also avail. in magnetic tape; back issues avail.) **Document type:** bulletin.
Formerly: Allensbacher Werbetraeger-Analyse.
Description: Market research and information on markets and media for advertising agencies and publishers.

658.8   UY
ALTA GERENCIA. 1982. m. $45 (foreign $90). C I E C C Universidad Abierta, Mario Cassinoni 1157, 11200 Montevideo, Uruguay. TEL 598-2-412174. FAX 598-2-487221. Ed. Edgardo Martinez Zimarioff. R&P contact: Edgardo Martinez Zimarioff. adv. contact: Laura Paz. circ. 9,000 (paid). (back issues avail.) **Document type:** academic/scholarly publication.
Former titles: Marketing Directo; Marketing S.

658 910.09   CN   ISSN 0843-462X
AM-CAN REPORT; marketing & trade journal. 1989. q. Can.$10($10) (effective 1991). (Am-Can International Club) Small Business World Magazine, 2433 Southvale Crescent, Ottawa, Ont. K1B 4T8, Canada. TEL 613-733-4260. Ed. Mohamed Talib. adv.; bk.rev. circ. 5,000. (tabloid format) **Document type:** trade publication.

658.8   US   ISSN 0065-8103
HF5421
AMERICAN DROP-SHIPPERS DIRECTORY. 1964. biennial. $15. World Wide Trade Service, Box 283, Medina, WA 98039. Ed. Randall Lucas. adv.; bk.rev.; circ. 8,500 (controlled). **Document type:** directory.
Description: Lists more than 500 wholesale sources of supply, of which 200 will make drop-shipments.

BUSINESS AND ECONOMICS — MARKETING AND PURCHASING

669 US ISSN 0002-9998
HD9506.U6 CODEN: AMMKA6
AMERICAN METAL MARKET. 1882. d. (Mon.-Fri.) $625 (Central & S. America and Europe $1050, elsewhere $1195) (effective 1996). Capital Cities - A B C, Inc., Diversified Publishing Group, 825 Seventh Ave., New York, NY 10019. TEL 212-887-8560. FAX 212-887-8493. (Subscr. to: Box 7701, Riverton, NJ 08077-7701) Ed. Michael G. Botta; Pub. John Lindsey. R&P contact: John Lindsey. adv. contact: Preston Gibson. bk.rev.; charts; illus.; mkt.; stat.; circ. 11,000 (paid). (tabloid format; also avail. in microfilm from FCM; microfiche; back issues avail.) **Indexed:** Alloys Ind., Bus.Ind., CAD CAM Abstr., Chem.Abstr., Eng.Mat.Abstr., Met.Abstr.Ind., Met.Abstr., Nonfer.Met.Alert, PCC Alert, Robomat., Steels Alert, Tr.& Indus.Ind., World Alum.Abstr. **Document type:** newspaper, trade publication.
● Also available online. Vendor(s): Information Access Co., Knight-Ridder Information, Inc.
—CASDDS; Linda Hall. **CCC.**
During 1972-1987 incorporated: Metalworking News (ISSN 0891-4036).
Description: Covers all aspects of metals business, including production, trade, activity on commodities markets, supply and demand; covers nonferrous, ferrous, precious metals, scrap and competing materials.

658.85 US ISSN 0003-0902
CODEN: AMSLB6
AMERICAN SALESMAN; the national magazine for sales professionals. 1955. m. $46.80 (foreign $57.20). National Research Bureau, 320 Valley St., Burlington, IA 52601-5513. TEL 319-752-5415. FAX 319-752-3421. Ed. Barbara Boeding; Pubs. Diane & Michael Darnall. R&P contact: Diane Darnell. bk.rev. circ. 1,500. (also avail. in microfilm) **Indexed:** ABI Inform., BPIA, Bus.Ind., Manage.Cont., Tr.& Indus.Ind. **Document type:** trade publication.
—BLDSC (0856.200000); UMI; UnCover. **CCC.**

658.8 384.6 US
AMERICAN TELEMARKETING ASSOCIATION. JOURNAL. Abbreviated title: J A T A. 10/yr. American Telemarketing Association, 4605 Lankersham Blvd., Ste. 824, N. Hollywood, CA 91602-1818. TEL 213-463-2330. FAX 213-462-3372. Ed. Roberta Black. adv. contact: Carole Morgan. circ. 1,200. **Document type:** newsletter.
Description: Provides legislative information, coverage of the association's activities, and educational information on topics relating to telemarketing as an industry.

ANALGESICS: THE INTERNATIONAL MARKET. see *PHARMACY AND PHARMACOLOGY*

380.1 II ISSN 0376-5512
HD4295.A5
ANDHRA PRADESH STATE TRADING CORPORATION LIMITED. ANNUAL REPORT. Key Title: Annual Report - Andhra Pradesh State Trading Corporation Limited. (Text in English) a. Andhra Pradesh State Trading Corporation Limited, 5-10-174 Fatchmaiden Rd., Hyderabad 500004, India.

338.43624 DK ISSN 0904-3616
ANLAEG BRUTTO. Variant title: V og S Priser, Anlaeg Brutto. 1972. a. DKK 1310 (effective 1997). V & S Byggedata A-S, Frederikssundsvej 194, DK-2700 Broenshoej, Denmark. TEL 45-38-60-77-11. FAX 45-38-60-77-44.
Former titles (until 1988): V og S Priser. Anlaeg (ISSN 0105-421X)

338.43624 DK ISSN 0904-3594
ANLAEG NETTO. Variant title: V & S Priser, Anlaeg Netto. 1990. a. DKK 1310 (effective 1997). V & S Byggedata A-S, Frederikssundsvej 194, DK-2700 Broenshoej, Denmark. TEL 45-38-60-77-11. FAX 45-38-60-77-44. Dir. Carl Friis Skovsen.

658.8 FR ISSN 0066-300X
ANUAIRE DU MARKETING. 1964. a. 580 F. Association Nationale du Marketing, Recherche, Strategie, Action, 221 Rue La Fayette, 75010 Paris, France. adv.; bk.rev. circ. 2,000.

658 US ISSN 1052-6838
HF5415.2
ANNUAL ADVANCED RESEARCH TECHNIQUES FORUM. 1991. a. $35 to non-members; members $25. American Marketing Association, 250 S. Wacker Dr., Ste. 200, Chicago, IL 60606. URL: http://www.ama.org. Ed. Francesca Van Gorp. R&P contact: Una Moon. adv. contact: Kathy Harp. **Document type:** proceedings.

658.8 US ISSN 0730-2606
HF5415
ANNUAL EDITIONS: MARKETING. 1973. a. $12.95. Dushkin Publishing Group, Sluice Dock, Guilford, CT 06437-9989. TEL 203-453-4351. FAX 203-453-6000. Ed. John E. Richardson; Pub. Ian Nielsen. illus. **Document type:** academic/scholarly publication.
Former titles: Readings in Marketing; Annual Editions: Readings in Marketing.
Refereed Serial

ANUNCIOS; semanario de la publicidad. see *ADVERTISING AND PUBLIC RELATIONS*

ANZEIGEN BEOBACHTER MOEBEL. see *INTERIOR DESIGN AND DECORATION — Furniture And House Furnishings*

APPAREL SALES - MARKETING COMPENSATION SURVEY. see *CLOTHING TRADE*

658 714 US ISSN 1041-388X
TH6485
AQUA: THE BUSINESS MAGAZINE FOR THE SPA AND POOL INDUSTRY. 1976. m. $48 (foreign $90) (effective 1996). A B Publications, 1846 Hoffman St., Madison, WI 53704. TEL 608-249-0186. FAX 608-249-1153. Ed. Alan Sanderfoot. circ. 14,000.
Incorporates (1972-1988): Flotation Sleep Industry (ISSN 0164-5749); **Former titles:** Spa and Sauna (ISSN 0886-9472); Spa and Sauna Trade Journal (ISSN 0164-4858)
Description: Contains market information, business management advice for retailers and builders.

658 BL
O ARAUTO DO VENDEDOR. 1953. q. free. Sindicato Empregados Vendedores e Viajantes do Comercio no Estado do Sao Paulo, Rua Santo Amaro No. 255 (Bela Vista), CEP 01315 Sao Paulo, Brazil. TEL 011-37-4531. FAX 011-36-2160. Ed. Lilly D. Portella. illus. circ. 10,000. (tabloid format)

ARGUS FUNDAMENTALS. see *PETROLEUM AND GAS*

ASIA: A DIRECTORY AND SOURCEBOOK. see *BUSINESS AND ECONOMICS — Trade And Industrial Directories*

658 UK
HF5415.12.A8
ASIA PACIFIC JOURNAL OF MARKETING LOGISTICS. 3/yr. £599($899) (effective 1998). (University of Queensland, Graduate School of Management, AT) M C B University Press Ltd., 60-62 Toller Ln., Bradford, W. Yorks BD8 9BY, England. TEL 44-1274-499821. FAX 44-1274-547143. TELEX 51317-MCBUNI-G. URL: http://www.mcb.co.uk. (N. American subscr. to: M C B University Press Limited, Box 1943, Birmingham, AL 35201) Ed. Oliver Yau. **Document type:** academic/scholarly publication.
—BLDSC (1742.260720); UMI.
Formerly (until 1993): Asia Pacific International Journal of Marketing (ISSN 0954-7517)
Description: Covers marketing issues relevant to Pacific rim countries.

ASIAN ADVERTISING AND MARKETING; the magazine for communication executives. see *ADVERTISING AND PUBLIC RELATIONS*

658 US
AUCTION BULLETIN. 1965. fortn. $460. John B. Tamke, Ed. & Pub., Box 5, Laconia, NH 03246. TEL 603-366-2553. FAX 603-366-5734. circ. 622. (looseleaf format; also avail. in video cassette) **Document type:** trade publication.

658 US
AUCTION PRICE GUIDE. s-a. $39.95. Cowles Publishing Co., 999 W. Riverside Ave., Box 2160, Spokane, WA 99201-1010. TEL 509-459-7000. FAX 509-459-5258.
Description: Lists actual prices paid at auction for merchandise.

658.84 US ISSN 0004-7465
THE AUCTIONEER. 1950. m. membership. National Auctioneers Association, 8880 Ballentine, Overland Park, KS 66214-1985. TEL 913-541-8084. FAX 913-894-5281. E-mail: naahq@aol.com. Ed. Ed Hiscock. R&P contact: Ed Hiscock. adv.; illus. circ. 5,900. **Document type:** trade publication.
Description: Provides members of NAA with information on association activities, industry issues and general auction news.

AUDIO: THE INTERNATIONAL MARKET. see *ELECTRONICS*

AUDIOVIDEO INTERNATIONAL. see *ELECTRONICS*

AUSTRALIA. BUREAU OF STATISTICS. NEW SOUTH WALES OFFICE. RETAILING IN NEW SOUTH WALES. see *BUSINESS AND ECONOMICS — Abstracting, Bibliographies, Statistics*

AUSTRALIA. BUREAU OF STATISTICS. RETAIL INDUSTRY, AUSTRALIA. see *BUSINESS AND ECONOMICS — Abstracting, Bibliographies, Statistics*

AUSTRALIA. BUREAU OF STATISTICS. RETAIL TRADE, AUSTRALIA: COMMODITY DETAILS. see *BUSINESS AND ECONOMICS — Abstracting, Bibliographies, Statistics*

AUSTRALIA. BUREAU OF STATISTICS. RETAILING IN AUSTRALIA. see *BUSINESS AND ECONOMICS — Abstracting, Bibliographies, Statistics*

AUSTRALIA. BUREAU OF STATISTICS. WHOLESALE INDUSTRY, AUSTRALIA. see *BUSINESS AND ECONOMICS — Abstracting, Bibliographies, Statistics*

AUSTRALIAN DENTAL PRACTICE MAGAZINE. see *MEDICAL SCIENCES — Dentistry*

651.2 AT ISSN 1037-6887
AUSTRALIAN NEWSAGENT AND STATIONER. 1921. m. Aus.$55. D.W. Thorpe, A member of the Reed Elsevier plc group, 18 Salmon St., Port Melbourne, Vic. 3207, Australia. TEL 61-3-9245-7370. FAX 61-3-9245-7395. E-mail: customer.service@thorpe.com.au; URL: http://www.reed-elsevier.com. Ed. John Leah. adv.; B&W page Aus.$680, color page Aus.$1820; 297 X 210. circ. 6,000. **Document type:** trade publication.
—CCC.
Former titles (until 1992): Australian Stationer and Newsagent (ISSN 1036-7969); (until 1991): Stationer and Newsagent (ISSN 1036-1200); Australian Stationer and Newsagent for Australia, New Zealand and the Pacific (ISSN 0004-9867); Ideas Newsagents and Stationers.
Description: Provides news, opinions, and information on new products of interest to these businesses, as well as sections on greeting cards, books.

658.8 AT ISSN 1038-9598
AUSTRALIAN PROFESSIONAL MARKETING. 1992. m. Aus.$55($105) (effective 1996). (Australian Marketing Institute) Reed Business Publishing Pty. Ltd. (Subsidiary of: Reed International PLC), P.O. Box 5487, W. Chatswood, N.S.W. 2057, Australia. TEL 61-2-699-2411. FAX 61-2-698-3920. circ. 12,390. **Document type:** trade publication.
—UnCover.
Description: Offers readers in-depth examination of marketing concepts, issues and strategies.

658 AT ISSN 0817-3192
HD2930.A1
AUSTRALIA'S TOP 500 COMPANIES. 1986. a. Aus.$265. Dun & Bradstreet Marketing Pty. Ltd., 19 Havilah St., Chatswood, N.S.W. 2065, Australia. TEL 61-2-9352700. FAX 61-2-9352777. URL: http://www.dbmarketing.com.au. adv. circ. 2,000.

AUTO DEALER. see *TRANSPORTATION — Automobiles*

AUTO PRICE ALMANAC. see *TRANSPORTATION — Automobiles*

BUSINESS AND ECONOMICS — MARKETING AND PURCHASING

658 388.3 US
AUTO RENTAL NEWS. 1988. bi-m. (plus Factbook in April). $25 (Canada $30; elsewhere $38). Bobit Publishing Company, 2512 Artesia Blvd., Redondo Beach, CA 90278-3210. TEL 310-376-8788. FAX 310-376-9043. E-mail: robert@bobit.com. Ed. Jon Le Sage. circ. 16,500 (controlled). **Document type:** trade publication.
 Description: For the car rental industry.

AUTO REVISTA. see *TRANSPORTATION — Automobiles*

658.8 UK
AUTO VENDING. 1991. m. £50 (Europe £65) (effective 1997). Rephoto Publishing Ltd., Rephoto House, 49a High St., Chislehurst, Kent BR7 5AF, England. TEL 44-181-295-0905. FAX 44-181-295-0659. Ed. Amanda Roberts; Pub. Phil Reynolds. adv. contact: Samantha Evans. circ. 7,000. **Document type:** trade publication.
 Formerly: Automatic Vending.

658.87 GW ISSN 0005-1039
AUTOMATEN-MARKT. 1949. m. DM.158. Sigert Verlag GmbH, Ekbertstr. 14, 38122 Braunschweig, Germany. TEL 0531-8092926. FAX 0531-8092937. Ed. Guenter Hennemann. adv.; bk.rev.; illus.; pat. circ. 5,500. **Document type:** trade publication.
 Description: Covers coin machines and the amusement business.

658.8 US ISSN 1061-1797
TJ1560
AUTOMATIC MERCHANDISER. 1958. m. $60 (Canada and Mexico $84; elsewhere $114) (effective 1997). Johnson Hill Press, Inc. (Subsidiary of: Cygnus Publishing), 1233 Janesville Ave., Ft. Atkinson, WI 53538. TEL 920-563-6388. FAX 920-563-1702. Ed. Elliot Maras; Pub. Gloria Cosby. adv. contact: Marsha Endres. bk.rev.; pat.; index. circ. 16,800. (also avail. in microform) **Document type:** trade publication.
 ●Also available online.
 —BLDSC (1829.205000). **CCC.**
 Formerly (until 1992): American Automatic Merchandiser (ISSN 0002-7545)
 Description: For vending machine operators, office coffee service operators and mobile caterers; features comprehensive reference of products, equipment, accessories and services.

AUTOMOTIVE WEEK. see *TRANSPORTATION — Automobiles*

AUTOMOTIVES: THE INTERNATIONAL MARKET. see *TRANSPORTATION — Automobiles*

B A G - HANDELSMAGAZIN. (Bundes Arbeitsgemeinschaft der Mittel- und Grossbetriebe des Einzelhandels e.V.) see *BUSINESS AND ECONOMICS — Domestic Commerce*

B & T; advertising, marketing & media weekly. (Broadcasting and Television) see *ADVERTISING AND PUBLIC RELATIONS*

B B I'S MONITOR OF TECHNOLOGY ASSESSMENT AND REIMBURSEMENT; cost, outcome and payment data critical to medical product markets. (Biomedical Business International) see *HOSPITALS — Computer Applications*

658.8 UK
B P M A NEWS. 1972. 6/yr. free. (British Promotional Merchandise Association) Headline Promotions, Osborn House, 21-25 Lower Stone St., Maidstone, Kent ME15 6YT, England. Ed. Leonard Baskett. adv.; bk.rev. circ. 15,400.
 Formerly: British Premium Merchandise Association News.

658 UK ISSN 0954-7746
B R A D DIRECT MARKETING. s.a. £200. (British Rate and Data) Maclean Hunter Ltd., Maclean Hunter House, Chalk Ln., Cockfosters Rd., Barnet, Herts EN4 0BU, England. TEL 081-242-3132. FAX 081-242-3134. TELEX 299072-MACHUN-G. **Document type:** trade publication.
 —BLDSC (2265.907000).

658 GW ISSN 0171-838X
B T E MARKETING-BERATER; Magazin fuer den Textileinzelhandel. 1967. m. DM.61.80. (Bundesverband des Deutschen Textileinzelhandels e.V.) Institut des Deutschen Textileinzelhandels GmbH, An Lyskirchen 14, 50676 Cologne, Germany. TEL 49-221-92150955. FAX 49-221-92150910. URL: http://www.bte.de. Ed. Kirsten Reinhardt. adv. contact: Sonja Vogel. bk.rev.; charts; illus.; tr.lit. circ. 15,500. **Document type:** trade publication.
 Incorporates: B T E - Werbedienst (ISSN 0005-3376)

B T H A BUYERS GUIDE. (British Toy & Hobby Association) see *GIFTWARE AND TOYS*

BABY CARE PRODUCTS: THE INTERNATIONAL MARKET. see *BEAUTY CULTURE*

BABY FOODS: THE INTERNATIONAL MARKET. see *FOOD AND FOOD INDUSTRIES*

BAKERY PRODUCTS: THE INTERNATIONAL MARKET. see *FOOD AND FOOD INDUSTRIES — Bakers And Confectioners*

BANK MARKETING. see *BUSINESS AND ECONOMICS — Banking And Finance*

658.8 PO
BAREME - IMPRENSA; base regular de meios. q. Esc.1660000 (effective Jan. 1994). Marktest, Rua de S. Jose 183-2, 1100 Lisbon, Portugal. (also avail. in magnetic tape)
 Formerly: Bareme - Base Regular de Meios.
 Description: Provides information on press audiences for analysis and advertising planning.

658.8 PO
BAREME - RADIO; base regular de meios. q. Esc.19200000 (effective 1994). Marktest, Rua de S. Jose 183-2, 1100 Lisbon, Portugal. (also avail. in magnetic tape)
 Formerly: Indice de Audience Semanal.
 Description: Radio audience studies used for analysis and advertising planning.

658 US ISSN 0882-6218
BARNARD'S RETAIL MARKETING REPORT. 1984. bi-m. $125. Barnard Enterprises, Inc., 1181 Raritan Rd., Ste. 200, Scotch Plains, NJ 07076-2820. TEL 908-561-2300. Ed. Kurt Barnard. bk.rev. (back issues avail.) **Document type:** newsletter.
 Description: Covers and forecasts retailing trends with emphasis on marketing.

BATH AND SHOWER PRODUCTS: THE INTERNATIONAL MARKET. see *BEAUTY CULTURE*

BEAUTY INC. see *BEAUTY CULTURE*

BEDROOM INDUSTRY; an information resource for the bedding industry. see *INTERIOR DESIGN AND DECORATION — Furniture And House Furnishings*

BEER HANDBOOK. see *BEVERAGES*

BEER: THE INTERNATIONAL MARKET. see *BEVERAGES*

658 GW
BERATUNGSBRIEF FUER PRODUKTMANAGER UND MARKETINGLEITER. 1984. fortn. DM.696. Verlag Norbert Mueller AG und Co. KG, Ingolstaedterstr. 20, 80807 Munich, Germany. TEL 49-89-3509302. FAX 49-89-35093218. Eds. Antje Fries, Michaela Hoess. index. circ. 800. (back issues avail.) **Document type:** newsletter.

658.7 GW ISSN 0341-4507
BESCHAFFUNG AKTUELL. (Supplement avail.: Der Beschaffungsmarkt) 1954. m. DM.182 (foreign DM.193.70) (effective 1997). (Bundesverband Materialwirtschaft und Einkauf e.V.) Konradin Verlag Robert Kohlhammer GmbH, Ernst-Mey-Str. 8, 70771 Leinfelden-Echterdingen, Germany. TEL 49-711-7594-0. FAX 49-711-7594-390. Ed. Heinz Kruse. adv. contact: B&W page DM.7560; trim 190 x 270; adv. contact: Klaus Paletta. bk.rev. circ. 19,984. (back issues avail.) **Document type:** trade publication.
 —SWETS. **CCC.**
 Formerly: Industrielle Einkauf (ISSN 0019-9265)
 Description: For materials management, industrial purchasing and logistics. Covers marketing, the economy, materials, quality control, and recycling. Includes reports and lists of events, positions available, and a list of suppliers and advertisers.

658 GW
BESCHAFFUNGS-MARKT. a. DM.182 (includes Beschaffung Aktuell) (effective 1997). Konradin Verlag Robert Kohlhammer GmbH, Ernst-Mey-Str. 8, 70771 Leinfelden-Echterdingen, Germany. TEL 49-711-7594-0. FAX 49-711-7594390. Ed. Heinz Kruse. adv.: B&W page DM.7560; trim 190 x 270; adv. contact: Klaus Paletta. circ. 20,000. **Document type:** trade publication.

658 SZ
BESCHAFFUNGSMANAGEMENT. (Text in French, German) 10/yr. 60 SFr. Schweizerischer Verband fuer Materialwirtschaft und Einkauf - Association Suisse pou l'Approvisionnement et l'Achat, Postfach, CH-8027 Zurich, Switzerland. TEL 41-1-2016606. FAX 41-1-2026175. Ed. J. Luzius Ruppert. adv. circ. 4,000. **Document type:** trade publication.
 Formerly: Einkaeufer Revue de l'Acheteur.

692.5 DK ISSN 0909-0452
BESKRIVELSESTEKSTER. Variant title: V & S Priser, Beskrivelsestekster. 1994. a. DKK 1310 (effective 1997). V & S Byggedata A-S, Frederikssundvej 194, DK-2700 Broenshoej, Denmark. TEL 45-38-60-77-11. FAX 45-38-60-77-44. Dir. Carl Friis Skovsen.

658.7 PH
BEST BALIK BUYS. (Special issue of: Balikbayan Program's Duty Free Catalogue) (Text in English) 1991. s-a. (Duty Free Philippines) Eastgate Publishing Corporation, Rms. 603-604, Emerald Bldg., Emerald Ave., Pasig, 1600 Metro Manila, Philippines. TEL 63-2-6312921. FAX 63-2-631-2992. Ed. Cecile G. Mauricio. adv. contact: Gina C. Sancaez. circ. 75,000. **Document type:** catalog.
 Description: Product and price listing catalogue informs readers of the many advantages of shopping at Duty Free Philippines outlets.

BESTSELLER. see *ADVERTISING AND PUBLIC RELATIONS*

BIBLIOGRAPHY ON LOGISTICS MANAGEMENT. see *BUSINESS AND ECONOMICS — Abstracting, Bibliographies, Statistics*

BICYCLE INDUSTRY INTERNATIONAL. see *SPORTS AND GAMES — Bicycles And Motorcycles*

BICYCLE RETAILER AND INDUSTRY NEWS. see *SPORTS AND GAMES — Bicycles And Motorcycles*

332.63 658 US
BIDNET LINK; communication between buyer and seller. 1985. q. $39.95 (foreign $69.95). International Data Base Corp., Box 5600, Albany, NY 12205. TEL 518-438-0092. FAX 518-438-0599. Ed. Stanley Newman. adv. contact: Karin Sheehan. circ. 5,000. **Document type:** newsletter.

658 US ISSN 1064-4180
BIOMEDICAL MARKET NEWSLETTER. 1991. m. $695 (foreign $790) (effective 1996 & 1997). David G. Anast, Ed.& Pub., 3237 Idaho Pl., Costa Mesa, CA 92626-2207. TEL 714-434-9500; 800-875-8181. FAX 714-434-9755. R&P contact: David G. Anast. adv. contact: Steve Baker. charts; illus.; stat.; tr.lit.; circ. paid (paid). **Document type:** newsletter, trade publication.
●Also available online. Vendor(s): CompuServe, Inc., Data-Star, Dow Jones News Retrieval, Information Access Co., Knight-Ridder Information, Inc., Lexis-Nexis.
  Description: Covers business, financial, regulations and marketing on medical equipment, devices, clinical tests, supplies and instruments.
  Refereed Serial

BOOK MARKETING UPDATE. see *PUBLISHING AND BOOK TRADE*

BOOK PUBLISHING RESOURCE GUIDE. see *PUBLISHING AND BOOK TRADE*

BOOKS: THE INTERNATIONAL MARKET. see *PUBLISHING AND BOOK TRADE*

658.8 US ISSN 0068-063X
HF5415.A2
BRADFORD'S DIRECTORY OF MARKETING RESEARCH AGENCIES AND MANAGEMENT CONSULTANTS IN THE UNITED STATES AND THE WORLD. 1944. biennial, 27th ed., 1997. $93. Bradford's Directory, Box 2300, Centerville, VA 20122-8945. TEL 703-830-1755. FAX 703-830-5303. E-mail: dford36975@aol.com. Ed. Douglas E. Ford. adv. circ. 5,000. pp./issue: 272. **Document type:** directory.
  Description: Contains over 1,800 listings, which include company name, address, phone and fax numbers, as well as short statement on expertise provided.

BRAIN/BUREIN. see *ADVERTISING AND PUBLIC RELATIONS*

BREAKFAST CEREALS: THE INTERNATIONAL MARKET. see *FOOD AND FOOD INDUSTRIES*

BRIDAL BUYER. see *MATRIMONY*

BRITAIN'S CATERING INDUSTRY. see *HOTELS AND RESTAURANTS*

BRITAIN'S D I Y INDUSTRY. see *COMPUTERS — Hardware*

BRITAIN'S DIRECT MARKETING INDUSTRY (YEAR). see *BUSINESS AND ECONOMICS — Trade And Industrial Directories*

BRITAIN'S DRINKS INDUSTRY. see *BEVERAGES*

658.8 UK
BRITISH COMMERCIAL AGENTS REVIEW. 1967. m. £48($80) British Agents Register (B.A.R.) Ltd., 24 Mount Parade, Harrogate, Yorks. HG1 1BP, England. FAX 01423-561204. Ed. M.A. Lewis. adv. circ. 6,000. **Document type:** trade publication.
  Formerly: British Agents Review (ISSN 0007-022X)
  Description: Promotion and enhancement of the services of manufacturers' agents in the United Kingdom.

BUILDING ECONOMIST. see *BUILDING AND CONSTRUCTION*

BUSINESS AIR TODAY. see *AERONAUTICS AND SPACE FLIGHT*

658.7 US ISSN 0021-0463
BUSINESS AND INDUSTRY; the management purchasing magazine. 1946. m. $24. Business Magazines, Inc., 1720 28th St., No.B, W. Des Moines, IA 50265-1436. FAX 515-225-2318. Ed. James V. Snyder; Pub. Robert J. Wagner. R&P contact: James V. Snyder. adv. contact: Robert J. Wagner. bk.rev.; charts; illus.; tr.lit. circ. 10,521. **Document type:** trade publication.
  Formerly: Iowa Business and Industry.

BUSINESS CREDIT. see *BUSINESS AND ECONOMICS — Banking And Finance*

BUSINESS DIRECTIONS; ideas & inspiration for better business. see *BUSINESS AND ECONOMICS — Small Business*

658 388.3 US
BUSINESS DRIVER. a. $5 (free to qualified personnel). Bobit Publishing Company, 2512 Artesia Blvd., Redondo Beach, CA 90278-3210. TEL 310-376-8788. FAX 310-376-9043. E-mail: robert@bobit.com. **Document type:** trade publication.
  Description: Car value issues and driver safety for business car drivers.

658 US
BUSINESS INFORMATION MARKETS (YEAR): THE STRATEGIC OUTLOOK. 1975. irreg., no.9, 1995. $2495 (Canada and Mexico $2505; elsewhere $2531); to subscribers of Electronic Information Report $1801 (Canada and Mexico $1815; elsewhere $1831) (effective 1996). Cowles - SIMBA Information (Subsidiary of: Cowles Business Media), 11 Riverbend Dr. S., Box 4949, Stamford, CT 06907-0949. TEL 203-358-9900; 800-307-2529. FAX 203-358-5811. E-mail: info@simbanet.com; URL: http://www.simbanet.com. **Document type:** trade publication.
  Description: Provides information on the $30 billion market, as well as profiles and forecasts for ten major industry segments: general business periodicals, trade magazines and newspapers, looseleafs, newsletters, print and online databases, business books, research services, report publishing, information on demand, face-to-face services, and audiovisual services.

658.8 US ISSN 0745-5933
HF5801 CODEN: BUMAED
BUSINESS MARKETING; news monthly concerning the how-to strategic and tactical marketing, sales and advertising of business-to-business products and services. 1916. m. $49. Crain Communications, Inc. (Chicago), 740 Rush St., Chicago, IL 60611-2590. TEL 312-649-5260. FAX 312-649-5228. E-mail: ckosek@crain.com; URL: http://www.crain.co.uk/crain/busmar.html. (Subscr. to: 965 E. Jefferson Ave., Detroit, MI 48207-3185. TEL 800-678-9595) Ed. Steve Yahn. adv.; bk.rev.; charts; illus.; tr.lit.; index; circ. 47,853 (controlled). (also avail. in microform from UMI,MIM; back issues avail.; reprint service avail. from UMI) **Indexed:** ABI Inform, Account.& Data Proc.Abstr., Account.Ind. (1974-), Anbar, ASEAN Manage.Abstr., B.P.I., BPIA, Bus.Ind., Comput.Indus.Up., INSPEC (1983-), Key to Econ.Sci., Manage.Cont., Mgmt.& Market.Abstr., Mid.East: Abstr.& Ind., P.A.I.S., Tr.& Indus.Ind. **Document type:** trade publication.
●Also available online. Vendor(s): Information Access Co.
  —BLDSC (2934.284000); AskIEEE; CASDDS; Genuine Article; KR SourceOne; SWETS; UMI. **CCC.**
  Formerly: Industrial Marketing (ISSN 0019-8498)

BUSINESS MONITOR: RETAIL SALES. see *BUSINESS AND ECONOMICS — Abstracting, Bibliographies, Statistics*

BUSINESS MONITOR: RETAILING. see *BUSINESS AND ECONOMICS — Abstracting, Bibliographies, Statistics*

BUSINESS MONITOR: WHOLESALING. see *BUSINESS AND ECONOMICS — Abstracting, Bibliographies, Statistics*

BUSINESS OF HERBS. see *GARDENING AND HORTICULTURE*

BUSINESS OPPORTUNITIES. see *BUSINESS AND ECONOMICS — International Commerce*

BUSINESS OPPORTUNITY WORLD. see *BUSINESS AND ECONOMICS — Small Business*

BUSINESS RATIO PLUS: ADVERTISING AGENCIES. see *ADVERTISING AND PUBLIC RELATIONS*

BUSINESS RATIO PLUS: THE AGRICULTURAL EQUIPMENT INDUSTRY. see *MACHINERY*

BUSINESS RATIO PLUS: BREWERS. see *BEVERAGES*

BUSINESS RATIO PLUS: CONFECTIONARY MANUFACTURERS. see *FOOD AND FOOD INDUSTRIES — Bakers And Confectioners*

BUSINESS RATIO PLUS: ELECTRONIC COMPONENT DISTRIBUTORS. see *ELECTRONICS*

BUSINESS RATIO PLUS: ENGINEERING DISTRIBUTORS. see *ENGINEERING*

BUSINESS RATIO PLUS: ESTATE AGENCIES. see *REAL ESTATE*

BUSINESS RATIO PLUS: FINANCE HOUSES. see *BUSINESS AND ECONOMICS — Banking And Finance*

BUSINESS RATIO PLUS: FREIGHT FORWARDERS. see *TRANSPORTATION*

BUSINESS RATIO PLUS: FROZEN FOOD DISTRIBUTORS. see *FOOD AND FOOD INDUSTRIES*

BUSINESS RATIO PLUS: FROZEN FOOD PRODUCERS. see *FOOD AND FOOD INDUSTRIES*

BUSINESS RATIO PLUS: INDUSTRIAL FASTENER DISTRIBUTORS. see *BUSINESS AND ECONOMICS — Production Of Goods And Services*

BUSINESS RATIO PLUS: INDUSTRIAL FASTNER MANUFACTURERS. see *BUSINESS AND ECONOMICS — Production Of Goods And Services*

658.8 UK ISSN 1354-3407
BUSINESS RATIO PLUS: MAIL ORDER & CATALOGUE HOUSES. 1981. a. I C C Business Publications (Subsidiary of: I C C Information Group), Field House, 72 Oldfield Rd., Hampton, Mddx. TW12 2HQ, England. TEL 44-181-783-0922. FAX 44-181-783-1940. charts; stat. **Document type:** directory.
  Formerly (until 1994): Business Ratio Report: Mail Order and Catalogue Houses (ISSN 0267-856X); Which superseded in part (1985-1993): Business Ratio Report. Direct Marketing (ISSN 0261-3859)

BUSINESS RATIO PLUS: MINING & QUARRYING. see *MINES AND MINING INDUSTRY*

BUSINESS RATIO PLUS: MINING EQUIPMENT MANUFACTURERS. see *MINES AND MINING INDUSTRY*

BUSINESS RATIO PLUS: NEWSPAPER PUBLISHERS. see *JOURNALISM*

BUSINESS RATIO REPORT: ADHESIVE MANUFACTURERS; an industry sector analysis. see *ENGINEERING — Chemical Engineering*

BUSINESS RATIO REPORT: AEROSPACE INDUSTRY; an industry sector analysis. see *AERONAUTICS AND SPACE FLIGHT*

BUSINESS RATIO REPORT: AIR CONDITIONING EQUIPMENT; an industry sector analysis. see *HEATING, PLUMBING AND REFRIGERATION*

BUSINESS RATIO REPORT: AIRFREIGHT AGENCIES; an industry sector analysis. see *TRANSPORTATION — Air Transport*

BUSINESS RATIO REPORT: ANTIQUES & FINE ART; an industry sector analysis. see *ANTIQUES*

BUSINESS RATIO REPORT: ARCHITECTURAL IRONMONGERS; an industry sector analysis. see *BUILDING AND CONSTRUCTION*

BUSINESS RATIO REPORT: BAKERIES; an industry sector analysis. see *FOOD AND FOOD INDUSTRIES — Bakers And Confectioners*

BUSINESS RATIO REPORT: BETTING AND GAMING; an industry sector analysis. see *SPORTS AND GAMES*

BUSINESS RATIO REPORT: THE BOAT BUILDING INDUSTRY; an industry sector analysis. see *TRANSPORTATION — Ships And Shipping*

BUSINESS RATIO REPORT: BOOKSELLERS; an industry sector analysis. see *PUBLISHING AND BOOK TRADE*

BUSINESS RATIO REPORT: BRICK & TILE MANUFACTURERS; an industry sector analysis. see *CERAMICS, GLASS AND POTTERY*

BUSINESS RATIO REPORT: BUILDERS MERCHANTS; an industry sector analysis. see *BUILDING AND CONSTRUCTION*

BUSINESS AND ECONOMICS — MARKETING AND PURCHASING

BUSINESS RATIO REPORT: BUILDING INSULATION CONTRACTORS; an industry sector analysis. see *BUILDING AND CONSTRUCTION*

BUSINESS RATIO REPORT: CAR DEALERS. INTERMEDIATE. see *TRANSPORTATION — Automobiles*

BUSINESS RATIO REPORT: CARPET MANUFACTURERS & DISTRIBUTORS; an industry sector analysis. see *INTERIOR DESIGN AND DECORATION — Furniture And House Furnishings*

658.8   UK   ISSN 0261-7560
BUSINESS RATIO REPORT: CASH & CARRY; an industry sector analysis. 1980. a. I C C Business Ratios Ltd., Freepost, Field House, Hampton, Mddx. TW12 1BR, England. TEL 081-783-0977. FAX 081-783-1940. charts; stat. **Document type:** trade publication.

BUSINESS RATIO REPORT: CERAMIC MANUFACTURERS; an industry sector analysis. see *CERAMICS, GLASS AND POTTERY*

BUSINESS RATIO REPORT: CHEMICAL DISTRIBUTORS; an industry sector analysis. see *CHEMISTRY*

BUSINESS RATIO REPORT: CLOTHING MANUFACTURERS. INTERMEDIATE; an industry sector analysis. see *CLOTHING TRADE*

BUSINESS RATIO REPORT: CLOTHING MANUFACTURERS. MAJOR; an industry sector analysis. see *CLOTHING TRADE*

BUSINESS RATIO REPORT: CLOTHING RETAILERS; an industry sector analysis. see *CLOTHING TRADE*

BUSINESS RATIO REPORT: CLOTHING WHOLESALERS; an industry sector analysis. see *CLOTHING TRADE*

BUSINESS RATIO REPORT: COMMERCIAL AND VIDEO EQUIPMENT; an industry sector analysis. see *COMMUNICATIONS — Video*

BUSINESS RATIO REPORT: COMMERCIAL HORTICULTURE AND GARDEN CENTRES; an industry sector analysis. see *GARDENING AND HORTICULTURE*

BUSINESS RATIO REPORT: COMMERCIAL VEHICLES; an industry sector analysis. see *TRANSPORTATION — Automobiles*

658.8   UK   ISSN 0261-7668
BUSINESS RATIO REPORT: COMPANY PERFORMANCE IRELAND; an industry sector analysis. 1979. a. I C C Business Ratios Ltd., Freepost, Field House, Hampton, Mddx. TW12 1BR, England. TEL 081-783-0977. FAX 081-783-1940. charts; stat. **Document type:** trade publication.

BUSINESS RATIO REPORT: COMPOUND ANIMAL FEEDSTUFFS; an industry sector analysis. see *AGRICULTURE — Feed, Flour And Grain*

BUSINESS RATIO REPORT: COMPUTER EQUIPMENT DISTRIBUTORS; an industry sector analysis. see *COMPUTERS — Computer Industry*

BUSINESS RATIO REPORT: COMPUTER SERVICES; an industry sector analysis. see *COMPUTERS — Computer Industry*

BUSINESS RATIO REPORT: COMPUTER SOFTWARE HOUSES; an industry sector analysis. see *COMPUTERS — Software*

658.8   UK   ISSN 0269-1035
BUSINESS RATIO REPORT: CONFECTIONERS, TOBACCONISTS AND NEWSAGENTS; an industry sector analysis. 1986. a. I C C Business Ratios Ltd., Freepost, Field House, Hampton, Mddx. TW12 1BR, England. TEL 081-783-0977. FAX 081-783-1940. charts; stat. **Document type:** trade publication.

BUSINESS RATIO REPORT: CONSTRUCTION EQUIPMENT; an industry sector analysis. see *BUILDING AND CONSTRUCTION*

BUSINESS RATIO REPORT: CONTRACT FURNITURE MANUFACTURERS; an industry sector analysis. see *INTERIOR DESIGN AND DECORATION — Furniture And House Furnishings*

BUSINESS RATIO REPORT: COTTON & MAN-MADE FIBRE PROCESSORS; an industry sector analysis. see *TEXTILE INDUSTRIES AND FABRICS*

BUSINESS RATIO REPORT: DAIRY PRODUCE; an industry sector analysis. see *AGRICULTURE — Dairying And Dairy Products*

BUSINESS RATIO REPORT: DEFENCE EQUIPMENT MANUFACTURERS; an industry sector analysis. see *MILITARY*

BUSINESS RATIO REPORT: DELIVERY AND DESPATCH SERVICES; an industry sector analysis. see *TRANSPORTATION — Trucks And Trucking*

658.8   UK   ISSN 0261-779X
BUSINESS RATIO REPORT: DEPARTMENT STORES; an industry sector analysis. 1980? a. I C C Business Ratios Ltd., Freepost, Field House, Hampton, Mddx. TW12 1BR, England. TEL 081-783-0977. FAX 081-783-1940. charts; stat. **Document type:** trade publication.

BUSINESS RATIO REPORT: DIE AND MOULD MANUFACTURERS AND DISTRIBUTORS.; an industry sector analysis. see *METALLURGY*

658.8   UK   ISSN 0267-8578
BUSINESS RATIO REPORT: DIRECT MARKETING SERVICES; an industry sector analysis. 1981. a. I C C Business Ratios Ltd., Freepost, Field House, Hampton, Mddx. TW12 1BR, England. TEL 0181-783-0977. FAX 0181-783-1940. charts; stat. **Document type:** trade publication.
Supersedes in part (1985-1993): Business Ratio Report. Direct Marketing (ISSN 0261-3859)

BUSINESS RATIO REPORT: DOMESTIC ELECTRIC APPLIANCES; an industry sector analysis. see *ELECTRONICS*

BUSINESS RATIO REPORT: DOMESTIC FURNITURE MANUFACTURERS; an industry sector analysis. see *INTERIOR DESIGN AND DECORATION — Furniture And House Furnishings*

BUSINESS RATIO REPORT: DROP FORGERS; an industry sector analysis. see *METALLURGY*

BUSINESS RATIO REPORT: DYERS & FINISHERS; an industry sector analysis. see *CLEANING AND DYEING*

BUSINESS RATIO REPORT: EDUCATIONAL EQUIPMENT INDUSTRY; an industry sector analysis. see *EDUCATION — Teaching Methods And Curriculum*

BUSINESS RATIO REPORT: ELECTRICAL CONTRACTORS; an industry sector analysis. see *ENGINEERING — Electrical Engineering*

BUSINESS RATIO REPORT: ELECTRICAL INSTALLATION EQUIPMENT MANUFACTURERS; an industry sector analysis. see *ENGINEERING — Electrical Engineering*

BUSINESS RATIO REPORT: ELECTRICAL WHOLESALERS; an industry sector analysis. see *ELECTRONICS*

BUSINESS RATIO REPORT: ELECTRONIC COMPONENT MANUFACTURERS; an industry sector analysis. see *ELECTRONICS*

BUSINESS RATIO REPORT: ELECTRONIC EQUIPMENT MANUFACTURERS; an industry sector analysis. see *ELECTRONICS*

BUSINESS RATIO REPORT: ELECTRONIC INSTRUMENT MANUFACTURERS; an industry sector analysis. see *ELECTRONICS*

BUSINESS RATIO REPORT: ENGINEERING DESIGN; an industry sector analysis. see *ENGINEERING*

BUSINESS RATIO REPORT: ENGINEERS HAND & SMALL TOOL MANUFACTURERS. see *ENGINEERING*

BUSINESS RATIO REPORT: EXHIBITION AND CONFERENCE ORGANISERS; an industry sector analysis. see *MEETINGS AND CONGRESSES*

BUSINESS RATIO REPORT: FIRE PROTECTION INDUSTRY; an industry sector analysis. see *FIRE PREVENTION*

BUSINESS RATIO REPORT: FOOD INGREDIENTS; an industry sector analysis. see *FOOD AND FOOD INDUSTRIES*

BUSINESS RATIO REPORT: FOOD PROCESSING & PACKAGING MACHINERY; an industry sector analysis. see *FOOD AND FOOD INDUSTRIES*

BUSINESS RATIO REPORT: FOOD PROCESSORS. INTERMEDIATE; an industry sector analysis. see *FOOD AND FOOD INDUSTRIES*

BUSINESS RATIO REPORT: FOOD PROCESSORS. MAJOR; an industry sector analysis. see *FOOD AND FOOD INDUSTRIES*

BUSINESS RATIO REPORT: FOOTBALL CLUBS; an industry sector analysis. see *SPORTS AND GAMES — Ball Games*

BUSINESS RATIO REPORT: FOOTWEAR DISTRIBUTORS; an industry sector analysis. see *SHOES AND BOOTS*

BUSINESS RATIO REPORT: FOOTWEAR MANUFACTURERS; an industry sector analysis. see *SHOES AND BOOTS*

BUSINESS RATIO REPORT: FRANCHISES; an industry sector analysis. see *BUSINESS AND ECONOMICS — Management*

BUSINESS RATIO REPORT: FRENCH & BRITISH FOOD PROCESSORS; an industry sector analysis. see *FOOD AND FOOD INDUSTRIES*

BUSINESS RATIO REPORT: GAS EQUIPMENT & SERVICES; an industry sector analysis. see *ENERGY*

BUSINESS RATIO REPORT: GREETING CARDS; an industry sector analysis. see *GIFTWARE AND TOYS*

BUSINESS RATIO REPORT: GROCERY WHOLESALERS; an industry sector analysis. see *FOOD AND FOOD INDUSTRIES — Grocery Trade*

BUSINESS RATIO REPORT: HEATING AND VENTILATING EQUIPMENT MANUFACTURERS; an industry sector analysis. see *HEATING, PLUMBING AND REFRIGERATION*

BUSINESS RATIO REPORT: HIGH STREET TRADING; an industry sector analysis. see *BUSINESS AND ECONOMICS — Domestic Commerce*

BUSINESS RATIO REPORT: HOUSEBUILDERS; an industry sector analysis. see *BUILDING AND CONSTRUCTION*

BUSINESS RATIO REPORT: HYDRAULIC & PNEUMATIC EQUIPMENT MANUFACTURERS; an industry sector analysis. see *ENGINEERING — Hydraulic Engineering*

BUSINESS RATIO REPORT: INDUSTRIAL CHEMICAL MANUFACTURERS. INTERMEDIATE; an industry sector analysis. see *CHEMISTRY*

BUSINESS RATIO REPORT: INDUSTRIAL CHEMICAL MANUFACTURERS. MAJOR; an industry sector analysis. see *CHEMISTRY*

BUSINESS RATIO REPORT: INDUSTRIAL ROBOTS; an industry sector analysis. see *COMPUTERS — Robotics*

BUSINESS RATIO REPORT: INSURANCE BROKERS; an industry sector analysis. see *INSURANCE*

BUSINESS RATIO REPORT: INSURANCE COMPANIES; an industry sector analysis. see *INSURANCE*

BUSINESS RATIO REPORT: INVESTMENT TRUSTS; an industry sector analysis. see *BUSINESS AND ECONOMICS — Investments*

BUSINESS RATIO REPORT: IRON FOUNDERS; an industry sector analysis. see *METALLURGY*

BUSINESS RATIO REPORT: JOINERY MANUFACTURERS; an industry sector analysis. see *BUILDING AND CONSTRUCTION — Carpentry And Woodwork*

BUSINESS RATIO REPORT: KITCHEN & BATHROOM FURNITURE AND FITTINGS; an industry sector analysis. see *INTERIOR DESIGN AND DECORATION*

BUSINESS RATIO REPORT: LAUNDERERS, DRY CLEANERS AND TEXTILE RENTAL; an industry sector analysis. see *CLEANING AND DYEING*

BUSINESS RATIO REPORT: LEATHER MANUFACTURERS & PROCESSORS; an industry sector analysis. see *LEATHER AND FUR INDUSTRIES*

BUSINESS RATIO REPORT: MACHINE TOOL MANUFACTURERS; an industry sector analysis. see MACHINERY

BUSINESS RATIO REPORT: MANAGEMENT CONSULTANTS; an industry sector analysis. see BUSINESS AND ECONOMICS — Management

658.8 UK ISSN 0952-5173
BUSINESS RATIO REPORT: MARKET RESEARCH; an industry sector analysis. 1987. a. I C C Business Ratios Ltd., Freepost, Field House, Hampton, Mddx. TW12 1BR, England. TEL 081-783-0977. FAX 081-783-0940. charts; stat. **Document type:** trade publication.

BUSINESS RATIO REPORT: MEDICAL EQUIPMENT MANUFACTURERS; an industry sector analysis. see MEDICAL SCIENCES

BUSINESS RATIO REPORT: METAL FINISHERS; an industry sector analysis. see METALLURGY

BUSINESS RATIO REPORT: MOTOR BODY BUILDERS & ENGINEERS; an industry sector analysis. see MACHINERY

BUSINESS RATIO REPORT: MOTOR GOODS DISTRIBUTORS; an industry sector analysis. see MACHINERY

BUSINESS RATIO REPORT: MUSICAL INSTRUMENTS; an industry sector analysis. see MUSIC

BUSINESS RATIO REPORT: NON-FERROUS FOUNDERS; an industry sector analysis. see METALLURGY

BUSINESS RATIO REPORT: NON-FERROUS METAL STOCKHOLDERS; an industry sector analysis. see METALLURGY

BUSINESS RATIO REPORT: OIL & GAS EXPLORATION & PRODUCTION; an industry sector analysis. see PETROLEUM AND GAS

BUSINESS RATIO REPORT: OIL & GAS REFINING & DISTRIBUTION; an industry sector analysis. see PETROLEUM AND GAS

BUSINESS RATIO REPORT: OPTICAL INDUSTRY; an industry sector analysis. see PHYSICS — Optics

BUSINESS RATIO REPORT: PAINT & PRINTING INK MANUFACTURERS; an industry sector analysis. see PAINTS AND PROTECTIVE COATINGS

BUSINESS RATIO REPORT: PAINTING AND DECORATING CONTRACTORS AND MERCHANTS; an industry sector analysis. see INTERIOR DESIGN AND DECORATION

BUSINESS RATIO REPORT: PAPER & BOARD MANUFACTURERS; an industry sector analysis. see PAPER AND PULP

BUSINESS RATIO REPORT: PAPER & BOARD PACKAGING; an industry sector analysis. see PACKAGING

BUSINESS RATIO REPORT: PAPER MERCHANTS; an industry sector analysis. see PAPER AND PULP

BUSINESS RATIO REPORT: PASSENGER SHIPPING; an industry sector analysis. see TRANSPORTATION — Ships And Shipping

BUSINESS RATIO REPORT: PERIODICAL PUBLISHERS; an industry sector analysis. see PUBLISHING AND BOOK TRADE

BUSINESS RATIO REPORT: PET FOOD MANUFACTURERS & DISTRIBUTORS; an industry sector analysis. see FOOD AND FOOD INDUSTRIES

BUSINESS RATIO REPORT: PHARMACEUTICAL MANUFACTURERS; an industry sector analysis. see PHARMACY AND PHARMACOLOGY

BUSINESS RATIO REPORT: PHOTOGRAPHIC EQUIPMENT AND PROCESSORS; an industry sector analysis. see PHOTOGRAPHY

BUSINESS RATIO REPORT: PLANT HIRE; an industry sector analysis. see BUILDING AND CONSTRUCTION

BUSINESS RATIO REPORT: PLASTICS PACKAGING; an industry sector analysis. see PACKAGING

BUSINESS RATIO REPORT: POULTRY PROCESSORS; an industry sector analysis. see AGRICULTURE — Poultry And Livestock

BUSINESS RATIO REPORT: PRE-CAST CONCRETE MANUFACTURERS; an industry sector analysis. see BUILDING AND CONSTRUCTION

BUSINESS RATIO REPORT: PRINT AND PACKAGING MACHINERY; an industry sector analysis. see PRINTING

BUSINESS RATIO REPORT: PRINTED CIRCUIT MANUFACTURERS; an industry sector analysis. see ELECTRONICS

BUSINESS RATIO REPORT: PRINTERS - INTERMEDIATE; an industry sector analysis. see PRINTING

BUSINESS RATIO REPORT: PRINTERS - MAJOR; an industry sector analysis. see PRINTING

BUSINESS RATIO REPORT: PROCESS PLANT; an industry sector analysis. see HEATING, PLUMBING AND REFRIGERATION

BUSINESS RATIO REPORT: PROPERTY DEVELOPERS, INVESTORS AND DEALERS; an industry sector analysis. see REAL ESTATE

BUSINESS RATIO REPORT: READY MIXED CONCRETE & AGGREGATES; an industry sector analysis. see BUILDING AND CONSTRUCTION

BUSINESS RATIO REPORT: REFRIGERATION EQUIPMENT; an industry sector analysis. see HEATING, PLUMBING AND REFRIGERATION

BUSINESS RATIO REPORT: RETAIL & WHOLESALE CHEMISTS; an industry sector analysis. see PHARMACY AND PHARMACOLOGY

658 AT ISSN 1031-1343
THE BUSINESS WHO'S WHO AUSTRALIAN PRODUCTS AND TRADENAMES GUIDE. 1967. a. Aus.$350. Dun & Bradstreet Marketing Pty. Ltd., 19 Havilan St., Chatswood, N.S.W. 2065, Australia. TEL 61-2-9352700. FAX 61-2-9352777. URL: http://www.dbmarketing.com.au. Ed. Peter Beck. adv. contact: Chris Pellegrinetti. circ. 2,000. (back issues avail.) **Document type:** directory.
●Also available on CD-ROM.
Former titles: Business Who's Who Australian Buying Reference (ISSN 0311-5070); Riddell's Australian Purchasing Yearbook (ISSN 0085-5715)
Description: Lists products and services divided into industry sectors, trade names and agencies, company address details.

658 UK
BUSINESSES & ASSETS. 1983. m. £85. Businesses & Assets Ltd., Business Marketplace, East Common, Gerrards Cross, Bucks. SL9 7AG, England. TEL 01753-891000. FAX 01753-880342. Ed. Lesley Carroll. adv.: B&W page £850, color page £1000; 257 x 180; adv. contact: Robert Spencer. bk.rev. circ. 15,000. (back issues avail.) **Document type:** trade publication.

BUSINESSMAN. see BUSINESS AND ECONOMICS — Management

658.8 SW
BUTIKS - SAELJAREN; den butiksnaera detaljhandelstidningen. 1927. 20/yr. SEK 720 (effective 1997); newsstand price: SEK 60. Kooperative Foerbundet, P.O. Box 15200, S-104 65 Stockholm, Sweden. TEL 46-8-743-10-00. FAX 46-8-743-15-26. Ed. Ulla Wallgren. adv.: color page SEK 46400; trim 210 x 297; adv. contact: Gustav Albo. circ. 20.000. cols./p.: 3; pp./issue: 83. **Document type:** trade publication.
Formerly: Kooperations - Saeljaren.

BUYING HABITS OF GOLF COURSE SUPERINTENDENTS. see SPORTS AND GAMES — Ball Games

658 US ISSN 0733-0103
BUYING STRATEGY FORECAST; the bi-weekly source of short-term buying forecasts and strategies. Alternate title: Purchasing Magazine's Buying Strategy Forecast. vol.10, 1985. bi-w. $238 (foreign $310). Cahners Publishing Company (Newton), Division of Reed Elsevier Inc., 275 Washington St., Newton, MA 02158-1630. TEL 617-558-4301. FAX 617-558-4700. (Subscr. to: Box 7610, Highlands Ranch, CO 80126. TEL 800-662-7776) Ed. Thomas Stundza; Pub. Jack O'Connor. circ. 425. **Document type:** trade publication, newsletter.
—CCC.
Description: News and graphic analysis of trends in and projections of commodities and products investments and pricing.

658 659.1 US ISSN 1063-3383
BUZZ (ROCHESTER); perspectives on marketing technology. 1992. m. free to qualified personnel. Buck & Pulleyn, Inc., 500 Helendale Rd., Rochester, NY 14609. TEL 716-288-6900. Ed. Cathy Rubino. R&P contact: Cecelia Stone. **Document type:** newsletter.
Description: Focuses on marketing communications trends and techniques.

658.8 694 SW ISSN 1103-3754
BYGG & JAERNHANDELN/BUILDING MATERIAL AND HARDWARE TRADE JOURNAL. 1914. 10/yr. SEK 250. Bygg och Jaernhandelns Foerlag, P.O. Box 24143, S-104 51 Stockholm, Sweden. TEL 46-8-663-69-05. FAX 46-8-661-54-20. E-mail: bygg-jarnhandeln@mbox300.swipnet.se. (Co-sponsors: Sveriges Jaernhandlarefoerbund, Sveriges Bygg & Traevaru-handelsfoerbund) Ed. Fredrik Dhejne. adv.: B&W page SEK 11800, color page SEK 18200; trim 185 x 262; adv. contact: Ulf Soederholm. bk.rev.; charts; illus.; tr.lit.; tr.mk.; circ. 3,400 (controlled). **Document type:** trade publication.
Formed by the 1993 merger of: Jaernhandlaren (ISSN 0021-552X) & Bygg- och Traevaruhandeln (ISSN 0347-5220)

658.8 380.14 UK
C B I DISTRIBUTIVE TRADES SURVEY. m. £320. Confederation of British Industry, 103 New Oxford St., London WC1A 1DU, England. TEL 44-71-379-7400. FAX 44-71-240-1578.
Formerly: Distributive Trades Survey (ISSN 0266-1802)

C C H MANAGEMENT MANUAL. see BUSINESS AND ECONOMICS — Management

658.8 IT
C E D E M NOTIZIE.* fortn. Centro di Documentazione Economica e di Marketing, Via Bruzzesi 27, 20146 Milan, Italy.

658.8 630 GH ISSN 0007-8611
C M B NEWSLETTER. 1956. q. free. Ghana Cocoa Marketing Board, P.O. Box 933, Accra, Ghana. Ed. Nana M.B. Sarpong 2nd. circ. 3,000. **Document type:** newsletter.

C P A ADMINISTRATOR'S REPORT & MANAGER'S REPORT; the resource successful CPA firms use in firm administration. see BUSINESS AND ECONOMICS — Personnel Management

C P A CLIENT BULLETIN. (American Institute of Certified Public Accountants) see BUSINESS AND ECONOMICS — Accounting

658 657 US ISSN 0279-1021
C P A MARKETING REPORT. 1981. m. $267 (Canada $297; elsewhere $322) (effective Oct. 1996). Strafford Publications, Inc., Specialized Information Services, 590 Dutch Valley Rd., N.E., Drawer 13729, Atlanta, GA 30324-0729. TEL 404-881-1141. FAX 404-881-0074. E-mail: custserv@straffordpub.com. Ed. Suzanne Verity; Pub. Richard M. Ossoff. R&P contact: Marianne Mueller. (looseleaf format; back issues avail.) **Document type:** newsletter.
Incorporates (1978-1987): C P A Proposal Alert.
Description: Helps public accounting firms design, implement and evaluate effective programs to attract new clients, enhance the firm's image, improve client relations and build sound practices.

BUSINESS AND ECONOMICS — MARKETING AND PURCHASING

660 670 US
C P I PURCHASING CHEMICALS YELLOW PAGES ANNUAL BUYING GUIDE. (Chemical Process Industries); an A to Z listing of over 10,000 chemicals and sources of supply. 1984. a. $85 (included in subscr. to CPI Purchasing magazine). Cahners Publishing Company (Newton), Division of Reed Elsevier Inc., 275 Washington St., Newton, MA 02158-1630. TEL 617-964-3030. FAX 617-558-4327. Ed. Kevin Fitzgerald; Pub. John O'Connor. adv. contact: Keith Guernsey. circ. 25,000. **Document type:** directory, trade publication.
Formerly (until 1992): C P I Purchasing Chemicals Directory.

THE C S R ADVISOR. (Customer Service Representative) see INSURANCE

658.8 AT
C T G GAZETTE. 1964. q. Aus.$0.24 per no. (Commercial Travellers' Guild) Paragon Publications, 9 Minyon St., Brunswick Heads, N.S.W. 2483, Australia. (Co-sponsor: New South Wales Sales Representatives)

CABLE THEFT NEWSLETTER. see COMMUNICATIONS — Television And Cable

658 FR ISSN 0249-5570
CAHIERS DE RECHERCHE EN GESTION DES ENTREPRISES. 1977. 2/yr. 160 Fr. Universite de Rennes I, Laboratoire Economie et Gestion des Entreprises, 7 place Hoche, 35000 Rennes, France. TEL 99-25-35-06. FAX 99-38-80-84. Ed. Alain Galesne. (back issues avail.) **Document type:** academic/scholarly publication.

CALIFORNIA. DEPARTMENT OF CONSUMER AFFAIRS. ANNUAL REPORT. see CONSUMER EDUCATION AND PROTECTION

658 US ISSN 1064-5543
CALL CENTER MAGAZINE. 1988. m. $14 (foreign $78). Telecom Library, Inc., 12 W. 21st St., New York, NY 10010. TEL 800-542-7279. (Subscr. to: Box 40706, Nashville, TN 37204) **Document type:** trade publication.
—KR SourceOne.
Formerly (until 1992): Inbound - Outbound Magazine (ISSN 1042-6116)
Description: For call center management; helps them choose and buy, implement and manage technology -- hardware, software and services used in telephone call centers.

CANADIAN ASSOCIATION OF EXPOSITION MANAGERS. COMMUNIQUE. see MEETINGS AND CONGRESSES

CANADIAN COMMERCIAL LAW GUIDE. see LAW — Corporate Law

658.8 CN
CANADIAN DIRECT MARKETING ASSOCIATION. ANNUAL FACT BOOK. a. Can.$195 (members Can.$95). Canadian Direct Marketing Association, One Concorde Gate, Ste. 607, Don Mills, ON M3C 3N6, Canada. TEL 416-391-2362. FAX 416-441-4062. Ed. Scott McClellan.

658.7 CN ISSN 0822-7799
CANADIAN DIRECTORY OF SHOPPING CENTRES. 1975. a. 260. Maclean-Hunter Ltd., Business Publication Division, Maclean-Hunter Bldg., 777 Bay St., Toronto, ON M5W 1A7, Canada. TEL 416-596-5939. Ed. Sandra Fabrizi. **Document type:** directory.

658 CN ISSN 0829-4836
HF5415.2
CANADIAN JOURNAL OF MARKETING RESEARCH. (Text in English, summaries in French) 1980. a. $25 to non-members. Professional Marketing Research Society, 2175 Sheppard Ave. E., Ste. 110, Willowdale, ON M2J 1W8, Canada. TEL 416-493-4080. Ed. Chuck Chakrapani. adv.; bk.rev. circ. 1,200. (back issues avail.) **Indexed:** Mark.Res.Abstr. (1991-). **Document type:** trade publication.
—BLDSC (3031.950000).
Refereed Serial

658 CN ISSN 1193-7513
CANADIAN PROFESSIONAL SALES ASSOCIATION. CONTACT. (Editions in English, French) 1940. 5/yr. Can.$92 membership. Canadian Professional Sales Association - Association Canadienne des Professionnels de la Vente, 145 Wellington St. W., Ste. 310, Toronto, ON M5J 1H8, Canada. TEL 416-408-2685. FAX 416-408-2684. E-mail: s.armstrong@eworld.com. Ed. Corinne Radake. R&P contact: Corinne Radake. bk.rev.; charts; illus.; stat.; tr.lit.; circ. 30,000 (controlled). (back issues avail.) **Document type:** newsletter, trade publication.
Description: Discusses upcoming events and news. Includes educational information for members.

658 CN
CANADIAN RETAILER (WINNIPEG). 1990. bi-m. August Communications, 200-388 Donald St., Winnipeg, MB R3B 2J4, Canada. TEL 204-957-0265. FAX 204-957-0217. Ed. Andrea Kuch. adv. contact: Gene Bruce. circ. 10,000. **Document type:** trade publication.

CANADIAN TRANSPORTATION & LOGISTICS. see TRANSPORTATION

658.87 CN ISSN 0008-5278
CANADIAN VENDING; the voice of automatic vending in Canada. 1952. 6/yr. Can.$26. N C C Publishing, 106 Lakeshore Rd. E., Ste. 209, Mississauga, Ont. L5G 1E3, Canada. TEL 416-271-1366. FAX 416-271-6373. Ed. Sandra Anderson. adv.: B&W page Can.$810; trim 8 1/8 x 10 7/8; adv. contact: Pete Wilkinson. charts; illus.; stat.; tr.lit. circ. 2,200. **Indexed:** Can.B.P.I.

CANNED FOODS: THE INTERNATIONAL MARKET. see FOOD AND FOOD INDUSTRIES

CAR AFTERMARKET: THE INTERNATIONAL MARKET. see TRANSPORTATION — Automobiles

CAR RENTAL: THE INTERNATIONAL MARKET. see TRANSPORTATION — Automobiles

CARD TALK. see ADVERTISING AND PUBLIC RELATIONS

CARTOON OPPORTUNITIES. see ART

658 SA
CASH 'N' CARRY NEWS. 1993. m. Complete Publishing (Pty.) Ltd., P.O. Box 87745, Houghton 2041, South Africa. TEL 27-11-7892112. FAX 27-11-7895347. adv.; illus. (tabloid format) **Document type:** trade publication.

658.8 US ISSN 1087-0601
HF5428
CHAIN STORE AGE; the newsmagazine for retail executives. 1924? m. $99 (foreign $165) (effective 1997). Lebhar-Friedman, Inc., 425 Park Ave., New York, NY 10022. TEL 212-756-5000. E-mail: isender@lf.com; URL: http://www.chainstoreage.com. Ed. Murray Forseter. adv. circ. 23,000. (also avail. in microfiche from CIS) **Indexed:** ABI Inform., B.P.I., Bus.Ind., Comput.Cont., INSPEC (1986-), PROMT, Ref.Pt.Food Indus.Abstr., SRI, Tr.& Indus.Ind. **Document type:** trade publication.
●Also available online. Vendor(s): Information Access Co., UMI.
—AskIEEE; KR SourceOne; UMI; UnCover. CCC.
Former titles (until Aug. 1995): Chain Store Age Executive with Shopping Center Age (ISSN 0193-1199); (until 1975): Chain Store Age Executives Edition Including Shopping Center Age (ISSN 0885-1425)
Description: Provides managers of chain retail stores with practical advice and news on trends.

CHANNELMARKER LETTER. see COMPUTERS — Computer Industry

THE CHARLESTON REPORT; business insights into the library market. see LIBRARY AND INFORMATION SCIENCES

658 IE ISSN 0790-438X
CHECKOUT. 1966. m. I£40. Checkout Publications Ltd., 22 Crofton Rd., Dunlaoire, Co. Dublin, Ireland. TEL 353-1-2808415. FAX 353-1-2808309. Ed. Mary Brophy; Pub. Kevin Kelly. adv. contact: Trisha Pender. circ. 5,500. **Indexed:** Key to Econ.Sci. **Document type:** trade publication.

CHEMICAL INDUSTRIES NEWSLETTER. see CHEMISTRY

CHEMICAL PEDDLER. see BUSINESS AND ECONOMICS — Trade And Industrial Directories

CHICAGO ARTISTS' NEWS. see ART

658.7 US ISSN 0009-367X
CHICAGO PURCHASOR. 1923. 4/yr. $15. Purchasing Management Association of Chicago, 2250 E. Devon Ave., Ste. 236, Des Plaines, IL 60018-4509. (Affiliate: National Association of Purchasing Management) Ed. John Pressley. adv.: B&W page $775, color page $1425; adv. contact: Jackie Stinson. circ. 5,000 (controlled). **Document type:** trade publication.

658.8 US ISSN 0734-8169
Z479
CHILDREN'S MEDIA MARKET PLACE. 1978. irreg., 4th ed., 1995. $49.95. Neal-Schuman Publishers, Inc., 100 Varick St., New York, NY 10013. TEL 212-925-8650. FAX 212-219-8916. Ed. Barbara Stein. R&P contact: Frederick Glasser. **Document type:** directory.
Description: Lists publishers, software and audio-visual producers and other media and services, primarily for grades K-8.

CHILE MARKETING AND FINANCIAL STATISTICS. see BUSINESS AND ECONOMICS — Abstracting, Bibliographies, Statistics

CHILLED AND DELICATESSEN FOODS: THE INTERNATIONAL MARKET. see FOOD AND FOOD INDUSTRIES

CHILTON'S AUTOMOTIVE MARKETING; a monthly publication for the retail jobber & distributor automotive aftermarket. see TRANSPORTATION — Automobiles

CHIMES (SUDBURY). see AGRICULTURE — Dairying And Dairy Products

CHINA AGRICULTURE. see AGRICULTURE

CIGARETTES: THE INTERNATIONAL MARKET. see TOBACCO

CIGARS, CIGARILLOS AND SMOKING TOBACCO: THE INTERNATIONAL MARKET. see TOBACCO

CLEANING APPLIANCES: THE INTERNATIONAL MARKET. see ELECTRONICS

658 US
CLOSEOUT NEWS. 1986. m. $44 (foreign $57). 500 Century Ln., No. 1, Holland, MI 49423-4287. TEL 616-392-9687; 800-600-7040. FAX 616-394-0102. Ed. Dennis Ende; Pub. Dennis Ende. R&P contact: Dennis Ende. adv. contact: Stacey Moomey. circ. 75,000. (tabloid format) **Document type:** newspaper, trade publication.
Description: Covers surplus and closeout merchandise of all types.

658.8 SP
CLUB DE DIRIGENTES DE VENTAS DE GIJON. BOLETIN. 12/yr. Club de Dirigentes de Ventas de Gijon - Sales Directors Club of Gijon, Instituto 17, 33201 Gijon, Spain. TEL 85-34-12-92. Ed. Javier Castro. **Document type:** bulletin.

658 531.64 US ISSN 1041-0988
HD9541
COALDAT MONTHLY (PRODUCING DISTRICT FORMAT). (Also avail.: Suppliers Format (ISSN 1041-097X) and Utility Format (ISSN 1041-0996)) 1986. m. $595 (foreign $635). Pasha Publications Inc., 1616 N. Ft. Myer Dr., Ste. 1000, Arlington, VA 22209-3107. TEL 703-528-1244. FAX 703-528-1253. stat. **Document type:** newsletter.
●Also available online.
Description: Monitors coal purchases by utilities.

658 531.64 US ISSN 1041-097X
HD9541
COALDAT MONTHLY (SUPPLIERS FORMAT). Variant title: Coaldat Marketing Report (Monthly). (Also avail.: Producing District Format (ISSN 1041-0988) and Utility Format (ISSN 1041-0996)) 1986. m. $595 (foreign $635). Pasha Publications Inc., 1616 N. Ft. Myer Dr., Ste. 1000, Arlington, VA 22209-3107. TEL 703-528-1244. FAX 703-528-1253. stat. **Document type:** newsletter.
●Also available online.
Description: Monitors all monthly utility coal purchases.

BUSINESS AND ECONOMICS — MARKETING AND PURCHASING

658 531.64   US   ISSN 1041-0996
HD9541
COALDAT MONTHLY (UTILITY FORMAT). (Also avail.: Suppliers Format (ISSN 1041-097X) and Producing District Format (ISSN 1041-0988)) 1986. m. $595 (foreign $635). Pasha Publications Inc., 1616 N. Ft. Myer Dr., Ste. 1000, Arlington, VA 22209-3107. TEL 703-528-1244. FAX 703-528-1253. stat. **Document type:** newsletter.
●Also available online.
Description: Monitors coal purchased by utilities.

658 531.64   US
COALDAT QUARTERLY. Variant title: Coaldat Marketing Report (Quarterly). (Avail. in Supplier Format, Utility Format) 1986. q. $395 (foreign $435). Pasha Publications Inc., 1616 N. Ft. Myer Dr., Ste. 1000, Arlington, VA 22209-3107. TEL 703-528-1244. FAX 703-528-1253. **Document type:** newsletter.
●Also available online.
Description: Monitors all utility coal purchases and determines market reach, size and share for coal based on quality, transportation and price.

378 658.8   US
THE COLLEGE STORE. 1933. a. $64 to non-members; members $54. National Association of College Stores, 500 E. Lorain St., Oberlin, OH 44074-1298. TEL 216-775-7777. FAX 216-775-4769. TELEX 856-850. E-mail: info@nacs.org; URL: http://www.nacs.org. Ed. Ron Stevens; Pub. Cynthia D'Angelo. R&P contact: Ron Stevens. adv. contact: Judy Pataky. charts; illus.; mkt.; index, cum.index. circ. 6,600. (also avail. in microform from UMI; reprint service avail. from UMI) **Indexed:** C.I.J.E. **Document type:** trade publication.
—UMI.
Formerly: College Store Journal (ISSN 0010-115X)

658.87   US   ISSN 0010-1141
COLLEGE STORE EXECUTIVE. 1970. 10/yr. $30. Executive Business Media, Inc., 825 Old Country Rd., Box 1500, Westbury, NY 11590. TEL 516-334-3030. Ed. Cathy Orobona. adv.; bk.rev.; charts; illus.; stat. (tabloid format)

658.8   US   ISSN 1065-0296
COLLEGIATE TRENDS. 1985. q. $95 (foreign $150) (effective 1997). Strategic Marketing Communications, Inc., 550 N. Maple Ave., Ridgewood, NJ 07450. TEL 201-612-8100. FAX 201-612-1444. URL: http://www.sancinc.com. Ed. Robert Doran; Pub. Eric Weil. charts; circ. 3,000 (paid). (back issues avail.) **Document type:** newsletter.
Description: Covers media marketing aimed at the college market.

658.8   US
COLLOQUY (MILFORD). 1990. q. Frequency Marketing Inc., Box 3920, Milford, OH 45150-3920. TEL 513-248-9184. FAX 513-248-9084. Ed. Kathleen Eardly; Pub. Richard Barlow. R&P contact: Kathleen Eardly. bk.rev. **Document type:** trade publication, newsletter.
Refereed Serial

658.7 338   US   ISSN 0095-3423
JK1673
COMMERCE BUSINESS DAILY; synopsis of United States government proposed procurement, sales, and contract awards. 1950. d. (Mon.-Fri.). $275 (priority mail $324) (foreign $343). U.S. International Trade Administration, U.S. and Foreign Commercial Service, U.S. Department of Commerce, Herbert C. Hoover Bldg., Rm. 3850, 14th St. & Constitution Ave., Washington, DC 20230. TEL 202-482-2867. (Subscr. to: Superintendent of Documents, U.S. Government Printing Office, Box 317954, Pittsburgh, PA 15250-7954. TEL 202-512-1800. FAX 202-512-2250) circ. 30,000.
●Also available online. Vendor(s): Knight-Ridder Information, Inc. (File nos.194 & 195), NewsNet, United Communications Group (CBD OnLine).
Description: Provides a synopsis of U.S. government-proposed procurement.

658.8 659.1   CN
COMMUNICATOR (DON MILLS). q. Can.$30 to non-members. Canadian Direct Marketing Association, One Concorde Gate, Ste. 607, Don Mills, ON M3C 3N6, Canada. TEL 416-391-2362. FAX 416-441-4062. Ed. Scott McClellan. adv. contact: katherine Brasch. circ. 2,500. **Document type:** newsletter.
Former titles: Direct Marketing Communicator (ISSN 0834-0722); (until 1986): Canadian Direct Marketing Communicator (ISSN 0831-7852); (until 1985): C D M A Update (ISSN 0831-7844); (until 1985): Direct Marketing Communicator (ISSN 0821-7602); (until 1983): Communicator (ISSN 0821-7599)

COMMUNITY PHARMACY. see PHARMACY AND PHARMACOLOGY

658.8 659.1   US   ISSN 0888-482X
KF2028.A15
COMPENDIUM OF GOVERNMENT ISSUES AFFECTING DIRECT MARKETING. a. $29.95. Direct Marketing Association (Washington), 1111 19th St. N.W., Ste. 1100, Washington, DC 20036-3603. TEL 202-955-5030. FAX 202-955-0085.

658   US   ISSN 0886-1994
THE COMPETITIVE ADVANTAGE; the newsletter for sales and marketing professionals. 1985. m. $99 (foreign $144). Competitive Advantage, Inc., 1901 N.W. 23rd Ave., Box 10828, Portland, OR 97296. TEL 503-274-2953. FAX 503-274-4349. Ed. Deirdre Hackett; Pub. James F. Moran. R&P contact: Dawn Drake. bk.rev. circ. 11,000. **Document type:** newsletter.
Description: Provides sales, marketing and management tools to make careers and companies more prosperous.

658.8 610   US   ISSN 1073-6816
COMPETITIVE HEALTHCARE MARKET REPORTER. 1993. s-m. $447 (effective 1997). (Managed Care Information Center) American Business Publishing, Brinley Professional Plaza, 3100 Hwy. 138, Box 1442, Wall Township, NJ 07719-1442. TEL 908-681-1133. FAX 908-681-0490. E-mail: 75673.624@compuserve.com. Ed. Melanie Jenkins; Pub. Robert K. Jenkins. R&P contact: Jillian Philipp. adv. contact: Judith Granholm. index. (back issues avail.) **Document type:** newsletter.
—CCC.
Description: Help keep you abreast of the fiercely competitive market. Get the facts and details you'll need on strategic issues, market facts, mergers and acquisitions, economics, network alliances and plan affiliations.

COMPOSANTS INSTRUMENTATION ELECTRONIQUES. see ELECTRONICS

COMPOSITES INDUSTRY MONTHLY. see ENGINEERING — Engineering Mechanics And Materials

658.7   IT
COMPRARE OGGI; rivista di management degli approvvigionamenti. 10/yr. L.145000 (foreign $120) (effective 1996). (Associazione Italiana di Management degli Approvvigionamenti (ADACI)) Societa Editoriale Farmaceutica s.r.l., Via Ausonio 12, 20123 Milan, Italy. TEL 39-2-89404545. FAX 39-2-89401168. Ed. Giancarlo Lubner. circ. 3,000.

658.7   SP   ISSN 0212-8268
COMPRAS Y EXISTENCIAS. 1980. 6/yr. (effective 1997). M. de Molina 44, 5o Dcha., 28006 Madrid, Spain. TEL 34-1-618263. FAX 34-1-5644091. (5900) Ed. Simon Pallares; Pub. Sonsoles Monis. adv. contact: M. Fernandez. bk.rev.; circ. 3,000 (paid). **Document type:** trade publication.

CONFECTIONERY: THE INTERNATIONAL MARKET. see FOOD AND FOOD INDUSTRIES — Bakers And Confectioners

658.7   CN
CONFERENCE BOARD OF CANADA. INDEX OF CONSUMER ATTITUDES. q. membership. (Contemporary Research Centre Ltd.) Conference Board of Canada, 255 Smyth Rd., Ste 100, Ottawa, ON K1H 8M7, Canada. TEL 613-526-3280. FAX 613-526-4857. charts; stat. **Indexed:** CS Ind.
Former titles: Conference Board of Canada. Consumer Attitudes and Buying Intentions (ISSN 0827-5831); Conference Board of Canada. Survey of Consumer Buying Intentions (ISSN 0381-7377)

658   US
CONFERENCE PROCEEDINGS MANUALS. 1988. a. avail. to conference attendees. International Ticketing Association, 250 W. 57th St., Ste. 722, New York, NY 10107. TEL 212-581-0600. FAX 212-581-0885. adv. contact: Patricia Spira. circ. 600. (back issues avail.) **Document type:** proceedings.
Formerly (until 1996): Conference Summary Manuals.
Description: Contains outlines of conference workshops on technology, management, marketing, and professional development.

658.8   US   ISSN 0573-665X
HC107.C8
CONNECTICUT MARKET DATA. 1957. biennial. $15 (diskette $10). Department of Economic Development, 865 Brook St., Rocky Hill, CT 06067-3405. TEL 203-258-4238. URL: http://www.state.ct.us. (also avail. in microfiche from CIS; diskette format) **Indexed:** SRI. **Document type:** government publication.

658   UK   ISSN 0962-113X
CONNECTIONS. 1990. q. membership. Chartered Institute of Marketing, Moor Hall, Cookham, Maidenhead, Berkshire SL6 9QH, England. TEL 44-1628-427500. FAX 44-1628-427499. TELEX 849462 TELFAC G. Ed. Louise Thompson. adv. contact: Louise Thompson. circ. 25,000. **Document type:** newsletter.

658   FR   ISSN 0767-0672
CONQUERIR. 10/yr. 4 et 6, rue Borromee, 75015 Paris, France. TEL 43-06-04-62. TELEX 201 746. Ed. Alain Gazo. circ. 20,000.
Description: For marketing and business directors.

658   UK
CONSUMER.* 6/yr. Akela House, Low Rd., Tasburgh, Norfolk NR15 1AR, England. Ed. Madeleine Munday. circ. 8,500.

658.8   UK
CONSUMER ASIA (YEAR). a. £415($930) (effective 1997). Euromonitor, 60-61 Britton St., London EC1M 5NA, England. TEL 44-171-251-8024. FAX 44-171-608-3149. E-mail: info@euromonitor.com; URL: http://www.euromonitor.com. (Addr. in N. America: Euromonitor International, 122 S. Michigan Ave., Ste. 1200, Chicago, IL 60603. TEL 800-577-3876. FAX 312-922-1157) **Document type:** trade publication.
Description: Analyzes the various consumer markets throughout Asian countries.

CONSUMER CATERING: THE INTERNATIONAL MARKET. see FOOD AND FOOD INDUSTRIES

658.8   UK
CONSUMER CHINA (YEAR). 1996. a. £395($790) (effective 1997). Euromonitor, 60-61 Britton St., London EC1M 5NA, England. TEL 44-171-251-8024. FAX 44-171-608-3149. E-mail: info@euromonitor.com; URL: http://www.euromonitor.com. (Addr. in N. America: Euromonitor International, Inc., 122 S. Michigan Ave., Ste. 1200, Chicago, IL 60603. TEL 800-577-3876. FAX 312-922-1157) charts; stat. **Document type:** trade publication.
Description: Evaluates the various consumer markets in China.

658.7   US   ISSN 1046-1876
CONSUMER CONFIDENCE SURVEY. 1968. m. $195 to non-members; members $95. Conference Board, Inc., 845 Third Ave., New York, NY 10022. TEL 212-759-0900. FAX 212-980-7014. charts; stat. circ. 1,000. **Indexed:** PROMT, SRI. **Document type:** newsletter.
Formerly (until 1987): Consumer Attitudes and Buying Plans (ISSN 0547-7204)
Description: Buyer appraisal of business conditions and employment.

BUSINESS AND ECONOMICS — MARKETING AND PURCHASING

658.8   UK   ISSN 0967-3601
CONSUMER EASTERN EUROPE (YEAR). 1992. a. £425($850) (effective 1997). Euromonitor, 60-61 Britton St., London EC1M 5NA, England. TEL 44-171-251-8024. FAX 44-171-608-3149. E-mail: info@euromonitor.com; URL: http://www.euromonitor.com. (Addr. in N. America: Euromonitor International, 122 S. Michigan Ave., Ste. 1200, Chicago, IL 60603. TEL 800-577-3876. FAX 312-922-1157) charts; stat. **Document type:** trade publication.
   Description: Analyzes economic and political trends that present business opportunities in Eastern Europe.

658.8   UK   ISSN 0308-4353
HD7022
CONSUMER EUROPE (YEAR). 1977. a. £525($1050) (effective 1997). Euromonitor, 60-61 Britton St., London EC1M 5NA, England. TEL 44-171-251-8024. FAX 44-171-608-3149. E-mail: info@euromonitor.com; URL: http://www.euromonitor.com. (Addr. in N. America: Euromonitor International, 122 S. Michigan Ave., Ste. 1200, Chicago, IL 60603. TEL 800-577-3876. FAX 312-922-1157) charts; stat. **Document type:** trade publication.
   Description: Provides a statistical guide to 250 consumer markets, with volume and value sales data broken down across 17 European countries. Presents statistical tables of production, sales, distribution, and consumption.

658.8   UK
CONSUMER INTERNATIONAL. 1994. biennial. £525($1050) (effective 1997). Euromonitor, 60-61 Britton St., London EC1M 5QU, England. TEL 44-171-251-8024. FAX 44-171-608-3149. E-mail: info@euromonitor.com; URL: http://www.euromonitor.com. (Addr. in N. America: Euromonitor International, 122 S. Michigan Ave., Ste. 1200, Chicago, IL 60603. TEL 800-577-3876. FAX 312-922-1157) charts; stat. **Document type:** trade publication.
   Description: Provides statistical coverage of the non-European consumer markets.

658.8 640.73   UK   ISSN 0959-5112
CONSUMER JAPAN (YEAR). 1989. biennial. £275($550) (effective 1996). Euromonitor, 60-61 Britton St., London EC1M 5NA, England. TEL 44-171-251-8024. FAX 44-171-608-3149. E-mail: info@euromonitor.com; URL: http://www.euromonitor.com. (Addr. in N. America: Euromonitor International, 122 S. Michigan Ave., Ste. 1200, Chicago, IL 60603. TEL 800-577-3876. FAX 312-922-1157) charts. **Document type:** trade publication.
   Description: Analyzes various national economic, social, and political trends that can affect marketing strategies in Japan.

658.8   UK
CONSUMER LATIN AMERICA (YEAR). 1993. biennial. £415($830) (effective 1997). Euromonitor, 60-61 Britton St., London EC1M 5NA, England. TEL 44-171-251-8024. FAX 44-171-608-3149. E-mail: info@euromonitor.com; URL: http://www.euromonitor.com. (Addr. in N. America: Euromonitor International, 122 S. Michigan Ave., Ste. 1200, Chicago, IL 60603. TEL 800-577-3876. FAX 312-922-1157) charts; stat. **Document type:** directory.
   Description: Covers all political and social trends that affect various consumer markets in South America.

CONSUMER PACKAGING: THE INTERNATIONAL MARKET. see *PACKAGING*

658.8   UK
CONSUMER SPAIN. 1991. biennial. £275($575) (effective 1997). Euromonitor, 87-88 Turnmill St., London EC1M 5Q, England. TEL 44-171-251-8024. FAX 44-171-608-3149. E-mail: info@euromonitor.com; URL: http://www.euromonitor.com. (Addr. in N. America: Euromonitor International, 122 S. Michigan Ave., Ste. 1200, Chicago, IL 60603. TEL 800-577-3876. FAX 312-922-1157) charts; stat. **Document type:** trade publication.
   Description: Analyzes the various consumer markets in Spain and the social, political, and economic trends that affect them.

658.8   UK   ISSN 0952-9543
HC101
CONSUMER U S A (YEAR). irreg. £375($750) (effective 1997). Euromonitor, 60-61 Britton St., London EC1M 5NA, England. TEL 44-171-251-8024. FAX 44-171-608-3149. E-mail: info@euromonitor.com; URL: http://www.euromonitor.com. (Addr. in N. America: Euromonitor International, 122 S. Michigan Ave., Ste. 1200, Chicago, IL 60603. TEL 800-577-3876. FAX 312-922-1157) **Document type:** directory, trade publication.
   Description: Provides key statistics and background information on U.S. businesses. Includes a comprehensive statistical database on market size for 350 market sectors, profiles of consumer goods manufacturers, a directory of U.S. retailers, and a guide to official and nonofficial business information sources.

CONTACT G E C. see *ENGINEERING — Electrical Engineering*

658.8   SZ
CONTEXT. (Text in French and German) 1896. bi-m. 78 SFr. (students 35 SFr.) (effective 1997). Schweizerischer Kaufmaennischer Verband - Societe Suisse des Employes de Commerce, Hans-Huber-Str. 4, CH-8027 Zurich, Switzerland. TEL 41-1-2834533. FAX 41-1-2015095. Ed. Leon Berger. R&P contact: Josef Kaelin. adv.; bk.rev.; charts; illus.; mkt.; stat.; tr.lit. circ. 65,000. **Document type:** newspaper.
   Former titles (until 1995): Schweizerische Kaufmaennische Zeitung; Schweizerisches Kaufmaennisches Zentralblatt (ISSN 0036-7866)

CONTINENTAL FRANCHISE REVIEW. see *BUSINESS AND ECONOMICS*

658   US   ISSN 0190-3063
KF842
CONTRACT MANAGEMENT. vol.10, 1970. m. $72. National Contract Management Association, 1912 Woodford Rd., Vienna, VA 22182-3728. Ed. Terry Hoskins. adv.: B&W page $2550. bibl.; charts; illus. **Indexed:** BPIA, Bus.Ind., Manage.Cont., Tr.& Indus.Ind.
   —BLDSC (3425.806000).
   Former titles: N C M A Magazine; N C M A Newsletter (ISSN 0027-6332)
   Description: Articles covering issues in contract management.

CONTRACTORS HOT LINE. see *BUILDING AND CONSTRUCTION*

658   SA
CONVENIENCE STORE RETAILING. 1988. m. R.60. Complete Publishing (Pty.) Ltd., P.O. Box 87745, Houghton 2041, South Africa. TEL 27-11-7892112. FAX 27-11-7895347. adv. circ. 15,000. **Document type:** trade publication.
   Formerly: Independent Retailer.

380.1   DK
COPENHAGEN BUSINESS SCHOOL. MARKETING INSTITUTE. WORKING PAPER. 1983. irreg., latest Oct. 7, 1996. free. Copenhagen Business School, Marketing Institute, Struenseegade 7-9, DK-2200 Copenhagen N, Denmark. TEL 45-38-15-21-00. FAX 45-38-15-21-01. Ed. Hans S. Solgaard. charts; cum.index. circ. 200. **Document type:** academic/scholarly publication.
   Formerly: Copenhagen School of Economics and Business Administration. Marketing Institute. Working Paper (ISSN 0109-3401)

658   US
COPY CHICAGO. m. membership. Business Marketing Association (Wilmette), Box 425, Wilmette, IL 60091. TEL 708-256-3883. Ed. Kirsten Reilly. **Document type:** newsletter.
   Description: Contains announcements of association events.

COUGH AND COLD REMEDIES: THE INTERNATIONAL MARKET. see *PHARMACY AND PHARMACOLOGY*

658.8   US   ISSN 0898-6614
COUNCIL OF LOGISTICS MANAGEMENT ANNUAL CONFERENCE PROCEEDINGS. (Supplement to: Bibliography on Logistics and Physical Distribution Management) vol.13, 1975. a. $35. Council of Logistics Management, 2803 Butterfield Rd., Ste. 380, Oak Brook, IL 60521. TEL 630-574-0985. FAX 630-574-0989. Ed. Elaine M. Winter. bk.rev.; charts. circ. 10,000. **Document type:** proceedings.
   Former titles: N C P D M Annual Conference Proceedings; National Council of Physical Distribution Management. Annual Conference Proceedings; National Council of Physical Distribution Management. Annual Meeting Proceedings.

COUNSEL. see *ADVERTISING AND PUBLIC RELATIONS*

658.8   US
COWLES - SIMBA REPORT ON DATABASE MARKETING. 1993. m. $329. Cowles - SIMBA Information (Subsidiary of: Cowles Business Media), 11 Riverbend Dr. S., Box 4949, Stamford, CT 06907-0949. TEL 203-358-9900; 800-307-2529. FAX 203-358-5811. E-mail: info@simbanet.com; URL: http://www.simbanet.com. **Document type:** newsletter.
   Formerly (until 1997): Cowles Report on Database Marketing (ISSN 1072-401X)
   Description: Includes comparisons, vital statistics, and real case studies on topics such as pricing, technology, and ethics.

658 659   US
CREATIVE MARKETING; incentives in retail promotion. 1979. q. Association of Retail Marketing Services, 3 Caro Ct., Red Bank, NJ 07701. TEL 908-842-5070. Ed. George Meredith. R&P contact: Gerri Hopkins. stat. circ. 4,200. (back issues avail.) **Document type:** newsletter.
   Incorporates (1978-1996): A R M S Register.
   Description: Covers incentive retail promotion, including trading stamps, continuities, tape plans, games and sweepstakes, traffic builders and direct premiums.

658.8 659.1   UK   ISSN 0262-1037
CREATIVE REVIEW. 1980. m. £30 (Europe £52; N. America £55). Centaur Communications Ltd., St. Giles House, 50 Poland St., London W1V 4AX, England. TEL 44-171-287-9800. FAX 44-171-439-1480. Ed. Lewis Blackwell. adv. (also avail. in microform from UMI) **Indexed:** Art Ind., DAAI. **Document type:** trade publication.
   —BLDSC (3487.245000); KR SourceOne; SWETS; UMI.

CREDIT AND CHARGE CARDS: THE INTERNATIONAL MARKET. see *BUSINESS AND ECONOMICS — Banking And Finance*

332.7 658   UK   ISSN 0265-2099
       CODEN: CEMNEJ
CREDIT MANAGEMENT. 1950. m. £50 (overseas £55). Institute of Credit Management, The Water Mill, Station Rd., S. Luffenham, Oakham, Leics. LE15 8NB, England. TEL 44-1780-721888. FAX 44-1780-721333. E-mail: info@icm.org.uk. Ed Ronald W. Aldridge. adv.: B&W page £900; color page £1225; adv. contact: Ronald W. Aldridge. bk.rev.; charts; illus. circ. 9,000. **Indexed:** ABI Inform, Anbar, INSPEC (1994-). **Document type:** trade publication.
   —BLDSC (3487.283000); AskIEEE; KR SourceOne; UMI.
   Description: Offers full coverage of consumer, trade, and export news and editorials.

CREDIT MANUAL OF COMMERCIAL LAWS. see *BUSINESS AND ECONOMICS — Banking And Finance*

THE CREDIT MEMO. see *BUSINESS AND ECONOMICS — Banking And Finance*

CRONER'S BUYING AND SELLING LAW. see *LAW*

CROSS AND TALK; for communications between you and the world. see *COMMUNICATIONS*

BUSINESS AND ECONOMICS — MARKETING AND PURCHASING

658   US
CUSTOMER PROFIT REPORT.* bi-w. $199. Marketing Publications Inc., 4120 Military Rd. NW, Washington, DC 20015-2930. TEL 301-585-0730. FAX 301-585-3084. Ed. Warren Blanding.
  Formerly: Customer Assurance Report.
  Description: Includes strategies for improving customer satisfaction, customer retention, profitability, and quality. For managers, directors, VP's of marketing, customer service and distribution.

658   UK
D & B EUROPA. 1989. a. £438. Dun & Bradstreet Ltd., Holmers Farm Way, High Wycombe, Bucks. HP12 4UL, England. TEL 44-1494-422000. FAX 44-1494-422260. Ed. Laura Morel. **Document type:** directory.
  Formerly: DunsEuropa.

338 658.8   US   ISSN 0746-6110
HF5001   CODEN: DBRED6
D & B REPORTS; the Dun & Bradstreet magazine for small business management. 1972. bi-m. $30. Dun & Bradstreet (Subsidiary of: Dun & Bradstreet Corporation), 299 Park Ave., New York, NY 10171. TEL 800-362-3425. FAX 212-593-6596. Ed. Patricia W. Hamilton. adv. contact: Margret McMahon. bk.rev.; charts; illus.; stat. circ. 67,682. **Indexed:** ABI Inform., B.P.I., BPIA, Bus.Ind., Manage.Abstr., Manage.Cont., PMR, PROMT, PSI, Tr.& Indus.Ind.
  —KR SourceOne; UMI; UnCover. **CCC**.
  Former titles (until 1979): Dun and Bradstreet Reports Magazine (ISSN 0164-517X); (until 1977): Dun and Bradstreet Reports (ISSN 0197-6982)

658.8   US   ISSN 1060-6106
D E C A DIMENSIONS. 1947. bi-m. $5. Distributive Education Clubs of America, 1908 Association Dr., Reston, VA 22091. TEL 703-860-5000. FAX 703-860-4013. E-mail: decainc@aol.com; URL: http://www.deca.org. Ed. Carol Lund; Pub. Ed Davis. R&P contact: Carol Lund. adv. contact: Cindy Allen. bk.rev.; illus. circ. 159,000. **Document type:** academic/scholarly publication.
  Former titles (until 1992): New Dimensions (Reston) (ISSN 0279-473X); (until 1982): D E C A Distributor (ISSN 0011-4847)
  Description: For students enrolled in a marketing education program at the high school and junior college level, and for college students preparing to teach marketing education. Topics include business and association news, career skills, and leadership development.

D I Y: THE INTERNATIONAL MARKET. (Do-It-Yourself) see INTERIOR DESIGN AND DECORATION — Furniture And House Furnishings

658   GW   ISSN 0416-5551
D M; Das private Wirtschaftsmagazin. Variant title: Deutsche Mark. (Supplement avail.: D M Aktuell (ISSN 0720-1109) 1960. m. DM.72 (foreign DM 80.40). Verlagsgruppe Handelsblatt GmbH, Kasernenstr. 67, 40213 Duesseldorf, Germany. TEL 49-211-8870. FAX 49-211-374955. (Subscr. to: Postfach 102717, 40018 Duesseldorf, Germany) circ. 178,376. (back issues avail.) **Document type:** bulletin.
  —SWETS. **CCC**.

658.8 659.1   US   ISSN 1049-6092
HF5415.126
D M A STATISTICAL FACT BOOK. a. $104.95 (members $79.95). Direct Marketing Association, Library & Resource Center, 1120 Ave. of the Americas, New York, NY 10036-6700. TEL 212-768-7277. FAX 212-768-4546. charts; stat. (reprint service avail. from UMI) **Indexed:** SRI.
  Formerly: Fact Book on Direct Marketing.
  Description: Covers many aspects of direct marketing including: media and market growth and usage trends, consumer and business attitudes and buying habits, expectations and outlooks, production and operating cost figures and environmental issues concerns.

658.8   IT
D M E COMMUNICAZIONE.* (Direct Marketing) 1991. m. L.124000 (Europe L.167000; elsewhere L.209000) (effective 1994). Deus Editore s.r.l., Via Breno 1, 20139 Milan, Italy. Ed. Ugo Canonici. adv.: B&W page L.4200000, color page L.7150000; trim 170 x 245. bk.rev.; circ. 7,467 (controlled). **Document type:** trade publication.
  Formerly: D M.

658.8   US   ISSN 0194-3588
HF5415.126
D M NEWS.* (Direct Marketing) 1979. w. (47/yr.). $75 (foreign $150) free to qualified personnel. D M News Corp. (Subsidiary of: Mill Hollow Publications), 100 Sixth Ave., 6th Fl., New York, NY 10013-1689. TEL 212-741-2095. FAX 212-633-9367. Ed. Larry Riggs. adv.; bk.rev.; circ. 31,000 (controlled). (tabloid format; reprint service avail. UMI,BLH) **Indexed:** Tel.Alert. **Document type:** newspaper.
  ●Also available online. Vendor(s): Lexis-Nexis.
  —KR SourceOne.

DAIRY PRODUCTS: THE INTERNATIONAL MARKET. see AGRICULTURE — Dairying And Dairy Products

DANSK PRESSE. see JOURNALISM

658 683.83   US
DEALERSCOPE MERCHANDISING FIRST OF THE MONTH. 1990. m. free to qualified personnel. North American Publishing Co., 401 N. Broad St., Philadelphia, PA 19108. TEL 215-238-5300. FAX 215-238-5284. Ed. Richard Sherwin. adv. circ. 30,000. **Document type:** trade publication.
  Description: Retail news about consumer electronics and major appliances for large chains and department store management.

DELANEY REPORT. see ADVERTISING AND PUBLIC RELATIONS

658   US   ISSN 1066-3843
   CODEN: DWORE8
DELPHI WORKFLOW REPORT; a monthly newsletter on workflow. 1993. m. $150 (foreign $200). Delphi Consulting Group, Inc., 100 City Hall Pl., 4th Fl., Boston, MA 02108-2105. TEL 617-247-1511. FAX 617-247-4957. E-mail: imw@delphigroup.com; URL: http://www.delphigroup.com. Ed. Thomas M. Koulopoulos. **Document type:** newsletter.
  Description: Provides current information on developments in the workflow market and insight into technologies, applications and methodologies for applying workflow analysis to your organization.

DEODORANTS: THE INTERNATIONAL MARKET. see BEAUTY CULTURE

658   CN
DETAIL. (Text in French) 1993. 5/yr. Can.$22 (in US Can.$50, elsewhere Can.$75). Editions Info Press, 4316 Blvd. St. Laurent Ste., 400, Montreal, PQ H2W 1Z3, Canada. TEL 514-842-2422. Ed. Romain Bedard. adv.: B&W page Can.$2500, color page Can.$3300; trim 8 1/2 x 11. circ. 15,000.

380.1   DK   ISSN 0109-1751
DETAIL-BLADET. 1983. 18/yr. DKK 11 per no. Erhvervs-Bladet A-S, Vesterbrogade 12, DK-1780 Copenhagen V, Denmark. Ed. Henrik Denman. illus. circ. 53,000.

381   NE   ISSN 0168-0021
DETAILHANDEL MAGAZINE. 1971. w. Hoofdbedrijfsschap Detailhandel, Postbus 90703, 2509 LS The Hague, Netherlands. TEL 31-70-3529800. FAX 31-70-3545435. **Document type:** trade publication.
  —SWETS.
  Formerly (until 1982): Detailhandelsbulletin (ISSN 0167-031X)

658   SZ
DETAILHANDEL UND GEWERBE. 10/yr. Neuengasse 20, Postfach 6335, CH-3001 Bern, Switzerland. TEL 031-220162. Ed. Bernhard Boegli. circ. 1,300.

658   US   ISSN 0149-7421
HF5415.1
DEVELOPMENTS IN MARKETING SCIENCE. 1977. a. $50 (effective 1997). Academy of Marketing Science, School of Business Administration, University of Miami, Box 248012, Coral Gables, FL 33124. TEL 305-284-6673. FAX 305-284-3762. Eds. Joseph F. Hair Jr., Elizabeth Wilson. adv. circ. 500. (back issues avail.) **Document type:** proceedings.
  —BLDSC (3579.084600).

DIGESTIVE REMEDIES: THE INTERNATIONAL MARKET. see PHARMACY AND PHARMACOLOGY

658   FR   ISSN 1147-7776
DIRECT. 1990. 9/yr. Marketing Mix S.A., 15 bis, rue Ernest Renan, B.P. 62, 92133 Issy-les-Moulineaux Cedex, France. TEL 40-93-01-02. FAX 40-93-03-40. Ed. Bruno Le Prat. circ. 5,500.

658   US   ISSN 1046-4174
HF5415.126
DIRECT (STAMFORD); the magazine for direct marketing management. 1988. m. $64 (free to qualified personnel). Cowles Business Media (Subsidiary of: Cowles Media Company), 11 River Bend Dr., S., Box 4949, Stamford, CT 06907-0949. TEL 203-358-9900. FAX 203-358-5811. Ed. Toni Angar. (reprint service avail from UMI) **Document type:** trade publication.
  Description: Reports on the latest developments in direct marketing.

658   BE
DIRECT EFFECT. (Text in Flemish) m. 3500 BEF. C E D Samsom (Subsidiary of: Wolters Samsom Belgie n.v.), Kouterveld 14, B-1831 Diegem, Belgium. TEL 32-2-7231111.
  Description: Explores direct marketing.

658.8 659.1   US   ISSN 0743-7625
DIRECT LINE. m. Direct Marketing Association, 1120 Ave. of the Americas, New York, NY 10036-6700. TEL 212-768-7277. FAX 212-768-4547.

658.8   US   ISSN 0012-3188
HF5861   CODEN: DIMADI
DIRECT MARKETING; using direct response advertising to enhance marketing database. 1938. m. $56. Hoke Communications, 224 Seventh St., Garden City, Long Island, NY 11530. TEL 516-746-6700; 800-229-6700. FAX 516-294-8141. E-mail: 71410.2423@compuserve.com; URL: http://netplaza.com/cgi-bin/document/plaza/business/1025/storepg2html?&uid429513. Ed. Edward Pasternack; Pub. Henry Hoke. R&P contact: Edward Pasternack. adv. contact: Henry Hoke. circ. 11,000. (also avail. in microform from UMI; reprint service avail. from UMI) **Indexed:** ABI Inform., ASEAN Manage.Abstr., B.P.I., BPIA, INSPEC. **Document type:** trade publication.
  ●Also available online. Vendor(s): Information Access Co., Lexis-Nexis, UMI.
  —BLDSC (3590.240000); AskIEEE; CASDDS; KR SourceOne; UMI; UnCover. **CCC**.
  Former titles (until 1968): Reporter of Direct Mail Advertising.
  Description: Regular departments, columns and special features provide timely insight on the people, organizations, trends and developments, strategies and tactics.

658.8 659.1   US
DIRECT MARKETING ASSOCIATION. ANNUAL REPORT. a. Direct Marketing Association, 1120 Ave. of the Americas, New York, NY 10036-6700. TEL 212-768-7277. FAX 212-768-4547. **Document type:** corporate report.

658   JA
DIRECT MARKETING IN JAPAN. (Text in English) irreg. $200 per no. Dodwell Marketing Consultants, Kowa No. 35 Bldg., 14-14, Akasaka 1-chome, Minato-ku, Tokyo 107, Japan. TEL 03-3589-0207. FAX 03-5570-7132. TELEX J22274 DODWELL. circ. 1,000. **Document type:** directory.
  Description: Covers 80 specialist and non-specialist direct marketers.

658   US   ISSN 0192-3137
HF5415.1
DIRECT MARKETING MARKET PLACE; the networking source of the direct marketing industry. Short title: D M M P. 1980. a. $199 (effective 1996). National Register Publishing, A Division of Reed Elsevier Inc., 121 Chanlon Rd., New Providence, NJ 07974. TEL 908-464-6800. FAX 908-665-6688. TELEX 13-8755. E-mail: info@reedref.com; URL: http://www.reedref.com. (Subscr. to: National Register Publishing, Order Dept., Box 31, New Providence, NJ 07974-9903. TEL 800-521-8110) Ed.Bd. adv.; stat.; tr.lit.; index. circ. 3,000. (back issues avail.) **Document type:** directory.
  Description: Lists over 31,000 key executives, leading direct marketing companies, major firms, suppliers, and creative sources in the US. Provides information on key decision makers, advertising budget, direct marketing expenditures, sales, and billing.

BUSINESS AND ECONOMICS — MARKETING AND PURCHASING

658.8   CN   ISSN 1187-7111
DIRECT MARKETING NEWS. 1988. 12/yr. Can.$60. C D M N Publishing, 1200 Markham Rd., Ste. 301, Scarborough, ON M1H 3C3, Canada. TEL 416-439-4083. FAX 416-439-4086. Ed. Dave Bosworth. adv.: B&W page Can.$2995, color page Can.$4195; trim 11 1/4 x 17 1/4; adv. contact: George Gadjovich. bk.rev.; circ. 7,000 (controlled).
   Formerly (until 1992): Canadian Direct Marketing News (ISSN 0844-3238)
   Description: Provides articles on telemarketing, direct marketing, database management and publishing management.

658   US   ISSN 1085-1321
DIRECT RESPONSE. 1971. m. $79 (foreign $88). Creative Direct Marketing Group, 1815 W. 213th St., Ste. 210, Torrance, CA 90501-2800. TEL 213-212-5727. FAX 213-212-5773. Ed. Craig Huey. R&P contact: Craig Huey. adv.: bk.rev. **Document type:** newsletter.
   Description: Contains original articles and a digest of the latest in direct marketing. Test results, new trends, case studies are outlined.

658.8   UK   ISSN 0952-9764
DIRECT RESPONSE. 1980. m. £45($125) (overseas £75). Brainstorm Publishing Co., 4 Market Pl., Hertford, Herts. SG14 1EB, England. TEL 01992-501177. FAX 01992-500387. Ed. P. Rowney. adv.: B&W page £1020, color page £1620; trim 297 x 210; adv. contact: Nicky Letts. bk.rev.; circ. 1,200 (paid); 7,400 (controlled). **Document type:** trade publication.
—BLDSC (3590.247000).
   Description: Covers direct marketing and mail order businesses specifically for clients and users. Contains news, views, interviews, and analyses.

DIRECT RESPONSE SPECIALIST. see ADVERTISING AND PUBLIC RELATIONS

658.8   US
DIRECT SELLING ASSOCIATION. INTERNATIONAL BULLETIN. 3/yr. membership only. (Direct Selling Association) World Federation of Direct Selling Associations, 1666 K St., N.W., Ste. 1010, Washington, DC 20006-2808. TEL 202-293-5760. FAX 202-463-4569. Ed. Joe Brinkler. illus. **Document type:** bulletin.

DIRECTION (ALLENDALE). see ADVERTISING AND PUBLIC RELATIONS

658.8 659.1   US   ISSN 0883-9727
DIRECTIONS (NEW YORK). bi-m. Direct Marketing Association, 1120 Ave. of the Americas, New York, NY 10036-6700. TEL 212-768-7277. FAX 212-768-4547. (reprint service avail. from UMI)
   Formerly (until 1985): Direct Marketing Journal (ISSN 0747-8100)

378   US   ISSN 0084-988X
DIRECTORY OF COLLEGE STORES. 1956. irreg. $90. B. Klein Publications, Box 6578, Delray Beach, FL 33482. TEL 407-496-3316. FAX 407-496-5546. Ed. Bernard Klein. **Document type:** directory.

658.83   UK   ISSN 0969-4587
DIRECTORY OF CONTINUOUS MARKET RESEARCH (YEAR). a. £48. N T C Publications Ltd., Farm Rd., Henley-on-Thames, Oxfordshire RG9 1EJ, England. TEL 01491-411000. FAX 01491-571188. **Document type:** directory.
   Description: Source of information about continuous and syndicated market surveys available in the UK.

DIRECTORY OF DISCOUNT AND GENERAL MERCHANDISE STORES (YEAR). see BUSINESS AND ECONOMICS — Trade And Industrial Directories

658.8   UK
DIRECTORY OF EUROPEAN RETAILERS & INTERNATIONAL BUYING AGENTS. 1953. biennial. £130 (overseas £140). Newman Books Ltd., 32 Vauxhall Bridge Rd., London SW1V 2SS, England. TEL 0171-973-6402. FAX 0171-233-5056. Ed. David Ricketts. adv. contact: Warren Brett. circ. 3,500 (paid). **Document type:** directory.
—BLDSC (3593.529000).
   Formerly: Stores of the World Directory (ISSN 0081-5829)
   Description: Lists major retailers in Europe.

DIRECTORY OF FRANCHISING ORGANIZATIONS. see BUSINESS AND ECONOMICS — Trade And Industrial Directories

DIRECTORY OF MAIL ORDER CATALOGS. see BUSINESS AND ECONOMICS — Trade And Industrial Directories

DIRECTORY OF MAJOR MALLS. see REAL ESTATE

DIRECTORY OF OPPORTUNITIES FOR GRADUATES. VOL. 6: BUYING, MARKETING, SELLING. see BUSINESS AND ECONOMICS — Trade And Industrial Directories

DIRECTORY OF PREMIUM, INCENTIVE & TRAVEL BUYERS. see BUSINESS AND ECONOMICS — Trade And Industrial Directories

DIRECTORY OF THE JAPANESE HEALTHCARE INDUSTRY. see MEDICAL SCIENCES

658   GW
DIREKT-KONTAKT BETRIEBSBEDARF. q. Konradin Verlag Robert Kohlhammer GmbH, Ernst-Mey-Str. 8, 70771 Leinfelden-Echterdingen, Germany. TEL 49-711-7594-0. FAX 49-711-7594390. adv.: B&W page DM.3200, color page DM.3600; trim 92 x 202; adv. contact: Vera Sebastian. circ. 25,000 (controlled). **Document type:** trade publication.
   Description: Direct mail booklet aimed at qualified buying influences in industry.

658.8   IT   ISSN 0012-3323
DIRETTORE COMMERCIALE; rivista di marketing per lo sviluppo delle vendite. 1957. m. (11/yr.). L.28000($30) Casa Editrice Edithema, Piazza della Repubblica 32, 20124 Milan, Italy. Dir. Paolo Bellavista. adv. circ. 6,300. (cards)

658.879   US   ISSN 0012-3579
HF5001   CODEN: DISMAD
DISCOUNT MERCHANDISER. 1961. m. $55 (foreign $100). (MacFadden Holdings, Inc.) Schwartz Publications, 233 Park Ave. S., New York, NY 10003. TEL 212-979-4860. FAX 212-474-7431. URL: http://screendoor.women.com/dun/. Ed. Steven Jacober. adv. circ. 35,000. (also avail. in microfiche from UMI; reprint service avail. from UMI) Indexed: ABI Inform, B.P.I., BPIA, P.A.I.S., PROMT, SRI. —BLDSC (3595.700000); KR SourceOne; UMI; UnCover.
   Description: Covers all phases of the mass merchandising retail industry.

658.879   US   ISSN 0012-3587
HF5001
DISCOUNT STORE NEWS. (Includes Apparel Merchandising) 1962. fortn. $100 (effective 1997). Lebhar-Friedman, Inc., 425 Park Ave. N., New York, NY 10022. TEL 212-756-5000; 800-766-6999. E-mail: dsn@lf.com; URL: http://www.discountstorenews.com. Ed. Tony Lisanti. adv.; illus.; tr.lit. circ. 26,051. (also avail. in microform from UMI; microfiche from CIS; reprint service avail. from UMI) Indexed: Bus.Ind., P.A.I.S, SRI, Tr.& Indus.Ind. **Document type:** trade publication.
●Also available online. Vendor(s): Information Access Co., Knight-Ridder Information, Inc., Lexis-Nexis. —BLDSC (3595.710000); UMI. CCC.
   Description: Covers merchandising and operational methods; includes reports on developments.

DISPOSABLE PAPER PRODUCTS: THE INTERNATIONAL MARKET. see PAPER AND PULP

658.8   SP
DISTRIBUCION ACTUALIDAD. 1975. m. (11/yr.). 15000 ptas. (foreign 25000 ptas.). Ediciones y Estudios, S.A., Enrique Larreta 9, 28036 Madrid, Spain. TEL 1-733-91-14. FAX 1-315-74-19. Ed. Alicia Davara; Pub. Miguel de Haro. adv. contact: Choni Velasco. bk.rev. **Document type:** trade publication.

658.7   US   ISSN 0894-7651
DISTRIBUTION CENTER MANAGEMENT. 1966. m. $129. Alexander Research & Communications, Inc., 215 Park Ave., S., Ste. 1301, New York, NY 10003. TEL 212-228-0246. FAX 212-228-0376. Ed. Anita Rosepka; Margaret/DeWitt. R&P contact: Mary Dalessandro. charts; illus.; stat. **Document type:** newsletter.
   Former titles (until 1979): Warehouse and Physical Distribution Productivity; (until 1973): Distribution-Warehouse Cost Digest (ISSN 0012-3927)
   Description: Provides practical strategies and industry news to help distribution center and warehouse professionals improve distribution center efficiency.

658.8   BE   ISSN 0012-3935
DISTRIBUTION D'AUJOURD'HUI; le mensuel des fabricants et commercants dynamiques. Flemish edition: Distributie Vandaag (ISSN 0773-1175) (Editions in Flemish, French) 1960. 10/yr. 10450 Fr. (effective 1997). Comite Belge de la Distribution - Belgisch Comite voor de Distributie, 34 rue Marianne, B-1180 Brussels, Belgium. TEL 02-3459923. FAX 02-3460204. Ed. Marcel Evrard. adv. **Indexed:** Key to Econ.Sci.
   Formerly (until 1968): Revue Belge de la Distribution (ISSN 0773-1183)
   Description: Examines the economic aspects, commercial techniques and marketing involved in distribution. Includes new product announcements.

658   US
DISTRIBUTION MANAGEMENT DIGEST. 1987. q. Business Marketing & Publishing Inc., Box 7457, Wilton, CT 06897. adv.: B&W page $855; adv. contact: George B. Young. **Document type:** newsletter.

DISTRIBUTIVE TRADES IN E C COUNTRIES. see BUSINESS AND ECONOMICS — Abstracting, Bibliographies, Statistics

658   IE   ISSN 0790-8776
DISTRIBUTIVE WORKER. 1904. 4/yr. Irish Distributive and Administrative Trade Union, 9 Cavendish Row, Dublin 1, Ireland. TEL 01-8746321. FAX 01-8729581. Ed. Owen Nulty. circ. 7,500. **Document type:** trade publication.
   Formerly (until 1921): Drapers' Assistant (ISSN 0790-8768)

DISTRIBUTOR MANAGEMENT DIGEST. see ELECTRONICS

658.7   US   ISSN 1043-7118
THE DISTRIBUTOR'S & WHOLESALER'S ADVISOR; reports for management in a competitive era. s-m. $197. Alexander Research & Communications, Inc., 215 Park Ave., S., Ste. 1301, New York, NY 10003. TEL 212-228-0246. FAX 212-228-0376. Ed. Anita Rosepka; Pub. Margarett DeWitt. R&P contact: Mary Dalessandro. **Document type:** newsletter.
   Description: Provides case studies, how-to reports and industry news to help wholesalers and distributors run their businesses more efficiently.

658   NE
DOCUMENTATIE REVUE. (2 editions avail.: Bouw, Techniek) s-a. free to qualified personnel. Misset (Subsidiary of: Reed Elsevier plc), Postbus 4, 7000 BA Doetinchem, Netherlands. TEL 31-8340-49911. FAX 31-8340-43839. TELEX 45481. Ed. J.F.F. van Bruggen. adv. contact: Cor van Nek. circ. 15,000 (controlled). **Document type:** trade publication.
   Description: Aimed at the purchasing department, management and executives of production and trade enterprises.

DOOR & WINDOW RETAILING. see BUILDING AND CONSTRUCTION

658   FR   ISSN 0769-5918
DOSSIERS DU MARKETING DIRECT. 1984. 11/yr. Centre Francais pour la Promotion du Marketing Direct, 4 rue de Commaille, 75007 Paris, France. TEL 42-22-90-33. FAX 42-22-23-89. Ed. M.C. Ferreira. circ. 2,000.
   Description: Educational review dedicated to direct marketing.

380.14   FR
DROGUERIE FRANCAISE LA COULEUR.* 1906. m. 4 F. (Federation Nationale des Syndicats de Droguistes) Editions P.B.M., 21 rue du Chateau d'Eau, 75010 Paris, France. Eds. Bernard Dentz & Paul Rouintru. adv. circ. 8,500. **Indexed:** Key to Econ.Sci.

BUSINESS AND ECONOMICS — MARKETING AND PURCHASING

658 US
DROP SHIPPING MARKETING METHODS. 1992. a. $18. Drop Shipping News, Box 7838, New York, NY 10150. TEL 212-688-8797. Ed. Nicholas T. Scheel. **Document type:** trade publication.
Description: Covers many facets of drop shipping and direct marketing.

658 US
DROP SHIPPING NEWS. 12/yr. Drop Shipping News, Box 7838, New York, NY 10150. TEL 212-688-8797. Ed. Nicholas T. Scheel.
Description: Covers all facets of drop shipping as a marketing function by shifting the risk of inventory possession backward through channels of distribution.

DROP SHIPPING SOURCE DIRECTORY OF MAJOR CONSUMER PRODUCT LINES. see *BUSINESS AND ECONOMICS — Trade And Industrial Directories*

DRUG STORE MARKET GUIDE; a detailed distribution analysis of chain and wholesale drug store industry. see *BUSINESS AND ECONOMICS — Trade And Industrial Directories*

381.45 US ISSN 0191-7587
HD9666.1
DRUG STORE NEWS. 1960. bi-w. $95 effective 1997). Lebhar-Friedman, Inc., 425 Park Ave., New York, NY 10022. TEL 212-756-5000. Ed. Marie Griffin. adv.; tr.lit. circ. 43,792. (also avail. in microform from UMI; microfiche from CIS; reprint service avail. from UMI) **Indexed:** I.P.A., SRI, Tr.& Indus.Ind. **Document type:** trade publication, newsletter.
●Also available online. Vendor(s): Information Access Co., Lexis-Nexis.
—UMI. **CCC.**
Supersedes: Chain Store Age Drug Magazine.

658 MP
DZAH DZEEL/MARKET. (Text in Mongolian) 1990. bi-m. Ministry of Trade and Industry, Ulan Bator, Mongolia.

E D M A - GRAM. (European Direct Marketing Association) see *ADVERTISING AND PUBLIC RELATIONS*

658.8 608 US
E P M ENTERTAINMENT MARKETING SOURCEBOOK. a. $295. E P M Communications, 160 Mercer St., 3rd Fl., New York, NY 10012-3212. TEL 212-941-0099. FAX 212-941-1622. Ed. Michael Schau; Pub. Ira Mayer. R&P contact: Ira Mayer. **Document type:** directory.
Description: Provides information on entertainment firms, sponsors, and service providers to the promotion and marketing industries.

658.8 620 UK ISSN 0144-476X
E R A TECHNOLOGY NEWS. (Electrical Research Association) 1979. s-a. free. E R A Technology Ltd., Cleeve Rd., Leatherhead, Surrey KT22 7SA, England. TEL 44-1372-367000. FAX 44-1372-367099. E-mail: info@era.co.uk. Ed.Bd. circ. 900 (controlled). **Indexed:** Alloys Ind., Eng.Mat.Abstr., INSPEC, Met.Abstr.Ind., Met.Abstr., Nonfer.Met.Alert, PCC Alert, Steels Alert, World Alum.Abstr. **Document type:** newspaper.
—BLDSC (3794.892000).
Description: Covers electrotechnology research, development, and testing.

658 NE ISSN 0928-1525
E R M. (Electro Radio Mercuur); het vakblad voor de elektrodetailhandel. 1928. 11/yr. fl.133.50 (effective 1997). Wegener Tijdschriften Groep B.V., Postbus 1860, 1110 CD Diemen, Netherlands. TEL 31-20-6603478. FAX 31-20-6956329. Ed. Anja van Dijk. bk.rev.; bibl.; charts; illus.; mkt.; pat.; stat.; tr.lit.; index. circ. 4,799. **Indexed:** Key to Econ.Sci. **Document type:** trade publication.
—SWETS.
Former titles (until 1992): E R M Journaal (ISSN 0921-5131); (until 1988): E R M (ISSN 0165-5205); Elektrotechnisch Vakblad E R M; (until 1976): Electro Radio Mercuur (ISSN 0013-4619); (until 1945): Electro Radio Techniek (ISSN 0926-6100).

658.8 NE
HF5415.2
E S O M A R DIRECTORY (YEAR). (In 3 vols.) 1965. a. 225 SFr. to non-members (effective 1997). European Society for Opinion and Marketing Research, J.J. Viottastraat 29, 1071 JP Amsterdam, Netherlands. TEL 31-20-664-2141. FAX 31-20-664-2922. E-mail: email@esomar.nl; URL: http://www.esomar.nl.
●Also available on CD-ROM.
Former Titles E S O M A R Handbook; E S O M A R Directory (ISSN 0923-8212); (until 1988): Handbook of Marketing Research (ISSN 0071-3074)

658.8 NE
E S O M A R MARKETING RESEARCH CONGRESS. (Text in English) a. 185 SFr. to non-members; members 165 SFr. European Society for Opinion and Marketing Research, J.J. Viottastraat 29, 1071 JP Amsterdam, Netherlands. TEL 31-20-664-2141. FAX 31-20-664-2922. E-mail: email@esomar.nl; URL: http://www.esomar.nl. **Indexed:** Mark.Res.Abstr. (1964-). **Document type:** proceedings.
—BLDSC (3811.276000).
Formerly: E S O M A R Congress. Proceedings (ISSN 0071-3082)

658.8 325 365 UK ISSN 0262-0456
HF1532.7
EAST EUROPEAN MARKETS; the East European business and financial briefing. fortn. £515($870) (overseas $580). Pearson Professional Ltd., Financial Times Newsletters and Management Reports (Subsidiary of: Financial Times Group), Maple House, 149 Tottenham Court Rd., London W1P 9LL, England. TEL 44-171-896-2325. FAX 44-171-896-2333. Eds. Trevor Petch, Simon Henderson; Pubs. John McLachlan, Carolyn White. (also avail. in microform from UMI) **Indexed:** Key to Econ.Sci. **Document type:** newsletter.
●Also available online. Vendor(s): Data-Star, Information Access Co., Lexis-Nexis.
—UMI.
Description: Provides a market intelligence service for international businessmen trading in Eastern Europe.

658.8 UK
EASTERN EUROPE: A DIRECTORY AND SOURCEBOOK. 1993. irreg. £195($390) (effective 1997). Euromonitor, 60-61 Britton St., London EC1M 5NA, England. TEL 44-171-251-8024. FAX 44-171-608-3149. E-mail: info@euromonitor.com; URL: http://www.euromonitor.com. (Addr. in N. America: Euromonitor International, 122 S. Michigan Ave., Ste. 1200, Chicago, IL 60603. TEL 800-577-3876. FAX 312-922-1157) stat. **Document type:** trade publication.
Description: Compiles statistics and data on the emerging East European consumer markets.

ECHO DES M.I.N.; mensuel de la filiere fruits et legumes. see *AGRICULTURE*

070.5
EDITOR & PUBLISHER MARKET GUIDE. 1924. a. $100 (CD-ROM $395). Editor & Publisher Co., Inc., 11 W. 19th St., New York, NY 10011. TEL 212-675-4380. FAX 212-929-1259. E-mail: edpub@mediainfo.com; URL: http://www.mediainfo.com. Ed. Ian Anderson. adv. circ. 4,000. (also avail. in microfiche from UMI,CIS; reprint service avail. from UMI) **Indexed:** SRI. **Document type:** directory.
●Also available online.
Also available on CD-ROM.
Description: Reference guide for US counties and daily newspaper cities in the US and Canada.

685 658 GW ISSN 0930-8458
EINKAEUFER IM MARKT. 1969. fortn. DM.210 (foreign DM.230.40). Wirtschaftsverlag GmbH, Im Weiher 10, 69121 Heidelberg, Germany. TEL 06221-489440. Ed. Horst Strache. index. **Document type:** trade publication.
—**CCC.**

658 SZ
EINKAUF - MATERIALWIRTSCHAFT - LOGISTIK. 1960. 11/yr. 70 SFr. (foreign 82 SFr.). Postfach 167, CH-6061 Sarnen, Switzerland. TEL 041-660766. FAX 041-660717. Ed. Benno Keller. adv.; bk.rev. circ. 6,500. **Document type:** trade publication.
Formerly: Einkaeufer - Materialwirtschaft - Logistik.

658.8 IE ISSN 0790-7508
ELECTRICAL MAIL. (Text mainly in English; occasionally in Irish) 1979. m. Electricity Supply Board, Lr. Fitzwilliam St., Dublin 2, Ireland. TEL 01-765831. FAX 01-760727. Ed. Alo Brady. circ. 15,500.
Incorporates: Electricity Supply Board. Marketing News.

658.8 621.3 US ISSN 0149-5771
ELECTRICAL MARKETING NEWSLETTER. 1975. s-m. $495. Intertec Publishing Corp., 9800 Metcalf, Overland Park, KS 66212-2215. TEL 913-341-1300. FAX 913-967-1898. Ed. Dale Funk. charts; pat. (also avail. in microform from UMI) **Document type:** newsletter.
—UMI. **CCC.**
Description: Electrical industry news and information.

658 US
ELECTRICAL PRODUCT NEWS. 1987. q. $29.50. Business Marketing & Publishing, Inc., Box 7457, Wilton, CT 06897. TEL 203-834-9959. Ed. George B. Young. adv.: B&W page $875. **Document type:** newsletter.

ELECTRICAL RETAILING. see *ENGINEERING — Electrical Engineering*

658 US
ELECTRICAL SALES BUILDERS. 1987. q. $29.50. Business Marketing & Publishing, Inc., Box 7457, Wilton, CT 06897. Ed. George B. Young. adv.: B&W page $875. **Document type:** newsletter.

658 683.83 US ISSN 0013-4430
TK1
ELECTRICAL WHOLESALING. 1920. m. $12. Intertec Publishing Corp., 9800 Metcalf, Overland Park, KS 66212-2215. TEL 913-341-1300. FAX 913-967-1898. Ed. Jim Lucy. adv.; illus.; tr.lit. circ. 23,000. (also avail. in microform from UMI; reprint service avail. from UMI) **Indexed:** SRI. **Document type:** trade publication.
—BLDSC (3691.971000); UMI. **CCC.**
Description: Current information on industry trends, business management, and sales techniques.

658 004 US
ELECTRONIC RETAILING. 1994. m. $44.95; newsstand price: $5. G P G Publishing, Inc. (Subsidiary of: R.J. Gordon & Co.), 9200 Sunset Blvd., Ste. 612, Los Angeles, CA 90069. TEL 818-782-7328. FAX 818-782-7450. E-mail: webmaster@elrond.worldshop.com; URL: http://www.eretail.com. Ed. Kathy St. Louis; Pub. Deborah Carver. adv.: B&W page $2450. circ. 21,500. **Document type:** trade publication.
●Also available online.
Description: Focuses on the new sales opportunities afforded by emerging electronic media such as commercial online services, the Internet, WWW, interactive kiosks, CD-ROM and more.

EMBROIDERY - MONOGRAM BUSINESS. see *NEEDLEWORK*

658 CN
EMERGING MARKETS ANALYST. m. $895. 1002 Sherbrooke St. W., 16th Fl., Montreal, PQ H3A 3L6, Canada. TEL 514-499-9706. FAX 514-499-9709. (Subscr. in U.S. to: Box 238, Chazy, NY 12921)
Formed by the merger of: Emerging Markets Analyst. Annual Backgrounders & Emerging Markets Analyst. Country Quarterlies & Emerging Markets Analyst. Monthly Bulletin.
Description: Provides a forecast and analysis of emerging capital markets.

658.8 US ISSN 0071-0695
PN1993
ENTERTAINMENT INDUSTRY SERIES. 1961. irreg. (approx. 1/yr.); latest vol.38. price varies. Seven Arts Press, Inc., 6253 Hollywood Blvd., Ste. 1100, Hollywood, CA 90028. TEL 213-469-1095. Ed. Joseph Yore. bk.rev. circ. 3,000. (back issues avail.) **Document type:** monographic series.

BUSINESS AND ECONOMICS — MARKETING AND PURCHASING

608 658.8 US ISSN 1048-5112
ENTERTAINMENT MARKETING LETTER. 1988. m. $319 (foreign $349). E P M Communications, 160 Mercer St., 3rd Fl., New York, NY 10012-3212. TEL 212-941-0099. FAX 212-941-1622. Ed. Michael Schau; Pub. Ira Mayer. R&P contact: Ira Mayer. s-a. index. (back issues avail.) **Document type:** newsletter.
●Also available online. Vendor(s): Information Access Co.
—CCC.
Description: Covers promotion, marketing, contests sponsorship, in-theater advertising, and product placement, for entertainment companies and sponsors.

ENTERTAINMENT SOFTWARE: THE INTERNATIONAL MARKET. see LEISURE AND RECREATION

ENVIRONMENT BUSINESS MAGAZINE. see ENVIRONMENTAL STUDIES

ENVIRONMENT NEWS. see ENVIRONMENTAL STUDIES

EQUINE OZ. see ADVERTISING AND PUBLIC RELATIONS

EQUIPMENT WORLD. see MACHINERY

658 796.72 US
ERNIE SAXTON'S MOTORSPORTS SPONSORSHIP - MARKETING NEWS; the latest marketing promotion & sponsorship news in all forms of motorsports. 1985. m. $69.95. Ernie Saxton Communications, 1448 Hollywood Ave., Langhorne, PA 19047-7417. TEL 215-752-7797. FAX 215-752-1518. Ed. Marilyn Saxton. adv.; bk.rev. **Document type:** newsletter.
Description: Lists motorsports marketing news and sponsorship opportunities and offers advice.

658.8 SP ISSN 0213-4950
ESMA INFORM. Variant title: Escuela Superior de Marketing y Administracion Inform. 1960. q. Escuela Superior de Marketing y Administracion Inform, Consejo de Ciento 42, 08014 Barcelona, Spain. TEL 3-426-99-88. FAX 3-426-76-21. Ed. Juan B. Renart. **Document type:** bulletin.
Former titles (until 1985): Boletin de Marketing y Administracion de Empresas (ISSN 0210-3508); (until 1976): Promoventas (ISSN 0212-6362); (until 1970): Ventas (ISSN 0505-2084)

ESSEX COUNTY COUNCIL. PLANNING. SUBJECT MONITORING REPORTS. RETAILING. see PUBLIC ADMINISTRATION — Municipal Government

658 FR ISSN 0984-774X
ETAT DE L'OPINION. 1984. a. (S O F R E S) Editions de Seuil, 27 rue Jacob, 75261 Paris Cedex 06, France. TEL 42-22-37-94. Eds. Olivier Duhamel, Jerome Jaffre.
Formerly (until 1987): Opinion Publique (ISSN 0980-2991)

ETAT-KALKULATOR. see ADVERTISING AND PUBLIC RELATIONS

THE EUROMONITOR BOOK REPORT (YEAR). see PUBLISHING AND BOOK TRADE

658 UK
EUROMONITOR EMERGING MARKET REPORT SERIES. irreg. £1950($3900) per no. Euromonitor, 60-61 Britton St., London EC1M 5NA, England. TEL 44-171-251-8024. FAX 44-171-608-3149. E-mail: info@euromonitor.com; URL: http://www.euromonitor.com. (Addr. in N. America: Euromonitor International, 122 S. Michigan Ave., Ste. 1200, Chicago, IL 60603. TEL 800-577-3876. FAX 312-922-1157) charts; stat.
Description: Assesses a specific consumer market in Latin America, Eastern Europe, or Asia.

658.8 UK
EUROPEAN CONSUMER LIFESTYLES. irreg., no.2, 1994. £495($990) Euromonitor, 60-61 Britton St., London EC1M 5NA, England. TEL 44-171-251-8024. FAX 44-171-608-3149. E-mail: info@euromonitor.com; URL: http://www.euromonitor.com. (N. American addr.: Euromonitor International Inc., 122 S. Michigan Ave., Ste. 1200, Chicago, IL 60603. TEL 800-577-3876. FAX 312-541-1567) **Document type:** trade publication.
Description: Reports on economic, demographic, and social trends in each major European nation.

EUROPEAN COSMETICS AND TOILETRIES MARKETING DIRECTORY. see BEAUTY CULTURE — Perfumes And Cosmetics

EUROPEAN COSMETICS AND TOILETRIES REPORT (YEAR). see BEAUTY CULTURE — Perfumes And Cosmetics

EUROPEAN DIRECTORY OF CONSUMER BRANDS AND THEIR OWNERS. see PATENTS, TRADEMARKS AND COPYRIGHTS

EUROPEAN DRINKS MARKETING DIRECTORY. see BEVERAGES

EUROPEAN ELECTRICAL APPLIANCES MARKETING DIRECTORY. see ELECTRONICS

EUROPEAN FOOD DATABOOK. see FOOD AND FOOD INDUSTRIES

EUROPEAN FOOD MARKETING DIRECTORY. see FOOD AND FOOD INDUSTRIES

EUROPEAN HOTEL AND CATERING MARKETING DIRECTORY. see HOTELS AND RESTAURANTS

658.8 UK
EUROPEAN INDUSTRIAL MARKETING RESEARCH PERSONAL CONTACT DIRECTORY. 1984. base vol. (plus irreg. updates). European Marketing Association - Association Europeene pour le Marketing, 18 St. Peters Steps, Brixham, Devon TQ5 9TE, England. Ed. D.W. Newill. adv.; bk.rev. (looseleaf format; back issues avail.)

658.8 UK ISSN 0309-0566
HF5410
EUROPEAN JOURNAL OF MARKETING. (Abstracts in English, French, German) 1967. m. £3329($5169) (foreign Aus.$6499) (effective 1998). M C B University Press Ltd., 60-62 Toller Ln., Bradford, W. Yorks BD8 9BY, England. TEL 44-1274-777700. FAX 44-1274-785200. TELEX 51317-MCBUNI-G. E-mail: akaminska@mcb.co.uk; URL: http://www.mcb.co.uk/liblink/ejm/jourhome.htm. Ed. David Carson. bk.rev.; abstr.; bibl.; charts; stat.; index. (reprint service avail. from SWZ) **Indexed:** ABI Inform, Account.& Data Proc.Abstr., Anbar, ASEAN Manage.Abstr., BPIA, Br.Hum.Ind., Bus.Ind., Cont.Pg.Manage., Curr.Cont., Manage.Cont., Mark.Res.Abstr. (1972-), Mgmt.& Market.Abstr., SCIMP (1978-), SSCI, Tr.& Indus.Ind. **Document type:** academic/scholarly publication.
●Also available online.
—BLDSC (3829.731000); SWETS; UMI; UnCover. CCC.
Incorporates: Journal of Advertising History (ISSN 0143-0793); Formerly: British Journal of Marketing (ISSN 0007-1099)
Description: Presents the practical applications of new ideas and developments in marketing research. Covers marketing planning, customer policy and service, marketing of services, history of advertising, and product development.

658 UK ISSN 0969-7012
EUROPEAN JOURNAL OF PURCHASING AND SUPPLY MANAGEMENT. 1994. q. fl.449($258) (effective 1998). Elsevier Science Ltd., Pergamon, P.O. Box 800, Kidlington, Oxford OX5 1DX, England. TEL 44-1865-843000. FAX 44-1865-843010. E-mail: nlinfo-f@elsevier.nl; usinfo-f@elsevier.com; forinfo-kuf@niftyserve.or.jp; URL: http://www.elsevier.nl/. (Suscr. to: elsevier Science, Regional Sales Office, P.O. Box 211, 1000 AE Amsterdam, Netherlands. TEL 31-20-4853757. FAX 31-20-4853432; Subscr. in the Americas to: Elsevier Science, Regional Sales Office, Box 945, New York, NY 10159-0945. TEL 212-633-3730. FAX 212-633-3680; Subscr. in Australasia and the Far East to: Elsevier Science (Singapore) Pte Ltd, No.1 Temasek Ave., No.17-01 Millenia Tower, Singapore 039192, Singapore. TEL 65-434-3727. FAX 65-337-4432) Ed. Richard Lamming. (also avail. in microform from UMI; back issues avail.) **Document type:** academic/scholarly publication.
—BLDSC (3829.738040); UMI. CCC.
Description: Covers every aspect of the purchasing of goods and services in all contexts.
Refereed Serial

EUROPEAN LEISURE AND ENTERTAINMENT MARKETING DIRECTORY. see LEISURE AND RECREATION

658 540 UK
EUROPEAN MARKET FOR HOUSEHOLD LAUNDRY DETERGENTS AND CONDITIONERS. 1994. irreg., latest 1995. £395. I A L Consultants, 109 Uxbridge Rd., Ealing, London W5 5TL, England. TEL 44-181-810-0919. FAX 44-181-566-4931. **Document type:** trade publication.

659.1 UK
EUROPEAN MARKETING ASSOCIATION. INTERNATIONAL MARKETING AND RESEARCH CONFERENCE. JOURNAL. irreg. European Marketing Association - Association Europeenne pour le Marketing, 18 St. Peters Steps, Brixham, Devon, England. **Document type:** academic/scholarly publication.

EUROPEAN MARKETING DATA AND STATISTICS (YEAR). see BUSINESS AND ECONOMICS — Abstracting, Bibliographies, Statistics

658 UK
EUROPEAN MARKETING NEWSLETTER. irreg. European Marketing Association - Association Europeenne pour le Marketing, 18 St. Peters Steps, Brixham, Devon, England. **Document type:** newsletter.

658 UK ISSN 0966-7717
EUROPEAN MARKETING POCKET BOOK (YEAR). a. £24. N T C Publications Ltd., Farm Rd., Henley-on-Thames, Oxfordshire RG9 1EJ, England. TEL 01491-411000. FAX 01491-571188. **Document type:** trade publication.
Description: Source of international marketing, media and advertising data covering 25 countries.

EUROPEAN MOTOR AND ALLIED TRADES MARKETING DIRECTORY. see TRANSPORTATION — Automobiles

EUROPE'S AUTOMOTIVE COMPONENTS BUSINESS. see TRANSPORTATION — Automobiles

EUROPE'S MEDIUM SIZED COMPANIES DIRECTORY (YEAR). see BUSINESS AND ECONOMICS — Trade And Industrial Directories

658 UK ISSN 0966-0259
EUROSLOT. 1990. m. £68 (Europe $135; Far East $210; rest of world $180. World's Fair Ltd., P.O. Box 57, Oldham OL1 4BB, England. TEL 061-624-3687. FAX 061-665-1260. Ed. Christine Butterworth. adv. circ. 13,500. **Document type:** trade publication.
Description: Coin-operated machine journal for Europe.

EVALUATING YOUR FIRM'S INJURY & ILLNESS RECORD. WHOLESALE & RETAIL TRADE INDUSTRIES. see OCCUPATIONAL HEALTH AND SAFETY

658 011 UK
EVENT ORGANISER. 1991. bi-m. £35 (foreign £50) (effective 1997). (Event Services Association) Trade Publications Ltd., 29 Market Pl., Wantage, Oxon. OX12 8BG, England. TEL 44-1235-772207. FAX 44-1235-769044. (Dist. by: Alpha Mail, 14 Victoria Way, West Sussex RH15 9NF, England. TEL 44-1444-071555. FAX 44-1444-071355) Ed. Jim Winship. adv.; B&W page £975; 296 x 210. tr.lit. circ. 7,000. (back issues avail.) **Document type:** trade publication.
Description: Publishes news and articles on the events industry for suppliers and organizers.

658 US ISSN 0887-6878
EXHIBIT BUILDER. 1983. bi-m. $25. Exhibit Builder, Inc., Box 4144, Woodland Hills, CA 91365. TEL 818-225-0100. FAX 818-225-0138. Ed. Judy Pomerantz. adv.; bk.rev. circ. 14,000. **Document type:** trade publication.
Description: Devoted to design and construction techniques. Provides successful case histories, new products and covers the services and products marketplace.

EXHIBIT BUILDER SOURCE BOOK DIRECTORY (YEAR). see BUSINESS AND ECONOMICS — Trade And Industrial Directories

658.8 US
EXHIBIT MARKETING MAGAZINE. 1989. 3/yr. Eaton Hall Publishing, 256 Columbia Tpke., Florham Park, NJ 07932. TEL 201-514-5900. FAX 201-514-5977. Ed. Scott Goldman. adv. contact: Gary Puro. circ. 31,000. **Document type:** trade publication.
Description: Offers advice to business trade show exhibitors to help them sell and exhibit.

BUSINESS AND ECONOMICS — MARKETING AND PURCHASING

EXHIBIT REVIEW. see *BUSINESS AND ECONOMICS — Trade And Industrial Directories*

658 338   US   ISSN 0739-6821
T391   CODEN: EXHIDV
EXHIBITOR MAGAZINE; the magazine for trade show and event marketing management. 1981. m. $68 (Canada & Mexico $115; elsewhere $150). Exhibitor Publications, Inc., 206 S. Broadway, Ste. 745, Rochester, MN 55904. TEL 507-289-6556. FAX 507-289-5253. E-mail: exhmag@aol.com; URL: http://www.exhibitornet.com. (Subscr. to: Box 368, Rochester, MN 55903-0368) Ed. Lee Knight; Pub. Lee Knight. adv.: B&W page $2529, color page $3379; trim 8 1/2 x 10 7/8; adv. contact: John Pavek. circ. 15,000. (back issues avail.) **Document type:** trade publication.
—CASDDS.
   Incorporates (in 1995): Buyers Guide: an Illustrated Guide to Trade Show Displays and Accessories.
   Description: For people who plan, implement or oversee trade show exhibiting programs. Highlights the strategic, logistical, and tactical aspects of trade show marketing and exhibit program management.

658.8   SW   ISSN 1103-436X
EXPOMARKETING; Nordens enda facktidning foer maessor och utstaellingar. 1984. q. SEK 200. Kellerman & Oeqvist, P.O. Box 515, S-611 10 Nykoeping, Sweden. TEL 46-155-21-98-15. FAX 46-155-21-98-59. E-mail: expomarketing@ett.se; URL: http://www.expomarketing.se. Ed. Roland Oeqvist; Pub. Roland Oeqvist. adv.: B&W page SEK12000, color page SEK16400; adv. contact: Roger Kellerman. circ. 5,000. **Document type:** trade publication.
   Formerly (until 1992): Maessor och Kongresser (ISSN 0282-793X)
   Description: Covers trade show and event marketing and management.

EXPOSURE! (YAKIMA). see *COMPUTERS — Computer Networks*

EYEWEAR: THE INTERNATIONAL MARKET. see *MEDICAL SCIENCES — Orthopedics And Traumatology*

657.04   SA
F A C T - TECHNICAL BULLETIN. (Text in Afrikaans) 1993. 4/yr. Instituut van Kommersiele en Finansiele Rekenmeesters van Suider-Afrika - Institute of Commercial and Financial Accountants of South Africa, P.O. Box 1791, Houghton 2041, South Africa. Ed. Simon Burdett. R&P contact: Simon Burdett. adv. contact: Simon Burdett. **Document type:** bulletin, newsletter.
   Formerly: Tegniese Bulletin.

658 664   US
F F P SERIES IN FOOD PRODUCTS MARKETING. (Food Products Press) irreg. price varies. Haworth Press, Inc., Food Products Press, 10 Alice St., Binghamton, NY 13904-9981. TEL 800-342-9678. FAX 607-722-6362. TELEX 7932599. Ed. John L. Stanton. **Document type:** monographic series.
   Description: Aims to develop a better understanding of food marketing by focusing attention on specific food industries and sectors and on specific food marketing activities.

F M A TODAY. (Fuel Merchants Association of New Jersey) see *PETROLEUM AND GAS*

658   SA
F M C G RETAILER. 1978. m. R.60. Complete Publishing (Pty.) Ltd., P.O. Box 87745, Houghton 2041, South Africa. TEL 27-11-7892112. FAX 27-11-7895347. adv.; illus. circ. 7,000. **Document type:** trade publication.

658.7   UK   ISSN 0014-6579
FACTORY EQUIPMENT NEWS. 1949. m. £35($159) (foreign £80). Wilmington Business Publishing, Apex House, London Rd., Northfleet, Kent DA11 9JA, England. TEL 44-1322-277788. FAX 44-1474-569418. E-mail: wbp@wilmington.co.uk. Ed. Judith Ruthven. circ. 50,058. (tabloid format) **Document type:** trade publication.

658   US
FAIR TRADER. m. free. Culture Clash Communications, E-mail: cclash@web.net; URL: http://www.izad.com/cultureclash. adv.
•Available only online.
   Description: Enables people around the globe to buy, sell and trade goods and services for a small fee.

658   US   ISSN 0071-3716
HG4961
FAIRCHILD'S FINANCIAL MANUAL OF RETAIL STORES.* 1923. a. $75 (effective Oct. 1990). Fairchild Books (Subsidiary of: Fairchild Publications Inc.), 7 W. 34th St., New York, NY 10001. TEL 212-630-4000. FAX 212-887-1946. TELEX 232666 FAPB. Ed. Robert Benjamin. stat. circ. 2,000. (also avail. in microfiche from CIS; back issues avail.) **Indexed:** SRI.

658 615   US
FAMILY ALMANAC. 1915. a. $41 (effective 1998). (National Association of Retail Druggists) Creative Comics Syndicate, 1608 South Dakota, Sioux Falls, SD 57105. TEL 800-423-7158. circ. 40,000.
   Former titles: N A R D Almanac and Health Guide; N A R D Almanac.

FARMERS HOT LINE. see *AGRICULTURE*

FAST FOOD: THE INTERNATIONAL MARKET. see *FOOD AND FOOD INDUSTRIES*

658 910.09   CN   ISSN 0836-6926
FETES ET FESTIVALS. 1982. q. Can.$23.54 (effective 1992). Societe des Fetes et Festivals du Quebec, 4545 Av. Pierre-de-Coubertin, P.O. Box 1000, succ.M, Montreal, PQ H1V 3R2, Canada. TEL 514-252-3037. FAX 514-254-1617. Ed. Pierre-Paul LeDuc. adv.; bibl.; illus.; stat. circ. 5,500. (back issues avail.)
   Formerly: Tam Ti Delam (ISSN 0705-3428)

FIBEROPTICS MARKETING INTELLIGENCE. see *PHYSICS — Optics*

658   IT   ISSN 1121-3906
FIERE NEL MONDO. 1981. a. L.45000. Centro Italiano Pubblicita s.r.l., Via G. Bruzzesi 35, Milan, Italy. Ed. Bonisolli Lanfranco. adv.

FINANCIAL MARKETING. see *BUSINESS AND ECONOMICS — Banking And Finance*

658.8   CN   ISSN 0227-6038
FINANCIAL POST CANADIAN MARKETS. 1925. a. Can.$79.75. Financial Post Co., Ltd., 333 King St., E., Toronto, ON M5A 4N2, Canada. TEL 416-350-6516. FAX 416-350-6501. Ed. Jean Graham. adv. circ. 6,000.
—CISTI.
   Formerly: Financial Post Survey of Markets (ISSN 0071-5077)

658.8   UK
FINANCIAL TIMES. MANAGEMENT REPORTS. irreg. price varies. Financial Times Business Information, Management Reports (Subsidiary of: Financial Times Group), 102 Clerkenwell Rd., London EC1M 5SA, England. TEL 44-171-814-9770. FAX 44-171-411-4415. (Orders to: F T B I, 126 Jermyn St., London SW1Y 4UJ, England. TEL 44-1209-612493. FAX 44-1209-612811) **Document type:** trade publication, monographic series.
   Description: Each volume researches a particular U.K. or international market.

FIREARMS BUSINESS. see *SPORTS AND GAMES*

FIRMA. see *BUSINESS AND ECONOMICS — Small Business*

FIZZZ; fuer die Szenengastronomie. see *BEVERAGES*

658 388.5   US
FLEET ASSOCIATION DIRECTORY. 1991. a. $20. Bobit Publishing Company, 2512 Artesia Blvd., Redondo Beach, CA 90278-3210. TEL 310-376-8788. FAX 310-376-9043. E-mail: robert@bobit.com. adv.: B&W page $1700; trim 8 x 10 7/8. **Document type:** directory.
   Description: Directory for car fleet associations.

658 388.5   US
FLEET FINANCIALS. 3/yr. $28 (Canada $34; elsewhere $42). Bobit Publishing Company, 2512 Artesia Blvd., Redondo Beach, CA 90278-3210. TEL 310-376-8788. FAX 310-376-9043. E-mail: robert@bobit.com. **Document type:** trade publication.
   Description: For top executives at companies having car fleets.

FLORAL MANAGEMENT; business news for the floral industry. see *GARDENING AND HORTICULTURE — Florist Trade*

658   CN   ISSN 1192-8573
FOCUS ON PROCUREMENT. 1992. 6/yr. Can.$24.95 (US Can.$29.95). MultiDirect Communications Inc., 786 Island Park Dr., Ottawa, ON K1Y 0C2, Canada. TEL 613-722-3940. FAX 613-722-3017. Ed. John Harrison. adv.: B&W page Can.$1725, color page Can.$2250; trim 8 1/4 x 10 3/4. circ. 11,500.

658   FR   ISSN 0997-7511
FONCTION G. 1989. 5/yr. 38 rue de Mathurins, 75008 Paris, France. TEL 42-66-25-54. FAX 47-42-06-17. circ. 8,500.

658.8   US   ISSN 0884-7185
FOOD BROKER QUARTERLY. 1985. q. $40. National Food Brokers Association, 2100 Reston Pkwy., Ste. 400, Reston, VA 22091-1218. TEL 202-789-2844. FAX 202-842-0839. Ed. Julie Legg. R&P contact: Julie Legg. adv. circ. 2,800. (back issues avail.) **Document type:** trade publication.
   Description: For management executives of food broker, retail and foodservice sales organizations and packaged goods manufacturers.

FOOD DISTRIBUTION RESEARCH SOCIETY. NEWSLETTER. see *FOOD AND FOOD INDUSTRIES*

FOOD MARKETING & TECHNOLOGY. see *FOOD AND FOOD INDUSTRIES*

FOOD, NONFOOD UND GETRAENKE. see *FOOD AND FOOD INDUSTRIES*

FOOD RETAILERS: THE INTERNATIONAL MARKET. see *FOOD AND FOOD INDUSTRIES — Grocery Trade*

FOOD TRADE NEWS. see *FOOD AND FOOD INDUSTRIES*

FOREIGN TRADE FAIRS NEW PRODUCTS NEWSLETTER. see *BUSINESS AND ECONOMICS — International Commerce*

658.8   UK
FRANCHISE INTERNATIONAL. 1985. 10/yr. £25 (foreign £95) (effective Jan. 1997). Franchise Development Services Ltd., Castle House, Castle Meadow, Norwich, Norfolk NR2 1PJ, England. TEL 44-1603-620301. FAX 44-1603-630174. E-mail: fds@norwich.com; URL: http://www.franchise-group.com. (Subscr. to: Rouen House, Rouen Rd., Norwich NR1 1RB) Ed. Dennis Chaplin; Pub. Roy Seaman. adv.: color page £3000 ($4500); trim 297 x 210; adv. contact: Paul Cairnie. bk.rev.; index. circ. 100,000. (back issues avail.) **Document type:** trade publication.
   Formerly (until 1993): Franchise Magazine (ISSN 0268-8395)
   Description: Provides news and on master franchise investment opportunities. Distributed to 180 countries worldwide.
   Refereed Serial

658   US
FRANCHISE NEWS. 1985. m. $315. Consultants America Corporation, 3820 Premier Ave., Memphis, TN 38118. TEL 901-368-3333. FAX 901-368-1144. Ed. R. Richey. R&P contact: R. Richey. circ. 10,000. (tabloid format) **Document type:** newsletter, trade publication.
   Description: Contains business reports, tips, law updates, and other information in the field of franchising.
   Refereed Serial

FRANCHISING RESEARCH. see *BUSINESS AND ECONOMICS*

BUSINESS AND ECONOMICS — MARKETING AND PURCHASING

341   US   ISSN 1041-7311
FRANCHISING WORLD. 1960. bi-m. $12 in U.S.; Canada $20; elsewhere $39. International Franchise Association, 1350 New York Ave., N.W., Ste. 900, Washington, DC 20005. TEL 202-628-8000. FAX 202-628-0812. TELEX 323175. Ed. Polly Larson. adv.; bibl.; stat. circ. 10,000. (also avail. in microform from UMI) **Indexed:** B.P.I.
●Also available online. Vendor(s): UMI.
—BLDSC (4032.782600); KR SourceOne; UMI.
    Former titles: Franchising Opportunities & International Franchise Association. Quarterly Legal Bulletin; International Franchise Association. Legal Bulletin (ISSN 0020-6792)
    Description: For franchisers and people interested in the industry; reports on news and trends in franchising.

FRASER'S CANADIAN TRADE DIRECTORY. see *BUSINESS AND ECONOMICS — Trade And Industrial Directories*

FREELANCERS OF NORTH AMERICA. see *PUBLISHING AND BOOK TRADE*

FRESH PRODUCE WORKSHOP. see *FOOD AND FOOD INDUSTRIES*

FRESHLINE. see *FOOD AND FOOD INDUSTRIES*

FRESNO DAILY LEGAL REPORT. see *CRIMINOLOGY AND LAW ENFORCEMENT*

658.5 659.1   US   ISSN 0046-5097
FRIDAY REPORT. 1961. w. $165 (foreign $215) (effective 1996). Hoke Communications, Inc., 224 Seventh St., Garden City, NY 11530-5771. TEL 516-746-6700. FAX 516-229-8141. Ed. Henry Hoke Jr. stat. circ. 900. (looseleaf format; back issues avail.) **Document type:** newsletter.
—CCC.
    Description: Covers the direct response advertising community; new campaigns, postal news, pertinent legislation, executive moves, new direct marketing lists, calendar of events.

658.8   US   ISSN 1057-5316
FROHLINGER'S MARKETING REPORT. 1987. bi-w. $200 (foreign $230) (effective through 1998). Marketing Strategist Communications, Ltd., 7 Coppel Dr., Tenafly, NJ 07670-2903. TEL 201-567-4447. FAX 201-568-8538. Ed. Joseph Frohlinger. bk.rev. circ. 5,000. **Document type:** newsletter.
●Also available online. Vendor(s): Information Access Co.
    Former titles (until Dec. 1990): Frohlinger's Marketing Strategist; (until Jun. 1988): Marketing Strategist (ISSN 0899-7993)
    Description: For multinational marketers, advertisers, and media firms.

FROZEN FOOD: THE INTERNATIONAL MARKET. see *FOOD AND FOOD INDUSTRIES*

FRUIT AND VEGETABLES: THE INTERNATIONAL MARKET. see *FOOD AND FOOD INDUSTRIES*

FRUIT JUICES: THE INTERNATIONAL MARKET. see *BEVERAGES*

658   UK
GALLOWAY GAZETTE AND STRANRAER NEWS. 1870. w. £21.30. Galloway Gazette Ltd., 71 Victoria St., Newton Stewart DG8 6PS, England. Ed. Alex Shand. adv.; film rev. circ. 9,580. (back issues avail.)

GARDENING: THE INTERNATIONAL MARKET. see *GARDENING AND HORTICULTURE*

658   PL   ISSN 0137-9550
GAZETA TARGOWA. 1971. m. Polish Institute of Fairs, Ul. K. Libelta 26, 61-707 Poznan, Poland. TEL 48-61-524897. FAX 48-61-526108. Ed. Kazimierz Marcinkowski; Pub. Alojzy A. Kuca. adv. contact: Krystyna Just. circ. 20,000. **Document type:** consumer publication, trade publication.

658   US   ISSN 0191-9421
GEORGIA RETAILING NEWS. 1969. m. free. Retailing Newspapers Inc., 3851 Wake Forest Rd., Decatur, GA 30034. adv. (tabloid format) **Document type:** newspaper.

GIFT BASKET REVIEW. see *ARTS AND HANDICRAFTS*

GLOBAL. see *ADVERTISING AND PUBLIC RELATIONS*

658.8   UK
GLOBAL STRATEGY 2000 SERIES. 1990. irreg. price varies. Euromonitor, 60-61 Britton St., London EC1M 5NA, England. TEL 44-171-251-8024. FAX 44-171-608-3149. E-mail: info@euromonitor.com; URL: http://www.euromonitor.com. (Addr. in N. America: Euromonitor International Inc., 122 S. Michigan Ave., Ste. 1200, Chicago, IL 60603. TEL 800-577-3876. FAX 312-922-1157) **Document type:** trade publication.
    Description: Each volume provides an in-depth analysis and forecast of a particular consumer market.

658.87   SW   ISSN 0046-6050
GOETEBORGS - KOEPMANNEN. 1941. m. SEK 10($2) Goeteborgs Koepmannafoerbund, P.O. Box 53 200, 400 15 Goeteborg 53, Sweden. Ed. Sten-Olof Palm. circ. 3,000.

658 796.352   US   ISSN 1072-1274
GOLF PRO MAGAZINE. 1988. 9/yr. $30 (effective Jan. 1995). Fairchild Fashion & Merchandising Group (Subsidiary of: Capital Cities - A B C, Inc.), 7 W. 34th St., New York, NY 10001. TEL 212-630-4199. FAX 212-630-4201. Ed. J.D. Kidd. circ. 11,000. **Document type:** trade publication.
    Formerly: Golf Pro Merchandiser (ISSN 1067-3415)
    Description: For professional on-course golf shop managers who buy and sell golf equipment, clothing, footwear and accessories.

658 352   CN   ISSN 1185-0337
GOVERNMENT BUSINESS. 1986. bi-m. Can.$18($30) Momentum Media Management, 4040 Creditview Rd., Unit 11, Box 1800, Mississauga, ON L5C 3Y8, Canada. TEL 905-813-7100. FAX 905-813-7117. E-mail: barwellj@momentummedia.com. Ed. Jay Barwell. adv.: B&W page Can.$2535, trim 8 x 11; adv. contact: Hugn Parkinson. bk.rev.; circ. 19,000 (controlled). (back issues avail.) **Document type:** trade publication.
    Formerly: Canadian Government Buyer (ISSN 0829-8629)
    Description: Examines trends, issues of government management, new products with specific government applications for administrators, facility managers and purchasers.

658   CN   ISSN 0840-870X
JL186
GOVERNMENT BUSINESS OPPORTUNITIES. (Text in English, French) 3/w. Can.$525 (foreign Can.$628.50). Canada Communication Group, 45 Sacre-Coeur Blvd., Rm. A-2411 E, Hull, PQ K1A 0S9, Canada. TEL 819-956-7864. FAX 819-956-5134. adv.: B&W page Can.$600. circ. 3,235. **Document type:** government publication.
    Formed by the 1989 merger of: Bulletin des Marches Publics (ISSN 0713-133X) & Bulletin of Business Opportunities (ISSN 0713-1321)

GOVERNMENT PRODUCT NEWS. see *PUBLIC ADMINISTRATION*

GOVERNMENT PURCHASING GUIDE. see *PUBLIC ADMINISTRATION*

GRAIN & FEED MARKETING. see *AGRICULTURE — Feed, Flour And Grain*

658   US   ISSN 8756-534X
HF5415.2
GREENBOOK; international directory of marketing research companies and services. 1963. a. $125. American Marketing Association, New York Chapter, 60 E. 42nd St., Ste. 1765, New York, NY 10165-0006. TEL 212-687-3280. FAX 212-557-9242. URL: http://www.greenbook.org. circ. 6,000. **Document type:** directory.
●Also available online.
    Description: Lists more than 2,200 marketing research companies and allied services from 90 countries.

338.4769   DK   ISSN 0907-1040
▼**GROENLAND.** Variant title: V & S Priser, Groenland. 1992. a. DKK 1680 (effective 1997). V & S Byggedata A-S, Frederikssundvej 194, DK-2700 Broenshoej, Denmark. TEL 45-38-60-77-11. FAX 45-38-60-77-44. Dir. Carl Friis Skovsen.

658   FR
GROUPE STRATEGIES. NEWSLETTER. 44/yr. Groupe Strategies, 15 bis, rue Ernest Renan, 92130 Issy-les-Moulineaux, France. TEL 40-93-01-02. FAX 40-93-01-81. TELEX 202 003. Ed. Marie-Lynn Librecht. circ. 300.

658   SP
GUIA DEL MARKETING. 1970. a. 4000 ptas. Ediciones y Estudios, S.A., Enrique Larreta 9, 28036 Madrid, Spain. TEL 91-315-98-45. FAX 91-315-56-28. Ed. Miguel de Haro. adv.; circ. 8,000 (paid). **Document type:** directory.
    Description: Guide for marketing and advertising professionals where one can find information on Spanish research institutes, advertising agencies, marketing schools, tele-sales, consultants, data banks and marketing models.

GUIA VENEZOLANA DE PUBLICIDAD Y MERCADEO. see *ADVERTISING AND PUBLIC RELATIONS*

GUIDA MARKETING. see *BUSINESS AND ECONOMICS — Trade And Industrial Directories*

658.8 338.025   GR   ISSN 1105-4964
GUIDE OF CONSUMER GOODS IN GREECE. (Text in Greek) 1978. biennial. Dr.30000($200) Report - D. Michaelidis, 8 Polytechniou, 104 33 Athens, Greece. TEL 30-1-5243-778. FAX 30-1-8222-040. Ed. Christine Shilioti; Pub. Vasso Michaelidis. R&P contact: Demetre Michaelidis. adv.: color page Dr. 650000; 230 x 300; adv. contact: Demetre Kontis. circ. 10,000 (paid). **Document type:** directory, trade publication.
    Description: Provides marketing data on the production, imports, consumption, and advertising of important consumer brands and lists the suppliers of these products.

GUIDELINES. see *COMMUNICATIONS — Telephone And Telegraph*

H C J COMMUNICATIONS REPORT. see *POLITICAL SCIENCE — International Relations*

658   US   ISSN 0746-9985
H S M A I MARKETING REVIEW. 1982. q. $20. Hospitality Sales and Marketing Association International, 1300 L St., Ste. 800, N.W., Washington, DC 20005. TEL 202-789-0089. FAX 202-765-0027. Ed. Ilsa Whittemore; Pub. Neil Ostergren. R&P contact: Ilsa Whittemore. adv. contact: Neil Ostergren. circ. 6,500. **Indexed:** Art.Hosp.& Tour., Lod.Restr.& Tour.Ind. **Document type:** trade publication.
    Formerly: H S M A Marketing Review (ISSN 0744-9011)

381 658   SW   ISSN 0345-4746
H T F - TIDNINGEN. 1930. 18/yr. SEK 180. (Handelstjaenstemannafoerbundet) Svenska Handelstjaenstemannafoerbundet, P.O. Box 30102, S-104 25 Stockholm, Sweden. TEL 46-8-737-80-00. Ed. Carl von Scheele. adv. circ. 143,100. cols./p.: 4; pp./issue: 32.

HAIR CARE PRODUCTS: THE INTERNATIONAL MARKET. see *BEAUTY CULTURE*

HANDBOOK OF MAGAZINE PRODUCTION. see *PUBLISHING AND BOOK TRADE*

658   JA
HANDBOOK OF MARKETING. a. Nihon Keizai Shimbun, Inc., 1-9-5 Ote-machi, Chiyoda-ku, Tokyo 100-66, Japan. TEL 81-3-3270-0251. FAX 81-3-5255-2661. TELEX J22308 NIKKEI. **Document type:** trade publication.
    Description: Provides detailed explanations of changes in the distribution industry during the year.

658   SZ
HANDEL HEUTE. 1978. 6/yr. 38.50 SFr. Handel Heute Verlags AG, Industriestr. 5, CH-3178 Boesingen, Switzerland. TEL 031-7479696. FAX 031-7479843. Ed. Ruedi Naef; Pub. Urs Bodmer. adv. contact: Walter Egli. bk.rev.; tr.lit. circ. 38,500. **Document type:** trade publication.
    Description: Trends and news of the international retail business.

HARDWARE MERCHANDISING. see *BUILDING AND CONSTRUCTION — Hardware*

HARDWARE RETAILER. see *BUILDING AND CONSTRUCTION — Hardware*

BUSINESS AND ECONOMICS — MARKETING AND PURCHASING

HEALTH & FITNESS BUSINESS. see *PHYSICAL FITNESS AND HYGIENE*

HEALTHCARE COMMUNITY RELATIONS & MARKETING LETTER. see *MEDICAL SCIENCES*

HEARTH & HOME; the magazine of specialty retailing. see *ENERGY*

658 US ISSN 1083-1428
HELLER REPORT: INTERNET STRATEGIES FOR EDUCATION MARKETS. m. $397. Nelson B. Heller & Associates, 1910 1st St., Ste 303, Highland Park, IL 60035-3146. TEL 847-441-2920. FAX 847-926-0202. E-mail: info@hellerreports.com. Ed. Anne Wujcik.
  Description: News and analysis of business opportunities in online content, hardware, software and services.

371.2 US ISSN 1047-5230
HELLER REPORT ON EDUCATION TECHNOLOGY AND TELECOMMUNICATIONS MARKETS. 1989. m. $395. Nelson B. Heller & Associates, 1910 1st St. Ste 303, Highland Park, IL 60035-3146. TEL 847-441-2920. FAX 847-926-0202. E-mail: info@hellerreports.com. Ed. Reida Oates; Pub. Nelson Heller. (back issues avail.)
  ●Also available online. Vendor(s): NewsNet (ED11).
  —CCC.

658 US
HI-TECH BUYERS GUIDE. 1946. a. $39.95. Directories of Industry, Inc., P.O. Box 456, Corona DelMar, CA 92625. TEL 714-792-1090. FAX 714-792-1095. adv. circ. 32,000. **Document type:** directory.
  Former titles: E I A Guide (ISSN 0070-7821); Western Industrial Purchasing Guide and Electronic - Sources.

HILDEBRANDT REPORT; a management and marketing newsletter for law firms. see *LAW*

HOME FURNISHINGS EXECUTIVE. see *INTERIOR DESIGN AND DECORATION — Furniture And House Furnishings*

HOME SCHOOL MARKET GUIDE; how to sell audiocassettes, books, educational toys and games, software programs, videos and other educational products to the home schoolmarket. see *EDUCATION*

HOMECARE. see *MEDICAL SCIENCES — Nurses And Nursing*

HOMECARE MONDAY. see *MEDICAL SCIENCES — Nurses And Nursing*

658 US
HONG KONG DIRECTORY TO 10,000 EXPORTERS & IMPORTERS. 1986. biennial. $155 includes updates. Howard Spriggle Publishers, Box 550, Ocean View, DE 19970-9801. Ed. Ken Wood. circ. 500. (also avail. in diskette format) **Document type:** directory.
  Formerly (until 1987): Hong Kong Bargain Guide to Factory Outlets.

658.8 US ISSN 1052-8733
HOSPITAL REVENUE REPORT. 1983. 25/yr. $379. United Communications Group, 11300 Rockville Pike, Ste. 1100, Rockville, MD 20852-3030. TEL 301-961-8777. FAX 301-816-8945. Ed. Lori Launi.
  —CCC.
  Incorporates (in 1990): Health Care Marketer (ISSN 0896-1204); Which incorporated (1985 - Sep. 1987): Urgent Care Business Report (ISSN 0883-8712); Health Care Marketer was formerly (until 1986): Health Care Marketer and Target Market (ISSN 0884-6596); Which incorporated: Cost Containment (ISSN 0198-9872).
  Description: Describes the necessary steps to designing and implementing specific marketing campaigns. Covers projections on costs and the response of patients and businesses.

HOT DRINKS: THE INTERNATIONAL MARKET. see *BEVERAGES*

658 668 US ISSN 0090-8878
HD9999.S7 CODEN: HPPIAB
HOUSEHOLD & PERSONAL PRODUCTS INDUSTRY; the magazine for the detergent, soap, cosmetic and toiletry, wax, polish and aerosol industries. Short title: H A P P I. 1964. m. $48 (Canada & Mexico $52; all others $64). Rodman Publications, Inc., 17 S. Franklin Trnpk., Ramsey, NJ 07446. TEL 201-825-2552. FAX 201-825-0553. Ed. Hamilton Carson. adv. contact: Matthew Montgomery. bk.rev.; charts; illus.; pat.; stat.; tr.lit.; tr.mk.; index. circ. 17,000. **Indexed:** Chem.Abstr., Curr.Pack.Abstr., Excerp.Med., PROMT. **Document type:** trade publication.
  —BLDSC (4334.880000); CASDDS; SWETS. **CCC**.
  Formerly: Detergents and Specialties (ISSN 0011-958X)

HOUSEHOLD CLEANING AGENTS: THE INTERNATIONAL MARKET. see *CLEANING AND DYEING*

HOUSEWARES CANADA. see *INTERIOR DESIGN AND DECORATION — Furniture And House Furnishings*

HOUSEWARES: THE INTERNATIONAL MARKET. see *INTERIOR DESIGN AND DECORATION — Furniture And House Furnishings*

658.8 HU ISSN 0237-1553
HC267.A2
HUNGARIAN BUSINESS HERALD. (Text in English, German) 1969. q. $17.50. Magyar Kereskedelmi Kamara, Kossuth L. ter 6-8, 1055 Budapest, Hungary. (Co-sponsor: Orszagos Piackutato Intezet) Ed. Gerd Biro. circ. 4,000. **Indexed:** Key to Econ.Sci., PROMT.
  Formerly (until 1985): Marketing in Hungary (ISSN 0025-3731)

338.4769 DK ISSN 0904-3632
HUSBYGNING BRUTTO. Variant title: V og S Priser, Husbygning Brutto. 1974. a. DKK 1310 (effective 1997). V & S Byggedata A-S, Frederikssundvej 194, DK-2700 Broenshoej, Denmark. TEL 45-38-60-77-11. FAX 45-38-60-77-44.
  Formerly (until 1989): V og S Priser, Husbygning (ISSN 0105-4201)

338.436 DK ISSN 0904-3624
HUSBYGNING NETTO. Variant title: V & S Priser, Husbygning Netto. 1987. a. DKK 1310 (effective 1997). V & S Byggedata A-S, Frederikssundvej 194, DK-2700 Broenshoej, Denmark. TEL 45-38-60-77-11. FAX 45-38-60-77-44. Dir. Carl Friis Skovsen.
  Formerly (until 1989): V og S Priser, Netto (ISSN 0902-2791)

HYPERMARKETS AND SUPERSTORES: THE INTERNATIONAL MARKET. see *FOOD AND FOOD INDUSTRIES — Grocery Trade*

658 660 UK
▼**I A L GLOBAL MARKET REPORT - METALLOCENES PATH TO THE FUTURE.** 1996. irreg. £850. I A L Consultants, 109 Uxbridge Rd., Ealing, London W5 5TL, England. TEL 44-181-810-0919. FAX 44-181-566-4931. **Document type:** trade publication.

658 US
I E G SPONSORSHIP REPORT; the international newsletter of event sponsorship and lifestyle marketing. 1982. bi-w. $390 (Canada & Mexico $410; elsewhere $465) (effective 1997). International Events Group, Inc., 640 N. LaSalle, Ste. 600, Chicago, IL 60610. TEL 312-944-1727. FAX 312-944-1897. E-mail: ieg@sponsorship.com; URL: http://www.sponsorship.com. Ed. Lesa Ukman; Pub. Jon Ukman. R&P contact: Jon Ukman. adv. contact: Meg Pound. index. circ. 12,000. (back issues avail.) **Document type:** directory, newsletter.
  Formerly: Special Events Report.
  Description: Presents case studies and quantitative analysis along with breaking news, positions available and agency action.

658 394.2 US
GT3930
I E G SPONSORSHIP SOURCEBOOK. 1984. a. $199 (Canada & Mexico $214; elsewhere $226) (effective 1997). International Events Group, Inc., 640 N. LaSalle, Ste. 600, Chicago, IL 60610. TEL 312-944-1727. FAX 312-944-1897. E-mail: ieg@sponsorship.com; URL: http://www.sponsorship.com. Ed. Lesa Ukman; Pub. Jon Ukman. adv. contact: Meg Pound. circ. 5,000. (also avail. in diskette format) **Document type:** directory.
  Former titles (until 1994): I E G Directory of Sponsorship Marketing (ISSN 1058-613X); (until 1990): Official (Year) Directory of Festivals, Sports and Special Events (ISSN 0894-0649); (until 1987): Official International Directory of Special Events and Festivals (ISSN 0743-4170)
  Description: Sourcebook on international events like the America's Cup and Los Angeles Marathon to regional crowd pleasers such as the Texas State Fair and Miami's Calle Ocho. Covers attendance, budget, sponsors and contacts of approximately 3,000 events, and lists suppliers and organizations that fuel the business.

658.7 US ISSN 0019-8285
TJ1
I E N: INDUSTRIAL EQUIPMENT NEWS; what's new in equipment, parts, materials. 1933. m. (free to qualified personnel). Thomas Publishing Company, Five Penn Plaza, 250 W. 34th St., New York, NY 10001. TEL 212-629-1551. Ed. Larry Burnstein. adv.: B&W page $15020. illus.; tr.lit. circ. 208,170. (also avail. in microform from UMI; reprint service avail. from UMI) **Indexed:** Br.Ceram.Abstr. **Document type:** trade publication.
  —Linda Hall.
  Description: Update on new industrial equipment.

658 SZ
I H A NEWS. q. I H A Institut fuer Marktanalysen, Obermattweg 9, CH-6052 Hergiswil, Switzerland. TEL 041-959111. FAX 041-959123. Ed. P. Hofer. circ. 10,000. **Document type:** trade publication.

658 RM ISSN 1221-6992
I M A S BULLETIN. 1991. m.? $196. Institutul de Marketing si Sondaje - Institute for Marketing and Public Opinion Polls, C.P. 56-52, 77750 Bucharest, Rumania.

658 IE ISSN 0791-6809
I M J - IRISH MARKETING JOURNAL. 1974. m. £75. Irish Marketing Journal, 31 Stillorgan Industrial Estate, Stillorgan, Co. Dublin, Ireland. TEL 01-2950088. FAX 01-2950089. Ed. Norman Barry. adv. contact: Kathy Moynihan. bk.rev.; illus. circ. 5,200. (tabloid format; back issues avail.) **Document type:** trade publication.

658 330 US
I N T I X NEWSLETTER. 1981. 8/yr. membership. International Ticketing Association, 250 W. 57th St., Ste. 722, New York, NY 10107. TEL 212-581-0600. FAX 212-581-0885. E-mail: info@intix.org. Ed. Patricia Spira. R&P contact: Patricia Spira. adv. contact: Patricia Spira. circ. 1,400 (controlled). **Document type:** newsletter.
  Formerly: B O M I Newsletter (ISSN 1071-6254)
  Description: Covers customer service, marketing, survey results, use of credit cards, and software for the ticketing industry worldwide.

658.8 659.1 SP ISSN 0214-7459
I.P. MARK. (Informacion de Publicidad y Marketing) 1962. 20/yr. 20000 ptas. (foreign 35000 ptas.) (effective 1995). Ediciones y Estudios, S.A. (Eyesa), Enrique Larreta 9-1o, 28036 Madrid, Spain. TEL 34-1-7339114. FAX 34-1-3157419. Ed. Manuel Carbado. adv.: page 275000 ptas.; adv. contact: Pilar Ramirez. bk.rev. circ. 5,500.
  —CINDOC.
  Formerly (until 1973): I.P. Informacion de la Publicidad (ISSN 0214-7483)
  Description: Contains advertising news, reports on advertising communications, public relations, services, launching of new products and campaigns.

I T COST MANAGEMENT SOURCEBOOK. see *COMPUTERS — Electronic Data Processing*

BUSINESS AND ECONOMICS — MARKETING AND PURCHASING

658   **UK**
I T MARKETING SOURCE BOOK. 1994. irreg. £75 (effective 1996). V N U Business Publications Ltd., 32-34 Broadwick St., London W1A 2HG, England. TEL 44-171-316-9000. FAX 44-171-316-9620. Ed. Peter Chare; Pub. Melanie Williams. adv. **Document type:** directory.
    Description: Guide to marketing in computer industry providing specialist help for sales and marketing professionals.

ICE CREAM, YOGHURTS AND CHILLED DESSERTS: THE INTERNATIONAL MARKET. see *FOOD AND FOOD INDUSTRIES*

658   **SZ**
IDEE A'JOUR. 10/yr. Vereinigung fuer Werbekommunikation, Froebelstr. 33, CH-8032 Zurich, Switzerland. Ed. Fridolin Kretz. circ. 3,000. **Document type:** bulletin.

338 658   **US**   **ISSN 1077-3045**
I'M TOO BUSY TO READ MARKETING REPORT SERVICE. 1992. m. $149 (foreign $169) (effective 1996). Win - Win Marketing, 662 Crestview Dr., San Jose, CA 95117. TEL 408-247-0122. FAX 408-249-5754. E-mail: towin@aol.com. Ed. Frankie Kangas. bk.rev. (back issues avail.) **Document type:** newsletter.
    Formerly (until 1994): Win - Win Marketing Newsletter for Small Business (ISSN 1063-5904)
    Description: Covers advertising, sales, public relations, and customer relations.

IMPORT CAR PRICES. see *TRANSPORTATION — Automobiles*

IN-CAR ENTERTAINMENT: THE INTERNATIONAL MARKET. see *ELECTRONICS*

IN-REGISTER NEWSLETTER. see *PRINTING*

658.85   **US**
INCENTIVE; managing & marketing through motivation. 1905. m. $48 (foreign $75). Bill Communications, Inc., 355 Park Ave. S., 5th Fl., New York, NY 10010-1789. TEL 212-592-6200. FAX 212-592-6339. Ed. Jennifer Juergens. adv.: B&W page $6330, color page $7240. circ. 40,050. (reprint service avail.) **Indexed:** ABI Inform., Bus.Ind., SRI. **Document type:** trade publication.
    ●Also available online. Vendor(s): UMI.
    —UMI; UnCover. CCC.
    Formerly (until 1988): Incentive Marketing (ISSN 0019-3364); Which incorporated: Incentive Travel.
    Description: Serves executives responsible for incentive programs geared to motivate employees, customers and dealers.

658   **GW**   **ISSN 0933-7849**
INCENTIVE JOURNAL; magazine for motivation and sales promotion. 1986. 4/yr. DM.85. E C - GmbH, Schulstr. 64, 65719 Hofheim, Germany. TEL 49-6192-39007. FAX 49-6192-39049. Ed. Gerald W. Huft. adv.: B&W page DM.4980, color page DM.6980; trim 190 x 265. bk.rev. circ. 12,000. (back issues avail.) **Document type:** consumer publication.
    Description: Examines incentives, motivation, sales promotion and meetings and congresses.

INCOME IN SALES - MARKETING MANAGEMENT. see *BUSINESS AND ECONOMICS — Labor And Industrial Relations*

658.8   **NE**
INCREASE YOUR SALES VOLUME; for businessmen and opportunity seekers. (Text in English) 1980. bi-m. fl.50($15) International Business & Information Services, Beukelsdijk 9a, 3021 AA Rotterdam, Netherlands. Ed. Roy K. Benschop. adv.; bk.rev.

658.8   **II**   **ISSN 0019-5316**
INDIAN JOURNAL OF MARKETING; journal of marketing, advertisement and sales management. (Text in English) 1968. m. Rs.60($25) Associated Management Consultants (P) Ltd., Y-21 Hauz Khas, New Delhi 110019, India. Ed. J. Gilani. adv.; bk.rev.; charts; stat. circ. 2,500.

658.5   **US**   **ISSN 0019-8153**
TJ1   **CODEN: INDDAZ**
INDUSTRIAL DISTRIBUTION; for industrial distributors and their sales personnel. 1911. m. $79.90 (Canada $104.90; Mexico $99.90; elsewhere $159.90). Cahners Publishing Company (Newton), Division of Reed Elsevier Inc., 275 Washington St., Newton, MA 02158-1630. TEL 617-558-4564. FAX 617-558-4677. E-mail: feedback@manufacturing.net; URL: http://www.manufacturing.net/magazine.id/. (Subscr to: 8773 S. Ridgeline Blvd., Highlands Ranch, CO 80126. TEL 303-470-4000) Ed. John J. Keough; Pub. Russell A. Piersons. R&P contact: John Keough. adv.: B&W page $6800, color page $8650; trim 7 7/8 x 10 1/2. bk.rev.; charts; illus.; mkt.; stat.; tr.lit.; index. circ. 42,000. (also avail. in microform; microfiche from CIS; reprint service avail. from UMI) **Indexed:** ABI Inform., B.P.I., BPIA, Bus.Ind., Manage.Cont., SRI, SRI, Tr.& Indus.Ind. **Document type:** trade publication.
    ●Also available online. Vendor(s): Information Access Co., Knight-Ridder Information, Inc.
    —BLDSC (4450.200000); Ei; KR SourceOne; Linda Hall; UMI; UnCover. CCC.
    Formerly: Industrial Distribution Marketplace.
    Description: For general line, specialist and combination industrial distributor firms. Provides how-to information and industry news, with an emphasis on increasing sales and profits.

658.7   **UK**   **ISSN 0019-8277**
INDUSTRIAL EQUIPMENT NEWS. 1951. m. £65 (foreign £80) (effective 1997). Nexus Media Ltd., Nexus House, Azalea Dr., Swanley, Kent BR8 8HY, England. TEL 44-1322-660070. FAX 44-1322-667633. Ed. Dawn Frosdick-Hopley. R&P contact: Dawn Frosdick-Hopley. adv. contact: Roy Kemp. bk.rev.; film rev.; illus.; mkt.; stat. circ. 39,721. (also avail. in microform from UMI; back issues avail.; reprint service avail. from UMI) **Indexed:** Agri.Eng.Abstr., BMT, Copper Abstr., Curr.Pack.Abstr., Fluidex, Tr.& Indus.Ind. **Document type:** trade publication.

INDUSTRIAL MACHINE TRADER. see *MACHINERY*

658.83   **US**   **ISSN 0019-8501**
HF5415.12.E8   **CODEN: IMMADX**
INDUSTRIAL MARKETING MANAGEMENT; the international journal of marketing for industrial and high tech firms. 1971. bi-m. fl.743($427) (effective 1998). Elsevier Science Inc., Box 945, New York, NY 10159-0945. TEL 212-633-3730. FAX 212-633-3680. TELEX 420643 AEP UI. E-mail: usinfo-f@elsevier.com; URL: http://www.elsevier.nl:80/inca/publications/store/5/0/7/2/0/505720.pub.shtml. (Subscr. outside the Americas to: Elsevier Science, Regional Sales Office, P.O. Box 211, 1000 AE Amsterdam, Netherlands. TEL 31-20-4853757. FAX 31-20-4853432; Subscr. in Australasia and the Far East to: Elsevier Science (Singapore) Pte Ltd, No.1 Temasek Ave., No.17-01 Millenia Tower, Singapore 039192, Singapore. TEL 65-434-3727. FAX 65-337-2230; Subscr. in Japan to: Elsevier Science Japan, 9-15 Higashi-Azabu 1-chome, Minato-ku, Tokyo 106, Japan. TEL 81-3-5561-5033. FAX 81-3-5561-5047) Ed. James Hlavacek. illus. (also avail. in microform from UMI; reprint service avail. from SWZ) **Indexed:** ABI Inform., Account.& Data Proc.Abstr., ASCA, B.P.I., BPIA, Bus.Ind., Cont.Pg.Manage., Curr.Cont., Intl.Mgmt.Info, Key to Econ.Sci., Manage.Abstr., Manage.Cont., Mgmt.& Market.Abstr., Risk Abstr., SCIMP, SSCI. **Document type:** academic/scholarly publication.
    —BLDSC (4457.750000); Genuine Article; KR SourceOne; SWETS; UMI; UnCover. CCC.
    Description: Provides in-depth case studies geared to the needs of managers, executives and professionals.
Refereed Serial

658.7   **US**   **ISSN 0019-8641**
INDUSTRIAL PURCHASING AGENT. 1956. m. $25. Publications for Industry, 21 Russell Woods Rd., Great Neck, NY 11021. TEL 516-487-0990. FAX 516-487-0809. Ed. Pearl Shaine Panes. adv.: B&W page $2087; trim 10 3/8 x 14 1/4. bk.rev.; film rev.; charts; illus.; stat.; tr.lit. circ. 25,000. (reprint service avail. from UMI) **Document type:** trade publication.
    Description: New product releases with or without photos for largest U.S. industrial concerns.

658.8   **UK**
INDUSTRIAL SELLING. 1980. q. membership. Institute of Industrial Selling, c/o European Marketing Association, 18 St. Peters Steps, Brixham, Devon, England. (Co-sponsors: Industrial Marketing Association, Sales Section; European Marketing Association, Selling Division) Ed. P. Allen. R&P contact: P. Allen. bk.rev. **Document type:** abstracting/indexing, newspaper, trade publication.
Refereed Serial

INDUSTRY WORLD. see *BEVERAGES*

INFO PRESSE COMMUNICATIONS; le seul magazine d'affaires francophones des communications au Canada. see *ADVERTISING AND PUBLIC RELATIONS*

658   **US**   **ISSN 1058-0344**
INFOMERCIAL MARKETING REPORT. 1991. m. $395 (Canada $435; elsewhere $445) (effective 1997 & 1998). Steven Dworman & Associates, 11533 Thurston Circle, Los Angeles, CA 90049. TEL 310-472-5253. FAX 310-472-6004. E-mail: clarkkent@aol.com; daliplanet@aol.com. Ed. Steve Dworman; Pub. Steve Dworman. R&P contact: Sandee Richardson. adv. contact: Sandee Richardson. bk.rev. circ. 3,000. (back issues avail.) **Document type:** newsletter.
    Description: Deals with all the behind-the-scenes-activities of the infomercial industry with quarterly media figures and an annual list of the top ten grossing infomercials.

658   **SZ**
INFORMATION FUER DEN KAUFMAENNISCHEN LEHRLING. m. Gerenstr. 16, CH-9400 Rorschach, Switzerland. Ed. W. Kurz. circ. 4,500.

INFORMATION SOLUTIONS; a newsletter of ideas and techniques about how to profit from information. see *BUSINESS AND ECONOMICS — Management*

INFORMATION SYSTEMS SPENDING; an analysis of trends and strategies. see *COMPUTERS — Electronic Data Processing*

658   **GW**   **ISSN 0940-7707**
INFORMATIONEN FUER DEN VERKAUFS INNENDIENST. (Text in Dutch, French and German) 1975. m. DM.237.60. Verlag Norbert Mueller AG und Co. KG, Ingolstaedterstr. 20, 80807 Munich, Germany. TEL 49-89-3509302. FAX 49-89-35093218. Ed. Hilger Veenema. circ. 2,500. (back issues avail.) **Document type:** trade publication.

INFORMATIONSDIENST GROSS- UND AUSSENHANDEL. see *BUSINESS AND ECONOMICS — International Commerce*

INLINE RETAILER & INDUSTRY NEWS. see *SPORTS AND GAMES*

INNOVATIVE LEADER; monthly tool to increase creativity and productivity. see *TECHNOLOGY: COMPREHENSIVE WORKS*

INSIDE SPORTING GOODS. see *SPORTS AND GAMES*

659.1 658   **US**
Z479
INTERACTIVE MARKETING & P R NEWS. 1994. bi-w. $495 (foreign $530) (effective 1996). Phillips Business Information, Inc., 1201 Seven Locks Rd., Potomac, MD 20854. TEL 301-424-3338. FAX 301-309-3847. E-mail: pbi@phillips.com. Ed. Diane Schwartz. bk.rev. (back issues avail.) **Document type:** newsletter.
    Formerly (until 1997): Interactive Marketing News (ISSN 1078-6821); Which incorporates (1996-1997): Interactive P R News (ISSN 1091-9090); (in 1995): Interactive Marketplace Regulatory Handbook (ISSN 1061-6780); Interactive Facts; Libby Direct Marketing Letter; Publishing Trends and Trendsetters; Which was formerly (1978-1991): Media Management Monographs (ISSN 0192-7663).
    Description: Provides news and advice on using interactive advertising and marketing.

384.55 US ISSN 1076-4526
TK6655.V5
INTERACTIVE VIDEO NEWS. 1991. bi-w. £697 (foreign $730) (effective 1997). Phillips Business Information, Inc., 1201 Seven Locks Rd., Potomac, MD 20854. TEL 301-424-3338. FAX 301-309-3847. E-mail: pbi@phillips.com. stat. (looseleaf format; back issues avail.) **Document type:** newsletter.
●Also available online. Vendor(s): Information Access Co., NewsNet (AD07).
—CCC.
Formed by the 1994 merger of: Video Services News (ISSN 1067-3849) & Video Marketing Newsletter (ISSN 0196-4429); **Incorporates in 1994:** On-Demand Video; **Incorporates (1989-1992):** Video News International (ISSN 1044-6354); (in 1990): Home Video Publisher (ISSN 0748-0822); Which **supersedes in part:** Home Video and Cable Report; **Incorporates (1970-1985):** VideoNews (ISSN 0145-9023); Which **incorporates (1971-1981):** Videocassette and CATV Newsletter; Which was **formerly:** Video Cassette Newsletter (ISSN 0049-6243).

658 US ISSN 1073-662X
HF1040.8
INTERNATIONAL CLOSEOUT DIRECTORY (YEAR); comprehensive buyers' reference. a. $100. Closeout Network, Box 707, Cherry Hill, NJ 08003-0707. **Document type:** directory.
Description: Lists more than 4,000 manufacturers, wholesalers, and importers who can provide closeout merchandise to retailers.

INTERNATIONAL JOURNAL OF ADVERTISING; the quarterly review of marketing communications. see ADVERTISING AND PUBLIC RELATIONS

INTERNATIONAL JOURNAL OF BANK MARKETING. see BUSINESS AND ECONOMICS — Banking And Finance

658.7 US ISSN 1055-6001
HF5437.A2 CODEN: JOPUAS
INTERNATIONAL JOURNAL OF PURCHASING & MATERIALS MANAGEMENT. (Text in English; summaries in French, German, Spanish) 1965. q. $59 (foreign $69). National Association of Purchasing Management, 2055 E. Centennial Circle, Box 22160, Tempe, AZ 85285-2160. TEL 602-752-6276. FAX 602-752-7890. URL: http://www.napm.org/pub/ijpmm.html. Ed. Phil Carter. R&P contact: Elizabeth M. O'Neall. bk.rev.; charts; illus.; index. circ. 3,000. (also avail. in microform from UMI; back issues avail. from UMI; reprint service avail. from SCH) **Indexed:** ABI Inform., Anbar, ASEAN Manage.Abstr., B.P.I, BPIA, Bus.Ind., Comput.Lit.Ind., Cont.Pg.Manage., Data Process.Dig., Intl.Mgmt.Info., Manage.Cont., Mgmt.& Market.Abstr., Tr.& Indus.Ind. **Document type:** academic/scholarly publication.
●Also available online. Vendor(s): Information Access Co., Knight-Ridder Information, Inc., UMI.
—BLDSC (4542.509400); KR SourceOne; SWETS; UMI; UnCover.
Former titles (until 1991): Journal of Purchasing and Materials Management (ISSN 0094-8594); Journal of Purchasing (ISSN 0022-4030)

658 NE ISSN 0167-8116
CODEN: IJRME6
INTERNATIONAL JOURNAL OF RESEARCH IN MARKETING. 1984. 5/yr. fl.735($422) (effective 1998). (European Marketing Academy) North-Holland (Subsidiary of: Elsevier Science B.V.), P.O. Box 211, 1000 AE Amsterdam, Netherlands. TEL 31-20-4853911. FAX 31-20-4853598. TELEX 18582 ESPA NL. URL: http://www.elsevier.nl:80/inca/publications/store/5/0/5/5/5/0/505550.pub.shtml. (Subscr. in the Americas to: Elsevier Science, Regional Sales Office, Box 945, New York, NY 10159-0945. TEL 212-633-3730. FAX 212-633-3680; Subscr. in Australasia and the Far East to: Elsevier Science (Singapore) Pte Ltd, No.1 Temasek Ave., No.17-01 Millenia Tower, Singapore 039192, Singapore. TEL 65-434-3727. FAX 65-337-2230; Subscr. in Japan to: Elsevier Science Japan, 9-15 Higashi-Azabu 1-chome, Minato-ku Tokyo 106, Japan. TEL 81-3-5561-5033. FAX 81-3-5561-5047) Ed. P. van den Abeele. adv.; bk.rev.; bibl.; charts. circ. 800. (also avail. in microform from UMI; back issues avail.; reprint service avail. from SWZ) **Indexed:** ABI Inform., Cont.Pg.Manage., Mark.Res.Abstr. (1984-), SCIMP (1985-). **Document type:** academic/scholarly publication.
—BLDSC (4542.535000); SWETS; UMI; UnCover. CCC.
Description: Communicates developments in marketing theory and thought, and results of empirical research.
Refereed Serial

658 UK ISSN 0959-0552
HF5429 CODEN: IRDMEQ
INTERNATIONAL JOURNAL OF RETAIL & DISTRIBUTION MANAGEMENT. 1986. 11/yr. £2879($4449) (foreign Aus.$5599) (effective 1998). M C B University Press Ltd., 60-62 Toller Ln., Bradford, W. Yorks BD8 9BY, England. TEL 44-1274-777700. FAX 44-1274-785200. TELEX 51317-MCBUNI-G. URL: http://www.mcb.co.uk. Ed. John Fernie. cum.index. (reprint service avail. from SWZ) **Indexed:** ABI Inform., Anbar, Cont.Pg.Manage., INSPEC (1990-), Mgmt.& Market.Abstr. **Document type:** academic/scholarly publication.
●Also available online. Vendor(s): Information Access Co.
Also available on CD-ROM.
—BLDSC (4542.537800); AskIEEE; KR SourceOne; SWETS; UMI. CCC.
Formerly: International Journal of Retailing (ISSN 0268-3903)
Description: Provides the directives needed to achieve success in a highly competitive field. Covers transnational developments, retailer-manufacturer relationships, management issues, and environmental and land use planning.

658 UK ISSN 0969-2495
INTERNATIONAL MARKETING; trade magazine for buyers of tax and duty-free goods. 1993. 10/yr. £65 (foreign £98) (effective 1997). Quest Magazines Ltd., Publishing House, 652 Victoria Rd., South Ruislip, Mddx. HA4 OSX, England. TEL 44-181-842-1010. FAX 44-181-841-2557. Ed. Veronica Simpson; Pub. Damian Riley-Smith. circ. 5,000. **Document type:** trade publication.

INTERNATIONAL MARKETING DATA AND STATISTICS (YEAR). see BUSINESS AND ECONOMICS — Abstracting, Bibliographies, Statistics

658 UK ISSN 0265-1335
HF1416
INTERNATIONAL MARKETING REVIEW. 1983. bi-m. £2559($3959) (foreign Aus.$4989) (effective 1998). M C B University Press Ltd., 60-62 Toller Ln., Bradford, W. Yorks BD8 9BY, England. TEL 44-1274-777700. FAX 44-1274-785200. TELEX 51317-MCBUNI-G. URL: http://www.mcb.co.uk/cgi-bin/mcb_serve/table1&imr&journal.html. Ed. Angela Rushton. adv.; bk.rev.; abstr.; charts; cum.index. circ. 900. (back issues avail.; reprint service avail. from SWZ) **Indexed:** ABI Inform., Cont.Pg.Manage., Mgmt.& Market.Abstr., SCIMP (1986-). **Document type:** academic/scholarly publication.
●Also available on CD-ROM.
—BLDSC (4543.976250); SWETS; UMI; UnCover. CCC.
Incorporates: Industrial Marketing and Purchasing (ISSN 0268-3911)
Description: Provides information about the latest developments in global marketing for practitioners, academics and students.

INTERNATIONAL NEW PRODUCT REPORT. see FOOD AND FOOD INDUSTRIES — Grocery Trade

INTERNATIONAL NEWSPAPER ADVERTISING AND MARKETING EXECUTIVES. SALES AND IDEA BOOK. see ADVERTISING AND PUBLIC RELATIONS

338.4 640.73 658.8 US ISSN 1086-1238
INTERNATIONAL PRODUCT ALERT. 1983. s-m. $600 (effective 1997). Marketing Intelligence Service Ltd., 6473D State Rt. 64, Naples, NY 14512-9726. TEL 716-374-6326. FAX 716-374-5217. E-mail: mktgintelsvc@cis.compuserve.com; URL: http://ourworld.compuserve.com/homepages/mktgintelsvc. Ed. Kim Cruise. index. (back issues avail.) **Document type:** newsletter.
●Also available online. Vendor(s): CompuServe, Inc., Data-Star, Dow Jones News Retrieval, Information Access Co., Knight-Ridder Information, Inc. (File no. 9), NewsNet (AD25).
Description: Reports new product launches throughout twenty countries overseas. Includes coverage of foods, beverages, health and beauty aids, household and pet products.

658 UK ISSN 0959-3969
HF5428
INTERNATIONAL REVIEW OF RETAIL, DISTRIBUTION AND CONSUMER RESEARCH. 1990. q. £80 (foreign $135) to individuals; institutions £175 (foreign $295); print & online eds. combined £210 (foreign $355) (effective 1998). Thomson Professional (Subsidiary of: International Thomson Publishing Group), 2-6 Boundary Row, London SE1 8HN, England. TEL 44-171-865-0066. FAX 44-171-522-9621. E-mail: journal@rapidcom.co.uk; URL: http://rdcr.thomsonprofessional.com. (Subscr. to: ITPS Ltd., Cheriton House, Andover, Hants SP10 5BE, England. TEL 44-1264-342713. FAX 44-1264-342807) Eds. John Dawson, Leigh Sparks. adv. contact: Gemma Heiseer. circ. 550. (back issues avail.) **Indexed:** Cont.Pg.Manage., Geo.Abstr. **Document type:** academic/scholarly publication.
●Also available online.
—BLDSC (4547.630000). CCC.
Description: Provides an international forum for theoretical research and reflection on practice for both retailing scholars and retailing professionals.
Refereed Serial

658 NE ISSN 0923-6716
INTERNATIONAL SERIES IN QUANTITATIVE MARKETING. (Text in English) 1989. irreg., vol.5, 1993. price varies. Kluwer Academic Publishers, Postbus 17, 3300 AA Dordrecht, Netherlands. TEL 31-78-6392392. FAX 31-78-6392254. TELEX 29245 KAPG NL. E-mail: services@wkap.nl; URL: http://www.wkap.nl. (Dist. by: Kluwer Academic Publishers Group, P.O. Box 322, 3300 AH Dordrecht, Netherlands. TEL 31-78-6392392. FAX 31-78-6546474; N. America dist. addr.: Box 358, Accord Sta., Hingham, MA 02018-0358. TEL 617-871-6600. FAX 617-871-6528) **Document type:** monographic series.
Refereed Serial

INTERNATIONAL TRADESHOW DIRECTORY. see BUSINESS AND ECONOMICS — Trade And Industrial Directories

658.8 US
INTERNATIONAL VENDING BUYER'S GUIDE AND DIRECTORY. 1946. a. $25 (effective 1997). Vending Times, Inc., 1375 Broadway, 6th Fl., New York, NY 10018-7001. TEL 212-302-4700. FAX 212-221-3311. Ed. Timothy Sanford. R&P contact: Victor Lavay. adv. contact: Steve Zarolnick. circ. 16,500. **Document type:** directory.
Incorporates: Vending Buyer's Guide.

658 GW ISSN 0170-3625
INTERNATIONALE BEITRAEGE ZUR MARKT-, MEINUNGS- UND ZUKUNFTSFORSCHUNG. 1972. irreg., vol.51. price varies. Wickert Institute Tuebingen, 89281 Altenstadt, Germany. adv.; bk.rev. circ. 2,700. **Document type:** monographic series.

INTERNET MARKETING & TECHNOLOGY REPORT. see COMPUTERS — Computer Networks

INTERNET MARKETING DIGEST. see COMPUTERS — Computer Networks

THE INTERNET TIMES. see COMPUTERS — Computer Networks

1532 BUSINESS AND ECONOMICS — MARKETING AND PURCHASING

INTERNET YELLOW PAGES: BUSINESS MODELS AND MARKET OPPORTUNITIES. see BUSINESS AND ECONOMICS — Computer Applications

INTERSERVICE. see MILITARY

658.8 SP ISSN 1131-6144
INVESTIGACION Y MARKETING. 3/yr. Urgell 152, Apdo. 37104, 08036 Barcelona, Spain. TEL 3-453-98-10. FAX 3-451-00-15. Ed. Gloria Batista. circ. 1,000.
—CINDOC.

658.8 332.6 PK ISSN 0021-0064
INVESTMENT & MARKETING. (Text in English) 1965. m. Rs.250($100) Business Promoters, 10-B Pak Chambers, West Wharf Rd., P.O. Box 7578, Karachi, Pakistan. TEL 92-21-201272. FAX 92-21-551959. TELEX SADIQ-PK-21404. Ed. S.B. Hassan. adv.; bk.rev.; charts; illus.; mkt.; stat. circ. 15,000.

658 IE ISSN 0791-3303
IRELAND. CENTRAL STATISTICS OFFICE. CONSUMER PRICE INDEX. m. I£24. Central Statistics Office, Skehard Rd., Cork, Ireland. TEL 353-21-359000. FAX 353-21-359090. E-mail: information@cso.ie; URL: http://www.cso.ie. **Document type:** government publication.
Description: Measures the change in the average level of prices paid for consumer goods and services purchased by Irish households.

658 IE ISSN 0791-315X
IRELAND. CENTRAL STATISTICS OFFICE. RETAIL SALES INDEX. m. I£24. Central Statistics Office, Skehard Rd., Cork, Ireland. TEL 353-21-359000. FAX 353-21-359090. E-mail: information@cso.ie; URL: http://www.cso.ie. (processed) **Document type:** government publication.
Description: Measures changes in both the value and volume levels of retail sales.

IRELAND. CENTRAL STATISTICS OFFICE. WHOLESALE PRICE INDEX. see BUSINESS AND ECONOMICS — Abstracting, Bibliographies, Statistics

658 IE ISSN 0790-7362
IRISH MARKETING REVIEW. 1986. 2/yr. I£40 to individuals; institutions I£85 (effective 1997 & 1998). (Dublin Institute of Technology, College of Marketing and Design) Mercury Publications Ltd., 37 Main St., Donnybrook, Dublin 4, Ireland. TEL 353-1-2602171. FAX 353-1-2696705. Ed. Aidan O'Driscoll. bk.rev. circ. 3,500. (also avail. in microform from UMI) **Indexed:** Cont.Pg.Manage. **Document type:** academic/scholarly publication.
—BLDSC (4572.908000); UMI.
Description: Examines research and practice in marketing from a generalist and international perspective.
Refereed Serial

658.7 IE
IRISH PURCHASING JOURNAL. 1971. 6/yr. £3. R O C Publishing Ltd., P.O. Box 14, Blackrock., Co. Dublin, Ireland. TEL 832341. TELEX 24447. Ed. Pat Leahne. adv.

658 JA
J E T R O MARKETING SERIES. irreg. Japan External Trade Organization, 2-5, Toranomon 2-chome, Minato-ku, Tokyo 105, Japan. TEL 81-3-3587-5521. FAX 81-3-3582-0504.

659.8 GW ISSN 0021-3985
HC79.C6
JAHRBUCH DER ABSATZ- UND VERBRAUCHSFORSCHUNG. 1955. q. DM.98. (Gesellschaft fuer Konsum-, Markt- und Absatzforschung) Duncker und Humblot GmbH, Postfach 410329, 12113 Berlin, Germany. TEL 49-30-7900060. FAX 49-30-79000631. Ed. F. Wimmer. bk.rev. **Indexed:** IBR, Key to Econ.Sci., P.A.I.S.For.Lang.Ind. **Document type:** academic/scholarly publication.
—BLDSC (4630.100000). **CCC.**

JAPAN MARKETING AND ADVERTISING YEARBOOK. see ADVERTISING AND PUBLIC RELATIONS

658.8 JA
JAPAN MARKETING DATA. (Text in English) a. $63. Intercontinental Marketing Corp., I.P.O. Box 5056, Tokyo 100-30, Japan. TEL 81-3-3661-7458. FAX 81-3-3667-9646.

JAPAN MEDICAL REVIEW; a monthly report on the Japanese healthcare industry. see MEDICAL SCIENCES

JAPAN STATISTICAL ASSOCIATION. MONTHLY REPORT OF RETAIL PRICES. CONSUMER PRICE INDEX. see BUSINESS AND ECONOMICS — Abstracting, Bibliographies, Statistics

JAPAN STATISTICAL ASSOCIATION. MONTHLY REPORT OF RETAIL PRICES. PRICES OF CONSUMER GOODS AND SERVICES. see BUSINESS AND ECONOMICS — Abstracting, Bibliographies, Statistics

658 361.73 UK
JOHNS HOPKINS NONPROFIT SECTOR SERIES. irreg., vol.2, 1996. Manchester University Press, Oxford Rd., Manchester M13 9NR, England. TEL 44-161-273-5539. FAX 44-161-274-3346. E-mail: mup@man.ac.uk. (Dist. in US & Canada by: St. Martin's Press, 175 Fifth Ave., New York, NY 10010) **Document type:** monographic series.

658 659.1 US ISSN 0889-485X
JONESREPORT FOR SHOPPING CENTER MARKETING. 1978. m. $125 (foreign $145) (effective 1997). Report Communications, 9595 Whitley Dr., Ste. 100, Indianapolis, IN 46240. TEL 317-844-9024. FAX 317-848-6953. E-mail: ctrmktg@jonesreport.com; URL: http://www.jonesreport.com/jonesreport/. Ed. Linda Lipp; Pub. Phil Stillerman. adv.; bk.rev.; index. circ. 1,500. (back issues avail.) **Document type:** newsletter.
—CCC.
Description: International newsletter about shopping center marketing and promotions for marketing directors of malls, strip centers, and other shopping facilities at the corporate level.

658 AT
JOURNAL OF AUSTRALIAN DIRECT MARKETING.* q. Aus.$48. Australian Direct Marketing Association, G.P.O. Box 3982, Sydney, N.S.W. 2001, Australia. TEL 02-2477744. Ed. Ian Mackay. adv. (back issues avail.)
Description: Looks at practitioners in direct marketing, as well as advertising agencies, merchandisers and retailers.

658 UK ISSN 1350-231X
THE JOURNAL OF BRAND MANAGEMENT. 1993. bi-m. £210 to Europe; U.S. & Canada $315; rest of world £225. Henry Stewart Publications, Russell House, 28-30 Little Russell St., London WC1A 2HN, England. TEL 44-171-404-3040. FAX 44-171-404-2081. E-mail: 100622.3264@compuserve.com. (Subscr. in US and Canada to: 810 E. 10th St., Box 1897, Lawrence, KS 66044. TEL 913-843-1221. FAX 913-843-1274) Ed. Daryn Moody. adv. contact: Fraser Tant. circ. 600. **Document type:** trade publication.
—BLDSC (4954.295000).
Description: For those concerned with the launch, development, management and evaluation of brands.

JOURNAL OF BUSINESS (SPOKANE). see BUSINESS AND ECONOMICS — Banking And Finance

658.8 UK ISSN 0885-8624
HF5415.1263
JOURNAL OF BUSINESS & INDUSTRIAL MARKETING. 1985. bi-m. £899($499) (foreign Aus.$1769) (effective 1998). M C B University Press Ltd., 60-62 Toller Ln., Bradford, W. Yorks BD8 9BY, England. TEL 44-1274-777700. FAX 44-1274-785200. TELEX 51317-MCBUNI-G. URL: http://www.mcb.co.uk/cgi-bin/mcb__serve/table1&jbi&journal1.html. Ed. W.J. Johnston. adv.; bk.rev.; index. circ. 3,000. **Indexed:** ABI Inform, Anbar, B.P.I. **Document type:** academic/scholarly publication.
—BLDSC (4954.661060); KR SourceOne; SWETS; UMI; UnCover. **CCC.**

658 001.6 US ISSN 0735-3766
HD38.5
JOURNAL OF BUSINESS LOGISTICS. 1978. s-a. $35. Council of Logistics Management, 2803 Butterfield, Oak Brook, IL 60521. TEL 630-574-0985. FAX 630-574-0989. Ed. John Coyle. bk.rev. circ. 10,000. **Indexed:** ABI Inform., HRIS. **Document type:** academic/scholarly publication.
●Also available online. Vendor(s): UMI.
—BLDSC (4954.703000); SWETS; UMI; UnCover.

658 US ISSN 1051-712X
HF5415.1263
JOURNAL OF BUSINESS-TO-BUSINESS MARKETING. 1993. q. $40 to individuals (Canada $52; elsewhere $56); institutions $60 (Canada $78; elsewhere $84); libraries $150 (Canada $195; elsewhere $210) (effective 1996-1997). Haworth Press, Inc., 10 Alice St., Binghamton, NY 13904. TEL 607-722-5857; 800-342-9676. FAX 607-722-6362. E-mail: getinfo@haworth.com; URL: http://www.haworth.com. Ed. J. David Lichtental; Pub. Bill Cohen. R&P contact: Ruthann Heath. adv.: B&W page $300; trim 4 3/8 x 7 1/8; adv. contact: Jackie Blakeslee. bk.rev. (also avail. in microform from UMI; reprint service avail. from HAW) **Indexed:** Cont.Pg.Manage., Human Resour.Abstr., Mgmt.& Market.Abstr., Oper.Res.Manage.Sci., Ref.Zh. **Document type:** academic/scholarly publication.
—BLDSC (4954.664000); Haworth.
Description: Features diverse approaches to business marketing theory development and problem solving.
Refereed Serial

658.8 UK ISSN 0736-3761
HF5410
JOURNAL OF CONSUMER MARKETING. 1983. bi-m. £899($499) (foreign Aus.$1769) (effective 1998). M C B University Press Ltd., 60-62 Toller Ln., Bradford, W. Yorks BD8 9BY, England. TEL 44-1274-777700. FAX 44-1274-785200. TELEX 51317-MCBUNI-G. E-mail: akamiaska@mcb.co.uk; URL: http://www.mcb.co.uk/cgi-bin/mcb__serve/table1.txt&jcm&journal1.html. Ed. Richard Leventhal. adv.; bk.rev.; index. circ. 4,000. (also avail. in microform from UMI; reprint service avail. from SWZ) **Indexed:** ABI Inform, B.P.I., Curr.Pack.Abstr., SCIMP (1991-). **Document type:** academic/scholarly publication.
●Also available on CD-ROM.
—BLDSC (4965.211600); KR SourceOne; SWETS; UMI; UnCover. **CCC.**
Incorporates (199?-1996): Journal of Product & Brand Management (ISSN 1061-0421)
Description: Provides action-oriented ideas and concepts to be put to practical use.

658.8 US ISSN 0093-5301
HF5415.3 CODEN: JCSRBL
JOURNAL OF CONSUMER RESEARCH; an interdisciplinary quarterly. 1973. q. $90 to institutions and non-member individuals (Canada $103.30; elsewhere $97); members $45 (Canada $55.15; elsewhere $52); students $25 (Canada $33.75; elsewhere $32) (effective 1998). University of Chicago Press, Journals Division, Box 37005, Chicago, IL 60637. TEL 773-753-3347. FAX 773-753-0811. E-mail: subscriptions@journals.uchicago.edu; URL: http://www.journals.uchicago.edu/JCR/home.html. Ed. Robert E. Burnkrant. adv.: page $500; trim 8 1/2 x 11. bk.rev.; index. circ. 3,200. (also avail. in microform from UMI; reprint service avail. from UMI) **Indexed:** ABI Inform, Arts & Hum.Cit.Ind., ASCA, B.P.I., Bibl.Agri., BPIA, Bus.Ind., Commun.Abstr., Curr.Cont., Curr.Pack.Abstr., Ergon.Abstr., Fam.Ind., Food Sci.& Tech.Abstr., HRIS, Int.Abstr.Oper.Res., J.Cont.Quant.Meth., J.of Econ.Lit., Lang.& Lang.Behav.Abstr., Manage.Cont., Mark.Res.Abstr. (1974-), Psychol.Abstr. (1974-), Psycscan, Ref.Zh., Sage Fam.Stud.Abstr., Sage Pub.Admin.Abstr., SCIMP (1978-), Sociol.Abstr., SSCI, Stud.Wom.Abstr., Tr.& Indus.Ind. **Document type:** academic/scholarly publication.
●Also available online. Vendor(s): Information Access Co., Knight-Ridder Information, Inc., Lexis-Nexis.
Also available on CD-ROM.
—BLDSC (4965.215000); Genuine Article; KR SourceOne; SWETS; UMI; UnCover. **CCC.**
Description: Focuses on scholarly research aimed at describing and explaining consumer behavior, in the broadest sense of that term.
Refereed Serial

658 US ISSN 0899-8620
JOURNAL OF CONSUMER SATISFACTION, DISSATISFACTION AND COMPLAINING BEHAVIOR. Variant title: C S - D & C B. 1988. a. Consumer Satisfaction, Dissatisfaction and Complaining Behavior, Inc., Marriott School of Management, 632 TNRB, Brigham Young University, Provo, UT 84602. TEL 801-378-2080. FAX 801-226-7650. E-mail: hkhunt@acd1.byu.edu. Ed. H. Keith Hunt. (back issues avail.)
—BLDSC (4965.216000); SWETS; UnCover.

THE JOURNAL OF DATABASE MARKETING. see BUSINESS AND ECONOMICS — Computer Applications

658.8 150 NE ISSN 0167-4870
HB74.P8
JOURNAL OF ECONOMIC PSYCHOLOGY. (Text in English) 1981. bi-m. fl.640($368) (effective 1998). (Society "European Research in Economic Psychology") North-Holland (Subsidiary of: Elsevier Science B.V.), P.O. Box 211, 1000 AE Amsterdam, Netherlands. TEL 31-20-4853911. FAX 31-20-4853598. TELEX 18582 ESPA NL. (Subscr. in the Americas to: Elsevier Science, Regional Sales Office, Box 945, New York, NY 10159-0945. TEL 212-633-3730. FAX 212-633-3680; Subscr. in Australasia and the Far East to: Elsevier Science (Singapore) Pte Ltd, No.1 Temasek Ave., No.17-01 Millenia Tower, Singapore 039192, Singapore. TEL 65-434-3727. FAX 65-337-2230; Subscr. in Japan to: Elsevier Science Japan, 9-15 Higashi-Azabu 1-chome, Minato-ku Tokyo 106, Japan. TEL 81-3-5561-5033. FAX 81-3-5561-5047) Ed. S.E.G. Lea. adv.; index. (also avail. in microform from UMI; back issues avail.; reprint service avail. from SWZ) Indexed: ABI Inform., ASCA, BPIA, C.R.E.J., Curr.Cont., Fam.Ind., Food Sci.& Tech.Abstr., HRIS, J.of Econ.Lit., Manage.Cont., PSI, Psychol.Abstr. (1981-), SSCI, Tr.& Indus.Ind. Document type: academic/scholarly publication.
—BLDSC (4973.054100); Genuine Article; SWETS; UMI; UnCover. CCC.
Description: Presents research on behavioral, especially socio-psychological, aspects of economic phenomena and processes.
Refereed Serial

658 AT ISSN 1326-4443
▼**JOURNAL OF EMPIRICAL GENERALISATIONS IN MARKETING SCIENCE.** 1996. irreg. University of South Australia, North Terrace, Marketing Science Centre, Adelaide, S.A. 5001, Australia. TEL 61-8-3020715. FAX 61-8-3020442. E-mail: Byron.Sharop@unisa.edu.au; URL: http://msc.citywest.unisa.edu.au/msc/Jems__Intro.html. Ed. Byron M. Sharp. Document type: academic/scholarly publication.
●Available only online.
Refereed Serial

658 382 US ISSN 1049-6483
CODEN: JEMAEN
JOURNAL OF EUROMARKETING. 1991. q. $45 to individuals (Canada 58.50; elsewhere $63); institutions $60 (Canada $78; elsewhere $84); libraries $225 (Canada $292.50; elsewhere $315) (effective 1996-1997). Haworth Press, Inc., 10 Alice St., Binghamton, NY 13904. TEL 607-722-5857; 800-342-9676. FAX 607-722-6362. E-mail: getinfo@haworth.com; URL: http://www.haworth.com. Ed. Erdener Kaynak; Pub. Bill Cohen. R&P contact: Ruthann Heath. adv.; B&W page $300; trim 4 3/8 x 7 1/8; adv. contact: Jackie Blakeslee. bk.rev. (also avail. in microfiche from UMI; microform from HAW; reprint service avail. from HAW) Indexed: Cont.Pg.Manage., Geo.Abstr.P.G., IDA, Mgmt.& Market.Abstr. Document type: academic/scholarly publication, trade publication.
—BLDSC (4979.602750); Haworth.
Description: Provides a forum that fosters a conceptual understanding of the European markets and marketing systems as well as analytical insights; highlights the past, present, and future of European marketing.
Refereed Serial

658 746.92 UK ISSN 1361-2026
▼**JOURNAL OF FASHION MARKETING AND MANAGEMENT.** 1996. q. £130 to Europe; U.S. & Canada $195; rest of world £145. Henry Stewart Publications, Russell House, 28-30 Little Russell St., London WC1A 2HN, England. TEL 44-171-404-3040. FAX 44-171-404-2081. E-mail: 100622.3264@compuserve.com. (Subscr. in US and Canada to: 810 E. 10th St., Box 1897, Lawrence, KS 66044. TEL 913-843-1221. FAX 913-843-1274) Ed. Daryn Moody. adv. contact: Fraser Tant. Document type: trade publication.
—BLDSC (4983.860000).
Description: Provides a forum for research in the marketing and management of clothing.
Refereed Serial

JOURNAL OF FOOD DISTRIBUTION RESEARCH. see FOOD AND FOOD INDUSTRIES

JOURNAL OF FOOD PRODUCTS MARKETING. see FOOD AND FOOD INDUSTRIES

657 US ISSN 0891-1762
HF1009.5 CODEN: JGMAE3
JOURNAL OF GLOBAL MARKETING. 1987. q. $50 to individuals (Canada $65; elsewhere $70); institutions $90 (Canada $117; elsewhere $126); libraries $250 (Canada $325; elsewhere $350) (effective 1996-1997). Haworth Press, Inc., 10 Alice St., Binghamton, NY 13904. TEL 607-722-9678; 800-342-9676. FAX 607-722-6362. E-mail: kax@psuvm.psu.edu; URL: http://web.spectra.net/cgi-bin/haworth/. Ed. Erdener Kaynak; Pub. Bill Cohen. R&P contact: Ruthann Heath. adv.; B&W page $300; trim 4 3/8 x 7 1/8; adv. contact: Jackie Blakeslee. bk.rev. circ. 350. (also avail. in microfiche from UMI; microform from HAW; reprint service avail. from HAW) Indexed: Anbar, B.P.I., Bus.Educ.Ind., Cont.Pg.Manage., Human Resour.Abstr., Int.Polit.Sci.Abstr., Mgmt.& Market.Abstr., P.A.I.S., Ref.Zh. Document type: academic/scholarly publication.
—BLDSC (4996.300000); Haworth; KR SourceOne; SWETS; UnCover.
Description: Addresses marketing challenges, opportunities, and problems encountered by firms, industries, and governments on a global scale.
Refereed Serial

658.8 613.7 US ISSN 0737-3252
RA410.A1
JOURNAL OF HEALTH CARE MARKETING. 1981. q. $70 to individual non-members; institutions $90; members $45. American Marketing Association, 250 S. Wacker Dr., Ste. 200, Chicago, IL 60606. TEL 312-648-0536. FAX 312-993-7542. URL: http://www.ama.org. Ed. Lynn Coleman. R&P contact: Una Moon. adv. contact: Kathy Harp. bk.rev.; abstr.; bibl.; charts; illus.; stat.; index. circ. 4,000. (also avail. in microfiche from MIM,UMI; reprint service avail. from UMI) Indexed: ABI Inform, B.P.I., Excerp.Med. Document type: academic/scholarly publication.
●Also available online. Vendor(s): Information Access Co., UMI.
—BLDSC (4996.738000); EMDOCS; KNAW; KR SourceOne; SWETS; UMI; UnCover. CCC.
Description: Geared to meet the needs of health care marketers with articles from professionals on provocative and relevant topics.

JOURNAL OF HIGH TECHNOLOGY MANAGEMENT RESEARCH. see BUSINESS AND ECONOMICS — Computer Applications

658.8 US ISSN 0883-7570
RA965.5
JOURNAL OF HOSPITAL MARKETING. 1987. s-a. $60 to individuals (Canada $78; elsewhere $84); institutions $85 (Canada $110.50; elsewhere $119); libraries $225 (Canada $292.50; elsewhere $315) (effective 1996-1997). Haworth Press, Inc., 10 Alice St., Binghamton, NY 13904. TEL 607-722-5857; 800-342-9676. FAX 607-722-6362. E-mail: getinfo@haworth.com; URL: http://www.haworth.com. Ed. William J. Winston; Pub. Bill Cohen. R&P contact: Ruthann Heath. adv.; B&W page $300; trim 4 3/8 x 7 1/8; adv. contact: Jackie Blakeslee. bk.rev. circ. 237. (also avail. in microfiche from UMI; microform from HAW; back issues avail.; reprint service avail. from HAW) Indexed: CINAHL, Curr.Cont., Excerp.Med., HMA, Hosp.Lit.Ind., Med.Care Rev. Document type: academic/scholarly publication.
—EMDOCS; Haworth.
Description: Presents new and effective ways of marketing hospital services. Shares current marketing applications and methodologies by professional hospital marketing consultants and educators.
Refereed Serial

JOURNAL OF HOSPITALITY & LEISURE MARKETING; the international forum for research, theory & practice. see HOTELS AND RESTAURANTS

658.8 US
HF5415.126
JOURNAL OF INTERACTIVE MARKETING. 1987. q. $440 (foreign $510) (effective 1998). (Direct Marketing Educational Foundation) John Wiley & Sons, Inc., Journals, 605 Third Ave., New York, NY 10158. TEL 212-850-6645. FAX 212-850-6021. TELEX 12-7063. E-mail: subinfo@jwiley.com; URL: http://www.wiley.co.uk. (Subscr. outside the Americas to: John Wiley & Sons Ltd., Baffins Ln., Chichester, W. Sussex PO19 1UD, England. TEL 44-1243-779777. FAX 44-1243-843232) Ed. Don Schultz. adv.; B&W page £640, color page £1515; trim 279 x 216. bk.rev.; software rev. circ. 1,000. (also avail. in microform from UMI; back issues avail.) Indexed: B.P.I. Document type: academic/scholarly publication.
●Also available online. Vendor(s): Knight-Ridder Information, Inc.
—BLDSC (4969.660000); KR SourceOne; UMI; UnCover. CCC.
Formerly: Journal of Direct Marketing (ISSN 0892-0591); Which incorporated (in 1987): Journal of Direct Marketing Research (ISSN 0888-9295)
Description: Offers an exchange of ideas in the field of direct marketing and the emerging field of interactive marketing. Designed to provide a bridge between direct-marketing practitioners and the academic research community.
Refereed Serial

658 640.73 US ISSN 0896-1530
HF5415.2 CODEN: JIMREY
JOURNAL OF INTERNATIONAL CONSUMER MARKETING. 1988. q. $45 to individuals (Canada $58.50; elsewhere $63); institutions $90 (Canada $117; elsewhere $126); libraries $225 (Canada $292.50; elsewhere $315) (effective 1997-1998). Haworth Press, Inc., 10 Alice St., Binghamton, NY 13904. TEL 607-722-5857; 800-342-9676. FAX 607-722-6362. E-mail: getinfo@haworth.com; URL: http://www.haworth.com. Ed. Erdener Kaynak; Pub. Bill Cohen. R&P contact: Ruthann Heath. adv.; B&W page $300; trim 4 3/8 x 7 1/8; adv. contact: Jackie Blakeslee. bk.rev. circ. 269. (also avail. in microfiche from UMI; microform from HAW; reprint service avail. from HAW) Indexed: Bus.Educ.Ind., Cont.Pg.Manage., Food Sci.& Tech.Abstr. Document type: academic/scholarly publication.
—BLDSC (5007.633000); Haworth; SWETS; UnCover.
Formerly: International Journal of Cross-Cultural Consumer Behavior.
Description: Publishes articles written by practitioners and public policymakers as well as academicians from a variety of countries. Offers managerial insights to practicing international business persons as well as to policymakers in governments and international agencies and organizations to enable them to formulate need-oriented action programs and policies.
Refereed Serial

658 UK ISSN 0262-1703
HF1009.5
JOURNAL OF INTERNATIONAL MARKETING. 1981-1982; N.S. 1993. 3/yr. $99.95. M C B University Press Ltd., 60-62 Toller Ln., Bradford, W. Yorks BD8 9BY, England. TEL 44-1274-777700. FAX 44-1274-785200. TELEX 51317-MCBUNI-G. URL: http://www.mcb.co.uk. Ed. John Peters; Pub. Jean Clarkson. Indexed: Account.& Data Proc.Abstr., ASCA, Curr.Cont., Food Sci.& Tech.Abstr. Document type: academic/scholarly publication.

658.8 US ISSN 1069-031X
HF1416
JOURNAL OF INTERNATIONAL MARKETING. 1993. q. $60 to individuals (foreign $65); institutions $115 (foreign $120). (Michigan State University, Center for International Business Education and Research) Michigan State University Press, Manly Miles Bldg., Ste. 25, 1405 S. Harrison Rd., East Lansing, MI 48823-5202. TEL 517-355-9543. FAX 517-432-2611. Ed. S. Tamer Cavusgil. bk.rev. circ. 400. (also avail. in microform from UMI) Document type: academic/scholarly publication.
—BLDSC (5007.673400); SWETS; UMI; UnCover.
Description: Dedicated to advancing international marketing practice, research and theory.
Refereed Serial

BUSINESS AND ECONOMICS — MARKETING AND PURCHASING

658 UK ISSN 1010-7347
JOURNAL OF INTERNATIONAL MARKETING & MARKETING RESEARCH. 1976. 3/yr. £65($110) European Marketing Association - Association Europeenne pour le Marketing, 18 St. Peters Steps, Brixham, Devon, England. (Co-sponsor: Commission Internationale de Marketing) Ed. David W. Newill. adv.; bk.rev.; cum.index; circ. controlled. (back issues avail.) **Indexed:** Mgmt.& Market.Abstr. **Document type:** academic/scholarly publication.
—BLDSC (5007.673600); SWETS.

658.8 UK ISSN 1356-0565
HF5438
▼**JOURNAL OF INTERNATIONAL SELLING & SALES MANAGEMENT.** 1995. s-a. £50. European Marketing Association, 18 St. Peters Steps, Brixham, Devon, England. (Co-sponsors: Federacion Internacional de Marketing; Institute of Industrial Selling) Ed. David W. Newill. adv.; bk.rev.; cum.index. **Document type:** academic/scholarly publication.
—BLDSC (5007.686430).
Refereed Serial

658 CN ISSN 1206-4890
▼**JOURNAL OF INTERNET PURCHASING.** 1997. bi-m. Box 5145, Station F, Ottawa, ON K2C 3H3, Canada. E-mail: jip-admin@arraydev.com; URL: http://www.arraydev.com/commerce/jip/. Ed. William Christensen.
●Available only online.
Description: Informs purchasing professionals and executives on principal developments, benchmark practices, and future trends in the Internet-based purchasing practices of governments and industry.

658 US ISSN 0276-1467
HF5410
JOURNAL OF MACROMARKETING. 1981. s-a. $33.60 to individuals (Canada and Mexico $38.85; elsewhere $44.10); institutions $53.55 (Canada and Mexico $57.75; elsewhere $63) (effective 1997). University of Colorado, Business Research Division, Campus Box 420, Boulder, CO 80309-0420. TEL 303-492-8227. FAX 303-492-3620. E-mail: nason@msu.edu. **Indexed:** ABI Inform., BPIA, Cont.Pg.Manage. **Document type:** academic/scholarly publication.
●Also available online. Vendor(s): UMI.
—BLDSC (5010.745000); SWETS; UMI; UnCover.

658 US ISSN 0022-2429
HF5415.A2 CODEN: JMKTAK
JOURNAL OF MARKETING. 1934. q. $75 to non-members; members $40; institutions $150. American Marketing Association, 250 S. Wacker Dr., Ste. 200, Chicago, IL 60606. TEL 312-648-0536. FAX 312-993-7542. URL: http://www.ama.org/pubs/jminfo/index.html. Ed. Robert Lusch. R&P contact: Una Moon. adv. contact: Kathy Harp. bk.rev.; abstr.; bibl.; charts; illus.; stat.; index. circ. 10,000. (also avail. in microform from UMI; reprint service avail. from UMI,KTO) **Indexed:** ABI Inform., Acad.Ind., Account.& Data Proc.Abstr., Account.Ind. (1974-), Anbar, ASCA, ASEAN Manage.Abstr., B.P.I., Bank.Lit.Ind., Bk.Rev.Ind. (1965-), BPIA, Bus.Ind., Child.Bk.Rev.Ind. (1965-), Commun.Abstr., Comput.Abstr., Cont.Pg.Manage., Curr.Cont., Curr.Pack.Abstr., IBR, Intl.Mgmt.Info., J.Cont.Quant.Meth., Key to Econ.Sci., Manage.Cont., Mark.Res.Abstr. (1963-), Mgmt.& Market.Abstr., P.A.I.S, PROMT, Psychol.Abstr., Ref.Pt.Food Indus.Abstr., SCIMP (1978-), SSCI, Tr.& Indus.Ind. **Document type:** academic/scholarly publication.
●Also available online. Vendor(s): Information Access Co., Lexis-Nexis, UMI.
—BLDSC (5012.100000); CASDDS; Genuine Article; KR SourceOne; SWETS; UMI; UnCover. **CCC.**

658 US ISSN 1046-669X
HF5415.129 CODEN: JMKCE7
JOURNAL OF MARKETING CHANNELS; distribution systems, strategy, and management. 1991. q. $45 to individuals (Canada $58.50; elsewhere $63); institutions $75 (Canada $97.50; elsewhere $105); libraries $160 (Canada $208; elsewhere $224) (effective 1996-1997). Haworth Press, Inc., 10 Alice St., Binghamton, NY 13904. TEL 607-722-5857; 800-342-9676. FAX 607-722-6362. E-mail: getinfo@haworth.com; URL: http://www.haworth.com. Ed. Bert Rosenbloom; Pub. Bill Cohen. R&P contact: Ruthann Heath. adv.: B&W page $300; trim 4 3/8 x 7 1/8; adv. contact: Jackie Blakeslee. bk.rev. (also avail. in microfiche from UMI; microform from HAW; reprint service avail. from HAW) **Indexed:** Cont.Pg.Manage., Human Resour.Abstr., INSPEC, Lang.& Lang.Behav.Abstr., Mgmt.& Market.Abstr., Sociol.Abstr., SOPODA. **Document type:** academic/scholarly publication.
—BLDSC (5012.113000); AskIEEE; Haworth; KR SourceOne; SWETS; UnCover.
Description: Focuses on distribution systems, strategy and management.
Refereed Serial

658 380 UK ISSN 1352-7266
HF5415.123
▼**JOURNAL OF MARKETING COMMUNICATIONS.** 1995. q. £45 (foreign $75) to individuals; institutions £195 (foreign $325); print & online eds. £235 (foreign $390) (effective 1998). Thomson Professional (Subsidiary of: International Thomson Publishing Group), 2-6 Boundary Row, London SE1 8HN, England. TEL 44-171-8650066. FAX 44-171-5229623. TELEX 290164 CHAPMA G. E-mail: journal@rapidcom.co.uk; URL: http://jmc.thomsonprofessional.com. (Subscr. to: International Thomson Publishing Services Ltd., Cheriton House, North Way, Andover, Hants. SP10 5BE, England. TEL 44-1264-342713. FAX 44-1264-342807; Subscr. in US & Canada to: 400 Market St., Philadelphia, PA 19106. TEL 800-552-5866) Ed. Philip J. Kitchen. adv. contact: Gemma Heiser. bibl. (back issues avail.; reprint service avail.) **Indexed:** Cont.Pg.Manage. **Document type:** academic/scholarly publication.
●Also available online.
—BLDSC (5012.114000).
Description: Devoted to publishing research papers and information articles on all aspects of marketing communications and promotion management.
Refereed Serial

658 US ISSN 0273-4753
HF5415
JOURNAL OF MARKETING EDUCATION. 1979. 3/yr. $34.65 to individuals (Canada and Mexico $39.90; elsewhere $45.15); institutions $57.75 (Canada and Mexico $64.05; elsewhere $69.30) (effective 1997). University of Colorado, Business Research Division, Campus Box 420, Boulder, CO 80309-0420. TEL 303-492-8227. FAX 303-492-3620. URL: http://bus.colorado.edu/BRD/JME.HTM. Ed. Robert Collins. circ. 400. **Indexed:** Bus.Educ.Ind. **Document type:** academic/scholarly publication.
—BLDSC (5012.115000); SWETS; UMI; UnCover.

658.8 378 US ISSN 0884-1241
LB2342.82 CODEN: JMHEEW
JOURNAL OF MARKETING FOR HIGHER EDUCATION. 1988. q. $40 to individuals (Canada $52; elsewhere $56); institutions $75 (Canada $97.50; elsewhere $105); libraries $175 (Canada $227.50; elsewhere $245) (effective 1997-1998). Haworth Press, Inc., 10 Alice St., Binghamton, NY 13904. TEL 607-722-5857; 800-342-9676. FAX 607-722-6362. E-mail: getinfo@haworth.com; URL: http://www.haworth.com. Ed. Thomas J. Hayes; Pub. Bill Cohen. R&P contact: Ruthann Heath. adv.: B&W page $300; trim 4 3/8 x 7 1/8; adv. contact: Jackie Blakeslee. bk.rev. circ. 124. (also avail. in microfiche from UMI; microform from HAW; reprint service avail. from HAW) **Indexed:** C.I.J.E., Cont.Pg.Educ., High.Educ.Abstr., Tech.Educ.Abstr. **Document type:** academic/scholarly publication.
—BLDSC (5012.118000); Haworth.
Description: Designed to provide guidance for marketing, admissions, public relations, development and planning professionals who have the responsibility for enrollments and image enhancements at institutions of higher education.
Refereed Serial

658 UK ISSN 0267-257X
JOURNAL OF MARKETING MANAGEMENT. 1985. q. £185 (effective 1997). Academic Press Ltd. (Subsidiary of: Harcourt Brace & Company Ltd.), 24-28 Oval Rd., London NW1 7DX, England. TEL 44-171-267-4466. FAX 44-171-482-2293. TELEX 25775 ACPRES G. URL: http://www.europe.idealibrary.com/. (Subscr. to: Harcourt Brace & Company Ltd., Foots Cray High St., Sidcup, Kent DA14 5HP, England. TEL 44-181-300-3322. FAX 44-181-309-0807) Ed. M.J. Baker. R&P contact: Catherine John. adv. contact: Nik Screen. **Indexed:** Cont.Pg.Manage. **Document type:** academic/scholarly publication.
—BLDSC (5012.125000); SWETS; UnCover. **CCC.**
Description: Concerned with all aspects of the management of the marketing mix and is intended to provide a forum for the exchange of the latest ideas and best practices in marketing.

658 UK ISSN 1355-2538
HF5410
▼**JOURNAL OF MARKETING PRACTICE: APPLIED MARKETING SCIENCE.** 1995. m. £199($299) (foreign Aus.$419) (effective 1998). M C B University Press Ltd., 60-62 Toller Ln., Bradford, W. Yorks BD8 9BY, England. TEL 44-1274-777700. FAX 44-1274-785200. E-mail: jclarkson@mcb.co.uk; URL: http://www.mcb.co.uk/liblink/jmpams/jourhome.htm. (Dist. in N. America by: MCB University Press Ltd., Box 10812, Birmingham, AL 35201-0812. TEL 800-633-4931. FAX 205-995-1588) Eds. Mark Jenkins, M. McDonald. **Indexed:** Cont.Pg.Manage. **Document type:** academic/scholarly publication.
●Also available online.
Also available on CD-ROM.
—UnCover. **CCC.**
Description: Studies the way in which marketing tools and techniques are applied in a live marketing environment; brings together the latest research and best practices from industry to show what is and isn't working the markeing today.

658.83 US ISSN 0022-2437
HF5415.2 CODEN: JMKRAE
JOURNAL OF MARKETING RESEARCH. 1964. q. $57 to non-members; members $40; institutions $150. American Marketing Association, 250 S. Wacker Dr., Ste. 200, Chicago, IL 60606. TEL 312-648-0536. FAX 312-993-7542. URL: http://www.ama.org/pubs/jmr/index.html. Ed. Russ Winer. R&P contact: Una Moon. adv. contact: Kathy Harp. bk.rev.; charts; index, cum.index every 5 yrs. circ. 9,000. (also avail. in microform from UMI; reprint service avail. from UMI,KTO,SCH) **Indexed:** ABI Inform., Account.Ind. (1974-), ASCA, B.P.I., BPIA, Bus.Ind., Commun.Abstr., Cont.Pg.Manage., Curr.Cont., Curr.Pack.Abstr., Food Sci.& Tech.Abstr., J.Cont.Quant.Meth., Key to Econ.Sci., Manage.Cont., Mark.Res.Abstr. (1964-), Mgmt.& Market.Abstr., Oper.Res.Manage.Sci., P.A.I.S., Psychol.Abstr. (1966-), Psycscan, Qual.Contr.Appl.Stat., SCIMP (1978-), SSCI, Tr.& Indus.Ind. **Document type:** academic/scholarly publication.
●Also available online. Vendor(s): Information Access Co., Lexis-Nexis.
—BLDSC (5012.150000); Genuine Article; KR SourceOne; SWETS; UMI; UnCover. **CCC.**
Description: Covers methodology and problems of research in marketing, discusses current trends and experiments in social psychology and other behavioral sciences as they affect marketing.

658.8 US ISSN 1069-6679
JOURNAL OF MARKETING THEORY AND PRACTICE. 1992. q. $60 to libraries (foreign $80) (effective 1997). Association of Marketing Theory and Practice, College of Business Administration, Department of Marketing, Georgia Southern University, Statesboro, GA 30460. TEL 912-681-5733. FAX 912-681-5655. E-mail: jrandall@gsaix2.cc.gasou.edu. (Subscr. to: Association of Marketing Theory and Practice, Box 8154, Georgia Southern University, Statesboro, GA 30460. TEL 912-681-5655) Ed. E. James Randall. **Document type:** academic/scholarly publication, trade publication.
—BLDSC (5012.155000).
Description: Reports on theory and practice in marketing and retail.

BUSINESS AND ECONOMICS — MARKETING AND PURCHASING

658.8 610 615   NR   ISSN 0331-0124
JOURNAL OF MEDICAL AND PHARMACEUTICAL MARKETING. 1972. bi-m. $115.20. Fred Atoki Publishing Co. Ltd., Plot 25 Kekere-Ekun St., Orile-Iganmu, Box 7313, Lagos, Nigeria. adv.; illus. circ. 16,000. Indexed: I.P.A.
●Also available online.

658.8   US   ISSN 1049-5142
CODEN: JNPMEZ
JOURNAL OF NONPROFIT & PUBLIC SECTOR MARKETING. 1986. q. $40 to individuals (Canada $52; elsewhere $56); institutions $60 (Canada $78; elsewhere $84); libraries $175 (Canada $227.50; elsewhere $245) (effective 1997-1998). Haworth Press, Inc., 10 Alice St., Binghamton, NY 13904. TEL 607-722-5857; 800-342-9676. FAX 607-722-6362. TELEX 4932599. E-mail: getinfo@haworth.com; URL: http://www.haworth.com. Ed. Donald R. Self; Pub. Bill Cohen. R&P contact: Ruthann Heath. adv.: B&W page $300; trim 4 3/8 x 7 1/8; adv. contact: Jackie Blakeslee. bk.rev. circ. 192. (also avail. in microfiche from UMI; microform from HAW; reprint service avail. from HAW) **Indexed:** Mgmt.& Market.Abstr., Soc.Work Res.& Abstr. **Document type:** academic/scholarly publication.
—BLDSC (5022.842300); Haworth.
Former titles (until 1991): Journal of Marketing for Mental Health; Psychotherapy Marketing and Practice Development Reports (ISSN 0883-7589)
Description: Provides a forum for the development of marketing thought and for the dissemination of marketing knowledge in the nonprofit and public sector of the economy.
Refereed Serial

658 361.73   UK   ISSN 1360-8576
▼**JOURNAL OF NONPROFIT AND VOLUNTARY SECTOR MARKETING.** 1996. q. £65($95) to small nonprofit organizations; £105($160) for large nonprofit organizations; £140 ($210) other institutions. Henry Stewart Publications, Russell House, 28-30 Little Russell St., London WC1A 2HN, England. TEL 44-171-404-3040. FAX 44-171-404-2081. E-mail: 100622.3264@compuserve.com. (Subscr. in US and Canada to: E. 10th St., Box 1897, Lawrence, KS 66044. TEL 913-843-1221. FAX 913-843-1274) Ed. Daryn Moody. adv. contact: Fraser Tant. **Document type:** trade publication.
Description: Forum for papers and case studies on marketing in the not-for-profit sector.
Refereed Serial

658   US   ISSN 0885-3134
JOURNAL OF PERSONAL SELLING AND SALES MANAGEMENT. 1980. q. $55 to individuals; institutions $75 (effective 1996). (Phi Sigma Epsilon) C T C Press, Box 1826, Clemson, SC 29631. TEL 800-844-2443. FAX 864-859-7002. E-mail: pse@exec.com. (Subscr. to: Phi Sigma Epsilon, 6560 S. 27th St., Oak Creek, WI 53154. TEL 414-761-9350) Ed. Alan J. Dubinsky. bk.rev.; bibl.; charts; cum.index: 1980-1994; circ. 500 (paid). (also avail. in microfilm from UMI; back issues avail.) **Document type:** academic/scholarly publication.
—BLDSC (5030.870000); UnCover.
Description: Covers most aspects of personal selling and sales management. Purpose is to bridge gap between academic and business communities involved in selling and sales management. Audience consists of academics, researchers, trainers, sales executives, and students.
Refereed Serial

JOURNAL OF PHARMACEUTICAL MARKETING AND MANAGEMENT. see *PHARMACY AND PHARMACOLOGY*

658.8 610   US   ISSN 1092-6801
JOURNAL OF PHARMACEUTICAL MARKETING PRACTICE. s-a. $36 to individuals; institutions $48; libraries $75 (effective 1997-1998). Haworth Press, Inc., 10 Alice St., Binghamton, NY 13904. TEL 607-722-5857; 800-342-9676. FAX 607-722-6362. E-mail: getinfo@haworth.com; URL: http://www.haworth.com. Ed. Mickey C. Smith, Lisa Ruby Basara; Pub. Bill Cohen. R&P contact: Ruthann Heath. adv.: B&W page $300; trim 4 3/8 x 7 1/8; adv. contact: Jackie Blakeslee. (also avail. in microform from HAW) **Document type:** academic/scholarly publication.
—Haworth.

658   US   ISSN 1045-8425
HF5416.5
JOURNAL OF PRICING MANAGEMENT. 1990. q. $140. Faulkner & Gray, Inc. (New York), 11 Penn Plaza, 17th Fl., New York, NY 10001. TEL 212-967-7000. FAX 212-967-7155. Ed. Pam Goett.
—UnCover.
Description: Covers rationale, implementation, and effects of pricing strategies. Reports on developments in pricing applications.

658.8   US   ISSN 0748-4623
JOURNAL OF PROFESSIONAL SERVICES MARKETING. 1985. s-a. (in 2 vols.). $48 to individuals (Canada $62.40; elsewhere $67.20); institutions $90 (Canada $117; elsewhere $126); libraries $225 (Canada $292.50; elsewhere $315) (effective 1996-1997). Haworth Press, Inc., 10 Alice St., Binghamton, NY 13904. TEL 607-722-5857; 800-342-9676. FAX 607-722-6362. TELEX 4932599. E-mail: getinfo@haworth.com; URL: http://www.haworth.com. Ed. William J. Winston; Pub. Bill Cohen. R&P contact: Ruthann Heath. adv.: B&W page $300; trim 4 3/8 x 7 1/8; adv. contact: Jackie Blakeslee. bk.rev. circ. 106. (also avail. in microfiche from UMI; microform from HAW; reprint service avail. from HAW) **Indexed:** ABI Inform, Abstr.Health Care Manage.Stud., Ind.Per.Art.Relat.Law, Psychol.Abstr. **Document type:** academic/scholarly publication.
—BLDSC (5042.720000); Haworth; SWETS.
Description: Critical journal for anyone interested in learning more about services marketing; covers current techniques and trends in the industry.
Refereed Serial

658.8   US   ISSN 0748-6766
HF5410
JOURNAL OF PUBLIC POLICY & MARKETING. 1982. s-a. $60 to non-members; members $40; institutions $90. American Marketing Association, 250 S. Wacker Dr., Chicago, IL 60606-5819. TEL 312-648-0536. URL: http://www.ama.org. Ed. Debra L. Scammon. R&P contact: Una Moon. adv. contact: Kathy Harp. circ. 1,000. **Indexed:** ABI Inform, ASCA, B.P.I., Curr.Cont., P.A.I.S., SSCI. **Document type:** academic/scholarly publication.
●Also available online. Vendor(s): Information Access Co., UMI.
—BLDSC (5043.645000); Genuine Article; KR SourceOne; SWETS; UMI; UnCover. **CCC.**
Formerly (until 1982): Journal of Marketing and Public Policy (ISSN 0743-9156)
Description: Covers the public policy, legal, and regulatory activities related to the marketing arena.

JOURNAL OF RESTAURANT & FOODSERVICE MARKETING. see *HOTELS AND RESTAURANTS*

658.87   US   ISSN 0022-4359
HF5001
JOURNAL OF RETAILING. 1925. q. $80 to individuals (foreign $100); institutions $205 (foreign $225) (effective 1998). (New York University, Stern School of Business) J A I Press Inc., 55 Old Post Rd., No. 2, Box 1678, Greenwich, CT 06830-1678. TEL 203-661-7602. FAX 203-661-0792. E-mail: jai@jaipress.net; URL: http://www.haas.berkeley.edu/~jrl. (Addr. in Europe: J A I Press Ltd., 38 Tavistock St., Covent Garden, London WC2E 7PB, England. TEL 44-171-379-8834. FAX 44-171-379-8835) Ed. Charles Ingene. adv.; bk.rev.; bibl.; charts; illus.; cum.index every 2 and 10 yrs. circ. 3,200. (also avail. in microform from UMI; back issues avail.; reprint service avail. from ISI,UMI,KTO) **Indexed:** ABI Inform, Account.& Data Proc.Abstr., Account.Ind. (1974-), Anbar, ASCA, ASEAN Manage.Abstr., B.P.I., BPIA, Bus.Ind., Comput.Lit.Ind., Cont.Pg.Manage., Curr.Cont., IBR, Key to Econ.Sci., Manage.Cont., Mgmt.& Market.Abstr., Oper.Res.Manage.Sci., P.A.I.S., Psychol.Abstr. (1982-), Ref.Pt.Food Indus.Abstr., SSCI, Tr.& Indus.Ind. **Document type:** academic/scholarly publication.
●Also available online. Vendor(s): Information Access Co., Knight-Ridder Information, Inc.
—BLDSC (5052.040000); Genuine Article; KR SourceOne; SWETS; UMI; UnCover. **CCC.**
Description: Presents scholarly articles on market trends, research developments, and relevant legislation.

658.8   UK   ISSN 0969-6989
HF5428
JOURNAL OF RETAILING AND CONSUMER SERVICES. 1994. q. fl.557($320) (effective 1998). Elsevier Science Ltd., Pergamon, P.O. Box 800, Kidlington, Oxford OX2 8DP, England. TEL 44-1865-843000. FAX 44-1865-843010. E-mail: nlinfo-f@elsevier.nl; usinfo-f@elsevier.com; forinfo-kyf04035@niftyserve.or.jp; URL: http://www.elsevier.nl/. (Subscr.to: Elsevier Science, Regional Sales Office, P.O. Box 211, 1000 AE Amsterdam, Netherlands. TEL 31-20-4853757. FAX 31-20-4853432; Subscr. in the Americas to: Elsevier Science, Regional Sales Office, Box 945, New York, NY 10159-0945. TEL 212-633-3730. FAX 212-633-3680; Subscr. in Australasia and the Far East to: Elsevier Science (Singapore) Pte Ltd, No.1 Temasek Ave., No.17-01 Millenia Tower, Singapore 039192, Singapore. TEL 65-434-3727. FAX 65-337-2230) Ed.Bd.; Pub. Lyndon Driscoll. (also avail. in microform from UMI; back issues avail.) **Indexed:** Geo.Abstr.P.G., IDA. **Document type:** academic/scholarly publication.
—BLDSC (5052.041000); EMDOCS; KR SourceOne; SWETS; UMI. **CCC.**
Refereed Serial

658   US   ISSN 1091-1340
▼**JOURNAL OF SEGMENTATION MARKETING;** innovations in market identification & targeting. 1997. s-a. $25 to individuals; institutions $40; libraries $65 (effective 1997-1998). Haworth Press, Inc., 10 Alice St., Binghamton, NY 13904. TEL 607-722-5857; 800-342-9676. FAX 607-722-6362. E-mail: getinfo@haworth.com; URL: http://www.haworth.com. Ed. Art T. Weinstein; Pub. Bill Cohen. R&P contact: Ruthann Heath. adv.: B&W page $300; trim 4 3/8 x 7 1/8; adv. contact: Jackie Blakeslee. (also avail. in microform from HAW,UMI; reprint service avail. from HAW) **Document type:** academic/scholarly publication.
—Haworth.

658.8   UK   ISSN 0887-6045
HD9980.1
JOURNAL OF SERVICES MARKETING. 1986. bi-m. £899($499) (foreign Aus.$1769) (effective 1998). M C B University Press Ltd., 60-62 Toller Ln., Bradford, W. Yorks BD8 9BY, England. TEL 44-1274-777700. FAX 44-1274-785200. TELEX 51317-MCBUNI-G. URL: http://www.mcb.co.uk/cgi-bin/meb__serve/table1.txt&jsm&journal1.htm. Ed. Charles Martin. adv.; bk.rev.; index. circ. 1,000. (back issues avail.) **Indexed:** ABI Inform. **Document type:** academic/scholarly publication.
●Also available on CD-ROM.
—BLDSC (5064.011000); SWETS; UMI; UnCover. **CCC.**

658   UK   ISSN 0965-254X
HF5415.13
JOURNAL OF STRATEGIC MARKETING. 1993. q. £50 (foreign $85) to individuals; institutions £205 (foreign $340); print & online eds. combined £245 (foreign $410) (effective 1998). Thomson Professional (Subsidiary of International Thomson Publishing Group), 2-6 Boundary Row, London SE1 8HN, England. TEL 44-171-8650066. FAX 44-171-5229623. TELEX 290164 CHAPMA G. E-mail: journal@rapidcom.co.uk; URL: http://jsm.thomsonprofessional.com. (Dist. by: International Thomson Publishing Services Ltd., Cheriton House, North Way, Andover, Hants. SP10 5BE, England. TEL 44-1264-342713. FAX 44-1264-342807; Subscr. in US & Canada to: 400 Market St., Philadelphia, PA 19106. TEL 800-552-5866) Ed. Gordon Greenley. adv. contact: Gemma Heiser. bibl. (reprint service avail.) **Indexed:** Cont.Pg.Manage. **Document type:** academic/scholarly publication.
●Also available online.
—BLDSC (5066.872950). **CCC.**
Description: Publishes articles and research dedicated to exploring the relationship between marketing and strategic management.
Refereed Serial

JOURNAL OF TRAVEL & TOURISM MARKETING. see *TRAVEL AND TOURISM*

JOURNAL OF VACATION MARKETING. see *TRAVEL AND TOURISM*

658.8   AU   ISSN 0022-6300
DER JUNGE KAUFMANN. 1968. m. S.616. Verlag Dr. Herta Ranner, Zeismannsbrunngasse 1, A-1070 Vienna, Austria. TEL 01-935387. Ed. H. Ranner. adv.; bk.rev. **Document type:** trade publication.

BUSINESS AND ECONOMICS — MARKETING AND PURCHASING

658   SZ
JUNGE KAUFMANN. 5/yr. Schweizerischer Kaufmannischer Verband, Hans-Huber Str. 4, CH-8027 Zurich, Switzerland. TEL 1-2024710.

659   NO   ISSN 0022-8214
KAMPANJE!. 1964. fortn. (20/yr.). NOK 745. Hjemmet-Mortensen AS, P.O. Box 5001, N-0301 Oslo, Norway. TEL 02-94-10-00. FAX 02-33-23-67. Ed. Johnny Gimmestad. adv. circ. 20,747.
—CCC.
Description: Articles on a variety of marketing subjects and media, information and communication in general.

658.7   US   ISSN 1056-6015
KANSAS CITY COMMERCE. 1990. m. (National Association of Purchasing Management) Printing & Publishing, Inc., 109 W. Washington, Millstadt, IL 62260-0030. TEL 618-476-7770. FAX 618-476-7616. Ed. Paul Stocklein. adv. circ. 5,583. **Document type:** trade publication.
Description: Presents features covering purchasing disciplines.

KART MARKETING INTERNATIONAL; the monthly trade magazine for the karting industry. see SPORTS AND GAMES

659   FI   ISSN 0783-5167
KEHITTYVAE KAUPPA. 1907. fortn. FIM 660. Kauppiaitten Kustannus Oy, Kanavakatu 3B, FIN-00160 Helsinki, Finland. TEL 358-0-228821. Ed. Kaisa Peutere. adv.; bk.rev.; tr.lit.; index; circ. 21,368 (controlled).
Former titles: Kauppias (ISSN 0355-3078); K-Kauppa Ja Myyja (ISSN 0047-3057)

KEY (BATTLEGROUND). see ADVERTISING AND PUBLIC RELATIONS

658   UK
KEY NOTE MARKET REPORT: AUTOMATIC VENDING. Variant title: Automatic Vending (Hampton). 1988. irreg., no.10, 1996. £205. Key Note Ltd., Field House, 72 Oldfield Rd., Hampton, Middlesex TW12 2HQ, England. TEL 44-181-783-0755. FAX 44-181-783-0049. **Document type:** trade publication.
●Also available online.
Also available on CD-ROM.
Formerly: Key Note Report: Automatic Vending (ISSN 1352-6138)

KEY NOTE MARKET REPORT: BICYCLES. see SPORTS AND GAMES — Bicycles And Motorcycles

KEY NOTE MARKET REPORT: BIOTECHNOLOGY. see BIOLOGY — Biotechnology

KEY NOTE MARKET REPORT: BROWN GOODS. see ELECTRONICS

KEY NOTE MARKET REPORT: BUS & COACH OPERATORS. see TRANSPORTATION

KEY NOTE MARKET REPORT: CABLE AND SATELLITE T V. see COMMUNICATIONS — Television And Cable

658   UK
KEY NOTE MARKET REPORT: CASH & CARRY OUTLETS. Variant title: Cash & Carry Outlets. irreg., no.12, 1995. £205. Key Note Ltd., Field House, 72 Oldfield Rd., Hampton, Middlesex TW12 2HQ, England. TEL 44-181-783-0755. FAX 44-181-783-0049. **Document type:** trade publication.
●Also available online.
Also available on CD-ROM.
Formerly (until 1995): Key Note Report: Cash and Carry Outlets (ISSN 0954-4283)

KEY NOTE MARKET REPORT: CLOTHING RETAILING. see CLOTHING TRADE

658   UK
KEY NOTE MARKET REPORT: CONVENIENCE RETAILING. Variant title: Convenience Retailing. irreg., vol.8, 1995. £205. Key Note Ltd., Field House, 72 Oldfield Rd., Hampton, Middlesex TW12 2HQ, England. TEL 44-181-783-0755. FAX 44-181-783-0049. Ed. Simon Howitt. **Document type:** trade publication.
●Also available online.
Also available on CD-ROM.
Formerly (until 1995): Key Note Report: Convenience Retailing (ISSN 1352-6537)

KEY NOTE MARKET REPORT: D I Y. see INTERIOR DESIGN AND DECORATION

658   UK
KEY NOTE MARKET REPORT: DIRECT MARKETING. Variant title: Direct Marketing. 1987. irreg., vol.8, 1995. £205. Key Note Ltd., Field House, 72 Oldfield Rd., Hampton, Middlesex TW12 2HQ, England. TEL 44-181-783-0755. FAX 44-181-783-0049. Ed. Phillippa Smith. **Document type:** trade publication.
●Also available online.
Also available on CD-ROM.
Formerly: Key Note Report: Direct Marketing (ISSN 0950-3765)

KEY NOTE MARKET REPORT: FAST FOOD AND HOME DELIVERY OUTLETS. see FOOD AND FOOD INDUSTRIES

KEY NOTE MARKET REPORT: HEALTH CLUBS AND LEISURE CENTRES. see SPORTS AND GAMES

658   UK
KEY NOTE MARKET REPORT: HOME SHOPPING. Variant title: Home Shopping. 1993. irreg., no.4, 1996. £205. Key Note Ltd., Field House, 72 Oldfield Rd., Hampton, Middlesex TW12 2HQ, England. TEL 44-181-783-0755. FAX 44-181-783-0049. **Document type:** trade publication.
●Also available online.
Also available on CD-ROM.
Formerly: Key Note Report: Home Shopping (ISSN 1354-2702)

KEY NOTE MARKET REPORT: INDUSTRIAL FASTENERS. see ENGINEERING — Engineering Mechanics And Materials

KEY NOTE MARKET REPORT: JEWELLERY, WATCHES & FASHION ACCESSORIES. see JEWELRY, CLOCKS AND WATCHES

658   UK
KEY NOTE MARKET REPORT: MAIL ORDER. Variant title: Mail Order. irreg., no.8, 1991. £185. Key Note Ltd., Field House, 72 Oldfield Rd., Hampton, Middlesex TW12 2HQ, England. TEL 44-181-783-0755. FAX 44-181-783-1940. **Document type:** trade publication.

KEY NOTE MARKET REPORT: MORTGAGE FINANCE. see BUSINESS AND ECONOMICS — Banking And Finance

658   UK
KEY NOTE MARKET REPORT: OWN BRANDS. Variant title: Own Brands. irreg., no.6, 1995. £205. Key Note Ltd., Field House, 72 Oldfield Rd., Hampton, Middlesex TW12 2HQ, England. TEL 44-181-783-0755. FAX 44-181-783-0049. **Document type:** trade publication.
●Also available online.
Also available on CD-ROM.
Formerly: Key Note Report: Own Brands.

KEY NOTE MARKET REPORT: PERISHABLE FAST-MOVING CONSUMER GOODS. see FOOD AND FOOD INDUSTRIES

KEY NOTE MARKET REPORT: PLASTICS PROCESSING. see PLASTICS

KEY NOTE MARKET REPORT: PREMIUM LAGERS, BEERS AND CIDERS. see BEVERAGES

KEY NOTE MARKET REPORT: SAUCES AND SPREADS. see FOOD AND FOOD INDUSTRIES

658   UK
KEY NOTE MARKET REPORT: SHOP FITTING. Variant title: Shop Fitting. irreg., no.5, 1995. £205. Key Note Ltd., Field House, 72 Oldfield Rd., Hampton, Middlesex TW12 2HQ, England. TEL 44-181-783-0755. FAX 44-181-783-0049. **Document type:** trade publication.
●Also available online.
Also available on CD-ROM.
Formerly: Key Note Report: Shop Fitting.

KEY NOTE MARKET REPORT: SOAPS & DETERGENTS. see CLEANING AND DYEING

KEY NOTE MARKET REPORT: T V & VIDEO RENTAL. see ELECTRONICS

KEY NOTE MARKET REVIEW: D I Y & HOME IMPROVEMENTS. see INTERIOR DESIGN AND DECORATION

658 052   UK
KEY NOTE MARKET REVIEW: GREY MARKET IN THE U K. Variant title: Grey Market in the U K. 1994. irreg. £410. Key Note Ltd., Field House, 72 Oldfield Rd., Hampton, Middlesex TW12 2HQ, England. TEL 44-181-783-0755. FAX 44-181-783-0049. Ed. Kim Thomasson. **Document type:** trade publication.
●Also available online.
Also available on CD-ROM.

658   UK
KEY NOTE MARKET REVIEW: RETAILING IN THE U K. Variant title: Retailing in the U K. irreg., no.6, 1997. £410. Key Note Ltd., Field House, 72 Oldfield Rd., Hampton, Middlesex TW12 2HQ, England. TEL 44-181-783-0755. FAX 44-181-783-0049. **Document type:** trade publication.
●Also available online.
Also available on CD-ROM.

658.8   UK
KEY NOTE MARKET REVIEW: U K PET MARKET. 1994. irreg. £410. Key Note Ltd., Field House, 72 Oldfield Rd., Hampton, Middlesex TW12 2HQ, England. TEL 44-181-783-0755. FAX 44-181-783-0049. Ed. Eleanor Hughes. **Document type:** trade publication.
●Also available online.
Also available on CD-ROM.

KEY NOTE MARKET REVIEW: U K PHARMACEUTICAL INDUSTRY. see PHARMACY AND PHARMACOLOGY

658   UK
KEY NOTE MARKET REVIEW: WHOLESALING IN THE U K. Variant title: Wholesaling in the U K. 1994. irreg. £410. Key Note Ltd., Field House, 72 Oldfield Rd., Hampton, Middlesex TW12 2HQ, England. TEL 44-181-783-0755. FAX 44-181-783-0049. Ed. Kim Thomasson. **Document type:** trade publication.
●Also available online.
Also available on CD-ROM.

KEY NOTE REPORT: HOME COMPUTERS - SOFTWARE. see COMPUTERS — Personal Computers

KEY NOTE REPORT: MEN'S CLOTHING RETAILERS. see CLOTHING TRADE

658   CN   ISSN 1205-7746
▼**KIDSCREEN.** 1996. m. Can.$79($59) (foreign $99). Brunico Communications Inc., 366 Adelaide St. W., Ste. 500, Toronto, ON M5V 1R9, Canada. TEL 416-408-2300. FAX 416-408-0870. E-mail: circ@brunico.com. Ed. Mark Symka; Pub. Ken Faier. adv.: B&W page Can.$3155; color page Can.$3985; trim 8 1/2 x 11. **Document type:** trade publication.
Description: Covers the business of children's entertainment production and programming and the marketing of child-oriented licensed products and services.

658   SZ
KIOSKINHABER. m. Postfach 330, CH-8401 Winterthur, Switzerland. TEL 052-821315. Ed. Peter Sutter. circ. 800.

380.14   NO
KJOEPMANNEN. m. (11/yr.). Bergens Kjoepmannsforening, Taarnplass 3, 5000 Bergen, Norway. adv. circ. 1,000.

658   SZ
KLARTEXT. 1981. 6/yr. 79 SFr. Postfach 7635, CH-3001 Bern, Switzerland. TEL 031-3824557. FAX 031-3824555. Ed. Klaus Bonanomi. adv. contact: Hannes Wieland. bk.rev. circ. 3,100. **Document type:** trade publication.

658.8   FI   ISSN 0023-3862
KOEPMANNEN. (Text in Swedish) 1928. 8/yr. FIM 100 for non-members. Finlands Svenska Koepmannafoerbund, Kaserngatan 23 A, 00130 Helsinki 13, Finland. Ed. P.H. Landen. adv.; illus.; stat. circ. 1,600.

KOEPMANNEN VAEST. see BUSINESS AND ECONOMICS — Domestic Commerce

BUSINESS AND ECONOMICS — MARKETING AND PURCHASING

658.8   SW   ISSN 1100-4924
KONFERENS VAERLDEN; en facktidskrift foer konferenser, motivation & incentive och affaersresor. 1989. 8/yr. SEK 420 (effective 1997); newsstand price: SEK 54. Foerlagshuset Stocom AB, P.O. Box 1106, S-172 22 Sundbyberg, Sweden. TEL 46--8-98-02-60. FAX 46-8-98-16-80. E-mail: konferensvaerlden@stocom.se; roger.kellerman@stocom.se; bjorn.stromberg@stocom.se; URL: http://www.stocom.se. Ed. Roger Kellerman; Pub. Bjorn A. Stromberg. adv. contact: Eva Svenander. bk.rev.
Document type: trade publication.

L M S; new developments in laboratory equipment. (Laboratory Marketing Spectrum) see *MEDICAL SCIENCES — Experimental Medicine, Laboratory Technique*

658   GW   ISSN 0171-015X
LAGERTECHNIK. 1967. a. Henrich Publikationen GmbH, Schwanheimerstr. 110, 60528 Frankfurt a.M., Germany. TEL 49-69-96777234. FAX 49-69-96777111. Ed. Martin Spiekermann. circ. 14,711. **Document type:** trade publication.

LARGE KITCHEN APPLIANCES: THE INTERNATIONAL MARKET. see *ELECTRONICS*

658.8   UK
LARGE MIXED RETAILERS: THE INTERNATIONAL MARKET. (Subseries of: Market Direction reports) a. £2250($4500) (effective 1997). Euromonitor, 60-61 Britton St., London EC1M 5NA, England. TEL 44-171-251-8024. FAX 44-171-608-3149. E-mail: info@euromonitor.com; URL: http://www.euromonitor.com. (Addr. in N. America: Euromonitor International, 122 S. Michigan Ave., Ste. 1200, Chicago, IL 60603. TEL 800-577-3876. FAX 312-922-1157) (looseleaf format) **Document type:** trade publication.
● Also available online. Vendor(s): Data-Star, Knight-Ridder Information, Inc.
Description: Analyzes the market for large department stores for France, Germany, Italy, Spain, the U.K., the U.S., and Japan.

658.8   CN   ISSN 0705-212X
LAWN & GARDEN TRADE. 4/yr. Can.$15($33) (effective 1997). 2585 Skymark Ave., Ste. 306, Mississauga, ON L4W 4L5, Canada. TEL 905-624-8218. FAX 905-624-6764. Ed. Peter Tasler. adv. contact: Norm Rosen. bk.rev.; circ. 14,000 (controlled). **Document type:** trade publication.
Description: Marketing news, trends, new products covering Canada's lawn, garden and outdoor power equipment industries.

LEADS. see *BUSINESS AND ECONOMICS — Economic Situation And Conditions*

LEARNING - FOUNTAIN REVIEWS. see *COMPUTERS — Computer Networks*

LESSONS OF YELLOW PAGES COMPETITION. see *BUSINESS AND ECONOMICS — Trade And Industrial Directories*

658   FR   ISSN 0759-0024
LETTRE DE LA COMMUNICATION. 47/yr. 5 rue Papillon, 75009 Paris, France. TEL 42-46-58-10. FAX 40-22-07-18. Ed. Nathalie Leclerc. circ. 1,200.

658.8 659.1   FR   ISSN 0298-9239
LETTRE DU SPONSORING ET DU MECENAT; le 1er support francais sur le parrainage d'entreprise. 1986. fortn. 3090 F.($482) (effective 1996). Editions L'Evenementiel France, 86, rue du President Wilson, 92300 Levallois Perret, France. TEL 1-47-39-45-19. FAX 1-40-38-02-97. Ed. Alain M. Chauveau. adv. contact: Jean Claude Roziv. **Document type:** newsletter.
Description: Devoted to sponsorship and project funding. For those involved in corporate techniques of marketing and communication as well as sports and cultural organizers, organizations and media.

LEWIS LETTER ON CABLE MARKETING. see *COMMUNICATIONS — Television And Cable*

658   UK   ISSN 0955-5455
LICENSED PRODUCT MARKETING. 1988. 4/yr. £16.50. c/o G.T. Portwin, 177 Hagden Lane, Watford WD1 8LN, England. TEL 0923-228577.
Formerly: Market Digest (ISSN 0953-704X)
Description: Covers charter merchandising and corporate licensing.

THE LICENSING BOOK. see *PATENTS, TRADEMARKS AND COPYRIGHTS*

LICENSING LETTER. see *PATENTS, TRADEMARKS AND COPYRIGHTS*

LIFESTYLE MARKET ANALYST. see *BUSINESS AND ECONOMICS — Abstracting, Bibliographies, Statistics*

LIGHTING MAGAZINE. see *INTERIOR DESIGN AND DECORATION — Furniture And House Furnishings*

LIMOUSINE & CHAUFFEUR. see *TRANSPORTATION — Automobiles*

658   US
LOGISTICS COMMENT. 1968. q. free to members. Council of Logistics Management, 2803 Butterfield Rd., Ste. 380, Oak Brook, IL 60521. TEL 630-574-0985. FAX 630-574-0989. Ed. Elaine M. Winter. bk.rev. circ. 10,000. **Document type:** bulletin.
Description: Provides information about the council of interest to members.

LOGISTICS MANAGEMENT; for buyers of logistics, transportation services, logistics technology and related equipment. see *TRANSPORTATION*

LUBES 'N' GREASES; the magazine of industry in motion. see *BUSINESS AND ECONOMICS — Management*

M A C NEWS. (Mid-Atlantic Council of Shopping Center Managers) see *BUSINESS AND ECONOMICS — Management*

658   GW
M D - MARKETING DIGEST; Fachbereichszeitschrift der Fachhochschule fuer Wirtschaft, Pforzheim. 1983. s-a. DM.10. Verein der Foerder und Absolventen (FAV), Fachhochschule fuer Wirtschaft, Tiefenbronner Str. 65, 75175 Pforzheim, Germany. TEL 07231-603-0. Ed. Philip Staehler. adv.; bk.rev. circ. 1,700. (back issues avail.) **Document type:** academic/scholarly publication.

658.8   US   ISSN 0092-4857
HC106.6
M E I MARKETING ECONOMICS GUIDE.* 1973. a. $30. Marketing Economics Institute, Ltd., 186-26 Avon Rd., Jamaica, NY 11432-5823. Ed. Alfred Hong. illus.; stat. (also avail. in magnetic tape; diskette format)

658.8   SP   ISSN 1130-8761
M K - MARKETING Y VENTAS PARA DIRECTIVOS. 1987. 11/yr. 19980 ptas. Grupo Especial Directivos, C. Orense 39 2o D, 28020 Madrid, Spain. TEL 34-1-5566411. FAX 34-1-5554118. Ed. Begona de Miguel. adv.: B&W page 230000 ptas., color page 275000 ptas.; trim 177 x 272; adv. contact: Juan Manuel Castro. circ. 9,637 (controlled). **Document type:** trade publication.

M L S. (Marketing Library Services) see *LIBRARY AND INFORMATION SCIENCES*

M P A NEWSLETTER OF RESEARCH. (Magazine Publishers of America) see *ADVERTISING AND PUBLIC RELATIONS*

M P R EXCHANGE. (American Society for Health Care Marketing and Public Relations) see *HOSPITALS*

M R A A NEWSLETTER. (Marine Retailers Association of America) see *SPORTS AND GAMES — Boats And Boating*

658   US
M R A BLUE BOOK RESEARCH SERVICES DIRECTORY. 1973. a. $70 to members; non-members $100 (effective 1997). Marketing Research Association, Inc., 2189 Silas Deane Hwy., Ste. 5, Box 230, Rocky Hill, CT 06067-0230. TEL 860-257-4008. FAX 860-257-3990. circ. 1,300. **Document type:** directory.
Formerly: M R A Research Service Directory.
Description: Outlines research and data-collection company capabilities and facilities.

MADE IN EUROPE. GENERAL MERCHANDISE. see *BUSINESS AND ECONOMICS — International Commerce*

MAGA SCENE. see *PUBLISHING AND BOOK TRADE*

THE MAGAZINE; everything you need to know to make it in the magazine business. see *PUBLISHING AND BOOK TRADE*

658.8 659.1   US
MAGNET MARKETING. 1976. q. free. Graham Communications, 40 Oval Rd., Quincy, MA 02170. TEL 617-328-0069. FAX 617-471-1504. Ed. Cindy Cantrell. circ. 3,500 (controlled). (some back issues avail.) **Document type:** newsletter.
Formerly (until 1991): Good Impressions.
Description: Features results-oriented articles and information on advertising, marketing, public relations, design, creative sales and fundraising for businesses.

658.8   UK
MAIL ORDER AND HOME SHOPPING: THE INTERNATIONAL MARKET. (Subseries of: Market Direction reports) a. £2250($4500) (effective 1997). Euromonitor, 60-61 Britton St., London EC1M 5NA, England. TEL 44-171-251-8024. FAX 44-171-608-3149. E-mail: info@euromonitor.com; URL: http://www.euromonitor.com. (Addr. in N. America: Euromonitor International, 122 S. Michigan Ave., Ste. 1200, Chicago, IL 60603. TEL 800-577-3876. FAX 312-922-1157) (looseleaf format) **Document type:** trade publication.
● Also available online. Vendor(s): Data-Star, Knight-Ridder Information, Inc.
Description: Analyzes the market for mail order and other forms of at-home shopping for France, Germany, Italy, Spain, the U.K., the U.S., and Japan.

MAIL ORDER BUSINESS DIRECTORY. see *BUSINESS AND ECONOMICS — Trade And Industrial Directories*

658.8   US   ISSN 0464-591X
MAINLY MARKETING; the Schoonmaker report to technical managements. 1962. m. $200. Schoonmaker Associates, Drawer 973, Coram, NY 11727. TEL 516-473-8741. Ed. W.K. Schoonmaker. bk.rev.; charts; stat.; cum.index. circ. 1,000. (back issues avail.)
Description: Attempts to help readers market better to and for high technology companies.

MAKE-UP AND COLOUR COSMETICS: THE INTERNATIONAL MARKET. see *BEAUTY CULTURE*

MANIPULACION DE MATERIALES EN LA INDUSTRIA. see *BUILDING AND CONSTRUCTION*

658.8   US   ISSN 1060-2712
MANUFACTURING AUTOMATION; the essential business resource on international manufacturing automation. m. $325 (overseas $345) (effective 1997 & 1998). Vital Information Publications, 754 Caravel Ln., Foster City, CA 94404. TEL 415-345-7018. FAX 415-345-7018. Ed. Peter Adrian; Pub. Peter Adrian. adv. contact: Lidia Bekker. charts; circ. 600 (paid). **Document type:** newsletter.
● Also available online. Vendor(s): Data-Star, Information Access Co., Knight-Ridder Information, Inc., NewsNet (MG17).
—BLDSC (5365.976000). CCC.
Formed by the 1991 merger of: Advanced Manufacturing; Manufacturing Automation News (ISSN 0957-0047); Incorporates (in 1991): Industrial Automation Outlook (ISSN 1051-9440); Advanced Manufacturing Newsletter; Manufacturing Automation News (ISSN 0950-5113) was formed by the 1987 merger of: F M S Update; Robot News International (ISSN 0262-1460); Industrial Automation Outlook was formerly: Factory Automation News (ISSN 1045-0554).
Description: Provides information on worldwide markets, products, technologies, and applications in key areas of manufacturing and industrial automation.

658   FR   ISSN 0183-3308
MARCHAND FORAIN. m. 2 place de l'Amirande, B.P. 52, 84000 Avignon Cedex, France. TEL 90-82-54-03. TELEX 432 770. Ed. Michel Pierre. circ. 24,000.

658 387
MARINE INDUSTRY RETAILER.* 11/yr. Box 50165, Denton, TX 76206-0165. TEL 602-838-9707. FAX 602-838-9745. Ed. Nicholas Blenkey. circ. 30,950.

MARKEDSFOERING. see *ADVERTISING AND PUBLIC RELATIONS*

BUSINESS AND ECONOMICS — MARKETING AND PURCHASING

658.8   SP
MARKERAMA. 6/yr. Consell de Cent 366, pra., 08009 Barcelona, Spain. TEL 3-302-25-27. FAX 3-412-33-26. Ed. Cesar Dutch. circ. 3,500.

658   UK   ISSN 0962-2039
MARKET DIRECTION REPORTS. (Consists of multiple sub-series) irreg. £1595($3190) per no. (effective 1997). Euromonitor, 60-61 Britton St., London EC1M 5NA, England. TEL 44-171-251-8024. FAX 44-171-608-3149. E-mail: info@euromonitor.com; URL: http://www.euromonitor.com. (Addr. in N. America: Euromonitor International, 122 S. Michigan Ave., Ste. 1200, Chicago, IL 60603. TEL 800-577-3876. FAX 312-922-1157) charts; stat. (looseleaf format) **Document type:** trade publication.
● Also available online. Vendor(s): Data-Star, Knight-Ridder Information, Inc.
Description: Analyzes the markets for a specific product in France, Germany, Italy, Spain, the U.K., the U.S., and Japan.

THE MARKET FOR CONSUMER HEALTHCARE IN LATIN AMERICA. see MEDICAL SCIENCES

THE WORLD MARKET FOR O T C HEALTHCARE IN CHINA. see PHARMACY AND PHARMACOLOGY

THE MARKET FOR O T C HEALTHCARE IN EASTERN EUROPE. see PHARMACY AND PHARMACOLOGY

THE MARKET FOR O T C HEALTHCARE IN LATIN AMERICA. see PHARMACY AND PHARMACOLOGY

THE MARKET FOR O T C HEALTHCARE IN SOUTH EAST ASIA. see PHARMACY AND PHARMACOLOGY

THE MARKET FOR PACKAGED FOODS IN LATIN AMERICA. see FOOD AND FOOD INDUSTRIES

THE MARKET FOR PACKAGED FOOD IN SOUTH EAST ASIA. see FOOD AND FOOD INDUSTRIES

THE MARKET FOR PACKAGING IN CHINA. see PACKAGING

THE MARKET FOR PACKAGING IN LATIN AMERICA. see PACKAGING

THE MARKET FOR PACKAGING IN SOUTH EAST ASIA. see PACKAGING

658.8   UK
THE MARKET FOR WHITE GOODS IN SOUTH EAST ASIA. (Part of Euromonitor Emerging Market Reports series) irreg., 1995 edition. £1950($3900) Euromonitor, 60-61 Britton St., London EC1M 5NA, England. TEL 44-171-251-8024. FAX 44-171-608-3149. E-mail: info@euromonitor.com; URL: http://www.euromonitor.com. (Addr. in N. America: 122 S. Michigan Ave., Ste. 1200, Chicago, IL 60603. TEL 800-577-3876. FAX 312-922-1157) **Document type:** trade publication.
Formerly: White Goods Markets in South East Asia.
Description: Reports on market conditions affecting the sales of major appliances in Southeast Asia.

380.14   UK
MARKET INTELLIGENCE. 1972. m. £1495 (effective 1996). Mintel International Group Ltd., 18-19 Long Ln., London EC1A 9HE, England. TEL 44-171-606-4533. FAX 44-171-606-5932. E-mail: mintel@cityscape.co.uk; URL: http://www.cityscape.co.uk/users/ca93/. Ed. Moira Paterson. index. circ. 600. (also avail. in microfiche; back issues avail.) **Indexed:** Food Sci.& Tech.Abstr., SCIMP (1984-). **Document type:** trade publication.
● Also available online.
Also available on CD-ROM.
Formerly: Mintel (ISSN 0305-3504)

052   SA
MARKET PLACE. 1978. fortn. R.155. Caxton Printing & Publishing Co., P.O. Box 1610, Parklands 2121, Johannesburg, South Africa. TEL 27-11-889-0600. FAX 27-11-889-0758. Ed. Heather Holt. R&P contact: Cliff Bucher. adv. contact: Adrienne Novis. bk.rev. circ. 3,500. **Document type:** trade publication.

658.83   UK   ISSN 0308-3446
MARKET RESEARCH EUROPE. 1968. m. £545($1090) (effective 1997). Euromonitor, 60-61 Britton St., London EC1M 5NA, England. TEL 44-171-251-8024. FAX 44-171-608-3149. E-mail: info@euromonitor.com; URL: http://www.euromonitor.com. (Addr. in N. America: Euromonitor International, 122 S. Michigan Ave. Ste. 1200, Chicago, IL 60603. TEL 800-577-3876. FAX 312-922-1157) charts; illus.; mkt.; stat.; index. (processed) **Indexed:** Art.Hosp.& Tour., BPIA, Cont.Pg.Manage., Int.Packag.Abstr., Key to Econ.Sci., PROMT, SCIMP (1984-). **Document type:** trade publication.
● Also available online. Vendor(s): Lexis-Nexis.
—BLDSC (5381.573000); SWETS.
Former titles: Euromonitor Review (ISSN 0014-2441); Which incorporates: Market Research in Benelux (ISSN 0047-598X); Market Research in Germany (ISSN 0047-5998); Market Research in Italy (ISSN 0047-6005)
Description: Covers the European food and nonfood markets, as well as the secondary consumer markets.

658.83   UK   ISSN 0308-3047
MARKET RESEARCH G B. 1960. m. £510($1020) Euromonitor, 60-61 Britton St., London EC1M 5NA, England. TEL 44-171-251-8024. FAX 44-171-608-3149. E-mail: info@euromonitor.com; URL: http://www.euromonitor.com. (Addr. in N. America: Euromonitor International, 122 S. Michigan Ave., Ste. 1200, Chicago, IL 60603. TEL 312-922-1115. FAX 312-922-1157) mkt.; stat. **Indexed:** Art.Hosp.& Tour., Cont.Pg.Manage., Food Sci.& Tech.Abstr., Int.Packag.Abstr., Key to Econ.Sci., SCIMP (1984-). **Document type:** trade publication.
—BLDSC (5381.585000); SWETS.
Formerly: Market Research (ISSN 0025-3588)

658.8   UK   ISSN 1352-1101
MARKET RESEARCH INTERNATIONAL. 1994. m. £545($1090) (effective 1997). Euromonitor, 60-61 Britton St., London EC1M 5QU, England. TEL 44-171-251-8024. FAX 44-171-608-3149. E-mail: info@euromonitor.com; URL: http://www.euromonitor.com/mri.html. (Addr. in N. America: Euromonitor International, 122 S. Michigan Ave., Ste. 1200, Chicago, IL 60603. TEL 800-577-3876. FAX 312-922-1157) charts; stat. **Document type:** trade publication.
Description: Covers a wide variety of international consumer markets.

658.8   UK   ISSN 0963-7257
MARKET RESEARCH REPORTER. 1992. 20/yr. £279($559) (effective 1996). Business Information Futures Ltd., One Henry Smith's Terr., Headland, Cleveland TS24 0PD, England. TEL 44-1429-231902. FAX 44-1249-861403. Ed. Anne P. Smith; Pub. Anne P. Smith. R&P contact: A.P. Smith. **Document type:** newsletter.
Description: Keeps market research professionals up to date on the findings of new market reports, covering both consumer and industrial markets.

658.8   UK   ISSN 0025-3618
HF5415.2   CODEN: JMRSBJ
MARKET RESEARCH SOCIETY. JOURNAL. vol.12, 1970. q. £99 (foreign £115.50) (effective 1998). Market Research Society, 15 Northburgh St., London EC1V 0AH, England. TEL 44-171-490-0608. (Subscr. to: NTC Publications Ltd., P.O. Box 69, Henley-on-Thames, Oxon RG9 1GB, England. TEL 44-1491-411000) Eds. Stephan Buck, James Rothman; Pub. Peter Greenwood. R&P contact: Nicola Potts. adv.; bk.rev.; bibl.; index. (also avail. in microfilm from UMI; SCH,UMI) **Indexed:** ABI Inform., Account.& Data Proc.Abstr., Anbar., BPIA, Bus.Ind., Commun.Abstr., Cont.Pg.Manage., Curr.Cont., HRIS, Manage.Cont., Mgmt.& Market.Abstr., P.A.I.S., Polit.Sci.Abstr., Psychol.Abstr. (1968-), Psyscsan., SCIMP (1978-), SSCI. **Document type:** trade publication.
● Also available online. Vendor(s): Information Access Co.
—BLDSC (4821.150000); Genuine Article; SWETS; UMI; UnCover.
Formerly: Commentary.
Description: Contains papers and shorter notes covering important technical advances, practical applications, appraisals of specific problem areas and issues of current concern, together with correspondence and reviews covering the broad field of marketing and social research.

658.8   UK   ISSN 0076-4523
MARKET RESEARCH SOCIETY. YEARBOOK. 1968. a. £65. Market Research Society, 15 Northburgh St., London EC1V 0AH, England. TEL 44-171-490-4911. FAX 44-171-490-0608. Ed. Phyllis Vangelder; Pub. Peter Greenwood. R&P contact: Nicola Potts. adv. circ. 6,500. **Document type:** corporate report.

MARKET RESEARCH SOURCEBOOK. see BUSINESS AND ECONOMICS — Trade And Industrial Directories

658 332.6   II
MARKET SURVEY CUM DETAILED TECHNO ECONOMIC FEASIBILITY REPORTS. (Text in English) irreg. Rs.2500($225) per no. Small Industry Research Institute, 4-43, Roop Nagar, P.O. Box 2106, New Delhi 110 007, India. TEL 91-11-2910805. FAX 91-11-2923955. TELEX 031-61028 SIRI IN.
Description: Describes in detail projects readily available, including market survey, manufacturing techniques, raw materials, plant and machinery, personnel requirements, land and building, and financial aspects.

658.8   US
MARKETEER. 1952. m. $25. c/o J. Cook, Ed., 1602 E. Glen Ave., Peoria, IL 61614. adv.; circ. 2,000 (controlled). **Document type:** trade publication.
Description: Covers new factory products on the market.

658.8   UK   ISSN 1351-6140
MARKETEER. 1983. w. £18.50 (foreign £45). P.O. Box 48, Northampton NN2 6BR, England. TEL 44-1604-710722. FAX 44-1604-791723. Ed. Phil Lymanth. R&P contact: Phil Lyman. adv. contact: Ros Byran. circ. 32,000. **Document type:** trade publication.
Formerly: Marketeer and Discount Trader (ISSN 0958-3750)
Description: Distributed to retail traders on outdoor, street, and covered markets in Britain.

658 350   AT
MARKETERS COMPLIANCE MANUAL. 1994. s-a. C C H Australia Ltd., P.O. Box 230, N. Ryde, N.S.W. 2113, Australia. TEL 61-1-300300244. FAX 61-1-300306224. (looseleaf format)
Description: For persons involved in marketing - provides explanation of how to keep advertising brochures, catalogues, price lists, promotional material, written warranties and any other representation of product or service within the law.

658 610   US   ISSN 1049-880X
MARKETER'S GUIDEPOST. 1990. bi-m. $72 to non-members; members $50 (effective 1997). Medical Group Management Association, 104 Inverness Terr. E., Englewood, CO 80112. TEL 303-397-7871. FAX 303-643-4427. Ed. Marilee Aust. circ. 500 (paid). **Document type:** newsletter.
Description: Aimed at medical practice administrators and marketers. Contains case studies from medical group practices, plus public-relations marketing tips and techniques.

MARKETER'S LEGAL GUIDE. see LAW — Corporate Law

658.8   BL   ISSN 0025-3634
MARKETING. * 1967. m. Rua Francois Coty, 228, CEP 01524 Sao Paulo, Brazil. Ed. Armando Ferrentini. adv.; illus.; stat. circ. 15,000. (looseleaf format; reprint service avail. from SCH) **Indexed:** B.P.I.

658.8   UK   ISSN 0025-3650
NOT IN LC   CODEN: MARKBC
MARKETING. 1980. w. £75. Haymarket Publishing Ltd., 174 Hammersmith Rd., London W6 7JP, England. TEL 44-171-413-4307. FAX 44-171-413-4509. (Subscr. to: P.O. Box 219, Woking, Surrey GU21 1ZW, England. TEL 44-1483-733800. FAX 44-1483-756792) Ed. Mike Hewitt. adv.; bk.rev.; abstr.; illus. circ. 40,291. (also avail. in microform from UMI; reprint service avail. from SCH) **Indexed:** ABI Inform., Account.& Data Proc.Abstr., Anbar., ASEAN Manage.Abstr., B.P.I., BPIA, Bus.Ind., Can.B.P.I., Ind.Bus.Rep., INSPEC (1983-), Manage.Cont., Mgmt.& Market.Abstr., PSI. **Document type:** trade publication.
● Also available online. Vendor(s): Information Access Co., MediaStream.
—BLDSC (5381.630000); AskIEEE; KR SourceOne; SWETS; UMI.

BUSINESS AND ECONOMICS — MARKETING AND PURCHASING

658.8   YU   ISSN 0581-1023
MARKETING. (Text in English, Serbian) 1970. q. $45 to individuals; institutions $65; libraries $90 (effective 1993). (Jugoslovensko Udruzenje za Marketing (JUMA) - Yugoslav Marketing Association (YUMA)) International Marketing Agency Ltd, Sarajevska 46, P.O. Box 937, 11000 Belgrade, Yugoslavia. TEL 644-743. FAX 38-11-146-605. Ed. Mile Jovic. adv.; bk.rev.; bibl. circ. 2,000. (reprint service avail. from SCH) **Indexed:** B.P.I.
—BLDSC (5381.630500).
    Description: Presents the theory and practice of marketing in Yugoslavia and all over the world.

658   GW   ISSN 0344-1369
MARKETING; Zeitschrift fuer Forschung und Praxis. 1979. q. DM.242 (students DM.174) (effective 1997). Verlag C.H. Beck, 80791 Munich, Germany. TEL 49-89-38189338. FAX 49-89-38189-398. Ed.Bd. adv.: B&W page DM.1800, color DM.3150; trim 260 x 186. circ. 1,200. (back issues avail.; reprint service avail. from SCH) **Indexed:** Account.& Data Proc.Abstr., B.P.I., SCIMP (1982-). **Document type:** trade publication.
—BLDSC (5381.630100); SWETS.

658.8   IE
MARKETING. 12/yr. Jetwood Ltd., 4 Arkendale Ct., Glengeary, Ireland. TEL 857087. Ed. Michael Cullen. circ. 4,000. (reprint service avail. from SCH) **Indexed:** B.P.I.

MARKETING ADDRESS DATA C D. see BUSINESS AND ECONOMICS — Trade And Industrial Directories

658.8   US   ISSN 0896-4742
MARKETING ADVENTS.* 1954. m. $125 membership only. Direct Marketing Association of Washington, 7702 Leesburg Pike, Ste. 400, Falls Church, VA 22043-2612. TEL 703-821-3629. FAX 703-821-3694. Ed. John Jay Daly. adv. circ. 1,500. **Indexed:** Manage.Cont., Tr.& Indus.Ind. **Document type:** newsletter.
    Description: Provides information on postal developments pertinent to the direct marketing industry, plus news and information about the Association.

658 659.1   UK
MARKETING & CREATIVE HANDBOOK. 1985. a. £25. Ste. 5, 74 Oak Rd., Horfield, Bristol BS7 8RZ, England. TEL 44-117-944-6144. URL: http://www.mch.co.uk. Ed. Nikki Bealing. adv.: page £1025; adv. contact: Clive Hicklin. circ. 65,000. **Document type:** directory.

658.8   IT
MARKETING & MANAGERS. 1988. 11/yr. L.70000 (foreign L.140000). Multispe s.r.l., Piazza Conciliazione 2, 20123 Milan, Italy. TEL 39-2-48007589. FAX 39-2-4984494. Ed. Giancarlo Spezia. adv.: B&W page L.5850000, color page L.9000000.

658.8   NE   ISSN 0923-5957
HF5415.2
MARKETING AND RESEARCH TODAY. 1966. 4/yr. 195 SFr. to non-members (foreign $210) (effective 1997). European Society for Opinion and Marketing Research, J.J. Viottastraat 29, 1071 JP Amsterdam, Netherlands. TEL 31-20-664-2141. FAX 31-20-664-2922. E-mail: email@esomar.nl; URL: http://www.esomar.nl. Ed. Bryan Bates. adv.; bk.rev.; charts; stat. circ. 2,100. (back issues avail.) **Indexed:** ABI Inform., Account.& Data Proc.Abstr., Anbar, ASSIA, BPIA, Cont.Pg.Manage., Key to Econ.Sci., Mark.Res.Abstr. (1989-), Mgmt.& Market.Abstr., PROMT, SCIMP (1979-). **Document type:** academic/scholarly publication.
—BLDSC (5381.636500); CISTI; SWETS; UMI; UnCover. **CCC.**
    Former titles (until 1989): European Research (ISSN 0304-4297); (until 1973): European Marketing Research Review (ISSN 0014-3014)
    Description: Disseminates latest developments in international markets with a focus on Western Europe.
    Refereed Serial

658   UK
MARKETING AND RETAILING WORKING PAPER SERIES. irreg. University of Ulster, Faculty of Business and Management, Coleraine BT52 1NA, N. Ireland. TEL 44-1265-324168. FAX 44-1265-324910. E-mail: b.quinn@ulst.ac.uk. Ed. Barry Quinn. **Document type:** monographic series.

MARKETING AND SALES CAREER DIRECTORY. see OCCUPATIONS AND CAREERS

MARKETING BOOK. see ADVERTISING AND PUBLIC RELATIONS

658   UK   ISSN 0954-1543
MARKETING BUSINESS. 1988. m. (Chartered Institute of Marketing) Premier Magazines Ltd., Haymarket House, 1 Oxendon St., London SW1Y 4EE, England. TEL 44-171-925-2544. FAX 44-171-839-4491. Ed. Jane Simms; Pub. David Fernando. adv. contact: Alistair Parkes. **Document type:** trade publication.
—BLDSC (5381.640500). **CCC.**
    Description: Covers marketing trends and techniques.

MARKETING COMPUTERS; communications, electronics and business systems. see COMPUTERS — Computer Industry

658   BL
MARKETING E NEGOCIOS. m. Cr.$70000 per no. Grupo Editorial Letter, Rua Otaviano Hudson 26, Copacabana, 22030-030 Rio de Janeiro RJ, Brazil. FAX 021-275-2346. circ. 40,000.

658.8   US   ISSN 0098-1397
HC102
MARKETING ECONOMICS KEY PLANTS;* guide to industrial purchasing power. 1960. biennial. $120. Marketing Economics Institute, Ltd., 186-26 Avon Rd., Jamaica, NY 11432-5823. Ed. Alfred Hong. stat. (also avail. in magnetic tape)
    Formerly: Market Statistics Key Plant Directory (ISSN 0076-4531)

658 378   US   ISSN 1052-8008
HF5415.1
MARKETING EDUCATION REVIEW. 1992-199?; resumed 1995. 3/yr. $40 to non-members; members $28. C T C Press, Box 1826, Clemson, SC 29633-1826. TEL 803-654-0510. FAX 803-654-7438. (Editorial addr.: Department of Marketing, College of Business and Public Administration, University of Louisville, Louisville, KY 40292. TEL 502-852-4849) Ed. Raymond LaForge. (also avail. in microform from UMI; back issues avail.) **Document type:** academic/scholarly publication.
—BLDSC (5381.641970); UMI. **CCC.**
    Description: Provides a communications network for marketing educators.

658   IT
MARKETING - ESPANSIONE; trimestrale di marketing e pubblicita. 1975. q. L.60000 (foreign L.64200). (Associazione Italiana per gli Studi di Marketing) Arnoldo Mondadori Editore S.p.A., Casella Postale 17135, 20170 Milan, Italy. TEL 3199345. Ed. Redento More. adv.; bk.rev.; charts; illus.; stat. circ. 7,076.
    Supersedes (in 1980): Giornale di Marketing.

MARKETING FOR LAWYERS NEWSLETTER. see LAW

658   US
MARKETING FORUM. bi-m. membership. American Society of Association Executives, Marketing Section, Eye St., N.W., Washington, DC 20006-1168. TEL 202-626-2850. FAX 202-408-9633. circ. 650.
    Description: Provides information on strategic marketing, marketing resources, successful marketing strategies; marketing case studies; 'how-to' articles; calendar of events.

658   UK   ISSN 0965-5328
THE MARKETING HANDBOOK. 1982. a. £55. Hollis Directories Ltd., Harlequin House, 7 High St., Teddington, Middlesex TW11 8EH, England. TEL 44-181-977-7711. FAX 44-181-977-1133. E-mail: hollis@hollis-pr.demon.co.uk; mhb@hollis-pr.demon.co.uk. Ed. Nesta Hollis. adv.: B&W page £1525, color page £2025; 270 x 130. circ. 5,000.
    Formerly (until 1990): U.K. Marketing Handbook.
    Description: Provides coverage in the UK within the following categories: marketing consultants, market research, design, direct marketing, sales promotion, creative services, print and related services, exhibition and conference services.

658.8   PL   ISSN 1231-7853
MARKETING I RYNEK. 1994. m. Polskie Wydawnictwo Ekonomiczne, Ul. Canaletta 4, 000-099 Warsaw, Poland. TEL 48-22-8278001. Ed. Ireneusz Rutkowski.

658.8   UK
MARKETING IN ACTION SERIES. irreg., no.5. £12.95. Kogan Page Ltd., 120 Pentonville Rd., London N1 9JN, England. TEL 44-171-278-0433. FAX 44-171-837-6348. TELEX 263088 KOGAN G. Ed. Norman Hart. R&P contact: Linda Batman. **Document type:** monographic series.

658.8   US   ISSN 0025-3723
MARKETING IN EUROPE; a monthly bulletin providing detailed analysis of the European market for consumer goods. (Issued in three groups: Food, Drink, Tobacco; Clothing, Furniture, Leisure Groups; Chemists and Household Goods, Domestic Appliances) m. £675($1080) for 3 groups (12 issues). Economist Intelligence Unit, 111 W. 57th St., New York, NY 10019. TEL 212-554-0600; 800-938-4685. FAX 212-586-1181. TELEX 175567. (UK addr.: Economist Intelligence Unit Ltd., Subscriptions Dept., P.O. Box 200, Harold Hill, Romford, Essex RM3 8UX, England. TEL 44-1708-381-444. FAX 44-1708-371-850) index. (also avail. in microform from WMP) **Indexed:** Cont.Pg.Manage., Ind.Bus.Rep., Key to Econ.Sci. **Document type:** bulletin.
—BLDSC (5381.642000); SWETS; UnCover.
    Description: Monitors consumer goods markets, marketing and distribution in Europe.

658.8   NR   ISSN 0331-8400
MARKETING IN NIGERIA; for business, economics, commerce, industry. 1972. m. £N10. Alpha Publications, 18 A Modele St., Surulere, Lagos State, Nigeria. Ed. Charles Boduko. adv.; bk.rev.; charts; illus.; stat.; tr.lit. circ. 30,000. **Document type:** trade publication.

658   UK   ISSN 0263-4503
HF5410
MARKETING INTELLIGENCE & PLANNING. 7/yr. £3589($5599) (foreign Aus.$6999) (effective 1998). M C B University Press Ltd., 60-62 Toller Ln., Bradford, W. Yorks BD8 9BY, England. TEL 44-1274-777700. FAX 44-1274-785200. TELEX 51317-MCBUNI-G. URL: http://www.mcb.co.uk. Ed. Michael Thomas. (reprint service avail. from SWZ) **Indexed:** ABI Inform., Mgmt.& Market.Abstr. **Document type:** academic/scholarly publication.
    ●Also available on CD-ROM.
—BLDSC (5381.646700); SWETS; UMI. **CCC.**
    Incorporates (1955-1989): Selling (ISSN 0037-1599); Journal of Sales Management.
    Description: Aims to help the marketing practitioner increase marketing effectiveness. Covers strategic planning, advertising effectiveness research, understanding buyer behavior, technological forecasting, the effective use of concept testing and more.

658.8   GW   ISSN 0025-3774
MARKETING JOURNAL. 1968. bi-m. DM.120. Marketing Journal Gesellschaft fuer angewandtes Marketing mbH, Koopstr. 20-22, 20144 Hamburg, Germany. TEL 49-40-4103148. FAX 49-40-4101276. Ed. Wolfgang K. A. Disch. adv.; bk.rev.; abstr.; bibl.; illus.; stat.; index. circ. 6,441. **Indexed:** Key to Econ.Sci. **Document type:** trade publication.
—SWETS.

MARKETING LAW REPORTING SERVICE. see LAW

658.8   US   ISSN 0923-0645
HF5415.2   CODEN: MLETEK
MARKETING LETTERS; a journal of research in marketing. 1990. q. fl.545 to institutions; $279.50 to institutions in U.S. (effective 1998). Kluwer Academic Publishers Boston, Box 358, Accord Sta., Hingham, MA 02018-0358. TEL 617-871-6600. FAX 617-871-6528. TELEX 200190. E-mail: services@wkap.nl; URL: http://www.wkap.nl/kapis/CGI-BIN/WORLDjournalhome.htm?0923-0645. (Dist. outside N. America by: Kluwer Academic Publishers Group, P.O. Box 322, 3300 AH Dordrecht, Netherlands. TEL 31-78-6392392. FAX 31-78-6546474) Ed. Donald Lehmann. (also avail. in microform from UMI; reprint service avail. from SWZ,UMI) **Document type:** academic/scholarly publication.
—BLDSC (5381.648050); SWETS; UMI; UnCover. **CCC.**
    Description: Publishes empirical findings, methodological papers and theoretical and conceptual insights across areas of research in marketing.
    Refereed Serial

BUSINESS AND ECONOMICS — MARKETING AND PURCHASING

658.8 659.1   CN   ISSN 0025-3642
HF5410
MARKETING MAGAZINE; Canada's weekly newspaper for marketing, advertising and sales executives. 1908. w. Can.$58 (foreign Can.$116). Maclean Hunter Ltd., Business Publication Division, Maclean Hunter Bldg., 777 Bay St., Toronto, ON M5W 1A7, Canada. TEL 416-596-5835. TELEX 062-19547. Ed. Wayne Gooding. adv.; bk.rev.; illus.; tr.lit.; index, cum.index. circ. 12,000. (tabloid format; also avail. in microform from UMI,MML) **Indexed:** B.P.I., Can.B.P.I., Can.Per.Ind., P.A.I.S., Tr.& Indus.Ind. **Document type:** newspaper.
—KR SourceOne; SWETS. **CCC**.
   Description: Serves the information needs of sales, advertising, and marketing executives in business, industry, and advertising agencies. Prepares a series of special reports on major media plus advertising and sales forecasts.

658.8   NZ   ISSN 0111-9044
MARKETING MAGAZINE. 1981. m. NZ.$78.50 (effective 1994). Profile Publishing Ltd., P.O. Box 5544, Wellesley St., Auckland, New Zealand. TEL 64-9-6308994. FAX 64-9-6301046. E-mail: sprofile@iconz.co.nz. Ed. Christine Joung. adv.; bk.rev. circ. 4,912. (back issues avail.) **Document type:** trade publication.
—BLDSC (5381.648400).
   Incorporates (1990-1992): Direct Marketing (ISSN 1170-3520)
   Description: Marketing strategy in practice for marketing-oriented executives.

658   US   ISSN 1061-3846
HF5415.13
MARKETING MANAGEMENT. 1992. q. $70 to non-members; members $45; institutions $90. American Marketing Association, 250 S. Wacker Dr., Chicago, IL 60606-5819. TEL 312-648-0536. FAX 312-993-7542. URL: http://www.ama.org. Ed. Carolyn Pollard Neal. R&P contact: Kathy Harp. adv.: B&W page $1200; adv. contact: Una Moon. circ. 5,000. (also avail. in microform from UMI) **Indexed:** B.P.I., C.R.I.Abstr., C.R.I.Curr.Cont. **Document type:** trade publication.
●Also available online. Vendor(s): UMI.
—BLDSC (5381.648420); KR SourceOne; SWETS; UMI. **CCC**.
   Description: For senior marketing management in the production and service markets; focuses on analysis, real marketplace applications, as well as insider and senior-level insights and opinions on the issues and trends facing today's business professionals.

658 658   UK   ISSN 0964-5454
THE MARKETING MANAGER'S YEARBOOK. 1991. a. £62.50. A P Information Services, Roman House, 296 Golders Green Rd., London NW11 9PZ, England. TEL 0181-455-4550. FAX 0181-455-6381. Ed. Karen Linch. adv.: B&W page £1,125, color page £ 1,575; trim 297 x 210. circ. 4,450. **Document type:** directory.
—BLDSC (5381.648450).
   Description: Profiles marketing departments of 9,000 U.K. companies and organizations.

658   SA   ISSN 0256-0348
MARKETING MIX. (Text in English) 1982. m. R.96. Systems Publishers (Pty) Ltd., P.O. Box 41345, Craighall 2024, South Africa. TEL 27-11-789-1808. FAX 27-11-789-4725. TELEX 4-24952. Ed. Gisele Wertheim-Aymes. adv.; bk.rev.; illus. circ. 7,530. **Indexed:** Ind.S.A.Per.

658.8   NE   ISSN 0025-3782
MARKETING MIX DIGEST. 1965. 11/yr. fl.365 (effective 1996). Kluwer Bedrijfswetenschappen B.V. (Subsidiary of: Wolters Kluwer N.V.), Postbus 23, 7400 GA Deventer, Netherlands. TEL 31-5700-48999. FAX 31-5700-11504. (Subscr. to: Intermedia bv, Postbus 4, 2400 MA Alphen aan den Rijn, Netherlands. TEL 31-172-466321. FAX 31-172-435527) adv.; bk.rev.; abstr.; illus.; stat.; index. **Document type:** trade publication.
—SWETS.

658.8   US   ISSN 0025-3790
HF5415   CODEN: MKNWAT
MARKETING NEWS; reporting on marketing and its association. 1967. bi-w. $75 to non-members; institutions $130. American Marketing Association, 250 S. Wacker Dr., Ste. 200, Chicago, IL 60606. TEL 312-648-0536. FAX 312-993-7542. URL: http://www.ama.org/pubs/mn/pub2.html. Ed. Gregg Cebrzynski. R&P contact: Una Moon. adv. contact: Kathy Harp. bk.rev.; charts; illus.; tr.lit. circ. 25,871. (tabloid format; also avail. in microform from UMI,MIM) **Indexed:** B.P.I, BPIA, Bus.Ind., INSPEC (1984-), Manage.Cont., PROMT, Tr.& Indus.Ind. **Document type:** newspaper, trade publication.
●Also available online. Vendor(s): Information Access Co., Lexis-Nexis, UMI.
—BLDSC (5381.648500); AskIEEE; CASDDS; KR SourceOne; UMI. **CCC**.

658   PH
MARKETING PROFILES OF STRATEGIC INDUSTRIES. (Text in English) 1991. a. Board of Investments, Industry & Investment Bldg., 385 Sen. Gil J. Puyat Ave., MCC P.O. Box 676, Makati, Metro Manila 3117, Philippines. TEL 818-1831. FAX 815-0702.

THE MARKETING PULSE; the exclusive insight provider to the entertainment, marketing, advertising and media industries. see *ADVERTISING AND PUBLIC RELATIONS*

MARKETING RECREATION CLASSES. see *EDUCATION — Guides To Schools And Colleges*

658.8   US   ISSN 1040-8460
HF5415.2
MARKETING RESEARCH; a magazine of management & applications. 1989. q. $70 to non-members (foreign $90); members $45; institutions $120 (foreign $140). American Marketing Association, 250 S. Wacker Dr., Ste. 200, Chicago, IL 60606. TEL 312-648-0536. FAX 312-993-7542. URL: http://www.ama.org/pubs/mr/index.html. Ed. Andrew Morrison. R&P contact: Una Moon. adv. contact: Kathy Harp. bk.rev. (back issues avail.) **Indexed:** B.P.I., Mark.Res.Abstr. (1989-). **Document type:** trade publication.
●Also available online. Vendor(s): UMI.
—BLDSC (5381.649700); KR SourceOne; SWETS; UMI; UnCover. **CCC**.
   Description: Promotes a new and broader AMA definition of marketing research that stresses developing and evaluating hypotheses and theories rather than merely analyzing data. For managers and practitioners of marketing research.
   Refereed Serial

MARKETING RESULTS; vakblad voor verkopers van drogisterijartikelen. see *PHARMACY AND PHARMACOLOGY*

658   US
MARKETING REVIEW. 1947. m. $40. American Marketing Association, New York Chapter, 60 E. 42nd St., Ste. 1765, New York, NY 10165-0006. TEL 212-687-3280. FAX 212-447-0994. Ed. Hal Marcus. adv.; index. circ. 5,000. **Indexed:** Hospit.Ind.
   Description: News magazine with articles on marketing and marketing research related practices and theories.

658   US   ISSN 0732-2399
HF5410
MARKETING SCIENCE. 1982. q. $80 to individuals (foreign $87) ; institutions $132 (foreign $139) (effective 1997). Institute for Operations Research and the Management Sciences, 901 Elkridge Landing Rd., Ste. 400, Linthicum, MD 21090-2909. TEL 410-850-0300. E-mail: iol-publications@mail.informs.org; URL: http://www.informs.org/Pubs/Market.html. Ed. Hau L. Lee. R&P contact: Fran Silverman. adv. contact: Kathye Long. charts; stat. circ. 1,744. (back issues avail.) **Indexed:** ABI Inform., ASCA, B.P.I., Compumath, Cont.Pg.Manage., Curr.Cont., Int.Abstr.Oper.Res., J.Cont.Quant.Meth., J.of Econ.Lit., Oper.Res.Manage.Sci., Qual.Contr.Appl.Stat., SSCI. **Document type:** trade publication.
—BLDSC (5381.665000); Genuine Article; KR SourceOne; SWETS; UMI; UnCover. **CCC**.

658.8306073   US   ISSN 0542-7398
MARKETING SCIENCE INSTITUTE. 1964. a. Marketing Science Institute, 1000 Massachusetts Ave., Cambridge, MA 02138-5396. TEL 617-491-2060. FAX 617-491-2065.

658.8   US   ISSN 0733-5768
MARKETING SCIENCE INSTITUTE. NEWSLETTER. Variant title: M S I Newsletter. 1969. s-a. free. Marketing Science Institute, 1000 Massachusetts Ave., Cambridge, MA 02138-5396. TEL 617-491-2060. FAX 617-491-2065. Ed. Marni Z. Clippinger. illus. circ. 8,000. **Document type:** newsletter.
   Description: Covers events, research findings, conferences, and membership of the Institute, a research center whose purpose is to advance marketing practice and knowledge.

658.8   US
MARKETING SCIENCE INSTITUTE. PUBLICATIONS. 1961. a. free. Marketing Science Institute, 1000 Massachusetts Ave., Cambridge, MA 02138-5396. TEL 617-491-2060. FAX 617-491-2065. circ. 8,000. **Document type:** catalog.

658.8   US
MARKETING SCIENCE INSTITUTE. RESEARCH PRIORITIES. biennial. free. Marketing Science Institute, 1000 Massachusetts Ave., Cambridge, MA 02138-5396. TEL 617-491-2060. FAX 617-491-2065. Ed. Marni Z. Clippinger. circ. 5,000. **Document type:** academic/scholarly publication.
   Formerly: Marketing Science Institute. Research Briefs.
   Description: Establishes research priorities for projects funded by the Institute, a non-profit research center whose purpose is to advance marketing practice and knowledge.

658.83   US   ISSN 0733-5733
MARKETING SCIENCE INSTITUTE - REPORT. 1969. irreg. Marketing Science Institute, 1000 Massachusetts Ave., Cambridge, MA 02138-5396. TEL 617-491-2060. FAX 617-491-2065. Ed. Marni S. Clippinger.
—BLDSC (7537.325000).

658   UK   ISSN 0967-0556
MARKETING SERIES. 1991. irreg. price varies. Natural Resources Institute, Central Ave., Chatham Maritime, Kent ME4 4TB, England. TEL 44-1634-880088. FAX 44-1634-880066. TELEX 263907-LDN-G. E-mail: publications@nri.org; URL: http://www.nri.org. **Document type:** monographic series.
●Also available online.
Also available on CD-ROM.
—BLDSC (5381.688000).
   Description: Covers marketing issues in developing countries, from initial analysis and methodology via policy formulation and monitoring to implementation.

658 380   US   ISSN 0897-6651
MARKETING SIGNS;* a newsletter at the crossroads of marketing, semiotics and consumer research. 1987. 3/yr. $10 (foreign $15) (effective 1992). Indiana University, School of Library & Information Science, Box 10, Bloomington, IN 47402-0010. TEL 812-855-2793. FAX 812-855-6166. Ed. Jean Umiker-Sebeok. bk.rev.; bibl. circ. 500. (back issues avail.) **Document type:** newsletter.
   Description: Covers signs and symbols in business communications, for professionals in marketing, consumer advertising research and university level semiotics and communications specialists.

658   UK   ISSN 0961-7752
MARKETING SUCCESS. 1990. q. £20 (foreign £25). Chartered Institute of Marketing, Moor Hall, Cookham, Maidenhead, Berkshire SL6 9QH, England. TEL 44-1628-427500. FAX 44-1628-427499. Ed. Angela Hatton. circ. 35,000. **Document type:** newsletter.

658   US   ISSN 1076-4879
HF5410
MARKETING TOOLS. 1994. 8/yr. $54. Cowles Business Media (Subsidiary of: Cowles Media Company), 11 River Bend Dr., S., Box 4949, Stamford, CT 06907-0949. TEL 203-358-9900. FAX 203-358-5811. Pub. Michelle DeChant. adv.: B&W page $2995. **Document type:** trade publication.
—BLDSC (5381.693100); UMI. **CCC**.

658   AT
▼**MARKETING UPDATE NEWSLETTER**. 1996. s-a. Exton Enterprises, P.O. Box 394, Mt. Ommaney, Qld. 4074, Australia. E-mail: exton@gil.com.au; URL: http://www.gil.com.au/comm/eemall. Ed. Rahan Exton. **Document type:** newsletter.
●Available only online.
   Description: Covers marketing and business information.

BUSINESS AND ECONOMICS — MARKETING AND PURCHASING

659   FR   ISSN 1251-1110
MARKETING VENTE. 10/yr. Marketing Mix, 15 bis, rue Ernest Renan, B.P. 62, 92133 Issy-les-Moulineaux, France. TEL 40-93-01-02. FAX 40-93-03-40. TELEX 202 003 F. Ed. Frederic Barillet. circ. 13,000.
    Formerly (until 1993): Marketing Mix (ISSN 0299-8076)

658.8   UK   ISSN 0141-9285
MARKETING WEEK. 1978. w. $175. Centaur Communications Ltd., 50 Poland St., London W1V 4AX, England. TEL 44-171-287-9800. FAX 44-171-439-1480. URL: http://www.marketing-week.co.uk/mw0001/. Ed. Stuart Smith. adv. (also avail. in microform from UMI) **Indexed:** Mgmt.& Market.Abstr., WPM. **Document type:** trade publication.
    ●Also available online. Vendor(s): UMI.
    —BLDSC (5381.694000); UMI.

658.8 380.1   US
MARKETING WITH TECHNOLOGY NEWS. 1997. m. Sarah Stambler, Ed. & Pub., 370 Central Park West, Ste. 210, New York, NY 10025. TEL 212-222-1713. FAX 212678-6357. E-mail: sarag@mwt.com. (only delivered by FAX)

658   CN   ISSN 0714-7422
MARKETNEWS. 1975. m. Can.$48.15($95) Bomar Publishing, 364 Supertest Rd., Ste. 200, North York, ON M3J 2M2. TEL 416-667-9945. FAX 416-667-0609. Ed. Robert Franner; Pub. Robert Grierson. adv. circ. 11,200.
    Formerly (until 1982): Audio Marketnews (ISSN 0382-6120)

MARKETOLOGY QUARTERLY. see BUSINESS AND ECONOMICS — Management

658   SA
MARKETPLACE; an insight into advertising, marketing, research, sales. 1976. 22/yr. R.121 (effective 1996). C T P Ltd., Parklands, P.O. Box 1610, Johannesburg 2121, South Africa. TEL 27-11-889-0600. FAX 27-11-889-0680. (Subscr. to: P.O. Box 1610, Parlands 2121, South Africa) Ed. Lynne Kloot. R&P contact: Lynne Kloot. adv. contact: B. Ferreira. bk.rev. circ. 3,000. (tabloid format) **Document type:** trade publication.
    Description: Covers all aspects of the South African advertising industry in print and broadcast media, with news of successful campaigns and analysis of trends in South Africa and the World.

658   US
MARKETPULSE.* 1985. irreg. (approx. 4/yr.). free to qualified personnel. (Dependable Lists, Inc.) Specialists Ltd., 1200 Harbor Blvd., 9th Fl., Weehawken, NJ 07087-6728. Ed. Ray Lewis.

658   MX
MARKETS IN MEXICO; location and logistics. (Text in English) irreg. $130. American Chamber of Commerce of Mexico, A.C., Lucerna 78, Col. Juarez, Del. Cuauhtemoc, 06600 Mexico DF, Mexico. TEL 52-5-724-3800. FAX 52-5-703-2911. R&P contact: Diana H. de Hernandez. **Document type:** directory.
    Description: Overview of logistical, geographic and market infrastructure for key industrial areas in Mexico.

658.8   UK   ISSN 0076-4647
MARKETS YEAR BOOK. 1955. a. £8.99. World's Fair Ltd., P.O. Box 57, Oldham OL1 4BB, England. TEL 061-624-3687. FAX 061-665-1260. circ. 10,000. **Document type:** trade publication.
    Description: Listing of different markets in England, Wales and Scotland providing market days, owners and superintendents.

658   SW   ISSN 1101-7961
MARKNADSTENDENSER; officielt organ foer Sveriges Marknadsfoerbund. 1983. 10/yr. SEK 250 (effective 1991). Aller Industripress, P.O. Box 601, S-251 05 Helsingborg, Sweden.
    Formerly (until 1991): Tendens; Incorporates: Marknadsvetande.

658.8   AU   ISSN 0025-3863
DER MARKT; Zeitschrift fuer Absatzwirtschaft und Marketing. 1962. q. S.400 (Germany DM.60; elsewhere S.435). Oesterreichische Gesellschaft fuer Absatzwirtschaft, Augasse 2-6, A-1090 Vienna, Austria. TEL 43-1-313364400. FAX 43-1-31336732. Ed.Bd. adv.: B&W page S.5000; trim 245 x 170. bk.rev.; charts; index. circ. 1,250. **Indexed:** IBR, SCIMP (1991-). **Document type:** trade publication.

658 635   GW   ISSN 0930-8741
MARKT IN GRUEN. 1985. 10/yr. DM.148 (effective 1997). Verlag Siegfried Rohn GmbH & Co. KG, Stolberger Str. 84, 50933 Cologne, Germany. TEL 49-221-54974. FAX 49-221-5497278. Ed. Ulrike Neugebauer. adv.: B&W page DM.4720, color page DM.8470; trim 185 x 270; adv. contact: Jenny Jones-Steinkamp. circ. 7,750. **Document type:** trade publication.

658.8   GW
MARKT INTERN. 1981. fortn. DM.167. Markt Intern Verlag GmbH, Grafenbergerallee 30, 40237 Duesseldorf, Germany. TEL 0211-6698-0. Ed. Erhard Liemen. (back issues avail.)

658.8   GW   ISSN 0933-7105
HF5415.2
MARKTFORSCHUNG UND MANAGEMENT; Zeitschrift fuer Marktorientierte Unternehmenspolitik. Variant title: M & M. 1957. bi-m. DM.126 (students DM.98) (effective 1997). Schaeffer - Poeschel Verlag, Postfach 103241, 70028 Stuttgart, Germany. TEL 49-711-2194102. FAX 49-711-2194119. Eds. Dr. Ulli Arnold, Dr. Fred Becker. adv.; bk.rev.; bibl. circ. 1,500. **Indexed:** Key to Econ.Sci. **Document type:** trade publication.
    —CCC.
    Former titles: Marktforschung (ISSN 0170-723X); Marktforscher (ISSN 0465-0166); Incorporated: G F M-Mitteilungen zur Markt- und Absatzforschung (ISSN 0016-3511)

658.7   UK   ISSN 0142-114X
MATERIALS HANDLING BUYERS GUIDE. 1963. a. £40 (foreign £45) (effective 1996). Turret Group Plc., Turret House, 171 High St., Rickmansworth, Herts WD3 1SN, England. TEL 44-1923-777000. FAX 44-1923-771297. adv.; index. **Document type:** directory.
    Formerly: Manual of Materials Handling and Ancilliary Equipment (ISSN 0076-4167)

658.7   II   ISSN 0543-0313
MATERIALS MANAGEMENT JOURNAL OF INDIA. (Text in English) 1960. m. Rs.32. P.G. Menon, Ed. & Pub., D-409 Defence Colony, New Delhi 110003, India. adv.; bk.rev. circ. 2,000.
    Incorporates: Eastern Purchasing Journal.

MATERIALWIRTSCHAFT UND LOGISTIK IM UNTERNEHMEN; Materialwirtschaft fuer Manager. see BUSINESS AND ECONOMICS — Management

MEAT AND POULTRY: THE INTERNATIONAL MARKET. see FOOD AND FOOD INDUSTRIES

658.8 615.19   US   ISSN 1067-733X
MED AD NEWS. 1982. 16/yr. $85. Engel Publishing Partners, 820 Bear Tavern Rd., W. Trenton, NJ 08628. TEL 609-530-0044. FAX 609-530-0207. Ed. Styli Engel. adv. circ. 10,300. **Document type:** trade publication.
    ●Also available online. Vendor(s): Information Access Co.
    —BLDSC (5424.621800); SWETS. **CCC.**
    Formerly: Medical Advertising News (ISSN 0745-0907)

MEDIA & MARKETING EUROPE. see ADVERTISING AND PUBLIC RELATIONS

MEDIA DIRECTORY. see ADVERTISING AND PUBLIC RELATIONS

659.1   US
MEDIA INC; Pacific Northwest marketing, media and creative services news. 1986. m. $25 (effective 1997). Media Index Publishing, Inc., Box 24365, Seattle, WA 98134-0365. TEL 206-382-9220. FAX 206-382-9437. Ed. Darcy Reinhart; Pub. Richard Woltjer. adv. contact: James Baker. charts; illus.; stat.; index. circ. 10,000. (tabloid format; back issues avail.) **Document type:** newspaper.
    Formerly: Aperture Northwest.
    Description: Contains news from the Pacific Northwest marketing, media and creative services industry.

658.8   IT
MEDIA KEY SYNTHESIS; mensile professionale di comunicazione, media e marketing. (Supplement avail. q.: Global) 1982. m. (10/yr.). L.200000 (foreign L.280000; $175) includes TV Key and Global. Media Key s.r.l., Via Filippino Lippi 33, 20131 Milan, Italy. TEL 39-2-70638348. FAX 39-2-2363662. Ed. Roberto Albano. adv. contact: Silvana Carazzina. circ. 10,500. **Document type:** trade publication.
    Description: Covers marketing, media research and planning, and advertising.

302.23 338.4   UK
MEDIA MAP DATAFILE. base vol. (plus m. updates). £545 (effective 1997). (Communications and Information Technology Research Ltd.) C I T Publications, 3 Colleton Cresc., Exeter, Devon EX2 4DG, England. TEL 44-1392-493-444. FAX 44-1392-493626. URL: http://www.telecoms-data.com. (looseleaf format)
    Supersedes in part: Media Map.
    Description: Contains profiles of over 150 companies including their latest financial results, contact details and media interests, plus circulation figures, viewing shares and media regulations. Includes a media directory.

302.23 338.4   UK
MEDIA MAP OF EASTERN EUROPE. a. £195 (effective 1997). (Communications and Information Technology Research Ltd.) C I T Publications, 3 Colleton Cresc., Exeter, Devon EX2 4DG, England. TEL 44-1392-493-444. FAX 44-1392-493-626. E-mail: talk2us@citpubs.zynet.co.uk; URL: http://www.telecomsdata.com.
    Supersedes in part: Media Map.
    Description: Provides an overview of the eastern European media market. Covers consumer media in 13 countries with profiles of all of the major players.

302.23 338.4   UK
MEDIA MAP OF WESTERN EUROPE. a. £195 (effective 1997). (Communications and Information Technology Research Ltd.) C I T Publications, 3 Colleton Cresc., Exeter, Devon EX2 4DG, England. TEL 44-1392-493-444. FAX 44-1392-493-656. E-mail: talk2us@citpubs.zynet.co.uk; URL: http://www.telecoms.data.com.
    Supersedes in part: Media Map.
    Description: Examines in detail the western European media market. Covers consumer media in 17 countries and contains details of national media regulations together with profiles of the major players. Includes a media directory.

658   BE
MEDIA MARKT. (Supplement avail.) (Text in Flemish) 11/yr. 3482 BEF. C E D Samsom (Subsidiary of: Wolters Samsom Belgie n.v.), Kouterveld 14, B-1831 Diegem, Belgium. TEL 32-2-7231111.
    Description: Depicts marketing and advertisement.

MEDICAL MARKETING & MEDIA. see PHARMACY AND PHARMACOLOGY

659.1   US   ISSN 1054-3066
MEDICAL NEWS REPORT. 1991. m. $150. Standish Publishing Co., Box 335, Ardmore, PA 19003. TEL 610-519-9220. FAX 610-519-9221. Ed. Kim Standish. circ. 500 (paid). **Document type:** newsletter.
    Description: Aimed at health care public relations professionals; reports on crisis communications, medical topics making news, media relations, and public relations management.

MEDICAL PRODUCTS SALES. see MEDICAL SCIENCES

MEDICATED SKINCARE: THE INTERNATIONAL MARKET. see PHARMACY AND PHARMACOLOGY

BUSINESS AND ECONOMICS — MARKETING AND PURCHASING

MEDIEN DIALOG; Gespraech - Diskussion - Meinung - Information. see COMMUNICATIONS — Television And Cable

MEDIENREPORT. see BUSINESS AND ECONOMICS — Management

658   SZ
MEDIENREPORT SCHWEIZ; Informationen fuer professionelle Medienanwender. 1980. m. 130 SFr. (Europe 150 SFr.; overseas 180 SFr.). Postfach 109, CH-4504 Solothurn, Switzerland. TEL 065-234940. FAX 065-234940. E-mail: 100336.546@compuserve.com. Ed. Udo Sollberger. adv.: page 660 SFr. bk.rev. circ. 1,000. **Document type:** trade publication.

MEDISTAT. see MEDICAL SCIENCES

MEMBERSHIP DEVELOPMENTS. see BUSINESS AND ECONOMICS — Management

MEN'S TOILETRIES: THE INTERNATIONAL MARKET. see BEAUTY CULTURE

658 380   US
MERCHANDISE MART RESOURCE GUIDE. 1952. a. $5. Merchandise Mart Properties, Inc., 470 Merchandise Mart, Chicago, IL 60654. TEL 312-527-4141. adv. circ. 60,000.
   Former titles: Merchandise Mart Buyers Guide; (until 1979): Merchandise Mart Directory (ISSN 0539-3876)

658.8   US
MERCHANDISING & OPERATING RESULTS OF DEPARTMENT AND SPECIALTY STORES. a. $100 to non-members; members $80. (National Retail Federation, Financial Executives Division) John Wiley & Sons, Inc., 605 Third Ave., New York, NY 10158-0012. TEL 212-850-6645. FAX 212-850-6021. stat. **Indexed:** SRI.
   Description: Survey report provides performance ratios by merchandise division for department and specialty stores and by volume group.

658 331   NZ   ISSN 0113-468X
THE MERCHANT. m. NZ$39.37 to non-members; members NZ$84.37. (Retail and Wholesale Merchants Association of New Zealand Inc.) Retailer Publishing Co., P.O. Box 12086, Wellington, New Zealand. TEL 04-4723-733. FAX 04-4721-071. Ed. Bill Lambert. adv.; bk.rev. circ. 2,800. (back issues avail.)
—CCC.
   Formerly (until 1987): Retail News.
   Description: Covers all aspects of retailing, wholesaling and distribution.

658.8   GW   ISSN 0935-7718
MESSE INDUSTRIESPIEGEL; Internationales Messe- und Ausstellungsorgan. Variant title: Industrie Spiegel. 1950. m. DM.87. Commerzia Verlag GmbH, Oxfordstr. 9, 53111 Bonn, Germany. FAX 030-7957781. TELEX 183676. adv.; bk.rev.; illus.; tr.lit.

658 669   ZA
METAL MARKETING CORPORATION OF ZAMBIA. ANNUAL REPORT.* (Text in English) a. Metal Marketing Corporation of Zambia Ltd., Menaco House, Sapele Rd., P.O.B. 35570, Lusaka.

METALCASTER. see BUSINESS AND ECONOMICS — Management

METALWORKING ENGINEERING AND MARKETING. see ENGINEERING — Engineering Mechanics And Materials

METROPOLITAN TORONTO BUSINESS AND MARKET GUIDE. see BUSINESS AND ECONOMICS

658.7   US   ISSN 0026-2412
MICHIGAN INDUSTRY. 1919. m. $20. Contractor Publishing Co., 1629 W. Lafayette, Detroit, MI 48216. TEL 313-962-3337. FAX 313-962-3655. Ed. Cheryl Van Houzen. adv.; charts; illus.; stat.; index. circ. 21,000. **Indexed:** Mich.Mag.Ind.
   Former titles (until 1967): Michigan Plant and Equipment; Michigan Purchasing Management; Detroit Purchasor.

MICHIGAN MANUFACTURERS DIRECTORY. see BUSINESS AND ECONOMICS — Trade And Industrial Directories

MICHIGAN STATE HORTICULTURAL SOCIETY. ANNUAL REPORT. see FOOD AND FOOD INDUSTRIES

MID-WEEK PETROLEUM ARGUS. see PETROLEUM AND GAS

658 659   FR   ISSN 0295-3943
MIDI MEDIA. 11/yr. Media Sud Communication, 5 rue Alsace-Lorraine, B.P. 27, 31012 Toulouse Cedex, France. TEL 61-55-54-94. FAX 61-25-03-09. Ed. Jean Paul Bobin. circ. 10,000.
   Description: Covers TV, radio, press, publicity and marketing in the South of France.

658   US
MIDWEST RETAILER. 1971. m. free. 8528 Columbus Ave., S. Bloomington, MN 55420-2460. TEL 612-854-7610. FAX 612-854-6460. Ed. Joan Thomasberg. R&P contact: Joan Thomasberg. adv.: B&W page $1456; adv. contact: John Thomasberg. circ. 6,200. **Document type:** trade publication.
   Description: Provides news of products, marketing changes, personnel and trends in the flooring industry.

MILCH-MARKETING. see AGRICULTURE — Dairying And Dairy Products

MILITARY EXCHANGE MAGAZINE. see MILITARY

338.4769   DK   ISSN 0908-3855
MILJOE. Variant title: V & S Priser, Miljoe. 1994. a. DKK 1310 (effective 1997). V & S Byggedata A-S, Frederikssundsvej 194, DK-2700 Broenshoej, Denmark. TEL 48-38-60-77-11. FAX 45-38-60-77-44. Dir. Carl Friis Skovsen.

MINERAL WATER: THE INTERNATIONAL MARKET. see BEVERAGES

658.8 683.8   AT
MINGAY'S ELECTRICAL RETAILER; covering sales and service in the home appliance radio and TV market. 1930. m. Aus.$65. Thomson Business Publishing, 47 Chippen St., Chippendale, N.S.W. 2008, Australia. TEL 02-699-2411. FAX 02-698-3920. Ed. Claire Moffatt. adv.; illus.; stat. circ. 5,583.
   Former titles: Mingay's Retailer and Merchandiser (ISSN 0728-9383); Mingay's News (ISSN 0026-5098); Mingay's Electrical Retail Weekly.

658   US   ISSN 1041-7524
MINORITY MARKETS ALERT. 1989. m. $295 (foreign $325). E P M Communications, 160 Mercer St., 3rd. Fl., New York, NY 10012-3212. TEL 212-941-0099. FAX 212-941-1622. Ed. Michael Schau; Pub. Ira Mayer. R&P contact: Ira Mayer. **Document type:** newsletter.
   ●Also available online. Vendor(s): Information Access Co., Knight-Ridder Information, Inc., Lexis-Nexis.
—CCC.
   Description: Presents facts, comprehensive overviews, projections and predictions, micromarketing information and shirtsleeve tidbits on how to best reach blacks, Hispanics, and Asian Americans.

790.13   US   ISSN 0191-6904
MODEL RETAILER. 1971. m. $35. Kalmbach Publishing Co., 210272 Crossroads Cir., Waukesha, WI 53187. TEL 414-796-8776. FAX 414-796-1142. Ed. Geoffrey A. Wheeler. adv.; bk.rev. circ. 6,330. **Document type:** trade publication.

658.7   CN   ISSN 0026-833X
HF5437
MODERN PURCHASING. 1959. 10/yr. Can.$30 (foreign Can.$65). Maclean Hunter Ltd., Business Publication Division, Maclean Hunter Bldg., 777 Bay St., Toronto, ON M5W 1A7, Canada. TEL 416-596-5000. FAX 416-596-5866. Ed. Joe Terrett. adv.: B&W page $2595, color page $3450; adv. contact: Karen James. illus. circ. 20,425. (also avail. in microform from UMI) **Indexed:** Can.B.P.I.
—BLDSC (5894.600000).

658 659.1   CN
MONDAY REPORT ON RETAILERS. 1973. w. Can.$330. Maclean-Hunter Ltd., Business Publication Division, Maclean-Hunter Bldg., 777 Bay St., Toronto, ON M5W 1A7, Canada. TEL 416-596-5915. Ed. Karen Orme. index. (processed)

338   US   ISSN 1040-6999
MUSEUM STORE. 1973. q. $30 (foreign $50) (effective 1997). Museum Store Association, Inc., 501 S. Cherry St., Ste. 460, Denver, CO 80222. TEL 303-329-6968. FAX 303-329-6134. Ed. Jenifer Merchant. adv. contact: Karen Ludwig. circ. 3,400. **Document type:** trade publication.
   Formerly: M U S T.
   Description: Provides information for museum store buyers and managers.

MUSIC AND SOUND RETAILER; the newsmagazine for musical instrument and sound product merchandisers. see MUSIC

MUSIC INC.. see MUSIC

MY LITTLE SALESMAN HEAVY EQUIPMENT CATALOG. see MACHINERY

MY LITTLE SALESMAN TRUCK CATALOG. see TRANSPORTATION — Trucks And Trucking

338.4   US   ISSN 0092-8410
HD9666.4
N A C D S LILLY DIGEST.* 1971. a. free. (National Association of Chain Drug Stores) Eli Lilly & Co., General Offices and Principal Laboratories, Lilly Corp. Center, Indianapolis, IN 46285. TEL 317-276-2000. illus.; stat. (also avail. in microfiche from CIS) **Indexed:** SRI.

658.8   II
N A F E D MARKETING REVIEW. (Text in English) 1971. m. Rs.18. National Agricultural Cooperative Marketing Federation of India Ltd., 1 Siddharth Enclave, (Nafed House), Ashram Chowk, New Delhi 110014, India. TEL 6845106. FAX 31-75347. TELEX 31-75358-NFD-IN. Eds. K. Janakiram, V. Mewawalla. adv.; bk.rev. circ. 1,500.

659.1   US
N A M A JOURNAL. 1990. 4/yr. $60 membership. National Account Management Association, 150 N. Wacker Dr., Ste. 960, Chicago, IL 60606-1607. TEL 312-251-3131. FAX 312-251-3132. Ed. Lisa Napolitano. adv.; bk.rev.; circ. 2,000 (controlled). **Document type:** trade publication.
   Formerly: N A M A News.
   Description: Covers strategies for successful customer management, including case studies of customer-supplier partnerships and benchmark data from Fortune 1000 companies.

N A P W NEWS/N V F G NUUS. (National Association of Pharmaceutical Wholesalers) see PHARMACY AND PHARMACOLOGY

N A U M D NEWS. (National Association of Uniform Manufacturers and Distributors) see CLOTHING TRADE

N A U M D OFFICE REPORTS. (National Association of Uniform Manufacturers and Distributors) see CLOTHING TRADE

658.87   DK   ISSN 1395-1831
N B. 1902. m. DKK 475 (effective 1997); newsstand price: DKK 50. Naerbutikkernes Landsforening, P.O. Box 13, Kochsgade 31, DK-5100 Odense C, Denmark. TEL 45-65-91-41-80. FAX 45-65-91-41-85-80. Ed. Hans Jorgen Staun. adv.: B&W page DKK 9500, color page DKK 4600; trim 265 x 185; adv. contact: Torben Pedersen. illus. circ. 7,300. (reprint service avail.) **Document type:** trade publication.
   Former titles (until 1995): Kiosk og Service (ISSN 0903-9287); Kioskejer-Bladet (ISSN 0023-172X)

N B W A HANDBOOK. (National Beer Wholesalers Association) see BEVERAGES

N B W A LEGISLATIVE AND REGULATORY ISSUES ALERT. (National Beer Wholesalers Association) see BEVERAGES

BUSINESS AND ECONOMICS — MARKETING AND PURCHASING

658.8 796   US   ISSN 1045-2087
GV743
N S G A RETAIL FOCUS. 1948. 10/yr. $50 to non-members; foreign $75. National Sporting Goods Association, 1699 Wall St., Mt. Prospect, IL 60056-5780. TEL 847-439-4000. FAX 847-439-0111. Ed. Brent Heathcott. adv.; bk.rev.; charts; illus.; stat.; circ. controlled. Indexed: Sportsearch. **Document type:** trade publication.
    Former titles: N S G A Sports Retailer (ISSN 0884-6278); Sports Retailer (ISSN 0279-6678); Selling Sporting Goods (ISSN 0037-1610)
    Description: Covers retail and industry news for corporate executive members of the Association.

688   US
N S S R A NEWSLETTER. (Former name of issuing body: National Ski Retailers Association) 1988. q. membership. National Ski & Snowboard Retailers Association, 1699 Wall St., Mt. Prospect, IL 60056. TEL 847-439-4293. FAX 847-439-0111. Ed. Thomas B. Doyle. circ. 500 (controlled). (back issues avail.) **Document type:** newsletter.
    Formerly: N S R A Newsletter.
    Description: Provides information to specialty ski shops on shop practices, financial management, and industry trends.

658   US
N Y AUCTION ADVERTISER. m. Brooklyn Journal Publications, Inc., 129 Montague St., Brooklyn, NY 11021. TEL 718-624-6033. FAX 718-875-5302.

NATIONAL AGRI-MARKETING ASSOCIATION NEWS. see AGRICULTURE

NATIONAL ASSOCIATION OF BEVERAGE RETAILERS. NEWS AND VIEWS. see BEVERAGES

NATIONAL ASSOCIATION OF DEALERS IN ANTIQUES. BULLETIN. see ANTIQUES

NATIONAL AUCTIONS & SALES. see BUSINESS AND ECONOMICS — Domestic Commerce

NATIONAL BEER WHOLESALERS ASSOCIATION. BEER PERSPECTIVES NEWSLETTER. see BEVERAGES

NATIONAL BEER WHOLESALERS ASSOCIATION. DISTRIBUTOR PRODUCTIVITY REPORT. see BEVERAGES

NATIONAL DIRECTORY OF MAILING LISTS. see BUSINESS AND ECONOMICS — Trade And Industrial Directories

NATIONAL GARDENING. see GARDENING AND HORTICULTURE

NATIONAL GARDENING SURVEY (YEAR); an exclusive market research report for the lawn and garden industry. see GARDENING AND HORTICULTURE

658.8   US
TX795.A1
NATIONAL ICE CREAM AND YOGURT RETAILERS ASSOCIATION. YEARBOOK. 1941. a. National Ice Cream and Yogurt Retailers Association, Inc., 1429 King Ave., Columbus, OH 43212. TEL 614-486-1444. FAX 614-486-4711. Ed. Don Buckley. R&P contact: Don Buckley. adv. contact: Jenny Carter. illus.; circ. 800 (paid). **Document type:** directory.
    Formerly: National Ice Cream Retailers Association. Yearbook (ISSN 8756-1719)

NATIONAL SPORTING GOODS ASSOCIATION BUYING GUIDE. see SPORTS AND GAMES

NATIONWIDE DIRECTORY OF SPORTING GOODS BUYERS. see SPORTS AND GAMES

641.1 658   US   ISSN 0164-338X
CODEN: NFMEEI
NATURAL FOODS MERCHANDISER; new ideas, trends, products for the natural and organic foods industry. 1979. 12/yr. $60 (free to qualified personnel). New Hope Communications, Inc., 1301 Spruce St., Boulder, CO 80302-4832. TEL 303-939-8440. FAX 303-939-9559. Ed. Frank Lampe; Pub. Rick Prill. adv.; bk.rev.; illus.; circ. 14,000 (controlled). **Document type:** trade publication.

NEA DIMOSSIOTIS. see ADVERTISING AND PUBLIC RELATIONS

658.87   US   ISSN 0028-1948
NEBRASKA RETAILER. 1906. bi-m. $50. Nebraska Retail Grocers Association, 5533 S. 27th St., Ste. 104, Lincoln, NE 68512-1611. Ed. Kathy Siefken; Pub. Kathy Siefken. R&P contact: Kathy Siefken. adv. contact: Kathy Siefken. circ. 500 (controlled). **Document type:** trade publication.

NEIL MUSCOTT'S SUCCESS NEWSLETTER; strategies and stories for successful people. see PSYCHOLOGY

338 658.8   GW
DER NEUE WEG. 1958. m. DM.39. (Deutscher Handelsvereinigung Spar) Verlag fuer Wirtschaftspraxis GmbH, Schumannstr. 27, Postfach 2625, 60325 Frankfurt, Germany. Ed. Eva-Maria Krome. circ. 9,400.

658.8   US
NEW ACCOUNT SELLING. 1991. bi-w. $68.90. Dartnell Corporation, 4660 N. Ravenswood Ave., Chicago, IL 60640. TEL 773-561-4000; 800-621-5463. FAX 773-561-3801. URL: http://www.dartnellcorp.com. Ed. Terry Breen. **Document type:** newsletter.
    Description: Offers effective techniques for building sales and improving profits.

NEW CAR PRICES - BUYER'S GUIDE REPORTS. see TRANSPORTATION — Automobiles

658.7   US
NEW ENGLAND PURCHASER. 1921. q. membership. Purchasing Management Association of Boston, Inc., 200 Baker Ave., Ste. 306, Concord, MA 01742-2112. TEL 508-371-2522. FAX 508-369-9130. Ed. Christiane Loup. bk.rev. circ. 1,600. **Document type:** trade publication, newsletter.
    Formerly: New England Purchaser - Connecticut Purchaser; Which was formed by the merger of: New England Purchaser (ISSN 0028-4858); Connecticut Purchaser (ISSN 0010-6208)
    Description: Includes information about association news, seminars, and events.

658   US
NEW JERSEY B M A NEWS; for business and marketing communicators. q. free. Business Marketing Association, New Jersey Chapter, c/o Disk Print, 625 Willow Grove Rd., Westfield, NJ 07090. TEL 908-654-6969. FAX 908-654-6435. Ed. Jean Benisch.
    Description: Provides members with commentary, advice, and association news.

658.8 790.1   UK   ISSN 0968-9400
NEW LEISURE MARKETS. 10/yr. £995($1990) (individual reports £195) (effective 1996). Business Information Futures Ltd., One Henry Smith's Terr., Headland, Cleveland, TS24 0PD, England. TEL 44-1429-231902. FAX 44-1429-861403. Ed. Anne P. Smith; Pub. Anne P. Smith. R&P contact: A.P. Smith. **Document type:** trade publication.
    Description: Each report analyzes a sector of the UK leisure market.

658   UK
NEW PRODUCT DEVELOPMENT NEWS. 1983. m. £450($695) (effective 1996). Mintel International Group Ltd., 18-19 Long Ln., London EC1A 9HE, England. TEL 44-171-606-4533. FAX 44-171-606-5932. Ed. David Jago. circ. 120. **Document type:** consumer publication.

658 346   NZ
▼**NEW ZEALAND GUIDE TO THE LAW FOR SALES & MARKETING.** 1995. 2/yr. NZ.$341 (effective 1997). C C H New Zealand Limited, P.O. Box 2378, Auckland, New Zealand. TEL 64-9-4839179. FAX 64-9-4834009.
    Description: Provides information about the legal requirements affecting sales and marketing to help reduce the risk of penalties and non-compliance.

658 338   US
NEWS & VIEWS (PORTLAND). m. membership only. Business Forms Management Association, Inc., 319 S.W. Washington St., Ste. 710, Portland, OR 97204-2604. TEL 503-227-3393. FAX 503-274-7667. E-mail: Paul@bfma.org; URL: http://www.bfma.org/-bfma/. Ed. Paul Telles. R&P contact: Paul Telles. adv. contact: Paul Telles. bk.rev. circ. 2,000. **Document type:** newsletter.
    Description: Discusses forms and systems management and current BFMA communications.

658   CN
NEWS CANADA. French edition: Actualite Canada. 1981. m. free. News Canada Inc., 366 Adelaide St., N.W., Ste. 606, Toronto, Ont. M5V 1R9, Canada. TEL 416-599-9900. FAX 416-599-9700. Ed. Linda Kroboth; Pub. Ruth Douglas. R&P contact: Angela Skura. adv. contact: Yvonne Larkin. circ. 1,546.

658.8   US
NEWS SCAN. m. General Merchandise Distributors Council, 1275 Lake Ave., Colorado Springs, CO 80906. TEL 303-576-4260.

658.8 070.172   US   ISSN 0745-5089
HF6107
NEWSPAPER MARKETING.* 10/yr. $50 to individuals; students $30. International Newspaper Advertising and Marketing Executives, 1921 Gallows Rd., No. 4, Vienna, VA 22182-3900. TEL 703-648-1168. FAX 703-476-6015. adv.; bk.rev.

658.8   US
NIELSEN ALLIANCE.* 1942. 3/yr. free. Nielsen Marketing Research (Subsidiary of: Dun & Bradstreet Corporation), 150 N. Martingale Rd., Schaumburg, IL 60173-2408. TEL 708-498-6300. Ed. Paul J.J. Payack. stat. circ. 20,000. Indexed: ABI Inform., PROMT.
—UMI.
    Supersedes (in 1992): Nielsen Researcher (ISSN 0885-6206)

658   BE
NIEUWSBRIEF DIREKT MARKETING EN VERKOOP. (Supplement avail.) (Text in Flemish) w. 5618 BEF. C E D Samsom (Subsidiary of: Wolters Samsom Belgie n.v.), Kouterveld 14, B-1831 Diegem, Belgium. TEL 32-2-7231111. **Document type:** newsletter.

NIKKEI BEST P C. see COMPUTERS — Computer Industry Directories

NIKKEI IMAGE CLIMATE FORECAST. see ADVERTISING AND PUBLIC RELATIONS

658   JA
NIKKEI QUARTERLY NEWSLETTER ON COMMODITIES. q. Nihon Keizai Shimbun, Inc., Nikkei Research Institute of Industry and Markets, 1-9-5 Ote-machi, Chiyoda-ku, Tokyo 100-66, Japan. TEL 81-3-5294-2574. FAX 81-3-5294-2593. TELEX J22308 NIKKEI. **Document type:** newsletter.
    Description: Contains price, demand, and sales trends of 500 categories from basic materials to consumer commodities.

658   JA
NIKKEI WEEKLY NEWSLETTER ON COMMODITIES. w. Nihon Keizai Shimbun, Inc., Nikkei Research Institute of Industry and Markets, 1-9-5 Ote-machi, Chiyoda-ku, Tokyo 100-66, Japan. TEL 81-3-5294-2574. FAX 81-3-5294-2593. TELEX J22308 NIKKEI. **Document type:** newsletter.
    Description: Contains pricing and demand forecasts for various commodities.

658   US   ISSN 0029-103X
NON-FOODS MERCHANDISING; for sales and distribution of non-foods. 1958. m. $85 (free to qualified personnel) (foreign $150). Cardinal Business Media, Inc., 200 Connecticut Ave., Ste. 5-D, Norwalk, CT 06854. TEL 203-838-9100. FAX 203-838-2550. (Subscr. to: Box 3055, Northbrook, IL 60065-3055. TEL 847-291-5212. FAX 847-291-4816) Ed. Chantal Tode; Pub. Marianne Howatson. adv. contact: Scott Zecker. charts; illus.; stat. circ. 20,000. (tabloid format) Indexed: Ref.Pt.Food Indus.Abstr. **Document type:** trade publication.
● Also available online. Vendor(s): Information Access Co.
    Formerly: Rack Merchandising.

331.88   NO   ISSN 0333-4570
NORSKE HANDELSREISENDE. 1907. m. (10/yr.). Norges Handelsreisendesforbund, Pilestredet 17, Oslo 1, Norway. circ. 4,200.

NORTH AMERICAN MEAT PROCESSORS ASSOCIATION. NEWSFAX. see FOOD AND FOOD INDUSTRIES

NOVA SCOTIA CRAFT NEWS. see ARTS AND HANDICRAFTS

BUSINESS AND ECONOMICS — MARKETING AND PURCHASING

658   SW   ISSN 1101-6779
OESTERGOETLANDS AFFAERER & SOEDERMANLAND; affaerstidningen i Oestergoetland. 1984. 11/yr. SEK 395 (effective 1991). Foeretagsmedia, P.O. Box 643, S-551 18 Joenkoeping, Sweden.
Formerly (until vol.8, 1990): Oestergoetlands Affaerer.

658   US
OFF-PRICE RETAIL DIRECTORY. a. $99 (members $79). (Off-Price Specialists, Inc.) Value Retail News, 11701 S. Belcher Rd., Ste. 130, Largo, FL 33773-5117. TEL 800-669-1020. Ed. Tom Kirwan; Pub. Dan Cochran. **Document type:** directory.

OFFICIAL INDUSTRIAL EQUIPMENT GUIDE. see AGRICULTURE — Agricultural Equipment

OFFICIAL SCHOOL BUS RESALE GUIDE. see TRANSPORTATION

OILS AND FATS: THE INTERNATIONAL MARKET. see FOOD AND FOOD INDUSTRIES

658.87   US   ISSN 0030-1841
OKLAHOMA RETAILER. 1961. m. $12. Oklahoma Retailer Publishing Co., Inc., 4500 N. Sewell, Ste. 12, Oklahoma City, OK 73118. TEL 405-528-0903. Ed. Fred Singleton. adv.; bk.rev.; illus. circ. 4,000. (tabloid format; also avail. in microfilm from UMI; reprint service avail. from UMI) **Document type:** trade publication.
—UMI.
Description: Covers appliances, electronics, plumbing, heating and air conditioning, furniture and home furnishings, and business in Oklahoma.

658.85   SA   ISSN 0030-2368
ON THE ROAD (CAPE TOWN). 1914. m. R.15. Southern Africa Commercial Travellers Association - Suidelike-Afrikaanse Handelsreisigersvereniging, Box 828, Cape Town, South Africa. TEL 27-21-216777. FAX 27-21-4197435. Ed. M. Silber. R&P contact: M. Silber. adv.; bk.rev. circ. 2,500. **Document type:** trade publication, newspaper.

ONLINE AND C D - R O M MANAGEMENT AND MARKETING DATABASES. see LIBRARY AND INFORMATION SCIENCES — Computer Applications

658.85   US   ISSN 0741-3750
HF5438
OPPORTUNITY MAGAZINE. 1923. m. $19.95 (foreign $27.95). Ashlee Publishing, 18 E. 41st St., New York, NY 10017. TEL 212-376-7722. FAX 212-376-7723. Ed. Donna Clapp; Pub. Shirrel Rhoades. adv.; bk.rev.; circ. controlled. (also avail. in microform from UMI; reprint service avail. from UMI) —UMI; UnCover.
Incorporates (1970-1983): Salesman's Opportunity Magazine (ISSN 0036-3510)
Description: Covers business opportunities for success seekers. Provides information about sales programs, franchises, and service businesses.

ORAL HYGIENE PRODUCTS: THE INTERNATIONAL MARKET. see BEAUTY CULTURE

658.7   US   ISSN 0030-4786
OREGON PURCHASOR.* 1928. m. $12 free. Purchasing Management Association of Oregon, c/o Decorators West, Box 25191, Portland, OR 97225-0191. TEL 503-245-2296. Eds. Annette Ross, Rick Drury. adv.; bk.rev.; circ. 2,200 (controlled).

364.4   US
OUNCE OF PREVENTION;* survey of security & loss prevention in the retail industry. a. $65 to non-members; members $35; institutions $13. International Mass Retail Association, 1700 N. Moore St., Ste. 2250, Arlington, VA 22209-1903. TEL 202-861-0774. FAX 202-785-4588. **Indexed:** SRI.

381.18   US
OUTDOOR BUSINESS & MARKET NEWS. 6/yr. $40 (effective 1996). Miller Freeman, Inc. (Subsidiary of: United News & Media), 600 Harrison St., San Francisco, CA 94107. TEL 415-905-2200. FAX 415-905-2233. (Subscr. to: Box 5058, Brentwood, TN 37024-5058. TEL 800-933-3321. FAX 615-371-8131)

OUTDOOR POWER EQUIPMENT OFFICIAL GUIDE. see AGRICULTURE — Agricultural Equipment

381.18   US   ISSN 0279-8107
OUTDOOR RETAILER. 1980. m. $40 (effective 1996). Pacifica Publishing Corporation, 310 Broadway, Laguna Beach, CA 92651. TEL 714-376-8155. FAX 714-497-2093. (Subscr. to: Box 5020, Brentwood, TN 37024-5020. TEL 800-933-3321. FAX 615-371-8131) Ed. Joan Alvarez; Pub. Joan Alvarez. adv.; B&W page $3058, color page $3909; 8 3/8 x 10 7/8. circ. 16,191 (controlled). **Document type:** trade publication.
—CCC.

658   US
OUTLET PROJECT DIRECTORY. a. $99 (members $79). (Off-Price Specialists, Inc.) Value Retail News, 11701 S. Belcher Rd., Ste. 130, Largo, FL 33773. TEL 813-536-4047. FAX 813-536-4384. Ed. Tom Kirwan; Pub. Terry Dunham. **Document type:** directory.

658   US
OUTLET RETAIL DIRECTORY. a. $99 (members $79). (Off-Price Specialists, Inc.) Value Retail News, 11701 S. Belcher Rd., Ste. 130, Largo, FL 33773. TEL 813-536-4047. FAX 813-536-4384. Ed. Tom Kirwan; Pub. Dan Cochran. **Document type:** directory.

658   US
OUTLET RETAILER. (Supplement to: Shopping Center World) 1992. m. Intertec Publishing Corp. (Atlanta), 6151 Powers Ferry Rd., N.W., Atlanta, GA 30339-2941. TEL 770-256-9800. FAX 770-256-3116. Ed. Teresa DeFranks. adv.: B&W page $2040, color page $2930; trim 8 1/8 X 10 7/8. circ. 34,718. **Document type:** trade publication.
Description: Provides information on the benefits of outlet centers and how to increase profits.

658.8   US
OVERCOMING OBJECTIONS. 1990. bi-w. $68.90. Dartnell Corporation, 4660 N. Ravenswood Ave., Chicago, IL 60640. TEL 773-561-4000; 800-621-5463. FAX 773-561-3801. URL: http://www.dartnellcorp.com. Ed. Christen Heide. **Document type:** newsletter.
Description: Provides salespeople practical responses to every objection they are likely to face and imparts proven techniques for turning every type of sales objection into a sales opportunity.

658.8   US
P M C OF N Y NEWSLETTER. 1950. m. $195 membership only. Premium Marketing Club of New York, Inc., 1620 Rte. 22 E., Ste. 300, Union, NJ 07083. TEL 908-687-3090. FAX 908-687-0977. E-mail: asnoff@ix.netcom.com. Ed. Marie Beyer. circ. 300 (paid). **Document type:** newsletter.
Description: Information regarding incentives.

658.7   US
P M NEWS.* 1926. m. membership only. Purchasing Management Association of Philadelphia, 656 E. Swedesford Rd., Ste. 208, Wayne, PA 19087-1606. TEL 610-337-1040. FAX 610-337-2232. Ed. Ginger Ale Baker. adv.; illus. circ. 3,000. **Document type:** newsletter.
Former titles (until 1991): Mid-Atlantic Purchasing (ISSN 0031-7322); Philadelphia Purchasor.

P-O-P TIMES. (Point-of-Purchase) see BUSINESS AND ECONOMICS — Economic Situation And Conditions

P S R S. (Publishing Sales Representative's Source) see PUBLISHING AND BOOK TRADE

PACE BUYER'S GUIDES. DOMESTIC & FOREIGN TRUCK, VAN, 4 X 4 PRICES, NEW & USED. see TRANSPORTATION — Automobiles

658   GW
PACK REPORT. m. DM.174.40 (E.U. DM.192.50; elsewhere DM.202.40) (effective 1997). Deutscher Fachverlag GmbH, Mainzer Landstr. 251, 60326 Frankfurt a.M., Germany. TEL 49-69-759501. FAX 49-69-75952999. (Subscr. to: Postfach 100606, 60006 Frankfurt a.M., Germany) Ed. Annette von der Heide. adv.: B&W page DM.4320, color page DM.6360; trim 185 x 270; adv. contact: Gudrun Bitterlich. circ. 12,074. **Indexed:** Food Sci.& Tech.Abstr., Int.Packag.Abstr., Key to Econ.Sci., Packag.Sci.Tech., Paper & Bd.Abstr. **Document type:** trade publication.
Incorporates (1960-1994): Verpackung (ISSN 0042-4269)

PAPIER, CARTON ET CELLULOSE. GUIDE DU PAPIER. see PAPER AND PULP

791.06 658   UK
PARK WORLD. 1985. m. £68 (Europe $135; Far East $210; rest of world $180). World's Fair Ltd., P.O. Box 57, Oldham OL1 4BB, England. TEL 061-624-3687. FAX 061-665-1260. Ed. Christine Butterworth. circ. 6,500. **Document type:** trade publication.
Description: Articles on amusement parks, suppliers and personalities.

PARTY & PAPER RETAILER. see LEISURE AND RECREATION

PASTA PRODUCTS: THE INTERNATIONAL MARKET. see FOOD AND FOOD INDUSTRIES

PENNSYLVANIA MARKETING BULLETIN. see FORESTS AND FORESTRY — Lumber And Wood

658 691   US   ISSN 0898-0047
PEOPLE & PROFITS; Bill Lee's tips, tactics and how-to's for the building supply, hardware and home center industry. 1988. m. $147. Lee Resources, Inc., Box 16711, Greenville, SC 29606. TEL 803-288-0461. FAX 803-234-6961. Ed. Beth White. charts; illus.; stat.; tr.lit.; index; circ. 1,100 (paid). (back issues avail.)

658   US
PERCEPTIVE REPORT. 1979. m. free to qualified personnel. Perceptive Marketers Agency, Ltd., 1100 E. Hector St., Ste. 301, Conshohocken, PA 19428. TEL 610-825-8710. FAX 610-825-9186. Ed. Bob Charkow; Pub. Allen P. Solowitz. circ. 500 (controlled). **Document type:** newsletter.

PERFUMES AND FRAGRANCES: THE INTERNATIONAL MARKET. see BEAUTY CULTURE

658   SZ
PERSOENLICH. 23/yr. Persoenlich Verlags AG, Hauptplatz 5, CH-8640 Rapperswil, Switzerland. TEL 055-261717. FAX 055-271593. Ed. Erich Liebi. circ. 1,600.

PERSONAL CARE APPLIANCES: THE INTERNATIONAL MARKET. see ELECTRONICS

658 001.6   UK
PERSONAL COMPUTER MARKETS. s-m. £882. Blackwell Publishers Ltd., 108 Cowley Rd., Oxford OX4 1JF, England. TEL 44-1865-791100. FAX 44-1865-791347. E-mail: jnlinfo@blackwellpublishers.co.uk; URL: http://www.blackwellpublishers.co.uk. **Document type:** trade publication.
•Also available online. Vendor(s): Data-Star, Information Access Co.
Description: Provides market information and interpretation on the professional personal computer industry.

PET BUSINESS. see PETS

PET FOODS AND PRODUCTS: THE INTERNATIONAL MARKET. see FOOD AND FOOD INDUSTRIES

381 636   US   ISSN 0162-8666
SF411
PET SUPPLIES MARKETING. 1947-1993; resumed. q. $250 (effective 1996). Fancy Publications, 2 Borroughs, Irvine, CA 92618-2804. TEL 714-855-8822. FAX 714-855-3045. URL: http://www.petchannel.com. (Subscr. to: Neodata, Box 58025, Boulder, CO 80322. TEL 800-365-4221. FAX 303-604-7455) Ed. Scott McElhaney; Pub. Norman Ridker. adv. contact: Andy Lamedman. illus. circ. 14,121. **Indexed:** Tr.& Indus.Ind. **Document type:** trade publication.
Former titles (until 1976): Pet Mass Marketing (ISSN 0095-6627); (until 1972): P S M (ISSN 0031-6180); Pet Shop Management.
Description: Covers news on manufacturing, management and sales techniques, store handling ideas, livestock and pet products and industry statistics.

PHARMA BUSINESS; the international magazine of pharmaceutical business and marketing. see PHARMACY AND PHARMACOLOGY

BUSINESS AND ECONOMICS — MARKETING AND PURCHASING

658 659.1   GW   ISSN 0721-5665
PHARMA-MARKETING JOURNAL. 1976. bi-m. DM.87.90. I F A M Institut, Kaiser-Wilhelm-Ring 13, 40545 Duesseldorf, Germany. TEL 49-211-55986-0. FAX 49-211-575043. adv.; bk.rev. circ. 1,100. **Document type:** trade publication. —SWETS.

PHARMACEUTICAL MARKETERS DIRECTORY. see *PHARMACY AND PHARMACOLOGY*

PHARMACIES AND DRUGSTORES: THE INTERNATIONAL MARKET. see *PHARMACY AND PHARMACOLOGY*

PHARMACY RETAILER. see *PHARMACY AND PHARMACOLOGY*

PHELON'S DISCOUNT - JOBBING TRADE. see *BUSINESS AND ECONOMICS — Trade And Industrial Directories*

PHONE SALES PRESENTATIONS FOR SERVICE-TYPE BUSINESSES, ETC. - A NEWSLETTER. see *COMMUNICATIONS*

PHOTO RETAILER. see *PHOTOGRAPHY*

PHOTOGRAPHY: THE INTERNATIONAL MARKET. see *PHOTOGRAPHY*

658.8   FI   ISSN 0032-0242
PIRKKA. 1933. m. FIM 190 free. Kauppiaitten Kustannus Oy, Kanavakatu 3.B, FIN-00160 Helsinki, Finland. TEL 358-0-1053010. FAX 358-0-105336235. E-mail: kaisa.peutere@kesto.fi; URL: http://www.pirkka.fi. Ed. Kaisa Peutere. adv.; illus. circ. 2,300,000 (controlled).

658   GW   ISSN 0724-9632
PLANUNG UND ANALYSE, Zeitschrift fuer Informationsmanagement, Markt-, Media- und Werbeforschung. 1973. 6/yr. (E.U. DM.177.50; elsewhere DM.180.70) (effective 1997). Deutscher Fachverlag GmbH, Mainzer Landstr. 251, 60326 Frankfurt a.M., Germany. TEL 49-69-759501. FAX 49-69-75952999. Ed. Karin Duerr. adv.; B&W page DM.3460, color page DM.5310; trim 175 x 272. bk.rev. circ. 2,000. (back issues avail.) **Document type:** trade publication. —SWETS.
  Formerly (until 1984): Interview und Analyse (ISSN 0343-9690)

PLASTICS BRIEF: THERMOPLASTICS MARKETING NEWSLETTER. see *PLASTICS*

PLUNKETT'S RETAIL INDUSTRY ALMANAC. see *BUSINESS AND ECONOMICS — Trade And Industrial Directories*

658   US   ISSN 1085-5009
▼**POINT OF PURCHASE MAGAZINE.** 1995. 9/yr. $60. Shore-Varrone, Inc., 6255 Barfield Rd. N.E., Ste. 200, Atlanta, GA 30328-4300. TEL 404-252-8831. FAX 404-252-4436. E-mail: Colleen_Moynahan@svi.ccmail.compuserve.com; URL: http://www.svi_atl.com. Ed. Colleen Mognahan; Pub. Stan Berman. **Document type:** trade publication.

658.8   FR   ISSN 0150-1844
POINTS DE VENTE. 1962. w. 588 F. (foreign 840 F.). Groupe Liaisons S.A., 1 av. Edouard Belin, 92856 Rueil Malmaison, France. TEL 33-1-41299899. FAX 33-1-41299908. adv.; bk.rev. **Indexed:** Key to Econ.Sci.
  Incorporates: Rayons Jardin (ISSN 0249-1605)

PORTUGAL. INSTITUTO NACIONAL DE ESTATISTICA. PRECOS RENDIMENTOS NA AGRICULTURA. see *AGRICULTURE*

POTATO COUNTRY. see *AGRICULTURE — Crop Production And Soil*

658.8   US   ISSN 0032-5619
HF5410
POTENTIALS IN MARKETING; promotion ideas for marketing professionals. 1968. 10/yr. $24 (Canada $27; elsewhere $50). Lakewood Publications, Inc., 50 S. Ninth St., Minneapolis, MN 55402. TEL 612-333-0471. FAX 612-333-6526. URL: http://www.lakewoodpub.com/pim/index.htm. Ed. Margaret Kaeter. adv.; illus. circ. 67,400. **Document type:** trade publication.
  ●Also available online. Vendor(s): Information Access Co.
  —KR SourceOne; UMI; UnCover. **CCC.**
  Incorporates (1976-1989): Marketing Communications (ISSN 0164-4343)
  Description: Contains ideas, products and services for boosting a company's competitive advantage.

PRACTICE BUILDER. see *ADVERTISING AND PUBLIC RELATIONS*

PREPARED SOUPS: THE INTERNATIONAL MARKET. see *FOOD AND FOOD INDUSTRIES*

PRESENTATIONS; technology and techniques for effective communication. see *ADVERTISING AND PUBLIC RELATIONS*

THE PRICE WATERHOUSE SALES AND MARKETING SOFTWARE HANDBOOK (YEAR). see *COMPUTERS — Software*

PRICING ADVISOR. see *CONSUMER EDUCATION AND PROTECTION*

658   UK   ISSN 0968-4905
HF5416
PRICING STRATEGY AND PRACTICE. 1993. q. £699($449) (effective 1997). M C B University Press Ltd., 60-62 Toller Ln., Bradford, W. Yorks BD8 9BY, England. TEL 44-1274-777700. FAX 44-1274-785200. TELEX 51317-MCBUNI-G. URL: http://www.mcb.co.uk. (N. American subscr. to: M C B University Press Limited, Box 1943, Birmingham, AL 35201) Ed. Kent Monroe. (reprint service avail. from SWZ) **Document type:** academic/scholarly publication.
  —BLDSC (6612.889040). **CCC.**

658   US   ISSN 0892-189X
PRING MARKET REVIEW.* 1984. m. $395. International Institute for Economic Research, Inc., Box 624, Gloucester, VA 23061-0624. TEL 203-868-7772. FAX 203-868-2683. Ed. Martin J. Pring. circ. 600.
  Description: Reviews the technical position of the world's major financial markets with special emphasis on U.S. debt and equities.

PRODUCT ALERT. see *FOOD AND FOOD INDUSTRIES*

659.1 615   US   ISSN 1078-6937
HF5415.15
PRODUCT MANAGEMENT TODAY. 1990. m. $45. Product Management Today, Inc., 28 Jones Ave., Flourtown, PA 19031. TEL 215-233-9384. FAX 215-233-9320. Ed. Peter Ciszewski; Pub. Thomas Lyons Drake. adv.; circ. 9,600 (controlled). **Document type:** trade publication.
  Description: Covers marketing, product management, managed care marketing and career development issues affecting the product management team, service healthcare manufacturers and service sector companies.

658   FR   ISSN 1150-5273
PROFESSION MARKETING. 1989. 24/yr. 2150 F. (foreign 2450 F.) (effective 1997). Ludmark France, 5 rue Fauvet, 75018 Paris, France. TEL 33-1-46273030. FAX 33-1-46272888. Ed. Jean-Luc Girardot; Pub. Denis Marcoullier. adv. contact: Denis Marcoullier. bk.rev.; circ. 1,750 (paid). **Document type:** bulletin.
  Description: Covers operational marketing.

PROFESSIONAL ADVISOR. see *ADVERTISING AND PUBLIC RELATIONS*

PROFESSIONAL CANDY BUYER. see *FOOD AND FOOD INDUSTRIES*

658   SA
PROFESSIONAL MANAGEMENT REVIEW. Cover title: P M R. (Text in English) 1990. m. R.110 (foreign R.190). P M R cc, P.O. Box 1200, Parklands 2121, South Africa. TEL 27-11-8804720. FAX 27-11-8804724. Ed. Ray Wood. adv. contact: Bob Stephen. bk.rev.; illus.; index. **Document type:** trade publication.
  Formerly: Professional Marketing Review (ISSN 1016-0051)
  Description: Presents expertise and intelligence on business and management issues affecting South Africa and the region.

658   UK   ISSN 0969-1847
PROFESSIONAL MARKETING. 1993. m. £100. Professional Marketing International, 99 Gresham St., London EC2V 7NA, England. TEL 0171-600-3335. FAX 0171-600-6252. Ed. Richard Chaplin. adv.; B&W page £700, color page £1000; adv. contact: Nadia Cristina. bk.rev. (back issues avail.) **Document type:** trade publication.

658   US   ISSN 1070-0455
PROFESSIONAL PURCHASING. 1972. m. $89 to non-members. American Purchasing Society, Inc., 11910 Oak Trail Way, Port Richey, FL 34668. TEL 813-862-7998. FAX 813-862-8199. Ed. Harry E. Hough. R&P contact: Harry E. Hough. adv. contact: Tammy Edwards. bk.rev.; index. circ. 3,000. (back issues avail.; reprint service avail.) **Document type:** newsletter.
  Description: Provides information on price, job openings in purchasing, and answers to purchasing problems.

658   US   ISSN 1077-436X
PROFESSIONAL SELLING. 1982. s-m. $137.88. Bureau of Business Practice, 24 Rope Ferry Rd., Waterford, CT 06386. TEL 860-442-4365. FAX 860-437-3555. URL: http://www.bbpnews.com. Ed. Paulette S. Kitchens; Pub. Peter Garabedian. R&P contact: Debra Ferraro. s-a. index. **Document type:** newsletter.
  Description: Provides field sales personnel with solutions for everyday sales problems.

658.7   CN
PROGRESSIVE PURCHASING. (Text in English and French) 1982. q. membership. Purchasing Management Association of Canada, 2 Carlton St., Suite 1414, Toronto, Ont. M5B 1J3, Canada. TEL 416-977-7111. FAX 416-977-8886. Ed. David Cameron. R&P contact: David Cameron. bk.rev. circ. 6,000. **Document type:** newsletter.
  Formerly: P M A C News; **Supersedes:** Action (ISSN 0319-5023)

658.8   US   ISSN 1047-1707
CODEN: PROMFN
PROMO; the international magazine for promotional marketing. 1987. m. $59. Cowles - SIMBA Information (Subsidiary of: Cowles Business Media), 11 Riverbend Dr. S., Box 4949, Stamford, CT 06907-0949. TEL 203-358-9900; 800-307-2529. FAX 203-358-5811. E-mail: info@simbanet.com; URL: http://www.simbanet.com. (Subscr. to: Box 682, Holmes, PA 19043-8112) Ed. Kerry E. Smith; Pub. Kerry Smith. adv. contact: Shirley Sax. charts. circ. 24,500. (back issues avail.) **Document type:** trade publication.
  ●Also available online. Vendor(s): Information Access Co.

PROMOTIONAL PRODUCTS BUSINESS. see *ADVERTISING AND PUBLIC RELATIONS*

658.85   UK   ISSN 0266-7991
HF5415
PROMOTIONS AND INCENTIVES. 1961. 10/yr. £52. Haymarket Publishing Ltd., 174 Hammersmith Rd., London W6 7JP, England. TEL 44-171-413-4328. FAX 44-171-413-4013. (Subscr. to: P.O. Box 219, Woking, Surrey GU21 1ZW, England. TEL 44-1483-733800. FAX 44-1483-756792) Ed. Max Cuff. adv.; bk.rev.; charts; illus.; stat.; tr.lit. circ. 7,000. (also avail. in microfilm from UMI; reprint service avail. from UMI) **Indexed:** Anbar. **Document type:** trade publication.
  —BLDSC (6925.500000); UMI. **CCC.**
  44Former titles: Incentive Marketing and Sales Promotion (ISSN 0305-2230); Incentive Marketing (ISSN 0019-3356)

BUSINESS AND ECONOMICS — MARKETING AND PURCHASING

658.8 US
PROOF. m. membership. Direct Marketing Club of New York, 224 Seventh St., Garden City, NY 11530-9619. Ed. Debra Ray. R&P contact: Debra Ray. **Document type:** newsletter.

PSYCHOLOGY & MARKETING. see PSYCHOLOGY

PUBBLICITA ITALIA. see ADVERTISING AND PUBLIC RELATIONS

658 US ISSN 1053-9751
HM261
PUBLIC PULSE. 1986. m. $297 (foreign $347). Roper Starch Worldwide, 205 E. 42nd St., New York, NY 10017. TEL 212-599-0700. FAX 212-867-7008. Ed. John Berry. **Document type:** newsletter.
●Also available online. Vendor(s): Lexis-Nexis.
Description: Tracks what people are thinking, doing and buying, through proprietary survey data.

PUBLICIDAD Y MERCADEO. see ADVERTISING AND PUBLIC RELATIONS

070.5 689.1 US
PUBLISHING POYNTERS; book and information marketing news and ideas from Dan Poynter. 1986. q. $9.95 for 8 issues (FAX delivery avail.). Para Publishing, Box 8206-462, Santa Barbara, CA 93118-8206. TEL 805-968-7277.
FAX 805-968-1379. E-mail: danpoynter@ parapublishing.com; URL: http://www. parapublishing.com/books/para/462. Ed. Patricia Finn; Pub. Dan Poynter. R&P contact: Jennifer Bond. bk.rev. circ. 13,000. (looseleaf format; back issues avail.) **Document type:** newsletter.

PURCHASER'S LEGAL ADVISER. see LAW

658.7 II ISSN 0014-6544
PURCHASING. 1964. m. Rs.25. India Publications Co., Denabank House, 2nd Fl., 31 Hamam St., Bombay 1, India. Ed. Eric Martin. adv.; bk.rev.; illus. **Indexed:** B.P.I., Tr.& Indus.Ind.
Formerly: Factory.

658.7 US ISSN 0033-4448
HF5001
PURCHASING (NEWTON). 1915. 19/yr. $95 (Canada $134; Mexico $125; elsewhere $155). Cahners Publishing Company (Newton), Division of Reed Elsevier Inc., 275 Washington St., Newton, MA 02158-1630. TEL 617-558-4291.
FAX 617-558-4327. E-mail: ptavares@cahners.com; URL: http://www.manufacturing.net/magazine/ purchasing/. (Subscr. to: 8773 S. Ridgeline Blvd., Highlands Ranch, CO 80126. TEL 800-662-7776) Ed. Kevin FitzGerald; Pub. Jack O'Connor. R&P contact: James Morgan. adv.: B&W page $10830, color page $12130. bk.rev.; charts; illus.; mkt.; tr.lit.; index. circ. 93,600. (also avail. in microform) **Indexed:** ABI Inform., B.P.I., BPIA, Bus.Ind., Eng.Ind., INSPEC, Key to Econ.Sci., Tr.& Indus.Ind. **Document type:** trade publication.
●Also available online. Vendor(s): Information Access Co.
—BLDSC (7160.500000); AskIEEE; KR SourceOne; Linda Hall; SWETS; UMI; UnCover. **CCC.**
Description: Provides price and market news and forecasts on industrial products, components and materials, office products, business systems, transportation. Reports latest purchasing tactics, strategies and techniques.

658 US ISSN 1077-4351
PURCHASING MANAGEMENT BULLETIN. s-m. $137.88. Bureau of Business Practice, 24 Rope Ferry Rd., Waterford, CT 06386. TEL 860-442-4365.
FAX 860-437-3555. URL: http://www.bbpnews.com. Ed. Lisa Goggins; Pub. Peter Garabedian. R&P contact: Debra Ferraro. s-a. index. **Document type:** newsletter.
Formerly: Purchasing Executive's Bulletin.
Description: Profiles noteworthy purchasing techniques in action at identified companies, including vendor selection and rating systems, vendor certification and partnering, sole sourcing, negotiations, value and cost analysis, and buyer training and development.

658.7 US ISSN 1086-5853
HD39.5
PURCHASING TODAY. m. membership. National Association of Purchasing Management, 2055 E. Centennial Circle, Tempe, AZ 85285.
TEL 602-752-6276. FAX 602-752-7890. Ed. Julie Murphree. adv.: B&W page $3706, color page $4731; trim 8 3/8 x 10 7/8; adv. contact: Jolene Gulley. circ. 40,000 (controlled).
Former titles: N A P M Insights (ISSN 1047-7470); (until 1990): Insight (Tempe).
Description: Publishes articles relating to purchasing and materials management.

QUICK PRINT PRODUCTS. see PRINTING

658 600 UK ISSN 0952-7532
QUIDDITY; polemical review of new developments in publishing. 1987. m. £60($140) 3 Abbey Orchard St., Ste. 20, Westminster, London SW1P 2JJ, England. TEL 01-222-1339. Ed. Graham Lea.
Description: For publishers and others concerned with electronic information, media and communication.

QUINCAILLERIE MATERIAUX. see BUILDING AND CONSTRUCTION — Hardware

658.8 US ISSN 0893-7451
CODEN: QMREEN
QUIRK'S MARKETING RESEARCH REVIEW. 1986. 10/yr. $60. (Quirk Enterprises) Quirk Enterprises, Box 23536, Minneapolis, MN 55423.
TEL 612-861-1836. FAX 612-861-8051. URL: http://www.quirks.com/. Ed. Joseph Rydholm; Pub. Tom Quirk. R&P contact: Daniel Quirk. adv. contact: Evan Tweed. bk.rev.; circ. 15,500 (controlled).
Document type: trade publication.
Description: Focuses on research techniques for the marketing industry. Includes case histories and industry product and personnel news.

658 US
R A C DIGEST.* bi-m. $65 membership. (Retail Advertising Conference) Retail Advertising and Marketing Association International, 333 N. Michigan Ave., Ste. 3000, Chicago, IL 60601-4105. TEL 312-245-9011. FAX 312-245-9015. **Document type:** bulletin.

658.8 GW
R B CONGRESS MARKETING. (Supplement to: R B Reisebuero-Marketing und R B Hotel-Marketing) 1967. m. DM.180($110) R B Redaktions Buero, Schraemelstr. 126, 81247 Munich, Germany.
TEL 089-88888888. FAX 089-8110655. Ed. Hans Nechleba. circ. 800. (looseleaf format) **Document type:** trade publication.

658 US
R N AND W P L ENCYCLOPEDIA. (Registered Number & Wool Products Label) a. $259.95. Salesman's Guide, A Division of Reed Elsevier Inc., 121 Chanlon Rd., New Providence, NJ 07974.
TEL 908-464-6800. FAX 609-665-2894. TELEX 138 755. E-mail: info@reedref.com; URL: http:// www.reedref.com. (Subscr. to: Salesman's Guide, Order Dept., Box 1009, Summit, NJ 07902. TEL 800-521-8110) Ed. Elizabeth Kizar; Pub. Peter Simon. (also avail. in magnetic tape) **Document type:** directory, trade publication.
Formerly: R N and W P L Encyclopedia and Yearbook.
Description: Lists RN and WPL identification numbers issued by the Federal Trade Commission.

910 658.8 US ISSN 0361-9923
G1019
RAND MCNALLY COMMERCIAL ATLAS AND MARKETING GUIDE. 1876. a. $395. Rand McNally & Co., 8255 N. Central Park, Skokie, IL 60076.
TEL 847-329-8100. (Orders to: Box 7600, Chicago, IL 60680) Ed. David Zapenski. R&P contact: Rebecca Engel King. TEL 847-329-2336. charts; stat.; index.

RECRUITMENT, RETENTION & RESTRUCTURING REPORT; strategies for recruiters, managers, R&R committees, & human resource directors. see MEDICAL SCIENCES — Nurses And Nursing

REGIONAL ECONOMIES AND MARKETS; a quarterly analysis from the Conference Board. see BUSINESS AND ECONOMICS — Economic Situation And Conditions

658 UK ISSN 0967-0068
REGIONAL MARKETING POCKET BOOK. a. £24. (Advertising Association) N T C Publications Ltd., Farm Rd., Henley-on-Thames, Oxfordshire RG9 1EJ, England. TEL 01491-411000.
FAX 01491-571188. **Document type:** trade publication.
Description: Guide to Britain's regional differences in relation to marketing.

REGIONAL OFFICIAL GUIDES: TRACTORS AND FARM EQUIPMENT. see AGRICULTURE — Agricultural Equipment

658 UK ISSN 1364-4424
REGIONAL SALES LEADS - CENTRAL MANCHESTER. 1995. a. £249 (disk format £395) (effective 1996). I C C Business Publications Ltd., Field House, 72 Oldfield Rd., Hampton, Middlesex TW12 2HQ, England. TEL 44-181-783-0922.
FAX 44-181-783-1940. (also avail. in diskette format)

338.4769 DK ISSN 1396-6812
RENOVERING OG DRIFT - NETTO. Variant title: V & S Priser, Renovering og Drift - Netto. 1989. a. DKK 1310 (effective 1997). V & S Byggedata A-S, Frederikssundsvej 194, DK-2700 Broenshoej, Denmark. TEL 45-38-60-77-11.
FAX 45-38-60-77-44. Dir. Carl Friis Skovsen.
Supersedes in part (in 1997): Renovering og Drift (ISSN 0905-9814); Which was formerly (until 1991): Drift og Vedligehold (ISSN 0904-3608)

658.8 640.73 US ISSN 1051-7057
RENTAL DEALER NEWS.* 1987. m. $36. Rental Dealer News, Inc., 4521 Campus Dr., Ste. 388, Irvine, CA 92612-2621. Ed. Marie May; Pub. Marie May. adv. circ. 13,000. **Document type:** trade publication.
Description: For the rent-to-own and rental dealer who merchandises video, audio, major appliances, furniture, accessory products, jewelry, computers, cellular phones, exercise equipment, tanning beds, portable spas, and peripheral products. Emphasis is on providing profiles of successful dealers, and information on running a successful store, including successful management and merchandising techniques.

338 US ISSN 0034-4524
RENTAL EQUIPMENT REGISTER. Short title: R E R. 1957. m. $75 in U.S.; Canada $85; elsewhere $190 (effective 1997). Miramar Communications Inc., 23815 Stuart Ranch Rd., Box 8987, Malibu, CA 90265-8987. TEL 310-337-9717. Ed. Chris Fletcher. adv.: B&W page $1810, color page $2505; trim 8 1/4 X 10 7/8. illus.; tr.lit.; circ. 17,500 (controlled).
Description: Edited for owners and managers of equipment rental and sales centers that are engaged in the rental of tools, contractor equipment, homeowner equipment, towing devices and outdoor power equipment.

658.8 338 US ISSN 1042-9085
HD9999.L438
RENTAL MANAGEMENT. 1970. m. $24 (foreign $60.50). American Rental Association, 1900 19th St., Moline, IL 61265. TEL 309-764-2475.
FAX 309-764-1533. URL: http://ararental.org. Ed. Brian Alm; Pub. F.I. Anderson. R&P contact: Brian Alm. adv. contact: Tamera Dawson. tr.lit. circ. 15,500. **Document type:** trade publication.
●Also available online.
Formerly: Rental Age (ISSN 0098-8529)
Description: Articles cover rental industry news, analyze operating philosophies of innovators, describe business strategies, interpret the effects of business, legislative and regulatory trends.

REP TALK. see BUSINESS AND ECONOMICS — Management

658.8 659.1 UK ISSN 0969-6709
RESEARCH. 1966. m. £78 to non-members. Market Research Society, 15 Northburgh St., London EC1V 0AH, England. TEL 44-171-490-4911.
FAX 44-171-490-0608. Ed. Peter Fiddick; Pub. Peter Greenwood. R&P contact: Nicola Potts. adv.; bk.rev. circ. 6,500. **Document type:** newsletter.
Formerly: M R S Newsletter (ISSN 0961-5172)

BUSINESS AND ECONOMICS — MARKETING AND PURCHASING

658.8 US ISSN 0739-358X
RESEARCH ALERT (NEW YORK); a bi-weekly report of consumer marketing studies. 1981. 24/yr. $369 (foreign $429). E P M Communications, 160 Mercer St., 3rd Fl., New York, NY 10012-3212. TEL 212-941-0099. FAX 212-941-1622. Ed. Michael Schau; Pub. Ira Mayer. R&P contact: Ira Mayer. index. (back issues avail.) **Document type:** newsletter.
●Also available online. Vendor(s): Information Access Co., Knight-Ridder Information, Inc., Lexis-Nexis.
—CCC.

658 US ISSN 0885-2111
HF5415.3
RESEARCH IN CONSUMER BEHAVIOR; a research annual. 1985. a. $73.25 to institutions. J A I Press Inc., 55 Old Post Rd., No. 2, Box 1678, Greenwich, CT 06830-1678. TEL 203-661-7602. FAX 203-661-0792. E-mail: jai@jaipress.com. Ed. Jagdish N. Sheth. **Document type:** monographic series.
—BLDSC (7737.005000); UnCover. **CCC.**

658.8 US ISSN 0191-3026
HF5415.2
RESEARCH IN MARKETING; an annual compilation of research. (Supplement avail.: Choice Models for Buyer Behavior) 1978. a. $73.25 to institutions. J A I Press Inc., 55 Old Post Rd., No. 2, Box 1678, Greenwich, CT 06836-1678. TEL 203-661-7602. Ed. Jagdish N. Sheth. **Indexed:** BPIA, Psychol.Abstr., Tr.& Indus.Ind.
—BLDSC (7741.916000); CISTI; UnCover. **CCC.**

658.8 659.1 UK ISSN 0969-6733
RESEARCHPLUS. 1992. m. Market Research Society, 15 Northburgh St., London EC1V 0AH, England. TEL 44-171-490-4911. FAX 44-171-490-0608. Ed. Val Stevenson; Pub. Peter Greenwood. R&P contact: Nicola Potts. adv. contact: Peter Greenwood. circ. 7,000. **Document type:** trade publication.

RESTAURANTS & INSTITUTIONS MARKETPLACE. see HOTELS AND RESTAURANTS

658 US ISSN 0951-9734
HF5429.6.G7
RETAIL BUSINESS: MARKET REPORTS.* 1958. m. £415($750) Corporate Intelligence on Retailing, 51 Doughty St., London WC1 N2LS, England. TEL 44-171-696-9006. **Indexed:** Food Sci.& Tech.Abstr.
●Also available online.
Superseded in part (in 1987): Retail Business (ISSN 0034-6012)
Description: Contains market surveys, consumer spending forecasts, a technology review and a product sector overview.

658 US ISSN 1086-2137
▼**RETAIL DELIVERY SYSTEMS NEWS.** 1996. bi-w. $595 (foreign $630) (effective 1997). Phillips Business Information, Inc., 1201 Seven Locks Rd., Potomac, MD 20854. TEL 301-424-3338. FAX 301-309-3847. E-mail: pbi@phillips.com. Ed. Lurdes da Maia-Abruscato. (back issues avail.) **Document type:** newsletter.
—CCC.
Incorporates in part (1987-1997): Financial Services Report (ISSN 0894-7260); Incorporates (in 1995): Securities Marketing News (ISSN 1074-8385); Which was formerly (until 1994): Bank Securities Report (ISSN 1071-2038); (1993-1994): Bank Securities News (ISSN 1068-3763); Financial Services Law Report; Financial Services Week (Potomac).

381.025 UK
RETAIL DIRECTORY. 1939. a. £150 (foreign £160). Newman Books Ltd., 32 Vauxhall Bridge Rd., London SW1V 2SS, England. TEL 0171-973-6402. FAX 0171-233-5056. Ed. David Ricketts. adv. contact: Warren Brett. circ. 4,000 (paid). **Document type:** directory.
—BLDSC (7785.502700).
Incorporates: London Shop Surveys (ISSN 0140-3206); **Former titles:** Stores, Shops, Hypermarkets Retail Directory (ISSN 0305-4012); Stores and Shops Retail Directory (ISSN 0081-5810)
Description: Directory of U.K. retailers with full company details including type of trade, number of branches, executives, and buyers.

RETAIL INFO SYSTEMS NEWS DIRECTORY. see BUSINESS AND ECONOMICS — Computer Applications

658.8 UK ISSN 0265-2536
RETAIL INTELLIGENCE. Key Title: Mintel Retail Intelligence Quarterly. 1980. bi-m. £1495 (effective 1996). Mintel International Group Ltd., 18-19 Long Ln., London EC1A 9HE, England. TEL 44-171-606-4533. FAX 44-171-606-5932. Ed. Neil Mason. circ. 150. (also avail. in microform; back issues avail.) **Document type:** trade publication.
●Also available online.
Also available on CD-ROM.
—BLDSC (7785.503300).
Description: Provides commercial insight into the retail trade using exclusive research.

658.8 UK ISSN 0968-8234
RETAIL MONITOR INTERNATIONAL. 1988. m. £510($1020) (effective 1997). Euromonitor, 60-61 Britton St., London EC1M 5NA, England. TEL 44-171-251-8024. FAX 44-171-608-3149. E-mail: info@euromonitor.com; URL: http://www.euromonitor.com. (Addr. in N. America: Euromonitor International, 122 S. Michigan Ave., Ste. 1200, Chicago, IL 60603. TEL 800-577-3876. FAX 312-922-1151) **Indexed:** Cont.Pg.Manage. **Document type:** trade publication.
—BLDSC (7785.503950).
Formerly (until 1990): Retail Monitor (ISSN 0952-9594)
Description: Covers European and international markets within the context of retailing; profiles retailers.

658 IE
RETAIL NEWS. 10/yr. I£35. (Retail Grocery Dairy and Allied Trades Association) Tara Publishing Co. Ltd., Poolbeg House, 1-2 Poolbeg St., Dublin 2, Ireland. TEL 01-6719244. FAX 01-6719263. Ed. Fergus Farrell. adv.: B&W page I£1225, color page I£1595; trim 297 x 210; adv. contact: Kathleen Belton. circ. 3,368. **Document type:** trade publication.
Description: Informs the independent retailer of new product lines.

658 IE
RETAIL NEWS DIRECTORY. a. I£20. Tara Publishing Co. Ltd., Poolbeg House, 1-2 Poolbeg St., Dublin 2, Ireland. TEL 01-6719244. FAX 01-6719263. Ed. Fergus Farrell. adv.: B&W page I£1290, color page I£1620; trim 263 x 183; adv. contact: Valerie Doyle. **Document type:** directory.

658 UK ISSN 0966-3711
RETAIL POCKET BOOK. a. £24. N T C Publications Ltd., Farm Rd., Henley-on-Thames, Oxfordshire RG9 1EJ, England. TEL 01491-411000. FAX 01491-571188. **Document type:** trade publication.
Description: Provides facts and figures on UK retail markets and retailers.

658.8 UK ISSN 0144-6835
RETAIL REVIEW. 1973. 10/yr. £93 (effective 1997). Co-operative Wholesale Society Ltd., Library & Information Unit, New Century House, Manchester M60 4ES, England. TEL 0161-827-6686. FAX 0161-834-4507. Ed. R.D. Hilton. bk.rev. circ. 2,000. (back issues avail.) **Document type:** newsletter.
Description: Covers a wide range of retail news.

RETAIL STATIONERY: THE INTERNATIONAL MARKET. see BUSINESS AND ECONOMICS — Office Equipment And Services

RETAIL STORE IMAGE. see INTERIOR DESIGN AND DECORATION

RETAIL TECHNOLOGY: A WORLD SURVEY. see BUSINESS AND ECONOMICS — Production Of Goods And Services

658.83 UK
RETAIL TRADE IN THE U K. (Subseries of: Euromonitor Market Reports) irreg. £450($900) Euromonitor, 60-61 Britton St., London EC1M 5NA, England. TEL 44-171-251-8024. FAX 44-171-608-3149. E-mail: info@euromonitor.com; URL: http://www.euromonitor.com. (Addr. in N. America: Euromonitor International, 122 S. Michigan Ave., Ste. 1200, Chicago, IL 60603. TEL 800-577-3876. FAX 312-922-1157) stat. **Document type:** trade publication.
Description: Contains statistical analyses examining trends in the retailing and distribution of consumer goods in the U.K., using time-series data.

658.83 UK ISSN 0966-7067
RETAIL TRADE INTERNATIONAL. (Subseries of: Euromonitor Market Reports) 1975. a. £795($1590) Euromonitor, 60-61 Britton St., London EC1M 5NA, England. TEL 44-171-251-8024. FAX 44-171-608-3149. E-mail: info@euromonitor.com; URL: http://www.euromonitor.com. (Addr. in N. America: Euromonitor International, 122 S. Michigan Ave., Ste. 1200, Chicago, IL 60603. TEL 800-577-3876. FAX 312-922-1157) stat. **Document type:** trade publication.
●Also available online.
Formerly: Retail Trade Europe
Description: Contains statistical analysis examining trends in retailing and the distribution of consumer goods in 70 countries throughout the world with time-series data from 1985-1990.

658.8 US
THE RETAILER. 1973. m. $18 (free to qualified personnel). Holco Communications Inc., Box 80727, Conyers, GA 30208-0727. TEL 404-483-4860. FAX 404-483-2447. adv. circ. 20,500. (tabloid format) **Document type:** trade publication.
Former titles: Carolina Retailer; Retail News Reporter; Retail Reporter (ISSN 0192-2475)
Description: Contains wholesale and manufacturing news and local distributor news. For owners and managers of businesses selling major appliances, consumer electronics, T.V.R.O. satellite, consumer outdoor power equipment, home office products and furniture.

658 MM
RETAILER. (Text in English and Maltese) m. $6 to non-members. Association of General Retailers and Traders, Republic St., Valletta, Malta. TEL 234170. FAX 246925. adv.; bk.rev.

658.87 US ISSN 0192-9151
RETAILER AND MARKETING NEWS. 1964. m. $12. R A M Nvest, Inc., c/o Michael J. Anderson, Ed., Box 191105, Dallas, TX 75219-1105. adv.; bk.rev.; illus. circ. 8,000. (tabloid format) **Document type:** trade publication.
Formerly: North Texas Retailer (ISSN 0029-2907)
Description: Regional business trade journal serving the appliance, consumer electronic and furniture industry in the northern half of Texas.

380.1 US
THE RETAILING IN THE 1990'S: A STRATEGIC AND FINANCIAL ANALYSIS. 1990. a. Dun & Bradstreet Information Services (Murray Hill) (Subsidiary of: Dun & Bradstreet, Inc.), One Diamond Hill Rd., Murray Hill, NJ 07974. TEL 908-665-5224. FAX 908-771-7599. Eds. Mel Feierstein, Pete Nevenglosky. **Document type:** trade publication.
Description: Examines major issues that have tremendous impact on retailing: leveraged buyouts, mergers and acquisitions, and business failures. Provides a financial analysis of industry norms and ratios, as well as sales and income by industry segment.

RETAILING NEWS. see ELECTRONICS

RETAILING TODAY. see BUSINESS AND ECONOMICS — Management

658 AG
REVISTA TIENDA. 1964. m. Carlos Pellegrini, 1175, piso 7A, 1009 Buenos Aires, Argentina. TEL 393-8526. Ed. Hernan Bianchi. circ. 9,000.

BUSINESS AND ECONOMICS — MARKETING AND PURCHASING

658.8   FR   ISSN 0035-3051
REVUE FRANCAISE DU MARKETING. 1964. 5/yr. 256 F. Association Nationale pour le Developpement des Techniques de Marketing, 221 rue Lafayette, 75010 Paris, France. TEL 40-38-97-11. FAX 40-38-05-08. Ed. Mme. Servant Chamoret. adv.; bk.rev.; abstr.; bibl.; charts; illus.; mkt. circ. 3,000. **Indexed:** Account.& Data Proc.Abstr., Cont.Pg.Manage., Mgmt.& Market.Abstr., P.A.I.S.For.Lang.Ind., SCIMP, SSCI. —BLDSC (7904.190000); SWETS.

658   IS
RIVON CHESHEV. q. Chesev Ltd., P.O. Box 40021, Tel Aviv 61 400, Israel. TEL (03)216291.

RUSSIA AND CHINA TRAVEL NEWS. see *TRAVEL AND TOURISM*

S A C I SLANTS. (Sales Association of the Chemical Industry, Inc.) see *CHEMISTRY*

658.8   GW   ISSN 0933-9469
S A Z. (Sport Artikel Zeitung); the leading sporting goods and sports fashion trade newspaper. 1974. fortn. DM.130. S A Z Verlag GmbH, Rumfordstr. 42, 80469 Munich, Germany. TEL 49-89-212110-0. FAX 49-89-2913435. Ed. Horst Frankl. circ. 10,000. **Document type:** trade publication.

658   GW
S B ARTIKEL. (Selbstbedienung); German self-service trade magazine. 1968. m. DM.80. Verlag fuer Handel und Marketing GmbH, Ruhrstr. 2, 58097 Hagen, Germany. TEL 02331-21044. FAX 02331-15213. Ed. Meno Schramm. circ. 21,000.

658 790.1   US
S G M A COMPREHENSIVE QUARTERLY SALES TRENDS REPORT. q. Sporting Goods Manufacturers Association, 200 Castlewood Dr., N. Palm Beach, FL 33408. TEL 561-842-4100. Ed. Sebastian DiCasoli. **Document type:** trade publication.

S N DISTRIBUTION STUDY OF GROCERY STORE SALES. see *FOOD AND FOOD INDUSTRIES*

S R D S: BULLET; the latest in list activity. (Standard Rate and Data Service) see *ADVERTISING AND PUBLIC RELATIONS — Abstracting, Bibliographies, Statistics*

381.2060489   DK   ISSN 0900-1891
SAELGEREN. 1901. s-m. DKK 200. Danske Saelgere, Noerre Farimagsgade, DK-1364 Copenhagen K, Denmark. Ed. Peter Hjort. adv. contact: Steen Weber Thomsen. circ. 25,500. **Document type:** trade publication.
Former titles (until 1972): Handelsrejsendebladet (ISSN 0900-2251); (until 1935): Organet for Danske Handelsrejsende.

658   SZ
ST. GALLISCH - APPENZELLISCHE GEWERBE ZEITUNG. m. Oberer Graben 12, CH-9000 St. Gallen 1, Switzerland. TEL 071-229191. Ed. A. Muehlematter. circ. 8,500.

658.8   JA
SALES. (Text in Japanese) 1956. m. 8160 Yen. Diamond Inc., 4-2, 1-chome, Kasumigaseki, Chiyoda-ku, Tokyo 100, Japan. Ed. Takeshi Sato.

658.8   US
SALES & MARKETING DIGEST (BELVIDERE). m. Marsili Publishing Inc., 2464 Circle Dr., Belvidere, IL 61008-9758. TEL 815-547-4311. Ed. Ray Marsili.

650   US
SALES & MARKETING DIGEST (NEW YORK). (Includes special bonus report) m. $19. Sales & Marketing Digest, 160 Fifth Ave., Ste. 812A, New York, NY 10010.

658 658   US
SALES AND MARKETING EXECUTIVE REPORT. 1978. bi-w. $179. Dartnell Corporation, 4660 N. Ravenswood Ave., Chicago, IL 60640. TEL 773-561-4000; 800-621-5463. FAX 773-561-3801. URL: http://www.dartnellcorp.com. Ed. Christen Heide. **Document type:** newsletter.
Description: Includes management reports, special surveys and trend analysis, and quarterly economic reports and analysis to help sales and marketing managers achieve sales and profit goals.

658.8   US
HF5438
SALES & MARKETING MANAGEMENT. 1918. 14/yr. $48 (Canada $66; elsewhere $77). Bill Communications, Inc., 355 Park Ave. S., 5th Fl., New York, NY 10010-1789. TEL 212-592-6200. FAX 212-592-6339. URL: http://www.edit.smmmag.com. Ed. Charles Butler. adv.; bk.rev.; illus.; tr.lit. circ. 60,000. (also avail. in microform from UMI; microfiche from CIS; reprint service avail. from UMI) **Indexed:** ABI Inform., ASEAN Manage.Abstr., B.P.I., BPIA, Chic.Per.Ind., INSPEC, Key to Econ.Sci., Mag.Ind., Manage.Cont., Mgmt.& Market.Abstr., P.A.I.S., PROMT, SRI. **Document type:** trade publication.
●Also available online. Vendor(s): Information Access Co., UMI.
—BLDSC (8070.670000); AskIEEE; KR SourceOne; SWETS; UMI; UnCover. **CCC**.
Former titles: S and M M Sales and Marketing Management (ISSN 0163-7517); (until 1976): Sales and Marketing Management (ISSN 0361-2570); (until 1975): Sales Management (ISSN 0036-3413)
Description: Supplies information to executives responsible for sales and marketing within their own organizations.

658.7   UK   ISSN 0264-3200
SALES AND MARKETING MANAGEMENT. 1976. m. £65 (foreign £75) (effective 1996). (Institute of Sales and Marketing Management) I S M Publishing Ltd., Nat West House, 31 Upper George St., Luton, Beds. LU1 2RD, England. TEL 44-1582-483232. FAX 44-1582-483232. Ed. Angela Jennings. R&P contact: Angela Jennings. adv.: B&W page £1150, color page £1600; 276 x 186; adv. contact: John Skillings. bk.rev.; illus. circ. 15,000. **Indexed:** Account.& Data Proc.Abstr., Account.Ind. (1974-), Bus.Ind., Cont.Pg.Manage., Mag.Ind., Tr.& Indus.Ind. **Document type:** consumer publication, trade publication.
●Also available online. Vendor(s): Knight-Ridder Information, Inc., UMI.
—BLDSC (8070.669000).
Formerly: Sales Management (ISSN 0140-5179); Incorporates: Sales Engineering (ISSN 0306-5618)
Description: Covers sales techniques, evaluation of markets for products and services, methods for attracting customers, sales team development, conference venues, business travel, and news in sales and marketing, video reviews, sales training, international trade news, and appointments.

SALES AND MARKETING PERSONNEL REPORT. see *BUSINESS AND ECONOMICS — Personnel Management*

SALES AND MARKETING SALARY SURVEY. see *BUSINESS AND ECONOMICS — Labor And Industrial Relations*

658   US   ISSN 1066-5463
HF5415.13
SALES AND MARKETING STRATEGIES & NEWS; comprehensive news source for successful sales & marketing strategies. 1991. 8/yr. $49. Hughes Communications, Inc., 211 W. State St., Box 197, Rockford, IL 61105. TEL 800-435-2937. FAX 815-963-7773. Ed. Bill E. Hughes; Pub. Bill Hughes. R&P contact: Kristi Nelson. adv. contact: Bruce Ericson. bk.rev.; circ. 62,000 (controlled). **Document type:** trade publication.
—KR SourceOne.

658   US   ISSN 0890-6912
SALES AND MARKETING TRAINING. 1987. q. $20. Executive Business Media, Inc., 825 Old Country Rd., Box 1500, Westbury, NY 11590. TEL 516-334-3030. Ed. Jim Rapp. adv.; bk.rev. circ. 7,500. **Document type:** trade publication.

658   US   ISSN 8756-8780
SALES AUTOMATION SUCCESS. 1985. 10/yr. $97 (effective 1994). Denali Group, Inc., 2815 N.W. Pine Cone Dr., Ste. 100, Issaquah, WA 98027-8698. TEL 206-392-3514. FAX 206-391-7982. E-mail: Rich_Bohn@msn.com. Ed. Steven P. Pokin; Pub. Richard N. Bohn. R&P contact: Richard N. Bohn. bk.rev.; index. (looseleaf format) **Document type:** newsletter.
●Also available online.
Description: Discusses how to use computer technology in direct sales to close more orders.

358   CN
SALES FORCE. 1994. 8/yr. Can.$38($60) C D M N Publishing, 1200 Markham Rd., Ste. 301, Scarborough, ON M1H 3C3, Canada. TEL 416-439-4083. FAX 416-439-4086. Ed. Brian Jeffrey; Pub. Steven Lloyd. adv.: B&W page Can.$3350, color page Can.$4300; trim 8 x 10 3/4. circ. 15,000.

658.81   US
SALES LEAD REPORT. 1990. q. free. Mac McIntosh Company, Inc., 1739 Havemeyer Lane, Redondo Beach, CA 90278-4716. TEL 310-376-1221; 800-944-5513. FAX 310-376-7722. E-mail: mac4leads@aol.com.

SALES MANAGEMENT. see *BUSINESS AND ECONOMICS — Management*

SALES MANAGEMENT. see *BUSINESS AND ECONOMICS — Management*

658.8   JA
SALES MANAGER. (Text in Japanese) 1966. m. 8160 Yen. Diamond Inc., 4-2, 1-chome, Kasumigaseki, Chiyoda-ku, Tokyo 100, Japan. Ed. Takeshi Sato. **Document type:** trade publication.

658.9   US   ISSN 0036-3421
SALES MANAGER'S BULLETIN. 1960. s-m. $187.80. Bureau of Business Practice, 24 Rope Ferry Rd., Waterford, CT 06386. TEL 860-442-4365. FAX 860-437-3555. URL: http://www.bbpnews.com. Ed. Paulette S. Kitchens; Pub. Peter Garabedian. R&P contact: Debra Ferraro. s-a. index. **Document type:** newsletter.
Description: Provides sales managers with personalized information via interviews with their peers in other companies and industries.

SALES MEMOS. see *BUSINESS AND ECONOMICS — Management*

658   GW
SALES PROFI; das Magazin fuer Top-Verkaeufer. 1991. m. DM.128 (foreign DM.145) (effective 1997). Betriebswirtschaftlicher Verlag Dr. Th. Gabler GmbH, Abraham-Lincoln-Str. 46, 65189 Wiesbaden, Germany. TEL 49-611-7878129. FAX 49-611-7878423. **Document type:** trade publication.

658.8   CN
SALES PROMOTION. q. Clifford Elliot & Associates Ltd., 3228 South Service Rd., Burlington, ON L7N 3H8, Canada. TEL 905-634-2100. FAX 905-634-2238. Ed. Todd Phillips. circ. 2,000 (controlled).
Description: Examines the leading areas of promotional expenditure, and their role in the marketing mix.

658 910.03   US
SALES WAYS. 1984. bi-m. free to qualified personnel. (National Alliance of Black Salesmen & Women) Time Crest Publishing, Box 2814, Manhattanville Sta., New York, NY 10027. TEL 212-409-4925. Ed. Franklyn Bryant. circ. 2,000. (looseleaf format) **Document type:** newsletter.
Formerly: National Alliance Report.
Description: Contains articles of interest to the black salesperson.

658   US
▼**SALESDOCTORS MAGAZINE**; seeking cures for the common close. 1995. m. SeaBird Associates, Inc., 5455 N. Federal Hwy., Ste. Q, Boca Raton, FL 33487. TEL 561-997-9345. FAX 561-997-9375. E-mail: salesdoctors@worldnet.att.net; URL: http://www.salesdoctors.com. Ed. Art Siegel; Pub. Art Siegel. R&P contact: Donna Siegel. adv. contact: Michael Berger. circ. 21,000 (controlled). **Document type:** trade publication.
●Available only online.
Formerly (until Sept. 1996): SalesDoctors (ISSN 1086-9476)
Description: Information for sales professionals, sales managers, trainers, marketing and customer service professionals and business owners. Includes section where readers can send individual questions directly to sales experts and receive free personal advice.

BUSINESS AND ECONOMICS — MARKETING AND PURCHASING

380.1 658.8 US ISSN 0738-6362
SALESMAN'S INSIDER. 1981. m. $48 in U.S.; Canada & Mexico $55; elsewhere $58 (effective 1997). Marv. Q. Modell Associates, 6009 Montgomery Corner, San Jose, CA 95135. TEL 408-270-4526. Ed. Marv. Q. Modell. bk.rev.; circ. 1,500 (paid). **Document type:** newsletter.
Description: Publishes tips, advice and strategies for successful sales negotiations.

658 US
SALESMANSHIP. 1972. bi-w. $68.90. Dartnell Corporation, 4660 N. Ravenswood Ave., Chicago, IL 60640. TEL 773-561-4000; 800-621-5463. FAX 773-561-3801. URL: http://www.dartnellcorp.com. Ed. Terry Breen. (reprint service avail. from UMI) **Document type:** newsletter.
Description: Enhances personal and corporate salespeople-training programs with instructive performance tips.

SATELLITE NEWS. see COMMUNICATIONS

SAVOURY SNACKS: THE INTERNATIONAL MARKET. see FOOD AND FOOD INDUSTRIES

640.73 IT ISSN 0036-570X
SCELTE DEL CONSUMATORE (MONTHLY); mensile di informazione e orientamento del consumatore. m. Unione Nazionale Consumatori, Via Andrea Doria 48, 00192 Rome, Italy. TEL 39-6-39737021. FAX 39-6-39733329. Ed. Vincenzo Dona. bk.rev. circ. 140,000. (tabloid format)
Formerly: Consumatore.

SCHOOL MARKETING NEWSLETTER. see EDUCATION — School Organization And Administration

658.8 370 US
▼**SCHOOL TECHNOLOGY MARKET REPORT.** 1997. bi-w. (24/yr.) $449. Cowles - SIMBA Information (Subsidiary of: Cowles Business Media), 11 Riverbend Dr. S., Box 4949, Stamford, CT 06907-0949. TEL 203-358-9900; 800-307-2529. FAX 203-358-5811. E-mail: info@simbanet.com; URL: http://www.simbanet.com.
Description: Contains news and analysis of how hardware and systems providers are marketing and selling their products to schools.

658 SZ
SCHWEIZERISCHE DETAILLISTEN ZEITUNG. m. Huebstr. 34, Postfach 97, CH-8307 Effretikon, Switzerland. TEL 052-325051. Ed. Hermann Keller. circ. 5,200.

658.8 SZ ISSN 0302-2048
SCHWEIZERISCHE GESELLSCHAFT FUER MARKTFORSCHUNG. GESCHAEFTSBERICHT. (Text in German) irreg., no.37, 1977. Schweizerische Gesellschaft fuer Marktforschung, Bleicherweg 21, 8022 Zurich, Switzerland. stat.

658 SZ
SCHWEIZERISCHE GEWERBE ZEITUNG. w. Schwarztorstr. 26, CH-3001 Bern, Switzerland. TEL 031-257785. FAX 031-262366. Ed. Ernst Tschanz. circ. 21,932.

658 910.09 UK
SCOTTISH COMMERCIAL TRAVELLERS' ASSOCIATION. NEWSCALL. 1903. a. £24 (effective 1997). Scottish Commercial Travellers' Association, 20 Anderson St., Airdrie ML6 0AA, Scotland. TEL 44-1236-756161. FAX 44-1236-766149. Ed. P. Neal. circ. 450. **Document type:** newsletter.

658.7 UK
SCOTTISH TRADES AND SHOPS HOLIDAYS. a. £1.75. William Culross & Son Ltd., Queen St., Coupar Angus, Perthshire, Scotland. **Document type:** consumer publication.

SE HABLA ESPANOL. see COMMUNICATIONS

658 US ISSN 1079-8307
▼**SEASON'S GREETINGS.** 1995. q. $36 (effective Feb. 1995). Byrne - McCoy Worldwide, Inc., 150 Fifth Ave., New York, NY 10011. TEL 212-691-1100. FAX 212-691-6185. E-mail: byrnemccoy@aol.com. (Subscr. to: Box 1284 JAF, New York, NY 10116-1284. TEL 212-691-1100. FAX 212-691-6185) Ed. Christopher Byrne; Pub. Robert McCoy. adv.: page $36; trim 8 1/8 x 10 7/8; adv. contact: Bruce Karaban. bk.rev. circ. 22,500. (back issues avail.) **Document type:** trade publication.

658.8 US ISSN 0049-0016
HD9999.S453
SECURITY DISTRIBUTING & MARKETING. Variant title: S D M Magazine. 1971. 13/yr. $79.95 (Canada $129.90; Mexico $119.95; elsewhere $179.90). Cahners Publishing Company (Des Plaines), Division of Reed Elsevier Inc., 1350 E. Touhy Ave., Box 5080, Des Plaines, IL 60018-5080. TEL 847-390-2116. FAX 847-635-9950. URL: http://www.sdmmag.com. (Subscr. to: 8773 S. Ridgeline Blvd., Highlands Ranch, CO 80126-2329. TEL 800-662-7776) (Co-sponsor: National Fire and Burglar Alarm Association) Ed. Bill Zalud; Pub. Susan A. Whitehurst. adv.; bk.rev.; charts; illus.; index. circ. 28,500. (also avail. in microform from UMI; microfiche from CIS; reprint service avail. from UMI) Indexed: CJPI, SRI. **Document type:** trade publication.
—UMI. **CCC.**
Description: For the security professional concerned with sales, installation, service and distribution of security, technology and management.

SECURITY INDUSTRY. see CRIMINOLOGY AND LAW ENFORCEMENT — Security

SECURITY RETAILER. see CRIMINOLOGY AND LAW ENFORCEMENT — Security

658 620.11 JA
SEISANZAI/INDUSTRIAL MARKETING. (Text in Japanese) 1964. m. 13000 Yen. News Digest Publishing Co. Ltd., 5-3, 3-chome, Uchiyama, Chikisa-ku, Nagoya 464, Japan. Ed. Shigeru Kobayashi; Pub. Shigeru Kabayashi. R&P contact: Shigeru Kabayashi. adv. contact: H. Higuchi. circ. 22,000. Indexed: B.P.I. **Document type:** trade publication.

658.8 GR ISSN 1105-4972
SELF SERVICE REVIEW. 1972. m. Dr.15000($75) Vasso Michaelidis Editions, 5 Polytechniou, 104 33 Athens, Greece. TEL 30-1-5222413. FAX 30-1-5222040. (Alt. addr.: 39 Spetson St., Xalandri, 152 32 Athens, Greece. TEL 30-1-6831342) Ed. Xenix Magliori; Pub. Vasso Michaelidis. R&P contact: Demetre Michaelidis. adv. contact: Vasso Michaelidis. bk.rev.; index; circ. 9,000. (paid). (back issues avail.) **Document type:** trade publication.
Description: Contains news and articles on retail and wholesale business and on the marketing of consumer goods.

658 US
HF5438
SELLING POWER; advisory for sales and marketing executives. 1981. 9/yr. $33 (Canada & Mexico $52; elsewhere $76) (effective 1997). Personal Selling Power, Inc., Box 5467, Fredericksburg, VA 22403-0467. TEL 540-752-7000. FAX 540-752-7001. E-mail: sellingpower@aol.com; URL: http://www.sellingpower.com. Ed. L.B. Gschwandtner; Pub. Gerhard Gschwandtner. R&P contact: Jeff Macharyas. adv. contact: Robert P. Benson. bk.rev.; charts; illus. circ. 125,000. (back issues avail.) **Document type:** trade publication.
Formerly: Personal Selling Power (ISSN 0738-8594)

658 US ISSN 1050-382X
SELLING TO SENIORS. 1987. m. $185. (Community Development Services, Inc.) C D Publications, 8204 Fenton St., Silver Spring, MD 20910. TEL 301-588-6380. FAX 301-588-6385. Ed. Len Curry. R&P contact: Mike Gerecht. index. **Document type:** newsletter.
Description: Practical advice on effective ways to reach the "over 50" market.

658.8 600 US ISSN 1060-1902
SENSOR BUSINESS DIGEST; the essential international business resource on sensors and instrumentation. m. $325 (overseas $345) (effective 1997 & 1998). Vital Information Publications, 754 Caravel Ln., Foster City, CA 94404. TEL 415-345-7018. FAX 415-345-7018. Ed. Peter Adrian; Pub. Peter Adrian. adv. contact: Lidia Bekker. circ. 500. **Document type:** newsletter.
●Also available online. Vendor(s): Data-Star, Information Access Co., Knight-Ridder Information, Inc., NewsNet (MG16).
—CCC.
Former titles: Measurement Chain (ISSN 1051-9432); Sensors Instrumentation News (ISSN 1045-6546); Sensors Newsletter.
Description: Reports on the sensor, instrumentation, and process-control industries. Analyzes market data and trends and highlights new products and technologies.

SERVICE STATIONS: THE INTERNATIONAL MARKET. see TRANSPORTATION — Automobiles

SHANGYE JINGJI, WUZI JINGJI. see BUSINESS AND ECONOMICS — Domestic Commerce

SHELDON'S MAJOR STORES & CHAINS. see BUSINESS AND ECONOMICS — Trade And Industrial Directories

658 US
SHICHANG BAO/MARKET NEWS. (Text in Chinese) 6/w. $168.50. China Books & Periodicals, Inc., 2929 24th St., San Francisco, CA 94110. TEL 415-282-2994. FAX 415-282-0994. **Document type:** newspaper.

SHOOTING SPORTS RETAILER. see SPORTS AND GAMES

658 US
SHOP-AT-HOME DIRECTORY. 1987. s-a. $6. Belcaro Group, Inc., 7100 E. Belleview Ave., Ste. 305, Greenwood Village, CO 80111-1636. TEL 303-843-0302. FAX 303-758-1926. adv. contact: Shelley Williamson. circ. 20,000,000 (paid). **Document type:** directory.

658 664 US
SHOPPER REPORT. 1979. m. $195. Consumer Network, Inc, 3624 Market St., Philadelphia, PA 19104. TEL 215-561-2921. FAX 215-557-7692. Ed. Mona Doyle. circ. 450. **Document type:** trade publication.
●Also available online. Vendor(s): Data-Star, Information Access Co., Knight-Ridder Information, Inc.
Description: Includes satisfaction polls drawn from a national panel of 5,000 shoppers. Most poll statements are taken directly from the consumer's own reports of their experiences.

658 JA
SHOPPING. (Text in Japanese) m. Nikkei Home Publishing, Inc. (Subsidiary of: Nihon Keizai Shimbun, Inc.), 2-2-7 Kanda Tsukasa-cho, Chiyoda-ku, Tokyo 101, Japan. TEL 03-3258-7818. **Document type:** consumer publication.
Description: Contains practical information on a broad range of consumer topics.

SHOPPING CENTER DIGEST; the locations newsletter. see REAL ESTATE

658.7 US ISSN 0559-9091
SHOPPING CENTER NEWSLETTER. 1959. m. National Research Bureau, 320 Valley St., Burlington, IA 52601-5513. TEL 319-752-5415. FAX 319-752-3421. Ed. Teresa Levinson; Pub. Michael Darnall. **Document type:** newsletter.

1550   BUSINESS AND ECONOMICS — MARKETING AND PURCHASING

658 333.33   US   ISSN 0049-0393
SHOPPING CENTER WORLD. (Supplement avail.: Outlet Retailer) 1972. m. (plus a. Directory) $74 (foreign $134). Intertec Publishing Corp. (Atlanta), 6151 Powers Ferry Rd., N.W., Atlanta, GA 30339-2941. TEL 770-955-2500. FAX 770-955-0400. Ed. Teresa DeFranks. adv.; charts; illus.; tr.lit. circ. 34,693. (also avail. in microform from UMI; reprint service avail. from UMI) **Document type:** trade publication.
  ●Also available online. Vendor(s): Information Access Co.
  —UMI. **CCC**.
  Incorporates (1975-1991): Shopping Center World Product and Service Directory.
  Description: Serves the fields of building, development, construction, design, financing, leasing, management and promotion of shopping centers, chain stores, and other related product and service industries.

658   UK   ISSN 0964-1793
SHOPPING CENTRE. 1991. m. £50 (Europe £65; elsewhere £90). William Reed Publishing Ltd., Broadfield Park, Crawley, W. Sussex RH11 9RT, England. TEL 44-1293-613400. FAX 44-1293-610345. Ed. Eric Williams. adv. **Document type:** trade publication.

658.8   SL   ISSN 0303-9315
SIERRA LEONE TRADE FAIRS AND EXHIBITIONS. 1974-1976; resumed 1988. a. $30. International Agencies, 9-9a Thunder Hill Rd., Box 1365, Kissy Mess, Freetown, Sierra Leone. Ed. Duncan Edem Archibong. adv.; bk.rev.; illus. circ. 10,000. **Document type:** trade publication.

SKI COST OF DOING BUSINESS SURVEY. see *SPORTS AND GAMES* — Abstracting, Bibliographies, Statistics

SKI INDUSTRY LETTER. see *SPORTS AND GAMES* — Outdoor Life

SKIN CARE: THE INTERNATIONAL MARKET. see *BEAUTY CULTURE*

SMALL KITCHEN APPLIANCES: THE INTERNATIONAL MARKET. see *ELECTRONICS*

SOFT DRINKS: THE INTERNATIONAL MARKET. see *BEVERAGES*

SOPHIA UNIVERSITY. INSTITUTE OF COMPARATIVE CULTURE. BUSINESS SERIES. see *BUSINESS AND ECONOMICS* — Management

658.7   US   ISSN 0049-1624
SOUTHERN PURCHASOR. 1970. bi-m. $6. Purchasing Management Association of Carolinas-Virginia, Inc., 5601 Roanne Way, No. 312-43, Greensboro, NC 27409-2915. TEL 919-272-6186. FAX 919-274-0716. Ed. V. Gilbert Snyder, Jr. adv.: B&W page $585, color page $1095; trim 7 x 10. illus. circ. 7,182. **Document type:** trade publication.
  Description: Covers buyer-seller relationships, purchasing and allied subjects, management, economic conditions, markets and trends, products, methods, association and personal news and news from suppliers.

658   US
SOUTHERN WHOLESALERS ASSOCIATION. NEWSLETTER. q. Southern Wholesalers Association, 3522 Habersham at Northlake, Tucker, GA 30084-4009. **Document type:** newsletter.

SPAIN: A DIRECTORY AND SOURCEBOOK. see *BUSINESS AND ECONOMICS* — Trade And Industrial Directories

SPECIAL EVENTS MAGAZINE. see *HOTELS AND RESTAURANTS*

658   CC
SPECIAL ISSUES FOR CHINESE EXPORT COMMODITIES FAIR/ZHONGGUO CHUKOU SHANGPIN JIAOYIHUI TEKAN. (Text in Chinese, English) s-a. HK.$60($33) Economic Information & Agency, 342 Hennessy Rd., 10th Fl., Wanchai, Hong Kong, People's Republic of China. TEL 5-738217. FAX 852-5-8388304. TELEX 86990 EIA HX.

659   US
SPECIALISTS' MARKETPLUS NEWSLETTER.* 1970. 6/yr. $36 (foreign $49). SpeciaLists Ltd., 1200 Harbor Blvd., 9th Fl., Weehawken, NJ 07087-6728. TEL 212-677-6760. Ed. Ray Lewis. adv.; bk.rev. circ. 9,500. (processed) **Document type:** newsletter.
  Former titles: Dependable's List Marketing Newsletter (ISSN 0399-7189); Dependable's List Letter.
  Description: Latest techniques for analyzing, evaluating and improving mailing lists, including the profitable marketing of those lists.

SPIELZEUG-MARKT; Hobby, Modellbau, Basteln. see *GIFTWARE AND TOYS*

SPIRITS: THE INTERNATIONAL MARKET. see *BEVERAGES*

658   IT
SPONSORNEWS. 12/yr. Imago s.r.l., Via Lanzone 22, 20123 Milan, Italy. TEL 2-72-010-054. FAX 2-72-010-095. Ed. Lorenzo Minoli.

SPORT CONSTRUCTION BUYER'S GUIDE. see *SPORTS AND GAMES*

SPORT MARKETING QUARTERLY; for professionals in the business of marketing sport. see *SPORTS AND GAMES*

SPORT UND MODE. see *SPORTS AND GAMES*

SPORTARTIKEL WIRTSCHAFT. see *SPORTS AND GAMES*

SPORTING GOODS BUSINESS; the national newsmagazine of the sporting goods industry. see *SPORTS AND GAMES*

SPORTING GOODS INTELLIGENCE; news and analysis of the international market. see *SPORTS AND GAMES*

SPORTING GOODS WHOLESALER. see *SPORTS AND GAMES*

SPORTS LICENSING INTERNATIONAL. see *SPORTS AND GAMES*

SPORTS MARKET PLACE. see *SPORTS AND GAMES*

SPORTS MARKETING LETTER. see *SPORTS AND GAMES*

SPORTS SHOP NEWS; national magazine for sporting goods buyers and retailers. see *SPORTS AND GAMES*

SPORTS TREND. see *SPORTS AND GAMES*

658 340   US
STATE CAPITOL WATCH.* 1987. 26/yr. International Mass Retail Association, 1700 N. Moore St., Ste. 2250, Arlington, VA 22209-1903. TEL 202-861-0774. FAX 202-785-4588. Ed. Jennifer Keehan. circ. 275. (back issues avail.) **Document type:** newsletter.

THE STATE OF THE MARKET. see *BUSINESS AND ECONOMICS* — Economic Situation And Conditions

STATS - MONTHLY STATISTICAL AND MARKETING DIGEST. see *STATISTICS*

STORE WINDOWS. see *ADVERTISING AND PUBLIC RELATIONS*

658   US   ISSN 0749-5153
STRATEGIC HEALTH CARE MARKETING. 1984. m. $249. Health Care Communications, 11 Heritage Lane, Box 594, Rye, NY 10580. TEL 914-967-6741. Ed. Michele von Dambrowski. bk.rev.; index. (back issues avail.) **Document type:** newsletter.
  —CCC.
  Description: Covers strategies and techniques in a wide range of service settings - from hospitals to physicians' offices.

658   CN   ISSN 1187-4309
STRATEGY; Canadian marketing report. 1989. 25/yr. Can.$59.50 (U.S. $93.50; elsewhere $186). Brunico Communications Inc., 366 Adelaide St. W., Ste. 500, Toronto, ON M5V 1R9, Canada. TEL 416-408-2300. FAX 416-408-0870. E-mail: circ@brunico.com. Ed. Patrick Allossery. adv.; B&W page Can.$3570; color page Can.$4465. circ. 18,000. **Indexed:** Can.B.P.I. **Document type:** trade publication.
  Formerly (until 1991): Playback Strategy (ISSN 0848-4457)
  Description: Covers the marketing and advertising industries in Canada.

658.8   GW   ISSN 0579-5923
STRUKTUR UND WACHSTUM. REIHE ABSATZWIRTSCHAFT. 1970. irreg., vol.14, 1994. DM.98. Duncker und Humblot GmbH, Postfach 410329, 12113 Berlin, Germany. TEL 49-30-790006-0. FAX 49-30-79000631. E-mail: duh-werbung@t-online.de. **Document type:** monographic series.

658   UN   ISSN 1014-1472
STUDIES IN THE PROCESSING, MARKETING AND DISTRIBUTION OF COMMODITIES. French edition: Etudes sur la Transformation, la Commercialisation et la Distribution des Produits de Base (ISSN 1014-1480); Spanish edition: Estudios sobre la Elaboracion, la Comercializacion y la Distribucion de los Productos Basicos (ISSN 1014-1529) 1984. irreg. $15 (effective 1997). (United Nations Conference on Trade and Development (UNCTAD)) United Nations Publications, Sales and Marketing Section, Room DC2-0853, New York, NY 10017. TEL 212-963-8302; 800-253-9646. FAX 212-963-3489. E-mail: publications@un.org; URL: http://www.un.org/publications. (Or: Distribution and Sales Section, Palais de Nations, 1211 Geneva 10, Switzerland)

SUBSCRIPTIONS STRATEGY; the direct marketing newsletter for publishers. see *PUBLISHING AND BOOK TRADE*

658.8   US
SUCCESS SOURCE MAGAZINE. 1992. bi-m. $10; newsstand price: $2.50. Ben Publishing, Box 137, Newbury, OH 44065-0137. TEL 216-564-7148. FAX 216-564-7148. Ed. Denise MacPherson. adv.: page $80; trim 7 1/2 x 10 1/2. charts; illus.; stat.; tr.lit. (back issues avail.) **Document type:** newsletter.
  Description: Provides useful information for those in mail order, network marketing, and those who are looking to enter these fields.

658.85   US
SUCCESSFUL CLOSING TECHNIQUES. 1984. bi-w. $68.90. Dartnell Corporation, 4660 N. Ravenswood Ave., Chicago, IL 60640. TEL 773-561-4000; 800-621-5463. FAX 773-561-3801. URL: http://www.dartnellcorp.com. Ed. Terry Breen. **Document type:** newsletter.
  Description: Provides fail-safe techniques for drumming up bigger sales and more frequent closings.

658.8   US   ISSN 0148-4052
HF5438   CODEN: SUMTEJ
SUCCESSFUL MEETINGS; the authority on meetings and incentive travel management. 1952. m. $48 (Canada $65; elsewhere $75). Bill Communications, Inc., 355 Park Ave. S., 5th Fl., New York, NY 10010-1789. TEL 212-592-6200. FAX 212-592-6339. Ed. Richard O'Connor; Pub. Richard O'Connor. adv.; bk.rev.; illus. circ. 40,050. (also avail. in microform from UMI; reprint service avail.) **Indexed:** ABI Inform., Account.& Data Proc.Abstr., BPIA, Bus.Ind., Hospit.Ind., Lod.Restr.& Tour.Ind., P.A.I.S., PROMT, PSI, Resour.Ctr.Ind., Tr.& Indus.Ind. **Document type:** trade publication.
  ●Also available online. Vendor(s): UMI.
  —BLDSC (8504.200000); CASDDS; KR SourceOne; UMI; UnCover. **CCC**.
  Former titles: S M - Successful Meetings (ISSN 0095-4241); S M - Sales Meetings (ISSN 0048-8917)
  Description: Serves corporate and association meeting planners primarily in North America, with emphasis on creating successful meetings.

BUSINESS AND ECONOMICS — MARKETING AND PURCHASING

658.8   SA
SUCCESSFUL SALESMANSHIP. m. R.161.40 (foreign R.259.40) (effective 1997). (Successful Salesmanship (Pty) Ltd.) Thomson Publications (Subsidiary of: Times Media Ltd.), P.O. Box 56182, Pinegowrie 2123, South Africa. TEL 27-11-789-2144. FAX 27-11-7893196. Ed. Richard Beynon. adv. **Document type:** trade publication.

658.8   US   ISSN 1050-1789
SULLIVAN'S RETAIL PERFORMANCE MONITOR.* 1972. s-w. $345. C S M Communications Co., Inc., 205 Regency Exec. Park Dr., Ste. 105, Charlotte, NC 28217-3989. TEL 516-265-3900. FAX 516-265-3281. Ed. Ralph Sullivan. adv.; bk.rev.; tr.lit.; index. circ. 7,916. **Indexed:** Tr.& Indus.Ind.
    Formerly (until 1990): Upscale Discounting (ISSN 1041-3219); (until 1987): C S M Merchandiser (ISSN 0898-7254); (until 1986): Catalog Showroom Merchandiser (ISSN 0194-3022)
    Description: Covers retail business and economics, sales and earnings, openings and closings, stock performance and more.

SUN CARE: THE INTERNATIONAL MARKET. see *BEAUTY CULTURE*

SUNSHINE ARTIST; America's premier show & festival guide for artists and craftspeople. see *ART*

658.878   SW   ISSN 0039-5781
SUPERMARKET. 1960. m. SEK 1225 (effective 1997). I C A Foerlaget AB, Storagatan 41, S-721 85 Vaesteraas, Sweden. Ed. Christina Berglund; Pub. Sven-Olof Rudenaas. adv. contact: Haakan Broberg. circ. 8,800. **Document type:** trade publication.
    Formerly: Sjaelvbetjaening.

658   BL
SUPERMERCADO MODERNO. 1969. m. $100. Informa Publicacoes Especializadas Ltda., Rua Brigadeiro Tobias 356, Andar 9o, Sao Paulo, SP, Brazil. TEL 55-11-227-1022. FAX 55-11-2289373. TELEX 30562 TLPB BR. Ed. Valdir Orsetti. adv. contact: Sergio Luis Alvim Veiga de Oliveira. circ. 15,500. **Document type:** trade publication.

658   US   ISSN 1046-3771
SUPPLIER SELECTION & MANAGEMENT REPORT. Abbreviated title: S S M R. 1989. m. $249 (outside N. America $273). Institute of Management & Administration, Inc., 29 W. 25th St., 5th Fl., New York, NY 10001-2299. TEL 212-244-0360. FAX 212-564-0465. URL: http://www.ioma.com. Ed. Joe Mazel; Pub. Perry Patterson. R&P contact: Sofie Kourkoutakis. index. (looseleaf format) **Document type:** newsletter.
    —CCC.
    Description: Shows purchasing and materials managers how to choose suppliers, achieve inventory accuracy, maintain JIT methods, develop procurement strategies that help achieve corporate business objectives.

658.7   UK
SUPPLY MANAGEMENT. 1973. fortn. £70 (foreign £95) (effective Mar. 1996). 17 Britton St., London EC1M 5NQ, England. TEL 44-171-880-6214. FAX 44-171-336-7635. Ed. Steve Crabb. adv.; charts; illus. circ. 22,000. **Indexed:** Mgmt.& Market.Abstr. **Document type:** trade publication.
    —AskIEEE; KR SourceOne.
    Formed by the Mar. 1996 merger of: Procurement Weekly (ISSN 0306-1922); Which was formerly: Purchasing Bulletin (ISSN 0033-4456) & Purchasing and Supply Management (ISSN 0265-2072); Which was formerly: Purchasing and Supply (ISSN 0309-7242); Purchasing Journal (ISSN 0033-4472)

658 001.6   US
SURVEY OF LOGISTICS SOFTWARE. 1980. a. $75 to members; non-members $100. Council of Logistics Management, 2803 Butterfield Rd., Oak Brook, IL 60521. TEL 630-574-0985. FAX 630-574-0989. **Document type:** directory.
    Description: Lists logistics-related software.

658.835 339.3   SW   ISSN 1102-2213
SVENSKA MARKNADEN, KNOW HOW; information och ideer. Variant title: D S M med Know How. 1945. 8/yr. SEK 300 to individuals; institutions SEK 600 (effective 1996). Jan Gillberg, Ed. & Pub., P.O. Box 5150, S-102 43 Stockholm, Sweden. TEL 46-8-667-68-42. FAX 46-33-68-82-39-13. adv.; bk.rev.; abstr.; illus.; index. circ. 10,769.
    Formed by the 1991 merger of: Know How (ISSN 0283-7870) & Svenska Marknaden (ISSN 0039-6850)
    Description: Based in France, the editorial staff strives to give a bird's-eye view of development and changes in Sweden.

SWEET & SAVOURY BISCUITS: THE INTERNATIONAL MARKET. see *FOOD AND FOOD INDUSTRIES — Bakers And Confectioners*

SWITZERLAND. CENTER FOR TRADE FAIRS. see *BUSINESS AND ECONOMICS — International Commerce*

658   GW
SYMBOLE; eine Zeitschrift fuer Abzeichen, Medaillen, Ehrenzeichen und Plaketten. 1987. q. free. Deumer GmbH und Co. KG, P.O. Box 1420, 58464 Luedenscheid, Germany. TEL 02351-184-0. (back issues avail.)

TAIWAN ELECTRONICS INDUSTRY. see *ELECTRONICS*

658.8 659.1   US
THE TARGET (WOODSIDE). vol.8, 1988. q. Metro Seliger Industries, Inc., 25-15 50th St., Woodside, NY 11377. TEL 718-278-2500. **Document type:** newsletter.
    Description: Contains news briefs and information about the company's activities in direct mail marketing, advertising and production.

658.8 659.1   US   ISSN 0889-5333
HF5410
TARGET MARKETING; the leading magazine for integrated database marketing. 1978. m. $65 (free to qualified personnel) (Canada $85; elsewhere $145). North American Publishing Co., 401 N. Broad St., Philadelphia, PA 19108. TEL 215-238-5300. FAX 215-238-5457. Ed. Denny Hatch; Pub. Peggy Hatch. R&P contact: Ned Borowsky. adv. contact: Peggy Hatch. bibl.; charts; stat.; tr.lit. circ. 36,796. (back issues avail.) **Indexed:** ABI Inform., BPIA, Graph.Arts Lit.Abstr., Manage.Cont. **Document type:** trade publication.
    ●Also available online. Vendor(s): Information Access Co.
    —BLDSC (8606.253500); KR SourceOne; UMI. CCC.
    Former titles: Zip Target Marketing; (until 1983): Zip (ISSN 0160-4090)
    Description: Covers all aspects of selling and marketing through the mail and other direct-response media. For writers, designers, catalogers, printers, list managers and those in allied industries for the latest news in regulations, direct-marketing techniques, equipment, and marketing strategy.

658.8 790.1   US
TEAM MARKETING REPORT. 1988. m. $179 (foreign $189). Team Marketing Report Inc., 660 W. Grand Ave., No. 100E, Chicago, IL 60610-3906. TEL 312-829-7060. FAX 312-733-4071. URL: http://www.teammarketing.com. Ed. Sean Brenner; Pub. Alan Friedman. R&P contact: Alan Friedman. adv. contact: Andrew Arkin. **Document type:** newsletter.
    Description: Reports on innovative and successful trends in sports marketing and sports sponsorships.

TECHKNOW TIMES. see *COMPUTERS — Computer Networks*

TECHNOLOGY TRANSFER WEEK. see *MILITARY*

TELCO BUSINESS REPORT; executive briefings on the Bell operating companies - regional holding companies and independent telcos. see *COMMUNICATIONS — Telephone And Telegraph*

TELECOM INDUSTRY ADVERTISING & MARKETING FORECAST (YEAR). see *ADVERTISING AND PUBLIC RELATIONS*

658   GW   ISSN 0940-7715
TELEFONMARKETING-PRAXIS. 1991. m. DM.240. Verlag Norbert Mueller AG und Co. KG, Ingolstaedterstr. 20, 80807 Munich, Germany. TEL 49-89-35093218. FAX 49-89-35093218. Ed. Gerlinde Guckelberger-Felix. index. circ. 700. (back issues avail.) **Document type:** newsletter.

658 338   US   ISSN 8750-9067
HF5415.1265
TELEMARKETER. 1980. s-m. $285. Actel Marketing, 163 Third Ave., Ste. 303, New York, NY 10003. TEL 212-674-2545. Ed. Aldyn McKean. adv.; bk.rev.; cum.index: 1980-1988. circ. 2,000. (back issues avail.)
    Formerly: A I S 800 Report.
    Description: Aspects of the telemarketing industry: sales, lead generation, fund raising.

TELEMARKETING UPDATE. see *COMMUNICATIONS*

658.8   US   ISSN 0882-1461
CODEN: TSERE4
TELEPHONE SELLING REPORT. 1984. m. $109. Business By Phone, Inc., 13254 Stevens St., Omaha, NE 68137-1728. TEL 402-895-9399. FAX 402-896-3353. URL: http://www.businessbyphone.com. Ed. Art Sobczak. bk.rev. (back issues avail.) **Document type:** newsletter.
    Description: Training newsletter with how-to ideas and tips on phone selling and prospecting.

658 621.38   US
TELEPROFESSIONAL INTERNATIONAL. 1994. 6/yr. $20 (Canada $25; elsewhere $30) (effective 1997). TeleProfessional Inc., 209 W. Fifth St., Ste. N, Waterloo, IA 50701-5420. TEL 319-235-4473; 888-835-3776. FAX 319-235-9850. URL: http://www.telemkt.com. Ed. Robert Van Voorhis, Jr.; Pub. Ross M. Scovotti. R&P contact: Robert E. Van Voorhis. **Document type:** trade publication.
    Description: Aims to provide a vehicle by which readers can learn about and contribute to the growth of the international call center marketplace.

658 621.38   US   ISSN 0886-9642
HF5415.1265
TELEPROFESSIONAL MAGAZINE. 1989. 11/yr. $39 (Canada $49; elsewhere $59). TeleProfessional Inc., 209 W. Fifth St., Ste. N, Waterloo, IA 50701-5420. TEL 319-235-4473; 888-835-3776. FAX 319-235-9850. URL: http://www.telemkt.com. Ed. Robert Van Voorhis, Jr.; Pub. Ross M. Scovotti. R&P contact: Robert E. Van Voorhis. adv.; bk.rev. circ. 35,000. **Document type:** trade publication.
    Description: For decision-makers actively involved in planning, managing, or operating a business call center. Provides a forum for new and business strategies and call-center technologies.

TELEVISION AND VIDEO: THE INTERNATIONAL MARKET. see *ELECTRONICS*

658.8   US
TEST AND MEASUREMENT SOURCE (YEAR). a. $545. Frost & Sullivan, 2525 Charleston St., Mountain View, CA 94043. TEL 415-961-9000. **Document type:** trade publication.
    Formerly: Test and Measurement World Yearbook.

TEXTILE AND FABRIC WASHING PRODUCTS: THE INTERNATIONAL MARKET. see *CLEANING AND DYEING*

658.8   SI   ISSN 0218-8139
TEXU JINGYING/ASIA FRANCHISE - BUSINESS OPPORTUNITIES MAGAZINE. (Text in Chinese, English) 1994. q. S.$77 (foreign $164) for 2 yrs. Asiawide Trends Pte. Ltd., 63 Robinson Rd., No. 04-06, Afro-Asia Bldg., Singapore 068894, Singapore. TEL 65-222-6228. FAX 65-226-1145. E-mail: fdsasia@cyberway.com.sg; URL: http://www.moneyasia.com/fransia. Ed. Albert Kong Chin-Hin. R&P contact: Helen Jieu. adv.: page S.$7380; trim 297 x 210; adv. contact: Leonard Yang. circ. 26,300. **Document type:** trade publication.
    Description: For CEOs, business development managers, venture capitalists looking to diversify into new areas; affluent individuals looking for new business opportunities; current operators of food, beverage, fashion and other retail business wanting to learn more about franchising.

THETA MARKET RESEARCH REPORTS. see *MEDICAL SCIENCES*

BUSINESS AND ECONOMICS — MARKETING AND PURCHASING

658   SZ   ISSN 0254-9697
THEXIS. 1984. 6/yr. 60 SFr. Forschungsinstitut fuer Absatz und Handel, Bodanstr. 8, CH-9000 St. Gallen, Switzerland. TEL 071-302820. FAX 071-232274. Ed. Peter Ritter. circ. 8,500.

658.8   US   ISSN 0362-7721
T12
THOMAS REGISTER OF AMERICAN MANUFACTURERS AND THOMAS REGISTER CATALOG FILE. (33 vol. set) 1908. a. $240. Thomas Publishing Company, Five Penn Plaza, New York, NY 10001. TEL 212-290-7277; 800-699-9822. FAX 212-290-7365. URL: http://www.thomasregister.com. index. **Document type:** directory, catalog.
● Also available online.
Also available on CD-ROM.
—CISTI.
Formerly: Thomas Register of American Manufacturers (ISSN 0082-4216)
Description: Lists nearly every industrial product or service offered in North America.

TIDINGS (CAMDEN). see BUSINESS AND ECONOMICS — Domestic Commerce

TIE LINES. see CLOTHING TRADE

658.8   NE   ISSN 0165-1439
TIJDSCHRIFT VOOR MARKETING. 1967. 11/yr. fl.199 (effective 1996). (Nederlands Instituut voor Marketing (NIMA)) Kluwer Bedrijfswetenschappen B.V. (Subsidiary of: Wolters Kluwer N.V.), Postbus 23, 7400 GA Deventer, Netherlands. TEL 31-570-648905. FAX 31-570-611504. (Subscr. to: Intermedia bv, Postbus 4, 2400 MA Alphen aan den Rijn, Netherlands. TEL 31-172-466321. FAX 31-172-435527) Ed. Ludo Koks. adv.: B&W page fl. 2765, color page fl.4915; trim 297 x 210; adv. contact: Ad Nuesink. bk.rev.; bibl.; charts; illus. circ. 11,245. **Indexed:** Key to Econ.Sci. **Document type:** trade publication.
—SWETS.
Formerly: N I A (ISSN 0027-6618)

658.8 679.7
TOBACCO MARKETS IN LATIN AMERICA. (Part of the Euromonitor Emerging Market Reports series) irreg., latest 1994 edition. £795($1590) Euromonitor, 60-61 Britton St., London EC1M 5NA, England. TEL 44-171-251-8024. FAX 44-171-608-3149. E-mail: info@euromonitor.com. URL: http://www.euromonitor.com. (Subscr. in N. America to: Euromonitor International Inc., 122 S. Michigan Ave., Ste. 1200, Chicago, IL 60603. TEL 800-577-3876. FAX 312-922-1157) **Document type:** trade publication.
Description: Analyzes business and economic trends in major Latin American nations affecting the tobacco market there.

TODAY FAX. see ADVERTISING AND PUBLIC RELATIONS

658   US   ISSN 0898-5561
TODAY'S DISTRIBUTOR. 1988. bi-m. $48 (Canada and Mexico $66; elsewhere $84; free to qualified personnel) (effective 1997). Johnson Hill Press, Inc. (Subsidiary of: Cygnus Publishing), 1233 Janesville Ave., Ft. Atkinson, WI 53538. TEL 920-563-6388. FAX 920-563-1702. Ed. Greg Udelhofen; Pub. Greg Udelhofen. circ. 42,000 (controlled). **Document type:** trade publication.
Description: Provides information to industrial and construction distributors which helps them deliver profitable customer solutions.

688 635.9   US   ISSN 1082-0434
TODAY'S HOSPITAL GIFT SHOP BUSINESS. 1978. 6/yr. Nason & Associates, Box 8204, Asheville, NC 28814. TEL 704-298-1322. FAX 704-298-1312. Ed. Marilyn Nason; Pub. Marilyn Nason. R&P contact: Marilyn Nason. adv. contact: Michelle Ramsey. circ. 8,000 (controlled). **Document type:** newsletter.
Description: For persons involved with hospital gift shops.

658   UK
TOP SELLING. 1991. 24/yr. £99. 125 High Holborn, London WC1V 6QA, England. TEL 071-404-1585. FAX 071-404-1580. Ed. Samantha Dawe. circ. 1,000. **Document type:** newsletter.
Description: Contains tips and ideas for improving selling skills with topical information on products and services.

TOP SOCIETY. see BUILDING AND CONSTRUCTION

658   US   ISSN 1062-2632
TOPICAL ISSUES IN PROCUREMENT SERIES. Abbreviated title: T I P S. 1989. m. $72. National Contract Management Association, 1912 Woodford Rd., Vienna, VA 22182. TEL 800-344-8096. FAX 703-448-0939. Ed. Amy Shotton-Peters. (looseleaf format; back issues avail.) **Document type:** bulletin.
Description: In-depth examination of issues facing contract management professionals in government and industry.

658.83   US
TOPLINE. 1978. q. free. McCollum-Spielman Worldwide, Inc., 235 Great Neck Rd., Great Neck, NY 11021. TEL 516-482-0310. FAX 516-482-3228. Ed. Paula Kay Pierce. charts; illus.; stat.; circ. 5,000 (controlled). (looseleaf format; back issues avail.) **Document type:** newsletter, trade publication.
Description: Contains market research information gleaned from McCollum Spielman studies of TV and print advertising.

TOYS AND GAMES: THE INTERNATIONAL MARKET. see GIFTWARE AND TOYS

658   IT
TRADE MARKETING; rivista di tecnica commerciale. 1991. 3/yr. L.69000 (foreign L.90000) (effective 1993). Franco Angeli Editore, Viale Monza, 106, Casella Postale 17175, 20100 Milan, Italy. TEL 02-2895762. Ed. Giampiero Lugli.

TRADE SHOWS & EXHIBITS SCHEDULE. see BUSINESS AND ECONOMICS — Trade And Industrial Directories

TRADESHOW. see ADVERTISING AND PUBLIC RELATIONS

TRADESHOW WEEK; since 1971, the only weekly source of news & statistics on the tradeshow industry. see ADVERTISING AND PUBLIC RELATIONS

658   US   ISSN 0000-1023
T394
TRADESHOW WEEK DATA BOOK; the annual statistical directory of US and Canadian tradeshows and public shows. 1985. a. £295($355) Tradeshow Week, A Division of Reed Elsevier Inc., 5700 Wilshire Blvd., Ste. 120, Los Angeles, CA 90036-3659. TEL 213-965-5300. E-mail: dgudea@tsweek; URL: http://www.tradeshowweek.com. (Subscr. to: E.S.P. Computer Services, Inc., Box 6340, Torrance, CA 90504. TEL 800-375-4212) Ed. Darlene Gudea. R&P contact: Darlene Gudea. TEL 213-965-5335. adv. contact: Irene Sperling. pp./issue: 2000. **Document type:** directory.
Description: Details trade and public shows in the US and Canada; lists marketing, statistical and historical data on expositions.

658   US   ISSN 0733-0189
TRADESHOW WEEK DATA BOOK - INTERNATIONAL EDITION. a. $255. Tradeshow Week, A Division of Reed Elsevier Inc., 5700 Wilshire Blvd., Ste. 120, Los Angeles, CA 90036-3659. TEL 213-965-5300. E-mail: dgudea@tsweek; URL: http://www.tradeshowweek.com. (Subscr. to: E.S.P. Computer Services, Inc., Box 6340, Torrance, CA 90504. TEL 800-375-4212) Ed. Darlene Gudea. R&P contact: Darlene Gudea. TEL 213-965-5335. adv. contact: Irene Sperling. **Document type:** directory.
Description: Contains detailed who, what, when, and where information on more than 3,700 trade fairs and exhibitions to be held in outside the US and Canada.

658 389   UK   ISSN 0953-8704
TRADING STANDARDS REVIEW. 1894. m. £42 (effective 1996). Institute of Trading Standards Administration, 4-5 Hadleigh Business Centre, 351 London Rd., Hadleigh, Essex SS7 2BT, England. TEL 44-1702-559922. FAX 44-1702-559902. Ed. A.J. Street. adv.; bk.rev.; illus.; index. circ. 2,300. **Document type:** trade publication.
—BLDSC (8881.051950); CISTI.
Former titles: Institute of Trading Standards Administration Monthly Review (ISSN 0302-3249); Institute of Weights and Measures Administration Monthly Review (ISSN 0020-319X)

658.7   US
TRAILS ADVOCATE. 1984. 6/yr. $15. Iowa Trails Council, Inc., Box 131, Center Point, IA 52213-0131. TEL 319-849-1844. FAX 319-849-2866. E-mail: tomneenan1@aol.com. Ed. Tom Neenan. adv.; maps, stat, tr.lit.; cum.index. circ. 1,400. (back issues avail.) **Document type:** newsletter.
Description: Discusses land acquisition, trail development and promotion.

TRAVEL AND TOURISM: THE INTERNATIONAL MARKET. see TRAVEL AND TOURISM

TRAVEL INDUSTRY MONITOR. see TRAVEL AND TOURISM

658   UK   ISSN 1357-3489
TRAVEL RETAILER INTERNATIONAL. 1991. bi-m. £60 (effective 1996). Euromoney Publications plc., Nestor House, Playhouse Yard, London EC4V 5EX, England. TEL 44-171-799-8935. FAX 44-171-779-8541. (Dist. in US by: American Educational Systems, 173 W. 81st St., New York, NY 10024. TEL 800-717-2669. FAX 212-501-8926) Ed. Liz Miller. circ. 5,000. **Document type:** trade publication.

TRAVELWRITER MARKETLETTER. see JOURNALISM

658.8   NE   ISSN 0165-537X
TREND; vakblad voor de eigentijdse ondernemer in glas, porselein, aardewerk, luxe- en huishoudelijke artiklen, kunstnijverheids- en geschenkartikelen. 1974. 11/yr. fl.99.50. Blauw Media Uitgeverij B.V., Postbus 1043, 3600 BA Maarssen, Netherlands. TEL 31-346-574040. FAX 31-346-576056. adv. circ. 6,000. **Document type:** trade publication.

658.8   NE   ISSN 0165-4438
TREND-BOUTIQUE; vakblad voor de eigentijdse ondernemer in lederwaren, bijoux en modeaccessories. 1980. 6/yr. fl.74.50. Blauw Media Uitgeverij B.V., Postbus 1043, 3600 BA Maarssen, Netherlands. TEL 31-346-574040. FAX 31-346-576056. adv. circ. 5,400. **Document type:** trade publication.

658   US   ISSN 1062-2330
TROUBLED COMPANY PROSPECTOR. 1992. w. $575 for 6 mos. Beard Group, Inc., Box 9867, Washington, DC 20016. TEL 301-951-6400. FAX 301-951-3621. E-mail: chris@bankrupt.com. Ed. Chris McHugh.

TRUCK SALES & LEASING MAGAZINE. see TRANSPORTATION — Trucks And Trucking

658   YU   ISSN 0564-3619
HG37.Y8
TRZISTE, NOVAC, KAPITAL. (Text mainly in Serbo-Croatian; occasionally in English) 1966. q. $70. Institut za Spoljnu Trgovinu, Mose Pijade 8, Belgrade, Serbia, Yugoslavia. Ed. Radovan Kovacevic.

658.8   US   ISSN 0300-6190
TUBE TOPICS. 1967. q. free. Tube Council of North America, 740 Broadway, No. 903, New York, NY 10003. TEL 212-477-9007. FAX 212-460-9028. Ed. Ted Klein. bk.rev.; charts; illus.; stat. circ. 3,500. **Indexed:** Curr.Pack.Abstr.; Graph.Arts Lit.Abstr. **Document type:** newsletter.

U D I WHO'S WHO IN POWER MARKETING. see ENERGY — Electrical Energy

U S D A EGG MARKET NEWS REPORT. (U.S. Department of Agriculture) see AGRICULTURE — Poultry And Livestock

U S D A POULTRY REPORT. (U.S. Department of Agriculture) see AGRICULTURE — Poultry And Livestock

658 304.6   US
▼ **U S MARKET FORECASTS.** 1996. a. Editor & Publisher Co., Inc., 11 W. 19th St., New York, NY 10011. TEL 212-675-4380. FAX 212-929-1259. E-mail: edpub@mediainfo.com; URL: http://www.mediainfo.com. **Document type:** directory.
● Also available on CD-ROM.
Description: Contains in-depth profiles of every US city with 2,500 residents or more, plus MSAs and NECMAs.

BUSINESS AND ECONOMICS — MARKETING AND PURCHASING

658 387   US   ISSN 1072-6098
UNDERWATER MAGAZINE. 1989. q. free in US; foreign $25. (Association of Diving Contractors) Doyle Publishing Co., 5222 FM 1960 W., Ste. 112, Houston, TX 77069. TEL 713-440-0278. FAX 713-580-4433. E-mail: underwater@diveweb.com; URL: http://diveweb.com/uw. Ed. Dee Hoffmann; Pub. Dowie Doyle. R&P contact: Dowie Doyle. adv. contact: Pamela Barnett. bk.rev.; illus.; tr.lit.; circ. 15,000 (controlled). **Document type:** trade publication.
   Description: Covers commercial diving for construction, engineering, the oil and gas industry, and scientific research.

658.8   SA
UNIVERSITY OF STELLENBOSCH. BUREAU FOR ECONOMIC RESEARCH. RETAIL SURVEY. (Text in English, summaries in Afrikaans) 1986. q. R.600 (effective 1996 & 1997). University of Stellenbosch, Bureau for Economic Research, Private Bag 5050, University, Stellenbosch 7599, South Africa. TEL 27-21-8872810. FAX 27-21-8839225. TELEX 520-383 SA. E-mail: odjs@maties.sun.ac.za. Ed. G Kershoff. circ. 600.
   Formerly (until vol.9, 1994): University of Stellenbosch. Bureau for Economic Research. Trade and Commerce (ISSN 0258-9311); Supersedes (in 1986): Consumer Survey Report (ISSN 0379-6086)
   Description: Discusses the latest market research on the behavior of South African consumers, including repercussions for wholesale and retail trade.

658   UK
UNIVERSITY OF STRATHCLYDE. DEPARTMENT OF MARKETING. WORKING PAPER SERIES. irreg. University of Strathclyde, Department of Marketing, Stenhouse Bldg., 173 Cathedral St., Galsgow G4 0RQ, Scotland. TEL 0141-552-4400. FAX 0141-552-2802. Ed. Susan Shaw. **Document type:** monographic series.

UOMO MANAGER. see *BUSINESS AND ECONOMICS — Management*

658   US
UP-TO-DATE PRICE MAGAZINE; published for distributors (wholesalers) of candy, tobacco, grocery, health & beauty aids, and sundry products. 1957. m. $35. 21 W. Delilah Rd., Pleasantville, NJ 08232. TEL 800-331-7061. FAX 609-646-2692. circ. 1,100.

USED CAR PRICES. see *TRANSPORTATION — Automobiles*

USED CARS INSIDER. see *TRANSPORTATION — Automobiles*

643.3   US
V D T A NEWS. m. free. Vacuum Dealers Trade Association, 2724 Second Ave., Des Moines, IA 50313-4933. TEL 515-282-9101. Ed. Judy Patterson. adv. contact: Judy Patterson. circ. 19,000. (tabloid format)

643.3   US
V D T A PHONE DIRECTORY AND PRODUCT GUIDE. a. Vacuum Dealers Trade Association, 2424 Second Ave., Des Moines, IA 50313-4933. TEL 515-282-9101. **Document type:** directory.

692.5   DK
▼**V & S GENERALBESKRIVELSE.** 1995. irreg. DKK 590 (effective 1997). V & S Byggedata, Frederikssundvej 194, DK-2700 Broensnhoej, Denmark. TEL 45-38-60-77-11. FAX 45-38-60-77-44. Dir. Carl Friis Skoven.

692.5   DK
▼**V OG S GENERALBESKRIVELSE, SUPPLEMENT.** 1995. irreg. DKK 200 (effective 1997). V &S Byggedata A-S, Frederikssundvej 194, DK-2700 Broensnhoej, Denmark. TEL 45-38-60-77-11. FAX 45-38-60-77-44. Dir. Carl Friis Skovsen.

692.3   DK
▼**V & S REGLER FOR OPMAALING AF BYGGERI.** 1994. irreg. DKK 200 (effective 1997). V & S Byggdata A-S, Frederikssundvej 194, DK-2700 Boensnhoej, Denmark. TEL 45-38-60-55-11. FAX 38-60-77-44. Dir. Carl Friis Skovsen.

658   SW   ISSN 0284-9984
VAESTERGOETLANDS AFFAERER; & Goeteborg - den regionala maanadstidningen foer foeretagsledare. Variant title: Regionala Vaestergoetlands Affaerer. 1985. m. SEK 395 (effective 1991). Foeretagsmedia, P.O. Box 643, S-551 18 Joenkoeping, Sweden.

658   SW   ISSN 0283-0892
VAESTRA SVERIGES AFFAERER & FOERETAG; Goeteborgs-postens regionala affaerstidning. 1986. 9/yr. SEK 392 (effective 1994). Vaestra Sveriges Affaerer & Foeretag, P.O. Box 411, S-401 26 Goeteborg, Sweden. TEL 46-031-624060. FAX 46-031-624066. Bosse Dahl. adv. contact: Ulf Niklasson. circ. 6,517 (paid); 7,530 (controlled).
●Also available online.
   Supersedes in part: Bra Foeretag.

658   US
VALUE RETAIL NEWS; the journal of outlet & off-price retailing & development. 1983. m. $144. Off-Price Specialists, Inc., 11701 Belcher Rd., S., Ste. 130, Largo, FL 33773-5117. TEL 813-536-4047. FAX 813-536-4389. Ed. Linda Humphers; Pub. Dan Cochran. adv. contact: Ronni O'Neil. bk.rev.; index. circ. 5,000. **Document type:** trade publication.
   Formerly: Off-Price News.
   Description: Covers real-estate leasing and related news of outlet and off-price retailers and developers.

658.8   UK   ISSN 0954-6235
VENDING INTERNATIONAL. 1967. m. £50. Dateam Publishing Ltd., Attn: Rob Foreman, Fairmeadow, Maidstone, Kent ME14 IN9, England. TEL 01622-687031. FAX 01622-757646. Ed. Geoff Manners; Pub. Nick Carpenter. adv. contact: Odell Gardner. Indexed: Art.Hosp.& Tour., PROMT. **Document type:** trade publication.
—BLDSC (9154.335000).
   Formerly: International Vending Times.

658   IT
VENDING MAGAZINE; of automatic merchandising. (Text in Italian; summaries in English and Italian) 1976. m. L.140000($80) in Europe; elsewhere L.190000. Vending Press s.r.l., Corso Mocalieri 21-A, 10131 Turin, Italy. TEL 39-11-6602900. FAX 39-11-6600120. Ed. Gian Franco Fassio. adv.: B&W page L.1315000, color page L.2200000; adv. contact: Silvana Ferrero. circ. 6,000. (back issues avail.) **Document type:** trade publication.

658   UK
VENDING: THE INTERNATIONAL MARKET. (Subseries of: Market Direction reports) a. £1595($3190) (effective 1997). Euromonitor, 60-61 Britton St., London EC1M 5NA, England. TEL 44-171-251-8024. FAX 44-171-608-3149. E-mail: info@euromonitor.com; URL: http://www.euromonitor.com. (Addr. in N. America: Euromonitor International, 122 S. Michigan Ave., Ste. 1200, Chicago, IL 60603. TEL 800-577-3876. FAX 312-922-1157) (looseleaf format) **Document type:** trade publication.
●Also available online. Vendor(s): Data-Star, Knight-Ridder Information, Inc.
   Description: Analyzes the market for vending machine sales in France, Germany, Italy, Spain, the U.K., the U.S., and Japan.

658.87   US   ISSN 0042-3327
VENDING TIMES; vending - feeding - coffee service - music & games. 1961. m. $35 (effective 1997). Vending Times, Inc., 1375 Broadway, 6th Fl., New York, NY 10018-7001. TEL 212-302-4700. FAX 212-221-3311. Ed. Timothy Sanford. R&P contact: Victor Lavay. adv. circ. 16,500. (also avail. in microform from UMI) Indexed: B.P.I., Bus.Ind., PROMT, SRI, Tr.& Indus.Ind. **Document type:** trade publication.
—UMI.
   Incorporates (as of 1974): Vend (ISSN 0042-3297); V-T Music and Games.

620   US
VENDOR PRODUCT COMPARISON (DESIGN ENGINEERING). 1984. m. $835. Information Handling Services, 15 Inverness Way E., Englewood, CO 80150. TEL 303-790-0600. FAX 303-799-4085. TELEX 4322083 IHS UI. Ed. Liz Maynard Prigge. adv. circ. 2,600.
   Formerly: Design Engineering Services Index.
   Description: Provides product and subject access to manufacturers of comparative products necessary for design engineering.

658.8   FR
VENDRE AUJOURD'HUI.* 1974. s-m. 190 F. 29, rue Violet, 75015 Paris, France. Ed. Jacques Aroud. adv.; bk.rev.; charts; stat.; tr.lit.

VENTE EQUIPEMENTS MENAGERS. see *ELECTRONICS*

658.87   GW   ISSN 0049-5999
DER VERSANDHAUSBERATER.* 1961. w. DM.720. Esternaystr. 32, 76337 Waldbronn, Germany. Ed. Klaus Prochazka. bk.rev. circ. 400. (processed) **Document type:** newsletter.
   Description: Weekly newsletter for catalog and mail order industries in German speaking countries.

380.1   IC   ISSN 1021-8467
VERZLUNARTIDINDI. 1950. bi-m. Kaupmannasamtoek Islands, Husi Verzlunarinnar, Kringlan 7, 103 Reykjavik. TEL 354-568-7811. FAX 354-568-5569. adv. circ. 1,500.

658 780 384.55   AT   ISSN 1033-4831
VIDEO & MUSIC BUSINESS. w. Aus.$385 (foreign Aus.$455). South Continent Corporation Pty. Ltd., P.O. Box 1024, Richmond North, Vic. 3121, Australia. TEL 03-429-5599. FAX 03-427-0332. Ed. Geoffrey M. Gold. adv. circ. 1,000.
   Formed by the merger of: Video Business & Music Business (ISSN 0815-2969)
   Description: Focuses on retailing, distribution and marketing of home video, films and prerecorded music.

VIDEOAGE. see *COMMUNICATIONS — Video*

VITAMINS AND DIETARY SUPPLEMENTS: THE INTERNATIONAL MARKET. see *PHARMACY AND PHARMACOLOGY*

658.8   IT   ISSN 0042-7837
VOCE DELLA FIERA; bisettimanale di economia e problemi di mercato. 1964. s-w. L.45000. Organizzazione "X" di Armando Rositani, C.so Cavour, 113, 70121 Bari, Italy. TEL 39-80-5214363. FAX 39-80-5214363. Ed. Armando Rositani. adv. contact: Mariuccia Verrone. bk.rev.; illus.; stat. circ. 10,000.

W E R A BROCHURE. (Western English Retailers Association) see *CLOTHING TRADE*

W E R A SPECIAL NEWSLETTER. (Western English Retailers Association) see *CLOTHING TRADE*

W S G A CHECKOUT. (Wine and Spirits Guild of America) see *BEVERAGES*

658   LE
WEEKLY OBSERVER. (Text in English) m. Dar Assayas S.A.L., P.O. Box 1038, Beirut, Lebanon. adv. circ. 7,000.

WEEKLY PETROLEUM ARGUS. see *PETROLEUM AND GAS*

WESTERN LUMBER (YEAR) BUYERS MANUAL. see *FORESTS AND FORESTRY — Lumber And Wood*

658   UK   ISSN 0265-296X
WHAT TO BUY FOR BUSINESS. m. £120 (not avail. in the U.S.). Reed Business Information, Quadrant House, The Quadrant, Sutton, Surrey SM2 5 AS, England. TEL 44-181-652-3500. FAX 44-181-652-8956. Ed. Sara Bean; Pub. Roger Williams. (back issues avail.) Indexed: Br.Ceram.Abstr., INSPEC (1983-), Intl.Polym.Sci.& Tech., RAPRA. **Document type:** trade publication.
—BLDSC (9309.625000); AskIEEE; KR SourceOne; SWETS. CCC.
   Formerly: Better Buys for Business.

WHAT'S NEW FOR FAMILY FUN CENTERS. see *BUSINESS AND ECONOMICS — Trade And Industrial Directories*

658.8 070.5   US
WHAT'S WORKING IN DIRECT MARKETING AND FULFILLMENT. 1982. bi-w. $182. United Communications Group, 11300 Rockville Pike, Ste. 1100, Rockville, MD 20852-3030. TEL 301-816-8950. FAX 301-816-8945. Ed. Barbara Weckstein Kaplowitz. cum.index: 1982-86. (back issues avail.)
   Description: Reports on innovative and unusual ways marketers are boosting response, cutting costs, and speeding fulfillment.

BUSINESS AND ECONOMICS — OFFICE EQUIPMENT AND SERVICES

658.8   UK   ISSN 0308-0021
HD9652.3
WHERE TO BUY: CHEMICALS & CHEMICAL PLANT (YEAR). 1930. a. (issued in Dec.) £86.60. Argus Business Media Ltd. (Subsidiary of: D M G Exhibitions Group Ltd.), Queensway House, 2 Queensway, Redhill, Surrey RH1 1QS, England. TEL 44-1737-768611. FAX 44-1737-761685. (reprint service avail. from UMI) **Document type:** directory.
    Description: Lists U.K. chemical traders and distributors.

WHITE PAGES & DIRECTORY LISTINGS (YEAR). see BUSINESS AND ECONOMICS — *Trade And Industrial Directories*

658.8   UK   ISSN 0083-9310
HG4538
WHO OWNS WHOM. NORTH AMERICA. 1969. a. £249. Dun & Bradstreet Ltd., Holmers Farm Way, High Wycombe, Bucks. HP12 4UL, England. TEL 44-1494-422000. FAX 44-1494-422260. Ed. Laura Morel. index. **Document type:** directory.
    ●Also available online.

658   US   ISSN 1049-0116
HF5465.5
WHOLESALE-BY-MAIL CATALOG. 1979. a. St. Martin's Press, 175 Fifth Ave., New York, NY 10010. TEL 212-674-5151.

659   US   ISSN 8755-2671
WHO'S MAILING WHAT!. 1984. m. $295 (effective 1997). North American Publishing Co., 401 N. Broad St., Philadelphia, PA 19108. TEL 215-238-5482. FAX 215-238-5412. Ed. Denison Hatch. circ. 2,000. **Document type:** newsletter.

WINDOW & DOOR FABRICATOR. see *BUILDING AND CONSTRUCTION*

WINE: THE INTERNATIONAL MARKET. see *BEVERAGES*

WIRTSCHAFT UND WETTBEWERB; Zeitschrift fuer Kartellrecht, Wettbewerbsrecht und Marktorganisation. see BUSINESS AND ECONOMICS — *Production Of Goods And Services*

WOLFF'S GUIDE TO THE LONDON METAL EXCHANGE. see *METALLURGY*

WOOD PRODUCTS: INTERNATIONAL TRADE AND FOREIGN MARKETS. see *AGRICULTURE — Agricultural Economics*

658.8   UK
HF5415.124
WORLD DIRECTORY OF MARKETING INFORMATION SOURCES. 1990. biennial. £275($550) (effective 1997). Euromonitor, 60-61 Britton St., London EC1M 5NA, England. TEL 44-171-251-8024. FAX 44-171-608-3149. E-mail: info@euromonitor.com; URL: http://www.euromonitor.com. (Addr. in N. America: Euromonitor International, 122 S. Michigan Ave., Ste. 1200, Chicago, IL 60603. TEL 800-577-3876. FAX 312-922-1157) **Document type:** directory.
    Formerly (until 1995): European Directory of Marketing Information Sources (ISSN 0950-656X)
    Description: Provides a guide to more than 3,000 sources of market and business information throughout the world.

WORLD DRINKS DATABOOK. see *BEVERAGES*

380   II
WORLD FAIRS GUIDE; devoted to industrial expansion, trade fairs, export, tourism and travel trade. (Text in English) 1959. m. Rs.140($25) (International Trade Fair Association) Trade Digest Publications, S-185 Greater Kailash II, New Delhi 48, India. TEL 6414185. Ed. C.L. Khanna. adv.; bk.rev.; tr.lit. circ. 7,500. (processed)
    Formerly: Trade Digest (ISSN 0041-042X)

658.87   US   ISSN 0049-8106
WORLD GIFT REVIEW MONTHLY NEWSLETTER.* 1965. m. $14. World Gift Review Co., 59 Hille Pl., Ridgefield Park, NJ 07660-2025. Ed. John W. Slawenski. adv.; bk.rev. circ. 9,600. (looseleaf format) **Document type:** newsletter.

WORLD HEALTHCARE MARKETING DIRECTORY. see *MEDICAL SCIENCES*

658.8   UK   ISSN 0043-9304
WORLD'S FAIR. 1904. w. £47 (Europe £57; Americas and Middle East £67; rest of world £72). World's Fair Ltd., P.O. Box 57, Oldham OL1 4BB, England. TEL 061-624-3687. FAX 061-665-1260. Ed. D.H. Snook. adv.; bk.rev.; charts; illus.; mkt.; pat.; tr.mk. circ. 30,000. **Document type:** newspaper.
    Incorporates: Coin Slot (ISSN 0010-0420); Market Trader.
    Description: News and features of interest to those involved in market trading, the amusement park, traveling fair and circus industries, steam preservation, and the coin machine industry.

WORLD'S MAJOR COMPANIES DIRECTORY. see BUSINESS AND ECONOMICS — *Trade And Industrial Directories*

380.14   UK   ISSN 0309-4960
WORLDWIDE MARKETING OPPORTUNITIES DIGEST. 1978. bi-m. $150 for 12 nos. International Commercial Network Ltd., 24 Mount Parade., Harrogate, Yorks. HG1 1BP, England. FAX 0423-561204. TELEX 94014165 AGTS G. Ed. M.A. Lewis. adv. circ. 2,000. **Document type:** trade publication.

658   US   ISSN 1041-7516
YOUTH MARKETS ALERT. 1989. m. $295 (foreign $325). E P M Communications, 160 Mercer St., 3rd Fl., New York, NY 10012-3212. TEL 212-941-0099. FAX 212-941-1622. Ed. Michael Schau; Pub. Ira Mayer. R&P contact: Ira Mayer. (back issues avail.) **Document type:** newsletter.
    ●Also available online. Vendor(s): Information Access Co., Knight-Ridder Information, Inc., Lexis-Nexis (AD12).
    —CCC.
    Description: Covers all the latest research on youth markets.

658.8   GW   ISSN 0170-1444
HF5415.2
ZEITSCHRIFT FUER MARKT, MEINUNGS- UND ZUKUNFTSFORSCHUNG. (Text in English, French, German; summaries in English, French, Spanish) 1957. q. DM.35($9) Demokrit Verlag, Postfach 2707, 72017 Tuebingen, Germany. Ed. Guenter Wickert. adv.; bk.rev.; bibl.; charts; illus. circ. 2,700. (also avail. in microfilm) **Indexed:** Key to Econ.Sci. **Document type:** bulletin.
    Formerly: Zeitschrift fuer Markt- und Meinungsforschung.

658 004.6   US
▼**1ST STEPS: DAILY MARKETING AND DESIGN**. 1995. d. Internet Business Network, 346 Starling Rd., Mill Valley, CA 94941. FAX 415-383-8676. E-mail: staff@interbiznet.com; URL: http://www.interbiznet.com/normad.html. Ed. John Sumser. **Document type:** newsletter.
    ●Available only online.
    Description: Focuses on tips, techniques, tools and resources for on-line marketing, advertising, customer service and promotion.
    Refereed Serial

BUSINESS AND ECONOMICS — Office Equipment And Services

651 376   PL   ISSN 0867-4175
A S - SEKRETARKA. Key Title: As Sekretarka. 1991. m. Conecta Ltd., Ul. Kosciuszki 61, 81-703 Sopot, Poland. TEL 48-58-517254. FAX 58-517674. TELEX 512528 BART PL. Ed. Malgorzata Lucewicz. adv. circ. 30,000.
    Description: Provides information for female secretaries.

AKTUELLT FOER KONTOR. see BUSINESS AND ECONOMICS — *Management*

651   FR   ISSN 0758-8763
ANNUAIRE BUREAUTIQUE INFORMATIQUE. 1972. a. 570 F. Editions Louis Johanet, 68 rue Boursault, 75017 Paris, France.
    Formerly: Annuaire de la Mecanographie, Materiel de Bureau, Informatique.

ARCHIV FUER STENOGRAFIE, TEXTVERARBEITUNG, BUEROTECHNIK. see *EDUCATION — Teaching Methods And Curriculum*

651 333.33   US
ARIZONA BUSINESS MAGAZINE. 1985. q. $19. 3111 N. Central Ave., Ste. 230, Phoenix, AZ 85012-2650. TEL 602-277-6045. Ed. Jessica McCann; Pub. Michael Atkinson. adv. contact: Earlene Miller. circ. 17,500. **Document type:** consumer publication.
    Former titles: Arizona Business and Development; Office Guide to Phoenix.
    Description: Focus on virtually every facet of the business community -- from development and construction to the environment, building management and architecture.

651.2   GW   ISSN 0722-3587
ASSISTENZ. 1951. 6/yr. DM.86 (foreign DM.92) (effective 1996). F B O - Fachverlag fuer Buero- und Organisationstechnik GmbH, Taunusstr. 54, 65183 Wiesbaden, Germany. TEL 49-611-534-0. FAX 49-611-534430. (back issues avail.) **Document type:** trade publication.
    —SWETS.

AUSTRALIAN NEWSAGENT AND STATIONER. see BUSINESS AND ECONOMICS — *Marketing And Purchasing*

004 330   US
AUTOMOTIVE MANAGEMENT INFORMATION SYSTEMS COUNCIL NEWSLETTER. 1979. s-a. free to members. Automotive Management Information Systems Council, Box 13966, Durham, NC 27709-3966. TEL 201-569-8500. circ. 150. **Document type:** newsletter.
    Formerly: Automotive Manufacturers E D T Council Newsletter.

651.2   GW   ISSN 0006-3843
B I T. (Buero und Informations Technik) 1964. 9/yr. DM.159.75 (foreign DM.177.75) (effective 1997). B I T Verlag Weinbrenner GmbH & Co. KG, Fasanenweg 18, 70771 Leinfelden-Echterdingen, Germany. TEL 49-711-75910. FAX 49-711-7591368. Pub. Karl-Heinz Weinbrenner. adv. contact: Christa Winkler. circ. 19,733. **Document type:** trade publication.
    —CCC.

651.2   US
B T A HOTLINE. 1968. s-m. (except. Feb. m.) $15 in Canada & Mexico $22; elsewhere $30. Business Technology Association, 12411 Wornall Rd., Kansas City, MO 64145. TEL 816-941-3100; 800-366-6950. FAX 816-941-8034. E-mail: btapubs@aol.com; URL: http://www.btanet.org. Ed. Brent Hoskins. adv.; circ. 4,000 (controlled). **Document type:** newsletter.
    Former titles: Business Equipment Hotline & Hotline (Kansas City).
    Description: Features industry news, association news and information on new products.

651.2 004.6   US   ISSN 1092-9169
B T A SOLUTIONS. 1949. m. $30 (Canada & Mexico $55; elsewhere $75). Business Technology Association, 12411 Wornall Rd., Kansas City, MO 64145-1166. TEL 816-941-3100. FAX 816-941-8034. E-mail: btapubs@aol.com; URL: http://www.btanet.org. Ed. Brent Hoskins. R&P contact: Brent Hoskins. adv.: page $1425; adv. contact: Cheri Deverey. illus.; circ. 10,000 (controlled). (back issues avail.) **Document type:** trade publication.
    Former titles: Business Technology Solutions (ISSN 1077-9353); (until 1994): N O M D A - L A N D A Spokesman (ISSN 1074-276X); (until 1993): N O M D A Spokesman (ISSN 0027-6871)
    Description: Published for business equipment dealers, networking systems integrators, and mailing system dealers. Dedicated to covering the latest trends and technologies in networking-business systems equipment.
    Refereed Serial

BUSINESS AND ECONOMICS — OFFICE EQUIPMENT AND SERVICES

651   GW   ISSN 0935-0276
HF5548.2
B T S. (Buero Technik Systeme) (Supplement avail.: Buero (ISSN 0177-7696)) 1987. m. DM.130. Basten Verlag, Eberstr. 30, 52134 Herzogenrath, Germany. TEL 02407-5003. FAX 02407-8902. Ed. Ingrid Steinwede. adv.; bk.rev.; pat.; stat.; cum.index. circ. 15,000. (processed; also avail. in looseleaf format) **Document type:** trade publication.
    Formed by 1987 merger of: B T S - Buerotechnische Sammlung (ISSN 0341-1370); Rationelle Buero (ISSN 0178-0549); Which was formerly (until 1985): Buero und E D V (ISSN 0340-3483); (until 1975): Rationelles Buero und E D V (ISSN 0340-3491); (until 1972): Rationelle Buero (ISSN 0034-0073)

653   GW   ISSN 0005-7010
BAYERISCHE BLAETTER FUER STENOGRAPHIE. 1867. bi-m. DM.24. Stenographen-Zentralverein Gabelsberger e.V., Uhlandstr. 16, 85521 Ottobrunn, Germany. Ed. Hans-Andreas Kroiss. adv.; bk.rev.; charts; illus.; stat.; index, cum.index. circ. 2,800.

BETRIEBSWIRTSCHAFTLICHE BLAETTER. see *BUSINESS AND ECONOMICS — Management*

651.2   US   ISSN 1084-2055
HF5548
BETTER BUYS FOR BUSINESS. 1986. 10/yr. $134 (Canada $141; elsewhere $235) (effective 1998). What to Buy for Business, Inc., Box 22857, Santa Barbara, CA 93121-2857. TEL 805-963-3539. FAX 805-963-3740. E-mail: orders@betterbuys.com; URL: http://www.betterbuys.com/betterbuys. Ed. Jon Bees; Pub. John Derrick. R&P contact: Michelle Gaitan. **Document type:** consumer publication.
    Formerly (until Jan. 1996): What to Buy for Business (ISSN 0886-6163); Which incorporates (in 1983): Better Buys for Business.
    Description: Consumer guide to all main types of business equipment services.

651.37   SA   ISSN 0378-9144
BOARDROOM. 1954. m. R.18. Southern African Institute of Chartered Secretaries and Administrators, P.O. Box 1917, Johannesburg 2000, Transvaal, South Africa. TEL 011-29-6116. Ed. Graham Hulley. adv.; bk.rev. circ. 9,444. **Indexed:** Ind.S.A.Per.
    Formerly (until 1976): Chartered Secretary.

651   GW   ISSN 0938-1511
BOSS; Fachzeitschrift fuer den PBS- und BBO-Handel. 1978. 10/yr. DM.148 (foreign DM.166.80) (effective 1997). B I T Verlag Weinbrenner GmbH & Co. KG, Fasanenweg 18, 70771 Leinfelden-Echterdingen, Germany. TEL 49-711-7591-0. FAX 49-711-7591368. illus. **Document type:** trade publication.

651.37   UK
BRISTOL SECRETARY MAGAZINE. 1988. m. £12. Media West Ltd., 30 Drakes Way, Portishead, Bristol BS20 9XA, England. TEL 01275-845846. Ed. H.B. Childs. adv.: B&W page £500, color page £750; trim 272 x 186; adv. contact: Rob McCabe. circ. 5,800 (paid). (back issues avail.) **Document type:** trade publication.

651.2   GW   ISSN 0007-3148
BUEROMARKT; Das Magazin der Buero-Wirtschaft. 1946. m. DM.101. Basten Verlag, Eberstr. 30, 52134 Herzogenrath, Germany. Ed. Werner Pohl. circ. 9,100.
    Incorporates: Buero-Wirtschaft (ISSN 0340-3009)
    Description: Publication for the office trade. Focuses on the latest information on office supplies, stationery, office technology, marketing, new products, international news.

330   GW
BUEROTECHNIK IM TEST; Fachzeitschrift fuer Automation, Buerotechnik, Datentechnik, EDV-Zubehoer. 6/yr. DM.168. Goeller Verlag GmbH, Hauptstr. 4, 76534 Baden-Baden, Germany. TEL 07221-71011-3. FAX 07221-75758. TELEX 781244. Ed. Hans-Juergen Goeller. circ. 2,000. (back issues avail.)
    Formerly: Bueromaschinen-Lexicon.

651   UK   ISSN 1352-5638
BUSINESS BASICS: PROPERTY. Key Title: Croner's Business Basics Bulletin. Property. 1994. base vol. (plus m. updates). £80.20 (updates £56.20) (effective 1995). Croner Publications Ltd (Subsidiary of: Wolters Kluwer N.V.), Croner House, 100 London Rd., Kingston-upon-Thames, Surrey TW2 6SR, England. TEL 44-181-547-3333. FAX 44-181-247-1300. TELEX 267778. (looseleaf format) **Document type:** trade publication.

651   US   ISSN 1078-2400
BUSINESS CONSUMER GUIDE. 1992. m. $159 (Canada $169; foreign $215). Beacon Research Group, 125 Walnut St., Watertown, MA 02172-4043. TEL 617-924-0044; 800-938-0088. FAX 617-924-0055. URL: http://www.buyerszone.com/. Ed. Mie-Yun Lee. R&P contact: Gregg Karet. (looseleaf format) **Document type:** newsletter.
    Description: Evaluates office products and services for the business community. Reviews the purchasing process and recommends brands and models offering the best combination of price, quality and service.

BUSINESS EDUCATION TODAY. see *EDUCATION — Teaching Methods And Curriculum*

651.2   UK   ISSN 0007-6708
BUSINESS EQUIPMENT DIGEST. 1961. m. £65 in the UK; Europe £120. I M L Group plc, Blair House, High St., Tonbridge, Kent TN9 1BQ, England. TEL 01732-359990. FAX 01732-770049. Ed. Eric Fordham; Pub. Peter Middup. R&P contact: M.T. Croucher. adv. contact: Andrea Church. bk.rev.; mkt.; tr.lit. circ. 33,400. **Indexed:** Anbar., Br.Ceram.Abstr., Build.Manage.Abstr., C.I.S. Abstr., Info.Media & Tech., INSPEC (1983-), Mgmt.& Market.Abstr., Print.Abstr., World Surf.Coat., WPM. **Document type:** trade publication.
    —BLDSC (2933.620000); AskIEEE; KR SourceOne.

686.2   US
BUSINESS PRODUCTS PROFESSIONAL. (Published in 2 regional editions) 1986. m. $90. Trade West Publishing, Inc., 4685 Brookhollow Cir., Riverside, CA 92509-3071. TEL 800-862-6100. FAX 800-862-6121. E-mail: info@tradewest.com; URL: http://www.tradewest.com. Ed. Dennis List; Pub. Paul J. Berardi. R&P contact: Dennis List. adv.: B&W page £2310, color page $3210 (both editions); 8 3/8 x 10 7/8; adv. contact: Dennis List. circ. 21,000. **Document type:** trade publication.
    Former titles (until Sep. 1994): Trade West (ISSN 1063-1275); (Sep. 1991-Sep. 1993): Business Products Professional.
    Description: Publishes trade articles for the independent business products distributor.

651   UK   ISSN 1356-0778
BUSINESS RATIO PLUS: STATIONERY DISTRIBUTORS. 1985. irreg., no.11, 1995. I C C Business Publications (Subsidiary of: I C C Information Group), Field House, 72 Oldfield Rd., Hampton, Middlesex TW12 2HQ, England. TEL 44-181-783-0922. FAX 44-181-783-1940.
    Formerly (until 1993): Business Ratio Report: Stationery Distributors (ISSN 0268-2427)

651   UK   ISSN 1356-0182
BUSINESS RATIO PLUS: STATIONERY MANUFACTURERS. 1972. irreg. I C C Business Publications (Subsidiary of: I C C Information Group), Field House, 72 Oldfield Rd., Hampton, Middlesex TW12 2HQ, England. TEL 44-181-783-0922. FAX 44-181-783-1940. **Document type:** trade publication.
    Formerly (until 1993): Business Ratio Report: Stationery Manufacturers (ISSN 0261-9571)

651.2   US   ISSN 1079-7467
BUSINESS SYSTEMS MAGAZINE. 1986. m. Corry Publishing, 2840 W. 21st St., Erie, PA 16506-2970. TEL 814-838-0025. FAX 814-838-0035. Ed. Shannan Lampe; Pub. Charles Mancino. adv.: B&W page $3800, color page $5000; trim 8 1/4 x 10 7/8; adv. contact: Michael Barbalaci. circ. 30,000 (controlled). **Indexed:** Tel.Abstr. **Document type:** trade publication.
    Former titles (until 1994): Business Systems Dealer (ISSN 1066-7997); (until 1992): Business Machine Dealer (ISSN 1055-7822); (until 1990): Business Electronics Dealer (ISSN 0893-6013); Business Electronics (ISSN 0889-4035)

651   US
BUYERS LABORATORY REPORT ON OFFICE PRODUCTS (FULL-O). 1962. m. $745. Buyers Laboratory Inc., 20 Railroad Ave., Hackensack, NJ 07601. TEL 201-488-0404. FAX 201-488-0461. E-mail: 76311.1067@compuserve.com; URL: http://www.buyers-lab.com. Ed. Daria Hoffman; Pub. Burt Meerow. R&P contact: Jane Lyons. adv. contact: John Ahrens. illus. circ. 2,300. (looseleaf format) **Document type:** newsletter.
    Formerly: Buyers Laboratory Test Reports. Series 1: Test Reports of Office Products.
    Description: The Full-Office Service combines three newsletters (Copier Review, Update, and FAXreporter), test findings for each product category, and printer specifications.

651 688   IT
C L. (CartoLibraio) 1965. m. L.60000($160) Solari e C. srl, Viale Stelvio 21, 20159 Milan, Italy. TEL 39-2-6686655. FAX 39-2-6886764. Ed. Mara Solari. adv.: B&W page L.2200000, color page L.3300000; trim 190 x 275. bk.rev. circ. 15,500. **Indexed:** CERDIC.
    Description: Covers the market of selling Italian school supplies, gift articles, stamps, stationery, office supplies and more both on the national and international scale.

651.2   CN   ISSN 0045-5210
C O M D A KEY. Key Title: COMDA Key. 1945. bi-m. membership. Canadian Office Machine Dealers Association, 3464 Kingston Rd., Ste. 204, Scarborough, ON M1M 1R5, Canada. TEL 416-261-1607. FAX 416-261-1679. Ed. Frank Stephen. adv.: B&W page $430; trim 8 1/2 x 11. circ. 1,837 (controlled).

651.2   CN   ISSN 1182-591X
C O P A CONVERSATION. (Text in English, French) 1982. 6/yr. 75 membership. Canadian Office Products Association, 1243 Islington Ave., Ste. 911, Toronto, ON M8X 1Y9, Canada. TEL 416-239-2737. FAX 416-239-1553. Ed. Darrell Townson. adv. contact: Susan Brown. circ. 4,900 (controlled). **Document type:** trade publication.

CANADIAN FACILITY MANAGEMENT & DESIGN. see *INTERIOR DESIGN AND DECORATION*

651.37 658   UK   ISSN 0268-8387
CAREER SECRETARY. 1970. q. £32 to non-members. Institute of Qualified Private Secretaries (I.Q.P.S.), 46 Kittiwake Dr., Kidderminster, Worcs. DY10 4RS, England. TEL 44-1562-822593. Ed. Susan Thomas. adv.: page £450. bk.rev. circ. 4,100. **Document type:** trade publication.
    Formerly: Institute of Qualified Private Secretaries. Journal.

676.282   IT
CARTOLERIA. 11/yr. L.48000 (foreign L.82000). Linea Commerciale, Via Andrea Doria 1, 20052 Monza (MI), Italy. TEL 39-39-737312. Ed. B. Nicola Giordano. adv.: page L.1800000. circ. 10,700.

651.2   SP   ISSN 0045-7116
CLAVE; revista del microordenador profesional, la informatica y el equipo de oficina. 1966. m. 5472 ptas. Pedeca Sociedad Cooperativa, Ltda., Maria Auxiliadora 5, 28040 Madrid, Spain. TEL 1-450-88-37. FAX 1-450-94-29. Ed. S. Sanchez de Ron. adv. circ. 15,000.
    —CCC.

CLERICAL SALARY REVIEW. see *BUSINESS AND ECONOMICS — Abstracting, Bibliographies, Statistics*

651 004   US   ISSN 1059-3470
QA76.9.C55
CLIENT - SERVER COMPUTING. 1991. m. $65 (Canada $75; elsewhere $125) (free to qualified personnel). Sentry Publishing Company, Inc., 1 Research Dr., Ste. 400B, Westborough, MA 01581-3907. TEL 508-366-2031. Ed. John Kerr; Pub. Donald Fagan. R&P contact: Barbara Gagne. adv. contact: Bill Orth. bk.rev.; circ. 90,000 (controlled). **Document type:** trade publication.
    —CISTI; KR SourceOne. CCC.
    Description: Aimed at information technology professionals and departmental managers who evaluate, buy, install, and run client-server systems at any level. Focuses on the management of the technology.

BUSINESS AND ECONOMICS — OFFICE EQUIPMENT AND SERVICES

338   US   ISSN 1043-0695
COMMUNIQUE (COLUMBUS, 1967). 1967. q. $7. Business Professionals of America, 5454 Cleveland Ave., Columbus, OH 43231-4021. TEL 614-895-7277. FAX 614-895-1165. E-mail: bpa@ix.netcom.com; URL: http://www.bpa.org/bpa.html. Ed. Stephen Dziura. R&P contact: Stephen Dziura. adv. contact: Stephen Dziura. charts; illus.; tr.lit. circ. 45,000. Indexed: Bus.Educ.Ind., Mgmt.& Market.Abstr. **Document type:** academic/scholarly publication.
   Former titles: O E A Communique (ISSN 0889-4817); Office Education Association. National Newsletter.
   Refereed Serial

651.3   BE
COMPTABILITE ET FISCALITE PRATIQUES. 1923. 10/yr. 9950 BEF (effective 1997). Kluwer Rechtwetenschappen Belgie - Ced Samson, Kouterveld 14, 1831 Diegem, Belgium. TEL 32-2-7231111. FAX 32-2-7231261. Ed. Inger Camps. adv. contact: Corry Govaerts. bk.rev. circ. 8,000. **Document type:** consumer publication.
   Formerly: Vie au Bureau.

004.7   GW
COMPUTER PERIPHERIE SOFTWARE; Produktinformation ueber Computer, Peripherie, Software OEM-Produkte und Kommunikations-Technik. 1986. 6/yr. free. Elsevier Thomas Fachverlag GmbH, Postfach 1869, 55008 Mainz, Germany. TEL 49-6131-8011-0. FAX 49-6131-831193. Ed. Rainer Sauer. adv.; bk.rev. circ. 40,000. **Document type:** trade publication.
   Former titles: Computer Produkte Software (ISSN 0939-1142); (until 1990): Buero Revue.
   Description: Focuses on new computer software and hardware, communications, peripherals and computer office equipment.

COMPUTERS & OFFICE EQUIPMENT: LATIN AMERICAN INDUSTRIAL REPORT. see *COMPUTERS*

651 380   GW   ISSN 1432-0401
▼**CONFERENCING**. 1996. q. DM.54 (foreign DM.62) (effective 1997). B I T Verlag Weinbrenner GmbH & Co. KG, Fasanenweg 18, 70771 Leinfelden-Echterdingen, Germany. TEL 49-711-7591-0. FAX 49-711-7591368. **Document type:** trade publication.

651   GW   ISSN 0947-1510
CONTROLLING INSTRUMENTE. 1994. bi-m. DM.98. Verlag Wirtschaft Recht und Steuern, Fraunhoferstr. 5, 82152 Planegg, Germany. TEL 49-89-89517-0. FAX 49-89-89517250. (Subscr. to: Postfach 1363, 82142 Planegg, Germany) (looseleaf format) **Document type:** trade publication.

651.2   IT
COPIA. 1986. 9/yr. L.60000 (foreign L.110000) (effective 1992). Edizioni Directa s.r.l., Via Paolo Sarpi 62, 20154 Milan, Italy. TEL 02-3313690. FAX 02-3313692. Ed. Giorgio De Monte. circ. 16,000. **Indexed:** Biol.& Agr.Ind.

621.38   US
COPIER. Variant title: Orion Copier Blue Book. 1991. a. $39 (effective 1996). Orion Research Corp., 14555 Scottsdale Rd., Ste. 330, Scottsdale, AZ 85254-3457. TEL 800-844-0759. FAX 800-375-1315. E-mail: orion@bluebook.com; URL: http://www.netzone.com/orion. (also avail. in diskette format) **Document type:** directory.
   Formerly (until 1996): Office Equipment (ISSN 1056-859X).

651.2   US
COPIER FAXTS. m. Dataquest, Inc., 1290 Ridder Park Dr., San Jose, CA 95131-2398. TEL 408-437-8000. FAX 408-437-0292. Ed. Lynn Ritter.

651.2   US   ISSN 0899-6164
COPIER REVIEW. m. $525. Buyers Laboratory, Inc., 20 Railroad Ave., Hackensack, NJ 07601-3309. TEL 201-488-0404. FAX 201-488-0461. E-mail: 76311.1067@compuserve.com; URL: http://www.buyers-lab.com. Ed. Daria Hofffman. R&P contact: Jane Lyons. adv. contact: John Ahrens. circ. 2,600. (looseleaf format) **Document type:** newsletter.
   Description: Provides news and analysis of copy machines, new products, new technologies, market trends and options for copiers.

651.37   US
CORPORATE SECRETARY'S GUIDE. 1950. m. $545. C C H Incorporated, 2700 Lake Cook Rd., Riverwoods, IL 60015. TEL 847-267-7000; 800-835-5224. FAX 800-224-8299. (looseleaf format)
   Formerly (until 1988): Stock Transfer Guide.

653   IT   ISSN 0010-9290
CORRIERE STENOGRAFICO. 1912. q. L.500. Unione Stenografica Italiana, Sala Stampa, Via Alfieri 10, Turin, Italy. Ed. Piero Molino. adv.; bk.rev. circ. 5,000.

651.3   US   ISSN 1079-1795
                     CODEN: CRSLEW
CREATIVE SECRETARY'S LETTER. 1960. s-m. $134.28. Bureau of Business Practice, 24 Rope Ferry Rd., Waterford, CT 06386. TEL 860-442-4365. FAX 860-437-3555. URL: http://www.bbpnews.com. Ed. Amy Keach; Pub. Peter Garabedian. R&P contact: Debra Ferraro. **Indexed:** Amer.Hist.& Life, Hist.Abstr. **Document type:** newsletter.
   Former titles (until 1994): Prentice Hall Creative Secretary's Letter (ISSN 1059-633X) & Professional Secretary - Administrative Support Letter; P.S. for Professional Secretaries (ISSN 0273-9682); P.S. for Private Secretaries (ISSN 0030-8285)
   Description: Includes interviews with experts in the business world that will help educate office professionals about the latest trends and innovations, as well as offer practical information they can apply on the job.

651.2   US
D I N: DEALER INFORMATION NETWORK. m. $725. Buyers Laboratory Inc., 20 Railroad Ave., Hackensack, NJ 07601. TEL 201-488-0404. FAX 201-488-0461. E-mail: 76311.1067@compuserve.com; URL: http://www.buyers-lab.com. Ed. Daria Hoffman; Pub. Burt Meerow. R&P contact: Jane Lyons. (looseleaf format) **Document type:** newsletter.
   Description: Combines two newsletters: Copier Review and FAXreporter, and tests findings for each product category and printer specifications.

653   GW   ISSN 0011-5169
D S T Z - DEUTSCHE STENOGRAFENZEITUNG. 1892. m. DM.42.50. (Deutscher Stenografenbund e. V.) Heckner Druck und Verlag, Postfach 1559, 38285 Wolfenbuettel, Germany. FAX 05331-800858. Ed. Helga Protz. index. **Document type:** trade publication.
   —CCC.

651.3   SW   ISSN 0349-3725
DAGENS SEKRETERARE. 1980. 9/yr. SEK 400. Today Press AB, P.O. Box 1413, S-751 44 Uppsala, Sweden. TEL 46-18-150-200. FAX 46-18-150-210. Ed. Birgitta Baecklund. adv.; B&W page SEK 15750, color page SEK 18900; adv. contact: Inger Kwammark. circ. 5,400. cols./p.: 3; pp./issue: 40.

DANSKE MOEBLER. see *INTERIOR DESIGN AND DECORATION — Furniture And House Furnishings*

651.2 621.381   IT
DEAL; il mensile di informatica e telecomunicazioni. m. (9/yr.). Gruppo Editoriale J C E, Via Ferri 6, 20092 Cinisello Balsamo (MI), Italy. TEL 39-2-660251. FAX 39-2-6127620. TELEX 352376 JCE MIL I. adv.: B&W page L.5400000, color page L.6900000; trim 210 x 276. circ. 13,500.
   Formerly: Future Office.

651.4   US
DISASTER RECOVERY JOURNAL; the journal dedicated to business continuity. 1987. q. free. Systems Support, Inc., Box 510110, St. Louis, MO 63151. TEL 314-894-0276. FAX 314-894-7474. URL: http://www.drj.com. Ed. David-Glen Smith; Pub. Richard Arnold. adv. contact: Rob Arnold. circ. 47,000 (controlled). **Document type:** trade publication.
   Description: Covers all aspects of business contingency planning and disaster recovery.

DISCRIMINATION CASE LAW DIGEST. see *BUSINESS AND ECONOMICS — Labor And Industrial Relations*

DOCUMENTATION SERVICES INDEX. see *BUSINESS AND ECONOMICS — Trade And Industrial Directories*

651   VE
E P O: CATALOGO DE EQUIPOS PARA OFICINA. 1976. a. M.G. Ediciones Especializadas, S.A., Av. Maturin, No. 15, Urb. Los Cedros, El Bosque, Caracas 1050, Venezuela. Ed. Montserrat Giol. adv.

651.2   US
E T CETERA. 1987. q. $20 in N. America; elsewhere $25. Early Typewriter Collectors Association, 2591 Military Ave., Los Angeles, CA 90064-1933. TEL 310-477-5229. E-mail: dcrehr@earthlink.net; URL: http://home.earthlink.net/~dcrehr/etc.html. Ed. Darryl Rehr. adv.; bk.rev. circ. 250. (back issues avail.)
   Description: Covers the history of typewriters, calculators and other office machines.

ELECTRONIC OFFICE; management and technology. see *BUSINESS AND ECONOMICS — Computer Applications*

EQUAL OPPORTUNITIES REVIEW. see *BUSINESS AND ECONOMICS — Labor And Industrial Relations*

651.4   GW   ISSN 0343-6691
ERFOLG. 1951. 6/yr. DM.110 (foreign DM.122). Hans Holzmann Verlag GmbH, Gewerbestr. 2, 86825 Bad Woerishofen, Germany. TEL 08247-35401. FAX 08247-354170. Ed. Erwin Stroebele. adv. circ. 15,400. **Document type:** consumer publication.

651   FR   ISSN 1148-5566
ESPACE BUREAU. (Supplement avail.: Guide Bureau) 1962. 6/yr. 350 F. (foreign 470 F.). Groupe Moniteur, 17 rue d'Uzes, 75002 Paris, France. FAX 33-1-42333819. TELEX UPRESSE 680876F. Ed. Patrick Cheruette. adv.; bk.rev. circ. 12,500.
   Formerly (until 1990): Bureaux de France (ISSN 0007-6074)

ETAGE; Chef-Informationen. see *BUSINESS AND ECONOMICS*

EUROPEAN BUSINESS SERVICES DIRECTORY. see *BUSINESS AND ECONOMICS — Trade And Industrial Directories*

651.2   US   ISSN 0894-5748
EXEC-U-TARY. 1975. m. $25 (foreign $35). National Association of Executive Secretaries, 900 S. Washington St., Ste. G-13, Falls Church, VA 22046. TEL 703-237-8616. Dir. Ruth Ludeman. adv.; bk.rev.; stat.; circ. 6,000 (paid). (back issues avail.) **Document type:** newsletter.

F M DATA MONTHLY. see *ARCHITECTURE*

651.2   GW
FACHZEITUNG FUER DEN BUEROFACHHANDEL. 1948. m. DM.88.50. (Verband Papier, Buerobedarf, Schreibwaren) Goeller Verlag GmbH, Hauptstr. 4, 76534 Baden-Baden, Germany. TEL 07221-71011. FAX 07221-75758. TELEX 781244. Eds. Manfred Fiehn, Christa Burghardt. adv.; bk.rev.; illus. circ. 8,000.
   Formerly: Fachzeitschrift fuer der Buerofachhandel (ISSN 0014-6412)

658.2   UK   ISSN 1351-668X
FACILITIES MANAGEMENT. 1994. bi-m. (plus q. supplement). £195 (foreign £205) (includes Management Guide) (effective 1997). Eclipse Group, Industrial Relations Services, 18-20 Highbury Pl., London N5 1QP, England. TEL 44-171-354-5858. FAX 44-171-354-8106. Ed. Frank Booty; Pub. Andrew Brode. R&P contact: Julia Gosling. adv. **Document type:** trade publication.
   —BLDSC (3863.455600).
   Description: Covers topics in strategic planning, property and building management, energy management, fire and security, health and safety, and the workplace.

FACILITIES PLANNING HANDBOOK. see *ARCHITECTURE*

FACSIMILE FACTS AND FIGURES. see *BUSINESS AND ECONOMICS — Abstracting, Bibliographies, Statistics*

651.2   US
FAX MAGAZINE.* 1987. q. Technical Data Publishing Corporation, 195A State Rte. 33, Hartfield, VA 23071. TEL 201-770-2633. Ed. William M. Rowe. adv. circ. 25,000.

651.3 US ISSN 0016-1616
OM NINE TO FIVE; tips and information for success in the office. 1960. bi-w. $68.90. Dartnell Corporation, 4660 N. Ravenswood Ave., Chicago, IL 60640. TEL 773-561-4000; 800-621-5463. FAX 773-561-3801. URL: http://www.dartnellcorp.com. Ed. Kim Andersen. bk.rev.; illus.; tr.lit.; index: 1960-62. circ. 31,000. (looseleaf format; also avail. in microform from UMI; reprint service avail. from UMI) **Document type:** newsletter.
—UMI. CCC.
Description: Provides office support staff tips on how to develop skills to overcome problems, how to work with other members of their team, and how to increase the company's success by increasing their own.

653 II
K ROUND-UP. (Text in English) 1977. m. Rs.27. Delhi Shorthand School, 2-58 Ramesh Nagar, New Delhi 110015, India. Ed. Dharma Vira. adv.; bk.rev. circ. 5,200.

T & STATIONERY BUSINESS. see GIFTWARE AND TOYS

651 688 IT
ORNALE IN CARTOLERIA. 1988. m. Radicchi Editore s.r.l., Via S.G.B. De la Salle 4, 20132 Milan, Italy. TEL 39-2-26300330. FAX 39-2-2566849. Ed. Rossella Radicchi. adv.: B&W page L.2050000, color page L.3050000; trim 180 x 274. circ. 13,786.

652 UK ISSN 0269-9486
REETINGS. 1970. bi-m. £30 (overseas £40) (effective 1997). (Greeting Card & Calendar Association) Lema Publishing Co., Unit 1, Queen Mary's Ave., Watford, Herts WD1 7JR, England. TEL 44-1293-250909. FAX 44-1293-250995. TELEX 8952440. Ed. Nicholas Eyriey; Pub. Malcolm Naish. adv. contact: Toni Sheppard. circ. 20,000. **Document type:** trade publication.

ABITAT UFFICIO. see INTERIOR DESIGN AND DECORATION

651.2 GW ISSN 0938-6556
ECKNERS HEFTE FUER TEXTVERARBEITUNG. bi-m. DM.42. Heckner Druck und Verlag, Postfach 1559, 38285 Wolfenbuettel, Germany. FAX 05331-800858. **Document type:** trade publication.
Formerly: Musterdiktate fuer Kurzschrift, Maschinenschreiben und Phonotypie.

OME BUSINESS MAGAZINE; the work from home magazine. see BUSINESS AND ECONOMICS — Small Business

SUISSE. see BUSINESS AND ECONOMICS — Management

E E E SYMPOSIUM ON MASS STORAGE SYSTEMS. DIGEST OF PAPERS. see COMPUTERS

651.505 004 AT ISSN 0816-200X
FORMAA QUARTERLY. 1985. q. Aus.$10 per issue. Records Management Association of Australia, Cnr. Scott St. & Parnell Pl., Newscastle, N.S.W. 2300, Australia. TEL 61-49-297766. FAX 61-49-297827. Ed. Ken Ridley. adv. contact: Sharon Lyons. bk.rev.; tr.lit.; index. circ. 2,500. (also avail. in microfiche; back issues avail.) **Document type:** consumer publication, trade publication.
—BLDSC (4478.890500).

651 SZ
FORMATIK UND BUERO TREND. q. Eulach Verlag AG, Wartstr. 6, CH-8401 Winterthur, Switzerland. TEL 052-2124021. FAX 052-2133207. Ed. Rene Donze; Pub. Willy Grueninger. adv. contact: Beda Schoenenberger. circ. 20,000. **Document type:** trade publication.

651 IT
FORMATION E TECHNOLOGY. 1966. m. L.80000 (foreign L.130000). Edizioni Scientifiche Tecniche Europee s.r.l., Via Giorgio Vasari 15, 20135 Milan, Italy. TEL 39-2-55018039. E-mail: edizioni.este@iol.it. Ed. Mario Grasso. R&P contact: Gianni Ceriani. adv. contact: Emma Samarati. bk.rev.; charts; illus.; index. circ. 9,500.
Former titles: E D P Telematica Notizie (ISSN 0391-6367) & E D P Notizie; Notizie Rapide (ISSN 0029-4454)

BUSINESS AND ECONOMICS — OFFICE EQUIPMENT AND SERVICES

INFORMATION SYSTEMS AUDIT & CONTROL ASSOCIATION. CONTROL OBJECTIVES; for information and related technology. see COMPUTERS — Electronic Data Processing

651.2 621.38 NE ISSN 1385-951X
▼**INFORMATION TECHNOLOGY & MANAGEMENT.** Announced for publication in 1998. q. 376 SFr. (effective 1998). Baltzer Science Publishers B.V., P.O. Box 221, 1400 AE Bussum, Netherlands. TEL 31-20-6370061. FAX 31-20-6323651. E-mail: subscribe@baltzer.nl; URL: http://www.baltzer.nl. **Document type:** academic/scholarly publication.

651.2 621.38 AT ISSN 1322-3526
INFORMATION TECHNOLOGY MANAGEMENT; non-technical report on IT and its applications. 1989. a. Aus.$425 (US & Europe Aus.$455) (effective 1998). Paul Budde Communication Pty. Ltd., 2643 George Downes Dr., Bucketty, N.S.W. 2250, Australia. TEL 61-49-988-144. FAX 961-49-988-247. E-mail: pbc@budde.com.au; URL: http://www.budde.com.au. Ed. Paul Budde. circ. 150. **Document type:** trade publication.
Description: Telecommunication and broadcasting technologies and applications, including pay TV, optical fiber, EDI, Videotex, ISDN and more.

651 GR
INNOVATIVE BUSINESS TECHNOLOGIES. (Text in Greek) 1986. m. Business Press S.A., 44 Syngrou, 117 42 Athens, Greece. TEL 30-1-9238-672. FAX 30-1-9216-847. Ed. Antonis Kassanos. circ. 10,000. **Document type:** trade publication.
Description: Covers office automation technologies in the Greek and international markets.

651 IT
INTERNATIONAL STATIONERY; events in the world of stationery. 1988. q. L.250. Radicchi Editore s.r.l., Via G.B. de la Salle 4, 20132 Milan, Italy. TEL 02-263-00-330. FAX 02-25-66-849. circ. 7,500.

651.2 FR
INTERNATIONAL STATIONERY GUIDE; European guide for stationery professionals. (Text in English, French, German, Italian) 1993. a. 510 F. Helios International, 14 bd. Montmartre, 75009 Paris, France. TEL 33-1-42469294. FAX 33-4-90882849. TELEX 432845. adv.: B&W page 11345 F., color page 16730 F.; trim 260 x 170; adv. contact: Sandrine Klein. circ. 24,000. **Document type:** directory.
Description: Lists manufacturers, suppliers, exporters and importers of stationery products at the international level are listed alphabetically, by brand name and product.

650 US ISSN 1049-9849
INVENTORY REDUCTION REPORT. Abbreviated title: I R R. 1986. m. $249 (outside N. America $273). Institute of Management & Administration, Inc., 29 W. 35th St., 5th Fl., New York, NY 10001-2299. TEL 212-244-0360. FAX 212-564-0465. URL: http://www.ioma.com. Ed. Joe Mazel; Pub. Perry Patterson. R&P contact: Sofie Kourkoutakis. index. (looseleaf format; back issues avail.) **Document type:** newsletter.
—CCC.

JAHRBUCH DER BUEROKOMMUNIKATION. see BUSINESS AND ECONOMICS — Abstracting, Bibliographies, Statistics

651.2 GW ISSN 0178-594X
K M I BUEROWIRTSCHAFT - LEHRE UND PRAXIS; Fachzeitschrift fuer Kurzschrift, Maschinenschreiben und Informationsverarbeitung. 1986. q. DM.20. Winklers Verlag, Postfach 111552, 64230 Darmstadt, Germany. TEL 49-6151-8768-0. FAX 49-6151-876860. adv.; bk.rev. circ. 3,600. **Document type:** trade publication.

651.2 NE ISSN 0022-8893
KANTOOR EN EFFICIENCY. 1962. m. fl.178. Brinkpoortstraat 38, 7411 HS Deventer, Netherlands. TEL 31-570-611044. FAX 31-570-612042. E-mail: kene@pi.net. Ed. Dick Overkleeft. adv.; bk.rev.; charts; illus.; stat.; index. circ. 7,500. **Indexed:** Key to Econ.Sci.
—KNAW; SWETS.
Description: Covers office organization and practice featuring the latest news and research in automation, software, programming, information processing, copymachines, office furnishings and more. Includes list of events and exhibitions.

651 NE ISSN 0022-8907
KANTOOR - SCHOOL - HUIS;* voorlichtingsblad voor gebruikers van kantoorartikelen. 1951. bi-m. Waldecklaan 41, Hilversum, Netherlands. Ed. B.W. De Veer. circ. 10,000.

651 NE ISSN 0929-7871
KANTOORMARKT BUSINESSMAGAZINE; vaktijdschrift voor de handel in kantoor- en schrijfartikelen, papeterie en wenskaarten. Short title: K B M. 1918. 10/yr. fl.148.50 (foreign fl.231.50) (effective 1997). Districomm B.V., Postbus 134, 6562 AD Groesbeek, Netherlands. TEL 31-24-3978081. FAX 31-24-3876071. Ed. Joost Heessels; Pub. Joost Heessels. adv.; illus.; stat.; index. circ. 4,500. **Document type:** trade publication.
Incorporates (1992-1993): Best of Seven (ISSN 0929-788X); **Former titles** (until 1993): K B M - Kantoormarkt (ISSN 0169-7285); (until 1984): K B M (ISSN 0169-3204); Formed by the 1980 merger of: Band (ISSN 0005-4909); K B (ISSN 0165-4403); Which was formerly: Kantoorboekhandel (ISSN 0039-0364).
Description: For the stationery, office supplies, and greeting card trade.

651 UK
KEY NOTE MARKET REPORT: OFFICE FURNITURE. Variant title: Office Furniture. irreg., no.12, 1996. £205. Key Note Ltd., Field House, 72 Oldfield Rd., Hampton, Middlesex TW12 2HQ, England. TEL 44-181-783-0755. FAX 44-181-783-0049. **Document type:** trade publication.
●Also available online.
Also available on CD-ROM.
Formerly: Key Note Report: Office Furniture (ISSN 0954-5085)

651 UK
KEY NOTE MARKET REPORT: PHOTOCOPIERS & FAX MACHINES. irreg., no.8, 1994. £205. Key Note Ltd., Field House, 72 Oldfield Rd., Hampton, Middlesex TW12 2HQ, England. TEL 44-181-783-0755. FAX 44-181-783-0049. **Document type:** trade publication.
●Also available online.
Also available on CD-ROM.
Formerly: Key Note Report: Photocopiers and Fax Machines (ISSN 1352-6995)

651 UK
KEY NOTE MARKET REPORT: STATIONERY (PERSONAL & OFFICE). Variant title: Stationery (Personal & Office). irreg., no.12, 1996. £205. Key Note Ltd., Field House, 72 Oldfield Rd., Hampton, Middlesex TW12 2HQ, England. TEL 44-181-783-0755. FAX 44-181-783-0049. **Document type:** trade publication.
●Also available online.
Also available on CD-ROM.
Formerly: Key Note Report: Stationery (Personal and Office) (ISSN 1354-2354)

651 UK ISSN 1357-1354
KEY NOTE MARKET REVIEW: U K OFFICE EQUIPMENT. Variant title: U K Office Equipment. irreg., no.3, 1996. £410. Key Note Ltd., Field House, 72 Oldfield Rd., Hampton, Middlesex TW12 2HQ, England. TEL 44-181-783-0755. FAX 44-181-783-0049. **Document type:** trade publication.
●Also available online.
Also available on CD-ROM.

651 DK ISSN 0026-8631
KONTORBLADET; tidsskrift for erhverv og kontor. 1964. m. DKK 395 (free within Denmark). Visholm Media AS, Sydvestvej 49, DK-2600 Glostrup, Denmark. Ed. Jann Larsen. adv.; tr.lit. circ. 85,000.
Formerly: Moderne Kontor.

651.8 651.3 SW ISSN 0023-3722
KONTORSVAERLDEN.* 1911. q. SEK 26. Sveriges Kontoristforerening, PO Box 1341, 11183 Stockholm, Sweden. Ed. Birger Ernblad. circ. 2,000.

651 GW
KULT AM PULT; das Journal fuer erlesene Schreibtischkultur. 3/yr. DM.24 (foreign DM.30) (effective 1997). B I T Verlag Weinbrenner GmbH & Co. KG, Fasanenweg 18, 70771 Leinfelden-Echterdingen, Germany. TEL 49-711-7591-0. FAX 49-711-7591368. **Document type:** trade publication.

BUSINESS AND ECONOMICS — OFFICE EQUIPMENT AND SERVICES

651.3 331.8   DK   ISSN 0903-7497
LAEGESEKRETAER NYT. 1968. m. Dansk Laegesekretaerforening - H K, H.C. Andersens Boulevard 50, DK-1780 Copenhagen V, Denmark. TEL 45-33-30-43-43. FAX 45-33-30-44-49. Ed. Niels Stoktoft Overgaard. circ. 9,600.

651.3   SW   ISSN 0345-746X
LAEKARSEKRETERAREN. 1964. 8/yr. SEK 225 (effective 1993). Sveriges Laekarsekreterarfoerbund (LSF), P.O. Box 7258, S-103 89 Stockholm, Sweden.

653   IT   ISSN 0024-1431
LETTURA STENOGRAFICA. 1928. bi-m. L.2000. Unione Stenografica Napoletana, Via L. Settembrini 9, 80138 Naples, Italy. Ed.Bd. adv.; bibl.

MAANEDSMAGASINET ERHVERV - NORDJYLLAND. see *BUSINESS AND ECONOMICS — Management*

651   NE   ISSN 1382-3590
MANAGEMENT SUPPORT MAGAZINE. (Text in Dutch) 1983. m. Samsom BedrijfsInformatie B.V. (Subsidiary of: Wolters Kluwer N.V.), Postbus 4, 2400 MA Alphen aan den Rijn, Netherlands. TEL 31-172-469954. FAX 31-172-422804. adv.; illus. circ. 11,000. **Document type:** trade publication. —SWETS.
Former titles (until 1995): Secretaresse Magazine (ISSN 0169-0582); (until 1985): Secretaresse Nieuwsbrief (ISSN 0926-8847)

651 658.403
621.381   US   ISSN 1070-4051
HF5547.A2   CODEN: MOTEE3
MANAGING OFFICE TECHNOLOGY; integrating technology & human resources for total office quality. 1956. m. $45 (free to qualified personnel). Penton Publishing Co. (Subsidiary of: Pittway Company), 1100 Superior Ave., Cleveland, OH 44114-2543. TEL 216-696-7000. FAX 216-696-7648. (Subscr. to: Box 95795, Cleveland, OH 44101) Ed. Lura K. Romei. adv.: page $7910; trim 8 x 10 3/4. bk.rev.; illus.; tr.lit.; index; circ. 110,000 (controlled). (also avail. in microform from UMI; back issues avail., reprint service avail. from UMI) **Indexed:** ABI Inform., Abstr.Bull.Inst.Pap.Chem., B.P.I., BPIA, Bus.Educ.Ind., Bus.Ind., CAD CAM Abstr., Comput.Cont., Comput.Dtbs., Comput.Lit.Ind., Consum.Ind., INSPEC, Intl.Civil Eng.Abstr., Intl.Mgmt.Info., Mag.Ind., Manage.Cont., Resour.Ctr.Ind., Soft.Abstr.Eng., Tel.Alert., Tr.& Indus.Ind. **Document type:** trade publication.
●Also available online. Vendor(s): Information Access Co., Knight-Ridder Information, Inc., UMI.
—AskIEEE; KR SourceOne; SWETS; UMI; UnCover. CCC.
Former titles (until June 1993): Modern Office Technology (ISSN 0746-3839); (until 1983): Modern Office Procedures (ISSN 0026-8208)
Description: An office magazine for managers and executives. Articles on office products, services and information systems.

651.2   US   ISSN 0164-4939
MARKING INDUSTRY MAGAZINE. 1907. m. $42 (includes a. buyer's guide Marking Products & Equipment) (effective 1997). Marking Devices Publishing, Inc., 136 W. Vallette St., Ste. 6, Elmhurst, IL 60126-4377. TEL 630-832-5200. FAX 630-832-5206. Ed. Kim Steiner; Pub. David Hochmeister. adv. contact: David Hochmeister. bk.rev.; illus.; tr.lit. circ. 1,400. **Document type:** trade publication.
Formerly: Marking Industry (ISSN 0025-3839)
Description: Designed for those firms engaged in the manufacturing, distribution and-or sales of marking products: rubber stamps and dies, steel stamps and dies; engraved plates and signs - plastic or metal.

651.2   US
MARKING PRODUCTS & EQUIPMENT. 1908. a. $24 (or included in subscr. to Marking Industry Magazine) (effective 1997). Marking Devices Publishing, Inc., 136 W. Vallette St., Ste. 6, Elmhurst, IL 60126-4377. TEL 630-832-5200. FAX 630-832-5206. Ed. Kim Steiner; Pub. David Hochmeister. adv.: B&W page $830, color page $1500; trim 8 3/8 x 10 7/8; adv. contact: David Hochmeister. **Document type:** trade publication.

651.2   GW   ISSN 0933-8241
MENSCH UND BUERO; ambience, architecture, communication, furnishing. 1987. bi-m. DM.102 (foreign DM.134) (effective 1997). Mensch und Buero Verlags GmbH, Lange Str. 94, 76530 Baden-Baden, Germany. TEL 49-7221-22416. FAX 49-7221-26684. E-mail: red.mub@t-online.de; URL: http://www.menschundbuero.de. Ed. Hans Ottomann. R&P contact: Hans Ottomann. adv.: B&W page DM.11236, color page DM.14836; trim 266 x 205; adv. contact: Roland Kuehn. bk.rev. circ. 40,000. **Document type:** trade publication.

651.2 333.33   US
METRO CHICAGO OFFICE GUIDE. q. Law Bulletin Publishing Co., 415 N. State St., Chicago, IL 60610-4674. TEL 312-644-7800. adv. circ. 10,000.

651.4   CN   ISSN 1182-0861
METRO OTTAWA OFFICE GUIDE.* 1989. q. Nortext (Nepean), 16 Concourse Gate, Ste. 200, Nepean, Ont. K2E 7S8, Canada. TEL 613-727-5466. FAX 613-727-6910. Ed. John Morrissy. circ. 25,000.

651 330   UK   ISSN 0143-1374
MIND YOUR OWN BUSINESS. 1978. 10/yr. £25. Market Place Publishing Ltd., 106 Church Rd., London SE19 2UB, England. TEL 44-181-771-3614. FAX 44-181-771-4592. E-mail: 101737.2100@compuserve.com. Ed. Bill Gledhill. R&P contact: Bill Gledhill. adv. contact: Neil Trim. bk.rev. circ. 32,134. (back issues avail.) **Indexed:** Info.Media & Tech., Mgmt.& Market.Abstr., Print.Abstr., WPM. **Document type:** trade publication.
—BLDSC (5775.574000); AskIEEE; KR SourceOne. *Refereed Serial*

651.2   US   ISSN 0196-3287
HD9800.U5
N O P A MEMBERSHIP DIRECTORY AND BUYER'S GUIDE (YEAR). 1906. a. $80 to non-members. National Office Products Association, 301 N. Fairfax St., Alexandria, VA 22314. TEL 703-549-9040. FAX 703-683-7552. Ed. Sandra Selva.

651.2   US   ISSN 1060-3522
HF5548
N O P A OFFICE MARKET UPDATE. (Includes annual Official Convention & Exhibit Guide) 1929. bi-m. $40 to non-members; members $10. National Office Products Association, 301 N. Fairfax St., Alexandria, VA 22314. TEL 703-549-9040. FAX 703-683-7552. Ed. Sandra Selva. adv.: B&W page $1395, color page $2205; trim 8 1/4 x 11. circ. 9,000. **Document type:** trade publication.
Former titles: Special Report to the Office Products Industry; Business Products (ISSN 0007-6988)

651   US
NATIONAL ASSOCIATION OF SECRETARIAL SERVICES. NEWSLETTER. m. $48. National Association of Secretarial Services, 3637 Fourth St. N., Ste. 330, St. Petersburg, FL 33704. TEL 813-823-3646. FAX 813-894-1277. Ed. Frank Fox. circ. 1,200. **Document type:** newsletter.
Description: Covers secretarial services industry. Includes industry news.

NATIONAL BUSINESS EDUCATION YEARBOOK. see *EDUCATION — Teaching Methods And Curriculum*

653   GW   ISSN 0028-3371
NEUE STENOGRAPHISCHE PRAXIS. 1953. q. DM.20. Verband der Parlaments- und Verhandlungsstenographen, Postfach 120409, 53046 Bonn, Germany. Ed. Dr. Karl Gutzler. adv.; bk.rev.; abstr.; illus.; stat. circ. 600.

651.2   AT
NEW OFFICE WORLD. m. Aus.$73. Thomson Business Publishing, 47 Chippen St., Chippendale, N.S.W. 2008, Australia. TEL 02-699-2411. FAX 02-698-3920. TELEX 122226. Ed. Nicola Grassie. adv. circ. 12,365.
Former titles: Office News (ISSN 1035-5316) & Office News and Automation (ISSN 0817-3672); Australasian Office News (ISSN 0727-7687)

651.2   NZ   ISSN 1171-8137
NEW ZEALAND OFFICE PRODUCTS NEWS. 1990. m. NZ.$29. Profile Publishing Ltd., P.O. Box 5544, Wellesley St., Auckland, New Zealand. TEL 64-9-6301040. FAX 64-9-6301046. E-mail: sprofile@iconz.co.nz. circ. 8,700.
Formerly (until 1992): Office Products News (ISSN 1170-4330)
Description: Focuses on the variety of goods and services that are incorporated into running a modern office.

380.1   NR   ISSN 0331-0973
HF5286.5.A3
NIGERIAN YELLOW PAGES. 1971. a. I C I C (Directory Publishers) Ltd., P.M.B. 3204, Surulere, Lagos State, Nigeria. Ed. Olu Adeyemi. **Document type:** directory.
Former titles (until 1979): Nigerian Office and Residential Directory; Nigerian Office and Quarters Directory (ISSN 0085-4190)

NOVA SCOTIA BUSINESS JOURNAL. see *BUSINESS AND ECONOMICS — Small Business*

651.37   US   ISSN 0893-1224
O N.* (Office Newsletter) 1986. m. $24. Lowen Publishing, 1379 W. Park Western Dr., 213, San Pedro, CA 90732-2217. Ed. Tod Snodgrass. bk.rev.
Description: Information and ideas to help office professionals on their jobs, focusing on such areas as communications, compensation, new products, office purchasing, and personal money-saving.

651.2 001.6 629.8   US
OBSERVER (APTOS); office systems trends. 1980. 6/yr. $95. Automated Office Resources, 812 Via Tornasol, Aptos, CA 95003-5624. Ed. Paula Cecil. circ. 2,500.
Formerly: Word Processing News.
Description: Contains information on office systems technology and educational computer use. Articles cover office automation, communications, information processing, microcomputers, hardware, software, industry news and technological developments.

OF COUNSEL; the monthly legal practice report. see *LAW*

651   GW
OFFICE; Magazin fuer das moderne Buero. 5/yr. DM.68 (effective 1997). Trend Medien Verlag GmbH, Herdweg 20, 70174 Stuttgart, Germany. TEL 49-711-18790-0. FAX 49-711-1879045. Ed. Sylvia Straetz; Pub. Klaus Vetterle. adv.: B&W page DM.8500, color page DM.11900; trim 184 x 278; adv. contact: Lothar Hofmann. circ. 45,000. **Document type:** trade publication.

651.2 629.8   IT
OFFICE AUTOMATION. 11/yr. Soiel International, Via Martiri Oscuri 3, 20125 Milan, Italy. TEL 39-2-26148855. FAX 39-2-26149333. Ed. Grazia Gargiulo. circ. 13,000.

651.2   UK
OFFICE BUYER. bi-m. £18.50 (foreign £30). Trade Media Ltd., Brookmead House, Thorney Leys Business Park, Witney, Oxon OX8 7GE, England. TEL 44-1993-775545. FAX 44-1993-778884. Ed. Ian Boughton. adv. contact: John Whittle. **Document type:** trade publication.
Formerly (until 1991): Office Supplies Buyer.

651.2   US   ISSN 1050-7612
OFFICE DEALER (YEAR); the industry's new products merchandizer. 1987. 6/yr. Office Systems, Box 908, Spring House, PA 19477-0908. TEL 215-628-7792. (Subscr. to: Box 3218, Lowell, MA 01853) Ed. Scott Cullen; Pub. Richard Kunkel. R&P contact: Scott Cullen. adv. contact: Diane Shapiro. **Indexed:** Comput.Lit.Ind.
—CCC.
Formerly: Office Systems Dealer (Year) (ISSN 0896-0852)

651   GW   ISSN 0937-4639
OFFICE DESIGN. 4/yr. DM.92 (foreign DM.96) (effective 1996). F B O - Fachverlag fuer Buero- und Organisationstechnik GmbH, Taunusstr. 54, 65183 Wiesbaden, Germany. TEL 49-611-534-0. FAX 49-611-534430. **Document type:** bulletin.

OFFICE EQUIPMENT AND PRODUCTS. see *ELECTRONICS*

BUSINESS AND ECONOMICS — OFFICE EQUIPMENT AND SERVICES

651.2 UK ISSN 0030-0187
OFFICE EQUIPMENT NEWS. 1956. m. £37/($119) (foreign £60). Wilmington Business Publishing, Apex House, London Rd., Northfleet, Kent DA11 9JA, England. TEL 44-1322-277788. FAX 44-1474-569418. E-mail: wbp@wilmington.co.uk. Ed. Andy Drew. adv.; bk.rev.; charts; illus.; tr.lit.; circ. 55,236 (controlled). (tabloid format) **Indexed:** BMT, Br.Ceram.Abstr., Info.Media & Tech., INSPEC (1984-). WPM. **Document type:** trade publication.
—BLDSC (6237.430000). **CCC.**

651 US ISSN 0743-5967
OFFICE GUIDE TO BROWARD & PALM BEACH COUNTIES.* 1982. q. $30. Office and Industrial Guide (Deerfield Beach), 2450 Hollywood Blvd., Ste. 701, Hollywood, FL 33020-6619. TEL 800-329-9696. Ed. Jackson Buck. adv. circ. 15,500.

651.2 747 IT ISSN 1120-012X
OFFICE LAYOUT. 1985. 6/yr. L.100000 (foreign L.240000) (effective 1996). Soiel International, Via Martiri Oscuri 3, 20125 Milan, Italy. TEL 39-2-26148855. FAX 39-2-26149333. E-mail: soiel.int@pn.itnet.it. Ed. Grazia Gargiulo. adv.: B&W page L.4000000, color page L.5600000; adv. contact: Claudia Gattelli. circ. 11,200. **Document type:** trade publication.
—BLDSC (6237.438000).
Description: Covers office organization, schemes and furnishings. Presents the best in production, design, furnishings, lighting, security and automation.

651 340 US
OFFICE MANAGEMENT NEWS. irreg. (2-4/yr.). membership. State Bar of Wisconsin, Office Management Section, 402 W. Wilson St., Madison, WI 53703. TEL 608-257-3838. FAX 608-257-5502. circ. 1,250. (back issues avail.) **Document type:** academic/scholarly publication.
Description: Covers the management of law offices.

651.2 621.381 US ISSN 0197-4602
HF5548
OFFICE PRODUCTS ANALYST; a monthly report devoted to the analysis of office products. Abbreviated title: O P A. 1976. m. $195 (foreign $210). Industry Analysts, Inc., 50 Chestnut St., Rochester, NY 14604. TEL 716-232-5320. FAX 716-454-5760. Ed. Kathy Dwyer; Pub. Louis E. Slawetjky. R&P contact: Alex Rockeffer. circ. 2,000. **Indexed:** Comput.Bus. **Document type:** newsletter.
—BLDSC (6237.670500).
Description: Provides comparisons of copying, duplicating, facsimile, word processing and microcomputer equipment. Tracks pricing, supplies, service and technology trends.

651.2 US
OFFICE PRODUCTS DEALER BUYING GUIDE AND DIRECTORY; for retailers of office supplies, office machines, computers and word processing systems, software and related supplies. 1904. s-m. $25. Hitchcock Publishing (Subsidiary of: Capital Cities - A B C, Inc.), 191 S. Gary Ave., Carol Stream, IL 60188. TEL 708-665-1000. FAX 708-462-2225. Ed. Al Lehto. adv.; illus.; pat.; tr.lit. circ. 26,000. (also avail. in microform from UMI; reprint service avail. from UMI)
—KR SourceOne; UMI. **CCC.**
Former titles: Office Products Dealer (ISSN 0199-1329); Office Products (ISSN 0030-0144); Office Appliances.
Description: For manufacturers, dealers and wholesalers of office supplies, furniture, computer and automation systems. Offers information on the office products industry, dealer management, marketing of equipment and systems.

651 US ISSN 0746-5467
OFFICE PRODUCTS INDUSTRY REPORT. 1970. bi-w. $40 to non-members; members $10. National Office Products Association, 301 N. Fairfax St., Alexandria, VA 22314. TEL 703-549-9040. FAX 703-683-7552. Ed. Sandra Selva. stat. circ. 9,000.

651 US ISSN 0739-3156
CODEN: OFPRDE
OFFICE PROFESSIONAL. 1981. m. $48. Professional Training Associates, Inc., 210 Commerce Blvd., Round Rock, TX 78664-2189. TEL 512-255-6006. FAX 512-255-7532. Ed. Marilyn C. Johnson; Pub. Dennis E. Murphy. R&P contact: Dennis E. Murphy. **Document type:** newsletter.
—**CCC.**

OFFICE SECRETARY. see BUSINESS AND ECONOMICS — Personnel Management

651 US ISSN 8750-3441
HF5548 CODEN: OFSYEH
OFFICE SYSTEMS (YEAR); the voice of the small to midsize company. 1984. m. $36 (free to qualified personnel). Office Systems, Bo 908, Spring House, PA 19477-0908. TEL 215-628-7792. Ed. Scott Cullen; Pub. Richard Kunkel. R&P contact: Scott Cullen. adv.: B&W page $5400, color page $6635; trim 7 x 10; adv. contact: Diane Shapiro. bk.rev. circ. 100,000. (also avail. in microform from UMI) **Indexed:** Bus.Educ.Ind.
—BLDSC (6237.684900); KR SourceOne; UMI; UnCover. **CCC.**

OFFICE SYSTEMS RESEARCH ASSOCIATION. CONFERENCE PROCEEDINGS. see COMPUTERS

OFFICE SYSTEMS RESEARCH JOURNAL. see COMPUTERS

651 UK ISSN 0269-2430
OFFICE TRADE NEWS. 1982. 11/yr. £37/($109) (foreign £55). Wilmington Business Publishing, Apex House, London Rd., Northfleet, Kent DA11 9JA, England. TEL 44-1322-277788. FAX 44-1474-569418. E-mail: wbp@wilmington.co.uk. Ed. Glynn Pritchard. circ. 9,012. **Document type:** trade publication.

651.2 US ISSN 0164-5951
CODEN: OWNEEH
OFFICE WORLD NEWS. Abbreviated title: O W N. 1972. m. $50 (free to qualified personnel). B U S Publications, 366 Ramtown Greenville Rd., Howell, NJ 07731-2789. TEL 908-785-1616. FAX 908-785-1347. Ed. Kim Chandlee McCabe; Pub. William P. Urban. R&P contact: Kim Chandlee McCabe. adv. contact: Kim Chandlee McCabe. bk.rev.; circ. 37,000 (controlled). **Indexed:** INSPEC (1985-), PROMT. **Document type:** trade publication.
—AskIEEE; KR SourceOne; UMI. **CCC.**
Formerly: Office Products News.
Description: For distributors, resellers, and dealers of office products, machines and systems. Concentrates on market and industry news, trends and analysis.

651 SP ISSN 0030-0624
OFICINA MODERNA; revista de papeleria, material, maquinas y muebles para oficina. 1961. bi-m. 6300 ptas. (foreign 10500 ptas.). (Asociacion Nacional de Empresarios de Papeleria y Objetos de Escritorio) Reclamo Tecnico, S.A., Casanova, 212, 08036 Barcelona, Spain. TEL 34-3-3212149. FAX 34-3-3223812. Ed. Jorge Foix Cusco. adv.: B&W page 87500 ptas., color page 139000 ptas.; trim 190 x 240. bk.rev.; bibl.; illus. circ. 6,000.
Description: Covers the world of stationery, includes sales, advertising and manufacturing of the industry.

651.2 SP ISSN 0030-0640
OFICINAS; mobiliario, instalacion, iluminacion, ergonomia, diseno oficinas. (Supplement avail.: Libro del Ano) 1968. 6/yr. 13400 ptas. (Europe 12600 ptas.; elsewhere 19500 ptas.) (effective 1997). Cetisa - Boixareu S.A., Concepcion Arenal, 5, 08027 Barcelona, Spain. TEL 34-3-3527061. FAX 34-3-3472350. TELEX 99417 CTISA. Ed. Santiago Pena. R&P contact: Lluis Lleida. adv. contact: Xavier Cuatracasas. circ. 6,500. **Document type:** consumer publication.
Description: Informs on all aspects of buildings, from architecture to ergonomics, including interior design and furnishings.

P B S AKTUELL. (Papierwaren, Buerobedarf, Schreibwaren) see PAPER AND PULP

652 GW
P B S AKTUELL. 1976. 10/yr. DM.48 (foreign DM.148) (effective 1997). B I T Verlag Weinbrenner GmbH & Co. KG, Fasanenweg 18, 70771 Leinfelden-Echterdingen, Germany. TEL 49-711-7591-0. FAX 49-711-7591368. index. **Document type:** trade publication.

651.2 GW ISSN 0344-726X
P B S REPORT. 1967. m. DM.116 (effective 1997). Umschau Zeitschriftenverlag Breidenstein GmbH, Stuttgarter Str. 18-24, 60329 Frankfurt a.M., Germany. TEL 49-69-2600-0. FAX 49-69-2600-619. Ed. Werner Stark. adv.: B&W page DM.4400, color page DM.6560; trim 170 x 270; adv. contact: Gisela Berg. bk.rev. circ. 8,952. **Document type:** trade publication.

676.282 SP ISSN 0212-8489
PAPELERIA. 1979. q. 3000 ptas. (foreign 5000 ptas.) (effective 1997). Ser-Graf, C. Vilamari 81, 08015 Barcelona, Spain. TEL 34-3-2260424. FAX 34-3-2263298. Pub. Antonio Palazon Serrano. adv.: color page 92000 ptas.; adv. contact: Javier Palazon Barriuso. circ. 5,000. **Document type:** consumer publication, directory.
Description: Covers office and school supplies, paper industry, and fine arts.

PAPETERIST/PAPETIER/CARTOLAIO. see PAPER AND PULP

651.2 FR ISSN 0031-1324
PAPETIER DE FRANCE; revue professionelle des papetiers detaillants fournituristes et grands magasins. 1947. m. (11/yr.). 635 F. Helios International, 14 bd. Montmartre, 75009 Paris, France. TEL 33-1-42469294. FAX 33-4-90882849. TELEX 432845. Ed. C. Durrieu. adv.; bk.rev.; rec.rev.; charts; illus.; pat.; tr.mk.; index. circ. 12,500. **Document type:** newspaper.
—**CCC.**

381.456762 DK ISSN 0031-143X
PAPIRHANDLEREN. 1949. m. DKK 400 (effective 1997). (Detail-Papirhandlerforeningen i Danmark) Pressto, P.O. Box 166, DK-6400 Soenderborg, Denmark. TEL 45-74-43-14-44. FAX 45-74-43-14-48. Ed. Bjarke Larsen. adv. contact: Kate Thygesen. bk.rev.; illus.; index. circ. 1,800. **Document type:** trade publication.

651.3 NE ISSN 0165-8867
PEN EN TOETS; algemeen tijdschrift voor stenografie, machineschrijven en kantoorpraktijk. 1914. 4/yr. fl.35. Associatie voor Stenografie, Machineschrijven en Kantoorpraktijk, Rechtestraat 26A, 5611 GP Eindhoven, Netherlands. FAX 040-449797. Ed. L.M.D. Ibes-Mansheym. adv.; bk.rev.; charts. circ. 1,500.
Former titles: Groote Schrijver-Genesiusblad (ISSN 0017-4564); Groote Schrijver.

651 US ISSN 0893-2549
CODEN: PRPSEB
PERSONAL REPORT FOR THE PROFESSIONAL SECRETARY.* 1972. m. $39. National Institute of Business Management, Box 9225, McLean, VA 22102-9664. TEL 703-905-8000. (Subscr. to: Box 25347, Alexandria, VA 22313) Ed. Barry Lenson. circ. 17,240. **Document type:** trade publication.
—CASDDS. **CCC.**
Formerly: Research Institute Personal Report for the Professional Secretary (ISSN 0276-6035)

651 UK ISSN 0965-4739
CODEN: PFMAES
PREMISES AND FACILITIES MANAGEMENT. 1986. m. £60 in the UK; Europe £80; elsewhere £110. I M L Group plc, Blair House, High St., Tonbridge, Kent TN9 1BQ, England. TEL 01732-359990. FAX 01732-770049. Ed. Richard Byatt; Pub. Peter Middup. R&P contact: M.T. Croucher. adv. contact: Mark Wiles. bk.rev. circ. 12,500. **Indexed:** INSPEC (1993-). **Document type:** trade publication.
—BLDSC (6607.644630); AskIEEE; KR SourceOne.

PRESTIGE CORPORATE INTERIORS. see INTERIOR DESIGN AND DECORATION

BUSINESS AND ECONOMICS — OFFICE EQUIPMENT AND SERVICES

651.2 US
PRINTER IMPRESSIONS. 1980. m. $385. Buyers Laboratory, Inc., 20 Railroad Ave., Hackensack, NJ 07601. TEL 201-488-0404. FAX 201-488-0461. Ed. Gail Stragusa; Pub. Gail Stragusa. R&P contact: Gail Stragusa. (looseleaf format) **Document type:** newsletter.
  Formerly: TypeLine.
  Description: Provides news and analysis of dot-matrix, ink-jet, laser and LED-array printers. Reports on new products, new technologies, market trends and options for each product category.

PRIVREDNO PRAVNI PRIRUCNIK; za pravnu opstu i kadrovsku sluzbu privrednih i ostalih radnih organizacija. see *LAW*

651.2 GW
PRODUKTUEBERSICHT: KOPIERER - VOLLFARB - GROSSFORMATKOPIERER. 1986. s-a. DM.41 (effective 1997). Comkotext GmbH, Blumenstr. 42, 40667 Meerbusch, Germany. TEL 49-2132-5951. FAX 49-2132-10217. Ed. Wolfgang Broetzmann. adv. circ. 5,000. (reprint service avail.) **Document type:** consumer publication.
  Formerly: Lexikon Buerotechnik.

651.2 GW
PRODUKTUEBERSICHT: MOBILTELEFONE - MOBILFAX. s-a. DM.41 (effective 1997). Comkotext GmbH, Blumenstr. 42, 40667 Meerbusch, Germany. TEL 49-2132-5951. FAX 49-2132-10217. Ed. Wolfgang Broetzmann. **Document type:** trade publication.

651.2 GW
PRODUKTUEBERSICHT: SEITEN - LASERDRUCKER. s-a. DM.41 (effective 1997). Comkotext GmbH, Blumenstr. 42, 40667 Meerbusch, Germany. TEL 49-2132-5951. FAX 49-2132-10217. Ed. Wolfgang Broetzmann. **Document type:** trade publication.

651.2 GW
PRODUKTUEBERSICHT: TELEFAX - MOBILFAX. s-a. DM.41 (effective 1997). Comkotext GmbH, Blumenstr. 42, 40667 Meerbusch, Germany. TEL 49-2132-5951. FAX 49-2132-10217. Ed. Wolfgang Broetzmann. **Document type:** trade publication.

651.2 GW
PRODUKTUEBERSICHT: THERMO - TINTEN - ZEILENDRUCKER- PLOTTER. s-a. DM.41 (effective 1997). Comkotext GmbH, Blumenstr. 42, 40667 Meerbusch, Germany. TEL 49-2132-5951. FAX 49-2132-10217. Ed. Wolfgang Broetzmann. **Document type:** trade publication.

651 VE
PROOFICINAS. 1978. a. Publicaciones Araguaney, Calle 8, Edificio Lec, piso 3, La Urbina, Caracas 107, Venezuela. adv.

651 US ISSN 8756-0089
RECORDS & RETRIEVAL REPORT; the newsletter for professional information managers. 1985. 10/yr. $145 (effective 1995). Greenwood Press, Inc., Subscription Publications (Subsidiary of: Greenwood Publishing Group Inc.), 88 Post Rd. W., Box 5007, Westport, CT 06881-5007. TEL 203-226-3571. FAX 203-222-1502. **Document type:** newsletter.
  —BLDSC (7325.353600).

648.5 NO ISSN 0802-2100
RENHOLDSNYTT. 1977. 6/yr. NOK 240. Selvig Publishing A-S, PO Box 9070 Vaterland, N-0134 Oslo, Norway. TEL 46-02-364440. FAX -46-02-360550. Ed. Marit Woehni. adv.; illus. circ. 4,100.

RESOURCE CENTER INDEX. see *BUSINESS AND ECONOMICS — Abstracting, Bibliographies, Statistics*

651.2 658.8 UK
RETAIL STATIONERY: THE INTERNATIONAL MARKET. (Subseries of: Market Direction reports) a. £1595($3190) (effective 1997). Euromonitor, 60-61 Britton St., London EC1M 5NA, England. TEL 44-171-251-8024. FAX 44-171-608-3149. E-mail: info@euromonitor.com; URL: http://www.euromonitor.com. (Addr. in N. America: Euromonitor International, 122 S. Michigan Ave., Ste. 1120, Chicago, IL 60603. TEL 800-577-3876. FAX 312-922-1157) (looseleaf format) **Document type:** trade publication.
  ●Also available online. Vendor(s): Data-Star, Knight-Ridder Information, Inc.
  Formerly (until 1995): Personal Stationery: The International Market.
  Description: Analyzes the personal stationery market for France, Germany, Italy, Spain, the U.K., the U.S., and Japan.

651 FR ISSN 0241-130X
LA REVUE DU SECRETARIAT ET DE LA COMPTABILITE. EDITION PROFESSEURS. 1919. q. 130 F. Union Professionnelle des Professeurs, Cadres et Techniciens du Secretariat et de la Comptabilite, 21 rue Croulebarbe, 75013 Paris, France. TEL 45-35-18-75. Ed. Jean Deslogis. adv.; illus.

651.2 US
S E R O M D A SCENE.* bi-m. South Eastern Regional Office Machine Dealers Association, Box 23670, Knoxville, TN 37933-1670. TEL 615-690-8996. FAX 615-690-3328. Ed. Betsy Morrow. circ. 1,000.

S I G O I S BULLETIN. (Special Interest Group for Office Information Systems) see *COMPUTERS — Computer Systems*

651.2 UK
S T N. (Stationery Trade News) 1983. m. £78 (foreign £110) (effective 1997). Trade Media Ltd., Brookmead House, Thorney Leys Business Park, Witney, Oxford OX8 7GE, England. TEL 44-1993-775545. FAX 44-1993-778884. Ed. Mark Devlin. adv. contact: John Whittle. bk.rev. circ. 8,200. **Document type:** trade publication.
  Formerly: Stationery Trade News (ISSN 0951-7820); Which incorporates: Office Dealer.

651 BE ISSN 0774-9104
SECRETARESSE; vakblad voor het dynamisch secretariaat. French edition: Secretaire (ISSN 0774-9112) (Supplement avail.) (Text in Flemish and French) 1984. m. (10/yr.). 2730 BEF. Kluwer Editorial (Subsidiary of: Wolters Kluwer Belgie n.v.), Kouterveld 2, B-1831 Diegem, Belgium. TEL 32-2-7231511. Ed. Biche Ehinger. adv.: color page 76000 BEF. bk.rev.; index; circ. 3,000 (paid); 5,500 (controlled). (back issues avail.) **Document type:** trade publication.
  Description: Details office automation, management, organization as well as features on personal health, literature and travel.

651.3 US ISSN 0037-0622
HF5547.A2 CODEN: SCTYA7
THE SECRETARY. 1942. 9/yr. $19. Stratton Publishing and Marketing Inc., 2800 Shirlington Rd., Ste. 706, Arlington, VA 22206. Ed. Susan L. Fitzgerald; Pub. Debra J. Stratton. adv.: B&W page $3500, color page $4500; trim 8 1/4 x 10 7/8; adv. contact: Eileen Warren. bk.rev.; illus.; stat.; index; circ. 40,000 (paid). (also avail. in microform from UMI; reprint service avail. from UMI) Indexed: Bus.Educ.Ind., ERIC, Pers.Lit.
  —CASDDS; CISTI; SWETS; UMI; UnCover. **CCC.**
  Description: Offers information and other tips for office professionals concerning office technology, productivity improvement, professional image-enhancement, and career advancement.

651 268 US ISSN 1070-9673
SECRETARY: F Y I. 1993. q. $16.08. Southern Baptist Convention, Sunday School Board, 127 Ninth Ave., N., Nashville, TN 37234. TEL 800-458-2772. FAX 615-251-5933. E-mail: customerservice@bssb.com.
  Description: Contains timely information and help on subjects of importance to secretaries, administrative assistants, and others who work in or manage the church or denominational office.

651 US ISSN 0164-3320
HD9999.S45 CODEN: SEDEEL
SECURITY DEALER. 1979. m. $50. P T N Publishing Corp., 445 Broad Hollow Rd., Ste. 21, Melville, NY 11747-4722. TEL 516-845-2700. FAX 516-845-7109. Ed. Susan A. Brady; Pub. Arnold B. Blumenthal. adv. circ. 23,050. **Document type:** trade publication.

651.3 GW ISSN 0171-4937
SEKRETARIAT; Fachmagazin fuer die Sekretaerin und Chefassistentin. 1955. m. DM.148 (foreign DM.170) (effective 1997). Betriebswirtschaftlicher Verlag Dr. Th. Gabler GmbH, Abraham-Lincoln-Str. 46, 65189 Wiesbaden, Germany. TEL 49-611-7878129. FAX 49-611-7878423. **Document type:** trade publication.
  —SWETS. **CCC.**
  Formerly: Gabriele (ISSN 0016-3708)

651 SZ
SIGNAL STENOGRAPHIQUE. 6/yr. Libellule 12, CH-1010 Lausanne, Switzerland. TEL 021-331453. Ed. Gabrielle Fasnacht. circ. 1,200.

651.2 IT
SISTEMI UOMINI MACCHINE ORGANIZZAZIONE. Short title: S U M O. 1958. 5/yr. Gruppo Editoriale J C E, Via Ferri 6, 20092 Cinisello Balsamo (MI), Italy. TEL 39-2-660251. FAX 39-2-6127620. Ed. Pasquale Satalino. circ. 30,000.

653 XO ISSN 0231-6978
SLOVENSKY STENOGRAF. 1945. 10/yr. (State Stenographical Institute in Bratislava) Slovenske Pedagogicke Nakladatelstvo, Sasinkova 5, 815 60 Bratislava, Slovakia. (Subscr. to: Slovart, Gottwaldovo nam. 6, 805-32 Bratislava, Slovakia) Ed. Marta Hajna. circ. 15,000.

SOCIETY OF DESIGN ADMINISTRATION. NATIONAL PUBLICATION. see *ARCHITECTURE*

651 US
SOUTH FLORIDA OFFICE GUIDE.* 1982. q. $30. South Florida Office Guides, Inc., 2632 Hollywood Blvd., Ste. 305, Hollywood, FL 33020-4857. TEL 305-570-7800. FAX 305-570-8380. Ed. Jann Sabin. adv. circ. 14,000. (reprint service avail.)
  Formerly: Office Guide to Miami (ISSN 0743-5983)

652.3 IT ISSN 0038-6863
SPECIALIZZAZIONE; trimestrale dell'Istituto I D I e di tecniche aziendali. 1963. q. membership. Istituto Dattilografico Italiano, Via Ricasoli 9, 50122 Florence, Italy. TEL 39-55-2398641. Ed. Flaviano Rodriguez. adv.: B&W page L.900000, color page L.1300000. circ. 7,000. (tabloid format)

653 II
SPEEDTYPE. (Text in English) 1978. q. Rs.12. Delhi Shorthand School, 2-58 Ramesh Nagar, New Delhi 110015, India. Ed. Dharma Vira. adv.; bk.rev. circ. 2,600.

653 II
SPEEDWRITER. (Text in English) 1975. m. Rs.55. Delhi Shorthand School, 2-58 Ramesh Nagar, New Delhi 110015, India. Ed. Dharma Vira. adv.; bk.rev. circ. 5,000.
  Description: Model test papers for various shorthand examinations.

651.2 SA
STATIONERY & OFFICE PRODUCTS S A. 1916. 8/yr. R.66 (foreign R.160). (National Office Products and Stationery Association of Southern Africa) R.D. Whales Associates, P.O. Box 73005, Fairland, Johannesburg 2030, South Africa. TEL 27-11-678-6317. FAX 27-11-476-7035. Ed. Robin Whales. adv. contact: Helen Norvall. bk.rev.; illus.; tr.lit. circ. 4,500. **Document type:** trade publication.
  Former titles: Office Products S A; Stationery; South African Stationery Trades Journal (ISSN 0038-2701)

651.2 CH
STATIONERY AND OFFICE SUPPLIES. (Text in English) s-a. $30. Taiwan Trade Pages Corp., P.O. Box 72-50, Taipei, Taiwan, Republic of China. TEL 02-3050759. FAX 886-2-3071000. TELEX 24838 TRADEPAG.

651.2 AT ISSN 1033-758X
STATIONERY NEWS. 1989. m. Aus.$50 (foreign Aus.$135) (effective Aug. 1996). Yaffa Publishing Group, 17-21 Bellevue St., Surry Hills, N.S.W. 2010, Australia. TEL 61-2-92812333. FAX 61-2-92812750. E-mail: yaffa@yaffa.com.au. Pub. Michael Merrick. adv.: B&W page Aus.$1975, color page Aus.$2745; trim 297 x 210; adv. contact: Rupert Merrick. circ. 6,000. **Document type:** trade publication.
 Description: Provides advertisers access to the buyers in each important link of the Australian stationery and office product reseller chain, including: office product dealers; stationery and office supply wholesalers; stationery retailers, superstores and mail order houses; newsagents throughout Australia; retail chain and department store buyers; manufacturers, importers and agents.

338 UK ISSN 0081-461X
STATIONERY TRADE REFERENCE BOOK AND BUYERS GUIDE. 1954. a. £50. Nexus Media Ltd., Nexus House, Azalea Dr., Swanley, Kent BR8 8HY, England. TEL 44-1322-660070. FAX 44-1322-667633. Pub. Tony De Bell. adv. contact: Douglas Muir. **Document type:** trade publication.
 —BLDSC (8447.298000).

651.2 UK ISSN 0039-0372
STATIONERY TRADE REVIEW. 1881. m. £78 (foreign £110) (effective 1997). Nexus Media Ltd., Nexus House, Azalea Dr., Swanley, Kent BR8 8HY, England. TEL 44-1322-660070. FAX 44-1322-667633. Ed. Maggie Gebbett. R&P contact: Maggie Gebbett. adv. contact: Douglas Muir. circ. 6,000. **Document type:** trade publication.

652 UK
STATIONERY UPDATE. 1990. m. £28 (Europe £50; elsewhere £70). Datateam Publishing Ltd., Fair Meadow, Maidstone, Kent ME14 1NG, England. TEL 44-1622-687031. FAX 44-1622-757646. Ed. Roger Hooper; Pub. Nick Carpenter. R&P contact: Bob Foreman. adv. contact: Sidney French. circ. 6,000. **Document type:** trade publication.
 Description: Contains news product information, literature, company profiles, overviews of market sectors, and industry trends.

653 DK ISSN 0039-1166
STENOGRAFISK TIDSSKRIFT. 1895. 4/yr. DKK 27($3) (effective 1996 & 1997). Dansk Stenografisk Forening, Grumstrupsalle 4, DK-8660 Skanderborg, Denmark. TEL 75-571073. Ed. K. Moerk-Hansen. adv.; bk.rev.; illus.; index; circ. controlled.

653 IT ISSN 0039-2960
STUDI GRAFICI. 1925. bi-m. L.500. Accademia Italiana di Stenografia, c/o Giuseppe Aliprandi, Ed., Via Soncin 17, 35100 Padua, Italy. (Co-sponsor: Primo Centro Italiano di Studi Dattilografici) adv.; bk.rev.; bibl.; illus.; stat.; index.

SYSDATA. see COMPUTERS

651.2 CH ISSN 1024-9001
TAIWAN STATIONERY AND OFFICE PRODUCTS BUYER'S GUIDE. (Text in English) a. $30. Trade Winds, Inc., No. 7, Lane 75, Yungkang St., P.O. Box 7-179, Taipei, Taiwan 10602, Republic of China. TEL 02-393-2718. FAX 02-396-4022. E-mail: tradwind@ms2.hinet.net; URL: http://www. tradewinds.com.tw. (Subscr. in U.S. to: Trade Winds Inc., Box 820519, Dallas, TX 75382. TEL 972-699-1188. FAX 972-699-1189) Ed. Donald Shapiro; Pub. Henry Ou. R&P contact: Donald Shapiro. adv. contact: Janice Hsieh. **Document type:** directory, catalog.
 Description: Covers stationery and office products produced in Taiwan for export.

651 GW ISSN 0946-6703
TEL-COM - BRIEF; Telekommunikation, Datenverarbeitung und Organisation. 1987. m. DM.420. Deutscher Wirtschaftsdienst, Marienburgerstr. 22, 50968 Cologne, Germany. TEL 49-221-93763-0. FAX 49-221-9376399. bk.rev.; index. circ. 500. **Document type:** bulletin.
 Former titles: Tel-Com D V und Orga-Brief; Former titles: Telcom-Brief (ISSN 0939-1649); D V und O R G A Brief (ISSN 0932-2698)

651 747 US ISSN 1059-0307
NA4170
TODAY'S FACILITY MANAGER; the magazine of facilities - interior planning team. 1988. m. $30. Group C Communications, 121 Monmouth St., Box 2060, Red Bank, NJ 07701. TEL 800-524-0337. FAX 908-758-6634. Ed. Heidi Schwartz. adv. contact: Victoria Jenks. bk.rev.; illus. circ. 38,000. (tabloid format; back issues avail.) **Document type:** trade publication.
 —KR SourceOne; UMI.
 Formerly (until 1993): Business Interiors (ISSN 1044-3584); Incorporates (1982-1987): Corporate Design (ISSN 0894-3575); Which was formerly (until 1987): Corporate Design and Realty (ISSN 8750-8206); (until 1984): Corporate Design (ISSN 0744-2750)

652 UK ISSN 0266-3295
TROPHY & ENGRAVING NEWS. Abbreviated title: T E N. 1984. m. £29.50 (overseas £48). Hill Media Ltd., Castle Chambers, 85 High St., Berkhamsted, Herts. HP4 2DF, England. TEL 44-1442-878787. FAX 44-1442-870888. Ed. Katie Thomas; Pub. Nigel Bean.
 Incorporates: Trophy and Incentive Marketing.
 Description: Provides a forum for the trophy engraving, industrial, and incentive marking trades.

651.2 US ISSN 0897-0939
UPDATE: THE EXECUTIVE'S PURCHASING ADVISOR. m. $175. Buyers Laboratory Inc., 20 Railroad Ave., Hackensack, NJ 07601. TEL 201-488-0404. FAX 201-488-0461. E-mail: 76311.1067@ compuserve.com; URL: http://www.buyers-lab.com. Ed. Daria Hoffman; Pub. Burt Meeraw. R&P contact: Jane Lyons. adv. contact: John Ahrens. circ. 2,200. (back issues avail.) **Document type:** newsletter.
 Description: Offers advice on purchasing and using office equipment, supplies and office services.

651.2 FI ISSN 0355-9912
UUDISTUVA KONTTORI; konttoritekniikan ja hallinnon ammattilehti. 1975. m. FIM 460. Oy Nantucket Ab, FIN-31640 Humppila, Finland. TEL 358-16-43-785-90. FAX 358-16-437-85-91. Ed. Risto Anttila. adv. contact: Leena Royna-Anttila. bk.rev.; illus.; index. circ. 13,500. (also avail. in microfiche) **Document type:** trade publication.

651.3 GW ISSN 0936-0700
V I T INFORMATIONSTECHNIK; Organisator. 1976. q. DM.24 (foreign DM.28.20). (Gesellschaft Deutscher Organisatoren) Fachschriften Verlag GmbH, Hoehenstr. 17, 70736 Fellbach, Germany. TEL 0711-5206-256. FAX 0711-5281424. Eds. Juergen Maler, Elmar O. Haaga. circ. 11,000. **Document type:** trade publication.

651 UK ISSN 0269-2996
WAREHOUSE COMPUTING. 6/yr. Turret House, 171 High St., Herts WD3 1SN, England. TEL 0923-777000. TELEX 888095-UKPUBS-G. Ed. Nick Allen. circ. 18,300.

651 US ISSN 1062-7650
HD9803.U6
THE WORKSTATION REPORT; (year) buyer's guide to office furniture. 1986. a. $49.95. Design Network International Ltd., P.O. Box 638, Highland Park, IL 60035-0638. TEL 708-831-0300. FAX 708-926-8230. Ed. Elizabeth Work. (back issues avail.)
 Description: Provides an overview of contract products, product services, and news digest for previous year.

ZEITSCHRIFT FUEHRUNG UND ORGANISATION. see BUSINESS AND ECONOMICS — Management

651.2 CC
ZHONGGUO WENFANG SIBAO/CHINESE FOUR TREASURES OF THE STUDY. (Text in Chinese) q. Zhongguo Wenfang Sibao Xiehui - Chinese Association of Four Treasures of the Study, 99 Liulichang, Xuanwu-qu, Beijing 100050, People's Republic of China. TEL 3017839. Ed. Huang He.
 Description: Features traditional Chinese office stationery: writing brush, ink stick, ink slab and paper.

653 II
40 MINUTES; an I Q monthly. (Text in English) 1981. m. Rs.27. Delhi Shorthand School, 2-58 Ramesh Nagar, New Delhi 110015, India. Ed. Dharma Vira. adv.; bk.rev. circ. 3,500.

BUSINESS AND ECONOMICS — Personnel Management

658.3 US ISSN 1068-0918
A C A JOURNAL; Perspectives in Compensation and Benefits. 4/yr. $65 (effective 1997). American Compensation Association, 14040 N. Northsight Blvd., Scottsdale, AZ 85260. TEL 605-951-9191. FAX 602-483-8352. Ed. Mike Bennett. (also avail. in microform from UMI) **Document type:** trade publication.
 ●Also available online. Vendor(s): UMI.
 —BLDSC (0570.452800); UMI.
 Description: Contains strategic articles on compensation and benefits.

658.3 331.2 US ISSN 1067-831X
HF5549.5.C67
A C A NEWS. 10/yr. $50 to non-members. American Compensation Association, 14040 N. Northsight Blvd., Scottsdale, AZ 85260. TEL 602-951-9191. FAX 602-483-8352. Ed. Rodney Platt. (also avail. in microform from UMI)
 ●Also available online. Vendor(s): UMI.
 —UMI.
 Incorporates (in 1992): Legislative Scene; (in 1992): Resources - News You Can Use.
 Description: Membership news magazine including features, news, and career-opportunity information.

658.3 345 US
A C J S EMPLOYMENT BULLETIN. 1993. m. (Oct.- Apr.). Academy of Criminal Justice Sciences, 402 Nunn Hall, Northern Kentucky University, Highland Heights, KY 41099-5998. TEL 606-572-5434; 800-757-ACJS. FAX 606-572-6665. circ. 3,400. **Document type:** bulletin.
 Description: Lists job vacancies in criminal justice field.

A D A COMPLIANCE MANUAL FOR EMPLOYERS. (Americans with Disabilities Act) see BUSINESS AND ECONOMICS — Labor And Industrial Relations

A P P A: THE ASSOCIATION OF HIGHER EDUCATION FACILITIES OFFICERS. PROCEEDINGS OF THE ANNUAL MEETING. see EDUCATION — School Organization And Administration

A S T D BUYERS GUIDE AND CONSULTANTS DIRECTORY. (American Society for Training and Development) see BUSINESS AND ECONOMICS — Trade And Industrial Directories

ABHIGYAN; the journal of foundation for organization research and education. see SOCIAL SCIENCES: COMPREHENSIVE WORKS

ACADEMY OF MANAGEMENT NEWSLETTER. see BUSINESS AND ECONOMICS — Management

ACCOUNTING AND AUDITING FOR EMPLOYEE BENEFITS. see BUSINESS AND ECONOMICS — Accounting

ADAM VEAVODA/MAN AND WORK; journal in labor studies. see OCCUPATIONS AND CAREERS

658.3 CN ISSN 1191-7881
ADMINISTRATIVE ASSISTANT'S UPDATE. 1986. m. Can.$139. M P L Communications Inc., 700-133 Richmond St. W., Toronto, ON M5H 3M8, Canada. TEL 416-869-1177. FAX 416-869-0456. **Document type:** trade publication.
 Formerly (until 1992): Secretary's Update (ISSN 0833-2878)
 Description: Professional newsletter for secretaries. Offers professional insights, tips and information designed to help secretaries in their daily tasks.

658.3 UK ISSN 0960-6580
ADULT AND YOUTH TRAINING. 1988. 12/yr. free. Training Agency, Employment Department, Information Services Branch, Rm. E810, Moorfoot, Sheffield S1 4PQ, England. TEL 01742-704289. FAX 01742-730982. Ed. Howard Woollin. circ. 35,000. **Document type:** government publication.
 Formed by the 1990 merger of: Employment Training News (ISSN 0955-4130); Youth Training News (ISSN 0952-9853)

BUSINESS AND ECONOMICS — PERSONNEL MANAGEMENT

658.3 UK
AFFILIATES DIRECTORY. a. C B I Employee Relocation Council, Centre Point, 103 New Oxford St., London WC1A 1DU, England. TEL 44-171-379-7400. FAX 44-171-240-8287. Ed. Sue Shortland. adv.: B&W page £1500, color page £2000; trim 303 x 213; adv. contact: Natalie Walton. circ. 2,000. **Document type:** directory.
 Description: Contains information about members.

658.3 US
AGENCY ISSUES. s-m. International Personnel Management Association, 1617 Duke St., Alexandria, VA 22314. TEL 703-549-7100. FAX 703-684-0948. Ed. Karen D. Smith. circ. 3,000. **Document type:** newsletter.
 Description: Short articles on trends in public personnel for agency members of IPMA.

658.3 US
ANNUAL EXECUTIVE COMPENSATION REPORT.* 1964. a. $225. Sibson & Company, Inc., c/o Ron Brandsdorfer, 504 Carnegie Ctr., CN 5211, Princeton, NJ 08543-5211. TEL 609-520-2700. circ. 1,000. (back issues avail.)
 Formerly: Annual Executive Compensation Study.

658.3 US
ANNUAL SURVEY OF HOURLY PAID EMPLOYEES IN ONTARIO. a. Can.$350. Central Ontario Industrial Relations Institute, 111 Richmond St., W., Ste. 1600, Toronto, ON M5H 2G4, Canada. TEL 416-368-2364. FAX 416-368-7217.

APPLIED H.R.M. RESEARCH. see PSYCHOLOGY

ARBEJDSMARKEDSPOLITISK AGENDA. see BUSINESS AND ECONOMICS — Labor And Industrial Relations

658.3 AT ISSN 1038-4111
HF5549.A2
ASIA PACIFIC JOURNAL OF HUMAN RESOURCES. Short title: Asia Pacific J H R. 1962. 3/yr. Aus.$60 to individuals (foreign Aus.$80); institutions Aus.$80 (foreign Aus.$100) (effective 1997). Australian Human Resources Institute, c/o Business Manager, P.O. Box 461, Mulgrave North, Vic. 3170, Australia. TEL 61-3-93444072. FAX 61-3-93444293. E-mail: infocent@ahri.com.au. Ed. Helen De Cieri. R&P contact: Ros Makris. adv. contact: Ros Makris. bk.rev. circ. 14,000. **Indexed:** Account.& Data Proc.Abstr., AESIS, ASEAN Manage.Abstr., Aus.P.A.I.S., B.P.I., Br.Hum.Ind., Bus.Ind., C.I.S. Abstr., Cont.Pg.Manage., High.Educ.Curr.Aware.Bull., Mgmt.& Market.Abstr., SCIMP. **Document type:** academic/scholarly publication.
 —BLDSC (1742.260690); UnCover.
 Former titles: Asia Pacific Human Resource Management (ISSN 1032-3627); (until 1989): Human Resource Management Australia (ISSN 0156-904X); Personnel Management (ISSN 0048-346X)
 Refereed Serial

658.3 AT
AUSTRALIAN & NEW ZEALAND TRAINING & DEVELOPMENT MANAGEMENT MANUAL. (In 3 vols.) 1993. q. C C H Australia Ltd., P.O. Box 230, North Ryde, N.S.W. 2113, Australia. TEL 61-1-300300224. FAX 61-1-300306224. (looseleaf format)
 Description: A reference resource specialising in the management of training activities in the workplace. Includes topics on the administration of training, core methods and techniques, needs analysis, design and evaluation, and competency-base training.

658.3 AT ISSN 1325-6858
AUSTRALIAN BENEFITS REVIEW. 1992. a. Aus.$425. Cullen Egan Dell, Level 8, 50 Bridge St., Sydney, N.S.W. 2000, Australia. TEL 61-2-93759800. FAX 61-2-92336800. Ed. Colin Hickling. charts; stat. table. 350. (looseleaf format)
 Description: Provides information on a range of benefits policies, remuneration and package designs.

658.3 AT ISSN 0314-4275
AUSTRALIAN SECRETARY.* q. Aus.$30. Institute of Professional Secretaries (Australia), P.O. Box 373, E. Kew, Vic. 3102, Australia. TEL 61-3-8185252. FAX 61-3-8196309. Ed. Veronica James. adv. circ. 2,500.
 Description: Addressed to persons in the secretarial and administration field and educators in secretarial and office procedures.

658.3 US ISSN 0005-3228
B N A POLICY AND PRACTICE SERIES. (Avail. in separate parts: Fair Employment Practices (ISSN 0149-2683); Labor Relations (ISSN 0149-2713); Wages and Hours (ISSN 0149-2691); Compensation (ISSN 0279-5418); Personnel Management (ISSN 0149-2675)) 1950. w. $1427 (effective July 1995). The Bureau of National Affairs, Inc., 1231 25th St., N.W., Washington, DC 20037. TEL 202-452-4200. FAX 202-822-8092. TELEX 285656 BANI WSH. URL: http://www.bna.com/. (Subscr. to: 9435 Key West Ave., Rockville, MD 20037. TEL 800-372-1033) Ed. Bill L. Manville. bibl.; charts; cum.index. (looseleaf format; back issues avail.) **Document type:** newsletter.
 ●Also available online. Vendor(s): Human Resources Information Network (BPP).
 —CCC.
 Formerly: Labor Policy and Practice.
 Description: Notification and reference service covering five major areas of employer-employee relations. Covered are personnel management, labor relations, fair employment practices, compensation, and wages and hours.

B N A POLICY AND PRACTICE SERIES. COMPENSATION. see BUSINESS AND ECONOMICS — Labor And Industrial Relations

658.3 US ISSN 0149-2675
KF3315
B N A POLICY AND PRACTICE SERIES. PERSONNEL MANAGEMENT. (Subseries of: B N A Policy and Practice Series (ISSN 0005-3228)) w. $683. The Bureau of National Affairs, Inc., 1231 25th St., N.W., Washington, DC 20037. TEL 202-452-4200. FAX 202-822-8092. TELEX 285656 BNAI WSH. URL: http://www.bna.com/. (Subscr. to: 9435 Key West Ave., Rockville, MD 20850. TEL 800-372-1033) Ed. Bill L. Manville. (looseleaf format; back issues avail.) **Document type:** newsletter.
 ●Also available online. Vendor(s): Human Resources Information Network.
 —CCC.
 Description: Practical guide to handling non-legal employee relations problems, in areas such as hiring, termination, workplace safety, grievances, training, and productivity.

B N A'S AMERICANS WITH DISABILITIES ACT MANUAL AND CASES. see LAW — Legal Aid

658.3 US ISSN 1072-1967
B N A'S EMPLOYMENT DISCRIMINATION REPORT. 1993. w. $802. The Bureau of National Affairs, Inc., 1231 25th St., N.W., Washington, DC 20037. TEL 202-452-4200. FAX 202-822-8092. TELEX 285656 BNAI WSH. URL: http://www.bna.com/. (Subscr. to: 9435 Key West Ave., Rockville, MD 20850. TEL 800-372-1033) Ed. James Fitzpatrick. (back issues avail.)
 ●Also available online.
 —CCC.
 Description: Covers decisional, legislative and regulatory developments of equal employment opportunity, including all facets of employment discrimination: race, national origin, religion, age, sex and disability.

BANK PERSONNEL NEWS. see BUSINESS AND ECONOMICS — Banking And Finance

BANQUES RESSOURCES HUMAINES. see BUSINESS AND ECONOMICS — Banking And Finance

658.3 GW ISSN 0174-6200
BASISTEXTE PERSONALWESEN. 1983. irreg. price varies. Ferdinand Enke Verlag, Postfach 300366, 70443 Stuttgart, Germany. TEL 49-711-25520-0. FAX 49-711-2552030. TELEX 07252275-GTV-D. Ed. Oswald Neuberger. adv. contact: Babette Kehrenberg. (reprint service avail. from IRC) **Document type:** monographic series.

658.3 US ISSN 1074-6293
KF1424.A15
BENEFITS & COMPENSATION UPDATE. 1974. m. $120.98 (foreign $167) (effective 1997). Warren, Gorham & Lamont, 395 Hudson St., New York, NY 10014. TEL 212-367-6300. FAX 212-367-6718. (Subscr. to: The Park Square Bldg., 31 St. James Ave., Boston, MA 02116-4112. TEL 800-950-1207) Ed. John D. Reynolds. (also avail. in microform from UMI; reprint service avail. from UMI; back issues avail.) **Indexed:** L.I.I. **Document type:** newsletter.
 —UMI. **CCC.**
 Former titles (until 1994): Employee Benefits Report (ISSN 0884-478X); (until 1984): Executive Compensation and Employee Benefits Report (ISSN 0273-9046); (until 1980): Executive Compensation Report (ISSN 0162-7503); Incorporates: Employee Benefit and ERISA Case Law Service.
 Description: Provides information on the latest ideas and developments in the field of employee benefits. Offers advice and up-to-date coverage on IRS actions, employment law, benefits planning, social security developments, and related topics.

658.3 CN ISSN 1191-0763
BENEFITS AND PENSIONS MONITOR. 1991. 6/yr. Can.$60 (foreign Can.$100) (effective 1997). Powershift Communications Inc., 245 Fairview Mall Dr., Ste. 501, North York, ON M2J 4T1, Canada. TEL 416-494-1066. FAX 416-494-2536. Ed. Patricia McCullagh. adv. contact: John McLaine. circ. 15,755. **Document type:** trade publication.
 Description: For those who invest pension funds, administer pension plans and-or manage employee benefit programs in Canada.

658.3 US ISSN 1063-9217
BENEFITS COMMUNICATOR. 1992. bi-m. $98. H R Communication Services, Box 671, Richmond, VA 23218. TEL 804-751-5003. Ed. Ann Black. R&P contact: Ann Black. **Document type:** newsletter.
 Description: Reports on trends and issues in benefits communication and administration.

658.3 US
BENEFITS GUIDE. base vol. (plus bi-m. updates and m. newsletter). $292 (effective 1995). Warren, Gorham & Lamont, One Penn Plaza, New York, NY 10119. TEL 212-971-5000. FAX 212-971-5113. (Subscr. to: The Park Square Bldg., 31 St. James Ave., Boston, MA 02116-4112. TEL 800-950-1207) (looseleaf format) **Document type:** trade publication, newsletter.
 Formerly: Managing Employee Benefits (ISSN 1057-3364)
 Description: Provides current information that deals with managed care (for AIDS and other catastrophic diseases), flexible benefits, cafeteria plans, family leave, COBRA, health care, continuation coverage and retiree health benefits. Includes federal and state laws.

BENEFITS LAW JOURNAL. see LAW — Legal Aid

658.3 US ISSN 0199-3100
HD4928.N62
BENEFITS NEWS ANALYSIS. 1979. 6/yr. $89 (effective Jan.1991). Benefits News Analysis, Inc., Box 4033, New Haven, CT 06525. TEL 203-393-2272. Ed. Faisal A. Saleh. adv. circ. 10,000.
 Description: Provides analysis of corporate employee benefit practices. Includes review of benefit program changes at a number of major corporations.

331 US ISSN 8756-1263
HD4928.N62
BENEFITS QUARTERLY. 1985. 4/yr. $100. International Society of Certified Employee Benefit Specialists, Inc., Box 209, Brookfield, WI 53008-0209. TEL 414-786-8771. FAX 414-786-8650. E-mail: iscbs@ifebp.org. Ed. Jack L. VanDerhei. R&P contact: Edye Biwer. bk.rev. circ. 17,000. **Indexed:** ABI Inform., P.A.I.S. **Document type:** trade publication
 ●Also available online. Vendor(s): UMI.
 —BLDSC (1891.485000); UMI. **CCC.**
 Description: In-depth articles on benefit-related topics, plus notes and comments; updates on current literature and legal-legislative-regulatory developments.

BUSINESS AND ECONOMICS — PERSONNEL MANAGEMENT

658 US
BENEFITS REPORT - ASIA. a. $1150. (Executive Compensation Service (ECS)) Wyatt Data Services, 218 Rte. 17, N., Roselle Park, NJ 07662-9832. TEL 201-843-1177. FAX 201-843-0101. charts.
  Description: Provides employee benefits information for 11 Asian countries.

658 US
BENEFITS REPORT - EUROPE. a. $940. (Executive Compensation Service (ECS)) Wyatt Data Services, 218 Rte. 17, N., Roselle Park, NJ 07662-9832. TEL 201-843-1177. FAX 201-843-0101.
  Description: Comprehensive guide to pensions and related employee benefits, both occupational and statutory; covers 17 Western European countries and Turkey.

BENEFITS SURVEY. see *BUSINESS AND ECONOMICS — Abstracting, Bibliographies, Statistics*

658.3 UK ISSN 1350-9845
BEST PRACTICE. 1993. bi-m. £150 (overseas £175($265)) (effective 1996). I F S International Ltd., Wolseley Business Park, Kempston, Bedford MK42 7PW, England. TEL 44-1234-853605. FAX 44-1234-854499. Ed. Rory L. Chase. R&P contact: David Watts. adv. contact: David Watts. Document type: trade publication.
  —CCC.
  Description: Assists executives and managers in business, government, and social services in introducing best-practice procedures in their organizations.

BETTER COMMUNICATION. see *COMMUNICATIONS*

658.3 UK
BLUEPRINT (NOTTINGHAM). 1970. 10/yr. free to current and retired employees. Boots Co., plc., 1 Thane Rd. W., Nottingham NG2 3AA, England. TEL 44-115-959-2365. FAX 44-115-959-5684. Ed. David Shelton. R&P contact: David Shelton. circ. 63,000 (controlled). (back issues avail.) Document type: newspaper.
  Formerly (until 1995): Boots Company News.
  Description: Informs employees and retirees of the Boots Company in the U.K. and overseas.

BOARD OF DIRECTORS REPORT. see *BUSINESS AND ECONOMICS — Management*

BRANCH OPERATIONS MANAGEMENT SERVICE. see *BUSINESS AND ECONOMICS — Banking And Finance*

658.3 GW ISSN 0937-2199
DAS BUERO. 1990. bi-m. DM.98. Verlag Wirtschaft Recht und Steuern, Fraunhoferstr. 5, 82152 Planegg, Germany. TEL 49-89-89517-0. FAX 49-89-89517250. (Subscr. to: Postfach 1363, 82142 Planegg, Germany) (looseleaf format) Document type: trade publication.

658.3 US
BUILDING BLOCKS IN TOTAL COMPENSATION. 1991. irreg. (5-10/yr.) $24.95 to non-members; members $19.95 per no. American Compensation Association, 14040 N. Northsight Blvd., Scottsdale, AZ 85260. TEL 602-951-9191. Ed. Mike Bennett. Document type: monographic series.
  Description: Provides instructional approaches to various aspects of compensation and benefits administration.

658.3 US ISSN 0525-2156
BULLETIN TO MANAGEMENT. (Subseries of: B N A Policy and Practice Series (ISSN 0005-3228)) 1947. w. $286. The Bureau of National Affairs, Inc., 1231 25th St., N.W., Washington, DC 20037. TEL 202-452-4200. FAX 202-822-8092. TELEX 285656 BNAI WSH. URL: http://www.bna.com/. (Subscr. to: 9435 Key West Ave., Rockville, MD 20850. TEL 800-372-1033) Ed. Bill L. Manville. charts; stat. (looseleaf format; back issues avail.) Indexed: Pers.Lit. Document type: newsletter.
  ●Also available online. Vendor(s): Human Resources Information Network (CDD, HDD).
  —CCC.
  Description: Summaries of current developments, discussions of real-life job situations, statistical charts and graphs, and ready-to-use policy studies.

658.3 UK ISSN 1352-5581
BUSINESS BASICS: STAFF. Key Title: Croner's Business Basics Bulletin. Staff. 1993. base vol. (plus m. updates). £80.80 (update service £56.80) (effective 1995). Croner Publications Ltd. (Subsidiary of: Wolters Kluwer N.V.), Croner House, 100 London Rd., Kingston-upon-Thames, Surrey TW2 6SR, England. TEL 44-181-547-3333. FAX 44-181-247-1300. TELEX 267778. (looseleaf format) Document type: trade publication.

C C H MANAGEMENT MANUAL. see *BUSINESS AND ECONOMICS — Management*

568.3 658 US
C P A ADMINISTRATOR'S REPORT & MANAGER'S REPORT; the resource successful CPA firms use in firm administration. 1981. m. $219 (effective 1997). Harcourt Brace Professional Publishing, 525 B St., Ste. 1900, San Diego, CA 92101-4495. TEL 619-699-6716. FAX 619-699-6593. Ed. Sidney Bernstein; Pub. Ken Rethmeier. R&P contact: Jenna Lake. TEL 619-699-6265. charts; stat.; tr.lit.; index, cum.index: 1981-1988. (looseleaf format; back issues avail.) Document type: newsletter.
  Formerly: C P A Administrative Report (ISSN 1047-5788)
  Description: Includes ways other firms smooth out workflow, hire and train staff, and stay competitive.

658.3 657 US ISSN 0745-0877
C P A PERSONNEL REPORT. 1982. m. $247 (Canada $277; elsewhere $302) (effective Oct. 1996). Strafford Publications, Inc., Specialized Information Services, 590 Dutch Valley Rd., N.E., Drawer 13729, Atlanta, GA 30324-0729. TEL 404-881-1141. FAX 404-881-0074. E-mail: custserv@straffordpub.com. Ed. Suzanne Verity; Pub. Richard M. Ossoff. R&P contact: Marianne Mueller. (looseleaf format; back issues avail.) Indexed: Account.Ind. (1986-). Document type: newsletter.
  Description: Helps firms excel in recruiting staff, competing with other firms to attract the best talent, making informed hiring and firing decisions and staying abreast of evaluation, compensation and benefits strategies, and management and motivational techniques.

658.3 374.8 UK
C P D LINK; a partnership in learning. 1994. m. free. Engineering Council, Continuing Professional Development Forum, 10 Maltravers St., London WC2R 3ER, England. TEL 0171-240-7891. FAX 0171-379-5586. Ed. John Lorriman. circ. 60,000. Document type: newsletter.
  Description: Profiles applications of continuing professional development programs in engineering settings.

658.3 378 US ISSN 1046-9508
LB2335.5.A1
C U P A JOURNAL. 1949. q. $75 to non-members; members $40. College and University Personnel Association, 1233 20th St., N.W., Washington, DC 20036. TEL 202-429-0311. FAX 202-429-0149. Ed. Daniel Julius. adv.; bk.rev.; bibl.; charts; stat.; index, cum.index: vol.1-15 (1949-1964). circ. 5,500. (also avail. in microform from UMI; reprint service avail. from UMI) Indexed: C.I.J.E., Cont.Pg.Educ., Curr.Cont., Educ.Admin.Abstr., Educ.Ind., High.Educ.Abstr., SSCI. Document type: academic/scholarly publication.
  —BLDSC (3493.245000); KR SourceOne; UMI; UnCover.
  Formerly: College and University Personnel Association. Journal (ISSN 0010-0935)
  Description: Focuses on human resource themes such as benefits, EEO, early retirement, administrative contracts, employee recruitment, and sexual harassment.

CALIFORNIA - FEDERAL PERSONNEL LAW UPDATE. see *LAW*

658.3 341 CN
CANADA - U.S. BUSINESS IMMIGRATION HANDBOOK. 1991. 2/yr. (plus updates). Can.$165. Carswell, One Corporate Plaza, 2075 Kennedy Rd., Scarborough, ON M1T 3V4, Canada. TEL 416-609-8000. FAX 416-298-5094. Ed. Joseph Grasmick. bibl.; charts; illus.; stat. circ. 1,000. (looseleaf format; back issues avail.)

CANADIAN ASSOCIATION OF SPECIAL LIBRARIES AND INFORMATION SERVICES. CALGARY CHAPTER. SALARY SURVEY. see *LIBRARY AND INFORMATION SCIENCES — Abstracting, Bibliographies, Statistics*

CANADIAN CASES ON EMPLOYMENT LAW. see *LAW*

658.3 CN ISSN 0838-228X
CANADIAN H R REPORTER; the national journal of human resource management. 1987. bi-w. Can.$98. M P L Communications Inc., 133 Richmond St., W., Ste. 700, Toronto, ON M5H 3M8, Canada. TEL 416-869-1177. FAX 416-869-0456. Ed. Chris Knight. adv. contact: Shelley Legault. bk.rev. circ. 8,000. (also avail. in microform from UMI; back issues avail.)
  —UMI.
  Description: For the human resources market including practitioners and related professionals. Covers news, developments, trends and products across Canada.

CANADIAN LEGAL & LEGISLATIVE BENEFITS REPORTER. see *LAW*

658.3 CN
CANADIAN PAYROLL MANAGEMENT GUIDE. 1985. m. Can.$395. C C H Canadian Ltd., 6 Garamond Ct., North York, ON M3C 1Z5, Canada. TEL 416-441-2992; 800-268-4522. FAX 416-444-9011. Document type: trade publication.
  Description: Provides information on all Federal and Provincial legislation and regulation pertaining to payroll preparation. Includes how-to information on a wide range of payroll related topics.

658.3 SP ISSN 1130-8117
CAPITAL HUMANO. 1988. 11/yr. 21650 ptas. (effective 1996). Grupo Especial Directivos, C. Orense 39 2o D, 28020 Madrid, Spain. TEL 1-556-64-11. FAX 1-555-41-18. Ed. Jose Antonio Carazo. adv.: B&W page 225000 ptas., color page 330000 ptas.; trim 189 x 260; adv. contact: Jorge Martinez. circ. 10,000.
  —CINDOC.

658.3 US
CAREER - OUTPLACEMENT; newsletter for human resource professionals, executives and managers. 1988. q. $24 (effective 1997). Career Management Consultants, Inc., 3207 N. Front St., Harrisburg, PA 17110. TEL 717-233-2272. FAX 717-233-2129. E-mail: jackate@darrington.net. (Edit. addr.: Box 1234, Darrington, WA 98241. TEL 360-436-0048. FAX 360-436-0048) Ed. Kate Duttro; Pub. Louis Persico. Document type: newsletter.
  Description: Each issue includes one feature article on topical subject, one case study, one book review, and chart of recent unemployment rates by state.

CATALYST DIRECTORY NEWSLETTER. see *NEW AGE PUBLICATIONS*

CENTRE I N F F O. GUIDES TECHNIQUES. see *EDUCATION — Adult Education*

CHARTERED SECRETARY. see *BUSINESS AND ECONOMICS — Small Business*

658 US
CHIEF EXECUTIVE OFFICERS' TOTAL COMPENSATION REPORT - MEXICO. a. $775. (Executive Compensation Service (ECS)) Wyatt Data Services, 218 Rte. 17, N., Roselle Park, NJ 07662-9832. TEL 201-843-1177. FAX 201-843-0101. charts.
  Description: Comprehensive source of information for the compensation practices and the prevalence and amount of fringe benefits for CEOs in Mexico.

658 US ISSN 1185-524X
CHIEF EXECUTIVES COMPENSATION IN CANADA. 1975. a. (Executive Compensation Service (ECS)) Wyatt Data Services, 218 Rte. 17, N., Roselle Park, NJ 07662-9832. TEL 201-843-1177. FAX 201-843-0101. Document type: trade publication.
  Former titles (until 1990): Remuneration of Chief Executives in Canada (ISSN 0707-3879); (until 1977): Remuneration of Chief Executive Officers in Canada (ISSN 0701-1059)

CHILE. INSTITUTO NACIONAL DE ESTADISTICAS. INDICE DE REMUNERACIONES. see *BUSINESS AND ECONOMICS — Abstracting, Bibliographies, Statistics*

BUSINESS AND ECONOMICS — PERSONNEL MANAGEMENT

658.3   UK
CHINA STAFF - HONG KONG STAFF. 10/yr. $270. Euromoney Publications plc., Nestor House, Playhouse Yard, London EC4V 5EX, England. TEL 44-171-779-8935. FAX 44-171-779-8541. (Dist. in US by: American Educational Systems, 173 W. 81st St, New York, NY 10024. TEL 800-717-2669. FAX 212-501-8926) **Document type:** trade publication.

658.3 384   CN   ISSN 0708-4471
CIRCUIT FERME; journal des employes de Radio-Canada. 1965. s-m. free. Canadian Broadcasting Corporation, 1400 E. Rene Levesque, Montreal, PQ H3C 3A8, Canada. TEL 514-597-4343. FAX 514-597-6000. Ed. Boris Volkoff. circ. 7,000.
 Description: Internal news for CBC radio and TV employees.

658.3   IT
CLASS. 1986. m. L.67200 (foreign L.110000) (effective 1997). Class Editori, Via Burigozzo 5, 20122 Milan, Italy. TEL 39-2-582191. FAX 39-2-58317429. Ed. Paolo Panerai. adv.: color page L.33500000. bk.rev.; circ. 90,000 (controlled).

658   US
COMPANY CAR REPORT - EUROPE. a. $940. (Executive Compensation Service (ECS)) Wyatt Data Services, 218 Rte. 17, N., Roselle Park, NJ 07662-9832. TEL 201-843-1177. FAX 201-843-0101. charts.
 Description: Provides information on how multinational companies set up and administer their company car policies in 17 Western European countries and Turkey.

658.3 352   US   ISSN 0732-5282
JS361
COMPENSATION (WASHINGTON, 1982); an annual report on local government executive salaries and fringe benefits. 1982. a. $180 (effective 1997). International City - County Management Assosiation, 777 N. Capitol St., N.E., Ste. 500, Washington, DC 20002-4201. TEL 202-962-3616; 800-745-8780. FAX 202-962-3500. Ed. Gwen Hall. R&P contact: Gwen Hall. circ. 900.

368   US   ISSN 0748-061X
HF5549.5.C67   CODEN: CBMAER
COMPENSATION & BENEFITS MANAGEMENT. 1984. q. $112 (effective 1992). Panel Publishers, Inc., 36 W. 44th St., No. 1316, New York, NY 10036-8102. TEL 212-790-2000. FAX 212-302-5119. Ed. Gerald Bush. charts. circ. 3,000. (also avail. in microform from UMI; back issues avail.) **Indexed:** ABI Inform., Account.Ind. (1984-), B.P.I.
 —BLDSC (3363.984000); CASDDS; KR SourceOne; UMI. **CCC.**
 Description: Articles directed to the executives, managers, or professionals responsible for the design, implementation and management of compensation programs.

COMPENSATION & BENEFITS SOFTWARE CENSUS. see *BUSINESS AND ECONOMICS — Computer Applications*

658   US
COMPENSATION AND BENEFITS SURVEY FOR EXECUTIVE LEVELS - MEXICO. a. $1030. (Executive Compensation Service (ECS)) Wyatt Data Services, 218 Rte. 17, N., Roselle Park, NJ 07662-9832. TEL 201-843-1177. FAX 201-843-0101. **Document type:** trade publication.
 Description: Contains compensation information on more than 60 executive positions in Mexico.

COMPENSATION IN THE HUMAN RESOURCES FIELD. see *BUSINESS AND ECONOMICS — Labor And Industrial Relations*

658   US
COMPENSATION REPORT - HONG KONG. a. $900. (Executive Compensation Service (ECS)) Wyatt Data Services, 218 Rte. 17, N., Roselle Park, NJ 07662-9832. TEL 201-843-1177. FAX 201-843-0101. charts. **Document type:** trade publication.

658   US
COMPENSATION REPORT - TAIWAN. a. $900. (Executive Compensation Service (ECS)) Wyatt Data Services, 218 Rte. 17, N., Roselle Park, NJ 07662-9832. TEL 201-843-1177. FAX 201-843-0101. **Document type:** trade publication.

658   US
COMPENSATION REPORT - THE PHILIPPINES. a. $900. (Executive Compensation Service (ECS)) Wyatt Data Services, 218 Rte. 17, N., Roselle Park, NJ 07662-9832. TEL 201-843-1177. FAX 201-843-0101. charts. **Document type:** trade publication.

658.3   UK   ISSN 1351-5802
COMPETENCY; the journal of performance through people. 1993. q. £185 (foreign £195) (effective 1997). Eclipse Group Ltd., Industrial Relations Services, 18-20 Highbury Pl., London N5 1QP, England. TEL 44-171-354-5858. FAX 44-171-226-8618. Ed. Neil Rankin. bk.rev.; software rev.; abstr.; tr.lit.; index. (back issues avail.) **Indexed:** Br.Educ.Ind., Mgmt.& Market.Abstr. **Document type:** trade publication.
 —BLDSC (3363.992245).
 Description: Discusses use of competencies by employers.

658.3 331   NE   ISSN 1384-6639
▼**CONCEPTS AND TRANSFORMATION;** international journal of action research and organizational renewal. (Text in English) 1996. 3/yr. fl.175 (effective 1998). John Benjamins Publishing Co., Amsteldijk 44, P.O. Box 75577, 1070 AN Amsterdam, Netherlands. TEL 31-20-6762325. FAX 31-20-6792956. URL: http://www.benjamins.nl. (In N. America: Box 27519, Philadelphia, PA 19118-0519. TEL 215-836-1200. FAX 215-836-1204) Eds. Hans van Beinum, Oeyvind Paalshaugen. bk.rev. (back issues avail.) **Document type:** academic/scholarly publication.
 —BLDSC (3399.412600).
 Refereed Serial

658.3   US
CORPORATE UNIVERSITY REVIEW. 1993. 6/yr. $49. Enterprise Communications Inc., 1483 Chain Bridge Rd., Ste. 202, McLean, VA 22101. TEL 703-448-0336. FAX 703-448-0270. (Subscr. to: 1165 Northchase Pkwy., N.E., Ste. 350, Marietta, GA 30067. TEL 770-988-9558) Ed. Lynn E. Densford. R&P contact: Lynn Densford. adv.: B&W page $3825; adv. contact: Jeff Watts. circ. 17,000. **Document type:** trade publication.
 Formerly: Workforce Training News.

CRONER'S EMPLOYMENT LAW. see *LAW*

658.3   UK   ISSN 0070-1580
CRONER'S REFERENCE BOOK FOR EMPLOYERS. 1947. base vol. (plus m. updates). £256.58 (updates £181.50) (effective 1995). Croner Publications Ltd. (Subsidiary of: Wolters Kluwer N.V.), Croner House, 100 London Rd., Kingston-upon-Thames, Surrey KT2 6SR, England. TEL 44-181-547-3333. FAX 44-181-547-2637. TELEX 267778. Ed. Clio Fisher. (looseleaf format)
 —BLDSC (3487.826000).
 Description: Provides comprehensive information on legal requirements and other information needed by employers.

658.3   US   ISSN 0145-8450
THE CUSTOMER COMMUNICATOR. m. $157. Alexander Research & Communications, Inc., 215 Park Ave. S., Ste. 1301, New York, NY 10003. TEL 212-228-0246. FAX 212-228-0376. Ed. Susan Hash; Pub. Margaret DeWitt. R&P contact: Mary Dalessandro. **Document type:** newsletter.
 Description: The training and motivation source for front-line customer service representatives.

658.3 331   NE
▼**DIALOGUES ON WORK AND INNOVATION.** (Text in English) 1996. irreg., vol.3, 1996. price varies. John Benjamins Publishing Co., Amsteldijk 44, P.O. Box 75577, 1070 AN Amsterdam, Netherlands. TEL 31-20-6762325. FAX 31-20-6792956. (In N. America: Box 27519, Philadelphia, PA 19118-0519. TEL 215-836-1200. FAX 215-836-1204) Ed. Hans van Beinum. (back issues avail.) **Document type:** monographic series.
 Description: Presents empirically based studies as well as theoretical reflections on the practice of organizational renewal.

658.3   US   ISSN 1067-7194
HF5549.5.M5
DIVERSITY FACTOR. 1992. q. $80 to libraries; corporations $195; foreign $205. P.O. Box 3188, Teaneck, NJ 07666. TEL 201-833-0011. FAX 201-833-4184. E-mail: mbwhite@mail.att.net. Ed. Margaret Blackburn White; Pub. Elise Y. Cross. R&P contact: Susan Levitt Whelan. bk.rev.; illus. circ. 1,500.
 —BLDSC (3604.271130). **CCC.**
 Description: Provides theoretical and practical information on the changing work force for corporations and public and private institutions.
 Refereed Serial

364 616   US   ISSN 1055-6281
DRUG DETECTION REPORT. 1991. 24/yr. $295. Pace Publications, 443 Park Ave. S., New York, NY 10016. TEL 212-685-5450. FAX 212-679-4701. Ed. Donald E. Veraska. **Document type:** newsletter.
 ●Also available online. Vendor(s): Information Access Co.

E B QUARTERLY. (Employee Benefits) see *BUSINESS AND ECONOMICS — Banking And Finance*

658.3 368   US   ISSN 0887-137X
HD4928.N6E27
E B R I ISSUE BRIEF. 1982. m. $1500 (includes Pension Investment Report). Employee Benefit Research Institute, 2121 K St., N.W., Ste. 600, Washington, DC 20037-1896. TEL 202-659-0670. FAX 202-775-6312. (Dist. by: Johns Hopkins University Press, EBRI Publications, Box 4866, Hampden Sta., Baltimore, MD 21211) R&P contact: Stephanie Robinson. cum.index. circ. 3,500. (also avail. in microform from UMI; back issues avail.) **Document type:** newsletter.
 —UMI. **CCC.**
 Description: Provides evaluations of evolving employee benefit issues and trends, including critical analyses of employee benefit program policies and proposals.

658.3   US   ISSN 0148-6934
HD4903.5.U58
THE E E O REVIEW. (Equal Employment Opportunity); a supervisor's guide to managing lawfully in the workplace. 1975. m. $189 (foreign $261) (effective 1998). John Wiley & Sons, Inc., Journals, 605 Third Ave., New York, NY 10158. TEL 212-850-6645. FAX 212-850-6021. E-mail: subinfo@jwiley.com; URL: http://www.wiley.co.uk. Ed. Sarah Magee. adv.: B&W page £640, color page £1515; trim 279 x 210. (looseleaf format) **Document type:** newsletter.
 —CCC.
 Formerly: Supervisor's E E O Review.
 Description: Contains practical information on how to handle E.E.O. and other personnel policies in hiring, promotion, discipline, and termination.

E M A REPORTER. (Employment Management Association) see *BUSINESS AND ECONOMICS — Labor And Industrial Relations*

E R I S A AND BENEFITS LAW JOURNAL. (Employee Retirement Income Security Act) see *LAW*

658.3   FR
ECOLE ET PROFESSIONS. 1982. 6/yr. 298 F. (effective 1997). Informations Developpement Entreprises, 24 rue de Lisbonne, 75008 Paris, France. TEL 33-1-53890289. FAX 33-1-53890290. Ed. Thierry Silvester. adv.; bk.rev. circ. 5,000.
 Former titles (until 1997): Relations Ecoles - Professions (ISSN 1143-354X); (until 1986): Cahiers des Relations Ecoles Professions (ISSN 0299-9625).
 Description: For personnel officers and training institutes.

658.3 004.6   US
▼**ELECTRONIC RECRUITING NEWS.** 1995. d. Internet Business Network, 346 Starling Rd., Mill Valley, CA 94941. TEL 415-380-8244. FAX 415-383-8676. E-mail: staff@interbiznet.com; URL: http://www.interbiznet.com/hrstart.html. Ed. John Sumser. R&P contact: Colleen Gildea. adv. contact: Colleen Gildea. **Document type:** newsletter.
 ●Available only online.
 Description: Targeted at human resource professionals, headhunters, placement firms and recruiting agencies on the Net.
 Refereed Serial

BUSINESS AND ECONOMICS — PERSONNEL MANAGEMENT

658.3 US ISSN 1042-1963
HF5549.5.E42
EMPLOYEE ASSISTANCE; solutions to the problems of EAPs. bi-m. $66. Stevens Publishing Corporation, 3700 J.H. Kultgen Frwy., Waco, TX 76706. TEL 817-776-9000. FAX 817-776-9018. Ed. Carole McMichael; Pub. Alan Stevens. adv. contact: Wes Jordan. circ. 23,000. **Document type:** trade publication.
—CCC.

658.3 US ISSN 1061-7728
EMPLOYEE ASSISTANCE PROFESSIONAL REPORT. 1990. m. $199. Stevens Publishing Corporation, 3700 J.H. Kultgen Frwy., Waco, TX 76706. TEL 817-776-9018. FAX 817-776-9018. Ed. Carole McMichael; Pub. L. Alan Stevens. **Document type:** newsletter.

658.3 157.6 US ISSN 0749-0003
HF5549.5.A4
EMPLOYEE ASSISTANCE QUARTERLY. (Former name of issuing body: National Council on Alcoholism) 1985. q. $45 to individuals (Canada $58.50; elsewhere $63); institutions $140 (Canada $182; elsewhere $196); libraries $300 (Canada $390; elsewhere $420) (effective 1996-1997). Haworth Press, Inc., 10 Alice St., Binghamton, NY 13904. TEL 607-722-5857; 800-342-9676. FAX 607-722-6362. E-mail: getinfo@haworth.com; URL: http://www.haworth.com. Ed. Keith McClellan; Pub. Bill Cohen. R&P contact: Ruthann Heath. adv.: B&W page $300; trim 4 3/8 x 7 1/8; adv. contact: Jackie Blakeslee. bk.rev. circ. 812. (also avail. in microfiche from UMI; microform from HAW; reprint service avail. from HAW) **Indexed:** Excerp.Med., IMFL, P.A.I.S., Psychol.Abstr. (1985-), Soc.Work Res.& Abstr.
—BLDSC (3737.032400); EMDOCS; Haworth; UnCover.
Formerly (until 1985): Labor Management Alcoholism Journal.
Description: Covers development of scholarly and research literature regarding work-based alcoholism programs and the employee assistance movement.
Refereed Serial

658.3 382 US ISSN 0194-3499
EMPLOYEE BENEFITS; survey data from benefit (year). 1947. a. $35. U.S. Chamber of Commerce, Research Center, 1615 H St., N.W., Washington, DC 20062. URL: http://www.uschamber.com.
Description: Serves as a reference guide for employees, employers, and benefits specialists.

EMPLOYEE BENEFITS ISSUES: THE MULTIEMPLOYER PERSPECTIVE; proceedings of the annual employee benefits conference with papers from other multi-employer conferences. see *BUSINESS AND ECONOMICS — Labor And Industrial Relations*

658.3 UK ISSN 1351-055X
EMPLOYEE DEVELOPMENT BULLETIN; practice and policy in training and development; recruitment, selection and retention. (Also avail. as part of: I R S Employment Review (ISSN 1358-2216)) 1990. m. £130 (foreign £144) (effective 1997). Eclipse Group Ltd., Industrial Relations Services, 18-20 Highbury Pl., London N5 1QP, England. TEL 44-171-354-5858. FAX 44-171-226-8618. Ed. Neil Rankin; Pub. Andrew Brode. index. (back issues avail.) **Indexed:** L.R.I. **Document type:** trade publication.
Formerly (until 1995): Recruitment and Development Report (ISSN 0959-146X)
Description: Provides practical coverage of issues relating to employers' skill needs: recruitment and selection, assessment, training, and development.

658.3 331.2 US ISSN 1061-2556
KF3512
EMPLOYEE FRINGE AND WELFARE BENEFIT PLANS. 1990. a. West Group, 620 Opperman Dr., Eagan, MN 55123. TEL 612-687-7000; 800-328-9352. FAX 612-687-7302. **Document type:** trade publication.

658.3 US
EMPLOYEE INVOLVEMENT ASSOCIATION. STATISTICAL REPORT. (Former name of issuing body: National Association of Suggestion Systems) 1943. a. $150 (Canada $210). Employee Involvement Association, 10565 Lee Hwy., Ste. 104, Fairfax, VA 22030-3135. TEL 703-383-1010. FAX 703-352-6767. E-mail: eia@washingtongroupinc.com; URL: http://www.eia.com. circ. 1,000.
Formerly: National Association of Suggestion Systems. Statistical Report (ISSN 0077-3441)

658.3 362.128 US ISSN 0889-5422
KF3457.3.A15
EMPLOYEE TESTING & THE LAW; reporting legal, technical, and business developments in employee testing. 1986. m. $295. Vanguard Information Publications, Box 667, Chapel Hill, NC 27514. TEL 919-967-2420. FAX 919-967-6294. Ed. Ted Shults. bk.rev.; index. circ. 2,000. (looseleaf format; also avail. in microform from UMI; back issues avail.)
—UMI.
Description: Covers legal and business issues involved in polygraphs, paper and pencil, drug and AIDS testing.

658.3 331 UK ISSN 0966-1662
EMPLOYMENT CASE DIGEST. (Supplement to: Personnel in Practice) 1992. m. Croner Publications Ltd. (Subsidiary of: Wolters Kluwer N.V.), Croner House, 100 London Rd., Kingston-upon-Thames, Surrey TW2 6SR, England. TEL 44-181-547-3333. FAX 44-181-247-1300. TELEX 267778. **Document type:** trade publication.
—BLDSC (3487.806500).

EMPLOYMENT DIGEST. see *BUSINESS AND ECONOMICS — Labor And Industrial Relations*

658.3 US
EMPLOYMENT DISCRIMINATION. 1987. base vol. (plus a. update). $105. Butterworth Legal Publishers (Salem) (Subsidiary of: Reed Elsevier plc), 8 Industrial Way, Bldg. C, Salem, NH 03079. TEL 800-548-4001. FAX 603-898-9858. Ed. Paul N. Cox. (looseleaf format)
Description: Covers defense, procedures, and remedies of employment discrimination.

344.01 658.3 US
EMPLOYMENT DISCRIMINATION. 1975. 9 base vols. (plus updates 3/yr.). $1090 for base vols.; updates $849. Matthew Bender & Co., Inc., 2 Park Ave., New York, NY 10016. TEL 212-448-2000. E-mail: international@bender.com; URL: http://www.bender.com.
Description: Discusses substantive and procedural law governing employment discrimination based on sex, age, race, religion, national origin and more.

658.3 331 US ISSN 0896-3452
EMPLOYMENT GUIDE. 1986. bi-w. $484. The Bureau of National Affairs, Inc., 1231 25th St., N.W., Washington, DC 20037. TEL 202-452-4200. FAX 202-822-8092. TELEX 285656 BNAI WSH. URL: http://www.bna.com/. (Subscr. to: 9435 Key West Ave., Rockville, MD 20850. TEL 800-372-1033) Ed. Bill L. Manville. index. (looseleaf format; back issues avail.) **Document type:** newsletter.
●Also available online. Vendor(s): Human Resources Information Network (EMPG, CDD, HDD).
Description: Easy-to-read, practical reference guide to a broad range of employment topics, designed for the small to medium-sized organization.

EMPLOYMENT IN THE MAINSTREAM. see *POLITICAL SCIENCE — Civil Rights*

EMPLOYMENT LAW UPDATE. see *LAW*

658.3 331 US
EMPLOYMENT MANAGEMENT TODAY. 1986. q. $40. Employment Management Association, 4101 Lake Boone Trail, Ste. 201, Raleigh, NC 27607. TEL 919-787-6010. FAX 919-787-4916. URL: http://www.cweb.com/ema/welcome.html. Ed. Carol Crane. R&P contact: Carol Crane. adv. contact: Tracy Williams. circ. 1,900. (back issues avail.)
Formerly (until 1996): E M A Journal.

THE EMPLOYMENT REPORT. see *BUSINESS AND ECONOMICS — Labor And Industrial Relations*

EMPLOYMENT STANDARDS HANDBOOK AND DIGEST SERVICE. see *LAW*

658 US
EMPLOYMENT TERMS AND CONDITIONS - EUROPE. a. $940. (Executive Compensation Service (ECS)) Wyatt Data Services, 218 Rte. 17, N., Roselle Park, NJ 07662-9832. TEL 201-843-1177. FAX 201-843-0101. **Document type:** trade publication.
Description: Guide to employment law and practice across Western Europe.

658 US
EMPLOYMENT TERMS AND CONDITIONS REPORT - ASIA. a. $1150. (Executive Compensation Service (ECS)) Wyatt Data Services, 218 Rte. 17, N., Roselle Park, NJ 07662-9832. TEL 201-843-1177. FAX 201-843-0101. **Document type:** trade publication.
Description: Provides information on terms and conditions of employment for 11 Asian nations.

658.3 UK ISSN 0968-4891
HD50.5
EMPOWERMENT IN ORGANIZATIONS. 1993. m. £499($759) (foreign Aus.$1029) (effective 1998). M C B University Press Ltd., 60-62 Toller Ln., Bradford, W. Yorks BD8 9BY, England. TEL 44-1274-777700. FAX 44-1274-785200. TELEX 51317-MCBUNI-G. URL: http://www.mcb.co.uk. (N. American subscr. to: M C B University Press Limited, Box 1943, Birmingham, AL 35201) Ed. Linda Logan. (reprint service avail. from SWZ) **Document type:** academic/scholarly publication.
—BLDSC (3737.863500). CCC.
Incorporates (1994-1996): Empowering Black Managers - The Southern African Experience (ISSN 0968-4921)

658.3 FR ISSN 0765-5762
LC1060
ENTREPRISES FORMATION. 1950. 8/yr. 440 F. (foreign 470 F.). Association Nationale pour la Formation Professionnelle des Adultes, 13 place du General de Gaulle, 93108 Montreuil, France. TEL 1-48-70-50-07. FAX 1-48-70-74-70. Ed. Didier Guibert. adv.; bk.rev.; bibl.; charts; illus.; stat. circ. 6,000.
Former titles: Notre Formation (ISSN 0029-4551); Objectif Formation.

658.3 FR ISSN 0071-2493
EUROPEAN ASSOCIATION FOR PERSONNEL MANAGEMENT. CONGRESS REPORTS. 1963. irreg., 1977, Madrid. European Association for Personnel Management, 29 av. Hoche, 75008 Paris, France.

EXECUTIVE COMPENSATION SURVEY REPORT. see *BUSINESS AND ECONOMICS — Labor And Industrial Relations*

658.3 US ISSN 8756-2308
HF5549.A2
EXECUTIVE EXCELLENCE; the newsletter of personal development, managerial effectiveness, and organizational productivity. 1983. m. $129 (foreign $149). Executive Excellence Publishing, 1344 E. 1120 S., Provo, UT 84606. TEL 801-375-4014. FAX 801-377-5960. E-mail: execexcl@itsnet.com; URL: http://www.eep.com. Ed. Kenneth M. Shelton. R&P contact: Noelle Ray. bk.rev. circ. 25,500. **Indexed:** ABI Inform. **Document type:** newsletter.
●Also available online. Vendor(s): UMI.
—BLDSC (3836.214100); SWETS; UMI.

EXECUTIVE GRAPEVINE, VOLUME 6: THE GRAPEVINE INDEX OF H R DIRECTORS, U K EDITION; recruitment library. see *BUSINESS AND ECONOMICS — Management*

EXECUTIVE PERQUISITES REPORT. see *BUSINESS AND ECONOMICS — Management*

F & W - FUEHREN UND WIRTSCHAFTEN IM KRANKENHAUS. see *HOSPITALS*

FAIR EMPLOYMENT COMPLIANCE; a confidential letter to management. see *BUSINESS AND ECONOMICS — Labor And Industrial Relations*

BUSINESS AND ECONOMICS — PERSONNEL MANAGEMENT

658.3 350 US ISSN 0163-7665
JK671
FEDERAL PERSONNEL GUIDE. 1979. a. $9.95. Uniformed Services Almanac, Inc., Box 4144, Falls Church, VA 22044. TEL 703-532-1631. FAX 703-532-1635. adv.: B&W page $3095; trim 9 1/2 x 7 1/4; adv. contact: Frank S. Joseph. circ. 60,000. Indexed: Pers.Lit. **Document type:** directory. —CCC.
Description: Provides a reference guide to federal employee pay, benefits, and organization.

658.3 US
FEDERAL QUALITY NEWS. bi-m. $13 (foreign $16.25). U.S. Office of Personnel Management, 1900 E St., N.W., Washington, DC 20415. TEL 202-606-2424. (Subscr. to: Superintendent of Documents, U.S. Government Printing Office, Box 371954, Pittsburgh, PA 15250-7954. TEL 202-512-1800. FAX 202-512-2250) (back issues avail.) **Document type:** government publication.

FICHES PRATIQUES DE LA FORMATION CONTINUE. MISE A JOUR. see EDUCATION — Adult Education

658.3 336 US
FINANCIAL INSTITUTIONS RETIREMENT FUND. ANNUAL REPORT. a. Financial Institutions Retirement Fund, Pentegra Group, 108 Corporate Park Dr., White Plains, NY 10604. TEL 914-694-1300. Ed. Gail E. Janensch. **Document type:** corporate report.

658 US
FINANCIAL PARTICIPATION - EUROPE. a. $545. (Executive Compensation Service (ECS)) Wyatt Data Services, 218 Rte. 17, N., Roselle Park, NJ 07662-9832. TEL 201-843-1177. FAX 201-843-0101. charts. **Document type:** trade publication.
Description: Provides survey data for 17 Western European countries regarding company practices on incentive programs that link awards to company performance.

658.3 US ISSN 0164-6397
HV8138
FIRE AND POLICE PERSONNEL REPORTER. 1975. m. $188 (effective Sep. 1997). Public Safety Personnel Research Institute, Inc., 5519 N. Cumberland Ave., Ste.1008, Chicago, IL 60656-1498. TEL 773-763-5259. FAX 773-763-3225. E-mail: aele@aol.com; URL: http://members.aol.com/fprptr. Ed. Wayne W. Schmidt. bk.rev.; index; circ. 1,300. (paid). **Document type:** newsletter.
Formerly: Fire Department Personnel Reporter.

FIRST DRAFT. see PUBLISHING AND BOOK TRADE

658.3 331 CN ISSN 0831-4535
KE3254.A13
FOCUS ON CANADIAN EMPLOYMENT AND EQUALITY RIGHTS. 1986. m. Can.$225. C C H Canadian Ltd., 6 Garamond Ct., North York, ON M3C 1Z5, Canada. TEL 416-441-2992; 800-268-4522. FAX 416-444-9011. **Document type:** trade publication.
Description: Reports on developments in the field including legislation and government programs and initiatives. Includes case notes and advice.

FORDYCE LETTER; commentary and information provided exclusively for those involved in the personnel, search, employment, recruiting and outplacement professions. see LAW — Corporate Law

658.3 SP ISSN 0213-2125
FORMACION Y EMPRESA. 1984. 4/yr. Aragon 204, 08011 Barcelona, Spain. TEL 323-12-08. FAX 323-73-17. TELEX 99398 EADA. Ed. Carlos Bascones. adv.; bk.rev. circ. 30,000.

FORMANDSBLADET. see BUILDING AND CONSTRUCTION

658 FR ISSN 0759-6340
HD5715.5.F8
FORMATION EMPLOI. 1983. q. 305 F. (Europe 325 F., elsewhere 350 F.) (effective 1997). (Centre d'Etudes et de Recherches sur les Qualifications) Documentation Francaise, 29-31 quai Voltaire, 75344 Paris Cedex 07, France. TEL 33-1-40157000. FAX 33-1-40157230. TELEX 215 666 DOCFRAN. (Subscr. to: 124 rue Henri Barbusse, 93308 Aubervilliers Cedex, France. TEL 33-1-48395600. FAX 33-1-48395601)

658.3 US ISSN 1061-7469
HD6983
GEOGRAPHIC REFERENCE REPORT (YEAR); annual report of costs, wages, salaries, and human resource statistics US and Canada. 1987. a. $349. E R I Economic Research Institute, 16770 N.E. 79th St., Ste. 104, Redmond, WA 98052. TEL 800-627-3697. FAX 800-753-4415. E-mail: eri_redmond@msn.com; URL: http://www.erieri.com. R&P contact: Briana Bennitt. **Document type:** academic/scholarly publication.
Former titles (until 1993): Geographic Reference (ISSN 1057-8498); (until 1990): Geographic Entry Level Salary Survey and Relocation Reference.

658.3 US
GETTING ALONG. 1990. bi-w. $68.90. Dartnell Corporation, 4660 N. Ravenswood Ave., Chicago, IL 60640. TEL 773-561-4000; 800-621-5463. FAX 773-561-3801. URL: http://www.dartnellcorp.com. Ed. David Dee. **Document type:** newsletter.
Description: Helps employees work with subordinates, superiors and co-workers as individuals to get things done effectively.

GEWERBEARCHIV; Zeitschrift fuer Gewerbe- und Wirtschaftsverwaltungsrecht. see LAW — Corporate Law

658.3 NE ISSN 0921-1896
GIDS VOOR PERSONEELSMANAGEMENT. 1958. 11/yr. fl.195 (effective 1996). Kluwer Bedrijfswetenschappen B.V. (Subsidiary of: Wolters Kluwer N.V.), Postbus 23, 7400 GA Deventer, Netherlands. TEL 31-5700-48999. FAX 31-5700-11504. (Subscr. to: Intermedia bv, Postbus 4, 2400 MA Alphen aan den Rijn, Netherlands. TEL 31-172-466321. FAX 31-172-435527) adv. circ. 8,500. **Document type:** trade publication.
—SWETS.
Formerly (until 1987): Gids voor Personeelsbeleid, Arbeidsvraagstukken, Sociale Verzekering (ISSN 0165-0289)

658.3 158.7 370.7 US ISSN 1059-6011
HM134   CODEN: GOSTDA
GROUP & ORGANIZATION MANAGEMENT; an international journal. 1976. q. $198 to institutions (effective Sep. 1996). Sage Publications, Inc., 2455 Teller Rd., Thousand Oaks, CA 91320. TEL 805-499-0721. FAX 805-499-0871. E-mail: libraries@sagepub.com; URL: http://www.sagepub.com. (Overseas subscr. to: Sage Publications Ltd., 6 Bonhill St., London EC2A 4PU, England; Sage Publications India Pvt. Ltd., Box 4215, New Delhi 110 048, India) Ed. Michael J. Kavanaugh. adv. contact: Margaret Travers. bk.rev.; index. circ. 1,300. (also avail. in microform from UMI; back issues avail.; reprint service avail. from UMI) **Indexed:** ABI Inform., ASCA, BPIA, Bus.Ind., C.I.J.E., CINAHL, Curr.Cont., Human Resour.Abstr., IMFL, Lang.& Lang.Behav.Abstr., Manage.Cont., Pers.Lit., Psychol.Abstr. (1976-), Psycscan, Sage Fam.Stud.Abstr., Sage Pub.Admin.Abstr., SSCI, Stud.Wom.Abstr., Tech.Educ.Abstr. **Document type:** academic/scholarly publication.
●Also available online. Vendor(s): Information Access Co.
—BLDSC (4220.173900); Genuine Article; SWETS; UMI; UnCover. **CCC.**
Formerly (until Mar. 1992): Group and Organization Studies (ISSN 0364-1082)
Description: Aims to bridge the gap between research and practice for psychologists, group facilitators, educators, and consultants involved in the broad field of human relations training.

GUIDE TO BACKGROUND INVESTIGATIONS. see CRIMINOLOGY AND LAW ENFORCEMENT — Security

658.3 US
GUIDE TO EMPLOYEE HANDBOOKS. a. $167.95 (overseas $244.35) (effective 1995). Warren, Gorham & Lamont, One Penn Plaza, New York, NY 10119. TEL 212-971-5000. FAX 800-971-5113. (Subscr. to: The Park Square Bldg., 31 St. James Ave., Boston, MA 02116-4112. TEL 800-950-1207) Ed. Robert J. Nobile. **Document type:** trade publication.
Description: Points out how to best update existing employee handbooks, covering key legal issues.

346 US
GUIDE TO TEXAS WORKERS' COMPENSATION REFORM. 1991. 2 base vols. (plus a. supplement). $225. Butterworth Legal Publishers (Subsidiary of: Reed Elsevier plc), 8 Industrial Way, Bldg. C, Salem, NH 03079. TEL 800-548-4001. FAX 603-898-9858. Ed.Bd. (looseleaf format)
Description: Analysis of the statutes producing recent changes in the workers' compensation and tort litigation system in Texas.

658.3 UK
GUIDES TO SUPPLIERS; series of guides to help personnel specialists in making purchasing choices. m. £126 (effective 1997). Incomes Data Services Ltd., 77 Bastwick St., London EC1V 3TT, England. TEL 44-171-250-3434. FAX 44-171-608-0949. **Document type:** trade publication.
Formerly: Personnel Products and Services (ISSN 1355-2961)
Description: Thoroughly guides managers in the purchasing of a particular product or service.

658.3 CC ISSN 1012-7887
H K STAFF; Hong Kong's human resources journal. 1988. 10/yr. HK.$1450 (foreign $200) (effective 1996). Asia Law & Practice Ltd., 2-F, 29 Hollywood Rd., Central, Hong Kong, People's Republic of China. TEL 544-9918. FAX 544-0040. (Dist. in US by: American Educational Systems, 173 W. 81st St., New York, NY 10024. TEL 800-717-2669. FAX 212-501-8926) **Document type:** trade publication.
Description: Covers employee benefits, contracts, employment law, migration, provident funds, salaries, tax, trade unions, training, and work permits.

658.3 US ISSN 1080-1847
H R BRIEFING. (Human Resources) 1972. s-m. $165.96. Bureau of Business Practice, 24 Rope Ferry Rd., Waterford, CT 06386. TEL 860-442-4365. FAX 860-437-3555. URL: http://www.bbpnews.com. Ed. Valeri Bolden-Barrett; Pub. Peter Garabedian. s-a.index. **Document type:** newsletter.
Former titles (until 1994): Personnel Manager's Letter (ISSN 0885-3037); Personnel Advisory Bulletin (ISSN 0164-5811)
Description: Covers a wide range of human resource topics, with emphasis on the human resource implications of current events and trends. Also includes interviews with HR pracititioners.

658 US ISSN 1072-0243
HF5549.2.U5   CODEN: HREREZ
H R EXECUTIVE REVIEW. q. $15 to members; non-members $60. Conference Board, Inc., 845 Third Ave., New York, NY 10022-6601. TEL 212-759-0900. FAX 212-980-7014.

658.3 US ISSN 1059-6038
HF5549.A2
H R FOCUS. 1919. m. $78.75 to non-members (foreign $113.75); members $70.88 (foreign $105.88). American Management Association, 1601 Broadway, New York, NY 10019. TEL 212-586-8100. E-mail: amapubs@aol.com. (Subscr. to: Box 57969, Boulder, CO 80322-7969) Ed. Bob Smith. adv.; bk.rev.; charts; illus.; index. circ 12,500. (also avail. in microform from UMI; reprint service avail. from UMI,SCH) **Indexed:** ABI Inform. (1971-), Acad.Ind., Account.Ind. (1974-), Anbar, ASEAN Manage.Abstr., B.P.I., BPIA, Comput.Lit.Ind., Cont.Pg.Manage., Curr.Cont., Educ.Admin.Abstr., Excerp.Med., Hosp.Lit.Ind., Key to Econ.Sci., Manage.Cont., Mgmt.& Market.Abstr., Oper.Res.Manage.Sci., Pers.Lit., Pers.Manage.Abstr. Psychol.Abstr., SSCI, Tr.& Indus.Ind., Work Rel.Abstr. **Document type:** trade publication.
●Also available online. Vendor(s): Information Access Co., UMI.
—BLDSC (4335.266800); Genuine Article; KR SourceOne; SWETS; UMI; UnCover. **CCC.**
Formerly (until 1991): Personnel (ISSN 0031-5702)
Description: Keeps human resources managers abreast of progressive personnel practices and current developments in the field.

H R I N REVIEW; the human resource information network newsletter. (Human Resource Information Network) see BUSINESS AND ECONOMICS — Computer Applications

658.3 NE ISSN 0923-1420
H R M SELECT. (Human Resource Management); het beste uit de internationale vakpers. 1989. 4/yr. fl.235 (effective 1996). Kluwer Bedrijfswetenschappen B.V. (Subsidiary of: Wolters Kluwer N.V.), Postbus 23, 7400 GA Deventer, Netherlands. TEL 31-5700-48999. FAX 31-5700-11504. (Subscr. to: Intermedia bv, Postbus 4, 2400 MA Alphen aan den Rijn, Netherlands. TEL 31-172-466321. FAX 31-172-435527) **Document type:** trade publication.
—SWETS.

658.3 346 US ISSN 1047-3149
HF5549.A2
H R MAGAZINE. (Human Resources) 1950. m. $60 to non-members. Society for Human Resource Management, 606 N. Washington St., Alexandria, VA 22314-1914. TEL 703-548-3440. FAX 703-836-0367. Ed. Ceel Pasternak; Pub. John T. Adams III. adv. contact: Gene Schuyler. bk.rev.; bibl.; charts; illus.; index. circ. 74,000. (also avail. in microform from UMI; microfiche; reprint service avail. from UMI) **Indexed:** ABI Inform., Account.& Data Proc.Abstr., Anbar, ASEAN Manage.Abstr., B.P.I., BPIA, Bus.Ind., C.I.J.E., Educ.Admin.Abstr., Manage.Cont., Mgmt.& Market.Abstr., P.A.I.S., Pers.Lit., Pers.Manage.Abstr., PROMT, Psychol.Abstr., Q.Abstr., Tr.& Dev.Alert, Tr.& Indus.Ind. **Document type:** trade publication.
●Also available online. Vendor(s): Human Resources Information Network, Information Access Co., UMI.
—BLDSC (4335.267450); KR SourceOne; SWETS; UMI; UnCover. **CCC.**
Former titles: Personnel Administrator (ISSN 0031-5729); (until 1954): Personnel News.
Description: Covers trends and legal issues of the human resource field.

658.3 US ISSN 1047-3157
H R NEWS. (Human Resources) 1990. m. Society for Human Resource Management, 606 N. Washington St., Alexandria, VA 22314-1914. TEL 703-548-3440. FAX 703-836-0367. **Document type:** trade publication.
—CCC.
Formerly (until 1989): Resource (Berea) (ISSN 0746-7850)

H R - P C; computer technology for human resource management. see BUSINESS AND ECONOMICS — Computer Applications

658.3 US
H R P S BEST PRACTICES SERIES. 1994. irreg. $32 to non-members; members $25. Human Resource Planning Society, 317 Madison Ave., Ste. 1509, New York, NY 10017. TEL 212-490-6387. FAX 212-682-6851. E-mail: info@hrps.org; URL: http://www.hrps.org.
Description: Provides a review and assessment of concepts, approaches, methods, and applications in subject areas of interest and value to HR executives and planners.

658.3 US
H R P S CORPORATE SPONSOR FORUM PROCEEDINGS. a. $32 to non-members; members $25. Human Resource Planning Society, 317 Madison Ave., Ste. 1509, New York, NY 10017. TEL 212-490-6387. FAX 212-682-6851. E-mail: info@hrps.org; URL: http://www.hrps.org. **Document type:** proceedings.

658.3 US
H R P S RESEARCH SYMPOSIUM PROCEEDINGS. biennial. $64 to non-members; members $50. Human Resource Planning Society, 317 Madison Ave., Ste. 1509, New York, NY 10017. TEL 212-490-6387. FAX 212-682-6851. E-mail: info@hrps.org; URL: http://www.hrps.org. **Document type:** proceedings.

658 US ISSN 0733-0332
R PLANNING NEWSLETTER. (Human Resources) (Former name of issuing body: Wargo & Company, Inc.) 1976. 10/yr. $180 (effective 1995). Alexander Consulting Group, 100 E. Wisconsin Ave., Ste. 1750, Milwaukee, WI 53202-4107. TEL 414-347-7750. FAX 414-347-7740. Ed. James W. Peters; Pub. James W. Peters. R&P contact: James W. Peters. TEL 414-347-7733. bk.rev.; bibl.; circ. 8,000 (paid). (back issues avail.) **Document type:** newsletter.
—CCC.
Formerly (until 1981): Manpower Planning (ISSN 0364-7358)
Description: Investigates business issues through strategic human resource management.

658.3 331 US ISSN 0741-6997
H R REPORTER. (Human Resources) (Includes Quarterly Specials) 1984. m. $325 (foreign $347) (effective 1997). L R P Publications, 747 Dresher Rd., Box 980, Horsham, PA 19044-0980. TEL 215-784-0941; 800-341-7874. FAX 215-784-9639. URL: http://www.lrp.com. Ed. Marilyn Schaefer. bk.rev.; charts; stat.; index. (looseleaf format; back issues avail.) **Document type:** newsletter.
—CCC.
Description: Reports on issues in human relations, corporate policies and programs, and new concepts, theories, and trends.

658.3 346.066 US
H R SERIES: COMPENSATION & BENEFITS. (Human Resources) 1990. 3 base vols. (plus m. update and newsletter). $473. Warren, Gorham & Lamont, One Penn Plaza, New York, NY 10119-4098. TEL 212-971-5000. FAX 212-971-5113. (Subscr. to: The Park Square Bldg., 31 St. James Ave., Boston, MA 02116-4112. TEL 800-950-1207) (looseleaf format)
Formerly: Compensation Strategy and Management (ISSN 1057-4859)
Description: Covers pay plan design, job evaluation, all types of benefits, executive compensation, and complex legal requirements.

658.3 US
H R SERIES: POLICIES AND PRACTICES. base vol. (plus fortn. updates). $473 (effective 1995). Warren, Gorham & Lamont, One Penn Plaza, New York, NY 10119. TEL 212-971-5000. FAX 212-971-5113. (Subscr. to: The Park Square Bldg., 31 St. James Ave., Boston, MA 02116-4112. TEL 800-950-1207) (looseleaf format)
Formerly: Human Resources Policies and Practices.
Description: Provides clear understanding of legal issues and contains key government required forms.

HAZARDS IN THE OFFICE. see PUBLIC HEALTH AND SAFETY

THE HEALTH & SAFETY MANAGER'S YEARBOOK. see OCCUPATIONAL HEALTH AND SAFETY

HEALTH AND WELFARE BENEFIT PLANS. see LAW

658.3 CN ISSN 0829-5700
HIRING & FIRING. French edition: Embaucher et Congedier (ISSN 1188-3863) 1985. 12/yr. Can.$135. Carswell, One Corporate Plaza, 2075 Kennedy Rd., Scarborough, ON M1T 3V4, Canada. TEL 416-609-8000. FAX 416-298-5094.
Formerly (until 1990): Hiring and Firing Newsletter (ISSN 1182-9338)
Description: Provides the information and knowledge needed to successfully perform the complex task of hiring and firing personnel.

HOOVER'S DIRECTORY OF HUMAN RESOURCES EXECUTIVES. see BUSINESS AND ECONOMICS — Trade And Industrial Directories

HOSPITAL AND HEALTH CARE REPORT. see HOSPITALS

658.3 US ISSN 1044-8004
HF5549.15 CODEN: HRDQER
HUMAN RESOURCE DEVELOPMENT QUARTERLY. 1990-199? q. $55 to individuals; institutions $106; sample issue free to librarians (effective 1997); newsstand price: $27. (American Society for Training and Development) Jossey-Bass Inc., Publishers, 350 Sansome St., 5th Fl., San Francisco, CA 94104. TEL 800-956-7734. FAX 800-605-2665. URL: http://www.josseybass.com. (Co-sponsor: Academy of Human Resource Development) Ed. Ronald L. Jacobs. bk.rev.; circ. 1,000. circ. 7,200 (paid). (also avail. in microfiche from UMI; back issues avail.) **Indexed:** Bus.Educ.Ind., C.I.J.E., Q.Abstr., Sociol.Abstr., Tr.& Dev.Alert. **Document type:** academic/scholarly publication.
—BLDSC (4336.432800); SWETS; UMI; UnCover.
Description: Draws together the work of scholars and practitioners in a range of related areas, including: training, management, industrial psychology, organizational behavior and adult education. Presents a comprehensive resource for information on the latest advances in human resource development theory and research.
Refereed Serial

658.3 US ISSN 1040-0443
HUMAN RESOURCE EXECUTIVE. 1987. m. $59.95. L R P Publications, Inc., 747 Dresher Rd., Ste. 500, Box 980, Horsham, PA 19044. TEL 215-784-0860. FAX 215-784-0870. Ed. David Shadovitz. adv. contact: Bill Corsini. circ. 45,117. **Indexed:** Q.Abstr., Tr.& Dev.Alert. **Document type:** trade publication.
●Also available online. Vendor(s): Human Resources Information Network.
—CCC.

658.3 US ISSN 0090-4848
HF5549.A2 CODEN: HRMAFP
HUMAN RESOURCE MANAGEMENT. 1962. q. $279 (foreign $341) (effective 1998). John Wiley & Sons, Inc., Journals, 605 Third Ave., New York, NY 10158. TEL 212-850-6645. FAX 212-850-6021. TELEX 12-7063. E-mail: subinfo@jwiley.com; URL: http://www.wiley.co.uk. Ed. D.O. Ulrich. adv.: B&W page £640, color page £1515; trim 279 x 210. (also avail. in microform from UMI; back issues avail.; reprint service avail. from UMI) **Indexed:** ABI Inform., Account.& Data Proc.Abstr., ASCA, ASEAN Manage.Abstr., B.P.I., BPIA, Bus.Ind., Cont.Pg.Manage., Curr.Cont., Educ.Admin.Abstr., Fam.Ind., Ind.S.A.Per., Manage.Cont., Pers.Lit., PSI, SCIMP, SSCI, Tr.& Dev.Alert, Tr.& Indus.Ind. **Document type:** academic/scholarly publication.
—BLDSC (4336.433000); CISTI; Genuine Article; KR SourceOne; SWETS; UMI; UnCover. **CCC.**
Description: Discusses new theories, techniques, case studies, models and research trends of significance to practicing managers.

658.3 UK ISSN 0967-0734
HF5549.A2
HUMAN RESOURCE MANAGEMENT INTERNATIONAL DIGEST. 1993. bi-m. £769($1269) (foreign Aus.$1599) (effective 1998). M C B University Press Ltd., 60-62 Toller Ln., Bradford, W. Yorks BD8 9BY, England. TEL 44-1274-777700. FAX 44-1274-785200. TELEX 51317-MCBUNI-G. URL: http://www.mcb.co.uk. (N. American subscr. to: M C B University Press Limited, Box 1943, Birmingham, AL 35201) Ed. Eric Sandelands. **Document type:** academic/scholarly publication.
—CCC.

658.3 UK ISSN 0954-5395
HUMAN RESOURCE MANAGEMENT JOURNAL. 1989? q. £130 foreign £140) (effective 1997). (Institute of Personnel Development) Eclipse Group Ltd., Industrial Relations Services, 18-20 Highbury Pl., London N5 1BR, England. TEL 44-171-354-5858. FAX 44-171-226-8618. (Co-publisher: Personnel Publications Ltd.) Ed.Bd. **Document type:** academic/scholarly publication, trade publication.
—BLDSC (4336.434050); SWETS. **CCC.**
Description: Covers topics in human resources management for practitioners and academics.

658.3 331.1 US
HUMAN RESOURCE MANAGEMENT NEWS; the weekly newsletter for the human resource management field. 1951. w. $240. Remy Publishing Co., 350 W. Hubbard St., No. 440, Chicago, IL 60610-4011. TEL 312-464-0300. Ed. John Hickey. index. **Document type:** newsletter.
Formerly: Industrial Relations News (ISSN 0019-8714)

658.3 US ISSN 1053-4822
HF5549.2.U5 CODEN: HRMRE7
HUMAN RESOURCE MANAGEMENT REVIEW. 1991. q. $85 to individuals (foreign $105); institutions $205 (foreign $225) (effective 1998). J A I Press Inc., 55 Old Post Rd., No. 2, Box 1678, Greenwich, CT 06830-1678. TEL 203-661-7602. FAX 203-661-0792. E-mail: jai@jaipress.com. (Addr. in Europe: J A I Press Ltd., 38 Tavistock St., Covent Garden, London WC2E 7PB, England. TEL 44-171-379-8834. FAX 44-171-379-8835) Eds. H. John Bernardin, Jeffrey S. Kane. (also avail. in microform from UMI; back issues avail.) **Indexed:** ASCA, Curr.Cont., Sociol.Abstr. **Document type:** trade publication.
—BLDSC (4336.434100); Genuine Article; SWETS; UnCover. **CCC.**
Description: Publishes conceptual and theoretical articles pertaining to human resource management and allied fields.

BUSINESS AND ECONOMICS — PERSONNEL MANAGEMENT

658.3   UK   ISSN 0957-7130
THE HUMAN RESOURCE MANAGEMENT YEARBOOK. 1988. a. £35.00. A P Information Services, Roman House, 296 Golders Green Rd., London NW11 9PZ, England. TEL 44-181-455-4550. FAX 44-181-455-6381. Eds. Michael Armstrong, Charlotte Evans. adv.: B&W page £525, color page £1,025; trim 210 x 148. bibl. circ. 700. (also avail. in diskette format) **Document type:** trade publication, directory, bibliography.
—BLDSC (4336.434200).
   Former titles: Personnel Yearbook; Personnel and Training Databook; Personnel and Training Management Yearbook (ISSN 0306-6673)
   Description: Includes a directory of consultancy service providers, a directory of official and public bodies in HRD, a section on legislative framework for employment and unions.

658.3   UK   ISSN 0957-6142
HUMAN RESOURCE MANAGER. 1989. 2/yr. free. Thorpe Park, Peterborough, Cambs. PE3 6JY, England. TEL 44-1733-555777. FAX 44-1733-312347. Ed. Diana Probert. R&P contact: Liz Phillips. bk.rev.; circ. 6,000 (controlled). **Document type:** trade publication.
   Formed by the merger of (1981-1988): Payroll Manager (ISSN 0262-981X); Personnel Matters.
   Description: Covers topical issues concerning payroll, personnel and pensions administration in the U.K., as well as related issues.

658.3   US   ISSN 0199-8986
HF5549.5.M3
HUMAN RESOURCE PLANNING. 1978. q. $90 (effective 1997). Human Resource Planning Society, 317 Madison Ave., Ste. 1509, New York, NY 10017. TEL 212-490-6387. FAX 212-682-6851. E-mail: info@hrps.org; URL: http://www.hrps.org. Ed. Beverly Bachtle Pinzon. adv. contact: Beverly Bachtle Pinzon. circ. 3,000. (also avail. in microfilm; back issues avail.) Indexed: ABI Inform., B.P.I., BPIA, Cont.Pg.Manage., Pers.Lit., Tr.& Indus.Ind. **Document type:** trade publication, academic/scholarly publication.
●Also available online. Vendor(s): Information Access Co., UMI.
—BLDSC (4336.434500); KR SourceOne; SWETS; UMI; UnCover.
   Description: Contains current theory, research and practice in strategic human resource management. Focuses on the HR practices that contribute to the achievement of organizational effectiveness.

658.3   US
HUMAN RESOURCE PROFESSIONAL. 1988. q. $99. Faulkner & Gray, Inc. (New York), 11 Penn Plaza, 17th Fl., New York, NY 10001. TEL 212-967-7000. FAX 212-967-7155. Ed. Christine Varholy. adv.: B&W page $1275, color page $2050; trim 8 1/8 x 10 7/8. circ. 10,853 (paid); 1,147 (controlled).
   Description: Tracks down, analyzes and reports on emerging human resources trends and highlights successful programs, policies and ideas.

658.3   UK   ISSN 0965-299X
HUMAN RESOURCES BRIEFING. 1992. m. Croner Publications Ltd. (Subsidiary of: Wolters Kluwer N.V.), Croner House, 100 London Rd., Kingston-upon-Thames, Surrey KT2 6SR, England. TEL 44-181-547-3333. FAX 44-181-547-2637. Ed. Paul Forrest. adv. contact: Paul Forrest. bk.rev. **Document type:** trade publication.

HUMAN RESOURCES JOURNAL. see BUSINESS AND ECONOMICS — Management

658.3   AT
HUMAN RESOURCES MANAGEMENT. (In 2 vols.) 1977. 10/yr. C C H Australia Ltd., P.O. Box 230, North Ryde, N.S.W. 2113, Australia. TEL 61-1-300300224. FAX 61-1-300306224. charts. (looseleaf format)
   Former titles: Human Resources; Australian Personnel Management.
   Description: Provides practical and theoretical information on a range of HR topics such as establishing staffing needs; recruitment and induction; training and development; equal employment opportunity; assessment and promotion; salaries and wages; superannuation; employee benefits; occupational health and safety; hours of work; productivity; communication; and termination and redundancy.

HUMAN RESOURCES MANAGEMENT. see BUSINESS AND ECONOMICS — Labor And Industrial Relations

658.3 331   US   ISSN 0745-063X
HUMAN RESOURCES MANAGEMENT - COMPENSATION. (Part of: Human Resources Management) 1981. 2 base vols. (plus m. updates). $370. C C H Incorporated, 2700 Lake Cook Rd., Riverwoods, IL 60015. TEL 847-267-7000; 800-835-5224. FAX 800-224-8299. (looseleaf format)
●Also available on CD-ROM.
   Description: Provides access to a wide range of compensation problems faced by personnel professionals. Includes the full text of federal wage laws and key regulations.

658.3 331   US
HUMAN RESOURCES MANAGEMENT - EMPLOYEE RELATIONS. (Part of: Human Resources Management) 1981. 2 base vols. (plus m. updates). $417. C C H Incorporated, 4025 W. Peterson Ave., Riverwoods, IL 60015. TEL 847-267-7000; 800-835-5224. FAX 800-224-8299. (looseleaf format)
●Also available on CD-ROM.
   Formerly: Human Resources Management - Employment Relations (ISSN 0745-2179)

658.3 323.4   US   ISSN 0745-2187
HUMAN RESOURCES MANAGEMENT - EQUAL EMPLOYMENT OPPORTUNITY. (Part of: Human Resources Management) 2 base vols. (plus m. updates). $417. C C H Incorporated, 2700 Lake Cook Rd., Riverwoods, IL 60015. TEL 847-267-7000; 800-835-5224. FAX 847-224-8299. (looseleaf format)
●Also available on CD-ROM.
   Description: Shows what companies and government contractors can do, can't do, and should do to comply with federal and state fair employment, affirmative action and equal pay rules.

HUMAN RESOURCES MANAGEMENT - O S H A COMPLIANCE. see OCCUPATIONAL HEALTH AND SAFETY

658.3   US   ISSN 0745-0621
HUMAN RESOURCES MANAGEMENT - PERSONNEL PRACTICES - COMMUNICATIONS. (Part of: Human Resources Management) 2 base vol. (plus m. updates). $417. C C H Incorporated, 2700 Lake Cook Rd., Riverwoods, IL 60015. TEL 847-267-7000; 800-835-5224. FAX 800-224-8299. (looseleaf format)
●Also available on CD-ROM.
   Description: Tells how to develop tested personnel policies to comply with the laws and get the workers and work you need.

658.3   CN   ISSN 0847-9453
HUMAN RESOURCES PROFESSIONAL; the magazine for Canadian human resources professionals. (Supplement avail.: HRPAO Sourcebook) 1985. 6/yr. Can.$45($50) (Europe $70) (effective 1996). (Human Resources Professionals Association of Ontario) Naylor Communications, 920 Yonge St., 6th Fl., Toronto, ON M4W 3C7, Canada. TEL 416-449-9321. FAX 416-449-9321. Ed. Katherine Came; Pub. Peter Waite. R&P contact: Katherine Came. adv.: B&W page Can.$1360, color page Can.$2559; trim 8 1/4 x 10 1/2; adv. contact: Allan Wheeler. bk.rev. circ. 8,105. Indexed: Can.B.P.I. **Document type:** trade publication.
—CCC.
   Formerly (until 1989): H R Professional (ISSN 0833-8892)
   Description: Provides timely and forthright information on human resources practices, including benefits and compensations, executive orientation, training, development and recruitment.

658.3   US   ISSN 1040-5232
HF5549.A2   CODEN: HRPREM
HUMAN RESOURCES PROFESSIONAL. 1988. q. $99. Faulkner & Gray, Inc. (New York), 11 Penn Plaza, 17th Fl., New York, NY 10001. TEL 212-967-7000. FAX 212-967-7155. Ed. Christine Varholy. Indexed: Q.Abstr., Tr.& Dev.Alert.
—BLDSC (4336.435700); SWETS; UMI. CCC.
   Incorporates (1989-1990): Journal of Staffing and Recruitment.
   Description: Helps the reader find and retain the right people in any labor market. Shows effective programs and policies.

658.3   AT
HUMAN RESOURCES REPORT. fortn. Aus.$355 (effective 1996). Newsletter Information Services, P.O. Box 693, Manly, N.S.W. 2095, Australia. TEL 61-2-9777500. FAX 61-2-9773310. E-mail: hww@hww.com.au; URL: http://www.hww.com.au. Ed. Peter Schwab. **Document type:** newsletter.
   Description: Provides analysis of trends in employment and human resource management.

HUMAN SIDE. see BUSINESS AND ECONOMICS — Labor And Industrial Relations

HUMANISME ET ENTREPRISE; revue informant des problemes humains, sociaux et economiques dans l'entreprise. see BUSINESS AND ECONOMICS — Labor And Industrial Relations

658.3 331   US   ISSN 1073-4627
HD38.25.U6
HUNT - SCANLON'S SELECT GUIDE TO HUMAN RESOURCE EXECUTIVES. 1992. a. $234.95 (effective 1997). Hunt - Scanlon Publishing Co., Inc., 1 East Putnam Ave., Greenwich, CT 06830. **Document type:** directory.
   Formerly (until 1994): Hunt - Scanlon's Directory of Human Resource Executives (ISSN 1067-4462)

658.3   UK   ISSN 1353-1573
I D S PENSIONS SERVICE; guidance through the law and company practice. a. vol. (plus news bulletin 10/yr.). £132 (effective 1997) (includes Pensions Manual). Incomes Data Services Ltd., 77 Bastwick St., London EC1V 3TT, England. TEL 44-171-250-3434. FAX 44-171-608-0949. **Document type:** trade publication, bulletin.
   Description: Covers the legal aspects of employee retirement-benefit packages.

658.3   US   ISSN 1089-991X
HF5549.A2
I H R I M - LINK. bi-m. $40. International Association for Human Resource Information Management, 14643 Dallas Parkway, No. 525, Dallas, TX 75240. TEL 972-661-3727. FAX 972-386-8180. E-mail: moreinfo@ihrim.org; URL: http://www.ihrim.org. R&P contact: Kevin Miles. circ. 6,000 (paid).
   Formerly: Association of Human Resource Systems Professionals. Review (ISSN 1075-2986)
   Refereed Serial

658.3   US   ISSN 1068-4239
I O M A'S REPORT ON COMPENSATION & BENEFITS FOR LAW OFFICES. Abbreviated title: CBLO. 1990. m. $295 (outside N. America $273). Institute of Management & Administration, Inc., 29 W. 35th St., 5th Fl., New York, NY 10001-2299. TEL 212-244-0360. FAX 212-564-0465. URL: http://www.ioma.com. Ed. Lisa Isom; Pub. Lee Rath. R&P contact: Sofie Kourkoutakis. index. (looseleaf format; back issues avail.) **Document type:** newsletter
—CCC.
   Former titles: I O M A's Report on Controlling Benefits Costs for Law, Design, C P A and Other Professional Services Firms (ISSN 1062-7936) & Professional Service Firms Report on Controlling Benefits and Deferred Compensation (ISSN 1053-5349)
   Description: Provide actionable information reader can use to manage their firms compensation and benefits program.

658.3   US   ISSN 1059-2741
I O M A'S REPORT ON MANAGING 401K PLANS. 1992. m. $257.95 (outside N. America $281.95). Institute of Management & Administration, Inc., 29 W. 35th St., 5th Fl., New York, NY 10001-2299. TEL 212-244-0360. FAX 212-564-0465. URL: http://www.ioma.com. Ed. Rebecca Morrow; Pub. Perry Patterson. R&P contact: Sofie Kourkoutakis. (looseleaf format) **Document type:** newsletter.
—CCC.
   Description: Covers how-to techniques for getting the maximum benefit from 401(k) plans while keeping costs to a minimum; includes surveys, trends, new products and service legislation.

BUSINESS AND ECONOMICS — PERSONNEL MANAGEMENT

658.3   US   ISSN 1056-7984
I O M A'S REPORT ON REDUCING BENEFITS COSTS. 1991. m. $249 (outside N. America $273). Institute of Management & Administration, Inc., 29 W. 35th St., 5th Fl., New York, NY 10001-2299. TEL 212-244-0360. FAX 212-564-0465. URL: http://www.ioma.com. Ed. Rebecca Morrow; Pub. Perry Patterson. R&P contact: Sofie Kourkoutakis. index. (looseleaf format; back issues avail.) **Document type:** newsletter.
—CCC.
    Description: Cost reduction strategies for HR, benefits managers in corporate environments.

658.3   US   ISSN 1067-4551
I O M A'S REPORT ON SALARY SURVEYS. 1993. m. $295 (outside N. America $273). Institute of Management & Administration, Inc., 29 W. 35th St., 5th Fl., New York, NY 10001-2299. TEL 212-244-0360. FAX 212-564-0465. URL: http://www.ioma.com. Ed. Laime Vaitkus; Pub. Perry Patterson. R&P contact: Sofie Kourkoutakis. index. (looseleaf format) **Document type:** newsletter.
—CCC.
    Description: Survey data and guidance on setting and managing compensation.

658.3   DK   ISSN 0109-2987
I P INFORMATION. bi-m. Dansk Institut for Personaleraadgivning, Hauser Plads 20, 1127 Copenhagen K, Denmark. Ed. Oluf Aagaard. adv. circ. 1,000.

658.3   US
I P M A NEWS. 1935. m. International Personnel Management Association, 1617 Duke St., Alexandria, VA 22314. TEL 703-549-7100. FAX 703-684-0948. Ed. Karen Smith. adv. contact: Karen Smith. illus. circ. 6,000. (tabloid format) **Document type:** newsletter.
—CCC.
    Formerly: International Personnel Management Association. Personnel News (ISSN 0031-5788)
    Description: News articles on national developments in the public personnel field.

658.3   US
I T A A COMPENSATION AND NON-CASH BENEFITS SURVEYS. a. price varies. Information Technology Association of America, 1616 N. Fort Myer Dr., Ste. 1300, Arlington, VA 22209-9998. TEL 703-284-5327. FAX 703-525-2279. (Subscr. to: c/o William M. Mercer, The National Survey Group, 1417 Lake Cook Rd., Deerfield, IL 60015. TEL 800-333-3070)

658.3   UK   ISSN 0954-7940
I T TRAINING. (Information Technology) 6/yr. £30 (overseas £50). 51 High St., Ruislip, Middx. HA4 7BG, England. TEL 0895-622112. FAX 0895-621582. Ed. Colin Steed. adv. contact: Sam Stevens. tr.lit. circ. 10,000. **Indexed:** Br.Educ.Ind. **Document type:** trade publication.
—BLDSC (4587.680000).
    Description: Discusses challenges and problems trainers in the computer profession are likely to encounter.
    Refereed Serial

IDEAS AND SOLUTIONS; magazine for businesses, products and services. see BUSINESS AND ECONOMICS — Production Of Goods And Services

IMPACT; labour law and management. see BUSINESS AND ECONOMICS — Labor And Industrial Relations

658.3   UK
IN CHARGE; a comprehensive approach to supervisory management. 1993. irreg. $29.95. Blackwell Publishers Ltd., 108 Cowley Rd., Oxford OX4 1JF, England. TEL 44-1865-791100. FAX 44-1865-791347. E-mail: jnlinfo@ blackwellpublishers.co.uk; URL: http://www. blackwellpublishers.co.uk. Ed.Bd. **Document type:** trade publication, monographic series.
    Description: Provides supervisors and frontline managers with the necessary skills to successfully fulfill the competencies outlined in the Management Charter Institute Supervisory Management Standards.

IN DEPTH (NEW YORK); report to management. see BUSINESS AND ECONOMICS — Labor And Industrial Relations

658.3   SZ
INDEX. m. Mapag Marketing Pool AG, Redingstr. 20, Postfach, CH-4028 Basel, Switzerland. TEL 061-3128888. FAX 061-3128884. Ed. Heinz Werner. adv.: B&W page 3400 SFr., color page 4900 SFr.; trim 184 x 250; adv. contact: Ruth Nebiker. circ. 10,500. **Document type:** trade publication.

658.3   II   ISSN 0970-3330
INDIAN JOURNAL OF TRAINING & DEVELOPMENT. (Text in English) 1971. q. Rs.150($30) Indian Society for Training & Development, B-41, Institutional Area, Behind Qutab Hotel, New Delhi 110 016, India. TEL 91-11-6867710. FAX 91-11-6867607. Ed. Krishan C. Sethi; Pub. K.N. Baqaya. adv. contact: K.N. Baqaya. bk.rev./; circ. 3,500 (paid). **Indexed:** C.R.I.Abstr., C.R.I.Curr.Cont., Mgmt.& Market.Abstr, Pub.Admin.Abstr. **Document type:** academic/scholarly publication.
    Former titles (until 1977): Training and Development (ISSN 0970-3322); (until 1976): I S T D Review (ISSN 0377-029X)
    Description: Leading professional journal devoted to the cause of human resources.
    Refereed Serial

658.5   UK   ISSN 0019-7858
HF5549.5.T7   CODEN: ILCTAU
INDUSTRIAL AND COMMERCIAL TRAINING; management of human resources. 1969. 7/yr. £2999($4629) (foreign Aus.$5849) (effective 1998). M C B University Press Ltd., 60-62 Toller Ln., Bradford, W. Yorks BD8 9BY, England. TEL 44-1274-777700. FAX 44-1274-785200. TELEX 51317-MCBUNI-G. URL: http://www.mcb.co.uk. Ed. Bryan Smith. bk.rev./; film rev.; charts; illus. (also avail. in microform from UMI; back issues avail.; reprint service avail. from SWZ,UMI) **Indexed:** ABI Inform., Account.& Data Proc.Abstr., Anbar, BPIA, Br.Educ.Ind., Bus.Ind., C.I.S. Abstr., Cont.Pg.Educ., Educ.Tech.Abstr., High.Educ.Curr.Aware.Bull., INSPEC, Mgmt.& Market.Abstr., Res.High.Educ.Abstr., SOMA, Tech.Educ.Abstr., Tr.& Dev.Alert, Work Rel.Abstr. **Document type:** academic/scholarly publication.
● Also available on CD-ROM.
—BLDSC (4444.970000); AskIEEE; KR SourceOne; SWETS; UMI. **CCC**.
    Description: Covers the role of today's trainer, computer-based training, new methods for learning and training, interactive video, continuing management education, recruitment, redundancy and retirement, applications of new technology and more.

INDUSTRIAL RELATIONS AND MANAGEMENT LETTER. see BUSINESS AND ECONOMICS — Labor And Industrial Relations

658   US
INDUSTRY REPORT ON PROFESSIONAL AND SCIENTIFIC PERSONNEL COMPENSATION. (Supplement to: Professional and Scientific Personnel Report - Geographic Edition) a. $690. (Executive Compensation Service (ECS)) Wyatt Data Services, 218 Rte. 17, N., Roselle Park, NJ 07662-9832. TEL 201-843-1177. FAX 201-843-0101. charts. **Document type:** trade publication.
    Description: Industry-by-industry examination of current professional employee compensation rates and policies.

INDUSTRY REPORT ON SUPERVISORY MANAGEMENT COMPENSATION. see BUSINESS AND ECONOMICS — Management

658   US   ISSN 1063-0058
TA158
INDUSTRY REPORT ON TECHNICIAN AND SKILLED TRADES PERSONNEL COMPENSATION. (Supplement to: Technician and Skilled Trades Personnel Report - Geographic Edition) 1992. a. $490. (Executive Compensation Service (ECS)) Wyatt Data Services, 218 Rte. 17, N., Roselle Park, NJ 07662-9832. TEL 201-843-1177. FAX 201-843-0101. charts. **Document type:** trade publication.
    Description: Technician and skilled trades personnel pay data reviewed from an industry-by-industry point of view.

INFO-LINE. see EDUCATION — Adult Education

658.3 336   IT
INFORMATORE PIROLA. 1964. w. (44/yr.). L.310000($195) (effective 1993). Pirola Editore S.p.A., Via Parabiago 19, 20151 Milan, Italy. TEL 2-30-221. FAX 2-380-112-05. Dir. Raffaele Rizzardi. bk.rev. circ. 14,500.

658.3   UK
INSIGHT (LONDON, 1984); journal of technical and vocational education initiative. 1984. 4/yr. free. Employment Department, Information Branch, Rm. E801, Moorfoot, Sheffield S1 4PQ, England. circ. 55,000.

658.3   FR
INTERESSEMENT DU PERSONNEL A L'ENTREPRISE; interessement, participation du personnel, actionnariat des salaries. a. 290 F. (effective 1993). Lamy S.A., 187-189 quai de Valmy, 75490 Paris Cedex 10, France. TEL 33-1-44721343. FAX 33-1-44721395.
    Description: Presents fiscal problems faced by corporate personnel.

658.3 011   US
INTERNATIONAL ASSOCIATION FOR HUMAN RESOURCE INFORMATION MANAGEMENT. CONFERENCE HIGHLIGHTS. a. International Association for Human Resource Information Management, 14643 Dallas Parkway, No. 525, Dallas, TX 75240. TEL 972-661-3727. FAX 972-386-8180. E-mail: moreinfo@ihrim.org; URL: http://www.ihrim.org. R&P contact: Kevin Miles.
    Formerly: Association of Human Resource Systems Professionals. Conference Highlights.
    Refereed Serial

658.3   UK   ISSN 0958-5192
HD4904.7   CODEN: IHMGEH
INTERNATIONAL JOURNAL OF HUMAN RESOURCES MANAGEMENT. 1990. bi-m. £50 (foreign $85) to individuals; institutions £165 (foreign $275); print & online eds. combined £200 (foreign $330) (effective 1998). Thomson Professional (Subsidiary of: International Thomson Publishing Group), 2-6 Boundary Row, London SE1 8HN, England. TEL 44-171-865-0066. FAX 44-171-522-9621. E-mail: journal@rapidcom.co.uk; URL: http://hrm. thomsonprofessional.com. (Subscr. to: ITPS Ltd., Cheriton House, Andover, Hants SP10 5BE, England. TEL 44-1264-342919. FAX 44-1264-342807) Ed. Michael Poole. adv. contact: Gemma Heiser. (back issues avail.) **Indexed:** Mgmt.& Market.Abstr. **Document type:** trade publication.
● Also available online.
—BLDSC (4542.288500); SWETS. **CCC**.
    Description: Provides a forum for human resource management scholars and professionals.
    Refereed Serial

658.3   UK   ISSN 0965-075X
HF5549.5.S38
INTERNATIONAL JOURNAL OF SELECTION AND ASSESSMENT. 1993. q. £125($173) (foreign £125) (effective 1997). Blackwell Publishers Ltd., 108 Cowley Rd., Oxford OX4 1JF, England. TEL 44-1865-791100. FAX 44-1865-791347. E-mail: jnlinfo@blackwellpublishers.co.uk; URL: http://www/blackwellpublishers.co.uk. Ed. Neil Anderson. (also avail. in microform from UMI) **Indexed:** ASCA, Curr.Cont. **Document type:** academic/scholarly publication.
—BLDSC (4542.544640); Genuine Article; UMI. **CCC**.
    Refereed Serial

658.3   UK   ISSN 1360-3736
HF5549.5.T7
INTERNATIONAL JOURNAL OF TRAINING & DEVELOPMENT. q. £125($150) (foreign £125) (effective 1997). Blackwell Publishers Ltd., 108 Cowley Rd., Oxford OX4 1JF, England. TEL 44-1865-791100. FAX 44-1865-791347. E-mail: jnlinfo@blackwellpublishers.co.uk; URL: http://www/blackwellpublishers.co.uk. **Document type:** academic/scholarly publication.
—CCC.
    Refereed Serial

INTERNATIONAL PRESS CUTTING SERVICE: LABOUR WELFARE - INDUSTRIAL LEGISLATION AND PERSONNEL MANAGEMENT. see BUSINESS AND ECONOMICS — Labor And Industrial Relations

BUSINESS AND ECONOMICS — PERSONNEL MANAGEMENT

658.3
HD69.C6 US ISSN 0749-2685
INTERNATIONAL REGISTRY OF ORGANIZATION DEVELOPMENT PROFESSIONALS AND ORGANIZATION DEVELOPMENT HANDBOOK. 1973. a. $25. Organization Development Institute (Chesterland), 11234 Walnut Ridge Rd., Chesterland, OH 44026-1299. TEL 216-461-4333. FAX 216-729-9319. E-mail: donwcole@aol.com; URL: http://members.aol.com/odinst. Ed. Donald W. Cole. circ. 500. **Document type:** directory.
Description: Listing of members' credentials; criteria for becoming a registered O.D. professional; descriptions of all O.D. and O.B. academic programs; accreditation criteria; O.D. networks worldwide; and the O.D. code of ethics, a statement on the knowledge and skill necessary to be competent in the field, and a variety of additional information.

658.3 US ISSN 0731-4531
INTERNATIONAL SOCIETY OF CERTIFIED EMPLOYEE BENEFIT SPECIALISTS. NEWSBRIEFS. 1982. bi-m. membership. International Society of Certified Employee Benefit Specialists, Inc., Box 209, Brookfield, WI 53008-0209. TEL 414-786-8771. FAX 414-786-8650. E-mail: iscebs@ifebp.org. Ed. Mary Brennan. R&P contact: Edye Biwer. bk.rev.; abstr. circ. 3,500. (tabloid format) **Document type:** newsletter.
Description: Contains news of society activities, articles on benefit-related topics, updates on current developments and literature in the field.

658.3 FR
JOURNAL AUX SYNDIQUES. 10/yr. Federation Nationale des Personnels des Organismes Sociales, 263 rue de Paris, 93515 Montreuil Cedex, France. circ. 50,000.
Formerly (until 1984): Voix des Employes et Cadres (ISSN 0766-2793)

658.3 FR ISSN 0184-0584
JOURNAL DU TRAVAIL TEMPORAIRE ET DES SERVICES. 1977. q. 100 F. Syndicat des Petites et Moyennes Entreprises de Travail Temporaire, 45 Rue de Turbigo, 75003 Paris, France. circ. 8,000. (back issues avail.) **Indexed:** RADAR.

658.3 US ISSN 1040-9602
HD66
JOURNAL FOR QUALITY AND PARTICIPATION. 1978. 7/yr. $60 (foreign $75) (effective 1997). Association for Quality and Participation, 801-B W. 8th St., Ste. 501, Cincinnati, OH 45203. TEL 513-381-1959. FAX 513-381-0070. Ed. Ned Hamson. adv.; bk.rev. circ. 11,000. (back issues avail.) **Indexed:** ABI Inform, Q.Abstr., Tr.& Dev.Alert. **Document type:** newsletter.
●Also available online. Vendor(s): UMI.
—BLDSC (5043.684000); SWETS; UMI; UnCover. **CCC.**
Formerly: Quality Circles Journal.
Description: Covers quality management, employee involvement, quality teams and continuous improvement.

JOURNAL OF CAREER PLANNING & EMPLOYMENT; the international magazine of placement and recruitment. see OCCUPATIONS AND CAREERS

658.3 US ISSN 0893-780X
KF3509.A15
JOURNAL OF COMPENSATION & BENEFITS. 1937. bi-m. $143.50 (overseas $222.05) (effective 1995). Warren, Gorham & Lamont, One Penn Plaza, New York, NY 10119. TEL 212-971-5000. FAX 212-971-5113. (Subscr. to: The Park Square Bldg., 31 St. James Ave., Boston, MA 02116-4112. TEL 800-950-1207) **Indexed:** ABI Inform, Account.Ind. (1985-), B.P.I. **Document type:** trade publication.
—BLDSC (4963.385000); KR SourceOne; UMI. **CCC.**
Description: Provides analysis of plan design, administration and record keeping, accounting, tax planning, fiduciary responsibilities, employment law affecting benefits, life and health insurance and legislation. Shows how to avoid legal or compliance problems.

JOURNAL OF EDUCATION AND WORK. see EDUCATION — Teaching Methods And Curriculum

658.3 US ISSN 1057-5073
HG9395
JOURNAL OF HEALTH CARE BENEFITS. 1991. bi-m. $131.98 (foreign $207.75) (effective 1995). Warren, Gorham & Lamont, One Penn Plaza, New York, NY 10119. TEL 212-971-5000. FAX 212-971-5113. (Subscr. to: The Park Square Bldg., 31 St. James Ave., Boston, MA 02116-4112. TEL 800-950-1207) Eds. Joseph W. Duva, Jeffrey D. Mamorsky. **Document type:** trade publication.
—**CCC.**
Description: Provides strategies for designing health care plans effectively and economically.

658.3 331 US ISSN 0022-166X
HD5701 CODEN: JHREA9
JOURNAL OF HUMAN RESOURCES; education, manpower and welfare economics. 1966. q. $45 to individuals; institutions $94. (University of Wisconsin at Madison, Industrial Relations Research Institute) University of Wisconsin Press, Social Science Bldg., 1180 Observatory Dr., Madison, WI 53706. TEL 608-262-4952. FAX 608-262-7560. (Subscr. to: Journal Division, 114 N. Murray St., Madison, WI 53715) (Co-sponsors: Institute for Research on Poverty) Ed. James Walker. adv.; bk.rev.; abstr.; bibl.; charts; stat.; index. circ. 2,500. (also avail. in microform from MIM,UMI; back issues avail.; reprint service avail. from UMI,KTO) **Indexed:** ABI Inform., Abstr.Health Care Manage.Stud., Adol.Ment.Hlth.Abstr., ASCA, ASSIA, BPIA, Bus.Ind.; C.I.J.E., CINAHL, CLOA, Curr.Cont., Educ.Admin.Abstr., Eng.Ind., Fam.Ind., Geo.Abstr.P.G., IDA, Ind.Med., J.of Econ.Lit., Manage.Cont., Med.Care Rev., Mid.East: Abstr.& Ind., Mult.Ed.Abstr., Pers.Lit., Pers.Manage.Abstr., Polit.Sci.Abstr., Soc.Sci.Ind., Soc.Work Res.& Abstr., Sociol.Educ.Abstr., SOMA, Sp.Ed.Needs Abstr., SSCI, Stud.Wom.Abstr., World Agri.Econ.& Rural Sociol.Abstr. **Document type:** academic/scholarly publication.
●Also available online. Vendor(s): Information Access Co., UMI.
—BLDSC (5003.430000); CISTI; Genuine Article; KR SourceOne; SWETS; UMI; UnCover. **CCC.**

658.3 332.6 US ISSN 1068-2309
HD4906
JOURNAL OF INTERNATIONAL COMPENSATION AND BENEFITS. 1992. bi-m. $223.75 (overseas $323.45) (effective 1995). Warren, Gorham & Lamont, One Penn Plaza, New York, NY 10119. TEL 212-971-5000. FAX 212-971-5113. (Subscr. to: The Park Square Bldg., 31 St. James Ave., Boston, MA 02116-4112. TEL 800-950-1207) Ed. Charles J. Boylan. **Document type:** trade publication.
—**CCC.**
Description: Analyzes issues in international company human resources management, covering major new laws and regulations that affect international compensation and benefits.

658.3 CN ISSN 1023-0467
▼**JOURNAL OF INTERNATIONAL HUMAN RESOURCE MANAGEMENT.** Abbreviated title: J I H R M. 1996. a. $50 (effective 1997-98). (Strategic Training Consultants) Universal Publications, P.O. Box 7305, Ottawa, ON K1L 8E4, Canada. TEL 613-831-1052; 888-659-4845. FAX 613-831-8452. E-mail: titles@upinfo.com; URL: http://www.upinfo.com/~up. Ed. Amarjit S. Sethi. R&P contact: Bob Smith. adv. contact: Bob Smith. bk.rev. circ. 500. **Indexed:** Sociol.Abstr. **Document type:** academic/scholarly publication.
Description: Provides articles on the development of strategic leadership in the new environment, matching corporate strategies with human resources management strategies.
Refereed Serial

JOURNAL OF MULTICULTURAL COUNSELING AND DEVELOPMENT. see PSYCHOLOGY

JOURNAL OF ORGANIZATIONAL BEHAVIOR MANAGEMENT. see PSYCHOLOGY

JOURNAL OF PERSONNEL EVALUATION IN EDUCATION. see EDUCATION

JOURNAL OF STAFF DEVELOPMENT. see EDUCATION — Adult Education

658.3 - UK
THE JOURNAL OF WORKPLACE LEARNING: EMPLOYEE COUNSELLING TODAY. 1989. 7/yr. £1499($2329) (foreign Aus.$2999) (effective 1998). M C B University Press Ltd., 60-62 Toller Ln., Bradford, W. Yorks BD8 9BY, England. TEL 44-1274-777700. FAX 44-1274-785200. TELEX 51317-MCBUNI-G. URL: http://www.mcb.co.uk. (N. American subscr. to: M C B University Press Limited, Box 1943, Birmingham, AL 35201) Ed. John Peters. (reprint service avail. from SWZ) **Document type:** academic/scholarly publication.
Formed by the merger of: Journal of Workplace Learning; (1989-1997): Employee Counselling Today (ISSN 0955-8217)

658.3 CC
JUNDUI ZHUANYE GANBU. (Text in Chinese) m. Guowuyuan, Jundui Zhuanye Bangongshi, 83, Fuxing Lu, Beijing 100856, People's Republic of China. TEL 6899280. Ed. Zhang Changsheng.

658.3 UK
KEY NOTE MARKET REPORT: CORPORATE GIFTWARE. Variant title: Corporate Giftware. irreg. £205. Key Note Ltd., Field House, 72 Oldfield Rd., Hampton, Middlesex TW12 2HQ, England. TEL 44-181-783-0755. FAX 44-181-783-0049. **Document type:** trade publication.

LAW OFFICE ADMINISTRATOR. see BUSINESS AND ECONOMICS — Management

LAWYER HIRING & TRAINING REPORT. see LAW

658.3 UK ISSN 0969-6474
THE LEARNING ORGANIZATION. 1994. 5/yr. £299($479) (foreign Aus.$599) (effective 1998). M C B University Press Ltd., 60-62 Toller Ln., Bradford, W. Yorks BD8 9BY, England. TEL 44-1274-777700. FAX 44-1274-785200. TELEX 51317-MCBUNI-G. URL: http://www.mcb.co.uk. (N. American subscr. to: M C B University Press Limited, Box 1943, Birmingham, AL 35201) Ed. John Peters. **Indexed:** Br.Educ.Ind., Cont.Pg.Educ., Mgmt.& Market.Abstr., Tech.Educ.Abstr. **Document type:** academic/scholarly publication.
●Also available on CD-ROM.
—BLDSC (5179.328300); SWETS. **CCC.**

658.3 GW ISSN 0024-0737
DER LEITENDE ANGESTELLTE; Zeitschrift fuer Fuehrungskraefte in der Wirtschaft. 1950. 10/yr. DM.59. MSK-Verlag GmbH, Schlehenstr. 45, 59063 Hamm, Germany. Ed. Jost J. Kroeger. adv.; bk.rev. circ. 43,500.

LIBRARY PERSONNEL NEWS. see LIBRARY AND INFORMATION SCIENCES

658.3 015 NE ISSN 0921-6154
LITERATUURINFORMATIE PERSONEELSBELEID EN ORGANISATIE. 1953. fortn. fl.240. K L M Royal Dutch Airlines, Information and Documentation Department, Postbus 7700, 1117 ZL Schiphol, Netherlands. bk.rev.; abstr.; bibl. circ. 2,850. (processed)
Former titles: Literatuurinformatie Personeelsaangelegenheden; Literatuur-Overzicht Personeelsaangelegenheden (ISSN 0024-4899)

658.3 GW ISSN 0941-9926
LOHN- UND GEHALTSPRAXIS. 1992. bi-m. DM.78. Verlag Wirtschaft Recht und Steuern, Fraunhoferstr. 5, 82152 Planegg, Germany. TEL 49-89-89517-0. FAX 49-89-89517250. (Subscr. to: Postfach 1363 82142 Planegg, Germany) (looseleaf format) **Document type:** trade publication.

658.311 US ISSN 0076-0889
LOOKING INTO LEADERSHIP SERIES. 1961. irreg. price varies. Leadership Resources Inc., Box 629, Luray, VA 22835-0629. TEL 703-876-8944. **Document type:** monographic series.

658.3 CN
MCDONALD QUARTERLY; the topical report on diversity issues. q. Can.$80. Cross Cultural Communications International, Inc., 200-275 Portage Ave., Winnipeg, MB R3B 2B3, Canada. TEL 204-949-1144; 800-665-4854. FAX 204-949-1372. adv. contact: Dayna Comeau Brown. pp./issue: 16. **Document type:** newsletter.
Description: Feature articles focus on media issues while in-depth articles advise readers of recent research findings.

BUSINESS AND ECONOMICS — PERSONNEL MANAGEMENT

658.3 NE ISSN 0925-806X
MAGAZINE OPLEIDINGEN; vakblad over lerende mensen in organisaties. (Includes q. supplement: Servicebrief) 1988. 8/yr. fl.160. Samsom BedrijfsInformatie B.V. (Subsidiary of: Wolters Kluwer N.V.), Postbus 4, 2400 MA Alphen aan den Rijn, Netherlands. TEL 31-172-466775. FAX 31-172-440681. Ed. Hanni Leenen. adv. contact: M. van den Akker. bk.rev.; software rev.; video rev. circ. 5,000. (back issues avail.) Document type: trade publication.
 Formerly (until 1989): Nieuwsmagazine Opleidingen (ISSN 0924-0802).
 Description: Covers issues relevant to personnel training and development in companies and organizations.

658.3 FR
MAITRISER (EDITION AERONAUTIQUE ET ESPACE). m. (10/yr.) 880 F. E S F Editeur, 17 rue Viete, 75854 Paris Cedex 17, France. TEL 44-15-62-00. adv.; bk.rev.; charts; illus.; stat.; index.

658.3 FR ISSN 1157-6065
MAITRISER (EDITION CHIMIE). m. (10/yr.). 880 F. E S F Editeur, 17 rue Viete, 75854 Paris Cedex 17, France. TEL 44-15-62-00. Ed. Gerard Didier.
 Former titles (until 1991): Travail et Maitrise (Edition Chimie) (ISSN 0758-4016); Travail et Maitrise (Edition Chimie - Techniciens) (ISSN 0758-4008)

658.3 FR ISSN 1157-6049
MAITRISER (EDITION GENERALE); information pour les agents de maitrise et l'encadrement de l'industrie. vol.33, 1977. m. (10/yr.). 880 F. E S F Editeur, 17 rue Viete, 75854 Paris Cedex 17, France. TEL 44-15-62-00. Ed. Gerard Didier. adv.; bk.rev.; charts; illus.; stat.; index. circ. 56,150.
 Formerly (until 1991): Travail et Maitrise (Edition Generale) (ISSN 0750-8964)

658.3 FR ISSN 1157-6057
MAITRISER (EDITION SIDERURGIE). m. (10/yr.). 880 F. E S F Editeur, 17 rue Viete, 75854 Paris Cedex 17, France. TEL 44-15-62-00. adv.; bk.rev.; charts; illus.; stat.; index.
 Formerly (until 1991): Travail et Maitrise (Edition Siderurgie) (ISSN 0750-8980)

658.3 US ISSN 0893-3189
MANAGEMENT COMMUNICATION QUARTERLY. 1987. q. $190 to institutions (effective Sep. 1996). Sage Publications, Inc., 2455 Teller Rd., Thousand Oaks, CA 91320. TEL 805-499-0721. FAX 805-499-0871. E-mail: libraries@sagepub.com; URL: http://www.sagepub.co.uk/journals/usdetails/j0025.htm. (Overseas subscr. to: Sage Publications Ltd., 6 Bonhill St., London EC2A 4PU, England; Sage Publications India Pvt. Ltd., P.O. Box 4215, New Delhi 110 048, India) Eds. Katherine I. Miller, Larry R. Smeltzer. adv. contact: Margaret Travers. bk.rev. circ. 1,100. (back issues avail.; reprint service avail.) Indexed: C.I.J.E., Commun.Abstr., Cont.Pg.Manage., Sociol.Abstr. Document type: academic/scholarly publication.
 —BLDSC (5359.013900); SWETS; UMI; UnCover. CCC.
 Description: Brings together communication research from many fields, with a focus on managerial and organizational effectiveness.

658.3
HD30.4 UK
MANAGEMENT DEVELOPMENT REVIEW. 1987. 7/yr. £629 includes CD-ROM (effective 1997). M C B University Press Ltd., 60-62 Toller Ln., Bradford, W. Yorks BD8 9BY, England. TEL 44-1274-777700. FAX 44-1274-785200. TELEX 51317-MCBUNI-G. URL: http://www.mcb.co.uk. Ed. Chris Ashton. circ. 2,000. Indexed: Br.Educ.Ind., Mgmt.& Market.Abstr., SOMA, Tech.Educ.Abstr. Document type: academic/scholarly publication.
 ●Also available on CD-ROM.
 —BLDSC (5359.019450); UMI. CCC.
 Incorporates (1993-1996): Financial Services Training Journal (ISSN 0967-4969); Formerly (until 1993): Target Management Development Review (ISSN 0962-2519)
 Description: Provides information on the realities and practice of management training and development.

658.3 UK
MANAGEMENT SKILLS AND DEVELOPMENT. 1992. m. £30 (overseas £50). Training Information Network Ltd., Jubilee House, The Oaks, Ruislip, Mddx. HA4 7LF, England. TEL 44-1895-622112. FAX 44-1895-621582. Ed. Anthony Landale. bk.rev.; video rev. circ. 28,000. Document type: trade publication.
 —BLDSC (5359.155700).
 Formerly: Management Training (ISSN 0966-4254)
 Description: Covers strategies and initiatives in professional training and development.

658.3 UK ISSN 1355-1515
MANAGING BEST PRACTICE. 1994. 10/yr. £275. Industrial Society, Robert Hyde House, 48 Bryanston Sq., London W1H 7LN, England. TEL 0171-262-2401. (Subscr. to: Sales Unit, Quadrant Ct., 49 Calthorpe Rd., Edgbaston, Birmingham B15 1TH, England. TEL 0121-454-6769) Ed. Patrick Burns. bk.rev. Document type: trade publication.
 —BLDSC (5359.284500).
 Description: Aims to provide best-practice advice, examples, options, and differing experience from a range of organizations, which together supply practical pointers to achieving excellence in managing personnel.

MANAGING FLEXIBLE BENEFITS PLANS. see BUSINESS AND ECONOMICS — Labor And Industrial Relations

MANAGING LEAVE AND HOLIDAYS. see LAW

MANNESMANN ILLUSTRIERTE. see BUSINESS AND ECONOMICS — Domestic Commerce

658.3 IS ISSN 0792-0970
MASHABEI EINOSH. (Text in Hebrew) 1988. m. IS.560($186) (effective 1997). Eush Ltd., P.O. Box 3202, Herzliya 46104, Israel. TEL 972-8-9500882. FAX 972-9-9582785. Eds. Chanoch Sadan, Nava Eldar; Pubs. Chanoch Sadan, Nava Eldar. adv. contact: Lang Nurith. bk.rev.; circ. 2,000 (paid).
 Refereed Serial

MATERIALIEN AUS DER ARBEITSMARKT- UND BERUFSFORSCHUNG. see BUSINESS AND ECONOMICS — Labor And Industrial Relations

MEDICAL BENEFITS. see INSURANCE — Abstracting, Bibliographies, Statistics

MIDDLE MANAGEMENT AND CLERICAL COMPENSATION REPORT - MEXICO. see BUSINESS AND ECONOMICS — Management

MIDDLE MANAGEMENT COMPENSATION - REGRESSION ANALYSIS REPORT. see BUSINESS AND ECONOMICS — Management

MIDDLE MANAGEMENT HI - COMP REPORT. see BUSINESS AND ECONOMICS — Management

MIDDLE MANAGEMENT REPORT. see BUSINESS AND ECONOMICS — Management

MINDPLAY; creativity & innovation in today's business environment. see BUSINESS AND ECONOMICS — Management

MOBILITY (WASHINGTON). see REAL ESTATE

658.3 388.324 US
MOTOR FLEET SUPERVISION; principles and practices. 1983. irreg. $20 per no. National Committee for Motor Fleet Supervisor Training, A-364 Engineering Bldg., Michigan State University, E. Lansing, MI 48824-1226. TEL 517-353-1790. Ed. Jack Burkert. Document type: academic/scholarly publication.

658.3 GW
MUSTERARBEITSVERTRAEGE UND ZEUGNISSE FUER DIE BETRIEBLICHE PRAXIS. 1992. q. DM.473.20. W E K A Management Fachverlage GmbH, Roemerstr. 16, 86438 Kissing, Germany. TEL 08233-23115. FAX 08233-23132. Ed. Wolf Hunold. circ. 1,100 (paid). (looseleaf format) Document type: trade publication.

N A S P A FORUM. (National Association of Student Personnel Administrators) see EDUCATION — Higher Education

N S S A NEWSLETTER. (National Science Supervisors Association) see SCIENCES: COMPREHENSIVE WORKS

658.3 US ISSN 0027-7150
N Y P M A BULLETIN. 1945. 10/yr. membership. New York Personnel Management Association, 245 Fifth Ave., Ste. 2103, New York, NY 10016. TEL 212-481-3038. FAX 212-481-3071. Ed. Rosemarie Sharpe. charts; illus. circ. 500. Document type: bulletin.
 Description: Contains organization news.

NATIONAL PUBLIC EMPLOYMENT REPORTER. see BUSINESS AND ECONOMICS — Labor And Industrial Relations

658.3 346 GW
NEUE ARBEITSRECHT VON A-Z FUER DEN GESCHAEFTSFUEHRER. 1992. q. DM.473.20. W E K A Management Fachverlage GmbH, Roemerstr. 16, 86438 Kissing, Germany. TEL 08233-23410. FAX 08233-23132. Eds. A. Mueller, W. Schoen. circ. 4,000 (paid). (looseleaf format) Document type: trade publication.

NEW HAMPSHIRE WORKERS' COMPENSATION MANUAL. see LAW — Corporate Law

658.3 340.5 US
NEW YORK CIVIL SERVICE UPDATE. m. $95. Nyper Publications, Box 662, Latham, NY 12110. TEL 518-786-1654. FAX 518-456-8582. URL: http://www.nyper.com. Ed. Harvey Randall. (back issues avail.) Document type: newsletter.
 Formerly: Civil Service Personnel Notes (ISSN 1071-7439)
 Description: Reports on civil service personnel matters.

658.3 340 NZ
NEW ZEALAND EMPLOYERS HANDBOOK. 1991. 2/yr. NZ.$293 (effective 1997). C C H New Zealand Limited, P.O. Box 2378, Auckland, New Zealand. TEL 64-9-483-9179. FAX 64-9-483-4009. (looseleaf format)
 Description: Provides up-to-date, practical information on the key facets of employment law, including details and practical implications of the new employment contracts legislation, and information on the day-to-day management of employment contracts, recruitment, training, accident compensation, taxation, health and safety and all the important areas of employee relations.

331.1 346.066 NZ
NEW ZEALAND EMPLOYMENT LAW LIBRARY. (In two vols.) 1985. 8/yr. NZ.$1199 (effective 1997). C C H New Zealand Limited, P.O. Box 2378, Auckland, New Zealand. TEL 64-9-483-9179. FAX 64-9-483-4009. (looseleaf format)
 Description: Provides information to help management and employees understand their rights and obligations under current labor laws.

NUOVO GOVERNO LOCALE. see BUSINESS AND ECONOMICS — Management

OF COUNSEL; the monthly legal practice report. see LAW

658 US
OFFICE PERSONNEL REPORT. a. $490. (Executive Compensation Service (ECS)) Wyatt Data Services, 218 Rte. 17, N., Roselle Park, NJ 07662-9832. TEL 201-843-1177. FAX 201-843-0101. charts. Document type: trade publication.
 Description: Complete information concerning office personnel salary.

658.3 651 UK ISSN 0951-6824
OFFICE SECRETARY. 1986. q. £9.50 (foreign £20). Trade Media Ltd., Brookmead House, Thorney Leys Business Park, Witney, Oxon OX8 6BH, England. TEL 44-1993-775545. FAX 44-1993-778884. Ed. Danusia Hutson. circ. 100,000. Document type: trade publication.

658.3 US ISSN 0078-4001
OHIO. DIVISION OF STATE PERSONNEL. ANNUAL REPORT. 1960. a. free. Division of State Personnel, Department of Administrative Services, 30 E. Broad St, Columbus, OH 43215. TEL 614-466-6341.

BUSINESS AND ECONOMICS — PERSONNEL MANAGEMENT

658.3 US
OKLAHOMA. PUBLIC EMPLOYEES RETIREMENT SYSTEM. ANNUAL REPORT. a. Public Employees Retirement System, 580 Jim Thorpe Bldg., Box 53007, Oklahoma City, OK 73152. TEL 405-521-2381.

658.3 US
ON THE HUMAN SIDE. q. Human Side Press, Ltd., 1800 Bering Dr., Ste. 1090, Houston, TX 77057. TEL 713-266-5388. FAX 713-266-5387. bk.rev.; charts; illus.

658.3 GW
OPEL POST. 10/yr. Adam Opel AG, 65423 Russelsheim, Germany. TEL 06142-664057. FAX 06142-61598. Ed. Norbert Giesen. circ. 80,000. (tabloid format; back issues avail.) **Document type:** bulletin.

658.3 NE ISSN 0922-0895
OPLEIDING & ONTWIKKELING; tijdschrift over human resource development. 1988. 10/yr. fl.174. Delwel Uitgeverij B.V., Postbus 19110, 2500 CC The Hague, Netherlands. TEL 31-70-3624800. FAX 31-70-3605606. Ed.Bd. **Document type:** trade publication.
—SWETS.
Description: Discussion of practical and theoretical issues in personnel management and development.

658.3 150 GW ISSN 0946-9834
ORGANISATIONSBERATUNG, SUPERVISION, CLINICAL MANAGEMENT. 1994. q. DM.81 (students DM.56; foreign DM.87) (effective 1997). Verlag Leske und Budrich GmbH, Postfach 300551, 51334 Leverkusen, Germany. TEL 49-2171-2079. FAX 49-2171-41209. **Document type:** academic/scholarly publication.

658.3 YU ISSN 0048-217X
ORGANIZACIJA I KADROVI/ORGANIZATION AND PERSONNEL. Slovenian edition: Organizacija in Kadri (ISSN 0350-1531) (Text in Serbocroatian; summaries in English and Russian) 1970. m. 950 din.($50.50) Institut za Organizaciju i Razvoj, Belgrade, Milana Rakica 35, Belgrade, Yugoslavia. (Co-sponsor: Ekonomski Institut, Zagreb) Ed. Jovo Brekic. adv.; bibl.; charts; illus.; stat.; tr.lit.
Formed by the merger of: Kadrovi i Rad & Samoupravna Organizacija.

658 XV ISSN 0350-1531
CODEN: ORKAEN
ORGANIZACIJA IN KADRI. (Text in Slovenian; summaries in English; edition also in Serbo-Croatian) 1972. m. 750 din.($50) Moderna Organizacija, Tomsiceva 7, 64001 Kranj, Slovenia. TEL 064-211-560. FAX 064-214-458. Ed. Peter Mikeln. adv.; bk.rev.; bibl.; charts. circ. 2,800. **Indexed:** Ergon.Abstr.
—AskIEEE; KR SourceOne.
Former titles: Moderna Organizacija (ISSN 0047-777X); Organizacija Kadrovska Politika (ISSN 0030-5022)

658.2 YU ISSN 0351-3440
ORGANIZACIJA POSLOVANJA. 1961. m. 500 din. Zavod za Organizaciju i Upravljanje Poslovnim Sistemom u Organizacijama Udruzenog Rada, Ul. 29 Novembra Br. 48-3, Belgrade, Yugoslavia. Ed. Dusanka Secerov.

ORGANIZATION DEVELOPMENT JOURNAL; guiding the future of people working together. see BUSINESS AND ECONOMICS — Management

658.3 UK ISSN 1350-9853
ORGANIZATIONAL EXCELLENCE NEWSLETTER. 1994. bi-m. £90 (overseas £105($157.50)) (effective 1996). (Best Practice Club) I F S International Ltd., Wolseley Business Park, Kempston, Bedford MK42 7PW, England. TEL 44-1234-853605. FAX 44-1234-854499. Ed. Chris Ashton; Pub. Rory Chase. R&P contact: David Watts. adv. contact: David Watts. **Document type:** newsletter.
—CCC.
Description: Provides executives and managers in business, government, and organizations with information to assist them in introducing best-practice procedures.

658.3 US
ORGANIZATIONS AND CHANGE. m. $110. Organization Development Institute (Chesterland), 11234 Walnut Ridge Rd., Chesterland, OH 44026-1299. TEL 216-461-4333. FAX 216-729-9319. E-mail: donwcole@aol.com; URL: http://members.aol.com/odinst. Ed. Donald W. Cole. **Document type:** newsletter.
Description: Lists meetings, jobs, and consulting opportunities in the field of organization development.

ORGANIZE YOUR LUCK!. see OCCUPATIONS AND CAREERS

658.3 BE ISSN 0030-543X
ORIENTATIONS; la revue du droit social et de la gestion du personnel. Flemish edition: Orientatie (ISSN 0773-350X) (Supplement avail.: Newsletter) 1971. m. 8268 BEF. C E D Samsom (Subsidiary of: Wolters Samsom Belgie n.v.), Kouterveld 14, B-1831 Diegem, Belgium. TEL 32-2-7231111. bk.rev.; bibl.; index. **Indexed:** HongKongiana.

658.3 UK ISSN 0966-7660
OVERSEAS JOBS EXPRESS. 1991. 26/yr. £52 (foreign $108) (effective 1996). Premier House, Shoreham Airport, Sussex BN43 5FF, England. TEL 44-1273-440220. FAX 44-1273-440229. E-mail: editor@oje.demon.co.uk; URL: http://www.overseasjobs.com. Ed. David Creffield. R&P contact: David Creffield. adv. contact: Mike Dorrinston. bk.rev.; circ. 20,000 (paid). (tabloid format) **Document type:** newspaper.
Description: Lists international employment opportunities and vacancies. Provides information to persons interested in living and/or working abroad.

658.3 US ISSN 0361-7467
HF5549.A2
P P F SURVEY. (Personnel Policies Forum) (Subseries of: B N A Policy and Practice Series) 1951. irreg. $50 per no. The Bureau of National Affairs, Inc., 1231 25th St., N.W., Washington, DC 20037. TEL 202-452-4200. FAX 202-822-8092. TELEX 285656 BNAI WSH. URL: http://www.bna.com/. (Subscr. to: 9435 Key West Ave., Rockville, MD 20850. TEL 800-372-1033) Ed. J. Michael Reidy. charts. (also avail. in microfilm; back issues avail.)
—CCC.
Formerly: Personnel Policies Forum (ISSN 0031-580X)
Description: Reports on human resources topics derived from responses to questionnaires sent to BNA's Personnel Policies Forum. Topics include recruiting and selection policies, promotion and transfer procedures, wage and salary administration, employee benefits and services, evaluation and motivation programs, grievance procedures, performance evaluation and motivation programs, training, and discipline and discharge policies.

658.3 NE ISSN 0165-3334
P W. (Personeelswerk); vakblad voor personeelsmanagement. Key Title: PW (Amsterdam). 1977. fortn. fl.208 includes 3 special guides. V N U Business Publications B.V., Postbus 9194, 1006 CC Amsterdam, Netherlands. TEL 31-20-4875417. FAX 31-20-4875732. Ed. Theo Eijspaart; Pub. Gert Jan Laurman. adv.; bk.rev.; stat.; illus.; index. circ. 15,000. (back issues avail.) **Document type:** trade publication.
Incorporates (1985-1993): P W Nieuws en Actualiteit (ISSN 0929-3280); **Incorporates** (1983-1985): Training en Opleiding (ISSN 0929-3272)
Description: Covers personnel management issues.

PARTNERS IN BUSINESS. see BUSINESS AND ECONOMICS — Management

331 UK ISSN 0143-8328
PAY AND BENEFITS BULLETIN. Short title: P A B B. (Also avail. as part of: I R S Employment Review (ISSN 1358-2216)) 1979. fortn. £175 (foreign £188) (effective 1997). Eclipse Group Ltd., Industrial Relations Services, 18-20 Highbury Pl., London N5 1QP, England. TEL 44-171-354-5858. FAX 44-171-226-8618. Ed. Paul Thompson. (reprint service avail. from UMI) **Indexed:** L.R.I. **Document type:** trade publication.
Description: Analyzes pay awards, surveys topical pay issues, summarizes pay-review settlements, and provides key negotiating statistics.

658.3 UK ISSN 0950-8147
PAYROLL MANAGER'S REVIEW. 1986. m. £65 (foreign £78). Tolley Publishing Co. Ltd., Tolley House, 2 Addiscombe Rd., Croydon, Surrey CR9 5AX, England. TEL 44-181-868-9141. FAX 44-181-686-3155. Eds. Ciarom Molloy, Mike Nicholas. circ. 4,000. **Document type:** trade publication.

658.3 657 US
PENSION COORDINATOR. 1987. 13 base vols. (w. supplements). $820. Research Institute of America, Inc., 90 Fifth Ave., New York, NY 10011. TEL 212-645-4800. FAX 212-337-4279. (Subscr. to: 117 E. Stevens Ave., Valhalla, NY 10595) (looseleaf format)
Description: Provides analysis of pension law, planning articles, official source materials and compliance tools.

658.3 331 UK ISSN 0959-8014
PENSIONS LAW REPORTS; the key pensions cases without delay. irreg. £282 (outside Europe £332) (effective 1997). Incomes Data Services Ltd., 77 Bastwick St., London EC1V 3TT, England. TEL 0171-250-3434. FAX 0171-608-0949.
Description: Provides the full text of legal decisions affecting pensions, along with a summary and commentary on the significance of each case.

658.3 UK ISSN 0269-7505
PENSIONS MANAGEMENT. 1985. m. £42 (overseas £63). Financial Times Business Information, Magazines (Subsidiary of: Financial Times Group), 2 Greystoke Pl., Fetter Ln., London EC4A 1ND, England. TEL 0171-405-6969. FAX 0171-405-5276. TELEX 296926 BUSINF G. (Subscr. to: 126 Jermyn St., London SW1Y 4UJ, England) adv.; bk.rev. circ. 12,087. (also avail. in microform from UMI) **Document type:** trade publication.
—BLDSC (6422.720170); UMI.
Description: Directed to pension professionals in the U.K. Covers all aspects of benefit planning and investment from personal and company pension schemes.

658.3 SA ISSN 1019-6196
PEOPLE DYNAMICS. (Text in English) 1973. m. (11/yr.) R.185 in South Africa; Southern Africa R.270; elsewhere R.323 (effective 1997). Institute of Personnel Management, P.O. Box 31390, Braamfontein 2017, South Africa. TEL 27-11-4824970. FAX 27-11-4825542. E-mail: alan.hosking@pixie.co.za. Ed. Alan Hosking. R&P contact: Linda Brims. adv.: B&W page R.3408, color page R.4912; trim 189 x 271; adv. contact: Barbara Spence. bk.rev.; illus. circ. 9,302. **Indexed:** Ind.S.A.Per. **Document type:** trade publication.
—BLDSC (6422.876530).
Former titles (until Feb. 1992): I P M Journal - I P B Joernaal (ISSN 1011-4149); (until 1985): I P M Manpower Journal (ISSN 1011-4270); (until 1982): People and Profits (ISSN 0301-6005)
Description: Discusses issues relating to all aspects of human resources administration and planning, with particular focus on the impact of changes in South Africa.
Refereed Serial

PERSONAL; Zeitschrift fuer Human Resource Management. see BUSINESS AND ECONOMICS — Labor And Industrial Relations

658.3 SW ISSN 0348-5242
PERSONAL; manniskor och arbete. 1961. 16/yr. SEK 410. Sveriges Personaladministrativa Foerening, P.O. Box 5757, 11487, 114 36 Stockholm, Sweden. Ed. Sven Janbrink. adv.; bk.rev.; index. circ. 14,500. (reprint service avail. from SCH)

658.3 GW ISSN 0937-3012
DAS PERSONAL. 1990. bi-m. DM.78. Verlag Wirtschaft Recht und Steuern, Fraunhoferstr. 5, 82152 Planegg, Germany. TEL 49-89-89517-0. FAX 49-89-89517250. (Subscr. to: Postfach 1363 82142 Planegg, Germany) (looseleaf format) **Document type:** trade publication.

PERSONAL & LEDARSKAP. see EDUCATION — Adult Education

BUSINESS AND ECONOMICS — PERSONNEL MANAGEMENT

658.3 GW ISSN 0723-3868
PERSONALFUEHRUNG. 1967. m. DM.238 (effective 1996). Deutsche Gesellschaft fuer Personalfuehrung e.V., Niederkasseler Lohweg 16, 40547 Duesseldorf, Germany. TEL 49-211-5978-0. Ed. Maria-Theresia Bittscheidt. adv.; bk.rev. circ. 6,000. (reprint service avail. from SCH) **Document type:** trade publication.
—SWETS.

658.3 GW ISSN 0476-3475
DIE PERSONALVERTRETUNG; Fachzeitschrift des gesamten Personalwesens fuer Personalvertretungen und Dienststellen. 1958. m. DM.154.80. Erich Schmidt Verlag GmbH & Co. (Bielefeld), Victoriastr. 44A, 33602 Bielefeld, Germany. TEL 49-521-58308-0. (Subscr. to: Postfach 102451, 33524 Bielefeld, Germany) **Document type:** trade publication.
—CCC.

658.3 GW ISSN 0341-4698
PERSONALWIRTSCHAFT; Zeitschrift fuer erfolgreiches Personalmanagement. 1974. m. DM.248. Luchterhand Verlag, Heddesdorferstr. 31, 56564 Neuwied, Germany. TEL 49-2631-801-0. FAX 49-2631-801210. Ed. Reiner Straub. adv. contact: Susanne Weigand. index. circ. 5,000. (back issues avail.; reprint service avail. from SCH) **Document type:** trade publication.
—SWETS. CCC.

658.3 NE ISSN 0031-5656
PERSONEELBELEID. 1965. m. (11/yr.). fl.175 to non-members (foreign fl.210). Nederlandse Vereniging voor Personeelbeleid, Postbox 19124, 3501 DC Utrecht, Netherlands. FAX 31-30-2343991. Ed. M. van de Wetering. adv.; bk.rev.; charts; illus. circ. 8,000. **Indexed:** Key to Econ.Sci. **Document type:** trade publication.
—SWETS.

658.3 FR
PERSONNEL. m. A N D C P - National Association of Directors and Personnel Officers, 29 av. Hoche, 75008 Paris, France. TEL 45-63-55-09. Ed. Jacques Laurioz. circ. 7,000. (reprint service avail. from SCH)

658.3 331.11 US ISSN 1044-2189
THE PERSONNEL ALERT (RAMSEY). 1989. s-m. $72.96. Alexander Hamilton Institute, 70 Hilltop Rd., Ramsey, NJ 07446-1119. TEL 201-825-3377. FAX 201-825-8696. TELEX 6402287386 MCI. Ed. Brian L.P. Zevnik. (back issues avail.) **Document type:** newsletter.
Description: Provides personnel managers with up-to-date information on important court decisions, government regulations, and trends in employment law.

658.3 UK ISSN 1351-0614
PERSONNEL ASSISTANT'S HANDBOOK BULLETIN. 1993. base vol. (plus m. updates). £88.25 (updates £63.50) (effective 1995). Croner Publications Ltd. (Subsidiary of: Wolters Kluwer N.V.), Croner House, 100 London Rd., Kingston-upon-Thames, Surrey TW2 6SR, England. TEL 44-181-547-3333. FAX 44-181-247-1300. TELEX 267778. (looseleaf format) **Document type:** trade publication.

PERSONNEL EXECUTIVES CONTACTBOOK. see BUSINESS AND ECONOMICS — Trade And Industrial Directories

658.3 346.066 US
PERSONNEL FORMS AND EMPLOYMENT CHECKLISTS. base vol. (plus supplement). $25. Butterworth Legal Publishers (Salem) (Subsidiary of: Reed Elsevier plc), 8 Industrial Way, Bldg. C, Salem, NH 03079. TEL 800-548-4001. FAX 603-898-9858. Ed. Maureen F. Moore. (looseleaf format)

658.3 331
PERSONNEL IN PRACTICE. (Supplement avail.: Employment Case Digest (ISSN 0966-1662)) base vol. (plus m. updates). £265.80 (updates £205.50) (effective 1995). Croner Publications Ltd. (Subsidiary of: Wolters Kluwer N.V.), Croner House, 100 London Rd., Kingston-upon-Thames, Surrey TW2 6SR, England. TEL 44-181-547-3333. FAX 44-181-247-1300. TELEX 267778. (looseleaf format) **Indexed:** Mgmt.& Market.Abstr. **Document type:** trade publication.

658.3 344.73 US ISSN 1082-9156
PERSONNEL MANAGEMENT GUIDEPOSTS FOR FEDERAL SUPERVISORS. 1989. m. $95 (effective 1997). L R P Publications, 747 Dresher Rd., Box 980, Horsham, PA 19044-0980. TEL 215-784-0941; 800-341-7874. FAX 215-784-9639. URL: http://www.lrp.com. Eds. Joanne Fiore, V. Nichols. q. index. (back issues avail.) **Document type:** newsletter.
—CCC.
Description: Keeps supervisors up-to-date on their personnel management responsibilities. Includes case decisions and policy changes that affect the federal sector.

658.3 UK ISSN 0265-704X
PERSONNEL MANAGER'S YEARBOOK. 1984. a. £65.00. A P Information Services, Roman House, 296 Golders Green Rd., London NW11 9PZ, England. TEL 0181-455-4550. FAX 0181-455-6381. Ed. Charlotte Evans; Pub. Alan Philipp. adv.; B&W page £915, color £1,500; trim 297 x 210. circ. 5,500. (also avail. in diskette format) **Document type:** directory.
—BLDSC (6428.089100).
Description: Lists key personnel, recruitment and training executives in the U.K.'s 5,000 largest companies and organizations. Also lists 5,000 providers of services to the industry.

658.3 US
THE PERSONNEL NEWS. 1984. m. $55. Personnel News, 2366 Walsh Ave., Santa Clara, CA 95051-1301. TEL 408-988-8991. FAX 408-988-8994. E-mail: pnews@scruznet.com. Ed. Judith H. Semas; Pub. Darrell Batchelder. R&P contact: Darrell Batchelder. adv. contact: Ken Whelan. bk.rev. circ. 10,000. **Document type:** newsletter, trade publication.
Description: Contains practical information to keep personnel and labor relations professionals current in their field and to assist them in the performance of their daily activities.

658.3 US
PERSONNEL POLICIES AND BENEFITS FOR THE APPAREL INDUSTRY. irreg. $60 to non-members; members $25. American Apparel Manufacturers Association, 2500 Wilson Blvd., Ste. 301, Arlington, VA 22201. TEL 703-524-1864. FAX 703-522-6741. **Document type:** trade publication.
Supersedes in part: Apparel Plant Wages and Personnel Policies (ISSN 0084-6678)

658.3 UK
PERSONNEL POLICIES IN EUROPE. q. £600. P-E International plc, Park House, Wick Rd., Egham, Surrey TW20 OHW, England. TEL 44-1784-434411. FAX 44-1784-476369. **Document type:** directory.
Refereed Serial

658.3 US
PERSONNEL PRACTICE IDEAS. m. $130.98 (overseas $187.45) (effective 1995). Warren, Gorham & Lamont, One Penn Plaza, New York, NY 10119. TEL 212-971-5000. FAX 212-971-5113. (Subscr. to: The Park Square Bldg., 31 St. James Ave., Boston, MA 02116-4112. TEL 800-950-1207) (also avail. in microform from UMI) **Document type:** newsletter.
Description: Addresses current employment law problems confronting human resources managers. Provides "how-to" information on complying with regulations, preparing employee handbooks, and interviewing job applicants in order to avoid costly errors.

PERSONNEL PSYCHOLOGY. see PSYCHOLOGY

658.3 UK ISSN 0048-3486
HF5549.A2
PERSONNEL REVIEW. 1971. bi-m. £3189($4949) (foreign Aus.$6239) (effective 1998). (Institute of Personnel Management) M C B University Press Ltd., 60-62 Toller Ln., Bradford, W. Yorks BD8 9BY, England. TEL 44-1274-777700. FAX 44-1274-785200. TELEX 51317 MCBUNI G. URL: http://www.mcb.co.uk. Ed. Margaret Reid. bk.rev.; bibl.; charts; illus.; cum.index. (also avail. in microform from UMI; back issues avail.; reprint service avail. from SWZ,UMI) **Indexed:** ABI Inform., Account.& Data Proc.Abstr., Anbar, ASCA, ASEAN Manage.Abstr., BPIA, Br.Educ.Ind., Bus.Ind., Cont.Pg.Manage., High.Educ.Curr.Aware.Bull., Manage.Cont., Mgmt.& Market.Abstr., SCIMP, SOMA, SSCI, Stud.Wom.Abstr., Tech.Educ.Abstr., Tr.& Dev.Alert, Work Rel.Abstr. **Document type:** academic/scholarly publication.
●Also available online. Vendor(s): Information Access Co.
Also available on CD-ROM.
—BLDSC (6428.098000); Genuine Article; SWETS; UMI. **CCC.**
Description: Seeks to present the latest research and developments in all disciplines of relevance to the personnel specialist. Covers organizational behavior and design, personnel and occupational psychology, education, training and development, staff planning and more.

PERSONNEL REWARDS. see BUSINESS AND ECONOMICS — Labor And Industrial Relations

658.3 330 US ISSN 1065-4615
HF5549.5.D37
PERSONNEL SOFTWARE CENSUS.* 1989. a. $79.95. Advanced Personnel Systems, 1873 Hidden View Ln., Roseville, CA 95661-5819. TEL 916-781-2900. FAX 916-781-2901. E-mail: frantz@hrcensus.com; URL: http://www.hrcensus.com. Ed. Richard B. Frantzreb. adv.; circ. 3,000 (paid). **Document type:** directory.
●Also available online. Vendor(s): Human Resources Information Network.
Description: Directory of HR software with 1,100 50-word listings (500-word listings for HR information systems) and complete vendor contact information. Covers micro, midrange, and mainframe systems for employment, benefits, payroll, training, HRIS, performance, health and safety.

658.3 331 II ISSN 0970-8405
PERSONNEL TODAY. (Text in English) 1949. q. $30. National Institute of Personnel Management, 45 Jhowtalla Rd., Calcutta 700 019, India. TEL 91-33-2475650. FAX 91-33-240-8179. Ed. B.D. Pande. adv.; bk.rev.; illus. circ. 6,000. **Document type:** academic/scholarly publication.
Formerly (until 1980): Industrial Relations (ISSN 0019-8684)

658.3 UK ISSN 0959-5848
PERSONNEL TODAY. 1987. fortn. £44 (Europe £60.50; rest of world £81.40). Reed Business Publishing Group, Horizon Division (Subsidiary of: Reed International PLC), Quadrant House, The Quadrant, Sutton, Surrey SM2 5AS, England. TEL 44-181-652-3946. FAX 44-181-652-8805. (Subscr. to: Freepost RCC 2619, P.O. Box 302, Haywards Heath, W. Sussex RH16 3BR, England) Ed. Toby Wolpe; Pub. Susan Downey. R&P contact: Toby Wolpe. adv. contact: Sally Collett. bk.rev. circ. 41,229. **Document type:** newspaper.
—BLDSC (6428.102100).
Description: Independent newspaper for professionals in personnel training and recruitment.

PETERSON'S INTERNSHIPS. see OCCUPATIONS AND CAREERS

PFEIFFER. ANNUAL; developing human resources. see BUSINESS AND ECONOMICS — Management

POLICIES, PRACTICES, AND EMPLOYEE BENEFITS SURVEY. see BUSINESS AND ECONOMICS — Labor And Industrial Relations

331 PO
PORTUGAL. MINISTERIO DAS CORPORACOES E PREVIDENCIA SOCIAL. GABINETE DE PLANEAMENTO. INGUERITO EMPREGO. (Subseries of its Serie Estatistica) (Summaries in English and French) irreg. Ministerio das Corporacoes e Previdencia Social, Gabinete de Planeamento, Lisbon, Portugal. stat.

BUSINESS AND ECONOMICS — PERSONNEL MANAGEMENT

658.3   US   ISSN 0742-7859
PRACTICAL SUPERVISION. 1984. m. $48. Professional Training Associates, Inc., 210 Commerce Blvd., Round Rock, TX 78664-2189. TEL 512-255-6006. FAX 512-255-7532. Ed. Robert Moskowitz; Pub. Dennis E. Murphy. R&P contact: Dennis E. Murphy. **Document type:** newsletter.
—CCC.

658.3   UK
PRACTICAL TRAINING. 1982. m. (except Aug.). £18.77. (Institute of Training and Development) Kay Davis Publishing, 166 Pullman Ct., Streatham Hill, London SW2 4S2, England. TEL 0171-671-2060. Ed. Eva Tyler; Pub. Kay Davis. adv. contact: Kay Davis. bk.rev. circ. 23,000. **Indexed:** Cont.Pg.Educ., Educ.Tech.Abstr., Tech.Educ.Abstr. **Document type:** trade publication.
Formerly (until 1995): Training and Development.
Description: Provides professional trainers with lively, in-depth, and accessible articles covering core training topics across all industry sectors, along with news and reviews.

658.3 336.2   NE
PRAKTIJKBLAD VOOR DE SALARISADMINISTRATIE. 1989. 10/yr. fl.365 includes Feiten en Cijfers (effective 1996). Uitgeverij Kluwer B.V., Postbus 23, 7400 GA Deventer, Netherlands. TEL 31-570-633155. FAX 31-570-633834. Ed. E. van Waaijen. (back issues avail.) **Document type:** trade publication.
Former titles: Loon en Salaris (ISSN 0928-0669); (until 1993): Nieuwsbrief Oort-wetgeving (ISSN 0923-9650)

THE PRESIDENT. see BUSINESS AND ECONOMICS — Management

658.3 388   US
PREVIEW (TROY). m. Chevrolet Motor Division, Box 500, Troy, MI 48007-0500. Ed. Duane Rose. adv. contact: Heidi Dilloway. software rev.; video rev.; charts; illus.; stat.
Description: Training and education publication for Chevrolet dealers and dealership managers.

PRIMA LIV; med Korpmotion. see SPORTS AND GAMES

PRIVREDNO PRAVNI PRIRUCNIK; za pravnu opstu i kadrovsku sluzbu privrednih i ostalih radnih organizacija. see LAW

658   US
PROFESSIONAL AND SCIENTIFIC PERSONNEL REPORT - GEOGRAPHIC EDITION. (Supplement to: Industry Report on Professional and Scientific Personnel Compensation) a. $690. (Executive Compensation Service (ECS)) Wyatt Data Services, 218 Rte. 17, N., Roselle Park, NJ 07662-9832. TEL 201-843-1177. FAX 201-843-0101. charts. **Document type:** trade publication.
Description: Provides geographic analyses of salaries and total cash compensation for a full spectrum of professional positions.

658.3   US   ISSN 0091-0260
HF5549.A2   CODEN: PPMNCX
PUBLIC PERSONNEL MANAGEMENT. 1940. q. $50 (foreign $75) (effective 1998). International Personnel Management Association, 1617 Duke St., Alexandria, VA 22314. TEL 703-549-7100. FAX 703-684-0948. E-mail: publications@ipma-hr.org; URL: http://www.ipma-hr.org. Ed. Karen D. Smith. adv. contact: Karen Smith. bk.rev.; abstr.; bibl.; index. circ. 7,000. (also avail. in microform from MIM,UMI; reprint service avail. from UMI) **Indexed:** A.B.C.Pol.Sci., ABI Inform., Account.& Data Proc.Abstr., Account.Ind. (1974-), Anbar, ASCA, B.P.I., Bk.Rev.Ind. (1965-1981, 1986-), BPIA, Bus.Ind., C.I.J.E., Child.Bk.Rev.Ind. (1965-1981, 1986-), Curr.Cont., Data Process.Dig., Educ.Admin.Abstr., Fam.Ind., Mid.East: Abstr.& Ind., P.A.I.S., Pers.Lit., Pers.Manage.Abstr., Psychol.Abstr. (1972-), Psycscan, Q.Abstr., Sage Pub.Admin.Abstr., SSCI, Tr.& Dev.Alert, Tr.& Indus.Ind., Work Rel.Abstr., Yrbk.Assoc.Educ.& Rehab.Blind. **Document type:** academic/scholarly publication.
●Also available online. Vendor(s): Information Access Co.
—BLDSC (6967.890000); Genuine Article; KR SourceOne; SWETS; UMI; UnCover. **CCC.**
Former titles: Public Personnel Review (ISSN 0033-3638); Personnel Administration.
Description: Articles on labor relations, assessment issues, comparative personnel policies, governmental reform and other areas of concern to personnel managers in the public sector.

658.3 332.2   US   ISSN 1047-224X
KF3512
QUALIFIED RETIREMENT AND OTHER EMPLOYEE BENEFIT PLANS. 1987. a. West Group, 620 Opperman Dr., Eagan, MN 55123. TEL 612-687-8000; 800-328-9352. FAX 612-687-7302. **Document type:** trade publication.

331 650   AT   ISSN 0314-2558
QUARTERLY SALARY REVIEW. 1968. q. Aus.$2200. Cullen Egan Dell, Level 8, 50 Bridge St., Sydney, N.S.W. 2060, Australia. TEL 61-2-93759800. FAX 61-2-93756800. Ed. Colin Hickling. circ. 550.
Description: Remuneration review covering positions at all levels of corporate, administrative and technical functions. Provides global view of salary movements in Australia.

658.3   GW
R K W KONTAKT. 1955. bi-m. Rationalisierungs-Kuratorium der Deutschen Wirtschaft e.V., Landesgruppe Bayern, Gustav-Heinemann-Ring 212, 81739 Munich, Germany. TEL 49-89-670040-0. FAX 49-89-67004040. Ed. Rudolf Donnert. bk.rev. circ. 2,500. **Document type:** newsletter.

658.3   US
RECRUITING AND SEARCH REPORT; the executive search information source. 1981. q. free to qualified personnel. Box 9433, Panama City Beach, FL 32417. TEL 904-235-3733. FAX 904-233-9695. Ed. Kenneth J. Cole; Pub. Kenneth J. Cole. bk.rev.; bibl.; charts; stat. circ. 7,000. (looseleaf format; back issues avail.)

658.3   US   ISSN 0034-1827
RECRUITING TRENDS; the monthly newsletter for the recruiting executive. 1962. m. $155. Remy Publishing Co., 350 W. Hubbard St., No. 440, Chicago, IL 60610-4011. TEL 312-464-0300. Ed. Catherine Davis. index. (looseleaf format) **Indexed:** Pers.Lit. **Document type:** newsletter.
Incorporates: Recruiting Engineers and Computer Professionals.

658.3   AT
RECRUITMENT AND TERMINATION GUIDE. 1994. q. C C H Australia Ltd., P.O. Box 230, North Ryde, N.S.W. 2113, Australia. TEL 61-1-300300224. FAX 61-1-300306224. (looseleaf format)
Description: Includes practical features such as checklists, sample forms and letters, comparative tables and calculations.

REGIONAL REPORT ON MIDDLE MANAGEMENT COMPENSATION. see BUSINESS AND ECONOMICS — Management

REGIONAL REPORT ON TOP MANAGEMENT COMPENSATION. see BUSINESS AND ECONOMICS — Management

658.3 333.33   US   ISSN 0275-7613
THE RELOCATION REPORT. 1983. s-m. $127 (effective 1996). Federal News Service, Box 13460, Silver Spring, MD 20911-0460. TEL 301-608-9322. Ed. Dona DeZube; Pub. L. Craig MacKown. (looseleaf format; back issues avail.) **Document type:** newsletter.
—CCC.
Description: Provides relocation industry news for real estate brokers, appraisers and relocation specialists.

658   US
REMUNERATION REPORT - AUSTRIA. a. $825. (Executive Compensation Service (ECS)) Wyatt Data Services, 218 Rte. 17, N., Rochelle Park, NJ 07662-9832. TEL 201-843-1177. FAX 201-843-0101. **Document type:** trade publication.

658   US
REMUNERATION REPORT - BELGIUM. a. $825. (Executive Compensation Service (ECS)) Wyatt Data Services, 218 Rte. 17, N., Rochelle Park, NJ 07662-9821. TEL 201-843-1177. FAX 201-843-0101. **Document type:** trade publication.

658   US
REMUNERATION REPORT - DENMARK. a. $825. (Executive Compensation Service (ECS)) Wyatt Data Services, 218 Rte. 17, N., Rochelle Park, NJ 07662-9832. TEL 201-843-1177. FAX 201-843-0101. **Document type:** trade publication.

658   US
REMUNERATION REPORT - FINLAND. a. $825. (Executive Compensation Service (ECS)) Wyatt Data Services, 218 Rte. 17, N., Rochelle Park, NJ 07662-9832. TEL 201-843-1177. FAX 201-843-0101. **Document type:** trade publication.

658   US
REMUNERATION REPORT - FRANCE. a. $825. (Executive Compensation Service (ECS)) Wyatt Data Services, 218 Rte. 17, N., Rochelle Park, NJ 07662-9832. TEL 201-843-1177. FAX 201-843-0101. **Document type:** trade publication.

658   US
REMUNERATION REPORT - GERMANY. a. $825. (Executive Compensation Service (ECS)) Wyatt Data Services, 218 Rte. 17, N., Rochelle Park, NJ 07662-9832. TEL 201-843-1177. FAX 201-843-0101. **Document type:** trade publication.

658   US
REMUNERATION REPORT - GREECE. a. $825. (Executive Compensation Service (ECS)) Wyatt Data Services, 218 Rte. 17, N., Rochelle Park, NJ 07662-9832. TEL 201-843-1177. FAX 201-843-0101. **Document type:** trade publication.

658   US
REMUNERATION REPORT - IRELAND. a. $825. (Executive Compensation Service (ECS)) Wyatt Data Services, 218 Rte. 17, N., Rochelle Park, NJ 07662-9832. TEL 201-843-1177. FAX 201-843-0101. **Document type:** trade publication.

658   US
REMUNERATION REPORT - ITALY. a. $825. (Executive Compensation Service (ECS)) Wyatt Data Services, 218 Rte. 17, N., Rochelle Park, NJ 07662-9832. TEL 201-843-1177. FAX 201-843-0101. **Document type:** trade publication.

658   US
REMUNERATION REPORT - LUXEMBOURG. a. $825. (Executive Compensation Service (ECS)) Wyatt Data Services, 218 Rte. 17, N., Rochelle Park, NJ 07622-9832. TEL 201-843-1177. FAX 201-843-0101. **Document type:** trade publication.

658   US
REMUNERATION REPORT - NETHERLANDS. a. $825. (Executive Compensation Service (ECS)) Wyatt Data Services, 218 Rte. 17, N., Rochelle Park, NJ 07662-9832. TEL 609-843-1177. FAX 201-843-0101. **Document type:** trade publication.

BUSINESS AND ECONOMICS — PERSONNEL MANAGEMENT

658   US
REMUNERATION REPORT - NORWAY. a. $825. (Executive Compensation Service (ECS)) Wyatt Data Services, 218 Rte. 17, N., Rochelle Park, NJ 07662-9832. TEL 201-843-1177. FAX 201-843-0101. **Document type:** trade publication.

658   US
REMUNERATION REPORT - PORTUGAL. a. $825. (Executive Compensation Service (ECS)) Wyatt Data Services, 218 Rte. 17, N., Rochelle Park, NJ 07662-9832. TEL 201-843-1177. FAX 201-843-0101. **Document type:** trade publication.

658   US
REMUNERATION REPORT - SPAIN. a. $825. (Executive Compensation Service (ECS)) Wyatt Data Services, 218 Rte. 17, N., Rochelle Park, NJ 07662-9832. TEL 201-843-1177. FAX 201-843-0101. **Document type:** trade publication.

658   US
REMUNERATION REPORT - SWEDEN. a. $825. (Executive Compensation Service (ECS)) Wyatt Data Services, 218 Rte. 17, N., Rochelle Park, NJ 07662-9832. TEL 201-843-1177. FAX 201-843-0101. **Document type:** trade publication.

658   US
REMUNERATION REPORT - SWITZERLAND. a. $825. (Executive Compensation Service (ECS)) Wyatt Data Services, 218 Rte. 17, N., Rochelle Park, NJ 07662-9832. TEL 201-843-1177. FAX 201-843-0101. **Document type:** trade publication.

658   US
REMUNERATION REPORT - TURKEY. a. $825. (Executive Compensation Service (ECS)) Wyatt Data Services, 218 Rte. 17, N., Rochelle Park, NJ 07662-9832. TEL 201-843-1177. FAX 201-843-0101. **Document type:** trade publication.

658   US
REMUNERATION REPORT - UNITED KINGDOM. a. $825. (Executive Compensation Service (ECS)) Wyatt Data Services, 218 Rte. 17, N., Rochelle Park, NJ 07622-9832. TEL 201-843-1177. FAX 201-843-0101. **Document type:** trade publication.

658.3   CC   ISSN 1000-7628
RENCAI KAIFA/TALENT EXPLOITATION. (Text in Chinese) 1986. m. $60. Shanghai Rencai Yanjiuhui, No.7, Alley 622, Huaihai Zhonglu, Shanghai 200020, People's Republic of China. TEL 021-3274690. Ed. Zuo Chao. adv.; bk.rev. circ. 50,000. **Document type:** academic/scholarly publication.
Description: Promotes reform on personnel management system.

RENTAL MANAGEMENT. see BUSINESS AND ECONOMICS — Marketing And Purchasing

REPORT ON CANADIAN EXECUTIVE AND MIDDLE MANAGEMENT REMUNERATION. see BUSINESS AND ECONOMICS — Management

658   US   ISSN 1060-0205
REPORT ON EXECUTIVE REMUNERATION. 1988. a. (Executive Compensation Service (ECS)) Wyatt Data Services, 218 Rte. 17, N., Rochelle Park, NJ 07662-9832. TEL 201-843-1177. FAX 201-843-0101. **Document type:** trade publication.

658   US   ISSN 1069-434X
HD4965.5.U6
REPORT ON EXPATRIATE COMPENSATION POLICIES AND PRACTICES. a. $680. (Executive Compensation Service (ECS)) Wyatt Data Services, 218 Rte. 17, N., Rochelle Park, NJ 07662-9832. TEL 201-843-1177. FAX 201-843-0101. charts. **Document type:** trade publication.
Former titles: Expatriate Compensation Policies and Practices (ISSN 1069-4420); (until 1985): Report on Expatriate Compensation Policies and Practices (ISSN 0885-2197)

658   US   ISSN 1063-1968
HF5549.2.U5
REPORT ON HUMAN RESOURCES COMPENSATION. a. $340. (Executive Compensation Service (ECS)) Wyatt Data Services, 218 Rte. 17, N., Rochelle Park, NJ 07622-9832. TEL 201-843-1177. FAX 201-843-0101. charts. **Document type:** trade publication.
Description: Provides a complete perspective on compensation in the human resources field.

658   US   ISSN 1057-9494
REPORT ON OFFICE PERSONNEL REMUNERATION.*
1981. a. $600. (Executive Compensation Service (ECS)) Wyatt Data Services, 218 State Rte. 17, N., Rochelle Park, NJ 07622-3333. TEL 201-585-9808. FAX 201-585-0127. **Document type:** trade publication.
Former titles (until 1990): Report on Canadian Office Personnel Remuneration (ISSN 1044-6028); (until 1987): Office Personnel Remuneration, Canada (ISSN 0835-6718); (until 1985): Report on Office Personnel Remuneration, Canada (ISSN 0829-5441); Office Personnel Canada (ISSN 0229-1649)
Description: Geographically focused pay information reported for 71 office personnel positions.

658.3   US   ISSN 0742-7301
HF5549.A2
RESEARCH IN PERSONNEL AND HUMAN RESOURCES MANAGEMENT. 1983. irreg., vol.14, 1996. $73.25. J A I Press Inc., 55 Old Post Rd., No. 2, Box 1678, Greenwich, CT 06830-1678. TEL 203-661-7602. FAX 203-661-0792. E-mail: jai@jaipress.com. (Subscr. in the UK and Europe to: JAI Press Ltd., 38 Tavistock St., Covent Garden, London WC2E 7PB, England. TEL 44-171-379-8834. FAX 44-171-379-8835) Ed. Gerald R. Ferris. **Document type:** monographic series.
—BLDSC (7755.071000); SWETS; UnCover. **CCC.**

658.3   UK
RESEARCH PAPERS IN MANAGEMENT STUDIES. irreg., no.8, 1993. £5. University of Cambridge, Judge Institute of Management Studies, Trumpington St., Cambridge CB2 1AG, England. TEL 44-1223-339700. FAX 44-1223-339701. Ed. C.N. Pitelis. **Document type:** monographic series.
Refereed Serial

336 346.066   US
RETIREMENT AND BENEFIT PLANNING; strategy and design for businesses and tax-exempt organizations. 1991. base vol. (plus a. supplement). $95. Butterworth Legal Publishers (Salem) (Subsidiary of: Reed Elsevier plc), 8 Industrial Way, Bldg. C, Salem, NH 03079. TEL 800-548-4001. FAX 603-898-9858. Ed. Randolph M. Goodman. (looseleaf format)
Description: Comprehensive review of laws and planning principles covering retirement plans from a legal perspective. Covers the emerging areas of retirement planning, and the benefits and responsibilities for employers and employees.

658.3   FR   ISSN 1163-913X
REVUE DE GESTION DES RESSOURCES HUMAINES. 1991. q. 385 F. (foreign 497 F.). (Association de la Gestion des Ressources Humaines) Editions E S K A, 27 rue Dunois, 75013 Paris, France. TEL 44-06-80-42. FAX 44-24-06-94. **Document type:** trade publication.
Description: Seeks to develop, verify, and advance knowledge in human resources management.

658.3   FR
REVUE RESSOURCES HUMAINES. 4/yr. Societe Formac, 45 rue de Turbigo, 75003 Paris, France. Ed. Brigitte Bouillon. circ. 7,500.

658 910.9   US   ISSN 0731-9150
RUNZHEIMER REPORTS ON RELOCATION. 1982. m. $354. Runzheimer International, Runzheimer Park, Rochester, WI 53167. TEL 414-767-2200. URL: http://www.runzheimer.com. Ed. Lori Hurst. (looseleaf format; back issues avail.) **Document type:** newsletter.
—CCC.

658 910.09   US   ISSN 0730-8663
RUNZHEIMER REPORTS ON TRAVEL MANAGEMENT. 1981. m. $295. Runzheimer International, Runzheimer Park, Rochester, WI 53167. TEL 414-767-2200. URL: http://www.runzheimer.com. Ed. Lori Hurst. (looseleaf format; back issues avail.) **Document type:** newsletter.
—CCC.
Description: Covers business travel management.

658.3   II   ISSN 0970-8731
S E N D O C BULLETIN. PART 3: MANAGEMENT AND BEHAVIORAL SCIENCES. (Text in English) 1973. m. Rs.150($75) National Institute of Small Industry Extension Training, Small Enterprises National Documentation Centre, Yousufguda, Hyderabad 500045, India. TEL 91-40-238544. FAX 91-40-238547. TELEX 425-6381-SIET-IN. Ed. M.B. Raju. **Document type:** abstracting/indexing.

658.3   US   ISSN 1063-1917
S E R AMERICA. (Service, Employment, Redevelopment) 1972. q. $25 to individuals; institutions $100. S E R - Jobs for Progress, Inc., 100 Decker Dr., Ste. 200, Irving, TX 75062-2206. TEL 214-541-0616. FAX 214-650-1860. Ed. Juan J. Constantino. adv. contact: Sherri Seidel. bibl.; stat. circ. 15,000.
Former titles (until 1986): S E R Network News; S E R News; Adelante S E R.
Description: Discusses the development and utilization of human resources with special emphasis on the needs of Hispanics in the areas of education, training, employment, business and economic opportunities.

658.3   US
S E R NETWORK DIRECTORY. (Service, Employment, Redevelopment) a. S E R - Jobs for Progress, Inc., 100 Decker Dr., Ste. 200, Irving, TX 75062-2206. TEL 214-541-0616. FAX 214-650-1860. (Co-sponsors: League of United Latin American Citizens (LULAC); American G.I. Forum) Ed. Obie Gonzalez. **Document type:** directory.
Description: Resource information guide in the areas of education, training, employment, business and economic opportunities for the development and utilization of America's human resources, with emphasis on the needs of Hispanics.

658.3   US
▼**S I REVIEW;** tools and techniques for staffing industry professionals. Cover title: Si Review. 1996. 6/yr. $48 in U.S. & Canada; elsewhere $72; free to qualified personnel. Staffing Industry Analysts, Inc., 2235 Grant Rd., No. 3, Los Altos, CA 94024. TEL 415-903-9494. FAX 415-903-9811. E-mail: editor@sireport; adsales@sireport; URL: http://www.sireport.com. Ed. Theresa Daly; Pub. Peter Yessne. adv. contact: Grant Landes. software rev.; illus.; tr.lit.; circ. 21,000 (controlled). **Document type:** trade publication.

658.3 331.2   US   ISSN 1041-6633
HD4973
SALARY BUDGET SURVEY. Key Title: Report on the Salary Budget Survey. a. $75 to non-members; members $55. American Compensation Association, 14040 N. Northsight Blvd., Scottsdale, AZ 85260. TEL 605-951-9191. **Indexed:** SRI. **Document type:** trade publication.
Description: Results of ACA annual survey of salary budgets, including trend information.

SALARY INCREASE SURVEY REPORT. see OCCUPATIONS AND CAREERS

658   US
SALES AND MARKETING PERSONNEL REPORT. a. $490. (Executive Compensation Service (ECS)) Wyatt Data Services, 218 Rte. 17, N., Rochelle park, NJ 07622-9832. TEL 201-843-1177. FAX 201-843-0101. charts. **Document type:** trade publication.
Description: Evaluates how the pay packages of the sales and marketing staff compare to the marketplace.

SALESMAN'S INSIDER. see BUSINESS AND ECONOMICS — Marketing And Purchasing

658.3   BE   ISSN 0774-7217
SAMSOM SOCIAAL OVERLEG. French edition: Samsom Concertation Sociale (ISSN 0774-7209) (Text in Flemish) 1986. m. 6360 BEF. C E D Samsom (Subsidiary of: Wolters Samsom Belgie n.v.), Kouterveld 14, B-1831 Diegem, Belgium. TEL 32-2-7231111. Ed.Bd.

B

BUSINESS AND ECONOMICS — PERSONNEL MANAGEMENT

658.3 340   GW   ISSN 0943-5980
SCHNELLBRIEF FUER PERSONALWIRTSCHAFT UND ARBEITSRECHT; aktuelle Gesetzgebung, neue Rechtsprechung und alle wichtigen Trends fuer die Personalarbeit. 1993. s-m. DM.236 (effective 1997). Verlag C.H. Beck, 80791 Munich, Germany. TEL 49-89-38189338. FAX 49-89-38189398. Ed.Bd. **Document type:** bulletin.

658.3   UK
SELECTION. 10/yr. free. Institute of Employment Consultants, 6 Guildford Rd., Woking, Surrey GU22 7PX, England. TEL 44-1483-766442. FAX 44-1483-714979. Ed. Susan Smith Meci. circ. 9,500. **Document type:** trade publication.

SHESHUNOFF TRAINING SERIES. see BUSINESS AND ECONOMICS — Banking And Finance

658.3   US
SMART WORKPLACE PRACTICES. 1981. m. $149. Independent Small Business Employers of America, 520 S. Pierce, Ste. 224, Mason City, IA 50401. TEL 515-424-3187. FAX 515-424-1673. Ed. Jim Collison. bk.rev.; circ. 1,200 (paid). (back issues avail.) **Document type:** newsletter.
Formerly: Employer Advocate.
Description: Focuses on how managers and supervisors can deal safely, effectively and profitably with their employees.

SOUNDVIEW EXECUTIVE BOOK SUMMARIES. see BUSINESS AND ECONOMICS — Management

658.3   UK
SPEAKING UP BY SECTOR. irreg, no.3, 1995. £20. Public Concern at Work, Lincoln's Inn House, 42 Kingsway, London WC2B 6EX, England. TEL 44-171-404-6609. FAX 44-171-404-6576. E-mail: whistle@pcaw.demon.co.uk. Ed. Guy Dehn. R&P contact: Guy Dehn. adv. contact: Guy Dehn. **Document type:** monographic series.

658.3   US   ISSN 1051-3051
HD5873
STAFFING INDUSTRY REPORT. (Monthly advertising supplement avail.) 1990. s-m. $345 in N. America: elsewhere £470 (includes annual Staffing Industry Resource Guide and 3 m. supplements). Staffing Industry Analysts, Inc., 2235 Grant Rd., No. 3, Los Altos, CA 94024. TEL 415-903-9494. FAX 415-903-9811. Ed. Theresa Daly; Pub. Peter Yessne. adv. contact: Grant Landes. index; circ. 3,000 (paid). (back issues avail.) **Document type:** newsletter.
Description: Reports company news, industry trends, and financial data regarding the temporary help, PEO, and employment services industry. Covers a variety of temporary-help staffing issues.

658.3   US
STAFFING INDUSTRY RESOURCE GUIDE. a. $42. Staffing Industry Analysts, Inc., 2235 Grant Rd., Ste.3, Los Altos, CA 94024. TEL 415-903-9494. FAX 415-903-9811. Ed. Doris Hisey; Pub. Peter Yessne. adv. contact: Grant Landes.

STATE CAPITALS. EMPLOYEE POLICY FOR THE PRIVATE & PUBLIC SECTORS. see PUBLIC ADMINISTRATION

658.3   US   ISSN 1052-4819
Z7164.C81
STERN'S SOURCEFINDER; human resources management. 1991. biennial. $169.95. Box 3233, Culver City, CA 90231-3233. TEL 310-838-4437. FAX 310-838-2344. Eds. Yvette Borcia, Gerry Stern; Pub. Michael Daniels. bk.rev.; circ. 500 (paid). (back issues avail.)
Description: Covers information sources for every aspect of human resource management, including organizations, compensation, benefits, career counseling, communication, law, health and safety, general management and labor and employee relations.

658.3 336.2   GW   ISSN 0944-5765
STEUER-BRIEF FUER DAS PERSONALBUERO. 1993. m. DM.9.85 per no. (effective 1997). Verlag Peter Deubner GmbH, Wolfgang-Mueller-Str. 14, 50968 Cologne, Germany. TEL 49-221-9370180. FAX 49-221-93701890. **Document type:** bulletin.

658   US
SUCCESSFUL BENEFITS COMMUNICATOR. 1992. m. $179. I O M A, 29 W. 35th St., 5th Fl., New York, NY 10001-2299. TEL 212-244-0360. **Document type:** newsletter.

SUPERVISORY MANAGEMENT REPORT - GEOGRAPHIC EDITION. see BUSINESS AND ECONOMICS — Management

SURVEY OF SALARIES. see BUSINESS AND ECONOMICS — Abstracting, Bibliographies, Statistics

658   US
SURVEY REPORT ON VARIABLE PAY PROGRAMS. a. $640. (Executive Compensation Service (ECS)) Wyatt Data Services, 218 Rte. 17, N., Roselle Park, NJ 07662-9832. TEL 201-843-1177. FAX 201-843-0101. charts. **Document type:** trade publication.
Description: Features annual survey data from over 400 variable-pay plans; provides information on the prevalence, eligibility, target and actual award levels of the country's most frequently used forms of alternative rewards.

658.3   UK
TEAM LEADER. s-m. 125 High Holborn, London WC1V 6QA, England. TEL 0171-404-1585. FAX 0171-404-1580. Ed. Jenny Hayes. **Document type:** newsletter.
Formerly: Foremanship.

658.3   US
TEAMWORK (CHICAGO). 1987. bi-w. $68.90 bi-w. Dartnell Corporation, 4660 N. Ravenswood Ave., Chicago, IL 60640. TEL 773-561-4000; 800-621-5463. FAX 773-561-3801. URL: http://www.dartnellcorp.com. Ed. Kim Andersen. **Document type:** newsletter.
Description: Offers insight, wisdom and new concepts that will have an immediate, positive impact on the relations between employees.

658.3   US   ISSN 1047-8388
TECHNICAL & SKILLS TRAINING. 1990. 8/yr. $59 (foreign $75). American Society for Training and Development, 1640 King St., Box 1443, Alexandria, VA 22313. TEL 703-683-8100. FAX 703-683-8103. (Subscr. to: Box 6871, Syracuse, NY 13217-9965) Ed. Ellen S. Carnevale. R&P contact: Roayn Ellis. adv.; charts; illus.; tr.lit.; index. circ. 20,000. (also avail. in microfilm; reprint service avail.; back issues avail.) Indexed: Cont.Pg.Educ., Q.Abstr., Tech.Educ.Abstr., Tr.& Dev.Alert. **Document type:** trade publication.
—KR SourceOne; SWETS. **CCC.**
Description: For technical and skills trainers; reports news and trends affecting the field, products available; and includes short articles on training topics, as well as articles on companies and techniques.

658   US
TA158
TECHNICIAN AND SKILLED TRADES PERSONNEL REPORT - GEOGRAPHIC EDITION. (Supplement to: Industry Report on Technician and Skilled Trades Personnel Compensation (ISSN 1063-0058)) a. $490. (Executive Compensation Service) Wyatt Data Services, 218 Rte. 17, N., Roselle Park, NJ 07662-9832. TEL 201-843-1177. FAX 201-843-0101. charts. **Document type:** trade publication.
Description: Provides data on salaries and total cash compensation for a full spectrum of technician and skilled trades personnel, analyzed from a geographic perspective.

658.3 621.381   US   ISSN 8756-7431
TELECOMMUTING REVIEW. 1984. m. $177 (foreign $197) (effective 1997). Gil Gordon Associates, 10 Donner Ct., Monmouth Junction, NJ 08852. TEL 908-329-2266. E-mail: 74375.1667@compuserve.com; URL: http://www.gilgordon.com. (Dist. by: TeleSpan Publishing Corp., 50 W. Palm St., Altadena, CA 91001) Ed. Gil Gordon. bk.rev. (back issues avail.) Indexed: Comput.Dtbs. **Document type:** newsletter.
● Also available online. Vendor(s): Information Access Co.
—BLDSC (8781.591000). **CCC.**
Description: Features case studies, legal, supervisory and technical issues; telecommuting (work-at-home) and virtual office programs sponsored by employers.

658.3 346.066   US   ISSN 0749-8233
TERMINATION OF EMPLOYMENT; employer and employee rights. base vol. (plus m. Report Bulletins and updates). $484.95 (foreign $639) (effective 1995). Warren, Gorham & Lamont, One Penn Plaza, New York, NY 10119. TEL 212-971-5000. FAX 212-971-5113. (Orders to: The Park Square Bldg., 31 St. James Ave., Boston, MA 02116-4112. TEL 800-950-1207) Ed. Kenneth McCulloch. (looseleaf format) **Document type:** trade publication.
Description: Emphasizes preventive measures and provides explanations of key federal laws and court cases that restrict an employer's rights to hire and fire at will.

658.3 338   AT
TIME MANAGEMENT. 1986. m. Aus.$195 (foreign Aus.$220) (effective 1996). c/o NGT Direct Marketing, 10-42 Garden Blvd., Dingley, Vic. 3172, Australia. TEL 61-2-4499994. FAX 61-2-445560. Ed. Lowell Tarling; Pub. Brad Tonini. **Document type:** newsletter.
Formerly: Timewatch (ISSN 0818-1918)

TIMING ANALYSIS PROJECTION. see STATISTICS

658.3   US   ISSN 0734-3302
HD7260
TODAY'S SUPERVISOR. 1935. m. $23 to non-members; members $18. National Safety Council, Periodicals Department, 1121 Spring Lake Dr., Itasca, IL 60143. TEL 708-775-2281. Ed. Kathleen Henderson; Pub. Kevin H. Axe. circ. 100,000. (also avail. in microform from UMI; reprint service avail. from UMI) **Document type:** trade publication.
—UMI.
Formerly (until 1982): Industrial Supervisor (ISSN 0019-879X)
Description: Addresses the many safety and health problems and issues that first-line supervisors face.

658.3 340   UK   ISSN 0969-6385
TOLLEY'S EMPLOYMENT LAW & PRACTICE. 1993. m. £95 (foreign £104). Tolley Publishing Co. Ltd., Tolley House, 2 Addiscombe Rd., Croydon, Surrey CR9 5AF, England. TEL 44-181-686-9141. FAX 44-181-686-3155. E-mail: julie_clarke@tolley.co.uk. Ed. Julie Clarke. adv. contact: Graham Joy. **Document type:** bulletin.
—BLDSC (8863.685800).

658.3   UK   ISSN 1365-5590
TOLLEY'S PAYROLL HANDBOOK. 1987. a. Tolley Publishing Co. Ltd., Tolley House, 2 Addiscombe Rd., Croydon, Surrey CR9 5AF, England. TEL 44-181-686-9141. FAX 44-181-686-3155. Ed. Mike Nicholas. **Document type:** trade publication.
—BLDSC (8863.686535).
Description: Comprehensive and practical guide to payroll department procedures.

TOP EXECUTIVE COMPENSATION. see BUSINESS AND ECONOMICS — Management

TOP MANAGEMENT COMPENSATION - REGRESSION ANALYSIS REPORT. see BUSINESS AND ECONOMICS — Management

TOP MANAGEMENT HI-COMP REPORT. see BUSINESS AND ECONOMICS — Management

TOP MANAGEMENT REMUNERATION REPORT - EUROPE. see BUSINESS AND ECONOMICS — Management

331   AT   ISSN 1325-6947
TOP MANAGEMENT REMUNERATION REVIEW. 1975. a. Aus.$1800 (avail. to Australian organizations only). Cullen Egan Dell, Level 8, 50 Bridge St., Sydney, N.S.W. 2000, Australia. TEL 61-2-3759800. FAX 61-2-2336800. Ed. Michelle Seddon. circ. 100
Description: Detailed remuneration review of senior management positions in Australia to contributors.

TOPICS (CAMBRIDGE). see BUSINESS AND ECONOMICS — Labor And Industrial Relations

658.3   US   ISSN 0888-6032
HF5549.5.C67
TOPICS IN TOTAL COMPENSATION. 1986. q. $72. (Human Resources Information Center) Panel Publishers, Inc., 36 W. 44th St., No. 1316, New York, NY 10036-2000. TEL 212-354-4545. FAX 212-302-5119. Ed. Robert McCaffery. circ. 1,800. (back issues avail.) Indexed: ABI Inform.
—UMI. **CCC.**
Description: Focuses on topics of interest to the compensation and benefits professional.

BUSINESS AND ECONOMICS — PERSONNEL MANAGEMENT

658.3 US
TOTAL COMPENSATION HANDBOOK. a. $276.45 (foreign $396.45) (effective 1995). Warren, Gorham & Lamont, One Penn Plaza, New York, NY 10119. TEL 212-971-5000. FAX 212-971-5113. (Subscr. to: The Park Square Bldg., 31 St. James Ave., Boston, MA 02116-4112. TEL 800-950-1207) **Document type:** trade publication.

TRAINING; the magazine covering the human side of business. see BUSINESS AND ECONOMICS — Management

331 US ISSN 1055-9760
HF5549.5.T7 CODEN: TRDEEL
TRAINING & DEVELOPMENT. 1945. m. $75 to non-members. American Society for Training and Development, 1640 King St., Box 1443, Alexandria, VA 22313. TEL 703-683-8100. FAX 703-683-8103. Ed. Patricia Galagan. R&P contact: Ryan Ellis. adv.; bk.rev.; charts; illus.; tr.lit.; index. circ. 35,000. (also avail. in microfilm from UMI; reprint service avail. from UMI) **Indexed:** ABI Inform., Account.& Data Proc.Abstr., Account.& Data Proc.Abstr., ASCA, B.P.I., Bus.Ind., C.I.J.E., Cont.Pg.Educ., Curr.Cont., INSPEC, Key to Econ.Sci., Lang.& Lang.Behav.Abstr., Manage.Cont., Oper.Res.Manage.Sci., Pers.Lit., Pers.Manage.Abstr., Psychol.Abstr., Psycscan, Q.Abstr., Risk Abstr., SSCI, Tr.& Dev.Alert, Tr.& Indus.Ind., Work Rel.Abstr. **Document type:** trade publication.
● Also available online. Vendor(s): Information Access Co.
—BLDSC (8883.500850); AskIEEE; CISTI; Genuine Article; KR SourceOne; SWETS; UMI; UnCover. **CCC.**
Former titles: A S T D Journal; Training Directors Journal; Training and Development Journal (ISSN 0041-0861); Incorporating: Training Research Abstracts (ISSN 0564-089X)

TRAINING AND DEVELOPMENT YEARBOOK. see BUSINESS AND ECONOMICS — Abstracting, Bibliographies, Statistics

658.3 UK ISSN 0968-4875
HD30.42.G7
TRAINING FOR QUALITY. 1993. q. £529($819) (effective 1997). M C B University Press Ltd., 60-62 Toller Ln., Bradford, W. Yorks BD8 9BY, England. TEL 44-1274-777700. FAX 44-1274-785200. TELEX 51317-MCBUNI-G. URL: http://www.mcb.co. uk. (N. American subscr. to: M C B University Press Limited, Box 1943, Birmingham, AL 35201) Ed. Matthew Hinds. (reprint service avail. from SWZ) **Indexed:** Br.Educ.Ind. **Document type:** academic/scholarly publication.
● Also available on CD-ROM.
—BLDSC (8883.509500). **CCC.**

658.3 UK
TRAINING NEWS. bi-m. P.O. Box 1, Atherstone, Warks. CV9 1BE, England. TEL 01827-718081. FAX 01926-413900. Ed. Paul Carter. **Document type:** trade publication.

658 UK ISSN 0041-090X
TRAINING OFFICER. 1965. 10/yr. £60 (foreign £75) (effective 1996). Marylebone Press Ltd., Lloyds House, 18 Lloyd St., Manchester M2 5WA, England. TEL 44-161-832-6541. FAX 44-161-832-8129. Ed. Sylvia Worth. adv.; bk.rev.; charts; illus. **Indexed:** Account.& Data Proc.Abstr., ASEAN Manage.Abstr., Br.Educ.Ind., Build.Manage.Abstr., Cont.Pg.Educ., High.Educ.Curr.Aware.Bull., INSPEC (1983-), Mgmt.& Market.Abstr., Stud.Wom.Abstr., Tr.& Dev.Alert. **Document type:** trade publication.
—BLDSC (8883.508500); AskIEEE; KR SourceOne; UMI.

658.3 UK ISSN 0952-0503
TRAINING TECHNOLOGY AND HUMAN RESOURCES. 1988. bi-m. £36 (foreign £44) (effective 1997 & 1998). M R Publishing Ltd., International Centre, Spindle Way, Crawley, W. Sussex RH10 1TG, England. TEL 44-1293-537003. FAX 44-1293-531105. Ed. Mike Randle; Pub. Mike Randle. adv. contact: Pat Randle. bk.rev. circ. 6,000. **Indexed:** Br.Educ.Ind., INSPEC (1994-). **Document type:** trade publication.
—AskIEEE; KR SourceOne.
Formerly (until 1992): Training Technology.

658.3 UK ISSN 0957-0004
TRAINING TOMORROW. 9/yr. £150 (foreign Aus.$299) (effective 1998). M C B University Press Ltd., 60-62 Toller Ln., Bradford, W. Yorks BD8 9BY, England. TEL 44-1274-777700. FAX 44-1274-785200. TELEX 51317-MCBUNI-G. URL: http://www.mcb.co. uk. Ed. Pete Maxted. adv.; bk.rev. circ. 1,600. **Indexed:** Br.Educ.Ind. **Document type:** bulletin.
—BLDSC (8883.583000); UMI. **CCC.**
Incorporates (1978-1996): Training Digest Europe (ISSN 1350-9489); (1994-1996): Training Network (ISSN 1351-1157)

658.3 UK ISSN 1353-5730
TRANSTERRA HUMAN RESOURCES REVIEW. 1993. bi-m. £110. Transterra Ltd., St. Julians, Kent TN15 0RX, England. TEL 44-1732-740850. FAX 44-1732-740849. Ed. M. Rigby. R&P contact: S. Klenke. adv. contact: S. Klenke. **Document type:** trade publication.

658.3 US ISSN 0272-569X
TRAVEL EXPENSE MANAGEMENT. 1979. 24/yr. $427 (effective 1997). American Business Publishing, Brinley Professional Plaza, 3100 Hwy. 138, Box 1442, Wall Township, NJ 07719-1442. TEL 908-681-1133. FAX 908-681-0490. E-mail: 75673.624@compuserve.com. Ed. Melanie Jenkins; Pub. Robert K. Jenkins. R&P contact: Jillian Philipp. adv. contact: Judith Granholm. index. circ. 425. (tabloid format; back issues avail.) **Document type:** newsletter.
—**CCC.**
Description: For travel managers of major corporations. Provides current information on developments in the field of travel and expense cost control.

U CO S D A BRIEFING PAPERS. (Universities' and Colleges' Staff Development Agency) see EDUCATION — Higher Education

U CO S D A GREEN PAPERS. (Universities' and Colleges' Staff Development Agency) see EDUCATION — Higher Education

U CO S D A HANDBOOKS. (Universities' and Colleges' Staff Development Agency) see EDUCATION — Higher Education

U CO S D A OCCASIONAL LONGER BRIEFING PAPERS. (Universities' and Colleges' Staff Development Agency) see EDUCATION — Higher Education

U CO S D A RESOURCE PACKS AND DISKS. (Universities' and Colleges' Staff Development Agency) see EDUCATION — Higher Education

658.3 II
UTPADAKTA. (Text in Hindi) m. Rs.25($13) National Productivity Council, Business Management Section, Uptadakta Bhawan, Lodi Rd., New Delhi 110003, India. TEL 4690331.
Description: Carries informative articles and features for supervisors and workers who want to achieve higher productivity.

658.3 US ISSN 0888-6628
WHAT TO DO ABOUT PERSONNEL PROBLEMS IN (STATE). 1985. m. $295. Business & Legal Reports, Inc., 39 Academy St., Madison, CT 06443-1513. TEL 203-245-7448; 800-727-5257. FAX 203-245-2559. Ed. Robert L. Brady. circ. 21,100 (paid). (looseleaf format; back issues avail.) **Document type:** newsletter.
—**CCC.**
Incorporates: Personnel Manager's Policy and Practice Update; What to do about Your Personnel Problems Today.
Description: Contains state-specific and federal information on human resource management, a 400 page answer book on all important policy and regulation topics and an annual wage and salary survey.

658.3 US
WHAT'S AHEAD IN HUMAN RESOURCES. 1973. s-m. $145. Remy Publishing Co., 350 W. Hubbard St., No. 440, Chicago, IL 60610-4011. TEL 312-464-0300. Ed. John Hickey. bk.rev. **Indexed:** Pers.Lit. **Document type:** newsletter.
Formerly: What's Ahead in Personnel (ISSN 0899-3076).

331 US ISSN 1075-8550
CODEN: WILRE2
THE WILLIAMS REPORT. 1982. m. $157. Joe Williams Communications, Inc., Box 924, Bartlesville, OK 74005. TEL 918-336-2267. Ed. Joe Williams; Pub. Joe Williams. bk.rev. (back issues avail.) **Document type:** newsletter.
Former titles: Communications Ideas, Plans and Strategies Report; Communication Illustrated; Employee Communication (ISSN 0736-7635)
Description: Reviews employee communications ideas, plans, and strategies.

WORK AND STRESS. see PSYCHOLOGY

658.3 US ISSN 1060-930X
HD4904.25
WORK-FAMILY ROUNDTABLE. 1991. q. $89 to non-members. Conference Board, Inc., 845 Third Ave., New York, NY 10022. TEL 212-759-0900. FAX 212-980-7014. **Document type:** newsletter.
—**CCC.**
Description: Provides information on how businesses are implementing work-family programs.

WORK TIMES. see BUSINESS AND ECONOMICS — Economic Situation And Conditions

WORKERS COMPENSATION; exposures, coverage, claims. see INSURANCE

658.3 331.1 US
HF5549.A2 CODEN: PEJOAA
WORKFORCE; the business magazine for leaders in human resources. 1922. m. $59 (foreign $99) (effective 1997). A C C Communications, Inc., Box 2440, Costa Mesa, CA 92628. TEL 714-751-1883. FAX 714-751-4106. E-mail: halcrowa@workforcemag.com; URL: http://www. HRHQ.com/. Ed. Dawn Anfuso; Pub. Allan Halcrow. R&P contact: Barbara Heckman. adv.; index. circ. 30,000. (also avail. in microfilm from UMI; reprint service avail. from UMI,KTO) **Indexed:** ABI Inform., Acad.Ind., Account.& Data Proc.Abstr., Anbar, ASCA, ASEAN Manage.Abstr., B.P.I., Bank.Lit.Ind., Bk.Rev.Ind. (1965-), BPIA, Bus.Ind., C.I.J.E., C.I.S.Abstr., Child.Bk.Rev.Ind. (1965-), Comput.Lit.Ind., Cont.Pg.Manage., Curr.Cont., Data Process.Dig., Educ.Admin.Abstr., Excerp.Med., Intl.Mgmt.Info., Key to Econ.Sci., Law Ofc.Info.Svc., Manage.Cont., Mgmt.& Market.Abstr., Oper.Res.Manage.Sci., P.A.I.S., Pers.Lit., Pers.Manage.Abstr., PROMT, PSI, Psychol.Abstr., Psycscan, Q.Abstr., Ref.Pt.Food Indus.Abstr., SCIMP, SSCI, Tech.Educ.Abstr., Tr.& Dev.Alert, Work Rel.Abstr. **Document type:** trade publication.
● Also available online. Vendor(s): Information Access Co., UMI.
—CASDDS; Genuine Article; KR SourceOne; SWETS; UMI; UnCover. **CCC.**
Former titles (until 1997): Personnel Journal (ISSN 0031-5745); (until 1927): Journal of Personnel Research (ISSN 0886-750X)

658.3 US
WORKING TOGETHER; a bulletin of inspiration and ideas for achievement-minded people. bi-w. $68.90. Dartnell Corporation, 4660 N. Ravenswood Ave., Chicago, IL 60640. TEL 773-561-4000; 800-621-5463. FAX 773-561-3801. URL: http:// www.dartnellcorp.com. Ed. Kim Andersen. circ. 25,000. **Document type:** bulletin.
Description: Helps employees appreciate the benefits of cooperation and involvement--for themselves and for their companies.

WORKLIFE REPORT. see BUSINESS AND ECONOMICS — Labor And Industrial Relations

658.3 SZ
WORKS. 12/yr. Badenerstr. 41, CH-8004 Zurich, Switzerland. TEL 41-1-2410757. FAX 41-1-2411409. Ed. Andreas Hubli. circ. 13,300. **Document type:** newspaper.
Formerly (until 1997): Schweizer Arbeitnehmer.

WORKSITE WELLNESS WORKS. see PUBLIC HEALTH AND SAFETY

1578 BUSINESS AND ECONOMICS — PRODUCTION OF GOODS AND SERVICES

658.3 UK
WORLDWIDE SURVEY OF INTERNATIONAL ASSIGNMENT POLICIES AND PRACTICES. EUROPEAN EDITION. 1981. a. Organization Resources Counselors, Inc., Buckingham Ct., 78 Buckingham Gate, London SW1E 6PE, England. TEL 44-171-222-9321. FAX 44-171-799-2018.
 Former titles: Survey of Policies and Practices for European Expatriates; Survey of Policies and Practices for U K Expatriates.

WRONGFUL DISMISSAL. see *LAW*

YOUR FINANCIAL FUTURE; Standard & Poor's guide to retirement planning. see *BUSINESS AND ECONOMICS — Investments*

658.3 GW ISSN 0179-6437
ZEITSCHRIFT FUER PERSONALFORSCHUNG. 1987. q. DM.74 (effective 1997). Rainer Hampp Verlag, Meringerzellerstr. 16, 86415 Mering, Germany. TEL 49-8233-4783. FAX 49-8233-30755. E-mail: rainer__hampp__verlag@t-online.de. **Document type:** trade publication.

BUSINESS AND ECONOMICS — Production Of Goods And Services

A B C BELGE POUR LE COMMERCE ET L'INDUSTRIE. see *BUSINESS AND ECONOMICS — Trade And Industrial Directories*

A B C LUXEMBOURGEOIS POUR LE COMMERCE ET L'INDUSTRIE. see *BUSINESS AND ECONOMICS — Trade And Industrial Directories*

388 US
A C M A NEWSLETTER. q. membership. American Cutlery Manufacturers Association, 209 Elden St., Ste. 202, Herndon, VA 20170-4815. TEL 703-709-8253. FAX 703-709-1036. E-mail: acma@erols.com. Dir. David W. Barrack. adv. **Document type:** newsletter.

338 658 US
A I M - R NEWS. m. Association of Industry Manufacturers Representatives, 222 Merchandise Mart Plaza, Ste. 1360, Chicago, IL 60654. TEL 312-464-0090. Ed. Betchie Bistrom. circ. 250.
 Description: Covers management and industry news.

338 PO ISSN 0870-287X
A I P INFORMACAO. 1975. 12/yr. $40 (effective 1995). Associacao Industrial Portuguesa, Praca das Industrias, 1399 Lisbon Codex, Portugal. TEL 351-1-3620100. FAX 351-1-3639047. TELEX 15650 AIPFIL P. Ed. Rui Ferreira Leite. adv. contact: Benvindo Teixeira. bk.rev. circ. 4,000. **Document type:** bulletin.
 —BLDSC (0773.452000).

A P I C S THE PERFORMANCE ADVANTAGE. (American Production and Inventory Control Society - The Educational Society for Resource Management) see *BUSINESS AND ECONOMICS — Management*

338.9 JA ISSN 0066-846X
HC415.I52
A P O ANNUAL REPORT. (Text in English) 1962. a. free. Asian Productivity Organization, 8-4-14 Akasaka, Minato-ku, Tokyo 107, Japan. FAX 81-3-3408-7220. TELEX J26477. E-mail: apo@gol.com; URL: http://www.apo-tokyo.com. Ed. Philip Mathews. circ. 2,500. (also avail. in microfiche from CIS) **Indexed:** IIS.

338 JA ISSN 0044-9229
A P O NEWS. 1971. m. free. Asian Productivity Organization, 8-4-14 Akasaka, Minato-ku, Tokyo 107, Japan. FAX 81-3-3408-7220. TELEX J26477. E-mail: apo@gol.com; URL: http://www.apo-tokyo.com. bk.rev. circ. 5,900. **Document type:** bulletin.
 Formerly: Asian Productivity Monthly Bulletin.

338 JA ISSN 0919-0589
HC415.I52
A P O PRODUCTIVITY JOURNAL. (Text in English) 1993. 2/yr. $10 in Asia & Oceania; elsewhere $23. Asian Productivity Organization, 8-4-14, Akasaka, Minato-ku, Tokyo 107, Japan. FAX 81-3-3408-7220. TELEX J26477. E-mail: apo@gol.com; URL: http://www.apo-tokyo.com. circ. 1,000.

A R W SUPPLIER NEWS. (Air-Conditioning & Refrigeration Wholesalers) see *HEATING, PLUMBING AND REFRIGERATION*

338 380 GW ISSN 0938-7927
ACQUISA; Zeitschrift fuer Verkauf, Marketing, Motivation. 1952. m. DM.98 (foreign DM.116). Max Schimmel Verlag GmbH, Im Kreuz 9, 97076 Wuerzburg, Germany. TEL 0931-2791400. FAX 0931-2791444. Ed. Martina Schimmel-Schloo; Pub. Annemarie Schimmel. adv. contact: Gudrun Schimmel-Wanner. circ. 34,348. **Document type:** trade publication.
 —BLDSC (0578.880250).
 Formerly: Industrie- und Handelsvertreter (ISSN 0019-9214)

338.7 GW ISSN 0002-3752
DIE AKTIENGESELLSCHAFT; Zeitschrift fuer das gesamte Aktienwesen. Abbreviated title: A G. m. DM.348. (Schutzvereinigung der Kleinaktionaere e.V.) Verlag Dr. Otto Schmidt KG, Unter den Ulmen 96-98, 50968 Cologne, Germany. TEL 49-221-9373801. FAX 49-221-93738943. E-mail: dr.otto.schmidt@t-online.de. Ed. K. Knauth. adv.; bk.rev.; index, cum.index: 1956-1965. circ. 2,000. (reprint service avail. from SCH) **Indexed:** ELLIS, IBr. **Document type:** trade publication.
 —SWETS. **CCC.**

338 GW
AKTIONAERSREPORT. m. DM.50 (effective 1997). Verlag Dr. Otto Schmidt KG, Unter den Ulmen 96-98, 50968 Cologne, Germany. TEL 49-221-9373801. FAX 49-221-93738943. E-mail: dr.otto.schmidt@t-online.de. **Document type:** bulletin.

ALFORJA; revista mensual de la produccion y distribucion moderna. see *FOOD AND FOOD INDUSTRIES*

338 PK
ALL PAKISTAN TEXTILE MILLS ASSOCIATION. CHAIRMAN'S REVIEW. (Text in English) a. free. All Pakistan Textile Mills Association, Muhammadi House, 3rd Fl., I.I. Chundrigar Rd., Karachi 2, Pakistan.
 Formerly: All Pakistan Textile Mills Association. Annual Report.

338 ISSN 0002-8908
AMERICAN INDUSTRY. 1946. m. $25. Publications for Industry, 21 Russell Woods Rd., Great Neck, NY 11021. TEL 516-487-0990. FAX 516-487-0809. Ed. Jack S. Panes. adv.; B&W page $2087; trim 10 3/8 x 14 1/4. bk.rev.; charts; illus.; tr.lit. circ. 25,000. (also avail. in microfilm from UMI; reprint service avail. from UMI) **Document type:** trade publication.
 —UMI.
 Description: New product releases with or without photos for largest U.S. industrial concerns.

621.75 US ISSN 1041-7958
TJ1 CODEN: AMMAAA
AMERICAN MACHINIST. 1877. m. $60 (Canada $80; elsewhere $100; free to qualified personnel). Penton Publishing Co. (Subsidiary of: Pittway Company), 1100 Superior Ave., Cleveland, OH 44114-2543. TEL 216-696-7000. FAX 216-696-0177. (Subscr. to: Box 95759, Cleveland, OH 44101) Ed. Ron Kohl. adv.; B&W page $4875. bk.rev.; charts; illus.; tr.lit.; index; circ. 82,000 (controlled). (also avail. in microform from UMI,PMC) **Indexed:** A.I.Abstr., A.S.& T.Ind., Alloys Ind., C.I.S.Abstr., CAD CAM Abstr., Cadscan, Chem.Abstr., Eng.Ind., Eng.Mat.Abstr., Fluidex, Ind.Sci.Rev., Int.Packag.Abstr., ISMEC, Lead Abstr., Met.Abstr.Ind., Met.Abstr., Nonfer.Met.Alert, PCC Alert, Robomat., SRI, Steels Alert, World Alum.Abstr., Zincscan. **Document type:** trade publication.
 —BLDSC (0841.000000); CASDDS; CISTI; Ei; Genuine Article; KR SourceOne; Linda Hall; SWETS; UMI; UnCover. **CCC.**
 Former titles: American Machinist and Automated Manufacturing (ISSN 0886-0335); (until 1986): American Machinist (ISSN 0002-9858); (until 1963): American Machinist - Metalworking Manufacturing (ISSN 0096-5154); (until 1960): American Machinist (ISSN 0360-5892)
 Description: Covers all aspects of manufacturing industry. Topics of articles include machine vision, computer-integrated manufacturing, robotics, lasers, computerized numerical control, and manufacturing systems.

AMERICAN STATISTICAL ASSOCIATION. SECTION ON QUALITY AND PRODUCTIVITY. PROCEEDINGS. see *BUSINESS AND ECONOMICS — Abstracting, Bibliographies, Statistics*

ANDHRA PRADESH PRODUCTIVITY COUNCIL. TARGET. see *PUBLIC ADMINISTRATION*

338 BE ISSN 0003-505X
LES ANNONCES DE L'INDUSTRIE. (Text in French) 1946. w. 1000 BEF per language edition (both editions 1600 BEF) (effective 1994). Kluwer Business Press (Subsidiary of: Wolters Kluwer N.V.), Kouterveld 2, 1831 Diegem, Belgium. TEL 32-2-7231111. FAX 32-2-7231512. Ed. Pierre d'Avistere. adv.; tr.lit. circ. 8,500. **Document type:** trade publication.

650 FR ISSN 0066-3379
ANNUAIRE NATIONAL DES FOURNISSEURS DES ADMINISTRATIONS FRANCAISES. 2nd ed., 1962. a. 825 Fr. Editions Le Fil D'Ariane, 98, rue de Miromesnil, 75008 Paris, France. TEL 42283813. FAX 46784191. Ed. Violaine Thielen; Pub. Marie Laure Cohen. adv. contact: Axel Gaud. **Document type:** directory.
 Description: Directory of companies by products and activities doing business with administrations and collectives.

338 660 UN ISSN 0251-0081
ANNUAL BULLETIN OF TRADE IN CHEMICAL PRODUCTS. 1974. a. price varies. Economic Commission for Europe (ECE), Chemical Section, Palais des Nations, 1211 Geneva 10, Switzerland. FAX 022-917-0036. (Orders in N. America to: United Nations Publications, Rm. DC2-863, New York, NY 10017. TEL 212-963-3489. FAX 212-963-8302; Or: Unipub, 4611-F Assembly Dr., Lanham, MD 20706. TEL 301-459-7666. FAX 301-459-0056) **Indexed:** IIS. **Document type:** government publication, bulletin.
 Description: Offers statistical data on world trade in chemical products among member nations.

ANNUAL EDITIONS: DEVELOPING THIRD WORLD. see *GEOGRAPHY*

ANNUAL REPORT ON THE NIGERIAN OIL INDUSTRY. see *PETROLEUM AND GAS*

ANNUAL SURVEY OF MANUFACTURES. see *BUSINESS AND ECONOMICS — Abstracting, Bibliographies, Statistics*

347.7 338 US ISSN 0003-6021
KF1632
ANTITRUST & TRADE REGULATION REPORT. 1961. w. $1125. The Bureau of National Affairs, Inc., 1231 25th St., N.W., Washington, DC 20037. TEL 202-452-4200. FAX 202-822-8092. TELEX 285656 BNAI WSH. URL: http://www.bna.com/. (Subscr. to: 9435 Key West Ave., Rockville, MD 20850. TEL 800-372-1033) Ed. Sheldon B. Richman. charts; stat.; cum.index. (looseleaf format; back issues avail.)
 ●Also available online. Vendor(s): Lexis-Nexis (TRADRG), West Group (BNA-ATRR).
 —**CCC.**
 Description: Covers significant competition and deceptive trade practice law developments on the federal, state and international levels.

330 SP ISSN 0301-7443
ANUARIO FINANCIERO Y DE SOCIEDADES ANONIMAS DE ESPANA. 1916. irreg., latest 1980. 4000 ptas. Editorial S O P E C S.A., Villanueva, 24 - 3o, 28001 Madrid, Spain. circ. 3,500.

APPROPRIATE TECHNOLOGY. see *AGRICULTURE — Agricultural Economics*

338 BA
ARAB INDUSTRY REVIEW. 1984. a. $35. Falcon Publishing, P.O. Box 5028, Manama, Bahrain. Ed. S Gangulyee. circ. 10,000.

338 US ISSN 0883-8984
HC107.A8
ARKANSAS JOURNAL. 1965. s-a. free. Industrial Development Commission, One Capitol Mall, Little Rock, AR 72201. TEL 501-682-1121. FAX 501-682-7341. Ed. Anna Landers. illus. circ. 13,000. **Indexed:** Phys.Ed.Ind. **Document type:** trade publication.
 Former titles (until 1985): Inside Arkansas (ISSN 0274-5887); This Is Arkansas.

BUSINESS AND ECONOMICS — PRODUCTION OF GOODS AND SERVICES

338   II   ISSN 0004-3567
HC431
ARTHA-VIKAS; a journal of economic development. (Text in English) 1965. s-a. Rs.75($30) to individuals; institutions Rs.100($35) (effective 1997). Sardar Patel University, Department of Economics, Vallabh Vidyanagar, Gujarat 388 120, India. FAX 91-2692-35238. E-mail: roo@patelernet. in. Ed.Bd. adv.: page Rs.2500. bk.rev. circ. 150.
Indexed: Trop.Oil Seeds Abstr., World Agri.Econ.& Rural Sociol.Abstr.
Description: Publishes research articles and reviews on economic development, particularly rural economic development.
Refereed Serial

338   CC   ISSN 0254-3729
HF3751
ASIAN BUSINESS. (Text in English) 1965. m. HK.$210 (Asia $55; elsewhere $105). Far East Trade Press Ltd., Kai Tak Commercial Bldg., 2nd Fl., 317 Des Voeux Rd., Central, Hong Kong, People's Republic of China. TEL 545-7200. FAX 544-6979. TELEX 83434-FETP-HX. E-mail: abeditor@asianbusiness.com.hk; URL: http://web3.asia1.com.sg/timesnet/navigatn/text/ab.html. (Subscr. to: Times Publishing Group, Block C, 10th Fl. Seaview Estate, 2-8 Watson Rd., North Point, Hong Kong, People's Republic of China. TEL 852-566-8381. FAX 852-508-0255) Ed. Jack Maisano. adv.: B&W page $9300, color page $13200; trim 205 x 275; adv. contact: Evelyn Leung. charts; illus.; tr.lit. circ. 104,503. (also avail. in microform from UMI; reprint service avail. from UMI) Indexed: ABI Inform., B.P.I., P.A.I.S., Per.Islam. (1996-), PROMT.
●Also available online. Vendor(s): UMI.
—BLDSC (1742.402800); KR SourceOne; SWETS; UMI; UnCover. CCC.
Former titles: Asian Business and Industry (ISSN 1013-9958); Asian Industry (ISSN 0004-458X)
Description: Authoritative business, industrial, financial information and analyses of the Asian region.

338 332.6   CC   ISSN 1015-504X
ASIAN MANUFACTURERS JOURNAL. 1988. bi-m. HK.$210 (other Asian areas $75; elsewhere $102). G.P.O. Box 6217, Hong Kong, People's Republic of China. TEL 852-2558-8131. FAX 852-2897-5087. TELEX HX82169. E-mail: enquiry@amj.com; URL: http://www.amj.com. Ed. Terence Hung. adv. contact: Joseph Cheng. circ. 32,000. Document type: trade publication.
●Also available online.
Description: Introduces made-in-Asia consumer goods including gifts, toys, electronics, fashion, and fashion accessories, and household items to buyers in Europe and North America.

338   CK   ISSN 0120-9515
ASOCIACION NACIONAL DE INDUSTRIALES. REVISTA BIMESTRAL. 1966. bi-m. Col.$10800. Asociacion Nacional de Industriales, Centro Coltejer, P. 8, Apartado Aereo 997, Medellin, Colombia. FAX 251-8830. TELEX 66631. Ed. Fabio Echeverri Correa. adv.; bk.rev.; bibl.; charts; stat. circ. 2,000.
Indexed: P.A.I.S.For.Lang.Ind.
—BLDSC (7840.870000).
Formerly: Asociacion Nacional de Industriales. Revista Trimestral (ISSN 0004-4865)

ASSOCIATION OF HOME APPLIANCE MANUFACTURERS. M A C A P STATISTICAL REPORT. (Major Appliance Consumer Action Panel) see *INTERIOR DESIGN AND DECORATION — Abstracting, Bibliographies, Statistics*

338   US
ASSOCIATION OF HOME APPLIANCE MANUFACTURERS. TRENDS AND FORECASTS. q. free (fax-on-demand). Association of Home Appliance Manufacturers, 20 N. Wacker Dr., Chicago, IL 60606. TEL 312-984-5800. FAX 312-984-5823. URL: http://www.aham.org. Document type: newsletter.
Description: Reports on shipment trends of major appliances. Includes ten-year summary and two-year forecast.

338   IT   ISSN 0004-5918
ASSOCIAZIONE DEGLI INDUSTRIALE DI AREZZO. NOTIZIARIO.* 1945. m. free. Associazione degli Industriali di Arezzo, Via Roma 2, C.P. 214, 52100 Arezzo, Italy. Ed. Dr. Guido Goti. stat.; index, cum.index. circ. 500. Indexed: Br.Ceram.Abstr., Fuel & Energy Abstr.

338   FR
ATLAS DES USINES DE FRANCE. a. 50 F. Groupe Usine Nouvelle, 59, rue du Rocher, 75008 Paris, France. TEL 44-69-59-55. circ. 70,000.

AUFBEREITUNGS-TECHNIK - MINERAL PROCESSING. see *MINES AND MINING INDUSTRY*

AUSTRALIA. BUREAU OF STATISTICS. CONSTANT PRICE ESTIMATES OF MANUFACTURING PRODUCTION, AUSTRALIA. see *BUSINESS AND ECONOMICS — Abstracting, Bibliographies, Statistics*

AUSTRALIA. BUREAU OF STATISTICS. MANUFACTURING PRODUCTION, AUSTRALIA, PRELIMINARY. see *BUSINESS AND ECONOMICS — Abstracting, Bibliographies, Statistics*

AUSTRALIA. BUREAU OF STATISTICS. MANUFACTURING PRODUCTION, AUSTRALIA: PRINCIPAL COMMODITIES PRODUCED. see *BUSINESS AND ECONOMICS — Abstracting, Bibliographies, Statistics*

AUSTRALIA. BUREAU OF STATISTICS. QUARTERLY INDEXES OF INDUSTRIAL PRODUCTION, AUSTRALIA. see *BUSINESS AND ECONOMICS — Abstracting, Bibliographies, Statistics*

AUSTRALIA. BUREAU OF STATISTICS. SOUTH AUSTRALIAN OFFICE. MANUFACTURING INDUSTRY, SOUTH AUSTRALIA. see *BUSINESS AND ECONOMICS — Abstracting, Bibliographies, Statistics*

AUSTRALIA. BUREAU OF STATISTICS. VICTORIAN OFFICE. MANUFACTURING INDUSTRY, VICTORIA. see *BUSINESS AND ECONOMICS — Abstracting, Bibliographies, Statistics*

338   AT
AUSTRALIAN BUSINESS NEWS. 1931. fortn. Aus.$36. Australian Business Ltd., 140 Arthur St., North Sydney, N.S.W. 2060, Australia. TEL 61-2-99277461. Ed. Ron Krueger. adv.; bk.rev. circ. 4,000. Document type: trade publication.
Former titles: Manufacturers' Bulletin (Sydney, 1991) (ISSN 1037-7271); (until 1991): A C M Bulletin (N.S.W. Edition) (ISSN 1035-3941); (until 1990): Manufacturers' Bulletin (Sydney, 1931) (ISSN 0816-9098)

AUSTRALIAN INDUSTRIAL & INTELLECTUAL PROPERTY. see *LAW*

AVANCE DE INFORMACION ECONOMICA. INDICADORES DE LA ACTIVIDAD INDUSTRIAL. see *BUSINESS AND ECONOMICS — Abstracting, Bibliographies, Statistics*

AVANCE DE INFORMACION ECONOMICA. INDICADORES DEL SECTOR MANUFACTURERO; 145 clases de actividad. see *BUSINESS AND ECONOMICS — Abstracting, Bibliographies, Statistics*

B A M A ANNUAL REPORT. (British Aerosol Manufacturers Association) see *CHEMISTRY*

330.9   MR   ISSN 0851-1934
HG3382.A8
BANQUE NATIONALE POUR LE DEVELOPPEMENT ECONOMIQUE. RAPPORT ANNUEL. (Text in Arabic, English, French) 1960. a. free. Banque Nationale pour le Developpement Economique, B.P. 407, Place des Alaouites, 12, Rabat 10000, Morocco. TEL 212-7-70-60-40. FAX 212-7-70-37-02. TELEX BADE MAROC 31942. illus.; stat. circ. 4,000. Document type: corporate report.

338 330.9   UK
BARCLAYS BANK. MANUFACTURING SURVEY. (Part of Industry Reports series) q. £120 (academic institutions and students £60). Barclays Bank plc., Economics Department, P.O. Box 12, Barclay's House, 1 Wimborne Rd., Poole, Dorset BH15 2BB, England. TEL 01202-344023. FAX 01202-402303.
Description: Surveys the economic condition and outlook of various manufacturing industries.

338   US
BAXTER; a world economic and investment service. 1924. s-m. $175. Baxter Brothers, Inc., 1030 E. Putnam Ave., Greenwich, CT 06830. TEL 203-637-4559. (Subscr. to: Rt. 25, Cutchogue, NY 11935) Ed. William J. Baxter, Jr. charts; stat. (back issues avail.)

338   GW
BEIERSDORF JOURNAL. 1960. q. Beiersdorf AG, Unnastr. 48, 20253 Hamburg, Germany. FAX 49-40-5696143. URL: http://www.beiersdorf.com. Ed. Dr. Matthias Schatz. R&P contact: Dr. Matthias Schatz. bk.rev.; circ. controlled. Document type: corporate report.
Formerly: Hauskurier.
Refereed Serial

338.8   US   ISSN 0196-7622
HD2868
BELGIAN - AMERICAN CHAMBER OF COMMERCE IN THE UNITED STATES. DIRECTORY;* listing of US firms in Belgium & Luxembourg. Variant title: U S - Belgium Trade Directory. biennial. $125. Belgian - American Chamber of Commerce in the U S, 1350 Ave. of the Americas, No. 26, New York, NY 10019-5400. Document type: directory.
Description: Directory of the membership of the Belgian American Chamber of Commerce in the US, plus addresses for doing business in the US and Belgium; also includes articles of practical interest.

338   BE
BELGIAN BUSINESS & INDUSTRIE. (Editions in Dutch, French) 1968. 10/yr. 1800 BEF. Business & Industrie (Subsidiary of: Roularta Media Group), Research Park Zellik, De Haak, 1731 Zellik (Brussels). TEL 32-2-4675740. FAX 32-2-4675969. E-mail: info@roularta.be; URL: http://www.innet.be/intermart/roularta. Dir. Wim Heirbaut. adv.; circ. 31,500 (controlled). Indexed: Key to Econ.Sci. Document type: trade publication.
●Also available on CD-ROM.
Former titles: Belgian Business Magazine (ISSN 0777-0987); Belgian Business.
Description: Business and economics: trends, key figures and reporting.

338.9   BE
BENELUX ECONOMIC UNION. CONSEIL CENTRAL DE L'ECONOMIE. RAPPORT DU SECRETAIRE SUR L'ACTIVITE DU CONSEIL. 1950. a. free. Benelux Economic Union, Conseil Central de l'Economie, Rue de la Regence, 39, 1000 Brussels, Belgium.
Formerly: Benelux Economic Union. Conseil Consultatif Economique et Social. Rapport du Secretaire Concernant les Activites du Conseil (ISSN 0522-8948)

BESTUUR EN BELEID V Z W. see *BUSINESS AND ECONOMICS*

338   GW   ISSN 0341-4477
BETRIEB UND MEISTER. 1968. m. DM.51.60 (foreign DM.57.60) (effective 1997). Konradin Verlag Robert Kohlhammer GmbH, Ernst-Mey-Str. 8, 70771 Leinfelden-Echterdingen, Germany. TEL 49-711-7594-0. FAX 49-711-7594-390. Ed. Rudolf Beyer. adv.: B&W page DM.6380, color page DM.8360; trim 190 x 270; adv. contact: Walter Schwager. bk.rev. circ. 23,538. (back issues avail.) Document type: trade publication.
—SWETS. CCC.
Description: Focuses on production aspects of goods and services for masterworkmen and technicians in industry.

354   AT
BETTER BUSINESS FOR QUEENSLAND. 1973. bi-m. Department of Tourism, Small Business and Industry, Library, P.O. Box 1141, Brisbane, Qld. 4001, Australia. TEL 61-7-2248568. FAX 61-7-2295289. Ed. Jim Kershaw. circ. 12,000. (tabloid format; back issues avail.) Document type: government publication.
Former titles: Queensland. Department of Tourism, Small Business and Industry. Industry; (until May. 1996): Queensland. Department of Business, Industry and Regional Development. Industry; Which incorporates (in Dec. 1992): Queensland. Department of Business, Industry and Regional Development. Client Update; (until Nov. 1990): Queensland. Department of Manufacturing and Commerce. Industry; (until Dec. 1989): Queensland. Department of Industry Development. Industry.
Description: Highlights Queensland's innovative manufacturers with stories of their achievements.

BUSINESS AND ECONOMICS — PRODUCTION OF GOODS AND SERVICES

338   GW   ISSN 0172-018X
BLAETTER FUER VORGESETZTE. 1957. m. DM.12. Dr. Curt Haefner Verlag, Bachstr. 14-16, 69121 Heidelberg, Germany. TEL 49-6221-6446-0. (Subscr. to: Postfach 106060, 69050 Heidelberg, Germany) Ed. Hans-Guenter Glass. abstr. circ. 41,000. (looseleaf format) **Document type:** newsletter.

338 658   BL   ISSN 0103-7528
TS156.A1
BOLETIM QUALIDADE E PRODUTIVIDADE: EVENTOS E CURSOS. q. $9.80. Instituto Brasileiro de Informacao em Ciencia e Tecnologia, SAS Quadro 5, Lote 6, Bloco H, 70070-000 Brasilia, D.F., Brazil. TEL 55-61-217-6161. FAX 55-61-226-2677. **Document type:** bulletin.

338.0972   MX   ISSN 0187-7321
BOLETIN INDUSTRIAL. 1983. m. free. Editorial Nova, S.A. de C.V., Goldsmith 37-401, Col. Polanco, 11550 Mexico, D.F., Mexico. TEL 52-5-2806080. FAX 52-5-2803194. E-mail: bolind@viernes.iwm.com.mx. Ed. Humberto Valades. adv. contact: Humberto Valades. circ. 36,000 (controlled). (tabloid format) **Document type:** trade publication. *Refereed Serial*

BOTSWANA MANUFACTURING DIRECTORY. see *BUSINESS AND ECONOMICS — Trade And Industrial Directories*

338   BL   ISSN 0045-2742
BRAZIL. SUPERINTENDENCIA DO DESENVOLVIMENTO DA AMAZONIA. S U D A M DOCUMENTA. (Text in Portuguese; summaries in English and Portuguese) 1970. irreg. free. Superintendencia do Desenvolvimento da Amazonia, Travessa Antonio Baena 1113, Caixa Postal 874, Belem-Para, Brazil. adv.

338.981   BL
BRAZIL DEVELOPMENT SERIES/SERIES DESENVOLVIMENTO BRASILEIRO. (Text in English and Portuguese) 1971. a. $20. (Brazilian Institute of Economic Studies) TELEPRESS Servicos de Imprensa, Ltda., Rua Albuquerque Lins, 1315, 01230 Sao Paulo, S.P., Brazil. Ed. Olavo G. Otero. illus. circ. 10,000.

338   GW
BUDERUS POST. 1950. q. Buderus Aktiengesellschaft, Postfach 1280, 35573 Wetzlar, Germany. TEL 49-6441-418-0. FAX 49-6441-418901. Ed. Hans Spiegelhalter. bk.rev. circ. 13,500. (back issues avail.) **Document type:** corporate report.

338   UK   ISSN 0955-3754
BULK MATERIALS INTERNATIONAL. 1988. 10/yr. 77A High Rd., Willesden Green, London NW10 2SU, England. TEL 081-451-6578. FAX 081-459-0712. Ed. Richard Miller. circ. 10,000.

BUSINESS EUROPE. see *BUSINESS AND ECONOMICS — International Commerce*

338   PL
BUSINESS FOUNDATION. PIERWSZY POLSKI ILUSTROWANY KATALOG TOWAROW/BUSINESS FOUNDATION. FIRST ILLUSTRATED DIRECTORY OF POLISH PRODUCTS. 1993. a. free. Business Foundation Co. Ltd., Ul. Krucza 38-42, 00-512 Warsaw, Poland. TEL 48-22-219993. FAX 48-22-219761. Ed. Wieslaw Szczepanek. **Document type:** directory, trade publication. **Description:** Presents Polish goods using various methods of photographic and graphic illustration. Medium through which companies may display and promote their products.

BUSINESS MONITOR: SERVICE TRADES. see *BUSINESS AND ECONOMICS — Abstracting, Bibliographies, Statistics*

BUSINESS RATIO PLUS: THE FORGING INDUSTRY. see *METALLURGY*

BUSINESS RATIO PLUS: FROZEN FOOD PRODUCERS. see *FOOD AND FOOD INDUSTRIES*

BUSINESS RATIO PLUS: THE HOTEL INDUSTRY. see *HOTELS AND RESTAURANTS*

338 658.8   UK   ISSN 1358-8060
BUSINESS RATIO PLUS: INDUSTRIAL FASTENER DISTRIBUTORS. 1979. a. I C C Business Publications Ltd., Field House, 72 Oldfield Rd., Hampton, Mddx. TW12 2HQ, England. TEL 44-181-783-0922. FAX 44-181-783-1940. charts; stat. **Document type:** trade publication.
Formerly (until 1995): Business Ratio Report: Industrial Fastener Distributors (ISSN 0261-846X)

338 658.8   UK   ISSN 1359-6020
BUSINESS RATIO PLUS: INDUSTRIAL FASTNER MANUFACTURERS. 1978. a. I C C Business Ratios Ltd., Field House, 72 Oldfield Rd., Hampton, Mddx. TW12 2HQ, England. TEL 44-181-783-0922. FAX 44-181-783-1940. charts; stat. **Document type:** trade publication.
Formerly (until 1995): Business Ratio Report: Industrial Fastener Manufacturers (ISSN 0261-8478)

338 678.2   UK
BUSINESS RATIO PLUS: THE RUBBER & TYRE INDUSTRY. a. £249. I C C Business Publications, Field House, 72 Oldfield Rd., Hampton, Middlesex TW12 2HQ, England. TEL 44-181-783-0922. FAX 44-181-783-1940.
Formerly: Business Ratio Report: Rubber Manufacturers and Processors.
Description: Analyses and compares the financial performance of companies within a given UK industry sector. Includes company and industry performance summaries, trends, and forecasts.

BUSINESS RATIO REPORT: DOMESTIC FURNITURE MANUFACTURERS; an industry sector analysis. see *INTERIOR DESIGN AND DECORATION — Furniture And House Furnishings*

BUSINESS RATIO REPORT: HEATING AND VENTILATING EQUIPMENT MANUFACTURERS; an industry sector analysis. see *HEATING, PLUMBING AND REFRIGERATION*

BUSINESS RATIO REPORT: HYDRAULIC & PNEUMATIC EQUIPMENT MANUFACTURERS; an industry sector analysis. see *ENGINEERING — Hydraulic Engineering*

BUSINESS RATIO REPORT: INDUSTRIAL CHEMICAL MANUFACTURERS. INTERMEDIATE; an industry sector analysis. see *CHEMISTRY*

BUSINESS RATIO REPORT: INDUSTRIAL CHEMICAL MANUFACTURERS. MAJOR; an industry sector analysis. see *CHEMISTRY*

BUSINESS RATIO REPORT: JOINERY MANUFACTURERS; an industry sector analysis. see *BUILDING AND CONSTRUCTION — Carpentry And Woodwork*

338.12   SW   ISSN 1102-8319
BUSINESS TENDENCY SURVEY FOR SERVICES SECTORS. (Text in English) 1991. q. SEK 280. Konjunkturinstitutet (KI), P.O. Box 3116, S-103 62 Stockholm, Sweden. TEL 46-8-453-59-00. FAX 46-8-453-59-80. circ. 300. **Description:** Consists of a survey of 1900 construction and services enterprises in Sweden.

650   PH   ISSN 0116-3930
BUSINESS WORLD. (Text in English) 1987. d. P.2080. BusinessWorld Publishing Corp., No. 95 Balete Drive Extension, New Manila, Quezon City 1112, Philippines. TEL 632-7270091. FAX 632-7276014. E-mail: marketng@bworld.com.ph. Ed. Raul L. Locsin; Pub. Raul L. Locsin. adv.: page P.92340; 69 x 58; adv. contact: Danilo Ocampo. bk.rev.; charts; illus.; mkt.; stat.; index. circ. 52,000. (looseleaf format; back issues avail.) **Document type:** newspaper.
● Also available online.
Formerly: Business Day (ISSN 0007-6635); Which incorporates: Asean's Largest Corporations; Philippines' Largest Exporters.
Description: Business and financial daily newspaper covering world economy, stock markets, commodities futures market, and corporate world.

338   US
C. BREWER TODAY. 1957. q. free. C. Brewer & Co. Ltd., Box 1826, Honolulu, HI 96805. TEL 808-536-4461. Ed. Kathy Oshiro. circ. 2,000 (controlled). (processed)
Formerly (until 1976): Brewer Monthly Letter.

338   AT   ISSN 0085-1280
HC601
C E D A GROWTH SERIES. 1961. irreg. price varies. Committee for Economic Development of Australia, 123 Lonsdale St., Melbourne, Vic. 3000, Australia. FAX 61-3-96637271. **Indexed:** Anim.Breed.Abstr., Aus.P.A.I.S., Biol.Abstr., Poult.Abstr., Vet.Bull.—UnCover.

338   EC   ISSN 0523-9141
HC204.5.I53
C E N D E S BOLETIN INDUSTRIAL. 1964. m. free. Centro de Desarrollo Industrial, Av. Orellana 1715, P.O. Box 2321, Quito, Ecuador. FAX 564502. TELEX 564502. Dir. Pablo Ourango. illus.; stat.

338   FR   ISSN 0399-8975
C N P F REVUE DES ENTREPRISES. no.142, 1956. m. 120 F. Conseil National du Patronat Francais, 31 av. Pierre 1er de Serbie, 75784 Paris, France. TEL 40-69-44-44. FAX 47-23-47-32. Ed. Michel Frois. adv.; bk.rev.; illus.; stat.; index. circ. 20,000. **Indexed:** C.I.S. Abstr.
—BLDSC (3287.313000).
Formerly: Patronat Francais (ISSN 0031-3165)

330   US   ISSN 0889-7395
C R A REVIEW. 1974. q. free. Charles River Associates, John Hancock Tower, 200 Clarendon St., Boston, MA 02116. TEL 617-425-3000. FAX 617-425-3132. (And: 1001 Pennsylvania Ave., N.W., Ste. 750, Washington, DC 20004) Ed. Charles Tuecker. R&P contact: Charles Tucker. charts; illus.; stat. circ. 15,000. (back issues avail.) **Indexed:** Alloys Ind., Eng.Mat.Abstr., Met.Abstr.Ind., Met.Abstr., Nonfer.Met.Alert, PCC Alert, Steels Alert, World Alum.Abstr. **Document type:** newsletter.
Formerly (until 1986): C R A Research Review.
Description: Highlights work CRA has done as economics management consultant in a wide range of industries.

338   BL
CADASTRO INDUSTRIAL DO PARA. irreg. Federacao das Industrias, Av. Nazare, 759, Belem, Para, Brazil.

338.025   CN
CALGARY MANUFACTURERS DIRECTORY. 1985. q. Can.$50. Calgary Economic Development Authority, P.O. Box 2100, Sta. M, Calgary, AB T2P 2M5, Canada. TEL 403-221-7821. FAX 403-221-7837. **Document type:** directory.

CAMARA DE INDUSTRIALES DE CARACAS. NOTI. see *BUSINESS AND ECONOMICS*

338   MX
CAMARA NACIONAL DE LA INDUSTRIA DE TRANSFORMACION. BOLETIN INFORMATIVO. m. free. Camara Nacional de la Industria de Transformacion, Apdo. Postal 60-468, Av. San Antonio 256, 03849 Mexico, D.F., Mexico. TEL 5-563-3500. Ed. Iris Arzate Rios. circ. controlled.

338.7   CM
CAMEROON DEVELOPMENT CORPORATION. ANNUAL REPORT AND ACCOUNTS/RAPPORT ANNUEL ET COMPTE-RENDU FINANCIER. Key Title: Annual Report and Accounts-Cameroon Development Corporation. (Text in English, French) 1947. a. free. Cameroon Development Corporation, Fako Division, Bota - Limbe, South West Province, Cameroon. TEL 332251. FAX 332654. TELEX 5242 KN. illus. circ. 5,000. **Document type:** corporate report.
Description: Purpose is to acquire lands for the planting of tropical crops and process semi-finished and finished products for local and overseas markets.

CANADIAN ENGINEERING & INDUSTRIAL YEAR BOOK. see *ENGINEERING*

338 330.9   CN
CANADIAN MANUFACTURERS ASSOCIATION. IN FOCUS. 6/yr. Canadian Manufacturers Association, 75 International Blvd., Toronto, ON M9W 6L9, Canada. TEL 416-798-8000. FAX 416-798-8050. E-mail: Gieg-MacDonald@cmaonline.com. Ed. Greg MacDonald. circ. 10,000.
Formerly: Canadian Manufacturers Association. President's Letter (ISSN 0849-2131)

BUSINESS AND ECONOMICS — PRODUCTION OF GOODS AND SERVICES

338   YU   ISSN 0008-8722
CELIK; casopis Udruzenja jugoslovenskih zelezara. (Summaries in English, Russian) 1965. bi-m. 420 din. Borba, Trg Marksa i Engelsa 7, Belgrade, Yugoslavia. Ed. Milena Stefanovic. **Indexed:** Met.Abstr., World Alum.Abstr.
—BLDSC (3097.580000).

CENSO DOS SERVICOS. see *BUSINESS AND ECONOMICS — Abstracting, Bibliographies, Statistics*

CENSO INDUSTRIAL. see *BUSINESS AND ECONOMICS — Abstracting, Bibliographies, Statistics*

338   US   ISSN 0090-7111
HC107.M2
CENSUS OF MAINE MANUFACTURES. (Subseries of: Maine. Bureau of Labor Standards. B L S Bulletin) 1948. a. free. Department of Labor, Bureau of Labor Standards, Technical Services Division, 45 State House Station, Augusta, ME 04333-0045. TEL 207-624-6440. FAX 207-624-6449. E-mail: webmaster_bls@state.me.us. Ed. Barbara Chenoweth. charts; stat. circ. 380. **Indexed:** Vert.File Ind. **Document type:** government publication.
Description: Covers Maine manufacturing establishments ranging from the single proprietorships to the largest corporations.

CENSUS OF MANUFACTURES: FINAL REPORTS. see *BUSINESS AND ECONOMICS — Abstracting, Bibliographies, Statistics*

CENSUS OF MANUFACTURES: PRELIMINARY REPORTS. see *BUSINESS AND ECONOMICS — Abstracting, Bibliographies, Statistics*

338.47   PR   ISSN 0552-5276
CENSUS OF MANUFACTURING INDUSTRIES OF PUERTO RICO. (Text in English, Spanish.) a. free. Department of Labor, Bureau of Labor Statistics, 505 Munoz Rivera Ave., Hato Rey, PR 00918. TEL 787-754-5351. Ed. Antonio Padilla Torres. stat. circ. 1,000. (tabloid format) **Document type:** government publication.

338.9   EC
CENTRO DE DESARROLLO INDUSTRIAL DEL ECUADOR. BOLETIN DE NOTICIAS TECNICAS. 1973. a. (with m. bulletins). free. Ministry of Industry, Centro de Desarrollo Industrial, Av. Orellana 1715, P.O. Box 2321, Quito, Ecuador. FAX 564502. TELEX 2350. circ. 600.
Formerly: Centro de Desarrollo Industrial del Ecuador. Noticias Tecnicas.

338   SP   ISSN 0214-6320
CENTRO DE INVESTIGACION Y CONTROL DE LA CALIDAD. 3/yr. free. Instituto Nacional del Consumo, Principe de Vergara 54, 28006 Madrid, Spain. **Indexed:** Ind.SST.

338   SZ   ISSN 1420-7230
CHEF-MAGAZIN FUER KLEIN- UND MITTELBETRIEBE. 1969. q. 67 SFr. (effective 1997); newsstand price: 18 SFr. Schweizerisches Institut fuer Unternehmerschulung im Gewerbe, Postfach 8166, CH-3001 Bern, Switzerland. TEL 41-31-3815151. FAX 41-31-3815765. Eds. B. Aellig, S. Guillet. adv.; stat. (looseleaf format) **Document type:** trade publication.
Formerly (until 1982): Unternehmungsfuehrung im Gewerbe (ISSN 1420-7249); **Incorporates:** Gewerbliche Rundschau (ISSN 0016-9412)

338 660   UN   ISSN 1020-0746
HD9656.A1
CHEMICAL INDUSTRY IN (YEAR) - ANNUAL REVIEW. 1971. a. price varies. Economic Commission for Europe (ECE), Palais des Nations, 1211 Geneva 10, Switzerland. TEL 41-22-917-2893. FAX 41-22-917-0036. (Or: United Nations Publications, Rm. DC2-853, New York, NY 10017. TEL 212-963-8302. FAX 212-963-3489) charts; stat. (also avail. in microfiche from CIS) **Indexed:** IIS.
—BLDSC (3148.270000). CCC.
Formerly (until 1992): Annual Review of the Chemical Industry (ISSN 0255-4291)

CHEMICAL INDUSTRY SOURCEBOOK AND STRATEGIC OVERVIEW. see *CHEMISTRY*

338   II
CHEMICAL PRODUCTS FINDER. (Text in English) 1982. m. Rs.1200($38) Business Press, Transmission House, Compartment No. 82, Plot No. 6-19, Marol Co-op Industrial Estate, M.V. Rd., Andheri East, Mumbai 400059, India. TEL 91-22-850-1871. FAX 91-22-850-2070. TELEX 011-78455 BPPL IN. Ed. A.G. Bhat. adv.: B&W page Rs.8500, color page Rs.12500; trim 280 x 205. bk.rev.; abstr.; charts; illus.
Description: Covers new products and news briefs.

CHILE. INSTITUTO NACIONAL DE ESTADISTICAS. INDICE DE PRODUCCION Y VENTA FISICA DE INDUSTRIAS MANUFACTURERAS. see *BUSINESS AND ECONOMICS — Abstracting, Bibliographies, Statistics*

CHILE. INSTITUTO NACIONAL DE ESTADISTICAS. INDUSTRIAS MANUFACTURERAS. see *BUSINESS AND ECONOMICS — Abstracting, Bibliographies, Statistics*

338   CH
CHINA DEVELOPMENT CORPORATION. ANNUAL REPORT. (Vols. for 1959-72 issued by the body under its English form of name) 1959. a. China Development Corporation, No. 125 Nanking E. Rd., Sec. 5, Taipei, Taiwan, Republic of China. illus.; stat.

338   US   ISSN 1047-1308
TS1033
CIRCLE Y OF YOAKUM. a. Circle Y, Inc., Box 797, 201 W. Morris St., Yoakum, TX 77995.

338   US
CITY PRODUCTS AND SERVICES GUIDE. 1983. a. League of Minnesota Cities, 145 University Ave. W., St. Paul, MN 55103-2044. TEL 612-281-1200. FAX 612-281-1299. URL: http://www.lmnc.org. Ed. Gayle Brodt. adv. contact: Gayle Brodt. **Document type:** government publication.
Description: Contains listings of businesses offering goods and services to Minnesota cities.

CLASSIFIED DIRECTORY OF WISCONSIN MANUFACTURERS. see *BUSINESS AND ECONOMICS — Trade And Industrial Directories*

CLEANER PRODUCTION. see *OCCUPATIONAL HEALTH AND SAFETY*

338   US   ISSN 1073-9602
CLEANER TIMES. 1989. m. $36. Advantage Publishing, 17319 Crystal Valley Rd., Little Rock, AR 72210-3608. TEL 501-455-1441. FAX 501-455-2479. Ed. Allison McGraw; Pub. Charlene Yarbrough. adv.: page $1319; trim 8 1/2 x 11; adv. contact: Chuck Prieur. bk.rev.; illus.; tr.lit.; index. circ. 14,000. (back issues avail.) **Document type:** trade publication.
Description: Emphasizes information, application, and productivity for persons engaged in the manufacturing, distribution, or use of high pressure water systems and accessories.

COLOMBIA. DEPARTAMENTO ADMINISTRATIVO NACIONAL DE ESTADISTICA. ANUARIO DE ESTADISTICAS INDUSTRIALES. see *BUSINESS AND ECONOMICS — Abstracting, Bibliographies, Statistics*

338   SP   ISSN 0213-0637
COMERCIO INDUSTRIA. 1970. m. 2500 ptas. Camara Oficial de Comercio e Industria de Madrid, Huertas 13, 28012 Madrid, Spain. TEL 1-429-31-93. Dir. Jose Diez Clavero. adv.; bk.rev.; bibl.; charts; illus.; index. circ. 158,773. **Indexed:** Chem.Abstr.
—CINDOC.
Formerly (until 1980): Comercio e Industria. Suplemento Quincenal (ISSN 0210-2595); Incorporated (in 1982): Comercio e Industria (ISSN 0210-2579); Which was formed by the merger of (1930-1970): Comercio (ISSN 0010-2261); (1923-1970): Industria (ISSN 0019-7432); Incorporated (1962-1969): Industria. Suplemento Quincenal (ISSN 0210-2587).

COMMERCE BUSINESS DAILY; synopsis of United States government proposed procurement, sales, and contract awards. see *BUSINESS AND ECONOMICS — Marketing And Purchasing*

338.6   EI   ISSN 0259-3157
COMMISSION OF THE EUROPEAN COMMUNITIES. REPORT ON COMPETITION POLICY. (Text in Dutch, English, French, German and Italian) 1972. a. newsstand price: $25. Office for Official Publications of the European Communities, L-2985 Luxembourg, Luxembourg. (Dist. in the U.S. by: Unipub, 4611-F Assembly Dr., Lanham, MD 20706-4391. TEL 800-274-4888. FAX 301-459-0056) **Indexed:** Chem.Abstr., IIS.
—BLDSC (7640.662000).

650   II   ISSN 0010-4027
COMPANY NEWS AND NOTES. 1962. m. Rs.42. Department of Company Affairs, Shastri Bhawan, Dr. Rajendraprasad Rd., New Delhi, India. (Dist. by: Controller of Publications, Civil Lines, Delhi 110 006, India) adv.; bk.rev.; bibl.; charts; stat.; index. circ. 12,000. **Indexed:** Pub.Admin.Abstr. **Document type:** trade publication, government publication.

338   US
COMPASS MAGAZINE.* 1965. 4/yr. $2 (free to businesses of Monmouth and Ocean counties, NJ). (Monmouth-Ocean Development Council) McLoughlin & Co. Publications, Box 7236, Shrewsbury, NJ 07702-7236. TEL 908-741-0547. FAX 908-842-5568. Ed. Carolann M. Perry. adv.; bk.rev.; charts; illus. circ. 7,000.
Former titles: Compass Quarterly; (until 1979): Compass (Asbury Park) (ISSN 0010-4191)

COMPETITION POLICY IN O E C D COUNTRIES. see *BUSINESS AND ECONOMICS — International Development And Assistance*

COMPUTERS IN FURNITURE AND CABINET MANUFACTURING. INTERNATIONAL SYMPOSIUM PROCEEDINGS. see *COMPUTERS — Automation*

338   CN
CONJONCTURE ECONOMIQUE DES REGIONS DU QUEBEC EN (YEAR). 1960. a. free. Ministere de l'Industrie, du Commerce et de la Technologie (Quebec), 710 place D'Youville, Quebec, PQ G1R 4Y4, Canada. TEL 418-691-5967. FAX 418-646-6435. R&P contact: Rose-Marie Auger. TEL 418-691-5950. circ. 1,500. **Document type:** government publication.
Former titles: Quebec (Province). Ministere de l'Industrie, du Commerce et de la Technologie. Direction de l'Analyse et de la Conjoncture Industrielle; Quebec (Province). Ministere de l'Industrie, du Commerce et de la Technologie. Direction de l'Analyse et de la Prevision Economique; Quebec (Province). Ministere de l'Industrie et du Commerce. Direction de l'Analyse et de la Prevision Economiques.
Description: Report on the economic situation of the Quebec economy.

338.6   US   ISSN 1070-9398
HF5429.3
CONSUMER GOODS MANUFACTURER; technology partnering for supply chain management. 1992. bi-m. Edgell Communications, Inc., Ten W. Hanover Ave., Ste. 107, Randolph, NJ 07869. TEL 973-895-3300. FAX 973-895-7711. Ed. Mark Frantz. R&P contact: Georgia Colicchio. adv.: B&W page $5850, color page $6950; trim 10 7/8 x 15; adv. contact: George Colicchio. circ. 25,000. (tabloid format) **Document type:** trade publication.

CONTACT TRANSPORT & LOGISTICS; le trait d'union industrie - prestataires de services - bindeteken tussen industrie en dienstverlenende sektor. see *BUSINESS AND ECONOMICS — Management*

338   CR
CORPORACION COSTARRICENSE DE FINANCIAMIENTO INDUSTRIAL. MEMORIA ANUAL. a. Corporacion Costarricense de Financiamiento Industrial, Apdo. 10067, San Jose, Costa Rica.

338   VE
CORPORACION DE LOS ANDES. REVISTA. 1966. q. free. Corporacion de los Andes, Edificio Sede, La Isla, Merida, Venezuela. charts; illus.; stat.
Formerly: Corpoandes (ISSN 0010-8944)

BUSINESS AND ECONOMICS — PRODUCTION OF GOODS AND SERVICES

338 US ISSN 1063-2735
THE COST CONTROLLER. 1991. m. $249 (effective 1997). Siefer Consultants, Inc., Box 1384, Storm Lake, IA 50588. TEL 712-732-7340. FAX 712-732-7906. Ed. Lynn Hardt. index. circ. 3,200. (back issues avail.) **Document type:** newsletter.
 Description: Covers specific examples of cost reduction strategies used in business and industry.

338 II
CURRENT DYNAMICS. (Text in English) 1971. m. Rs.24($14) Space Age Publishers, 237 Netaji Subhas Rd., Calcutta 47, India. Ed. J. Chakravarty. adv.; charts.

338 US ISSN 0498-8477
CURRENT INDUSTRIAL REPORTS. (Consists of 70 series.) m. and q. online. a. consolidated report in printed format and online. U.S. Bureau of the Census, Customer Services, Washington, DC 20233. TEL 301-457-4100. FAX 301-457-4714. URL: http://www.census.gov/. charts; stat. (also avail. in microfiche from CIS; back issues avail.) reprint service avail. from CIS and the Census Bureau) **Indexed:** Abstr.Bull.Inst.Pap.Chem., Amer.Stat.Ind. (1975-), Curr.Pack.Abstr., World Surf.Coat. **Document type:** government publication.
●Also available online.

338 US ISSN 0364-1880
HD9724
CURRENT INDUSTRIAL REPORTS: MANUFACTURERS' SHIPMENTS, INVENTORIES, AND ORDERS AND UNITED STATES DEPARTMENT OF COMMERCE NEWS: ADVANCE REPORT ON DURABLE GOODS MANUFACTURERS' SHIPMENTS AND ORDERS. (Series M3-1) m. (plus a. summary). $38 (foreign $47.50). U.S. Bureau of the Census, Customer Services, Washington, DC 20233. TEL 301-457-4100. FAX 301-457-4714. URL: http://www.census.gov/. (Subscr. to: Superintendent of Documents, U.S. Government Printing Office, Box 371954, Pittsburgh, PA 15250-7954. TEL 202-512-1800. FAX 202-512-2250) charts; stat. (back issues avail.) **Indexed:** Abstr.Bull.Inst.Pap.Chem., Amer.Stat.Ind. (1975-), Curr.Pack.Abstr., World.Surf.Coat. **Document type:** government publication.
●Also available online.
 Description: Compiles data on the total production, value, shipment, and consumption of various products manufactured by U.S. industries.

338 US
CURRENT INDUSTRIAL REPORTS: MANUFACTURING TECHNOLOGY - FACTORS AFFECTING ADOPTION (YEAR). (Series SMT) irreg. price varies. U.S. Bureau of the Census, Customer Services, Washington, DC 20233. TEL 301-457-4100. FAX 301-457-4714. URL: http://www.census.gov/. (Subscr. to: Superintendent of Documents, U.S. Government Printing Office, Box 371954, Pittsburgh, PA 15250-7954. TEL 202-512-3238. FAX 202-512-2250) **Document type:** government publication.
●Also available online.

CYPRUS. DEPARTMENT OF STATISTICS AND RESEARCH. ECONOMIC INDICATORS. see *BUSINESS AND ECONOMICS — Economic Situation And Conditions*

CYPRUS TIME OUT; tourist and business guide. see *TRAVEL AND TOURISM*

D I S P. (Dokumente und Informationen zur Schweizerischen Orts-, Regional- und Landesplanung) see *HOUSING AND URBAN PLANNING*

338 330.9 US ISSN 1051-5933
HC101
D R I - MCGRAW-HILL U S MARKETS REVIEW: INDUSTRY FOCUS. Key Title: U S Markets Review: Industry Focus. s-a. D R I - McGraw-Hill, 24 Hartwell Ave., Lexington, MA 02173. TEL 617-863-5100. FAX 617-860-6332. TELEX 200 284. Ed. Vivien Singer. (back issues avail.) **Document type:** trade publication.
 Former titles: U S Industry Review; Interindustry Review.

338 330.9 US ISSN 1069-6482
HC107.A13
D R I - MCGRAW-HILL U S MARKETS REVIEW: METRO FOCUS. Key Title: U S Markets Review: South. Metro Focus. 1992. q. D R I - McGraw-Hill, 24 Hartwell Ave., Lexington, MA 02173. TEL 617-863-5100. FAX 617-860-6332. TELEX 200 284. Ed. Sara Johnson. **Document type:** trade publication.

338 330.9 US ISSN 1069-6431
HC107.A14
D R I - MCGRAW-HILL U S MARKETS REVIEW: MIDWEST. STATE FOCUS. Key Title: U S Markets Review: Midwest. State Focus. q. D R I - McGraw-Hill, 24 Hartwell Ave., Lexington, MA 02173. TEL 617-863-5100. FAX 617-860-6332. TELEX 200 284. Ed. Sara Johnson. **Document type:** trade publication.
 Formerly (until 1992): D R I - McGraw-Hill U S Markets Review: Midwestern Focus (ISSN 1051-4422)

338 330.9 US ISSN 1069-6466
HC107.A115
D R I - MCGRAW-HILL U S MARKETS REVIEW: NORTHEAST. METRO FOCUS. Key Title: U S Markets Review: Northeast. Metro Focus. 1992. q. D R I - McGraw-Hill, 24 Hartwell Ave., Lexington, MA 02173. TEL 617-863-5100. FAX 617-860-6332. TELEX 200 284. Ed. Sara Johnson. **Document type:** trade publication.

338 330.9 US ISSN 1069-6423
HC107.A115
D R I - MCGRAW-HILL U S MARKETS REVIEW: NORTHEAST. STATE FOCUS. Key Title: U S Markets Review: Northeast. State Focus. q. D R I - McGraw-Hill, 24 Hartwell Ave., Lexington, MA 02173. TEL 617-863-5100. FAX 617-860-6332. TELEX 200 284. Ed. Sara Johnson. **Document type:** trade publication.
 Formerly (until 1992): D R I - McGraw-Hill U S Markets Review: Northeastern Focus (ISSN 1051-4430)

338 330.9 US ISSN 1056-6058
HC101
D R I - MCGRAW-HILL U S MARKETS REVIEW: REGIONAL FORECAST SUMMARY. Key Title: U S Markets Review: Regional Forecast Summary. q. D R I - McGraw-Hill, 24 Hartwell Ave., Lexington, MA 02173. TEL 617-860-5100. FAX 617-860-6332. TELEX 200 284. Ed. Sara Johnson. **Document type:** trade publication.

338 330.9 US ISSN 1056-6066
HC101
D R I - MCGRAW-HILL U S MARKETS REVIEW: REGIONAL PREVIEW. Key Title: U S Markets Review: Regional Preview. q. D R I - McGraw-Hill, 24 Hartwell Ave., Lexington, MA 02173. TEL 617-863-5100. FAX 617-860-6332. TELEX 200 284. Ed. Sara Johnson. **Document type:** trade publication.

338 330.9 US ISSN 1069-6458
HC107.A13
D R I - MCGRAW-HILL U S MARKETS REVIEW: SOUTH. STATE FOCUS. Key Title: U S Markets Review: South. State Focus. q. D R I - McGraw-Hill, 24 Hartwell Ave., Lexington, MA 02173. TEL 617-860-6332. FAX 617-860-6332. TELEX 200 284. Ed. Sara Johnson. **Document type:** trade publication.
 Formerly (until 1992): D R I - McGraw-Hill U S Markets Review: Southern Focus (ISSN 1051-4449)

338 330.9 US ISSN 1069-6474
HC107.A17
D R I - MCGRAW-HILL U S MARKETS REVIEW: WEST. METRO FOCUS. Key Title: U S Markets Review: West. Metro Focus. 1992. q. D R I - McGraw-Hill, 24 Hartwell Ave., Lexington, MA 02173. TEL 617-863-5100. FAX 617-860-6332. TELEX 200 284. Ed. Sara Johnson. **Document type:** trade publication.

338 330.9 US ISSN 1069-644X
HC107.A17
D R I - MCGRAW-HILL U S MARKETS REVIEW: WEST. STATE FOCUS. Key Title: U S Markets Review: West. State Focus. q. D R I - McGraw-Hill, 24 Hartwell Ave., Lexington, MA 02173. TEL 617-863-5100. FAX 617-860-6332. TELEX 200 284. Ed. Sara Johnson. **Document type:** trade publication.
 Formerly (until 1992): D R I - McGraw-Hill U S Markets Review: Western Focus (ISSN 1051-4457)

338 US
DATELINE. bi-m. membership only. Association of Home Appliance Manufacturers, 20 N. Wacker Dr., Chicago, IL 60606. TEL 312-984-5800. FAX 312-984-5823. URL: http://www.aham.org. **Document type:** newsletter.
 Formerly: Exec-U-Letter.

DEFENCE AND PEACE ECONOMICS. see *MILITARY*

DELAWARE VALLEY REGIONAL PLANNING COMMISSION. ANNUAL REPORT. see *TRANSPORTATION*

338 JA
DENKYU KOGYOKAIHO/JAPAN ELECTRIC LAMP MANUFACTURERS ASSOCIATION. BULLETIN. (Text in Japanese) 1952. m. Nihon Denkyu Kogyokai - Japan Electric Lamp Manufactures Association, 7-1, Yuraku-cho 1-chome, Chiyoda-ku, Tokyo 100, Japan.

338 AG ISSN 0046-001X
HD85.S7
DESARROLLO ECONOMICO; revista de ciencias sociales. 1961. q. Arg.$60 (America $74; Europe $76; elsewhere $80) (effective 1997). Instituto de Desarrollo Economico y Social, Araoz 2836, 1425 Buenos Aires, Argentina. TEL 54-1-804-4949. FAX 54-1-804-5856. Ed. Juan Carlos Torre. adv.; bk.rev.; bibl.; charts; cum.index: 1958-1990. circ. 2,000. (back issues avail.) **Indexed:** Amer.Hist.& Life (1978-), ASCA, Geo.Abstr.H.G., Hisp.Amer.Per.Ind. (1970-), Hist.Abstr. (1978-), IBR, Int.Lab.Doc., J.of Econ.Lit., Lang.& Lang.Behav.Abstr., P.A.I.S.For.Lang.Ind., Rural Recreat.Tour.Abstr., Sociol.Abstr., SSCI, World Agri.Econ.& Rural Sociol.Abstr.
—BLDSC (3555.727000); Genuine Article; SWETS

385 CK ISSN 0418-7547
DESARROLLO INDOAMERICANO. 1966. m. Col.$2000($120) Desarrollo Indoamericano, Carrera 54 No. 58-132, Apdo. Aereo 50122, Barranquilla, Colombia. TEL 341-606. Dir. Jose Consuegra. **Indexed:** Hisp.Amer.Per.Ind. (1970-), IBR, P.A.I.S.For.Lang.Ind.

338.9 JO
DEVELOPMENT/TANMIYAH.* (Text in Arabic) 1973. m. Ministry of Information, P.O. Box 1794, Amman, Jordan. Ed. George Bandak.

338 PH
DEVELOPMENT ACADEMY OF THE PHILIPPINES. PRESIDENT'S REPORT TO THE BOARD OF TRUSTEES. (Text in English) 1974. a. Development Academy of the Philippines, Office of Special Services, P.O. Box 5160 MCC, Makati, Metro Manila, Philippines. illus. circ. controlled.
 Formerly: Development Academy of the Philippines. Annual Report.

338 IO ISSN 0125-9970
DINAMIKA. (Text in Javanese) 1972. q. Rps.250 per no. West Java Chamber of Commerce and Industry - Kamar Dagang dan Industri Jawa Barat, Suniaraja 3, Bandung, West Java, Indonesia. Ed. Ajan Sujana. adv.; charts; stat. circ. 2,500.

338 US
DIRECTORY OF APPLIANCES, EQUIPMENT, CONSTRUCTION MATERIALS, AND COMPONENTS EVALUATED IN ACCORDANCE WITH INTERNATIONAL PUBLICATIONS. a. Underwriters Laboratories Inc., Publications, 333 Pfingsten Rd., Northbrook, IL 60062-2096. TEL 708-272-8800. FAX 708-272-8129. **Document type:** directory.

DIRECTORY OF MANUFACTURERS. see *GARDENING AND HORTICULTURE*

338 SI
DIRECTORY OF S P S B PRODUCTS & COMPANIES & ACCREDITED LABORATORIES. (Former name of issuing body: Singapore Institute of Standards and Industrial Research) (Text in English) 1976. a. Singapore Productivity and Standards Board, One Science Park Dr., Singapore Science Park, Singapore 118221, Singapore. TEL 65-7729792. FAX 65-8720531. circ. 6,000. **Document type:** directory.
 Former titles: Directory of S I S I R Certified Products and Companies and Accredited Laboratories; Directory of Certified Products and Companies and Accredited Laboratories in Singapore (ISSN 0218-3021); Directory of Certified Products in Singapore (ISSN 0217-8311)

BUSINESS AND ECONOMICS — PRODUCTION OF GOODS AND SERVICES

338   JA
DIRECTORY OF THE NATIONAL PRODUCTIVITY ORGANIZATIONS IN A P O MEMBER COUNTRIES. (Text in English) 1962. irreg., latest 1996. Asian Productivity Organization, 8-4-14 Akasaka, Minato-ku, Tokyo 107, Japan. FAX 81-3-3408-7220. TELEX J26477. E-mail: apo@gol.com; URL: http://www.apo-tokyo.com. Ed. Philip Mathews. circ. 1,500. **Document type:** directory.
   Former titles: Profiles of the National Productivity Organizations in A P O Member Countries; Asian Productivity Organization. Review of Activities of National Productivity Organizations (ISSN 0571-3005)

338   AO
DIVULGACAO. 1969. a. Camara Municipal du Lobito, Caixa Postal Tres, Lobito, Angola. charts; illus.

DOMINICAN REPUBLIC. SECRETARIA DE ESTADO DE INDUSTRIA Y COMERCIO. REVISTA. see *BUSINESS AND ECONOMICS — Domestic Commerce*

338   IO
DUNIA USAHA.* 1972. m. Rps.1000. Jalan Kembang Jepun 25-27, Surabaya, Indonesia. Ed. Bd. charts; illus.

338   PK
E I P INDUSTRIAL RESEARCH SERVICE. (Text in English) 1977. w. Rs.4000($400) Economic and Industrial Publications, Al-Masiha, 47 Abdullah Haroon Rd., P.O. Box 7843, Karachi 74400, Pakistan. Ed. Bd.; Pub. Iqbal Haidari. charts; stat. circ. 1,000. (looseleaf format) **Document type:** trade publication.

338   US   ISSN 0012-8147
T1
EARLY AMERICAN INDUSTRIES ASSOCIATION. CHRONICLE. 1933. q. $30 includes Shavings from the Chronicle of the Early American Industries Association. Early American Industries Association, 167 Bakerville Rd., S. Dartmouth, MA 02748. (Alt. addr.: 1234 Yardley Ave., Linden, PA 19067) Ed. Daniel B. Rubel. bk.rev.; illus.; index. circ. 3,300. (reprint service avail. from UMI) **Indexed:** Amer.Hist.& Life, Hist.Abstr.

L'EAU, L'INDUSTRIE, LES NUISANCES. see *WATER RESOURCES*

338.9   SP   ISSN 0422-2784
ECONOMIA INDUSTRIAL. 1964. s-m. $95. Ministerio de Industria, Comercio, y Turismo, Dr. Fleming 7, 2o, 28036 Madrid, Spain. TEL 250-0202. Ed. Arcadio Lopez. adv.; charts; illus.; stat.; tr.lit.; cum.index. circ. 5,000. **Indexed:** Key to Econ.Sci., SCIMP (1989-).
—BLDSC (3650.710000); CINDOC.

338   IT   ISSN 0390-6140
HC301
ECONOMIA PUBBLICA. 1971. m. (8/yr.). L.110000 (foreign L.145000) (effective 1993). (Centro Italiano di Ricerche e Informazione Sull'Economia delle Imprese Pubbliche e di Pubblico Interesse) Franco Angeli Editore, Viale Monza 106, 20127 Milan, Italy. TEL 02-28-27-651. Ed. Alberto Mortara. adv.; bk.rev.; abstr.; bibl.; charts; stat.; index. circ. 6,000. **Indexed:** ELLIS, P.A.I.S.For.Lang.Ind.
—BLDSC (3651.090000).
   Formerly: Bollettino dell'Economia Pubblica (ISSN 0390-6159)

338   US   ISSN 0742-3713
ECONOMIC DEVELOPMENT REVIEW. 1983. 4/yr. $60 (foreign $75) to individuals; institutions $48 (foreign $63). American Economic Development Council, 9801 W. Higgins Rd., Ste. 540, Rosemont, IL 60018-4726. TEL 847-692-9944. FAX 847-696-2990. E-mail: aedc@interaccess.com; URL: http://www.aedc.org/hqtrs. Ed. Mark Waterhouse. R&P contact: Marion Morgan. adv.: page $950; trim 8 1/2 x 11; adv. contact: Marion Morgan. bk.rev. circ. 3,000. (also avail. in microform from UMI; reprint service avail. from UMI) **Indexed:** ABI Inform., BPIA, J.of Econ. Lit., Manage.Cont., P.A.I.S., Tr.& Indus.Ind. **Document type:** academic/scholarly publication.
   ●Also available online. Vendor(s): UMI.
—BLDSC (3652.740000); SWETS; UMI; UnCover.
   Former titles (1965-1981): American Industrial Development Council Journal; **Supersedes:** American Economic Development Council. Newsletter; American Industrial Development Council Newsletter; American Industrial Development Council. Professional Notes.

338   US   ISSN 0739-8956
HC107.T3
ECONOMIC GROWTH IN TENNESSEE, ANNUAL REPORT. a. (with q. updates). free. Department of Economic and Community Development, Rachel Jackson Bldg., 8th Fl., Nashville, TN 37243-0405. TEL 615-741-1995. Ed. Ray Dickerson. stat. **Document type:** government publication.
   Formerly (until 1981): Industrial Growth in Tennessee, Annual Report (ISSN 0099-1872)

338.473621   UK   ISSN 1356-9007
▼**ECONOMICS, MEDICINES, & HEALTH.** 1995. q. £37.50 (free to qualified personnel); newsstand price: £9.50. Catalyst Healthcare Communications, 5 Bennell Ct., Comberton, Cambridge CB3 7DS, England. TEL 44-1233-2664918. Ed. Mark Greener; Pub. Dr. Julian Guest. adv. contact: Jacqui Pope.
—BLDSC (3657.060000).

338   EC
ECUADOR. CENTRO DE DESARROLLO INDUSTRIAL. BOLETIN ESTADISTICAS. ECONOMICAS. 1983. q. free. Centro de Desarrollo Industrial, Av. Orellana 1715, P.O. Box 2321, Quito, Ecuador. FAX 564502. TELEX 2350. charts; illus.; stat. circ. 500.
   Former titles: Ecuador. Centro de Desarrollo Industrial. Boletin Estadisticas; Ecuador. Centro de Desarrollo Industrial. Boletin Industrial (ISSN 0045-611X)

338   EC   ISSN 0070-8887
ECUADOR. CENTRO DE DESARROLLO INDUSTRIAL. INFORME DE LABORES. 1959. a. free. Centro de Desarrollo Industrial, Av. Orellana 1715, P.O. Box 2321, Quito, Ecuador. FAX 564502. TELEX 2350. circ. 600.

338   EC
ECUADOR. MINISTERIO DE INDUSTRIAS, COMERCIO E INTEGRACION. BOLETIN DE INFORMACION DE LAS EMPRESAS ACOGIDAS A LA LEY DE FOMENTO INDUSTRIAL. 1974. a. Ministerio de Industrias, Comercio e Integracion, Quito, Ecuador.

338   AU
EINKAUFSFUEHRER FUER WISSENSCHAFT UND FORSCHUNG. bi-m. Sommerhaidenweg 124, A-1190 Vienna, Austria. TEL 01-443295. FAX 01-442825. circ. 9,000.

338 658.1   SW   ISSN 1102-2922
EKONOMI & STYRNING. 1990. 6/yr. SEK 624; newsstand price: SEK 140. Svenska Civilekonomfoereningen, Dalagatan 34, S-113 24 Stockholm, Sweden. TEL 46-8-30-02-50. FAX 46-8-34-81-08. Ed. Inge Wennberg; Pub. Marika Markland. adv.: B&W page SEK 11500, color page SEK 16400; trim 186 x 264; adv. contact: Haakan Hansson. circ. 7,400. cols./p.: 3; pp./issue: 48. **Document type:** trade publication.

338   BW
HD70.S632
EKONOMIKA PROMYSHLENNOGO PROIZVODSTVA. (Subseries of: Respublikanskie Mezhvedomstvennye Sborniki) 1970. a. 3 Rub. (Belorusskii Gosudarstvennyi Izdatel'stvo Vysheishaya Shkola, Pr. Masherava 11, 22600 Minsk, Belarus. TEL 0172-236494. **Indexed:** Curr.Dig.Sov.Press.
   Former titles (until no.20, 1991): Ekonomika, Organizatsiya i Planirovanie Promyszlennogo Proizvodstva (ISSN 0235-2427); (until 1986): Ekonomika i Organizatsiya Promyshlennogo Proizvodstva (ISSN 0321-4990)

338   RU   ISSN 0869-4672
EKONOMIST. 1923. m. $94 (effective 1998). Gosplan, Smolenskii Blvd., D. 3-5, 119898 Moscow, Russia. TEL 7-95-246-1637. Ed. N.D. Kovalenko. bk.rev.; stat.; index. circ. 23,380. **Indexed:** Chem.Abstr., Curr.Dig.Sov.Press, Geo.Abstr., Maize Abstr., Potato Abstr., Rural Recreat.Tour.Abstr., Triticale Abstr., World Agri.Econ.& Rural Sociol.Abstr. **Document type:** government publication, academic/scholarly publication.
—BLDSC (0397.796000).
   Formerly (until 1992): Planovoe Khozyaistvo (ISSN 0370-0356)

338   II   ISSN 0970-7441
ELECTRONIC PRODUCTS FINDER. (Text in English) 1985. m. Rs.800($28) Business Press, Transmission House, Compartment No. 82, Plot No. 6-19, Marol Co-op Industrial Estate, M.V. Rd., Andheri East, Mumbai 400 059, India. TEL 91-22-850-9100. FAX 91-22-850-2070. TELEX 011-78455 BPPL IN. Ed. K.S. Pai. adv.: B&W page Rs.6000, color page Rs.10600; trim 280 x 205. bk.rev.; abstr.; charts; illus. circ. 8,000. **Description:** Covers new products and news briefs.

338   AG
ENERGIA INDUSTRIAL. 6/yr. Editorial Golova s.r.l., Av. de Mayo 963, Buenos Aires, Argentina. circ. 4,000.

ENQUETE SUR LES ENTREPRISES INDUSTRIELLES ET COMMERCIALES DU TOGO. see *BUSINESS AND ECONOMICS — Domestic Commerce*

338.7   CN
ENTERPRISE P E I. 1966. a. free. Prince Edward Island Development Agency, West Royalty Industrial Park, Charlottetown, PE C1E 1B0, Canada. TEL 902-368-5800. FAX 902-566-4030. TELEX 014-44109.
   Former titles: Prince Edward Island Development Agency. Annual Report; (until 1985): Industrial Enterprises Incorporated. Annual Report.

338   FR   ISSN 0751-588X
ENTREPRISES RHONE ALPES. 1942. 10/yr. 200 F. Editions S.M.E., 55 Montee de Choulans, 69323 Lyon Cedex 05, France. TEL 78-42-29-53. FAX 78-42-09-14. Ed. Jean Mochon. adv.; illus.; mkt.; tr.lit.; index. circ. 3,012. **Indexed:** Cadscan, Chem.Abstr., Lead Abstr., Zincscan.
   Supersedes: Metallurgie (ISSN 0026-0878)

EQUIPMENT MANUFACTURERS INSTITUTE. FIRST OF THE WEEK NEWSLETTER. see *AGRICULTURE — Agricultural Equipment*

EQUIPMENT MANUFACTURERS INSTITUTE. RETAIL SALES REPORTS. see *AGRICULTURE — Agricultural Equipment*

EQUIPMENT MANUFACTURERS INSTITUTE. STATE OF THE INDUSTRY. see *AGRICULTURE — Agricultural Equipment*

338 621.9   SP   ISSN 1130-9571
EQUIPOS Y PRODUCTOS INDUSTRIALES. 1991. 9/yr. Elsevier Prensa S.A., Avda. Paral.lel 180, 0815 Barcelona, Spain. TEL 34-3-3255350. FAX 34-3-4252880. Ed. Lluis Lahoz. adv. contact: Manuel Fernandez de Liencres. circ. 27,000. **Document type:** trade publication. **Description:** Covers new products for industry.

338.9   SP   ISSN 0084-5132
ESCUELA DE GERENTES DE COOPERATIVAS. CARTILLAS DE COOPERACION. 1971. irreg., latest issue 1978. 25 ptas. (Escuela de Gerentes de Cooperativas) Centro Nacional de Educacion Cooperativa, Palacio de la Cooperacion, Apdo. de Correos 15, San Felix 9, Zaragoza, Spain. (Affiliate: Federacion Nacional de Cooperativas de Espana) Ed. Joaquin Mateo.

338   IT   ISSN 0014-0554
ESPANSIONE. 1969. m. L.35700 (foreign L.83400). Arnoldo Mondadori Editore S.p.A., Casella Postale 1833, 20101 Milan, Italy. TEL 39-2-3199345. Ed. Redento Mori. adv.: B&W page L.13200000, color page L.19800000. circ. 42,000.

338 650   FR
T12.5.F7
ESSOR FRANCAIS DE L'INDUSTRIE. a. 600 F. Union Francaise d'Annuaires Professionnels, 130 av. des Bouleaux, B.P. 36, 78192 Trappes Cedex, France. TEL 01-30-13-82-00. FAX 01-30-13-82-11. **Document type:** directory.
   Formerly: Dictionnaire de l'Industrie Francaise (ISSN 0070-4741)

338.9   ET   ISSN 0378-0813
ETHIOPIAN JOURNAL OF DEVELOPMENT RESEARCH. (Former name of issuing body: Haile Selassie I University) (Text in English) 1974. s-a. $7 per no. Addis Ababa University, Institute of Development Research, P.O. Box 1176, Addis Ababa, Ethiopia. TELEX 21205. Ed. T. Mulat. bk.rev.; charts; stat. circ. 1,000. **Indexed:** P.L.E.S.A. (1987-).

EUROPEAN ELECTRONIC CHEMICALS MARKET. see *ENGINEERING — Chemical Engineering*

BUSINESS AND ECONOMICS — PRODUCTION OF GOODS AND SERVICES

338   UK   ISSN 1352-9633
EUROPEAN RETAIL DIGEST. q. £95 to academic institutions; commercial institutions £125. Oxford Institute of Retail Management, Templeton College, Kennington, Oxford OX1 5NY, England. TEL 01865-735422. FAX 01865-736374. Ed. Wendy Wood. **Indexed:** Cont.Pg.Manage. **Document type:** trade publication.
—BLDSC (3829.924900).
   Description: Provides a guide to trends and developments in retailing within Europe.

338   US
EUROPEAN SERVICES INDUSTRY. 1994. bi-m. $65. Association for Services Management International, 1342 Colonial Blvd., Ste. 25, Ft. Myers, FL 33907. TEL 813-275-7887. FAX 813-275-0794. Ed. Leonard Mafrica. adv.: B&W page $3150. circ. 8,500. (tabloid format) **Document type:** trade publication.

EUROPEAN SIGN MAGAZINE. see ADVERTISING AND PUBLIC RELATIONS

338   UK   ISSN 0800-0638
HD2356.E9
EUROPE'S 15000 LARGEST COMPANIES. 1975. a. £185. E L C Publishing Ltd., 109 Uxbridge Rd., Ealing, London W5 STL, England. TEL 0181-566-2288. FAX 0181-566-4931. (Dist. in the U.S. by: Dun's Marketing Services, 3 Century Dr., Parsippany, NJ 07054) Ed. D. Wildey. circ. 4,000.
—BLDSC (3830.397000); CISTI.
   Former titles (until 1985): Europe's 10000 Largest Companies; (until 1984): Europe's 5000 Largest Companies.

338   AU
EUROTEC. 1975. m. S.520. Bohmann Druck und Verlag GmbH & Co. KG, Leberstr. 122, A-1110 Vienna, Austria. TEL 43-1-74095-0. FAX 43-1-74095-183. TELEX 132312. E-mail: output@inmedias.ping.at. adv.; illus.; tr.lit. circ. 15,000. **Document type:** trade publication.
   Formerly: Output Oesterreich (ISSN 0254-5306)

338   FR   ISSN 0014-4703
HC271
EXPANSION. 1967. bi-m. 482 F. Groupe Expansion, 25 rue Leblanc, 75842 Paris Cedex 15, France. TEL 40-60-40-60. FAX 40-60-41-22. TELEX 205 581. Ed. Gerard Moatti. adv. circ. 200,565. (also avail. in microform from UMI; reprint service avail. from UMI) **Indexed:** ELLIS, Key to Econ.Sci., Mgmt.& Market.Abstr., P.A.I.S.For.Lang.Ind., SCIMP (1986-).
—BLDSC (3836.430000); SWETS; UMI. **CCC.**

338   SA
EXPANSION. 1975. m. R.6. Business Week Holdings Ltd, Sakers Corner, 34 Eloff St., Johannesburg, South Africa. illus.

338   MX   ISSN 0185-2728
EXPANSION. 1969. fortn. $98 in US & Canada; Latin America $106; Europe & Asia $116 (effective 1997). Grupo Editorial Expansion (Subsidiary of: Capital Cities - A B C, Inc.), Salamanca 35, Col. Roma, 06700 Mexico D.F., Mexico. TEL 207-20-66. FAX 208-28-19. Ed. Diego Arrazola. R&P contact: David Estrello. adv. contact: Manuel Mier y Concha. illus. circ. 23,516. **Document type:** consumer publication.
   Description: Covers business news of Mexico.

338 640.73   BE   ISSN 0771-2987
F E B BULLETIN. Dutch edition: V B O Bulletin. (Editions in Dutch and French) 1895. m. 3950 BEF($89) Federation des Entreprises de Belgique - Verbond van Belgische Ondernemingen, 4 Ravenstein, 1000 Brussels, Belgium. adv.; bk.rev.; charts; illus.; index. circ. 14,000 (French ed. 6,500; Dutch ed. 7,500). **Document type:** bulletin.
   Formerly (until 1972): Federation des Industries Belges. Bulletin (ISSN 0014-9349)

F E W A TIPS. (Farm Equipment Wholesalers Association) see AGRICULTURE — Agricultural Equipment

338   NR
F I I R O TECHNICAL INFORMATION BULLETIN FOR INDUSTRY. 1972. q. £N10 free to research organizations. Federal Institute of Industrial Research, Oshodi, P.M.B. 21023, Ikeja, Lagos State, Nigeria. TELEX 26006. Ed.Bd. charts; illus. circ. 1,000. **Document type:** bulletin, government publication.

338.4
F T C NEWSNOTES. 1974. w. free. U.S. Federal Trade Commission, Office of Public Affairs, Sixth St. and Pennsylvania Ave., N.W., Washington, DC 20580. TEL 202-655-4000. (Subscr. to: Superintendent of Documents, U.S. Government Printing Office, Box 371954, Pittsburgh, PA 15250-7954. TEL 202-512-1800. FAX 202-512-2250) Ed. Murfy Alexander. (also avail. in microfiche from CIS; back issues avail.; reprint service avail. from CIS) **Indexed:** Amer.Stat.Ind. (1982-), PROMT. **Document type:** government publication.
   Formerly (until 1990): Quarterly Financial Report for Manufacturing, Mining and Trade Corporations (ISSN 0098-681X); U.S. Federal Trade Commission. Quarterly Financial Report: United States Manufacturing Corporations (ISSN 0033-5509)
   Description: Summarizes rulemaking procedures, speeches, and other noteworthy occurrences.

338   AT   ISSN 0312-973X
FACTORY MANAGEMENT. 1973. m. Aus.$24. Finecraft Publishing Co., P.O. Box 260, Neutral Bay Junction, N.S.W. 2089, Australia. Ed. John Walters.
   Formerly: Manufacturing News in Australia (ISSN 0311-2160)

353 650   US   ISSN 0014-9063
KF849.A1
FEDERAL CONTRACTS REPORT. 1964. w. $1098. The Bureau of National Affairs, Inc., 1231 25th St., N.W., Washington, DC 20037. TEL 202-452-4200. FAX 202-822-8092. TELEX 285656 BNAI WSH. URL: http://www.bna.com/. (Subscr. to: 9435 Key West Ave., Rockville, MD 20850. TEL 800-372-1033) Ed. Melainie I. Dooley. bk.rev.; index. (looseleaf format; back issues avail.)
   ●Also available online. Vendor(s): Lexis-Nexis (FDCONT), West Group.
—**CCC.**
   Description: Reporting service providing comprehensive coverage of the current developments affecting federal contracts and grants.

338   US
FEDERAL SUPPLY CODE FOR MANUFACTURERS, UNITED STATES AND CANADA.* (In 2 parts: Cataloging Handbook H 4-1, Name to Code; Cataloging Handbook H 4-2, Code to Name) bi-m. $24. U.S. Defense Logistics Agency, 8725 John J. Kingman Rd., Ste. 2533, Fort Belvoir, VA 22060-6221. TEL 202-274-6000. (Dist. by: Supt. of Documents, Washington, DC 20402) (microfiche)

338 640.73   BE   ISSN 0773-1884
FEDERATION DES ENTREPRISES DE BELGIQUE. RAPPORT ANNUEL. Dutch edition: Verbon van Belgische Ondernemingen. Jaarlijks Verslag (ISSN 0773-1892) a. Federation des Entreprises de Belgique - Verbond van Belgische Ondernemingen, 4 Ravenstein, 1000 Brussels, Belgium. **Document type:** corporate report.
   Formerly: Federation des Industries Belges. Rapport Annuel (ISSN 0071-4178)

338   UA
FEDERATION OF EGYPTIAN INDUSTRIES. MONTHLY BULLETIN. (Text in English) m. Federation of Egyptian Industries - Ittihad al-Sinaat al-Misriyah, 26a, Sherif Pasha St., Cairo, Egypt. **Document type:** bulletin.

338   US   ISSN 0171-5062
FERTIGUNG UND BETRIEB. (Text in German) 1974. irreg. price varies. Springer-Verlag, 175 Fifth Ave., New York, NY 10010. TEL 212-460-1500. FAX 212-473-6272. (Also: Berlin, Heidelberg, Tokyo and Vienna) (reprint service avail. from ISI) **Document type:** academic/scholarly publication.
   Supersedes: Werkstattbuecher fuer Betriebsfachleute Konstrukteure und Studenten (ISSN 0083-8055)

FINANCIAL SURVEY. THE FISH INDUSTRY; company data for success. see BUSINESS AND ECONOMICS — Trade And Industrial Directories

FINITE ELEMENTS IN ANALYSIS AND DESIGN; the international journal of applied finite elements and computer-aided engineering. see ENGINEERING — Computer Applications

338   GW   ISSN 0938-8044
FIRMEN DER NEUEN BUNDESLAENDER. 1990. a. DM.448 (effective 1997). Verlag Hoppenstedt GmbH, Havelstr. 9, 64295 Darmstadt, Germany. TEL 49-6151-380-0. FAX 49-6151-380-360. circ. 23,000. **Document type:** directory.
   ●Also available online. Vendor(s): Data-Star, Knight-Ridder Information, Inc.
   Also available on CD-ROM.
   Incorporates: Offizielles Verzeichnis der Treuhandanstalt.

FLAGSTAFF INSTITUTE. JOURNAL. see BUSINESS AND ECONOMICS — International Commerce

338   SW   ISSN 1100-6331
FOERETAG & NAERINGSLIV. 1988. q. SEK 100 (effective 1991). Mellansvenska Fackfoerlaget, P.O. Box 14239, S-104 40 Stockholm, Sweden.

338   SW   ISSN 0348-7830
FOERETAG OCH SAMHAELLE. 1975. q. SEK 120 (effective 1990). S N S - Studiefoerbundet Naeringsliv och Samhaelle, Skoeldungag. 2, S-114 27 Stockholm, Sweden.

338   SW   ISSN 0284-2807
FOERETAGSMAGASINET. 1987. q. Foeretagsmagasinet, P.O. Box 19064, S-400 12 Goeteborg, Sweden.

650   SP   ISSN 0015-6035
FOMENTO DE LA PRODUCCION; revista de la industria, el comercio y las finanzas. 1946. s-m. 5500 ptas. Casanova, 57, 08011 Barcelona, Spain. TEL 3-253-06-97. FAX 3-323-38-85. Ed. Ramon Carlos Baratech. illus.; stat.
—CINDOC.

330   FR   ISSN 0071-6847
FONDS DE DEVELOPPEMENT ECONOMIQUE ET SOCIAL. CONSEIL DE DIRECTION. RAPPORT. a. (Ministere de l'Economie et des Finances) Imprimerie Nationale, B.P. 514, 59505 Douai Cedex, France. TEL 27-93-70-90. FAX 27-93-70-96. TELEX 120 389 F.

614   US   ISSN 0362-6466
FOOD AND DRUG LETTER. 1976. bi-m. $895. Washington Business Information, Inc., c/o Karen Harrington, 1117 N. 19th St., Ste. 200, Arlington, VA 22209. TEL 703-247-3434. FAX 703-247-3421. Ed. Michael Dolan. bk.rev.; charts. (looseleaf format) **Document type:** newsletter.
   ●Also available online. Vendor(s): Ovid Technologies, Inc. (DIOG), Data-Star, Knight-Ridder Information, Inc.
—**CCC.**
   Incorporating: Nutrition Intelligence.
   Description: Focuses on major regulatory issues of foods, drugs and cosmetics.

338.8   JA
FOREIGN-AFFILIATED ENTERPRISES IN JAPAN.* (Text in English) 1967. a. 13000 Yen. Ministry of International Trade and Industry, 1-3-1 Kasumigaseki, Chiyoda-ku, Tokyo 100, Japan. TEL 03-501-1511. illus.; stat.

338 658   US
FOREMAN'S PRODUCTION PLANNER; a monthly production guide to better leadership and supervision. m. $28.32. Dartnell Corporation, 4660 N. Ravenswood Ave., Chicago, IL 60640. TEL 773-561-4000; 800-621-5463. FAX 773-561-3801. URL: http://www.dartnellcorp.com. Ed. Linda Segall.
   Description: A time management instrument and training aid that will give foremen and the company the production edge to increase efficiency, supervise staff and promote gook work habits.

330   FI   ISSN 0533-070X
FORUM FOER EKONOMI OCH TEKNIK. (Text in Swedish) 1968. fortn. FIM 250. Foerlags Ab Forum foer Ekonomi och Teknik, Mannerheimintie 18, 00100 Helsinki 10, Finland. Ed. Ragnhild Artimo. adv.; bk.rev.; charts; illus.; tr.lit.; index. circ. 12,841. **Indexed:** INIS Atomind.
—Linda Hall.
   Formed by the merger of: Mercator (ISSN 0025-9837) & Tekniskt Forum (ISSN 0040-2362)

BUSINESS AND ECONOMICS — PRODUCTION OF GOODS AND SERVICES

338   **FR**
FRANCE. DIRECTION GENERALE DE LA CONCURRENCE ET DE LA CONSOMMATION. BULLETIN OFFICIEL - SERVICE DES PRIX. 1941. irreg. 86 F. (foreign 153 F.) per no. Direction des Journaux Officiels, 26 rue Desaix, 75727 Paris Cedex 15, France. TEL 1-45-78-61-44. (also avail. in microfiche)
Formerly: France. Direction Generale de la Concurrence et des Prix. Bulletin Officiel des Services des Prix (ISSN 0071-870X)

338   **FR**   ISSN 0242-3456
FRANCE INDUSTRIE. 1976. m. (11/yr.). 280 F. Societe Nouvelle Meridionale d'Imprimerie et d'Edition (S N M I E), Centre d'Affaires CAP SUD, Immeuble Orion, Route de Marseille, 84000 Avignon, France. TEL 90-89-90-91. FAX 90-89-31-62. Ed. Marie-Claire Forcina. adv.: B&W page 8300 F., color page 16600 F.; trim 373 x 243; adv. contact: Christian Hodapp. circ. 15,000.

G K N PLC. REPORTS & ACCOUNTS (YEAR). see *BUSINESS AND ECONOMICS — Economic Situation And Conditions*

330   **GW**   ISSN 0072-159X
GERMANY. SACHVERSTAENDIGENRAT ZUR BEGUTACHTUNG DER GESAMTWIRTSCHAFTLICHEN ENTWICKLUNG. JAHRESGUTACHTEN. 1964. a. DM.45. Statistisches Bundesamt, 65180 Wiesbaden, Germany. TEL 49-611-75-1. FAX 49-611-724000. TELEX 61186-STBA-D. URL: http://www.statistik-bund.de. circ. 3,300. **Document type**: government publication.

338   **BE**   ISSN 0773-0543
HD28
GESTION 2000; management & prospective. (Text in English, French) 1985. 6/yr. 5900 BEF (Europe 6500 BEF; elsewhere 6800 BEF). Recherches et Publications en Management a.s.b.l., Verte Voie 20, B-1348 Louvain-la-Neuve, Belgium. TEL 32-10-453435. FAX 32-10-454060. Ed. Etienne Cracco. R&P contact: Brigitte Evrard. adv. contact: Ctistina Soster. bk.rev.; bibl.; index. circ. 3,500. Indexed: Geo.Abstr., Key to Econ.Sci., Mgmt.& Market.Abstr., SCIMP (1981-). **Document type**: academic/scholarly publication.
—BLDSC (4163.790000); SWETS.
Former titles: Demain; Etudes et Expansion (ISSN 0037-9263); Annales des Sciences Economiques Appliquees.
Description: Covers all aspects of management, including strategy, marketing, finance, human resources and production, from an international perspective.

338   **GH**
GHANA MANUFACTURER. 1974. q. free. Association of Ghana Industries, P.O. Box 8624, Accra - North, Ghana. TEL 233-21-777283. FAX 233-21-773143. Ed. Eddie Imbeah-Amoakuh. adv. circ. 1,200. **Document type**: trade publication.

GOLF CLUBMAKER. see *SPORTS AND GAMES — Ball Games*

350   **US**
GOODS AND SERVICES BULLETIN. 1984. w. $45. State Bookstore, Commonwealth of Massachusetts, State House, Rm. 116, Boston, MA 02133. circ. 1,950. **Document type**: bulletin.

353   **PL**   ISSN 1231-2037
TS149
GOSPODARKA MATERIALOWA I LOGISTYKA. 1949. m. $160 (effective 1998). Polskie Wydawnictwo Ekonomiczne, Ul. Canaletta 4, 00-099 Warsaw, Poland. TEL 48-22-8278001. (Dist. by: Mezhdunarodnaya Kniga, B. Yakimanka 39, 117049 Moscow, Russia. TEL 7-095-2384967. FAX 7-095-2384634) Ed. Stanislaw Wesolowski. bk.rev.; charts; illus.; stat.; index.
Formerly (until 1994): Gospodarka Materialowa (ISSN 0017-2405)

338   **PL**   ISSN 0867-0005
HC337.P7
GOSPODARKA NARODOWA; analizy, prognozy, strategia. (Text and summaries in English, Polish) 1946. m. $132 (effective 1998). Instytut Rozwoju i Studiow Strategicznych, Plac Trzech Krzyzy 5, 00-507 Warsaw, Poland. TEL 48-2-6285895. FAX 48-2-6250676. (Dist. by: Ars Polona-Ruch, Krakowskie Przedmiescie 7, Warsaw, Poland. TEL 48-22-261201; Dist. also by: Mezhdunarodnaya Kniga, B. Yakimanka 39, 117049 Moscow, Russia. TEL 7-095-2384967. FAX 7-095-2384634) (Co-sponsors: Cetnralny Urzad Planowania; Glowny Urzad Statystyczny) Ed. Danuta Hubner. adv. contact: Wladyslawa Czech Matuszewska. bk.rev.; charts; stat.; index. circ. 1,000. **Indexed**: AgroLibrex. **Document type**: academic/scholarly publication.
—BLDSC (4201.655000).
Formerly (until 1990): Gospodarka Planowa (ISSN 0017-2421)
Description: Covers national economy from a theoretical and political perspective.

338   **US**   ISSN 0072-5137
HD3858
GOVERNMENT CONTRACTS DIRECTORY. 1964. a. $89.50. Government Data Publications, Inc., 1155 Connecticut Ave., N.W., Washington, DC 20036. Ed. Siegfried Lobel. **Document type**: directory.

338   **US**   ISSN 0887-4085
HD3858
GOVERNMENT PRIMECONTRACTS MONTHLY. 1976. m. $96. Government Data Publications, Inc., 1155 Connecticut Ave., N.W., Washington, DC 20036. Ed. Siegfried Lobel.

GREECE. NATIONAL STATISTICAL SERVICE. PRODUCTION OF MANUFACTURED ITEMS. see *BUSINESS AND ECONOMICS — Abstracting, Bibliographies, Statistics*

338   **GW**
GROSSUNTERNEHMEN IN OESTERREICH. 1979. a. DM.420 (effective 1997). Verlag Hoppenstedt GmbH, Havelstr. 9, 64295 Darmstadt, Germany. TEL 49-6151-380-0. FAX 49-6151-380-360. circ. 10,000. **Document type**: directory.
Formerly: Oesterreich 2000.

338   **GW**   ISSN 1215-7481
GROSSUNTERNEHMEN IN UNGARN. Hungarian edition: Magyarorszag Nagy Vallalatai es Vallalkozasai (ISSN 1215-6906) 1992. a. DM.350 (effective 1997). Verlag Hoppenstedt GmbH, Havelstr. 9, 64295 Darmstadt, Germany. TEL 49-6151-380-0. FAX 49-6151-380-360. circ. 10,000. **Document type**: directory.

338   **US**   ISSN 0017-4815
HT390   CODEN: GRCHDH
GROWTH AND CHANGE; a journal of urban and regional policy. 1970. q. $39 to individuals (foreign $56); institutions $83.50 (foreign 101.50) (effective 1997). (University of Kentucky, College of Business and Economics, Center for Business and Economic Research) Blackwell Publishers, 238 Main St., Cambridge, MA 02141. TEL 617-547-7110. FAX 617-547-0789. E-mail: subscript@blackwellpub.com. Eds. Richard E. Gift, Thomas R. Leinbach. adv. contact: Scottie Kenkel. bk.rev.; index; circ. 850 (paid); 150 (controlled). (also avail. in microform from UMI) **Indexed**: A.B.C.Pol.Sci., ABI Inform., Arts & Hum.Cit.Ind., ASCA, BPIA, Bus.Ind., Curr.Cont., Energy Ind., Energy Info.Abstr., Geo.Abstr.H.G., Human Resour.Abstr., IDA, Int.Polit.Sci.Abstr., J.of Econ.Abstr., J.of Econ.Lit., Key to Econ.Sci., Mid.East: Abstr.& Ind., Mkt.Inform.Guide, P.A.I.S., Popul.Ind., Rural Recreat.Tour.Abstr., Sage Pub.Admin.Abstr., Sage Urb.Stud.Abstr., Sel.Water Res.Abstr., Soils & Fert., SSCI, SSCI, Tr.& Indus.Ind., Urb.Aff.Abstr., Work Rel.Abstr., World Agri.Econ.& Rural Sociol.Abstr. **Document type**: academic/scholarly publication.
●Also available online. Vendor(s): Information Access Co., UMI.
—BLDSC (4223.020000); Genuine Article; SWETS; UMI; UnCover. **CCC**.
Description: Interdisciplinary journal focusing on regional economic development and related policy issues.
Refereed Serial

338   **SP**   ISSN 1130-5185
GRUPO I N I (RESUMEN DE ACTIVIDADES). 1940. a. free. Instituto Nacional de Industria, Plaza de Salamanca, 8, 28006 Madrid, Spain. TEL 341-401 40 04. illus.
Formerly (until 1980): Spain. Instituto Nacional de Industria. Resumen de Actividades - Memoria (ISSN 1130-5177)

330.9   **SG**
GUIDE DE L'INVESTISSEUR INDUSTRIEL AU SENEGAL. irreg. 3000 Fr.CFA. Societe Nationale d'Etude et de Promotion Industrielle, 4, rue Maunoury, B.P. 100, Dakar, Senegal. illus.

338   **II**
GUJARAT INDUSTRIAL DEVELOPMENT CORPORATION. ANNUAL REPORT. (Text in English) a. Gujarat Industrial Development Corporation, Ashram Rd., Ahmedabad 9, India. illus.; stat.

338.7409489   **DK**   ISSN 0905-5878
HD28
GULDNUMMERET. DANMARKS 500 STOERSTE VIRKSOMHEDER. 1975. a. DKK 10. A-S Boersens Magasiner, Moentergade 19, DK-1140 Copenhagen K, Denmark. Ed. Kristian Lund. adv. contact: Willy Joergensen. **Document type**: directory.
Formerly (until 1989): Danmarks 200 Stoerste Virksomheder (ISSN 0106-9977)

338 628.5   **BA**
GULF INDUSTRY & SAUDI ARABIA REVIEW. (Text in English) bi-m. $48. Al Hilal Publishing & Marketing Group, P.O. Box 224, Manama, Bahrain. TEL 973-293131. FAX 973-293400. TELEX 8981 HILAL BN. (In U.K: Hilal International (UK) Ltd., Crescent Ct., 102 Victor Rd., Teddington, Middx TW11 8SS, England. TEL 44-181-9433630. FAX 44-181-9433701) Ed. Fermin D'Souza. adv.: B&W page $2625, color page $3290. circ. 7,167. **Document type**: trade publication.
Description: For individuals with an involvement or interest in the industrial development of the Gulf region, including industrialists, factory managers, major distributors of industrial products, and government officials.

338   **GW**   ISSN 0073-0068
HANDBUCH DER GROSSUNTERNEHMEN. 1953. a. (2 vols.) DM.765 for 2 vols. (effective 1997). Verlag Hoppenstedt GmbH, Havelstr. 9, 64295 Darmstadt, Germany. TEL 49-6151-380-0. FAX 49-6151-380-360. adv. circ. 23,500. **Document type**: directory.
●Also available online. Vendor(s): Data-Star, GBI, Knight-Ridder Information, Inc.

HARRIS CONNECTICUT MANUFACTURERS DIRECTORY. see *BUSINESS AND ECONOMICS — Trade And Industrial Directories*

HARRIS DELAWARE MANUFACTURERS DIRECTORY. see *BUSINESS AND ECONOMICS — Trade And Industrial Directories*

HARRIS GEORGIA MANUFACTURERS DIRECTORY. see *BUSINESS AND ECONOMICS — Trade And Industrial Directories*

HARRIS MASSACHUSETTS MANUFACTURERS DIRECTORY. see *BUSINESS AND ECONOMICS — Trade And Industrial Directories*

HARRIS NATIONAL MANUFACTURERS DIRECTORY (YEAR). see *BUSINESS AND ECONOMICS — Trade And Industrial Directories*

HARRIS NATIONAL MANUFACTURERS DIRECTORY MIDWEST EDITION (YEAR). see *BUSINESS AND ECONOMICS — Trade And Industrial Directories*

HARRIS NATIONAL MANUFACTURERS DIRECTORY NORTHEAST EDITION (YEAR). see *BUSINESS AND ECONOMICS — Trade And Industrial Directories*

HARRIS NATIONAL MANUFACTURERS DIRECTORY SOUTHEAST EDITION (YEAR). see *BUSINESS AND ECONOMICS — Trade And Industrial Directories*

HARRIS NATIONAL MANUFACTURERS SOUTH CENTRAL DIRECTORY ON DISC. see *BUSINESS AND ECONOMICS — Trade And Industrial Directories*

HARRIS NEW ENGLAND MANUFACTURERS DIRECTORY. see *BUSINESS AND ECONOMICS — Trade And Industrial Directories*

BUSINESS AND ECONOMICS — PRODUCTION OF GOODS AND SERVICES

HARRIS RHODE ISLAND MANUFACTURERS DIRECTORY. see *BUSINESS AND ECONOMICS — Trade And Industrial Directories*

HARRIS SOUTH CAROLINA MANUFACTURERS DIRECTORY. see *BUSINESS AND ECONOMICS — Trade And Industrial Directories*

HARRIS TEXAS MANUFACTURERS DIRECTORY. see *BUSINESS AND ECONOMICS — Trade And Industrial Directories*

338.9   US
HAWAII. DEPARTMENT OF BUSINESS, ECONOMIC DEVELOPMENT & TOURISM. ANNUAL REPORT. 1962. a. free. Department of Business, Economic Development & Tourism, Communications & Publications, Box 2359, Honolulu, HI 96804. TEL 808-586-2404. FAX 808-586-2427. circ. 1,500. **Document type:** government publication.
Former titles: Hawaii. Department of Business and Economic Development. Annual Report (ISSN 1041-0635); (until 1987): Hawaii. Department of Planning and Economic Development. Annual Report (ISSN 0073-1072)

HAZARDOUS WASTE TREATMENT AND DISPOSAL MARKET IN EUROPE. see *ENVIRONMENTAL STUDIES — Waste Management*

338   JA
HOKKAIDO KOGYO KAIHATSU SHIKENJO NENPO/GOVERNMENT INDUSTRIAL DEVELOPMENT LABORATORY, HOKKAIDO. ANNUAL REPORT. 1961. a. Hokkaido Kogyo Kaihatsu Shikenjo - Government Industrial Development Laboratory, Hokkaido, 41-2 Higashi-Tsukisamu, Toyohira-ku, Sapporo 061-01, Hokkaido, Japan. abstr.

338   JA
HOKKOHKEN NEWS. bi-m. free. Hokkaido National Industrial Research Institute, 2-17 Tsukisamu-higashi, Toyohira-ku, Sapporo 062, Hokkaido, Japan. FAX 81-11-857-8901. E-mail: tonooka@nniri.go.jp. **Document type:** newsletter.
Formerly: Hokkaishi News.

338   CC
HONG KONG PRODUCTIVITY COUNCIL ANNUAL REPORT. (Text in Chinese, English) 1968. annual. Hong Kong Productivity Council, HKPC Bldg., 78 Tat Chee Ave., Kowloon, Hong Kong, People's Republic of China. TEL 852-2788-5678. FAX 852-2788-5900. TELEX 32842 HKPC HX. Ed. Betty Lee. circ. 5,000.
Formerly: Hong Kong Productivity Council and Centre Annual Report.

338   CC
HONG KONG PRODUCTIVITY NEWS. (Text in Chinese and English) 1967. m. Hong Kong Productivity Council, 2-F, HKPC Bldg., 78 Tat Chee Ave., Kowloon, Hong Kong, People's Republic of China. TEL 852-2788-5678. FAX 852-2788-5052. Ed. Wendy Tsang. adv.: B&W page HK.$5600, color page HK.$8300; 370 x 266. circ. 7,000.

HUNGARY. KOZPONTI STATISZTIKAI HIVATAL. IPARSTATISZTIKAI EVKONYV. see *BUSINESS AND ECONOMICS — Abstracting, Bibliographies, Statistics*

338   IE
I B E C - E S R I BUSINESS FORECAST. 1974. m. Irish Business and Employers Confederation, Confederation House, 84-86 Lower Baggot St., Dublin 2, Ireland. TEL 353-1-6601011. FAX 353-1-6601717. URL: http://www.iol.ie/ibec. Ed. David Croughan. circ. controlled. **Document type:** bulletin.
Formerly: C I I - E S R I Business Forecast.

338   IE
I B E C NEWS. 1965. m. Irish Business and Employers Confederation, Confederation House, 84-86 Lower Baggot St., Dublin 2, Ireland. TEL 353-1-6601011. FAX 353-1-6601717. URL: http://www.iol.ie/ibec. Ed. Karin Mac Arthur. circ. 6,000. circ. controlled. (looseleaf format) **Document type:** newsletter.
Formerly (until 1992): C I I Newsletter.

I D E OCCASIONAL PAPERS SERIES. (Institute of Developing Economies) see *BUSINESS AND ECONOMICS*

338   GW   ISSN 0170-5660
I F O STUDIEN ZUR INDUSTRIEWIRTSCHAFT. 1967. irreg., vol.51, 1995. price varies. I F O Institut fuer Wirtschaftsforschung, Poschingerstr. 5, 81679 Munich, Germany. TEL 49-89-9224-0. FAX 49-89-985369. circ. 500. **Document type:** monographic series.

I I R R REPORT. (International Institute of Rural Reconstruction) see *BUSINESS AND ECONOMICS — International Development And Assistance*

338   US
I S O 9000 REGISTERED FIRMS DIRECTORY. (International Organization for Standarization) s-a. (2 vols./yr.). Underwriters Laboratories Inc., Publications, 333 Pfingsten Rd., Northbrook, IL 60062-2096. TEL 708-272-8800. FAX 708-272-8129. **Document type:** directory.
Description: Lists firms complying with ISO 9000 standards.

338 658.3
IDEAS AND SOLUTIONS; magazine for businesses, products and services. 1986. m. $35. Gibbs Publishing Company, Box 600927, N. Miami Beach, FL 33160. Ed. James Calvin Gibbs. adv.; bk.rev. circ. 2,500. **Document type:** trade publication.

338   US
ILLINOIS MANUFACTURER. 1991. bi-m. $30. Illinois Manufacturer, 220 E. Adams St., Springfield, IL 62701-1123. TEL 217-522-1240. FAX 217-522-8469. E-mail: jfrech95@aol.com; URL: http://www.ima.net.org. Ed. Jane C. Frech. R&P contact: Max Montgomery. adv.: page $1340; trim 8 1/2 x 11; adv. contact: Max Montgomery. circ. 7,000. (back issues avail.) **Document type:** trade publication.
Description: Featuring articles on manufacturing related issues.

600 338   FR   ISSN 1244-5819
INDEX S V P; publication hebdomadaire d'informations. 1960. w. 960 F. (effective 1992). Societe S V P, 70 rue des Rosiers, 93585 Saint-Ouen Cedex, France. TEL 47-87-11-11. FAX 47-87-70-70. TELEX 233 999 SVP F. Dir. Brigitte de Gastines. adv.; bk.rev. circ. 17,500.

338   II   ISSN 0970-6119
INDIAN CEMENT REVIEW. (Text in English) 1986. m. $100. Wadhera Publications, General Assurance Bldg., 232 Dr. D.N. Rd., Mumbai 400 001, India. TEL 91-22-2046918. Ed. Roshanlal Wadhera. circ. 3,500. **Indexed:** C.R.I.Abstr., C.R.I.Curr.Cont. **Document type:** trade publication.

338   UY   ISSN 0376-9941
HC231
INDICE INDUSTRIAL - ANUARIO DE LA INDUSTRIA URUGUAYA. 1957. a. Sarandi 456, Montevideo, Uruguay. TEL 2-951963. Dir. W.M. Trias. circ. 6,000.

338 621.9   SP   ISSN 0213-6295
INDUEQUIPO. 1986. 6/yr. Pza. Republica del Ecuador 6, 28016 Madrid, Spain. TEL 2509943. FAX 1-4582606. Ed. Sergio R. Sanchez. circ. 7,000. **Description:** Covers industrial equipment.

338   GT   ISSN 0019-7408
INDUSTRIA. 1957. m. newsstand price: $1. Camara de Industria de Guatemala, Ruta 6, 9-21, Zona 4, Guatemala, Guatemala. TEL 502-2-340849. FAX 502-2-341090. Dir. Luis Anibal Blanco. adv. contact: Ana Graciela Lopez de Ruiz. bibl.; charts; illus.; mkt.; stat.; tr.lit.; index, cum.index. circ. 3,000. **Document type:** newspaper.
Formerly: Revista Industria.

338   PO
INDUSTRIA. 12/yr. Confederacao Industria Portuguesa, Av. 5 de Outubro, 35 - 1o, 1000 Lisbon, Portugal. TEL 54-70-20.

338   BO
INDUSTRIA BOLIVIANA. vol.23, 1973. s-m. Camara Nacional de Industrias, Casilla 611, La Paz, Bolivia.

338   BL   ISSN 0019-7602
HC186
INDUSTRIA E DESENVOLVIMENTO. 1968. m. Federacao e Centro das Industrias do Estado de Sao Paulo, Av. Paulista 1313, andar 10, Sao Paulo, SP, Brazil. Ed. Ney Lima Figueiredo. adv.; bk.rev.; abstr.; bibl.; charts; illus.; stat. circ. 27,000.

338   SP
INDUSTRIA ESPANOLA (MADRID). 4/yr. 5,000 ptas. Ministerio de Industria, Paseo de la Castellana, 210, 28046 Madrid, Spain. TEL 1-457-08-03. FAX 1-457-29-38. Ed. Fernando Escribano.

338   SP   ISSN 0210-1815
INDUSTRIA INTERNACIONAL. 1965. m. 3895 ptas. Publicaciones Internacionales S.A., Paseo de Castellana 210, 28046 Madrid, Spain. TEL 1-457-08-06. FAX 1-457-29-38. Ed. F. Escribano. circ. 6,000 (controlled).

338   IT   ISSN 0019-7661
INDUSTRIA LOMBARDA. 1947. w. L.7500. Associazione Industriale Lombarda, Via Pantano 9, 20122 Milan, Italy. TEL 39-2-583701. Ed. Giuliano Faliva. circ. 16,000. **Document type:** newsletter.

338   PE
INDUSTRIA PERUANA. 1896. m. $100. Sociedad de Industrias, Los Laureles 365, San Isidro, Lima, Peru. Ed. Rolando Celi Burneo. adv. circ. 6,000.

338   IT
INDUSTRIA: RIVISTA DI ECONOMIA POLITICA INDUSTRIALE. 1980. 4/yr. Lit.128000 (foreign L.190000) (effective 1997). Societa Editrice Il Mulino, Strada Maggiore, 37, Bologna 40125, Italy. TEL 39-51-256011. FAX 39-51-256034. E-mail: riviste@mulino.it. Ed. Patrizio Bianchi. adv.: B&W page L.3400000. charts; index. circ. 1,600. (back issues avail.) **Indexed:** ELLIS, P.A.I.S.For.Lang.Ind. —BLDSC (4438.250000); SWETS.
Formed by the merger of (1887-1979): Industria (ISSN 0019-7416); (1975-1979): Rivista di Economia e Politica Industriale (ISSN 0390-041X)

338   IT   ISSN 0019-7769
INDUSTRIA TOSCANA. 1944. w. L.35000. S I N E C, Via Valfonda 9, 50123 Florence, Italy. adv.

338   CE   ISSN 0019-8064
INDUSTRIAL CEYLON. (Text in English) 1960-1980; resumed 19?? 32/yr. Ceylon National Chamber of Industries, Flat No. 20, 1st. Fl., Galle Face Court, Columbo, Sri Lanka. Ed. P. Sangarapillai. adv.; charts; stat.; tr.lit. circ. 800. **Indexed:** Sri Lanka Sci.Ind.

338   II   ISSN 0019-8099
INDUSTRIAL COURIER. (Text in English) 1969. q. Rs.2.50 per copy. N. K. Lahiri, Ed. & Pub., 45-9 Choudhurypara Lane, Howrah 711104, India. adv.; bk.rev.; charts; illus.; stat. circ. 3,000.

338   PK
INDUSTRIAL DEVELOPMENT. (Text in English) 1972. bi-m. Rs.20. Press Corporation of Pakistan, P.O. Box 3138, Karachi 75400, Pakistan. TEL 21-455-3703. FAX 21-7736198. Ed. Saeed Hafeez. adv.; bk.rev. circ. 5,000. (also avail. in microfiche from UMI) **Indexed:** Tr.& Indus.Ind.

338   II   ISSN 0019-8188
INDUSTRIAL ECONOMIST. (Text in English) 1968. fortn. Rs.200 (foreign $50). S-15 Industrial Estate, Guindy, Chennai 600 032, India. TEL 91-44-234-2248. FAX 91-44-234-9382. E-mail: sangitav@giasmda.vsnl.net.in. Ed. S. Viswanathan; Pub. S. Viswanathan. R&P contact: Bala Swaminathan. adv.: B&W page Rs.10000, color page Rs.15000; trim 205 x 280; adv. contact: Bala Swaminathan. bk.rev.; charts; illus.; stat. circ. 10,000.
Description: Contains analysis of corporate performance, stock markets, policy critique, global glimpses, information technology and politicao-economic policy issues.
Refereed Serial

338   UA   ISSN 0019-820X
INDUSTRIAL EGYPT. (Text in Arabic and English) 1924. q. Federation of Egyptian Industries - Ittihad al-Sinaa al-Misriyah, 26A Sharia Sherif Pasha, P.O. Box 251, Cairo, Egypt. TEL 02-3928317. FAX 02-3928075. TELEX 92624. Ed. Darwish M. Darwish. adv. circ. 900. **Indexed:** Key to Econ.Sci.

338   II   ISSN 0019-8269
INDUSTRIAL ENTERPRISE.* (Text in English) 1968. m. Rs.15. Cactus Publications, 55-1-2 Sastitola Rd., Calcutta 11, India. Ed. B.N. Nobis. adv.; bk.rev.; charts; illus.; tr.lit.

BUSINESS AND ECONOMICS — PRODUCTION OF GOODS AND SERVICES

338   UK
INDUSTRIAL EQUIPMENT NEWS PRODUCT INFORMATION SERVICE. 1964. 10/yr. Nexus Media Ltd., Nexus House, Azalea Dr., Swanley, Kent BR8 8HY, England. TEL 44-1322-660070. FAX 44-1322-667633. Ed. Dawn Frosdick-Hopley. R&P contact: Dawn Frosdick-Hopley. adv. contact: Roy Kemp. circ. 33,000. **Document type:** trade publication.

338   II
INDUSTRIAL EXPANSION. (Text in English) 1969. q. Rs.10. K.S. South Extension, Part 1, New Delhi, India. Ed. Usha Datta. adv.; charts; tr.lit.

338   II   ISSN 0377-0036
T1
INDUSTRIAL HERALD. (Text in English) vol.20, 1965. m. Rs.150. (Industrial & Scientific Research Association) Gopali and Co., 407-408 Mount Rd., Madras 600 035, India. TEL 91-44-4330979. FAX 91-44-4332413. Ed. R. Kalidasan. adv.; bk.rev.; illus. circ. 22,000.
   Formerly: Indsearch.

338   II   ISSN 0019-8412
INDUSTRIAL INDIA. (Text in English) 1950. m. Rs.60. (All-India Manufacturers' Organization) Chary Publications, 14 Sidh Prasad, Ghatkopar Mahul Rd., Tilak Nagar, Bombay 400089, India. Ed. G.S. Pohekar. adv.; bk.rev.; illus. **Indexed:** PROMT.
   Incorporating: Index Port.

338   CN   ISSN 0836-737X
INDUSTRIAL PROCESS PRODUCTS AND TECHNOLOGY. 1987. 6/yr. Swan Erickson Publishing Inc., 1011 Upper Middle Rd., E., Ste. 1235, Oakville, ON L6H 5Z9, Canada. TEL 905-475-4231. FAX 905-475-3512. Ed. Bob Erickson; Pub. Bob Erickson. adv.: B&W & color, B&W page Can.$2910; trim 11 1/4 x 16 1/2; adv. contact: Michael Swan. circ. 25,745. **Document type:** trade publication.
   Description: For the chemical process industries and other primary and secondary manufacturing industries utilizing chemicals or chemical engineering processes.

338   PR   ISSN 0019-8633
INDUSTRIAL PUERTO RICO. (Text in English) 1965. bi-m. Antilles Publishing, 721 Hernandez St., Miramar Towers, Apt. 12B, Santurce 00908, PR 00901. Ed. Mary Kay Murphy-Aivaziar. adv.; bk.rev.; charts; illus.; stat.; circ. 7,500 (controlled).

338   UK   ISSN 0263-7952
INDUSTRIAL RESEARCH IN UNITED KINGDOM. 1946. biennial, 16th ed., 1995. £190. Longman Group UK Ltd., Longman House, Burnt Mill, Harlow, Essex CM20 2JE, England. TEL 44-1279-426721. FAX 44-1279-431059. (Subscr. to: Pearson Professional, P.O. Box 77, Fourth Ave., Harlow, Essex CM19 5BQ, England. TEL 44-1279-623924. FAX 44-1279-639609; Dist. in U.S. and Canada by: Gale Research Co. Ltd., Book Tower, Detroit, MI 48226) index. **Document type:** monographic series.
—BLDSC (4461.810000).

338   GR
INDUSTRIAL REVIEW. (Supplement to: Viomichaniki Epitheorissis (ISSN 0042-6415)) (Text in English) 1991 (Dec.). q. Dr.7500($40); newsstand price: Dr.1900. 7 Valaoritou St., 106 71 Athens, Greece. TEL 30-1-3625-666. FAX 30-1-3623-879. Ed. Dimitrios Karamanos; Pub. Alexandra C. Vovolini-Laskaridis. adv. contact: Lydie Chapel. bk.rev.; charts; illus.; tr.mk. (back issues avail.) **Document type:** trade publication.
   Description: Covers a particular Greek industrial sector.

338   II
INDUSTRIAL SITUATION IN INDIA. (Text in English) 1972. q. $5. Manjari Chaudhuri, 188-78. Prince Anwar Shah Rd., Calcutta 45, India.

338   CM
INDUSTRIE CAMEROUNAISE. a. Syndicat des Industries du Cameroun, B.P. 673, Douala, Cameroon.

338   FR
INDUSTRIE EUROPEENNE.* 1957. m. 40 F. 14 allee du Quebec, 91430 Igny, France. Ed. Andre de Gendre. circ. 6,000.

338   GW   ISSN 0940-8436
INDUSTRIE MEISTER. 1971. m. DM.104. Vogel Verlag und Druck GmbH & Co. KG, Max-Planck-Str. 7-9, 97082 Wuerzburg, Germany. TEL 49-931-4182145. FAX 49-931-4182905. (Subscr. to: Vogel Verlag, 97064 Wuerzburg, Germany; Dist. in US bu: Vogel Europublishing, Inc., 632 Sunflower Ct., San Ramos, CA 94583. TEL 510-648-1170. FAX 510-648-1171) Ed. Dietmar Kuhn. adv.: B&W page DM.5850, color page DM.8400; trim 270 x 190; adv. contact: Helmut Sieber. circ. 15,922 (controlled). **Document type:** trade publication.
—SWETS. **CCC.**
   Formerly: Meister - Zeitung (ISSN 0341-759X)

338   CN
INDUSTRIE NOUVELLE. 1985. 4/yr. $12. 1001 Rue de Maisonneuve Ouest, Montreal, PQ H3A 3E1, Canada. TEL 514-845-5141. Ed. Antoine Di-Lillo. adv. circ. 17,809.

338   GW   ISSN 0174-6146
INDUSTRIE SERVICE. 1960. m. DM.114 (foreign DM.130) (effective 1997). Verlag fuer Technik und Wirtschaft GmbH & Co., Lise-Meitner-Str. 2, 55129 Mainz, Germany. TEL 49-6131-992-0. FAX 49-6131-992100. (Subscr. to: Postfach 4029, 55030 Mainz, Germany) Ed. Michaela Heider-Peschel. adv.: B&W page DM.10450, color page DM.13150; trim 265 x 185; adv. contact: Michael Spahn. illus. circ. 55,000. **Document type:** trade publication.

338   SZ   ISSN 0253-8539
INDUSTRIEARCHAEOLOGIE; zeitschrift fuer industrielle Kulturgueter, Kunst und Reisen. (Text mainly in German, occasionally in English and French) 1977. q. 69 SFr. c/o Oskar Baldinger, Ed. & Pub., Aarestr. 83, CH-5222 Umiken, Switzerland. TEL 41-56-4410043. FAX 41-56-4414854. adv.; bk.rev.; illus. circ. 800. **Document type:** academic/scholarly publication.

338   FR   ISSN 1167-7287
INDUSTRIES. m. free. (Ministere de l'Industrie de la Poste et des Telecommunications) Delegation a la Communication, 20 Av. de Segur, 75353 Paris 07 SP, France. TEL 33-1-43-19-66-83. FAX 33-1-43-19-31-24. Ed. Janine Toffin. charts. circ. 44,500.
   Formerly: Lettre 101 (ISSN 0294-0620); Which was formed by the merger of: Recherche et Technologie (ISSN 0752-5575) & Industrie et Energie Francaises (ISSN 0249-9819)
   Description: Each issue concentrates on a particular industry indigenous to certain regions of France.

338 332.6   US
INDUSTRIES IN TRANSITION. 1974. m. $375. Business Communications Co., Inc. (Norwalk), 25 Van Zant St., Norwalk, CT 06855. TEL 203-853-4266. FAX 203-853-0348. TELEX 6502934929 WUI. Ed. Betsy Du Walt. circ. 200.
● Also available online. Vendor(s): Data-Star, Information Access Co., Knight-Ridder Information, Inc., NewsNet (GB46).
—CCC.
   Formerly (until 1977): Growth Industry News (ISSN 0160-1083).

338   JA   ISSN 0446-1266
INDUSTRIES OF JAPAN. (Text in English) 1958. a. 800 Yen. (Mainichi Daily News) Mainichi Newspapers, 1-1-1, Hitotsubashi, Chiyoda-ku, Tokyo 100-51, Japan. TEL 03-3212-0321. FAX 03-3211-0895. TELEX 22324. stat.

338   SW   ISSN 0283-4197
INDUSTRIFOERBUNDET HANDELSPOLITIK; information fraan Industriforbundets handelspolitiska avdeling. 1981. 6-7/yr. Industriforbundet, P.O. Box 5501, S-114 85 Stockholm, Sweden.

338   YU   ISSN 0019-9419
INDUSTRIJSKA ISTRAZIVANJA;* casopis za pitanja primene metoda operacionih i drugih istrazivanja. (Text in Serbo-Croatian; summaries in English and Russian) 1963. 6/yr. 200 din. Ogranomatik, Institut a Organizacija Rada i Automatizaciju Pioslovanja, Milana Rakica 35, Box 999, Belgrade, Yugoslavia. Ed. Dragutin Boskovic.

INDUSTRY AND HIGHER EDUCATION. see
EDUCATION — Higher Education

338 916.76   KE   ISSN 0073-781X
HC517.E2
INDUSTRY IN EAST AFRICA.* 1962. a. $10. P.O. Box 30339, Nairobi, Kenya. Ed. C.N. Bhatt.

338   UK   ISSN 0264-4932
INDUSTRY NORTHWEST. 1973. m. £25. Industry Northwest Publications Ltd., Ste. 1E, 3 The Parsonage, Manchester M3 2HB, England. TEL 061-832-2143. FAX 061-832-5589. Ed. Deborah Humphreys. adv. circ. 14,200.

338   PO   ISSN 0871-5157
INFORMACAO INDUSTRIAL. 1989. 10/yr. C T - Informacao Cientifica e Tecnica Lda., R. do 4 de Infantaria 36-4o, 1300 Lisbon, Portugal. TEL 1-691103. FAX 1-691131. Ed. Joao Aguas.

338   IT
INFORMAZIONE INDUSTRIALE (SIENA); industria Toscana. 1944. w. L.120000 membership. Associazione degli Industriali della Provincia di Siena, Via dei Rossi 2, 53100 Siena, Italy. TEL 39-577-283005. FAX 39-577-283025. Ed. Guglielmo Centini. charts; mkt.; stat.; tr.mk.; index, cum.index. circ. 1,000. **Document type:** newsletter.
   Formerly: Informatore Industriale; Supersedes (in 1980): Notizie per gli Industriali della Provincia di Siena (ISSN 0029-4446)

338   IT   ISSN 0020-0786
INFORMAZIONE INDUSTRIALE (TURIN). 1920. s-m. Unione Industriale di Torino, Via Fanti 17, Turin, Italy. Dir. Giancarlo Forconi. bk.rev.; illus. circ. 5,000.

602.94489   DK   ISSN 0446-2491
INGENIOERENS INDKOEBSBOG. 1960. a. DKK 408. Teknisk Forlag A-S, Skelbaekgade 4, DK-1780 Copenhagen V, Denmark. TEL 45-31-21-68-01. FAX 45-31-21-04-01. adv. circ. 6,000.

338   US   ISSN 1058-8523
INNOVATIVE PRODUCTS. Variant title: Innovative Products Letter. 1988. q. $19 (effective 1997). Innovation Groups, Inc., Box 16645, Tampa, FL 33687. TEL 813-622-8484. FAX 813-664-0051. Ed. Nicole Wooden. R&P contact: Nicole Wooden. adv. contact: Nicole Wooden. bk.rev. circ. 13,500.
   Description: Discusses new and existing products of interest to local governments.

338   AT   ISSN 0310-5660
INSIDE RETAILING. 1971. w. Aus.$417. Ian Huntley Pty. Ltd., 233 Military Rd., Cremorne, N.S.W. 2090, Australia. TEL 61-2-9953-5788. FAX 61-2-9953-2280. (Subscr. to: P.O. Box 99, Cremorne, N.S.W. 2090, Australia) Ed. Murray White. charts; stat.; index. (back issues avail.) **Document type:** newsletter.
   Description: Covers retailing in general.

INSTITUTE OF PUBLIC ENTERPRISE. JOURNAL. see
BUSINESS AND ECONOMICS — Management

338 629.8   US   ISSN 1080-2576
▼**INTELLIGENT MANUFACTURING.** 1995. m. $115 (effective 1997). Lionheart Publishing, Inc., P.O. Box 159, Kent, OH 44240-0003. TEL 330-677-4210. FAX 330-678-9011. E-mail: blanchard@lionhrtpub.com; URL: http://lionhrtpub.com/IM/IM-welcome.html. Ed. David Blanchard; Pub. John Llewellyn. R&P contact: David Blanchard. **Document type:** newsletter.
● Also available online.
—CCC.
   Description: Covers advanced manufacturing technologies, focusing on applications, case studies, and real world solutions.

352   FR   ISSN 0240-9925
INTER REGIONS; les cahiers de l'expansion regionale. 1979. 11/yr. 380 F. (foreign 335 F.) (effective 1998). Conseil National des Economies Regionales et de la Productivite (C.N.E.R.P.), 219 bd. Saint-Germain, 75007 Paris, France. TEL 33-1-42223529. FAX 33-1-45499446. Anne-France Braquehais. adv. contact: Elisabeth Cornu. **Indexed:** P.A.I.S.For.Lang.Ind. **Document type:** bulletin.
   Formed by the merger of: Inter Region; (1961-1979): Cahiers de l'Expansion Regionale (ISSN 0014-4711)

BUSINESS AND ECONOMICS — PRODUCTION OF GOODS AND SERVICES

338 006.6   US   ISSN 1053-8291
TR835
INTERNATIONAL IMAGING SOURCE BOOK (LARCHMONT). 1972. biennial. $99.50. Microfilm Publishing, Inc., Box 950, Larchmont, NY 10538-0950. TEL 914-834-3044. FAX 914-834-3993. Ed. Mitchell M. Badler. adv.; bk.rev.; illus.; stat. circ. 3,500. **Document type:** directory.
—BLDSC (4541.038860); CISTI.
Former titles: International Micrographics Source Book (ISSN 0272-0310); International Microfilm Source Book (ISSN 0362-4498); Microfilm Source Book (ISSN 0090-2861)
Description: Gives sources of supply for products and services in twenty areas related to business imaging.

INTERNATIONAL JOURNAL FOR MANUFACTURING SCIENCE AND PRODUCTION. see *TECHNOLOGY: COMPREHENSIVE WORKS*

INTERNATIONAL JOURNAL OF ENVIRONMENTALLY CONSCIOUS MANUFACTURING. see *ENVIRONMENTAL STUDIES*

INTERNATIONAL JOURNAL OF INDUSTRIAL ERGONOMICS. see *ENGINEERING*

INTERNATIONAL JOURNAL OF PRODUCTION ECONOMICS; an international journal for industry. see *ENGINEERING — Industrial Engineering*

338 620   UK   ISSN 0020-7543
TS155.A1   CODEN: IJPRB8
INTERNATIONAL JOURNAL OF PRODUCTION RESEARCH. Online edition (UK ISSN 1366-588X) (Text and summaries in English, French, German) 1961. m. £921($1520) to institutions (£1105($1824) with online ed.) (effective 1998). Taylor & Francis Ltd., 1 Gunpowder Sq., London EC4A 3DE, England. TEL 44-171-583-0490. FAX 44-171-583-0585. TELEX 858540. E-mail: info@tandf.co.uk; URL: http://www.tandf.co.uk/e-pub.cwonline.htm#prs. (Subscr. in N. America to: Taylor & Francis Inc., 1900 Frost Rd., Ste. 101, Bristol, PA 19007-1598. TEL 800-821-8312. FAX 215-785-5515) (Co-sponsors: Institution of Production Engineers; American Institute of Industrial Engineers; Society of Manufacturing Engineers) Eds. R.J. Sury, J.E. Middle. adv.; bk.rev.; bibl.; charts; illus.; index. (also avail. in microform from MIM,KTO) **Indexed:** ASCA, Br.Tech.Ind., CAD CAM Abstr., Cadscan, Cont.Pg.Manage., Curr.Cont., Cyb.Abstr., Eng.Ind., Ergon.Abstr., INSPEC, Int.Abstr.Oper.Res., ISMEC, J.Cont.Quant.Meth., Lead Abstr., Mid.East: Abstr.& Ind., Oper.Res.Manage.Sci., PROMT, Psychol.Abstr., SSCI, Zent.Math., Zincscan. **Document type:** academic/scholarly publication.
●Also available online.
—BLDSC (4542.486000); AskIEEE; CISTI; Ei; Genuine Article; KR SourceOne; Linda Hall; SWETS; UnCover. **CCC.**
Description: Publishes papers on the technology and fundamental behavior of production resources, with the complex and cross-disciplinary problems of analysis and control that arise in combining these resources within the design of production systems.

INTERNATIONAL JOURNAL OF SERVICE INDUSTRY MANAGEMENT. see *BUSINESS AND ECONOMICS — Management*

338   NE   ISSN 0924-6363
INTERNATIONAL STUDIES IN THE SERVICE ECONOMY. (Text in English) 1990. irreg., vol.4, 1993. Kluwer Academic Publishers, Postbus 17, 3300 AA Dordrecht, Netherlands. TEL 31-78-6392392. FAX 31-78-6392254. TELEX 29245 KAPG NL. E-mail: services@wkap.nl; URL: http://www.wkap.nl. (Dist. by: Kluwer Academic Publishers Group, P.O. Box 322, 3300 AH Dordrecht, Netherlands. TEL 31-78-6392392. FAX 31-78-6546474; N. America dist. addr.: Box 358, Accord Sta., Hingham, MA 02018-0358. TEL 617-871-6600. FAX 617-871-6528) (back issues avail.) **Document type:** monographic series.
—BLDSC (4549.818000).
Refereed Serial

338   HU   ISSN 0021-0749
IPARGAZDASAG.* (Text in Hungarian; contents page in German and Russian) 1947. m. $36. Szerzesi es Vezetesi Tudomanyos Tarsasag, Fo u. 68, 1027 Budapest, Hungary. TEL 2021456. (Subscr. to: Kultura, Box 149, H-1389 Budapest, Hungary) Ed. Dr. Istvan Harsanyi. charts; illus.; stat.
Formerly (until 1959): Tobbtermeles (ISSN 0369-0075)

338   IR   ISSN 0578-6959
IRAN. MINISTRY OF ECONOMY. REPORT ON COMMENCEMENT AND OPERATION PERMITS FOR INDUSTRIAL ESTABLISHMENTS.* (Text in English) q. free. Ministry of Finance and Economic Affairs, Teheran, Iran. stat.

JABATAN PERANGKAAN MALAYSIA. PENYIASATAN TAHUNAN INDUSTRI PEMBUATAN/MALAYSIA. DEPARTMENT OF STATISTICS. ANNUAL SURVEY OF MANUFACTURING INDUSTRIES. see *BUSINESS AND ECONOMICS — Abstracting, Bibliographies, Statistics*

338   JA   ISSN 0075-3289
JAPAN CENSUS OF MANUFACTURES: REPORT BY COMMODITIES.* 1909. a. 4600 Yen. Ministry of International Trade and Industry, Research and Statistics Division - Tsusho Sangyo Chosakai, 1-3-1 Kasumigaseki, Chiyoda-ku, Tokyo 100, Japan. TEL 03-501-1511. circ. 800.

600 330   JA   ISSN 0910-8300
HC461
JAPAN ECONOMIC ALMANAC; an annual in-depth report on the state of the Japanese economy. (Text in English) 1962. a. 9800 Yen($59.50) Nihon Keizai Shimbun, Inc., 1-9-5 Otemachi, Chiyoda-ku, Tokyo 100-66, Japan. TEL 81-3-3270-0251. FAX 81-3-5255-2661. TELEX J22308 NIKKEI. Ed. Norimichi Okai. adv. contact: Kazuo Onodera. circ. 5,000. **Document type:** trade publication.
●Also available online.
—CISTI.
Formerly (until 1985): Industrial Review of Japan (ISSN 0537-5452)

650   JA   ISSN 0916-877X
HC461   CODEN: BUJAEW
JAPAN 21ST. (Text in English) 1955. m. 14,400 Yen (foreign $168). Japan Industrial Journal, Publication Bureau - Nihon Kogyo Shimbun, Sankei Bldg., 1-7-2 Ohte-machi, Chiyoda-ku, Tokyo 100, Japan. TEL 81-3-3231-7111. FAX 81-3-3667-9646. (Dist. by: International Marketing Corp., I.P.O. Box 5056, Tokyo 100-30, Japan. TEL 81-3-3661-7458) Ed. Shinji Umemura. adv.; bk.rev.; illus. circ. 65,000. (also avail. in microform from UMI) **Indexed:** ABI Inform., B.P.I., BPIA, JTA, Mgmt.& Market.Abstr., P.A.I.S., PROMT, SSCI, Tr.& Indus.Ind.
—KR SourceOne; UMI; UnCover.
Former titles (until Dec. 1991): Business Japan (ISSN 0300-4341); Asia Scene (ISSN 0004-4504)

JAPANESE FINANCE AND INDUSTRY: QUARTERLY SURVEY. see *BUSINESS AND ECONOMICS — Banking And Finance*

338   TZ   ISSN 0021-5872
HG3729.T352
JENGA; N D C's industrial magazine. 1968. q? Sh.10 per no. National Development Corporation, P.O. Box 2669, Dar es Salaam, Tanzania. TEL 255-51-26271. TELEX 41068. charts; illus. circ. 6,000. **Document type:** trade publication.

338   CC   ISSN 1002-5626
JIAYONG DIANQI/HOUSEHOLD APPLIANCE. 1980. m. Y8.64. Ministry of Light Industry, Beijing Household Electric Appliances Research Institute, 6 Yuetan Beixiaojie, Beijing 100037, People's Republic of China. TEL 86-11-8311220. FAX 86-11-8312464. Ed. Zhang You-liang. adv.; index. circ. 400,000. pp./issue: 40. **Document type:** consumer publication.
Description: Covers popular science, especially the practical knowledge and information to serve household appliance customers, amateurs, and maintenance personnels.

338   US   ISSN 0746-8881
JOB SHOP TECHNOLOGY. 1984. q. free to qualified personnel. Edwards Publishing, 16 Waterbury Rd., Box 7193, Prospect, CT 06712-1237. TEL 203-758-4474; 800-317-0474. FAX 203-758-4475. URL: http://www.jobshoptechnology.com. Ed. John P. Wright; Pub. Dave Edwards. R&P contact: John Wright. adv. contact: Rob Eichner. circ. 100,000 (controlled). **Document type:** trade publication.
Description: Dedicated to help product manufacturers understand parts and services provided by job shops

JOURNAL OF CLEANER PRODUCTION. see *ENGINEERING — Industrial Engineering*

JOURNAL OF COMMERCE, INDUSTRY & TRANSPORTATION. see *BUSINESS AND ECONOMICS — Domestic Commerce*

JOURNAL OF ENGINEERING AND TECHNOLOGY MANAGEMENT. see *BUSINESS AND ECONOMICS — Management*

338 380   II
TN860
JOURNAL OF INDUSTRY & COMMERCE; oil and coal news. (Text in English) 1964. m. $300. K. Kumar, Ed. & Pub., D-34 South Extension Part 1, New Delhi 49, India. adv.; bk.rev.; illus.; stat. circ. 1,000.
Formerly: Fortnightly Journal of Industry and Commerce (ISSN 0015-8127)

338 380   II   ISSN 0022-1880
HC431
JOURNAL OF INDUSTRY AND TRADE.* (Text in English) 1951. m. Rs.22($10.30) Ministry of Commerce and Supply, Vdyog Bhavan, New Delhi 110 011, India. TEL 11-3016664. Ed. A.C. Banerjee. adv.; bk.rev.; charts; mkt.; stat.; index; cum.index. circ. 2,000.

JOURNAL OF MATERIALS PROCESSING AND MANUFACTURING SCIENCE. see *TECHNOLOGY: COMPREHENSIVE WORKS*

338 658   US   ISSN 0737-6782
HF5415.153   CODEN: JPIMDD
JOURNAL OF PRODUCT INNOVATION MANAGEMENT. 1984. bi-m. fl.611($351) (effective 1998). (Product Development & Management Association) Elsevier Science Inc., Box 945, New York, NY 10159-0945. TEL 212-633-3730. FAX 212-633-3680. TELEX 420643 AEP UI. E-mail: usinfo-f@elsevier.com; URL: http://www.elsevier.nl:80/inca/publications/store/. (Subscr. outside the Americas to: Elsevier Science, Regional Sales Office, P.O. Box 211, 1000 AE Amsterdam, Netherlands. TEL 31-20-4853757. FAX 31-20-4853432; Subscr. in Australasia and the Far East to: Elsevier Science (Singapore) Pte Ltd, No.1 Temasek Ave., No.17-01 Millenia Tower, Singapore 039192, Singapore. TEL 65-434-3727. FAX 65-337-2230; Subscr. in Japan to: Elsevier Science Japan, 9-15 Higashi-Azabu 1-chome, Minato-ku, Tokyo 106, Japan. TEL 81-3-5561-5033. FAX 81-3-5561-5047) Ed. Thomas P. Hustad. (reprint service avail. from SWZ) **Indexed:** ABI Inform., ASCA, BPIA, Commun.Abstr., Cont.Pg.Manage., Curr.Cont., Eng.Ind., INSPEC, Manage.Cont., Mgmt.& Market.Abstr., Oper.Res.Manage.Sci., Qual.Contr.Appl.Stat., SSCI. **Document type:** academic/scholarly publication.
—BLDSC (5042.650000); AskIEEE; CISTI; Ei; Genuine Article; KR SourceOne; Linda Hall; SWETS; UMI; UnCover. **CCC.**
Description: Dedicated to the advancement of management practice in all of the functions involved in the total process of product innovation.
Refereed Serial

JOURNAL OF PRODUCTIVITY ANALYSIS. see *BUSINESS AND ECONOMICS — Management*

BUSINESS AND ECONOMICS — PRODUCTION OF GOODS AND SERVICES

338 UK ISSN 0967-3237
JOURNAL OF TARGETING, MEASUREMENT AND ANALYSIS. 1992. q. £145($210) (effective 1996). Henry Stewart Publications, Russell House, 28-30 Little Russell St., London WC1A 2HN, England. TEL 44-171-404-3040. FAX 44-171-486-2081. Ed. May Corfield. bk.rev. **Document type:** academic/scholarly publication.
—BLDSC (5068.185000). **CCC.**
 Description: Publishes rigorous papers on practical matters that allow marketers to measure and target their prospective and existing customers more effectively and efficiently.
Refereed Serial

338 340 GW ISSN 0931-6000
DAS JURISTISCHE BUERO. m. DM.276. Luchterhand Verlag, Heddesdorferstr. 31, 56564 Neuwied, Germany. TEL 49-2631-801-0. FAX 49-2631-801210. adv. contact: Margret Sock-Freiberg. **Document type:** bulletin.

650 AU ISSN 0022-9253
KASTNER & OEHLER FIRMEN ZEITUNG. 1951. q. free. Kastner und Oehler, Sackstr. 7-13, 8012 Graz, Austria. Ed. Martin Kastner. bk.rev.; charts; illus. circ. 3,500.

KELLY'S LINK. see *BUSINESS AND ECONOMICS — Trade And Industrial Directories*

THE KENTUCKY MANUFACTURER. see *BUSINESS AND ECONOMICS*

KENYA. CENTRAL BUREAU OF STATISTICS. DEVELOPMENT ESTIMATES. see *BUSINESS AND ECONOMICS — Abstracting, Bibliographies, Statistics*

KENYA. CENTRAL BUREAU OF STATISTICS. ESTIMATES OF RECURRENT EXPENDITURES. see *BUSINESS AND ECONOMICS — Abstracting, Bibliographies, Statistics*

KENYA. CENTRAL BUREAU OF STATISTICS. ESTIMATES OF REVENUE EXPENDITURES. see *BUSINESS AND ECONOMICS — Abstracting, Bibliographies, Statistics*

KENYA. CENTRAL BUREAU OF STATISTICS. SURVEYS OF INDUSTRIAL PRODUCTION. see *BUSINESS AND ECONOMICS — Abstracting, Bibliographies, Statistics*

338 KE
KENYA ASSOCIATION OF MANUFACTURERS. MEMBERS LIST AND INTERNATIONAL STANDARD INDUSTRIAL CLASSIFICATION. 1959. biennial, latest 1996. $50. Kenya Association of Manufacturers, P.O. Box 30225, Nairobi, Kenya. TELEX 25715. adv. circ. 500. **Document type:** directory.
 Formerly: Kenya Association of Manufacturers. Industrial Index and Members List.
 Description: Contains contact information and export markets for members and information about the association as well as an overview of the Kenyan manufacturing sector, agencies that assist manufacturing and export enterprises in Kenya, trends of Kenyan exports form 1963, the top ten sources of Kenyan imports and the top ten export markets for Kenyan goods.

338 II ISSN 0047-3359
KERALA INDUSTRY; journal of industry & trade. (Text in English) 1956. m. Rs.50. Department of Industries and Commerce, Box 108, Trivandrum 695001, India. TEL 91-471-330995. FAX 91-471-330995. E-mail: nicker1!jaitha@ren.nic.in. Ed. Anuj Krishnan Nair. adv.; bk.rev.; abstr.; bibl.; charts; illus.; stat.; tr.lit. circ. 1,500. (also avail. in microform from UMI; reprint service avail. from UMI) **Document type:** trade publication.
—UMI.

338 UK
THE KEY NOTE GUIDE TO TELEWORKING. irreg. £205. Key Note Ltd., Field House, 72 Oldfield Rd., Hampton, Middlesex TW12 2HQ, England. TEL 44-181-783-0755. FAX 44-181-783-0049. **Document type:** trade publication.

388 UK
KEY NOTE MARKET REPORT: CUTLERY. Variant title: Cutlery. irreg., no.8, 1991. £185. Key Note Ltd., Field House, 72 Oldfield Rd., Hampton, Middlesex TW12 2HQ, England. TEL 44-181-783-0755. FAX 44-181-783-1940. **Document type:** trade publication.

338 UK
KEY NOTE MARKET REPORT: OFF-LICENSE TRADE.
Variant title: Off-License Trade. irreg., no.10, 1992. £185. Key Note Ltd., Field House, 72 Oldfield Rd., Hampton, Middlesex TW12 2HQ, England. TEL 44-181-783-0755. FAX 44-181-783-1940. **Document type:** trade publication.
 ●Also available online.
 Also available on CD-ROM.
 Formerly: Key Note Report: Off-License Trade.

338 UK
KEY NOTE MARKET REPORT: PROCESS PLANT. Variant title: Process Plant. irreg., no.6, 1994. £205. Key Note Ltd., Field House, 72 Oldfield Rd., Hampton, Middlesex TW12 2HQ, England. TEL 44-181-783-0755. FAX 44-181-783-0049. **Document type:** trade publication.
 ●Also available online.
 Also available on CD-ROM.
 Formerly: Key Note Report: Process Plant (ISSN 1352-7118)

338 UK
KEY NOTE MARKET REPORT: SLIMMING MARKET. irreg., no.6, 1993. £205. Key Note Ltd., Field House, 72 Oldfield Rd., Hampton, Middlesex TW12 2HQ, England. TEL 44-181-783-0755. FAX 44-181-783-0049. **Document type:** monographic series.
 ●Also available online.
 Also available on CD-ROM.
 Former titles: Key Note Report: Slimming Market; (until 1989): Key Note Report: Slimming Products (ISSN 0265-7953)

338 UK
KEY NOTE MARKET REPORT: THE TAKE HOME TRADE. Variant title: The Take Home Trade. irreg. £205. Key Note Ltd., Field House, 72 Oldfield Rd., Hampton, Middlesex TW12 2HQ, England. TEL 44-181-783-0755. FAX 44-181-783-0049. **Document type:** trade publication.

338 UK
KEY NOTE MARKET REVIEW: U K DISTRIBUTION. Variant title: U K Distribution. irreg., no.4, 1995. £410. Key Note Ltd., Field House, 72 Oldfield Rd., Hampton, Middlesex TW12 2HQ, England. TEL 44-181-783-0755. FAX 44-181-783-0049. **Document type:** trade publication.
 ●Also available online.
 Also available on CD-ROM.

KHADI GRAMODYOG; journal of rural economy. see *AGRICULTURE — Agricultural Economics*

338 NO
KOEFFBLADET - I N. m. (10/yr.). NOK 120. (Kjoepmennenes Oekonomiske Fellesforetagende A-L) K Oe F F-Gruppen A-S, Jappe Ippesvei 3, 6500 Kristiansund N, Norway. FAX 073-70950. Ed. Per Gunnar Aakvik. adv. circ. 11,117.

338 AU
KONJUNKTUR. 1950. w. S.350 per month. Austria Presse Agentur (APA), Gunoldstr. 14, A-1199 Vienna, Austria. Ed. H. Jaros. (processed)
 Formerly: Konjunkturdienst (ISSN 0023-3455)

338 GW ISSN 0023-3439
KONJUNKTUR VON MORGEN. 1959. fortn. DM.174 (effective 1996). (H W W A - Institut fuer Wirtschaftsforschung, Hamburg) Nomos Verlagsgesellschaft mbH und Co. KG, Waldseestr. 3-5, 76530 Baden-Baden, Germany. TEL 49-7221-2104-0. FAX 49-7221-210427. Ed. G. Grosser. charts; stat. (reprint service avail. from ISI) **Document type:** bulletin.
—CCC.

338.12 SW ISSN 0345-6390
KONJUNKTURBAROMETERN; business tendency survey. 1954. q. SEK 520 (effective 1994). Konjunkturinstitutet, P.O. Box 3116, S-103 62 Stockholm, Sweden. TEL 46-8-453-59-00. FAX 46-8-453-59-80. circ. 400.
 Description: Consists of a survey of 1900 business enterprizes in Sweden.

338 SW ISSN 0282-9967
KONJUNKTUREN; rapport fraan Industrifoerbundets ekonomiskpolitiska avdeling. 1980. q. SEK 400 (effective 1991). Industrifoerbundet, P.O. Box 5501, S-114 85 Stockholm, Sweden.

658.83 YU ISSN 0023-3471
KONJUNKTURNI BAROMETAR.* (Text in Serbo-Croatian) 1962. m. 600 din. Zavod za Trzisna Istrazivanja, Mose Pijade 8-I, 11001 Belgrade, Yugoslavia. Ed. Julije Drasinover. stat.; circ. controlled.

338 GW ISSN 0023-3498
HC10
KONJUNKTURPOLITIK/APPLIED ECONOMICS QUARTERLY; Zeitschrift fuer angewandte Wirtschaftsforschung. (Supplements avail.) (Text in English and German; summaries in English) 1954. q. DM.156. Duncker und Humblot GmbH, Postfach 410329, 12113 Berlin, Germany. TEL 49-30-79000001. FAX 49-30-79000631. E-mail: duh-werbung@t-online.de. adv.; bk.rev.; charts; stat.; index. **Indexed:** IBR, J.of Econ.Lit., Key to Econ.Sci., P.A.I.S.For.Lang.Ind., P.A.I.S. **Document type:** academic/scholarly publication.
—BLDSC (5110.900000); SWETS. **CCC.**

338.9 KO
KOREA (REPUBLIC). NATIONAL STATISTICAL OFFICE. ANNUAL REPORT ON CURRENT INDUSTRIAL PRODUCTION SURVEY. (Text in English, Korean) 1970. a. 22000 Won($46) National Statistical Office, Hanta Bldg., 647-15, Yoksam-dong, Kangnam-gu, Seoul 135-080, S. Korea. TEL 82-2-222-1971. (Subscr. to: Korean Statistical Association, Statistics Training Center Bldg., 90 Kyoungun-dong, Chongro-gu, Seoul 110-310, Korea. TEL 82-2-517-0382. FAX 82-2-725-4347) circ. 400. **Document type:** government publication.
 Formerly: Korea (Republic). Economic Planning Board. Annual Report on Current Industrial Production Survey.

KOTHARI'S INDUSTRIAL DIRECTORY OF INDIA. see *BUSINESS AND ECONOMICS — Trade And Industrial Directories*

338 JA
KYUSHU KOGYO GIJUTSU SHIKENJO NENPO/GOVERNMENT INDUSTRIAL RESEARCH INSTITUTE, KYUSHU. ANNUAL REPORT. (Text in Japanese) a. Kyushu Kogyo Gijutsu Shikenjo - Government Industrial Research Institute, Kyushu, 807-1 Shuku-machi, Tosu-Kyushu 841, Japan. abstr.

338 GW ISSN 0023-6268
L G A RUNDSCHAU. 1874. q. free. Landesgewerbeanstalt Bayern, Postfach 3022, 90014 Nuernberg, Germany. TEL 49-911-6555-0. FAX 49-911-6554235. TELEX 622229. Ed. D. Balzer. adv.: B&W page DM.1260; trim 210 x 297; adv. contact: Thomas Wolkensteorfer. bk.rev.; index. circ. 3,000. **Document type:** consumer publication.

338 JA ISSN 0287-2404
L T C B RESEARCH; review of Japanese industry. (Text in English) 1970. q. free. Long Term Credit Bank of Japan Ltd., Economics Division, 2-4 Otemachi, 1-chome, Chiyoda-ku, Tokyo, Japan. Ed. Sawako Hagtwara. charts; stat. **Indexed:** Key to Econ.Sci., P.A.I.S.
 Formerly: Chogin Research (ISSN 0009-4951)

368.5 US ISSN 0733-513X
KF1296.A15
LEADER'S PRODUCT LIABILITY LAW AND STRATEGY. 1982. m. $195. New York Law Publishing Co., 111 Eighth Ave., New York, NY 10011. TEL 212-463-5721. FAX 212-463-5623. URL: http://www.ljx.com. Ed. Leslie Nicholson. index. (looseleaf format; back issues avail.) **Document type:** newsletter.
 Formerly (until 1988): Leader's Product Liability Newsletter.
 Description: Publishes tips and strategies for product liability practitioners, with reports on trends, court decisions, administrative rulings, legislative proposals, and news of settlements.

LEBENSMITTEL MARKT. see *FOOD AND FOOD INDUSTRIES*

330 FR ISSN 0399-8606
LETTRE DE L'EXPANSION. 1970. w. 4950 F. Groupe Expansion, 25 rue LeBlanc, 75015 Paris, France. TEL 40-60-40-60. Ed. Philippe Bauchard. charts.

BUSINESS AND ECONOMICS — PRODUCTION OF GOODS AND SERVICES

338 380.5 LB
LIBERIA. MINISTRY OF COMMERCE, INDUSTRY AND TRANSPORTATION. ANNUAL REPORT.* a. Ministry of Commerce, Industry and Transportation, P.O. Box 9041, Monrovia, Liberia.

338 LB
LIBERIA. MINISTRY OF PLANNING AND ECONOMIC AFFAIRS. ANNUAL REPORT TO THE PEOPLE'S REDEMPTION COUNCIL.* 1965. a. $5. Ministry of Planning and Economic Affairs, P.O. Box 9016, Monrovia, Liberia.
   Formerly: Liberia. Ministry of Planning and Economic Affairs. Annual Report to the Session of the Legislature of the Republic of Liberia (ISSN 0459-2182); Which supersedes: Liberia. Department of Planning and Economic Affairs. Annual Report.

338 II ISSN 0076-0269
LOCATIONS OF INDUSTRIES IN GUJARAT STATE. (Text in English) 1956. irreg. Rs.7.30. Bureau of Economics and Statistics, Sector No. 18, Gandhinagar, India.

LOOKOUT - FOODS. see FOOD AND FOOD INDUSTRIES

LUBRICANTS WORLD. see PETROLEUM AND GAS

LYS; miljoe-design-teknik. see ENGINEERING — Electrical Engineering

338 II ISSN 0541-5357
HC431
M B I'S INDIAN INDUSTRIES ANNUAL. (Text in English) 1963. a. Rs.20. Chary Publications, 14 Sidh Prasad, Ghatkopar Mahul Rd., Tilak Nagar, Bombay 400089, India.

338 US
M E M A MARKET ANALYSIS; a bimonthly report on the vehicle parts industry. 1976. bi-m. $250 (effective 1997). Motor & Equipment Manufacturers Association, Box 13966, Research Triangle Park, NC 27709. TEL 919-549-4800. FAX 919-549-4824. URL: http://www.Afmkt.com/ME.MA. Ed. F. Hampshire. bk.rev. circ. 750. **Document type:** trade publication.

MAANEDSMAGASINET ERHVERV - NORDJYLLAND. see BUSINESS AND ECONOMICS — Management

338 NE ISSN 0024-8843
MAATSCHAPPIJBELANGEN. 1832. m. fl.105. Nederlandsche Maatschappij voor Nijverheid en Handel - Netherlands Society for Industry and Trade, P.O. Box 205, 2000 AE Haarlem, Netherlands. TEL 31-23-5360624. FAX 31-23-5360122. E-mail: info@nmnh.nl; URL: http://www.nmnh.nl. (Dist. by: Wyt Uitgeefgroep, P.O. Box 6438, 3002 AK Rotterdam, Netherlands) Ed. E.A. Nieuwenhuijzen Kruseman. adv.; bk.rev.; bibl.; charts; illus.; stat.; tr.lit.; index. circ. 10,500. (back issues avail.) **Indexed:** ELLIS, Excerp.Med.
—SWETS.

338 SP ISSN 0210-0762
MAESTRIA INDUSTRIAL. 1963. m. 600 ptas. Federacion de Asociaciones de Maestros Industriales de Espana - Federation of Industrial Managers' Associations of Spain, Lillo, 1, 2o Acia 3, 28041 Madrid, Spain. TEL 1-217-96-59. Dir. Fidel Astudillo Jimenez. adv.; bk.rev.; bibl.; charts; illus. circ. 5,000.

MAGAZINE RECYCLING BENELUX. see ENVIRONMENTAL STUDIES — Waste Management

338 US ISSN 1045-6317
HD9727.M2
MAINE MANUFACTURING DIRECTORY. 1965. a. $55. Tower Publishing Co., 588 Saco Rd., Standish, ME 04084-6239. TEL 207-642-5400; 800-969-8693. FAX 207-642-5463. adv. **Document type:** directory.
   Former titles (until 1985): Maine Marketing Directory (ISSN 0145-9007); (until 1975): Directory of Maine Manufacturers.
   Description: Lists manufacturers in Maine, organized alphabetically, geographically and by product.

338 US
MAJOR INDUSTRIAL RESEARCH UNIT STUDIES. 1928. irreg. University of Pennsylvania, Wharton School, Industrial Research Unit, 3733 Vance Hall, Philadelphia, PA 19104-6358. TEL 215-898-5605. **Document type:** academic/scholarly publication.
   Formerly: University of Pennsylvania. Wharton School of Finance and Commerce. Industrial Research Unit Studies (ISSN 0083-9094)

MALAYSIA. DEPARTMENT OF STATISTICS. INDEX OF INDUSTRIAL PRODUCTION, MALAYSIA. see BUSINESS AND ECONOMICS — Abstracting, Bibliographies, Statistics

MALAYSIA. DEPARTMENT OF STATISTICS. MONTHLY MANUFACTURING STATISTICS, MALAYSIA. see BUSINESS AND ECONOMICS — Abstracting, Bibliographies, Statistics

338 MX
MANUFACTURA. m.? $55 in US & Canada; Latin America $60; elsewhere $64 (effective 1997). Grupo Editorial Expansion, Salamanca 35, Col. Roma, 06700 Mexico DF, Mexico. TEL 2072066. **Document type:** consumer publication.
   Description: Provides product news, industry news and in-depth features on plant operations, design and development, processing, and automation - instrumentation.

338 US ISSN 0191-7234
MANUFACTURERS' MART. 1978. m. $18. Manufacturers Mart Publications, 16 High St., Westerly, RI 02891-1850. TEL 401-348-0797. FAX 401-348-0799. Ed. Philip G. Cannon Sr. adv. contact: Jeane Caseley. bk.rev. circ. 30,000. **Document type:** trade publication, directory.

338 AT ISSN 0025-2530
MANUFACTURERS' MONTHLY. 1961. m. $80. Peter Isaacson Publications Pty. Ltd., 46-50 Porter St., Prahran, Vic. 3181, Australia. TEL 61-3-2457777. FAX 61-3-2457840. Ed. Roger Harrison. adv.; bk.rev.; illus.; stat. circ. 15,068. (tabloid format)

330 US
MANUFACTURERS REPRESENTATIVES OF AMERICA. NEWSLINE. 1978. q. membership. Manufacturers Representatives of America, Box 150229, Arlington, TX 76015-6229. TEL 817-561-7272. FAX 817-561-7275. Ed. William R. Bess.
   Description: News for members of the association.

338 US
MANUFACTURING ENGINEERING AND MATERIALS PROCESSING SERIES. 1977. irreg., vol.50, 1997. price varies. Marcel Dekker, Inc., 270 Madison Ave., New York, NY 10016. TEL 212-696-9000. FAX 212-685-4540. TELEX 421419. Pub. Graham Garratt. R&P contact: Julia Mulligan. **Indexed:** INSPEC. **Document type:** monographic series.

338 US ISSN 1078-2397
▼**MANUFACTURING NEWS.** 1995. bi-m. $395 (foreign $445) (effective 1996). Publishers & Producers, Box 30, Annandale, VA 22003. TEL 703-750-2664. FAX 703-750-0064. E-mail: 104355.3100@compuserve.com. Ed. Richard McCormack; Pub. Richard McCormack. R&P contact: Anne Anderson. adv. contact: Anne Anderson. bk.rev.; abstr.; bibl.; illus.; index. (back issues avail.) **Document type:** trade publication.
●Also available online. Vendor(s): Information Access Co.
—CCC.
   Description: Covers advanced manufacturing, trends, manufacturing research and development, and government policies affecting manufacturing.

338 NE
MANUFACTURING RESEARCH AND TECHNOLOGY. 1985. irreg., vol.19, 1993. price varies. Elsevier Science B.V., Books Division, P.O. Box 211, 1000 AE Amsterdam, Netherlands. TEL 31-20-4853911. FAX 31-20-4853705. TELEX 18582 ESPA NL. E-mail: nlinfo-f@elsevier.nl; usinfo-f@elsevier.com; forinfo-kyf04035@niftyserve.or.jp; URL: http://www.elsevier.nl/. (Subscr. in the Americas to: Elsevier Science, Regional Sales Office, Box 945, New York, NY 10159-0945. TEL 212-633-3730. FAX 212-633-3680; Subscr. in Australasia and the Far East to: Elsevier Science (Singapore) Pte Ltd, No.1 Temasek Ave., No.17-01 Millenia Tower, Singapore 039192, Singapore. TEL 65-434-3727. FAX 65-337-2230; Subscr. in Japan to: Elsevier Science Japan, 9-15 Higashi-Azabu 1-chome, Minato-ku, Tokyo 106, Japan. TEL 212-633-3680. FAX 81-5-5561-5047) **Document type:** monographic series.
   Refereed Serial

MANUFACTURING REVIEW. see TECHNOLOGY: COMPREHENSIVE WORKS

338 US
MANUFACTURING SURVEY. m. $30. Dun & Bradstreet, Economic Analysis Department, 220 E. 42nd St., 9th Fl., New York, NY 10017-4717. FAX 212-883-3400. (Subscr. to: Box 1861, New York, NY 10163-1861)
   Description: Nationwide survey of 1,000 manufacturing firms regarding their production, new orders, unfilled orders, exports and finished goods inventories for the upcoming three months.

338 US ISSN 0748-948X
TS155.A1 CODEN: MASYES
MANUFACTURING SYSTEMS; the management magazine of integrated manufacturing. 1983. m. $75 (free to qualified personnel). Hitchcock Publishing (Subsidiary of: Capital Cities - A B C, Inc.), 191 S. Gary Ave., Carol Stream, IL 60188-2292. TEL 708-665-1000. FAX 708-462-2225. TELEX 72-0404. Ed. Tom Inglesby. adv.; bk.rev.; circ. 115,000 (controlled). (also avail. in microform from UMI) **Indexed:** A.I.Abstr., ABI Inform, Alloys Ind., CAD CAM Abstr., Comput.Lit.Ind., Eng.Mat.Abstr., Met.Abstr.Ind., Met.Abstr., Nonfer.Met.Alert, Oper.Res.Manage.Sci., PCC Alert, Qual.Contr.Appl.Stat., Steels Alert, Text.Tech.Dig., World Alum.Abstr.
—BLDSC (5367.284100); CISTI; Linda Hall; SWETS; UMI; UnCover. **CCC.**
   Formerly: Manufacturing Operations.

338 US ISSN 1044-7024
HD9721
MANUFACTURING U S A. biennial. $175. Gale Research, 835 Penobscot Bldg., 645 Griswold St., Detroit, MI 48226-4094. TEL 313-961-2242; 800-877-4253. FAX 800-414-5043. E-mail: daniel_snyder@gale.com. Ed. Arsen Darnay.
—CISTI.
   Description: Presents complete statistical profiles on 450 manufacturing industries.

338 II
MARCH OF KARNATAKA. (Text in English) m. Rs.3. Department of Information and Tourism, 5 Infantry Rd., Bangalore, India. Ed.Bd. adv.; charts; illus.; stat.
   Formerly (Nov. 1973): March of Mysore.

338 PK ISSN 0464-9974
MARKET BULLETIN. (Text in English, Gujarati) 1952. 2/w. Rs.400($75) Kazgi Bazar, P.O. Box 4553, Karachi 74000, Pakistan. TEL 2416735. Ed. A.D. Karim. adv.; bk.rev. circ. 2,000. **Document type:** bulletin.

THE MARKET FOR CONSUMER HEALTHCARE IN LATIN AMERICA. see MEDICAL SCIENCES

THE WORLD MARKET FOR O T C HEALTHCARE IN CHINA. see PHARMACY AND PHARMACOLOGY

THE MARKET FOR O T C HEALTHCARE IN EASTERN EUROPE. see PHARMACY AND PHARMACOLOGY

THE MARKET FOR O T C HEALTHCARE IN LATIN AMERICA. see PHARMACY AND PHARMACOLOGY

THE MARKET FOR O T C HEALTHCARE IN SOUTH EAST ASIA. see PHARMACY AND PHARMACOLOGY

MEDICAL PRODUCT MANUFACTURING NEWS. see INSTRUMENTS

BUSINESS AND ECONOMICS — PRODUCTION OF GOODS AND SERVICES

338   AU
MEGA TECH.* 10/yr. Erb Verlag GmbH, Eichenstr. 38, A-1120 Vienna, Austria. TEL 01-5871381. FAX 01-58713816. Ed. Alfred Bartolitius. circ. 17,000.

338   BL   ISSN 0104-3234
MELHORES E MAIORES. (Special edition of: Exame) 1973. a. $3.59. Editora Abril, S.A., Av. Octaviano Alves de Lima 4400, 02909-900 Sao Paulo SP, Brazil. TEL 011-877-1322. FAX 011-877-1437. Ed. Jose Roberto Guzzo. adv.; charts; illus.; stat. circ. 11,700. **Document type:** consumer publication.
    Description: Annual balance of the 500 major businesses in Brazil.

330   US
MID-AMERICA BANNER. 1986. 6/yr. free. Mid-America Machine Dealers Association, 40625 N. Sunset Dr., Antioch, IL 60002. TEL 847-395-6922; 800-822-4546. FAX 847-395-6922. Ed. Karen Brainard. R&P contact: Dorothy Foley. adv. contact: Dorothy Foley. circ. 1,000 (controlled).
    Description: Focus on the business equipment industry. Provides members with association news.

658.5   IS   ISSN 0017-7059
HA-MIFAL/ENTERPRISE. (Text in Hebrew) 1952. m. 120. Israel Institute of Productivity, 4 Henrietta Szold St., P.O. Box 33010, Tel-Aviv, Israel. Ed. Oded Kor-al. **Indexed:** Ind.Heb.Per.

338 658   HU   ISSN 0580-4485
TS156.A1
MINOSEG ES MEGBIZHATOSAG. (Text in Hungarian; summaries in English, French, German, Russian; 4 special issues in English, German, Russian, Spanish) 1966. bi-m. $38.50. Prodinform Muszaki Tanacsado Vallalat - Prodinform Technical Consulting Company, Munkacsy Mihaly u. 16, P.O. Box 453t 5, 1372 Budapest 5, Hungary. TEL 323-770. TELEX 22-7750 PROD-H. (Subscr. to: Kultura Foreign Trade Company, P.O. Box 149, Budapest H-1389, Hungary) Ed. Gabriel Gyozo. adv.; bk.rev.; abstr. circ. 4,000. **Indexed:** INSPEC.
—CISTI.

338   US   ISSN 0540-4193
MISSOURI'S NEW AND EXPANDING INDUSTRY. 1952. a. free. Department of Economic Development, Box 118, Jefferson City, MO 65102. TEL 573-751-9072. FAX 573-751-7385. E-mail: gbeahan@mail.state.mo.us. Ed. Gary W. Beahan. bk.rev.; circ. 400 (controlled). **Document type:** government publication.
    Formerly: Missouri New and Expanding Manufacturers.
    Description: Data and graphs on annual measures of manufacturing growth and development in the state, based on qualified activities announced by companies.

338   GW   ISSN 0930-3618
MITTELSTAENDISCHE UNTERNEHMEN. 1986. a. DM.530 for 2 vols. (effective 1997). Verlag Hoppenstedt GmbH, Havelstr. 9, 64295 Darmstadt, Germany. TEL 49-6151-380-0. FAX 49-6151-380-360. circ. 50,000. **Document type:** trade publication.
    ●Also available online. Vendor(s): Data-Star, GBI, Knight-Ridder Information, Inc.
    Also available on CD-ROM.

338   US
MODERN CORPORATION CHECKLISTS (SUPPLEMENT). a. $151.45 (foreign $241.95) (effective 1995). Warren, Gorham & Lamont, One Penn Plaza, New York, NY 10119. TEL 212-971-5000. FAX 212-971-5113. (Subscr. to: The Park Square Bldg., 31 St. James Ave., Boston, MA 02116-4112. TEL 800-950-1207) (looseleaf format) **Document type:** trade publication.
    Description: Covers all aspects of company practices with checklists from firms and law departments.

MOFET. see *MACHINERY*

338   II
MONTHLY PRODUCTION OF SELECTED INDUSTRIES OF INDIA. (Text in English) m. Rs.64.80($23.40) Ministry of Planning, Department of Statistics, Central Statistical Organisation, Industrial Statistics Wing, Calcutta 700 001, India. **Document type:** government publication.

MOROCCO. DIRECTION DE LA STATISTIQUE. INDICE DES PRIX A LA PRODUCTION INDUSTRIELLE, ENERGETIQUE ET MINIERE. see *BUSINESS AND ECONOMICS — Abstracting, Bibliographies, Statistics*

MOROCCO. DIRECTION DE LA STATISTIQUE. INDICE DES PRIX DE GROS. see *BUSINESS AND ECONOMICS — Abstracting, Bibliographies, Statistics*

MOROCCO. DIRECTION DE LA STATISTIQUE. INDICE DU COUT DE LA VIE. see *BUSINESS AND ECONOMICS — Abstracting, Bibliographies, Statistics*

388   SP
MOVICARGA. 12/yr. Venezuela 2, 10 D, Pol. Vallaeguado, Apdo. 115, 28820 Coslada (Madrid), Spain. TEL 1-673-58-12. FAX 1-673-59-11. Ed. D. Luis Garcia Sanchez. circ. 6,000.

338   SP
MUNDO INDUSTRIAL. 1967. 11/yr. 10000 ptas. Ediciones Roda S.L., Corcega, 204 bajos, 08036 Barcelona, Spain. TEL 3-322-39-51. FAX 3-419-24-63. Ed. Antonio Castro. adv.: B&W page 112000 ptas., color page 180000 ptas.; 375 x 255. index. circ. 10,000. (tabloid format) **Document type:** newspaper.

338   FI   ISSN 0355-3256
MYYNTINEUVOJA. 11/yr. FIM 350. Suomen Spar oy, Tyoepajakatu 13, 00580 Helsinki 13, Finland. FAX 6197882. circ. 12,200.

338   US
N A P S A RESULTS.* bi-m. $50. National Appliance Parts Suppliers Association, 14415 S.E. MCU Plain Blvd., Ste. 105-B-205, Vancouver, WA 98684. TEL 312-922-6222. FAX 312-922-2734. adv. circ. 500. **Document type:** newsletter.
    Description: Provides news of the appliance parts aftermarket and other items of interest to association members.

N A U M D NEWS. (National Association of Uniform Manufacturers and Distributors) see *CLOTHING TRADE*

N A U M D OFFICE REPORTS. (National Association of Uniform Manufacturers and Distributors) see *CLOTHING TRADE*

N A U M D POSTAL UPDATE. (National Association of Uniform Manufacturers and Distributors) see *CLOTHING TRADE*

338   NR
N N D C NEWSLETTER. 1978. q. New Nigeria Development Company Ltd., P.M.B. 2120, Kaduna, Nigeria. illus. **Document type:** newsletter.

338   NO   ISSN 0047-8601
NAERING I NORD.* 1971. 10/yr. NOK 200. Icon A-S, Naering i Nord, 8001 Bodoe, Norway. Ed. Odd Gjerstad. circ. 4,000.

338   NO   ISSN 0804-4597
HC361
NAERINGSLIVETS UKEAVIS. 1919. fortn. NOK 150. Naeringslivets Forlag, P.O. Box 5145, Majorstua, N-0302 Oslo, Norway. adv.; illus.; tr.lit.; index. circ. 4,200.
    Formerly (until 1993): Apropos (ISSN 0802-247X); Which superseded in part (in 1988): Norges Industri (ISSN 0029-1706)

NAPETCOR. see *PETROLEUM AND GAS*

338.9   XR
NARODNI HOSPODARSTVI - INDIKATOR/NATIONAL ECONOMY - INDICATOR. 1948. m. $62.40. (Statni Planovaci Komise) Orbis, Vinohradska 46, 120 41 Prague 2, Czech Republic. TEL 42-2-24247575. FAX 42-2-24247575. Ed. Jitka Blahova. adv.; bk.rev.; bibl.; charts. circ. 10,000. **Indexed:** Rural Recreat.Tour.Abstr., World Agri.Econ.& Rural Sociol.Abstr.
    Former titles (until 1995): Narodni Hospodarstvi (ISSN 0862-7037); (until 1990): Planovane Hospodarstvi (ISSN 0032-0749)
    Description: Brings together economists and the business community, government conceptions, entrepreneurial expertise.

338   DK
NATIONAL AGENCY OF INDUSTRY AND TRADE. ANNUAL REPORTS (YEAR)/AARSBERETNINGER. 1982. a. free. National Agency of Industry and Trade, P.O. Box 983, Soendergade 25, DK-8600 Silkeborg, Denmark. TEL 86-825655. FAX 45-86-801629. TELEX 63346. circ. 5,000.
    Former titles: Investering i Produktion (ISSN 0108-2329) & Denmark. Egnsudviklingsraadet. Beretning.

NATIONAL HOUSEWARES MANUFACTURERS ASSOCIATION. STATE OF THE INDUSTRY REPORT. see *BUSINESS AND ECONOMICS — Abstracting, Bibliographies, Statistics*

338   CN
NATIONAL INDUSTRIAL NEWS. 1976. m. Brymell Publications, Inc., 801 York Mills Rd., Ste. 201, Don Mills, ON M3B 1X7, Canada. TEL 416-446-1404; 800-624-2776. FAX 416-446-0502. Ed. W.R. Bryson; Pub. W.R. Bryson. adv.: page Can.$3900; trim 10 7/8 x 16 1/2; adv. contact: Ken Muir. circ. 24,500 (controlled). **Document type:** trade publication.
    Former titles: National Industrial Magazine; Ontario Industrial Magazine.

338   II
NATIONAL PRODUCTS NEWS. (Text in English) 1989. m. Rs.150; newsstand price: Rs.15. Seven Hills Publications Pvt. Ltd., Nahar & Seth Industrial Estate, A-Wing, Gala No. 3061, 3rd Fl., Pannalal Silk Mills Compound, L.B.S. Marg, Bhandup (W), Bombay 400 078, India. TEL 5645479. Ed. A.S. Mani. adv.: B&W page Rs.8000, color page Rs.18000; trim 280 x 200; adv. contact: P.V. Murali. circ. 12,700. **Document type:** trade publication.

NATIONAL QUALITY MANUFACTURING GUIDE. see *BUSINESS AND ECONOMICS — Trade And Industrial Directories*

NEDERLANDS A B C DIENSTVERLENERS. see *BUSINESS AND ECONOMICS — Trade And Industrial Directories*

NEDERLANDS A B C VOOR HANDEL EN INDUSTRIE. see *BUSINESS AND ECONOMICS — Trade And Industrial Directories*

338.9   NP   ISSN 0077-6548
NEPAL INDUSTRIAL DEVELOPMENT CORPORATION. ANNUAL REPORT. (Text in English) 1959. a. free. Nepal Industrial Development Corporation, N.I.D.C. Bldg., Durbar Marg, Box 10, Kathmandu, Nepal. TEL 977-1-228322. FAX 977-1-227428. **Document type:** corporate report.

338.9   NP   ISSN 0077-6556
HC497.N5
NEPAL INDUSTRIAL DEVELOPMENT CORPORATION. INDUSTRIAL DIGEST. (Text in English) 1966. a. Rs.30($5) Nepal Industrial Development Corporation, N.I.D.C. Bldg., Durbar Marg, Box 10, Kathmandu, Nepal. Ed. Ramesh Nath Dhungel.

330   NE   ISSN 0166-9478
NETHERLANDS. CENTRAAL PLANBUREAU. CENTRAAL ECONOMISCH PLAN. Key Title: Centraal Economisch Plan. English edition: Central Economic Plan (ISSN 0926-8235) (Includes the National Budget) 1946. a. fl.69. (Centraal Planbureau) S D U Uitgeverij, Chr. Plantijnstraat 2, 2515 TZ The Hague, Netherlands. TEL 31-70-3789911. FAX 31-70-3475778. **Document type:** government publication.
—SWETS.

338   AU
NEUHEITEN. 6/yr. Postfach 2, A-2332 Hennersdorf, Austria. TEL 2235-81565. Ed. Alfred Vejchar. circ. 130,000.

338.9   CN
T177.C2
NEW BRUNSWICK. RESEARCH AND PRODUCTIVITY COUNCIL. ANNUAL REPORT. 1962. a. free. Research and Productivity Council, Fredericton, NB, Canada. TEL 506-452-8994. FAX 506-452-1395. Ed. Peter Lewell. circ. 500. **Document type:** government publication.
—CISTI.
    Formerly: New Brunswick. Research and Productivity Council. Report (ISSN 0077-8117)

BUSINESS AND ECONOMICS — PRODUCTION OF GOODS AND SERVICES

338 US ISSN 0028-4378
NEW BUSINESS INCORPORATIONS. 1947. m. $25. Dun & Bradstreet, Economic Analysis Department, 220 E. 42nd St., 9th Fl., New York, NY 10017-4717. FAX 212-883-3400. (Subscr. to: Box 1861, New York, NY 10163-1861) (also avail. in microfiche from CIS) **Indexed:** SRI.
Description: Provides the number of new incorporations in each of the 50 states, with commentary and comparisons to previous periods.

380 US
NEW HAMPSHIRE MANUFACTURING DIRECTORY. a. $55. Tower Publishing Co., 588 Saco Rd., Standish, ME 04084-6239. TEL 207-642-5400; 800-969-8693. FAX 207-642-5463. **Document type:** directory.
Formerly: New Hampshire Marketing Directory (ISSN 0276-2110)
Description: Lists manufacturers in New Hampshire alphabetically, geographically and by product.

338 US ISSN 0028-5560
HC107.N5
NEW JERSEY BUSINESS; the magazine of industry and business. 1954. m. $20. New Jersey Business Magazine, 310 Passaic Ave., Fairfield, NJ 07004. TEL 201-882-5004. Ed. James T. Prior. adv.; charts; illus. circ. 15,693. **Indexed:** Oper.Res.Manage.Sci., P.A.I.S. **Document type:** consumer publication.
●Also available online. Vendor(s): Lexis-Nexis, UMI.
—UMI.

NEW JERSEY MANUFACTURERS DIRECTORY. see BUSINESS AND ECONOMICS — Trade And Industrial Directories

338 NR ISSN 0189-1316
NEW NIGERIA DEVELOPMENT COMPANY LIMITED. ANNUAL REPORT AND ACCOUNTS. 1969. a. free. New Nigeria Development Company Ltd., P.M.B. 2120, Kaduna, Nigeria. **Document type:** corporate report.
Supersedes (in 1978): Northern Nigeria Development Corporation. Report.

338 UK
NEW PRODUCT NEWSLETTER. m. New Product Newsletter Co. Ltd., 1A Chesterfield St., London W1, England.

NEW YORK MANUFACTURERS DIRECTORY. see BUSINESS AND ECONOMICS — Trade And Industrial Directories

NEWS & VIEWS (PORTLAND). see BUSINESS AND ECONOMICS — Marketing And Purchasing

338 JA
NIKKEI SANGYO SHIMBUN/NIKKEI INDUSTRIAL DAILY. (Text in Japanese) 1973. d. (except Sun.). Nihon Keizai Shimbun, Inc., 1-9-5 Ote-machi, Chiyoda-ku, Tokyo 100-66, Japan. TEL 81-3-3270-0251. FAX 81-3-5255-2661. TELEX J22308 NIKKEI. Ed. Masayuki Shimada. adv.; B&W page 2460000 Yen; trim 385 x 533; adv. contact: Hideaki Nakajima. circ. 255,500. **Document type:** newspaper.
Description: Provides in-depth coverage of developments in industry, including new products and technologies.

338 JA
NIKKEI TRENDY. (Text in English) m. Nikkei Home Publishing, Inc. (Subsidiary of: Nihon Keizai Shimbun, Inc.), 2-2-7 Kanda Tsukasa-cho, Chiyoda-ku, Tokyo 101, Japan. TEL 03-5256-6924. **Document type:** consumer publication.
Description: Contains information on current hit products and services.

338 JA ISSN 0388-709X
NIKKO FORAMU/NIKKO PRODUCER - GOODS FORUM. (Text in Japanese) 1980. m. 400 Yen per no. Nihon Kogyo Shinbunsha, 7-2, Otemachi 1-chome, Chiyoda-ku, Tokyo 100, Japan.

338 FR ISSN 0078-0960
NOMENCLATURE DES ENTREPRISES NATIONALES A CARACTERE INDUSTRIEL OU COMMERCIAL ET DES SOCIETIES D'ECONOMIE MIXTE D'INTERET NATIONAL. irreg. price varies. (Ministere de l'Economie et des Finances) Imprimerie Nationale, B.P. 514, 59505 Douai Cedex, France. TEL 27-93-70-90. FAX 27-93-70-96. TELEX 120 389 F.

338.948 NO ISSN 0802-8818
DL55
NORD REVY; tidsskrift for regional udvikling, naeringsliv og miljoe. (Text in Danish, Norwegian, Swedish; summaries in English) 1990. bi-m. NOK 608 in Nordic countries; elsewhere $116 (effective 1997). (Nordic Institute for Regional Research (NordREFO).) Scandinavian University Press, P.O. Box 2959 Toeyen, N-0608 Oslo, Norway. TEL 47-22-57-54-00. FAX 47-22-57-53-53. E-mail: mail@scup.no; URL: http://www.scup.no. (US addr.: 875 Massachusetts Ave., Ste. 84, Cambridge, MA 02139. TEL 617-497-6515. FAX 617-354-6875) Ed. Lars Hedegaard. **Indexed:** Geo.Abstr.P.G. **Document type:** academic/scholarly publication.
Description: Focuses on regional development, business and environment in the Scandinavian countries.

338 GW
NORDDEUTSCHES HANDWERK. 1895. s-m. DM.84 (effective 1997). Schluetersche GmbH und Co. KG, Hans-Boeckler-Allee 7, 30173 Hannover, Germany. TEL 49-511-8550-0. FAX 49-511-8550402. (Subscr. to: Postfach 5440, 30054 Hannover, Germany) Ed. Irmke Froemling. adv.; bk.rev. circ. 75,561. **Document type:** bulletin.
—CCC.
Formerly: Nordwestdeutsches Handwerk (ISSN 0029-1617)

NORTH CAROLINA MANUFACTURERS DIRECTORY. see BUSINESS AND ECONOMICS — Trade And Industrial Directories

338 DR ISSN 0254-2153
NOTAS DE DESARROLLO. 1967. q. free. Fundacion Dominicana de Desarrollo, Apdo. 857, Santo Domingo, Z.P.1, Dominican Republic. illus. circ. 2,000.

338 XV ISSN 0029-5051
T4 CODEN: NOVPAJ
NOVA PROIZVODNJA; obzornik napredka v tehniki in gospodarstvu. (Text in Slovenian; summaries in English) 1950. q. 100 din.($25) Zveza Inzenirjev in Tehnikov Slovenije, Erjavceva 15, Ljubljana, Slovenia. Ed. Albert Nicic. adv.; bk.rev.; index. **Indexed:** Chem.Abstr.
—CASDDS; Linda Hall.

338 620 PL ISSN 0208-6891
NOWATOR; pismo poswiecone tworczosci technicznej. 1954. m $51. Wydawnictwo Czasopism i Ksiazek Technicznych SIGMA - NOT, Ul. Ratuszowa 11, P.O. Box 1004, 00-950 Warsaw, Poland. TEL 48-22-180918. FAX 48-22-192187. TELEX 814550 SIGMA PL. (Dist. by: Zaklad Kolportazu SIGMA-NOT, ul. Bartycka 20, P.O. Box 1004, 00-950, Warsaw, Poland) Ed. Bronislaw Pilawski. adv.; bk.rev. circ. 5,700. (tabloid format)
Former titles: Temat - Wynalazczosc i Racjonalizacja (ISSN 0137-379X); (until 1974): Wynalazczosc i Racjonalizacja (ISSN 0043-9649)

341.1 FR ISSN 0029-7038
O E C D LIAISON BULLETIN BETWEEN RESEARCH AND TRAINING INSTITUTES. (Editions in English, French) irreg. price varies. Organization for Economic Cooperation and Development, 2 rue Andre-Pascal, 75775 Paris Cedex 16, France. (U.S. orders to: O.E.C.D. Publications and Information Center, 2001 L St., N.W., Ste. 650, Washington, DC 20036-4922. TEL 202-785-6323) (back issues avail.)

338 NO ISSN 0332-5555
HC361
OEKONOMISK RAPPORT. 1962. 22/yr. NOK 745. A-S Hjemmet, Kristian IV. Gt. 13, N-0107 Oslo, Norway. Ed. Kjell Thompson. adv.; bk.rev.; charts; illus.; stat.; index. circ. 30,000.
Formerly (until 1975): Bedriftsoekonomisk Informasjon (ISSN 0045-1606)

OFFICIAL IOWA MANUFACTURERS DIRECTORY. see BUSINESS AND ECONOMICS — Trade And Industrial Directories

338 NE ISSN 1383-3391
ONDERNEMEN!; magazine voor de ondernemd Nederland. 1995. 10/yr. fl.72.50. Wegener Tijdschriften Groep B.V., Postbus 1860, 1110 CD Diemen, Netherlands. TEL 31-20-6603335. FAX 31-20-6956329. adv.; bk.rev.; stat. circ. 119,725. **Document type:** trade publication.
Formed by the merger of (1979-1995): Ondernemers-Visie (ISSN 0165-1897); (1979-1995): Ondernemer (Rijswijk) (ISSN 0927-3611); Which was formerly (1975-1979): Zelfstandig Ondernemerschap (ISSN 1383-4142); Which was formed by the merger of (1968-1975): Ondernemer (ISSN 1383-4150); (1947-1975): Modern Ondernemerschap (ISSN 0026-8216)

338 NE ISSN 0030-3488
OPENBARE UITGAVEN. 1968. 6/yr. fl.93 to individuals; institutions fl.148 (effective 1995). (Instituut voor Onderzoek van Overheidsuitgaven) Vuga Uitgeverij B.V., Postbus 16400, 2500 BK The Hague, Netherlands. TEL 31-70-3614011. FAX 31-70-3625468. Ed. H. de Groot. adv.: B&W page fl.1050, color page fl.3010; trim 160 x 240. charts; stat. circ. 1,000. **Indexed:** Key to Econ.Sci. **Document type:** academic/scholarly publication.
—SWETS.

338 FR
OPTION QUALITE; reglementation, technologie, controle des produits. 1983. m. 730 F. (effective 1994). Lamy S.A., 187-189 quai de Valmy, 75490 Paris Cedex 10, France. TEL 33-1-44721343. FAX 33-1-44721395.
Description: Provides information on how to track and improve the quality of products for professionals in the food industry.

338 NR
OYO STATE. MINISTRY OF ECONOMIC PLANNING AND COMMUNITY DEVELOPMENT. ANNUAL REPORT.* a. Government Printer, Ibadan, Oyo State, Nigeria. **Document type:** government publication.
Formerly: Western State. Ministry of Economic Planning and Community Development. Annual Report.

338 330 CN
P M E AU QUEBEC. ETAT DE LA SITUATION. (Petite et Moyenne Entreprise) a. free. Ministere de l'Industrie, du Commerce, de la Science et de la Technologie, 710 place D'Youville, 9e etage, Quebec, PQ G1R 4Y4, Canada. TEL 418-691-5993. FAX 418-646-6435. URL: http://www.micst.gouv.qc.ca. circ. 1,000. **Document type:** government publication.
Formerly: Quebec (Province). Ministere de l'Industrie, du Commerce, de la Science et de la Technologie. Direction de l'Analyse des P M E et des Regions.
Description: Reports on the situation of the small and medium businesses in Quebec in the previous year.

PADDLER'S PRINT. see SPORTS AND GAMES — Boats And Boating

338 PK ISSN 0078-8392
PAKISTAN. OFFICE OF THE ECONOMIC ADVISER. GOVERNMENT SPONSORED CORPORATIONS AND OTHER INSTITUTIONS. (Text in English) 1965. a. free. Office of the Economic Adviser, Islamabad, Pakistan. circ. controlled.

338.9 PK ISSN 0078-8414
PAKISTAN. PLANNING AND DEVELOPMENT DIVISION. DEVELOPMENT PROGRAMME. (Text in English) 1971. a. $20. Planning and Development Division, Block "P", Islamabad, Pakistan.

338.9 PK ISSN 0078-8201
PAKISTAN INDUSTRIAL DEVELOPMENT CORPORATION. REPORT. (Text in English) 1952. a. Pakistan Industrial Development Corporation, PIDC House, Dr. Ziauddin Ahmad Rd., Karachi 4, Pakistan.

PARAGUAY INDUSTRIAL Y COMERCIAL. see BUSINESS AND ECONOMICS — Domestic Commerce

PATENT DIGEST. see PATENTS, TRADEMARKS AND COPYRIGHTS

338 US
PEOPLE AND PRODUCTS. m. General Merchandise Distributors Council, 1275 Lake Ave., Colorado Springs, CO 80906.

BUSINESS AND ECONOMICS — PRODUCTION OF GOODS AND SERVICES

338   **UK**
PERFORMANCE MATERIALS TECHNOLOGY. m. Britannia House, 960 High Rd., London N12 9RY, England. TEL 0181-446-5141. FAX 0181-446-3659. Ed. Nick C. Dellow. **Document type:** newsletter.
  Formerly: New Materials World.

338.9   **BL**   **ISSN 0100-0551**
HC186
PESQUISA E PLANEJAMENTO ECONOMICO. 1971. 3/yr. R.20. Instituto de Pesquisa Economica Aplicada, Av. Presidente Antonio Carlos, 51, 13 andar, 20020-010 Rio de Janeiro, RJ, Brazil. TEL 55-21-2205533. FAX 55-21-2401920. E-mail: ppe@ipea.gov.br; URL: http://www.ipea.gov.br. Ed. Octavio Augusto Fontes Tourinho. adv.; bk.rev. circ. 1,000. Indexed: Hisp.Amer.Per.Ind. (1980-), IBR, J.of Econ.Lit., P.A.I.S.For.Lang.Ind. **Document type:** academic/scholarly publication.
  Formerly: Pesquisa e Planejamento (ISSN 0304-2308)
  Description: Presents research and studies in economic and social planning.
  Refereed Serial

PESQUISA INDUSTRIAL. see *BUSINESS AND ECONOMICS — Abstracting, Bibliographies, Statistics*

PHARMACEUTICAL MANUFACTURING REVIEW. see *PHARMACY AND PHARMACOLOGY*

338   **PH**   **ISSN 0116-6891**
PHILIPPINES. NATIONAL STATISTICS OFFICE. INDUSTRY TRENDS. m. National Statistics Office, Ramon Magsaysay Blvd., Box 779, Manila, Philippines. FAX 63-2-610794. pp./issue: 32. **Document type:** government publication.
  Description: Discusses the results of the Survey of Key Enterprises in Manufacturing, a special study conducted by NSO to provide flash indicators on the performance of growth-oriented industries.

338   **SA**
PLANT EQUIPMENT HIRE & RATE REVIEW. (Text in English) 1977. m. (11/yr.). R.99 (Southern Africa R.125; elsewhere R.260) (effective Aug. 1995). Brooke Pattrick (Pty) Ltd., P.O. Box 422, Bedfordview 2008, South Africa. TEL 27-11-6224666. FAX 27-11-6167196. Ed. Marge Murray. adv. contact: John Pattrick. circ. 4,100 (controlled). **Document type:** trade publication.
  Formerly: Plant.
  Description: Features company news, information on manufactured parts, articles on people in the profession, plant news, and listings of manufacturers and hire equipment and services available.

338   **US**   **ISSN 1083-5636**
▼**PLANT PROSPECTOR.** 1995. w. $575 for 6 mos. Beard Group, Inc., Box 8867, Washington, DC 20016. TEL 310-951-6400. FAX 301-951-3621. E-mail: chris@bankrupt.com.

338   **ISSN 0191-2933**
HC79.D5
▼**PLANTS, SITES & PARKS.** 1974. bi-m. $30 (effective 1997). B P I Communications, 49 Music Sq., W., Nashville, TN 37203. TEL 615-329-4940. FAX 615-329-4733. E-mail: info@bpicom.com; URL: http://www.bizsites.com. Ed. Ken Ibold; Pub. Len/Scaffidi. R&P contact: Ken Ibold. adv. contact: Nancy Kay. illus.; stat.; circ. 40,500 (controlled). (also avail. in microfilm from UMI; reprint service avail. from UMI) **Document type:** trade publication.
  ●Also available online. Vendor(s): Information Access Co.
  —UMI. CCC.
  Description: Offers site relocation advice for companies looking to relocate or expand.

338.9   **GW**   **ISSN 0079-2284**
▼**PLANUNGSSTUDIEN.** 1969. irreg., vol.21, 1984. price varies. Nomos Verlagsgesellschaft mbH und Co. KG, Waldseestr. 3-5, 76530 Baden-Baden, Germany. TEL 49-7221-21040. FAX 49-7221-210427. (Subscr. to: Postfach 610, 76484 Baden-Baden, Germany) Ed. Joseph H. Kaiser. **Document type:** monographic series.

▼**PLASTICS: LATIN AMERICAN INDUSTRIAL REPORT.** see *PLASTICS*

338   **PL**   **ISSN 0239-9415**
POLITECHNIKA POZNANSKA. ZESZYTY NAUKOWE. ORGANIZACJA I ZARZADZANIE. 1969. irreg., latest no.19. price varies. Politechnika Poznanska, Pl. Curie Sklodowskiej 2, 60-965 Poznan, Poland. TEL 48-61-313216. Ed. Leszek Pacholski. **Document type:** academic/scholarly publication.
  Formerly: Politechnika Poznanska. Zeszyty Naukowe. Ekonomika i Organizacja Przemyslu (ISSN 0137-690X)
  Description: Covers ergonomics, quality engineering, production engineering and management, marketing and infomatics, economics, business law.

POLYURETHANE CHEMICALS AND PRODUCTS IN EUROPE. see *ENGINEERING — Chemical Engineering*

338 680   **AT**
POOL & SPA REVIEW. 1973. q. Aus.$45 (foreign Aus.$85). Wallacia (Sales) Pty. Ltd., 4 Coppabella Rd., Dural, N.S.W. 2158, Australia. TEL 61-2-651-2044. FAX 61-9-651-2825. Ed. Ben Smith. adv.; tr.lit. circ. 2,900. **Document type:** trade publication.
  Former titles: Pool and Spa Industry Review; (until Mar. 1983): Caspa (ISSN 0311-0001)

PORTUGAL. INSTITUTO NACIONAL DE ESTATISTICA. INDICE DA PRODUCAO INDUSTRIAL. see *MINES AND MINING INDUSTRY*

338 621.9   **US**
POWER PRODUCTS BUSINESS. 1975. m. $365. Power Systems Research, 1301 Corporate Center Dr., Ste. 113, St. Paul, MN 55121. TEL 612-454-0144. FAX 612-454-0760. Ed. Gordon Gilbert; Pub. Geroge Zirnhelt. R&P contact: George Zirnhelt. stat.; circ. 150 (paid). (looseleaf format) **Document type:** newsletter.
  Former titles: Engine Power Perspective (ISSN 1056-4063); Diesel Power Perspective (ISSN 0743-0787)
  Description: News and market information regarding engine manufacturers, components and engine-powered equipment.

338   **IV**
PRINCIPALES INDUSTRIES INSTALLEES EN COTE D'IVOIRE. 1968. a. free. Chambre d'Industrie de Cote d'Ivoire, B.P. 1758, Abidjan, Ivory Coast.
  Formerly: Principales Industries Ivoiriennes.

338   **PH**   **ISSN 0115-4419**
PRIVATE DEVELOPMENT CORPORATION OF THE PHILIPPINES. INDUSTRY DIGEST. (Text in English) 1977. bi-m. $55. Private Development Corporation of the Philippines - Pribadong Korporasyon sa Pagpapaunlad ng Pilipinas, P.O. Box 757 Makati, Metro Manila 3117, Philippines. TEL 02-8100231. FAX 02-8195376. TELEX RCA-22080.

338   **US**   **ISSN 0190-9851**
PRIVATE LABEL; the magazine for house brands and generics. 1979. bi-m. $33 (foreign $75) (effective 1997). E.W. Williams Publications Co., 2125 Center Ave., Ste. 305, Fort Lee, NJ 07024-5859. TEL 201-592-7007. FAX 201-592-7171. Ed. Peter Berlinski; Pub. Andrew H. Williams. R&P contact: Tony Faber. adv. contact: Charles Loomer. bk.rev. circ. 28,000. Indexed: Ref.Pt.Food Indus.Abstr. **Document type:** trade publication.
  ●Also available online.
  Incorporates (in 1990): Private Label Executive Edition.

338 658.8   **US**   **ISSN 0886-5582**
PRIVATE LABEL INTERNATIONAL; the magazine for store labels (own brands) and generics. (Text in English; summaries in French, German) 1986. s-a. $20 (foreign $45) (effective 1997). E.W. Williams Publications Co., 2125 Center Ave., Ste. 305, Fort Lee, NJ 07024-5859. TEL 201-592-7007. FAX 201-592-7171. Ed. Peter Berlinski; Pub. Andrew H. Williams. R&P contact: Tony Faber. adv. contact: Charles Loomer. **Document type:** trade publication.

330   **BN**   **ISSN 0350-9788**
PRIVREDNE NOVINE.* 1972. w. 1000 din. Oslobodjenje, Dzemala Bijedica 185, 71000 Sarajevo, Bosnia Hercegovina. Ed. Ljubomir Solomunovic.

338   **UK**
PROCESSING TECHNOLOGY FOR CHINA. (Text in Chinese) a. £55. Sterling Publications Ltd., 86-88 Edgware Rd., London W2 2YW, England. TEL 44-171-915-9600. FAX 44-171-915-9619. circ. 10,000. **Document type:** trade publication.

338   **US**
PRODUCT DEVELOPMENT BEST PRACTICES REPORT. m. Management Roundtable, Inc., 95 Sawyer Rd., Ste. 510, Waltham, MA 02154-3471. Ed. Alexander J. Cooper. **Document type:** newsletter.
  Formerly: Design for Manufacture Alert (ISSN 1049-8400)
  Description: Provides case studies, and perspectives on strategies for manufacturing excellence.

PRODUCT SAFETY LETTER. see *PUBLIC HEALTH AND SAFETY*

PRODUCTION AND OPERATIONS MANAGEMENT. see *BUSINESS AND ECONOMICS — Management*

PRODUCTION PLANNING & CONTROL. see *ENGINEERING — Computer Applications*

338   **PE**   **ISSN 0032-9908**
PRODUCTIVIDAD. 1961. a. free. Ministerio de Trabajo y Promocion Social, Centro Nacional de Productividad (CENIP), Apdo. 5442, Av. Paseo de la Republica 3101, piso 9, San Isidro, Lima 100, Peru. TEL 417033. Dir. Alfonso Luna Victoria Sanchez. adv.; abstr.; charts; illus. circ. 2,500. **Document type:** government publication.

658.5   **II**   **ISSN 0032-9924**
PRODUCTIVITY. (Text in English) 1959. q. Rs.300($80) (National Productivity Council, Business Management Section) New Age International Pvt. Ltd., Journals Division, 4835-24, Ansari Rd., Daryaganj, New Delhi 110 002, India. TEL 91-11-3261487. FAX 91-11-3267437. Ed. D.P. Upadhyay. adv.; bk.rev.; illus, stat.; index, cum.index: vols.1-17 (1959-1976). circ. 3,000. Indexed: C.R.I.Abstr., C.R.I.Curr.Cont., Int.Lab.Doc., Pub.Admin.Abstr., Text.Tech.Dig. **Document type:** academic/scholarly publication.
  Description: Provides research based techno-managerial expertise for invigorating the economy.

PRODUCTIVITY; techniques and technologies supporting lean manufacturing. see *BUSINESS AND ECONOMICS — Management*

338   **II**   **ISSN 0970-5597**
PRODUCTIVITY NEWS. (Text in English) 1963. m. Rs.50($24) National Productivity Council, Business Management Section, Utpadakta Bhawan, Lodi Rd., New Delhi 110003, India. Ed. Harkirat Singh. adv.; bk.rev.; illus. circ. 2,500.
  Description: Provides a wide coverage of significant developments in all sectors of national economy.

338   **US**
PRODUCTS & SERVICES. a. $49 (free with purchase of any other Value Retail News Directory). Value Retail News, 11701 S. Belcher Rd., Ste. 130, Largo, FL 33773. TEL 813-536-4047; 800-669-1020. FAX 813-536-4047. Ed. Kris Hundley; Pub. Dan Cochran. adv. contact: Fran Tolson. **Document type:** directory.

338.0294   **US**
PRODUCTS CERTIFIED FOR CANADA DIRECTORY. s-a. (2 vols./yr.) Underwriters Laboratories Inc., Publications, 333 Pfingsten Rd., Northbrook, IL 60062-2096. TEL 708-272-8129. FAX 708-272-8129. **Document type:** directory.

338   **UY**
PRODUCTS OF URUGUAY. 1899. m. free. Camara de Industrias del Uruguay, Av. Lib. Brig. Gral. Lavalleja 1672, Montevideo, Uruguay. adv.
  Former titles: Camara de Industrias del Uruguay. Guia de Socios y de Productos; Union Industrial Uruguaya. Guia de Socios y de Productos (ISSN 0041-6908)

BUSINESS AND ECONOMICS — PRODUCTION OF GOODS AND SERVICES

338   GW   ISSN 0344-6166
PRODUKTION; Wochenzeitung fuer das Technische Management. 1962. w. DM.112. Verlag Moderne Industrie, Justus-von-Liebig-Str. 1, 86899 Landsberg, Germany. TEL 49-8191-125-0. FAX 49-8191-125-312. Ed. Guenter Koegel. adv.: B&W page DM.19120; trim 365 x 255; adv. contact: Gerald Zasche. charts; illus. circ. 39,458. **Document type:** trade publication.

658.5   YU   ISSN 0032-9975
PRODUKTIVNOST. 1958. m. 700 din.($44.20) Jugoslovenski Zavod za Produktivnost Rada, Uzum Mirkova 1, Belgrade, Yugoslavia. Ed. Miodrag Zivkovic. adv.; bk.rev.; abstr.; charts; stat.

338   US
PROFILE (SKOKIE); a newsmagazine for the people of Brunswick. 1964. q. free. Brunswick Corporation, One N. Field Ct., Lake Forest, IL 60045-4811. TEL 847-735-4457. FAX 847-735-4765. Ed. Eugene Fisher. R&P contact: Eugene Fisher. circ. 30,000 (controlled). (back issues avail.) **Description:** News of the activities of Brunswick Corporation and its people.

338   IT   ISSN 0391-8351
PROGRAMMAZIONE IN SARDEGNA. 1966. 6/yr. free. Centro Regionale di Programmazione, Via Mameli, 88, Cagliari, Italy. TEL 070-6064659. FAX 070-6064684. bk.rev.; stat. circ. 5,500.

338   RU   ISSN 0033-1163
T4   CODEN: PAKBAG
PROMYSHLENNOST' ARMENII. (Text in Russian) 1958. m. 16.20 Rub. Izdatel'stvo Kniga, 50, Gorky St., 125047 Moscow, Russia. charts; index. **Indexed:** Chem.Abstr.
—CASDDS.

338   RU   ISSN 0033-1171
HD28
PROMYSHLENNOST' BELORUSSII. (Text in Russian) 1958. m. 19.20 Rub. Izdatel'stvo Kniga, 50, Gorky St., 125047 Moscow, Russia. charts; index. **Indexed:** Chem.Abstr.

338.9   VE
PROSPECCION SIGLO 21. VENEZUELA ANO 2000.* 1969. q. Universidad Catolica Andres Bello, Centro de Estudios del Futuro de Venezuela, Apdo. 29068, Caracas 1021, Venezuela. bibl.; stat.

333.7   US   ISSN 0079-7634
PUBLIC POLICY ISSUES IN RESOURCE MANAGEMENT. 1965. irreg., latest 1986. price varies. (University of Washington, Graduate School of Public Affairs) University of Washington Press, Box 50096, Seattle, WA 98105. TEL 206-543-4050. **Document type:** monographic series.
Refereed Serial

PUMP INDUSTRY ANALYST. see *MACHINERY*

338.7   II
PUNJAB STATE INDUSTRIAL DEVELOPMENT CORPORATION. ANNUAL REPORT.* (Text in English) a. Punjab State Industrial Development Corporation, United Commercial Bank Bldg., 3rd Fl., Sector 17-B, Chandigarh, India. illus.; stat.

338   IT   ISSN 0391-6146
QUALE IMPRESA. 1974. m. L.60000 (foreign L.90000). Servizio Italiano Pubblicazioni Internazionali s.r.l., Viale L. Pasteur, 6, 00144 Rome, Italy. TEL 39-6-5920509. FAX 39-6-5924819. Ed. Francesco Guidi. adv.: color page L.4000000. circ. 10,000. **Document type:** trade publication.

QUALITY NEW ZEALAND. see *BUSINESS AND ECONOMICS — Management*

380.14   US   ISSN 1003-5915
QUANGUO XINCHANPIN/NEW PRODUCTS OF THE P R C. (Text in Chinese) m. $33.20. China Books & Periodicals, Inc., 2929 24th St., San Francisco, CA 94110. TEL 415-282-2994. FAX 415-282-0994.

QUARTERLY BUSINESS FAILURES. see *BUSINESS AND ECONOMICS — Economic Situation And Conditions*

338.5   JA   ISSN 0913-1841
HC462.9
QUARTERLY FORECAST OF JAPANESE ECONOMY. (Text in Japanese; summaries in English) 1967. 4/yr. 24000 Yen. Japan Center for Economic Research, Economic Analysis Division, Nikkei Kayabacho Bldg., 6-1 Nihonbashi Kayabacgi 2-chome, Chuo-ku, Tokyo 103, Japan. TEL 81-3-3639-2801. FAX 81-3-3639-2839. stat.; circ. controlled. **Indexed:** PROMT.
Former titles: Quarterly Forecast of Japan's Economy by the S A Method (ISSN 0910-075X); Eighteen Month Forecast of Japan's Economy (ISSN 0013-2594)
Description: Provides an unbiased short-term forecast of Japanese business and economy.

338 330   CN
QUEBEC (PROVINCE). MINISTERE DE L'ANALYSE DE LA CONJONCTURE INDUSTRIELLE. SECTEUR MANUFACTURIER ET LE COMMERCE. free. Ministere de l'Industrie, du Commerce, de la Science et de la Technologie, 710 place D'Youville, 9e etage, Quebec, PQ G1R 4Y4. TEL 418-691-5967. FAX 418-646-6435. URL: http://www.micst.gouv.qc.ca. circ. 1,500. **Document type:** government publication.
Description: Report on the Quebec manufacturing and trade sectors in the past year.

354   AT
QUEENSLAND. DEPARTMENT OF TOURISM, SMALL BUSINESS AND INDUSTRY. ANNUAL REPORT. 1963. a. free. Department of Tourism, Small Business and Industry, Library, G.P.O. Box 1141, Brisbane, Qld. 4001, Australia. illus. circ. 4,000. **Document type:** government publication.
Former titles (until Mar. 1996): Queensland. Department of Business, Industry and Regional Development. Annual Report; (until Nov. 1990): Queensland. Department of Manufacturing and Commerce. Annual Report; (until Dec. 1989): Queensland. Department of Industry Development. Annual Report; Queensland. Department of Commercial and Industrial Development. Annual Report.

R N AND W P L ENCYCLOPEDIA. (Registered Number & Wool Products Label) see *BUSINESS AND ECONOMICS — Marketing And Purchasing*

338   GW   ISSN 0931-8801
R W I - KONJUNKTURBERICHTE. 1949. s-a. price varies. (Rheinisch-Westfaelisches Institut fuer Wirtschaftsforschung, Essen) Duncker und Humblot GmbH, Postfach 410329, 12113 Berlin, Germany. TEL 49-30-7900060. FAX 49-30-79000631. E-mail: duh-werbung@t-online.de. Ed. R. Doehm, B. Puecker. stat. **Indexed:** INIS Atomind. **Document type:** academic/scholarly publication.

338   GW   ISSN 0939-2335
R W I KONJUNKTURBRIEF. 1952. irreg. DM.8 per no. Rheinisch-Westfaelisches Institut fuer Wirtschaftsforschung, Essen, Hohenzollernstr. 1-3, 45128 Essen, Germany. TEL 49-201-8149-0. FAX 49-201-8149200. E-mail: schmidtj@rwi-essen.de; URL: http://www.rwi-essen.de. circ. 400. (looseleaf format; back issues avail.) **Indexed:** ELLIS. **Document type:** academic/scholarly publication.

338.7   II
RAJASTHAN STATE WAREHOUSING CORPORATION. ANNUAL REPORT AND ACCOUNTS. (Text in English) a. Rajasthan State Warehousing Corporation, Govind Bhavan, Subhash Marg, C-Scheme, Jaipur 1, India. stat.

338.9   RU   ISSN 0131-8330
REGIONAL'NAYA NAUKA O RAZMESHCHENII PROIZVODITEL'NYKH SIL;* sbornik referativnykh rabot. irreg. Rossiiskaya Akademiya Nauk, Sibirskoe Otdelenie, Institut Ekonomiki i Organizatsii Promychlennogo Proizvodstva, Pr. Akademika Lavrenteva 17, 640090 Novosibirsk, Russia. illus.

REHABILITATION INDUSTRIES CORPORATION. ANNUAL REPORT. see *EDUCATION — Special Education And Rehabilitation*

338   US
RENTAL PRODUCT NEWS. 1978. 7/yr. $48 (Canada and Mexico $66; elsewhere $84) (effective 1997). Johnson Hill Press, Inc. (Subsidiary of: Cygnus Publishing), 1233 Janesville Ave., Ft. Atkinson, WI 53538. TEL 920-563-6388. FAX 920-563-1699. Ed. Jennifer Lescohier; Pub. David Davel. adv. contact: David Davel. circ. 20,500 (controlled). **Former titles:** Rental (ISSN 0898-7106); Rental Product News (ISSN 0163-3112)
Description: Provides a complete source of product news and information for businesses involved in construction, industrial equipment, lawn maintenance gear and do-it-yourself tools.

338 650   FR   ISSN 0080-1089
REPERTOIRE DICTIONNAIRE INDUSTRIEL. 1956. a. 4550 F. Service de Renseignements du Repertoire Industriel, 18, rue Leon, 75018 Paris, France. TEL 42-54-52-52. adv.

784   US   ISSN 0360-7348
ML1
REPLAY; a monthly publication for the coin-operated amusement machine industry. Key Title: RePlay Magazine. 1975. m. $65 (Canada & Mexico $85; elsewhere $220 by airmail). Replay Publishing, Inc., Box 2550, Woodland Hills, CA 91365. TEL 818-347-3820. FAX 818-347-2112. E-mail: replayol@aol.com; URL: http://www.replaymag.com. Ed. Marcus Webb; Pub. Ed Adlum. adv. contact: Barry Zweben. illus. circ. 5,900. **Document type:** trade publication.

REPRESENTATIVE. see *AGRICULTURE — Agricultural Equipment*

338.767   II   ISSN 0304-811X
HD9745.I44
REPUBLIC FORGE COMPANY. ANNUAL REPORT. Key Title: Annual Report - Republic Forge Company. (Text in English) 14th, 1971. a. Republic Forge Company, Maula Ali, Hyderabad 40, India. stat.

RESEARCH DISCLOSURE. see *PATENTS, TRADEMARKS AND COPYRIGHTS*

338.5   EI   ISSN 0378-4479
HC241.2
RESULTS OF THE BUSINESS SURVEY CARRIED OUT AMONG MANAGEMENTS IN THE COMMUNITY. (Text in Dutch, English, French, German and Italian) 1962. m. $130. (Commission of the European Communities) Office for Official Publications of the European Communities, L-2985 Luxembourg, Luxembourg. (Dist. in the U.S. by: Unipub, 4611-F Assembly Dr., Lanham, MD 20706-4391. TEL 800-274-4888. FAX 301-459-0056) **Indexed:** EC Ind., IIS.
—BLDSC (7780.308000).
Formerly: Results of the Business Survey Carried Out Among Heads of Enterprises in the Community (ISSN 0034-5857)

330.9 658.8   UK
RETAIL TECHNOLOGY: A WORLD SURVEY. irreg. £3950 (U.S. $7,900). Euromonitor, 60-61 Britton St., London EC1M 5NA, England. TEL 44-171-251-8024. FAX 44-171-608-3149. E-mail: info@euromonitor.com; URL: http://www.euromonitor.com. (Addr. in Americas: Euromonitor International, 122 S. Michigan Ave., Ste. 1200, Chicago, IL 60603. TEL 312-922-1115. FAX 312-922-1157) charts, stat.
Description: Covers supplier and retailer profiles and studies on operating factors and new technology. Includes analyses of the market with background information and attention to emerging markets.

338   CK   ISSN 0034-8686
HC10
REVISTA DE PLANEACION Y DESARROLLO. Variant title: Planeacion y Desarrollo. 1969. irreg. $5. Departamento Nacional de Planeacion, Biblioteca, Calle 26, No. 13-19, 2o piso, Bogota, D.E., Colombia. circ. 2,000. **Indexed:** Amer.Hist.& Life (1969-1972), Hisp.Amer.Per.Ind. (1970-), Hist.Abstr. (1969-1972), IBR, Int.Lab.Doc., P.A.I.S.For.Lang.Ind.

REVUE D'ECONOMIE INDUSTRIELLE. see *BUSINESS AND ECONOMICS — Economic Situation And Conditions*

RIVISTA DELLE SOCIETA. see *LAW — Constitutional Law*

RIVISTA DI DIRITTO INDUSTRIALE. see *PATENTS, TRADEMARKS AND COPYRIGHTS*

RUMANIA. COMISIA NATIONALA PENTRU STATISTICA. BULETIN STATISTIC INDUSTRIE/RUMANIA. NATIONAL COMMISSION FOR STATISTICS. STATISTICAL BULLETIN - INDUSTRY. see *BUSINESS AND ECONOMICS* — Abstracting, Bibliographies, Statistics

338   IT
S L - RIVISTA DI ORGANIZZAZIONE. 4/yr. Via E. Cornalia 19, 20124 Milan, Italy. TEL 2-66-92-908. FAX 2-66-98-75-92. Ed. Ennio Baldini. circ. 23,000.

690 658.2   US   ISSN 0270-8779
SALES PROSPECTOR.* (In 14 U.S. regional editions) 1958. m. $495 for one regional edition. Prospector Research Services, Inc., Box 185, Lake Bluff, IL 60044-0185. **Document type:** trade publication, newsletter.
Incorporates: Commercial Expansion Reporter (ISSN 0010-2954)
Description: Reports on expansions and new construction in business, industry, retail outlets, institutions and hotels.

SAMSOM BESLOTEN VENNOOTSCHAPPEN MET BEPERKTE AANSPRAKELIJKHEID. see *BUSINESS AND ECONOMICS*

338   BE   ISSN 0778-6158
SAMSOM SUBSIDIE-INFO. (Text in Flemish) 1990. s-m. 4770 BEF. C E D Samsom (Subsidiary of: Wolters Samsom Belgie n.v.), Kouterveld 14, B-1831 Diegem, Belgium. TEL 32-2-7231111.
Description: Highlights sources of financing and support measures.

338   SZ
SCHWEIZER INDUSTRIE. 1988. q. 75 SFr. Verlag Schweizer Journal AG, Kreuzstr. 11, CH-8712 Staefa, Switzerland. Ed. Dr. Hans Frey. **Document type:** trade publication.

338   SZ
SCHWEIZER INDUSTRIE UND VERKEHRS REVUE. q. Verlag Hugo Zwerger, Stationsstr. 9, Postfach, CH-8355 Aadorf, Switzerland. TEL 052-473738. Ed. H. Zwerger. circ. 4,000.

338   CG   ISSN 0377-5135
T175   CODEN: STICD8
SCIENCES, TECHNIQUES, INFORMATIONS C R I A C. irreg. Centre de Recherches Industrielles en Afrique Centrale, B.P. 54, Lubumbashi, Democratic Republic of the Congo. illus.
Formerly: Centre de Recherche Industrielles en Afrique Centrale. Bulletin d'Information.

338   GW   ISSN 0048-9735
SCOPE; Industrie-Magazin fuer Fuehrungskraefte. 1961. m. free. Verlag Hoppenstedt GmbH, Havelstr. 9, 64295 Darmstadt, Germany. TEL 49-6151-380-0. FAX 49-6151-380-360. Ed. Dieter Capelle. circ. 80,000. **Document type:** trade publication.
Formerly: Scope - Journal.

SECOM ANNUAL REPORT (YEAR). see *CRIMINOLOGY AND LAW ENFORCEMENT* — Security

338   SG
SENEGAL. MINISTERE DE L'ECONOMIE ET DES FINANCES. INDICE DES PRIX. m. free. Ministere de l'Economie et des Finances, Direction de la Statistique, B.P. 116, Dakar, Senegal. TEL 221-21-03-01. **Document type:** government publication.

338   SG
SENEGAL. MINISTERE DE L'ECONOMIE ET DES FINANCES. INDICE ET LA PRODUCTION INDUSTRIELLE. q. 2000 Fr.CFA (foreign 4000Fr.CFA). Ministere de l'Economie et des Finances, Direction de la Statistique, B.P. 116, Dakar, Senegal. TEL 221-21-03-01. **Document type:** government publication.

338   US   ISSN 1058-1626
HD9981.1
SERVICE INDUSTRIES U S A; industry analyses, statistics and leading organizations. 1992. biennial. Gale Research, 835 Penobscot Bldg., 645 Griswold St., Detroit, MI 48226-4094. TEL 313-961-2242; 800-877-4253. FAX 800-414-5043. E-mail: daniel__snyder@gale.com. Ed. Arsen J. Darnay.

338   FR
SERVICES-MARCHE COMMUN EUROPEEN. 1965. q. (with 4 supplements). 36 F.($8) for 3 years. Services G.E.C.E., 23 rue de l'Esperance, 75013 Paris, France. adv. bk.rev. circ. 40,000. (also avail. in magnetic tape)

658   JA
SEVEN - ELEVEN JAPAN. (YEAR) ANNUAL REPORT. (Text in English) 1974. a. Seven - Eleven Japan Co., Ltd. (Subsidiary of: Ito-Yokado Co., Ltd.), 1-4 Shiba Koen 4-chome, Minato-ku, Tokyo 105, Japan. TEL 03-3459-3711. FAX 03-3438-3724. charts; illus.; mkt.; stat. **Document type:** corporate report.

338   CC
SHANGHAI ZHILIANG/SHANGHAI QUALITY. (Text in Chinese) bi-m. Shanghai Zhiliang Guanli Xiehui - Shanghai Quality Administration Society, 988 Yan'an Zhonglu, Shanghai 200040, People's Republic of China. TEL 2475711. Ed. Guan Zhaokang.

338   US
SHAVINGS FROM THE CHRONICLE OF THE EARLY AMERICAN INDUSTRIES ASSOCIATION. 1971. 6/yr. $30 includes Chronicle. Early American Industries Association, 167 Bakerville Rd., S. Dartmouth, MA 02748-0143. bk.rev. circ. 3,300. (reprint service avail. from UMI) **Document type:** newsletter.

338   CH
SHIH TAI CHI YEH/TIMES ENTERPRISE. (Text in Chinese; some articles in English) 1973. m. $20. Times Enterprise Corp., 219 Hsining S. Rd., 10th Fl., Taipei, Taiwan, Republic of China. illus.

SIGNALS. see *BUSINESS AND ECONOMICS* — Small Business

SINERGIE; rivista di studi e ricerche. see *BUSINESS AND ECONOMICS* — Management

338.9   SI   ISSN 0080-9683
HC445.8
SINGAPORE. ECONOMIC DEVELOPMENT BOARD. ANNUAL REPORT. (Text in English) 1962. a. price varies. Economic Development Board, 250 N. Bridge Rd., 24-00 Raffles City Tower, Singapore 0617, Singapore. TEL 336-2288. Ed.Bd. circ. 10,000.

338   SI
TA368
SINGAPORE STANDARDS CATALOGUE. (Text in English) 1977. biennial. Singapore Productivity and Standards Board, One Science Park Dr., Singapore Science Park, Singapore 118221, Singapore. TEL 65-7729786. FAX 65-7761280. circ. 1,500. **Document type:** catalog.

333   US   ISSN 1080-7799
HD58
SITE SELECTION. 1956. bi-m. $20 per vol., $75 per set. Conway Data, Inc., 35 Technology Pkwy., Ste. 150, Norcross, GA 30092. TEL 770-446-6996. FAX 770-263-8825. TELEX 80-4468ATL. URL: http://www.sitenet.com. Ed. Jack C. Lyne. adv.; illus.; cum.index: 1956-1994. circ. 40,500. (also avail. in microform from UMI; reprint service avail. from ISI, UMI) **Indexed:** B.P.I., BPIA, Bus.Ind., Manage.Cont., PROMT, Tr.& Indus.Ind. **Document type:** trade publication.
—BLDSC (8286.424950); KR SourceOne; UMI; UnCover. **CCC**.
Formerly (until 1994): Site Selection and Industrial Development (ISSN 1041-3073); Incorporates: Industrial Development (US 0192-0901); Which was formerly: Industrial Development and Manufacturers Record (US 0097-3033); Which was formed by the merger of: Manufacturers Record; Industrial Development; Former titles: Site Selection Handbook (US 0080-9810); Industrial Development's Site Selection Handbook (US 0149-9810).
Description: Focuses on business expansion planning with original research and analysis, interviews, case studies and industry reports. Features major reference guides to new plant construction, area economic development agencies, R&D centers, and office-industrial parks. Covers quality of life and political-business climates.

SITEWORLD. see *BUSINESS AND ECONOMICS* — International Development And Assistance

338   NO   ISSN 0333-3868
SKATTEBETALEREN. 1952. 7/yr. NOK 145 (effective 1997). Skattebetalerforeningen, P.O. Box 213 Sentrum, N-0103 Oslo, Norway. TEL 47-22-42-07-27. FAX 47-22-33-71-80. Ed. Erik Stenbeck. adv.: B&W page NOK 7500, color page NOK 17500. bk.rev. circ. 24,000. **Document type:** consumer publication.
Formerly: Skatt og Budsjett.

338   SG
SOCIETE NATIONALE D'ETUDE ET DE PROMOTION INDUSTRIELLE. BULLETIN D'INFORMATION INDUSTRIELLE. bi-m. 3000 Fr.CFA. Societe Nationale d'Etude et de Promotion Industrielle, 14, rue Maunoury, B.P. 100, Dakar, Senegal.

338   US   ISSN 1055-906X
SORKINS DIRECTORY OF BUSINESS & GOVERNMENT (CHICAGO EDITION). Sorkins Directory of Business & Government (St. Louis Edition) (ISSN 0748-0458); Sorkins Directory of Business & Government (Kansas City Edition) (ISSN 0894-1033) 1991. a. (print edition); q. (electronic editions). $1550 for Chicago edition (electronic $1895); St. Louis edition $845 (electronic $1295); Kansas City edition $845 (electronic $1295). Sorkins Directories, Inc., 1001 Craig Rd., Ste. 260, St. Louis, MO 63146. TEL 314-872-2101; 800-758-3228. FAX 314-872-2102. URL: http://www.sorkins.com. Eds. Pam & Murray Sorkin; Pubs. Pam & Murray Sorkin. adv. contact: Darin Tubb. (also avail. in diskette format) **Document type:** directory.
●Also available online.
Also available on CD-ROM.
Description: Features profiles of major companies in the region, and their executives. Includes government and non-profit organizations.

338 330.968   SA   ISSN 1023-652X
SOUTH AFRICAN INDUSTRY. 1994. m. £240($399) Ion Publishers, P.O. Box 1951, Houghton 2041, South Africa. Ed. Alex van den Heever. **Indexed:** Ind.S.A.Per.

SOUTHERN FARM EQUIPMENT MANUFACTURERS. NEWSLETTER. see *AGRICULTURE* — Agricultural Equipment

338   SP
SPAIN. MINISTERIO DE INDUSTRIA. RESULTADOS DE LA ENCUESTA DE COYUNTURA INDUSTRIAL: SECTOR INDUSTRIAL. 1963. irreg. included with the review Economia Industrial. Ministerio de Industria, Paseo de la Castellana 160, Madrid 28046, Spain. bk.rev. circ. 10,000.

SPORTING GOODS AGENTS ASSOCIATION. MEMBERSHIP ROSTER. see *SPORTS AND GAMES*

STANDARD & POOR'S REGISTER OF CORPORATIONS, DIRECTORS AND EXECUTIVES. see *BUSINESS AND ECONOMICS* — Management

338 794.8   US   ISSN 0739-1048
STAR TECH JOURNAL. 1979. m. $81. Star Tech Journal, Inc., Box 35, Medford, NJ 08055. TEL 609-654-5544. FAX 609-654-1441. E-mail: info@startechjournal.com; URL: http://www.cyberenet.net/~startech. Ed. James Calore; Pub. James Calore. adv. circ. 4,500. **Document type:** trade publication.
Description: Provides information on the technology of the coin-op entertainment industry.

STATE CAPITALS. ECONOMIC DEVELOPMENT. see *PUBLIC ADMINISTRATION*

338   GR   ISSN 0072-7458
HC295
STATE OF GREEK INDUSTRY IN (YEAR). (Text in English) 1940-1977; resumed 1984. a. free. Federation of Greek Industries, 5 Xenophontos Str., 105 57 Athens, Greece. circ. 4,000.

BUSINESS AND ECONOMICS — PRODUCTION OF GOODS AND SERVICES

338 HU ISSN 1215-2463
HD28
STRUKTURAK, SZERVEZETEK, STRATEGIAK. (Editions in English, Hungarian) 1961. q. 500 Ft.($30) M T A Ipar-es Vallalatgazdasag-kutato Intezet - Research Institute of Industrial Economics, Budaorsi ut. 45, 1112 Budapest, Hungary. TEL 361-1853-774. FAX 361-1853-779. Ed. Adam Torok. bk.rev.; stat. circ. 1,500. **Document type:** academic/scholarly publication.
—BLDSC (8479.475000).
Former titles (until 1990): Ipargazdasagi Szemle (ISSN 0133-6452); (until 1970): Magyar Tudomanyos Akademia. Ipargazdasagtani Kutatocsoport (Year) (ISSN 0200-1934).

STUDIES IN INDUSTRIAL ORGANIZATION. see *BUSINESS AND ECONOMICS — Economic Systems And Theories, Economic History*

STUDIES IN PRODUCTION AND ENGINEERING ECONOMICS. see *BUSINESS AND ECONOMICS*

338 SP
SUMINISTROS INDUSTRIALES. 6/yr. Via Augusta 59, 8o Of. 812, 08006 Barcelona, Spain. TEL 3-2378865. FAX 3-4158688. Ed. Salvador Beltran Nunez. circ. 5,000.
Description: Covers professional hardware and associated industries.

SUPPLY, DISTRIBUTION, MANUFACTURING & SERVICE; supply and service companies & equipment manufacturers. see *PETROLEUM AND GAS*

338 IS ISSN 0081-9743
SURVEYS AND DEVELOPMENT PLANS OF INDUSTRY IN ISRAEL/HATA'ASIYAH BE-YISRAEL. (Editions in English, Hebrew) 1964. a. free. Ministry of Industry and Trade, Jerusalem, Israel. Ed. H. Ross. circ. 1,000. **Document type:** government publication.
Formerly: Survey of Industry in Israel.

338 SW ISSN 0281-6989
SVENSKT NAERINGSLIV. 1984. q. SEK 120 (effective 1990). Svenskt Naeringsliv, P.O. Box 19064, S-400 12 Goeteborg, Sweden.

SVERIGES STOERSTA FOERETAG/LARGEST COMPANIES IN SWEDEN; med nyckeltal foer naeringslivet under (aar); with financial data for Swedish companies in (year). see *BUSINESS AND ECONOMICS — Trade And Industrial Directories*

T V NEWS. see *COMMUNICATIONS — Television And Cable*

338 CH ISSN 0039-9108
TAIWAN INDUSTRIAL PANORAMA. 1962. m. free. Ministry of Economic Affairs, Industrial Development & Investment Center, 7 Roosevelt Rd., Sec. 1, 10th Fl., Taipei, Taiwan, Republic of China. TEL 02-3947213. FAX 02-3926835. TELEX 10634-INVEST. Ed. Ming Ching Su. stat. circ. 5,000. Indexed: Key to Econ.Sci.

TAIWAN SPORTS GOODS BUYER'S GUIDE. see *SPORTS AND GAMES*

TAIWAN STATIONERY AND OFFICE PRODUCTS BUYER'S GUIDE. see *BUSINESS AND ECONOMICS — Office Equipment And Services*

TAIWAN TOY BUYER'S GUIDE. see *GIFTWARE AND TOYS*

338 II
TAMIL NADU INDUSTRIAL DEVELOPMENT CORPORATION. ANNUAL REPORT. (Report year ends Mar. 31) (Text in English) 7th edt., 1972. a. Tamil Nadu Industrial Development Corporation, Local Library Authority Building, 3rd Fl., 150-A Anna Salai, Madras, India. illus.; stat. **Document type:** corporate report.

TAMIL NADU TOURISM DEVELOPMENT CORPORATION. ANNUAL REPORT. see *TRAVEL AND TOURISM*

338.5 JA ISSN 0916-670X
HC462.9
TANKAN - SHORT-TERM ECONOMIC SURVEY OF ENTERPRISES IN JAPAN; records and forecasts. (Text in Japanese) 1957. q. 1200 Yen per no. Bank of Japan, Research and Statistics Department - Nippon Ginko, c/o Public Relations Department, 2-1-1 Hongoku-Cho, Nihonbashi, Chuo-ku, Tokyo 103, Japan. TEL 81-3-3279-1111.
FAX 81-3-5203-8703. TELEX JPTCO J27161. (Dist. by: Tokiwa Sohgoh Service Co., Ltd., Kyodo Bldg., 2-4, 3-chome, Hongokucho, Chuo-ku, Tokyo 103, Japan. TEL 81-3-3270-5713. FAX 81-33270-5710; Overseas dist. by: Japan Publications Trading Co., Ltd., Book Export No.2 Dept., P.O. Box 5030 Tokyo International, Tokyo 100-31, Japan) stat. circ. 250. pp./issue: 190. (microform)
Formerly (until 1990): Kigyo Tanki Keizai Kansoku Chosa - Short-Term Economic Survey of Enterprises in Japan (ISSN 0387-0642); Which incorporates: Shuyo Kigyo Tanki Keizai Kansoku Chosa - Short-Term Economic Survey of Principal Enterprises in Japan (ISSN 0387-0634); Supersedes (in 1974): Shuyo Kigyo, Chusho Kigyo Tanki Keizai Kansoku (ISSN 0387-0626); Which was formed by the 1970 merger of: Shuyo Kigyo Tanki Keizai Kansoku (ISSN 0549-3188) and Chusho Kigyo Tanki Keizai Kansoku (ISSN 0387-0618); Which was formerly (until 1966): Chusho Kigyo no Gyokyo Yosoku (ISSN 0387-060X).
Description: Reports quarterly business surveys tracing short-term economic trends.

338 TZ
TANZANIA. PLANNING COMMISSION. MACRO PLANNING DEPARTMENT. HALI YA UCHUMI WA TAIFA - ANNUAL ECONOMIC SURVEY. 1973. a. $3. Planning Commission, Macro Planning Department, P.O. Box 9242, Dar es Salaam, Tanzania. TEL 255-51-29418. TELEX 41651 DEPLAN TZ. (Subscr. to: Government Publications Agency, P.O. Box 1801, Dar es Salaam, Tanzania) stat. circ. 1,000. **Document type:** government publication.
Former titles: Tanzania. Ministry of Planning and Economic Affairs. Hali Ya Uchumi Wa Taifa - Annual Economic Survey; Tanzania. Ministry of Economic Affairs and Development Planning. Hali Ya Uchumi Wa Taifa - Annual Economic Survey.

322 US ISSN 1065-3015
TAPE - DISC BUSINESS. 1987. m. $74. Knowledge Industry Publications, Inc., 701 Westchester Ave., White Plains, NY 10604-3002.
TEL 914-328-9157. FAX 914-328-9093. Ed. Pat Casey; Pub. Barbara Stockwell. R&P contact: Janet Moore. adv. contact: Pam King. charts; illus.; stat. circ. 8,000. (back issues avail.) **Document type:** trade publication.
●Also available online. Vendor(s): Information Access Co.
—KR SourceOne. **CCC.**
Description: News publications on magnetic and optical media duplication.

338 US ISSN 1051-1636
TS155.A1
TARGET (WHEELING); innovation at work. 1985. 5/yr. membership only; free to libraries. Association for Manufacturing Excellence, 380 W. Palatine Rd., Wheeling, IL 60090-5863. TEL 847-520-3282. FAX 847-520-0163. Ed. Robert W. Hall. R&P contact: JoAnn Weitzenfled. bk.rev.; cum.index: 1983-1994. circ. 6,500. (back issues avail.) **Document type:** trade publication.

338 JA ISSN 0911-5544
T1
TECHNO JAPAN; a monthly survey of Japanese technology and industry. (Text in English) 1968. m. 24000 Yen. (Fuji Marketing Research Co., Ltd. - Fuji Gaikoku Shijo Chosa K.K.) Fuji Technology Press Ltd., Daini Bldg., 11-17 Toranomon, 1-chome, Minato-ku, Tokyo 105, Japan.
TEL 81-3-3508-0051. FAX 81-3-592-0648. Ed. Keiji Hayashi. adv.; s-a. index. circ. 18,756. (back issues avail.) Indexed: Abstr.J.Earthq.Eng., JCT, JTA. —BLDSC (8755.460800); CISTI; SWETS.
Formerly (until 1985): Technocrat (ISSN 0040-1609)

TECHNOLOGY, RISK AND SOCIETY; an international series in risk analysis. see *BUSINESS AND ECONOMICS — Economic Systems And Theories, Economic History*

TECNOINDUSTRIA. see *TECHNOLOGY: COMPREHENSIVE WORKS*

338.3 KR ISSN 0233-9897
TEKHNICHESKII PROGRESS I EFFEKTIVNOST' PROIZVODSTVA. (Subseries of: Kharkivskyi Politekhnichnyi Instytut. Vestnik) (Text in Russian) irreg. price varies. Kharkivskyi Politekhnichnyi Instytut, Ul. Frunze 21, Kharkov 310002, Ukraine. illus.
Formerly (until 1981): Ekonomika Promyslovosti.

TEKNIK OCH KULTUR. see *TECHNOLOGY: COMPREHENSIVE WORKS*

332 338 UK ISSN 0267-1484
TELECOM MARKETS. 1984. fortn. £665($997) Financial Times Telecoms & Media Publishing (Subsidiary of: Financial Times Group), Maple House, 149 Tottenham Court Rd., London W1P 9LL, England. TEL 44-171-896-2234.
FAX 44-171-896-2256. Ed. Neil McCartney; Pub. Helen Nicol. (also avail. in microform from UMI) **Document type:** newsletter.
●Also available online. Vendor(s): Data-Star, Information Access Co., Lexis-Nexis.
—BLDSC (3927.027000); SWETS; UMI.
Description: Provides information and analysis on telecommunications markets: convergence between deregulation and free markets, telephony and computing, voice, image and data, state monopoly, and private capital.

338 BL ISSN 0495-0879
TENDENCIA. 1973. m. $26. Bloch Editores S.A., Rua do Russell, 766-804, 22210-000 Rio de Janeiro, RJ, Brazil. TEL 021-5554000. FAX 021-2059998. TELEX 2121525 BLOC. Ed. Antonio Cunha. illus. circ. 50,000. **Document type:** consumer publication.

338 AT ISSN 0812-2288
TENDERS AUSTRALIA. 1905. w. Aus.$244. Thomson Business Publishing, 47 Chippen St., Chippendale, N.S.W. 2008, Australia. TEL 02-699-2411.
FAX 02-698-3920. Ed. Val Pablovic. adv. circ. 2,215.
Formerly: Tenders (ISSN 0040-3113)

338 US ISSN 0040-4365
TEXAS INDUSTRIAL EXPANSION. (Supplement to: Directory of Texas Manufacturers) 1950. m. $50 (effective 1995). University of Texas at Austin, Bureau of Business Research, Box 7459, Austin, TX 78713. TEL 512-471-1616. FAX 512-471-1063. E-mail: dhardy@mail.utexas.edu. Ed. Elaine Pinckard. circ. 3,200. (reprint service avail. from UMI) **Document type:** newsletter.
—CCC.
Description: Tracks information on new and expanding manufacturing plants in Texas.

338 US
TEXAS INDUSTRIAL PRODUCTION INDEX. 1958. m. free. Federal Reserve Bank of Dallas, Sta. K, Dallas, TX 75222. TEL 214-651-6289. circ. 1,000.
Description: Measures the output of the industrial sector of the Texas economy.

THAI JOURNAL OF DEVELOPMENT ADMINISTRATION. see *PUBLIC ADMINISTRATION*

TIE LINES. see *CLOTHING TRADE*

TIME MANAGEMENT. see *BUSINESS AND ECONOMICS — Personnel Management*

650 UK ISSN 0082-4429
TIMES 1000; lists leading companies in Britain and overseas. 1966. a. £29.50. Times Books Ltd., 77-85 Fulham Palace Rd., Hammersmith, London W6 8JB, England. TEL 081-741-7070.
FAX 081-307-4440. Ed. Margaret Allen. adv. circ. 9,000. **Document type:** directory.
—BLDSC (8855.300000).

338 621.9 US
TOOLING AND MANUFACTURING ASSOCIATION. PURCHASING GUIDE. biennial. $125 (free to qualified personnel). Tooling and Manufacturing Association, 1177 S. Dee Rd., Park Ridge, IL 60068. TEL 708-825-1120. Ed. Jeffrey Hayes. adv. circ. 18,000. **Document type:** directory.
Formerly: Tool and Die Institute Purchasing Guide

BUSINESS AND ECONOMICS — PRODUCTION OF GOODS AND SERVICES

338 664   AT
TOOWOOMBA - QUEENSLAND'S GROWTH CENTRE. irreg. Aus.$2. Downs Printing Co., Margaret St., Toowoomba, Qld., Australia. TEL 324011.
   Description: Includes a brief history of the area. Focuses on educational facilities and industries.

338   SA   ISSN 0563-8895
TOP COMPANIES. (Supplement to: Financial Mail) 1967. a. Times Media Limited, P.O. Box 1138, Johannesburg 2000, South Africa. TEL 27-11-497-2711. FAX 27-11-834-1408. illus. circ. 35,000.
   Description: Provides detailed financial and production information on South Africa's top 300 industrial companies, with additional information on other sectors of the economy, including mining, life insurance, health care, banking and the financial markets.

338   PK   ISSN 0041-0411
HF41
TRADE CHRONICLE; Pakistan's leading magazine of commerce, industry and public affairs. (Text in English) 1953. m. $90. Chronicle Publications, P.O. Box 5257, Iftikhar Chambers, Altaf Hussain Rd., Karachi 74000, Pakistan. TEL 92-21-218129. FAX 92-21-219190. Ed. Abdul Rauf Siddiqi. adv. contact: Mushtaq Ali. bk.rev.; illus.; mkt.; pat.; tr.lit.; tr.mk.; circ. 1,100 (paid); 5,500 (controlled). **Document type:** trade publication.

TRADEWINDS. see SPORTS AND GAMES — Outdoor Life

338   MX   ISSN 0041-1124
TRANSFORMACION. 1957. m. Mex.$35. Camara Nacional de la Industria de Transformacion, Apdo. Postal 60-468, Av. San Antonio 256, 03849 Mexico, D.F., Mexico. TEL 5-563-3500. Ed. Iris Arzate Rios. adv.; bk.rev.; charts; illus.; stat. circ. 25,000.

338.9   TU   ISSN 0082-6944
TURKEY. DEVLET PLANAMA TESKILATI. YILI PROGRAMI UCUNCU BES YIL/TURKEY. STATE PLANNING ORGANIZATION. ANNUAL PROGRAM OF THE FIVE YEAR DEVELOPMENT PLAN. 1963. a. State Planning Organization - Devlet Planlama Teskilati, Ankara, Turkey. circ. 5,000.

338   UK
U K S M A COUNCIL'S REPORT AND FINANCIAL STATEMENTS. a. U K Spring Manufacturers' Association, Henry St., Sheffield S3 7EQ, England. TEL 44-114-2760542. FAX 44-114-2760554. E-mail: uksma@uksma.org.uk. **Document type:** corporate report.
   Formerly (until 1996): S R A M A Council's Report and Financial Statements.

338   US
U S SURVEY OF BUSINESS EXPECTATIONS. 1947. q. $40. Dun & Bradstreet, Economic Analysis Department, 220 E. 42nd St., 9th Fl., New York, NY 10017-4717. FAX 212-883-3400. (Subscr. to: Box 1861, New York, NY 10017-1861) **Indexed:** SRI.
   Formerly: Business Expectations (ISSN 0007-7178)
   Description: Nationwide survey of 3,000 business executives regarding their expectations for sales, profits, prices, inventories, employment, new orders and exports in the upcoming quarter.

354   UG
UGANDA ESTIMATES OF DEVELOPMENT EXPENDITURES. a., latest 1977. Sh.20 price varies. Government Printer, Box 33, Entebbe, Uganda. (Subscr. to: Chief Government Statistician, Ministry of Planning and Economic Development, P.O. Box 7086, Kampala, Uganda)

338.094   DK
UGEMAGASINET INDUSTRIEN. 1900. 40/yr. DKK 600 to non-members. Dansk Industri (DI) - Confederation of Danish Industries, DK-1787 Copenhagen V, Denmark. TEL 45-33-77-33-77. FAX 45-33-77-37-70. TELEX 1122 17 DI DK. Ed. Poul Scheuer. adv.; bk.rev.; charts; illus.; circ. 14,600 (controlled). **Document type:** newsletter, trade publication.
   Former titles (until 1993): Industrien (Ugebrevet) (ISSN 0907-7332); (until 1992): Industriens Ugebrev (ISSN 0906-9267); (until 1991): Dansk Industri (ISSN 0045-9623); (until 1972): Tidsskrift for Industri (ISSN 0040-7070)
   Description: Focuses on Danish industry and economy as well as worldwide markets as they relate to Danish commerce.

UNIVERSITY OF YORK. CENTRE FOR DEFENCE ECONOMICS. RESEARCH MONOGRAPH SERIES. see MILITARY

UNIWERSYTET GDANSKI. WYDZIAL EKONOMIKI PRODUKCJI. ZESZYTY NAUKOWE. EKONOMIKA I ORGANIZACJA TURYSTYKI I USLUG. see TRAVEL AND TOURISM

338   PL   ISSN 0860-0171
UNIWERSYTET GDANSKI. WYDZIAL EKONOMIKI PRODUKCJI. ZESZYTY NAUKOWE. FINANSE I RACHUNEK EKONOMICZNY (NO.). (Text in Polish; summaries in English and Russian) 1974. irreg., latest no.19. price varies. Uniwersytet Gdanski, Wydzial Ekonomiki Produkcji, c/o Biblioteka Glowna, Ul. Armii Krajowej 110, 81-824 Sopot, Poland. TEL 51-0061. TELEX 051 2247 BMOR PL. (Dist. by: Ars Polona-Ruch, Krakowskie Przedmiescie 7, 00-680 Warsaw, Poland) **Document type:** academic/scholarly publication.
—BLDSC (9512.432600).
   Formerly (until 1980): Uniwersytet Gdanski. Wydzial Ekonomiki Produkcji. Zeszyty Naukowe. Zagadnienia Finansowe (ISSN 0208-4775)
   Description: Covers theoretical and practical financial problems (budget, banks, enterprises), economic analysis and planning in economy, reports on scientific conferences, and chronicle of the Chair of Finances.

338   PL   ISSN 0208-4783
UNIWERSYTET GDANSKI. WYDZIAL EKONOMIKI PRODUKCJI. ZESZYTY NAUKOWE. ZAGADNIENIA EKONOMIKI PRZEMYSLU. (Text in Polish; summaries in English and Russian) 1972. irreg., latest no.15. price varies. Uniwersytet Gdanski, Wydzial Ekonomiki Produkcji, c/o Biblioteka Glowna, Ul. Armii Krajowej 110, 81-824 Sopot, Poland. TEL 51-0061. TELEX 051 2247 BMOR PL. (Dist. by: Ars Polona-Ruch, Krakowskie Przedmiescie 7, 00-680 Warsaw, Poland) Ed. Jan Wojewnik. illus. **Document type:** academic/scholarly publication.
—BLDSC (9512.433270).
   Description: Covers development problems of programming industry, such as production efficiency, fixed assets, quality of production, and prices.

338   MY   ISSN 0126-8937
USAHALUAN. (Text in English) 1972. 4/yr. free. Malaysian Industrial Development Finance Berhad, Bangunan MIDF, Jalan Tun Razak, Kuala Lumpur, Malaysia. TEL 60-3-2613908. FAX 60-3-2613908. TELEX MIDFKL MA 30534. Ed. Bd. adv.; charts; illus. circ. 3,000.
   Formerly: M I D F Reports.

338   BE
USINE/BEDRIJF. (Text in Dutch, French) 1924. 10/yr. 1750 BEF. Benefalux S.A., Rue Jorez 21-23, 1070 Brussels, Belgium. TEL 32-2-5560356. FAX 32-2-5230355. Ed. B. Droulez. adv.; bk.rev. circ. 17,000. **Document type:** trade publication.

330   SW   ISSN 0503-6127
VAART EKONOMISKA LAEGE. 1948. a. SEK 180 (effective 1989). Sparfraemjandet, P.O. Box 16425, S-103 27 Stockholm, Sweden.

338   FI   ISSN 0356-8091
VALTIONYHTIOT. 1969. a. FIM 35. Valtionyhtioiden Neuvottelukunta, Aleksanterinkatu 10, Helsinki 17, Finland. Wd. Ritva Hainari. circ. 8,000.

338   SW   ISSN 0506-4406
HD70.S8
VECKANS AFFAERER; den aktuella affarstidningen. (Supplement avail.: Maanadens Affaerer) 1965. w. SEK 1038 (effective 1995). Affaersfoerlaget, P.O. Box 3188, S-103 63 Stockholm, Sweden. Ed. Bengt Ericson. adv.; charts; illus.; stat. circ. 33,800.
Indexed: Paper & Bd.Abstr.

338   US
HC107.V53
VERMONT ECONOMIC DEVELOPMENT AUTHORITY. ANNUAL REPORT. * 1975. a. free. Economic Development Authority, 58 E. State St., Montpelier, VT 05602-3043. TEL 802-223-7226. FAX 802-223-4205. circ. 400 (controlled). **Document type:** corporate report, government publication.
   Formerly: Vermont Industrial Development Authority. Annual Report (ISSN 0363-2067)

338   US
VERMONT MANUFACTURING & WHOLESALE - DISTRIBUTOR DIRECTORY. a. $55 (effective 1997). Tower Publishing Co., 588 Saco Rd., Standish, ME 04084. TEL 207-642-5400; 800-969-8693. FAX 207-642-5463. Ed. Mary Ann Hildreth; Pub. Michael L. Lyons. adv. **Document type:** directory.
   Former titles: Vermont Manufacturing Directory & Vermont Business Phone Book and Manufacturers Directory; Vermont Marketing Directory.
   Description: Lists more than 1,000 manufacturing and wholesale firms in Vermont in three sections: alphabetical, geographical and product.

338   NP
VIKAS: NEPAL JOURNAL OF DEVELOPMENT. (Text in English) 1975. s-a. National Planning Commission, Secretariat, Kathmandu, Nepal.

338   GR   ISSN 0042-6415
VIOMICHANIKI EPITHEORISSIS; miniaio oikonomiko periodiko. (Supplement avail.: Industrial Review) 1934. m. (11/yr.), plus 4 English-language supplements. Dr.9500($85) to individuals; institutions Dr.17500 (includes supplements); newsstand price: Dr.1000. 4 Zalokost St., 10671 Athens, Greece. TEL 30-1-3626360. FAX 30-1-3626388. Ed. Dimitris Karamanos; Pub. Alexandra C. Vovolini-Laskaridis. adv. contact: Maria F. Kelepouri. bk.rev.; charts; illus.; stat.; tr.lit.; tr.mk.; index; circ. 25,000 (paid). **Document type:** trade publication.
—BLDSC (9237.770000).
   Description: Covers Greek financial and political current events, industrial and technological advances.

VOLONTE DE L'INDUSTRIE, DU COMMERCE ET DES PRESTATAIRES DE SERVICES. see BUSINESS AND ECONOMICS — Domestic Commerce

338   BE   ISSN 0773-4778
VRAAG EN AANBOD. (Text in Dutch) 1954. w. 7000 BEF. Kluwer Business Press (Subsidiary of: Wolters Kluwer N.V.), Kouterveld 2, 1831 Diegem, Belgium. TEL 32-2-7231511. FAX 32-2-7231212. E-mail: joris.de.vroey@infoboard.be. Ed. Michel Verstrepen; Pub. Bernard Lefevre. adv. contact: Gisela Buggenhout. bk.rev. circ. 20,000. **Document type:** trade publication.

338   NE   ISSN 0165-3954
VRAAG & AANBOD. Regional edition: Vraag en Aanbod Regio Noord. Regional edition: Vraag en Aanbod Regio Oost. Regional edition: Vraag en Aanbod Regio West. Regional edition: Vraag en Aanbod Regio Zuid. (Supplements avail.: Bedrijfsgoed; Bedrijfsvervoer; Kwaliteitskrant; Wie Levert Merken (ISSN 0928-7930); Wie Levert Produkten en Diensten (ISSN 0928-7949); Wie Levert Regio) 1898. w. (Fri.). fl.299 (Belgium fl.345; elsewhere fl.550) (effective 1996). Kluwer BedrijfsInformatie B.V. (Subsidiary of: Wolters Kluwer N.V.), Postbus 23, 7400 GA Deventer, Netherlands. TEL 31-570-648705. FAX 31-570-643015. E-mail: 102212.3636@compuserve.com. Ed. D. van der Meulen. adv.: B&W page fl. 4395; trim 420 x 300; adv. contact: Ad Nuesink. circ. 20,000. (tabloid format) **Document type:** trade publication.
   Description: Covers news, market developments, technology, economics, management and entrepreneurial information for small and medium-sized industrial companies, commercial, construction and professional service firms.

VYAVASAYA KERALAM. see *BUSINESS AND ECONOMICS — Domestic Commerce*

W E P Z A NEWSLETTER. (World Export Processing Zones Association) see *BUSINESS AND ECONOMICS — International Commerce*

WASHINGTON DRUG LETTER (WASHINGTON, 1979). see *PHARMACY AND PHARMACOLOGY*

WHO OWNS WHOM. CONTINENTAL EUROPE. see *BUSINESS AND ECONOMICS — Management*

338 628.5   US
WIRELINE (ALEXANDRIA). q. membership only. American Wire Producers Association, 515 King St., Ste. 420, Alexandria, VA 22314-3137. TEL 703-549-6003. FAX 703-684-6048. (tabloid format; back issues avail.) **Document type:** newsletter.

658 340 338   GW   ISSN 0043-6151
WIRTSCHAFT UND WETTBEWERB; Zeitschrift fuer Kartellrecht, Wettbewerbsrecht und Marktorganisation. 1952. m. DM.396. Verlagsgruppe Handelsblatt GmbH, Kasernenstr. 67, 40213 Duesseldorf, Germany. TEL 49-211-8870. FAX 49-211-374955. (Subscr. to: Postfach 102717, 40018 Duesseldorf, Germany) Ed.Bd. adv.; bk.rev.; abstr.; bibl.; index. (reprint service avail. from UMI) **Indexed:** ELLIS, IBR, Key to Econ.Sci., P.A.I.S.For.Lang.Ind. **Document type:** bulletin. —BLDSC (9325.480000); SWETS. **CCC.**

WOOD LEADER. see *FORESTS AND FORESTRY — Lumber And Wood*

338   UK
WORLD MARKET FOR CONVENIENCE STORE RETAILING. irreg. £4500($8950) (effective 1997). Euromonitor, 60-61 Turnmill St., London EC1M 5NA, England. TEL 44-171-251-8024. FAX 44-171-608-3149. E-mail: info@euromonitor.com; URL: http://www.euromonitor.com. (U.S. subscr. to: Euromonitor International, 122 S. Michigan Ave., Ste. 1200, Chicago, IL 60603. TEL 800-577-3876. FAX 312-922-1157) **Document type:** directory.

WORLD MARKET FOR HOT DRINKS. see *BEVERAGES*

WORLD STEEL STATISTICS MONTHLY. see *METALLURGY — Abstracting, Bibliographies, Statistics*

338   UK   ISSN 0955-6060
WORLD'S NEW PRODUCTS. 1982. m. $425. World Business Publications Ltd., Britannia House, 4th Fl., 960 High Rd., London N12 9RY, England. TEL 44-181-446-5141. FAX 44-181-446-3659. Ed. George Mills. **Document type:** trade publication.

338.9689   ZA
ZAMBIA. MINISTRY OF PLANNING AND FINANCE. ANNUAL REPORT. 1971. a. 20 n. Ministry of Planning and Finance, P.O. Box RW 62, Lusaka, Zambia. (Subscr. to: Government Printer, Box 136, Lusaka, Zambia) **Document type:** government publication.
Formed by the merger of: Zambia. Ministry of Development and National Guidance. Annual Report; Zambia. Ministry of Finance. Annual Report (ISSN 0084-4896)

338   CC
ZHILIANG GUANLI/QUALITY CONTROL. (Text in Chinese) m. Zhiliang Guanli Zazhishe, No. 12, Zhongjing Jidao, Xidan, Beijing 100032, People's Republic of China. TEL 667131. Ed. Liu Yuanzhang.

338 690   RU   ISSN 0044-4464
ZHILISHCHNOE I KOMMUNAL'NOE KHOZYAISTVO. (Text in Russian) 1951. m. $92 (effective 1998). Furkasovskii per. 12-5, 101819 Moscow, Russia. TEL 7-095-9231107. FAX 7-095-9231107. (Dist. by: Mezhdunarodnaya Kniga, B. Yakimanka 39, 117049 Moscow, Russia. TEL 7-095-2384967. FAX 7-095-2384634) (C) Ed. Margarita Nazarenko. bk.rev.; bibl.; charts; illus.; stat.; tr.lit.; index. circ. 12,700. **Indexed:** Chem.Abstr.

729.39 645.3   NE
ZONVAK. 8/yr. Misset (Subsidiary of: Reed Elsevier plc), Postbus 4, 7000 BA Doetinchem, Netherlands. TEL 31-8340-49911. FAX 31-8340-63638. adv.: B&W page fl.2075, color page fl.3265; trim 210 x 297; adv. contact: Cor van Nek. circ. 2,840. **Document type:** trade publication.

338   SP
132 EXPRES. 1973. a. free. Subdireccion de Estudios Economicos y Marketing, Avda. Generalisimo, 146, 28016 Madrid, Spain. charts; illus.; stat.; tr.lit. (tabloid format)

BUSINESS AND ECONOMICS — Public Finance, Taxation

A I P T EMPLOYER TAX GUIDE. (Association for International Practical Training) see *EDUCATION — International Education Programs*

ABAPA FREER. see *BUSINESS AND ECONOMICS — Small Business*

336   US   ISSN 0163-1241
KF6369.8.C5
ABINGDON CLERGY INCOME TAX GUIDE. 1972. a. $12.95. Abingdon Press, 201 Eighth Ave., S., Box 801, Nashville, TN 37202-0801. TEL 800-251-3320. FAX 615-749-6417.
Formerly (until 1978): Clergy's Federal Income Tax Guide (ISSN 0090-9866)
Description: Offers clergy of all denominations information on filling out federal income tax forms.

336   CN   ISSN 1198-2632
ACCESS A L'IMPOT. 1994. m. Can.$425. Dacfo Publications Inc., 1255 University, Ste. 1500, Montreal, PQ H3B 3W9, Canada. TEL 514-392-9229; 800-763-2236. FAX 514-392-9240.
Description: Reports and explains the technical interpretations of the administrative practices of Revenue Canada as they relate to revenue taxes.

336   CN   ISSN 1201-303X
▼**ACCESS TO CANADIAN COMMODITY TAXES.** 1995. m. Can.$425. Dacfo Publications Inc., 1255 University, Ste. 1500, Montreal, PQ H3B 3W9, Canada. TEL 514-392-9229; 800-763-2236. FAX 514-392-9240. **Document type:** newsletter.
Description: Provides tax practitioners with a systematic examination of Revenue Canada's policies and practices as they relate to commodity tax matters. Reports and comments on internal documents obtained from Revenue Canada through the Access to Information Act.

336   CN   ISSN 1183-3831
ACCESS TO CANADIAN INCOME TAX. Key Title: Access Letter. 1989. m. Can.$875. Dacfo Publications Inc., 1255 University, Ste. 1500, Montreal, PQ H3B 3W9, Canada. TEL 514-392-9229; 800-763-2236. FAX 514-392-9240. Ed. Claude Desy.
Description: Provides tax practitioners with a systematic examination of Revenue Canada's policies and practices as they relate to tax matters.

336   BE   ISSN 0773-2163
ACCOUNTANCY THEMA'S; veertiendaagse nieuwsbrief voor bedrijfsrevisoren, accountants, en administratieve en financiele managers. (Supplement avail.) 1983. s-m. 6042 BEF. C E D Samsom (Subsidiary of: Wolters Samsom Belgie n.v.), Kouterveld 14, B-1831 Diegem, Belgium. TEL 32-2-7231111. bk.rev.; index. circ. 1,500.
Description: Contains articles on up-to-date accountancy, practical accountancy and financial analysis.

336.2 657   US   ISSN 1059-7654
ACCOUNTANT'S TAX WEEKLY. w. $211 (effective 1997). Harcourt Brace Professional Publishing, 525 B St., Ste. 1900, San Diego, CA 92101-4495. TEL 619-699-6716. FAX 619-699-6593. Ed. Sidney Bernstein; Pub. Ken Rethmeier. R&P contact: Jenna Lake. TEL 619-699-6265. **Document type:** newsletter.
Description: Informs accountants and financial executives of important new developments in such areas as fringe benefits, business deductions, payroll and benefits costs, executive compensation, travel and entertainment, and corporate tax returns.

ACCOUNTING AND TAX INDEX. see *BUSINESS AND ECONOMICS — Abstracting, Bibliographies, Statistics*

ACCOUNTING TECHNICIAN. see *BUSINESS AND ECONOMICS — Accounting*

336 333.33 340   US
ADVANCED TAX PLANNING FOR REAL PROPERTY TRANSACTIONS. a. $40 softcover. Continuing Education of the Bar - California, University of California Extension, 2300 Shattuck Ave., Berkeley, CA 94704. TEL 510-642-6211. FAX 510-642-3788. (Co-sponsor: State Bar of California)

336.2   NE
AFRICAN TAX SYSTEMS. French edition: Systemes Fiscaux Africains. (Text in English) 1971. 6 base vols. (plus q. updates). $1035 (renewal $535) (effective 1997). (United Nations Economic Commission for Africa, UN) I B F D Publications B.V., P.O. Box 20237, 1000 HE Amsterdam, Netherlands. TEL 31-20-6267726. FAX 31-20-6228658. TELEX 13217 INTAX NL. (In US: IBFD Publications USA, Inc., 4 Maple Ln., Valatie, NY 12184. TEL 800-299-6330. FAX 518-758-2246) Ed. elizabeth de Brauw-Itay. (looseleaf format)
Description: Provides essential information to help overcome obstacles to international trade, including in-depth description of tax systems and investment regulations.

AGRICULTURAL TAXATION STUDIES. see *AGRICULTURE — Agricultural Economics*

ALABAMA. DEPARTMENT OF REVENUE. ANNUAL REPORT. see *PUBLIC ADMINISTRATION — Municipal Government*

ALABAMA. DEPARTMENT OF REVENUE. COUNTY LINES NEWSLETTER. see *PUBLIC ADMINISTRATION — Municipal Government*

ALABAMA. DEPARTMENT OF REVENUE. GENERAL SUMMARY OF STATE TAXES. see *PUBLIC ADMINISTRATION — Municipal Government*

ALABAMA. DEPARTMENT OF REVENUE. REVENUE REVIEW NEWSLETTER. see *PUBLIC ADMINISTRATION — Municipal Government*

336   US
ALASKA. DEPARTMENT OF REVENUE. REVENUE SOURCES. 1975? q. Department of Revenue, Research Section, Pouch SA, Juneau, AK 99801. TEL 907-465-3682. Ed. Vincent D. Wright. **Document type:** government publication.
Formerly: Alaska. Department of Administration. Revenue Sources.

ALASKA. DEPARTMENT OF REVENUE. STATE INVESTMENT PORTFOLIO. see *BUSINESS AND ECONOMICS — Investments*

336.2   CN
ALBERTA, N.W.T. & YUKON TAX REPORTER. m. Can.$335. C C H Canadian Ltd., 6 Garamond Ct., North York, ON M3C 1Z5, Canada. TEL 416-441-2992; 800-268-4522. FAX 416-444-9011. **Document type:** trade publication.
Formerly: Alberta, N.W.T. & Yukon Tax Reports.
Description: Covers every aspect of taxation for Alberta, N.W.T. and the Yukon.

ALGEMEEN FISKAAL TIJDSCHRIFT; informatie voor de belastingkundige en de administratieve en financiele managers. see *BUSINESS AND ECONOMICS — Accounting*

336   AE
ALGERIA. DIRECTION DES DOUANES. BULLETIN COMPARATIF TRIMESTRIEL. q. Direction des Douane 119, rue du Docteur Saadane, Algiers, Algeria.

336.2   US   ISSN 0148-9976
KF6750
ALL STATES TAX HANDBOOK (YEAR). a. $30. Research Institute of America, Inc, 90 Fifth Ave., New York, N 10011. TEL 212-645-4800.
Description: Provides comparisons of different tax rates and structures for all fifty states and the District of Columbia.

BUSINESS AND ECONOMICS — PUBLIC FINANCE, TAXATION

336 UK ISSN 0268-1269
ALLIED DUNBAR TAX HANDBOOK. 1984. a. £19.99. Longman Group Ltd., Law, Tax and Finance Division, 21-27 Lamb's Conduit St., London WC1N 3NJ, England. TEL 071-242-2548. FAX 071-831-8119. **Document type:** bulletin.
Formerly (until 1985): Allied Dunbar Tax Guide (ISSN 0268-0254)
Description: Advice and information on the workings of income tax, capital gains tax, corporate tax, inheritance tax and value added tax in the United Kingdom.

336.2 US ISSN 1043-6960
KF6369
ALTERNATIVE MINIMUM TAX. 1993. a. $166.45 (foreign $240.45) (effective 1995). Warren, Gorham & Lamont, One Penn Plaza, New York, NY 10119. TEL 212-971-5000. FAX 212-971-5113. (Subscr. to: The Park Square Bldg., 31 St. James Ave., Boston, MA 02116-4112. TEL 800-950-1207) Ed. Daniel J. Lathorpe. (looseleaf format) **Document type:** trade publication.
Description: Analyzes the complexities of the alternative minimum tax and how it applies in both corporate and individual situations.

336.76 AG ISSN 0325-2582
AMBITO FINANCIERO. d. (5/w.). Arg.$275($800) (effective Mar. 1995). Editorial Amfin, S.A., Paseo Colon 1196, 1063 Capital Federal BA, Argentina. FAX 54-1-349-1505. Ed. Julio A. Ramos. adv.: B&W page Arg.$18270. circ. 133,300. (also avail. in microfilm)

AMERICA REPORT. see *BUSINESS AND ECONOMICS — Economic Situation And Conditions*

AMERICAN BAR ASSOCIATION. SECTION OF TAXATION. NEWSLETTER. see *LAW*

AMERICAN HORSE COUNCIL TAX BULLETIN. see *SPORTS AND GAMES — Horses And Horsemanship*

336 US ISSN 0739-7569
K1
AMERICAN JOURNAL OF TAX POLICY. 1981. s-a. $22. American College of Tax Counsel, Box 870382, Tuscaloosa, AL 35487-0382. TEL 205-348-7372. FAX 205-348-3917. E-mail: JBRYCE@UA1VM.UA.EDU. Ed. James D. Bryce. R&P contact: James D. Bryce. circ. 1,300. (also avail. in microfiche from WSH; back issues avail.; reprint service avail. from WSH) **Indexed:** L.R.I., Leg.Per. **Document type:** academic/scholarly publication.
●Also available online. Vendor(s): Lexis-Nexis, West Group.
—KR SourceOne; UnCover.

336 AS
AMERICAN SAMOA GOVERNMENT. COMPREHENSIVE ANNUAL FINANCIAL REPORT. a. American Samoa Government, Treasury Department, Pago Pago, 96799, American Samoa. **Indexed:** So.Pac.Per.Ind. **Document type:** government publication.

336 US ISSN 0198-9073
HF5681.T3
AMERICAN TAXATION ASSOCIATION. JOURNAL. 1979. s-a. $30. (American Taxation Association) American Accounting Association, 5717 Bessie Dr., Sarasota, FL 34233. TEL 941-921-7747. FAX 941-923-4093. URL: http://omer.actg.uic.edu:800/Jata/JATA.html. Ed. Sandy Kramer. R&P contact: Mary Cole. bk.rev.; software rev.; abstr. **Indexed:** Account.Ind. (1979-), Account.Ind.
—UMI; UnCover.
Description: Provides articles on tax topics. *Refereed Serial*

336 II
ANDHRA PRADESH STATE FINANCIAL CORPORATION. REPORT AND ACCOUNTS. (Text in English) 1956. a. Andhra Pradesh State Financial Corporation, 5-9-194 Chirag Ali Lane, Hyderabad 500001, India. TELEX 0425-6428-ASFC-IN. stat.
Formerly: Andhra Pradesh State Financial Corporation. Report.

ANNUAL EDITIONS: DEVELOPING THIRD WORLD. see *GEOGRAPHY*

ARGUS (DALAROE), aarsbok foer Tullmuseum och Tullhistoriska Foereningen. see *MUSEUMS AND ART GALLERIES*

336 NE ISSN 1385-3082
ASIA - PACIFIC TAX BULLETIN. Cover title: A P T B. (Text in English) 1983; N.S. 1995. m. $250 (effective 1997). (International Bureau of Fiscal Documentation) I B F D Publications B.V., P.O. Box 20237, 1000 HE Amsterdam, Netherlands. TEL 31-20-6267726. FAX 31-20-6228658. (In US: IBFD Publications USA, Inc., 4 Maple Ln., Valatie, NY 12184. TEL 800-299-6330. FAX 518-758-2246) Ed. Victor T. Chew. (back issues avail.) **Document type:** bulletin.
—BLDSC (1742.261900); UnCover.
Supersedes (in 1995): A P T I R C Bulletin (ISSN 0218-3536); Formerly (until 1991): Asian-Pacific Tax and Investment Research Centre Bulletin (ISSN 0217-6661)
Description: Provides news and analysis of taxation and investment issues in Asia and the Pacific region, including significant reports and documents.

AURA WEALTH NEWSLETTER; economic survival in perilous times. see *BUSINESS AND ECONOMICS — Economic Situation And Conditions*

AUSTRALIA. BUREAU OF STATISTICS. PUBLIC SECTOR FINANCIAL ASSETS AND LIABILITIES, AUSTRALIA. see *BUSINESS AND ECONOMICS — Abstracting, Bibliographies, Statistics*

AUSTRALIA. BUREAU OF STATISTICS. TASMANIAN OFFICE. GOVERNMENT FINANCE STATISTICS, TASMANIA. see *BUSINESS AND ECONOMICS — Abstracting, Bibliographies, Statistics*

AUSTRALIA. BUREAU OF STATISTICS. TAXATION REVENUE, AUSTRALIA. see *BUSINESS AND ECONOMICS — Abstracting, Bibliographies, Statistics*

336.2 AT
AUSTRALIA. DEPARTMENT OF INDUSTRY, SCIENCE AND TOURISM. ANNUAL REPORT. 1954. a. free. Department of Industry, Science and Tourism, P.O. Box 9839, Canberra City, A.C.T. 2601, Australia. TEL 61-6-2136000. FAX 61-6-2137000. Ed.Bd. circ. 8,000.
Former titles (until Mar. 1996): Australia. Department of Industry, Science and Technology. Annual Report; (until July 1994): Australia. Department of Industry, Technology and Regional Development. Annual Report; (until 1992): Australia. Department of Industry, Technology and Commerce. Annual Report (ISSN 0728-6856); (until 1981): Australia. Department of Police and Customs. Review of Activities; Australia. Department of Industry and Commerce. Annual Report (ISSN 0067-1347)

336 AT ISSN 0157-0730
AUSTRALIAN & NEW ZEALAND CONVEYANCING REPORT. 1979. 8/yr. C C H Australia Ltd., P.O. Box 230, North Ryde, N.S.W. 2113, Australia. TEL 61-1-300300224. FAX 61-1-300306224. charts. (looseleaf format)
—CCC.
Description: Covers case reporting and analyses, practice pointers, drafting comments and precedents.

336 AT
AUSTRALIAN CAPITAL GAINS TAX PLANNER. 1989. q. C C H Australia Ltd., P.O. Box 230, North Ryde, N.S.W. 2113, Australia. TEL 61-1-300300224. FAX 61-1-300306224. (looseleaf format)
Description: Provides practical commentary on CGT on a transactional basis and keeps up-to-date with changes in legislation and with cases and ruling.

336.2 AT ISSN 0310-7817
AUSTRALIAN FEDERAL TAX REPORTER. (In 11 vols.) 1969. w. C C H Australia Ltd., P.O. Box 230, North Ryde, N.S.W. 2113, Australia. TEL 61-1-300300224. FAX 61-1-300306224. (looseleaf format)
●Also available on CD-ROM.
—CCC.
Description: Contains detailed commentary on virtually every provision of the Australian income tax and fringe benefits tax legislation, including reference to relevant regulations, cases and Tax Office rulings. Includes commentary on superannuation legislation.

AUSTRALIAN FRINGE BENEFITS TAX GUIDE FOR EMPLOYERS. see *LAW — Corporate Law*

336 AT
AUSTRALIAN INCOME TAX BILLS. 1993. irreg. C C H Australia Ltd., P.O. Box 230, North Ryde, N.S.W. 2113, Australia. TEL 61-1-300300224. FAX 61-1-300306224. (looseleaf format)
Description: Provides full text of all new Income Tax Bills introduced into Federal Parliament, plus explanation, memoranda, and second reading speeches.

336 AT
AUSTRALIAN INCOME TAX GUIDE. (In 3 vols.) 1969. fortn. C C H Australia Ltd., P.O. Box 230, North Ryde, N.S.W. 2113, Australia. TEL 61-1-300300224. FAX 61-1-300306224. charts. (looseleaf format)
Description: Provides practical explanations of income tax implications on business actions and everyday transactions. Includes step-by-step examples, tables, diagrams and checklists.

336.2 AT ISSN 0810-5480
KU2832.A27
AUSTRALIAN INCOME TAX LEGISLATION; including regulations, rates and international agreements. (In 4 vols.) 1969. irreg., as necessary for all legislative changes. C C H Australia Ltd., P.O. Box 230, North Ryde, N.S.W. 2113, Australia. TEL 61-1-300300224. FAX 61-1-300306224. (looseleaf format)
●Also available on CD-ROM.
—CCC.
Formerly (until 1976): Australian Income Tax Assessment Act and Regulations.
Description: Contains the full text of the Income Tax Assessment Act and Regulations and related legislation. Includes detailed history notes of amendments made to the legislation in the last seven years.

AUSTRALIAN INCOME TAX RULINGS. see *LAW*

AUSTRALIAN INTERNATIONAL TAX AGREEMENTS. see *LAW*

336.2 AT ISSN 0810-5596
AUSTRALIAN MASTER TAX GUIDE. a. C C H Australia Ltd., P.O. Box 230, North Ryde, N.S.W. 2113, Australia. TEL 61-1-300300224. FAX 61-1-300306224.

336 AT
AUSTRALIAN MASTER TAX GUIDE UPDATER. 1984. q. C C H Australia Ltd., P.O. Box 230, North Ryde, N.S.W. 2113, Australia. TEL 61-1-300300224. FAX 61-1-330306224. (looseleaf format)
Description: Designed to update the Australian Master Tax Guide. Summarises all the tax developments during the year, including legislation and proposed legislation, cases, rulings and deteminations.

336 AT
AUSTRALIAN PAY-ROLL TAX MANUAL. (In 2 vols.) 1979. 10/yr. C C H Australia Ltd., P.O. Box 230, North Ryde, N.S.W. 2113, Australia. TEL 61-1-300300224. FAX 61-1-300306224.
Description: Explains the application of pay-roll tax in the Sates and Territories. Contains legislation, official rulings and case notes.

336.2 AT
AUSTRALIAN SALES TAX GUIDE. (In 4 vols.) 1973. irreg., (approx. every 3 wks.). C C H Australia Ltd., P.O. Box 230, North Ryde, N.S.W. 2113, Australia. TEL 61-1-300300224. FAX 61-2-300306224. index. (looseleaf format)
Description: Provides a comprehensive analysis of sales tax law in Australia. Includes detailed commentary, cases and legislation as well as analysis on exemptions and classifications.

336 AT
AUSTRALIAN STAMP DUTIES LAW. 4 base vols. (plus m. updates). Aus.$950 (effective 1997). Butterworths, Division of Reed International Books Australia Pty. Ltd. (Subsidiary of: Reed Elsevier Australia Pty. Ltd.), 271-273 Lane Cove Rd., North Ryde, N.S.W. 2113, Australia. TEL 61-2-93354444. FAX 61-2-93354655. (Dist. in N. America by: Wm. W. Gaunt & Sons, Inc., Law Book Dealers & Subscription Agents, Gaunt Bldg., 3011 Gulf Dr., Homes Beach, FL 34217-2199) Ed. Sarah Davis. R&P contact: Deanne Castellino. adv. contact: Melinda Smith. (looseleaf format)
Formerly: Australian Revenue and Stamp Duties.

BUSINESS AND ECONOMICS — PUBLIC FINANCE, TAXATION

336 340   AT
▼**AUSTRALIAN SUPER NEWS.** 1995. m. C C H Australia Ltd., P.O. Box 230, N. Ryde, N.S.W. 2113, Australia. TEL 61-1-300300224. FAX 61-1-300306224.
    Description: Discusses latest developments in superannuation law and practice and its impact in areas such as industrial law, discrimination law, bankruptcy law and family law.

336   AT
▼**AUSTRALIAN SUPERANNUATION: TAXATION MATERIALS.** 1995. irreg., as required for all legislative changes. C H Australia Ltd., P.O. Box 230, North Ryde, N.S.W. 2113, Australia. TEL 61-1-300300224. FAX 61-1-300306224. (looseleaf format)
    Description: Contains source materials for areas of superannuation administered by the Australian Taxation Office and other agencies.

336 340   AT
AUSTRALIAN TAX CASES. (In 2 vols., bound annually) 1969. w. C C H Australia Ltd., P.O. Box 230, North Ryde, N.S.W. 2113, Australia. TEL 61-1-300300224. FAX 61-1-300306224. (looseleaf format) Indexed: Curr.Aus.N.Z.Leg.Lit.Ind.
    Description: Reports tax cases in full text, covering income tax and indirect taxes from the Administrative Appeals Tribunal and the Courts in all Australian jurisdictions.

336 340   AT   ISSN 0812-695X
AUSTRALIAN TAX FORUM; a journal of taxation policy, law and reform. 1984. q. Aus.$67 to individuals; libraries Aus.$86. Taxation Institute of Australia, 7th Fl., 64 Castlereagh St., Sydney, N.S.W. 2000, Australia. TEL 61-2-92323422. FAX 61-2-92216953. E-mail: tline@taxia.asn.au; URL: http://www.taxia/asn.au/. Ed. Richard Vann. adv.; index; circ. 500 (paid). (also avail. in microfiche from UMI; reprint service avail. from WSH; back issues avail.) Indexed: Account.Ind. (1984-), C.L.I., J.of Econ.Lit., L.R.I. **Document type:** academic/scholarly publication.
    ●Also available online. Vendor(s): UMI.
    —UMI; UnCover.
    Description: Publishes papers on tax analysis and policy, tax law and tax reform in Australia.
    Refereed Serial

336.2 340   AT   ISSN 0311-094X
K1
AUSTRALIAN TAX REVIEW. 1971. q. Aus.$225. L B C Information Services, 50 Waterloo Rd., N. Ryde, N.S.W. 2113, Australia. TEL 61-2-99366444. FAX 61-2-8889706. TELEX ASBOOK 27995. Ed. A.H. Slater. charts; stat. (reprint service avail. from WSH) Indexed: Aus.P.A.I.S., C.L.I., Curr.Aus.N.Z.Leg.Lit.Ind., L.R.I., Leg.Cont., Leg.Per., P.A.I.S.
    —BLDSC (1822.500000); KR SourceOne; UMI; UnCover.
    Description: Provides discussion of tax issues and problems from recent cases or legislation.

336   NE   ISSN 0166-8528
B & G. (Bank en Gemeenten) 1974. 10/yr. fl.60 (effective 1997). Bank Nederlandse Gemeenten N. V., Koninginnegracht 2, 2514 AA The Hague, Netherlands. TEL 31-70-3750820. FAX 31-70-3454743. URL: http://www.bng.nl. (Co-sponsor: Vereniging van Nederlandse Gemeenten) Ed. J.G. Klaassens. R&P contact: J.G. Klaassens. adv.; bk.rev. circ. 9,000.
    —SWETS.
    Formerly: Gemeentefinancien (ISSN 0016-6057)
    Description: Publishes in-depth articles concerning financial and organizational matters affecting local and regional authorities.

B N A'S BANKING REPORT; legal and regulatory developments in the financial services industry. see *LAW*

336.2714   NE   ISSN 0922-9566
B T W BRIEF. (Belasting Toegevoegde Waarde) 1989. 10/yr. fl.273 (effective 1996). Uitgeverij Fed bv (Subsidiary of: Wolters Kluwer N.V.), Postbus 23, 7400 GA Deventer, Netherlands. TEL 31-570-633155. FAX 31-570-633834. Eds. S.T.M. Beelen, J.L.M.J. Vervloed. (back issues avail.) **Document type:** trade publication.
    Description: Covers practical issues, recent jurisprudence and developments relating to value added taxation in the Netherlands.

336   BA
BAHRAIN. MONETARY AGENCY. ANNUAL REPORT. a. Monetary Agency, P.O. Box 27, Manama, Bahrain. TEL 535535. FAX 533342. TELEX BN9191. charts; stat. **Document type:** government publication.

336 382   SL   ISSN 0067-2998
BALANCE OF PAYMENTS OF SIERRA LEONE. a. free. Bank of Sierra Leone, Siaka Stevens St., P.O. Box 30, Freetown, Sierra Leone. TEL 232-22-226501. FAX 232-22-224766. TELEX 3232 FREETOWN. **Document type:** corporate report.

BALANCE OF PAYMENTS OF TRINIDAD AND TOBAGO. see *BUSINESS AND ECONOMICS* — *Abstracting, Bibliographies, Statistics*

336 382   SP   ISSN 1136-5331
BALANZA DE PAGOS DE ESPANA. 1971. a. $4.50. (Ministerio de Economia y Hacienda, Secretaria General de Comercio) Banco de Espana, Seccion de Publicaciones, Negociado de Distribucion y Gestion, Alcala 50, 28014 Madrid, Spain. TEL 338-51-80. circ. 1,500.

336   PN
BANCO NACIONAL DE PANAMA. INFORMACION ECONOMICA Y FINANCIERA DE LA REPUBLICA DE PANAMA. 1978. a. free. Banco Nacional de Panama, Gerencia de Planificacion Economica y Financiera, Apdo. 5220, Panama 5, Panama.
FAX 507-69-5645. charts; stat. circ. 1,000.

BANGLADESH BANK. STATISTICS DEPARTMENT. ANNUAL BALANCE OF PAYMENTS. see *BUSINESS AND ECONOMICS* — *Abstracting, Bibliographies, Statistics*

BANGLADESH BANK. STATISTICS DEPARTMENT. BALANCE OF PAYMENTS. see *BUSINESS AND ECONOMICS* — *Abstracting, Bibliographies, Statistics*

THE BANK INCOME TAX RETURN MANUAL. see *BUSINESS AND ECONOMICS* — *Banking And Finance*

382 336   JA
BANK OF JAPAN. BALANCE OF PAYMENTS MONTHLY. (Text in English, Japanese) 1965. m. 900 Yen per no. Bank of Japan, International Department - Nippon Ginko, c/o Public Relations Department, 2-1-1 Hongoku-cho, Nihonbashi, Chuo-ku, Tokyo 103, Japan. TEL 81-3-3292-3753. FAX 81-3-3292-0410. (Dist. by: Tokiwa Shinyo Chosa Ltd., Hayakawa Bldg., 6-1 Kobuna-cho, Nihonbashi, Chuo-ku, Tokyo 103, Japan. TEL 81-3-3270-5713; Overseas dist. by: Tokiwa Sogo Co. Ltd., Kyodo Bldg., 3-2-4, Hongoky-cho, Nihonbashi, Chuo-ku, Tokyo 103, Japan)
    Formerly: Bank of Japan. Japan's Balance of Payments. Summary Report (ISSN 0549-317X)
    Description: Contains summary table, trade services, income, current transfers, financial account and capital account, changes in short-term external assets and liabilities of authorized foreign exchange banks, exports and imports by principal commodity, exports and imports by principal country.

336 382   LY   ISSN 0075-921X
BANK OF LIBYA. BALANCE OF PAYMENTS.* (Text in Arabic and English) 1954. a. free. Bank of Libya, P.O.B. 1103, Sharia al-Mahik Scoud, Tripoli, Libya.

336 382.1   FR
BANQUE DE FRANCE. BALANCE DES PAIEMENTS ET LA POSITION EXTERIEURE DE LA FRANCE. 1982. a. 200 F. (Ministere de l'Economie, des Finances et du Budget, Direction du Tresor) Banque de France, Service de l'Information, 48 rue Croix des Petits Champs, 75001 Paris, France. TEL 42-92-39-31. charts; stat. **Document type:** government publication.
    Former titles: France. Ministere de l'Economie, des Finances et du Budget. Balance des Paiements de la France (ISSN 0292-6733); France. Ministere de l'Economie et des Finances. Balance des Paiements entre la France et l'Exterieur (ISSN 0071-8890)
    Description: Presents a statistical and macroeconomic panorama of the economic, financial and monetary climates beyond France.

336   BB
BARBADOS. MINISTRY OF FINANCE AND ECONOMIC AFFAIRS. FINANCIAL STATEMENT AND BUDGETARY PROPOSALS. 1974. bi-m. $6 (effective 1995). Ministry of Finance and Economic Affairs, Government Printery, Bay St., St. Michael, Barbados, W.I. circ. 500. **Document type:** government publication.
    Formerly (until 1988): Barbados. Ministry of Finance and Planning. Financial Statement and Budgetary Proposals.

336   SP
BASQUE REGION. OGASUN ETA FINANTZA SAILA. (YEAR) RAKO AURREKONTUAK/BASQUE REGION. DEPARTAMENTO DE HACIENDA Y FINANZAS. PRESUPUESTOS (YEAR). a. (Ogasun eta Finantza Saila, Aurrekontu Zuzendaritza - Departamento de Hacienda y Finanzas, Direccion de Presupuestos) Eusko Jaurlaritzaren Argitalpen-Zerbitzu Nagusia - Servicio Central de Publicaciones del Gobierno Vasco, C. Duque de Wellington, 2, 01010 Vitoria-Gasteiz, Spain. circ. 500.

336   GW   ISSN 1431-293X
BECK'SCHES NACHSCHLAGEWERK DER ENTSCHEIDUNGEN DES BUNDESFINANZHOFS. Variant title: B F H - N. 1966. bi-m. DM.154 (effective 1997). Verlag C.H. Beck, 80791 Munich, Germany. TEL 49-89-38189340. FAX 49-89-38189398. Ed.Bd. **Document type:** academic/scholarly publication.

336.2   NE   ISSN 0167-4293
BELASTINGBLAD. 1982. bi-w. fl.0.56 per page (approx. fl.476) (effective 1996). Uitgeverij Kluwer B.V., Postbus 23, 7400 GA Deventer, Netherlands. TEL 31-570-633155. FAX 31-570-633834. adv. (back issues avail.) **Document type:** trade publication.
    —SWETS.

336.2   BE   ISSN 0005-853X
BELGIUM. MINISTERE DES FINANCES. ADMINISTRATION DES CONTRIBUTIONS. BULLETIN DES CONTRIBUTIONS. Dutch edition: Belgium. Ministerie van Financien. Hoofdbestuur van de Directe Belastingen. Bulletin der Belastingen (ISSN 0772-7208) (Text in French) 1925. m. 2300 BEF (foreign 3600 BEF) (effective 1996). Ministere des Finances, Administration Centrale des Contributions Directes - Ministerie van Financien, Hoofdbestuur van de Directe Belastingen, Rijksadministratief Centrum, Financietoren - Bus 32, Kruidtuinlaan 50, B-1010 Brussels, Belgium. TEL 32-2-2103816.
FAX 32-2-2104118. charts; stat. circ. 4,312 (1,856 French ed.; 2,456 Dutch ed.). **Document type:** government publication.

336   BE   ISSN 0779-8601
BELGIUM. MINISTERIE VAN FINANCIEN. DOCUMENTATIEBLAD/BELGIUM. MINISTERE DES FINANCES. BULLETIN DE DOCUMENTATION. (Text in Dutch, English, French) 1941. bi-m. 2500 BEF (3000 BEF in EU; elsewhere 3100 BEF). Ministerie van Financien, Studie- en Documentatiedienst - Ministere des Finances, Services d'Etudes et de Documentation, RAC Financietoren Bus 30, Kruidtuinlaan 50, 1010 Brussels, Belgium. TEL 32-2-2103902. FAX 32-2-2103946. circ. 1,150. **Document type:** bulletin.
    Description: Covers issues and topics relating to Belgian public finance and economic policy.

BERKELEY JOURNAL OF INTERNATIONAL LAW. see *LAW* — *International Law*

336.2   NE   ISSN 0165-0130
BESLISSINGEN IN BELASTINGZAKEN. Key Title: B N B. Beslissingen in Belastingzaken. Nederlandse Belastingrechtspraak. 1953. bi-w. fl.0.31 per page (approx. fl.930) (effective 1996). Uitgeverij Kluwer B.V., Postbus 23, 7400 GA Deventer, Netherlands. TEL 31-570-633155. FAX 31-570-633834. circ. 3,000.
    —SWETS.

336   GW   ISSN 0174-5395
BETRIEBSPRUEFUNG; besser vorbereiten-erfolgreicher verhandeln-weniger nachzahlen. 1984. q. DM.170. Rudolf Haufe Verlag GmbH & Co. KG, Hindenburgstr. 64, 79102 Freiburg, Germany. TEL 49-761-3683-0. FAX 49-761-3683-195. (looseleaf format) **Document type:** trade publication.

BUSINESS AND ECONOMICS — PUBLIC FINANCE, TAXATION

336 US
...ND TELLER. 1971. 2/yr. free. U.S. Department of the Treasury, Bureau of the Public Debt, 999 E St., N.W., Washington, DC 20239-0001. TEL 202-219-3302. Ed. Sheila E. Nelson. R&P contact: Sheila E. Nelson. charts. circ. 205,000. **Document type:** government publication, newsletter.

336 BS ISSN 0068-0451
HJ80N
...TSWANA. ANNUAL STATEMENTS OF ACCOUNTS. a. P.11. Government Printer, Private Bag 0081, Gaborone, Botswana.

336.2 BS
...TSWANA. DEPARTMENT OF INCOME TAX. ANNUAL REPORT. 1972. a. free. Department of Taxes, Private Bag 0013, Gaborone, Botswana. TEL 267-352444. FAX 267-374642. **Document type:** corporate report, government publication.

336 BL ISSN 0103-1090
...AZIL. TRIBUNAL DE CONTAS DA UNIAO. REVISTA. 1970. q. price varies. Imprensa Nacional, SIG, Quadra 6, Lote 800, Caixa Postal 30000, 70604-900 Brasilia DF, Brazil. TEL 55-61-3139905. FAX 55-61-3139528. index. **Document type:** government publication.

336.2 CN ISSN 0045-3056
...ITISH COLUMBIA TAX REPORTER. m. Can.$335. C C H Canadian Ltd., 6 Garamond Ct., North York, ON M3C 1Z5, Canada. TEL 416-441-2992; 800-268-4522. FAX 416-444-9011. index. **Document type:** trade publication.
Formerly: British Columbia Tax Reports.
Description: Covers every aspect of taxation in British Columbia.

336.2 US ISSN 0007-1862
...ITISH TAX GUIDE. 1963. m. $530. C C H Incorporated, 2700 Lake Cook Rd., Riverwoods, IL 60015. TEL 847-267-7000; 800-835-5224. FAX 800-224-8299. (looseleaf format)
—CCC.

336.2 UK ISSN 0007-1870
K2
...ITISH TAX REVIEW. 1956. bi-m. £80. Sweet & Maxwell, South Quay Plaza, 7th Fl., 183 Marsh Wall, London E14 9FT, England. TEL 071-538-8686. FAX 071-538-9508. Ed. J. Patterson. adv. contact: Jackie Wood. bk.rev. (reprint service avail. from RRI,WSH) Indexed: Account.Ind. (1974-), C.L.I., C.R.E.J., Curr.Cont., L.R.I., Leg.Cont., Leg.Per., LJI, P.A.I.S., Rural Recreat.Tour.Abstr., SSCI, World Agri.Econ.& Rural Sociol.Abstr., World Bank.Abstr. **Document type:** bulletin.
—BLDSC (2345.350000); KR SourceOne; SWETS; UMI; UncoVer. **CCC.**

336 PK
...JDGET OF THE GOVERNMENT OF PAKISTAN. DEMANDS FOR GRANTS AND APPROPRIATIONS. (Text in English) a. free to qualified personnel. Finance Division, Islamabad, Pakistan.
Supersedes: Pakistan. Ministry of Finance. Budget of the Central Government (ISSN 0078-8317)

...JILDING SOCIETY TAXATION MANUAL. see LAW — Estate Planning

336 FR ISSN 0242-5912
...JLLETIN FISCAL. vol.43, 1977. m. 450 F. (effective 1997). Editions Francis Lefebvre, 42 rue de Villiers, 92300 Levallois, France. TEL 41-05-22-00. FAX 41-05-22-30. adv. **Document type:** bulletin.
Former titles: Bulletin de Documentation Pratique des Taxes sur le Chiffre d'Affaires (ISSN 0007-4276); Bulletin de Documentation Pratiques des Impots Directs et des Taxes sur le Chiffre d'Affaires (ISSN 0007-4268)

336.2 NE ISSN 0007-4624
HJ101
BULLETIN FOR INTERNATIONAL FISCAL DOCUMENTATION. (Text in English) 1946. m. $390 (effective 1997). (International Bureau of Fiscal Documentation) I B F D Publications B.V., P.O. Box 20237, 1000 HE Amsterdam, Netherlands. TEL 31-20-6267726. FAX 31-20-6228658. TELEX 13217 INTAX NL. (In US: IBFD Publications USA, Inc., 4 Maple Ln., Valatie, NY 12184. TEL 800-299-6330. FAX 518-758-2246) (Co-sponsor: International Fiscal Association) Ed. David Hughes. adv.; bk.rev.; bibl.; index. (looseleaf format; back issues avail.) Indexed: Account.Ind. (1974-), C.R.E.J., Curr.Cont., ELLIS, Ind.Per.Art.Relat.Law, J.of Econ.Lit., Key to Econ.Sci., Mid.East: Abstr.& Ind., P.A.I.S., SSCI. **Document type:** bulletin.
—BLDSC (2865.050000); SWETS; UncoVer.
Description: Provides detailed analysis of developments in tax policy and law

336 FR ISSN 0427-2129
BULLETIN OFFICIEL DES DOUANES. 1954. d. 1105 F. (Direction Generale des Douanes et Droits Indirects) Imprimerie Nationale, B.P. 514, 59505 Douai Cedex, France. TEL 27-93-70-70. FAX 27-93-70-96. TELEX 120 389 F. **Document type:** bulletin.

336 FR ISSN 0982-801X
BULLETIN OFFICIEL DES IMPOTS. (In 14 series) d. 710 F. for the series. Imprimerie Nationale, B.P. 514, 59505 Douai Cedex, France. TEL 27-93-70-70. FAX 27-93-70-96. TELEX 120 389 F.

336 GW ISSN 0175-5366
BUNDESSTEUERBLATT. s-m. DM.79.60 (effective 1997). Stollfuss Verlag Bonn, Postfach 2428, 53014 Bonn, Germany. TEL 49-228-724-0. FAX 49-228-659223. **Document type:** bulletin.
—SWETS.

336 US ISSN 0738-5765
BUSBY PAPERS.* 1981. s-m. $300. Horace W. Busby & Associates, 401 Montana Ave., No. 4, Santa Monica, CA 90403-1303. Ed. Margaret Mayer. circ. 360. (back issues avail.)
Description: Informs business clients of trends in socio-political demographics; analyzes developments in government and politics.

BUSINESS BASICS: TAX A - Z. see BUSINESS AND ECONOMICS — Management

336.2 US
BUSINESS ORGANIZATIONS WITH TAX PLANNING. (Issued in 16 base vols. with supplements) 1963. irreg. $2220. Matthew Bender & Co., Inc., 2 Park Ave., New York, NY 10016. TEL 212-448-2000. E-mail: international@bender.com; URL: http://www.bender.com. Ed. Zolman Cavitch.
Description: Provides in-depth analysis of corporation law and all relevant aspects of federal corporate taxation.

336.207 UK ISSN 1351-0819
BUSINESS TAX PLANNING. 1993. m. £120. Longman Group Ltd., Law, Tax and Finance Division, 21-27 Lamb's Conduit St., London WC1N 3NJ, England. TEL 071-242-2548. FAX 071-831-8119. Indexed: Euro.LJI, LJI.

336.2 UK ISSN 0525-3063
BUTTERWORTHS BUDGET TAX TABLES. 1966. a. £4.95($10) Butterworth & Co. (Publishers) Ltd., Part of the Reed Elsevier group, Halsbury House, 35 Chancery Ln., London WC2A 1EL, England. TEL 071-400-2500. FAX 071-400-2842. (U.S. addr.: Butterworth Legal Publishers, 90 Stiles Rd., Salem, NH 03079-9981. TEL 603-898-9664) Ed. Derek Bond. circ. 13,000.
Description: Contains details and explanations of the budget proposals, set out under distinctive headings.

336.2 UK ISSN 0141-1500
BUTTERWORTHS ORANGE TAX HANDBOOK. 1976. a. £21($40) Butterworth & Co. (Publishers) Ltd., Part of the Reed Elsevier group, Halsbury House, 35 Chancery Ln., London WC2A 1EL, England. TEL 071-400-2500. FAX 071-400-2842. (U.S. addr.: Butterworth Legal Publishers, 90 Stiles Rd., Salem, NH 03079-9981. TEL 603-898-9664) Ed. Moiz Sadikali. adv. **Document type:** trade publication.
—BLDSC (2935.633000).
Description: Contains up-to-date text of all legislation and other material relating to inheritance tax, national insurance contributions, stamp duty and value added tax.

BUTTERWORTHS REGIONAL LEVIES REPORT. see LAW

336 SA
BUTTERWORTHS TAX ALERT. m. R.222.30. Butterworth Publishers (Pty.) Ltd., Part of the Reed Elsevier group, P.O. Box 792, Durban 4000, South Africa. TEL 27-31-2683111. FAX 27-31-2683110. (looseleaf format) **Document type:** abstracting/indexing.
Description: Update service containing details of all changes to the tax law, as well as summaries and commentary covering all tax cases, legislation, fiscal rulings, and other relevant tax developments.

336 NZ
BUTTERWORTHS TAXATION LIBRARY. 3 base vols. (plus updates 8/yr.) NZ.$99. Butterworths of New Zealand Ltd., A member of the Reed Elsevier plc group, P.O. Box 472, 205-207 Victoria St., Wellington, New Zealand. TEL 64-4-3851479. FAX 64-4-3851598. Ed. Stephen Gibbs. (looseleaf format)
Description: Contains consolidated statutes, regulations and case references.

336 UK ISSN 0264-2174
BUTTERWORTHS U K TAX GUIDE. a. £19.95($51) Butterworth & Co. (Publishers) Ltd., Part of the Reed Elsevier group, Halsbury House, 35 Chancery Ln., London WC2A 1EL, England. TEL 071-400-2500. FAX 071-400-2842. (U.S. addr.: Butterworth Legal Publishers, 90 Stiles Rd., Salem, NH 03079-9981. TEL 603-898-9664) Ed.Bd. **Document type:** trade publication.
—BLDSC (2935.645000).
Description: Examines in detail all the principal taxes, including stamp duty and national insurance contributions, showing how they work and the policy behind the statutory provisions.

336 SA
BUTTERWORTHS V A T GRAM. (Value Added Tax); early information about changes to V A T. (Text in English) q. Butterworths (Pty.) Ltd. (Subsidiary of: Part of the Reed Elsevier group), P.O. Box 792, Durban 4000, South Africa. TEL 27-31-294247. FAX 27-31-283255. Eds. Anne Bennett, Des Kruger. (looseleaf format)
Supersedes (in 1995): Juta's V A T News.

336.2 UK ISSN 0141-3856
BUTTERWORTHS YELLOW TAX HANDBOOK. 1962. a. £21($40) Butterworth & Co. (Publishers) Ltd., Part of the Reed Elsevier group, Halsbury House, 35 Chancery Ln., London WC2A 1EL, England. TEL 071-400-2500. FAX 071-400-2842. (U.S. addr.: Butterworth Legal Publishers, 90 Stiles Rd., Salem, NH 03079-9981. TEL 603-898-9664) Ed. Moiz Sadikali. adv.
—BLDSC (2935.675000).
Formerly: Butterworths Tax Handbook (ISSN 0068-452X)
Description: Provides the text of the legislation relating to income tax, capital gains tax and corporation tax in the amended and updated form needed for accurate assessments.

336.2 US
KF6285.B45
C C H FEDERAL TAX WEEKLY. (Commerce Clearing House) 1951. w. $252. C C H Incorporated, 2700 Lake Cook Rd., Riverwoods, IL 60015. TEL 847-267-7000; 800-835-5224. FAX 800-224-8299. index. (looseleaf format) **Document type:** newsletter.
●Also available on CD-ROM.
—CCC.
Former titles: Bender's Federal Tax Week; U S Tax Week (ISSN 0041-8129)

BUSINESS AND ECONOMICS — PUBLIC FINANCE, TAXATION

336   AT   ISSN 1032-1810
C C H JOURNAL OF AUSTRALIAN TAXATION. 1989. bi-m. C C H Australia Ltd., P.O. Box 230, North Ryde, N.S.W. 2113, Australia. TEL 61-1-300300224. FAX 61-1-300306224. —UnCover.
    Description: Contains articles and regular features which are authored by top tax professionals from all over Australia.

C C H MANAGEMENT MANUAL. see *BUSINESS AND ECONOMICS — Management*

C P A DIGEST; ideas for the busy C P A. see *BUSINESS AND ECONOMICS — Accounting*

336   US
C S E A ANNUAL REPORT. a. membership. California Society of Enrolled Agents, 3200 Ramos Circle, Sacramento, CA 95827. TEL 916-366-6646. FAX 916-366-6674. adv.; circ. 3,500 (controlled). (back issues avail.) **Document type:** corporate report.
    Description: Informs members and other interested parties of society activities, progress and financial standing.

CAHIERS DE DROIT FISCAL INTERNATIONAL. see *LAW — International Law*

336   CC   ISSN 1005-4375
CAIZHENG YU SHUIWU/PUBLIC FINANCE AND TAXATION. (Subseries of: Fuyin Baokan Ziliao) (Text in Chinese) m. $65.19. Zhongguo Renmin Daxue, Shubao Ziliao Zhongxin - China People's University, Book & Newspaper Information Center, 3 Zhang Zizhong Rd., P.O. Box 1122, Beijing 100007, People's Republic of China. TEL 86-10-4015080. (Dist. in US by: China Publications Service, Box 49614, Chicago, IL 60649. TEL 312-288-3291. FAX 312-288-8570) pp./issue: 96.
    Description: Covers the systems, policies and regulations of Chinese taxation, and government budget and expenditure.

336.2   US
CAL - TAX DIGEST. 1960. m. $59. California Taxpayers Association, 921 11th St., Ste. 800, Sacramento, CA 95814. TEL 916-441-0490. URL: http://www.caltax.org. Ed. Ronald W. Roach. R&P contact: Ronald W. Roach. bk.rev.; charts; stat. circ. 5,000. **Indexed:** Cal.Per.Ind. (1978-). **Document type:** academic/scholarly publication.
    Formerly (until 1997): Cal - Tax News (ISSN 0008-0543)

336   US   ISSN 0068-5801
CALIFORNIA. STATE BOARD OF EQUALIZATION. ANNUAL REPORT. 1879. a. free. State Board of Equalization, Box 942879, Sacramento, CA 94279-0058. TEL 916-322-8825. FAX 916-324-1258. URL: http://www.boe.ca.gov/boe/. Ed. Katherine Evatt. circ. 4,000. **Indexed:** SRI. **Document type:** government publication.
    Description: Includes information on tax revenue, programs, operations, court decisions, and legislation for California property taxes, sales and use taxes, excise taxes, fuel taxes, and environmental fees.

336.24 345
CALIFORNIA CLOSELY HELD CORPORATIONS: TAX PLANNING AND PRACTICE GUIDE. 1987. 3 base vols. with irreg. supplements. $525. Matthew Bender & Co., Inc., 2 Park Ave., New York, NY 10016. TEL 212-448-2000. E-mail: international@bender.com; URL: http://www.bender.com. Ed. Robert W. Wood. (looseleaf format)
    Description: Examines all appropriate federal and California securities laws and corporate law. Provides complete tax planning guidance and how-to advice on structuring corporate transactions with shareholders.

CALIFORNIA COMMUNITY PROPERTY WITH TAX ANALYSIS. see *LAW — Family And Matrimonial Law*

336   US
THE CALIFORNIA ENROLLED AGENT. 1977. m. (11/yr.). $35. California Society of Enrolled Agents, 3200 Ramos Circle, Sacramento, CA 95827. TEL 916-366-6646. FAX 916-366-6674. E-mail: eupcsea@aol.com; CAEAS@aol.com. Ed. William G. Sprague. R&P contact: Bill Sprague. adv. contact: Kitty Steacy. circ. 4,400. (back issues avail.)
    Description: Professional tax preparation topics, technical articles and organization news.

336.2   US
CALIFORNIA FAMILY TAX PLANNING. 1963. 2 base vols. with irreg supplements. $400. Matthew Bender & Co., Inc., 2 Park Ave., New York, NY 10016. TEL 212-448-2000. E-mail: international@bender.com; URL: http://www.bender.com. Eds. Ralph S. Rice, Terence R. Rice. (looseleaf format)
    Description: Provides plans, methods, procedures and sample forms for optimum family tax savings under California and federal income, estate and gift tax law.

336   US
CALIFORNIA PUBLIC FINANCE. 48/yr. $495 for new subscr. (foreign $545); renewal $545 (foreign $595). American Banker - Bond Buyer, Newsletter Division (Subsidiary of: Thomson Financial Services Company), One State St. Plaza, New York, NY 10004-1549. TEL 800-733-4371. FAX 212-943-2224. (Subscr. to: Box 28315, Washington, DC 20038-8315. TEL 202-347-2665) **Document type:** newsletter.
    ●Also available online. Vendor(s): Information Access Co., NewsNet (Fl65).
    Description: Latest developments affecting municipal bonds in the state that issues more municipal bonds than any other state. Reports on new issues by the state's 457 cities and 58 counties and follows legislative developments affecting public finance in Sacramento and Washington.

336   US
CALIFORNIA STATE ASSOCIATION OF COUNTIES FINANCE; corporation newsletter. irreg. $10. California State Association of Counties, 1100 K St., Ste. 101, Sacramento, CA 95814. TEL 916-327-7500. **Document type:** newsletter.
    Description: Reports on issues of importance in public finance. Explores creative financing for capital improvements.

336 350   US
CALIFORNIA TAX ANALYSIS. 1983. 5 base vols. (plus m. updates). $529. C C H Incorporated, 2700 Lake Cook Rd., Riverwoods, IL 60015. TEL 847-267-7000; 800-835-5224. FAX 800-224-8299. Eds. Robert A. Peterson, Philip Plant. (looseleaf format)
    ●Also available on CD-ROM.
    Formerly: California Taxation.

336.2   US
CALIFORNIA TAX HANDBOOK (YEAR). a. $25. Research Institute of America, Inc., 90 Fifth Ave., New York, NY 10011. TEL 212-645-4800.
    Description: Explains all of California's state taxes, with tips, suggestions and cautions.

345   US
CALIFORNIA TAX LAWYER. 1991. q. $45 (effective 1996). State Bar of California, Taxation Section, 555 Franklin St., San Francisco, CA 94102. TEL 415-561-8808. FAX 415-561-8368. Ed. John Arao. R&P contact: John Arao. adv. contact: John Arao. circ. 4,100. **Document type:** academic/scholarly publication.
    Formerly: Tax Section News.

336   CN   ISSN 0708-9031
CANADA. DEPARTMENT OF NATIONAL REVENUE. EXCISE NEWS. (Text in English and French) 1971. q. free. Department of National Revenue, Customs and Excise Branch, 191 Laurier Ave. W., Ottawa, Ont. K1A 0L5, Canada. TEL 613-994-7990. circ. 80,000.
    Formerly: Federal Sales Tax News.

336.02   CN
CANADA. DEPARTMENT OF NATIONAL REVENUE. REPORT: CUSTOMS, EXCISE AND TAXATION. (Text in English, French) a. Department of National Revenue, Finance Directorate, 191 Laurier Ave. W., Ottawa, Ont. K1A 0L5, Canada. TEL 613-995-6447.

336.71   CN   ISSN 0847-0359
CANADA. STATISTICS CANADA. PROVINCIAL ECONOMIC ACCOUNTS ANNUAL ESTIMATES/CANADA. STATISTIQUE CANADA. COMPTES ECONOMIQUES PROVINCIAUX ESTIMATIONS ANNUELLES. (Print edition ceased) 1961. a. Can.$80 (foreign $80) (effective 1998). Statistics Canada, Operations and Integration Division, Circulation Management, Jean Talon Bldg., 2-C12, Tunney's Pasture, Ottawa, ON K1A 0T6, Canada. TEL 800-267-6677. URL: http://www.statcan.ca. (only avail. on diskette) **Document type:** government publication.
    Description: Provides a regional perspective on Canadian economic developments. Includes separate sets of statistical tables for each of the twelve provinces and territories.

336.24   CN   ISSN 0008-2694
CANADA INCOME TAX GUIDE. 1952. m. Can.$360. C C H Canadian Ltd., 6 Garamond Ct., North York, ON M3C 1Z5, Canada. TEL 416-441-2992; 800-268-4522. FAX 416-444-9011. index. **Document type:** trade publication.
    Description: Provides a concise and basic explanation of the federal income tax law with illustrative examples.

336   CN
CANADA INCOME TAX GUIDE WITH CANADIAN INCOME TAX ACT. REGULATIONS & RULINGS. m. Can.$620. C C H Canadian Ltd., 6 Garamond Ct., North York, ON M3C 1Z5, Canada. TEL 416-441-2992; 800-268-4522. FAX 416-444-9011. **Document type:** trade publication.
    Description: Explanation of the federal income tax law with illustrative examples. Consolidated texts of the income tax act and regulations with historical notes, references to related sections, summaries of amendments.

336.2   CN   ISSN 0008-2740
KE5665.8
CANADA TAX CASES. 1948. 24/yr. Can.$465. Carswell, One Corporate Plaza, 2075 Kennedy Rd., Scarborough, ON M1T 3V4, Canada. TEL 416-609-8000. FAX 416-298-5094. Ed. H. Heward Stikeman. index.
    Description: Reports all judgments concerning federal taxation handed down by the Supreme Court of Canada, the Federal Court, the Tax Court, and the upper courts of the provinces. Includes comprehensive headnotes, editorial notes regarding significant decisions, topical and statutory indexes and tables of appeals.

336.2   CN   ISSN 0008-2759
CANADA TAX SERVICE; a loose-leaf tax information service. 1948. 24/yr. Can.$1000. Carswell, One Corporate Plaza, 2075 Kennedy Rd., Scarborough, ON M1T 3V4, Canada. TEL 416-609-8000. FAX 416-298-5094. Ed. H. Heward Stikeman. charts; index. (looseleaf format)
    Description: Provides section-by-section treatment of the Income Tax Act. All relevant information follows each statutory provision and includes full historical notes, detailed commentary and analysis, precedent-setting cases, numerical examples where appropriate, interpretation bulletins, information circulars, and income tax regulations.

CANADA'S TAX TREATIES. see *LAW*

336   CN
CANADIAN CURRENT INCOME TAX PROPOSALS. irreg. Can.$200. C C H Canadian Ltd., 6 Garamond Ct., North York, ON M3C 1Z5, Canada. TEL 416-441-0086; 800-268-4522. FAX 416-444-9011. **Document type:** trade publication.
    Description: Reproduces all proposed amendments to the federal Income Tax Act and Regulations.

336.2   CN   ISSN 0317-6495
CANADIAN CURRENT TAX. 1974. m. Can.$300. Butterworths Canada Ltd., Part of the Reed Elsevier group, 75 Clegg Rd., Markham, ON L6G 1A1, Canada. TEL 905-479-2665. FAX 905-479-2826. Ed. Vern Krishna. (looseleaf format) **Indexed:** Ind.Can.L.P.I. **Document type:** trade publication.
    Description: Discusses developments in all aspect of tax law for lawyers and accountants.

BUSINESS AND ECONOMICS — PUBLIC FINANCE, TAXATION

336   CN
CANADIAN G S T & COMMODITY TAX CASES. m. Can.$280. C C H Canadian Ltd., 6 Garamond Ct., North York, ON M3C 1Z5, Canada. TEL 416-441-0086; 800-268-4522. FAX 416-444-9011. **Document type:** trade publication.
   Description: Contains full-text decisions pertaining to the GST, FST, Provincial Sales Tax, gasoline tax and tobacco tax.

336   CN
CANADIAN GOODS AND SERVICES TAX REPORTER. m. Can.$420. C C H Canadian Ltd., 6 Garamond Ct., North York, ON M3C 1Z5, Canada. TEL 416-441-2992; 800-268-4522. FAX 416-444-9011. **Document type:** trade publication.
   Description: Provides up-to-date developments concerning the goods and services tax as they occur. Includes detailed commentary on and analysis of the tax.

336   CN
CANADIAN GOODS & SERVICES TAX REPORTER, COMMENTARY. m. Can.$260. C C H Canadian Ltd., 6 Garamond Ct., North York, ON M3C 1Z5, Canada. TEL 416-441-0086; 800-268-4522. FAX 416-444-9011. **Document type:** trade publication.
   Description: Provides detailed commentary on and analysis of the GST.

340 336.2   CN
CANADIAN INCOME TAX ACT, REGULATIONS & RULINGS. m. Can.$360. C C H Canadian Ltd., 6 Garamond Ct., North York, ON M3C 1Z5, Canada. TEL 416-441-2992; 800-268-4522. FAX 416-444-9011. **Document type:** trade publication.
   Description: Consolidated texts of the Income Tax Act and Regulations with historical notes, references to related sections, summaries of amendments, interpretation bulletins and advance rulings.

336   CN
CANADIAN INCOME TAX DESKTOP REFERENCE. a. Can.$60. Carswell, One Corporate Plaza, 2075 Kennedy Rd., Scarborough, ON M1T 3V4, Canada. TEL 416-609-8000. FAX 416-298-5094. (looseleaf format)

CANADIAN INDUSTRIAL INCENTIVES LEGISLATION. see *LAW*

336.2   CN   ISSN 0316-1331
CANADIAN MASTER TAX GUIDE. a. Can.$42.95. C C H Canadian Ltd., 6 Garamond Ct., North York, ON M3C 1Z5, Canada. TEL 416-441-2992; 800-268-4522. FAX 416-444-9011. (also avail. in diskette format) **Document type:** trade publication.
   Description: Explains Canadian federal income taxation.

CANADIAN MONEYSAVER; your personal finance guide. see *BUSINESS AND ECONOMICS — Investments*

336 333.33   CN
CANADIAN REAL ESTATE INCOME TAX GUIDE. q. Can.$245. C C H Canadian Ltd., 6 Garamond Ct., North York, ON M3C 1Z5, Canada. TEL 416-441-2992; 800-268-4522. FAX 416-444-9011. **Document type:** trade publication.
   Description: Covers tax implications associated with the acquisition, ownership and disposition of Canadian real estate.

CANADIAN SMALL BUSINESS FINANCING AND TAX PLANNING GUIDE. see *BUSINESS AND ECONOMICS — Small Business*

336.2   CN   ISSN 0316-3571
HJ2449
CANADIAN TAX FOUNDATION. TAX CONFERENCE. REPORT OF PROCEEDINGS. Title varies slightly. 1947. a. Canadian Tax Foundation - L'Association Canadienne d'Etudes Fiscales, One Queen St., E., Ste. 1800, Toronto, ON M5C 2Y2, Canada. TEL 416-863-9784. FAX 416-863-9585. Ed. Laurel Amalia. R&P contact: Laurel Amalia. adv. contact: Pat Hillmer. **Indexed:** C.L.I., L.R.I., Leg.Per. **Document type:** proceedings.
   —KR SourceOne.
   Description: Technical papers reflecting the notable public finance and tax developments of the year.

336   CN   ISSN 1192-2672
HJ13
CANADIAN TAX HIGHLIGHTS. 1993. m. Can.$160 (effective 1997). Canadian Tax Foundation - L'Association Canadienne d'Etudes Fiscales, One Queen St., E., Ste. 1800, Toronto, ON M5C 2Y2, Canada. TEL 416-863-9784. FAX 416-863-9585. Eds. Vivien Morgan, Laurel Amalia. R&P contact: Laurel Amalia. circ. 9,000. **Document type:** newsletter.
   Description: Fast-breaking tax information, including matters of particular importance to small and medium-sized businesses.

336.2   CN   ISSN 0008-5111
CANADIAN TAX JOURNAL. 1953. 6/yr. Can.$150 (effective 1997). Canadian Tax Foundation - L'Association Canadienne d'Etudes Fiscales, One Queen St., E., Ste. 1800, Toronto, ON M5C 2Y2, Canada. TEL 416-863-9784. FAX 416-863-9585. Ed. Laurel Amalia. R&P contact: Laurel Amalia. adv. contact: Pat Hillmer. bk.rev.; bibl.; charts; index. circ. 9,000. **Indexed:** Account.Ind. (1974-), BPIA, C.L.I., Can.B.P.I., Can.Per.Ind., Ind.Can.L.P.L., L.I.I., L.R.I., Leg.Per., P.A.I.S. **Document type:** academic/scholarly publication.
   —BLDSC (3044.930000); KR SourceOne; SWETS; UnCover.
   Description: Disseminates the results of research in and informed comment on taxation and public finance, with particular reference to Canada.

336   CN   ISSN 0319-2431
CANADIAN TAX NEWS. (Editions in English and French) 1973. 8/yr. Can.$165. Carswell, One Corporate Plaza, 2075 Kennedy Rd., Scarborough, ON M1T 3V4, Canada. TEL 416-609-8000. FAX 416-298-5094. Ed. Donald R. Huggott. index, cum.index. **Indexed:** Ind.Can.L.P.L. **Document type:** newsletter.
   Description: Reports and comments on significant legislative and regulatory activities in Canadian taxation policy and practice.

336 340   CN
CANADIAN TAX OBJECTIONS AND APPEAL PROCEDURES. 1991. q. Can.$235. C C H Canadian Ltd., 6 Garamond Ct., North York, ON M3C 1Z5, Canada. TEL 416-441-2992; 800-268-4522. FAX 416-444-9011. **Document type:** trade publication.
   Description: Deals with objections and appeals relating to federal income tax, the Goods and Services Tax and other federal taxes.

336.2   CN   ISSN 0008-512X
CANADIAN TAX PAPERS. irreg., no.100, 1995. price varies. Canadian Tax Foundation - L'Association Canadienne d'Etudes Fiscales, One Queen St., E., Ste. 1800, Toronto, ON M5C 2Y2, Canada. TEL 416-863-9784. FAX 416-863-9585. Ed. Laurel Amalia. R&P contact: Laurel Amalia. **Indexed:** Can.Per.Ind. **Document type:** monographic series.

336   CN   ISSN 0227-8375
CANADIAN TAX PLANNERS NEWSLETTER. 1979. bi-m. Can.$75. Canadian Tax Planners Ltd., Box 6489, London, ON N5W 3S5, Canada. TEL 519-641-7369. Ed. D.C. Pollock. (looseleaf format; back issues avail.) **Document type:** newsletter.
   Description: Reviews Canadian income tax.

336.2   CN   ISSN 0008-5138
CANADIAN TAX REPORTER. 1939. w. Can.$1340. C C H Canadian Ltd., 6 Garamond Ct., North York, ON M3C 1Z5, Canada. TEL 416-441-2992; 800-268-4522. FAX 416-444-9011. index. **Document type:** trade publication.
   Description: Reports on federal corporate and personal income tax laws, regulations and rulings with comprehensive digests of all court decisions relating to federal income tax with a list of appeals filed.

336.2   CN
CANADIAN TAX REPORTER, COMMENTARY. m. Can.$425. C C H Canadian Ltd., 6 Garamond Ct., North York, ON M3C 1Z5, Canada. TEL 416-441-0086; 800-268-4522. FAX 416-444-9011. **Document type:** trade publication.
   Description: Contains commentary on the Canadian Income Tax Act with legislation.

336.2   CN   ISSN 0225-0608
THE CANADIAN TAXPAYER. 1979. 24/yr. Can.$265. Carswell, One Corporate Plaza, 2075 Kennedy Rd., Scarborough, ON M1T 3V4, Canada. TEL 416-609-8000. FAX 416-298-5094. Ed. Arthur B.C. Drache.

336.2 332.6   US   ISSN 0008-5855
CAPITAL CHANGES REPORTS. 1928. w. $1199 (CD-ROM ed. $1415). C C H Incorporated, 2700 Lake Cook Rd., Riverwoods, IL 60015. TEL 847-267-7000; 800-835-5224. FAX 800-224-8299. cum.index. (looseleaf format)
   ●Also available on CD-ROM.
   —CCC.

336.2   UK
CAPITAL GAINS TAX HANDBOOK (YEAR). 1978. a. £18.70 (effective 1995). Croner Publications Ltd. (Subsidiary of: Wolters Kluwer N.V.), Croner House, 100 London Rd., Kingston-upon-Thames, Surrey TW2 6SR, England. TEL 44-181-547-3333. FAX 44-181-247-1300. TELEX 267778. **Document type:** trade publication.
   —BLDSC (8863.685400).
   Formerly (until 1992): Tolley's Capital Gains Tax (Year) (ISSN 0143-1633)

336   UK
CAPITAL TAX PLANNING. 1979. m. £145($222) Longman Group UK Ltd., Law, Tax and Finance Division, 21-27 Lamb's Conduit St., London WC1N 3NJ, England. TEL 0171-242-2548. FAX 0171-831-8119. Ed. Roy Greenfield. **Indexed:** Euro.LJI, LJI. **Document type:** bulletin.
   —UMI. **CCC.**
   Former titles: Capital Taxes News and Reports (ISSN 0264-7834); C T T News and Reports; Capital Transfer Tax News.
   Description: Information on all aspects of capital taxation.

336   SP
CARTA TRIBUTARIA. 1985. 22/yr. 68975 ptas. Grupo Especial Directivos, C. Orense, 39 2o D, 28020 Madrid, Spain. TEL 34-1-5566411. FAX 34-1-5554118. Ed. Jose Antonio Cortes.

336   CJ   ISSN 0303-8718
CAYMAN ISLANDS. CURRENCY BOARD. REPORT. 1972. a. free. Currency Board, Government Administration Bldg., George Town, Grand Cayman, Cayman Islands, British W.I. TEL 809-949-7900. FAX 809-945-1145. TELEX 4260 CP. Ed.Bd. adv. contact: Cindy Bush. illus. circ. 250. **Document type:** corporate report.

336   NE   ISSN 1385-2159
CENTRAL AND EAST EUROPEAN TAX DIRECTORY. (Text in English) 1994. a. $150 (effective 1997). I B F D Publications B.V., P.O. Box 20237, 1000 HE Amsterdam, Netherlands. TEL 31-20-6267726. FAX 31-20-6228658. TELEX 13217 INTAX NL. (In US: IBFD Publications USA, Inc., 4 Maple Ln., Valatie, NY 12184. TEL 800-299-6330. FAX 518-758-2246) Ed. Maria Veghely. **Document type:** directory.
   Description: Provides reference information on corporate income tax, personal income tax, social security and VAT in the entire Central and East European region.

336   BH   ISSN 1025-1618
CENTRAL BANK OF BELIZE. ANNUAL REPORT AND ACCOUNTS. a. free. Central Bank of Belize, P.O. Box 852, Belize City, Belize. TEL 501-2-77216. FAX 501-2-76383. TELEX 225 MONETARY BZ. E-mail: orlandoa@cenbank.gov.bz. **Document type:** corporate report.
   Formerly (until 1982): Monetary Authority of Belize. Annual Report and Accounts.

CENTRAL BANK OF BELIZE. ANNUAL STATISTICAL DIGEST. see *BUSINESS AND ECONOMICS — Abstracting, Bibliographies, Statistics*

336   BH
CENTRAL BANK OF BELIZE. QUARTERLY ECONOMIC REVIEW. 1977. 3/yr. free. Central Bank of Belize, P.O. Box 852, Belize City, Belize. TEL 501-2-77216. FAX 501-2-76383. TELEX 225 MONETARY BZ. E-mail: orlandoa@cenbank.gov.bz.
   Former titles (until 1982): Central Bank of Belize. Quarterly Review (ISSN 1025-1634); Belize. Monetary Authority. Quarterly Review.

BUSINESS AND ECONOMICS — PUBLIC FINANCE, TAXATION

336.73   US   ISSN 0272-6017
HJ275
CHANGING PUBLIC ATTITUDES ON GOVERNMENTS AND TAXES; a commission survey. a. $10. U.S. Advisory Commission on Intergovernmental Relations, 800 K St., N.W., Ste. 450-S, Washington, DC 20575. TEL 202-653-5640. **Document type:** government publication.

336   US   ISSN 0278-0593
CHARITABLE GIVING AND SOLICITATION. 1981. base vol. (plus m. bulletin). $425. Warren, Gorham & Lamont, One Penn Plaza, New York, NY 10119-4098. TEL 212-971-5000. FAX 212-971-5113. (Subscr. to: The Park Square Bldg., 31 St. James Ave., Boston, MA 02116-4112. TEL 800-950-1210) Ed.Bd. (looseleaf format)
Description: Focuses on laws governing charitable giving and solicitation, with numerous tips and proven fund-raising ideas.

336   UK
CHARTERED INSTITUTE OF PUBLIC FINANCE AND ACCOUNTANCY. PUBLIC FINANCE FOUNDATION. DISCUSSION PAPERS. 1985. irreg. (3-6/yr.). price varies. Chartered Institute of Public Finance and Accountancy, Public Finance Foundation, 3 Robert St., London WC2N 6BH, England. TEL 0171-895-8823. FAX 0171-895-8825. (back issues avail.) **Document type:** monographic series.
Description: Discusses various aspects of public finance in government and among regulated industries and utilities.

336   UK
CHARTERED INSTITUTE OF PUBLIC FINANCE AND ACCOUNTANCY. PUBLIC FINANCE FOUNDATION. PRIVATISATION SERIES. 1988. irreg., no.5, 1989. price varies. Chartered Institute of Public Finance and Accountancy, Public Finance Foundation, 3 Robert St., London WC2N 6BH, England. TEL 0171-895-8823. FAX 0171-895-8825. (back issues avail.) **Document type:** monographic series.
Description: Discusses various issues concerning the privatization of public utilities and nationalized industries.

336   UK
CHARTERED INSTITUTE OF PUBLIC FINANCE AND ACCOUNTANCY. PUBLIC FINANCE FOUNDATION. WORKING PAPERS. irreg. free. Chartered Institute of Public Finance and Accountancy, Public Finance Foundation, 3 Robert St., London WC2N 6BH, England. TEL 0171-895-8823. FAX 0171-895-8825. (back issues avail.) **Document type:** monographic series.
Description: Disseminates research on various aspects of public financing of regulated industries.

CHARTERED INSTITUTE OF PUBLIC FINANCE AND ACCOUNTANCY. RATING REVIEW (SCOTLAND). ACTUALS. see BUSINESS AND ECONOMICS — Abstracting, Bibliographies, Statistics

CHARTERED INSTITUTE OF PUBLIC FINANCE AND ACCOUNTANCY. RATING REVIEW (SCOTLAND) STATISTICS. ESTIMATES. see BUSINESS AND ECONOMICS — Abstracting, Bibliographies, Statistics

336   UK
CHECK YOUR TAX AND MONEY FACTS. a. £2.50. W. Foulsham & Co. Ltd., Yeovil Rd., Slough SL1 4JH, England.
Formerly: Check Your Tax.
Description: Addresses public finance, taxation and general economic topics.

336   CL
CHILE. DIRECCION DE PRESUPUESTOS. CALCULO DE ENTRADAS DE LA NACION. a. Direccion de Presupuestos, Piso 12, Of. 24-25, Teatinos 120, Santiago, Chile. FAX 56-2-6713-814. charts.

336   CL
CHILE. DIRECCION DE PRESUPUESTOS. EXPOSICION SOBRE EL ESTADO DE LA HACIENDA PUBLICA. 1914. a. Direccion de Presupuestos, Piso 12, Of. 24-25, Teatinos 120, Santiago, Chile. FAX 56-2-6713-814. charts; stat.

336   CL
CHILE. DIRECCION DE PRESUPUESTOS. INSTRUCCIONES PARA LA EJECUCION DE LA LEY DE PRESUPUESTOS. a. Direccion de Presupuestos, Piso 12, Of. 24-25, Teatinos 120, Santiago, Chile. FAX 56-2-6713-814. charts.

336   CL
CHILE. DIRECCION DE PRESUPUESTOS. LEY DE PRESUPUESTOS PARA EL SECTOR PUBLICO. 1884. a. Direccion de Presupuestos, Piso 12, Of. 24-25, Teatinos 120, Santiago, Chile. FAX 56-2-6713-814. charts.

336   CL
CHILE. SERVICIO DE IMPUESTOS INTERNOS. BOLETIN OFICIAL. (Includes annuals: Indice de Materias del Boletin, Textos Legales Actualizados) 1954. m. Esc.83000($219) to individuals; institutions Esc.98000($258) (effective 1995). Servicio de Impuestos Internos, Teatinos 120, 1o Piso, Oficina de Comunicaciones, Santiago, Chile. TEL 56-2-6921330. FAX 56-2-6921353. Ed. Bernardo Lara Berrios; Pub. Gonzalo Vergara Gomez. index. circ. 4,000. **Document type:** government publication, bulletin.
Formerly: Chile. Servicio de Impuestos Internos. Boletin (ISSN 0716-145X)
Description: Covers administration and jurisprudence on taxes.

336.2   CC
CHINA TAX REVIEW. (Text in English) 1994. 10/yr. HK.$2500 in Hong Kong; elsewhere $350. Ashton - Brooke Asia Publishing Ltd., G.P.O. Box 12261, Central, Hong Kong, People's Republic of China. TEL 852-2982-0590. FAX 852-2982-0590. **Document type:** newsletter.
Description: Provides up-to-date information on developments related to individual and corporate taxation in China.

336   PO
CIENCIA E TECNICA FISCAL. no.169, 1973. bi-m. Esc.180. Ministerio das Financas, Direccao Geral da Administracao Publica, Av. 24 de Julho 80-D, 1200 Lisbon, Portugal. Ed.Bd. adv.; bk.rev.; charts. circ. 3,400. **Document type:** government publication.

CLIENT TAX NEWSLETTER. see BUSINESS AND ECONOMICS — Accounting

CLIENT'S MONTHLY ALERT; monthly roundup of significant business & tax developments. see BUSINESS AND ECONOMICS — Accounting

336   FR   ISSN 0294-1546
CODE GENERAL DES IMPOTS. 1975. a. 240 F. (Direction Generale des Impots) Imprimerie Nationale, B.P. 514, 59505 Douai Cedex, France. TEL 27-93-70-90. FAX 27-93-70-96.
Description: Allows access to regulatory and legislative texts concerning French fiscal law.

336.2 340   CN
COLLECTION FISCALE DU QUEBEC. (Text in French) m. Can.$1016. C C H - F M Ltd., 33 Racine, Farnham, PQ J2N 3A3, Canada. TEL 800-363-8304. FAX 514-293-2644. Ed. Pierrette Gregoire.
Formerly: Fiscalite Quebecoise.
Description: Publishes the full texts of statutes and detailed commentary of federal and provincial income taxes.

336   US
COLLEGE OF WILLIAM AND MARY. MARSHALL-WYTHE SCHOOL OF LAW. TAX CONFERENCE. 1955. a. College of William and Mary, Marshall-Wythe School of Law, Williamsburg, VA 23185. TEL 757-221-9833. (Dist. by: Wm. W. Gaunt & Sons, Inc., Gaunt Bldg., 3011 Gulf Dr., Homes Beach, FL 34217-2199. TEL 813-778-5211. FAX 813-778-5252)

336   CK
COLOMBIA. MINISTERIO DE HACIENDA Y CREDITO PUBLICO. PROYECTO DE PRESUPUESTO GENERAL DE LA NACION. a. Ministerio de Hacienda y Credito Publico, Direccion General del Presupuesto, Carrera 7a, 6-45, pisos 1o, 7o, 8o, Santa Fe de Bogota, Colombia. FAX 91-286-53-45. charts. **Document type:** government publication.
Formerly: Colombia. Direccion General del Presupuesto. Proyecto de Presupuesto (ISSN 0588-3598)

336 341   NE
A COMMENTARY TO THE U S - NETHERLANDS INCOME TAX CONVENTION. (Text in English) base vol. (plus irreg. supplement). Kluwer Law International (Subsidiary of: Wolters Kluwer N.V.), Postbus 85889, 2508 CN The Hague, Netherlands. TEL 31-70-3081500. E-mail: services@wkap.nl; URL: http://www.wkap.nl. (Dist. by: Libresso Distribution Centre, P.O. Box 23, 7400 GA Deventer, Netherlands. TEL 31-570-633155. FAX 31-570-633834; In N. America: Kluwer Law International, 675 Massachusetts Ave., Cambridge, MA 02139. TEL 617-354-0140. FAX 617-354-8595) (looseleaf format)
Description: Publishes commentary, case law and relevant literature pertaining to the 1994 U.S.-Netherlands tax treaty.

336.2   EI   ISSN 0377-0192
HJ2599.5
COMMISSION OF THE EUROPEAN COMMUNITIES. DIRECTORATE OF TAXATION. INVENTORY OF TAXES. (Text in English) a. $110. Office for Official Publications of the European Communities, L-2985 Luxembourg, Luxembourg.
—BLDSC (4557.702300).

336   UK
COMMODITY WEEK. 1760. w. £250 (Europe £290; rest of world £290) (effective 1996). U K Publications, 10 Little College St., London SW1, England. TEL 44-171-976-7772. FAX 44-171-976-0775. **Document type:** trade publication.
Former titles: Public Ledger and Commodity Week; Public Ledger Commodity Year Book.

COMPANY CAR TAX. see TRANSPORTATION — Automobiles

354.67   CM
COMPTES NATIONAUX DU CAMEROUN. a. 4000 Fr.CFA. Direction de la Statistique et de la Comptabilite Nationale - Department of Statistics and National Accounts, B.P. 660, Yaounde, Cameroon. **Document type:** government publication.

332   US
COMPTROLLER'S HANDBOOK. (Supplementary vols. avail.: Comptroller's Handbook for Fiduciary Activities; Comptroller's Handbook for Compliance) base vol. (plus irreg. updates). $120 (effective 1997). U.S. Office of the Comptroller of the Currency, Administrator of National Banks, Washington, DC 20219. FAX 202-874-5263. (Subscr. to: Box 7004, Chicago, IL 60673-0004) **Document type:** trade publication, government publication.
Description: Presents policies and procedures for the examination of the commercial activities of national banks.

COMPUTER LAW & TAX REPORT; monthly newsletter covering computer-related law and tax issues. see COMPUTERS

354   CG
CONSEILLER COMPTABLE. Variant title: Revue Zairoise de la Comptabilite. 1974. q. 10 Fr.CFA($13). Conseil Permanent de la Comptabilite, Departement des Finances et du Budget, 17, av. du Port, Building S.N.C.Z., B.P. 308, Kinshasa, Democratic Republic of the Congo. Ed. Kinzonzi Mvutukidi Ngindu K. adv.; bk.rev.; illus. circ. 1,000.

350   US   ISSN 0148-009X
CONSOLIDATED TAX RETURN (SUPPLEMENT). a. $201.45 (foreign 306.95) (effective 1995). Warren, Gorham & Lamont, One Penn Plaza, New York, NY 10119. TEL 212-971-5000. FAX 212-971-5113. (Subscr. to: The Park Square Bldg., 31 St. James Ave., Boston, MA 02116-4112. TEL 800-950-1207) **Document type:** trade publication.

CONSTRUCTION ACCOUNTING MANUAL. see BUSINESS AND ECONOMICS — Accounting

BUSINESS AND ECONOMICS — PUBLIC FINANCE, TAXATION

336 690   US   ISSN 1047-5796
CONSTRUCTION NICHE BUILDER. 1989. m. $196 (effective 1997). Harcourt Brace Professional Publishing, 525 B St., Ste. 1900, San Diego, CA 92101-4495. TEL 619-699-6716. FAX 619-699-6593. Ed. Dan Shiffrin; Pub. Ken Rethmeier. R&P contact: Jenna Lake. TEL 619-699-6265. **Document type:** newsletter.
   Description: Devoted to strategies and techniques for CPAs serving the construction industry.

336   SP   ISSN 0069-9292
CONTABILIDAD NACIONAL DE ESPANA. a. Instituto Nacional de Estadistica, P. de la Castellana, 183, 28071 Madrid, Spain.

CORPORATE BUSINESS LAW REPORT; a practical business review for corporate administrators. see *LAW — Corporate Law*

336.2   CN   ISSN 0070-0282
KE5884
CORPORATE MANAGEMENT TAX CONFERENCE. 1959. a. price varies. Canadian Tax Foundation - L'Association Canadienne d'Etudes Fiscales, One Queen St., E., Ste. 1800, Toronto, ON M5C 2Y2, Canada. TEL 416-863-9784. FAX 416-863-9585. Ed. Laurel Amalia. R&P contact: Laurel Amalia. **Indexed:** C.L.I., L.R.I., Leg.Per. **Document type:** proceedings.
—KR SourceOne. **CCC.**
   Description: Technical papers with analysis of a tax topic of interest to the corporate sector.

336.2   UK
CORPORATION TAX HANDBOOK (YEAR). 1978? a. £18.70 (effective 1995). Croner Publications Ltd. (Subsidiary of: Wolters Kluwer N.V.), Croner House, 100 London Rd., Kingston-upon-Thames, Surrey TW2 6SR, England. TEL 44-181-547-3333. FAX 44-181-247-1300. TELEX 267778. **Document type:** trade publication.
—BLDSC (8863.685700).
   Formerly (until 1992): Tolley's Corporation Tax (Year) (ISSN 0305-8921)

336   US
HD30.28
COST MANAGEMENT UPDATE. 1985. m. $75. Institute of Management Accountants, 10 Paragon Dr., Montvale, NJ 07645-1760. TEL 201-573-9000. Ed. Karen Sanders. bk.rev. circ. 1,400. (back issues avail.) **Indexed:** Account.Ind. (1985-).
●Also available online. Vendor(s): UMI.
   Formerly (until 1991): Business and Tax Planning Quarterly (ISSN 0898-1841)
   Description: Information for financial management executives.

336   CR
COSTA RICA. DIRECCION GENERAL DE LA TRIBUTACION DIRECTA. ESTADISTICA DEMOGRAFIA FISCAL DEL IMPUESTO SOBRE LA RENTA. PERIODOS. no.71, 1974. irreg. free. Direccion General de Tributacion Directa, San Jose, Costa Rica. circ. 250.

336   CR   ISSN 0070-0576
COSTA RICA. MINISTERIO DE HACIENDA OFICINA DEL PRESUPUESTO. INFORME.* a. Ministerio de Hacienda, Oficina del Presupuesto, San Jose, Costa Rica.

RED-ALERT. see *BUSINESS AND ECONOMICS — Banking And Finance*

336   UK
RONER'S GUIDE TO CORPORATION TAX. Variant title: Guide to Corporation Tax. 1978. base vol. (plus q. updates). £218.30 (updates £163.30) (effective 1995). Croner Publications Ltd. (Subsidiary of: Wolters Kluwer N.V.), Croner House, 100 London Rd., Kingston-upon-Thames, Surrey KT2 6SR, England. TEL 44-181-547-3333. FAX 44-181-547-2637. TELEX 267778. Ed. Robert Piper. (looseleaf format) **Document type:** trade publication.
   Description: Covers computation and administration of corporation tax.

336.2   UK
CRONER'S REFERENCE BOOK FOR THE SELF-EMPLOYED AND SMALLER BUSINESS. 1976. base vol. (plus m. updates). £147.50 (updates £89) (effective 1995). Croner Publications Ltd. (Subsidiary of: Wolters Kluwer N.V.), Croner House, 100 London Road, Kingston-upon-Thames, Surrey KT2 6SR, England. TEL 44-181-547-3333. FAX 44-181-547-2637. TELEX 267778. Ed. Robert Piper. (looseleaf format) **Document type:** trade publication.
—BLDSC (3487.832500).
   Formerly: Croner's Reference Book for the Self-Employed (ISSN 0141-707X)
   Description: Includes comprehensive coverage of current information about VAT, taxation, health and safety issues, National Insurance, employment, consumer and company law.

336.2   UK
CRONER'S REFERENCE BOOK FOR V A T. 1973. base vol. (plus m. updates). £254.90 (updates £199.90) (effective 1995). Croner Publications Ltd. (Subsidiary of: Wolters Kluwer N.V.), Croner House, 100 London Rd., Kingston-upon-Thames, Surrey KT2 6SR, England. TEL 44-181-547-3333. FAX 44-181-547-2637. TELEX 267778. Ed. Katherine Besomi. (looseleaf format)
   Formerly: Croner's Reference Book for Value Added Tax.
   Description: Provides in-depth coverage of the Value Added Tax.

336.2   SP   ISSN 0210-2919
CRONICA TRIBUTARIA. 1972. q. 8000 ptas. Instituto de Estudios Fiscales, Avda. de Cardenal Herrera Oria 378, 28035 Madrid, Spain. TEL 34-1-3398800. FAX 34-1-3398964. (Subscr. to: Ministerio de Economia y Hacienda, Centro de Publicaciones, Plaza del Campillo del Mundo Nuevo 3, 28005 Madrid, Spain. TEL 91-527-1437)
—CINDOC.

336   NR
CROSS RIVER STATE. MINISTRY OF ECONOMIC DEVELOPMENT AND RECONSTRUCTION. STATE DEVELOPMENT PLAN.* 1970? irreg. 5p. Ministry of Economic Development and Reconstruction, Calabar, South-Eastern State, Nigeria. (Dist. by: Cross River State Government Printer, Calabar, South-Eastern Nigeria) illus.; stat. **Document type:** government publication.
   Formerly: South-Eastern State. Ministry of Economic Development and Reconstruction. State Development Plan.

336
CUMULATIVE LIST OF ORGANIZATIONS. a. plus q. supplements. $90. U.S. Internal Revenue Service, I R S Bldg., 1111 Constitution Ave., N.W., Washington, DC 20224. (Dist. by: Bernan Press, 4611-F Assembly Dr., Lanham, MD 20706-4391. TEL 800-274-4447. FAX 301-459-0056; And: Superintendent of Documents, U.S. Government Printing Office, Box 371954, Pittsburgh, PA 15250. TEL 202-512-1800. FAX 202-512-2250) **Document type:** government publication.
   Description: Lists the names of tax-exempt organizations.

336.73   US   ISSN 0082-9439
HJ9011
CURRENT GOVERNMENTS REPORTS: CITY GOVERNMENT FINANCES. (Series GF-4) 1965. a. price varies. U.S. Bureau of the Census, Governments Division, Washington, DC 20233. TEL 301-457-1523. (also avail. in microfiche; back issues avail.) **Document type:** government publication.
●Available only online.

336   US   ISSN 0098-678X
HJ9011
CURRENT GOVERNMENTS REPORTS: COUNTY GOVERNMENT FINANCES. (Series GF-8) a. price varies. U.S. Bureau of the Census, Governments Division, Washington, DC 20233. TEL 202-457-1523. (also avail. in microfiche) **Document type:** government publication.
●Available only online.

336 331 350   US   ISSN 0096-3224
JK2474
CURRENT GOVERNMENTS REPORTS: FINANCES OF EMPLOYEE RETIREMENT SYSTEMS OF STATE AND LOCAL GOVERNMENTS. (Series GF-2) a. price varies. U.S. Bureau of the Census, Governments Division, Washington, DC 20233. TEL 202-457-1523. (also avail. in microfiche) **Indexed:** Amer.Stat.Ind. **Document type:** government publication.
●Available only online.

336   US   ISSN 0095-3741
HJ257.2
CURRENT GOVERNMENTS REPORTS: GOVERNMENT FINANCES. Key Title: Governmental Finances (Washington). (Series GF-5) a. price varies. U.S. Bureau of the Census, Governments Division, Washington, DC 20233. TEL 301-457-1523. FAX 301-457-4714. stat. (also avail. in microfiche; back issues avail.) **Document type:** government publication.
●Available only online. Vendor(s): CompuServe, Inc., Knight-Ridder Information, Inc.

336.2   US
CURRENT GOVERNMENTS REPORTS: STATE AND LOCAL GOVERNMENT SPECIAL STUDIES. (Series GSS) irreg. U.S. Bureau of the Census, Governments Division, Washington, DC 20233. TEL 301-457-1586. (also avail. in microfiche) **Document type:** government publication.

336   US   ISSN 0270-0808
HJ2385
CURRENT GOVERNMENTS REPORTS: STATE GOVERNMENT TAX COLLECTIONS. (Series GF-1. Print edition ceased 1992.) 1965. a. price varies. U.S. Bureau of the Census, Customer Services, Washington, DC 20233. TEL 202-457-4100. URL: http://www.census.gov/. **Document type:** government publication.
●Available only online.
   Formerly (until 1977): State Tax Collections (ISSN 0095-4152)

336.2 340   II
CURRENT INCOME TAX LAW. (Text in English) no. 75, 1973. m. Current Law Publishers, Box 1268 G.P.O., Delhi 110006, India. Ed. J.D. Jain. charts. (looseleaf format)

336   US
CURRENT LEGAL FORMS WITH TAX ANALYSIS. 1948. 23 base vols. (plus updates 4/yr.). $1595 for base vols.; updates $1195. Matthew Bender & Co., Inc., 2 Park Ave., New York, NY 10016. TEL 212-448-2000. E-mail: international@bender.com; URL: http://www.bender.com.
   Description: Highly annotated forms, agreements, and legal documentation with tax introductions, practice backgrounds and annotations to case law and tax code.

336.2   II   ISSN 0971-0043
CURRENT TAX REPORTER. (Text in English) 1972. w. Rs.2160 (effective 1997). G-315 Shastri Nagar, Jodhpur 342 003, Rajasthan, India. TEL 291-33300. FAX 91-291-612621. URL: http://www.ctr-india.com. Ed. Raman Bissa; Pub. K. Kumar. R&P contact: K. Kumar. adv.; bk.rev.; bibl. circ. 10,000. **Document type:** newspaper.
   Formerly: Current Tax Reporter (Supreme Court).
   Description: Contains Supreme Court and High Court decisions.

336   US   ISSN 0011-4146
KF6687.A2
CUSTOMS BULLETIN AND DECISIONS; regulations, rulings, decisions, and notices concerning customs and related matters and decisions of Court of Customs and Patent Appeals and Customs Court. 1967. w. $144 (foreign $180) (effective 1995). U.S. Customs Service, National Support Staff, Rm. B338, 1301 Constitution Ave. N.W., Washington, DC 20229. (Subscr. to: Superintendent of Documents, U.S. Government Printing Office, Box 371954, Pittsburgh, PA 15250-7954. TEL 202-512-1800. FAX 202-512-2250) (also avail. in microform from UMI; back issues avail.; reprint service avail. from UMI) **Document type:** government publication, bulletin.
   Formerly: Weekly Treasury Decisions.
   Description: Contains regulations, rulings, decisions, and notices concerning U.S. Customs and related matters of the U.S. Customs Service.

BUSINESS AND ECONOMICS — PUBLIC FINANCE, TAXATION

CUSTOMS IMPORTS AND EXPORTS JOURNAL. see BUSINESS AND ECONOMICS — *International Commerce*

336   US   ISSN 1063-7443
CUSTOMS RECORD. 1988. w. $550 (outside N. America $750). International Business Reports, Box 1425, Vienna, VA 22183-1425. TEL 703-998-2927. FAX 703-998-0019. Eds. Emilio G. Collado, Edward P. Kemp. **Document type:** newsletter.
    Description: Reports on all activity at the US Customs Service; changes in special tariff programs; federal court cases and decisions; and Congressional legislation and reports.

336   JA
CUSTOMS TARIFF SCHEDULES. (Text in Japanese, English) a. 23301 Yen. Japan Tariff Association, c/o Jibiki Daini Bldg., 4-7-8 Kojimachi, Chiyoda-ku, Tokyo, Japan. **Document type:** government publication.

336   CY   ISSN 0070-2323
HJ68
CYPRUS. BUDGET: ESTIMATES OF REVENUE AND EXPENDITURE. (Text in English) a. £6($24) Government Printing Office, Nicosia, Cyprus. TEL 357-2-302202. FAX 357-2-303175. **Document type:** government publication.

336   CY   ISSN 0084-9510
HJ68
CYPRUS. DEVELOPMENT ESTIMATES. a. £C4($14.40) Government Printing Office, Nicosia, Cyprus. TEL 357-2-302202. FAX 357-2-303175. **Document type:** government publication.

336   CY   ISSN 0574-8305
HG3729.C85
CYPRUS. LOAN COMMISSIONERS. ACCOUNTS AND STATISTICS FOR THE YEAR. 1954. a. £C1.50. Loan Commissioners, Nicosia, Cyprus. FAX 357-2-365580. stat. circ. 350. **Document type:** government publication.

336 355   US   ISSN 1058-076X
UC267   CODEN: DCAEEV
D C A A CONTRACT AUDIT MANUAL. s-a. $40 (foreign $50) (effective 1997). U.S. Defense Contract Audit Agency, c/o Superintendent of Documents, U.S. Government Printing Office, Washington, DC 20402. (Subscr. to: Superintendent of Documents, U.S. Government Printing Office, Box 371954, Pittsburgh, PA 15250-7954. TEL 202-512-1800. FAX 202-512-2250) **Document type:** government publication.
    Description: Establishes auditing policies and procedures for Department of Defense D.C.A.A. personnel.

336   US   ISSN 0092-6884
KF6289.A1
DAILY TAX REPORT; from today's daily report for executives. 1954. d. (Mon.-Fri.) $2063. The Bureau of National Affairs, Inc., 1231 25th St., N.W., Washington, DC 20037. TEL 202-452-4200. FAX 202-822-8092. TELEX 285656 BNAI WSH. URL: http://www.bna.com/. (Subscr. to: 9435 Key West Ave., Rockville, MD 20850. TEL 800-372-1033) Ed. Nancee L. Simonson. bi-w. & bi-m. indexes. (looseleaf format; back issues avail.)
    ●Also available online. Vendor(s): Bureau of National Affairs, Lexis-Nexis (BNADTR), NewsNet, West Group (BNA-DTR).
    —CCC.
    Description: Tax notification service designed to give tax professionals rapid notification and comprehensive coverage of national legislative, regulatory, judicial, and policy developments.

336   US
DAILY TAXFAX. (Supplement to: Highlights & Documents (ISSN 0889-3055)) d. $2249 ($1249 to subscribers of Highlights & Documents). Tax Analysts, 6830 N. Fairfax Dr., Arlington, VA 22213. TEL 800-955-2444. FAX 703-533-4444. (only avail. by fax) **Document type:** trade publication.
    Description: Summarizes the day's tax news developments, including court decisions and congressional announcements, classified by Internal Revenue Code section, state, and country.

336   US   ISSN 0145-0239
DAILY TREASURY STATEMENT; cash and debt operations of the United States Treasury. d. (weekdays only). $463 (foreign $579) (effective 1995). U.S. Department of the Treasury, Bureau of the Public Debt, Rm. 553, 999 E St., Washington, DC 20239-0001. TEL 202-219-3300. (Subscr. to: Superintendent of Documents, U.S. Government Printing Office, Box 371954, Pittsburgh, PA 15250-7954. TEL 202-512-1800. FAX 202-512-2250) **Document type:** government publication.

336   UA
DALIL AL-DARA'IB/TAX GUIDE. (Text in Arabic) 1989. irreg. Mu'assasat al-Ahram, Sharia al-Galaa, Cairo, Egypt. TEL 02-758333. FAX 02-745888. TELEX 20185 AHRAM UN.

336.2   NE
DATABASE OF CORPORATE TAXATION AND CROSS-BORDER PAYMENTS IN O E C D COUNTRIES. (Text in English) 3/yr. $565 (renewals $345) (effective 1997). I B F D Publicatons B.V., P.O. Box 20237, 1000 HE Amsterdam, Netherlands. TEL 31-20-6267726. FAX 31-20-6228658. TELEX 13217 INTAX NL. (In US: IBFD Publications USA, Inc., 4 Maple Ln., Valatie, NY 12184. TEL 800-299-6330. FAX 518-758-2246) (diskette format)
    Description: Contains developments in corporate taxation in developed countries. Includes information on taxation of resident and non-resident companies and holding companies, as well as taxation of foreign-source income.

336.2   NE
DATABASE OF TAXATION OF PRIVATE INCOME IN O E C D COUNTRIES. (Text in English) 3/yr. $565 (renewals $345) (effective 1997). I B F D Publications B.V., P.O. Box 20237, 1000 HE Amsterdam, Netherlands. TEL 31-20-6267726. FAX 31-20-6228658. TELEX 13217 INTAX NL. (In US: IBFD Publications USA, Inc., 4 Maple Ln., Valatie, NY 12184. TEL 800-299-6330. FAX 518-758-2246) (diskette format)
    Description: Contains information on the taxation of resident and non-resident individuals, with particular reference to dividends and interest. Features a transitional comparison of taxes borne on dividends and a list of tax-exempt government bonds.

336   UK
DE VOIL: VALUE ADDED TAX. 3 base vols. (plus m. updates). £225($450) Butterworth & Co. (Publishers) Ltd., Part of the Reed Elsevier group, Halsbury House, 35 Chancery Ln., London WC2A 1EL, England. TEL 071-400-2500. FAX 071-400-2842. (U.S. addr.: Butterworth Legal Publishers, 90 Stiles Rd., Salem, NH 03079-9981. TEL 603-898-9664) (looseleaf format) **Document type:** trade publication.

336   DK   ISSN 0905-7544
HJ56
DENMARK. FINANSMINISTERIET. UDGIFTSANALYSER. 1979. a. DKK 90. (Finansministeriet, Budgetdepartementet) Official Danish Information Service, P.O. Box 1103, Bredgade 20, DK-1009 Copenhagen K, Denmark. (Dist. by: Danske Boghendleres Kommissionsanstalt, Siljangade 6, DK-2300 Copenhagen S, Denmark) **Document type:** government publication.
    Former titles (until 1990): Denmark. Finansministeriet. Redegoerelse om den Offentlige Sektor (ISSN 0904-3098); (until 1988): Denmark. Finansministeriet. Budgetdepartementet. Budgetredegoerelse (ISSN 0106-3006)

336   US
DEPRECIATION & CAPITAL PLANNING. 1987. base vol. (plus supplements). $145 (effective 1995). Warren, Gorham & Lamont, One Penn Plaza, New York, NY 10119. TEL 212-971-5000. FAX 212-971-5113. (Subscr. to: The Park Square Bldg., 31 St. James Ave., Boston, MA 02116-4112. TEL 800-950-1207) **Document type:** trade publication.
    Description: Complete planning reference to all changes in depreciation and investment credits.

336.2   GW   ISSN 0724-5637
DEUTSCHE STEUER-ZEITUNG. 1913. s-m. DM.348 (effective 1997). (Bundesministerium der Finanzen) Stollfuss Verlag Bonn, Postfach 2428, 53014 Bonn, Germany. TEL 49-228-724-0. FAX 49-228-659223. Ed. E. Stoecker. charts; illus.; index. circ. 3,800. **Indexed:** IBR. **Document type:** government publication.
    —CCC.
    Formerly: Deutsche Steuer-Zeitung: Ausgabe A (ISSN 0012-0774)

343.04   GW   ISSN 0012-1347
DEUTSCHES STEUERRECHT; Wochenschrift fuer Steuerrecht, Gesellschaftsrecht und Betriebswirtschaft. Variant title: D St R. Cassette edition: D St R - Cassetten (ISSN 0949-4774) 1962. w. DM.306 (cassette edition DM.372; CD-ROM edition DM.798) (effective 1997). (Bundessteuerberaterkammer) Verlag C.H. Beck, 80791 Munich, Germany. TEL 49-89-38189-338. FAX 49-89-38189-398. Ed.Bd. adv.: B&W page DM.4800, color page DM.8400; trim 260 x 186. bk.rev.; index, cum.index covering 10 yrs.; circ. 25,135 (controlled). (also avail. in audio cassette; back issues avail.) **Indexed:** IBR. **Document type:** trade publication.
    ●Also available on CD-ROM.

336   FR   ISSN 0012-2491
DICTIONNAIRE PERMANENT: FISCAL. 1947. 3 base vols. plus w. updates. 1730 F. for base vols. (updates 520 F.) (effective 1995). Editions Legislatives et Administratives, 80 av. de la Marne, 92546 Montrouge Cedex, France. TEL 40-92-68-68. FAX 46-56-00-15. TELEX 632 855 F. bibl.; index, cum.index. circ. 9,000. (looseleaf format)
    Description: Covers fiscal laws for individuals and businesses.

336.2   II
DIRECT TAXES BULLETIN. (Text in English, Hindi) 1961. q. Rs.114($41.04) Government of India, Department of Publications, Civil Lines, Delhi 110 054, India. TEL 11-2517409. **Document type:** government publication, bulletin.

336 355   US   ISSN 1058-0158
UC267
DIRECTORY OF D C A A OFFICES. s-a. $10 (foreign $12.50) (effective 1997). U.S. Defense Contract Audit Agency, c/o Superintendent of Documents, U.S. Government Printing Office, Washington, DC 20402. (Subscr. to: Superintendent of Documents, U.S. Government Printing Office, Box 371954, Pittsburgh, PA 15250-7954. TEL 202-512-1800. FAX 202-512-2250) **Document type:** directory, government publication.
    Description: Lists personnel at the Defense Contract Audit Agency headquarters and regional offices, as well as those working at the Defense Contract Audit Institute.

DIRECTORY OF WISCONSIN LEGISLATIVE AND CONGRESSIONAL DISTRICTS. see *PUBLIC ADMINISTRATION*

336 346.01   US   ISSN 0730-6555
DIVORCE TAXATION. 1981. base vol. (plus m. Report Bulletins and updates). $465. Warren, Gorham & Lamont, 395 Hudson St., New York, NY 10014. TEL 212-367-6300; 212-971-5000. FAX 212-367-6718. (Subscr. to: The Park Square Bldg., 31 St. James Ave., Boston, MA 02116-4112. TEL 800-950-1210) Ed. Marjorie A. O'Connell. (looseleaf format)
    Description: Explains tax consequences of spousal and child support payments, property rights and interests, and special marital assets. Highlights provisions of new legislation.

336.2   CN   ISSN 0046-0567
KE5665.8
DOMINION TAX CASES. s-m. Can.$565. C C H Canadian Ltd., 6 Garamond Ct., North York, ON M3C 1Z5, Canada. TEL 416-441-2992; 800-268-4522. FAX 416-444-9011. index. (also avail. in diskette format) **Document type:** trade publication.
    ●Also available on CD-ROM.
    Description: Digests full texts of federal income ta judgments from the Tax, Federal and Supreme Courts of Canada and selected provincial courts.

BUSINESS AND ECONOMICS — PUBLIC FINANCE, TAXATION

336.2 338   PL   ISSN 1231-3084
DORADCA PODATNIKA. 1993. w. 509.60 Zl.; newsstand price: 9.80 Zl. (Biuro Informacji Organizacyjno-Prawnej INFOR) Wydawnictwo INFOR Sp. z o.o., Ul. Woycickiego 1-3, 01-930 Warsaw, Poland. TEL 48-22-354999. FAX 48-22-354999. Ed. Grazyna Gonciarska. adv. (back issues avail.)
    Formerly (until 1994): Jak Prowadzic Ksiegi Podatkowe (ISSN 1231-3076)
    Description: Deals with income taxes (individual and corporate), value added tax, revenue fees and charges.

DUTCH BUSINESS LAW. see *LAW — Corporate Law*

336   US
KF6272
E A JOURNAL. (Enrolled Agents) 1983. bi-m. $48 (effective 1996). National Association of Enrolled Agents, 200 Orchard Ridge Dr., Ste. 302, Gaithersburg, MD 20878-1978. TEL 301-212-9608. FAX 301-990-1611. E-mail: naea1@aol.com; URL: http://www.naea.org. Ed. Cliff Weiss. R&P contact: Cliff Weiss. adv. contact: Cliff Weiss. circ. 9,000. Document type: trade publication.
    ●Also available online.
    Formerly: E A (ISSN 8750-7072)
    Description: Provides timely and informative articles on the technical aspects of taxation, IRS policies and procedures, and tax practice.
    Refereed Serial

336   US   ISSN 0891-592X
E ALERT. 1985. s-m. $16 to members only. National Association of Enrolled Agents, 200 Orchard Ridge Dr., Ste. 302, Gaithersburg, MD 20878-1978. TEL 301-212-9608. FAX 301-990-1611. E-mail: naea1@aol.com. Ed. Cliff Weiss. R&P contact: Cliff Weiss. circ. 9,000. Document type: newsletter.

B QUARTERLY. (Employee Benefits) see *BUSINESS AND ECONOMICS — Banking And Finance*

336   NE
C CORPORATE TAX LAW. (Text in English) 3 base vols. (plus s-a. updates). $875 (renewals $390) (effective 1997). I B F D Publications B.V., P.O. Box 20237, 1000 HE Amsterdam, Netherlands. TEL 31-20-6267726. FAX 31-20-6228658. TELEX 13217 INTAX NL. (In US: IBFD Publications USA, Inc., 4 Maple Ln., Valatie, NY 12184. TEL 800-299-6330. FAX 518-758-2246) Ed. Otmat Thommes. (looseleaf format)
    Description: Provides detailed coverage and assessment of EC corporate tax directives and their impact on multinational companies doing business in Europe.

336   EI   ISSN 1011-4637
C S C FINANCIAL REPORT. (European Coal and Steel Community) (Editions in Dutch, French, German, Italian) 1956. a. Commission of the European Communities, L-2985 Luxembourg, Luxembourg. (Dist. in the U.S. by: European Community Information Service, 2100 M St., N.W., Ste. 707, Washington, DC 20037) circ. controlled. (also avail. in microfiche from CIS) Indexed: IIS. Document type: newsletter.
    —BLDSC (3659.633700).

336   UK   ISSN 1350-1089
E C TAX JOURNAL. 1995. 3/yr. £99 (effective 1997). Key Haven Publications plc., 7 Crescent Stables, 139 Upper Richmond Rd., London SW15 2TN, England. TEL 44-181-780-2522. FAX 44-181-780-1693. Ed. Timothy Lyons. Document type: bulletin.
    —BLDSC (3647.257755).
    Description: Provides a forum to discuss E.C. tax issues related to both particular member states and to the E.C. as a whole.

336 341   NE   ISSN 0928-2750
E C TAX REVIEW. (European Communities) (Supplement to: Intertax (ISSN 0165-2826)) 1992. q. fl.794 to institutions (effective 1998). Kluwer Law International (Subsidiary of: Wolters Kluwer N.V.), Postbus 85889, 2508 CN The Hague, Netherlands. TEL 31-70-3081500. FAX 31-70-3081515. (Dist. by: Libresso Distribution Centre, P.O. Box 23, 7400 GA Deventer, Netherlands. TEL 31-570-633155. FAX 31-570-633834; In N. America: Kluwer Law International, 675 Massachusetts Ave., Cambridge, MA 02139. TEL 617-354-0140. FAX 617-354-8595) Ed. Frans Vanistendael. (back issues avail.) Indexed: Euro.LJI.
    —BLDSC (3647.257770). **CCC.**
    Description: Covers current developments in taxation in the EC, including current cases before the European Court of Justice and relevant national EC tax cases.

336   UK   ISSN 0268-2265
ECONOMIC PRIORITIES - BUDGET REPRESENTATIONS. 1965. a. £10 to non-members. Confederation of British Industry, Centre Point, 103 New Oxford St., London WC1A 1DU, England. TEL 44-71-379-7400. FAX 44-71-240-1578. TELEX 21332.
    Formerly: Budget Representatives to the Chancellor.

336   EC
ECUADOR. CORPORACION FINANCIERA NACIONAL. MEMORIA. a. free. Corporacion Financiera Nacional, Direccion de Relaciones Publicas, Robles 731 y Amazonas, Apdo. de Correos 163, Quito, Ecuador. charts; illus.; stat. Document type: corporate report.
    Formerly (until 1977): Ecuador. Comision de Valores. Corporacion Financiera Nacional. Memoria (ISSN 0589-7688)
    Description: Reviews the activities of the association. Includes statistics on the financial status of the CFN.

336   EC
ECUADOR. DIRECCION GENERAL DE RECAUDACIONES. BOLETIN.* irreg. Direccion General de Recaudaciones, Quito, Ecuador. charts; stat. Document type: government publication, bulletin.

336   IS
EIDKUNAI MISIM. (Text in Hebrew) 1982. q. Hamachone Lemisim Veletautz Kalkalei, 9 Peretz St., Tel Aviv 66 853, Israel. TEL 03-375982. Ed. Menachem Cohen.

336 331   RU   ISSN 0869-7302
EKSPRESS - ZAKON. (Text in Russian) 1992. 52/yr. $712 (effective 1998). Izdatel'stvo I N F R A - M, Dmitrovskoe shosse, 107, 127247 Moscow, Russia. TEL 7-095-4855779. FAX 7-095-4855318. E-mail: relcom-contract@infram.msk.ru. Ed. Vladimir N. Prudnikov. adv.; index; circ. 3,000. (controlled). (back issues avail.)
    Description: Collection of legal and normative acts.
    Refereed Serial

336   US
EMPLOYMENT TAX FORMS. 1991. 2 base vols. (plus irreg. updates). $255. C C H Incorporated, 2700 Lake Cook Rd., Riverwoods, IL 60015. TEL 847-267-7000; 800-835-5224. FAX 800-224-8299. (looseleaf format)

ENVIRONMENT AND PLANNING C: GOVERNMENT & POLICY. see *PUBLIC ADMINISTRATION*

336.2 657   UK   ISSN 1361-0104
ENVIRONMENTAL TAXATION AND ACCOUNTING. 1996. q. £95 (foreign £105). Cameron May Ltd., 69-71 Bondway, London SW8 1SQ, England. TEL 44-171-582-7567. FAX 44-171-793-8353. E-mail: 100615.1547@compuserve.com.
    —BLDSC (3791.698200).

ERNST & YOUNG FINANCIAL PLANNING REPORTER. see *BUSINESS AND ECONOMICS — Investments*

336   US
ERNST & YOUNG'S OIL AND GAS TAX REPORTER. (Supplement avail.: Tax Trends) 1993. base vol. (plus q. updates). $329. C C H Incorporated, 2700 Lake Cook Rd., Riverwoods, IL 60015. TEL 847-267-7000; 800-835-5224. FAX 800-224-8299. (looseleaf format) Document type: newsletter.
    Description: Covers the federal tax aspects of the oil and gas industry.

336 382   PN   ISSN 0378-7397
HG3883.P25
ESTADISTICA PANAMENA. SITUACION ECONOMICA. SECCION 341. BALANZA DE PAGOS. 1954. a. Bl.0.50 (effective 1997). Direccion de Estadistica y Censo, Contraloria General, Apdo. 5213, Panama 5, Panama. FAX 507-269-7294. circ. 900. Document type: government publication, bulletin.
    Description: Presents statistics on goods, services, rents, and other exchanges.

336   LO
ESTIMATES OF THE REVENUE AND EXPENDITURE OF THE KINGDOM OF LESOTHO. a. Government Printer, Maseru, Lesotho.

ESTUDIOS ECONOMICOS. see *BUSINESS AND ECONOMICS — Economic Systems And Theories, Economic History*

332   FR
ETUDES JURIF. s-a. (with 2 updates). price varies per no. (Societe Jurif) Cahiers Fiscaux Europeens, 51 Avenue Reine Victoria, 06000 Nice, France. TEL 93-81-03-26. FAX 93-53-66-28. TELEX 461682 FONTANE. (looseleaf format)

336   GW
EURO STEUER TELEX; Spezialdienst mit Kennziffen Service. 1987. s-m. DM.42.80 per mo. (effective 1997). Verlag Peter Deubner GmbH, Wolfgang-Mueller-Str. 14, 50968 Cologne, Germany. TEL 49-221-9370180. FAX 49-221-93701890. Ed. Peter Deubner. adv.; bk.rev.; index. (back issues avail.) Document type: trade publication.
    Formerly: Steuer Telex International (ISSN 0930-7656)

336.2
EUROFISC. 6/yr. fl.160 (effective 1996). Uitgeverij Fed bv (Subsidiary of: Wolters Kluwer N.V.), Postbus 23, 7400 GA Deventer, Netherlands. TEL 31-570-633155. FAX 31-570-633834. (back issues avail.) Document type: newsletter.

336   NE   ISSN 0925-9759
KJC7101.3
EUROPEAN TAX HANDBOOK. (Text in English) 1990. a. $175 (effective 1997). I B F D Publications B.V., P.O. Box 20237, 1000 HE Amsterdam, Netherlands. TEL 31-20-6267726. FAX 31-20-6228658. TELEX 13217 INTAX NL. (In US: IBFD Publications USA, Inc., 4 Maple Ln., Valatie, NY 12184. TEL 800-299-6330. FAX 518-758-2246)
    Description: Provides extensive up-to-date summaries of the taxation of corporations and individuals in 35 countries in Western, Central and Eastern Europe, including a chapter on the EC.

336.2   NE   ISSN 0014-3138
EUROPEAN TAXATION. (Text in English) 1961. m. $640 (effective 1997). (International Bureau of Fiscal Documentation) I B F D Publications B.V., P.O. Box 20237, 1000 HE Amsterdam, Netherlands. TEL 31-20-6267726. FAX 31-20-6228658. TELEX 13217 INTAX NL. (In US: IBFD Publications USA, Inc., 4 Maple Ln., Valatie, NY 12184. TEL 800-299-6330. FAX 518-758-2246) (Co-sponsor: Confederation Fiscale Europeenne) Ed. M.R. Nettinga-Arnheim. adv.; index. (reprint service avail. from SWZ) Indexed: C.R.E.J., ELLIS, Euro.LJI, Key to Econ.Sci., P.A.I.S., SCIMP (1983-).
    ●Also available on CD-ROM.
    —BLDSC (3830.250000); SWETS; UnCover.
    Description: Comprehensive analysis of current issues in European tax law, including topical articles, case law, discussions of rulings and decisions.

336.2   NE
EUROPEAN TAXATION DATA BASE ON C D - R O M. (Text in English) 3/yr. $3375 (effective 1997). I B F D Publications B.V., P.O. Box 20237, 1000 HE Amsterdam, Netherlands. TEL 31-20-6267726. FAX 31-20-6228658. TELEX 13217 INTAX NL. (In US: IBFD Publications USA, Inc., 4 Maple Ln., Valatie, NY 12184. TEL 800-299-6330. FAX 518-758-2246)
    ●Available only on CD-ROM.
    Description: Provides a comprehensive description of tax systems of European countries, with original texts (and translations) of laws, and EC draft directives.

BUSINESS AND ECONOMICS — PUBLIC FINANCE, TAXATION

336   BE
EUROPEAN UPDATE. 1981. bi-m. free. Deloitte Touche Tohmatsu Europe Services, 326 Rue Royale, 1210 Brussels, Belgium. TEL 32-2-2195696. FAX 32-2-2231995. E-mail: 106372.3145@compuserve.com. Ed. Graham Branton; Pub. Graham Branton. R&P contact: Graham Branton. adv. contact: Graham Branton. circ. 16,000. **Document type:** newsletter.
   Former titles (until June 1982): Touche Ross European Commentary (ISSN 0254-9166); Fideurope European Commentary.
   Description: Covers political, legal and business related developments in the EC and Eastern Europe.

EXCISE TAX QUARTERLY. see *TRANSPORTATION — Trucks And Trucking*

336   US   ISSN 0273-7612
EXECUTIVE COMPENSATION & TAXATION COORDINATOR. 1978. 3 base vols. (plus m. supplements). $450 includes m. Executive Compensation Alert. Research Institute of America, Inc., 90 Fifth Ave., New York, NY 10011. TEL 212-645-4800. (Subscr. to: 117 E. Stevens Ave., Valhalla, NY 10595. TEL 800-431-9025) Ed.Bd. (looseleaf format)
   —CCC.
   Description: Provides an analysis of tax laws affecting executive compensation, and official source materials.

336.2   US
EXECUTIVE'S TAX & MANAGEMENT REPORT. w. $195 (effective 1997). Harcourt Brace Professional Publishing, 525 B St., Ste. 1900, San Diego, CA 92101-4495. TEL 619-699-6716. FAX 619-699-6593. Ed. Terence Meyers; Pub. Ken Rethmeier. R&P contact: Jenna Lake. TEL 619-699-6265. **Document type:** newsletter.
   Formerly: Executive's Tax Report (ISSN 1063-0481)
   Description: Informs business owners and top executives of tax law changes, IRS rulings, and court decisions that can affect both their own income and their company's earnings.

336.2   US
EXEMPT ORGANIZATION MASTER LIST ON C D - R O M. q., a. versions avail. $149 for a., q. $199. Tax Analysts, 6830 N. Fairfax Dr., Arlington, VA 22213. TEL 800-955-2444. FAX 703-533-4444.
   ●Available only on CD-ROM.
   Description: Includes over 1 million official IRS descriptions of organizations that qualify for exempt status. Provides information such as deductibility of contributions, addresses, accounting periods, and principal activities.

336   US   ISSN 0899-3831
KF6449.A15
THE EXEMPT ORGANIZATION TAX REVIEW. 1988. m. $649. Tax Analysts, 6830 N. Fairfax Dr., Arlington, VA 22213. TEL 703-533-4400; 800-955-2444. FAX 703-533-4444. Ed. Carolyn Wright; Pub. Thomas F. Field. (back issues avail.) **Document type:** trade publication.
   —UnCover. **CCC.**
   Description: Provides news and commentary on tax developments affecting nonprofit organizations and includes full-text documents of important court cases and rulings.

332.6   US   ISSN 0279-2427
EXEMPT ORGANIZATIONS REPORTS. 1971. bi-w. $846. C C H Incorporated, 2700 Lake Cook Rd., Riverwoods, IL 60015. TEL 847-267-7000; 800-835-5224. FAX 800-224-8299.
   Formerly: Private Foundations Reports (ISSN 0273-5873)

336   UK   ISSN 1362-0053
EXTEL CAPITAL GAINS TAX SERVICE. 1966. a. vol. plus m. updates. £390 for base volume; £450 with updates. Financial Times Information Ltd., Extel, Fitzroy House, 13-17 Epworth St., London EC2A 4DL, England. TEL 44-171-825-8000. FAX 44-171-608-2032. TELEX 884319. URL: http://www.info.ft.com/.
   Formerly (until 1995): Capital Gains Tax Service.
   Description: Details the CGT position on all UK securities quoted on the London and Republic of Ireland Stock Exchanges and authorised unit trusts existing on and after the base date of 31 March 1982.

EXTEL DIVIDEND & INTEREST RECORD. see *BUSINESS AND ECONOMICS — Banking And Finance*

336   GW   ISSN 0174-3163
F L F. (Finanzierung, Leasing, Factoring) 1954. bi-m. DM.140. Verlag fuer Absatzwirtschaft GmbH, Ulrich-von-Hassell-Str. 64, 53123 Bonn, Germany. TEL 49-228-252023. FAX 49-228-255093. Ed.Bd. adv.; bk.rev. circ. 2,000. (back issues avail.) **Document type:** trade publication.
   Formerly (until 1980): Teilzahlungswirtschaft (ISSN 0492-5661)

336   DK   ISSN 0907-7723
F.S.R.S AFGIFTSLOVE. 1993. a. DKK 250. Foreningen af Statsautoriserede Revisorer, Revisorernes Hus, Kronprinsessegade 8, DK-1306 Copenhagen K, Denmark. TEL 45-33-93-91-91. FAX 45-33-11-09-13. TELEX 22491. Ed. Jens Drejer.

336   DK   ISSN 0905-4367
F.S.R.S SKATTELOVE MED NOTER. 1958. a. DKK 700. Foreningen af Statsautoriserede Revisorer, Kronprinsessegade 8, 1306 Copenhagen K, Denmark. TEL 45-33 93 91 91. FAX 45-33-11-09-13. TELEX 22491.
   Formerly (until 1990): Skattelove (ISSN 0108-6022)

336.73   US   ISSN 0071-3678
HJ257
FACTS AND FIGURES ON GOVERNMENT FINANCE. 1941. a. $60. Tax Foundation, Inc., 1250 H St., N.W., Ste. 750, Washington, DC 20005. TEL 202-783-2760. FAX 202-942-7675. Ed. Patrick Frenor. stat. (also avail. in microfiche from CIS) **Indexed:** SRI.
   —BLDSC (3864.132000).

336.2   SW   ISSN 1104-9405
FAKTA OM SVERIGES SKATTER OCH SOCIALA. 1981. triennial. SEK 75 (effective 1997). Svenska Arbetsgivarefoereningen (SAF), S-103 30 Stockholm, Sweden.
   Formerly (until 1994): Fakta om Sveriges Skatter (ISSN 0281-8469)

FARM INCOME TAX MANUAL. see *AGRICULTURE — Agricultural Economics*

336 338.1   UK   ISSN 0268-9863
KD5494.F37
FARM TAX BRIEF; practical guidance on effective tax planning and the law relating to agricultural land. 1986. 10/yr. £170 (foreign $340) (effective 1997). (Country Landowners' Association) Monitor Press Ltd., Suffolk House, Church Field Rd., Sudbury, Suffolk CO10 6YA, England. TEL 44-1787-378607. FAX 44-1787-881147. Ed. Richard Williams. (back issues avail.) **Indexed:** Euro.LJI, LJI. **Document type:** bulletin.
   Description: Provides expert analysis and comment, practical articles and planning points, comprehensive news coverage and guidance on tax planning and the law relating to agricultural land.

FARM TAX SAVER. see *AGRICULTURE — Agricultural Economics*

336.2   NE
FED FISCALE BROCHURES. 1964. irreg., latest 1996. price varies. Uitgeverij Fed bv (Subsidiary of: Wolters Kluwer N.V.), Postbus 23, 7400 GA Deventer, Netherlands. TEL 31-570-633155. FAX 31-570-633834. Ed.Bd. (back issues avail.) **Document type:** monographic series.

336.2   NE
FED FISCALE STUDIESERIE. irreg., no.30, 1996. price varies. Uitgeverij Fed bv (Subsidiary of: Wolters Kluwer N.V.), Postbus 23, 7400 GA Deventer, Netherlands. TEL 31-570-633155. FAX 31-570-633834. Ed.Bd. (back issues avail.) **Document type:** monographic series.

FEDERAL ESTATE AND GIFT TAX REPORTS. see *LAW — Estate Planning*

353 145   US
FEDERAL ESTATE AND GIFT TAXATION (SUPPLEMENT). base vol. (plus s-a. supplements). $161.45 (foreign $254.95) (effective 1995). Warren, Gorham & Lamont, One Penn Plaza, New York, NY 10119. TEL 212-971-5000. FAX 212-971-5113. (Subscr. to: The Park Square Bldg., 31 St. James Ave., Boston, MA 02116-4112. TEL 800-950-1207) **Document type:** trade publication.
   Formerly: Stephens, Maxfield and Lind's Federal Estate and Gift Taxation (Supplement).

336   US   ISSN 0414-0141
FEDERAL EXCISE TAX REPORTS. 1913. m. $362. C C H Incorporated, 2700 Lake Cook Rd., Riverwoods, IL 60015. TEL 847-267-7000; 800-835-5224. FAX 800-224-8299. Ed. D. Newquist. (looseleaf format)
   ●Also available on CD-ROM.

353   US   ISSN 1066-1972
KF6369
FEDERAL INCOME TAX LAW. a. $104.95 (overseas $162.45) (effective 1995). Warren, Gorham & Lamont, One Penn Plaza, New York, NY 10119. TEL 212-971-5000. FAX 212-971-5113. (Subscr. to: The Park Square Bldg., 31 St. James Ave., Boston, MA 02116-4112. TEL 800-950-1207) **Document type:** trade publication.
   Former titles: Federal Income Tax Law (Supplement); Stanley and Kilcullen's Federal Income Tax Law (Supplement).

336   US   ISSN 1043-7371
KF6356.99
FEDERAL INCOME TAX REGULATIONS (NEW YORK). 1988. s-a. $52. Research Institute of America, Inc., 90 Fifth Ave., New York, NY 10011. TEL 212-645-4800. FAX 212-337-4279. (Subscr. to: 117 E.. Stevens Ave., Valhalla, NY 10595)

353 332   US
FEDERAL INCOME TAXATION OF BANKS AND FINANCIAL INSTITUTIONS (SUPPLEMENT). base vol. (plus q. supplements). $205 for base vol. plus supplements (foreign $266.50). Warren, Gorham & Lamont, One Penn Plaza, New York, NY 10119. TEL 212-971-5000. FAX 212-971-5113. (Subscr. to: The Park Square Bldg., 31 St. James Ave., Boston, MA 02116-4112. TEL 800-950-1207) **Document type:** trade publication.

FEDERAL INCOME TAXATION OF REAL ESTATE. see *REAL ESTATE*

FEDERAL SOCIAL SECURITY LAWS. see *INSURANCE*

336   US   ISSN 0162-1092
FEDERAL TAX ARTICLES. 1962. m. $516. C C H Incorporated, 2700 Lake Cook Rd., Riverwoods, IL 60015. TEL 847-267-7000; 800-835-5224. FAX 800-224-8299.

336 346.066   US
FEDERAL TAX COLLECTIONS, LEINS AND LEVIES.* 1988. base vol. (plus supplements). Maxwell Macmillan, Rosenfeld Launer, 90 Fifth Ave., New York, NY 07632-3310. TEL 800-562-0245. FAX 201-816-3569. Ed. William D. Elliott.

336.2   US   ISSN 0738-8632
FEDERAL TAX COORDINATOR 2D. 1970. 35 base vols. (plus w. supplements). $1375 (includes Weekly Alert newsletter & Internal Revenue Bulletin. Research Institute of America, Inc., 90 Fifth Ave., New York, NY 10011. TEL 212-645-4800. FAX 212-337-4279. (Subscr. to: 117 E. Stevens Ave., Valhalla, NY 10595. TEL 800-431-9025) (looseleaf format)
   ●Also available online. Vendor(s): Lexis-Nexis. Also available on CD-ROM.
   —CCC.
   Former titles: Federal Tax Coordinator; Tax Coordinator (ISSN 0039-999X)
   Description: Provides analysis of federal tax law, including commentary and practical guidance, and official source materials.

336   US   ISSN 0163-996X
FEDERAL TAX COORDINATOR 2D. WEEKLY ALERT. (Supplement to: Federal Tax Coordinator 2d) w. $175. Research Institute of America, Inc., 90 Fifth Ave., New York, NY 10011. TEL 212-645-4800. FAX 212-337-4279. (Subscr. to: 117 E. Stevens Ave., Valhalla, NY 10595) **Document type:** newsletter.
   —CCC.

BUSINESS AND ECONOMICS — PUBLIC FINANCE, TAXATION 1609

336   US   ISSN 0274-6298
ERAL TAX FORMS. 1973. irreg. $350. C C H ncorporated, 2700 Lake Cook Rd., Riverwoods, IL 0015. TEL 847-267-7000; 800-835-5224. AX 800-224-8299.

36   US   ISSN 0162-1661
ERAL TAX GUIDE REPORTS. 1958. 8 base vols. plus m. updates). $802 (CD-ROM ed. $798). C C H Incorporated, 2700 Lake Cook Rd., Riverwoods, IL 60015. TEL 847-267-7000; 800-835-5224. AX 800-224-8299. (looseleaf format)
Also available on CD-ROM.

350 347
ERAL TAX LITIGATION (SUPPLEMENT). a. $152.95 foreign $244.55) (effective 1995). Warren, Gorham & Lamont, One Penn Plaza, New York, NY 0119. TEL 212-971-5000. FAX 212-971-5113. Subscr. to: The Park Square Bldg., 31 St. James Ave., Boston, MA 02116-4112. TEL 800-950-1207) **Document type:** trade publication.
Former titles: Federal Tax Litigation; Tax Court Practice (Supplement).

336.2   US   ISSN 0888-0522
ERAL TAX MANUAL. 1960. m. $299. C C H ncorporated, 2700 Lake Cook Rd., Riverwoods, IL 0015. TEL 847-267-7000; 800-835-5224. AX 800-224-8299. (looseleaf format)
Former titles: Federal Tax Compliance Reports; until 1986): Federal Tax Compliance Manual (ISSN 0748-1462); Federal Tax Return Manual (ISSN 0071-4143)

336 340   US   ISSN 1076-2280
KF6276.99
ERAL TAX REGULATIONS. 1957. 5 base vols. (plus m. Report Bulletins and irreg. update). $310. Research Institute of America, Inc., 90 Fifth Ave., New York, NY 10011. TEL 212-645-4800. (looseleaf format; also avail. in microfiche from WSH)
Also available online. Vendor(s): Research Institute of America.
Formerly: Federal Income Tax Regulations (Paramus).
Description: Presents full text of income tax regulations and details regulatory activity following tax reform legislation.

ERAL TAX VALUATION DIGEST. see LAW — Estate Planning

336   US
KF6272.I44
ERAL TAXATION. 1954. q. $18 to members; non-members $68. Illinois State Bar Association, Section of Federal Taxation, Illinois Bar Center, Springfield, IL 62701. TEL 217-525-1760. FAX 217-525-0712. Eds. John Truskowski, George Marifian. (looseleaf format) **Document type:** newsletter.

336   US
ERAL TAXATION OF BANKRUPTCY WORKOUTS. base vol. (plus a. supplement). $171.45 (overseas $246.95) (effective 1995). Warren, Gorham & Lamont, One Penn Plaza, New York, NY 10119. TEL 212-971-5000. FAX 212-971-5113. (Subscr. to: The Park Square Bldg., 31 St. James Ave., Boston, MA 21116-4112. TEL 800-950-1207) Ed. Chris Trower. (looseleaf format) **Document type:** trade publication.
Description: Provides comprehensive coverage of bankruptcy and tax issues.

ERAL TAXATION OF OIL AND GAS TRANSACTIONS. see PETROLEUM AND GAS

336   FR   ISSN 0150-5467
UILLET RAPIDE FISCAL SOCIAL. vol.33, 1978. bi-w. 685 F. (effective 1997). Editions Francis Lefebvre, 42 rue de Villiers, 92300 Levallois, France. TEL 41-05-22-00. FAX 41-05-22-30.

336.2   SW   ISSN 0284-5024
CKDATA - SKATTEFOERVALTNINGEN, RIKSSKATTEVERKET. 1981. a. SEK 60 (effective 1996). (Riksskatteverket, Taxering- och Revisionsavdeling) Fritzes, S-106 47 Stockholm, Sweden. **Document type:** government publication.

336 336.73   US
FIDUCIARY TAX GUIDE. 1990. m. $417. C C H Incorporated, 2700 Lake Cook Rd., Riverwoods, IL 60015. TEL 847-267-7000; 800-835-5224. FAX 800-224-8299. (looseleaf format)

FIJI. BUREAU OF STATISTICS. ECONOMIC AND FUNCTIONAL CLASSIFICATION OF GOVERNMENT ACCOUNTS. see BUSINESS AND ECONOMICS — Abstracting, Bibliographies, Statistics

336   UK   ISSN 0267-4424
FINANCIAL ACCOUNTABILITY & MANAGEMENT. 1985. q. £84($167) (foreign £108) (effective 1997). Blackwell Publishers Ltd., 108 Cowley Rd., Oxford OX4 1JF, England. TEL 44-1865-791100. FAX 44-1865-791347. E-mail: jnlinfo@ blackwellpublishers.co.uk; URL: http:///www.blackwellpublishers.co.uk. Ed. Irvine Lapsley. adv. (also avail. in microform; reprint service avail. from SWZ,UMI) **Indexed:** ABI Inform., Account.Ind. (1985-), Cont.Pg.Manage., PSI, SCIMP (1991-). **Document type:** trade publication.
—BLDSC (3926.932000); SWETS; UMI; UnCover. **CCC.**
Refereed Serial

FINANCIAL AND MONETARY POLICY STUDIES. see BUSINESS AND ECONOMICS — Banking And Finance

FINANCIAL INSTITUTIONS RETIREMENT FUND. ANNUAL REPORT. see BUSINESS AND ECONOMICS — Personnel Management

336 332   US
FINANCIAL SERVICES DOCUMENT WATCH - PUBLIC FINANCE EDITION. (Consists of 4 eds.: Banking; Insurance; Public Finance; Thrift) m. $180. American Banker - Bond Buyer, Newsletter Division (Subsidiary of: Thomson Financial Services Company), One State St. Plaza, New York, NY 10004-1549. TEL 800-733-4371. FAX 212-943-2224. (Subscr. to: Box 28315, Washington, DC 20038-8315. TEL 202-347-2665) **Document type:** newsletter.
Supersedes in part: Insurance Document Watch.
Description: Real-time delivery of key documents in the public finance sector.

336.2   UK   ISSN 0141-0741
FINANCIAL TIMES WORLD TAX REPORT. Variant title: World Tax Report. 1972. m. £405 (foreign £435 ($689)) (effective 1997). Financial Times Professional Publishing (Subsidiary of: Financial Times Group), Maple House, 149 Tottenham Court Rd., London W1P 9LL, England. TEL 44-171-896-2222. FAX 44-171-896-2276. Ed. Jonathan Schwarz; Pub. John McLachlan. bk.rev.; stat.; index. (also avail. in microfiche; back issues avail.) **Document type:** newsletter.
Also available online. Vendor(s): Information Access Co., Knight-Ridder Information, Inc., Lexis-Nexis.
—UMI.
Formerly (until 1977): Financial Times Tax Newsletter (ISSN 0306-3089)
Description: Provides a survey of world developments in taxation divided by country. Contains news and commentary about international tax issues, including tax reform, proposals, double-taxation treaties, compliance, tax havens, and government budgets worldwide.

FINANSOVYE BUKHALTERSKIE KONSYL'TATSII. see BUSINESS AND ECONOMICS — Accounting

336.2   GW
KK7163.A13
FINANZ-RUNDSCHAU FUER EINKOMMENSTEUER. 1946. s-m. DM.342 (effective 1997). Verlag Dr. Otto Schmidt KG, Unter den Ulmen 96-98, 50968 Cologne, Germany. TEL 49-221-9373801. FAX 49-221-93738943. E-mail: dr.otto.schmidt@t-online.de. Ed. M. Lopau. bk.rev.; bibl.; index. circ. 3,500. (reprint service avail. from SCH) **Document type:** trade publication.
—CCC.
Former titles: Finanz-Rundschau (ISSN 0940-4538); Finanz-Rundschau. Ausgabe A (ISSN 0176-7771); Finanz-Rundschau (ISSN 0015-2196)

350 336   IT   ISSN 0394-8307
FINANZA LOCALE; rivista mensile de contabilita e tributi degli enti locale e delle regioni. 1981. m. (11/yr.). L.120000 to individuals; institutions L.218000 (effective 1994). Maggioli Editore, Viale Vespucci 12-n, Casella Postale 290, 47037 Rimini, Italy. TEL 0541-626777. FAX 0541-622020. Dirs. Franceso Tesauro, Mario Trimeloni. adv.: B&W page L.1200000, color page L.1800000; trim 115 x 195.

332   GW   ISSN 0015-2218
HJ105
FINANZARCHIV. 1884. 4/yr. DM.278 (effective 1998). Verlag Mohr Siebeck, Wilhelmstr. 18, 72074 Tuebingen, Germany. TEL 49-7071-923-0. FAX 49-7071-51104. E-mail: mohr-siebeck@t-online.de; URL: http://www.mohr.de. (Subscr. to: Postfach 2040, 72010 Tuebingen, Germany) Ed. Norbert Andel. R&P contact: Jill Sopper. adv. contact: Tilman Gaebler. bk.rev.; index. **Indexed:** ELLIS, IBR, Key to Econ.Sci., P.A.I.S., P.A.I.S.For.Lang.Ind. **Document type:** academic/scholarly publication.
—SWETS. **CCC.**
Description: Covers all aspects of public finance.

FINANZAS PUBLICAS ESTATALES Y MUNICIPALES DE MEXICO. see BUSINESS AND ECONOMICS — Abstracting, Bibliographies, Statistics

336   IT   ISSN 0015-2242
FINANZIERE. 1886. m. L.28000. (Fondo di Assistenza per i Finanzieri) Comando Generale della Guardia di Finanza, Ufficio Stampa, Viale XX1 Aprile 55, 00162 Rome, Italy. TEL 39-6-44221. Ed. Daniele Caprino. adv.: page L.4000000. bk.rev.; bibl.; illus.; stat.; index. circ. 46,000.

336.2 340   AU   ISSN 0015-2277
FINANZRECHTLICHE ERKENNTNISSE DES VERWALTUNGSGERICHTSHOFES; Beilage zur Oesterreichischen Steuer-Zeitung. 1948. s-m. S.3600. Verlag Orac GesmbH & Co. KG, Graben 17, A-1010 Vienna, Austria. TEL 43-1-53452-0. FAX 43-1-53452141. circ. 12,100. **Document type:** bulletin.

336   FI   ISSN 0533-1099
HC340.2.A1
FINLAND. KANSANTALOUSOSASTO. KANSANTALOUDEN KEHITYSARVIO. SUMMARY: NATIONAL BUDGET FOR FINLAND. (Text in Finnish; summaries in English) 1966. a. Valtion Painatuskeskus - Government Printing Centre; Ministry of Finance, Annankatu 44, 00100 Helsinki 10, Finland.

343.05 336.2   BE
FISCAAL JAAROVERZICHT. (Text in Dutch) a. 1710 BEF. Kluwer Rechtswetenschappen Belgie (Subsidiary of: Wolters Kluwer N.V.), Santvoortbeeklaan 21-25, 2100 Antwerp, Belgium. FAX 32-3-3600467. **Document type:** trade publication.
Description: Reviews developments in taxation and revenue law during the preceding year.

336.2 340   NE   ISSN 0927-5746
FISCAAL ONDERNEMINGSRECHT. Variant title: Tijdschrift Fiscaal Ondernemingsrecht. 1992. bi-m. fl.267.80 (effective 1996). Uitgeverij Kluwer B.V., Postbus 23, 7400 GA Deventer, Netherlands. TEL 31-570-633155. FAX 31-570-633834. adv.; circ. 800 (paid). **Document type:** academic/scholarly publication.

343.05   BE
FISCAAL PRAKTIJKBOEK DIRECTE BELASTINGEN. (Text in Dutch) a. 2465 BEF. Kluwer Rechtswetenschappen Belgie (Subsidiary of: Wolters Kluwer N.V.), Santvoortbeeklaan 21-25, 2100 Antwerp, Belgium. FAX 32-3-3600467. Ed. Willy Maeckelbergh. (back issues avail.) **Document type:** trade publication.

336.2   NE   ISSN 0165-0335
FISCAAL WEEKBLAD FED. 1940. w. fl.0.42 per page (effective 1996). Uitgeverij Fed bv (Subsidiary of: Wolters Kluwer N.V.), Postbus 23, 7400 GA Deventer, Netherlands. TEL 31-570-633155. FAX 31-570-633834. (looseleaf format; back issues avail.) **Document type:** trade publication.
Formerly (until 1985): Losbladig Fiscaal Weekblad Fed (ISSN 1382-4902)

BUSINESS AND ECONOMICS — PUBLIC FINANCE, TAXATION

336   US   ISSN 0197-288X
FISCAL LETTER. 6/yr. $35 (Canada $37.50). National Conference of State Legislatures, 1560 Broadway, Ste. 700, Denver, CO 80202. TEL 303-830-2200. FAX 303-863-8003. Ed. Scott Mackey. **Document type:** newsletter.
    Description: Monitors state tax and budget actions, appropriations issues, tax reform and tax revolt measures.

336   UK   ISSN 0143-5671
FISCAL STUDIES. 1979. q. £43($84) to individuals (U.S. & Canada $131; elsewhere £56); institutions £65 (U.S. & Canada $87; elsewhere $85). Institute of Fiscal Studies, 7 Ridgmount St., London WC1E 7AE, England. TEL 44-171-636-3784. FAX 44-171-323-4780. E-mail: mailbox@ifs.org.uk; URL: http://www1.ifs.org.uk/ifsinfo/fiscalStudies.htm. (Dist. by: Worldwide Subscription Services Ltd., Unit 4, Gibbs Reed Farm, Ticehurst, E. Sussex TN5 7HE, England) Ed.Bd.; Pub. Robert Markless. adv. contact: Robert Markless. circ. 1,350. (also avail. in microfilm from UMI) **Indexed:** ABI Inform., C.R.E.J., Cont.Pg.Manage., J.of Econ.Lit., Rural Recreat.Tour.Abstr., World Agri.Econ. & Rural Sociol.Abstr., World Bank.Abstr. **Document type:** academic/scholarly publication.
    ● Also available online. Vendor(s): UMI.
    —BLDSC (3934.479000); SWETS; UMI. **CCC**.
    Refereed Serial

343.05 336.2   BE   ISSN 0772-733X
FISCALE JURISPRUDENTIE/JURISPRUDENCE FISCALE. (Text in Dutch, French) 1982. 10/yr. 8350 BEF. Kluwer Rechtswetenschappen Belgie (Subsidiary of: Wolters Kluwer N.V.), Santvoortbeeklaan 21-25, 2100 Antwerp, Belgium. FAX 32-3-3600467. (back issues avail.) **Document type:** trade publication.
    Description: Covers Belgian, European and international taxation law, local and regional tax issues, and relevant judicial decisions.

343.05 336.2   BE   ISSN 0774-658X
DE FISCALE KOERIER. French edition: Courrier Fiscal (ISSN 0774-9775) (Text in Dutch) 1986. fortn. 7980 BEF includes Fiscaal Jaaroverzicht. Kluwer Rechtswetenschappen Belgie (Subsidiary of: Wolters Kluwer N.V.), Santvoortbeeklaan 21-25, 2100 Antwerp, Belgium. FAX 32-3-3600467. Ed. Stefan Sablon. **Document type:** newsletter.
    Description: Covers the latest developments in taxation law.

336   NE   ISSN 1382-3507
FISCALE PRAKTIJKVRAGEN. 1946. 10/yr. fl.205 (effective 1996). Gouda Quint B.V. (Subsidiary of: Wolters Kluwer N.V.), Postbus 1148, 6801 MK Arnhem, Netherlands. (Dist. by: Libresso Distribution Centre, P.O. Box 23, 7400 GA Deventer, Netherlands. TEL 31-570-633155. FAX 31-570-633834) Ed. E.P.J. Wasch. adv. **Indexed:** Key to Econ.Sci.
    Formerly (until 1995): Fiscale en Administratieve Praktijkvragen (ISSN 0165-2966)
    Description: Questions and answers for the tax law practice.

332   FR   ISSN 0242-5599
FISCALITE EUROPEENNE. (Editions avail. for 9 regions: Allemagne, Belgique, Espagne, France, Grande-Bretagne, Italie, Luxembourg, Monaco, Pays-Bas) 1968. q. price varies. Cahiers Fiscaux Europeens, 51 Avenue Reine Victoria, 06000 Nice, France. TEL 93-81-03-26. FAX 93-53-66-28. TELEX 461682 FONTANE. Ed. Pierre Fontaneau. (looseleaf format)
    —SWETS.

336   FR
FISCALITE EUROPEENNE: DROIT INTERNATIONAL DES AFFAIRES. 1970. q. 518 F. Cahiers Fiscaux Europeens, 51 Avenue Reine Victoria, 06000 Nice, France. TEL 93-81-03-26. FAX 93-53-66-28. TELEX 461682. Ed. Pierre Fontaneau. (looseleaf format) **Indexed:** ELLIS.
    Formerly: Fiscalite Europeenne Revue.

336   IT
FISCO. 1977. w. L.410000. Editoriale Tributaria Italiana S.p.A., Viale Mazzini 25, 00195 Rome, Italy. TEL 39-6-3217578. FAX 39-6-3217808. Ed. Pasquale Marino. adv. B&W page L.6500000. bk.rev./ abstr.; bibl.; index. circ. 49,615.
    Description: Offers laws, rules and regulations involved with the Ministry of Finance.

343.05   BE
FISCOLEX REGIONALE EN PROVINCIALE BELASTINGEN/FISCOLEX IMPOTS REGIONIAUX ET PROVINCIAUX. (Text in Dutch, French) a. 3850 BEF. Kluwer Rechtswetenschappen Belgie (Subsidiary of: Wolters Kluwer N.V.), Santvoortbeeklaan 21-25, 2100 Antwerp, Belgium. FAX 32-3-3600467. Ed. Paul Van Orshoven. (back issues avail.) **Document type:** trade publication.

343.05   BE
FISCOLEX W.I.B.. French edition: Fiscolex C.I.R. (Text in Dutch) a. 3850 BEF. Kluwer Rechtswetenschappen Belgie (Subsidiary of: Wolters Kluwer N.V.), Santvoortbeeklaan 21-25, 2100 Antwerp, Belgium. FAX 32-3-3600467. Ed. Stefan Sablon. **Document type:** trade publication.

336   BE   ISSN 0772-4845
LE FISCOLOGUE. Dutch edition: Fiskoloog (ISSN 0772-4837) (Text in French) 1980. w. 9920 BEF in Belgium; Europe 10230 BEF. Biblo N.V., Brasschaatsteenweg 308, 2920 Kalmthout, Belgium. Ed. Jan Van Dyck. index. (also avail. in microfiche; back issues avail.) **Document type:** newsletter.

336   BE   ISSN 0772-1463
LE FISCOLOGUE INTERNATIONAL. Dutch edition: Fiskoloog Internationaal (ISSN 0771-7520) (Text in French) 1983. m. 7710 BEF in Belgium; Europe 7805 BEF. Biblo N.V., Brasschaatsteenweg 308, 2920 Kalmthout, Belgium. Ed. Jan Van Dyck. index. (also avail. in microfiche; back issues avail.) **Document type:** newsletter.

336   US
FLORIDA BAR. TAX SECTION BULLETIN. irreg. (2-4/yr.). membership. Florida Bar, 650 Apalachee Pkwy., Tallahassee, FL 32399-2300. TEL 904-561-5630. circ. 1,900. **Document type:** newsletter.

336   US
FLORIDA STATE & LOCAL TAXATION. 1983. 2 base vols. (plus suppl. 2-3/yr.) $120. Butterworth Legal Publishers (Salem) (Subsidiary of: Reed Elsevier plc), 8 Industrial Way, Bldg. C, Salem, NH 03079. TEL 800-548-4001. FAX 603-898-9858. (looseleaf format)

FOREIGN TAX LAW BI-WEEKLY BULLETIN. see *LAW*

336   GW   ISSN 0933-8497
FORMELN FUER DIE STEUER- UND WIRTSCHAFTSPRAXIS. irreg. DM.86. Erich Schmidt Verlag GmbH & Co. (Berlin), Genthiner Str. 30G, 10785 Berlin, Germany. TEL 49-30-250085-0. FAX 49-30-25008521. (looseleaf format) **Document type:** bulletin.

336.2   FR   ISSN 0997-4768
FRANCE. CONSEIL DES IMPOTS. RAPPORT AU PRESIDENT DE LA REPUBLIQUE. irreg. price varies. Direction des Journaux Officiels, 26 rue Desaix, 75727 Paris Cedex 15, France. TEL 16-1-40-58-78-78. (Co-sponsor: Ministere de l'Environnement et du Cadre de Vie) (also avail. in microfiche)

336   FR   ISSN 0071-8637
FRANCE. DIRECTION GENERALE DES DOUANES ET DROITS INDIRECTS. ANNUAIRE ABREGE DE STATISTIQUES. a. 270 F. Imprimerie Nationale, B.P. 514, 59505 Douai Cedex, France. TEL 27-93-70-70. FAX 27-93-70-96. TELEX 120 389 F. (also avail. in microfilm from BHP)
    Description: Presents the results of trade for France for the preceding year by product or group of products and for each trading partner broken down by product.

336.1   FR
FRANCE. DIRECTION GENERALE DES IMPOTS. BULLETIN OFFICIEL D'ANNONCES DES DOMAINES. 1947. s-m. 40 F. Direction des Impots, Service des Domaines, 17 rue Scribe, 75436 Paris Cedex 09, France. TEL 94-94-78-78. Ed. J. Gaillard; adv.; bk.rev.; illus. circ. 38,000.

336 340   FR   ISSN 0767-1237
FRANCE. DIRECTION GENERALE DES IMPOTS. PRECIS DE FISCALITE. 1980. a. 250 F. (Direction Generale des Impots) Imprimerie Nationale, B.P. 514, 59505 Douai Cedex, France. TEL 27-93-70-90. FAX 27-93-70-96.
    Formerly (until 1980): France. Direction Generale des Impots. Precis de Fiscalite Cadastre Domaine Publicite Fonciere (ISSN 0767-1229)

336   FR   ISSN 0071-8742
FRANCE. INSPECTION GENERALE DES FINANCES. ANNUAIRE. 1952. a. Imprimerie Nationale, B.P. 514, 59505 Douai Cedex, France. TEL 27-93-70-90. FAX 27-93-70-96. TELEX 120 389 F.

336   FR   ISSN 0244-1179
FRANCE. MINISTERE DE L'ECONOMIE, DES FINANCES ET DU BUDGET. NOTES BLEUES; revue d'information economique et financiere. 1952. a. price varies. Ministere de l'Economie, des Finances et du Budget, Direction de la Communication, 139 rue de Bercy, 75012 Paris, France. TEL 40-24-88-15. (Dist. by: Documentation Francaise, 29-31 Quai Voltaire, Paris Cedex 07, France) **Indexed:** ELLIS.
    Former titles: France. Ministere du Budget. Notes Bleues & France. Ministere du Budget. Budget (ISSN 0071-8904); France. Ministere de l'Economie et des Finances. Budget.

336   US
FRANCHISING & LICENSING OF PUBLIC SERVICES IN FLORIDA. 1985. base vol. (plus suppl.). $80. Butterworth Legal Publishers (Salem) (Subsidiary of: Reed Elsevier plc), 8 Industrial Way, Bldg. C, Salem, NH 03079. TEL 800-548-4001. FAX 603-898-9858. (looseleaf format)

336   US
FRINGE BENEFITS TAX GUIDE. 1985. m. $461. C C H Incorporated, 2700 Lake Cook Rd., Riverwoods, IL 60015. TEL 847-267-7000; 800-835-5224. FAX 800-224-8299.

336   GW   ISSN 0944-291X
FUER SIE PRIVAT. 1985. m. DM.96. V S R W Verlag, Annabergerstr. 283, 53175 Bonn, Germany. TEL 49-228-95124-0. FAX 49-228-9512490. E-mail: vsrw@aol.com. Ed. Hagen Pruehs. R&P contact: Hagen Pruehs. adv.: page DM.2400; trim 210 x 297; adv. contact: Christiane Hellwig. circ. 9,500. **Document type:** newsletter.

336   US
G A A F R REVIEW. (Governmental Accounting, Auditing and Financial Reporting) m. $75 to non-members; members $40. Government Finance Officers Association, 180 N. Michigan Ave., Ste. 800, Chicago, IL 60601. TEL 312-977-9700. FAX 312-977-4806. **Document type:** newsletter.

336   CN   ISSN 0847-3528
G S T & COMMODITY TAX. (Goods and Services Tax) 1987. 10/yr. Can.$190. Carswell, One Corporate Plaza, 2075 Kennedy Rd., Scarborough, ON M1T 3V4, Canada. TEL 416-609-8000. FAX 416-298-5094. Eds. Allan Taitz, Jack Millar. **Document type:** newsletter.
    Formerly (until 1989): De Boo Commodity Tax Reports (ISSN 0835-6726)

336   CN
G S T GUIDE FOR BUSINESS. 1991. 6/yr. Can.$150. Carswell, One Corporate Plaza, 2075 Kennedy Rd., Scarborough, ON M1T 3V4, Canada. TEL 416-609-8000. FAX 416-298-5094. Ed. Bart Singh. charts, stat.; index. circ. 3,000. (looseleaf format; back issues avail.)

GABLERS - MAGAZIN; Zeitschrift fuer innovative Fuehrungskraefte. see *BUSINESS AND ECONOMICS — Management*

354.67   GO
GABON. DIRECTION GENERALE DES FINANCES ET DU BUDGET. PROJET DU BUDGET GENERAL. irreg. Direction Generale des Finances et du Budget, Ministere de l'Economie et des Finances, Libreville, Gabon. stat.

336   GW   ISSN 0941-1976
GELD UND STEUERN. 1992. bi-m. DM.39.80. Verlag Wirtschaft Recht und Steuern, Fraunhoferstr. 5, 82152 Planegg, Germany. TEL 49-89-89517-0. FAX 49-89-89517250. (looseleaf format) **Document type:** consumer publication.

BUSINESS AND ECONOMICS — PUBLIC FINANCE, TAXATION

336 GW ISSN 0947-658X
GERMAN TAX NEWS. bi-m. DM.65. Luchterhand Verlag, Heddesdorferstr. 31, 56564 Neuwied, Germany. TEL 49-2631-801-0. FAX 49-2631-801210. **Document type:** newsletter.

354.667 GH
GHANA. SUPREME MILITARY COUNCIL. BUDGET PROPOSALS. a. NC.1. Supreme Military Council, Ministry of Finance, Accra, Ghana. stat. **Document type:** government publication.

GILBERT LAW SUMMARIES. INCOME TAX 1 (INDIVIDUAL). see LAW

GILBERT LAW SUMMARIES. INCOME TAX 2 (CORPORATE). see LAW — Corporate Law

336.2 IT ISSN 0391-1853
GIURISPRUDENZA DELLE IMPOSTE. 1953. bi-m. Lit.135000 (foreign Lit.200000) (effective 1997). Casa Editrice Dott. A. Giuffre, Via Busto Arsizio 40, 20151 Milan, Italy. TEL 39-2-38089200. FAX 39-2-38009582. Ed. C. Berliri. adv. circ. 5,800.

336 GW ISSN 0939-5547
DIE GMBH. 1991. bi-m. DM.98. Verlag Wirtschaft Recht und Steuern, Fraunhoferstr. 5, 82152 Planegg, Germany. TEL 49-89-89517-0. FAX 49-89-89517250. (Subscr. to: Postfach 1363, 82142 Planegg, Germany) (looseleaf format) **Document type:** trade publication.

336 US ISSN 0731-583X
KF1432.1
GOING PUBLIC HANDBOOK; going public, the integrated disclosure system and exempt financing. 1982. a. $140. Clark - Boardman - Callaghan, 375 Hudson St., New York, NY 10014. TEL 212-929-7500; 800-422-2101. FAX 212-924-0460. Ed. Harold S. Bloomenthal.
Description: Provides practitioners with the basics of public financing and with numerous hard-to-find and crucial sample documents and forms.

352.1 US ISSN 0883-7856
HJ9103
GOVERNMENT FINANCE REVIEW. (Former name of issuing organization: Municipal Finance Officers Association of the U.S. and Canada) 1985. bi-m. $30. Government Finance Officers Association, 180 N. Michigan Ave., Ste. 800, Chicago, IL 60601. TEL 312-977-9700. FAX 312-977-4806. Eds. Karen Utterback, Barbara Weiss. adv.; bk.rev.; index. circ. 15,000. (also avail. in microform from UMI; back issues avail.; reprint service avail. from UMI) **Indexed:** A.B.C.Pol.Sci., ABI Inform., Account.Ind. (1985-), B.P.I., BPIA, Manage.Cont., P.A.I.S., PROMT, Sage Pub.Admin.Abstr., Tr.& Indus.Ind. **Document type:** trade publication.
●Also available online. Vendor(s): Information Access Co.
—BLDSC (4204.102500); KR SourceOne; UMI; UnCover.
Formed by the merger of (197?-1985): Government Financial Management Resources in Review (ISSN 0272-6823); (1926-1985): Governmental Finance (ISSN 0091-4835); Which was formerly (until 1971): Municipal Finance (ISSN 0027-3473)
Description: Covers the spectrum of public finance issues.

336.1 352.7 US
GRANT AND REGULATION ALERT. (Supplement to: Local - State Funding Report) w. Government Information Services, 4301 Fairfax Dr., Ste. 875, Arlington, VA 22203-1627. TEL 703-528-1000. FAX 703-528-6060. (reprint service avail.)
Formerly: Grant Alert.
Description: Funding news, rule changes and other announcements from the Federal Register and Commerce Business Daily.

339.20941 UK
GREAT BRITAIN. BOARD OF INLAND REVENUE. SURVEY OF PERSONAL INCOMES. Key Title: Survey of Personal Incomes. 1972. irreg. £4.95. H.M.S.O., Publications Centre, P.O. Box 276, London SW8 5DT, England. (Subscr. to: H.M.S.O, c/o Liaison Officer, Atlantic House, Holborn Viaduct, London EC1P 1BN, England) stat. **Document type:** government publication.

336 UK
GREAT BRITAIN. H M CUSTOMS & EXCISE. BUSINESS NEWS. 1990. bi-m. H M Customs and Excise, Business Unit, New King's Beam House, 11th Fl., 22 Upper Ground, London SE1 9PJ, England. TEL 44-171-865-5570. FAX 44-171-865-5626. Ed. Martin Stevens. **Document type:** government publication.
Formed by the 1995 merger of: Customs News (ISSN 0968-414X) & Single Market Report (ISSN 0968-073X)
Description: Reports changes in U.K. customs procedures and legislation implemented and under review.

336 UK
GREAT BRITAIN. H M CUSTOMS & EXCISE. MANAGEMENT PLAN. biennial. H M Customs & Excise, Business Unit, New King's Beam House, 22 Upper Ground, London SE1 9PJ, England. TEL 44-171-865-5570. FAX 44-171-865-5626. **Document type:** government publication.

336 UK
GREAT BRITAIN. H M TREASURY. GOVERNMENT PROCUREMENT: PROGRESS REPORT TO THE PRIME MINISTER (YEAR). a. Stationery Office, 51 Nine Elms Ln., London SW8 5DR, England. TEL 44-171-873-0011. FAX 44-171-873-8247. (Subscr. to: Stationery Office, Publication Centre, P.O. Box 276, London SW8 5DT, England. TEL 44-171-873-8466. FAX 44-171-873-8222) **Document type:** government publication.
Formerly (until 1993): Great Britain. H M Treasury. Government Purchasing: Progress Report to the Prime Minister (Year).

336 UK
GREAT BRITAIN. TREASURY. SUPPLY ESTIMATES. 1850. a. price varies. H.M.S.O., 51 Nine Elms Ln., London SW8 5DR, England. TEL 44-171-873-0011. FAX 44-171-873-8247. stat.; index. circ. 500. **Document type:** government publication.

GREECE. NATIONAL STATISTICAL SERVICE. PROVISIONAL NATIONAL ACCOUNTS OF GREECE. see BUSINESS AND ECONOMICS — Abstracting, Bibliographies, Statistics

GREECE. NATIONAL STATISTICAL SERVICE. QUARTERLY NATIONAL ACCOUNTS OF GREECE. see BUSINESS AND ECONOMICS — Abstracting, Bibliographies, Statistics

336 GW ISSN 0946-0489
DAS GROSSE RECHNUNGSWESEN A B C. 1994. bi-m. DM.78. Verlag Wirtschaft Recht und Steuern, Fraunhoferstr. 5, 82152 Planegg, Germany. TEL 49-89-89517-0. FAX 49-89-89517250. (Subscr. to: Postfach 1363, 82142 Planegg, Germany) (looseleaf format) **Document type:** trade publication.

336.2 GU ISSN 0072-7873
GUAM. DEPARTMENT OF REVENUE AND TAXATION. REPORT. 1969. a. $2. Department of Revenue and Taxation, Office of the Director, 855 West Marine Dr., Agana, Guam 96910. TEL 671-477-1040. circ. 100.

336 CC
GUANGXI SHENJI/GUANGXI AUDIT. (Text in Chinese) bi-m. Guangxi Shenji Ju, Xinghu Lu, Nanning, Guangxi 530022, People's Republic of China. TEL 42327. Ed. Cui Chusheng.

336 CC
GUANGXI SHUIWU/GUANGXI TAXATION. (Text in Chinese) bi-m. Guangxi Shuiwu Ju - Guangxi Bureau of Taxation, 82 Taoyuan Lu, Nanning, Guangxi 530021, People's Republic of China. TEL 28920. Ed. Li Qiaoyu.

336 CN ISSN 0432-9368
LE GUIDE DU CONTRIBUABLE CANADIEN. 1954. a. Can.$58.95. C C H - F M Ltd., 33 Racine, Farnham, PQ J2N 3A3, Canada. TEL 800-363-8304. FAX 514-293-2644. Ed. Pierrette Gregoire.

GUIDE TO FEDERAL FUNDING FOR EDUCATION. see EDUCATION — School Organization And Administration

336.2 JA ISSN 0072-8551
GUIDE TO JAPANESE TAXES. (Editions in English, Japanese) 1965. a. 7000 Yen. Zaikei Shoho Sha. Co., Ltd., 1-2-14 Higashi Shimbashi, Minato-ku, Tokyo, Japan. TEL 03-3572-0624. FAX 03-3572-5189. (Dist. in US by: Fred B. Rothman & Co., 10368 W. Centennial Rd., Littleton, CO 80123) Ed. Hiroaki Nagahata. circ. 5,000.
Description: Provides extensive and up-to-date information on Japanese taxes based on laws, regulations and circulars.

336.2 US
GUIDE TO SALES AND USE TAXES (YEAR). (Supplement to: State and Local Taxes - Sales and Use Taxes) a. $60. Research Institute of America, Inc., 90 Fifth Ave., New York, NY 10011. TEL 212-645-4800. (Subscr. to: 117 E. Stevens Ave., Valhalla, NY 10595. TEL 800-562-0245) Ed. George Wohar, Jr.
Description: Provides state-by-state coverage of sales and use taxes in every state and the District of Columbia.

336 NE
GUIDE TO THE EUROPEAN V A T DIRECTIVES; commentary on the Value Added Tax of the European Community. (Text in English, other European languages) 1993. 5 base vols. (plus q. updates). $1065 (renewals $550) (effective 1997). I B F D Publications B.V., P.O. Box 20237, 1000 HE Amsterdam, Netherlands. TEL 31-20-6267726. FAX 31-20-6228658. TELEX 13217 INTAX NL. (In US: IBFD Publications USA, Inc., 4 Maple Ln., Valatie, NY 12184. TEL 800-299-6330. FAX 518-758-2246) Eds. B.J.M. Terra, Julie Kajus. (looseleaf format)
Description: Provides comprehensive information on VAT legislation within the EC, including historical background and general introduction, and title-by-title commentary on the VAT Directives. Text of the Directives is presented in the nine working languages of the EC.

336.2 US ISSN 0072-8837
GUIDEBOOK TO CALIFORNIA TAXES. 1950. a. $32. C C H Incorporated, 2700 Lake Cook Rd., Riverwoods, IL 60015. TEL 847-267-7000; 800-835-5224. FAX 800-224-8299.

336.2 US ISSN 0093-8637
KFF470.A73
GUIDEBOOK TO FLORIDA TAXES. a. $32. C C H Incorporated, 2700 Lake Cook Rd., Riverwoods, IL 60015. TEL 847-267-7000; 800-835-5224. FAX 800-224-8299.

336.2 US ISSN 0072-8845
KFI1670.A73
GUIDEBOOK TO ILLINOIS TAXES. 1971. a. $32. C C H Incorporated, 2700 Lake Cook Rd., Riverwoods, IL 60015. TEL 847-267-7000; 800-835-5224. FAX 800-224-8299.

336.2 US ISSN 0072-8861
GUIDEBOOK TO MASSACHUSETTS TAXES. 1967. a. $32. C C H Incorporated, 2700 Lake Cook Rd., Riverwoods, IL 60015. TEL 847-267-7000; 800-835-5224. FAX 800-224-8299.

336.2 US ISSN 0072-887X
GUIDEBOOK TO MICHIGAN TAXES. 1968. a. $32. C C H Incorporated, 2700 Lake Cook Rd., Riverwoods, IL 60015. TEL 847-267-7000; 800-835-5224. FAX 800-224-8299.

336.2 US ISSN 0072-8888
GUIDEBOOK TO NEW JERSEY TAXES. 1969. a. $32. C C H Incorporated, 2700 Lake Cook Rd., Riverside, IL 60015. TEL 847-267-7000; 800-835-5224. FAX 800-224-8299.

336.2 US ISSN 0072-8896
KFN5860.Z9
GUIDEBOOK TO NEW YORK TAXES. 1965. a. $32. C C H Incorporated, 2700 Lake Cook Rd., Riverwoods, IL 60015. TEL 847-267-7000; 800-835-5224. FAX 800-224-8299. (also avail. in diskette format (ISSN 1068-2694))

336.2 US ISSN 0091-1186
KFN7870.A73
GUIDEBOOK TO NORTH CAROLINA TAXES. 1972. a. $32. C C H Incorporated, 2700 Lake Cook Rd., Riverwoods, IL 60015. TEL 847-267-7000; 800-835-5224. FAX 800-224-8299.

BUSINESS AND ECONOMICS — PUBLIC FINANCE, TAXATION

336.2   US   ISSN 0091-4010
KF0470.A73
GUIDEBOOK TO OHIO TAXES. 1972. a. $32. C C H Incorporated, 2700 Lake Cook Rd., Riverwoods, IL 60015. TEL 847-267-7000; 800-835-5224. FAX 800-224-8299.

336.2   US   ISSN 0072-890X
GUIDEBOOK TO PENNSYLVANIA TAXES. 1965. a. $32. C C H Incorporated, 2700 Lake Cook Rd., Riverwoods, IL 60015. TEL 847-267-7000; 800-835-5224. FAX 800-224-8299. —CCC.

336.2   US   ISSN 0093-8645
KFW2870.A73
GUIDEBOOK TO WISCONSIN TAXES. a. $32. C C H Incorporated, 2700 Lake Cook Rd., Riverwoods, IL 60015. TEL 847-267-7000; 800-835-5224. FAX 800-224-8299.

336.2   NE
GUIDES TO EUROPEAN TAXATION: TAXATION & INVESTMENT IN CENTRAL AND EAST EUROPEAN COUNTRIES. (Text in English) 1983. 3 base vols. (plus updates 3/yr.). $1035 (renewals $500) (effective 1997). I B F D Publications B.V., P.O. Box 20237, 1000 HE Amsterdam, Netherlands. TEL 31-20-6267726. FAX 31-20-6228658. TELEX 13217 INTAX NL. (In US: IBFD Publications USA, Inc., 4 Maple Ln., Valatie, NY 12184. TEL 800-299-6330. FAX 518-758-2246) Ed. G.M.M. Michielse. (looseleaf format)
    Formerly: Guides to European Taxation: Taxation in European Socialist Countries.
    Description: Details the taxation systems for companies and individuals in Hungary, Poland, the Czech Republic, Slovakia, Bulgaria, Romania, Croatia and Russia, and includes profiles of taxation systems in Albania, Belarus, Estonia, and other states of the region

336.2   NE
GUIDES TO EUROPEAN TAXATION: TAXATION OF COMPANIES IN EUROPE. (Text in English) 5 base vols. (plus bi-m updates). $1750 (renewals $940) (effective 1997). I B F D Publications B.V., P.O. Box 20237, 1000 HE Amsterdam, Netherlands. TEL 31-20-6267726. FAX 31-20-6228658. TELEX 13217 INTAX NL. (In U.S.: IBFD Publications USA, Inc., 4 Maple Ln., Valatie, NY 12184. TEL 800-299-6330. FAX 518-758-2246) Ed. L.J. Kesti. (looseleaf format)
    Description: Systematically examines all forms of taxation at each stage of a company's life.

336.2   NE
GUIDES TO EUROPEAN TAXATION: TAXATION OF INDIVIDUALS IN EUROPE. (Text in English) 1991. 2 base vols. (plus s-a. updates). $965 (renewals $390) (effective 1997). I B F D Publications B.V., P.O. Box 20237, 1000 HE Amsterdam, Netherlands. TEL 31-20-6267726. FAX 31-20-6228658. TELEX 13217 INTAX NL. (In US: IBFD Publications USA, Inc., 4 Maple Ln., Valatie, NY 12184. TEL 800-299-6330. FAX 518-758-2246) Ed. Catherine S. Bobbett. (looseleaf format)
    Description: Analyzes and compares the taxation of resident and non-resident individuals in the 12 EC countries, Austria, Finland, Norway, Sweden, Switzerland and Turkey.

336.2   NE
GUIDES TO EUROPEAN TAXATION: TAXATION OF PATENT ROYALTIES, DIVIDENDS, INTEREST IN EUROPE. (Text in English) 1963. base vol. (plus updates 3/yr.). $565 (renewals $315) (effective 1997). I B F D Publications B.V., P.O. Box 20237, 1000 HE Amsterdam, Netherlands. TEL 31-20-6267726. FAX 31-20-6228658. TELEX 13217 INTAX NL. (In US: IBFD Publications USA, Inc., 4 Maple Ln., Valatie, NY 12184. TEL 800-299-6330. FAX 518-758-2246) Ed. P.M. Smit. bibl. (looseleaf format)
    Description: Provides a country by country description of all withholding taxes (with base and rates) on corporate cross border payments in Europe.

336.2   NE
GUIDES TO EUROPEAN TAXATION: TAXATION OF PRIVATE INVESTMENT INCOME. (Text in English) base vol. (plus updates 3/yr.). $565 (renewals $315) (effective 1997). I B F D Publications B.V., P.O. Box 20237, 1000 HE Amsterdam, Netherlands. TEL 31-20-6267726. FAX 31-20-6228658. TELEX 13217 INTAX NL. (In US: IBFD Publications USA, Inc., 4 Maple Ln., Valatie, NY 12184. TEL 800-299-6330. FAX 518-758-2246) Ed. Bernard P. Dik. (looseleaf format)
    Description: Provides country by country outlines of the taxation of investment and investment income for resident and non-resident individuals in the 12 EC countries, Austria, Finland, Norway, Sweden, Switzerland and the USA.

336.2   NF
GUIDES TO EUROPEAN TAXATION: VALUE ADDED TAXATION IN EUROPE. (Text in English) 3 base vols. (plus q. updates). $1000 (renewals $455) (effective 1997). I B F D Publications B.V., P.O. Box 20237, 1000 HE Amsterdam, Netherlands. TEL 31-20-6267726. FAX 31-20-6228658. TELEX 13217 INTAX NL. (In US: IBFD Publications USA, Inc., 4 Maple Ln., Valatie, NY 12184. TEL 800-299-6330. FAX 518-758-2246) Ed. Julie Kajus. bibl. (looseleaf format)
    Description: Analyzes VAT structures and their effect on international trade.

336   II   ISSN 0533-649X
GUJARAT STATE FINANCIAL CORPORATION. ANNUAL REPORT. (Text in English) a. Gujarat State Financial Corporation, Jaladarshan Bldg., Ashram Rd., Navrangpura, P.O. Box 4030, Ahmedabad 380009, India. illus.; stat.

GUYANA. AUDITOR GENERAL. REPORT ON THE PUBLIC ACCOUNTS. see *BUSINESS AND ECONOMICS — Abstracting, Bibliographies, Statistics*

336   UK
H M CUSTOMS AND EXCISE OFFICIAL V A T GUIDES. irreg. £147. Longman Group UK Ltd., Law, Tax and Finance Division, 21-27 Lamb's Conduit St., London WC1N 3NJ, England. TEL 0171-242-2548. FAX 0171-831-8119. (looseleaf format) **Document type:** bulletin.
    Description: Reproduction of official VAT leaflets with index, table of cases and table of statutes.

336   SP   ISSN 0210-1173
HJ1244
HACIENDA PUBLICA ESPANOLA. 1970. 9/yr. 12500 ptas. Instituto de Estudios Fiscales, Avda. de Cardenal Herrera Oria 378, 28035 Madrid, Spain. TEL 34-1-3398800. FAX 34-1-3398964. (Subscr. to: Ministerio de Economia y Hacienda, Centro de Publicaciones, Plaza del Campillo del Mundo Nuevo 3, 28005 Madrid, Spain. TEL 91-527-1437) bk.rev.; bibl.; index. Indexed: P.A.I.S.For.Lang.Ind. —CINDOC.

HAIGUAN TONGJI/CUSTOMS STATISTICS. see *BUSINESS AND ECONOMICS — Abstracting, Bibliographies, Statistics*

343.05 336.2   BE   ISSN 0779-1186
HANDBOEK VOOR FISCAAL RECHT. French edition: Manuel de Droit Fiscal (ISSN 0779-1178) (Text in Dutch) 1955. a. 6214 BEF. Kluwer Rechtswetenschappen Belgie (Subsidiary of: Wolters Kluwer N.V.), Santvoortbeeklaan 21-25, 2100 Antwerp, Belgium. FAX 32-3-3600467. **Document type:** trade publication.
    Description: Provide general reference information relating to taxation in Belgium.

336   US   ISSN 0163-4615
HG61
HANDBOOK OF BUSINESS FINANCE AND CAPITAL SOURCES.* 1979. a. $145. Interfinance Corporation, Box 15183, Minneapolis, MN 55415-0183. TEL 612-588-6067. Ed. Dileep Rao.

336.2   NE
HANDBOOK ON THE 1989 DOUBLE TAXATION CONVENTION BETWEEN THE FEDERAL REPUBLIC OF GERMANY AND THE UNITED STATES OF AMERICA. (Text in English, German) 1966. 2 base vols. (plus s-a. updates). $625 (renewals $125) (effective 1997). I B F D Publications B.V., P.O. Box 20237, 1000 HE Amsterdam, Netherlands. TEL 31-20-6267726. FAX 31-20-6228658. TELEX 13217 INTAX NL. (In US: IBFD Publications USA, Inc., 4 Maple Ln., Valatie, NY 12184. TEL 800-299-6330. FAX 518-758-2246) Ed. J.C. Amico. (looseleaf format)
    Formerly (until 1989): Handbook on the U.S. - German Tax Convention.

HANDBUCH DER AUSLANDSZOELLE. see *BUSINESS AND ECONOMICS — International Commerce*

336   GW   ISSN 0171-2365
HANDBUCH DER STEUERVERANLAGUNGEN: EINKOMMENSTEUER, KOERPERSCHAFTSTEUER, GEWERBESTEUER, UMSATZSTEUER. (Subseries of the institute's Schriften) 1964. a. price varies. (Deutsches Wissenschaftliches Steuerinstitut der Steuerberater und Steuerbevollmaechtigten e.V.) C.H. Beck'sche Verlagsbuchhandlung, Wilhelmstr. 9, 80801 Munich, Germany. TEL 089-38189-338. FAX 089-38189-398. **Document type:** bulletin.
    ●Also available on CD-ROM.

336   US
HANDY - WHITMAN INDEX OF PUBLIC UTILITY CONSTRUCTION COSTS. (Issued separately by subject area: Electric, Gas, Water) 1924. s-a. price varies. Whitman, Requardt & Associates, 2315 St. Paul St., Baltimore, MD 21218. TEL 410-235-3450. FAX 410-243-5716. Ed. Dennis R. Funk. stat.; index. circ. 600. **Document type:** bulletin.
    Description: Compiles construction cost indices for various categories of plant capital for the electric, gas, and water utility industries.

350.827   US   ISSN 1066-0925
KF6654.599
HARMONIZED TARIFF SCHEDULE OF THE UNITED STATES ANNOTATED. (Subseries of: U S I T C Publication (ISSN 0196-9153)) 1963. base vol. plus a. update. $66 (foreign $82.50) (effective 1995). U.S. International Trade Commission, Office of Tariff Affairs and Trade Agreements, International Trade Commission Bldg., 500 E St., S.W., Washington, DC 20436. (Subscr. to: Superintendent of Documents, U.S. Government Printing Office, Box 371954, Pittsburgh, PA 15250-7954. TEL 202-512-1800. FAX 202-512-2250) (looseleaf format) **Document type:** government publication.
    Formerly (until 1987): Tariff Schedules of the United States Annotated (ISSN 0082-173X)
    Description: Shows the American nomenclature for imported articles and their rates of duty. Includes the text of N.A.F.T.A.

336   UK
HARRISON'S INLAND REVENUE INDEX TO TAX CASES. irreg. £233. (Solicitor's Office of the Inland Revenue) Longman Group UK Ltd., Law, Tax and Finance Division, 21-27 Lamb's Conduit St., London WC1N 3NJ, England. TEL 0171-242-2548. FAX 0171-831-8119. (looseleaf format) **Document type:** bulletin.
    Description: Synopsis of all Inland Revenue reports of tax cases back to 1875, indexed alphabetically and by subject.

HAWAII. LEGISLATIVE AUDITOR. SPECIAL REPORTS. see *PUBLIC ADMINISTRATION*

HEALTH CARE FINANCING REVIEW. see *MEDICAL SCIENCES*

HEALTH CARE FINANCING REVIEW. SUPPLEMENT. see *PUBLIC HEALTH AND SAFETY*

336   US   ISSN 0889-3055
KF6272
HIGHLIGHTS AND DOCUMENTS. Key Title: Today's Highlights and Documents. Variant title: Daily Tax Highlights and Documents. (Annual compilation avail.: Highlights & Documents on Microfiche) 1986-1987; resumed 198? a. $2249. Tax Analysts, 6830 N. Fairfax Dr., Arlington, VA 22213. TEL 800-433-4400; 800-955-2444. FAX 703-533-4444. (back issues avail.) **Document type**: trade publication.
—CCC.
   Description: Covers IRS, congressional, judicial, state, and international tax news, and contains the full texts of documents relating to tax regulations released within the previous 24-48 hours.

336   US
HIGHLIGHTS & DOCUMENTS ON MICROFICHE. (Compilation of: Highlights & Documents (ISSN 0889-3055) a. Tax Analysts, 6830 N. Fairfax Dr., Arlington, VA 22213. TEL 800-955-2444. FAX 703-533-4444. (microfiche) **Document type**: trade publication.

336 790.13   US
HOBBY - BUSINESS WORLD. 1976. w. Cricket Communications, Inc., Box 527, Ardmore, PA 19003. TEL 215-789-2480. FAX 215-747-6684. TELEX 6505179983. Ed. Mark E. Battensby. bk.rev. (tabloid format; back issues avail.) **Document type**: newsletter.

HORSE OWNERS AND BREEDERS TAX MANUAL. see SPORTS AND GAMES — Horses And Horsemanship

336   CC
HUBEI CAISHUI. (Text in Chinese) m. Hubei Sheng Shuiwu Ju, Hongshan Lu, Wuchang-qu, Wuhan, Hubei 430071, People's Republic of China. TEL 813317. Ed. Chen Tai'an.

I D W FACHNACHRICHTEN. (Institut der Wirtschaftspruefer in Deutschland e.V.) see BUSINESS AND ECONOMICS — Accounting

336   UK
I F A C INTERNATIONAL PUBLIC SECTOR GUIDELINE (NO.). 1990. irreg., no.3, 1992. Chartered Institute of Public Finance and Accountancy, 3 Robert St., London WC2N 6BH, England. TEL 44-171-543-5600. FAX 44-171-543-5700. (back issues avail.)

336   UK
I F A C PUBLIC SECTOR COMMITTEE STUDY REPORT (NO.). 1991. irreg., no.2, 1993. price varies. Chartered Institute of Public Finance and Accountancy, 3 Robert St., London WC2N 6BH, England. TEL 44-171-895-8823. FAX 44-171-895-8825. (back issues avail.) **Document type**: monographic series, trade publication.

336   NE   ISSN 1016-7560
I F A CONGRESS SEMINAR SERIES. 1977. a. price varies. (International Fiscal Association) Kluwer Law International (Subsidiary of: Wolters Kluwer N.V.), Postbus 85889, 2508 CN The Hague, Netherlands. TEL 31-70-3081500. FAX 31-70-3081515. (Dist. by: Libresso Distribution Centre, P.O. Box 23, 7400 GA Deventer, Netherlands. TEL 31-570-633155. FAX 31-570-633834; N. America dist. addr.: Kluwer Law International, 675 Massachusetts Ave., Cambridge, MA 02139. TEL 617-354-0140. FAX 617-354-8595) (back issues avail.) **Document type**: proceedings.
—BLDSC (4363.260000).

336   NZ
I R D TAX RULINGS. 1991. bi-m. NZ.$692 (effective 1997). C C H New Zealand Limited, P.O. Box 2378, Auckland, New Zealand. TEL 64-9-483-9179. FAX 64-0-483-4009. (looseleaf format)
   Description: Helps accountants, tax advisors and lawyers understand how the IRD will approach particular issues regarding New Zealand income tax laws.

336   US   ISSN 0148-1940
KF6282.A2
I R S LETTER RULINGS. (Internal Revenue Service) base vol. (plus w. reports). $1308. C C H Incorporated, 2700 Lake Cook Rd., Riverwoods, IL 60015. TEL 847-267-7000; 800-835-5224. FAX 800-224-8299.
—CCC.

336.2   US
I R S LETTER RULINGS AND TECHNICAL ADVICE MEMORANDUMS (1980-YEAR). a. $1299 for print service and CD-ROM; CD-ROM only $99. Tax Analysts, 6830 N. Fairfax Dr., Arlington, VA 22213. TEL 800-955-2444. FAX 703-533-4444.
● Also available on CD-ROM.
   Description: Contains the full text of over 70,000 private letter rulings and technical advice memorandums issued by the IRS from 1980-1996. Documents include summary prepared by Tax Analysts staff.

336   US
I R S PUBLICATIONS. (Internal Revenue Service) 1977. irreg. $307 (CD-ROM ed. $241). C C H Incorporated, 2700 Lake Cook Rd., Riverwoods, IL 60015. TEL 847-267-7000; 800-835-5224. FAX 800-224-8299. (looseleaf format)
● Also available online. Vendor(s): Wilsonline. Also available on CD-ROM.

336   US   ISSN 1060-9520
HJ4652
I R S RESEARCH BULLETIN. 1985. a. $10. U.S. Internal Revenue Service, 1111 Constitution Ave., N.W., Washington, DC 20224. TEL 202-783-3238. Ed. Bryan L. Musselman. circ. 3,250. **Document type**: government publication, bulletin.
   Formerly (until 1991): Trends Analyses and Related Statistics.
   Description: Serves as a major vehicle for communicating recent tax administration research to I.R.S. executives and to the general public.

336   CN
I T A SERIES. (Income Tax Act) 1991. q. Can.$450. C C H Canadian Ltd., 6 Garamond Ct., North York, ON M3C 1Z5, Canada. TEL 416-441-2992; 800-268-4522. FAX 416-444-9011. (also avail. in diskette format) **Document type**: trade publication.
   Description: Provides full consolidated text of Canadian Income Tax Act, Regulations, Bulletins, Circulars, Rulings.

ILLINOIS PROPERTY TAX STATISTICS. see BUSINESS AND ECONOMICS — Abstracting, Bibliographies, Statistics

336   RM   ISSN 1223-5180
IMPOZITE SI TAXE. m. Tribuna Economica s.r.l., Bd. Gh. Magheru 28-30, Sec. 1, 70159 Bucharest, Rumania. TEL 40-0-6592060. (Subscr. to: Rodipet S.A., P.O. Box 33-57, Bucharest, Rumania) adv.

336   AG   ISSN 0325-3635
IMPUESTOS; revista critica mensual de jurisprudencia y legislacion. (Includes: a. compilation) 1942. m. $600. Ediciones la Ley S.A., 1471 Tucuman, 1050 Buenos Aires, Argentina. TEL 541-495481. FAX 541-4760953. Ed. Marcelo Lascano.
   Description: Critical review of tax jurisprudence and legislation.

336   CN
INCOME TAX AND FAMILY LAW HANDBOOK. 1988. 3/yr. Can.$180. Butterworths Canada Ltd., Part of the Reed Elsevier group, 75 Clegg Rd., Markham, ON L6G 1A1, Canada. TEL 905-479-2665. FAX 905-479-2826. Ed. Mary Lou Benotto. (looseleaf format) **Document type**: trade publication.
   Description: Explains the Federal Income Tax Act and provincial tax statutes relevant to family law issues in Canada.

336   SA
INCOME TAX IN SOUTH AFRICA. 3 base vols. (plus a. supplement). R.615. Butterworth Publishers (Pty.) Ltd., Part of the Reed Elsevier group, P.O. Box 792, Durban 4000, South Africa. TEL 27-31-2683111. FAX 27-31-2683110. (looseleaf format)
   Formerly: Income Tax Service.
   Description: Provides comprehensive coverage of the legal principles of income tax, and practical advice on tax planning and tax solutions.

336.24   II   ISSN 0019-3453
INCOME TAX REPORTS; a journal of the law of income tax, wealth tax, gift tax and estate duty. (Text in English) 1933. w. Rs.940. Company Law Institute of India Pvt. Ltd., 88 Thayagaraya Rd., Madras 600017, India. Ed. Bd. circ. 16,500.

336 340   US   ISSN 1057-4824
KF6482
INCOME TAXATION OF NATURAL RESOURCES. bi-m. $550. Research Institute of America, Inc., 90 Fifth Ave., New York, NY 10011. TEL 212-645-4800. Ed. C.W. Russell.
   Description: Provides comprehensive explanations of tax regulations governing intangible costs and their impact on exploration, development, and exploitation of oil, gas, solid minerals, and timber resources.

336   GU   ISSN 1057-5456
HJ98.2.K6
INDEPENDENT AUDITORS' REPORT ON GENERAL PURPOSE FINANCIAL STATEMENTS - KOSRAE. 1989. a. Touche Ross & Co., GCIC Bldg., Ste. 810, 414 W. Soledad Ave., Agana, Guam 96910-5014.

336.2   II   ISSN 0073-6120
INDIA. CENTRAL BOARD OF REVENUE. CENTRAL EXCISE MANUAL.* (Text in English) a. Rs.6.25($2.85) Central Board of Revenue, Ministry of Finance, New Delhi, India.

336   II
INDIA. FINANCE DEPARTMENT. BUDGET OF THE CENTRAL GOVERNMENT. a. Finance Department, New Delhi, India. charts; stat.
   Supersedes: India. Ministry of Finance. Budget (ISSN 0536-9290)

336.2   CC
INDONESIA & PHILIPPINES TAX REVIEW. (Text in English) 10/yr. HK.$2800 in Hong Kong; elsewhere $380. Ashton - Brooke Asia Publishing Ltd., G.P.O. Box 12261, Central, Hong Kong, People's Republic of China. TEL 852-2982-0590. FAX 852-2982-0590. **Document type**: newsletter.
   Description: Provides advice on complicated tax issues and developments for companies operating in Indonesia and the Philippines.

(YEAR) INFLUENZA IMMUNIZATIONS PAID FOR BY MEDICARE; state and county rates. see PUBLIC HEALTH AND SAFETY

INFORMACION DINAMICA DE CONSULTA. see LAW — Corporate Law

336   US
INFORMATION RETURNS GUIDE. 1987. m. $296. C C H Incorporated, 2700 Lake Cook Rd., Riverwoods, IL 60015. TEL 847-267-7000; 800-835-5224. FAX 800-224-8299. (looseleaf format)

INFORMATORE PIROLA. see BUSINESS AND ECONOMICS — Personnel Management

336 340   SA
▼**INFOTAX**. (Not avail. in print format. System requirements: 6Mb Hard Disk Space, Windows (3.1, NT or 95); Includes: S A Tax Review (1019-8474)) 1997. q. R.600($140) (effective 1997); R.1000 ($230) (effective 1998). InfoMedia Technologies (Pty) Ltd., P.O. Box 44597, Claremont 7735, South Africa. TEL 27-21-689 5075. FAX 27-21-689-5025. E-mail: infomedia@iafrica.com; URL: http://www.pix.za/taxfax/taxfax.html. Ed. Marius van Blerck. (also avail. in diskette format)
● Also available on CD-ROM.
   Description: Aims to provide complete information on South African taxation.

336   US
INHERITANCE, ESTATE AND GIFT TAX REPORTS FEDERAL - ALL STATES. 1928. w. $1231. C C H Incorporated, 2700 Lake Cook Rd., Riverwoods, IL 60015. TEL 847-267-7000; 800-835-5224. FAX 800-224-8299.
   Description: Covers estate-gift tax law on federal and state levels.

336   US
INHERITANCE, ESTATE AND GIFT TAX REPORTS, HOME STATE. (In 2 vols.) m. $428. C C H Incorporated, 2700 Lake Cook Rd., Riverwoods, IL 60015. TEL 847-267-7000; 800-835-5224. FAX 800-224-8299.

BUSINESS AND ECONOMICS — PUBLIC FINANCE, TAXATION

336   **UK**
INLAND REVENUE OFFICIAL TAX GUIDES. irreg. Longman Group UK Ltd., Law, Tax and Finance Division, 21-27 Lamb's Conduit St., London WC1N 3NJ, England. TEL 44-171-242-2548. FAX 44-171-831-8119.
Description: Reproduces all current Inland Revenue leaflets; indexed, with tables of cases and statutes.

336   **UK**   **ISSN 1350-410X**
INLAND REVENUE PRACTICES AND CONCESSIONS YEARBOOK. 1992. irreg. £160. Longman Group UK Ltd., Law, Tax and Finance Division, 21-27 Lamb's Conduit St., London WC1N 3NJ, England. TEL 0171-242-2548. FAX 0171-831-8119. (looseleaf format) **Document type:** bulletin.
Description: Commentary on the Inland Revenue's interpretation of tax legislation.

336 336.1   **GW**
INSTITUT "FINANZEN UND STEUERN." I F ST SCHRIFTEN. 1954. irreg., no.351, 1996. price varies. Institut "Finanzen und Steuern" e.V., Postfach 7269, 53072 Bonn, Germany. TEL 49-228-982210. FAX 49-228-9822150. index, cum.index. (back issues avail.) **Document type:** monographic series.
Formerly: Institut "Finanzen und Steuern." Gruene Briefe (ISSN 0067-9941)

336 336.1   **GW**   **ISSN 0067-995X**
INSTITUT "FINANZEN UND STEUERN." SCHRIFTENREIHE. 1950. irreg., no.126, 1989. price varies. Institut "Finanzen und Steuern" e.V., Postfach 7269, 53072 Bonn, Germany. TEL 49-228-982210. FAX 49-228-9822150. index, cum.index. (back issues avail.) **Document type:** monographic series.

336 332   **AU**
INSTITUT FUER FINANZWISSENSCHAFT UND STEUERRECHT. GELBE BRIEFE. 1960. 6/yr. membership. Institut fuer Finanzwissenschaft und Steuerrecht, Seilerstaette 24, A-1010 Vienna, Austria. TEL 01-5129910. Ed. Anton Matzinger. abstr. circ. 730. **Document type:** bulletin.

336 332   **AU**
INSTITUT FUER FINANZWISSENSCHAFT UND STEUERRECHT. MITTEILUNGSBLATT. 1960. 4/yr. membership. Institut fuer Finanzwissenschaft und Steuerrecht, Seilerstaette 24, A-1010 Vienna, Austria. TEL 01-5129910. Ed. Anton Matzinger. **Document type:** newsletter.

336   **UK**   **ISSN 0260-6496**
INSTITUTE OF CHARTERED ACCOUNTANTS IN ENGLAND AND WALES. TAX DIGEST. 1980. irreg. £175 (overseas £192.50). (Institute of Chartered Accountants) Accountancy Books, 399 Silbury Blvd., Central Milton Keynes, Bucks. MK9 2HL, England. TEL 44-1908-248000. FAX 44-1908-248001. circ. 1,500. **Document type:** trade publication.
—BLDSC (8611.590000).

336 368   **US**   **ISSN 0890-9164**
KF6495.I5
THE INSURANCE TAX REVIEW. 1986. m. $649. Tax Analysts, 6830 N. Fairfax Dr., Arlington, VA 22213. TEL 703-533-4400; 800-955-2444. FAX 703-533-4444. (back issues avail.) **Document type:** trade publication.
—CCC.
Description: Covers federal and state taxation of insurance companies, products and policyholders with full text documents and commentary.

336   **AG**
INTER-AMERICAN CENTER OF TAX ADMINISTRATORS. INFORMATIVO - NEWSLETTER.* (Text in English and Spanish) 1968. bi-m. $12. Inter-American Center of Tax Administrators - Centro Interamericano de Administradores Tributarios, San Jose 83, 2do piso, Buenos Aires, Argentina. bk.rev.; illus. circ. 2,500. (back issues avail.)

336   **US**   **ISSN 0885-0437**
KF6275.99
INTERNAL REVENUE ACTS. 1954. a. West Group, 620 Opperman Dr., Eagan, MN 55123. TEL 612-687-8000; 800-328-9352. FAX 612-687-7302. (also avail. in microfiche from WSH) **Document type:** trade publication.

336.2   **US**   **ISSN 0020-5761**
INTERNAL REVENUE BULLETIN. (Semiannual Cummulative Bulletins avail.) 1919. w. $137 (foreign $171.25). U.S. Internal Revenue Service, 1111 Constitution Ave., N.W., Washington, DC 20224. TEL 800-829-1040. (Subscr. to: Superintendent of Documents, U.S. Government Printing Office, Box 371954, Pittsburgh, PA 15250-7954. TEL 202-512-1800. FAX 202-512-2250) circ. 25,057. (also avail. in microform from UMI,PMC; back issues avail.; reprint service avail. from UMI) **Document type:** bulletin, government publication.
Description: Announces official I.R.S. rulings, Treasury Decisions, Executive Orders, legislation, and court decisions pertaining to internal revenue matters.

336   **US**   **ISSN 0163-7177**
KF6276.526.A19
INTERNAL REVENUE CODE. Cover title: Complete Internal Revenue Code. s-a. $35.50. Research Institute of America, Inc., 90 Fifth Ave., New York, NY 10011. TEL 212-645-4800. FAX 212-337-4279. (Subscr. to: 117 E. Stevens Ave., Valhalla, NY 10595. TEL 800-431-9025)
—CCC.

336   **US**
INTERNAL REVENUE CUMULATIVE BULLETIN. a. $47. U.S. Internal Revenue Service, I R S Bldg., 1111 Constitution Ave., N.W., Washington, DC 20224. (Dist. by: Bernan Press, 4611-F Assembly Dr., Lanham, MD 20706-4391. TEL 800-274-4447. FAX 301-459-0056; And: Superintendent of Documents, U.S. Government Printing Office, Box 371954, Pittsburgh, PA 15250-7954. TEL 202-512-1800. FAX 202-512-2250) (also avail. in microfiche from WSH) **Document type:** government publication.

336   **US**
INTERNAL REVENUE MANUAL: ABRIDGED AND ANNOTATED. 3 base vols. (plus q. updates). $350. Clark - Boardman - Callaghan, 375 Hudson St., New York, NY 10014. TEL 212-929-7500; 800-422-2101. FAX 212-924-0460.
Description: Provides a selected abridgement, supplemented with annotations, of the IRS's massive official Internal Revenue Manual.

336   **US**
INTERNAL REVENUE MANUAL - AUDIT AND ADMINISTRATION. 1977. irreg. $1101. C C H Inc., 2700 Lake Cook Rd., Riverwoods, IL 60015. TEL 847-267-7000. Ed. J. Rooney. **Document type:** government publication.
● Also available online.
Also available on CD-ROM.

336   **SZ**   **ISSN 0074-1744**
INTERNATIONAL ASSOCIATION OF STATE LOTTERIES. (REPORTS OF CONGRESS). (Reports published in host country) 1974. biennial, 12th, 1976, Nairobi. 8 Fr.($300) International Association of State Lotteries, Hirschengraben 62, P.O. Box 644, 8021 Zurich, Switzerland. adv.; bk.rev. circ. 1,000.

336   **NE**   **ISSN 0074-2104**
INTERNATIONAL BUREAU OF FISCAL DOCUMENTATION. ANNUAL REPORT. (Text in English) 1953. a. free. I B F D Publications B.V., P.O. Box 20237, 1000 HE Amsterdam, Netherlands. TEL 31-20-6267726. FAX 31-20-6228658. TELEX 13217 INTAX NL. (In US: IBFD Publications USA, Inc., 4 Maple Ln., Valatie, NY 12184. TEL 800-299-6330. FAX 518-758-2246) Ed. H.M.A.L. Hamaekers. **Document type:** corporate report.
—BLDSC (1309.900000).

INTERNATIONAL CHARITABLE GIVING: LAWS AND TAXATION. see *LAW — International Law*

336.2   **BE**   **ISSN 0074-4476**
INTERNATIONAL CUSTOMS JOURNAL/BULLETIN INTERNATIONAL DES DOUANES. (Text in English, French, German, Italian, Spanish) 1891. irreg. price varies. International Customs Tariffs Bureau - Bureau International des Tarifs Douaniers, Rue de l'Association 38, B-1000 Brussels, Belgium. (Dist. in the U.S. by: National Technical Information Service, U.S. Department of Commerce, Springfield, VA 22161) circ. 4,500.

336   **NE**
INTERNATIONAL GUIDE TO MERGERS AND ACQUISITIONS. (Text in English) 1992. 2 base vols. (plus s-a. updates). $900 (renewals $390) (effective 1997). I B F D Publications B.V., P.O. Box 20237, 1000 HE Amsterdam, Netherlands. TEL 31-20-6267726. FAX 31-20-6228658. TELEX 13217 INTAX NL. (In US: IBFD Publications USA, Inc., 4 Maple Ln., Valatie, NY 12184. TEL 800-299-6330. FAX 518-758-2246) Ed. Claudia Daiber. (looseleaf format) **Document type:** trade publication.
Description: Provides practical advice for tax specialists involved in domestic and transnational mergers, acquisitions and re-organizations, covering relevant tax regulations, legislation, and company law.

336   **NE**
THE INTERNATIONAL GUIDE TO PARTNERSHIPS. (Text in English) 1996. base vol. (plus s-a. updates). $375 (effective 1997). I B F D Publications B.V., P.O. Box 20237, 1000 HE Amsterdam, Netherlands. TEL 31-20-6267726. FAX 31-20-6228658. TELEX 13217 INTAX NL. (In US: IBFD Publications USA, Inc., 4 Maple Ln., Valatie, NY 12184. TEL 800-299-6330. FAX 518-758-2246) Ed. Kees van Raad. (looseleaf format)
Description: Provides complete coverage of the company and tax law applying to partnerships, including international aspects.

336.2 332.6   **UK**
THE INTERNATIONAL GUIDE TO TAXATION OF LIFE ASSURANCE AND MUTUAL FUNDS. base vol. plus a. update. £429($858) for base vol.; update £195 ($390). Monitor Press, Suffolk House, Churchfield Rd., Sudbury, Suffolk CO10 6YA. TEL 44-1787-378607. FAX 44-1787-881147. (Subscr. in the U.S. to: IBC (USA), 290 Eliot St., Box 91004, Ashland, MA 01721-9104. TEL 508-881-2800. FAX 508-881-0982) Ed. Tony Wickenden. **Document type:** trade publication.
Description: Answers questions on taxation that buyers and sellers of financial services products raise.

336 341   **US**
INTERNATIONAL INCOME TAX RULES OF THE UNITED STATES. 1989. base vol. (plus suppl.). $125. Butterworth Legal Publishers (Salem) (Subsidiary of: Reed Elsevier plc), 8 Industrial Way, Bldg. C, Salem, NH 03079. TEL 800-548-4001. FAX 603-898-9858. Ed. Michael J. McIntyre. (looseleaf format)
Description: Describes international tax rules of the United States, concentrating on the tax rules that resolve potential conflicts between the US claims for tax revenue from transnational income and the claims of other national tax jurisdictions.

336   **GW**   **ISSN 0074-6533**
INTERNATIONAL INSTITUTE OF PUBLIC FINANCE. PAPERS AND PROCEEDINGS.* (Supplement to: Public Finance (ISSN 0033-3476)) (Text in English, French, German) 1938. a. price varies. International Institute of Public Finance, Universitaet Saarbruecken, 66000 Saarbruecken, Germany. circ. 1,700. **Document type:** academic/scholarly publication.
Description: Presents selected papers from the annual meetings of the institute.

336   **US**
INTERNATIONAL PERSONAL TAX PLANNING ENCYCLOPEDIA. Variant title: Lawrence International Personal Tax Planning Encyclopaedia. 1990. 2 base vols. (plus a. supplement). $175. Butterworth Legal Publishers (Salem) (Subsidiary of: Reed Elsevier plc), 8 Industrial Way, Bldg. C, Salem, NH 03079. TEL 800-548-4001. FAX 603-898-9858. (U.K. and European orders to: Borough Green, Sevenoaks, Kent TN15 8PH, England. TEL 44-732-882566) Ed. Robert C. Lawrence, III. (looseleaf format)

336   **II**
INTERNATIONAL PRESS CUTTING SERVICE: CENTRAL EXCISE NOTIFICATIONS AND NEWS. (Text in English) w. Rs.625($75) International Press Cutting Service, P.O. Box 121, Allahabad 211001, India. **Document type:** newsletter.

BUSINESS AND ECONOMICS — PUBLIC FINANCE, TAXATION

336.2 332 II ISSN 0047-1097
INTERNATIONAL PRESS CUTTING SERVICE: TAXATION - FINANCE - COMPANY LAW. 1967. w. Rs.635($75) International Press Cutting Service, P.O. Box 121, Allahabad 211001, India. Ed. N. Khanna. bk.rev.; index. circ. 1,200. (processed) **Document type:** newsletter.

336 US ISSN 0927-5940
HJ2240 CODEN: ITPFEB
INTERNATIONAL TAX AND PUBLIC FINANCE. 1993. q. fl.545 to institutions; $279.50 to institutions in U.S. (effective 1998). Kluwer Academic Publishers Boston, Box 358, Accord Sta., Hingham, MA 02018-0358. TEL 617-871-6600. FAX 617-871-6528. TELEX 200190. E-mail: services@wkap.nl; URL: http://www.wkap.nl. (Dist. outside N. America by: Kluwer Academic Publishers Group, P.O. Box 322, 3300 AH Dordrecht, Netherlands. TEL 31-78-6392392. FAX 31-78-6546474) Eds. Jack Mintz, Michael Keen. (back issues avail.; reprint service avail. from SWZ) **Document type:** academic/scholarly publication.
—BLDSC (4550.392500); UnCover. **CCC.**
Description: Publishes theoretical and empirical studies of tax policies, including expenditure and financial policies.
Refereed Serial

336.2 US ISSN 0097-7314
HJ2240
INTERNATIONAL TAX JOURNAL. 1974. q. $136 (effective 1992). Panel Publishers, Inc., 36 W. 44th St., No. 1316, New York, NY 10036-8102. TEL 212-790-2000. FAX 212-302-5119. URL: http://www.aspenpulo.com/index.htm. Ed. Tom Whitehill. adv.; bk.rev.; charts. (also avail. in microform from UMI; back issues avail.; reprint service avail. from WSH) **Indexed:** ABI Inform., Account.Ind. (1974-), B.P.I., BPIA, Bus.Ind., C.L.I., IBR, L.R.I., Leg.Cont., Leg.Per., P.A.I.S., Tr.& Indus.Ind.
—BLDSC (4550.398000); KR SourceOne; SWETS; UMI; UnCover. **CCC.**
Description: Articles, columns and tax notes pertaining to the international tax market.

336 AT
INTERNATIONAL TAX PLANNING - EXPATRIATES & MIGRANTS. (Complements: International Tax Planning Manual - Corporations; International Offshore Financial Centres) 1992. q. C C H Australia Ltd., P.O. Box 230, North Ryde, N.S.W. 2113, Australia. TEL 61-1-300300224. FAX 61-1-300306224. (looseleaf format) **Document type:** trade publication.
Description: Explaining the personal taxation issues raised when expatriates and migrants leave their home country and relocate under a new tax regime. Adopting a country-by-country approach, the service covers over 20 countries.

336 US
INTERNATIONAL TAX PLANNING MANUAL; corporations. 8/yr. (in 2 vols.) $575. C C H Incorporated, 2700 Lake Cook Rd., Riverwoods, IL 60015. TEL 847-267-7000; 800-835-5224. FAX 800-224-8299.

336 382 AT
INTERNATIONAL TAX PLANNING MANUAL - CORPORATIONS. (Complements: International Tax Planning - Expatriates & Migrants; International Offshore Financial Centres) 1986. 8/yr. C C H Australia Ltd., P.O. Box 230, North Ryde, N.S.W. 2113, Australia. TEL 61-1-300300224. FAX 61-1-300306224. (looseleaf format)
Formerly: International Tax Planning Manual.
Description: Explains the principles of international tax planning for corporations when they invest in any one or more of 42 different countries.

336.2 UK ISSN 0300-1628
K9
INTERNATIONAL TAX REPORT; maximizing tax opportunities worldwide. 1972. m. £460($920) Monitor Press Ltd., Suffolk House, Church Field Rd., Sudbury, Suffolk CO10 6YA, England. TEL 44-1787-378607. FAX 44-1787-881147. Ed. Richard P. Casna. bk.rev.; bibl.; charts; stat.; index. circ. 850. (back issues avail.) **Document type:** trade publication.
● Also available online. Vendor(s): Data-Star, Lexis-Nexis, UMI.
—UMI. **CCC.**
Incorporates: International Tax Digest (ISSN 0955-498X)
Description: Reports changes in international tax legislation and gives practical advice on tax planning strategies. Contains a conference calendar and a summary of world tax developments.

INTERNATIONAL TAX REVIEW. see *BUSINESS AND ECONOMICS — International Commerce*

336 UK
INTERNATIONAL TAX SYSTEMS AND PLANNING TECHNIQUES. irreg. £165. Longman Group UK Ltd., Law, Tax and Finance Division, 21-27 Lamb's Conduit St., London WC1N 3NJ, England. TEL 0171-242-2548. FAX 0171-831-8119. (looseleaf format) **Document type:** bulletin.
Description: Advice on tax management and planning for multi-national businesses.

INTERNATIONAL TAX TREATIES OF ALL NATIONS. SERIES A. see *LAW — International Law*

INTERNATIONAL TAX TREATIES OF ALL NATIONS. SERIES B. see *LAW — International Law*

336.2 UK
▼**INTERNATIONAL TAXATION OF LOW TAX TRANSACTIONS.** 1996. s-a. $450. B N A International, Inc. (Subsidiary of: The Bureau of National Affairs, Inc.), Heron House, 6th Fl., 10 Dean Farrar St., London SW1H 0DX, England. TEL 44-171-222-8831. FAX 44-171-222-0294. TELEX 262570 BNALDN G. Ed. S. Joel Kolko. (looseleaf format; back issues avail.)

341.57 665.5 US
INTERNATIONAL TAXATION SERIES. base vols. (plus q. supplements). $4100 (renewal $1700). Barrows Co., Inc., 116 E. 66th St., New York, NY 10021. TEL 212-772-1199. FAX 212-288-7242. TELEX 4971238 BARROWS. Eds. G.H. Barrows, Marta Guerra.
Description: Presents an overview of the taxation of oil and gas, with a summary and analysis for every country.

INTERNATIONAL TRANSFER PRICING JOURNAL. see *BUSINESS AND ECONOMICS — Banking And Finance*

336.2 NE ISSN 0925-0832
INTERNATIONAL V A T MONITOR. (Value Added Taxation) (Text in English) 1990. 6/yr. $520 (effective 1997). I B F D Publications B.V., P.O. Box 20237, 1000 HE Amsterdam, Netherlands. TEL 31-20-6267726. FAX 31-20-6228658. TELEX 13217 INTAX NL. (In US: IBFD Publications USA, Inc., 4 Maple Ln., Valatie, NY 12184. TEL 800-299-6330. FAX 518-758-2246) Eds. Ben Terra, Servaas van Thiel. (also avail. in microfiche; back issues avail.)
Description: Covers current issues in VAT, including outlines of VAT policy and legislation within particular countries, case reviews, and relevant EC developments.

336.2 GW ISSN 0020-9368
INTERNATIONALE WIRTSCHAFTS-BRIEFE; Zeitschrift fuer internationales Steuer- und Wirtschaftsrecht, Euratom, OECD, Steuern und Zoelle im gemeinsamen Markt. 1954. fortn. DM.434.40. (Deutsche Vereinigung fuer Internationales Steuerrecht) Verlag Neue Wirtschafts-Briefe GmbH, Eschstr. 22, 44629 Herne, Germany. stat.; index, cum.index. circ. 3,500. (looseleaf format) **Document type:** trade publication.
—SWETS. **CCC.**

336 GW ISSN 0942-6744
INTERNATIONALES STEUERRECHT; Monatsschrift fuer europaeische und internationale Steuer- und Wirtschaftsberatung. Abbreviated title: I St R. 1992. bi-m. DM.596 (students DM.498) (effective 1997). (Bundessteuerberaterkammer) Verlag C.H. Beck, 80791 Munich, Germany. TEL 49-89-38189338. FAX 49-89-38189398. Ed.Bd. adv.: B&W page DM.2200, color page DM.3850; trim 260 x 186. circ. 2,700. **Indexed:** IBR. **Document type:** trade publication.

336 US
KF6763.A15
INTERSTATE TAX INSIGHTS. 1981. m. $175 (effective 1997). Interstate Tax Corporation, 193 East Ave., Norwalk, CT 06855-1109. TEL 203-854-0704. FAX 203-853-9510. Ed. Caryl Nackenson-Sheiber. bk.rev.; index. circ. 1,050. (looseleaf format; back issues avail.) **Document type:** newsletter.
Formerly (until Dec. 1996): Interstate Tax Report (ISSN 0731-5651)

INTERTAX; international tax review. see *BUSINESS AND ECONOMICS — International Commerce*

INVESTING, LICENSING AND TRADING. AMERICAS. see *BUSINESS AND ECONOMICS — International Commerce*

INVESTING, LICENSING AND TRADING. ARGENTINA. see *BUSINESS AND ECONOMICS — International Commerce*

INVESTING, LICENSING AND TRADING. ASIA. see *BUSINESS AND ECONOMICS — International Commerce*

INVESTING, LICENSING AND TRADING. AUSTRALIA. see *BUSINESS AND ECONOMICS — International Commerce*

INVESTING, LICENSING AND TRADING. AUSTRIA. see *BUSINESS AND ECONOMICS — International Commerce*

INVESTING, LICENSING AND TRADING. BELGIUM. see *BUSINESS AND ECONOMICS — International Commerce*

INVESTING, LICENSING AND TRADING. BRAZIL. see *BUSINESS AND ECONOMICS — International Commerce*

INVESTING, LICENSING AND TRADING. BRITAIN. see *BUSINESS AND ECONOMICS — International Commerce*

INVESTING, LICENSING AND TRADING. CANADA. see *BUSINESS AND ECONOMICS — International Commerce*

INVESTING, LICENSING AND TRADING. CENTRAL AMERICA; including El Salvador, Guatemala, Honduras and Costa Rica. see *BUSINESS AND ECONOMICS — International Commerce*

INVESTING, LICENSING AND TRADING. CHILE. see *BUSINESS AND ECONOMICS — International Commerce*

INVESTING, LICENSING AND TRADING. CHINA. see *BUSINESS AND ECONOMICS — International Commerce*

INVESTING, LICENSING AND TRADING. COLOMBIA. see *BUSINESS AND ECONOMICS — International Commerce*

INVESTING, LICENSING AND TRADING. CZECH REPUBLIC. see *BUSINESS AND ECONOMICS — International Commerce*

INVESTING, LICENSING AND TRADING. DENMARK. see *BUSINESS AND ECONOMICS — International Commerce*

INVESTING, LICENSING AND TRADING. ECUADOR. see *BUSINESS AND ECONOMICS — International Commerce*

INVESTING, LICENSING AND TRADING. EGYPT. see *BUSINESS AND ECONOMICS — International Commerce*

BUSINESS AND ECONOMICS — PUBLIC FINANCE, TAXATION

INVESTING, LICENSING AND TRADING. EUROPEAN UNION. see *BUSINESS AND ECONOMICS — International Commerce*

INVESTING, LICENSING AND TRADING. FINLAND. see *BUSINESS AND ECONOMICS — International Commerce*

INVESTING, LICENSING AND TRADING. FRANCE. see *BUSINESS AND ECONOMICS — International Commerce*

INVESTING, LICENSING AND TRADING. GERMANY. see *BUSINESS AND ECONOMICS — International Commerce*

INVESTING, LICENSING AND TRADING. GLOBAL EDITION. see *BUSINESS AND ECONOMICS — International Commerce*

INVESTING, LICENSING AND TRADING. GREECE. see *BUSINESS AND ECONOMICS — International Commerce*

INVESTING, LICENSING AND TRADING. HONG KONG. see *BUSINESS AND ECONOMICS — International Commerce*

INVESTING, LICENSING AND TRADING. HUNGARY. see *BUSINESS AND ECONOMICS — International Commerce*

INVESTING, LICENSING AND TRADING. INDIA. see *BUSINESS AND ECONOMICS — International Commerce*

INVESTING, LICENSING AND TRADING. INDONESIA. see *BUSINESS AND ECONOMICS — International Commerce*

INVESTING, LICENSING AND TRADING. IRELAND. see *BUSINESS AND ECONOMICS — International Commerce*

INVESTING, LICENSING AND TRADING. ISRAEL. see *BUSINESS AND ECONOMICS — International Commerce*

INVESTING, LICENSING AND TRADING. ITALY. see *BUSINESS AND ECONOMICS — International Commerce*

INVESTING, LICENSING AND TRADING. JAPAN. see *BUSINESS AND ECONOMICS — International Commerce*

INVESTING, LICENSING AND TRADING. KENYA. see *BUSINESS AND ECONOMICS — International Commerce*

INVESTING, LICENSING AND TRADING. LUXEMBOURG. see *BUSINESS AND ECONOMICS — International Commerce*

INVESTING, LICENSING AND TRADING. MALAYSIA. see *BUSINESS AND ECONOMICS — International Commerce*

INVESTING, LICENSING AND TRADING. MEXICO. see *BUSINESS AND ECONOMICS — International Commerce*

INVESTING, LICENSING AND TRADING. MIDDLE EAST - AFRICA. see *BUSINESS AND ECONOMICS — International Commerce*

INVESTING, LICENSING AND TRADING. NETHERLANDS. see *BUSINESS AND ECONOMICS — International Commerce*

INVESTING, LICENSING AND TRADING. NEW ZEALAND. see *BUSINESS AND ECONOMICS — International Commerce*

INVESTING, LICENSING AND TRADING. NIGERIA. see *BUSINESS AND ECONOMICS — International Commerce*

INVESTING, LICENSING AND TRADING. NORWAY. see *BUSINESS AND ECONOMICS — International Commerce*

INVESTING, LICENSING AND TRADING. PAKISTAN. see *BUSINESS AND ECONOMICS — International Commerce*

INVESTING, LICENSING AND TRADING. PANAMA. see *BUSINESS AND ECONOMICS — International Commerce*

INVESTING, LICENSING AND TRADING. PERU. see *BUSINESS AND ECONOMICS — International Commerce*

INVESTING, LICENSING AND TRADING. PHILIPPINES. see *BUSINESS AND ECONOMICS — International Commerce*

INVESTING, LICENSING AND TRADING. POLAND. see *BUSINESS AND ECONOMICS — International Commerce*

INVESTING, LICENSING AND TRADING. PORTUGAL. see *BUSINESS AND ECONOMICS — International Commerce*

INVESTING, LICENSING AND TRADING. PUERTO RICO. see *BUSINESS AND ECONOMICS — International Commerce*

INVESTING, LICENSING AND TRADING. RUSSIA. see *BUSINESS AND ECONOMICS — International Commerce*

INVESTING, LICENSING AND TRADING. SAUDI ARABIA. see *BUSINESS AND ECONOMICS — International Commerce*

INVESTING, LICENSING AND TRADING. SINGAPORE. see *BUSINESS AND ECONOMICS — International Commerce*

INVESTING, LICENSING AND TRADING. SLOVAKIA. see *BUSINESS AND ECONOMICS — International Commerce*

INVESTING, LICENSING AND TRADING. SOUTH AFRICA. see *BUSINESS AND ECONOMICS — International Commerce*

INVESTING, LICENSING AND TRADING. SOUTH KOREA. see *BUSINESS AND ECONOMICS — International Commerce*

INVESTING, LICENSING AND TRADING. SPAIN. see *BUSINESS AND ECONOMICS — International Commerce*

INVESTING, LICENSING AND TRADING. SWEDEN. see *BUSINESS AND ECONOMICS — International Commerce*

INVESTING, LICENSING AND TRADING. SWITZERLAND. see *BUSINESS AND ECONOMICS — International Commerce*

INVESTING, LICENSING AND TRADING. TAIWAN. see *BUSINESS AND ECONOMICS — International Commerce*

INVESTING, LICENSING AND TRADING. THAILAND. see *BUSINESS AND ECONOMICS — International Commerce*

INVESTING, LICENSING AND TRADING. TURKEY. see *BUSINESS AND ECONOMICS — International Commerce*

INVESTING, LICENSING AND TRADING. UNITED STATES OF AMERICA. see *BUSINESS AND ECONOMICS — International Commerce*

INVESTING, LICENSING AND TRADING. URUGUAY. see *BUSINESS AND ECONOMICS — International Commerce*

INVESTING, LICENSING AND TRADING. VENEZUELA. see *BUSINESS AND ECONOMICS — International Commerce*

INVESTING, LICENSING AND TRADING. VIETNAM. see *BUSINESS AND ECONOMICS — International Commerce*

INVESTMENT BLUE BOOK. see *BUSINESS AND ECONOMICS — Investments*

336.2   NE
▼**INVESTMENT FUNDS.** (Text in English) 1996. 2 base vols. (plus a. update). $750 (renewals $250) (effective 1997). I B F D Publications B.V., P.O. Box 20237, 1000 HE Amsterdam, Netherlands. TEL 31-20-6267726. FAX 31-20-6228658. TELEX 13217 INTAX NL. (In US: IBFD Publications USA, Inc., 4 Maple Ln., Valatie, NY 12184. TEL 800-299-6330. FAX 518-758-2246) Ed. Dali Bouzoraa. (looseleaf format)
   Description: International guide to the taxation and regulation of mutual investment funds and their investors.

INVESTMENT LIMITED PARTNERSHIPS HANDBOOK. see *BUSINESS AND ECONOMICS — Investments*

IRELAND. CENTRAL STATISTICS OFFICE. BALANCE OF INTERNATIONAL PAYMENTS. see *BUSINESS AND ECONOMICS — Abstracting, Bibliographies, Statistics*

IRELAND. CENTRAL STATISTICS OFFICE. NATIONAL INCOME AND EXPENDITURE. see *BUSINESS AND ECONOMICS — Abstracting, Bibliographies, Statistics*

336   IE   ISSN 0075-0670
IRELAND (EIRE) DEPARTMENT OF FINANCE. FINANCIAL STATEMENT OF THE MINISTER FOR FINANCE. a. Department of Finance, Dublin, Ireland.

ISRAEL. CENTRAL BUREAU OF STATISTICS. LOCAL AUTHORITIES IN ISRAEL: FINANCIAL DATA. see *BUSINESS AND ECONOMICS — Abstracting, Bibliographies, Statistics*

336   IS
ISRAEL. DEPARTMENT OF CUSTOMS AND V A T. YALKUT. (Value Added Tax) (Text in Hebrew; occasional summaries in English and other languages) 1955. irreg. IS.30($20) Department of Customs and V A T, Publication & Instruction Section, 32 Agron St., P.O. Box 320, Jerusalem 91002, Israel. circ. 1,500.
   Document type: government publication.
   Formerly: Israel. Department of Customs and Excise. Yalkut (ISSN 0578-8250)

336   IS
ISRAEL. KNESSET. VA'ADAT HA-KESAFIM MISPARIM AL VA'ADAT HA-KESAFIM/ISRAEL. KNESSET. FINANCE COMMITTEE. DATA ON ACTIVITIES. 1972. a. Knesset, Finance Committee, Jerusalem, Israel. Ed. Ivor Kershner. circ. controlled. (processed)

336.2   IT   ISSN 1122-4436
HD671
ITALY. DIPARTIMENTO DEL TERRITORIO. RIVISTA. Key Title: Rivista del Dipartimento del Territorio. (Text in Italian; summaries in English, French, German and Italian) 1934. 3/yr. L.50000 (foreign L.72000) (effective 1993). Ministero delle Finanze, Dipartimento del Territorio, Largo Leopardi 5, 00185 Rome, Italy. TEL 34-6-48168432. (Subscr. to: Istituto Poligrafico e Zecca dello Stato, Piazza Verdi 10, 00198 Rome, Italy. TEL 34-6-85081) Ed. Enrico Vitelli. adv.; bk.rev.; bibl.; charts; illus.; tr.lit.; index. **Indexed:** GeoRef.
—CISTI.
   Formerly (until 1993): Rivista del Catasto e dei Servizi Tecnici Erariali (ISSN 0035-5860)

336   US
IT'S YOUR MONEY (JEFFERSON CITY). 1981. w. Department of the Treasury, State Capitol, Jefferson City, MO 65101. TEL 314-751-2411. Ed. John Robinson. circ. 700.

336   IV
IVORY COAST. MINISTERE DE L'ECONOMIE, DES FINANCES ET DU PLAN. COMPTES DE LA NATION. 1966. a. 20000 Fr.CFA. Ministere de l'Economie, des Finances et du Plan, B.P. V 125, Abidjan, Ivory Coast. TEL 225-21-48-92.
   Formerly: Ivory Coast. Ministere du Plan. Comptes de la Nation (ISSN 1013-5863)

336.2   US   ISSN 1056-3121
J.K. LASSER'S MONTHLY TAX LETTER. m. $24. (J.K. Lasser Tax Institute) Prentice Hall, 113 Sylvan Ave. Rte. 9W, Englewood Cliffs, NJ 07632. **Document type:** newsletter.
   Former titles (until 1991): J.K. Lasser's Monthly Tax Service (ISSN 0895-3147); (until 1987): Monthly Tax Service (ISSN 0736-1505)

BUSINESS AND ECONOMICS — PUBLIC FINANCE, TAXATION

336.24   US   ISSN 0084-4314
J.K. LASSER'S YOUR INCOME TAX. 1937. a. $14.95. (J.K. Lasser Institute) Macmillan General Reference, 1633 Broadway, New York, NY 10019. TEL 212-654-8500. Ed. Bernard Greisman.

336.2   US   ISSN 0075-2061
KF6369
J.K. LASSER'S YOUR INCOME TAX, PROFESSIONAL EDITION. 1962. a. $50. (J.K. Lasser Institute) Macmillan General Reference, 1633 Broadway, New York, NY 10019. TEL 212-654-8500.

343.05   BE
JAARBOEK PERSONENBELASTING. (Text in Dutch) a. 6395 BEF. Kluwer Rechtswetenschappen Belgie (Subsidiary of: Wolters Kluwer N.V.), Santvoortbeeklaan 21-25, 2100 Antwerp, Belgium. FAX 32-3-3600467. Ed. Ludo Dillen. **Document type:** trade publication.

336.2 343.04   NE   ISSN 0925-5133
JAARBOEK VOOR DE BELASTINGDIENST EN DE BELASTINGADVIESPRAKTIJK. 1833. a. fl.80. (Kluwer Fiscole en Financiele Uitgers) Noorduijn, Staverenstraat 32015, 7418 CJ Deventer, Netherlands. TEL 31-570-647111. FAX 31-570-634740. (Dist by: P.O. Box 23, 7400 GA Deventer, Netherlands. TEL 31-570-647407. FAX 31-570-632411; Subscr. to: V. Spilbergenstraat 32, 8023 XM Zwolle, Netherlands. TEL 31-38-4549586. FAX 31-38-4528392) Ed. Jan Hoogewag. circ. 4,000 (paid). **Document type:** directory.
   Former titles (until 1988): Jaarboek voor de Ambtenaren van de Belastingdienst (ISSN 0922-7482); (until 1987): Jaarboekje voor de Ambtenaren van's Rijks Belasttingen (ISSN 0922-730X)
   Description: Lists names and employees of the Dutch Department of Finance including the IRS and tax advisers.

336   US
JACOBS REPORT ON ASSET PROTECTION STRATEGIES. irreg. (10-12/yr.) $145 for 12 issues (effective 1997). Research Press Inc., 4500 W. 72nd Terrace, Prairie Village, KS 66208. TEL 913-362-9667. Ed. Vernon K. Jacobs. R&P contact: Vernon K. Jacobs. **Document type:** newsletter.
   Formerly (until Mar. 1993): Jacobs Report on Investment and Retirement Tax Planning.

336   GW
JAHRBUCH DER FACHANWAELTE FUER STEUERRECHT. a. DM.82. Verlag Neue Wirtschafts-Briefe GmbH, Eschstr. 22, 44629 Herne, Germany. (back issues avail.) **Document type:** trade publication.

JAHRESFACHKATALOG RECHT - WIRTSCHAFT - STEUERN. see BUSINESS AND ECONOMICS

336   US
JAPANESE INTERNATIONAL TAXATION. 1983. base vol. plus a. supplements. $165 for base vol. Juris Publishing, Executive Park, One Odell Plaza, Yonkers, NY 10701. TEL 800-887-4064. FAX 914-375-6047. Ed.Bd. (looseleaf format)

JOURNAL D'ECONOMIE MEDICALE. see MEDICAL SCIENCES

JOURNAL DE DROIT FISCAL. see LAW

JOURNAL OF ACCOUNTING AND PUBLIC POLICY. see BUSINESS AND ECONOMICS — Accounting

JOURNAL OF BANK TAXATION. see BUSINESS AND ECONOMICS — Banking And Finance

JOURNAL OF CONSTRUCTION ACCOUNTING AND TAXATION. see BUSINESS AND ECONOMICS — Accounting

338 336.2   US   ISSN 0094-0593
K10
JOURNAL OF CORPORATE TAXATION. 1973. q. $146.50 (overseas $225.95) (effective 1995). Warren, Gorham & Lamont, One Penn Plaza, New York, NY 10119. TEL 212-971-5000. FAX 212-971-5113. URL: http://www.wgl.com/tax/jct.html. (Subscr. to: The Park Square Bldg., 31 St. James Ave., Boston, MA 02116-4112. TEL 800-950-1205) Ed. Gersham Goldstein. (also avail. in microform from UMI,MIM; reprint service avail. from RRI,WSH) **Indexed:** ABI Inform., Account.Ind. (1974-), ASCA, B.P.I., Bank.Lit.Ind., BPIA, Bus.Ind., C.L.I., Curr.Cont., Fam.Ind., L.R.I., Leg.Per., Manage.Cont, P.A.I.S., SSCI, Tr.& Indus.Ind.
   —BLDSC (4965.338000); Genuine Article; KR SourceOne; SWETS; UMI; UnCover. **CCC.**
   Description: Provides analysis and guidance for practitioners who must stay on top of all the latest developments and their planning implications. Covers corporate reorganizations, compensation and fringe benefits, tax accounting, international developments, closely held corporations, and consolidated tax returns.

JOURNAL OF FINANCIAL PLANNING. see BUSINESS AND ECONOMICS — Investments

JOURNAL OF INTERNATIONAL ACCOUNTING, AUDITING AND TAXATION. see BUSINESS AND ECONOMICS — Accounting

336   US   ISSN 1049-6378
K4464.A13
JOURNAL OF INTERNATIONAL TAXATION. 1990. m. $277.25 (foreign $388.45) (effective 1995). Warren, Gorham & Lamont, One Penn Plaza, New York, NY 10119. TEL 212-971-5000. FAX 212-971-5113. URL: http://www.wgl.com/tax/joit.html. (Subscr. to: The Park Square Bldg., 31 St. James Ave., Boston, MA 02116-4112. TEL 800-950-1207) Ed. Robert Gallagher. adv. contact: Margaret Lord-York. charts. circ. 2,500. (also avail. in microform from UMI; reprint service avail. from WSH) **Document type:** trade publication.
   ●Also available online. Vendor(s): Lexis-Nexis.
   —BLDSC (5007.686800); UMI; UnCover. **CCC.**
   Description: Offers broad-based, in-depth coverage of U.S. taxation issues as they relate to international transactions. Also covers foreign taxation matters.

343.05   US   ISSN 1076-0865
K10
JOURNAL OF LIMITED LIABILITY COMPANIES; a national journal covering the business, legal, and tax aspects of limited liability companies. 1994. q. $160 (overseas $208). Warren, Gorham & Lamont, One Penn Plaza, New York, NY 10119-4098. TEL 212-971-5423. FAX 212-971-5113. (Subscr. to: The Park Square Bldg., 31 St. James Ave., Boston, MA 02116-4112. TEL 800-950-1207) Ed. Sandra K. Lewis. adv.; bk.rev.; charts; index. circ. 4,500. **Document type:** trade publication.
   —UMI; UnCover. **CCC.**
   Description: Contains articles on all aspects of operating a limited-liability company, with emphasis on the planning potential of such entities.
   Refereed Serial

336   US   ISSN 1054-8394
KF6750.A15
JOURNAL OF MULTISTATE TAXATION. 1991. bi-m. $214.75 (overseas $310.45) (effective 1995). Warren, Gorham & Lamont, One Penn Plaza, New York, NY 10119. TEL 212-971-5000. FAX 212-971-5113. (Subscr. to: The Park Square Bldg., 31 St. James Ave., Boston, MA 02116-4112. TEL 800-950-1216) Pub. Thomas J. Kelly. circ. 2,200. (also avail. in microform from UMI; reprint service avail. from WSH) **Document type:** trade publication.
   —UMI. **CCC.**
   Description: Covers developments on planning in-state and local taxation nationwide; of interest to those involved in multistate operations and individuals with assets or investments in more than one state.
   Refereed Serial

336   US   ISSN 0749-4513
K10
JOURNAL OF PARTNERSHIP TAXATION. 1984. q. $146.50 (overseas $225.95) (effective 1995). Warren, Gorham & Lamont, One Penn Plaza, New York, NY 10119. TEL 212-971-5000. FAX 212-971-5113. (Subscr. to: The Park Square Bldg., 31 St. James Ave., Boston, MA 02116-4112. TEL 800-950-1205) (reprint service avail. from RRI,WSH) **Indexed:** ABI Inform., Account.Ind. (1984-).
Document type: trade publication.
   ●Also available online. Vendor(s): Lexis-Nexis (TAXRIA-Library), West Group (WGL-JPTAX).
   —BLDSC (5029.300000); UMI; UnCover. **CCC.**
   Description: Covers trends and developments in partnership taxation, including recent legislation, regulations, and case law.

336.2 331   US   ISSN 0148-2181
K16
JOURNAL OF PENSION PLANNING AND COMPLIANCE. 1974. q. $136 (effective 1992). Panel Publishers, Inc., 36 W. 44th St., No. 1316, New York, NY 10036-8102. TEL 212-790-2000. FAX 212-302-5119. Ed. Bruce J. McNeil. (also avail. in microform from UMI; microfiche from WSH; back issues avail.; reprint service avail. from WSH) **Indexed:** ABI Inform., Account.Ind. (1974-), BPIA, Bus.Ind., C.L.I., L.I.I., L.R.I., Leg.Cont., Leg.Per., Manage.Cont, P.A.I.S., Tr.& Indus.Ind.
   —BLDSC (5030.520000); UMI. **CCC.**
   Formerly: Pension and Profit-Sharing Tax Journal.
   Description: Technical articles on major issues confronting the pension community.

336   PH   ISSN 0115-9143
HC451
JOURNAL OF PHILIPPINE DEVELOPMENT. (Formerly published by: National Economic Development Authority) (Text in English) 1974. s-a. $46 (effective 1996). Philippine Institute for Development Studies, NEDA sa Makati Bldg., 3rd Fl., Rm. 304, 106 Amorsolo St., Legaspi Village, Makati 1229, Metro Manila, Philippines. TEL 632-893-5705. FAX 632-8161091. Ed. Jennifer P.T. Liguton. adv.; bk.rev. circ. 500. **Indexed:** Asian-Pac.Econ.Lit. **Document type:** academic/scholarly publication.
   —UnCover.
   Formerly: N E D A Journal of Development.
   Description: Studies economics in business, sociology, politics, public administration and foreign relations as they relate to the development of the Philippines.
   Refereed Serial

336 333.33   UK   ISSN 1357-1419
JOURNAL OF PROPERTY TAX ASSESSMENT & ADMINISTRATION. 1994. 3/yr. University of Ulster, School of the Built Environment, Coleraine BT52 1SA, N. Ireland. Eds. William McCluskey, Alastair Adair. **Document type:** academic/scholarly publication.
   —BLDSC (5042.781200).

336   US   ISSN 1041-4797
K10
JOURNAL OF PROPERTY TAX MANAGEMENT. 1989. q. $136 (effective 1992). Panel Publishers, Inc., 36 W. 44th St., No. 1316, New York, NY 10036-8102. TEL 212-790-2000. FAX 212-302-5119. Ed. Sheree L. Nelson. (back issues avail.)
   —CCC.
   Description: Commentary on issues and legislation affecting property tax, property valuation and property appraisal.

JOURNAL OF REAL ESTATE TAXATION. see REAL ESTATE

336   US   ISSN 1045-1471
K10
JOURNAL OF S CORPORATION TAXATION. 1989. q. $146.50 (overseas $225.95) (effective 1995). Warren, Gorham & Lamont, One Penn Plaza, New York, NY 10119. TEL 212-971-5000. FAX 212-971-5113. (Subscr. to: The Park Square Bldg., 31 St. James Ave., Boston, MA 02116-4112. TEL 800-950-1205) Ed. Jerald D. August. (also avail. in microform from UMI; reprint service avail. from WSH) **Indexed:** L.R.I., Leg.Per. **Document type:** trade publication.
   —KR SourceOne; UMI. **CCC.**
   Description: Provides current analysis, commentary, and planning guidance regarding the taxation of S corporations.

BUSINESS AND ECONOMICS — PUBLIC FINANCE, TAXATION

336　　　　　US　　ISSN 0744-6713
K10
JOURNAL OF STATE TAXATION. q. $136 (effective 1992). Panel Publishers, Inc., 36 W. 44th St., No. 1316, New York, NY 10036-8102. TEL 212-790-2000. FAX 212-302-5119. Ed. James T. Collins. (also avail. in microform from UMI; back issues avail.; reprint service avail. from WSH) **Indexed:** Account.Ind. (1986-), B.P.I., BPIA, C.L.I., L.R.I., Leg.Cont., Leg.Per., P.A.I.S.
—KR SourceOne; UMI. **CCC.**
　Description: Articles on state and local tax planning and compliance for tax management professionals.

336.2　　　　US　　ISSN 0022-4863
HJ2360　　　　　　CODEN: JOTAAM
THE JOURNAL OF TAXATION; a national journal of current developments, analysis, and commentary for tax professionals. 1954. m. $185 (overseas $264.95) (effective 1995). Warren, Gorham & Lamont, One Penn Plaza, New York, NY 10119. TEL 212-971-5185. FAX 212-971-5113. URL: http://www.wgl.com/tax/jtax.html. (Subscr. from: The Park Square Bldg., 31 St. James Ave., Boston, MA 02116-4112. TEL 800-950-1207) Ed. Joseph Graf. adv.; bk.rev.; charts; index. circ. 14,000. (also avail. in microform from UMI; reprint service avail. from RRI,UMI,WSH) **Indexed:** ABI Inform., Account.Ind. (1974-), ASCA, B.P.I., Bank.Lit.Ind., BPIA, Bus.Ind., C.L.I., Curr.Cont., L.R.I., Law Ofc.Info.Svc., Leg.Cont., Leg.Per., Manage.Cont., P.A.I.S., Risk Abstr., SSCI, Tr.& Indus.Ind. **Document type:** trade publication.
●Also available online. Vendor(s): Lexis-Nexis (TAXRIA-Library), West Group (WGL-JTAX).
—BLDSC (5068.200000); Genuine Article; KR SourceOne; SWETS; UMI; UnCover. **CCC.**
　Description: Contains articles on every key tax development. Provides analysis of every court and revenue ruling, as well as advice in daily tax problems.
　Refereed Serial

336　　　　　US　　ISSN 1069-1294
KF6410.A15
JOURNAL OF TAXATION OF EMPLOYEE BENEFITS. 1993. bi-m. $168.25 (foreign $247.95) (effective 1995). Warren, Gorham & Lamont, One Penn Plaza, New York, NY 10119. TEL 212-971-5000. FAX 212-971-5113. (Subscr. to: The Park Square Bldg., 31 St. James Ave., Boston, MA 02116-4112. TEL 800-950-1207) Ed. Deborah Walker. (also avail. in microform from UMI; reprint service avail. from WSH) **Document type:** trade publication.
—UMI. **CCC.**

336　　　　　US　　ISSN 1040-7839
KF6449.A15
JOURNAL OF TAXATION OF ESTATES AND TRUSTS. 1988. q. $125. Faulkner & Gray, Inc. (New York), 11 Penn Plaza, 17th Fl., New York, NY 10001. TEL 212-967-7000. FAX 212-967-7155. Ed. Leslie Laffie. (reprint service avail. from WSH) **Indexed:** Account.Ind. (1988-).
　Description: Covers new developments from the IRS, the Treasury, and the courts.

336　　　　　US　　ISSN 1043-0539
KF6449.A15
JOURNAL OF TAXATION OF EXEMPT ORGANIZATIONS. 1989. bi-m. $173.25 (overseas $251.95) (effective 1995). Warren, Gorham & Lamont, One Penn Plaza, New York, NY 10119. TEL 212-971-5000. FAX 212-971-5113. (Subscr. to: Park Square Bldg., 31 St. James Ave., Boston, MA 02116-4112. TEL 800-950-1207) Ed. Joseph E. Lundy. (reprint service avail. from WSH) **Indexed:** Account.Ind. (1989-). **Document type:** trade publication.
—UMI. **CCC.**
　Description: Gives advice, strategies, and analysis of the current tax situation for tax-exempt organizations.

336　　　　　US　　ISSN 0747-9115
K10
JOURNAL OF TAXATION OF INVESTMENTS. 1983. q. $146.50 (overseas $325.95) (effective 1995). Warren, Gorham & Lamont, One Penn Plaza, New York, NY 10119. TEL 212-971-5000. FAX 212-971-5113. (Subscr. to: The Park Square Bldg., 31 St. James Ave., Boston, MA 02116-4112. TEL 800-950-1207) Ed. James N. Calvin. (reprint service avail. from WSH) **Indexed:** ABI Inform., Account.Ind. (1985-), L.R.I., Leg.Per. **Document type:** trade publication.
—BLDSC (5068.210000); KR SourceOne; UMI; UnCover. **CCC.**
　Description: Devoted to tax issues affecting investments. Offers advice for new investment opportunities and brings new perspectives on traditional investment techniques.

336 330　　　US　　ISSN 1040-502X
KF6491.A15
JOURNAL OF TAXATION OF S CORPORATIONS. 1988. q. $125. Faulkner & Gray, Inc. (New York), 11 Penn Plaza, 17th Fl., New York, NY 10001. TEL 212-967-7000. FAX 212-967-7155. Ed. Leslie Laffie. (reprint service avail. from WSH) **Indexed:** Account.Ind. (1989-).
—UMI.
　Description: Focuses on S Corporations' status and its area of taxation.

KANO (STATE) PUBLIC FINANCE STATISTICS OF KANO STATE & LOCAL GOVERNMENT COUNCILS. see BUSINESS AND ECONOMICS — Abstracting, Bibliographies, Statistics

336　　　　　JA　　ISSN 0286-1933
**　　　　　　　　　　CODEN: KCBSDI**
KANZEI CHUO BUNSEKIJOHO/CENTRAL CUSTOMS LABORATORY. REPORTS. (Text in Japanese; summaries in English, Japanese) 1965. a. Okurasho, Kanzei Chuo Bunsekijo - Ministry of Finance, Central Customs Laboratory, 531, Iwase, Matsudo-shi, Chiba-ken 271, Japan. **Indexed:** Food Sci.& Tech.Abstr.
—BLDSC (7395.428000); CASDDS.

336
KARNATAKA. FINANCE DEPARTMENT. ANNUAL REPORT. (Text in English) a. Finance Department, Bangalore, Karnataka, India.
　Supersedes: Mysore. Finance Department. Annual Report.

336.3　　　　US　　ISSN 0095-1498
HJ9243.4
KENTUCKY LOCAL DEBT REPORT; a detailed statement of the bonded indebtedness of all Kentucky units of local government. 1971. a. Office of the Controller, State Local Debt Office, 702 Capital Ave., Rm. 069, Capitol Annex, Frankfort, KY 40601. TEL 502-564-3710. Ed. Nancy Rodgers. **Document type:** government publication.
　Description: Contains comprehensive data for all local government bonded indebtedness (county, city, school, special district) presented for each unit of local government by purpose.

336　　　　　KE　　ISSN 0075-5931
KENYA. PUBLIC ACCOUNTS COMMITTEE. ANNUAL REPORT. a. (Public Accounts Committee) Government Printing and Stationery Department, P.O. Box 30128, Nairobi, Kenya. **Document type:** government publication.

343.73 347.3　　US　　ISSN 0023-1762
HJ9
KIPLINGER TAX LETTER. 1925. fortn. $56. Kiplinger Washington Editors, Inc., 1729 H St. N.W., Washington, DC 20006. TEL 202-887-6400. FAX 202-778-8976. URL: http://www.kiplinger.com/newsletter/tax.html. Ed. Steven Ivins.
●Also available online.
—CCC.
　Description: News focusing on tax issues and problems associated with personal or business financial management.

336.2　　　　NE　　ISSN 0923-5051
KLUWER BELASTINGGIDS. 1971. a. fl.21.75 (effective 1996). Uitgeverij Kluwer B.V., Postbus 23, 7400 GA Deventer, Netherlands. TEL 31-570-633155. FAX 31-570-633834. adv.; circ. 80,000 (paid). **Document type:** trade publication.

336.2　　　　NE　　ISSN 0923-8468
KLUWER LOONBELASTINGGIDS. Variant title: Loonbelastinggids. 1982. a. fl.39 (effective 1996). Uitgeverij Kluwer B.V., Postbus 23, 7400 GA Deventer, Netherlands. TEL 31-570-633155. FAX 31-570-633834. adv.; circ. 2,500 (paid).

336.249　　　　NE
KLUWER SOVAC SERIES ON SOCIAL SECURITY. irreg. price varies. Kluwer Law International (Subsidiary of: Wolters Kluwer N.V.), Postbus 85889, 2508 CN The Hague, Netherlands. TEL 31-70-3081500. FAX 31-70-3081515. E-mail: services@wkap.nl URL: http://www.wkap.nl. (Dist. in N. America by: Kluwer Law International, 675 Massachusetts Ave., Cambridge, MA 02139. TEL 617-354-0140. FAX 617-354-8595) **Document type:** monographic series.

LAND AND LIBERTY; bi-monthly journal for land value taxation and free trade. see REAL ESTATE

336.2　　　　NE
LATIN AMERICAN TAXATION DATA BASE ON C D - R O M. a. $1500 (effective 1997). I B F D Publications B.V., P.O. Box 20237, 1000 HE Amsterdam, Netherlands. TEL 31-20-6267726. FAX 31-20-6228658. (In US: IBFD Publications USA, Inc., 4 Maple Ln., Valatie, NY 12184. TEL 800-299-6330. FAX 518-758-2246) (also avail. in looseleaf format)
●Also available on CD-ROM.
　Description: Covers international taxation issues pertaining to Latin America.

LAWYERS TAX COMPANION. see LAW

336 343.05　　US
HJ3698.A295T38
LEGISLATIVE TAX BILL SERVICE.* 1966. w. during legislature session. $1000. Tax Foundation of Hawaii, 126 Queen St., Ste. 304, Honolulu, HI 96813-4415. Ed. Lowell L. Kalapa. s-a. index. circ. 415.
　Description: Covers tax legislation introduced during the legislative session.

336　　　　　LO　　ISSN 0075-8817
LESOTHO. TREASURY. REPORT ON THE FINANCES AND ACCOUNTS. a. R.4. Treasury, P.O. Box 401, Maseru, Lesotho. **Document type:** government publication.

LETTER OF CREDIT UPDATE. see LAW

LEXIKON DES STEUER- UND WIRTSCHAFTSRECHTS. see LAW

336　　　　　LB　　ISSN 0304-727X
HJ89.L5
LIBERIA. MINISTRY OF FINANCE. ANNUAL REPORT.* 1972. a. Ministry of Finance, Broad St., Monrovia, Liberia. charts; stat.

336.666　　　　LB
LIBERIA. MINISTRY OF PLANNING AND ECONOMIC AFFAIRS. GOVERNMENT ACCOUNTS.* a. latest 1980. $3. Ministry of Planning and Economic Affairs, PO Box 9016, Monrovia, Liberia. stat.

336　　　　　US
LIFE AND TAXES. 1968. a. free. New England War Tax Resistance, Box 397174, Cambridge, MA 02139. TEL 617-859-0662. Ed.Bd. bk.rev. circ. 800. **Document type:** newsletter.
　Formerly: New England War Tax Resistance Newsletter.
　Description: Covers recent regional gatherings, future events and activities. Includes anti-tax articles.

336　　　　　US　　ISSN 0892-516X
LIMITED PARTNERSHIP INVESTMENT REVIEW. 1980. m. $197. Limited Partnership Investment Review, Inc., 55 Morris Ave., Springfield, NJ 07081. TEL 201-467-8700. FAX 201-467-0368. Ed. David W. Kennedy. adv.; bk.rev.; charts; stat.; index. (back issues avail.)
●Also available online. Vendor(s): NewsNet.
　Formerly (until June 1987): Tax Shelter Investment Review.
　Description: Offers detailed analyses of risks, tax consequences, general partners' track records.

BUSINESS AND ECONOMICS — PUBLIC FINANCE, TAXATION

336   US
LIQUOR CONTROL LAW REPORTS; federal and all states. 9 base vols. (plus bi-w. updates). $3042 (or avail. separately by states or federal). C C H Incorporated, 2700 Cook Rd., Riverwoods, IL 60015. TEL 847-267-7000; 800-835-5224. FAX 800-224-8299.

LIST OF PARTIES EXCLUDED FROM FEDERAL PROCUREMENT AND NONPROCUREMENT PROGRAMS. see PUBLIC ADMINISTRATION

336   UK
LLOYDS BANK TAX GUIDE. 1987. a. Lloyds Bank plc., Economics Department, P.O. Box 19, Hays Lane House, 1 Hays Ln., London SE1 2HA, England. TEL 0171-407-1000. FAX 0171-357-4378. Eds. Sara Williams, John Willman.

336   US   ISSN 0085-2821
HJ9011.M3
LOCAL GOVERNMENT FINANCES IN MARYLAND. 1948. a. free. Department of Fiscal Services, 90 State Circle, Annapolis, MD 21401. TEL 410-841-3710. FAX 410-841-3722. stat.; circ. controlled. (processed; also avail. in microfiche from UMI) **Indexed:** SRI. **Document type:** government publication. **Description:** Gives a financial report on the counties, incorporated municipalities, and special districts of Maryland.

336   UK   ISSN 1356-9805
LOCAL MANAGEMENT AND FINANCE. fortn. £95 (overseas £110). London Research Centre, Research Library, 81 Black Prince Rd., London SE1 7SZ, England. TEL 44-171-627-9666. FAX 44-171-627-9674. Ed. Mark Cousins. adv. contact: Annabel Davies.
Formerly: Find - Financial Digest (ISSN 0269-2503)
Description: Current awareness bulletin covering local government finance and management.

336.1 360   US   ISSN 0741-3173
LOCAL - STATE FUNDING REPORT. (Includes w. supplement: Grant and Regulation Alert) 1972. w. (50/yr.). $299. Government Information Services, 4301 Fairfax Dr., Ste. 875, Arlington, VA 22203-1627. TEL 703-528-1000. FAX 703-528-6060. Eds. Jeanne Williams, Lisa Hayes.
—CCC.
Formerly (until 1983): Local Government Funding Report (ISSN 0273-4451)
Description: Summarizes information on funding from federal and private sector sources. Covers developments in Congress, the White House and federal agencies.

336.2   CN   ISSN 0710-1759
LOI DE L'IMPOT SUR LE REVENU DU CANADA ET REGLEMENT. a. Can.$64.95 paperbound; Can.$74.95 hardbound. C C H - F M Ltd., 33 Racine, Farnham, PQ J2N 3A3, Canada. TEL 800-363-8304. FAX 514-293-2644. Ed. Pierrette Gregoire. index.
Former titles: Loi de l'Impot sur le Revenu du Canada; Loi de l'Impot sur le Revenu Canadien (ISSN 0076-048X)

336   UK   ISSN 0951-7618
LONGMAN TAX DIGEST. 1987. m. £50($95) Longman Group UK Ltd., Law, Tax and Finance Division, 21-27 Lamb's Conduit St., London WC1N 3NJ, England. TEL 0171-242-2548. FAX 0171-831-8119. Ed. Mike Truman.
—UMI. CCC.
Description: Digests all developments in taxation.

336.2   NE
LOONBRIEF. 10/yr. fl.273 (effective 1996). Uitgeverij Fed bv (Subsidiary of: Wolters Kluwer N.V.), Postbus 23, 7400 GA Deventer, Netherlands. TEL 31-570-633155. FAX 31-570-633834. Eds. G.J.M Jacobs, W. Seijbel. index. (back issues avail.) **Document type:** trade publication.

336.17   CN   ISSN 0709-5724
HG6149.Q4
LOTO - QUEBEC. RAPPORT ANNUEL. English edition: Loto - Quebec. Annual Report (ISSN 0709-5740) 1970. a. Societe des Loteries du Quebec, Public Affairs, 500 Sherbrooke St. W., Montreal, PQ H3A 3G6, Canada. TEL 514-282-8000. FAX 514-873-8999. TELEX 05560178. illus. circ. 15,000. **Document type:** corporate report.

LOTTERY & CASINO NEWS. see SPORTS AND GAMES

336   DK   ISSN 0106-8466
KJR7
LOVTIDENDE B FOR KONGERIGET DANMARK. 1896. s-a. DKK 200 (effective 1997). Justitsministeriet, Sekretariatet for Retsinformation, Axeltorv 6, 5. sal, D-1609 Copenhagen V, Denmark. TEL 45-33-32-52-22. FAX 45-33-91-28-01. Dir. Nina Koch. adv. contact: Nina Koch. index. circ. 575. **Document type:** government publication. **Description:** Official organ for promulgating the State Budget in accordance with Danish law.

336   US
LOW-INCOME HOUSING TAX CREDIT HANDBOOK. a. $150. Clark - Boardman - Callaghan, 375 Hudson St., New York, NY 10014. TEL 212-929-7500; 800-422-2101. FAX 212-924-0460. Eds. Michael J. Novogradac, Eric J. Fortenbach.
Description: Offers guidance through laws, regulations, and judicial decisions concerning the low-income housing tax credit.

336   LU   ISSN 0076-1559
LUXEMBOURG. MINISTERE DES FINANCES. BUDGET DE L'ETAT. a. free. Ministere des Finances, 3 rue de la Congregation, L-1352 Luxembourg, Luxembourg. (Subscr. to: Service Central des Imprimes, Dept. Diffusion, B.P. 1302, L-1013 Luxembourg, Luxembourg) circ. controlled. **Document type:** government publication.

336   LU
LUXEMBOURG. MINISTERE DES FINANCES. PROJET DE LOI CONCERNANT LE BUDGET DES RECETTES ET DES DEPENSES DE L'ETAT. a. free. Ministere des Finances, 3 rue de la Congregation, L-2931 Luxembourg, Luxembourg. (Subscr. to: Service Central des Imprimes, Dept. Diffusion, B.P. 1302, L-1013 Luxembourg, Luxembourg) **Document type:** government publication.

336.2   NE   ISSN 0005-8335
K13
MAANDBLAD BELASTING BESCHOUWINGEN; onafhankelijk maandblad voor belastingrecht en belastingpraktijk. vol. 42, 1973. m. fl.250 (foreign fl.215). Koninklyke Vermande, P.O. Box 20, 8200 AA Lelystad, Netherlands. TEL 31-320-237723. Ed. Dr. H.P.A.M. van Arendonk. adv.; bk.rev.; abstr.; bibl.; index. circ. 3,000.
—SWETS.

336.2 341   NE
MAASTRICHTSE FISCALE SYMPOSIA. 1992. a. price varies. Gouda Quint B.V. (Subsidiary of: Wolters Kluwer N.V.), Postbus 1148, 6801 MK Arnhem, Netherlands. (Dist. by: Libresso Distribution Centre, P.O. Box 23, 7400 GA Deventer, Netherlands. TEL 31-570-633155. FAX 31-570-633834) (back issues avail.) **Document type:** proceedings.

MCGOLDRICK'S CANADIAN CUSTOMS GUIDE "HARMONIZED SYSTEM". see BUSINESS AND ECONOMICS — International Commerce

MAGAZINE AFFAIRES PLUS. see BUSINESS AND ECONOMICS — Investments

336   II   ISSN 0076-2555
MAHARASHTRA STATE BUDGET IN BRIEF. (Text in English, Marathi) 1960. a. free. Directorate of Economics and Statistics, MHADA Bldg., Kalanagar, Bandra (E), Bombay 400051, India. Ed. V.B. Mujumdar. circ. controlled.

336   MW   ISSN 0076-3020
MALAWI. ACCOUNTANT GENERAL. REPORT. a. (Accountant General) Malawi. Government Printer, P.O. Box 37, Zomba, Malawi. **Document type:** government publication.

336   MW
MALAWI. DEPARTMENT OF TAXES. ANNUAL REPORT OF THE COMMISSIONER OF TAXES. (Text in English) a. Department of Taxes, P.O. Box 162, Blantyre, Malawi. TEL 265-620277. (Orders to: Government Printer, P.O. Box 37, Zomba, Malawi. TEL 265-50-523155) **Document type:** government publication.

MALAWI. ECONOMIC PLANNING DIVISION. MID-YEAR ECONOMIC REVIEW. see PUBLIC ADMINISTRATION

336   MW   ISSN 0076-3195
HJ83.2
MALAWI. MINISTRY OF FINANCE. BUDGET STATEMENT. a. Ministry of Finance, P.O. Box 30049, Lilongwe 3, Malawi. TEL 265-782199. (Orders to: Government Printer, P.O. Box 37, Zomba, Malawi. TEL 265-50-523155) **Document type:** government publication.

336   MW
MALAWI. MINISTRY OF FINANCE. FINANCIAL STATEMENT. (Subseries of its Budget Document) a. Ministry of Finance, P.O. Box 30049, Lilongwe 3, Malawi. TEL 265-782199. (Orders to: Government Printer, P.O. Box 37, Zomba, Malawi. TEL 265-50-523155) **Document type:** government publication.

MALAWI. NATIONAL STATISTICAL OFFICE. BALANCE OF PAYMENTS. see BUSINESS AND ECONOMICS — Abstracting, Bibliographies, Statistics

336   MW   ISSN 0076-3314
MALAWI. OFFICE OF THE AUDITOR GENERAL. REPORT. a. K2. (Office of the Auditor General) Malawi. Government Printer, P.O. Box 37, Zomba, Malawi. **Document type:** government publication.

336.2   CC
MALAYSIA TAX REVIEW. (Text in English) 10/yr. HK.$2500 in Hong Kong; elsewhere $350. Ashton - Brooke Asia Publishing Ltd., G.P.O. Box 12261, Central, Hong Kong, People's Republic of China. TEL 852-2982-0590. FAX 852-2982-0590. **Document type:** newsletter. **Description:** Provides advice on tax planning measures on areas including taxation of foreign-sourced income, double taxation avoidance treaties, expatriate personnel remuneration, the practical difficulties surrounding the recent schedular tax payment and developments in real property gains tax.

336   AT
MANAGING PAYROLL ADMINISTRATION. 1992. q. C C H Australia Ltd., P.O. Box 230, North Ryde, N.S.W. 2113, Australia. TEL 61-1-300300224. FAX 61-1-300306224. (looseleaf format)
Formerly: Australian Payroll Administration Manual.
Description: Contains information necessary for the setting-up and day-to-day administration of a pay office.

336.2   CN
MANITOBA AND SASKATCHEWAN TAX REPORTER. m. Can.$335. C C H Canadian Ltd., 6 Garamond Ct., North York, ON M3C 1Z5, Canada. TEL 416-441-2992; 800-268-4522. FAX 416-444-9011. index. **Document type:** trade publication.
Formerly: Manitoba and Saskatchewan Tax Reports.
Description: Current reporting covers every aspect of provincial taxation in Manitoba and Saskatchewan.

336.2   CN   ISSN 0047-5971
MARITIMES TAX REPORTER. 1950. m. Can.$335. C C H Canadian Ltd., 6 Garamond Ct., North York, ON M3C 1Z5, Canada. TEL 416-441-2992; 800-268-4522. FAX 416-444-9011. **Document type:** trade publication.
Formerly: Maritimes Tax Reports.
Description: Current reporting covers every aspect of provincial taxation in the Maritime provinces.

345 336.2   US
MARYLAND TAX COURT SERVICE. 1990. m. $375. Hawkins Publishing Co., Inc., Box 480, Mayo, MD 21106. TEL 410-798-1677. FAX 410-798-1098. Ed. Carl R. Eyler. cum.index. circ. 50. (looseleaf format) **Document type:** abstracting/indexing.

336   US   ISSN 0732-0825
KFM2870
MASSACHUSETTS APPELLATE TAX BOARD REPORTER. 1982. 4/yr. $65. Butterworth Legal Publishers (Salem) (Subsidiary of: Reed Elsevier plc), 8 Industrial Way, Bldg. C, Salem, NH 03079. TEL 800-548-4001. FAX 603-898-9858. cum.index. (looseleaf format; back issues avail.)
Description: Includes full-text opinions of the Tax Board with case abstracts.

BUSINESS AND ECONOMICS — PUBLIC FINANCE, TAXATION

336   US
MASSACHUSETTS CORPORATE TAX MANUAL. (3rd ed., 1992) 2nd ed., 1986. 2 base vols. (plus irreg. supplements). $160. Butterworth Legal Publishers (Salem) (Subsidiary of: Reed Elsevier plc), 8 Industrial Way, Bldg. C, Salem, NH 03079. TEL 800-548-4001. FAX 603-898-9858. Ed. Jay L. Horowitz. (looseleaf format)

336 340   US
MASSACHUSETTS SALES AND USE TAX MANUAL. irreg., 2nd ed., 1991. $175. Butterworth Legal Publishers (Salem) (Subsidiary of: Reed Elsevier plc), 8 Industrial Way, Bldg. C, Salem, NH 03079. TEL 800-548-4001. FAX 603-898-9858. Ed. Joseph X. Donovan. (looseleaf format)

MAURITIUS. CENTRAL STATISTICAL OFFICE. DIGEST OF PUBLIC FINANCE STATISTICS. see BUSINESS AND ECONOMICS — Abstracting, Bibliographies, Statistics

MAURITIUS. CENTRAL STATISTICAL OFFICE. NATIONAL ACCOUNTS OF MAURITIUS. see BUSINESS AND ECONOMICS — Abstracting, Bibliographies, Statistics

336   MF   ISSN 0076-549X
MAURITIUS. CUSTOMS AND EXCISE DEPARTMENT. ANNUAL REPORT. 1938. a. Rs.325. Customs and Excise Department, Port Louis, Mauritius. TEL 230-240-9702. (Subscr. to: Government Printing Officer, Sir Seewoosagur Ramgoolam St., Atchia Bldg., Port Louis, Mauritius. TEL 230-2088274) Ed. N. Bissessur. circ. 350. **Document type:** government publication.

336   MF   ISSN 0543-1565
MAURITIUS. DIRECTOR OF AUDIT. REPORT. 1912. a. Rs.75. Audit Department, Port Louis, Mauritius. circ. 500. **Document type:** government publication.

336   MF
MAURITIUS. MINISTRY OF FINANCE. UNIFIED REVENUE BOARD. REPORT. a. Ministry of Finance, Unified Revenue Board, Port Louis, Mauritius. Ed. M. Baguant.

336   MF   ISSN 0076-5562
MAURITIUS. PUBLIC ACCOUNTS COMMITTEE. REPORT.★ a. price varies. Government Printing Office, Elizabeth II Ave., Port Louis, Mauritius.

340 336   US   ISSN 0279-9286
MERTENS LAW OF FEDERAL INCOME TAXATION: CURRENT TAX HIGHLIGHTS. Key Title: Mertens Current Tax Highlights. 1982. m. $222. Clark - Boardman - Callaghan Company, Inc., 155 Pfingsten Rd., Deerfield, IL 60015. TEL 800-323-1336. Ed. Jim Fegen.

336.2   US   ISSN 1060-1856
KF6491.Z9
MILLER S CORPORATION TAX GUIDE. 1993. a. $119 (effective 1997). (Miller Accounting Publications, Inc.) Harcourt Brace Professional Publishing, 525 B St., Ste. 1900, San Diego, CA 92101-4495. TEL 619-699-6716. FAX 619-699-6593. Ed. Robert Jamison.
Description: Covers the latest S corporation tax rules and regulations.

336.776   US
HJ11
MINNESOTA. DEPARTMENT OF REVENUE. BIENNIAL REPORT. 1940. biennial. Department of Revenue, Communications Division, MS 3310, St. Paul, MN 55146. TEL 612-296-3781. stat. **Document type:** government publication.
Former titles: Minnesota. Department of Revenue. Annual Report (ISSN 0095-0645); Supersedes: Minnesota. Department of Taxation. Biennial Report.

MINNESOTA. DEPARTMENT OF REVENUE. PETROLEUM DIVISION. ANNUAL REPORT. see PETROLEUM AND GAS

MINNESOTA LEGAL REGISTER: MINNESOTA TAX COURT DECISIONS. see LAW — Judicial Systems

336.2   US
MINNESOTA SALES AND USE TAX ANNUAL REPORT BULLETIN. 1971. a. Department of Revenue, MS 2230, St. Paul, MN 55146. charts; stat. **Document type:** government publication, bulletin.
Formerly: Minnesota Sales and Use Tax Quarterly Report Bulletin.
Description: Summary of data reported on state sales and tax returns, broken down by major industry and geographic area.

336   US
MINNESOTA TAX APPEALS. 1989. base vol. (plus suppl.). $65. Butterworth Legal Publishers (Salem) (Subsidiary of: Reed Elsevier plc), 8 Industrial Way, Bldg. C, Salem, NH 03079. TEL 800-548-4001. FAX 603-898-9858. Ed. Earl B. Gustafson. (looseleaf format)
Description: Provides an overview of Minnesota state tax appeals.

336   IS
MISIM. (Text in Hebrew) 1987. bi-m. Ronen Publishing Company, P.O. Box 36665, Tel Aviv 61366, Israel. TEL 03-375912. FAX 03-615460.

366.778   US
MISSOURI. DEPARTMENT OF REVENUE. COMPREHENSIVE ANNUAL FINANCIAL REPORT. 1919. a. price varies. Department of Revenue, Financial and General Services, Box 475, Jefferson City, MO 65105. TEL 314-751-3530. FAX 314-751-8405. (Co-sponsor: Missouri State Treasurer) Ed. Nancy Holtschneider. stat. circ. 300. (also avail. in microfiche from CIS) **Indexed:** SRI. **Document type:** government publication.
Former titles: Missouri. Department of Revenue. Component Unit Financial Report; Missouri. Department of Revenue. Annual Combined Financial Report.

336   NE   ISSN 0924-4956
MONETARY MONOGRAPHS. Dutch edition: Monetaire Monografieen (ISSN 0924-4964) (Text in English) 1984. irreg. price varies. Kluwer Academic Publishers, Postbus 17, 3300 AA Dordrecht, Netherlands. TEL 31-78-6392392. FAX 31-78-6392254. TELEX 29245 KAPG NL. E-mail: services@wkap.nl; URL: http://www.wkap.nl. (Dist. by: Kluwer Academic Publishers Group, P.O. Box 322, 3300 AH Dordrecht, Netherlands. TEL 31-78-6392392. FAX 31-78-6546474; N. America dist. addr.: Box 358, Accord Sta., Hingham, MA 02018-0358. TEL 617-871-6600. FAX 617-871-6528) **Document type:** monographic series.

336   PL   ISSN 1231-1855
MONITOR PODATKOWY. 1994. m. Wydawnictwo C.H. Beck, Ul. Tyniecka 38a, 02-621 Warsaw, Poland. (Co-publisher: Verlag C.H. Beck) **Document type:** academic/scholarly publication.

336.2   US   ISSN 0027-0385
MONTHLY DIGEST OF TAX ARTICLES. 1950. m. $60. Newkirk Products, Inc., 15 Corporate Circle, Albany, NY 12203. TEL 518-862-3200. Ed. James H. Blake. R&P contact: James H. Blake. abstr.; circ. 9,000 (paid). **Document type:** academic/scholarly publication.
Description: Covers federal income, estate and gift taxes.

336.2   UK
MOORES ROWLAND'S ORANGE TAX GUIDE. 1978. a. £31.95($62) Butterworth & Co. (Publishers) Ltd., Part of the Reed Elsevier group, Halsbury House, 35 Chancery Ln., London WC2A 1EL, England. TEL 071-400-2500. FAX 071-400-2842. (U.S. addr.: Butterworth Legal Publishers, 90 Stiles Rd., Salem, NH 03079-9981. TEL 603-898-9664) Ed. John Jeffrey-Cook. **Document type:** trade publication.
Former titles: Moores and Rowland's Tax Guide (ISSN 0267-8829); Rowland's Tax Guide (ISSN 0143-280X)
Description: Deals with inheritance tax, national insurance contribution, stamp duty and value added tax.

336   UK
MOORES ROWLAND'S YELLOW TAX GUIDE. a. £31.95($87) Butterworth & Co. (Publishers) Ltd., Part of the Reed Elsevier group, Halsbury House, 35 Chancery Ln., London WC2A 1EL, England. TEL 071-400-2500. FAX 071-400-2842. (U.S. addr.: Butterworth Legal Publishers, 90 Stiles Rd., Salem, NH 03079-9981. TEL 603-898-9664) Ed. John Jeffrey-Cook. **Document type:** trade publication.
Formerly: Moores Rowland's Orange and Yellow Tax Guides.
Description: Deals with income tax, corporation tax and capital gains tax.

336   US   ISSN 1065-5972
MULTI-STATE SALES TAX GUIDE. 1940. w. $1286 (CD-ROM ed. $1320). C C H Incorporated, 2700 Lake Cook Rd., Riverwoods, IL 60015. TEL 847-267-7000; 800-835-5224. FAX 800-224-8299. (looseleaf format)
• Also available on CD-ROM.
Former titles: Multi-State Sales Tax Reports; All State Sales Tax Reports (ISSN 0414-0109)

336   US   ISSN 1051-1555
HD2753.U6
MULTISTATE CORPORATE INCOME TAX GUIDE. 1985. m. $709. C C H Incorporated, 2700 Lake Cook Rd., Riverwoods, IL 60015. TEL 312-583-8500; 800-835-5224. FAX 800-224-8299. (looseleaf format)
• Also available on CD-ROM.
—CCC.

336   US
MULTISTATE TAX COMMISSION REVIEW. 1981. irreg. $35 for 4 issues. Multistate Tax Commission, 444 N. Capitol St., N.W., Ste. 425, Washington, DC 20001. TEL 202-624-8699. FAX 202-624-8819. Ed. Michael Mazerov. bk.rev. circ. 2,200. **Document type:** government publication, newsletter.
Description: Covers policy issues and current developments in state taxation of multijurisdictional business activity.

336 352   US   ISSN 0199-6134
HJ9103
MUNICIPAL FINANCE JOURNAL. q. $142 (effective 1992). Panel Publishers, Inc., 36 W. 44th St., No. 1316, New York, NY 10036-8102. TEL 212-790-2000. FAX 212-302-5119. Ed. W. Bartley Hildreth. (also avail. in microform from UMI; microfiche from WSH; back issues avail.; reprint service avail. from WSH) **Indexed:** Account.Ind. (1986-), Bank.Lit.Ind., BPIA, C.L.I., Leg.Cont., Leg.Per., Manage.Cont.
—UMI; UnCover. CCC.
Description: Articles and columns covering recent tax and legal trends affecting large and small municipalities.

336 350   US
N C B A REPORTS. 1979. m. $70. National Commodity & Barter Association, Box 2255, Longmont, CO 80502. TEL 303-833-3333. index. (tabloid format)
Document type: newsletter.
Description: Covers government abuse of citizens, IRS abuses, how to defend yourself against the IRS, and issues pertaining to the abolition of the IRS and the Federal Reserve system and money reform.

N J W ENTSCHEIDUNGSDIENST FAMILIEN- UND ERBRECHT. (Neue Juristische Wochenschrift) see LAW — Civil Law

336   CC
NASHUI REN. (Text in Chinese) m. Hubei Sheng Shuiwu Ju, Hongshan Lu, Wuchang-qu, Wuhan, Hubei 430071, People's Republic of China. TEL 712970. Ed. Liu Xiaohui.

NATIONAL ACCOUNTANT. see BUSINESS AND ECONOMICS — Accounting

NATIONAL ACCOUNTS OF THE MALTESE ISLANDS. see BUSINESS AND ECONOMICS — Abstracting, Bibliographies, Statistics

NATIONAL CUSTOMS TARIFF GUIDEBOOK - AUSTRIA. see BUSINESS AND ECONOMICS — International Commerce

NATIONAL CUSTOMS TARIFF GUIDEBOOK - BRAZIL. see BUSINESS AND ECONOMICS — International Commerce

BUSINESS AND ECONOMICS — PUBLIC FINANCE, TAXATION

NATIONAL CUSTOMS TARIFF GUIDEBOOK - CANADA. see BUSINESS AND ECONOMICS — International Commerce

NATIONAL CUSTOMS TARIFF GUIDEBOOK - CZECH AND SLOVAK REPUBLICS. see BUSINESS AND ECONOMICS — International Commerce

NATIONAL CUSTOMS TARIFF GUIDEBOOK - EUROPEAN UNION. see BUSINESS AND ECONOMICS — International Commerce

NATIONAL CUSTOMS TARIFF GUIDEBOOK - FINLAND. see BUSINESS AND ECONOMICS — International Commerce

NATIONAL CUSTOMS TARIFF GUIDEBOOK - HUNGARY. see BUSINESS AND ECONOMICS — International Commerce

NATIONAL CUSTOMS TARIFF GUIDEBOOK - INDIA. see BUSINESS AND ECONOMICS — International Commerce

NATIONAL CUSTOMS TARIFF GUIDEBOOK - ISRAEL. see BUSINESS AND ECONOMICS — International Commerce

NATIONAL CUSTOMS TARIFF GUIDEBOOK - JAPAN. see BUSINESS AND ECONOMICS — International Commerce

NATIONAL CUSTOMS TARIFF GUIDEBOOK - MEXICO. see BUSINESS AND ECONOMICS — International Commerce

NATIONAL CUSTOMS TARIFF GUIDEBOOK - NORWAY. see BUSINESS AND ECONOMICS — International Commerce

NATIONAL CUSTOMS TARIFF GUIDEBOOK - PEOPLE'S REPUBLIC OF CHINA. see BUSINESS AND ECONOMICS — International Commerce

NATIONAL CUSTOMS TARIFF GUIDEBOOK - POLAND. see BUSINESS AND ECONOMICS — International Commerce

NATIONAL CUSTOMS TARIFF GUIDEBOOK - REPUBLIC OF KOREA. see BUSINESS AND ECONOMICS — International Commerce

NATIONAL CUSTOMS TARIFF GUIDEBOOK - ROMANIA. see BUSINESS AND ECONOMICS — International Commerce

NATIONAL CUSTOMS TARIFF GUIDEBOOK - SWEDEN. see BUSINESS AND ECONOMICS — International Commerce

NATIONAL CUSTOMS TARIFF GUIDEBOOK - SWITZERLAND. see BUSINESS AND ECONOMICS — International Commerce

NATIONAL CUSTOMS TARIFF GUIDEBOOK - TURKEY. see BUSINESS AND ECONOMICS — International Commerce

NATIONAL CUSTOMS TARIFF GUIDEBOOK - UNITED STATES OF AMERICA. see BUSINESS AND ECONOMICS — International Commerce

336.2   US   ISSN 1066-8608
NATIONAL TAX ASSOCIATION - TAX INSTITUTE OF AMERICA. PROCEEDINGS OF THE ANNUAL CONFERENCE ON TAXATION. 1907. a. $30 (or membership). National Tax Association - Tax Institute of America, 725 15th St., N.W., Ste. 600, Washington, DC 20005-2109. TEL 202-737-3325. R&P contact: Joan Casey. index. circ. 3,300. **Document type:** proceedings.
  Formerly: Annual Conference on Taxation. Proceedings.
  Description: Papers from the annual conference on the theory and practice of federal, state and local taxation.

336.2   US   ISSN 0028-0283
HJ2240   CODEN: NTXJAC
NATIONAL TAX JOURNAL. 1948. q. $60 to individuals (foreign $65); libraries $90 (foreign $95). National Tax Association - Tax Institute of America, 725 15th St., N.W., Ste. 600, Washington, DC 20005-2109. TEL 202-737-3325. URL: http://www.cob.asu.edu/nta/NTJ.html. Ed. Joel B. Slemrod. R&P contact: Joan Casey. abstr.; bibl.; charts. circ. 3,300. (also avail. in microform from UMI; microfiche from WSH; reprint service avail. from KTO,WSH) **Indexed:** ABI Inform., Account.Ind. (1974-), ASCA, B.P.I., Bank.Lit.Ind., BPIA, Bus.Ind., C.L.I., C.R.E.J., Curr.Cont., IBR, Int.Polit.Sci.Abstr., J.of Econ.Lit., L.R.I., Leg.Cont., Leg.Per., P.A.I.S., Risk Abstr., SSCI, Tr.& Indus.Ind., World Bank.Abstr. **Document type:** academic/scholarly publication.
  ●Also available online. Vendor(s): Information Access Co.
  —BLDSC (6033.115000); Genuine Article; KR SourceOne; SWETS; UMI; UnCover. **CCC.**
  Description: Articles on taxation and public finance in the United States and foreign countries.

340 336   CN
NATIONAL TRADE AND TARIFF SERVICE. 6/yr. Can.$660. Butterworths Canada Ltd., Part of the Reed Elsevier group, 75 Clegg Rd., Markham, ON L6G 1A1, Canada. TEL 905-479-2665. FAX 905-479-2826. Ed. A. de Lotbiniere Panet. index. (looseleaf format) **Document type:** trade publication.
  Formerly (until 1990): Canadian Customs and Excise Reports (ISSN 0228-3409)
  Description: Contains legislation and full text of cases decided in the area of trade and tariffs, customs and exercise taxes and special import measures.

336.2   NE
NEDERLANDSE JURISPRUDENTIE INZAKE INTERNATIONAAL BELASTINGRECHT; directe belastingen van internationaal opererende ondernemingen. 1993. base vol. (plus irreg. updates, 1-2/yr.) $125 (renewals $65) (effective 1997). (Rijksuniversiteit Groningen, Juridische Faculteit, Vakgroep Belastingrecht) I B F D Publications B.V., P.O. Box 20237, 1000 HE Amsterdam, Netherlands. TEL 31-20-6267726. FAX 31-20-6228658. TELEX 13217 INTAX NL. (In US: IBFD Publications USA, Inc., 4 Maple Ln., Valatie, NY 12184. TEL 800-299-6330. FAX 518-758-2246) Ed. A. Nooteboom. (looseleaf format)
  Description: Basic analysis of Dutch jurisprudence relating to the taxation of international firms.

NETHERLANDS. CENTRAAL BUREAU VOOR DE STATISTIEK. NATIONALE REKENINGEN/NETHERLANDS. CENTRAL BUREAU OF STATISTICS. NATIONAL ACCOUNTS. see BUSINESS AND ECONOMICS — Abstracting, Bibliographies, Statistics

NETHERLANDS. CENTRAAL BUREAU VOOR DE STATISTIEK. STATISTIEK DER RIJKSFINANCIEN/NETHERLANDS. CENTRAL BUREAU OF STATISTICS. STATISTICS OF THE STATE FINANCES OF THE NETHERLANDS. see BUSINESS AND ECONOMICS — Abstracting, Bibliographies, Statistics

336.2   GW   ISSN 0939-5881
NEUE STEUER-INFORMATIONEN. 1991. s-m. DM.238 (effective 1997). Verlag Peter Deubner GmbH, Wolfgang-Mueller-Str. 14, 50968 Cologne, Germany. TEL 49-221-9370180. FAX 49-221-93701890. **Document type:** bulletin.

336.2   SZ   ISSN 0028-338X
NEUE STEUERPRAXIS. 1946. m. 67 SFr. (Kantonale Steuerverwaltung) Paul Haupt AG, Falkenplatz 14, CH-3001 Bern, Switzerland. TEL 41-31-3012345. FAX 41-31-3015469. adv.; bk.rev.; charts. circ. 600. **Document type:** government publication.
  —**CCC.**

336.1 340   GW   ISSN 0028-3460
NEUE WIRTSCHAFTS-BRIEFE; Zeitschrift fuer Steuer- und Wirtschaftsrecht. 1947. w. DM.354.60. Verlag Neue Wirtschafts-Briefe GmbH, Eschstr. 22, 44629 Herne, Germany. TEL 49-2323-141-0. FAX 49-2323-141123. adv.; bk.rev.; abstr.; bibl.; charts; stat.; index, cum.index. circ. 89,000. (looseleaf format) **Indexed:** CERDIC. **Document type:** trade publication.
  ●Also available on CD-ROM.
  —**CCC.**

336   US
NEW ENGLAND WAR TAX RESISTANCE. ANNUAL REPORT. a. New England War Tax Resistance, Box 397174, Cambridge, MA 02139. TEL 617-859-0662. **Document type:** corporate report.
  Description: Information and news on financial affairs, activities and events of the organization.

336   UK
NEW EQUITABLE LIFE TAX GUIDE. 1896? a. $39.95 in N. America. Blackwell Publishers Ltd., 108 Cowley Rd., Oxford OX4 1JF, England. TEL 44-1865-791100. FAX 44-1865-791347. E-mail: jnlinfo@blackwellpublishers.co.uk; URL: http://www.blackwellpublishers.co.uk. Eds. Clive Steward, Anthony Taylor.
  Formerly: Smith's Taxation.
  Description: Covers U.K. law and practice relating to income, capital gains, corporation, value-added, inheritance and Council taxes.
  Refereed Serial

NEW HAMPSHIRE MUNICIPAL PRACTICE SERIES. VOL. 2: MUNICIPAL FINANCE AND TAXATION. see PUBLIC ADMINISTRATION — Municipal Government

NEW IN DUTY FREE. see BUSINESS AND ECONOMICS — International Commerce

336   US   ISSN 0733-1584
HJ11
NEW JERSEY. DEPARTMENT OF THE TREASURY. DIVISION OF TAXATION. ANNUAL REPORT. 1945. a. free. Department of the Treasury, Division of Taxation, Technical Services T S B - O C E, CN 281, Trenton, NJ 08646-0281. TEL 609-633-8426. circ. 2,000. **Indexed:** SRI. **Document type:** government publication.
  Description: Contains detailed descriptions of the division organization and taxes administered by the division, and various tax statistical tables.

336.2   US   ISSN 1073-6808
HJ2422
NEW JERSEY STATE TAX NEWS. 1972. q. free. Department of the Treasury, Division of Taxation, Technical Services T S B - O C E, CN 281, Trenton, NJ 08646-0281. TEL 609-633-8426. FAX 609-777-4319. Ed. Linda B. Hickey. charts; stat. circ. 21,000. **Document type:** government publication, newsletter.
  Description: Information for tax practitioners.

336   US   ISSN 0279-6481
NEW JERSEY TAX COURT REPORTS. 1980. bi-m. West Group, 620 Opperman Dr., Eagan, MN 55123. TEL 612-687-8000. FAX 612-687-7302.

336   AT
NEW SOUTH WALES AND A.C.T. STAMP DUTIES. 1985. bi-m. C C H Australia Ltd., P.O. Box 230, North Ryde, N.S.W. 2113, Australia. TEL 61-1-300300224. FAX 61-1-300306224. (looseleaf format)
  Supersedes in part (in 1991): Australian Stamp Duties.
  Description: Contains explanation of the law governing stamp duties, financial institutions duty and debits tax and commentary on dutiable instruments applicable in New South Wales and Australian Capital Territory.

NEW SOUTH WALES CONVEYANCING LAW AND PRACTICE. see LAW

336   AT
NEW SOUTH WALES LAND TAX. 1984. q. C C H Australia Ltd., P.O. Box 230, North Ryde, N.S.W. 2113, Australia. TEL 61-1-300300224. FAX 61-1-300306224. (looseleaf format)
  Description: Covers the law and practice of land tax in New South Wales. Includes up-to-date full text legislation, reports relevant cases, reproduces relevant revenue rulings, and contains in-depth commentary with extensive worked examples.

336   US
NEW YORK (CITY). COMPTROLLERS REPORT. 1976. m. free. Comptrollers Office, Municipal Building, New York, NY 10007. TEL 212-566-7231. Ed. Henry Walter. charts; stat. circ. 29,000. **Document type:** government publication.

BUSINESS AND ECONOMICS — PUBLIC FINANCE, TAXATION

336 333.33   US
NEW YORK CITY. REAL PROPERTY TAX. ANNUAL REPORT. a. City of New York, Department of Finance, Municipal Bldg., New York, NY 10007. TEL 212-669-4855.
Description: Covers New York City's property market and property tax policy.

336   US
NEW YORK UNIVERSITY. INSTITUTE ON FEDERAL TAXATION. CONFERENCE ON CHARITABLE FOUNDATIONS. 1955. biennial. $205. (New York University, School of Continuing Education in Law and Taxations) Matthew Bender & Co., Inc., 2 Park Ave., New York, NY 10016. TEL 212-448-2000. E-mail: international@bender.com; URL: http://www.bender.com. Ed. Nicolas Liakas. index, cum.index: vols.1-10. (also avail. in microfilm from RRI; back issues avail.; reprint service avail. from WSH)
Indexed: C.L.I., L.R.I.

336   NZ
NEW ZEALAND. AUDIT OFFICE. REPORT ON THE PUBLIC ACCOUNTS. 1856. a. NZ.$8. Government Printing Office, Private Bag, Wellington, New Zealand. TEL 09-737-320. Ed. A.M. Spencer. circ. 1,000. (back issues avail.)
Description: Audit report on financial statements of the New Zealand Government.

NEW ZEALAND ASSET PLANNING AND DUTIES GUIDE. see *LAW*

336 346.066   NZ
NEW ZEALAND BUSINESS LAW GUIDE. 1985. 8/yr. NZ.$1203 (effective 1997). C C H New Zealand Limited, P.O. Box 2378, Auckland, New Zealand. TEL 64-9-483-9179. FAX 64-9-483-4009. (looseleaf format)
Description: Information on all facets of business law. Includes full text legislation, full text or extracts of cases, and new developments covering proposed legislation, reports and government statements.

336   NZ   ISSN 0545-7572
NEW ZEALAND CURRENT TAXATION. 52/yr. NZ.$432. Butterworths of New Zealand Ltd., A member of the Reed Elsevier plc group, P.O. Box 472, 205-207 Victoria St., Wellington, New Zealand. TEL 64-4-385-1479. FAX 64-4-385-1598. Ed. Stephen Gibbs.
—CCC.
Description: Tax intelligence service offering up-to-date information in the taxation field.

336 346.066   NZ
NEW ZEALAND GOODS AND SERVICES TAX GUIDE. 1985. 6/yr. NZ.$806 (effective 1997). C C H New Zealand Limited, P.O. Box 2378, Auckland, New Zealand. TEL 64-9-483-9179. FAX 64-9-483-4009. (looseleaf format)
Formerly: New Zealand Sales, Goods and Service Taxes Guide.
Description: Provides information on goods and services tax. Includes full text legislation, government papers, case digests and new developments on legislative proposals.

336   NZ
NEW ZEALAND INCOME TAX GUIDE. 1973. 8/yr. NZ.$727 (effective 1997). C C H New Zealand Limited, P.O. Box 2378, Auckland, New Zealand. TEL 64-9-483-9179. FAX 64-9-483-4009. (looseleaf format)
Formerly: New Zealand Master Tax Guide Manual.
Description: Practical guide to income tax in New Zealand. Extensive indexes and thorough examination of important topics.

336.2   NZ
NEW ZEALAND INCOME TAX LAW AND PRACTICE. 1973. 10/yr. NZ.$2562 (effective 1997). C C H New Zealand Limited, P.O. Box 2378, Auckland, New Zealand. TEL 64-9-483-9179. FAX 64-9-483-4009. (looseleaf format) *Indexed:* Curr.Aus.N.Z.Leg.Lit.Ind.
Description: A comprehensive guide to income tax in New Zealand. Includes up-to-date new developments section, budget night tax reports, and special dispatch letters on major tax developments.

336 346.066   NZ   ISSN 0112-9791
NEW ZEALAND INCOME TAX LEGISLATION. 1984. 7/yr. NZ.$843 (effective 1997). C C H New Zealand Limited, P.O. Box 2378, Auckland, New Zealand. TEL 64-9-483-9179. FAX 64-9-483-4009. (looseleaf format)
Description: All significant legislation affecting income tax and land tax in New Zealand, reproduced in full text.

336.2   NZ   ISSN 1322-4417
NEW ZEALAND JOURNAL OF TAXATION LAW AND POLICY. 1994. q. NZ.$218.43. Brooker's Limited, Level 1 - Telecom Networks House, 68-86 Jervois Quay, Wellington, New Zealand. TEL 64-4998178. FAX 64-4-4998173. E-mail: publishing@brookers.co.nz. Eds. Garth Harris, Christopher Ohms. R&P contact: Geoff Adlam.
Description: Carries articles dealing with all aspects of taxation law and policy.
Refereed Serial

336   NZ
NEW ZEALAND LOTTERY BOARD. REPORT. (Title varies slightly) 1963. a. price varies. (New Zealand Lottery Board) Government Printing Office, Private Bag, Wellington, New Zealand. stat. circ. 200.
Formerly (until 1977): New Zealand. Lottery Board of Control. Report (ISSN 0545-7297)

336.2   NZ
NEW ZEALAND MASTER TAX GUIDE UPDATER. 1994. 3/yr. NZ.$179 (effective 1997). C C H New Zealand Limited, P.O. Box 2378, Auckland, New Zealand. TEL 64-9-4839179. FAX 64-9-4834009.
Description: Practical guide to income tax in New Zealand.

336 346.066   NZ
NEW ZEALAND SUPERANNUATION GUIDE. 1983. 2/yr. NZ.$755 (effective 1997). C C H New Zealand Limited, P.O. Box 2378, Auckland, New Zealand. TEL 64-9-483-9179. FAX 64-9-483-4009. (looseleaf format)
Description: A practical manual designed to assist in the planning and maintenance of superannuation schemes. Includes commentary and relevant legislation and cases.

336 346.066   NZ   ISSN 0112-3823
NEW ZEALAND TAX CASES. 1984. 22/yr. NZ.$1086 (effective 1997). C C H New Zealand Limited, P.O. Box 2378, Auckland, New Zealand. TEL 64-9-483-9179. FAX 64-9-483-4009.
—CCC.
Description: Comprehensive full text reporting of relevant New Zealand tax decisions.

336   NZ   ISSN 0110-4233
NEW ZEALAND TAX PLANNING REPORT. 1979. 6/yr. NZ.$390 (effective 1997). C C H New Zealand Limited, P.O. Box 2378, Auckland, New Zealand. TEL 64-9-483-9179. FAX 64-9-483-4009. Ed. D. Simcock. (looseleaf format)
Description: Articles by New Zealand tax practitioners on tax planning issues.

NIGERIA FINANCE YEAR-BOOK. see *BUSINESS AND ECONOMICS — Banking And Finance*

336.2   US   ISSN 1066-1018
KF6449.A73
NON-PROFIT LEGAL & TAX LETTER.* 1962. 18/yr. $235 (effective 1996). Organization Management Inc., 8081 Emerald Pool Ct., Mechanicsville, VA 23111. TEL 703-968-7039. FAX 703-818-0259. Ed.Bd. bk.rev.; bibl. (looseleaf format; back issues avail.) *Document type:* newsletter.
—CCC.
Incorporates (in 1996): NonProfit Insight (ISSN 1056-4594); Which was formerly (1980-1991): Tax-Exempt News (ISSN 0194-228X); (until June 1992): Non-Profit Organization Tax Letter (ISSN 0550-8401)
Description: provides up-to-date information for non-profit organizations and their professional advisors on legal and tax issue affecting the tax-exempt sector.

336.2   US   ISSN 1075-3532
NONPROFIT TAX LETTER. s-m. $149 (effective 1997). Harcourt Brace Professional Publishing, 525 B St., Ste. 1900, San Diego, CA 92101-4495. TEL 619-699-6716. FAX 619-699-6593. Eds. Dorinda DeScherer, Terence Meyers; Pub. Ken Rethmeier. R&P contact: Jenna Lake. TEL 619-699-6265. *Document type:* newsletter.
Description: Timely tax and financial strategies for nonprofit organizations.

336   NO   ISSN 0333-1423
NORSK SKATTELOVSAMLING. 1954. a. NOK 600. Jacob Jaroey, Vraasgt. 18, N-3701 Skien, Norway. TEL 47-35-59-92-26. Ed. Erik Friis Faehn; Jacob Jaroey.
● Also available on CD-ROM.

336.2   US
NORTH CAROLINA. DEPARTMENT OF REVENUE. FRANCHISE TAX AND CORPORATE INCOME TAX RULES AND BULLETINS. 1964. irreg., latest 1995. free. Department of Revenue, Corporate Income and Franchise Tax Division, Box 871, Raleigh, NC 27602-0871. TEL 919-733-8510. FAX 919-733-1821. circ. 7,500. *Document type:* government publication, bulletin.
Former titles (until 1992): North Carolina. Department of Revenue. Franchise Tax and Corporate Income Tax Rules and Regulations; (until 1976?): North Carolina. Department of Revenue. Franchise Tax and Corporate Income Tax Bulletins for Taxable Years (ISSN 0078-138X)
Description: Guide in the interpretation and administration of the corporate income and franchise tax laws, covering the major provisions and the laws relating to corporate income and franchise taxes.

336   UK
NORTHERN IRELAND. DEPARTMENT OF FINANCE AND PERSONNEL. NORTHERN IRELAND ESTIMATES (YEAR); for services under the Government of Northern Ireland. a. £15.40 per no. Department of Finance and Personnel, Stormont, Belfast, N. Ireland. (Subscr. to: H.M.S.O., 80 Chichester St., Belfast BT1 4JY, N. Ireland. TEL 0232-238451)
Formerly (until 1987): Northern Ireland. Department of Finance and Personnel. Estimates for Services under the Government of Northern Ireland (Year).

336   NO
NORWAY. ROYAL NORWEGIAN MINISTRY OF FINANCE. FINAL BUDGET PROPOSAL. (YEAR); Norwegian economy. a. Ministry of Finance, P6 8008 Dep., 0030 Oslo 1, Norway. circ. 1,700.

336   NO   ISSN 0803-5962
NORWAY. ROYAL NORWEGIAN MINISTRY OF FINANCE. THE NATIONAL BUDGET. (YEAR). (Text in English and Norwegian) 1946. a. free. Ministry of Finance, P6 8008 Dep., 0030 Oslo 1, Norway. circ. 1,700. *Document type:* government publication.
Supersedes in part (in 1986): National Budget of Norway (ISSN 0077-3573)

336   NO
NORWAY. ROYAL NORWEGIAN MINISTRY OF FINANCE. THE REVISED NATIONAL BUDGET. (YEAR). (Text in English and Norwegian) 1946. a. free. Ministry of Finance, P6 8008 Dep., 0030 Oslo 1, Norway. circ. 1,700. *Document type:* government publication.
Supersedes in part (in 1986): National Budget of Norway (ISSN 0077-3573)

336   US   ISSN 1086-5551
NOT-FOR-PROFIT FINANCIAL STRATEGIES. m. $125 (effective 1997). Harcourt Brace Professional Publishing, 525 B St., Ste.1900, San Diego, CA 92101-4495. TEL 619-699-6716. FAX 619-699-6593. Ed. Warren Ruppell; Pub. Ken Rethmeier. R&P contact: Jenna Lake. TEL 619-699-6265.
Description: Provides financial, tax and management strategies for not-for profit organizations.

BUSINESS AND ECONOMICS — PUBLIC FINANCE, TAXATION

336.3   MX
NUEVO CONSULTORIO FISCAL; juridico, laboral y contable-financiero. 1987. s-m. Mex.$415 (effective 1997). Universidad Nacional Autonoma de Mexico, Facultad de Contaduria y Administracion, Apartado Postal 70-287, Edificio de la Direccion, 2o. Piso, Cub. 21, Circuito Exterior, Ciudad Universitaria, 04510 Mexico, D.F., Mexico. TEL 52-5-6228396. FAX 52-5-6161355. Ed. Ma. Antonieta Martin Granados.
    Formerly: Consultorio Fiscal (ISSN 0187-6724)
    Description: Disseminates Mexican fiscal law procedures in the private and public sector.

332   US
O C C BULLETINS. m. $150 (effective 1997). U.S. Office of the Comptroller of the Currency, Administrator of National Banks, Washington, DC 20219. FAX 202-874-5263. (Subscr. to: Box 70004, Chicago, IL 60673-0004) **Document type:** bulletin, government publication.
    Description: Provides information of continuing concern regarding O.C.C. or O.C.C.-supported policies and guidelines; informs readers of pending regulation changes and other general information.

336   FR
O E C D AGRICULTURAL POLICIES, MARKETS AND TRADE. MONITORING AND OUTLOOK. a. price varies. Organization for Economic Cooperation and Development, 2 rue Andre-Pascal, 75775 Paris Cedex 16, France. (U.S. orders to: O.E.C.D. Publications and Information Center, 2001 L St., N.W., Ste. 650, Washington D.C. 20036-4922. TEL 202-785-6323) charts; stat. **Indexed:** IIS.
    Formerly: O E C D Agricultural Policy Reports.

O E C D EXTERNAL DEBT STATISTICS. see *BUSINESS AND ECONOMICS — Abstracting, Bibliographies, Statistics*

336   FR   ISSN 0304-3738
HC79.I5
O E C D QUARTERLY NATIONAL ACCOUNTS/O C D E BULLETIN DES COMPTES NATIONAUX TRIMESTRIELS. q. 300 F.($72) Organization for Economic Cooperation and Development, 2 rue Andre-Pascal, 75775 Paris Cedex 16, France. (U.S. orders to: O.E.C.D. Publications and Information Center, 2001 L St., N.W., Ste. 650, Washington, DC 20036-4922. TEL 202-785-6323) **Indexed:** IIS.
    Description: Presents, in standard tables, the components of GDP by expenditure, cost structure and type of activity, the financing and composition of gross capital formation and the components of private final consumption expenditure for member countries.

336   SZ   ISSN 1013-5774
OEFFENTLICHE FINANZEN DER SCHWEIZ/FINANCES PUBLIQUES EN SUISSE. (Text in French and German) 1972. a. 22 SFr. Bundesamt fuer Statistik, Schwarztorstr. 96, CH-3003 Bern, Switzerland. TEL 41-31-3236060. FAX 41-31-3236061. URL: http://www.admin.ch/bfs. **Document type:** government publication.

336.2   AU   ISSN 0029-9529
OESTERREICHISCHE STEUERZEITUNG. 1948. fortn. S.2200. Verlag Orac GesmbH & Co. KG, Graben 17, A-1010 Vienna, Austria. TEL 43-1-53452-0. FAX 43-1-53452141. adv.: B&W page S.16000; trim 167 x 249; adv. contact: Christian Braun. bk.rev.; index. circ. 12,100. **Document type:** bulletin.

336 341   AU   ISSN 0379-4407
K15
OESTERREICHISCHE ZEITSCHRIFT FUER WIRTSCHAFTSRECHT. 1974. q. S.440 (effective 1996). (Institut fuer Angewandte-, Sozial-, und Wirtschaftsforschung) Wilhelm Braumueller, Universitaets-Verlagsbuchhandlung GmbH, Servitengasse 5, A-1092 Vienna, Austria. TEL 43-1-3191159. FAX 43-1-3102805. Eds. Karl Korinek, Karl Wenger. adv. contact: Susanne Mondl. circ. 1,500. **Indexed:** IBR. **Document type:** trade publication.

336.2   AU   ISSN 0029-9685
OESTERREICHISCHE ZOLL UND STEUER NACHRICHTEN; Informationen fuer Zoll und Wirtschaft. 1956. m. S.1550. Grenz Verlag, Flossgasse 6, A-1025 Vienna, Austria. TEL 43-1-2141715. FAX 43-1-214171530. adv.; bk.rev.; abstr.; bibl.; stat.; tr.mk.; index, cum.index. **Document type:** trade publication.

336   US
OFFICIAL I R S PUBLICATIONS. 1991. w. (Dec.-Mar.); m. (Apr.-Nov.). $260. Research Institute of America, Inc., 90 Fifth Ave., New York, NY 10011. TEL 212-645-4800. FAX 212-337-4279. (Subscr. to: 117 E. Stevens Ave., Valhalla, NY 10595) (looseleaf format)
    Description: Consists of more than 140 taxpayer information publications

OFFSHORE INVESTMENT. see *BUSINESS AND ECONOMICS — Banking And Finance*

344.1034   UK   ISSN 1366-7564
OFFSHORE TAXATION REVIEW. 1990. 3/yr. £140 (effective 1997). Key Haven Publications plc., 7 Crescent Stables, 139 Upper Richmond Rd., London SW15 2TN, England. TEL 44-181-780-2522. FAX 44-181-780-1693. Ed. David Ewart. **Document type:** bulletin.
—BLDSC (6244.249200).
    Formerly: Offshore Tax Planning Review (ISSN 0961-1363)

OIL AND GAS ACCOUNTING. see *BUSINESS AND ECONOMICS — Accounting*

336.278 665   US   ISSN 0030-1396
K15
OIL AND GAS TAX QUARTERLY. vol.36, 1981. q. $157. Matthew Bender & Co., Inc., 2 Park Ave., New York, NY 10016. TEL 212-448-2000. E-mail: international@bender.com; URL: http://www.bender.com. Ed. L. Crumbley. bibl.; index. (also avail. in microform from UMI; microfilm from RRI,WSH; reprint service avail. from RRI,UMI,WSH) **Indexed:** Account.Ind. (1990-), C.L.I., L.R.I., Leg.Per. —KR SourceOne; UMI; UnCover. CCC.

336.2   US
OKLAHOMA. AD VALOREM TAX DIVISION. (YEAR) PROGRESS REPORT TO THE LEGISLATURE ON PROPERTY REVALUATION. 1968. a. free. Tax Commission, Ad Valorem Tax Division, 2501 Lincoln Blvd., Oklahoma City, OK 73194. TEL 405-521-3178. FAX 405-521-3991. Ed. Jeff Spelman. stat. circ. 500. **Document type:** government publication.

336.2   US
ONEDISC. m., q., and a. versions avail. $279 for monthly; q. $169; a. $99. Tax Analysts, 6830 N. Fairfax Dr., Arlington, VA 22213. TEL 800-955-2444. FAX 703-533-4444.
    ●Available only on CD-ROM.
    Description: Includes the complete Internal Revenue Code, all IRS regulations, IRS taxpayer information publications, revenue rulings and procedures since 1954, technical advice notices and announcements, key court decisions and more. Subscribers receive annual reference discs with annual IRS Letter Rulings since 1980 and Court Opinions dating back to 1942.

336.2   CN   ISSN 0048-1866
ONTARIO TAX REPORTS. 1950. m. Can.$345. C C H Canadian Ltd., 6 Garamond Ct., North York, ON M3C 1Z5, Canada. TEL 416-441-2992; 800-268-4522. FAX 416-444-9011. index. **Document type:** trade publication.
    Description: Current reporting covers every aspect of taxation.

336   DK   ISSN 0108-9722
OPGAVESAMLING I SKAT 1. Cover title: Opgavesamling i Skatteret I. 1980. a. DKK 160. Alternativ Revisions Forlag, Riddergade 7, DK-4700 Naesved, Denmark.

336   DK   ISSN 0108-9730
OPGAVESAMLING I SKAT 2 OG ERHVERVSJURA. Cover title: Opgavesamling i Skatteret II og Erhvervsjura. 1980. a. DKK 160. Alternativ Revisions Forlag, Riddergade 7, DK-4700 Naesved, Denmark.

336   US
OREGON. DEPARTMENT OF REVENUE. INCOME, INHERITANCE AND GIFT TAX LAW BOOK. biennial. $22. Department of Revenue, Revenue Bldg., Salem, OR 97310. TEL 503-945-8635. FAX 503-945-8738. **Document type:** government publication.
    Description: Oregon laws and administrative rules on personal income taxes, corporation income and excise taxes, inheritance and gift taxes.

336   US
OREGON. DEPARTMENT OF REVENUE. INCOME TAX AND PROPERTY TAX LAWS AND ADMINISTRATIVE RULES. a. $5. Department of Revenue, Revenue Bldg., Salem, OR 97310. TEL 503-945-8635. FAX 503-945-8738. **Document type:** government publication.

336   US
OREGON. DEPARTMENT OF REVENUE. PROPERTY ASSESSMENT AND TAXATION ADMINISTRATIVE RULE BOOK. biennial. Department of Revenue, Revenue Bldg., Salem, OR 97310. TEL 503-945-8635. FAX 503-945-8738. **Document type:** government publication.
    Formerly: Oregon. Department of Revenue. Property Assessment and Taxation Law Book.
    Description: Contains Oregon property tax administrative rules.

336   US
OREGON. DEPARTMENT OF REVENUE. SUMMARY OF OREGON TAXES. a. Department of Revenue, Revenue Bldg., Salem, OR 97310. TEL 503-945-8635. FAX 503-945-8738. **Document type:** government publication.

OREGON PERSONAL INCOME TAX STATISTICS. see *BUSINESS AND ECONOMICS — Abstracting, Bibliographies, Statistics*

OREGON PROPERTY TAX STATISTICS. see *BUSINESS AND ECONOMICS — Abstracting, Bibliographies, Statistics*

336.2   JA   ISSN 0078-7094
OUTLINE OF JAPANESE TAX. 1953. a. 3100 Yen. (Ministry of Finance - Okura-sho) Government Publications Service Center, 2-1, 1-chome, Kasumigaseki, Chiyoda-ku, Tokyo 100, Japan. **Document type:** government publication.

336   US   ISSN 1059-2032
P B C FEDERAL TAX GUIDE.* 1991. q. $29.99. Publishing & Business Consultants, 101 W. 64th St., Unit 3-2, Inglewood, CA 90302-1255. TEL 213-732-3477. FAX 213-732-9123. (Subscr. to: Box 75392, Los Angeles, CA 90075) Ed. Andeson Napoleon Atia. **Document type:** consumer publication.

336   UK
P T C ASSESSMENT. 1979. m. (11/yr.). £12 (overseas £18). Public Services, Tax and Commerce Union, 5 Great Suffolk St., London SE1 0NS, England. TEL 44-171-960-3000. FAX 44-171-960-3001. E-mail: ptc-editorial@geo2.poptel.org.uk. Ed. Richard Upton. adv. contact: Ron Hall. bk.rev. circ. 50,000. **Indexed:** Psychol.Abstr. (1994-). **Document type:** newsletter.
    Formerly: Assessment.
    Description: Covers issues and events relevant to PTC Revenue Group members, including developments in taxation, employee relations, and technology.

336   PK
P.T.D. ANNUAL TAX DIGEST. (Pakistan Tax Decisions) (Text in English) a., latest 1994. Rs.450. P.L.D. Publishers, 35 Nabha Rd., Lahore 1, Pakistan. TEL 92-42-213497. FAX 92-42-7238113. (back issues avail.)

336   PK   ISSN 0304-6478
HJ67.5
PAKISTAN. FINANCE DIVISION. ANNUAL BUDGET STATEMENT (FINAL). (Text in English) a. Finance Division, Islamabad, Pakistan. stat.

336   PK
PAKISTAN. FINANCE DIVISION. BUDGET IN BRIEF. (Text in English) 1964. a. free to qualified personnel. Finance Division, Islamabad, Pakistan.
    Formerly: Pakistan. Ministry of Finance. Budget in Brief (ISSN 0078-8309)

336   PK   ISSN 0376-9208
HJ67.5
PAKISTAN. FINANCE DIVISION. ECONOMIC ANALYSIS OF THE BUDGET. (Text in English) a. free to qualified personnel. Finance Division, Islamabad, Pakistan. **Document type:** government publication.
    Formerly (until 1973): Pakistan. Ministry of Finance. Economic Analysis of the Central Government (ISSN 0078-8325)

BUSINESS AND ECONOMICS — PUBLIC FINANCE, TAXATION

338.9   PK   ISSN 0376-9011
HC440.5
PAKISTAN. FINANCE DIVISION. ESTIMATES OF FOREIGN ASSISTANCE. (Text in English) 1976. irreg. Finance Division, Islamabad, Pakistan.
    Supersedes (in 1977): Pakistan. Ministry of Finance. Estimates of Foreign Assistance (ISSN 0555-8786)

336   PK
PAKISTAN. FINANCE DIVISION. SUPPLEMENTARY DEMANDS FOR GRANTS AND APPROPRIATIONS. (Text in English) 1973. irreg. free to qualified personnel. Finance Division, Islamabad, Pakistan. charts; stat.; circ. controlled.

336   PK   ISSN 0078-7892
HC440.5.A1
PAKISTAN BASIC FACTS. (Text in English) a. Rs.5. Office of the Economic Adviser, Islamabad, Pakistan.
    Formerly: Pakistan. Ministry of Finance. Basic Facts About the Budget (ISSN 0078-8295)

PAKISTAN CUSTOMS TARIFF. see *BUSINESS AND ECONOMICS — International Commerce*

336.2   PK   ISSN 0031-0115
PAKISTAN TAX DECISIONS; a comprehensive monthly journal of Pakistan on taxation. 1959. m. Rs.1000($55) (effective 1995). P.L.D. Publishers, 35 Nabha Rd., Lahore 1, Pakistan. TEL 92-42-213497. FAX 92-42-7238113. Ed. Malik Muhammad Saeed. (back issues avail.; reprint service avail. from UMI)
    Description: Reports relevant tax law, Federal Government legislation and case decisions in the Supreme Court of Pakistan and the High Courts.

336 382   PK   ISSN 0078-852X
PAKISTAN'S BALANCE OF PAYMENTS. (Text in English) 1948. a. Rs.13($4) State Bank of Pakistan, Central Directorate, Public Relations Department, I.I. Chundrigar Rd., P.O. Box 4456, Karachi, Pakistan. TEL 92-2414141. FAX 92-2417865. TELEX 2754 SBPK PK. **Document type:** government publication.

382   PK
PAKISTAN'S BALANCE OF PAYMENTS (QUARTERLY). (Text in English) q. free. State Bank of Pakistan, Central Directorate, Public Relations Department, I.I. Chundrigar Rd., P.O. Box 4456, Karachi, Pakistan. TEL 92-2414141. FAX 92-2417865. TELEX 2754 SBPK PK. **Document type:** government publication.

336.2   PN
PANAMA. CONTRALORIA GENERAL. INFORME TRIMESTRAL DE RENTAS Y GASTOS. Cover title: Panama. Contraloria General. Boletin de Contabilidad. 1965. q. free. Contraloria General, Direccion de Contabilidad, Apdo. 5213, Panama 5, Panama. stat. circ. 1,000.
    Description: Provides statistics on the revenue and expenditures of Panama.

336   AT
PAPUA NEW GUINEA INCOME TAX LEGISLATION. 1977. irreg., as required for legislative changes. C C H Australia Ltd., P.O. Box 230, North Ryde, N.S.W. 2113, Australia. TEL 61-1-300300224. FAX 61-1-300306224. (looseleaf format)
    Description: Consolidates PNG's income tax legislation with an explanation of the historical background to the legislation.

PARTNERSHIP AND S CORPORATION COORDINATOR. see *BUSINESS AND ECONOMICS — Investments*

336   US
PARTNERSHIP TAX PLANNING & PRACTICE. 1987. m. $417. C C H Incorporated, 2700 Lake Cook Rd., Riverwoods, IL 60015. TEL 847-267-7000; 800-835-5224. FAX 800-224-8299. (looseleaf format)
    Formerly (until 1993): Partnership Tax Reporter.

336.2   US
PATRIOT CANNON; booming for the tax patriot community. 1980. bi-m. $25. Patriot Cannon, Box 2368, Anderson, SC 29622. circ. 500. **Document type:** newsletter.
    Description: Covers taxpayers' rights, tax issues, governmental corruption and legal issues.

336.2   US   ISSN 0895-7975
PAYROLL MANAGER'S LETTER. 1984. s-m. $199. Bureau of Business Practice, 24 Rope Ferry Rd., Waterford, CT 06386. TEL 860-442-4365. FAX 860-437-3555. URL: http://www.bbpnews.com. Ed. Joanne Mitchell-George; Pub. Peter Garabedian. R&P contact: Debra Ferraro. **Document type:** newsletter.
    Description: Examines new tax laws and regulations, IRS announcements, news from the Social Security Administration and the Department of Labor, and the latest payroll-related court cases.

PAYROLL PRACTITIONER'S COMPLIANCE HANDBOOK; year-end and quarterly reporting. see *BUSINESS AND ECONOMICS — Accounting*

PEACE TAX FUND NEWSLETTER. see *POLITICAL SCIENCE — Civil Rights*

336   US
PENNSYLVANIA. STATE TAX EQUALIZATION BOARD. ANNUAL CERTIFICATION.* vol.28, 1975. a. State Tax Equalization Board, Fulton Bldg., 5th Fl., 200 N. 3rd St., Harrisburg, PA 17101. TEL 717-787-5950.

336 340   US
PENNSYLVANIA CHAMBER OF BUSINESS AND INDUSTRY. TAX BULLETIN.* fortn. $215 to non-members; members $165. Pennsylvania Chamber of Business and Industry, 417 Walnut St., Harrisburg, PA 17101. TEL 800-326-3252. FAX 717-255-3298.
    Description: Covers Pennsylvania business tax developments.

336 362.6   US
PENSION AND BENEFITS UPDATE. bi-m. $50 to non-members; active members $35. Government Finance Officers Association, 180 N. Michigan Ave., Ste. 800, Chicago, IL 60601. TEL 312-977-9700. FAX 312-977-4806. **Document type:** newsletter.
    Description: Covers current topics in the areas of public pension and benefits.

336   UK   ISSN 0964-6744
PERSONAL TAX PLANNING REVIEW. 1991. 3/yr. £99 (effective 1997). Key Haven Publications plc., 7 Crescent Stables, 139 Upper Richmond Rd., London SW15 2TN, England. TEL 44-181-780-2522. FAX 44-181-780-1693. Ed. Peter Vaines. **Document type:** bulletin.
    —BLDSC (6427.895000).

336   US   ISSN 0740-0624
HJ9103
PERSPECTIVES ON LOCAL PUBLIC FINANCE AND PUBLIC POLICY. 1983. irreg., vol.4, 1997. $73.25 to institutions. J A I Press Inc., 55 Old Post Rd., No. 2, Box 1678, Greenwich, CT 06830-1678. TEL 203-661-7602. FAX 203-661-0792. E-mail: jai@jaipress.com. (Subscr. in the UK and Europe to: JAI Press Ltd., 38 Tavistock St., Covent Garden, London WC2E 7PB, England. TEL 44-171-379-8834. FAX 44-171-379-8835) Ed. John Anderson. **Document type:** monographic series.

336   US
PEYRON TAX ACCOUNTANT'S COMMUNIQUE. 1978. m. $44 (effective 1996). Peyron Associates Inc., 3212 Preston St., Louisville, KY 46213. TEL 502-637-7483. Ed. Dan Peyron. R&P contact: Dan Peyron. circ. 1,000. **Document type:** newsletter.
    Description: Tax preparation advice for accountants, including relevant tax cases, tax code changes, IRS and state tax audits and tips on operating tax preparation offices.

336 340   US
PEYRON TAX LETTER & SOCIAL SECURITY REPORT. 1980. m. $44 (effective 1997). Peyron Associates Inc., 3212 Preston St., Louisville, KY 46213. TEL 502-637-7483. Ed. Dan Peyron. R&P contact: Dan Peyron. circ. 1,000. **Document type:** newsletter.
    Description: Tax saving advice for income and social security taxes.

336   PH   ISSN 0116-3426
PHILIPPINE REVENUE JOURNAL. 1963. m. free. Bureau of Internal Revenue, National Office Bldg., 1st Fl., Quezon City, Philippines. Ed. Manuel F. Almario. bk.rev. circ. 6,000.

336.2   PH   ISSN 0031-7845
PHILIPPINE TAX JOURNAL;* the magazine for lawyers, accountants and businessmen. (Text in English) 1956. m. P.24($24) R-203 University Center Bldg., 1985 Recto Ave., Manila, Philippines. Ed. Cirilo G. Montejo. index. circ. 1,000.

336.2   GR
PHOROLOGIKE EPITHEORESIS. (Some numbers issued in combined form) m. Dr.500. Ekdosis Panelleniou Henoseos Ephoriakon Hypallelon, Akadimias 76, Athens, Greece.

PLANNING TAX-DEFERRED PROPERTY TRANSACTIONS. see *LAW — Estate Planning*

336   PO   ISSN 0079-4201
PORTUGAL. MINISTERIO DAS FINANCAS. RELATORIO DO ORCAMENTO GERAL DO ESTADO.* a. price varies. Ministerio das Financas, Rua da Alfandega, 1100 Lisbon Codex, Portugal.

POSTBUECHL. see *COMMUNICATIONS — Postal Affairs*

THE PRACTICAL TAX LAWYER. see *LAW*

336   CN
PRACTITIONER'S PROVINCIAL TAX SERVICE - ALBERTA. 1992. m. Can.$170. Carswell, One Corporate Plaza, 2075 Kennedy Rd., Scarborough, ON M1T 3V4, Canada. TEL 416-609-8000. FAX 416-298-5094. (looseleaf format)
    Description: Provides accurate up-to-date consolidations of provincial tax law, including all statutes and regulations affecting individual and corporate, retail sales, property, commodity and mining and logging taxes, where applicable.

336   CN
PRACTITIONER'S PROVINCIAL TAX SERVICE - ATLANTIC PROVINCES. 1992. m. Can.$1170. Carswell, One Corporate Plaza, 2075 Kennedy Rd., Scarborough, ON M1T 3V4, Canada. TEL 416-609-8000. FAX 416-298-5094. (looseleaf format)
    Description: Provides up-to-date consolidations of provincial tax law, including all statutes and regulations affecting individual and corporate, retail sales, property, commodity and mining and logging taxes, where applicable.

336   CN
PRACTITIONER'S PROVINCIAL TAX SERVICE - BRITISH COLUMBIA. 1992. m. Can.$190. Carswell, One Corporate Plaza, 2075 Kennedy Rd., Scarborough, ON M1T 3V4, Canada. TEL 416-609-8000. FAX 416-298-5094. (looseleaf format)
    Description: Provides accurate up-to-date consolidations of provincial tax law, including all statutes and regulations affecting individual and corporate, retail sales, property, commodity and mining and logging taxes, where applicable.

336   CN
PRACTITIONER'S PROVINCIAL TAX SERVICE - MANITOBA AND SASKATCHEWAN. 1992. m. Can.$170. Carswell, One Corporate Plaza, 2075 Kennedy Rd., Scarborough, ON M1T 3V4, Canada. TEL 416-609-8000. FAX 416-298-5094. (looseleaf format)
    Description: Provides accurate up-to-date consolidations of provincial tax law, including all statutes and regulations affecting individual and corporate, retail sales, property, commodity and mining and logging taxes, where applicable.

336   CN
PRACTITIONER'S PROVINCIAL TAX SERVICE - ONTARIO. 1992. m. Can.$190. Carswell, One Corporate Plaza, 2075 Kennedy Rd., Scarborough, ON M1T 3V4, Canada. TEL 416-609-8000. FAX 416-298-5094. (looseleaf format)
    Description: Provides accurate, up-to-date consolidations of provincial tax law, including all statutes and regulations affecting individual and corporate, retail sales, property, commodity and mining and logging taxes, where applicable.

336 CN
PRACTITIONER'S PROVINCIAL TAX SERVICE - QUEBEC. 1992. m. Can.$210. Carswell, One Corporate Plaza, 2075 Kennedy Rd., Scarborough, ON M1T 3V4, Canada. TEL 416-609-8000. FAX 416-298-5094. (looseleaf format)
   Description: Provides accurate up-to-date consolidations of provincial tax law, including all statutes and regulations affecting individual and corporate, retail sales, property, commodity, mining and logging taxes, where applicable.

336 340 US ISSN 1056-9952
KF6369
PRACTITIONERS 1040 DESKBOOK. 1989. a. $135. Practitioners Publishing Co., Box 966, Fort Worth, TX 76101-0966. Ed. Jim Reeves.

PRAKTIJKBLAD VOOR DE SALARISADMINISTRATIE. see BUSINESS AND ECONOMICS — Personnel Management

336 US
PRESIDENT'S FISCAL YEAR (YEAR) BUDGET. 1991. a. $5. Tax Foundation, Inc., 1250 H St., N.W., Ste. 750, Washington, DC 20005. TEL 202-783-2760. FAX 202-942-7375.
   Description: Discusses the current administration's budget.

336 SP ISSN 0210-5977
HJ60
PRESUPUESTO Y GASTO PUBLICO. 1979. 3/yr. 5000 ptas. Instituto de Estudios Fiscales, Avda. de Cardenal Herrera Oria 378, 28035 Madrid, Spain. TEL 34-1-3398800. FAX 34-1-3398964. (Subscr. to: Ministerio de Economia y Hacienda, Centro de Publicaciones, Plaza del Campillo del Mundo Nuevo 3, 28005 Madrid, Spain. TEL 91-527-1437)
—CINDOC.

343 US ISSN 1056-7690
KF6297.Z9
THE PRICE WATERHOUSE INVESTOR'S TAX ADVISER. 1991. a. Pocket Books, 1230 Ave. of the Americas, New York, NY 10020.

336 UK ISSN 0967-229X
PRIVATE CLIENT BUSINESS. bi-m. £118. Sweet & Maxwell, South Quay Plaza, 7th Fl., 183 Marsh Wall, London E14 9FT, England. TEL 071-538-8686. FAX 071-538-9508. Ed. Jeanette Culleton. adv. contact: Jackie Wood. Indexed: Euro.LJI, LJI. Document type: bulletin.
—BLDSC (6617.061520).
   Formerly: Capital Taxes and Estate Planning Quarterly.

PROFESSIONAL PRACTICE MANAGEMENT; the business monthly for the professions. see BUSINESS AND ECONOMICS — Banking And Finance

336 PL ISSN 0867-7514
PRZEGLAD PODATKOWY. 1991. m. Oferta dla Kazdego, Spolka z o.o., Wiejska 12, 00-490 Warsaw, Poland. TEL 48-22-272466. FAX 48-22-267584. Ed. Witold Konieczny. circ. 20,000.
   Description: Covers taxation, foreign capital, banking, customs duties.

330 US ISSN 0275-1100
HJ2052.A2
PUBLIC BUDGETING AND FINANCE. 1981. q. $48 to individuals (foreign $80); institutions $104 (foreign $136) (effective 1997). (American Association for Budget and Program Analysis) Transaction Publishers, Transaction Periodicals Consortium, Department 3092, Rutgers University, New Brunswick, NJ 08903. TEL 908-445-2280. FAX 908-445-3138. (Co-sponsor: American Society for Public Administration, Section on Budgeting and Financial Management) Ed. John L. Mikesell. adv.: page $500; 5 1/4 x 8 1/2; adv. contact: Alicja Garbie. circ. 2,400. (back issues avail.) Indexed: ABI Inform., BPIA, C.R.E.J., Cont.Pg.Manage., Int.Polit.Sci.Abstr., J.of Econ.Lit., P.A.I.S., Sage Pub.Admin.Abstr., Sage Urb.Stud.Abstr. Document type: academic/scholarly publication.
●Also available online. Vendor(s): UMI.
—BLDSC (6962.825000); SWETS; UMI; UnCover. CCC.
   Description: Fundamental journal of theory and practice in financial management and budgeting at all levels of U.S. government.

336 US ISSN 0048-5853
HJ101 CODEN: PFQADD
PUBLIC FINANCE QUARTERLY. 1973. q. $248 to institutions (effective Sep. 1996). Sage Publications, Inc., 2455 Teller Rd., Thousand Oaks, CA 91320. TEL 805-499-0721. FAX 805-499-0871. E-mail: libraries@sagepub.com; URL: http://www.sagepub.com. (Overseas subscr. to: Sage Publications Ltd., 6 Bonhill St., London EC2A 4PU, England; Sage Publications India Pvt. Ltd., P.O. Box 4215, New Delhi 110 048, India) Ed. J. Ronnie Davis. adv. contact: Margaret Travers. bk.rev.; abstr.; charts; illus. circ. 1,400. (also avail. in microfilm from UMI; back issues avail.; reprint service avail. from UMI) Indexed: ABI Inform., ASCA, BPIA, Bus.Ind., C.R.E.J., Curr.Cont., J.of Econ.Lit., Manage.Cont., Mid.East: Abstr.& Ind., P.A.I.S., Sage Urb.Stud.Abstr., SSCI, Tr.& Indus.Ind. Document type: academic/scholarly publication.
●Also available online. Vendor(s): Information Access Co.
—Genuine Article; UMI; UnCover. CCC.
   Description: Explores the theory, policy, and institutions related to the allocation, distribution, and stabilization functions within the public sectors of the economy.

336 UK
PUBLIC MONEY. w. St. Giles House, 50 Poland St., London W1V 4AX, England. TEL 071-287-9800. FAX 071-287-8873. Ed. J. Jackson.
   Description: Directed to all public finance professionals.

PUBLIC SECTOR. see PUBLIC ADMINISTRATION

PUBLIC SERVICES YEARBOOK. see PUBLIC ADMINISTRATION

336 332.6 UK ISSN 1350-2697
PUBLIC TREASURER. 1993. m. £35. L G C Communications, 33-39 Bowling Green Ln., London EC1R 0DA, England. TEL 44-171-505-8400. FAX 44-171-837-2725. URL: http://www.emap.com/lgc. (Subscr. to: 196 High St., Tonbridge, Kent TN9 1EF, England. TEL 01732-770377. FAX 01732-361708) Ed. Belinda Fowler; Pub. Crispin Derby. adv.: B&W page £1450, color page £2325; trim 300 x 220; adv. contact: Lisa Edwards. circ. 10,256 (paid). (back issues avail.)
●Also available online.
—BLDSC (6969.492000).
   Refereed Serial

336 340 US
PUERTO RICO TAX REPORTS. (In 2 vols; Vol.1: General Index; Income, Property, Sales, Excise and City Taxes; Vol.2: The Law; Cumulative Index; New Matters; Case Table; Tax Articles; Income Tax Regulations (Spanish)) (Text in English, Spanish; summaries in English) 1964. m. $489. C C H Incorporated, 2700 Lake Cook Rd., Riverwoods, IL 60015. TEL 847-267-7000; 800-835-5224. FAX 800-224-8299. (looseleaf format)

336.2 CN ISSN 0048-6299
QUEBEC TAX REPORTS. 1950. m. Can.$345. C C H Canadian Ltd., 6 Garamond Ct., North York, ON M3C 1Z5, Canada. TEL 416-441-2992; 800-268-4522. FAX 416-444-9011. index. Document type: trade publication.
   Description: Current reporting covers every aspect of consumer and income taxes in Quebec.

336 AT
QUEENSLAND STAMP DUTIES. 1985. q. C C H Australia Ltd., P.O. Box 230, North Ryde, N.S.W. 2113, Australia. TEL 61-2-8571555. FAX 61-2-8571601. (looseleaf format)
   Supersedes in part (in 1991): Australian Stamp Duties.
   Description: Contains general explanation of law governing stamp duties and debits tax that applies in Queensland and commentary on dutiable instruments. Includes all relevant Queensland stamp duties and related revenue legislation and official rulings.

336.2 378 AT ISSN 1325-2135
QUESTION BUDGET, INCOME TAX LAW FOR ACCOUNTANTS, INCOME TAX LAW FOR TAX AGENTS. 1985. a. Aus.$17.50 (effective 1996). Alan Kirby, Ed. & Pub., P.O. Box 632, Hurstville, N.S.W. 2232, Australia. TEL 61-2-5794959. Document type: academic/scholarly publication.
   Formerly: Question Budget, Taxation Law and Practice (Year) (ISSN 1034-5159)
   Description: Provides questions on taxation for students taking taxation as part of an accounting or law course.

336.2 378 657 AT ISSN 1325-2143
QUESTION BUDGET, INCOME TAX LAW FOR ACCOUNTANTS, INCOME TAX LAW FOR TAX AGENTS. ANSWERS TO QUESTIONS (YEAR). 1985. a. Aus.$28 (effective 1996). Alan Kirby, Ed. & Pub., P.O. Box 632, Hurstville, N.S.W. 2232, Australia. TEL 61-2-5794959.
   Formerly: Question Budget, Taxation Law and Practice. Answers to Questions (Year) (ISSN 1034-5167)

336 US
R I A ANALYSIS OF FEDERAL TAXES: EXCISE. 1991. base vol. (plus bi-w. supplements). $275. Research Institute of America, Inc., 90 Fifth Ave., New York, NY 10011. TEL 212-645-4800. FAX 212-337-4279. (Subscr. to: 117 E. Stevens Ave., Valhalla, NY 10595) (looseleaf format)

336 US
R I A ANALYSIS OF FEDERAL TAXES: INCOME. 1991. 14 base vols. (plus w. & bi-w. supplements). $650 includes Weekly Alert, Special Studies, R I A Federal Tax Handbook. Research Institute of America, Inc., 90 Fifth Ave., New York, NY 10011. TEL 212-645-4800. FAX 212-337-4279. (Subscr. to: 117 E. Stevens Ave., Valhalla, NY 10595) (looseleaf format)

336 US
R I A COMPLETE FEDERAL TAX FORMS. 1991. 3 base vols. (plus bi-w. supplements). $300. Research Institute of America, Inc., 90 Fifth Ave., New York, NY 10011. TEL 212-645-4800. FAX 212-337-4279. (Subscr. to: 117 E. Stevens Ave., Valhalla, NY 10595) (looseleaf format)

336 US
R I A FEDERAL TAX HANDBOOK. 1975. a. $25. Research Institute of America, Inc., 90 Fifth Ave., New York, NY 10011. TEL 212-645-4800. FAX 212-337-4279. (Subscr. to: 117 E. Stevens Ave., Valhalla, NY 10595) Ed.Bd. (looseleaf format)
   Formerly: Master Federal Tax Manual.

336 US
R I A INTERNAL REVENUE CODE AND REGULATIONS. 1991. 7 base vols. (plus bi-w. supplements). $275. Research Institute of America, Inc., 90 Fifth Ave., New York, NY 10011. TEL 212-645-4800. FAX 212-337-4279. (Subscr. to: 117 E. Stevens Ave., Valhalla, NY 10595) (looseleaf format)
   Description: Presents the full text of the Internal Revenue Code and all final, temporary and proposed regulations.

336 US
HJ2425
R I A TAX GUIDE. 1966. 2 vols. (m. supplements). $350 includes Weekly Alert newsletter. Research Institute of America, Inc., 90 Fifth Ave., New York, NY 10011. TEL 212-645-4800. FAX 212-337-4279. (Subscr. to: 117 E. Stevens Ave., Valhalla, NY 10595. TEL 800-431-9025) (looseleaf format)
●Also available on CD-ROM.
   Formerly: Tax Guide.

336 II ISSN 0079-9556
HJ66.R3
RAJASTHAN, INDIA. DIRECTORATE OF ECONOMICS AND STATISTICS. BUDGET STUDY. (Text in English and Hindi) 1959. a. free. Directorate of Economics and Statistics, Tilak Marg, Jaipur, Rajasthan, India. Document type: government publication.

336.2 IT ISSN 0033-9458
RASSEGNA DELLA STAMPA; problemi fiscali. 1955. m. L.100000. Associazione fra le Societa Italiane per Azioni, Piazza Venezia 11, 00187 Rome, Italy. bk.rev.; abstr.; bibl.; index. (looseleaf format; also avail. in cards)

BUSINESS AND ECONOMICS — PUBLIC FINANCE, TAXATION

336   IT   ISSN 0393-4098
RASSEGNA MENSILE DELLA IMPOSTE DIRETTE. 1952. m. L.16000. c/o Antonino La Mattina, Ed., Via Fregene N. 14, 00183 Rome, Italy. adv.

336.2   IT
RASSEGNA TRIBUTARIA. 1958. m. L.114000. E T I S.p.A., Viale Mazzini 25, 00195 Rome, Italy. FAX 350108. Ed. Dr. Gianni Carbone. adv.; bk.rev.; abstr.; bibl.; index. circ. 6,000.
    Formerly: Imposte Dirette Erariali e l'Iva.

REAL ESTATE TAX DIGEST. see *REAL ESTATE*

REAL ESTATE TAX IDEAS. see *REAL ESTATE*

336   SY   ISSN 0080-0309
RECUEIL COMPLET DES BUDGETS DE LA SYRIE. a. $85. Office Arabe de Presse et de Documentation, P.O. Box 3550, 67 Place Chahbandar, Damascus, Syria. Ed. Adnan Khani.

REGIONAL LEVIES SERVICE. see *LAW*

336   LO   ISSN 0085-2740
REPORT BY THE AUDITOR GENERAL ON THE ACCOUNTS OF LESOTHO. 1966. a., latest issue 1972-73. $0.50. Auditor General, P.O. Box 502, Maseru, Lesotho.

336   TR
REPORT OF THE AUDITOR GENERAL ON THE PUBLIC ACCOUNTS OF THE REPUBLIC OF TRINIDAD AND TOBAGO. 1962. a. $1.80. (Auditor General of Trinidad and Tobago) Government Printery, Sales Section, 48 St. Vincent St., Port-of-Spain, Trinidad & Tobago, W.I. stat. circ. 500.

336   US   ISSN 0731-2954
KFN2270
REPORTS OF CASES ARGUED AND DETERMINED IN THE TAX COURT OF NEW JERSEY. 1981. a. West Group, 620 Opperman Dr., Eagan, MN 55123. TEL 612-687-8000; 800-328-9352. FAX 612-687-7302.

336   SE
REPUBLIC OF SEYCHELLES. TRADES TAX REGULATIONS (YEAR). a.? Ministry of Finance and Information, Trade and Commerce Section, Victoria, Mahe, Seychelles. **Document type:** government publication.

RESEARCH INSTITUTE OF AMERICA. SPECIAL STUDIES. see *BUSINESS AND ECONOMICS — Accounting*

RETIREMENT AND BENEFIT PLANNING; strategy and design for businesses and tax-exempt organizations. see *BUSINESS AND ECONOMICS — Personnel Management*

336   CN
REVENUE CANADA ROUND TABLE ANNOTATED. irreg. Can.$350. C C H Canadian Ltd., 6 Garamond Ct., North York, ON M3C 1Z5, Canada. TEL 416-441-0086; 800-268-4522. FAX 416-444-9011. **Document type:** trade publication.
    Description: Consolidates questions and answers from the annual Revenue Canada Round Tables and Corporate Round Tables.

REVISTA DE ADMINISTRACAO MUNICIPAL. see *PUBLIC ADMINISTRATION — Municipal Government*

REVISTA DE DERECHO FINANCIERO Y DE HACIENDA PUBLICA. see *LAW*

336   MZ
REVISTA FISCAL. 1989-1992; resumed 1996. q. Ministerio das Financas, Av. 25 de Setembro 1008, 5o, C.P. 272 Maputo, Mozambique. TEL 20982. circ. 2,000.

REVUE DU TRESOR; organe d'etudes et d'informations professionnelles. see *BUSINESS AND ECONOMICS — Accounting*

336   FR   ISSN 0294-0833
REVUE FRANCAISE DE FINANCES PUBLIQUES. 1983. q. 490 F. (foreign 510 F.) (effective 1997). (Librairie Generale de Droit et de Jurisprudence) Editions Juridiques Associees, 14 rue Pierre et Marie Curie, 75005 Paris, France. TEL 3-1-44419710. FAX 33-1-43547821. TELEX EJA 203 918 F. Eds. Michel Bouvier, Marie-Christine Esclassan. bk.rev. (reprint service avail. from SCH) **Indexed:** ELLIS. —BLDSC (7904.137000); SWETS.
    Description: For professors, finance professionals, public administrators, private business managers.

REVUE GENERALE DE FISCALITE; information a l'usage des conseillers fiscaux, gestionnaires administratifs et financiers. see *BUSINESS AND ECONOMICS — Accounting*

336.2   IS   ISSN 0334-3065
RIVAON HA-YISRAELI L'MISIM/ISRAELI TAX REVIEW. 1965. q. IS.140($46) (effective July 1996). State Revenue Administration, Custom Sq., 32 Agron St., Jerusalem, Israel. TEL 972-2-6703201. FAX 972-2-6258602. Ed. Mira Dror. adv.; bk.rev.; abstr.; bibl.; charts; stat.; index. circ. 1,800. (tabloid format) **Indexed:** Ind.Heb.Per. **Document type:** government publication.
    Formerly: Riv'on l'Inyanei Misim - Quarterly Tax Journal (ISSN 0035-7138)
    Refereed Serial

336.2   IT   ISSN 0035-709X
RIVISTA TRIBUTARIA; rassegna bimestrale di dottrina giurisprudenza e legislazione. 1931. bi-m. Via Tronto 20, 00198 Rome, Italy. Ed. Pietro Adomino. index.

336   US   ISSN 1040-2241
KF6272
RUXTON REPORT.* 1982. m. $75. Ruxton Company, Box 20090, Santa Barbara, CA 93120. TEL 303-481-4389. Ed. Jack Kennedy, Sr. adv.; bk.rev. circ. 900. (back issues avail.)
    Formerly: B M E Tax Newsletter (ISSN 0740-2376)
    Description: Covers tax planning and compliance for small business and tax practitioners.

336 340   SA   ISSN 1019-8474
S A TAX REVIEW. (Print edition ceased 1997. System requirements: 6Mb Hard Disk Space, Windows (3.1, NT or 95); Also avail. as part of InfoTax) 1988. q. R.420($100) (effective 1997); R.460 ($100) (effective 1998). InfoMedia Technologies (Pty) Ltd., P.O. Box 44597, Claremont 7735, South Africa. TEL 27-21-689 5075. FAX 27-21-689-5025. E-mail: infomedia@iafrica.com; URL: http://www.pix.za/taxfax/taxfax.html. Ed. Ray Eskinazi. charts; stat. circ. 360. (also avail. in diskette format) **Indexed:** Ind.S.A.Per. **Document type:** academic/scholarly publication.
    ●Also available on CD-ROM.
    Description: Provides in depth coverage of international tax developments relevant to Southern African readers, and Southern African tax matters relevant to foreign investors.

336   US   ISSN 0738-2448
S CORPORATIONS (NEW YORK, 1983). 1983. base vol. (plus m. Report Bulletins and updates). $395. Warren, Gorham & Lamont, One Penn Plaza, New York, NY 10119-4098. TEL 212-971-5000. FAX 212-971-5113. (Subscr. to: The Park Square Bldg., 31 St. James Ave., Boston, MA 02116-4112. TEL 800-950-1210) Ed. Robert W. Wood. (looseleaf format)
    Description: Provides in-depth explanations and new ideas from experts in the field. Includes updates on latest developments, official documents and relevant legislative history.

336   US
S CORPORATIONS GUIDE. 1983. m. $472. C C H Incorporated, 2700 Lake Cook Rd., Riverwoods, IL 60015. TEL 847-267-7000; 800-835-5224. FAX 800-224-8299. (looseleaf format; back issues avail.)
    Description: Covers revised rules that alter significantly the manner in which shareholders of a small business electing "S Corporation" status are taxed on income earned by the corporation.

336   DK
S R - SKAT. 1989. 7/yr. DKK 450. Foreningen af Statsautoriserede Revisorer, Revisorernes Hus, Kronprinsessegade 8, DK-1306 Copenhagen K, Denmark. TEL 45-33-93-91-91. FAX 45-33-11-09-13. TELEX 22491. Ed. Soeren Rasmussen.

336   US
SALES AND USE TAX REVIEW. 1991. m. $195. Corporate Tax Publishers, Inc., Box 261, Leonia, NJ 07605. TEL 201-461-6619. FAX 201-461-6619. Eds. Michael Fishbein, Jonathan Skiba. bk.rev. (looseleaf format) **Document type:** newsletter.

SALES OF A BUSINESS IN MINNESOTA. see *LAW*

336.271   II   ISSN 0036-3472
SALES TAX ADVICES. (Text in English) 1969. m. Rs.300($40) Nahar Sales Tax Advices Private Limited, 20-1 Maharshi Debendra Rd., 2nd Fl., Calcutta 700 007, India. TEL 39-7218. Ed. M.L. Nahar. adv.; bk.rev.; index. circ. 1,000. (processed)

336.2   US
SALES TAX NEWSLETTER. 1973. s-a. free. Department of Taxation and Finance, Technical Services Bureau, State Campus, Albany, NY 12227. Ed. M. Edwards. circ. 500,000. **Document type:** government publication, newsletter.
    Description: Contains articles concerning interpretations, policies and procedures related to the administration of the New York State sales and use tax laws.

336   GW   ISSN 0342-197X
SAMMLUNG DER ENTSCHEIDUNGEN DES BUNDESFINANZHOFS. 1950. 18/yr. DM.456. Stollfuss Verlag Bonn, Postfach 2428, 53014 Bonn, Germany. TEL 0228-724-0. FAX 0228-659723. **Document type:** bulletin.

SAMSOM ACTUALITE COMPTABLE; lettre bimensuelle a l'usage des experts-comptables, reviseurs d'enterprises, directeurs financiers et administratifs. see *BUSINESS AND ECONOMICS — Accounting*

336   BE   ISSN 0776-1465
SAMSOM FISCALE WENKEN. French edition: Samsom Signaux Fiscaux (ISSN 0776-1473) (Text in Flemish) 1988. s-m. 4770 BEF. C E D Samsom (Subsidiary of: Wolters Samsom Belgie n.v.), Kouterveld 14, B-1831 Diegem, Belgium. TEL 32-2-7231111.
    Description: Gives financial advice for those not in the accounting or finance field.

332.1   SU   ISSN 0558-7220
HG1213
SAUDI ARABIAN MONETARY AGENCY. ANNUAL REPORT. Arabic edition: Al-Taqrir al-Sanawi - S.A.M.A. (ISSN 1319-1845) (Text in English) 1961. a. Saudi Arabian Monetary Agency, Research and Statistics Department, P.O. Box 2992, Riyadh 11169, Saudi Arabia. TEL 966-1-463-3000. TELEX 401734. charts. **Document type:** government publication. —BLDSC (1432.015000).
    Description: Reviews economic developments and major trends of the past year.

336   US   ISSN 1075-9832
KF6335.A29
SELECTED FEDERAL TAXATION STATUTES AND REGULATIONS. 1975. a. West Group, 620 Opperman Dr., Eagan, MN 55123. TEL 612-687-7000; 800-328-9352. FAX 612-687-7302. **Document type:** trade publication.

336   NE   ISSN 0924-4654
SERIES ON INTERNATIONAL TAXATION. 1979. irreg., no.15, 1993. price varies. Kluwer Law International (Subsidiary of: Wolters Kluwer N.V.), Postbus 85889, 2508 CN The Hague, Netherlands. TEL 31-70-3081500. FAX 31-70-3081515. (Dist. by: Libresso Distribution Centre, P.O. Box 23, 7400 GA Deventer, Netherlands. TEL 31-570-633155. FAX 31-570-633834; In N. America: Kluwer Law International, 675 Massachusetts Ave., Cambridge, MA 02139. TEL 617-354-0140. FAX 617-354-8595) (back issues avail.) **Document type:** monographic series. —BLDSC (8250.161600).
    Description: Discusses specific countries' tax policies, theoretical issues in tax law and tax treaty negotiation.

BUSINESS AND ECONOMICS — PUBLIC FINANCE, TAXATION

336   SE
SEYCHELLES. MINISTRY OF FINANCE. BUDGET ADDRESS. (Text in Creole, English and French) a. $50. Ministry of Finance, P.O. Box 313, Victoria, Mahe, Seychelles. TEL 0248-25252. FAX 0248-25265. TELEX 2363 FINTUR SZ.
    Formerly: Seychelles. Office of the President. Budget Address.

336   CC
SHANGHAI CAISHUI/SHANGHAI FINANCIAL TAXATION. (Text in Chinese) m. Shanghai Caizheng Kexue Yanjiusuo - Shanghai Institute of Financial Science, 60 Jiujiang Road, Room 518, Shanghai 200002, People's Republic of China. TEL 3233208.

336   US   ISSN 0732-7714
KF6280.5
SHEPARD'S FEDERAL TAX CITATIONS. 1980. 11 base vols. (plus bi-m. supplement). $450. Shepard's (Subsidiary of: Reed Elsevier plc & The Times Mirror Company), Box 35300, Colorado Springs, CO 80935-3530. TEL 800-525-2474.

336   CC   ISSN 1003-448X
SHUIWU YANJIU/TAXATION RESEARCH. (Text in Chinese) 1985. m. Y60 (foreign $26) (effective 1998). (Guojia Shuiwu-ju - State Taxation Bureau) Zhongguo Shuiwu Zazhishe, No.5 Yangfangdian Xilu, Haidian District, Beijing 100038, People's Republic of China. TEL 86-10-6318-3035. FAX 86-10-63183007. Ed. Zhang Musheng. R&P contact: Zhang Musheng. circ. 12,000. Document type: academic/scholarly publication.

336   SL
SIERRA LEONE. MINISTRY OF FINANCE. BUDGET SPEECH. a. Ministry of Finance, Freetown, Sierra Leone. Document type: government publication.

336.2   UK   ISSN 0308-8030
SIMON'S TAX CASES. Alternate title: Simon's Weekly Tax Service: Cases. (Is subseries of : Simon's Weekly Tax Service) 1973. w. £250($375) for entire series. Butterworth & Co. (Publishers) Ltd., Part of the Reed Elsevier group, Halsbury House, 35 Chancery Ln., London WC2A 1EL, England. TEL 071-405-6900. FAX 071-405-1332. (U.S. addr.: Butterworth Legal Publishers, 90 Stiles Rd., Salem, NH 03079-9981. TEL 603-898-9664) (looseleaf format) Document type: trade publication.
    Description: Provides record of changes in the law and practice affecting the major U.K. taxes. Includes full reports of all tax cases decided in the High Court, the Court of Appeal, the Court of Session in Scotland, the Court of Appeal in Northern Ireland, the House of Lords, and selected European cases.

336.2   UK   ISSN 0308-8049
SIMON'S TAX INTELLIGENCE. Alternate title: Simon's Weekly Tax Service: Intelligence. (Is subseries of: Simon's Weekly Tax Service) w. £250($345) for entire series. Butterworth & Co. (Publishers) Ltd., Part of the Reed Elsevier group, Halsbury House, 35 Chancery Ln., London WC2A 1EL, England. TEL 071-400-2500. FAX 071-400-2842. (U.S. addr.: Butterworth Legal Publishers, 90 Stiles Rd., Salem, NH 03079-9981. TEL 603-898-9664) (looseleaf format)
    Description: Provides record of changes in the law and practice affecting the major U.K. taxes. Covers statutory instruments, Inland Revenue press releases, V.A.T. press releases, official concessions and statements of practice, Parliamentary proceedings, E.C. material, notes and news, tax case digests, V.A.T. tribunal decisions, Budget tax coverage, Finance Bill summaries and reports on progress.

336   UK
SIMON'S TAXES. 10 base vols. (plus m. updates). £645. Butterworth & Co. (Publishers) Ltd., Part of the Reed Elsevier group, Halsbury House, 35 Chancery Ln., London WC2A, England. TEL 071-400-2500. FAX 071-400-2842. (U.S. addr.: Butterworth Legal Publishers, 90 Stiles Rd., Salem, NH 03079. TEL 603-898-9664) Ed.Bd. Document type: trade publication.
    Description: Features detailed explanation to the law and practice relating to U.K. income tax, corporate tax and capital gains tax.

336.2   CC
SINGAPORE TAX REVIEW. (Text in English) 10/yr. HK.$2500 in Hong Kong; elsewhere $350. Ashton - Brooke Asia Publishing Ltd., G.P.O. Box 12261, Central, Hong Kong, People's Republic of China. TEL 852-2980-0590. FAX 852-2982-0590.
    Document type: newsletter.
    Description: Provides advice on complicated tax issues and developments for all companies operating in Singapore.

SKATTE- OCH TAXERINGSFOERFATTNINGARNA; saadan de lyder den 1 januari... see LAW

336.2   SW   ISSN 1103-3738
SKATTEBOK FOER DIG. 1971. a. SEK 195 (effective 1992). L. T., Box 14171, S-104 41 Stockholm, Sweden. Eds. F. Nilson, P. Kindlund, O. Stenman.
    Former titles (until 1991): Lilla Deklarationsboken; (until 1983): Deklaration foer Loentagar och Villaaegare.

336.2 343.04   SW   ISSN 0280-5014
SKATTEFRAGOR KRING BOKSLUTET; handbok i foeretagsbeskattning. 1956. a. SEK 150 (effective 1993). S-E Banken, S-106 40 Stockholm, Sweden.
    Formerly (until 1992): Skattefraagor Kring ... Aars Bokslut.

336.2   SW   ISSN 1103-3037
SKATTEHANDBOK FOER CHEFER. 1991. a. SEK 640 (effective 1992). Liber Ekonomi, S-205 10 Malmoe, Sweden.

SKATTELAGSTIFTNING; lagar och andra foerfattningar som de lyder den ... see LAW

336   DK   ISSN 0106-8024
SKATTEN.* 1946. a. DKK 38. Aktuelle Boeger, Birkedammervej 31, DK-2400 Copenhagen NV, Denmark.

336   DK   ISSN 0107-3885
SKATTEN. ERHVERV. 1981. a. DKK 36. Aktuelle Boeger, c/o Danske Boghendleres Kommissionanstalt, Siljangade 6, 2300 Copenhagen S, Denmark. Ed. Jens Stubkjaer.
    Formerly: Afskrivning.

336.2   SW   ISSN 0346-1254
SKATTENYTT. Variant title: S N. 1951. m. SEK 440 (effective 1991). c/o P. Melz, Lundgatan 36, S-117 27 Stockholm, Sweden. (Subscr. to: Skattenytt Foerlags AB, Oestra Aagatan 9, S-753 22 Uppsala, Sweden)

343.48904   DK   ISSN 0108-6049
SKATTEPOLITISK OVERSIGT. 1944. 8/yr. DKK 496. Erhvervenes Skattesekretariat, H.C. Andersens Boulevard 37, DK-1553 Copenhagen V., Denmark. TEL 33-127748. FAX 33-328202. adv.: B&W page DKK 3500; trim 202 x 130. circ. 3,021. (back issues avail.) Document type: trade publication.
    Description: Highlights tax policies for lawyers and auditors.

SKATTERETT; Tidsskrift for skatt og avgift. see LAW

336   US
SMALL BUSINESS TAX PLANNER. 1986. m. $215. Research Institute of America, Inc., 90 Fifth Ave., New York, NY 10011. TEL 212-645-4800. FAX 212-337-4279. (Subscr. to: 117 E. Stevens Ave., Valhalla, NY 10595) (looseleaf format)
    Description: Publishes tax planning articles geared to the small business.

336   US   ISSN 0276-5322
KF6491.A15
SMALL BUSINESS TAX REVIEW. 1980. m. $84. A-N Group, Inc., Box 895, Melville, NY 11747-0895. TEL 516-549-4090. E-mail: angroup@pb.net; URL: http://www.smbiz.com. Ed. Steven A. Hopfenmuller. (looseleaf format; back issues avail.) Document type: newsletter.
    ●Also available online. Vendor(s): NewsNet (TX15).
    Description: Focuses on federal taxes and recent developments aimed at small businesses and individuals.

343.04   US   ISSN 1048-521X
SOFTWARE TAXATION LETTER.* 1990. 10/yr. $275. (Software Taxation Institute) Kutish Publications, Inc., Box 10170, Reno, NV 89510-0170. TEL 800-342-9621. FAX 800-803-9623. Ed. L.J. Kutten. index. (looseleaf format; back issues avail.) Document type: newsletter.
    —CCC.

350   SA
SOUTH AFRICA. OFFICE OF THE AUDITOR-GENERAL. REPORT OF THE AUDITOR-GENERAL. (Text in Afrikaans, English) 1993. a. (Office of the Auditor-General) Government Printer, Private Bag X85, Pretoria 0001, South Africa. Document type: government publication.

336   AT
SOUTH AUSTRALIA AND NORTHERN TERRITORY STAMP DUTIES. 1985. q. C C H Australia Ltd., P.O. Box 230, North Ryde, N.S.W. 2113, Australia. TEL 61-1-300300224. FAX 61-1-300306224. (looseleaf format)
    Supersedes in part (in 1991): Australian Stamp Duties.
    Description: Covers stamp duty and related revenue legislation, with editorial commentary discussing what is dutiable, how much duty is payable, when and how duty is payable, and whether there are concessions and exemptions from duty.

336   US
SOUTH CAROLINA MONTHLY REVENUE LETTER. m. free. Budget and Control Board, Board of Economic Advisors, Ste. 442, Rembert Dennis Bldg., 1000 Assembly St., Columbia, SC 29201. TEL 803-734-3805. FAX 803-734-4719. Ed. M. Greg DiBiase. Document type: government publication.

336.2   NE
▼**SOUTHEAST ASIAN TAX HANDBOOK.** (Text in English) 1996. a. $125 (effective 1997). I B F D Publications B.V., P.O. Box 20237, 1000 HE Amsterdam, Netherlands. TEL 31-20-6267726. FAX 31-20-6228658. TELEX 13217 INTAX NL. (In US: IBFD Publications USA, Inc., 4 Maple Rd., Valatie, NY 12184. TEL 800-299-6330. FAX 518-758-2246) Ed. Victor T. Chew. Document type: directory.
    Description: Comprehensive guide to taxation in the seven ASEAN countries.

336   SP
SPAIN. MINISTERIO DE ECONOMIA Y HACIENDA. DIRECCION GENERAL DE SEGUROS. BALANCES Y CUENTAS; seguros privados. a. 9500 ptas. (effective 1997). Ministerio de Economia y Hacienda, Direccion General de Seguros, Paseo de la Castellana 44, 28046 Madrid, Spain. TEL 34-1-3397000. FAX.34-1-3397113. charts. Document type: government publication.

336   US   ISSN 0194-8237
SPIDELL'S CALIFORNIA TAXLETTER. 1979. m. $97. Spidell Publishing, Inc., 1110 N. Gilbert, Anaheim, CA 92801. TEL 714-776-7850. FAX 714-776-9906. Ed. Robert A. Spidell; Pub. Robert A. Spidell. circ. 7,000. (looseleaf format; back issues avail.) Document type: newsletter.

336.26   PL   ISSN 0038-7746
SPOLEM. 1906. s-m. 72 Zl. Krajowy Zwiazek Rewizyjny Spoldzielni Spozywcow - Spolem - National Supervision Committee of Consumer Cooperatives, Grazyny 13, 02-548 Warsaw, Poland. TEL 48-22-452323. FAX 48-22-452581. TELEX 817611. bk.rev.; illus. circ. 55,000.

336 340   AT   ISSN 0727-7970
STAMP DUTIES N.S.W. & A.C.T.. 1979. 4/yr. in 2 vols. Aus.$395. L B C Information Services, 50 Waterloo Rd., N. Ryde, N.S.W. 2113, Australia. TEL 61-2-99366444. FAX 61-2-98889706. TELEX ASBOOK 27995. Ed. D. Graham Hill. (looseleaf format)
    Description: Concentrates on N.S.W. Stamp Duties Act 1920 and regulations, the A.C.T. Taxation (Administration) Act 1969 and other relevant stamp duties legislation.

BUSINESS AND ECONOMICS — PUBLIC FINANCE, TAXATION

340 336   AT
STAMP DUTIES SOUTH AUSTRALIA. 1991. 3/yr. Aus.$275. L B C Information Services, 50 Waterloo Rd., N. Ryde, N.S.W. 2113, Australia. TEL 61-299366444. FAX 61-2-98889706. TELEX ASBOOK 27995. Ed. M. Quinlan. (looseleaf format)
Description: Features a comprehensive coverage of all stamp duties legislation and Stamp Duties Office practice in South Australia.

336   AT
▼**STAMP DUTIES VICTORIA.** 1995. 4/yr. Aus.$275. L B C Information Services, 50 Waterloo Rd., N. Ryde, N.S.W. 2113, Australia. TEL 61-2-99366444. FAX 61-2-98889706. TELEX ASBOOK 27995. Ed. M. Hines. (looseleaf format)
Description: Covers the law of stamp duty in Victoria.

336 340   AT
STAMP DUTIES W.A. 1992. 3/yr. Aus.$275. L B C Information Services, 50 Waterloo Rd., N. Ryde, N.S.W. 2113, Australia. TEL 61-2-99366444. FAX 61-2-98889706. TELEX ASBOOK 27995. Ed. Michael Quinlan. (looseleaf format)
Description: Features a comprehensive coverage of all stamp duties legislation and Stamp Duties Office practice in Western Australia.

336   US   ISSN 0162-3494
STANDARD FEDERAL TAX REPORTS. 22 base vols. (plus w. update). $1869 (CD-ROM ed. $1704). C C H Incorporated, 2700 Lake Cook Rd., Riverwoods, IL 60015. TEL 847-267-7000; 800-835-5224. FAX 800-224-8299. (looseleaf format)
●Also available online. Vendor(s): UMI.
Also available on CD-ROM.
—CCC.

336   SA
STANDARD TRUST INCOME TAX GUIDE. a. R.60. Butterworth Publishers (Pty.) Ltd., Part of the Reed Elsevier group, P.O. Box 792, Durban 4000, South Africa. TEL 27-31-2683111. FAX 27-31-2683110.
Description: Reference guide for the layman and specialist, covering the Income Tax Act, relevant tax legislation, principles and practical advice for tax planning.

336.2   NZ   ISSN 0111-9370
STAPLES' GUIDE TO NEW ZEALAND INCOME TAX PRACTICE. 1936. a. Aus.$99. Brooker's Limited, Level 1 - Telecom Networks House, 68-86 Jervois Quay, Wellington, New Zealand. TEL 64-4-4998178. FAX 64-4-4998173. E-mail: publishing@brookers.co.nz. (Dist. by: Carswell, One Corporate Plaza, 2075 Kennedy Rd., Scarborough, Ont. M1T 3V4, Canada) Eds. Clifford Mancer, John Veal. adv. circ. 8,200.
●Also available on CD-ROM.
Formerly: Guide to New Zealand Income Tax Practice (ISSN 0072-8616)

350   US   ISSN 0742-0498
STATE BUDGET AND TAX NEWS. s-m. $220. State Policy Research, Inc., 182 W. Royal Forest Blvd., Columbus, OH 43214-2029. (Subscr. to: Box 11806, Birmingham, AL 35202. TEL 205-995-1567) Ed. Harold A. Hovey.
Description: Reporting of actions by state governments and legislatures on their budgets and taxes.

STATE CAPITALS. LOTTERY, PARIMUTUEL & CASINO REGULATION. see *PUBLIC ADMINISTRATION*

STATE CAPITALS. TAXATION AND REVENUE POLICIES. see *PUBLIC ADMINISTRATION*

STATE CAPITALS. TAXES - PROPERTY. see *PUBLIC ADMINISTRATION*

336   US   ISSN 1042-6027
HJ10.3
STATE FISCAL CAPACITY AND EFFORT. 1986. biennial. U.S. Advisory Commission on Intergovernmental Relations, 800 K St., N.W., Ste. 450-S., Washington, DC 20575. TEL 202-653-5640. **Document type:** government publication.

350   US   ISSN 8750-6637
STATE POLICY REPORTS. 1983. s-m. $415. State Policy Research, Inc., 182 W. Royal Forest Blvd., Columbus, OH 43214-2029. (Subscr. to: Box 11806, Birmingham, AL 35202. TEL 205-995-1567) Ed. Harold A. Hovey. bk.rev.; s-a. index, cum.index. circ. 500. **Indexed:** SRI.
Description: Analytical reporting on all aspects of state government policies of economic significance.

STATE TAX ACTION COORDINATOR. see *BUSINESS AND ECONOMICS — Accounting*

336   US
STATE TAX CASES REPORTS. base vol. (plus m. updates). $450 includes w. State Tax Review. C C H Incorporated, 2700 Lake Cook Rd., Riverwoods, IL 60015. TEL 847-267-7000; 800-835-5224. FAX 800-224-8299.

336   US   ISSN 0162-1777
STATE TAX GUIDE. 1937. bi-w. $923 (CD-ROM ed. $929). C C H Incorporated, 2700 Lake Cook Rd., Riverwoods, IL 60015. TEL 847-267-7000; 800-835-5224. FAX 800-224-8299. (looseleaf format)
●Also available on CD-ROM.
—CCC.

336.2   US   ISSN 0081-4598
STATE TAX HANDBOOK. 1964. a. $32. C C H Incorporated, 2700 Lake Cook Rd., Riverwoods, IL 60015. TEL 847-267-7000; 800-835-5224. FAX 800-224-8299.

336   US   ISSN 1057-8404
KF6750
STATE TAX NOTES. 1991. w. (plus a. CD-ROM). $949. Tax Analysts, 6830 N. Fairfax Dr., Arlington, VA 22213. TEL 703-533-4400; 800-955-2444. FAX 703-533-4444. (also avail. in microfiche; back issues avail.) **Document type:** trade publication.
●Also available online. Vendor(s): Knight-Ridder Information, Inc., Lexis-Nexis.
Also available on CD-ROM.
—CCC.
Description: Covers state and local tax developments in all 50 states.

336 343.05   US
▼**STATE TAX ONEDISC.** 1996. m., q., and a. versions avail. $399 for m., $299 for q., $199 for a. Tax Analysts, 6830 N. Fairfax Dr., Arlington, VA 22213. TEL 703-503-4600; 800-955-2444. FAX 703-533-4444. Ed. David Brunori.
●Available only on CD-ROM.
Description: Contains complete tax statutes and regulations for all fifty states and DC. Also all U.S. Supreme court decisions concerning state and local taxes, and an archive of special reports published in State Tax Notes magazine.

336   US
STATE TAX REPORTS. 1937. m. price varies. C C H Incorporated, 2700 Lake Cook Rd., Riverwoods, IL 60015. TEL 847-267-7000; 800-835-5224. FAX 800-224-8299. (looseleaf format)
●Also available on CD-ROM.

336.2   US   ISSN 0162-1750
HJ2385
STATE TAX REVIEW. 1941. w. $89. C C H Incorporated, 2700 Lake Cook Rd., Riverwoods, IL 60015. TEL 847-267-7000; 800-835-5224. FAX 800-224-8299. (also avail. in microform from UMI)
●Also available online. Vendor(s): NewsNet, UMI.
—UMI. CCC.

336   DK   ISSN 0106-2905
HJ56
STATENS OG KOMMUNERNES BUDGETTER. 1986. a. Budgetdepartementet, Direktoratet for Statens Indkoeb, Copenhagen, Denmark.

336   AT
STEP-BY-STEP PRECEDENTS & PROCEDURES - COMPANIES, TRUSTS, SUPERANNUATION FUNDS. (In 3 vols.) 1980. irreg. C C H Australia Ltd., P.O. Box 230, North Ryde, N.S.W. 2113, Australia. TEL 61-1-300300224. FAX 61-1-300306224. (looseleaf format)
Description: A practical guide to procedures encountered in the daily administration of proprietary companies, trusts and superannuation funds. Explains the procedures required under the corporation law and includes all the relevant forms for each step.

336   GW   ISSN 0172-7214
DAS STEUER A B C. 1979. bi-m. DM.78. Verlag Wirtschaft Recht und Steuern, Fraunhoferstr. 5, 82152 Planegg, Germany. TEL 49-89-89517-0. FAX 49-89-89517250. (Subscr. to: Postfach 1363, 82142 Planegg, Germany) (looseleaf format)
Document type: bulletin.

336   GW   ISSN 0179-0161
STEUER AKTUELL. 1986. s-m. DM.93.60. Erich Fleischer Verlag, Postfach 1264, 28818 Achim, Germany. TEL 49-4202-5170. FAX 49-4202-51741. Ed. Thomas Holzer. adv. contact: Manfred Becker. **Document type:** bulletin.
Description: Covers legal issues pertaining to business administration.

336.2   AU
STEUER-AUSLANDDIENST. 1973. 4/yr. membership. Institut fuer Finanzwissenschaft und Steuerrecht, Seilerstaette 24, A-1010 Vienna, Austria. TEL 01-5129910. Ed. Anton Matzinger. **Document type:** bulletin.

STEUER-BRIEF FUER AERZTE UND ZAHNAERZTE. see *MEDICAL SCIENCES*

STEUER-BRIEF FUER ARCHITEKTEN UND INGENIEURE. see *ENGINEERING*

STEUER-BRIEF FUER DAS BAU- UND BAUNEBENGEWERBE. see *BUILDING AND CONSTRUCTION*

STEUER-BRIEF FUER DAS HOTEL- UND GASTSTAETTENGEWERBE. see *HOTELS AND RESTAURANTS*

STEUER-BRIEF FUER DAS KFZ-GEWERBE. see *TRANSPORTATION — Automobiles*

STEUER-BRIEF FUER DAS PERSONALBUERO. see *BUSINESS AND ECONOMICS — Personnel Management*

STEUER-BRIEF FUER DEN GMBH-GESCHAEFTSFUEHRER. see *BUSINESS AND ECONOMICS — Management*

STEUER-BRIEF FUER HANDELS- UND VERSICHERUNGSVERTRETER. see *INSURANCE*

STEUER-BRIEF FUER HAUS- UND GRUNDBESITZER. see *REAL ESTATE*

STEUER-BRIEF FUER PERSONENGESELLSCHAFTEN. see *CLUBS*

STEUER-BRIEF FUER VEREINE. see *CLUBS*

336.2   GW   ISSN 0937-1680
STEUER-EILDIENST. 1913. w. DM.319 (effective 1997). (Bundesministerium der Finanzen) Stollfuss Verlag Bonn, Postfach 2428, 53014 Bonn, Germany. TEL 49-228-724-0. FAX 49-228-659223. Ed. H. Hoellig. charts; illus.; index. circ. 1,300. (back issues avail.) **Document type:** government publication.
—CCC.
Former titles: Deutsche Steuer-Zeitung. Eildienst (ISSN 0724-553X); Deutsche Steuer-Zeitung. Ausgabe B (ISSN 0012-0782)

336   GW   ISSN 0177-9664
STEUER-LEXIKON TEIL II. 1954. m. DM.246. Erich Fleischer Verlag, Postfach 1264, 28818 Achim, Germany. TEL 49-4202-517-0. FAX 49-4202-51741. Ed. Thomas Holzer. adv. contact: Manfred Becker. index. **Document type:** bulletin.
Description: Contains essays, commentary, and decrees concerning financial administration and related legal issues.

BUSINESS AND ECONOMICS — PUBLIC FINANCE, TAXATION

336   GW
STEUER QUINTESSENZ. m. DM.330 (effective 1997). Stollfuss Verlag Bonn, Postfach 2428, 53014 Bonn, Germany. TEL 49-228-724-0. FAX 49-228-659223. **Document type:** bulletin.

336   SZ
STEUER REVUE/REVUE FISCALE. (Text in French, German) 1946. m. 178 SFr. Cosmos Verlag AG, Oberer Wehrliweg 5, Postfach 425, CH-3074 Muri-Bern, Switzerland. TEL 41-31-9516611. FAX 41-31-9516659. Ed. H.R. Aeberli. adv.; bk.rev. circ. 3,500. (back issues avail.) **Indexed:** IBR. **Document type:** bulletin.

336   GW   ISSN 0177-9656
STEUER SEMINAR; praktische Faelle des Steuerrechts. 1955. m. DM.84. Erich Fleischer Verlag, Postfach 1264, 28818 Achim, Germany. TEL 49-4202-517-0. FAX 49-4202-51741. Ed. Thomas Holzer. adv. contact: Manfred Becker. index. **Document type:** bulletin. **Description:** Covers legal issues related to business administration.

336.2   GW   ISSN 0170-7620
STEUER TELEX; Spezialdienst fuer den Steuerfachmann. 1974. w. DM.42.80 per mo. (effective 1997). Verlag Peter Deubner GmbH, Wolfgang-Mueller-Str. 14, 50968 Cologne, Germany. TEL 49-221-9370180. FAX 49-221-93701890. bk.rev.; index. **Document type:** trade publication. **Superseded:** Aktuelle Steuer-Informationen (ISSN 0002-385X)

STEUER UND STUDIUM; Zeitschrift fuer die Aus- und Fortbildung im Steuerrecht. see *LAW*

336.2   GW   ISSN 0341-2954
STEUER UND WIRTSCHAFT; Zeitschrift fuer die gesamte Steuerwissenschaft. 1924. q. DM.258 (effective 1997). Verlag Dr. Otto Schmidt KG, Unter den Ulmen 96-98, 50968 Cologne, Germany. TEL 49-221-9373801. FAX 49-221-93738943. E-mail: dr.otto.schmidt@t-online.de. Ed. Dr. Wissinger. adv.; bk.rev. circ. 1,500. (reprint service avail. from SCH) **Indexed:** CERDIC, ELLIS, IBR. **Document type:** trade publication. —SWETS. CCC.

336.2   SZ
STEUERBELASTUNG IN DER SCHWEIZ - KANTONSHAUPTORTE, KANTONSZIFFERN/CHARGE FISCALE EN SUISSE - CHEFS-LIEUX DES CANTONS, NOMBRES CANTONAUX. (Text in French and German) a. 13 SFr. Bundesamt fuer Statistik, Schwarztorstr. 96, CH-3003 Bern, Switzerland. TEL 41-31-3236060. FAX 41-31-3236061. URL: http://www.admin.ch/bfs. **Document type:** government publication. **Formerly:** Steuerbelastung in der Schweiz.

336.2   GW   ISSN 0049-223X
DER STEUERBERATER; Zeitschrift fuer Beruf und Praxis des Steuerberaters. 1949. m. DM.168 (effective 1997). Verlag Recht und Wirtschaft GmbH, Haeusserstr. 14, 69115 Heidelberg, Germany. TEL 49-6221-906-1. (Subscr. to: Postfach 105960, 69049 Heidelberg, Germany) adv.; bk.rev.; index. circ. 4,500. (reprint service avail. from SCH) **Document type:** trade publication. —CCC.

336.2   GW   ISSN 0081-5519
STEUERBERATER-JAHRBUCH; zugleich Bericht ueber den jaehrlich stattfindenden Fachkongress der Steuerberater der BRD. 1950. a. price varies. (Fachinstitut der Steuerberater) Verlag Dr. Otto Schmidt KG, Unter den Ulmen 96-98, 50968 Cologne, Germany. TEL 49-221-9373801. FAX 49-221-93738943. E-mail: dr.otto.schmidt@t-online.de. circ. 1,500. **Document type:** trade publication.

336   GW   ISSN 0490-9658
DIE STEUERBERATUNG. 1958. m. DM.218 (effective 1997). Stollfuss Verlag Bonn, Postfach 2428, 53014 Bonn, Germany. TEL 49-228-724-0. FAX 49-228-659223. **Document type:** bulletin. —CCC.

336.2   GW
DIE STEUERFACHANGESTELLTEN. 1966. m. DM.66. Friedrich Kiehl Verlag GmbH, Pfaustr. 13, 67063 Ludwigshafen, Germany. TEL 49-621-63502-0. FAX 49-621-6350222. Ed. Adolf Schmidt; Pub. Ernst Kleyboldt. adv. contact: Joern Mueller-Grote. bk.rev. circ. 23,500. **Document type:** academic/scholarly publication. —CCC. **Former titles:** Steuerfachgehilfen (ISSN 0936-6164); Briefe fuer Junge Steuerfachleute (ISSN 0007-0009)

336   GW   ISSN 0943-5735
DIE STEUERGESETZE. 1949. irreg. DM.228. Erich Schmidt Verlag GmbH & Co. (Berlin), Genthiner Str. 30G, 10785 Berlin, Germany. TEL 49-30-250085-0. FAX 49-30-25008521. (looseleaf format) **Document type:** bulletin.

336   GW
STEUERGESETZE PLUS. a. (plus irreg. updates). DM.168 (effective 1997). Verlag C.H. Beck, 80791 Munich, Germany. TEL 49-89-38189338. FAX 49-89-38189398. **Document type:** abstracting/indexing. ●Available only on CD-ROM.

336   GW   ISSN 0340-9503
DIE STEUERLICHE BETRIEBSPRUEFUNG; Fachorgan fuer die Wirtschafts- und Pruefungspraxis. m. DM.177.60. Erich Schmidt Verlag GmbH & Co. (Bielefeld), Viktoriastr. 44A, 33602 Bielefeld, Germany. TEL 49-521-583080. (Subscr. to: Postfach 102451, 33524 Bielefeld, Germany) **Document type:** trade publication. —SWETS. CCC.

STEUERRECHT - FUNDSTELLEN; Rechtsprechung, Verwaltung, Schrifttum. see *LAW* — Abstracting, Bibliographies, Statistics

336   GW
STEUERVERANLAGUNGEN C D - R O M. a. DM.798 (effective 1997). Verlag C.H. Beck, 80791 Munich, Germany. TEL 49-89-38189338. FAX 49-89-38189398. **Document type:** abstracting/indexing. ●Available only on CD-ROM.

336   AU
STEUERZAHLER. bi-m. Staudgasse 83, A-1180 Vienna, Austria. TEL 01-473183. circ. 10,000.

336   GW
DER STEUERZAHLER. m. Steuerzahler Service GmbH, Schillerstr. 14, 40237 Duesseldorf, Germany. TEL 0211-689868. FAX 0211-681289. Ed. Dieter Lau; Pub. Susanne Tiemann. adv. contact: Karl-Heinz Daeke. circ. 363,592. **Document type:** bulletin.

STOCK VALUES AND DIVIDENDS FOR TAX PURPOSES. see *BUSINESS AND ECONOMICS* — Investments

STORA SKATTEBOKEN; foerfattningar, rekommendationer och tabeller per den ... see *LAW*

STRUCTURING BUY - SELL AGREEMENTS; tax and legal analysis with forms. see *LAW* — Corporate Law

336   US
STUDIES IN FEDERAL TAXATION. 1969. irreg., latest 1990. price varies. American Institute of Certified Public Accountants, Harborside Financial Ctr., 201 Plaza Three, NJ 07311-9801. TEL 201-938-3796; 800-862-4272. FAX 201-329-1112. URL: http://www.aicpa.org. (Alt. addr.: 1211 Ave. of the Americas, New York, NY 10036. TEL 212-596-6200) **Document type:** trade publication.

336   UK
STUDIES IN LEASING LAW & TAX. (Supplement to: World Leasing Yearbook; Airfinance Annual) a. £20($35) (effective 1997). Euromoney Publications plc., Books, Nestor House, Playhouse Yard, London EC4V 5EX, England. TEL 44-171-779-8935. FAX 44-171-779-8541. **Description:** Provides in-depth reviews of the legal and taxation implications of various asset financing and leasing structures.

336   IS
SUGEOT BIDINAI MISIM. (Text in Hebrew) 1978. irreg. Hamachone Lemisim Veleyautz Kalkalei, 9 Peretz St., Tel Aviv 66 853, Israel. TEL 03-375982. Ed. Menachem Cohen. **Description:** Problems and solutions to exams for tax advisors and accountants.

336.1   SW   ISSN 0039-5455
SUNT FOERNUFT; skattebetalarnas tidning. 1921. 8/yr. SEK 175 (effective 1991). Skattebetalarnas Foerening - Swedish Taxpayers' Association, S-114 95 Stockholm, Sweden. FAX 46-8-213858. Ed. Bengt Gustafson. adv.; bk.rev.; illus.; index. circ. 185,000. (also avail. in audio cassette)

336.2   NE   ISSN 0039-5927
SUPPLEMENTARY SERVICE TO EUROPEAN TAXATION. (Text in English) 1963. 15 base vols. (plus m. updates). $1815 (renewals $1095) (effective 1997). I B F D Publications B.V., P.O. Box 20237, 1000 HE Amsterdam, Netherlands. TEL 31-20-6267726. FAX 31-20-6228658. TELEX 13217 INTAX NL. (In US: IBFD Publications USA, Inc., 4 Maple Ln., Valatie, NY 12184. TEL 800-299-6330. FAX 518-758-2246) Ed. Juhani Kesti. bk.rev.; bibl.; charts. (looseleaf format) **Description:** Summarizes the taxation of individuals and corporations in the majority of European countries, followed by full texts of most double taxation treaties concluded by European countries with others.

336   US
SURVEY OF STATE TAX RATES AND COLLECTIONS. 1991. a. $5. Tax Foundation, Inc., 1250 H St., N.W., Ste. 750, Washington, DC 20005-3908. TEL 202-783-2760. FAX 202-942-7675. **Indexed:** SRI. **Description:** Details the trends in state tax collections by type of tax and provides major tax rates for each state.

336.2   SW   ISSN 0346-2218
SVENSK SKATTETIDNING. 1934. irreg.(8-10/yr.). SEK 782 (effective 1995). Fritzes Foerlag, P.O. Box 6472, S-113 82 Stockholm, Sweden. Ed. Arne Baeckvold. bk.rev.

336.2   SW   ISSN 0282-4108
SVENSK TULL. 1946. 10/yr. SEK 248 (effective 1997). Generaltullstyrelsen, P.O. Box 2267, S-103 17 Stockholm, Sweden. (Subscr. to: C.E. Fritzes AB, S-106 47 Stockholm, Sweden) **Document type:** newspaper. **Former titles** (until 1985): Generaltullstyrelsens Meddelanden; (until 1968): Kungl. General Tullstyrelsens Meddelanden.

336   SW   ISSN 0347-7169
SWEDEN. FINANSDEPARTEMENTET. REGERINGENS BUDGETFOERSLAG. Cover title: Sweden. Finansdepartementet Presenterar Regeringens Budgetfoerslag: Finansplan, Sammandrag. 1971. a. Fritzes, S-106 47 Stockholm, Sweden. TEL 46-8-6909090. FAX 46-8-205021. **Document type:** government publication. **Formerly** (until 1972): Sweden. Finansdepartementet. Sammandrag av Statsverkspropositionen.

336   SW   ISSN 1100-9403
SWEDEN. MINISTRY OF FINANCE. REVISED BUDGET STATEMENT. (Text in English) 1975. a. Ministry of Finance, Roedbodgatan 6, S-103 33 Stockholm, Sweden. stat. **Former titles** (until 1988): Revised Finance Bill (ISSN 0282-4841); (until 1982): Swedish Economy (ISSN 0347-5646); (until 1977): Svenska Ekonomin.

336   SW   ISSN 0347-7312
SWEDEN. RIKSREVISIONSVERKET. STATENS FINANSER; Riksrevisionsverkets aarsbok. 1921. a. free. P.O. Box 45070, S-104 30 Stockholm, Sweden. Ed. Tina Granath. circ. 5,200. **Document type:** government publication. **Former titles** (until 1971): Sweden. Riksrevisionsverket. Riksrevisionsverkets Aarsbok; (until 1962): Sweden. Riksraekenskapsverket. Riksraekenskapsverkets Aarsbok; (until 1930): Sweden. Riksraekenskapsverket. Riksraekenskapsverkets Revisionsberaettelse.

T M A TOBACCO BAROMETER. see *TOBACCO*

1630 BUSINESS AND ECONOMICS — PUBLIC FINANCE, TAXATION

T M A TOBACCO WEEKLY. see *TOBACCO*

336   **US**
TABLES OF REDEMPTION VALUES FOR U.S. SAVINGS BONDS, SERIES E AND TABLES OF REDEMPTION VALUES FOR U.S. SAVINGS BONDS, SERIES EE. s-a. U.S. Department of the Treasury, Bureau of Public Debt, 13th & C Sts., S.W., Washington, DC 20226. TEL 202-566-2000. (Dist. by: Supt. of Documents, Washington, DC 20402)
Formerly: Tables of Redemption Values for U.S. Savings Bonds, Series A-E (ISSN 0039-8829)

336.2 346 640   **FI**   **ISSN 0788-9135**
TALOUSTAITO. 1948. m. FIM 285; newsstand price: FIM 35. Verotieto Oy, Kalevankatu 4, FIN-00100 Helsinki, Finland. TEL 358-0-618-87319. FAX 358-0-608087. Ed. Heikki Hakala. adv.: B&W page FIM 16870, color page FIM 21900; adv. contact: Raimo Nevalainen. bk.rev. circ. 161,239.

TARIF AKTUELL. see *BUSINESS AND ECONOMICS — International Commerce*

336.946   **AT**
TASMANIA. DEPARTMENT OF THE TREASURY. BUDGET PAPERS; summary of estimated expenditure (including expenditure reserved by law) and estimated revenue. irreg. Aus.$55 (foreign Aus.$65). Printing Authority of Tasmania, G.P.O. Box 307-C, Hobart, Tas. 7001, Australia. TEL 61-3-62333168. FAX 61-3-62332460. E-mail: bookshop@pat.tas.gov.au. stat. **Document type:** government publication.
Formerly: Tasmania. Department of the Treasury. Consolidated Revenue Fund.

TAX ACCOUNTING. see *BUSINESS AND ECONOMICS — Accounting*

336   **US**
TAX ACTION COORDINATOR. 10 base vols. (bi-w. updates). $575. Research Institute of America, Inc., 90 Fifth Ave., New York, NY 10011. TEL 212-645-4800. FAX 212-337-4279. (Subscr. to: 117 E. Stevens Ave., Valhalla, NY 10595. TEL 800-431-9025) Ed.Bd. (looseleaf format)
Description: Provides tax planning guidance and compliance tools.

336   **AG**
TAX ADMINISTRATION REVIEW.* (Text in English, Spanish) 1985. a. $20. Inter-American Center of Tax Administrators, San Jose 83, 2do piso, Buenos Aires, Argentina. (Co-sponsor: Institute of Fiscal Studies of Spain)

336.2   **US**   **ISSN 0039-9949**
HJ2360
TAX ADMINISTRATORS NEWS. 1937. m. $35. Federation of Tax Administrators, 444 N. Capitol St., N.W., Ste. 348, Washington, DC 20001. TEL 202-624-5890. URL: http://sso.org/fta/fta.html. Ed. Audrey Maynard. bk.rev.; illus.; stat. circ. 2,000. **Document type:** newsletter.

TAX-ADVANTAGED SECURITIES LAW REPORT. see *LAW — Corporate Law*

336.2   **US**   **ISSN 0039-9957**
K24   **CODEN: TAADDJ**
THE TAX ADVISER; a magazine of tax planning, trends and techniques. 1970. m. $94. American Institute of Certified Public Accountants, Harborside Financial Ctr., 201 Plaza Three, Jersey City, NJ 07311-9801. TEL 201-938-3796; 800-862-4272. FAX 201-329-1112. URL: http://www.aicpa.org. (Alt. addr.: 1211 Ave. of the Americas, New York, NY 10036. TEL 212-596-6200) Ed. N. Fiore. cum.index. circ. 30,000. (also avail. in microform from UMI,WSH; reprint service avail. from UMI,WSH) **Indexed:** ABI Inform., Account.Ind. (1974-), B.P.I., BPIA, Bus.Ind., C.L.I., Fam.Ind., Ind.Per.Art.Relat.Law, L.R.I., Leg.Per., Manage.Cont., PSI, Tr.& Indus.Ind. **Document type:** trade publication.
●Also available online. Vendor(s): Information Access Co., UMI.
—BLDSC (8611.566000); KR SourceOne; UMI; UnCover. **CCC.**

336   **US**
TAX ANALYST MICROFICHE DATABASE. w. $2249. Tax Analysts, 6830 Fairfax Dr., Arlington, VA 22213. TEL 703-533-4400; 800-955-2444. FAX 703-533-4444. (microfiche) **Document type:** trade publication.
●Also available on CD-ROM.
Formerly: Tax Notes Microfiche Database (ISSN 0730-8604); Incorporates (1992-1996): State Tax Notes Microfiche Database (ISSN 1060-491X) & Tax Notes International Microfiche Database (ISSN 0887-5626)
Description: Contains all pages of Tax Notes, State Tax Notes, and Tax Notes International magazines, and all the supporting full-text documents cited.

336 343.05   **US**
TAX ANALYSTS LETTER RULING SERVICE. 1988. w. $1249. Tax Analysts, 6830 N. Fairfax Dr., Arlington, VA 22213. TEL 703-553-4400; 800-955-2444. FAX 703-553-4444. Ed. (back issues avail.)
●Also available on CD-ROM.
—**CCC.**
Formerly: I R S Letter Rulings and Technical Advice Memorandums (ISSN 1066-6303); Incorporates (in 1995): Letter Ruling Review (ISSN 1047-1596); Which was formerly (in 1988): Letter Ruling Alert (ISSN 0898-4409)
Description: Contains U.S. Internal Revenue Service letter rulings and technical advice, weekly memoranda, and copyrighted summaries and indexes.

TAX & BUSINESS ADVISER. see *BUSINESS AND ECONOMICS — Accounting*

343.05   **US**
TAX AND BUSINESS PLANNING OF LIMITED LIABILITY COMPANIES. 1993. a. $156.45 (foreign $227.45) (effective 1995). Warren, Gorham & Lamont, One Penn Plaza, New York, NY 10119. TEL 212-971-5000. (Subscr. to: The Park Square Bldg., 31 St. James Ave., Boston, MA 02116-4112. TEL 800-950-1207) Eds. Carter B. Bishop, Daniel S. Kleinberger. **Document type:** trade publication.
Description: Analyzes all aspects of tax law as it applies to limited-liability corporations and includes annotated sample forms.

336   **FR**   **ISSN 1011-4688**
TAX - BENEFIT POSITION OF PRODUCTION WORKERS/SITUATION DES OUVRIERS AU REGARD DE L'IMPOT ET DES TRANSFERTS SOCIAUX. 1984? a. price varies. Organization for Economic Cooperation and Development, 2 rue Andre-Pascal, 75775 Paris Cedex 16, France. (U.S. orders to: O.E.C.D. Publications and Information Center, 2001 L St., N.W., Ste. 650, Washington, DC 20036-4922. TEL 202-785-6323) **Indexed:** IIS.

336   **SA**
TAX BREAKS. 1986. m. $190 (effective through Oct. 1997). Prescon Publishing Corporation (Pty) Ltd, P.O. Box 84004, Greenside 2034, South Africa. TEL 27-11-646-9750. FAX 27-11-646-4617. E-mail: prescon@aztec.co.za. Ed. Kathy Thersby. **Document type:** newsletter.
Description: Tax advice and opportunities for individuals.

TAX BURDEN ON TOBACCO. see *TOBACCO — Abstracting, Bibliographies, Statistics*

336   **UK**   **ISSN 0262-7639**
TAX CASE ANALYSIS. 1980. m. £245($375) Longman Group UK Ltd., Law, Tax and Finance Division, 21-27 Lamb's Conduit St., London WC1N 3NJ, England. TEL 0171-242-2548. FAX 0171-831-8119. Ed. Peter White. **Document type:** bulletin.
—UMI. **CCC.**
Description: Tax case decisions and their impact on tax planning.

336   **UK**
TAX CASE REPORT. irreg. £41 (effective 1994). H.M.S.O., 51 Nine Elms Ln., London SW8 5DR, England. TEL 44-171-873-0011. FAX 44-171-873-8463. (Subscr. to: H.M.S.O. Publications Centre, P.O. Box 276, London SW8 5DT, England. TEL 44-171-873-9090. FAX 44-171-873-8200) circ. 5,250. **Document type:** government publication.

336   **US**   **ISSN 0162-1815**
TAX COURT REPORTS. 3 base vols. (plus w. updates). $967. C C H Incorporated, 2700 Lake Cook Rd., Riverwoods, IL 60015. TEL 847-267-7000; 800-835-5224. FAX 800-224-8299. (also avail. in microfiche from WSH)
—**CCC.**

336   **US**   **ISSN 0162-1823**
TAX COURT REPORTS (DECISIONS EDITION). 1924. w. $714. C C H Incorporated, 2700 Lake Cook Rd., Riverwoods, IL 60015. TEL 847-267-7000. FAX 800-224-8299. (looseleaf format)

336   **US**   **ISSN 0888-1243**
HJ9
THE TAX DIRECTORY. 1984. a. (plus q. updates). $299 for print or CD-ROM; $399 for both. Tax Analysts, 6830 N. Fairfax Dr., Arlington, VA 22213. TEL 703-553-4400; 800-955-2444. FAX 703-533-4444. Ed. Tamera Wells-Lee. (back issues avail.) **Document type:** directory.
●Also available online. Vendor(s): Knight-Ridder Information, Inc., Lexis-Nexis.
Also available on CD-ROM.
—**CCC.**
Description: Lists names, addresses, and telephone information for 17,000 tax officials at the state, federal, and international levels, plus worldwide listings of private tax professionals and corporate tax managers.

336.2   **US**   **ISSN 0040-0025**
K24
THE TAX EXECUTIVE. 1944. bi-m. $105 (foreign $130) (effective 1997). Tax Executives Institute, Inc., 1001 Pennsylvania Ave., N.W., No. 320, Washington, DC 20004-2505. TEL 202-638-5601. FAX 202-638-5607. (Subscr. to: Box 96129, Washington, DC 20090-6129) Ed. Timothy J. McCormally; Pub. Michael J. Murphy. R&P contact: Timothy J. McCormally. adv. contact: Kurt Larrick. bk.rev.; charts; illus.; stat.; index. circ. 5,500. (also avail. in microform from UMI; back issues avail.; reprint service avail. from RRI,UMI,WSH) **Indexed:** ABI Inform., Abstr.Bk.Rev.Curr.Leg.Per., Account.Ind. (1974-), BPIA, Bus.Ind., C.L.I., Ind.Per.Art.Relat.Law, L.R.I., Leg.Per., P.A.I.S, Tr.& Indus.Ind. **Document type:** trade publication.
●Also available online. Vendor(s): Information Access Co., UMI.
Also available on CD-ROM.
—BLDSC (8611.600000); UMI; UnCover.
Description: Devoted to publishing and reprinting position papers reflecting innovative, creative thinking; sets forth proposals for change and improvement in tax systems and unique solutions to problems; critically analyzes recent legislation and regulations; and explores means by which the professionalism of corporate tax operations can be enhanced.

336.2   **US**   **ISSN 0883-1335**
TAX FEATURES. (Supplement avail.) 1957. 11/yr. $15 Tax Foundation, Inc., 1250 H St., N.W., Ste.750, Washington, DC 20005. TEL 202-783-2760. FAX 202-942-7675. Ed. Stephen Gold. charts; illus. stat. circ. 8,000. (also avail. in microfiche from CIS) **Indexed:** SRI. **Document type:** newsletter.
—UMI.
Formerly: Monthly Tax Features (ISSN 0047-8040)
Description: Reports on Tax Foundation analyses and studies.

TAX FILE. see *BUSINESS AND ECONOMICS — Accounting*

336   **US**
TAX FOUNDATION. FEDERAL TAX BURDEN BY STATE. a. $5. Tax Foundation, Inc., 1250 H St., N.W., Ste.750, Washington, DC 20005. TEL 202-783-2760. FAX 202-942-7675. **Indexed:** SRI.
Former titles: Tax Foundation. Memorandum on the Allocation of the Federal Tax Burden and Federal Grants-in-Aid by State; Tax Foundation. Annual Memorandum.
Description: Computes the percentage of federal taxes each state bears, and compares this with federal spending in each state.

350 US
TAX FRAUD AND EVASION. a. (in 2 vols.). $160.95 for vol.1 (foreign $254.95); vol.2 $161.45 (foreign $254.95) (effective 1995). Warren, Gorham & Lamont, One Penn Plaza, New York, NY 10119. TEL 212-971-5000. FAX 212-971-5113. (Subscr. to: The Park Square Bldg., 31 St. James Ave., Boston, MA 02116-4112. TEL 800-950-1207) **Document type:** trade publication.

336 SA
TAX HANDBOOK. a. R.85. Butterworth Publishers (Pty.) Ltd., Part of the Reed Elsevier group, P.O. Box 792, Durban 4000, South Africa. TEL 27-31-2683111. FAX 27-31-2683110.
Formerly (until 1991): Income Tax Handbook.
Description: Provides practitioners with compact and accessible information on tax legislation currently in force.

332.6 BF
TAX HAVEN REPORTER NEWSLETTER. 1985. m. $150. New Providence Press, P.O. Box CB 11552, Nassau, Bahamas. TEL 242-327-7359. FAX 242-327-7359. Ed. Thomas P. Azzara. adv. contact: Linda Veri. circ. 1,000. **Document type:** newsletter.
Description: Covers various popular tax havens, including the Bahamas, Cayman Islands and Panama.

332.6 BF
TAX HAVENS OF THE WORLD. 1987. a., 6th ed., 1996. $75. Tax Haven Reporter, P.O. Box CB 11552, Nassau, Bahamas. TEL 242-327-7359. FAX 242-327-7359. Ed. Thomas P. Azzara. circ. 8,000. **Document type:** bulletin.
Description: Covers over 28 tax havens used by businesspeople to cut and eliminate taxes.

336.2 640.75 US ISSN 0279-4446
TAX HOTLINE; the inside report for people who need to be on top of every tax break the law allows. 1981. m. $59. 55 R.R. Ave., Greenwich, CT 06836. TEL 203-625-5900. FAX 203-861-7443. (Subscr. to: Subscriber Service Center, Box 58477, Boulder, CO 80322. TEL 800-288-1051) Ed. David Ellis; Pub. Martin Edelston. circ. 165,000. (looseleaf format) **Document type:** newsletter.

336 US ISSN 0279-2109
TAX IDEAS. 2 base vols. (plus m. bulletin). $415 (foreign $540) (effective 1994-1995). Warren, Gorham & Lamont, One Penn Plaza, New York, NY 10119. TEL 212-971-5000. FAX 212-971-5113. (Subscr. to: The Park Square Bldg., 31 St. James Ave., Boston, MA 02116-4112. TEL 800-950-1207) (looseleaf format) **Document type:** trade publication.
Description: Compiles the most important ideas and strategies.

336 UK ISSN 0263-9076
TAX INSIGHT. 1982. m. £120. Templegate Press Ltd., P.O. Box 3, Woking, Surrey GU21 1AA, England. TEL 09323-51991. Ed. Alan Rook. circ. 1,000. (back issues avail.)

336 340 UK ISSN 0954-7274
K24
TAX JOURNAL. 1988. w. Butterworth & Co. (Publishers) Ltd., Part of the Reed Elsevier group, Halsbury House, 35 Chancery Ln., London WC2A 1EL, England. TEL 071-400-2500.
FAX 071-400-2842. (U.S. addr.: Butterworth Legal Publishers, 90 Stiles Rd., Salem, NH 03079. TEL 603-898-9664) (also avail. in microform from UMI; reprint service avail. from WSH) Indexed: Euro.LJI, LJI. **Document type:** trade publication.
—BLDSC (8611.604980). **CCC**.
Description: Examines and comments on tax cases and explores their wider implications, providing details on transcripts for tax specialists in practice, commerce and public service.

TAX LAW REVIEW. see *LAW*

336 UK
TAX LAW REVIEW COMMITTEE. INTERIM REPORT ON TAX LEGISLATION. a. Institute for Fiscal Studies, Tax Law Review Committee, 7 Ridgmount St., London WC1E 7AE, England. TEL 44-171-636-3784.
FAX 44-171-323-4780. E-mail: mailbox@ifs.org.uk; URL: http://www.ifs.org.uk. **Document type:** bulletin.

TAX LAWS OF THE WORLD. see *LAW*

336 SA ISSN 1017-1193
TAX LIBRARY/BELASTINGBIBLIOTEEK. 1989. q. R.1630. Juta & Co. Ltd., P.O. Box 14373, Kenwyn 7790, South Africa. TEL 27-21-7975101. FAX 27-21-7970121.
●Available only on CD-ROM.
Description: Presents all relevant South African statutes and reports pertaining to taxation and revenue.

336 US
TAX MANAGEMENT COMPENSATION PLANNING. (Subseries of: Tax Management Compensation Series) 1973. m. $879 (subscr. includes Compensation Planning Journal). Tax Management, Inc. (Subsidiary of: The Bureau of National Affairs, Inc.), 1250 23rd St., N.W., Washington, DC 20037-1166. TEL 202-833-7240.
FAX 202-833-7297. TELEX 285656 BNAI WSH. URL: http://www.bna.com/. (Subscr. to: 9435 Key West Ave., Rockville, MD 20850. TEL 800-372-1033) Ed. Glenn Davis. bibl. (back issues avail.) **Document type:** trade publication.
●Also available online. Vendor(s): West Group (File TM-CP, TM-CP-OLD, TM-CPJ).
Formerly: Tax Management Executive Compensation.
Description: Covers the areas of pensions, employee benefits, profit sharing and welfare plans, and deferred compensation planning.

336 382 UK
TAX MANAGEMENT COUNTRY PORTFOLIOS. (Subseries of: Tax Management International Series) 1972. irreg. £456. Tax Management, Inc. (Subsidiary of: The Bureau of National Affairs, Inc.), Heron House, 10 Dean Farrar St., London SW1H 0DX, England. TEL 44-171-222-8831. FAX 44-171-222-5550. (back issues avail.) **Document type:** bulletin.
●Also available on CD-ROM.
Formerly: Tax Management International Portfolios.
Description: Each portfolio covers an individual country, with complete tax planning guidance on conducting successful business operations in that country.

336 US
TAX MANAGEMENT ESTATES, GIFTS AND TRUSTS. (Subseries of: Tax Management Estates, Gifts and Trusts Series) 1967. m. $902 (subscr. includes Estates Gifts and Trusts Journal). Tax Management, Inc. (Subsidiary of: The Bureau of National Affairs, Inc.), 1250 23rd St., N.W., Washington, DC 20037-1166. TEL 202-833-7240.
FAX 202-833-7297. TELEX 285656 BNAI WSH. (Subscr. to: 9435 Key West Ave., Rockville, MD 20850. TEL 800-372-1033) Ed. Glenn Davis. bibl. (looseleaf format; back issues avail.) **Document type:** trade publication.
●Also available online. Vendor(s): West Group (Files TM-EGT, TM-EGT-OLD, TM-EGTJ).
Description: Covers specific areas of estate planning and administration.

336 US
TAX MANAGEMENT ESTATES, GIFTS AND TRUSTS REFERENCE FILES. (Subseries of: Tax Management Estates, Gifts and Trusts Series) 1984. bi-w. $643. Tax Management, Inc. (Subsidiary of: The Bureau of National Affairs, Inc.), 1250 23rd St., N.W., Washington, DC 20037-1166. TEL 202-833-7240. FAX 202-833-7297. TELEX 285656-BNAI-WSH. (Subscr. to: 9435 Key West Ave., Rockville, MD 20850. TEL 800-372-1033) Ed. Glenn B. Davis. (looseleaf format; back issues avail.) **Document type:** trade publication.
Description: Compilation of basic textual material (including the IRS Code, regulations, and rulings) relating to estates, gifts, and trusts.

336 US
TAX MANAGEMENT FINANCIAL PLANNING (SUPPLEMENT). (Supplement to ISSN 8756-1360) 1985. bi-w. $700 includes Tax Management Financial Planning Journal. Tax Management, Inc. (Subsidiary of: The Bureau of National Affairs, Inc.), 1250 23rd St., N.W., Washington, DC 20037-1166. TEL 202-833-7240.
FAX 202-833-7297. TELEX 285656-BNAI-WSH. (Subscr. to: 9435 Key West Ave., Rockville, MD 2850. TEL 800-372-1033) Ed. Glenn Davis. (looseleaf format; back issues avail.) **Document type:** trade publication.
Description: Notification and reference service to be used as a practical guide to financial planning. For financial planners in a wide variety of disciplines.

336.2 US ISSN 1087-2922
▼**TAX MANAGEMENT FINANCIAL PRODUCTS REPORT**. 1996. s-m. $973. Tax Management, Inc. (Subsidiary of: The Bureau of National Affairs, Inc.), 1231 25th St., N.W., Washington, DC 20037. TEL 202-833-7240; 800-372-1033.
FAX 202-833-7297. TELEX 285656 BNAI WSH. URL: http://www.bna.com/. (Subscr. to: 9435 Key West Ave., Rockville, MD 20850) Ed. Glenn B. Davis. (back issues avail.)
●Also available online.
Description: Focuses on the taxation of financial products.

336 US
TAX MANAGEMENT FOREIGN INCOME PORTFOLIOS. (Subseries of: Tax Management Foreign Income Series) 1964. bi-m. $1276 (subscr. includes Tax Management International Journal). Tax Management, Inc. (Subsidiary of: The Bureau of National Affairs, Inc.), 1250 23rd St., N.W., Washington, DC 20037-1166. TEL 202-833-7240. FAX 202-833-7297. TELEX 285656-BNAI-WSH. (Subscr. to: 9435 Key West Ave., Rockville, MD 20850. TEL 800-372-1033) Ed. Glenn B. Davis. bibl. (back issues avail.) **Document type:** trade publication.
●Also available online. Vendor(s): West Group (File TM-FOR).
Description: Portfolio service covering tax and related corporate problems arising from the U.S. taxation of foreign income and the conduct of business in selected countries around the world.

336 US
TAX MANAGEMENT I R S FORMS. 1988. base vol. (plus irreg. updates). $363. Tax Management, Inc. (Subsidiary of: The Bureau of National Affairs, Inc.), 1250 23rd St., N.W., Washington, DC 20037-1166. TEL 202-833-7240.
FAX 202-833-7297. TELEX 285656 BNAI WSH. (Subscr. to: 9435 Key West Ave., Rockville, MD 20850. TEL 800-372-1033) Ed. Glenn B. Davis. (looseleaf format; back issues avail.)

336 US
TAX MANAGEMENT I R S PRACTICE AND POLICY. 1990. m. $951. Tax Management, Inc. (Subsidiary of: The Bureau of National Affairs, Inc.), 1250 23rd St., N.W., Washington, DC 20037-1166. TEL 202-833-7240. FAX 202-833-7297. TELEX 285656-BNAI-WSH. (Subscr. to: 9435 Key West Ave., Rockville, MD 20850. TEL 800-372-1033) Ed. Glenn B. Davis. (looseleaf format; back issues avail.) **Document type:** trade publication.
Description: Comprehensive discussion of IRS practice from audits through collections. Covers IRS directories and industry specific handbooks that help facilitate dealings with the IRS.

336 US
TAX MANAGEMENT I R S PRACTICE & POLICY BULLETIN. 1990. m. $357. Tax Management, Inc. (Subsidiary of: The Bureau of National Affairs, Inc.), 1250 23rd St., N.W., Washington, DC 20037-1166. TEL 202-833-7240. FAX 202-833-7297. TELEX 285656-BNAI-WSH. (Subscr. to: 9435 Key West Ave., Rockville, MD 20850. TEL 800-372-1033) Ed. Glenn B. Davis. (back issues avail.) **Document type:** trade publication.

336 UK ISSN 0143-7941
K4456.2
TAX MANAGEMENT INTERNATIONAL FORUM. (Subseries of: Tax Planning International) 1980. q. £216($370) B N A International, Inc. (Subsidiary of: The Bureau of National Affairs, Inc.), Heron House, 10 Dean Farrar St., London SW1H 0DX, England. TEL 44-171-222-8831. FAX 44-171-222-0294. E-mail: bnai@bna.com; URL: http://www.bna.com. Ed. Deborah Russell. index. (back issues avail.) **Document type:** newsletter.
●Also available online.
—SWETS. **CCC**.
Description: Practitioners in major industrial nations discuss problems in international tax law.

BUSINESS AND ECONOMICS — PUBLIC FINANCE, TAXATION

336.2   US   ISSN 0090-4600
K24
TAX MANAGEMENT INTERNATIONAL JOURNAL; a monthly professional review of current international tax developments. (Subseries of: Tax Management Foreign Income Series) 1972. m. $389. Tax Management, Inc. (Subsidiary of: The Bureau of National Affairs, Inc.), 1250 23rd St., N.W., Washington, DC 20037-1166. TEL 202-833-7240. FAX 202-833-7297. TELEX 285656-BNAI-WSH. (Subscr. to: 9435 Key West Ave., Rockville, MD 20850. TEL 800-372-1033) Ed. Glenn B. Davis. bk.rev.; s-a. index. (back issues avail.) **Indexed:** ABI Inform., Account.Ind. (1979-), BPIA, Bus.Ind., C.L.I., L.R.I. **Document type:** trade publication.
●Also available online. Vendor(s): Knight-Ridder Information, Inc. (Files 15, 485), UMI.
—UMI. **CCC.**
   Description: Review of current international tax, fiscal, and economic developments affecting worldwide business operations.

336   US   ISSN 0148-8295
TAX MANAGEMENT MEMORANDUM. 1979. bi-w. $306. Tax Management, Inc. (Subsidiary of: The Bureau of National Affairs, Inc.), 1231 23rd St., N.W., Washington, DC 20037-1166. TEL 202-833-7240. FAX 202-833-7297. TELEX 285656-BNAI-WSH. (Subscr. to: 9435 Key West Ave., Rockville, MD 20850. TEL 800-372-1033) Ed. Glenn B. Davis. index. (back issues avail.) **Indexed:** C.L.I., L.R.I. **Document type:** trade publication.
●Also available online. Vendor(s): UMI, West Group (File TM-TMM).
—UMI. **CCC.**
   Description: Contains an analysis of a current tax development by Tax Management's Advisory Board.

336.2   US
▼**TAX MANAGEMENT MULTISTATE TAX ELECTRONIC WEEKLY REPORT.** 1997. w. $625. Tax Management, Inc. (Subsidiary of: The Bureau of National Affairs, Inc.), 1231 25th St., N.W., Washington, DC 20037. TEL 202-833-7240; 800-372-1033. FAX 202-833-7297. TELEX 285656 BNAI WSH. URL: http://www.bna.com/. Ed. Glenn B. Davis. (diskette format)

336   US   ISSN 0738-5285
TAX MANAGEMENT PRIMARY SOURCES. (Subseries of: Tax Management Primary Sources) 1982. m. $1060 includes Washington Tax Review. Tax Management, Inc. (Subsidiary of: The Bureau of National Affairs, Inc.), 1250 23rd St., N.W., Washington, DC 20037-1166. TEL 202-833-7240. FAX 202-833-7297. TELEX 285656-BNAI-WSH. (Subscr. to: 9435 Key West Ave., Rockville, MD 20850. TEL 800-372-1033) Ed. Glenn Davis. (looseleaf format; back issues avail.) **Document type:** trade publication.
—**CCC.**
   Description: Covers legislative history of the Internal Revenue Code.

336   US   ISSN 0887-2562
KF6272
TAX MANAGEMENT PRIMARY SOURCES WASHINGTON TAX REVIEW. (Subseries of: Tax Management Primary Sources) 1979. m. $162. Tax Management, Inc. (Subsidiary of: The Bureau of National Affairs, Inc.), 1250 23rd St., N.W., Washington, DC 20037-1166. TEL 202-833-7240. FAX 202-833-7297. TELEX 285656-BNAI-WSH. (Subscr. to: 9435 Key West Ave., Rockville, MD 20850. TEL 800-372-1033) Ed. Glenn B. Davis. index. (back issues avail.) **Indexed:** Bus.Ind. **Document type:** trade publication.
—UMI. **CCC.**
   Formerly: Washington Tax Review (ISSN 0737-5875)
   Description: Analysis of tax legislative developments.

336   US   ISSN 1044-7261
TAX MANAGEMENT TAX PRACTICE SERIES. 1989. w. $875. Tax Management, Inc. (Subsidiary of: The Bureau of National Affairs, Inc.), 1250 23rd St., N.W., Washington, DC 20037-1166. TEL 202-833-7240. FAX 202-833-7297. TELEX 285656-BNAI-WSH. (Subscr. to: 9435 Key West Ave., Rockville, MD 20850. TEL 800-372-1033) Ed. Glenn B. Davis. (looseleaf format; also avail. in diskette format; back issues avail.) **Document type:** trade publication.
—**CCC.**
   Description: Covers the spectrum of taxation, including U.S. income, foreign income, estates, gifts, and trusts, with hundreds of practice applications.

336   US   ISSN 1083-7345
TAX MANAGEMENT TAX PRACTICE SERIES BULLETIN. 1990. bi-w. $102. Tax Management, Inc. (Subsidiary of: The Bureau of National Affairs, Inc.), 1250 23rd St., N.W., Washington, DC 20037-1166. TEL 202-833-7240. FAX 202-833-7297. TELEX 285656-BNAI-WSH. (Subscr. to: 9435 Key West Ave., Rockville, MD 20850. TEL 800-372-1033) Ed. Glenn B. Davis. (back issues avail.) **Document type:** newsletter.
—**CCC.**

336   US   ISSN 0494-8270
▼**TAX MANAGEMENT TRANSFER PRICING PORTFOLIO SERIES.** 1995. bi-w. $1969. Tax Management, Inc. (Subsidiary of: The Bureau of National Affairs, Inc.), 1250 23rd St., N.W., Washington, DC 20037-1166. TEL 202-833-7240. FAX 202-833-7297. TELEX 285656-BNAI-WSH. (Subscr. to: 9435 Key West Ave., Rockville, MD 20850. TEL 800-372-1033) Ed. Glenn B. Davis. (back issues avail.)
—**CCC.**

336   US   ISSN 1063-2069
KF6461.5
TAX MANAGEMENT TRANSFER PRICING REPORT; a biweekly update on transfer pricing and related issues. 1992. bi-w. $973. Tax Management, Inc. (Subsidiary of: The Bureau of National Affairs, Inc.), 1250 23rd St., N.W., Washington, DC 20037-1166. TEL 202-833-7240. FAX 202-833-7297. TELEX 285656-BNAI-WSH. (Subscr. to: 9435 Key West Ave., Rockville, MD 20850. TEL 800-372-1033) Ed. Glenn B. Davis. (back issues avail.) **Document type:** trade publication.
—**CCC.**
   Description: Focuses exclusively on transfer pricing. Includes regulatory activity, legislative developments, court cases and analysis with practical insight into developments in the area of transfer pricing.

336   US
TAX MANAGEMENT U S INCOME. (Subseries of: Tax Management U S Income Series) 1959. bi-w. $1867 includes Tax Management Weekly Report, Tax Management Revenue Forms Service and Tax Management Memorandum. Tax Management, Inc. (Subsidiary of: The Bureau of National Affairs, Inc.), 1250 23rd St., N.W., Washington, DC 20037-1166. TEL 202-833-7240. FAX 202-833-7297. TELEX 285656-BNAI-WSH. (Subscr. to: 9435 Key West Ave., Rockville, MD 20850. TEL 800-372-1033) Ed. Glenn B. Davis. bibl. (back issues avail.) **Document type:** trade publication.
●Also available online. Vendor(s): West Group (Files TM-US, TM-US-OLD, TM-TMWR).
   Description: Portfolio and journal service covering tax planning problems related to federal taxation of domestic income.

336   US   ISSN 0884-6057
KF6272
TAX MANAGEMENT WEEKLY REPORT. 1982. w. $996. Tax Management, Inc. (Subsidiary of: The Bureau of National Affairs, Inc.), 1250 23rd St., N.W., Washington, DC 20037-1166. TEL 202-833-7240. FAX 202-833-7297. TELEX 285656-BNAI-WSH. (Subscr. to: 9435 Key West Ave., Rockville, MD 20850. TEL 800-372-1033) Ed. Glenn Davis. (back issues avail.) **Document type:** trade publication.
●Also available online. Vendor(s): Human Resources Information Network (File DD), NewsNet (File TMWEEK), West Group (File TM-TMWR).
—**CCC.**
   Formerly: B N A's Weekly Tax Report (ISSN 0733-0405)
   Description: Reports developments affecting taxation and the tax aspects of accounting. Covers summaries of federal cases including the U.S. Tax Court, synopses of the I.R.S. general counsel and technical advice memoranda, analysis of noteworthy I.R.S. revenue ruling, procedures and private letter ruling, and status reports of Treasury Department actions on pending regulations.

336   US   ISSN 1083-2289
TAX MANAGEMENT'S MULTISTATE TAX PORTFOLIO SERIES. 1994. m. $1012 (CD-ROM $1050). Tax Management, Inc. (Subsidiary of: The Bureau of National Affairs, Inc.), 1250 23rd St., N.W., Washington, DC 20037-1166. TEL 202-833-7240. FAX 202-833-7297. TELEX 285656-BNAI-WSH. (Subscr. to: 9435 Key West Ave., Rockville, MD 20850. TEL 800-372-1033) Ed. Glenn B. Davis. (back issues avail.) **Document type:** trade publication.
●Also available on CD-ROM.
   Description: Provides a comprehensive multi-state discussion of all aspects of a particular state tax planning problems. Also contains detailed citations to state code and regulations, state administrative and judicial court decisions, and state administrative pronouncements.

336.2   CN   ISSN 0576-6230
KE5662
TAX MEMO. 1954. irreg., latest 1990. price varies. Canadian Tax Foundation - L'Association Canadienne d'Etudes Fiscales, One Queen St., E., Ste. 1800, Toronto, ON M5C 2Y2, Canada. TEL 416-863-9784. FAX 416-863-9585. Ed. Laurel Amalia. R&P contact: Laurel Amalia. charts; stat. **Document type:** academic/scholarly publication.
   Description: Intermittent reports on tax developments of topical interest.

336 343.05   US   ISSN 0279-0211
TAX NEWS. 2/yr. membership. State Bar of Wisconsin, Taxation Section, 402 W. Wilson St., Madison, WI 53703. TEL 608-257-3838. FAX 608-257-5502. circ. 1,000. (back issues avail.) **Document type:** newsletter.

336.2   NE   ISSN 0040-0076
K4456.2
TAX NEWS SERVICE. (Text in English) 1965. w. $435 (online $600) (effective 1997). I B F D Publications B.V., P.O. Box 20237, 1000 HE Amsterdam, Netherlands. TEL 31-20-6267726. FAX 31-20-6228658. TELEX 13217 INTAX NL. (In US: IBFD Publications USA, Inc., 4 Maple Ln., Valatie, NY 12184. TEL 800-299-6330. FAX 518-758-2246) q. index, cum.index. (looseleaf format) **Document type:** newsletter.
●Also available online. Vendor(s): I B F D Pubns. BV, Lexis-Nexis.
   Description: Covers current developments in international taxation.

BUSINESS AND ECONOMICS — PUBLIC FINANCE, TAXATION

336 320 US ISSN 0270-5494
KF6272
TAX NOTES; the weekly tax service. 1972. w. (plus a CD-ROM). $1699 (includes a. and 1985-1996 compilations on CD-ROM). Tax Analysts, 6830 N. Fairfax Dr., Arlington, VA 22213. TEL 703-533-4400; 800-955-2444. FAX 703-533-4444. Ed. Christopher Bergin. index; circ. controlled. **Indexed:** Bus.Ind., C.L.I., L.R.I., Leg.Cont., Tr.& Indus.Ind. **Document type:** trade publication.
●Also available online. Vendor(s): Knight-Ridder Information, Inc., Lexis-Nexis.
Also available on CD-ROM.
—UMI. **CCC.**
Description: Provides in-depth coverage of tax news from all federal sources, together with summaries of all tax documents and decisions released each week, and analytical articles and commentary.

336 US ISSN 1058-3971
K4471.2
TAX NOTES INTERNATIONAL. 1989. w. $949. Tax Analysts, 6830 N. Fairfax Dr., Arlington, VA 22213. TEL 703-533-4646; 800-533-4400. FAX 703-533-4444. Ed. Susan M. Lyons; Pub. Thomas F. Field. R&P contact: Susan M. Lyons. TEL 703-533-4640. (back issues avail.) **Indexed:** L.R.I.
●Also available online. Vendor(s): Knight-Ridder Information, Inc., Lexis-Nexis.
—BLDSC (8611.608100). **CCC.**
Description: Features international tax news and commentary from a worldwide reporting staff along with summaries of statutes, regulations, rulings, court decisions and tax treaties.

336 US
TAX PENALTIES AND INTEREST HANDBOOK. 1990. base vol. (plus a. suppl.). $80. Butterworth Legal Publishers (Salem) (Subsidiary of: Reed Elsevier plc), 8 Industrial Way, Bldg. C, Salem, NH 03079. TEL 800-548-4001. FAX 603-898-9858. Eds. Howard Davidoff, David Minars. (looseleaf format)
Description: Covers all federal and state penalty and interest sections of the Internal Revenue Code.

336.2 II
TAX PLANNING. (Text in English and Gujarati) 1975. m. Rs.250. Swati Prakashan, Purvalaya Building, 14-15 Ramkrishna Nagar, Rajkot 360002, India. Ed. P.C. Parekh. adv.

336 346.066 US
TAX PLANNING FOR CORPORATE ACQUISITIONS.* 1988. base vol. (plus suppl.). Maxwell Macmillan, Rosenfeld Launer, 90 Fifth Ave., New York, NY 10011-7629. TEL 800-562-0245. FAX 201-816-3569. Ed. George Brode, Jr.

336.2 US ISSN 0040-0092
KF6296.A15
TAX PLANNING IDEAS.* (In 3 vols.) vol.17, 1970. s-m. $66. Macmillan Information Company Inc., 90 Fifth Ave., New York, NY 10011-7629. TEL 800-562-0245. FAX 201-816-3569. adv.; bk.rev.; charts. (also avail. in microform from UMI; reprint service avail. from UMI) **Indexed:** L.I.I.

336 UK ISSN 0309-7900
K4464.A13
TAX PLANNING INTERNATIONAL REVIEW; a monthly journal of international tax planning, development and opportunities. (Subseries of: Tax Planning International) 1981. m. £432($780) B N A International, Inc. (Subsidiary of: The Bureau of National Affairs, Inc.), Heron House, 10 Dean Farrar St., London SW1H 0DX, England.
TEL 44-171-222-8831. FAX 44-171-222-0294. E-mail: bnai@bna.com; URL: http://www.bna.com. Ed. Deborah Russell. index. (back issues avail.) **Indexed:** Account.Ind. (1988-). **Document type:** academic/scholarly publication.
●Also available online.
—SWETS. **CCC.**
Former titles: Tax Haven Review; Tax Planning International.
Description: Covers international tax-planning developments and opportunities, including country surveys and tax treaty developments.

336 US ISSN 0892-8649
HJ10.3
TAX POLICY AND THE ECONOMY. 1987. a. $30 hardcover (foreign $40); paperback $15 (foreign $25) (effective 1997). (National Bureau of Economic Research) M I T Press, 5 Cambridge Center, Cambridge, MA 02142.
TEL 617-253-2889. FAX 617-577-1545. E-mail: journals-orders@mit.edu; URL: http://www-mitpress.mit.edu. (Editorial addr.: 1050 Massachusetts Ave., 3rd Fl., Cambridge, MA 02138) Ed. James M. Poterba; Paul/Dzus. (back issues avail.; reprint service avail. from UMI) **Indexed:** J.of Econ.Lit. **Document type:** academic/scholarly publication.
—BLDSC (8611.611000). **CCC.**
Description: Covers issues in the current tax debate, focusing on the economic effects of tax policies. Geared toward policymakers, corporate managers, lawyers and economists.

336 US ISSN 1086-0088
TAX PRACTICE. w. $199. Tax Analysts, 6830 N. Fairfax Dr., Arlington, VA 22213. TEL 703-533-4400; 800-955-2444. FAX 703-533-4444. Ed. Robert Manning; Pub. Thomas Field. q. index. (back issues avail.) **Document type:** trade publication.
—CCC.
Formerly (until 1995): Tax Practice and Controversies (ISSN 1074-5858); Which was formed by the merger of (1991-1993): I R S Tax Practice Insider (ISSN 1063-4932); (1992-1993): Tax-Related Documents (ISSN 1062-9106); Which was formerly: Tax-Related Administrative Documents (ISSN 1060-9865)
Description: Provides a weekly guide to tax developments including IRS rulings and regulations, tax developments in congress and tax decisions from the courts.

350 US
TAX PRACTICE DESKBOOK. base vol. (plus a. supplement). $105. Warren, Gorham & Lamont, One Penn Plaza, New York, NY 10119.
TEL 212-971-5000. FAX 212-971-5113. (Subscr. to: The Park Square Bldg., 21 St. James Ave., Boston, MA 02116-4112. TEL 800-950-1207) **Document type:** trade publication.
Formerly: Freeman and Freeman's Tax Practice Deskbook (Supplement).

336.2 UK ISSN 0269-3720
TAX PRACTITIONER'S DIARY. a. £16.50($28) (effective 1995-1996). Butterworth & Co. (Publishers) Ltd., Part of the Reed Elsevier group, Halsbury House, 35 Chancery Ln., London WC2A 1EL, England. TEL 0171-400-2500. FAX 0171-400-2842. (U.S. addr.: Butterworth Legal Publishers, 90 Stiles Rd., Salem, NH 03079-9981. TEL 603-898-9664) Ed.Bd. **Document type:** trade publication.
Description: Covers income including corporate, inheritance, and value-added taxes, as well as national insurance contributions and duties. Also included is a comprehensive list of tax district addresses and collection offices throughout the U.K.

332.6 US ISSN 1075-5780
TAX PRACTITIONERS JOURNAL. 1994. q. $30. National Association of Tax Practitioners, 720 Association Dr., Appleton, WI 54914. TEL 414-749-1040. FAX 414-749-1062. Ed. Alan S. Prahl. R&P contact: Cindy Van Beckum. adv. contact: Cindy Van Beckum. circ. 16,000. (back issues avail.) **Document type:** trade publication.
Description: Tax preparation for EAs, CPAs, CFPs, and attorneys.

336.2 CN ISSN 0227-1265
HJ4661.A2
TAX PRINCIPLES TO REMEMBER. 1972. a. price varies. Canadian Institute of Chartered Accountants, 277 Wellington St. W., Toronto, Ont. M5V 3H2, Canada. TEL 416-977-3222. FAX 416-977-8585. circ. 9,000.
Description: Source of reference for office, university or home study use. Includes changes to the Canadian Income Tax Act, and interpretive bulletins and information circulars of the Department of National Revenue.

336 CN ISSN 0827-3677
KE5662
TAX PROFILE. m. Can.$165. C C H Canadian Ltd., 6 Garamond Ct., North York, ON M3C 1Z5, Canada. TEL 416-441-2992; 800-268-4522.
FAX 416-444-9011. **Document type:** trade publication.
●Also available online. Vendor(s): QL Systems Ltd.
Description: Comments on items of interest regarding federal income tax and other federal and provincial taxes.

336.2 US ISSN 1059-6356
TAX RETURN PREPARER'S LETTER. s-m. $129 (effective 1997). Harcourt Brace Professional Publishing, 525 B St., Ste. 1900, San Diego, CA 92101-4495. TEL 619-699-6716. FAX 619-699-6593. Ed. Sidney Bernstein; Pub. Ken Rethmeier. R&P contact: Jenna Lake. TEL 619-699-6265. **Document type:** newsletter.
Description: Covers new tax developments, and critical information on new tax forms and procedures.

336 US
TAX SAVINGS REPORT. 1982. 10/yr. $39 (effective 1995). National Taxpayers Union, 108 N. Alfred St., Alexandria, VA 22314. TEL 703-683-5700. FAX 703-683-5722. Ed. Ellen Katz. index; circ. 22,000 (paid). (looseleaf format; back issues avail.) **Document type:** newsletter.
Description: Provides income tax advice for individuals and small business owners, including filing and deduction strategies, recordkeeping, and dealing with audits.

336.2 II ISSN 0040-0122
TAX TIMES. (Text in Hindi) 1965. w. Rs.45($2) Tax Times Trust - Nathoo Rem Jain, Sarafa, Jhansi, Uttar Pradesh, India. adv.; bk.rev.; illus. circ. 2,000. (looseleaf format)

336 US
TAX TREATIES (NEW YORK). 1969. 3 base vols. (plus m. Report Bulletins and updates). $410. Warren, Gorham & Lamont, One Penn Plaza, New York, NY 10119-4098. TEL 212-971-5000. FAX 212-971-5113. (Subscr. to: The Park Sqare Bldg., 31 St. James Ave., Boston, MA 02116-4112. TEL 800-950-1200) (looseleaf format) **Document type:** trade publication.
Description: Provides up-to-date analysis of international tax agreements. Includes full official text of every treaty and protocol relating to income, gift and estate taxes.

538 US ISSN 0414-0176
TAX TREATIES (RIVERWOODS). m. $470 (CD-ROM ed. $516). C C H Incorporated, 2700 Lake Cook Rd., Riverwoods, IL 60015. TEL 847-267-7000; 800-835-5224. FAX 800-224-8299. (looseleaf format)
●Also available on CD-ROM.

336.2 NE
TAX TREATIES DATA BASE ON C D - R O M. (Not avail. in printed format) (Text in English) 2/yr. $1500 (effective 1997). I B F D Publications B.V., P.O. Box 20237, 1000 HE Amsterdam, Netherlands. TEL 31-20-6267726. FAX 31-20-6228658. TELEX 13217 INTAX NL. (In US: IBFD Publications USA, Inc., 4 Maple Ln., Valatie, NY 12184. TEL 800-299-6330. FAX 518-758-2246)
●Also available online. Vendor(s): I B F D Pubns. BV, Lexis-Nexis.
Also available on CD-ROM.
Description: Provides full text of tax treaties and protocols, including OECD and UN draft and model conventions, in searchable format.

336 NE
TAX TREATMENT OF CROSS-BORDER DONATIONS; including the tax status of charities and foundations. (Text in English) 1994. base vol. (plus a. update). $190 (renewals $65) (effective 1997). I B F D Publications B.V., P.O. Box 20237, 1000 HE Amsterdam, Netherlands. TEL 31-20-6267726. FAX 31-20-6228658. TELEX 13217 INTAX NL. (In US: IBFD Publications USA, Inc., 4 Maple St., Valatie, NY 12184. TEL 800-299-6330. FAX 518-758-2246) Ed. Paul Bater. (looseleaf format)
Description: Studies the treatment of charitable non-governmental organizations in over 25 countries, covering tax status and the taxation of donations, and international aspects such as the relevant provisions of tax treaties.

BUSINESS AND ECONOMICS — PUBLIC FINANCE, TAXATION

336 NE
TAX TREATMENT OF TRANSFER PRICING. (Text in English) 1987. 5 base vols. (plus s-a. updates). $1315 (renewals $515) (effective 1997). I B F D Publications B.V., P.O. Box 20237, 1000 HE Amsterdam, Netherlands. TEL 31-20-6267726. FAX 31-20-6228658. TELEX 13217 INTAX NL. (In US: IBFD Publications USA, Inc., 4 Maple Ln., Valatie, NY 12184. TEL 800-299-6330. FAX 518-758-2246) Ed. Rijkele Betten. (looseleaf format)
Description: Provides in-depth, country-by-country surveys of transfer pricing compiled by leading international tax experts for 20 nations.

336.2 II
TAX-VYAPAR; periodical devoted to problems of commerce and taxes. (Editions in English, Gujarati and Hindi) 1968. m. Rs.200. Swati Prakashan, Purvalaya Building, 14-15 Ramkrishna Nagar, Rajkot 360002, India. Ed. P.C. Parekh. adv.; index.

TAX WATCH. see POLITICAL SCIENCE

336 AT ISSN 1320-9426
TAX WEEK; C C H federal and state tax news. Variant title: C C H Tax Week. 1994. w. C C H Australia Ltd., P.O. Box 230, North Ryde, N.S.W. 2113, Australia. TEL 61-1-300300224. FAX 61-1-300306224. **Document type:** newsletter.
●Also available online.
Description: Reports on tax issues including income tax, fringe benefits tax, superannuation, sales tax and stamp duties. 0

336.2 PK ISSN 0040-0157
TAXATION. (Text and summaries in English) 1959. m. Rs.110. Taxation Publishers, 6 Liaquat Rd., Lahore 6, W. Pakistan. Ed. S.M. Raza Nqvi. charts. **Indexed:** L.R.I.

336.2 UK ISSN 0040-0149
HJ2600
TAXATION; leading authority on tax law practice and administration in the UK. 1927. w. £111. Tolley Publishing Co. Ltd., Tolley House, 2 Addiscombe Rd., Croydon, Surrey CR9 5AF, England. TEL 44-181-686-9141. FAX 44-181-686-3155. Ed. M. Gunn. adv.; bk.rev.; stat.; s-a. index. circ. 13,000. **Indexed:** C.L.I., Euro.LJI, L.R.I., LJI, RICS. **Document type:** trade publication.
—BLDSC (8611.650000).

336.2 II
TAXATION. (Text in English) 1948. m. Rs.425. 174 Jorbagh, New Delhi 110003, India. Ed. B.B. Bhargava. adv.; bk.rev. circ. 6,000.

336.2 NE
TAXATION & INVESTMENT IN CANADA. (Text in English) base vol. (plus s-a. updates). $290 (renewals $135) (effective 1997). I B F D Publications B.V., P.O. Box 20237, 1000 HE Amsterdam, Netherlands. TEL 31-20-6267726. FAX 31-20-6228658. TELEX 13217 INTAX NL. (In US: IBFD Publications USA, Inc., 4 Maple Ln., Valatie, NY 12184. TEL 800-299-6330. FAX 518-758-2246) (looseleaf format)
Formerly: Taxes and Investment in Canada and the U S A.
Description: Outlines and clarifies the laws and systems of both federal and provincial governments.

336 NE
TAXATION & INVESTMENT IN MEXICO. (Text in English) 1994. base vol. (plus s-a. updates). $290 (renewals $135) (effective 1997). I B F D Publications B.V., P.O. Box 20237, 1000 HE Amsterdam, Netherlands. TEL 31-20-6267726. FAX 31-20-6228658. TELEX 13217 INTAX NL. (In US: IBDF Publications USA, Inc., 4 Maple Ln., Valatie, NY 12184. TEL 800-299-6330. FAX 518-758-2246) (looseleaf format)
Description: Covers taxation of resident and non-resident individuals and businesses in Mexico, including taxation of capital and capital transfers.

336.2 332.6 NE
TAXATION & INVESTMENT IN SOUTH AFRICA. (Text in English) 1994. base vol. (plus s-a. update). $290 (renewals $135) (effective 1997). I B F D Publications B.V., P.O. Box 20237, 1000 HE Amsterdam, Netherlands. TEL 31-20-6267726. FAX 31-20-6228658. TELEX 13217 INTAX NL. (In US: IBFD Publications USA, Inc., 4 Maple Ln., Valatie, NY 12184. TEL 800-299-6330. FAX 518-758-2246) (looseleaf format)
Description: Provides detailed information on business and taxation in South Africa, including income tax, VAT, capital transfer taxes and exchange controls.

336.2 NE
TAXATION & INVESTMENT IN THE CARIBBEAN. (Text in English) 4 base vols. (plus s-a. updates). $1035 (renewals $370) (effective 1997). I B F D Publications B.V., P.O. Box 20237, 1000 HE Amsterdam, Netherlands. TEL 31-20-6267726. FAX 31-20-6228658. TELEX 13217 INTAX NL. (In US: IBFD Publications USA, Inc., 4 Maple Ln., Valatie, NY 12184. TEL 800-299-6330. FAX 518-758-2246) Ed. Elizabeth de Brauw. (looseleaf format)
Description: Provides a description of the economic situation in each country, a detailed account of the income tax systems and the incentives available for investment.

336.2 NE
TAXATION & INVESTMENT IN THE PEOPLE'S REPUBLIC OF CHINA. (Text in English) base vol. (plus s-a. updates). $290 (renewals $135) (effective 1997). I B F D Publications B.V., P.O. Box 20237, 1000 HE Amsterdam, Netherlands. TEL 31-20-6267726. FAX 31-20-6228658. TELEX 13217 INTAX NL. (In US: IBFD Publications USA, Inc., 4 Maple Ln., Valatie, NY 12184. TEL 800-299-6330. FAX 518-758-2246) Ed. Peter Hann. (looseleaf format)
Incorporates: Foreign - Related Tax Laws and Regulations of the People's Republic of China.
Description: Provides an in-depth analysis of the economy and of the various openings for economic development and business expansion. Allows opportunities and risks to be calculated, potential problems to be identified and provides necessary background information to formulate investment strategies.

336.2 657 US ISSN 0040-0165
HF5681.T3
TAXATION FOR ACCOUNTANTS. 1966. m. $114.98 (overseas $186.95) (effective 1995). Warren, Gorham & Lamont, One Penn Plaza, New York, NY 10119. TEL 212-971-5000. FAX 212-971-5113. URL: http://www.wgl.com/tax/txac.html. (Subscr. to: The Park Square Bldg., 31 St. James Ave., Boston, MA 02116-4112. TEL 800-950-1207) Ed. Sandra K.Lewis. adv. circ. 8,544. (also avail. in microform from UMI; reprint service avail. from RRI,WSH) **Indexed:** ABI Inform., Account.Ind. (1974-), B.P.I., BPIA, Bus.Ind., L.I.I., Manage.Cont., P.A.I.S. **Document type:** trade publication.
●Also available online. Vendor(s): Lexis-Nexis.
—KR SourceOne; SWETS; UMI; UnCover. **CCC.**
Formerly (until 1993): I R S Practice Alerts.
Description: Covers current tax developments and their implications and offers solutions to tax problems that arise frequently in general accounting practice.

343.73 336.2 US ISSN 0161-178X
K24
TAXATION FOR LAWYERS. 1972. bi-m. $114.98 (overseas $183.95) (effective 1995). Warren, Gorham & Lamont, One Penn Plaza, New York, NY 10119. TEL 212-971-5000. FAX 212-971-5240. (Subscr. to: The Park Square Bldg., 31 St. James Ave., Boston, MA 02116-4112. TEL 800-950-1207) Ed. Thomas Harding. adv.; illus. circ. 1,400. (also avail. in microform from UMI; reprint service avail. from RRI, UMI,WSH) **Indexed:** Account.Ind. (1974-), BPIA, C.L.I., L.I.I., L.R.I. **Document type:** trade publication.
●Also available online. Vendor(s): Lexis-Nexis.
—UMI; UnCover. **CCC.**
Description: Helps attorneys in general practice develop and maintain up-to-date tax awareness in legal matters.
Refereed Serial

336.2 AT ISSN 0494-8343
TAXATION IN AUSTRALIA (BLUE EDITION). 1963. m. membership. Taxation Institute of Australia, 7th Fl., 64 Castlereagh St., Sydney, N.S.W. 2000, Australia. TEL 61-2-92323422. FAX 61-2-92216953. E-mail: tline@taxia.ana.au; URL: http://www.taxia.asn.au. Ed. David Evans. adv.; bk.rev.; index; circ. 10,000 (controlled). (tabloid format; back issues avail.) **Indexed:** Account.Ind. (1989-), Aus.P.A.I.S. **Document type:** academic/scholarly publication.
Description: Provides tax information for members of the institute including tax rulings, determinations and cases.
Refereed Serial

336.2 AT ISSN 1039-2572
TAXATION IN AUSTRALIA (RED EDITION). 1991. bi-m. Aus.$165. Taxation Institute of Australia, 7th Fl., 64 Castlereagh St., Sydney, N.S.W. 2000, Australia. TEL 61-2-92323422. FAX 61-2-92216953. E-mail: tline@taxia.ans.au; URL: http://www.taxia.asn.au. Ed. David Evans. index; circ. 1,200 (paid). (back issues avail.) **Document type:** academic/scholarly publication.
Description: Provides academic and specialist articles on taxation.
Refereed Serial

336.1 NE
TAXATION IN LATIN AMERICA. (Text in English) 4 base vols. (plus updates 4/yr.). $1035 (renewals $535) (effective 1997). I B F D Publications B.V., P.O. Box 20237, 1000 HE Amsterdam, Netherlands. TEL 31-20-6267726. FAX 31-20-6228658. TELEX 13217 INTAX NL. (In US: IBFD Publications USA, Inc., 4 Maple Ln., Valatie, NY 12184. TEL 800-299-6330. FAX 518-758-2246) Ed. David Hughes. bibl. (looseleaf format)
●Also available on CD-ROM.
Formerly: Corporate Taxation in Latin America.
Description: Documents the legal and taxation systems in full, includes practical, detailed sections on investment.

336.2 II
TAXATION LAW REPORTS. 1971. m. Rs.288($96) All India Reporter Ltd., P.O. Box 209, Nagpur 440012, India. Ed. V.R. Manohar. adv.; bk.rev.; bibl. circ. 1,500.

336 SA
TAXATION OF EMPLOYEES. base vol. (plus a. supplement). R.228. Butterworth Publishers (Pty.) Ltd., Part of the Reed Elsevier group, P.O. Box 792, Durban 4000, South Africa. TEL 27-31-2683111. FAX 27-31-2683110. (looseleaf format)
Description: Comprehensive guide to planning tax-effective remuneration packages for employers, employees and the self-employed. Provides practical advice on matters including different approaches to providing fringe benefits, as well as share incentive schemes, deferred compensation and other retirement benefits.

336 NE
TAXATION OF PERMANENT ESTABLISHMENTS. (Text in English) 1993. 2 base vols. (plus s-a. updates). $750 (renewals $190) (effective 1997). I B F D Publications B.V., P.O. Box 20237, 1000 HE Amsterdam, Netherlands. TEL 31-20-6267726. FAX 31-20-6228658. TELEX 13217 INTAX NL. (In US: IBFD Publications USA, Inc., 4 Maple Ln., Valatie, NY 12184. TEL 800-758-1411. FAX 518-758-2246) Ed. Irene J.J. Burgers. (looseleaf format)
Description: Provides a systematic analysis of the role of permanent establishments in international tax law, including commentary on articles 5, 7 and 24 of the OECD Model Tax Convention, and the influence of the EC.

350 US
TAXATION OF THE CLOSELY HELD CORPORATION (SUPPLEMENT). biennial supplements to base vol. $155 for base vol. (foreign $218.95) (effective 1994). Warren, Gorham & Lamont, One Penn Plaza, New York, NY 10119. TEL 212-971-5000. FAX 212-971-5113. (Subscr. to: The Park Square Bldg., 31 St. James Ave., Boston, MA 02116-4112. TEL 800-950-1207) **Document type:** trade publication.
Formerly: Taxation of Closely Held Corporations (Supplement).

BUSINESS AND ECONOMICS — PUBLIC FINANCE, TAXATION

336   UK
TAXATION PRACTITIONER. 1976. m. £62 (effective 1997). Chartered Institute of Taxation, 12 Upper Belgrave St., London SW1X 8BB, England. TEL 44-171-235-9381. FAX 44-171-235-2562. Ed. Andrew Flint; Pub. Sarah Hine. adv. contact: Roger THomas. bk.rev. circ. 23,000. **Indexed:** Euro.LJI, LJI. **Document type:** academic/scholarly publication.
    Refereed Serial

336   AT
TAXATION PRECEDENTS, PROCEDURES AND ELECTIONS. 1988. irreg. (approx. 2/yr.). C C H Australia Ltd., P.O. Box 230, N. Ryde, N.S.W. 2113, Australia. TEL 61-1-300300224. FAX 61-1-300306224. (looseleaf format)
    Description: Provides step-by-step procedures and precedents for elections, notices and options required under the Income Tax Assessment Act and Fringe Benefits Tax Assessment Act. Covers income tax, capital gains, fringe benefits and superannuation.

336.2   AT   ISSN 0040-0173
TAXATION RECORD JOURNAL.* 1954. m. free. Federated Clerks' Union, Taxation Officers Branch, 155 Castlereagh St., Sydney, N.S.W. 2000, Australia, Australia. TEL 03-62-3921. TELEX AA30625 ME 979. Ed. R. Markham. adv. circ. 16,000.

336.2   PK
TAXATION STRUCTURE OF PAKISTAN. (Text in English) 1974. a. Finance Division, Islamabad, Pakistan.

336   US
TAXES (MADISON). a. $2.25. Wisconsin Taxpayers Alliance, 335 W. Wilson St., Madison, WI 53703-3694. TEL 608-255-4581. Ed. Ren Kiemel. **Indexed:** B.P.I.
    Description: Contains information on all federal, state, and local taxes paid by Wisconsin taxpayers. Includes federal and state income tax filing guides.

336.2   US   ISSN 0040-0181
KF6272   CODEN: TAXSA6
TAXES (RIVERWOODS); the tax magazine. 1923. m. $186. C C H Incorporated, 2700 Lake Cook Rd., Riverwoods, IL 60015. TEL 847-267-7000; 800-836-5224. FAX 800-224-8299. bk.rev.; charts; illus.; index. (also avail. in microform from UMI; reprint service avail. from KTO,WSH) **Indexed:** Account.Ind. (1974-), ASCA, B.P.I., BPIA, Bus.Ind., C.L.I., Curr.Cont., L.I.I., L.R.I., Leg.Cont., Leg.Per., P.A.I.S., SSCI, Tr.& Indus.Ind.
    ●Also available online. Vendor(s): UMI.
    —CASDDS; KR SourceOne; SWETS; UnCover. **CCC.**
    Former titles (until 1939): Tax Magazine (ISSN 8755-2221); (until 1931): National Tax Magazine (ISSN 8755-223X); (until 1930): National Income Tax Magazine (ISSN 8755-2248)

336   NE
TAXES AND INVESTMENT IN ASIA AND THE PACIFIC. (Text in English) 1978. 10 base vols. (plus m. updates). $1815 (renewals $1095) (effective 1997). (United Nations Economic and Social Commission for Asia and the Pacific (ESCAP), UN) I B F D Publications B.V., P.O. Box 20237, 1000 HE Amsterdam, Netherlands. TEL 31-20-6267726. FAX 31-20-6228658. TELEX 13217 INTAX NL. (In US: IBFD Publications USA, Inc., 4 Maple Ln., Valatie, NY 12184. TEL 800-299-6330. FAX 518-758-2246) Ed. Peter Hann. (looseleaf format)
    Description: Offers information on tax policies and systems for foreign and intraregional investors, governments and policy makers.

336   NE
TAXES AND INVESTMENT IN THE MIDDLE EAST. 1977. 2 base vols. (plus q. updates). $775 (renewals $390) (effective 1997). I B F D Publications B.V., P.O. Box 20237, 1000 HE Amsterdam, Netherlands. TEL 31-20-6267726. FAX 31-20-6228658. TELEX 13217 INTAX NL. (In US: IBFD Publications USA, Inc., 4 Maple Ln., Valatie, NY 12184. TEL 800-299-6330. FAX 518-758-2246) Ed. Peter Hann. (looseleaf format)
    Description: Outlines background information on the economy and political structure, and provides the relevant legal, administrative, economic and tax measures.

336   US   ISSN 0162-3486
KF6285
TAXES ON PARADE. w. $97. C C H Incorporated, 2700 Lake Cook Rd., Riverwoods, IL 60015. TEL 847-267-7000; 800-835-5224. FAX 800-224-8299.
    —UMI. **CCC.**

336   CN   ISSN 0821-3704
THE TAXLETTER. 1983. m. Can.$89. Hume Publishing Company Ltd., 604-2200 Yonge St., Toronto, ON M4S 2C6, Canada. TEL 800-733-4863. FAX 416-440-8268. Ed. David Louis. adv. contact: Barbara Ritchie. index. **Document type:** newsletter.
    Description: Tax planning strategies and consumer news on personal tax planning.

336.24   SA   ISSN 0040-0270
TAXPAYER; a monthly journal devoted to the law, practice and incidence of income tax and other revenue laws. 1952. m. R.410.40 (effective 1993). Taxpayer C C, P.O. Box 3191, 4 Church Sq., 8000 Cape Town, South Africa. TEL 21-21-452592. FAX 27-21-4617488. Ed.Bd. adv.; bk.rev.; charts; index. circ. 2,000. **Indexed:** Ind.S.A.Per.

336 657   AT   ISSN 0728-554X
TEACHER'S TAX GUIDE. 1978. a. Aus.$5. Victorian Affiliated Teachers Federation, P.O. Box 7644, Melbourne, Vic. 3150, Australia. TEL 61-3-8200766. FAX 61-3-8200766. Ed. Alan W. Kidd. circ. 2,000.

336   US   ISSN 0742-0757
HJ11
TENNESSEE TAX GUIDE. 1982. a. $12.75. M. Lee Smith Publishers LLC, 5201 Virginia Way, Brentwood, TN 37024-5094. TEL 615-373-5717; 800-274-6774. FAX 615-373-5183. Ed. Bradford N. Forrister; Pub. M. Lee Smith.
    Description: Comprehensive survey of major Tennessee state and local taxes.

336   US
TENNESSEE TAX SERVICE. 1989. m. M. Lee Smith Publishers LLC, 5201 Virginia Way, Brentwood, TN 37024-5094. TEL 615-373-5717; 800-274-6774. FAX 615-373-5183. Ed. Bradford N. Forrister; Pub. M. Lee Smith.
    Formerly (until 1992): Tennessee Tax Review (ISSN 1044-0798)
    Description: Updates developments in Tennessee state and local taxes.

336   IT
TESTATA: RIVISTA DELLA GUARDIA DI FINANZA. 1952. bi-m. L.8000 (foreign L.14000). (Guardia di Finanza) Comando Generale della Guardia di Finanza, Ufficio Stampa, Via Sicilia 178, 00187 Rome, Italy. Ed. Daniele Caprino. bibl.; illus.; stat.; index. circ. 6,000. **Indexed:** ELLIS, P.A.I.S.For.Lang.Ind.
    —BLDSC (7986.630000).
    Formerly: Rivista della Guardia di Finanza (ISSN 0035-595X)

336   TH
THAILAND'S BUDGET IN BRIEF. (Text in English and Thai) 1960 (Thai ed.); 1962 (Eng. ed.). irreg. free. Bureau of the Budget, Bangkok, Thailand. FAX 2713662. circ. 1,500.

343.489   DK   ISSN 0908-8431
TIDSSKRIFT FOR SKATTER OG AFGIFTER. 1984. m. DKK 545. (Skatteministeriet, Told- og Skattestyrelsen) A-S Skattekartoteket, Palaegade 4, P.O. Box 9026, DK-1022 Copenhagen K, Denmark. TEL 45-33-11-78-74. FAX 45-33-93-80-09. Eds. Peter Taarnhoej, Ib Elligsoee. adv. **Document type:** government publication.
    Formed by the merger of (1984-1994): Tidsskrift for Skatteret (ISSN 0109-2383) & Told Skat Nyt (ISSN 0906-1517); Which was formerly (until 1991): Skat (ISSN 0900-0178); Which incorporates (1939-1986): Meddelelser fra Landsskatteretten (ISSN 0108-5751); (1967-1985): Meddelelser fra Skattedepartementet (ISSN 0108-576X)
    Description: Presents a complete set of Danish tax court decisions, rulings and decisions from the National Tax Tribunal and the administration. Also features articles on current tax topics.

336.2   UK   ISSN 0143-294X
TOLLEY'S PRACTICAL TAX NEWSLETTER. 1940. bi-w. £123 (foreign £144). Tolley Publishing Co. Ltd., Tolley House, 2 Addiscombe Rd., Croydon, Surrey CR9 5AF, England. TEL 44-181-686-9141. FAX 44-181-686-3155. Ed. Ian Dodds. bk.rev. **Indexed:** Euro.LJI, LJI. **Document type:** newsletter.
    —BLDSC (8863.686540).
    Former titles: Fiscal Press (ISSN 0956-3954); Tax Partner (ISSN 0954-6537); Income Tax Digest and Accountants' Review (ISSN 0308-7883)
    Description: Provides updates on all forms of taxes in the United Kingdom.

336.2   UK   ISSN 0951-175X
TOLLEY'S PRACTICAL V A T. (Value Added Tax) 1987. m. £113 (foreign £129). Tolley Publishing Co. Ltd., Tolley House, 2 Addiscombe Rd., Croydon, Surrey CR9 5AX, England. TEL 44-181-686-9141. FAX 44-181-686-3155. Ed. Debbie Russell. circ. 1,200. **Indexed:** Euro.LJI, LJI. **Document type:** bulletin.

336   UK   ISSN 0261-8664
TOUCHE ROSS & COMPANY. TAX NEWSLETTER. 1981. q. Touche Ross & Co. (Subsidiary of: Deloitte Touche Tohmatsu International), 1 Little New St., London EC4A 3TR, England. TEL 0171-936-3000. FAX 0171-583-8517. circ. 10,000. **Document type:** newsletter.

TRENDS, TIPS AND TAX. see *BUSINESS AND ECONOMICS — Management*

336   US   ISSN 1084-8320
TRI-STATE LETTER PLUS. m. $198. Harcourt Brace Professional Publishing, 525 B St., Ste 1900, San Diego, CA 92101-4495. TEL 619-699-6716. FAX 619-699-6593. Ed. Joseph L. Goldman; Pub. Ken Rethmeier. R&P contact: Jenna Lake. TEL 619-699-6265.
    Description: News on how to comply with changing tax laws, avoid penalties, and maximize planning opportunities in Connecticut, New York and New Jersey.

TRUSTS AND ESTATES (ATLANTA). see *BUSINESS AND ECONOMICS — Investments*

336.2   US   ISSN 0564-4402
KF6289.A1
TULANE TAX INSTITUTE. 1951. a. $479. Totaltape Publishing, 9417 Princess Palm Ave., Ste. 400, Tampa, FL 33619. TEL 800-874-7877. FAX 800-345-8273. E-mail: bisk@bisk.com; URL: http://www.bisk.com. Ed. Steve Galloway; Pub. Nathan M. Bisk. R&P contact: Andrew Titen. adv. contact: Vicki Mosen. (also avail. in microfiche from WSH,PMC; microfilm from WSH,PMC; audio cassette; video cassette; back issues avail.; reprint service avail. from WSH) **Indexed:** C.L.I., Leg.Per. **Document type:** proceedings.

336.2   SW   ISSN 0346-2854
TULLINFORMATION; tidskrift. 1974. 50/yr. SEK 340 (effective 1997). Generaltullstyrelsen, P.O. Box 2267, S-103 17 Stockholm. (Subscr. to: C.E. Fritzes AB, S-106 47 Stockholm, Sweden) **Document type:** newsletter.

336   TI   ISSN 0082-6820
TUNISIA. MINISTERE DU PLAN. BUDGET ECONOMIQUE. a. free. Ministere du Plan, Tunis, Tunisia. **Document type:** government publication.

336.2   US   ISSN 0083-0534
U S EXCISE TAX GUIDE. a. $22.50 paperback. C C H Incorporated, 2700 Lake Cook Rd., Riverwoods, IL 60015. TEL 847-267-7000; 800-835-5224. FAX 800-224-8299.

336   US   ISSN 1069-8914
KF6419.A65
U S INTERNATIONAL TAX FORMS MANUAL. a. $230.95 (foreign $325.45) (effective 1995). Warren, Gorham & Lamont, One Penn Plaza, New York, NY 10119. TEL 212-971-5000. FAX 212-971-5113. (Subscr. to: The Park Square Bldg., 31 St. James Ave., Boston, MA 02116-4112. TEL 800-950-1207) Ed. Stuart Singer. (looseleaf format) **Document type:** trade publication.
    Description: Provides a comprehensive guide to U.S. international tax reporting and compliance.

U S INTERNATIONAL TRANSFER PRICING. see *BUSINESS AND ECONOMICS — Banking And Finance*

BUSINESS AND ECONOMICS — PUBLIC FINANCE, TAXATION

336.2 US ISSN 0083-1700
KF6369.A1
U S MASTER TAX GUIDE. irreg. $160. C C H Incorporated, 2700 Lake Cook Rd., Riverwoods, IL 60015. TEL 847-267-7000; 800-835-5224. FAX 800-224-8299. (looseleaf format)
—CCC.

336 US ISSN 0745-8894
U S TAXATION OF INTERNATIONAL OPERATIONS. 1973. base vol. (plus s-m. Report Bulletins and articles). $495. Warren, Gorham & Lamont, One Penn Plaza, New York, NY 10110-4098. TEL 212-971-5000. FAX 212-971-5113. (Subscr. to: The Park Square Bldg., 31 St. James Ave., Boston, MA 02116-4112. TEL 800-950-1210) (looseleaf format)
Description: Examines special concerns of U.S. corporations and American citizens operating or investing abroad.

382 NE ISSN 0167-4064
U T C. (Uitspraken van de Tariefcommissie) (Supplement to: In- en Uitvoernieuws (ISSN 0019-3178)) 1953. bi-m. (Tariefcommissie) Uitgeverij Kluwer B.V., Postbus 23, 7400 GA Deventer, Netherlands. TEL 31-570-633155. FAX 31-570-633834. Ed.Bd. index. circ. 1,300. (looseleaf format)
—SWETS.
Formerly (until 1979): Uitspraken van de Tariefcommissie (ISSN 0041-5588).

336 GW ISSN 0937-387X
UMSATZSTEUER-KARTEI. irreg. DM.96. Erich Schmidt Verlag GmbH & Co. (Berlin), Genthiner Str. 30G, 10785 Berlin, Germany. TEL 49-30-250085-0. FAX 49-30-25008521. (looseleaf format) **Document type:** bulletin.

336.2 GW ISSN 0341-8669
KK7290.A13
UMSATZSTEUER-RUNDSCHAU. 1952. m. DM.208 (effective 1997). Verlag Dr. Otto Schmidt KG, Unter den Ulmen 96-98, 50968 Cologne, Germany. TEL 49-221-9373801. FAX 49-221-93738943. E-mail: dr.otto.schmidt@t-online.de. Ed.Bd. circ. 4,200. (reprint service avail. from SCH) **Document type:** bulletin.
—SWETS. CCC.

336 GW ISSN 0935-7998
UMSATZSTEUER- UND VERKEHRSTEUER-RECHT. 1909. m. DM.249 (effective 1997). Stollfuss Verlag Bonn, Postfach 2428, 53014 Bonn, Germany. TEL 49-228-724-0. FAX 49-228-659223. Ed. Friedrich Klenk. bk.rev.; index. circ. 900. **Document type:** bulletin.
—CCC.
Formerly: Deutsche Verkehrsteuer-Rundschau (ISSN 0341-8766)

336 GW ISSN 0940-8738
UMSATZSTEUERGESETZ. irreg. DM.196. Erich Schmidt Verlag GmbH & Co. (Berlin), Genthiner Str. 30G, 10785 Berlin, Germany. TEL 49-30-250085-0. FAX 49-30-25008521. (looseleaf format) **Document type:** bulletin.

336 CN ISSN 0838-8393
UNDERSTANDING INCOME TAX; for practitioners. a. Can.$49.95. Carswell, One Corporate Plaza, 2075 Kennedy Rd., Scarborough, ON M1T 3V4, Canada. TEL 416-609-8000. FAX 416-298-5094.
Description: Straightforward, non-technical guide to Canadian federal income tax law for the non-specialist.

330.9 TS
UNITED ARAB EMIRATES. AL-MASRAF AL-MARKAZI. AL-TAQRIR AL-SANAWI/UNITED ARAB EMIRATES. CENTRAL BANK. ANNUAL REPORT. (Text in Arabic, English) 1974. a. Central Bank, P.O. Box 854, Abu Dhabi, United Arab Emirates. TEL 652220. FAX 668483. TELEX 24173 MARKAZI EM. circ. controlled.
Description: Examines economic, financial and banking trends in the U.A.E. and in the international business climate.

336.3 US ISSN 0091-3553
HJ275
U.S. COMMUNITY SERVICES ADMINISTRATION. FEDERAL OUTLAYS IN SUMMARY.* Key Title: Federal Outlays in Summary. 1967. a. U.S. Community Services Administration, 1200 19th St., N.W., Washington, DC 20506. TEL 202-244-5840. (Orders to: National Technical Information Service, Springfield, VA 22151) stat. (also avail. in microfiche from NTI)
Formerly: U.S. Office of Economic Opportunity. Federal Outlays in Summary.

336 US ISSN 0884-1063
HJ10
U.S. DEPARTMENT OF THE TREASURY. FINANCIAL MANAGEMENT SERVICE. UNITED STATES GOVERNMENT ANNUAL REPORT AND APPENDIX. a. U.S. Department of the Treasury, Financial Management Service, Budget Reports Branch, 941 N. Capitol St., Rm. 749, Washington, DC 20227. TEL 202-208-1434. (Subscr. to: Supt. of Documents, Washington D.C. 20402) (back issues avail.) **Document type:** government publication.
Former titles: U.S. Department of the Treasury. Bureau of Government Financial Operations. Treasury Combined Statement of Receipts, Expenditures and Balances of the United States; U.S. Department of the Treasury. Combined Statement of Receipts, Expenditures and Balances of the United States.

336 US ISSN 0083-1476
U.S. INTERNAL REVENUE SERVICE. ANNUAL REPORT. Variant title: Commissioner's and Chief Counsel's. Annual Report. 1863. a. $5 4.060. U.S. Internal Revenue Service, 1111 Constitution Ave., N.W., Washington, DC 20224. TEL 800-829-1040. (Subscr. to: Superintendent of Documents, U.S. Government Printing Office, Box 371954, Pittsburgh, PA 15250-7954. TEL 202-512-1800. FAX 202-512-2250; Or: Bernan, 4611-F, Assembly Dr., Lanham, MD 20706. TEL 800-274-4447. FAX 301-459-0056) charts; illus.; maps; stat. **Document type:** government publication.
Description: Describes changes at the I.R.S. in 1990 and includes statistics on the number of tax returns received, amount of money the government raised, number and amount of tax refunds, and number of tax audits; also provides a list of officials.

336.2 US ISSN 0363-3594
KF6362.3
U.S. INTERNAL REVENUE SERVICE. BULLETIN INDEX - DIGEST SYSTEM: PART 1. INCOME TAX. base vol. plus irreg. supplements. $42 (foreign $52.50). U.S. Internal Revenue Service, 1111 Constitution Ave., N.W., Washington, DC 20024. (Subscr. to: Superintendent of Documents, U.S. Government Printing Office, Box 371954, Pittsburgh, PA 15250-7954. TEL 202-512-1800. FAX 202-512-2250) **Document type:** government publication.

336.2 345.05 US ISSN 0363-8456
KF6571.A65
U.S. INTERNAL REVENUE SERVICE. BULLETIN INDEX - DIGEST SYSTEM: PART 2. ESTATE AND GIFT TAXES. base vol. plus irreg. supplements. $23 (foreign $28.75). U.S. Internal Revenue Service, 1111 Constitution Ave., N.W., Washington, DC 20024. (Subscr. to: Superintendent of Documents, U.S. Government Printing Office, Box 371954, Pittsburgh, PA 15250-7954. TEL 202-512-1800. FAX 202-512-2250) **Document type:** government publication.

336.2 US ISSN 0363-8502
KF6362.3
U.S. INTERNAL REVENUE SERVICE. BULLETIN INDEX - DIGEST SYSTEM: PART 3. EMPLOYMENT TAXES. base vol. plus irreg. supplements. $22 (foreign $27.50). U.S. Internal Revenue Service, 1111 Constitution Ave., N.W., Washington, DC 20224. (Subscr. to: Superintendent of Documents, U.S. Government Printing Office, Box 371954, Pittsburgh, PA 15250-7954. TEL 202-512-1800. FAX 202-512-2250) **Document type:** government publication.

336.2 US ISSN 0363-8499
KF6600.A57
U.S. INTERNAL REVENUE SERVICE. BULLETIN INDEX - DIGEST SYSTEM: PART 4. EXCISE TAXES. base vol. plus irreg. supplements. $21 (foreign $26.25). U.S. Internal Revenue Service, 1111 Constitution Ave., N.W., Washington, DC 20224. (Subscr. to: Superintendent of Documents, U.S. Government Printing Office, Box 371954, Pittsburgh, PA 15250-7954. TEL 202-512-1800. FAX 202-512-2250) **Document type:** government publication.

336 US
U.S. INTERNAL REVENUE SERVICE. CONTROLLER'S MONTHLY FINANCIAL REPORT. m. U.S. Internal Revenue Service, 1111 Constitution Ave., N.W., Washington, DC 20224. (Subscr. to: Superintendent of Documents, U.S. Government Printing Office, Box 371954, Pittsburgh, PA 15250-7954. TEL 202-512-1800. FAX 202-512-2250) **Document type:** government publication.

U.S. INTERNAL REVENUE SERVICE. STATISTICS OF INCOME, FINAL CORPORATION INCOME TAX RETURNS. see BUSINESS AND ECONOMICS — Abstracting, Bibliographies, Statistics

U.S. INTERNAL REVENUE SERVICE. STATISTICS OF INCOME, FINAL INDIVIDUAL INCOME TAX RETURNS. see BUSINESS AND ECONOMICS — Abstracting, Bibliographies, Statistics

336.2 US ISSN 0083-1484
KF6491.A73
U.S. INTERNAL REVENUE SERVICE. TAX GUIDE FOR SMALL BUSINESS. 1956. a. U.S. Internal Revenue Service, 1111 Constitution Ave., N.W., Washington, DC 20224. TEL 800-829-1040.

336 US
U.S. INTERNAL REVENUE SERVICE. TAX MANAGEMENT PORTFOLIOS. irreg., no.384, 1992. price varies. U.S. Internal Revenue Service, I R S Bldg., 1111 Constitution Ave., Washington, DC 20224. (Dist. by: Bernan Press, 4611-F Assembly Dr., Lanham, MD 20706-4391. TEL 800-274-4447. FAX 301-459-0056; And: Superintendent of Documents, U.S. Government Printing Office, Box 371954, Pittsburgh, PA 15250-7954. TEL 202-512-1800. FAX 202-512-2240) **Document type:** government publication.

336 US
U.S. INTERNAL REVENUE SERVICE. TAX RULES OF PRACTICE. a. U.S. Internal Revenue Service, I R S Bldg., 1111 Constitution Ave., N.W., Washington, DC 20224. (Dist. by: Bernan Press, 4611-F Assembly Dr., Lanham, MD 20706-4391. TEL 800-274-4447. FAX 301-459-0056; And: Superintendent of Documents, U.S. Government Printing Office, Box 371954, Pittsburgh, PA 15250-7954. TEL 202-512-1800. FAX 202-512-2250) **Document type:** government publication.

332 US
U.S. OFFICE OF THE COMPTROLLER OF THE CURRENCY. INTERPRETATIONS AND ACTIONS. base vol. plus irreg. updates. $175 (effective 1996). U.S. Office of the Comptroller of the Currency, Administrator of National Banks, Washington, DC 20219. FAX 202-874-5263. (Subscr. to: Box 70004, Chicago, IL 60673-0004) **Document type:** trade publication, government publication.
Description: Includes legal staff interpretations, trust interpretive letters, securities letters, and bank accounting advisory series. Announces final enforcement actions against national banks and public evaluation, as well as final decisions under the Community Reinvestment Act.

BUSINESS AND ECONOMICS — PUBLIC FINANCE, TAXATION

332 US ISSN 0738-2146
HG2543
U.S. OFFICE OF THE COMPTROLLER OF THE CURRENCY. QUARTERLY JOURNAL. 1981. q. $100 (effective 1997). U.S. Office of the Comptroller of the Currency, Administrator of National Banks, Washington, DC 20219. FAX 202-874-5263. (Subscr. to: Box 70004, Chicago, IL 60673-0004) stat. circ. 6,000. (also avail. in microfiche from CIS; back issues avail.; reprint service avail. from CIS) **Indexed:** Amer.Stat.Ind. (1982-). **Document type:** government publication, academic/scholarly publication.
   Description: Records the most important O.C.C. actions and policies. Includes policy statements, decisions on banking structure, selected speeches, testimony, material released in the interpretive letters series, summaries of enforcement actions, and other information of interest to administrators of national banks.

336 341 NE
UNITED STATES INCOME TAX TREATIES. (Text in English) 1989. base vol. (plus s-a. updates). $247 (effective 1996). Kluwer Law International (Subsidiary of: Wolters Kluwer N.V.), Postbus 85889, 2508 CN The Hague, Netherlands. TEL 31-70-3081500. FAX 31-70-3081515. (Dist. by: Libresso Distribution Centre, P.O. Box 23, 7400 GA Deventer, Netherlands. TEL 31-570-633155. FAX 31-570-633834; In N. America: Kluwer Law International, 675 Massachusetts Ave., Cambridge, MA 02139. TEL 617-354-0140. FAX 617-354-8595) Ed.Bd. (looseleaf format)
   Description: Comprehensive reference to the more than 40 bilateral U.S. tax treaties in force, with expert commentary and analysis.

336 341 NE
UNITED STATES INTERNAL REVENUE SERVICE INTERNATIONAL TAX COMPLIANCE INFORMATION. (Text in English) 1992. 5 base vols. (plus irreg. updates, 1-2/yr.). fl.575($300) (effective 1993). Kluwer Law International (Subsidiary of: Wolters Kluwer N.V.), Postbus 85889, 2508 CN The Hague, Netherlands. TEL 31-70-3081500. FAX 31-70-3081515. (Dist. by: Libresso Distribution Centre, P.O. Box 23, 7400 GA Deventer, Netherlands. TEL 31-570-633155. FAX 31-570-633834; In N. America: Kluwer Law International, 675 Massachusetts Ave., Cambridge, MA 02139. TEL 617-354-0140. FAX 617-354-8595) Ed. Charles M. Bruce. (looseleaf format)
   Description: Contains coursework designed by agents of the I.R.S. Provides insight into what I.R.S. examiners have been taught to look for when reviewing international tax case.

336.2 340 US ISSN 0040-0017
HJ10
UNITED STATES TAX COURT REPORTS. 1924. m. $29 (foreign $36.25) (effective fall 1993). U.S. Tax Court, 400 Second St., N.W., Washington, DC 20217. TEL 202-783-3238. FAX 202-606-8704. (Subscr. to: Superintendent of Documents, U.S. Government Printing Office, Box 371954, Pittsburgh, PA 15250-9754. TEL 202-512-1800. FAX 202-512-2250) Ed. John T. Fee. index. circ. 2,663. (also avail. in microform from UMI,BHP,PMC; microfiche from BHP,WSH; back issues avail.) **Indexed:** L.I.I. **Document type:** government publication. ●Also available online. Vendor(s): West Group.
   Formerly: Board of Tax Appeals Reports.
   Description: Presents judicial decisions on points of law in cases heard in open court, for subsequent citation as precedent.

336 UK ISSN 0263-9947
V A T INTELLIGENCE. (Value Added Tax) 1983. m. £125. Gee & Co. Ltd., South Quay Plaza, 183 Marsh Wall, London E14 9FS, England. TEL 071-538-5386. FAX 071-538-8623. Eds. Ernest Hoskin, Victor Durkacz. **Indexed:** Euro.LJI, LJI. **Document type:** newsletter.

336 UK ISSN 0964-5985
V A T PLANNING. 1991. m. Butterworth & Co. (Publishers) Ltd., Part of the Reed Elsevier group, Halsbury House, 35 Chancery Ln., London WC2A 1EL, England. TEL 071-400-2500. FAX 071-400-2842. (U.S. addr.: Butterworth Legal Publishers, 90 Stiles Rd., Salem, NH 03079-9981. TEL 603-898-9664) Ed. Alan Buckett. **Indexed:** Euro.LJI, LJI.

336.2 NE ISSN 0042-2258
VAKSTUDIE NIEUWS; dokumentatie op het gebied van het fiscaal recht. 1945. fortn. Uitgeverij Kluwer B.V., Postbus 23, 7400 GA Deventer, Netherlands. TEL 31-570-633155. FAX 31-570-633834. Ed.Bd. adv.; bk.rev.; index. circ. 9,000. (looseleaf format) —SWETS.

336.2 UK
VALUE ADDED TAX AND DUTIES TRIBUNALS REPORTS. irreg. £18.50. (V A T and Duties Tribunal) Stationery Office, 51 Nine Elms Ln., London SW8 5DR, England. TEL 44-171-873-9090. FAX 44-171-873-8200. (Subscr. to: Publications Centre, P.O. Box 276, London SW8 5DT, England. TEL 44-171-873-8466. FAX 44-171-873-8222) **Document type:** government publication.
   Formerly (until 1996): Value Added Tax and Duties Reports.

336 AT
VICTORIA AND TASMANIA STAMP DUTIES. 1985. bi-m. C C H Australia Ltd., P.O. Box 230, North Ryde, N.S.W. 2113, Australia. TEL 61-1-300300224. FAX 61-1-300306224. (looseleaf format)
   Supersedes in part (in 1991): Australian Stamp Duties.
   Description: Covers stamp duty and related revenue legislation, with editorial commentary discussion on what is dutiable, how much duty is payable, and whether there are concessions and exemptions from duty.

336 US ISSN 0735-9004
K26
VIRGINIA TAX REVIEW. 1981. q. $45 (effective 1994-1995). Virginia Tax Review Association, University of Virginia, School of Law, Charlottesville, VA 22901. TEL 804-924-4726. FAX 804-924-7536. Ed. Kevin Cunningham. R&P contact: David Coolidge. adv. contact: Kimberly A. Crowder. circ. 750. (back issues avail.; reprint service avail. from RRI,WSH) **Indexed:** ABI Inform., Account.Ind. (1989-), C.L.I., L.R.I., Leg.Per. **Document type:** academic/scholarly publication. ●Also available online. Vendor(s): West Group. —KR SourceOne; UMI; UnCover.
   Description: Focuses on tax and tax-related matters; written by legal academics and practioners from scholarly and practical perspectives. Notes and comments by students.
   Refereed Serial

336 II
VYAPARI-MITRA. (Text in Marathi) 1950. m. Rs.100 (effective 1995). 106-9 Parashram Kuti, Erandawana J, Poona 4, India. TEL 647200. Ed. G.D. Sharma. adv.; bk.rev.; bibl. circ. 36,500. **Document type:** trade publication.

336 US
W G L TAX AUDIO ALERT. (Not avail. in printed format.) m. $225 (includes Audio Alert Quizzer) (foreign $292.50) (effective 1995). Warren, Gorham & Lamont, One Penn Plaza, New York, NY 10119. TEL 212-971-5000. FAX 212-971-5113. (Subscr. to: The Park Square Bldg., 31 St. James Ave., Boston, MA 02116-4112. TEL 800-950-1207) (audio cassette) **Document type:** trade publication.
   Description: Provides tax and tax law reports, analysis, and commentary.

336 US
W G L TAX JOURNAL DIGEST. 1981. a. $58.95 (overseas $115.65) (effective 1995). Warren, Gorham & Lamont, One Penn Plaza, New York, NY 10119. TEL 212-971-5000. FAX 212-971-5113. (Subscr. to: The Park Square Bldg., 31 St. James Ave., Boston, MA 02116-4112. TEL 800-950-1207) **Document type:** abstracting/indexing, trade publication.
   Description: Summarizes articles on federal taxation from other W.G.L. publications published during the previous year.

336 UK
WAKEFORD'S MANUAL OF EMPLOYEE TAXATION. base vol. (plus updates 3/yr.). £150($140) Butterworth & Co. (Publishers) Ltd., Part of the Reed Elsevier group, Halsbury House, 35 Chancery Ln., London WC2A 1EL, England. TEL 071-400-2500. FAX 071-400-2842. (U.S. addr.: Butterworth Legal Publishers, 90 Stiles Rd., Salem, NH 03079-9981. TEL 603-898-9664) Ed. A.H. Wakeford. (looseleaf format) **Document type:** trade publication.
   Description: Covers expenses and benefits, lump-sum payments and pensions, residence and domicile, and tax rules for overseas workers.

336.2 634.9 US
WASHINGTON (STATE). DEPARTMENT OF REVENUE. FOREST TAX SECTION. FOREST TAX ANNUAL REPORT. 1973. a. free. Department of Revenue, Box 47472, Olympia, WA 98504-7472. TEL 360-753-7086. FAX 360-664-8438. Ed. Bill Justis. **Document type:** corporate report, government publication.
   Former titles: Washington (State). Department of Revenue. Forest Tax Annual Report; Washington (State). Department of Revenue. Forest Tax Report (ISSN 0362-7462)

336.2 US
WASHINGTON (STATE). DEPARTMENT OF REVENUE. RESEARCH DIVISION. COMPARATIVE STATE - LOCAL TAXES. 1970. a. Department of Revenue, Research Division, Box 47459, Olympia, WA 98504-7459. TEL 360-753-2087. FAX 360-664-0972. stat.; circ. controlled. **Document type:** government publication.
   Formerly: Washington (State). Department of Revenue. Research and Information Division. Comparative State-Local Taxes.

WASHINGTON (STATE). DEPARTMENT OF REVENUE. RESEARCH DIVISION. PROPERTY TAX STATISTICS. see BUSINESS AND ECONOMICS — Abstracting, Bibliographies, Statistics

WASHINGTON (STATE). DEPARTMENT OF REVENUE. RESEARCH DIVISION. TAX STATISTICS. see BUSINESS AND ECONOMICS — Abstracting, Bibliographies, Statistics

336 US
WASHINGTON TAX DECISIONS. 1987. irreg. (approx. 3 vols./yr.). $60 per vol. Butterworth Legal Publishers (Salem) (Subsidiary of: Reed Elsevier plc), 8 Industrial Way, Bldg. C, Salem, NH 03079. TEL 800-548-4001. FAX 603-898-9858. Ed.Bd. (looseleaf format)

336 US
WASHINGTON TAX REPORTER. 1984. irreg. free. Ernst & Young (Washington), Box 33337, Washington, DC 20033-0337. TEL 202-663-9500. FAX 202-663-9510. Ed. S.T. Reiner. circ. 240,000.

336 346 US
WASHINGTON TAXES; a taxpayer's manual for practice before the Department of Revenue. 1992. base vol. (plus supplements). $95. Butterworth Legal Publishers (Salem) (Subsidiary of: Reed Elsevier plc), 8 Industrial Way, Bldg. C, Salem, NH 03079. TEL 800-548-4001. FAX 603-898-9858. Ed. Martin Silver. (looseleaf format)
   Description: Problem solving guide for accountants, attorneys and small business owners, covering current policies and practices of the Washington State Department of Revenue.

336 US
WEST VIRGINIA TAX CALENDAR. 1950. a. $10. West Virginia Chamber of Commerce, Box 2789, Charleston, WV 25330. TEL 304-342-1115. **Document type:** trade publication.

336 AT
WESTERN AUSTRALIA STAMP DUTIES. 1985. q. C C H Australia Ltd., P.O. Box 230, North Ryde, N.S.W. 2113, Australia. TEL 61-1-300300224. FAX 61-1-300306224. (looseleaf format)
   Supersedes in part (in 1991): Australian Stamp Duties.
   Description: Covers stamp duty and related revenue legislation, with editorial commentary discussing what is dutiable, how much duty is payable, when and how duty is payable, and whether there are concessions and exemptions from duty.

BUSINESS AND ECONOMICS — PUBLIC FINANCE, TAXATION

336   US
WEST'S TAX LAW DICTIONARY. 1992. a. West Group, 620 Opperman Dr., Eagan, MN 55123. TEL 612-687-8000; 800-328-9352. FAX 612-687-7302. **Document type:** trade publication.

343.055   BE
WETBOEK FISCAAL RECHT - B.T.W/CODE DE DROIT FISCAL - TAXE SUR LA VALEUR AJOUTEE. (Text in Dutch, French) 7 base vols. (plus updates 3/yr.). 7350 BEF. Kluwer Rechtswetenschappen Belgie, Editions Story-Scientia (Subsidiary of: Wolters Kluwer N.V.), Santvoortbeeklaan 21-25, 2100 Antwerp, Belgium. FAX 32-3-3600467. Eds. Frans Vanistendael, Inge Van De Woesteyne. (looseleaf format) **Document type:** trade publication.
   Description: Covers value added taxation (VAT) in Belgium.

343.052   BE
WETBOEK FISCAAL RECHT - INKOMSTENBELASTING. (Text in Dutch, French) 5 base vols. (plus updates 3/yr.). 13500 BEF. Kluwer Rechtswetenschappen Belgie, Editions Story-Scientia (Subsidiary of: Wolters Kluwer N.V.), Santvoortbeeklaan 21-25, 2100 Antwerp, Belgium. FAX 32-3-3600467. Eds. Frans Vanistendael, Peter Verbanck. (looseleaf format) **Document type:** trade publication.

336 352   US   ISSN 1083-1347
WHAT'S WORKING IN STATE AND LOCAL GOVERNMENT. 1977. bi-m. $247 (effective 1996). Government Information Services, 4301 Fairfax Dr., Ste. 875, Arlington, VA 22203-1627. TEL 703-528-1000. FAX 703-528-6060. Ed. Donald Hoffman. (back issues avail.)
   Formerly (until 1995): Financing Local Government; Incorporated (1977-1994): Urban Outlook (ISSN 0732-8265); Which incorporated: Urban Futures Idea Exchange (ISSN 0147-7137); Incorporated (in 1990): Privatization Report (ISSN 1042-9395); Which was formerly (until 1988): Privitization (ISSN 0888-7446); (until 1986): Privitization Report (ISSN 0887-7718); Former titles (until June 1988): Survival News for Cities and Towns (ISSN 0892-3612); Which was formed by the Feb. 1987 merger of: Revenue Enhancement Reporter (ISSN 0886-053X); And: Cost Cutting Digest (Arlington) (ISSN 0886-4128); Which both superseded (in Dec. 1986): Shared Revenues Report (ISSN 0273-4494); Which incorporated (in 1985): Revenue Raising and Cost Cutting Report (ISSN 0742-6437); Which was formed by the 1984 merger of: Cost Cutting Digest (ISSN 0740-4905) & Revenue Raising Report (ISSN 0740-4891).
   Description: Shows proven techniques that other governments have used to cut the cost of local government and expand their revenue base through innovative tax levies, user fees and portfolio management.

336.2   UK   ISSN 0260-3926
WHILLANS'S TAX TABLES. 1948. a. £3.50($6) Butterworth & Co. (Publishers) Ltd., Part of the Reed Elsevier group, Halsbury House, 35 Chancery Ln., London WC2A 1EL, England. TEL 071-400-2500. FAX 071-400-2842. (U.S. addr.: Butterworth Legal Publishers, 90 Stiles Rd., Salem, NH 03079-9981. TEL 603-898-9664) Ed. Sheila Parrington. circ. 24,000.
   Formerly: Whillan's Tax Tables and Tax Reckoner (ISSN 0308-7948)
   Description: Covers income tax, inheritance tax, capital gains tax, corporation tax, and other related subjects.

336   CN
WINDOW ON CANADIAN TAX. 1991. m. Can.$595. C C H Canadian Ltd., 6 Garamond Ct., North York, ON M3C 1Z5, Canada. TEL 416-441-2992; 800-268-4522. FAX 416-444-9011. (also avail. in diskette format) **Document type:** trade publication.
   Description: Summarizes and comments on the most important Revenue Canada income tax documents obtained under the Access to Information Act.

THE WISCONSIN TAXPAYER. see *PUBLIC ADMINISTRATION*

336   GW
WOHNEN-ZEITSCHRIFT FUER DAS WOHNUNGSWESEN IN BAYERN. 1903. m. DM.60. Verband Bayerischer Wohnungsunternehmen e.V., Stollbergstr. 7, 80539 Munich, Germany. FAX 089-2285940. adv.; bk.rev. circ. 2,000. **Document type:** consumer publication.
   Formerly: Zeitschrift fuer das Gemeinnuetzige Wohnungswesen in Bayern.

336   UK
WORLD DIRECTORY OF TAX ADVISERS (YEAR). 1993. a. Euromoney Publications plc., Nestor House, Playhouse Yard, London EC4V 5EX, England. TEL 0171-779-8935. FAX 0171-779-8541. Ed. Matt Morgan; Pub. Dominic Carman. **Document type:** trade publication.

336.3   US   ISSN 0363-4795
HJ7469
WORLD MILITARY AND SOCIAL EXPENDITURES. 1974. a. $7. World Priorities, Inc., Box 25140, Washington, DC 20007. TEL 202-965-1661. Ed. Ruth Leger Sivard. charts; circ. 20,000 (paid). **Indexed:** SRI. **Document type:** academic/scholarly publication.
—BLDSC (9356.674600).
   Description: Report on the use of world resources for two kinds of priorities: military power and human needs. Includes background data for 142 countries.

336   UK
WORLD TAX NEWS. q. Touche Ross & Co. (Subsidiary of: Deloitte Touche Tohmatsu International), 1 Little New St., London EC4A 3TR, England. TEL 0171-936-3000. FAX 0171-583-8517. **Document type:** trade publication.
   Formerly: International Tax News.

336   UK
WORLDWIDE LIVING COSTS. 1973. 2/yr. £650. P-E International plc, Park House, Wick Rd., Egham, Surrey TW20 0HW, England. TEL 44-1784-434411. FAX 44-1784-476369. **Document type:** corporate report.
   Formerly: International Taxation & Cost of Living. *Refereed Serial*

336.2   US
WORLDWIDE TAX TREATIES ON C D - R O M. m., q., and a. versions avail. $999 for m.; q. $949; a. $919. Tax Analysts, 6830 N. Fairfax Dr., Arlington, VA 22213. TEL 800-955-2444. FAX 703-533-4444.
● Available only on CD-ROM.
   Description: Contains the full text of more than 2,600 U.S. and non U.S. tax treaties, legislative histories of U.S. treaties, and treaty-related news and commentary.

336.2   US
HJ11
WYOMING. DEPARTMENT OF REVENUE. ANNUAL REPORT. 1973. a. $4. Department of Revenue, Herschler Bldg., Cheyenne, WY 82002-0110. TEL 307-777-7961. stat. circ. 150. **Indexed:** SRI. **Document type:** government publication.
   Formerly: Wyoming. Department of Revenue and Taxation. Annual Report (ISSN 0094-9019)

336   IS   ISSN 0333-5666
YEDA LEMEIDA; journal on taxation, law and economics. 1977. m. Raayonote Ltd., P.O. Box 26051, Tel Aviv 61 260, Israel. TEL 03-295749.

336   GW
Z T R. (Zeitschrift fuer Tarifrecht) m. DM.312. Verlagsgruppe Jehle Rehm GmbH, Einsteinstr. 172, 81675 Munich, Germany. TEL 49-89-41979-0. FAX 49-89-41979230. Ed. Winrich Bolck. **Document type:** trade publication.

336   SZ
ZAHLUNGSBILANZ DER SCHWEIZ.* French edition: Balance Suisse des Paiements. (Supplement to: Switzerland. Eidgenoessisches Volkswirtschaftsdepartement. Volkswirtschaft und Schweizerische Nationalbank. Monatsbericht) a. Schweizerische Nationalbank, Postfach, CH-8002 Zurich, Switzerland. **Document type:** government publication.
   Formerly: Ertragsbilanz der Schweiz.

336   CG
ZAIRE. DIRECTION GENERALE DES FINANCES. BULLETIN DES FINANCES. no.9, 1975. bi-m. K.10. Direction Generale des Finances, Division des Etudes et de la Documentation, B.P. 12997, Kinshasa, Democratic Republic of the Congo. illus.; stat. **Document type:** bulletin.

336.2   NE   ISSN 0923-5531
ZAKBOEKJE VOOR DE BELASTINGCONTROLE. 1986. a. fl.34. Gouda Quint B.V. (Subsidiary of: Wolters Kluwer N.V.), Postbus 1148, 6801 MK Arnhem, Netherlands. (Dist. by: Libresso Distribution Centre, P.O. Box 23, 7400 GA Deventer, Netherlands. TEL 31-570-633155. FAX 31-570-633834) Eds. R.N.J. Kamerling, H.L. Haxe.
   Description: Presents reference information relating to taxation and fiscal control.

336   ZA
ZAMBIA. DEPARTMENT OF CUSTOMS AND EXCISE. ANNUAL REPORT OF THE CONTROLLER OF CUSTOMS AND EXCISE. (Text in English) a. Zambia Government Printing Department, P.O. Box 30136, Lusaka, Zambia. **Document type:** government publication.
   Description: Reports on imposition, collection and management of customs, excise and other duties in Zambia.

336.2   ZA   ISSN 0084-4675
ZAMBIA. DEPARTMENT OF TAXES. ANNUAL REPORT OF THE COMMISSIONER OF TAXES. 1964. a. K.150. Zambia Government Printing Department, P.O. Box 30136, Lusaka, Zambia. **Document type:** government publication.
   Description: Covers collecting of income taxes in Zambia.

336   ZA   ISSN 0084-4683
ZAMBIA. DEPARTMENT OF THE ADMINISTRATOR-GENERAL AND OFFICIAL RECEIVER. REPORT. 1964. a. K.100. Zambia Government Printing Department, P.O. Box 30136, Lusaka, Zambia. **Document type:** government publication.

336   ZA   ISSN 0303-2760
ZAMBIA. OFFICE OF THE AUDITOR-GENERAL. REPORT OF THE AUDITOR-GENERAL. 1963. a. K.100. Zambia Government Printing Department, P.O. Box 30136, Lusaka, Zambia. **Document type:** government publication.
   Description: Reports on government accounting principles.

336.2   JA
ZEIMU TOKEI KARA MITA HOJIN KIGYO NO JITTAI. Short title: Hojin Kigyo no Jittai. (Text in Japanese) 1963. a. 1800 Yen. (Ministry of Finance - Okura-sho) Government Publications Service Center, 2-1, 1-chome, Kasumigaseki, Chiyoda-ku, Tokyo 100, Japan. **Document type:** government publication.

ZEITSCHRIFT FUER ERBRECHT UND VERMOEGENSNACHFOLGE; Erbrecht - Gesellschaftsrecht - Steuerrecht. see *LAW — Civil Law*

336   GW   ISSN 0940-6867
ZEITSCHRIFT FUER VERMOEGENS- UND INVESTITIONSRECHT; Privatisierung - Restitution - Rehabilitierung in den neuen Bundeslaendern. Abbreviated title: V I Z. 1991. m. DM.366 (effective 1997). Verlag C.H. Beck, 80791 Munich, Germany. TEL 49-89-38189338. FAX 49-89-38189398. Ed.Bd. adv.: B&W page DM.2300, color DM.4025; trim 260 x 186. circ. 3,000. (back issues avail.) **Document type:** bulletin.
● Also available on CD-ROM.

336   GW
ZEITSCHRIFT FUER ZOELLE; Aussenwirtschaft, Finanzpolitik, Marktordnung. 1925. m. DM.310 (effective 1997). Stollfuss Verlag Bonn, Postfach 2428, 53014 Bonn, Germany. TEL 49-228-724-0. FAX 49-228-659223. Eds. Prof. Hampel, Prof. Arendt. **Indexed:** ELLIS. **Document type:** bulletin.
—BLDSC (9496.400000); SWETS. **CCC.**
   Formerly: Zeitschrift fuer Zoelle und Verbrauchersteuern (ISSN 0342-3484)

BUSINESS AND ECONOMICS — SMALL BUSINESS

336   CC   ISSN 1003-4471
ZHONGGUO SHUIWU/CHINA TAXATION. (Text in Chinese) m. Y54 (foreign $26) (effective 1998). (Guojia Shuiwu-ju) Zhongguo Shuiwu Zazhishe, 68 Zaolin Qianjie, Beijing 100053, People's Republic of China. TEL 86-10-6318-2991.
FAX 86-10-6318-3007. (Dist. overseas by: China International Book Trading Corp., P.O. Box 399, Beijing 100044, P.R. China; Dist. in US by: China Books & Periodicals, Inc., 2929 24th St., San Francisco, CA 94110. TEL 415-282-2994) Ed. Zhang Musheng. **Document type:** trade publication.
    Description: Covers Chinese policies and regulations on taxation.

336.2   CC
ZHONGGUO SHUIWU BAO/CHINA TAXATION NEWS. (Text in Chinese) 1991. 3/w. (Guojia Shuiwu Ju) Zhongguo Shuiwu Bao Bianjibu, Ganshiqiao, Guang'anmen Wai, Xuanwu Qu, Beijing 100055, People's Republic of China. TEL 86-10-3269646. (Dist. overseas by: China International Book Trading Corp., P.O. Box 399, Beijing 100044, P.R. China) Ed. Yang Youjun; Pub. Guan Yongning. **Document type:** newspaper.

336   RH
ZIMBABWE. MINISTRY OF FINANCE. BUDGET ESTIMATES. 1940. a. Z.$12. Ministry of Finance, Private Bag 7705, Causeway, Harare, Zimbabwe. TEL 263-4-722101. FAX 263-4-796563. (Subscr. to: Government Printer, P.O. Box CY 341, Causeway, Zimbabwe) circ. 1,200. **Document type:** government publication.
    Former titles (until 1995): Zimbabwe. Ministry of Finance. Estimates of Expenditure; (until 1992): Zimbabwe. Ministry of Finance. Financial Statement; Rhodesia. Ministry of Finance. Budget Statement.

336   RH
ZIMBABWE. MINISTRY OF FINANCE. ESTIMATES OF EXPENDITURE. Cover title: Estimates of Expenditure - Zimbabwe. a. $3 (effective 1992). Department of Printing and Stationery, P.O. Box 8062, Causeway, Harare, Zimbabwe. **Document type:** government publication.

350.724 382.7   DK   ISSN 0105-8355
ZISE; told- og skattehistorisk tidsskrift. 1978. 3/yr. DKK 60. Told- og Skattehistorisk Selskab, Oestbanegade 123, DK-2100 Copenhagen Oe, Denmark. TEL 45-35-29-73-00.
FAX 45-35-29-29-18. Ed. Mikael Venge. R&P contact: Gunnar Jakobsen. bk.rev. circ. 2,400.

350.724   SZ
ZOLL - RUNDSCHAU/REVUE DES DOUANES/RIVISTA DELLE DOGANE; Fachzeitschrift des Schweizerischen Zollpersonals. (Text in German, French and Italian) 1956. 4/yr. Directorate General of Customs, Section Information, Monbijoustr. 40, CH-3003 Bern, Switzerland. TEL 41-31-3226743.
FAX 41-31-3224294. TELEX 911100-OZD-CH. E-mail: roger.gauderon@ezv.admin.ch. Ed. Roger Gauderon. illus. **Document type:** government publication.

336   GW   ISSN 0939-2165
ZOLLRECHT. irreg. DM.148. Erich Schmidt Verlag GmbH & Co. (Berlin), Genthiner Str. 30G, 10785 Berlin, Germany. TEL 49-30-250085-0.
FAX 49-30-25008521. (looseleaf format) **Document type:** bulletin.

336   US
ZONDERVAN CHURCH AND NONPROFIT ORGANIZATION TAX AND FINANCIAL GUIDE. 1991. a. $14.99. Zondervan Publishing House, 5300 Patterson Ave. S.E., Grand Rapids, MI 49530. TEL 616-698-6900; 800-727-3480. FAX 616-698-3439. Ed. Stan Gundry; Pub. Scott Bolinder. R&P contact: Carolyn Weidmayer. circ. 20,000. **Document type:** consumer publication.
    Description: A complete tax and financial guide for churches and other organizations to help prepare their tax returns each year.

336   US
ZONDERVAN MINISTER'S TAX & FINANCIAL GUIDE. 1991. a. $14.99. Zondervan Publishing House, 5300 Patterson Ave. S.E., Grand Rapids, MI 49530. TEL 616-698-6900; 800-727-3480.
FAX 616-698-3439. Ed. Stan Gundry. R&P contact: Carolyn Weidmayer. circ. 20,000.
    Description: A complete guide to help ministers prepare their tax returns each year and plan their financial futures.

336.2   US   ISSN 0363-2997
1040 PREPARATION. a. $37.50. C C H Incorporated, 2700 Lake Cook Rd., Riverwoods, IL 60015. TEL 847-267-7000; 800-835-5224.
FAX 800-224-8299. illus.
    Formerly (until 1976): Practical Guide to Individual Income Tax Return Preparation (ISSN 0098-1575)

336   US   ISSN 0897-4306
1040 REPORT. 1979. m. $20. National Association of Tax Practitioners, 720 Association Dr., Appleton, WI 54914-1483. TEL 414-749-1040.
FAX 414-749-1062. Ed. David Mellem. R&P contact: David Mellem. circ. 16,000. (back issues avail.) **Document type:** newsletter.
    Description: Tax preparation information for accountants, attorneys and CPAs.

BUSINESS AND ECONOMICS — Small Business

A B C DIALOGUE. (Association of Bridal Consultants) see MATRIMONY

338   US
A S B A TODAY. bi-m. $18. American Small Businesses Association, Box 3323, Oakton, VA 22124. TEL 202-628-6316. Ed. Kristin Liercke. R&P contact: Kristin Liercke. bk.rev.; circ. 65,000 (controlled).

336   US
ABAPA FREER. 1992. q. $7 for 5 nos. Correspan, Box 759-ULR, Veneta, OR 97487. Ed. Pat Underhill. bk.rev. circ. 3,000. (back issues avail.) **Document type:** consumer publication.
    Description: Forum about places with fewer taxes and restrictions and more tolerance, and about decentralized networking techniques.

ACCOUNTING FORUM. see BUSINESS AND ECONOMICS — Accounting

AGENDA. see ART

ALASKA BUSINESS MONTHLY. see BUSINESS AND ECONOMICS

AMERICAN OSTRICH. see AGRICULTURE

AMERICAN WINDOW CLEANER; voice of the professional window cleaner. see OCCUPATIONAL HEALTH AND SAFETY

650   IT   ISSN 0004-3737
ARTIGIANO MODENESE. 1960. m. L.1000. Libero Artigianato e Piccole Aziende Modenesi, Via Emilia Ouest 101, 41100 Modena, Italy. Ed. Jacobbe Giovanni. circ. 6,000.

338   FR   ISSN 0153-2006
ARTISANAT BATIMENT 34. 1975. q. Syndicat des Artisans et des Petites Entreprises du Batiment de l'Herault, 44 av. St. Lazare, 34000 Montpellier, France. Ed. Jose Maldonado. adv.

338   FR
ARTISANAT FRANCAIS. 1947. m. 2 F. per no. 30 rue Vinaigriers, 75010 Paris, France. adv.

338   CC   ISSN 1019-2239
ASIA INC. (Text in English) 1992. m. HK.$349($79) Asia, Inc. Ltd., 8-F Kinwick Centre, 32 Hollywood Rd., Central, Hong Kong, People's Republic of China. TEL 852-2581-8088. FAX 852-2851-0302. E-mail: adsales@asia-inc.com; editors@asia-inc.com; URL: http://www.asia-inc.com/. Ed. William Mellor; Pub. Anne Lim. adv.: B&W page $8850, color page $11500; trim 205 x 270; adv. contact: Anne Lim. circ. 75,000. Indexed: Manage.Cont. Tr.& Indus.Ind.
● Also available online.
    Description: Covers Asian business, economic and political issues, travel, leisure and self-improvement.

338   US
ATLANTA SMALL BUSINESS MONTHLY.* 1987. 12/yr. $15. Media 3 Publications, Inc., 4721 Chamblee Dunwoody Rd., 100-B, Atlanta, GA 30338-6000. TEL 404-394-2811. FAX 404-394-2719. Ed. Millann Funk. adv.; bk.rev.; circ. 25,000 (controlled). (tabloid format) **Document type:** newspaper.
    Formerly: Atlanta Small Business Journal.
    Description: Provides "how to" information for owners of small to mid-size businesses; presents such topics as advertising, marketing, finance management, selling and customer service.

AUSTRALIA. BUREAU OF STATISTICS. SMALL BUSINESS IN AUSTRALIA. see BUSINESS AND ECONOMICS — Abstracting, Bibliographies, Statistics

338   UK
B R A V E. 3/yr. Coach House Small Business Centre, 2 Upper York St., Bristol BS2 8QN, England. TEL 0272-272222. FAX 0272-445661. Ed. Neil Pickford. circ. 4,000.

338   BG
BANGLADESH SMALL AND COTTAGE INDUSTRIES CORPORATION. BULLETIN. (Text in Bengali) m. Bangladesh Small and Cottage Industries Corporation, 137-138, Motijheel Commercial Area, Dhaka 2, Bangladesh. **Document type:** bulletin.

BANQUES DES PROFESSIONNELS. see BUSINESS AND ECONOMICS — Banking And Finance

338   US   ISSN 0736-1904
BARTER UPDATE. 1983. a. $4. Update Publicare Co., c/o Prosperity & Profits Unlimited, Distribution Services, Box 416, Denver. TEL 303-575-5676. Ed. A. Doyle. adv.; bibl. circ. 1,000. (looseleaf format; also avail. in microfiche; back issues avail.) **Document type:** newsletter.
—CCC.

338 658.8   US   ISSN 1085-7974
▼**BASKETELL**; the quarterly newsletter for savvy gift basket professionals. 1996. q. $14.95 (effective 1997). Sweet Survival, Box 31, River Street Sta., Paterson, NJ 07544-0031. TEL 973-279-2799. FAX 973-742-0700. E-mail: survival@ix.netcom. com. Ed. Shirley Frazier. circ. 125 (paid). (back issues avail.) **Document type:** newsletter, trade publication.
    Description: Provides ideas and information for gift basket professionals in all stages of development.

338.6   BE   ISSN 0067-5393
BELGIUM. CONSEIL SUPERIEUR DES CLASSES MOYENNES. RAPPORT ANNUEL DU SECRETAIRE GENERAL. Dutch edition: Belgium. Hoge Raad voor de Middenstand. Jaarverslag van de Secretaris Generaal. (Text in French) 1951. a. free. Conseil Superieur des Classes Moyennes, Tour Sablon, 7 rue J. Stevens, B-1000 Brussels, Belgium. **Document type:** government publication.

338   US   ISSN 0740-5669
BETTER BUSINESS. 1981. s-a. $12. National Minority Business Council, Inc., 235 E. 42nd St., New York, NY 10017. TEL 212-573-2385. Ed. John F. Robinson. adv.; bk.rev. circ. 10,000.

338 371.42   CN   ISSN 1198-8819
BIG DREAMS. Online edition (CN ISSN 1200-5460) 1994. m. $20. 2202 Haversley Ave., Coquitlam, BC V3J 1W4, Canada. TEL 604-760-1631.
FAX 604-931-2135. E-mail: duncans@wimsey.com; URL: http://www.wimsey.com/~duncans/BigDreams. Ed. Duncan Stickings. (back issues avail.)
● Also available online.

650   II   ISSN 0006-2219
BIHAR INDUSTRIES; quarterly bulletin for small industries. (Text in English and Hindi) 1962. q. Rs.5. Directorate of Industries, Department of Industries and Technical Education, Patna, Bihar, India. Ed. S. Krishnan. adv.; bk.rev.; charts; pat.; stat. circ. 2,500. **Document type:** bulletin.

338   US
BIZ TIPS NEWSLETTER. m. free. E-mail: bizinfo@bizresource.com; URL: http://www.bizresource.com. **Document type:** newsletter.
● Available only online.
    Description: Full of tips, ideas and motivation for entrepreneurs.

BUSINESS AND ECONOMICS — SMALL BUSINESS

338 US ISSN 1063-3561
BOOTSTRAPPIN' ENTREPRENEUR; the newsletter for individuals with great ideas and a little bit of cash. 1992. q. $30 (effective 1994). Research Done Write, 6308 W. 89th St., Ste. 306-UI, Los Angeles, CA 90045. TEL 310-568-9861. E-mail: ibootstrap@aol.com. Ed. Kimberly Stansell. (looseleaf format) **Document type:** newsletter.
Description: Covers starting and building a business on a mini-budget, including low-cost marketing strategies, management ideas, success stories.

338 FR ISSN 0755-1541
BULLETIN DES METIERS ET DE L'ARTISANAT. 1940. 11/yr. 62 rue La Boetie, 75008 Paris, France. TEL 45-61-04-61. FAX 45-63-95-43. Ed. Josette Lapierre. circ. 25,000. **Document type:** bulletin.

338 US
BUSINESS DIGEST OF DELAWARE VALLEY. 1977. 12/yr. $20. Business Digest of Philadelphia Inc., 2449 Golf Rd., Philadelphia, PA 19131. TEL 215-477-8620. adv. circ. 25,000.
•Also available online. Vendor(s): Knight-Ridder Information, Inc.
Description: Focuses on small business.

338 658.8 AT ISSN 1031-2315
BUSINESS DIRECTIONS; ideas & inspiration for better business. 1987. 8/yr. Aus.$49; newsstand price: Aus.$6.25. Victory Press Pty. Ltd., P.O. Box 565, Victoria Park, W.A. 6100, Australia. TEL 61-9-4702353. FAX 61-9-4702363. E-mail: bosubs@business.com.au; URL: http://www.business.com.au/business. Ed. Richard Keeves. adv. contact: David Dell. circ. 10,000. (back issues avail.) **Document type:** consumer publication.
•Also available online.
—UnCover.

BUSINESS EXCHANGE. see *BUSINESS AND ECONOMICS — Investments*

338 CN
BUSINESS EXECUTIVE. 1994. m. Can.$48 (effective 1997). Business Executive Inc., 466 Speers Rd., Ste. 220, Oakville ON L6K 3W9, Canada. TEL 905-845-8300. FAX 905-845-9086. E-mail: wendyp@interlog.com; URL: http://www.busexec.com. Ed. Wendy Peters; Pub. Thomas Peters. R&P contact: Thomas Peters. adv.: B&W page Can.$2200; trim 10 x 14; adv. contact: Thomas Peters. bk.rev.; software rev.; circ. 30,000 (controlled). cols./p.: 4; pp./issue: 20. (tabloid format) **Document type:** newspaper.
Description: Contains local business news coverage, columns on human resources, law, computers, finance, and physical fitness submitted by local business people. Also automobile column and local government pages.

338 UK ISSN 0955-789X
BUSINESS FRANCHISE. 10/yr. £20 (foreign £40) (effective 1996). Blenheim House, 630 Chiswick High Rd., London W4 5BG, England. TEL 0181-742-7828. FAX 0181-742-0387. Ed. Lynne Lister. adv. contact: Sara Caitlin. circ. 20,000. **Document type:** consumer publication.

338 346.066 US ISSN 0274-8991
BUSINESS FRANCHISE GUIDE. 2 base vols. (plus m. reports). $794. C C H Incorporated, 2700 Lake Cook Rd., Riverwoods, IL 60015. TEL 847-267-7000; 800-835-5224. FAX 800-224-8299. **Document type:** consumer publication.

BUSINESS GAZETTE. see *BUSINESS AND ECONOMICS — Management*

338 UK ISSN 1355-6347
▼**BUSINESS, GROWTH & PROFITABILITY.** 1995. q. £115 (outside European Union £130). Henry Stewart Publications, Russell House, 28-30 Little Russell St., London WC1A 2HN, England. TEL 44-171-404-3040. FAX 44-171-404-2081. E-mail: 100622.3264@compuserve.com. (Subscr. in US and Canada to: 810 E. 10th St., Box 1897, Lawrence, KS 66044. TEL 913-843-1221. FAX 913-843-1274) Ed. Daryn Moody. adv. contact: Fraser Tant. **Document type:** trade publication.
Description: Publishes detailed advice, research and opinion on topics of direct use to small and medium-sized businesses.
Refereed Serial

338 US
BUSINESS HOTLINE ONLINE. m. E-mail: webmaster@bizhotline.com; URL: http://www.bizhotline.com.
•Available only online.
Description: Covers topics facing today's small and home based businesses: accounting and finance, legal issues, direct mail, public speaking, personal finance, marketing tips, import & export, business opportunities, franchising information and marketing on the internet.

338 US
BUSINESS IN BROWARD. 1987. 8/yr. $32 (effective 1997). Lauderdale Publishing, 1301 Andrews Ave., P.O. Box 7375, Ft. Lauderdale, FL 33316. TEL 954-763-3338. FAX 954-763-4481. E-mail: SFBIZ@mindspring.com. Ed. Cathy Duber; Pub. Sherry Friedlander. adv.: B&W page $1900, color page $2400; trim 8 1/2 x 11; adv. contact: Fran Salis. bk.rev. circ. 30,000. (also avail. in microform from UMI)
•Also available online. Vendor(s): Lexis-Nexis, UMI.
Description: Covers local business and features local people.

338 UK ISSN 0266-8297
BUSINESS INFORMER. 1984. bi-m. £24 (foreign £29) (effective Sep. 1995). Denholme Publishing, P.O. Box 39, Hartlepool, Cleveland TS24 1SJ, England. TEL 44-191-518-4281. Ed. Alan K. Roxborough; Pub. Alan K. Roxborough. bk.rev.; circ. 70,000 (paid). (also avail. in diskette format; back issues avail.)
Description: Digests UK and EU business legislation and provides associated business information for small- and medium-sized businesses, trade bodies, and business-support groups.

338 US ISSN 1056-6244
BUSINESS INSIGHT (RICHLAND). 1985. m. $24 (free to qualified personnel). B C O Marketing Communications, Inc., Box 347, Richland, MI 49083-0347. TEL 616-629-3131. FAX 616-629-0803. Ed. Amy Scoville; Pub. Robert Beardsley. R&P contact: Robert Beardsley. adv. contact: Melanie DeVries. bk.rev.; circ. 8,692 (controlled). (back issues avail.) **Document type:** trade publication.
Formerly (until 1991): Business Digest (ISSN 0897-5221)
Description: Provides local small-business executives with information to help them effectively participate in the local business community.

THE BUSINESS JOURNAL (LIMA); West Central Ohio's leading business publication. see *BUSINESS AND ECONOMICS — Domestic Commerce*

338 US
THE BUSINESS NEWS. 1990. fortn. $24. American City Business Journals, Inc. (Dayton), 322 S. Patterson Blvd., Dayton, OH 45402-2866. TEL 513-222-6900. FAX 513-222-9967. Ed. Tim Tresslar; Pub. Dave Smith. adv. contact: Dave Smith. bk.rev. circ. 12,000. **Document type:** newspaper.
Formerly: Miami Valley Business News.

338 US ISSN 0279-4276
HC107.N8
BUSINESS NORTH CAROLINA. 1981. m. $30. News and Observer Publishing Co., 5435 77 Center Dr., Ste. 50, Charlotte, NC 28217-0711. TEL 704-523-6987. FAX 704-523-4211. Ed. David Kinney. adv.; circ. 26,000 (paid). (also avail. in microform from UMI) **Indexed:** Tr.& Indus.Ind. **Document type:** trade publication.
•Also available online. Vendor(s): Information Access Co., Knight-Ridder Information, Inc., Lexis-Nexis, UMI. —UMI.

338 UK ISSN 0265-3591
BUSINESS OPPORTUNITIES DIGEST. 1982. m. £15. Institute of Small Business, Centre for Business Development, 95 Kippling Ave., Goring-by-Sea, W. Sussex BN12 6LJ, England. TEL 44-1903-430439. FAX 44-1903-530441. (Alt. addr. Columbus Press Chartsearch (Advertising Office), 28 Charles Sq., London N1 6HT, England. TEL 44-171-417-0700. FAX 44-171-417-0702) Ed. H. Churchill Semple. adv.; bk.rev. circ. 25,000. **Document type:** newsletter.
—BLDSC (2934.478000).
Description: Aims to provide subscribers with the most extensive coverage of new opportunities of any monthly.

338 US ISSN 1042-6175
HF5429.235.U5
BUSINESS OPPORTUNITIES HANDBOOK. q. $19.95 (effective Nov. 1993). Enterprise Magazines, Inc., 1020 N. Broadway, Ste. 111, Milwaukee, WI 53202. TEL 414-272-9977. FAX 414-272-9973. E-mail: info@ezines.com; URL: http://www.ezines.com. **Document type:** directory.
•Also available online.
Description: Contains detailed listings on over 2,500 companies selling franchises and other business opportunities.

338 658 UK ISSN 1356-1723
BUSINESS OPPORTUNITY WORLD. 1992. m. £29.97 (effective 1996). Merlin Publications Ltd., 14 Hove Business Centre, Fonthill Rd., Hove, E. Sussex BN3 6HA, England. TEL 44-1273-888992. (Dist. by: UMD, 16-28 Tabernacle St., London EC2A 4PN, England. TEL 44-171-638-4666) Ed. Sarah Sendall; Pub. Rodney Thomas. R&P contact: Sarah Sendall. adv.: color page £1645; trim 297 x 210; adv. contact: Mark Forsyth. circ. 40,000 (paid). (back issues avail.) **Document type:** consumer publication.
Description: Information for people seeking business opportunities and start-up advice.

338 US
BUSINESS ORGANIZATIONS: FRANCHISING. 1969. 4 base vols. (plus supplements). $790. Matthew Bender & Co., Inc., 2 Park Ave., New York, NY 10016. TEL 212-448-2000. E-mail: international@bender.com; URL: http://www.bender.com. Ed. Gladys Glickman.
Description: Synthesizes legal, business and tax considerations of modern franchising.

338 US ISSN 1084-4473
HD62.7
BUSINESS PLANS HANDBOOK. 1994. a. Gale Research, 835 Penobscot Bldg., 645 Griswold St., Detroit, MI 48226-4094. TEL 313-961-2242; 800-877-4253. FAX 800-414-5043. E-mail: daniel__snyder@gale.com. Ed. Angela Shupe.

338 UK
BUSINESS SERVICES RESEARCH MONOGRAPH. 1994. irreg. Open University, Small Business Research Trust, Business School, Walton Hall, Milton Keynes, Bucks. MK7 6AA, England. TEL 44-1908-655831. FAX 44-1908-655898. E-mail: small.business.research.trust@ac.open.uk; URL: http://www-iet.open.ac.uk/iet/sbrt/sbrt.htm. **Document type:** monographic series.

338 US ISSN 1069-5818
BUSINESS START-UPS. 1989. m. $9.97 (Canada $24.97; elsewhere $29.97); newsstand price: $2.50. Entrepreneur Inc., 2392 Morse Ave., Irvine, CA 92614. TEL 714-261-2083. FAX 714-755-4211. Ed. Donna Clapp. circ. 240,000. **Document type:** trade publication.
Formerly (until 1993): New Business Opportunities (ISSN 1041-3707)
Description: Presents articles and information geared toward persons starting their own business.

BUYING AND SELLING BUSINESSES - PERSONAL PROPERTY. see *BUSINESS AND ECONOMICS — Banking And Finance*

C C A NEWS. (Consumer Credit Association) see *BUSINESS AND ECONOMICS — Banking And Finance*

C P A CLIENT BULLETIN. (American Institute of Certified Public Accountants) see *BUSINESS AND ECONOMICS — Accounting*

338.9 CK
CAJA DE CREDITO AGRARIO, INDUSTRIAL Y MINERO. FINANCIAMIENTO DE LA PEQUENA Y MEDIANA INDUSTRIA. 1973. a. Caja de Credito Agrario, Industrial y Minero, Bogota, Colombia. charts; stat.

338 US ISSN 0883-6159
CALIFORNIA BROKER. 1982. m. $42. McGee Publishers, Inc., 217 E. Alameda Ave., Ste. 301, Burbank, CA 91502-2622. TEL 818-843-3485. Ed. Kate Kinkade. adv. circ. 25,000. (back issues avail.)

338 US
CAMPGROUNDATA; national newsletter for campground buyers & owners. 1983. bi-m. $30. Campground Data Resource, 225 E. Stuart Ave., Lake Wales, FL 33853. TEL 813-676-0009. Ed. Dale S. Bourdette. circ. 2,000. **Document type:** newsletter.

BUSINESS AND ECONOMICS — SMALL BUSINESS

338 CN ISSN 1192-4012
NADIAN ENTREPRENEUR. q. $20. Abaco Communications Ltd., 20 Crown Steel Dr., Unit 10, Markham, ON L3R 9X9, Canada. TEL 416-477-4349. Ed. Elizabeth Harris. circ. 100,000. **Document type:** trade publication.

336 338 CN
NADIAN SMALL BUSINESS FINANCING AND TAX PLANNING GUIDE. 1984. m. Can.$430. C C H Canadian Ltd., 6 Garamond Ct., North York, ON M3C 1Z5, Canada. TEL 416-441-2992; 800-268-4522. FAX 416-444-9011. **Document type:** trade publication.
Description: Covers all aspects of small business financing and tax planning.

338 CN
NADIAN SMALL BUSINESS MANAGEMENT MANUAL. bi-m. Can.$315. C C H Canadian Ltd., 6 Garamond Ct., North York, ON M3C 1Z5, Canada. TEL 416-441-2992; 800-268-4522. FAX 416-444-9011. **Document type:** trade publication.
Formerly (until 1995): Canadian Small Business Guide.
Description: Provides a handy, practical reference for owners and administrators of businesses in Canada. Covers finance, marketing and personnel.

338 US
CASHFLOW. 1996. bi-m. MarketLynx, 462 Boston St., Topsfield, MA 01983. TEL 508-887-7900. Ed. Barry Harrigan. adv.; circ. controlled. **Document type:** trade publication.

790.13 US
AST POLYMER CONNECTION. (Former name of the issuing body: Cultured Marble Institute) 1975. bi-m. $75 to non-members (foreign $90); members $35 (foreign $50) (effective 1997). International Cast Polymer Association, 8201 Greensboro Dr., Ste. 300, McLean, VA 22102. TEL 703-610-9034. FAX 703-610-9005. E-mail: ICPA@icpa-hq.com; URL: http://www.icpa-hq.com. Ed. Julie Underwood. R&P contact: Julie Underwood. adv.: B&W page $767, color page $1413; trim 8 1/2 x 111; adv. contact: Julie Underwood. circ. 2,000. **Document type:** trade publication.
Formerly: Cultured Marble News.
Description: Contains association news and promotions, government regulatory updates, technical articles as well as news items that affect the cast materials industry.

CELLULAR SALES & MARKETING; cell the world! see COMMUNICATIONS — Telephone And Telegraph

338 US
THE CHANGEWINDS LETTER. 1997. m. $30 for 1st class mail; e-mail $18; fax $24. Northwind Publications, 439 Ponderosa Way, Jemez Springs, NM 87025. TEL 505-829-3448. FAX 505-829-3449. Ed. Paula & David Oliver. (also avail. by fax)
Description: Designed for the small business person, self-employed person, or the general reader interested in the major trends shaping our lives. For anyone who cares about the future and wants to see that it is a peaceful and productive one.

338 658 UK
CHARTERED SECRETARY. m. Institute of Chartered Secretaries & Administrators, 16 Park Crescent, London W1N 4AM, England. TEL 44-171-580-4741. bk.rev.

CHIEF EXECUTIVE OFFICERS NEWSLETTER; for the entrepreneurial manager and the professionals who advise him. see BUSINESS AND ECONOMICS — Management

658 338 US
CLEANING BUSINESS; published monthly for the self-employed cleaning & maintenance professional. 1980. m. $20 (foreign $36) (effective 1996). Wm. R. Griffin, Pub., Box 1273, Seattle, WA 98111-1273. TEL 206-622-4241. FAX 206-622-6876. E-mail: wgriffin@seanet; URL: http://www.cleaningconsultants.com. Ed. Robert Kearney. adv.: B&W page $400; trim 8 1/4 x 10 7/8; adv. contact: Nanette Bordner. bk.rev.; index. circ. 5,000. (back issues avail.) **Document type:** trade publication.
●Also available online.
Formerly: Service Business (ISSN 0736-5764)
Description: Trade journal for small cleaning and maintenance contractors. Covers janitorial, house cleaning, fire restoration, high pressure washing, carpet and upholstery cleaning, window washing and commercial buildings.

338 613.7 US ISSN 1043-9692
CLUB BUSINESS INTERNATIONAL.* 1982. m. $27 membership only. I R S A, The Association of Quality Clubs, 263 Summer St., Boston, MA 02210-1114. TEL 617-951-0055. FAX 617-951-0056. adv. circ. 7,000. Indexed: Sportsearch (1987-). **Document type:** trade publication.
Description: Concerned with the quality and profitability of racquet and fitness clubs. Includes club profiles, how-to articles and product information.

338 741.5 US ISSN 1059-9401
COMICS RETAILER. 1992. m. $29.95 (free to qualified personnel) (effective 1997). Krause Publications, Inc., 700 E. State St., Iola, WI 54990. TEL 715-445-2214. FAX 715-445-4087. Ed. John Jackson Miller, Jr.; Pub. Greg Loescher. adv. contact: Jim Felhofer. circ. 6,768. **Document type:** trade publication.
Description: Covers managing a comics shop and creating profit.

338 FR
COMMERCANT. bi-m. 15 F. Confederation des Commercants-Detaillants de France et d'Outre Mer, 21 rue du Chateau d'Eau, 75010 Paris, France. Ed. Roger Stoll. adv.

338 US ISSN 1089-2664
▼THE COMPLETE GIFT BASKET INDUSTRY REFERENCE DIRECTORY. 1996. a. $25. Sweet Survival, Box 31, River Street Sta., Paterson, NJ 07544-0031. TEL 973-279-2799. FAX 973-742-0700. E-mail: survival@ix.netcom.com. Ed. Shirley Frazier. **Document type:** directory, trade publication.
Description: Contains categories of service-related resources for gift basket businesses in all stages of development.

338 621.39 US ISSN 1089-5825
▼CONTRACT PROFESSIONAL; the magazine for career contractors and consultants. 1996. bi-m. $24 (Canada $34; foreign $45). Skinner - James Publishing, 125 Walnut St., Watertown, MA 02172. Ed. Michelle Bates Deakin; Pub. Stephanie Skinner. R&P contact: Stephanie Skinner. adv. contact: Adrienne Adler. illus, tr.lit. **Document type:** trade publication.

338 US CODEN: MIVEE5
CORPORATE REPORT VENTURES. 1989. q. American City Business Journals, Inc. (Austin), 505 Powell St., Austin, TX 78703-5121. circ. 13,364. **Document type:** trade publication.
●Also available online. Vendor(s): UMI.
—UMI.
Formerly (until 1995): Minnesota Ventures (ISSN 1058-3653)
Description: Provides how-to information for small to mid-sized companies.

338 US
COTTAGE CONNECTION (CHICAGO). 1982. bi-m. $45. National Association for the Cottage Industry, Box 14850, Chicago, IL 60614. TEL 773-472-8116. Ed. Virginia McCullough; Pub. Caralee Smith Kern. adv.; bk.rev.; charts; illus.; stat.; tr.lit. circ. 8,000. (tabloid format; back issues avail.) **Document type:** newsletter.
—UnCover.
Description: Profiles home-based businesses; articles on legal, accounting, and zoning issues.

338 II ISSN 0970-7387
COTTAGE INDUSTRIES; an industrial monthly journal. (Text in English) 1967. m. Rs.72($25) Small Industry Research Institute, 4-43, Roop Nagar, P.O. Box 2106, New Delhi 110 007, India. TEL 91-11-2910805. FAX 91-11-2923955. TELEX 031 61028 SIRI IN. Ed. D.C. Gupta. bk.rev. circ. 10,000. (back issues avail.) **Document type:** trade publication.
Description: Features industrial technical projects for entrepreneurs.

COUNTRY COTTAGE PENPALS. see HOBBIES

COUNTRY SAMPLER'S COUNTRY BUSINESS. see GIFTWARE AND TOYS

CRAFT MARKETING NEWS. see ARTS AND HANDICRAFTS

CREATIVE OUTLETS. see ARTS AND HANDICRAFTS

338 686.2 US
THE CROUSER REPORT. 1986. m.; online ed. w. $195. Crouser & Associates, 235 Dutch Rd., Charleston, WV 25302. TEL 304-342-5100. FAX 304-342-5187. E-mail: crouser@ibm.net; URL: http://www.crouser.com. Ed. Thomas P. Crouser; Pub. Thomas P. Crouser. software rev.; stat. circ. 1,000. (back issues avail.) **Document type:** newsletter.
●Also available online.

338 SP ISSN 1131-6985
CUADERNOS DE ESTUDIOS EMPRESARIALES. 1991. a. 1000 ptas.($12) (effective 1997). Universidad Complutense, Escuela Universitaria de Estudios Empresariales, Servicio de Publicaciones, Calle Isaac Peral s-n, Ciudad Universitaria, 28040 Madrid, Spain. TEL 34-1-3946934. FAX 34-1-3946954. (back issues avail.)
—CINDOC.
Description: Promotes university and business relationships.

DAILY JOURNAL OF COMMERCE. see BUSINESS AND ECONOMICS — Domestic Commerce

DIGITAL IMAGING DIGEST. see PHOTOGRAPHY

DORADCA PODATNIKA. see BUSINESS AND ECONOMICS — Public Finance, Taxation

658.2 US ISSN 0279-4039
DYNAMIC BUSINESS; image building for small business. 1945. 10/yr. $25 (foreign $45). S M C Business Councils, 1400 S. Braddock Ave., Pittsburgh, PA 15218-1264. TEL 412-371-1500. FAX 412-371-0460. URL: http://www.smc.org. Ed. Cliff Shannon; Pub. Leo R. McDonough. R&P contact: Mary L. Heindl. adv. contact: Terry Mohr. bk.rev.; circ. 10,000. (controlled). Indexed: Ind.Hyg.Dig. **Document type:** trade publication.
●Also available online.
Formerly: Smaller Manufacturer.
Description: Publishes material that helps small business owners promote and enhance their operations.

E B; Handbuch fuer Selbstaendige und Unternehmer. see BUSINESS AND ECONOMICS

338 NE ISSN 0928-222X
E I M IN DE MARKT. (Economisch Instituut voor het Midden- en Kleinbedrijf) 1962. q. fl.25. Research Institute for Small & Medium Sized Businesses - Economisch Instituut voor het Midden- en Kleinbedrijf, Postbus 7001, 2701 AA Zoetermeer, Netherlands. TEL 31-79-413634. FAX 31-79-415024. bk.rev.; abstr.; charts; stat. circ. 2,500. Indexed: Key to Econ.Sci.
Formerly (until 1992): E I M Mededelingen (ISSN 0012-768X)

338 NE ISSN 0070-8836
E I M YEAR REPORT. 1961. a. free. Economisch Instituut voot het Midden- en Kleinbedrijf - Research Institute for Small & Medium Sized Businesses, Postbus 7001, 2701 AA Zoetermeer, Netherlands. TEL 31-79-3413634. FAX 31-79-3425786.

338
ELECTRONIC MONEY TREE. (Print edition ceased) 1969. m. free. E-mail: emt@soos.com; URL: http://www.soos.com/$tree. Ed. Richard Soos.
●Available only online.

BUSINESS AND ECONOMICS — SMALL BUSINESS

ENRICH!; information bank briefings for network members. see *BUSINESS AND ECONOMICS — Chamber Of Commerce Publications*

338   II   ISSN 0013-8673
ENTERPRISE. (Text in English) 1967. m. Rs.18($3) Vidarbha Industries Association, Bank of Maharashtra Bldg., 2nd Floor, Sitabuldi, Nagpur 440 012, Maharashtra, India. Ed. B.G. Dave. adv.: bk.rev.; charts; illus.; stat. circ. 2,000.

338   US   ISSN 0163-3341
HF5001
ENTREPRENEUR (IRVINE). 1973. m. $19.97 (foreign $39.97); newsstand price: $4. Entrepreneur Media, Inc., 2392 Morse Ave., Irvine, CA 92614. TEL 714-261-2325. FAX 714-755-4211. (Subscr. to: Box 50368, Boulder, CO 80321-0368. TEL 800-274-6229) Ed. Rieva Lesonsky; Pub. Lee Jones. R&P contact: Peggy Castillo. adv. contact: Steve Olson. circ. 510,000. (also avail. in microfiche; back issues avail.) Indexed: B.P.I., P.A.I.S., PMR. **Document type:** consumer publication.
—KR SourceOne; SWETS; UMI; UnCover.
Formerly (until 1977): Insider's Report.
Description: Provides information on running a small business.
Refereed Serial

338   CN   ISSN 1188-8997
THE ENTREPRENEURIAL SPIRIT. m. A F A B Publishing, 339 10th Ave., S.E., Ste. 125, Calgary, AB T2G 0W2, Canada. TEL 403-255-9387. FAX 403-264-2540. Ed. Doug Kipp. **Document type:** newsletter.
Description: Provides advice, information and company profiles while building a network of small businesses throughout North America.

338   US
ENTREPRENEUR'S DIGEST.* 8/yr. 400 Granite St., Waupaca, WI 54981-1019. TEL 414-233-2674. Ed. Raymond Hipp.

338   US
ENTREPRENEUR'S FRANCHISE SPECIAL. 1986. a. $2.95 (Canada $3.50). Entrepreneur Inc., 2392 Morse Ave., Irvine, CA 92614. TEL 714-261-2325. FAX 714-755-4211. Ed. Rieva Lesonsky; Pub. Lee Jones. R&P contact: Tracey Collins. adv. contact: Steve Olson. **Document type:** consumer publication.
Former titles: Entrepreneur's Guide to Franchise and Business Opportunities & Entrepreneur's Franchise Yearbook (ISSN 0889-4310)
Description: Comprehensive listings of franchise and business opportunities and information on investing in an opportunity.

ENTREPRENEURSHIP, INNOVATION AND CHANGE. see *BUSINESS AND ECONOMICS — Management*

338   US   ISSN 1042-2587
HD2346.U5
ENTREPRENEURSHIP: THEORY AND PRACTICE. 1976. q. $50 to individuals (foreign $66); institutions $85 (foreign $100) (effective 1997). Baylor University, Hankamer School of Business, BU Box 98006, Waco, TX 76798-8006. TEL 817-755-1111 ext.156. FAX 817-755-2271. E-mail: ray_bagby@baylor.edu; URL: http://hsb.baylor.edu/html/dept/bcpr/HSB/genmf.htm. Ed. D. Ray Bagby. charts, stat.; index. circ. 1,600. (also avail. in microform from UMI; reprint service avail. from UMI) **Indexed:** ABI Inform., Account.& Data Proc.Abstr., Account.Ind. (1983-), ASEAN Manage.Abstr., B.P.I., BPIA, Bus.Ind., Cont.Pg.Manage., INSPEC, Manage.Cont., P.A.I.S., Tr.& Indus.Ind. **Document type:** academic/scholarly publication.
●Also available online. Vendor(s): Information Access Co., UMI.
Also available on CD-ROM.
—BLDSC (3790.548000); KR SourceOne; SWETS; UMI; UnCover. **CCC.**
Formerly (until vol.12): American Journal of Small Business (ISSN 0363-9428)
Description: Publishes results of research in entrepreneurship, small business, and family business.

338   AU
ERFOLG IM BERUF. q. Matzleinsdorfer Hochhaus 12-67, A-1050 Vienna, Austria. TEL 01-551351. FAX 01-544458. Ed. Elvira Fischhof. circ. 4,000.

338.7   NE
EUROPEAN OBSERVATORY FOR S M ES. ANNUAL REPORT. a. E I M, P.O. Box 7001, 2701 AA Zoetermeer, Netherlands. TEL 31-79-3413634. FAX 31-79-3425786.
Description: Studies the structure, developments, and determinants of success of SMEs.

338   SP   ISSN 0214-5820
EUROPYME. 11/yr. Prensa Hispanoamericana, S.A., Gasquena 21, 28022 Madrid, Spain. TEL 1-747-80-00. FAX 1-747-90-56. Ed. Rafael de Otero. circ. 30,000.

338   UK   ISSN 0014-4460
EXCHANGE AND MART. 1868. w. £82 (Europe £130; rest of world £225). Link House Advertising Periodicals Ltd., 25 West St., Poole, Dorset BH15 1LL, England. TEL 44-1202-445000. FAX 44-1202-445189. (Subscr. to: Garrard House, 2-6 Homesdale Rd., Bromley, Kent BR2 9WL, England. TEL 44-181-402-8181. FAX 44-181-402-8383) R&P contact: Michael Peden. adv. contact: Michael James. circ. 114,000. **Document type:** consumer publication.
Description: Advertisements of various products.

338   US   ISSN 0279-1382
EXECUTIVE REPORT. 1981. m. $30. Riverview Publications, Inc., 3 Gateway Center, 5th Fl., Pittsburgh, PA 15222-1004. TEL 412-471-4585. FAX 412-644-3006. E-mail: er_editor@execreport.com. Ed. Jane A. Black. adv. contact: Patrick Wood. bk.rev.; tr.lit. circ. 27,000. (reprint service avail.) **Indexed:** Tr.& Indus.Ind.
●Also available online. Vendor(s): Knight-Ridder Information, Inc., Lexis-Nexis, UMI.
—UMI. **CCC.**

EXHIBITOR MAGAZINE; the magazine for trade show and event marketing management. see *BUSINESS AND ECONOMICS — Marketing And Purchasing*

338   US   ISSN 0888-367X
EXTRA INCOME. 1984. bi-m. $11.95 (effective 1997-1998). Business Concepts, Inc., Box 21957, Santa Barbara, CA 93121-1957. TEL 805-687-7712. FAX 805-569-0861. E-mail: 74434.2471@compuserve.com. (Subscr. to: Box 573, Mt. Morris, IL 61054) Ed. Petie Hall Maher; Pub. J. Scott Maher. R&P contact: Jeff O'Mahoney. adv.: B&W page $3480, color page $4500; trim 5 3/8 x 7 7/16; adv. contact: Scott Maher. circ. 350,000 (paid). **Document type:** consumer publication.
Description: For home and self-employed business opportunity seekers.

338   UK
F C C NEWS. 1986. q. membership. 14 East St., Alresford, Hants. SO24 9EE, England. TEL 01962-732777. FAX 01962-733637. Ed. Adrian Hunt. circ. 4,000. **Document type:** newsletter.

338   UK
F P B QUARTERLY REPORT. 1988. q. Forum of Private Business, Ruskin Chambers, Drury Ln., Knutsford, Ches. WA6 6HA, England. TEL 44-1565-634467. FAX 44-1565-650059. Ed. James Redman. **Document type:** academic/scholarly publication.
Formerly: F P B Action Report.

338   US   ISSN 1047-255X
HD62.25
FAMILY BUSINESS. 1989. bi-m. $39.97. Family Business Publishing Company, Inc. (Subsidiary of: M L R Enterprises, Inc.), 229 S. 18th St., Philadelphia, PA 19103. TEL 215-790-7000. FAX 215-790-7005. Ed. Steven Solomon. adv. circ. 60,000.
Description: Designed to meet the special needs and interests of America's family-owned companies.

338   US   ISSN 0894-4865
FAMILY BUSINESS REVIEW. 1988. q. $52 to individuals; institutions $82. Family Firm Institute, 12 Harris St., Brookline, MA 02146. TEL 617-738-1591. URL: http://www.ffi.org/. Ed. Ivan Lansberg. bk.rev. circ. 1,300. (back issues avail.) **Document type:** academic/scholarly publication.
—BLDSC (3865.559220); UMI.
Description: For professionals and scholars who work with family businesses, the latest ideas and strategies for effectively meeting the needs of today's family-run businesses.
Refereed Serial

658   NO   ISSN 0802-7129
FIRMA. 1984. 6/yr. NOK 680 (effective 1997). Mir D A, P.O. Box 23, N-7904 Lundamo, Norway. TEL 47-72-85-40-30. FAX 47-72-85-47-80. E-mail folven@online.no. Ed. Reiel Folven. R&P contact: Reiel Folven. adv. contact: Astrid Wiig. circ. 5,000. **Document type:** newsletter.
Incorporates (1995-1997): God Leder (ISSN 0805-3677); *Formerly* (until 1990): Kreaktiv (ISSN 0800-7403)

338   UK   ISSN 0959-8375
FIRST VOICE. Key Title: First Voice of Small Business. bi-m. membership. (Federation of Small Businesses N F S E Sales Ltd., 140 Lower Marsh, Westminster Bridge, London SE1 7EA, England. TEL 44-171-928-9272. FAX 44-171-401-2544. Ed. Sarah Beevers. adv.: B&W page £2150, color page £2750; adv. contact: James Parker. circ. 63,262. **Document type:** trade publication.

338   US   ISSN 0882-5505
HF5429.235.U5
THE FRANCHISE HANDBOOK. 1985. q. $19.95. Enterprise Magazines, Inc., 1020 N. Broadway, Ste 111, Milwaukee, WI 53202. TEL 414-272-9977. FAX 414-272-9973. E-mail: info@franchise.com; URL: http://www.franchise1.com. **Document type:** consumer publication.
●Also available online.
Description: Contains information on more than 1700 franchises currently being marketed, as well as articles and expert advice.

338   US
FRANCHISE OPPORTUNITIES GUIDE. 1962. s-a. $30. International Franchise Association, 1350 New York Ave., N.W., Ste. 900, Washington, DC 20005-4709. TEL 202-628-8000. FAX 202-628-0812. adv.; circ. 62,000 (paid). **Document type:** directory.

338   US
▼**FRANCHISE TIMES.** 1995. w. $35. Crain Communications, Inc. (Chicago), 740 N. Rush St., Chicago, IL 60611-2590. TEL 800-281-7713. bk.rev.; circ. 100,000 (paid). **Document type:** trade publication.
Formerly: Franchise Buyer.
Description: Covers all aspects of purchasing and running a franchise. Profiles franchisors and franchisees, analyzes market trends, and reports pertinent legislation.

338   UK   ISSN 0144-0543
FRANCHISE WORLD. 1978. q. £20. Franchise Publications, James House, 37 Nottingham Rd., London SW17 7EA, England. Ed. Robert Riding. adv. illus.

338 363.49   US
▼**FRANCHISEWISE.** 1995. q. $400 membership (foreign $500). International Gay & Lesbian Franchise Association, 2765 N. Scottsdale Rd., Ste. 104D, Scottsdale, AZ 85257. TEL 602-949-7848. FAX 602-990-1958. E-mail: gayfranch@aol.com. Ed. Thomas A. Cutler; Pub. Thomas A. Cutler. adv.; bk.rev.; circ. 10,000 (paid). **Document type:** newsletter.
Formerly: International Gay and Lesbian Franchise News.
Description: For gay and lesbian franchisees or potential franchisees wishing to know which franchisors are receptive to the gay community.

338   AT   ISSN 1321-408X
FRANCHISING; and win your own business magazine. 1987. bi-m. Aus.$50. (Franchises Association of Australia and New Zealand) Hassel Hunt & Moore Pty. Ltd., Level 1, 5 Vuko Pl., Warriewood, N.S.W. 2102, Australia. TEL 61-2-99700688. FAX 61-2-99796979. E-mail: hhm@franchise.net.au; URL: http://www.franchise.net.au. (Subsc. addr.: P.O. Box 900, Mona Vale, N.S.W. 2103, Australia) Ed. Geoff Hill. R&P contact: Geoff Hill. adv.: B&W page Aus.$1725, color page Aus.$2275; trim 275 x 205; adv. contact: Ken Lane. circ. 13,000. (back issues avail.) **Document type:** consumer publication, trade publication.
●Also available online.

BUSINESS AND ECONOMICS — SMALL BUSINESS 1643

338 US
FREENTERPRISE;* America's journal of income opportunities. 1991. m. $24.95. Free Enterprise Inc., 4725 E. Sunrise Dr., Ste. 352, Tucson, AZ 85718-4534. TEL 602-296-6777. FAX 602-296-2705. (Subscr. to: Box 17988, Tucson, AZ 85731-7988. TEL 800-364-2990) Ed. Bonnie Webber. adv. contact: Deborah Twyman. circ. 55,000. (back issues avail.) **Document type:** trade publication.
  Description: Provides updated information on the multi-level marketing industry, including legal and postal regulations.

338 JA ISSN 0285-8460
GEKKAN CHUSHO-KIGYO/MONTHLY SMALLER BUSINESSES. Key Title: Chusho Kigyo. (Text in Japanese) 1976. m. 3600 Yen. Diamond Inc., 4-2, 1-chome, Kasumigaseki, Chiyoda-ku, Tokyo 100, Japan. Ed. Yoshizumi Saito.

338 659.1 GW ISSN 0344-2292
DIE GESCHAEFTSIDEE; Fachmagazin fuer Unternehmensgruendung und neue Maerkte. (Editions in French and German) 1976. bi-m. DM.297.60. Verlag Norman Rentrop, Theodor-Heuss-Str. 4, 53177 Bonn, Germany. TEL 49-228-8205-0. FAX 49-228-364411. TELEX 17228309. Ed. Norman Rentrop. bk.rev. (back issues avail.) **Document type:** bulletin.
  Description: Market studies, franchise news, new products and how-to articles for German entrepreneurs.

338 332.6 AT ISSN 1035-6606
GET RICH NEWS. 1987. bi-m. $40. Southern Media Services, P.O. Box 529, Kiama, N.S.W 2533, Australia. Ed. Nic van Oudtshoorn. adv.; bk.rev. circ. 53,000.
  Description: Provides business opportunity news for entrepreneurs.

338 GW
GEWERBE REPORT. 1964. m. DM.30. Europaverband der Selbstaendigen, Oberbexbacherstr. 7, 66450 Bexbach, Germany. TEL 49-6826-1470. FAX 49-6826-50904. Ed. Karl Kunrath. adv. contact: Doris Hahn. bk.rev.; abstr.; illus.; stat.; index. circ. 20,000. (back issues avail.) **Document type:** consumer publication.

338 IT
GIORNALE DELL'INDUSTRIA MINORE. m. Via Mozart 1, 20122 Milan, Italy. Ed. G.N. Mariani.

GOVERNMENT PROGRAMS. see SOCIAL SERVICES AND WELFARE

338 CN
GUIDE TO ESTABLISHING A BUSINESS IN CALGARY. 1985. a. Can.$5. Calgary Economic Development Authority, P.O. Box 2100, Sta. M, Calgary, AB T2P 2M5, Canada. TEL 403-221-7821. FAX 403-221-7837. **Document type:** bulletin.
  Description: Detailed reference source for those interested in joining Calgary's business community.

338 371.42 651 US
HOME BUSINESS MAGAZINE; the work from home magazine. 1993. bi-m. $15 (foreign $30); newsstand price: $3.95. United Marketing & Research Company, Inc., Box 2712, 9582 Hamilton Ave., No. 368, CA 92646. TEL 714-968-0331. FAX 714-968-7722. E-mail: sysadmin@qi3.com; URL: http://www.homebusinessmag.com. Ed. Stacy Ann Henderson; Pub. Richard Henderson. R&P contact: Richard Henderson. TEL 714-968-0331. adv.: page $890; trim 7 x 10; adv. contact: Richard Henderson. bk.rev.; software rev.; pat.; stat.; tr.lit. circ. 70,000. **Document type:** consumer publication.
●Also available online.
  Description: Provides information on home business opportunities. Includes a directory, case histories, and articles on getting started, creating a home office, franchising, etc.

338 UK ISSN 0968-2066
HOME RUN; for all who want to work effectively from home. 1992. 10/yr. £72 (other EC countries £82; elsewhere £92). Active Information, Cribau Mill, The Cwm, Llanvair Discoed, Chepstow, Gwent NP6 6RD, Wales. TEL 44-1291-641777. FAX 44-1291-641222. E-mail: info@homerun.co.uk; URL: http://homerun.co.uk. Ed. Sophie Chalmers; Pub. Andrew James. R&P contact: Sophie Chalmers. adv. contact: Andrew James. bk.rev.; index. (back issues avail.) **Document type:** newsletter.
  Description: Contains practical articles on such small-business marketing, office management, personnel development for persons working from home. Also covers tax law and technology updates.

338 US ISSN 1067-0300
HOMEBASED BUSINESS NEWS REPORT; turning your idea into a reality. 1992. bi-m. $14. Home Office Management Services, 1151 N.E. Todd George Rd., Lee's Summit, MO 64086-5332. TEL 816-525-4484. FAX 816-525-4484. E-mail: bob-bethsmith@worldnet.att.nett. Ed. Beth Smith. R&P contact: Beth Smith. adv. contact: Beth Smith. bk.rev. circ. 1,000. (tabloid format) **Document type:** newsletter.

HOW TO BE YOUR OWN PUBLISHER UPDATE. see PUBLISHING AND BOOK TRADE

HOW TO DOUBLE YOUR INCOME; monthly report for hairstylists. see BEAUTY CULTURE

338 IE
HOW TO START YOUR OWN BUSINESS WITH 2000 TO 5000 DOLLARS. (Text in English) 1985. a. $100. Royal University, Ltd., 6 Lower Hatch St., Dublin 2, Ireland. FAX 353-1-6686632. Ed. C.V. Ramasastry. adv.; bk.rev.; circ. 20 (controlled). (looseleaf format) **Document type:** trade publication, newsletter.
  Formerly: Worldwide Directory of East Indians (ISSN 0748-223X)

338 746.5 CI
HRVATSKI OBRTNIK. (Text in Croatian) 1947. m. $26. (Savez Udruzenja Samostalnih Privrednika Hrvatske) Magos d.o.o., Kaciceva 9, 41000 Zagreb, Croatia. TEL 041-422-182. FAX 041-423-793. (Subscr. to: Trg. Ivana Mazuranica 5-II, 41000 Zagreb, Croatia) Ed. Zoraw Zokovic. circ. 15,000. (back issues avail.)
  Former titles: Obrtnicki Vjesnik; (until Nov., 1990): Zanatski List.

I D A DOWNTOWN NEWSBRIEFS. (International Downtown Association) see HOUSING AND URBAN PLANNING

I'M TOO BUSY TO READ MARKETING REPORT SERVICE. see BUSINESS AND ECONOMICS — Marketing And Purchasing

338 IT
IMPRENDITORE. 1948. m. L.60000 (foreign L.80000) (effective 1995). Servizio Italiano Pubblicazioni Internazionali s.r.l., Viale L. Pasteur, 6, 00144 Rome, Italy. TEL 39-6-5918586. FAX 39-6-5924819. Ed. Paolo Mazzanti. adv.: color page L.6000000. circ. 54,000. **Document type:** trade publication.
  Formerly (until 1994): Gazzetta della Piccola Industria (ISSN 0391-6138)

338 US ISSN 0190-2458
HF5001 CODEN: INBSD5
IN BUSINESS (EMMAUS); the magazine for environmental entrepreneuring. 1979. bi-m. $29 (foreign $37) (effective 1997). J G Press, Inc., 419 State Ave., Emmaus, PA 18049. TEL 610-967-4135. Ed. Jerome Goldstein. adv.; bk.rev.; index. circ. 3,000. (also avail. in microfilm; back issues avail.) **Indexed:** BPIA, Bus.Ind., Environ.Per.Bibl. (1990-), INSPEC, Tr.& Indus.Ind. —BLDSC (4371.696000); CISTI; UMI; UnCover. CCC.
  Description: Discusses methods of incorporating environmentally sound processes and products into business practice.

338 US ISSN 0162-8968
HD2346.U5 CODEN: INCCDU
INC.; the magazine for growing companies. (In 12 regional editions) 1979. m. $19 (effective 1996). Goldhirsh Group, Inc., 38 Commercial Wharf, Boston, MA 02110. TEL 617-248-8000. FAX 617-248-8090. TELEX 710-321-0523. URL: http://www.incmag.com. (Subscr. to: Box 54129, Boulder, CO 80322. TEL 800-234-0999) Ed. George Gendron; Pub. J. Riley McDonough. R&P contact: Diana Bukaty. TEL 212-326-2600. adv. contact: Gary Mirkin. circ. 650,000 (paid). (also avail. in microfiche from CIS; reprint service avail. from UMI) **Indexed:** ABI Inform, Account.Ind. (1983-), B.P.I., Bk.Rev.Ind. (1984-), Bus.Ind., C.I.S. Abstr., CAD CAM Abstr., Child.Bk.Rev.Ind. (1984-), Environ.Abstr., INSPEC (1983-), Mag.Ind., PROMT, PSI, Rehabil.Lit., SRI, Tel.Abstr., Tr.& Indus.Ind. **Document type:** consumer publication.
●Also available online. Vendor(s): Information Access Co., Knight-Ridder Information, Inc., Lexis-Nexis. —BLDSC (4374.760000); AskIEEE; CIS; Genuine Article; KR SourceOne; SWETS; UMI; UnCover. CCC.

338 US ISSN 0019-3429
INCOME OPPORTUNITIES; America's best money-making ideas. 1952. m. $19.95 (effective 1996). Essence Communications Inc., 1500 Broadway, Ste. 600, New York, NY 10036-4015. TEL 212-642-0600. FAX 212-302-8269. URL: http://www.incomeops.com/. (Subscr. to: Box 55026, Boulder, CO 80322) Ed. Linda Molnar. adv.; abstr.; charts; pat.; tr.lit.; tr.mk. circ. 350,349. (also avail. in microform from UMI; reprint service avail. from UMI) **Document type:** consumer publication.
●Also available online.
—UMI.

338 US ISSN 0147-5924
INFO FRANCHISE NEWSLETTER. 1977. m. $96 (outside N. America $120) (effective 1997). Info Press, Inc., 728 Center St., Box 550, Lewiston, NY 14092-0550. TEL 716-754-4669. FAX 905-688-7728. E-mail: infopress@infonews.com; URL: http://infonews.com/franchise. (Or: 9 Duke St., St. Catharines, ON L2R 6W8, Canada) Ed. Ted Dixon; Pub. Ted Dixon. adv. **Document type:** newsletter.
  Description: Covers business format franchising: list of new franchises, recent legislation and litigation, trends and forecasts.

338 FR ISSN 0292-4765
INFORMATIONS ENTREPRISE. 10/yr. 18 rue Tiphaine, 75015 Paris, France. TEL 45-75-21-21. FAX 45-75-12-77. Ed. Antoine Silber. circ. 37,000.

658.02 SW ISSN 0282-4655
INITIATIV; tidningen for dig som driver eget foeretag. 1983. bi-m. SEK 225 (foreign SEK 260). Tryckerifoerlaget, Tumstocksvaagen 19, P.O. Box 7093, S-183 07 Taaby, Sweden. TEL 046-08-756-74-45. FAX 046-08-756-03-95. Ed. Leif Lindberg. adv. circ. 15,000. (back issues avail.) **Document type:** trade publication.
  Description: Covers economics, finance, marketing, public relations, franchising, mail order, interviews and portrayals.

INLINE RETAILER & INDUSTRY NEWS. see SPORTS AND GAMES

338 US
INSIDE SELF-STORAGE.* 1991. m. Virgo Publishing, Inc., 3300 N. Central Ave., Ste. 2500, Phoenix, AZ 85012. TEL 602-990-1101. FAX 602-990-0819. Ed. John Baragona. adv.: B&W page $1690; trim 8 1/8 x 19 7/8. circ. 20,000.
  Description: Covers aspects of the self-storage industry for owners, operators, managers, investors, vendors and lenders.

338 UK ISSN 1355-2554
HB615
▼**INTERNATIONAL JOURNAL OF ENTREPRENEURIAL BEHAVIOUR & RESEARCH.** 1995. m. £199($299) (foreign Aus.$419) (effective 1998). M C B University Press Ltd., 60-62 Toller Ln., Bradford, W. Yorks BD8 9BY, England. TEL 44-1274-777700. FAX 44-1274-785200. URL: http://www.mcb.co.uk. Ed. John Pheby. **Document type:** trade publication. —BLDSC (4542.240400). CCC.

BUSINESS AND ECONOMICS — SMALL BUSINESS

338   UK   ISSN 0266-2426
INTERNATIONAL SMALL BUSINESS JOURNAL. 1982. q. £89($122) Woodcock Publications Ltd., P.O. Box 1, Macclesfield, Cheshire SK10 4YQ, England. TEL 44-1625-528516. FAX 44-1625-532644. Ed. Clive Woodcock. R&P contact: Clive Woodcock. adv. contact: Clive Woodcock. bk.rev. **Indexed:** B.P.I., Cont.Pg.Manage., P.A.I.S., SCIMP (1984-). **Document type:** academic/scholarly publication.
●Also available online. Vendor(s): Information Access Co., UMI.
—BLDSC (4549.406500); KR SourceOne; SWETS; UMI.
Incorporates: European Small Business Journal.
Refereed Serial

650   GW   ISSN 0020-9481
INTERNATIONALES GEWERBEARCHIV; Zeitschrift fuer Klein- und Mittelunternehmen. (Supplements avail.) 1953. q. DM.72. (Schweizerisches Institut fuer Gewerbliche Wirtschaft, SZ) Duncker und Humblot GmbH, Postfach 410329, 12113 Berlin, Germany. TEL 49-30-7900060. FAX 49-30-79000631. E-mail: duh-werbung@t-online.de. (Co-sponsor: Hochschule St. Gallen fuer Wirtschafts-und Sozialwissenschaft) Ed. Dr. A. Gutersohn. adv.; bk.rev.; index. **Indexed:** IBR, Key to Econ.Sci. **Document type:** academic/scholarly publication.
—CCC.

338   659.1   US
INTRODUCTION TO MAIL ORDER. 1976. q. $10. G & B Records, Box 10150, Terra Bella, CA 93270-0150. TEL 209-535-5722. Ed. Glenn C. Bridgeman. adv. circ. 5,000.

IOWA HOME-BASED BUSINESS DIRECTORY. see BUSINESS AND ECONOMICS — Trade And Industrial Directories

ISRAEL. CENTRAL BUREAU OF STATISTICS. INDUSTRY AND CRAFTS SURVEY. see BUSINESS AND ECONOMICS — Abstracting, Bibliographies, Statistics

338   US
ITEM.* 1958. m. free to employees. (Itek Corporation) Itek Optical Systems (Subsidiary of: Litton Corporation), 4 Hartwell Pl., Lexington, MA 02173-3122. TEL 617-276-2000. FAX 617-276-2000. Ed. Diana Tempel. pat. circ. 850. (tabloid format; back issues avail.)
Formerly: Itek News.
Description: House organ.

338.6   II   ISSN 0447-2500
JAGRITI; fortnightly news magazine on rural reconstruction. (Editions in English and Hindi) 1957? fortn. Rs.10. Khadi and Village Industries Commission, Directorate of Publicity, Gramodaya, Irla Rd., Vile Parle (West), Bombay 400056, India. Ed. M.P. Sharma. bk.rev.; illus.

338   GW   ISSN 0938-7056
JAHRBUCH FRANCHISING. 1990. biennial. DM.68. (Deutscher Franchise Verband e.V.) Deutscher Fachverlag GmbH, Mainzer Landstr. 251, 60326 Frankfurt a.M., Germany. TEL 49-69-7595-2124. FAX 49-69-7595-2110.

JOURNAL OF BUSINESS (SPOKANE). see BUSINESS AND ECONOMICS — Banking And Finance

JOURNAL OF BUSINESS VENTURING. see BUSINESS AND ECONOMICS

338   US
HG4027.7
THE JOURNAL OF ENTREPRENEURIAL AND SMALL FIRM FINANCE. 1991. 3/yr. $80 to individuals (foreign $100); institutions $195 (foreign $215) (effective 1998). J A I Press Inc., 55 Old Post Rd., No. 2, Box 1678, Greenwich, CT 06830-1678. TEL 203-661-7602. FAX 203-661-0792. E-mail: jai@jaipress.com. (Addr. in Europe: J A I Press Ltd., 38 Tavistock St., Covent Garden, London WC2E 7PB, England. TEL 44-171-379-8834. FAX 44-171-379-8835) Ed. Rassoul Yazdipour. (also avail. in microform from UMI; back issues avail.) **Document type:** academic/scholarly publication.
—BLDSC (5064.709000); SWETS. **CCC.**
Formerly: Journal of Small Business Finance (ISSN 1057-2287)
Description: Focuses on the financial, economic, and accounting aspects of small firms.

658   US   ISSN 0047-2778
HD69.S6   CODEN: JSBMAU
JOURNAL OF SMALL BUSINESS MANAGEMENT. 1963. q. $45 to individuals (foreign $60); institutions $70 (foreign $85) (effective 1997). West Virginia University, Bureau of Business and Economic Research, Box 6025, Morgantown, WV 26506-6025. TEL 304-293-7534. E-mail: jsbm@wvube1.be.wvu.edu; URL: http://www.wvu.edu/~colbe/research/bureau/jsbm.htm. (Co-sponsor: International Council for Small Business)) Ed. Frederick C. Scherr. adv. contact: Lynn Reinke. bk.rev.; abstr.; bibl.; index. circ. 3,500. (also avail. in microform; reprint service avail. from SCH,SWZ,UMI) **Indexed:** ABI Inform., Account.& Data Proc.Abstr., ASCA, ASEAN Manage.Abstr., B.P.I., BPIA, Bus.Ind., Cont.Pg.Manage., Curr.Cont., Mag.Ind., Manage.Cont., P.A.I.S., Pers.Manage.Abstr., Tr.& Indus.Ind. **Document type:** academic/scholarly publication.
●Also available online. Vendor(s): Information Access Co., UMI.
—BLDSC (5064.710000); Genuine Article; KR SourceOne; SWETS; UMI; UnCover.
Description: Articles, features and editorials on small business and entrepreneurship.

338   US   ISSN 1081-8510
JOURNAL OF SMALL BUSINESS STRATEGY.* 1990. s-a. $20. Small Business Institute Directors' Association, Wittenberg University, Box 720, Springfield, OH 45501. Ed. Pam Schinder. illus.; index. **Document type:** academic/scholarly publication.
Refereed Serial

338   II
K V I C ANNUAL REPORT. (Editions in English and Hindi) 1957. a. Khadi and Village Industries Commission, Directorate of Publicity, Gramodaya, Irla Rd., Vile Parle (West), Bombay 400056, India. charts; illus.; stat.
Formerly: India. Khadi and Village Industries Commission. Report (ISSN 0073-6198)

338   US
KANSAS CITY SMALL BUSINESS MONTHLY. m. E-mail: kcsmbiz@kcsmallbiz.com; URL: http://www.kcsmallbiz.com.
●Available only online.
Description: Covers new ideas in management, marketing, legal matters, finance, human resources, and office technology.

658.5   FI   ISSN 0022-9229
KASITYO JA TEOLLISUUS. 1908. m. FIM 45. Pienteollisuuden Keskusliitto, Kansakoulukatu 10 A 21, Helsinki 10, Finland. Ed.Bd. adv.; bk.rev.; charts; illus.; stat.; cum.index. circ. 10,000.

338   UK
KEY NOTE MARKET REPORT: EQUIPMENT LEASING. Variant title: Equipment Leasing. irreg., no.10, 1995. £205. Key Note Ltd., Field House, 72 Oldfield Rd., Hampton, Middlesex TW12 2HQ, England. TEL 44-181-783-0755. FAX 44-181-783-0049. **Document type:** trade publication.
●Also available online.
Also available on CD-ROM.
Formerly: (until 1995): Key Note Report: Equipment Leasing (ISSN 0954-4526)

338   UK
KEY NOTE MARKET REPORT: FRANCHISING. Variant title: Franchising. irreg., no.4, 1991. £185. Key Note Ltd., Field House, 72 Oldfield Rd., Hampton, Middlesex TW12 2HQ, England. TEL 44-181-783-0755. FAX 44-181-783-1940. **Document type:** trade publication.

338   658   PL   ISSN 1230-9427
KOBIETA I BIZNES/WOMEN & BUSINESS; akademicko-gospodarcze forum. (Text in English, Polish) 1993. q. Szkola Glowna Handlowa, Kolegium Gospodarki Swiatowej, Al. Niepodleglosci 162, 02-554 Warsaw, Poland. TEL 48-22-495084. FAX 48-22-495084. (Co-sponsor: Miedzynarodowe Forum Kobiet - International Forum for Women) Ed. Ewa Lisowska. adv. contact: Ewa Lisowska. (also avail. in diskette format; back issues avail.) **Document type:** academic/scholarly publication.
Description: Presents studies on small and medium businesses run by women.
Refereed Serial

338   CN   ISSN 0842-098X
KOOTENAY BUSINESS MAGAZINE. 1986. m. Can.$20. Kootenay Advertiser Ltd., 1510 2nd St. N., Cranbrook, BC V1C 3L2, Canada. TEL 604-489-3455. FAX 604-489-3743. Ed. Daryl Shellborn. adv. contact: Keith G. Powell. circ. 7,500. **Document type:** consumer publication.
Description: Business information about the Kootenays.

338   GW
KREISHANDWERKERSCHAFT MOENCHENGLADBACH. MITTEILUNGSBLATT. 1968. m. membership. Kreishandwerkerschaft Moenchengladbach, Pescher Str. 111-119, 41065 Moenchengladbach, Germany. TEL 02161-45021-23. circ. 4,000. (back issues avail.)

338   FR
LAMY ASSOCIATIONS. (Supplements avail.) a. 1020 F. (with supplements 1430 F.)(effective 1993). Lamy S.A., 187-189 quai de Valmy, 75490 Paris Cedex 10, France. TEL 33-1-44721343. FAX 33-1-44721395. (looseleaf format)
Description: Aids in daily management and development of partnerships.

338   US   ISSN 1071-0426
LEGACIES; family business newsletter. 1989. q. $15.95 in Texas; outside Texas free. Baylor University, Institute for Family Business, Box 98011, Waco, TX 76798-8011. TEL 254-755-2265. FAX 254-755-2271. E-mail: Doris__Sandberg@baylor.edu; URL: http://hsb.baylor.edu/html/cel/ifb/ifb__home.htm. Ed. Doris Sandberg. bk.rev. circ. 7,000. pp./issue: 8. **Document type:** newsletter.
Description: Looks at family business forums, conferences, awards, succession problems.

338   UK   ISSN 0968-4638
MACHINE KNIT TODAY. South African edition (ISSN 1019-7508) 1988. m. £21.60 (foreign £31) (effective 1996). Aspen Litharne Publishing (Subsidiary of: Aspen Communications plc), P.O. Box 9, Stratford-upon-Avon, Warwickshire CV37 8RS, England. TEL 44-1789-720604. FAX 44-1789-720888. Ed. Carol Chambers. adv. contact: Maggie Michaells. circ. 20,000. **Document type:** consumer publication.
Formerly: (until 1993): Profitable Machine Knitting (ISSN 0954-5468)
Description: Informs and instructs how to run a knitting machine business at home.

338   GW   ISSN 0177-7491
MAERKTE IM SAARLAND. 1947. a. DM.10. Statistisches Amt des Saarland, Postfach 103044, 66030 Saarbruecken, Germany. circ. 600. **Document type:** bulletin.

338   CN   ISSN 0828-8089
HD2346.C2
MAGAZINE P M E; le magazine de l'entrepreneurship du Quebec. 1984. m. (10/yr.) Can.$24.16. Publications Transcontinental Inc., 1100 Boul. Rene Levesque W., 24th Fl., Montreal, PQ H3B 4X9, Canada. TEL 514-392-9000. FAX 514-393-9430. Ed. Guy Paradis. adv. contact: Richard Barbeau. circ. 28,003. **Indexed:** Pt.de Rep. (1989-).

338   DK   ISSN 0107-8305
MARKEDS-BOG. 1982. a. DKK 100 (effective 1993). Dixit, Industrivej 12, 8653 Them, Denmark. TEL 86-84-70-22. FAX 86-84-71-15. Ed. Torben Kahr. illus.
Formerly: Markedskalender.

338   US   ISSN 0888-3327
MARKETERS FORUM MAGAZINE. 1981. m. $30. Forum Publishing Co., 383 E. Main St., Centerport, NY 11721-1538. TEL 516-754-5000. TELEX 804294. Ed. Martin Stevens. adv.; bk.rev. circ. 70,000. **Document type:** trade publication.
Description: For owners of retail stores who buy goods for resale through retail outlets.

BUSINESS AND ECONOMICS — SMALL BUSINESS

338   US   ISSN 0025-6137
MAY TRENDS; marketing and economic trends for business executives. 1967. s-a. free. George S. May International Company, Management Consultants, 303 S. Northwest Hwy., Park Ridge, IL 60068-4265. TEL 847-825-8806. FAX 847-825-8806. Ed. Roz Angell. R&P contact: Roz Angell. circ. 30,000 (controlled). **Document type:** consumer publication.
  Description: Emphasizes economic, marketing, government trends which affect small business operations. Presents ideas and viewpoints of leading authorities familiar with the field.

THE MERCHANT. see *BUSINESS AND ECONOMICS — Marketing And Purchasing*

MINI LAB FOCUS. see *PHOTOGRAPHY*

338 305.896073   US   ISSN 1048-0919
MINORITY BUSINESS ENTREPRENEUR. 1984. bi-m. $15. 3528 Torrance Blvd., Ste. 101, Torrance Blvd., Ste. 101, CA 90503-4803. TEL 310-540-9398. FAX 310-792-8263. E-mail: mbewbe@ix.netcom.com; URL: http://www.mbemag.com. Ed. Jeanie Barnett; Pub. Ginger Conrad. R&P contact: Barbara Daley. adv. contact: Barbara Daley. bk.rev. circ. 40,000. (back issues avail.) **Document type:** trade publication.
  Description: Creates opportunities for minority and women owned businesses to do business with majority-owned businesses and government.

338   US
MISSOURI BUSINESS. 1952. 10/yr. $3. Missouri Chamber of Commerce, Box 149, Jefferson City, MO 65102. Ed. Nancy Sell. circ. 5,000.

338   US   ISSN 1050-5652
MONEY MAKER'S MONTHLY. 1986. m. $19.95 in U.S.; Canada $46.95; elsewhere $67.95 (effective 1997). 6827 W. 171st St., Tinley Park, IL 60477-3447. TEL 708-633-8888. FAX 708-633-8889. E-mail: mmm1@ais.net; URL: http://www.mmmonthly.com. Ed.Bd.; Pub. Keith B. Laggos. R&P contact: Keith B. Laggos. adv.: B&W page $3600, color page $5760; trim 10 1/4 x 15 7/8; adv. contact: Marvin Bohannan. bk.rev. circ. 71,000. **Document type:** trade publication.
  Description: Devoted to direct sales, network and multilevel marketing.

338   US
MOST LIKELY TO SUCCEED. 1990. bi-m. $29. Richard Siedlecki Consulting, 4767 Lake Forrest Dr., N.E., Atlanta, GA 30342-2539. TEL 404-303-9900. Ed. Richard Siedlecki; Pub. Richard Siedlecki. bk.rev. circ. 1,000. (back issues avail.) **Document type:** newsletter.
  Former titles: Siedlecki's Right-to-the-Point; (until 1994): Siedlecki on Business; Siedlecki on Marketing; Siedlecki Letter.
  Description: Provides business facts on management and marketing; aimed at owners of small and growing businesses.

338   US   ISSN 0196-3171
HF5429.3
N A R D A'S COST OF DOING BUSINESS SURVEY. 1947. a. $250. North American Retail Dealers Association, 10 E. 22nd St., Ste. 310, Lombard, IL 60148-6191. TEL 630-953-8950. FAX 630-953-8957. E-mail: nardahdq@aol.com. circ. 1,000. Indexed: SRI. **Document type:** trade publication.

N A S B I C NEWS. (National Association of Small Business Investment Companies) see *BUSINESS AND ECONOMICS — Investments*

338   US   ISSN 0195-1513
N F I B. m. National Federation of Independent Business, 53 Century Blvd., Ste. 205, Nashville, TN 37214. Ed. David Cullen. charts; illus.

NATIONAL ACCOUNTANT. see *BUSINESS AND ECONOMICS — Accounting*

NATIONAL DIPPER; the magazine for ice cream retailers. see *FOOD AND FOOD INDUSTRIES*

NATIONAL DIRECTORY OF MINORITY - OWNED BUSINESS FIRMS. see *BUSINESS AND ECONOMICS — Trade And Industrial Directories*

338 531.54   US
NETWORKER (CLEVELAND). 1986. bi-m. $95. Network of Small Businesses, 5420 Mayfield Rd., Cleveland, OH 44124. TEL 216-442-5600. FAX 216-449-3227. Ed. Irwin Friedman. R&P contact: Irwin Friedman. adv. circ. 625. **Document type:** trade publication.
  Description: Directed to small business owners interested in getting funding from private investors, acquiring government contracts, and networking with other businesses, also investors seeking high-yield investments.

338   US   ISSN 0279-4527
HF3163.N5
NEW ORLEANS CITYBUSINESS. 1943. w. $52. New Orleans City Business, 111 Veterans Blvd., Ste. 1810, Metairie, LA 70005. TEL 504-834-9292. FAX 504-837-2258. (Subscr. to: Box 19308, New Orleans, LA 70179) Ed. Kathy Finn; Pub. William Metcalf. adv. contact: Lisa Blossman. bk.rev.; charts; stat. circ. 14,000. (tabloid format; also avail. in microfiche from UMI; back issues avail.) Indexed: Tr.& Indus.Ind.
  ●Also available online. Vendor(s): Knight-Ridder Information, Inc., Lexis-Nexis, UMI.
  —UMI.
  Former titles: Citybusiness (Metairie); Citybusiness; Supersedes (in 1980): New Orleans Business (ISSN 0094-3622); Which was formerly: Jefferson Business - New Orleans; Jefferson Business.

338   JA   ISSN 0289-6516
NIKKEI VENTURE. 1984. m. 12840 Yen. Nikkei Business Publications, Inc. (Subsidiary of: Nihon Keizai Shimbun, Inc.), 2-7-6 Hirakawa-cho, Chiyoda-ku, Tokyo 102, Japan. TEL 81-3-5210-8041. FAX 81-3-5210-8119. URL: http://www.nikkeibp.co.jp/. (Subscr. to: Nikkei Business Pub. Inc., P.O. Box 20, Kasai Post Office, Tokyo 134-70, Japan) Ed. Katsuro Miyashima; Pub. Toshio Onda. adv.: B&W page 483000 Yen, color page 725000 Yen; trim 208 x 280; adv. contact: Yoshio Kato. circ. 72,548. **Document type:** publication.
  Description: Focuses on small and medium-sized growth business, with practical information on management, risks, and opportunities.

338   FR   ISSN 0992-3144
NOTE D'INFOS. (Supplement avail.: Lettre Sociale de Note d'Infos Fiscales, Sociales et Juridiques (ISSN 1143-8894)) 11/yr. S I D Communications, 19 rue Gay Lussac, B.P. 221, 86000 Poitiers, France. TEL 49-61-20-20. FAX 49-01-68-19. Ed. Claude Fouchier. circ. 200,000.
  Formerly (until 1988): Note d'Infos Fiscales, Sociales et Juridiques (ISSN 0988-6400)

338 388.321   UK   ISSN 0260-8294
NOTTINGHAM LICENSED TAXI OWNERS & DRIVERS ASSOCIATION. NEWSLETTER. 1980. q. Nottingham Licensed Taxi Owners & Drivers Association, 63a Derby Rd., Nottingham, England.

338   CN   ISSN 0820-2737
NOVA SCOTIA BUSINESS JOURNAL. 1986. m. Can.$24($22.50) (foreign Can.$30). Bilby Holdings Ltd., 6029 Cunard St., Halifax, NS B3K 1E5, Canada. TEL 902-420-0437. FAX 902-423-8212. Ed. Ken Partridge. R&P contact: Barry Herold. adv. contact: Norm Duncan. bk.rev. circ. 15,685. (also avail. in microform from UMI) **Document type:** trade publication.
  —UMI.

NOVA SCOTIA CRAFT NEWS. see *ARTS AND HANDICRAFTS*

NOVOGRADISKI GLASNIK. see *AGRICULTURE*

O P A S T C O ROUNDTABLE; the magazine of ideas for small telephone companies. (Organization for the Promotion and Advancement of Small Telecommunications Companies) see *COMMUNICATIONS — Telephone And Telegraph*

338 658   US
OPERATING RESULTS OF INDEPENDENT SUPERMARKETS. a. $75 to non-members; members $30. Food Marketing Institute, 800 Connecticut Ave., N.W., Washington, DC 20006. TEL 202-452-8444. Indexed: SRI. **Document type:** trade publication.
  Description: Managerial tool for independent supermarket retailers to evaluate their own store's operating results.

330   IT
ORIZZONTI INDUSTRIALI. 1968. m. (10/yr.). L.5000. Associazione Piccole e Medie Industrie, Via S. Serlio 26, 40128 Bologna, Italy. TEL 51-374-893. FAX 51-356-118. TELEX 511299 APIBO I. Ed. Paolo Beghelli. adv.; bk.rev. circ. 15,000.

338   FR
P M I FRANCE. 5/yr. 23 rue de Clery, 75002 Paris, France. TEL 45-08-91-88. Ed. Lazaro Gecsges. circ. 10,000.
  Description: Provides general economic information relevant to small and medium sized industrial enterprises.

P R C NEWS; a weekly news in brief for the video industry. (Pre Recorded Cassette) see *COMMUNICATIONS — Video*

338   UK   ISSN 0961-2602
PARTY TIMES. 1991. bi-m. £22.50 (effective 1997). Plaza Publishing Ltd., 1A Tradescant Rd., London SW8 1XD, England. TEL 44-171-793-0001. FAX 44-171-735-2009. Ed. Andrew Maiden; Pub. Andrew Maiden. adv.: B&W page £1095, color page £1295; adv. contact: Alice Frackelton. **Document type:** trade publication.
  Formerly (until 1997): BalloonWorld.
  Description: Provides an effective communications link between several tiers of the party industry.

658.041   US
THE PAY DAY TABLOID. 1983. m. $5. Graphico Publishing, Box 488, Bluff City, TN 37618-0488. TEL 423-652-2307. FAX 423-652-2307. (Edit. addr.: Box 792, Woodbine, NJ 08270-0792. TEL 609-628-4711) adv.: page $125. circ. 15,000. (tabloid format) **Document type:** trade publication.
  Description: Presents information on books, reports, advertising, printing and small home-based businesses.

THE PENSION ACTUARY. see *INSURANCE*

338   US
PERSPECTIVES (ALEXANDRIA). 1990. q. membership only. International Sign Association, 801 N. Fairfax St., Ste. 205, Alexandria, VA 22314. TEL 703-836-4012. FAX 703-836-8353. E-mail: shane@signs.org; URL: http://www.signs.org. Ed. Shane Artim. charts; illus.; stat.; tr.lit.; circ. 1,200 (paid). (looseleaf format; back issues avail.) **Document type:** newsletter.
  Description: Covers governmental relations issues on Capitol Hill affecting the on-premise sign industry.

338   UK   ISSN 1350-5017
PET BUSINESS WORLD. 1951. m. £12 (rest of Europe £20; elsewhere £30). Dog World Ltd., 9 Tufton St., Ashford, Kent TN23 1QN, England. TEL 44-1233-621877. FAX 44-1233-645669. Ed. Margaret Ferris. adv. contact: Gwen M. Neilg. bk.rev. circ. 5,000. **Document type:** trade publication.
  Formerly: Pet Store Trader.

PET SERVICES JOURNAL. see *PETS*

338.021   PO   ISSN 0870-2640
PORTUGAL. INSTITUTO NACIONAL DE ESTATISTICA. INQUERITO AO EMPREGO. 1974. q. Esc.4100. Instituto Nacional de Estatística, Ave. Antonio Jose de Almeida, 1078 Lisbon, Portugal. TEL 351-1-8470050. FAX 351-1-8478578. TELEX 351-1-63738 PCDINE P.

PRINTING BUSINESS REPORT. see *PRINTING*

338   US
PROFITS. 1970. bi-m. free. Howard University, Small Business Development Center, School of Business & Public Administration, 2600 6th St., N.W., Box 748, Washington, DC 20059. TEL 202-806-1550. Ed. Emma J. O'Neal. bk.rev.; charts; illus. circ. 2,000.

PRZEGLAD HANDLOWY. see *BUSINESS AND ECONOMICS — Domestic Commerce*

QIYE GUANLI/ENTERPRISE MANAGEMENT. see *BUSINESS AND ECONOMICS — Management*

BUSINESS AND ECONOMICS — SMALL BUSINESS

338   CC
QIYE YANJIU/ENTERPRISE STUDIES. (Text in Chinese) m. $39.50. Diyi Qiche Zhizao Chang, 39-1 Dongfeng Dajie, Chaoyang-qu, Changchun, Jilin 130011, People's Republic of China. TEL 503526. (Distr. by: China Books & Periodicals, Inc., 2929 24th St., San Francisco, CA 94110. TEL 415-282-2994) Ed. Lei Liulong.

338 330   US
QUICK SOLUTIONS. 1993. 3/yr. E-mail: vince14@aol.com; URL: http://www.idsonline.com/quick/. Ed. Vince Shelton. **Document type:** trade publication. ●Available only online.
 Description: Provides small business information and computer guidance.

338   GW   ISSN 0931-0622
R W I HANDWERKSBERICHTE. 1954. a. DM.40. Rheinisch-Westfaelisches Institut fuer Wirtschaftsforschung, Essen, Hohenzollernstr. 1-3, 45128 Essen, Germany. TEL 49-201-8149-0. FAX 49-201-8149200. E-mail: schmidtj@rwi-essen.de; URL: http://www.rwi-essen.de. circ. 500. (back issues avail.) **Document type:** trade publication.

338   UK
REFERENDUM. 8/yr. Ruskin Chambers, Drury Ln., Knutsford, Ches. WA16 6HA, England. TEL 01565-634467. FAX 01565-650059. Ed. Dave Harrop. circ. 18,278.

REGIONAL DIRECTORY OF MINORITY- AND WOMEN-OWNED BUSINESS FIRMS: CENTRAL EDITION. see BUSINESS AND ECONOMICS — Trade And Industrial Directories

REGIONAL DIRECTORY OF MINORITY- AND WOMEN-OWNED BUSINESS FIRMS: EASTERN EDITION. see BUSINESS AND ECONOMICS — Trade And Industrial Directories

REGIONAL DIRECTORY OF MINORITY- AND WOMEN-OWNED BUSINESS FIRMS: WESTERN EDITION. see BUSINESS AND ECONOMICS — Trade And Industrial Directories

REP TALK. see BUSINESS AND ECONOMICS — Management

338   US   ISSN 0893-4347
RESEARCH RECOMMENDATIONS; * economics, political & tax advisory letter. 1937. w. $125. National Institute of Business Management, Box 9286, McLean, VA 22102-9658. TEL 703-905-8000. (Subscr. to: Box 25287, Alexandria, VA 22313) Ed. Paul Hencke. circ. 55,000. **Document type:** newsletter.

338   US
RETAIL INK. 1992. m. International Specialty Shops Association, Box 14456, 915 Canterbury Rd., N.E., Atlanta, GA 30324. TEL 404-237-2907. adv. circ. 10,000. **Document type:** newspaper.
 Description: Addresses the problems, solutions and particular operational situations of specialty stores.

338   CN   ISSN 0776-5436
REVUE INTERNATIONALE P M E. (Petite et Moyenne Entreprise) (Summaries in English, French, Spanish) 1977. q. 1200 Fr. Universite du Quebec a Trois Rivieres, C.P. 500, Trois-Rivieres, PQ G9A 5H7, Canada. TEL 819-376-5079. FAX 819-376-5079. Ed. Pierre-Andre Julien. **Indexed:** Pt.de Rep.—BLDSC (7925.119500).
 Formerly (until 1988): P M E: Revue de la Petite et Moyenne Entreprise (ISSN 0705-0674)

RISK MANAGEMENT FOR EXECUTIVE WOMEN. see INSURANCE

338   US
▼**THE ROTHMAN REPORT.** 1996. fortn. 1280 E. Easter Ave., Littleton, CO 80122. E-mail: hrothman@ecentral.com; URL: http://www.ecentral.com/business/rothman/. Ed. Howard Rothman. **Document type:** trade publication.
 Description: Reportage and analysis of current ideas, news and tools of interest to wired small business owners and operators.

338   US   ISSN 8750-3158
S B A N E ENTERPRISE. 1984. m. $49 (foreign $95). Smaller Business Association of New England, 204 Second Ave., Waltham, MA 02154. TEL 617-890-9070. FAX 617-890-4567. Ed. Julie Scofield. R&P contact: Julie Scofield. adv.: Jean/Peckham. bk.rev.; charts; illus.; stat. circ. 2,700. (tabloid format) **Document type:** newsletter.
 Refereed Serial

338   US
S B I C DIRECTORY AND HANDBOOK OF SMALL BUSINESS FINANCE. 1970. a. $15. International Wealth Success, Inc., Box 186, Merrick, NY 11566. TEL 516-766-5850. FAX 516-766-5919. Ed. Tyler G. Hicks. adv. **Document type:** directory.
 Description: Lists over 400 SBIC's including name, address, types of preferred financing, details of their capital structure.

658   II   ISSN 0970-8464
S E D M E. (Small Enterprises Development, Management and Extension) (Text in English) 1966. 4/yr. Rs.150($60) National Institute of Small Industry Extension Training, Yousufguda, Hyderabad 500045, India. TEL 91-40-238544. FAX 91-40-238547. TELEX 425-6381-SIET-IN. Ed. M.B. Raju. bk.rev.; charts; stat. circ. 400. **Indexed:** Int.Lab.Doc. **Document type:** academic/scholarly publication.
 Formerly: S I E T Studies (ISSN 0036-1518)

338   II   ISSN 0970-8723
S E N D O C BULLETIN. PART 2: ECONOMIC AND DEVELOPMENT. (Text in English) 1973. m. Rs.80($40) National Institute of Small Industry Extension Training, Small Enterprises National Documentation Centre, Yousufguda, Hyderabad 500045, India. TEL 91-40-238544. FAX 91-40-238547. TELEX 425-6381-SIET-IN. Ed. K. Subashini. **Document type:** abstracting/indexing.

338   US
S O H O JOURNAL. (Small Office Home Office) 1981. q. $25 (membership $45; libraries $35). National Association for the Cottage Industry, Box 14850, Chicago, IL 60614. TEL 312-472-8116. Ed. Virginia McCollough; Pub. Coralee Smith Kern. adv.; bk.rev.; charts; illus.; stat.; tr.lit.; circ. 16,000 (paid). (tabloid format; back issues avail.) **Indexed:** Br.Ceram.Abstr., INSPEC. **Document type:** newsletter, trade publication.
 Formerly: Mind Your Own Business at Home (ISSN 0277-6820)
 Description: Covers legal taxes, zoning, marketing and licensing concerns pertaining to home-based businesses.

338   II
S S I. (Small Scale Industries) (Text in English) 1976. m. Rs.80($30) Eastern Trade Press Co., 43 Sunder Mahal, Churchgate, Bombay 400020, India. Ed. Bhojan Krishnan. adv.; bk.rev. circ. 10,000.

338   US   ISSN 0278-5048
SALES REP'S ADVISOR. 1981. s-m. $127. Alexander Research & Communications, Inc., 215 Park Ave., S., Ste. 1301, New York, NY 10003. TEL 212-228-0246. FAX 212-228-0376. Ed. Carol Carangelo; Pub. Shirley Alexander. R&P contact: Mary Dalessandro. bk.rev. **Document type:** newsletter.
 Description: Provides information on handling crises with power buyers. Includes tax information and strategies, business management, partnering with principals, sales management, legal issues and more.

338   US   ISSN 1053-1696
HF5482.4
THE SAN FRANCISCO ALMANAC. 1990. bi-m. $18. 1657 Waller St., Ste. A, San Francisco, CA 94117. TEL 415-751-0357. Ed. Walter Biller. adv.; bk.rev. **Document type:** consumer publication.
 —CCC.
 Description: Contains general-interest articles about local people, places, and opportunities.

SELBSTAENDIG IN DER WIRTSCHAFT. see BUSINESS AND ECONOMICS — Economic Situation And Conditions

338   US   ISSN 1041-8741
SELF-EMPLOYED AMERICA. 1989. bi-m. $12. National Association for the Self-employed, 2121 Precinct Line Rd., Hurst, TX 76054. TEL 817-428-4243; 800-232-6273. FAX 817-428-4210. Ed. Heidi Williams. adv. contact: Karen Jones. circ. 320,000 (controlled). **Document type:** trade publication.

338   US   ISSN 0736-1912
SELF-EMPLOYMENT UPDATE. 1983. a. $6. Update Publicare Co., c/o Prosperity & Profits Unlimited, Distribution Services, Box 416, Denver, CO 80201-0416. TEL 303-575-5676. Ed. A. Doyle. circ. 1,500. **Document type:** newsletter.
 —CCC.

338   US   ISSN 1044-9590
SELF STORAGE JOURNAL. m. Self Storage Association, 60 Revere Dr., Ste. 500, Northbrook, IL 60062-1577. TEL 312-480-9627. FAX 312-480-9282. Ed. Charles Laughlin. circ. 1,043. **Document type:** trade publication.
 Formerly: Self-Service Storage (ISSN 0892-5062)

SEMINARS, WORKSHOPS & CLASSES. see EDUCATION — Adult Education

338   US
▼**A SERIOUS BUSINESS.** 1996. bi-w. $15 (effective 1997 & 1998). Gabriel Publishing Company, 1469 Rosena Ave., Madison, OH 44051. TEL 216-428-6163; 800-359-5166. FAX 216-428-5509. E-mail: editor@earthone.com; URL: http://earthone.com. Ed. Ray Gabriel. bk.rev. circ. 4,000. **Document type:** newsletter.
 ●Available only online.
 Description: Contains new marketing ideas, how-tos, common problem solutions, valuable resources, tips and tricks by and for successful business people in over 70 countries.

SERVICE QUARTERLY. see TRANSPORTATION — Automobiles

SERVICE TECHNICIAN. see ENGINEERING — Chemical Engineering

338   US
SIGNALS. 1944. bi-m. membership only. International Sign Association, 801 N. Fairfax St., Ste. 205, Alexandria, VA 22314. TEL 703-836-4012. FAX 703-836-8353. E-mail: shane@signs.org; URL: http://www.signs.org. Ed. Shane Artim. R&P contact: Chery Haser. bk.rev.; charts; illus.; stat.; tr.lit. circ. 1,600. (looseleaf format) **Document type:** newsletter.
 Description: Covers issues of importance to small business owners in the on-premise sign industry.

338   UK   ISSN 0262-3102
SMALL BUSINESS. 1976. 6/yr. £115 (foreign £150). Small Business Bureau, Curzon House, Church Rd., Windlesham, Surrey GU20 6BH, England. TEL 44-1276-452010. FAX 44-1276-451602. E-mail: sbb@compuserve.com; URL: http://www.smallbusinessbureau.org.uk. Ed. Arthur Bell. adv.; bk.rev. circ. 20,000. (also avail. in microform from UMI) **Document type:** newspaper.
 Incorporates: S B B Tax News (ISSN 0263-3817)

338   US   ISSN 1069-9619
SMALL BUSINESS ADVISOR. 1993. m. $45 (effective 1997). Small Business Advisors, Inc., Box 436, Woodmere, NY 11598. TEL 516-374-1387; 800-295-1325. FAX 516-374-1175. E-mail: smalbusadv@aol.com. Ed. Ann Liss; Pub. Joseph Gelb. R&P contact: Arthur Van Dam. bk.rev.; circ. 2,000 (paid). (back issues avail.) **Document type:** newsletter.
 Description: Allows small-business owners easy access to specialized information their growing companies need; topics include finance and cash flow, human resources management, insurance, law, marketing, technology, and taxation.
 Refereed Serial

THE SMALL BUSINESS ADVISOR: SOFTWARE NEWS. see BUSINESS AND ECONOMICS — Computer Applications

338   US
SMALL BUSINESS ADVOCATE (BROOKLYN). m. Brooklyn Journal Publications, Inc., 129 Montague St., Brooklyn, NY 11201. TEL 718-624-6033. FAX 718-875-5302.

BUSINESS AND ECONOMICS — SMALL BUSINESS

338 US ISSN 1045-7658
HD62.7
SMALL BUSINESS ADVOCATE (WASHINGTON). 1982. m. free. U.S. Small Business Administration, Office of Advocacy, Mail Code 3114, 409 Third St., S.W., Washington, DC 20416. TEL 202-205-6531. FAX 202-205-6928. Ed. John Ward. bk.rev.; stat.; circ. 9,800 (controlled). (looseleaf format; also avail. in microfiche). **Document type:** government publication, newsletter.
Formerly (until 1988): Advocacy Notes.
Description: Covers regulatory and legislative issues pertaining to small business with economic research and other items of interest.

338 658 UK ISSN 0968-1000
HD2346.G7
SMALL BUSINESS AND ENTERPRISE DEVELOPMENT. 1994. 3/yr. £95 (foreign $150) (effective 1997). John Wiley & Sons Ltd., Journals, Baffins Ln., Chichester, W. Sussex PO19 1UD, England. TEL 44-1243-779777. FAX 44-1243-775878. E-mail: info-assets@wiley.co.uk; URL: http://www.wiley.co.uk. (Subscr. in the Americas to: John Wiley & Sons, Inc., 605 Third Ave., New York, NY 10158-0012. TEL 212-850-6645. FAX 212-850-6021) Ed. Peter Jennings. adv.: B&W page £595, color page £1495; trim 297 x 210; adv. contact: Bob Kern. bk.rev. **Document type:** trade publication.
—CCC.
Description: Discusses various aspects of developing and managing a small business.

338 US ISSN 0893-8326
HF5001
SMALL BUSINESS BULLETIN (WORCESTER). 1978. 6/yr. $85. Small Business Service Bureau, Inc., Box 1441, 554 Main St., Worcester, MA 01601. TEL 508-756-3513. FAX 508-791-4709. Ed. Bernard Weiss. bk.rev.; illus.; circ. 35,000 (controlled). **Document type:** bulletin, trade publication.
Former titles: Small Business Report; Small Business.

338 US
SMALL BUSINESS CHRONICLE.* 1988. m. $18. Philadelphia Small Business Chronicle, Inc., 3012 Butler Pike, Conshohocken, PA 19428-2115. Ed. John Hayes. adv.; bk.rev. circ. 35,000. (tabloid format; back issues avail.) **Document type:** trade publication.
Formerly: Philadelphia Small Business Chronicle.
Description: For executives of small to medium sized businesses.

SMALL BUSINESS COMPUTER NEWS. see COMPUTERS — Microcomputers

338 NE ISSN 0921-898X
HD2341 CODEN: SBECEX
SMALL BUSINESS ECONOMICS; an international journal. (Text in English) 1989. 8/yr. fl.1000 to institutions; $513 to institutions in U.S. (effective 1998). Kluwer Academic Publishers, Postbus 17, 3300 AA Dordrecht, Netherlands. TEL 31-78-6392392. FAX 31-78-6392254. TELEX 29245 KAPG NL. E-mail: services@wkap.nl; URL: http://www.wkap.nl. (Dist. by: Kluwer Academic Publishers Group, P.O. Box 322, 3300 AH Dordrecht, Netherlands. TEL 31-78-6392392. FAX 31-78-6546474; N. America dist. addr.: Box 358, Accord Sta., Hingham, MA 02018-0358. TEL 617-871-6600. FAX 617-871-6528) Eds. Zoltan J. Acs, David B. Audertsch. (also avail. in microform from UMI; back issues avail.; reprint service avail. from SWZ)
Indexed: ASCA, Asian-Pac.Econ.Lit., Curr.Cont., IBR, SSCI. **Document type:** academic/scholarly publication.
—BLDSC (8309.975880); Genuine Article; SWETS; UMI. **CCC.**
Description: Provides a forum for the economic analysis of the role of small business.
Refereed Serial

338 US
SMALL BUSINESS EXECUTIVE REPORT. m. $52 (effective 1997). Charles Moore Associates, Inc., Stump Rd., Box 6, Southampton, PA 18966-0006. TEL 215-355-6084. FAX 215-364-2212. Ed. Fred Bird. **Document type:** trade publication.

338 340 US ISSN 1084-3639
▼**SMALL BUSINESS JOURNAL.** 1995. bi-m. $60 (effective 1996). Small Business Association of Michigan, 222 N. Washington Sq., Box 16158, Lansing, MI 48901-6158. TEL 517-482-8788. FAX 517-482-4205. Ed. Dennis Larson. adv.: page $935; trim 8 1/2 x 11; adv. contact: Donna Gardner. charts; illus. circ. 8,300. **Document type:** trade publication.
●Also available online.
Formerly: Journal of Small Business.
Description: Focuses on trends and issues which affect small businesses in Michigan. Includes coverage of state government initiatives.

338 US
SMALL BUSINESS MAGAZINE. 1979. m. $60. Richboro Press, Box 947, Southampton, PA 18966-0947. TEL 215-355-6084. FAX 215-364-2212. Ed. George Moore; Pub. Charles Moore. adv.; bk.rev.

338 AT ISSN 1035-3097
SMALL BUSINESS, MARKETING AND SOCIETY. 1992. s.a. $120 to individuals; institutions $260. James Nicholas Publishers, P.O. Box 224, Alber Park, Vic. 3206, Australia. TEL 61-3-6965545. FAX 61-3-6992040. URL: http://www.jamesnicholaspublishers.com.au. Ed. Joseph Zajda; Pub. Rea Zajda. R&P contact: Mary Berchmann. adv. contact: Dorothy Murphy. bk.rev.; index. **Document type:** academic/scholarly publication.
Description: Examines relationships between business, marketing and society, including the economic roles of small business, human factors, state policies and planning, and small business in Russia, new independent states of the former Soviet Union, Europe and the world.
Refereed Serial

338 US
SMALL BUSINESS NEWS - AKRON. 1991. m. $20; newsstand price: 2. Small Business News, Inc. (Akron), 86 W. Bowery St., Akron, OH 44308-1101. TEL 330-535-6397. FAX 330-535-6491. E-mail: sbnpubak@interramp.com; URL: http://www.sbnpub.com. Dir. Mike Marzec; Pub. Fred Koury. adv. contact: Brent Fickle. circ. 18,000 (controlled). (tabloid format; also avail. in microform from UMI) **Document type:** newspaper.
●Also available online. Vendor(s): UMI.
Description: Contains business news for entrepreneurs in Akron and surrounding counties.

338 US ISSN 1080-4803
SMALL BUSINESS NEWS - CLEVELAND. 1989. m. $20; newsstand price: 2. Small Business News, Inc. (Cleveland), 14725 Detroit Ave., Ste. 300, Cleveland, OH 44107-4103. TEL 216-228-6397. FAX 216-529-8924. E-mail: 74631.3631@compuserve.com; URL: http://www.sbnpub.com. Ed. Mike Marcek; Pub. Fred Koury. adv. contact: Brent Fickle. circ. 29,000 (controlled). (also avail. in microform from UMI; back issues avail.) **Document type:** newspaper.
●Also available online. Vendor(s): UMI.
Description: Contains company profiles, news, and information for small business owners and managers in Cuyahoga, Lake, Geauga and Lorain counties.

338 US ISSN 1071-8087
SMALL BUSINESS OPPORTUNITIES. 1988. bi-m. $9.97. Harris Publications, Inc., 1115 Broadway, 8th fl., New York, NY 10010. TEL 212-807-7100. FAX 212-627-4678. adv. circ. 250,000. **Document type:** trade publication.
Description: Provides how-to information on starting and operating a business. Includes profiles on successful entrepreneurs.

338 US
SMALL BUSINESS OR ENTREPRENEURIAL RELATED NEWSLETTERS, PUBLICATIONS & PERIODICALS, ETC.; an updating reference. 1990. biennial. $11.95 (Canada $12.95; elsewhere $14.95). Update Publicare Co., c/o Prosperity & Profits Unlimited, Distribution Services, Box 416, Denver, CO 80201. TEL 303-575-5676. Ed. A. Doyle. **Document type:** newsletter.

338 US ISSN 1076-8483
HD2346.U5
SMALL BUSINESS PROFILES. 1994. a. Gale Research, 835 Penobscot Rd., 645 Griswold St., Detroit, MI 48226-4094. TEL 313-961-2242; 800-877-4253. FAX 800-414-5043. E-mail: daniel_snyder@gale.com. Ed. Susan M. Bourgoin.

338 CN
SMALL BUSINESS QUARTERLY. 4/yr. Can.$30 (effective 1997). Ministry of Finance and Corporate Relations, B C Stats, P.O. Box 9410, Stn. Prov. Govt., Victoria, BC V8W 9V1, Canada. TEL 250-387-0359. FAX 250-387-0380. E-mail: bcstats@fincc04.fin.gov.bc.ca; URL: http://www.bcstats.gov.bc.ca. **Document type:** government publication.
Supersedes: Business Formations and Failures (ISSN 1184-9223)

338 US ISSN 0883-3397
HD2346.U5
SMALL BUSINESS SOURCEBOOK. (Supplement avail.) 1983. biennial. $220 (supplement $90) (effective Apr. 1993). Gale Research, 835 Penobscot Bldg., 645 Griswold St., Detroit, MI 48226-4094. TEL 313-961-2242; 800-877-4253. FAX 800-414-5043. E-mail: daniel_snyder@gale.com. Ed. Carol A. Schwartz.
Description: Highlights live and basic print sources of information such as associations, federal and state government agencies, and consulting firms.

SMALL BUSINESS START-UP INDEX. see BUSINESS AND ECONOMICS — Abstracting, Bibliographies, Statistics

338 US ISSN 0162-8658
SMALL BUSINESS TAX CONTROL. 1970. m. $127. Inside Mortgage Finance Publications, Box 42387, Washington, DC 20015. TEL 301-951-1240. FAX 301-656-1709. URL: http://users.aol.com/imfpubs. Ed. Guy D. Cecala; Pub. Guy D. Cecala. R&P contact: Didi Parks. circ. 5,000. **Document type:** newsletter.
Description: Tax guide designed to assist small business owners in preparing their taxes and staying abreast of major issues which could affect their companies' operations.

SMALL BUSINESS TAX PLANNER. see BUSINESS AND ECONOMICS — Public Finance, Taxation

SMALL BUSINESS TAX REVIEW. see BUSINESS AND ECONOMICS — Public Finance, Taxation

650 US ISSN 0898-4972
SMALL BUSINESS U S A.* 1937. m. $125 membership. National Small Business United, 1156 15th St., N.W., Ste. 1100, Washington, DC 20005-1704. TEL 202-293-8830. FAX 202-872-8543. Ed. Gwen Fry. adv.; bk.rev.; illus.; circ. 11,000 (paid). **Document type:** newsletter.
Former titles (until 1987): Voice of Small Business (ISSN 0037-7198); Small Business Bulletin.
Description: Information on wages and benefits, employee quality, healthcare and financing. Focuses on legislation affecting small business.

338 SA
SMALL BUSINESS WORLD; committed to small business growth. 1993. m. R.28.80. Damont Publishers, P.O. Box 490, Newtown, Johannesburg 2113, South Africa. adv.; illus. **Indexed:** Ind.S.A.Per. **Document type:** trade publication.

338 CN ISSN 0835-4251
SMALL BUSINESS WORLD MAGAZINE. 1987. bi-m. Can.$10($15) 2433 Southvale Crescent, Ottawa, Ont. K1B 4T8, Canada. TEL 613-733-4260. Ed. Astrid Robinson. adv.; bk.rev. circ. 10,000. (back issues avail.)

338 UK ISSN 0957-1329
SMALL ENTERPRISE DEVELOPMENT. 1990. q. £36($60) to individuals; institutions £60 ($100) (effective 1996). Intermediate Technology Publications Ltd., 103-105 Southampton Row, London WC1B 4HH, England. TEL 44-171-436-9761. FAX 44-171-436-2013. E-mail: itpubs@gn.apc.org; URL: http://www.oneworld.org/itdg/publications.html. Ed. Clare Tawney. adv.; bk.rev. circ. 1,000. **Indexed:** Abstr.Rural Dev.Trop., Geo.Abstr.P.G., IBR, IDA. **Document type:** academic/scholarly publication.
—BLDSC (8309.983800); SWETS. **CCC.**
Refereed Serial

338 TZ
SMALL INDUSTRIES DEVELOPMENT ORGANIZATION. ANNUAL REPORT. (Editions in English and Swahili) 1975. a. Small Industries Development Organization (SIDO), P.O. Box 2476, Dar es Salaam, Tanzania. Ed.Bd. circ. 1,000. **Document type:** corporate report.

BUSINESS AND ECONOMICS — SMALL BUSINESS

338   II
SMALL INDUSTRIES GUIDE.* irreg., no.2, 1969. Rs.2 per issue. Ministry of Industrial Development, Development Commissioner-Small Scale Industries, Internal Trade and Company Affairs, New Delhi, India. charts; stat.

381
SMALL SCALE INDUSTRIES ENVOY. (Text in English) 1972. m. Rs.10. Maharashtra Small Scale Industries Association, 0-10 Bhavana Prabhadevi, Bombay 25, India. Ed. Samuel Valiyaparampil. adv.; bk.rev. circ. 5,000.

338   NR
SMALL-SCALE INDUSTRIES: SOUTH EASTERN AND BENUE PLATEAU STATES OF NIGERIA. a. University of Nigeria, Department of Economics, Nsukka, Enugu State, Nigeria. Eds. E.C. Iwuji, A.E. Okorafor.

338
SMALL TIME OPERATOR; how to start your own small business, keep your books, pay your taxes and stay out of trouble. 1976. a. $16.95. Bell Springs Publishing, Box 1240, Willits, CA 95490. TEL 707-459-6372. Ed. Bernard Kamoroff. bk.rev. circ. 40,000. **Document type:** consumer publication.

THE SOURCE (ABINGTON). see FOOD AND FOOD INDUSTRIES — Grocery Trade

338   US
SOUTHEAST ALASKA BUSINESS JOURNAL.* 1990. m. $15.60. Summit Services, Inc., 1910 Alex Holden Way, Juneau, AK 99801. TEL 907-789-0829. FAX 907-789-0987. Ed. Renda Heimbinger. adv. contact: Kristen Hammond. circ. 5,000. (back issues avail.) **Document type:** trade publication.
    Description: Informs owners of southeastern Alaska businesses on bankruptcies, liens, and business licences.

SOUVENIR. see GIFTWARE AND TOYS

338   US   ISSN 0735-1437
HD2346.U5
THE STATE OF SMALL BUSINESS: A REPORT OF THE PRESIDENT TRANSMITTED TO THE CONGRESS. a. price varies. U.S. Small Business Administration, Attn.: John Ward, Ed., MC-3114, 409 Third St., S.W., Washington, DC 20416. TEL 202-205-6531. URL: http://www.sba.gov/ADVO/stats/state.html. (Subscr. to: Superintendent of Documents, U.S. Government Printing Office, Box 371954, Pittsburgh, PA 15250-7954. TEL 202-512-1800. FAX 202-512-2250) R&P contact: John Ward. charts; stat. (also avail. in microfiche from NTI) **Document type:** government publication.
—BLDSC (8438.279000).
    Description: Compiles statistics on small businesses in the U.S. in an annual report to Congress.

338   US   ISSN 0742-843X
HD2346.U5
THE STATES AND SMALL BUSINESS: A DIRECTORY OF PROGRAMS AND ACTIVITIES. 1979. s-a. $12. U.S. Small Business Administration, Office of Advocacy, Mail Code 3114, Washington, DC 20416. TEL 202-205-6531. (Subscr to: Superintendent of Documents, U.S. Government Printing Office, Box 371954, Pittsburgh, PA 15250-7954. TEL 202-512-1800. FAX 202-512-2250) Ed. John Ward. circ. 2,500 (paid). (also avail. in microfiche) **Document type:** government publication, directory.
    Formerly: States and Small Business: Programs and Activities.
    Description: Lists more than 1,000 state programs for help in financing a small-business venture.

381.109489   DK   ISSN 0903-868X
SUPERMARKEDSHAANDBOGEN (YEAR)/SUPERMARKETS AND OTHER LARGE GROCERY STORES. 1965. a. DKK 1095. Stockmann-Gruppen A-S, Gammel Lundtoftevej 1C, DK-2800 Lyngby, Denmark. TEL 45-93-92-00. FAX 45-93-92-97-48. Dir. Henning Bahr. **Document type:** trade publication.
    Formerly (until 1995): Supermarkeder og Andre Store Dagligvarebutikker (Year); Formed by the merger of (1965-1988): Supermarkeder (ISSN 0586-9005); (1982-1988): Discountbutikker (ISSN 0108-5255); Formerly (1980-1982): Lavprisbutikker (ISSN 0107-4342)
    Description: Contains up-to-date information about the Danish everyday commodities market.

338   US   ISSN 1083-6691
SVOBODA'S HOME & SMALL BUSINESS; the magazine for the independent business professional. 1993. m. $24. American Business Communicators, 3553 W.Peterson Ave., Ste. 40, Chicago, IL 60659. TEL 773-588-4410. FAX 773-588-4415. E-mail: jcs@svobodamag.com; URL: http://www.svobodamag.com. Ed. Jill V. Cleary Svoboda; Pub. Albert J. Svoboda. adv.; B&W page $2290; trim 10 1/8 x 13 5/8; adv. contact: Albert J. Svoboda. bk.rev.; illus.; circ. 29,500 (controlled). (back issues avail.) **Document type:** trade publication.
    Former titles: Svoboda's Home and Small Business Reporter; Home and Small Business Reporter.

338   US
SWAP MEET. 1990. m. $30. Forum Publishing Co., 383 E. Main St., Centerport, NY 11721-1538. TEL 516-754-5000. FAX 516-754-0630. Ed. Sheri Stevens. adv. contact: Martin Stevens. circ. 70,000. **Document type:** trade publication.
    Description: Connects wholesalers and flea market vendors. Provides merchandise sources.

338 677   US   ISSN 1053-6493
T-SHIRT BUSINESS INFO MAPPING NEWSLETTER. 1990. biennial. $6.50 (foreign $8). Continnuus, c/o Prosperity & Profits Unlimited Distribution Services, Box 416, Denver, CO 80201-0416. TEL 303-575-5676. Ed. A.C. Doyle. R&P contact: A. Doyle. circ. 1,500. (looseleaf format) **Document type:** newsletter.
    Description: Provides information on the t-shirt business.

TABAK PLUS BENELUX; vakblad voor de tabaksdetailhandel. see TOBACCO

338   UK
TAKING UP A FRANCHISE; the Daily Telegraph guide. a. £9.99. Kogan Page Ltd., 120 Pentonville Rd., London N1 9JN, England. TEL 44-171-278-0433. FAX 44-171-837-6348. TELEX 263088 KOGAN G. R&P contact: Linda Batman. **Document type:** trade publication.

338   US   ISSN 0885-1522
TANNING TRENDS; the news journal for the indoor tanning industry. 1985. 10/yr. $56 (foreign $76) (effective 1996). Tanning Trends Inc., 3101 Page Ave., Jackson, MI 49203. TEL 517-784-1772. FAX 517-787-3940. E-mail: tantrends@voyager.net. (Subscr. addr.: Box 1630, Jackson, MI 49204) Ed. Bonnie Gretzner; Pub. Matt D. Russell. R&P contact: Matt D. Russell. adv.; B&W page $1635, color page $2315; trim 8 1/4 x 10 3/4; adv. contact: Victoria Moss. circ. 20,000 (controlled). (back issues avail.) **Document type:** trade publication.

TELEMARKETER. see BUSINESS AND ECONOMICS — Marketing And Purchasing

338 330.9   US   ISSN 0735-1135
HC107.T3
TENNESSEE'S BUSINESS. 1974. 3/yr. free. Middle Tennessee State University, College of Business, 1301 E. Main St., MTSU Box 102, Murfreesboro, TN 37132. TEL 615-898-2610. FAX 615-898-5045. E-mail: pawells@mtsu.edu; URL: http://www.mtsu/-berc/. Ed. Horace E. Johns. R&P contact: Reuben Kyle. adv. contact: Reuben Kyle. circ. 5,500. Indexed: P.A.I.S. **Document type:** academic/scholarly publication.
    Formerly (until 1990): Tennessee Business and Economic Review.
    Description: Provides a forum for exchange of ideas in the field of economics and business among businesspersons, academicians, and government officials.

338   CN   ISSN 0834-3497
THUNDER BAY BUSINESS. 1984. m. Can.$25. North Superior Publishing Inc., 1145 Barton St., Thunder Bay, ON P7B 5N3, Canada. TEL 807-623-2348. FAX 807-623-7515. Ed. Scott A. Sumnr; Pub. Scott A. Sumnr. circ. 10,000. (tabloid format; back issues avail.) **Document type:** trade publication.

338   SW   ISSN 1101-7872
TIDNINGEN FOERETAGARNA. (Supplement avail.: Marknad) 1991. 13/yr. SEK 295 (effective 1991). (Foeretagarnas Riksorganisation) Foeretagarna Foerlags AB, Vegagatan 14, S-113 93 Stockholm, Sweden. FAX 46-8-32-71-68. Ed. Rolf Bromme. adv. circ. 85,000. **Document type:** trade publication.
    Formed by the merger of (1936-1991): Smaafoertagartidningen Hantverck och Industri (ISSN 0283-9652); (1898-1991): Foeretagaren (ISSN 0015-5276)

TIME MANAGEMENT. see BUSINESS AND ECONOMICS — Personnel Management

TOOWOOMBA INDUSTRIAL PROFILE. see BUSINESS AND ECONOMICS — Economic Situation And Conditions

338   CN   ISSN 0831-4160
TORONTO BUSINESS MAGAZINE. 1975. s-a. Can.$33. Zanny Publications Ltd., 11966 Woodbine Ave., Gormley, ON L0H 1G0, Canada. TEL 905-887-5048. FAX 905-479-4839. Ed. Amy Margaret; Pub. Janet Gardiner. adv.; B&W page Can.$3017, color page Can.$3960; trim 8 1/4 x 10 3/4; adv. contact: B. Baker. circ. 41,000. **Document type:** trade publication.

338 388.324   US   ISSN 0894-962X
TRUCKSTOP WORLD. 1987. q. $18. Newport Communications, Box W, Newport Beach, CA 92658. TEL 714-261-1636. Ed. Jack Thiessen. adv. circ. 9,821.
—CCC.

U.S. INTERNAL REVENUE SERVICE. TAX GUIDE FOR SMALL BUSINESS. see BUSINESS AND ECONOMICS — Public Finance, Taxation

338   US   ISSN 0083-3274
HC106.5
U.S. SMALL BUSINESS ADMINISTRATION. ANNUAL REPORT. 1953. a. free. U.S. Small Business Administration, c/o John Ward, Ed., MC-3114, 409 Third St., S.W., Washington, DC 20416. TEL 202-205-6740. R&P contact: John Ward. circ. 2,000 (controlled). (also avail. in microfiche from NTI) **Document type:** government publication.
    Description: Summary of activities and accomplishments of the Small Business Administration's numerous program areas.

338   US   ISSN 0742-3802
HD2346.U5
U.S. SMALL BUSINESS ADMINISTRATION. OFFICE OF THE INSPECTOR GENERAL. SEMI-ANNUAL REPORT. 1978. s-a. free. U.S. Small Business Administration, Office of the Inspector General, 409 Third St. S.W., Washington, DC 20416. FAX 202-205-7382. circ. 300. **Document type:** government publication.

UNIVERSITY OF NEW ENGLAND. DEPARTMENT OF ACCOUNTING & FINANCIAL MANAGEMENT. WORKING PAPERS. see BUSINESS AND ECONOMICS — Accounting

338 630   US
THE UPRIGHT OSTRICH.* 10/yr. $25 (foreign $35). Order of the Upright Ostrich, 3585 County Rd. O, Milwaukee, WI 53080-1435. TEL 414-332-5075. Ed. Peggy Poor.
    Description: Supports independent farmers, small business, and the return to a sound money system.

VENTURE CAPITAL JOURNAL; the only financial analyst of small business investment companies and venture capital companies. see BUSINESS AND ECONOMICS — Investments

338 332.6   UK   ISSN 0265-6248
VENTURE CAPITAL REPORT. 1978. m. £300. Venture Capital Report Ltd., The Magdalen Centre, Oxford Science Park, Oxford OX4 4GA, England. TEL 44-1865-784411. FAX 44-1865-784412. E-mail: vcr@vcr1978.demon.co.uk; URL: http://www.demon.co.uk/vcr1978. Ed. Lucius Cary. adv.; bk.rev.; charts; illus.; index, cum.index. circ. 800. (back issues avail.) **Document type:** bulletin.
—BLDSC (9154.535000).

BUSINESS AND ECONOMICS — TRADE AND INDUSTRIAL DIRECTORIES

338   UK
VENTURE CAPITAL REPORT GUIDE TO VENTURE CAPITAL IN THE U K AND EUROPE. 1983. biennial. £125. Venture Capital Report Ltd., The Magdalen Centre, Oxford Science Park, Oxford OX4 4GA, England. TEL 44-1865-784411. FAX 44-1865-784412. E-mail: vcr@vcr1978.demon.uk; URL: http://www.demon.co.uk/vcr1978. Ed. Lucius Cary. circ. 2,000. **Document type:** trade publication.
    Formerly: Venture Capital Report Guide to Venture Capital in Europe.

338   CN   ISSN 0830-8713
VICTORIA'S BUSINESS REPORT. 1983. 18/yr. Can.$18. Monday Publications Ltd., 1609 Blanshard St., Victoria, BC V8W 2J5, Canada. TEL 604-382-6188. FAX 604-381-2662. Ed. Gery Lemon. adv.: B&W page Can.$750; adv. contact: John Meloche. circ. 14,000. **Document type:** consumer publication.

338   US
VIRTUALBUSINESS NEWS. w. E-mail: paulm@virtualbusiness.news; URL: http://www.virtualbusiness.net/vbnews/.
    •Available online only.
    Description: Dedicated to small and home-based businesses.

338   FR
VOLONTE. 11/yr. Societe d'Edition et de Publication des Petites et Moyennes Entreprises, 23 rue de Clery, 75002 Paris, France. TEL 45-08-91-88. Ed. Lucien Rebuffel. circ. 45,000.

338 621.38   US
W E S A NEWSLETTER. 1973. bi-m. free to qualified personnel. Wisconsin Electronic Sales and Service Association, Box 531, Butler, WI 53007-0531. TEL 414-246-6495. Ed. Larry Neuens. adv.: page $50; adv. contact: Larry Neuens. circ. 250 (controlled). **Document type:** newsletter.

WHAT'S BREWING. see *BEVERAGES*

338   US   ISSN 0897-5116
WISCONSIN SMALL BUSINESS COUNSELOR. 1985. 10/yr. $44.97. Counselor Publishing Co., Inc., Business Research Center, Box 1896, Green Bay, WI 54305-1896. TEL 414-435-0808. FAX 414-432-8581. Ed. Philip C. Hauck. adv.; bk.rev.; cum.index: 1986-1992. circ. 3,000. (back issues avail.) **Document type:** trade publication.
    Description: Practical ideas and techniques for business owners.

338   SA
WOMEN ENTREPRENEURS IN SOUTH AFRICA. (Text in English) 1993. a. Dictum Publishers, P.O. Box 40704, Cleveland 2022, South Africa. illus.

WORCESTER BUSINESS JOURNAL. see *BUSINESS AND ECONOMICS — Domestic Commerce*

WORK-AT-HOME SOURCEBOOK; how to find "at-home" work that's right for you. see *OCCUPATIONS AND CAREERS*

338   UK
WORKS MANAGEMENT SPECIAL REPORT FOR SMALLER COMPANIES. q. Franks Hall, Horton Kirby, Kent DA4 9LL, England. TEL 0322-222222. FAX 0322-289577. Ed. John Dwyer.

338.7 658   CC   ISSN 1005-4340
XIANGZHEN QIYE YU NONGCHANG GUANLI. (Subseries of: Fuyin Baokan Ziliao) (Text in Chinese) m. $65.19. Zhongguo Renmin Daxue, Shubao Ziliao Zhongxin - China People's University, Book & Newspaper Information Center, 3 Zhang Zizhong Rd., P.O. Box 1122, Beijing 100007, People's Republic of China. TEL 86-10-4015080. (Dist. in US by: China Publications Service, Box 49614, Chicago, IL 60649. TEL 312-288-3291. FAX 312-288-8570) pp./issue: 96.

346.066   US   ISSN 0731-1109
KF889.A1
YOU AND THE LAW;* executive guide to legal problems. 1973. m. $125. National Institute of Business Management, Box 9206, McLean, VA 22102-9666. TEL 703-905-8000. (Subscr. to: Box 25348, Alexandria, VA 22313) Ed. Dan Moskowitz. bibl. circ. 14,000. (looseleaf format) **Document type:** newsletter.
    Formerly (until 1978): Your Business and the Law (ISSN 0093-3503)

334   US   ISSN 0736-4865
HG4027.7
YOU AND YOUR BUSINESS.* 1977. m. Thomas J. Martin, Ed. & Pub., 16 Fox LN, Locust Valley, NY 11560-1119. TEL 516-681-2111. circ. controlled.

338   US   ISSN 1064-2544
HD62.7
YOUR COMPANY; a small-business resource for the 90s. 1993. q. free to qualified personnel. American Express Publishing Corp. (New York), 1120 Ave. of the Americas, New York, NY 10036. TEL 212-382-5600. FAX 212-768-1568. Ed. Mary Ellen Ward.

338   SA   ISSN 1023-5213
YOUR OWN BUSINESS. (Text in English) 1994. m. R.76.45. P.O. Box 16557, Vlaeberg 8018, South Africa. adv.; illus. **Document type:** consumer publication.

338   BE
ZELFSTANDIG ONDERNEMEN. w. N.C.M.V., Spastraat 8, 1040 Brussels, Belgium. TEL 238-05-11. FAX 230-93-54. Ed. Ronny Lannoo. adv.: B&W page 87400 BEF, color page 129000 BEF; trim 280 x 410. circ. 28,000.
    Description: Provides information on trade management for small businesses.

338   CC
ZHONGGUO QIYEJIA/CHINESE ENTREPRENEURS. (Text in Chinese) m. $50.30. Jingji Ribao She - Economic Daily, 277 Wangfujing Dajie, Beijing 100746, People's Republic of China. (Dist. in US by: China Books & Periodicals, Inc., 2929 24th St., San Francisco, CA 94110) Ed. Feng Bing.

338   CC
ZHONGGUO XIANGZHEN QIYE/CHINA'S TOWNSHIP ENTERPRISES. (Text in Chinese) m. Nongye Bu, Xiangzhen Qiye Ju - Ministry of Agriculture, Bureau of Township Enterprises, No. 11, Nongzhanguan Nanli, Beijing 100026, People's Republic of China. TEL 5003366. (Dist. in US by: China Books & Periodicals, Inc., 2929 24th St., San Francisco, CA 94110. TEL 415-282-2994) Ed. Zhang Yi. **Document type:** government publication.

BUSINESS AND ECONOMICS — Trade And Industrial Directories

338 340   US
A B A JOURNAL ANNUAL BUYERS GUIDE. 1993. a. American Bar Association, 750 N. Lake Shore Dr., Chicago, IL 60611. TEL 312-988-5000. FAX 312-988-6014. adv.: B&W page $3000, color page $4500; trim 8 3/16 x 10 3/4. circ. 38,000. **Document type:** directory.

338.025   BE   ISSN 0775-6178
A B C BELGE POUR LE COMMERCE ET L'INDUSTRIE. (Text in Dutch, French; summaries in English, German) 1981. a. A B C pour le Commerce et l'Industrie C.V., Doornveld 1B28, B-1731 Asse, Belgium. TEL 32-2-4630273. FAX 32-2-4630885. Ed. Daniel Labbeke. (also avail. in diskette format) **Document type:** directory.
    •Also available online.
    Also available on CD-ROM.
    Description: Business information on Belgian companies, including manufacturers and producers, importers, and professional services.

380   GW
A B C DER DEUTSCHEN WIRTSCHAFT - QUELLENWERK FUR EINKAUF-VERKAUF. (Text in German; indexed in English, French, Spanish) a. $147 (effective 1997). A B C Publishing Group, Postfach 100262, 64202 Darmstadt, Germany. TEL 49-6151-3892-0. FAX 49-6151-33164. TELEX 419257. (Dist. in US by: Western Hemisphere Publishing Corp., Box 847, Hillsboro, OR 97123. TEL 503-640-3736. FAX 503-640-2748) Ed. Margit Selka. R&P contact: Margit Selka. circ. 30,000. **Document type:** directory.
    •Also available online. Vendor(s): Data-Star, FIZ Technik.
    Also available on CD-ROM.

338.025   BE   ISSN 0776-9954
A B C LUXEMBOURGEOIS POUR LE COMMERCE ET L'INDUSTRIE. (Text in French) 1989. a. A B C pour le Commerce et l'Industrie C.V., Doornveld 1B28, B-1731 Asse, Belgium. TEL 32-2-4630273. FAX 32-2-4630885. adv. avail. in diskette format; magnetic tape) **Document type:** directory.
    •Also available online.
    Also available on CD-ROM.
    Description: Provides information on businesses in Luxembourg in the manufacturing and service sectors.

A B D. (Aviation Buyers Directory) see *AERONAUTICS AND SPACE FLIGHT*

A B H I DIRECTORY. (Association of British Health-Care Industries) see *MEDICAL SCIENCES*

380   JA
A C C J DIRECTORY. (Text in English) 1950. a. (plus 3 updates). 5000 Yen($45) to members; non-members 10000 Yen($95). American Chamber of Commerce in Japan, Bridgestone Toranomon Bldg., 5-F, 3-25-2 Toranomon, Minato-ku, Tokyo 105, Japan. TEL 03-3433-5381. FAX 03-3436-1446. E-mail: info@accj.or.jp. Ed. Jeanmarie Todd. R&P contact: Jeanmarie Todd. adv. (also avail. in diskette format) **Document type:** directory.
    Description: Listing of Chamber members, member firms, supporting associates and companies of the American Chamber of Commerce in Japan.

338.025   US
A D S C MEMBERSHIP DIRECTORY. a. $75 (foreign $90). Association of Drilled Shaft Contractors, Box 280379, Dallas, TX 75228. TEL 214-343-2091. FAX 214-343-2384. Ed. Scot Litke. adv.: bk.rev. circ. 2,000. **Document type:** directory.
    Description: Listings of all contractor, supplier and technical members involved in drilled shaft and anchored earth retention construction and design throughout the world.

338.476   US
A F I BUYING DIRECTORY. a. $35. (National Association of Federally Licensed Firearms Dealers) A F I Communications Group Inc., 2455 E. Sunrise Blvd., 9th Fl., Ft. Lauderdale, FL 33304-3118. TEL 954-561-3505. FAX 954-561-4129. URL: http://www.amfire.com. Ed. Robert Lesmeister; Pub. Andrew Molchan. adv.: B&W page $3275; 7 x 10; adv. contact: Jim VanBuren. circ. 60,000. **Document type:** directory.
    Formerly: A F I Buying Directory and Who's Who.

388.324   US
A M C SCALE DIRECTORY (YEARS); United States and Canada. biennial. $20. American Movers Conference, 1611 Duke St., Alexandria, VA 22314. TEL 703-683-7410. FAX 703-548-1845. **Document type:** directory, trade publication.
    Description: Contains listing of 1700 scales for weighing trucks in U.S. and Canada.

338.025 665.6   US
A O S C DIRECTORY. 1963. a. $50 to non-members; members $20. Association of Oilwell Servicing Contractors, 6060 N. Central Expy., Ste. 428, Dallas, TX 75206. TEL 214-692-0771. Ed. Katherine Leidy. adv. contact: Katherine Leidy. circ. 1,000. (back issues avail.) **Document type:** directory.

388.025   US
A P R A (YEAR) MEMBERSHIP ROSTER AND TRADE DIRECTORY. a. $400. Automotive Parts Rebuilders Association, 4401 Fair Lakes Court, Ste. 210, Fairfax, VA 22033. Ed. Judith W. Chandler. circ. 2,100. (back issues avail.) **Document type:** directory, trade publication.
    Description: Lists rebuilders and suppliers within the automotive aftermarket industry that are members of APRA.

A P R O DIRECTORY. see *TRAVEL AND TOURISM*

A P T YEARBOOK. (Asia - Pacific Telecommunity) see *COMMUNICATIONS — Telephone And Telegraph*

B

BUSINESS AND ECONOMICS — TRADE AND INDUSTRIAL DIRECTORIES

670 696 US
A S A MEMBERSHIP DIRECTORY. 1980. a. $70 to non-members; members $40. American Supply Association, 222 Merchandise Mart Pl., Ste. 1360, Chicago, IL 60654. TEL 312-464-0090. FAX 312-464-0091. E-mail: asaemail@interserv.com. Ed. Brad Fridell; Pub. Brad Fridell. adv. contact: Molly Frank-Stewart. circ. 3,200. **Document type:** directory.

380 658.31 US
A S T D BUYERS GUIDE AND CONSULTANTS DIRECTORY. a. $45 to non-members. American Society for Training and Development, 1640 King St., Box 1443, Alexandria, VA 22313. TEL 703-683-8100. FAX 703-683-8103. Ed. Jan Throckmorton. adv. contact: Jan Throckmorton. **Document type:** directory.
Former titles: Training Resources; A S T D Consultant Directory (ISSN 0098-5619)

A T & T NATIONAL TOLL-FREE DIRECTORY - BUSINESS BUYER'S GUIDE - BUSINESS EDITION. see COMMUNICATIONS — Telephone And Telegraph

658 US
A W M A BUYING GUIDE & ANNUAL MEMBERSHIP DIRECTORY. a. $125. American Wholesale Marketers Association, 1128 16th St., N.W., Washington, DC 20036. TEL 202-463-2124. FAX 202-467-0559. Pub. Joyce A./Grimley. R&P contact: Joyce A. Grimley. adv. contact: Mary Ann Paniccia. **Document type:** directory.
Description: Complete guide to the wholesale candy, tobacco and snack food distribution industry.

382 TS
A - Z: UNITED ARAB EMIRATES BUSINESS LOCATIONS GUIDE. 1988. a. Al- Saqr Publishing House, P.O. Box 198, Ajman, United Arab Emirates. TEL 425135. FAX 421876.

380.1 389.6 US ISSN 1043-0121
A 2 L A (YEAR) ANNUAL REPORT. 1987. a. American Association for Laboratory Accreditation, 656 Quince Orchard Rd., Ste. 620, Gaithersburg, MD 20878-1409. TEL 301-670-1377. FAX 301-869-1495. Ed. Theresa Adams; Pub. Peter Unger. **Document type:** corporate report.

380.1 389.6 US ISSN 1040-9181
TA416.5.U6
A 2 L A (YEAR) DIRECTORY OF ACCREDITED LABORATORIES. 1980. a. free. American Association for Laboratory Accreditation, 656 Quince Orchard Rd., Ste. 620, Gaithersburg, MD 20878-1409. TEL 301-670-1377. FAX 301-869-1495. Ed. Theresa Adams; Pub. Peter Unger. index. **Document type:** directory.
Description: Provides scope of testing capability for 900 laboratories found competent to perform specific tests or types of tests.

380.1 389.6 US ISSN 1040-9157
A 2 L A NEWS. 1980. q. free. American Association for Laboratory Accreditation, 656 Quince Orchard Rd., Ste. 620, Gaithersburg, MD 20878-1409. TEL 301-670-1377. FAX 301-869-1495. Ed. Percy Pan; Pub. Peter Unger. **Document type:** newsletter.
Formerly: A 2 L A Update.
Description: Presents updating information on accredited labs.

ACCESS (SEATTLE); a guide to the visual arts in Washington State. see ART

690 US
ACCESS CONTROL & SECURITY INTEGRATION BUYERS' GUIDE. 1958. a. $59.95. Intertec Publishing Corp. (Atlanta), 6151 Powers Ferry Rd., N.W., Atlanta, GA 30339-2941. TEL 770-955-2500. FAX 770-955-0400. Ed. Barbara Katinsky. adv. **Document type:** trade publication.
Former titles: Access Control Buyers' Guide & Fence Industry - Access Control Directory; Fence Industry Directory.

ADAM FILM WORLD GUIDE DIRECTORY OF ADULT FILM. see MOTION PICTURES

380 659.1 AT ISSN 0819-6648
ADBRIEF REGISTER: AGENCIES & MARKETERS. 1986. 3/yr. Aus.$345($220) (effective 1996). Newsletter Information Services, P.O. Box 693, Manly, N.S.W. 2095, Australia. TEL 61-2-9777500. E-mail: hww@hww.com.au; URL: http://www.hww.com.au. Ed. Simon Canning. R&P contact: Sue Mitchell. adv.: B&W page Aus.$500; adv. contact: Janice Garrett. circ. 500. (also avail. in diskette format) **Document type:** directory.
Description: Directory of advertising agencies, advertising consultancies, media-buying and sales promotion companies and national and regional advertisers.

668.3 UK
ADHESIVES AND SEALANTS DIRECTORY. 1966. a. £37 (rest of world £41) (effective 1996). Turret Group Plc., Turret House, 171 High St., Rickmansworth, Herts WD3 1SN, England. TEL 44-1923-777000. FAX 44-1923-771297. adv.; charts. **Document type:** directory.
Formerly: Adhesives Directory (ISSN 0305-3199)

ADRESSBUCH FUER DEN DEUTSCHSPRACHIGEN BUCHHANDEL C D - R O M. see PUBLISHING AND BOOK TRADE

001.642 620 US ISSN 0749-4874
T12.3.W2
ADVANCED TECHNOLOGY IN WASHINGTON STATE. 1984. a. $34 (diskette $48) (effective 1995 & 1996). Commerce Publishing Corp. (Seattle), Box 9805, Seattle, WA 98109-0805. TEL 206-286-1498. Ed. Glenn Avery. R&P contact: Glenn Avery. bk.rev.; circ. 12,500 (paid). (also avail. in diskette format) **Document type:** directory.
Description: Provides information on over 1500 technology based firms, including address, size by sales and employees, key personnel, market areas, and product data. Includes general information on the technology and software industry in Washington State.

382 659.1 US ISSN 1055-8950
ADWEEK AGENCY DIRECTORY. (Supplement to: Client - Brand Directory, Major Media Directory) a. $275. A S M Communications, Inc. (New York), 1515 Broadway, New York, NY 10036. TEL 212-536-5263. (Subscr. to: Box 2006, Lakewood, NJ 08701. TEL 800-468-2395) Ed. Michael Battaglia; Pub. Mitch Tego. adv. contact: Julie Azons. **Document type:** directory.
Description: Directory of US advertising agencies, public relations firms, and media buying services, providing key facts and personnel.

659.1 US ISSN 1049-7064
HF6182.U5
ADWEEK CLIENT - BRAND DIRECTORY. (Suppl. to: Adweek Agency Directory) 1988. a. $235. B P I Communications Inc. (New York), 1515 Broadway, New York, NY 10036. TEL 212-765-7300; 800-468-2395. (Subscr. to: Box 2006, Lakewood, NJ 08701) adv. **Document type:** directory.
Description: Directory of US brand-name products and services and the organizations that market them. Provides key facts and personnel.

380 US
AFFILIATED WAREHOUSE COMPANIES DIRECTORY. 1953. biennial. free. Affiliated Warehouse Companies, Inc., Box 295, Hazlet, NJ 07730. TEL 908-739-2323. Ed. Jim McBride. circ. 16,000 (controlled). **Document type:** directory.
Description: Lists third party warehouses, contacts, phone and fax numbers, location and size, and what type of storage each warehouse has. For organizations seeking public warehouse space or outsource warehousing.

AFFILIATES DIRECTORY. see BUSINESS AND ECONOMICS — Personnel Management

338.025 792 UK ISSN 0964-7244
AFRO-ASIAN ARTISTS' REGISTER. 1990. biennial. (British Actors' Equity) Spotlight, 7 Leicester Pl., London WC2H 7BP, England. TEL 44-171-437-7631. FAX 44-171-437-5881. E-mail: info@spotlightcd.com. Ed. Christine Barry. **Document type:** directory.

338 778.534 US ISSN 1069-3890
PN2289
AGENCIES: WHAT THE ACTOR NEEDS TO KNOW. 1984. m. $50. Acting World Books, Box 3899, Hollywood, CA 90078. TEL 818-905-1345; 800-210-1197. Ed. Lawrence Parke. adv. contact: Lawrence Parke. tr.lit. circ. 7,000. **Document type:** directory, trade publication.
Description: Update of franchised talent agencies in Hollywood, with full descriptions of representation and staffs; also includes appraisals by industry consultants and career guidance editorials.

780 SP
AGENDA CLAVE; guia practica de la industria musical y del espectaculo. 1993. a. 12000 ptas.($98) (effective 1997). Clave Professional, Av. Gaudi 10, 2o, 1a, 08025 Barcelona, Spain. TEL 34-3-3475199. FAX 34-3-4561729. Pub. Jordi Rueda. adv.: B&W page 120000 ptas ($1000), color page 160000 ptas. ($1400); 190 x 270. **Document type:** directory.
Description: Provides about 15000 addresses of organizations and professionals in the music and show business industries in Spain and Spanish-speaking countries.

AGRICULTURE, HORTICULTURE AND FORESTRY; a directory of New Zealand contacts. see AGRICULTURE

AIR FREIGHT DIRECTORY. see TRANSPORTATION — Air Transport

338.025 US ISSN 1043-7924
HF5065.A37
ALABAMA BUSINESS DIRECTORY. 1988. a. $350 (effective 1997). American Business Directories (Subsidiary of: American Business Information, Inc.), 5711 S. 86th Cir., Box 27347, Omaha, NE 68127. TEL 402-593-4600; 800-555-6124. FAX 401-331-5481. E-mail: jerr.venner@abii.com. index. (also avail. in magnetic tape; diskette format) **Document type:** directory.
●Also available online.
Also available on CD-ROM.
Description: Includes all businesses in the state compiled from the yellow pages and telephone-verified. Each listing includes company name, complete address, phone number, name of owner, manager, and employee size, sales volume codes, credit rating codes.

670 US ISSN 1061-9585
T12
ALABAMA INDUSTRIAL DIRECTORY. biennial. $55. Development Office, c/o State Capitol, 401 Adams Ave., Montgomery, AL 36130. TEL 205-242-0400. FAX 205-242-2414. Ed. Steve Nix. adv.; index. circ. 5,000. **Document type:** directory, government publication.
Formerly (until 1991): Alabama Directory of Mining and Manufacturing (ISSN 0145-4048); Supersedes (in 1976): Industrial Alabama (ISSN 0073-7321)

670 US ISSN 1045-2664
HF5065.A37
ALABAMA MANUFACTURERS REGISTER. a. $79 (diskette $445; CD-Rom $445) (effective 1997). Manufacturers' News, Inc., 1633 Central St., Evanston, IL 60201. TEL 847-864-7000. FAX 847-332-1100. Ed. Louise M. West. adv.: B&W page $1843; adv. contact: Charles Scherer. (also avail. in diskette format) **Document type:** directory.
●Also available on CD-ROM.
Description: Profiles 6,847 manufacturers, listed ways: by product, alphabetically, by city, by S.I.C. and by parent company. Complete addresses, phone numbers and flags for new businesses in city, alphabetical and SIC sections.

338.025 US ISSN 1060-7943
ALAMEDA COUNTY COMMERCE AND INDUSTRY DIRECTORY. a. $75. Database Publishing Company, 1590 S. Lewis St., Anaheim, CA 92805-6423. TEL 714-778-6400. FAX 714-778-6811. (Subscr. to: Box 70024, Anaheim, CA 92825-0024. TEL 800-888-8434) (also avail. in diskette format) **Document type:** directory.
●Also available on CD-ROM.
Description: Lists 3,800 manufacturers, wholesalers and service companies; and 8,900 owners and key executives.

BUSINESS AND ECONOMICS — TRADE AND INDUSTRIAL DIRECTORIES

338   US   ISSN 1048-7069
HF5065.A4
ALASKA BUSINESS DIRECTORY. 1990. a. $295 (effective 1997). American Business Directories (Subsidiary of: American Business Information, Inc.), 5711 S. 86th Cir., Box 27347, Omaha, NE 68127. TEL 402-593-4600; 800-555-6124. FAX 402-331-5481. E-mail: jerry.venner@abii.com. index. (also avail. in magnetic tape; diskette format)
Document type: directory.
●Also available online.
Also available on CD-ROM.
  Description: Includes all businesses in the state compiled from the yellow pages and telephone-verified. Each listing includes company name, complete address, phone number, name of owner, manager, and employee size and sales volume codes, and credit rating codes.

ALASKA BUSINESS MONTHLY. see *BUSINESS AND ECONOMICS*

338.025   US   ISSN 1085-746X
ALASKA MANUFACTURERS REGISTER. 1994. a. $45 (diskette $195;CD-ROM $195) (effective 1997). Manufacturers' News, Inc., 1633 Central St., Evanston, IL 60201-1569. TEL 847-864-7000. FAX 847-332-1100. (also avail. in diskette format)
Document type: directory.
  Supersedes in part (in 1996): Alaska - Hawaii Manufacturers Directory (ISSN 1074-2468)
  Description: Profiles 611 companies.

380 340   CN   ISSN 0823-2350
ALBERTA LEGAL TELEPHONE DIRECTORY. a. Can.$17.50 (effective 1997). Canada Law Book Inc., 240 Edward St., Aurora, ON L4G 3S9, Canada. TEL 905-841-6472; 800-263-2037. FAX 905-841-5085. Ed. Judy Antoniadis. adv. contact: Mary Powell. **Document type:** directory.

380 622   CN   ISSN 0831-019X
ALBERTA OIL & GAS DIRECTORY. 1980. a. Can.$95. Armadale Publications Inc., Box 1193, MPO, Edmonton, Alta. T5J 2M4, Canada. TEL 403-429-1073. FAX 403-425-5844. Ed. Winston Mohabir. adv.; tr.lit. circ. 7,000. (back issues avail.) **Document type:** directory.
—CISTI.

338   US   ISSN 1049-8257
HF5035
ALL-IN-ONE BUSINESS CONTACTBOOK (YEAR). 1990. a. $49.95. Gale Research, 835 Penobscot Bldg., 645 Griswold St., Detroit, MI 48226-4094. TEL 313-961-2243; 800-877-4253. FAX 800-414-5043. E-mail: daniel__snyder@gale.com. Ed. Karen Hill.
  Description: Provides dial-up listings for 10,000 US companies.

338.025   II
ALL INDIA INDUSTRIAL YELLOW PAGES. Short title: A I I T P. (Text in English) 1991. irreg. Rs.500($80) Kanishka Industrial Consultants Pvt. Ltd., 12, Community Centre, Mayapuri Phase-I, New Delhi 110064, India. TEL 5413209. Ed. R.K. Verma. adv. **Document type:** directory.
  Description: Directory on various Indian industries with name, addresses, telephone, and products.

338   SA   ISSN 1016-6327
AMANZIMTOTI DIRECTORY. 1981. a. $20. Braby's (Subsidiary of: Kohler Packaging Ltd.), P.O. Box 1426, Pinetown 3600, South Africa. TEL 27-31-7017021. FAX 27-31-7017036. **Document type:** directory.

AMERICAN ART DIRECTORY. see *ART*

380.1   US
AMERICAN ASSOCIATION OF MEAT PROCESSORS. GOLD BOOK MEMBERSHIP DIRECTORY AND BUYERS' GUIDE. s-a. $95. American Association of Meat Processors, Box 269, Elizabethtown, PA 17022. TEL 717-367-1168. FAX 717-367-9096. E-mail: aamp@aamp.com. Ed. Anne B. Tantum. circ. 2,300. **Document type:** directory.
  Former titles: American Association of Meat Processors. Gold Book Members & American Association of Meat Processors. Directory of Suppliers and Wholesalers.
  Description: Lists location of meat businesses, products and suppliers.

388   US   ISSN 1069-8442
HF5035
AMERICAN BIG BUSINESSES DIRECTORY. a. $595 (effective 1997). American Business Directories (Subsidiary of: American Business Information, Inc.), 5711 S. 86th Circle, Box 27347, Omaha, NE 68127. TEL 402-593-4600; 800-555-6124. FAX 402-331-5481. E-mail: jerry.venner@abii.com. (also avail. in magnetic tape; diskette format)
Document type: directory.
  Former titles (until 1993): Big Businesses Directory (ISSN 1061-2173); (until 1990): Blue Chip Companies Directory.
  Description: Lists over 177,000 companies with 100 or more employees, alphabetically and by city. Includes company name, complete address and phone number, executive names and titles, up to 3 SIC codes, number of employees and sales volume, and credit rating codes.

380 614.6   US   ISSN 0065-7565
AMERICAN BLUE BOOK OF FUNERAL DIRECTORS. 1932. biennial. $75 (effective 1997). Kates - Boylston Publications, Inc., 100 Wood Av. South, Iselin, NJ 08830-2716. TEL 212-398-9266. FAX 212-768-9140. E-mail: ktsboylstn@aol.com. Ed. Patrick W. Purcell; Pub. Thomas Hughes. R&P contact: Thomas Hughes. adv.: B&W page $1150, color page $1925; trim 8 1/4 x 11; adv. contact: Patrick Purcell. bk.rev.; circ. 10,000 (paid). **Document type:** directory.

AMERICAN BOOK TRADE DIRECTORY. see *PUBLISHING AND BOOK TRADE*

338.025   US   ISSN 1062-5119
HF5035
THE AMERICAN BUSINESS DISC. a. American Business Directories (Subsidiary of: American Business Information), 5711 S. 86th Circle, Box 27347, Omaha, NE 68127. TEL 402-593-4523; 800-555-6124. FAX 402-331-6681. E-mail: jerry.venner@abii.com. **Document type:** directory.
●Available only on CD-ROM.
  Description: Lists 10 million U.S. businesses by name, S.I.C. code, yellow page heading, and geographic location.

338   AG
AMERICAN CHAMBER OF COMMERCE IN ARGENTINA. DIRECTORY. (Text in English) 1974. a. $100. American Chamber of Commerce in Argentina, Viamonte 1133, p.8, 1153 Buenos Aires, Argentina. TEL 54-1-3714500. FAX 54-1-3718400. adv.: page $1000; adv. contact: Mariana Urrestarazu. illus. **Document type:** directory.
  Former titles (until 1993): American Business in Argentina; (until 1977): Directory of American Business in Argentina.
  Description: Lists American businesses in Argentina. Contains information on the authorities, committees and companies which are members.

AMERICAN COMPANIES: GUIDE TO SOURCES OF INFORMATION/SOCIETES AMERICAINES: REPERTOIRE DES SOURCES DE DOCUMENTATION/AMERICANISCHE HANDELSGESELLSCHAFTEN: HANDBUCH DER INFORMATIONSQUELLEN. see *BUSINESS AND ECONOMICS — Abstracting, Bibliographies, Statistics*

AMERICAN DROP-SHIPPERS DIRECTORY. see *BUSINESS AND ECONOMICS — Marketing And Purchasing*

AMERICAN EXPORT REGISTER (YEAR). see *BUSINESS AND ECONOMICS — International Commerce*

AMERICAN FINANCIAL DIRECTORY. see *BUSINESS AND ECONOMICS — Banking And Finance*

677   US
AMERICAN FLOCK ASSOCIATION DIRECTORY. 1987. biennial. free. American Flock Association, 230 Congress St., Boston, MA 02110. TEL 617-542-8220. FAX 617-542-2199. E-mail: amerflock@aol.com; URL: http://www.flocking.org. Ed. David Trumbull. **Document type:** directory.
  Description: Lists companies which are flock users, flock producers, raw material suppliers, adhesive manufacturers, machinery suppliers, and consultants to the industry.

382   GR   ISSN 0065-8537
AMERICAN - HELLENIC CHAMBER OF COMMERCE. BUSINESS DIRECTORY. SPECIAL ISSUE. (Supplement to: American - Hellenic Chamber of Commerce. Business Directory (ISSN 0065-8529)) (Text in English) 1960. a. $250. American - Hellenic Chamber of Commerce, 16 Kanari St., 106 74 Athens, Greece. TEL 363-6407. Ed. Sotiris Yannopoulos; Pub. Sotiris Yannopoulos. adv. circ. 5,000. **Document type:** directory, trade publication.

380.1   US   ISSN 1061-219X
HD9723
AMERICAN MANUFACTURERS DIRECTORY. 1989. a. $595 (effective 1997). American Business Directories (Subsidiary of: American Business Information, Inc.), 5711 S. 86th Circle, Box 27347, Omaha, NE 68127. TEL 402-593-4600; 800-555-6124. FAX 402-331-5481. E-mail: jerry.venner@abii.com. index. (also avail. in magnetic tape; diskette format) **Document type:** directory.
●Also available online.
Also available on CD-ROM.
—CISTI.
  Formerly (until 1991): U S Manufacturers Directory (ISSN 1042-1742)
  Description: Includes all manufacturers across the US with 25 or more employees compiled from surveys. Each listing includes company name, complete address, phone number, name of owner and/or manager, and employee size and sales volume codes, credit rating codes.

AMERICAN RECOVERY ASSOCIATION. NEWS AND VIEWS. see *BUSINESS AND ECONOMICS — Banking And Finance*

AMERICAN SHOEMAKING DIRECTORY OF SHOE MANUFACTURERS. see *SHOES AND BOOTS*

AMERICAN SHOWCASE ILLUSTRATION. see *ART*

338.4   US
AMERICAN SPORTSWEAR & KNITTING TIMES BUYERS' GUIDE (YEAR); and knitwear apparel directory. a. $25. National Knitwear and Sportswear Association, 386 Park Ave. S., New York, NY 10016. TEL 212-683-7520. FAX 212-532-0766. **Document type:** trade publication, directory.
  Former titles: Knitting Times Buyers' Guide (Year) & Knitting Times Buyers' Guide and Knitwear Apparel Directory; Knitting Times Buyers' Guide and Knitwear Directory; Knitting Times Buyers' Guide Directory; Knitted Outerwear Times Buyer's Guide Directory.

380.1   US   ISSN 1061-2114
HF5421
AMERICAN WHOLESALERS AND DISTRIBUTORS DIRECTORY. 1992. irreg., 4th ed., 1996. $180 (effective 1997). Gale Research, 835 Penobscot Bldg., 645 Griswold St., Detroit, MI 48226-4094. TEL 313-961-2242; 800-877-4253. FAX 800-414-5043. E-mail: daniel__snyder@gale.com. Eds. Holly Selden, Jane Malonis. **Document type:** directory.

382   US   ISSN 0740-4018
HG4057
AMERICA'S CORPORATE FAMILIES AND INTERNATIONAL AFFILIATES. (In 3 vols.) a. $900 to commercial institutions; libraries $810. Dun and Bradstreet (Subsidiary of: Dun & Bradstreet Corporation), 3 Sylvan Way, Parsippany, NJ 07054-3896. TEL 201-605-6000.
  Description: Links U.S. parent companies with their foreign subsidiaries and foreign parent companies and their U.S. subsidiaries.

BUSINESS AND ECONOMICS — TRADE AND INDUSTRIAL DIRECTORIES

380.1 332　　　　US
HG4057
AMERICA'S CORPORATE FINANCE DIRECTORY. 1983. a. $575. National Register Publishing, A Division of Reed Elsevier Inc., 121 Chanlon Rd., New Providence, NJ 07974. TEL 908-464-6800. FAX 908-665-2870. TELEX 138 755. E-mail: info@reedref.com; URL: http://www.reedref.com. (Subscr. to: National Register Publishing, Order Dept., Box 31, New Providence, NJ 07974-9903. TEL 800-521-8110) (also avail. in magnetic tape) **Document type:** directory.
●Also available on CD-ROM. Producer(s): Bowker Electronic Publishing.
Formerly (until 1994): Corporate Finance Bluebook (ISSN 0740-2546)
Description: Lists 5,000 leading companies and 20,000 subsidiaries. Entries include information on sales, earnings, assets, liabilities, pension plan and assets, contact information, major suppliers, and US subsidiaries. Each entry also lists up to 23 financial service firms, including insurance brokers, insurers, pension managers, auditors, legal counsel, and master trustees.

338　　　　US　　ISSN 1057-5642
HG4915
AMERICA'S FINEST COMPANIES. 1991. a. $39.95. Staton Institute Inc., 300 East Blvd., Ste. B-4, Charlotte, NC 28203-4784. TEL 704-332-7514. FAX 704-332-0427. URL: http://www.statoninstitute.com. Ed. Bill Staton. stat. circ. 33,000.
Description: Lists all US companies with 10 or more straight years of higher earnings and dividends. Provides quality ratings, addresses and other valuable investment information.

AMERICA'S NETWORK DIRECTORY. see COMMUNICATIONS — Telephone And Telegraph

AMERICA'S PAY-PER-CALL DIRECTORY; a billion dollar baby. see COMMUNICATIONS — Telephone And Telegraph

ANGLO - AMERICAN TRADE DIRECTORY (YEAR). see BUSINESS AND ECONOMICS — Chamber Of Commerce Publications

382　　　　FR
ANNUAIRE DES EXPORTATEURS FRANCAIS COMMERCANT AVEC L'U.R.S.S. 1976. a. 270 F. to non-members. Chambre de Commerce Franco-Rousse, 22 av. F.D. Roosevelt, 75008 Paris, France.

380　　　　AT
ANNUAIRE FRANCAIS D'AUSTRALIE. (Text in French) 1957. biennial. Aus.$50. Courrier Australien, 506-149 Castlereagh St., Sydney, N.S.W. 2000, Australia. Ed. J.P. Sourdin. R&P contact: J.P. Soudrin. adv. contact: J.P. Soudrin. circ. 6,000. (back issues avail.) **Document type:** directory.
Description: Directory of French business associations and people in Australia, as well as interested Australian companies and personalities.

ANNUAL REGISTRARS SERVICE. see BUSINESS AND ECONOMICS — Investments

338 617.7　　　　IT
ANNUARIO OTTICO ITALIANO. quadrennial. L.120000 (foreign L.135000) (effective 1996 ed.) Edizioni Ariminum, Via Negroli 51, 20133 Milan, Italy. TEL 39-2-70123727. FAX 39-2-717346. **Document type:** directory.
Description: Covers optics, frame industry and optical instruments in Italy.

382　　　　IT
ANNUARIO UFFICIALE DELLE IMPRESES ITALIANE IN CINA. A. Promit s.r.l., Corso G. Ferraris 149, 10128 Turin, Italy. TEL 011-318-69-16. FAX 011-3186917. Ed. Luciano Canobbio. adv.: B&W page L.3300000, color page L.4800000; 180 x 240.

338　　　　BE
ANTWERP PORT ANNUAL. 1905. a. 2495 BEF. Lloyd Anversois S.A., Vlemickstraat 18, 2000 Antwerp, Belgium. TEL 32-3-2340550. FAX 32-3-2340850. URL: http://www.portofantwerp.be/. Ed. Bernard van den Bossche; Pub. Guy Dubois. adv. contact: Koen Heinen. illus. circ. 7,000. **Document type:** directory.
Formerly: Annuaire Maritime.

670　　　　BL　　ISSN 0100-9745
ANUARIO DAS INDUSTRIAS. 1952. a. Editora Pesquisa e Industria Ltda., Rua Martin Fontes 230, 01050 São Paulo SP, Brazil. TEL 011-259-0333. FAX 011-256-8681. **Document type:** directory.

380.1　　　　SP
ANUARIO DE EMPRESAS EXPORTADORAS. 1974. a. Organizacion Sindical Espanola, Servicio de Accion Exterior Empresarial, Casa Sindical, Paseo del Prado 18, Madrid, Spain.

668.8　　　　CK
ANUARIO DEL EMPAQUE. a. free. Publicar S.A., Av. 68 No. 75A-50, piso 2, A.A. 8010, Bogota, Colombia. TEL 2255555. FAX 2254015. **Document type:** directory.

338　　　　CK
ANUARIO EMPRESARIAL DE COLOMBIA; registro nacional de comerciantes. 1972. a. Col.2500($50) (Confederacion Colombiana de Camaras de Comercio) Editorial Prensa Moderna, Carrera 13-No. 27-47, Of.502, Bogota, Colombia. Ed. Gaston E. Abello. circ. 15,000. (magnetic tape; microfiche)

669　　　　CK
ANUARIO METAL; guia especializada de compras del sector metalurgico y metalmecanico. a. free. (Fedemetal) Publicar S.A., Av. 68 No. 75A-50, piso 2, A.A. 8010, Bogota, Colombia. TEL 2255555. FAX 2254015. **Document type:** directory.

338 347.016　　　GW　　ISSN 0944-212X
ANWALT- UND NOTARVERZEICHNIS. a. (in 2 vols.). DM.148 (CD-ROM DM.298) (effective 1997). Verlag Dr. Otto Schmidt KG, Unter den Ulmen 96-98, 50968 Cologne, Germany. TEL 49-221-9373801. FAX 49-221-93738943. E-mail: dr.otto.schmidt@t-online.de. **Document type:** directory.
●Also available on CD-ROM.
Former titles (until 1992): Anwalts- und Notarverzeichnis der Bundesrepublik Deutschland (ISSN 0172-7621); (until 1978): Anwalts- und Notarverzeichnis der Bundesrepublik (ISSN 0341-2547).

677　　　　NZ
APPAREL TRADE DIRECTORY. 1969. a. NZ.$58 (in US NZ.$85). Apparel Publishing Ltd., P.O. Box 56071, Dominion Rd., Auckland 3, New Zealand. TEL 64-9-6315685. FAX 64-9-6303706. E-mail: apparel@iprolink.co.nz. Ed. Val Blomfield; Pub. Paul Blomfield. R&P contact: Paul Blomfield. adv. contact: Paul Blomfield. circ. 2,000. **Document type:** directory, trade publication.
Formerly: Apparel Buyers Guide Year Book.

382　　　FR　　ISSN 0066-5398
APPEL SERVICE; REPERTOIRE D'ADRESSES UTILES POUR LE COMMERCE ET L'INDUSTRIE.* 1968. irreg. price varies. Editions Publiplast, 55 rue du Faubourg-Montmartre, 75009 Paris, France.

380　　　　US
APPLIANCE MANUFACTURER BUYERS GUIDE. 1953. a. $25. Business News Publishing Company, 755 W. Big Beaver, Ste. 1000, Troy, MI 48084. TEL 810-362-3700. FAX 810-362-0317. URL: http://www.bnp.com. (Subscr. to: Box 3212, Northbrook, IL 60065) Ed. Norman C. Remich; Pub. Linda Calkins. adv. contact: Tim Johnson. circ. 35,200. **Document type:** directory.

380　　　UK　　ISSN 0958-2339
ARAB BUYERS' GUIDE TO BRITISH INDUSTRY. (Text in Arabic) 1951. a. Exact Communications Ltd., 90 Moorsom St., Birmingham B6 4NT, England. TEL 44-121-333-4644. FAX 44-121-333-5823. adv. contact: Michael Burgess. **Document type:** directory.
Description: Promotes British and other products or services in the Middle East and North Africa.

380　　　　UK
ARAB TRADE DIRECTORY. (Text in Arabic, English and French) biennial. $120. New Product Newsletter Co. Ltd., 1A Chesterfield St., London W1, England. adv. **Document type:** directory.

380　　　　UK
ARABIAN YEARBOOK. 1978. a. $135. New Product Newsletter Co. Ltd., 1A Chesterfield St., London W1, England. (Dist. in U.S. by: Croner Publications, Inc., 34 Jericho Tpke., Jericho, NY 11753)

338 691 721　　　　US
ARCHITECTS CATALOG.* 1993. a. free. Architects Catalog, Inc., 1305 Post Rd., Ste. 305, Fairfield, CT 06430-6016. TEL 203-256-1600. FAX 203-254-8166. adv.; circ. 40,000 (controlled). **Document type:** directory.
Description: Lists over 6200 national and international building product manufacturers organized by product type and firm name.

338　　　　BL
ARGENTINA COMPANY HANDBOOK. a. I M F Editora Ltda., Av. Erasmo Braga 227, Grupo 404, 20020-000 Rio de Janeiro RJ, Brazil. TEL 55-21-2404347. FAX 55-21-2627570. **Document type:** directory.

338.025　　　US　　ISSN 1046-3011
HC107.A6
ARIZONA BUSINESS DIRECTORY. 1988. a. $350 (effective 1996). American Business Directories (Subsidiary of: American Business Information, Inc.), 5711 S. 86th Circle, Box 27347, Omaha, NE 68127. TEL 402-593-4600; 800-555-6124. FAX 402-331-5481. E-mail: jerry.venner@abii.com. index. (also avail. in magnetic tape; diskette format) **Document type:** directory.
●Also available online.
Also available on CD-ROM.
Description: Includes all businesses in the state compiled from the yellow pages and telephone-verified. Each listing includes company name, complete address, phone number, name of owner, manager, and employee size, sales volume codes, credit rating codes.

670.25791　　　US　　ISSN 1071-3514
T12
ARIZONA INDUSTRIAL DIRECTORY; manufacturers, wholesalers. 1982. a. $97 (diskette & CD-ROM $457) (effective 1997). Phoenix Chamber of Commerce, 201 N. Central Ave., 27th Fl., Phoenix, AZ 85073. TEL 602-495-2195. FAX 602-495-8913. circ. 5,000. (also avail. in diskette format) **Document type:** directory.
●Also available on CD-ROM.
Formerly (until 1988): Arizona Directory of Manufacturers.
Description: Provides information about existing manufacturers and wholesalers in Arizona.

338.025　　　US　　ISSN 1048-7190
HF5065.A8
ARKANSAS BUSINESS DIRECTORY. 1988. a. $325 (effective 1997). American Business Directories (Subsidiary of: American Business Information, Inc.), 5711 S. 86th Circle, Box 27347, Omaha, NE 68127. TEL 402-593-4600; 800-555-6124. FAX 402-331-5481. E-mail: jerry.venner@abii.com. index. (also avail. in magnetic tape; diskette format) **Document type:** directory.
●Also available online.
Also available on CD-ROM.
Description: Includes all businesses in the state compiled from the yellow pages and telephone-verified. Each listing includes company name, complete address, telephone number, name of owner, manager, and employee size, sales volume codes, and credit rating codes.

670　　　　US
ARKANSAS DIRECTORY OF MANUFACTURERS. 1955. a. $65 (effective Apr. 1996). Industrial Development Foundation, Box 1784, Little Rock, AR 72203. TEL 501-682-7341. (Dist. by: Manufacturers' News, Inc., 1633 Central St., Evanston, IL 60201. TEL 708-864-7000) Ed. Patricia F. Brown. adv.; illus. circ. 5,400. **Document type:** directory.
Formerly: Directory of Manufacturers in Arkansas (ISSN 0361-2996)
Description: Profiles approximately 2,600 manufacturers. Includes alphabetical, geographical, exporters, product index, SIC and parent company sections.

338.025　　　US　　ISSN 1082-0264
HF5065.A8
ARKANSAS MANUFACTURERS REGISTER. a. $56 (diskette or CD-ROM $295) (effective 1997). Manufacturers' News, Inc., 1633 Central St., Evanston, IL 60201-1569. TEL 847-864-7000. FAX 847-332-1100. (also avail. in diskette format) **Document type:** directory.
●Also available on CD-ROM.
Description: Profiles 3416 companies.

BUSINESS AND ECONOMICS — TRADE AND INDUSTRIAL DIRECTORIES

ARKANSAS PRESS ASSOCIATION DIRECTORY. see *JOURNALISM*

380 700 069 US
N8710
ART MARKETING SOURCEBOOK. 1990. biennial. $21.95. ArtNetwork Press, 18757 Wildflower Dr., Box 1268, Penn Valley, CA 95946. TEL 916-432-7630. FAX 916-432-7633. **Document type:** directory.
  Formerly (until 1995): Directory of Artist Associations and Exhibition Spaces, Art Commissions, Museum Curators and Art Critics (ISSN 1057-7203)
  Description: Gives fine artists direct insight to sales contacts and target markets. Listings of artwork professionals are complete with name, address, telephone number and other detailed information. Each of the 2500 specialty listings provides information on dealers' policies, target markets, review standards, commissions and more.

658.8 UK
ASIA: A DIRECTORY AND SOURCEBOOK. 1992. irreg. £215($430) (effective 1997). Euromonitor, 60-61 Britton St., London EC1M 5NA, England. TEL 44-171-251-8024. FAX 44-171-608-3149. E-mail: info@euromonitor.com; URL: http://www.euromonitor.com. (Addr. in N. America: Euromonitor International, 122 S. Michigan Ave., Ste. 1200, Chicago, IL 60603. TEL 800-577-3876. FAX 312-922-1157) stat. **Document type:** trade publication.
  Description: Compiles statistics and information on the expanding consumer markets in the region and provides useful sources of information for 13 Asian countries.

ASIA - PACIFIC SATELLITE DIRECTORY. see *COMMUNICATIONS*

ASIAN AND AUSTRALASIAN COMPANIES. see *BUSINESS AND ECONOMICS — Abstracting, Bibliographies, Statistics*

338 JA
ASIAN COMPANY HANDBOOK. (Text in English) a. 5800 Yen($65) Toyo Keizai Inc., 1-2-1 Nihombashi Hongoku-cho, Chuo-ku, Tokyo 103, Japan. TEL 03-3246-5655. FAX 03-3241-5543. **Document type:** directory.
  Description: Provides detailed information on selected corporations on the stock exchanges in Hong Kong, Indonesia, the Republic of Korea, Malaysia, Singapore, Taiwan and Thailand.

ASIAN MARKETS; a guide to company and industry information sources. see *BUSINESS AND ECONOMICS — International Commerce*

ASIAN PRINTING DIRECTORY. see *PRINTING*

670 UK ISSN 0961-7132
ASIAN TRADER. (Text in English, Gujarati, Urdu) 1985. fortn. £65. (Garavi Gujarat Group) Asian Trade Publications Ltd., Garavi Gujarat House, 1-2 Silex St., London SE1 0DW, England. TEL 44-171-928-1234. FAX 44-171-261-0055. TELEX 8955335-GUJRAT-G. Ed. K.R. Solanki. adv. contact: Paul Gray. circ. 45,713 (controlled). (back issues avail.) **Document type:** trade publication.
  Description: Magazine for independent, Asian-owned retail outlets; carries trade and information, supported by all major manufacturers in UK.

380.1 ES
ASOCIACION SALVADORENA DE INDUSTRIALES DIRECTORIO DE ASOCIADOS. (Text in Spanish) a. Asociacion Salvadorena de Industriales, Apartado Postal No. (06) 48, Calles Roma y Liverpool, Colonia Roma, San Salvador, El Salvador. **Document type:** directory.

382 UK ISSN 0260-2474
ASPIS; the classified Greek commercial directory. (Text in English and Greek) 1980. a. Aspis Publications, 89 Tottenham Ln., London N8 9BE, England. illus. **Document type:** directory.

380.1 663.6 II
ASSAM DIRECTORY & TEA AREAS HANDBOOK. 1928. a. Rs.975($60) Assam Review Publishing Co., 29 Waterloo St., Calcutta 700 069, India. Ed. G.L. Banerjee. adv.: B&W page $150; trim 180 x 245; adv. contact: U. Bhatta. bk.rev. colc. 7,500. **Document type:** directory.
  Formerly: Assam Directory of Tea Areas.
  Description: Directory of tea producing gardens, tea companies, and tea exporters of India, Bangladesh, Sri Lanka, Kenya, and Nepal.

338 670 MW
ASSOCIATED CHAMBERS OF COMMERCE AND INDUSTRY OF MALAWI. INDUSTRIAL AND TRADE DIRECTORY. (Text in English) 1974. biennial, 6th 1982. K.5. Associated Chamber of Commerce and Industry of Malawi, P.O. Box 258, Blantyre, Malawi. TEL 265-671988. FAX 265-671147. TELEX 43992. adv. circ. 1,000. **Document type:** directory.
  Formerly: Industrial Directory and Brand Names Index of Malawi.

280.4 016 US ISSN 0066-8710
Z7753
ASSOCIATED CHURCH PRESS. DIRECTORY. 1947. a. $30 to individuals; libraries $22. Associated Church Press, Box 30215, Phoenix, AZ 85046-0215. TEL 602-569-6371. FAX 602-569-6180. Ed. John Stapert. adv. circ. 700. **Document type:** directory.
  Description: Lists Ecumenical religious publications in the United States and Canada.

ASSOCIATION OF M B AS ADDRESS BOOK. see *BUSINESS AND ECONOMICS — Management*

678.2 668.4 FR
ASSOCIATION POUR LA PROMOTION DE LA PROFESSION DU CAOUTCHOUC ET DE PLASTIQUES. GUIDE. 1978. biennial. 500 F. Association pour la Promotion de la Profession du Caoutchouc et de Plastiques, 1 Square la Bruyere, 75009 Paris, France. TEL 33-1-42821022. FAX 33-1-42805545. Ed. P. Mercier. circ. 3,000.
  Former titles: Union des industries et de la Distribution des Plastiques et du Caoutchouc. Guide & Syndicat General des Commerces et Industries du Caoutchouc et des Plastiques. Guide (ISSN 0224-2435)

380 US ISSN 1054-4070
HD2425
ASSOCIATIONS YELLOW BOOK; who's who at the leading U.S. trade and professional associations. 1991. s-a. $200 (effective 1997). Leadership Directories, Inc., 104 Fifth Ave., 2nd Fl., New York, NY 10011. TEL 212-627-4140. FAX 212-645-0931. Ed. Chris Muntone. **Document type:** directory.
  ●Also available on CD-ROM. Producer(s): Chadwyck-Healey Inc.
  —CISTI. **CCC.**

340.025 340 CN ISSN 0826-2896
ATLANTIC LEGAL TELEPHONE DIRECTORY. a. Can.$18 (effective 1997). Canada Law Book Inc., 240 Edward St., Aurora, ON L4G 3S9, Canada. TEL 905-841-6472; 800-263-2037. FAX 905-841-5085. adv. **Document type:** directory.

AUDARENA STADIUM INTERNATIONAL GUIDE & FACILITY BUYERS GUIDE. see *THEATER*

AUDIOTEX DIRECTORY & BUYER'S GUIDE. see *COMMUNICATIONS — Telephone And Telegraph*

338 674.2 AT
AUSTRALASIAN FURNISHING DIRECTORY (YEAR). a. Aus.$55 in Australia & New Zealand; elsewhere Aus.$60. Furnishing Publications Pty. Ltd., Courtyard, Monash Homemaker Centre, 1207 Princes Hwy., Clayton, Vic. 3168, Australia. TEL 61-3-95629177. FAX 61-3-95629477. Ed. Keith Dunn; Pub. Keith Dunn. R&P contact: Keith Dunn. adv. contact: Grahame Waterson. **Document type:** directory, trade publication.
  Description: Provides information on Australasian furniture, soft furnishings and floorcoverings, retailers, manufacturers, suppliers, and interior designers. Provides the names of key people, addresses, and phone numbers.

338 665.7 665.5 AT
AUSTRALASIAN OIL & GAS EXPLORERS DIRECTORY. 1991. s-a. Aus.$80 (effective 1995). Business Intelligence (W.A.), P.O. Box 210, Claremont, W.A. 6010, Australia. TEL 61-9-4487665. FAX 61-9-4485011. Ed. Steve Whitfield. circ. 300. **Document type:** directory.
  Description: Provides contact details for oil and gas explorers and technical service companies involved in Australia, New Zealand and Papua New Guinea.

338 387.7 AT ISSN 1321-4012
AUSTRALIAN AEROSPACE INDUSTRY CAPABILITY DIRECTORY. 1994. irreg. Aus.$10. (Department of Industry, Science and Technology) Peter Isaacson Publications Pty. Ltd., 46-50 Porter St., Prahran, Vic. 3181, Australia. TEL 61-3-2457777. FAX 61-3-2457840. adv. contact: Joseph Dagher. **Document type:** directory.
  Description: Comprehensive reference on Australian companies offering products and services to the aerospace industry. Originally designed for display at international air shows.

AUSTRALIAN AND NEW ZEALAND WINE INDUSTRY DIRECTORY. see *BEVERAGES*

338 382 AT ISSN 1039-9208
AUSTRALIAN EXPORTS. 1964. a. Aus.$295. (Australian Trade Commission) Peter Isaacson Publications Pty. Ltd., 46-50 Porter St., Prahran, Vic. 3181, Australia. TEL 61-3-2457777. FAX 61-3-2457840. adv. contact: Josepg Dagher. circ. 5,000. (back issues avail.) **Document type:** directory.
  —UMI.
  Supersedes in part (in 1992): Australian Exports and Imports (ISSN 1032-2116); Which was formed by the merger of (1979-1988): Australian Exports (ISSN 0156-3661); Which was formerly: Australian Directory of Exports (ISSN 0084-7305); (1982-1988): Australian Imports (ISSN 0813-3409); Which was formerly: Australian Importers (ISSN 0156-367X); Index of Australian Importers (ISSN 0155-7009).
  Description: List companies who export their Australian products and services to overseas markets.

338 610 AT ISSN 1323-0824
AUSTRALIAN HEALTH AND MEDICAL INDUSTRY DIRECTORY. 1992. a. Aus.$85. (Austrade) Peter Isaacson Publications Pty. Ltd., 46-50 Porter St., Prahran, Vic. 3181, Australia. TEL 61-3-2457777. FAX 61-3-2457840. adv. contact: Joseph Dagher. circ. 8,000. **Document type:** directory.
  Formerly: Australian Health and Medical Exports.
  Description: Outlines exporters of Australian health and medical equipment and services. Indicates areas of expertise, contact details, where they export to, etc.

338 382 AT
AUSTRALIAN IMPORTS. 1964. a. Aus.$95. Peter Isaacson Publications Pty. Ltd., 46-50 Porter St., Prahran, Vic. 3181, Australia. TEL 61-3-2457777. FAX 61-3-2457840. adv. contact: Joseph Dagher. **Document type:** directory.
  Supersedes in part (in 1992): Australian Exports and Imports (ISSN 1032-2116); Which was formed by the merger of (1979-1988): Australian Exports (ISSN 0156-3661); Which was formerly: Australian Directory of Exports (ISSN 0084-7305); (1982-1988): Australian Imports (ISSN 0813-3409); Which was formerly: Australian Importers (ISSN 0156-367X); Index of Australian Importers (ISSN 0155-7009).
  Description: Lists companies who import their products and services into Australia.

340.06294 AT ISSN 0155-297X
AUSTRALIAN LEGAL DIRECTORY. 1977. a. Aus.$105 (foreign Aus.$150). (Law Council of Australia) Australian Document Exchange Pty. Ltd., 153 Phillip St., 1st Fl., Sydney, N.S.W. 2000, Australia. TEL 61-2-2212677. FAX 61-2-2212372. Ed. Bruce Rose. circ. 2,000 (paid). **Document type:** directory.

AUSTRALIAN MARKET GUIDE. see *BUSINESS AND ECONOMICS — Investments*

BUSINESS AND ECONOMICS — TRADE AND INDUSTRIAL DIRECTORIES

338.025   AT
AUSTRALIAN MINING SPECIFICATION GUIDE. a. Aus.$75 (effective 1996). Reed Business Publishing Pty. Ltd. (Subsidiary of: Reed International PLC), P.O. Box 5487, W. Chatswood, N.S.W. 2057, Australia. TEL 61-2-699-2411. FAX 61-2-698-3920. **Document type:** directory, trade publication. **Description:** Provides a fully cross-indexed guide to mining equipment, services and suppliers.

338.025   CH
AUTO & MOTORCYCLE PARTS BUYERS' GUIDE. s-a. $50. Trade Winds, Inc., No. 7, Lane 75, Yungkang St., P.O. Box 7-179, Taipei, Taiwan 10602, Republic of China. TEL 886-2-3932718. FAX 886-2-3964022. E-mail: tradewind@ms2.hinet.net; URL: http://www.tradewinds.com.tw. (Subscr. in U.S. to: Trade Winds Inc., Box 820519, Dallas, TX 75382. TEL 972-699-1188. FAX 972-699-1189) Ed. Donald Shapiro. **Document type:** directory, catalog. **Description:** Covers suppliers of automobile and motorcycle parts and accessories in Taiwan and elsewhere in East and Southeast Asia.

AUTOBUSINESS. see *TRANSPORTATION — Automobiles*

AUTOMOTIVE INDUSTRIES (YEAR). see *TRANSPORTATION — Automobiles*

AUTOMOTIVE MARKETING WHO'S WHO A P A A SHOW DIRECTORY. see *TRANSPORTATION — Automobiles*

380   US
AUTOMOTIVE RECYCLERS BUYERS GUIDE - MEMBERSHIP ROSTER. a. $150 to non-members. Automotive Recyclers Association, 3975 Fair Ridge Dr., Ste. 20 N., Fairfax, VA 22033-2924. TEL 703-385-1001. Ed. Christopher Murphy. adv. circ. 1,600. **Document type:** directory. **Formerly:** Automotive Dismantlers and Recyclers Buyers Guide - Membership Roster.

AUTOPART; a directory of companies supplying the motor trade. see *TRANSPORTATION — Automobiles*

380   UK
B A C B MEMBERSHIP AND SERVICES DIRECTORY (YEAR). (Former name of issuing body: British Association of Industrial Editors) 1978. a. £250. British Association of Communicators in Business, 3 Locks Yard., High St, Sevenoaks, Kent TN13 1LT, England. TEL 44-1732-459331. FAX 44-1732-461757. adv. circ. 1,250. **Document type:** directory. **Former titles:** B A I E Membership and Services Directory (Year); B A I E Membership Directory; Who's Who in Industrial Editing (ISSN 0068-1296); British Association of Industrial Editors. B A I E Directory of Members.

380.1 794.6   US
B B I A MEMBERSHIP AND PRODUCT INFORMATION GUIDE. a. free. Billiard and Bowling Institute of America, 200 Castlewood Dr., N. Palm Beach, FL 33408. TEL 407-840-1120. Ed. Sebastian Dicasoli. circ. 2,000.

380.1   CN   ISSN 0843-8021
B C DAIRY DIRECTORY. 1982. a. Can.$10 (effective 1997). RR 1, Boothe Rd., Naramata, BC, V0H 1N0, Canada. TEL 250-496-5707. FAX 250-496-5132. Pub. Mike McCarthy. adv.; circ. 1,600 (controlled). **Document type:** directory. **Description:** Edited for commercial and purebred dairy producers and the dairy industry in British Columbia.

B C LABOUR DIRECTORY. see *BUSINESS AND ECONOMICS — Labor And Industrial Relations*

380 796   UK
B F S S COUNTRY SPORTS HANDBOOK AND TRADE DIRECTORY. 1978. a. British Field Sports Society, Old Town Hall, 367 Kennington Rd., London SE11 4PT, England. TEL 44-171-928-4742. FAX 44-171-928-4742. E-mail: info@bfss.org; URL: http://www.bfss.org. Ed. Derek Bingham. adv.; bk.rev.; illus. circ. 80,000. **Document type:** directory. **Former titles:** Country Sports Directory; (until 1989): B F S S Members Handbook; (until 1988): B F S S Reference Book; British Field Sports Society. Annual Journal. **Description:** Supplies information on country sports.

B H A B INFORMATION HANDBOOK. (British Helicopter Advisory Board) see *AERONAUTICS AND SPACE FLIGHT*

683   UK
B H F DIRECTORY. a. free. British Hardware Federation, 225 Bristol Rd., Edgbaston, Birmingham B5 7UB, England. TEL 44-121-446-6688. FAX 44-121-446-5215. Ed. John Morgan; Pub. Michael I. Weedon. R&P contact: Michael I. Weedon. adv. contact: Roger Loweth. circ. 10,000. **Document type:** directory, trade publication. **Description:** Lists members, officers, products, and services.

659.1 301.16   US
B M A MEMBERSHIP DIRECTORY AND RESOURCE GUIDE. 1986. a. $100 to non-members. Business Marketing Association, 150 N. Wacker Dr., Chicago, IL 60606. TEL 312-409-4262. FAX 312-409-4266. Ed. Barbara Waldorf. circ. 5,000. **Document type:** directory. **Former titles:** B M A Membership Directory and Yellow Pages & B - P A A Membership Directory and Yellow Pages. **Description:** Includes company addresses, phone numbers, titles, and a yellow pages section of services for business communications professionals.

B M R A RUBBER AND POLYURETHANE DIRECTORY. (British Rubber Manufacturers' Association Ltd.) see *RUBBER*

B N A'S DIRECTORY OF STATE & FEDERAL COURTS, JUDGES, AND CLERKS. see *LAW*

B T B. (Branchevejviser for Traelast og Byggemarkeder) see *FORESTS AND FORESTRY — Lumber And Wood*

BABY SHOP; the magazine for independent juvenile product retailers. see *GIFTWARE AND TOYS*

659.2   US   ISSN 1089-0971
HF5813.E79
BACON'S INTERNATIONAL MEDIA DIRECTORY. 1974. a. $280. Bacon's Publishing Company, Inc., 332 S. Michigan Ave., Ste. 900, Chicago, IL 60604. TEL 312-922-2400. FAX 312-922-3127. Ed. Ruth McFarland. circ. 1,200. **Document type:** directory. **Formerly** (until 1992): Bacon's International Publicity Checker (ISSN 0161-4363) **Description:** Directory of print media for Western Europe.

659.1   US
BACON'S NEWSPAPER - MAGAZINE DIRECTORY. (In 2 vols.: Magazines & Newspapers) 1952. a. (plus q. update). $280. Bacon's Publishing Company, Inc., 332 S. Michigan Ave., Chicago, IL 60604. TEL 312-922-2400. FAX 312-922-3127. Ed. Ruth McFarland. circ. 10,200. **Document type:** directory. **Formerly** (until 1992): Bacon's Publicity Checker (ISSN 0162-3125) **Description:** Directory of print media in US and Canada.

BACON'S RADIO & T V CABLE DIRECTORIES. see *COMMUNICATIONS — Television And Cable*

380   BA   ISSN 0408-215X
BAHRAIN TRADE DIRECTORY. (Text in Arabic and English) a. P.O. Box 524, Manama, Bahrain. Ed. A.E. Ashir. **Document type:** directory.

799.2   UK   ISSN 0067-2947
BAILY'S HUNTING DIRECTORY. 1897. a. £29.95. Pearson Publishing, Chesterton Mill, French's Rd., Cambridge CB4 3NP, England. TEL 44-1223-350555. FAX 44-1223-356484. Ed. Karen Alexander. adv. contact: Susan Philo. bk.rev. circ. 1,750. **Document type:** directory. **Description:** Contains details on hunts and hunting throughout the U.K., Europe, the U.S., and Canada. *Refereed Serial*

BAKING INDUSTRY DIRECTORY. see *FOOD AND FOOD INDUSTRIES — Bakers And Confectioners*

BAKING, SNACK DIRECTORY & BUYERS GUIDE. see *AGRICULTURE — Feed, Flour And Grain*

380   II
BANGLADESH DIRECTORY AND YEAR BOOK. (Text in English) 1976. a. Rs.75($15) Associated Book Promoters, 9-2A Ekbalpur Ln., Calcutta 700023, India. **Document type:** directory.

382   BB
BARBADOS. EXPORT DIRECTORY. 1982. irreg. free. Export Promotion Corporation, Pelican Industrial Park, St. Michael, Barbados, W.I. TEL 246-427-5752. FAX 246-427-5867. Ed.Bd. adv. **Document type:** directory.

380 659   US
BARTER COMMUNIQUE. 1975; N.S. 1997. q. $30 (foreign $59) (effective Mar. 1997). Full Circle Marketing Corp., Box 2527, Sarasota, FL 34230-2527. TEL 941-349-3300; 888-550-7500. FAX 941-365-6642. E-mail: murleybird@aol.com. Ed. Robert Murley; Pub. Robert Murley. adv.: B&W page $2700; trim 7 3/4 x 10. bk.rev.; circ. 52,000 (controlled). (tabloid format) **Description:** Includes articles on why, where, with whom, and how to barter, how others have barterd successfully, how to use barter to incease sales and profits, and getting what you otherwise can't afford by bartering.

658   UK   ISSN 0067-5342
BELFAST AND NORTHERN IRELAND DIRECTORY. 1852. a. £49.50. Century Newspapers Ltd., 46-56 Boucher Cresc., Belfast BT12 6QY, N. Ireland. TEL 44-1232-680000. FAX 44-1232-664412. Ed. Geoff Martin. adv. contact: Gary Hamilton. circ. 3,000. **Document type:** directory, newspaper.

BENN'S MEDIA: EUROPE. see *JOURNALISM*

BENN'S MEDIA: U K. see *JOURNALISM*

BENN'S MEDIA: WORLD. see *JOURNALISM*

650 382   GW   ISSN 0067-6063
BERLINER HANDELSREGISTER VERZEICHNIS. a. DM.76. Adressbuch-Gesellschaft Berlin mbH, Friedrichstr. 210, 1000 Berlin 61, Germany. adv.; index.

380   US
BEST 900 NUMBERS. 1991. a. $3.50 in U.S.; $4.50 Canada. (Philip Leif Group) St. Martin's Press, 175 Fifth Ave., New York, NY 10010. **Description:** Guide to "900" (dial-it, pay-per-call, audiotex) services in the United States. Explains the types of 900 services, how they work, who operates them, and typical charges.

338.025 378   US
HD5724
BIG BOOK OF MINORITY OPPORTUNITIES. 1974. irreg., 6th ed., 1995. $39. Garrett Park Press, Box 190F, Garrett Park, MD 20896. TEL 301-946-2553. Ed. Willis L. Johnson. bibl. **Document type:** directory. **Formerly** (until 1995): Directory of Special Programs for Minority Group Members: Career Information Services, Employment Skills, Banks, Financial Aid Sources (ISSN 0093-9501) **Description:** Lists 2900 educational programs for minorities in specific fields, 580 programs of support for students in any field, and 800 programs for specific minority groups.

380   US
BILINGUAL SERVICES DIRECTORY. 1989. a. free. 1135 Sunbury Rd., South Elgin, IL 60177. TEL 708-697-3533. FAX 708-697-3533. Ed. Laura Carillo Barth. adv.: B&W page $500; trim 7 x 10. circ. 10,000. **Document type:** directory.

338.025 780   US
BILLBOARD'S TAPE - DISC DIRECTORY. a. $32. B P I Communications, Inc. (New York), 1515 Broadway, New York, NY 10036. TEL 212-764-7300; 800-344-7119. FAX 212-944-1719. (And: 5055 Wilshire Blvd., Los Angeles, CA 90036) (also avail. in microfilm; reprint service avail. from UMI). **Document type:** directory. **Former titles:** Billboard's International Directory of Manufacturing and Packaging; Billboard's Audio-Video-Tape Sourcebook; Billboard International Tape Directory (ISSN 0090-645X) **Description:** Professional services and supplies for CD, record and video manufacturers, audio and videotape manufacturers, video program suppliers and buyers, video music producers and production facilities.

BINGO NEWS & GAMING HI-LITES. see *CONSUMER EDUCATION AND PROTECTION*

338.025 663   UK
BINSTED'S BOTTLING DIRECTORY (YEAR). a. £40. Binsted Publications, Ltd., Walton House, 90 London Rd., Hook, Hants. RG27 9LF, England. TEL 01256-764180. FAX 01256-766102. Ed. Edward C. Binsted; Pub. Edward C. Binsted. **Document type:** directory.

BIOSCAN; the worldwide biotech industry reporting service. see *BIOLOGY — Biotechnology*

338 660   UK   ISSN 1059-7352
TP248.3
BIOTECHNOLOGY DIRECTORY (YEAR). 1984. a. £155. Macmillan Reference Ltd., 25 Eccleston Pl., London SW1W 9NF, England. TEL 44-171-881-8000. FAX 44-171-881-8000. (U.S. addr: Stockton Press, 345 Park Ave. S., New York, NY 10010. TEL 212-689-9200) Ed. Jim Coombs. adv. **Document type:** directory.
—BLDSC (4537.195000); CISTI. **CCC.**
 Formerly: International Biotechnology Directory (ISSN 0265-3877)
 Description: Provides information on companies, research centers, and academic institutions involved in new and established technologies.

338 910.03   US
BLACK PAGES - CHICAGO. a. free. Black Pages - Chicago, 407 E. 25th St., Ste. 610, Chicago, IL 60616-2433. TEL 213-808-1800. Pub. Arnette French. **Document type:** directory.
 Description: Profiles and lists black-owned business establishments and services in Chicago.

338.025 621.38   UK   ISSN 0960-5142
BLUE BOOK OF BRITISH BROADCASTING. 1974. a. £75. Tellex Monitors Ltd., Communications House, 210 Old St., London EC1V 9UN, England. TEL 44-171-566-3100. FAX 44-171-566-3152. E-mail: sales@tellex.press.net; URL: http://www.tellex.press.net. Ed. Robin Mann. R&P contact: Joanne Ferris. adv.: page £750; adv. contact: Joanne Ferris. circ. 2,000 (paid); 500. **Document type:** directory.
—BLDSC (2114.003000).

BLUE BOOK: THE DIRECTORY OF THE LAW SOCIETY OF SCOTLAND. see *LAW*

338.025   TH
BOARD OF TRADE OF THAILAND. TRADE DIRECTORY. (Text in English) a. Board of Trade of Thailand, 150 Rajbopit Rd., Bangkok 10200, Thailand. TEL 66-2-221-0555. FAX 66-2-225-3995. Ed. Rachanee Watchareewong. **Document type:** directory.
 Description: Lists the top 50 Thai importers and exporters of the top 50 important products to about 40 countries of destination.

BOAT & MOTOR DEALER. see *SPORTS AND GAMES — Boats And Boating*

BOAT GUIDE. see *SPORTS AND GAMES — Boats And Boating*

796.9 387   US
BOATING INDUSTRY MARINE BUYERS' GUIDE. 1937. a. $54.95. Intertec Publishing Corp. (Atlanta), 6151 Powers Ferry Rd., N.W., Atlanta, GA 30339-2941. TEL 770-955-2500. FAX 770-955-0400. Ed. Richard W. Porter. adv. circ. 31,334. (also avail. in microform from UMI; reprint service avail. from UMI) **Document type:** trade publication, directory.
 Description: Comprehensive recreational marine industry sourcebook, including directories of suppliers' addresses, distributors, marine manufacturers' representatives, stock boatbuilders (classified by type), marine product manufacturers and services.

382   BO
BOLIVIA EXPORT DIRECTORY/BOLIVIA DIRECTORIO DE EXPORTADORES. a. Instituto Nacional de Promocion de la Exportaciones (INPEX), Av. Arce esq. Goitia 2021, Casilla 10871, La Paz, Bolivia. TEL 378000. FAX 391226. TELEX 3643 INPEX BV. **Document type:** directory.
 Description: Guide book for producing and exporting firms.

332.6   US   ISSN 1053-8658
HG4907
BOND BUYER'S MUNICIPAL MARKETPLACE. a. $180. Thomson Financial Publishing, 4709 W. Golf Rd., Skokie, IL 60076-1256. TEL 847-676-9600; 800-321-3373. FAX 847-933-8101. Ed. Beth Swann. R&P contact: Beth Swann. adv. contact: Hugh Boyd. **Document type:** directory.
—CCC.
 Formerly: Directory of Municipal Bond Dealers of the United States (ISSN 0094-100X)

BOOK PUBLISHING RESOURCE GUIDE. see *PUBLISHING AND BOOK TRADE*

338   SA
BOTSWANA BUSINESS DIRECTORY. 1981. a. R.60 (effective 1997). Braby's (Subsidiary of: Kohler Packaging Ltd.), P.O. Box 1426, Pinetown 3600, South Africa. TEL 27-31-7017021. FAX 27-31-7017036. adv. **Document type:** directory.

338   BS
BOTSWANA MANUFACTURING DIRECTORY. 1984. biennial. free. Ministry of Commerce and Industry, Department of Trade and Investment Promotion (T I P A), Private Bag 00367, Gaborone, Botswana. TEL 267-351790. FAX 267-305375. TELEX 2674 TRADE BD. Ed. Mukram Sheikh. circ. 10,000. **Document type:** government publication, directory.
 Description: Gives information about manufacturers and the range of manufactured products in Botswana.

380   BS
BOTSWANA TRADE DIRECTORY. 1982. biennial. free. Ministry of Commerce and Industry, Department of Trade and Investment Promotion (T I P A), Private Bag 00367, Gaborone, Botswana. TEL 267-351790. FAX 267-305375. TELEX 2674 TRADE BD. Ed. Mukram Sheikh. circ. 10,000. **Document type:** directory, government publication.
 Description: Gives information about importers, exporters and service organizations of Botswana.

338   FR   ISSN 0299-5921
BOTTIN ENTREPRISES. (Text in French; summaries in English) 1895. a. (3 vols.) $500. Bottin S A, 4 rue Andre Boulle, 94961 Cretil Cedex 9, France. TEL 49-81-56-56. FAX 49-81-56-76. TELEX 262 407. index.
●Also available online.
 Formed by the 1987 merger of: Bottin Professions. Liste Alphabetique Nationale des Entreprises (ISSN 0759-383X); Which was formerly (until 1983): Bottin. Liste Alphabetique Nationale des Entreprises (ISSN 0294-9997); (1976-1981): Bottin Professions. Liste Alphabetique Nationale des Entreprises (ISSN 0294-9989); And: Bottin Professions. Rubriques Professionelles (ISSN 0759-3848); Which was formerly (until 1983): Bottin. Produits et Services (ISSN 0752-7012); (1976-1980): Bottin Professions. Rubriques (ISSN 0752-7004).
 Description: Classifies the 100,000 most important French companies by departments and towns, with addresses, telephone, fax, number of employees, capital, executives, and activity.

BOXWOOD BUYER'S GUIDE. see *GARDENING AND HORTICULTURE*

338   SA   ISSN 0520-7010
BRABY'S BLOEMFONTEIN DIRECTORY. (Text in English) a. R.50 (effective 1997). Braby's (Subsidiary of: Kohler Packaging Ltd.), P.O. Box 1426, Pinetown 3600, South Africa. TEL 27-31-7017021. FAX 27-31-7017036. Ed. A. Stagg. (also avail. in diskette format) **Document type:** directory.

338   SA
BRABY'S BORDER DIRECTORY AND SURROUNDING AREAS. Variant title: Border Directory. a. R.25 (effective 1997). Braby's (Subsidiary of: Kohler Packaging Ltd.), P.O. Box 1426, Pinetown 3600, South Africa. TEL 27-31-7017021. FAX 27-31-7017036. **Document type:** directory.
 Formed by the 1993 merger of: Braby's King William's Town Directory & Braby's Queenstown Directory & Braby's Ciskei Buyer's Guide.

338   SA
BRABY'S CAPE DIRECTORY. Variant title: Cape Directory. (Text in English) a. R.102 (effective 1997). Braby's (Subsidiary of: Kohler Packaging Ltd.), P.O. Box 1426, Pinetown 3600, South Africa. TEL 27-31-7017021. FAX 27-31-7017036. Ed. A. Stagg. **Document type:** directory.
 Formerly: Braby's Cape Province Directory (ISSN 0378-9179)

338   SA   ISSN 0259-5729
BRABY'S CHATSWORTH DIRECTORY. 1980. a. R.25 (effective 1996). Braby's (Subsidiary of: Kohler Packaging Ltd.), P.O. Box 1426, Pinetown 3600, South Africa. TEL 27-31-7017021. FAX 27-31-7017036. **Document type:** directory.

338   SA
BRABY'S COMMERCIAL DIRECTORY OF SOUTHERN AFRICA. (In 2 vols.) 1924. a. $250 (effective 1996). Braby's (Subsidiary of: Kohler Packaging Ltd.), P.O. Box 1426, Pinetown 3600, South Africa. TEL 27-31-7017021. FAX 27-31-7017036. Ed. A. Stagg. adv. circ. 20. **Document type:** directory.
 Formerly: Braby's Commercial Directory of South, East and Central Africa (ISSN 0378-9187); **Incorporates:** Cape Times Directory of Southern Africa (ISSN 0379-4601)
 Description: Provides alphabetical and classified listings of all businesses in Southern Africa.

338 968   SA
BRABY'S DIRECTORY ON DISK. (Avail. in 9 regional editions: Durban, East London, Port Elizabeth, Bloemfontein, Cape Peninsula, Johannesburg, Pietermaritzburg, East Rand, Pretoria; Not avail. in print format) (Text in English) 1993. a. $495. Braby's (Subsidiary of: Kohler Packaging Ltd.), P.O. Box 1426, Pinetown 3600, South Africa. TEL 27-31-7017021. FAX 27-31-7017036. adv. (also avail. in diskette format) **Document type:** directory.
●Also available on CD-ROM.

338   SA
BRABY'S DUNDEE - NEWCASTLE - VRYHEID DIRECTORY. 1965. a. R.35 (effective 1996). Braby's (Subsidiary of: Kohler Packaging Ltd.), P.O. Box 1426, Pinetown 3600, South Africa. TEL 27-31-7017021. FAX 27-31-7017036. **Document type:** directory.
 Formed by the merger of: Braby's Dundee Directory (ISSN 0378-9209) & Braby's Newcastle Directory (ISSN 0378-9284) & Braby's Vryheid Directory (ISSN 0378-9330)

338   SA   ISSN 0378-9217
BRABY'S EAST LONDON DIRECTORY. (Text in English) 1961. a. R.40 (effective 1996). Braby's (Subsidiary of: Kohler Packaging Ltd.), P.O. Box 1426, Pinetown 3600, South Africa. TEL 27-31-7017021. FAX 27-31-7017036. Ed. A. Stagg. (also avail. in diskette format) **Document type:** directory.

338   SA
DT891
BRABY'S FREE STATE - NORTHERN CAPE DIRECTORY. Variant title: O F S - Northern Cape Directory. (Text in English) a. R.50 (effective 1996). Braby's (Subsidiary of: Kohler Packaging Ltd.), P.O. Box 1426, Pinetown 3600, South Africa. TEL 27-31-7017021. FAX 27-31-7017036. Ed. A. Stagg. adv. **Document type:** directory.
 Former titles: Braby's Orange Free State Northern Cape Directory; Braby's Orange Free State Directory (ISSN 0378-9292)

338   SA
BRABY'S GAUTENG - NORTH WEST - P W V - DIRECTORY. a. R.180 (effective 1996). Braby's (Subsidiary of: Kohler Packaging Ltd.), P.O. Box 1426, Pinetown 3600, South Africa. TEL 27-31-7017021. FAX 27-31-7017036. Ed. A. Stagg. adv. **Document type:** directory.
 Formerly (until 1994): Braby's Transvaal Directory (ISSN 0068-0621)

338   SA   ISSN 0378-9241
BRABY'S GREYTOWN DIRECTORY. 1974. a. R.25 (effective 1996). Braby's (Subsidiary of: Kohler Packaging Ltd.), P.O. Box 1426, Pinetown 3600, South Africa. TEL 27-31-7017021. FAX 27-31-7017036. **Document type:** directory.

BUSINESS AND ECONOMICS — TRADE AND INDUSTRIAL DIRECTORIES

338　　　　　　　SA　　ISSN 0259-4692
BRABY'S HIGHWAY DIRECTORY. 1977. a. R.35 (effective 1996). Braby's (Subsidiary of: Kohler Packaging Ltd.), P.O. Box 1426, Pinetown 3600, South Africa. TEL 27-31-7017021. FAX 27-31-7017036. **Document type:** directory.

338　　　　　　　SA　　ISSN 0378-925X
BRABY'S HOWICK DIRECTORY. 1973. a. R.20 (effective 1996). Braby's (Subsidiary of: Kohler Packaging Ltd.), P.O. Box 1426, Pinetown 3600, South Africa. TEL 27-31-7017021. FAX 27-31-7017036. **Document type:** directory.

338　　　　　　　SA　　ISSN 1016-6602
BRABY'S KIMBERLEY BUYERS' GUIDE/BRABY'S KIMBERLEY KOOPGIDS. 1984. a. R.20 (effective 1996). Braby's (Subsidiary of: Kohler Packaging Ltd.), P.O. Box 1426, Pinetown 3600, South Africa. TEL 27-31-7017021. FAX 27-31-7017036. **Document type:** directory.

338　　　　　　　SA
BRABY'S NAMIBIA DIRECTORY. 1969. a. R.60 (effective 1996). Braby's (Subsidiary of: Kohler Packaging Ltd.), P.O. Box 1426, Pinetown 3600, South Africa. TEL 27-31-7017021. FAX 27-31-7017036. adv. **Document type:** directory.
　Formerly: Braby's South West Africa Directory (ISSN 0378-9322)

338　　　　　　　SA
BRABY'S NORTH COAST AND ZULULAND DIRECTORY. Variant title: North Coast and Zululand Directory. 1958. a. R.50 (effective 1996). Braby's (Subsidiary of: Kohler Packaging Ltd.), P.O. Box 1426, Pinetown 3600, South Africa. TEL 27-31-7017021. FAX 27-31-7017036. **Document type:** directory.
　Formerly (until 1994): Braby's Natal North Coast and Zululand Directory (ISSN 0520-7037)

338　　　　　　　SA　　ISSN 0378-9306
BRABY'S PIETERMARITZBURG DIRECTORY. (Text in English) 1957. a. R.60 (effective 1996). Braby's (Subsidiary of: Kohler Packaging Ltd.), P.O. Box 1426, Pinetown 3600, South Africa. TEL 27-31-7017021. FAX 27-31-7017036. Ed. A. Stagg. (also avail. in diskette format) **Document type:** directory.

338　　　　　　　SA　　ISSN 0378-9314
BRABY'S PRETORIA DIRECTORY. 1974. a. R.65 (effective 1996). Braby's (Subsidiary of: Kohler Packaging Ltd.), P.O. Box 1426, Pinetown 3600, South Africa. TEL 27-31-7017021. FAX 27-31-7017036. **Document type:** directory.

338　　　　　　　SA　　ISSN 1016-6378
BRABY'S SOUTH COAST AND SOUTHERN NATAL DIRECTORY. 1957. a. R.50 (effective 1996). Braby's (Subsidiary of: Kohler Packaging Ltd.), P.O. Box 1426, Pinetown 3600, South Africa. TEL 27-31-7017021. FAX 27-31-7017036. **Document type:** directory.

338　　　　　　　SA
BRABY'S UMTATA & BUTTERWORTH. 1972. a. R.30 (effective 1996). Braby's (Subsidiary of: Kohler Packaging Ltd.), P.O. Box 1426, Pinetown 3600, South Africa. TEL 27-31-7017021. FAX 27-31-7017036. **Document type:** directory.
　Formerly: Braby's Transkei Business Directory (ISSN 1016-7080)

380.1　　　　　US
BRAZILIAN AMERICAN WHO'S WHO; companies in the United States and their subsidiaries and affiliates in Brazil. 1980. a. $100. Brazilian - American Chamber of Commerce, Inc., 22 W. 48th St., Ste. 404, New York, NY 10036-1886. TEL 212-575-9030. FAX 212-921-1078. **Document type:** directory.
　Formerly (until 1992): Brazil - U S Business Listing.

BRAZILIAN EXPORT MARKET. see *BUSINESS AND ECONOMICS — International Commerce*

380　　　　　　IC
BREF TIL STORKAUPMANNA. no.1, vol.5, 1969. irreg. (approx. 6/yr.). membership. Felag Islenskra Storkaupmanna - Association of Icelandic Importers, Exporters and Wholesale Merchants, Hus Verslunarinnar, 103 Reykjavik, Iceland. TEL 354-552-7066. FAX 354-568-8441. Ed. Arni Reynisson. circ. 700 (controlled).
　Formerly: F I S Frettabref.

BREWERS DIGEST ANNUAL BUYERS GUIDE AND BREWERY DIRECTORY. see *BEVERAGES*

BREWERS GUILD DIRECTORY. see *BEVERAGES*

BREWERY MANUAL & WHO'S WHO IN BRITISH BREWING & SCOTCH WHISKEY DISTILLING. see *BEVERAGES*

338.025 687　　　　UK
BRITAIN'S CLOTHING AND FOOTWEAR INDUSTRY. irreg., latest 1991. £50. Jordan & Sons Ltd., 21 St. Thomas St., Bristol BS1 6JS, England. TEL 44-117-923-0600. FAX 44-117-923-0063. **Document type:** directory.

380　　　　　　UK
BRITAIN'S DIRECT MARKETING INDUSTRY (YEAR). 1988. irreg., latest 1991. £50. Jordan & Sons Ltd., 21 St. Thomas St., Bristol BS1 6JS, England. TEL 44-117-923-0600. FAX 44-117-923-0063. charts; stat. **Document type:** directory.
　Description: Financial data and addresses for top U.K. direct marketing companies and market analysis.

380　　　　　　UK
BRITAIN'S FRANCHISING INDUSTRY. 1986. irreg., latest 1991. £50. Jordan & Sons Ltd., 21 St. Thomas St., Bristol BS1 6JS, England. TEL 44-117-923-0600. FAX 44-117-923-0063. charts; stat. (back issues avail.) **Document type:** directory.
　Description: Financial data and addresses for franchising operations in U.K. with market analysis.

338.025　　　　　UK
BRITAIN'S GUARDING INDUSTRY. irreg., latest 1991. £50. Jordan & Sons Ltd., 21 St. Thomas St., Bristol BS1 6JS, England. TEL 44-117-923-0600. FAX 44-117-923-0063. **Document type:** directory.

380　　　　　　UK
BRITAIN'S PAINT INDUSTRY. 1986. irreg., latest 1994. £125. Jordan & Sons Ltd., 21 St. Thomas St., Bristol BS1 6JS, England. TEL 44-117-923-0600. FAX 44-117-923-0063. abstr.; charts; stat. (back issues avail.) **Document type:** directory.
　Description: Financial data and addresses for British paint companies with market analyses.

380.1 332.64　　　UK
BRITAIN'S SECURITY INDUSTRY. 1978. irreg. £50. Jordan & Sons Ltd., 21 St. Thomas St., Bristol BS1 6JS, England. TEL 44-117-923-0600. FAX 44-117-923-0063. **Document type:** directory.
　Formerly: British Security Companies (ISSN 0263-3655)
　Description: Profiles the latest three years' profit and loss accounts and balance sheets for security companies. Provides director's name, registered office address, and business description.

380　　　　　　UK
BRITAIN'S SPORTING GOODS INDUSTRY: INTO THE 1990'S. 1986. irreg., latest 1993. £75. Jordan & Sons Ltd., 21 St. Thomas St., Bristol BS1 6JS, England. TEL 44-117-923-0600. FAX 44-117-923-0063. **Document type:** directory.
　Formerly: Britain's Sports Industry Equipment, Clothing and Footwear.
　Description: Financial data and addresses of 78 U.K. sports goods companies.

338.025 384　　　UK
BRITAIN'S TELEVISION AND RADIO INDUSTRY. irreg., latest 1991. £50. Jordan & Sons Ltd., 21 St. Thomas St., Bristol BS1 6JS, England. TEL 44-117-923-0600. FAX 44-117-923-0063. **Document type:** directory.

380.1　　　　　UK
BRITAIN'S TOP FOREIGN-OWNED COMPANIES. 1979. a. (in 2 vols.). £190 (£125 per vol.). Jordan & Sons Ltd., 21 St. Thomas St., Bristol BS1 6JS, England. TEL 44-117-923-0600. FAX 44-117-923-0063. **Document type:** directory.
　Former titles: Britain's Top 2500 Foreign-Owned Companies; Britain's Top 1000 Foreign-Owned Companies (ISSN 0263-242X)

380　　　　　　UK
BRITAIN'S TOP JAPANESE-OWNED COMPANIES. 1987. irreg., latest 1991. £50. Jordan & Sons Ltd., 21 St. Thomas St., Bristol BS1 6JS, England. TEL 44-117-923-0600. FAX 44-117-923-0063. (back issues avail.) **Document type:** directory.
　Formerly: Japanese Companies in the U.K.
　Description: Financial data on top Japanese companies in U.K. including addresses.

338.025 646.7　　UK
BRITAIN'S TOP TOILETRY AND DETERGENT COMPANIES. irreg., latest 1991. £50. Jordan & Sons Ltd., 21 St. Thomas St., Bristol BS1 6JS, England. TEL 44-117-923-0600. FAX 44-117-923-0063. **Document type:** directory.

338.025　　　　　UK
BRITAIN'S TOP U S OWNED COMPANIES. irreg., latest 1991. £50. Jordan & Sons Ltd., 21 St. Thomas St., Bristol BS1 6JS, England. TEL 44-117-923-0600. FAX 44-117-923-0063. **Document type:** directory.

380　　　　　　UK
BRITAIN'S TOP 10,000 PRIVATELY OWNED COMPANIES. a. (in 5 vols.). £395 (£130 per vol.). Jordan & Sons Ltd., 21 St. Thomas St., Bristol BS1 6JS, England. TEL 44-117-923-0600. FAX 44-117-923-0063. adv.; bk.rev.; charts; stat. circ. 2,000. **Document type:** directory.
　Incorporates: British Privately Owned Companies. The Third 2000; British Privately Owned Companies. The Second 2000; Which superseded: Britain's Top Private Companies. The First and Second Thousand; Former titles: Britain's Privately Owned Companies. The Top 2000; Britain's Top 2000 Private Companies; Britain's Top 1000 Private Companies (ISSN 0263-3671).

338.025 690　　　UK
BRITAIN'S TOP 1000 CONSTRUCTION COMPANIES. irreg., 1992. £75. Jordan & Sons Ltd., 21 St. Thomas St., Bristol BS1 6JS, England. TEL 44-117-923-0600. FAX 44-117-923-0063. **Document type:** directory.

380　　　　　　UK
BRITAIN'S TOP 1000 MOTOR DISTRIBUTORS. 1988. irreg., latest 1991. £50. Jordan & Sons Ltd., 21 St. Thomas St., Bristol BS1 6JS, England. TEL 44-117-923-0600. FAX 44-117-923-0063. **Document type:** directory.
　Formerly: Britain's Top 300 Motor Distributors.
　Description: Financial data and addresses for top 1000 motor distributor companies in U.K.

338.025 688.8　　UK
BRITAIN'S TOP 300 PACKAGING MANUFACTURERS. irreg., latest 1991. £50. Jordan & Sons Ltd., 21 St. Thomas St., Bristol BS1 6JS, England. TEL 44-117-923-0600. FAX 44-117-923-0063. **Document type:** directory.

380　　　　　　UK
BRITAIN'S TOP 300 PRINTERS. 1988. irreg., latest 1992. £50. Jordan & Sons Ltd., 21 St. Thomas St., Bristol BS1 6JS, England. TEL 44-117-923-0600. FAX 44-117-923-0063. **Document type:** directory.
　Description: Financial data and addresses of Britain's top 300 printing companies.

338.025 333.33　　UK
BRITAIN'S TOP 300 PROPERTY DEVELOPERS. irreg., latest 1991. £50. Jordan & Sons Ltd., 21 St. Thomas St., Bristol BS1 6JS, England. TEL 44-117-923-0600. FAX 44-117-923-0063. **Document type:** directory.

338.025 660　　　UK
BRITAIN'S TOP 500 CHEMICAL COMPANIES. irreg., 1992. £50. Jordan & Sons Ltd., 21 St. Thomas St., Bristol BS1 6JS, England. TEL 44-117-923-0600. FAX 44-117-923-0063. **Document type:** directory.

338.025 628.4　　UK
BRITAIN'S WASTE MANAGEMENT INDUSTRY. irreg., latest 1992. £50. Jordan & Sons Ltd., 21 St. Thomas St., Bristol BS1 6JS, England. TEL 44-117-923-0600. FAX 44-117-923-0063. **Document type:** directory.

BUSINESS AND ECONOMICS — TRADE AND INDUSTRIAL DIRECTORIES

380 340   CN   ISSN 0521-0585
BRITISH COLUMBIA LEGAL TELEPHONE DIRECTORY. a. Can.$22 (effective 1997). Canada Law Book Inc., 240 Edward St., Aurora, ON L4G 3S9, Canada. TEL 905-841-6472; 800-263-2037. FAX 905-841-5085. adv. contact: Mary Powell. **Document type:** directory.
  Formerly (until 1958): British Columbia Legal Directory and Telephone List (ISSN 0317-3305).

BRITISH COLUMBIA PORTS HANDBOOK (YEAR). see TRANSPORTATION — Ships And Shipping

BRITISH CONFERENCE DESTINATIONS DIRECTORY (YEAR). see MEETINGS AND CONGRESSES

382   UK   ISSN 1350-6986
BRITISH EXPORTS/EXPORTATIONS BRITANNIQUES/BRITISCHER EXPORT/EXPORTACIONES BRITANICAS. (Text in English; indexes in French, German, Spanish) 1969. a. £145 (free to qualified personnel outside U.K.). Kompass (Subsidiary of: Reed Information Services Ltd.), Part of the Reed Elsevier group, Windsor Ct., E. Grinstead House, E. Grinstead, W. Sussex RH19 1XD, England. TEL 44-1342-326972. FAX 44-1342-335747. TELEX 95127-INFSER-G. Ed. Dawn Ingram; Pub. Derek Barley. adv. contact: Julie Mason. circ. 40,000 (controlled). **Document type:** directory.
● Also available online. Vendor(s): Reed Information Services Ltd.
   —BLDSC (5105.611100); CISTI.
  Former titles: British Exports. Export Services. (ISSN 0305-7682); British Exports (ISSN 0068-1970)
  Description: Directory of UK companies with specific interests in exporting outside the UK.

670   UK   ISSN 0957-6754
BRITISH HEALTH & FITNESS CLUB DIRECTORY. 1990. a. £54. John S. Turner & Associates Ltd., Victoria House, 25 High St., Over, Cambridge CB4 5NB, England. TEL 0954-30940. FAX 0954-31886. Ed. Judy Richardson. adv. circ. 2,000. **Document type:** directory.

670   UK   ISSN 0957-8730
BRITISH LEISURE & SWIMMING POOL DIRECTORY. 1990. a. £54. John S. Turner & Associates Ltd., Victoria House, 25 High St., Over, Cambridge CB4 5NB, England. TEL 0954-30940. FAX 0954-31886. Ed. Judy Richardson. circ. 2,000. **Document type:** directory.

670   UK   ISSN 0950-0308
BRITISH LEISURE CENTRE DIRECTORY. 1986. a. £54. John S. Turner & Associates Ltd., Victoria House, 25 High St., Over, Cambridge CB4 5NB, England. TEL 0954-30940. FAX 0954-30940. Ed. Judy Richardson. circ. 2,000. **Document type:** directory.
  —BLDSC (2327.654500).

670   UK   ISSN 0955-4025
BRITISH OUTDOOR AMENITIES DIRECTORY. 1989. a. £64. John S. Turner & Associates Ltd., Victoria House, 25 High St., Over, Cambridge CB4 5NB, England. TEL 0954-30940. FAX 0954-31886. Ed. Judy Richardson. circ. 2,000. **Document type:** directory.

BRITISH THEATRE DIRECTORY. see THEATER

338.025   UK   ISSN 0968-2716
BRITON'S INDEX: FINANCIAL INSTITUTIONS. 1993. 3/yr. £235. Two-Ten Communications Ltd., Communications House, 210 Old St., London EC1V 9UN, England. TEL 44-171-490-8111. FAX 44-171-490-1255. Ed. Victoria Caulton. **Document type:** directory.

338.025   UK   ISSN 0968-2708
BRITON'S INDEX: INVESTMENT RESEARCH ANALYSTS. 1989. 3/yr. £235. Two-Ten Communications Ltd., Communications House, 210 Old St., London EC1V 9UN, England. TEL 44-171-490-8111. FAX 44-171-490-1255. Ed. Victoria Caulton. **Document type:** directory.

BROADCAST PRODUCTION GUIDE. see COMMUNICATIONS — Television And Cable

(YEAR) BROKERS 1000. see BUSINESS AND ECONOMICS — Investments

679.6   UK
BRUSH AND ALLIED TRADES INTERNATIONAL DIRECTORY. a. £30 (foreign £33) (effective 1996). Turret Group Plc., Turret House, 171 High St., Rickmansworth, Herts WD3 1SN, England. TEL 44-1923-777000. FAX 44-1923-771297. adv. **Document type:** directory.
  Former titles: Brushes International Directory (ISSN 0966-4890); Brush and Allied Trades Directory (ISSN 0305-4861); Directory of Brush and Allied Trades (ISSN 0070-5179)

BUILDING, HARDWARE AND HOUSEWARES (YEAR). see BUILDING AND CONSTRUCTION

BUILDING MATERIALS DIRECTORY. see BUILDING AND CONSTRUCTION

670 690   US
BUILDING PRODUCTS FILE. 1970. bi-m. $495. Information Handling Services, 15 Inverness Way, E., Englewood, CO 80150. TEL 303-790-0600. FAX 303-799-4085. TELEX 4322083 IHS UI. Ed. Liz Maynard Prigge. adv. circ. 780.
  Description: Provides vendor, brand name and CSI 16-division subject access to major manufacturers of construction-related products.

BUILDING SUPPLY DEALERS ASSOCIATION OF BRITISH COLUMBIA. BUYER'S GUIDE AND PRODUCT SOURCE DIRECTORY. see BUILDING AND CONSTRUCTION

338.025 384.55   UK   ISSN 1365-9677
▼**BURGUNDY BOOK OF EUROPEAN BROADCASTING.** 1996. a. £95 (effective 1997). Tellex Monitors Ltd., Communications House, 210 Old St., London EC1V 9UN, England. TEL 44-171-566-3100. FAX 44-171-566-3152. E-mail: sales@tellex.press.net; URL: http://www.tellex.press.net. Ed. Robin Mann. R&P contact: Joanne Ferris. adv.: page £750. circ. 1,000 (paid). **Document type:** directory.

338   CN   ISSN 1205-0431
BURNABY B O A R D. irreg. Can.$10. (Burnaby Chamber of Commerce) DoMac Publications Ltd., 108-10721-139 St., Surrey, BC V3T 4L8, Canada. TEL 604-582-7288. FAX 604-583-3000. adv.: B&W page Can.$1795, color page Can.$2295; trim 8 1/4 x 10 7/8. circ. 7,000. **Document type:** directory.
  Formerly: Burnaby Centennial B O A R D (ISSN 1188-8075)
  Description: Provides business-to-business references in the area.

BURRELLE'S MEDIA DIRECTORY. see COMMUNICATIONS

659.1   US   ISSN 0883-9999
BURRELLE'S NEW ENGLAND MEDIA DIRECTORY (YEAR). 1975. a. $95. Burrelle's Media Directories, 75 E. Northfield Rd., Livingston, NJ 07039. TEL 201-992-6600. (Affiliate: New England Newsclip Agency, Inc.) Ed. James L. Hayes. adv. contact: James L. Hayes. circ. 3,000. **Document type:** directory.
  Incorporates (1979-1986): Maine Media Directory; **Former titles:** New England Media Directory; Directory of New England Newspapers, College Publications, Periodicals, and Radio and Television Stations (ISSN 0195-7619)

382   FI   ISSN 0355-0346
HD9735.F49
BUSINESS CONTACTS IN FINLAND. 1974. irreg. free. Yritystieto Oy, Box 148, 00181 Helsinki, Finland. Ed. Borje Thilman. adv. circ. 15,000.

338.025   HU
BUSINESS DATA HUNGARY. (Text in Hungarian, English, German) 1994. a. 5200 Ft. (effective May 1995). Magyar Herold Business Data kft., Szechenyi u. 14, 1054 Budapest, Hungary. TEL 01-2694540. FAX 01-1127201. (Subscr. to: Herold Business Data GmbH, Guntramsdorferstr. 105, 2340 Modling, Austria. TEL 2236-4010. FAX 2236-4018) Ed. Martina Bedi. adv. contact: Karin Schumach. circ. 25,000. **Document type:** directory.
  Formerly: Company Data Hungary.

BUSINESS DESK REFERENCE. see BUSINESS AND ECONOMICS — Chamber Of Commerce Publications

338.4   CC
BUSINESS DIRECTORY OF HONG KONG. (Text in English) 1977. a. HK.$900 (foreign $160) (effective 1996). Current Publications Ltd., 1503 Enterprise Bldg., 228 Queen's Rd., Central, G.P.O. Box 9848, Hong Kong, People's Republic of China. TEL 5434702. FAX 8158396. Ed. Charles Lau. adv.: B&W page $1,200, color page $2,000; trim 10 x 7. **Document type:** trade publication.
  Description: Provides information on general business facilities in Hong Kong. Lists over 2900 manufacturers, 3600 importers and exporters, and 5500 services, professional firms and government departments. Includes personnel names, and telephone and fax numbers.

338.09897 658.1   FI   ISSN 0785-5540
HC340.2
BUSINESS FINLAND. (Text in English) 1988. a. FIM 170. (Central Chamber of Commerce in Finland) Helsinki Media Special Magazines, P.O. Box 16, FIN-00381 Helsinki, Finland. TEL 358-0-120-5911. FAX 358-0-120-5959. (Co-sponsor: Finnish Foreign Trade Association) Ed. Veijo Kayhty. R&P contact: Anneli Italvoma-Alanen. adv. contact: Anneli Italvoma-Alanen. circ. 30,000. **Document type:** directory, trade publication.
● Also available on CD-ROM.
  Description: Business, economy and trade in Finland. Includes list of major Finnish exporters.

338.025   PL
BUSINESS FOUNDATION. POLAND. INNOVATION, RESEARCH & DEVELOPMENT. (Text in English) 1993. biennial. $20. Business Foundation Co. Ltd., Ul. Krucza 38-42, 00-512 Warsaw, Poland. TEL 48-22-219993. FAX 48-22-219761. Eds. Monika Chojna, Waldemar Latoszek. circ. 4,000 (controlled). (also avail. in diskette format) **Document type:** directory, trade publication.
  Description: Directory of offerings from Polish scientific research organizations and institutions.

338.025   PL
BUSINESS FOUNDATION BOOK. GENERAL TRADE INDEX & BUSINESS GUIDE. (Text in English; cross-reference indexes in English, German, French, Polish, Russian) 1991. a. $245. Business Foundation Co. Ltd., Ul. Krucza 38-42, 00-512 Warsaw, Poland. TEL 48-22-219993. FAX 48-22-219761. E-mail: business@sam.nask.com.pl. Ed. Jerzy Oledzki. adv. contact: Monika Lechowska. circ. 20,000 (controlled). (also avail. in diskette format) **Document type:** directory, trade publication.
● Also available online.
  Description: Provides listings of over 5000 Polish companies looking for partners to expand their business domestically and abroad. Includes a business guide providing readers with basic knowledge of Polish economy, market and politics with articles by eminent business specialists and politicians.

338   IO
BUSINESS GUIDE BOOK TO JAKARTA. (Text in English) 1969. a. Gabungan Importir Nasional Seluruh Indonesia - National Importers Association of Indonesia, Jl. Kesejahteraan No. 98 APRJ, Jakarta 10110, Indonesia. TEL 021-360-643. FAX 62-021-367269. adv.; illus. circ. 10,000.
  Formerly: Djakarta Business Guide Book.

338   GW
BUSINESS GUIDE CENTRAL - EAST EUROPE. (Text in English) a. DM.48($30) (effective 1998). Dr. Harnisch Verlagsgesellschaft mbH, Blumenstr. 15, 90402 Nuernberg, Germany. TEL 49-911-2018-0. FAX 49-911-2018100. E-mail: uepost@aol.com. circ. 13,000 (paid). **Document type:** directory.

338.025   UK
BUSINESS INFORMATION BASICS. q. £185($345) (effective 1997). Headland Business Information (Subsidiary of: Bowker-Saur), Customer Services Department, Maypole House, Maypole Rd., E. Grinstead, W. Sussex RH19 1HU, England. TEL 44-1342-330-100. FAX 44-1342-330-191. E-mail: custserv@bowker-saur.co.uk. Ed. Sylvia Piggott. **Document type:** directory, trade publication.
  Former titles (until 1992): Business Information Yearbook (ISSN 0953-9263); (until 1988): Business Information Sourcebook.
  Description: Contains evaluative surveys of resources and an insider's analysis of the major resources. Outlines important trends in business information. Includes up-to-date directory of business information sources.

BUSINESS AND ECONOMICS — TRADE AND INDUSTRIAL DIRECTORIES

380   UK   ISSN 0266-3821
CODEN: BIREEY
BUSINESS INFORMATION REVIEW. 1984. q. £170 (effective 1996). Headland Business Information (Subsidiary of: Bowker-Saur), Customer Services Department, Maypole House, Maypole Rd., E. Grinstead, W. Sussex RH19 1HU, England. TEL 44-1342-330-100. FAX 44-1342-330-191. E-mail: custserv@bowker-saur.co.uk. (Subscr. to: World Wide Subscription Services, Unit 4, Gibbs Reed Farm, Ticehurst, East Sussex TN5 7HE, England) Ed. Pamela Foster. adv.; bk.rev.; abstr.; bibl.; charts; stat.; index. circ. 750. (also avail. in microform from UMI; back issues avail.) **Indexed:** Anbar, Curr.Cont., INSPEC (1987-), LISA, Mgmt.& Market.Abstr., P.I.R.A., WPM. **Document type:** trade publication.
●Also available on CD-ROM.
—BLDSC (2933.805000); AskIEEE; KR SourceOne; SWETS; UMI.
   Description: Includes articles written by field experts about business information sources - print and electronic. Analyzes information sources in specific industry sectors and countries, and the use of business information.

670   US
BUSINESS JOURNAL'S DIRECTORY OF MANUFACTURING.* a. $115. Corfacts, Business Information Division, c/o Business Journal of New Jersey, Box 920, Morristown, NJ 07751. Ed. Kathleen Barbarello. **Document type:** directory.
   Description: Lists over 10,000 manufacturing firms in New Jersey. Provides address, telephone and fax numbers, year founded, sales or revenues, number of employees, SIC code, description, and names and titles of key executives. Includes indexes grouped by industry, geographically, by annual revenues, and by number of employees.

380   US   ISSN 0888-1413
HF3010
BUSINESS ORGANIZATIONS, AGENCIES, AND PUBLICATIONS DIRECTORY. 1980. biennial. $375. Gale Research, 835 Penobscot Bldg., 645 Griswold St., Detroit, MI 48226-4094. TEL 313-961-2242; 800-877-4253. FAX 800-414-5043. E-mail: daniel__snyder@gale.com. **Document type:** directory.
●Also available online.
   Formerly: Business Organizations and Agencies Directory (ISSN 0749-0801)
   Description: Comprehensive guide to business-related resources.

338.025   US
BUSINESS PHONE BOOK U S A. a. $140. Omnigraphics, Inc., 2500 Penobscot Bldg., Detroit, MI 48226. TEL 313-961-1340; 800-234-1340. FAX 800-875-1340. (Dist. by: Reference Press, Inc., 6448 Hwy. 290 E., Ste. E-104, Austin, TX 78723. TEL 512-454-7778. FAX 512-454-9401) Pub. Frederick G. Ruffner, Jr. **Document type:** directory.
—CISTI.
   Formerly: National Directory of Addresses and Telephone Numbers (ISSN 0740-7203)
   Description: Lists more than 122000 verified listings for businesses, government offices, associations, educational institutions and other organizations.

BUSINESS REVIEW - DIRECTORY. see BUSINESS AND ECONOMICS — Chamber Of Commerce Publications

THE BUSINESS TELEVISION DIRECTORY. see COMMUNICATIONS — Television And Cable

658.8   AT   ISSN 0068-4503
HF5292
THE BUSINESS WHO'S WHO OF AUSTRALIA. 1964. a. Aus.$795 for 2 vols. Dun & Bradstreet Marketing Pty. Ltd., 19 Havilah St., Chatswood, N.S.W. 2067, Australia. TEL 61-2-9352700. FAX 61-2-9352777. URL: http://www.dbmarketing.com.au. adv. circ. 5,700. **Document type:** directory.
●Also available online. Vendor(s): AUSINET.
—CISTI. **CCC.**
   Formerly: Business Who's Who of Australia and Australian Purchasing Yearbook.
   Description: Alphabetical listings of major Australian companies. Listings include company names and addresses, affiliated and subsidiary company names, key personnel, products and services, and annual sales figures.

338   PH
BUSINESSDAY'S CORPORATE PROFILES.* 1981. a. P.300($70) Businessday Corporation, 113 West Ave., Quezon City 3010, Philippines. circ. 8,400.

380.1   CH
BUSINESSMAN'S DIRECTORY, THE REPUBLIC OF CHINA. (Text in Chinese and English) 1971. a. $80. Taiwan Enterprise Press, Ltd., Box 73-4, Taipei, Taiwan, Republic of China. Ed. Henry K.C. Lee. adv.; bk.rev. circ. 30,000. **Document type:** directory.

BUTTERWORTHS LAW DIRECTORY. see LAW

382   II   ISSN 0304-968X
HF3783
BUY FROM INDIA; world trade directory & handbook. (Text in English) 1974. biennial. Rs.300($50) per no. 10, Mangal Baugh, Pushpa Park, Daftary Rd., Malad (East), Bombay 400 097, India. TELEX 011-4220. Ed. S.L. Varma. adv.; illus. circ. 4,000. **Document type:** directory.

380.1   KO
BUYERS' GUIDE.* (Text in Korean) 1973. a. $90. Buyers Guide Ltd., Korea World Trade Center, 159-1 Samsung-dong, Kangnam-ku, Seoul, S. Korea. TEL 02-551-2376. FAX 02-551-2377. (Subscr. to: C.P.O. Box 4922, Seoul, S. Korea) circ. 30,000.

BUYERS GUIDE FOR THE HEALTH CARE MARKET; a directory of products and service for health care institutions. see HOSPITALS

380   US
BUYER'S GUIDE TO THE NEW YORK MARKET. 1930. a. included with Earnshaw's magazine. Earnshaw Publications, Inc., 225 W. 34th St., Ste. 1212, New York, NY 10001. Ed. Thomas W. Hudson, Sr. adv. circ. 10,000.

338   IT   ISSN 1122-8636
C D MONACI. (Compact Disc) s-a. Guida Monaci S.p.A., Via Vitorchiano 107, 00189 Rome, Italy. TEL 39-6-3331333. FAX 39-6-3335555. **Document type:** directory.
●Available only on CD-ROM.
   Description: Complete business data bank of the Italian industrial and service sectors.

C F I INTERNATIONAL DIRECTORY. see CLOTHING TRADE

C I DIRECTORY. (Cosmetics International) see BEAUTY CULTURE — Perfumes And Cosmetics

C P I PRODUCT PROFILES. see CHEMISTRY

C Q RADIO AMATEUR. see ENGINEERING — Electrical Engineering

384.55   US
CABLE INDUSTRY DIRECTORY. a. $249 (effective 1997). Phillips Business Information, Inc., 1201 Seven Locks Rd., Potomac, MD 20854. TEL 301-424-3338. FAX 301-309-3847. E-mail: pbi@phillips.com. **Document type:** directory.

338.025   CN
CALGARY ADVANCED TECHNOLOGY DIRECTORY. 1991. q. Can.$10. Calgary Economic Development Authority, P.O. Box 2100, Sta. M, Calgary, AB T2P 2M5, Canada. TEL 403-221-7821. FAX 403-221-7837. **Document type:** directory.

CALGARY EXPORTERS DIRECTORY. see BUSINESS AND ECONOMICS — International Commerce

CALGARY MANUFACTURERS DIRECTORY. see BUSINESS AND ECONOMICS — Production Of Goods And Services

338.025   US
CALIFORNIA BUSINESS DIRECTORY. 1992. a. $995 (effective 1996). American Business Directories (Subsidiary of: American Business Information, Inc.), 5711 S. 86th Circle, Box 27347, Omaha, NE 68127. TEL 402-593-4600; 800-555-6124. FAX 402-331-5481. E-mail: jerry.venner@abii.com. (also avail. in magnetic tape; diskette format) **Document type:** directory.
●Also available online.
Also available on CD-ROM.
   Description: Includes all businesses in the state compiled from the yellow pages and telephone-verified. Each listing includes company name, complete address, phone number, name of owner or manager, employee size, sales volume codes, and credit rating codes.

380.1 382   US   ISSN 0270-4862
HF5065.C2
CALIFORNIA INTERNATIONAL TRADE REGISTER. 1980-1981; resumed 1989. a. $129 (diskette $495) (effective 1996). (California State World Trade Commission) Database Publishing Company, 1590 S. Lewis St., Anaheim, CA 92805-6423. TEL 714-778-6400. FAX 714-778-6811. (Subscr. to: Box 70024, Anaheim, CA 92825-0024-7440. TEL 800-888-8434) Ed. Ken Gregory. adv. circ. 750. (also avail. in diskette format) **Document type:** directory.
   Description: Provides key facts on 7,900 California importers and exporters.

670 338   US   ISSN 0068-5739
CALIFORNIA MANUFACTURERS REGISTER. 1948. a. $169 (diskette $795) (effective 1996). (California Manufacturers Association) Database Publishing Company, 1590 S. Lewis St., Anaheim, CA 92805-6423. TEL 714-778-6400. FAX 714-778-6811. (Subscr. to: Box 70024, Anaheim, CA 92825-0024. TEL 800-888-8434) Ed. Ken Gregory. adv.; tr.lit. circ. 3,500. (also avail. in diskette format) **Document type:** directory.
●Also available on CD-ROM.
   Description: Provides information on over 30,000 manufacturers. Includes products and services, alphabetical and geographical sections; address, phone and SIC in all three sections.

770   JA
CAMERART PHOTO TRADE DIRECTORY. 1958. a. $88. Intercontinental Marketing Corp., I.P.O. Box 5056, Tokyo 100-30, Japan. TEL 81-3-3661-7458. FAX 81-3-3667-9646. illus. **Document type:** directory.

338.2728 622
665.5   CN   ISSN 0824-4766
CANADA A-Z; oil, gas, mining directory. 1980. a. Can.$95. Armadale Publications Inc., Box 1193, MPO, Edmonton, Alta. T5J 2M4, Canada. TEL 403-429-1073. FAX 403-425-5844. Ed. Winston Mohabir. adv.; tr.lit. circ. 7,000. (back issues avail.)
   Description: Lists oil, gas and mining companies in Canada, geographically by cities and by types of activity.

670   CN
CANADIAN CHEMICAL DIRECTORY. (In 2 vols.: Products, Companies) 1917. a. Can.$95 per vol. Camford Information Services Inc., 801 York Mills Rd., Ste. 201, Don Mills, ON M3B 1X7, Canada. TEL 416-291-3215. Pub. Bob Douglas. **Document type:** directory.
—Linda Hall.
   Formerly: Chemical Buyer's Guide (ISSN 0069-2891)

670   CN   ISSN 0068-8452
HD9655.C2
CANADIAN CHEMICAL, PHARMACEUTICAL AND PRODUCT DIRECTORY. 1948. a. Can.$35($45) Lloyd Publications of Canada, 66 Falby Ct., Ste. 1603, Ajax, Ont. L1S 3L2, Canada. TEL 416-619-0421. Ed. J. Lloyd. adv.; index. circ. 7,000. **Document type:** directory.
—CISTI.
   Formerly (until 1967): Canadian Chemical Directory (ISSN 0381-5749)
   Description: Listing of Canadian manufacturers, distributors and services for chemical raw materials products, pharmaceuticals, and equipment. Contain three sections arranged alphabetically by name, products and trade names.

670 664　　　　　CN　　ISSN 0068-8754
CANADIAN FOOD AND PACKAGING DIRECTORY. 1924. a. Can.$35($45) Lloyd Publications of Canada, 66 Falby Ct., Ste. 1603, Ajax, Ont. L1S 3L2, Canada. TEL 416-619-0421. Ed. J. Lloyd. adv.; index. circ. 8,500. **Document type:** directory.
—CISTI.
　Description: Listing of Canadian manufacturers, distributors and wholesalers of foods, packaging, and equipment. Contains three sections arranged alphabetically by name, products and trade names.

380.1 685　　　　CN　　ISSN 0068-8762
CANADIAN FOOTWEAR & LEATHER DIRECTORY. 1924. a. Can.$30($40) Lloyd Publications of Canada, 66 Falby Ct., Ste. 1603, Ajax, Ont. L1S 3L2, Canada. TEL 416-619-0421. Ed. J. Lloyd. adv.; index. circ. 5,500. **Document type:** directory.
　Description: Listing of Canadian manufacturers, distributors and wholesalers of footwear, leather goods, and equipment. Contains three sections arranged alphabetically by name, products and trade names.

380　　　　　　　　CN
CANADIAN FORCES BASE KINGSTON OFFICIAL DIRECTORY. (Text in English or French) a. Kingston Publications, P.O. Box 1352, Kingston, ON K7L 5C6, Canada. TEL 613-549-8442. Ed. Mary Laflamme. adv. contact: Ruth Kirkby. **Document type:** directory.
　Description: Published for exclusive distribution to all military personnel of C.F.B. Kingston and its associated units. Provides correct information on the area phone numbers, shops, services, accommodations, entertainment and restaurants.

380.1 749　　　　CN　　ISSN 0068-8789
CANADIAN FURNITURE & FURNISHINGS DIRECTORY. 1924. a. Can.$30($40) Lloyd Publications of Canada, 66 Falby Ct., Ste. 1603, Ajax, Ont. L1S 3L2, Canada. TEL 416-619-0421. Ed. J. Lloyd. adv.; index. circ. 5,700. **Document type:** directory.
　Description: Listing of Canadian manufacturers, distributors and wholesalers of furniture, and house furnishings. Contains three sections arranged alphabetically by name, products and trade names.

380 621.3 683.8　　CN　　ISSN 0456-3867
TS26
CANADIAN HARDWARE, ELECTRICAL & BUILDING SUPPLY DIRECTORY. 1949. a. Can.$35($45) Lloyd Publications of Canada, 66 Falby Ct., Ste. 1603, Ajax, Ont. L1S 3L2, Canada. TEL 416-619-0421. Ed. J. Lloyd. adv.; index. circ. 8,500. **Document type:** directory.
—CISTI.
　Description: Listing of Canadian manufacturers, wholesalers and distributors of hardware, electrical and building products. Contains three sections: alphabetical by name, product and trade name.

647.9　　　　　　　CN　　ISSN 0381-5765
CANADIAN HOTEL, RESTAURANT, INSTITUTION & STORE EQUIPMENT DIRECTORY. 1925. a. Can.$35($45) Lloyd Publications of Canada, 66 Falby Ct., Ste. 1603, Ajax, Ont. L1S 3L2, Canada. TEL 416-619-0421. Ed. J. Lloyd. adv.; index. circ. 8,300. **Document type:** directory.
　Description: Listing of Canadian manufacturers, distributors and wholesalers of hotel, restaurant, institution and store equipment. Contains three sections: alphabetical by name, products and trade names.

382　　　　　　　CN　　ISSN 1180-0828
CANADIAN INTERNATIONAL TRADE DIRECTORY. 1990. q. Can.$200 (effective 1997). Intratech (Subsidiary of: E L LittleJohn and Associates), Minto Place Postal Outlet, Box 56067, Ottawa, ON K1R 7Z1, Canada. TEL 613-235-9183. FAX 613-594-3857. Ed. G.D. Cann. circ. 200. **Document type:** directory.
　Description: Examines the world trade scene from a Canadian perspective.

380.1 658.8　　　CN　　ISSN 0068-9041
CANADIAN JEWELLERY & GIFTWARE DIRECTORY. 1924. a. Can.$35($45) Lloyd Publications of Canada, 66 Falby Ct., Ste. 1603, Ajax, Ont. L1S 3L2, Canada. TEL 416-619-0421. Ed. J. Lloyd. adv.; index. circ. 7,000. **Document type:** directory.
　Description: Listing of Canadian manufacturers, distributors and wholesalers of jewellery, giftware, equipment and supplies. Contains three sections arranged alphabetically by name, products and trade name.

338　　　　　　　CN　　ISSN 0315-0879
HF3223
CANADIAN KEY BUSINESS DIRECTORY. 1974. a. $450. Dun & Bradstreet Canada, 5770 Hurontario St., Mississauga, ON L5R 3GH, Canada. TEL 416-568-6147. FAX 416-568-6197. Ed. Raymond Martin. circ. 2,500. **Document type:** directory.
—CISTI.

380 340　　　　　CN　　ISSN 0843-7084
CANADIAN LEGAL FAX DIRECTORY. 1989. irreg. Can.$42 per no. (effective 1997). Canada Law Book Inc., 240 Edward St., Aurora, ON L4G 3S9, Canada. TEL 905-841-6472; 800-263-2037. FAX 905-841-5085. **Document type:** directory.

780　　　　　　　CN　　ISSN 0381-5730
CANADIAN MUSIC DIRECTORY. 1926. a. Can.$30($40) Lloyd Publications of Canada, 66 Falby Ct., Ste. 1603, Ajax, Ont. L1S 3L2, Canada. TEL 416-619-0421. Ed. J. Lloyd. adv.; index. circ. 5,300. **Document type:** directory.
　Description: Listing of Canadian manufacturers, distributors and wholesalers of music, musical instruments, supplies and more. Contains three sections: alphabetical by name, products and trade names.

CANADIAN PETROLEUM INDUSTRY. see *PETROLEUM AND GAS*

382　　　　　　　CN　　ISSN 1183-1677
CANADIAN R & D DIRECTORY. 1990. base vol. plus q. updates. Can.$200 (effective 1997). Intratech (Subsidiary of: E L LittleJohn and Associates), Minto Place Postal Outlet, Box 56067, Ottawa, ON K1R 7Z1, Canada. TEL 613-235-9183. FAX 613-594-3857. Ed. G.D. Cann. circ. 300. **Document type:** directory.
　Description: Lists R&D facilities in Canada, government, universities. Includes R&D tax incentives, government R&D funding programs.

670 790.1　　　　CN　　ISSN 0316-7771
CANADIAN SPORTING GOODS & PLAYTHINGS. DIRECTORY. 1949. a. Can.$35($45) Lloyd Publications of Canada, 66 Falby Ct., Ste. 1603, Ajax, Ont. L1S 3L2, Canada. TEL 416-619-0421. Ed. J. Lloyd. adv.; index. circ. 8,000. **Document type:** directory.
　Description: Listing of Canadian manufacturers, distributors and wholesalers of sporting goods, playthings, and recreational equipment. Contains three sections arranged alphabetically by name, products and trade names.

677　　　　　　　CN　　ISSN 0068-9858
CANADIAN TEXTILE DIRECTORY. 1924. a. Can.$35($45) Lloyd Publications of Canada, 66 Falby Ct., Ste. 1603, Ajax, Ont. L1S 3L2, Canada. TEL 416-619-0421. Ed. J. Lloyd. adv.; index. circ. 7,500. **Document type:** directory.
—CISTI.

380　　　　　　　CN　　ISSN 0068-9904
HF3223
CANADIAN TRADE INDEX.* 1900. a. Can.$140. Canadian Manufacturers Association, 75 International Blvd., Toronto, ON M9W 6L9, Canada. TEL 416-798-8000. FAX 416-798-8050. Ed. Fran Chung. adv.; index. circ. 13,000. **Document type:** abstracting/indexing.
●Also available online. Vendor(s): Southam Electronic Publishing.
Also available on CD-ROM.
—CISTI.

380.1　　　　　　CN　　ISSN 0068-9955
CANADIAN VARIETY MERCHANDISE DIRECTORY. 1924. a. Can.$35($45) Lloyd Publications of Canada, 66 Falby Ct., Ste. 1603, Ajax, Ont. L1S 3L2, Canada. TEL 416-619-0421. Ed. J. Lloyd. adv.; index. circ. 6,000. **Document type:** directory.
　Formerly: Canadian Toy, Notion and Stationery Directory.
　Description: Listing of Canadian manufacturers, distributors and wholesalers of toys, notions, stationery, and office equipment. Contains three sections arranged alphabetically by name, products and trade names.

664.15 380.1　　　　　US
CANDY BUYERS DIRECTORY. (Includes: Directory of Candy Brokers) 1932. a. $55 (effective 1997). Manufacturing Confectioner Publishing Co., Directory Division, 175 Rock Rd., Glen Rock, NJ 07452. TEL 201-652-2655. Ed. Allen R. Allured. adv. circ. 12,000. (tabloid format) **Document type:** directory.

CAPTAIN LILLIE'S BRITISH COLUMBIA COAST GUIDE AND RADIOTELEPHONE DIRECTORY. see *TRANSPORTATION — Ships And Shipping*

380 796.5　　　　　AT
CARAVAN CAMPING DIRECTORY. a. membership. (National Roads and Motorists Association) N R M A Ltd., 151 Clarence St., Sydney, N.S.W. 2000, Australia. TEL 64-2-2922631. FAX 64-2-2922639. R&P contact: Stephen Salter. adv. contact: Vicky Syrace. **Document type:** directory.

388.3　　　　　　　UK
CARAVAN INDUSTRY SUPPLIES & SERVICES DIRECTORY. 1980. a. £9 (or included in Caravan Business) (effective 1998). A.E. Morgan Publications Ltd., Stanley House, 9 West St., Epsom, Surrey KT18 7RL, England. TEL 44-1372-741411. FAX 44-1372-744493. adv. circ. 2,500. **Document type:** directory.
　Description: Lists suppliers of camping trailers and motorhomes.

382　　　　　　　　US
CARIBBEAN BASIN PROFILE. 1979. a. Caribbean Publishing Co. Ltd., 2655 Le Jeune Rd., Ste. 800, Coral Gables, FL 33134-5814. TEL 305-442-4205. FAX 305-442-8329. Ed. Sam Skogstad; Pub. Sam Skogstad. adv. contact: Sam Skogstad. maps; stat. circ. 10,000. **Document type:** trade publication.
　Former titles: Caribbean Basin Commercial Profile & Caribbean Business Directory; Caribbean Directory.
　Description: Covers economy, tourism, government, politics, and business climate.

382　　　　　　　　PR
CARIBBEAN BUSINESS - TO - BUSINESS GUIDE, THE SOURCE. 1988. a. $23.95 (effective 1995). Casiano Communications, Inc., 1700 Fernandez Juncos Ave., Stop 25, San Juan, PR 00909-2999. TEL 787-728-3000. FAX 787-728-7325. Ed. Manuel Casiano, Jr. **Document type:** directory.
　Formerly (until 1989): Puerto Rico Business - to - Business Executive Guide.
　Description: Complete study of all business areas, backed up with a compendium of tables and charts.

382　　　　　　　　US
CARIBBEAN YELLOW PAGES. 1980. a. Caribbean Publishing Co. Ltd., 2655 Le Jeune Blvd., Ste. 800, Coral Gables, FL 33134-5814. TEL 305-442-4505. FAX 305-442-8329. circ. 40,000. **Document type:** directory.
　Description: Lists 50,000 businesses from the Caribbean and 900 US companies which do business in the region, classed by product or service.

CARROLL'S FEDERAL DIRECTORY; executive, legislative, and judicial. see *PUBLIC ADMINISTRATION*

CARROLL'S FEDERAL REGIONAL DIRECTORY. see *PUBLIC ADMINISTRATION*

CARROLL'S STATE DIRECTORY. see *PUBLIC ADMINISTRATION — Municipal Government*

CARROLL'S STATE DIRECTORY (YEAR) ANNUAL. see *PUBLIC ADMINISTRATION — Municipal Government*

070.5　　　　　　　UK
CASSELL, PUBLISHERS ASSOCIATION AND THE FEDERATION OF EUROPEAN PUBLISHERS ASSOCIATIONS. DIRECTORY OF PUBLISHING IN CONTINENTAL EUROPE. 1991. a. £65. Cassell plc., Villiers House, 41-47 Strand, London WC2N 5JE, England. (Dist. in the U.S. by: Cassell, PCS Data Processing Inc., 360 W. 31st St., New York, NY 10001) (Co-sponsors: Publishers Association; Federation of European Publishers Associations) **Document type:** directory.

BUSINESS AND ECONOMICS — TRADE AND INDUSTRIAL DIRECTORIES

671.2 US
CASTING SOURCE DIRECTORY. 1991. a. $99. American Foundrymen's Society, Inc., 505 State St., Des Plaines, IL 60016-8399. TEL 708-824-0181. FAX 708-824-7848. adv. circ. 27,000. **Document type:** catalog.
   Description: For buyers, designers and specifiers of cast metal components.

338.025 US ISSN 1042-6167
HF5465.5
CATALOG HANDBOOK; catalog of catalogs. 1989. q. $19.95. Enterprise Magazines, Inc., 1020 N. Broadway, Ste. 111, Milwaukee, WI 53202. TEL 414-272-9977. FAX 414-272-9973. E-mail: info@ezines.com. **Document type:** consumer publication, directory.
   Description: Directory of retail mail-order catalogs.

670 621.9 US
CATALOG OF U.S. VALVES. triennial. $20 (free to qualified personnel). Valve Manufacturers Association of America, 1050 17th St., N.W., Ste. 701, Washington, DC 20036. TEL 202-331-8105. FAX 202-296-0378. E-mail: vma@vma.org; URL: http://www.industry.net/vma. Ed. Lisa Cherubini. tr.lit. circ. 20,000. **Document type:** catalog.
   Description: Reference to valve and actuator products and services offered by industrial valve manufacturers in the United States for end users and purchasers.

CATALOGO MOTORISTICO. see *TRANSPORTATION — Automobiles*

380 MX
CATALOGO PRODUCTOS Y SERVICIOS DEL ESTADO DE MEXICO. 1973. a. Asociacion de Industriales del Estado de Mexico, Diagonal Jose T. Cuellar 99 A, Mexico 8, D.F., Mexico.

CATERING BUYERS' GUIDE. see *FOOD AND FOOD INDUSTRIES*

338 CJ
CAYMAN ISLANDS YEARBOOK AND BUSINESS DIRECTORY. 1987. a. $34. Cayman Free Press Ltd., P.O. Box 1365, Grand Cayman, Cayman Islands, British W.I. TEL 345-949-5111. FAX 345-949-7033. Ed. Ursula Gill; Pub. Brian Uzzell. R&P contact: Brian Uzzell. adv. contact: Valerie Kempter. circ. 5,000. **Document type:** directory.

382 NA
CENTRAL BUREAU OF STATISTICS. QUARTERLY TRADE REPORT OF CURACAO AND BONAIRE. (Text and summaries in English) 1954. q. fl.35. Central Bureau of Statistics, Fort Amsterdam z/n, Willemstad, Curacao, Netherlands Antilles. TEL 599-9-611031. FAX 599-9-611696. E-mail: ank0004@ibm.net. circ. 250. **Document type:** government publication.
   Former titles (until 1992): Im- and Export Quarterly Statistics of Curacao and Bonaire by Commodity - Country; (until 1987): Kwartaalstatistiek van de In- en Uitvoer per Land - Goederensoort van Curacao en Bonaire.

CENTRE RANKINGS. see *BUSINESS AND ECONOMICS — Abstracting, Bibliographies, Statistics*

016 332 UK ISSN 1365-4322
CENTRES, BUREAUS & RESEARCH INSTITUTES; the directory of UK concentrations of effort, information, and expertise. 1987. irreg., no.3, 1996. £115($200) C.B.D. Research Ltd., 15 Wickham Rd., Beckenham, Kent BR3 5JS, England. TEL 44-181-650-7745. FAX 44-181-650-0768. E-mail: 100702.32@compuserve.com. Ed. Simone Riley. **Document type:** directory.
   Formerly (until 1993): Centres and Bureaux (ISSN 1352-3228)
   Description: Lists 1,800 centers of research and expertise in the U.K.

380 US
CERTIFIED IRRIGATION SPECIALISTS AND TECHNICIANS DIRECTORY. a. free. Irrigation Association, 8260 Willow Oaks Corp. Dr., Ste. 120, Fairfax, VA 22031. TEL 703-573-3551. FAX 703-573-1913. URL: http://www.irrigation.org. circ. 1,000. **Document type:** directory.
   Description: Lists certified landscape irrigation auditors, designers, contractors and managers.

380 PK
CHAMBER'S TRADE DIRECTORY. (Text in English) irreg. Rs.150. Chamber of Commerce and Industry, Aiwan-e-Tijarat, Box 4158, Nicol Rd., Karachi 2, Pakistan. **Document type:** directory.

382 540 US
CHEM SOURCES INTERNATIONAL. 1987. s-a. $285. Chemical Sources International, Inc., Box 1824, Clemson, SC 29633. TEL 803-646-7840. FAX 803-646-9938. Ed. Dale A. Krohn. **Document type:** directory.
   ●Also available online. Vendor(s): STN International. Also available on CD-ROM.
   Description: List of chemical compounds and distributors produced by foreign firms.

660 US ISSN 0094-6567
TP12
CHEM SOURCES U S A. 1958. a. $295. Chemical Sources International, Inc., Box 1824, Clemson, SC 29633-1824. TEL 803-646-7840. FAX 803-646-9938. Ed. Dale A. Krohn. adv. contact: Dale A. Krohn. **Document type:** directory.
   ●Also available online. Vendor(s): STN International. Also available on CD-ROM.
   —CISTI.
   Description: Chemical source directory listing compounds of U.S. chemical firms.

CHEMICAL ENGINEERING BUYER'S GUIDE. see *ENGINEERING — Chemical Engineering*

CHEMICAL INDUSTRIES ASSOCIATION. DIRECTORY OF CHEMICAL PRODUCTS AND BUYERS GUIDE. see *CHEMISTRY*

CHEMICAL INDUSTRY EUROPE. see *ENGINEERING — Chemical Engineering*

051 US ISSN 0069-2999
CHEMICAL PEDDLER. 1921. a. free. Sales Association of the Chemical Industry, Inc., 66 Morris Ave., Ste. 2A, Springfield, NJ 07081-1450. TEL 201-379-1100. FAX 201-379-6507. adv. contact: Dale Nieves. index. circ. 3,500. **Document type:** trade publication.
   Description: Contains photographs by and of the Association's members, with captions.

CHEMICALS. see *CHEMISTRY*

670 660 JA
CHEMINDEX; chemical buyers' guide for Japan. 1988. irreg. 22427 Yen (other Asian countries $208; elsewhere $213). Chemical Daily Co., Ltd., International Affairs, 3-16-8, Nihonbashi Hama-cho, Chuo-ku, Tokyo 103, Japan. TEL 81-3-3663-7932. FAX 81-3-3663-7275. TELEX 2422362 NIPPO J. E-mail: chemnews@tky.threewebnet.or.jp; URL: http://www.chemnews-japan.com/. pp./issue: 640.
   Description: Lists over 16,000 chemical products, major manufacturers, code numbers, addresses, and traders.

CHEMIST & DRUGGIST DIRECTORY. see *PHARMACY AND PHARMACOLOGY*

338.025 US ISSN 1048-7239
HF5068.C4
CHICAGO AREA BUSINESS DIRECTORY. 1985. a. $495 (effective 1997). American Business Directories (Subsidiary of: American Business Information, Inc.), 5711 S. 86th Circle, Box 27347, Omaha, NE 68127. TEL 402-593-4600; 800-555-6124. FAX 402-331-5481. E-mail: jerry.venner@abii.com. (also avail. in magnetic tape; diskette format) **Document type:** directory.
   ●Also available online.
   Also available on CD-ROM.
   Description: Includes all businesses in the Chicago area compiled from the yellow pages and telephone-verified. Each listing includes company name, complete address, name of owner or manager, employer size, sales volume rating codes.

338.025 CC
CHINA FAX & TELEX DIRECTORY. (Text in English) 1989. a. China Phone Book Company Ltd. (Subsidiary of: Review Publishing Co. Ltd.), G.P.O. Box 11581, 24-F Citicorp Centre, 18 Whitfield Rd., Causeway Bay, Hong Kong, People's Republic of China. TEL 852-2508-4408. FAX 852-2503-1526. **Document type:** directory.
   Description: Lists major organizations in China alphabetically, geographically, numerically by fax and telex, and by industry.

338.025 CC
CHINA LEADING COMPANIES. (Text in English, Chinese) 1992. a. $70. China Statistical Information and Consultancy Service Center, 38 Yuetan Nanjie, Sanlihe, Beijing 100826, People's Republic of China. TEL 86-10-8015074. FAX 86-10-8015078. adv. **Document type:** directory.

338 CC ISSN 0250-4170
HF5260.A3
CHINA PHONE BOOK & ADDRESS DIRECTORY. (Text in Chinese and English) a. China Phone Book Company Ltd., G.P.O. Box 11581, 24-F Citicorp Centre, 18 Whitfield Rd., Hong Kong, People's Republic of China. TEL 852-508-4405. FAX 852-503-1526. Ed. Mary Ng Wai-Yuen. (back issues avail.) **Document type:** directory.

338.025 CC
CHINA PHONE BOOK & BUSINESS DIRECTORY. (Text in Chinese, English) 1978. s-a. $79 per no. China Phone Book Company Ltd. (Subsidiary of: Review Publishing Co. Ltd.), G.P.O. Box 11581, 24-F Citicorp Centre, 18 Whitfield Rd., Causeway Bay, Hong Kong, People's Republic of China. TEL 852-2508-4408. FAX 852-2503-1526. adv.: B&W page $4800, color page $6700; trim 200 x 276; adv. contact: Vincci Yu. circ. 15,000. **Document type:** directory.
   Description: Over 19,000 listings of significant organizations in China with full contact details. Classified by provinces and by major industry groups.

338.025 659.1 CN ISSN 1191-3568
CHINESE TELEPHONE DIRECTORY. (Text in Chinese, English) 1935. a. $25. Chinese Publicity Bureau Ltd., 459 East Hastings St., Vancouver, BC V6A 1P5, Canada. TEL 604-254-2533. FAX 604-254-3033. Ed. Wanda Chow. R&P contact: Patrick Li. adv. contact: Marty Ng. circ. 30,000. (back issues avail.) **Document type:** directory.
   Description: Features index to advertisers, classified buyer's guide, and classified Chinese businesses.

338.025 677 UK
▼**CHINESE TEXTILE INDUSTRY DIRECTORY.** 1995. s-a. £80 (foreign £90) (effective 1997). World Textile Publications Ltd., Perkin House, 1 Longlands St., Bradford, W. Yorkshire BD1 2TP, England. TEL 44-1274-378800. FAX 44-1274-378811. E-mail: 104470.3070@compuserve.com; URL: http://www.vitalo.com/worldtextile. **Document type:** directory.

338.025 SI
CHINESE YELLOW PAGES. (Editions in Chinese, English) a. Integrated Information Pte. Ltd. (Subsidiary of: Singapore Telecom), Orchard P.O. Box 389, Singapore. adv.: B&W page $17600, color page $21725; 188 x 260. circ. 175,000.

380 788.53 US ISSN 0894-8674
PN1998.A1
CINEMATOGRAPHERS, PRODUCTION DESIGNERS, COSTUME DESIGNERS & FILM EDITORS GUIDE. 1988. a. $55 (effective 1996). Lone Eagle Publishing Co., 2337 Roscomare Rd., No. 9, Los Angeles, CA 90077-1851. TEL 310-471-8066. FAX 310-471-4969. Ed. Ed Stockly. adv. circ. 2,500. **Document type:** directory.
   Description: Lists film craftspeople and technicians in the motion picture industry.

001.6 621.381 CN
CINFOLINK ANNUAL REVIEW OF INFORMATION SERVICES IN CHINA. biennial. Can.$60($50) Cinfolink Services, 85 Roe Ave., Toronto, ON M5M 2H6, Canada. TEL 416-485-8063. E-mail: cinfo@ican.net; URL: http://www.pneumatic.com/cinfolink. Ed. H.C. Campbell. circ. 500 (paid); 150. **Document type:** directory.
   Formerly: Cinfolink Directory of Information Services in China.
   Description: Covers 230 selected electronic databases, 15 information networks and 412 key sources of current publications in the People's Republic of China and Hong Kong and 74 Internet information services. Contains review articles by leading members of information industry in China.

338   UK   ISSN 0142-5072
DA679
CITY OF LONDON DIRECTORY & LIVERY COMPANIES GUIDE. 1863. a. £19 (effective 1997). City Press Ltd., 42 North Sta. Rd., Colchester, Essex CO1 1RB, England. TEL 44-1206-545121. FAX 44-1206-545190. TELEX 98517 DISOP G. Ed. Patricia M. Hetherington; Pub. Patricia M. Hetherington. R&P contact: Christopher Hayman. adv. contact: Annabel Palmer. circ. 1,500. **Document type:** directory.
   Description: Lists names and addresses of liverymen of London, by company.

CITYFILE. see *BUSINESS AND ECONOMICS — Banking And Finance*

670   US   ISSN 0069-4525
T12
CLASSIFIED DIRECTORY OF WISCONSIN MANUFACTURERS. 1921. a. $136. (Wisconsin Manufacturers & Commerce) W M C Service Corporation, 501 E. Washington Ave., Box 352, Madison, WI 53701-0352. TEL 608-258-3400. FAX 608-258-3413. Eds. M.A. Lange, J.L. Mandt. adv.; index. (also avail. in diskette format) **Document type:** directory.
   ● Also available on CD-ROM.

382   CC
CLASSIFIED INTERNATIONAL BUSINESS DIRECTORY FOR CHINA. 1981. biennial. HK.$180. China Council for the Promotion of International Trade, G.P.O. Box 3724, Hong Kong, People's Republic of China. Ed. Richard L.C. Wong. adv.; bk.rev. circ. 40,000. **Document type:** directory.

622   US   ISSN 1045-6430
TN805.A4
COAL MINE DIRECTORY. 1972. a. $149 in US & Canada; elsewhere $157.50. Intertec, 29 N. Wacker Dr., Chicago, IL 60606. TEL 312-726-2802. FAX 312-726-2574. Ed. Arthur P. Sanda; Pub. Ken Hughes. adv. contact: Daria Shariari. circ. 800 (paid). **Document type:** directory.
   Description: Lists all operating coal mines and processing plants in the United States and Canada, including names, addresses, phone and fax numbers, production tonnages, mining types and personnel.

COFFEE INTERNATIONAL DIRECTORY. see *FOOD AND FOOD INDUSTRIES*

COLE'S REGISTER OF BRITISH ANTIQUARIAN & SECONDHAND BOOKDEALERS. see *PUBLISHING AND BOOK TRADE*

380   642.58   US
COLLEGE - UNIVERSITY FOODSERVICE WHO'S WHO. triennial. $310 (diskette $1000). Information Central Inc., Box 3900, Prescott, AZ 86302. TEL 520-778-1513. FAX 520-778-1513. E-mail: woodman@bslnet.com. Ed. Julie Woodman. stat.; index. (looseleaf format; also avail. in diskette format) **Document type:** directory.
   Description: Provides food service data and listings for 2700 two- and four-year academic institutions, including sport facilities.

338.025   US   ISSN 1048-7204
HF3161.C6
COLORADO BUSINESS DIRECTORY. 1987. a. $375 (effective 1997). American Business Directories (Subsidiary of: American Business Information, Inc.), 5711 S. 86th Circle, Box 27347, Omaha, NE 68127. TEL 402-593-4600; 800-555-6124. FAX 402-331-5481. E-mail: jerry.venner@abii.com. index. (also avail. in magnetic tape; diskette format) **Document type:** directory.
   ● Also available online.
   Also available on CD-ROM.
   Description: Includes all businesses in the state compiled from the yellow pages and telephone-verified. Each listing includes company name, complete address, phone number, name of owner, manager, and employee size, sales volume code and credit rating codes.

338.7   US   ISSN 1081-3942
COLORADO MANUFACTURERS REGISTER. 1995. a. $75 (diskette $295) (effective 1997). 1590 S. Lewis St., Anaheim, CA 92805-6423. TEL 714-778-6400. FAX 714-778-6811. **Document type:** directory.
   Description: Publishes complete profiles of 4909 manufacturing, mining and selected service firms.

COMBINED INDEPENDENTS HOLDINGS DIRECTORY. see *BUSINESS AND ECONOMICS — International Commerce*

COMEDY U S A INDUSTRY GUIDE. see *THEATER*

380   UK   ISSN 0966-0542
COMMERCE BUSINESS DIRECTORIES. BLACK COUNTRY NORTH. 1988. a. £20 (diskette ed. £150). Commerce Publications, Commerce Business Directories, Station House, Station Rd., Newport Pagnell, Milton Keynes, Bucks. MK16 0AG, England. TEL 44-1908-614477. FAX 44-1908-616441. Ed. Steve Brennan. circ. 7,000. (also avail. in diskette format) **Document type:** directory.
   Supersedes (in 1990): Black Country North Business Directory (ISSN 0963-1348); Which supersedes in part (in 1989): Black Country Business Directory (ISSN 0957-1035)
   Description: Lists and describes companies in the northern Midlands region of England and provides contact persons.

380   UK
COMMERCE BUSINESS DIRECTORIES. BLACK COUNTRY SOUTH. 1988. a. £27 (diskette ed. £150). Commerce Publications, Commerce Business Directories, Station House, Station Rd., Newport Pagnell, Milton Keynes, Bucks. MK16 0AG, England. TEL 44-1908-614477. FAX 44-1908-616441. Ed. Steve Brennan. circ. 7,000. (also avail. in diskette format) **Document type:** directory.
   Supersedes (in 1990): Black Country South Business Directory (ISSN 0963-133X); Which supersedes in part (in 1989): Black Country Business Directory (ISSN 0957-1035)
   Description: Lists businesses and contact persons in the southern Midlands region of England.

380   UK   ISSN 0957-1051
COMMERCE BUSINESS DIRECTORIES. MILTON KEYNES. 1981. a. £30 (diskette ed. £150). Commerce Publications, Commerce Business Directories, Station House, Station Rd., Newport Pagnell, Milton Keynes, Bucks. MK16 0AG, England. TEL 01908-614477. FAX 01908-616441. Ed. Steve Brennan. circ. 7,500. (also avail. in diskette format) **Document type:** directory.
   Description: Lists businesses and contact persons in Milton Keynes and the surrounding area.

380   UK   ISSN 0966-0550
COMMERCE BUSINESS DIRECTORIES. NORTHAMPTON. 1988. a. £25 (diskette ed. £150). Commerce Publications, Commerce Business Directories, Station House, Station Rd., Newport Pagnell, Milton Keynes, Bucks. MK16 0AG, England. TEL 44-1908-614477. FAX 44-1908-616441. circ. 3,000. (also avail. in diskette format) **Document type:** directory.
   Description: Lists businesses and contact persons for the Northamptonshire region of England.

380   UK   ISSN 0963-1356
COMMERCE BUSINESS DIRECTORIES. OXFORD. 1991. a. £25 (diskette ed. £150). Commerce Publications, Commerce Business Directories, Station House, Station Rd., Newport Pagnell, Milton Keynes, Bucks. MK16 0AG, England. TEL 44-1908-614477. FAX 44-1908-616441. Ed. Steve Brennan. (also avail. in diskette format) **Document type:** directory.
   Description: Lists companies and contact persons for Oxfordshire.

380   UK   ISSN 0957-1078
COMMERCE BUSINESS DIRECTORIES. PETERBOROUGH. 1985. a. £25 (diskette ed. £150). Commerce Publications, Commerce Business Directories, Station House, Station Rd., Newport Pagnell, Milton Keynes, Bucks. MK16 0AG, England. TEL 44-1908-614477. FAX 44-1908-616441. Ed. Steve Brennan. circ. 3,000. (also avail. in diskette format) **Document type:** directory.
   Description: Lists businesses and contact persons in Peterborough.

380   UK   ISSN 1355-1582
COMMERCE BUSINESS DIRECTORIES. READING. 1989. a. £25 (diskette ed. £150). Commerce Publications, Commerce Business Directories, Station House, Station Rd., Newport Pagnell, Milton Keynes, Bucks. MK16 0AG, England. TEL 44-1908-614477. FAX 44-1908-616441. Ed. Steve Brennan. circ. 5,000. (also avail. in diskette format) **Document type:** directory.
   Supersedes (in 1991): Reading Business Directory (ISSN 0957-1086)
   Description: Lists businesses and contact persons in the Reading area.

380   UK   ISSN 0964-8585
COMMERCE BUSINESS DIRECTORIES. REDDITCH. 1986. a. £23 (diskette ed. £150). Commerce Publications, Commerce Business Directories, Station House, Station Rd., Newport Pagnell, Milton Keynes, Bucks. MK16 0AG, England. TEL 44-1908-614477. FAX 44-1908-616441. Ed. Steve Brennan. circ. 4,000. (also avail. in diskette format) **Document type:** directory.
   Supersedes (in 1990): Redditch and District Business Directory (ISSN 0957-1094)
   Description: Lists businesses and contact persons in Redditch and the surrounding area.

380   UK   ISSN 0957-1116
COMMERCE BUSINESS DIRECTORIES. TELFORD. 1985. a. £28 (diskette ed. £150). Commerce Publications, Commerce Business Directories, Station House, Station Rd., Newport Pagnell, Milton Keynes, Bucks. MK16 0AG, England. TEL 44-1908-614477. FAX 44-1908-217425. circ. 6,500. (also avail. in diskette format) **Document type:** directory.
   Description: Lists businesses and contact persons in Telford.

380   UK   ISSN 0967-1501
COMMERCE BUSINESS DIRECTORIES. WATFORD & HEMEL HEMPSTEAD. 1992. a. £25 (diskette ed. £150). Commerce Publications, Commerce Business Directories, Station House, Station Rd., Newport Pagnell, Milton Keynes, Bucks. MK16 0AG, England. TEL 44-1908-614477. FAX 44-1908-217425. Pub. Maria Luisi. circ. 3,000. (also avail. in diskette format) **Document type:** directory.
   Formed by the merger of (1988-1992): Hemel Hempstead Business Directory (ISSN 0957-1043); (1989-1992): Watford Business Directory (ISSN 0957-1124)
   Description: Lists businesses and contact persons in Watford and Hemel Hempstead.

338.025   SI
COMMERCIAL & INDUSTRIAL GUIDE. a. Integrated Databases India Ltd., II , c/o Orchard P.O. Box 389, Singapore, Singapore. adv.: B&W page $17600, color page $21725; trim 210 x 275. circ. 200,000.

380.1   ET
COMMERCIAL BANK OF ETHIOPIA. TRADE DIRECTORY. irreg. free. Commercial Bank of Ethiopia, P.O. Box 255, Addis Ababa, Ethiopia. **Document type:** directory.

602.9   US   ISSN 1047-6393
T223.V4
COMPANIES AND THEIR BRANDS. (Supplement avail.) a. $369 (in 2 vols.). Gale Research, 835 Penobscot Bldg., 645 Griswold St., Detroit, MI 48226-4094. TEL 313-961-2242; 800-877-4253. FAX 800-414-5043. E-mail: daniel_snyder@gale.com. Ed. Susan Stetler.
   ● Also available online. Vendor(s): Knight-Ridder Information, Inc.
   —CISTI
   Formerly: Trade Names Dictionary: Company Index (ISSN 0277-0369)
   Description: Lists over 47,000 company entries including the brand-name products they manufacture or distribute.

BUSINESS AND ECONOMICS — TRADE AND INDUSTRIAL DIRECTORIES

670 US ISSN 1057-9222
UC267
COMPANIES PARTICIPATING IN THE DEPARTMENT OF DEFENSE SUBCONTRACTING PROGRAM.* q. $23 (foreign $28.75) (effective 1995). U.S. Department of Defense, Defense Logistics Agency, 8725 John J. Kingman Rd., Ste. 2533, Fort Belvoir, VA 22060-6221. (Subscr. to: Superintendent of Documents, U.S. Government Printing Office, Box 371954, Pittsburgh, PA 15250-7954. TEL 202-512-1800. FAX 202-512-2250) (also avail. in microfiche from CIS; back issues avail.; reprint service avail. from CIS) Indexed: Amer.Stat.Ind. (1980-). **Document type:** government publication.

338.025 AU
COMPANY DATABASE C D. 2/yr. S.32000. (Kreditschutz von 1870) Herold Business Data AG, Guntramsdorferstr. 105, A-2340 Moedling, Austria. TEL 43-2236-401. FAX 43-2236-4018. E-mail: kundendienst@herold.co.at; URL: http://www.herold.co.at/home. **Document type:** directory.
●Available only on CD-ROM.

338 AU
DER COMPASS - BAND HANDEL UND DIENSTLEISTUNGEN. a. S.2000 (effective 1996). Compass Verlag, Matznergasse 17, A-1141 Vienna, Austria. TEL 43-1-98116-0. FAX 43-1-9811698. E-mail: office@compass.co.at; URL: http://www.compass.co.at. Ed. Werner Futter. R&P contact: Werner Futter. adv. contact: Michael Bayer. **Document type:** directory.
Formerly: Handels - Compass (ISSN 0253-7087)
Description: Describes business structure of Austrian trading and services industry enterprises.

670 AU
DER COMPASS - BAND INDUSTRIE. 1867. a. S.2000. (Austrian Chamber of Commerce) Compass Verlag, Matznergasse 17, A-1141 Vienna, Austria. TEL 43-1-98116-0. FAX 43-1-9811698. E-mail: office@compass.co.at; URL: http://www.compass.co.at. Ed. Werner Futter. R&P contact: Werner Futter. adv. contact: Michael Bayer. **Document type:** directory.
Formerly: Industrie-Compass Oesterreich (ISSN 0073-7712)
Description: Provides description of business structure of approximately 18,000 manufacturing enterprises of any corporative type classified in lines of production and, within these categories, grouped according to location.

380 US
COMPLETE COMMODITY FUTURES DIRECTORY. 1980. irreg. $195. Christopher Resources, Inc., 34 N. White St., Box 488, Frankfort, IL 60423-0488. TEL 800-332-3441. FAX 815-485-2499. Ed. M.C. Marasco. R&P contact: Martin Fabish. adv. contact: Martin Fabish. circ. 3,500. (looseleaf format; also avail. in magnetic tape; diskette format; back issues avail.) **Document type:** directory.

THE COMPLETE GIFT BASKET INDUSTRY REFERENCE DIRECTORY. see BUSINESS AND ECONOMICS — Small Business

COMPOSITE CATALOG OF OIL FIELD EQUIPMENT & SERVICES. see PETROLEUM AND GAS

COMPUTER LISTING SERVICE'S MACHINERY & EQUIPMENT GUIDE. see MACHINERY

COMPUTER SECURITY BUYERS GUIDE. see COMPUTERS — Computer Security

338.025 UK ISSN 0951-2705
CONFERENCES AND EXHIBITIONS DIARY. 1986. q. £75 (foreign £85). Themetree Ltd., 2 Prebendal Ct., Oxford Rd., Aylesbury, Bucks. HP19 3EY, England. TEL 44-1296-428585. FAX 44-1296-436622. Ed. John Charlton. circ. 1,080. (looseleaf format) **Document type:** directory.

338.025 US ISSN 1048-7212
HC107.C8
CONNECTICUT BUSINESS DIRECTORY. 1988. a. $350 (effective 1997). American Business Directories (Subsidiary of: American Business Information, Inc.), 5711 S. 86th Cir., Box 27347, Omaha, NE 68127. TEL 402-593-4600; 800-555-6124. FAX 402-331-5481. E-mail: jerry.venner@abii.com. index. (also avail. in magnetic tape; diskette format) **Document type:** directory.
●Also available online.
Also available on CD-ROM.
Description: Includes all businesses in the state compiled from the yellow pages and telephone-verified. Each listing includes company name, complete address, phone number, name of owner, manager, and employee size, sales volume codes and credit rating codes.

670 US ISSN 0193-5909
HD9727.C8
CONNECTICUT - RHODE ISLAND DIRECTORY OF MANUFACTURERS. 1979. a. $72.50 (diskette $495) (effective 1996). Commerce Register, Inc., 190 Godwin Ave., Midland Park, NJ 07432. TEL 201-445-3000. FAX 201-445-5806. adv. (also avail. in magnetic tape; diskette format) **Document type:** directory.
Description: Profiles more than 6,000 companies and all key executives; includes alphabetical, geographical and product line by SIC sections.

CONNECTICUT - RHODE ISLAND TELEPHONE TICKLER FOR INSURANCE MEN & WOMEN. see INSURANCE

670 690 US
CONSTRUCCION PAN-AMERICANA INTERNATIONAL BUYER'S GUIDE.* (Text in Spanish) 1981. a. International Construction Publishing, Inc., 9500 S. Dadeland Blvd., Ste. 550, Miami, FL 33156-2819. TEL 305-670-4818. FAX 305-670-4820. Ed. Juan Escalante. circ. 11,780.
Description: Lists manufacturers of construction equipment, accessories and supplies from all over the world.

338.025 690 CC
CONSTRUCTION AND INTERIOR DIRECTORY. (Text in English) 1992. a. HK.$350. Press Mark Media Ltd., Flat 3, 1-F Prospect Mansion, 66-72 Paterson St., Causeway Bay, Hong Kong, People's Republic of China. TEL 852-8822-230. FAX 852-8823-949. TELEX 49505 EMART HX. Ed. Kenneth Li Kam Man. adv.: color page HK$6800; adv. contact: Jackie Ho. circ. 10,000. **Document type:** directory.
Description: Covers every aspect relating to the construction industry and domestic interiors for architects, contractors, designers and developers.

380 625.7 690 US
CONSTRUCTION INDUSTRIES OF MASSACHUSETTS DIRECTORY; a directory and catalog of highway and heavy construction in New England. 1948. a. $15. Construction Industries of Massachusetts, Inc., 1500 Providence Hwy., Ste. 14, Box 667, Norwood, MA 02062. **Document type:** directory.
Formerly: Construction Directory (ISSN 0099-8281)

338.025 620 UK
CONSULTANT ENGINEERS 500. 1991. a. £37.50 (effective 1997). Anchorage Press Ltd., 9 Hartington Rd., Twickenham TW1 3EL, England. TEL 44-181-892-9905. FAX 44-181-891-2462. E-mail: anchorage@compuserve.com; URL: http://www.ourworld.compuserve.com/homepages/anchorage. Ed. Simon Fullalove; Pub. Simon Fullalove. R&P contact: Simon Fullalove. adv. contact: Simon Fullalove. Indexed: I.M.M.Abstr. **Document type:** directory.

CONSULTANTS AND CONSULTING ORGANIZATIONS DIRECTORY; a reference guide to concerns and individuals engaged in consultation for business, industry and government. see BUSINESS AND ECONOMICS — Management

338 US ISSN 1042-153X
HD69.C6
CONSULTANTS DIRECTORY FOR BUSINESS AND INDUSTRY; a practical guide for finding needed expertise. a. Gale Research, 835 Penobscot Bldg., 645 Griswold St., Detroit, MI 48226-4094. TEL 313-961-2242; 800-877-4253. FAX 800-414-5043. E-mail: daniel_snyder@gale.com. Ed. Martin Connors. **Document type:** directory.

CONSULTING ENGINEER INTERNATIONAL. see ENGINEERING

352 SA
CONTAC. (Text in English) 1981. a. R.233.70. McGregors Informations Services Pty Ltd., P.O. Box 651302, Benimore 2010, South Africa. TEL 884-3301. adv. circ. 850. **Document type:** directory.
Formerly: Kontak.

338.025 US ISSN 1059-7093
CONTRA COSTA COUNTY COMMERCE AND INDUSTRY DIRECTORY. 1992. a. $75. Database Publishing Company, 1590 S. Lewis St., Anaheim, CA 92805-6423. TEL 714-778-6400. FAX 714-778-6811. (Subscr. to: Box 70024, Anaheim, CA 92825-0024. TEL 800-888-8434) (also avail. in diskette format) **Document type:** directory.
●Also available on CD-ROM.
Description: Covers 2,700 manufacturing, wholesale, and service firms; and 5,300 top executives.

380 331.1 US ISSN 1063-9268
CONTRACT EMPLOYMENT WEEKLY. 1969. w. $65 (effective Jul. 1995). C.E. Publications, Inc., Box 97000, Kirkland, WA 98083. TEL 206-823-2222. FAX 206-821-0942. Ed. Janice Erickson; Pub. Jerry Erickson. R&P contact: Jerry Erickson. adv. contact: Carol McDaniel. **Document type:** trade publication.
Formerly: Contract Engineer Weekly.

CONTRACT FURNISHING DIRECTORY. see INTERIOR DESIGN AND DECORATION — Furniture And House Furnishings

380 629.8 US
CONTROL SOFTWARE DIRECTORY FOR PROCESS CONTROL. 1988. a. Putman Publishing Co., 301 E. Erie St., Chicago, IL 60611. TEL 312-644-2020. FAX 312-644-1131. Ed. Paul Studebaker. circ. 72,000. **Document type:** directory.
Description: Lists names, addresses, and phone numbers of suppliers of software for industrial process control applications.

CONVERTER DIRECTORY; suppliers and services to the U.K. converting industry. see PAPER AND PULP

CO-OP ADVERTISING PROGRAM SOURCEBOOK (YEAR). see ADVERTISING AND PUBLIC RELATIONS

COOPERATIVE TRADE DIRECTORY FOR SOUTHEAST ASIA. see BUSINESS AND ECONOMICS — Cooperatives

659.1 US
CORPORATE AFFILIATIONS PLUS. q. $1995. National Register Publishing, A Division of Reed Elsevier Inc., 121 Chanlon Rd., New Providence, NJ 07974. TEL 908-464-6800. FAX 908-771-7704. TELEX 138 755. E-mail: info@reedref.com; URL: http://www.reedref.com. (Subscr. to: National Register Publishing, Order Dept., Box 31, New Providence, N 07974-9903. TEL 800-521-8110)
●Available only on CD-ROM. Producer(s): Bowker Electronic Publishing.
Description: Includes the entire Corporate Affiliations Library (public, private, and international) as well as America's Corporate Finance Directory. Allows for the research of corporate statistics and current financials for over 15,000 domestic and foreign companies and their 100,000 subsidiaries, affiliates, divisions, and joint ventures; review profiles of more than 190,000 influential decision makers; locate solid sales leads; discover new investment opportunities.

380 US ISSN 0589-7920
CORPORATE REPORT FACT BOOK; a directory of publicly held companies in the Ninth Federal Reserve District. 1967. a. $127. American City Business Journals, Inc. (Austin), 505 Powell St., Austin, TX 78703-5121. Ed. Tom Smith. adv.: B&W page $1450. circ. 3,200 (paid). **Document type:** directory.
Incorporates: Corporate Report Who's Who in Upper Midwest Business.

670 600   US
HG4057
CORPTECH DIRECTORY OF TECHNOLOGY COMPANIES. (In 4 vols.) 1986. a. $545 softcover; hardcover $595 (diskette $4950; CD-ROM $2450) (effective 1997). Corporate Technology Information Services Inc., c/o Eileen Kenney, 12 Alfred Ave., Ste. 200, Woburn, MA 01801. TEL 617-932-3939. FAX 617-932-6335. E-mail: sales@corptech.com; URL: http://www.corptech.com. Ed. Steven W. Parker. circ. 45,000. (diskette format; back issues avail.) **Document type:** directory.
●Also available online. Vendor(s): Questel Orbit Inc. (CORP).
Also available on CD-ROM.
—CISTI. CCC.
   Formerly: Corporate Technology Directory (ISSN 0887-1930)
   Description: Comprehensive source of company information on America's 45,000

670 600   US
CORPTECH - TECHNOLOGY SPOTLIGHT. m. Corporate Technology Information Services Inc., 12 Alfred St., Ste. 200, Woburn, MA 01801. TEL 617-932-3939. FAX 617-932-6335. E-mail: sales@corptech.com; URL: http://www.corptech.com:3600/spotmenu.htm. **Document type:** trade publication.
●Available only online.
   Description: Offers reports on the level of employment for high technology industry in the U.S.

380   US
CORRECTIONAL FOODSERVICE WHO'S WHO. 1997. triennial. $295 (diskette $950). Information Central Inc., Box 3900, Prescott, AZ 86302. TEL 520-778-1513. FAX 520-778-1513. E-mail: woodman@bslnet.com. Ed. Julie Woodman. stat.; index. (looseleaf format; also avail. in diskette format) **Document type:** directory.
   Description: Provides foodservice data on all jails, prisons, juvenile facilities with 125 or more inmates.

338.025   AT
▼**COUNTERPOINT DIRECTORY.** 1996. a. Aus.$80. Reed Business Publishing Pty. Ltd. (Subsidiary of: Reed International PLC), P.O. Box 5487, W. Chatswood, N.S.W. 2057, Australia. TEL 61-2-699-2411. FAX 61-2-698-8138. **Document type:** directory, trade publication.
   Description: A comprehensive listing of names, addresses and contact numbers of leading electrical appliance manufacturers, agents, branches, store groups, service agents, industry associations, regulatory bodies and research companies.

THE COWLES - SIMBA REPORT ON DIRECTORY PUBLISHING. see *PUBLISHING AND BOOK TRADE*

CRANFIELD SCHOOL OF MANAGEMENT ADDRESS BOOK. see *COLLEGE AND ALUMNI*

CRAWFORD'S DIRECTORY OF CITY CONNECTIONS. see *BUSINESS AND ECONOMICS — Banking And Finance*

CREATIVE OPTIONS FOR BUSINESS AND ANNUAL REPORTS; photography, illustration & graphic design. see *ART*

381   NA
CURACAO PROFESSIONAL GUIDE. a. Know How Group N.V., Schottegatweg Oost 56, P.O. Box 473, Curacao, Netherlands Antilles. TEL 367079. FAX 367080. **Document type:** directory.

380   NA
CURACAO TRADE AND INDUSTRY DIRECTORY.* (Text in Dutch, English or Spanish.) a. (Curacao Trade and Industry Association) Citroen-Daal, Pietermaai 21, P.O.B. 49, Willemstad, Curacao, Netherlands Antilles. illus.

CURRENT BRITISH DIRECTORIES. see *BUSINESS AND ECONOMICS — Abstracting, Bibliographies, Statistics*

CURRENT EUROPEAN DIRECTORIES/REPERTOIRE DES ANNUAIRES EUROPEENS/HANDBUCH DER EUROPAEISCHEN ADRESSBUECHER. see *BUSINESS AND ECONOMICS — Abstracting, Bibliographies, Statistics*

338   UK
CUSTOM CHEMICAL SYNTHESIS SERVICES IN FRANCE. 1984. irregr., latest 1993. £200. I A L Consultants, 109 Uxbridge Rd., Ealing, London W5 5TL, England. TEL 44-181-810-0919. FAX 44-181-566-4931. **Document type:** trade publication.

CYCLISTS' YELLOW PAGES. see *SPORTS AND GAMES — Bicycles And Motorcycles*

381   CY   ISSN 0070-2331
CYPRUS CHAMBER OF COMMERCE AND INDUSTRY DIRECTORY;* guide to commerce, industry, tourism and agriculture. (Text in English) 1967. irreg., 2nd ed., 1970. $25. D. Couvas & Sons Ltd., Box 35, Limassol, Cyprus. (Dist. by: International Publications Service, 114 E. 32nd St., New York, NY 10016). **Document type:** directory.

D C C TRADE DIRECTORY. (Delhi Chamber of Commerce) see *BUSINESS AND ECONOMICS — Chamber Of Commerce Publications*

338.025 070.5   UK
D P A MEMBERSHIP BOOK. 1989. a. free. (Directory Publishers Association) A P Information Services, Roman House, 296 Golders Green Rd., London NW11 9PZ. TEL 44-181-455-4550. FAX 44-181-455-6381. Ed. Rosemary Pettit. adv.: page £300; trim 195 x 135; adv. contact: Anthony Margolis. stat.; index. circ. 3,000. **Document type:** directory.
●Also available on CD-ROM.
   Description: Lists and provides information on members and publications. Compiles statistics and contains the Code of Professional Practice.

338.025 070.5   UK   ISSN 1351-251X
D P A NEWS. 1992. q. Directory Publishers Association, 93a Blenheim Cresc., London W11 2EQ, England. TEL 44-171-221-9089. URL: http://www.d-net.com. Ed. Rosemary Pettir. **Document type:** newsletter.

DAIRY FOODS MARKET DIRECTORY. see *FOOD AND FOOD INDUSTRIES*

DALIL AL-MUSADDIRIN/DIRECTORY OF EXPORTERS. see *BUSINESS AND ECONOMICS — International Commerce*

338   US
DALTON'S ALLENTOWN, BETHLEHEM, LANCASTER READING METROPOLITAN DIRECTORY: BUSINESS - INDUSTRY. 1991. a. $85 ($325 on diskette). Dalton Directory, 410 Lancaster Ave., Haverford, PA 19041. TEL 800-221-1050. FAX 610-649-3596. Ed. Patrick Dalton. (also avail. in diskette format) **Document type:** directory.
   Description: Lists over 5,000 companies with company names, addresses, phone and fax numbers, names and titles of key executives.

338   US
DALTON'S BALTIMORE - WASHINGTON METROPOLITAN DIRECTORY: BUSINESS - INDUSTRY. a. $95 (diskette $350). Dalton Directory, 410 Lancaster Ave., Haverford, PA 19041. TEL 800-221-1050. FAX 610-649-3596. Ed. Patrick Dalton. (also avail. in diskette format) **Document type:** directory.
   Description: Lists more than 8,000 companies with addresses, phone and fax numbers, names and titles of key executives.

338   US   ISSN 1052-6609
HF5068.N5
DALTON'S NEW YORK METROPOLITAN DIRECTORY: BUSINESS - INDUSTRY. 1984. a. $129 (diskette $475). Dalton Directory, 410 Lancaster Ave., Haverford, PA 19041. TEL 800-221-1050. FAX 610-649-3596. Ed. Patrick Dalton. (also avail. in diskette format) **Indexed:** Excerp.Med. **Document type:** directory.
   Description: Lists over 14,000 companies with addresses, phone and fax numbers, names and titles of key executives.

338   US   ISSN 1053-685X
HF3163.P5
DALTON'S PHILADELPHIA METROPOLITAN DIRECTORY: BUSINESS - INDUSTRY. 1964. a. $129 (diskette $475). Dalton Directory, 410 Lancaster Ave., Haverford, PA 19041. TEL 800-221-1050. FAX 610-649-3596. Ed. Patrick Dalton. (also avail. in diskette format)
   Former titles (until 1986): Dalton's Delaware Valley Directory (ISSN 0733-2416); (until 1982): Dalton's Directory of Business and Industry (ISSN 0732-6955)
   Description: Lists more than 14,000 companies with addresses, phone and fax numbers, names and titles of key executives.

DATA COMMUNICATIONS BUYERS' GUIDE. see *COMPUTERS — Data Communications And Data Transmission Systems*

DATA ENTRY - DATA CONVERSION SERVICES DIRECTORY. see *COMPUTERS — Electronic Data Processing*

338.025   UK   ISSN 1358-8974
DATAPACK; buyer's directory for the tax and duty free industry. 1993. s-a. £130 (effective 1997). Quest Magazines Ltd., Publishing House, 652 Victoria Rd., South Ruislip, Mddx. HA4 0SX, England. TEL 44-181-842-1010. FAX 44-181-841-2557. Ed. Veronica Simpson; Pub. Chris Mitchell. circ. 3,000. **Document type:** directory.

677   US   ISSN 0363-5252
TS1312
DAVISON'S SALESMAN'S BOOK. 1916. a. $60. Davison Publishing Co., Inc., Box 1289, Concord, NC 28026-1289. TEL 704-785-8700; 800-328-4766. FAX 704-785-8701. E-mail: textiles@davisonbluebook.com; URL: http://www.davisonbluebook.com. Ed. Bruce W. Nealy; Pub. Bruce W. Nealy. adv. contact: Carol H. Nealy. **Document type:** directory, trade publication.
●Also available online.
   Description: Lists all textile mills, dyers and finishers in the U.S., Canada and Mexico.

677   US   ISSN 0070-2951
DAVISON'S TEXTILE BLUE BOOK. 1866. a. $120. Davison Publishing Co., Inc., Box 1289, Concord, NC 28026-1289. TEL 704-785-8700. FAX 704-785-8701. E-mail: textiles@davisonbluebook.com; URL: http://www.davisonbluebook.com. Ed. Bruce W. Nealy.
●Also available online.
—CISTI.
   Description: Lists all mills, dyers and finishers in the U.S., Canada and Mexico, plus sales offices, yarn dealers, and cotton dealers, etc.

DEFENSE INDUSTRY CHARTS. see *MILITARY*

338.025   US   ISSN 1048-7085
HF5065.D3
DELAWARE BUSINESS DIRECTORY. 1990. a. $295 (effective 1997). American Business Directories (Subsidiary of: American Business Information, Inc.), 5711 S. 86th Circle, Box 27347, Omaha, NE 68127. TEL 402-593-4600; 800-555-6124. FAX 402-331-5481. E-mail: jerry.venner@abii.com. index. (also avail. in magnetic tape; diskette format) **Document type:** directory.
●Also available online.
Also available on CD-ROM.
   Description: Includes all businesses in the state compiled from the yellow pages and telephone-verified. Each listing includes company name, complete address, phone number, name of owner, manager, and employee size, sales volume codes and credit rating codes.

380   US   ISSN 0272-8117
HD9727.D3
DELAWARE DIRECTORY OF COMMERCE AND INDUSTRY. 1950. a. $75. Delaware State Chamber of Commerce, 1201 N. Orange St., Box 671, Wilmington, DE 19899. TEL 302-655-7221. FAX 302-654-0691. (Dist. by: Manufacturers' News, Inc., 1633 Central St., Evanston, IL 60201. TEL 708-864-7000) adv. (also avail. in diskette format) **Document type:** directory.
   Formerly: Delaware Manufacturers Directory.
   Description: Company profiles of more than 6,000 firms; includes five sections -- alphabetically by company name, SIC, geographical, alphabetical listing of manufacturing and manufacturing industries.

BUSINESS AND ECONOMICS — TRADE AND INDUSTRIAL DIRECTORIES

338.025 US ISSN 1087-1896
HF5065.D3
DELAWARE MANUFACTURERS REGISTER. a. $45 (diskette or CD-ROM $195) (effective 1997). Manufacturers' News, Inc., 1633 Central St., Evanston, IL 60201-1569. TEL 847-864-7000. FAX 847-332-1100. (also avail. in diskette format) **Document type:** directory.
  Description: Profiles 791 companies.

THE DESIGN FIRM DIRECTORY - ENVIRONMENTAL AND INTERIOR DESIGN EDITION. see *INTERIOR DESIGN AND DECORATION*

THE DESIGN FIRM DIRECTORY - GRAPHIC AND INDUSTRIAL DESIGN EDITION; a listing of firms and consultants in industrial and graphic design in the U.S. and Canada. see *INTERIOR DESIGN AND DECORATION*

DESIGN NEWS O E M DIRECTORY. see *MACHINERY*

338.025 677 UK ISSN 0951-3930
DESKBOOK OF U K AGENTS. 1970. biennial. £20 (effective 1997). World Textile Publications Ltd., Perkin House, 1 Longlands St., Bradford, W. Yorkshire BD1 2TP, England. TEL 44-1274-378800. FAX 44-1274-378811. E-mail: 104470.3070@compuserve.com; URL: http://www.vitalo.com/worldtextile. **Document type:** directory.
  Description: Guide to the world's textile machinery makers and their representatives in the UK.

380 663.2 US ISSN 1056-523X
TP548.5.A6
DESKTOP PRODUCTS GUIDE. 1970. a. $25. Vineyard and Winery Services, Inc., 103 Third St., Box 231, Watkins Glen, NY 14891. TEL 607-535-7133. FAX 607-535-2998. Ed. J. William Moffett. R&P contact: J. William Moffett. adv. contact: Hope Merletti. circ. 2,000. **Document type:** directory, trade publication.
  Description: Lists suppliers for the wine and grape industry. Includes universities, research centers, seminars, competitions, and wineries by state, including Canada.

338 380 GW ISSN 0418-8381
DAS DEUTSCHE FIRMEN-ALPHABET; Industrie, Handel, Verkehr, Organisationen. a. DM.26. Deutscher Adressbuch Verlag, Arheilger Weg 17, 64380 Rossdorf, Germany. TEL 06154-699500. FAX 06154-6995490. adv. circ. 8,000. **Document type:** directory.

380.1 GW
DEUTSCHER VERSAND-EINKAUFSFUEHRER; erstes und einziges Versandfirmenregister in Deutschland. 1984. a. DM.50($30) Horst Ludwig Verlag, Jenseitsstr. 10, 50127 Bergheim, Germany. TEL 02271-92791. adv. circ. 1,500.
  Description: Presents all kinds of mail order products.

338 GW ISSN 0724-6633
DEUTSCHES BUNDES-ADRESSBUCH: INDUSTRIE, GROSS- UND AUSSENHANDEL, DIENSTLEISTUNGEN, ORGANISATIONEN. a. DM.96. Deutscher Adressbuch Verlag, Arheilger Weg 17, 64380 Rossdorf, Germany. TEL 49-6154-699500. FAX 49-6154-6995490. adv.; illus. circ. 6,000. **Document type:** directory.
  Formerly: Deutsches Bundes-Adressbuch der Firmen aus Industrie, Handel und Verkehr (ISSN 0343-589X)

338.025 US ISSN 1046-7262
DIAL-A-FAX DIRECTORY; world's largest resource of fax services. 1987. a. Dial-A-Fax Directories, Benjamin Fox Pavilion, Ste. 930, Jenkintown, PA 19046. **Document type:** directory.
  Formerly (until 1989): Fax Phone Book (ISSN 0896-9434)

380 PN
DIRECTORIO COMERCIAL E INDUSTRIAL DE PANAMA/COMMERCIAL AND INDUSTRIAL DIRECTORY OF PANAMA. 1958. a. $30 (effective 1997). Camara de Comercio, Industrias y Agricultura de Panama, P.O. Box 74, Panama 1, Panama. E-mail: cciap@panama.phoenix.net; URL: http://www.panacamara.com. Ed. Francia de Rojas. R&P contact: Jorge Carney. adv. contact: Victor A. Ortiz. circ. 2,000. **Document type:** directory.

380 MX
DIRECTORIO DE CENTROS DE INFORMACION. 1973. irreg., 14th ed., 1997. $200 (effective 1997). Ibcon, S.A., Gutenberg 224, Col. Anzures, 11590 Mexico D.F., Mexico. TEL 52-5-2554577. FAX 52-5-2554577. E-mail: ibcon@infosel.net.mx; URL: http://www.dirsainf.com.mx/ibom1.htm. Ed. Gabriel Zaid. **Document type:** directory.
  Description: Lists a thousand associations, government agencies, universities, embassies, information publishers, specialized libraries, and other sources of information for marketing research. Indexed by topics.

382 MX
DIRECTORIO DE CLIENTES PARA EXPORTAR A LOS ESTADOS UNIDOS. (Text in English) 1981. irreg., 11th ed., 1997. $280 (effective 1997). Ibcon, S.A., Gutenberg 224, Col. Anzures, 11590 Mexico D.F., Mexico. TEL 52-5-2554577. FAX 52-5-2554577. E-mail: ibcon@infosel.net.mx; URL: http://www.dirsainf.com.mx/ibcm1.htm. Ed. Gabriel Zaid. **Document type:** directory.
  Description: Lists 4000 American, Puerto Rican and Canadian importers interested in Mexican products, indexed by product.

350 MX
▼**DIRECTORIO DE EJECUTIVAS.** (Includes a diskette index) 1996. irreg., 2nd ed., 1997. $200 (effective 1997). Ibcon, S.A., Gutenberg 224, Col. Anzures, 11590 Mexico D.F., Mexico. TEL 52-5-2554577. FAX 52-5-554577. E-mail: ibcon@infosel.net.mx; URL: http://www.dirsainf.com.mx.ibcon1.htm. Ed. Gabriel Zaid. index. **Document type:** directory.
  Description: Lists over 3000 women executives in business, government and charities in Mexico City.

380 MX
DIRECTORIO DE EMPRESAS - DIRECTORIO DE PROVEEDORES - DIRECTORIO POR COLONIAS. 1992. irreg., 5th ed., 1997. $400 for 3 vol. set (effective 1997). Ibcon, S.A., Gutenberg 224, Col. Anzures, 11590 Mexico D.F., Mexico. TEL 52-5-2554577. FAX 52-5-2554577. E-mail: ibcon@infosel.net.mx; URL: http://www.dirsainf.com.mx/ibcon1.htm. Ed. Gabriel Zaid. **Document type:** directory.
  Description: Lists 15,000 incorporated companies located in Mexico City and greater Mexico City. Provides address, phone and fax numbers, and trade area.

380 UY
DIRECTORIO DE FAX DEL URUGUAY. 3rd ed., 1991. a. Urufax, s.r.l., Rio Branco 1358 Of. 308, 11100 Montevideo, Uruguay. TEL 98-54-19. **Document type:** directory.

380 MX
▼**DIRECTORIO DE FUNCIONARIOS.** 1995. irreg. 5th ed., 1997. $200 (effective 1997). Ibcon, S.A., Gutenberg 224, Col. Anzures, 11590 Mexico DF, Mexico. TEL 52-5-2554577. FAX 52-5-2554577. E-mail: ibcon@infosel.net.mx; URL: http://www.dirsainf.com.mx/ibon1.htm. Ed. Gabriel Zaid. **Document type:** directory.
  Description: Lists over 7000 government officers with address, phone and fax.

380 MX
DIRECTORIO DE GRANDES COMPRADORES. 1982. irreg., 12th ed., 1997. $200 (effective 1997). Ibcon, S.A., Gutenberg 224, Col. Anzures, 11590 Mexico D.F., Mexico. TEL 52-5-2554577. FAX 52-5-2554577. E-mail: ibcon@infosel.net.mx; URL: http://www.dirsainf.com.mx/ibcon1.htm. Ed. Gabriel Zaid. **Document type:** directory.
  Description: Lists the top 2500 Mexican purchasing departments (business and government). Includes executives, titles, addresses, phones, and faxes, indexed by products bought.

382 MX
DIRECTORIO DE IMPORTADORES. 1991. irreg., 5th ed., 1997. $200 (effective 1997). Ibcon, S.A., Gutenberg 224, Col. Anzures, 11590 Mexico D.F., Mexico. TEL 52-5-2554577. FAX 52-5-2554577. E-mail: ibcon@infosel.net.mx; URL: http://www.dirsainf.com.mx/ibcon1.htm. Ed. Gabriel Zaid. **Document type:** directory.
  Description: Lists 2000 Mexican companies importing at least one million dollars per year. Includes executive name, address, phone, fax, and products imported, indexed by products imported.

300 MX
DIRECTORIO DE JURISTAS. 1997. irreg., 1st ed., 1997. Mex.$200 (effective 1997). Ibcon, S.A., Gutenberg 224, Col. Anzures, 11590 Mexico, D.F., Mexico. TEL 52-5-2554577. FAX 52-5-2554577. E-mail: ibcon@infosel.net.mx; URL: http://www.dirsainf.com.mx/ibcon.htm. **Document type:** directory.
  Description: Lists corporation legal managers, law firms, notary offices, depository companies, collecting services, experts, translators, law and arbitral courts, law makers, law schools, libraries, associations, and publishers. Indexed by companies, agencies and jurists.

664.9 MX ISSN 0187-7631
DIRECTORIO DE LA INDUSTRIA CARNICA. 1987. a. $25 (foreign $55). Alfa Editores Tecnicos S.A., Libertad No. 107-402, 03660 Mexico DF, Mexico. TEL 525-579-3333. FAX 525-532-9504. adv.: B&W page $572, color page $800; 215 x 280. circ. 5,000 (controlled). **Document type:** directory.
  Description: Lists 520 producers and 230 suppliers in the meat industry.

663 MX ISSN 0187-764X
DIRECTORIO DE LA INDUSTRIA MEXICANA DE BEBIDAS. 1987. a. $25 (foreign $55). Alfa Editores Tecnicos S.A., Libertad No. 107-402, 03660 Mexico DF, Mexico. TEL 525-579-3333. FAX 525-532-9504. adv.: B&W page $572, color page $800; 215 x 280. circ. 5,000 (controlled). **Document type:** directory.
  Description: Lists 1900 beverage producers and 740 goods and services suppliers.

637 MX ISSN 0187-7623
DIRECTORIO DE LACTEOS MEXICANOS. 1988. a. $25 (foreign $55). Alfa Editores Tecnicos S.A., Libertad No. 107-402, 03660 Mexico DF, Mexico. TEL 525-579-3333. FAX 525-532-9504. adv.: B&W page $572, color page $800; 215 x 280. circ. 5,000 (controlled). **Document type:** directory.
  Description: Lists 550 manufacturers and 300 goods and services suppliers in the dairy industry.

380 360 MX
DIRECTORIO DE OBRAS SOCIALES. 1984. irreg., 7th ed., 1997. $60 (effective 1997). Ibcon, S.A., Gutenberg 224, Col. Anzures, 11590 Mexico D.F., Mexico. TEL 52-5-2554577. FAX 52-5-2554577. E-mail: ibcon@infosel.net.mx; URL: http://www.dirsainf.com.mx/ibcon1.htm. Ed. Gabriel Zaid. **Document type:** directory.
  Description: Lists 250 private charities in Mexico City looking for company patrons. Brief description of their social work and needs.

380 MX
DIRECTORIO DE SERVICIOS PARA EL EXPORTADOR. 1980. irreg., 11th ed., 1996. $130 (effective 1997). Ibcon, S.A., Gutenberg 224, Col. Anzures, 11590 Mexico D.F., Mexico. TEL 52-5-255-4577. FAX 52-5-2554577. E-mail: ibcon@infosel.net.mc; URL: http://www.dirsainf.com.mx/ibon1.htm. Ed. Gabriel Zaid. **Document type:** directory.
  Description: Lists 400 companies, associations and government agencies offering every kind of service needed by exporters in Mexico City, indexed by services.

350 MX
DIRECTORIO DEL GOBIERNO. (Supplement avail. by fax: Suscrifax) 1983. irreg., 20th ed., 1997. $200 (effective 1997). Ibcon, S.A., Gutenberg 224, Col. Anzures, 11590 Mexico D.F., Mexico. TEL 52-5-2554577. FAX 52-5-2554577. E-mail: ibcon@infosel.net.mx; URL: http://www.dirsainf.com.mx/ibcon1.htm. Ed. Gabriel Zaid. **Document type:** directory.
  Description: Lists names, with job titles, phone and fax numbers, of federal, state and municipal government personnel and executive, legislative and judicial branch personnel. Indexed by surname and keyword of agencies.

332.025 CK ISSN 0123-1162
DIRECTORIO DEL SECTOR FINANCIERO. s-a. $350 (effective 1998). Asociacion Bancaria y de Entidades Financieras, Apdo. Aereo 13994, Bogota D.C., Colombia. TEL 57-1-2114811. FAX 57-1-2119915. E-mail: info@asobancaria.com; URL: http://www.asobancaria.com. **Document type:** directory.
  Description: Provides financial information as well as 7450 CEO's and VIP's names and addresses.

BUSINESS AND ECONOMICS — TRADE AND INDUSTRIAL DIRECTORIES

380   EC
DIRECTORIO ECUATORIANO; industrial y comercial. a. O M C Publicaciones, Foch 635 y Reina Victoria, Edif. Johnson, 4to piso, Quito, Ecuador. TEL 548432. Dir. Rocio Gonzalez de Moreno. **Document type:** directory.

338   US
DIRECTORIO HISPANO; the Hispanic yellow page directory. 1988. a. 685 S. Hwy. 427, Longwood, FL 32750-6403. TEL 407-767-0070. FAX 407-767-5478. Ed. Dora Casanova de Toro; Pub. Manuel A. Toro. adv.: B&W page $4800, color page $5200; adv. contact: Alicia Ramirez. maps; circ. 50,000 (controlled). **Document type:** directory.
   Description: Business telephone directory and source of information for the Hispanic community.

670   CL
DIRECTORIO INDUSTRIAL DE CHILE; fabricantes, productos y servicios. 1987? biennial. (Sociedad de Fomento Fabril) Publicaciones Lo Castillo S.A., Perez Valenzuela 1620, Santiago, Chile. TEL 223-8031. **Document type:** directory.

338   CK   ISSN 0122-0217
DIRECTORIO INDUSTRIAL Y COMERCIAL; de America Latina. 1966. a. $50. Legis S.A., Av. Eldorado 81-10, Apdo. Aereo 98888, Bogota, Colombia. TEL 91-263-2990. FAX 91-410-0628. TELEX 43300 LEGIS CO. Ed. Roberto Escobar. R&P contact: Roberto Escobar. circ. 50,000 (controlled). **Document type:** directory.
   Formerly: Directorio Industrial de Colombia.

639.2   MX
DIRECTORIO INTERNACIONAL DE LA INDUSTRIA PESQUERA Y LA AQUACULTURA. a. $25 (foreign $55). Alfa Editores Tecnicos S.A., Libertad No. 107-402, 03660 Mexico DF, Mexico. TEL 525-579-3333. FAX 525-5329504. adv.: B&W page $572, color page $800; 215 x 280. circ. 5,000 (controlled). **Document type:** directory.
   Description: Lists over 1350 companies and individuals devoted to fishing and aquaculture activities and over 300 suppliers of equipment, goods and services.

658.8   CL
DIRECTORIO NACIONAL DE ABASTECIMIENTO E INSUMOS PARA SUPERMERCADOS. 1992. a. (Asociacion Gremial de Supermercados y Autoservicios de Chile) Publicaciones Lo Castillo S.A., Perez Valenzuela 1620, Santiago, Chile. TEL 2352606. FAX 2352007. Ed. Alberto Gana D. **Document type:** directory.

338   NQ
DIRECTORIO NACIONAL DE EMPRESAS. biennial. Vistazo Economico, Camino de Oriente, Contiguo Rest., Las Brasas, Managua, Nicaragua. TEL 70738. **Document type:** directory.

DIRECTORIO NACIONAL DE ENTIDADES COOPERATIVOS. see BUSINESS AND ECONOMICS — Cooperatives

332   ES
DIRECTORIO Y SERVICIOS DE INSTITUCIONES DEL SISTEMA FINANCIERO DE EL SALVADOR. a. Banco Central de Reserva de El Salvador, Gerencia de Instituciones Financieras, Apdo. Postal (06) 106, San Salvador, El Salvador. **Document type:** directory.

380.1   LB
DIRECTORY AND WHO'S WHO IN LIBERIA.* 1971. irreg. A & A Enterprises Inc., Box 103, Monrovia, Liberia. adv.; illus.

DIRECTORY IN RUSSIAN OF BRITISH FIRMS INTERESTED IN TRADE WITH THE F S U. see BUSINESS AND ECONOMICS — International Commerce

DIRECTORY MARKETPLACE. see PUBLISHING AND BOOK TRADE

338.025 659.1   UK
DIRECTORY OF ADVERTISING AGENCIES. s-a. Ethical Publications Ltd., Vincent House, Vincent Ln., Dorking, Surrey RH4 3JD, England. TEL 44-1306-740777. FAX 44-1306-741069. Ed. Stephen Lederer; Pub. Mark Savage. R&P contact: Ian Williams. adv. contact: Zoe Almeida. **Document type:** directory, trade publication.

DIRECTORY OF AGING RESOURCES. see GERONTOLOGY AND GERIATRICS

DIRECTORY OF AGRICULTURAL CO-OPERATIVES IN THE UNITED KINGDOM. see AGRICULTURE — Agricultural Economics

DIRECTORY OF ALBERTA'S AGRICULTURAL PROCESSING INDUSTRY. see AGRICULTURE — Agricultural Economics

380.1   US
HD9940.U3
DIRECTORY OF APPAREL SPECIALITY STORES (YEAR); includes: family wear, sporting goods, and activewear retailers. a. $240 (effective 1997). C S G Information Services (Subsidiary of: Lebhar-Friedman, Inc.), 3922 Coconut Palm Dr., Tampa, FL 33619. TEL 813-664-6800. FAX 813-664-6882. Ed. Chris Anderson. (also avail. in magnetic tape; diskette format) **Document type:** directory.
   Formed by the merger of: Directory of Women's and Children's Wear Speciality Stores (Year) (ISSN 0277-9617); Which was formerly: Directory of Apparel Speciality Stores. Women's and Children's (ISSN 0272-1104) & Directory of Men's and Boys' Wear Speciality Stores (Year) (ISSN 0277-9625); Which was formerly: Directory of Men's and Boys' Speciality Stores (ISSN 0272-1112)
   Description: Details over 5,200 women's, men's, family, and sporting goods retailers operating approximately 55,000 stores. Listings identify sales volume, number of stores, price lines, product lines, resident buyers, and over 18,000 key executive, buying, merchandising, and administrative personnel.

DIRECTORY OF APPLIANCES, EQUIPMENT, CONSTRUCTION MATERIALS, AND COMPONENTS EVALUATED IN ACCORDANCE WITH INTERNATIONAL PUBLICATIONS. see BUSINESS AND ECONOMICS — Production Of Goods And Services

720   US
DIRECTORY OF ARCHITECTS IN METROPOLITAN WASHINGTON. 1991. biennial. price varies. American Institute of Architects, Washington Chapter, 1777 Church St., N.W., Washington, DC 20036. TEL 202-667-1798. FAX 202-667-4327. R&P contact: Julienne Nelson. adv. circ. 3,500. **Document type:** directory.
   Formerly (until 1991): D C - A I A Member Handbook.

382   US
DIRECTORY OF ARIZONA EXPORTERS. 1977. q. $35 (diskette $100). Department of Commerce, 3800 N. Central Ave., Ste. 1500, Phoenix, AZ 85012. TEL 602-280-1371. FAX 602-280-1305. Ed. Dan Bjerk. adv. contact: Dorothy A. Bigg. circ. 5,000. (also avail. in diskette format) **Document type:** directory, government publication.
   Formerly: Arizona U S A International Trade Directory.
   Description: Lists Arizona companies that currently export or would like to export their products or services.

380   CN   ISSN 0316-0734
AS40
DIRECTORY OF ASSOCIATIONS IN CANADA/REPERTOIRE DES ASSOCIATIONS DE CANADA. 1973. a. price varies. Micromedia Ltd., 20 Victoria St., Toronto, ON M5C 2N8, Canada. TEL 416-362-5211. FAX 416-362-6161. E-mail: info@micromedia.on.ca; URL: http://www.mmltd.com. Eds. Jane Maxwell, Susan Vilhena. R&P contact: Gail Dykstra. **Document type:** directory.
   ●Also available online.
   —CISTI.

011   AT   ISSN 0110-666X
DIRECTORY OF AUSTRALIAN ASSOCIATIONS. (Supplement published between editions) 1978. bi-m. Aus.$195. Margaret Gee Media Group, 45 Flinders Ln., Melbourne, Vic. 3000, Australia. TEL 03-654-2800. FAX 03-650-6261. adv. **Document type:** directory.

381.45   US   ISSN 0736-0452
HD9710.3.U5
DIRECTORY OF AUTOMOTIVE AFTERMARKET SUPPLIERS (YEAR). 1973. a. $260 (effective 1997). C S G Information Services (Subsidiary of: Lebhar-Friedman, Inc.), 3922 Coconut Palm Dr., Tampa, FL 33619. TEL 813-664-6800. FAX 813-664-6882. Ed. Arthur Rosenberg. (also avail. in magnetic tape; diskette format) **Document type:** directory.
   Former titles: Directory of Auto Supply Chains (ISSN 0730-2533) Supersedes in part: Directory: Home Centers and Hardware Chains, Auto Supply Chains (ISSN 0094-8667); Directory-Hardware and Home Improvement Center Chains, Auto Supply Chains (ISSN 0092-1483); Directory-Auto Supplies and Hardware Chains.
   Description: Profiles approximately 1,250 jobber-retailers operating over 19,400 two-or-more unit stores; approximately 1,100 warehouse distributors-branch offices serving over 1.4 million accounts; 17 major buying-programming distribution groups serving over 47,000 members; names and titles of over 7,700 key personnel and decision makers.

DIRECTORY OF BOOK PRINTERS (YEAR). see PUBLISHING AND BOOK TRADE

338.025 340   UK
DIRECTORY OF BRITISH AND IRISH LAW LIBRARIES. irreg., 5th ed., 1995. £50. (British and Irish Association of Law Libraries) Legal Information Resources Ltd., The Hatcheries, Hall Bank Ln., Mytholmroyd, Hebden Bridge, W. Yorks HX7 5HQ, England. TEL 44-1422-888000. FAX 44-1422-888001. E-mail: dominic@legalinfo.co.uk. Ed. Pauline Fothergill. adv. contact: Julie Lord. **Document type:** directory.

380   UK   ISSN 0070-5152
DIRECTORY OF BRITISH ASSOCIATIONS. 1965. biennial. £142.50($285) C.B.D. Research Ltd., 15 Wickham Rd., Beckenham, Kent BR3 2JS, England. TEL 44-181-650-7745. FAX 44-181-650-0768. Eds. A.J.W. Henderson, S.P.A. Henderson. index. circ. 6,000. **Document type:** directory.
   —CISTI.
   Description: Lists 6,700 national organizations in the U.K. and Ireland.

660   UK   ISSN 0265-8275
TP248.17
DIRECTORY OF BRITISH BIOTECHNOLOGY. 1984. biennial. £65. Longman Group UK Ltd., Longman House, Burnt Mill, Harlow, Essex CM20 2JE, England. TEL 44-1279-442601. FAX 44-1279-431059. (Subscr. to: Pearson Professional, P.O. Box 77, Fourth Ave., Harlow, Essex CM19 5BQ, England. TEL 44-1279-623924. FAX 44-1279-639609) Ed. M.G. Burdon. adv. (back issues avail.)
   —BLDSC (3592.766250); CISTI.

382   UK   ISSN 0958-6520
DIRECTORY OF BRITISH IMPORTERS. 1974. a. £150. Trade Research Publications, 2 Wycliffe Grove, Werrington, Peterborough, Cambs. PE4 5DE, England. TEL 44-1733-573975. FAX 44-1733-328323. Ed. Sara Macleod. adv.: page £560; adv. contact: Sara Macleod. circ. 800. **Document type:** directory.
   —BLDSC (3592.900000).

380.1   US
DIRECTORY OF BUILDING PRODUCTS & HARDLINES DISTRIBUTORS. a. $260 (effective 1997). C S G Information Services (Subsidiary of: Lebhar-Friedman, Inc.), 3922 Coconut Palm Dr., Tampa, FL 33619. TEL 813-664-6800. FAX 813-664-6882. (also avail. in magnetic tape; diskette format) **Document type:** directory.
   —CCC.
   Formerly: Directory of Hardlines Distributors (Year); Incorporates: Directory of Hardware and Housewares Distributors (ISSN 0882-536X)
   Description: Profiles over 2,300 houseware, paint, electrical, heating, cooling, plumbing, and lumber companies, building supplies distributors (minimum $2 million annual sales), serving over 6.3 million retailers, contractors and commercial accounts. Listings identify sales volume, product lines, markets served, distribution centers, buying/marketing groups and more. Also includes names and titles of over 9,000 key executives and decision makers.

BUSINESS AND ECONOMICS — TRADE AND INDUSTRIAL DIRECTORIES

338   US
DIRECTORY OF BUSINESS INFORMATION RESOURCES. a. $165. Grey House Publishing, Pocket Knife Sq., Lakeville, CT 06039. TEL 860-435-0868; 800-562-2139. FAX 860-435-0867. Ed. Amy E. Lignor; Pub. Leslie E. Mackenzie. R&P contact: Leslie K. Mackenzie. **Document type:** directory.
   Description: Lists over 2200 associations, over 2400 newsletters, over 2400 magazines, over 2000 trade shows, over 2200 databases and directories for over 90 industries.

338   US
DIRECTORY OF BUSINESS TO BUSINESS CATALOGS. a. $125. Grey House Publishing, Pocket Knife Sq., Lakeville, CT 06039. TEL 860-435-0868; 800-562-2139. FAX 860-435-0867. Ed. Amy E. Lignor; Pub. Leslie E. Mackenzie. **Document type:** directory.
   Description: Lists over 5000 business catalog companies in 35 different product areas.

332.1   US   ISSN 1066-9736
HG65
DIRECTORY OF BUYOUT FINANCING SOURCES. 1982. a. $295. (Securities Data Company, Inc.) Securities Data Publishing, 40 W. 57th St., 11th Fl., New York, NY 10019. TEL 212-765-5311. FAX 212-765-6123. Ed. Daniel Bokser. **Document type:** directory.
   Former titles (until 1992): Buyouts Directory of L B O Financing Sources (ISSN 1050-4915); (until 1990): Buyouts Directory of Financing Sources (ISSN 1040-5739); (until 1989): Directory of Financing Sources for Buyouts and Acquisitions (ISSN 0898-1108)

338.025 600   US
HF5065.C2
DIRECTORY OF CALIFORNIA TECHNOLOGY COMPANIES. a. $145 (diskette $495) (effective 1996). Database Publishing Company, 1590 S. Lewis St., Anaheim, CA 92805-6423. TEL 714-778-6400. FAX 714-778-6811. (Subscr. to: Box 70024, Anaheim, CA 92625-0024. TEL 800-888-8434) (also avail. in diskette format) **Document type:** directory.
   Formerly: California Technology Register (ISSN 1059-7085)
   Description: Identifies 10,500 manufacturers, R & D firms, research laboratories, telecommunications companies, distributors of technology components and products, and aerospace and defense companies in California that utilize medium and high technologies in the operation of their business.

338.025   US
HD9981.7.C2
DIRECTORY OF CALIFORNIA WHOLESALERS AND SERVICE COMPANIES. 1979. a. $169 (diskette $795) (effective 1996). Database Publishing Company, 1590 S. Lewis St., Anaheim, CA 92805-6423. TEL 714-778-6400. FAX 714-778-6811. (Subscr. to: Box 70024, Anaheim, CA 92625-0024. TEL 800-888-8434) Ed. Ken Gregory. circ. 750. (also avail. in diskette format) **Document type:** directory.
   Formerly: California Services Register (ISSN 0271-6615)
   Description: Provides information on 40,000 California service businesses, including contractors, wholesalers, transportation, finance, and business services companies.

DIRECTORY OF CANADIAN CHARTERED ACCOUNTANTS. see BUSINESS AND ECONOMICS — Accounting

700   US
DIRECTORY OF CARTOONISTS - GAGWRITERS - SHORT HUMOR MARKETS. 1960. a. $12. Gag Recap Publishers, 12 Hedden Pl., New Providence, NJ 07974-1724. TEL 908-464-1158. Ed. Al Gottlieb. **Document type:** directory.
   Description: Lists names and addresses of cartoonists and gagwriters seeking and supplying gags for cartoons and markets for short humor.

647.95   US   ISSN 0411-7085
TX907
DIRECTORY OF CHAIN RESTAURANT OPERATORS (YEAR); includes: leading chain hotel companies operating foodservice units. a. $290 (effective 1997). C S G Information Services (Subsidiary of: Lebhar-Friedman, Inc.), 3922 Coconut Palm Dr., Tampa, FL 33619. TEL 813-664-6800. FAX 813-664-6882. Ed. Terry Ponder. (also avail. in magnetic tape; diskette format)
   ●Also available on CD-ROM.
   Description: Profiles over 4,000 three-or-more unit chain restaurant companies operating or franchising more than 350,000 restaurants, drive-ins, cafeterias, hotels, motels, contract feeders, industrial feeders, as well as food units in drug chains, general merchandise chains, and discount stores. Identifies sales volume, national franchise headquarter location, number of units operated, primary wholesaler, type of liquor menu and foodservice offered, trading area, and more.

DIRECTORY OF CHEMICAL PRODUCERS - CANADA. see CHEMISTRY

DIRECTORY OF CHEMICAL PRODUCERS - CHINA. see CHEMISTRY

DIRECTORY OF CHEMICAL PRODUCERS - EAST ASIA. see CHEMISTRY

DIRECTORY OF CHEMICAL PRODUCERS - MEXICO. see CHEMISTRY

DIRECTORY OF CHEMICAL PRODUCERS - MIDDLE EAST. see CHEMISTRY

DIRECTORY OF CHEMICAL PRODUCERS - SOUTH AMERICA. see CHEMISTRY

DIRECTORY OF CHEMICAL PRODUCERS - UNITED STATES. see CHEMISTRY

DIRECTORY OF CHEMICAL PRODUCERS - WESTERN EUROPE. see CHEMISTRY

380   CC
DIRECTORY OF CHINESE ENTERPRISES FOR FOREIGN ECONOMIC RELATIONS AND TRADES. (Text in Chinese, English) 1993. biennial. $165. Han Consultants Inc., P.O. Box 71006, Wuhan, Hubei 430071, People's Republic of China. TEL 86-27-7838532. FAX 86-27-7878343. circ. 7,000. **Document type:** directory.
   Description: Lists import and export corporations and enterprises subordinate to Chinese ministries and commissions at the national level.

380   CC   ISSN 0259-1146
DIRECTORY OF CHINESE EXTERNAL ECONOMIC ORGANIZATIONS & INDUSTRIAL - COMMERCIAL ENTERPRISES. 1982. irreg. HK.$450($78) Economic Information & Agency, 342 Hennessy Rd., 10th Fl., Wanchai, Hong Kong, People's Republic of China. TEL 852-573-8217. FAX 852-838-8304. TELEX 86990 EIA HX. **Document type:** directory.

338 630   IO
DIRECTORY OF COCONUT TRADERS AND EQUIPMENT MANUFACTURERS. (Text in English) irreg. Asian and Pacific Coconut Community, Lina Bldg., 3rd Fl., Jl. H.R. Rasuna Said Kav. B-7, Kuningan, Jakarta 12920, Indonesia. TEL 62-21-5221712. FAX 62-21-5221714. TELEX 62863 APCC IA. E-mail: apcc@indo.net.id; URL: http://www.idrc.org.sg/pan/apcc. **Document type:** directory.
   Formed by the merger of: Directory of Coconut Processing Machinery, Equipment, Manufacturers and Suppliers & Directory of Coconut Products Importers & Directory of Coconut Products Exporters.
   Description: Lists more than 800 exporters, 400 importers and 60 equipment manufacturers including name of companies, addresses, contact numbers and products they are dealing with.

338   US   ISSN 0084-9898
T12
DIRECTORY OF COLORADO MANUFACTURERS. 1948. every 18 months. $80. University of Colorado, Business Research Division, Campus Box 420, Boulder, CO 80309-0420. TEL 303-492-8227. FAX 303-492-3620. Ed. Gin S. Hayden. circ. 2,500. **Document type:** directory.
   Description: Lists 6,500 manufacturers in alphabetic, geographic and S.I.C. sections. Phone number, top marketing official's name and title, area of distribution and product description in geographical and S.I.C. sections.

380   SY
DIRECTORY OF COMMERCE & INDUSTRY. 1979. a. $60. Arab Advertising Organization, 28 Mountanabbi St., P.O. Box 2842-3034, Damascus, Syria. TEL 225219. TELEX 411923. Dir. Mouhammed Qatian. adv. circ. 20,000. **Document type:** directory.

332.6 380   US   ISSN 1045-0041
HG4028.D5
DIRECTORY OF COMPANIES OFFERING DIVIDEND REINVESTMENT PLANS. 1982. a. $32.45. Evergreen Enterprises, Box 763, Laurel, MD 20725-0763. Ed. S. Kinoshita. **Document type:** directory, consumer publication.

DIRECTORY OF COMPOSITE MANUFACTURERS, SUPPLIERS, AND SERVICES. see ENGINEERING — Engineering Mechanics And Materials

DIRECTORY OF COMPUTER RETAILERS, DEALERS & DISTRIBUTORS (YEAR). see COMPUTERS — Computer Industry Directories

380 001.642   US   ISSN 0748-1543
QA76.6
DIRECTORY OF COMPUTER SOFTWARE. a. $59 (foreign $75). U.S. National Technical Information Service, 5285 Port Royal Rd., Springfield, VA 22161. TEL 703-487-4650. FAX 703-321-8547. TELEX 64617.
   —CISTI.
   Formerly (until 1983): Directory of Computer Software and Related Technical Reports (ISSN 0278-257X)
   Description: Describes software applications and tools available from NTIS.

380.1   US
HD9696.C63
DIRECTORY OF COMPUTER V A R'S & SYSTEM INTEGRATORS (YEAR). Variant title: Directory of V A Rs. a. $290 (effective 1997). C S G Information Services (Subsidiary of: Lebhar-Friedman, Inc.), 3922 Coconut Palm Dr., Tampa, FL 33619. TEL 813-664-6800. FAX 813-664-6882. Ed. Michael Jarvis. (also avail. in magnetic tape; diskette format) **Document type:** directory.
   ●Also available on CD-ROM.
   Formerly: Directory of Value Added Resellers (Year) (ISSN 0884-8300)
   Description: Profiles nearly 3,800 VARs, including value added dealers, non-storefront VARs, system houses, and system integrators serving a wide variety of end users. Listings identify type of applications, sales volume, percentage of sales in hardware, software, and peripherals, operating systems, products resold, services provided, ability to network, and more. Includes nearly 11,250 key executive, buying, and administrative personnel.

DIRECTORY OF CONNECTICUT LIBRARIES AND MEDIA CENTERS. see LIBRARY AND INFORMATION SCIENCES

338   US   ISSN 1087-0741
HD69.C6
DIRECTORY OF CONSULTANTS AND CONTRACTORS ACTIVE IN EASTERN EUROPE. 1991. biennial. $40 (foreign $45) (effective 1996 & 1997). Projects Research, Inc., Box 2558, Falls Church, VA 22042. TEL 703-698-9330. FAX 703-698-9837. Pub. Joe Lill. **Document type:** directory.
   Formerly (until 1996): International Directory of Consultants and Contractors Active in Eastern Europe (ISSN 1053-2501)
   Description: Lists architects, consulting engineers, planners and contractors engaged in construction activities, urban and rural development, and environmental engineering.

BUSINESS AND ECONOMICS — TRADE AND INDUSTRIAL DIRECTORIES

338 US ISSN 1087-0717
HD69.C6
DIRECTORY OF CONSULTANTS AND CONTRACTORS ACTIVE IN LATIN AMERICA AND THE CARIBBEAN. 1992. biennial. $40 (foreign $45) (effective 1996 & 1997). Projects Research, Inc., Box 2558, Falls Church, VA 22042. TEL 703-698-9330. FAX 703-698-9837. Ed. Joe Lill. **Document type:** directory.
Formerly (until 1996): International Directory of Consultants and Contractors Active in Latin America and the Caribbean (ISSN 1058-5788)
Description: Lists architects, consulting engineers, planners and contractors engaged in construction activities, urban and rural development, and environmental engineering.

338 US ISSN 1087-0768
TA12
DIRECTORY OF CONSULTANTS AND CONTRACTORS ACTIVE IN THE FAR EAST. 1987. biennial. $65 (foreign $70) (effective 1996 & 1997). Projects Research, Inc., Box 2558, Falls Church, VA 22042. TEL 703-698-9330. FAX 703-698-9837. Ed. Joe Lill. **Document type:** directory.
Formerly (until 1996): International Directory of Consultants and Contractors Active in the Far East (ISSN 1051-435X)
Description: Lists architects, consulting engineers, planners and contractors engaged in construction activies, urban and rural development, and environmental engineering.

338 US ISSN 1087-075X
HD69.C6
DIRECTORY OF CONSULTANTS AND CONTRACTORS ACTIVE IN THE MIDDLE EAST AND AFRICA. 1986. biennial. $60 (foreign $65) (effective 1996 & 1997). Projects Research, Inc., Box 2558, Falls Church, VA 22042. TEL 703-698-9330. FAX 703-698-9837. Ed. Joe Lill. **Document type:** directory.
Former titles (until 1996): International Directory of Consultants and Contractors Active in the Middle East and Africa (ISSN 1058-580X); (until 1989): International Directory of Consultants and Contractors Active in the Middle East (ISSN 1060-5770)
Description: Lists architects, consulting engineers, planners and contractors engaged in construction activities, urban and rural development, and environmental engineering.

338 US ISSN 1087-0725
HD69.C6
DIRECTORY OF CONSULTANTS AND CONTRACTORS ACTIVE IN THE UNITED STATES AND CANADA. 1992. biennial. $60 (foreign $65) (effective 1996 & 1997). Projects Research, Inc., Box 2558, Falls Church, VA 22042. TEL 703-698-9330. FAX 703-698-9837. Ed. Joe Lill. **Document type:** directory.
Formerly (until 1996): International Directory of Consultants and Contractors Active in the United States and Canada (ISSN 1058-5796)
Description: Lists architects, consulting engineers, planners and contractors engaged in construction activities, urban and rural development, and environmental engineering.

338 US ISSN 1087-0733
TA12
DIRECTORY OF CONSULTANTS AND CONTRACTORS ACTIVE IN WESTERN EUROPE. 1991. biennial. $65 (foreign $70) (effective 1996 & 1997). Projects Research, Inc., Box 2558, Falls Church, VA 22042. TEL 703-698-9330. FAX 703-698-9837. Ed. Joe Lill. **Document type:** directory.
Formerly (until 1996): International Directory of Consultants and Contractors Active in Western Europe (ISSN 1056-1099)
Description: Lists architects, consulting engineers, planners and contractors engaged in construction activities, urban and rural development, and environmental engineering.

DIRECTORY OF CONSULTING ENGINEERING SERVICES IN NORTH CAROLINA. see *ENGINEERING*

670 747 US
DIRECTORY OF CONTRACT WALLCOVERINGS AND SPECIFICATIONS. 1984. a. $15.95. Wall Publications, Inc., 570 Seventh Ave., Ste. 500, New York, NY 10018. TEL 212-869-4960. FAX 212-869-1141. Ed. Maurice S. Murray. adv. circ. 16,000. **Document type:** trade publication.
Description: Lists firms supplying wall coverings for commercial and nonresidential applications. Also contains a glossary, how-to articles, technical data, and wallcovering specifications for nonresidential and commercial USASP.

380 US ISSN 0736-9778
HG4057
DIRECTORY OF CORPORATE AFFILIATIONS. (Consists of 5 vols.: Vols. 1 & 2: Master Index; Vol. 3: U.S. Public Companies; Vol. 4: U.S. Private Companies; Vol. 5: International Public and Private Companies) 1981. a. £825. National Register Publishing, A Division of Reed Elsevier Inc., 121 Chanlon Rd., New Providence, NJ 07974. TEL 908-464-6800. FAX 908-771-7704. TELEX 138 755. E-mail: info@reedref.com; URL: http://www.reedref.com. (Subscr. to: National Register Publishing, Order Dept., Box 31, New Providence, NJ 07974-9903. TEL 800-521-8110) adv.; stat.; index. circ. 2,500. pp./issue: 11000. (also avail. in magnetic tape) **Document type:** directory.
●Also available online. Vendor(s): Knight-Ridder Information, Inc. (File no.513, Corporate Affiliations), Lexis-Nexis.
Also available on CD-ROM. Producer(s): Bowker Electronic Publishing.
—CISTI.
Supersedes (in 1992): International Directory of Corporate Affiliations (ISSN 0730-9465); International Directory of Corporate Affiliations: U S Parent Companies; International Directory of Corporate Affiliations: Non-U S Parent Companies.
Description: Five volume corporate reference tool comprised of three distinct titles and a comprehensive master index.

DIRECTORY OF CREMATORIA. see *FUNERALS*

(YEAR) DIRECTORY OF CUSTOM FINISHERS, VENDORS AND CONSULTANTS. see *ENGINEERING — Engineering Mechanics And Materials*

338 US
HF5465.U4
DIRECTORY OF DEPARTMENT STORES & MAIL ORDER FIRMS (YEAR); includes: resident buyers, mail order firms. a. $290 (effective 1997). C S G Information Services (Subsidiary of: Lebhar-Friedman, Inc.), 3922 Coconut Palm Dr., Tampa, FL 33619. TEL 813-664-6800; 800-927-9292. FAX 813-664-6882. Ed. Chris Anderson; Pub. Robert H. Wenning. (also avail. in magnetic tape; diskette format) **Document type:** directory.
●Also available on CD-ROM.
Formerly: Directory of Department Stores (Year) (ISSN 0419-2508)
Description: Provides complete profiles on over 375 department store companies. Includes over 15,000 names and titles of key executives and buyers. Listings identify sales volume, trading area, private label, products line, store location types, furniture styles and price lines, resident buyers and more.

DIRECTORY OF DEVELOPMENT AND TRAINING INSTITUTES IN AFRICA. see *BUSINESS AND ECONOMICS — International Development And Assistance*

658.8 US
HF5035
DIRECTORY OF DISCOUNT AND GENERAL MERCHANDISE STORES (YEAR). 1961. a. $325 (effective 1997). C S G Information Services (Subsidiary of: Lebhar-Friedman, Inc.), 3922 Coconut Palm Dr., Tampa, FL 33619. TEL 813-664-6800. FAX 813-664-6810. Ed. Janice Backer. (also avail. in magnetic tape; diskette format) **Document type:** directory.
●Also available on CD-ROM.
Former titles: Directory of Discount Department Stores (Year) (ISSN 0897-5442); Directory of Discount Department Stores, Catalog Showrooms (Year) (ISSN 0897-1765); Directory of Discount Department Stores (ISSN 0736-931X); Directory of Discount Centers (ISSN 0070-5446)
Description: Provides complete company profiles on approximately 4,700 total retailers operating over 55,000 stores. Identifies sales volume, square footage, store locations, speciality departments, and more than 29,000 key executives, buying and administrative personnel are included.

338 US ISSN 0730-2703
HD9666.3
DIRECTORY OF DRUG STORE AND H B C CHAINS (YEAR); includes: drug wholesalers. 1945. a. $290 (effective 1997). C S G Information Services (Subsidiary of: Lebhar-Friedman, Inc.), 3922 Coconut Palm Dr., Tampa, FL 33619. TEL 813-664-6800. FAX 813-664-6882. Eds. Michael Jarvis, Debbie Scruggs. illus. (also avail. in magnetic tape; diskette format) **Document type:** directory.
●Also available on CD-ROM.
Former titles: Directory of Drug Store and H B C Chains (Year); Directory of Drug Store Chains.
Description: Provides complete company profiles on over 1,800 two-or-more store chains, and nearly 100 drug wholesale companies. Listings identify sales volume, trading area, primary wholesaler, product lines carried, prescriptions filled daily, and distribution centers. Over 9,000 key executives, buying and administrative personnel.

382 BE
DIRECTORY OF E U TRADE AND PROFESSIONAL ASSOCIATIONS AND THEIR INFORMATION - THE BLUE BOOK. (European Union) 5100 BEF. Euroconfidentiel s.a., Rue de Rixensart 18, 1332 Genval, Belgium. TEL 32-2-6520284. FAX 32-2-6530180. **Document type:** directory.
Description: Lists address, telephone and fax numbers, chairman and contact person, and working languages of 650 European Union associations.

338 II
DIRECTORY OF ECONOMIC RESEARCH CENTRES IN INDIA. (Supplements issued annually) 1972. irreg., 2nd edition, 1975. Rs.85($13.20) Information Research Academy, 37 Amir Ali Ave., Calcutta 700019, India. Ed. Partha Subir Guha. adv. circ. 2,500. **Document type:** directory.

DIRECTORY OF ELECTRIC UTILITY INDUSTRY. see *ENGINEERING — Electrical Engineering*

380.1 US
DIRECTORY OF ELECTRICAL WHOLESALE DISTRIBUTORS. 1930. biennial. $695. Intertec Publishing Corp., Electrical Publishing Group, 9800 Metcalf Ave., Overland Park, KS 66212-2215. TEL 913-341-1300. FAX 913-967-1898. Ed. Andrea W. Herbert; Pub. Richard A. Hathaway. adv. contact: Evelyn W. Hornaday. **Document type:** directory.

338 UK
DIRECTORY OF ENGINEERING CAPACITY. 1958. a. $14. Coventry Chamber of Commerce & Industry, 123 St. Nicholas St., Coventry CV1 4FD, England. Ed. June Morden. adv. circ. 5,000. **Document type:** directory.
Description: Lists plants, capacity and contract machining facilities.

DIRECTORY OF ENGINEERS AND LAND SURVEYORS REGISTERED IN SOUTH CAROLINA. see *ENGINEERING*

DIRECTORY OF ENVIRONMENTAL INFORMATION SOURCES. see *ENVIRONMENTAL STUDIES*

BUSINESS AND ECONOMICS — TRADE AND INDUSTRIAL DIRECTORIES

380   **UK**
DIRECTORY OF EUROPEAN BUSINESS. 1992. irreg. £124. Bowker - Saur Ltd., A member of Reed Elsevier plc group, Maypole House, Maypole Rd., E. Grinstead, W. Sussex RH19 1HU, England. TEL 44-1342-330100. FAX 44-1342-330191. E-mail: custserv@bowker-saur.co.uk; URL: http://www.reed-elsevier.com. (also avail. in magnetic tape) **Document type:** directory.
Description: Provides all the key contact data for anyone doing cross-border business, or researching the new Europe. Covers the 40 countries of Western and Eastern Europe, including the Baltic Republics, Russia and Turkey.

338   **BE**   **ISSN 0771-7865**
DIRECTORY OF EUROPEAN COMMUNITY TRADE AND PROFESSIONAL ASSOCIATIONS/REPERTOIRE DES ORGANISATIONS PROFESSIONNELLES DE LA COMMUNAUTE EUROPEENNE/VERZEICHNIS DER VERBAENDE IN DER EUROPAEISCHEN GEMEINSCHAFT. (Text English, French, German) 1980. biennial, 5th ed. 1992. 3500 BEF. (European Communities Commission) Editions Delta, Rue Scailquin 55, B-1210 Brussels, Belgium. TEL 32-2-217-55-55. FAX 32-2-217-93-93. (Dist. by: Bernan, 4611-F Assembly Dr., Lanham, MD 20706-4391) Ed. Georges-Francis Seingry. **Document type:** directory.
—CISTI.
Description: Lists over 500 lobbies at the European level in the following sectors of activity: industry, small- and medium-sized enterprises, trade, transport, professions, other activities, trade unions, and consumer organizations. Includes telephone, fax and telex numbers, names of general secretary and chairman, year established, and the more than 5,000 member organizations with addresses, telephone and fax numbers.

338.025 677   **UK**   **ISSN 0965-6030**
DIRECTORY OF EUROPEAN DYERS, PRINTERS AND FINISHERS. 1987. biennial. £27.50 (effective 1997). World Textile Publications Ltd., Perkin House, 1 Longlands St., Bradford, W. Yorkshire BD1 2TP, England. TEL 44-1274-378800. FAX 44-1274-378811. E-mail: 104470.3070@compuserve.com; URL: http://www.vitalo.com/worldtextile. **Document type:** directory.
Formerly (until 1992): Directory of U K Dyers and Finishers (ISSN 0951-4074)

011   **UK**   **ISSN 0952-3626**
HD2429.E87   **CODEN: DEIAE5**
DIRECTORY OF EUROPEAN INDUSTRIAL & TRADE ASSOCIATIONS. 1971. irreg., 6th, 1997. £195($390) C.B.D. Research Ltd., 15 Wickham Rd., Beckenham, Kent BR3 2JS, England. TEL 44-181-650-7745. FAX 44-181-650-0768. Ed. R.W. Adams. circ. 4,000. **Document type:** directory.
—BLDSC (3593.528000); CASDDS; CISTI.
Formerly: Directory of European Associations. Part 1: National Industrial Trade and Professional Associations (ISSN 0070-5500)
Description: Lists 6,000 European national trade and industrial organizations outside the U.K.

DIRECTORY OF EUROPEAN RETAILERS & INTERNATIONAL BUYING AGENTS. see *BUSINESS AND ECONOMICS — Marketing And Purchasing*

382   **UK**   **ISSN 0142-4769**
DIRECTORY OF EXPORT BUYERS IN THE U K. 1978. a. £85. Trade Research Publications, 2 Wycliffe Grove, Werrington, Peterborough, Cambs. PE4 5DE, England. TEL 44-1733-573975. FAX 44-1733-328323. Ed. Sara Macleod. adv.: page £560; adv. contact: Sara Macleod. circ. 500. **Document type:** directory.
—BLDSC (3593.535000).

380.1   **US**
DIRECTORY OF EXPORTERS. biennial. free. Iowa Department of Economic Development, 200 E. Grand Ave., Des Moines, IA 50309. TEL 515-242-4743. FAX 515-242-4918. **Document type:** directory.
Former titles: Iowa International Directory; Iowa Manufacturer's Export Directory; Iowa Directory of Exporting Companies; Iowa International Directory.

382   **US**
DIRECTORY OF FEDERAL AND STATE BUSINESS ASSISTANCE. biennial. $29 in N. America; elsewhere $58. U.S. National Technical Information Service, 5285 Port Royal Rd., Springfield, VA 22161. TEL 703-487-4630. FAX 703-321-8547. TELEX 64617. Ed. Ed Lehmann. **Document type:** directory.
Description: Describes and summarizes over 180 federal and 400 state programs designed to assist growing companies in effectively competing in national and international markets.

338.025   **UK**   **ISSN 0968-0152**
DIRECTORY OF FIRMS. 1992. a. £60. Structural Engineers Trading Organisation Ltd., 11 Upper Belgrave St., London SW1X 8BH, England. TEL 44-171-235-4535. FAX 44-171-235-4294. adv.; circ. 5,000. **Document type:** directory.
Description: Lists firms of consulting structural engineers in the U.K.

338   **US**   **ISSN 1076-3694**
T12
DIRECTORY OF FLORIDA INDUSTRIES. 1935. a. $106.10 (effective 1998). (Florida Chamber of Commerce Management Corp., Inc.) Harris InfoSource International, 2057-2 Aurora Rd., Twinsburg, OH 44087-1999. TEL 216-425-9000; 800-888-5900. FAX 216-425-7150. E-mail: catknapp@aol.com. Ed. Gary Cliett. adv.; circ. 5,000 (controlled). **Document type:** directory.
● Also available on CD-ROM.

380.1   **US**   **ISSN 0271-7662**
HD9321.3
DIRECTORY OF FOODSERVICE DISTRIBUTORS (YEAR); includes: full-line food, equipment, supplies, specialty distributors. 1973. a. $290 (effective 1997). C S G Information Services (Subsidiary of: Lebhar-Friedman, Inc.), 3922 Coconut Palm Dr., Tampa, FL 33619. TEL 813-664-6800. FAX 813-664-6882. Ed. Jeffrey Huggins. (also avail. in magnetic tape; diskette format) **Document type:** directory.
Formerly: Chain Store Guide Directory: Food Service Distributors (ISSN 0091-9152)
Description: Companion to the restaurant database. Profiles 5,100 distributors (with minimum annual sale of $500,000). Identifies sales volume, product lines carried, buying and marketing group affiliations, number of accounts served; type of restaurants and institutions served, trading area and more. Names and titles of over 23,000 key personnel and decision makers.

332.673   **US**   **ISSN 1050-8694**
HG4057
DIRECTORY OF FOREIGN INVESTMENT IN THE U S; real estate and business. a. Gale Research, 835 Penobscot Bldg., 645 Griswold St., Detroit, MI 48226-4094. TEL 313-961-2242; 800-414-5043. FAX 800-877-4253. E-mail: daniel_snyder@gale.com. Ed. Nancy Garman.

650 658.8   **US**   **ISSN 0070-556X**
HF5429
DIRECTORY OF FRANCHISING ORGANIZATIONS.* 1959. a. $7.95 (effective 1997). Pilot Books, Box 2102, Greenport, NY 11944-0893. TEL 516-422-2225. FAX 516-422-2227. Ed. R. Ungerleider. R&P contact: Anne Small. **Document type:** directory.
Description: Comprehensive listings of top franchises with descriptions and approximate investment. Includes facts about the business and evaluation checklists.

338.025 658   **US**   **ISSN 1049-9253**
DIRECTORY OF HEALTH CARE PROFESSIONALS. 1990. a. American Hospital Association, One North Franklin, Chicago, IL 60606. TEL 312-422-3395. FAX 312-422-4583. **Document type:** directory.

338.025 610   **US**   **ISSN 1064-8496**
DIRECTORY OF HEALTHCARE GROUP PURCHASING ORGANIZATIONS. 1983. a. $315 (effective 1997). Medical Economics Co., 5 Paragon Dr., Montvale, NJ 07645-1742. TEL 201-358-7657; 800-745-2601. FAX 201-722-2662. E-mail: tom_young@medec.com. Ed. Thomas B. Young. adv. **Document type:** directory.
● Also available online. Vendor(s): Lexis-Nexis.
Description: Provides information on over 550 group purchasing organizations.

338 615   **US**   **ISSN 1054-3082**
HD9666.3
DIRECTORY OF HIGH VOLUME INDEPENDENT DRUG STORES (YEAR). 1992. a. $290 (effective 1997). C S G Information Services (Subsidiary of: Lebhar-Friedman, Inc.), 3922 Coconut Palm Dr., Tampa, FL 33619. TEL 813-664-6800. FAX 813-664-6882. Ed. Debbie Scruggs. (also avail. in magnetic tape; diskette format) **Document type:** directory.
Description: Profiles approximately 8,000 one-unit drug retailers and the names and titles of over 15,000 key executives within those companies (including owner, president, head pharmacist and general buyer). Company listings provide sales volume, product lines carried, square footage, indicates computerized Rx, year founded and more.

380.1   **US**   **ISSN 0888-0166**
TX907
DIRECTORY OF HIGH VOLUME INDEPENDENT RESTAURANTS (YEAR). 1987. a. $300 (effective 1998). C S G Information Services (Subsidiary of: Lebhar-Friedman, Inc.), 3922 Coconut Palm Dr., Tampa, FL 33619. TEL 813-664-6800. FAX 813-664-6882. Eds. Jeffrey Huggins, Terry Ponder. (also avail. in magnetic tape; diskette format) **Document type:** directory.
Description: Provides complete information on over 6,000 one-or-two unit independents, each with a minimum $1 million in annual sales. Listings identify type of foodservice, liquor served, type of menu, sales volume, number of seats, and more. Also includes names and titles of over 19,000 key decision makers.

380.1   **US**   **ISSN 0272-0167**
HD9745.U4
DIRECTORY OF HOME CENTER OPERATORS & HARDWARE CHAINS (YEAR); includes: home center warehouses, lumber/building material outlets, farm & home stores & specialty paint chains. 1948. a. $290 (effective 1997). C S G Information Services (Subsidiary of: Lebhar-Friedman, Inc.), 3922 Coconut Palm Dr., Tampa, FL 33619. TEL 813-664-6800. FAX 813-664-6882. Ed. Arthur Rosenberg. (also avail. in magnetic tape; diskette format) **Document type:** directory.
● Also available on CD-ROM.
Supersedes in part: Directory: Home Centers and Hardware Chains, Auto Supply Chains (ISSN 0094-8667)
Description: Details over 4,500 home centers, warehouses, and lumber-building material companies (minimum $1 million in annual sales); over 100 two-or-more-unit farm and home store chains operating more than 1,700 units; and 23 buying groups serving over 106,000 accounts. Listings identify sales volume, product lines carried, distribution centers, percentage of sales to D-I-Y consumers, buying-marketing groups amd more. Also includes names and titles of over 20,000 key executives and buyers.

380.1   **US**   **ISSN 0888-0158**
HD9773.U4
DIRECTORY OF HOME FURNISHINGS RETAILERS (YEAR); includes: full-line home furnishing stores, and wholesalers. 1987. a. $325 (effective 1997). C S G Information Services (Subsidiary of: Lebhar-Friedman, Inc.), 3922 Coconut Palm Dr., Tampa, FL 33619. TEL 813-664-6800. FAX 813-664-6882. Ed. Ashley Valdes. (also avail. in magnetic tape; diskette format) **Document type:** directory.
Description: Provides selling information on approximately 4,800 furniture and home furnishings retail companies, and nearly 250 major wholesalers, each with minimum $1 million annual sales. Include information on sales volume, price lines, furniture styles, distribution centers, number of stores operated, year founded, and names and titles of over 15,500 key decision makers.

382 380.1   **CC**
DIRECTORY OF HONG KONG IMPORT & EXPORT TRADE.* a. HK.$200. Hong Kong Trade and Industry Promotion Centre, 23/F, Wu Sang House, 655 Nathan Rd., Mongkok, Kowloon, Hong Kong, People' Republic of China. TEL 852-2399-3100. FAX 852-2381-2492. **Document type:** directory.

BUSINESS AND ECONOMICS — TRADE AND INDUSTRIAL DIRECTORIES

338.025 CC
▼DIRECTORY OF HONG KONG INDUSTRIAL SUPPLIERS (YEAR). (Text in Chinese, English) 1996. a. HK.$600 (S.E. Asia $115; elsewhere $130). Hong Kong Productivity Council, HKPC Bldg., 78 Tat Chee Ave., Kowloon, Hong Kong, People's Republic of China. TEL 852-2788-5814. FAX 852-2788-5959. E-mail: isd@hkpc.org; URL: http://www.hkpc.org. circ. 5,000. Document type: directory.
   Description: Lists over 3,000 industrial suppliers in Hong Kong; contains essential information for sourcing raw materials, semi-manufactures, parts and components, machinery, equipment and tools.

338.4 CC
DIRECTORY OF HONG KONG INDUSTRIES. (Text in English) 1976. a. HK.$750 (S.E. Asia $155; elsewhere $170). Hong Kong Productivity Council, HKPC Bldg., 78 Tat Chee Ave., Kowloon, Hong Kong, People's Republic of China. TEL 852-788-5821. FAX 852-788-5959. TELEX 32842 HKPC HX. E-mail: isd@hkpc.org; URL: http://www.hkpc.org. adv. circ. 3,000. Document type: directory.
   Description: Lists about 6,400 major manufacturing companies in Hong Kong as well as relevant government departments and major industrial and trade associations.

380 CC
DIRECTORY OF HONG KONG TRADE AND INDUSTRY.* (In three vols.) (Text in Chinese and English) a. HK.$1180 (HK.$420 per vol.). Hong Kong Trade and Industry Promotion Centre, 23/F, Wu Sang House, 655 Nathan Rd., Mongkok, Kowloon, Hong Kong, People's Republic of China. TEL 852-2399-3100. FAX 852-2381-2492. Ed. Eddie Lam. stat. Document type: directory.

362.11025 US ISSN 0885-9671
DIRECTORY OF HOSPITAL PERSONNEL. 1986. a. Medical Economics Co., 5 Paragon Dr., Montvale, NJ 07645-1742. TEL 201-358-7657; 800-745-2601. FAX 201-722-2662. E-mail: mdr@medec.com. Document type: directory.
   ●Also available online. Vendor(s): Lexis-Nexis.

DIRECTORY OF HOSPITALS AND N H S TRUSTS (YEAR). see HOSPITALS

382.45 621 II ISSN 0417-5964
DIRECTORY OF INDIAN ENGINEERING EXPORTERS. 1957. irreg., 11th ed., 1995. Rs.300($10) Engineering Export Promotion Council, World Trade Centre, 3rd Fl., 14-1B Ezra St., Calcutta 700001, India. TEL 91-33-250442. FAX 91-33-2319968. adv.; illus. circ. 3,000. Document type: directory.

338 PK
DIRECTORY OF INDUSTRIAL ESTABLISHMENTS IN PUNJAB. (Text in English) 1975. a. Rs.40. Directorate of Industries and Mineral Development, Lahore, Punjab, Pakistan. Document type: directory.

DIRECTORY OF INDUSTRIAL LABORATORIES IN ISRAEL. see ENGINEERING

382 TS
DIRECTORY OF INDUSTRIAL PRODUCTS: MADE IN SHARJAH, UNITED ARAB EMIRATES/DALEEL AL MONTAJAT AL SINA'IAH: SON'I FI AL SHARIQAH. (Text in Arabic, English) 1988. irreg., 4th ed., 1996-1997. Sharjah Chamber of Commerce and Industry, P.O. Box 580, Sharjah, United Arab Emirates. TEL 971-6-541444. FAX 971-6-541119. Document type: directory.
   Description: Provides names, addresses, and activities for Sharjah's indistrial firms. Also includes information about development of the industrial sector of Sharjah.

338.025 332.96 US ISSN 1050-3218
JK791
DIRECTORY OF INSTITUTIONAL INVESTMENT FUNDS. 1989. a. Corporate Profiles, Inc., Database Services Group, 27 Janci St., Metuchen, NJ 08840. TEL 908-321-0708. Document type: directory.
   Description: Covers two broad categories of institutional investment funds: employee benefit - pension, savings, and deferred compensation; non-employee benefit funds - endowment, specific-purpose, board-designated and foundation.

334 302.14 US ISSN 1054-500X
HX654
DIRECTORY OF INTENTIONAL COMMUNITIES. 1990. triennial, latest 1996 ed. $25 to individuals; institutions $35. Fellowship for Intentional Community, Rte. 1, Box 155, Rutledge, MO 63563. TEL 816-883-5545. Ed. Laird Schaub. R&P contact: Laird Schaub. adv. contact: Diana Christian. circ. 20,000. (also avail. in microfiche from UMI) Document type: directory.
   Description: An ecumenical guidebook for those interested in alternative, cooperative lifestyles.

338 630 IO
DIRECTORY OF INTERNATIONAL COCONUT RESEARCH WORKERS. (Text in English) irreg. $25. Asian and Pacific Coconut Community, Wisma Bakrie, 3rd Fl., Jl. H.R. Rasuna Said, Kuningan, Jakarta 12920, Indonesia. TEL 510073. FAX 0062-21-5205160. TELEX 62863 APCC IA. Document type: directory.
   Description: Lists more than 255 experts in Asia, Pacific and other regions, which are classified under 24 disciplines and countries.

338 US ISSN 1046-4263
HG4028.C6
DIRECTORY OF INTERNATIONAL CORPORATE GIVING IN AMERICA AND ABROAD. a. $180. Gale Research, 835 Penobscot Bldg., 645 Griswold St., Detroit, MI 48226-4094. TEL 313-961-2242; 800-877-4253. FAX 800-414-5043. E-mail: daniel__snyder@gale.com. Ed. Deborah Morad; Pub. Karen Hill. Document type: directory.
   Formerly (until 1990): Directory of International Corporate Giving in America.

338 UK
DIRECTORY OF INTERNATIONAL SOURCES OF BUSINESS INFORMATION. 1989. irreg. Pitman Publishing, 128 Long Acre, London WC2E 9AN, England. TEL 44-171-447-2000. FAX 44-171-240-5771. Ed. Sarah Ball. Document type: directory.

330 IS
DIRECTORY OF ISRAEL. (Text in English) 1953. a. $45. N.A. Etrogy Publishing Company, Box 815, Tel-Aviv, Israel. TEL 293451. (Dist. by: International Publications Service, 303 Park Ave. S., New York, N.Y. 10010) Ed. A. Etrogy. adv.; bk.rev.
   Formerly: Directory of Israeli Merchants and Manufacturers (ISSN 0070-5705)

382 GW
DIRECTORY OF JAPANESE ADDRESSES IN EUROPE. a. DM.108. Japaninfo Verlag, Bismarckring 40, 89077 Ulm, Germany. TEL 0731-68093. FAX 0731-68095. Document type: directory.

382 JA
DIRECTORY OF JAPANESE AFFILIATED COMPANIES IN ASIA (YEAR). 1982. triennial, latest 1994-95. $165. Japan External Trade Organization, Publications Department, 2-5 Toranomon 2-chome, Minato-ku, Tokyo 105, Japan. TEL 03-3582-3518. FAX 03-3587-2485. Document type: directory.
   Formerly: Directory of Japanese Affiliated Companies in A S E A N Countries (Year).
   Description: Lists 3,574 Japanese-affiliated companies in Asian countries in alphabetical order and by type of products or business.

382 JA
DIRECTORY OF JAPANESE AFFILIATED COMPANIES IN THE E U (YEAR). triennial, latest 1996-97. $240. Japan External Trade Organization, Publications Department, 2-5, Toranomon 2-chome, Minato-ku, Tokyo 105, Japan. TEL 03-3582-3518. FAX 03-3587-2485. Document type: directory.
   Description: Lists 2,988 Japanese-affiliated companies in the EU, alphabetically grouped by country and city, and by the type of products or businesses.

382 JA
DIRECTORY OF JAPANESE AFFILIATED COMPANIES IN THE U S A AND CANADA. 1969. triennial, latest 1995-96. $260. Japan External Trade Organization, Publications Department, 2-2-5 Toranomon, Minato-ku, Tokyo 105, Japan. TEL 03-3582-3518. FAX 03-3587-2485. TELEX J24378 JETRO. adv. Document type: directory.
   Former titles (until 1986): Directory of Japanese Firms, Offices and Other Organizations in the United States; Directory of Japanese Firms, Offices and Subsidiaries in the United States.
   Description: Lists 7,900 Japanese-affiliated enterprises in alphabetical order by country and state or province.

739.27 JA
DIRECTORY OF JAPANESE JEWELERS (YEAR). 1990. w. 150000 Yen. Yano Research Institute Ltd., Pola Ebisu Bldg., 9-19 Higashi 3-chome, Shibuya-ku, Tokyo 150, Japan. TEL 03-548-5461. FAX 03-548-5468. Document type: directory.
   Description: Data on retailers, wholesalers, and manufacturers in Japan.

380 600 US
DIRECTORY OF JAPANESE TECHNICAL RESOURCES IN THE UNITED STATES. a. $40 in N. America; elsewhere $80. U.S. National Technical Information Service, 5285 Port Royal Rd., Springfield, VA 22161. TEL 703-487-4630. FAX 703-321-8547. TELEX 64617. (also avail. in microform from NTI) Document type: directory.
   Formerly: Directory of Japanese Technical Resources.
   Description: Includes a list of commercial organizations which abstract Japanese technical information, government agencies involved with Japanese technical information as well as libraries with extensive holdings. Also contains a list of reports translated by the U.S. Government and available to the public.

670 US
T12
DIRECTORY OF KANSAS BUSINESSES. 1940. a. $50. Department of Commerce and Housing, Research and Analysis Section, 700 S.W. Harrison, Ste. 1300, Topeka, KS 66603-3712. TEL 913-296-3481. FAX 913-296-5055. (Dist. by: Manufacturers' News, Inc., 1633 Central St., Evanston, IL 60201. TEL 708-864-7000) Ed. Rhonda Egans. circ. 2,000. (also avail. in diskette format) Document type: directory.
   Former titles: Directory of Kansas Manufacturers and Products (ISSN 0070-5721); (until 1954): Made in Kansas (ISSN 0415-9586); (until 1953): It's Made in Kansas (ISSN 0198-8336)
   Description: Profiles Kansas businesses including service-oriented companies and manufacturers.

DIRECTORY OF LANDFILL TECHNOLOGY AND ORGANIC WASTE (YEAR). see ENVIRONMENTAL STUDIES — Waste Management

380 US ISSN 0415-9594
HF5468
DIRECTORY OF LEADING CHAIN STORES (YEAR). a. $325 (effective 1997). C S G Information Services (Subsidiary of: Lebhar-Friedman, Inc.), 3922 Coconut Palm Dr., Tampa, FL 33619. TEL 813-664-6800. FAX 813-664-6882. (also avail. in magnetic tape; diskette format) Document type: directory.
   ●Also available on CD-ROM.
   —CCC.
   Description: Listings include prototype size, projected openings, closings and remodelings, as well as names and titles of thousands of key executives and administors.

670 338 US ISSN 0275-1089
T12
DIRECTORY OF LOUISIANA MANUFACTURERS. 1942. a. $57 (diskette & CD-ROM $299) (effective 1998). Harris InfoSource International, 2057-2 Aurora Rd., Twinsburg, OH 44087. TEL 216-425-9000; 800-888-5900. FAX 216-425-7150. E-mail: catknapp@aol.com. Ed. Frances L. Carlsen. index. circ. 3,500. (also avail. in diskette format) Document type: directory.
   ●Also available on CD-ROM.
   Formerly: Louisiana Directory of Manufacturers (ISSN 0076-1028)

BUSINESS AND ECONOMICS — TRADE AND INDUSTRIAL DIRECTORIES

330 298   US   ISSN 1066-9744
HD2746.5
DIRECTORY OF M & A INTERMEDIARIES. 1987. a. $295. (Securities Data Company, Inc.) Securities Data Publishing, 40 W. 57th St., 11th Fl., New York, NY 10019. TEL 212-765-5311. FAX 212-765-6123. Ed. Yong Lim. adv.; index. **Document type:** directory.
    Formerly: Merger Directory.
    Description: Lists corporate acquirers and their criteria, as well as professional service firms and their services.

380   US   ISSN 0899-5710
HF5465.5
DIRECTORY OF MAIL ORDER CATALOGS. 1981. a. $165. Grey House Publishing, Pocket Knife Sq., Lakeville, CT 06039. TEL 860-435-0868; 800-562-2139. FAX 860-435-0867. Ed. Amy E. Lignor; Pub. Leslie E. Mackenzie. **Document type:** directory.
    Description: Lists over 7500 catalog companies, their presidents, production managers, marketing managers, buyers, and list managers, as well as catalog information.

DIRECTORY OF MAILING LIST COMPANIES. see ADVERTISING AND PUBLIC RELATIONS

659.1   US   ISSN 1045-6201
HF5465.5
DIRECTORY OF MAJOR MAILERS & WHAT THEY MAIL (YEAR). 1990. a. $495 (effective 1997). North American Publishing Co., 401 N. Broad St., Philadelphia, PA 19108. TEL 215-238-5300. FAX 215-238-5457. Ed. Paul Bobrakch. adv.; index. circ. 1,000. (also avail. in magnetic tape) **Document type:** directory.
    •Also available on CD-ROM.
    Description: Directory of 6,000 major mailers (names, addresses, phone numbers, list sizes) plus descriptions of 18,000 mailings in 200 categories.

DIRECTORY OF MANAGEMENT CONSULTANTS IN THE UK. see BUSINESS AND ECONOMICS — Management

338.025 690   II
DIRECTORY OF MANUFACTURERS & DEALERS OF BUILDING INDUSTRY. (Text in English) 1994. irreg. $15. Architects Publishing Corp. of India, 51 Sujata, Ground Fl., Rani Sati Marg, Malad East, Mumbai 400 097, India. TEL 91-22-883-4442. Ed. A.K. Gupta. adv. circ. 5,000. **Document type:** directory, trade publication.
    Description: Alphabetical listing of manufacturers and dealers of building products and materials in India, including name, address, phone number, details of products, and annual sales.

DIRECTORY OF MEMBERSHIP & PRECAST CONCRETE PRODUCTS. see BUILDING AND CONSTRUCTION

380.1 669   US
DIRECTORY OF METALLURGICAL CONSULTANTS & TRANSLATORS. 1984. biennial. $70 in US, Canada, Mexico; elsewhere $80. A S M International, Materials Information, Materials Park, OH 44073. TEL 216-338-5151. FAX 216-338-4634. TELEX 980-619. (UK addr.: Institute of Materials, Materials Information, 1 Carlton House Terr., London SW1Y 5DB, England. TEL 071-839-4071) **Document type:** directory.

380   MX
DIRECTORY OF MEXICAN CORPORATIONS. (Text in English) 1992. irreg., 4th ed., 1997. $200 (effective 1997). Ibcon, S.A., Gutenberg 224, Col. Anzures, 11590 Mexico D.F., Mexico. TEL 52-5-2554577. FAX 52-5-2554577. E-mail: ibcon@infosel.net.mx; URL: http://www.dirsainf.com.mx/ibcon1.htm. Ed. Gabriel Zaid. **Document type:** directory.
    Description: Lists 1200 corporations selling at least ten million US dollars per year. Indexed by CEO, SIC code, foreign associates, location, and products imported and exported.

388   UK
DIRECTORY OF MULTINATIONALS. biennial. £325. Macmillan Reference Ltd., Houndmills, Basingstoke, Hants RG21 2XS, England. TEL 44-1256-817245. FAX 44-1256-812589. (Dist. in the U.S. by: Stockton Press, 49 E. 24th St., New York, NY 10010. TEL 212-673-4400. FAX 212-673-9842) Ed. John Stopford. **Document type:** directory.
    Formerly: World Directory of Multinational Enterprises (ISSN 0265-3893)
    Description: Profiles 450 major multinational companies. Lists all directors and major shareholders, summarizes products produced, describes the organizational structure, and provides background details on the strategic development of the company, its principal subsidiaries, and its financial performance over the past five years.

DIRECTORY OF MUSEUMS AND SPECIAL COLLECTIONS IN THE UNITED KINGDOM. see MUSEUMS AND ART GALLERIES

670   US   ISSN 0070-5926
T12
DIRECTORY OF NEBRASKA MANUFACTURERS. 1960. biennial. $50. Department of Economic Development, Box 94666, Lincoln, NE 68509. TEL 402-471-3111. FAX 708-322-1100. (Dist. by: Manufacturers' News, Inc., 1633 Central St., Evanston, IL 60201-1505. TEL 708-864-7000) Ed. Tom Hanson. circ. 5,000. **Document type:** directory.
    Description: Comprehensive information on 1,849 manufacturers with an average total employment of 94,816; includes alphabetical, geographical and SIC sections, plus alphabetical index to product classification.

670   US   ISSN 0889-0382
HD9723
DIRECTORY OF NEW ENGLAND MANUFACTURERS; * CT, ME, MA, NH, RI, VT. a. $128. George D. Hall Co., Inc., 50 Franklin St., 4th Fl., Boston, MA 02110-1306. TEL 617-523-3745. FAX 708-322-1100. (Dist. by: Manufacturers' News, Inc., 1633 Central St., Evanston, IL 60201-1505. TEL 708-864-7000) **Document type:** directory.
    Description: Profiles 22,000 manufacturers in Connecticut, Maine, Massachusetts, New Hampshire, Rhode Island and Vermont; includes alphabetical, geographical and product sections.

670   US
HD9727.N9
DIRECTORY OF NORTH DAKOTA MANUFACTURERS AND FOOD PROCESSORS. 1959. biennial. $50. Department of Economic Development and Finance, 1833 E. Bismarck Expressway, Bismarck, ND 58504-6708. TEL 701-328-5300. FAX 701-328-5320. E-mail: ccmail.ndef@ranch.state.nd.us. (Dist. by: Manufacturers' News, Inc., 1633 Central St., Evanston, IL 60201-1505. TEL 708-864-7000) Eds. Leigh Ann Huether, Linda Fiectner. circ. 2,500. (also avail. in diskette format) **Document type:** directory.
    Former titles: Directory of North Dakota Manufacturers (ISSN 0090-5577); Directory of North Dakota Industrial and Manufacturing Plants.
    Description: Lists approximately 790 manufacturers in three color-coded sections: product (by SIC), alphabetical, and geographic.

338.025 658   UK
DIRECTORY OF OPPORTUNITIES FOR GRADUATES. VOL. 6: BUYING, MARKETING, SELLING.* 1980. a. free to qualified personnel. Newpoint Publishing Ltd., Windsor Ct., E. Grinstead House, E. Grinstead, W. Sussex RH19 1XA, England. Ed. Jane York. adv.; charts. circ. 20,000. **Document type:** directory.
    Former titles: Directory of Opportunities for Graduates. Vol. 6: Administration, Management, Marketing and Sales; (until 1984): Graduate Careers in Sales and Marketing for Graduates and Postgraduates (ISSN 0260-0706); Graduate Careers in Sales and Marketing.

338.025 331.1   UK   ISSN 0070-6051
HD6270
DIRECTORY OF OVERSEAS SUMMER JOBS; your complete guide to thousands of summer employment opportunities abroad. Variant titles: Vacation Work's Overseas Summer Jobs. Overseas Summer Jobs. 1969. a. $14.95. Vacation Work, 9 Park End St., Oxford OX1 1HJ, England. (Dist. in U.S. by: Peterson's Guides, 202 Carnegie Ctr., Princeton, NJ 08543. TEL 800-338-3282) Ed. David Woodworth. **Document type:** directory.
    Description: Lists jobs outside the UK and offers advice on landing one of them.

658.8   US   ISSN 0196-8262
HF6146.P7
DIRECTORY OF PREMIUM, INCENTIVE & TRAVEL BUYERS. 1970. a. $259.95. Salesman's Guide, A Division of Reed Elsevier Inc., 121 Chanlon Rd., New Providence, NJ 07974. TEL 908-464-6800. FAX 908-665-2894. TELEX 138 755. E-mail: info@reedref.com; URL: http://www.reedref.com. (Subscr. to: Salesman's Guide, Order Dept., Box 1009, Summit, NJ 07902. TEL 800-521-8110) Ed. Elizabeth Kizar; Pub. Peter Simon. (also avail. in magnetic tape) **Document type:** directory, trade publication.
    Former titles (until 1992): Nationwide Directory of Premium, Incentive and Travel Buyers; Directory of Premium and Incentive Buyers (ISSN 0070-6124)
    Description: Profiles 20,000 buyers of premiums, incentives, and travel programs in over 12,000 companies.

338 352   US   ISSN 0887-4042
DIRECTORY OF PRIMES. 1983. a. $15. Government Data Publications, Inc., 1155 Connecticut Ave., N.W., Washington, DC 20036. **Document type:** directory.

380 628.5   US
DIRECTORY OF PRODUCTS AND SERVICES FOR THE VACUUM INDUSTRY. 1994. a. $10 (foreign $15) (effective 1997). Association of Vacuum Equipment Manufacturers, 440 Live Oak Loop, Albuquerque, NM 87122. TEL 505-856-6924. FAX 505-856-6716. E-mail: avemfo@avem.org; URL: http://www.avem.org. Ed. Vivienne Harwood Mattox. adv. contact: Vivienne Harwood Mattox. circ. 1,000. **Document type:** directory.
    Description: Describes products and services of the major vacuum equipment manufacturers.
    Refereed Serial

333.33   US   ISSN 1051-1768
DIRECTORY OF PROFESSIONAL APPRAISAL SERVICES. a. $12. American Society of Appraisers, Box 17265, Washington, DC 20041-0265. TEL 703-478-2228. FAX 703-742-8471. E-mail: asainfo@apo.com. Ed. Rebecca Ewing. R&P contact: Rebecca Ewing. TEL 703-733-2103. adv.: page $1000; adv. contact: Amy Starliper. circ. 8,000. **Document type:** directory.
    Formerly (until 1990): Professional Appraisal Services Directory (ISSN 0196-4097)
    Description: Lists appraisers accredited by ASA.

338.025   CC
DIRECTORY OF PROFESSIONAL ASSOCIATION AND LEARNED SOCIETIES IN HONG KONG. (Text in English) 1988. irreg., 4th ed., 1996. HK.$300($40) Hong Kong Polytechnic Library, Hung Hom, Kowloon, Hong Kong, People's Republic of China. TEL 852-2766-6863. FAX 852-2765-8274. TELEX 38964-POLYX-HX. E-mail: lbinf@polyu.edu.hk. Eds. Barry Burton, Nancy Wong. **Document type:** directory.
    Description: Provides information on the professional associations and learned societies in Hong Kong, including their contact information, organization, membership requirements, publications, activities, and services.

332.67   AT
DIRECTORY OF PROPERTY INVESTORS AND DEVELOPERS. irreg. Davies and Dalziel Investment Service, G.P.O. Box 1392m, Melbourne, Vic. 3001, Australia. **Document type:** directory.

BUSINESS AND ECONOMICS — TRADE AND INDUSTRIAL DIRECTORIES

338.025 070.5 US
DIRECTORY OF PUBLISHING: A PRACTICAL GUIDE. irreg., 4th ed., 1996. $44.95. Cowles - SIMBA Information (Subsidiary of: Cowles Business Media), 11 Riverbend Dr. S., Box 4949, Stamford, CT 06907-0949. TEL 203-358-9900; 800-307-2529. FAX 203-358-5811. E-mail: info@simbanet.com; URL: http://www.simbanet.com. **Document type:** directory.
Description: Covers nature and function of directories, editorial techniques, circulation marketing and production for directory publishers.

384 371 US
BV655
DIRECTORY OF RELIGIOUS MEDIA. 1972. a. $69.95 (foreign $89.95). National Religious Broadcasters, Inc., 7839 Ashton Ave., Manassas, VA 20109. TEL 703-330-7000. FAX 703-330-6996. Ed. Karen M. Hawkins; Pub. E. Brandt Gustavson. adv.: B&W page $975, color page $1575; trim 8 3/8 x 10 7/8; adv. contact: Dick Reynolds. index; circ. 2,500 (paid). **Document type:** directory.
Formerly: Directory of Religious Broadcasting (ISSN 0731-0331)
Description: Covers the worldwide Christian religious broadcasting industry, listing more than 4000 radio and television stations, program producers, manufacturers, and related suppliers and services.

DIRECTORY OF RESTAURANT & FAST FOOD CHAINS IN CANADA (YEAR). see FOOD AND FOOD INDUSTRIES

338 380.1 CN ISSN 0225-9443
DIRECTORY OF RETAIL CHAINS IN CANADA. 1975. a. Can.$250. Maclean Hunter Ltd., Business Publication Division, Maclean-Hunter Bldg., 777 Bay St., Toronto, ON M5W 1A7, Canada. TEL 416-596-5939. Ed. Sandra Fabrizi. **Document type:** directory.

338 663.895 678 UK
DIRECTORY OF RUBBER ORGANIZATIONS (YEAR). 1995. a. £15 (diskette £25) (effective 1997). International Rubber Study Group, 8th Fl., York House, Empire Way, Wembley, Mddx. HA9 OPA, England. TEL 44-181-903-2848. FAX 44-181-903-2848. (also avail. in diskette format)

DIRECTORY OF SIMULATION SOFTWARE. see COMPUTERS — Computer Simulation

387 SI ISSN 0218-4400
DIRECTORY OF SINGAPORE SHIPBUILDING & OFFSHORE INDUSTRIES (YEAR). (Text in English) a. $50. Times Trade Directories Pte. Ltd., Times Centre, One New Industrial Rd., Singapore 536196, Singapore. TEL 65-2848844. FAX 65-2850161. TELEX RS 25713 TIMES. Pub. Leslie Lim. R&P contact: Leslie Lim. adv. contact: Joseph Liang. **Document type:** directory.
Description: Lists marine and offshore industries. Provides information on shipbuilders and repairers, oil rig builders, marine equipment and supplies, offshore equipment and supplies, and other marine-related products and services.

380.1 658.878 US ISSN 0896-2162
HF5469.23.U6
DIRECTORY OF SINGLE UNIT SUPERMARKET OPERATORS (YEAR). a. $280 (effective 1997). C S G Information Services (Subsidiary of: Lebhar-Friedman, Inc.), 3922 Coconut Palm Dr., Tampa, FL 33619. TEL 813-664-6800. FAX 813-664-6882. Ed. Sam Sadler. (also avail. in magnetic tape; diskette format) **Document type:** directory.
Description: Provides selling information on over 6,400 single unit supermarket operators with minimum $1 million in annual sales. Identifies sales volume, square footage, type of store operated (including superstores, supermarkets, warehouse, box, combo and gourmet stores), whether scanning equipment is used, type of specialty departments operated, whether beer, wine or liquor is carried, year founded. Also includes names and titles of over 24,000 key executives and buyers.

380 CE
DIRECTORY OF STATE CORPORATIONS. (Text in English) a. Rs.10. Sri Lanka Institute for the Study of State Corporations, 380 Bauddhaloka Mawatha, Colombo 7, Sri Lanka.

338 672 US
DIRECTORY OF STEEL FOUNDRIES AND BUYER'S GUIDE. 1930. biennial. $95 (diskette $325). Steel Founders' Society of America, 455 State St., Des Plaines, IL 60016. TEL 847-299-9160. FAX 847-299-3105. Ed. Kathleen J. Reese. adv. circ. 1,500. (also avail. in diskette format) **Document type:** directory.
Formerly: Directory of Steel Foundries in the United States, Canada and Mexico.

338.025 371.42 UK ISSN 0308-7123
DIRECTORY OF SUMMER JOBS ABROAD. 1970. a. £7.99. Vacation - Work, 9 Park End St., Oxford OX1 1HJ, England. Ed. David Woodworth. **Document type:** directory.
Description: Geared toward British citizens.

338.025 371.4 UK ISSN 0143-3490
HF5382.5.G7
DIRECTORY OF SUMMER JOBS IN BRITAIN. 1970. a. $15.95. Vacation - Work, 9 Park End St., Oxford OX1 1HJ, England. (Dist. in U.S. by: Peterson's Guides, 202 Carnegie Ctr., Princeton, NJ 08543-2123. TEL 800-338-3282) Ed. David Hatchell. **Document type:** directory.

380.1 658.8 US ISSN 0196-1845
HD9321.3
DIRECTORY OF SUPERMARKET, GROCERY & CONVENIENCE STORE CHAINS (YEAR); includes: market share. a. $300 (effective 1997). C S G Information Services (Subsidiary of: Lebhar-Friedman, Inc.), 3922 Coconut Palm Dr., Tampa, FL 33619. TEL 813-664-6800. FAX 813-664-6882. Ed. Ron Bock. (also avail. in magnetic tape; diskette format) **Document type:** directory.
●Also available on CD-ROM.
Description: Profiles approximately 2,300 two-or-more supermarkets and grocery store chains (minimum $2 million annual sales) operating nearly 35,000 units including superstores, warehouse, combo stores; nearly 1,700 convenience store chains operating over 72,000 stores. Listings identify sales volume, store location type, type of store operated, specialty departments, scanning equipment and more. Also includes names and titles of over 28,000 executives and buyers.

382 CH
(YEAR) DIRECTORY OF TAIWAN'S LEADING EXPORTERS. a. NT.$800($50) in Asia, Middle East, Oceania; elsewhere $60. China Economic News Service, 561 Chunghsiao E. Rd., Sec. 4, Taipei, Taiwan 10516, Republic of China. TEL 02-642-2629. FAX 02-642-7422. TELEX 27110-CENSPC. **Document type:** directory.
Formerly: Directory of Exhibitors Taipei International Trade Fairs.

670 US ISSN 0070-6450
T2
DIRECTORY OF TEXAS MANUFACTURERS. (In 2 vols.; supplement avail.: Texas Industrial Expansion) 1933. a. $130 includes supplement (effective 1997). University of Texas at Austin, Bureau of Business Research, Box 7459, Austin, TX 78713. TEL 512-471-1616. FAX 512-471-1063. E-mail: dhardy@mail.utexas.edu. Ed. Lois Shrout. R&P contact: Lois Shrout. circ. 5,000. (also avail. in diskette format; back issues avail.) **Document type:** directory.
●Also available on CD-ROM.
Description: Provides information on more than 16,000 manufacturing plants. Cross-indexed four ways: locate firms by company name, by product, by location (county and city), or numerically by S.I.C. code.

664 US ISSN 1063-9756
HD9321.3
DIRECTORY OF THE CANNING, FREEZING, PRESERVING INDUSTRIES. 1966. biennial. $165 standard ed.; deluxe ed. $265 (effective 1997). Edward E. Judge & Sons, Inc., Box 866, Westminster, MD 21158. TEL 410-876-2052. FAX 410-848-2034. Ed. Daniel P. Judge. (also avail. in diskette format; back issues avail.) **Document type:** directory.
Description: Covers North American commercial food canners, freezers and preservers. Includes detailed company profiles, showing division and subsidiary relationships, management personnel; factory addresses and products, etc.

674 US ISSN 0070-6477
DIRECTORY OF THE FOREST PRODUCTS INDUSTRY. 1919. biennial. $217 (Business Travel Edition of Primary Producers $167; Business Travel Edition of Secondary Manufacturer $167). Miller Freeman, Inc. (Subsidiary of: United Newspapers), 600 Harrison St., San Francisco, CA 94107. TEL 415-905-2200. FAX 415-905-2232. Ed. Vincent M. Ridley. (reprint service avail. from UMI) **Document type:** directory.
—CCC.

670 US
DIRECTORY OF THE REFRACTORIES INDUSTRY (YEAR). 1954. quadrennial, latest 1997. $85 to non-members; members $45; foreign $100. Refractories Institute, 650 Smithfield St., Ste. 1160, Pittsburgh, PA 15222-3907. TEL 412-281-6787. FAX 412-281-6881. R&P contact: Robert W. Crolius. circ. 1,500. **Document type:** directory.
Formerly: Product Directory of the Refractories Industry of the United States (ISSN 0196-2388)

DIRECTORY OF THE SCIENTISTS, TECHNOLOGISTS, AND ENGINEERS OF THE P C S I R. see SCIENCES: COMPREHENSIVE WORKS

DIRECTORY OF THE SPANISH COTTON-SYSTEM TEXTILE ENTERPRISES/DIRECTORIO EMPRESAS TEXTILES DE PROCESO ALGODONERO/DIRECTORI EMPRESES TEXTILS DE PROCES COTONER/DIRECTOIRE ENTREPRISES TEXTILES DE PROCESSUS COTONNIER. see TEXTILE INDUSTRIES AND FABRICS

332.6 US ISSN 1014-8507
HD9980.1
DIRECTORY OF THE WORLD'S LARGEST SERVICE COMPANIES. irreg. $295. (United Nations, Center on Transnational Corporations) Moody's Investors Service (Subsidiary of: Dun & Bradstreet Corporation), 99 Church St., New York, NY 10007-0300. TEL 212-553-0300. **Document type:** directory.
Description: Provides information on over 200 of the world's largest transnational public and private corporations in service industries.

380.1 674 MY ISSN 0126-6330
HD9766.M3
DIRECTORY OF TIMBER TRADE. (Text in English) 1970. biennial. M.$200($87) per no. Malaysian Timber Industry Board - Lembaga Perindustrian Kayu Malaysia, P.O. Box 10887, 50728 Kuala Lumpur, Malaysia. FAX 03-2929834. TELEX MALTIM MA 30993. E-mail: mtib@po.jaring.my. Ed. Tuan Haji Jahaya bin Mat. circ. 5,000. **Document type:** directory.
Description: Lists names, addresses, certificate numbers, end colors and shipping marks of timber exporters, sawmillers and manufacturers of timber products in Malaysia. Also includes timber graders, packers, timber preservation and kiln-dry operators.

380 338 US ISSN 1063-9748
QA76.6
DIRECTORY OF U.S. GOVERNMENT SOFTWARE FOR MAINFRAMES AND MICROCOMPUTERS. a. $62 (foreign $82). U.S. National Technical Information Service, 5285 Port Royal Rd., Springfield, VA 22161. TEL 703-487-4650. FAX 703-321-8547. TELEX 64617. (also avail. in microfiche; magnetic tape)
—CISTI.
Former titles (until 1992): Directory of Computerized Data Files (ISSN 0738-4610); (until 1982): Directory of Computerized Datafiles and Related Technical Reports (ISSN 0731-3322)
Description: Describes software applications available. With more than 2,000 programs arranged under 21 subject headings, each entry contains full bibliographic information, software descriptions, and ordering instructions. Indexed by subject, hardware, language, and sponsoring agency.

664.9 380 US
DIRECTORY OF U.S. MEAT SUPPLIERS.* a. United States Meat Export Federation, 1050 17th St., No. 2200, Denver, CO 80265-2073. TEL 303-399-7151. FAX 303-321-7075. **Document type:** directory.

DIRECTORY OF U.S. SUBSIDIARIES OF BRITISH COMPANIES. see BUSINESS AND ECONOMICS — Chamber Of Commerce Publications

BUSINESS AND ECONOMICS — TRADE AND INDUSTRIAL DIRECTORIES

668.4 US
DIRECTORY OF U S AND CANADIAN SCRAP PLASTICS PROCESSORS AND BUYERS. a. $40 (effective 1993). Resource Recycling, Inc., Box 10540, Portland, OR 97296-0540. TEL 503-227-1319. FAX 503-227-6135. charts. **Document type:** directory.
  Description: Provides information on more than 400 plastics scrap reclaimers, with company addresses, contact names, and specific scrap plastic preferences. Also includes information on manufacturers of plastics recycling equipment.

DIRECTORY OF UNITED STATES EXPORTERS. see *BUSINESS AND ECONOMICS — International Commerce*

DIRECTORY OF UNITED STATES IMPORTERS. see *BUSINESS AND ECONOMICS — International Commerce*

384.554 US ISSN 1053-9069
HD9697.V543
DIRECTORY OF VIDEO RETAILERS. 1990. a. $175. Palm Springs Media, Inc., Box 2740, Palm Springs, CA 92263-2740. TEL 619-322-3050. Ed. Steve Tolin. **Document type:** directory.
  Description: Lists 100,000 US retailers of video hardware and software.

381.45 US ISSN 1068-7157
HD9321.3
DIRECTORY OF WHOLESALE GROCERS (YEAR); includes: service merchandisers. a. $300 (effective 1997). C S G Information Services (Subsidiary of: Lebhar-Friedman, Inc.), 3922 Coconut Palm Dr., Tampa, FL 33619. TEL 813-664-6800. FAX 813-664-6882. Ed. Jeffrey Huggins. (also avail. in magnetic tape; diskette format) **Document type:** directory.
  ●Also available on CD-ROM.
  Former titles: Directory of Cooperatives, Voluntaries and Wholesale Grocers (ISSN 0277-1969); Directory of Retailer Owned Cooperative Chains, Wholesaler Sponsored Voluntary Chains, Wholesale Grocers (ISSN 0271-8006); Retailer Owned Cooperative Chains, Voluntary Chains and Wholesale Grocers (ISSN 0196-1810)
  Description: Companion to supermarket database. Profiles over 2,200 headquarters, divisions and branches for over 40 coops; 80 voluntary groups; 1,100 non-sponsoring wholesalers; 40 cash-and-carry warehouse operations; over 230 service merchandisers. Identifies sales volume, product line carried, number of accounts and store served, location, distribution centers, and warehouse type. Also includes 13,000 names and titles of key executives and buyers.

338 US
DIRECTORY OF WIRE COMPANIES OF NORTH AMERICA. 1973. a. $119 (foreign $150). C R U International, 7500 Greenway Center Dr., Ste. 480, Greenbelt, MD 20770. TEL 301-441-8997. FAX 301-441-9091. Ed. Karen Chasez. adv. contact: Clifton Crawford. circ. 5,000. **Document type:** directory.
  Description: Profiles over 950 wire companies, ferrous-nonferrous and insulated wire, principal personnel, supplier data and fiber optic firms.

DIRECTORY OF WORLD CHEMICAL PRODUCERS (YEAR). see *CHEMISTRY*

DIRECTORY TO THE FURNITURE & FURNISHING INDUSTRY. see *INTERIOR DESIGN AND DECORATION — Furniture And House Furnishings*

338.025 659.1 US
DIRECTORY WORLD. 1989. bi-m. $60 (Canada $75; elsewhere $120) (effective 1997). Cowles - SIMBA Information (Subsidiary of: Cowles Business Media), 11 Riverbend Dr. S., Box 4949, Stamford, CT 06907-0949. TEL 203-358-9900; 800-307-2529. FAX 203-358-5811. E-mail: info@simbanet.com; URL: http://www.simbanet.com. **Document type:** trade publication.
  Description: Covers news and strategic planning on challenges facing the yellow pages and directory industry such as sales and marketing, new technologies and production.

338.025 659.1 US
DIRECTORY WORLD'S YELLOW PAGES INDUSTRY SOURCE BOOK. 1988. a. $155.95 (Canada and Mexico $169.95; elsewhere $189.95) (effective 1997-98). Cowles - SIMBA Information (Subsidiary of: Cowles Business Media), 11 Riverbend Dr. S., Box 4949, Stamford, CT 06907-0949. TEL 203-358-9900; 800-327-2529. FAX 203-358-5811. E-mail: info@simbanet.com; URL: http://www.simbanet.com. **Document type:** directory.
  Formerly (until 1995): Yellow Pages Industry Source Book.
  Description: Lists key officers, revenues, leading books, major accounts, sales offices, and suppliers for more than 500 firms involved in all aspects of yellow pages publishing.

670 651.2 US
DOCUMENTATION SERVICES INDEX. (In 3 vols.: A, Vendor Name; B, Brand-Trade Name; C, Locator Code) 1964. bi-m. $695. Information Handling Services, 15 Inverness Way East, Englewood, CO 80150. TEL 303-790-0600. FAX 303-799-4085. TELEX 4322083 IHS UI. Ed. Liz Maynard Prigge. adv. circ. 889. **Document type:** abstracting/indexing.
  Description: Provides vendor and Brand-Trade name access to OEMs servicing aerospace and design engineering fields.

338.025 US
DOING BUSINESS IN BOSTON. 1994. biennial. $55. American City Business Journals, Inc. (Austin), 505 Powell St., Austin, TX 78703-5121. (Editorial addr.: 200 High St., Boston, MA 02110. TEL 617-330-1000. FAX 617-330-1016) Ed. Jeffrey P. Levine; Pub. James C. Mcnneto. adv.: B&W page $1900. circ. 5,000 (paid). **Document type:** directory.
  Description: Profiles 1,280 major public, private, foreign, mutual, nonprofit and subsidiary companies with headquarters in the Boston metropolitan area, encompassing Essex, Middlesex, Norfold, Plymouth and Suffolk counties in Massachusetts, or companies with significant operations in the region.

338.025 610 US ISSN 1074-9640
Z6658
DOODY'S RATING SERVICE.* 1993. irreg. Doody Publishing, Inc., 1101 Lake St., Ste. 306, Oak Park, IL 60301-1047. TEL 708-386-9500; 800-219-9500. FAX 708-386-9500. **Document type:** trade publication.

338.025 US ISSN 1048-7247
HF5065.I3
DOWNSTATE ILLINOIS BUSINESS DIRECTORY. 1985. a. $430 (effective 1997). American Business Directories (Subsidiary of: American Business Information, Inc.), 5711 S. 86th Circle, Box 27347, Omaha, NE 68127. TEL 402-593-4600; 800-555-6124. FAX 402-331-5481. E-mail: jerry.verrer@abii.com. (also avail. in magnetic tape; diskette format) **Document type:** directory.
  ●Also available online.
  Also available on CD-ROM.
  Description: Includes all businesses in downstate Illinois compiled from the yellow pages and telephone-verified. Includes company name, complete address, employee size and sales volume, name of owner or manager and credit rating codes.

DRILLING & WELL SERVICING CONTRACTORS; drilling & well servicing contractors, equipment manufacturers & supply companies. see *PETROLEUM AND GAS*

380 658.8 US
DROP SHIPPING SOURCE DIRECTORY OF MAJOR CONSUMER PRODUCT LINES. 1977. a. $12. Drop Shipping News, Box 7838, New York, NY 10150. TEL 212-688-8797. Ed. Nicholas T. Scheel.
  Description: Lists over 700 supply sources for over 200,000 consumer products for mail order and other middlemen.

670 330 US ISSN 0277-3716
HD9666.3
DRUG STORE MARKET GUIDE; a detailed distribution analysis of chain and wholesale drug store industry. 1981. a. $299 (effective 1997). Melnor Publishing, Inc., 1739 Horton Ave., Mohegan Lake, NY 10547. TEL 914-528-7147. FAX 914-528-1369. Ed. Melanie R. Buse. **Document type:** directory.

670 UK ISSN 0960-8338
DUDLEY CHAMBER OF INDUSTRY & COMMERCE DIRECTORY. 1980. a. £8. Coventry Chamber of Commerce & Industry, St. Nicholas St., Coventry CV1 4FD, England. TEL 0203-27586. circ. 3,000. **Document type:** directory.
  Description: Lists services and products of members in classified order.

338 US
DUN & BRADSTREET STANDARD REGISTER. Variant title: Dun and Bradstreet - Seyd's Register. (Published in 5 volumes: Vol.1, Northern Counties, Vol.2. Midlands, Vol.3. London, Vol.4. Southern Counties and Wales, Vol.5. Scotland and North Ireland) 1965. a. L.1.24. Dun's Marketing Services (Subsidiary of: Dun & Bradstreet, Inc.), 3 Sylvan Way, Parsippany, NJ 07054-3896. TEL 201-455-0900. (And: 26-32 Clifton St., London EC2P 2LY, England)
  Former titles: Dun and Bradstreet Register (ISSN 0070-7635); Bradstreet's Register; Incorporates: Seyd's Commercial Lists (ISSN 0080-911X)

380 US ISSN 0734-2845
HG4057
DUN'S BUSINESS RANKINGS. 1982. a. $485 to commercial institutions; libraries $355. Dun and Bradstreet (Subsidiary of: Dun & Bradstreet Corporation), 3 Sylvan Way, Parsippany, NJ 07054-3896. TEL 201-605-6000.
  Description: Ranks the top 25000 public and private U.S. companies according to both sales volume and number of employees within 67 industry categories, within each state, by size, and by public and private designation.

669 380 US ISSN 0278-8799
TS203
DUN'S INDUSTRIAL GUIDE - THE METALWORKING DIRECTORY. 1961. a. $795 to commercial institutions; libraries $485. Dun and Bradstreet (Subsidiary of: Dun & Bradstreet Corporation), 3 Sylvan Way, Parsippany, NJ 07054-3896. TEL 201-605-6000. (also avail. in magnetic tape) **Document type:** directory.
  —CISTI.
  Formerly: Dun and Bradstreet Metalworking Directory (ISSN 0070-7597)
  Description: Data on over 71,000 equipment manufacturers and metal distributors.

338 US ISSN 1061-0723
HG4057.A6
DUN'S REGIONAL BUSINESS DIRECTORY. ALABAMA AREA. a. $495. Dun and Bradstreet (Subsidiary of: Dun & Bradstreet Corporation), 3 Sylvan Way, Parsippany, NJ 07054-3896. TEL 201-455-0900. **Document type:** directory.
  Description: Provides information on the service, performance and operations of companies in Alabama.

338.7 US ISSN 1051-3876
HG4058.A85
DUN'S REGIONAL BUSINESS DIRECTORY. ATLANTA AREA. 1990. a. $495. Dun & Bradstreet (Subsidiary of: Dun & Bradstreet Corporation), 3 Sylvan Way, Parsippany, NJ 07054-3896. TEL 201-455-0900. **Document type:** directory.
  Description: Provides information on the services, performance and operations of Atlanta companies.

338.7 US ISSN 1051-1326
HG4058.B7
DUN'S REGIONAL BUSINESS DIRECTORY. BOSTON AREA. 1990. a. $495. Dun & Bradstreet (Subsidiary of: Dun & Bradstreet Corporation), 3 Sylvan Way, Parsippany, NJ 07054-3896. TEL 201-455-0900. **Document type:** directory.
  Description: Provides information on the services, performance and operations of Boston area businesses.

338 US ISSN 1061-1126
HG4057.I6
DUN'S REGIONAL BUSINESS DIRECTORY. CENTRAL INDIANA AREA. 1991. a. $495. Dun & Bradstreet (Subsidiary of: Dun & Bradstreet Corporation), 3 Sylvan Way, Parsippany, NJ 07054-3896. TEL 201-455-0900. **Document type:** directory.
  Description: Provides information on the services, performance and operations of companies in central Indiana.

BUSINESS AND ECONOMICS — TRADE AND INDUSTRIAL DIRECTORIES

338　　　　US　　ISSN 1061-0820
HG4057.P4
DUN'S REGIONAL BUSINESS DIRECTORY. CENTRAL PENNSYLVANIA AREA. 1991. a. $495. Dun & Bradstreet (Subsidiary of: Dun & Bradstreet Corporation), 3 Sylvan Way, Parsippany, NJ 07054-3896. TEL 201-455-0900. **Document type:** directory.
   Description: Provides information on the services, performance and operations of companies in central Pennsylvania.

338　　　　US　　ISSN 1061-1134
HG4058.C27
DUN'S REGIONAL BUSINESS DIRECTORY. CHARLOTTE - GREENSBORO AREA. 1991. a. $495. Dun & Bradstreet (Subsidiary of: Dun & Bradstreet Corporation), 3 Sylvan Way, Parsippany, NJ 07054-3896. TEL 201-455-0900. **Document type:** directory.
   Description: Provides information on the services, performance and operations of companies in and around Charlotte and Greensboro.

338　　　　US　　ISSN 1061-074X
DUN'S REGIONAL BUSINESS DIRECTORY. CHICAGO METROPOLITAN AREA. 1990. a. $495. Dun & Bradstreet (Subsidiary of: Dun & Bradstreet Corporation), 3 Sylvan Way, Parsippany, NJ 07054-3896. TEL 201-455-0900. **Document type:** directory.
   Description: Provides information on the services, performance and operations of companies in the Chicago metropolitan area.

338.7　　　US　　ISSN 1051-161X
HG4058.C5
DUN'S REGIONAL BUSINESS DIRECTORY. CHICAGO SUBURBAN AREA. 1990. a. $495. Dun & Bradstreet (Subsidiary of: Dun & Bradstreet Corporation), 3 Sylvan Way, Parsippany, NJ 07054-3896. TEL 201-455-0900. **Document type:** directory.
   Description: Provides information on the services, performance and operations of suburban Chicago businesses.

338.7　　　US　　ISSN 1051-1288
HG4058.C55
DUN'S REGIONAL BUSINESS DIRECTORY. CINCINNATI AREA. 1990. a. $495. Dun & Bradstreet (Subsidiary of: Dun & Bradstreet Corporation), 3 Sylvan Way, Parsippany, NJ 07054-3896. TEL 201-455-0900. **Document type:** directory.
   Description: Provides information on the services, performance and operations of companies in Cincinnati.

338.7　　　US　　ISSN 1051-1083
HG4058.C6
DUN'S REGIONAL BUSINESS DIRECTORY. CLEVELAND. 1989. a. $495. Dun & Bradstreet (Subsidiary of: Dun & Bradstreet Corporation), 3 Sylvan Way, Parsippany, NJ 07054-3896. TEL 201-455-0900. **Document type:** directory.
   Description: Provides information on the services, performance and operations of Cleveland businesses.

338　　　　US　　ISSN 1061-0758
HG4058.C64
DUN'S REGIONAL BUSINESS DIRECTORY. COLUMBUS AREA. 1992. a. $495. Dun & Bradstreet (Subsidiary of: Dun & Bradstreet Corporation), 3 Sylvan Way, Parsippany, NJ 07054-3896. TEL 201-455-0900. **Document type:** directory.
   Description: Provides information on the services, performance and operations of companies in the Columbus, Ohio area.

338.7　　　US　　ISSN 1051-1180
HG4058.D2
DUN'S REGIONAL BUSINESS DIRECTORY. DALLAS - FORT WORTH AREA. 1990. a. $495. Dun & Bradstreet (Subsidiary of: Dun & Bradstreet Corporation), 3 Sylvan Way, Parsippany, NJ 07054-3896. TEL 201-455-0900. **Document type:** directory.
   Description: Provides information on the services, performance and operations of Dallas and Fort Worth area businesses.

338　　　　US　　ISSN 1061-1142
HG4058.D46
DUN'S REGIONAL BUSINESS DIRECTORY. DENVER AREA. 1990. a. $495. Dun & Bradstreet (Subsidiary of: Dun & Bradstreet Corporation), 3 Sylvan Way, Parsippany, NJ 07054. TEL 201-455-0900. **Document type:** directory.
   Description: Provides information on the services, performance and operations of companies in the Denver area.

338.7　　　US　　ISSN 1051-1628
HG4058.D6
DUN'S REGIONAL BUSINESS DIRECTORY. DETROIT. a. $495. Dun & Bradstreet (Subsidiary of: Dun & Bradstreet Corporation), 3 Sylvan Way, Parsippany, NJ 07054-3896. TEL 201-455-0900. **Document type:** directory.
   Description: Provides information on the services, performance and operations of Detroit businesses.

338　　　　US　　ISSN 1061-1207
HG4057.G4
DUN'S REGIONAL BUSINESS DIRECTORY. GEORGIA (EXCLUDING ATLANTA) AREA. 1992. a. $495. Dun & Bradstreet (Subsidiary of: Dun & Bradstreet Corporation), 3 Sylvan Way, Parsippany, NJ 07054-3896. TEL 201-455-0900. **Document type:** directory.
   Description: Provides information on the services, performance and operations of Georgia companies outside Atlanta.

338　　　　US　　ISSN 1051-2586
HG4057.C8
DUN'S REGIONAL BUSINESS DIRECTORY. HARTFORD, NEW HAVEN, SPRINGFIELD AREA. 1990. a. $495. Dun & Bradstreet (Subsidiary of: Dun & Bradstreet Corporation), 3 Sylvan Way, Parsippany, NJ 07054-3896. TEL 201-455-0900. **Document type:** directory.
   Description: Provides information on the services, performance and operations of Connecticut businesses.

338.7　　　US　　ISSN 1051-1172
HG4058.H68
DUN'S REGIONAL BUSINESS DIRECTORY. HOUSTON AREA. 1990. a. $495. Dun & Bradstreet (Subsidiary of: Dun & Bradstreet Corporation), 3 Sylvan Way, Parsippany, NJ 07054-3896. TEL 201-455-0900. **Document type:** directory.
   Description: Provides information on the services, performance and operations of Houston area businesses.

338　　　　US　　ISSN 1061-1150
HG4057.I8
DUN'S REGIONAL BUSINESS DIRECTORY. IOWA METROS AND OMAHA, NEBRASKA AREA. 1990. a. $495. Dun & Bradstreet (Subsidiary of: Dun & Bradstreet Corporation), 3 Sylvan Way, Parsippany, NJ 07054. TEL 201-455-0900. **Document type:** directory.
   Description: Provides information on the services, performance and operations of companies in the Iowa and Omaha areas.

338　　　　US　　ISSN 1061-0766
HG4057.K2
DUN'S REGIONAL BUSINESS DIRECTORY. KANSAS CITY AREA. 1992. a. $495. Dun & Bradstreet (Subsidiary of: Dun & Bradstreet Corporation), 3 Sylvan Way, Parsippany, NJ 07054-3896. TEL 201-455-0900. **Document type:** directory.
   Description: Provides information on the services, performance and operations of companies in the Kansas City area.

338　　　　US　　ISSN 1061-1169
HG4057.K4
DUN'S REGIONAL BUSINESS DIRECTORY. KENTUCKY METROS (INCLUDING EVANSVILLE, IN). 1989. a. $495. Dun & Bradstreet (Subsidiary of: Dun & Bradstreet Corporation), 3 Sylvan Way, Parsippany, NJ 07054-3896. TEL 201-455-0900. **Document type:** directory.
   Description: Provides information on the services, performance and operations of companies in Kentucky's metropolitan areas.

338.7　　　US　　ISSN 1051-1202
HG4057.N7
DUN'S REGIONAL BUSINESS DIRECTORY. LONG ISLAND, NEW YORK. 1990. a. $495. Dun & Bradstreet (Subsidiary of: Dun & Bradstreet Corporation), 3 Sylvan Way, Parsippany, NJ 07054-3896. TEL 201-455-0900. **Document type:** directory.
   Description: Provides information on the services, performance and operations of companies on Long Island.

338.7　　　US　　ISSN 1051-158X
HG4057.C2
DUN'S REGIONAL BUSINESS DIRECTORY. LOS ANGELES COUNTY AREA. 1990. a. $495. Dun & Bradstreet (Subsidiary of: Dun & Bradstreet Corporation), 3 Sylvan Way, Parsippany, NJ 07054-3896. TEL 201-455-0900. **Document type:** directory.
   Description: Provides information on the services, performance and operations of Los Angeles businesses.

338　　　　US　　ISSN 1051-2594
DUN'S REGIONAL BUSINESS DIRECTORY. LOS ANGELES SUBURBAN AREA. 1990. a. Dun & Bradstreet, Inc. (Subsidiary of: Dun & Bradstreet, Inc.), 3 Sylvan Way, Parsippany, NJ 07054-3896. TEL 201-455-0900. **Document type:** directory.
   Description: Provides information on the services, performance and operations of businesses in suburban Los Angeles.

338　　　　US　　ISSN 1051-256X
HG4058.M45
DUN'S REGIONAL BUSINESS DIRECTORY. MEMPHIS AREA. 1990. a. $495. Dun & Bradstreet (Subsidiary of: Dun & Bradstreet Corporation), 3 Sylvan Way, Parsippany, NJ 07054-3896. TEL 201-455-0900. **Document type:** directory.
   Description: Provides information on the services, performance and operations of Memphis businesses.

338　　　　US　　ISSN 1051-2551
DUN'S REGIONAL BUSINESS DIRECTORY. MIAMI - FORT LAUDERDALE - WEST PALM BEACH. 1990. a. $495. Dun & Bradstreet (Subsidiary of: Dun & Bradstreet Corporation), 3 Sylvan Way, Parsippany, NJ 07054-3896. TEL 201-455-0900. **Document type:** directory.
   Description: Provides information on the services, performance and operations of businesses in the greater Miami area.

338　　　　US　　ISSN 1061-1177
HG4057.M5
DUN'S REGIONAL BUSINESS DIRECTORY. MICHIGAN METROS (EXCLUDING DETROIT) AREA. 1991. a. $495. Dun & Bradstreet (Subsidiary of: Dun & Bradstreet Corporation), 3 Sylvan Way, Parsippany, NJ 07054-3896. TEL 201-455-0900. **Document type:** directory.
   Description: Provides information on the services, performance and operations of Michigan companies outside Detroit.

338.7　　　US　　ISSN 1051-130X
HG4058.M6
DUN'S REGIONAL BUSINESS DIRECTORY. MILWAUKEE - MADISON AREA. 1990. a. $495. Dun & Bradstreet (Subsidiary of: Dun & Bradstreet Corporation), 3 Sylvan Way, Parsippany, NJ 07054-3896. TEL 201-455-0900. **Document type:** directory.
   Description: Provides information on the services, performance and operations of Milwaukee and Madison businesses.

338　　　　US　　ISSN 1051-2535
HG4058.M63
DUN'S REGIONAL BUSINESS DIRECTORY. MINNEAPOLIS - ST. PAUL AREA. 1990. a. $495. Dun & Bradstreet (Subsidiary of: Dun & Bradstreet Corporation), 3 Sylvan Way, Parsippany, NJ 07054-3896. TEL 201-455-0900. **Document type:** directory.
   Description: Provides information on the services, performance and operations of companies in the Twin Cities.

380　　　　US　　ISSN 1061-0774
HG4057.N35
DUN'S REGIONAL BUSINESS DIRECTORY. NEW ENGLAND AREA. a. $495. Dun & Bradstreet (Subsidiary of: Dun & Bradstreet Corporation), 3 Sylvan Way, Parsippany, NJ 07054. TEL 201-455-0900. **Document type:** directory.
   Description: Provides information on the services, performance and operations of New England companies.

B

BUSINESS AND ECONOMICS — TRADE AND INDUSTRIAL DIRECTORIES

338.7 — US — ISSN 1051-1318
HG4058.N4
DUN'S REGIONAL BUSINESS DIRECTORY. NEW ORLEANS AREA. 1990. a. $495. Dun & Bradstreet (Subsidiary of: Dun & Bradstreet Corporation), 3 Sylvan Way, Parsippany, NJ 07054-3986. TEL 201-455-0900. **Document type:** directory.
 Description: Provides information on the services, performance and operations of New Orleans businesses.

338 — US — ISSN 1051-2543
DUN'S REGIONAL BUSINESS DIRECTORY. NEW YORK METROPOLITAN AREA. 1990. a. $495. Dun & Bradstreet (Subsidiary of: Dun & Bradstreet Corporation), 3 Sylvan Way, Parsippany, NJ 07054-3896. TEL 201-455-0900. **Document type:** directory.
 Description: Provides information on the services, performance and operations of businesses in the New York metropolitan area.

338 — US — ISSN 1051-2608
DUN'S REGIONAL BUSINESS DIRECTORY. NEW YORK SUBURBAN AREA. 1990. a. $495. Dun & Bradstreet (Subsidiary of: Dun & Bradstreet Corporation), 3 Sylvan Way, Parsippany, NJ 07054-3896. TEL 201-455-0900. **Document type:** directory.
 Description: Provides information on the services, performance and operations of suburban New York businesses.

338 — US — ISSN 1061-0782
HG4058.N67
DUN'S REGIONAL BUSINESS DIRECTORY. NORFOLK - RICHMOND AREA. a. $495. Dun & Bradstreet (Subsidiary of: Dun & Bradstreet Corporation), 3 Sylvan Way, Parsippany, NJ 07054-3896. TEL 201-455-0900. **Document type:** directory.
 Description: Provides information on the services, performance and operations of companies in the Norfolk - Richmond area.

338 — US — ISSN 1061-1185
HG4057.C2
DUN'S REGIONAL BUSINESS DIRECTORY. NORTHERN CALIFORNIA AREA. 1991. a. $495. Dun & Bradstreet (Subsidiary of: Dun & Bradstreet Corporation), 3 Sylvan Way, Parsippany, NJ 07054-3896. TEL 201-455-0900. **Document type:** directory.
 Description: Provides information on the services, performance and operations of businesses in Northern California.

338.7 — US — ISSN 1051-1296
HG4057.N5
DUN'S REGIONAL BUSINESS DIRECTORY. NORTHERN NEW JERSEY AREA. 1990. a. $495. Dun & Bradstreet (Subsidiary of: Dun & Bradstreet Corporation), 3 Sylvan Way, Parsippany, NJ 07054-3896. TEL 201-455-0900. **Document type:** directory.
 Description: Provides information on the services, performance and operations of companies in northern New Jersey.

338 — US — ISSN 1061-0804
HF5065.N7
DUN'S REGIONAL BUSINESS DIRECTORY. NORTHERN NEW YORK STATE AREA. 1991. a. $495. Dun & Bradstreet (Subsidiary of: Dun & Bradstreet Corporation), 3 Sylvan Way, Parsippany, NJ 07054-3896. TEL 201-455-0900. **Document type:** directory.
 Description: Provides information on the services, performance and operations of businesses in northern New York State.

338 — US — ISSN 1061-0790
HG4057.O5
DUN'S REGIONAL BUSINESS DIRECTORY. OKLAHOMA - ARKANSAS AREA. 1991. a. $495. Dun & Bradstreet (Subsidiary of: Dun & Bradstreet Corporation), 3 Sylvan Way, Parsippany, NJ 07054-3896. TEL 201-455-0900. **Document type:** directory.
 Description: Provides information on the services, performance and operations of companies in Arkansas and Oklahoma.

338 — US — ISSN 1061-1347
HG4057.O7
DUN'S REGIONAL BUSINESS DIRECTORY. OREGON AREA. 1991. a. $495. Dun & Bradstreet (Subsidiary of: Dun & Bradstreet Corporation), 3 Sylvan Way, Parsippany, NJ 07054-3896. TEL 201-455-0900. **Document type:** directory.
 Description: Provides information on the services, performance and operations of Oregon businesses.

338 — US — ISSN 1061-1193
HG4058.O74
DUN'S REGIONAL BUSINESS DIRECTORY. ORLANDO - JACKSONVILLE AREA. 1991. a. $495. Dun & Bradstreet (Subsidiary of: Dun & Bradstreet Corporation), 3 Sylvan Way, Parsippany, NJ 07054-3896. TEL 201-455-0900. **Document type:** directory.
 Description: Provides information on the services, performance and operations of businesses in the Orlando and Jacksonville area.

338 — US — ISSN 1051-2519
HG4058.P542
DUN'S REGIONAL BUSINESS DIRECTORY. PHILADELPHIA AREA. 1990. a. $495. Dun & Bradstreet (Subsidiary of: Dun & Bradstreet Corporation), 3 Sylvan Way, Parsippany, NJ 07054-3896. TEL 201-455-0900. **Document type:** directory.
 Description: Provides information on the services, performance and operations of Philadelphia area businesses.

338.7 — US — ISSN 1051-1571
HG4058.P545
DUN'S REGIONAL BUSINESS DIRECTORY. PHOENIX - TUCSON. 1990. a. $495. Dun & Bradstreet (Subsidiary of: Dun & Bradstreet Corporation), 3 Sylvan Way, Parsippany, NJ 07054-3896. TEL 201-455-0900. **Document type:** directory.
 Description: Provides information on the services, performance and operations of Phoenix and Tucson area businesses.

338.7 — US — ISSN 1051-1210
HG4058.P6
DUN'S REGIONAL BUSINESS DIRECTORY. PITTSBURGH AREA. 1990. a. $495. Dun & Bradstreet (Subsidiary of: Dun & Bradstreet Corporation), 3 Sylvan Way, Parsippany, NJ 07054-3896. TEL 201-455-0900. **Document type:** directory.
 Description: Provides information on the services, performance and operations of Pittsburgh businesses.

338 — US — ISSN 1051-2578
HG4058.R34
DUN'S REGIONAL BUSINESS DIRECTORY. RALEIGH - DURHAM - FAYETTEVILLE AREA. 1990. a. $495. Dun & Bradstreet (Subsidiary of: Dun & Bradstreet Corporation), 3 Sylvan Way, Parsippany, NJ 07054-3896. TEL 201-455-0900. **Document type:** directory.
 Description: Provides information on the services, performance and operations of North Carolina companies in the Durham, Raleigh and Fayetteville areas.

338 — US — ISSN 1061-1355
HG4058.S24
DUN'S REGIONAL BUSINESS DIRECTORY. ST. LOUIS AREA. 1991. a. $495. Dun & Bradstreet (Subsidiary of: Dun & Bradstreet Corporation), 3 Sylvan Way, Parsippany, NJ 07054-3896. TEL 201-455-0900. **Document type:** directory.
 Description: Provides information on the services, performance and operations of companies in the St. Louis area.

338 — US — ISSN 1061-0812
HG4058.S26
DUN'S REGIONAL BUSINESS DIRECTORY. SAN ANTONIO AREA. 1991. a. $495. Dun & Bradstreet (Subsidiary of: Dun & Bradstreet Corporation), 3 Sylvan Way, Parsippany, NJ 07054-3896. TEL 201-455-0900. **Document type:** directory.
 Description: Provides information on the services, performance and operations of companies in the San Antonio area.

338.7 — US — ISSN 1051-1563
HG4057.C2
DUN'S REGIONAL BUSINESS DIRECTORY. SAN DIEGO AREA. 1990. a. $495. Dun & Bradstreet (Subsidiary of: Dun & Bradstreet Corporation), 3 Sylvan Way, Parsippany, NJ 07054-3896. TEL 201-455-0900. **Document type:** directory.
 Description: Provides information on the services, performance and operations of businesses in San Diego.

338.7 — US — ISSN 1051-1598
HG4058.S4
DUN'S REGIONAL BUSINESS DIRECTORY. SAN FRANCISCO AREA. 1990. a. $495. Dun & Bradstreet (Subsidiary of: Dun & Bradstreet Corporation), 3 Sylvan Way, Parsippany, NJ 07054-3896. TEL 201-455-0900. **Document type:** directory.
 Description: Provides information on the services, performance and operations of businesses in San Francisco and its environs.

338 — US — ISSN 1051-2527
HG4058.S53
DUN'S REGIONAL BUSINESS DIRECTORY. SEATTLE AREA. 1990. a. $495. Dun & Bradstreet (Subsidiary of: Dun & Bradstreet Corporation), 3 Sylvan Way, Parsippany, NJ 07054-3896. TEL 201-455-0900. **Document type:** directory.
 Description: Provides information on the services, performance and operations of Seattle businesses.

338 — US — ISSN 1061-1215
HG4057.S6
DUN'S REGIONAL BUSINESS DIRECTORY. SOUTH CAROLINA AREA. 1990. a. $495. Dun & Bradstreet (Subsidiary of: Dun & Bradstreet Corporation), 3 Sylvan Way, Parsippany, NJ 07054-3896. TEL 201-455-0900. **Document type:** directory.
 Description: Provides information on the services, performance and operations of companies in South Carolina.

338.7 — US — ISSN 1051-1199
HG4058.T35
DUN'S REGIONAL BUSINESS DIRECTORY. TAMPA - ST. PETERSBURG AREA. 1990. a. $495. Dun & Bradstreet (Subsidiary of: Dun & Bradstreet Corporation), 3 Sylvan Way, Parsippany, NJ 07054-3896. TEL 201-455-0900. **Document type:** directory.
 Description: Provides information on the services, performance and operations of businesses in the Tampa - St. Petersburg area.

338 — US — ISSN 1061-0731
HG4057.T2
DUN'S REGIONAL BUSINESS DIRECTORY. TENNESSEE METROS AREA. 1992. a. $495. Dun & Bradstreet (Subsidiary of: Dun & Bradstreet Corporation), 3 Sylvan Way, Parsippany, NJ 07054-3896. TEL 201-455-0900. **Document type:** directory.
 Description: Provides information on the services, performance and operations of companies in Tennessee.

338.7 — US — ISSN 1051-1601
HG4058.W3
DUN'S REGIONAL BUSINESS DIRECTORY. WASHINGTON D.C. - BALTIMORE AREA. 1990. a. $495. Dun & Bradstreet (Subsidiary of: Dun & Bradstreet Corporation), 3 Sylvan Way, Parsippany, NJ 07054-3896. TEL 201-455-0900. **Document type:** directory.
 Description: Provides information on the services, performance and operations of businesses in Baltimore and Washington, DC.

384.54 380 — US — ISSN 0743-7498
HF6146.R3
DUNCAN'S RADIO MARKET GUIDE. 1984. a. $330. Duncan's American Radio, Box 8446, Cincinnati, OH 45208-0446. TEL 513-731-1800. Ed. James H. Duncan.

DUNDEE AND TAYSIDE CHAMBER OF COMMERCE AND INDUSTRY. BUYER'S GUIDE AND TRADE DIRECTORY.
 see BUSINESS AND ECONOMICS — Chamber Of Commerce Publications

BUSINESS AND ECONOMICS — TRADE AND INDUSTRIAL DIRECTORIES

380   SA
DURBAN CHAMBER OF COMMERCE AND INDUSTRY. MEMBERSHIP DIRECTORY. 1926. a. R.30. Durban Chamber of Commerce and Industry, P.O. Box 1506, Durban 4000, South Africa. TEL 27-31-3013692. FAX 27-31-3045255. Ed. N. Thomson; Pub. Graham Cleveland. R&P contact: N. Thomson. adv. contact: Colleen Grant. circ. 7,500. **Document type:** directory.
   Former titles: Durban Regional Chamber of Business. Membership Directory & Natal Chamber of Industries. Yearbook and Directory; Natal Chamber of Industries. Annual Report; Natal Manufacturers Association. Annual Report.

338   SA
DURBAN METROPOLITAN DIRECTORY. (Text in English) 1953. a. free to qualified personnel. Braby's (Subsidiary of: Kohler Packaging Ltd.), P.O. Box 1426, Pinetown 3600, South Africa. TEL 27-31-7017021. FAX 27-31-7017036. Ed. A. Stagg. adv. (also avail. in diskette format) **Document type:** directory.
   Formerly: Durban Corporation Directory (ISSN 0378-9195)

380   CN
DURHAM BUSINESS DIRECTORY & CONSUMERS' GUIDE. 1976. a. Can.$30($40) Lloyd Local Directory (Subsidiary of: Lloyd Publications of Canada), 66 Falby Ct., Ste. 1603, Ajax, Ont. L1S 3L2, Canada. TEL 416-619-0421. Ed. J. Lloyd. adv.; index. circ. 30,000.
   Former titles: Durham Classified Business Directory and Consumers' Guide; Durham Yellow Directory.
   Description: Complete listing of all businesses and services within the Durham Region of Ontario arranged in three sections, i.e. alphabetically by company name, products and postal codes.

540 660   NE
DUTCH CHEMICAL INDUSTRY HANDBOOK/HANDBOEK VOOR DE NEDERLANDSE CHEMISCHE INDUSTRIE. (Text in Dutch, English, French, German) 1977. a. fl.200. (Vereniging van de Nederlandse Chemische Industrie) Samsom H.D. Tjeenk Willink B.V. (Subsidiary of: Wolters Kluwer N.V.), Postbus 316, 2400 AH Alphen aan den Rijn, Netherlands. TEL 31-1720-66822. FAX 31-1720-66639. circ. 2,000. (looseleaf format) **Document type:** directory.
   Description: Directory of all chemical and pharmaceutical producers in the Netherlands, with product registers.

338 550   FR   ISSN 0257-053X
E A R S E L DIRECTORY. (Text in English) 600 F. (effective 1998). European Association of Remote Sensing Laboratories - Association Europeenne de Laboratoires de Teledetection, 2 av. Rapp, 75340 Paris Cedex 07, France. TEL 33-1-45567360. FAX 33-1-45567361. E-mail: earsel@meteo.fr. **Document type:** directory.
   Description: Lists member and observer laboratories, their activities and equipment.

622   US
E & M J INTERNATIONAL DIRECTORY OF MINING. (Engineering & Mining Journal) 1983. a. $140 in US & Canada; elsewhere $165. Intertec, Mining Information Services, 29 N. Wacker Dr., Chicago, IL 60606. TEL 312-726-2802. FAX 312-726-2574. adv. contact: Daria Shahriari. circ. 1,000 (paid). **Indexed:** Tr.& Indus.Ind. **Document type:** directory.
   Formerly: E & M J International Directory of Mining and Mineral Processing Operations.
   Description: Lists major metal, non-metal, and coal mines and processing plants, as well as company headquarters throughout the world. Includes addresses, phone and fax numbers, minerals produced and key personnel names.

384.3 005   US
E D I YELLOW PAGES. (Electronic Data Interchange) a. $99 (effective 1996). Phillips Business Information, Inc., 1201 Seven Locks Rd., Potomac, MD 20854. TEL 301-424-3338. FAX 301-309-3847. E-mail: pbi@phillips.com. **Document type:** directory.
   Formerly: E D I Directory.
   Description: Comprehensive information on all technical and marketing aspects of EDI, including software, international and financial EDI, trade associations and user groups.

F Y DIRECTORY. (Electronics For You) see ELECTRONICS

338.025 621.3   US
E G S A BUYERS GUIDE AND MEMBER SERVICES DIRECTORY. a. free. Electrical Generating Systems Association, 1650 S. Dixie Hwy., Boca Raton, FL 33432-7462. TEL 305-755-2677. FAX 305-755-2679. Ed. Jim McMullen. **Document type:** directory.

E M R DIRECTORY OF CONSTRUCTION INFORMATION RESOURCES. see BUILDING AND CONSTRUCTION

E N R DIRECTORY OF CONTRACTORS - MIDWEST. see BUILDING AND CONSTRUCTION

E N R DIRECTORY OF CONTRACTORS - NORTHEAST. see BUILDING AND CONSTRUCTION

E N R DIRECTORY OF CONTRACTORS - SOUTH. see BUILDING AND CONSTRUCTION

E N R DIRECTORY OF CONTRACTORS - WEST. see BUILDING AND CONSTRUCTION

E N R DIRECTORY OF DESIGN FIRMS. see ENGINEERING

630 334.683   UK
EAST EUROPE AGRICULTURE & FOOD. m. £390 (rest of Europe £730; elsewhere £470) (effective 1997). Agra Europe (London) Ltd., 25 Frant Rd., Tunbridge Wells, Kent TN2 5JT, England. TEL 44-1892-533813. FAX 44-1892-544895. TELEX 95114 AGRATW G. E-mail: 100637.3460@compuserve.com. s-a. index. **Indexed:** Dairy Sci.Abstr., Maize Abstr., Potato Abstr., Soils & Fert., Triticale Abstr., World Agri.Econ.& Rural Sociol.Abstr. **Document type:** trade publication.
   ●Also available online. Vendor(s): Information Access Co.
   —SWETS.
   Former titles: East Europe and U S S R Agriculture and Food; East Europe and China Agriculture and Food; East Europe Agriculture (ISSN 0263-3205)
   Description: Covers production, policy, prices, trade and investment from the former U.S.S.R and Eastern Europe.

338.025 687   UK
EAST EUROPEAN CLOTHING INDUSTRY DIRECTORY. a. World Textile Publications Ltd., Perkin House, 1 Longlands St., Bradford, W. Yorkshire BD1 2TP, England. TEL 44-1274-378800. FAX 44-1274-378811. E-mail: 104470.3070@compuserve.com; URL: http://www.vitalo.com/worldtextile. **Document type:** directory.

338.025 677   UK
▼**EAST EUROPEAN TEXTILE INDUSTRY DIRECTORY.** 1995. a. £97.50 (foreign £102) (effective 1997). World Textile Publications Ltd., Perkin House, 1 Longlands St., Bradford, W. Yorkshire BD1 2TP, England. TEL 44-1274-378800. FAX 44-1274-378811. E-mail: 104470.3070@compuserve.com; URL: http://www.vitalo.com/worldtextile. **Document type:** directory.

380   UK
EAST MERCIA CHAMBER OF COMMERCE & INDUSTRY DIRECTORY. a. £35. Kemps Publishing Ltd., 11 The Swan Courtyard, Charles Edward Rd., Birmingham B26 1BU, England. TEL 44-121-765-4144. FAX 44-121-706-6210. **Document type:** directory.
   Formerly: Walsall Chamber of Commerce & Industry Directory (ISSN 0141-6626)

380   EC
ECUADOR. MINISTERIO DE INDUSTRIAS, COMERCIO E INTEGRACION. DIRECTORIO INDUSTRIAL DE LAS EMPRESAS ACOGIDAS A LA LEY DE FOMENTO INDUSTRIAL. 1957. irreg. Ministerio de Industrias, Comercio e Integracion, Quito, Ecuador. **Document type:** government publication, directory.

LES EDITEURS BELGES DE LANGUE FRANCAISE. see PUBLISHING AND BOOK TRADE

EDITOR & PUBLISHER MARKET GUIDE. see BUSINESS AND ECONOMICS — Marketing And Purchasing

380 070.5   CN   ISSN 1196-8362
EDITORS' ASSOCIATION OF CANADA. DIRECTORY OF EDITORS. Short title: E A C Directory of Editors. (Text in English and French) 1980. a. Editors' Association of Canada - Association Canadienne des Redacteurs - Reviseurs, 35 Spadina Rd., Toronto, ON M5R 2S9, Canada. TEL 416-975-1379. Ed. Susan Bridges. adv.; bk.rev. circ. 3,000. **Document type:** directory.
   Formerly: Freelance Editors' Association of Canada. Directory of Members (ISSN 0226-9031)

371.6   ISSN 0193-1067
EDUCATIONAL DEALER. 1977. 5/yr. $15 (free to qualified personnel). Fahy - Williams Publishing, Inc., Box 1080, Geneva, NY 14456-8080. TEL 315-789-0458. Ed. Kevin Fahy. adv. contact: Tim Braden. bk.rev.; circ. 13,712 (controlled). **Document type:** trade publication.
   Description: For school supply dealers or distributors. Covers warehousing, merchandising, catalog publishing, etc.

338 380   GW   ISSN 0724-6625
HF3563
EINKAUFS 1X1 DER DEUTSCHEN INDUSTRIE. 1961. a. DM.110. Deutscher Adressbuch Verlag, Arheilger Weg 17, 64380 Rossdorf, Germany. TEL 06154-699500. FAX 06154-6995490. adv.; index in English and French. circ. 20,000. **Document type:** directory.
   ●Also available online. Vendor(s): Data-Star, FIZ Technik.
   Also available on CD-ROM.
   Formerly (until 1981): Deutsches Bundes-Adressbuch. Bezugsquellenteil (ISSN 0343-5881)

ELECTRICAL APPLIANCE AND UTILIZATION EQUIPMENT DIRECTORY. see ELECTRONICS

ELECTRICAL CONSTRUCTION MATERIALS DIRECTORY. see ENGINEERING — Electrical Engineering

338.025   AT
ELECTRICAL WORLD BUYERS' GUIDE TO SUPPLIERS. a. Aus.$75 (effective 1996). Reed Business Publishing Pty. Ltd. (Subsidiary of: Reed International PLC), P.O. Box 5487, W. Chatswood, N.S.W. 2057, Australia. TEL 61-2-372-5222. FAX 61-2-419-7399. **Document type:** directory, trade publication.
   Description: Comprehensive directory of manufacturers, distributors and agencies in Australia's electrical industry.

ELECTRICAL WORLD DIRECTORY OF ELECTRIC POWER PRODUCERS. see ENERGY — Electrical Energy

ELECTRICAL WORLD DIRECTORY OF ELECTRIC UTILITIES IN CANADA. see ENERGY — Electrical Energy

ELECTRICAL WORLD DIRECTORY OF ELECTRIC UTILITIES IN LATIN AMERICA, BERMUDA AND THE CARIBBEAN ISLANDS. see ENERGY — Electrical Energy

ELECTRONIC BUYERS' NEWS; the electronic industry's purchasing newsweekly. see ELECTRONICS

643   US
ELECTRONIC DISTRIBUTION SHOW DIRECTORY. 1937. a. Electronic Industry Show Corp., 222 S. Riverside Plaza, Ste. 2160, Chicago, IL 60606. TEL 312-648-1140. FAX 312-648-4282. Ed. Gretchen Oie. adv.: B&W page $1620, color page $2270; bleed 8 1/2 x 11 1/4. circ. 6,000. (back issues avail.) **Document type:** directory.
   Description: Lists electronic distributors, show exhibitions and program of events.

380.1 643   US   ISSN 0091-9519
TK7800
ELECTRONIC INDUSTRIES ASSOCIATION. TRADE DIRECTORY AND MEMBERSHIP LIST.* a. $200 to non-members; members $85. Electronic Industries Association, 2500 Wilson Blvd., Arlington, VA 22201. TEL 703-907-7500. Ed. Carol S. Benda. **Document type:** directory.
   —CISTI.
   Formerly: Electronic Industries Association. Membership List.
   Description: Lists more than 1,000 member companies in the electronics manufacturing industry. Includes corporate and division locations, phone numbers and executive level personnel, and product and services.

BUSINESS AND ECONOMICS — TRADE AND INDUSTRIAL DIRECTORIES

338 643 US ISSN 0422-9053
HD9696.A3
ELECTRONIC INDUSTRY TELEPHONE DIRECTORY (YEAR).* 1963. a. $55. Chilton Co., Chilton Way, Radnor, PA 19089. TEL 215-964-4082. adv. contact: Loretta K. Witt. circ. 101,000. **Document type:** directory.
—CISTI.

380 643 US ISSN 0070-7589
ELECTRONIC MARKETING DIRECTORY. 1959. a. (National Credit Office) Dun's Marketing Services (Subsidiary of: Dun & Bradstreet, Inc.), 3 Sylvan Way, Parsippany, NJ 07054-3896. TEL 201-455-0900. **Document type:** directory.
Formerly: Dun and Bradstreet Electronic Marketing Directory.

ELECTRONICS BUYERS' GUIDE. see *ELECTRONICS*

920 621.38 US ISSN 1060-2100
HD9696.A3
ELECTRONICS MANUFACTURERS DIRECTORY; a marketer's guide to manufacturers in the United States and Canada. 1949. a. $245 (diskette & CD-ROM $595). Harris InfoSource International, 2057-2 Aurora Rd., Twinsburg, OH 44087. TEL 216-425-9000; 800-888-5900. FAX 216-425-7150. E-mail: catknapp@aol.com. Ed. Frances L. Carlsen; Pub. Mark Sabourin. adv.; index. circ. 2,000. (also avail. in diskette format) **Document type:** directory.
—CISTI.
Former titles: U S Electronic Industry Directory (ISSN 1047-5583); (until 1990): Who's Who in Electronics (ISSN 1047-6709)

338.4 643 UK
ELECTRONICS 150. 1979; N.S. 1995. a. $630 (effective Sep. 1995). Elsevier Science Ltd., P.O. Box 800, Kidlington, Oxford OX5 1DX, England. TEL 44-1865-843000. FAX 44-1865-843010. E-mail: nlinfo-f@elsevier.nl; usinfo-f@elsevier.com; forinfo-kyf04035@niftyserve.or.jp; URL: http://www.elsevier.nl/. (Subscr. to: Elsevier Science, Regional Sales Office, P.O. Box 211, 1000 AE Amsterdam, Netherlands. TEL 31-20-4853757. FAX 31-20-4853432; Subscr. in the Americas to: Elsevier Science, Regional Sales Office, Box 945, New York, NY 10159-0945. TEL 212-633-3730. FAX 212-633-3680; Subscr. in Australasia and the Far East to: Elsevier Science (Singapore) Pte Ltd, No.1 Temasek Ave., No.17-01 Millenia Tower, Singapore 039192, Singapore. TEL 65-434-3727. FAX 65-337-2230) Ed. A. Fletcher. abstr.; index. circ. 250. (back issues avail.) **Document type:** directory.
—CCC.
Former titles (until 1995): World Electronics Companies File (ISSN 0951-5747); Incorporates (in 1988): World Electronics Bulletin (ISSN 0954-1268); (until 1988): European Electronics Companies File; Mackintosh European Electronics Companies File (ISSN 0142-9671); Which incorporates: Mackintosh European Electronics Companies Bulletin (ISSN 0143-0696); Mackintosh Yearbook of European Electronics Companies.
Description: Provides full corporate information on the world's top 150 electronics manufacturers.

EMBROIDERY DIRECTORY. see *TEXTILE INDUSTRIES AND FABRICS*

338.025 657 US
EMERSON'S DIRECTORY OF LEADING ACCOUNTING FIRMS WORLDWIDE. 1988. biennial. latest 4th ed. $275. Emerson Company, 12356 Northup Way, Ste. 103, Bellevue, WA 98005. TEL 206-869-0655. FAX 206-869-0746. index. **Document type:** directory.
Formerly: Emerson's Directory of Leading U.S. Accounting Firms.
Description: Provides comprehensive information on the top CPA firms worldwide.

338 SA ISSN 0259-868X
EMPANGENI - RICHARDS BAY DIRECTORY. 1987. a. R.30 (effective 1997). Braby's (Subsidiary of: Kohler Packaging Ltd.), P.O. Box 1426, Pinetown 3600, South Africa. TEL 27-31-7017021. FAX 27-31-7017036. **Document type:** directory.

EMPLOYMENT LAW DESK BOOK FOR TENNESSEE EMPLOYERS. see *LAW*

338 BL
EMPRESAS JAPONESAS DO BRASIL. ANNUARIO/BURAJIRU NIKKEI KIGYO NENKAN. (Text in Japanese and Portuguese) a. Selecoes Economicas, Av. Paulista 807, Sao Paulo, Brazil.

ENCYCLOPAEDIA OF HONG KONG TRADE & INDUSTRY (YEAR). see *ENCYCLOPEDIAS AND GENERAL ALMANACS*

338.025 US ISSN 1086-4768
▼**ENCYCLOPEDIA OF BUSINESS.** 1995. triennial. Gale Research, 835 Penobscot Bldg., 645 Griswold St., Detroit, MI 48226-4094. TEL 313-961-2242; 800-877-4253. FAX 800-414-5043. E-mail: daniel__snyder@gale.com. Ed.Bd. **Document type:** trade publication.

382 US ISSN 1084-8614
HD2324
▼**ENCYCLOPEDIA OF GLOBAL INDUSTRIES.** 1996. biennial. Gale Research, 835 Penobscot Bldg., 645 Grsiwold St., Detroit, MI 48226-4094. TEL 313-961-2242; 800-877-4253. FAX 800-877-4253. E-mail: daniel__snyder@gale.com. Eds. Diane M. Sawinski, Wendy H. Mason. **Document type:** directory.

790.1 US
▼**ENCYCLOPEDIA OF SPORTS CONTACTS;** the sports networking reference guide. 1996. a. $45.95 (effective Dec. 1996). Global Sports Productions Ltd., 1223 Broadway, Ste. 102, Santa Monica, CA 90404-2707. TEL 310-454-9480. FAX 310-454-6590. Ed. Greg Andrews; Pub. Edward T. Kobak, Jr. adv. contact: Tina Evans. circ. 7,500 (paid). **Document type:** directory.
Description: Provides a business and sports administration view of the field of sports management, sports media, sports event management and sponsorships, sports marketing and public relations. Includes a directory of contacts from sports facilities, professional, amateur, collegiate, scholastic and international sports.

338.025 621.042 UK ISSN 0263-9971
ENERGY-SAVING MARKETGUIDE. 1982. biennial. £15 (effective 1995). Aydee Marketing Ltd., Nithsdale House, 159 Cambridge St., Aylesbury, Bucks HP20 1BQ, England. TEL 44-1296-434381. FAX 44-1296-436936. Ed. Jean Payne; Pub. Richard Salmon. adv.: page £1195; trim 260 x 184; adv. contact: Richard Salmon. circ. 6,000. **Document type:** directory.

THE ENGINEER BUYER'S GUIDE. see *ENGINEERING*

380.1 669 US
ENGINEERED MATERIALS DIRECTORY OF CONSULTANTS & TRANSLATORS. 1988. biennial. $70 in US, Canada, Mexico; elsewhere $80. A S M International, Materials Information, Materials Park, OH 44073. TEL 216-338-5151. FAX 216-338-4634. TELEX 980-619. (UK addr.: Institute of Materials, Materials Information, 1 Carlton House Terr., London SW1Y 5DB, England. TEL 071-839-4071) **Document type:** directory.

620 005.3 US ISSN 1043-6944
TA345
ENGINEERING & INDUSTRIAL SOFTWARE DIRECTORY. 1985. irreg. Engineering Information, Inc., Castle Point on the Hudson, Hoboken, NJ 07030. TEL 201-216-8500; 800-221-1044. FAX 201-216-8532.
—CISTI.

ENGINEERING INDUSTRIES. see *MINES AND MINING INDUSTRY*

ENGINEERING INDUSTRIES ASSOCIATION. CLASSIFIED DIRECTORY AND BUYERS GUIDE. see *ENGINEERING*

339 620 NZ ISSN 0110-3571
ENGINEERING REFERENCE HANDBOOK. 1976. irreg., approx. 18/yr. NZ.$99. Engineering Handbook Ltd., P.O. Box 26-269, Epsom, Auckland, New Zealand. TEL 64-9-3582749. FAX 64-9-3582741. Ed. Des Snell. R&P contact: Des Snell. adv.: page NZ.$720; trim 210 x 297. circ. 500 (paid). (back issues avail.) **Document type:** directory.
Description: Listings of workshop engineering and related companies, including machine capacities, products made, maintenance and design areas.

ENTEC DIRECTORY OF ENVIRONMENTAL TECHNOLOGY. see *ENVIRONMENTAL STUDIES*

613.1 US ISSN 1061-2122
HD9718.U6
ENVIRONMENTAL INDUSTRIES MARKETPLACE. 1992. a. $175. Gale Research, 835 Penobscot Bldg., 645 Griswold St., Detroit, MI 48226-4094. TEL 313-961-2242; 800-877-4253. FAX 800-414-5043. E-mail: daniel__snyder@gale.com. Ed. Karin Napoleon Meech. **Document type:** directory.
Description: Lists over 10,000 companies in the industry.

ENVIRONMENTAL TELEPHONE DIRECTORY. see *ENVIRONMENTAL STUDIES*

670 US
EQUIPOS PRODUCTOS INDUSTRIALES. 9/yr. Thomas Publishing Company, Five Penn Plaza, 8th fl., New York, NY 10001. TEL 212-629-1546. FAX 212-629-1542. (In Spain: Elsevier Prensa S.A., Av. Parallel 180, 08015 Barcelona, Spain. TEL 3-32-55-350) Ed. Ignacio Orteu Gimenez. adv. circ. 26,344.
Description: Features news about industrial and engineering products and services around the world.

ESSOR FRANCAIS DE L'INDUSTRIE. see *BUSINESS AND ECONOMICS — Production Of Goods And Services*

ESTATES GAZETTE DIRECTORY. see *REAL ESTATE*

380 ET
HF3889.A48
ETHIOPIAN TRADE DIRECTORY. 1954. a., latest 1990. Ethiopian Chamber of Commerce, P.O. Box 517, Addis Ababa, Ethiopia. (Co-sponsor: Addis Ababa Chamber of Commerce) (reprint service avail. from ISI) **Document type:** directory.
Supersedes: Trade Directory and Guide Book to Ethiopia (ISSN 0564-0490)

EURO - WHO'S WHO; who is who in the institutions of the European Union and in the other European Organizations. see *BIOGRAPHY*

EUROFILE ARTISTS, VENUES AND TOURING DIRECTORY. see *MUSIC*

780 NE
EUROFILE MUSIC INDUSTRY DIRECTORY. (Text in English) 1989. a. fl.135($90) B P I Communications, Rijnsburgstraat 11, 1059 AT Amsterdam, Netherlands. TEL 31-20-669-1961. FAX 31-20-669-1941. Ed. Cesco van Gool. circ. 7,000. (also avail. in diskette format) **Document type:** directory.
Description: Lists 15000 companies active in the music industry in Western and Eastern Europe.

384.5 NE
EUROFILE RADIO INDUSTRY DIRECTORY. (Text in English) 1991. a. fl.135($90) B P I Communications, Rijnsburgstraat 11, 1059 AT Amsterdam, Netherlands. TEL 31-20-669-1961. FAX 31-20-669-1941. Ed. Cesco van Gool. circ. 5,000. (also avail. in diskette format) **Document type:** directory.
Description: Provides information on 2500 Western and Central European radio stations and 4500 radio related companies worldwide.

382 FR ISSN 0982-3360
EUROPAGES. 1983. a. 320 F. (CD-ROM ed. 560 F.) (effective 1997). Euredit s.a., 9 av. de Friedland, 75008 Paris, France. TEL 33-1-53775400. FAX 33-1-42893473. E-mail: comments@europages.com; URL: http://www.europages.com. R&P contact: Helmut Rieder. adv. contact: Katia Maddalena. **Document type:** directory.
●Also available online.
Also available on CD-ROM.
—BLDSC (3829.341210); CISTI.
Description: Lists European suppliers in 18 industries and market sectors.

EUROPEAN ADHESIVES & SEALANTS YEARBOOK AND DIRECTORY. see *PAINTS AND PROTECTIVE COATINGS*

BUSINESS AND ECONOMICS — TRADE AND INDUSTRIAL DIRECTORIES

338.025 UK ISSN 0964-8550
EUROPEAN BUSINESS INFORMATION SOURCEBOOK. biennial. £160 (effective 1997). Headland Business Information (Subsidiary of: Bowker-Saur), Customer Services Department, Maypole House, Maypole Rd., E. Grinstead, W. Sussex RH19 1HU, England. TEL 44-1342-330-100. FAX 44-1342-330-191. E-mail: custserv@bowker-saur.co.uk. bk.rev. **Document type:** directory.
Description: Covers European business information sources in the E.C., as well as the members of E.F.T.A. and Eastern Europe.

338 651 US ISSN 1063-5718
HF5152
EUROPEAN BUSINESS SERVICES DIRECTORY. 1993. irreg. Gale Research, 835 Penobscot Bldg., 645 Griswod St., Detroit, MI 48226-4094. TEL 313-961-2242; 800-877-4253. FAX 800-414-5043. E-mail: daniel__snyder@gale.com. Ed. Michael B. Huellmantel. **Document type:** directory.

EUROPEAN COIL COATING ASSOCIATION DIRECTORY. see PAINTS AND PROTECTIVE COATINGS

EUROPEAN COMPANIES; guide to sources of information. see BUSINESS AND ECONOMICS — Abstracting, Bibliographies, Statistics

658 382 US ISSN 1060-1880
HD69.C6
EUROPEAN CONSULTANTS DIRECTORY. 1992. a. $225. Gale Research, 835 Penobscot Bldg., 645 Griswold St., Detroit, MI 48266-4094. TEL 313-961-2242; 800-877-4253. FAX 800-414-5043. E-mail: daniel__snyder@gale.com. Ed. Karin E. Koek. **Document type:** directory.

EUROPEAN COSMETICS AND TOILETRIES MARKETING DIRECTORY. see BEAUTY CULTURE — Perfumes And Cosmetics

EUROPEAN DEVELOPMENT DIRECTORY. see BUSINESS AND ECONOMICS — International Development And Assistance

EUROPEAN DIRECTORY OF CONSUMER BRANDS AND THEIR OWNERS. see PATENTS, TRADEMARKS AND COPYRIGHTS

THE EUROPEAN DIRECTORY OF MANAGEMENT CONSULTANTS. see BUSINESS AND ECONOMICS — Management

EUROPEAN ELECTRICAL APPLIANCES MARKETING DIRECTORY. see ELECTRONICS

EUROPEAN ELECTRONIC COMPONENT DISTRIBUTOR DIRECTORY. see ELECTRONICS

EUROPEAN ELECTRONIC PRODUCTION DIRECTORY - SMART GROUP YEARBOOK. see ELECTRONICS

621.381 UK
EUROPEAN ELECTRONICS DIRECTORY (YEAR) - COMPONENTS & SUB-ASSEMBLIES; the guide to manufacturers, distributors and agents. 1991. irreg., 3rd ed., 1995. $375 (effective Sep. 1995). Elsevier Science Ltd., Books Division, The Boulevard, Langford Ln., Kidlington, Oxford OX5 1GB, England. TEL 44-1865-843000. FAX 44-1865-843010. E-mail: nlinfo-f@elsevier.nl; usinfo-f@elsevier.com; forinfo-kyf04035@niftyserve.or.jp; URL: http://www.elsevier.nl/. (Subscr. to: Elsevier Science, Regional Sales Office, P.O. Box 211, 1000 AE Amsterdam, Netherlands. TEL 31-20-4853757. FAX 31-20-4853432; Subscr. in the Americas to: Elsevier Science, Regional Sales Office, Box 945, New York, NY 10159-0945. TEL 212-633-3730. FAX 212-633-3680; Subscr. in Australasia and the Far East to: Elsevier Science (Singapore) Pte Ltd, No.1 Temasek Ave., No.17-01 Millenia Tower, Singapore 039192, Singapore. TEL 65-434-3727. FAX 65-337-2230) Ed. Andrew Fletcher. **Document type:** trade publication, directory.
Incorporates (in 1991): European Electronics Component Distributors Directory.
Description: Comprehensive reference to companies and products manufactured and distributed in Eastern and Western Europe.

EUROPEAN FOOD DATABOOK. see FOOD AND FOOD INDUSTRIES

EUROPEAN FOOD MARKETING DIRECTORY. see FOOD AND FOOD INDUSTRIES

EUROPEAN GENERATING SET DIRECTORY. see ENGINEERING — Electrical Engineering

EUROPEAN GLASS DIRECTORY AND BUYER'S GUIDE. see CERAMICS, GLASS AND POTTERY

338.025 614 UK ISSN 0962-385X
EUROPEAN HEALTH & SAFETY MARKETGUIDE. (Text in English; summaries in French, German, Italian, Spanish) 1981. a. £35 (effective 1995). Aydee Marketing Ltd., 159 Cambridge St., Aylesbury, Bucks HP20 1BQ, England. TEL 44-1296-434381. FAX 44-1296-436936. Ed. Jean Payne; Pub. Richard Salmon. adv.: page £1195; trim 260 x 184; adv. contact: Richard Salmon. circ. 6,000 (paid). (back issues avail.) **Document type:** directory.
Formerly (until 1990): Health and Safety Marketguide (ISSN 0261-8036)

EUROPEAN HOTEL AND CATERING MARKETING DIRECTORY. see HOTELS AND RESTAURANTS

338.025 677 UK
▼**EUROPEAN INDEX OF YARNS AND FIBRES.** 1995. a. £30. World Textile Publications Ltd., Perkin House, 1 Longlands St., Bradford, W. Yorkshire BD1 2TP, England. TEL 44-1274-378800. FAX 44-1274-378811. E-mail: 104470.3070@compuserve.com; URL: http://www.vitalo.com/worldtextile. **Document type:** directory.
Description: Guide to the wide range of natural and man-made fibers and yarns available to European textile manufacturers.

EUROPEAN INDUSTRIAL MARKETING RESEARCH PERSONAL CONTACT DIRECTORY. see BUSINESS AND ECONOMICS — Marketing And Purchasing

EUROPEAN LEISURE AND ENTERTAINMENT MARKETING DIRECTORY. see LEISURE AND RECREATION

EUROPEAN MARKETS: A GUIDE TO COMPANY AND INDUSTRY INFORMATION SOURCES. see BUSINESS AND ECONOMICS — International Commerce

EUROPEAN MEDIA DIRECTORY. see JOURNALISM

EUROPEAN MOTOR AND ALLIED TRADES MARKETING DIRECTORY. see TRANSPORTATION — Automobiles

EUROPEAN RESEARCH CENTRES; a directory of organizations in science, technology, agriculture and medicine. see SCIENCES: COMPREHENSIVE WORKS

384.5 US ISSN 1080-4242
EUROPEAN SATELLITE DIRECTORY. 1994. a. $159 (effective 1995). Phillips Business Information, Inc., 1201 Seven Locks Rd., Potomac, MD 20854. TEL 301-424-3338. FAX 301-309-3847. E-mail: pbi@phillips.com. **Document type:** directory.

070.5 UK
EUROPEAN SPECIALIST PUBLISHERS DIRECTORY. irreg. Gale Research International Ltd., P.O. Box 699, Cheriton House, North Way, Andover, Hants SP10 5YE, England. Ed. Sarah M. Hall. **Document type:** directory.

THE EUROPEAN UNION ENCYCLOPEDIA AND DIRECTORY (YEAR). see ENCYCLOPEDIAS AND GENERAL ALMANACS

338.025 658.8 UK
EUROPE'S MEDIUM SIZED COMPANIES DIRECTORY (YEAR). irreg., latest 1997. £295($590) (effective 1997). Euromonitor, 60-61 Britton St., London EC1M 5NA, England. TEL 44-171-251-8024. FAX 44-171-608-3149. E-mail: info@euromonitor.com; URL: http://www.euromonitor.com. (Addr. in N. America: Euromonitor International, 122 S. Michigan Ave., Ste. 1200, Chicago, IL 60603. TEL 800-577-3876. FAX 312-922-1157) **Document type:** directory.
Formerly: European Directory of Medium Sized Companies.

380.1 NE
EVENTLINE; an international database of conferences, symposia, trade fairs & exhibitions. (Not avail. in printed format) m. Elsevier Science B.V., P.O. Box 521, 1000 AM Amsterdam, Netherlands. TEL 31-20-4853911. FAX 31-20-4853598. E-mail: nlinfo-f@elsevier.nl; usinfo-f@elsevier.com; forinfo-kyf04035@niftyserve.or.jp; URL: http://www.elsevier.nl/. (Subscr. in the Americas to: Elsevier Science, Regional Sales Office, Box 945, New York, NY 10159-0945. TEL 212-633-3730. FAX 212-633-3680; Subscr. in Australasia and the Far East to: Elsevier Science (Singapore) Pte Ltd, No.1 Temasek Ave., No.17-01 Millenia Tower, Singapore 039192, Singapore. TEL 65-434-3727. FAX 65-337-2230; Subscr. in Japan to: Elsevier Science Japan, 9-15 Higashi-Azabu 1-chome, Minato-ku, Tokyo 106, Japan. TEL 81-3-5561-5033. FAX 81-3-5561-5047) (diskette format) **Document type:** directory.
● Also available online. Vendor(s): Data-Star, European Space Agency, Knight-Ridder Information, Inc.
Description: Provides a full geographic listing of future events held worldwide, by country, state and city, with a contact address.

338.025 664 US ISSN 1082-2011
HF5428
EXCLUSIVE BRANDS SOURCEBOOK (YEAR). a. $150 ($160 in Canada; elsewhere $175). Exclusive Brands Publications, 23 W. 35th St., New York, NY 10001. TEL 212-695-5118. FAX 212-643-8396. E-mail: excbrands@aol.com; URL: http://www.incadinc.com/pl-eb. Ed. Philip Fitzell; Pub. William Fitzell. R&P contact: Philip Fitzell. bk.rev. **Document type:** directory.

670 658 US
EXHIBIT BUILDER SOURCE BOOK DIRECTORY (YEAR). 1985. a. $50. Exhibit Builder, Inc., Box 4144, Woodland Hills, CA 91365. TEL 818-225-0100. FAX 818-225-0138. adv. circ. 20. **Document type:** directory.

338 US ISSN 1046-2872
EXHIBIT REVIEW. 1989. a. $59.95 (foreign $69.95) (effective 1994). Phoenix Communications, Inc., Box 5808, Beaverton, OR 97006-0808. TEL 503-244-8677. FAX 503-244-8745. Ed. Deborah King. adv.; bk.rev. circ. 10,000. **Document type:** directory.
Description: Lists more than 8,000 trade and consumer shows. Contains articles on new products, how-to information for exhibitors, and business travel.

EXHIBITIONS ROUND THE WORLD. see MEETINGS AND CONGRESSES

380.5 US
(YEAR) EXPEDITED CARRIERS NETWORK GUIDE. a. Air and Expedited Motor Carriers Conference, 2200 Mill Rd., Alexandria, VA 22314. TEL 703-838-7978. Ed. Dave Osiecki. circ. 400. **Document type:** directory.
Description: Provides the user with a complete listing of the expedited services provided by members of the conference.

380.102 DK ISSN 0908-9659
HF3643
EXPORT DENMARK. 1883. a. DKK 95. Export Denmark, Kongeriget Danmarks Handels & Exportkalender, Gl. Kongevej 86 A, DK-1850 Frederiksberg C, Denmark.
Former titles (until 1993): Kongeriget Danmarks Handelskalender (ISSN 0302-5403); (until 1962): Kongeriget Danmarks Handels-Kalender med Postadresse-Register; (until 1936): Kongeriget Danmarks Officielle Post- og Telegraf-Adressebog samt Handels-Kalender (ISSN 0105-0230)

382 684.1 UK
EXPORT DIRECTORY; members and buyers guide. a.? £5. Association of Suppliers to the Furniture Industry Export Club, P.O. Box 10, Epping, Essex CM16 7RR, England. TEL 44-992-578873. FAX 44-992-572217. **Document type:** directory.

BUSINESS AND ECONOMICS — TRADE AND INDUSTRIAL DIRECTORIES

380　　　　　　　CL　　　ISSN 0717-005X
EXPORT DIRECTORY CHILE/DIRECTORIO DE LA EXPORTACION. (Text in English, French, German, Spanish) 1976. a. free. Ministerio de Relaciones Exteriores, Direccion de Promocion de Exportaciones, Alameda Bernardo O'Higgins 1315, 2o piso, Santiago, Chile. FAX 56-2-6960639. TELEX 340120 PROCH CL. adv. circ. 15,000. **Document type:** directory.
　　Description: Contains background material on exporters, and includes companies that have exported over US$30,000 in the previous year.

338.025　332.6　　　　　IR
EXPORT DIRECTORY, ISLAMIC REPUBLIC OF IRAN. a. Export Promotion Centre of Iran, P.O. Box 11-48, Tadjrish, Tehran, Iran. **Document type:** directory.

382　　　　　　　BL
EXPORT DIRECTORY OF BRAZIL/GUIA BRASILEIRO DE EXPORTACAO. (Text in English, French, Portuguese, and Spanish) 1964. a. Cr.$50. Banco do Brasil, Eixo Rodoviario Sul, Sector Bancario Sul, Lote 23, C.P. 562, Brasilia, D.F., Brazil. (Co-sponsor: Emprendimentos Brasileiros de Informacoes Dirigidas Ltda.) Ed. Gilberto Huber. bk.rev.; illus. circ. 25,000. **Document type:** directory.
　　Formerly: G B E: Export Directory of Brazil.

382　　　　　　　FR　　　ISSN 1263-5456
▼**EXPORT SERVICES.** 1995. a. 750 F. (effective 1995). Librairie du Commerce International, 24 bd. de l'Hopital, B.P. 438, 75233 Paris Cedex 05, France. TEL 33-1-40-73-34-86. FAX 33-1-43-36-47-98. TELEX 206-811-F. Ed. Gerard Le Coz. adv.; circ. 10,000 (paid). (also avail. in diskette format) **Document type:** directory.
　　Description: Lists 8000 French firms specializing in international services business, classified according to their main activity. Indexed by service company location.

338　　　　　　　IR
EXPORTS DIRECTORY OF IRAN INDUSTRIES. a. IRI.10000($50) (effective 1994). Iran Exports Publication Co. Ltd., P.O. Box 15815-3373, Tehran 15956, Iran. TEL 98-21-8801999. FAX 98-21-890547. adv. **Document type:** directory.
　　Description: Provides information about Iranian industries, agriculture and the economy, with classified listing of Iranian industrial companies.

THE F I S DIRECTORY OF U K EXPORTERS. see BUSINESS AND ECONOMICS — International Commerce

THE F I S DIRECTORY OF U K IMPORTERS. see BUSINESS AND ECONOMICS — International Commerce

338.025　　　　　UK
F M YEARBOOK. (Facilities Management) 1992. a. £45 (foreign £52) (effective 1997). Faversham House Group Ltd., Faversham House, 232a Addington Rd., South Croydon, Surrey CR2 8LE, England. TEL 44-181-651-7100. FAX 44-181-651-7117. adv. contact: Mark Houghton. **Document type:** directory.
　　Description: Reference guide for buyers and services in the facilities management profession.

FAIRPLAY CONTAINER OPERATORS DIRECTORY (YEAR). see TRANSPORTATION — Ships And Shipping

338　687　　　　　US
FASHION MARKET DIRECTORY. 1986. 7/yr. Fashion Market Directory Group, Ltd., 330 W. 38th St., 15th Fl., New York, NY 10018. TEL 212-760-5100. FAX 212-760-5112. adv. circ. 83,817. **Document type:** directory.
　　Description: Aimed at the trade apparel market in New York; combined with a collection of original photos of apparel items currently offered on the wholesale market. Includes women's, men's and children's ready-to-wear, sportswear and accessories.

382　　　　　US　　　ISSN 1055-2421
HF3491
FAULKNER & GRAY'S EUROPEAN BUSINESS DIRECTORY. 1992. a. $345 (effective 1995). Faulkner & Gray, Inc. (New York), 11 Penn Plaza, 17th Fl., New York, NY 10001. TEL 212-967-7000. FAX 212-967-7155. **Document type:** directory.

338　　　　　　　SA
FAX DIRECTORY OF SOUTHERN AFRICA. a. R.85 (effective 1997). Braby's (Subsidiary of: Kohler Packaging Ltd.), P.O. Box 1426, Pinetown 3600, South Africa. TEL 27-31-7017021. FAX 27-31-7017036. adv. **Document type:** directory.
　　Formerly: Communications (Fax) Directory.

338.025　　　　　US　　　ISSN 1075-7112
HE7771
FAX U S A; a directory of facsimile numbers for business and organizations nationwide. 1993. a. $90. Omnigraphics, Inc., 2500 Penobscot Bldg., Detroit, MI 48226. TEL 313-961-1340; 800-234-1340. FAX 800-875-1340. Ed. Kay Gill; Pub. Frederick G. Ruffner, Jr. R&P contact: Kay Gill. **Document type:** directory.
　　—CISTI.
　　Description: Provides more than 116000 fax numbers for America's largest corporations, educational institutions, organizations and government agencies. Includes complete addresses and telephone numbers.

380.1　　　　　US　　　ISSN 1043-7568
HD9715.25.U6
FEDERAL BUYERS GUIDE.* 1987. 2/yr. $20. Federal Buyers Guide, Inc., Box 22507, Santa Barbara, CA 93121-2507. TEL 805-683-6181. FAX 805-683-8593. Ed. Rick Flores. adv.; bk.rev. circ. 10,128. **Document type:** directory.
　　Description: Assists federal government buyers in locating businesses wanting to contract to the federal government.

660　　　　　BE　　　ISSN 0425-9076
FEDERATION DES INDUSTRIES CHIMIQUES DE BELGIQUE. ANNUAIRE. (Text in Dutch, English, French, German) irreg., latest 1996. 4400 BEF. Federation des Industries Chimiques de Belgique, Square Marie-Louise 49, 1000 Brussels, Belgium. TEL 32-2-2389711. FAX 32-2-2311301. adv. circ. 4,500. **Document type:** directory.
　　Description: Alphabetical list of the members of the Federation of Industries Chimiques de Belgique and index to their products.

382　　　　　　　PK
FEDERATION OF PAKISTAN CHAMBERS OF COMMERCE AND INDUSTRY. DIRECTORY OF EXPORTERS. (Text in English) 1977. a. Rs.150($20) Federation of Pakistan Chambers of Commerce and Industry, St-28, Block 5, Scheme-V, Share-Firdousi Kehkashan, Clifton, Karachi, Pakistan. **Document type:** directory.

FEED INDUSTRY RED BOOK; reference manual for the feed industry. see AGRICULTURE — Feed, Flour And Grain

380　　　　　　　CE
FERGUSON'S SRI LANKA DIRECTORY (YEAR). (Text in English) 1859. biennial. $24. Associated Newspapers of Ceylon Ltd., Lake House, D.R. Wijewardena Mawatha, Colombo 10, Sri Lanka. TEL 94-1-421181. FAX 94-1-449069. TELEX 22262 CE. adv.; stat. circ. 10,000. **Document type:** directory.
　　Formerly: Ferguson's Ceylon Directory.

FIJI CLASSIFICATION & DICTIONARY OF OCCUPATIONS. see BUSINESS AND ECONOMICS — Labor And Industrial Relations

380　778.53　　　US　　　ISSN 1055-081X
ML128.M7
FILM COMPOSERS GUIDE. 1990. a. $50 (effective 1996). Lone Eagle Publishing Co., 2337 Roscomare Rd., No. 9, Los Angeles, CA 90077-1851. TEL 310-471-8066. FAX 310-471-4669. Ed. Vincent Jacquet-Francillon. adv. circ. 2,500. **Document type:** directory.
　　Description: Lists film composers, their motion picture credits, contact information, releasing company and year.

380　778.53　　　US　　　ISSN 0740-2872
PN1998.A2
FILM DIRECTORS: A COMPLETE GUIDE. 1983. a. $65 (effective 1996). Lone Eagle Publishing Co., 2337 Roscomare Rd., No. 9, Los Angeles, CA 90077-1851. TEL 310-471-8066. FAX 310-471-4969. Ed. Michael Singer. adv. circ. 5,000. **Document type:** directory.
　　Description: Lists over 4500 motion picture directors, their credits, contact information, Oscar awards and nominations, and includes interviews. 41,000 film listings.

380　778.53　　　US　　　ISSN 1058-2630
PN1998.A1
FILM PRODUCERS, STUDIOS, AGENTS AND CASTING DIRECTORS GUIDE. 1989. a. $55. Lone Eagle Publishing, 2337 Roscomare Rd., No. 9, Los Angeles, CA 90077-1851. TEL 310-471-8066. FAX 310-471-4969. (Dist. in Europe by: Gazelle Book Services, Falcon Hse. Queen Sq., Lancaster, LA1 1RN, England. TEL 44-52468765) Ed. David Kipen. adv. contact: Jeff Black. circ. 3,000. **Document type:** directory.
　　Formerly (until 1990): Film Producers, Studios and Agents Guide (ISSN 0894-8666)
　　Description: Film industry credit and contact directory. Lists film producers, studios, production companies, casting directors, managers and agents.

380.1　778　　　　　US
FILM WORLD DIRECTORY OF ADULT FILM & VIDEO. a. $10.95 (effective 1997). Knight Publishing Corp., 8060 Melrose Ave., Los Angeles, CA 90046. TEL 213-653-8060. FAX 213-655-9452. **Document type:** directory.

380　778.53　　　US　　　ISSN 0894-864X
PN1996
FILM WRITERS GUIDE. 1989. a. $60. Lone Eagle Publishing Co., 2337 Roscomare Rd., No. 9, Los Angeles, CA 90077-1851. TEL 310-471-8066. FAX 310-471-4969. Ed. Susan Avallone. adv. circ. 3,000. **Document type:** directory.
　　Description: Lists over 7300 screenwriters, their contact information, credits and companies. Includes interviews. Lists 2,000 film titles and listings of unproduced screenplays.

365　　　　　　　UK
FINANCIAL SURVEY. AGRICULTURAL GROWERS & MERCHANTS. LONDON & SOUTH; company data for success. a. I C C Business Publications Ltd., Field House, 72 Oldfield Rd., Hampton, Mddx. TW12 2HQ, England. TEL 44-181-783-0922. FAX 44-181-783-1940. charts; stat. (also avail. in diskette format) **Document type:** trade publication, directory.
　　Formerly (until 1991): Financial Survey Company Directory. Agricultural Growers and Merchants. London and South (ISSN 0952-0015)
　　Description: Contains financial information and contact data for companies in the industry.

630　　　　　　　UK
FINANCIAL SURVEY. AGRICULTURAL GROWERS & MERCHANTS. MIDLANDS & NORTH. a. I C C Business Publications Ltd., Field House, 72 Oldfield Rd., Hampton, Mddx. TW12 2HQ, England. TEL 44-181-783-0922. FAX 44-181-783-1940. charts; stat. (also avail. in diskette format) **Document type:** trade publication, directory.
　　Formerly (until 1991): Financial Survey Company Directory. Agricultural Growers and Merchants. Midlands and North (ISSN 0952-0112)

621.9　　　　　　　UK
FINANCIAL SURVEY. AUTOMATIC VENDING; company data for success. a. I C C Business Publications Ltd., Field House, 72 Oldfield Rd., Hampton, Mddx. TW12 2HQ, England. TEL 44-181-783-0922. FAX 44-181-783-1940. charts; stat. **Document type:** trade publication, directory.
　　Formerly (until 1991): Financial Survey Company Directory. Automatic Vending (ISSN 0952-0163)
　　Description: Contains financial information and contact data.

BUSINESS AND ECONOMICS — TRADE AND INDUSTRIAL DIRECTORIES

664.752   UK
FINANCIAL SURVEY. BAKERY PRODUCTS MANUFACTURERS; company data for success. a. I C C Business Publications Ltd., Field House, 72 Oldfield Rd., Hampton, Mddx. TW12 2HQ, England. TEL 44-181-783-0922. FAX 44-181-783-1940. charts; stat. (also avail. in diskette format) **Document type:** trade publication, directory.
   Formerly (until 1991): Financial Survey Company Directory. Bakery Products Manufacturers (ISSN 0952-0058)

621.9   UK
FINANCIAL SURVEY. BEARING MANUFACTURERS & DISTRIBUTORS; company data for success. a. I C C Business Publications Ltd., Field House, 72 Oldfield Rd., Hampton, Mddx. TW12 2HQ, England. TEL 44-181-783-0922. FAX 44-181-783-1940. charts; stat. (also avail. in diskette format) **Document type:** trade publication.
   Former titles (until 1989): Financial Survey Company Directory. Bearing Manufacturers and Distributors (ISSN 0953-7686); (until 1988): Financial Survey Company Directory. Bearing Manufacturers (ISSN 0952-0007)
   Description: Contains financial information and contact data on companies.

623.82   UK
FINANCIAL SURVEY. BOAT BUILDERS & MARINE ENGINEERS; company data for success. a. I C C Business Publications Ltd., Field House, 72 Oldfield Rd., Hampton, Mddx. TW12 2HQ, England. TEL 44-181-783-0922. FAX 44-181-783-1940. charts; stat. (also avail. in diskette format) **Document type:** trade publication, directory.
   Formerly (until 1990): Financial Survey Company Directory. Boat Builders and Marine Engineers (ISSN 0952-5289)
   Description: Contains financial information and contact data for companies in the industry.

670 658.8   UK   ISSN 1358-8117
FINANCIAL SURVEY. BRICK & TILE MANUFACTURERS AND DISTRIBUTORS. a. I C C Business Publications Ltd., Field House, 72 Oldfield Rd., Hampton, Mddx. TW12 2HQ, England. TEL 44-181-783-0922. FAX 44-181-783-1940. (also avail. in diskette format) **Document type:** directory.
   Former titles (until 1995): I C C Financial Survey. Brick and Tile Manufacturers & Financial Survey Company Directory. Brick and Tile Manufacturers (ISSN 0953-1866)

338.025 609   UK
FINANCIAL SURVEY. BUILDERS MERCHANTS. a. I C C Business Publications Ltd., Field House, 72 Oldfield Rd., Hampton, Mddx. TW12 2HQ, England. TEL 44-181-783-0922. FAX 44-181-783-1940. (diskette format) **Document type:** directory.
   Formed by the merger of: Financial Survey. Builders Merchants. London and South; Which was formerly: Financial Survey Company Directory. Builders Merchants. London and South & Financial Survey. Builders Merchants. Midlands and North; Which was formerly: Financial Survey Company Directory. Builders Merchants. Midlands and North.

338 392.8   UK
FINANCIAL SURVEY. BUILDING CONTRACTORS; company data for success. a. I C C Business Publication Ltd., Field House, 72 Oldfield Rd., Hampton, Mddx. TW12 2HQ, England. TEL 44-181-783-0922. FAX 44-181-783-1940. (also avail. in diskette format) **Document type:** directory.
   Formed by the merger of: Financial Survey. Building Contractors. London and South; Which was formerly: Financial Survey Company Directory. Building Contractors. London and South (ISSN 0952-1356); I C C Financial Survey and Directory. Building Contractors. London and South & Financial Survey. Building Contractors. Midlands and North; Which was formerly: Financial Survey Company Directory. Building Contractors. Midlands and North (ISSN 0952-1348); I C C Financial Survey and Directory. Building Contractors. Midlands and North.

677   UK
FINANCIAL SURVEY. CARPET MANUFACTURERS & WHOLESALE DISTRIBUTORS; company data for success. a. I C C Business Publications Ltd., Field House, 72 Oldfield Rd., Hampton, Mddx. TW12 2HQ, England. TEL 44-181-783-0922. FAX 44-181-783-1940. charts; stat. **Document type:** trade publication, directory.
   Formerly (until 1991): Financial Survey Company Directory. Carpet Manufacturers and Wholesale Distributors (ISSN 0952-0090)
   Description: Contains financial information and contact data.

670 380 664   UK
FINANCIAL SURVEY. CATERING EQUIPMENT MANUFACTURERS AND DISTRIBUTORS; company data for success. 1979. a. I C C Business Publications Ltd., Field House, 72 Oldfield Rd., Hampton, Mddx. TW12 2HQ, England. FAX 44-181-783-1940. (also avail. in diskette format) **Document type:** directory.
   Description: Contains financial information and contact data for companies in the industry.

330   UK
FINANCIAL SURVEY. COMMODITY BROKERS. ENGLAND AND WALES; company data for success. 1978. a. I C C Business Publications Ltd., Field House, 72 Oldfield Rd., Hampton, Mddx. TW12 2HQ, England. TEL 44-181-783-0922. FAX 44-181-783-0940. (also avail. in diskette format) **Document type:** directory.
   Formerly (until 1995): Financial Survey. Commodity and Futures Brokers. England and Wales (ISSN 0261-5819)
   Description: Contains financial information and contact data for companies in the industry.

690   UK
FINANCIAL SURVEY. CONSTRUCTION EQUIPMENT MANUFACTURERS & DISTRIBUTORS; company data for success. a. I C C Business Publications Ltd., Field House, 72 Oldfield Rd., Hampton, Mddx. TW12 2HQ, England. TEL 44-181-783-0922. FAX 44-181-783-1940. charts; stat. (also avail. in diskette format) **Document type:** trade publication, directory.
   Formerly (until 1991): Financial Survey Company Directory. Construction Equipment Manufacturers and Distributors (ISSN 0952-0244)
   Description: Contains financial information and contact data.

620   UK
FINANCIAL SURVEY. DIE & MOLD MANUFACTURERS & DISTRIBUTORS; company data for success. a. I C C Business Publications Ltd., Field House, 72 Oldfield Rd., Hampton, Mddx. TW12 2HQ, England. TEL 44-181-783-0922. FAX 44-181-783-1940. charts; stat. (also avail. in diskette format) **Document type:** trade publication, directory.
   Formerly (until 1990): Financial Survey Company Directory. Die and Mould Manufacturers and Distributors (ISSN 0952-780X)
   Description: Contains financial information and contact data for companies in the industry.

621.3   UK
FINANCIAL SURVEY. ELECTRONIC MANUFACTURERS & DISTRIBUTORS; company data for success. a. I C C Financial Surveys Ltd., Field House, 72 Oldfield Rd., Hampton, Mddx. TW12 2HQ, England. TEL 44-181-783-0922. FAX 44-181-783-1940. charts; stat. (also avail. in diskette format) **Document type:** trade publication, directory.
   Formerly (until 1990): Financial Company Directory. Electronic Manufacturers and Distributors (ISSN 0952-5025)
   Description: Contains financial information and contact data for companies in the industry.

338 639.2   UK   ISSN 1358-7897
FINANCIAL SURVEY. THE FISH INDUSTRY; company data for success. a. I C C Business Publications Ltd., Field House, 72 Oldfield Rd., Hampton, Mddx. TW12 2HQ, England. TEL 44-181-783-0922. FAX 44-181-783-1940. **Document type:** directory.
   Formerly: Financial Survey. Fish Trawling, Processing and Merchanting.

664 380   UK   ISSN 1361-4827
FINANCIAL SURVEY. FOOD PROCESSORS; company data for success. 1995. a. I C C Business Publications Ltd., Field House, 72 Oldfield Rd., Hampton, Mddx. TW12 2HQ, England. TEL 44-181-783-0922. FAX 44-181-783-1940. (also avail. in diskette format) **Document type:** directory.
   Description: Contains financial information and contact data for companies in the industry.

664
FINANCIAL SURVEY. THE FROZEN FOOD INDUSTRY; company data for success. a. I C C Business Publications Ltd., Field House, 72 Oldfield Rd., Hampton, Mddx. TW12 2HQ, England. TEL 44-181-783-0922. FAX 44-181-783-1940. **Document type:** trade publication, directory.
   Former titles (until 1996): Financial Survey. Company Data for Success: Frozen Food Processors, Distributors and Centres (ISSN 0952-9454); (until 1986): I C C Financial Survey and Directory. Frozen Food Processors, Distributors, and Centres.
   Description: Contains financial information and contact data for companies in the industry.

658.8   UK   ISSN 1363-8912
FINANCIAL SURVEY. FRUIT, FLOWER & VEGETABLE MERCHANTS. 1995. a. I C C Business Publications Ltd., Field House, Hampton, Mddx. TW12 2HQ, England. TEL 44-181-783-0977. FAX 44-181-783-1940. charts; stat. (also avail. in diskette format) **Document type:** trade publication, directory.
   Formerly (until 1996): I C C Financial Survey. Fruit, Flower and Vegetable Merchants (ISSN 1363-8661); Which was formed by the 1995 merger of: I C C Financial Survey. Fruit, Flower and Vegetable Merchants. London and South; Which was formerly: Financial Survey Company Directory. Fruit, Flower, and Vegetable Merchants. London and South (ISSN 0953-5896) & I C C Financial Survey. Fruit, Flower, and Vegetable Merchants. Midlands and North; Which was formerly: Financial Survey Company Directory. Fruit, Flower, and Vegetable Merchants. Midlands and North (ISSN 0953-4733)
   Description: Contains financial information and contact data for companies in the industry.

338 658   UK   ISSN 1363-9056
FINANCIAL SURVEY. THE HAND AND SMALL TOOL INDUSTRY. a. I C C Business Publications Ltd., Field House, 72 Oldfield Rd., Hampton, Mddx. TW12 2HQ, England. TEL 44-181-783-0922. FAX 44-181-783-1940. charts; stat.
   Former titles (in 1995): I C C Financial Survey. Hand and Small Tool Industry (ISSN 1359-2629); (until 1994): I C C Financial Survey. Engineers Hand and Small Tool Industry.

674.94   UK
FINANCIAL SURVEY. HOTELS & LEISURE COMPLEXES; company data for success. a. I C C Business Publications Ltd., Field House, 72 Oldfield Rd., Hampton, Mddx. TW12 2HQ, England. TEL 44-181-783-0922. FAX 44-181-783-1940. charts; stat. (also avail. in diskette format) **Document type:** trade publication, directory.
   Formerly (until 1991): Financial Survey Company Directory. Hotels and Leisure Complexes (ISSN 0952-1259)
   Description: Contains financial information and contact data for companies in the industry.

338 332   UK
FINANCIAL SURVEY. INSTALLMENT, CREDIT, AND FINANCE; company data for success. a. I C C Business Publications Ltd., Field House, 72 Oldfield Rd., Hampton, Mddx. TW12 2HQ, England. TEL 44-181-783-0977. FAX 44-181-783-1940. (also avail. in diskette format) **Document type:** directory.
   Formerly: Financial Survey Company Directory. Installment, Credit and Finance (ISSN 0952-7273)
   Description: Contains financial information and contact data for companies in the industry.

338.025 645   UK
FINANCIAL SURVEY. THE LIGHTING EQUIPMENT INDUSTRY. a. I C C Business Publications Ltd., Field House, 72 Oldfield Rd., Hampton, Middlesex TW12 2HQ, England. TEL 44-181-783-0922. FAX 44-181-783-1940. (diskette format) **Document type:** directory.
   Formerly: Financial Survey. Lighting Devices and Systems.
   Description: Contains financial information and contact data for companies in the industry.

B

BUSINESS AND ECONOMICS — TRADE AND INDUSTRIAL DIRECTORIES

636 UK
FINANCIAL SURVEY. MEAT AND POULTRY. SCOTLAND; company data for success. a. I C C Business Publications Ltd., Field House, 72 Oldfield Rd., Hampton, Mddx. TW12 2HQ, England. TEL 44-181-783-0922. FAX 44-181-783-1940. charts; stat. (also avail. in diskette format) **Document type:** trade publication, directory.
Formerly (until 1990): Financial Company Directory. Meat and Poultry. Scotland (ISSN 0952-5017)
Description: Contains financial information and contact data for companies in the industry.

338.025 332.6 UK
FINANCIAL SURVEY. METAL STOCKHOLDERS. 1986. a. I C C Business Publications Ltd., Field House, 72 Oldfield Rd., Hampton, Middlesex TW12 2HQ, England. TEL 44-181-783-0922. FAX 44-181-783-0922. (diskette format) **Document type:** directory.
Formerly: Financial Survey Company Directory. Metal Stockholders (ISSN 0953-4687)
Description: Contains financial information and contact data for companies in the industry.

669 UK
FINANCIAL SURVEY. NON-FERROUS METAL FOUNDERS; company data for success. a. I C C Business Publications Ltd., Field House, 72 Oldfield Rd., Hampton, Mddx. TW12 2HQ, England. TEL 44-181-783-0922. FAX 44-181-783-1940. charts; stat. (also avail. in diskette format) **Document type:** trade publication, directory.
Former titles (until 1986): Financial Survey. Company Data for Success: Metal Founders. Non-Ferrous (ISSN 0952-0120); I C C Financial Survey and Directory: Metal Founders - Non-Ferrous.
Description: Contains financial information and contact data for companies in the industry.

789.56 UK
FINANCIAL SURVEY. PHARMACEUTICAL MANUFACTURERS & DISTRIBUTORS. a. I C C Business Publications Ltd., Field House, 72 Oldfield Rd., Hampton, Mddx. TW12 2HQ, England. TEL 44-181-783-0922. FAX 44-181-783-1940. charts; stat. (also avail. in diskette format) **Document type:** trade publication, directory.
Formerly (until 1991): Financial Survey Company Directory. Pharmaceutical Manufacturers and Distributors (ISSN 0952-4819)
Description: Contains financial information and contact data for companies in the industry.

770 UK
FINANCIAL SURVEY. PHOTOGRAPHIC EQUIPMENT MANUFACTURERS & DISTRIBUTORS; company data for success. a. I C C Business Publications Ltd., Field House, 72 Oldfield Rd., Hampton, Mddx. TW12 2HQ, England. TEL 44-181-783-0922. FAX 44-181-783-1940. charts; stat. (also avail. in diskette format) **Document type:** trade publication, directory.
Formerly (until 1991): Financial Survey Company Directory. Photographic Equipment Manufacturers and Distributors (ISSN 0951-7065)
Description: Contains financial information and contact data for companies in the industry.

690 UK
FINANCIAL SURVEY. PLANT HIRE; company data for success. a. I C C Business Publications Ltd., Field House, 72 Oldfield Rd., Hampton, Mddx. TW12 2HQ, England. TEL 44-181-783-0922. FAX 44-181-783-1940. charts; stat. (also avail. in diskette format) **Document type:** trade publication, directory.
Formed by the 1995 merger of: Financial Survey. Company Data for Success: Plant Hire. London and South; Which was formerly: Financial Survey Company Directory: Plant Hire. London and South (ISSN 0953-1963); Financial Survey. Company Data for Success: Plant Hire. Midlands and North; Which was formerly: Financial Survey Company Directory. Plant Hire. Midlands and North (ISSN 0953-1939)
Description: Contains financial information and contact data for companies in industry.

338.025 686.2 UK ISSN 1363-5409
FINANCIAL SURVEY. PRINTERS. 1996. a. I C C Business Publications Ltd., Field House, 72 Oldfield Rd., Hampton, Mddx. TW12 2HQ, England. TEL 44-181-783-0922. FAX 44-181-783-1940.
Formed by the merger of: Financial Survey. Printers. London and South; Which was formerly (until 1992): Financial Survey Company Directory (ISSN 0959-3187) & Financial Survey. Printers. Midlands and North; Which was formerly (1986-1992): Financial Survey Company Directory. Printers. Midlands and North (ISSN 0953-1769)

659.1 UK
FINANCIAL SURVEY. SIGN & STREET FURNITURE MANUFACTURERS & DISTRIBUTORS; company data for success. a. I C C Business Publications Ltd., Field House, 72 Oldfield Rd., Hampton, Mddx. TW12 2HQ, England. TEL 44-181-783-0922. FAX 44-181-783-1940. charts; stat. (also avail. in diskette format) **Document type:** trade publication, directory.
Formerly (until 1991): Financial Survey Company Directory. Sign and Street Furniture Manufacturers and Distributors (ISSN 0952-0147)
Description: Contains financial information and contact data for companies in the industry.

330.9 658 UK ISSN 1363-8947
FINANCIAL SURVEY. TEXTILE RENTAL, LAUNDERERS AND DRY CLEANERS. a. I C C Business Publications Ltd., Field House, 72 Oldfield Rd., Hampton, Mddx. TW12 2HQ, England. TEL 44-181-783-0922. FAX 44-181-783-1940.
Formerly (until 1995): I C C Financial Survey. Textile Rental, Launderers and Dry Cleaners (ISSN 1363-8696); Which was formed by the 1994 merger of: I C C Financial Survey. Laundry and Textile Rental Industry. London and South & I C C Financial Survey. Laundry and Textile Rental Industry. Midlands and North.

674 UK
FINANCIAL SURVEY. TIMBER MERCHANTS; company data for success. a. I C C Business Publications Ltd., Field House, 72 Oldfield Rd., Hampton, Mddx. TW12 2HQ, England. TEL 44-181-783-0977. FAX 44-181-783-1940. charts; stat. (also avail. in diskette format) **Document type:** trade publication, directory.
Formerly (until 1991): Financial Survey Company Directory. Timber Merchants (ISSN 0953-5934)
Description: Contains financial information and contact data for companies in the industry.

633.71 664.752 UK
FINANCIAL SURVEY. TOBACCO AND CONFECTIONARY WHOLESALERS; company data for success. a. I C C Business Publications Ltd., Field House, 72 Oldfield Rd., Hampton, Mddx. TW12 2HQ, England. TEL 44-181-783-0922. FAX 44-181-783-1940. charts; stat. (also avail. in diskette format) **Document type:** trade publication, directory.
Formerly (until 1991): Financial Survey Company Directory. Tobacco and Confectionary Wholesalers (ISSN 0953-5926)
Description: Contains financial information and contact data for companies in the industry.

668.5 UK
FINANCIAL SURVEY. THE TOILETRIES AND COSMETICS INDUSTRY; company data for success. a. I C C Business Publications, Field House, 72 Oldfield Rd., Hampton, Mddx. TW12 2HQ, England. TEL 44-181-783-0922. FAX 44-181-783-1940. charts; stat. (also avail. in diskette format) **Document type:** trade publication, directory.
Former titles (until 1994): Financial Survey. Company Data for Success: Toiletry and Cosmetic Industry; (until 1991): Financial Survey Company Directory. Toiletry and Cosmetic Manufacturers and Distributors (ISSN 0953-5918)
Description: Contains financial information and contact data for companies in the industry.

384.55 UK
FINANCIAL SURVEY. THE VIDEO AND AUDIO VISUAL INDUSTRY; company data for success. a. I C C Business Publications Ltd., Field House, 72 Oldfield Rd., Hampton, Mddx. TW12 2HQ, England. TEL 44-181-783-0922. FAX 44-181-783-1940. charts; stat. (also avail. in diskette format) **Document type:** trade publication, directory.
Formerly: Financial Survey Company Directory. Audio Visual.
Description: Contains financial information and contact data for companies in the industry.

338.025 660 UK
FINANCIAL TIMES INDUSTRIAL COMPANIES: CHEMICALS. a. Longman Group UK Ltd., Longman House, Burnt Mill, Harlow, Essex CM20 2JE, England. TEL 44-1279-426721. FAX 44-1279-431059. (Subscr. to: Pearson Professional, P.O. Box 77, Fourth Ave., Harlow, Essex CM19 5BQ, England. TEL 44-1279-623924. FAX 44-1279-639609) Ed. Deborah Lyttelton. **Document type:** directory.

FINDEX (YEAR); the worldwide directory of market research reports, studies & surveys. see *BUSINESS AND ECONOMICS — Abstracting, Bibliographies, Statistics*

382 UK
FINDING EXPORT MARKETS. 1988. irreg. £15. Trade Research Publications, 2 Wycliffe Grove, Werrington, Peterborough, Cambs. PE4 5DE, England. TEL 44-1733-573975. FAX 44-1733-328323. Ed. Douglas Tookey. **Document type:** directory.

FIRE DIRECTORY. see *FIRE PREVENTION*

FIRE PROTECTION EQUIPMENT DIRECTORY. see *FIRE PREVENTION*

FIRE RESISTANCE DIRECTORY. see *FIRE PREVENTION*

380 AU
FIRMENBUCH OESTERREICH; mit dem genauen Wortlaut der amtlichen Protokollierung. 1947. a. S.4200 (effective 1996). Jupiter Verlag GmbH, Robertgasse 2, A-1020 Vienna, Austria. **Document type:** directory.
● Also available on CD-ROM.
Formerly: Handelsregister Oesterreich.

338.025 GW ISSN 0428-478X
FIRMENHANDBUCH CHEMISCHE INDUSTRIE. BUNDESREPUBLIK DEUTSCHLAND. 1953. biennial. DM.198 (CD-ROM DM.598). E C O N Verlag GmbH, Postfach 300321, 40403 Duesseldorf, Germany. TEL 49-211-4359746. FAX 49-211-4359781. Ed. Diethelm Krull. R&P contact: Cita Wendt. adv.: B&W page DM.2950, color page DM.4950; trim 180 x 265; adv. contact: Barbara Lampe. circ. 4,500. **Document type:** directory.
● Also available on CD-ROM.
— CISTI.
Description: Handbook of the chemical industry in Germany listing 25,000 products, 2,000 manufacturers, and 1,500 brand names.

FITECH INTERNATIONAL; the international equipment guide for the emergency services. see *FIRE PREVENTION*

THE FITZHUGH DIRECTORY OF INDEPENDENT HEALTHCARE AND LONG TERM CARE. FINANCIAL INFORMATION. see *MEDICAL SCIENCES*

FLIGHT INTERNATIONAL DIRECTORY. PART 1: U K AND IRELAND. see *TRANSPORTATION — Air Transport*

FLIGHT INTERNATIONAL DIRECTORY. PART 2: MAINLAND EUROPE. see *TRANSPORTATION — Air Transport*

FLIGHT INTERNATIONAL DIRECTORY OF BRITISH AVIATION. see *TRANSPORTATION — Air Transport*

FLIGHT INTERNATIONAL DIRECTORY OF EUROPEAN AVIATION. see *TRANSPORTATION — Air Transport*

338 US ISSN 1048-7093
HC107.F6
FLORIDA BUSINESS DIRECTORY. 1989. a. $795 (effective 1997). American Business Directories (Subsidiary of: American Business Information, Inc.), 5711 S. 86th Circle, Box 27347, Omaha, NE 68127. TEL 402-593-4600; 800-555-6124. FAX 402-331-5481. E-mail: jerry.venner@abii.com. index. (also avail. in magnetic tape; diskette format) **Document type:** directory.
● Also available online.
Also available on CD-ROM.
Formed by the 1990 merger of: Tampa and North Florida Business Directory (ISSN 1047-2703) & Miami and South Florida Business Directory (ISSN 1047-1804)
Description: Includes all businesses in the state compiled from the yellow pages and telephone verified. Each listing includes company name, complete address, phone number, name of owner, manager, and employee size and sales volume codes and credit rating codes.

BUSINESS AND ECONOMICS — TRADE AND INDUSTRIAL DIRECTORIES

338 350   US
FLORIDA DIRECTORY. 1991. a. $65. Florida Communications Network, Inc., Box 2099, Gainesville, FL 32602. Ed. John Hotaling; Pub. Jon Mills. circ. 350. **Document type:** directory.
   Description: Lists the state's elected and appointed officials at all levels. Includes demographic and media information for each county including one or more major city.

917.502   US   ISSN 0882-9438
HD9727.F6
FLORIDA MANUFACTURERS REGISTER. a. $143 (diskette and CD-ROM $745) (effective 1997). Manufacturers' News, Inc., 1633 Central St., Evanston, IL 60201. TEL 847-864-7000. FAX 847-332-1100. Ed. Louise M. West. adv.: B&W page $1843; adv. contact: Charles Scherer. illus. (diskette format) **Document type:** directory.
   Description: Profiles 19,950 manufacturers; five different sections list companies by product, alphabetically, by city, by SIC, and by parent company.

532   US
FLUID POWER CERTIFICATION BOARD. CERTIFICATION DIRECTORY; accredited fluid power educational institutions and instructors and certified fluid power mechanics, technicians, specialists and engineers. 1991. a. $100 to non-members (effective 1997). Fluid Power Society, Fluid Power Certification Board, 2433 N. Mayfair Rd., Ste. 111, Milwaukee, WI 53226. TEL 414-257-0910. FAX 414-257-4092. circ. 3,200. **Document type:** directory.

FLUID POWER HANDBOOK & DIRECTORY. see ENGINEERING — Engineering Mechanics And Materials

664 663   US
▼**FOOD AND BEVERAGE MARKETPLACE.** 1996. a. $225. Grey House Publishing, Pocket Knife Sq., Lakeville, CT 06039. TEL 860-435-0868; 800-562-2139. FAX 860-435-0867. **Document type:** directory.

664 338   US
FOOD INDUSTRY DIRECTORY. 1974. a. National Food Distribution Network Inc., Box 4607, Clearwater, FL 34618-4607. circ. 34,000. **Document type:** directory.

338.025 664 688.9   UK
FOOD PACKER INTERNATIONAL DIRECTORY (YEAR). a. £40. Binsted Publications Ltd., Walton House, 90 London Rd., Hook, Hants. GR27 9LF, England. TEL 01256-764180. FAX 01256-766102. Ed. Edward C. Binsted; Pub. Edward C. Binsted. **Document type:** directory.

664   US
FOOD PROCESSING FOOD PROCESSORS' RESOURCE. 1977. a. $59. Putman Publishing Co., 301 E. Erie, Chicago, IL 60611. TEL 312-644-2020. FAX 312-644-7870. Ed. Bob Messenger; Pub. James Powers. R&P contact: Bob Messenger. adv.: B&W page $2710; trim 8 x 10 7/8; adv. contact: James Powers. circ. 66,033. **Document type:** trade publication.

338.025   US
FOODSERVICE GAS EQUIPMENT CATALOG. 1946. biennial, latest 25th ed. $15. C P Publishing, Inc., Box 267, Fond du Lac, WI 54936. TEL 414-923-3700. FAX 414-923-6805. Pub. Colleen A. Phalen. illus. **Document type:** catalog.
   Description: A comprehensive guide to gas foodservice equipment in the industry. Contains over 40 categories of commercial equipment from broilers, fryers and ovens to ranges and water heaters.

382 664   US   ISSN 1062-7324
FOODSERVICE YEARBOOK INTERNATIONAL. 1991. a. $65. Keller International Publishing Corporation, 150 Great Neck Rd., Great Neck, NY 11021. TEL 516-829-9210. FAX 516-829-7265. Ed. Howard Stone. adv. contact: Jennifer Zepnick. circ. 15,700. **Document type:** directory, trade publication.
   Description: Lists products, suppliers, associations, exhibitions, publications and country data.

FOREIGN PRESS ASSOCIATION LIST OF MEMBERS. see PUBLISHING AND BOOK TRADE

671.2   UK   ISSN 0264-5319
FOUNDRY YEAR BOOK AND CASTING BUYERS' DIRECTORY. 1972. a. (issued in December). £114.90 (overseas $173.40) (effective 1997). Argus Business Media Ltd. (Subsidiary of: D M G Exhibitions Group Ltd.), Queensway House, 2 Queensway, Redhill, Surrey RH1 1QS, England. TEL 44-1737-768611. FAX 44-1737-761685. **Indexed:** Copper Abstr. **Document type:** directory, trade publication.
   Formerly (until 1982): Foundry Year Book (ISSN 0306-4212)
   Description: Contains the names, addresses, and telephone and fax numbers of U.K. operators of foundries and forges. Lists suppliers of materials and equipment.

670   FR   ISSN 0759-5689
LA FRANCE DE L'INDUSTRIE ET SES SERVICES. Variant title: Kompass France. (Text in French; classifications and summaries in English, French, German, Spanish) 1923. a. 1820 F. (effective 1997). Kompass France, 66 quai du Marechal Joffre, 92415 Courbevoie Cedex, France. Ed. Bertrand Macabeo; Pub. Bertrand Macabeo. R&P contact: Bertrand Macabeo. adv. contact: Mireille Girault. illus. circ. 10,000. (also avail. in magnetic tape) **Document type:** directory.
   Former titles: Repertoire General de la Production Francaise (ISSN 0337-5714); Annuaire Industriel. Repertoire General de la Production Francaise (ISSN 0075-6652)

338   FR
HF3553
FRANCE TELEXPORT. (Text in English, French, German, Spanish) 1979. a. 900 F.($195) (effective 1996). Librairie du Commerce International, 24 Bd. de l'Hopital, B.P. 438, 75233 Paris Cedex 05, France. TEL 33-1-40-73-34-86. FAX 33-1-43-36-47-98. TELEX 206 811 LICOMIN F. Ed. Gerard Le Coz; Pub. M. Moulet. adv./ circ. 15,000 (paid). **Document type:** directory.
   Formerly (until 1995): Francexport (ISSN 0244-710X)
   Description: Lists 37,000 French firms doing business abroad, classified by the products they export or import.

338   US   ISSN 0318-8752
HF5429.3
FRANCHISE ANNUAL; complete handbook and directory. 1969. a. $39.95 (outside N. America $44.95) (effective 1997). (International Franchise Opportunities) Info Press, Inc., 728 Center St., Box 550, Lewiston, NY 14092-0550. TEL 716-754-4669. FAX 905-688-7728. E-mail: infopress@infonews.com; URL: http://infonews.com/franchise. Ed. Ted Dixon. bk.rev.; index. circ. 15,000. **Document type:** directory.

FRANCO-BRITISH CHAMBER OF COMMERCE AND INDUSTRY. TRADE DIRECTORY. see BUSINESS AND ECONOMICS — Chamber Of Commerce Publications

382   US   ISSN 0071-917X
FRANCO-BRITISH TRADE DIRECTORY. 1883. a. £57. French Chamber of Commerce in Great Britain, 197 Knightsbridge, London SW7, England. Ed. Ms. T. Penketh. circ. 2,000. **Document type:** directory.
   Description: Annual publication of the French Chamber of Commerce, with a directory of members, activities and useful Franco-British information.

380.1 658   CN   ISSN 0071-9277
FRASER'S CANADIAN TRADE DIRECTORY. 1913. a. Can.$110. Maclean-Hunter Ltd., Business Publication Division, Maclean-Hunter Bldg., 777 Bay St., Toronto, ON M5W 1A7, Canada. TEL 416-596-5086. **Document type:** directory.
   —CISTI.

338.025   US
FREE IN AMERICA CATALOG; the First Coast's business guide for free and inexpensive items. 1991. q. free in the U.S. Vaughan Publishing Co., Box 23401, 3478 Fairbanks Rd., Jacksonville, FL 32241. TEL 904-260-9198. FAX 904-260-9198. E-mail: freestuff@aol.com. Ed. Nan Ramey. adv.: B&W page $275; trim 8 x 10 1/2; adv. contact: C.H. Taylor. bk.rev. circ. 20,000. (tabloid format) **Document type:** directory, catalog.
   Formerly: Jaguar.
   Description: Lists Jacksonville-area businesses, hotels, and resorts; contains news pertaining to free and inexpensive consumer items.

380   FR   ISSN 0759-3694
FRENCH COMPANY HANDBOOK; for evaluating key listed French companies. (Text in English) 1981. a. $75. International Business Development (Subsidiary of: International Herald Tribune), 181 av. Charles-de-Gaulle, 92125 Neuilly Cedex, France. TEL 33-1-41439494. FAX 33-1-41439393. (U.S. subscr. to: Reference Press, Inc., 6448 Highway 290 E., Ste. E-104, Austin, TX 78723. TEL 800-486-8666) Ed. Bruce Singer; Pub. Richard McClean. R&P contact: Karen Diot. adv. contact: Patricia Goupy. circ. 15,000. **Document type:** directory.
   Description: Guide to over 130 major French companies, published with the Paris stock exchange. Offers detailed financial, economic and commercial profile of each company, key facts on doing business in France, and the operations of the Paris financial markets.

FROZEN AND CHILLED FOODS YEAR BOOK. see FOOD AND FOOD INDUSTRIES

382   GW   ISSN 0344-0079
FRUCHTHANDEL ADRESSBUCH. (Text in English, French and German) 1962. a. DM.99.50. Dr. Rolf Wolf Verlag GmbH, Postfach 105551, 40046 Duesseldorf, Germany. TEL 49-211-991040. FAX 49-211-663162. Ed. Eva Schmeiss; Pub. Robert Broadfoot. R&P contact: Robert Broadfoot. adv.: B&W page DM.2900, color page DM.5075; trim 125 x 210; adv. contact: Juergen Meier. circ. 2,700 (paid). **Document type:** directory.
   Description: Directory of import and wholesale trade in fruit, vegetables, dried fruit and potatoes in Germany, Austria, Belgium, Switzerland and Eastern Europe.

338.76606   US   ISSN 1063-0341
TP248.17
G E N GUIDES TO BIOTECHNOLOGY COMPANIES. (Genetic Engineering News) a. $280 (foreign $295) (effective 1997). Mary Ann Liebert, Inc. Publishers, 2 Madison Ave., Larchmont, NY 10538. TEL 914-834-3100. FAX 914-834-3688. E-mail: liebert@pipeline.com. adv. (also avail. in diskette format) **Document type:** directory.
   —CISTI.
   Description: Contains business information on biotechnology companies for executives, investors, directors and all biotechnology professionals.

380.1   GM
GAMBIA. CENTRAL STATISTICS DEPARTMENT. DIRECTORY OF ESTABLISHMENTS. (Formerly issued by Central Statistics Division) a. D.8. Central Statistics Department, Wellington St., Banjul, Gambia. **Document type:** government publication, directory.

338.025 790.1   US
GAMING SYSTEMS SOURCE DIRECTORY. 1983. s-a. $10. Gibbs Publishing Company, Box 600927, N. Miami Beach, FL 33160. Ed. James Calvin Gibbs. adv. circ. 200,000. **Document type:** directory.

GAS AND OIL EQUIPMENT DIRECTORY. see HEATING, PLUMBING AND REFRIGERATION

GAS INDUSTRY DIRECTORY (YEAR). see PETROLEUM AND GAS

GAS UTILITY INDUSTRY. see PETROLEUM AND GAS

338   SA
GAUTENG DIRECTORY. a. R.165. Braby's (Subsidiary of: Kohler Packaging Ltd.), P.O. Box 1426, Pinetown 3600, South Africa. TEL 27-31-7017021. FAX 27-31-7017036. adv. (also avail. in diskette format) **Document type:** directory.
   Former titles (until 1995): P W V Directory; (until 1994): Rand - Pretoria Directory; Incorporates: Johannesburg - West Rand Directory; Which was formerly: Braby's Business Directory of Johannesburg.

GAYELLOW PAGES; classified directory of lesbian and gay U S A and Canada organizations and businesses. see HOMOSEXUALITY

BUSINESS AND ECONOMICS — TRADE AND INDUSTRIAL DIRECTORIES

380 301.16   US   ISSN 0097-8175
P88.8
GEBBIE PRESS ALL-IN-ONE DIRECTORY. 1972. a. $95 (effective 1998). Gebbie Press, Box 1000, New Paltz, NY 12561. TEL 914-255-7560. FAX 914-256-1239. Ed. Amalia Gebbie. index. (also avail. in diskette format) **Document type:** directory. **Description:** Lists all public relations outlets in the United States, including daily, weekly, Black and Hispanic newspapers, radio and television stations, general consumer magazines, business papers, trade press, Black press and radio, Hispanic press and radio, farm publications, and news syndicates.

GENERAL MEDICAL COUNCIL. MEDICAL REGISTER. see *MEDICAL SCIENCES*

338.025   UK   ISSN 1354-2818
GENERATION IN EUROPE. irreg. £195. O X E R A Press, Blue Boar Ct., Alfred St., Oxford OX1 4EH, England. TEL 44-1865-251142. FAX 44-1865-201080. **Document type:** directory. **Description:** Up-to-date source of information on the electricity industries in 26 western and eastern European countries.

670   US   ISSN 0743-4502
HD9981.7.C8
GEORGE D. HALL'S CONNECTICUT SERVICE DIRECTORY.* 1984. every 18 mos. $64. George D. Hall Co., Inc., 50 Franklin St., 4th Fl., Boston, MA 02110-1306. TEL 617-523-3745. FAX 708-332-1100. (Dist. by: Manufacturers' News, Inc., 1633 Central St., Evanston, IL 60201-1505. TEL 708-864-7000) (also avail. in magnetic tape; diskette format) **Document type:** directory. **Description:** Provides specific information for more than 9,200 service-oriented businesses; includes alphabetical, geographical and service by SIC sections.

670   US   ISSN 0889-0390
T12
GEORGE D. HALL'S DIRECTORY OF CENTRAL ATLANTIC STATES MANUFACTURERS;* Maryland, Delaware, Virginia, West Virginia, North Carolina, South Carolina. every 18 mos. $83. George D. Hall Co., Inc., 50 Franklin St., 4th Fl., Boston, MA 02110-1306. TEL 617-523-3745. FAX 708-322-1100. (Dist. by: Manufacturers' News, Inc., 1633 Central St., Evanston, IL 60201-1505. TEL 708-864-7000) **Document type:** directory. **Description:** Profiles over 14,000 manufacturers in Maryland, Delaware, Virginia, West Virginia, and North and South Carolina; includes alphabetical, geographical, and product sections.

670 915.5   US   ISSN 0196-8270
HD9727.C8
GEORGE D. HALL'S DIRECTORY OF CONNECTICUT MANUFACTURERS.* every 18 months. $60. George D. Hall Co., Inc., 50 Franklin St., 4th Fl., Boston, MA 02110-1306. TEL 617-523-3745. FAX 708-322-1100. (Dist. by: Manufacturers' News, Inc., 1633 Central St., Evanston, IL 60201. TEL 708-864-7000) **Document type:** directory. **Description:** Profiles over 6,500 manufacturers; includes alphabetical, geographical and product sections.

670   US   ISSN 0149-6913
HD9727.M4
GEORGE D. HALL'S DIRECTORY OF MASSACHUSETTS MANUFACTURERS.* a. $60. George D. Hall Co., Inc., 50 Franklin St., 4th Fl., Boston, MA 02110-1306. TEL 617-523-3745. FAX 708-322-1100. (Dist. by: Manufacturers' News, Inc., 1633 Central St., Evanston, IL 60201-1505. TEL 708-864-7000) **Document type:** directory. **Description:** Profiles over 8,000 manufacturers listed alphabetically, geographically, and by product.

670   US   ISSN 0892-8282
HD9727.N8
GEORGE D. HALL'S DIRECTORY OF NORTH CAROLINA MANUFACTURERS.* irreg., latest 1990. $49. George D. Hall Co., Inc., 50 Franklin St., 4th Fl., Boston, MA 02110-1306. TEL 617-523-3745. FAX 708-322-1100. (Dist. by: Manufacturers' News, Inc., 1633 Central St., Evanston, IL 60201-1505. TEL 708-864-7000) **Document type:** directory. **Description:** Profiles over 5,700 manufacturers; includes alphabetical, geographical and product sections.

670   US   ISSN 0196-7185
HD9981.7.M4
GEORGE D. HALL'S MASSACHUSETTS SERVICE DIRECTORY.* a. $68. George D. Hall Co., Inc., 50 Franklin St., 4th Fl., Boston, MA 02110-1306. TEL 617-523-3745. FAX 708-322-1100. (Dist. by: Manufacturers' News, Inc., 1633 Central St., Evanston, IL 60201-1505. TEL 708-864-7000) **Document type:** directory. **Description:** Provides information on about 11,800 service-oriented companies; includes alphabetical, geographical and service by SIC sections.

670   US   ISSN 0278-9124
HD9727.N5
GEORGE D. HALL'S NEW JERSEY MANUFACTURERS DIRECTORY.* biennial. $74. George D. Hall Co., Inc., 50 Franklin St., 4th Fl., Boston, MA 02110-1306. TEL 617-523-3745. FAX 708-322-1100. (Dist. by: Manufacturers' News, Inc., 1633 Central St., Evanston, IL 60201-1505. TEL 708-864-7000) **Document type:** directory. **Description:** Profiles over 11,400 manufacturers arranged alphabetically, geographically and by product sections.

670   US   ISSN 0272-1074
HD9727.N7
GEORGE D. HALL'S NEW YORK MANUFACTURERS DIRECTORY.* 1980. biennial. $74. George D. Hall Co., Inc., 50 Franklin St., 4th Fl., Boston, MA 02110-1306. TEL 617-523-3745. FAX 708-322-1100. (Dist. by: Manufacturers' News, Inc., 1633 Central St., Evanston, IL 60201-1505. TEL 708-864-7000) **Document type:** directory. **Description:** Provides information on over 14,000 manufacturers; includes alphabetical, geographical, and product sections.

338   US   ISSN 1048-7220
HF5065.G4
GEORGIA BUSINESS DIRECTORY. 1988. a. $425 (effective 1997). American Business Directories (Subsidiary of: American Business Information, Inc.), 5711 S. 86th Circle, Box 27347, Omaha, NE 68127. TEL 402-593-4600; 800-555-6124. FAX 402-331-5481. E-mail: jerry.venner@abii.com. index. (also avail. in magnetic tape; diskette format) **Document type:** directory.
●Also available online.
Also available on CD-ROM.
Description: Includes all businesses in the state compiled from the yellow pages and telephone-verified. Each listing includes company name, complete address, phone number, name of owner, manager, and employee size and sales volume codes and credit rating codes.

670   US   ISSN 0896-4009
HD9727.G4
GEORGIA MANUFACTURERS REGISTER. a. $103 (diskette and CD-ROM $545) (effective 1997). Manufacturers' News, Inc., 1633 Central St., Evanston, IL 60201. TEL 847-864-7000. FAX 847-332-1100. Ed. Louise M. West. adv. contact: Charles Scherer. (diskette format) **Document type:** directory. **Description:** Profiles 10,388 manufacturers listed in product, alphabetical, geographical, SIC and computer brand sections.

330   US   ISSN 0435-5482
HC107.G4
GEORGIA MANUFACTURING DIRECTORY. a. $55. Department of Industry, Trade and Tourism, Marquis II Tower, Ste. 1100, 285 Peachtree Center Ave., Box 1776, Atlanta, GA 30301. TEL 404-656-3607. FAX 404-656-3567. TELEX 211988 GAINTL ATL. Ed. Deborah Battle. circ. 3,500. **Document type:** directory.

GERMAN-THAI CHAMBER OF COMMERCE HANDBOOK AND DIRECTORY. see *BUSINESS AND ECONOMICS — Chamber Of Commerce Publications*

338.025   GW
GERMANY'S TOP 500. (Text in English) a. newsstand price: DM.195. Frankfurter Allgemeine Zeitung GmbH, Information Services, Hellerhofstr. 2-4, 60327 Frankfurt a.M., Germany. TEL 49-69-75912219. FAX 49-69-75912188. (Dist. in U.S. and Canada by: European Business Publications, Inc., Box 891, Darien, CT 06820. TEL 203-656-2701. FAX 203-655-8332) (also avail. in diskette format) **Document type:** directory.
●Also available online.
Formerly: Germany's Top 300.
Description: Provides detailed information on Germany's leading companies, insurers and banks.

GHANA NATIONAL CHAMBER OF COMMERCE. BUSINESS DIRECTORY. see *BUSINESS AND ECONOMICS — Chamber Of Commerce Publications*

670   UK
GLASS AGE DIRECTORY. 1986. a. £36.50. Spotlight Publications Ltd., Ludgate House, 245 Blackfriars Rd., London SE1 9UR, England. TEL 071-620-3636. FAX 071-401-8036. Ed. Peter Butler. adv. contact: Debbie Sheppard. circ. 8,000. (back issues avail., reprint service avail.) **Document type:** directory.

666.1 380   US   ISSN 1057-5405
TP847
GLASS FACTORY DIRECTORY OF NORTH AMERICA AND U.S. INDUSTRY FACTBOOK. 1884. a. $25 (effective through 1998). (National Glass Budget) L J V, Inc., Box 2267, Hempstead, NY 11551-2267. TEL 516-481-2188. Ed. Liz Scott. adv.; charts; illus.; mkt. circ. 1,650. (also avail. in diskette format) **Indexed:** Chem.Abstr., PROMT. **Document type:** directory.
—Linda Hall; UMI.
Former titles: Glass News Directory; Glass News (ISSN 0890-3743); (until 1985): National Glass Budget (ISSN 0027-9390).
Description: Lists glass factories in the US, Canada, and Mexico, with information on personnel, equipment, and product lines.

GOLDEN STATES FINANCIAL DIRECTORY. see *BUSINESS AND ECONOMICS — Banking And Finance*

338   SA
GOLDFIELDS BUYER'S GUIDE. (Text in Afrikaans, English) 1993. a. R.20. Braby's (Subsidiary of: Kohler Packaging Ltd.), P.O. Box 1426, Pinetown 3600, South Africa. TEL 27-31-7017021. FAX 27-31-7017036. adv.; illus.; maps. **Document type:** directory.
Formerly: Free State Goldfields Development Region Buyer's Guide.

GOLF COURSE BUILDERS ASSOCIATION OF AMERICA. DIRECTORY. see *BUILDING AND CONSTRUCTION*

380.1 363.6   AT   ISSN 0728-0874
GOVERNMENT EQUIPMENT NEWS. 1981. m. Aus.$88($120) (effective 1996). Reed Business Publishing Pty. Ltd. (Subsidiary of: Reed International PLC), P.O. Box 5487, W. Chatswood, N.S.W. 2057, Australia. TEL 61-2-372-5222. FAX 61-2-419-7399. circ. 11,096.
Description: Provides independent, up-to-date information on new products, news and technolgoy.

338 658.8   US
HD3861.U6
GOVERNMENT PRIME CONTRACTORS DIRECTORY. 1966. a. $15. Government Data Publications, Inc., 1155 Connecticut Ave., N.W., Washington, DC 20036. Ed. Siegfried Lobel. **Document type:** directory.
Former titles: Government Production Prime Contractors Directory (ISSN 0887-4107); Directory of Government Production Prime Contractors (ISSN 0070-5594).

GRAPHIC ARTISTS GUILD. DIRECTORY OF ILLUSTRATIONS. see *ART*

GREAT BRITAIN. GOVERNMENT OPPORTUNITIES. see *PUBLIC ADMINISTRATION*

GREAT BRITAIN. MINISTRY OF DEFENCE. WORKS SERVICES OPPORTUNITIES. see *PUBLIC ADMINISTRATION*

GREAT YARMOUTH PORT AND INDUSTRY HANDBOOK. see *TRANSPORTATION — Ships And Shipping*

BUSINESS AND ECONOMICS — TRADE AND INDUSTRIAL DIRECTORIES

338 US
GREATER BATON ROUGE MANUFACTURERS DIRECTORY. biennial. $25. Greater Baton Rouge Chamber of Commerce, 564 Laurel St., Box 3217, Baton Rouge, LA 70821. TEL 504-381-7125. Ed.Bd. circ. 5,000. **Document type:** directory.

670 US
GREATER BUFFALO PARTNERSHIP MEMBERSHIP DIRECTORY. a. $75. Greater Buffalo Partnership, 300 Main Place Tower, Buffalo, NY 14202-3797. TEL 716-852-7100. URL: http://www.gbpartnership.org. Ed. Julie Hazzan; Pub. Andrew J. Rudnick. circ. 6,000. (also avail. in diskette format) **Document type:** directory.
Former titles: Greater Buffalo Business Directory & Western New York Business Directory; Western New York Buyer's Guide and Roster; Directory-Metropolitan Buffalo; Buffalo Area Chamber of Commerce Buyer's Guide.

330 US
GREATER ORLANDO CHAMBER OF COMMERCE MEMBERSHIP DIRECTORY. a. $15. Greater Orlando Chamber of Commerce, Box 1234, Orlando, FL 32802. TEL 407-425-1234. FAX 407-839-5020.

380 US
GREATER WASHINGTON - MARYLAND SERVICE STATION AND AUTOMOTIVE REPAIR ASSOCIATION. MEMBERSHIP DIRECTORY & BUYER'S GUIDE. 1985. a. Greater Washington - Maryland Service Station and Automotive Repair Association, 9420 Annapolis Rd., Ste. 307, Lanham, MD 20706-3021. TEL 301-577-2875. circ. 7,000. **Document type:** directory.

631 US
GREEN MARKETS WORLD DIRECTORY OF THE FERTILIZER INDUSTRY. a. $135 (foreign $150) (effective 1995). Pike & Fischer, Inc., 4600 East-West Hwy., Ste. 200, Bethesda, MD 20814. TEL 301-654-6262. FAX 301-654-6297. **Document type:** directory.
Description: Comprehensive information for purchasing or marketing fertilizer worldwide, including names and addresses of organizations, management personnel, production capacities, fertilizer and related products produced and purchased.

338 370 US
GREEN PAGES; California's school business directory. 1991. s-a. free to qualified personnel. Murdoch, Walrath & Holmes, 1130 K St., Ste. 210, Sacramento, CA 95814. TEL 916-441-3883. Ed. Laura Mastrangelo. adv.; circ. 6,000 (controlled).

380 DK ISSN 0901-6201
HC351
GREENS; haandbogen om dansk erhvervsliv. 1884. a. DKK 3840 (effective 1997). Forlaget Boersen A-S, Moentergade 19, 1140 Copenhagen K, Denmark, Denmark. circ. 3,000.

GROCERY STORES DIRECTORIES. see BUSINESS AND ECONOMICS — Domestic Commerce

338 GW
DAS GROSSE EINKAUFS 1X1 DER DEUTSCHEN WIRTSCHAFT. a. (3 vols.). DM.148 (effective 1997). Deutscher Adressbuch Verlag, Arheilger Weg 17, 64380 Rossdorf, Germany. TEL 49-6154-69950-0. FAX 49-6154-6995490. E-mail: einkaufs1x1@t-online.de; URL: http://www.einkaufs1x1.de. circ. 75,000 (paid). **Document type:** directory.
●Also available on CD-ROM.

338.025 GW
DIE GROSSEN 500. 1976. m. DM.298. Luchterhand Verlag, Heddesdorferstr. 31, 56564 Neuwied, Germany. TEL 49-2631-801-0. FAX 49-2631-801210. Ed. Ernst Schmacke. (looseleaf format; also avail. in diskette format) **Document type:** directory.

338.025 GW
GROSSUNTERNEHMEN DER TSCHECHISCHEN REPUBLIK. (Text in English, German) 1994. a. DM.335 (effective 1997). Verlag Hoppenstedt GmbH, Havelstr. 9, 64295 Darmstadt, Germany. TEL 49-6151-380-0. FAX 49-6151-380360. **Document type:** directory.
Description: Provides information on 8,000 major companies in the Czech Republic.

338 UK ISSN 0959-9959
TA715
GROUND ENGINEERING YEARBOOK. 1990. a. £62.50 (foreign £79) (effective 1996). Thomas Telford Ltd., 1 Heron Quay, London E14 4JD, England. TEL 44-171-987-6999. FAX 44-171-538-4101. TELEX 289105-CIVILS-G. Ed. David Sanders. R&P contact: Peter Bealing. adv. contact: Mark Ostrowski. **Document type:** directory.
—BLDSC (4219.210000).
Description: Directory of addresses and information on suppliers of materials and machinery for geotechnical engineering, addresses for major contractors and geotechnical engineers, mainly UK and Europe.

382 CK
GUIA DE COMERCIO EXTERIOR EXPORTADORES/GUIDE TO FOREIGN TRADE EXPORTERS. biennial. (Analdex) Publicar S.A., Av. 68 No. 75A-50, piso 2, A.A. 8010, Bogota, Colombia. TEL 222-55-55. FAX 225-15-45. **Document type:** directory.

070.5 SP
GUIA DE LA DISTRIBUCION EN ESPANA; libros y publicaciones. 1981. a. $40. Federacion de Asociaciones Nacionales de Distribuidores de Ediciones, Santiago Rusinol 8, 28040 Madrid, Spain. TEL 533-51-49. adv. **Document type:** directory.

GUIA DE LA INDUSTRIA ALIMENTARIA/MEXICAN FOOD & FEED INDUSTRY GUIDE. see FOOD AND FOOD INDUSTRIES

GUIA DE LA INDUSTRIA: EQUIPO Y APARATOS/PLANT AND LABORATORY EQUIPMENT GUIDE; para laboratorios y plantas. see MACHINERY

GUIA DE LA INDUSTRIA QUIMICA/MEXICAN CHEMICAL INDUSTRY GUIDE; productos quimicos-chemicals. see ENGINEERING — Chemical Engineering

380 PY
GUIA DE LA INDUSTRIA: REPUBLICA DEL PARAGUAY. irreg., no.2, 1983. Editora Guia de la Industria, Alberdi 454, 1 piso, Of. 10, Edif. Cardinal, Asuncion, Paraguay.

GUIA DEL ENVASE Y EMBALAJE/CONTAINER AND PACKAGING GUIDE. see PACKAGING

GUIA DOS EDITORES ASOCIADOS. see PUBLISHING AND BOOK TRADE

380.1 666 SP
GUIA GENERAL DE LAS INDUSTRIAS CERAMICAS Y AFINES DE ESPANA. a. L.33000 (effective 1996). Faenza Editrice Iberica S.L., C. San Vicente 62, entlo., 12001 Castellon, Spain. TEL 34-64-216570. FAX 34-64-241010. adv.: B&W page L.2050000, color page L.227000. **Document type:** directory.
Formerly: Guia General de las Industrias Azulejeras y Auxiliares de Espana.

670 MX
GUIA INDUSTRIAL MEXICANA. 1967. s-a. Augustan Melgar, No. 44-5, Condesa, 06140 Mexico DF, Mexico. Ed. Jose Flores Sedano. circ. 10,000. **Document type:** directory.

387 VE ISSN 1315-5792
GUIA MARITIMA, PORTUARIA Y DE LA INDUSTRIA NAVAL DE VENEZUELA/MARITIME, PORT AND NAVAL INDUSTRY GUIDE OF VENEZUELA. (Text in English, Spanish) a. Bs.10000 (effective 1998). Urbanizacion Vista Alegre, Calle 11, Quinta Maria Teresa, Caracas, Venezuela. TEL 58-02-4724885. FAX 58-02-4723711. E-mail: ajguzman@etheron.net. Ed. Perdo J. Guzman Quevedo. adv.: B&W page Bs.150000, color page Bs.400000; adv. contact: Enrique Andreiny Guzman. **Document type:** directory.
Formerly: Derrotero de los Puertos y Costas de Venezuela.

380 PE
▼**GUIA VERDE INDUSTRIAL Y COMERCIAL.** vol.53, 1994. a. Sirob Ediciones, Av. Del Parque Norte 299, Of.02, 3o, Urb. Corpac, San Isidro, Lima, Peru. TEL 51-14-422980.

659.1 IT
GUIDA AGENZIE. 1990. a. L.90000. Marketing Finanza Italia s.r.l., Via Stradella 3, 20129 Milan, Italy. TEL 2-29-40-05-54. FAX 2-29-40-18-16. Ed. Lillo Perri. circ. 4,500. **Document type:** directory.

350 IT
GUIDA AGLI ACQUISTI PER GLI ENTI PUBBLICI. 1991. a. L.60000. Kompass Italia, Via Privata Filippa 14, 10139 Turin, Italy. TEL 39-11-797404. FAX 39-11-797464. (Subscr. to: Kompass Italia, Via S. Rita da Cascia 33, 20143 Milan, Italy) **Document type:** directory.

382 IT ISSN 0391-8246
GUIDA DELLE REGIONI D'ITALIA. 1971. a. L.240000 (effective 1997). SEAT, Via Saffi 18, 10138 Turin, Italy. TEL 39-6-855691. FAX 39-6-85569817. Ed. Filiberto Dani. adv. contact: Dina Drago. circ. 10,000. **Document type:** directory.
●Also available on CD-ROM.

658.8 IT
GUIDA MARKETING. 1990. a. L.90000. Marketing Finanza Italia s.r.l., Via Stradella 3, 20129 Milan, Italy. TEL 2-29-40-05-54. FAX 2-29-40-18-16. Ed. Lillo Perri. circ. 4,500. **Document type:** directory.

338.0961 TI ISSN 0330-9290
GUIDE ECONOMIQUE DE LA TUNISIE. 1976. a. $150. Societe I E A, 16 rue de Rome, 1015 Tunis, Tunisia. FAX 216-1-353172. illus. **Document type:** directory.
Description: Covers all aspects of the Tunisian economy, including government ministries, commercial legislation, the banking system, and detailed information on more than 8,000 Tunisian companies.

674 US
GUIDE FOR BUYERS OF QUALITY HARDWOODS.* 1960. a. free. Hardwood Manufacturers Association, 400 Penn Center Blvd., Ste. 530, Pittsburgh, PA 15235-5605. Ed. Susan M. Regan. circ. 10,000.

380 668.55 FR
GUIDE INTERNATIONAL DE LA PARFUMERIE/GENERAL DIRECTORY OF THE PERFUME AND COSMETIC INDUSTRY. (Text in English, French) 1948. biennial. 390 F. Editions Publi-Guid, 195 Quai de la Gourdine, 77400 Lagny, France. FAX 33-1-64-02-48-81. Ed. Gilbert Hieblot. adv.; index in English and French. circ. 3,000. **Document type:** directory.
Formerly: Guide de la Parfumerie (ISSN 0072-7989)

GUIDE OF CONSUMER GOODS IN GREECE. see BUSINESS AND ECONOMICS — Marketing And Purchasing

GUIDE TO AMERICAN EDUCATIONAL DIRECTORIES. see EDUCATION — Abstracting, Bibliographies, Statistics

GUIDE TO AMERICAN SCIENTIFIC AND TECHNICAL DIRECTORIES. see TECHNOLOGY: COMPREHENSIVE WORKS — Abstracting, Bibliographies, Statistics

GUIDE TO ELECTRONICS INDUSTRY IN INDIA. see ELECTRONICS

THE GUIDE TO EUROPEAN BUSINESS MEDIA. see ADVERTISING AND PUBLIC RELATIONS

GUIDE TO EUROPEAN PRODUCERS OF POLYURETHANE PAINTS & COATINGS. see PAINTS AND PROTECTIVE COATINGS

338 MK
GUIDE TO INDUSTRY (SULTANATE OF OMAN). (Text in English) 1989. a. $30. Apex Publishing, P.O. Box 2616, Ruwi 112, Muscat, Sultanate of Oman. TEL 968-799388. FAX 968-793316. Ed. Anju Visen Singh; Pub. Saleh M. Talib. adv. circ. 20,000. **Document type:** directory.
Description: Covers the expanding manufacturing sector in Oman.

380 US
GUIDE TO KEY BRITISH ENTERPRISES I AND II. a. Dun's Marketing Services (Subsidiary of: Dun & Bradstreet, Inc.), 3 Sylvan Way, Parsippany, NJ 07054-3896. TEL 201-455-0900. (And: 26-32 Clifton St., London EC2P 2LY, England) **Document type:** directory.
Formerly: British Middle Market Directory (ISSN 0068-2268)

BUSINESS AND ECONOMICS — TRADE AND INDUSTRIAL DIRECTORIES

332   CN   ISSN 0827-0864
HG2701
GUIDE TO THE CANADIAN FINANCIAL SERVICES INDUSTRY. a. Can.$349.95. Globe Information Services, 444 Front St. W., Toronto, ON M5V 2S9, Canada. TEL 416-585-5250. FAX 416-585-5249. Ed. Alan Husdal; Pub. Michael J. Ryan. **Document type:** directory.
●Also available online.
   Description: Provides essential facts and figures on over 900 financial services industries.

338   UK
GUIDEBOOK TO THE EUROPEAN ADHESIVES INDUSTRY. 1981. irreg., latest Jan. 1994. £250. I A L Consultants, 109 Uxbridge Rd., Ealing, London W5 5TL, England. TEL 44-181-810-0919. FAX 44-181-566-4931. **Document type:** directory.
   Formerly: Adhesives Euro-Guide.

GUIDEBOOK TO THE EUROPEAN PRINTING INKS INDUSTRY. see *PRINTING*

658.8 380   FR
GUIDOR. (Guide Annuaire Officiel du Complexe de Rungis) a. Compagnie de Documentation, 1 rue Ambroise Thomas, 75009 Paris, France. TEL 45-23-07-40. charts. **Document type:** directory.

338.025 665.5   US   ISSN 0739-3547
HD9567.A13
GULF COAST OIL DIRECTORY. 1952. a. $65. I.E.I. Publishing Division, 1635 W. Alabama, Houston, TX 77006-4196. TEL 713-529-1616. FAX 713-529-0936. Ed. Janis Johnson; Pub. Shawn Wymes. adv. contact: Rob Garza. circ. 9,500. (also avail. in diskette format; back issues avail.) **Document type:** directory.
   Description: Contains listings of oil related companies within the 5 state Gulf Coast area, plus listings of PEMEX offices and personnel within Mexico.

338   BA
GULF DIRECTORY. 1977. a. 15 din.($85) Tele-Gulf Directory Publications W L L, Bahrain Tower, 3rd Fl., P.O. Box 2378, Manama, Bahrain. TEL 973-213301. FAX 973-210503. adv.: B&W page $3928, color page $6955; trim 220 x 290; adv. contact: Hazel Irving. circ. 30,000. **Document type:** directory.
   Formerly: Gulf Telephone Directory.
   Description: Reference for businesses in the Gulf region, covering virtually every commercial, industrial, and service company in the six gulf states, including importers and manufacturers agents, and other commercial data.

382   US   ISSN 1056-3105
HG4235.53.Z65
GULF RECONSTRUCTION BUSINESS GUIDE. 1990. bi-m. MacQueen & Associates, 4944 Platt Springs Rd., W. Colombia, SC 29170.

382   UK
GUYANA TRADE DIRECTORY. 1981. a. £1. Arthur H. Thrower Ltd., 44-46 S. Ealing Rd., London W5, England. **Document type:** directory.

H I D A MANUFACTURERS DIRECTORY. (Health Industry Distributors Association) see *MEDICAL SCIENCES*

338.025 332 332.6   UK
HAMBROS DEALERS DIRECTORY (YEAR); foreign exchange treasury and bullion. Hambros, 41 Tower Hill, London EC3N 4HA, England. TEL 44-171-865-1676. FAX 44-171-265-0800. Ed. Margaret Wood. adv. **Document type:** directory.
   Description: Banks whose names appear in the directory are reasonably active in quoting two way prices in the international foreign exchange market, the deposit market, or both; their dealers are members of the Association Cambiste Internationale.

HANDBOOK OF LIVE ANIMAL TRANSPORT. see *TRANSPORTATION — Abstracting, Bibliographies, Statistics*

HANDBUCH FUER DAS GESUNDHEITSWESEN IN SCHLESWIG-HOLSTEIN. see *MEDICAL SCIENCES*

683 670   US
HARDWARE AGE "WHO MAKES IT" BUYERS' GUIDE. 1922. a. $25 included in subscr. to Hardware Age. Chilton Co., Chilton Way, Radnor, PA 19089. TEL 215-964-4269. Ed. Debra Hoover. adv.; tr.lit.; circ. controlled. (reprint service avail. from UMI) **Document type:** directory.
   Formerly: Hardware Age "Who Makes It" Directory.

380.1   US
HARDWARE AGE WHO'S WHO; verified directory of hardlines distributors. 1925. biennial. $195. Chilton Co., 1 Chilton Way, Radnor, PA 19089. TEL 215-964-4269. Ed. Debra Hoover. **Document type:** directory.

HARPERS GUIDE TO SPORTS TRADE. see *SPORTS AND GAMES*

338   US   ISSN 1080-2614
▼**HARRIS CONNECTICUT MANUFACTURERS DIRECTORY.** 1995. a. $65 (diskette & CD-ROM $349) (effective 1998). Harris InfoSource International, 2057-2 Aurora Rd., Twinsburg, OH 44087. TEL 216-425-9000; 800-888-5900. FAX 800-643-5997. E-mail: catknapp@aol.com. Ed. Frances L. Carlsen. (also avail. in diskette format) **Document type:** directory.
●Also available on CD-ROM.

338   US   ISSN 1080-2592
▼**HARRIS DELAWARE MANUFACTURERS DIRECTORY.** 1995. a. $29 (diskette & CD-ROM $149) (effective 1998). Harris InfoSource International, 2057-2 Aurora Rd., Twinsburg, OH 44087. TEL 216-425-9000; 800-888-5900. FAX 216-425-7150. E-mail: catknapp@aol.com. Ed. Frances L. Carlsen. (also avail. in diskette format) **Document type:** directory.
●Also available on CD-ROM.

338   US   ISSN 1065-4755
HARRIS GEORGIA MANUFACTURERS DIRECTORY. 1994. a. $89 (diskette & CD-ROM $395) (effective 1998). Harris InfoSource International, 2057-2 Aurora Rd., Twinsburg, OH 44087. TEL 216-425-9000; 800-888-5900. FAX 800-643-5997. E-mail: catknapp@aol.com. Ed. Frances L. Carlsen. (also avail. in diskette format) **Document type:** directory.
●Also available on CD-ROM.

380.1   US   ISSN 0734-3256
HD9727.I3
HARRIS ILLINOIS INDUSTRIAL DIRECTORY (YEAR). a. $154 (diskette & CD-ROM $695) (effective 1998). Harris InfoSource International, 2057-2 Aurora Rd., Twinsburg, OH 44087. TEL 216-425-9000; 800-888-5900. FAX 216-425-7150. E-mail: catknapp@aol.com. (also avail. in diskette format) **Document type:** directory.
●Also available on CD-ROM.

338 670   US   ISSN 0888-8175
T12
HARRIS INDIANA INDUSTRIAL DIRECTORY (YEAR). 1924. a. $99 (diskette & CD-ROM $549) (effective 1998). Harris InfoSource International, 2057-2 Aurora Rd., Twinsburg, OH 44087. TEL 216-425-9000; 800-888-5900. FAX 216-425-7150. E-mail: catknapp@aol.com. Ed. Frances L. Carlsen. (also avail. in diskette format) **Document type:** directory.
●Also available on CD-ROM.
   Former titles (until 1984): Harris Indiana Marketers Industrial Directory; Indiana Industrial Directory (ISSN 0073-6910)

380.1   US   ISSN 0887-4255
HD9727.K4
HARRIS KENTUCKY INDUSTRIAL DIRECTORY (YEAR). a. $76 (diskette & CD-ROM $325) (effective 1998). Harris InfoSource International, 2057-2 Aurora Rd., Twinsburg, OH 44087. TEL 216-425-9000; 800-888-5900. FAX 216-425-7150. E-mail: catknapp@aol.com. (also avail. in diskette format) **Document type:** directory.
●Also available on CD-ROM.

670   US   ISSN 1065-7231
HF5065.M25
HARRIS MARYLAND MANUFACTURERS DIRECTORY (YEAR). 1963. a. $65 (diskette & CD-ROM $325) (effective 1998). (Department of Economic and Employment Development) Harris InfoSource International, 2057-2 Aurora Rd., Twinsburg, OH 44087. TEL 216-425-9000; 800-888-5900. FAX 216-425-7150. E-mail: catknapp@aol.com. (also avail. in diskette format) **Document type:** directory.
   Former titles (until 1993): Harris Maryland Industrial Directory (ISSN 1055-5617); (until 1990): Maryland Manufacturers Directory (ISSN 1050-2718); (until 1989): Directory, Maryland Manufacturers (ISSN 0070 5802)

338   US   ISSN 1078-6341
HF5065.M3
▼**HARRIS MASSACHUSETTS MANUFACTURERS DIRECTORY.** 1995. a. $70 (diskette & CD-ROM $395) (effective 1998). Harris InfoSource International, 2057-2 Aurora Rd., Twinsburg, OH 44087. TEL 216-425-9000; 800-888-5900. FAX 216-425-7150. E-mail: catknapp@aol.com. Ed. Frances L. Carlsen. (also avail. in diskette format) **Document type:** directory.
●Also available on CD-ROM.

338.4   US   ISSN 0888-8167
HD9727.M5
HARRIS MICHIGAN INDUSTRIAL DIRECTORY (YEAR). 1974. a. $149 (diskette & CD-ROM $695) (effective 1998). InfoSource International, 2057-2 Aurora Rd., Twinsburg, OH 44087. TEL 216-425-9000; 800-888-5900. FAX 216-425-7150. E-mail: catknapp@aol.com. (also avail. in diskette format) **Document type:** directory.
●Also available on CD-ROM.
   Former titles: Harris Michigan Marketers Industrial Directory; Harris Michigan Manufacturers Industrial Directory (ISSN 0363-1869)

338   US   ISSN 0895-2469
T12
HARRIS MISSOURI DIRECTORY OF MANUFACTURERS. 1947. a. $99 (diskette & CD-ROM $549) (effective 1998). Harris InfoSource International, 2057-2 Aurora Rd., Twinsburg, OH 44087. TEL 216-425-9000; 800-888-5900. FAX 216-425-7150. E-mail: catknapp@aol.com. (also avail. in diskette format) **Document type:** directory.
●Also available on CD-ROM.
   Formerly: Missouri Directory of Manufacturing and Mining (ISSN 0076-9584)

338 917.3   US   ISSN 1061-2076
HARRIS NATIONAL MANUFACTURERS DIRECTORY (YEAR). a. $495 (diskette & CD-ROM $3900) (effective 1998). Harris InfoSource International, 2057 Aurora Rd., Twinsburg, OH 44087. TEL 216-425-9000; 800-888-5900. FAX 216-425-7150. E-mail: catknapp@aol.com. Ed. Frances L. Carlsen. (also avail. in diskette format) **Document type:** directory.
●Also available on CD-ROM.

338 917.3   US   ISSN 1061-2025
HF5047
HARRIS NATIONAL MANUFACTURERS DIRECTORY MIDWEST EDITION (YEAR). a. $205 (diskette & CD-ROM $1695) (effective 1998). Harris InfoSource International, 2057-2 Aurora Rd., Twinsburg, OH 44087. TEL 216-425-9000; 800-888-5900. FAX 216-425-7150. E-mail: catknapp@aol.com. (also avail. in diskette format) **Document type:** directory.
●Also available on CD-ROM.

338 917.4   US   ISSN 1061-2041
HF5041
HARRIS NATIONAL MANUFACTURERS DIRECTORY NORTHEAST EDITION (YEAR). a. $205 (diskette & CD-ROM $1295) (effective 1998). Harris InfoSource International, 2057-2 Aurora Rd., Twinsburg, OH 44087. TEL 216-425-9000; 800-888-5900. FAX 216-425-7150. E-mail: catknapp@aol.com. (also avail. in diskette format) **Document type:** directory.
●Also available on CD-ROM.

BUSINESS AND ECONOMICS — TRADE AND INDUSTRIAL DIRECTORIES

338 917.5   US   ISSN 1061-2033
HF5044
HARRIS NATIONAL MANUFACTURERS DIRECTORY SOUTHEAST EDITION (YEAR). a. $205 (diskette & CD-ROM $1195) (effective 1998). Harris InfoSource International, 2057-2 Aurora Rd., Twinsburg, OH 44087. TEL 216-425-9000; 800-888-5900. FAX 216-425-7150. E-mail: catknapp@aol.com. (also avail. in diskette format) **Document type**: directory.
●Also available on CD-ROM.

338 917.8   US
HF5050
HARRIS NATIONAL MANUFACTURERS SOUTH CENTRAL DIRECTORY ON DISC. a. diskette $595 (effective 1998). Harris InfoSource International, 2057-2 Aurora Rd., Twinsburg, OH 44087. TEL 216-425-9000; 800-888-5900. FAX 216-425-7150. E-mail: catknapp@aol.com. (diskette format) **Document type**: directory.
  Formerly: Harris National Manufacturers Directory (West and Southwest Edition) (ISSN 1061-205X)

338   US   ISSN 1080-3467
HF5041
▼**HARRIS NEW ENGLAND MANUFACTURERS DIRECTORY**. 1995. a. $168 (diskette & CD-ROM $895) (effective 1998). Harris InfoSource International, 2057-2 Aurora Rd., Twinsburg, OH 44087. TEL 216-425-9000; 800-888-5900. FAX 216-425-7150. E-mail: catknapp@aol.com. Ed. Frances L. Carlsen. (also avail. in diskette format) **Document type**: directory.
●Also available on CD-ROM.

670   US   ISSN 0888-8140
HD9727.03
HARRIS OHIO INDUSTRIAL DIRECTORY (YEAR). 1918. a. $149 (diskette & CD-ROM $695) (effective 1998). Harris InfoSource International, 2057-2 Aurora Rd., Twinsburg, OH 44087. TEL 216-425-9000; 800-888-5900. FAX 216-425-7150. E-mail: catknapp@aol.com. (also avail. in diskette format) **Document type**: directory.
●Also available on CD-ROM.
  Former titles: Harris Ohio Marketers Industrial Directory (ISSN 0733-4664); Ohio Industrial Directory (ISSN 0161-4878); Ohio Manufacturers Industrial Directory; Directory of Ohio Manufacturers (ISSN 0070-5985)

382   US   ISSN 0734-8541
HC107.P4
HARRIS PENNSYLVANIA INDUSTRIAL DIRECTORY (YEAR). 1913. a. $149 (diskette $695) (effective 1998). Harris InfoSource International, 2057-2 Aurora Rd., Twinsburg, OH 44087. TEL 216-425-9000; 800-888-5900. FAX 216-425-7150. E-mail: catknapp@aol.com. (also avail. in diskette format) **Document type**: directory.
  Former titles (until 1982): Pennsylvania Industrial Directory; Harris Pennsylvania Marketing Directory; Industrial Directory of the Commonwealth of Pennsylvania.

338 917.4   US   ISSN 1078-6333
HF5065.R5
▼**HARRIS RHODE ISLAND MANUFACTURERS DIRECTORY**. 1995. a. $49 (diskette & CD-ROM $249). Harris Publishing Co. (Twinsburg), 2057-2 Aurora Rd., Twinsburg, OH 44087. TEL 216-425-9000; 800-888-5900. FAX 800-643-5997. E-mail: catknapp@aol.com. Ed. Frances L. Carlsen. (also avail. in diskette format) **Document type**: directory.
●Also available on CD-ROM.

338   US   ISSN 1065-4747
HD9727.S6
HARRIS SOUTH CAROLINA MANUFACTURERS DIRECTORY. 1994. a. $60 (diskette & CD-ROM $299) (effective 1998). Harris InfoSource International, 2057-2 Aurora Rd., Twinsburg, OH 44087. TEL 216-425-9000; 800-888-5900. FAX 216-425-7150. E-mail: catknapp@aol.com. Ed. Frances L. Carlsen. (also avail. in diskette format) **Document type**: directory.
●Also available on CD-ROM.

338   US   ISSN 1076-5123
HF5065.T4
▼**HARRIS TEXAS MANUFACTURERS DIRECTORY**. 1995. a. $135 (diskette & CD-ROM $695) (effective 1998). Harris InfoSource International, 2057-2 Aurora Rd., Twinsburg, OH 44087. TEL 216-425-9000; 800-888-5900. FAX 216-425-7150. E-mail: catknapp@aol.com. Ed. Frances L. Carlsen. (also avail. in diskette format) **Document type**: directory.
●Also available on CD-ROM.

670   US   ISSN 0887-4247
HD9727.W4
HARRIS WEST VIRGINIA MANUFACTURING DIRECTORY (YEAR). 1980. a. $49 (diskette & CD-ROM $249). Harris Publishing Co. (Twinsburg), 2057-2 Aurora Rd., Twinsburg, OH 44087. TEL 216-425-9000; 800-888-5900. FAX 216-425-7150. E-mail: catknapp@aol.com. (also avail. in diskette format) **Document type**: directory.
●Also available on CD-ROM.

HARVARD BUSINESS SCHOOL CLUB OF LONDON ADDRESS BOOK. see COLLEGE AND ALUMNI

338.025   US   ISSN 1048-7107
HF5065.H3
HAWAII BUSINESS DIRECTORY. 1990. a. $295 (effective 1997). American Business Directories (Subsidiary of: American Business Information, Inc.), 5711 S. 86th Circle, Box 27347, Omaha, NE 68127. TEL 402-593-4600; 800-555-6124. FAX 402-331-5481. E-mail: jerry.venner@abii.com. index. (also avail. in magnetic tape; diskette format) **Document type**: directory.
●Also available on CD-ROM.
Also available online.
  Description: Includes all businesses in the state. Each listing includes company name, complete address, name of owner, and employee size and sales volume codes and credit rating codes.

380   US
HAWAII BUYER'S GUIDE; an authoritative guide to industrial products and services in Hawaii. a. Hawaii Business Publishing Corp., Box 913, Honolulu, HI 96808. TEL 808-946-3978. Ed. Jeff Barrus; Pub. Kim Jacobsen. R&P contact: Ethel Murphy. adv. contact: Ethel Murphy. **Document type**: directory.

338.025   US   ISSN 1085-7451
HF5065.H3
HAWAII MANUFACTURERS DIRECTORY. 1994. a. $49 (diskette or CD-ROM $195) (effective 1997). Manufacturers' News, Inc., 1633 Central St., Evanston, IL 60201-1569. TEL 847-864-7000. FAX 847-332-1100. (also avail. in diskette format) **Document type**: directory.
  Supersedes in part (in 1996): Alaska - Hawaii Manufacturers Directory (ISSN 1074-2468)
  Description: Profiles 1103 companies.

HAZARDOUS WASTE SERVICES DIRECTORY. see ENVIRONMENTAL STUDIES — Waste Management

382 642.5   US
HEALTHCARE FOODSERVICE WHO'S WHO. 1979. triennial. $630 (diskette $2150). Information Central Inc., Box 3900, Prescott, AZ 86302. TEL 520-778-1513. FAX 520-778-1513. E-mail: woodman@bslnet.com. Ed. Julie Woodman. stat.; index. (looseleaf format; also avail. in diskette format) **Document type**: directory.
  Description: Provides food service data on hospitals with over 140 beds and nursing homes and long-term psychiatric and short-term mental health institutions in the U.S. with more than 170 beds.

371 796   US   ISSN 8756-310X
SB486.V64
HELPING OUT IN THE OUTDOORS; a directory of volunteer jobs and internships in parks and forests nationwide. 1980. a. $7 per issue. American Hiking Society, Box 20160, Washington, DC 20041-2160. TEL 301-565-6704. FAX 301-565-6714. Ed. Shirley Hearn. R&P contact: Lura Loftus. circ. 15,000. **Document type**: directory.

338   SA
HIGHWAY DIRECTORY. a. R.20 (effective 1996). Braby's (Subsidiary of: Kohler Packaging Ltd.), P.O. Box 1426, Pinetown 3600, South Africa. TEL 27-31-7017021. FAX 27-31-7017036. **Document type**: directory.
  Incorporates: Queensburgh Buyer's Guide.

338   US
HISPANIC YELLOW PAGES (ATLANTA). (Text in Spanish) 1989. a. free. Casablanca Publications, Inc., Box 870175, Stone Mountain, GA 30087-0005. TEL 770-413-1431. FAX 770-413-9908. Ed. Zaida Gonzalez. adv.: B&W page $950. circ. 50,000. **Document type**: directory.
  Description: Includes Hispanic and non-Hispanic businesses and professionals in the Atlanta metro area.

338   US
HISPANIC YELLOW PAGES (MCLEAN).* Variant title: Paginas Amarillas. (Text in Spanish) 1986. a. free. Vega and Associates, 2071 Chain Bridge Rd., Ste. 50, Vienna, VA 22182-2622. TEL 703-903-9779. FAX 703-903-9788. Ed. Martha Loque; Pub. Francisco Vega, Jr. adv.: B&W page $1700; adv. contact: Robert Kershaw. circ. 100,000 (controlled). **Document type**: directory.

HOLLIS BUSINESS ENTERTAINMENT (YEAR). see HOTELS AND RESTAURANTS

HOLLIS EUROPE; the directory of European public relations & PR networks. see ADVERTISING AND PUBLIC RELATIONS

HOLLIS PRESS & PUBLIC RELATIONS ANNUAL. see ADVERTISING AND PUBLIC RELATIONS

HOLLIS SPONSORSHIP & DONATIONS YEARBOOK. see ADVERTISING AND PUBLIC RELATIONS

HOLLIS SPONSORSHIP NEWSLETTER. see ADVERTISING AND PUBLIC RELATIONS

338.025   CC
HONG KONG BUSINESS & INDUSTRIAL DIRECTORY (YEAR). (In 2 vols.) a. $230 per vol. (free to qualified personnel). Hong Kong T & I Publishing Company, P.O. Box 95709, Tsim Sha Tsui P.O., Kowloon, Hong Kong, People's Republic of China. adv. **Document type**: directory.
  Description: Provides a listing of over 38,000 major commercial and manufacturing companies under 66 divided topics.

338.025 005.302   CC
HONG KONG COMPUTER DIRECTORY (YEAR). (Text in English) 1992. a. HK.$550 (S.E. Asia $95; elsewhere $105). Hong Kong Productivity Council, HKPC Bldg., 78 Tat Chee Ave., Yau Yat Chuen, Kowloon, Hong Kong, People's Republic of China. TEL 852-2788-5963. FAX 852-2788-5959. E-mail: isd@hkpc.org; URL: http://www.hkpc.org. circ. 5,000. **Document type**: directory.
  Description: Lists over 2,000 software products and about 1,100 IT related companies.

338.025 382   CC
HONG KONG IMPORTERS' DIRECTORY (YEAR). (Text in Chinese, English) 1993. a. HK.$250 (S.E. Asia $80; elsewhere $100). Hong Kong Productivity Council, HKPC Bldg., 78 Tat Chee Ave., Yau Yat Chuen, Kowloon, Hong Kong, People's Republic of China. TEL 582-2788-5814. FAX 852-2788-5959. E-mail: isd@hkpc.org; URL: http://www.hkpc.org. circ. 5,000. **Document type**: directory.
  Description: Lists major importers in Hong Kong with full address, telephone, telex and fax numbers, number of employees, sales turnover, major products and brand names. Covers over 8,000 products and 7,000 brand names.

338.025   CC
HONG KONG LINKAGE INDUSTRY DIRECTORY (YEAR). (Text in Chinese, English) 1989. a. HK.$500 (S.E. Asia $90; elsewhere $100). Hong Kong Productivity Council, HKPC Bldg., 78 Tat Chee Ave., Yau Yat Chuen, Kowloon, Hong Kong, People's Republic of China. TEL 852-2788-5954. FAX 852-2788-5959. E-mail: isd@hkpc.org; URL: http://www.hkpc.org. circ. 5,000. **Document type**: directory.
  Description: Lists of major workshops and suppliers in Hong Kong in various metal sectors including: mould and tool making, surface finishing, industrial machinery repair and maintenance, and more.

382   CC   ISSN 0073-3245
HONG KONG MANUFACTURERS AND EXPORTERS REGISTER. 1963. irreg., 8th ed., 1975. $18. Oriental Publicity Service, P.O. Box 4366, N.P., Hong Kong, People's Republic of China. Ed. Anthony Leung. adv. circ. 5,000. **Document type**: directory.

BUSINESS AND ECONOMICS — TRADE AND INDUSTRIAL DIRECTORIES

338.025 621   CC
▼HONG KONG MECHATRONICS DIRECTORY (YEAR). (Text in Chinese, English) 1988. a. HK.$150 (S.E. Asia $33; elsewhere $38). Hong Kong Productivity Council, HKPC Bldg., 78 Tat Chee Ave., Yau Yat Chuen, Kowloon, Hong Kong. TEL 852-2788-5954. FAX 852-2788-5959. E-mail: isd@hkpc.org; URL: http://www.hkpc.org. circ. 5,000. **Document type:** directory.
   Description: Lists major local manufacturers, sales agents and retailers engaged in the field of mechatronics.

658.3   US
▼HOOVER'S DIRECTORY OF HUMAN RESOURCES EXECUTIVES. 1995. a. $39.95. Reference Press, Inc., Box 140375, Austin, TX 78714-0375. TEL 512-454-7778. FAX 512-454-9401. E-mail: orders@hoovers.com; URL: http://www.hoovers.com. **Document type:** directory.
   ●Also available online.
   Description: Lists names and addresses of human resources executives at the top 5000 US employers.

HOOVER'S GUIDE TO COMPUTER COMPANIES. see COMPUTERS — Computer Industry Directories

338   US
HOOVER'S GUIDE TO PRIVATE COMPANIES. 1994. 2/yr. $79.95. Reference Press, Inc., Box 140375, Austin, TX 78714-0375. TEL 512-454-7778. FAX 512-454-9401. E-mail: orders@hoovers.com; URL: http://www.hoovers.com. **Document type:** directory.
   ●Also available online.
   Description: Profiles the 500 largest privately owned companies in the US, including histories, financial data, and pertinent names and addresses.

070.5 338.4
HOOVER'S GUIDE TO THE BOOK BUSINESS. 1993. 2/yr. $9.95. Reference Press, Inc., Box 140375, Austin, TX 78714-0375. TEL 512-454-7778. FAX 512-454-9401. E-mail: orders@hoovers.com; URL: http://www.hoovers.com. **Document type:** directory.
   ●Also available online.
   Also available on CD-ROM.
   Description: Profiles the leading firms in the book business.

338   US
▼HOOVER'S GUIDE TO THE TOP CHICAGO COMPANIES. 1996. 2/yr. $24.95. Reference Press, Inc., Box 140375, Austin, TX 78714-0375. TEL 512-454-7778. FAX 512-454-9401. E-mail: orders@hoovers.com; URL: http://www.hoovers.com. (also avail. in diskette format) **Document type:** directory.
   ●Also available online.
   Description: Profiles the top 615 companies in the Chicago area.

338   US
▼HOOVER'S GUIDE TO THE TOP NEW YORK COMPANIES. 1996. 2/yr. $24.95. Reference Press, Inc., Box 140375, Austin, TX 78714-0375. TEL 512-454-7778. FAX 512-454-9401. E-mail: orders@hoovers.com; URL: http://www.hoover.com. (also avail. in diskette format) **Document type:** directory.
   ●Also available online.
   Also available on CD-ROM.
   Description: Profiles the top 1350 companies in the metropolitan New York area.

338   US
▼HOOVER'S GUIDE TO THE TOP SOUTHERN CALIFORNIA COMPANIES. 1996. 2/yr. $24.95. Reference Press, Inc., Box 140375, Austin, TX 78714-0375. TEL 512-454-7778. FAX 512-454-9401. E-mail: orders@hoovers.com; URL: http://www.hoovers.com. (also avail. in diskette format) **Document type:** directory.
   ●Also available online.
   Also available on CD-ROM.
   Description: Profiles the top 870 companies in southern California.

338   US
HOOVER'S GUIDE TO THE TOP TEXAS COMPANIES. 1993. 2/yr. $24.95. Reference Press, Inc., Box 140375, Austin, TX 78714-0375. TEL 512-454-7778. FAX 512-454-9401. E-mail: orders@hoovers.com; URL: http://www.hoovers.com. (also avail. in diskette format) **Document type:** directory.
   ●Also available online.
   Description: Profiles the top 850 companies in Texas.

380   US   ISSN 1055-7202
HG4057
HOOVER'S HANDBOOK OF AMERICAN BUSINESS. 1991. a. $39.95. Reference Press, Inc., Box 140375, Austin, TX 78714-0375. TEL 512-454-7778. FAX 512-454-9401. E-mail: orders@hoovers.com; URL: http://www.hoovers.com. **Document type:** directory.
   ●Also available online.
   Also available on CD-ROM.
   —CISTI.
   Supersedes in part: Hoover's Handbook (ISSN 1056-6229)
   Description: Profiles over 750 major U.S. companies, including histories, financial data, pertinent names and addresses.

338   US   ISSN 1069-7519
HG4057
HOOVER'S HANDBOOK OF EMERGING COMPANIES. 1993. a. $39.95. Reference Press, Inc., Box 140375, Austin, TX 78714-0375. TEL 512-454-7778. FAX 512-454-9401. E-mail: orders@hoovers.com; URL: http://www.hoovers.com. **Document type:** directory.
   ●Also available online.
   Also available on CD-ROM.
   Description: Profiles 250 growth companies, including high-profile and lesser-known companies. Contains financial data, an overview of operations and pertinent names and addresses.

338   US   ISSN 1055-7199
HG4009
HOOVER'S HANDBOOK OF WORLD BUSINESS. 1991. 2/yr. $37.95 (effective Oct. 1994). Reference Press Inc., Box 140375, Austin, TX 78714-0375. TEL 512-454-7778. FAX 512-454-9401. E-mail: orders@hoovers.com; URL: http://www.hoovers.com. Ed.Bd. **Document type:** directory.
   ●Also available online.
   Also available on CD-ROM.
   Supersedes in part: Hoover's Handbook (ISSN 1056-6229)
   Description: Profiles 227 major non-U.S. public, private and state-owned companies, including histories, financial data, and pertinent names and addresses.

382   US
▼HOOVER'S MASTERLIST OF MAJOR LATIN AMERICAN COMPANIES. 1996. s-a. $79.95. Reference Press, Inc., Box 140375, Austin, TX 78714-0375. TEL 512-454-7778. FAX 512-454-9401. E-mail: orders@hoovers.com; URL: http://www.hoovers.com. **Document type:** directory.
   ●Also available online.
   Description: Profiles more than 1,400 Latin American public and private companies.

338.025   US   ISSN 1066-291X
HOOVER'S MASTERLIST OF MAJOR U S COMPANIES (YEAR). 1993. a. Reference Press, Inc., Box 140375, Austin, TX 78714-0375. TEL 512-454-7778. FAX 512-454-9401. E-mail: orders@hoovers.com; URL: http://www.hoovers.com. (also avail. in diskette format) **Document type:** directory.
   ●Also available online.
   Description: Profiles more than 10000 U.S. public and private companies.

338 798.2   CN   ISSN 0828-4679
HORSE INDUSTRY DIRECTORY OF CANADA.* 1989. a. Can.$9.95. Whitehouse Publishing, P.O. Box 1778, Vernon, BC V1T 8C3, Canada. TEL 403-640-4975. FAX 604-545-9896. **Document type:** directory.
   Description: Features names and addresses of breed groups, clubs and organizations, farriers, instructors, colleges, universities, publications, and commercial listings.

HOUSTON OIL DIRECTORY. see PETROLEUM AND GAS

HOUSTON PETROLEUM INDUSTRY. see PETROLEUM AND GAS

HOW TO FIND INFORMATION ABOUT COMPANIES; the corporate intelligence source book. see BUSINESS AND ECONOMICS

HUDSON VALLEY TELEPHONE TICKLER. see INSURANCE

338.025   US
HUMAN FACTORS AND ERGONOMICS SOCIETY DIRECTORY AND YEARBOOK. 1958. a. $50 to non-members. Human Factors and Ergonomics Society, Box 1369, Santa Monica, CA 90406-1369. TEL 310-394-1811. FAX 310-304-2410. E-mail: hfes@compuserve.com; URL: http://www.hfes.org. adv. contact: Lois Smith. circ. 5,200 (paid). (back issues avail.) **Document type:** directory.
   —CISTI.
   Formerly: Human Factors Society. Directory and Yearbook (ISSN 0270-5311)
   Description: Contains descriptions of activities that took place among the Society's major committees, local and student chapters and technical interest groups during the previous year; contacts; geographical member index.

I A L PLASTICS YEARBOOK. see PLASTICS

338.025 613.62   US
I A Q PRODUCT & SERVICE GUIDE. (Indoor Air Quality); the directory of products and services for control of indoor air quality. 1992. a. $75. Cutter Information Corp., 37 Broadway, Arlington, MA 02174-5552. TEL 617-648-8700. FAX 617-648-1950. Ed. Charles Gibbs; Pub. Karen Fine Coburn. R&P contact: Carolyn Licata. adv. contact: Tomlin Coggeshall. (back issues avail.) **Document type:** directory.
   Description: Lists over 2,500 products and services to aid in the detection, mitigation, and prevention of indoor air quality problems.

338 666   US
I C A TRADE JOURNAL. 1958. q. International Ceramic Association, Box 39, Glen Burnie, MD 21061. **Document type:** trade publication.

I C ALTERNATE SOURCES & REPLACEMENTS D.A.T.A. DIGEST. see ELECTRONICS

380.1 658.8   US   ISSN 0731-518X
HD9003
I D HANDBOOK OF FOODSERVICE DISTRIBUTION (YEAR). (Institutional Distribution) 1981. a. $330. Bill Communications, Inc., 355 Park Ave. S., 5th Fl., New York, NY 10010-1789. TEL 212-592-6200. FAX 212-592-6339. Ed. Edith Fried Walker. circ. 1,000.
   —CCC.
   Description: Directory of foodservice distributors in the US, Canada and the Caribbean.

I D SYSTEMS BUYERS GUIDE. see BUSINESS AND ECONOMICS — Computer Applications

338.025 665   US
I O G C C MEMBERS AND OIL AND GAS AGENCIES DIRECTORY. a. $11. Interstate Oil and Gas Compact Commission, Box 53127, Oklahoma City, OK 73152-3127. TEL 405-525-3556. **Document type:** directory.

I S O 9000 REGISTERED FIRMS DIRECTORY. (International Organization for Standarization) see BUSINESS AND ECONOMICS — Production Of Goods And Services

I T A A MEMBERSHIP DIRECTORY. (Information Technology Association of America) see COMPUTERS — Electronic Data Processing

BUSINESS AND ECONOMICS — TRADE AND INDUSTRIAL DIRECTORIES

338.025   US   ISSN 1048-3357
HF5065.I2
IDAHO BUSINESS DIRECTORY. 1989. a. $295 (effective 1997). American Business Directories (Subsidiary of: American Business Information, Inc.), 5711 S. 86th Circle, Box 27347, Omaha, NE 68127. TEL 402-593-4600; 800-555-6124. FAX 402-331-5481. E-mail: jerry.venner@abii.com. index. (also avail. in magnetic tape; diskette format) **Document type:** directory.
●Also available online.
Also available on CD-ROM.
    Description: Includes all businesses in the state, listing addresses, phone numbers, key personnel, with employee size and sales volume codes and credit rating codes.

338.025   US   ISSN 1081-3950
HF5065.I2
▼**IDAHO MANUFACTURERS REGISTER.** 1995. a. $65 (diskette $245) (effective 1996). (Association of Idaho Manufacturers) Database Publishing Company, 1590 S. Lewis St., Anaheim, CA 92805. TEL 714-778-6400. FAX 714-778-6611. Ed. Kathie Scott; Pub. James H. Holly. R&P contact: Ken Gregory. (also avail. in diskette format) **Document type:** directory.

670   US   ISSN 1057-347X
HD9727.I2
IDAHO MANUFACTURING DIRECTORY. 1972. triennial. $50. University of Idaho, Center for Business Development and Research, College of Business and Economics, Moscow, ID 83844-3227. TEL 208-885-6611. FAX 208-885-5580. (Dist. by: Manufacturers' News, Inc., 1633 Central St., Evanston, IL 60201. TEL 708-864-7000) Ed. Tisha Egashina; Pub. Tisha Egashina. circ. 1,400. (also avail. in diskette format) **Document type:** directory.
    Former titles: High Tech and Manufacturing Directory of Idaho; (until 1982): Manufacturing Directory of Idaho.
    Description: Contains information on more than 1,200 companies listed in three principal sections - S.I.C., geographic, and alphabetical.

338.025   US   ISSN 1048-504X
HF5065.I3
ILLINOIS BUSINESS DIRECTORY. 1985. a. $695 (effective 1997). American Business Directories (Subsidiary of: American Business Information, Inc.), 5711 S. 86th Circle, Box 27347, Omaha, NE 68127. TEL 402-593-4600; 800-555-6124. FAX 402-331-5481. E-mail: jerry.venner@abii.com. index. (also avail. in magnetic tape; diskette format) **Document type:** directory.
●Also available online.
Also available on CD-ROM.
    Description: Includes all businesses in the state, listing addresses and phone numbers, key personnel, with employee size and sales volume codes, and credit rating codes.

670   US   ISSN 0160-3302
T12
ILLINOIS MANUFACTURERS DIRECTORY. 1912. a. $169 (diskette and CD-ROM $745) (effective 1997). Manufacturers' News, Inc., 1633 Central St., Evanston, IL 60201. TEL 847-864-7000. FAX 847-332-1100. Ed. Louise M. West. adv.: B&W page $1843; adv. contact: Charles Scherer. illus. (also avail. in magnetic tape; diskette format) **Document type:** directory.
●Also available on CD-ROM.
    Description: Profiles 23,346 manufacturers listed in six sections -- product, alphabetical, geographical, SIC, parent company and Chicago zip code.

670   US   ISSN 0092-3818
HC107.I3
ILLINOIS SERVICES DIRECTORY. a. $179 (diskette or CD-ROM $995) (effective 1997). Manufacturers' News, Inc., 1633 Central St., Evanston, IL 60201-1505. TEL 847-864-7000. FAX 847-332-1100. Ed. Louise M. West. adv. contact: Charles Scherer. illus. (diskette format) **Document type:** directory.
●Also available on CD-ROM.
    Description: Profiles 28,778 non-manufacturing firms; includes product-service, alphabetical, geographical, SIC, and parent company.

IMMEDIATE ARTS - WRITERS' DIRECTORY; independent & small press publishers. see *PUBLISHING AND BOOK TRADE*

663 338.47   US
HD9350.3
IMPACT WORLD DIRECTORY; leading spirits, wine & beer companies; who's who of industry executives. 1990. a. $310. M. Shanken Communications, Inc., 387 Park Ave. S., New York, NY 10016. TEL 212-684-4224. FAX 212-684-5424. TELEX 422687 MSHANK UI. Ed. Marvin R. Shanken. adv.; index. **Document type:** directory.
    Formerly: Impact International Directory (ISSN 1048-2253)
    Description: Lists more than 750 suppliers, agents and importers, distributors and wholesalers, and duty free operators in the wine, beer and spirits industry.

INDEPENDENT LIQUID TERMINALS ASSOCIATION. DIRECTORY OF BULK LIQUID TERMINAL AND ABOVEGROUND STORAGE TANK EQUIPMENT AND SERVICES: SUPPLIERS OF EQUIPMENT & SERVICES. see *PETROLEUM AND GAS*

INDEPENDENT LIQUID TERMINALS ASSOCIATION. DIRECTORY OF BULK LIQUID TERMINAL AND STORAGE FACILITIES. see *PETROLEUM AND GAS*

338.025   GR   ISSN 1105-8390
INDEX HELLAS; odegos demosion hyperesion trapezon kai diethon organision. 1993. biennial. Dr.20000 (diskette Dr.25000). Ekdoseis tis Europis, Stournara 47 & 3 Septembriou, 104 32 Athens, Greece. TEL 30-1-5200-321. FAX 30-1-5200-324. (also avail. in diskette format) **Document type:** directory.
    Description: Lists 75,000 addresses of Greek firms, along with 100,000 telephone, fax, and telex numbers.

INDIAN ARCHITECTS DIRECTORY & REFERENCE BOOK. see *ARCHITECTURE*

INDIAN HOSIERY DIRECTORY. see *CLOTHING TRADE*

338.025   II
INDIAN IMPORT EXPORT DIRECTORY.* irreg. $50. Tele Direct (Informatics) India Pvt. Ltd., S-351, Panchsheel Park, New Delhi 110 017, India. TEL 647-2323. TELEX 031-62746 TEDI IN. **Document type:** directory.

338.025   II
INDIAN INDUSTRIAL SOURCES. (Text in English) 1985. m. Rs.150. Industrial Magazines (Bombay) Pvt. Ltd., 309 Vasan Udyog Bhavan, Tulsi Pipe Rd., Lower Parel, Bombay 400013, India. TEL 4937718. Ed. Deepak Sule. adv.: B&W page Rs.5500, color page Rs.11000; trim 275 x 205; adv. contact: T.N. Hariharan. **Document type:** directory.

INDIANA. STATE BOARD OF REGISTRATION FOR ARCHITECTS. ROSTER OF REGISTERED ARCHITECTS. see *ARCHITECTURE*

338.025   US   ISSN 1048-7255
HF5065.I6
INDIANA BUSINESS DIRECTORY. 1987. a. $395 (effective 1997). American Business Directories (Subsidiary of: American Business Information, Inc.), 5711 S. 86th Circle, Box 27347, Omaha, NE 68127. TEL 402-593-4600; 800-555-6124. FAX 402-331-5481. E-mail: jerry.venner@abii.com. index. (also avail. in magnetic tape; diskette format) **Document type:** directory.
●Also available online.
Also available on CD-ROM.
    Description: Includes all businesses in the state, listing address and phone numbers, key personnel, with employee size and sales volume codes, and credit rating codes.

670   US   ISSN 0735-2417
HD9727.I6
INDIANA MANUFACTURERS DIRECTORY. a. $109 (diskette and CD-ROM $545) (effective 1997). Manufacturers' News, Inc., 1633 Central St., Evanston, IL 60201. TEL 847-864-7000. FAX 847-332-1100. Ed. Louise M. West. adv. contact: Charles Scherer. illus. (diskette format) **Document type:** directory.
●Also available on CD-ROM.
    Description: Profiles 11,926 manufacturers listed in five sections -- product, alphabetical, geographical, SIC, and parent company.

380.1 382   IO   ISSN 0216-1052
INDONESIAN IMPORTERS DIRECTORY. (Supplement avail.: List of Goods Allocated) (Text in English) 1978. biennial. $100. Gabungan Importir Nasional Seluruh Indonesia - National Importers Association of Indonesia, Jl. Kesejahteraan No. 98 APRJ, Jakarta 10110, Indonesia. TEL 021-360-643. FAX 62-021-367269. Eds. Zahri Achmad, S. Hoesin. charts; stat.; tr.lit. circ. 3,000. **Document type:** directory.
    Description: General information and lists importers in Indonesia.

747   DK   ISSN 0106-7346
INDRETNINGSHAANDBOGEN; idebog for indretning af virksomheder, institutioner og offentligt miljøe. 1980. a. DKK 95 (effective 1997). NOVA Kommunikation A-S, P.O. Box 146, DK-3450 Alleroed, Denmark. TEL 45-48-17-00-78. FAX 45-48-17-13-65. adv.: Color page DKK 17200; trim 235 x 175 x 184. illus.; circ. 12,000 (controlled). **Document type:** directory.
    Description: Lists furniture and furnishing suppliers, interior designers and architects.

380 330   KE
INDUSTRIAL & TRADE DIRECTORY. a. EAs.200. Translinkers Publishing Co., P.O. Box 44169, Nairobi, Kenya. Ed. George C. Kimani. adv.; bk.rev. circ. 60,000. **Document type:** directory.
    Formerly (until 1981): Kenya Enterprise.

330   JA
INDUSTRIAL GOODS DISTRIBUTION IN JAPAN. (Text in English) Irreg., latest Oct. 1991. $750 per copy. Dodwell Marketing Consultants, Kowa No. 35 Bldg., 14-14, Akasaka 1-chome, Minato-ku, Tokyo 107, Japan. TEL 03-3589-0207. FAX 03-5570-7132. TELEX J22274 DODWELL. index. **Document type:** directory.
    Description: Directory featuring chemical, electronic and other industrial material distributors and trade associations in Japan.

INDUSTRIAL MARKET PLACE. see *MACHINERY*

380 621.9 600   II   ISSN 0970-6895
INDUSTRIAL PRODUCTS FINDER. (Text in English) 1972. m. Rs.2250($70) Business Press, Transmission House, Compartment No. 82, Plot No. 6-19, Marol Co-op Industrial Estate, M.V. Rd., Andheri East, Mumbai 400 059, India. TEL 91-22-850-9100. FAX 91-22-850-2070. TELEX 011-78455 BPPL IN. Ed. K.S. Pai. adv.; bk.rev.; abstr.; charts; illus. circ. 20,710. **Document type:** trade publication.
    Description: Covers new products and news briefs.

380   US   ISSN 1045-3652
INFORMATION CATALOG. bi-m. free. Find - S V P, 625 Ave. of the Americas, New York, NY 10114-0354. TEL 212-645-4500; 800-346-3787. FAX 212-807-2716. E-mail: catalog@find/sup.com; URL: http://www.findsvp.com. Ed. Lynn Christie; Pub./ Michael Shoi. **Document type:** catalog.

INFORMATION MARKETPLACE DIRECTORY. see *PUBLISHING AND BOOK TRADE*

INGENIOERENS INDKOEBSBOG. see *BUSINESS AND ECONOMICS — Production Of Goods And Services*

INSEAD ALUMNI ASSOCIATION ADDRESS BOOK. see *BUSINESS AND ECONOMICS — Management*

INSTITUTE OF CHARTERED ACCOUNTANTS OF SCOTLAND. OFFICIAL DIRECTORY. see *BUSINESS AND ECONOMICS — Accounting*

INSURANCE ALMANAC: WHO, WHAT, WHEN AND WHERE IN INSURANCE. see *INSURANCE*

338.025 006.6   US
▼**THE INTERACTIVE MULTIMEDIA SOURCEBOOK (YEAR).** 1996. a. £115($135) R.R. Bowker, A Division of Reed Elsevier Inc., 121 Chanlon Rd., New Providence, NJ 07974. TEL 908-464-6800; 888-269-5372. FAX 908-665-6688. E-mail: info@bowker.com; URL: http://www.reedref.com. pp./issue: 800. **Document type:** directory.
    Description: Provides details on more than 2,500 US companies, businesses, and professionals involved in the multimedia industry.

BUSINESS AND ECONOMICS — TRADE AND INDUSTRIAL DIRECTORIES

384.3 US
(YEAR) INTERACTIVE TELEVISION INDUSTRY DIRECTORY.
1994. irreg., no.2, 1995. $65 (Canada and Mexico $105; elsewhere $120). Cowles - SIMBA Information (Subsidiary of: Cowles Business Media), 11 Riverbend Dr. S., Box 4949, Stamford, CT 06907-0949. TEL 203-358-9900; 800-307-2529. FAX 203-358-5811. E-mail: info@simbanet.com; URL: http://www.simbanet.com. **Document type:** directory.
Description: Lists companies and key personnel in the interactive-television industry.

747 US
INTERIOR DESIGN BUYERS GUIDE. 1970. a. $20. Cahners Publishing Company (New York), Design Division, Division of Reed Elsevier Inc., 245 W. 17th St., New York, NY 10011. TEL 212-645-0067. FAX 212-463-6667. (Subscr. to: Box 7820, Torrance, CA 90504-9220) Ed. Benjamin Velez. adv.; tr.lit.; index. circ. 44,372. (back issues avail.) **Document type:** consumer publication, directory.

382 US
▼**INTERNATIONAL BUSINESS AND TRADE DIRECTORIES.**
1996. a. $125. Grey House Publishing, Pocket Knife Sq., Lakeville, CT 06039. TEL 860-435-0868; 800-562-2139. FAX 860-435-0867. **Document type:** directory.
Description: Lists over 4000 worldwide industry-specific business directories.

330 IR
INTERNATIONAL BUSINESS DIRECTORY OF IRAN. 1989. a. IRl.3000($10) Iran Exports Publication Co. Ltd., P.O. Box 15815-3373, Teheran 15956, Iran. TEL 98-21-4401800. FAX 98-21-890547. **Document type:** directory.

382 US ISSN 1050-8384
HF54.U5
INTERNATIONAL COMPANIES AND THEIR BRANDS.
1989. a. Gale Research, 835 Penobscot Bldg., 645 Griswold St., Detroit, MI 48266-4094. TEL 313-961-2242; 800-877-4253. FAX 800-414-5043. E-mail: daniel__snyder@gale.com. Ed. Donna Wood.
—CISTI
Formerly (until 1991): International Trade Names Dictionary: Company Index (ISSN 0899-7594)

338.025 US
INTERNATIONAL COMPANIES IN SOUTH CAROLINA. base vol. plus a. update. $20. Department of Commerce, Research and Communications, Box 927, Columbia, SC 29202. TEL 803-737-0400. FAX 803-737-1652. Ed. Nikki Edwards. R&P contact: Nikki Edwards. TEL 803-737-3864. adv. contact: Dennis Craighead. **Document type:** directory.
Description: Gives information on companies in South Carolina owned entirely or partially by non-U.S. companies. Provides a section on international capital investment, a parent company section and three indices.

THE INTERNATIONAL DIRECTORY OF BUSINESS INFORMATION SOURCES & SERVICES. see BUSINESS AND ECONOMICS — International Commerce

INTERNATIONAL DIRECTORY OF ELECTRIC UTILITIES. see ENERGY — Electrical Energy

INTERNATIONAL DIRECTORY OF ENGINEERING SOCIETIES AND RELATED ORGANIZATIONS. see ENGINEERING

382 980 US
INTERNATIONAL DIRECTORY OF IMPORTERS. (In 9 vols.) 1979. a. Interdata, 1741 Kekamek N.W., Poulsbo, WA 98370. TEL 360-779-1511. FAX 360-697-4696. (looseleaf format) **Document type:** directory.
Description: Designed and compiled for manufacturers, exporters and trading firms who wish to expand overseas sales. Lists importing firms and major wholesalers in Europe, the Middle East, North America, Central and South America, Africa, and the Asia-Pacific region.

382 980 US ISSN 1050-5520
HF3873.I58
INTERNATIONAL DIRECTORY OF IMPORTERS: AFRICA.
irreg., 7th ed., 1996-97. $225 (effective 1997). Interdata, 1741 Kekamek N.W., Poulsbo, WA 98370. TEL 360-779-1511. FAX 360-697-4696. (looseleaf format) **Document type:** directory.
Description: Features more than 11,000 importing firms from 42 different countries in Africa - from Algeria to Zimbabwe. Contains detailed company information, as well as a comprehensive commodity index.

382 980 US ISSN 1050-5539
HF3751.8
INTERNATIONAL DIRECTORY OF IMPORTERS: ASIA - PACIFIC. (In 2 vols.) irreg., 7th ed., 1996-97. $350 (effective 1997). Interdata, 1741 Kekamek N.W., Poulsbo, WA 98370. TEL 360-779-1511. FAX 360-697-4696. (looseleaf format) **Document type:** directory.
Description: Covers Australia, Bangladesh, China, Hong Kong, India, Indonesia, Japan, Malaysia, Nepal, New Zealand, Pakistan, Philippines, Singapore, South Korea, Sri Lanka, Taiwan and Thailand. Includes comprehensive index and details company information; over 30,000 entries.

382 980 US ISSN 1050-5555
HF3493
INTERNATIONAL DIRECTORY OF IMPORTERS: EUROPE.
(In 3 vols.) irreg., 9th ed., 1997. $450 (effective 1997). Interdata, 1741 Kekamek N.W., Poulsbo, WA 98370. TEL 360-779-1511. FAX 360-697-4696. (looseleaf format) **Document type:** directory.
Description: Covers over 54,000 importers in 36 countries in Western and Eastern Europe. Details company information and comprehensive commodity index.

382 980 US ISSN 1050-5563
HF3756.A48
INTERNATIONAL DIRECTORY OF IMPORTERS: MIDDLE EAST. irreg., 8th ed., 1996-97. $225 (effective 1997). Interdata, 1741 Kekamek N.W., Poulsbo, WA 98370. TEL 360-779-1511. FAX 360-697-4696. (looseleaf format) **Document type:** directory.
Description: Covers over 14,000 importers in Bahrain, Egypt, Iran, Israel, Jordan, Kuwait, Lebanon, Malta, Oman, Qatar, Saudi Arabia, Syria, Turkey, United Arab Emirates and Yemen. Provides detailed company information and index.

382 980 US ISSN 1050-5466
HF3012
INTERNATIONAL DIRECTORY OF IMPORTERS: NORTH AMERICA. 1982. irreg., 7th ed., 1996-97. $185. Interdata, 1741 Kekamek N.W., Poulsbo, WA 98370. TEL 360-779-1511. FAX 360-697-4696. (looseleaf format) **Document type:** directory.
—CISTI
Description: Covers the North American continent with 20,000 entries of importing firms from the United States and Canada. Details company information and includes commodity index.

382 980 US ISSN 1050-5547
HF3230.5.A48
INTERNATIONAL DIRECTORY OF IMPORTERS: SOUTH - CENTRAL AMERICA. irreg., 7th ed., 1997-98. $225 (effective 1997). Interdata, 1741 Kekamek N.W., Poulsbo, WA 98370. TEL 360-779-1511. FAX 360-697-4696. (looseleaf format) **Document type:** directory.
Description: Covers 22,000 importers in Argentina, Bolivia, Brazil, Chile, Colombia, Costa Rica, Ecuador, El Salvador, Guatemala, Honduras, Mexico, Nicaragua, Panama, Paraguay, Peru, Uruguay, Venezuela and the West Indies. Details company information and index.

659.152 US ISSN 1081-6879
INTERNATIONAL DIRECTORY OF MODEL - TALENT AGENCIES AND SCHOOLS. 1970. a. $29.95 (effective 1996 ed.). Peter Glenn Publications, Inc., 42 W. 38th St., Ste. 802, New York, NY 10018. TEL 212-869-2020; 888-332-6700. FAX 212-354-4099. Ed. David Vando; Pub. Chip Brill. adv. contact: Tricia Mazzilli. circ. 15,000. **Document type:** directory.
Former titles: Directory of Talent and Modeling Agencies and Schools International (ISSN 0742-5570); (until 1984): Directory of Model - Talent Agencies and Schools International (ISSN 0730-9953); (until 1982): Models Mart Directory of Modeling Agencies, Talent Agencies and Model Schools (ISSN 0272-8206)
Description: Lists agencies and schools around the world. Includes related service companies.

INTERNATIONAL DIRECTORY OF NEW AND RENEWABLE ENERGY INFORMATION SOURCES AND RESEARCH CENTRES. see ENERGY

380.1 US ISSN 0894-7104
INTERNATIONAL DIRECTORY OF PRIVATE PRESSES.
1978. a., 7th ed., 1995. $50. Educators Research Service, 2443 Fair Oaks Blvd., Ste. 316, Sacramento, CA 95825. TEL 916-924-1151. Ed. Budd Westreich; Pub. Budd Westreich. (back issues avail.) **Document type:** directory.

INTERNATIONAL ENVIRONMENTAL TECHNOLOGY. ANNUAL BUYERS DIRECTORY. see ENVIRONMENTAL STUDIES — Pollution

639.9 622 US ISSN 1074-0104
INTERNATIONAL EROSION CONTROL ASSOCIATION. PRODUCTS & SERVICES DIRECTORY. 1990. a. $19 to non-members; members $15. International Erosion Control Association, Box 4904, Steamboat Springs, CO 80477-4904. TEL 970-879-3010; 800-455-4322. FAX 970-879-8563. E-mail: ecinfo@ieca.org; URL: http://www.ieca.org. **Document type:** directory.
Description: Lists 500 manufacturers, suppliers, consultants, contractors, organizations, and government agencies specializing in erosion control.

INTERNATIONAL FOOD DIRECTORY. see FOOD AND FOOD INDUSTRIES

382 332.6 US ISSN 1040-6921
HG4509
INTERNATIONAL INVESTOR'S DIRECTORY; sourcebook for international investor. (In 6 vols.) 1988. a. $75 per vol. Asset International, Inc., 125 Greenwich Ave., Greenwich, CT 06830. TEL 203-629-5014. FAX 203-629-5024. TELEX 262356 ASIN UR. Ed. Eric Laursen. adv. circ. 2,000. (also avail. in diskette format; back issues avail.) **Document type:** directory.
—CCC

INTERNATIONAL KEY PERSONNEL LIST. see ENGINEERING — Engineering Mechanics And Materials

338.025 341.025 UK ISSN 0309-0825
THE INTERNATIONAL LAW LIST. 1866. a. £54($85) (effective 1997). L. Corper-Mordaunt & Co., 57 Fitzhardinge House, 14 Portman Sq., London W1H 9HB, England. TEL 44-171-935-3853. FAX 44-171-487-3836. **Document type:** directory.
Former titles (until 1936): Reference Register and International Law List; (until 1911): Reference Register.

INTERNATIONAL LEATHER GUIDE. see LEATHER AND FUR INDUSTRIES

INTERNATIONAL MED-TECH DIRECTORY; the international financial guide to over 800 publicly traded healthcare companies. see MEDICAL SCIENCES

665.5 380 US
INTERNATIONAL OIL SCOUTS ASSOCIATION DIRECTORY.
1956. a. $35. International Oil Scouts Association, Box 272949, Houston, TX 77277-2949. circ. 400. **Document type:** directory.

INTERNATIONAL PESTICIDE DIRECTORY. see AGRICULTURE — Crop Production And Soil

INTERNATIONAL PETROLEUM INDUSTRY. see PETROLEUM AND GAS

BUSINESS AND ECONOMICS — TRADE AND INDUSTRIAL DIRECTORIES

338.025 621.3   UK
INTERNATIONAL POWER GENERATION DIRECTORY OF EUROPEAN MANUFACTURERS. 1995. a. £55 (foreign £60). Argus Business Media Ltd. (Subsidiary of: D M G Exhibitions Group Ltd.), Queensway House, 2 Queensway, Redhill, Surrey RH1 1QS, England. TEL 44-1737-768611. FAX 44-1737-760564.
  Description: Provides detailed information for power industry specifiers and purchasers.

380.1   US
HD999.L173
INTERNATIONAL PRIVATE LABEL DIRECTORY (YEAR). 1981. a. $75 (foreign $125) (effective 1997). E.W. Williams Publications Co., 2125 Center Ave., Ste. 305, Fort Lee, NJ 07024-5859. TEL 201-592-7007. FAX 201-592-7171. Ed. Olga Gudal; Pub. Andrew H. Williams. R&P contact: Tony Faber. adv. contact: Charles Loomer. bk.rev. circ. 10,000. Document type: directory.
  Formerly: Private Label Directory (ISSN 1047-2266)
  Description: Lists suppliers to private and generic labels. Reaches food, drug and general merchandise buyers.

INTERNATIONAL PULP & PAPER DIRECTORY. see *PAPER AND PULP*

INTERNATIONAL RADCURE YEARBOOK & DIRECTORY. see *PAINTS AND PROTECTIVE COATINGS*

INTERNATIONAL REFRACTORIES HANDBOOK & DIRECTORY. see *CERAMICS, GLASS AND POTTERY*

INTERNATIONAL RELATIONS RESEARCH DIRECTORY. see *POLITICAL SCIENCE — International Relations*

380   CE
INTERNATIONAL TRADE DIRECTORY OF SRI LANKA AND MALDIVES. 1989. a. $50. Trans Publishing House, 39 Canal Rd., P.O. Box 489, Fort Colombo 1, Sri Lanka. TEL 545124. FAX 575599. TELEX 22082 XPOINT CE. Ed. M. Faizer Mackeen. adv. **Document type:** directory.

380.1   GW
INTERNATIONAL TRADESHOW DIRECTORY. (Text in English) 1985. s-a. DM.450 (foreign DM.490) (effective 1997). M und A Verlag fuer Messen, Ausstellungen und Kongresse GmbH (Subsidiary of: Deutscher Fachverlag GmbH), Postfach 101528, 60015 Frankfurt a.M., Germany. TEL 49-69-759502. FAX 49-69-75951280. Ed. Dorit Vogel-Seib. adv.: B&W page DM.4220, color page DM.5720; trim 210 x 280; adv. contact: Jutta Fautz. circ. 2,863 (paid). (also avail. in diskette format; back issues avail.) **Document type:** directory.
  ●Also available online. Vendor(s): Data-Star, Knight-Ridder Information, Inc., Lexis-Nexis.
  Description: Schedule of fairs and exhibitions worldwide listing approximately 7,500 trade fair and exhibition dates in 103 countries.

INTERNATIONAL VENDING BUYER'S GUIDE AND DIRECTORY. see *BUSINESS AND ECONOMICS — Marketing And Purchasing*

380.1   GW   ISSN 0302-2196
HD2421
INTERNATIONALES VERZEICHNIS DER WIRTSCHAFTSVERBAENDE/WORLD GUIDE TO TRADE ASSOCIATIONS. irreg., 4th ed., 1995. DM.598. K.G. Saur Verlag KG, A member of the Reed Elsevier plc group, Ortlerstr. 8, 81373 Munich, Germany. TEL 49-89-76902-0. FAX 49-89-76902150. E-mail: 100730.1341@compuserve.com; URL: http://www.reed-elsevier.com. (Subscr. to: Postfach 701620, 81316 Munich, Germany; Dist. in US by: R.R. Bowker, 121 Chanlon Rd., Box 31, New Providence, NJ 07974. TEL 908-665-6719) **Document type:** directory.
  —CISTI.
  Description: Provides over 31,000 names and addresses of national and international trade associations, arranged according to category (commercial, economic, industrial and professional).

INTERNET YELLOW PAGES: BUSINESS MODELS AND MARKET OPPORTUNITIES. see *BUSINESS AND ECONOMICS — Computer Applications*

338   US   ISSN 0193-8541
HC107.A11
INTERSTATE MANUFACTURERS AND INDUSTRIAL DIRECTORY BUYERS GUIDE. 1936. a. Interstate Publishers Corp., 1841 Broadway, Ste. 713, New York, NY 10023-5876. TEL 212-246-8484. FAX 212-246-8821. Ed. Frank Masorana; Pub. Ralph Kass. R&P contact: Michael Green. adv. contact: Paul Levine. **Document type:** directory.
  Formerly (until 1977): Eastern Manufacturers and Industrial Directory Buyers Guide (ISSN 0731-9223)

INVESTIGATOR'S INTERNATIONAL ALL-IN-ONE DIRECTORY OF THE INVESTIGATIVE INDUSTRY. see *CRIMINOLOGY AND LAW ENFORCEMENT*

INVESTMENT JAPAN (YEAR). see *BUSINESS AND ECONOMICS — Investments*

338   NR
INVESTMENTS AND CREDIT CORPORATION OF OYO STATE. INDUSTRIAL DIRECTORY. 1970. irreg. Investments and Credit Corporation of Oyo State, P.M.B. 5085, Ibadan, Oyo State, Nigeria. **Document type:** directory.
  Formerly: Western Nigeria Development Corporation. Industrial Directory.

338.025 332.6   PH
INVESTOR'S GUIDE TO THE PHILIPPINES. (Text in English) a. Mahal Kong Philippinas Inc., P.O. Box EA-414, Ermita, Manila, Philippines. TEL 632-911-4665. FAX 632-911-4619. Ed. Michael G. Say. adv. contact: Zorahayda A. Banigan.

338.025   US   ISSN 1048-7263
HF5065.I8
IOWA BUSINESS DIRECTORY. 1984. a. $340 (effective 1997). American Business Directories (Subsidiary of: American Business Information, Inc.), 5711 S. 86th Circle, Box 27347, Omaha, NE 68127. TEL 402-593-4600; 800-555-6124. FAX 402-331-5481. E-mail: jerry.venner@abii.com. index. (also avail. in magnetic tape; diskette format) **Document type:** directory.
  ●Also available online.
  Also available on CD-ROM.
  Description: Includes all businesses in the state compiled from the yellow pages and telephone verified. Each listing includes company name, address, name of owner, employee size, sales volume codes, and credit rating codes.

338 659.1   US
IOWA HOME-BASED BUSINESS DIRECTORY.* 1994. a. $15. Integrity Communications, 535 Hayward Ave., Ames, IA 50014-7345. TEL 515-292-7154. FAX 515-292-7154. Ed. Clare Bills. adv.: B&W page $250. circ. 2,000 (paid). (also avail. in diskette format) **Document type:** directory.

338.4767   US   ISSN 0737-7940
HD9727.I8
IOWA MANUFACTURERS REGISTER. 1983. a. $74 (diskette and CD-ROM $445) (effective 1997). Manufacturers' News, Inc., 1633 Central St., Evanston, IL 60201. TEL 847-864-7000. FAX 847-332-1100. Ed. Louise M. West. adv.: B&W page $1843; adv. contact: Charles Scherer. illus. (also avail. in magnetic tape; diskette format) **Document type:** directory.
  ●Also available on CD-ROM.
  Description: Lists 6,632 manufacturers by company name, location, SIC, and product.

380   UK
IRELAND: A DIRECTORY (YEAR). a. £65($130) (effective 1997). Euromonitor, 60-61 Britton St., London EC1M 5NA, England. TEL 44-171-251-8024. FAX 44-171-608-3149. E-mail: info@euromonitor.com; URL: http://www.euromonitor.com. (Addr. in N. America: Euromonitor International, 122 S. Michigan Ave., Ste. 1200, Chicago, IL 60603. TEL 800-577-3876. FAX 312-922-1157) **Document type:** directory.
  Description: Lists more than 2,000 organizations in Ireland, presenting a comprehensive guide to the public, economic, political, and commercial scene in that nation.

IRON AND STEEL INTERNATIONAL (REDHILL). see *METALLURGY*

IRRIGATION ASSOCIATION. MEMBERSHIP DIRECTORY AND BUYERS' GUIDE. see *AGRICULTURE — Agricultural Equipment*

380   IC   ISSN 1011-5323
ISLENSK FYRIRTAEKI/ICELANDIC FIRMS. 1983. a. Frodi Ltd., Seljavegur 2, IS-101 Reykjavik, Iceland. TEL 354-515-5500. FAX 354-515-5599. Ed. Berghildur Erla Bernhardsdottir.
  Description: Contains information about firms and institutions in Iceland.

ISRAEL CONVENTIONS, TRADE SHOWS, FESTIVALS & SPECIAL EVENTS. see *MEETINGS AND CONGRESSES*

670 676   IS
ISRAEL INSTITUTE OF PACKAGING. PACKAGING DIRECTORY. 1976. a. free. Israel Center for Packaging and Product Design, P.O. Box 20038, Tel Aviv, Israel. TEL 03-5614431. Ed. Zvi Ben-Nun. adv. contact: Nira Cohen. circ. 5,000. **Document type:** directory.

338.0962   UA
ITTIHAD AL-SINAAT AL-MISRIYAH. YEAR BOOK/FEDERATION OF EGYPTIAN INDUSTRIES. YEAR BOOK. (Text in English) 1961. a. £E5. Federation of Egyptian Industries - Ittihad al-Sinaat al-Misriyah, 26A Sharia Sherif Pasha, P.O. Box 251, Cairo, Egypt. TEL 02-3928317. FAX 02-3928075. TELEX 92624. Ed. Darwish M. Darwish. adv.; stat. circ. 900. **Document type:** directory.

382   JA
J B I A DIRECTORY. (Text in English, Japanese) 1972. a. 8000 Yen. Japan Book Importers Association, Chiyoda Kaikan, 21-4 Nihonbashi 1-chome, Chuo-ku, Tokyo 103, Japan. TEL 81-3-3271-6901. FAX 81-3-3271-6920. Ed. Makoto Kobayashi. circ. 2,000. **Document type:** directory.

338.7   IO   ISSN 0215-8590
JAKARTA BUSINESS DIRECTORY. (Text in English or Indonesian) 1974. irreg. Kamar Dagang dan Industri Jakarta, Jalan W. Jakarta Fair, Tromol Post 3077, Jakarta, Indonesia. illus. **Document type:** directory.

380.1   IO
JAKARTA METROPOLITAN BUYERS' GUIDE. (Text in English) a. C.V. Taro & Co., Jalan Samanhudi ZB, Box 3472, Jakarta, Indonesia.

382 629.1   JA   ISSN 0286-0635
JAPAN AVIATION DIRECTORY. (Text in English) 1968. a. $163. Koku Shinbunsha - Wing Aviation Press, Kanda Kitamura Bldg., Kanda Higashi-Konya-cho, Chiyoda-ku, Tokyo 101, Japan. TEL 03-3258-9840. FAX 03-3258-5044. TELEX J27117-WINGKOKU. (Dist. by: Intercontinental Marketing Corp., I.P.O. Box 5056, Tokyo 100-30, Japan. TEL 81-3-3661-6458. FAX 81-3-3667-9646) Ed. Hitoshi Ohashi. adv.: B&W page 400000 Yen, color page 680000 Yen; trim 210 x 298; adv. contact: Hitoshi Ohashi. circ. 5,000. **Document type:** directory. —CISTI.
  Formerly (until 1978): Japan Aerospace Directory.

JAPAN CHEMICAL DIRECTORY (TOKYO, 1963). see *ENGINEERING — Chemical Engineering*

338   JA
JAPAN COMPANY DATAFILE (YEAR). (Supplement to: Japan Company Handbook.) (Text in English) 1991. irreg. 60000 Yen($520) in Asia; U.S. $550; Europe $565. Toyo Keizai Inc., 1-2-1 Nihonbashi Hongoku-cho, Chuo-ku, Tokyo 103, Japan. TEL 03-3246-5655. FAX 03-3241-5543. (Dist. in US by: Moody's Investors Service, 99 Church St., New York, NY 10007) Ed. Toshimasa Shibata.
  Description: Covers 1178 top Japanese companies and contains a wealth of in-depth data on each company, including corporate history, product range, directors, subsidiaries, complete balance sheets for 1980, 1985 and 1991.

BUSINESS AND ECONOMICS — TRADE AND INDUSTRIAL DIRECTORIES

915.2 338   JA   ISSN 0288-9307
HC461
JAPAN COMPANY HANDBOOK. FIRST SECTION. (The Japan Company Profile Service provides d. & w. electronic updates on the handbook through Reuters Monitor.) (Text in English) 1974. q. 18400 Yen($222) Toyo Keizai Inc. - Oriental Economist, 1-2-1 Nihombashi Hongoku-cho, Chuo-ku, Tokyo 103, Japan. TEL 03-3246-5621. FAX 03-3241-5543. (Dist. by: Japan Publications Trading Co., Ltd., Box 5030, Tokyo International, Tokyo 100-31, Japan; Dist. in US by: Moody's Investors Service, 99 Church St., New York, NY 10007) Ed. Fusakazu Izumura. adv. (also avail. in microform from MIS)
Supersedes: Japan Company Directory (Tokyo, 1974) (ISSN 0075-3211)
Description: First section covers Blue Chip companies. Provides corporate names, addresses, telephone numbers, business descriptions, names and titles of senior officers, shareholders' equities and major stockholders, and overseas offices and subsidiaries. Includes financial analyses and historical data.

915.2   JA
JAPAN COMPANY HANDBOOK. SECOND SECTION. (The Japan Company Profile Service provides d. & w. electronic updates on the handbook through Reuters Monitor.) (Text in English) 1982. q. 18400 Yen($222) Toyo Keizai Inc., 1-2-1 Nihombashi Hongoku-cho, Chuo-ku, Tokyo 103, Japan. TEL 03-3246-5655. FAX 03-3241-5543. (Subscr. to: Japan Publications Trading Co., Ltd., Box 5030, Tokyo International, Tokyo 100-31, Japan; Dist. in US by: Moody's Investors Service, 99 Church St., New York, NY 10007) Ed. Fusakazu Izumura. adv.; bk.rev. circ. 15,000. (also avail. in microform from MIS)
Formerly: Second Section Firms (ISSN 0288-9315)
Description: Second section covers younger growth companies. Provides corporate names, addresses, telephone numbers, business descriptions, names and titles of senior officers, shareholders' equities and major stockholders, overseas offices and subsidiaries. Includes financial analyses and historical data.

338   JA
JAPAN DIRECTORY: BUSINESS & SOCIETY. (Text in English) 1931. a. 50000 Yen (Asia 62000 Yen; Europe 68000 Yen; N. America 68000 Yen). Japan Press, Ltd., Japan Directory Division, C.P.O. Box 6, Tokyo 100-91, Japan 100. TEL 81-3-3404-5161. FAX 81-3-3404-5152. Ed. Yoshio Wada. adv. circ. 25,000. Document type: directory.
Formed by the merger of: Japan Business Directory (Year) (ISSN 0910-1780) & Japan Society Directory (ISSN 0075-322X)
Description: Contains comprehensive information on foreign firms and related organs, foreign residents in Japan, hotels, stores, restaurants, schools, hospitals, clubs, embassies, consulates, government agencies, and classified telephone and fax directories.

380.1 621.38   JA
JAPAN ELECTRONICS BUYERS' GUIDE. Short title: E B G. 1968. a. $220. Dempa Publications, Inc., 1-11-15, Higashi Gotanda, Shinagawa-ku, Tokyo 141, Japan. TEL 81-3-3445-6111. FAX 81-3-3445-6110. (U.S. addr.: 275 Madison Ave., New York, NY 10016. TEL 212-682-4755. FAX 212-682-2730) adv. Document type: directory.
●Available only on CD-ROM.
Description: Directory of Japanese manufacturers and trading firms and product listing classified by 24 product categories.

382   JA
JAPAN TRADE DIRECTORY (YEAR)/NIHON BOEKI SHINKOKAI. (Text in English) 1982. a. 34000 Yen ($335) Japan External Trade Organization, Publication Department, 2-5 Toranomon, 2-chome, Minato-ku, Tokyo 105, Japan. TEL 03-3582-3518. FAX 03-3587-2485. TELEX J24378. (Dist. in US by: Business Network Corporation, 245 Peach Tree Center Ave., Ste. 2206, Atlanta, GA 30303) adv. circ. 10,000. Document type: directory.
Description: Provides detailed information on Japanese companies in export, import and service trades and international transactions.

338
JAPANESE OVERSEAS INVESTMENTS (YEAR); a complete listing by firms and countries. (Text in English) 1992. irreg. 60000 Yen (Asia $520; U.S. $550; Europe $565). Toyo Keizai Inc., 1-2-1 Nihombashi Hongoku-cho, Chuo-ku, Tokyo 103, Japan. TEL 03-3246-5655. FAX 03-3241-5543. Document type: directory.
Description: Covers over 10,000 overseas affiliates of more than 1,000 Japanese companies in over 100 nations around the world.

338   US
JAPANESE TELEPHONE DIRECTORY AND GUIDE OF SOUTHERN CALIFORNIA. 1981. a. free. Japan Publicity, 19300 S. Hamilton Ave., Ste. 110, Gardena, CA 90248-4408. TEL 310-515-7100. FAX 310-515-7188. E-mail: info@japanpub.com; URL: http://www.japanpub.com. Ed. Yoshiko Miller; Pub. Chieko Mori. adv.: B&W page $2490, color page $5600; trim 8 1/4 x 10 3/4; adv. contact: Paul M. Whitney. circ. 65,000 (controlled). Document type: directory.

380   UK
JORDAN'S REGIONAL DIRECTORIES OF KEY BUSINESS PROSPECTS - YORKSHIRE AND HUMBERSIDE (YEAR). 1988. irreg., latest 1992. £50. Jordan & Sons Ltd., 21 St. Thomas St., Bristol BS1 6JS, England. TEL 44-117-923-0600. FAX 44-117-923-0063. stat. Document type: directory.
Description: Financial details and addresses of 1000 companies in Yorkshire and Humberside, England.

380 796.5   US
K O A DIRECTORY ROAD ATLAS AND CAMPING GUIDE. 1970. a. free. (Kampgrounds of America, Inc.) Meredith Corporation, 1716 Locust St., Des Moines, IA 50336. TEL 515-284-3412. FAX 515-284-2700. adv.: B&W page $21375, color page $26725; 8 5/16 x 10 7/8. maps; circ. 1,900,000 (controlled). Document type: directory.
Formerly: K O A Handbook and Directory for Campers.
Description: Features product and service-related information on camping. Lists KOA facilities.

338.025   US   ISSN 1048-7271
HF5065.K2
KANSAS BUSINESS DIRECTORY. 1983. a. $325 (effective 1997). American Business Directories (Subsidiary of: American Business Information, Inc.), 5711 S. 86th Circle, Box 27347, Omaha, NE 68127. TEL 402-593-4600; 800-555-6124. FAX 402-331-5481. E-mail: jerry.venner@abii.com. index. (also avail. in magnetic tape; diskette format) Document type: directory.
●Also available online.
Also available on CD-ROM.
Description: Includes all businesses in the state compiled from the yellow pages and telephone verified. Each listing includes company name, address, phone number, name of owner, and employee size and sales volume codes, and credit rating codes.

380   US   ISSN 1042-0355
HF5065.K2
THE KANSAS DIRECTORY OF COMMERCE. 1989. a. $70. Wichita Eagle-Beacon, Box 820, Wichita, KS 67201-0820. TEL 800-825-6397. FAX 316-268-6646. (Dist. by: Manufacturers' News, Inc., 1633 Central St., Evanston, IL 60201. TEL 708-864-7000. FAX 708-332-1100) adv. contact: Kate Stillie. (also avail. in diskette format) Document type: directory.
Description: Includes information on more than 4,500 manufacturers and other major employers organized alphabetically, geographically, by S.I.C. code of products made, and by S.I.C. code of products purchased.

338.025   US   ISSN 1082-0256
HF5065.K2
KANSAS MANUFACTURERS REGISTER. a. $69 (diskette or CD-ROM $345) (effective 1997). Manufacturers' News, Inc., 1633 Central St., Evanston, IL 60201-1569. TEL 847-864-7000. FAX 847-332-1100. (also avail. in diskette format) Document type: directory.
●Also available on CD-ROM.
Description: Profiles 3991 companies.

KASHRUTH DIRECTORY. see FOOD AND FOOD INDUSTRIES

670 338   UK   ISSN 1350-4150
HF54.G7
KELLY'S DIRECTORY; list of 82,000 of UK's business classified. 1877. a. £159 (foreign £270). Kelly's Directories (Subsidiary of: Reed Information Services), Part of the Reed Elsevier group, Windsor Court, E. Grinstead House, E. Grinstead, W. Sussex RH19 1XB, England. TEL 01342-326972. FAX 01342-335747. TELEX 95127-INFSER-G. URL: http://www.reedinfo.co.uk. Ed. Jan Brazier; Pub. Derek Barley. adv. contact: Julie Mason. circ. 12,250. Document type: directory.
●Also available online. Vendor(s): Reed Information Services Ltd.
Also available on CD-ROM.
—BLDSC (5089.256193).
Former titles (until 1993): Kelly's Business Directory (ISSN 0269-9265); Kelly's Manufacturers and Merchants Directory (ISSN 0075-5370)

380   UK   ISSN 1350-4169
KELLY'S LINK. 1987. a. free. Kelly's Directories (Subsidiary of: Reed Information Services), Part of the Reed Elsevier group, Windsor Court, E. Grinstead House, E. Grinstead, W. Sussex RH19 1XB, England. TEL 01342-326972. FAX 01342-335747. URL: http://www.reedinfo.co.uk. Ed. Jan Brazier; Pub. Derek Barley. adv. contact: Julie Mason. circ. 50,000 (controlled). Document type: directory.
●Also available online. Vendor(s): Reed Information Services Ltd.
Formerly (until 1993): Kelly's Business Link (ISSN 0269-9281)
Description: Information on over 14,000 businesses throughout the UK which promote their products and services.

380   UK   ISSN 0269-9273
KELLY'S OIL & GAS DIRECTORY. a. free. Kelly's Directories (Subsidiary of: Reed Information Services), Part of the Reed Elsevier group, Windsor Court, E. Grinstead House, E. Grinstead, W. Sussex RH19 1XB, England. TEL 01342-326972. FAX 01342-335747. URL: http://www.reedinfo.co.uk. Ed. Jan Brazier; Pub. Derek Barley. adv. contact: Julie Mason. circ. 7,000 (controlled). Document type: directory.
●Also available online. Vendor(s): Reed Information Services Ltd.
Formerly (until 1993): Kelly's Oil & Gas Industry Directory.
Description: Over 4,000 companies listed under more than 1,600 classified headings.

338.025   US   ISSN 1048-728X
HF5065.K4
KENTUCKY BUSINESS DIRECTORY. 1985. a. $340 (effective 1997). American Business Directories (Subsidiary of: American Business Information, Inc.), 5711 S. 86th Circle, Box 27347, Omaha, NE 68127. TEL 402-593-4600; 800-555-6124. FAX 402-331-5481. E-mail: jerry.venner@abii.com. index. (also avail. in magnetic tape; diskette format) Document type: directory.
●Also available online.
Also available on CD-ROM.
Description: Includes all businesses in the state compiled from the yellow pages and telephone-verified. Each listing includes company name, address, phone number, name of owner, and employee size and sales volume code, and credit rating codes.

670   US   ISSN 0075-5494
KENTUCKY DIRECTORY OF MANUFACTURERS. 1948. a. $40. Cabinet for Economic Development, Division of Research, 500 Mero St., Frankfort, KY 40601. TEL 502-564-4886. FAX 502-564-3256. Ed. Beck McGaughey. circ. 3,000. Document type: directory.
Formerly: Kentucky Industrial Directory (ISSN 0075-5516)
Description: Includes company name and address, parent company and home office name and address, chief executive at plant location, employment, products and SIC codes.

BUSINESS AND ECONOMICS — TRADE AND INDUSTRIAL DIRECTORIES

670　　　　　　　　US　　ISSN 0741-9031
T12.3.K4
KENTUCKY MANUFACTURERS REGISTER. a. $74.50 (diskette and CD-ROM $345) (effective 1997). Manufacturers' News, Inc., 1633 Central St., Evanston, IL 60201. TEL 847-864-7000. FAX 847-332-1100. Ed. Louise M. West. adv.: B&W page $1843; adv. contact: Charles Scherer. illus. (diskette format) **Document type:** directory.
• Also available on CD-ROM.
Description: Lists 5,694 manufacturers by product, alphabetically, geographically, by SIC, and by parent company.

KENTUCKY STATE AGENT HANDBOOK. see *INSURANCE*

338.4　　　　　　KE　　ISSN 0376-8481
HD9737.K4
KENYA. CENTRAL BUREAU OF STATISTICS. DIRECTORY OF INDUSTRIES. Key Title: Directory of Industries. (Former name of issuing body: Kenya. Ministry of Planning and National Development) irreg., latest 1986. KShs.120. Ministry of Finance and Planning, Central Bureau of Statistics, P.O. Box 30266, Nairobi, Kenya. (Subscr. to: Government Press, Haile Selaissie Ave., P.O. Box 30128, Nairobi, Kenya. TEL 254-2-334075) stat. **Document type:** government publication, directory.
Supersedes: Kenya. Ministry of Finance and Economic Planning. Statistics Division. Register of Manufacturing Firms.

KENYA ASSOCIATION OF MANUFACTURERS. MEMBERS LIST AND INTERNATIONAL STANDARD INDUSTRIAL CLASSIFICATION. see *BUSINESS AND ECONOMICS — Production Of Goods And Services*

KENYA EXPORT DIRECTORY. see *BUSINESS AND ECONOMICS — International Commerce*

KENYA NATIONAL CHAMBER OF COMMERCE AND INDUSTRY. TRADE AND INDUSTRY GUIDE. see *BUSINESS AND ECONOMICS — Chamber Of Commerce Publications*

338　　　　　　　　SI
KEY BUSINESS DIRECTORY OF INDONESIA - THAILAND. (Text in English) a. Dun & Bradstreet (Singapore) Pte. Ltd., Publications Department, Park Mall, 9 Penang Rd., No. 09-20, Singapore 0923, Singapore. **Document type:** directory.

338.025　　　　　SI
KEY BUSINESS DIRECTORY OF MALAYSIA. (Text in English) a. Dun & Bradstreet (Singapore) Pte. Ltd., Publications Department, Park Mall, 9 Penang Rd., No. 09-20, Singapore 0923, Singapore. **Document type:** directory.

338.025　　　　　SI
KEY BUSINESS DIRECTORY OF SINGAPORE. (Text in English) a. Dun & Bradstreet (Singapore) Pte. Ltd., Publications Department, Park Mall, 9 Penang Rd., No. 09-20, Singapore 0923, Singapore. **Document type:** directory.

338.025 330　　　UK
KEY NOTE MARKET REVIEW: BUSINESS INFORMATION IN THE U K. Variant title: Business Information in the U K. irreg. £410. Key Note Ltd., Field House, 72 Oldfield Rd., Hampton, Middlesex TW12 2HQ, England. TEL 44-181-783-0755. FAX 44-181-783-0049. **Document type:** trade publication.

338.025　　　　　UK　　ISSN 1357-0463
KEY NOTE MARKET REVIEW: CORPORATE SERVICES IN THE U K. Variant title: Corporate Services in the U K. 1994. irreg. £410. Key Note Ltd., Field House, 72 Oldfield Rd., Hampton, Middlesex TW12 2HQ, England. TEL 44-181-783-0755. FAX 44-181-783-0049. **Document type:** trade publication.
• Also available online.
Also available on CD-ROM.

622　　　　　　　　US
KEYSTONE COAL INDUSTRY MANUAL. 1918. a. $260 in US & Canada; elsewhere $310. Intertec, Mining Information Services, 29 N. Wacker Dr., Chicago, IL 60606. TEL 312-726-2802. FAX 312-726-2574. Ed. Arthur P. Sanda. adv. contact: Daria Shahriari. **Document type:** directory.
Description: Lists all operating coal mines and processing plants in U.S. and Canada. Also includes essential information on coal sales, coal exporters, coal transportation companies, users of coal and coal seam geology.

KLIK! SHOWCASE PHOTOGRAPHY. see *PHOTOGRAPHY*

380.1025489　　　DK　　ISSN 0075-661X
HF3643
KOMPASS; indeks over Danmarks industri og naegringsliv. Variant title: Kompass Danmark. (Text in Danish; classifications in Danish, English, French, German, Spanish; summaries in Danish, English, German) 1961. s-a. DKK 1470. Forlaget Kompass Danmark, Oeveroedvej 5, DK-2840 Holte, Denmark. TEL 45-45-41-21-00. FAX 45-45-41-06-65. adv.; bk.rev. circ. 6,000. **Document type:** directory.
• Also available on CD-ROM.
—BLDSC (5105.601000).

380　　　　　　　　UK
KOMPASS ADVERTISING EXTRACTS. Variant title: U K Kompass Buyers Guides. (In 5 vols.) 1978. a. Kompass (Subsidiary of: Reed Information Services Ltd.), Part of the Reed Elsevier group, Windsor Ct., E. Grinstead House, E. Grinstead, W. Sussex RH19 1XD, England. TEL 44-1342-326972. FAX 44-1342-335992. TELEX 95127-INSFER-G. Ed. Dawn Ingram. circ. 6,000. **Document type:** directory.
Former titles: Kompass Industrial Sections; Kompass Buyers Guides; Euro Kompass U K Buyers Guides; Euro Kompass U K Industrial Sections.

338 664 663　　　AT
KOMPASS AGRIBUSINESSS AND FOOD AND BEVERAGE. 1996. a. $80. (Australian Trade Commission) Peter Isaacson Publications Pty. Ltd., 46-50 Porter St., Prahran, Vic. 3181, Australia. TEL 61-3-2457777. FAX 61-3-2457840. adv. contact: Joseph Dagher. circ. 3,000. **Document type:** directory.
• Also available online.
Formed by the 1996 merger of: Agriculture Australia (ISSN 1039-6187) & Kompass Food and Beverage (ISSN 1322-2813); Which was formerly: Hospitality Industry Suppliers Index (ISSN 0817-0398); (until 1986): Hospitality Buyers Guide (ISSN 0156-3688); Hospitality Buyers Guide and Diary (ISSN 0314-1551); Hospitality Yearbook (ISSN 0311-2969).
Description: Details companies in agricultural and food industry in Australia.

670　　　　　　　　AT
KOMPASS AUSTRALIA. 1970. a. (in 2 vols.). $495. (Associated Chambers of Manufacturers of Australia) Peter Isaacson Publications Pty. Ltd., 46-50 Porter St., Prahran, Vic. 3181, Australia. TEL 61-3-2457777. FAX 61-3-2457840. adv. contact: Joseph Dagher. **Document type:** directory.
• Also available online.
Also available on CD-ROM.
—BLDSC (5105.603000); CISTI. **CCC**.
Former titles: Kompass Register; Kompass Australia (ISSN 0075-6628)
Description: Lists products and services in Australia, with cross-references to the companies that supply them.

670　　　　　　　　BE　　ISSN 0778-4147
HF5181.B3
KOMPASS BELGIUM; repertoire de l'economie de la Belgique. (Text in Dutch and French; classifications and summaries in Dutch, English, French, German) 1961. a. free. (Foundation for Promoting International Economic Information, SZ) Editus Belgium S.A., Av. Moliere 256, 1060 Brussels, Belgium. TEL 32-2-3459070. FAX 32-2-3473340. TELEX 62903 KMPPS B. (Dist. in the U.S. and Canada by: Croner Publications, 211-03 Jamaica Ave., Queens Village, NY 11428) Ed. C. Somville. adv. circ. 4,700. **Document type:** directory.
• Also available online.
Also available on CD-ROM.
—BLDSC (5105.606000).
Formerly (until 1990): Kompass Belgium - Luxembourg (ISSN 0075-6636)

338 330　　　　　AT
KOMPASS BUSINESS SERVICES AND TRANSPORT. 1996. a. Aus.$85. Peter Isaacson Publications Pty. Ltd., 46-50 Porter St., Prahran, Vic. 3181, Australia. TEL 61-3-2457777. FAX 61-3-2457840. adv. contact: Joseph Dagher. circ. 3,000. **Document type:** directory.
Formed by the merger of (1994-1996): Kompass Logistic Services and Equipment (ISSN 1322-2821); (1993-1996): Kompass Business and Commercial Services (ISSN 1320-5404)
Description: Lists companies in Australia in the transport industry and who provide products and services to businesses.

338 668.4 678.2　AT
KOMPASS CHEMICAL, PLASTIC AND RUBBER PRODUCTS. 1993. a. Aus.$85. Peter Isaacson Publications Pty. Ltd., 46-50 Porter St., Prahran, Vic. 3181, Australia. TEL 61-3-2457777. FAX 61-3-2457840. adv. contact: Joseph Dagheriuti. circ. 1,000. **Document type:** directory.
• Also available online.
Formerly: Kompass Plastic, Rubber and Chemical Products.
Description: Details companies who provide products and services to the plastics, rubber and chemical industries. Full contact details provided for each company.

338 643　　　　　AT　　ISSN 1320-5412
KOMPASS ELECTRONIC AND ELECTRICAL PRODUCTS. 1993. a. Aus.$85. Peter Isaacson Publications Pty. Ltd., 46-50 Porter St., Prahran, Vic. 3181, Australia. TEL 61-3-2457777. FAX 61-3-2457840. adv. contact: Joseph Dagher. circ. 1,000. **Document type:** directory.
• Also available online.
Description: Details Australian electronics and electrical products suppliers and their associated companies who service the industry. Full contact details are also provided.

670　　　　　　　　NE　　ISSN 0075-6660
KOMPASS HOLLAND; informatiewerk over het Nederlandse Bedrijfsleven. (Text in Dutch; classifications and summaries in Dutch, English, German, French, Spanish) 1964. a. fl.325. (Foundation for Promoting International Economic Information, SZ) Kompass Nederland BV, Hogehilweg 15, 1101 CB Amsterdam Z.O., Netherlands. (Subscr. to: Croner Publications, Inc., 211-03 Jamaica Ave., Queens Village, NY 11428) adv.; bk.rev. circ. 8,600. **Document type:** directory.

338.025　　　　　IE
KOMPASS IRELAND (YEAR). 1988. a. I£140. (Irish Business and Employers Confederation) Kompass Ireland Publishers Ltd., Kompass House, Parnell Ct., 1 Granby Row, Dublin 1, Ireland. TEL 353-1-8728800. FAX 353-1-8733711. E-mail: postmaster@kompass.ie. (Co-sponsor: Northern Ireland Chamber of Commerce and Industry) Ed. Carol Delany. adv. contact: Michael McGowan. circ. 4,000. **Document type:** directory.

670　　　　　　　　IT　　ISSN 0075-6687
HF3583
KOMPASS ITALIA; repertorio generale dell'economia italiana. (Text in Italian; classifications and summaries in Italian, French, English, German) 1962. a. L.500000. (Kompass International S.A., SZ) Kompass Italia S.p.A., Via Seruais, 125, 10146 Turin, Italy. adv. circ. 12,000. **Document type:** directory.
• Also available on CD-ROM. Producer(s): SilverPlatter Information, Inc.

670　　　　　　　　MR　　ISSN 0075-6695
KOMPASS MAROC; register of Moroccan industry and commerce. (Text and classifications in French; summaries in English, French) 1966. a. $150. (Foundation for Promoting International Economic Information, SZ) Kompass Maroc-Veto, Boite Postale 11100, MA Casablanca, Morocco. FAX 2-266056. (Affiliate: Kompass International AG, Zurich) Ed. Eric Verdavainne. adv. circ. 7,000. (also avail. in diskette format) **Document type:** directory.

BUSINESS AND ECONOMICS — TRADE AND INDUSTRIAL DIRECTORIES

338   NO   ISSN 0075-6709
HC362.2
KOMPASS NORGE; indeks over Norges industri og Naeringsliv. (Text in English, French, German, Norwegian, Spanish; summaries in English, German, Norwegian) 1970. a. NOK 1460. (Export Council of Norway) Kompass Norge A-S, Hillevaagsveien 107, N-4004 Stavanger, Norway. Ed. Irene Fjelde Asboernsen. adv. circ. 6,000. **Document type:** directory.

338.025   PH
KOMPASS PHILIPPINES; register of industry and commerce of the Republic of the Philippines. (Text in English) 1990. a. $130 (effective 1996). Belgosa Business Communication Inc., 6-F, PDCP Bank Center, Alfaro cor. Herrera Sts., Salcedo Villge, Makati City, Philippines. TEL 632-8925462. FAX 632-8136837. E-mail: kompass@globe.com. ph. circ. 500. **Document type:** directory.
    Description: Lists 15500 companies and 50000 products and services.

338 618   AT
KOMPASS PRECISION EQUIPMENT. 1993. a. Aus.$80. (Austrade) Peter Isaacson Publications Pty. Ltd., 46-50 Porter St., Prahran, Vic. 3181, Australia. TEL 61-3-2457777. FAX 61-3-2457840. adv. contact: Nicholas Ricciuti. circ. 7,500. **Document type:** directory.
    Former titles: Australian Scientific and Industrial Equipment Catalogue (ISSN 1322-2805) & Australian Scientific and Laboratory Exports.
    Description: Details Australian exporters of scientific and industrial equipment, products and services.

338.025 663   FR   ISSN 0299-6154
KOMPASS PROFESSIONNEL. AGRICULTURE, ALIMENTATION. 1969. a. (effective 1997). Kompass France, 66 quai du Marechal Joffre, 92415 Courbevoie Cedex, France. Ed. Bertrand Macabeo; Pub. Bertrand Macabeo. R&P contact: Bertrand Macabeo. adv. contact: Mireille Girault. **Document type:** directory.
    Former titles (until 1986): Kompass. L'Alimentation Francaise (ISSN 0337-5242); (until 1973): Annuaire Industriel. L'Alimentation Francaise (ISSN 0337-5234).

338.025 624   FR   ISSN 0299-6162
KOMPASS PROFESSIONNEL. BATIMENT ET GENIE CIVIL, MANUTENTION - LEVAGE, BOIS - MEUBLES. 1971. a. Kompass France, 66 quai du Marechal Joffre, 92415 Courbevoie Cedex, France. Ed. Bertrand Macabeo; Pub. Bertrand Macabeo. R&P contact: Bertrand Macabeo. adv. contact: Mireille Girault. **Document type:** directory.
    Former titles (until 1986): Kompass. Genie Civil, Manutention - Levage, Stockage (ISSN 0396-0021); (until 1976): Kompass. Equipements de Genie Civil, Manutention, Levage (ISSN 0337-5498); (until 1975): Kompass. Batiment, Travaux Publics, Manutention Levage (ISSN 0337-548X); (until 1973): Annuaire Industriel. Batiment, Travaux Publics, Manutention, Levage (ISSN 0337-5471).

338.025 690   FR   ISSN 1143-8606
KOMPASS PROFESSIONNEL. CHAUDRONNERIE, CONSTRUCTIONS METALLIQUES, TOLERIES, TUBES, CHAUFFAGE. 1969. a. Kompass France, 66 quai du Marechal Joffre, 92415 Courbevoie Cedex, France. Ed. Bertrand Macabeo; Pub. Bertrand Macabeo. R&P contact: Bertrand Macabeo. **Document type:** directory.
    Former titles (until 1987): Kompass. Chaudronnerie, Constructions Metalliques, Tolerie, Tubes, Chauffage (ISSN 0337-5269); (until 1973): Annuaire Industriel. Chaudronnerie, Constructions Metalliques, Tolerie, Tubes, Chauffage (ISSN 0337-5250).

338.025 540   FR   ISSN 0299-6111
KOMPASS PROFESSIONNEL. CHIMIE, PLASTIQUES, CAOUTCHOUC, PRODUITS MINERAUX. 1971. a. Kompass France, 66 quai du Marechal Joffre, 92415 Courbevoie Cedex, France. Ed. Bertrand Macabeo; Pub. Bertrand Macabeo. R&P contact: Bertrand Macabeo. adv. contact: Mireille Girault. **Document type:** directory.
    Former titles (until 1987): Kompass. Chimie, Petrole, Plastiques, Caoutchouc (ISSN 0337-5285); (until 1974): Annuaire Industriel. Chimie, Petrole, Plastique, Caoutchouc (ISSN 0337-5277).

338.025 658.86   FR   ISSN 0990-8536
KOMPASS PROFESSIONNEL. DISTRIBUTION, COMMERCE DE GROS. 1988. a. Kompass France, 66 quai du Marechal Joffre, 92415 Courbevoie Cedex, France. Pub. Bertrand Macabeo. R&P contact: Bertrand Macabeo. adv. contact: Mireille Girault. **Document type:** directory.

338.025 530   FR   ISSN 0299-612X
KOMPASS PROFESSIONNEL. ELECTRICITE, ELECTRONIQUE, INFORMATIQUE. 1969. a. Kompass France, 66 quai du Marechal Joffre, 92415 Courbevoie Cedex, France. Ed. Bertrand Macabeo; Pub. Bertrand Macabeo. R&P contact: Bertrand Macabeo. adv. contact: Mireille Girault. **Document type:** directory.
    Former titles (until 1987): Kompass. Electricite, Electronique, Nucleaire (ISSN 0337-5307); (until 1974): Annuaire Industriel. Electricite, Electronique, Nucleaire (ISSN 0337-5293).

338.025   FR   ISSN 0990-8544
KOMPASS PROFESSIONNEL. INDUSTRIES EN MATIERES MULTIPLES. 1988. a. Kompass France, 66 quai du Marechal Joffre, 92415 Courbevoie Cedex, France. Ed. Bertrand Macabeo; Pub. Bertrand Macabeo. R&P contact: Bertrand Macabeo. adv. contact: Mireille Girault. **Document type:** directory.

338.025 621   FR   ISSN 0299-6103
KOMPASS PROFESSIONNEL. MACHINES - OUTILS, ROBOTIQUE, MECANIQUE GENERALE. 1971. a. Kompass France, 66 quai du Marechal Joffre, 92415 Courbevoie Cedex, France. Ed. Bertrand Macabeo; Pub. Bertrand Macabeo. R&P contact: Bertrand Macabeo. adv. contact: Mireille Girault. **Document type:** directory.
    Former titles (until 1983): Kompass. Machine-Outil (ISSN 0337-5463); (until 1973): Annuaire Industriel. Machine-Outil (ISSN 0337-5455).

338.025 389.6   FR   ISSN 0299-6081
KOMPASS PROFESSIONNEL. PRECISION. 1971. a. Kompass France, 66 quai du Marechal Joffre, 92415 Courbevoie Cedex, France. Ed. Bertrand Macabeo; Pub. Bertrand MAcabeo. R&P contact: Bertrand Macabeo. adv. contact: Mireille Girault. **Document type:** directory.
    Former titles (until 1987): Kompass. Precision (ISSN 0337-5447); (until 1974): Annuaire Industriel. Precision, Mesure, Controle, Regulation, Essais, Optique, Horlogerie (ISSN 0337-5439).

338.025 669   FR   ISSN 0299-6138
KOMPASS PROFESSIONNEL. PRODUITS DU METAL. 1969. a. Kompass France, 66 quai du Marechal Joffre, 92415 Courbevoie Cedex, France. Ed. Bertrand Macabeo; Pub. Bertrand Macabeo. R&P contact: Bertand Macabeo. adv. contact: Mireille Girault. **Document type:** directory.
    Former titles (until 1987): Kompass. Petite Metallurgie, Composants Mecaniques (ISSN 0337-5323); (until 1975): Annuaire Industriel. Petite Metallurgie (ISSN 0337-5315).

380   FR   ISSN 0299-609X
KOMPASS PROFESSIONNEL. SERVICES, INDUSTRIES GRAPHIQUES. 1969. a. 270 F. Kompass France, 66 quai du Marechal Joffre, 92415 Courbevoie Cedex, France. Ed. Bertrand Macabeo; Pub. Bertrand Macabeo. R&P contact: Bertrand Macabeo. adv. contact: Mireille Girault. **Document type:** directory.
    Former titles (until 1987): Kompass. Special Services (ISSN 0337-5366); (until 1975): Annuaire Industriel. Special Services (ISSN 0337-5358).

338.025 669   FR   ISSN 0299-6170
KOMPASS PROFESSIONNEL. SIDERURGIE, METALLURGIE, FONDERIE. 1969. a. Kompass France, 66 quai du Marechal Joffre, 92415 Courbevoie Cedex, France. Ed. Bertrand Macabeo; Pub. Bertrand Macabeo. R&P contact: Bertrand Macabeo. adv. contact: Mireille Girault. **Document type:** directory.
    Former titles (until 1987): Kompass. Siderurgie, Metallurgie, Fonderie, Travail des Metuax (ISSN 0337-534X); (until 1975): Annuaire Industriel. Siderurgie, Metallurgie, Fonderie, Travail des Metaux (ISSN 0337-5331).

338.025 627   FR   ISSN 0299-6197
KOMPASS PROFESSIONNEL. TECHNIQUES HYDRAULIQUES ET PNEUMATIQUES, CLIMATISATION. 1975. a. Kompass France, 66 quai du Marechal Joffre, 92415 Courbevoie Cedex, France. Ed. Bertrand Macabeo; Pub. Bertrand Macabeo. R&P contact: Bertrand Macabeo. adv. contact: Mireille Girault. **Document type:** directory.
    Formerly (until 1986): Kompass. Techniques Hydrauliques et Pneumatiques (ISSN 0396-003X)

670 687   FR   ISSN 0299-6146
KOMPASS PROFESSIONNEL. TEXTILE, HABILLEMENT, CUIRS ET PEAUX. (Text and summaries in English, French, German and Spanish) 1974. a. 270 F. (effective 1997). Kompass France, 66 quai du Marechal Joffre, 92415 Courbevoie Cedex, France. Ed. Bertrand Macabeo; Pub. Bertrand Macabeo. R&P contact: Bertrand Macabeo. adv. contact: Mireille Girault. illus. **Document type:** directory.
    Former titles (until 1987): Kompass. Le Textile et l'Habillement (ISSN 0396-1931); (until 1975): Kompass. L'Industrie Francaise du Textile, de l'Habillement, de la Chaussure (ISSN 0396-1923)

338.025 380.5   FR   ISSN 0990-8552
KOMPASS PROFESSIONNEL. TRANSPORTS, MOYENS DE TRANSPORTS. 1988. a. Kompass France, 66 quai du Marechal Joffre, 92415 Courbevoie Cedex, France. Ed. Bertrand Macabeo; Pub. Bertrand Macabeo. R&P contact: Bertrand Macabeo. adv. contact: Mireille Girault. **Document type:** directory.

670 664   FR
KOMPASS PROFESSIONNELS. (In 15 sections: Agriculture, Alimentation; Batiment et Genie Civil, Manutention-Levage, Bois-Meubles; Chaudronnerie, Constructions Metalliques, Toleries, Tubes, Chauffage; Chimie, Plastiques, Caoutchouc, Produits Mineraux; Distribution, Commerce de Gros; Electricite, Electronique, Informatique; Industries en Matieres Multiples; Machines-Outils, Robotique, Mecanique Generale; Precision; Produits du Metal; Services, Industries Graphiques; Siderurgie, Metallurgie, Fonderie; Techniques Hydrauliques et Pneumatiques, Climatisation; Textile, Habillement, Cuirs et Peaux; Transports, Moyens de Transports) (Text and summaries in English, French, German, Spanish) 1974. a. price varies. Kompass France, 66 quai du Marechal Joffre, 92415 Courbevoie Cedex, France. Ed. Bertrand Macabeo; Pub. Bertrand Macabeo. R&P contact: Bertrand Macabeo. adv. contact: Mireille Girault. illus. **Document type:** directory.
    Description: Fifteen sectional directories covering whole French industry.

338.025   KO
KOMPASS REPUBLIC OF KOREA. (Text in English) 2nd ed., 1990. a.? Global Industrial Survey Co., Ltd., Kolon Bldg., 5F, 45, Mugyo-dong, Chung-gu, Seoul, S. Korea. TEL 02-758-6820. FAX 02-755-1776.

670   SZ   ISSN 0075-6717
KOMPASS SCHWEIZ - LIECHTENSTEIN; informationswerk der Schweizerischen Wirtschaft. (Text in French, German, Italian; classifications in English, French, German, Italian; summaries in English, French, and German) 1947. a. $150. Schweiz Verlag AG, In Grosswiesen 14, 8044 Zurich, Switzerland. (Dist. in the U.S. and Canada by: Croner Publications, Inc., 211-03 Jamaica Ave., Queens Village, NY 11428) adv. circ. 10,000. **Document type:** directory.

338.025   SI   ISSN 0217-0604
KOMPASS SINGAPORE. (Text in English) 1971. a., 15th ed., 1992. Kompass South East Asia Ltd., 326C King George's Ave., Singapore 0820, Singapore. TEL 296-9684. FAX 296-2561. TELEX RS 20013 KMPSS.
—BLDSC (5105.627000).

330   SA   ISSN 1022-3568
KOMPASS SOUTH AFRICA. 1993. a. R.620 (effective 1997). Reed Business Information South Africa (Pty.) Ltd., P.O. Box 653207, Benmore 2010, South Africa. TEL 27-11-774-1110. FAX 27-11-883-4729. URL: http://africa.cis.co.za. adv. contact: Rohini Bawa. **Document type:** directory.
●Also available online.
Also available on CD-ROM.
    Description: Lists information on more than 15,000 South African businesses and manufacturers, including addresses, telephone and fax numbers, and their products and services.

BUSINESS AND ECONOMICS — TRADE AND INDUSTRIAL DIRECTORIES   1693

670　　　　　　SW　　ISSN 0075-6725
HF3673
KOMPASS SVERIGE; handbok oever Sveriges industri och Naeringsliv. (Text in Swedish; classifications in Swedish, English, French, German, Spanish; summaries in Swedish, English, German) 1958. a. SEK 1780 (effective 1997). Kompass Sverige AB, Torsgatan 21, S-113 90 Stockholm, Sweden. FAX 46-8-7363022. (U.S. dist.: Reed Business Publishing, 121 Chanlon Rd., New Providence, NJ 07974. TEL 908-464-6800) adv. circ. 6,000. **Document type:** directory.
●Also available online. Vendor(s): Knight-Ridder Information, Inc.
Also available on CD-ROM.

338.025　　　　CH　　ISSN 0259-4021
HC430.5.A1
KOMPASS TAIWAN. (Text in English) 1973. a. (in 2 vols.). $300. Trade Winds, Inc., No. 7, Lane 75, Yungkang St., P.O. Box 7-179, Taipei, Taiwan 10602, Republic of China. TEL 886-2-3932718. FAX 886-2-3963345. E-mail: tradwind@ms2.hinet. net; URL: http://www.tradewinds.comtw. (Subscr. in U.S. to: Trade Winds Inc., Box 820519, Dallas, TX 75382. TEL 972-699-1188. FAX 972-699-1189) Ed. Don Shapiro. R&P contact: Lloyd Tan. adv. **Document type:** directory.
Description: Provides information on 25,000 companies in Taiwan and their products or services.

380 658　　　　　UK
KOMPASS U.K. REGIONAL SALES GUIDE (YEAR). (In 4 vols.) a. £125 per vol.; set £340. Kompass (Subsidiary of: Reed Information Services Ltd.), Part of the Reed Elsevier group, Windsor Ct., E. Grinstead House, E. Grinstead, W. Sussex RH19 1XD, England. TEL 01342-326972. FAX 01342-335992. TELEX 95127-INFSER-G. Pub. Gemma Hamel-Smith. circ. 16,000. **Document type:** directory.
Formerly: Kompass U.K. Management Register.

670　　　　　　UK　　ISSN 0959-6976
KOMPASS UNITED KINGDOM; register of British industry and commerce. (In 5 vols.) 1962. a. £964. (Confederation of British Industry) Kompass (Subsidiary of: Reed Information Services Ltd.), Part of the Reed Elsevier group, Windsor Ct., E. Grinstead House, E. Grinstead, W. Sussex RH19 1XD, England. TEL 44-1342-326972. FAX 44-1342-335992. TELEX 95127-INFSER-G. Ed. Dawn Ingram; Pub. Derek Barley. adv. contact: Brian Higgins. circ. 8,500. **Document type:** directory.
●Also available online. Vendor(s): Reed Information Services Ltd.
Also available on CD-ROM.
—CISTI; Linda Hall.
Formerly: Kompass United Kingdom - C B I (ISSN 0075-6733)

338　　　　　　PH　　ISSN 0117-5718
KONTAKS PHILIPPINES (YEAR). (Supplement to: Philippines Business Directory) (Text in English) 1977. biennial. P.950 (foreign $70). Massmark Philippines, P.O. Box 3333, Manila 1073, Philippines. TEL 805-0955. Ed. J.C. Borja. adv.: B&W page $250. (reprint service avail.) **Document type:** directory.
Formerly: Kontaks (ISSN 0115-513X)
Description: Provides marketing guide, marketing indices, business profiles and marketing insights of leading opinion writers and business people.

338.025　　　　GW　　ISSN 0935-0241
KONZERNE IN SCHAUBILDERN. 1974. 8/yr. Verlag Hoppenstedt GmbH, Havelstr. 9, 64295 Darmstadt, Germany. TEL 49-6151-380-0. FAX 49-6151-380360. (looseleaf format; also avail. in diskette format) **Document type:** directory.
●Also available online. Vendor(s): Lexis-Nexis.
Also available on CD-ROM.
Description: Information on 700 international holding companies and their relation to over 70,000 affiliated companies.

380 659　　　　KO　　ISSN 1225-0147
KOREA ANNUAL; comprehensive handbook on Korea. Korean edition: Hapdong Yongam (ISSN 0073-0335) (Text in English) 1963. a. $42 for 1996 ed. Yonhap News Agency, 85-1 Soosong-Dong, Chongro-ku, Box Kwangwhamoon 1039, Seoul, S. Korea. TEL 02-398-3590. FAX 02-398-3631. TELEX YONHAP K23618. (U.S. addr.: Western Publications Service, 1359 20th Ave., San Francisco, CA 94122. TEL 415-566-3550) Ed. Young-Il Kim; Pub. So-Whan Hyon. adv. circ. 30,000.
—BLDSC (5113.450000).
Description: Contains reviews of major events in the past year, including government activities, economic indices and statistics, education and social affairs.

338.025 643　　　KO　　ISSN 1227-5336
KOREA BUYERS GUIDE ELECTRONICS. (Text in English) m. $70 in Asia; elsewhere $95. (Korea Foreign Trade Association) Buyers Guide Corp., Korea World Trade Center, 159-1, Samsung-dong, Kangnam-gu, Seoul 135-729, S. Korea. TEL 82-2-551-2376. FAX 82-2-551-2377. (Subscr. to: Trade Center, P.O. Box 8, Seoul, S. Korea; Dist. in US by: Charles Lee, Korea Buyers Guide of America Ltd., 612 S. Wheeling Rd., Wheeling, IL 60090. TEL 800-732-3572. FAX 708-459-0995) Ed. Sung-Hwan Park.

380 659　　　　KO　　ISSN 0075-6814
KOREA DIRECTORY. (Text in English) 1958. a. $78. Korea Directory Company, C.P.O. Box 3955, Seoul 100-639, S. Korea. (Dist. in US by: Croner Publications, Inc., 34 Jericho Tpke., Jericho, NY 11753. TEL 516-333-9085) adv. contact: O.R. Kim. **Document type:** directory.
Description: Lists manufacturers, business firms and trading companies in Korea.

338.025　　　　KO
KOREA YELLOW PAGES (YEAR). (Text in English) 1983. a. $50. Korea Yellow Pages Ltd., K.P.O. Box 1525, Seoul 110-615, S. Korea. TEL 02-332-5942. FAX 02-333-5264. Ed. M.E. Chong. adv. **Document type:** directory.
Description: Lists major Korean businesses and services.

380　　　　　　KO
KOREAN BUSINESS DIRECTORY. (Text in English) 1970. a. $110. Korea Chamber of Commerce and Industry, 45, Namdaemunno 4-ga, Chung-gu, C.P.O. Box 25, Seoul 100-743, S. Korea. TEL 82-2-316-3114. FAX 82-2-757-9475. Ed. Kim Chung-Tai. adv. **Document type:** directory.
Description: Lists about 9,700 of Korea's manufacturers, traders, service industries, economic organizations. Also provides a thorough guide book for conducting profitable business with Korea.

338　　　　　　KO
KOREAN SOURCES (YEAR). s-a. $66. C.P.O. Box 3955, Seoul, S. Korea. TEL 737-9451. **Document type:** directory.
Description: Covers major export industries.

382　　　　　　KO
KOREAN TRADE DIRECTORY. (Text in English) 1959. biennial. 30000 Won($40) (effective 1991). Korea Foreign Trade Association, 159-1 Samsung-dong, Dang-nam-ku, Seoul 135-729, S. Korea. TEL 02-551-5267. FAX 02-551-5161. TELEX KOTRASO K 24265. Ed. Yong-Hak Park. circ. 5,000. **Document type:** directory.
Description: Covers Korean company information indexed by products and import and export items.

338 332.6　　　　II
KOTHARI'S INDUSTRIAL DIRECTORY OF INDIA. (Text in English) 1936. every 18 mos., 40th ed., 1996. $225. Kothari Enterprises, Kothari Bldgs., 144, Mahatma Gandhi Salai, Madras 600 034, India. TEL 91-44-8272131. FAX 91-44-8256464. TELEX 041-8325 KS IN. Ed. S. Arokiasamy. adv. circ. 5,000. **Document type:** directory.
Formerly: Kothari's Economic and Industrial Guide of India; Continues: Kothari's Economic Guide and Investor's Handbook of India.
Description: Covers economic, financial, industrial and business decision makers in India and all over the world.

338　　　　　　DK　　ISSN 0900-2243
HF3643
KRAK; industrial and trade directory for Denmark. (Issued in 4 vols.) (Text in English) 1770. a. DKK 3025. Kraks Forlag AS, Virumgaardsvej 21, DK-2830 Virum, Denmark. TEL 45-45-83-45-83. FAX 45-45-83-10-11. adv. circ. 30,000. **Document type:** directory.

382　　　　　　SW　　ISSN 1400-1489
KRITISKA E U FAKTA. 1989. 10/yr. SEK 10 per no. Nej til E U, Torsg. 2, S-111 23 Stockholm, Sweden. (Subscr. to: P.O. Box 31124, S-400 32 Goeteborg, Sweden)
Formerly (until 1994): Kritiska Europafakta.

338.025　　　　GW
KUENSTLER JAHRBUCH. 1994. a. DM.48 (US DM.56). Verlag Disco Post GmbH, Oststr. 2, 56424 Staudt, Germany. TEL 49-2602-70044. FAX 49-2602-69939. Ed. Karl-Heinz Busch. R&P contact: Karl-Heinz Busch. adv.: B&W page DM.1250, color page DM.1875; trim 120 x 180; adv. contact: Karin Ostrowski. circ. 10,000. **Document type:** directory.

338　　　　　　SA
KWAZULU - NATAL BUSINESS REGISTER. 1983. a. R.102 (effective 1997). Braby's (Subsidiary of: Kohler Packaging Ltd.), P.O. Box 1426, Pinetown 3600, South Africa. TEL 27-31-7017021. FAX 27-31-7017036. adv. **Document type:** directory.
Former titles (until 1994): Natal - KwaZulu Business Register (ISSN 0259-2304); (until 1987): Natal Business Register (ISSN 0258-5006)

338　　　　　　SA
KWAZULU - NATAL DIRECTORY. Spine title: Braby's KwaZulu Natal Directory. (Text in English) 1902. a. R.180 (effective 1997). Braby's (Subsidiary of: Kohler Packaging Ltd.), P.O. Box 1426, Pinetown 3600, South Africa. TEL 27-31-7017021. FAX 27-31-7017036. Ed. A. Stagg. adv. **Document type:** directory.
Formerly (until 1994): Braby's Natal Directory (ISSN 0378-9276)

338　　　　　　SA
KWAZULU - NATAL MIDLANDS DIRECTORY. a. R.25 (effective 1997). Braby's (Subsidiary of: Kohler Packaging Ltd.), P.O. Box 1426, Pinetown 3600, South Africa. TEL 27-31-7017021. FAX 27-31-7017036. **Document type:** directory.
Formerly: Natal Midlands Directory.

670 542　　　　CN
LABORATORY YELLOW PAGES. 1990. a. Can.$40. Jesmar Communications Inc., 30 E. Beaver Creek Rd., Ste. 220, Richmond Hill, Ont. L4B 1J2, Canada. TEL 416-886-5040. FAX 416-886-6615. Ed. Kathleen Hurd. adv. circ. 32,140. **Document type:** directory.

338　　　　　　SA　　ISSN 0378-9268
LADYSMITH DIRECTORY. (Text in English) a. R.25 (effective 1996). Braby's (Subsidiary of: Kohler Packaging Ltd.), P.O. Box 1426, Pinetown 3600, South Africa. TEL 27-31-7017021. FAX 27-31-7017036. Ed. A. Stagg. **Document type:** directory.

338 362.15　　　UK　　ISSN 0953-9050
LAING'S REVIEW OF PRIVATE HEALTHCARE (YEAR); and directory of independent hospitals and nursing and residential homes. 1987. a. £130. Laing & Buisson, Lymehouse Studios, 38 Georgiana St., London NW1 0EB, England. TEL 44-171-284-1268. FAX 44-171-267-8269. E-mail: laingb@dial.pipex.com. Ed. William Laing. adv.; stat. circ. 4,000. **Document type:** directory.
●Also available on CD-ROM.
—BLDSC (5143.788000).

LASER FOCUS WORLD BUYERS' GUIDE. see PHYSICS — Optics

380　　　　　　CR
LATIN AMERICAN IMPORT - EXPORT DIRECTORY. (Text in English, Spanish) 1983. a. $23.50. International Trade Council, Box 73, 1007 San Jose, Costa Rica. TEL 33-8697. **Document type:** directory.

LAW FIRMS YELLOW BOOK; who's who in the management of the leading U.S. law firms. see LAW

LEADERSHIP DIRECTORIES ON C D - R O M. see PUBLIC ADMINISTRATION

B

BUSINESS AND ECONOMICS — TRADE AND INDUSTRIAL DIRECTORIES

LEATHER MANUFACTURER DIRECTORY. see *LEATHER AND FUR INDUSTRIES*

670   LE   ISSN 0075-8353
LEBANESE INDUSTRIAL AND COMMERCIAL DIRECTORY/ANNUAIRE DES PROFESSIONS AU LIBAN. (Text in French; index in Arabic, English and French) 1953. biennial. $30. Middle East Commercial Information Center, Box 6466, Beirut, Lebanon. (Dist. by: UNIPUB, 345 Park Ave. S., New York, NY 10010) Ed. Charles G. Gedeon. adv. circ. 10,000. **Document type:** directory.

338.025 320   US
▼**THE LEFT GUIDE;** a guide to liberal, progressive, and left-of-center organizations. 1996. s-a. $74.95. Economics Americam Inc., 612 Church St., Ann Arbor, MI 48104. TEL 313-995-0865. FAX 313-747-7258. E-mail: wilcoxdl@aol.com. Ed. Derk Arend Wilcox. **Document type:** directory.
Description: Lists over 2,000 think tanks, lobbying groups, publishers, and public-interest litigation organizations. Includes financial information on organizations including revenues, salaries, lobbying expenditures and sources of funding.

388   US   ISSN 1068-686X
HE5623
LEONARD'S GUIDE. NATIONAL CONTRACT CARRIERS DIRECTORY. 1989. a. $75 (effective 1997). G.R. Leonard & Co., 2121 Shermer Rd., Northbrook, IL 60062. TEL 847-498-2121. **Document type:** directory.

388   US
LEONARD'S GUIDE. NATIONAL THIRD PARTY LOGISTICS DIRECTORY. a. $75 (effective 1997). G.R. Leonard & Co., 2121 Shermer Rd., Northbrook, IL 60062. TEL 847-498-2121.
Formerly: Leonard's Guide. National Transportation Brokers Directory.

388   US
LEONARD'S GUIDE. NATIONAL WAREHOUSE AND DISTRIBUTION DIRECTORY. a. $75 (effective 1997). G.R. Leonard & Co., 2121 Shermer Rd., Northbrook, IL 60062. TEL 847-498-2121. **Document type:** directory.

338   SA   ISSN 1016-3999
LESOTHO BUSINESS DIRECTORY. 1973. a. R.48 (effective 1997). Braby's (Subsidiary of: Kohler Packaging Ltd.), P.O. Box 1426, Pinetown 3600, South Africa. TEL 27-31-7017021. FAX 27-31-7017036. adv. **Document type:** directory.

338.025 658   US
LESSONS OF YELLOW PAGES COMPETITION. 1993. irreg. $1501 (Canada and Mexico $1515; elsewhere $1535) (effective 1997). Cowles - SIMBA Information (Subsidiary of: Cowles Business Media), 11 Riverbend Dr. S., Box 4949, Stamford, CT 06907-0949. TEL 203-358-9900; 800-307-2529. FAX 203-358-5811. E-mail: info@simbanet.com; URL: http://www.simbanet.com. **Document type:** trade publication.
Description: Analyzes the succcesses and failures among yellow pages directories launched during the previous five years.

382.025   LB
LIBERIAN TRADE DIRECTORY;* basic trade information, exporters & importers. irreg. Ministry of Commerce, Industry and Transportation, Director of Foreign Trade, Box 9041, Monrovia, Liberia. **Document type:** directory.

THE LIBRARIES DIRECTORY. see *LIBRARY AND INFORMATION SCIENCES*

380   GW   ISSN 0941-6072
LIEFERN UND LEISTEN; firms classified according to trades. (Text in German; index in English and French) 1926. a. DM.140. Deutscher Adressbuch Verlag, Arheilger Weg 17, 64380 Rossdorf, Germany. TEL 06154-699500. FAX 06154-6995490. adv. circ. 5,000. **Document type:** directory.
●Also available on CD-ROM.
Formerly: Deutsche Branchen-Fernsprechbuch (ISSN 0170-284X)

LIGHTWAVE BUYERS GUIDE. see *COMMUNICATIONS*

LIST OF SHIPOWNERS, MANAGERS AND MANAGING AGENTS. see *TRANSPORTATION — Ships And Shipping*

LITERARY MARKET PLACE; the directory of American book publishing industry. see *PUBLISHING AND BOOK TRADE*

LLOYD'S A S E A N SHIPPING DIRECTORY. see *TRANSPORTATION — Ships And Shipping*

LLOYD'S MARINE EQUIPMENT BUYERS' GUIDE. see *TRANSPORTATION — Ships And Shipping*

LLOYD'S MARITIME DIRECTORY (YEAR); international shipping & shipbuilding directory. see *TRANSPORTATION — Ships And Shipping*

338.025 387   UK   ISSN 0960-6017
LLOYD'S SHIPPING CONNECTIONS. 1976. a. $65. L L P Limited, Sheepen Pl., Colchester, Essex CO3 3LP, England. TEL 44-1206-772277. FAX 44-1206-772118. Ed. Suzanne Hooke; Pub. Alan Condron. adv.: page £590; trim 210 x 147; adv. contact: Jacqueline Raven. bk.rev.; index; circ. 1,000. (also avail. in diskette format; back issues avail.) **Document type:** directory.

LOCKSMITH LEDGER - INTERNATIONAL DIRECTORY. see *CRIMINOLOGY AND LAW ENFORCEMENT — Security*

LOCKWOOD - POST'S DIRECTORY OF THE PULP, PAPER AND ALLIED TRADES. see *PAPER AND PULP*

LONDON PORT HANDBOOK (YEAR). see *TRANSPORTATION — Ships And Shipping*

LONG ISLAND TELEPHONE TICKLER FOR INSURANCE MEN & WOMEN. see *INSURANCE*

338.025 610   UK
LONG TERM CARE OF ELDERLY AND PHYSICALLY DISABLED PEOPLE - DIRECTORY OF MAJOR PROVIDERS. 1987. a. £120 (effective 1997). Laing & Buisson, Lymehouse Studios, 38 Georgiana St., London NW1 0EB, England. TEL 44-171-284-1268. FAX 44-171-267-8269. E-mail: laingb@dial.pipex.com. Ed. Jon Windus. adv. contact: Aidan Merritt. **Document type:** directory.
Formerly (until 1996): Long Term Care - Directory of Major Providers (ISSN 0957-5553)

338.025   US   ISSN 1048-7298
HF5065.L8
LOUISIANA BUSINESS DIRECTORY. 1988. 375. $375 (effective 1997). American Business Directories (Subsidiary of: American Business Information, Inc.), 5711 S. 86th Circle, Box 27347, Omaha, NE 68127. TEL 402-593-4600; 800-555-6124. FAX 402-331-5481. E-mail: jerry.venner@abii.com. index. (also avail. in magnetic tape; diskette format) **Document type:** directory.
●Also available online.
Also available on CD-ROM.
Description: Includes all businesses in the state compiled from the yellow pages and telephone-verified. Each listing includes company name, address, phone number, name of owner, and employee size and sales volume codes, and credit rating codes.

670   US   ISSN 1053-8992
HF5065.L8
LOUISIANA MANUFACTURERS REGISTER. 1991. a. $64 (diskette and CD-ROM $345)(effective 1997). Manufacturer's News, Inc., 1633 Central St., Evanston, IL 60201-1505. TEL 847-864-7000. FAX 847-332-1100. (diskette format) **Document type:** directory.
●Also available on CD-ROM.
Description: Lists 5,313 Louisiana manufacturers by their industrial product or service, alphabetically and geographically by city.

LOUISIANA - MISSISSIPPI STATE AGENT HANDBOOK. see *INSURANCE*

670   GW   ISSN 0932-3317
M UND A - MESSEPLANER INTERNATIONAL; schedule for fairs and exhibitions worldwide. 1919. s-a. DM.246.10 (foreign DM.310). M und A Verlag fuer Messen, Ausstellungen und Kongresse GmbH (Subsidiary of: Deutscher Fachverlag GmbH), Postfach 101528, 60015 Frankfurt a.M., Germany. TEL 49-69-759502. FAX 49-69-75951280. E-mail: muamesseplaner-redaktion@dfv.de. Ed. Dorit Vogel-Seib. adv.: B&W page DM.4730, color page DM.6020; trim 210 x 297; adv. contact: Jutta Fautz. circ. 8,098. (also avail. in diskette format) **Document type:** directory.
●Also available online.
Formerly: M und A Kalender.
Description: Contains basic data on approximately 7,500 fairs and exhibitions worldwide.

332.6   NE   ISSN 1350-1143
MCGREGOR'S WHO OWNS WHOM (SOUTHERN AFRICAN EDITION). 1980. a. $480 (effective 1993). Kluwer Law International (Subsidiary of: Wolters Kluwer N.V.), Postbus 85889, 2508 CN The Hague, Netherlands. TEL 31-70-3081500. FAX 31-70-3081515. E-mail: services@wkap.nl; URL: http://www.wkap.nl. (Dist. by: Libresso Distribution Centre, P.O. Box 3, 7400 GA Deventer, Netherlands. TEL 31-5700-33155. FAX 31-5700-33834; In N. America: Kluwer Law International, 675 Massachusetts Ave., Cambridge, MA 02139. TEL 617-354-0140. FAX 617-354-8595) Ed. R. McGregor. **Document type:** directory.
Description: Provides summary financial and ownership information for all companies listed on the Johannesburg, Harare, Windhoek and Gaborone stock exchanges.

338.025   UK   ISSN 0267-4378
HG4135
MACMILLAN'S UNQUOTED COMPANIES (YEAR). 1985. a. £350. Macmillan Reference Ltd., 25 Eccleston Pl., London SW1W 9NF, England. TEL 44-171-881-8000. FAX 44-171-881-8001. (Dist. in the U.S. by: Stockton Press, 345 Park Ave. S., 10th Fl., New York, NY 10010. TEL 212-689-9200. FAX 212-689-9711) **Document type:** directory.
—BLDSC (5330.393200).
Description: Keeps readers up to date with key developments among the top 20,000 unquoted U.K. companies.

338   US   ISSN 0886-9189
T12
MACRAE'S BLUE BOOK; serving the original equipment market. 1893. a. $170 (diskette $295) (effective 1996). (MacRae's Blue Book) Business Research Publications, Inc., 65 Bleecker St., 5th Fl., New York, NY 10012. TEL 800-673-4700. FAX 212-475-1790. URL: http://www.d-net.com/macraes. (Dist. by: Manufacturers' News, Inc., 1633 Central St., Evanston, IL 60201-1505. TEL 708-864-7000) Ed. Mary O'Hara Smith. R&P contact: Mary O'Hara Smith. (also avail. in diskette format) **Document type:** directory.
Former titles (until 1985): MacRae's Industrial Directory (ISSN 0749-5986); (until 1984): MacRae's Blue Book (ISSN 0076-2067)
Description: Provides buyers and specifiers with quick and easy access to approximately 45,000 leading manufacturers and their products.

382 642.47   GW
▼**MADE IN EUROPE - HOTEL AND CATERING SUPPLY GUIDE.** (Text in English) 1995. a. DM.75($50) (effective 1997). Made in Europe Marketing Organisation GmbH, Hahnstr. 70, 60528 Frankfurt a.M., Germany. TEL 49-69-668038. FAX 49-69-66803838. E-mail: 100734.3642@compuserve.com; URL: http://www.miesys.com. Ed. Martin Romer. circ. 25,000 (paid). **Document type:** catalog, directory.
●Also available on CD-ROM.
Description: Information for those involved in the purchasing of hotel and catering supplies as well as community care catering services.

338   BA
MADE IN THE ARAB WORLD. (Text in Arabic, English) a Falcon Publishing, P.O. Box 5028, Manama, Bahrain. TEL 253162. FAX 259694. TELEX 8917 FALPUB BN. Ed. V.N. Gopalakrishnan. circ. 22,000. **Document type:** directory.
Description: Provides statistical and detailed information on the industrial sector in the Arab countries.

BUSINESS AND ECONOMICS — TRADE AND INDUSTRIAL DIRECTORIES

670 TI
MADE IN TUNISIA; guide des industries Tunisiennes. 1974. biennial. $50 (effective Oct. 1992). CERES Productions, 6 Ave. A. Azzam, 1002 Tunis, Tunisia. TEL 216-1-782033. FAX 216-1-787516. Ed. Nadra ben Smail. adv. circ. 10,000. **Document type:** directory.

380 674 CN ISSN 0316-6414
MADISON'S CANADIAN LUMBER DIRECTORY. 1952. a. Can.$119.99. Madison's Canadian Lumber Reporter (1973) Ltd., Box 2486, Vancouver, BC V6B 3W7, Canada. TEL 604-681-6838. FAX 604-681-6585. E-mail: madisons@dowco.com; URL: http://www.com/cmd/madisons. Ed. Leah McNutt; Pub. Laurence Cater. R&P contact: Laurence Cater. adv. contact: Debbie Fach. charts; stat. **Document type:** directory.
—CISTI.

338.0294 HU ISSN 1218-1927
MAI PIAC; a sikeres kereskedo lapja. (Text in German, Hungarian; summaries in English, German, Hungarian) 1994. m. 2218 Ft. (effective 1998). Magyar Szakkkiado Kft (Subsidiary of: Deutscher Fachverlag Gmbh), Pozsonyi ut 54, 1133 Budapest, Hungary. TEL 36-1-3443235. FAX 36-1-3443237. Ed. Gabor Kovecs; Pub. Tamas Buga. R&P contact: Tamas Buga. adv. contact: Zoltan Toth. bk.rev. circ. 12,000. **Document type:** trade publication.
Description: Presents information about food and drug market, mainly for retail and wholesale traders. *Refereed Serial*

380 658.8 US ISSN 0085-2953
HF5466
MAIL ORDER BUSINESS DIRECTORY. 1955. a. $85. B. Klein Publications, Box 6578, Delray Beach, FL 33482. TEL 407-496-3316. FAX 407-496-5546. Ed. Bernard Klein. **Document type:** directory.

MAIL ORDER PRODUCT GUIDE. see *ADVERTISING AND PUBLIC RELATIONS*

338.025 US ISSN 1048-7115
HF5065.M2
MAINE BUSINESS DIRECTORY. 1990. a. $295 (effective 1997). American Business Directories (Subsidiary of: American Business Information, Inc.), 5711 S. 86th Circle, Box 27347, Omaha, NE 68127. TEL 402-593-4600; 800-555-6124. FAX 402-331-5481. E-mail: jerry.venner@abii.com. index. (also avail. in magnetic tape; diskette format) **Document type:** directory.
●Also available online.
Also available on CD-ROM.
Description: Includes all businesses in the state compiled from the yellow pages and telephone verified. Each listing includes company name, address, phone number, name of owner, and employee size and sales volume codes, and credit rating codes.

MAINE MANUFACTURING DIRECTORY. see *BUSINESS AND ECONOMICS — Production Of Goods And Services*

670 US ISSN 0197-1220
T12
MAINE, VERMONT AND NEW HAMPSHIRE DIRECTORY OF MANUFACTURERS. 1979. a. $62.50 (diskette $295) (effective 1996). Commerce Register, Inc., 190 Godwin Ave., Midland Park, NJ 07432. TEL 201-445-3000. FAX 201-445-5806. (also avail. in magnetic tape; diskette format) **Document type:** directory.
Description: Profiles about 4000 manufacturers; includes alphabetical, geographical and product line by SIC sections, as well as a key executive list.

332.6 NE ISSN 0966-0372
HF5154.7.A3
MAJOR BUSINESS ORGANISATIONS OF EASTERN EUROPE AND THE COMMONWEALTH OF INDEPENDENT STATES. 1991. a. $685 (effective 1994). Kluwer Law International (Subsidiary of: Wolters Kluwer N.V.), Postbus 85889, 2508 CN The Hague, Netherlands. TEL 31-70-3081500. FAX 31-70-3081515. E-mail: services@wkap.nl; URL: http://www.wkap.nl. (Dist. by: Libresso Distribution Centre, P.O. Box 23, 7400 GA Deventer, Netherlands. TEL 31-5700-33155. FAX 31-5700-33834; In N. America: Kluwer Law International, 675 Massachusetts Ave., Cambridge, MA 02139. TEL 617-354-0140. FAX 617-354-8595) Ed.Bd. **Document type:** directory.
Formerly (until 1992): Major Business Organisations of Eastern Europe and the Soviet Union (ISSN 0963-052X)
Description: Provides data on the most important business organizations in the Baltic Republics, Commonwealth of Independent States and other nations in Central Europe.

338 UK ISSN 0960-5711
MAJOR COMPANIES OF EUROPE. VOLUME 1. MAJOR COMPANIES OF THE CONTINENTAL EUROPEAN COMMUNITY. 1982. a. £640($1280) for the 3-vol. set. Graham & Whiteside, Tuition House, 5-6 Francis Grove, Wimbledon, London SW19 4DT, England. Ed. Ruth Whiteside. adv. (also avail. in microfiche) **Document type:** directory.
Formerly (until 1986): Major Companies of Europe. Volume 1. Companies in the European Economic Community (ISSN 0266-934X)
Description: Provides information on more than 9,000 Western European companies and subsidiaries.

338 UK ISSN 0268-4667
MAJOR COMPANIES OF EUROPE. VOLUME 2. MAJOR COMPANIES OF THE UNITED KINGDOM. 1986. a. £640($1280) for the 3-vol. set. Graham & Whiteside, Tuition House, 5-6 Francis Grove, Wimbledon, London SW19 4DT, England. Ed. Ruth Whiteside. **Document type:** directory.

338 UK ISSN 0268-4675
MAJOR COMPANIES OF EUROPE. VOLUME 3. MAJOR COMPANIES OF WESTERN EUROPE OUTSIDE THE EUROPEAN ECONOMIC COMMUNITY. 1982. a. £640($1280) for the 3-vol. set. Graham & Whiteside, Tuition House, 5-6 Francis Grove, Wimbledon, London SW19 4DT, England. Ed. Ruth Whiteside. **Document type:** directory.
—BLDSC (5353.603950); CISTI.
Formerly (until 1986): Major Companies of Europe. Volume 2. Companies in Western Europe Outside the European Economic Community (ISSN 0266-9358)

382 NE ISSN 0144-0594
HF3866
MAJOR COMPANIES OF THE ARAB WORLD. 1977. a. £360($720) Kluwer Law International (Subsidiary of: Wolters Kluwer N.V.), Postbus 85889, 2508 CN The Hague, Netherlands. TEL 31-70-3081500. FAX 31-70-3081515. (Dist. by: Libresso Distribution Centre, P.O. Box 23, 7400 GA Deventer, Netherlands. TEL 31-5700-33155. FAX 31-5700-33834; In N. America: Kluwer Law International, 675 Massachusetts Ave., Cambridge, MA 02139. TEL 617-354-0140. FAX 617-354-8595) Ed. G.C. Bricault. adv. (also avail. in microform from UMI) **Document type:** directory.
—BLDSC (5353.603600); CISTI.
Description: Provides corporate information on some 6,700 Arab companies in more than 20 countries.

382 NE ISSN 0961-3226
HG4244.6
MAJOR COMPANIES OF THE FAR EAST AND AUSTRALASIA. VOLUME 1. SOUTH EAST ASIA. (Also avail.: Vol.2 - East Asia (ISSN 0961-3234) and Vol.3 - Australia and New Zealand (ISSN 0961-3013)) 1983. a. £570($1140) for the 3-vol. set. Kluwer Law International (Subsidiary of: Wolters Kluwer N.V.), Postbus 85889, 2508 CN The Hague, Netherlands. TEL 31-70-3081500. FAX 31-70-3081515. (Dist. by: Libresso Distribution Centre, P.O. Box 23, 7400 GA Deventer, Netherlands. TEL 31-5700-33155. FAX 31-5700-33834; In N. America: Kluwer Law International, 675 Massachusetts Ave., Cambridge, MA 02139. TEL 617-354-0140. FAX 617-354-8595) Ed. J.C. Carr. adv. (also avail. in microform from UMI) **Document type:** directory.
—CISTI.
Formerly (until 1990): Major Companies of the Far East. Volume 1. South East Asia (ISSN 0267-2251)

382 NE ISSN 0961-3234
MAJOR COMPANIES OF THE FAR EAST AND AUSTRALASIA. VOLUME 2. EAST ASIA. (Also avail.: Vol.1 - South East Asia (ISSN 0961-3226) and Vol.3 - Australia and New Zealand (ISSN 0961-3013)) 1983. a. £570($1140) for the 3-vol. set. Kluwer Law International (Subsidiary of: Wolters Kluwer N.V.), Postbus 85889, 2508 CN The Hague, Netherlands. TEL 31-70-3081500. FAX 31-70-3081515. E-mail: services@wkap.nl; URL: http://www.wkap.nl. (Dist. by: Libresso Distribution Centre, P.O. Box 23, 7400 GA Deventer, Netherlands. TEL 31-5700-33155. FAX 31-78-5700-33834; In N. America: Kluwer Law International, 675 Massachusetts Ave., Cambridge, MA 02139. TEL 617-354-0140. FAX 617-354-8595) Ed. J.C. Carr. adv. (also avail. in microform from UMI) **Document type:** directory.
—BLDSC (5353.603975).
Formerly (until 1990): Major Companies of the Far East. Volume 2. East Asia (ISSN 0267-226X)

382 NE ISSN 0961-3013
MAJOR COMPANIES OF THE FAR EAST AND AUSTRALASIA. VOLUME 3. AUSTRALIA AND NEW ZEALAND. (Also avail.: Vol.1 - South East Asia (ISSN 0961-3226) and Vol.2 - East Asia (ISSN 0961-3234)) 1983. a. £570($1140) for the 3 vol. set. Kluwer Law International (Subsidiary of: Wolters Kluwer N.V.), Postbus 85889, 2508 CN The Hague, Netherlands. TEL 31-70-3381500. FAX 31-70-3381515. E-mail: services@wkap.nl; URL: http://www.wkap.nl. (Dist. by: Libresso Distribution Centre, P.O. Box 23, 7400 GA Deventer, Netherlands. TEL 31-5700-33155. FAX 31-5700-33834; In N. America: Kluwer Law International, 675 Massachusetts Ave., Cambridge, MA 02139. TEL 617-354-0140. FAX 617-354-8595) Ed. J.C. Carr. adv. (also avail. in microform from UMI) **Document type:** directory.
Formerly (until 1990): Major Companies of the Far East. Volume 3. Australasia.
Description: Provides information on more than 6,000 of the principal companies of the Far East and Australasia.

338 US
MAJOR CORPORATIONS DIRECTORY: CENTRAL PUGET SOUND. biennial. $39.50. Greater Seattle Chamber of Commerce, 1301 Fifth Ave., Ste. 2400, Seattle, WA 98101-2603. TEL 206-389-7200. FAX 206-389-7288. URL: http://www.seattlechamber.com. Ed. Gina Morales. (also avail. in diskette format) **Document type:** directory.
Formerly: Major Employers Directory: Central Puget Sound.
Description: Lists companies of 100 or more employees in King, Pierce and Snohomish counties. Includes address, phone, fax, key contacts, number of employees and products-service description.

BUSINESS AND ECONOMICS — TRADE AND INDUSTRIAL DIRECTORIES

333.79   NE
MAJOR ENERGY COMPANIES OF EUROPE. 1985. a. £185($315) Kluwer Law International (Subsidiary of: Wolters Kluwer N.V.), Postbus 85889, 2508 CN The Hague, Netherlands. TEL 31-70-3081500. FAX 31-70-3081515. E-mail: services@wkap.nl; URL: http://www.wkap.nl. (Dist. by: Libresso Distribution Centre, P.O. Box 23, 7400 GA Deventer, Netherlands. TEL 31-5700-33155. FAX 31-5700-33834; In N. America: Kluwer Law International, 675 Massachusetts Ave., Cambridge, MA 02139. TEL 617-351-0140. FAX 617-354-8595) Ed. Ruth Whiteside. **Document type:** directory.
—CISTI.
    Former titles: Major Energy Companies of Western Europe; Major Energy Companies of Europe (ISSN 0268-2311)

382 332   NE
MAJOR FINANCIAL INSTITUTIONS OF CONTINENTAL EUROPE (YEAR). 1985. a. £195($360) Kluwer Law International (Subsidiary of: Wolters Kluwer N.V.), Postbus 85889, 2508 CN The Hague, Netherlands. TEL 31-70-3081500. FAX 31-70-3081515. E-mail: services@wkap.nl; URL: http://www.wkap.nl. (Dist. by: Kluwer Academic Publishers Group, P.O. Box 322, 3300 AH Dordrecht, Netherlands. TEL 31-5700-33155. FAX 31-5700-33834; In N. America: Kluwer Law International, 675 Massachusetts Ave., Cambridge, MA 02139. TEL 617-354-0140. FAX 617-354-8595) Ed. Ruth Whiteside. **Document type:** directory.
    Formerly: Major Banks, Finance and Investment Companies of Continental Europe (ISSN 0268-232X)
    Description: Offers data on more than 1,000 financial firms in 17 countries of Western Europe, including locations, finances, and senior personnel.

338.025   SI   ISSN 1394-1313
MALAYSIA CONSTRUCTION AND EQUIPMENT CATALOGUE (YEAR). (Text in English) a. $50. Times Trade Directories Pte. Ltd., Times Centre, One New Industrial Rd., Singapore 536196, Singapore. TEL 65-2850161. FAX 65-2881186. TELEX RS 25713 TIMES. Pub. Leslie Lim. R&P contact: Leslie Lim. adv. contact: Joseph Liang. **Document type:** catalog.
    Formerly: Malaysia Industrial and Equipment Catalogue (Year).
    Description: A comprehensive buying guide for the construction, marine and timber industries.

338 720 747   SI   ISSN 1394-1291
MALAYSIA SOURCE BOOK FOR ARCHITECTS AND DESIGNERS (YEAR). (Text in English) a. $50. Times Trade Directories Pte. Ltd., Times Centre, One New Industrial Rd., Singapore 536196, Singapore. TEL 65-2850161. FAX 65-2881186. TELEX RS 25713 TIMES. Pub. Leslie Lim. R&P contact: Leslie Lim. adv. contact: Joseph Liang. **Document type:** directory.
    Description: Guide for the building and furnishing industries. Offers the widest range of products, materials and services available in Malaysia.

381.0025   MM
MALTA TRADE DIRECTORY (YEAR). 1968. a. $48. Malta Chamber of Commerce, The Exchange, Republic St., Valletta VLT 05, Malta. FAX 356-245223. Ed. Anthony Borg-Cardona. R&P contact: Anthony Borg-Cardonna. adv.; bk.rev. circ. 1,500. **Document type:** directory.
    Former titles: Trade Directory (Year); Malta Chamber of Commerce. Trade Directory; Malta Trade Directory (ISSN 0076-3446); Malta Chamber of Commerce Classified Directory.
    Description: Lists of members, economic information on Malta, and tourist and trade statistics.

MANAGED HEALTH CARE DIRECTORY. see *HOSPITALS*

380   UK
MANAGEMENT CONSULTANCY - FINANCIAL SURVEY (YEAR). 1986. irreg., latest 1992. £50. Jordan & Sons Ltd., 21 St. Thomas St., Bristol BS1 6JS, England. TEL 44-117-923-0600. FAX 44-117-923-0063. **Document type:** monographic series.

THE MANAGEMENT TRAINING DIRECTORY. see *BUSINESS AND ECONOMICS — Management*

670   US
▼**MANUFACTURERS PHONE BOOK U S A (YEAR).** 1997. a. $125. Omnigraphics, Inc., 2500 Penobscot Bldg., Detroit, MI 48226. TEL 313-961-1383; 800-234-1340. FAX 313-961-1340.
    Description: Lists approximately 41,300 manufacturers in the U.S. by company name, by state, and by product type.

338.025   SI
MANUFACTURERSLINK; a mini directory. (Text in English) 1993. biennial. free. Singapore Confederation of Industries, S.M.A. House, 20 Orchard Rd., Singapore 238830, Singapore. TEL 65-3388787. FAX 65-3365385. E-mail: scihq@sci.org.sg; URL: http://www.sci.org.sg/sci. Ed. Grace Yu. circ. 8,000. **Document type:** directory, trade publication.
    Description: Names and addresses of manufacturers and companies in the service industry.

384   US   ISSN 0076-4418
MARCONI'S INTERNATIONAL REGISTER; linking buyers and sellers worldwide through fax and business listings. (In 4 sections: Alphabetical, International Trade, Legal, Index of Trade & Legal Headings) 1898. a. $150. Telegraphic Cable & Radio Registrations, Inc., 19 Dogwood Ln., Box 14, Larchmont, NY 10538. TEL 914-632-8171. FAX 914-698-8171. Ed. Joanne Clark; Pub. L.G. Smith. R&P contact: Joanne Clark. adv.; index. circ. 5,000. **Document type:** directory.
—CISTI.
    Formerly: International Register of Telegraphic and Trade Addresses.
    Description: Lists more than 40,000 firms in over 100 countries who are seeking new international business contacts for importing or exporting and manufacturing.

301.16   AT   ISSN 1036-9201
MARGARET GEE'S AUSTRALIAN MEDIA GUIDE. 1978. 3/yr. Aus.$350. Information Australia Group, 45 Flinders Ln., Melbourne, Vic. 3000, Australia. TEL 61-3-654-2800. FAX 61-3-650-5261. Ed. Jayne Mahoney; Pub. Michael Wilkinson. (also avail. in diskette format) **Document type:** directory.
    Formerly (until 1992): Margaret Gee's Media Guide (ISSN 0158-0779)
    Description: Directory of Australian media: newspapers, magazines, newsletters, radio, television.

MARINE PRODUCTS DIRECTORY. see *SPORTS AND GAMES — Boats And Boating*

658.8   UK
MARKET RESEARCH SOURCEBOOK. 1984. a. £175. Headland Business Information (Subsidiary of: Bowker-Saur), Customer Services Department, Maypole House, Maypole Rd., E. Grinstead, W. Sussex RH19 1HU, England. TEL 44-1342-330-100. FAX 44-1342-330-191. E-mail: custserv@bowker-saur.co.uk; URL: http://www.bowker-saur.co.uk. Ed. David Mort.
    Incorporates (in 1997): Market Information (ISSN 0966-212X)
    Description: Provides an up-to-date information source for market researchers, business librarians, business information users and information producers.

338.025 658   AU
MARKETING ADDRESS DATA C D. (Text in English) 2/yr. S.19900. Herold Business Data AG, Guntramsdorferstr. 105, A-2340 Moedling, Austria. TEL 43-2236-401. FAX 43-2236-4018. E-mail: kundendienst@herold.co.at; URL: http://www.herold.co.at/home. **Document type:** directory.
    ●Available only on CD-ROM.

380   US
▼**MARKETING IN NEW JERSEY: A GUIDE TO TRADE AND PROFESSIONAL ASSOCIATIONS IN NEW JERSEY.** 1996. a. $49.95. Resource Communications Group, 3011 N. Lamar Blvd., Ste. 302, Austin, TX 78705. TEL 512-458-2021; 800-331-5076. FAX 512-458-2059. E-mail: rcg_NetConnect@austintx.net; URL: http://www.austintx.net/users/ResourceComm/NetConnectPage.htm. Ed. Jeanne Graves. circ. 500. **Document type:** directory.
    Description: Lists trade and professional associations in New Jersey with addresses, fax numbers, web page addresses, and publications

MARTINDALE-HUBBELL BAR REGISTER OF PREEMINENT LAWYERS. see *LAW*

MARTINDALE-HUBBELL CANADIAN LAW DIRECTORY. see *LAW*

MARTINDALE-HUBBELL DISPUTE RESOLUTION DIRECTORY. see *LAW*

MARTINDALE-HUBBELL INTERNATIONAL ARBITRATION AND DISPUTE RESOLUTION DIRECTORY (YEAR). see *LAW*

MARTINDALE-HUBBELL INTERNATIONAL LAW DIRECTORY (YEAR). see *LAW*

MARTINDALE-HUBBELL LAW DIRECTORY. see *LAW*

MARTINDALE-HUBBELL LAW DIRECTORY ON C D - R O M. see *LAW*

338.025   US   ISSN 1048-7123
HF5065.M25
MARYLAND BUSINESS DIRECTORY. 1990. a. $350 (effective 1997). American Business Directories (Subsidiary of: American Business Information, Inc.), 5711 S. 86th Circle, Box 27347, Omaha, NE 68127. TEL 402-593-4600; 800-555-6124. FAX 402-331-5481. E-mail: jerry.venner@abii.com. index. (also avail. in magnetic tape; diskette format) **Document type:** directory.
    ●Also available online.
    Also available on CD-ROM.
    Description: Includes all businesses in the state compiled from the yellow pages and telephone verified. Listings include company name, complete address, phone number, name of owner or manager, employee size and sales volume, and credit rating codes.

338.025   US   ISSN 1065-2507
HF5065.M25
MARYLAND - D.C. MANUFACTURERS REGISTER. 1994. a. $68 (diskette or CD-ROM $345) (effective 1997). Manufacturers' News, Inc., 1633 Central St., Evanston, IL 60201-1569. TEL 847-864-7000. FAX 847-332-1100. (also avail. in diskette format) **Document type:** directory.
    ●Also available on CD-ROM.
    Description: Profiles 5716 companies.

670   US
MARYLAND - DELAWARE DIRECTORY OF MANUFACTURERS. 1993. a. $62.50. Commerce Register, Inc., 190 Godwin Ave., Midland Park, NJ 07432. TEL 201-445-3000. FAX 201-445-5806. **Document type:** directory.
    Description: Profiles about 4000 companies alphabetically, geographically, and by product line. Contains listings of all key executives.

338.025 600   US
MASS HIGH TECH DIRECTORY. 1983. a. $175. Mass Tech Communications, 200 High St., 4th Fl., Boston MA 02110-3036. TEL 617-478-0630. URL: http://www.boston.com/mht. adv.; B&W page $2500. circ. 1,000 (paid). **Document type:** directory.

338   US   ISSN 1048-7131
HF5065.M3
MASSACHUSETTS BUSINESS DIRECTORY. 1990. a. $425 (effective 1997). American Business Directories (Subsidiary of: American Business Information, Inc.), 5711 S. 86th Circle, Omaha, NE 68127. TEL 402-593-4600; 800-555-6124. FAX 402-331-5481. E-mail: jerry.venner@abii.com. index. (also avail. in magnetic tape; diskette format) **Document type:** directory.
    ●Also available online.
    Also available on CD-ROM.
    Description: Includes all businesses in the state compiled from the yellow pages and telephone-verified. Each listing includes company name, address, phone number, name of owner or manager, and employee size-sales volume codes and credit rating codes.

BUSINESS AND ECONOMICS — TRADE AND INDUSTRIAL DIRECTORIES

670 US ISSN 0195-5810
HD9727.M4
MASSACHUSETTS DIRECTORY OF MANUFACTURERS. 1975. a. $72.50 (diskette $495) (effective 1996). Commerce Register, Inc., 190 Godwin Ave., Midland Park, NJ 07432. TEL 201-445-3000. FAX 201-445-5806. adv. (also avail. in magnetic tape; diskette format) **Document type:** directory.
 Description: Profiles over 6000 manufacturers listed alphabetically, geographically, and by product line, and SIC. Also lists key executives.

MATERIALS RESEARCH CENTRES; a world directory of organizations and programmes in materials science. see ENGINEERING — Engineering Mechanics And Materials

338 SA
MAURITIUS, REUNION & SEYCHELLES DIRECTORY. 1969. a. R.48 (effective 1997). Braby's (Subsidiary of: Kohler Packaging Ltd.), P.O. Box 1426, Pinetown 3600, South Africa. TEL 27-31-7017021. FAX 27-31-7017036. adv. **Document type:** directory.

670 621.3 US
MECTRONIC BUYERS DIRECTORY. (In 2 editions: Northern California and Southern California) 1981. a. M B D Publishing, 491 Macara Ave., Ste. 1014, Sunnyvale, CA 94086. TEL 408-738-3020. FAX 408-738-1213. adv. circ. 26,000. **Document type:** directory.
 Description: Lists purchasing sources of electronic and electromechanical components and sub-assemblies, materials and services for buyer-specifiers, designers and engineers.

380 US
Z6951
MEDIA CALENDAR DIRECTORY. 1982. a. $280. Bacon's Publishing Company, Inc., 332 S. Michigan Ave., Ste. 900, Chicago, IL 60604. TEL 312-922-2400. FAX 312-922-3127. Ed. Ruth McFarland. circ. 2,000. **Document type:** directory.
 Formerly (until 1992): Bacon's Media Alerts (ISSN 0736-4644)
 Description: Editorial calendars and profiles of major newspapers and magazines.

338.025 659.1 GW ISSN 0943-1764
MEDIA DATEN: DEUTSCHLAND OST. 1991. 2/yr. DM.270. Media Daten Verlag GmbH, Klingenweg 4, 65396 Walluf, Germany. TEL 49-6123-700-0. FAX 49-6123-700122. circ. 1,500 (paid). **Document type:** directory.

MEDIA MAP DATAFILE. see BUSINESS AND ECONOMICS — Marketing And Purchasing

MEDIA MAP OF EASTERN EUROPE. see BUSINESS AND ECONOMICS — Marketing And Purchasing

MEDIA MAP OF WESTERN EUROPE. see BUSINESS AND ECONOMICS — Marketing And Purchasing

380 070 AT ISSN 0811-8892
MEDIA OWNERSHIP IN AUSTRALIA. a. Aus.$49.95. (Information Australia) Margaret Gee Media Group, 45 Flinders Lane, Melbourne, Vic. 3000, Australia. TEL 03-654-2800. FAX 03-650-5261. Ed. G.R. Brown.

THE MEDIAMAP (YEAR); the European Media Yearbook. see ADVERTISING AND PUBLIC RELATIONS

MEDIAMAP WEEKLY UPDATE. see ADVERTISING AND PUBLIC RELATIONS

338.7 US ISSN 0146-8022
HD9994.U5
MEDICAL AND HEALTHCARE MARKETPLACE GUIDE. 1973. a. $670 (foreign $745); (effective 1997). Legal Communications, Ltd., 1617 JFK Blvd., Ste. 960, Philadelphia, PA 19103. TEL 215-557-2300. FAX 215-557-2301. Ed. Robert C. Smith, Jr. adv. contact: Todd Milller. circ. 1,000. **Document type:** directory.
 •Also available on CD-ROM.
 —CISTI. CCC.
 Formerly (until 1975): Medical and Healthcare Stock Market Guide (ISSN 0097-4870)
 Description: Profiles approximately 5,500 "high visibility" manufacturers, service organizations, dealers and distributors in the medical and healthcare marketplace. Analyzes over 100 market segments.

MEDICAL PRODUCTS OF JAPAN; medical equipment directory. see MEDICAL SCIENCES

MEDITERRANEAN SHIPPING DIRECTORY. see TRANSPORTATION — Ships And Shipping

338 NE ISSN 0960-1449
HF5152.A3
MEDIUM COMPANIES OF EUROPE. VOLUME 1. MEDIUM COMPANIES OF THE CONTINENTAL EUROPEAN ECONOMIC COMMUNITY. (Also avail. Vol.2 - Medium Companies of the United Kingdom (ISSN 0961-2920) and Vol.3 - Medium Companies of Western Europe Outside the European Economic Community (ISSN 0961-2939)) 1990. a. £599($1198) for the 3-vol. set. Kluwer Law International (Subsidiary of: Wolters Kluwer N.V.), Postbus 85889, 2508 CN The Hague, Netherlands. TEL 31-70-3081500. FAX 31-70-3081515. E-mail: services@wkap.nl; URL: http://www.wkap.nl. (Dist. by: Libresso Distribution Centre, P.O. Box 23, 7400 GA Deventer, Netherlands. TEL 31-5700-33155. FAX 31-5700-33834; In N. America: Kluwer Law International, 675 Massachusetts Ave., Cambridge, MA 02139. TEL 617-354-0140. FAX 617-354-8595) Ed. Ruth Whiteside. adv. **Document type:** directory.
 Description: As a companion set to Major Companies of Europe, lists more than 7,000 prominent European businesses.

338 NE ISSN 0961-2920
MEDIUM COMPANIES OF EUROPE. VOLUME 2. MEDIUM COMPANIES OF THE UNITED KINGDOM. (Also avail.: Vol.1 - Medium Companies of the Continental European Economic Community (ISSN 0960-1449) and Vol.3 - Medium Companies of Western Europe Outside the European Economic Community (ISSN 0961-2939)) 1990. a. £599($1198) for the 3-vol. set. Kluwer Law International (Subsidiary of: Wolters Kluwer N.V.), Postbus 85889, 2508 CN The Hague, Netherlands. TEL 31-70-3081500. FAX 31-70-3081515. E-mail: services@wkap.nl; URL: http://www.wkap.nl. (Dist. by: Libresso Distribution Centre, P.O. Box 23, 7400 GA Deventer, Netherlands. TEL 31-5700-33155. FAX 31-5700-33834; In N. America: Kluwer Law International, 675 Massachusetts Ave., Cambridge, MA 02139. TEL 617-354-0140. FAX 617-354-8595) Ed. Ruth Whiteside. **Document type:** directory.
 Description: A companion set to Major Companies of Europe, lists more than 7,000 prominent European businesses.

338 NE ISSN 0961-2939
MEDIUM COMPANIES OF EUROPE. VOLUME 3. MEDIUM COMPANIES OF WESTERN EUROPE OUTSIDE THE EUROPEAN ECONOMIC COMMUNITY. (Also avail: Vol.1 - Medium Companies of the Continental European Economic Community (ISSN 0960-1449) and Vol.2 - Medium Companies of the United Kingdom) 1990. a. £599($1198) for the 3-vol. set. Kluwer Law International (Subsidiary of: Wolters Kluwer N.V.), Postbus 85889, 2508 CN The Hague, Netherlands. TEL 31-70-3081500. FAX 31-70-3081515. E-mail: services@wkap.nl; URL: http://www.wkap.nl. (Dist by: Kluwer Academic Publishers Group, P.O. Box 322, 3300 AH Dordrecht, Netherlands. TEL 31-5700-33155. FAX 31-5700-33834; In N. America: Kluwer Law International, 675 Massachusetts Ave., Cambridge, MA 02139. TEL 617-354-0140. FAX 617-354-8595) Ed. Ruth Whiteside. **Document type:** directory.
 Description: As a companion set to Major Companies of Europe, lists more than 7,000 prominent European businesses.

669 FR
MEILLEURES ADRESSES (YEAR); fonderie, moules, machines-outils. 1988. a. 955 F. (foreign 1170 F.) (effective 1998). Revue Francaise des Metallurgistes, 32 rue Saint-Marc, 75002 Paris, France. TEL 33-1-42603151. FAX 33-1-42603842. URL: http://www.cgn.fr. **Document type:** directory.
 Formely: Meilleures Adresses de la Fonderie (Year) (ISSN 1164-1711)
 Description: Lists full addresses of French founderies, suppliers and molds.

669 FR ISSN 1240-9863
MEILLEURES ADRESSES DES TRAITEMENTS DE SURFACE. 1991. a. 240 F. (foreign 390 F.) (effective 1998). Revue Francaise des Metallurgistes, 32 rue Saint-Marc, 75002 Paris, France. TEL 33-1-42603151. FAX 33-1-42603842. URL: http://www.cgn.fr. **Document type:** directory.

669 FR ISSN 0992-2164
MEILLEURES ADRESSES DES TRAITEMENTS THERMIQUES. 1988. a. 180 F. (foreign 295 F.) (effective 1998). Revue Francaise des Metallurgistes, 32 rue Saint-Marc, 75002 Paris, France. TEL 33-1-42603151. FAX 33-1-42603842. URL: http://www.cgn.fr. **Document type:** directory.
 Description: Lists heat treatment sites.

338 387 AT ISSN 0267-7350
MELBOURNE PORT AND SHIPPING HANDBOOK. 1985. a. Charter Pacific Publications Pty. Ltd., P.O. Box 356, Mount Martha, Vic. 3934, Australia. TEL 61-3-59771668. FAX 61-3-59771670. E-mail: charpac@ozemail.com.au. Ed. Gerry Cansdale. circ. 6,000. **Document type:** trade publication.

MERCHANDISE MART RESOURCE GUIDE. see BUSINESS AND ECONOMICS — Marketing And Purchasing

670 US ISSN 0317-252X
METRO NEW YORK DIRECTORY OF MANUFACTURERS. 1955. a. $92.50 (diskette $395) (effective 1996). Commerce Register, Inc., 190 Godwin Ave., Midland Park, NJ 07432. TEL 201-445-3000. FAX 201-445-5806. adv. (also avail. in magnetic tape; diskette format) **Document type:** directory.
 Description: Profiles more than 8,000 manufacturers and key executives from Manhattan, Bronx, Queens, Brooklyn, Staten Island, and Nassau, Suffolk, Westchester, Rockland, Orange and Putnam counties; includes alphabetical, geographical, and product line by SIC sections.

338.025 US
METROPOLITAN MILWAUKEE ASSOCIATION OF COMMERCE. MEMBERSHIP DIRECTORY & BUYERS' GUIDE (YEAR). a. $10 to members; non-members $55. Metropolitan Milwaukee Association of Commerce, Council of Small Business Executives, 756 N. Milwaukee St., Milwaukee, WI 53202. TEL 414-287-4100. **Document type:** directory.
 Description: Lists Milwaukee companies' names, products, services, addresses, phones, contact names and range of employees.

338.025 382 US ISSN 1055-9124
HF3233
MEXICAN PRODUCT GUIDE. 1990. a. De Paula Publishing and Services Corp., 421 Seventh Ave., Ste. 1206, New York, NY 10001. TEL 212-629-4541.

338.025 US ISSN 1047-1790
HC107.M5
MICHIGAN BUSINESS DIRECTORY. 1987. a. $430 (effective 1997). American Business Directories (Subsidiary of: American Business Information, Inc.), 5711 S. 86th Circle, Box 27347, Omaha, NE 68127. TEL 402-593-4600; 800-555-6124. FAX 402-331-5481. E-mail: jerry.venner@abii.com. index. (also avail. in magnetic tape; diskette format) **Document type:** directory.
 •Also available online.
 Also available on CD-ROM.
 Description: Includes all businesses in the state compiled from the yellow pages and telephone verified. Listings include company name, complete address, phone number, name of owner or manager, employee sizes and sales volume, and credit rating codes.

338.025 US ISSN 1057-3062
MICHIGAN CENTRAL REGION BUSINESS REGISTER. 1991. a. $175. Pick Publications, Inc., 24293 Telegraph, Ste. 140, Southfield, MI 48034-7924. TEL 810-827-7111. FAX 810-827-7119. E-mail: pickinc1@aol.com. (also avail. in magnetic tape) **Document type:** directory.
 Incorporates (in 1993): Michigan Bay - Midland - Saginaw Counties Business Register (ISSN 1057-3054) & Michigan Ingham - Jackson Counties Business Register (ISSN 1057-3119)

BUSINESS AND ECONOMICS — TRADE AND INDUSTRIAL DIRECTORIES

338.025 US ISSN 1068-8722
MICHIGAN DETROIT REGION BUSINESS REGISTER. 1991. a. $175. Pick Publications, Inc., 24293 Telegraph, Ste. 140, Southfield, MI 48034-7924. TEL 810-827-7111. FAX 810-827-7119. E-mail: pickinc1@aol.com. (also avail. in magnetic tape) **Document type:** directory.
  Formerly (until 1993): Michigan City of Detroit Business Register (ISSN 1057-3194)

380 US ISSN 0890-4049
HF3161.M5
MICHIGAN DISTRIBUTORS DIRECTORY; distributors, wholesalers, jobbers, manufacturing agents. 1987. a. $146. Pick Publications, Inc., 24293 Telegraph Rd., Ste. 140, Southfield, MI 48034-7924. TEL 810-827-7111. FAX 810-443-5191. E-mail: pickinc1@aol.com. Ed. P.S. Pickell. adv. circ. 1,000. (also avail. in magnetic tape) **Document type:** directory.
  —CCC.
  Description: Provides a complete list of company profiles.

338.025 US ISSN 1068-8781
MICHIGAN EAST OAKLAND COUNTY BUSINESS DIRECTORY. 1991. a. $175. Pick Publications, Inc., 24293 Telegraph, Ste. 140, Southfield, MI 48034-7924. TEL 810-827-7111. FAX 810-827-7119. E-mail: pickinc1@aol.com. (also avail. in magnetic tape) **Document type:** directory.
  Formerly (until 1993): Michigan North Oakland County Business Directory (ISSN 1057-3178)

338.025 US ISSN 1057-3143
MICHIGAN KENT COUNTY BUSINESS REGISTER. 1991. a. $175. Pick Publications, Inc., 24293 Telegraph, Ste. 140, Southfield, MI 48034-7924. TEL 810-827-7111. FAX 810-827-7119. E-mail: pickinc1@aol.com. (also avail. in magnetic tape) **Document type:** directory.

338.025 US ISSN 1057-316X
MICHIGAN MACOMB COUNTY BUSINESS REGISTER. 1991. a. $175. Pick Publications, Inc., 24293 Telegraph, Ste. 140, Southfield, MI 48034-7924. TEL 810-827-7111. FAX 810-827-7119. E-mail: pickinc1@aol.com. (also avail. in magnetic tape) **Document type:** directory.

670 US ISSN 0736-2889
HD9723
MICHIGAN MANUFACTURERS DIRECTORY. 1937. a. $149.50 (diskette and CD-ROM $795) (effective 1996). Pick Publications, Inc., 24293 Telegraph Rd., Ste. 140, Southfield, MI 48034-7924. TEL 810-827-7111. FAX 810-443-5191. E-mail: pickinc1@aol.com. (Dist. by: Manufacturers' News, Inc., 1633 Central St., Evanston, IL 60201. TEL 708-864-7000) Ed. P.S. Pickell. adv. circ. 4,000. (also avail. in magnetic tape; diskette format) **Document type:** directory.
  ●Also available on CD-ROM.
  —CCC.
  Formerly: Directory of Michigan Manufacturers (ISSN 0070-5845)
  Description: Provides a complete list of company profiles.

338.025 US ISSN 1068-8730
MICHIGAN NORTHERN LOWER PENINSULA REGION BUSINESS REGISTER. 1991. a. $175. Pick Publications, Inc., 24293 Telegraph, Ste. 140, Southfield, MI 48034-7924. TEL 810-827-7111. FAX 810-827-7119. E-mail: pickinc1@aol.com. (also avail. in magnetic tape) **Document type:** directory.
  Formed by the 1993 merger of: Michigan Northeastern Region Business Register (ISSN 1057-3046) & Michigan Northwestern Region Business Register (ISSN 1057-3038)

338.025 US ISSN 1068-8765
MICHIGAN SOUTHEAST REGION BUSINESS REGISTER. 1991. a. $175. Pick Publications, Inc., 24293 Telegraph, Ste. 140, Southfield, MI 48034-7924. TEL 810-827-7111. FAX 810-827-7119. E-mail: pickinc1@aol.com. (also avail. in magnetic tape) **Document type:** directory.
  Formed by the 1993 merger of: Michigan Branch - Hillsdale - Lenawee - Monroe Counties Business Register (ISSN 1057-3135) & Michigan Livingston - Washtenaw Counties Business Register (ISSN 1057-3127)

338.025 US ISSN 1068-8773
MICHIGAN SOUTHWEST REGION BUSINESS REGISTER. 1991. a. $175. Pick Publications, Inc., 24293 Telegraph, Ste. 140, Southfield, MI 48034-7924. TEL 810-827-7111. FAX 810-827-7119. E-mail: pickinc1@aol.com. (also avail. in magnetic tape) **Document type:** directory.
  Formed by the 1993 merger of: Michigan Berrien - Cass - St. Joseph - Van Buren Counties Business Register (ISSN 1057-3097) & Michigan Clahoun - Kalamazoo Counties Business Directory (ISSN 1057-3100)

338.025 US ISSN 1057-3070
MICHIGAN THUMB REGION BUSINESS REGISTER. 1991. a. $175. Pick Publications, Inc., 24293 Telegraph, Ste. 140, Southfield, MI 48034-7924. TEL 810-827-7111. FAX 810-827-7119. E-mail: pickinc1@aol.com. (also avail. in magnetic tape) **Document type:** directory.
  Incorporates (in 1993): Michigan Genesee County Business Register (ISSN 1057-3151)

338.025 US ISSN 1057-302X
MICHIGAN UPPER PENINSULA REGION BUSINESS REGISTER. 1991. a. $175. Pick Publications, Inc., 24293 Telegraph Rd., Ste. 140, Southfield, MI 48034-7924. TEL 810-827-7111. FAX 810-827-7119. E-mail: pickinc1@aol.com. Ed. Steve Schwartz. R&P contact: Paul S. Pickell. (also avail. in diskette format; magnetic tape) **Document type:** directory.
  Description: For businesses in Michigan's Upper Peninsula.

338.025 US ISSN 1068-8749
MICHIGAN WEST CENTRAL REGION BUSINESS REGISTER. 1991. a. $175. Pick Publications, Inc., 24293 Telegraph, Ste. 140, Southfield, MI 48034-7924. TEL 810-827-7111. FAX 810-827-7119. E-mail: pickinc1@aol.com. (also avail. in magnetic tape) **Document type:** directory.
  Formerly (until 1993): Michigan Allegan - Muskegon - Ottawa Counties Business Register (ISSN 1057-3089)

338.025 US ISSN 1068-879X
MICHIGAN WEST OAKLAND COUNTY BUSINESS REGISTER. 1991. a. $175. Pick Publications, Inc., 24293 Telegraph, Ste. 140, Southfield, MI 48034-7924. TEL 810-827-7111. FAX 810-827-7119. E-mail: pickinc1@aol.com. (also avail. in magnetic tape) **Document type:** directory.
  Formerly (until 1993): Michigan South Oakland County Business Register (ISSN 1057-3186)

338.025 US ISSN 1057-3208
MICHIGAN WESTERN WAYNE COUNTY BUSINESS REGISTER. 1991. a. $175. Pick Publications, Inc., 24293 Telegraph, Ste. 140, Southfield, MI 48034-7924. TEL 810-827-7111. FAX 810-827-7119. E-mail: pickinc1@aol.com. (also avail. in magnetic tape) **Document type:** directory.

MICROCOMPUTER MARKET PLACE (YEAR); the complete guide to PC software and hardware vendors, service providers, and information sources. see COMPUTERS — Microcomputers

MIDCONTINENT PETROLEUM INDUSTRY. see PETROLEUM AND GAS

MIDDLE EAST AND WORLD WATER DIRECTORY. see WATER RESOURCES

382 332 US
MIDWEST CLEARING CORPORATION AND MIDWEST SECURITIES TRUST COMPANY. DIRECTORY OF PARTICIPANTS. bi-m. Midwest Clearing Corporation, One Financial Place, 440 S. LaSalle St., Chicago, IL 60605. TEL 312-663-2278. (Co-sponsor: Midwest Securities Trust Co.) **Document type:** directory.

355 US ISSN 1073-5909
MILITARY FACILITIES LISTING. 1993. s-a. $125. Carroll Publishing, 1958 Thomas Jefferson St., N.W., Washington, DC 20007. TEL 202-333-8620. FAX 202-337-7020. **Document type:** directory.
  Description: Lists contact information and key decision-makers at 550 military installations throughout the U.S. Includes a brief sketch of each installation.

338.7 US ISSN 1051-3442
HF5035
MILLION DOLLAR DIRECTORY. 1959. a. $1310 to commercial institutions; libraries $1250. Dun and Bradstreet (Subsidiary of: Dun and Bradstreet Corporation), 3 Sylvan Way, Parsippany, NJ 07054-3896. TEL 201-605-6000. (also avail. in magnetic tape) **Document type:** directory.
  ●Also available online. Vendor(s): Knight-Ridder Information, Inc. (File no.517), Questel Orbit Inc. Also available on CD-ROM. Producer(s): Dun & Bradstreet Information Services.
  Formerly (until 1985): Dun and Bradstreet Million Dollar Directory (ISSN 0734-2861); **Incorporating:** Dun and Bradstreet Middle Market Directory (ISSN 0070-7600)
  Description: Detailed information on more than 390,000 of America's largest companies in both public and private sectors.

MINING DIRECTORY: MINING AND MINE EQUIPMENT COMPANIES WORLDWIDE; the standard reference work for the mining industry. see MINES AND MINING INDUSTRY

338.025 US ISSN 1047-3181
HC107.M6
MINNESOTA BUSINESS DIRECTORY. 1984. a. $395 (effective 1997). American Business Directories (Subsidiary of: American Business Information, Inc.), 5711 S. 86th Circle, Box 27347, Omaha, NE 68127. TEL 402-593-4600; 800-555-6124. FAX 402-331-5481. E-mail: jerry.venner@abii.com. index. (also avail. in magnetic tape; diskette format) **Document type:** directory.
  ●Also available online.
  Also available on CD-ROM.
  Description: Includes all businesses in the state compiled from the yellow pages and telephone verified. Listings include company name, complete address, phone number of owner or manager, employee size and sales volume, and credit rating codes.

670 US ISSN 0364-1570
T12
MINNESOTA DIRECTORY OF MANUFACTURERS. 1991. a. $107. K & G Publishing, Inc., P.O. Box 46473, 250 Prairie Center Dr., Ste. 202, Eden Prairie, MN 55344-0558. TEL 612-941-1535. FAX 612-941-2012. Ed. Katherine J. Mohrenweiser. circ. 3,500. **Document type:** directory.

670 US ISSN 0738-1514
HD9727.M6
MINNESOTA MANUFACTURERS REGISTER. a. $105 (diskette and CD-ROM $545) (effective 1997). Manufacturers' News, Inc., 1633 Central St., Evanston, IL 60201. TEL 847-864-7000. FAX 847-332-1100. Ed. Louise M. West. adv.: B&W page $1843; adv. contact: Charles Scherer. illus. (diskette format) **Document type:** directory.
  ●Also available on CD-ROM.
  Description: Profiles 11,236 manufacturers in five different sections; listings by product, alphabetical, geographical by city, SIC and parent company.

MINNESOTA WOMEN'S DIRECTORY. see WOMEN'S INTERESTS

338 US
MINORITY BUSINESS INFORMATION RESOURCES DIRECTORY. a. $32. Try Us Resources, Inc., 2105 Central Ave., N.E., Minneapolis, MN 55418. TEL 612-781-6819. FAX 612-781-0109. Ed. Leslie Smith-Bonds. **Document type:** directory.
  Supersedes (in 1994): Guide to Obtaining Minority Business Directories; **Formerly:** Guide to Minority Business Directories (ISSN 0362-3459)
  Description: Lists legislation and compliance regulations, S.B.A., M.B.D.A. and other federal programs; local minority business directories; and a calendar of trade fairs and conferences.

338.025 600 US
MINORITY - OWNED HIGH TECH BUSINESSES. (Print version ceased 1995) 1992. a. Business Research Services, Inc., 4201 Connecticut Ave., N.W., Ste. 610, Washington, DC 20008. TEL 202-364-6473 FAX 202-686-3228. (diskette format) **Document type:** directory.
  Description: Lists over 6,000 minority-owned companies in high technology industries.

BUSINESS AND ECONOMICS — TRADE AND INDUSTRIAL DIRECTORIES

380.1 US
MINORITY SUPPLIERS REPORT AND DIRECTORY; industrial reference guide. 1971. a. $65. Project Magazine Inc., Box 8214, Philadelphia, PA 19101. TEL 215-387-1600. Ed. Emory Washington. index. (looseleaf format) **Document type:** directory.
  Formerly: Minority Suppliers Directory.

338.025 US ISSN 1046-056X
HF5065.M7
MISSISSIPPI BUSINESS DIRECTORY. 1988. a. $325 (effective 1997). American Business Directories (Subsidiary of: American Business Information, Inc.), 5711 S. 86th Circle, Box 27347, Omaha, NE 68127. TEL 402-593-4600; 800-555-6124. FAX 402-331-5481. E-mail: jerry.venner@abii.com. index. (also avail. in magnetic tape; diskette format) **Document type:** directory.
●Also available online.
Also available on CD-ROM.
  Description: Includes all businesses in the state compiled from the yellow pages and telephone verified. Listings include company name, complete address, phone number of owner of manager, employee size and sales volume, and credit rating codes.

670 US
MISSISSIPPI MANUFACTURERS - CROSS-MATCH DIRECTORY. 1964. biennial. $50. Department of Economic and Community Development, Box 849, Jackson, MS 39205. TEL 601-359-3958. FAX 601-359-2832. URL: http://www.mississippi.org. Ed. Lanny F. McKay. (also avail. in diskette format) **Document type:** directory.
  Formerly: Mississippi Manufacturers Directory.
  Description: Company profiles of 2,808 manufacturers listed alphabetically, geographically and by product.

338.025 US ISSN 1078-2249
HF5065.M7
▼**MISSISSIPPI MANUFACTURERS REGISTER.** 1995. a. $65 (diskette or CD-ROM $345) (effective 1997). Manufacturers' News, Inc., 1633 Central St., Evanston, IL 60201-1569. TEL 847-864-7000. FAX 847-332-1100. (also avail. in diskette format) **Document type:** directory.
●Also available on CD-ROM.
  Description: Profiles 3670 companies.

338.025 US ISSN 1048-7301
HF5065.M8
MISSOURI BUSINESS DIRECTORY. 1983. a. $425 (effective 1997). American Business Directories (Subsidiary of: American Business Information, Inc.), 5711 S. 86th Circle, Box 27347, Omaha, NE 68127. TEL 402-593-4600; 800-555-6124. FAX 402-331-5481. E-mail: jerry.venner@abii.com. index. (also avail. in magnetic tape; diskette format) **Document type:** directory.
●Also available online.
Also available on CD-ROM.
  Description: Includes all businesses in the state compiled from the yellow pages and telephone verified. Listings include company name, complete address, phone number, name of owner or manager, employee size and sales volume, and credit rating codes.

670 917 US ISSN 0893-2816
HD9727.M8
MISSOURI MANUFACTURERS REGISTER. a. $99 (diskette and CD-ROM $545) (effective 1997). Manufacturers' News, Inc., 1633 Central St., Evanston, IL 60201. TEL 847-864-7000. FAX 847-332-1100. Ed. Louise M. West. adv.: B&W page $1843; adv. contact: Charles Scherer. illus. (diskette format) **Document type:** directory.
●Also available on CD-ROM.
  Description: Lists 9,553 manufacturers by product, alphabetically, geographically, by SIC, and parent company.

338 621.389 US
MIX ANNUAL DIRECTORY OF RECORDING INDUSTRY FACILITIES AND SERVICES. Running title: Mix Annual Recording Industry Directory. Short title: Master Directory. a. $24.95. Cardinal Business Media Inc., 6400 Hollis, Ste. 12, Emeryville, CA 94608. TEL 510-653-3307. FAX 510-653-5142. Ed. Blair Jackson; Pub. Hillel Resner. adv. contact: Brad Borkhart. **Document type:** trade publication, directory.

664 US
MODERN GROCER INDUSTRY DIRECTORY. biennial. $80. Griffin Publishing Company, Inc., P.O Box 2025, Dennis, MA 02638. TEL 508-385-5700. FAX 508-385-8134. **Document type:** trade publication, directory.
  Description: Directory of retailers, vendors, brokers, wholesalers and distributors serving New York, New Jersey and lower Connecticut. Includes cross reference indexes linking products by brand to corporate company names.

667.6 380.1 US ISSN 0090-5402
TP934.5
MODERN PAINT & COATINGS PAINT RED BOOK; directory of the paint and coatings industry. a. $58.95. Intertec Publishing Corp. (Atlanta), 6151 Powers Ferry Rd., N.W., Atlanta, GA 30339-2941. TEL 770-955-2500. FAX 770-955-0400. Ed. Barbara Katinsky. circ. 18,712. **Document type:** directory.
—CCC.

338.025 US ISSN 1048-731X
HF5065.M9
MONTANA BUSINESS DIRECTORY. 1989. a. $295 (effective 1997). American Business Directories (Subsidiary of: American Business Information, Inc.), 5711 S. 86th Circle, Box 27347, Omaha, NE 68127. TEL 402-593-4600; 800-555-6124. FAX 402-331-5481. E-mail: jerry.venner@abii.com. index. (also avail. in magnetic tape; diskette format) **Document type:** directory.
●Also available online.
Also available on CD-ROM.
  Description: Lists all businesses in the state; includes company name, complete address, phone number, name of owner, manager, and employee size, sale volume codes, and credit rating codes.

670 US ISSN 1057-6681
HD9727.M9
MONTANA MANUFACTURERS DIRECTORY. 1955. irreg., latest 1991. $50. Department of Commerce, Trade Program, 1424 Ninth Ave., Helena, MT 59620. TEL 406-444-4780. FAX 406-444-1872. (Subscr. to: Rebcca Baumann, Montana Department of Commerce Trade Program, 1324 9th Ave., Helena, MT 59620-0501. TEL 406-444-4392) stat. circ. 3,000. **Document type:** directory, government publication.
  Former titles: Montana Manufacturers and Products Directory; Directory of Montana Manufacturers (ISSN 0544-8794)
  Description: Profiles over 1,250 manufacturers comprising a $2 billion industrial market.

380 301.412 CN ISSN 0823-0188
MONTREAL WOMEN'S DIRECTORY/ANNUAIRE DES FEMMES DE MONTREAL. (Text in English and French) 1973. a. Can.$19.95. Editions Communiqu'elles, 3585 St. Urbain, Montreal, Que. H2X 2N6, Canada. TEL 514-844-1761. FAX 514-842-1067. Ed. Jacquie Manthorne. adv. circ. 2,000. (back issues avail.) **Document type:** directory.
  Formerly: (until 1982): Montreal Women's Yellow Pages (ISSN 0705-8934)
  Description: Provides a directory of services, groups and resources for women in the greater Montreal area.

MONTSERRAT. STATISTICS OFFICE. OVERSEAS TRADE REPORT. see *STATISTICS*

332 UK
MORGAN STANLEY CENTRAL BANK DIRECTORY (YEAR). 1991. a. £120 (foreign £129 ($200)) (effective 1997). Central Banking Publications, 27 Chancery Lane, London WC2A 1PA, England. E-mail: centralbank@easynet.co.uk; URL: easyweb.easynet.co.uk/centralbank/. (Dist. in N. America by: European Business Publications Inc., Box 891, Darien, CT 06820. TEL 203-656-2701. FAX 203-655-8332) Ed. Robert Pringle. R&P contact: Robert Pringle. **Document type:** directory.
  Description: Comprehensive guide to the world's central banks and the people who run them. For each of the 173 banks, the directory offers a run-down of its recent history, providing insights into the bank's current concerns and duties.

333.33 US
MORTGAGE INDUSTRY 5000. 1990. a. $350 (effective 1997). Inside Mortgage Finance Publications, Box 42387, Washington, DC 20015. TEL 301-951-1240. FAX 301-656-1709. URL: http://users.aol.com/imfpubs. Ed. Guy D. Cecala; Pub. Guy D. Cecala. R&P contact: Didi Parks. (also avail. in diskette format) **Document type:** directory.
  Formerly: Mortgage Lender Directory.
  Description: Features more than 4,000 lenders that originate, service or hold one- to four-family residential mortgages.

338 US ISSN 0580-0412
MOTION PICTURE, TV & THEATRE DIRECTORY; for services & products. 1960. s-a. $15.20. M.P.E. Publications, Inc., Box 276, Tarrytown, NY 10591. TEL 212-245-0969. FAX 212-245-0974. Ed. John Low. adv. contact: Michael Graves. circ. 80,300. (back issues avail.) **Document type:** directory.
  Description: Directory of the motion picture and television industries. Primarily concerns pre-production, production and post-production (products, services, equipment) of film and video.

388
MOTOR FREIGHT DIRECTORY. (In regional eds.: Southeast, Central States, Chicago, Western States, New England, New York, Mid-Atlantic, Southwest) a. $75 per ed. (effective 1997). G.R. Leonard & Co., 2121 Shermer Rd., Northbrook, IL 60062. TEL 847-498-2121. **Document type:** directory.

629.227
MOTORCYCLE PRODUCT NEWS TRADE DIRECTORY.* 1973. a. M H West, Inc. (Subsidiary of: Maclean Hunter Publishing Co.), 3000 Town Ctr., Ste. 2750, Southfield, MI 48075-1212. TEL 818-997-0644. FAX 818-997-1058. (Subscr. to: 29 N. Wacker Dr., Chicago, IL 60606) adv. **Document type:** directory.

338 SA
MPUMALANGA DIRECTORY. 1976. a. R.30 (effective 1997). Braby's (Subsidiary of: Kohler Packaging Ltd.), P.O. Box 1426, Pinetown 3600, South Africa. TEL 27-31-7017021. FAX 27-31-7017036. **Document type:** directory.
  Former titles: Eastern Transvaal Buyer's Guide & Lowveld - Nelspruit Buyer's Guide; Supersedes: Buyers' Guide, Directory. Lowveld (ISSN 1016-4006)

MUIR'S ORIGINAL LOG HOME GUIDE FOR BUILDERS & BUYERS. see *BUILDING AND CONSTRUCTION*

384.1 US
TK6011
MULTIMEDIA TELECOMMUNICATIONS SOURCEBOOK.* (Former name of issuing body: North American Telecommunications Association) 1976. a. $95 (effective 1996). MultiMedia Telecommunications Association, 2500 Wilson Blvd., Ste. 3, Arlington, VA 22201-3834. TEL 202-296-9800. FAX 202-296-4993. E-mail: info@mmta.org; URL: http://www.mmta.org. Ed. Guy Walden. adv. contact: Mary Bradshaw. circ. 10,000. Indexed: SRI. **Document type:** directory.
  Formerly: Telecommunications Sourcebook (ISSN 0730-9872)
  Description: Buyer's guide to companies that manufacture and distribute business and public communications systems, with company profiles, market reviews and forecasts for the U.S. telecommunications marketplace. Lists products and services provided by each company.

MUSIC BUSINESS DIRECTORY. see *MUSIC*

338.025 US
THE N A F T A REGISTER. (North American Free Trade Agreement) a. $150 (free to libraries). Global Contact, Inc., 383 Kings Hwy. N., Ste. 210, Cherry Hill, NJ 08034. TEL 609-482-2011. FAX 609-482-2066. E-mail: globalc@ix.netcom.com. adv. contact: Michael A. Ruccolo. **Document type:** directory.
  Description: Directory of companies located within the NAFTA region that have a specific interest in exporting their products and services.

BUSINESS AND ECONOMICS — TRADE AND INDUSTRIAL DIRECTORIES

380   US
N A S C O GUIDE TO CAMPUS CO-OPS. 1974. biennial. $3. North American Students of Cooperation, Box 7715, Ann Arbor, MI 48107. TEL 313-663-0889. E-mail: NASCO@umich.edu. adv. circ. 2,000. **Document type:** directory.
    Former titles: N A S C O Campus Co-Op Directory; Cooperatives in Campus Areas of North America.

N D A PIPELINE. (New Drug Approval) see *PHARMACY AND PHARMACOLOGY*

332.6   US   ISSN 1062-0907
HG4907
N I M A - NELSON DIRECTORY OF MINORITY & WOMAN-OWNED INVESTMENT MANAGERS. 1992. a. $125 (effective 1993). (National Investment Managers Association) Nelson Publications, 1 Gateway Plaza, Box 591, Port Chester, NY 10573. TEL 914-937-8400. FAX 914-937-8908. stat. **Document type:** directory.
    Description: Profiles 150 minority and woman-owned money management firms, with investment performance statistics.

380   GW
N N. (Nicht Notierten Deutschen Aktiengesellschaften) a. DM.985. Verlag Hoppenstedt GmbH, Havelstr. 9, 64295 Darmstadt, Germany. TEL 49-6151-380436. FAX 49-6151-380-360. **Document type:** directory.
    Description: Information about roughly 2,700 public limited companies in Germany.

695 338.025   US   ISSN 1053-8305
TH2430
N R C A MEMBERSHIP DIRECTORY. 1949. a. $55 to non-members; members $5. National Roofing Contractors Association, 10255 W. Higgins Rd., Ste. 600, Rosemont, IL 60018. TEL 847-299-9070. FAX 847-299-1183. E-mail: nrca@roofonline.org; URL: http://www.roofonline.org. Ed. Alison LaValley. circ. 4,500. **Document type:** directory.
    Description: Lists associate, international, contractors, and architects as well as engineers and consultants who are members of NRCA.

338 381   AT
N S W TRADE DIRECTORY. a. Aus.$85. A P N Specialist Publishing, 46-50 Porter St., Prahran, Vic. 3181, Australia. adv. contact: Joseph Dagher. **Document type:** directory, trade publication.
    Description: Record of companies in New South Wales and their products and services. Distributed by government and industry officials on all trade and diplomatic missions.

338 968   SX
NAMIBIA TRADE DIRECTORY; an overview of Namibia trade and industry. 1991. a. n.$40. Namibia Trade Directory CC, P.O. Box 21593, Windhoek, Namibia. TEL 264-61-225665. FAX 264-61-220410. E-mail: paul@apple.com.na. Ed. Paul van Schalkwyk; Pub. Paul van Schalkwyk. adv. contact: Svignet Swit. illus. circ. 10,000. **Document type:** trade publication, directory.
    ●Also available online.
    Description: Includes background on Namibia, and contact names and address for all ministries, educational institutions, chambers of commerce, and service, financial and manufacturing companies.

NATIONAL BIOTECH REGISTER. see *BIOLOGY — Biotechnology*

338.025   US
THE NATIONAL BOOK OF BUSINESS LISTS; top 40 businesses in 50 categories. 1992. a. $19.95. Reference Press, Inc., Box 140375, Austin, TX 78714-0375. TEL 512-454-7778. FAX 512-454-9401. E-mail: orders@hoovers.com; URL: http://www.hoovers.com. Ed. Bartholomew K. Cronin. charts. (back issues avail.) **Document type:** directory.
    ●Also available online.
    Description: Lists the top companies in each of 50 categories, giving addresses and names of key personnel.

338   SA
HF3901.A48
NATIONAL CLASSIFIED DIRECTORY OF SOUTH AFRICA. 1972. a. R.150 (effective 1996). Braby's (Subsidiary of: Kohler Packaging Ltd.), P.O. Box 1426, Pinetown 3600, South Africa. TEL 27-31-7017021. FAX 27-31-7017036. adv. **Document type:** directory.
    Formerly: Commercial and Industrial Register of South Africa (ISSN 0379-9816)

671   US
NATIONAL COIL COATERS ASSOCIATION. PRODUCT CAPABILITY DIRECTORY. a. $10. National Coil Coaters Association, 401 N. Michigan Ave., Ste. 2200, Chicago, IL 60611. TEL 312-321-6894. FAX 312-527-6640. E-mail: leslie_harris@SBA.COM. **Document type:** directory.
    Description: Describes coil coating and the capabilities and facilities of NCCA members.

389.6   US
NATIONAL CONFERENCE OF STANDARDS LABORATORIES. DIRECTORY OF STANDARDS LABS. biennial. $100 to non-members; members $25. National Conference of Standards Laboratories, 1800 30th St., Ste. 305B, Boulder, CO 80301. TEL 303-440-3339. FAX 303-440-3384. E-mail: ncsl-staff@ncsl-hq.org; URL: http://www.NCSL-Hq.org. **Document type:** directory.

388   US   ISSN 1049-4995
HJ6685
NATIONAL CUSTOMS BROKERS & FORWARDERS ASSOCIATION OF AMERICA. MEMBERSHIP DIRECTORY. a. $25. National Customs Brokers & Forwarders Association of America, Inc., 1200 18th St., N.W., Ste. 901, Washington, DC 20036. TEL 202-466-0222. FAX 202-466-0226. URL: http://www.ncbfaa.org/ncbfaa. adv. circ. 4,000. **Document type:** directory.

338 615.534   US
NATIONAL DIRECTORY OF CHIROPRACTIC. 1989. a. $45. National Directory of Chiropractic Foundation, Box 10056, Olathe, KS 66051. TEL 800-888-7914. FAX 913-780-0658. Ed. Ross S. Trivas; Pub. Ross S. Trivas. R&P contact: Larry Glavas. adv.; circ. 9,000 (paid); 31,000 (controlled). (also avail. in diskette format) **Document type:** directory.
    Description: Provides information on the chiropractic profession: lists providers of chiropractic supplies and services; chiropractic colleges; information on chiropractors; state by state information on licensing, examination, societies and organizations.

338   US   ISSN 1060-6025
HG3766
NATIONAL DIRECTORY OF CORPORATE DISTRESS SPECIALISTS. 1992. a. $245 (effective 1997). Lustig Data Research Inc., 653 Arbuckle Ave., Woodmere, NY 11598-2701. TEL 516-295-4165. FAX 516-295-4165. Ed. Joel W. Lustig. R&P contact: Joel Lustig. adv. **Document type:** directory.
    Description: Lists firms and professionals providing services in bankruptcies, problem-loan workouts, turnarounds, and distressed securities investing.

320 330   US   ISSN 0749-9736
HD59
NATIONAL DIRECTORY OF CORPORATE PUBLIC AFFAIRS. Abbreviated title: C P A. 1983. a. $95. Columbia Books Inc., 1212 New York Ave., N.W., Ste. 330, Washington, DC 20005. TEL 202-898-0662. FAX 202-898-0775. E-mail: cbibooks@worldnet.att.net; URL: http://www.d-net.com/columbia/. Ed. J. Valerie Steele. **Document type:** directory.
    Description: Comprehensive overview of corporate civic responsibility and public relations carried out by 15,000 leaders in 2,000 companies, with lists by corporation including the office and officers responsible for public and community relations, policy formulation, advocacy advertising, state and federal lobbying, political action, and corporate contributions.

NATIONAL DIRECTORY OF FIRE CHIEFS, RESCUE & EMERGENCY DEPARTMENTS. see *FIRE PREVENTION*

658   US
NATIONAL DIRECTORY OF MAILING LISTS. 1990. a. $495. Oxbridge Communications, Inc., 150 Fifth Ave., Ste. 302, New York, NY 10011. TEL 212-741-0231. FAX 212-633-2938. **Document type:** directory.
    ●Also available online.
    Also available on CD-ROM.
    Description: Contains information on more than 15000 mailing lists.

338 380.1   US   ISSN 0886-3881
HD2346.U5
NATIONAL DIRECTORY OF MINORITY - OWNED BUSINESS FIRMS. 1985. a. $275. Business Research Services, Inc., 4201 Connecticut Ave., N.W., Ste. 610, Washington, DC 20008. TEL 202-364-6473. FAX 202-686-3228. Ed. Thomas D. Johnson. (also avail. in magnetic tape; diskette format) **Document type:** directory.
    Description: Lists over 25,000 minority-owned firms. Organized by SIC code and geographical location. Includes owner's name, telephone, line of business, certification status, start date and sales volume.

338 331.4   US   ISSN 0886-389X
HD2346.U5
NATIONAL DIRECTORY OF WOMAN - OWNED BUSINESS FIRMS. 1986. a. $275. Business Research Services, Inc., 4201 Connecticut Ave., N.W., Ste. 610, Washington, DC 20008. TEL 202-364-6473. FAX 202-686-3228. Ed. Thomas D. Johnson. R&P contact: Thomas D. Johnson. (magnetic tape; also avail. in diskette format) **Document type:** directory.
    Description: Lists over 10,000 woman-owned firms, nationwide, arranged by SIC code, geographical area, with owner's name, telephone, line of business, and certification status noted.

384   US   ISSN 1045-9499
TK6710
NATIONAL FAX DIRECTORY. 1989. a. $89 (effective Nov. 1993). Gale Research, 835 Penobscot Bldg., 645 Griswold St., Detroit, MI 48226-4094. TEL 313-961-2242; 800-877-4253. FAX 800-414-5043. E-mail: daniel_snyder@gale.com. Ed. Karin E. Koek. (also avail. in magnetic tape; diskette format) **Document type:** directory.
—CISTI.
    Description: Provides the fax numbers of over 160,000 of the nation's most important companies and organizations.

380.1
NATIONAL FITNESS TRADE JOURNAL. 1982. q. $25 (foreign $72). (National Health Club Association) Wally Bayko Productions, Inc., Box 2378, Corona, CA 91718-2378. TEL 909-371-0606. FAX 909-371-0608. Ed. Greta Blackburn. adv.; charts; illus.; stat.; tr.lit. circ. 20,000. (back issues avail.) **Document type:** trade publication.

THE NATIONAL FREIGHT AND TRANSPORT GUIDE (YEAR). see *TRANSPORTATION*

380 674   US
NATIONAL HARDWOOD LUMBER ASSOCIATION MEMBERSHIP DIRECTORY. 1912. a. $85. National Hardwood Lumber Association, Box 34518, Memphis, TN 38184-0518. TEL 901-377-1818. Ed. Rebecca Stevens. R&P contact: Rebecca Stevens adv. contact: Rebecca Stevens. circ. 2,000. **Document type:** directory.
    Formerly: National Hardwood Lumber Association Yearbook.
    Description: Includes products, species, facilities, salesmen.

380 659.1   CN   ISSN 0077-5177
HF5808.C2
NATIONAL LIST OF ADVERTISERS. 1936. a. Can.$107.50. Maclean-Hunter Ltd., Business Publication Division, Maclean-Hunter Bldg., 777 Bay St., Toronto, ON M5W 1A7, Canada. TEL 416-867-9500. FAX 416-867-1505. Ed. Nancy Remnant. **Document type:** directory.
—CISTI.
    Description: Lists names, addresses, brand names, personnel, etc. of over 3,000 national advertisers.

NATIONAL ORGANIC DIRECTORY. see *AGRICULTURE*

BUSINESS AND ECONOMICS — TRADE AND INDUSTRIAL DIRECTORIES

338 620   UK
NATIONAL QUALITY ENGINEERING GUIDE. 1994. a. £25 (diskette ed. £150). Commerce Publications, Commerce Business Directories, Station House, Station Rd., Newport Pagnell, Milton Keynes, Bucks MK16 OAG, England. TEL 44-1908-614477. FAX 44-1908-217425. Pub. Maria Luisi. (also avail. in diskette format) **Document type**: directory.

338   UK
NATIONAL QUALITY MANUFACTURING GUIDE. 1994. a. £25 (diskette ed. £150). Commerce Publications, Commerce Business Directories, Station House, Station Rd., Newport Pagnell, Milton Keynes, Bucks MK16 OAG, England. TEL 44-1908-614477. FAX 44-1908-217425. Pub. Maria Luisi. circ. 14,000. (also avail. in diskette format) **Document type**: directory.

NATIONAL REFERRAL ROSTER; the nation's directory of residential real estate firms. see REAL ESTATE

380.1   US   ISSN 0734-354X
HD2425
NATIONAL TRADE AND PROFESSIONAL ASSOCIATIONS OF THE UNITED STATES. Abbreviated title: N T P A Directory. 1966. a. $85 paperback. Columbia Books Inc., 1212 New York Ave., N.W., Ste. 330, Washington, DC 20005. TEL 202-898-0662. FAX 202-898-0775. E-mail: cbibooks@worldnet.att.net; URL: http://www.d-net.com/columbia/. Ed. John Russell. circ. 7,200. **Document type**: directory. —CISTI; UnCover.
Former titles: National Trade and Professional Association of the United States and Labor Unions; (until 1982): National Trade and Professional Associations of the United States and Canada and Labor Unions (ISSN 0094-8284); (until 1975): Directory of National Trade and Professional Associations of the United States (ISSN 0070-5918); (until 1974): National Trade and Professional Associations of the United States and Labor Unions (ISSN 0090-5038)
Description: Compiles more than 7,500 trade associations, professional societies, and labor unions, with information on the names of executive officers; memberships, staff and budget size; periodic publications; future events, and historical background, primary index alphabetically by organization name, subsidiary indexes by subject, budget, region, executive name, and acronym.

363.7502573   US   ISSN 1054-8238
HD9999.U53
THE NATIONAL YELLOW BOOK OF FUNERAL DIRECTORS. (Supplement avail.: Catalog of Funeral Home Supplies (ISSN 1054-2426)) 1974. a. $70. Nomis Publications, Inc., Box 5122, Youngstown, OH 44514. TEL 330-788-9608; 800-321-7479. FAX 330-788-1112. Ed. Margaret Rouzzo; Pub. Margaret Rouzzo. R&P contact: Margaret Rouzzo. adv. contact: Margaret Rouzzo. illus. circ. 23,000. **Document type**: directory.
Former titles (until 1988): Yellow Book of Funeral Directors and Suppliers (ISSN 1054-822X); (until 1984): Yellow Book of Funeral Directors and Services (ISSN 0098-3322)

NATIONWIDE OVERNIGHT STABLING DIRECTORY & EQUESTRIAN VACATION GUIDE. see SPORTS AND GAMES — Horses And Horsemanship

NATURAL GAS INDUSTRY DIRECTORY. see PETROLEUM AND GAS

338.025   US   ISSN 1048-7328
HF5065.N2
NEBRASKA BUSINESS DIRECTORY. 1981. a. $300 (effective 1997). American Business Directories (Subsidiary of: American Business Information, Inc.), 5711 S. 86th Circle, Box 27347, Omaha, NE 68127. TEL 402-593-4600; 800-555-6124. FAX 402-331-5481. E-mail: jerry.verrer@abii.com. index. (also avail. in magnetic tape; diskette format) **Document type**: directory.
●Also available online.
Also available on CD-ROM.
Description: Lists all businesses in the state; includes company name, complete address, phone number, name of owner, manager, and employee size, sales volume codes, and credit rating codes.

338.025   US   ISSN 1059-7727
NEBRASKA MANUFACTURERS REGISTER. 1993. a. $65 (diskette or CD-ROM $345) (effective 1997). Manufacturers' News, Inc., 1633 Central St., Evanston, IL 60201-1569. TEL 847-864-7000. FAX 847-332-1100. (also avail. in diskette format) **Document type**: directory.
●Also available on CD-ROM.
Description: Profiles 3183 companies.

338.025   NE   ISSN 0923-6902
NEDERLANDS A B C DIENSTVERLENERS. 1987. a. fl.395 (effective Sep. 1997). A B C voor Handel en Industrie C.V., P.O. Box 190, 2000 AD Haarlem, Netherlands. TEL 31-23-5319031. FAX 31-23-5327033. E-mail: info@abs-d.nl; URL: http://www.abc-d.nl. circ. 7,000. **Document type**: directory.
●Also available online. Vendor(s): Data-Star.
Description: Provides information on more than 23,000 professional service firms in the Netherlands, including branch offices of foreign firms.

338.025   NE
NEDERLANDS A B C VOOR HANDEL EN INDUSTRIE. 1952. a. fl.399 (effective Sep. 1997). A B C voor Handel en Industrie C.V., P.O. Box 190, 2000 AD Haarlem, Netherlands. TEL 31-23-5319031. FAX 31-23-5327033. E-mail: info@abc-d.nl; URL: http://www.abc-d.nl. circ. 19,250. **Document type**: directory.
●Also available online. Vendor(s): Data-Star.
Description: Provides business information on producers, importers and merchandisers.

333.33   US   ISSN 1060-5789
HD251
NELSON'S DIRECTORY OF INSTITUTIONAL REAL ESTATE. 1992. a. $275 (effective 1993). Nelson Publications, 1 Gateway Plaza, Box 591, Port Chester, NY 10573. TEL 914-937-8400. FAX 914-937-8908. Ed. Walter R. Nelson. **Document type**: directory.
Description: Information for pension fund, institutional and foundation investors, sponsors and consultants on institutional real estate investors, real estate investment management services and related support services.

332 338   US   ISSN 0896-0143
HG4907
NELSON'S DIRECTORY OF INVESTMENT MANAGERS. 1988. a. $435 (effective 1993). Nelson Publications, 1 Gateway Plaza, Box 591, Port Chester, NY 10573. TEL 914-937-8400. FAX 914-937-8908. Ed. Walter R. Nelson. adv.; stat. circ. 3,000. **Document type**: directory.
Incorporates: Nelson's Guide to Investment Consultants (ISSN 1049-5630)
Description: Contains information on over 2,000 money management firms, including company profiles, investment executives, fees, performance statistics.

332.6   US   ISSN 0896-0135
HG4907
NELSON'S DIRECTORY OF INVESTMENT RESEARCH. 1975. a. $495 ($550 with Nelson's Guide to Institutional Research) (effective 1993). Nelson Publications, 1 Gateway Plaza, Box 591, Port Chester, NY 10573. TEL 914-937-8400. FAX 914-937-8908. Ed. Walter R. Nelson. adv.; stat.
Former titles: Nelson's Directory of Wall Street Research (ISSN 0896-3851); Investment Decisions Directory of Wall Street Research (ISSN 0897-5388); Nelson's Directory of Wall Street Research (ISSN 0740-8714); Nelson Directory of Securities Research (ISSN 0272-5355); Directory of Securities Research (ISSN 0277-8343); National Directory of Wall Street Research.
Description: Comprehensive guide to stock research, including corporate profiles, securities analysts covering each stock, and key executives for over 12000 companies worldwide.

380 332.6   US
HD7105.45.U6
NELSON'S DIRECTORY OF PLAN SPONSORS. 1990. a. $475 (effective 1993). Nelson Publications, 1 Gateway Plaza, Box 591, Port Chester, NY 10573. TEL 914-937-8400. FAX 914-937-8908. **Document type**: directory.
Formerly: Nelson's Directory of Plan Sponsors and Tax Exempt Funds (ISSN 1053-0312)
Description: Profiles the investments of more than 10,000 sponsors of pension and endowment funds.

332.6   US   ISSN 1053-2536
HG4907
NELSON'S GUIDE TO PENSION FUND CONSULTANTS. 1990. a. $295 (effective 1993). Nelson Publications, 1 Gateway Plaza, Box 591, Port Chester, NY 10573. TEL 914-937-8400. FAX 914-937-8908. **Document type**: directory.
Description: Provides descriptions of more than 350 professional investment consulting firms serving sponsors of employee benefit funds, foundations, and endowments.

NETHERLANDS-AMERICAN TRADE DIRECTORY. see BUSINESS AND ECONOMICS — Chamber Of Commerce Publications

382   UK   ISSN 0308-1273
NETHERLANDS-BRITISH TRADE DIRECTORY. 1961. a. £15 to non-members. Netherlands-British Chamber of Commerce, The Dutch House, 307-308 High Holborn, London WC1V 7LS, England. adv. circ. 5,000. **Document type**: directory.

NEUMANN - HANDBUCH FUER DEN PRESSEVERTRIEB. see PUBLISHING AND BOOK TRADE

338.025   US   ISSN 1048-7336
HF5065.N3
NEVADA BUSINESS DIRECTORY. 1989. a. $295 (effective 1997). American Business Directories (Subsidiary of: American Business Information, Inc.), 5711 S. 86th Circle, Box 27347, Omaha, NE 68127. TEL 402-593-4600; 800-555-6124. FAX 402-331-5481. E-mail: jerry.venner@abii.com. index. (also avail. in magnetic tape; diskette format) **Document type**: directory.
●Also available online.
Also available on CD-ROM.
Description: Includes all businesses in the state compiled from the yellow pages and telephone-verified. Each listing includes company name, complete address, phone number, name of owner, manager, and employee size, sales volume codes, and credit rating codes.

670   US   ISSN 1057-5243
NEVADA INDUSTRIAL DIRECTORY. 1974. a. $99. Gold Hill Publishing Co., Drawer F, Virginia City, NV 89440. TEL 702-847-0222. Pub. David W. Toll. adv. contact: John Ponzo. circ. 3,500. (also avail. in diskette format) **Document type**: directory.
Former titles (until 1987): Compleat Nevada Industrial Directory (ISSN 0898-8226); Nevada Industrial Directory (ISSN 1047-1766); Directory of Nevada Businesses (ISSN 0098-0501)
Description: Provides information on over 6,500 companies arranged alphabetically, geographically, and by SIC.

338.7   US   ISSN 1083-317X
HF5065.N3
▼**NEVADA MANUFACTURERS REGISTER**. 1996. a. $55 (diskette $195) (effective 1996). Database Publishing Company, 1590 S. Lewis St., Anaheim, CA 92825-0024. TEL 714-778-6400. FAX 714-778-6811. (diskette format) **Document type**: directory.
Description: Provides complete profiles of 1736 manufacturing, mining and selected service firms.

338.025   US   ISSN 1048-714X
HF5065.N4
NEW HAMPSHIRE BUSINESS DIRECTORY. 1990. a. $295 (effective 1997). American Business Directories (Subsidiary of: American Business Information, Inc.), 5711 S. 86th Circle, Box 27347, Omaha, NE 68127. TEL 402-593-4600; 800-555-6124. FAX 402-331-5481. E-mail: jerry.venner@abii.com. index. (also avail. in magnetic tape; diskette format) **Document type**: directory.
●Also available online.
Also available on CD-ROM.
Description: Lists all businesses in the state; includes company name, complete address, phone number, name of owner, manager, and employee size, sales volume codes, and credit rating codes.

NEW HAMPSHIRE MANUFACTURING DIRECTORY. see BUSINESS AND ECONOMICS — Production Of Goods And Services

BUSINESS AND ECONOMICS — TRADE AND INDUSTRIAL DIRECTORIES

338.025　　　US　　ISSN 1048-7158
HF5065.N5
NEW JERSEY BUSINESS DIRECTORY. 1990. a. $425 (effective 1997). American Business Directories (Subsidiary of: American Business Information, Inc.), 5711 S. 86th Circle, Box 27347, Omaha, NE 68127. TEL 402-593-4600; 800-555-6124. FAX 402-331-5481. E-mail: jerry.venner@abi.com. index. (also avail. in magnetic tape; diskette format) **Document type:** directory.
●Also available online.
Also available on CD-ROM.
　Description: Lists all businesses in the state; includes complete address, phone number, name of owner, manager, and employee size, sales volume codes, and credit rating codes.

380　　　　　　US　　
HF5065.N5
NEW JERSEY BUSINESS SOURCE BOOK. (In 2 vols.; Vol.2: New Jersey Labor Unions) 1987. biennial. $89.95 (effective 1997). Resource Communications Group, 3011 N. Lamar Blvd., Ste. 302, Austin, TX 78705. TEL 512-458-2021; 800-331-5076. FAX 512-458-2059. E-mail: rcg__NetConnect@austintx.net; URL: http://www.austintx.net/users/ResourceComm/NetConnectPage.htm. Ed. Jeanne Graves. circ. 800. **Document type:** directory.
　Description: Lists larger corporations, all professional and trade associations, local and international assistance programs for New Jersey businesses and New Jersey chambers of commerce.

670　　　　　　US　　ISSN 0195-9352
HD9727.N5
NEW JERSEY DIRECTORY OF MANUFACTURERS. 1979. a. $92.50 (diskette and CD-ROM $495) (effective 1996). Commerce Register, Inc., 190 Godwin Ave., Midland Park, NJ 07432. TEL 201-445-3000. FAX 201-446-5806. adv. circ. 3,000. (also avail. in magnetic tape; diskette format) **Document type:** directory.
●Also available on CD-ROM.
　Description: Profiles approximately 9,000 manufacturers and their key executives; includes alphabetical, geographical and product line sections.

331.3　　　　　US　　ISSN 1081-9134
NEW JERSEY LABOR UNIONS. (Vol.2 of: New Jersey Business Source Book) 1992. a. $39.95 (effective 1997). Resource Communications Group, 3011 N. Lamar Blvd., Ste. 302, Austin, TX 78705. TEL 512-458-2021; 800-331-5076. FAX 512-458-2059. E-mail: rcg__NetConnect@austintx.net; URL: http://www.austintx.net/users/ResourceComm/NetConnectPage.htm. Ed. Jeanne Graves. circ. 300. **Document type:** directory.
　Description: Lists personnel in all unions in New Jersey. Indexed by county and municipality.

338　　　　　　US　　ISSN 1078-6325
HF5065.N5
▼**NEW JERSEY MANUFACTURERS DIRECTORY.** 1995. a. $109 (diskette & CD-ROM $595). Harris InfoSource International, 2057-2 Aurora Rd., Twinsburg, OH 44087. TEL 216-425-9000; 800-888-5900. FAX 800-6423-5997. E-mail: catknapp@aol.com. Ed. Frances L. Carlsen. (also avail. in diskette format) **Document type:** directory.
●Also available on CD-ROM.

380　　　　　　US　　ISSN 1054-5190
P88.8
NEW JERSEY MEDIA GUIDE. 1989. a. $89.95 (effective 1997). Resource Communications Group, 3011 N. Lamar Blvd., Ste. 302, Austin, TX 78705. TEL 512-458-2021; 800-331-2059. FAX 512-458-2059. E-mail: rcg__NetConnect@austintx.net; URL: http://www.austintx.net/users/ResourceComm/NetConnectPage.htm. Ed. Jeanne Graves. circ. 500. **Document type:** directory.
　Description: Details all media in the state: newspapers, radio and TV stations, publications, news bureaus and syndicates. Includes details on staffing, address, fax and e-mail addresses.

NEW JERSEY STATE AGENT HANDBOOK. see *INSURANCE*

NEW MEDIA SHOWCASE; the digital sourcebook. see *ART — Computer Applications*

338.025　　　US　　ISSN 1048-7344
HF5065.N6
NEW MEXICO BUSINESS DIRECTORY. 1989. a. $295 (effective 1997). American Business Directories (Subsidiary of: American Business Information, Inc.), 5711 S. 86th Circle, Box 27347, Omaha, NE 68127. TEL 402-593-4600; 800-555-6124. FAX 402-331-5481. E-mail: jerry.venner@abii.com. index. (also avail. in magnetic tape; diskette format) **Document type:** directory.
●Also available online.
Also available on CD-ROM.
　Description: Lists all businesses in the state; includes company name, complete address, phone number, name of owner, manager, and employee size, sale volume codes, and credit rating codes.

670　　　　　　US
NEW MEXICO MANUFACTURERS DIRECTORY. 1992. biennial. $50 (effective Mar. 1996). Center for Economic Development, Research, and Assistance, Box 30001, Dept. 3CR, Las Cruces, NM 88003-8001. TEL 505-646-6315. FAX 505-646-7037. Ed. Heidi Young. R&P contact: Heidi Young. TEL 505-646-5868. stat.; tr.lit. (also avail. in diskette format; back issues avail.) **Document type:** directory.
　Description: Lists manufacturers located in New Mexico. Includes company name, address, phone number, year established, contact person, up to 4 products, and SIC codes.

380　640.73　　　AT　　ISSN 0817-024X
NEW SOUTH WALES & AUSTRALIAN CAPITAL TERRITORY RETAIL DIRECTORY. a. Aus.$125. Jared Publishing, P.O. Box 51, Mitcham, Vic. 3132, Australia. TEL 61-3-8742415. FAX 61-3-8735951. Ed. Bruce Atkinson. **Document type:** directory.

338　387　　　　AT　　ISSN 0266-0652
NEW SOUTH WALES PORTS HANDBOOK. 1985. a. Charter Pacific Publications Pty. Ltd., P.O. Box 356, Mount Martha, Vic. 3934, Australia. TEL 61-3-59771668. FAX 61-3-59771670. E-mail: charpac@ozemail.com.au. Ed. Gerry Cansdale. circ. 6,000. **Document type:** trade publication, directory.

338.025　　　　US
NEW YORK BUSINESS DIRECTORY. 1993. a. $795 (effective 1997). American Business Directories (Subsidiary of: American Business Information, Inc.), 5711 S. 86th Circle, Box 27347, Omaha, NE 68127. TEL 402-593-4600; 800-555-6124. FAX 402-331-5481. E-mail: jerry.venner@abi.com. index. (also avail. in magnetic tape; diskette format) **Document type:** directory.
●Also available online.
Also available on CD-ROM.
　Description: Lists all businesses in the state; includes company name, complete address, phone number, name of owner, manager, and employee size, sales volume codes, and credit rating codes.

338　　　　　　US
NEW YORK CITY MODEL AGENCY DIRECTORY. 1987. a. $11.95 (effective 1996 ed.). Peter Glenn Publications, Inc., 42 W. 38th St., Ste. 802, New York, NY 10018. TEL 212-869-2020; 888-332-6700. FAX 212-354-4099. Pub. Chip Brill. adv. contact: Tricia Mazzilli. circ. 3,500. **Document type:** directory.
　Description: Presents a breakdown of the New York model agencies with names, addresses, telephone numbers, physical requirements, interview policies, types of modeling done and specialty types looked for. Designed for aspiring models.

338　　　　　　US　　ISSN 1078-6384
HF5065.N7
▼**NEW YORK MANUFACTURERS DIRECTORY.** 1995. a. $109 (diskette & CD-ROM $695). Harris InfoSource International, 2057-2 Aurora Rd., Twinsburg, OH 44087. TEL 216-425-9000; 800-888-5900. FAX 216-425-7150. E-mail: catknapp@aol.com. Ed. Frances L Carlsen. (also avail. in diskette format) **Document type:** directory.
●Also available on CD-ROM.

338.025　　　　US
NEW YORK METRO BUSINESS DIRECTORY. 1993. a. $595 (effective 1997). American Business Directories (Subsidiary of: American Business Information, Inc.), 5711 S. 86th Circle, Box 27347, Omaha, NE 68127. TEL 402-593-4600; 800-555-6124. FAX 402-331-5481. E-mail: jerry.venner@abii.com. (also avail. in magnetic tape; diskette format) **Document type:** directory.
●Also available online.
Also available on CD-ROM.
　Description: Includes all businesses in the New York City metropolitan area compiled from the yellow pages and telephone-verified. Listings include company name, complete address, phone number, name of owner or manager, employee size and sales volume and credit rating codes.

NEW YORK STATE AGENT HANDBOOK. see *INSURANCE*

NEW YORK TELEPHONE TICKLER FOR INSURANCE MEN AND WOMEN. see *INSURANCE*

650　　　　　　NZ　　ISSN 0077-9571
NEW ZEALAND BUSINESS WHO'S WHO. 1935. a. NZ.$279 (CD-ROM NZ.$588); foreign NZ.$305 (CD-ROM NZ.$598). New Zealand Financial Press Ltd., P.O. Box 1881, Auckland 1, New Zealand. TEL 64-9-3071287. FAX 64-9-3732734. Ed. Peter Clark. R&P contact: Peter Clark. adv. contact: Peter Clark. circ. 5,000. **Document type:** directory.
●Also available on CD-ROM.
　Description: Provides up-to-date facts and all the communication data needed to reach New Zealand manufactures, trade suppliers, importers and exporters.

382　　　　　　NZ　　ISSN 1172-7136
NEW ZEALAND EXPORT YEARBOOK. 1967. a. NZ.$49.95. Profile Publishing Ltd., P.O. Box 5544, Wellesley St., Auckland, New Zealand. TEL 64-9-6308940. FAX 64-9-6301046. Ed. M. Wheeler. adv. circ. 3,000. **Document type:** directory.
　Former titles: Cranwell New Zealand Export Yearbook (ISSN 1171-6991); (until 1986): Cranwells New Zealand Export Year Book (ISSN 1170-6201); (until 1982): New Zealand Export Year Book (ISSN 0549-0278)
　Description: Represents New Zealand exporters to the world markets.

670　　　　　　NZ　　ISSN 0112-2606
NEW ZEALAND PACKAGING YEARBOOK. 1970. a. NZ.$36 (Australian NZ.$53). Profile Publishing Ltd., P.O. Box 5544, Wellesley St., Auckland, New Zealand. TEL 64-9-6308940. FAX 64-9-6301046. E-mail: sprofile@iconz.co.nz. adv. circ. 3,000. **Document type:** directory.
　Description: For the packaging industry of New Zealand, containing information on products and services available to the industry.

670　　　　　　NZ
NEW ZEALAND TRAVEL INDUSTRY DIRECTORY. 1968. a. NZ.$14. Mercantile Gazette Marketing, P.O. Box 20-034, Christchurch 5, New Zealand. FAX 64-3-3584490. Ed. G. Everts. adv.
　Formerly (until 1996): Travel Executives of New Zealand (ISSN 1172-3084)

338　　　　　　US　　ISSN 1071-8931
PN4899.W304
NEWS MEDIA YELLOW BOOK; who's who among reporters, writers, editors and producers in the nation's government and business capitals. 1989. $265 (effective 1997). Leadership Directories, Inc. 104 Fifth Ave., 2nd Fl., New York, NY 10011. TEL 212-627-4140. FAX 212-645-0931. Ed. Michele Barile. **Document type:** directory.
●Also available on CD-ROM. Producer(s): Chadwyck-Healey Inc.
—CCC.
　Formerly: News Media Yellow Book of Washington and New York (ISSN 1043-2620)
　Description: Lists reporters, writers, and editors at various media organizations. Provides information on news desks, bureaus, and sections, gives telephone and FAX numbers. Includes indexes referencing columnists, programs, periodicals, personnel, and organizations.

BUSINESS AND ECONOMICS — TRADE AND INDUSTRIAL DIRECTORIES

338.4   NR   ISSN 1116-1027
NIGERIA INDUSTRIAL DIRECTORY. 1975. irreg. £N200. Malthouse Press Ltd., 8 Amore St. (off Toyin St.), P.O. Box 8917, Ikeja, Lagos State, Nigeria. adv.; circ. 5,000 (controlled). **Document type:** directory.
   Formerly: Manufacturers Association of Nigeria. Industrial Directory.

NIGERIAN YELLOW PAGES. see BUSINESS AND ECONOMICS — Office Equipment And Services

338.025   JA
NIKKEI CORPORATE GUIDE. (Text in Japanese) a.? Nihon Keizai Shimbun, Inc., 1-9-5 Ote-machi, Chiyoda-ku, Tokyo 100, Japan. TEL 81-3-3270-0251. FAX 81-3-5255-2661. TELEX J22308 NIKKEI.
   Description: Provides detailed data and analysis on 2,600 companies, as well as information on securities and life insurance companies.

338.025 677   UK   ISSN 0963-701X
NONWOVENS REPORT YEARBOOK. 1978. a. £30 (foreign £35). World Textile Publications Ltd., Perkin House, 1 Longlands St., Bradford, W. Yorkshire BD1 2TP, England. TEL 44-1274-378800. FAX 44-1274-378811. E-mail: 104470.3070@compuserve.com; URL: http://www.vitalo.com/worldtextile. **Document type:** directory.

NORDIC NETWORK. see SPORTS AND GAMES — Outdoor Life

670   US   ISSN 1052-0716
HD9696.A3
NORTH AMERICAN DIRECTORY OF CONTRACT MANUFACTURERS IN ELECTRONICS. 1989. irreg. $177 (diskette $197). Miller Freeman, Inc. (Subsidiary of: United Newspapers), 600 Harrison St., San Francisco, CA 94107. TEL 415-905-2200. FAX 415-905-2232. Ed. Vincent M. Ridley. (also avail. in diskette format) **Document type:** directory.

NORTH AMERICAN GRAIN & MILLING ANNUAL. see AGRICULTURE — Feed, Flour And Grain

338.025 792   UK   ISSN 1351-8429
NORTH AMERICAN REGISTER. 1994. a. Spotlight, 7 Leicester Pl., London WC2H 7BP, England. TEL 44-171-437-7631. FAX 44-171-437-5881. E-mail: info@spotlightcd.com. Ed. Christine Barry. **Document type:** directory.

338.025   US   ISSN 1046-9060
HC107.N8
NORTH CAROLINA BUSINESS DIRECTORY. 1988. a. $430 (effective 1997). American Business Directories (Subsidiary of: American Business Information, Inc.), 5711 S. 86th Circle, Box 27347, Omaha, NE 68127. TEL 402-593-4600; 800-555-6124. FAX 402-331-5481. E-mail: jerry.venner@abii.com. index. (also avail. in magnetic tape; diskette format) **Document type:** directory.
•Also available online.
Also available on CD-ROM.
   Description: Includes all businesses in the state compiled from the yellow pages and telephone-verified. Each listing includes company name, complete address, phone number, name of owner, manager, and employee size, sales volume codes, and credit rating codes.

380   US
NORTH CAROLINA DIRECTORY OF TRADE AND PROFESSIONAL ASSOCIATIONS. 1976. biennial. $64.50. University of North Carolina at Greensboro, Center for Applied Research, 301 Bryan Bldg., Greensboro, NC 27412-5001. TEL 910-334-3088. FAX 910-334-4272. E-mail: redmondj@iago.uncg.edu. Ed. John G. Redmond. R&P contact: John G. Redmond. **Document type:** directory.

338   US
HF5065.N8
NORTH CAROLINA MANUFACTURERS DIRECTORY. 1993. a. $75 (diskette & CD-ROM $395) (effective 1998). Harris InfoSource International, 2057-2 Aurora Rd., Twinsburg, OH 44087. TEL 216-425-9000; 800-888-5900. FAX 216-425-7150. E-mail: catknapp@aol.com. Ed. Frances L. Carlsen. (also avail. in diskette format) **Document type:** directory.
•Also available on CD-ROM.
   Formerly: Directory of North Carolina Manufacturing Firms (ISSN 1065-4720)

338.025   US   ISSN 1073-2128
NORTH CAROLINA MANUFACTURERS REGISTER. 1994. a. $104 (diskette and CD-ROM $545) (effective 1997). Manufacturers' News, Inc., 1633 Central St., Evanston, IL 60201-1569. TEL 847-864-7000. FAX 847-332-1100. (also avail. in diskette format) **Document type:** directory.
•Also available on CD-ROM.
   Description: Profiles 11202 companies.

338   US
NORTH CAROLINA METALWORKING DIRECTORY. 1975. quinquennial, latest 1992. $25. North Carolina State University, Industrial Extension Service, Box 7902, Raleigh, NC 27695-7902. TEL 919-515-5408. FAX 919-515-6159. Ed. Robert L. Edwards. circ. 600. **Document type:** directory.
   Description: Lists metalworking firms and contractors in N. Carolina, with information on specializations.

338.025   US   ISSN 1046-8129
HF5065.N9
NORTH DAKOTA BUSINESS DIRECTORY. 1984. a. $295 (effective 1997). American Business Directories (Subsidiary of: American Business Information, Inc.), 5711 S. 86th Circle, Box 27347, Omaha, NE 68127. TEL 402-593-4600; 800-555-6124. FAX 402-331-5481. E-mail: jerry.venner@abii.com. index. (also avail. in magnetic tape; diskette format) **Document type:** directory.
•Also available online.
Also available on CD-ROM.
   Description: Lists all businesses in the state; company name, complete address, phone number, name of owner, manager, and employee size, sales volume codes, and credit rating codes.

338.025   US   ISSN 1087-8343
HF5065.N9
NORTH DAKOTA MANUFACTURERS REGISTER. a. $54 (diskette or CD-ROM $195) (effective 1997). Manufacturers' News, Inc., 1633 Central St., Evanston, IL 60201-1569. TEL 847-864-7000. FAX 847-332-1100. (also avail. in diskette format) **Document type:** directory.
•Also available on CD-ROM.
   Description: Profiles 963 companies.

670   US   ISSN 1042-5535
T12
NORTH JERSEY REGIONAL INDUSTRIAL BUYING GUIDE. 1976. a. free to qualified personnel. Thomas Publishing Company, Five Penn Plaza, New York, NY 10001. TEL 212-629-2100. FAX 212-629-2195. Ed. Marie McGurk. adv. circ. 35,000. **Document type:** directory.
   Formerly (until 1988): North Jersey Regional Industrial Purchasing Guide (ISSN 0737-0989)

NORTH - SOUTH CAROLINA STATE AGENT HANDBOOK. see INSURANCE

388   US
NORTHEAST DIRECTORY OF TRANSPORTATION SERVICES. 1992. a. $60 (effective 1995). Northeast Journal of Transportation, 31 Fargo St., S. Boston, MA 02127. TEL 617-695-1660. FAX 617-695-1665. Ed. George Lauriat; Pub. William Bourbon. adv. contact: William Bourbon. circ. controlled. **Document type:** trade publication, directory.
   Description: Covers transportation services in the Northeast, from Montreal to the Port of New York-New Jersey, including New England.

NORTHEAST STATES PETROLEUM INDUSTRY. see PETROLEUM AND GAS

338.025   US   ISSN 1063-4177
HF5065.C2
NORTHERN CALIFORNIA BUSINESS DIRECTORY. 1992. a. $695 (effective 19967. American Business Directories (Subsidiary of: American Business Information, Inc.), 5711 S. 86th Circle, Box 27347, Omaha, NE 68127. TEL 402-593-4600; 800-555-6124. FAX 402-331-5481. E-mail: jerry.venner@abii.com. index. (also avail. in magnetic tape; diskette format) **Document type:** directory.
•Also available on CD-ROM.
Also available online.
   Description: Includes all businesses in the Northern California area compiled from the yellow pages and telephone-verified. Each listing includes company name, complete address, phone number, name of owner, manager, and employee size, sales volume codes, and credit rating codes.

338   US   ISSN 1052-8822
HF5065.C2
NORTHERN CALIFORNIA BUSINESS DIRECTORY AND BUYERS GUIDE. 1991. a. $169 (diskette $795) (effective 1996). Database Publishing Company, 1590 S. Lewis St., Anaheim, CA 92805-6423. TEL 714-778-6400. FAX 714-778-6811. (Subscr. to: Box 70024, Anaheim, CA 92825-0024. TEL 800-888-8434) Ed. Ken Gregory. circ. 750. (also avail. in diskette format) **Document type:** directory.
   Description: Contains profiles of 26,000 manufacturers, wholesalers, distributors and service companies in Northern California.

380.1   UK
▼**NORTHERN IRELAND TRADE DIRECTORY.** 1997. biennial. £60. Business to Business Publications, The King Bldg., Ste. 11, 152 Albertbridge Rd., Belfast BT5 4GS, N. Ireland. TEL 44-1232-455775. FAX 44-1232-461924. E-mail: nitradedirectory@unite.co.uk. Ed. J.V. Herron. adv.: page £1900; adv. contact: Lorna Thomson. circ. 5,000. **Document type:** directory.
•Also available on CD-ROM.

338   SA
NORTH WEST DIRECTORY. a. R.30 (effective 1997). Braby's (Subsidiary of: Kohler Packaging Ltd.), P.O. Box 1426, Pinetown 3600, South Africa. TEL 27-31-7017021. FAX 27-31-7017036. **Document type:** directory.
   Formerly: North West Buyer's Guide; Supersedes: Bophuthatswana Buyer's Guide.

NORTHWEST GAY GUIDE; directory of gay - lesbian businesses. see HOMOSEXUALITY

NORTHWEST HIGH TECH (YEAR). see COMPUTERS — Computer Industry Directories

NORTHWESTERN LUMBER ASSOCIATION DEALER REFERENCE MANUAL. see FORESTS AND FORESTRY — Lumber And Wood

338.025 610.73   US   ISSN 0192-2394
RT82
NURSING (YEAR) CAREER DIRECTORY. 1979. a. free. Springhouse Corporation (Subsidiary of: Reed Elsevier Medical group plc.), 1111 Bethlehem Pike, Box 908, Springhouse, PA 19477-0908. TEL 215-646-8700; 800-346-7844. FAX 215-646-4399. adv.; charts; illus.; tr.lit.; circ. 100,000 (controlled). **Document type:** directory.
—CCC.
   Description: Directed to Registered Nurses and nursing graduate students seeking employment in American hospitals.

635   US
O A N DIRECTORY & BUYER'S GUIDE. 1961. a. $7.50 (effective 1993). Oregon Association of Nurserymen, 2780 S.E. Harrison, Ste. 102, Milwaukie, OR 97222. TEL 503-653-8733. FAX 503-653-1528. Ed. Don Grey. adv.; illus.; circ. 6,500 (controlled). **Document type:** trade publication, directory.
   Description: Provides more than 20000 listings of plants, products and services for the national nursery, greenhouse and landscape gardening trades.

BUSINESS AND ECONOMICS — TRADE AND INDUSTRIAL DIRECTORIES

660.029   US   ISSN 0276-539X
TP12   CODEN: OCBDDH
O P D CHEMICAL BUYERS DIRECTORY. (Companion volume to: Schnell Red Book of Chemical Services) 1913. a. (included in Chemical Marketing Reporter). Schnell Publishing Co., Inc., 80 Broad St., New York, NY 10004-2203. TEL 212-248-4177. FAX 212-248-4903. circ. 17,000. **Document type:** directory.
— BLDSC (6265.850000); CASDDS; CISTI. **CCC.**
   Formerly: Chemical Buyers Directory.

382 659.1   UK
O P M A OVERSEAS MEDIA GUIDE. 1965. a. £25. Overseas Press and Media Association, c/o Sinclairs, 32 Queen Anne St., London W1M 9LB, England. adv.; circ. 5,000 (controlled). **Document type:** directory.
   Formerly (until 1987): Overseas Media Guide (ISSN 0078-7132)

OCCUPATIONAL HEALTH & SAFETY NEWS. see *OCCUPATIONAL HEALTH AND SAFETY*

338.025 380   US   ISSN 0149-1091
HD59
O'DWYER'S DIRECTORY OF CORPORATE COMMUNICATIONS. 1975. a. $110. J.R. O'Dwyer Co., Inc., 271 Madison Ave., New York, NY 10016. TEL 212-679-2471. FAX 212-683-2750. Ed. Jack O'Dwyer. adv.; stat.; index. **Document type:** directory.

338 659.1   US   ISSN 0191-0051
HD59
O'DWYER'S DIRECTORY OF PUBLIC RELATIONS EXECUTIVES. 1979. a. $90. J.R. O'Dwyer Co., Inc., 271 Madison Ave., New York, NY 10016. TEL 212-679-2471. FAX 212-683-2750. Ed. Jack O'Dwyer. **Document type:** directory.

380 659.1   US   ISSN 0078-3374
HM263
O'DWYER'S DIRECTORY OF PUBLIC RELATIONS FIRMS. 1969. a. $145. J.R. O'Dwyer Co., Inc., 271 Madison Ave., New York, NY 10016. TEL 212-679-2471. FAX 212-683-2750. adv. circ. 2,000. **Document type:** directory.

OFF-PRICE RETAIL DIRECTORY. see *BUSINESS AND ECONOMICS — Marketing And Purchasing*

OFFICE DEALER (YEAR); the industry's new products merchandiser. see *BUSINESS AND ECONOMICS — Office Equipment And Services*

OFFICIAL BRITISH THEATRE DIRECTORY SEATING PLAN GUIDE. see *THEATER*

OFFICIAL DIRECTORY OF NEW JERSEY LIBRARIES AND MEDIA CENTERS. see *LIBRARY AND INFORMATION SCIENCES*

380   US
OFFICIAL INTERMODAL GUIDE; directory of intermodal services, facilities and personnel. 1983. 2/yr. $241 (effective 1996). K - III Directory Corp., 10 Lake Dr., Highstown, NJ 08520. TEL 800-221-5488. FAX 609-371-7879. adv. circ. 2,200. **Document type:** directory.
   Description: Profiles most intermodal facilities. Company names, contact personnel, addresses and phone numbers are provided.

338   US
OFFICIAL INTERNATIONAL BUSINESS DIRECTORY OF THE LATIN AMERICAN WORLD. (Text in English, Portuguese, Spanish) 1982. a. $150 per m. Aquino Productions, Box 125, Rochester, VT 05767. Ed. Andres C. Aquino. adv. **Document type:** directory.
   Formerly: Official International Business Directory of the Spanish Speaking World (ISSN 0735-5513)

338   US   ISSN 1056-6872
OFFICIAL IOWA MANUFACTURERS DIRECTORY. 1994. a. $67 (diskette & CD-ROM $325). Harris InfoSource International, 2057-2 Aurora Rd., Twinsburg, OH 44087. TEL 216-425-9000; 800-888-5900. FAX 216-425-7150. E-mail: catknapp@aol.com. Ed. Frances L. Carlsen. (also avail. in diskette format) **Document type:** directory.
   ●Also available on CD-ROM.

384.55 380   US   ISSN 0890-782X
HD9696.V533
OFFICIAL VIDEO DIRECTORY & BUYER'S GUIDE. 1987. a. $125. Palm Springs Media, Inc., Box 2740, Palm Springs, CA 92263. TEL 619-322-3050. FAX 619-322-1260. Ed. Steve Tolin. adv. circ. 6,000. **Document type:** directory.
   Description: Sourcebook of suppliers and manufacturers of video hardware and software.

338.025   US   ISSN 1048-7360
HF5065.O3
OHIO BUSINESS DIRECTORY. 1989. a. $495 (effective 1997). American Business Directories (Subsidiary of: American Business Information, Inc.), 5711 S. 86th Circle, Box 27347, Omaha, NE 68127. TEL 402-593-4600; 800-555-6124. FAX 402-331-5481. E-mail: jerry.venner@abii.com. index. (also avail. in magnetic tape; diskette format) **Document type:** directory.
   ●Also available online.
   Also available on CD-ROM.
   Description: Includes all business in the state compiled from the yellow pages and telephone-verified. Each listing includes company name, complete address, phone number, name of owner, manager, and employee size, sales volume codes, and credit rating codes.

670   US   ISSN 0737-7495
HD9727.O3
OHIO MANUFACTURERS DIRECTORY. 1983. a. $149 (diskette or CD-ROM $745) (effective 1997). Manufacturers' News, Inc., 1633 Central St., Evanston, IL 60201. TEL 847-864-7000. FAX 847-332-1100. Ed. Louise M. West. adv.: B&W page $1843; adv. contact: Charles Scherer. (also avail. in diskette format) **Document type:** directory.
   ●Also available on CD-ROM.
   Description: Lists 22,572 manufacturers by product, alphabetically, geographically by SIC and parent co.

670   US   ISSN 0884-173X
HD9727.O3
OHIO REGISTER OF MANUFACTURERS. 1983. a. $92.50. Commerce Register, Inc., 190 Godwin Ave., Midland Park, NJ 07432. TEL 201-445-3000. FAX 201-445-5806. adv.; illus. (also avail. in magnetic tape; diskette format) **Document type:** directory.
   Formerly: Ohio Directory of Manufacturers (ISSN 0738-3711)
   Description: Profiles over 12,000 manufacturers and their key executives in five different sections: alphabetically, geographically by city, by SIC.

OIL & GAS DIRECTORY. see *PETROLEUM AND GAS*

OILS AND FATS INTERNATIONAL DIRECTORY. see *CHEMISTRY — Organic Chemistry*

338.025   II
OKHLA & NEHRU PLACE DIRECTORY; the authentic industrial & business intelligence. (Text in English) 1986. irreg., 4th ed., 1995. Rs.225($15) Businesslinks, 3, DSIDC Complex, Okhla Phase 1, New Delhi 110 020, India. TEL 6819111. Ed. A. Azim Siddigui. adv.: page Rs.3000; 160 x 210. circ. 10,000. **Document type:** trade publication, directory.

338.025   US   ISSN 1048-7379
HF5065.O5
OKLAHOMA BUSINESS DIRECTORY. 1987. a. $350 (effective 1997). American Business Directories (Subsidiary of: American Business Information, Inc.), 5711 S. 86th Circle, Box 27347, Omaha, NE 68127. TEL 402-593-4600; 800-555-6124. FAX 402-331-5481. E-mail: jerry.venner@abii.com. index. (also avail. in magnetic tape; diskette format) **Document type:** directory.
   ●Also available online.
   Also available on CD-ROM.
   Description: Includes all businesses in the state compiled from the yellow pages and telephone-verified. Each listing includes company name, complete address, phone number, name of owner, manager, and employee size, sales volume codes and credit rating codes.

338   US   ISSN 1051-919X
HD9727.O5
OKLAHOMA DIRECTORY OF MANUFACTURERS AND PROCESSORS. 1957. a. $69. Department of Commerce, Box 26980, Oklahoma City, OK 73126-0980. TEL 405-815-6552. FAX 405-815-5199. circ. 4,000. **Document type:** government publication, directory.

670   US   ISSN 1059-4523
HF5065.O5
OKLAHOMA MANUFACTURERS REGISTER. 1992. a. $71 (diskette or CD-ROM $345) (effective 1997). Manufacturers' News, Inc., 1633 Central St., Evanston, IL 60201-1505. TEL 847-864-7000. FAX 847-332-1100. Ed. Louise M. West. adv.: B&W page $1843; adv. contact: Charles Scherer. circ. 1,429. (also avail. in diskette format) **Document type:** directory.
   ●Also available on CD-ROM.
   Description: Lists 5,645 manufacturers by industrial product, alphabetically, by SIC code and geographically.

OMEGA NEW AGE DIRECTORY. see *NEW AGE PUBLICATIONS*

THE ONE MILLION PLUS CHARITIES DIRECTORY. see *SOCIAL SERVICES AND WELFARE*

338.025 339   UK
HF54.5
ONLINE - C D - R O M BUSINESS SOURCEBOOK. 1986. a. £155 (effective 1997). Headland Business Information (Subsidiary of: Bowker-Saur), Customer Services Department, Maypole House, Maypole Rd., East Grinstead, W. Sussex RH19 1HH, England. TEL 44-1429-231902. FAX 44-1429-861403. Ed. Pamela Foster. **Document type:** directory.
— BLDSC (6260.761490).
   Formerly (until 1993): Online Business Sourcebook (ISSN 0953-5055)
   Description: Provides a one-stop guide to more than 700 business databases and 59 leading hosts.

338 670   UK
OPUS DESIGN FILE. 1984. a. £55 (overseas £65) (effective 1995). Builder Group plc., Builder House, 1 Millharbour, London E14 9RA, England. TEL 44-171-560-4000. FAX 44-171-560-4100. (Subscr. to: Building, Freepost (LE6522), Leicester LE87 4DH, England. TEL 01858-468811) circ. 13,900. **Document type:** trade publication.
— CISTI.
   Formerly: Opus Building Services Design File (ISSN 0266-1063)

338.025   US   ISSN 1059-7077
ORANGE COUNTY BUSINESS AND INDUSTRIAL DIRECTORY. a. $75 (diskette $295) (effective 1996). (Orange County Business Council) Database Publishing Company, 1590 S. Lewis St., Anaheim, CA 92805-6423. TEL 714-778-6400. FAX 714-778-6811. (Subscr. to: Box 70024, Anaheim, CA 92825-0024. TEL 800-888-8434) (also avail. in diskette format) **Document type:** directory.
   Former titles: Orange County Business Directory & Orange County Commerce and Industry Directory.
   Description: Lists 6,500 companies including 3,000 manufacturing firms and 15,250 top executives.

670 600   US
HC107.C22
ORANGE COUNTY TECHNOLOGY GUIDE (YEAR). 1992. a. $90. Corporate Technology Information Services Inc., 12 Alfred St., Ste. 200, Woburn, MA 01801. TEL 617-932-3939. FAX 617-932-6335. **Document type:** directory.
— CCC.
   Formerly (until 1995): Greater Orange County Technology Resource Guide (Year) (ISSN 1060-1627)
   Description: Profiles thousands of technology manufacturers - firms involved in such high growth high-tech activities as lasers, computers, advanced materials, and biotech. Listed alphabetically and cross indexed by city and over 250 product categories.

338.025 US ISSN 1047-8809
HF5065.O7
OREGON BUSINESS DIRECTORY. 1989. a. $350 (effective 1997). American Business Directories (Subsidiary of: American Business Information, Inc.), 5711 S. 86th Circle, Box 27347, Omaha, NE 68127. TEL 402-593-4600; 800-555-6124. FAX 402-331-5481. E-mail: jerry.venner@abii.com. index. (also avail. in magnetic tape; diskette format) **Document type:** directory.
●Also available online.
Also available on CD-ROM.
Description: Includes all businesses in the state compiled from the yellow pages and telephone-verified. Each listing includes company name, complete address, phone number, name of owner, manager, and employee size, sales volume codes and credit rating codes.

338.025 US ISSN 1071-6890
HF5065.O7
OREGON MANUFACTURERS REGISTER. 1994. a. $99 (diskette $395) (effective 1996). Database Publishing Company, 1590 S. Lewis St., Anaheim, CA 92805-6423. TEL 714-778-6400. FAX 714-778-6811. Ed. Kathie Scott. adv. contact: Ken Gregory. circ. 2,000. (also avail. in diskette format) **Document type:** directory.
Formerly: Oregon Manufacturers Directory.
Description: Profiles 5,500 manufacturing firms and 13,300 CEO's and key executives.

338.025 327 US ISSN 0250-6211
F1402
ORGANIZATION OF AMERICAN STATES. DIRECTORY. q. $3 per no. Organization of American States, General Secretariat, 1889 F St., N.W., Washington, DC 20006. TEL 703-941-1617. **Document type:** directory.

OUTLET PROJECT DIRECTORY. see *BUSINESS AND ECONOMICS — Marketing And Purchasing*

380 687 US
OUTLET REPORT. a. $12.95. Lazar Media Group, Inc., 108 E. 38th St., Ste. 2000, New York, NY 10016. TEL 212-683-7612. FAX 212-683-7704. Ed. Ann Rizzo.
Description: Contains information on outlet centers around the country. Includes over 300 outlet centers and lists the address, directions, days and hours and a listing of all the individual outlets at these centers.

OUTLET RETAIL DIRECTORY. see *BUSINESS AND ECONOMICS — Marketing And Purchasing*

OUTLOOK MAGAZINE. see *INTERIOR DESIGN AND DECORATION — Furniture And House Furnishings*

380 UK
OVERSEAS TRADE DIRECTORIES; who's who, press guides, year books. 1947. irreg. £38($50) New Product Newsletter Co. Ltd., 1A Chesterfield St., London W.1., England. Ed. H.R. Vaughan. adv. circ. 5,000. (also avail. in microfilm from UMI) **Document type:** directory.

338.025 AT
A C E BUYERS' GUIDE. (Process and Control Engineering) a. Aus.$75 (effective 1996). Reed Business Publishing Pty. Ltd. (Subsidiary of: Reed International PLC), P.O. Box 5487, W. Chatswood, N.S.W. 2057, Australia. TEL 61-2-372-5222. FAX 61-2-419-7399. **Document type:** directory, trade publication.
Description: A comprehensive directory of people, companies, products, and brand names within the Australian process and control engineering market.

C P C I MEMBERSHIP DIRECTORY AND PRODUCT LISTING. (Power Conversion Products Council International) see *ENGINEERING — Electrical Engineering*

E M: PLANT ENGINEERING AND MAINTENANCE SOURCEBOOK. see *BUSINESS AND ECONOMICS — Management*

333.33 658 US
M A DIRECTORY. 1968. a. $50. Property Management Association, 8811 Colesville Rd., Ste. G106, Silver Spring, MD 20910. TEL 301-587-6543. Ed. Samia Abdel-Malak; Pub. John P. Bachner. adv. contact: Stacy Johnson. circ. 2,500. **Document type:** directory.
Description: Listing of members and property management resources.

382 659 UK
P R PLANNER - EUROPE. 1974. a. £485. Media Information Ltd., Hale House, 290-296 Green Lanes, London N13 5TP, England. FAX 44-181-886-0703. Ed. Ernest Wedgwood. (looseleaf format) **Document type:** directory.
●Also available on CD-ROM.

382 659 UK
P R PLANNER - U.K. 1966. a. £350. Media Information Ltd., Hale House, 290-296 Green Lanes, London N13 5TP, England. TEL 44-181-882-0155. FAX 44-181-886-0703. Ed. Maureen Gunter. (looseleaf format) **Document type:** trade publication.

338 665.538 US ISSN 1042-4865
HD9567.A17
PACIFIC - MOUNTAIN OIL DIRECTORY. (Includes Buyer's Guide) 1988. a. I.E.I., Publishing Division, 1635 W. Alabama, Houston, TX 77006. TEL 713-529-1616. FAX 713-520-0936. Ed. Janis Johnson; Pub. Shawn Wymes. adv. contact: Rob Garza. circ. 7,750. (back issues avail.) **Document type:** directory.

380.1 US ISSN 0555-8581
PACIFIC SOUTHWEST DIRECTORY. 1951. a. $60 to non-members. California Grain & Feed Association, 1521 I St., Sacramento, CA 95814-2016. FAX 916-446-1063. Ed. D.J. Gutioriez. adv. circ. 1,200. **Document type:** directory.
Description: Covers Arizona, California, Hawaii, Nevada and Utah.

380 915 AT ISSN 0311-0826
PACIFIC TRAVEL DIRECTORY. 1973. a. Aus.$7.50. c/o Pacific Airlines News, Box 1, Surfers Paradise, Qld. 4217, Australia. Ed. A. H. McRobbie. **Document type:** directory.

PACKAGING INDUSTRY DIRECTORY. see *PACKAGING*

PACKAGING SUPPLIER SOURCE GUIDE. see *PACKAGING*

PACKAGING USERS DIRECTORY. see *PACKAGING*

382 332.4 UK
HG3851
THE PAINE WEBBER EUROMONEY DIRECTORY. US edition: Euromoney Directory. 1973. a. £280($440) Euromoney Publications plc., Nestor House, Playhouse Yard, London EC4V 5EX, England. TEL 0171-779-8935. FAX 0171-779-8541. **Document type:** directory.
Former titles: Merrill Lynch - Euromoney Directory (ISSN 0953-1181); (until 1987): Hambro Euromoney Directory (ISSN 0306-3933)

382 PK
PAKISTAN TRADE DIRECTORY - EXPORTERS AND MANUFACTURERS. (Text in English) 1952. irreg. Rs.400($42) Publishers International, Bandukwala Bldg., No. 4, I.I. Chundrigar Rd, Karachi, Pakistan. Ed. Kamaluddin Ahmed. adv. circ. 10,000. **Document type:** directory.
Former titles: Directory of Exporters and Manufacturers; Directory of Pakistan Exporters.

PAN-EUROPEAN ASSOCIATIONS; a directory of multi-national organisations in Europe. see *POLITICAL SCIENCE — International Relations*

380 FR
PARIS-ANGLOPHONE. 1989. a. $14.95. Anglophone S.A., 32 rue Edouard Vaillant, 93100 Montreuil, France. TEL 33-1-48596658. FAX 33-1-48596668. E-mail: http://www.paris-anglo.com. R&P contact: Frank D. Cluck. adv. contact: David Applefield. circ. 10,000 (controlled). **Document type:** directory.
●Also available online.
Description: Provides a complete listing of English-speaking commercial, professional companies and organizations, and cultural activities in France.

338.025 US ISSN 1048-7395
HF5065.P4
PENNSYLVANIA BUSINESS DIRECTORY. 1989. a. $495 (effective 1997). American Business Directories (Subsidiary of: American Business Information, Inc.), 5711 S. 86th Circle, Box 27347, Omaha, NE 68127. TEL 402-593-4600; 800-555-6124. FAX 402-331-5481. E-mail: jerry.venner@abii.com. index. (also avail. in magnetic tape; diskette format) **Document type:** directory.
●Also available online.
Also available on CD-ROM.
Description: Includes all businesses in the state compiled from the yellow pages and telephone-verified. Each listing includes company name, complete address, phone number, name of owner, manager, and employee size, sales volume codes, and credit rating codes.

670 US ISSN 0733-5237
HD9727.P4
PENNSYLVANIA DIRECTORY OF MANUFACTURERS. 1980. a. $92.50. Commerce Register, Inc., 190 Godwin Ave., Midland Park, NJ 07432. TEL 201-445-3000. FAX 201-445-5806. adv. (also avail. in magnetic tape; diskette format) **Document type:** directory.
Description: Profiles approximately 12,000 companies alphabetically, geographically, and by product line. Also lists key executives.

917.402 US ISSN 0887-3682
HD9727.P4
PENNSYLVANIA MANUFACTURERS REGISTER. a. $149 (diskette or CD-ROM $745) (effective 1997). Manufacturers' News, Inc., 1633 Central St., Evanston, IL 60201. TEL 847-864-7000. FAX 847-332-1100. Ed. Louise M. West. adv.: B&W page $1843; adv. contact: Charles Scherer. illus. (diskette format) **Document type:** directory.
●Also available on CD-ROM.
Description: Profiles 19,868 manufacturers; includes product, alphabetical, geographical by city, SIC, and parent company sections.

PERIOD BUILDING RESTORATION TRADES & SUPPLIERS DIRECTORY. see *ARCHITECTURE*

PERMIAN BASIN PETROLEUM INDUSTRY. see *PETROLEUM AND GAS*

658.3 US ISSN 1068-4751
HF5549.2.U5
PERSONNEL EXECUTIVES CONTACTBOOK. 1993. a. $149. Gale Research, 835 Penobscot Bldg., 645 Griswold St., Detroit, MI 48226-4094. TEL 313-961-2242; 800-877-4253. FAX 800-414-5043. E-mail: daniel_snyder@gale.com. Ed. Cynthia Russell Spomer. **Document type:** directory.
Description: Lists human resources professionals at more than 30,000 U.S. companies.

380.1 004 AT
PERTH COMPUTING DIRECTORY. 1987. a. Aus.$75 (effective 1997). Business Intelligence (W.A.), P.O. Box 210, Claremont, W.A. 6010, Australia. TEL 61-9-4487665. FAX 61-9-4475011. Ed. Steve Whitfield. **Document type:** directory.
Description: Provides contact details and summary of products and services for computer products retailers and wholesalers in Perth, Western Australia.

PETERHEAD PORT HANDBOOK. see *TRANSPORTATION — Ships And Shipping*

338 US ISSN 1080-2541
▼**PETERSON'S CONTRACT SERVICES FOR HIGHER EDUCATION.** 1995. a. Peterson's, 202 Carnegie Center, Box 2123, Princeton, NJ 08543-2123. TEL 609-243-9111; 800-338-3282. FAX 609-243-9150. URL: http://www.petersons.com. Ed. Barbara Lawrence. **Document type:** trade publication, directory.
Description: Lists more than 100 areas - from bookstore management to food service - and 2,000 vendors that currently provide these services to colleges and universities in the U.S.

PETERSON'S HIDDEN JOB MARKET. see *OCCUPATIONS AND CAREERS*

PETROCHEMICAL INDUSTRY; petrochemical plants, engineering, construction, equipment manufactures & supply companies. see *PETROLEUM AND GAS*

BUSINESS AND ECONOMICS — TRADE AND INDUSTRIAL DIRECTORIES

670 615.19   JA
PHARMACEUTICAL MANUFACTURERS OF JAPAN. 1981. biennial. 15000 Yen. Yakugyo Jiho Co., Ltd., 2-36 Kanda Jimbo-cho, Chiyoda-ku, Tokyo 101, Japan.
    Description: Addresses and research figures of Japanese pharmaceutical companies.

381.1 658   US   ISSN 1072-2572
PHELON'S DISCOUNT - JOBBING TRADE. a. $175 (effective 1997). Phelon Sheldon & Marsar, Inc., 330 Main St., Ridgefield Park, NJ 07660-1228. TEL 201-440-9096; 800-234-8804. FAX 201-440-8568. **Document type:** directory.

746.92   US   ISSN 1072-2564
PHELON'S WOMEN'S APPAREL AND ACCESSORY SHOPS. biennial, 11th ed. $175 (effective 1997). Phelon Sheldon & Marsar, Inc., 330 Main St., Ridgefield Park, NJ 07660-1228; 800-234-8804. FAX 201-440-8568. Ed. Kenneth W. Phelon Jr. circ. 1,000 (paid). **Document type:** directory.
    Formerly: Phelon's Women's Apparel Shops (ISSN 0737-3430)

380   US
PHILADELPHIA STOCK EXCHANGE GUIDE. 1965. m. $378. C C H Incorporated, 2700 Lake Cook Rd., Riverwoods, IL 60015. TEL 847-267-7000; 800-835-5224. FAX 800-224-8299. (looseleaf format)

338   PH
PHILIPPINES BUSINESS DIRECTORY. (Text in English) a. P.300($75) Massmark Philippines, P.O. Box 3333, Manila 1073, Philippines. TEL 805-0955. adv. **Document type:** directory.

PHILIPPINES YEARBOOK OF THE FOOKIEN TIMES. see BUSINESS AND ECONOMICS — Banking And Finance

PHILLIPS' INTERNATIONAL PAPER DIRECTORY. see PAPER AND PULP

384.5   US
PHILLIPS WORLD SATELLITE ALMANAC. 1985. a. $257. Phillips Business Information, Inc., 1201 Seven Locks Rd., Potomac, MD 20854. TEL 301-424-3338; 800-777-5006. FAX 301-309-3847. E-mail: pbi@phillips.com. **Document type:** directory.
—CISTI
    Formerly: World Satellite Almanac (ISSN 0885-1611); Which incorporates (1993-1995): Satellite Systems Handbook (ISSN 1078-8298)
    Description: Presents technical and operating details of all commercial satellite systems and operators. Shows areas of coverage, and signal strengths, and lists contacts and brokers.

338   SA   ISSN 1016-6793
PHOENIX - VERULAM & TONGAAT BUYERS' GUIDE. 1987. a. R.20 (effective 1996). Braby's (Subsidiary of: Kohler Packaging Ltd.), P.O. Box 1426, Pinetown 3600, South Africa. TEL 27-31-7017021. FAX 27-31-7017036. **Document type:** directory.
    Formerly: Phoenix Verulam Buyer's Guide (ISSN 1016-4022)

338   UK   ISSN 0953-7597
PIMS EUROPEAN TRADE & TECHNICAL DIRECTORY. 1988. 2/yr. £185 (effective 1997). PIMS (UK) Ltd., PIMS House, Mildmay Ave., London N1 4RS, England. TEL 44-171-226-1000. FAX 44-171-354-7053. **Document type:** directory.
    Formerly: Pims European Directory.
    Description: Directory of European trade and technical presses indexed by subject and publication.

PIMS U K A-Z TOWNS. see PUBLISHING AND BOOK TRADE

PIMS U K MEDIA DIRECTORY. see PUBLISHING AND BOOK TRADE

PIPELINE & GAS JOURNAL ANNUAL DIRECTORY OF PIPELINES AND EQUIPMENT. see PETROLEUM AND GAS

PIPELINE INDUSTRY (TULSA). see PETROLEUM AND GAS

338.025   US
▼**PITTSBURGH BUSINESS DIRECTORY.** 1996. a. $44.95. American City Business Journals, Inc. (Austin), 505 Powell St., Austin, TX 78703-5121. (Subscr. to: Pittsburgh Business Times, 2313 E. Carson St., Ste. 200, Pittsburgh, PA 15203-2109. TEL 412-481-6397. FAX 412-481-9956) adv.: B&W page $1700. circ. 3,000 (paid). **Document type:** directory.

PIXEL - THE COMPUTER ANIMATION DIRECTORY. see ART — Computer Applications

338   US   ISSN 0895-4682
AS29.N5
PLACES: A DIRECTORY OF PUBLIC PLACES FOR PRIVATE EVENTS AND PRIVATE PLACES FOR PUBLIC FUNCTIONS. 1978. biennial. $24.95. Tenth House Enterprises, Inc., Box 810, Gracie Sta., New York, NY 10028. TEL 212-737-7536. FAX 212-737-9469. Ed. Tatiana Stoumen; Pub. Hannelore Hahn. adv. contact: Peter Donoso. circ. 15,000. **Document type:** directory.
    Description: Lists close to 1,000 public and private facilities in New York and its environs.

338.025   AT
PLANTLINE BUYERS' GUIDE. a. Aus.$75 (effective 1996). Reed Business Publishing Pty. Ltd. (Subsidiary of: Reed International PLC), P.O. Box 5487, W. Chatswood, N.S.W. 2057, Australia. TEL 61-2-372-5222. FAX 61-2-419-7399. **Document type:** directory, trade publication.
    Description: A complete guide to products and equipment for Australia's manufacturing industry.

PLASTICS & PACKAGING. see PACKAGING

668.4   UK
PLASTICS, RUBBER & CHEMICAL PRODUCTS; an advertising extract from Kompass. a. (in 5 vols.). Kompass (Subsidiary of: Reed Information Services Ltd.), Part of the Reed Elsevier group, Windsor Ct., E. Grinstead House, E. Grinstead, W. Sussex RH19 1XD, England. TEL 44-1342-326972. FAX 44-1342-317241. TELEX 95127-INSFER-G. **Document type:** directory.
    Formerly (until 1995): Buyer's Guide. Plastics, Rubber and Chemical Products (Year).

688.72   US
PLAYTHINGS BUYERS GUIDE. 1903. a. included in subscr. to Playthings. Geyer-McAllister Publications, Inc., 51 Madison Ave., New York, NY 10010. TEL 212-689-4411. Ed. Frank Reysen, Jr. adv. circ. 15,000. **Document type:** directory.
    Formerly: Playthings Directory (ISSN 0079-2349)
    Description: Alphabetical listing of manufacturers, importers, trade associations, licensors, trademarks and trade names, designers and inventors, suppliers and showrooms.

338 696   US
PLUMBING AND MECHANICAL DIRECTORY. 1992. a. $25. Business News Publishing Company, 55 W. Big Beaver Rd., Ste. 1000, Troy, MI 48084. TEL 810-362-3700. FAX 810-362-0317. URL: http://www.bnp.com. (Subscr. to: Box 3212, Northbrook, IL 60065) Ed. Jim Olsztynski; Pub. George Zebrowski. adv.: B&W page $1885, color page $1935; trim 5 3/8 x 8 1/2; adv. contact: Patty Podboy. circ. 41,000. **Document type:** directory.
●Also available online.
    Description: For the plumbing - pipe, valves, fittings - hydronic heating industry.

380   US
▼**PLUNKETT'S ENTERTAINMENT AND MEDIA INDUSTRY ALMANAC.** 1997. a. $149.99. Plunkett Research, Ltd., P.O. Drawer 8270, Galveston, TX 77553-8270. TEL 409-765-8530. FAX 409-765-8571. Ed. Jack W. Plunkett; Pub. Jack W. Plunkett. **Document type:** directory.

338.025 332   US
▼**PLUNKETT'S FINANCIAL SERVICES INDUSTRY ALMANAC.** 1996. a. $136.49 (effective 1996). Plunkett Research, Ltd., P.O. Drawer 8270, Galveston, TX 77553-8270. TEL 409-765-8530. FAX 409-765-8571. Ed. Jack W. Plunkett; Pub. Jack W. Plunkett. **Document type:** directory.
    Description: Complete guide to the size, scope and potential of every segment of the financial services industry.

338.025 610   US
PLUNKETT'S HEALTH CARE INDUSTRY ALMANAC. 1985. a. $156.49 (effective 1997). Plunkett Research, Ltd., P.O. Drawer 8270, Galveston, TX 77553-8270. TEL 409-765-8530. FAX 409-765-8571. Ed. Jack W. Plunkett; Pub. Jack W. Plunkett. **Document type:** directory.
    Description: Complete reference guide to the American health care industry and its leading corporations.

338.025 621   US
▼**PLUNKETT'S INFOTECH INDUSTRY ALMANAC.** 1996. a. $131.50. Plunkett Research, Ltd., P.O. Drawer 8270, Galveston, TX 77553-8270. TEL 409-765-8530. FAX 409-765-8571. Ed. Jack W. Plunkett; Pub. Jack W. Plunkett. **Document type:** directory.
    Description: Provides an in-depth analysis of the burgeoning InfoTech revolution, each industry segment, and the most outstanding corporations within those industries.

338.025 658   US
▼**PLUNKETT'S RETAIL INDUSTRY ALMANAC.** 1997. a. $136.49 (effective 1996). Plunkett Research, Ltd., P.O. Drawer 8270, Galveston, TX 77553-8270. TEL 409-765-8530. FAX 409-765-8571. Ed. Jack W. Plunkett; Pub. Jack W. Plunkett. **Document type:** directory.
    Description: Presents the trends and a thorough analysis of careers, suppliers, finances, and future growth within the retail industry.

380 332.1   US   ISSN 1058-0603
HG1536
POLK BANK DIRECTORY. INTERNATIONAL EDITION. 1894. a. $243. R.L. Polk & Co., Bank Services Division, Box 305100, Nashville, TN 37230-5100. TEL 615-889-3350. FAX 615-885-3081. adv.; bk.rev.; charts; stat. circ. 17,500. **Document type:** directory.
    Formerly: Polk's World Bank Directory. International Edition (ISSN 0085-4999)

380 332.1   US   ISSN 1058-0611
HG1536
POLK BANK DIRECTORY. NORTH AMERICAN EDITION. 1894. 2/yr. $276.75 per no. R.L. Polk & Co., Bank Services Division, Box 305100, Nashville, TN 37230-5100. TEL 615-889-3350. FAX 615-885-3081. TELEX 554344 ENCYCOBANK NAS. adv.; bk.rev. circ. 18,500. (also avail. in magnetic tape; diskette format) **Document type:** directory.
    Formerly: Polk's World Bank Directory. North American Edition.

380 332   US
POLK'S FINANCIAL INSTITUTIONS BUYER'S GUIDE AND SERVICES DIRECTORY.* 1991. a. $95. R.L. Polk & Co., 1321 Murfreesboro Pike No. 731, Nashville, TN 37217-2626. TEL 615-889-3350. Ed. Jerry Eimbinder. adv. circ. 15,000. **Document type:** directory.
    Description: Categorizes the products and services useful for executives in banking, credit card and securities industries.

POLLUTION ENGINEERING PRODUCT - SERVICE LOCATOR. see ENVIRONMENTAL STUDIES — Waste Management

POLYMERS PAINT COLOR YEAR BOOK. see PAINTS AND PROTECTIVE COATINGS

797.21   US   ISSN 0194-5351
HD9993.S953
POOL & SPA NEWS; the national trade magazine for the swimming pool & spa industry. 1961. s-m. $17.97 (effective 1997). Leisure Publications, Inc., 3923 W 6th St., Los Angeles, CA 90020. TEL 213-385-3926. FAX 213-383-1152. Ed. Anne Blakey. adv.; tr.lit. circ. 16,000. **Document type:** trade publication.
    Formerly: Pool News (ISSN 0032-4280)
    Description: For pool and spa professionals.

380.1   US
POOL & SPA NEWS SOURCE BOOK. 1968. a. $49.50 (effective 1997). Leisure Publications, Inc., 3923 W 6th St., Los Angeles, CA 90020. TEL 213-385-3926. FAX 213-383-1152. Ed. Anne Blakey. adv. circ. 16,000. **Document type:** trade publication.
    Former titles: Pool and Spa News Directory; Pool News Directory (ISSN 0194-1380)

BUSINESS AND ECONOMICS — TRADE AND INDUSTRIAL DIRECTORIES

338   SA
PORT ELIZABETH - UITENHAGE DIRECTORY. (Text in English) a. R.50. Braby's (Subsidiary of: Kohler Packaging Ltd.), P.O. Box 1426, Pinetown 3600, South Africa. TEL 27-31-7017021. FAX 27-31-7017036. Ed. A. Stagg. (also avail. in diskette format) **Document type:** directory.
  Former titles: Donaldson's Port Elizabeth, Uitenhage and Despatch Directory; Donaldson's Port Elizabeth Directory (ISSN 0416-2706)

PORTFOLIO OF BLACK BUSINESS IN SOUTHERN AFRICA. see BUSINESS AND ECONOMICS

POWER AGENT. see ASTROLOGY

380.1 384.55   US
PRE-RECORDED VIDEO SUPPLIERS DIRECTORY. 1993. irreg. $215 (foreign $255). Corbell Publishing, 4676 Admiralty Way, Ste. 300, Marina Del Rey, CA 90292. TEL 310-574-5337. FAX 301-574-5383. Ed. Deborah Rolfe; Pub. Maureen Healy. R&P contact: Maureen Healy. adv. contact: Joseph Daneshrad. **Document type:** directory.
  Description: Lists the major studios, video suppliers. Also contains valuable statistics on the business yesterday, today and tomorrow.

PREPARED FOODS FOOD INDUSTRY SOURCEBOOK. see FOOD AND FOOD INDUSTRIES

PRINT BUYERS DIRECTORY. see PRINTING

PRINTING TRADES DIRECTORY. see PRINTING

PRINTWORLD DIRECTORY OF CONTEMPORARY PRINTS AND PRICES. see ART

338.025   IE
PRIVATE RESEARCH TOP 2000 IRISH COMPANIES. 1982. a. I£95($150) Private Research Ltd., 7-8 Mount St. Crescent, Dublin 2, Ireland. TEL 353-1-6760774. FAX 353-1-6760773. Ed. John O'Neill. adv. contact: James Treacy. (also avail. in diskette format; back issues avail.) **Document type:** corporate report.
  Formerly: Aspect Top 2000 Irish Companies.

382 332.6   US   ISSN 0094-3134
HG4907
PROBE DIRECTORY OF FOREIGN DIRECT INVESTMENT IN THE UNITED STATES.* 1974. irreg., latest 1989. $250. Probe International, Inc., 1047 Sunset Rd., Stamford, CT 06903-2429. TEL 203-329-9595. FAX 203-329-8054. Ed. Evalyn Weiner. **Document type:** directory.
  Description: Lists U.S. manufacturers which are partly or wholly foreign-owned and lists foreign owners by country. Includes addresses, telephone numbers, key product line and key executives.

338.025 663 664   II
PROCESSED FOODS & BEVERAGES DIRECTORY (YEAR). (Text in English) biennial. Rs.500 (foreign $50). Amalgamated Press, Narang House, 41 Ambalal Doshi Marg, Fort, Mumbai 400001, India. TEL 91-22-2650268. FAX 91-22-2641275. Ed. Norman J. Dasilva; Pub. Norman J. Dasilva. **Document type:** directory.
  Description: Covers food & beverage manufacturers, raw materials suppliers, food and beverage processing and packaging machinery suppliers, importers and exporters of processed food, food associations and institutes.

382 670   SP   ISSN 0079-5836
PRODEI; catalogue of Spanish manufacturers, exporters and importers. (Text and summaries in English, French, German, Spanish) 1945. biennial. 20000 ptas.($150) (effective 1996-97 ed.). Capel Editorial Distribuidora, S.A., Almirante, 21, Apdo. 562, 28004 Madrid, Spain. TEL 34-1-3080644. FAX 34-1-3105141. adv. circ. 15,000. **Document type:** directory.
  Description: Provides information on the Spanish market. All sectors of the Spanish economy from the most qualified precision enterprise to the modest craftsman.

PRODUCCION QUIMICA MEXICANA/MEXICAN CHEMICAL PRODUCTION. see ENGINEERING — Chemical Engineering

382 778.5   US   ISSN 0732-6653
PN1993.5.U77
PRODUCER'S MASTERGUIDE; the international production manual for motion pictures, television, commercials, cable and videotape industries in the United States, Canada, the United Kingdom, Bermuda, the Caribbean Islands, Mexico, South America, Europe, the Far East, Australia and New Zealand. 1979. a. $125 (Canada $125; elsewhere $155). Producer's Masterguide, 60 E. 8th St., 31st Fl., New York, NY 10003-6514. TEL 212-777-4002. FAX 212-777-4101. E-mail: producers@masterguide.com; URL: http://www.producers.masterguide.com. Ed. Shmuel Bension. adv.; charts; stat. circ. 18,000. **Document type:** directory.
  Formerly (until 1982): New York Production Manual (ISSN 0163-1276)

382   CH   ISSN 1026-9525
▼**PRODUCTOS DE TAIWAN.** (Text in Spanish) 1996. a. $30. Trade Winds, Inc., No. 7, Lane 75, Yungkang St., P.O. Box 7-179, Taipei, Taiwan, Republic of China. TEL 886-2-3913251. FAX 886-2-3964022. E-mail: tradwind@ms2.hinet.net; URL: http://www.tradewinds.comtw. (Subscr. in US to: Trade Winds, Inc., Box 820519, Dallas, TX 75382. TEL 972-699-1188. FAX 972-699-1189)
  Description: Covers all types of products made in Taiwan for the Latin American market.

PRODUCTS CERTIFIED FOR CANADA DIRECTORY. see BUSINESS AND ECONOMICS — Production Of Goods And Services

620   NE
PRODUKT JAARBOEK. a. fl.39 (effective 1996). Wyt Uitgeefgroep B.V., Postbus 6438, 3002 AK Rotterdam, Netherlands. TEL 31-10-4657771. FAX 31-10-4780904. E-mail: 101630.2235@compuserve.com. adv. **Document type:** directory.
  Description: Product and company information in the industrial design sector.

650 338   II   ISSN 0079-5925
PROFESSIONAL AND TRADE ORGANISATIONS IN INDIA. 1963. irreg. Rs.5 (foreign $10). Kothari Publications, 12 India Exchange Pl., Calcutta 700 001, India. TEL 91-33-220-9563. Ed. H. Kothari. adv. **Document type:** directory.
  Description: Provides information about leading professional and scientific employers, cultural, and trade organizations in India.

380.1 770   UK   ISSN 0263-3159
PROFESSIONAL PHOTOGRAPHER DIRECTORY AND BUYER'S GUIDE. 1961. a. £7.50. E M A P Vision Ltd., Maclaren House, Scarbrook Rd., Croydon, Surrey CR9 1QH, England. TEL 081-760-9690. FAX 081-681-1672. TELEX 946665. Ed. David Warr. adv.; bk.rev. circ. 7,718. (also avail. in microfilm) **Document type:** directory.
  Description: Directory to professional photographic equipment and services.

380.1 664   US   ISSN 0890-7986
HF5429.3
PROGRESSIVE GROCER'S DIRECTORY OF MASS MERCHANDISERS. a. $220. Trade Dimensions, 263 Tresser Blvd., Stamford, CT 06901. TEL 203-977-7600. FAX 203-977-7645. URL: http://www.tradedimensions.com. Ed. Jane Sherlin; Pub. Garrett Van Siclen. R&P contact: Garett Van Siclen. **Document type:** directory.
  Description: Profiles retail mass merchandising companies, with information on chains, including product lines, names of buyers and other key personnel.

PROGRESSIVE GROCER'S MARKET SCOPE. see FOOD AND FOOD INDUSTRIES

PUBLIC RELATIONS OFFICE OF THE SUGAR INDUSTRY. ANNUAIRE. see FOOD AND FOOD INDUSTRIES

380.1 659.1   US
PUBLIC RELATIONS SOCIETY OF AMERICA DIRECTORY. Variant title: Public Relations Journal Register Issue. (Published as 13th issue of Public Relations Journal) 1945. a. Public Relations Society of America, Inc., 33 Irving Pl., New York, NY 10003-2376. TEL 212-460-1468. adv.; bibl. circ. 11,800.
Indexed: B.P.I., P.A.I.S. **Document type:** directory.
  Formerly: Public Relations Register.

070.5   US   ISSN 0000-0671
Z475   CODEN: PDWSEG
PUBLISHERS, DISTRIBUTORS & WHOLESALERS OF THE UNITED STATES; a directory of publishers, distributors, associations, wholesalers, software producers and manufacturers listing editorial and ordering addresses, and an ISBN publisher prefix index. (Issued in 2 vols.) 1979. a. £165. R.R. Bowker, A Division of Reed Elsevier Inc., 121 Chanlon Rd., New Providence, NJ 07974. TEL 908-464-6800. FAX 908-665-3502. TELEX 138 755. E-mail: info@bowker.com; URL: http://www.reedref.com. (Subscr. to: Order Dept., Box 31, New Providence, NJ 07974-9903. TEL 800-521-8110) pp./issue: 3300. (also avail. in magnetic tape) **Document type:** bibliography, directory.
  ●Also available online. Vendor(s): Knight-Ridder Information, Inc. (File no.450), Lexis-Nexis (PDW). Also available on CD-ROM. Producer(s): Bowker Electronic Publishing.
  —BLDSC (7156.068000); CASDDS; CISTI. **CCC.**
  Formerly (until 1980): Publishers and Distributors of the United States (ISSN 0000-0620)
  Description: Includes subsidiaries, imprints and divisions, inactive and out-of-business companies, and specialized publishers. Lists ISBN prefixes and toll-free phone and fax numbers. Also includes discount schedule.

338   PR   ISSN 0090-3612
HC157.P8
PUERTO RICO OFFICIAL INDUSTRIAL DIRECTORY. (Text in English) 1966. a. $129 (effective 1997). (Economic Development Administration) Direct Marketing and Media Group, Inc., P.O. Box 9024182, San Juan, PR 00902-4182. TEL 787-268-1111. FAX 787-268-7044. E-mail: dmmg@caribe.net; URL: http://www.prid.com. (Dist. in the U.S. by: Manufacturers' News, Inc., 1633 Central St., Evanston, IL 60201-1505. TEL 708-864-7000) Ed. Howard G. Patterson; Pub. Lilia Molina-Ruiz. R&P contact: Howard G. Patterson. adv.: B&W page $5475, color page $6200; adv. contact: Diana Lopez. stat.; circ. 5,000 (paid). **Document type:** directory.
  Description: Contains information on more than 8,000 manufacturers, distributors, wholesalers and service firms. Covers the business environment, economic trends, key industry profiles, market and industrial sector statistics, government programs, and industrial parks.

PULP & PAPER BUYERS GUIDE. see PAPER AND PULP

PULSE BUYERS GUIDE. see ELECTRONICS

380 910.9   IT
Q T DIRECTORY.* (Quality Travel) (Text in English, German, Italian) 1988. a. L.100000 per no. A P I Editrice s.r.l., Corso di Porta Romana 122, 20122 Milan, Italy. TEL 02-58314981. FAX 02-8323710. Ed. Antonio Spagnoli. circ. 16,000.

338   BL   ISSN 0102-7115
QUEM E QUEM NA ECONOMIA BRASILEIRA. 1967. a. $10. Editora Visao Ltda., Rua Alvaro de Carvalho, 350, 2o andar, C.P. 3082, 01050 Sao Paulo, Brazil. TEL 256-5011. FAX 258-1919. TELEX 1121436. Ed. Hamilton Lucas de Oliveira. adv. circ. 140,000.

382   FR   ISSN 0079-9262
QUI REPRESENTE QUI. (Text and summaries in English, French, German, Spanish) 1956. a. 450 F. Kompass France, 66 quai du Marechal Joffre, 92415 Courbevoie Cedex, France. Ed. Bertrand Macabeo; Pub. Bertrand Macabeo. R&P contact: Bertrand Macabeo. adv. contact: Mireille Girault. illus. **Document type:** directory.
  Description: Lists 16,000 branches or foreign representatives of importers in France and 6,840 French importers.

650   FR   ISSN 0079-9270
QUI VEND ET ACHETE QUOI?; annuaire industriel de Haute Normandie. 1970. 3/yr. 480 F. Chambre Regionale de Commerce et d'Industrie de Haute-Normandie, 9, rue Robert Schuman, Rouen, France. TEL 35-88-44-42. FAX 35-88-06-52. circ. 2,500.
  Description: Discusses 2000 factories located in the region.

QUICK GUIDE TO THE NEW TELECOM LINGO. see COMMUNICATIONS — Telephone And Telegraph

BUSINESS AND ECONOMICS — TRADE AND INDUSTRIAL DIRECTORIES

382   SP
QUIEN VENDE EN ESPANA LOS PRODUCTOS EXTRANJEROS/WHO SELLS FOREIGN PRODUCTS IN SPAIN. 1966. biennial. 12000 ptas. Prointer-Ediciones, Puerta del Sol 11, Madrid, Spain.

338 669   US
R & I BLUE BOOK. (Recognition & Identification) 1991. a. (Recognition & Promotions Business) Engravers Journal, Inc., Box 318, Brighton, MI 48116. TEL 313-229-5725. FAX 313-229-8320. Eds. James J. Farrel, Michael J. Davis.

338.025   US
HF5068.S3
R C G A ROSTER AND MEMBERSHIP SERVICES DIRECTORY.* 1983. a. $50 to non-members. St. Louis Regional Commerce and Growth Association, 1 Metropolitan Sq., Ste. 1300, St. Louis, MO 63102-2733. Ed. Laura Barlow. R&P contact: Laura Barlow.
   Formerly: Buyer's Guide of Products and Services in St. Louis Region (ISSN 0741-8205)

977   US
R C G A'S DIRECTORY OF ST. LOUIS LARGE EMPLOYERS.* 1957. biennial. $20 (diskette $59). St. Louis Regional Commerce and Growth Association, 1 Metropolitan Sq., Ste. 1300, St. Louis, MO 63102-1300. Ed. Laura Barlow. circ. 3,600. (also avail. in diskette format) **Document type:** directory.
   Formerly: Large Employers Directory of Metropolitan St. Louis.
   Description: Lists companies with 100 or more employees located in the St. Louis metropolitan area by groupings, SIC codes, employee size, alpha-order, and zip code.

380 760   US
R S V P: THE DIRECTORY OF ILLUSTRATION AND DESIGN. 1975. a. $21 (effective 1995). 253 Washington Ave., Box 050314, Brooklyn, NY 11205-0314. TEL 718-857-9267. FAX 718-783-2376. E-mail: RSVPdirectory@acornis.com. Eds. Richard Lebenson, Kathleen Creighton. adv.; illus. circ. 18,000. (back issues avail.) **Document type:** directory.
   Formerly (until 1991): R S V P: The Directory of Creative Talent.
   Description: National illustrated directory of illustration and design.
   Refereed Serial

338 790.01   US
R VERS GUIDE TO FLORIDA. 1992. a. Florida Recreational Vehicle Trade Association, 401 N. Parsons Ave., No. 107, Brandon, FL 33510-4538. TEL 813-684-7882. Ed. David Kelly. circ. 80,000. **Document type:** directory.
   Formerly: F R V T A Membership Directory.
   Description: Lists members, their addresses, phone numbers and products and services.

RADIO CO-OP SOURCES. see *COMMUNICATIONS — Radio*

RADIO CONTACTS (YEAR). see *COMMUNICATIONS — Radio*

RAW MATERIALS FOR THE REFRACTORIES INDUSTRY. see *METALLURGY*

338 691   NZ   ISSN 0813-5207
RAWLINSONS NEW ZEALAND CONSTRUCTION HANDBOOK. 1986. a. NZ.$144 (foreign NZ.$194) (effective 1996). Rawlinsons New Zealand Construction Handbook Ltd., Rawlinson House, 4th Fl., 25-27 Broadway, Newmarket, Auckland, New Zealand. TEL 64-9-5290061. FAX 64-9-5244977. Ed. Cathy Giddens. adv.; bk.rev. circ. 1,200. (back issues avail.) **Document type:** trade publication.
●Also available on CD-ROM.
   Description: A comprehensive guide to building construction costs in New Zealand.

338 780   US
RECORD RETAILING DIRECTORY. 1991. a. $99. B P I Communications, Inc. (New York), 1515 Broadway, New York, NY 10036. TEL 212-536-5025; 800-344-7119. FAX 212-536-5358. adv.; B&W & color, B&W page $1100; trim 6 x 9. circ. 1,150.
   Description: Lists major independent record dealers and chain headquarters, owners and buyers.

380 790   US
RECREATION AND OUTDOOR LIFE DIRECTORY; a guide to national and international organizations. 1979. irreg., 2nd ed., 1983. $160. Gale Research, 835 Penobscot Bldg., 645 Griswold St., Detroit, MI 48226-4094. TEL 313-961-2242; 800-877-4253. FAX 800-414-5043. E-mail: daniel__snyder@gale.com. Ed. Paul Wasserman. **Document type:** directory.
   Description: Directory of outdoor recreation associations and groups.

RECRUITING AND SEARCH REPORT; the executive search information source. see *BUSINESS AND ECONOMICS — Personnel Management*

338.025   GW
RED BOX. (Text in English, German) 1970. a. DM.290. Red Box Verlag GmbH, Abteistr. 49, 20149 Hamburg, Germany. TEL 49-40-4501500. FAX 49-40-45015099. Ed. Margit Bethge; Pub. Margit Bethge. adv.; B&W page DM.4680. circ. 10,000 (paid). **Document type:** directory.

380.1 070.5   GW   ISSN 0173-959X
REDAKTIONS ADRESS. 1979. 2/yr. DM.340. Media Daten Verlag GmbH, Klingenweg 4, 65396 Walluf, Germany. TEL 49-6123-700-0. FAX 49-6123-700122. cum.index. circ. 1,500. **Document type:** directory.
   Description: Editorial addresses of German media (approximately 5000 publications).

382
REFERENCE BOOK FOR WORLD TRADERS. base vols. (plus m. suppl.). $160. Croner Publications, Inc., 10951 Sorrento Valley Rd., Ste. 1-D, San Diego, CA 92121-1613. TEL 619-546-1894; 800-441-4033. FAX 619-546-1955. Ed. Elizabeth Duffy. (looseleaf format) **Document type:** directory.
   Description: Basic information on and for those participating in international trade.

REFLECTIONS MAGAZINE - DIRECTORY. see *NEW AGE PUBLICATIONS*

332 364   UK   ISSN 0080-0538
REGENCY INTERNATIONAL DIRECTORY; of private investigators, process servers, private detectives & debt collecting agencies. 1967. a. $50. Regency International Publications Ltd., 325 Canterbury Road, Densole, Folkestone, Kent CT18 7BB, England. TEL 0303-893488. FAX 0303-893488. Ed. Alan L. Valle. adv.; circ. controlled.

387.7   US
REGIONAL AIRLINE DIRECTORY. a. $247 (effective 1996). Phillips Business Information, Inc., 1201 Seven Locks Rd., Potomac, MD 20854. TEL 301-424-3338. FAX 301-340-3847. E-mail: pbi@phillips.com. **Document type:** directory.
   Description: Up-to-date facts and figures in the U.S. and international commuter regional airline industries, including airlines, manufacturers, consultants, attorneys, air taxi operators, suppliers, trade associations, and more.

338.025   UK
REGIONAL DIRECTORIES OF KEY BUSINESS PROSPECTS. MIDLANDS. irreg., latest 1991. £50. Jordan & Sons Ltd., 21 St. Thomas St., Bristol BS1 6JS, England. TEL 44-117-923-0600. FAX 44-117-923-0063. **Document type:** directory.

338.025   UK
REGIONAL DIRECTORIES OF KEY BUSINESS PROSPECTS. NORTH EAST. irreg., latest 1991. £50. Jordan & Sons Ltd., 21 St. Thomas St., Bristol BS1 6JS, England. TEL 44-117-923-0600. FAX 44-117-923-0063. **Document type:** directory.

338.025   UK
REGIONAL DIRECTORIES OF KEY BUSINESS PROSPECTS. WALES. irreg., latest 1991. £50. Jordan & Sons Ltd., 21 St. Thomas St., Bristol BS1 6JS, England. TEL 44-117-923-0600. FAX 44-117-923-0063. **Document type:** directory.

338.025   US   ISSN 1047-7799
HD2346.U52
REGIONAL DIRECTORY OF MINORITY- AND WOMEN-OWNED BUSINESS FIRMS: CENTRAL EDITION. a. $175. Business Research Services, Inc., 4201 Connecticut Ave., N.W., Ste. 610, Washington, DC 20008. TEL 800-325-8720. FAX 202-686-3228. **Document type:** directory.

338.025   US   ISSN 1047-7802
HD2346.U52
REGIONAL DIRECTORY OF MINORITY- AND WOMEN-OWNED BUSINESS FIRMS: EASTERN EDITION. a. $175. Business Research Services, Inc., 4201 Connecticut Ave., N.W., Ste. 610, Washington, DC 20008. TEL 800-845-8420. FAX 202-686-3228. Ed. Thomas D. Johnson. R&P contact: Thomas D. Johnson. **Document type:** directory.

338.025   US   ISSN 0886-3946
HD2346.U52
REGIONAL DIRECTORY OF MINORITY- AND WOMEN-OWNED BUSINESS FIRMS: WESTERN EDITION. a. $175. Business Research Services, Inc., 4201 Connecticut Ave., N.W., Ste. 610, Washington, DC 20008. TEL 800-325-8720. FAX 202-686-3228. Ed. Thomas D. Johnson; Pub. Thomas D. Johnson. R&P contact: Thomas D. Johnson. **Document type:** directory.

670 600   US   ISSN 1070-5600
HF5047
REGIONAL TECHNOLOGY GUIDE - CENTRAL U S REGION. Cover title: Central U S Regional Technology Guide. s-a. $175. Corporate Technology Information Services Inc., c/o Eileen Kenney, 12 Alfred St., Ste. 200, Woburn, MA 01801-1915. TEL 617-932-3939. FAX 617-932-6335. E-mail: sales@corptech.com; URL: http://www.corptech.com. **Document type:** directory.
—CCC.
   Formed by the 1994 merger of: Sales Guide to High Tech Companies - South Central Region (ISSN 1040-0532) & Sales Guide to High Tech Companies - North Central Region (ISSN 1040-0540)
   Description: Profiles thousands of technology manufacturers and developers in OH, IN, KY and WV. Covers 17 different high-tech industries, offering detailed information on each company, including key contacts, and a description of products manufactured and employment growth.

670 600   US   ISSN 1070-5597
HF5041
REGIONAL TECHNOLOGY GUIDE - EASTERN LAKES REGION. Cover title: Eastern Lakes Regional Technology Guide. s-a. $175. Corporate Technology Information Services Inc., c/o Eileen Kenney, 12 Alfred St., Ste. 200, Woburn, MA 01801-1915. TEL 617-932-3939. FAX 617-932-6335. E-mail: sales@corptech.com; URL: http://www.corptech.com. **Document type:** directory.
—CCC.
   Formerly (until 1994): Sales Guide to High Tech Companies - Eastern Great Lakes (ISSN 1040-0559)
   Description: Profiles thousands of technology manufacturers and developers in Upstate NY, PA excluding Philadelphia. Covers 17 different high-tech industries, offering detailed information on each company, including key contacts and a description of products manufactured and employment growth.

670 600   US   ISSN 1070-5589
HF5047
REGIONAL TECHNOLOGY GUIDE - GREAT LAKES REGION. Cover title: Great Lakes Regional Technology Guide. 1994. s-a. $175. Corporate Technology Information Services Inc., c/o Eileen Kenney, 12 Alfred St., Ste. 200, Woburn, MA 01801-1915. TEL 617-932-3939. FAX 617-932-6335. E-mail: sales@corptech.com; URL: http://www.corptech.com. **Document type:** directory.
—CCC.
   Description: Profiles thousands of technology manufacturers and developers in WI, MI and IL. Covers 17 different high-tech industries, offering detailed information on each company, including key contacts and a description of products manufactured and employment growth.

670 600   US   ISSN 1070-5554
HF5041
REGIONAL TECHNOLOGY GUIDE - MID ATLANTIC REGION. Cover title: Mid-Atlantic Regional Technology Guide. 1988. s-a. $175. Corporate Technology Information Services Inc., c/o Eileen Kenney, 12 Alfred St., Ste. 200, Woburn, MA 01801-1915. TEL 617-932-3939. FAX 617-932-6335. E-mail: sales@corptech.com; URL: http://www.corptech.com. **Document type:** directory.
—CCC.
  Formerly (until 1994): Sales Guide to High Tech Companies - Mid Atlantic Region (ISSN 1040-0575)
  Description: Profiles thousands of technology manufacturers and developers in DC, VA, and MD. Covers 17 different high-tech industries, offering detailed information on each company, including key contacts and a description of products manufactured and employment growth.

670 600   US   ISSN 1070-5570
HF5047
REGIONAL TECHNOLOGY GUIDE - MIDWEST REGION. Cover title: Mid-West Regional Technology Guide. 1994. s-a. $175. Corporate Technology Information Services Inc., c/o Eileen Kenney, 12 Alfred St., Ste. 200, Woburn, MA 01801-1915. TEL 617-932-3939. FAX 617-932-6335. E-mail: sales@corptech.com; URL: http://www.corptech.com. **Document type:** directory.
—CCC.
  Description: Profiles thousands of technology manufacturers and developers in MN, IA, MO, KS, ND, SD and NE. Covers 17 different high-tech industries, offering detailed information on each company, including key contacts and description of products manufactured and employment growth.

670 600   US   ISSN 1070-552X
HF5041
REGIONAL TECHNOLOGY GUIDE - NEW ENGLAND REGION. Cover title: New England Regional Technology Guide. 1988. s-a. $175. Corporate Technology Information Services Inc., c/o Eileen Kenney, 12 Alfred St., Ste. 200, Woburn, MA 01801-1915. TEL 617-932-3939. FAX 617-932-6335. E-mail: sales@corptech.com; URL: http://www.corptech.com. **Document type:** directory.
—CCC.
  Formerly (until 1994): Sales Guide to High Tech Companies - New England Region (ISSN 1040-0591)
  Description: Profiles thousands of technology manufacturers and developers in MA, NH, RI, VT and ME. Covers 17 different high-tech industries, offering detailed information on each company, including key contacts and a description of products manufactured and employment growth.

670 600   US   ISSN 1070-5546
HF5065.N5
REGIONAL TECHNOLOGY GUIDE - NEW JERSEY AND DELAWARE VALLEY REGION. 1992. s-a. $175. Corporate Technology Information Services Inc., c/o Eileen Kenney, 12 Alfred St., Ste. 200, Woburn, MA 01801-1915. TEL 617-932-3939. FAX 617-932-6335. E-mail: sales@corptech.com; URL: http://www.corptech.com. **Document type:** directory.
—CCC.
  Formerly (until 1994): New Jersey Technology Resource Guide (ISSN 1060-1589)
  Description: Profiles thousands of technology manufacturers and developers in NJ, DE and Philadelphia. Covers 17 different high-tech industries, offering detailed information on each company, including key contacts and a description of products manufactured and employment growth.

670 600   US   ISSN 1070-5538
HC108.N72
REGIONAL TECHNOLOGY GUIDE - NEW YORK METRO REGION. Cover title: New York Metro Regional Technology Guide. 1988. s-a. $175. Corporate Technology Information Services Inc., c/o Eileen Kenney, 12 Alfred St., Ste. 200, Woburn, MA 01801-1915. TEL 617-932-3939. FAX 617-932-6335. E-mail: sales@corptech.com; URL: http://www.corp.tech.com. **Document type:** directory.
—CCC.
  Formerly (until 1994): Sales Guide to High Tech Companies - New York Metro (ISSN 1040-0583)
  Description: Profiles thousands of technology manufacturers and developers in New York City, Long Island, CT and Westchester County. Covers 17 different high-tech industries, offering detailed information on each company, including key contacts and a description of products manufactured and employment growth.

670 600   US   ISSN 1070-5635
HF5065.C2
REGIONAL TECHNOLOGY GUIDE - NORTHERN CALIFORNIA REGION. Cover title: Northern California Regional Technology Guide. s-a. $175. Corporate Technology Information Services Inc., c/o Eileen Kenney, 12 Alfred St., Ste. 200, Woburn, MA 01801-1915. TEL 617-932-3939. FAX 617-932-6335. E-mail: sales@corptech.com; URL: http://www.corptech.com. **Document type:** directory.
—CCC.
  Supersedes in part (in 1994): Sales Guide to High Tech Companies - California (ISSN 1041-0260)
  Description: Profiles thousands of technology manufacturers and developers in Greater San Francisco and Silicon Valley. Covers 17 different high-tech industries, offering detailed information on each company, including key contacts and a description of products manufactured and employment growth.

670 600   US   ISSN 1070-5619
HF5050
REGIONAL TECHNOLOGY GUIDE - NORTHWEST REGION. Cover title: Northwest U S Regional Technology Guide. s-a. $175. Corporate Technology Information Services Inc., c/o Eileen Kenney, 12 Alfred St., Ste. 200, Woburn, MA 01801-1915. TEL 617-932-3939. FAX 617-932-6335. E-mail: sales@corptech.com; URL: http://www.corptech.com. **Document type:** directory.
—CCC.
  Formerly (until 1994): Sales Guide to High Tech Companies - Northwest Region (ISSN 1040-0516)
  Description: Profiles thousands of technology manufacturers and developers in OR, WA, MT, AK, NV, WY and ID. Covers 17 different high-tech industries, offering detailed information on each company, including key contacts and a description of products manufactured and employment growth.

670 600   US   ISSN 1070-5562
HF5044
REGIONAL TECHNOLOGY GUIDE - SOUTHEAST REGION. Cover title: Southeast U S Regional Technology Guide. s-a. $175. Corporate Technology Information Services Inc., c/o Eileen Kenney, 12 Alfred St., Ste. 200, Woburn, MA 01801-1915. TEL 617-932-3939. FAX 617-932-6335. E-mail: sales@corptech.com; URL: http://www.corptech.com. **Document type:** directory.
—CCC.
  Formerly (until 1994): Sales Guide to High Tech Companies - Southeast Region (ISSN 1040-0567)
  Description: Profiles thousands of technology manufacturers and developers in MS, LA, AR, AL, GA, TN, NC, SC, FL and Puerto Rico. Covers 17 different high-tech industries, offering detailed information on each company, including key contacts and a description of products manufactured and employment growth.

670 600   US   ISSN 1070-5627
HF5065.C2
REGIONAL TECHNOLOGY GUIDE - SOUTHERN CALIFORNIA REGION. Cover title: Southern California Regional Technology Guide. s-a. $175. Corporate Technology Information Services Inc., c/o Eileen Kenney, 12 Alfred St., Ste. 200, Woburn, MA 01801-1915. TEL 617-932-3939. FAX 617-932-6335. E-mail: sales@corptech.com; URL: http://www.corptech.com. **Document type:** directory.
—CCC.
  Supersedes in part (in 1994): Sales Guide to High Tech Companies - California (ISSN 1041-0260)
  Description: Profiles thousands of technology manufacturers and developers in Los Angeles, Orange County, San Diego and Hawaii. Covers 17 different high-tech industries, offering detailed information on each company, including key contacts and a description of products manufactured and employment growth.

670 600   US   ISSN 1070-5643
HF5050
REGIONAL TECHNOLOGY GUIDE - SOUTHWEST REGION. Cover title: Southwest U S Regional Technology Guide. s-a. $175. Corporate Technology Information Services Inc., c/o Eileen Kenney, 12 Alfred St., Ste. 200, Woburn, MA 01801-1915. TEL 617-932-3939. FAX 617-932-6335. E-mail: sales@corptech.com; URL: http://www.corptech.com. **Document type:** directory.
—CCC.
  Formerly (until 1994): Sales Guide to High Tech Companies - Southwest Region (ISSN 1040-0524)
  Description: Profiles thousands of technology manufacturers and developers in UT, CO, NM, AZ, TX and OK. Covers 17 different high-tech industries, offering detailed information on each company, including key contacts and a description of products manufactured and employment growth.

380 968   RH
REGISTER & BUYERS GUIDE. Variant title: C Z I Register and Buyer's Guide. 1980. a. Z.$69.80 (foreign Z.74.30) (effective 1997). (Confederation of Zimbabwe Industries) Thomson Publications Zimbabwe (Pvt) Ltd., Thomson House, P.O. Box 1683, Harare, Zimbabwe. TEL 263-4-736835. FAX 263-4-752390. **Document type:** directory.

338   BL
REGISTRO INDUSTRIAL BRASILEIRO. 1979. a. $120. Publicacoes Industriais Ltda., Rua Brigadeiro Tobias 356, 5 Andar, 01032 Sao Paulo SP, Brazil. FAX 11-228-9373. TELEX 11-30562. Ed. Raul Gonzalez Simon. adv.; illus. circ. 20,000. (back issues avail.)

670   MX
REGISTRO INDUSTRIAL MEXICANO. 1986. a. $80 (effective 1993). Reportero Industrial Mexicano, S.A., Goldsmith 38-301, 11560 Mexico, D.F., Mexico. TEL 525-280-6122. FAX 525-280-8697. Ed. Antonio Rojo. circ. 10,000.

658.403   FR   ISSN 1147-7814
REPERTOIRE DES BANQUES DE DONNEES PROFESSIONNELLES/THE PROFESSIONAL DATABASES DIRECTORY. irreg. 650 F. (effective 1997). Association des Professionnels de l'Information et de la Documentation (ADBS) - Association of Information and Documentation Professionals, 25 rue Claude Tillier, 75012 Paris, France. TEL 33-1-43722525. FAX 33-1-43723041. E-mail: adbs@adbs.fr; URL: http://www.adbs.fr. Ed. Jean-Michel Rauzier. **Document type:** directory.
●Also available online.
  Formerly (until 1989): Repertoire des Banques de Donnees en Conversationnel (ISSN 0758-816X)
  Description: Describes 2000 professional databases available online in France, indexed by subject, producer and vendor.

BUSINESS AND ECONOMICS — TRADE AND INDUSTRIAL DIRECTORIES

380   CN   ISSN 1184-9916
HD9734.C3
REPERTOIRE DES PRODUITS DISPONIBLES AU QUEBEC. (Text in French; glossary in English and French) 1978. a. Can.$169 (effective 1997). Centre de Recherche Industrielle du Quebec, 333 rue Franquet, Sainte-Foy, PQ G1P 4C7, Canada. TEL 418-652-2234. FAX 418-652-2212. E-mail: bturgeon@criq.qc.ca. Ed. Bernard Turgeon. R&P contact: Francois Lauziere. adv. contact: Louise Lajeunesse. circ. 5,250. (also avail. in diskette format) **Document type:** directory.
●Also available on CD-ROM.
— CISTI.
Formerly (until 1991): Repertoire des Produits Fabriques au Quebec (ISSN 0704-7940)
Description: Directory of Quebec industries. Lists products and services, trade marks, manufacturers and distributors.

661   SP
REPERTORIO DE LA INDUSTRIA QUIMICA ESPANOLA/DIRECTORY OF THE SPANISH CHEMICAL INDUSTRY. triennial. Federacion Empresarial de la Industria Quimica Espanola, Hermosilla, 31, 28001 Madrid, Spain. TEL 4317964. FAX 576-33-81. **Document type:** directory.

669   CL
REPERTORIO SIDERURGICO LATINOAMERICANO. 1960. irreg., 11th ed., 1995. $100 to non-members in America; elsewhere $110; members $80 in America; elsewhere $85 (effective 1995). Instituto Latinoamericano del Fierro y el Acero, Av. Providencia 2285, 4o Piso, Of. 401, Casilla 16065, Santiago 9, Chile. TEL 56-2-2330545. FAX 56-2-2330768. **Document type:** directory.
Description: Provides data on companies in the sector: addresses, personnel, products and services.

670   MX
REPORTERO INDUSTRIAL MEXICANO. (Text in Spanish) 1980. m. $55. Keller International Publishing Corporation, 150 Great Neck Rd., Great Neck, NY 11021. Ed. Felicia Morales. adv. circ. 16,000. (tabloid format)

380   PO   ISSN 0872-0223
REPORTORIO DA INDUSTRIA, COMERCIO E SERVICOS DE PORTUGAL/REGISTER OF PORTUGUESE INDUSTRY, COMMERCE AND SERVICES/REPERTOIRE GENERAL DE L'ECONOMIE PORTUGAISE/INFORMATIONSWERK FUER DIE WIRTSCHAFT VON PORTUGAL. (Text in English and Portuguese) 1992. a. Interpropo - Sociedade de Propaganda Internacional de Produtos Portugueses, Ltda., Rua Coronel Bento Roma, 28, 1700 Lisbon, Portugal. TEL 80-28-80. FAX 80-96-58. **Document type:** directory.

RESEARCH & DEVELOPMENT PRODUCT SOURCE TELEPHONE DIRECTORY. see *TECHNOLOGY: COMPREHENSIVE WORKS*

380.1   US   ISSN 0278-1743
Q179.98
RESEARCH SERVICES DIRECTORY; a one-step guide to contract research firms and laboratories. 1981. biennial. $305. Gale Research, 835 Penobscot Bldg., 645 Griswold St., Detroit, MI 48226-4094. TEL 313-961-2242; 800-877-4253. FAX 800-414-5043. E-mail: daniel_snyder@gale.com. Ed. Annette Piccirelli. **Document type:** directory.
●Also available online. Vendor(s): Knight-Ridder Information, Inc.
— CISTI.
Description: Details the services, facilities, and expertise offered by more than 4,000 research and development companies in the United States.

RETAIL DIRECTORY. see *BUSINESS AND ECONOMICS — Marketing And Purchasing*

RETAIL INFO SYSTEMS NEWS DIRECTORY. see *BUSINESS AND ECONOMICS — Computer Applications*

380   US
RETIREMENT HOUSING FOODSERVICE WHO'S WHO. 1997. triennial. $200 (diskette $950). Information Central Inc., Box 3900, Prescott, AZ 86302. TEL 520-778-1513. FAX 520-778-1513. E-mail: woodman@bslnet.com. Ed. Julie Woodman. stat.; index. (looseleaf format; also avail. in diskette format) **Document type:** directory.
Description: Provides foodservice data on 1700 largest retirement housing facilities in the US.

338.025   US   ISSN 1048-7166
HF5065.R5
RHODE ISLAND BUSINESS DIRECTORY. 1990. a. $295 (effective 1997). American Business Directories (Subsidiary of: American Business Information, Inc.), 5711 S. 86th Circle, Box 27347, Omaha, NE 68127. TEL 402-593-4600; 800-555-5124. FAX 402-331-5481. E-mail: jerry.venner@abii.com. index. (also avail. in magnetic tape; diskette format) **Document type:** directory.
●Also available online.
Also available on CD-ROM.
Description: Includes all businesses in the state compiled from the yellow pages and telephone-verified. Each listing includes company name, complete address, phone number, name of owner, manager, and employee size, sales volume codes, and credit rating codes.

670   US   ISSN 0361-5103
RHODE ISLAND DIRECTORY OF MANUFACTURERS. 1951. a. $45 (effective 1996). Department of Economic Development, 1 W. Exchange St., Providence, RI 02903-1058. TEL 401-277-2601. FAX 401-277-2102. (Dist. by: Manufacturers' News, Inc., 1633 Central St., Evanston, IL 60201-1505. TEL 708-864-7000) circ. 3,000. **Document type:** directory.
Formerly: Rhode Island Directory of Manufacturers and List of Commercial Establishments (ISSN 0080-2743)
Description: Profiles over 2,500 firms; includes SIC section, as well as alphabetic and geographical indexes.

338.025 320   US   ISSN 1064-7414
HS2321
THE RIGHT GUIDE; a guide to conservative, free-market, and traditional organizations. 1992. s-a. $74.95. Economics America, Inc., 612 Church St., Ann Arbor, MI 48104. TEL 313-995-0865. FAX 313-747-7258. E-mail: wilcoxdl@aol.com. Ed. Derk Arend Wilcox. **Document type:** directory.
Description: Lists over 3,000 think tanks, lobbying groups, publishers, and public-interest litigation organizations. Includes financial information on organizations including revenues, salaries, lobbying expenditures and sources of funding.

ROANOKE REGIONAL CHAMBER OF COMMERCE. INDUSTRIAL DIRECTORY. see *BUSINESS AND ECONOMICS — Chamber Of Commerce Publications*

338.4767025   US   ISSN 0883-8046
T12.3.W47
ROCKY MOUNTAIN HIGH TECHNOLOGY DIRECTORY. 1985. a. $159 (effective 1997). Leading Edge Communications, Inc., 1121 Old Siskiyou Hwy., Ashland, OR 97520. TEL 541-482-4990. FAX 541-482-4993. Eds. Philip Boesche, Kimberley Boesche. circ. 1,500. **Document type:** directory.
Description: Lists profiles of about 4,500 manufacturers and research and development firms in Arizona, Colorado, Montana, Nevada, New Mexico, Utah and Wyoming engaged in high-technology activities.

ROCKY MOUNTAIN STATES PETROLEUM INDUSTRY. see *PETROLEUM AND GAS*

ROOFING MATERIALS AND SYSTEMS DIRECTORY. see *BUILDING AND CONSTRUCTION*

380.1   NR
ROTA TRADE AND INDUSTRIAL DIRECTORY. NORTH CENTRAL STATE.* s-a. £N50. Rota Publishing Co. Ltd., A.C. 5 Lagos St., 2nd Fl., P.O. Box 497, Kaduna, Nigeria. adv.

620   SA
S A A C E DIRECTORY OF FIRMS/S A V R I FIRMAGIDS. (Text in Afrikaans and English) 1967. irreg. R.8. South African Association of Consulting Engineers - Suid-Afrikaanse Vereniging van Raadgewende Ingenieurs, P.O. Box 1644, Randburg 2125, South Africa. TEL 27-11-7875944. FAX 27-11-7895264. E-mail: saace@iafrica.com. Ed. Linda Waterford. adv. contact: Linda Waterford. circ. 3,000. **Document type:** directory.
Former titles: South African Association of Consulting Engineers. Directory of Registered Firms; South African Association of Consulting Engineers. Directory of Members' Firms - Suid-Afrikaanse Vereniging van Raadgewende Ingenieurs. Gids van Lede Se Firmas.

338   SA
S A D C TRADE DIRECTORY. (Southern African Development Coordination Conference) a. R.120 (effective 1996). Braby's (Subsidiary of: Kohler Packaging Ltd.), P.O. Box 1426, Pinetown 3600, South Africa. TEL 27-31-7017021. FAX 27-31-7017036. adv. **Document type:** directory.
Formerly: S A D C C Directory.

338 658   SA
S A DIRECTORY OF BLACK MANAGERS. 1994. a. R.25. Black Enterprise Publishing and Marketing, P.O. Box 2185, Houghton 2041, South Africa. Ed. Thami Mazwai. adv.; illus. **Document type:** directory.

338 381   AT
S A TRADE DIRECTORY. (South Australia) a. Aus.$85. A P N Specialist Publishing, 46-50 Porter St., Prahran, Vic. 3181, Australia. adv. contact: Joseph Dagher. **Document type:** directory.
Description: Record of companies in South Australia and their products and services. Distributed by government and industry officials on all trade and diplomatic missions.

332.6   US
S I A DIRECTORY & GUIDE. a. free. Securities Industry Association, 120 Broadway, 35th Fl., New York, NY 10271. TEL 212-608-1500. Ed. Rosalie Pepe. **Document type:** directory.
Description: Provides a guide to the membership, organization and services of the association.

S I E (YEAR) GUIDE TO INVESTMENT SERVICES. (Select Information Exchange) see *BUSINESS AND ECONOMICS — Investments*

S P I MEMBERSHIP DIRECTORY AND BUYER'S GUIDE. (Society of the Plastics Industry, Inc.) see *PLASTICS*

380.1   US   ISSN 1047-9619
SAN DIEGO COUNTY BUSINESS DIRECTORY. 1990. a. $75 (diskette $295) (effective 1996). (San Diego Economic Development Corporation) Database Publishing Company, 1590 S. Lewis St., Anaheim, CA 92805-6423. TEL 714-778-6400. FAX 714-778-6811. (Subscr. to: Box 70024, Anaheim, CA 92825-0024. TEL 800-888-8434) Ed. Ken Gregory. (diskette format) **Document type:** directory.
Description: Profiles over 4700 manufacturers, wholesalers, importers, exporters, and service companies.

338.025 659   US   ISSN 1063-9144
SAN DIEGO CREATIVE DIRECTORY. 1981. every 18 mos. $44.50 (effective Aug. 1996); newsstand price: $49.95. Blue Book Publishers, Inc., 7807 Girard Ave., Ste. 200, La Jolla, CA 92037. TEL 619-454-7939. FAX 619-454-8032. Pub. Richard L. Levin. R&P contact: Richard L. Levin. adv. color page $4500; trim 8 1/2 x 11; adv. contact: Susan Davidson. circ. 5,000. (back issues avail.) **Document type:** directory.
Description: Portfolio of creative services by San Diego area advertisers, plus a directory of those and related services provided by the communications and creative community.

338.025 381   US
SAN FRANCISCO COUNTY COMMERCE AND INDUSTRY DIRECTORY. a. $75 (diskette $295) (effective 1996). (San Francisco Chamber of Commerce) Database Publishing Company, 1590 S. Lewis St., Anaheim, CA 92805-6423. TEL 714-778-6400. FAX 714-778-6811. (Subscr. to: Box 70024, Anaheim, CA 92825-0024. TEL 800-888-8434) (also avail. in diskette format) **Document type:** directory.
Description: Lists 3,700 companies; profiles 650 large companies (200 plus employees) in the 5-county Bay area.

SAN JOSE FILM & VIDEO PRODUCTION BINDER. see *MOTION PICTURES*

BUSINESS AND ECONOMICS — TRADE AND INDUSTRIAL DIRECTORIES

338.025 381   US   ISSN 1060-7951
SAN MATEO COUNTY COMMERCE AND INDUSTRY DIRECTORY. a. $75. (San Mateo Chamber of Commerce) Database Publishing Company, 1590 S. Lewis St., Anaheim, CA 92805-6423. TEL 714-778-6400. FAX 714-778-6811. (Subscr. to: Box 70024, Anaheim, CA 92825-0024. TEL 800-888-8434) (also avail. in diskette format) **Document type:** directory.
● Also available on CD-ROM.
Description: Lists 2,800 companies, and 7,000 executives, managers and owners. Profiles 650 large companies (200 plus employees) in the 5-county Bay area.

338.015 381   US
SANTA CLARA COUNTY COMMERCE AND INDUSTRY DIRECTORY. a. $75 (diskette $295) (effective 1996). Database Publishing Company, 1590 S. Lewis St., Anaheim, CA 92805-6423. TEL 714-778-6400. FAX 714-778-6811. (Subscr. to: Box 70024, Anaheim, CA 92825-0024. TEL 800-888-8434) (also avail. in diskette format) **Document type:** directory.
Description: Contains 4,700 manufacturers, wholesalers, and services firms.

670   CN   ISSN 0080-6536
HD9734.C3
SASKATCHEWAN MANUFACTURERS GUIDE.* 1971. biennial. Government Printing Co., 2005 8th St., Regina, Sask. S4P 3V7, Canada. TEL 306-566-9393. circ. controlled.
Former titles: Saskatchewan Index. Manufacturers' Edition; Saskatchewan Trade Directory.

384   US
TK5104
SATELLITE INDUSTRY DIRECTORY. 1979. a. $257 (effective 1996). Phillips Business Information, Inc., 1201 Seven Locks Rd., Potomac, MD 20854. TEL 301-424-3338. FAX 301-309-3847. E-mail: pbi@phillips.com. Ed. Monica L. Kenny. **Document type:** directory.
● Also available online. Vendor(s): NewsNet (TE83E).
—CISTI.
Former titles (until 18th ed., 1996): World Satellite Directory (ISSN 1046-0950); Satellite Directory.
Description: Comprehensive guide to the world-wide satellite communications systems and all related manufacturing and service industries.

THE SCHNELL RED BOOK OF CHEMICAL SERVICES. see *CHEMISTRY*

382 642.58   US
SCHOOL FOODSERVICE WHO'S WHO. 1973. triennial. $675 (diskettes $2100). Information Central Inc., Box 3900, Prescott, AZ 86302. TEL 520-778-1513. FAX 520-778-1513. E-mail: woodman@bsInet.com. Ed. Julie Woodman. stat.; index. (looseleaf format; also avail. in diskette format) **Document type:** directory.
Description: Provides food service data on all U.S. school districts with enrollments of 1500 or more.

380   UK   ISSN 0965-5344
SCOTLAND'S TOP 2000 COMPANIES (YEAR). 1989. a. (in 2 vols.). £190 (£125 per vol.). Jordan & Sons Ltd., 21 St. Thomas St., Bristol BS1 6JS, England. TEL 44-117-923-0600. FAX 44-117-923-0063. **Document type:** directory.
—BLDSC (8205.975811).
Formerly: Scotland's Top 1000 Companies.
Description: Financial data and addresses for top 2000 Scottish companies.

338.025   UK   ISSN 0954-1039
SCOTTISH LICENSEE. 1988. m. £29.95 to non-members. (S L T A) Scotmedia Magazines Ltd., 3 Park St. S., Glasgow G3 6BG, Scotland. TEL 44-141-332-3255. FAX 44-141-332-2012. Ed. Susan Young; Pub. Noel Young. R&P contact: Susan Young. adv. contact: Mark Besson. bk.rev. circ. 6,000. **Document type:** trade publication.

338   CN   ISSN 1204-7619
SCOTT'S DIRECTORIES - ATLANTIC INDUSTRIAL DIRECTORY. 1977. a. Can.$175($175) (effective 1997). Southam Information Products Ltd., Scott's Directories, 1450 Don Mills Rd., Don Mills, ON M3B 2X7, Canada. TEL 416-442-2122. FAX 416-510-6875. (also avail. in diskette format) **Document type:** directory.
● Also available on CD-ROM.
Former titles (until 1995): Scott's Directories - Atlantic Manufacturing (ISSN 0831-1854); (until 1985): Scott's Industrial Directory - Atlantic Manufacturers (ISSN 0706-5167)
Description: Accesses information on 5,500 manufacturing, wholesale and distribution companies and 10,081 executives and agents in New Brunswick, Nova Scotia, P.E.I. and Newfoundland.

380   CN   ISSN 1199-7494
SCOTT'S DIRECTORIES, GREATER TORONTO BUSINESS DIRECTORY. 1980. a. (in 2 vols.). Can.$315($315) (effective 1997). Southam Information Products Ltd., Scott's Directories, 1450 Don Mills Rd., Don Mills, ON M3B 2X7, Canada. TEL 416-442-2122. FAX 416-510-6875. Ed. Cindy Gardiner. adv. contact: Doug Finley. (also avail. in diskette format) **Document type:** directory.
● Also available on CD-ROM.
—CISTI.
Former titles (until 1993): Scott's Directories, Metropolitan Toronto and Toronto Vicinity Trade (ISSN 0828-914X); (until 1985): Scott's Trade Directory (ISSN 0228-6920)

338   CN   ISSN 0830-9272
HC117.O6
SCOTT'S DIRECTORIES - ONTARIO MANUFACTURERS. 1957. a. Can.$295 (effective 1997). Southam Information Products Ltd., Scott's Directories, 1450 Don Mills Rd., Don Mills, ON M3B 2X7, Canada. TEL 416-442-2122. FAX 416-510-6875. (also avail. in diskette format) **Document type:** directory.
● Also available on CD-ROM.
—CISTI.
Former titles (until 1984): Scott's Industrial Directory - Ontario Manufacturers (ISSN 0316-7879); (until 1972): Scott's Industrial Directory - Ontario Section (ISSN 0316-7860)
Description: Details 21,053 companies and over 50,094 executives and contacts.

338   CN   ISSN 0829-2221
SCOTT'S DIRECTORIES - QUEBEC MANUFACTURERS/SCOTT'S REPERTOIRES - FABRICANTS DU QUEBEC. (Text in English, French) 1963. a. Can.$260($260) (effective 1997). Southam Information Products Ltd., Scott's Directories, 1450 Don Mills Rd., Don Mills, ON M3B 2X7, Canada. TEL 416-442-2122. FAX 416-510-6875. (also avail. in diskette format) **Document type:** directory.
● Also available on CD-ROM.
Formerly (until 1983): Scott's Quebec Industrial Directory (ISSN 0582-3080)
Description: Information on 16,360 companies and 37,090 top executives.

338   CN   ISSN 1200-8540
SCOTT'S DIRECTORIES - WESTERN INDUSTRIAL DIRECTORY. 1969. a. Can.$240 (effective 1997). Southam Information Products Ltd., Scott's Directories, 1450 Don Mills Rd., Don Mills, ON M3B 2X7, Canada. TEL 416-442-2122. FAX 416-510-6875. (also avail. in diskette format) **Document type:** directory.
● Also available on CD-ROM.
—CISTI.
Former titles (until 1994): Scott's Directories - Western Manufacturers (ISSN 0829-2248); (until 1986): Scott's Industrial Directory. Western Manufacturers (ISSN 0317-879X); Scott's Industrial Directory. Western Section (ISSN 0317-8781)
Description: Profiles 17,250 companies and 29,645 executives in British Columbia, Alberta, Saskatchewan and Manitoba.

SCREEN INTERNATIONAL EUROGUIDE; the definitive guide to film, television and video in Europe. see *MOTION PICTURES*

381   US   ISSN 1079-3712
HF5482
SECONDARY MARKET GUIDE. 1994. a. $100 (foreign $110). Penton Publishing Co. (Hasbrouck Heights) (Subsidiary of: Pittway Company), 611 Rte. 46 W., Hasbrouck Heights, NJ 07604. TEL 201-393-9558; 800-526-6052. FAX 201-393-9553. **Document type:** directory.

SECURITECH; the international guide to security equipment. see *CRIMINOLOGY AND LAW ENFORCEMENT*

338   PH
SECURITIES & EXCHANGE COMMISSION. BUSINESS DAY'S 1000 TOP CORPORATIONS IN THE PHILIPPINES.* (Text in English) 1969. a. 400p.($67) (Securities & Exchange Commission) Businessday Corporation, 113 West Ave., Quezon City 3010, Philippines. circ. 25,000.
Formerly: S E C - B D Top 1000 Corporations in the Philippines.

338 364.4   US
SECURITY INDUSTRY BUYERS GUIDE. 1987. a. $169 (effective 1996). (American Society for Industrial Security) Phillips Business information, Inc., 1201 Seven Locks Rd., Potomac, MD 20854. TEL 301-424-3338. FAX 301-309-3847. E-mail: pbi@phillips.com. adv.: B&W page $4800; trim 8 1/4 x 10 7/8. **Document type:** directory.
Description: Consolidates purchasing information on industrial-commercial security products, services and systems.

030 380   US   ISSN 0080-8512
SEEKER'S GUIDE; a directory of unusual organizations. 1961. irreg., latest ed., 1970. $5.60. Aurea Publications, 207 Allen Ave., Allenhurst, NJ 07711. TEL 908-531-4535. Ed. Alex Sandri White.

338   GW   ISSN 0723-3159
SEIBT INDUSTRIEKATALOG. English edition: Seibt Directory of German Industry (ISSN 0940-9831); French edition: Seibt Repertoire de l'Industrie Allemande (ISSN 0940-984X) 1921. a. DM.50. Seibt Verlag GmbH, Leopoldstr. 208, 80804 Munich, Germany. TEL 49-89-360903-0. FAX 49-89-364317. URL: http://www.seibt.com. adv. circ. 25,000. **Document type:** directory.
● Also available online. Vendor(s): GBI.
Also available on CD-ROM.

SELL'S MARINE INDUSTRY BUYERS' GUIDE. see *SPORTS AND GAMES — Boats And Boating*

338   UK   ISSN 0261-5584
SELL'S PRODUCTS & SERVICES DIRECTORY. 1885. a. £86.50 (Europe £97; rest of world £107) (effective 1997). Miller Freeman Information Services (Subsidiary of: United News & Media), Riverbank House, Angel Ln., Tonbridge, Kent TN9 1SE, England. TEL 44-1732-362666. FAX 44-1732-767301. URL: http://www.mfplc.com. Ed. Gwen Young. adv. contact: Elaine Soni. bk.rev. circ. 5,000. **Document type:** directory.
● Also available on CD-ROM.
Incorporates (1984-1993): Sell's Scottish Directory; Which was formerly: Scottish National Register of Classified Trades (ISSN 0080-8148);
Former titles: Sell's Directory of Products and Services (ISSN 0080-8725); Sell's Directory of British Industry and Commerce.
Description: Lists products and services for commerce and industry.

SEMICONDUCTOR INDUSTRY ASSOCIATION. STATUS REPORT & INDUSTRY DIRECTORY (YEAR). see *ELECTRONICS*

380 670   US   ISSN 1042-1866
HF5549.5.T7
SEMINARS DIRECTORY; a guide to approximately 10,000 seminars and workshops held in the United States and Canada on subjects of interest to business, industry, and government. 1989. irreg., 2nd ed., 1991. $130. (Seminar Clearinghouse International, Inc.) Gale Research, 835 Penobscot Bldg., 645 Griswold St., Detroit, MI 48226-4094. TEL 313-961-2242; 800-877-4253. FAX 800-414-5043. E-mail: daniel_snyder@gale.com. Ed. Karin E. Koek.

BUSINESS AND ECONOMICS — TRADE AND INDUSTRIAL DIRECTORIES

382 **TS**
SHARJAH COMMERCIAL DIRECTORY/DALIL AL-SHARQAH AL-TIJARI. (Text in Arabic, English) 1980. a. $45 in Arab countries; elsewhere $75. Sharjah Chamber of Commerce and Industry, P.O. Box 580, Sharjah, United Arab Emirates. TEL 971-6-541444. FAX 971-6-541119. Ed. Ahmed Mohamed Al Midfa'a. R&P contact: Saeed O. Al Jarwan. adv. contact: Saeed Al Najjar. **Document type:** directory.
Description: Provides general information on economic development in the U.A.E. and more detailed information on Sharjah, including current projects, commercial, trade and industrial activity. Lists Sharjah-based and other U.A.E. firms by activity type and company name.

382 **TS**
▼**SHARJAH EXPORTER - IMPORTER DIRECTORY/DALEEL AL SARIQAH LIL MOSADDIREEN WA AL-MOSTAWRIDEEN.** (Text in Arabic, English) 1995. a. free. Sharjah Chamber of Commerce and Industry, P.O. Box 580, Sharjah, United Arab Emirates. TEL 971-6-541444. FAX 971-6-541119. **Document type:** directory.
Description: Includes names, addresses, activities, and other information for Sharjah's exporters and inporters. Also presents information about ports and customs.

381.1 658.8 **US**
SHELDON'S MAJOR STORES & CHAINS. a. $175 (effective 1997). Phelon Sheldon & Marsar, Inc., 330 Main St., Ridgefield Park, NJ 07660-1228. TEL 201-440-9096; 800-234-8804. FAX 201-440-8568. **Document type:** directory.

380 **IS**
SHERUT MAEDA EISKEI. (Text in Hebrew) m. Dun and Bradstreet (Israel) Ltd., P.O. Box 20001, Tel Aviv 61 200, Israel. TEL (03)216121.

SHOE FACTORY BUYER'S GUIDE; directory of suppliers to the shoe manufacturing industry. see SHOES AND BOOTS

380 **JA**
SHOKURYO KEIZAI NENKAN/FOOD ECONOMICS YEARBOOK.* a. 2500 Yen. Shokuryo Keizai Shinbun Sha, 35-12 Ishigatsuji-machi, Tennoji-ku, Osaka 543, Japan. illus.
Formerly: Sogo Keizai Nenkan.

380.1 **US** **ISSN 0037-4210**
HF5035
SHOPPING CENTER DIRECTORY. (In 5 vols.) 1957. a. $765 (includes Top Contacts). National Research Bureau, Inc. (Chicago), 150 N. Wacker Dr., Ste. 2222, Chicago, IL 60606-1608. TEL 312-541-0100. FAX 312-541-1492. (Orders to: National Research Bureau, 263 Tresser Blvd., 5th Fl., Stamford, CT 06901. TEL 800-456-4555. FAX 203-977-7645) Ed. Patricia Kelly; Pub. Nancy Veatch. **Document type:** directory.
●Also available on CD-ROM.
Description: Provides descriptive information regarding U.S. shopping centers, including ownership, leasing information, anchor stores, tenant listings, and more.

SHORTLINER. see AGRICULTURE — Agricultural Equipment

380 **UK**
SHOWDATES. (Supplement to: Showman's Directory) 1981. a. £25 includes Showman's Directory. Lance Publications, 45 Bridge St., Godalming, Surrey GU7 1HL, England. TEL 44-1483-422184. FAX 44-1483-425697. Ed. Valerie Wright; Pub. Stephen Lance. adv. contact: Justin Lance. circ. 3,500. **Document type:** directory.
Description: Examines shows such as: agricultural, county, town, air, dog shows, steam engine rallies, and festivals.

380 **UK**
SHOWMAN'S DIRECTORY. (Supplement avail.: Showdates) 1968. a. £15. Lance Publications, 45 Bridge St., Godalming, Surrey GU7 1HL, England. TEL 44-1483-422184. FAX 44-1483-425697. Ed. Valerie Wright; Pub. Stephen Lance. adv. contact: Justin Lance. circ. 6,500. **Document type:** directory.

338 **UK** **ISSN 0261-8974**
SIGNMAKERS AND SUPPLIERS DIRECTORY. 1971. a. £6.50 (effective 1998). A.E. Morgan Publications Ltd., Stanley House, 9 West St., Epsom, Surrey KT18 7RL, England. TEL 44-1372-741411. FAX 44-1372-744493. Ed. Mike Connolly; Pub. Terence Morgan. adv.: B&W page £490, color page £770; trim 190 x 130; adv. contact: Julia Dempster. illus.; index. **Document type:** directory.
Formerly (until 1978): Sign Makers and Suppliers Year Book and Directory.
Description: Lists suppliers of goods and services for the sign industry.

380.1 **SI** **ISSN 0218-2831**
SINGAPORE CONTRACTORS' EQUIPMENT CATALOGUE. 1990. a. $40. Times Trade Directories Pte. Ltd., Times Centre, One New Industrial Rd., Singapore 536196, Singapore. TEL 65-285-0161. FAX 65-2881186. TELEX RS 25713 TIMESS. Pub. Leslie Lim. R&P contact: Leslie Lim. adv. contact: Joseph Liang. circ. 20,000 (controlled). **Document type:** catalog.
Description: Caters to the building, marine and oil field industry.

382 **SI** **ISSN 0217-5428**
SINGAPORE EXPORTERS. (Text in English) 1984. a. S.$50. (Trade Development Board) Singapore Information Services Pte. Ltd., 1 Maritime Sq., 11-17 World Trade Centre, Telok Blangah Rd., Singapore 0409, Singapore. TEL 2723390. FAX 2783391. **Document type:** trade publication.

382 **SI**
SINGAPORE INDIAN CHAMBER OF COMMERCE. ANNUAL REPORT & DIRECTORY. (Text in English) 1948. a. S.$20($25) Singapore Indian Chamber of Commerce, 101 Cecil St., 23-01 Tong Eng Bldg., Singapore 0106, Singapore. FAX 65-223-1707. TELEX RS 22336 SINDCC. circ. 700.
Formerly: Singapore Indian Chamber of Commerce. Directory.

338.025 720 747 **SI** **ISSN 0218-3153**
SINGAPORE SOURCE BOOK FOR ARCHITECTS & DESIGNERS. 1989. a. $60. Times Trade Directories Pte. Ltd., Times Centre, One New Industrial Rd., Singapore 536196, Singapore. TEL 65-2850161. FAX 65-2850161. TELEX RS 25713 TIMESS. Pub. Leslie Lim. R&P contact: Leslie Lim. adv. contact: Joseph Liang. circ. 15,000 (controlled). **Document type:** directory.
Description: Provides a comprehensive catalogue of building and decorative products and services.

SKANDINAVISKE SKIPSREDERIER/YEARBOOK OF SCANDINAVIAN SHIPOWNERS. see TRANSPORTATION — Ships And Shipping

338 **US** **ISSN 0887-4050**
SMALL BUSINESS PREFERENTIAL SUBCONTRACTS OPPORTUNITIES MONTHLY. m. $84. Government Data Publications, Inc., 1155 Connecticut Ave., N.W., Washington, DC 20036. Ed. Siegfried Lobel.

338 **PK**
SMAR'S INDUSTRIAL DIRECTORY OF PAKISTAN. (Text in English) 1971. a. Rs.25($20) Smar International, 6 Afshan Chambers, Tariq Rd., P.E.C.H.S., Karachi 29, Pakistan. Ed. Mahmud-Ul-Hassan. adv. circ. 5,000. **Document type:** directory.

SOCIETY OF GLASS AND CERAMIC DECORATORS. MEMBERSHIP DIRECTORY. see CERAMICS, GLASS AND POTTERY

685.31 **US**
SOLE SOURCE; the footwear industry directory. 1994. a. $45. Footwear Industries of America, 1420 K St., N.W., Ste. 600, Washington, DC 20005. TEL 202-789-1420; 800-688-7653. FAX 202-789-4058. URL: http://www.fia.org. Ed. Angela Kluwin. adv.; circ. 1,000 (paid). **Document type:** directory.
Description: Lists manufacturers, importers, distributors and suppliers of goods and services in the US & Canada, with product categories.

616.99 **BP**
SOLOMON ISLANDS TRADE DIRECTORY (YEAR). a.? Ministry of Commerce and Primary Industries, Foreign Investment Board, P.O. Box G26, Honiara, Solomon Islands. TEL 677-23015. **Document type:** directory, trade publication, government publication.

SORKINS DIRECTORY OF BUSINESS & GOVERNMENT (CHICAGO EDITION). see BUSINESS AND ECONOMICS — Production Of Goods And Services

338.025 690 **US**
THE SOURCE (PRINCETON). a. Construction Financial Management Association, 707 State Rd., Ste. 223, Princeton, NJ 08540-1413. TEL 609-683-5000. FAX 609-683-4821. Ed. Paula A. Wristen. adv.: B&W page $1250; adv. contact: Sarah G. Patt. circ. 5,500 (controlled). **Document type:** directory.

301.16 **CN** **ISSN 0700-480X**
SOURCES. 1977. s-a. Can.$60. 4 Phipps St., Ste. 109, Toronto, ON M4Y 1J5, Canada. TEL 416-964-7799. FAX 416-964-8763. E-mail: R; URL: http://www.sources.com. Ed. Kate MacDougall; Pub. Barrie Zwicker. adv. contact: Kate MacDougall. bk.rev.; circ. 14,000 (paid). **Document type:** directory.
●Also available online.
—CISTI.
Description: Helps journalists, newsmakers and others find expert contacts.

671.52 **SA**
SOUTH AFRICAN INSTITUTE OF WELDING. NATIONAL REGISTER/SUID-AFRIKAANSE INSTITUUT VIR SWEIWESE. NASIONALE REGISTER. (Text in Afrikaans, English) 1994. a. South African Institute of Welding - Suid-Afrikaanse Instituut vir Sweiwese, P.O. Box 527, City West 2025, South Africa. illus. **Document type:** directory.

SOUTH CAROLINA BUILDER. see BUILDING AND CONSTRUCTION

338.025 **US** **ISSN 1046-0934**
HF5065.S6
SOUTH CAROLINA BUSINESS DIRECTORY. 1988. a. $340 (effective 1997). American Business Directories (Subsidiary of: American Business Information, Inc.), 5711 S. 86th Circle, Box 27347, Omaha, NE 68127. TEL 402-593-4600; 800-555-6124. FAX 402-331-5481. E-mail: jerry.venner@abii.com. index. (also avail. in magnetic tape; diskette format) **Document type:** directory.
●Also available online.
Also available on CD-ROM.
Description: Includes all businesses in the state compiled from the yellow pages and telephone-verified. Each listing includes company name, complete address, phone number, name of owner, manager, and employee size, sales volume codes, and credit rating codes.

670 **US**
SOUTH CAROLINA INDUSTRIAL DIRECTORY. a. $65 (diskette $199). Department of Commerce, Research and Communications, Box 927, Columbia, SC 29202. TEL 803-737-0400. FAX 803-737-1652. Pub. Nikki Edwards. R&P contact: Nikki Edwards. TEL 803-737-3864. adv. contact: Dennis Craighead. stat. (also avail. in diskette format) **Document type:** government publication, directory.
Description: Provides information on 4,100 manufacturing and research firms in 5 sections and through various statistical data sections.

338.025 **US** **ISSN 1074-2476**
▼**SOUTH CAROLINA MANUFACTURERS REGISTER.** 1995. a. $62 (diskette or CD-ROM $345) (effective 1997). Manufacturers' News, Inc., 1633 Central St. Evanston, IL 60201-1569. TEL 847-864-7000. FAX 847-332-1100. (also avail. in diskette format) **Document type:** directory.
●Also available on CD-ROM.
Description: Profiles 4806 companies.

338.4767025 **US** **ISSN 1090-5073**
▼**SOUTH CENTRAL HIGH TECHNOLOGY DIRECTORY.** 1996. a. $90 (effective 1997). Leading Edge Communications, Inc., 1121 Old Siskiyou Hwy., Ashland, OR 97520. TEL 541-482-4990. FAX 541-482-4993. Eds. Philip Boesche, Kimberly Boesche. circ. 300. **Document type:** directory.
Description: Lists profiles of about 1,600 manufacturers and research and development firms in Arkansas, Louisiana and Oklahoma engaged in high-technology activities.

BUSINESS AND ECONOMICS — TRADE AND INDUSTRIAL DIRECTORIES

338   **SA**
SOUTH COAST DIRECTORY. 1979. a. R.20. Braby's (Subsidiary of: Kohler Packaging Ltd.), P.O. Box 1426, Pinetown 3600, South Africa. TEL 27-31-7017021. FAX 27-31-7017036. **Document type:** directory.
Incorporates: Scottburgh Directory - Buyer's Guide & Port Shepstone - Margate Directory; Which was formerly: Port Shepstone Directory (ISSN 1016-6823)

339.025   **US**   **ISSN 1048-7409**
HF5065.S8
SOUTH DAKOTA BUSINESS DIRECTORY. 1984. a. $295 (effective 1997). American Business Directories (Subsidiary of: American Business Information, Inc.), 5711 S. 86th Circle, Box 27347, Omaha, NE 68127. TEL 402-593-4600; 800-555-6124. FAX 402-331-5481. E-mail: jerry.venner@abii.com. index. (also avail. in magnetic tape; diskette format) **Document type:** directory.
●Also available online.
Also available on CD-ROM.
Description: Includes all businesses in the state compiled from the yellow pages and telephone-verified. Each listing includes company name, complete address, phone number, name of owner, manager, and employee size, sales volume codes, and credit rating codes.

338   **US**
HC107.S8
SOUTH DAKOTA MANUFACTURERS REGISTER. 1975. a. $54 (diskette and CD-ROM $195) (effective 1997). Manufacturers' News, Inc., 1633 Central St., Evanston, IL 60201. TEL 847-864-7000. FAX 847-332-1100. Ed. Louise M. West. adv.: B&W page $1843; adv. contact: Charles Scherer. (diskette format) **Document type:** directory.
Former titles (until 1997): South Dakota Manufacturers and Processors Directory (ISSN 1075-6825); (until 1994): Manufacturers and Processors Directory. South Dakota (ISSN 1049-3050); (until 1990): Directory of Manufacturers and Processors (ISSN 0743-5940); (until 1984): Manufacturers and Processors Directory (ISSN 0094-2758)
Description: Profiles approximately 1,101 manufacturers; includes SIC, geographical, alphabetical and export sections.

368   **US**
SOUTH TEXAS INSURANCE DIRECTORY.* a. $55. Insurance Field Company, Box 18630, Louisville, KY 40218. TEL 502-491-5857. FAX 502-491-5905. adv.: B&W page $250.
Description: Details the facilities and services of licensed property, liability and life companies and agencies in the region.

338 387   **UK**   **ISSN 0268-6511**
SOUTHAMPTON PORT HANDBOOK. 1985. a. £25. Compass Publications Ltd., Abbot House, Castle Acre, King's Lynn, Norfolk PE32 2BQ, England. TEL 01760-755783. FAX 01760-755782. Ed. James P. Moriarty. circ. 6,000. **Document type:** directory.

SOUTHEAST STATES PETROLEUM INDUSTRY. see *PETROLEUM AND GAS*

338.4 916.8   **SA**
SOUTHERN AFRICAN TOURISM UPDATE'S BUYERS' GUIDE & WHO'S WHO FOR SOUTHERN AFRICAN TOURISM PRODUCTS. 1994. a. (Southern African Tourism and Safari Association) Travel & Trade Publishing (Pty) Ltd., P.O. Box 662, Auckland Park 2006, South Africa. adv.; illus.; maps. **Document type:** directory.

338.025   **US**   **ISSN 1061-2181**
HF5065.C2
SOUTHERN CALIFORNIA BUSINESS DIRECTORY. 1992. a. $795 (effective 1997). American Business Directories (Subsidiary of: American Business Information, Inc.), 5711 S. 86th Circle, Box 27347, Omaha, NE 68127. TEL 402-593-4600; 800-555-6124. FAX 402-331-5481. E-mail: jerry.venner@abii.com. index. (also avail. in magnetic tape; diskette format) **Document type:** directory.
●Also available online.
Also available on CD-ROM.
Description: Includes all businesses in the Southern California area compiled from the yellow pages and telephone-verified. Each listing includes company name, complete address, phone number, name of owner, manager, and employee size, sales volume codes, and credit rating codes.

380.1   **US**   **ISSN 0093-3090**
HF5065.C2
SOUTHERN CALIFORNIA BUSINESS DIRECTORY AND BUYERS GUIDE. 1964. a. $169 (diskette $795) (effective 1996). (Los Angeles Area Chamber of Commerce) Database Publishing Company, 1590 S. Lewis St., Anaheim, CA 92805-6423. TEL 714-778-6400. FAX 714-778-6811. (Subscr. to: Box 70024, Anaheim, CA 92825-0024. TEL 800-888-8434) Ed. Ken Gregory. adv.; illus. circ. 3,500. (also avail. in diskette format) **Document type:** directory.
Description: Details profiles of 29,000 manufacturers, wholesalers, and service companies in 13 Southern California counties.

670 600   **US**
HC107.C22
SOUTHLAND TECHNOLOGY LEADER. 1993. a. $90. Corporate Technology Information Services Inc., 12 Alfred St., Ste. 200, Woburn, MA 01801. TEL 617-932-3939. FAX 617-932-6335. **Document type:** directory.
—CCC.
Formerly (until 1995): Greater Los Angeles Technology Resource Guide (Year) (ISSN 1060-1619)
Description: Profiles thousands of technology manufacturers - firms involved in such high growth, high-tech activities as lasers, computers, advanced materials, and biotech. Listed alphabetically and cross indexed by city and over 250 product categories.

SPACE AND EDUCATION. see *AERONAUTICS AND SPACE FLIGHT*

SPACE AND INDUSTRY; (year) directory of U K capabilities. see *AERONAUTICS AND SPACE FLIGHT*

658.8   **UK**
SPAIN: A DIRECTORY AND SOURCEBOOK. irreg., latest 1993. £195($390) (effective 1997). Euromonitor, 60-61 Britton St., London EC1M 5NA, England. TEL 44-171-251-8024. FAX 44-171-608-3149. E-mail: info@euromonitor.com; URL: http://www.euromonitor.com. (Addr. in N. America: Euromonitor International, 122 S. Michigan Ave., Ste. 1200, Chicago, IL 60603. TEL 800-577-3876. FAX 312-922-1157) **Document type:** trade publication, directory.
Description: Provides the market data and company information marketers need to enter the growing consumer markets of Spain.

380 778.53   **US**   **ISSN 1045-0750**
TR847.5
SPECIAL EFFECTS & STUNTS GUIDE. 1989. a. $50 (effective through 1997). Lone Eagle Publishing Co., 2337 Roscomare Rd., No.9, Ed. Tassilo Baur, CA 90077-1851. TEL 310-471-8066. FAX 310-471-4969. circ. 3,000. **Document type:** directory.
Description: Lists motion picture coordinators of special effects and stunts.

338.025 380.52   **GW**   **ISSN 0471-1858**
SPEDITEUR ADRESSBUCH. 1950. a. DM.164 (effective 1997). Deutscher Verkehrs Verlag GmbH, Nordkanalstr. 36, 20097 Hamburg, Germany. TEL 49-40-23714165. FAX 49-40-23714123. **Document type:** directory.

338.025 790.1   **US**
▼**SPORT SUMMIT SPORTS BUSINESS DIRECTORY.** 1995. a. International Sport Summit, 6550 Rock Spring Dr., Ste. 500, Bethesda, MD 20817-1126. FAX 301-718-0981. circ. 1,000. **Document type:** directory.
Description: Comprehensive resource guide providing information on over 9,000 companies in every aspect of the sports business industry.

SPORTS MARKET PLACE. see *SPORTS AND GAMES*

338   **SA**   **ISSN 1016-6904**
SPRINGS BUYERS' GUIDE. 1990. a. R.25 (effective 1996). Braby's (Subsidiary of: Kohler Packaging Ltd.), P.O. Box 1426, Pinetown 3600, South Africa. TEL 27-31-7017021. FAX 27-31-7017036. **Document type:** directory.

STAINLESS STEEL BUYER'S GUIDE (YEAR). see *METALLURGY*

380 659.1   **US**   **ISSN 1048-2415**
HF5805
STANDARD DIRECTORY OF ADVERTISERS (BUSINESS CLASSIFICATIONS EDITION). (Also avail. Geographic Edition (ISSN 0081-4229)) 1964. a. $499.95. National Register Publishing, A Division of Reed Elsevier Inc., 121 Chanlon Rd., New Providence, NJ 07974. TEL 908-464-6800. FAX 908-464-3553. E-mail: info@reedref.com; URL: http://www.reedref.com. (Subscr. to: National Register Publishing, Order Dept., Box 31, New Providence, NJ 07974-9903. TEL 800-521-8110) circ. 25,000. **Document type:** directory.
●Also available online. Vendor(s): Lexis-Nexis.
—CCC.
Description: Lists advertisers alphabetically by industry or by state and city; listings include address and telephone numbers, advertising appropriations and agencies.

380 659.1   **US**   **ISSN 0081-4229**
HF5805
STANDARD DIRECTORY OF ADVERTISERS (GEOGRAPHIC EDITION). (Also avail. Business Classifications Edition (ISSN 1048-2415)) 1915. a. $499.95 for each ed.; including Advertiser/Agency Supplement published 3/yr. National Register Publishing, A Division of Reed Elsevier Inc., 121 Chanlon Rd., New Providence, NJ 07974. TEL 908-464-6800. FAX 908-464-3553. TELEX 138 755. E-mail: info@reedref.com; URL: http://www.reedref.com. (Subscr. to: National Register Publishing, Order Dept., Box 31, New Providence, NJ 07974-9903. TEL 800-521-8110) adv. circ. 25,000. (also avail. in magnetic tape) **Document type:** directory.
●Also available on CD-ROM. Producer(s): Bowker Electronic Publishing.
Description: Lists advertisers alphabetically by industry or by state and city; listings include address and telephone numbers, advertising appropriations and agenices.

380 659.1   **US**   **ISSN 0085-6614**
STANDARD DIRECTORY OF ADVERTISING AGENCIES; the agency red book. 1917. 2/yr. $499.95 including Advertiser/Agency supplement published 2/yr. National Register Publishing, A Division of Reed Elsevier Inc., 121 Chanlon Rd., New Providence, NJ 07974. TEL 908-464-6800. FAX 908-464-3500. TELEX 138 755. E-mail: info@reedref.com; URL: http://www.reedref.com. (Subscr. to: National Register Publishing, Order Dept., Box 31, New Providence, NJ 07974-9903. TEL 800-521-8110) adv. circ. 9,200. (also avail. in magnetic tape) **Document type:** directory.
●Also available on CD-ROM. Producer(s): Bowker Electronic Publishing.
—CCC.
Description: Lists current facts on over 9,000 advertising agencies in the USA. Includes key management, creative, account, and production people.

BUSINESS AND ECONOMICS — TRADE AND INDUSTRIAL DIRECTORIES

335   US
STANDARD DIRECTORY OF INTERNATIONAL ADVERTISERS AND AGENCIES; the international red book. 1984. a. $399.95. National Register Publishing, A Division of Reed Elsevier Inc., 121 Chanlon Rd., New Providence, NJ 07974. TEL 908-464-6800. FAX 908-665-6688. TELEX 138 755. E-mail: info@reedref.com; URL: http://www.reedref.com. (Subscr. to: National Register Publishing, Order Dept., Box 31, New Providence, NJ 07974. TEL 800-521-8110) adv. (also avail. in magnetic tape) **Document type:** directory.
●Also available on CD-ROM. Producer(s): Bowker Electronic Publishing.
Former titles (until 1991): Macmillan Directory of International Advertisers and Agencies (ISSN 1056-0947); (until 1990): Standard Directory of Worldwide Marketing (ISSN 0895-514X); Standard Directory of International Advertisers and Advertising Agencies.
Description: In-depth profiles of over 1,600 international advertisers and over 1,800 international advertising agencies from more than 90 countries.

380   JA   ISSN 0585-0444
STANDARD TRADE INDEX OF JAPAN. Title varies: Japan Register of Merchants, Manufacturers and Shippers. (Text in English) 1957. a. $284. (Japan Chamber of Commerce and Industry) Intercontinental Marketing Corp., 2-2, Marunouchi 3-chome, Chiyoda-ku, Tokyo 100, Japan. FAX 03-3211-4859. (Dist. by: Intercontinental Marketing Corp., I.P.O. Box 5056, Tokyo 100-31, Japan. TEL 81-3-3661-7458. FAX 81-3-3667-9646) **Document type:** directory, trade publication.
—BLDSC (8430.287000); CISTI.
Description: Reference guide covering information on firms in Japan, manufacturers, importers, and exporters, government agencies, overseas establishments, brand names classified by commodity and more.

338   SA   ISSN 1016-6912
STANGER DIRECTORY. 1982. a. R.25 (effective 1996). Braby's (Subsidiary of: Kohler Packaging Ltd.), P.O. Box 1426, Pinetown 3600, South Africa. TEL 27-31-7017021. FAX 27-31-7017036. **Document type:** directory.

380.1   US   ISSN 1044-324X
HD2425
STATE AND REGIONAL ASSOCIATIONS OF THE UNITED STATES. Abbreviated title: S R A Directory. 1988. a. $65 paperback. Columbia Books Inc., 1212 New York Ave., N.W., Ste. 330, Washington, DC 20005. TEL 202-898-0662. FAX 202-898-0775. E-mail: cbibooks@worldnet.att.net; URL: http://www.d-net.com/columbia/. Ed. John Russell. **Document type:** directory.
Description: Compilation of 7,300 major state and regional societies and labor organizations in the US. Includes information on names and titles of executive officers, membership, staff and budget size, future membership meetings, and historical background.

700   US
STATE ARTS AGENCY DIRECTORY. m. $10 per no. National Assembly of State Arts Agencies, 1010 Vermont Ave., N.W., Ste. 920, Washington, DC 20005. TEL 202-347-6352. FAX 202-737-0562. E-mail: nasaa@tmn.com. Ed. Glorious Pitt. **Document type:** directory.
Description: Lists state arts agency executive directors and chairs alphabetically including addresses. Also includes names, addresses, and phone numbers for the seven regional arts organizations.

STATE SOURCES OF COMPANY INTELLIGENCE. see BUSINESS AND ECONOMICS

380 332.6   II   ISSN 0971-3808
STOCK EXCHANGE OFFICIAL DIRECTORY. (Text in English) 1966. w. Rs.3000. Stock Exchange Foundation, Dalal St., Fort, Bombay 400 001, India. TEL 22-274170. FAX 22-2028121. TELEX 011-5925-STEXIN. Ed. R.R. Nair. adv.; charts; stat. **Document type:** corporate report.

STOCK PHOTO DESKBOOK. see PHOTOGRAPHY

STONE FEDERATION HANDBOOK. see BUILDING AND CONSTRUCTION

380.1   US
SUCCESSFUL MEETINGS SOURCE BOOK. (Special issue of: Successful Meetings Magazine) a. $35. Bill Communications, Inc., 355 Park Ave. S., 5th Fl., New York, NY 10010-1789. TEL 212-592-6200. FAX 212-592-6339.
Former titles: Successful Meetings Facilities Directory; International Convention Facilities Directory.
Description: Annual source book for successful sales meetings.

338   MK
SULTANATE OF OMAN BUSINESS DIRECTORY (YEAR). 1978. a. $50. Apex Publishing, P.O. Box 2616, Ruwi 112, Muscat, Sultanate of Oman. TEL 968-799388. FAX 968-793316. Ed. Jane Gartside; Pub. Saleh M. Talib. R&P contact: Jane Gartside. adv.; stat.; tr.lit.; index. circ. 40,000. (back issues avail.) **Document type:** directory.
Description: Business directory covering the entire country and detailing company information.

338   MK
SULTANATE OF OMAN TELEPHONE DIRECTORY. a. free. Tele-Gulf Directory Publications, P.O. Box 3030, Ruwi 112, Muscat, Sultanate of Oman. TEL 968-605815. FAX 968-605825. Ed. Sreekumar Nair. adv. circ. 156,000. **Document type:** directory.

338.025   AT
SUPER REVIEW TOP 1500 DIRECTORY. a. $2850 (includes diskette). Reed Business Publishing Pty. Ltd. (Subsidiary of: Reed International PLC), P.O. Box 5487, W. Chatswood, N.S.W. 2057, Australia. TEL 61-2-372-5222. FAX 61-2-419-7399. (also avail. in diskette format) **Document type:** directory, trade publication.
Description: Information on Australia's 1,500 largest superannuation funds including contact details, data on fund type, assets under management, service providers and the percentage allocation of funds to investment managers.

SUPPLIER'S SOURCE DIRECTORY. see TRANSPORTATION — Automobiles

SUPPLY, DISTRIBUTION, MANUFACTURING & SERVICE; supply and service companies & equipment manufacturers. see PETROLEUM AND GAS

380.1   UK   ISSN 0268-9766
SURFACE COATING & RAW MATERIAL DIRECTORY. 1986. a. £40 (effective June 1991). (Oil and Colour Chemists' Association) Industrial Trade Journals Ltd., Stakes House, Quebec Sq., Westerham, Kent TN16 1TD, England. TEL 0959-564212. FAX 0959-562325. Ed. Cathy Neal. index. circ. 3,000. (back issues avail.)

380 338   SW   ISSN 0282-5813
SVERIGES STOERSTA FOERETAG/LARGEST COMPANIES IN SWEDEN; med nyckeltal foer naeringslivet under (aar); with financial data for Swedish companies in (year). 1968. a. SEK 1280 (effective 1997). Ekonomisk Litteratur AB, P.O. Box 14113, S-161 14 Bromma, Sweden. TEL 46-8-26-70-30. FAX 46-8-26-70-42. Ed. Krister Wellros. R&P contact: Berit von Sydow. adv. contact: Gunnar Larsson. (also avail. in diskette format) **Document type:** directory.
Former titles (until 1984): Sveriges 4000 Stoersta Foeretag; (until 1983): Sveriges 3000 Stoersta Foeretag; (until 1982): Sveriges 2000 Stoersta Foeretag; (until 1980): Sveriges 1000 Stoersta Foeretag; (until 1973): Sveriges 500 Stoersta Foeretag.

338   SA   ISSN 1016-7072
HF5280.A3
SWAZILAND BUYERS' GUIDE. 1986. a. R.30 (effective 1997). Braby's (Subsidiary of: Kohler Packaging Ltd.), P.O. Box 1426, Pinetown 3600, South Africa. TEL 27-31-7017021. FAX 27-31-7017036. **Document type:** directory.

338   SZ
SWISS EXPORT DIRECTORY; products and services of Switzerland. (Text in English, French, German, Spanish) biennial. $37. Swiss Office for Trade Promotion, Stampfenbachstr. 85, CH-8035 Zurich, Switzerland. TEL 41-1-3655151. FAX 41-1-3655221. **Document type:** directory.

T C S & D YEARBOOK. (Temperature Controlled Storage and Distribution) see FOOD AND FOOD INDUSTRIES

338   US
THE T E I DIRECTORY OF U.S. COMPANIES DOING BUSINESS IN CENTRAL & EASTERN EUROPE & NEWLY INDEPENDENT STATES. a. Technology Exchange International, Inc., 9914 Broadview Dr., No. 210, Fairfax, VA 22030-2007. TEL 703-671-4367. FAX 703-671-6379. **Document type:** directory.
Formerly: Wetherby Directory.

339.025 333.79   II
T E R I ENERGY DATA DIRECTORY AND YEARBOOK; a comprehensive resource on energy, environment and economy. Short title: T E D D Y. (Text in English) Rs.700 for paperback; hardcover Rs.850. Tata Energy Research Institute, India Habitat Centre, Lodi Rd., New Delhi 110 003, India. TEL 91-11-4622246. FAX 91-11-4621770. E-mail: mailbox@teri.ernet.in. circ. 4,000. **Document type:** directory.
Description: Contains the latest information on energy supply and demand, costs and prices, and sales and consumption.

T M A DIRECTORY OF CIGARETTE BRANDS. (Tobacco Merchants Association of the United States, Inc.) see TOBACCO

133.5 338.025   US   ISSN 1065-7533
TAAFFE O'CONNELL'S ASTRO CASTER; a comprehensive listing of over 700 Hollywood casting agents, their astrological signs, address & phone numbers, sign descriptions, show assignments and studio breakdowns. (Part of: The Industry's Edge Series) 1991. 4/yr. $25. Canoco Publishing, 11611 Chenault St., Ste. 118, Los Angeles, CA 90049. TEL 310-471-2287. FAX 310-471-1944. E-mail: industryedge@earthlink.net; URL: http://www.hollywoodnetwork.com/astrohollywood. Ed. Taaffe O'Connell. R&P contact: Taaffe O'Connell. adv.: B&W page $600; adv. contact: Susan Moore. circ. 20,000. (back issues avail.) **Document type:** directory.
Description: Comprehensive listing of Hollywood's casting directors, studio breakdowns, show assignments, astrological signs; and information on how to deal with them in the casting process.

382   CH
TAIPEI TRADERS INFORMATION SYSTEM. (Text in English) 1963. a. $60. Importers & Exporters Association of Taipei, 5th Fl., 350 Sungkiang Rd., Taipei, Taiwan 104, Republic of China. TEL 02-581-3521. FAX 02-542-3704. TELEX 23339. (diskette format)
Formerly (until 1991): Taiwan Trade Directory.

380.1   CH   ISSN 1024-8943
TAIWAN BICYCLES & PARTS GUIDE (YEAR). a. $50 (CD-ROM $20). Trade Winds, Inc., No. 7, Lane 75, Yungkang St., P.O. Box 7-179, Taipei, Taiwan 10602, Republic of China. TEL 02-393-2718. FAX 02-396-4022. E-mail: tradwind@ms2.hinet.net; URL: http://www.tradewinds.com.tw. (Subscr. in U.S. to: Trade Winds Inc., Box 820519, Dallas, TX 75382. TEL 972-699-1188. FAX 972-699-1189) Ed. Donald Shapiro; Pub. Henry Ou. R&P contact: Donald Shapiro. adv.: page $1400; adv. contact: Janice Hsieh.
●Also available on CD-ROM.
Description: Covers bicycles, parts, accessories and machines.

338 670   CH   ISSN 0082-1470
TAIWAN BUYERS' GUIDE; alphabetical and classified lists of 15000 Taiwan manufacturers, importers, exporters and services. (Editions in Chinese and English) 1958. a. NT.$3800($200) China Productivity Center, Box 769, Taipei, Taiwan, Republic of China. TEL 886-2-6982989. FAX 886-2-6982976. TELEX 22954-CPTC. adv.; bk.rev. circ. 20,000. **Document type:** directory.

380.1 739.27   CH   ISSN 1024-8951
TAIWAN GIFTS & HOUSEWARES BUYERS' GUIDE. a. $30 Trade Winds, Inc., No. 7, Lane 75, Yungkang St., P.O. Box 7-179, Taipei, Taiwan 10602, Republic of China. TEL 02-391-3251. FAX 02-396-4022. E-mail: tradwind@ms2.hinet.net; URL: http://www.tradewinds.com.tw. (Subscr. in U.S. to: Trade Winds Inc., Box 820519, Dallas, TX 75382. TEL 972-699-1188. FAX 972-699-1189) Ed. Donald Shapiro; Pub. Henry Ou. R&P contact: Donald Shapiro. adv. contact: Janice Hsieh. **Document type:** directory.
Description: Covers giftware products and housewares produced in Taiwan.

BUSINESS AND ECONOMICS — TRADE AND INDUSTRIAL DIRECTORIES

338.025 CH ISSN 1024-8978
TAIWAN HAND TOOLS BUYERS' GUIDE. (Text in English) a. $30. Trade Winds, Inc., No. 7, Lane 75, Yungkang St., P.O. Box 7-179, Taipei, Taiwan 10602, Republic of China. TEL 02-393-2718. FAX 02-396-4022. E-mail: tradwind@ms2.hinet.net; URL: http://www.tradewinds.com.tw. (Subscr. in U.S. to: Trade Winds Inc., Box 820519, Dallas TX 75382. TEL 972-699-1188. FAX 972-699-1189) Ed. Donald Shapiro; Pub. Henry Ou. R&P contact: Donald Shapiro. adv. contact: Janice Hsieh. pp./issue: 250. **Document type:** directory, catalog.
  Description: Product catalogs and supplier directories for all kinds of tools and related products.

380.1 CH ISSN 1024-8986
TAIWAN HARDWARE BUYERS' GUIDE. a. $30. Trade Winds, Inc., No. 7, Lane 75, Yungkang St., P.O. Box 7-179, Taipei, Taiwan 10602, Republic of China. TEL 02-391-3251. FAX 02-396-4022. E-mail: tradwind@ms2.hinet.net; URL: http://www.tradewinds.com.tw. (Subscr. in U.S. to: Trade Winds Inc., Box 820519, Dallas, TX 75382. TEL 972-699-1188. FAX 972-699-1189) Ed. Donald Shapiro; Pub. Henry Ou. R&P contact: Donald Shapiro. adv. contact: Janice Hsien. **Document type:** directory, catalog.
  Description: Includes building materials, locks, tools, fasteners, and other hardware.

338.025 CH
TAIWAN INDUSTRIAL SUPPLIERS; a buyer's best resource. 1992. a. $30 in N. America, Europe & Africa; elsewhere $25. China Economic News Service, 561 Chunghsiao E. Rd., Sec. 4, Taipei, Taiwan 10516, Republic of China. TEL 886-2-642-2629. FAX 886-2-642-7422. TELEX 27710 CENSPC.
  Description: Lists manufacturers of rubber and plastics, transportation equipment, electrical appliances, machinery, hardware parts and components and accessories.

338.025 610 CH
▼**TAIWAN MEDICAL & HEALTH EQUIPMENT BUYERS' GUIDE.** (Text in English) 1995. a. $30. Trade Winds, Inc., No. 7, Lane 75, Yungkang St., P.O. Box 7-179, Taipei, Taiwan, Republic of China. TEL 886-2-3913251. FAX 886-2-3964022. E-mail: tradwind@ms2.hinet.net; URL: http://www.tradewinds.com.tw. (Subscr. in US to: Trade Winds Inc., Box 820519, Dallas, TX 75382. TEL 972-699-1188. FAX 972-699-1189) **Document type:** catalog.
  Description: Product catalogs and supplier directories for all kinds of medical and health-related equipment and supplies.

338.025 US ISSN 1055-9116
HF3846.8
TAIWAN PRODUCT GUIDE (YEAR). 1990. a. De Paula Publishing and Services Corp., 421 Seventh Ave., Ste. 1206, New York, NY 10001. TEL 212-629-4541. Ed. Carlos de Paula.

380.1 CH ISSN 0379-7910
TAIWAN YELLOW PAGES. a. NT.$1200($155) (CD-ROM $155). Taiwan Yellow Pages Corp., Chouwoo House 2F, P.O. Box 84-84, 57 Tunhwa S. Rd., Sec. 1, Taipei, Taiwan, Republic of China. TEL 886-2-570-9966. FAX 886-2-578-2739. URL: http://www.twn-online.com.tw. Ed. Lee Chung; Pub. Kingman Sheih. R&P contact: Gary Man. adv. contact: Edwin Chiang. circ. Gary/Man. **Document type:** trade publication.
●Also available on CD-ROM.
  Description: Lists over 65,000 entries on Taiwan manufacturers and traders.

338 670 TZ
TANZANIA. BUREAU OF STATISTICS. DIRECTORY OF INDUSTRIES. 1968 (not published 1972-1974). irreg. Bureau of Statistics, P.O. Box 796, Dar es Salaam, Tanzania. (Orders to: Government Publications Agency, P.O. Box 1801, Dar es Salaam, Tanzania) **Document type:** directory, government publication.

TANZANIA IMPORT AND EXPORT DIRECTORY. see BUSINESS AND ECONOMICS — International Commerce

670 AT ISSN 0314-8696
TASMANIAN MANUFACTURERS DIRECTORY. 1978. irreg. Aus.$25 (diskette Aus.$150). Tasmania Development and Resources, G.P.O. Box 646, Hobart, Tas. 7001, Australia. TEL 61-03-62335888. FAX 61-03-62335800. URL: http://www.tdr.tas.gov.au. circ. 10,000. (also avail. in diskette format) **Document type:** government publication, directory.

338.025 615 UK
TECHNOMARK REGISTER. CONTRACT PACKAGERS & MANUFACTURERS - EUROPE. a. £275($500) (CD-ROM £475($800)) (effective 1997). Technomark Consulting Services Ltd., King House, London W2 4UA, England. TEL 44-171-229-9239. FAX 44-171-792-2587. E-mail: info@technomark.com; URL: http://www.technomark.com/technomark. Ed. R.G. Hughes. R&P contact: Marianne Searle. adv. contact: Jill Bracey. **Document type:** directory.
●Also available on CD-ROM.
  Description: Listing of organizations which undertake as a primary objective medical, scientific or technical work on a commercial basis involving packaging and manufacturing in the European pharmaceutical and healthcare industries.

338.025 615.9 UK
TECHNOMARK REGISTER. CONTRACT RESEARCH ORGANISATIONS - NORTH AMERICA. a. £350($625) (CD-ROM £600($1000)) (effective 1997). Technomark Consulting Services Ltd., King House, London W2 4UA, England. TEL 44-171-229-9239. FAX 44-171-792-2587. E-mail: info@technomark; URL: http://www.dashnet.com/technomark. Ed. R.G. Hughes. R&P contact: Marianne Searle. adv. contact: Jill Bracey. **Document type:** directory.
  Description: Listing of organizations which undertake as a primary objective medical, scientific or technical work on a commercial basis in the North American pharmaceutical or healthcare industries.

338.025 615.9 UK
TECHNOMARK REGISTER. EUROPEAN CONTRACT RESEARCH ORGANISATIONS. CLINICAL RESEARCH. 1988. a. £350($625) (CD-ROM £600($1000)) (effective 1997). Technomark Consulting Services Ltd., King House, London W2 4UA, England. TEL 44-171-229-9239. FAX 44-171-792-2587. E-mail: info@technomark.com; URL: http://www.dashnet.com/technomark. Ed. R.G. Hughes. R&P contact: Marianne Searle. adv. contact: Jill Bracey. circ. 250. **Document type:** directory.
●Also available on CD-ROM.
  Description: Listing of organizations which undertake as a primary objective medical, scientific or technical work on a commercial basis.

338.025 615 UK
TECHNOMARK REGISTER. EUROPEAN CONTRACT RESEARCH ORGANISATIONS. TOXICOLOGY & ANALYSIS. a. £275($500) (CD-ROM £475($800)) (effective 1997). Technomark Consulting Services Ltd., King House, London W2 4UA, England. TEL 44-171-229-9239. FAX 44-171-792-2587. E-mail: info@technomark.com; URL: http://www.dashnet.com/technomark. Ed. R.G. Hughes. R&P contact: Marianne Searle. adv. contact: Jill Bracey. **Document type:** directory.
●Also available on CD-ROM.
  Description: Listing of organizations which undertake as a primary objective medical, scientific or technical work on a commercial basis in the fields of toxicology and analysis.

621.38 001.6 600 US ISSN 1055-8454
TK5102.5 CODEN: TDIREL
TELECOMMUNICATIONS DIRECTORY; an international descriptive guide to approximately 2,300 telecommunications organizations, systems, and services. 1983. biennial. $325 (effective June 1993). Gale Research, 835 Penobscot Bldg., 645 Griswold St., Detroit, MI 48226-4094. TEL 313-961-2242; 800-877-4253. FAX 800-414-5043. E-mail: daniel_snyder@gale.com. Ed. John Krol. (also avail. in magnetic tape; diskette format) **Document type:** directory.
—CISTI
  Formerly: Telecommunications Systems and Services Directory (ISSN 0738-3045)

384.5 US
TELEPHONE INDUSTRY DIRECTORY. a. $249 (effective 1996). Phillips Business Information, Inc., 1201 Seven Locks Rd., Potomac, MD 20854. TEL 301-424-3338. FAX 301-309-3847. E-mail: pbi@phillips.com. **Document type:** directory.
●Also available online. Vendor(s): NewsNet (TE83E).
  Description: Covers all areas of telecommunications, from telephones and payphones to microwave, fiber optics, voice processing, cellular and mobile phones, data transmission.

384.55 US ISSN 1055-0828
PN1992
TELEVISION DIRECTORS GUIDE. 1990. a. $45 (effective 1996). Lone Eagle Publishing Co., 2337 Roscomare Rd., No. 9, Los Angeles, CA 90077-1851. TEL 310-471-8066. FAX 310-471-4969. Ed. Lynne Naylor. adv. circ. 2,500. **Document type:** directory.
  Description: Covers network, syndication, cable, MOWs, comedy, drama and specials.

658.8 384.554 US ISSN 0049-3317
TELEVISION SPONSORS DIRECTORY; product cross-reference directory. Cover title: Television Sponsors Product Cross-Reference Directory. 1970. q. $19.40. Everglades Publishing Co., Drawer Q, Everglades, FL 33929. Ed. Roger C. Foss. circ. 1,200. (processed)

384.55 791.457 US ISSN 0894-8658
TELEVISION WRITERS GUIDE. a. $50 (effective 1996). Lone Eagle Publishing Co., 2337 Roscomare Rd., No. 9, Los Angeles, CA 90077-1851. TEL 310-471-8066. FAX 310-471-4969. Ed. Lynne Naylor. adv. circ. 3,000. **Document type:** directory.
  Description: Lists people who write for television. Includes contacts, credits, networks and genres.

338.025 US ISSN 1042-8801
HF5065.T2
TENNESSEE BUSINESS DIRECTORY. 1987. a. $395 (effective 1997). American Business Directories (Subsidiary of: American Business Information, Inc.), 5711 S. 86th Circle, Box 27347, Omaha, NE 68127. TEL 402-593-4600; 800-555-6124. FAX 402-331-5481. E-mail: jerry.venner@abii.com. index. (also avail. in magnetic tape; diskette format) **Document type:** directory.
●Also available online.
Also available on CD-ROM.
  Description: Includes all businesses in the state compiled from the yellow pages and telephone-verified. Each listing includes company name, complete address, phone number, name of owner, manager, and employee size, sales volume codes, and credit rating codes.

670 US ISSN 0360-5477
T12
TENNESSEE MANUFACTURERS DIRECTORY. 1943. a. $92 (diskette $395) (effective 1996). (Department of Economic and Community Development) M. Lee Smith Publishers LLC, 5201 Virginia Way, Box 5094, Brentwood, TN 37024-5094. TEL 615-373-5717; 800-274-6774. FAX 615-373-5183. (Dist. by: Manufacturers' News, Inc., 1633 Central St., Evanston, IL 60201-1505. TEL 708-864-7000) Pub. M. Lee Smith. circ. 12,000. (also avail. in magnetic tape; diskette format) **Document type:** directory.
  Former titles: Tennessee Directory of Manufacturers (ISSN 0070-6442); Directory of Tennessee Industries.
  Description: Provides up to 30 facts about each of more than 5,500 manufacturers in Tennessee and neighboring states.

TENNESSEE STATE AGENT HANDBOOK. see INSURANCE

670 FI ISSN 0781-6987
TEOLLISUUDEN KESKUSLIITTO. JASENLUETTELO/FINLANDS INDUSTRIFOERBUND. MEDLEMSFOERTECKNING/CONFEDERATION OF FINNISH INDUSTRIES. LIST OF MEMBERS. biennial. membership. Teollisuusden Keskusliitto, Etelaranta 10, PL 220, 00131 Helsinki 13, Finland. circ. 5,000.
  Formerly: Suomen Teollisuusliittoo. Jasenluettelo.

BUSINESS AND ECONOMICS — TRADE AND INDUSTRIAL DIRECTORIES

380 HF5065.T4 US ISSN 1053-6698
TEXAS BUSINESS DIRECTORY. 1991. a. $795 (effective 1997). American Business Directories (Subsidiary of: American Business Information, Inc.), 5711 S. 86th Circle, Box 27347, Omaha, NE 68127. TEL 402-593-4600; 800-555-6124. FAX 402-331-5481. E-mail: jerry.venner@abii.com. index. (also avail. in magnetic tape; diskette format) **Document type:** directory.
●Also available online.
Also available on CD-ROM.
Description: Includes all businesses in the state compiled from the yellow pages and telephone-verified. Each listing includes company name, complete address, phone number, name of owner or manager, and employee size and sales volume codes, and credit rating codes.

338.4767025 US ISSN 0896-9779
TEXAS HIGH TECHNOLOGY DIRECTORY. 1988. a. $139 (effective 1997). Leading Edge Communications, Inc., 1121 Old Siskiyou Hwy., Ashland, OR 97520. TEL 541-482-4990. FAX 541-482-4993. Eds. Philip Boesche, Kimberley Boesche. circ. 800. **Document type:** directory.
Description: Lists profiles of about 4,300 manufacturers and research and development firms in Texas engaged in high-technology activities.

670 HD9727.T4 US ISSN 0743-1163
TEXAS MANUFACTURERS REGISTER. a. $149 (diskette or CD-ROM $745) (effective 1997). Manufacturers' News, Inc., 1633 Central St., Evanston, IL 60201. TEL 847-864-7000. FAX 847-332-1100. Ed. Louise M. West. adv.; B&W page $1843; adv. contact: Charles Scherer. illus. (diskette format) **Document type:** directory.
●Also available on CD-ROM.
Description: Profiles 22,789 manufacturers listed five different ways by product, alphabetically, geographically, by SIC, and parent company.

338.4 ML14.T3 US ISSN 1062-6646
THE TEXAS MUSIC INDUSTRY DIRECTORY. 1991. a. $15. Office of the Governor, Texas Music Office, Box 13246, Austin, TX 78711. TEL 512-463-6666. FAX 512-463-4114. Ed. Deb Freeman. circ. 15. **Document type:** directory, government publication.
Description: Lists more than 5,000 Texas music businesses cross-referenced among 86 categories. Also lists classical music organizations, schools, songwriters, and events.

TEXAS PETROLEUM INDUSTRY. see *PETROLEUM AND GAS*

THE TEXAS RECORDING AND PRODUCTION GUIDE. see *SOUND RECORDING AND REPRODUCTION*

TEXAS STATE AGENT HANDBOOK. see *INSURANCE*

650 HD2428.T4 US ISSN 0362-7519
TEXAS TRADE AND PROFESSIONAL ASSOCIATIONS AND OTHER SELECTED ORGANIZATIONS. 1951. biennial. $15 for 1996 edition. University of Texas at Austin, Bureau of Business Research, Box 7459, Austin, TX 78713. TEL 512-471-1616. FAX 512-671-1063. E-mail: dhardy@mail.utexas.edu. Ed. Rita J. Wright. R&P contact: Lois Shrout. circ. 1,750. (back issues avail.; reprint service avail. from UMI) **Document type:** directory.
Formerly (until 1972): Selected Trade and Professional Associations in Texas (ISSN 0080-8644).
Description: Lists officers, along with their addresses and phone numbers; number of members; titles and frequency of association publications.

338 690 TH
THAI BUILDERS DIRECTORY. (Text in English) 1970. a. Advertising and Media Consultants Ltd., Silom Condominium, 12th Fl., 52-38 Soi Saladaeng 2, Bangkok, Thailand. TEL 2-2338126. FAX 2-2366764. TELEX 82463 LOOKEAS TH. Ed. Satish Sehgal. adv.; B&W page B.22000, color page B.45000; trim 190 x 254; adv. contact: Ravi Sehgal. circ. 20,000. **Document type:** directory.
Description: Information on the Thai building and construction industry.

THAI CHAMBER OF COMMERCE. DIRECTORY (YEAR). see *BUSINESS AND ECONOMICS — Chamber Of Commerce Publications*

338.025 TH
THAI FURNITURE INDUSTRIES ASSOCIATION DIRECTORY. 1992. a. $24 per no. Cosmic Group of Companies, 4th Fl., Phyathai Bldg., 31 Phyathai Rd., Rajthevi, Bangkok 10400, Thailand. TEL 245-3850. FAX 246-4737. adv.: color page $1200. circ. 5,000 (controlled). **Document type:** directory.
Description: Covers furniture and timber industries.

382 TH ISSN 0857-1155
THAI INDUSTRIAL DIRECTORY. (Text in English and Thai) 1970. a. Advertising and Media Consultants Ltd., Silom Condominium, 12th Fl., 52-38 Soi Saladaeng 2, Bangkok 10500, Thailand. TEL 2-333401. FAX 2-366764. TELEX 82463 LOOKEAS TH. Ed. Arthit Sehgal. adv. contact: Satish Sehgal. circ. 15,000. **Document type:** directory.

THAI-KOREAN CHAMBER OF COMMERCE HANDBOOK & DIRECTORY. see *BUSINESS AND ECONOMICS — Chamber Of Commerce Publications*

670 615.1 TH
THAI PHARMACEUTICAL DIRECTORY. (Text in English) 1970. a. Advertising and Media Consultants Ltd., Silom Condominium, 12th Fl., 52-38 Soi Saladaeng 2, Bangkok, Thailand. TEL 235-6186. FAX 236-6764. TELEX 82463-LOOKEAS-TH. Ed.Bd. circ. 20,000. **Document type:** directory.
Description: Aimed at doctors, pharmacists and health officials.

THAILAND COMPANY INFORMATION (YEAR). see *BUSINESS AND ECONOMICS — Domestic Commerce*

380.1 TH ISSN 0857-2984
THAILAND INDUSTRIAL BUYER'S GUIDE. 1981. a. $85. The Business Publications (1985) Co. Ltd., 9-42 Soi Kingpetch, Petchburi Rd., P.O. Box 2729, Bangkok 10400, Thailand. TEL 662-2150926-9. FAX 662-2156865. **Document type:** directory.
Description: Lists Thai manufacturers, exporters, products, and export-related services.

380 UK
THAMES VALLEY BUSINESS DIRECTORY. a. £40. (Thames Valley Chamber of Commerce & Industry) Kemps Publishing Ltd., 11 The Swan Courtyard, Charles Edward Rd., Birmingham B26 1BU, England. TEL 44-121-765-4144. FAX 44-121-706-6210. adv.; illus.; tr.lit. **Document type:** directory.
Former titles: Thames Valley Chamber of Commerce and Industry Directory; Thames-Chiltern Chamber of Commerce and Industry Directory; South Bucks and East Berks Chamber of Commerce and Industry Directory.

380.1 II
THAPAR'S INDIAN INDUSTRIAL DIRECTORY AND IMPORT AND EXPORT DIRECTORY OF THE WORLD. (Text in English) 1960. a. $120. Sunderdas Gianchand, 644 Jss. Rd., Bombay 400 002, India. TEL 22-310518. Ed. Ramesh Shetty. adv. circ. 50,000. **Document type:** directory.
Formerly: Calcutta Market.

338 350 US ISSN 1063-3340
▼**THINK TANK DIRECTORY;** guide to nonprofit public policy research organizations. 1996. a. $125 (effective 1996-97 ed.). Government Research Service, 214 S.W. Sixth Ave., Ste. 301, Topeka, KS 66603-3719. TEL 913-232-7720. FAX 913-232-1615. **Document type:** directory.
Description: Includes name, address, tel and fax, e-mail, website, chief executive officer, mission statement, board members, budget categories, and areas of research interest for over 1200 think tanks.

THOMAS FOOD INDUSTRY REGISTER. see *FOOD AND FOOD INDUSTRIES*

THOMAS REGISTER OF AMERICAN MANUFACTURERS AND THOMAS REGISTER CATALOG FILE. see *BUSINESS AND ECONOMICS — Marketing And Purchasing*

381 IE ISSN 0082-4224
THOM'S COMMERCIAL DIRECTORY. 1844. a. $200. Thom's Directories Ltd., 38 Merrion Sq., Dublin 2, Ireland. TEL 353-1-6767481. FAX 353-1-6762620. Ed. J.L. Wootton, Sr. **Document type:** directory.
●Also available on CD-ROM.

332.1 US ISSN 1057-8986
HG2441
THOMSON BANK DIRECTORY. 1876. a. $335. Thomson Financial Publishing, 4709 W. Golf Rd., Skokie, IL 60076-1256. TEL 847-676-9600; 800-321-3373. FAX 847-933-8101. Ed. Beth Swann. R&P contact: Beth Swann. adv. contact: Hugh Boyd. stat. **Document type:** directory.
Former titles (until 1991): Rand McNally Bankers Directory (ISSN 0895-4623); (until 1986): Rand McNally International Bankers Directory (ISSN 0360-7445).
Description: Provides a comprehensive listing of more than 130,000 banks, covering North American and international banks and their branches.

380 332.3 US ISSN 1062-1717
HG2150
THOMSON SAVINGS DIRECTORY. 1982. a. $195. (United States League of Savings Institutions) Thomson Financial Publishing, 4709 W. Golf Rd., Skokie, IL 60076. TEL 847-676-9600; 800-321-3373. FAX 847-933-8101. Ed. Beth Swann. R&P contact: Beth Swann. adv. contact: Hugh Boyd. **Document type:** directory.
Former titles (until 1991): U S Savings Institutions Directory (ISSN 1045-8883); (until 1989): U S Savings and Loan Directory (ISSN 0734-9203).
Description: Supplies up-to-date information on all U.S. savings institutions and their branches, with addresses, key officers, and comparative financial data.

670 666 IT
TILE BOOK; Italian repertory of ceramic firms. 1973. a. Lit.35000 (effective 1997). Gruppo Editoriale Faenza Editrice s.p.a., Via Pier. de Crescenzi, 44, 48018 Faenza, Italy. TEL 39-546-663488. FAX 39-546-660440. E-mail: gefe.vendita@uno.dinamica.it; gefe.info@uno.dinamica.it. Ed. Franco Rossi. adv.; B&W page Lit.2520000, color page Lit.2930000. circ. 5,000.
Formerly: Annuario delle Ceramiche Italiane per l'Edilizia.

666 IT
TILE BRICKS REFRACTORIES SUPPLIERS BOOK. 1976. a. Lit.30000 (effective 1997). Gruppo Editoriale Faenza Editrice S.p.A., Via Pier. de Crescenzi, 44, 48018 Faenza RA, Italy. TEL 39-546-663488. FAX 39-546-660440. E-mail: gefe.vendita@uno.dinamica.it; gefe.info@uno.dinamica.it. Ed. Franco Rossi. adv.; B&W page Lit.2540000, color page Lit.2930000. circ. 5,000.
Former titles: Suppliers Ceramics Book; Annuario de Fornitori.

TIMBER TRADES ADDRESS BOOK. see *FORESTS AND FORESTRY — Lumber And Wood*

338.025 SI ISSN 1394-1321
TIMES BUSINESS DIRECTORY OF MALAYSIA (YEAR). (Text in English) a. $80. Times Trade Directories Pte. Ltd., Times Centre, One New Industrial Rd., Singapore 536196, Singapore. TEL 65-2848844. FAX 65-2850161. TELEX RS 25713 TIMES. Pub. Leslie Lim. adv. contact: Leslie Lim. **Document type:** directory.
Description: Contains comprehensive listings of key local and foreign companies operating in Malaysia.

338.025 SI ISSN 0217-6009
TIMES BUSINESS DIRECTORY OF SINGAPORE. (Text in English) 1880. a. $100. Times Trade Directories Pte. Ltd., Times Centre, One New Industrial Rd., Singapore 536196, Singapore. TEL 65-2848844. FAX 65-2850161. TELEX RS-25713-TIMESS. Pub. Leslie Lim. R&P contact: Leslie Lim. adv. contact: Joseph Liang. bk.rev.; circ. 25,000 (controlled). **Document type:** directory.
Formerly: Straits Times Directory of Singapore; Supersedes in part: Straits Times Directory of Malaysia and Singapore (ISSN 0585-3931).
Description: Provides information on nature of business, contact telephone, fax, addresses, and key personnel for each company listed.

BUSINESS AND ECONOMICS — TRADE AND INDUSTRIAL DIRECTORIES

380   SI   ISSN 0218-1002
TIMES GUIDE TO COMPUTERS. 1985. a. $25. Times Trade Directories Pte. Ltd., Times Centre, One New Industrial Rd., Singapore 536196, Singapore. TEL 65-2848844. FAX 65-2850161. TELEX RS 25713 TIMESS. Pub. Leslie Lim. R&P contact: Leslie Lim. adv. contact: Joseph Liang. circ. 30,000 (controlled). **Document type:** directory.
    Description: Directory of computer manufacturers, agents, distributors and dealers in Singapore.

338   NR
TIMES TRADE AND INDUSTRIAL DIRECTORY. 1972. irreg. price varies. Daily Times of Nigeria Ltd., Publications Division, New Isheri Rd., P.M.B. 21340, Agidingbi, Ikeja, Lagos State, Nigeria. TEL 234-64-900850-9. FAX 234-64-21333. Ed. James O. Ojiako. illus. **Document type:** directory.

659.1   301.412   US
TODAY'S ARIZONA WOMAN BUSINESS DIRECTORY; a directory of women's businesses and businesses interested in reaching the women's market. 1975. a. $12. Publishers West, Inc., 4425 N. Saddlebag Tr., Scottsdale, AZ 85251. TEL 602-945-5000. FAX 602-941-5196. Ed. Charlotte Hodel; Pub. Eleanore Klein. adv.: page $1790; trim 8 3/8 x 10 3/8; adv. contact: Alison Lee. index. circ. 30,000. **Document type:** directory.
    Former titles: Women's Yellow Pages Arizona (ISSN 1042-8488); (until 1989): Women's Pages Arizona (ISSN 0894-0703).
    Description: Serves as a guide of services and products. Lists women's businesses, and other businesses and professions providing services to women.

338   US   ISSN 0363-2962
HE8811
TOLL-FREE DIGEST.* 1976. a. $17.95. Toll-Free Digest Co., Inc., Box 291, Kinderhook, NY 12106-0291. FAX 518-828-9635. Ed. Paul R. Montana.

338.025   US
▼**TOLL - FREE PHONE BOOK U S A (YEAR).** 1997. a. $75. Omnigraphics, Inc., 2500 Penobscot Bldg., Detroit, MI 48226. TEL 313-961-1383; 800-234-1340. FAX 313-961-1340.
    Description: Lists toll-free numbers for nearly 33,000 companies associations, educational institutions, travel providers, and government agencies across the country.

TOOLING AND MANUFACTURING ASSOCIATION. PURCHASING GUIDE. see BUSINESS AND ECONOMICS — Production Of Goods And Services

TOOLROOM DIRECTORY. see MACHINERY

690   380.1   US
TOP CONTACTS. Variant title: Shopping Center Directory's Top Contacts. (Vol. 5 of: Shopping Center Directory) 1988. a. $305. National Research Bureau, Inc. (Chicago), 150 N. Wacker Dr., Ste. 2222, Chicago, IL 60606-1608. TEL 312-541-0100. FAX 312-541-1492. (Orders to: National Research Bureau, 263 Tresser Blvd., 5th Fl., Stamford, CT 06901. TEL 800-456-4555. FAX 203-977-7645) **Document type:** directory.
    Formerly (until 1994): Shopping Center Developer Directory (ISSN 1040-1911).
    Description: Provides headquarters information on the top 1500 owners, leasing agents and management companies who control three or more shopping centers in the U.S.

338   340   CN   ISSN 0317-588X
TORONTO LEGAL DIRECTORY. 1925. a. $25.92. University of Toronto Press, Directories Departement, 10 St. Mary St., Ste. 700, Toronto, ON M4Y 2W8, Canada. TEL 416-978-2239. FAX 416-978-4738. E-mail: utpbooks@gpu.utcc. utoronto.ca. Ed. Kieran Simpson. adv. **Document type:** directory.

338.4   916.8   SA
TOURISM TRADE DIRECTORY: SOUTH AFRICA. 1994. a. Satour, Private Bag X164, Pretoria 0001, South Africa. Ed. Jill Archer. **Document type:** directory.

688   CN   ISSN 0317-9443
TOY AND DECORATION FAIR DIRECTORY. (Text in English, French) 1941. a. Can.$10.70. Canadian Toy Association, Box 294, Kleinburg, ON L0J 1C0, Canada. TEL 416-893-1689. FAX 416-893-2392. Ed. Sheila Edmondson. adv. circ. 3,500. **Document type:** directory.
    Formerly: Canadian Toy Fair. Trade Show Directory (ISSN 0068-9890)

670   US
TRADE AND PROFESSIONAL ASSOCIATIONS IN CALIFORNIA; a directory. 1979. irreg., 6th ed., 1995. $50 to individuals; libraries $25. California Institute of Public Affairs, Box 189040, Sacramento, CA 95818. TEL 916-442-CIPA. FAX 916-442-2478. (Affiliate: The Claremont Graduate School) **Document type:** directory.
    Description: Lists the addresses and telephone numbers of over 2,200 business and professional organizations in the state, alphabetized, numbered, and indexed by subject and key words.

382   US   ISSN 0564-0482
TRADE DIRECTORIES OF THE WORLD. base vol. plus m. supplements. $90 (foreign $125) (effective 1997). Croner Publications, Inc., 10951 Sorrento Valley Rd., Ste. 1-D, San Diego, CA 92121-1613. TEL 619-546-1894. FAX 619-546-1955. Ed. Elizabeth Duffy. (looseleaf format) **Document type:** directory.
—CISTI.
    Description: Lists trade, industrial and professional directories.

380.102   DK   ISSN 0109-467X
T12.5.D4
TRADE DIRECTORY FOR DENMARK/DAENISCHER HANDELSKALENDER/ANNUAIRE DE L'EXPORTATION DU DANEMARK/ANNUARIO DE LA EXPORTATION DE DINAMARCA/ANUARIO DE LA EXPORTACION DE DINAMARCA. (Text in English, French, German and Spanish) 1956. biennial. Information Office of the Danish Foreign Trade, Hellerupvej 78, 2900 Hellerup, Denmark. illus.
    Formerly (until 1984): Udenrigshandelskalenderen for Danmark (ISSN 0532-1360)

TRADE DIRECTORY OF MEXICO. see BUSINESS AND ECONOMICS — International Commerce

TRADE OPPORTUNITY. see BUSINESS AND ECONOMICS — Chamber Of Commerce Publications

381   607.34   US
TRADE SHOWS & EXHIBITS SCHEDULE. 1925. s-a. $170. Bill Communications, Inc., 355 Park Ave. S., 5th Fl., New York, NY 10010-1789. TEL 212-592-6200. FAX 212-592-6339. Ed. Jean Jaworek. adv. circ. 2,500. **Document type:** directory.
—CISTI.
    Formerly (until 1954): Exhibits Schedule (ISSN 0531-5360)
    Description: Directory listing of trade shows and exhibits scheduled for the published and following year.

382   CH
TRADE YELLOW PAGES (YEAR). 1990. a. NT.$1200($65) (N. America & Europe $90). Taiwan Trade Pages Corp., P.O. Box 72-50, Taipei, Taiwan, Republic of China. TEL 02-3053960. FAX 02-3071000. Ed. Valerie Liu.
    Description: Lists 30,000 suppliers under 604 product categories in 20 main industrial groups.

338.025   332.6   SI
TRADELINK - CHINESE. (Text in English) a. $80. Times Trade Directories Pte. Ltd., Times Centre, One New Industrial Rd., Singapore 536196, Singapore. TEL 65-2848844. FAX 65-2850161. TELEX RS 25713 TIMES. Pub. Leslie Lim. R&P contact: Leslie Lim. adv. contact: Joseph Liang. **Document type:** directory.
    Description: Lists Singapore companies engaged in exporting Singapore-manufactured products and services to China.

338.025   332.6   SI
TRADELINK - ENGLISH. (Text in English) a. $90. Times Trade Directories Pte. Ltd., Times Centre, One New Industrial Rd., Singapore 536196, Singapore. TEL 65-2848844. FAX 65-2850161. TELEX RS 25713 TIMES. Pub. Leslie Lim. R&P contact: Leslie Lim. adv. contact: Joseph Liang. **Document type:** directory.
    Description: Lists Singapore companies engaged in the exporting of Singapore-manufactured products and services to the world market.

670   SI
TRADELINK - S C I ANNUAL DIRECTORY (YEAR). (Former name of issuing body: Singapore Manufacturers' Association) (Text in English) 1960. a. free. Singapore Confederation of Industries, S.M.A. House, 20 Orchard Road, Singapore 238830, Singapore. TEL 65-3388787. FAX 65-3365385. E-mail: scihq@sci.org.sg; URL: http://www.sci.org.sg/sci. Ed. Grace Yu. adv. circ. 5,000. **Document type:** directory, trade publication.
    Former titles: Tradelink - S M A Annual Directory (Year) (ISSN 0217-7447); (until 1986): Singapore Manufacturers' Association Directory (ISSN 0129-9867); Directory of Singapore Manufacturers (ISSN 0070-6337)
    Description: Names and addresses of manufacturers as well as names and addresses of companies in the service industry.

380   011   JA   ISSN 0285-3809
TRADESCOPE. (Text in English) 1981. w. free. Japan External Trade Organization, International Communication Department, 2-5 Toranomon 2-chome, Minato-ku, Tokyo 104, Japan. TEL 03-3582-5521. FAX 03-3582-0504. TELEX J 24378. Ed. Naohiko Taguchi. circ. 6,000. **Document type:** trade publication.
●Also available online.
—BLDSC (8881.036500).

382.6   II   ISSN 0082-5824
TRADO: ASIAN - AFRICAN DIRECTORY OF EXPORTERS, IMPORTERS AND MANUFACTURERS.* (Text in English) 1956. a. $115. Trado Publications Pvt. Ltd., c/o Bansi Hse, 1/24 Asaf Ah Rd., New Delhi 110001, India. Ed. J.K. Chug. adv.; index. circ. 10,000.

917   US
TRAILER LIFE CAMPGROUND AND R V SERVICES DIRECTORY. Running title: Campground & R V Services Guide. 1971. a. $15.95. Affinity Group, Ic., T L Enterprises, 2575 Vista Del Mar Dr., Ventura, CA 93001-3920. TEL 805-667-4100; 800-234-3450. Pub. Joe Daquino. adv.; illus. circ. 375,000. **Document type:** directory.
    Former titles: Good Sam Club's Recreational Vehicle Owners Directory (ISSN 0090-3256); Trailer Life's Recreational Vehicle Campground and Services Guide (ISSN 0093-4283)
    Description: Lists 25,000 private and public campgrounds, recreational vehicle service and accessory centers, and liquid propane gas locations in North America.

TRAINING AND ENTERPRISE DIRECTORY. see EDUCATION

338.025   380.5   UK
TRANSPORT E-MAIL DIRECTORY. a. £20. P T R C Education and Research Services Ltd., Glenthorne House, Hammersmith Grove, London W6 0LG, England. TEL 44-181-741-1516. FAX 44-181-741-5993. E-mail: ptrc@cityscape.co.uk. **Document type:** directory.

380.5   US   ISSN 0447-9181
TRANSPORTATION TELEPHONE TICKLER. (Published in a national edition in 4 vols. and 11 regional editions) 1950. a. $94.95 (effective 1997). Journal of Commerce, Inc. (Subsidiary of: Economist Group), 2 World Trade Center, 27th fl., New York, NY 10048-0203. TEL 212-837-7000. (Subscr. to: 445 Marshall St., Phillipsburg, NJ 08865. TEL 908-859-1300) adv.; index. circ. 130,000.
●Also available on CD-ROM.
—CCC.

380   910.2   US   ISSN 0082-6146
G155.A1
TRAVEL INDUSTRY PERSONNEL DIRECTORY.* 1951. a. $25. Fairchild Books (Subsidiary of: Fairchild Publications Inc.), 7 W. 34th St., New York, NY 10001. TEL 212-630-4000. FAX 212-887-1946. Ed. Marsheela Evans. adv.; index. circ. 7,000.

BUSINESS AND ECONOMICS — TRADE AND INDUSTRIAL DIRECTORIES

TRAVEL TRADE GAZETTE DIRECTORY. see *TRAVEL AND TOURISM*

380 910.09   US
TRAVELODGE NORTH AMERICAN - INTERNATIONAL TRAVEL DIRECTORY. 1963. s-a. free. H F S, Inc., 339 Jefferson Rd., Parsippany, NJ 07054. TEL 201-428-9700. circ. 550,000. **Document type:** directory.
   Former titles: Travelodge and Viscount Hotels North American Travel Directory; Travelodge - Forte Viscount Hotels Travel Directory; TraveLodge - Viscount Hotels Vacation Travel Directory.

380.1 910   AT
TRAVELTRADE YEARBOOK. 1966. s-a. Aus.$37($53) per issue (effective 1996). Reed Business Publishing Pty. Ltd. (Subsidiary of: Reed International PLC), P.O. Box 5487, W. Chatswood, N.S.W. 2057, Australia. TEL 61-2-372-5222. FAX 61-2-419-7064. E-mail: 100252,147@compuserve.com; URL: http://www.traveltrade.com.au. Ed. Doug Kujovic; Pub. Michael Woolley. adv.: B&W page Aus.$2500, color page Aus.$3400; trim 297 x 210; adv. contact: John McGaulley. circ. 3,936 (paid). **Document type:** directory, trade publication.
   Description: Comprehensive manual of travel industry suppliers, principals and retailers.

675.058   US
TRAVELWARE RESOURCES DIRECTORY. a. $20. Business Journals, 50 Day St., Box 5550, Norwalk, CT 06856. TEL 203-853-6015. illus. **Document type:** directory, trade publication.
   Former titles: Luggage and Travelware Directory and Market Guide; Luggage and Travelware Directory; Luggage and Leather Goods Directory.

TRINIDAD AND TOBAGO TRADE DIRECTORY. see *BUSINESS AND ECONOMICS — International Commerce*

TRUCKING TIMES. see *TRANSPORTATION — Trucks And Trucking*

650   US   ISSN 0191-6106
HD2346.U5
TRY US; national minority business directory. 1969. a. $58. Try Us Resources, Inc., 2105 Central Ave., N.E., Minneapolis, MN 55418. TEL 612-781-6819. FAX 612-781-0109. Ed. Leslie Smith-Bonds. R&P contact: Leslie Smith-Bonds. **Document type:** directory.
   Formerly: National Minority Business Directory (ISSN 0077-5231)
   Description: Provides names of contact personnel and information on company capabilities, years in business, certifications held, number of employees, previous year's sales and more.

U D I WHO'S WHO IN ELECTRIC TRANSMISSION & DISTRIBUTION. (Utility Data Institute) see *ENERGY — Electrical Energy*

332   NE   ISSN 1352-4461
HG4135.5
U K BUSINESS FINANCE DIRECTORY (YEAR); the guide to sources of U K corporate finance. 1984. a. £154($290) Kluwer Law International (Subsidiary of: Wolters Kluwer N.V.), Postbus 85889, 2508 CN The Hague, Netherlands. TEL 31-70-3081500. FAX 31-70-3081515. (Dist. by: Libresso Distributions Centre, P.O. Box 23, 7400 GA Deventer, Netherlands. TEL 31-5700-33155. FAX 31-5700-33834; In N. America: Kluwer Law International, 675 Massachusetts Ave., Cambridge, MA 02139. TEL 617-354-0140. FAX 617-354-8595) Eds. G.C. Bricault, J.C. Carr. adv. **Document type:** directory.
   Former titles: (until 1990): Sunday Telegraph Business Finance Directory (ISSN 0268-2249); (until 1985): Sunday Telegraph U K Finance Directory (ISSN 0267-2464); U K Finance Directory.
   Description: Lists more than 1,500 accountants, banks, finance houses, insurance companies, stockbrokers, and other financial institutions.

670   UK
U K INDUSTRIAL TRADE NAMES; including imported items. 1966. a. £235. Kompass (Subsidiary of: Reed Information Services Ltd.), Part of the Reed Elsevier group, Windsor Ct., E. Grinstead House, E. Grinstead, W. Sussex RH19 1XD, England. TEL 44-1342-326972. FAX 44-1342-335992. TELEX 95127-INFSER-G. circ. 2,200. **Document type:** directory.
   ●Also available online. Vendor(s): Reed Information Services Ltd.
   Formerly: U K Trade Names (ISSN 0082-7142)

338.025   UK
U K KOMPASS REGISTER. 1962. a. £299. Kompass (Subsidiary of: Reed Information Services Ltd.), Part of the Reed Elsevier group, Windsor Ct., E. Grinstead House, E. Grinstead, W. Sussex RH19 1XD, England. TEL 44-1342-326972. FAX 44-1342-335747. **Document type:** directory.

U K MEDIA DIRECTORY. see *JOURNALISM*

U K MEDIA TOWN BY TOWN. see *JOURNALISM*

338.025 322   UK   ISSN 1356-6369
THE U K WEALTH DIRECTORY. 1994. biennial. £81 (overseas £86). Rowland Lybrand of London, 28 Weatley Ct., Mixenden, Halifax, W. Yorks. HX2 8QL, England. TEL 01422-241197. **Document type:** directory.
   Description: List the names, addresses, and assets of multi-millionaires in the U.K., most owning major quantities of shares in public and private companies.

338   US
U S A TODAY SOURCE GUIDE. a. U S A Today (Subsidiary of: Gannett Newspapers), 1000 Wilson Blvd., Arlington, VA 22229. TEL 800-USA-1415. **Document type:** directory.
   Description: Lists trade and professional organizations, colleges and other institutions, social service and advocacy groups, and a wide range of public and private companies.

338.025 304.6   UK   ISSN 1356-6377
THE U S A WEALTH DIRECTORY. 1994. biennial. £47 (overseas £52). Rowland Lybrand of London, 28 Weatley Ct., Mixenden, Halifax, W. Yorks. HX2 8QL, England. TEL 01422-241197. **Document type:** directory.
   Description: Lists the names, addresses, and assets of multi-millionaires in the U.S., most of whom own a substantial percentage of shares in major U.S. corporations.

382   US
U S - ARGENTINA TRADE PAGES.* (Text in English, Spanish) 1992. a. $59.95. Global Source, Inc., 9717 Longview Dr., Ellicott City, MD 21042-2335. TEL 202-429-5582. FAX 202-638-1284. Ed. Kara Kent. adv.: color page $3000. circ. 10,000. **Document type:** directory.
   Description: Contains trade statistics, detailed export information and thousands of contacts in US and Argentina.

382   US
U S - BRAZIL TRADE PAGES.* (Text in English, Portuguese) 1992. a. $59.95. Global Source, Inc., 9717 Longview Dr., Ellicott City, MD 21042-2335. TEL 202-429-5582. FAX 202-638-1284. Ed. Kara Kent. adv.: color page $3000-5000. circ. 10,000. **Document type:** directory.
   Description: Contains country specific trade statistics, detailed export information and thousands of contacts in US and Brazil.

382   US
U S - CANADA TRADE PAGES.* (Text in English, French) 1992. a. $59.95. Global Source, Inc., 9717 Longview Dr., Ellicott City, MD 21042-2335. TEL 202-429-5582. FAX 202-638-1284. Ed. Kara Kent. adv.: color page $3000. circ. 10,000. **Document type:** directory.
   Description: Contains trade statistics, detailed export information and thousands of contacts in US and Canada.

382   US
U S - CHILE TRADE PAGES.* (Text in English, Spanish) 1992. a. $59.95. Global Source, Inc., 9717 Longview Dr., Ellicott City, MD 21042-2335. TEL 202-429-5582. FAX 202-638-1284. Ed. Kara Kent. adv.: color page $3000. circ. 10,000. **Document type:** directory.
   Description: Contains trade statistics, detailed export information and thousands of contacts in US and Chile.

380.1   GW   ISSN 0946-1477
U S E M A C NEWSLETTER. (Text in English, German) 10/yr. DM.180. Verlag Dr. Grueb Nachf., Oelbergweg 8, 79283 Bollschweil, Germany. TEL 49-7633-7025. FAX 49-7633-82129. Ed. Rainer Grueb. adv.; bk.rev.; charts; illus.; pat.; stat. circ. 10,000. (tabloid format) **Document type:** newsletter.
   Formerly: Exporama (ISSN 0176-540X)

U S EXPORT DIRECTORY. see *BUSINESS AND ECONOMICS — International Commerce*

382   US
U S FIRMS IN GERMANY/AMERIKANISCHE UNTERNEHMEN IN DEUTSCHLAND. biennial. DM.160($100) (effective 1994). German American Chamber of Commerce, Publication Services, 40 W. 57th St., 31st Fl., New York, NY 10019. TEL 212-974-8830. FAX 212-974-8867. Ed. Sven Oehme. adv. contact: Benigna Kirsten. (also avail. in diskette format) **Document type:** directory.
   Description: Provides information on subsidiaries of U.S. owned firms active in Germany.

338   US
U S INDUSTRIAL DIRECTORY. (In 2 vols.: Vol.1: Catalogue Showcase; Vol.2: Product Directory) 1940. a. $195. Reed Information Services, Division of Reed Elsevier Inc., 121 Chanlon Rd., New Providence, NJ 07974. TEL 908-464-6800. (Subscr. to: 200 Clearwater Dr., Oakbrook, IL 60521. TEL 708-574-7081. FAX 708-390-2850) adv. circ. 100,000. **Document type:** directory.
   Description: For manufacturers and suppliers of every kind of industrial product.

U S KEY PERSONNEL LIST. see *ENGINEERING — Engineering Mechanics And Materials*

U S - MEXICO BORDER ENVIRONMENTAL DIRECTORY. see *ENVIRONMENTAL STUDIES*

382   US
U S - MEXICO TRADE PAGES.* (Text in English, Spanish) 1992. a. $59.95. Global Source, Inc., 9717 Longview Dr., Ellicott City, MD 21042-2335. TEL 202-429-5582. FAX 202-638-1284. Ed. Kara Kent. adv.: color page $3000. circ. 10,000. **Document type:** directory.
   Description: Contains trade statistics, detailed export information, and thousands of contacts in US and Mexico.

U S POWERPLANT EQUIPMENT DIRECTORY. see *ENERGY — Electrical Energy*

382   US
U S - VENEZUELA TRADE PAGES.* (Text in English, Spanish) 1992. a. $59.95. Global Source, Inc., 9717 Longview Dr., Ellicott City, MD 21042-2335. TEL 202-429-5582. FAX 202-638-1284. Ed. Kara Kent. adv.: color page $3000. circ. 10,000. **Document type:** directory.
   Description: Contains trade statistics, detailed export information and thousands of contacts in US and Venezuela.

380   US
U S 1 DIRECTORY. a. U S 1 Publishing Co., 12 Roszel Rd., Princeton, NJ 08540. TEL 609-452-0038. FAX 609-452-0033. adv.: B&W page $835; trim 8 1/2 x 11. circ. 5,000. **Document type:** directory.

338   US
UNDERGROUND CONSTRUCTION. ANNUAL DIRECTORY. 1952. a. $75. Oildom Publishing Co. of Texas, Inc., Box 219368, Houston, TX 77218-9368. TEL 713-558-6930. FAX 713-558-7029. Ed. Robert Carpenter; Pub. O.L. Klinger III. adv. contact: Lori Laxen-Brown. circ. 34,500. **Indexed:** AESIS. **Document type:** directory.
   Former titles: Pipeline and Utilities Construction. Annual Directory & Pipeline and Underground Utilities Construction. Annual Directory.

UNDERWRITERS LABORATORIES. ANNUAL PRODUCT DIRECTORIES. see ENVIRONMENTAL STUDIES — Waste Management

338   TS
UNITED ARAB EMIRATES. BUSINESS DIRECTORY. 1986. a. $90. Frontline Advertising & Marketing, P.O. Box 5151, Sharjah, United Arab Emirates. TEL 6-371177. FAX 6-373366. TELEX 68844 UNIGET EM. Dir. Rajeev Lal. circ. 15,000. **Document type:** directory.

UNITED STATES GOVERNMENT MANUAL. see *PUBLIC ADMINISTRATION*

338.025 382   US   ISSN 1062-8339
UNITED STATES IMPORTERS PRODUCT GUIDE. a. De Paula Publishing and Services Corp., 421 Seventh Ave., Ste. 1206, New York, NY 10001. TEL 212-629-4541. Ed. Carlos De Paula. **Document type:** directory.

382   US   ISSN 0502-5842
UNITED STATES - ITALY TRADE DIRECTORY. 1950. a. $150. Italy - America Chamber of Commerce, Inc., 730 Fifth Ave., Ste. 600, New York, NY 10019. TEL 212-459-0044. FAX 212-459-0090. adv. circ. 5,000. **Document type:** directory.

650 338   AT
UNIVERSAL BUSINESS DIRECTORIES. ADELAIDE BUSINESS TO BUSINESS DIRECTORY. 1942. a. Aus.$40. Universal Press Pty. Ltd., 64 Talavera Rd., Macquarie Park, N.S.W. 2113, Australia. TEL 02-8881877. FAX 02-8889850. adv. **Document type:** directory.
    Former titles: Universal Business Directories. Adelaide Business and Street Directory; Universal Business Directories. Adelaide and South Australia Country Trade and Business Directory (ISSN 0083-3797)

650 338   AT
UNIVERSAL BUSINESS DIRECTORIES. BRISBANE BUSINESS TO BUSINESS DIRECTORY. 1934. a. Aus.$40. Universal Press Pty. Ltd., 64 Talavera Rd., Macquarie Park, N.S.W. 2113, Australia. TEL 02-8881877. FAX 02-8889850. adv. **Document type:** directory.
    Former titles: Universal Business Directories, Brisbane and Suburban Business and Street Directory; Universal Business Directories, Brisbane and Suburban Business and Trade Directory (ISSN 0083-369X)

650 338   AT
UNIVERSAL BUSINESS DIRECTORIES. MELBOURNE BUSINESS TO BUSINESS DIRECTORY. 1948. a. Aus.$70. Universal Press Pty. Ltd., 64 Talavera Rd., Macquarie Park, N.S.W. 2113, Australia. TEL 02-8881877. FAX 02-8889850. adv. **Document type:** directory.
    Formerly: Universal Business Directories, Melbourne and Suburban Business and Trade Directory (ISSN 0083-3746)

650   AT
UNIVERSAL BUSINESS DIRECTORIES. NEW SOUTH WALES. CENTRAL WEST BUSINESS TO BUSINESS DIRECTORY. a. Universal Press Pty. Ltd., 64 Talavera Rd., Macquarie Park, N.S.W. 2113, Australia. TEL 02-8881877. FAX 02-8889850. **Document type:** directory.

650   AT
UNIVERSAL BUSINESS DIRECTORIES. NEW SOUTH WALES. HUNTER REGION BUSINESS TO BUSINESS DIRECTORY. a. Universal Press Pty. Ltd., 64 Talavera Rd., Macquarie Park, N.S.W. 2113, Australia. TEL 02-8881877. FAX 02-8889850. **Document type:** directory.

650   AT
UNIVERSAL BUSINESS DIRECTORIES. NEW SOUTH WALES. ILLAWARRA REGION BUSINESS TO BUSINESS DIRECTORY. a. Universal Press Pty. Ltd., 64 Talavera Rd., Macquarie Park, N.S.W. 2113, Australia. TEL 02-8881877. FAX 02-8889850. **Document type:** directory.

650   AT
UNIVERSAL BUSINESS DIRECTORIES. NEW SOUTH WALES. NEW ENGLAND REGION BUSINESS TO BUSINESS DIRECTORY. a. Universal Press Pty. Ltd., 64 Talavera Rd., Macquarie Park, N.S.W. 2113, Australia. TEL 02-8881877. FAX 02-8889850. **Document type:** directory.

650 338   AT
UNIVERSAL BUSINESS DIRECTORIES. NEW SOUTH WALES. NORTH COAST REGION BUSINESS TO BUSINESS DIRECTORY. a. Universal Press Pty. Ltd., 64 Talavera Rd., Macquarie Park, N.S.W. 2113, Australia. TEL 02-8881877. FAX 02-8889850. **Document type:** directory.

650   AT
UNIVERSAL BUSINESS DIRECTORIES. NEW SOUTH WALES. RIVERINA REGION BUSINESS TO BUSINESS DIRECTORY. a. Universal Press Pty. Ltd., 64 Talavera Rd., Macquarie Park, N.S.W. 2113, Australia. TEL 02-8881877. FAX 02-8889850. **Document type:** directory.

650   AT
UNIVERSAL BUSINESS DIRECTORIES. NEW SOUTH WALES. SOUTH EASTERN REGION BUSINESS TO BUSINESS DIRECTORY. a. Universal Press Pty. Ltd., 64 Talavera Rd., Macquarie Park, N.S.W 2113, Australia. TEL 02-8881877. FAX 02-8889850. **Document type:** directory.

650   AT
UNIVERSAL BUSINESS DIRECTORIES. NORTHERN TERRITORY BUSINESS TO BUSINESS DIRECTORY. a. Aus.$30. Universal Press Pty. Ltd., 64 Talavera Rd., Macquarie Park, N.S.W. 2113, Australia. TEL 02-8881877. FAX 02-8889850. **Document type:** directory.

650   AT
UNIVERSAL BUSINESS DIRECTORIES. PAPUA NEW GUINEA BUSINESS TO BUSINESS DIRECTORY. A. Aus.$30. Universal Press Pty. Ltd., 64 Talavera Rd., Macquarie Park, N.S.W. 2113, Australia. TEL 02-8881877. FAX 02-8889850. **Document type:** directory.

650 338   AT
UNIVERSAL BUSINESS DIRECTORIES. PERTH BUSINESS TO BUSINESS DIRECTORY. 1960. a. Aus.$40. Universal Press Pty. Ltd., 64 Talavera Rd., Macquarie Park, N.S.W. 2113, Australia. TEL 02-8881877. FAX 02-8889850. **Document type:** directory.
    Formerly: Universal Business Directories, Perth and Fremantle and Suburbs Business and Trade Directory (ISSN 0083-3789)

650   AT
UNIVERSAL BUSINESS DIRECTORIES. QUEENSLAND. BUNDABERG BUSINESS TO BUSINESS DIRECTORY. a. Universal Press Pty. Ltd, 64 Talavera Rd., Macquarie Park, N.S.W. 2113, Australia. TEL 02-8881877. FAX 02-8889850. **Document type:** directory.

650   AT
UNIVERSAL BUSINESS DIRECTORIES. QUEENSLAND. CAIRNS BUSINESS TO BUSINESS DIRECTORY. a. Universal Press Pty. Ltd., 64 Talavera Rd., Macquarie Park, N.S.W 2113, Australia. TEL 02-8881877. FAX 02-8889850. **Document type:** directory.

650   AT
UNIVERSAL BUSINESS DIRECTORIES. QUEENSLAND. GLADSTONE BUSINESS TO BUSINESS DIRECTORY. a. Universal Press Pty. Ltd., 64 Talavera Rd., Macquarie Press, N.S.W. 2113, Australia. TEL 02-881877. FAX 02-8889850. **Document type:** directory.

650   AT
UNIVERSAL BUSINESS DIRECTORIES. QUEENSLAND. GYMPIE BUSINESS TO BUSINESS DIRECTORY. a. Universal Press Pty. Ltd., 64 Talavera Rd., Macquarie Park, N.S.W. 2113, Australia. TEL 02-8881877. FAX 02-8889850. **Document type:** directory.

650   AT
UNIVERSAL BUSINESS DIRECTORIES. QUEENSLAND. MACKAY BUSINESS TO BUSINESS DIRECTORY. a. Universal Press Pty. Ltd., 64 Talavera Rd., Macquarie Park, N.S.W. 2113, Australia. TEL 02-8881877. FAX 02-8889850. **Document type:** directory.

650   AT
UNIVERSAL BUSINESS DIRECTORIES. QUEENSLAND. MARYBOROUGH BUSINESS TO BUSINESS DIRECTORY. a. Universal Press Pty. Ltd., 64 Talvera Rd., Macquarie Park, N.S.W. 2113, Australia. TEL 02-8881877. FAX 02-8889850. **Document type:** directory.

650   AT
UNIVERSAL BUSINESS DIRECTORIES. QUEENSLAND. REDCLIFFE BUSINESS TO BUSINESS DIRECTORY. a. Universal Press Pty. Ltd., 64 Talavera Rd., Macquarie Park, N.S.W. 2113, Australia. TEL 02-8881877. FAX 02-8889850. **Document type:** directory.

650   AT
UNIVERSAL BUSINESS DIRECTORIES. QUEENSLAND. ROCKHAMPTON BUSINESS TO BUSINESS DIRECTORY. a. Universal Press Pty. Ltd., 64 Talavera Rd., Macquarie Park, N.S.W. 2113, Australia. TEL 02-8881877. FAX 02-8889850. **Document type:** directory.

650   AT
UNIVERSAL BUSINESS DIRECTORIES. QUEENSLAND. SUNSHINE COAST BUSINESS TO BUSINESS DIRECTORY. a. Universal Press Pty. Ltd., 64 Talavera Rd., Macquarie Park, N.S.W. 2113, Australia. TEL 02-8881877. FAX 02-8889850. **Document type:** directory.

650   AT
UNIVERSAL BUSINESS DIRECTORIES. QUEENSLAND. TOOWOOMBA BUSINESS TO BUSINESS DIRECTORY. a. Universal Press Pty. Ltd., 64 Talavera Rd., Macquarie Park, N.S.W. 2113, Australia. TEL 02-8881877. FAX 02-8889850. **Document type:** directory.

650   AT
UNIVERSAL BUSINESS DIRECTORIES. QUEENSLAND. TOWNSVILLE BUSINESS TO BUSINESS DIRECTORY. a. Universal Press Pty. Ltd., 64 Talavera Rd., Macquarie Park, N.S.W. 2113, Australia. TEL 02-881877. FAX 02-8889850. **Document type:** directory.

650   AT
UNIVERSAL BUSINESS DIRECTORIES. SOUTH AUSTRALIA BUSINESS TO BUSINESS DIRECTORY. a. Aus.$30. Universal Press Pty. Ltd., 64 Talavera Rd., Macquarie Park, N.S.W 2113, Australia. TEL 02-8881877. FAX 02-8889850. **Document type:** directory.

338 650   AT
UNIVERSAL BUSINESS DIRECTORIES. SYDNEY BUSINESS TO BUSINESS DIRECTORY. 1948. a. Aus.$70. Universal Press Pty. Ltd., 64 Talavera Rd., Macquarie Park, N.S.W. 2113, Australia. TEL 02-8881877. FAX 02-8889850. adv. **Document type:** directory.
    Former titles: Universal Business Directories, Sydney and Suburban Business and Street Directory; Universal Business Directories, Sydney and Suburban Business and Trade Directory (ISSN 0083-3819)

338 650   AT
UNIVERSAL BUSINESS DIRECTORIES. TASMANIA BUSINESS TO BUSINESS DIRECTORY. 1950. a. Aus.$17. Universal Press Pty. Ltd., 64 Talavera Rd., Macquarie Park, N.S.W. 2113, Australia. TEL 02-8881877. FAX 02-8889850. adv. **Document type:** directory.
    Former titles: Universal Business Directories. Tasmania Business and Street Directory; Universal Business. Tasmania Business and Trade Directory (ISSN 0083-3827)

650   AT
UNIVERSAL BUSINESS DIRECTORIES. VICTORIA. BALLARAT BUSINESS TO BUSINESS DIRECTORY. a. Universal Press Pty. Ltd., 64 Talavera Rd., Macquarie Park, N.S.W 2113, Australia. TEL 02-8881877. FAX 02-8889850. **Document type:** directory.

640   AT
UNIVERSAL BUSINESS DIRECTORIES. VICTORIA. BENDIGO BUSINESS TO BUSINESS DIRECTORY. a. Universal Press Pty. Ltd., 64 Talavera Rd., Macquarie Park, N.S.W 2113, Australia. TEL 02-8881877. FAX 02-8889850. **Document type:** directory.

650   AT
UNIVERSAL BUSINESS DIRECTORIES. VICTORIA. GEELONG BUSINESS TO BUSINESS DIRECTORY. a. Universal Press Pty. Ltd., 64 Talavera Rd., Macquarie Park, N.S.W. 2113, Australia. TEL 02-8881877. FAX 02-8889850. **Document type:** directory.

BUSINESS AND ECONOMICS — TRADE AND INDUSTRIAL DIRECTORIES

650　　　　　　　AT
UNIVERSAL BUSINESS DIRECTORIES. VICTORIA. GOULBURN VALLEY BUSINESS TO BUSINESS DIRECTORY. a. Universal Press Pty. Ltd., 64 Talavera Rd., Macquarie Park, N.S.W. 2113, Australia. TEL 02-2881877. FAX 02-2889850. **Document type:** directory.

650　　　　　　　AT
UNIVERSAL BUSINESS DIRECTORIES. VICTORIA. LATROBE VALLEY BUSINESS TO BUSINESS DIRECTORY. a. Universal Press Pty. Ltd., 64 Talavera Rd., Macquarie Park, N.S.W. 2113, Australia. TEL 02-2881877. FAX 02-2889850. **Document type:** directory.

650　　　　　　　AT
UNIVERSAL BUSINESS DIRECTORIES. VICTORIA. NORTH EAST VICTORIA BUSINESS TO BUSINESS DIRECTORY. a. Universal Press Pty. Ltd., 64 Talavera Rd., Macquarie Park, N.S.W. 2113, Australia. TEL 02-2881877. FAX 02-2889850. **Document type:** directory.

650　　　　　　　AT
UNIVERSAL BUSINESS DIRECTORIES. VICTORIA. SUNRAYSIA-MALLEE BUSINESS TO BUSINESS DIRECTORIES. a. Universal Press Pty. Ltd., 64 Talavera Rd., Macquarie Park, N.S.W. 2113, Australia. TEL 02-2881877. FAX 02-2889850. **Document type:** directory.

650　　　　　　　AT
UNIVERSAL BUSINESS DIRECTORIES. VICTORIA. WEST DISTRICT BUSINESS TO BUSINESS DIRECTORY. a. Universal Press Pty. Ltd., 64 Talavera Rd., Macquarie Park, N.S.W. 2113, Australia. TEL 02-2881877. FAX 02-2889850. **Document type:** directory.

650　　　　　　　AT
UNIVERSAL BUSINESS DIRECTORIES. VICTORIA. WIMMERA BUSINESS TO BUSINESS DIRECTORY. a. Universal Press Pty. Ltd., 64 Talavera Rd., Macquarie Park, N.S.W. 2113, Australia. TEL 02-2881877. FAX 02-2889850. **Document type:** directory.

338.025　　　　　US
UPSTATE NEW YORK BUSINESS DIRECTORY. 1993. a. $430 (effective 1997). American Business Directories (Subsidiary of: American Business Information, Inc.), 5711 S. 86th Circle, Box 27347, Omaha, NE 68127. TEL 402-593-4600; 800-555-6124. FAX 402-331-5481. E-mail: jerry.venner@abii.com. (also avail. in magnetic tape; diskette format) **Document type:** directory.
●Also available online.
Also available on CD-ROM.
Description: Includes all businesses in the upstate New York area compiled from the yellow pages and telephone-verified. Listings include company name, complete address, phone number, name of owner or manager, employee size, sales volume, and credit rating codes.

670　　　　　US　　ISSN 0732-2860
HD9727.N7
UPSTATE NEW YORK DIRECTORY OF MANUFACTURERS. 1981. a. $62.50 (diskette $295) (effective 1996). Commerce Register, Inc., 190 Godwin Ave., Midland Park, NJ 07432. TEL 201-445-3000. FAX 201-445-5806. adv. (also avail. in magnetic tape; diskette format) **Document type:** directory.
Description: Profiles approximately 5,100 manufacturers; features alphabetical, geographical, and product line by SIC sections.

USED EQUIPMENT DIRECTORY. see *MACHINERY*

338.025　　　　　US　　ISSN 1048-7417
HF5065.U8
UTAH BUSINESS DIRECTORY. 1989. a. $295 (effective 1997). American Business Directories (Subsidiary of: American Business Information, Inc.), 5711 S. 86th Circle, Box 27347, Omaha, NE 68127. TEL 402-593-4600; 800-555-6124. FAX 402-331-5481. E-mail: jerry.venner@abii.com. index. (also avail. in diskette format) **Document type:** directory.
●Also available online.
Also available on CD-ROM.
Description: Includes all businesses in the state compiled from the yellow pages and telephone-verified. Each listing includes company name, complete address, phone number, name of owner, manager, and employee size, sales volume codes, and credit rating codes.

670　　　　　US　　ISSN 8755-2841
HD9727.U8
UTAH DIRECTORY OF BUSINESS AND INDUSTRY. 1951. a. $34. Department of Employment Security, Division of Economic Development, 324 S. State St., Ste. 500, Salt Lake City, UT 84111. TEL 801-538-8700; 800-848-0688. FAX 801-538-8773. (Dist. by: Manufacturers' News, Inc., 1633 Central St., Evanston, IL 60201-1505. TEL 708-864-7000) circ. 2,500. (also avail. in diskette format) **Document type:** directory, government publication.
Formerly: Directory of Utah Manufacturers (ISSN 0070-6566)
Description: Includes standard industrial code, county and alphabetical listing of all manufacturing firms and nonmanufacturing firms with 20 or more employees.

380.1　　　　　UK　　ISSN 1358-7927
V A R WORLD. (Value Added Reselling) 1992. m. £24 (foreign £50) (effective 1996). V N U Business Publications BV, VNU House, 32-34 Broadwick St., London W1A 2HG, England. TEL 44-171-439-4242. FAX 44-171-437-7001. **Document type:** trade publication.

VADEMEKUM DER GESCHICHTSWISSENSCHAFTEN. see *HISTORY — History Of Europe*

VANCOUVER PORT HANDBOOK. see *TRANSPORTATION — Ships And Shipping*

670 620　　　　　US
VENDOR CATALOG SERVICES INDEX. (In 3 vols. - A: Vendor Name; B: Brand-Trade Name; C: Locator-Subject Index) 1979. bi-m. $1165. Information Handling Services, 15 Inverness Way E., Englewood, CO 80150. TEL 303-790-0600. FAX 303-799-4085. TELEX 4322083 IHS UI. Ed. Liz Maynard Prigge. adv. circ. 2,500.
●Also available on CD-ROM.
Formerly: Master Catalog Services Index.
Description: Provides vendor, brand name and subject access to major manufacturers in all fields including aerospace and engineering components and products.

VENDOR PRODUCT COMPARISON (DESIGN ENGINEERING). see *BUSINESS AND ECONOMICS — Marketing And Purchasing*

338.025　　　　　GW
VERBAENDE, BEHOERDEN, ORGANISATIONEN DER UNGARISCHEN WIRTSCHAFT. (Text in English, German, Hungarian) 1993. a. DM.220. Verlag Hoppenstedt GmbH, Havelstr. 9, 64295 Darmstadt, Germany. TEL 49-6151-380-0. FAX 49-6151-380360. **Document type:** directory.
Description: Provides information on economic organizations, companies and institutions in Hungary.

338　　　　　US　　ISSN 1048-7174
HF5065.V5
VERMONT BUSINESS DIRECTORY. 1990. a. $295 (effective 1997). American Business Directories (Subsidiary of: American Business Information, Inc.), 5711 S. 86th Circle, Box 27347, Omaha, NE 68127. TEL 402-593-4600; 800-555-6124. FAX 402-331-5481. E-mail: jerry.venner@abii.com. index. (also avail. in magnetic tape; diskette format) **Document type:** directory.
●Also available online.
Also available on CD-ROM.
Description: Includes all businesses in the state compiled from the yellow pages and telephone-verified. Each listing includes company name, address, phone number, name of owner or manager, and employee size and sales volume codes, and credit rating codes.

670　　　　　US
VERMONT BUYER'S GUIDE. a. Agency of Development and Community Affairs, Pavilion Office Bldg., Montpelier, VT 05602. TEL 802-828-3211. FAX 802-828-3339. Ed. Lori McAllister. adv. contact: Geriame Smart. circ. 15,000. **Document type:** consumer publication.
Formerly: Vermont Directory of Manufacturers.

VERMONT MANUFACTURING & WHOLESALE - DISTRIBUTOR DIRECTORY. see *BUSINESS AND ECONOMICS — Production Of Goods And Services*

338　　　　　US　　ISSN 0083-5781
JK3030
VERMONT YEAR BOOK. 1818. a. $31.65 (effective 1995). National Survey, Chester, VT 05143. TEL 802-875-2121. FAX 802-875-2123. Ed. James A. Graham, Jr. R&P contact: James A. Graham, Jr. adv.: B&W page $410; adv. contact: James A. Graham, Jr. maps. circ. 2,000. **Document type:** directory.
Formerly: Walton's Register.
Description: Comprehensive directory of federal, state, and local government departments and officials in Vermont, with additional listings of businesses, manufacturing, travel and media companies, organizations and professionals.

382.025945　　　　　AT
VICTORIAN INTERNATIONAL TRADE DIRECTORY. 1994. a. Aus.$45. (Victorian Employers' Chamber of Commerce and Industry) Peter Isaacson Publications Pty. Ltd., 46-50 Porter St., Prahran, Vic. 3181, Australia. TEL 61-3-2457777. FAX 61-3-2457840. adv. contact: Joseph Dagher. **Document type:** directory.
Formerly: Victorian International Trade Directory and Handbook (ISSN 1321-7585)
Description: Details Victorian companies and their products and services.

380 640.73　　　　AT　　ISSN 0812-2970
VICTORIAN TASMANIAN RETAIL DIRECTORY. 1982. a. Aus.$145 (effective 1996). Jared Publishing, P.O. Box 51, Mitcham, Vic. 3132, Australia. TEL 61-3-8742415. FAX 61-38735951. Ed. Bruce Atkinson. circ. 1,000. **Document type:** directory.
Description: Lists leasing managers, shopping centers, retailers and suppliers to retail industry.

VIDEO BUSINESS. see *COMMUNICATIONS — Video*

380.1 384.55　　　　US
VIDEO DISTRIBUTOR'S DIRECTORY (YEAR). 1991. a. $170. Corbell Publishing, 4676 Admiralty Way, Ste. 300, Marina Del Rey, CA 90292. TEL 310-574-5337. FAX 310-574-5383. Pub. Maureen/Healy. **Document type:** directory.
Description: Complete guide to video distributors, rackjobbers, and direct response companies in North America.

380.1 384.55　　　　US
VIDEO DUPLICATION DIRECTORY. 1992. a. $207. Corbell Publishing, 4676 Admiralty Way, Ste. 300, Marina Del Rey, CA 90292. TEL 310-574-5337. FAX 310-574-5383. Pub. Maureen Healy. **Document type:** directory.
Description: Complete guide to video duplicators in the United States and Canada.

BUSINESS AND ECONOMICS — TRADE AND INDUSTRIAL DIRECTORIES

338.025 US ISSN 1047-2711
HC107.V8
VIRGINIA BUSINESS DIRECTORY. 1988. a. $395 (effective 1997). American Business Directories (Subsidiary of: American Business Information, Inc.), 5711 S. 86th Circle, Box 27347, Omaha, NE 68127. TEL 402-593-4600; 800-555-6124. FAX 402-331-5481. E-mail: jerry.venner@abii.com. index. (also avail. in magnetic tape; diskette format) **Document type:** directory.
●Also available online.
Also available on CD-ROM.
 Description: Includes all businesses in the state compiled from the yellow pages and telephone-verified. Each listing includes company name, complete address, phone number, name of owner or manager, and employee size and sales volume codes, and credit rating codes.

622 622 US ISSN 0882-3219
HC107.V8
VIRGINIA INDUSTRIAL DIRECTORY. 1940. a. $75 to non-members; members $60. Virginia Chamber of Commerce, 9 S. Fifth St., Richmond, VA 23219. TEL 800-477-7682. FAX 804-783-6112. Ed. Lou Ann Ladin. circ. 7,000. (also avail. in diskette format) **Document type:** directory.
●Also available on CD-ROM.
 Formerly (until 1980): Directory of Virginia Manufacturing and Mining (ISSN 0070-6574)
 Description: Provides a resource for locating sales contacts, products and services in Virginia.

670 US ISSN 1065-2493
HF5065.V8
VIRGINIA MANUFACTURERS DIRECTORY. 1993. a. $77 (diskette or CD-ROM $445) (effective 1997). Manufacturers' News, Inc., 1633 Central St., Evanston, IL 60201. TEL 847-864-7000. FAX 847-332-1100. Ed. Louise M. West. adv.: B&W page $1843; adv. contact: Charles Scherer. circ. 1,000. (diskette format) **Document type:** directory.
●Also available on CD-ROM.
 Description: Profiles 7,030 manufacturers listed 5 different ways; by product, alphabetically, geographically, by SIC and parent company.

VIRGINIA STATE AGENT HANDBOOK. see *INSURANCE*

W M D A MEMBERSHIP DIRECTORY AND BUYERS GUIDE; who's who in woodworking machinery distribution. (Woodworking Machinery Distributors Association) see *BUILDING AND CONSTRUCTION — Carpentry And Woodwork*

687 US ISSN 1067-6325
W W D SUPPLIER'S GUIDE. (Women's Wear Daily); women's apparel and accessories manufacturers. a. Fairchild Fashion & Merchandising Group (Subsidiary of: Capital Cities - A B C, Inc.), 7 W. 34th St., New York, NY 10001. TEL 212-630-3880. FAX 212-630-3868.

WALDEN'S A B C GUIDE AND PAPER PRODUCTION YEARBOOK. see *PAPER AND PULP*

338.7 UK ISSN 0306-185X
WALES BUSINESS DIRECTORY (CARDIFF). a. £12.95. Invest, Pearl Assurance House, Greyfriars Rd., Cardiff CF1 3AG, Wales. Ed. Mrs. G. Grace. adv. circ. 2,500. **Document type:** directory.
 Formerly: Industrial Directory of Wales.

380 UK
WALES BUSINESS DIRECTORY (SOLIHULL). a. £40. (Federation of Welsh Chambers of Commerce Inc.) Kemps Publishing Ltd., 11 The Swan Courtyard, Charles Edward Rd., Birmingham B26 1BU, England. TEL 44-121-765-4144. FAX 44-121-706-6210. **Document type:** directory.
 Formerly: Available from Wales.

347.73025 US ISSN 0742-1095
KF8700.A19
WANT'S FEDERAL - STATE COURT DIRECTORY (YEAR). 1984. a. $35. Want Publishing Co., 420 Lexington Ave., Rm. 300, New York, NY 10170-0399. TEL 212-687-3774. E-mail: rwant@msn.com. Ed. Robert S. Want. circ. 5,000. **Document type:** directory.
 —CCC.
 Description: Lists federal and state judges and court clerks, with explanations of each state's court system.

330 US ISSN 1048-8707
HG4057
WARD'S BUSINESS DIRECTORY OF U S PRIVATE AND PUBLIC COMPANIES. (Consists of 5 vols.; Vol.1: Alphabetic Listing A-F; Vol.2: Alphabetic Listing G-O; Vol.3: Alphabetic Listing P-Z; Vol.4: Special Features and Geographic Listing; Vol.5: Ranked by Sales Within 4-Digit SIC) 1961. a. $1210 for entire set; vols.1-4 $1045; vol.5 only $710 (effective 1993). Gale Research, 835 Penobscot Bldg., 645 Griswold St., Detroit, MI 48226-4094. TEL 313-961-2242; 800-877-4253. FAX 800-414-5043. E-mail: daniel__snyder@gale.com. Ed. Julie E. Towell. (also avail. in magnetic tape; diskette format)
 —CISTI.
 Formed by the 1989 merger of: Ward's Business Directory of U S Private and Public Companies. Vol.1; Over 11.5 Million Dollars in Sales (ISSN 1042-816X) & Ward's Business Directory of U S Private and Public Companies. Vol.2; From .5 to 11.5 Million Dollars (ISSN 1042-9190) & Ward's Business Directory of U S Private and Public Companies. Vol.3; Ranked by Sales within Industry (ISSN 1042-9204); Vol.1 was formerly (until 1989): Ward's Business Directory, Vol.1, U S Private Companies, Largest Private Plus Selected Public (ISSN 0897-1633); (until 1987): Ward's Directory of Largest U S Companies (ISSN 0882-7900); (until 1984): Ward's Directory of Largest U S Corporations (ISSN 0730-3122); (until 1980): Leading U S Corporations (ISSN 0270-1804). Vol.2 was formerly (until 1989): Ward's Business Directory, Vol.2, U S Private Companies up to 11 Million Dollars in Sales (ISSN 0897-1641); (until 1987): Ward's Business Directory of Major U S Private Companies (ISSN 0882-8008); (until 1984): Ward's Directory of Private U S Companies (ISSN 0737-4445). Vol.3 was formerly (1988-1989): Ward's Business Directory of U S Private Companies by Industry (ISSN 0897-1625).

380 US ISSN 1059-9266
HG4057
WARD'S SALES PROSPECTOR; a directory of leads by state and by industry. (5 vol. set) 1992. a.? Gale Research, 835 Penobscot Bldg., 645 Griswold St., Detroit, MI 48226-4094. TEL 313-961-2242; 800-877-4253. FAX 800-414-5043. E-mail: daniel__snyder@gale.com. Ed. Kenneth Estell. **Document type:** directory.

338.025 US ISSN 1043-9781
HF5065.W2
WASHINGTON BUSINESS DIRECTORY. 1988. a. $395 (effective 1997). American Business Directories (Subsidiary of: American Business Information, Inc.), 5711 S. 86th Circle, Box 27347, Omaha, NE 68127. TEL 402-593-4600; 800-555-6124. FAX 402-331-5481. E-mail: jerry.venner@abii.com. index. (also avail. in magnetic tape; diskette format) **Document type:** directory.
●Also available online.
Also available on CD-ROM.
 Description: Includes all businesses in the state compiled from the yellow pages and telephone-verified. Each listing includes company name, complete address, phone number, name of owner, manager, and employee size, sales volume codes, and credit rating codes.

338.025 US ISSN 1048-7077
HF5068.W3
WASHINGTON D.C. AREA BUSINESS DIRECTORY. 1990. a. $340 (effective 1997). American Business Directories (Subsidiary of: American Business Information, Inc.), 5711 S. 86th Circle, Box 27347, Omaha, NE 68127. TEL 402-593-4600; 800-555-6124. FAX 402-331-5481. E-mail: jerry.venner@abii.com. index. (also avail. in magnetic tape; diskette format) **Document type:** directory.
●Also available online.
Also available on CD-ROM.
 Description: Includes all businesses in the DC metro area compiled from the yellow pages and telephone-verified. Each listing includes company name, complete address, phone number, name of owner, manager, and employee size, sales volume codes, and credit rating codes.

670 US ISSN 0148-5687
T12
WASHINGTON MANUFACTURERS REGISTER. 1965. a. $99 (diskette $395) (effective 1996). (Washington Department of Community, Trade and Economic Development) Database Publishing Company, 1590 S. Lewis St., Anaheim, CA 92805-6423. TEL 714-778-6400. FAX 714-778-6811. (Subscr. to: Box 70024, Anaheim, CA 92825-0024. TEL 800-888-8434) Ed. Ken Gregory. adv. circ. 2,000. **Document type:** directory.
●Also available on CD-ROM.
 Former titles: Directory of Washington Manufacturers (ISSN 0148-3641); Directory of Washington State Manufacturers, Products, Industry, Location (ISSN 0419-3857)
 Description: Provides updated profiles on 6,500 manufacturers, assemblers, and fabricators in Washington state.

WASHINGTON TELECOM DIRECTORY. see *COMMUNICATIONS — Telephone And Telegraph*

328.025 GW ISSN 0171-9688
WER GEHOERT ZU WEM. triennial. Commerzbank AG, Neue Mainzer Str. 32-36, 60261 Frankfurt a.M., Germany. TEL 49-69-13622379. FAX 49-69-13622008. (U.S. subscr. to: European Business Publications Inc., Box 891, Darien, CT 06820. TEL 203-656-2701. FAX 203-655-8332) **Document type:** directory.

670 GW ISSN 0171-5674
WER LIEFERT WAS?. (Text in Dutch, English, French, German, Italian, Spanish) 1932. a. DM.268 (CD-ROM version DM.248) (effective 1997). Wer Liefert Was? GmbH, Normannenweg 16-20, 20537 Hamburg, Germany. TEL 49-40-25440-0. FAX 49-40-25440100. E-mail: info@wlonline.de; URL: http://www.wlwonline.de. adv. circ. 80,000. **Document type:** directory.
●Also available online. Vendor(s): FIZ Technik, Knight-Ridder Information, Inc., Lexis-Nexis.
Also available on CD-ROM.
 Description: Business-to-business directory in six languages covering approximately 184,000 companies located in Germany, Austria, Switzerland, Belgium, Luxembourg and the Netherlands.

338.025 GW
WER LIEFERT WAS? C D - MARKETING. (Text in Dutch, English, French, German, Italian, Spanish) 1986. s-a. DM.1600($1000) Wer Liefert Was? GmbH, Normannenweg 16-20, 20537 Hamburg, Germany. TEL 49-40-25440-0. FAX 49-40-25440100. E-mail: info@wlwonline.de; URL: http://www.wlwonline.de. circ. 12,500 (paid). **Document type:** directory.
 Description: Covers approximately 210,000 companies located in Germany, Austria, Switzerland, Belgium, Luxembourg, the Netherlands, the Czech Republic, Slovenia, Slovakia and Croatia.

670 GW
WER LIEFERT WAS? CENTRAL EUROPE. (Text in Croatian, Czech, English, French, German, Italian, Slovenian) 1992. a. (in 2 vols.). DM.98 (CD-ROM DM.148) (effective 1997). Wer Liefert Was? GmbH, Normannenweg 16-20, 20537 Hamburg, Germany. TEL 49-40-25440-0. FAX 49-40-25440100. E-mail: info@wlwonline.de; URL: http://www.wlwonline.de. circ. 20,000 (paid). **Document type:** directory.
●Also available on CD-ROM.
 Description: Business-to-business directory covering approximately 20,000 companies and their products and services in The Czech Republic, Slovenia, and Slovakia.

338.025 GW
▼**WER LIEFERT WAS? LIGHT.** (Text in Dutch, English, French, German, Italian, Spanish) 1996. a. DM.85. Wer Liefert Was? GmbH, Normannenweg 16-20, 20537 Hamburg, Germany. TEL 49-40-25440-0. FAX 49-40-25440100. E-mail: info@wlwonline.de; URL: http://www.wlwonline.de. circ. 10,000 (paid). **Document type:** directory.
●Available only on CD-ROM.
 Description: Business-to-business directory covering approximately 184,000 companies located in Germany, Austria, Switzerland, Belgium, Luxembourg and the Netherlands.

BUSINESS AND ECONOMICS — TRADE AND INDUSTRIAL DIRECTORIES

338.025 664   GW   ISSN 0171-4368
WER UND WAS IN DER DEUTSCHEN SUESSWARENINDUSTRIE. 1949. a. DM.186 (effective 1997). B. Behr's Verlag GmbH, Averhoffstr. 10, 22085 Hamburg, Germany. TEL 49-40-2270080. FAX 49-40-2201091. E-mail: behrs@behrs.de; URL: http://www.behrs.de. **Document type:** directory.
   Formerly (until 1974): Suesswaren Jahrbuch (ISSN 0448-1380)

338.025   US   ISSN 1047-9007
HC107.W5
WEST VIRGINIA BUSINESS DIRECTORY. 1988. a. $295 (effective 1997). American Business Directories (Subsidiary of: American Business Information, Inc.), 5711 S. 86th Circle, Box 27347, Omaha, NE 68127. TEL 402-593-4600; 800-555-6124. FAX 402-331-5481. E-mail: jerry.venner@abii.com. index. (also avail. in magnetic tape; diskette format) **Document type:** directory.
●Also available on CD-ROM.
   Description: Includes all businesses in the state compiled from the yellow pages and telephone-verified. Each listing includes company name, complete address, phone number, name of owner, manager, and employee size, sales volume codes, and credit rating codes.

670   US   ISSN 0893-2824
HD9727.W4
WEST VIRGINIA MANUFACTURERS REGISTER. 1987. a. $54 (diskette or CD-ROM $295) (effective 1997). Manufacturers' News, Inc., 1633 Central St., Evanston, IL 60201. TEL 847-864-7000. FAX 847-332-1100. Ed. Louise M. West. adv.: B&W page $1843; adv. contact: Charles Scherer. (diskette format) **Document type:** directory.
●Also available on CD-ROM.
   Description: Profiles 2,364 manufacturers by product, geographically by city, by SIC code, and alphabetically.

338   SA
WESTERN CAPE BUSINESS REGISTER. (Text in English) 1964. a. $130 (effective 1994). Braby's (Subsidiary of: Kohler Packaging Ltd.), P.O. Box 1426, Pinetown 3600, South Africa. TEL 27-31-7017021. FAX 27-31-7017036. Ed. A. Stagg. adv. (also avail. in diskette format) **Document type:** directory.
   Former titles: Cape Peninsula Directory & Cape Times Peninsula Directory (ISSN 0379-461X)

WESTERN STATES PETROLEUM INDUSTRY. see PETROLEUM AND GAS

792 380   US   ISSN 1090-7564
WHAT'S NEW FOR FAMILY FUN CENTERS. 1993. 9/yr. $24 (Canada $27; elsewhere $50) (effective 1997). Hunter Publishing Limited Partnership, 2101 S. Arlington Heights Rd., Ste. 150, Arlington Heights, IL 60005. TEL 847-427-9512. FAX 847-427-2097. Ed. Galynn Nordstrom. **Document type:** trade publication, consumer publication.
   Description: New products and services for owners and managers of family entertainment businesses.

670   UK   ISSN 0142-4971
WHAT'S NEW IN INDUSTRY. m. Miller Freeman Technical Ltd. (Subsidiary of: Miller Freeman plc), Miller Freeman House, 30 Calderwood St., London SE18 6QH, England. TEL 44-181-855-7777. FAX 44-181-854-7476. Ed. David Keighley. adv. contact: Paul Connolly. circ. 41,037. **Indexed:** Br.Ceram.Abstr., Int.Packag.Abstr. **Document type:** trade publication.

WHAT'S NEW IN INTERIORS. see INTERIOR DESIGN AND DECORATION

WHERE TO BUILD - WHERE TO REPAIR. see TRANSPORTATION — Ships And Shipping

WHERE TO BUY: CHEMICALS & CHEMICAL PLANT (YEAR). see BUSINESS AND ECONOMICS — Marketing And Purchasing

338.025 658   US
WHITE PAGES & DIRECTORY LISTINGS (YEAR). 1993. irreg., 3rd ed., July 1997. $2001 (Canada and Mexico $2015; elsewhere $2035) (effective 1997). Cowles - SIMBA Information (Subsidiary of: Cowles Business Media), 11 Riverbend Dr. S., Box 4949, Stamford, CT 06907-0949. TEL 203-358-9900; 800-307-2529. FAX 203-358-5811. E-mail: info@simbanet.com; URL: http://www.simbanet.com. **Document type:** trade publication.
   Description: Aims to provide insight into the regulatory and legislative changes surrounding white pages listings, and data on the policies and prices of the major telephone companies.

659.1   US   ISSN 0511-8794
WHITMARK DIRECTORY;* source book of talent, production and audio visual in the Southwest. 1967-68. a. $50. Whitmark Associates, Inc., 2908 McKinney Ave., Dallas, TX 75204-2431. adv. circ. 2,500. (back issues avail.)
   Description: Contains pictorial talent pages plus seven-state southwestern film-video industry producers and support services.

338   US   ISSN 0149-0281
HF5616.U5
WHO AUDITS AMERICA; a directory of publicly held corporations and the accounting firms who audit them. 1976. s-a. $125 hardcover. Data Financial Press, Box 668, Menlo Park, CA 94026. TEL 415-321-4553. Ed. S.P. Harris. circ. 2,500. (back issues avail.)

338.025   SZ
WHO OWNS WHOM; der schweizerische Beteiligungsatlas. a. (Schweizerischer Adressbuchverleger Verband) Orell Fuessli Verlag, Dietzingerstr. 3, CH-8036 Zurich, Switzerland. TEL 41-1-4667432. FAX 41-1-4667412. Eds. Ulrich Baer, Hansjuerg Saager. **Document type:** directory.

338   UK   ISSN 0302-4091
HD2927   CODEN: WOWFET
WHO OWNS WHOM. AUSTRALASIA AND FAR EAST. (In 2 vols.) 1971. a. £239. Dun & Bradstreet Ltd., Holmers Farm Way, High Wycombe, Bucks. HP12 4UL, England. TEL 44-1494-422000. FAX 44-1494-422260. Ed. Laura Morel. index. **Document type:** directory.
●Also available online.
—BLDSC (9311.917000).
   Formerly: Who Owns Whom. Australia and Japan International.

658   UK   ISSN 0140-4040
HG4135.Z5   CODEN: WOWREV
WHO OWNS WHOM. UNITED KINGDOM AND REPUBLIC OF IRELAND. (In 2 vols.) 1958. a. £338. Dun & Bradstreet Ltd., Holmers Farm Way, High Wycombe, Bucks. HP12 4UL, England. TEL 44-1494-422000. FAX 44-1494-422260. Ed. Laura Morel. index. **Document type:** directory.
●Also available online.
—BLDSC (9311.950000); CISTI.
   Formerly: Who Owns Whom. United Kingdom (ISSN 0083-9329)

380 700   US
WHOLE ARTS DIRECTORY. 1987. irreg., approx. triennial. $12.95 (effective 1997). Midmarch Arts Press, 300 Riverside Dr., New York, NY 10025. TEL 212-666-6990. Ed. Sylvia Moore. R&P contact: Cynthia Navaretta. **Document type:** directory.

WHO'S WHO; the MASA buyers' guide to blue ribbon mailing services. see ADVERTISING AND PUBLIC RELATIONS

WHO'S WHO IN CORRUGATED. see PAPER AND PULP

WHO'S WHO IN INSURANCE. see INSURANCE

WHO'S WHO IN LIVE ANIMAL TRADE & TRANSPORT. see TRANSPORTATION

338 332.3   UK   ISSN 0962-9017
WHO'S WHO IN MORTGAGE FINANCE. 1949. biennial. £50. Franey and Co. Ltd., South Quay Plaza, 183 Marsh Wall, London E14 9FS, England. **Document type:** directory.
   Former titles: Who's Who in Housing Finance; Building Societies Who's Who.

WHO'S WHO IN RISK MANAGEMENT. see INSURANCE

338.025   UK   ISSN 0956-3016
HG172.A2
WHO'S WHO IN THE CITY. a. £99. (Stock Exchange Council, London) Macmillan Reference Ltd., 25 Eccleston Pl., London SW1W 9NF, England. TEL 44-171-881-8000. FAX 44-171-881-8001. (Dist. in the U.S. by: Stockton Press, 345 Park Ave. S., 10th Fl., New York, NY 10010. TEL 212-689-9200. FAX 212-689-9711) **Document type:** directory.
—BLDSC (9312.320000).
   Description: Provides information on key London companies and their senior management.

338.025 613.1   UK
WHO'S WHO IN THE ENVIRONMENT: SCOTLAND. a. £6 (diskette £25). Environment Council, 21 Elizabeth St., London SW1W 9RP, England. TEL 44-171-824-8411. FAX 44-171-730-9941. URL: http://www.envirocom.com/tec. (also avail. in diskette format)
   Description: Guide for all who are concerned about the environment in Scotland.

WHO'S WHO IN THE FISH INDUSTRY. see FISH AND FISHERIES

WHO'S WHO IN THE MOTION PICTURE INDUSTRY; directors, producers, writers, & studio executives. see MOTION PICTURES

380.1 639.2   UK
WHO'S WHO IN THE TACKLE TRADE. a. £20($35) includes Tackle Talk International. Pendragon Publishing, The Red House, High St., Bushey, Watford, Herts WD2 3DE, England. TEL 44-181-950-6360. FAX 44-181-420-4163. Ed. Ron Sorkin; Pub. Ron Sorkin. R&P contact: Ron Sorkin. adv. contact: John Furlong. **Document type:** directory.

338   NE   ISSN 0928-7930
WIE LEVERT MERKEN. (Supplement to: Vraag en Aanbod (ISSN 0165-3954)) 1984. a. Kluwer BedrijfsInformatie B.V., Postbus 23, 7400 GA Deventer, Netherlands. TEL 31-570-648705. FAX 31-570-643015. adv.; illus. **Document type:** directory.
   Supersedes in part (in 1992): Merkenwijzer (ISSN 0921-9285)

338   NE   ISSN 0928-7949
WIE LEVERT PRODUKTEN EN DIENSTEN. (Supplement to: Vraag en Aanbod (ISSN 0165-3954)) 1937. a. Kluwer BedrijfsInformatie B.V., Postbus 23, 7400 GA Deventer, Netherlands. TEL 31-570-648705. FAX 31-570-643015. adv. **Document type:** directory
   Supersedes in part (in 1993): Wie Levert (Year) (ISSN 0922-4718)

338   NE
WIE LEVERT REGIO. (Supplement to: Vraag en Aanbod (ISSN 0165-3954)) a. Kluwer BedrijfsInformatie B.V., Postbus 23, 7400 GA Deventer, Netherlands. TEL 31-570-648705. FAX 31-570-643015. adv.; illus. **Document type:** directory.
   Supersedes in part (in 1993): Wie Levert (Year) (ISSN 0922-4718)

WINE AND SPIRIT INTERNATIONAL YEAR BOOK. see BEVERAGES

WINE & SPIRITS INDUSTRY MARKETING. see BEVERAGES

663.1   US
WINES AND VINES: DIRECTORY OF THE WINE INDUSTRY IN NORTH AMERICA. 1941. a. $50 (Canada & Mexico $60; elsewhere $70) (effective 1997). Hiaring Co., 1800 Lincoln Ave., San Rafael, CA 94901-1298. TEL 415-453-9700. FAX 415-453-2517. circ. 4,500. **Document type:** directory.
   Supersedes: Wines and Vines - Annual Directory of the Wine Industry (ISSN 0084-0351)

BUSINESS AND ECONOMICS — TRADE AND INDUSTRIAL DIRECTORIES

384.5 US
TK6570.M6
WIRELESS INDUSTRY DIRECTORY. a. $249 (effective 1996). Phillips Business Information, Inc., 1201 Seven Locks Rd., Potomac, MD 20854. TEL 301-424-3338. FAX 301-309-3847. E-mail: pbi@phillips.com. Ed. Bill Gelfield. **Document type:** directory.
Former titles: Cellular - Mobile Communications Directory (ISSN 1076-1837); Mobile Communications Directory (ISSN 1055-1980)
Description: Lists over 4,000 manufacturers, distributors, and service providers in the mobile communications industry. Includes names, addresses, telephone numbers, contact information and product information.

338.025 US ISSN 1048-7433
HF5065.W6
WISCONSIN BUSINESS DIRECTORY. 1985. a. $395 (effective 1997). American Business Directories (Subsidiary of: American Business Information, Inc.), 5711 S. 86th Circle, Box 27347, Omaha, NE 68127. TEL 402-593-4600; 800-555-6124. FAX 402-331-5481. E-mail: jerry.venner@abii.com. index. (also avail. in magnetic tape; diskette format) **Document type:** directory.
●Also available online.
Also available on CD-ROM.
Description: Includes all businesses in the state compiled from the yellow pages and telephone-verified. Each listing includes company name, complete address, phone number, name of owner, manager, and employee size, sales volume codes, and credit rating codes.

670 US
WISCONSIN BUSINESS SERVICE DIRECTORY. 1987. a. $136 (diskette $550) (effective 1996). (Wisconsin Manufacturers & Commerce) W M C Service Corporation, 501 E. Washington Ave., Box 352, Madison, WI 53701-0352. TEL 608-258-3400. FAX 608-258-3413. Eds. M.A. Lange, J.L. Mandt. adv. (also avail. in diskette format) **Document type:** directory.
Formerly: Wisconsin Services Directory.
Description: Profiles 16,000 business-to-business service firms listed alphabetically, geographically by city, product or service, and S.I.C. codes.

670 US ISSN 0738-0070
HD9727.W6
WISCONSIN MANUFACTURERS REGISTER. a. $109 (diskette or CD-ROM $545) (effective 1997). Manufacturers' News, Inc., 1633 Central St., Evanston, IL 60201. TEL 847-864-7000. FAX 847-332-1100. Ed. Louise M. West. adv.: B&W page $1843; adv. contact: Charles Scherer. illus. (diskette format) **Document type:** directory.
●Also available on CD-ROM.
Description: Profiles 11,775 manufacturers; includes product, alphabetical, geographical, SIC, and parent company.

380 301.412 US
WOMEN'S YELLOW PAGES.* 1977. a. $6. 13601 Ventura Blvd., Ste. 374, Sherman Oaks, CA 91423-3788. TEL 310-398-5761. Ed. Nancy Sardella. adv. circ. 20,000. (back issues avail.)

338.025 677 UK ISSN 0268-3601
WOOL TRADE DIRECTORY OF THE WORLD. 1985. biennial. £150. World Textile Publications Ltd., Perkin House, 1 Longlands St., Bradford, W. Yorkshire BD1 2TP, England. TEL 44-1274-378800. FAX 44-1274-378811. E-mail: 104470.3070@compuserve.com; URL: http://www.vitalo.com/worldtextile. **Document type:** directory.

382 US ISSN 1062-1172
HF54.U5
WORLD BUSINESS DIRECTORY. 1992. a. 395. (World Trade Centers Association) Gale Research, 835 Penobscot Bldg., 645 Griswold St., Detroit, MI 48266-4094. TEL 313-961-2242; 800-877-4253. FAX 800-414-5043. E-mail: daniel_snyder@gale.com. Eds. Meghan A. O'Meara, Kimberly A. Peterson. **Document type:** directory.
—CISTI.
Description: Compiles information on over 100,000 companies in 190 countries.

WORLD DIRECTORY OF ADVERTISING AGENCIES. see ADVERTISING AND PUBLIC RELATIONS

WORLD DIRECTORY OF BUSINESS INFORMATION LIBRARIES. see LIBRARY AND INFORMATION SCIENCES

WORLD DIRECTORY OF EXHIBITIONS AND TRADE FAIRS. see MEETINGS AND CONGRESSES

338.025 323.4 UN
WORLD DIRECTORY OF HUMAN RIGHTS RESEARCH AND TRAINING INSTITUTIONS. (Subseries of: World Social Science Information Directories) 1987. triennial. price varies. UNESCO Publishing, 7 Place de Fontenoy, 75352 Paris 07 SP, France. TEL 33-1-45684300. FAX 33-1-45685741. URL: http://www.unesco.org/publications. (Dist. in the U.S. by: Bernan Associates, 4611-F Assembly Dr., Lanham MD 20706-4391. TEL 800-274-4888. FAX 800-865-3450) (also avail. in microfiche) **Document type:** directory.
●Also available online.
Also available on CD-ROM.
Formerly: World Directory of Human Rights Teaching and Research.

382 387 UK ISSN 0951-5879
WORLD DIRECTORY OF LINER SHIPPING AGENTS. 1987. a. £50($85) E M A P - Finance & Freight Ltd., 151 Rosebery Ave., London EC1R 4QX, England. TEL 44-171-505-3516. FAX 44-171-505-3535. Ed. Mark Lambert. circ. 1,000. (back issues avail.) **Document type:** directory.
Description: A shippers' guide to who-represents-whom in the intermodal shipping industry.

WORLD DIRECTORY OF MARKETING INFORMATION SOURCES. see BUSINESS AND ECONOMICS — Marketing And Purchasing

WORLD DIRECTORY OF NON-OFFICIAL STATISTICAL SOURCES. see STATISTICS

WORLD DIRECTORY OF NON-OFFICIAL STATISTICS SOURCES. see BUSINESS AND ECONOMICS — Abstracting, Bibliographies, Statistics

WORLD DRINKS DATABOOK. see BEVERAGES

333.79 FR
WORLD ENERGY CONFERENCE. DIRECTORY OF ENERGY INFORMATION CENTRES IN THE WORLD. (Text in English, French) 1976. triennial, latest 3rd, 1983. 185 F. Institut Francais de l'Energie, 3 rue Henri Heine, 75016 Paris, France. FAX 40-50-07-54. TELEX IFENERG 615867. **Document type:** directory.

666.1 IT
WORLD GLASSWARE INDUSTRY DIRECTORY. (Text in English) 1990. a. $130 (effective 1997). Artech Publishing s.r.l., Via Gramsci 63, 20032 Cormano (MI), Italy. TEL 39-2-66302904. FAX 39-2-66302914. Ed. Marco Pinetti. **Document type:** directory.
Description: Provides company profiles, addresses, officers, plants, number of employees, capital, trademarks, areas of activity, and innovations.

WORLD HEALTHCARE MARKETING DIRECTORY. see MEDICAL SCIENCES

WORLD JEWELOGUE (YEAR). see JEWELRY, CLOCKS AND WATCHES

WORLD LEASING YEARBOOK (YEAR). see BUSINESS AND ECONOMICS — Economic Situation And Conditions

WORLD MARKET FOR CONVENIENCE STORE RETAILING. see BUSINESS AND ECONOMICS — Production Of Goods And Services

WORLD PHARMACEUTICAL DIRECTORY. see PHARMACY AND PHARMACOLOGY

WORLD TIME CATALOGUE (YEAR). see JEWELRY, CLOCKS AND WATCHES

WORLD TOBACCO DIRECTORY. see TOBACCO

338 US
WORLD TRADE CENTERS ASSOCIATION. DIRECTORY. 1972. s-a. $450 to non-members; members $150. World Trade Centers Association, 1 World Trade Center, Ste. 7701, New York, NY 10048. TEL 212-432-7626. (Subscr. to: Gale Research Inc., 935 Penobscot Bldg., Detroit, MI 48226. TEL 800-877-GALE) Ed. J. Squasoni. circ. 10,000. **Document type:** directory.

382 US ISSN 1058-1618
HF54.U5
WORLD TRADE RESOURCES GUIDE; a guide to resources on importing from and exporting to the major trading nations of the world. 1992. s-a. Gale Research, 835 Penobscot Bldg., 645 Griswold St., Detroit, MI 48226-4094. TEL 313-961-2242; 800-877-4253. FAX 800-414-5043. E-mail: daniel_snyder@gale.com. Ed. Kenneth Estell. **Document type:** directory.

338.025 658.8 UK
WORLD'S MAJOR COMPANIES DIRECTORY. irreg., latest 1994. £275($550) (effective 1997). Euromonitor, 87-88 Turnmill St., London EC1M 5QU, England. TEL 44-171-251-8024. FAX 44-171-608-3149. E-mail: info@euromonitor.com; URL: http://www.euromonitor.com. (Addr. in N. America: Euromonitor International, 122 S. Michigan Ave., Ste. 1200, Chicago, IL 60603. TEL 800-577-3876. FAX 312-922-1157) **Document type:** directory.
Description: Lists major national and multinational companies, arranged by country.

WORLD'S MAJOR SOFT DRINK COMPANIES. see BEVERAGES

338 US ISSN 1058-5818
HD69.C6
WORLDWIDE DIRECTORY OF CONSULTANTS AND CONTRACTORS. 1992. biennial. $110 (foreign $115) (effective 1996 & 1997). Projects Research, Inc., Box 2558, Falls Church, VA 22042. TEL 703-698-9330. FAX 703-698-9837. Ed. Joe Lill. **Document type:** directory.
Description: Lists architects, consulting engineers, planners and contractors engaged in construction activities, urban and rural development, and environmental engineering.

338.025 547.5 US
WORLDWIDE DIRECTORY OF MULTICHIP MODULE VENDORS AND RELATED COMPANIES. a. International Society for Hybrid Microelectronics, 1850 Centennial Park Dr., Ste. 105, Reston, VA 22091-1517. TEL 703-758-1060. FAX 703-758-1066. **Document type:** directory.
Description: Lists up-to-date compilation of finished module and substrate suppliers, MCM design houses, CAD tool vendors, base substrate suppliers, thin film dielectric materials, contract assembly services, bare die sources, testing and inspection services and equipments, and selected academic and research organizations.

382 US ISSN 1056-456X
HF5429.23
WORLDWIDE FRANCHISE DIRECTORY. 1991. irreg. Gale Research, 835 Penobscot Bldg., 645 Griswold St., Detroit, MI 48266-4094. TEL 313-961-2242; 800-877-4253. FAX 800-414-5043. E-mail: daniel_snyder@gale.com. Ed. Susan Boyles Martin.

350.6 US ISSN 0894-1521
JF37
WORLDWIDE GOVERNMENT DIRECTORY. 1981. a. (plus q. updates). $357 for base vol.; including q. updates $497 (effective 1997). Keesing's Worldwide, LLC, 7979 Old Georgetown Rd., Ste. 900, Bethesda, MD 20814. TEL 301-718-8770. FAX 301-718-8494. E-mail: keesings.com; URL: http://www.keesings.com. Ed. Charlie Liang; Stephen Orlofsky. adv. circ. 2,000. **Document type:** directory.
●Also available on CD-ROM. Producer(s): Knight-Ridder, Inc.
—CISTI.
Formerly: Lambert's Worldwide Government Directory (ISSN 0276-900X)
Description: Contains the names and addresses of government officials in every country in the world. Includes data on international organizations and foreign embassies abroad.

CALCULATING MACHINES

338.025 659.1   US
WORLDWIDE YELLOW PAGES MARKETS (YEAR). biennial, latest no.4, Sept. 1997. $7006 (Canada and Mexico $7020; elsewhere $7040) (effective Sept. 1997). Cowles - SIMBA Information (Subsidiary of: Cowles Business Media), 11 Riverbend Dr. S., Box 4949, Stamford, CT 06907-0949. TEL 203-358-9900; 800-307-2529. FAX 203-358-5811. E-mail: info@simbanet.com; URL: http://www.simbanet.com. **Document type:** trade publication.
   Former titles: Worldwide Yellow Pages Opportunities (Year); (until 1995): New Opportunities in Talking Yellow Pages (Year).
   Description: Assesses the opportunities and pitfalls in the global yellow pages marketplace.

920 011   US   ISSN 0084-2699
PS1
WRITERS DIRECTORY. 1970. biennial. $130. Gale Research, 835 Penobscot Bldg., 645 Griswold St., Detroit, MI 48226-4094. TEL 313-961-2242; 800-877-4253. FAX 800-414-5043. E-mail: daniel_snyder@gale.com. circ. 7,500. **Document type:** directory.
   —BLDSC (9364.701000).
   Description: Contains biographical, bibliographical, and contact information for more than 15,000 living authors with their professional addresses, pen names, genres, career information, and titles with publication dates.

338.025   US   ISSN 1048-7425
HF5065.W8
WYOMING BUSINESS DIRECTORY. 1989. a. $295 (effective 1997). American Business Directories (Subsidiary of: American Business Information, Inc.), 5711 S. 86th Circle, Box 27347, Omaha, NE 68127. TEL 402-593-4600; 800-555-6124. FAX 402-331-5481. E-mail: jerry.venner@abii.com. index. (also avail. in magnetic tape; diskette format) **Document type:** directory.
   ●Also available online.
   Also available on CD-ROM.
   Description: Includes all businesses in the state compiled from the yellow pages and telephone-verified. Each listing includes company name, complete address, phone number, name of owner, manager, and employee size, sales volume codes, and credit rating codes.

670   US   ISSN 0511-0289
HD9727.W8
WYOMING DIRECTORY OF MANUFACTURING AND MINING. 1956. a. $39 (diskette or CD-ROM $195) (effective 1997). Manufacturers' News, Inc., 1633 Central St., Evanston, IL 60201-1505. TEL 847-864-7000. FAX 847-322-1100. Ed. Louise M. West. **Document type:** directory.
   Description: Profiles approximately 1200 manufacturing firms.

YEARBOOK OF EUROPEAN TELECOMMUNICATIONS. see *COMMUNICATIONS*

338.025 659.1   US   ISSN 1071-2461
YELLOW PAGES & DIRECTORY REPORT; the newsletter for the yellow page & directory publishing industry. 1985. bi-w. (22/yr.). $549 (outside N. America $549) (effective 1997). Cowles - SIMBA Information (Subsidiary of: Cowles Business Media), 11 Riverbend Dr. S., Box 4949, Stamford, CT 06907-0949. TEL 203-358-9900; 800-307-2529. FAX 203-358-5811. E-mail: simbainfo@simbanet.com; URL: http://www.simbanet.com. Ed. Natalie Schwartz. adv. **Document type:** newsletter.
   ●Also available online. Vendor(s): Information Access Co.
   —CCC.
   Description: Covers the activities of utility and independent yellow pages publishers, certified marketing representatives, sales agents, and yellow pages associations.

338.025 659.1   US
YELLOW PAGES MARKET FORECAST (YEAR). 1986. a. $2001 (Canada and Mexico $2015; elsewhere $2035) (effective 1997). Cowles - SIMBA Information (Subsidiary of: Cowles Business Media), 11 Riverbend Dr. S., Box 4949, Stamford, CT 06907-0949. TEL 203-358-9900; 800-307-2529. FAX 203-358-5811. E-mail: simbainfo@simbanet.com; URL: http://www.simbanet.com. **Document type:** trade publication.
   Description: Reviews the significant developments in the yellow pages market, and provides revenue and market share statistics, analysis on new media products and international ventures, litigation, acquisitions, and divestitures at leading companies.

YELLOW PAGES OF GOLF; for North America. see *SPORTS AND GAMES — Ball Games*

338.025 659.1   US
YELLOW PAGES SALES & MARKETING (YEAR). irreg., no.2, 1996. $2495 (Canada and Mexico $2515; elsewhere $2531) (effective 1997). Cowles - SIMBA Information (Subsidiary of: Cowles Business Media), 11 Riverbend Dr. S., Box 4949, Stamford, CT 06907-0949. TEL 203-358-9900; 800-307-2529. FAX 203-358-5811. E-mail: info@simbanet.com; URL: http://www.simbanet.com. **Document type:** trade publication.
   Description: Analyzes the sales and marketing of yellow pages directories as well as technological developments in the industry.

338.025 659.1   US
YELLOW PAGES 2000: FORECAST & ANALYSIS. 1994. $4995 (effective 1997). Cowles - SIMBA Information (Subsidiary of: Cowles Business Media), 11 Riverbend Dr. S., Box 4949, Stamford, CT 06907-0949. TEL 203-358-9900; 800-307-2529. FAX 203-358-5811. E-mail: info@simbanet.com; URL: http://www.simbanet.com. **Document type:** trade publication.
   Description: Assesses the growth potential of the yellow pages through the year 2000.

382   YU   ISSN 0084-4349
YUGOSLAV EXPORT - IMPORT DIRECTORY. (Text in English) 1956. irreg. free. (Yugoslav Chamber of Economy) Yugoslaviapublic, Knez Mihailova 10, P.O. Box 447, 11001 Belgrade, Yugoslavia. FAX 011-622-858. TELEX 11-125. adv. circ. 7,000. **Document type:** directory.

338   SA
ZAMBIA TRADE DIRECTORY. a. R.60 (effective 1996). Braby's (Subsidiary of: Kohler Packaging Ltd.), P.O. Box 1426, Pinetown 3600, South Africa. TEL 27-31-7017021. FAX 27-31-7017036. adv. **Document type:** directory.

382   RH
ZIMBABWE EXPORT DIRECTORY. Running title: C Z I Zimbabwe Export Directory. 1983. a. Z.$75.15 (foreign Z.$79.25) (effective 1997). (Confederation of Zimbabwe Industries) Thomson Publications Zimbabwe (Pvt) Ltd., P.O. Box 1683, Harare, Zimbabwe. TEL 263-4-736835. FAX 263-4-752390. circ. 2,500. **Document type:** directory.
   Description: Includes alphabetical listings of local manufacturing companies and products, as well as all matters related to import and export in the Zimbabwean context.

382   RH
ZIMBABWE NATIONAL CHAMBER OF COMMERCE DIRECTORY. Abbreviated title: Z N C C Directory. (Text in English) 1983. a. Z.$69.80 (foreign Z.$74.30) (effective 1997). (Zimbabwe National Chamber of Commerce) Thomson Publications Zimbabwe (Pvt) Ltd., P.O. Box 1683, Harare, Zimbabwe. TEL 263-4-736835. FAX 263-4-752390. adv. circ. 1,800. **Document type:** directory.
   Description: Gives alphabetical and classified index of products and services offered by the ZNCC and its members, as well as procedural information on all aspects of local commercial business activity.

800 & FAX TRAVEL DIRECTORY. see *TRAVEL AND TOURISM*

380   CN
1000 PLUS TRADE AND PROFESSIONAL ASSOCIATIONS IN THE TORONTO REGION. 1987. irreg. Can.$50 to non-members; members Can.$40 (effective 1997). Board of Trade of Metropolitan Toronto, P.O. Box 60, 1 First Canadian Place, Toronto, ON M5X 1C1, Canada. TEL 416-366-6811. Ed. Mary de Reus. **Document type:** directory.
   Former titles: Directory of Trade and Professional Associations in the Toronto Region; Directory of Trade and Professional Association in Metropolitan Toronto (ISSN 0836-4958); Directory of Local and National Business, Trade and Professional Associations in Metropolitan Toronto.
   Description: Lists 1,200 local, provincial, national and international associations serving the interests of the business community in the Toronto region.

382   FI   ISSN 0786-5546
3000 LARGEST COMPANIES IN FINLAND (YEAR). (Text in English, Finnish) a. FIM 395. Yritystieto Oy, PL 148, 00181 Helsinki 18, Finland. TEL 358-0-648292. FAX 358-0-648250. Ed. Borje Thilman. stat.
   Description: Provides financial, sales, addresses and other information on 3000 companies, ranked by sales volume.

CALCULATING MACHINES

see Computers–Calculating Machines

CARDIOVASCULAR DISEASES

see Medical Sciences–Cardiovascular Diseases

CARPENTRY AND WOODWORK

see Building and Construction–Carpentry and Woodwork

CERAMICS, GLASS AND POTTERY

see also Art

666   UK   ISSN 0268-9847
ADVANCED CERAMICS REPORT; an international newsletter. 1986. m. £387($637) (effective 1998) International Newsletters, P.O. Box 133, Witney OX8 6ZH, England. TEL 44-1993-824130. FAX 44-1993-824150. E-mail: in@intnews.com. Ed Jon Binner. bk.rev.; charts; stat. (also avail. in microform from UMI; back issues avail.) **Indexed:** Alloys Ind., Eng.Mat.Abstr., Met.Abstr.Ind., Met.Abstr. Nonfer.Met.Alert, PCC Alert, Steels Alert, World Alum.Abstr. **Document type:** newsletter.
   —BLDSC (0696.836000); CISTI; SWETS. **CCC.**
   Description: Focuses on microprocessor applications and their implications for commerce and industry.

ADVANCED COMPOSITES BULLETIN; an international newsletter. see *PLASTICS*

ADVANCED MATERIALS NEWS. see *ENGINEERING — Engineering Mechanics And Materials*

AIRBRUSH ACTION. see *ART*

AMERICAN ASSOCIATION FOR CRYSTAL GROWTH NEWSLETTER. see *CHEMISTRY — Crystallography*

666.1   US   ISSN 0738-3290
AMERICAN CARNIVAL GLASS NEWS. 1966. q. $15 membership. American Carnival Glass Association, c/o Larry Yung, Jr., Sec., 9621 Springwater Ln., Miamisburg, OH 45342. TEL 513-439-0697. Ed. Joan Anderson. adv. circ. 900. (back issues avail.) **Document type:** newsletter.

CERAMICS, GLASS AND POTTERY

666   US   ISSN 0002-7812
CODEN: ACSBA7
AMERICAN CERAMIC SOCIETY. BULLETIN. Variant title: Ceramic Bulletin. 1922. m. $50 to non-members. American Ceramic Society, 735 Ceramic Pl., Westerville, OH 43081. TEL 614-794-5890. FAX 614-794-5854. Ed. Patricia Janeway; Pub. Paul Holbrook. R&P contact: Patricia Janeway. adv. contact: Annette Delagrange. bk.rev.; charts; illus.; tr.lit.; index. circ. 15,000. (reprint service avail.) Indexed: A.S.& T.Ind., AESIS, Alloys Ind., Art & Archaeol.Tech.Abstr., ASCA, Br.Ceram.Abstr., C.R.I.Abstr., C.R.I.Curr.Cont., Cadscan, Ceram.Abstr., Chem.Abstr., Concr.Abstr., Curr.Cont., Energy Info.Abstr., Eng.Ind., Eng.Mat.Abstr., Environ.Abstr., Excerp.Med., Fuel & Energy Abstr., GeoRef., Ind.Sci.Rev., INIS Atomind., INSPEC (1968-), Lead Abstr., Mat.Sci.Cit.Ind., Met.Abstr.Ind., Nonfer.Met.Alert, PCC Alert, PROMT, Sci.Cit.Ind., SSCI, Steels Alert, World Alum.Abstr., Zincscan. Document type: bulletin, trade publication.
—BLDSC (0812.000000); AskIEEE; CASDDS; CISTI; Ei; Genuine Article; KR SourceOne; Linda Hall; SWETS; UMI; UnCover. **CCC.**

666 016   US   ISSN 0002-7820
TP785   CODEN: JACTAW
AMERICAN CERAMIC SOCIETY. JOURNAL. 1899. m. $425 to non-members; members $92 (effective 1998). American Ceramic Society, 735 Ceramic Pl., Westerville, OH 43081. TEL 614-794-5890. FAX 614-794-5854. Ed. John B. Wachtman, Jr.; Pub. Paul Holbrook. R&P contact: Russ Jordon. adv. contact: Annette Delagrange. charts; illus.; index; circ. 4,000 (paid). (also avail. in microform from PMC,UMI; reprint service avail. from UMI; back issues avail.) Indexed: A.S.& T.Ind., AESIS, Alloys Ind., Appl.Mech.Rev., Art & Archaeol.Tech.Abstr., ASCA, Br.Ceram.Abstr., Bull.Thermodyn.& Thermochem., C.R.I.Abstr., C.R.I.Curr.Cont., Cadscan, Ceram.Abstr., Chem.Cit.Ind., Chem.Infd., Compumath, Concr.Abstr., Curr.Cont., Energy Info.Abstr., Eng.Ind., Eng.Mat.Abstr., Environ.Abstr., Excerp.Med., IBR, Ind.Sci.Rev., INIS Atomind., INSPEC (1968-), Lead Abstr., Met.Abstr., Met.Abstr.Ind., Mineral.Abstr., Nonfer.Met.Alert, Steels Alert, World Alum.Abstr., Zincscan. Document type: academic/scholarly publication.
—BLDSC (4684.000000); AskIEEE; CASDDS; CIS; CISTI; Ei; Genuine Article; KR SourceOne; Linda Hall; SWETS; UMI; UnCover. **CCC.**
Supersedes (in 1918): American Ceramic Society. Transactions (ISSN 0096-7394)
Description: Contains records of original research that provide or lead to fundamental principles of ceramics. Papers explore mechanisms, stuctures, and behaviors as they relate to ceramic materials.
Refereed Serial

AMERICAN CLAY EXCHANGE. see ANTIQUES

666.1   US   ISSN 0002-8649
HD6350.G5   CODEN: AGLRAE
AMERICAN GLASS REVIEW. 1882. 7/yr. $25 includes American Glass Review Glass Factory Directory as 7th issue. Doctorow Communications, Inc., 1011 Clifton Ave., Ste. B1, Clifton, NJ 07013-3518. TEL 201-779-1600. FAX 201-779-3242. Ed. Susan Grisham. adv.; bk.rev.; charts; illus.; mkt.; pat.; stat.; tr.lit. circ. 2,000. (also avail. in microform from UMI) Indexed: Alloys Ind., Chem.Abstr., Eng.Mat.Abstr., Int.Packag.Abstr., Met.Abstr., Met.Abstr.Ind., Nonfer.Met.Alert, PCC Alert, Steels Alert, World Alum.Abstr.
—CASDDS; CISTI; Linda Hall; UMI. **CCC.**

666   IT   ISSN 0391-5816
ANDAR PER CERAMICHE NEL MONDO. (Text in English, French, German, Italian, Portuguese, Spanish) 1969. a. L.200000($200) Via Statutaria 46-C, 42013 Casalgrande, Reggio Emilia, Italy. TEL 0522-846239. FAX 0522-841063. Ed. Mirko A. Montanari. adv.; index, cum.index; circ. 8,000 (controlled).
Formerly: Andar per Ceramiche (ISSN 0003-2891)

ANNUAL BOOK OF A S T M STANDARDS. VOLUME 15.01. REFRACTORIES, MANUFACTURED CARBON AND GRAPHITE PRODUCTS; ACTIVATED CARBON. see ENGINEERING — Engineering Mechanics And Materials

666 621.9   IT
ANNUARIO A N D I L (YEAR). 1990. a. Lit.35000 (effective 1997). (Associazione Nazionale degli Industriali dei Laterizi) Gruppo Editoriale Faenza Editrice S.p.A., Via Pier. de Crescenzi, 44, 48018 Faenza RA, Italy. TEL 39-546-663688. FAX 39-546-660440. E-mail: gefe.vendita@uno. dinamica.it; gefe.info@uno.dinamica.it. Ed. Franco Rossi. adv.; B&W page Lit.1830000, color page Lit.2040000. circ. 5,000. **Document type:** directory.
Description: Publishes news about brick industry.

666   BL   ISSN 0100-8633
ANNUARIO BRASILEIRO DE CERAMICA.* 1978. a. $15. Associacao Brasileira de Ceramica, Rua Pedro de Toledo 282, Vila Clementino, 04039 Sao Paulo, Brazil.

666   IT   ISSN 0066-4472
ANNUARIO CERAMICA. 1970. a. L.6000($20) Casa Editrice Palazzo Vecchio, Via Vittorio Emanuele, 155, 50134 Florence, Italy. adv.

APPLIED CLAY SCIENCE; an international journal on the application and technology of clays and clay minerals. see EARTH SCIENCES — Geology

ARCHITECTS' GUIDE TO GLASS, METAL & GLAZING. see ARCHITECTURE

ARS CERAMICA. see ANTIQUES

ART CALENDAR. see ART

666   IT   ISSN 0004-3478
ARTEREGALO; rivista bimestrale della cristalleria, porcellana, ceramica, articoli da regalo e di qualita per la casa. (In 3 rotating editions: Artedregalo Tavola, Artedregalo Oggettistica, Artedregalo International) (Text in English, French, German, Italian and Spanish) 1966. bi-m. (8/yr.). L.240000 (effective 1996). Pubbliemme International s.r.l., Via Caracciolo 77, 20155 Milan, Italy. TEL 39-2-33100954. FAX 39-2-313864. Ed. Giorgio Brautigam; Pub. Massimo Martini. adv.: B&W page L.2400000, color page L.3200000; 220 x 290; adv. contact: Graziella Giobbi Martini. illus. circ. 23,700. **Document type:** trade publication.
Description: For dealers of ceramics, porcelain, crystalware, silverware, gift items and high quality goods for the home.

ARTICOLI CASALINGHI ED ELETTROCASALINGHI. see INTERIOR DESIGN AND DECORATION — Furniture And House Furnishings

ARTSFOCUS. see MUSEUMS AND ART GALLERIES

666.1   JA
CODEN: AGKHAD
ASAHI GLASS COMPANY. RESEARCH CENTER. REPORTS/ASAHI GARASU KENKYU HOKOKU. (Text in English, Japanese; summaries in English) 1950. s-a. exchange basis. Asahi Glass Co., Ltd., Research Center - Asahi Garasu K.K. Chuoh-Kenkyusho, 1150 Hazawa-cho, Kanagawa-ku, Yokohama 221, Japan. TEL 045-334-6111. FAX 045-334-6187. Ed. Kimihiko Satoh. cum.index. circ. 1,000. Indexed: Alloys Ind., Chem.Abstr., Eng.Mat.Abstr., INIS Atomind., JCT, JTA, Met.Abstr.Ind., Nonfer.Met.Alert, PCC Alert, Steels Alert, World Alum.Abstr. **Document type:** corporate report.
—BLDSC (7592.420000); CASDDS; Linda Hall.
Formerly: Asahi Glass Company. Research Laboratory. Reports (ISSN 0004-4210)

666.1   NE   ISSN 0589-2546
ASSOCIATION INTERNATIONALE POUR L'HISTOIRE DU VERRE. ANNALES DES CONGRES. 1958. triennial, 13th, 1995. price varies. Association Internationale pour l'Histoire du Verre - International Association for the History of Glass, AIHV Secretariat, P.O. Box 177, 7240 AD Lochem, Netherlands. TEL 31-573-256272. FAX 31-573-256272. Ed. Annet van Wiechen. (back issues avail.) **Document type:** proceedings.

666   NE   ISSN 0447-9823
ASSOCIATION INTERNATIONALE POUR L'HISTOIRE DU VERRE. BULLETIN. (Text in English, French and German) 1962. irreg., no.9, 1983. price varies. Association Internationale pour l'Histoire du Verre - International Association for the History of Glass, AIHV Secretariat, P.O. Box 177, 7240 AD Lochem, Netherlands. TEL 31-573-256272. FAX 31-573-256272. Ed. A. van Wiechmen. bk.rev. circ. 200. Indexed: Br.Archaeol.Abstr. **Document type:** bulletin.

666   AT   ISSN 1018-6689
TP785   CODEN: JAUSEL
AUSTRALASIAN CERAMIC SOCIETY. JOURNAL. 1965. s-a. Aus.$108 (effective 1998). Australasian Ceramic Society, c/o ANSTO, PMBI, Menai, N.S.W. 2234, Australia. TEL 61-2-7173477. FAX 61-2-5439205. Ed. C. Sorrell. adv.; bk.rev.; charts; illus.; cum.index. circ. 700. (also avail. in microfiche; back issues avail.; reprint service avail. from ISI) Indexed: AESIS, Alloys Ind., C.R.I.Abstr., Cadscan, Ceram.Abstr., Chem.Abstr., Curr.Cont., Eng.Mat.Abstr., INIS Atomind., INSPEC, Lead Abstr., Met.Abstr., Met.Abstr.Ind., Nonfer.Met.Alert, PCC Alert, Met.Zh., Steels Alert, World Alum.Abstr., Zincscan. **Document type:** bulletin.
—AskIEEE; CASDDS; CISTI; Genuine Article; KR SourceOne; Linda Hall; SWETS. **CCC.**
Formerly (until 1992): Australian Ceramic Society. Journal (ISSN 0004-881X)
Description: Covers the fields of ceramic technology, basic science and related materials, including new advances in ceramic materials.
Refereed Serial

388.3   US   ISSN 0005-0717
AUTO AND FLAT GLASS JOURNAL. 1953. m. $35 (foreign $68) (effective Jan. 1996). Grawin Publications, Inc., 303 Harvard E., No. 101, Box 12099, Seattle, WA 98102. TEL 206-322-5120. Ed. Jeff Martin; Pub. J.P. Whinihan. adv. contact: Sally Swendt. bk.rev. circ. 5,700. **Document type:** trade publication.
Description: Step-by-step installation procedures for current model cars with business and tax advice, product information, and industry news.

666.1 629.286   US   ISSN 1047-2061
HD9710.3.A1
AUTOGLASS. Variant title: Auto Glass Magazine. 1990. bi-m. $19.95. National Glass Association, 8200 Greensboro Dr., Ste. 302, McLean, VA 22102-3881. TEL 703-442-4890. FAX 703-442-0630. E-mail: nga@glass.org; URL: http://ourworld.compuserve.com/homepages/nga. Ed. Jennifer Cetta; Pub. Nicole Harris. R&P contact: Nicole Harris. adv. contact: Mike Gribbin. circ. 7,000. **Document type:** trade publication.
—CISTI.
Description: Serving the automotive glass industry, both OEM and aftermarket segments. Reports the latest industry news, insurance and legislative regulations, installation methods, and new product information.

666 690   SP   ISSN 0211-7967
AZULEJO; ceramica noble. (Text in English, Spanish) 1979. 4/yr. 10000 ptas.($115) (effective 1997). Publica, S.A., Ecuador, 75, entlo., 08029 Barcelona, Spain. TEL 34-3-3215046. FAX 34-3-3221972. Ed. Carlos Romagosa. adv. circ. 10,000. **Document type:** trade publication.
Description: Covers the industry of ceramic tiles.

666   GW   ISSN 0341-3608
BAUKERAMIK; Information des Fachhandels ueber fein- und grobkeramische Erzeugnisse. 1973. q. DM.24. Gert Wohlfarth GmbH Verlag Fachtechnik und Mercator-Verlag, Stresemannstr. 20-22, 47051 Duisburg, Germany. TEL 49-203-30527-0. FAX 49-203-337765. E-mail: wohlfarth@t-online.de. Ed. Gerd Rottstegge; Pub. Gert Wohlfarth. adv.; bk.rev. circ. 21,000. **Document type:** trade publication.

666.1   UK   ISSN 0967-3121
BLUE BOOK (YEAR). a. T B B Publications Ltd., 4 Simon Campion Ct., High St., Epping, Essex CM16 4AU. TEL 01992-560215. FAX 01992-560216. adv.: B&W page £890, color page £1520; adv. contact: Simon Edwards. **Document type:** directory.
Formerly (until 1990): Flat Glass International Blue Book (ISSN 0960-9296)

CERAMICS, GLASS AND POTTERY

666   CC   ISSN 1000-2871
CODEN: BYTAE8
BOLI YU TANGCI. (Text in Chinese) 1973. bi-m. $45 (effective 1995). Zhongguo Qinggong Zonghui, Boli Tangci Yanjiusuo, No.6, Xinhua Lu, Shanghai 200052, People's Republic of China. TEL 2403230. Ed. Wang Nanning; Pub. Zhang Bin. adv. contact: Pan Yukun. bk.rev.; circ. 5,000 (paid).
—BLDSC (4190.421000); CASDDS.
Refereed Serial

666   UK   ISSN 0268-4373
TP790   CODEN: BCPREL
BRITISH CERAMIC PROCEEDINGS. 1964. irreg., no.49, 1992. price varies. Institute of Ceramics, Shelton House, Stoke Rd., Shelton, Stoke-on-Trent ST4 2DR, England. TEL 44-1782-202116. FAX 44-1782-202421. (Affiliate: Institute of Materials) **Indexed:** Alloys Ind., Br.Ceram.Abstr., Chem.Abstr., Eng.Mat.Abstr., INSPEC (1984-), Met.Abstr.Ind., Met.Abstr., Nonfer.Met.Alert, PCC Alert, Steels Alert. **Document type:** proceedings.
—BLDSC (2293.440000); AskIEEE; CASDDS; CISTI; KR SourceOne; Linda Hall; SWETS; UnCover.
Supersedes (in 1984): British Ceramic Society. Proceedings (ISSN 0524-5141)

666   UK   ISSN 0144-2147
CODEN: SBCRDX
BRITISH CERAMIC RESEARCH. SPECIAL PUBLICATIONS. 1948. irreg. (2-3/yr.), latest no.136, 1993. British Ceramic Research Ltd., Queen's Rd., Penkhull, Stoke-on-Trent ST4 7LQ, England. bibl.; charts; illus. circ. 1,000. **Indexed:** Chem.Abstr., GeoRef.
—BLDSC (8373.930000); CASDDS; CISTI; Linda Hall.

666.1   UK
BRITISH GLASS MANUFACTURERS CONFEDERATION. ANNUAL REVIEW. 1955. a. membership or exchange basis. British Glass Manufacturers Confederation, Northumberland Rd., Sheffield S10 2UA, England. Ed. D.K. Barlow. circ. 500. **Document type:** corporate report.
Formerly (until 1987): British Glass Industry Research Association. Annual Report (ISSN 0068-2020)

666.1   UK   ISSN 0962-032X
BRITISH GLASS MANUFACTURERS CONFEDERATION. DIGEST OF INFORMATION AND PATENT REVIEW. 1956. q. £100 to non-members. British Glass Manufacturers Confederation, Northumberland Rd., Sheffield S10 2UA, England. **Indexed:** Int.Packag.Abstr. **Document type:** abstracting/indexing.
—BLDSC (3587.630000).
Former titles (until 1988): British Glass Industry Research Association Review; (until 1987): British Glass Industry Research Association. Digest of Information and Patent Review.

666 658.8   UK   ISSN 0950-2408
BUSINESS RATIO REPORT: BRICK & TILE MANUFACTURERS; an industry sector analysis. 1986. a. I C C Business Ratios Ltd., Freepost, Field House, Hampton, Mddx. TW12 1BR, England. TEL 081-783-0977. FAX 081-783-1940. charts; stat. **Document type:** trade publication.

666 658.8   UK   ISSN 0261-7579
BUSINESS RATIO REPORT: CERAMIC MANUFACTURERS; an industry sector analysis. 1974. a. I C C Business Ratios Ltd., Freepost, Field House, Hampton, Mddx. TW12 1BR, England. TEL 081-783-0977. FAX 081-783-1940. charts; stat. **Document type:** trade publication.

666.1   SW   ISSN 0280-7076
BYGGGLAS;* tidskrift om glas i funktion, yta och miljoe. 1933. 8/yr. SEK 260 (effective 1991). (Glasmaesterifoerbundet) L M P Editorial, P.O. Box 5384, S-102 46 Stockholm, Sweden.

666.1   SP   ISSN 0214-6592
C I C - VIDRIO. 6/yr. 7000 ptas. (Europe 8500 ptas.; elsewhere 10000 ptas.). Centro Informativo de la Construccion, Roger de Lluria 117, 08037 Barcelona, Spain. TEL 4870455. FAX 215-84-15. Ed. Ferran Cabellos Romero. adv.: B&W page 88000 ptas., color page 135000 ptas.; trim 210 x 297. circ. 4,000. **Document type:** trade publication.
Description: Technical review on materials and equipment.

CAHIERS DE LA CERAMIQUE EGYPTIENNE. see ARCHAEOLOGY

666   CN   ISSN 0068-8444
CODEN: JCCSA9
CANADIAN CERAMIC SOCIETY. JOURNAL. 1928. a. Can.$40 (US Can.$45; elsewhere Can.$50) (effective 1996). Canadian Ceramic Society, 2175 Sheppard Ave. E., Ste. 310, Willowdale, ON M2J 1W8, Canada. TEL 416-491-2886. FAX 416-491-1670. Ed. M. Sayer. adv. contact: B.L. Howell. circ. 800. (also avail. in microfilm from PMC) **Indexed:** Alloys Ind., ASCA, Br.Ceram.Abstr., Cadscan, Chem.Abstr., Curr.Cont., Eng.Mat.Abstr., Lead Abstr., Met.Abstr.Ind., Met.Abstr., Nonfer.Met.Alert, PCC Alert, Steels Alert, World Alum.Abstr., Zincscan. **Document type:** newsletter, proceedings, trade publication, academic/scholarly publication.
—BLDSC (3018.878000); CASDDS; CISTI; Genuine Article; Linda Hall; UnCover. **CCC.**
Incorporates: Canadian Ceramics Quarterly (ISSN 0831-2974); Which was formed by 1985 merger of: Ceramic Hobbyist (ISSN 0707-5197); Canadian Clay and Ceramics Quarterly (ISSN 0624-2658); Which was formerly: Canadian Clay and Ceramics (ISSN 0009-8566); Clay Products News and Ceramic Record.

666.1   US
CARNIVAL PUMP. 1967. q. $15 membership. International Carnival Glass Association, Box 306, Mentone, IN 46539. TEL 219-353-7678. Ed. Carl Booker. **Document type:** newsletter.
Description: Provides information for individuals interested in collecting, trading, and learning about antique carnival glass.

666   US   ISSN 0363-8642
Z5853.M4   CODEN: CRPRDY
CEMENTS RESEARCH PROGRESS. 1974. irreg., latest 1995. $70 to non-members; members $56. American Ceramic Society, 735 Ceramic Pl., Westerville, OH 43081. TEL 614-794-5890. FAX 614-794-5854. Ed. Leslie J. Struble. cum.index: 1974-1983. (back issues avail.; reprint service avail.) **Document type:** monographic series.
—BLDSC (3102.150000); CASDDS; CISTI. **CCC.**

666   II   ISSN 0008-9397
CODEN: CGCRAP
CENTRAL GLASS AND CERAMIC RESEARCH INSTITUTE. BULLETIN. (Text in English; summaries in English, French and German) 1954. q. Rs.35($24) Central Glass and Ceramic Research Institute, 196 Raja S.C. Mullick Rd., Calcutta 700 032, India. TEL 33-463496. (Affiliate: Council of Scientific and Industrial Research) adv.; bk.rev.; charts; illus.; stat.; index. circ. 650. (reprint service avail. from UMI) **Indexed:** Br.Ceram.Abstr., Ceram.Abstr., Chem.Abstr., Curr.Cont., INIS Atomind.
—CASDDS; Linda Hall; UMI.

666   IT   ISSN 0392-6842
CER; il mensile dell'assopiastrelle. 1974. 9/yr. L.70000 (Europe L.130000, elsewhere L.190000) (effective 1995-96). (Ceramic Tile and Refractories Association) Edi. Cer. S.p.A., Viale Monte Santo 40, 41049 Sassuolo (Modena), Italy. TEL 39-536-804585. FAX 39-536-806510. Ed. Francesco Genitoni. adv.: B&W page L.1500000, color page L.1600000. bk.rev. circ. 7,000. **Document type:** trade publication.

666   IT   ISSN 0392-6834
CER ANNUARIO. a. (Associazione Nazionale dei Produttori di Piastrelle di Ceramica) Edi. Cer S.r.l., Viale Monte Santo, 40, 41049 Sassuolo (Modena), Italy. TEL 0536-804585. FAX 0536-806510. TELEX 511050 ASSCER I. **Document type:** trade publication.

666   IT   ISSN 0392-6850
CER FORNITORI. a. (Associazione Nazionale dei Produttori di Piastrelle di Ceramica) Edi. Cer S.r.l., Viale Monte Santo, 40, 41049 Sassuolo (Modena), Italy. TEL 0536-804585. FAX 0536-806510. TELEX 511050 ASSCER I. **Document type:** trade publication.

666   US   ISSN 0196-6219
TP785   CODEN: CESPDK
CERAMIC ENGINEERING AND SCIENCE PROCEEDINGS. 1980. bi-m. $180 to non-members; members $132. American Ceramic Society, 735 Ceramic Pl., Westerville, OH 43081. TEL 614-794-5890. FAX 614-794-5854. Ed. John B. Wachtman, Jr. charts; illus. (reprint service avail. from UMI) **Indexed:** Alloys Ind., Br.Ceram.Abstr., C.R.I.Abstr., C.R.I.Curr.Cont., Ceram.Abstr., Chem.Abstr., Eng.Mat.Abstr., INIS Atomind., Met.Abstr.Ind., Met.Abstr., Nonfer.Met.Alert, PCC Alert, Steels Alert, World Alum.Abstr. **Document type:** proceedings.
—BLDSC (3115.240000); CASDDS; CISTI; Ei; Linda Hall; SWETS; UMI; UnCover. **CCC.**

666   GW   ISSN 0173-9913
TP785   CODEN: CCFDD7
CERAMIC FORUM INTERNATIONAL; journal for the ceramic industries and ceramic research. (Suppl. avail.: Deutsche Keramische Gesellschaft. Fortschrittsberichte (ISSN 0177-6983)) (Text in English, German) 1923. 10/yr. DM.312 (foreign DM.332) (effective 1998). (Deutsche Keramische Gesellschaft e.V.) Bauverlag GmbH, Postfach 1460, 65004 Wiesbaden, Germany. TEL 49-6123-700-0. FAX 49-6123-700122. E-mail: bauverlag.zeitschr.-journals@t-online.de. Ed. H. Reh. adv. contact: P. Schaetzko. bk.rev.; abstr.; bibl.; charts; illus.; pat.; index. circ. 5,000. **Indexed:** Art & Archaeol.Tech.Abstr., Br.Ceram.Abstr., Ceram.Abstr., Chem.Cit.Ind., INIS Atomind., INSPEC (1980-), Mat.Sci.Cit.Ind., SSCI. **Document type:** trade publication.
—BLDSC (3115.502000); AskIEEE; CASDDS; CISTI; Ei; Genuine Article; KR SourceOne; Linda Hall; SWETS. **CCC.**
Formerly: Deutsche Keramische Gesellschaft. Berichte (ISSN 0365-9542)
Description: Trade publication for the ceramics industry. Covers the latest information on research in ceramic materials. Includes abstracts of scientific papers.

666   UK   ISSN 0958-9899
TP785
CERAMIC INDUSTRIES INTERNATIONAL. 1891. bi-m. £68 (foreign £80) (effective 1997). Turret Group Plc., Turret House, 171 High St., Rickmansworth, Herts WD3 1SN, England. TEL 44-1923-777000. FAX 44-1923-771297. (Subscr. to: P.O. Box 77, Watford, Herts WD1 8UT, England. TEL 44-1923-228577. FAX 44-1923-221346) Ed. Alan Cartwright; Pub. Peter de Lacey. adv.: B&W page £810, color page £1300; trim 298 x 210; adv. contact: Tony Marchant. bk.rev.; abstr.; pat.; stat. **Indexed:** AESIS, Artbibl.Mod., Br.Ceram.Abstr., Br.Tech.Ind., Key to Econ.Sci., Met.Abstr., World Alum.Abstr. **Document type:** trade publication.
—BLDSC (3115.540000); CISTI; Linda Hall; SWETS UMI.
Formerly: Ceramics Industries Journal (ISSN 0305-7623); Which incorporated: British Clayworker (ISSN 0300-4325); Ceramics (ISSN 0009-0301)

666   US   ISSN 0009-0220
TP785   CODEN: CEINAT
CERAMIC INDUSTRY; the magazine for refractories, traditional & advanced ceramic manufacturers. (Includes: Data Book Buyers Guide; Materials Handbook; Economic Forecast; Giants in Ceramics) 1923. 13/yr. $65 (Mexico $77; Canada $79.55; elsewhere $135). Business News Publishing Company, 755 W. Big Beaver Rd., Ste. 1000, Troy, MI 48084. TEL 810-362-3700. FAX 810-362-0317. URL: http://www.bnp.com. (Subscr. to: Box 3212, Northbrook, IL 60065) Ed. Laurel Sheppard; Pub. Myra Smitley. adv. contact: Carol Lawrence. bk.rev.; charts; illus.; tr.lit.; index. circ. 13,030. (also avail. in microfilm) **Indexed:** A.S. & T.Ind., AESIS, Alloys Ind., Br.Ceram.Abstr., Ceram.Abstr., Chem.Abstr., Eng.Ind., Eng.Mat.Abstr. Excerp.Med., Ind.Sci.Rev., Met.Abstr., Met.Abstr.Ind., Nonfer.Met.Alert, PCC Alert, PROMT, Steels Alert, World Alum.Abstr. **Document type:** trade publication.
●Also available online. Vendor(s): Information Access Co.
—BLDSC (3116.000000); CISTI; Ei; KR SourceOne Linda Hall; SWETS; UMI; UnCover. **CCC.**
Description: Serves manufacturers in the refractories, traditional, and advanced ceramic markets with industry news, technology, equipment and market trends coverage.

CERAMICS, GLASS AND POTTERY 1727

666 US
CERAMIC INDUSTRY DATA BOOK BUYERS GUIDE. 1922. a. $25. Business News Publishing Company, 755 W. Big Beaver Rd., Ste. 1000, Troy, MI 48084. TEL 810-362-3700. FAX 810-362-4932. (Subscr. to: Box 3212, Northbrook, IL 60065) Ed. Pat Janeway. adv.; charts. circ. 13,000. **Document type:** directory.
—Linda Hall.
Formerly (until 1984): Ceramic Data Book (ISSN 0162-5330)

666 UK ISSN 0144-1825
TP808
CERAMIC REVIEW. 1970. bi-m. £32 (overseas £37($70)) (effective 1998). Ceramic Review Publishing Ltd., 21 Carnaby St., London W1V 1PH, England. TEL 44-171-439-3377. FAX 44-171-287-9954. Eds. Emmanuel Cooper, Eileen Lewenstein. adv. contact: Daphne Matthews. bk.rev.; illus.; tr.lit.; index. circ. 9,200. **Indexed:** Art Ind., Artbibl.Mod., DAAI, Pinpointer. **Document type:** trade publication.
—BLDSC (3116.400000); KR SourceOne; UnCover.

666 JA ISSN 0912-9200
TA455.C43
CERAMIC SOCIETY OF JAPAN. JOURNAL (INTERNATIONAL EDITION). Japanese edition: Seramikkusu Kyokaishi (ISSN 0914-5400) (Text in English) 1987. m. 200000 Yen. (Ceramic Society of Japan - Nippon Seramikkusu Kyokai Gakujutsu Ronbunshi) Fuji Technology Press Ltd., 7F Daini Bunsei Bldg., 11-7, Toranomon 1-chome, Minato-ku, Tokyo 105, Japan. TEL 81-3-3508-0051. FAX 81-3-3592-0648. Ed. Keiji Hayashi.
—BLDSC (4725.102000); CISTI; SWETS.

666 US ISSN 8756-8187
TP785 CODEN: CESOEI
CERAMIC SOURCE. 1985. a. $25. American Ceramic Society, 735 Ceramic Pl., Westerville, OH 43081. TEL 614-794-5890. FAX 614-794-5854. Ed. Patricia Janeway. adv.; charts; illus. circ. 14,000. (reprint service avail. from UMI) **Indexed:** C.R.I.Abstr., C.R.I.Curr.Cont., INSPEC.
—CISTI. **CCC.**

738 AT
CERAMIC STUDY GROUP. NEWSLETTER. 1960. 10/yr. Aus.$35 (effective 1996). Ceramic Study Group Inc, P.O. Box 1528, Macquarie Centre, Sydney, N.S.W. 2113, Australia. URL: http://www.zip.com.au/~bobf. Ed. Kay Alliband. R&P contact: Paquita Farmer. adv. contact: P. Farmer. bk.rev. circ. 600. **Document type:** newsletter.

666 GW ISSN 0944-9825
CERAMIC SUPPLIERS INTERNATIONAL (YEAR). 1981. a. DM.96. Verlag Schmid GmbH (Freiburg), Postfach 6609, 79042 Freiburg, Germany. TEL 49-761-89609-0. FAX 49-761-8960980. Pub. Hagen Dettmer. adv. **Document type:** directory.
Formerly (until 1993): International Buyers' Guide (ISSN 0935-6444)

620.14 UK ISSN 0964-9735
CERAMIC TECHNOLOGY INTERNATIONAL. 1992. a. £55. Sterling Publications Ltd., 86-88 Edgware Rd., London W2 2YW, England. TEL 44-171-915-9600. FAX 44-171-915-9619. R&P contact: Sandy Tucker. circ. 10,000. **Document type:** trade publication.

666 SP ISSN 0214-8994
CERAMIC TILES OF SPAIN.* 1989. 4/yr. Faenza Editrice Iberica S.L., C. San Vicente 62 entlo., 12001 Castellon de la Plana, Spain. TEL 64-21-65-70. FAX 64-21-10-10. Ed. Benjamin Cervera.
Description: Covers exporting of Spanish tiles.

666 BL ISSN 0366-6913
CODEN: CMCAAG
CERAMICA.* 1954. 12/yr. $90. Associacao Brasileira de Ceramica, Rua Pedro de Toledo 282, Vila Clementino, 04039 Sao Paulo, Brazil. adv.; bk.rev.; illus.; tr.lit. circ. 7,000. **Indexed:** Alloys Ind., Br.Ceram.Abstr., Ceram.Abstr., Chem.Abstr., Eng.Mat.Abstr., INIS Atomind., Met.Abstr., Met.Abstr.Ind., Nonfer.Met.Alert, PCC Alert, Steels Alert, World Alum.Abstr.
—BLDSC (3117.200000); CASDDS; CISTI.

666 IT ISSN 0366-5801
CODEN: CERMA3
CERAMICA. 1948. bi-m. $70. Casa Editrice Palazzo Vecchio, Via Vittorio Emanuele 155, Florence, Italy. Ed. Carlo Voltolini. adv. circ. 3,000. **Indexed:** Br.Ceram.Abstr., Ceram.Abstr., Chem.Abstr.
—CASDDS; CISTI.

666 SP ISSN 0210-010X
CERAMICA; keramos. 1978. q. 3000 ptas.($25) Paseo Acacias 9, 28005 Madrid, Spain. TEL 39-1-8843073. Ed. Antonio Vivas. adv.: page $380; trim 240 x 175. bk.rev.; software rev.; bibl.; tr.lit.; index. circ. 10,000. **Document type:** academic/scholarly publication.
—CINDOC.

666 IT ISSN 1121-6093
CERAMICA ACTA. (Text in English, Italian) 1989. bi-m. L.180000 (Europe L.300000; elsewhere L.440000) (effective 1997). Centro Ceramico Bologna, Via Martelli 26, 40138 Bologna, Italy. TEL 39-51-534015. FAX 39-51-530085. E-mail: centro.ceramico@cencerbo.it. Ed. Giorgio Timellini. adv.; bk.rev. **Indexed:** Alloys Ind., Eng.Mat.Abstr., Met.Abstr.Ind., Met.Abstr., Mineral.Abstr., Nonfer.Met.Alert, PCC Alert, Steels Alert, World Alum.Abstr. **Document type:** academic/scholarly publication.
—BLDSC (3117.250000).
Description: Covers traditional ceramics, advanced technical ceramics, glass, bioceramics, energy and processes and quality.

666 SP
CERAMICA INFORMACION. 1974. m. (10/yr.). L.130000 (foreign L.190000) (effective 1996). Faenza Editrice Iberica S.L., C. San Vicente 62 entlo., 12001 Castellon de la Plana, Spain. TEL 34-64-216570. FAX 34-64-241010. Ed. B. Cervera Carceller. adv.: B&W page L.1250000, color page L.1440000. bk.rev. circ. 3,350. **Indexed:** Ind.SST.

666 IT ISSN 0009-0271
CODEN: CINFDR
CERAMICA INFORMAZIONE; periodico tecnico specializzato. 1966. m. (9/yr.). Lit.160000 in Europe; Oceania Lit.295000; elsewhere Lit.245000 (effective 1997). (Societa Italiana per la Ceramica) Gruppo Editoriale Faenza Editrice s.p.a., Via Pier. de Crescenzi, 44, Faenza, Italy. TEL 39-546-663488. FAX 39-546-660440. E-mail: gefe.vendita@uno.dinamica.it; gefe.info@uno.dinamica.it. Ed. Gastone Vecchi. R&P contact: Luisa Teston. adv.: B&W page Lit.1750000, color page Lit.1930000; adv. contact: Elvio Meri. bk.rev.; adv.; bibl.; charts; illus.; tr.lit.; index. **Indexed:** Br.Ceram.Abstr., Chem.Abstr. **Document type:** corporate report.
—BLDSC (3117.300000); CASDDS.
Description: Covers the ceramic sector in Italy. Includes articles about tiles, raw materials and equipment.

666 IT
CERAMICA PER L'ARCHITETTURA. Short title: C A. 1987. 3/yr. Lit.70000 in Europe; Oceania Lit.120000; elsewhere Lit.90000 (effective 1997). Gruppo Editoriale Faenza Editrice S.p.A., Via Pier. de Crescenzi, 44, Faenza, Italy. TEL 39-546-663488. FAX 39-546-660440. E-mail: gefe.vendita@uno.dinamica.it; gefe.info@uno.dinamica.it. Ed. I. Bondi. R&P contact: Luisa Teston. adv.: color page L.4640000; adv. contact: Orieta Merliak. circ. 12,000. (back issues avail.) **Document type:** academic/scholarly publication.
Description: Supports ceramics and tiles as artistic expression in architecture and urban design.
Refereed Serial

747 AG ISSN 0325-0229
CODEN: CECRBC
CERAMICA Y CRISTAL. 1961. 5/yr. Arg.$25($100) Editorial Ciclo, Av. Melian 2208, 1430 Buenos Aires, Argentina. TEL 54-1-5421612. FAX 54-1-5447007. Ed. Arnoldo Alonso Ibanez; Pub. Marcelo Alonso Marasco. adv.: B&W page $100, color page $750; adv. contact: Carla Alonso Marasco. bk.rev.; illus. circ. 2,500. **Indexed:** Alloys Ind., Eng.Mat.Abstr., INIS Atomind., Met.Abstr.Ind., Met.Abstr., Nonfer.Met.Alert, PCC Alert, Steels Alert, World Alum.Abstr. **Document type:** trade publication.
—BLDSC (3117.350000); CASDDS.
Former titles (until 1965): Estilo (ISSN 0014-133X); (until 1961): Ceramica y Cristal (ISSN 0325-0210)

CERAMICS. see CHEMISTRY — Physical Chemistry

666 AT ISSN 1035-1841
NK3700
CERAMICS; art and perception. 1991. q. $50 (foreign $55) (effective 1997). Ceramic Art, 35 William St., Paddington, Sydney, NSW 2021, Australia. TEL 61-2-93615286. FAX 61-2-93615402. Ed. Janet Mansfield. adv.; illus.
—BLDSC (3118.200000); UnCover.

666 US
CERAMICS (LIVONIA). 1963. m. $19.60 (foreign $26.60). Scott Publications, 30595 Eight Mile Rd., Livonia, MI 48152-1798. TEL 248-477-6650. FAX 248-477-6795. Ed. Bill Thompson; Pub. Robert Keessen. adv. contact: Jim Mac. bk.rev. circ. 16,000. **Document type:** consumer publication.
Formed by the 1988 merger of: Ceramic Projects; Ceramics, the Magazine of Techniques; Ceramic Teaching Projects and Trade News (ISSN 0162-7090); Ceramic Trade News and Catalog File (ISSN 0009-0263)

666 UK ISSN 0272-8842
TP785 CODEN: CINNDH
CERAMICS INTERNATIONAL. (Text and summaries in English) 1974. 8/yr. fl.1644($945) (effective 1998). Elsevier Science Ltd., P.O. Box 800, Kidlington, Oxford OX5 1DX, England. TEL 44-1865-843000. FAX 44-1865-843010. E-mail: nlinfo-f@elsevier.nl; usinfo-f@elsevier.com; forinfo-kyf04035@niftyserve.or.jp; URL: http://www.elsevier.nl/. (Subscr. to: Elsevier Science, Regional Sales Office, P.O. Box 211, 1000 AE Amsterdam, Netherlands. TEL 31-20-4853757. FAX 31-20-4853432; Subscr. in the Americas to: Elsevier Science, Regional Sales Office, Box 945, New York, NY 10159-0945. TEL 212-633-3730. FAX 015492488680; Subscr. in Australasia and the Far East to: Elsevier Science (Singapore) Pte Ltd, No.1 Temasek Ave., No.17-01 Millenia Tower, Singapore 039192, Singapore. TEL 65-434-3727. FAX 65-337-2230) Ed. Pietro Vincenzini. adv.; bk.rev. circ. 450. (back issues avail.) **Indexed:** Alloys Ind., Appl.Mech.Rev., ASCA, Br.Ceram.Abstr., Chem.Abstr., Chem.Cit.Ind., Curr.Cont., Eng.Mat.Abstr., INSPEC (1981-), Mat.Sci.Cit.Ind., Met.Abstr., Met.Abstr.Ind., Nonfer.Met.Alert, PCC Alert, Steels Alert, World Alum.Abstr. **Document type:** academic/scholarly publication.
—BLDSC (3119.015000); AskIEEE; CASDDS; CISTI; Ei; Genuine Article; KR SourceOne; Linda Hall; SWETS; UnCover. **CCC.**
Formerly (until 1981): Ceramurgia International (ISSN 0390-5519)
Description: Deals with the fundamental aspects of ceramic science and its application to the development of improved traditional and non-traditional ceramic products.
Refereed Serial

666 US
CERAMICS: LATIN AMERICAN INDUSTRIAL REPORT. (Avail. for each of 22 Latin American countries) 1985. a. $435 per country report. Aquino Productions, Box 125, Rochester, VT 05767. Ed. Andres C. Aquino.

666 US ISSN 0009-0328
TP785
CERAMICS MONTHLY. 1953. 10/yr. $26. American Ceramic Society, 735 Ceramic Pl., Box 6102, Westerville, OH 43086-6102. TEL 614-794-5890. FAX 614-794-5854. Ed. Ruth C. Butler; Pub. Mark J. Mecklenburg. R&P contact: Mark J. Mecklenburg. adv. contact: Steve Hecker. bk.rev.; illus.; index; circ. 37,000. (paid). (also avail. in microfiche from NBI,UMI; reprint service avail. from UMI) **Indexed:** Access (1980-1988), Art & Archaeol.Tech.Abstr., Art Ind., Artbibl.Mod., Biog.Ind., Ceram.Abstr., DAAI, Ind.How To Do It (1990-), Mag.Ind., Pinpointer. **Document type:** trade publication.
●Also available online. Vendor(s): Information Access Co., UMI.
—BLDSC (3119.050000); KR SourceOne; SWETS; UMI; UnCover.
Description: Serves potters, ceramic sculptors, schools, craft centers, galleries, collectors and others with interest in ceramics.

666 AT ISSN 1324-4175
CERAMICS TECHNICAL. s-a. Aus.$35 (foreign $35). Ceramic Art, 35 William St., Paddington, N.S.W. 2021, Australia. TEL 61-2-93615286. FAX 61-2-93615402.
—BLDSC (3119.059000).

CERAMICS, GLASS AND POTTERY

666 — FR — ISSN 0009-0336
CERAMIQUE MODERNE. 1959. m.(except Jul.-Aug. combined). 205 F. (foreign 240 F.). Editions Techniques et Artistiques, 22 rue Le Brun, 75013 Paris, France. TEL 45-87-17-48. Ed. Milutin Krstic. adv.: B&W page 4348 F.; trim 190 x 276. bk.rev.; bibl.; charts; illus.; stat.; index. circ. 3,700.
Description: Devoted to the materials and accessories, as well as the fashioning, baking, enamelling and decoration of ceramics.

666 — IT — ISSN 0045-6152
TP785 CODEN: CRGIAR
CERAMURGIA. (Text in Italian; summaries in English and Italian) 1971. q. $225 foreign (effective 1997). Techna s.r.l., Casella Postale 174, 48018 Faenza, Italy. TEL 39-546-22461. FAX 39-546-664138. Ed. Dr. Pietro Vincenzini. adv.: B&W page L.1300000, color page L.1850000. bk.rev.; abstr.; bibl.; illus.; pat. circ. 2,100. **Indexed:** Alloys Ind., Br.Ceram.Abstr., Chem.Abstr., Eng.Ind., Eng.Mat.Abstr., Fuel & Energy Abstr., Met.Abstr., Met.Abstr.Ind., PCC Alert, Steels Alert, World Alum.Abstr.
—BLDSC (3119.300000); CASDDS; CISTI; Ei; Linda Hall.

666 — IT — ISSN 1121-6956
CERMICANTICA; mensile sull'arte della maiolica, dell porcellana e del vetro. 1991. m. (11/yr.). L.95000 (Europe L.150000; elsewhere L.200000 (effective 1995 & 1996). Editrice Belriguardo, Via Montebello 18, 44100 Ferrara, Italy. TEL 39-532-202170. FAX 39-532-205332. Ed. Romolo Magnani. **Document type:** consumer publication.

666 — US — ISSN 0009-4382
CHINA GLASS & TABLEWARE. 1892. 7/yr. $25 (includes Red Book Directory). Doctorow Communications, Inc., 1011 Clifton Ave., Ste. B1, Clifton, NJ 07013-3518. TEL 201-779-1600. FAX 201-779-3242. Ed. Susan Grisham. adv.; bk.rev.; charts; illus.; mkt.; pat.; tr.lit. circ. 4,500.
—CCC.

666 — UK
CLAY TECHNOLOGY.* bi-m. Newton Mann Ltd., Stretton Rd., Tansley, Matlock, Derbyshire DE4 5GE, England. Ed. Charles Mann. circ. 2,000.

666 — FR — ISSN 0763-0018
COMPOSITES ET NOUVEAUX MATERIAUX (PARIS, 1980). 18/yr. 2200 F. A Jour, 11 rue du Marche St. Honore, 75001 Paris, France. TEL 42-96-76-22. FAX 40-20-07-75. TELEX 615 887 AJOUR F. Ed. Juliette Fauchet.

666 — FR — ISSN 0069-830X
CONFEDERATION DES INDUSTRIES CERAMIQUES DE FRANCE. ANNUAIRE. 1953. biennial. 288 F. Septima, 14 rue Falguiere, 75015 Paris, France. adv. **Document type:** directory.
Description: More than 1000 addresses of ceramics industry manufacturers and suppliers, and others.

666 — CN — ISSN 1194-6377
CONTACT (CALGARY); ceramics from a Canadian perspective. 1976. q. Can.$30($30) (foreign $33) (effective 1997). Ceramic Contacts Inc., P.O. Box 56599, 8601 Warden Ave., Box 56599, Markham, ON L3R 0M6, Canada. TEL 403-270-3252; 800-334-4054. FAX 403-270-3252. E-mail: btipton@cadvision.com; URL: http://www.cadvision.com/ceramics. Ed. Barbara Tipton. adv. contact: Frank Tucker. bk.rev.; circ. 2,000 (paid).
Description: Exhibition reviews, artist profiles, commentary, technical information.

666 — IT — ISSN 1120-5822
D'A; la prima rivista italiana d'artigianato e di arti applicate. 1990. q. L.40000 (foreign L.75000). Editrice Milo s.a.s., Piazza Roma 12, 01030 Vitorchiano (VT), Italy. TEL 39-761-370590. FAX 39-761-370733. Ed. Giovanni Milani. adv.: B&W page L.2700000, color page L.3500000; 210 x 285. circ. 12,300. **Document type:** trade publication.

666.1 748 — US — ISSN 0895-3961
THE DAZE INC.; the nation's market place for glass and china. 1971. m. $21 (Canada $22). Box 57, Otisville, MI 48463. TEL 810-631-4593. FAX 810-631-4567. bk.rev. circ. 20,000.
Formerly (until 1984): Depression Glass Daze (ISSN 0270-8485)

666 — GW
DEUTSCHE KERAMIK. 1973. triennial. DM.45. (Kreisverwaltung des Westerwaldkreises in Montabaur) Verlag der Museen des Westerwaldkreises, 56410 Montabaur, Germany. TEL 49-2602-124226. FAX 49-2602-124542. TELEX 869619-KVMO-D. **Document type:** catalog.

666 — GW — ISSN 0070-4199
CODEN: DKGFBF
DEUTSCHE KERAMISCHE GESELLSCHAFT. FACHAUSSCHUSSBERICHTE. 1953. irreg., no.30, 1992. DM.40 to members; non-members DM.80. Deutsche Keramische Gesellschaft e.V., Frankfurter Str. 196, 51147 Cologne, Germany. TEL 02203-69069. FAX 02203-69301. Ed.Bd. **Indexed:** Chem.Abstr. **Document type:** trade publication.
—CASDDS.

666 — GW — ISSN 0177-6983
CODEN: FDKGFF
DEUTSCHE KERAMISCHE GESELLSCHAFT. FORTSCHRITTSBERICHTE. (Supplement to: Ceramic Forum International (ISSN 0173-9913)) 1985. irreg. Bauverlag GmbH, Postfach 1460, 65004 Wiesbaden, Germany. TEL 06123-700-0. FAX 06123-700122. **Indexed:** Alloys Ind., Eng.Mat.Abstr., Met.Abstr.Ind., Met.Abstr., Nonfer.Met.Alert, PCC Alert, Steels Alert, World Alum.Abstr. **Document type:** monographic series.
—BLDSC (4024.036300); CASDDS; CISTI. **CCC.**

666.1 — GW
DEUTSCHER GLASERKALENDER; Ratgeber und Helfer fuer Glaser und Fensterbauer. 1950. a. DM.21.80 (effective 1997). Verlag Karl Hofmann, Postfach 1360, 73603 Schorndorf, Germany. TEL 49-7181-402-0. FAX 49-7181-402111. adv.; stat. circ. 5,500. **Document type:** trade publication.

666 — GW
EHRENPREIS DEUTSCHE KERAMIK. 1983. irreg. DM.64. Verlag der Museen des Westerwaldkreises, 56410 Montabaur, Germany. TEL 49-2602-124226. FAX 49-2602-124542. TELEX 869619-KVMOD. Ed.Bd. **Document type:** catalog.

666.2 — CI — ISSN 0350-3607
CODEN: EKESDN
EMAJL, KERAMIKA, STAKLO. (Text in Serbo-Croatian; summaries in English and German) 1964. q. $20. Udruzenje Emajliraca Jugoslavije - Yugoslavian Enamellers Association, Srebrnjak 169, 41000 Zagreb, Croatia. Ed. Robert Laslo. adv.; bk.rev.; circ. 1,000 (controlled). **Indexed:** Chem.Abstr.
—CASDDS.
Formerly (until 1969): Emajl (ISSN 0013-6506)

666 — UK — ISSN 0071-0547
ENGLISH CERAMIC CIRCLE. TRANSACTIONS. 1927. a. price varies. English Ceramic Circle, c/o Mrs. J. Bennett, Secy., 5 The Drive, Beckenham, Kent BR3 1EE, England. Ed. Tom Walford. cum.index. circ. 500. **Indexed:** Art & Archaeol.Tech.Abstr., Artbibl.Mod., Br.Archaeol.Abstr., RILA. **Document type:** academic/scholarly publication, proceedings.
—BLDSC (8931.523000).

666 — UK
EUROGLASS. 1990. q. £30. Spotlight Publications Ltd. (Subsidiary of: Morgan-Grampian plc) Ludgate House, 245 Blackfriars Rd., London SE1 9UR, England. TEL 0171-620-3636. FAX 0171-401-8036. Ed. Peter Butler. adv. contact: Debbie Shepherd. circ. 4,300. **Document type:** trade publication.

620.14 — UK — ISSN 0955-2219
CODEN: JECSER
EUROPEAN CERAMIC SOCIETY. JOURNAL. Key Title: Journal of the European Ceramic Society. 1985. 16/yr. fl.3118($1792) (effective 1998). Elsevier Science Ltd., P.O. Box 800, Kidlington, Oxford OX5 1DX, England. TEL 44-1865-843000. FAX 44-1865-843010. E-mail: nlinfo-f@elsevier.nl; usinfo-f@elsevier.com; forinfo-kyf04035@niftyserve.or.jp; URL: http://www.elsevier.nl/. (Subscr. to: Elsevier Science, Regional Sales Office, P.O. Box 211, 1000 AE Amsterdam, Netherlands. TEL 31-20-4853757. FAX 31-20-4853432; Subscr. in the Americas to: Elsevier Science, Regional Sales Office, Box 945, New York, NY 10159-0945. TEL 212-633-3730. FAX 212-633-3680; Subscr. in Australasia and the Far East to: Elsevier Science (Singapore) Pte Ltd, No.1 Temasek Ave., No.17-01 Millenia Tower, Singapore 039192, Singapore. TEL 65-434-3727. FAX 65-337-2230) Ed. R.J. Brook. adv. (back issues avail.) **Indexed:** Alloys Ind., Appl.Mech.Rev., ASCA, Ceram.Abstr., Chem.Cit.Ind., Curr.Cont., Eng.Mat.Abstr., INSPEC (1989-), Mat.Sci.Cit.Ind., Met.Abstr.Ind., Met.Abstr., Nonfer.Met.Alert, PCC Alert, Steels Alert, World Alum.Abstr. **Document type:** academic/scholarly publication.
—BLDSC (4741.629000); AskIEEE; CASDDS; CISTI; Ei; EMDOCS; Genuine Article; KR SourceOne; Linda Hall; SWETS; UnCover. **CCC.**
Formerly (until 1989): International Journal of High Technology Ceramics (ISSN 0267-3762)
Description: Publishes the results of original research relating to the structure, properties and processing of ceramic materials.
Refereed Serial

380 666.1 — UK — ISSN 0306-204X
HD9623.E8
EUROPEAN GLASS DIRECTORY AND BUYER'S GUIDE. 1970. a. (issued in Jan.). £138.50 (overseas $191) (effective 1997). Argus Business Media Ltd. (Subsidiary of: D M G Exhibitions Group Ltd.), Queensway House, 2 Queensway, Redhill, Surrey RH1 1QS, England. TEL 44-1737-768611. FAX 44-1737-761685. Ed. K. Tolley. adv. **Document type:** directory.
—BLDSC (3829.716700).
Formerly: Glass Directory and Buyer's Guide.
Description: Provides detailed, up-to-date information on manufacturers, processors, and manipulators of glass products and materials in Europe.

666 — US
EXPANDED SHALE, CLAY AND SLATE INSTITUTE. SPECIAL BULLETINS. irreg. Expanded Shale, Clay and Slate Institute, 2225 E. Murray Holladay Rd., Ste. 102, Salt Lake City, UT 84117. TEL 801-272-7070. FAX 801-272-3377. **Document type:** consumer publication.

666 — UK — ISSN 0964-6779
FABRICATION & GLAZING INDUSTRIES. 1981. m. £25 (rest of Europe £40, elsewhere £75). T B B Publications Ltd., 4 Simon Campion Ct., High St., Epping, Essex CM16 4AU, England. TEL 01992-560215. FAX 01992-560216. Ed. John Roper. adv. contact: Gerald Batt. bk.rev.; illus.; circ. 8,329. **Document type:** trade publication.
Formerly (until 1991): Flat Glass International (ISSN 0262-3315)
Description: Contains articles and industry news of interest to glazing contractors, specifiers, glaziers, and window and door fabricators, installers, and architects.

666 738 — IT — ISSN 0014-679X
FAENZA; rivista di studi di storia e di tecnica dell'arte ceramica. (Text in Italian; summaries in English, French, German) 1913. 6/yr. L.60000 (foreign L.70000) (effective 1997). Museo Internazionale delle Ceramiche, Via Campidori 2, 48018 Faenza, Italy. TEL 39-546-21240. FAX 39-546-27141. E-mail: http://racine.ra.it. Ed. Gian Carlo Bojani. adv.; bk.rev.; bibl.; charts; illus.; index. circ. 1,028. **Indexed:** Art & Archaeol.Tech.Abstr., Artbibl.Mod., Ceram.Abstr., IBR, RILA. **Document type:** bulletin, bibliography.
—SWETS.

CERAMICS, GLASS AND POTTERY

666   IT
FASHION CERAMIC TILES. Variant title: Ceramic Tile Fashion. (Supplement to: Ceramica Per l'Edilizia (ISSN 0392-4890)) 1983. s-a. (foreign L.27000). Gruppo Editoriale Faenza Editrice S.p.A., Via de Crescenzi 44, 48018 Faenza, Italy. TEL 39-546-663488. FAX 39-546-660440. E-mail: gefe.vendita@uno.dinamica.it; gefe.info@uno.dinamica.it. Ed. Rolando Giovannini. R&P contact: Luisa Teston. adv.: color page Lit.2120000; adv. contact: Elvio Neri. **Document type:** trade publication.

FLASH POINT. see *ANTIQUES*

666.122   US   ISSN 0016-3155
FUSION.* 1954. q. $32. American Scientific Glassblowers Society, 1835 Saint Clair Ave., Saint Paul, MN 55105-1642. TEL 612-696-9286. FAX 419-478-0636. Ed. Brenda Cloninger. adv.; bk.rev.; abstr.; illus. circ. 1,200. **Indexed:** Chem.Abstr., Tr.& Indus.Ind.
—CISTI.
Description: Educational material pertaining to the field of scientific glassblowing.

666   CN   ISSN 0832-9656
FUSION MAGAZINE. 1985. 3/yr. Can.$55 to individuals; institutions Can.$75. Ontario Clay & Glass Association, Gardener's Cottage, 225 Confederation Dr., Scarborough, ON M1G 1B2, Canada. TEL 416-438-8946. FAX 416-438-0192. E-mail: fusion@aracnet.net. Ed. Elizabeth Dingman; Pub. Robert Tetu. adv. contact: Brian Truscott. bk.rev. circ. 900. (back issues avail.) **Indexed:** DAAI. **Document type:** trade publication.
Description: Provides a range of subject matter on ceramics and glass from reviews, exhibitions and listings to technical articles and profiles.

666 745.5   AT   ISSN 1322-5103
FUSIONS. 1968. q. Aus.$45 membership. Queensland Potters Association, Cnr. Malt & Brunswick Sts., Fortitude Valley, Qld. 4006, Australia. TEL 61-7-33585122. FAX 61-7-33584540. Ed. Bernice Gerrand. R&P contact: Bernice Gerrand. adv.; bk.rev. circ. 850. **Document type:** newsletter.
Formerly: Q P A News (ISSN 1038-2240)
Description: Reports on the association's exhibitions, workshops and coming events. Includes technical notes.

666.1   GW   ISSN 1432-6264
G F F - ZEITSCHRIFT FUER GLAS, FENSTER, FASSADE. 1950. s-m. DM.153.60 (students DM.120) (effective 1997). Verlag Karl Hofmann, Postfach 1360, 73603 Schorndorf, Germany. TEL 49-7181-402-0. FAX 49-7181-402111. Ed. Klauspeter Schroeder. adv.; bk.rev.; charts; illus.; tr.lit. circ. 6,500. **Document type:** trade publication.
—CCC.
Former titles: Glas und Rahmen (ISSN 0342-5142); St. Lucas Allgemeine Glaserzeitung (ISSN 0036-3065)

G P MAGAZIN. (Gewerkschaftpost) see *ENGINEERING — Chemical Engineering*

666   NE
GEMENGDE BRANCHE; vakblad voor de handel in huishoudelijke en luxe artikelen, glas, porselein, aardewerk en kunstnijverheidsartikelen. 1948. m. fl.120. Stichting Vakbladen Gemengde en Gespecialiseerde Branches, Postbus 7105, 2701 AC Zoetermeer, Netherlands. FAX 079-514811. Ed. K. Clay. adv.; bk.rev.; illus.; tr.lit. circ. 6,000. **Indexed:** Key to Econ.Sci.
Former titles (until 1978): Vakblad Gemengde Branche; Gemengde Branche (ISSN 0016-6235)

GIFT AND DECORATIVE ACCESSORIES BUYERS DIRECTORY. see *GIFTWARE AND TOYS*

658.7   UK   ISSN 0016-9854
GIFT BUYER INTERNATIONAL. 1964. m. £58($90) Ralph Sadgrove, M1 Victoria House, Southampton Row, London WC1B 4EW, England. FAX 01-2424996. Ed. Josie Hawkins. adv.; bk.rev. circ. 4,750.

GIFTS & DECORATIVE ACCESSORIES; the international business magazine of gifts, tabletop, gourmet, home accessories, greeting card and social stationery. see *GIFTWARE AND TOYS*

GLAS; Architektur und Technik. see *ARCHITECTURE*

666.1 666.5   SW   ISSN 0017-078X
GLAS OCH PORSLIN. 1930. bi-m. SEK 225 (effective 1990). Sveriges Glas- och Porslinshandlarefoerbund (SGPF), P.O. Box 53200, S-400 15 Goeteborg, Sweden. Ed. N.A. Holmgren. adv.; illus. circ. 800. **Document type:** trade publication.

666.1   AU
GLAS - OESTERREICHISCHE GLASERZEITUNG. vol.23, 1970. m. S.580. (Bundes- und Landesinnungen der Glaser) Oesterreichischer Wirtschaftsverlag, Nikolsdorfergasse 7-11, A-1051 Vienna, Austria. TEL 0222-555585. TELEX 1-11669. Ed. Peter Hauer. adv.; bk.rev.; illus. circ. 1,700.
Formerly: Oesterreichische Glaserzeitung (ISSN 0029-9162)

666.122   SZ   ISSN 0017-0836
GLASBLAESER.* 1947. bi-m. 12 Fr.($2.80) Glasblaeser-Vereinigung, Schuetzenrainweg 10, 4125 Riehen, Switzerland. Ed. Alfred Zollinger. adv.; bk.rev.; illus. circ. 200. **Document type:** trade publication.

666.1   DK   ISSN 0907-1423
GLASMAGASINET. 1917. q. free to qualified personnel. (Danish Flat Glass Association) Glasbranche Foreningen, Gothersgade 160, DK-1123 Copenhagen K, Denmark. TEL 45-33-32-23-11. FAX 45-33-13-65-60. Ed. Poul Thorsen. R&P contact: Poul Thorsen. adv. contact: Poul Thorsen. bk.rev.; illus.; index. circ. 7,500. **Document type:** bulletin.
Formerly (until 1992): Glarmestertidende (ISSN 0017-0755)

666.1   UK   ISSN 0017-0984
TP845   CODEN: GLASAT
GLASS (REDHILL); the monthly journal. 1923. m. £113.05 (foreign £135.665 (effective 1997). Argus Business Media Ltd. (Subsidiary of: D M G Exhibitions Group Ltd.), Queensway House, 2 Queensway, Redhill, Surrey RH1 1QS, England. TEL 44-1737-768611. FAX 44-1737-761685. Ed. J. Phillips. (also avail. in microform from UMI) **Indexed:** Br.Tech.Ind., Chem.Abstr., Excerp.Med., Int.Packag.Abstr., Packag.Sci.Tech. **Document type:** trade publication.
●Also available online. Vendor(s): Information Access Co.
—BLDSC (4190.000000); CASDDS; CISTI; Ei; Linda Hall; SWETS; UMI.
Description: Informs professionals in the European glass manufacturing industry. Covers the container, flat, domestic, and specialty glassware sectors.

GLASS AGE DIRECTORY. see *BUSINESS AND ECONOMICS — Trade And Industrial Directories*

666   US   ISSN 0361-7610
TP845   CODEN: GLCEAV
GLASS AND CERAMICS. English translation of: Steklo i Keramika (RU ISSN 0131-9582) 1956. m. $1595 (foreign $1865) (effective 1998). (Russian Academy of Sciences, RU) Plenum Publishing Corp., Consultants Bureau, 233 Spring St., New York, NY 10013-1578. TEL 212-620-8468. FAX 212-463-0742. TELEX 23-421139. Ed. L.V. Sokolova. (also avail. in microfilm from UMI; back issues avail.) **Indexed:** Acoust.Abstr., Alloys Ind., ASCA; Cadscan, Chem.Titles, Curr.Cont., Eng.Ind., Eng.Mat.Abstr., Excerp.Med., INIS Atomind., ISMEC, Lead Abstr., Mat.Sci.Cit.Ind., Met.Abstr., Met.Abstr.Ind., Nonfer.Met.Alert, PCC Alert, Steels Alert, World Alum.Abstr., Zincscan. **Document type:** academic/scholarly publication.
—BLDSC (0412.000000); CISTI; Genuine Article; SWETS; UMI. CCC.
Refereed Serial

666.1   UK   ISSN 0260-6321
GLASS AND GLAZING NEWS. 1980. irreg. (3-4/yr.). free. Glass and Glazing Federation, 44-48 Borough High St., London SE1 1XB, England. TEL 44-171-403-7177. Ed. Catherine Hogan. illus. circ. 36,500. **Document type:** newsletter.

666 693   UK   ISSN 0269-0659
GLASS & GLAZING PRODUCTS. 1985. m. £30 (effective 1994). E M A P Maclaren Ltd., 19 Scarbrook House, Croydon, Surrey CR9 1QH, England. TEL 0181-688-7788. FAX 0181-680-5892. Ed. Damon Geesley. adv. contact: Dennis Johnson. circ. 8,500. (back issues avail.) **Document type:** trade publication.
Description: Contains product updates in glass products for doors and windows.

GLASS ART SOCIETY JOURNAL. see *ART*

666.1   UK   ISSN 0951-3108
GLASS ASSOCIATION. JOURNAL. Key Title: Journal of the Glass Association. biennial. membership. Glass Association, c/o Roger Dodsworth, Broadfield House Glass Museum, Barnett Ln., Kingswinford, W. Midlands DY6 9QA, England. TEL 44-1384-273011. FAX 44-1384-453576. Eds. Ian Wolfenden, Richard Gray. **Indexed:** DAAI. **Document type:** trade publication.
Description: Reflects the breadth of interest of current glass studies in the design, social, industrial, and economic contexts of glass, as well as its aesthetic and art historical aspects.

666.1   CN   ISSN 0843-7041
GLASS CANADA. 1989. 6/yr. $39. A I S Communications Ltd., 145 Thames Rd. W., Exeter, ON N0M 1S3, Canada. TEL 519-235-2400. FAX 519-235-0798. Ed. Craig Power. adv. contact: Bill Branderhorst. circ. 4,742. **Document type:** trade publication.
—CISTI.

666.1   US   ISSN 0893-8660
NK5100
GLASS COLLECTOR'S DIGEST. 1987. bi-m $22 (foreign $30) (effective 1997 & 1998). Glass Press, Inc., 217 Union St., Box 553, Marietta, OH 45750. TEL 614-373-6146. FAX 614-373-6917. Ed. D. Thomas O'Connor; Pub. David E. Richardson. R&P contact: David E. Richardson. adv. contact: Terry Ellen Nutter. bk.rev.; charts; illus.; cum.index; circ. 7,000 (paid). (back issues avail.) **Document type:** consumer publication.
Description: Covers all areas of collectible glass, with features on glassmakers, dealers and collectors.

666.1   UK   ISSN 0265-9654
NK5100
GLASS CONE. s-a. membership. Glass Association, Broadfield House Glass Museum, Barnett La., Kingswinford, West Midlands DY6 9QA, England. TEL 0384-273011. FAX 0384-453576. Ed. Charles Hajdamach.

666 380.1   US   ISSN 0017-1018
TP845   CODEN: GLDIAE
GLASS DIGEST; management magazine serving the flat glass, architectural metal and allied products industry. 1922. m. $40 (foreign $50). Ashlee Publishing Co., Inc., 18 E. 41st St., Phse., New York, NY 10017-6222. TEL 212-376-7722. FAX 212-376-7723. Ed. Charles B. Cumpston. adv.; charts; illus.; mkt.; stat.; tr.lit.; index; circ. 12,000 (paid). (also avail. in microform from UMI; reprint service avail. from UMI) **Indexed:** Chem.Abstr. **Document type:** trade publication.
—CASDDS; CISTI; Ei; UMI. CCC.

666 669   US
GLASS DIGEST BUYER'S GUIDE. 1958. a. $35 (or included with Glass Digest). Ashlee Publishing Co., Inc., 18 E. 41st St., Phse., New York, NY 10017-6222. TEL 212-376-7722. FAX 212-376-7723. Ed. Charles B. Cumpston. adv. circ. 11,000. **Document type:** catalog, trade publication.
—CISTI.
Former titles: International Glass - Metal Catalog (ISSN 0147-300X); (until 1973): Glass-Metal Catalog (ISSN 0072-4645); Glass-Metal Directory.

GLASS FACTORY DIRECTORY OF NORTH AMERICA AND U.S. INDUSTRY FACTBOOK. see *BUSINESS AND ECONOMICS — Trade And Industrial Directories*

666   US   ISSN 0017-1026
TP845   CODEN: GLINAK
GLASS INDUSTRY. (Includes Annual Directory Issue) 1920. m. $40 (foreign $50). Ashlee Publishing Co., Inc., 18 E. 41st St., Phse., New York, NY 10017-6222. TEL 212-376-7722. FAX 212-376-7723. Ed. Charles B. Cumpston. adv.; bk.rev.; illus.; pat.; stat.; index; circ. 2,600 (paid). (also avail. in microform from UMI; reprint service avail. from UMI) **Indexed:** A.S.& T.Ind., Br.Ceram.Abstr., Ceram.Abstr., Eng.Ind., Ind.Sci.Rev., Int.Packag.Abstr., PROMT. **Document type:** trade publication.
—BLDSC (4191.000000); CASDDS; CISTI; Ei; KR SourceOne; Linda Hall; SWETS; UMI; UnCover. CCC.

CERAMICS, GLASS AND POTTERY

666   UK   ISSN 0143-7836
 CODEN: GLINDN
GLASS INTERNATIONAL. 1978. q. £91.20 (foreign £129.20) (effective 1997). Argus Business Media Ltd. (Subsidiary of: D M G Exhibitions Group Ltd.), Queensway House, 2 Queensway, Redhill, Surrey RH1 1QS, England. TEL 44-1737-768611. FAX 44-1737-761685. Ed. J. Phillips. **Indexed:** Br.Tech.Ind., Int.Packag.Abstr. **Document type:** trade publication.
●Also available online. Vendor(s): Information Access Co.
—BLDSC (4191.150000); CASDDS; CISTI; SWETS.
 Description: Covers the glass manufacturing industry worldwide.

666   US
GLASS: LATIN AMERICAN INDUSTRIAL REPORT. (Avail. for each of 22 Latin American countries) 1985. a. $435 per country report. Aquino Productions, Box 125, Rochester, VT 05767. Ed. Andres C. Aquino.

666.1   IT   ISSN 0394-9893
GLASS MACHINERY PLANTS & ACCESSORIES; bi-monthly glass industry international magazine. (Text in English) 1988. bi-m. $160 (effective 1997). Artech Publishing s.r.l., Via Gramsci 63, 20032 Cormano (MI), Italy. TEL 39-2-66302904. FAX 39-2-66302914. Ed. Marco Pinetti. adv. contact: Oliver Marra. **Document type:** trade publication.
—BLDSC (4191.230000).
 Description: For glassworks involved in production and processing of hollow and pressed glass: bottles and containers, household, lighting, technical, scientific, medical and industrial glassware.

338.4 666.1   US   ISSN 0747-4261
HD9623.U44
GLASS MAGAZINE. 1948. m. $34.95. National Glass Association, 8200 Greensboro Dr., Ste. 302, McLean, VA 22102. TEL 703-442-4890. FAX 703-442-0630. E-mail: nga@glass.org; URL: http://ourworld.compuserve.com/homepages.nga. Ed. Sean McKenna; Pub. Nicole Harris. R&P contact: Nicole Harris. adv. contact: Mike Gribbin. circ. 17,000. **Indexed:** Art Ind. **Document type:** trade publication.
—BLDSC (4191.242000); CISTI.
 Formerly: Glass Dealer (ISSN 0094-3746)
 Description: Serves the architectural glass industry, architectural metal, building, remodeling, and related architectural industries. Reports the latest industry developments, technical information, management strategies, and new product information.

666   NO   ISSN 0802-5428
GLASS & PORSELEN; special magazine for glass, porcelain, gifts and kitchenware. 1946. 5/yr. NOK 350. (Forbundet for Glass og Porselen) A-S Ursus Forlag og Pressbyraa, Odins gt. 26, 0266 Oslo, Norway. TEL 47-22-43-40-60. FAX 47-22-43-61-43. Ed. Vigdis L'Orsa. adv.: B&W page NOK 5750, color page NOK 8750. bk.rev.; illus.; circ. 3,000 (controlled). **Document type:** trade publication.
—CCC.
 Formerly (until 1990): Glassposten (ISSN 0046-6018)

738.4   US   ISSN 1083-6888
NK4997
GLASS ON METAL; the enamelist's magazine. 1982. 5/yr. $45 (Canada & Mexico $52; Europe $59.10; elsewhere $62.50). Enamelist Society, Box 310, Newport, KY 41072. TEL 606-291-3800. FAX 606-291-1849. Ed. Tom Ellis. R&P contact: Tom Ellis. adv. contact: Tom Ellis. bk.rev.; illus.; circ. 1,100 (paid). pp./issue: 24. (back issues avail.) **Document type:** academic/scholarly publication.
 Description: Covers the history of enameling, contemporary uses, people and places, techniques, technology, and research on new products.

GLASS PATTERNS QUARTERLY. see ARTS AND HANDICRAFTS

666.1   RU   ISSN 1087-6596
TP845
GLASS PHYSICS AND CHEMISTRY. English translation of: Fizika i Khimiya Stekla (RU ISSN 0132-6651) 1975. bi-m. $995 in US; elsewhere $1165 (effective 1998). (Russian Academy of Sciences) Maik Nauka - Interperiodica, Mezhdunarodnyi Otdel, Ul. Profsoyuznaya, 90, 117864 Moscow, Russia. TEL 7-095-3360066. FAX 7-095-3360066. TELEX 23-421139. (Dist. by: Plenum Publishing Corp., 233 Spring St., New York, NY 10013-1578, U.S.A. TEL 212-620-8468. FAX 212-463-0742) Ed. O.V. Mazurin. (also avail. in microfilm from UMI; back issues avail.) **Indexed:** ASCA, Chem.Cit.Ind., Eng.Ind., INSPEC, Mat.Sci.Cit.Ind. **Document type:** academic/scholarly publication.
—AskIEEE; CISTI; Ei; Genuine Article; KR SourceOne; Linda Hall; SWETS; UMI; UnCover. **CCC.**
 Formerly (until 1994): Soviet Journal of Glass Physics and Chemistry (ISSN 0360-5043)
 Refereed Serial

666.1   UK   ISSN 0959-0838
GLASS PRODUCTION TECHNOLOGY INTERNATIONAL. 1990. a. £55. Sterling Publications Ltd., 86-88 Edgware Rd., London W2 2YW, England. TEL 44-171-915-9600. FAX 44-171-915-9619. R&P contact: Sandy Tucker. circ. 6,000. **Document type:** trade publication.
—BLDSC (4191.813000).

666.1   US   ISSN 1077-517X
GLASS REFLECTIONS. 1983. q. $20 (foreign $40) (effective 1997). Glass Association of North America, 3310 S.W. Harrison St., Topeka, KS 66611-2279. TEL 913-266-7013. FAX 913-266-0272. Ed. Vicki Louvier; Pub. Wn.J. Birch. circ. 500. **Document type:** newsletter.

666.1   GW   ISSN 0946-7475
TP845   CODEN: GLBEAQ
GLASS SCIENCE AND TECHNOLOGY; Glastechnische Berichte. (Text in English; index in English and German) 1923. m. DM.545 (effective 1998). Deutsche Glastechnische Gesellschaft e.V., Mendelssohnstr. 75-77, 60325 Frankfurt a.M., Germany. TEL 49-69-975861-0. FAX 49-69-97586199. E-mail: 76105.1464@compuserve.com. Ed. H.A. Schaeffer. adv.: B&W page DM.1870, color page DM.3250; trim 250 x 171. bk.rev.; abstr.; bibl.; charts; illus.; pat.; index, cum.index: vols.1-30, 31-40, 41-50. circ. 2,000. (back issues avail.) **Indexed:** Art & Archaeol.Tech.Abstr., ASCA, Br.Ceram.Abstr., C.I.S. Abstr., Chem.Abstr., Chem.Cit.Ind., Curr.Cont., Eng.Ind., Ind.Sci.Rev., INIS Atomind., Int.Packag.Abstr., Mat.Sci.Cit.Ind., Sci.Cit.Ind. **Document type:** academic/scholarly publication.
—BLDSC (4192.060000); AskIEEE; CASDDS; CISTI; Ei; Genuine Article; KR SourceOne; Linda Hall; SWETS. **CCC.**
 Formerly (until 1994): Glastechnische Berichte (ISSN 0017-1085)
 Description: News about glass science and technology.
 Refereed Serial

666.1   NE   ISSN 0927-4472
 CODEN: GSCTER
GLASS SCIENCE AND TECHNOLOGY. (Text in English) 1977. irreg., vol.13, 1993. price varies. Elsevier Science B.V., Books Division, P.O. Box 211, 1000 AE Amsterdam, Netherlands. TEL 31-20-4853911. FAX 31-20-4853705. TELEX 18582 ESPA NL. E-mail: nlinfo-f@elsevier.nl; usinfo-f@elsevier.com; forinfo-kyf04035@niftyserve.or.jp; URL: http://www.elsevier.nl/. (Subscr. in the Americas to: Elsevier Science, Regional Sales Office, Box 945, New York, NY 10159-0945. TEL 212-633-3730. FAX 212-633-3680; Subscr. in Australasia and the Far East to: Elsevier Science (Singapore) Pte Ltd, No.1 Temasek Ave., No.17-01 Millenia Tower, Singapore 039192, Singapore. TEL 65-434-3727. FAX 65-337-2230; Subscr. in Japan to: Elsevier Science Japan, 9-15 Higashi-Azabu 1-chome, Minato-ku, Tokyo 106, Japan. TEL 81-3-5561-5033. FAX 81-3-5561-5047) **Indexed:** Chem.Abstr. **Document type:** monographic series.
—BLDSC (4192.050000); CASDDS.
 Refereed Serial

666.1   IT   ISSN 1120-6748
GLASS - TECHNOLOGY INTERNATIONAL. (Text in English) 1989. bi-m. $160 (effective 1997). Artech Publishing s.r.l., Via Gramsci 63, 20032 Cormano (MI), Italy. TEL 39-2-66302904. FAX 39-2-66302914. adv. contact: Oliver Marra. **Document type:** trade publication.
 Formerly: Automotive Glass.
 Description: For people involved in the flat glass industry from building to automotive, furniture to household electric appliances.

GLASS WORKSHOP. see ARTS AND HANDICRAFTS

666.1   SW   ISSN 0017-1093
 CODEN: GLTIAQ
GLASTEKNISK TIDSKRIFT. (Text in English, Swedish; occasionally in Danish, German, Norwegian) 1946. 3/yr. SEK 600 in Scandinavia; Europe SEK 650; elsewhere SEK 700. Glasforskningsinstitutet (Glafo) - Glass Research Institute, P.O. Box 3093, S-350 33 Vaexjoe, Sweden. TEL 46-470-100-90. Ed. Elisabeth Flygt. adv.; bk.rev.; abstr.; illus.; index. circ. 400. **Indexed:** Ceram.Abstr., Chem.Abstr. **Document type:** academic/scholarly publication.
—CASDDS; CISTI; Linda Hall.
 Formerly (until vol.4, 1947): Medlemsskrift - Stiftelsen Glasinstitutet i Vaexjoe.
 Description: Features articles on the glass industry.

666.1   GW   ISSN 0017-1107
GLASWELT: DEUTSCHE GLASERZEITUNG; Fachzeitschrift fuer Handwerk, Handel und Industrie. 1947. m. DM.199.20 (foreign DM.254.40) (effective 1996). Gentner Verlag Stuttgart, Forststr. 131, 70193 Stuttgart, Germany. TEL 49-711-63672-0. FAX 49-711-63672-11. Eds. U. Baete, M. Brown. adv. contact: Walter Eder. bk.rev.; charts; illus.; pat.; tr.lit.; index. circ. 7,316. **Indexed:** Chem.Abstr., IBR. **Document type:** trade publication.
—CISTI. **CCC.**
 Formerly: Glaswelt.

666   UK   ISSN 0261-0329
GLAZED EXPRESSIONS. 1981. 2/yr. £18 to individuals (foreign £24); institutions £24 (foreign £30). Tiles & Architectural Ceramics Society, Liverpool Museum, William Brown St., Liverpool L3 8EN, England. TEL 44-151-2070001. (Subscr. to: Kathy Huggins, Reabrook Lodge, 8 Sutton Rd., Shrewsbury SY2 6DD, England. TEL 44-1743-236127) Ed. Hans van Lemmen. bk.rev.; illus. circ. 500. **Indexed:** Br.Ceram.Abstr., DAAI. **Document type:** bulletin.
 Description: News, research and features pertaining to tiles and architectural ceramics.

666   UK
GLOBAL CERAMIC REVIEW. 1966. q. £55 (foreign £80) (includes supplement) (effective Jan. 1997). British Ceramic Plant & Machinery Manufacturers' Association, 44 Kingsway, Stoke-on-Trent, Staffs ST4 1JH, England. TEL 44-1782-411433. FAX 44-1782-747061. Ed. Charles R. Wallin. R&P contact: Charles Wallin. adv.: B&W page $825, color page $1550; trim 297 x 210. bk.rev.; charts; illus. circ. 8,000. (back issues avail.) **Indexed:** Alloys Ind., Br.Ceram.Abstr., Eng.Mat.Abstr., Met.Abstr.Ind., Met.Abstr., Nonfer.Met.Alert, PCC Alert, Steels Alert, World Alum.Abstr. **Document type:** trade publication.
—CISTI.
 Formerly (until 1991): British Ceramic Review (ISSN 0306-7076)
 Description: Concentrates on ceramic production technology for all sectors of the industry. Features articles on applied technology, case histories, personnel moves, a calendar of events, a quarterly round-up of ceramic industry patents, and information on suppliers.

GROUPE INTERNATIONAL D'ETUDE DE LA CERAMIQUE EGYPTIENNE. BULLETIN DE LIAISON. see ARCHAEOLOGY

GUIA GENERAL DE LAS INDUSTRIAS CERAMICAS Y AFINES DE ESPANA. see BUSINESS AND ECONOMICS — Trade And Industrial Directories

HANDBOOK FOR CERAMIC TILE INSTALLATION. see BUILDING AND CONSTRUCTION

CERAMICS, GLASS AND POTTERY

666 **CC** ISSN 1003-319X
HEBEI TAOCI/HEBEI CERAMICS. (Text in Chinese) 1973. q. $15. Hebei Taoci Gongye Keji Qingbaozhan - Hebei Scientific and Technical Information Centre of Ceramic Industry, Taoci Yanjiusuo, Tangshan, Hebei 063020, People's Republic of China. TEL 71414. Ed. Liu Deli. adv.: B&W page$1000, color page $1500. circ. 1,200.

HEISEY NEWS. see *ANTIQUES*

666 **US** ISSN 1045-2397
HIGH TECH CERAMICS NEWS. 1989. m. $395. Business Communications Co., Inc (Norwalk), 25 Van Zant St., Ste. 13, Norwalk, CT 06855. TEL 203-853-4266. FAX 203-853-0348. TELEX 6502934929 WUI. Ed. Thomas Abraham. (back issues avail.) Indexed: Alloys Ind., Eng.Mat.Abstr., Met.Abstr.Ind., Met.Abstr., Nonfer.Met.Alert, PCC Alert, Steels Alert, World Alum.Abstr.
●Also available online. Vendor(s): Data-Star, Information Access Co., Knight-Ridder Information, Inc., NewsNet (ML05).
—BLDSC (4307.361055). **CCC**.
Description: Provides current analysis of new products, patents and industry trends. Written for materials companies and materials scientists.

HOBSTAR. see *ANTIQUES*

I C A TRADE JOURNAL. (International Ceramic Association) see *BUSINESS AND ECONOMICS — Trade And Industrial Directories*

I M M E BOLETIN. (Instituto de Materiales y Modelos Estructurales) see *ENGINEERING — Civil Engineering*

IBIDEN COMPANY. ANNUAL REPORT. see *CHEMISTRY*

666 **II** ISSN 0371-750X
TP785
INDIAN CERAMIC SOCIETY. TRANSACTIONS. (Text in English) 1942. bi-m. Rs.200($40) Indian Ceramic Society, c/o Central Glass and Ceramic Research Institute, Calcutta 700 032, India. TEL 91-33-473-3496. FAX 91-33-473-0957. Ed. H.S. Maiti. R&P contact: A.K. Banerjee. adv. contact: A.K. Banerjee. bk.rev.; bibl.; charts; illus. circ. 1,500. (also avail. in microfiche from UMI; reprint service avail. from UMI) Indexed: Anal.Abstr., Br.Ceram.Abstr., C.R.I.Abstr., C.R.I.Curr.Cont., Ceram.Abstr., Chem.Abstr., Eng.Mat.Abstr., Met.Abstr., Met.Abstr.Ind., Nonfer.Met.Alert, PCC Alert, Steels Alert, World Alum.Abstr. Document type: academic/scholarly publication.
—BLDSC (8937.000000); CASDDS; CISTI; Linda Hall; UMI.
Description: Devoted to the advancement of ceramic science, arts and technologies.
Refereed Serial

666 **II** ISSN 0019-4492
NK3700 CODEN: IDCMAL
INDIAN CERAMICS. (Text in English) 1938-1988 (Aug.); resumed 1994. 4/yr. Rs.450($100) 10 Sourin Roy Rd., Behala, Calcutta 700 034, India. TEL 91-33-478-9101. FAX 91-33-468-2612. Ed. Ambar Roy. R&P contact: Ambar Roy. adv.: page $100; 220 x 180. bk.rev.; abstr.; charts; tr.lit.; stat.; index. circ. 500. Indexed: Br.Ceram.Abstr., C.R.I.Abstr., C.R.I.Curr.Cont., Ceram.Abstr., Chem.Abstr. Document type: academic/scholarly publication.
—CASDDS; CISTI; Linda Hall.
Description: Covers glass, cement, refractory, pottery, oxides, abrasive, fine ceramics and special ceramics.

666 **IT** ISSN 1121-7588
TP785 CODEN: INCEE3
INDUSTRIAL CERAMICS. 1981. 3/yr. $165 foreign (effective 1997). Techna s.r.l., Casella Postale 174, 48018 Faenza, Italy. TEL 39-546-22461. FAX 39-546-664138. Ed. Pietro Vincenzini. adv.: B&W page L.2300000; trim 210 x 297; adv. contact: Gianantonio Bertoni. bk.rev.; pat.; stat.; tr.lit. circ. 4,000. (back issues avail.) Indexed: Alloys Ind., ASCA, Br.Ceram.Abstr., Chem.Abstr., Eng.Ind., Eng.Mat.Abstr., INSPEC, Met.Abstr.Ind., Met.Abstr., Nonfer.Met.Alert, PCC Alert, Steels Alert, World Alum.Abstr. Document type: academic/scholarly publication, newsletter.
—BLDSC (4447.080000); AskIEEE; CASDDS; CISTI; Ei; Genuine Article; KR SourceOne; SWETS; UnCover.
Former titles: Industrial Ceramic - C I News; (until 1987): C I News (ISSN 0392-2960)
Description: Covers fine ceramics, heavy clay products and refractories. Includes activities of research labs throughout the world.

666 **FR** ISSN 1169-873X
CODEN: INCVEK
INDUSTRIE CERAMIQUE ET VERRIERE. (Text in English, French) 1947. m. (except Aug.) 847.43 F. (foreign 1051 F.) (effective 1997). Septima, 14 rue Falguiere, 75015 Paris, France. TEL 33-1-44384800. FAX 33-1-44384809. Ed. Mme. D. Lecat. adv.; bk.rev.; abstr.; bibl.; charts; illus.; stat.; tr.lit.; index. circ. 3,000. Indexed: Alloys Ind., Br.Ceram.Abstr., C.I.S. Abstr., Cadscan, Ceram.Abstr., Chem.Abstr., Eng.Mat.Abstr., Excerp.Med., GeoRef., INIS Atomind., INSPEC, Lead Abstr., Met.Abstr.Ind., Met.Abstr., Nonfer.Met.Alert, PCC Alert, Steels Alert, World Alum.Abstr., Zincscan. Document type: trade publication.
—BLDSC (4465.050000); CASDDS; CISTI; Ei; Linda Hall; SWETS. **CCC**.
Formerly: Industrie Ceramique (ISSN 0019-9044); Incorporating (1948-1981): Societe Francaise de Ceramique. Bulletin (ISSN 0037-931X); (1972-1981): Societe Francaise de Ceramique. Traductions Brevets.
Description: Covers the fields of ceramic and glass-works.

666 **GW** ISSN 0020-5214
TP785 CODEN: ITCRAC
INTERCERAM; international ceramic review. (Text in English; abstracts in French, German, Spanish) 1951. 6/yr. DM.370. Verlag Schmid GmbH (Freiburg), Postfach 6609, 79042 Freiburg, Germany. TEL 49-761-8960940. FAX 49-761-8960980. circ. 14,500. Indexed: Alloys Ind., Br.Ceram.Abstr., Chem.Abstr., Eng.Mat.Abstr., Met.Abstr., Met.Abstr.Ind., Nonfer.Met.Alert, PCC Alert, Steels Alert, World Alum.Abstr. Document type: trade publication.
—BLDSC (4532.000000); CASDDS; CISTI; Ei; Linda Hall; SWETS. **CCC**.
Description: Focuses on research and development, innovative technology, new products, market analyses, company profiles, and information about conferences, symposiums and fairs.

666 **FR** ISSN 0074-218X
INTERNATIONAL CERAMIC CONGRESS. PROCEEDINGS. (Proceedings published by host country) irreg., 13th, 1974, Amsterdam. European Ceramic Association, 44 rue Copernic, 75116 Paris, France. TEL 45-00-18-56. TELEX 611913 F CERAFRA.

666 **UK** ISSN 0266-9374
INTERNATIONAL CERAMIC DIRECTORY. 1984. quinquennial. £40. London and Sheffield Publishing Co. Ltd., 291 Cricklewood Ln., Childs Hill, London NW2 2JL, England. TEL 44-181-446-3445. FAX 44-181-446-3445. Document type: directory.
Description: Lists all ceramic manufacturers from brick and tile to pottery worldwide, containing descriptions, directions and products. Does not include refractory manufacturers.

666 **IT**
INTERNATIONAL CERAMICS JOURNAL. (Text in English) 1978. 6/yr. Lit.81000 in Europe; Oceania Lit.144000; elsewhere Lit.107000 (effective 1997). Faenza Editrice S.p.A., Via Pier de Crescenzi 44, 48018 Faenza (RA), Italy. TEL 39-546-663488. FAX 39-546-660440. E-mail: gefe.vendita@uno.dinamica.it; gefe.info@uno.dinamica.it. Ed. Franco Roni. adv.: B&W page Lit.2630000, color page Lit.2860000; adv. contact: Elvio Neri. circ. 3,297. Document type: trade publication.
Description: Disseminates information on traditional and new Italian technology in the area of plant, machinery, equipment, raw materials and products for the ceramic sector.

666.1 **IT**
INTERNATIONAL GLASS JOURNAL. (Text in English) 1937. q. Lit.90000 (Europe Lit.115000; Oceania Lit.165000; elsewhere Lit.140000) (effective 1997). Gruppo Editoriale Faenza Editrice s.p.a., Via Pier. de Crescenzi, 44, 48018 Faenza RA, Italy. TEL 39-546-663488. FAX 39-546-660440. E-mail: gefe.vendita@uno.dinamica.it; gefe.info@uno.vendita.it. Ed. Franco Roni. adv.: B&W page Lit.1560000, color page Lit.1740000. circ. 3,750. Document type: trade publication.
—Ei.
Formerly: Vetro Informazione (ISSN 0392-8241)

666.1 **UK** ISSN 1359-4974
CODEN: IGREFU
▼**INTERNATIONAL GLASS REVIEW.** 1995. s-a. Euromoney Publications plc., Nestor House, Playhouse Yard, London EC4V 5EX, England. TEL 44-171-779-8935. FAX 44-171-779-8541. (Dist. in US by: American Educational Systems, 173 W. 81st St., New York, NY 10024. TEL 800-717-2669. FAX 212-501-8926) Document type: trade publication.
—CASDDS.

666 382 **UK**
INTERNATIONAL REFRACTORIES HANDBOOK & DIRECTORY. 1976. quadrennial. £75. London and Sheffield Publishing Co. Ltd., 291 Cricklewood Ln., Childs Hill, London NW2 2JL, England. TEL 44-181-446-3445. FAX 44-181-446-3445. Document type: directory.
Description: Comprehensive list of names, addresses, telephone and fax numbers, and products of all refractory manufacturers and engineers worldwide.

ISENKRAMBRANCHEN. see *INTERIOR DESIGN AND DECORATION — Furniture And House Furnishings*

666.5 **CC** ISSN 1001-9545
JINGDEZHEN TAOCI/JINGDEZHEN CERAMICS. (Text in Chinese) q. Jiangxi Sheng Taoci Yanjiusuo - Jiangxi Ceramics Research Institute, Zhangshusha, Jingdezhen Dongjiao (East Suburb), Jiangxi 333001, People's Republic of China. TEL 225514. (Co-sponsor: Jiangxi Sheng Taoci Keji Qingbao Zhan) Ed. Wang Deji.

666.5 **CC** ISSN 1000-2278
JINGDEZHEN TAOCI XUEYUAN XUEBAO/JINGDEZHEN CERAMICS INSTITUTE. JOURNAL. (Text in Chinese; abstracts in English) 1980. q. Y10. Jingdezhen Taoci Xueyuan - Jingdezhen Ceramic Institute, Jingdezhen, Jiangxi 333001, People's Republic of China. TEL 0798-441845. FAX 0798-441837. Ed. Lin Yunwan. adv.: bk.rev. circ. 2,000. Document type: academic/scholarly publication.
Description: Contains research papers and reviews on silicate engineering, ceramics machinery, art & design for ceramics and ceramics history.

JOURNAL OF ELECTROCERAMICS. see *ENGINEERING — Engineering Mechanics And Materials*

666 **IS**
KADAROT. (Text in Hebrew) a. Association of Ceramic Artists in Israel, P.O. Box 8378, Jerusalem 91083, Israel. TEL 02-249575.

666.1 II ISSN 0971-3751
CODEN: GLUDDJ
KANCH; the quarterly of the All India Glass Manufacturers' Federation. (Text in English) 1972. q. All India Glass Manufacturers' Federation, 812 New Delhi House, 27 Barakhamba Rd., New Delhi 110 001, India. Ed. N.D. Shetty. adv. **Document type:** trade publication.
—BLDSC (5085.324500); CASDDS.
Formerly (until 1992): Glass Udyog (ISSN 0379-0460)

666 738 GW ISSN 0023-0561
TP785 CODEN: KERZAS
KERAMISCHE ZEITSCHRIFT. 1948. m. DM.340. Verlag Schmid GmbH (Freiburg), Postfach 6609, 79042 Freiburg, Germany. TEL 49-761-8960940. FAX 49-761-8960980. circ. 4,100. **Indexed:** Alloys Ind., Art & Archaeol.Tech.Abstr., Br.Ceram.Abstr., C.I.S. Abstr., Ceram.Abstr., Chem.Abstr., Eng.Ind., Eng.Mat.Abstr., Excerp.Med., Fuel & Energy Abstr., INIS Atomind., Met.Abstr., Met.Abstr.Ind., Nonfer.Met.Alert, PCC Alert, Steels Alert, World Alum.Abstr. **Document type:** trade publication.
—BLDSC (5089.725000); CASDDS; CISTI; Ei; Linda Hall; SWETS. **CCC.**
Description: Focuses on research and development, innovative technology, new products, market analyses, company portraits, and information on congresses, symposiums and trade fairs for the complete ceramics industry.

KEY ENGINEERING MATERIALS. see *METALLURGY*

666 UK
KEY NOTE MARKET REPORT: CHINA & EARTHENWARE. Variant title: China & Earthenware. irreg., no.13, 1996. £205. Key Note Ltd., Field House, 72 Oldfield Rd., Hampton, Middlesex TW12 2HQ, England. TEL 44-181-783-0755. FAX 44-181-783-0049. **Document type:** trade publication.
●Also available online.
Also available on CD-ROM.
Formerly: Key Note Report: China and Earthenware.

666.1 UK
KEY NOTE MARKET REPORT: GLASSWARE. Variant title: Glassware. irreg., no.8, 1992. £185. Key Note Ltd., Field House, 72 Oldfield Rd., Hampton, Middlesex TW12 2HQ, England. TEL 44-181-783-0755. FAX 44-181-783-1940. **Document type:** trade publication.
●Also available online.
Also available on CD-ROM.
Formerly: Key Note Report: Glassware (ISSN 0954-5220)

KEY NOTE MARKET REPORT: PACKAGING (GLASS). see *PACKAGING*

666 NE ISSN 0167-5001
CODEN: KLEIDW
KLEI, GLAS, KERAMIEK. 1950. 10/yr. fl.63.60 includes Keramisch Jaarboek. (Nederlandse Keramische Federatie - Dutch Ceramic Federation) Pressefoon Uitgeverij bv, Postbus 2093, 1960 GB Heemskerk, Netherlands. TEL 31-2510-35150. FAX 31-2510-35150. Pub. J. Wiegers. adv.; bk.rev.; charts; illus.; index. circ. 1,500. **Indexed:** Br.Ceram.Abstr., Chem.Abstr., Excerp.Med., Key to Econ.Sci. **Document type:** trade publication.
—BLDSC (5099.076000); CASDDS; CISTI; Linda Hall; SWETS.
Formerly: Klei en Keramiek (ISSN 0023-2041)

KOVELS ON ANTIQUES AND COLLECTIBLES; the newsletter for dealers, collectors and investors. see *ANTIQUES*

666.3 GW
LANDESINNUNG DER BAYERISCHEN TOEPFER. MITTEILUNGEN. irreg. (3-4/yr.). Landesinnung der Bayerischen Toepfer, Toepferweg 16, 87527 Altstaedten, Germany.

666 688 IT
MAGAZINE PREMIERE. (Text in English, Italian) 1987. 4/yr. L.100000 (Europe $100; elsewhere $160). Eva Rutter Editore s.r.l., Casa Corni, 27047 Santa Maria della Versa (PV), Italy. TEL 39-385-798086. Ed. Eva Rutter. adv.: color page L.2500000. circ. 9,000. **Document type:** trade publication.
Formerly: Premiere.

666 913 GW ISSN 0076-5171
MATERIALIEN ZUR ROEMISCH-GERMANISCHEN KERAMIK. 1914. irreg., no.12, 1993. price varies. (Deutsches Archaeologisches Institut, Roemisch-Germanische Kommission) Dr. Rudolf Habelt GmbH, Am Buchenhang 1, 53115 Bonn, Germany. TEL 49-228-9238322. FAX 49-228-923836. **Document type:** monographic series.

666 GW ISSN 0171-399X
MESSE DIGEST; Einkaufsplaner. 1972. s-a. DM.95 (effective 1997). Verlag Wareninformation GmbH, Niederwallstr. 25, 41460 Neuss, Germany. TEL 49-2131-222027. FAX 49-2131-275549. Ed. Gerhard Fass; Pub. Frank Hetzenecker. adv. contact: Ildiko Schiller. circ. 8,500. **Document type:** trade publication.

MINES, MINERALS, ENERGY, ECOLOGY, POLLUTION, CERAMICS, REFRACTORY, CEMENT, GLASS. see *MINES AND MINING INDUSTRY*

666 GW ISSN 0933-2367
NK3930
NEUE KERAMIK. 1987. bi-m. DM.66 (Europe DM.72) (effective 1996). Verlag Neue Keramik GmbH, Unter den Eichen 90, 12205 Berlin, Germany. TEL 49-30-84109216. FAX 49-30-84109217. Ed. Gustav Weiss. adv.; bk.rev. circ. 8,000. (back issues avail.) **Document type:** trade publication.

666 XR ISSN 1210-2741
TP485
NEW GLASS REVIEW; glass, china and ceramics magazine. German edition: Neue Glasrevue (ISSN 1210-2733) (Text in English, German; summaries in French) 1945. m. $89. Efekt, Co. Ltd., Ciklova 3, 128 00 Prague 2, Czech Republic. TEL 42-2-6926207. (Dist. by: Abont Ltd., Chlumova 17, 1300 Prague 3, Czech Republic. TEL 420-2-22781521) Ed. Ludmila Halkovova. R&P contact: Ludmila Halkovova. adv.: B&W page $1613, color page $2581; adv. contact: T. Rashanova. illus. circ. 7,000. **Indexed:** Artbibl.Mod., RILA.
Former titles (until 1992): Glass Review (ISSN 0323-0635); Czechoslovak Glass Review (ISSN 0034-9127)
Description: Brings a survey of novelties, new trends and technologies, exhibitions and designers, new offers and business deals.
Refereed Serial

666 SZ
OFENBAU PLATTENBELAEGE. m. (11/yr.). 49 SFr. (foreign 64 SFr.) (effective 1996). Verband Schweizerischer Hafner- und Plattengeschaefte, Solothurnerstr. 236, CH-4600 Olten, Switzerland. TEL 41-62-324735. FAX 41-62-320508. Eds. Rene Hayoz, Heidi Staeheli. adv.: B&W page 575 SFr., color page 975 SFr.; trim 182 x 266. circ. 875. **Document type:** newspaper.

666 RU
CODEN: OGNPA2
OGNEUPORY I TEKHNICHESKAYA KERAMIKA. English translation: Refractories and Industrial Ceramics (US ISSN 1083-4877) (Text in Russian; summaries in English, Russian) 1933. m. 20000 Rub. Izdatel'stvo Metallurgiya, 2-i Obydenskii per., 14, 119857 Moscow, Russia. TEL 7-095-2025740. FAX 7-095-2025752. Ed. A.V. Serafinovich. adv.; bk.rev. (back issues avail.) **Indexed:** Chem.Abstr., Chem.Titles. **Document type:** academic/scholarly publication.
—AskIEEE; CASDDS; CISTI; KR SourceOne; Linda Hall. **CCC.**
Formerly (until May 1995): Ogneupory (ISSN 0369-7290)

PERSPECTIVE. see *BUILDING AND CONSTRUCTION — Hardware*

666 PL ISSN 0079-3264
CODEN: PPKCBN
POLSKA AKADEMIA NAUK. ODDZIAL W KRAKOWIE. KOMISJA CERAMICZNA. PRACE: CERAMIKA. (Text in Polish; summaries in English, Russian) 1964. irreg., no.40, 1992. price varies. Polska Akademia Nauk, Oddzial w Krakowie, Komisja Ceramiczna, Ul. Slawkowska 21, 31-016 Krakow, Poland. TEL 48-12-224853. FAX 48-12-222791. Ed. Roman Pampuch. circ. 520. **Indexed:** Chem.Abstr., Eng.Ind. **Document type:** monographic series.
—BLDSC (6588.013000); CASDDS; CISTI.

POLYTECHNICAL UNIVERSITY OF BUCHAREST. SCIENTIFIC BULLETIN. SERIES B: CHEMISTRY AND MATERIALS SCIENCE. see *CHEMISTRY*

666 US ISSN 0032-4477
TP785
POPULAR CERAMICS. Spanish edition: Artes de la Ceramica. 1949. m. $24.95 (effective 1997). Jones Publishing Inc., Box 5000, N. 7450 Aanstad Rd., Iola, WI 54945. TEL 715-445-5000. E-mail: jonespub@gglbbs.com. Ed. Barbara Tobias. adv.; bk.rev.; illus.; index. circ. 17,000. (also avail. in microform from UMI) **Indexed:** Ind.How To Do It (1990-). **Document type:** consumer publication.
—UMI.
Description: Published for people who truly enjoy creating unique ceramic pieces. A variety of color projects offered for all skill levels.

POTTERY SOUTHWEST; news, queries & views on archaeological ceramics by Southwesternists. see *ARCHAEOLOGY*

POWDER METALLURGY AND METAL CERAMICS. see *METALLURGY*

PREVISIONS GLISSANTES DETAILLEES EN PERSPECTIVES SECTORIELLES (VOL.24): INDUSTRIE DU VERRE. see *BUSINESS AND ECONOMICS — Economic Situation And Conditions*

666 PL ISSN 1232-9703
PRZEGLAD DOKUMENTACYJNY MATERIALOW OGNIOTRWALYCH. 1963. m. $216. Instytut Materialow Ogniotrwalych, Ul. Toszecka 99, 44-101 Gliwice, Poland. TEL 48-3-1701801. FAX 48-3-1701934. TELEX 036172 JMO PL. Ed. Jerzy Czechowski. bk.rev.; abstr.; index. circ. 300. (processed)

666 AT ISSN 0728-0858
QUEENSLAND POTTERS ASSOCIATION. ANNUAL REPORT OF THE DIRECTORS. 1979. a. Queensland Potters Association, Cnr Malt & Brunswick Sts., Fortitude Valley, Qld. 4006, Australia. TEL 61-7-33585122. FAX 61-7-33854540. Ed. Bernice Gerrand. R&P contact: Bernice Gerrand. **Document type:** corporate report.

666 668.4 UK ISSN 0955-212X
RAW MATERIALS FOR PIGMENTS, FILLERS AND EXTENDERS. 1988. irreg., vol.2, 1995. £87($155) Industrial Minerals Information Ltd., Park House, Park Terrace, Worcester Park, Surrey KT4 7HY, England. TEL 44-171-827-9977.
FAX 44-181-337-8943. adv. contact: Phillip Owen. charts; mkt. **Document type:** trade publication.

666 UK ISSN 0952-598X
RAW MATERIALS FOR THE GLASS AND CERAMICS INDUSTRIES. 1990. triennial. $125. Metal Bulletin plc, Park House, Park Terrace, Worcester Park, Surrey KT4 7HY, England. TEL 44-171-827-9977. FAX 44-181-337-8943. Ed. Karen Harries-Rees. adv. contact: Phil Owen. bk.rev. **Document type:** trade publication.

666 US ISSN 1083-4877
TN677.A1 CODEN: RICEFY
REFRACTORIES AND INDUSTRIAL CERAMICS. English translation of: Ogneupory i Tekhnicheskaya Keramika. 1960. m. $1360 (foreign $1590) (effective 1997). (Ministerstvo Chernoi Metallurgii, Tsentralnyi Sovet Nauchno-Tekhnicheskogo Obshchestvo po Chernoi Metallurgii, RU) Plenum Publishing Corp., Consultants Bureau, 233 Spring St., New York, NY 10013-1578. TEL 212-620-8468. FAX 212-463-0742. TELEX 23-421139. (Co-sponsors: American Institute of Mining, Metallurgical, and Petroleum Engineers; American Society for Testing and Materials) Ed. V.S. Antipov. charts, illus.; index. (also avail. in microform from UMI; back issues avail.) **Indexed:** Alloys Ind., Chem.Titles, Curr.Cont., Energy Res.Abstr., Eng.Ind., Eng.Mat.Abstr., INSPEC (1969-), Met.Abstr.Ind., Met.Abstr., Nonfer.Met.Alert, PCC Alert, Steels Alert, World Alum.Abstr. **Document type:** academic/scholarly publication.
—BLDSC (0420.726800); CISTI; Ei; Linda Hall; UMI; UnCover. **CCC.**
Formerly (until vol.37, 1996): Refractories (ISSN 0034-3102)
Refereed Serial

CERAMICS, GLASS AND POTTERY

666   UK   ISSN 1362-4547
REFRACTORIES ENGINEER. 1972. q. £23.50 to non-members. (Institute of Refractories Engineers) Poulton Ltd., Station House, Cannock Rd., Hednesford, Staffs. WS12 4AF, England. TEL 44-1543-422217. FAX 44-1453-877725. E-mail: 101364.61@compuserve.com. Ed. J.B. Traynor. adv. contact: J.B. Traynor. **Indexed:** Alloys Ind., Eng.Mat.Abstr., Met.Abstr.Ind., Met.Abstr., Nonfer.Met.Alert, PCC Alert, Steels Alert, World Alum.Abstr. **Document type:** trade publication.
—BLDSC (7332.985000).
    Formerly (until 1996): Institute of Refractories Engineers. Journal (ISSN 0269-6924)

666.1   CC   ISSN 1000-985X
                         CODEN: REJIEIt
RENGONG JINGTI XUEBAO/JOURNAL OF SYNTHETIC CRYSTALS. (Text in Chinese) 1972. q. $56.5. (Chinese Ceramic Society, Committee on Crystal Growth and Materials) Chemical Industry Press - Huaxue Gongye Chubanshe, No. 3 Huixinli, Chaoyangpu, Beijing 100029, People's Republic of China. TEL 86-10-4918318. FAX 86-10-4918318. (Co-sponsor: Research Institute of Synthetic Crystals) pp./issue: 82. **Document type:** academic/scholarly publication.
—CASDDS.
    Formerly (until 1989): Rengong Jingti (ISSN 1001-0904)
    Description: Reports the recent researches and developments in the field of crystal growth and synthetic crystal materials in China.

666.1   SP
REVISTA DEL VIDRIO HUECO. (Supplement avail.: Anuario Espanol del Vidrio Hueco) 4/yr. 12720 ptas. includes Anuario; foreign 9000 ptas.($90) for magazine, 7000 ptas($70) for Anuario (effective 1994). Proporcion 3, S.A., Bruc. 48, 2o, 08010 Barcelona, Spain. TEL 3-412-07-64. FAX 3-412-49-25. Ed. Agustin Calvo.

666.1   SP
REVISTA DEL VIDRIO PLANO. (Supplement avail.: Anuario Espanol del Vidrio Plano) 6/yr. 14840 ptas. includes Anuario; foreign 10000 ptas. for magazine, 8000 ptas. for anuario. Proporcion 3, S.A., Bruc 48, 2o, 08010 Barcelona, Spain. TEL 3-412-07-64. FAX 3-412-49-25. Ed. Agustin Calvo.
    Description: Covers plate glass industry and machinery.

666   FR   ISSN 0758-3389
REVUE DE LA CERAMIQUE ET DU VERRE. 1981. bi-m. 365 F. (Europe 400 F.) (effective 1997). 61 rue Marconi, B.P. 3, 62880 Vendin-le-Vieil, France. TEL 33-3-21794444. FAX 33-3-21794445. Ed. Sylvie Girard; Pub. Sylvie Girard. adv.: B&W page 3300 F., color page 6600 F.; 300 x 220. bk.rev. circ. 6,200. **Indexed:** DAAI. **Document type:** trade publication.
    Formerly (until 1982): Revue de la Ceramique (ISSN 0294-202X)
    Description: Deals with every feature in ceramics and glass.
    Refereed Serial

666.1   IT
RIVISTA DEL VETRO. 8/yr. L.40000 (foreign L.100000). Editrice Editas s.r.l., Via G. Washington 50, 20146 Milan, Italy. TEL 39-2-48012921. FAX 39-2-48012293. Ed. Fulvio Golob. adv. contact: Mimma Piola. circ. 10,000. **Document type:** consumer publication.

666 330   GW
DER ROSENTHALER. 1970. q. free. Rosenthal AG, Postfach 1520, 95085 Selb, Germany. FAX 09287-72225. Ed. Roland Raithel. bk.rev. circ. 10,000.

SANITARY TABLEWARE, ARTISTIC CERAMICS SUPPLIERS BOOK. see *HEATING, PLUMBING AND REFRIGERATION*

666   GW   ISSN 0036-5947
DIE SCHAULADE; international trade magazine for table top, household goods, giftware and living accessories. 1925. m. DM.128 (foreign DM.135) (effective 1997). Meisenbach GmbH, Hainstr. 18, 96047 Bamberg, Germany. TEL 49-951-861135. FAX 49-951-861158. (Subscr. to: Postfach 2069, 96011 Bamberg, Germany) Ed. Beate Schraml. adv.: B&W page DM.3890, color page DM.5873.90; trim 184 x 260; adv. contact: Sabine Botta. abstr.; illus.; stat.; index. circ. 7,777. **Indexed:** Key to Econ.Sci. **Document type:** trade publication.

666   GW   ISSN 0343-9445
SCHOTT INTERN. English edition (ISSN 0720-1087); French edition (ISSN 0936-2878) 1953. m. Schott Glaswerke, Hattenbergstr. 10, 55122 Mainz, Germany. Ed. Hermann-Josef Berg.

SCIENCE OF SINTERING. see *METALLURGY*

666.1   HU   ISSN 0237-2169
SCIENTIFIC SOCIETY OF THE SILICATE INDUSTRY. CONFERENCE ON SILICATE INDUSTRY AND SILICATE SCIENCE. (Text in English, German, Hungarian, Russian) 1973. quadrennial. $64. OMIKK Technoinform, Muzeum u. 17, Budapest VIII, Hungary. (Subscr. to: H-1428 Budapest, Pf.12, Hungary) Ed. Maria Palocz. (also avail. in microfiche)

666.3   UK   ISSN 0260-7972
SCOTTISH POTTERY STUDIES. 1982. irreg. £1.95. Scottish Pottery Society, c/o Graeme Cruickshank, 21 Warrender Park Terrace, Edinburgh, Scotland. circ. 1,000.
—BLDSC (8211.088000).

666   JA   ISSN 0009-031X
                         CODEN: SERAA7
SERAMIKKUSU/CERAMICS JAPAN. (Text in Japanese; titles and key words in English) 1966. m. 24000 Yen (foreign 29500 Yen). Ceramic Society of Japan - Nippon Seramikkusu Kyokai, 22-17 Hyakunin-cho 2-chome, Shinjuku-ku, Tokyo 169, Japan. Ed. Yoshiro Suzuki. adv.; bk.rev.; illus. circ. 6,000. **Indexed:** Alloys Ind., Br.Ceram.Abstr., Ceram.Abstr., Chem.Abstr., Eng.Mat.Abstr., JCT, JTA, Met.Abstr., Met.Abstr.Ind., Nonfer.Met.Alert, PCC Alert, Steels Alert, World Alum.Abstr. **Document type:** bulletin.
—BLDSC (3119.030000); CASDDS; CISTI; Linda Hall. **CCC.**

666   JA   ISSN 0914-5400
TP785   CODEN: NSKRE2
SERAMIKKUSU KYOKAISHI/CERAMIC SOCIETY OF JAPAN. JOURNAL. International edition (ISSN 0912-9200) (Text in English and Japanese) 1891. m. 36000 Yen (foreign 41500 Yen). Ceramic Society of Japan - Nippon Seramikkusu Kyokai, 22-17 Hyakunin-cho 2-chome, Shinjuku-ku, Tokyo 169, Japan. Ed. Yoshiro Suzuki. adv.; bk.rev. circ. 6,000. **Indexed:** Alloys Ind., ASCA, Br.Ceram.Abstr., Ceram.Abstr., Chem.Abstr., Chem.Cit.Ind., Eng.Ind., Eng.Mat.Abstr., INSPEC, JTA, Met.Abstr., Met.Abstr.Ind., Nonfer.Met.Alert, PCC Alert, Steels Alert, World Alum.Abstr. **Document type:** academic/scholarly publication.
—BLDSC (4725.100000); AskIEEE; CASDDS; CISTI; Ei; Genuine Article; KR SourceOne; Linda Hall. **CCC.**
    Formerly (until 1988): Yogyo Kyokaishi (ISSN 0009-0255); (until 1950): Yogyo Kyokai Zasshi (ISSN 0372-7769)

666   BE   ISSN 0037-5225
TP785   CODEN: SIINAT
SILICATES INDUSTRIELS; ceramic science and technology. (Text in English, French, German) 1930. 6/yr. 4900 BEF (foreign 6500 BEF) (effective 1998). Belgian Ceramic Society, 4 ave. Gouverneur Cornez, 7000 Mons, Belgium. TEL 32-65-348000. FAX 32-65-348005. E-mail: bcrcins@mail.interpac.be. Ed. F. Cambier; Pub. F. Cambier. R&P contact: J. Tirlocq. adv. contact: F. Trautes. bk.rev.; abstr.; bibl.; charts; illus.; tr.lit.; index. circ. 1,000. **Indexed:** Alloys Ind., ASCA, Br.Ceram.Abstr., C.R.I.Library, C.R.I.Curr.Cont., Ceram.Abstr., Chem.Abstr., Eng.Mat.Abstr., HRIS, Met.Abstr., Met.Abstr.Ind., Nonfer.Met.Alert, PCC Alert, Steels Alert, World Alum.Abstr. **Document type:** bulletin.
—BLDSC (8279.000000); CASDDS; CISTI; Ei; Genuine Article; Linda Hall.
    Refereed Serial

666   SP   ISSN 0366-3175
TP785   CODEN: BSCVB9
SOCIEDAD ESPANOLA DE CERAMICA Y VIDRIO. BOLETIN. 1961. bi-m. 13800 ptas. Sociedad Espanola de Ceramica y Vidrio - Spanish Society of Ceramics and Glass, Ctra. Antigua de Valencia, km. 24300, 28500 Arganda del Rey (Madrid), Spain. TEL 34-1-871-18-00. FAX 34-1-870-05-50. E-mail: secu@icu.csic.es. Ed. Emilio Criado Herrero. adv.: B&W page 70000 ptas., color page 90000 ptas.; 180 x 260. bk.rev.; abstr.; bibl.; charts; illus.; pat.; index; circ. 1,500. (controlled). (also avail. in microform) **Indexed:** Br.Ceram.Abstr., Ceram.Abstr., Chem.Abstr., Ind.SST. **Document type:** bulletin.
—BLDSC (2191.520000); CASDDS; CISTI. **CCC.**
    Former titles: Ceramica y Vidrio; Sociedad Espanola de Ceramica y Vidrio. Boletin; Sociedad Espanola de Ceramica. Boletin (ISSN 0037-8550)
    Refereed Serial

338 666   US
SOCIETY OF GLASS AND CERAMIC DECORATORS. MEMBERSHIP DIRECTORY. 1964. a. $250 to non-members. Society of Glass and Ceramic Decorators, 1627 K St., N.W., Ste. 800, Washington, DC 20006-1702. TEL 202-728-4132. FAX 202-728-4133. Ed. Andrew Bopp; Pub. Sandra Spence. R&P contact: Andrew Bopp. adv. contact: Andrew Bopp. circ. 700. **Document type:** directory.
    Formerly: Society of Glass Decorators. Membership Directory.
    Description: Lists companies and individuals involved in all aspects of decorating glass and ceramicware worldwide. Decorators are identified by type of product and by decorating technique through 350 indexes, which also list suppliers.

748   US
SOCIETY OF GLASS AND CERAMIC DECORATORS. TECHNOTEBOOK. 1964. a. $495 to non-members; members $195; corporate members 1 copy free. Society of Glass and Ceramic Decorators, 1627 K St., N.W, Ste. 800, Washington, DC 20006-1702. TEL 202-728-4132. FAX 202-728-4133. Ed. Andrew Bopp; Pub. Sandra Spence. R&P contact: Andrew Bopp. circ. 700. **Document type:** proceedings.
    Former titles (until 1994): Society of Glass and Ceramic Decorators. Seminar Proceedings; Society of Glass Decorators. Seminar Proceedings; Society of Glass Decorators. Papers Presented at Annual Seminar (ISSN 0081-1602)
    Description: Serves as a technical and regulatory manual for the decorating industry. Includes sections on inks, colors and pigments, drying, firing and annealing, precious metals, screen printing, ceramic decorating and other subjects. Articles are compiled from SGCD seminar presentations and other sources.

666.1 645   UK   ISSN 1357-4752
SPECCHECK. q. T B B Publications Ltd., 4 Simon Campion Ct., High St., Epping, Essex CM16 4AU, England. TEL 01992-560215. FAX 01992-560216. adv.: page £995; trim 297 x 210. circ. 10,000. **Document type:** directory.

666   UK   ISSN 0082-0954
TP785
SPECIAL CERAMICS. (Subseries of: British Ceramic Proceedings (ISSN 0268-4373)) 1960. irreg., no.9, 1992. price varies. Institute of Ceramics, Shelton House, Stoke Rd., Shelton, Stoke-on-Trent ST4 2DR, England. TEL 44-782-202116. FAX 44-782-202421. (Affiliate: Institute of Materials) **Document type:** proceedings.
    Supersedes (in 1975): Symposium on Special Ceramics, Stoke-on-Trent, England. Special Ceramics, Proceedings.

CERAMICS, GLASS AND POTTERY

666   GW   ISSN 0341-0676
CODEN: SPREAS
SPRECHSAAL; fuer Betriebsmanagement und Technologie. (Text in German; summaries in English) 1868. m. DM.477 (overseas DM.549) (effective 1997). Sprechsaal Publishing Group, Mauer 2, 96450 Coburg, Germany. TEL 49-9561-80730. FAX 49-9561-90009. Ed. Christoph Mueller. adv.: B&W page DM.3234; trim 270 x 185. bk.rev.; abstr.; charts; illus.; mkt.; pat.; tr.lit.; tr.mk.; index. circ. 7,591. **Indexed**: Alloys Ind., Br.Ceram.Abstr., C.I.S. Abstr., Ceram.Abstr., Chem.Abstr., Eng.Mat.Abstr., Excerp.Med., Int.Packag.Abstr., Met.Abstr.Ind., Met.Abstr., Nonfer.Met.Alert, PCC Alert, Steels Alert, World Alum.Abstr. **Document type**: trade publication.
—BLDSC (8822.950000); CASDDS; CISTI; Linda Hall; SWETS. **CCC**.
   Former titles: Sprechsaal fuer Keramik, Glas, Baustoffe (ISSN 0340-5133); Sprechsaal fuer Keramik, Glas, Email, Silikate (ISSN 0038-8548)

666.1   IT   ISSN 0391-4259
CODEN: RSSVDT
STAZIONE SPERIMENTALE DEL VETRO. RIVISTA. 1971. bi-m. Lit.108000 in Europe; Oceania Lit.185000; elsewhere Lit.146000 (effective 1997). (Stazione Sperimentale del Vetro) Gruppo Editoriale Faenza Editrice S.p.A., Via Pier Crescenzi, 44, 48018 Faenza (RA), Italy. TEL 39-546-663488. FAX 39-546-660440. E-mail: gefe.vendita@uno.dinamica.it; gefe.info@uno.dinamica.it. Ed. Giovanni Bonetti. adv.: B&W page Lit.880000, color page Lit.1540000. bk.rev.; abstr.; bibl.; pat.; index. circ. 1,500.
—BLDSC (7978.800000); CASDDS; CISTI; Linda Hall.

666.6   US   ISSN 1052-6994
STONE WORLD. 1984. m. $65 (Canada $81.55; Mexico $77; elsewhere $101). Business News Publishing Company, 755 W. Big Beaver, Ste. 1000, Troy, MI 48084. TEL 810-362-3700. FAX 810-362-0317. URL: http://www.stoneworld.com. (Subscr. to: Box 3212, Northbrook, IL 60065) Ed. Mike Reis; Pub. John Sailor. adv. contact: Alex Bachrach. circ. 16,530. **Document type**: trade publication.
●Also available online.
—CISTI. **CCC**.
   Description: Covers the subject of granite, marble, limestone, sandstone, onyx, and other natural stone products for producers and users.

666.1   US   ISSN 0569-7468
CODEN: PSAGB6
SYMPOSIUM ON THE ART OF SCIENTIFIC GLASSBLOWING PROCEEDINGS.* 1956. a. price varies. American Scientific Glassblowers Society, 1835 Saint Clair Ave., Saint Paul, MN 55105-1642. TEL 612-696-9286. FAX 419-478-0636. Ed. Brenda Cloninger. bibl.; illus. circ. 1,000. **Document type**: proceedings.
—BLDSC (6849.460000).
   Description: Technical papers presented at the annual ASGS symposium.

666   PL   ISSN 0039-8144
TP785   CODEN: SZKCAN
SZKLO I CERAMIKA. (Text in Polish; summaries in English, French, Russian) 1935. bi-m. $41. Wydawnictwo Czasopism i Ksiazek Technicznych SIGMA - NOT, Ul. Ratuszowa 11, P.O. Box 1004, 00-950 Warsaw, Poland. TEL 48-22-182918. FAX 48-22-192187. TELEX 814550 SIGMA PL. (Dist. by: SIGMA - NOT Ltd., Ul. Bartycka 20, 00-716 Warsaw, Poland) adv.; bk.rev. circ. 600. **Indexed**: Br.Ceram.Abstr., Ceram.Abstr., Chem.Abstr., Fuel & Energy Abstr., INSPEC.
—CASDDS; CISTI; Linda Hall.

666   AU
T U K INFORM. (Tisch und Kueche Informationen) w. S.400. Johann L. Bondi und Sohn, Industriestr. 2, A-2380 Perchtoldsdorf, Austria. TEL 01-864921. FAX 01-86492144. adv.; bk.rev.; abstr.; illus.; stat. circ. 13,060. **Document type**: trade publication.
   Formerly: Tisch und Kueche (ISSN 0040-8123)

666   AT   ISSN 1321-3679
TABLE & KITCHEN. 1994. bi-m. Aus.$40 (foreign Aus.$110) (effective Aug. 1996). Yaffa Publishing Group, 17-21 Bellevue St., Surry Hills, N.S.W. 2010, Australia. TEL 61-2-92812333. FAX 61-2-92812750. E-mail: yaffa@yaffa.com.au. Ed. Stuart Loch; Pub. Michael Merrick. adv.: B&W page Aus.$1235, color page Aus.$1645; trim 297 x 210; adv. contact: Rupert Merrick. circ. 3,500. **Document type**: trade publication.
   Description: Provides advertisers with direct access to all retail buyers of tabletop and kitchenware throughout Australia.

TABLE ET CADEAU. see *INTERIOR DESIGN AND DECORATION — Furniture And House Furnishings*

666   UK   ISSN 0143-7755
TP785
TABLEWARE INTERNATIONAL. 1877. m. £77 (overseas £92) (effective 1997). Argus Business Media Ltd. (Subsidiary of: D M G Exhibitions Group Ltd.), Queensway House, 2 Queensway, Redhill, Surrey RH1 1QS, England. TEL 44-1737-768611. FAX 44-1737-761989. Ed. Eric Ickinger. adv.; bk.rev. circ. 10,500. **Indexed**: Br.Ceram.Abstr., Key to Econ.Sci. **Document type**: trade publication.
—SWETS.
   Former titles: Tableware International and Pottery Gazette (ISSN 0039-8853); Pottery Gazette and Glass Trade Review.

666   CC   ISSN 1000-9892
TAOCI YANJIU/CERAMICS STUDIES JOURNAL. (Text in Chinese) q. Y18. Jiangxi Sheng Taoci Yanjiusuo - Jiangxi Ceramics Research Institute, Zhangshusha, Jingdezhen Dongjiao (East Suburb), Jiangxi 333001, People's Republic of China. TEL 443186. (Dist. outside China by: Guoji Shudian - China International Book Trading Corp., P.O. Box 399, Beijing, P.R.C.) (Co-sponsor: Jiangxi Sheng Taoci Keji Qingbao Zhan) Ed. Tai Xilin.
—BLDSC (3116.655000).

TECHNICAL CERAMICS INTERNATIONAL. see *ENGINEERING*

666   SP   ISSN 0211-7290
TECNICA CERAMICA. 1971. 10/yr. 8800 ptas.($95) (effective 1997). Publica S.A., Ecuador, 75, entlo., 08029 Barcelona, Spain. TEL 34-3-3215046. FAX 34-3-3221972. Ed. Juan Balague Castella. adv.; bk.rev.; bibl.; charts; illus. circ. 3,000. **Indexed**: Alloys Ind., Eng.Mat.Abstr., Ind.SST, Met.Abstr., Met.Abstr.Ind., Nonfer.Met.Alert, PCC Alert, Steels Alert, World Alum.Abstr.

666   GW   ISSN 0938-9806
TILE & BRICK INTERNATIONAL. (Text in English; summaries in French, German, Spanish) 1984. bi-m. DM.310. Verlag Schmid GmbH (Freiburg), Postfach 6609, 79042 Freiburg, Germany. TEL 49-761-8960940. FAX 49-761-8960980. **Document type**: trade publication.
—BLDSC (8845.620000); Ei.
   Formerly (until 1989): Interbrick (ISSN 0178-2223)
   Description: Focuses on research and development, innovative technology, new products, market analyses, company profiles, and information about conferences, symposiums and fairs.

666 691.4   US   ISSN 0192-9550
TILE AND DECORATIVE SURFACES. 1954. m. $50 (Canada and Mexico $55; overseas $60). 6300 Variel Ave., Ste. I, Woodland Hills, CA 91367-2513. TEL 818-704-5555. FAX 818-704-6500. TELEX 181545-TILE-MAG-CD. Ed. Ken Echard; Pub. Jerry Fisher. R&P contact: Ken Echard. adv.: B&W page $2360, color page $3210; trim 8 1/4 x 10 7/8; adv. contact: Steve Fisher. bk.rev.; illus.; index. circ. 17,046. **Document type**: trade publication.
—CCC.
   Formerly: Tile and Architectural Ceramics (ISSN 0040-7666)

TILE BOOK; Italian repertory of ceramic firms. see *BUSINESS AND ECONOMICS — Trade And Industrial Directories*

TILE BRICKS REFRACTORIES SUPPLIERS BOOK. see *BUSINESS AND ECONOMICS — Trade And Industrial Directories*

666   US   ISSN 1077-6974
TILE DESIGN & INSTALLATION. 1987. q. $55 (Canada $70.85; elsewhere $91). Business News Publishing Company, 755 W. Big Beaver, Ste. 1000, Troy, MI 48084. TEL 810-362-3700. FAX 810-362-0317. URL: http://www.bnp.com. (Subscr. to: Box 3212, Northbrook, IL 60065) Ed. John Maynard; Pub. Myra Smitley. adv. contact: Myra Smitley. circ. 17,530. **Document type**: trade publication.
   Formerly (until 1994): Tile World (ISSN 1074-455X)
   Description: For professionals who design, specify, distribute, install and buy quality tile products.

TILE ITALIA. see *INTERIOR DESIGN AND DECORATION*

666 690   US
TILE NEWS. 1980. 3/yr. free. (Italian Tile Center) Italian Trade Commission, 499 Park Ave., New York, NY 10022. TEL 212-980-1500. FAX 212-758-1050. TELEX 423792-ITCO UI. E-mail: itc@westnet.com; URL: http://www.westnet.com.itatrade/. R&P contact: Jacqueline Greaves. circ. 22,000. **Document type**: trade publication.
   Description: Presents new uses, ideas and designs for the Italian tile industry in the U.S.

666   UK   ISSN 0264-5157
TILES & ARCHITECTURAL CERAMICS SOCIETY JOURNAL. biennial. Tiles & Architectural Ceramics Society, Leeds Metropolitan University, Leeds LS1 3HE, England. TEL 44-113-2832600. **Indexed**: DAAI. **Document type**: bulletin.

666   UK   ISSN 1355-6738
TILES & ARCHITECTURAL CERAMICS SOCIETY NEWSLETTER. 1985. q. Tiles & Architectural Ceramics Society, Leeds Metropolitan University, Leeds LS1 3HE, England. TEL 44-113-2832600. **Document type**: newsletter.

666   SA
TILING NEWS. (Text in English) 1993. bi-m. membership. (South African Ceramic Tile Manufacturers Association) Association Services, P.O. Box 19139, Fisher's Hill 1408, South Africa. illus. **Document type**: newsletter.

U S GLASS, METAL & GLAZING. see *BUILDING AND CONSTRUCTION*

UMSCHAU. see *ENGINEERING — Chemical Engineering*

748   FR   ISSN 0180-0078
VERRE ACTUALITES; le magazine des materiaux verriers. 7/yr. 270 F. (foreign 370 F.) (effective 1997). Publicat, 17 bd. Poissonniere, 75082 Paris Cedex 02, France. TEL 33-1-40391313. FAX 33-1-40391454. Ed. Yvan Floch. adv.: B&W page 7800 F., color page 13800 F.; trim 215 x 285. illus. **Document type**: trade publication.

666.1   FR   ISSN 1268-2616
▼**VERRE INTERNATIONAL.** Key Title: Revue Technique Verre International. (Text in French, English) 1995. q. 195 F. (foreign 260 F.) (effective 1998). Revue Francaise des Metallurgistes, 32, rue Saint Marc, 75002 Paris, France. TEL 33-1-42603151. FAX 33-1-42603842. URL: http://www.cgn.fr. **Document type**: trade publication.
   Description: Specializes in the glass industry.

666.1 724   IT
VETRO SPAZIO; magazine on glass in architecture - facades, energy, renewal, interiors, new technologies. 1985. 4/yr. L.40000 (foreign L.70000) (effective 1996). Miller Freeman Editas s.r.l., Via Washington 50, 20146 Milan, Italy. TEL 39-2-48012911. FAX 39-2-48012293. Ed. Maria Grazia Marchelli. adv.: B&W page L.1800000, color page L.2500000; trim 210 x 297; adv. contact: Mimma Piola. circ. 6,000. **Document type**: trade publication.

VJESNIK ZA ARHEOLOGIJU I HISTORIJU DALMATINSKU. see *ARCHAEOLOGY*

666 690   UK   ISSN 0263-1784
WINDOW INDUSTRIES. 1975. m. £18. Comprint Ltd., Penn House, Penn Pl., Rickmansworth, Herts. WD3 1SN, England. Ed. Simon Napper. adv.; bk.rev. circ. 2,500. **Indexed**: Alloys Ind., Eng.Mat.Abstr., Met.Abstr., Met.Abstr.Ind., Nonfer.Met.Alert, PCC Alert, Steels Alert, World Alum.Abstr.
—BLDSC (9319.324000).
   Formerly: Double Glazing - Domestic, Industrial and Commercial (ISSN 0306-3879)

CERAMICS, GLASS AND POTTERY — ABSTRACTING, BIBLIOGRAPHIES, STATISTICS

WINDOW TRADE NEWS. see *BUILDING AND CONSTRUCTION*

666   UK   ISSN 0959-6127
TP785   CODEN: WCREEJ
WORLD CERAMICS & REFRACTORIES. 1990. bi-m. £148 in Europe; elsewhere £170 (effective 1997). London and Sheffield Publishing Co. Ltd., 291 Cricklewood Ln., Childs Hill, London NW2 2JL, England. TEL 44-181-446-3445. FAX 44-181-446-3445. E-mail: 106062.531@compuserve.com. Ed. B.G.R. Lohan. adv.; bk.rev.; abstr.; illus.; tr.lit. circ. 4,700. **Indexed:** AESIS, Alloys Ind., Br.Ceram.Abstr., Br.Tech.Ind., C.R.I.Abstr., C.R.I.Curr.Cont., Chem.Abstr., Eng.Mat.Abstr., Met.Abstr.Ind., Met.Abstr., PCC Alert, Steels Alert, World Alum.Abstr. **Document type:** trade publication.
—BLDSC (9353.132000); CASDDS; CISTI; Linda Hall; SWETS.
   Formed by the 1990 merger of: Euroclay (ISSN 0306-1841); Refractories Journal (ISSN 0034-3110); Incorporates (in 1988): Metals International (ISSN 0265-0983); Formerly (until 1973): Claycraft (ISSN 0009-8582)
   Description: Trade publication covering all aspects of ceramics, refractories, heavy clay, brick, pipe and tile and industrial ceramic industries, from manufacturers to suppliers.

WORLD GLASSWARE INDUSTRY DIRECTORY. see *BUSINESS AND ECONOMICS — Trade And Industrial Directories*

666 624   GW   ISSN 0341-0552
TP785   CODEN: ZIIND7
Z I INTERNATIONAL. (Ziegelindustrie; journal for the brick and tile, structural ceramics, refractory and clay pipe industries. (Text in English and German; summaries in French, Italian, and Spanish) 1948. 11/yr. DM.329 (foreign DM.390) (effective 1998). Bundesverband der Deutschen Ziegelindustrie e.V.) Bauverlag GmbH, Postfach 1460, 65004 Wiesbaden, Germany. TEL 49-6123-700-0. FAX 49-6123-700122. E-mail: bauverlag.zeitschr.-journals@t-online.de. Ed. U. Gerhards. adv. contact: A. Hoepfl. bk.rev.; charts; illus.; pat.; stat.; tr.lit.; index, cum.index. circ. 5,000. **Indexed:** Br.Ceram.Abstr., C.I.S. Abstr., Ceram.Abstr., Chem.Abstr., Fuel & Energy Abstr. **Document type:** trade publication.
—BLDSC (9512.950000); CASDDS; CISTI; Ei; Linda Hall. **CCC.**
   Formerly: Z I: Ziegelindustrie (ISSN 0044-4693)
   Description: Trade publication for the brick and tile, structural ceramics, refractory and clay pipe industries. Includes calendar of events, industry and company news, topical news, preview of events, and positions available.

666   CC   ISSN 1001-9642
ZHONGGUO TAOCI/CHINESE CERAMICS. (Text in Chinese) 1959. bi-m. Y24. Qinggong Zhonghui, Taoci Kexue Yanjiusuo - Ministry of Light Industry, Research Institute of Ceramics, 203 Xinchang Xilu, Jingdezhen, Jiangxi 333001, People's Republic of China. TEL 86-798-443138. FAX 86-798-442642. Ed. Fanhao Zeng. R&P contact: Fanhao Zeng. adv. contact: Ziyin Xu. circ. 3,500 (paid). **Document type:** academic/scholarly publication.

CERAMICS, GLASS AND POTTERY — Abstracting, Bibliographies, Statistics

666 016   YU   ISSN 0351-2509
BILTEN DOKUMENTACIJE. PRERADA NEMETALNIH MINERALA-PROIZVODNJA GRADJEVINSKOG MATERIJALA/BULLETIN OF DOCUMENTATION. MANUFACTURE OF NON-METALLIC MINERAL PRODUCTS-MANUFACTURE OF CONSTRUCTION MATERIALS. 1950. bi-m. $264. Jugoslovenski Centar za Tehniku i Naucnu Dokumentaciju - Yugoslav Center for Technical and Scientific Documentation (YCTSD), Sl. Penezica-Krcuna 29-31, Box 724, 11000 Belgrade, Yugoslavia. Ed. Ljiljana Kojic-Bogdanovic.
   Formerly: Bilten Dokumentacije. Silikatna Industrija (ISSN 0006-2693)

666 016   UK   ISSN 0307-7357
TP785   CODEN: TJBCAD
BRITISH CERAMIC SOCIETY. TRANSACTIONS. 1971. bi-m. £135 (outside the E.U. £161 ($274)) (effective 1996). Institute of Materials, 1 Carlton House Terr., London SW1Y 5DB, England. TEL 44-171-839-4071. FAX 44-171-839-2078. E-mail: instmat@Cityscape.co.uk. Ed. Mary Chim. adv.; bk.rev.; abstr.; bibl.; charts; illus.; pat.; index. circ. 3,000. **Indexed:** AESIS, ASCA, Br.Ceram.Abstr., Br.Tech.Ind., C.R.I.Abstr., C.R.I.Curr.Cont., Chem.Abstr., Chem.Cit.Ind., Eng.Ind., Fuel & Energy Abstr., GeoRef., IBR, INSPEC, Mat.Sci.Cit.Ind., Met.Abstr., Sci.Cit.Ind., SSCI, World Alum.Abstr. **Document type:** academic/scholarly publication.
—AskIEEE; CASDDS; CISTI; KR SourceOne; UnCover.
   Incorporates: British Ceramic Society. Journal (ISSN 0266-7606); Which superseded: British Ceramic Society. Publications (ISSN 0007-0394)

540 666   US   ISSN 0895-5948
CODEN: CSCMEU
C A SELECTS. CERAMIC MATERIALS (JOURNALS). 1988. s-w. $240 to non-members; members $70 (effective 1998). Chemical Abstracts Service (Subsidiary of: American Chemical Society), 2540 Olentangy River Rd., Box 3012, Columbus, OH 43210-0012. TEL 614-447-3600. FAX 614-447-3713. TELEX 6842086. **Document type:** abstracting/indexing.
   Description: Covers the chemistry, production, and use of oxide and nonoxide ceramics and glass ceramics as structural and building materials, refractories, thermal and electrical insulators, membranes, solid electrolytes, cutting tools, and dishware.

666   US   ISSN 0885-0100
CODEN: CSCPE5
C A SELECTS. CERAMIC MATERIALS (PATENTS). s-w. $240 to non-members; members $70 (effective 1998). Chemical Abstracts Service (Subsidiary of: American Chemical Society), 2540 Olentangy River Rd., Box 3012, Columbus, OH 43210-0012. TEL 614-447-3600. FAX 614-447-3713. TELEX 6842086. **Document type:** abstracting/indexing.
   Description: Covers patents on the chemistry and technology of the ceramic industry, including cermets.

338.4   CN   ISSN 0835-0167
HD9585.A3
CANADA. STATISTICS CANADA. NON-METALLIC MINERAL PRODUCTS INDUSTRIES/INDUSTRIES DES PRODUITS MINERAUX NON-METALLIQUES. (Text in English and French) 1927. a. Can.$40 (foreign $40) (effective 1998). Statistics Canada, Operations and Integration Division, Circulation Management, Jean Talon Bldg., 2-C12, Tunney's Pasture, Ottawa, ON K1A 0T6, Canada. TEL 613-951-7277; 800-267-6677. FAX 613-951-1584. URL: http://www.statcan.ca. (also avail. in microform from MML) **Document type:** government publication.
   Formerly: Canada. Statistics Canada. Non-Metallic Products Industries; Supersedes: Canada. Statistics Canada. Glass and Glass Products Industries; Which was formerly: Canada. Statistics Canada. Glass and Glass Products Manufacturers-Fabricants de Verre et d'Articles en Verre (ISSN 0575-8661)
   Description: Provides an annual census of manufacture.

666   US   ISSN 0095-9960
TP785   CODEN: CEAUAA
CERAMIC ABSTRACTS. CD-ROM edition (US ISSN 1056-3490) 1922. bi-m. $295 to non-members; members $95. (American Ceramic Society) Cambridge Scientific Abstracts, Attn: Angela Hitti, 7200 Wisconsin Ave., 6th Fl., Bethesda, MD 20814. TEL 301-961-6750. FAX 301-961-6720. E-mail: market@csa.com; URL: http://www.csa.com. Ed. Marian Swirtski; Pub. Ted Caris. R&P contact: Barbara Inkellis. TEL 301-961-6718. adv. contact: Bart DeCastro. index. circ. 1,500. (back issues avail.; reprint service avail.) **Indexed:** Br.Ceram.Abstr., C.R.I.Abstr., C.R.I.Curr.Cont. **Document type:** abstracting/indexing.
●Also available online. Vendor(s): Knight-Ridder Information, Inc. (File no.335), Questel Orbit Inc. (CERM), STN International (CERAB).
Also available on CD-ROM. Producer(s): NISC.
—CISTI; Linda Hall; UMI. **CCC.**
   Description: Includes over 200,000 abstracts and patents on ceramics and related fields.

016.666   US   ISSN 1056-3490
CERAMIC ABSTRACTS (C D - R O M). s-a. $695. (American Ceramic Society, Inc.) National Information Services Corporation (NISC), 3100 St. Paul St., Ste. 806, Baltimore, MD 21218. TEL 410-243-0797. FAX 410-243-0982. **Document type:** abstracting/indexing.
●Available only on CD-ROM. Producer(s): NISC.

666   US   ISSN 1049-1252
C2C ABSTRACTS: JAPAN - CERAMICS. (Text in English) 1990. m. $200. Scan C2C, 1001 Pennsylvania Ave., N.W., No.1300, Washington, DC 20024-2505. TEL 800-525-3865. FAX 202-863-3855. **Document type:** abstracting/indexing.
●Also available online. Vendor(s): Data-Star (JPTC), European Space Agency (File no.241), Knight-Ridder Information, Inc. (File no.582), Questel Orbit Inc. (JTEC).
Also available on CD-ROM. Producer(s): Knight-Ridder, Inc.
   Description: Contains abstracts of articles from Japanese scientific, business, and technical journals. Each entry lists title, author, author affiliation, journal title, issue number, page numbers, date, abstract, number of bibliographic references, and language (if not Japanese). Covers crystallography, glass, industrial and fine ceramics, and processing.

666.1   FR
FRANCE. SERVICE D'ETUDE DES STRATEGIES ET DES STATISTIQUES INDUSTRIELLES. RESULTATS MENSUELS DES ENQUETES DE BRANCHE. INDUSTRIE DU VERRE. m. 260 F. (foreign 310 F.)(effective 1991). Service d'Etude des Strategies et des Statistiques Industrielles (SESSI), 85 Bd. du Montparnasse, 75270 Paris Cedex 06, France. TEL 45-56-42-34. FAX 45-56-40-71. stat.
   Description: Follows developments in the glass industry through the performance of selected indicators.

666.1   FR
FRANCE. SERVICE D'ETUDE DES STRATEGIES ET DES STATISTIQUES INDUSTRIELLES. RESULTATS TRIMESTRIELS DES ENQUETES DE BRANCHE. INDUSTRIE DU VERRE. q. 180 F. (foreign 210 F.)(effective 1991). Service d'Etude des Strategies et des Statistiques Industrielles (SESSI), 85 Bd. du Montparnasse, 75270 Paris Cedex 06, France. TEL 45-56-42-34. FAX 45-56-40-71. stat.
   Description: Provides detailed industry-wide performance statistics for comparative evaluations.

666.1 016   UK   ISSN 0017-1050
TP845   CODEN: GLSTAK
GLASS TECHNOLOGY. (Section A of Journal of the Society of Glass Technology) 1960. bi-m. £132 (effective 1996). Society of Glass Technology, Thornton, 20 Hallam Gate Rd., Sheffield S10 5BT, England. TEL 44-1742-663168. FAX 44-1742-665252. E-mail: gt@glass.demon.co.uk. Ed. David Moore. R&P contact: Jenny Lawless. adv. contact: David Moore. bk.rev.; abstr.; index. circ. 1,500. (also avail. in microform from PMC) **Indexed:** A.S.& T.Ind., Alloys Ind., ASCA, Br.Archaeol.Abstr., Br.Ceram.Abstr., Br.Tech.Ind., Cadscan, Ceram.Abstr., Chem.Abstr., Chem.Cit.Ind., Curr.Cont., Eng.Mat.Abstr., Excerp.Med., Ind.Sci.Rev., INIS Atomind., INSPEC, Int.Packag.Abstr., Lead Abstr., Mat.Sci.Cit.Ind., Met.Abstr., Nonfer.Met.Alert, PCC Alert, Sci.Cit.Ind., Steels Alert, World Alum.Abstr., Zincscan. **Document type:** trade publication.
—BLDSC (4192.100000); AskIEEE; CASDDS; CISTI; Ei; KR SourceOne; Linda Hall; SWETS; UnCover.
   Formerly: Society of Glass Technology. Journal.

CHAMBER OF COMMERCE PUBLICATIONS

666.1 016   UK   ISSN 0031-9090
TA450   CODEN: PCGLA6
PHYSICS AND CHEMISTRY OF GLASSES. (Section B of Journal of the Society of Glass Technology) 1960. bi-m. £138.50 (effective 1996). Society of Glass Technology, Thornton, 20 Hallam Gate Rd., Sheffield S10 5BT, England. TEL 44-1742-663168. FAX 44-1742-665252. E-mail: pardc@glass.demon.co.uk. Ed. David Moore. R&P contact: Jenny Lawless. adv. contact: David Moore. bk.rev.; abstr.; charts; illus.; pat.; index. circ. 1,100. **Indexed:** Alloys Ind., ASCA, Br.Ceram.Abstr., Br.Tech.Ind., Cadscan, Ceram.Abstr., Chem.Abstr., Chem.Cit.Ind., Curr.Cont., Eng.Mat.Abstr., GeoRef., Ind.Sci.Rev., INSPEC, Lead Abstr., Met.Abstr., Met.Abstr.Ind., Nonfer.Met.Alert, PCC Alert, Phys.Ber., Sci.Cit.Ind., Steels Alert, World Alum.Abstr., Zincscan. **Document type:** trade publication.
—BLDSC (6478.100000); AskIEEE; CASDDS; CISTI; Ei; KR SourceOne; Linda Hall; SWETS; UnCover.

666 681   AU
SACHGUETERERZEUGUNG SCHNELLBERICHT. 1971. q. S.140. Oesterreichisches Statistisches Zentralamt, Hintere Zollamtsstr. 2b, A-1033 Vienna, Austria. TEL 43-1-71128-7628. FAX 43-1-71128-7728. circ. 130. (looseleaf format; also avail. in magnetic tape) **Document type:** government publication.
Description: Data on manufacturing.

666 016   UK   ISSN 0957-8897
WORLD CERAMICS ABSTRACTS. 1958. m. £290 (in the UK and rest of Europe; elsewhere £330) (effective 1996). (British Ceramic Research Limited) Ceram Research Ltd., Queens Rd., Penkhull, Stoke-on-Trent, Staffs. ST4 7LQ, England. Ed. Pauline Russell. index. circ. 1,000. **Indexed:** AESIS, Br.Ceram.Abstr., Int.Packag.Abstr. **Document type:** abstracting/indexing.
●Also available online. Vendor(s): Questel Orbit Inc.
—CISTI; Linda Hall; UMI. **CCC.**
Formerly (until 1989): British Ceramic Abstracts (ISSN 0300-4570)
Refereed Serial

CHAMBER OF COMMERCE PUBLICATIONS

see Business and Economics—Chamber of Commerce Publications

CHEMICAL ENGINEERING

see Engineering—Chemical Engineering

CHEMISTRY

see also Chemistry—Analytical Chemistry; Chemistry—Computer Applications; Chemistry—Crystallography; Chemistry—Electrochemistry; Chemistry—Inorganic Chemistry; Chemistry—Organic Chemistry; Chemistry—Physical Chemistry

540   HU   ISSN 1217-8969
QD1   CODEN: ACMECEI
A C H - MODELS IN CHEMISTRY; an international forum for all aspects of chemistry-related models and modelling. (Text in English) 1951. 6/yr. $234 (effective 1998). (Magyar Tudomanyos Akademia) Akademiai Kiado Rt., P.O. Box 245, H-1519 Budapest, Hungary. TEL 36-1-2043976. FAX 36-1-2043973. Ed. Andras P. Schubert. adv.; bk.rev.; bibl.; charts; illus.; index, cum.index. (also avail. in microform; microfiche from BHP) **Indexed:** Apic.Abstr., ASCA, Biol.Abstr., Biotech.Abstr., Chem.Abstr., Chem.Cit.Ind., Chem.Eng.Abstr., Chem.Infd., Curr.Adv.Ecol.Sci., Curr.Chem.React., Curr.Cont., Excerp.Med., Food Sci.& Tech.Abstr., Helminthol.Abstr., Ind.Chem., Ind.Sci.Rev., Mass Spectr.Bull., Mat.Sci.Cit.Ind., Met.Abstr., Sci.Cit.Ind., Sci.Cit.Ind., T.C.E.A., World Alum.Abstr. **Document type:** academic/scholarly publication.
—BLDSC (0575.400000); CASDDS; CISTI; Ei; Genuine Article; KNAW; Linda Hall; SWETS; UnCover. **CCC.**
Former titles (until 1993): Acta Chimica Hungarica (ISSN 0231-3146); (until 1982): Academiae Scientiarum Hungaricae. Acta Chimica (ISSN 0001-5407); Superseded in part (1946-1949): Hungarica Acta Chimica (ISSN 0367-634X).
Description: Reports original research focused on models or modeling in any area of chemistry.

540   US   ISSN 0065-7751
                            CODEN: ACMOAG
A C S MONOGRAPHS. 1924. irreg., no.185, 1986. American Chemical Society, 1155 16th St., N.W., Washington, DC 20036. TEL 800-227-5558. FAX 202-872-4615. Ed. M. Joan Comstock. **Indexed:** Biol.Abstr., Chem.Abstr. **Document type:** academic/scholarly publication, monographic series.
—BLDSC (0578.890000); CASDDS; CISTI.

540   US   ISSN 0097-6156
                            CODEN: ACSMC8
A C S SYMPOSIUM SERIES. 1974. irreg., no.518, 1993. price varies. American Chemical Society, 1155 16th St. N.W., Washington, DC 20036. TEL 800-227-5558. FAX 202-872-4615. Ed. M. Joan Comstock. (reprint service avail. from ISI) **Indexed:** API Abstr., API Catal., API Hlth.& Environ., API Oil., API Pet.Ref., API Pet.Subst., API Transport., ASCA, Biol.Abstr., Chem.Abstr., Chem.Cit.Ind., Chem.Infd., Cott.& Trop.Fibr.Abstr., Dairy Sci.Abstr., Food Sci.& Tech.Abstr., GeoRef., I.M.M.Abstr., Ind.Sci.Rev., Ind.Sci.Rev., INIS Atomind., INSPEC, Maize Abstr., Plant Grow.Reg.Abstr., Rice Abstr., Sci.Cit.Ind., Sci.Cit.Ind., Sel.Water Res.Abstr., Soyabean Abstr., Sugar Ind.Abstr., Triticale Abstr., Weed Abstr. **Document type:** academic/scholarly publication.
—BLDSC (0578.895000); CASDDS; CISTI; Ei; Genuine Article; KNAW; SWETS. **CCC.**
Refereed Serial

540   HU   ISSN 0075-5397
QD1   CODEN: KUERDK
A KEMIA UJABB EREDMENYEI. 1970. irreg., vol.80, 1996. price varies. (Magyar Tudomanyos Akademia) Akademiai Kiado Rt., P.O. Box 245, H-1519 Budapest, Hungary. TEL 36-1-2043976. FAX 36-1-2043973. Ed. Bela Csakvari. **Document type:** academic/scholarly publication.
—CASDDS.

A S B C NEWSLETTER. (American Society of Brewing Chemists) see BEVERAGES

ACADEMIA DE STIINTE A REPUBLICII MOLDOVA. BULETINUL. STIINTE BIOLOGICE SI CHIMICE/AKADEMIYA NAUK RESPUBLIKI MOLDOVA. IZVESTIYA. BIOLOGICHESKIE I KHIMICHESKIE NAUKI. see BIOLOGY

540   CH   ISSN 0001-3927
ACADEMIA SINICA. INSTITUTE OF CHEMISTRY. BULLETIN. 1959. a. exchange basis. Academia Sinica, Institute of Chemistry - Chung Yang Yen Chiu Yuan Hua Hsueh Yen Chiu So, Nankang, Taipei, Taiwan 11529, Republic of China. TEL 866-2-782-1889. FAX 866-2-783-1237. TELEX 17414 ACADSINA. Ed. Ling-Kang Liu. charts; illus. circ. 1,000. **Indexed:** Chem.Abstr., Plant Breed.Abstr. **Document type:** academic/scholarly publication.
—BLDSC (2580.200000); CISTI.

540   US
ACADEMIC DIGEST. 3/yr. American Chemical Society, 1155 16th St., N.W., Washington, DC 20036. TEL 800-227-5558. FAX 202-872-4615. **Document type:** academic/scholarly publication.

ACADEMIE SERBE DES SCIENCES ET DES ARTS. CLASSE DES SCIENCES MATHEMATIQUES ET NATURELLES. BULLETIN. SCIENCES NATURELLES. see SCIENCES: COMPREHENSIVE WORKS

540 660   US   ISSN 0001-4478
ACCELERATOR NEWSLETTER. 1916. m. (Sep.-May). $5. American Chemical Society, Indiana Section, Box 1291, Indianapolis, IN 46206-1291. TEL 317-253-8136. Ed. Norman Hudson. adv.; bk.rev.; illus. circ. 1,200.
Description: Contains reviews on chemistry software.

540   US   ISSN 0001-4842
QD1   CODEN: ACHRE4
ACCOUNTS OF CHEMICAL RESEARCH. 1968. m. $252 to institutional non-members; members $33 (effective 1997). American Chemical Society, 1155 16th St., N.W., Washington, DC 20036. TEL 202-872-4363. FAX 614-447-3671. (Subscr. to: Membership and Subscription Services, Box 3337, Columbus, OH 43210. TEL 614-447-3776) Ed. F.W. McLafferty. index. circ. 6,920. (also avail. in microform; back issues avail.; reprint service avail. from ISI) **Indexed:** Abstr.Bull.Inst.Pap.Chem., ASCA, Cadscan, Chem.Abstr., Chem.Cit.Ind., Curr.Adv.Biochem., Curr.Adv.Ecol.Sci., Curr.Cont., Dairy Sci.Abstr., Energy Info.Abstr., Environ.Abstr., Excerp.Med., GeoRef., Ind.Sci.Rev., INIS Atomind., Lead Abstr., Mass Spectr.Bull., Mat.Sci.Cit.Ind., Sci.Cit.Ind., Zincscan. **Document type:** academic/scholarly publication.
●Also available online. Vendor(s): STN International (CJACS).
—BLDSC (0573.529660); CASDDS; CISTI; Genuine Article; KNAW; Linda Hall; SWETS; UMI; UnCover. **CCC.**
Description: Contains information on major advances in basic research and applications. Brief, critical articles cover various areas of chemical research.
Refereed Serial

540 660   XV   ISSN 1318-0207
QD1   CODEN: ACSLE7
ACTA CHIMICA SLOVENICA. (Text in English; summaries in English, Slovenian) 1954. q. $50. Slovensko Kemijsko Drustvo, Hajdrihova 19, 61115 Ljubljana, Slovenia. TEL 386-61-176-0200. FAX 386-61-125-9244. E-mail: chem.soc@ki.si. Ed.Bd. adv.; bk.rev.; index. circ. 1,400. **Indexed:** Chem.Abstr. **Document type:** academic/scholarly publication.
—BLDSC (0611.015000); CASDDS; CISTI; Linda Hall; UnCover.
Formerly (until 1993): Slovensko Kemijsko Drustvo. Vestnik (ISSN 0560-3110)
Refereed Serial

CHEMISTRY

540 — **II** — **ISSN 0253-7338**
QD1 — **CODEN: ACICDV**
ACTA CIENCIA INDICA. CHEMISTRY. (Text in English) 1974. q. Rs.150($100) (effective 1998). (Society for the Progress of Science) Pragati Prakashan, c/o K.K. Mittal, Business Manager, Box 62, Meerut 250001, India. TEL 91-121-640642. FAX 91-121-541852. Ed. V.P. Kudesia. R&P contact: K.K. Mittal. adv. contact: K.K. Mittal. bk.rev. **Document type:** academic/scholarly publication.
—BLDSC (0611.371000); CASDDS; CISTI; Ei; Linda Hall.
Supersedes in part (in 1979): Acta Ciencia Indica (ISSN 0379-5411)

540 — **GW** — **ISSN 0323-7648**
TS1300 — **CODEN: ACPODY**
ACTA POLYMERICA. (Text in English) 1950. m. DM.175 (foreign DM.199) to individuals; institutions DM.1055 (foreign DM.1105) (effective 1997). Wiley - V C H, Postfach 101161, 69451 Weinheim, Germany. TEL 49-6201-606-147. FAX 49-6201-606117. E-mail: subservice@vchgroup.de; URL: http://www.vchgroup.de. (Subscr. in the Americas to: John Wiley & Sons, Inc., 605 Third Ave., New York, NY 10158. TEL 212-850-6645. FAX 212-850-6021) Ed.Bd. illus.; index. circ. 1,200. **Indexed:** Abstr.Bull.Inst.Pap.Chem., Alloys Ind., Anal.Abstr., ASCA, Cadscan, Chem.Abstr., Chem.Cit.Ind., Curr.Cont., Eng.Mat.Abstr., Ind.Sci.Rev., INIS Atomind., Intl.Polym.Sci.& Tech, Lead Abstr., Mat.Sci.Cit.Ind., Met.Abstr., Met.Abstr.Ind., Nonfer.Met.Alert, Paper & Bd.Abstr., PCC Alert, RAPRA, Sci.Cit.Ind., Steels Alert, Text.Tech.Dig., World Alum.Abstr., World Text.Abstr., Zincscan. **Document type:** academic/scholarly publication.
—BLDSC (0660.500000); CASDDS; CISTI; Ei; Genuine Article; Linda Hall; SWETS. **CCC.**

669 540 — **FI** — **ISSN 1239-0518**
CODEN: ASCMA4
ACTA POLYTECHNICA SCANDINAVICA. CHEMICAL TECHNOLOGY SERIES. (Text and summaries in English) irreg. (5-7/yr.) FIM 450 (effective 1997). Teknillisten Tieteiden Akatemia - Finnish Academy of Technology, Tekniikantie 12, Fin-02150 Espoo, Finland. Ed. Seppo Palosaari. index, cum.index: 1958-1994. circ. 500. (also avail. in microfilm from UMI; back issues avail.; reprint service avail. from UMI) **Indexed:** Alloys Ind., ASCA, Cadscan, Chem.Abstr., Curr.Cont., Eng.Mat.Abstr., I.M.M.Abstr., INIS Atomind., INSPEC (1984-), Lead Abstr., Met.Abstr.Ind., Met.Abstr., Nonfer.Met.Alert, PCC Alert, Steels Alert, World Alum.Abstr., Zincscan. **Document type:** monographic series.
—BLDSC (0661.255100); AskIEEE; CASDDS; CISTI; KR SourceOne; Linda Hall; UMI; UnCover.
Former titles (until 1995): Acta Polytechnica Scandinavica. Chemical Technology and Metallurgy Series (ISSN 0781-2698); Acta Polytechnica Scandinavica. Chemistry and Metallurgy Series (ISSN 0001-6853)
Description: Presents research results in chemical engineering.

540 370 — **PL** — **ISSN 0208-6182**
CODEN: AULCD2
ACTA UNIVERSITATIS LODZIENSIS: FOLIA CHIMICA. (Text in Polish; summaries in various languages) 1955-1974; N.S. 1982. irreg. Wydawnictwo Uniwersytetu Lodzkiego, Ul. Jaracza 34, Lodz, Poland. TEL 331671. (Dist. by: Ars Polona-Ruch, Krakowskie Przedmiescie 7, Warsaw, Poland) **Indexed:** Chem.Abstr. **Document type:** academic/scholarly publication.
—BLDSC (0585.206200); CASDDS; CISTI; KNAW; Linda Hall.
Supersedes in part: Uniwersytet Lodzki. Zeszyty Naukowe. Seria 2: Nauki Matematyczno-Przyrodnicze (ISSN 0076-0366)
Description: Provides scientific research papers on physical, organic, inorganic and general chemistry.

ACTA UNIVERSITATIS SZEGEDIENSIS DE ATTILA JOZSEF NOMINATAE. ACTA PHYSICA ET CHEMICA. see PHYSICS

540 — **FR** — **ISSN 0151-9093**
CODEN: ACCHDG
ACTUALITE CHIMIQUE. 1973. 11/yr. 1050 F. (foreign 1260 F.) (effective 1997). Societe Francaise de Chimie, 250 rue Saint Jacques, 75005 Paris, France. TEL 33-1-40467160. FAX 33-1-40467161. adv.; bk.rev.; bibl.; charts; illus.; circ. 2,378 (controlled). (back issues avail.) **Indexed:** Alloys Ind., ASCA, C.I.S. Abstr., Chem.Abstr., Chem.Cit.Ind., Chem.Infd., Eng.Mat.Abstr., Excerp.Med., INIS Atomind., Met.Abstr.Ind., Met.Abstr., Nonfer.Met.Alert, PCC Alert, SSCI, Steels Alert, World Alum.Abstr.
—BLDSC (0677.102000); CASDDS; CISTI; Ei; Genuine Article; Linda Hall; SWETS.

540 — **JA** — **ISSN 0917-9917**
ADSORPTION NEWS. (Text in English, Japanese) 1987. q. Nihon Kyuchaku Gakkai - Japan Society on Adsorption, c/o M. Suzuki, Gen. Sect., University of Tokyo, Institute of Industrial Science, 6-22-1, Roppongi, Minato-ku, Tokyo 106, Japan. TEL 03-3408-1483. Ed. Katsumi Kaneko. **Document type:** newsletter.
—BLDSC (0696.626000).

540 — **US** — **ISSN 1062-0044**
QD320 — **CODEN: ACANEP**
ADVANCES IN CARBOHYDRATE ANALYSIS, a research annual. 1992. a. $97.50. J A I Press Inc., 55 Old Post Rd., No. 2, Box 1678, Greenwich, CT 06830-1678. TEL 203-661-7602. FAX 203-661-0792. E-mail: jai@jaipress.com. **Indexed:** Chem.Abstr. **Document type:** monographic series.
—CASDDS.

540 — **US** — **ISSN 0065-2393**
QD1 — **CODEN: ADCSAJ**
ADVANCES IN CHEMISTRY SERIES. 1950. irreg., no.232, 1993. price varies. American Chemical Society, 1155 16th St., N.W., Washington, DC 20036. TEL 800-227-5558. FAX 202-872-4615. Ed. M. Joan Comstock. (reprint service avail. from ISI) **Indexed:** API Abstr., API Catal., API Hlth.& Environ., API Oil., API Pet.Ref., API Pet.Subst., API Transport., ASCA, Biol.Abstr., Chem.Abstr., Chem.Cit.Ind., Chem.Ind., Dairy Sci.Abstr., Excerp.Med., Food Sci.& Tech.Abstr., Geo.Abstr., GeoRef., Ind.Sci.Rev., INIS Atomind., Mat.Sci.Cit.Ind., Nutr.Abstr., Sci.Cit.Ind. **Document type:** academic/scholarly publication.
—BLDSC (0703.700000); CASDDS; CISTI; Genuine Article; KNAW; SWETS; UnCover. **CCC.**
Refereed Serial

660 — **US** — **ISSN 1063-0619**
ADVANCES IN DETAILED REACTION MECHANISMS. 1991. irreg., vol.5, 1997. $109.50. J A I Press Inc., 55 Old Post Rd., No.2, Box 1678, Greenwich, CT 06830-1678. TEL 203-661-7602. FAX 203-661-0792. E-mail: jai@jaipress.com. (In Europe: JAI Press Ltd., 38 Tavistock St., Covent Garden, London WC2E 7PB, England. TEL 44-171-379-8834. FAX 44-171-379-8835) Ed. James Coxon. **Document type:** academic/scholarly publication, monographic series.
Description: Highlights selected approaches which have led to advances in the study of detailed reaction mechanisms.

540 — **UK**
ADVANCES IN DYNAMIC STEREOCHEMISTRY. (Text in English) 1985. a. $60. Freund Publishing House Ltd., Ste. 500, Chesham House, 150 Regent St., London W1R 5FA, England. (And: P.O. Box 35010, Tel Aviv, Israel. TEL 972-3-5628540. FAX 972-3-5628538) Ed. Marcel Gielen. **Document type:** academic/scholarly publication.

540 — **US**
ADVANCES IN FREE RADICAL CHEMISTRY. 1990. irreg., vol.2, 1997. $109.50. J A I Press Inc., 55 Old Post Rd., No.2, Box 1678, Greenwich, CT 06830-1678. TEL 203-661-7602. FAX 203-661-0792. E-mail: jai@jaipress.com. (In Europe: JAI Press Ltd., 38 Tavistock St., Covent Garden, London WC2E 7PB, England. TEL 44-171-379-8834. FAX 44-171-379-8835) Ed. Dennis Tanner. **Document type:** academic/scholarly publication, monographic series.
Description: Provides a vehicle in which investigators, who have demonstrated a high degree of competence in some aspect of free radical chemistry, can present a particular area of interest.

540 — **US**
▼**ADVANCES IN MACROMOLECULAR CARBOHYDRATE RESEARCH.** 1997. irreg. $112.50. J A I Press Inc., 55 Old Post Rd., No.2, Box 1678, Greenwich, CT 06830-1678. TEL 203-661-7602. FAX 203-661-0792. E-mail: jai@jaipress.com. (In Europe: JAI Press Ltd., 38 Tavistock St., Covent Garden, London WC2E 7PB, England. TEL 44-171-379-8834. FAX 44-171-379-8835) Ed. Robert Sturgeon. **Document type:** academic/scholarly publication, monographic series.

ADVANCES IN MEDICINAL CHEMISTRY. see MEDICAL SCIENCES

660 — **US** — **ISSN 1075-1629**
ADVANCES IN METAL AND SEMICONDUCTOR CLUSTERS. 1993. irreg., vol.4, 1997. $109.50. J A I Press Inc., 55 Old Post Rd., No.2, Box 1678, Greenwich, CT 06830-1678. TEL 203-661-7602. FAX 203-661-0792. E-mail: jai@jaipress.com. (In Europe: JAI Press Ltd., 38 Tavistock St., Covent Garden, London WC2E 7PB, England. TEL 44-171-379-8834. FAX 44-171-379-8835) Ed. Michael Duncan. **Document type:** academic/scholarly publication, monographic series.
Description: Focuses on spectroscopic measurements of molecular structure, kinetic and dynamic measurements of cluster chemistry, quantum theoretical models of cluster bonding, synthesis of new materials from clusters, and attempts to synthesize and isolate clusters in macroscopic quantities.

541.28 — **US** — **ISSN 0065-3276**
QD453 — **CODEN: AQCHA9**
ADVANCES IN QUANTUM CHEMISTRY. 1964. irreg., vol.28, 1997. Academic Press, 525 B St., Ste. 1900, San Diego, CA 92101-4495. TEL 619-231-0926. FAX 619-699-6715. (Subscr. to: Order Dept., 6277 Sea Harbor Dr., 4th Fl., Orlando, FL 32887. TEL 800-321-5068) Ed. Per-Olov Lowdin. index. (reprint service avail. from ISI) **Indexed:** ASCA, Chem.Abstr., Chem.Cit.Ind., Ind.Sci.Rev., INSPEC, Phys.Ber., Sci.Cit.Ind. **Document type:** academic/scholarly publication.
—CASDDS; CISTI; Linda Hall; SWETS; UnCover. **CCC.**
Refereed Serial

540 — **US** — **ISSN 1046-5723**
QD478 — **CODEN: ASCHER**
ADVANCES IN SOLID-STATE CHEMISTRY. irreg., vol.4, 1997. $109.50. J A I Press Inc., 55 Old Post Rd., No. 2, Box 1678, Greenwich, CT 06830-1678. TEL 203-661-7602. FAX 203-661-0792. E-mail: jai@jaipress.com. (Addr. in the U.K. and rest of Europe: J A I Press Ltd., 38 Tavistock St., Covent Garden, London WC2E 7PB, England. TEL 44-171-379-8834. FAX 44-171-379-8835) Ed. C.R.A. Catlow. **Indexed:** Chem.Cit.Ind., Mat.Sci.Cit.Ind. **Document type:** monographic series.
—BLDSC (0711.425000); CASDDS; CISTI. **CCC.**

540 — **US** — **ISSN 1068-7459**
ADVANCES IN SUPRAMOLECULAR CHEMISTRY. 1990. irreg., vol.4, 1997. $109.50. J A I Press Inc., 55 Old Post Rd., No.2, Box 1678, Greenwich, CT 06830-1678. TEL 203-661-7602. FAX 203-661-0792. E-mail: jai@jaipress.com. (In Europe: JAI Press Ltd., 38 Tavistock St., Covent Garden, London WC2E 7PB, England. TEL 44-171-379-8834. FAX 44-171-379-8835) Ed. George Gokel. **Document type:** academic/scholarly publication, monographic series.

540 — **US** — **ISSN 1046-5766**
QD255.4 — **CODEN: ATIMEB**
ADVANCES IN THEORETICALLY INTERESTING MOLECULES. 1989. irreg., vol.4, 1997. $109.50. J A I Press Inc., 55 Old Post Rd., No. 2, Box 1678, Greenwich, CT 06830-1678. TEL 203-661-7602. FAX 203-661-0792. E-mail: jai@jaipress.com. (Subscr. in the UK and Europe to: JAI Press Ltd., 38 Tavistock St., Covent Garden, London WC2E 7PB, England. TEL 44-171-379-8834. FAX 44-171-379-8835) Ed. Randolph Thummel. **Document type:** monographic series.
—BLDSC (0711.620500); CASDDS; CISTI.

CHEMISTRY

540 US ISSN 0278-6826
TP244.A3 CODEN: ASTYDQ
AEROSOL SCIENCE AND TECHNOLOGY. 1982. m. fl.1549($890) (effective 1998). (American Association for Aerosol Research) Elsevier Science Inc., Box 945, New York, NY 10159-0945. TEL 212-633-3730. FAX 212-633-3680. TELEX 420643 AEP Ul. E-mail: usinfo-f@elsevier.com; URL: http://www.elsevier.nl/. (Subscr. outside the Americas to: Elsevier Science, Regional Sales Office, P.O. Box 211, 1000 AE Amsterdam, Netherlands. TEL 31-20-4853757. FAX 31-20-4853432; Subscr. in Australasia and the Far East to: Elsevier Science (Singapore) Pte Ltd, No.1 Temasek Ave., No.17-01 Millenia Tower, Singapore 039192, Singapore. TEL 65-434-3727. FAX 65-337-2230; Subscr. in Japan to: Elsevier Science Japan, 9-15 Higashi-Azabu 1-chome, Minato-ku, Tokyo 106, Japan. TEL 81-3-5561-5033. FAX 81-3-5561-5047) Ed.Bd. bk.rev. (also avail. in microform from UMI) **Indexed:** ASCA, Chem.Abstr., Chem.Cit.Ind., Chem.Eng.Abstr., Compumath, Curr.Cont., Ecol.Abstr., Energy Ind., Energy Info.Abstr., Energy Rev., Eng.Ind., Environ.Per.Bibl., Excerp.Med., Geo.Abstr.P.G., Ind.Sci.Rev., INIS Atomind., INSPEC (1983-), Pollut.Abstr., Sci.Cit.Ind., T.C.E.A. **Document type:** academic/scholarly publication.
—BLDSC (0729.835400); AskIEEE; CASDDS; CISTI; Ei; EMDOCS; Genuine Article; KR SourceOne; Linda Hall; SWETS; UnCover. **CCC.**
Incorporates (1985-1988): Atomisation and Spray Technology (ISSN 0266-3481)
Description: Covers theoretical and experimental investigations of aerosol and closely related phenomena.
Refereed Serial

541 660 SP ISSN 0001-9704
TP1 CODEN: AFINAE
AFINIDAD; revista de quimica teorica y aplicada. (Text in English and Spanish; summaries in Catalan, English and Spanish) 1921. 6/yr. 6000 ptas. in Iberia and Latin America; elsewhere $80. Instituto Quimico de Sarria, Asociacion de Quimicos, Via Augusta 390, 08017 Barcelona, Spain. TEL 34-3-2804276. FAX 34-3-2804276. E-mail: aiqs@iqs.url.es. Ed. Jaume Arboles. adv. contact: Lluis Agullo. bk.rev.; charts; illus.; index; circ. 2,500 (controlled). **Indexed:** ASCA, Cadscan, Chem.Abstr., Chem.Cit.Ind., Curr.Cont., Ind.Sci.Rev., Ind.SST, Lead Abstr., Mass Spectr.Bull., Sci.Cit.Ind., Weed Abstr., World Surf.Coat., Zincscan. **Document type:** academic/scholarly publication.
—BLDSC (0732.000000); CASDDS; CISTI; Genuine Article; Linda Hall; SWETS; UnCover. **CCC.**
Refereed Serial

AG-CHEM AGE/NOYAKU JIDAI. see *AGRICULTURE*

AGROCHEMIA/AGRICULTURAL CHEMICALS. see *AGRICULTURE*

AGROCHEMIA; poradnik nawozenia i ochrony roslin. see *AGRICULTURE*

AGROCHIMICA; rivista internazionale di chimica vegetale, pedologia e fertilizzazione del suolo. see *AGRICULTURE*

AKADEMIA ROLNICZA, POZNAN. ROCZNIKI. FIZYKA, CHEMIA. see *PHYSICS*

540 GS
QD1 CODEN: IGSKDH
AKADEMIYA NAUK GRUZII. SERIYA KHIMICHESKAYA. (Text in Georgian, Russian) 1975. q. 18.20 Rub. Akademiya Nauk Gruzii, Rustaveli prosp., 52, 380008 Tbilisi, Georgia. **Indexed:** Alloys Ind., Anal.Abstr., Chem.Abstr., Eng.Mat.Abstr., INIS Atomind., Maize Abstr., Met.Abstr., Met.Abstr.Ind., Nonfer.Met.Alert, PCC Alert, Steels Alert, World Alum.Abstr. **Document type:** academic/scholarly publication.
—CASDDS; CISTI; KNAW; Linda Hall.
Formerly: Akademiya Nauk Gruzinskoi S.S.R. Izvestiya. Seriya Khimicheskaya (ISSN 0132-6074)

540 KZ
QD1 CODEN: IKAKAK
AKADEMIYA NAUK KAZAKHSTANA. IZVESTIYA. SERIYA KHIMICHESKAYA. (Text in Russian) 1947. bi-m. Gylym, Ul. Pushkina 111-113, 480100 Alma-Ata, Kazakhstan. TEL 3272-611877. (Subscr. to: G.R. Kondubayeva, ul. Shevchenko 28, 480021 Alma-Ata, Kazakhstan) Ed. E.E. Ergozhin. charts; index. **Indexed:** Anal.Abstr., Chem.Abstr., INIS Atomind., Mass Spectr.Bull., Met.Abstr., World Alum.Abstr. **Document type:** academic/scholarly publication.
—CASDDS; CISTI; Linda Hall. **CCC.**
Formerly (until 1992): Akademiya Nauk Kazakhskoi S.S.R. Izvestiya. Seriya Khimicheskaya (ISSN 0002-3205)

540 570 KG
CODEN: INKSAD
AKADEMIYA NAUK RESPUBLIKI KYRGYZSTAN. IZVESTIYA. KHIMIKO-TEKHNOLOGICHESKIE I BIOLOGICHESKIE NAUKI. (Text in Russian) 1955. bi-m. Izdatel'stvo Ilim, Lininsky pr. 265 A, 720071 Bishkek, Kyrgyzstan. TEL 7-3312-253874. Ed. K.S. Sylaimankulov.
—CASDDS; CISTI; Linda Hall.
Formerly (until 1991): Akademiya Nauk Kirgizskoi S.S.R. Izvestiya. Khimiko-tekhnologicheskie i Biologicheskie Nauki (ISSN 0235-0084); Which superseded in part (in 1985): Akademiya Nauk Kirgizskoi S.S.R. Izvestiya (ISSN 0002-3221)

AKADEMIYA NAUK TAJIKISTANA. IZVESTIYA. OTDELENIE FIZIKO-MATEMATICHESKIKH I GEOLOGO-KHIMICHESKIKH NAUK. see *PHYSICS*

AKADEMIYA NAUK TURKMENISTANA. IZVESTIYA. SERIYA FIZIKO-TEKHNICHESKIKH, KHIMICHESKIKH I GEOLOGICHESKIKH NAUK. see *PHYSICS*

540 BW
QD1 CODEN: VBSKAK
AKADEMIYA NAVUK BELARUSI. VESTSI. SERIYA KHIMICHNYKH NAVUK/NATIONAL ACADEMY OF SCIENCES OF BELARUS. PROCEEDINGS. CHEMICAL SERIES. 1965. bi-m. 30000 Rub.($65) (effective 1998). Vydavetstvo Belaruskaya Navuka, Zhodzinskaya, 18, 220141 Minsk 41, Belarus. TEL 268-33-24. FAX 268-252277. TELEX 252277 NAUKA. (Dist. by: Mezhdunarodnaya Kniga, B. Yakimanka 39, 117049 Moscow, Russia. TEL 7-095-2384967. FAX 7-095-2384634) Ed. I.I. Lishtvan. bibl.; charts; illus.; index. circ. 200. **Indexed:** Copper Abstr. **Document type:** academic/scholarly publication.
—CASDDS; CISTI; KNAW; Linda Hall.
Formerly (until 1992): Akademiya Navuk Belarusskai S.S.R. Vestsi. Seriya Khimichnykh Navuk (ISSN 0002-3590)
Description: Presents papers on analytical, physical, inorganic, organic, bioorganic chemistry, chemistry of high-molecular compounds, applied chemistry and chemical technology.

540 YU ISSN 0002-4961
ALBUS. (Text in Serbo-Croatian) vol.5, 1966. m. Albus (Fabrika Sapuna i Hemijskih Proizvoda), Novi Sad, Yugoslavia. Ed. Ilija Lemajic. index.

ALMANAK NUKLIR BIOLOGI DAN KIMIA. see *ENERGY — Nuclear Energy*

540.1 UK ISSN 0002-6980
QD1 CODEN: AMBXAO
AMBIX. 1937. 3/yr. (in 1 vol., 3 nos./vol.) £44($90) (Society for the History of Alchemy and Chemistry) Black Bear Press Ltd., Kings Hedges Rd., Cambridge CB4 2PQ, England. TEL 44-1223-424571. FAX 44-1223-426877. Ed. Dr. G.K. Roberts. adv. contact: N.G. Coley. bk.rev.; illus.; index, cum.index. circ. 500. **Indexed:** Amer.Hist.& Life (1967-), Chem.Abstr., Hist.Abstr. (1967-). **Document type:** academic/scholarly publication.
—BLDSC (0809.000000); CASDDS; CISTI; Linda Hall; SWETS; UnCover. **CCC.**
Refereed Serial

341.37 628.53 US
AMERICAN ASSOCIATION FOR FUEL CELLS. NEWSLETTER. no.5, Spring 1994. irreg. American Association for Fuel Cells, 50 San Miguel Ave, Daly City, CA 94015. **Document type:** newsletter, proceedings.
Description: Discusses research into fuel cells for use in cleaner modes of transportation.

AMERICAN CHEMICAL SOCIETY. DIRECTORY OF GRADUATE RESEARCH. see *EDUCATION — Guides To Schools And Colleges*

540 US ISSN 0740-0667
QD1 CODEN: ACEPCF
AMERICAN CHEMICAL SOCIETY. DIVISION OF ENVIRONMENTAL CHEMISTRY. PREPRINTS OF EXTENDED ABSTRACTS. 1961. 2/yr. $30 (effective 1998). American Chemical Society, Division of Environmental Chemistry, 1810 Georgia St., Cape Girardeau, MO 63701. TEL 573-334-3827. FAX 573-334-2551. E-mail: scifair@semovm.semo.edu. Ed. Ruth Hathaway; Pub. Ruth Hathaway. R&P contact: Ruth Hathaway. adv. contact: Robert Paddock. abstr.; illus. circ. 6,000. **Indexed:** API Abstr., API Catal., API Hlth.& Environ., API Oil., API Pet.Ref., API Pet.Subst., API Transport., Chem.Abstr., INIS Atomind. **Document type:** proceedings.
—BLDSC (6027.140000); CASDDS; CISTI; Linda Hall.
Formerly: American Chemical Society. Division of Environmental Chemistry. Preprints of Papers (ISSN 0093-3066)

540 US ISSN 0002-7863
QD1 CODEN: JACSAT
AMERICAN CHEMICAL SOCIETY. JOURNAL. 1879. bi-w. $1695 to institutional non-members; members $125 (effective 1997). American Chemical Society, 1155 16th St., N.W., Washington, DC 20036. TEL 800-333-9511. (Subscr. to: Membership and Subscription Services, Box 3337, Columbus, OH 43210. TEL 614-447-3776. FAX 614-447-3671) Ed. Allen J. Bard. adv.; bk.rev.; charts; illus.; index. circ. 12,800. (also avail. in microform from PMC; back issues avail.) **Indexed:** A.S.& T.Ind., Abstr.Bull.Inst.Pap.Chem., Apic.Abstr., Appl.Mech.Rev., ASCA, Biol.Abstr., Biotech.Abstr., Biwk.Pap.Rad.Chem.& Photochem., Br.Ceram.Abstr., Bull.Thermodyn.& Thermochem., Cadscan, Chem.Abstr., Chem.Cit.Ind., Chem.Infd., Curr.Adv.Biochem., Curr.Adv.Ecol.Sci., Curr.Adv.Genetics & Molec.Biol., Curr.Chem.React., Curr.Cont., Dairy Sci.Abstr., Eng.Ind., Excerp.Med., Food Sci.& Tech.Abstr., Gen.Sci.Ind., Hort.Abstr., Ind.Chem., Ind.Med., Ind.Sci.Rev., INIS Atomind., INSPEC (1968-), Lead Abstr., Mass Spectr.Bull., Mat.Sci.Cit.Ind., Met.Abstr., NRN, Nutr.Abstr., Petrol.Abstr., RAPRA, Sci.Cit.Ind., Soils & Fert., Sugar Ind.Abstr., Zincscan. **Document type:** academic/scholarly publication.
●Also available online. Vendor(s): STN International (CJACS).
—BLDSC (4685.000000); AskIEEE; CASDDS; CISTI; Ei; Genuine Article; KR SourceOne; Linda Hall; SWETS; UMI; UnCover. **CCC.**
Description: Documents advances in all areas of chemical research.

540 020 US
AMERICAN CHEMICAL SOCIETY PUBLICATIONS QUARTERLY; a newsletter for librarians and information specialists. vol.5, no.1, 1993. q. American Chemical Society, 1155 16th St., N.W., Washington, DC 20036. TEL 800-333-9511. FAX 614-447-3671. (Subscr. to: Membership and Subscription Services, Box 3337, Columbus, OH 43210. TEL 614-447-3776) **Document type:** newsletter.

540 US
AMERICAN INSTITUTE OF CHEMISTS. PROFESSIONAL DIRECTORY. 1969. a. $65. American Institute of Chemists, Inc., 501 Wythe St., Alexandria, VA 22314-1917. TEL 703-836-2090. Ed. Sharon Dobson. adv. circ. 5,000. **Document type:** directory.
Formerly: American Institute of Chemists. Membership Directory (ISSN 0084-6376)

AMERICAN LEATHER CHEMISTS ASSOCIATION. JOURNAL. see *LEATHER AND FUR INDUSTRIES*

AMERICAN SOCIETY OF BREWING CHEMISTS. JOURNAL. see *BEVERAGES*

540 SP ISSN 1130-2283
CODEN: ANQUEX
ALES DE QUIMICA; international edition. (Text in English; summaries in English, Spanish) 1903. bi-m. 9800 Ptas. (effective 1997). (Real Sociedad Espanola de Quimica) Springer-Verlag Iberica, S.A., Provenca, 388, 1a planta, 08025 Barcelona, Spain. TEL 39-3-4570227. FAX 39-3-4571502. (Subscr. in N. America to: Springer-Verlag New York, Inc., 333 Meadowlands Pkwy., Secaucus, NJ 07094. TEL 212-460-1500. FAX 212-473-6272) Ed. Jaume Casabo Gispert. adv.; bk.rev.; bibl.; charts; illus.; index. **Indexed**: ASCA, Chem.Abstr., Chem.Cit.Ind., Curr.Chem.React., Curr.Cont., Ind.Chem., Ind.SST, Mat.Sci.Cit.Ind, Met.Abstr., SSCI, Sugar Ind.Abstr. **Document type**: academic/scholarly publication.
●Also available online.
—BLDSC (0890.200000); CASDDS; CISTI; Genuine Article; Linda Hall; SWETS. **CCC**.
Formed by the 1990 merger of: Anales de Quimica. Serie A. Quimica Fisica e Ingeniera Quimica (ISSN 0214-9397); Which was formerly (until 1989): Anales de Quimica. Serie A. Quimica Fisica y Quimica Tecnica (ISSN 0211-1330); Anales de Quimica. Serie B. Quimica Inorganica y Quimica Analitica (ISSN 0211-1349); Anales de Quimica. Serie C. Quimica Organica y Bioquimica (ISSN 0211-1357); Which had superseded (in 1980): Anales de Quimica (ISSN 0365-4990); Which was formerly (until 1967): Real Sociedad Espanola de Fisica y Quimica. Anales. Serie B: Quimica (ISSN 0034-088X); Which superseded in part (in 1948): Anales de Fisica y Quimica (ISSN 0365-2351).
Description: Provides a forum for chemical research in many areas.
Refereed Serial

543 JA ISSN 0910-6340
CODEN: ANSCEN
ALYTICAL SCIENCES. (Text in English) 1985. bi-m. £39 to individuals (US $70); institutions £79 (US $142) (effective 1997). Japan Society for Analytical Chemistry - Nihon Bunseki Kagaku Kai, 26-2 Nishigotanda 1-chome, Shinagawa-ku, Tokyo 141, Japan. TEL 81-3-3490-3351.
FAX 81-3-3490-3572. (Subscr. to: Turpin Distribution Services Ltd., Blackhorse Rd., Letchworth, Herts., SG6 1HN, England. TEL 44-1462-672555. FAX 44-1462-480947) Ed. Mitsugi Senda. circ. 3,600. (back issues avail.) **Indexed**: Alloys Ind., ASCA, Chem.Abstr., Chem.Cit.Ind., Curr.Cont., Eng.Mat.Abstr., INIS Atomind., Mass Spectr.Bull., Mat.Sci.Cit.Ind., Met.Abstr., Met.Abstr.Ind., Nonfer.Met.Alert, PCC Alert, Sci.Cit.Ind., Steels Alert, World Alum.Abstr. **Document type**: academic/scholarly publication.
—BLDSC (0897.139500); CASDDS; CISTI; Genuine Article; KNAW; Linda Hall; SWETS; UnCover. **CCC**.
Description: Covers fundamental and applied aspects of analytical chemistry.

540 GW ISSN 0044-8249
QD1 CODEN: ANCEAD
GEWANDTE CHEMIE. 1888. 22/yr. DM.2371 (foreign DM.2481) (effective 1997). (Gesellschaft Deutscher Chemiker, GW) Wiley - V C H, Postfach 101161, 69451 Weinheim, Germany.
TEL 49-6201-606-0. FAX 49-6201-606328.
TELEX 465516-VCHWH-D. E-mail: subservice@vchgroup.de; URL: http://www.vchgroup.de. (Subscr. in the Americas to: John Wiley & Sons, Inc., 605 Third Ave., New York, NY 10158. TEL 212-850-6645. FAX 212-850-6021) Ed. P. Goelitz. adv.; bk.rev./ illus. circ. 4,400. (also avail. in microfilm from KTO,VCI; back issues avail.) **Indexed**: Abstr.Bull.Inst.Pap.Chem., Art & Archaeol.Tech.Abstr., ASCA, Biol.Abstr., Biotech.Abstr., Biwk.Pap.Rad.Chem.& Photochem., Cadscan, Chem.Abstr., Chem.Infd., Curr.Adv.Ecol.Sci., Curr.Chem.React., Curr.Cont., Deep Sea Res.& Oceanogr.Abstr., Excerp.Med., GeoRef., Ind.Chem., Ind.Med., Ind.Sci.Rev., INIS Atomind., Lead Abstr., Nutr.Abstr., Sci.Cit.Ind., SSCI, Zincscan. **Document type**: academic/scholarly publication.
●Also available online. Vendor(s): STN International (CJVCH).
—BLDSC (0902.000000); CASDDS; CISTI; Linda Hall; SWETS. **CCC**.

540 GW ISSN 0570-0833
QD1 CODEN: ACIEAY
ANGEWANDTE CHEMIE: INTERNATIONAL EDITION. Includes supplement in every second issue: Chemistry - A European Journal (ISSN 0947-6539) (Text in English) 1961. 22/yr. DM.2371 (foreign DM.2481) (effective 1997). Wiley - V C H, Postfach 101161, 69451 Weinheim, Germany.
TEL 49-6201-606-0. FAX 49-6201-606-328.
TELEX 465516-VCHWH-D. E-mail: subservice@vchgroup.de; URL: http://www.vchgroup.de. (Subscr. in the Americas to: John Wiley & Sons, Inc., 605 Third Ave., New York, NY 10158. TEL 212-850-6645. FAX 212-850-6021) Ed. P. Goelitz. circ. 3,390. (also avail. in microfilm from VCI) **Indexed**: Abstr.Bull.Inst.Pap.Chem., ASCA, Chem.Cit.Ind., Curr.Cont., Food Sci.& Tech.Abstr., Ind.Chem., Ind.Sci.Rev., Mat.Sci.Cit.Ind. **Document type**: academic/scholarly publication.
●Also available online.
—BLDSC (0902.000500); AskIEEE; CASDDS; CISTI; Ei; EMDOCS; Genuine Article; KR SourceOne; Linda Hall; SWETS; UnCover. **CCC**.

542 US ISSN 0172-4967
ANLEITUNG FUER DIE CHEMISCHE LABORATORIUMSPRAXIS - CHEMICAL LABORATORY PRACTICE. 1970. irreg., vol.24, 1989. price varies. Springer-Verlag, 175 Fifth Ave., New York, NY 10010. TEL 212-460-1500. FAX 212-473-6272. (Also: Berlin, Heidelberg, Tokyo and Vienna) Ed. H. Mayer-Kaupp. (reprint service avail. from ISI) **Document type**: monographic series.
Formerly: Anleitung fuer die Chemische Laboratoriumspraxis (ISSN 0066-1910)

540 FI ISSN 1239-6311
QD1 CODEN: AAFCAX
ANNALES ACADEMIAE SCIENTIARUM FENNICAE. CHEMICA. (Text in English, French, German) 1909. irreg. price varies. Suomalainen Tiedeakatemia - Academia Scientiarum Fennica, Mariankatu 5, FIN-00170 Helsinki, Finland. (Subscr. to: The Bookstore Tiedekirja, Kirkkokatu 14, FIN-00170 Helsinki, Finland) Ed. Jouko Koskikallio. circ. 330. (also avail. in microform; back issues avail.) **Indexed**: Anal.Abstr., Bibl.Agri., Biol.Abstr., Bull.Signal., Chem.Abstr., Excerp.Med., GeoRef., Hort.Abstr., Ind.Med., INIS Atomind., INSPEC (1968-), Ref.Zh. **Document type**: academic/scholarly publication.
—AskIEEE; CASDDS; CISTI; KNAW; KR SourceOne; Linda Hall.
Formerly (until 1995): Annales Academiae Scientiarum Fennicae. Series A, II: Chemica (ISSN 0066-1961); Which superseded in part (in 1941): Annales Academiae Scientiarum Fennicae. Series A (ISSN 0365-673X)

540 FR ISSN 0151-9107
QD1 CODEN: ANCPAC
ANNALES DE CHIMIE: SCIENCE DES MATERIAUX. (Text and summaries in English, French) 1789. 8/yr. 1342 F. to individuals; institutions 1815F. (effective 1998). (International Union of Testing and Research Laboratories for Materials and Structures) Masson - Periodiques, 120 bd. St. Germain, 75006 Paris, France. TEL 33-1-40466200.
FAX 33-1-40466201. (Subscr. to: Societe de Periodiques Specialises, B.P. 22-F, 41354 Vineuil Cedex, France. TEL 33-2-54504612. FAX 33-2-54504611) Ed. D. Dimitrov. adv.; bk.rev.; illus.; index. circ. 1,160. (also avail. in microform from UMI,PMC; reprint service avail. from ISI) **Indexed**: Alloys Ind., Anal.Abstr., ASCA, Cadscan, Chem.Abstr., Chem.Cit.Ind., Chem.Infd., Curr.Chem.React., Curr.Cont., Eng.Mat.Abstr., Excerp.Med., Ind.Chem., Ind.Sci.Rev., INIS Atomind., INSPEC (1991-), Lead Abstr., Mat.Sci.Cit.Ind., Met.Abstr.Ind., Met.Abstr., Nonfer.Met.Alert, PCC Alert, Sci.Cit.Ind., Soils & Fert., Steels Alert, World Alum.Abstr., Zincscan. **Document type**: academic/scholarly publication.
—BLDSC (0970.000000); AskIEEE; CASDDS; CISTI; Ei; Genuine Article; KR SourceOne; Linda Hall; SWETS; UMI; UnCover. **CCC**.
Former titles: Rilem Bulletin; (until vol.3, 1978): Annales de Chimie (ISSN 0003-3936)
Description: Publishes original reports and developments in the fields of metal manufacturing, solid mineral compounds, macromolecular organic compounds, thermodynamic properties, reactivity, and reactive kinetics, geochemistry.

540 PL ISSN 0137-6853
QC1 CODEN: AUMCD7
ANNALES UNIVERSITATIS MARIAE CURIE-SKLODOWSKA. SECTIO AA. CHEMIA. (Text in English, French, Polish; summaries in English, Polish) 1946. a. price varies. Uniwersytet Marii Curie-Sklodowskiej, Wydawnictwo, Pl. M. Curie-Sklodowskiej 5, 20-031 Lublin, Poland. TEL 48-81-375304. FAX 48-81-336699. TELEX 0643223. Ed. Kazimierz Sykut. circ. 550. **Indexed**: Chem.Abstr., INIS Atomind. **Document type**: academic/scholarly publication.
—BLDSC (0956.006000); CASDDS; CISTI; Linda Hall.

540 IT ISSN 0003-4592
CODEN: ANCRAI
ANNALI DI CHIMICA. (Text in English) 1914. bi-m. L.270000 (Europe L.450000; elsewhere L.500000) (effective 1995). Societa Chimica Italiana, Viale Liegi, 48, 00198 Rome, Italy. TEL 39-6-8549691. FAX 39-6-8548734. Ed. Guido Saini. circ. 450. **Indexed**: Anal.Abstr., ASCA, Biol.Abstr., Biotech.Abstr., Cadscan, Chem.Abstr., Chem.Cit.Ind., Chem.Infd., Curr.Chem.React., Curr.Cont., Dairy Sci.Abstr., Excerp.Med., Ind.Chem., Ind.Sci.Rev., INIS Atomind., Lead Abstr., Mass Spectr.Bull., Sci.Cit.Ind., Zincscan. **Document type**: academic/scholarly publication.
—BLDSC (1012.000000); CASDDS; CISTI; Ei; Genuine Article; Linda Hall; SWETS; UnCover.
Description: Covers analytical and environmental chemistry, applied chemistry, mass spectrometry and electrochemistry.

ANNUAL BULLETIN OF TRADE IN CHEMICAL PRODUCTS.
see *BUSINESS AND ECONOMICS — Production Of Goods And Services*

540 UK ISSN 0268-2605
QD410 CODEN: AOCHEX
APPLIED ORGANOMETALLIC CHEMISTRY. 1987. m. $1095 (foreign $1095) (effective 1998). John Wiley & Sons Ltd., Journals, Baffins Ln., Chichester, W. Sussex PO19 1UD, England.
TEL 44-1243-779777. FAX 44-1243-843232.
E-mail: cs-journals@wiley.co.uk; URL: http://www.wiley.co.uk. (Subscr. in the Americas to: John Wiley & Sons, Inc., 605 Third Ave., New York, NY 10158. TEL 212-850-6645. FAX 212-850-6021) Ed. P.J. Craig. adv.: B&W page £595, color page £1495; 230 x 170; adv. contact: Bob Kern. circ. 400. (also avail. in microform from UMI; back issues avail.; reprint service avail. from SWZ) **Indexed**: ASCA, Chem.Cit.Ind., Curr.Cont., Mat.Sci.Cit.Ind. **Document type**: academic/scholarly publication.
—BLDSC (1576.270000); CASDDS; CISTI; Ei; Genuine Article; SWETS; UMI. **CCC**.
Description: Contains regular papers, short communications of some urgency, and the occasional review in the organometallic area.

APPLIED SPECTROSCOPY. see *PHYSICS — Optics*

ARCHEIA TES PHARMAKEUTIKES (ATHENS). see *PHARMACY AND PHARMACOLOGY*

ARCHIVUM COMBUSTIONIS. see *ENGINEERING*

540 UK ISSN 0960-2739
CODEN: APCHF7
ASIA PACIFIC CHEMICALS. 1990. m. £75($135) Reed Business Information (Subsidiary of: Reed Elsevier group), Quadrant House, The Quadrant, Sutton, Surrey SM2 5AS, England. TEL 44-181-652-8146. FAX 44-181-652-8918. (Subscr. to: Stuart House, Perrymount Rd., Haywards Heath, W. Sussex RH16 3BN, England. TEL 44-1444-445355) Ed. Naresh Gupta. adv.: B&W page $2845, color page $4000; 178 x 254. circ. 7,514 (controlled). (back issues avail.) **Indexed**: Intl.Polym.Sci.& Tech., RAPRA, World Surf.Coat. **Document type**: trade publication.
—BLDSC (1742.257800); CASDDS; SWETS. **CCC**.

540 II ISSN 0970-7077
CODEN: AJCHEW
ASIAN JOURNAL OF CHEMISTRY. (Text in English) 1989. q. Rs.250($60) to individuals; institutions Rs.600($175). Chemic Publishing Co., c/o Mrs. Pushpa Agarwal, Circ. Mgr., 11-100, Rajendra Nagar, Sector 3, Sahibabad 201 005 (Ghaziabad), India. TEL 91-575-630138. Ed. R.K. Agarwal. R&P contact: Pushpa Agarwal. **Indexed**: ASCA, Chem.Cit.Ind., Mat.Sci.Cit.Ind. **Document type**: academic/scholarly publication.
—BLDSC (1742.473000); CASDDS; Genuine Article; KNAW; UnCover.

CHEMISTRY

540   AG   ISSN 0365-0375
                         CODEN: AAQAAE
ASOCIACION QUIMICA ARGENTINA. ANALES. (Text in English or Spanish; abstracts in English and Spanish) 1912. bi-m. (Consejo Nacional de Investigaciones Cientificas y Tecnicas) Fernando Garcia Cambeiro (Dist.), Cochabamba 244, 1150 Buenos Aires, Argentina. Ed. Alicia B. Pomilio. **Indexed:** Chem.Cit.Ind., Food Sci.& Tech.Abstr., Ind.Chem., INIS Atomind.
—BLDSC (0870.000000); CASDDS; CISTI; Genuine Article; KNAW; Linda Hall.

ASSOCIATION OF MARINE LABORATORIES OF THE CARIBBEAN. NEWSLETTER. see *EARTH SCIENCES — Oceanography*

ASSOCIATION OF MARINE LABORATORIES OF THE CARIBBEAN. PROCEEDINGS. see *EARTH SCIENCES — Oceanography*

ATELIERS. see *CHILDREN AND YOUTH — For*

540   GW
AUSBILDER IN DER CHEMISCHEN INDUSTRIE. 1970. bi-m. DM.9. (Bundesarbeitgeberverband Chemie) Dr. Curt Haefner Verlag, Bachstr. 14-16, 69121 Heidelberg, Germany. TEL 49-6221-6446-0. (Subscr. to: Postfach 106060, 69050 Heidelberg, Germany) circ. 8,000. **Document type:** trade publication.

540   AT   ISSN 1031-8305
AUSTRALIAN CHEMISTRY RESOURCE BOOK. 1982. a. Aus.$10($7) (Royal Australian Chemical Institute) Charles Stuart University - Mitchell, School of Applied Sciences, Bathurst, N.S.W. 2795, Australia. TEL 61-63-315125. FAX 61-63-384-649. Ed. C.L. Fogliani. circ. 2,500. **Document type:** academic/scholarly publication.
    Description: Directed to secondary and higher-level teachers of chemistry.

540   AT   ISSN 0004-9425
QD1   CODEN: AJCHAS
AUSTRALIAN JOURNAL OF CHEMISTRY. 1948. m. Aus.$670($670) for print ed.; online ed. Aus.$640 ($640); both Aus.$700($700) (effectie 1998). (C.S.I.R.O. Australia) C.S.I.R.O. Publishing, 150 Oxford St., Collingwood, Vic. 3066, Australia. TEL 61-3-96627500. FAX 61-3-96627611. E-mail: john.zdysiewicz@publish.csiro.au; URL: http://www.publish.csiro.au/journals/ajc/index.html. Eds. J.R. Zdysiewicz, J.M. Cameron. adv.; bibl.; charts; illus.; index. circ. 750. (also avail. in microform from UMI; back issues avail.) **Indexed:** Abstr.Bull.Inst.Pap.Chem., AESIS, Alloys Ind., Anal.Abstr., ASCA, Biol.Abstr., Biotech.Abstr., Biwk.Pap.Rad.Chem.& Photochem., Bull.Thermodyn.& Thermochem., Cadscan, Chem.Abstr., Chem.Cit.Ind., Chem.Infd., Curr.Adv.Ecol.Sci., Curr.Chem.React., Curr.Cont., Curr.Leather Lit., Dairy Sci.Abstr., Eng.Mat.Abstr., Excerp.Med., Field Crop.Abstr., Food Sci.& Tech.Abstr., Forest.Abstr., Herb.Abstr., Hort.Abstr., Ind.Chem., Ind.Sci.Rev., INIS Atomind., Lead Abstr., Mass Spectr.Bull., Met.Abstr., Met.Abstr.Ind., Nonfer.Met.Alert, Sci.Cit.Ind., Steels Alert, World Alum.Abstr., World Text.Abstr., Zincscan. **Document type:** academic/scholarly publication.
●Also available online.
—BLDSC (1806.000000); CASDDS; CISTI; Ei; Genuine Article; Linda Hall; SWETS; UMI; UnCover. **CCC.**
    Description: Covers all aspects of chemistry, and chemical technology, e.g. theoretical, physical, inorganic, organic, organometallic.

540   AJ   ISSN 0005-2531
                         CODEN: AZKZAU
AZERBAIDZHANSKII KHIMICHESKII ZHURNAL. (Text in Azerbaidzhani, Russian) 1959. bi-m. 22.80 Rub. (Akademiya Nauk Azerbaijana) Izdatel'stvo Elm, Ul. Narimanova, 37, 370073 Baku, Azerbaijan. Ed. M.F. Nagiev. charts; index. circ. 3,000. **Indexed:** Chem.Abstr., INIS Atomind.
—CASDDS; CISTI; Linda Hall. **CCC.**

540   UK
B A M A ANNUAL REPORT. a. British Aerosol Manufacturers Association, Kings Bldg., Smith Sq., London SW1P 3JJ, England. TEL 0171-828-5111. FAX 0171-834-8436. TELEX 916672 CHEMIN G. Ed. Sarah Ross. R&P contact: Sarah Ross. **Document type:** corporate report.

BAYER BERICHTE. see *PHARMACY AND PHARMACOLOGY*

540   GW   ISSN 0301-0457
RM31   CODEN: BHIMA2
BEHRING INSTITUTE MITTEILUNGEN; Behring Institute Research Communications. (Text in English; summaries in English, German) 1907. irreg., no.96, 1995. price varies. Medizinische Verlagsgesellschaft mbH, Postfach 1732, 35007 Marburg, Germany. TEL 49-6421-293-0. FAX 49-6421-22910. Ed. F.R. Seiler. R&P contact: F.R. Seiler. circ. 4,000. (back issues avail.) **Indexed:** Chem.Abstr., Diar.Dis.Res., Excerp.Med., Ind.Med. **Document type:** academic/scholarly publication.
—BLDSC (1878.109000); CASDDS; CISTI; KNAW; Linda Hall. **CCC.**
    Description: Original observations of topics in laboratory and clinical research in immunology, microbiology, and blood protein chemistry. Includes proceedings of scientific meetings and workshops sponsored by Behring Institute.

BEIKOKU TOKKYO SHOROKU. KAGAKU IPPAN, ORIMONO HEN/U.S. PATENT ABSTRACTS. GENERAL CHEMISTRY, TEXTILE. see *PATENTS, TRADEMARKS AND COPYRIGHTS — Abstracting, Bibliographies, Statistics*

540   GW   ISSN 0943-3104
DER BENZOLRING. 1980. 3/yr. free. (Chemischen Instituts Dr. Flad) W E G R A Verlags-Gesellschaft mgH, Breitscheidstr. 127, 70176 Stuttgart, Germany. TEL 0711-634760. FAX 0711-634768. TELEX 721779-CHF-D. circ. 10,000. **Document type:** academic/scholarly publication.

BIORESOURCE TECHNOLOGY. see *BIOLOGY — Biotechnology*

660   GW   ISSN 0006-4750
BLICK VOM HOCHHAUS. 1960. m. free. Huels AG, 45764 Marl, Germany. Ed. Georg Heinze. bk.rev. **Document type:** trade publication.

540 660   II   ISSN 0067-9925
BOMBAY TECHNOLOGIST. (Text in English) 1951. a. Rs.50($5) Technological Association, University of Bombay, Department of Chemical Technology, N.M. Parekh Marg, Matunga, Bombay 400 019, India. FAX 91-22-4145614. Ed. S.D. Samant. adv. circ. 1,000. **Indexed:** Biol.Abstr., Chem.Abstr.

643   US
HD9585.B67
BORAX PIONEER. 1987. 3/yr. U.S. Borax, Inc., 26877 Torney Rd., Valencia, CA 91355. (U.K. addr.: Borax Consolidated Ltd., 170 Priestly Rd., Guildford, Surrey GU2 5RQ, England. TEL 44-1483-734000. FAX 44-1483-4576764) Eds. Nicolais Gordon-Brown, Tana Burrows. circ. 6,000 (controlled). **Document type:** trade publication.
    Formerly (until 1994): Borax Review (ISSN 0951-8452)
    Description: Devoted to the customers of Borax.

BRAGANTIA. see *AGRICULTURE*

BROMIDES IN AGRICULTURE. see *AGRICULTURE*

540   BU   ISSN 0861-9808
QD1   CODEN: IZKHDX
BULGARIAN CHEMICAL COMMUNICATIONS. (Text in English; summaries in Bulgarian) 1968. q. $196. Bulgarian Academy of Sciences, Chemical Institute, Block 11, Office 105, 1113 Sofia, Bulgaria. TEL 359-2-7132576. FAX 359-2-720038. TELEX 22729 ECHBAN-BG. E-mail: bnachem@bgearn.bitnet. (Co-sponsor: Bulgarian Chemical Society) Ed. V. Beshkov. index. circ. 700. (back issues avail.; reprint service avail. from IRC) **Indexed:** Chem.Abstr., Met.Abstr., MLA Intl.Bibl.
—AskIEEE; CASDDS; CISTI; KNAW; KR SourceOne.
    Formerly (until 1992): Izvestiia po Khimiia (ISSN 0324-1130)

540   BE   ISSN 0037-9646
QD1   CODEN: BSCBAG
BULLETIN DES SOCIETES CHIMIQUES BELGES. (Text in Dutch, English, French, German) 1887. m. 5250 BEF. Comite van Beheer van het Bulletin v.z.w., Krijgslaan 281, S-12, B-9000 Ghent, Belgium. TEL 32-9-2644831. FAX 32-9-2644992. TELEX 12754 RUGENT. E-mail: Harry.Thun@rug.ac.be. Ed. Harry P. Thun. adv.; bk.rev.; abstr.; charts; illus. circ. 3,000. **Indexed:** Alloys Ind., ASCA, Cadscan, Chem.Abstr., Chem.Cit.Ind., Chem.Infd., Chem.Titles, Curr.Adv.Ecol.Sci., Curr.Chem.React., Curr.Cont., Eng.Mat.Abstr., Excerp.Med., GeoRef., Ind.Chem., Ind.Sci.Rev., Lead Abstr., Met.Abstr., Met.Abstr.Ind., Nonfer.Met.Alert, PCC Alert, Sci.Cit.Ind., Steels Alert, World Alum.Abstr., Zincscan. **Document type:** bulletin, academic/scholarly publication.
—BLDSC (2758.200000); CASDDS; CISTI; Ei; Genuine Article; Linda Hall; SWETS; UnCover. **CCC.**
    Description: Original research and critical reviews in the field of chemistry.
    Refereed Serial

BULLETIN OF MAGNETIC RESONANCE. see *PHYSICS*

540   II   ISSN 0970-4620
                         CODEN: BPAAS:C
BULLETIN OF PURE & APPLIED SCIENCES. SECTION C: CHEMISTRY. 1982. 2/yr. Rs.300($50) Dr. A.K. Sharma, Ed. & Pub., 140 (RPS) D.D.A. Flat, Mansarovar Park, Shahdara, New Delhi 110 032, India. TEL 91-11-2117408. R&P contact: A.K. Sharma. adv. contact: A.K. Sharma. bk.rev. circ. 600. **Document type:** academic/scholarly publication, bulletin.
—CISTI; Linda Hall. **CCC.**

540 658.8   UK   ISSN 0268-4284
BUSINESS RATIO REPORT: CHEMICAL DISTRIBUTORS; an industry sector analysis. 1985. a. I C C Business Ratios Ltd., Freepost, Field House, Hampton, Mddx. TW12 1BR, England. TEL 081-783-0977. FAX 081-783-1940. charts; stat. **Document type:** trade publication.

540 338 658.8   UK   ISSN 0267-0011
BUSINESS RATIO REPORT: INDUSTRIAL CHEMICAL MANUFACTURERS. INTERMEDIATE; an industry sector analysis. 1974. a. I C C Business Ratios Ltd., Freepost, Field House, Hampton, Mddx. TW12 1BR, England. TEL 081-783-0977. FAX 081-783-1940. charts; stat. **Document type:** trade publication.
    Supersedes in part (in 1984): Business Ratio Report: Chemical Manufacturers (ISSN 0261-7587)

540 338 658.8   UK   ISSN 0267-002X
BUSINESS RATIO REPORT: INDUSTRIAL CHEMICAL MANUFACTURERS. MAJOR; an industry sector analysis. 1974. a. I C C Business Ratios Ltd., Freepost, Field House, Hampton, Mddx. TW12 1BR, England. TEL 081-783-0977. FAX 081-783-1940. charts; stat. **Document type:** trade publication.
    Supersedes in part (in 1984): Business Ratio Report: Chemical Manufacturers (ISSN 0261-7587)

540   JA   ISSN 0913-3747
C I C S J BULLETIN. (Text in English, Japanese) 1983. bi-m. Chemical Society of Japan, Chemical Information and Computer Sciences - Nippon Kagakkai Joho Kagaku Bunkai, 1-5, Kanda Surugadai, Chiyoda-ku, Tokyo 101, Japan. **Document type:** bulletin.

540   CN
C P I PRODUCT PROFILES. irreg. Can.$72.50($65) (foreign $65) per no. Camford Information Services Inc., 801 York Mills Rd., Ste. 201, Don Mills, ON M3B 1X7, Canada. TEL 416-291-3215. FAX 416-291-3406. Ed. George Deligiannis. **Document type:** trade publication.
    Description: Provides basic market information for chemical products.

C P I PURCHASING CHEMICALS YELLOW PAGES ANNUAL BUYING GUIDE; an A to Z listing of over 10,000 chemicals and sources of supply. (Chemical Process Industries) see *BUSINESS AND ECONOMICS — Marketing And Purchasing*

540 530   US   ISSN 0147-6262
QD65
C R C HANDBOOK OF CHEMISTRY AND PHYSICS. 1978. a. $99.50 (foreign $120). C R C Press, Inc., 2000 Corporate Blvd., N.W., Boca Raton, FL 33431. TEL 561-994-0555; 800-272-7737. FAX 561-997-0949. TELEX 568689-CRC PRESS. Ed. David R. Lide. **Document type:** academic/scholarly publication.
—BLDSC (3487.096270); CISTI. **CCC.**
    Description: Offers a broad coverage of all types of data commonly encountered by physical scientists.

660   US
C S M A EXECUTIVE NEWSWATCH. 1977. w. membership only. Chemical Specialties Manufacturers Association, 1913 Eye St., N.W., Washington, DC 20006. TEL 202-872-8110. Ed. Anastasia Ralph; Pub. Raysh Engel. circ. 1,000. **Document type:** newsletter.

C S M C R I NEWSLETTER. (Central Salt and Marine Chemicals Research Institute) see *EARTH SCIENCES — Oceanography*

CADASTRO BRASILEIRO DE QUIMICA. see *ENGINEERING — Chemical Engineering*

540   CN   ISSN 1187-8746
CAMFORD CHEMICAL REPORT. 1969. w (50/yr.). Can.$749 (foreign Can.$769). Camford Information Services Inc., 801 York Mills Rd., Ste. 201, Don Mills, ON M3B 1X7, Canada. TEL 416-291-3215. FAX 416-291-3406. Ed. Joe Piccione. circ. 200 (paid). **Indexed:** PROMT. **Document type:** newsletter.
—BLDSC (3016.193500); CISTI. **CCC.**
    Former titles: Corpus Chemical Report (ISSN 0228-653X); C P I Management Service (ISSN 0315-257X); Polyfacts (ISSN 0315-2588)

540   CN   ISSN 0823-5228
TP1   CODEN: CCHNEE
CANADIAN CHEMICAL NEWS/ACTUALITE CHIMIQUE CANADIENNE. (Text in English and French) 1949. 10/yr. Can.$50 (foreign $70) (effective 1997). Chemcan Publishers Limited, 130 Slater St., Ste. 550, Ottawa, ON K1P 6E2, Canada. TEL 613-232-6252. FAX 613-232-5862. Ed. Nola Haddadian. adv. contact: Allison McLear. bk.rev.; charts; illus.; tr.lit.; index. circ. 7,000. **Indexed:** Biol.Abstr., C.I.S. Abstr., Can.B.P.I., Can.B.P.I., Chem.Abstr., Energy Info.Abstr., Environ.Abstr., Excerp.Med., INIS Atomind., Telegen. **Document type:** trade publication.
●Also available online. Vendor(s): Information Access Co.
—BLDSC (3018.990000); CASDDS; CISTI; Ei; Linda Hall; UMI; UnCover. **CCC.**
    Formerly (until 1984): Chemistry in Canada (ISSN 0009-3114)

540   CN   ISSN 0008-4042
QD1   CODEN: CJCHAG
CANADIAN JOURNAL OF CHEMISTRY/JOURNAL CANADIEN DE CHIMIE. (Text mainly in English, occasionally in French) 1929. m. Can.$172 to individuals (foreign $182); institutions Can.$545 (foreign $545) (effective 1996). National Research Council of Canada, Research Journals, Ottawa, ON K1A 0R6, Canada. TEL 613-993-9084. FAX 613-952-7656. URL: http://www.cisti.nrc.ca/cisti/journals/. Ed. Dr. T. Chivers. adv.: B&W page Can.$600; trim 8 1/2 x 11; adv. contact: Hoda Jabbour. bibl.; illus.; index. circ. 1,800. (also avail. in microform from UMI,PMC; back issues avail.; reprint service avail. from UMI) **Indexed:** Abstr.Bull.Inst.Pap.Chem., ASCA, Biol.Abstr., Biotech.Abstr., Biwk.Pap.Rad.Chem.& Photochem., Cadscan, Chem.Abstr., Chem.Cit.Ind., Chem.Infd., Curr.Adv.Biochem., Curr.Adv.Ecol.Sci., Curr.Chem.React., Curr.Cont., Dairy Sci.Abstr., Deep Sea Res.& Oceanogr.Abstr., Excerp.Med., Forest.Abstr., Forest Prod.Abstr., GeoRef., Helminthol.Abstr., Herb.Abstr., Hort.Abstr., Ind.Chem., Ind.Sci.Rev., Ind.Vet., INIS Atomind., INSPEC (1968-), Lead Abstr., Mass Spectr.Bull., Mat.Sci.Cit.Ind., Met.Abstr., Nutr.Abstr., Petrol.Abstr., Sci.Cit.Ind., Soils & Fert., World Alum.Abstr., World Text.Abstr., Zincscan. **Document type:** academic/scholarly publication.
—BLDSC (3031.000000); ADONIS; AskIEEE; CASDDS; CISTI; Ei; EMDOCS; Genuine Article; KR SourceOne; Linda Hall; SWETS; UMI; UnCover. **CCC.**
    Refereed Serial

540 660   NE   ISSN 1011-372X
                     CODEN: CALEER
CATALYSIS LETTERS. (Text in English) 1988. 28/yr. (in 7 vols., 4 nos./vol.). 2730 SFr. (effective 1998). Baltzer Science Publishers B.V., P.O. Box 221, 1400 AE Bussum, Netherlands. TEL 31-20-6370061. FAX 31-20-6323651. E-mail: subscribe@baltzer.nl; URL: http://www.baltzer.nl. (Subscr. in N. America to: Baltzer Science Publishers, Box 8577, Red Bank, NJ 07701-8577) Eds. Gabor Somorjai, John Thomas. adv. **Indexed:** ASCA, Chem.Abstr., Chem.Cit.Ind., Curr.Cont., Mat.Sci.Cit.Ind., Sci.Cit.Ind. **Document type:** academic/scholarly publication.
—BLDSC (3090.907000); CASDDS; CISTI; Ei; Genuine Article; KNAW; Linda Hall; SWETS; UnCover. **CCC.**
    Description: Covers the science of catalysis and sub-disciplines.

660   US
CATALYSIS: SCIENCE AND TECHNOLOGY. 1981. irreg. price varies. Springer-Verlag, 175 Fifth Ave., New York, NY 10010. TEL 212-460-1500. FAX 212-473-6272. (Also: Berlin, Heidelberg, Tokyo and Vienna) Eds. J.R. Anderson, M. Boudart. (reprint service avail. from ISI) **Document type:** academic/scholarly publication.

CATALYSIS TODAY; a serial publication dealing with topical themes in catalysis and related subjects. see *ENGINEERING — Chemical Engineering*

540   US   ISSN 0008-767X
QD1   CODEN: CATLAG
CATALYST (PHILADELPHIA). 1916. m. (Sep.-Jun.) $4.25 (foreign $5.25). American Chemical Society, Philadelphia Section, University of Pennsylvania, Department of Chemistry, Philadelphia, PA 19104-6323. TEL 215-382-1589. Ed. Robert C. Benedict. R&P contact: E.H. Harper. adv.: B&W page $267.50; trim 4 1/2 x 7 3/16; adv. contact: Victor Tortorelli. bk.rev.; charts; illus. circ. 5,200. **Indexed:** Amer.Hist.& Life (1969-1985), Hist.Abstr. (1969-1985). **Document type:** newsletter.

660   II   ISSN 0008-8579
CAUSTIC. (Text in English and Malayalam) 1967. q. free. Travancore-Cochin Chemicals Ltd., Udyogamandal 683501, Alwaye, Kerala, India. Ed. G.P.C. Nayar. adv.; bk.rev.; illus. circ. 1,200.

540   UK
CHEM-FACTS: EUROPEAN REVIEW. 1992. irreg. £100. Chem-Intell, Reed Information Services (Subsidiary of: Reed Telepublishing Ltd.), Windsor Ct., East Grinstead House, E. Grinstead, W. Sussex RH19 1XA, England. TEL 44-1342-335831. FAX 44-1342-335612. TELEX 95127 INFSER G. **Document type:** directory.
●Also available online. Vendor(s): Data-Star, Knight-Ridder Information, Inc.
    Description: Lists and profiles more than 800 major chemical manufacturers in 17 European nations.

540   UK
CHEM-FACTS: FRANCE. 1991. irreg. £75. Chem-Intell, Reed Information Services (Subsidiary of: Reed Telepublishing Ltd.), Windsor Ct., East Grinstead House, E. Grinstead, W. Sussex RH19 1XA, England. TEL 44-1342-335831. FAX 44-1342-335612. TELEX 95127 INFSER G. **Document type:** directory.
●Also available online. Vendor(s): Data-Star, Knight-Ridder Information, Inc.
    Description: Surveys the French chemical industry and more than 120 companies. Also gives ten-year trends on production and trade.

540   UK
CHEM-FACTS: GERMANY. 1988. irreg., latest 1992. £100. Chem-Intell, Reed Information Services (Subsidiary of: Reed Telepublishing Ltd.), Windsor Ct., East Grinstead House, E. Grinstead, W. Sussex RH19 1XA, England. TEL 44-1342-335831. FAX 44-1342-335612. TELEX 95127 INFSER G.
●Also available online. Vendor(s): Data-Star, Knight-Ridder Information, Inc.
    Formerly (until 1992): Chem-Facts: Federal Republic of Germany.
    Description: Presents the findings of a detailed survey of more than 120 major industrial chemicals and over 90 chemical manufacturing companies.

CHEMISTRY   1741

540   UK
CHEM-FACTS: UNITED KINGDOM. 1987. irreg. £75. Chem-Intell, Reed Information Services (Subsidiary of: Reed Telepublishing Ltd.), Windsor Ct., East Grinstead House, E. Grinstead, W. Sussex RH19 1XA, England. TEL 44-1342-335831. FAX 44-1342-335612. TELEX 95127 INFSER G. **Document type:** directory.
●Also available online. Vendor(s): Data-Star, Knight-Ridder Information, Inc.
    Description: Presents the findings of a detailed survey of more than 100 major industrial chemicals.

540   US   ISSN 0736-4687
CHEM MATTERS. 1983. 4/yr. $8. American Chemical Society, Office of High School Chemistry, 1155 16th St., N.W., Washington, DC 20036. TEL 202-872-4600. FAX 202-833-7732. URL: http://www.chemcenter.org. (Subscr. to: ACS Education Products, Box 2537, Kearneysville, WV 25430) R&P contact: Janet Boese. TEL 202-872-6164. adv. contact: Michael John Tinnesand. circ. 45,000 (paid). **Document type:** academic/scholarly publication.
●Also available on CD-ROM.

CHEM SOURCES INTERNATIONAL. see *BUSINESS AND ECONOMICS — Trade And Industrial Directories*

CHEM SOURCES U S A. see *BUSINESS AND ECONOMICS — Trade And Industrial Directories*

540   CN   ISSN 0703-1157
CHEM 13 NEWS. 1968. 9/yr. Can.$11($14) (foreign Can.$16) (effective 1996-1997). University of Waterloo, Department of Chemistry, Waterloo, ON N2L 3G1, Canada. TEL 519-888-4567. FAX 519-746-0435. E-mail: lbrubacher@uwaterloo.ca. Ed. Lewis J. Brubacher. R&P contact: Lewis Brubacher. adv.; bk.rev.; illus.; circ. 4,400 (paid). **Indexed:** Chem.Abstr. **Document type:** academic/scholarly publication.
—CISTI.
    Description: Contains teaching ideas, experiments, demonstrations, humor and background articles for high school chemistry teachers.

540   US   ISSN 0736-6019
TP202
CHEMCYCLOPEDIA. 1982. a. $60. American Chemical Society, 1155 16th St., N.W., Washington, DC 20036. TEL 800-227-5558. FAX 202-872-4615. Ed. Joseph Kuney. adv. circ. 62,000. **Document type:** catalog.
—CISTI. **CCC.**

CHEMECOLOGY; covering health, safety and the environment. see *ENVIRONMENTAL STUDIES*

540   PL   ISSN 0411-8634
                     CODEN: CHSZAY
CHEMIA W SZKOLE. 1954. 5/yr. $10. (Ministerstwo Edukacji Narodowej) Wydawnictwa Szkolne i Pedagogiczne, Pl. Dabrowskiego 8, 00-696 Warsaw, Poland. TEL 48-22-265451. FAX 48-22-268971. (Dist.by: Ars Polona, Krakowskie Przedmiescie 7, Warsaw, Poland) Ed. Andrzej Rubaszkiewicz. circ. 8,000.
—CASDDS.
    Description: Discusses the latest achievements in chemistry and chemical technology, and presents new concepts in teaching chemistry.

660   II   ISSN 0009-2320
TP1   CODEN: CHAIAT
CHEMICAL AGE OF INDIA. (Text in English) 1949. m. Rs.500($75) (Chemical Process Industries of India) Technical Press Publications, 5-1 Convent St., Colaba, Mumbai 400 039, India. TEL 91-22-2021446. FAX 91-22-2871499. TELEX 011-83479 CHEM IN. Ed. J.P. de Sousa. bk.rev.; abstr.; charts; illus.; tr.lit.; index. circ. 6,400. (also avail. in microform from UMI) **Indexed:** Chem.Abstr., Chem.Eng.Abstr., CLOSS, Fluidex, Fuel & Energy Abstr., INIS Atomind., Soils & Fert., T.C.E.A. **Document type:** academic/scholarly publication.
—CASDDS; CISTI; Linda Hall; SWETS; UMI. **CCC.**

ULRICH'S INTERNATIONAL PERIODICALS DIRECTORY 1998

CHEMISTRY

540 613.1   II   ISSN 0971-2151
CODEN: CEREEH
CHEMICAL & ENVIRONMENTAL RESEARCH. (Text in English) 1992. q. Rs.450 to individuals (foreign $60); institutions Rs.750 (foreign $100). (Muslim Association for the Advancement of Science) 44, Ahmad Nagar, Dodhpur, Aligarh 202 001, India. TEL 91-571-401209. FAX 91-571-400466. Ed. Ali Mohammad. circ. 300. **Document type:** academic/scholarly publication.
—CASDDS.
Description: Contains research papers dealing with all aspects of environmental research and research in chemistry.

540 615   JA   ISSN 0009-2363
RS1.N56   CODEN: CPBTAL
CHEMICAL & PHARMACEUTICAL BULLETIN. (Text in English) 1953. m. $125 to members. Pharmaceutical Society of Japan - Nihon Yakugakkai, 12-15, Shibuya 2-chome, Shibuya-ku, Tokyo 150, Japan. Ed. Koichi Shudo. adv.; charts; index. circ. 3,600. (also avail. in microfilm from PMC) **Indexed:** Anal.Abstr., ASCA, Biol.Abstr., Biotech.Abstr., Chem.Abstr., Chem.Cit.Ind., Chem.Infd., Crop Physiol.Abstr., Curr.Adv.Cancer Res., Curr.Adv.Ecol.Sci., Curr.Chem.React., Curr.Cont., Dairy Sci.Abstr., Dent.Ind., Excerp.Med., Forest.Abstr., Forest Prod.Abstr., Helminthol.Abstr., Herb.Abstr., I.P.A., Ind.Chem., Ind.Med., Ind.Sci.Rev., INIS Atomind., Mass Spectr.Bull., Mat.Sci.Cit.Ind., Nutr.Abstr., Protozool.Abstr., Rev.Med.& Vet.Mycol., Sci.Cit.Ind., Seed Abstr., Sugar Ind.Abstr., Weed Abstr.
●Also available online.
—BLDSC (3138.800000); CASDDS; CISTI; Genuine Article; KNAW; Linda Hall; SWETS; UnCover. **CCC.**
Formerly: Pharmaceutical Bulletin.

540   US   ISSN 0009-2398
CHEMICAL BOND. 1950. 9/yr. $5. American Chemical Society, St. Louis Section, c/o Messenger Printing Co., 125 W. Argonne Dr., St. Louis, MO 63122. Ed. John Bornmann. adv.; bk.rev. circ. 1,850. **Document type:** newsletter.
Description: Lists events and member news.

540   US   ISSN 0009-2401
CODEN: CHEBAS
CHEMICAL BULLETIN. 1914. m. (Sep.-Jun.). $15. American Chemical Society, Chicago Section, 7173 N. Austin Ave., Niles, IL 60714. TEL 847-647-8405. Ed. Fran Karen Kravitz. adv. circ. 5,800. **Document type:** newsletter.
—Linda Hall.
Description: Contains organization news.

540   UK   ISSN 1359-7345
QD1   CODEN: CHCOFS
CHEMICAL COMMUNICATIONS; a journal for urgent preliminary accounts of important chemical research. Variant title: ChemComm. Online edition (UK ISSN 1364-548X) 1965. s-m. £623 to institutions (US $1121) (effective 1997). The Royal Society of Chemistry, Thomas Graham House, Science Park, Milton Rd., Cambridge CB4 4WF, England. TEL 44-1223-420066. FAX 44-1223-423429. E-mail: chemcomm@rsc.org; URL: http://chemistry.rsc.org/rsc/. (Subscr. to: Turpin Distribution Services Ltd., Blackhorse Rd., Letchworth, Herts. SG6 1HN, England. TEL 44-1462-672555. FAX 44-1462-480947) adv.; charts; illus.; index. circ. 4,000. (also avail. in microform from UMI,PMC; reprint service avail. from UMI) **Indexed:** Abstr.Bull.Inst.Pap.Chem., Agroforest.Abstr., ASCA, Biol.Abstr., Chem.Abstr., Chem.Cit.Ind., Chem.Infd., Chem.Titles, Curr.Cont., Deep Sea Res.& Oceanogr.Abstr., Excerp.Med., Ind.Chem., Ind.Sci.Rev., INIS Atomind., Mass Spectr.Bull., Mat.Sci.Cit.Ind., Ref.Zh., Sci.Cit.Ind. **Document type:** academic/scholarly publication.
●Also available online. Vendor(s): STN International (CJRSC).
—BLDSC (3139.350000); ADONIS; CASDDS; CISTI; Ei; EMDOCS; Genuine Article; Linda Hall; SWETS; UMI; UnCover. **CCC.**
Former titles: Journal of the Chemical Society - Chemical Communications (ISSN 0022-4936); **Supersedes:** Chemical Communications (ISSN 0009-241X)
Description: Covers developments in all branches of chemistry.
Refereed Serial

540   II   ISSN 0970-9525
CHEMICAL DIGEST; industrial trends and opportunities. (Text in English) 1971. m. Rs.60($20) Small Business Publications, P.O. Box 2131, 4-45 Roop Nagar, Delhi 110007, India. TEL 91-11-2523701. FAX 91-11-2924673. Ed. R.K. Gupta. adv.; bk.rev. **Document type:** newsletter.

540   US
CHEMICAL DISTILLATIONS. (Subseries of: Chemical Follow-up) 1977. m. avail. to qualified personnel only. Cyrus J. Lawrence, Inc., 1290 Ave. of the Americas, New York, NY 10104. TEL 212-468-5000. circ. controlled. (back issues avail.)

540   US   ISSN 1430-4171
▼**CHEMICAL EDUCATOR.** 1996. bi-m. $24.95 to individuals; institutions $100 (effective 1996). Springer-Verlag, 175 Fifth Ave., New York, NY 10010. TEL 212-460-1500. FAX 212-473-6272. E-mail: orders@springer-ny.com; URL: http://journals-springer-ny.com/chedr/. Ed. Clifford LeMaster. **Document type:** academic/scholarly publication.
●Available only online.
Description: Provides resources and information for chemical education professionals.
Refereed Serial

540   II   ISSN 0009-2533
CODEN: CHERDB
CHEMICAL ERA. (Text in English) 1964. m. Rs.150. O. N. Pandeya, Ed. & Pub., 105-C Block F, New Alipore, Calcutta 700053, India. Ed. L.K. Pandeya. **Indexed:** Chem.Abstr., Excerp.Med.
—CASDDS; CISTI.

CHEMICAL HAZARDS IN INDUSTRY. see OCCUPATIONAL HEALTH AND SAFETY

540   US   ISSN 1066-5315
QD11   CODEN: CHHEEM
CHEMICAL HERITAGE. 1982. 2/yr. $25 (effective 1996 & 1997). Chemical Heritage Foundation, 315 Chestnut St., Philadelphia, PA 19106. TEL 215-925-2222. FAX 215-925-1954. Ed. Mary Virginia Orna. R&P contact: Frances Kohler. adv.: page $1000; trim 7 1/2 x 9 3/4; adv. contact: Laurel Adelman. bk.rev. circ. 20,000. (back issues avail.) **Document type:** academic/scholarly publication.
—CASDDS; Linda Hall.
Former titles (until Winter 1992-93): Beckman Center News and Othmer Library News; Beckman Center News (ISSN 1052-0414); B C H O C News (ISSN 0736-4555)
Description: For chemists, chemical engineers, teachers, and scholars. Reports on developments in history of the chemical sciences and technologies and on programs of the foundation and its constituent parts: Beckman Center, Othmer Library, and public outreach.

540 338.025   UK   ISSN 0961-270X
CHEMICAL INDUSTRIES ASSOCIATION. DIRECTORY OF CHEMICAL PRODUCTS AND BUYERS GUIDE. a. £110 (foreign £130). (Chemical Industries Association Ltd.) Hamlet Information Services Ltd., Padlock Rd., West Wratting, Cambridge CB1 5LS, England. TEL 01223-290838. FAX 01223-290687. Ed. C.E. Freer; Pub. Peter G. Lewis. circ. 3,500. **Document type:** directory.
Formerly (until 1991): Chemicals. Text - Intro.

540 658.8   US   ISSN 1051-9041
CHEMICAL INDUSTRIES NEWSLETTER. 1960. bi-m. free. S R I International, Process Industries Division, Chemical Marketing Research Center, Menlo Park, CA 94025. TEL 415-859-3346. E-mail: webmaster@methane.sri.com; URL: http://www-cmrc.sri.com/CIN/. Ed. Elizabeth Johnson. abstr.; stat. **Indexed:** Intl.Polym.Sci.& Tech., RAPRA. **Document type:** newsletter.
●Also available online.
—BLDSC (3147.150000); Linda Hall.
Former titles: Chemical Industries Centers Newsletter; Chemical Industries Division Newsletter; Chemical Industries Center Newsletter; Chemical Economics Newsletter.

CHEMICAL INDUSTRY IN (YEAR) - ANNUAL REVIEW. see BUSINESS AND ECONOMICS — Production Of Goods And Services

540   US
CHEMICAL INDUSTRY MONITOR. (Subseries of: Chemical Follow-up) 1976. s-m. avail. to private clients only. Cyrus J. Lawrence, Inc., 1290 Ave. of the Americas, New York, NY 10104. TEL 212-468-5000. circ. controlled. (looseleaf format; back issues avail.)

338.4   US   ISSN 1054-4941
HD9651.1
CHEMICAL INDUSTRY SOURCEBOOK AND STRATEGIC OVERVIEW.* a.? Lavely Associates, 5 Prospect St., Acton, MA 01720-3620.

540   UK   ISSN 0045-6403
CHEMICAL INSIGHT. 1972. s-m. £575. Reed Business Information (Subsidiary of: Reed Elsevier group), Quadrant House, The Quadrant, Sutton, Surrey SM2 5AS, England. TEL 44-181-652-3396. FAX 44-181-652-8952. Ed. Nigel Davis. bk.rev.; index. **Indexed:** PROMT. **Document type:** newsletter.

540   US   ISSN 0947-0662
QD1
▼**THE CHEMICAL INTELLIGENCER.** 1995. q. $78 (effective 1998). Springer-Verlag, Life Science Journals, 175 Fifth Ave., New York, NY 10010. TEL 212-460-1500. FAX 212-473-6272. E-mail: orders@springer-ny.com; URL: http://www.springer-ny.com. (Subscr. to: Springer-Verlag, Journals Fulfillment Services, Box 2845, Secaucus, NJ 07906-2485. TEL 800-777-4643. FAX 201-348-4505; Subscr. overseas to: Heidelberger Platz 3, 14197 Berlin, Germany. TEL 49-30-82072-0. FAX 49-30-8207448) Ed. Istvan Hargittai. R&P contact: Ian Gross. adv. contact: Robert Vrooman. (reprint service avail.)
—BLDSC (3148.325000); CISTI; SWETS. **CCC.**
Description: Informs a broad audience of the history of chemistry and where it is headed with discoveries, interviews, experiments, and new applications.
Refereed Serial

660 667.6 615   US   ISSN 0090-0907
TP1   CODEN: CMKRA5
CHEMICAL MARKETING REPORTER. 1871. w. $99 (Europe $295; elsewhere $245). Schnell Publishing Co., Inc., 80 Broad St., New York, NY 10004-2203. TEL 212-248-4177. FAX 212-248-4903. TELEX 226113 CMR UR. URL: http://www.chemexpo.com; http://elsevier.nl:80/inca/publications/store. Ed. Harry Van; Pub. Clifford Hannan. adv. contact: Clifford Johnson. bk.rev.; charts; mkt.; stat.; circ. 17,000 (paid). (tabloid format; also avail. in microfilm from UMI,PMC) **Indexed:** Abstr.Bull.Inst.Pap.Chem., Acid Rain Abstr., Acid Rain Ind., B.P.I., BPIA, Bus.Ind., Chem.Abstr., Fuel & Energy Abstr., I.P.A., Intl.Polym.Sci.& Tech., Key to Econ.Sci., PROMT, RAPRA, Tr.& Indus.Ind. **Document type:** trade publication.
●Also available online. Vendor(s): Information Access Co., Knight-Ridder Information, Inc., UMI.
—CASDDS; CISTI; KR SourceOne; Linda Hall; SWETS; UMI. **CCC.**
Formerly (until 1972): Oil, Paint and Drug Reporter (ISSN 0030-1469)

540   US
CHEMICAL MONOGRAPHS REVIEW.* 1985. q. free. Chemists' Club Library, 40 W. 45th St., New York, NY 10036-4203. TEL 212-679-6383. FAX 212-779-0349. (And: 52 E. 41st St., New York, NY 10016) bk.rev. circ. 600. (looseleaf format; back issues avail.) **Document type:** monographic series.
Description: Covers review of new chemistry books and chemistry related books.

CHEMICAL NEWSLETTER. see OCCUPATIONAL HEALTH AND SAFETY

CHEMICAL PEDDLER. see BUSINESS AND ECONOMICS — Trade And Industrial Directories

540   UK
CHEMICAL PLANT FILE. a. (plus m. updates). price varies. Chem-Intell, Reed Information Services (Subsidiary of: Reed Telepublishing Ltd.), Windsor Ct., East Grinstead House, E. Grinstead, W. Sussex RH19 1XA, England. TEL 44-1342-335831. FAX 44-1342-335612. TELEX 95127 INFSER G. **Document type:** directory.
●Also available online. Vendor(s): Data-Star, Knight-Ridder Information, Inc., Reed Information Services Ltd.
Formerly: Chemical Age Project File.

540 US
CHEMICAL PROCESSING'S PROBLEM SOLVER'S RESOURCE FOR THE C P I. 1938. a. Putman Publishing Co., 301 E. Erie St., Chicago, IL 60611. TEL 312-644-2020. FAX 312-644-1131. Ed. John McCallion. adv. circ. 80,037.
 Formerly: Chemical Processing Guide and Directory.

CHEMICAL REGULATION REPORTER; a weekly review of activity affecting chemical users and manufacturers. see ENVIRONMENTAL STUDIES

540 378   CC   ISSN 1005-9040
     CODEN: CRCUED
CHEMICAL RESEARCH IN CHINESE UNIVERSITIES. (Text in English) 1984. q. $60. Jilin Daxue, Like Xuebao Bianjibu, 83, Jiefang Lu, Changchun, Jilin 130021, People's Republic of China. TEL 86-431-8923189. FAX 86-431-8923907. TELEX 83040 JLU CN. (Dist. by: Science Press New York, Ltd., 63-117 Alderton St., Rego Park, NY 11374. TEL 718-459-4638) Ed. Tang Aoqing. Indexed: ASCA, Chem.Cit.Ind., Curr.Cont., Mat.Sci.Cit.Ind. Document type: academic/scholarly publication.
 —BLDSC (3150.441000); CASDDS; Ei.
 Formerly (until vol.7, 1991): Chemical Journal of Chinese Universities (ISSN 1000-9213)
 Description: Comprehensive academic journal on chemistry. Contains theses, research notes, letters and reviews by teachers, researchers, postgraduates and graduate students.

540   US   ISSN 0009-2665
     CODEN: CHREAY
CHEMICAL REVIEWS. 1924. 8/yr. $520 to institutional non-members; members $41 (effective 1997). American Chemical Society, 1155 16th St., N.W., Washington, DC 20036. TEL 800-333-9511. FAX 614-447-3671. (Subscr. to: Membership and Subscription Services, Box 3337, Columbus, OH 43210. TEL 614-447-3776) Ed. Josef Michl. adv.; bibl.; charts; index. circ. 4,800. (also avail. in microform from RPI,PMC; microfiche from IDC; reprint service avail. from ISI) Indexed: A.S.& T.Ind., Abstr.Bull.Inst.Pap.Chem., Appl.Mech.Rev., ASCA, Biol.Abstr., Biotech.Abstr., Cadscan, Chem.Abstr., Chem.Cit.Ind., Chem.Infd., Curr.Adv.Ecol.Sci., Curr.Chem.React., Curr.Cont., Dairy Sci.Abstr., Excerp.Med., Ind.Chem., Ind.Mat., Ind.Sci.Rev., INIS Atomind., Lead Abstr., Mass Spectr.Bull., Mat.Sci.Cit.Ind., Nutr.Abstr., RAPRA, Sci.Cit.Ind., Soils & Fert., World Surf.Coat., World Text.Abstr., Zincscan. Document type: academic/scholarly publication.
 ●Also available online. Vendor(s): STN International (CJACS).
 —BLDSC (3151.000000); CASDDS; CISTI; Ei; Genuine Article; KR SourceOne; Linda Hall; SWETS; UMI; UnCover. CCC.
 Description: Provides comprehensive critical analyses in all fields of chemistry -- organic, inorganic, physical, analytical, theoretical, and biological.

540 660   NE   ISSN 0927-0841
CHEMICAL SAFETY SHEETS. (Text in English) 1991. a. price varies. (Nederlandse Instituut voor Arbeidsomstandigheden) Kluwer Academic Publishers, Postbus 17, 3300 AA Dordrecht, Netherlands. TEL 31-78-6392392. FAX 31-78-6392254. E-mail: services@wkap.nl; URL: http://www.wkap.nl. (Dist. by: Kluwer Academic Publishers Group, P.O. Box 322, 3300 AH Dordrecht, Netherlands. TEL 31-78-6392392. FAX 31-78-6546474; N. America dist. addr.: Box 358, Accord Sta., Hingham, MA 02018-0358. TEL 617-871-6600. FAX 617-871-6528) (Co-sponsor: Vereniging van de Nederlandse Chemische Industrie) stat. circ. 5,000.
 Description: Specifies health hazards and precautionary measures associated with more than 950 chemicals.

CHEMICAL SCIENCES GRADUATE SCHOOL FINDER. see EDUCATION — Guides To Schools And Colleges

540   ET   ISSN 1011-3924
     CODEN: BCETE6
CHEMICAL SOCIETY OF ETHIOPIA. BULLETIN. 1986. s-a. Br.22 to individuals (foreign $29); institutions Br.33 (foreign $40). Chemical Society of Ethiopia, P.O. Box 32934, Addis Ababa, Ethiopia. TEL 251-1-121201. FAX 251-1-551244. E-mail: chemistry@padis.gn.apc.org. Ed. Wendimagegn Mammo. adv.; bk.rev.; index. circ. 1,100. (back issues avail.) Indexed: ASCA, Chem.Abstr., Chem.Cit.Ind., Curr.Cont., Environ.Abstr. Document type: academic/scholarly publication, bulletin.
 —BLDSC (2442.950000); CASDDS; Genuine Article.
 Refereed Serial

540   JA   ISSN 0009-2673
QD1   CODEN: BCSJA8
CHEMICAL SOCIETY OF JAPAN. BULLETIN. (Text in English) 1926. m. $114 to members; non-members N. America $552; elsewhere $522 (effective 1995). Chemical Society of Japan - Nippon Kagakukai, 1-5, Kanda-Surugadai, Chiyoda-ku, Tokyo 101, Japan. TEL 03-3292-6161. FAX 03-3292-6318. Ed. Hideki Sakurai. index. circ. 4,100. (also avail. in microfilm from UMI,PMC; reprint service avail. from UMI) Indexed: Abstr.Bull.Inst.Pap.Chem., Anal.Abstr., API Abstr., API Catal., API Hlth.& Environ., API Oil., API Pet.Ref., API Pet.Subst., API Transport., Appl.Mech.Rev., ASCA, Biol.Abstr., Biotech.Abstr., Biwk.Pap.Rad.Chem.& Photochem., Cadscan, Chem.Abstr., Chem.Cit.Ind., Chem.Infd., Curr.Adv.Ecol.Sci., Curr.Chem.React., Curr.Cont., Dairy Sci.Abstr., Deep Sea Res.& Oceanogr.Abstr., Energy Ind., Energy Info.Abstr., Excerp.Med., GeoRef., Ind.Chem., Ind.Sci.Rev., INIS Atomind., JCT, JTA, Lead Abstr., Mass Spectr.Bull., Petrol.Abstr., RAPRA, Sci.Cit.Ind., Soils & Fert., SSCI, Sugar Ind.Abstr., World Surf.Coat., Zincscan. Document type: bulletin, academic/scholarly publication.
 —BLDSC (2443.000000); CASDDS; CISTI; EMDOCS; Genuine Article; Linda Hall; SWETS; UMI; UnCover. CCC.
 Description: Publishes original research papers in the all-around field of chemistry.

540   JA
CHEMICAL SOCIETY OF JAPAN. DIVISION OF COLLOID AND SURFACE CHEMISTRY. NEWSLETTER. (Text in English, Japanese) bi-m. Chemical Society of Japan, Division of Colloid and Surface Chemistry - Nippon Kagakkai Koroido Oyobi Kaimen Kagaku Bukai, 1-5, Kanda Surugadai, Chiyoda-ku, Tokyo 101, Japan. Document type: newsletter.

540 530 616.075   JA
CHEMICAL SOCIETY OF JAPAN. SYMPOSIUM ON PHYSICAL AND CHEMICAL ASPECTS OF ULTRASOUND. PROCEEDINGS/ONPA NO BUSSEI TO KAGAKU TORONKAI KOEN RONBUNSHU. (Text in Japanese) a. Chemical Society of Japan - Nippon Kagakukai, 1-5, Kanda Surugadai, Chiyoda-ku, Tokyo 101, Japan. Document type: proceedings.

540   PK   ISSN 0253-5106
QD1   CODEN: JCSPDF
CHEMICAL SOCIETY OF PAKISTAN. JOURNAL. (Text in English, French and German; summaries in English) 1979. q. Rs.100($30) Chemical Society of Pakistan, H.E.J. Research Institute of Chemistry, University of Karachi, Karachi 75280, Pakistan. FAX 92-21-466896. TELEX 28095 HEJRI PK. Ed. Atta-Ur-Rahman. bk.rev. circ. 1,000. (back issues avail.) Indexed: ASCA, Chem.Abstr., Chem.Cit.Ind., Curr.Cont., Food Sci.& Tech.Abstr., Ind.Chem. Document type: academic/scholarly publication.
 —BLDSC (4729.082000); CASDDS; CISTI; Ei; Genuine Article; UnCover.

540   US   ISSN 0411-8871
CHEMICAL SPOTLIGHT. 1950. m. $227. Chemical Spotlight Inc., 203 Oak St., Ridgewood, NJ 07450-2512. TEL 201-444-7810. FAX 201-444-7939. Ed. Harry E. Whitmore.

540 660   II   ISSN 0045-6497
CHEMICAL TAKE-OFF; monthly journal of chemical and chemical-based industries. (Text in English) 1971. m. Rs.40($11) G-77 Himalaya House, Curzon Rd., New Delhi, India. Ed. S. Chopra. adv.; bk.rev.; charts. circ. 6,000. (back issues avail.)

CHEMICAL THERMODYNAMICS. see PHYSICS

540   US   ISSN 0149-2381
TP1   CODEN: CTTRDY
CHEMICAL TIMES & TRENDS. 1977. q. $27 (foreign $39) (effective 1997). Chemical Specialties Manufacturers Association, 1913 Eye St., N.W., Washington, DC 20006. TEL 202-872-8110. FAX 202-872-8114. Ed. Connie Neuman. R&P contact: Connie Neuman. adv.; bk.rev.; charts; illus. circ. 7,000. Indexed: Chem.Abstr., Resour.Ctr.Ind. Document type: trade publication.
 —BLDSC (3151.790000); CASDDS; CISTI; Ei; KNAW; UnCover.

540   UK
CHEMICAL WEEK (INTERNATIONAL EDITION). 1914. w. $115 (Europe & Asia $399; Canada $145; Mexico, Caribbean & S. America $255) (effective 1996). 24-25 Scala St., London W1P 1LU, England. TEL 44-171-436-7676. FAX 44-171-436-3749. URL: http://www.chemweek.com. (U.S. addr.: Chemical Week Associates, 888 Seventh Ave., 26th Fl., New York, NY 10106-2698. TEL 212-621-4900) Ed. David Hunter; Pub. Michael Silber. bk.rev.; circ. 36,165 (paid). Indexed: Int.Packag.Abstr., World Surf.Coat. Document type: trade publication.
 Description: Provides global news and analysis for the chemical industry.

540 660   II   ISSN 0045-6500
     CODEN: CHWEBQ
CHEMICAL WEEKLY. (Text in English) 1956. w. Rs.600($75) (effective 1997). Sevak Publications, 306 Shri Hanuman Industrial Estate, G.D. Ambekar Rd., Post Box No. 7110, Wadala, Bombay 400 031, India. Ed. Ravi Raghavan; Pub. N.R. Rajagopalan. adv.; pat.; stat. circ. 25,000. Indexed: Chem.Abstr., W.R.C.Inf.
 —BLDSC (3153.030000); CASDDS.

540   UK
CHEMICALS. (Text in English; introduction in French, German, Spanish) 1920. a. £110 (foreign £130). (Chemical Industries Association Ltd.) Hamlet Information Services Ltd., Padlock Rd., West Wratting, Cambridge CB1 5LS, England. TEL 01223-290838. FAX 01223-290687. Ed. C.E. Freer; Pub. Peter G. Lewis. circ. 13,000. Document type: directory.
 Formerly: British Chemicals and Their Manufacturers.

CHEMICALS AND ALLIED PRODUCTS EXPORT PROMOTION COUNCIL. EXPORTERS DIRECTORY. see BUSINESS AND ECONOMICS — International Commerce

540   II   ISSN 0009-2746
CHEMICALS - INTERNATIONAL. (Text in English) 1965. m. Rs.25. Encee Technical Publications Corporation, 1-E-22 Jhandewalan Extension, New Delhi, India. Eds. V. Navin, S.K. Nanda. adv.; charts; illus.; stat. circ. 5,760.

540   US
CHEMICALS: LATIN AMERICAN INDUSTRIAL REPORT. (Avail. for each of 22 Latin American countries) 1985. a. $435 per country report. Aquino Productions, Box 125, Rochester, VT 05767. Ed. Andres C. Aquino.

CHEMICALS TODAY. see ENGINEERING — Chemical Engineering

CHEMISTRY

540   XR   ISSN 0009-2770
CODEN: CHLSAC
CHEMICKE LISTY/CHEMICAL PAPERS. (Text in Czech, Slovak or English; contents page and summaries in English) 1876. m. 744 Kc.($91) (foreign DM 440) (effective 1998). Ceska Spolecnost Chemicka - Czech Chemical Society, Pelleova 24, 160 00 Prague 6, Czech Republic. TEL 42-2-3114756. FAX 42-2-329265. E-mail: mblahova@iic.cas.cz; URL: http://www.uochb.cas.cz/ChemListy/chemilisty.html. (Dist. by: Mezhdunarodnaya Kniga, B. Yakimanka 39, 117049 Moscow, Russia. TEL 7-095-2384967. FAX 7-095-2384634; Dist. in Western countries by: Kubon & Sagner, P.O. Box 34 01 08, 8000 Munich 34, Germany) (Co-sponsor: Institute of Chemical Technology, Prague) Ed. Bohumil Kratochvil. adv. contact: Pavel Drasar. bk.rev.; abstr.; charts; illus.; index. circ. 1,000. **Indexed:** Alloys Ind., Anal.Abstr., Art & Archaeol.Tech.Abstr., ASCA, Biol.Abstr., C.I.S. Abstr., Cadscan, Chem.Abstr., Chem.Cit.Ind., Compumath, Curr.Cont., Eng.Mat.Abstr., Food Sci.& Tech.Abstr., Ind.Sci.Rev., INIS Atomind., Lead Abstr., Mat.Sci.Cit.Ind., Met.Abstr.Ind., Met.Abstr., Nonfer.Met.Alert, Nutr.Abstr., PCC Alert, Sci.Cit.Ind., SSCI, Steels Alert, World Alum.Abstr., World Surf.Coat., Zincscan.
—BLDSC (3154.000000); CASDDS; CISTI; Ei; Genuine Article; Linda Hall; UMI. **CCC**.
Description: Review of articles on progress in chemistry, papers on laboratory techniques and instruments, book reviews, discussions, reports on selected meetings and personal reports.

540 660   XR   ISSN 0009-2789
TP1   CODEN: CHPUA4
CHEMICKY PRUMYSL/CHEMICAL INDUSTRY. (Text in Czech; summaries in English) 1925. m. 432 Kc. (effective 1997). Enonomia, a.s., Na Florenci 3, 115 43 Prague 1, Czech Republic. TEL 421-2-2823845. Ed. Sarka Spevakova. R&P contact: Sarka Spevakova. adv. contact: L. Varbuchta. bk.rev.; charts; illus.; index. circ. 3,400. **Indexed:** Abstr.Bull.Inst.Pap.Chem., Abstr.Bull.Inst.Pap.Chem., Anal.Abstr., C.I.S. Abstr., Chem.Abstr., Chem.Eng.Abstr., INIS Atomind., Intl.Polym.Sci.& Tech., Met.Abstr., RAPRA, T.C.E.A., World Alum.Abstr., World Surf.Coat.
—BLDSC (3155.400000); CASDDS; CISTI; Linda Hall; SWETS.
Refereed Serial

540   GW   ISSN 0009-2843
CODEN: CHSCBY
CHEMIE IN DER SCHULE. (Contents page in English, French, German, Russian) 1953. 11/yr. DM.89.10 (effective 1997); newsstand price: DM.10.20. Paedagogischer Zeitschriftenverlag, Postfach 269, 10107 Berlin, Germany. TEL 49-30-20183592. FAX 49-30-20183593. (Subscr. to: CVK Cornelsen Verlagskontor, Postfach 100271, 33260 Bielefeld, Germany) Ed. Kurt Pittelkau. adv.; bk.rev.; bibl.; charts; index. circ. 2,400. **Indexed:** Chem.Abstr. **Document type:** academic/scholarly publication.
—CASDDS.

540   GW   ISSN 0009-2851
CODEN: CUNZAW
CHEMIE IN UNSERER ZEIT. 1967. bi-m. DM.110 (foreign DM.122) to individuals; institutions DM. 160 (foreign DM.172); students DM.75 (foreign DM.87) (effective 1997). (Gesellschaft Deutscher Chemiker) Wiley - V C H, Postfach 101161, 69451 Weinheim, Germany. TEL 49-6201-606167. FAX 49-6201-606117. TELEX 465516-VCHWH-D. E-mail: subservice@vchgroup.de; URL: http://www.vchgroup.de. (Subscr. in the Americas to: John Wiley & Sons, Inc., 605 Third Ave., New York, NY 10158. TEL 212-850-6645. FAX 212-850-6021) Ed. G. Karger. adv.; bk.rev.; index. circ. 15,100. (reprint service avail. from ISI) **Indexed:** Art & Archaeol.Tech.Abstr., ASCA, Biol.Abstr., Cadscan, Chem.Abstr., Chem.Cit.Ind., Curr.Cont., Excerp.Med., Food Sci.& Tech.Abstr., Ind.Sci.Rev., INIS Atomind., Lead Abstr., Risk Abstr., Sci.Cit.Ind., Zincscan. **Document type:** academic/scholarly publication.
—BLDSC (3157.550000); CASDDS; CISTI; Ei; Genuine Article; Linda Hall; SWETS. **CCC**.

CHEMIEARBEITER. see *BUSINESS AND ECONOMICS — Labor And Industrial Relations*

540   PL   ISSN 0009-2886
CODEN: CHGLAY
CHEMIK; miesiecznik naukowo-techniczny. 1947. m. 96 Zl.($71.50) (Stowarzyszenie Inzynierow i Technikow Przemyslu Chemicznego) Zaklad Wydawniczy Chempress, Ul. Gornych Walow 25, 44-100 Gliwice, Poland. TEL 48-32-316135. FAX 48-32-316135. (Co-sponsor: Ministerstwo Przemyslu Chemicznego) Ed. Edward Buntner. R&P contact: Edward Buntner. adv.: B&W page 1000 Zl. bk.rev.; illus.; index. circ. 650. **Indexed:** Chem.Abstr. **Document type:** proceedings, trade publication.
—CASDDS; CISTI; Linda Hall.
Description: Addressed to engineers and economists in the chemical and related industries, as well as to the workers of scientific-research units.

CHEMINDEX; chemical buyers' guide for Japan. see *BUSINESS AND ECONOMICS — Trade And Industrial Directories*

540   NE   ISSN 0167-2746
CODEN: CMAGDR
CHEMISCH MAGAZINE. 1903. m. fl.347 (foreign fl.400) includes Chemisch Weekblad (effective 1996). (Koninklijke Nederlandse Chemische Vereniging - Royal Netherlands Chemical Society) Ten Hagen & Stam b.v. (Subsidiary of: Wolters Kluwer N.V.), Postbus 34, 2501 AG The Hague, Netherlands. TEL 31-70-3045700. FAX 31-70-3045812. Ed. Edwin Kisman. adv.: B&W page fl.3940, color page fl.6765; trim 297 x 210; adv. contact: Herman Voois. bk.rev.; bibl.; charts; illus.; stat.; index. circ. 15,987 (paid). **Indexed:** Anal.Abstr., Art & Archaeol.Tech.Abstr., Biol.Abstr., Biotech.Abstr., C.I.S. Abstr., Chem.Abstr., Chem.Titles, Excerp.Med., Key to Econ.Sci. **Document type:** trade publication.
—BLDSC (3158.750000); CASDDS; CISTI; Linda Hall; SWETS; UMI.
Formerly (until 1980): Chemisch Weekblad Magazine (ISSN 0378-1895); Supersedes in part (in Jan. 1976): Chemisch Weekblad (ISSN 0009-2932)
Description: Reports on a survey of chemical developments, including Dutch research, new processes, instrumentation and automation techniques.

540   NE   ISSN 0378-1887
QD1
CHEMISCH WEEKBLAD. 1903. w. (Sat.) fl.347 (foreign fl.400) includes Chemisch Magazine (effective 1996). (Koninklijke Nederlandse Chemische Vereniging - Royal Netherlands Chemical Society) Ten Hagen & Stam b.v. (Subsidiary of: Wolters Kluwer N.V.), Postbus 34, 2501 AG The Hague, Netherlands. TEL 31-70-3045700. FAX 31-70-3045812. Ed. Edwin Kisman. adv.: trim 420 x 300; adv. contact: Herman Voois. circ. 15,996 (paid). **Indexed:** Key To Econ.Sci. **Document type:** trade publication.
—CISTI; Linda Hall.
Formerly: Chemisch Weekblad - Chemische Courant; Supersedes in part (in Jan. 1976): Chemisch Weekblad (ISSN 0009-2932)
Description: Covers developments in chemistry and in the chemical industry, including economic and policy news, and working conditions.

540 660   GW   ISSN 0009-2940
QD1   CODEN: CHBEAM
CHEMISCHE BERICHTE; inorganic and organometallic chemistry. (Text in English) 1868. m. DM.1595 (foreign DM.1655) (effective 1997). (Gesellschaft Deutscher Chemiker) Wiley - V C H, Postfach 101161, 69451 Weinheim, Germany. TEL 49-6201-606147. FAX 49-6201-606117. TELEX 465516-VCHWH-D. E-mail: chember@vchgroup.de; URL: http://www.vchgroup.de. (Subscr. in the Americas to: John Wiley & Sons, Inc., 605 Third Ave., New York, NY 10158. TEL 212-850-6645. FAX 212-850-6021) Ed. R. Temme. adv. contact: R. Roth. charts; illus.; index, cum.index: 1868-1956 (in 2 vols.). circ. 1,900. (also avail. in microform from VCI; reprint service avail. from ISI) **Indexed:** Abstr.Bull.Inst.Pap.Chem., ASCA, Biol.Abstr., Biotech.Abstr., Cadscan, Chem.Abstr., Chem.Cit.Ind., Chem.Infd., Curr.Adv.Ecol.Sci., Curr.Chem.React., Curr.Cont., Dairy Sci.Abstr., Excerp.Med., Ind.Chem., Ind.Sci.Rev., Lead Abstr., Mass Spectr.Bull., Mat.Sci.Cit.Ind., Sci.Cit.Ind., Zincscan. **Document type:** academic/scholarly publication.
•Also available online.
—BLDSC (3160.000000); CASDDS; CISTI; Ei; Genuine Article; Linda Hall; SWETS; UnCover. **CCC**.

540 660 615   SZ   ISSN 0009-2983
CODEN: CHRUAE
CHEMISCHE RUNDSCHAU; Wochenzeitung fuer Chemie, Pharmazie, und Lebensmitteltechnik. (Text in German) 1947. w. 105 SFr. (foreign 150 SFr.). Vogt-Schild AG, Zuchwilerstr. 21, CH-4501 Solothurn, Switzerland. TEL 065-247247. FAX 065-247235. Ed. Alfred Widmer. adv.: B&W page 6230.40 SFr., color page 7330.40 SFr.; trim 290 x 440; adv. contact: Andreas Benz. bk.rev.; illus.; mkt.; circ. 18,500 (controlled). **Indexed:** C.I.S. Abstr., Chem.Abstr., Key to Econ.Sci., PROMT. **Document type:** newspaper.
—BLDSC (3161.900000); CASDDS.

540   US   ISSN 0009-3025
CODEN: CHESAB
CHEMIST. 1923. 6/yr. $30. American Institute of Chemists, Inc., 501 Wythe St., Alexandria, VA 22314. TEL 703-836-2090. FAX 703-836-2091. Ed. Sharon Dobson. adv.: B&W page $560; trim 8 1/2 x 11; adv. contact: Sharon Dobson. bk.rev.; charts; illus.; tr.lit. circ. 5,000. (also avail. in microform from UMI; reprint service avail. from UMI) **Indexed:** Abstr.Bull.Inst.Pap.Chem., Chem.Abstr. **Document type:** trade publication.
—BLDSC (3165.000000); Linda Hall; UMI.
Description: Contains organization news.
Refereed Serial

540 577   NE   ISSN 0275-7540
QH545.A1   CODEN: CHECDY
CHEMISTRY AND ECOLOGY. 1982. 4/yr. (in 1 vol., 4 nos./vol.). $373 (effective 1998). Gordon and Breach - Harwood Academic, Amsteldisk 166, 1st Fl., 1079 LH Amsterdam, Netherlands. URL: http://www.gbhap.com/Chemistry_Ecology/. (Subscr. to: International Publishers Distributor, Box 32160, Newark, NJ 07102. TEL 800-545-8398. FAX 215-750-6343) Ed. Gwyneth Howells. (also avail. in microform) **Indexed:** Chem.Abstr., Ecol.Abstr., Food Sci.& Tech.Abstr., Geo.Abstr.H.G., Geo.Abstr.P.G., Geol.Abstr., IDA, Sport Fish.Abstr., Wild.Rev., Zoo.Rec.
•Also available online.
Also available on CD-ROM.
—BLDSC (3169.500000); CASDDS; CISTI; SWETS. **CCC**.
Refereed Serial

540 660   UK   ISSN 0009-3068
TP1   CODEN: CHINAG
CHEMISTRY AND INDUSTRY. 1881. s-m. £221 to institutions in the EU (N. America $422; elsewhere £249) (effective 1997). Society of Chemical Industry, 14 Belgrave Sq., London SW1X 8PS, England. TEL 44-171-235-3681. FAX 44-171-235-9410. E-mail: enquiries@chemind.demon.co.uk; URL: http://ci.mond.org. (Dist. by: Turpin Distribution Services Ltd., Blackhorse Rd., Letchworth, Herts. SG6 1HN, England. TEL 44-1462-672555. FAX 44-1462-480947; Subscr. to: Society of Chemical Industry, Distribution Centre, Blackhorse Rd., Letchworth, Herts. SG6 1HN, England; Subscr. in Japan to: Usaco Corp., Tsutsumi Bldg., 13-12 Shimbashi 1-chome, Minato-ku, Tokyo 105, Japan) Ed. Andrew Miller. R&P contact: Andrew Miller. adv. contact: Hugh Jenkins. bk.rev.; bibl.; charts; illus.; index; circ. 9,161 (paid). **Indexed:** A.S.& T.Ind., Agri.Eng.Abstr., Anal.Abstr., API Abstr., API Catal., API Hlth.& Environ., API Oil., API Pet.Ref., API Pet.Subst., API Transport., ASCA, Biodet.Abstr., Biol.Abstr., Biotech.Abstr., Br.Tech.Ind., C.I.S. Abstr., C.R.I.Abstr., Cadscan, Chem.Abstr., Chem.Cit.Ind., Chem.Eng.Abstr., Chem.Infd., Cott.& Trop.Fibr.Abstr., Curr.Biotech.Abstr., Curr.Chem.React., Dairy Sci.Abstr., Energy Info.Abstr., Environ.Abstr., Excerp.Med., Field Crop Abstr., Fluidex, Food Sci.& Tech.Abstr., Fuel & Energy Abstr., Herb.Abstr., High.Educ.Curr.Aware.Bull., Hort.Abstr., Ind.Chem., Ind.Sci.Rev., Ind.Vet., INIS Atomind., Int.Packag.Abstr., Intl.Polym.Sci.& Tech., Lab.Haz.Bull., Lead Abstr., Maize Abstr., Mass Spectr.Bull., Met.Abstr., Nutr.Abstr., Packag.Sci.Tech Petrol.Abstr., Plant Breed.Abstr., PROMT, Protozool.Abstr., RAPRA, Res.High.Educ.Abstr., Risk Abstr., Sci.Cit.Ind., Soils & Fert., SSCI, T.C.E.A., Telegen, Triticale Abstr., Vet.Bull., W.R.C.Inf., Weed Abstr., World Alum.Abstr., World Surf.Coat., World Surf.Coat., World Text.Abstr., Zincscan. **Document type:** trade publication.
•Also available online.
—BLDSC (3170.000000); CASDDS; CISTI; Ei; Genuine Article; KR SourceOne; Linda Hall; SWETS; UMI; UnCover.
Description: Covers applied science and related issues within the chemical, pharmaceutical and biotechnology industries.

540 370 II ISSN 0970-597X
CHEMISTRY EDUCATION. (Text in English) 1984. q. Rs.120($40) (University Grants Commission) New Age International Pvt. Ltd., Journals Division, 4835-24 Ansari Rd., Daryaganj, New Delhi 110 002, India. TEL 91-11-3267996. FAX 91-11-3267437. TELEX 031-66507-WELIN. circ. 1,000.
—BLDSC (3171.225000).

540 JA ISSN 0911-9566
CODEN: CHEXEU
CHEMISTRY EXPRESS. (Text in English, Japanese) 1986. m. 500 Yen per no. Kinki Chemical Society - Kinki Kagaku Kyokai, 8-4, Utsubohon-machi 1-chome, Nishi-ku, Osaka 550, Japan. **Indexed:** Abstr.Bull.Inst.Pap.Chem., ASCA, Chem.Abstr., Eng.Ind.
—CASDDS; CISTI. **CCC.**

CHEMISTRY FOR THE FUTURE (YEAR); first degree courses in chemistry and related sciences. see EDUCATION — Guides To Schools And Colleges

540 US
CHEMISTRY FOR THE 21ST CENTURY SERIES. Variant title: I U P A C Chemistry for the 21st Century Series. irreg., latest 1994. (International Union of Pure and Applied Chemistry) C R C Press, Inc., 2000 Corporate Blvd., N.W., Boca Raton. TEL 561-998-9784; 800-272-7737. FAX 561-994-0555. TELEX 568689-CRC PRESS. **Document type:** monographic series.

540 AT ISSN 0314-4240
TP1 CODEN: CHAUDY
CHEMISTRY IN AUSTRALIA. 1931. m. Aus.$113 (overseas Aus.$155) to non-members (effective 1995). Royal Australian Chemical Institute, 1-21 Vale St., N. Melbourne, Vic. 3051, Australia. TEL 61-3-93266285. FAX 61-3-93294398. E-mail: chemaust@raci.org.au. Ed. Kathy Hutton. R&P contact: Kathy Hutton. adv. contact: George Crawford. bk.rev.; charts; illus.; stat.; index. circ. 7,830. (also avail. in microfiche) **Indexed:** AESIS, Aus.Sci.Ind., Cadscan, Chem.Abstr., Dairy Sci.Abstr., Food Sci.& Tech.Abstr., INIS Atomind., Lead Abstr., Res.High.Educ.Abstr., Zincscan. **Document type:** academic/scholarly publication.
—BLDSC (3170.230000); CISTI; Ei; KNAW; Linda Hall; UnCover. **CCC.**
Formerly (until July 1977): Royal Australian Chemical Institute. Proceedings (ISSN 0035-8746).
Description: Provides topical science articles, news conference listings, and reports on new products.

540 UK ISSN 0009-3106
QD1 CODEN: CHMBAY
CHEMISTRY IN BRITAIN. 1965. m. £265($477) (effective 1997). The Royal Society of Chemistry, Thomas Graham House, Science Park, Milton Rd., Cambridge CB4 4WF, England. TEL 44-1223-420066. FAX 44-1223-423429. E-mail: sales@rsc.org; URL: http://chemistry.rsc.org/rsc/. (Subscr. to: Turpin Distribution Services Ltd., Blackhorse Rd., Letchworth, Herts. SG6 1HN, England. TEL 44-1462-672555. FAX 44-1462-480947) Ed. Richard Stevenson. adv.; bk.rev. circ. 45,000. **Indexed:** Abstr.Hyg., Acid Rain Ind., AESIS, Alloys Ind., Anal.Abstr., Art & Archaeol.Tech.Abstr., ASCA, Biol.Abstr., Br.Ceram.Abstr., Br.Tech.Ind., C.I.S. Abstr., Cadscan, Chem.Abstr., Chem.Cit.Ind., Chem.Infd., Curr.Biotech.Abstr., Curr.Cont., Dairy Sci.Abstr., Eng.Mat.Abstr., Environ.Abstr., Excerp.Med., Food Sci.& Tech.Abstr., GeoRef., High.Educ.Curr.Aware.Bull., Ind.Sci.Rev., INIS Atomind., Lab.Haz.Bull., Lead Abstr., Mass Spectr.Bull., Met.Abstr., Met.Abstr.Ind., Nonfer.Met.Alert, PCC Alert, PROMT, Res.High.Educ.Abstr., Risk Abstr., Sci.Cit.Ind., Soils & Fert., SSCI, Steels Alert, Trop.Dis.Bull., W.R.C.Inf., World Alum.Abstr., World Surf.Coat., Zincscan. **Document type:** academic/scholarly publication.
—BLDSC (3170.300000); CASDDS; CISTI; Ei; Genuine Article; Linda Hall; SWETS; UMI; UnCover. **CCC.**
Description: Contains scientific articles of general chemical interest and keeps the scientist up-to-date on economic, political, and social factors and their effects on the scientific community.

540 660 UK ISSN 0193-6484
QD1 CODEN: CINRDT
CHEMISTRY INTERNATIONAL; the news magazine of IUPAC. 1979. bi-m. £75($116) (foreign £75) (effective 1998). (International Union of Pure and Applied Chemistry) Blackwell Science Ltd., Osney Mead, Oxford OX2 OEL, England. TEL 44-1865-206206. FAX 44-1865-721205. E-mail: journals.cs@blacksci.co.uk; URL: http://www.black.co.uk. Ed. J.H. Williams; Pub. Allen Stevens. R&P contact: Sarah Pollard. adv. contact: Martine Cariou-Keen. circ. 6,665. (also avail. in microform from UMI) **Indexed:** Chem.Abstr., Deep Sea Res.& Oceanogr.Abstr., Excerp.Med., INIS Atomind., Intl.Polym.Sci.& Tech., RAPRA, World Surf.Coat. **Document type:** academic/scholarly publication.
—BLDSC (3172.010000); ADONIS; CASDDS; CISTI; KNAW; Linda Hall; SWETS; UMI. **CCC.**
Formerly: I U P A C Information Bulletin (ISSN 0145-5672); Which superseded (1956-1977): International Union of Pure and Applied Chemistry. Information Bulletin (ISSN 0539-1148)

540 JA ISSN 0366-7022
QD1 CODEN: CMLTAG
CHEMISTRY LETTERS. (Text in English) 1972. m. $75 to members; non-members N. America $298; elsewhere $276 (effective 1994). Chemical Society of Japan - Nippon Kagakukai, 5, 1-chome, Kanda-Surugadai, Chiyoda-ku, Tokyo 101, Japan. Ed. Shun-ichi Murahashi. circ. 4,600. (also avail. in microfiche; reprint service avail. from UMI) **Indexed:** Anal.Abstr., ASCA, Biwk.Pap.Rad.Chem.& Photochem., Cadscan, Chem.Abstr., Chem.Cit.Ind., Chem.Infd., Curr.Adv.Ecol.Sci., Curr.Chem.React., Curr.Cont., Dairy Sci.Abstr., Excerp.Med., Ind.Chem., Ind.Sci.Rev., INIS Atomind., JCT, JTA, Lead Abstr., Mass Spectr.Bull., Sci.Cit.Ind., Soils & Fert., Sugar Ind.Abstr., Zincscan. **Document type:** academic/scholarly publication.
—BLDSC (3172.020000); CASDDS; CISTI; Ei; Genuine Article; Linda Hall; SWETS; UMI; UnCover. **CCC.**

540 US ISSN 0069-3146
CHEMISTRY OF FUNCTIONAL GROUPS. 1965. irreg., latest 1993. price varies. John Wiley & Sons, Inc., 605 Third Ave., New York, NY 10158. TEL 212-850-6000. FAX 212-850-6088. TELEX 12-7063. Ed. Saul Patai. **Indexed:** Chem.Cit.Ind. **Document type:** monographic series.
Refereed Serial

540 581 US ISSN 0937-2148
CODEN: CPLPET
CHEMISTRY OF PLANT PROTECTION SERIES. 1986. irreg., vol.12, 1995. price varies. Springer-Verlag, 175 Fifth Ave., New York, NY 10010. TEL 212-460-1500. FAX 212-473-6272. (Also: Berlin, Heidelberg, Tokyo, Vienna) (reprint service avail. from ISI) **Document type:** monographic series.
—BLDSC (3172.118400); CASDDS; CISTI. **CCC.**

540 UK ISSN 0959-8464
CODEN: CEEVE3
CHEMISTRY REVIEW. 1991. 5/yr. (Sept.-May). £20.95 (Europe £29.50; rest of world £34.50) (effective 1997 & 1998). Philip Allan Publishers Ltd., Market Pl., Deddington, Oxon. OX15 OSE, England. TEL 44-1869-338652. FAX 44-1869-338803. R&P contact: Ceri Jenkins. adv. contact: Ceri Jenkins. **Document type:** academic/scholarly publication.
—BLDSC (3172.155000); CASDDS; CISTI. **CCC.**

540 NE ISSN 1071-6114
QD1 CODEN: SSRRDN
CHEMISTRY REVIEWS. 1979. 4/yr. $197 (effective 1998). Gordon and Breach - Harwood Academic, Amsteldisk 166, 1st Fl., 1079 LH Amsterdam, Netherlands. (Subscr. to: International Publishers Distributor, Box 32160, Newark, NJ 07102. TEL 800-545-8398. FAX 215-750-6343) Eds. M.E. Vol'pin, D. Phillips. (also avail. in microform) **Indexed:** Chem.Abstr., Curr.Cont. **Document type:** academic/scholarly publication.
—CASDDS; CISTI. **CCC.**
Formerly (until vol.18): Soviet Scientific Reviews. Section B: Chemistry Reviews (ISSN 0143-0408)
Refereed Serial

540 UK
CHEMISTRY TODAY; Web's daily chemistry news and jobs source. d. Society of Chemical Industry, 14 Belgrave Sq., London SW1X 8PS, England. TEL 44-171-235-3681. FAX 44-171-235-9410. E-mail: webmaster@chemind.demon.co.uk; URL: http://chemistry.mond.org.
● Available only online.
Description: Covers the latest news in chemical sciences and employment opportunities in the field.

540 920 NE ISSN 0921-8629
CHEMISTS AND CHEMISTRY. 1984. irreg. price varies. Kluwer Academic Publishers, Postbus 17, 3300 AA Dordrecht, Netherlands. TEL 31-78-6392392. FAX 31-78-6392254. TELEX 29245 KAPG NL. E-mail: services@wkap.nl; URL: http://www.wkap.nl. (Dist. by: Kluwer Academic Publishers Group, P.O. Box 322, 3300 AH Dordrecht, Netherlands. TEL 31-78-6392392. FAX 31-78-6546474; N. America dist. addr.: Box 358, Accord Sta., Hingham, MA 02018-0358. TEL 617-871-6600. FAX 617-871-6528) **Document type:** monographic series.
—BLDSC (3172.235000); CISTI.
Refereed Serial

540 GW ISSN 0944-5846
CHEMKON - CHEMIE KONKRET; Forum fuer Unterricht und Didaktik. 1994. q. DM.95 (foreign DM.115) (effective 1997). Wiley - V C H, Postfach 101161, 69451 Weinheim, Germany. TEL 49-6201-606147. FAX 49-6201-606117. E-mail: subservice@vchgroup.de; URL: http://www.vchgroup.de. (Subscr. in the Americas to: John Wiley & Sons, Inc., 605 Third Ave., New York, NY 10158. TEL 212-850-6645. FAX 212-850-6021) Ed. Dr. Walter Jansen. adv. contact: Norbert Schippel. circ. 1,200. **Document type:** academic/scholarly publication.
—BLDSC (3172.252000).
Description: Helps teachers and professors make the world of chemistry more tangible to their students.

CHEMOSPHERE; chemistry, biology and toxicology as related to environmental problems. see ENVIRONMENTAL STUDIES — Toxicology And Environmental Safety

660 661 KO
QD1 CODEN: HKKCAZ
CHEMWORLD.* (Text in Korean) 1946. 12/yr. Korean Chemical Society - Daehan Hwahak Hoe, 35, 5-ka, Anam-dong, Sungbuk-ku, Seoul, S. Korea. TEL 2-3453-3781. FAX 2-3453-3785. Ed. Young Bok Chae. adv.: B&W page $250, color page $1000; trim 188 x 258; adv. contact: Byung Hun Ahn. circ. 6,000.
—CASDDS; CISTI; Linda Hall.
Formerly (until 1992): Progress in Chemistry and Chemical Industry (ISSN 0439-9838)

540 SZ ISSN 0009-4293
TP1 CODEN: CHIMAD
CHIMIA. (Text in English, French, German) 1947. m. 220 SFr. Neue Schweizerische Chemische Gesellschaft, c/o Ciba, K-25.5.02, CH-4002 Basel, Switzerland. TEL 41-61-6966626. FAX 41-61-6966985. URL: http://sgich1.unifr.ch/chimia/home/chimia.html. Ed. C. Ganter. R&P contact: C. Ganter. adv.; bk.rev.; abstr.; charts; illus.; cum.index every 10 yrs. circ. 3,600. (also avail. in microfilm from PMC) **Indexed:** Alloys Ind., Anal.Abstr., ASCA, Biol.Abstr., Biotech.Abstr., C.I.S. Abstr., Chem.Abstr., Chem.Cit.Ind., Chem.Eng.Abstr., Chem.Infd., Curr.Chem.React., Curr.Cont., Dairy Sci.Abstr., Eng.Mat.Abstr., Excerp.Med., Food Sci.& Tech.Abstr., GeoRef., Ind.Chem, Ind.Sci.Rev., INIS Atomind., Mat.Sci.Cit.Ind., Met.Abstr., Met.Abstr.Ind., Nonfer.Met.Alert, PCC Alert, Risk Abstr., Sci.Cit.Ind, SSCI, Steels Alert, T.C.E.A., World Alum.Abstr. **Document type:** academic/scholarly publication.
—BLDSC (3173.000000); CASDDS; CISTI; Ei; Genuine Article; Linda Hall; SWETS; UnCover.

CHEMISTRY

540 TU ISSN 0379-5896
CODEN: CATUA9
CHIMICA ACTA TURCICA. (Text in English, French, German; summaries in English) 1973. 3/yr. Istanbul Universitesi, Muhendislik Fakultesi Dekanligi - Istanbul University, Faculty of Engineering, Dean's Office, 34850 Avcilar - Istanbul, Turkey. TEL 90-212-5911998. FAX 90-212-5911997. E-mail: iuchemeng@magnet.com.tr. Eds. Murat Orbay, Murat Orbay. circ. 300. **Indexed:** Chem.Abstr. **Document type:** academic/scholarly publication.
—BLDSC (3174.030000); CASDDS; CISTI; Linda Hall.
Description: Publishes original research papers and short notes in all fields of pure and applied chemistry and chemical engineering.
Refereed Serial

540 371.3 IT ISSN 0392-8942
CODEN: CSCUDJ
CHIMICA NELLA SCUOLA. 1983. 5/yr. L.50000 (foreign $40) (effective 1994). Editrice di Chimica s.r.l., Viale Liegi 48, 00198 Rome, Italy. TEL 39-6-8549691. FAX 39-6-8548734.
—CASDDS.

540 IT ISSN 0392-839X
CODEN: CHOGDS
CHIMICA OGGI/CHEMISTRY TODAY. 1982. 10/yr. L.150000 to individuals; institutions L.185000; foreign $190 (effective 1995 & 1996). Teknoscienze s.r.l., Via Aurelio Saffi, 23, 20123 Milan, Italy. TEL 39-2-4818118. FAX 39-2-4818070. Ed. Carla Scesa; Pub. Gianna Lorenzini. adv.: B&W page $1860; adv. contact: Michaela Carmagnola. bk.rev. circ. 8,000. **Indexed:** ASCA, Chem.Abstr., Curr.Biotech.Abstr., I.P.A. **Document type:** trade publication.
—BLDSC (3175.100000); CASDDS; CISTI; Ei; Genuine Article; KNAW.
Refereed Serial

540 GR ISSN 0366-5526
CODEN: CCGEAC
CHIMIKA CHRONIKA. GENERAL EDITION. (Text in Greek; summaries in English) m. Dr.2000($35) to individuals; institutions Dr.4000($35); students Dr.500. Association of Greek Chemists, 27 Kaningos, 106 82 Athens, Greece. Ed.Bd. charts; illus. **Indexed:** Abstr.Bull.Inst.Pap.Chem.
—CASDDS; CISTI; Linda Hall.

540 GR ISSN 0366-693X
QD1 CODEN: CMCRCZ
CHIMIKA CHRONIKA. NEW SERIES. (Text in English; summaries in Greek) q. Dr.2500($40) Association of Greek Chemists, 27 Kaningos St., 106 82 Athens, Greece. Ed. P. Dimotakis. charts; illus. **Indexed:** Food Sci.& Tech.Abstr., INIS Atomind.
—BLDSC (3180.050000); CASDDS; CISTI; Linda Hall; SWETS.

540 CC ISSN 1001-8417
CODEN: CCLEE7
CHINESE CHEMICAL LETTERS; preliminary chemical communications in English. 1991. 12/yr. $29 (effective 1997). Chinese Chemical Society, P.O. Box 2709, Beijing 100080, People's Republic of China. TEL 86-10-6256-8157. FAX 86-10-6256-8157. E-mail: qiuxb@infoc3.icas.cn. index. (also avail. in microform from UMI; back issues avail.) **Indexed:** ASCA, Chem.Abstr., Mat.Sci.Cit.Ind. **Document type:** academic/scholarly publication.
—BLDSC (3180.274300); CASDDS.
Description: Publishes preliminary accounts of important Chinese chemical research not previously published in Chinese literature.
Refereed Serial

540 CH ISSN 0009-4536
QD1 CODEN: JCCTAC
CHINESE CHEMICAL SOCIETY. JOURNAL (TAIPEI). (Text in English and other languages) 1954. bi-m. NT.$1000 to non-members; members NT.$400 ($48 in Hong Kong; elsewhere $60). Chinese Chemical Society - Chung-kuo Hua Hsueh Hui, P.O. Box 609, Taipei, Taiwan 10099, Republic of China. TEL 035-715131-5548. (Editorial addr.: P.O. Box 2-55, Hsinchu, Taiwan 30098, R.O.C.) (Co-sponsor: National Science Council) Ed. Chun-Chen Liao. adv.; abstr.; bibl.; charts. circ. 2,000. **Indexed:** Anal.Abstr., ASCA, Biol.Abstr., Cadscan, Chem.Abstr., Chem.Cit.Ind., Chem.Infd., Curr.Cont., Lead Abstr., Mass Spectr.Bull., Zincscan.
—BLDSC (4729.250000); CASDDS; CISTI; Ei; Genuine Article; Linda Hall; UnCover.
Supersedes in part: Chinese Chemical Society. Journal (Peiping) (ISSN 0375-8745)
Description: Contains both experimental and theoretical research on fundamental aspects of chemistry.

540 CC ISSN 1000-0518
CODEN: YIHUED
CHINESE JOURNAL OF APPLIED CHEMISTRY. (Text in Chinese; abstracts in English) 1983. bi-m. $88.20 (effective 1997). Chinese Chemical Society - Zhongguo Huaxuehui, P.O. Box 2709, Beijing 100080, People's Republic of China. TEL 86-10-6256-8157. FAX 86-10-6256-8157. E-mail: qiuxb@infoc2.icas.cn.
—BLDSC (3180.294000); CASDDS; CISTI.

CHINESE JOURNAL OF CHEMICAL ENGINEERING. see ENGINEERING — Chemical Engineering

540 CC ISSN 1001-604X
QD1 CODEN: CJOCEV
CHINESE JOURNAL OF CHEMISTRY. Chinese edition: Huaxue Xuebao (ISSN 0567-7351) (Text in English) 1983. bi-m. DM.660($364) (effective 1997). (Chinese Chemical Society - Zhongguo Huaxuehui) Science Press, Marketing and Sales Department, 16 Donghuangchenggen North St., Beijing 100717, People's Republic of China. TEL 4010642. FAX 4019810. (Dist. in Europe by: V S P, P.O. Box 346, 3700 AH Zeist, Netherlands. TEL 31-30-6925790. FAX 31-30-6932081; Dist. in N. America by: Science Press New York, Ltd., 84-04 58th Ave., Elmhurst, NY 11373. TEL 718-476-0238. FAX 718-476-0273) (Co-publisher: V S P) Ed. Huang Wei-Yuan. adv. circ. 6,000. pp./issue: 96. **Indexed:** Alloys Ind., ASCA, Chem.Cit.Ind., Eng.Mat.Abstr., INIS Atomind., Mat.Sci.Cit.Ind., Met.Abstr.Ind., Met.Abstr., Nonfer.Met.Alert, PCC Alert, Steels Alert, World Alum.Abstr. **Document type:** academic/scholarly publication.
—BLDSC (3180.299500); CASDDS; CISTI; Ei; Genuine Article; KNAW; Linda Hall.
Formerly (until 1989): Acta Chimica Sinica (English Edition) (ISSN 0256-7660)
Description: Presents research on organic, inorganic, physical, and analytical chemistry in mainland China.
Refereed Serial

CHINESE JOURNAL OF GEOCHEMISTRY. see EARTH SCIENCES — Geology

CLINICA CHIMICA ACTA; international journal of clinical chemistry and medical biochemistry. see MEDICAL SCIENCES

CLINICAL CHEMISTRY; clinical chemistry reference edition (the institutional edition). see MEDICAL SCIENCES

CLINICAL CHEMISTRY AND ENZYMOLOGY COMMUNICATIONS. see BIOLOGY — Biological Chemistry

540 XR ISSN 0010-0765
QD1 CODEN: CCCCAK
COLLECTION OF CZECHOSLOVAK CHEMICAL COMMUNICATIONS. (Text in English) 1919. m. £518 (effective 1997). Ceska Akademie Ved, Ustav Organicke Chemie a Biochemie - Czech Academy of Sciences, Institute of Organic Chemistry and Biochemistry, Flemingovo nam. 2, 166 10 Prague 6, Czech Republic. TEL 420-2-3312111. FAX 420-2-24310090. (Dist. by: Harcourt Brace & Company Ltd., Foots Cray High St., Sidcup, Kent DA14 5HP, England. TEL 44-181-3003322. FAX 44-181-3090807) Ed. M. Soucek. bk.rev.; bibl.; charts; illus.; index. circ. 2,550. (also avail. in microfilm from PMC) **Indexed:** Abstr.Bull.Inst.Pap.Chem., Alloys Ind., Anal.Abstr., ASCA, Biodet.Abstr., Biol.Abstr., C.I.S. Abstr., Cadscan, Chem.Abstr., Chem.Cit.Ind., Chem.Eng.Abstr., Chem.Infd., Compumath, Curr.Adv.Biochem., Curr.Adv.Ecol.Sci., Curr.Chem.React., Curr.Cont., Dairy Sci.Abstr., Eng.Mat.Abstr., Excerp.Med., F.A.C.T., Field Crop Abstr., Food Sci.& Tech.Abstr., Herb.Abstr., Ind.Chem., Ind.Sci.Rev., Lead Abstr., Mass Spectr.Bull., Mat.Sci.Cit.Ind., Met.Abstr., Met.Abstr.Ind., Nonfer.Met.Alert, Nutr.Abstr., PCC Alert, RAPRA, Sci.Cit.Ind., Soils & Fert., Steels Alert, T.C.E.A., World Alum.Abstr., World Surf.Coat., World Text.Abstr., Zincscan. **Document type:** academic/scholarly publication.
—BLDSC (3310.500000); CASDDS; CISTI; Ei; EMDOCS; Genuine Article; KNAW; KR SourceOne; Linda Hall; SWETS; UnCover. CCC.
Description: Publishes theoretical and experimental results achieved at research institutes and universities in the Czech Republic, covering research in all branches of chemistry, including chemical physics, physical, and quantum chemistry.

COLOR. see PHYSICS — Optics

540 US ISSN 1386-2073
COMBINATORIAL CHEMISTRY & HIGH THROUGHPUT SCREENING. Announced for publication in 1998. q. fl.262 to individuals (outside Europe $119); institutions fl.627 (outside Europe $285 (effective 1998). Bentham Science Publishers, 7436 S.W. 117 Ave., Box 130, Miami, FL 33183. FAX 305-596-5120. adv. contact: T. Lucas. **Document type:** academic/scholarly publication.
Description: Publishes original research articles describing various topics in combinatorial chemistry and/or high throughput screening. Ancillary subjects, such as robotics and informatics, are also covered.
Refereed Serial

COMMENTATIONES PHYSICO-MATHEMATICAE ET CHEMICO-MEDICAE. see PHYSICS

540 US
CONCEPTS IN CHEMISTRY.* irreg. price varies. Houghton Mifflin Co., 222 Berkeley St., Boston, MA 02116-3764. TEL 617-725-5000. FAX 617-277-5409.

540 XO ISSN 0139-9535
CODEN: PCCHDB
CONFERENCE ON COORDINATION CHEMISTRY PROCEEDINGS. irreg., 6th, 1976, Bratislava. price varies. Slovenska Vysoka Skola Technicka, Janska 1 812 37 Bratislava, Slovakia. **Indexed:** Chem.Abstr.
—BLDSC (6843.131000); CASDDS.

540 US ISSN 1064-2811
TP12
CONSULTING SERVICES. 1928. biennial. $25 (foreign $70). Association of Consulting Chemists and Chemical Engineers, Inc., 40 W. 45th St., New York NY 10036. TEL 212-983-3160. FAX 212-983-3161. Ed. Elizabeth K. Jones. circ. 500. **Document type:** directory.
—CISTI.
Description: Directory containing one-page "scope sheet" for each member and an extensive classified directory.

541.224　　　US　　ISSN 0069-9845
　　　　　　　　　　CODEN: CCHEDK
COORDINATION CHEMISTRY. (Subseries of: I U P A C Chemical Data Series (ISSN 0275-0910)) (Text in English; occasionally in French or German) 9th, 1968. irreg., 15th 1973, Moscow; 16th 1974, Dublin. price varies. (International Union of Pure and Applied Chemistry) C R C Press, Inc., 2000 Corporate Blvd., N.W., Boca Raton. TEL 561-994-0555; 800-272-7737. FAX 561-998-9784. TELEX 568689-CRC PRESS. **Indexed:** Cadscan, Lead Abstr., Zincscan. **Document type:** monographic series.

541.224　　　SZ　　ISSN 0010-8545
QD475　　　　　　CODEN: CCHRAM
COORDINATION CHEMISTRY REVIEWS; an international journal. (Text in English, French and German) 1966. 11/yr. fl.5717($3286) (effective 1998). Elsevier Science S.A., P.O. Box 564, CH-1001 Lausanne 1, Switzerland. TEL 41-21-3207381. FAX 41-21-3235444. TELEX 450620-ELSA-CH. (Subscr. to: Elsevier Science, Regional Sales Office, P.O. Box 211, 100 AE Amsterdam, Netherlands. TEL 31-20-4853757. FAX 31-20-4853432; Subscr. in the Americas to: Elsevier Science, Regional Sales Office, Box 945, New York, NY 10159-0945. TEL 212-633-3730. FAX 212-633-3680; Subscr. in Australasia to: Elsevier Science (Singapore) Pte. Ltd., No. 1 Temasek Ave., No. 17-01 Millenia Tower, Singapore 039192, Singapore. TEL 65-434-3727. FAX 65-337-2230) Ed. Dr. A.B.P. Lever. adv.; bk.rev.; charts; illus.; index. (also avail. in microform from UMI) **Indexed:** ASCA, Chem.Abstr., Chem.Cit.Ind., Chem.Infd., Curr.Adv.Ecol.Sci., Curr.Cont., Ind.Sci.Rev., Mat.Sci.Cit.Ind., Sci.Cit.Ind. **Document type:** academic/scholarly publication.
—BLDSC (3465.500000); CASDDS; CISTI; Genuine Article; Linda Hall; SWETS; UnCover. **CCC.**
Description: Offers rapid publication of review articles on topics of current interest and importance in coordination chemistry. Includes aspects on organometallic, theoretical and bioinorganic chemistry.
Refereed Serial

540　　　CI　　ISSN 0011-1643
　　　　　　　　CODEN: CCACAA
CROATICA CHEMICA ACTA. (Text in English) 1927. q. $75. Hrvatsko Kemijsko Drustvo - Croatian Chemical Society, Marulicev trg 19, Zagreb, Croatia. TEL 041-44-65-28. FAX 38-41-446528. (Co-sponsor: University of Zagreb) Ed. Vladimir Simeon. adv.; bk.rev.; abstr.; bibl.; illus.; index. circ. 1,100. (also avail. in microform from UMI; reprint service avail. from UMI) **Indexed:** Anal.Abstr., ASCA, Biol.Abstr., Bull.Signal., Cadscan, Chem.Abstr., Chem.Cit.Ind., Curr.Adv.Ecol.Sci., Curr.Cont., Ind.Sci.Rev., INIS Atomind., Lead Abstr., Phys.Ber., Ref.Zh., Sci.Cit.Ind., Zincscan.
—BLDSC (3487.500000); CASDDS; CISTI; Genuine Article; Linda Hall; UMI; UnCover.

541.28　　　US　　ISSN 0145-6814
　　　　　　　　　CODEN: CPQCDE
CURRENT AWARENESS PROFILE ON QUANTUM CHEMISTRY. 1973. fortn. $50. Indiana University, QCPE, Creative Arts 181, Bloomington, IN 47405. TEL 812-855-4784. FAX 812-855-5539. E-mail: qcpe@ucs.indiana.edu. Ed. Richard W. Counts. bk.rev. circ. 150. **Document type:** abstracting/indexing.
—CASDDS.
Refereed Serial

540 616　　　US　　ISSN 0929-8673
　　　　　　　　　　CODEN: CMCHE7
CURRENT MEDICINAL CHEMISTRY. (Text in English) 1994. 6/yr. fl.480 to individuals (outside Europe $218); institutions fl.1298 (outside Europe $590) (effective 1998). Bentham Science Publishers, 7436 S.W. 117 Ave., Box 130, Miami, FL 33183. FAX 305-596-5120. adv. contact: T. Lucas. (back issues avail.) **Indexed:** ASCA, Bull.Signal., Chem.Abstr., Excerpt.Med. (1995-), Int.Abstr.Biol.Sci. **Document type:** academic/scholarly publication.
—BLDSC (3500.304000); CASDDS; CISTI; Genuine Article; SWETS. **CCC.**
Description: Publishes reviews on developments in medicinal chemistry and rational drug design.
Refereed Serial

540　　　NE　　ISSN 0732-4391
QD1
CURRENT TOPICS IN CHINESE SCIENCE. SECTION B: CHEMISTRY. 1982. irreg., vol.3, 1984. Gordon and Breach - Harwood Academic, Amsteldisk 166, 1st Fl., 1079 LH Amsterdam, Netherlands. (Subscr. to: International Publishers Distributor, Box 32160, Newark, NJ 07102. TEL 800-545-8398. FAX 215-750-6343) (also avail. in microfilm) **Document type:** monographic series.
—CCC.
Refereed Serial

CURRENT TOPICS IN ENVIRONMENTAL AND TOXICOLOGICAL CHEMISTRY. see *ENVIRONMENTAL STUDIES — Toxicology And Environmental Safety*

CUSTOM CHEMICAL SYNTHESIS SERVICES IN FRANCE. see *BUSINESS AND ECONOMICS — Trade And Industrial Directories*

540　　　PL
　　　　　　CODEN: CZTEAY
CZASOPISMO TECHNICZNE. SERIA C: CHEMIA. (Content page in 4 languages) 1877. irreg. 20 Zl. (effective 1997). Politechnika Krakowska, Ul. Warszawska 24, 31-155 Krakow, Poland. TEL 48-12-37-42-89. FAX 48-12-335773. TELEX 322468 PK PL. E-mail: Marcinek@biblos.pk.edu.pl. bk.rev.; charts; illus.; index. circ. 12,000. **Document type:** academic/scholarly publication.
—CASDDS.
Supersedes in part: Czasopismo Techniczne (ISSN 0011-4561); Which was formerly (until 1883): Dzwignia (ISSN 1230-2791).

DAHLEM WORKSHOP REPORTS. PHYSICAL, CHEMICAL, AND EARTH SCIENCES RESEARCH REPORT. see *PHYSICS*

540　　　DK　　ISSN 0011-6335
　　　　　　　　CODEN: DAKEAT
DANSK-KEMI. 1920. m. DKK 475. Jante-Forlaget ApS, Box 15, Kongstrupvej 3, DK-4390 Vipperoed, Denmark. TEL 45-53-48-28-00. FAX 45-53-48-22-05. Ed. Styhr Petersen. adv.; bk.rev. circ. 5,289. (reprint service avail.) **Indexed:** C.I.S. Abstr., Chem.Abstr., INIS Atomind. **Document type:** academic/scholarly publication, trade publication.
—CASDDS; CISTI; Linda Hall.
Formerly (until 1962): Kemisk Maanedsblad og Nordisk Handelsblad (ISSN 0368-5233)

540　　　CC　　ISSN 1000-8438
　　　　　　　　CODEN: DAHUEW
DAXUE HUAXUE/UNIVERSITY CHEMISTRY. (Text in Chinese) 1986. bi-m. $36 (effective 1997). Zhongguo Huaxue Xuehui, Daxue Huaxue Bianjibu - Chinese Chemical Society, Editorial Office of University Chemistry, Beijing University, Chemistry Bldg., Haidian-qu, Beijing 100871, People's Republic of China. TEL 861-6275-1721. FAX 861-6275-4096. E-mail: qiuxb@infoc3.icas.cn. (Co-sponsor: Research Center of Higher Chemical Education) Ed. Tongwen Hua. **Document type:** academic/scholarly publication.
—BLDSC (9106.450000); CASDDS.
Description: Provides a forum for issues relating to higher chemical education. Reports new trends in chemistry and related disciplines.
Refereed Serial

540　　　US　　ISSN 0095-8387
QD1　　　　　　CODEN: DCBUAC
DEL-CHEM BULLETIN. 1944. 9/yr. $2. American Chemical Society, 1155 16th St., N.W., Washington, DC 20036. TEL 202-872-4363. FAX 202-872-4615. Ed. Ann Moffett. adv.; bk.rev. circ. 3,000. **Document type:** bulletin.
—CASDDS.

DEUTSCHES KUNSTSTOFF-INSTITUT. MITTEILUNGEN. see *PLASTICS*

DICCIONARIO DE ESPECIALIDADES AGROQUIMICAS. see *AGRICULTURE*

DIMENSIO. see *MATHEMATICS*

DIQIU HUAXUE. see *EARTH SCIENCES — Geology*

540 690　　　US　　ISSN 1045-5256
HD9655.C2
DIRECTORY OF CHEMICAL PRODUCERS - CANADA. 1988. a. $725 (renewals $475; CD-ROM edition $1090). S R I International, Process Industries Division, Chemical Marketing Research Center, Menlo Park, CA 94025. TEL 415-859-3627. FAX 415-859-4623. Ed. J. Hardy. stat. **Document type:** directory.
●Also available on CD-ROM.
—CISTI.
Description: Lists commercial chemical manufacturers in Canada.

660　　　US
▼**DIRECTORY OF CHEMICAL PRODUCERS - CHINA.** 1995. a. $1500 (renewals $1000; CD-ROM edition $2250). S R I International, Process Industries Division, Chemical Marketing Research Center, Menlo Park, CA 94025. TEL 415-859-3627. FAX 415-859-4623. **Document type:** directory.
●Also available on CD-ROM.

660　　　US　　ISSN 1049-6068
HD9657.E182
DIRECTORY OF CHEMICAL PRODUCERS - EAST ASIA. 1989. a. $1875 (renewals $13.25; CD-ROM edition $2815). S R I International, Process Industries Division, Chemical Marketing Research Center, Menlo Park, CA 94025. TEL 415-859-3627. FAX 415-859-4623. Ed. J. Hardy. **Document type:** directory.
●Also available on CD-ROM.

338.7 660　　　US
▼**DIRECTORY OF CHEMICAL PRODUCERS - MEXICO.** 1995. a. $850 (renewals $575; CD-ROM edition $1275). S R I International, Process Industries Division, Chemical Marketing Research Center, Menlo Park, CA 94025. TEL 415-859-3627. FAX 415-859-4623. **Document type:** directory.
●Also available on CD-ROM.

338.7 660　　　US
▼**DIRECTORY OF CHEMICAL PRODUCERS - MIDDLE EAST.** 1995. a. $1000 (renewals $675; CD-ROM edition $1500). S R I International, Process Industries Division, Chemical Marketing Research Center, Menlo Park, CA 94025. TEL 415-859-3627. FAX 415-859-4623. **Document type:** directory.
●Also available on CD-ROM.

338.7 660　　　US
▼**DIRECTORY OF CHEMICAL PRODUCERS - SOUTH AMERICA.** 1995. a. $1200 (renewals $780; CD-ROM edition $1800). S R I International, Process Industries Division, Chemical Marketing Research Center, Menlo Park, CA 94025. TEL 415-859-3627. FAX 415-859-4623. **Document type:** directory.
●Also available on CD-ROM.

660　　　US　　ISSN 0012-3277
HD9651.3
DIRECTORY OF CHEMICAL PRODUCERS - UNITED STATES. 1961. a. $1600 (renewals $1020; CD-ROM edition $2400). S R I International, Process Industries Division, Chemical Marketing Research Center, Menlo Park, CA 94025. TEL 415-859-3627. FAX 415-859-4623. Ed. J. Hardy. charts; stat. **Document type:** directory.
●Also available on CD-ROM.
—CISTI.

660　　　US
DIRECTORY OF CHEMICAL PRODUCERS - WESTERN EUROPE. 1978. a. $2200 (renewals $1380; CD-ROM edition $3300). S R I International, Process Industries Division, Chemical Marketing Research Center, Menlo Park, CA 94025. TEL 415-859-3627. FAX 415-859-4623. Ed. J. Hardy. charts; stat. **Document type:** directory.
●Also available on CD-ROM.

1748 CHEMISTRY

540   US   ISSN 0196-0555
TP12
DIRECTORY OF WORLD CHEMICAL PRODUCERS (YEAR). Standard edition (ISSN 1078-0548); Limited edition (ISSN 1078-053X) 1980. triennial. $950 for standard ed.; limited ed. $600; single-user diskette $1800; network diskette $3000 (effective 1995-96). Chemical Information Services, Inc., Box 8344, University Sta., Dallas, TX 75205. TEL 214-340-4345. FAX 214-340-4346. E-mail: cheminfo@connect.net. (Diskettes avail. from: CIS Data Services, Inc., 4111 N. Central Expressway, Ste. 203, Dallas, TX 75204. TEL 214-520-2680) (also avail. in diskette format) Document type: directory.
—CISTI.
   Description: Contains 56,831 alphabetically listed product titles (including cross-references), manufactured by 7,076 chemical producers in 81 countries on 6 continents.

560   RU   ISSN 0012-5008
QD1   CODEN: DKCHAY
DOKLADY CHEMISTRY. English translation of: Rossiiskaya Akademiya Nauk. Doklady. 1956. m. $1375 in US; elsewhere $1610 (effective 1998). (Russian Academy of Sciences, Chemical Section) Maik Nauka - Interperiodica, Mezhdunarodnyi Otdel, Ul. Profsoyuznaya, 90, 117864 Moscow, Russia. TEL 7-095-3360066. FAX 7-095-3360666. (Dist. by: Plenum Publishing Corp., 233 Spring St., New York, NY 10013-1578, U.S.A. TEL 212-620-6468. FAX 212-463-0742) Ed. V.A. Kabanov. (also avail. in microfilm from UMI; back issues avail.) Indexed: Alloys Ind., Chem.Eng.Abstr., Chem.Titles, Energy Res.Abstr., Eng.Mat.Abstr., INIS Atomind., Mass Spectr.Bull., Met.Abstr.Ind., Met.Abstr., Nonfer.Met.Alert, PCC Alert, Steels Alert, T.C.E.A., World Alum.Abstr. Document type: academic/scholarly publication.
—BLDSC (0411.320000); CISTI; SWETS; UMI; UnCover. CCC.
   Refereed Serial

DUPONT MAGAZINE. see *BUSINESS AND ECONOMICS*

DUTCH CHEMICAL INDUSTRY HANDBOOK/HANDBOEK VOOR DE NEDERLANDSE CHEMISCHE INDUSTRIE. see *BUSINESS AND ECONOMICS — Trade And Industrial Directories*

540 530   UK   ISSN 0143-7208
TP890   CODEN: DYPIDX
DYES AND PIGMENTS. 1980. m. fl.2386($1371) (effective 1998). Elsevier Science Ltd., P.O. Box 800, Kidlington, Oxford OX5 1DX, England. TEL 44-1865-843000. FAX 44-1865-843010. E-mail: nlinfo-f@elsevier.nl; usinfo-f@elsevier.com; forinfo-kyf04035@niftyserve.or.jp; URL: http://www.elsevier.nl/. (Subscr. to: Elsevier Science, Regional Sales Office, P.O. Box 211, 1000 AE Amsterdam, Netherlands. TEL 31-20-4853757. FAX 31-20-4853432; Subscr. in the Americas to: Elsevier Science, Regional Sales Office, Box 945, New York, NY 10159-0945. TEL 212-633-3730. FAX 212-633-3680; Subscr. in Australasia and the Far East to: Elsevier Science (Singapore) Pte Ltd, No.1 Temasek Ave., No.17-01 Millenia Tower, Singapore 039192, Singapore. TEL 65-434-3727. FAX 65-337-2230) Ed. A.T. Peters. adv.; bk.rev.; charts; illus.; index. (also avail. in microform from UMI; back issues avail.) Indexed: ASCA, Cascadan, Chem.Abstr., Chem.Cit.Ind., Chem.Infd., Curr.Cont., Eng.Ind., Ind.Sci.Rev., Lead Abstr., Mat.Sci.Cit.Ind., Met.Abstr., Sci.Cit.Ind., Text.Tech.Dig., World Surf.Coat., Zincscan. Document type: academic/scholarly publication.
—BLDSC (3635.600000); CASDDS; CISTI; Ei; Genuine Article; Linda Hall; SWETS; UnCover. CCC.
   Description: Covers the scientific and technical aspects of the chemistry and physics of dyes, pigments and their intermediates.
   Refereed Serial

E C N CHEMSCOPE. see *ENGINEERING — Chemical Engineering*

540 530   BL   ISSN 0100-4670
                      CODEN: ECQUDX
ECLETICA QUIMICA; serie quimica. (Text in Portuguese; summaries in English and Portuguese) 1976. a. $30 or exchange basis. Universidade Estadual Paulista, Av. Vicente Ferreira 1278, Caixa Postal 71, 17515-901 Marilia SP, Brazil. TEL 55-144-222504. FAX 55-144-222504. E-mail: uespr@brfapesp.bitnet. Ed.Bd. bibl.; charts. circ. 1,000. Indexed: Anal.Abstr., ASCA, Biol.Abstr., Chem Abstr., Chem.Cit.Ind., Curr.Adv.Ecol.Sci., INIS Atomind. Document type: academic/scholarly publication.
—BLDSC (3647.895000); CASDDS; CISTI; Genuine Article; KNAW.
   Description: Presents results of chemical research.

540   MX   ISSN 0187-893X
EDUCACION QUIMICA. (Text in English, French, Portuguese, Spanish) 1989. q. Mex.$80($30) (effective 1997). Universidad Nacional Autonoma de Mexico, Facultad de Quimica, Apartado Postal 70-197, 04510 Mexico, D.F., Mexico. TEL 52-5-6162604. FAX 52-5-6161868. E-mail: andoni@servidor.unam.mx; URL: http://hunabku.pquim.unam.mx/eq/index.html. Ed. Andoni Garritz Ruiz.
   Description: Presents original papers on chemistry. Designed for college teachers.

540   UK   ISSN 0013-1350
                      CODEN: EDCHAU
EDUCATION IN CHEMISTRY. 1964. bi-m. £116 (US $210) (effective 1997). The Royal Society of Chemistry, Thomas Graham House, Science Park, Milton Rd., Cambridge CB4 4WF, England. TEL 44-1223-420066. FAX 44-1223-423429. E-mail: sales@rsc.org; URL: http://chemistry.rsc.org/rsc/. (Subscr. to: Turpin Distribution Services Ltd., Blackhorse Rd., Letchworth, Herts. SG6 1HN, England. TEL 44-1462-672555. FAX 44-1462-480947) Ed. Kathryn Roberts. adv.; bk.rev.; film rev.; charts; illus.; index. circ. 2,500. (also avail. in microform from UMI; reprint service avail. from UMI) Indexed: Br.Educ.Ind., C.I.J.E., Chem.Abstr., Curr.Biotech.Abstr., Educ.Tech.Abstr., Excerp.Med., High.Educ.Curr.Aware.Bull., INIS Atomind., Lab.Haz.Bull., Media Rev.Dig., Res.High.Educ.Abstr., Tech.Educ.Abstr. Document type: academic/scholarly publication.
—BLDSC (3661.226000); CASDDS; CISTI; Linda Hall; SWETS; UMI; UnCover. CCC.
   Description: Devoted to the problems of chemical education at all levels from the secondary school to the university. Covers a broad range of pertinent topics of interest to teachers.

540   UA   ISSN 0449-2285
EGYPTIAN JOURNAL OF CHEMISTRY. (Text in English; summaries in Arabic and English) 1958. 6/yr. $157 (effective 1997). (Egyptian Chemical Society, Research Department) National Information and Documentation Centre (NIDOC), Tahrir St., Dokki, Awqaf P.O., Cairo, Egypt. TEL 20-2-3371696. Ed. M.M. Sidky. bibl.; charts. (reprint service avail. from IRC) Indexed: Biol.Abstr., Chem.Abstr., Chem.Infd., Curr.Adv.Ecol.Sci., Field Crop Abstr., GeoRef., Herb.Abstr., Hort.Abstr., Mass Spectr.Bull. Document type: academic/scholarly publication.
—CISTI; SWETS.

540   JA
EKITAI KUROMATOGURAFU KENKYUKAI KOEN YOSHISHU/RESEARCH GROUP OF LIQUID CHROMATOGRAPHY. PROCEEDINGS. (Text in English) 1966. a. Ekitai Kuromatogurafu Kenkyukai - Research Group of Liquid Chromatography, c/o Ms. Iwase, Pasutsuru Kenkyujo, 103-5, Tanaka Monzencho, Sakyo-ku, Kyoto 606, Japan. Document type: proceedings.

ELECTRONIC CHEMICALS NEWS. see *ELECTRONICS*

540   GW   ISSN 0173-0835
QD79.E44   CODEN: ELCTDN
ELECTROPHORESIS. (Text in English) 1980. 18/yr. DM.350 (foreign DM.380) to individuals; institutions DM.1895 (foreign DM.1970) (effective 1997). Wiley - V C H, Postfach 101161, 69469 Weinheim, Germany. TEL 49-6201-606147. FAX 49-6201-606117. TELEX 465516-VCHWH-D. E-mail: subservice@vchgroup.de; URL: http://www.vchgroup.de. (Subscr. in the Americas to: John Wiley & Sons, Inc., 605 Third Ave., New York, NY 10158. TEL 212-850-6645. FAX 212-850-6021) Ed. B.J. Radola. adv.; bk.rev.; illus. circ. 1,250. (also avail. in microfilm from VCI; reprint service avail. from ISI) Indexed: Anal.Abstr., ASCA, Biol.Abstr., Chem.Abstr., Chem.Cit.Ind., Curr.Adv.Biochem., Curr.Adv.Ecol.Sci., Curr.Adv.Genetics & Molec.Biol., Curr.Cont., Dairy Sci.Abstr., Excerp.Med., Food Sci.& Tech.Abstr., Ind.Sci.Rev., Mat.Sci.Cit.Ind., Sci.Cit.Ind. Document type: academic/scholarly publication.
—BLDSC (3706.378000); CASDDS; CISTI; Ei; Genuine Article; KNAW; Linda Hall; SWETS; UnCover. CCC.

540   NE   ISSN 1024-2430
                      CODEN: EANTE2
▼**ENANTIOMER.** 1997. bi-m. $76 (effective 1998). Gordon and Breach - Harwood Academic, Amsteldisk 166, 1st Fl., 1079 LH Amsterdam, Netherlands. URL: http://www.gbhap.com/Enantiomer/. (Subscr. to: International Publishers Distributor, Box 32160, Newark, NJ 07102. TEL 800-545-8398. FAX 215-750-6343) (microform)
●Also available online.
Also available on CD-ROM.
—CASDDS.
   Description: Dedicated to the chemistry and biochemistry of enantiomers.

ENERGY & FUELS. see *ENERGY*

540 333.7   NE
▼**ENVIRONMENT & CHEMISTRY.** (Text in English) 1995. irreg. price varies. Kluwer Academic Publishers, Postbus 17, 3300 AA Dordrecht, Netherlands. TEL 31-78-6392392. FAX 31-78-6392254. E-mail: services@wkap.nl; URL: http://www.wkap.nl. (Dist. by: Kluwer Academic Publishers Group, P.O. Box 322, 3300 AH Dordrecht, Netherlands. TEL 31-78-6392392. FAX 31-78-6546474; N. America dist. addr.: Box 358, Accord Sta., Hingham, MA 02018-0358. TEL 617-871-6600. FAX 617-871-6528) Document type: monographic series.

540   ER   ISSN 1406-0124
QD1   CODEN: ENTKDR
ESTONIAN ACADEMY OF SCIENCES. PROCEEDINGS. CHEMISTRY. (Text in English; summaries in English and Estonian) 1956. s-a. $78 (effective 1998). Teaduste Akadeemia Kirjastus, Estonia pst.7, 0001 Tallinn, Estonia. TEL 372-2-454156. FAX 372-6-466026. E-mail: virve@kirj.ee. (Dist. by: Mezhdunarodnaya Kniga, B. Yakimanka 39, 117049 Moscow, Russia. TEL 7-095-2384967. FAX 7-095-2384634; Subscr. to: Akateeminen Kirjakauppa 128 SF, 00101 Helsinki, Finland; or to: Bibliotekstajanst AB 200 S22100 Lund, Sweden) circ. 550. Indexed: Alloys Ind., Eng.Mat.Abstr., INIS Atomind., Met.Abstr.Ind., Met.Abstr., Nonfer.Met.Alert, PCC Alert, Steels Alert, World Alum.Abstr. Document type: academic/scholarly publication, proceedings.
—BLDSC (6699.205000); CASDDS; CISTI; KNAW; Linda Hall; UnCover. CCC.
   Former titles: Eesti Teaduste Akadeemia. Toimetised. Keemia; (until: 1990): Akademiya Nauk Estonskoi S.S.R. Izvestiya. Khimiya (ISSN 0201-8128); Supersedes in part (in 1978): Akademiya Nauk Estonskoi S.S.R. Izvestiya. Khimiya i Geologiya.

EURO COURSES. CHEMICAL AND ENVIRONMENTAL SCIENCES. see *ENVIRONMENTAL STUDIES*

540 341   UK   ISSN 0967-7844
EUROCHEM MONITOR. base vol. plus irreg. updates. £1200 (rest of Europe £1250; elsewhere £1300); updates (renewals only) £600 (rest of Europe £640; elsewhere £680) (effective 1997). Agra Europe (London) Ltd., 25 Frant Rd., Tunbridge Wells, Kent TN2 5JT, England. TEL 44-1892-533813. FAX 44-1892-544895. TELEX 95114 AGRATW G. E-mail: 100637.3460@compuserve.com. (looseleaf format) **Document type:** trade publication.
   Description: Contains complete and consolidated texts of EU legislation on the marketing and use of dangerous chemical substances.

EUROPEAN MARKET FOR HOUSEHOLD LAUNDRY DETERGENTS AND CONDITIONERS. see BUSINESS AND ECONOMICS — Marketing And Purchasing

540   UK
EUROPEAN RADIATION CURING MARKET. 1990. irreg., latest 1995. £850. I A L Consultants, 109 Uxbridge Rd., Ealing, London W5 5TL, England. TEL 44-181-810-0919. FAX 44-181-566-4931. **Document type:** trade publication.

F A C E N A. (Facultad de Ciencias Exactas y Naturales y Agrimensura) see BIOGRAPHY

541.28   SP   ISSN 0378-4843
QD450   CODEN: FCTLDW
F C T L (Folia Chimica Theoretica Latina); publicacion periodica de los quimicos cuanticos de expresion latina. (Text in French, Italian, Spanish) 1973. q. 2500 ptas.($25) annual laboratory subscription 6000 ptas.($60). Consejo Superior de Investigaciones Cientificas (C.S.I.C.), Instituto de Estructura de la Materia, Serrano, 119, 28006 Madrid, Spain. TEL 341-5855404. FAX 341-5642431. Ed. Yves G. Smeyers. adv.; bk.rev.; abstr.; bibl. circ. 200. (back issues avail.) **Indexed:** Chem.Abstr., Ind.SST. **Document type:** government publication, monographic series, bulletin.
—BLDSC (3969.252000); CASDDS. **CCC.**

540   GW   ISSN 0933-5927
               CODEN: FSFSES
F & S. (Filtrieren und Separieren) 1987. bi-m. DM.85.20 (effective 1997). Umschau Zeitschriftenverlag Breidenstein GmbH, Stuttgarter Str. 18-24, 60329 Frankfurt a.M., Germany. TEL 49-69-2600-0. FAX 49-69-2600-609. Ed. Dr. Siegfried Ripperger. adv.; B&W page DM.5439, color page DM.8430; trim 176 x 247; adv. contact: Isabelle Sinhoff. bk.rev. circ. 5,905. **Document type:** academic/scholarly publication.
—CASDDS; CISTI.

FARBE AKTUELL PLUS. see PHARMACY AND PHARMACOLOGY

FARM CHEMICALS. see AGRICULTURE — Crop Production And Soil

FARMACI. see PHARMACY AND PHARMACOLOGY

540   US   ISSN 0014-5920
FL A C S.* (Florida Section of American Chemical Society) 1948. m. (except July, Aug., Sep.). $2. American Chemical Society, Florida Section, c/o Harold Van Wart, Department of Chemistry, Florida State University, Tallahassee, FL 32306. adv.; bk.rev.; illus.; circ. 2,350 (controlled). (tabloid format)

FLAME RETARDANCY OF POLYMERIC MATERIALS PROCEEDINGS (YEAR). see FIRE PREVENTION

541.39   UK   ISSN 1351-4180
FOCUS ON CATALYSTS. 1994. m. £245($450) (effective 1997). The Royal Society of Chemistry, Thomas Graham House, Science Park, Milton Rd., Cambridge DB4 4WF, England. TEL 44-1223-420066. FAX 44-1223-423429. E-mail: sales@rsc.org; URL: http://chemistry.rsc.org/rsc/. (Subscr. to: Turpin Distribution Services Ltd., Blackhorse Rd., Letchworth, Herts. SG6 1HN, England. TEL 44-1462-672555. FAX 44-1462-480947) Ed. Alan Comyns. **Document type:** newsletter.
   Description: Monitors all important developments for catalysts and chemical processing.

540   UK   ISSN 1360-5879
▼**FOCUS ON ORGANIC DYES AND COLOURS.** 1996. m. £245($450) (effective 1997). The Royal Society of Chemistry, Thomas Graham House, Science Park, Milton Rd., Cambridge CB4 4WF, England. TEL 44-1223-420066. FAX 44-1223-423429. E-mail: sales@rsc.org; URL: http://chemistry.rsc.org/rsc/. (Subscr. to: Turpin Distribution Services Ltd., Blackhorse Rd., Letchworth, Herts SG6 1HN, England. TEL 44-1462-480947. FAX 44-1462-480947) Ed. Peter Bamfield. **Document type:** newsletter.
   Description: Provides analysis and comment on all technical and commercial developments in organic dyes and colorants worldwide.

FOCUS ON PIGMENTS. see PAINTS AND PROTECTIVE COATINGS

660   UK   ISSN 1351-4210
FOCUS ON SURFACTANTS. 1994. m. £245($450) (effective 1997). The Royal Society of Chemistry, Thomas Graham House, Science Park, Milton Rd., Cambridge CB4 4WF, England. TEL 44-1223-420066. FAX 44-1223-423429. E-mail: sales@rsc.org. (Subscr. to: Turpin Distribution Services Ltd., Blackhorse Rd., Letchworth, Herts. SG6 1HN, England. TEL 44-1462-672555. FAX 44-1462-480947) Ed. Gordon Hollis. **Document type:** newsletter.
   Description: Covers all developments in the manufacture of surfactants.

540   XR
FOLIA FACULTATIS SCIENTIARUM NATURALIUM UNIVERSITATIS MASARYKIANAE BRUNENSIS: CHEMIA. a. price varies. Masarykova Universita, Prirodovedecka Fakulta - Masaryk University, Faculty of Sciences, Kotlarska 2, 611 37 Brno, Czech Republic. Ed. Josef Havel. **Indexed:** Biol.Abstr. **Document type:** academic/scholarly publication, monographic series.
—CISTI; Linda Hall.
   Formerly: Folia Facultatis Scientiarum Naturalium Universitatis Purkynianae Brunensis: Chemia (ISSN 0323-0236)

FOOD AND CHEMICAL TOXICOLOGY. see ENVIRONMENTAL STUDIES — Toxicology And Environmental Safety

664   UK   ISSN 0308-8146
TX501   CODEN: FOCHDJ
FOOD CHEMISTRY. 1976. m. fl.3544($2037) (effective 1998). Elsevier Science Ltd., P.O. Box 800, Kidlington, Oxford OX5 1DX, England. TEL 44-1865-843000. FAX 44-1865-843010. E-mail: nlinfo-f@elsevier.nl; usinfo-f@elsevier.com; forinfo-kyf04035@niftyserve.or.jp; URL: http://www.elsevier.nl:80/inca/publications/store/4/0/5/8/5/7/405857.pub.shtml. (Subscr. to: Elsevier Science, Regional Sales Office, P.O. Box 211, 1000 AE Amsterdam, Netherlands. TEL 31-20-4853757. FAX 31-20-4853432; Subscr. in the Americas to: Elsevier Science, Regional Sales Office, Box 945, New York, NY 10159-0945. TEL 212-633-3730. FAX 212-633-3680; Subscr. in Australasia and the Far East to: Elsevier Science (Singapore) Pte Ltd, No.1 Temasek Ave., No.17-01 Millenia Tower, Singapore 039192, Singapore. TEL 65-434-3727. FAX 65-337-2230) Eds. G.G. Birch, R.S. Shallenberger. adv.; bk.rev.; illus.; index. (also avail. in microform from UMI; back issues avail.) **Indexed:** Agri.Eng.Abstr., Anal.Abstr., Apic.Abstr., Art & Archaeol.Tech.Abstr., ASCA, Biodet.Abstr., Biol.Abstr., Chem.Abstr., Chem.Cit.Ind., Crop Physiol.Abstr., Curr.Adv.Ecol.Sci., Curr.Cont., Curr.Pack.Abstr., Dairy Sci.Abstr., Eng.Ind., Excerp.Med., Fababean Abstr., Field Crop Abstr., Food Sci.& Tech.Abstr., Herb.Abstr., Hort.Abstr., Ind.Sci.Rev., Int.Packag.Abstr., Maize Abstr., Mass Spectr.Bull., Nutr.Abstr., Plant Grow.Reg.Abstr., Potato Abstr., Sci.Cit.Ind., Seed Abstr., Sorghum & Millets Abstr., Soyabean Abstr., Sugar Ind.Abstr., Triticale Abstr., Trop.Oil Seeds Abstr., Weed Abstr. **Document type:** academic/scholarly publication.
—BLDSC (3977.284000); CASDDS; CISTI; EMDOCS; Genuine Article; Linda Hall; SWETS; UnCover. **CCC.**
   Incorporates (1985-1991): Journal of Micronutrient Analysis (ISSN 0266-349X)
   Description: Concerned with the chemistry and biochemistry of foods, and chemical and biochemical changes occurring in them.
   Refereed Serial

GALAXIA. see TEXTILE INDUSTRIES AND FABRICS

540   CC   ISSN 1003-3874
               CODEN: GACAFF
GANGUANG CAILIAO/PHOTOSENSITIVE MATERIALS. (Text in Chinese) 1973. bi-m. Y15 (foreign $10) (effective 1997). Huagong Bu, Ganguang Cailiao Xinxi Zhan - Ministry of Chemical Industry, Information Center for Photographic Materials, c/o Zhongguo Lekai Jiaopian Gongsi, Jianshe Rd., Baoding, Hebei 071054, People's Republic of China. TEL 86-312-3033279. FAX 86-312-3026296. E-mail: hjbdlkqb@public.sj.hj.cn. Ed. Rongguo Yao. R&P contact: Fengqi Wang. adv. contact: Licheng Du. bk.rev.; circ. 5,000 (paid). **Document type:** academic/scholarly publication.
—CASDDS.
   Description: Provides information on the development, manufacture and application of photosensitive materials. Covers new products, technologies and trends of the market and industrial circle.
   Refereed Serial

540 378   CC   ISSN 0251-0790
QD1   CODEN: KTHPDM
GAODENG XUEXIAO HUAXUE XUEBAO/CHEMICAL JOURNAL OF CHINESE UNIVERSITIES. (Text in Chinese) 1980. m. $30. Jilin Daxue, Like Xuebao Bianjibu, 83, Jiefang Lu, Changchun, Jilin 130021, People's Republic of China. TEL 86-431-8923189. FAX 86-431-8923907. (Dist. overseas by: China International Book Trading Corp., P.O. Box 399, Beijing, P.R. China) Ed. Tang Aoqing. **Indexed:** ASCA, Chem.Abstr. **Document type:** academic/scholarly publication.
—BLDSC (3148.330000); CASDDS; CISTI; Ei; Genuine Article.
   Description: Contains theses, research notes, letters and reviews by teachers, researchers, postgraduates, and graduate students at Jilin University.

547.7   CC   ISSN 1003-3726
               CODEN: GATOE5
GAOFENZI TONGBAO/POLYMER BULLETIN. (Text in Chinese; abstracts in English) 1988. q. $30 (effective 1997). (Chinese Chemical Society - Zhongguo Huaxuehui) Chemical Industry Press - Huaxue Gongye Chubanshe, No. 3 Huixinli, Chaoyangqu, Beijing 100029, People's Republic of China. TEL 86-10-4918318. FAX 86-10-4918089. **Document type:** academic/scholarly publication.
—BLDSC (6547.702400); CASDDS.

540   IT   ISSN 0016-5603
QD1   CODEN: GCITA9
GAZZETTA CHIMICA ITALIANA; an international journal of chemistry. (Text in English) 1871. m. L.380000 (Europe L.550000; elsewhere L.600000) (effective 1995). Societa Chimica Italiana, Viale Liegi 48, 00198 Rome, Italy. TEL 39-6-8549691. FAX 39-6-8548734. Ed. Fausto Calderazzo. **Indexed:** Art & Archaeol.Tech.Abstr., ASCA, Biol.Abstr., Biotech.Abstr., Cadscan, Chem.Abstr., Chem.Cit.Ind., Curr.Chem.React., Curr.Cont., Ind.Chem., Ind.Sci.Rev., INIS Atomind., Lead Abstr., Mass Spectr.Bull., Mat.Sci.Cit.Ind., Met.Abstr., Numis.Lit., Sci.Cit.Ind., Zincscan.
—BLDSC (4095.000000); CASDDS; CISTI; Ei; Genuine Article; Linda Hall; SWETS; UnCover.
   Description: Multi-disciplinary research of fundamental aspects of chemistry.

540   JA   ISSN 0386-961X
               CODEN: GNKGAN
GENDAI KAGAKU/CHEMISTRY TODAY. (Text in Japanese) 1971. m. 780 Yen per no. Tokyo Kagaku Dojin, 36-7, Sengoku 3-chome, Bunkyo-ku, Tokyo 112, Japan. **Indexed:** Chem.Abstr.
—CASDDS; CISTI.

540   JA   ISSN 0910-4747
               CODEN: GKZOE3
GENDAI KAGAKU. ZOKAN/CHEMISTRY TODAY. SPECIAL NUMBER. (Text in Japanese) 1984. bi-m. Tokyo Kagaku Dojin, 36-7, Sengoku 3-chome, Bunkyo-ku, Tokyo 112, Japan. **Indexed:** Chem.Abstr.
—BLDSC (4096.399720); CASDDS.

GEOCHEMICAL SOCIETY. SPECIAL PUBLICATION. see EARTH SCIENCES — Geology

GEOKHIMIYA. see EARTH SCIENCES — Geology

CHEMISTRY

540 660 BN ISSN 0367-4444
CODEN: GHTBAB
GLASNIK HEMICARA I TEHNOLOGA BOSNE I HERCEGOVINE. (Subseries of: Documenta Chemica Yugoslavica) irreg. Akademija Nauka i Umjetnosti Bosne i Hercegovine, Hemijski Institut, Vojvode Putnika 43, Sarajevo, Bosnia Hercegovina. Ed. Franjo Krleza. **Indexed:** Chem.Abstr.
—BLDSC (4184.950000); CASDDS.

540 UK ISSN 0072-6524
GREAT BRITAIN. LABORATORY OF THE GOVERNMENT CHEMIST. ANNUAL REPORT OF THE GOVERNMENT CHEMIST. 1959. a. price varies. H.M.S.O., 51 Nine Elms Ln., London SW8 5DR, England. TEL 44-171-873-0011. FAX 44-171-873-8247. (reprint service avail. from UMI) **Document type:** government publication.

540 FR
GUIDE DE LA CHIMIE INTERNATIONAL. a. 490 F. S.E.P Edition, 194-196 rue Marcadet, 75018 Paris, France. Ed. Robert Frappa.

GUIDEBOOK TO THE EUROPEAN ADHESIVES INDUSTRY. see BUSINESS AND ECONOMICS — Trade And Industrial Directories

HACETTEPE FEN VE MUHENDISLIK BILIMLERI DERGISI. SERI C: KIMYA, FIZIK VE MUHENDISLIK/HACETTEPE BULLETIN OF NATURAL SCIENCES AND ENGINEERING. SERIES C: CHEMISTRY, PHYSICS AND ENGINEERING. see SCIENCES: COMPREHENSIVE WORKS

540 JA
HAII KAGOBUTSU NO KOKAGAKU TORONKAI KOEN YOSHISHU/PROCEEDINGS OF THE SYMPOSIUM ON PHOTOCHEMISTRY OF COORDINATION COMPOUNDS. (Text in Japanese) a. Rikagaku Kenkyujo - Institute of Physical and Chemical Research, 2-1, Hirosawa, Wako-shi, Saitama-ken 351-01, Japan. **Document type:** proceedings.

HANDBOOK OF CHEMICAL NEUROANATOMY. see MEDICAL SCIENCES — Psychiatry And Neurology

540 614.7 US
HANDBOOK OF ENVIRONMENTAL CHEMISTRY. 1980. irreg., vol.4-D, 1995. price varies. Springer-Verlag, 175 Fifth Ave., New York, NY 10010. TEL 212-460-1500. FAX 212-473-6272. (reprint service avail. from ISI) **Document type:** academic/scholarly publication.

HANDBOOK OF ENVIRONMENTAL ISOTOPE GEOCHEMISTRY. see EARTH SCIENCES

540 JA
HANDBOOK OF EXISTING & NEW CHEMICAL SUBSTANCES. (Editions in English, Japanese) irreg., 7th ed., 1996. 24466 Yen (other Asian countries $289; elsewhere $308). (Ministry of International Trade & Industry) Chemical Daily Co., Ltd., International Affairs, 3-16-8, Nihonbashi Hama-cho, Chuo-ku, Tokyo 103, Japan. TEL 81-3-3663-7932. FAX 81-3-3663-7275. TELEX 2422362 NIPPO J. E-mail: chemnews@tky.threewebnet.or.jp; URL: http://www.chemnews-japan.com/. pp./issue: 850.
Description: Lists chemical substances based on Chemical Substance Control Law in Japan.

540 NE
HANDBOOK OF NATURAL PRODUCTS DATA. (Text in English) 1990. irreg., vol.3, 1994. price varies. Elsevier Science B.V., Books Division, P.O. Box 211, 1000 AE Amsterdam, Netherlands. TEL 31-20-4853911. FAX 31-20-4853705. TELEX 18582 ESPA NL. E-mail: nlinfo-f@elsevier.nl; usinfo-f@elsevier.com; forinfo-kyf04035@niftyserve.or.jp; URL: http://www.elsevier.nl/. (Subscr. in the Americas to: Elsevier Science, Regional Sales Office, Box 945, New York, NY 10159-0945. TEL 212-633-3730. FAX 212-633-3680; Subscr. in Australasia and the Far East to: Elsevier Science (Singapore) Pte Ltd, No.1 Temasek Ave., No.17-01 Millenia Tower, Singapore 039192, Singapore. TEL 65-434-3727. FAX 65-337-2230; Subscr. in Japan to: Elsevier Science Japan, 9-15 Higashi-Azabu 1-chome, Minato-ku, Tokyo 106, Japan. TEL 81-3-5561-5033. FAX 81-3-5561-5047) Ed. Prof. Atta-ur-Rahman. (back issues avail.) **Document type:** monographic series.
Refereed Serial

HANDBOOK ON THE PHYSICS AND CHEMISTRY OF RARE EARTHS. see PHYSICS

HANDBOOK ON THE PHYSICS AND CHEMISTRY OF THE ACTINIDES. see PHYSICS

HANGUK NONGHWAHAKHOECHI/AGRICULTURAL CHEMISTRY AND BIOTECHNOLOGY. see AGRICULTURE — Crop Production And Soil

540 AI
QD1.A3515 CODEN: AYKZAN
HAYASTANI CHIMIKAKAN HANDES. (Text and summaries in Armenian, English, Russian) 1947. 4/yr. 400 dram. Akademiya Nauk Armenii, Pr. Marshala Bagramayana, 24, 375019 Erevan, Armenia. TEL 78852-524580. FAX 78852-151087. Ed. S.A. Vartanian. index. **Indexed:** Alloys Ind., Chem.Abstr., Eng.Mat.Abstr., Mass Spectr.Bull., Met.Abstr., Met.Abstr.Ind., Nonfer.Met.Alert, PCC Alert, Steels Alert, World Alum.Abstr. **Document type:** academic/scholarly publication.
—CASDDS; CISTI; Linda Hall.
Formerly: Armyanskii Khimicheskii Zhurnal - Aikakan Himiakan Amsagir (ISSN 0515-9628)

HAZMAT PACKAGER AND SHIPPER; hazardous materials transportation. see PACKAGING

540 CC ISSN 1003-5095
HEBEI HUAGONG/HEBEI CHEMICAL ENGINEERING. (Text in Chinese) 1978. q. Hebei Sheng Huagong Xuehui - Hebei Society of Chemical Engineering, 1 Jianhuamian Dajie, Shijiazhuang, Hebei 050031, People's Republic of China. TEL 741853. Ed. Rong Wenzhong.

540 SZ ISSN 0018-019X
CODEN: HCACAV
HELVETICA CHIMICA ACTA. (Text in German, English, French and Italian) 1918. 8/yr. DM.1075 (foreign DM.1115) (effective 1997). (Schweizerische Chemische Gesellschaft - Swiss Chemical Society) Verlag Helvetica Chimica Acta, P.O. Box 313, CH-4010 Basel, Switzerland. (Subscr. to: Wiley - V C H, Postfach 101161, 69451 Weinheim, Germany. TEL 49-6201-606147. FAX 49-6201-606117; Subscr. in the Americas to: John Wiley & Sons, Inc., 605 Third Ave., New York, NY 10158. TEL 212-850-6645. FAX 212-850-6021) Ed. M.V. Kisakurek. adv.; abstr.; charts; index. circ. 2,400. (also avail. in microfilm from PMC) **Indexed:** Abstr.Bull.Inst.Pap.Chem., Anal.Abstr., ASCA, Biol.Abstr., Biotech.Abstr., Bull.Thermodyn.& Thermochem., Chem.Abstr., Chem.Cit.Ind., Chem.Infd., Crop Physiol.Abstr., Curr.Cont., Excerp.Med., Forest.Abstr., Forest Prod.Abstr., Helminthol.Abstr., Ind.Chem., Ind.Sci.Rev., INIS Atomind., Mass Spectr.Bull., Mat.Sci.Cit.Ind., Met.Abstr., Nutr.Abstr., Sci.Cit.Ind., SSCI. **Document type:** academic/scholarly publication.
—BLDSC (4287.000000); CASDDS; CISTI; Ei; EMDOCS; Genuine Article; Linda Hall; SWETS; UnCover. **CCC**.

540 YU ISSN 0440-6826
CODEN: HMPGAI
HEMIJSKI PREGLED/CHEMICAL REVIEW. (Text in Serbo-Croatian; abstracts in English) 1950. bi-m. $30. Srpsko Hemijsko Drustvo - Serbian Chemical Society, Karnegijeva 4, Box 462, 11001 Belgrade, Yugoslavia. TEL 011 328-583. (Subscr. to: Jugoslovenska Knjiga, Export-Import, Trg Republike 5, 11000 Belgrade, Yugoslavia) Ed. Stanimir Arsenijevic. **Indexed:** Chem.Abstr.
—CASDDS.

540 GW ISSN 0720-941X
HENKEL - REFERATE; Veroeffentlichungen aus der Henkel-Forschung. International edition: Henkel Referate, Excerpts of Henkel Research Papers (ISSN 0720-9428) 1964. a. free. Henkel KGaA, 40191 Duesseldorf, Germany. TEL 49-211-797-2787. FAX 49-211-7985598. Ed. Dr. Ulrich Zeidler. R&P contact: Dr. Ulrich Zeidler. circ. 15,000. **Document type:** trade publication.
Description: Excerpts of papers on chemical research, process development and technology, and product development and applications technology.

540 UK ISSN 0793-0283
CODEN: HCOMEX
HETEROCYCLIC COMMUNICATIONS; an international journal in heterocyclic chemistry. 1994. bi-m. $280 (effective 1997). Freund Publishing House Ltd., Ste. 500, Chesham House, 150 Regent St., London W1R 5FA, England. (And: P.O. Box 35010, Tel Aviv, Israel. TEL 972-3-5628540. FAX 972-3-5625838) Ed. R.R. Gupta. (reprint service avail.) **Document type:** academic/scholarly publication.
—BLDSC (4301.259000); CASDDS.
Description: Publishes preliminary research reports and full-length research papers conveying important developments on all phases of heterocyclic chemistry, including inorganic-ring systems.

540 US ISSN 1068-6983
QD506.A1 CODEN: HCREEO
HETEROGENEOUS CHEMISTRY REVIEWS; the review journal devoted to the chemistry and molecular physics of surfaces, interfaces, materials, colloids, polymers and biopolymers. 1994. q. $325 to institutions (effective 1996). John Wiley & Sons, Inc., Journals, 605 Third Ave., New York, NY 10158-0012. TEL 212-850-6645. FAX 212-850-6021. TELEX 12-7063. E-mail: SUBINFO@JWILEY.COM. (Subscr. outside the Americas to: John Wiley & Sons Ltd., Baffins Ln., Chichester, W. Sussex P019 1UD, England. TEL 44-1243-779777. FAX 44-1243-776128) Ed. David Avnir. adv.: B&W page £475, color page £1325; trim 279 x 210; adv. contact: Michael J. Levermore. bk.rev. (also avail. in microform from UMI; back issues avail.) **Indexed:** ASCA, Curr.Cont. **Document type:** academic/scholarly publication.
—BLDSC (4301.351000); CASDDS; CISTI; Genuine Article. **CCC**.
Description: Devoted to the chemistry and molecular physics of surfaces, interfaces, materials, colloids, polymers, and biopolymers.
Refereed Serial

540 US ISSN 0164-6109
THE HEXAGON. 1910. q. $5. Alpha Chi Sigma Fraternity, G R L Consultants, 12814 Kings Forest, San Antonio, TX 78230-1511. TEL 210-492-4290; 800-357-5944. FAX 210-492-5330. E-mail: geegeel@aol.com. (Subscr. to: 2114 N. Franklin Rd., Indianapolis, IN 46219. TEL 317-357-5944) Ed. Robert E. Lyle; Pub. Maury Boyd. R&P contact: Robert Boyle. bk.rev.; illus. circ. 30,000. **Document type:** academic/scholarly publication.
Description: Covers the history of chemistry.

HIGH - TC UPDATE. see PHYSICS

HINDUSTAN LATEX. VARSHIKA RIPORTA/HINDUSTAN LATEX. ANNUAL REPORTS. see PLASTICS

HOKKAIDO KYOIKU DAIGAKU KIYO. DAI-2-BU, A. SUGAKU, BUTSURI, KAGAKU, KOGAKU-HEN/HOKKAIDO UNIVERSITY OF EDUCATION. JOURNAL. SECTION 2 A. MATHEMATICS, PHYSICS, CHEMISTRY, ENGINEERING. see MATHEMATICS

338.4766 660 CC ISSN 1000-6613
CODEN: HUJIEK
HUAGONG JINZHAN/CHEMICAL INDUSTRY AND ENGINEERING PROGRESS. (Text in Chinese) 1982. bi-m. $70. (Chemical Industry and Engineering Society of China) Chemical Industry Press - Huaxue Gongye Chubanshe, No. 3 Huixinli, Chaoyangqu, Beijing 100029, People's Republic of China. TEL 86-10-4918318. FAX 86-10-4918318. Ed. Chengwei Shi. adv. contact: Yanhong Dai. pp./issue: 64. **Document type:** academic/scholarly publication.
—CASDDS.
Description: Features the current developments and advances in the field of chemical industry and engineering. Topics include chemical industry, technology, engineering, machinery, process automation, environmental protection, economy and management.

540 662.6 CC ISSN 1004-0862
HUAGONG ZHI YOU/FRIEND OF CHEMICAL INDUSTRY. (Text in Chinese) q. $2 per no. Hebei Shiyou Huagong Guihua Shejiyuan - Hebei Institute of Petrochemical Industry, 11 Jichang Lu, Shijiazhuang Hebei 050071, People's Republic of China. TEL 0312-311486. Ed. Jiang Ximing. adv. contact: Zhao Tina-Hong. **Document type:** academic/scholarly publication.

540 614.7   CC   ISSN 0254-6108
QD1   CODEN: HUHUDB
HUANJING HUAXUE/JOURNAL OF ENVIRONMENTAL CHEMISTRY. (Text in Chinese; summaries in English) 1982. bi-m. $5 per no. (Chinese Academy of Sciences, Ecology and Environment Research Centre) Science Press, Marketing and Sales Department, 16 Donghuangchenggen North St., Beijing 100717, People's Republic of China. TEL 4010642. FAX 4012180. TELEX 210247-SPBJ-CN. (US office: Science Press New York, Ltd., 63-117 Alderton St., Rego Park, NY 11374. TEL 718-459-4638) adv. circ. 21,000.
—CASDDS; CISTI; Linda Hall.
Description: Contains original theses and reviews on environmental analytic chemistry, pollution chemistry, pollution prevention chemistry, and recent research results.
Refereed Serial

540   CC   ISSN 1001-7631
             CODEN: HFGGEU
HUAXUE FANYING GONGCHENG YU GONGYI/CHEMICAL REACTION ENGINEERING AND TECHNOLOGY. (Text in Chinese) 1985. q. $48. Zhejiang Daxue, Huagong Xi - Zhejiang University, Department of Chemical Engineering, Zheda Lu, Hangzhou, Zhejiang 310027, People's Republic of China. TEL 0571-572244. FAX 0571-571797. TELEX 35040 ZUFAO CN. Ed. Chen Gantang. **Document type:** academic/scholarly publication.
—BLDSC (3150.332000); CASDDS; CISTI; Ei.

540 370   CC
HUAXUE JIAOXUE/CHEMISTRY TEACHING. (Text in Chinese) 1978. bi-m. Y19.20 (effective 1994). Huadong Shifan Daxue, Huaxue Xi - East China Normal University, Chemistry Department, 3663 Zhongshan Beilu, Shanghai 200062, People's Republic of China. TEL 021-2577577. FAX 021-2576217. Ed. Jin Litong. adv. circ. 30,000. **Document type:** academic/scholarly publication.
Description: Covers teaching and learning methods, practices and experiments in education reform.

540   CC   ISSN 1005-281X
             CODEN: HJINEL
HUAXUE JINZHAN/PROGRESS IN CHEMISTRY. 1989. q. $50. Zhongguo Kexueyuan, Wenxian Qingbao Zhongxin - Chinese Academy of Sciences, Documentation and Information Center, 8 Kexueyuan Nanlu, Zhongguancun, Beijing 100080, People's Republic of China. TEL 86-10-6256-2547. FAX 81-10-6256-6846. E-mail: scinfo@bib10.las.ac.cn. Ed. Hua Yanwen. **Document type:** academic/scholarly publication.
●Also available on CD-ROM.
—CASDDS.
Description: Reports on the latest development in the field of chemistry.

540   CC   ISSN 0441-3776
QD1   CODEN: HHTPAU
HUAXUE TONGBAO/CHEMISTRY BULLETIN. (Text in Chinese) 1933. m. $144 (effective 1997). Science Press, Marketing and Sales Department, Donghuangchenggen North St., Beijing 100717, People's Republic of China. TEL 4010642. FAX 4019810. adv. contact: Yuanyaun Liu. circ. 41,000. **Indexed:** Chem.Abstr., Mass Spectr.Bull. **Document type:** academic/scholarly publication.
—BLDSC (3168.840000); CASDDS; CISTI; Ei; Linda Hall.
Description: Presents trends and developments in pure and applied chemistry in China and abroad. Contains review articles, notes and communications, experimental techniques, basic knowledge, history of chemistry, and academic activities.

HUAXUE WULI XUEBAO/CHINESE JOURNAL OF CHEMICAL PHYSICS. see *PHYSICS*

540   CC   ISSN 0567-7351
QD1   CODEN: HHHPA4
HUAXUE XUEBAO/ACTA CHIMICA SINICA. English edition: Chinese Journal of Chemistry (ISSN 1001-604X) (Text in Chinese; summaries in English) 1933. m. $252 (effective 1997). (Chinese Chemical Society) Science Press, Marketing and Sales Department, 16 Donghuangchenggen North St., Beijing 100717, People's Republic of China. TEL 4010642. FAX 4019810. adv. circ. 8,000. **Indexed:** Anal.Abstr., Apic.Abstr., ASCA, Biol.Abstr., Chem.Abstr., Chem.Cit.Ind., Corros.Abstr., Curr.Adv.Ecol.Sci., Curr.Cont., INIS Atomind., Mat.Sci.Cit.Ind., Met.Abstr., Sci.Cit.Ind. **Document type:** academic/scholarly publication.
—BLDSC (0611.000000); CASDDS; CISTI; Ei; Genuine Article; Linda Hall.
Supersedes in part: Chinese Chemical Society. Journal (Peiping) (ISSN 0375-8745)
Description: Presents original research on organic, inorganic, physical, and analytical chemistry in mainland China.
Refereed Serial

HUNGARIAN ACADEMY OF SCIENCES. CENTRAL RESEARCH INSTITUTE FOR PHYSICS. YEARBOOK/MAGYAR TUDOMANYOS AKADEMIA. KOZPONTI FIZIKAI KUTATO INTEZET. EVKONYV. see *PHYSICS*

540 338 660   HU   ISSN 0133-0276
TP1   CODEN: HJICAI
HUNGARIAN JOURNAL OF INDUSTRIAL CHEMISTRY. (Text in English) 1973. q. $110 (effective 1997). Hungarian Academy of Sciences, Research Institute of Chemical Engineering, Egyetem u. 2, P.O. Box 125, H-8201 Veszprem, Hungary. TEL 36-88-421-663. FAX 36-88-424-424. E-mail: hjic@mukki.richem.hu; URL: http://www.vein.hu/HJIC. (Subscr. to: Kultura, P.O. Box 149, H-1389 Budapest 62, Hungary) Ed. E. Bador. adv.; bk.rev.; charts; stat.; index. circ. 1,200. (back issues avail.) **Indexed:** Alloys Ind., API Abstr., API Catal., API Hlth.& Environ., API Oil., API Pet.Ref., API Pet.Subst., API Transport., ASCA, Cadscan, Chem.Abstr., Chem.Cit.Ind., Chem.Eng.Abstr., Curr.Cont., Eng.Mat.Abstr., Gas Abstr., INIS Atomind., Lead Abstr., Met.Abstr., Met.Abstr.Ind., Nonfer.Met.Alert, PCC Alert, Risk Abstr., Steels Alert, T.C.E.A., World Alum.Abstr., Zincscan.
—BLDSC (4337.025000); CASDDS; CISTI; Ei; Genuine Article; Linda Hall; SWETS.

HYOMEN KAGAKU KISO KOZA/TEXTBOOK OF LECTURES ON SURFACE SCIENCE. see *PHYSICS*

HYOMEN KAGAKU KOEN TAIKAI KOEN YOSHISHU/SURFACE SCIENCE SOCIETY OF JAPAN. ABSTRACTS OF MEETINGS. see *PHYSICS*

HYOMEN KAGAKU SEMINA/TEXTBOOK OF SEMINAR ON SURFACE SCIENCE. see *PHYSICS*

540   JA   ISSN 1342-0321
             CODEN: IAREFM
I C R ANNUAL REPORT. (Text in English) Kyoto University, Institute for Chemical Research - Kyoto Daigaku Kenkyusho, Gokasho, Goko-sho, Uji-shi, Kyoto 611, Japan. TEL 81-774-38-3010. FAX 81-774-38-4370. Ed. Misae Hiramoto. **Document type:** academic/scholarly publication.

I N A VJESNIK INDUSTRIJE NAFTE. see *PETROLEUM AND GAS*

540   US   ISSN 0897-8026
TP669   CODEN: IFRMEC
I N F O R M: INTERNATIONAL NEWS ON FATS, OILS & RELATED MATERIALS. 1990. m. $110 (foreign $125). (American Oil Chemists' Society) A O C S Press, 1608 Broadmoor Dr., Box 3489, Champaign, IL 61821-0489. TEL 217-359-2344. FAX 217-351-8091. E-mail: general@aocs.org; URL: http://www.aocs.org. Ed. T.L. Mounts. R&P contact: Connie Winslow. TEL 217-357-5401. adv. contact: Lisa Spencer. **Indexed:** Abstr.Bull.Inst.Pap.Chem., Food Sci.& Tech.Abstr. **Document type:** trade publication.
—BLDSC (4478.882000); CASDDS; CISTI; Ei; Linda Hall; SWETS; UMI. **CCC.**
Description: News and information of interest to professionals interested in the science and technology of fats and oils, surfactants, detergents, proteins, oleochemicals, and related substances.

540   SP   ISSN 0210-508X
I.Q.S.; trabajos de fin de carrera. 1971. a. $10. Institut Quimic de Sarria, 08017 Barcelona, Spain. FAX 2056266. Ed.Bd. circ. controlled. (back issues avail.) **Indexed:** Chem.Abstr., Ind.SST.

540 666   JA
IBIDEN COMPANY. ANNUAL REPORT. 1989. a. Ibiden Company Ltd., Somubu, 2-1 Kanda-machi, Ogaki-shi, Gifu-ken 503, Japan. TEL 0584-813111. FAX 0584-814574.
Description: Information on electronics-related products, fine ceramics, and building materials.

THE IMMUNOASSAY KIT DIRECTORY. SERIES A: CLINICAL CHEMISTRY. see *MEDICAL SCIENCES — Allergology And Immunology*

THE IMMUNOASSAY KIT DIRECTORY. SERIES B: INFECTIOUS DISEASES. see *MEDICAL SCIENCES — Allergology And Immunology*

540   II   ISSN 0253-4134
QD1   CODEN: PIAADM
INDIAN ACADEMY OF SCIENCES. PROCEEDINGS. CHEMICAL SCIENCES. (Text in English) 1934. 6/yr. Rs.150($150) (effective 1997). Indian Academy of Sciences, C.V. Raman Avenue, P.B. No. 8005, Bangalore 560 080, India. TEL 91-80-3342546. FAX 91-80-3346094. TELEX 0845-2178-ACAD-IN. E-mail: chemsci@ias.ernet.in. Ed. V. Krishnan. bibl.; illus.; index. circ. 1,000. (also avail. in microfilm from UMI; reprint service avail. from ISI,UMI) **Indexed:** Alloys Ind., ASCA, Chem.Abstr., Chem.Cit.Ind., Curr.Cont., Energy Info.Abstr., Eng.Mat.Abstr., Environ.Abstr., Ind.Sci.Rev., INSPEC (1980-), Met.Abstr., Met.Abstr.Ind., Nonfer.Met.Alert, PCC Alert, Phys.Ber., Sci.Cit.Ind., Steels Alert, World Alum.Abstr. **Document type:** academic/scholarly publication, proceedings.
—BLDSC (6709.920000); AskIEEE; CASDDS; CISTI; Ei; Genuine Article; KNAW; KR SourceOne; SWETS; UMI; UnCover.

INDIAN CHEMICAL DIRECTORY. see *ENGINEERING — Chemical Engineering*

540   II   ISSN 0019-4522
QD1   CODEN: JICSAH
INDIAN CHEMICAL SOCIETY. JOURNAL. 1924. m. $250 (effective 1996); Rs.1000($300) (effective 1997). Indian Chemical Society, 92 Acharya Prafulla Chandra Rd., Calcutta 700009, India. TEL 91-33-350-3478. Ed. Prabir K. Gupta. adv.; bk.rev.; index. circ. 2,500. (also avail. in microfilm from UMI,PMC; reprint service avail. from UMI) **Indexed:** Anal.Abstr., ASCA, Biol.Abstr., Biotech.Abstr., Cadscan, Chem.Cit.Ind., Chem.Infd., Curr.Chem.React., Curr.Cont., Dairy Sci.Abstr., Excerp.Med., Food Sci.& Tech.Abstr., Helminthol.Abstr., Ind.Chem., INIS Atomind., Lead Abstr., Mass Spectr.Bull., Nutr.Abstr., Zincscan. **Document type:** academic/scholarly publication.
—BLDSC (4763.000000); CASDDS; CISTI; Ei; Genuine Article; Linda Hall; SWETS; UMI; UnCover.
Incorporates: Indian Journal of Applied Chemistry (ISSN 0019-5065)
Refereed Serial

| 540 | II | ISSN 0971-457X |
| TP1 | | CODEN: ICHTEU |

INDIAN JOURNAL OF CHEMICAL TECHNOLOGY. (Text in English) 1963. bi-m. Rs.250($120) (Council of Scientific and Industrial Research, Publications & Information Directorate) Scientific Publishers, P.O. Box 91, 5A, New Pali Rd., Jodhpur 342 001, India. TEL 91-291-33323. E-mail: pid@sirnetd.erbet.in. (Dist. by: HPC Publishers' Distributors Pvt. Ltd., 4805-24, 1st Fl., Bharat Ram Rd., Darya Ganj, New Delhi 110 002, India. TEL 91-11-3254401. FAX 91-11-6863511) Ed. G.P. Phondke. adv.; bibl.; charts; illus.; index. circ. 1,200. (also avail. in microform from UMI; back issues avail.; reprint service avail. from UMI) **Indexed:** Alloys Ind., Anal.Abstr., Appl.Mech.Rev., ASCA, Biol.Abstr., CAD CAM Abstr., Cadscan, Ceram.Abstr., Chem.Abstr., Chem.Eng.Abstr., Curr.Cont., Dairy Sci.Abstr., Energy Ind., Energy Info.Abstr., Eng.Ind., Eng.Mat.Abstr., Environ.Abstr., Excerp.Med., Fluidex, Food Sci.& Tech.Abstr., Gas Abstr., Geotech.Abstr., INIS Atomind., INSPEC (1968-), Lead Abstr., Met.Abstr., Met.Abstr.Ind., Mineral.Abstr., Nonfer.Met.Alert, Nutr.Abstr., PCC Alert, Soils & Fert., Steels Alert, Sugar Ind.Abstr., T.C.E.A., World Alum.Abstr., World Text.Abstr., Zincscan. **Document type:** academic/scholarly publication.
—BLDSC (4410.595000); AskIEEE; CASDDS; CISTI; Genuine Article; KR SourceOne; Linda Hall; UMI; UnCover.
Supersedes in part (in 1994): Indian Journal of Technology (ISSN 0019-5669)

| 540 | II | ISSN 0376-4710 |
| | | CODEN: IJCADU |

INDIAN JOURNAL OF CHEMISTRY. SECTION A: INORGANIC, PHYSICAL, THEORETICAL AND ANALYTICAL CHEMISTRY. (Text in English) 1976. m. Rs.500($240) (Council of Scientific and Industrial Research, Publications & Information Directorate) Scientific Publishers, P.O. Box 91, 5A, New Pali Rd., Jodhpur 342 001, India. TEL 91-291-33323. FAX 91-291-613480. (Co-sponsor: Indian National Science Academy) Ed. S.S. Saksena. adv.; charts; illus.; index. circ. 1,400. (back issues avail.) **Indexed:** Anal.Abstr., ASCA, Biol.Abstr., C.R.I.Abstr., C.R.I.Curr.Cont., Cadscan, Ceram.Abstr., Chem.Abstr., Chem.Cit.Ind., Chem.Infd., Curr.Chem.React., Curr.Cont., Ind.Chem., Ind.Sci.Rev., INIS Atomind., INSPEC, Lead Abstr., Mat.Sci.Cit.Ind., Met.Abstr., Nutr.Abstr., Sci.Cit.Ind., World Alum.Abstr., World Text.Abstr. **Document type:** academic/scholarly publication.
—BLDSC (4410.601000); CASDDS; CISTI; Ei; EMDOCS; Genuine Article; KNAW; KR SourceOne; Linda Hall; SWETS; UnCover.
Supersedes in part (1963-1976): Indian Journal of Chemistry (ISSN 0019-5103)

| 540 | II | ISSN 0376-4699 |
| | | CODEN: IJSBDB |

INDIAN JOURNAL OF CHEMISTRY. SECTION B: ORGANIC AND MEDICINAL CHEMISTRY. (Text in English) 1976. m. Rs.500($240) (Council of Scientific and Industrial Research, Publications & Information Directorate) Scientific Publishers, P.O. Box 91, 5A, New Pali Rd., Jodhpur 342 001, India. TEL 91-291-33323. (Co-sponsor: Indian National Science Academy) Ed. S.S. Saksena. (back issues avail.) **Indexed:** Anal.Abstr., ASCA, Biol.Abstr., Chem.Abstr., Chem.Cit.Ind., Chem.Infd., Curr.Adv.Ecol.Sci., Curr.Chem.React., Curr.Cont., Helminthol.Abstr., Hort.Abstr., Ind.Chem., Ind.Sci.Rev., INIS Atomind., INSPEC, Mass Spectr.Bull., Nutr.Abstr., Sci.Cit.Ind., SSCI, World Text.Abstr. **Document type:** academic/scholarly publication.
—BLDSC (4410.610000); CASDDS; CISTI; Ei; EMDOCS; Genuine Article; KNAW; KR SourceOne; Linda Hall; SWETS; UnCover.
Supersedes in part (1963-1976): Indian Journal of Chemistry (ISSN 0019-5103)

| 540 | II | ISSN 0971-1627 |
| QD399 | | CODEN: IJCHEI |

INDIAN JOURNAL OF HETEROCYCLIC CHEMISTRY. (Text in English) 1991. q. Rs.500($150) C-85, Sector B, Aliganj Scheme, Lucknow 226 024, India. TEL 91-22-323421. Ed. Dr. R.S. Varma. R&P contact: R.S. Varma. bk.rev. circ. 200. **Indexed:** ASCA, Chem.Cit.Ind., Curr.Cont. **Document type:** academic/scholarly publication.
—BLDSC (4414.350000); CASDDS; CISTI; Genuine Article.
Description: Publishes review articles and original research papers pertaining to structure and synthesis, mechanism of reactions, spectral studies, biologically active compounds, bio-chemical studies, physicochemical work and phytochemistry.
Refereed Serial

| 540 | US | ISSN 0019-6924 |

INDICATOR. 1920. m. (Sep.-June). $20. American Chemical Society, New York & North Jersey Sections, 43 Reservoir Place, Cedar Grove, NJ 07009. TEL 201-239-1975. Ed. Lilian H. Sello. adv. contact: Herman Burwasser. illus. circ. 13,000. **Document type:** academic/scholarly publication, newsletter.

INDUSTRIA QUIMICA EN CIFRAS. see *CHEMISTRY — Abstracting, Bibliographies, Statistics*

| 660 628.5 | NE | ISSN 0926-9614 |
| | | CODEN: ICHLE6 |

INDUSTRIAL CHEMISTRY LIBRARY. (Text in English) 1989. irreg., vol.5, 1993. price varies. Elsevier Science B.V., Books Division, P.O. Box 211, 1000 AE Amsterdam, Netherlands. TEL 31-20-4853911. FAX 31-20-4853705. TELEX 18582 ESPA NL. E-mail: nlinfo-f@elsevier.nl; usinfo-f@elsevier.com; forinfo-kyf04035@niftyserve.or.jp; URL: http://www.elsevier.nl/. (Subscr. in the Americas to: Elsevier Science, Regional Sales Office, Box 945, New York, NY 10159-0945. TEL 212-633-3730. FAX 212-633-3680; Subscr. in Australasia and the Far East to: Elsevier Science (Singapore) Pte Ltd, No.1 Temasek Ave., No.17-01 Millenia Tower, Singapore 039192, Singapore. TEL 65-434-3727. FAX 65-337-2230; Subscr. in Japan to: Elsevier Science Japan, 9-15 Higashi-Azabu 1-chome, Minato-ku, Tokyo 106, Japan. TEL 81-3-5561-5033. FAX 81-3-5561-5047) Ed. S.T. Sie. (back issues avail.) **Document type:** monographic series.
—BLDSC (4448.310000); CASDDS. CCC.
Refereed Serial

INDUSTRIAL LASER BUYERS GUIDE. see *PHYSICS — Optics*

| 540 | FR | ISSN 0020-045X |
| | | CODEN: INFCA8 |

INFORMATIONS - CHIMIE. 1963. m. 1240 F. (foreign 1755 F.) (effective 1996). Societe d'Expansion Technique et Economique S.A., 4 rue de Seze, 75009 Paris, France. TEL 44-94-50-60. FAX 44-94-50-75. Ed. Dmitri Savostianoff. adv.; charts; illus.; mkt.; stat.; index. circ. 7,500. (also avail. in microfilm from PMC; back issues avail.) **Indexed:** Alloys Ind., API Abstr., API Catal., API Hlth.& Environ., API Oil., API Pet.Ref., API Pet.Subst., API Transport., Art & Archaeol.Tech.Abstr., Chem.Abstr., Chem.Infd., Eng.Mat.Abstr., Excerp.Med., INIS Atomind., Key to Econ.Sci., Met.Abstr.Ind., Met.Abstr., Nonfer.Met.Alert, PCC Alert, Steels Alert, World Alum.Abstr.
—BLDSC (4496.529000); CASDDS; CISTI; Ei; SWETS. CCC.
Incorporating: Chimie et Industrie; Genie Chimique; Hauts Polymeres.

| 540 | FR | ISSN 0339-6045 |
| | | CODEN: ICHEDI |

INFORMATIONS CHIMIE HEBDO. (Supplement to: Informations - Chimie) w. (42/yr.). 3680 F. (foreign 4150 F.) (effective 1996). Societe d'Expansion Technique et Economique S.A., 4 rue de Seze, 75009 Paris, France. Ed. Dmitri Savostianoff. **Indexed:** Chem.Abstr.
—BLDSC (4496.531500); CASDDS.

| 540 | GW | |

INSTITUT FUER THEORETISCHE CHEMIE. UNIVERSITAET STUTTGART. ARBEITSBERICHT. 1966. biennial. Universitaet Stuttgart, Institut fuer Theoretische Chemie, Pfaffenwaldring 55, 70569 Stuttgart, Germany. TEL 0711-6854401. FAX 0711-6854442. Ed. H. Preuss. circ. 350. **Document type:** academic/scholarly publication.

INSTITUTE OF PHYSICAL AND CHEMICAL RESEARCH. SCIENTIFIC PAPERS. see *PHYSICS*

| 540 | II | ISSN 0020-3254 |
| TP1 | | CODEN: JOICA7 |

INSTITUTION OF CHEMISTS (INDIA). JOURNAL. (Text in English) 1929. bi-m. $25. Institution of Chemists (India), 11-4, Dr. Biresh Guha Road, Calcutta 700 017, India. TEL 91-33-240-3832. Ed. Debi Chakravarti. R&P contact: Arun K. Chakravarti. adv.: B&W page $30; trim 180 x 234; adv. contact: Hony Secretary. bk.rev.; charts; illus.; index. circ. 1,500. (back issues avail.) **Indexed:** Chem.Abstr., Dairy Sci.Abstr., Food Sci.& Tech.Abstr. **Document type:** academic/scholarly publication, proceedings.
—BLDSC (4791.300000); CASDDS; CISTI; Ei; Linda Hall; UnCover.
Supersedes in part: Institution of Chemists (India). Journal and Proceedings.
Refereed Serial

| 540 | II | ISSN 0369-8599 |

INSTITUTION OF CHEMISTS (INDIA). PROCEEDINGS. (Text in English) q. Institution of Chemists (India), 11-4, Dr. Biresh Guha Rd., Calcutta 700 017, India. TEL 91-33-240-3832. Ed. Debi Chakravarti. R&P contact: Arun R. Chakravarti. circ. 2,000. **Indexed:** Chem.Abstr. **Document type:** academic/scholarly publication, proceedings.
Supersedes in part: Institution of Chemists (India). Journal and Proceedings.

| 540 | RM | |

INSTITUTUL DE SUBINGINERI ORADEA. LUCRARI STIINTIFICE: SERIA CHIMIE. (Text in Rumanian, occasionally in English or French; summaries in English, French, German, or Rumanian) 1967. a. Institutul de Subingineri Oradea, Calea Armatei Rosii Nr. 5, 3700 Oradea, Rumania.
Formerly: Institutul Pedagogic Oradea. Lucrari Stiintifice Seria Chimie; which continues in part (in 1973): Institutul Pedagogic Oradea. Lucrari Stiintifice: Seria Matematica, Fizica, Chimie; which superseded in part (in 1971): Institutul Pedagogic Oradea. Lucrari Stiintifice: Seria A and Seria B; which was formerly (until 1969): Institutul Pedagogic Oradea. Lucrari Stiintifice.

| 540 660 | RM | ISSN 1223-8147 |
| | | CODEN: BPICDV |

INSTITUTUL POLITEHNIC DIN IASI. BULETINUL. SECTIA 2: CHIMIE. (Text in English, French, German, Italian, Russian, Spanish) 1946. s-a. exchange basis. Institutul Politehnic din Iasi, Bd. Copou 11, 6600 Jassy, Rumania. TEL 40-1-46577. FAX 40-81-47923. Eds. Alfred Braier, Hugo Rosman. adv.; bk.rev.; bibl. circ. 450. **Indexed:** Appl.Mech.Rev., Chem.Abstr., INSPEC, Math.R., Met.Abstr., Ref.Zh.
—BLDSC (2366.102500); CASDDS; CISTI; Linda Hall.
Former titles: Institutul Politehnic din Iasi. Buletinul. Sectia 2: Chimie si Inginerie Chimica (ISSN 0254-7104); Institutul Politehnic Iasi. Buletinul. Sectia 2: Chimie (ISSN 0373-3246)

INTERMETALLICS. see *METALLURGY*

| 540 | US | ISSN 1056-9480 |
| TS695 | | |

INTERNATIONAL CONFERENCE ON CHEMICAL VAPOR DEPOSITION. PROCEEDINGS. (Subseries of: Electrochemical Society. Proceedings (ISSN 0161-6374)) 1967. irreg., 12th, 1993, Honolulu. price varies. Electrochemical Society, Inc., 10 S. Main St., Pennington, NJ 08534-2896. TEL 609-737-1902. FAX 609-737-2743. (Co-sponsor: American Nuclear Society) R&P contact: Mary E. Yess. (also avail. in microform from UMI; back issues avail.) **Document type:** proceedings —CCC.
Description: Covers all aspects of CVD technology including fundamental chemistry studies and microelectronic and photonic applications.

CHEMISTRY 1753

540 US
INTERNATIONAL FEDERATION OF CLINICAL CHEMISTRY. JOURNAL. 1989. 5/yr. International Scientific Communications, Inc., 30 Controls Dr., Box 42, Shelton, CT 06484-0042. TEL 203-926-9300. FAX 203-926-9310. (U.K. subscr. to: I.S.C. House, Progress Business Centre, 5 Whittle Pkwy., Slough, Berks. SL1 6DQ, England. TEL 44-1628-668881. FAX 44-1628-669199) Ed. Brian Howard. adv. circ. 26,000. **Document type:** trade publication.
Description: Covers laboratory practices, clinical applications, and the evaluation of advances in technology for laboratory testing.

INTERNATIONAL GUIDE TO SCIENTIFIC INSTRUMENTS & CHEMICALS. see INSTRUMENTS

541.28 US ISSN 0020-7608
QD462 CODEN: IJQCB2
INTERNATIONAL JOURNAL OF QUANTUM CHEMISTRY. (Supplement avail.: Quantum Chemistry Symposium (ISSN 0161-3642)) (Text mainly in English; occasionally in French and German; summaries in English, French and German) 1966. 30/yr. $4439 (foreign $4964) (effective 1998). John Wiley & Sons, Inc., Journals, 605 Third Ave., New York, NY 10158. TEL 212-850-6645. FAX 212-850-6021. TELEX 12-7063. E-mail: subinfo@jwiley.com; URL: http://www.wiley.co.uk. (Subscr. outside the Americas to: John Wiley & Sons Ltd., Baffins Ln., Chichester, W. Sussex PO19 1UD, England. TEL 44-1243-779777. FAX 44-1243-776128) Ed. Per Olov Lowdin. adv. B&W page £640, color page £1515; trim 254 x 165. bk.rev.; cum.index. circ. 850. (also avail. in microform from UMI; back issues avail.) **Indexed:** ASCA, Chem.Abstr., Chem.Cit.Ind., Chem.Titles, Curr.Cont., Excerp.Med., Ind.Sci.Rev., INIS Atomind., INSPEC, Mass Spectr.Bull., Mat.Sci.Cit.Ind., Phys.Ber., Sci.Cit.Ind. **Document type:** academic/scholarly publication.
—BLDSC (4542.512000); AskIEEE; CASDDS; CISTI; Ei; Genuine Article; KR SourceOne; Linda Hall; SWETS; UMI; UnCover. **CCC.**
Description: Publishes information on quantam mechanics: fundamental concepts; mathematical structure; applications to atoms, molecules, crystals and molecular biology.
Refereed Serial

541.28 US ISSN 0161-3642
QD462 CODEN: IJQSDI
INTERNATIONAL JOURNAL OF QUANTUM CHEMISTRY. QUANTUM CHEMISTRY SYMPOSIUM. 1967. s-a. price varies. John Wiley & Sons, Inc., Journals, 605 Third Ave., New York, NY 10158-0012. TEL 212-650-8000. **Document type:** proceedings.
—BLDSC (4542.515000); AskIEEE; CASDDS; CISTI; KR SourceOne; SWETS; UMI. **CCC.**
Formerly (until 1977): International Journal of Quantum Chemistry. Symposium (ISSN 0538-821X)

540 370 US ISSN 0306-7696
CODEN: INCECZ
INTERNATIONAL NEWSLETTER ON CHEMICAL EDUCATION. 1974. s-a. £6 for 2 yrs. to individuals; institutions £12. (International Union of Pure and Applied Chemistry, Committee on Teaching and Chemistry, UK) C R C Press, Inc., 2000 Corporate Blvd, N.W., Boca Raton, FL 33431. TEL 561-994-0555; 800-272-7737. FAX 561-998-9784. TELEX 568689-CRC PRESS. (U.K. editorial addr.: Centre for Studies in Science and Mathematics Education, University of Leeds, School of Education, Leeds LS2 9JT, England. TEL 01132-334614. FAX 01132-334683) Ed. Peter Towse. circ. 3,500. **Indexed:** High.Educ.Curr.Aware.Bull. **Document type:** newsletter.
—BLDSC (4544.446500); CASDDS; Linda Hall.

INTERNATIONAL POLYMER SCIENCE AND TECHNOLOGY. see PLASTICS

540 UK ISSN 0958-661X
CODEN: ISMCEE
INTERNATIONAL SERIES OF MONOGRAPHS ON CHEMISTRY. 1977. irreg. vol.27, 1995. price varies. Oxford University Press, Walton St., Oxford OX2 6DP, England. TEL 44-1865-56767. FAX 44-1865-56646. (Subscr. in U.S. to: Oxford University Press Inc., 2001 Evans Rd., Cary, NC 27513. TEL 919-677-0977. FAX 919-677-1714) Ed.Bd. **Indexed:** INSPEC. **Document type:** monographic series.
—BLDSC (4549.259600).
Refereed Serial

541.28 US
CODEN: IJQBDZ
INTERNATIONAL SYMPOSIUM ON ATOMIC, MOLECULAR AND SOLID-STATE THEORY, COLLISION PHENOMENA AND COMPUTATIONAL METHODS. PROCEEDINGS. Represents: International Journal of Quantum Chemistry. Symposium. Variant title: Lowdin Symposia. 1967. irreg. latest no.26, 1992. $30. John Wiley & Sons, Inc., 605 Third Ave., New York, NY 10158. TEL 212-850-6000. Ed. Per-Olov Lowdin. (also avail. in microform from UMI; reprint service avail. from UMI) **Indexed:** Biol.Abstr., Chem.Abstr., INSPEC. **Document type:** proceedings.
—BLDSC (4542.513000); AskIEEE; CASDDS; CISTI; KR SourceOne; SWETS; UMI. **CCC.**
Former titles (until 1977): International Symposium on Atomic, Molecular and Solid-State Theory and Quantum Statistics. Proceedings (ISSN 0360-8832); (until 1973): International Symposium on Atomic, Molecular and Solid-State Theory and Quantum Biology. Proceedings (ISSN 0076-1370); (1967): International Symposium on Atomic, Molecular and Solid-State Theory. Proceedings.
Refereed Serial

660 JA
INTERNATIONAL SYMPOSIUM ON THE CHEMISTRY OF CEMENT. PROCEEDINGS.* irreg., 5th, 1968, Tokyo. $22. Cement Association of Japan, Hattori Bldg., No. 1, 1-chome, Kyobashi, Chuo-ku, Tokyo, Japan. **Document type:** proceedings.

660 US
INTERNATIONAL U V - E B PROCESSING CONFERENCE AND EXHIBITION. PROCEEDINGS. 1988. biennial, latest 1996. $130 (effective 1996). RadTech International North America, 60 Revere Dr., Ste. 500, Northbrook, IL 60062. TEL 847-480-9576. FAX 847-480-9282. E-mail: uveb@radtech.com; URL: http://www.radtech.com. (back issues avail.) **Document type:** proceedings.

540 UK ISSN 1362-671X
▼**INTERNET JOURNAL OF VIBRATIONAL SPECTROSCOPY.** 1996. bi-m. E-mail: ijvs@soton.ac.uk; URL: http://www.teamworks.co.uk/ijvs/. Ed. Patrick Hendra.
●Available only online.

540 US
INTRODUCTION TO GRAVITATION CHEMISTRY; experimental and theoretical reviews. 1974. 2/yr. free. Ensanian Physicochemical Institute, Box 98, Eldred, PA 16731. TEL 814-225-3296. Ed. Minas Ensanian. bk.rev.; bibl.; charts; illus.; circ. 100 (controlled). (processed) **Document type:** corporate report.

540 660 IR ISSN 1021-9986
CODEN: IJCEE9
IRANIAN JOURNAL OF CHEMISTRY AND CHEMICAL ENGINEERING (INTERNATIONAL ENGLISH EDITION). Persian edition: Nashriyyah-i Shimi va-Muhandisi-i Shimi-i Iran (ISSN 1022-7768) 1981. 2/yr. IRl.5000 to individuals (Asia, Africa & Europe $40; Australia, Japan, N. & S. America $50); institutions IRl.7000 (Asia, Africa & Europe $60; Australia, Japan, N. & S. America $70) (effective 1998). Jihad Danishgahi, P.O. Box 14155-4364, Tehran, Iran. TEL 98-21-6497572. FAX 98-21-6400730. TELEX 214259 DMJD IR. Ed. Mohammad N. Sarbolouki. R&P contact: Mohammad S. Haji-Tarverdi. bk.rev. circ. 2,000. **Indexed:** ASCA, Chem.Abstr., Chem.Cit.Ind., MLA Intl.Bibl. **Document type:** academic/scholarly publication.
—CASDDS: Genuine Article.
Description: Publishes original research articles, reviews and short communications on all areas of pure and applied chemistry and chemical engineering (theoretical and experimental). Serves as medium for exchange between Iranian academia and industry and the world scientific community.
Refereed Serial

540 IQ ISSN 0379-8321
QD1 CODEN: JICSDK
IRAQI CHEMICAL SOCIETY. JOURNAL. 1976. s-a. ID.10($30) Iraqi Chemical Society, Box 8011 Salihiyah, Baghdad, Iraq. Ed. Fouad I. Kanbour. abstr. circ. 1,000. **Indexed:** Chem.Abstr. **Document type:** academic/scholarly publication.
—CASDDS; CISTI; Linda Hall.

541.388 NE ISSN 1025-6016
CODEN: IPRXA9
ISOTOPES IN ENVIRONMENTAL AND HEALTH STUDIES. (Text in English, German or Russian) 1966. 8/yr. (in 2 vols., 4 nos./vol.) $151 (effective 1998). Gordon and Breach - Harwood Academic, Amsteldisk 166, 1st Fl., 1079 LH Amsterdam, Netherlands. (Subscr. to: International Publishers Distributor, Box 32160, Newark, NJ 07102. TEL 800-545-8398. FAX 215-750-6343) Ed. P. Krumbiegel. adv.; bk.rev.; charts; illus.; index. **Indexed:** Anal.Abstr., ASCA, Biwk.Pap.Rad.Chem.& Photochem., Chem.Abstr., Chem.Cit.Ind., Curr.Cont., Excerp.Med., Ind.Sci.Rev., INIS Atomind., Risk Abstr., Sci.Cit.Ind. **Document type:** academic/scholarly publication.
—BLDSC (4583.413000); CASDDS; CISTI; Linda Hall; SWETS. **CCC.**
Formerly (until 1995): Isotopenpraxis (ISSN 0021-1915)

541.3 610.28 NE ISSN 0927-4510
QD607.I86
ISOTOPES IN THE PHYSICAL AND BIOMEDICAL SCIENCES. (Text in English) 1987. irreg. v.2, 1991. price varies. Elsevier Science B.V., Books Division, P.O. Box 211, 1000 AE Amsterdam, Netherlands. TEL 31-20-4853911. FAX 31-20-4853705. TELEX 18582 ESPA NL. E-mail: nlinfo-f@elsevier.nl; usinfo-f@elsevier.com; forinfo-kyf04035@niftyserve.or.jp; URL: http://www.elsevier.nl/. (Subscr. in the Americas to: Elsevier Science, Regional Sales Office, Box 945, New York, NY 10159-0945. TEL 212-633-3730. FAX 212-633-3680; Subscr. in Australasia and the Far East to: Elsevier Science (Singapore) Pte Ltd, No.1 Temasek Ave., No.17-01 Millenia Tower, Singapore 039192, Singapore. TEL 65-434-3727. FAX 65-337-2230; Subscr. in Japan to: Elsevier Science Japan, 9-15 Higashi-Azabu 1-chome, Minato-ku, Tokyo 106, Japan. TEL 81-3-5561-5033. FAX 81-3-5561-5047) Eds. E. Buncel, J.R. Jones. (back issues avail.) **Document type:** monographic series.
—KNAW.
Refereed Serial

540 IS ISSN 0021-2148
QD1 CODEN: ISJCAT
ISRAEL JOURNAL OF CHEMISTRY. (Text in English) 1951. 4/yr. $295 (effective 1996). Laser Pages Publishing (1992) Ltd., P.O. Box 50257, Jerusalem 91502, Israel. TEL 972-2-370699. FAX 972-2-370625. Ed. H. Levanon. adv.; charts; illus.; index. circ. 700. (also avail. in microfilm from PMC) **Indexed:** Anal.Abstr., ASCA, Biol.Abstr., Biotech.Abstr., Biwk.Pap.Rad.Chem.& Photochem., Cadscan, Chem.Abstr., Chem.Cit.Ind., Chem.Infd., Curr.Chem.React., Curr.Cont., Dairy Sci.Abstr., Ind.Chem., Ind.Sci.Rev., INIS Atomind., INSPEC, Lead Abstr., Mass Spectr.Bull., Mat.Sci.Cit.Ind., Nutr.Abstr., Sci.Cit.Ind., Zincscan. **Document type:** academic/scholarly publication.
—BLDSC (4583.802000); AskIEEE; CASDDS; CISTI; Ei; Genuine Article; KNAW; KR SourceOne; Linda Hall; SWETS; UnCover. **CCC.**
Description: Publishes current research in chemistry from around the world. Each issues presents papers on a single topic.
Refereed Serial

541.3 615.8 HU ISSN 0865-0497
TK9400 CODEN: IZDIE2
IZOTOPTECHNIKA, DIAGNOSZTIKA/ISOTOPE TECHNICS, DIAGNOSTICS. Short title: I T D. (Text in Hungarian; summaries in English) 1958. 4/yr. $30 (effective Jan. 1994). Izotop Intezet Kft., P.O. Box 77, 1525 Budapest, Hungary. TEL 361-169-9499. FAX 361-169-5087. TELEX 225360. Ed. Istvan Mucha. adv.: page $100. bk.rev.; circ. 350 (controlled). **Indexed:** Biol.Abstr., Chem.Abstr., INIS Atomind., INSPEC. **Document type:** academic/scholarly publication.
—BLDSC (4588.535000); AskIEEE; CASDDS; CISTI; KR SourceOne.
Former titles (until 1989): Izotoptechnika (ISSN 0004-7201); Atomtechnikai Tajekoztato.
Description: Covers the application of stable and radio-isotopes in medicine, industry, agriculture and basic research.

540 JA ISSN 0388-5186
CODEN: JAFODZ
J A I C I FORAMU. (Text in Japanese) 1979. q. free. Japan Association for International Chemical Information - Kagaku Joho Kyokai, 6-25-4 Honkomagome, Bunkyo-ku, Tokyo 113, Japan. TEL 81-3-5978-3631. FAX 81-3-5978-3600. Ed. Osamu Suzuki. **Document type:** newsletter.

CHEMISTRY

540   SZ
JAHRBUCH CHEMISCHE RUNDSCHAU; Jahresausgabe zur Wochenzeitung fuer Chemie, Pharmazie und Lebensmitteltechnik. (Text in German) 1961. a. 25 SFr. Vogt-Schild AG, Zuchwilerstr. 21, CH-4501 Solothurn, Switzerland. TEL 065-247247. FAX 065-247235. Ed. Alfred Widmer. adv.: B&W page 2750 SFr., color page 3850 SFr.; trim 185 x 260; adv. contact: Andreas Benz. bk.rev. circ. 5,800. (tabloid format) **Document type:** academic/scholarly publication.

540   JA   ISSN 0914-6415
JAPANESE SYMPOSIUM ON PLASMA CHEMISTRY. NEWS/PURAZUMA KAGAKU GODO SHINPOJUMU. (Text in English, Japanese) 1988. s-a. Organizing Committee of Japanese Symposium on Plasma Chemistry - Purazuma Kagaku Godo Shinpojumu Soshiki Iinkai, Kyoto Daigaku Kogakubu Denshi Kogakka, Yoshida Honmachi, Sakyo-ku, Kyoto-shi, Kyoto 606, Japan.

JAPANESE WEEKLY ON PHARMACY AND CHEMISTRY/YAKUGYO SHINBUN. see *PHARMACY AND PHARMACOLOGY*

540   CC   ISSN 0254-5861
                CODEN: JHUADF
JIEGOU HUAXUE/CHINESE JOURNAL OF STRUCTURAL CHEMISTRY. (Text in Chinese and English) 1982. bi-m. (4/yr. in English; 2/yr. in Chinese). Y30 (foreign $98) (effective 1997). Chinese Academy of Sciences, Fujian Institute of Research on the Structure of Matter, P.O. Box 143, Fuzhou, Fujian 350002, People's Republic of China. TEL 86-591-3711368. FAX 86-591-3714946. TELEX 92219 FIRSM CN. Ed. Lu Jiaxi. circ. 1,000. **Document type:** academic/scholarly publication.
—BLDSC (5066.876000); CASDDS.
     Description: Publishes original research papers on new experimental and theoretical investigations and outstanding achievements in the area of structural chemistry, particularly molecular and crystal structure, quantum chemistry calculations, IR spectroscopy, NMR, EPR and mass spectroscopy.

660   GW   ISSN 0941-1216
QD1   CODEN: JPCCEM
JOURNAL FUER PRAKTISCHE CHEMIE. CHEMIKER-ZEITUNG. (Text in English, German) 1828. 8/yr. DM.636 (foreign $398) (effective 1997). Huethig GmbH, Postfach 102869, 69018 Heidelberg, Germany. TEL 49-6221-489261. FAX 49-6221-489623. E-mail: matthieb@huethig.de. Ed. H.G.O. Becker. adv.: B&W page DM.1530; trim 178 x 236; adv. contact: Michael Loebach. bk.rev.; charts; illus.; index. circ. 1,100. (also avail. in microfilm from UMI,PMC; microfiche from BHP; reprint service avail. from UMI) **Indexed:** ASCA, Cadscan, Chem.Abstr., Chem.Cit.Ind., Chem.Infd., Curr.Chem.React., Excerpt.Med., Food Sci.& Tech.Abstr., GeoRef., Ind.Chem., Ind.Sci.Rev., INIS Atomind., Lead Abstr., Sci.Cit.Ind. **Document type:** academic/scholarly publication.
—BLDSC (5042.010000); AskIEEE; CASDDS; CISTI; Genuine Article; KR SourceOne; Linda Hall; SWETS; UnCover. **CCC.**
     Formerly: Journal fuer Praktische Chemie (ISSN 0021-8383); Which incorporated: Chemiker-Zeitung (ISSN 0009-2894)
     Description: Scientific journal covering all fields of applied chemistry (synthetic and physical organic chemistry, natural product chemistry, analytical and technical chemistry, element organic and inorganic chemistry).

JOURNAL OF ALLOYS AND COMPOUNDS; an interdisciplinary journal of materials science and solid-state chemistry and physics. see *METALLURGY*

540   NE   ISSN 0165-2370
TP156.P9   CODEN: JAAPDD
JOURNAL OF ANALYTICAL AND APPLIED PYROLYSIS. (Text in English) 1979. 8/yr. fl.2800($1609) (effective 1998). Elsevier Science B.V., P.O. Box 211, 1000 AE Amsterdam, Netherlands. TEL 31-20-4853911. FAX 31-20-4853908. TELEX 18582 ESPA NL. E-mail: nlinfo-f@elsevier.nl; usinfo-f@elsevier.com; forinfo-kyf04035@niftyserve.or.jp; URL: http://www.elsevier.nl/. (Subscr. in the Americas to: Elsevier Science, Regional Sales Office, Box 945, New York, NY 10159-0945. TEL 212-633-3730. FAX 81-3-5561-5033; Subscr. in Australasia and the Far East to: Elsevier Science (Singapore) Pte Ltd, No.1 Temasek Ave., No.17-01 Millenia Tower, Singapore 039192, Singapore. TEL 65-434-3727. FAX 65-337-2230; Subscr. in Japan to: Elsevier Science Japan, 9-15 Higashi-Azabu 1-chome, Minato-ku, Tokyo 106, Japan. TEL 81-3-5561-5033. FAX 81-3-5561-5047) Eds. H.R. Schulten, R.P. Lattimer. adv.; bk.rev.; illus. (also avail. in microform from UMI) **Indexed:** Anal.Abstr., Art & Archaeol.Tech.Abstr., ASCA, Biol.Abstr., Chem.Abstr., Chem.Cit.Ind., Curr.Cont., Deep Sea Res.& Oceanogr.Abstr., Gas Abstr., Geophys.Abstr., Ind.Sci.Rev., Mass Spectr.Bull., Sci.Cit.Ind. **Document type:** academic/scholarly publication.
—BLDSC (4928.100000); CASDDS; CISTI; Ei; Genuine Article; Linda Hall; SWETS; UnCover. **CCC.**
     Description: Devoted to the publication of qualitative and quantitative results relating to: controlled thermal degradation and pyrolysis of technical and biological macromolecules; environmental, geochemical, biological and medical applications of analytical pyrolysis; basic studies in high temperature chemistry, reaction kinetics and pyrolysis mechanisms.
     Refereed Serial

540 551.5   NE   ISSN 0167-7764
QC879.6   CODEN: JATCE2
JOURNAL OF ATMOSPHERIC CHEMISTRY. 1983. 9/yr. fl.1260 to institutions; $646.50 to institutions in U.S. (effective 1998). Kluwer Academic Publishers, Postbus 17, 3300 AA Dordrecht, Netherlands. TEL 31-78-6392392. FAX 31-78-6392254. TELEX 29245 KAPG NL. E-mail: services@wkap.nl; URL: http://www.wkap.nl. (Dist. by: Kluwer Academic Publishers Group, P.O. Box 322, 3300 AH Dordrecht, Netherlands. TEL 31-78-6392392. FAX 31-78-6546474; N. America dist. addr.: Box 358, Accord Sta., Hingham, MA 02018-0358. TEL 617-871-6600. FAX 617-871-6528) Ed.Bd. adv.; bk.rev.; illus.; index. (also avail. in microform from UMI; reprint service avail. from SWZ) **Indexed:** Acid Rain Abstr., Acid Rain Ind., ASCA, Chem.Abstr., Chem.Cit.Ind., Curr.Cont., Deep Sea Res.& Oceanogr.Abstr., Environ.Abstr., Environ.Per.Bibl. (1993-), Excerp.Med., Geo.Abstr.P.G., Ind.Sci.Rev., Int.Abstr.Biol.Sci., Int.Aerosp.Abstr., Meteor.& Geoastrophys.Abstr., Pollut.Abstr., Ref.Zh., Sci.Cit.Ind., Sel.Water Res.Abstr. **Document type:** academic/scholarly publication.
—BLDSC (4949.050000); CASDDS; CIS; Ei; EMDOCS; Genuine Article; KR SourceOne; Linda Hall; SWETS; UMI; UnCover. **CCC.**
     Description: Publishes interdisciplinary studies of the chemistry of the Earth's atmosphere.
     Refereed Serial

540   US   ISSN 0732-8303
QD320   CODEN: JCACDM
JOURNAL OF CARBOHYDRATE CHEMISTRY. 1974. 9/yr. $995 (foreign $1028.75) (effective 1998). Marcel Dekker Journals, 270 Madison Ave., New York, NY 10016. TEL 212-696-9000. FAX 212-685-4540. TELEX 421419. (Subscr. to: Box 5017, Monticello, NY 12701) Ed. D. Kiely. (also avail. in microform from RPI) **Indexed:** Abstr.Bull.Inst.Pap.Chem., ASCA, Biol.Abstr., Chem.Abstr., Chem.Cit.Ind., Chem.Infd., Curr.Chem.React, Curr.Cont., Dairy Sci.Abstr., Excerp.Med., Ind.Chem., Ind.Sci.Rev., Mass Spectr.Bull., Nutr.Abstr., Sci.Cit.Ind. **Document type:** academic/scholarly publication.
—BLDSC (4954.855000); ADONIS; CASDDS; CISTI; Ei; Genuine Article; Linda Hall; SWETS; UMI; UnCover. **CCC.**
     Supersedes in part (in 1982): Journal of Carbohydrates, Nucleosides, Nucleotides (ISSN 0094-0585)
     Refereed Serial

JOURNAL OF CELLULOSE SCIENCE AND TECHNOLOGY. see *PAPER AND PULP*

540   US   ISSN 1058-5834
QD502   CODEN: JCBKEI
JOURNAL OF CHEMICAL AND BIOCHEMICAL KINETICS. 1991. q. $195 (effective 1996). Nova Science Publishers, Inc., 6080 Jericho Tpke., Ste. 207, Commack, NY 11725-2808. TEL 516-499-3103. FAX 516-499-3146. E-mail: novasci1@aol.com. Ed. Gennady E. Zaikov. **Document type:** academic/scholarly publication.
—CASDDS; CISTI; KNAW; Linda Hall.
     Description: Presents original research on the development and use of kinetic methods, in the study of mechanisms and kinetics of chemical and biochemical processes.

540 660   US   ISSN 0021-9568
QD1   CODEN: JCEAAX
JOURNAL OF CHEMICAL AND ENGINEERING DATA. 1959. q. $496 to institutional non-members; members $43 (effective 1997). American Chemical Society, 1155 16th St. N.W., Washington, DC 20036. TEL 800-333-9511. FAX 614-447-3671. E-mail: marsh@jced.com; URL: http://pubs.acs.org/journals/jceaax/index.html. (Subscr. to: Membership and Subscription Services, Box 3337, Columbus, OH 43210. TEL 614-447-3776) Ed. Dr. Kenneth N. Marsh. adv.; bibl.; charts; index. circ. 1,591. (also avail. in microform from RPI; back issues avail.) **Indexed:** A.S.& T.Ind., Abstr.Bull.Inst.Pap.Chem., API Abstr., API Catal., API Hlth.& Environ., API Oil., API Pet.Ref., API Pet.Subst., API Transport., ASCA, Cadscan, Chem.Abstr., Chem.Cit.Ind., Chem.Eng.Abstr., Chem.Infd., Curr.Chem.React., Curr.Cont., E&P Hlth. (1993-), Eng.Ind., Fuel & Energy Abstr., Gas Abstr., Gas Process.& Ppl. (1993-), Ind.Chem., Ind.Sci.Rev., INIS Atomind., Lead Abstr., Off.Tech. (1993-), Petrol.Abstr. (1961-), RAPRA, Sci.Cit.Ind., Soils & Fert., T.C.E.A., W.R.C.Inf., Zincscan. **Document type:** academic/scholarly publication.
●Also available online. Vendor(s): STN International (CJACS).
—BLDSC (4955.800000); CASDDS; CISTI; Ei; Genuine Article; KR SourceOne; Linda Hall; PADDS; SWETS; UMI; UnCover. **CCC.**
     Description: International source for experimental data on pure compounds and their mixtures in the gaseous, liquid, and soild-state, as well as semi-empirical and theoretical correlations for predicting properties of scientific and technological importance.

JOURNAL OF CHEMICAL ECOLOGY. see *ENVIRONMENTAL STUDIES*

540   US   ISSN 0021-9584
QD1   CODEN: JCEDA8
JOURNAL OF CHEMICAL EDUCATION. 1924. m. $32 to individuals (foreign $40); institutions $64 (foreign $80). American Chemical Society, Division of Chemical Education, Inc., c/o Dept. of Chemistry, Montana State University, Bozeman, MT 59717-0340. TEL 406-994-5393. FAX 406-994-5407. E-mail: uchke@earth.oscs.montana.edu; jceonline@chem.wisc.edu; URL: http://jchemed.chem.wisc.edu/. (Subscr. to: Subscription Fulfillment Dept., 1991 Northampton St., Easton, PA 18042. TEL 215-250-7264) Ed. Dr. J.J. Lagowski adv.; bk.rev.; abstr.; charts; film rev.; illus.; stat.; tr.lit.; index. circ. 20,000. (also avail. in microform from UMI,PMC; reprint service avail. from UMI) **Indexed:** Abstr.Bull.Inst.Pap.Chem., Art & Archaeol.Tech.Abstr., Biol.Abstr., C.I.J.E., C.I.S. Abst Chem.Abstr., Chem.Cit.Ind., Chem.Infd., Curr.Cont., Dairy Sci.Abstr., Deep Sea Res.& Oceanogr.Abstr., Educ.Ind., Educ.Tech.Abstr., Excerp.Med., Gen.Sci.Ind., GeoRef., High.Educ.Curr.Aware.Bull., Ind.Sci.Rev., INIS Atomind., INSPEC, Lab.Haz.Bull., Mass Spectr.Bull., Mat.Sci.Cit.Ind., Res.High.Educ.Abstr., Risk Abstr., Sci.Cit.Ind., SSCI. **Document type:** academic/scholarly publication.
●Also available online. Vendor(s): UMI.
—BLDSC (4956.000000); CASDDS; CISTI; Ei; Genuine Article; KR SourceOne; Linda Hall; SWETS; UMI; UnCover. **CCC.**
     Description: Publishes articles and notes, surveyi the state of the art in such wide ranging areas as computers, thermodynamic engines and cryoscopy
     Refereed Serial

540 370   CC   ISSN 1003-3807
JOURNAL OF CHEMICAL EDUCATION. (Text in Chinese; abstracts in English) 1980. bi-m. $63 (effective 1997). Chinese Chemical Society - Zhongguo Huaxuehui, P.O. Box 2709, Beijing 100080, People's Republic of China. TEL 86-10-6256-8157. FAX 86-10-6256-8157. E-mail: qiuxb@infoc3.icas.cn.

JOURNAL OF CHEMICAL EDUCATION: SOFTWARE. SERIES B; for MS-DOS - IBM PC compatible computers. see EDUCATION — Computer Applications

JOURNAL OF CHEMICAL EDUCATION: SOFTWARE. SERIES C; for Apple Macintosh computers. see EDUCATION — Computer Applications

JOURNAL OF CHEMICAL EDUCATION: SOFTWARE. SERIES D; for Windows. see EDUCATION — Computer Applications

JOURNAL OF CHEMICAL EDUCATION: SOFTWARE. SPECIAL ISSUE SERIES. see EDUCATION — Computer Applications

540   UK   ISSN 0308-2342
QD40   CODEN: JRPSDC
JOURNAL OF CHEMICAL RESEARCH. Microfiche and Miniprint edition (UK ISSN 0308-2350) (In two parts: Part S (Synopses) (ISSN 0308-2342) and Part M (Microfiche or Miniprint) (ISSN 0308-2350)) (Text in English, French and German) 1977. m. £437($787) for part S and either Part M (Microfiche) or Part M (Miniprint) (effective 1997). The Royal Society of Chemistry, Thomas Graham House, Science Park, Milton Rd., Cambridge CB4 4WF, England. TEL 44-1223-420066. FAX 44-1223-423429. E-mail: sales@rsc.org; URL: http://chemistry.rsc.org/rsc/. (Subscr. to: Turpin Distribution Services Ltd., Blackhorse Rd., Letchworth, Herts. SG6 1HN, England. TEL 44-1462-672555. FAX 44-1462-480947; And: Postfach 101161, 69451 Weinheim, Germany) (Co-publisher: Wiley - V C H) (Co-sponsors: Societe Francaise de Chimie, Gesellschaft Deutscher Chemiker) Ed. M. Ennis. index. (also avail. in microfiche) Indexed: Anal.Abstr., ASCA, Biol.Abstr., Cadscan, Chem.Abstr., Chem.Cit.Ind., Chem.Infd., Curr.Chem.React., Curr.Cont., Deep Sea Res.& Oceanogr.Abstr., GeoRef., Ind.Chem., Ind.Sci.Rev., INIS Atomind., Lead Abstr., Mass Spectr.Bull., Sci.Cit.Ind., Zincscan. Document type: academic/scholarly publication.
●Also available online. Vendor(s): STN International (CJRSC).
—BLDSC (4957.030000); CASDDS; CISTI; Genuine Article; Linda Hall; SWETS. CCC.
Description: Covers all areas of chemistry. Part S consists of synopses of research papers. Part M contains reproductions of the full texts of the authors' original typescripts corresponding to the synopses appearing in Part S.
Refereed Serial

660   II   ISSN 0021-9622
JOURNAL OF CHEMICALS AND ALLIED INDUSTRIES. (Text in English) bi-m. $30. Ad International, Sayajiganj, Baroda 390005, India. Ed. C.M. Pandit. circ. 2,500.

544.92   NE   ISSN 0378-4347
QD271   CODEN: JCBADL
JOURNAL OF CHROMATOGRAPHY - BIOMEDICAL APPLICATIONS; an international journal devoted to new developments and advances in biomedical applications of chromatography and electrophoresis. Variant title: Journal of Chromatography B. (Subseries of: Journal of Chromatography) (Text in English, French and German; summaries in English) 1977. 26/yr. fl.6225($3578) (effective 1998). Elsevier Science B.V., P.O. Box 211, 1000 AE Amsterdam, Netherlands. TEL 31-20-4853911. FAX 31-20-4853598. TELEX 18582 ESPA NL. E-mail: nlinfo-f@elsevier.nl; usinfo-f@elsevier.com; forinfo-kyf04035@niftyserve.or.jp; URL: http://www.elsevier.nl/. (Subscr. in the Americas to: Elsevier Science, Regional Sales Office, Box 945, New York, NY 10159-0945. TEL 212-633-3730. FAX 212-633-3680; Subscr. in Australasia and the Far East to: Elsevier Science (Singapore) Pte Ltd, No.1 Temasek Ave., No.17-01 Millenia Tower, Singapore 039192, Singapore. TEL 65-434-3727. FAX 65-337-2230; Subscr. in Japan to: Elsevier Science Japan, 9-15 Higashi-Azabu 1-chome, Minato-ku, Tokyo 106, Japan. TEL 81-3-5561-5033. FAX 81-3-5561-5047) Ed. Karel Macek. adv.; bk.rev.; charts; illus.; index. circ 3,463. (also avail. in microform from UMI; back issues avail.) Indexed: Anal.Abstr., ASCA, Biol.Abstr., Biotech.Abstr., C.I.S. Abstr., Chem.Abstr., Chem.Cit.Ind., Chem.Titles, Curr.Adv.Biochem., Curr.Cont., Curr.Cont., Curr.Leather Lit., Dairy Sci.Abstr., Environ.Per.Bibl., Excerp.Med., Food Sci.& Tech.Abstr., Helminthol.Abstr., I.P.A., Ind.Med., Ind.Sci.Rev., Mass Spectr.Bull., Neurosci.Cit.Ind., Ref.Zh., Rev.Plant Path., Sci.Cit.Ind., THA. Document type: academic/scholarly publication.
—BLDSC (4958.350300); ADONIS; CASDDS; CISTI; EMDOCS; Genuine Article; KNAW; Linda Hall; SWETS; UnCover. CCC.
Description: Deals with developments in and applications of chromatographic and electrophoretic techniques related to clinical diagnosis or alterations during medical treatment.
Refereed Serial

540   US   ISSN 1040-7278
QD921   CODEN: JCSCEB
JOURNAL OF CLUSTER SCIENCE. 1989. q. $345 (foreign $405) (effective 1998). Plenum Publishing Corp., 233 Spring St., New York, NY 10013-1578. TEL 212-620-8000. FAX 212-463-0742. TELEX 23-421139. Ed.Bd. adv. (back issues avail.) Indexed: Alloys Ind., Eng.Mat.Abstr., INSPEC (1990-), Met.Abstr., Met.Abstr.Ind., Nonfer.Met.Alert, PCC Alert, Steels Alert, World Alum.Abstr. Document type: academic/scholarly publication.
—BLDSC (4958.792500); AskIEEE; CASDDS; CISTI; KR SourceOne; Linda Hall; SWETS; UMI; UnCover. CCC.
Description: Interdisciplinary exploration of the chemical and physical properties, bonding and structure, mathematics, and molecular biology of clusters.
Refereed Serial

JOURNAL OF COATED FABRICS. see TEXTILE INDUSTRIES AND FABRICS

540   US   ISSN 0192-8651
QD39.3.E46   CODEN: JCCHDD
JOURNAL OF COMPUTATIONAL CHEMISTRY. 1980. 16/yr. $1196 (foreign $1476) (effective 1998). John Wiley & Sons, Inc., Journals, 605 Third Ave., New York, NY 10158. TEL 212-850-6645. FAX 212-850-6021. TELEX 12-7063. (Subscr. outside the Americas to: John Wiley & Sons Ltd., Baffins Ln., Chichester, W. Sussex PO19 1UD, England. TEL 44-1243-779777. FAX 44-1243-776128) Eds. Norman L. Allinger, Paul von Schleyer. adv.: B&W page £640, color page £1515; trim 279 x 210. circ. 1,200. (also avail. in microform from UMI; back issues avail.; reprint service avail. from UMI) Indexed: Abstr.Bull.Inst.Pap.Chem., ASCA, Cadscan, Chem.Abstr., Chem.Cit.Ind., Curr.Cont., Ind.Sci.Rev., INSPEC, Lead Abstr., Math.R., Sci.Cit.Ind., Zincscan. Document type: academic/scholarly publication.
—BLDSC (4963.460000); ADONIS; AskIEEE; CASDDS; CISTI; Ei; Genuine Article; KR SourceOne; Linda Hall; SWETS; UMI; UnCover. CCC.
Description: Covers all aspects of computational chemistry: organic, inorganic, physical, analytical, and molecular mechanics. Also explores quantum chemistry.
Refereed Serial

541.224   NE   ISSN 0095-8972
QD471   CODEN: JCCMBQ
JOURNAL OF COORDINATION CHEMISTRY. 1971. 12/yr. (in 3 vols., 4 nos./vol.). $359 (effective 1998). Gordon and Breach - Harwood Academic, Amsteldisk 166, 1st Fl., 1079 LH Amsterdam, Netherlands. URL: http://www.gbhap.com/Coordination_Chemistry/. (Subscr. to: International Publishers Distributor, Box 32160, Newark, NJ 07102. TEL 800-545-8398. FAX 215-750-6343) Eds. Peter A. Williams, Jim D. Atwood. adv. (also avail. in microform) Indexed: ASCA, Cadscan, Chem.Cit.Ind., Curr.Cont., Ind.Sci.Rev., INIS Atomind., INSPEC, Lead Abstr., Mass Spectr.Bull., Sci.Cit.Ind., Zincscan. Document type: academic/scholarly publication.
●Also available online.
Also available on CD-ROM.
—BLDSC (4965.320000); CASDDS; CISTI; Ei; EMDOCS; KR SourceOne; Linda Hall; SWETS; UnCover. CCC.
Refereed Serial

JOURNAL OF FLUORESCENCE. see CHEMISTRY — Inorganic Chemistry

JOURNAL OF FOOD COMPOSITION AND ANALYSIS; an international journal. see FOOD AND FOOD INDUSTRIES

540   US   ISSN 1082-6076
QD79.C454   CODEN: JLCTFC
JOURNAL OF LIQUID CHROMATOGRAPHY & RELATED TECHNOLOGIES. 1978. 20/yr. $1875 (foreign $1950) (effective 1998). Marcel Dekker Journals, 270 Madison Ave., New York, NY 10016. TEL 212-696-9000. FAX 212-685-4540. TELEX 421419 MARDEEK. (Subscr. to: Box 5017, Monticello, NY 12701) Ed. Jack Cazes. adv.: B&W page $765, color page $1665. charts; illus.; index. (also avail. in microform from RPI; back issues avail.) Indexed: Abstr.Bull.Inst.Pap.Chem., Anal.Abstr., ASCA, Biol.Abstr., Chem.Abstr., Chem.Cit.Ind., Curr.Adv.Biochem., Curr.Adv.Ecol.Sci., Curr.Cont., Dairy Sci.Abstr., Deep Sea Res.& Oceanogr.Abstr., Excerp.Med., Food Sci.& Tech.Abstr., Hort.Abstr., Ind.Sci.Rev., Ind.Vet., INIS Atomind., Mat.Sci.Cit.Ind., Plant Grow.Reg.Abstr., Protozool.Abstr., Sci.Cit.Ind., Small Anim.Abstr., Soils & Fert., Vet.Bull., W.R.C.Inf., Weed Abstr. Document type: academic/scholarly publication.
—BLDSC (5010.510500); ADONIS; CASDDS; CISTI; Ei; Genuine Article; Linda Hall; SWETS; UMI; UnCover. CCC.
Formerly (until 1996): Journal of Liquid Chromatography (ISSN 0148-3919)
Description: Publishes a selection of critical papers dealing with analytical, preparative and process-scale liquid chromatography of all types and technologies.
Refereed Serial

JOURNAL OF LUMINESCENCE; an interdisciplinary journal of research on excited state processes in condensed matter. see PHYSICS — Optics

540   UK   ISSN 0959-9428
TA401   CODEN: JMACEP
JOURNAL OF MATERIALS CHEMISTRY. Online edition (UK ISSN 1364-5501) 1991. m. £560 to institutions (US $1008) (effective 1997). The Royal Society of Chemistry, Thomas Graham House, Science Park, Milton Rd., Cambridge CB4 4W, England. TEL 44-1223-420066. FAX 44-1223-423429. E-mail: sales@rsc.org; URL: http://chemistry.rsc.org/rsc/. (Dist. by: Turpin Distribution Services Ltd., Blackhorse Rd., Letchworth, Herts. SG6 1HN, England. TEL 44-1462-672555. FAX 44-1462-480947) Ed. Janet Leader. (also avail. in microform from UMI) Indexed: Alloys Ind., ASCA, Chem.Cit.Ind., Curr.Cont., Eng.Mat.Abstr., Ind.Sci.Rev., Intl.Polym.Sci.& Tech., Mat.Sci.Cit.Ind., Met.Abstr., Met.Abstr.Ind., Nonfer.Met.Alert, PCC Alert, RAPRA, Sci.Cit.Ind., Steels Alert, World Alum.Abstr. Document type: academic/scholarly publication.
—BLDSC (5012.205000); CASDDS; CISTI; Genuine Article; SWETS; UMI; UnCover. CCC.
Description: Focuses on areas of materials chemistry associated with advanced technology.

JOURNAL OF MATHEMATICAL CHEMISTRY. see MATHEMATICS

JOURNAL OF MATHEMATICAL SCIENCES. see MATHEMATICS

CHEMISTRY

541.2 NE ISSN 0022-2860
QD471 CODEN: JMOSB4
JOURNAL OF MOLECULAR STRUCTURE. (Text in English, French, German) 1967. 45/yr. fl.7680($4414) (effective 1998). Elsevier Science B.V., P.O. Box 211, 1000 AE Amsterdam, Netherlands. TEL 31-20-4853911. FAX 31-20-4853598. TELEX 18582 ESPA NL. E-mail: nlinfo-f@elsevier.nl; usinfo-f@elsevier.com; forinfo-kyf04035@niftyserve.or.jp; URL: http://www.elsevier.nl/. (Subscr. in the Americas to: Elsevier Science, Regional Sales Office, Box 945, New York, NY 10159-0945. TEL 212-633-3730. FAX 212-633-3680; Subscr. in Australasia and the Far East to: Elsevier Science (Singapore) Pte Ltd, No.1 Temasek Ave., No.17-01 Millenia Tower, Singapore 039192, Singapore. TEL 65-434-3727. FAX 65-337-2230; Subscr. in Japan to: Elsevier Science Japan, 9-15 Higashi-Azabu 1-chome, Minato-ku, Tokyo 106, Japan. TEL 81-3-5561-5033. FAX 81-3-5561-5047) Ed.Bd. adv.; bk.rev.; charts; illus. (also avail. in microform from UMI) **Indexed:** ASCA, Bull.Thermodyn.& Thermochem., Cadscan, Chem.Abstr., Chem.Cit.Ind., Chem.Infd., Curr.Cont., Ind.Sci.Rev., INIS Atomind., INSPEC, Lead Abstr., Mass Spectr.Bull., Mat.Sci.Cit.Ind., Phys.Ber., Sci.Cit.Ind., Zincscan. **Document type:** academic/scholarly publication.
—BLDSC (5020.800000); AskIEEE; CASDDS; CISTI; Ei; EMDOCS; Genuine Article; KR SourceOne; Linda Hall; SWETS; UnCover. **CCC.**
Description: Provides new information on molecular stucture, regardless of the physical method or methods used in the study.
Refereed Serial

541.2 CC
JOURNAL OF MOLECULAR STRUCTURE. (Text in English) 1985. q. $218 (effective 1997). Chinese Chemical Society - Zhongguo Huaxuehui, P.O. Box 2709, Beijing 100080, People's Republic of China. TEL 86-10-6256-8157. FAX 86-10-6256-8157. E-mail: qiuxb@infoc3.icas.cn.

540 NE ISSN 0166-1280
QD471 CODEN: THEODJ
JOURNAL OF MOLECULAR STRUCTURE: THEOCHEM; applications of theoretical chemistry to organic, inorganic and biological problems. (Text in English, French or German) 1981. 48/yr. fl.8640($4966) (effective 1998). Elsevier Science B.V., P.O. Box 211, 1000 AE Amsterdam, Netherlands. TEL 31-20-4853911. FAX 31-20-4853598. TELEX 18582 ESPA NL. E-mail: nlinfo-f@elsevier.nl; usinfo-f@elsevier.com; forinfo-kyf04035@niftyserve.or.jp; URL: http://www.elsevier.nl/. (Subscr. in the Americas to: Elsevier Science, Regional Sales Office, Box 945, New York, NY 10159-0945. TEL 212-633-3730. FAX 212-633-3680; Subscr. in Australasia and the Far East to: Elsevier Science (Singapore) Pte Ltd, No.1 Temasek Ave., No.17-01 Millenia Tower, Singapore 039192, Singapore. TEL 65-434-3727. FAX 65-337-2230; Subscr. in Japan to: Elsevier Science Japan, 9-15 Higashi-Azabu 1-chome, Minato-ku, Tokyo 106, Japan. TEL 81-3-5561-5033. FAX 81-3-5561-5047) Ed.Bd. (also avail. in microform from UMI; back issues avail.) **Indexed:** Chem.Abstr., Chem.Cit.Ind., Chem.Infd., Compumath, Curr.Cont., Ind.Sci.Rev., INSPEC (1981-), Mass Spectr.Bull., Mat.Sci.Cit.Ind., Sci.Cit.Ind. **Document type:** academic/scholarly publication.
—AskIEEE; CASDDS; CISTI; Genuine Article; KR SourceOne; SWETS. **CCC.**
Formerly: Theochem.
Description: For chemical physicists, chemists, and biochemists concerned with the application of theoretical methods for the resolution of practical chemical problems.
Refereed Serial

JOURNAL OF NATURAL & PHYSICAL SCIENCES. see *BIOLOGY*

JOURNAL OF NATURAL SCIENCES AND MATHEMATICS. see *SCIENCES: COMPREHENSIVE WORKS*

JOURNAL OF NON-CRYSTALLINE SOLIDS; a journal on the physical, chemical and structural properties of glasses, amorphous semiconductors and metals, including the liquid state. see *PHYSICS*

547 669 NE ISSN 0378-5203
CODEN: JOCLD7
JOURNAL OF ORGANOMETALLIC CHEMISTRY LIBRARY. (Text in English) 1976. irreg., vol.22, 1990. price varies. Elsevier Science B.V., Books Division, P.O. Box 211, 1000 AE Amsterdam, Netherlands. TEL 31-20-4853911. FAX 31-20-4853705. TELEX 18582 ESPA NL. E-mail: nlinfo-f@elsevier.nl; usinfo-f@elsevier.com; forinfo-kyf04035@niftyserve.or.jp; URL: http://www.elsevier.nl/. (Subscr. in the Americas to: Elsevier Science, Regional Sales Office, Box 945, New York, NY 10159-0945. TEL 212-633-3730. FAX 212-633-3680; Subscr. in Australasia and the Far East to: Elsevier Science (Singapore) Pte Ltd, No.1 Temasek Ave., No.17-01 Millenia Tower, Singapore 039192, Singapore. TEL 65-434-3727. FAX 65-337-2230; Subscr. in Japan to: Elsevier Science Japan, 9-15 Higashi-Azabu 1-chome, Minato-ku, Tokyo 106, Japan. TEL 81-3-5561-5033. FAX 81-3-5561-5047) index. **Indexed:** Chem.Abstr., Chem.Infd., Curr.Adv.Ecol.Sci., Curr.Cont., Mass Spectr.Bull. **Document type:** monographic series.
—BLDSC (5027.102000); CASDDS; CISTI; KNAW; SWETS. **CCC.**
Refereed Serial

541 US ISSN 0047-2689
Q199 CODEN: JPCRBU
JOURNAL OF PHYSICAL AND CHEMICAL REFERENCE DATA. (Monographic supplement avail. (ISSN 1063-0651)) 1972. 6/yr. $615 to institutional non-members; members $98 (effective 1997). American Institute of Physics, One Physics Ellipse, College Park, MD 20740-3843. TEL 301-209-3000. (Subscr. to: American Chemical Society, 1155 16th St., N.W., Washington, DC 20036. TEL 516-576-2411. FAX 516-576-2374) (Co-sponsors: American Chemical Society; U.S. National Institute for Standards and Technology) Ed. David R. Lide, Jr. charts; illus.; index. circ. 220. (also avail. in microfilm from AIP; microfiche from AIP; back issues avail.; reprint service avail.) **Indexed:** A.S.& T.Ind., Alloys Ind., Appl.Mech.Rev., ASCA, Bull.Thermodyn.& Thermochem., Cadscan, Chem.Abstr., Chem.Cit.Ind., Curr.Cont., Eng.Mat.Abstr., Gen.Phys.Adv.Abstr., Ind.Sci.Rev., INIS Atomind., INSPEC (1973-), Lead Abstr., Mass Spectr.Bull., Met.Abstr.Ind., Met.Abstr., Nonfer.Met.Alert, Nucl.Sci.Abstr., PCC Alert, Phys.Ber., Soils & Fert., Steels Alert, World Alum.Abstr., Zincscan. **Document type:** academic/scholarly publication.
—BLDSC (5035.700000); AskIEEE; CASDDS; CISTI; Genuine Article; KR SourceOne; Linda Hall; SWETS; UnCover. **CCC.**
Description: Presents compilations of critically evaluated data on physical and chemical properties.
Refereed Serial

541 US ISSN 1063-0651
CODEN: JPCMEI
JOURNAL OF PHYSICAL AND CHEMICAL REFERENCE DATA. MONOGRAPH. 1989. irreg. price varies. American Institute of Physics, 1 Physics Ellipse, College Park, MD 20740-3843. TEL 301-209-3000. (Subscr. to: American Chemical Society, 1155 16th St., N.W., Washington, DC 20036. TEL 516-576-2411. FAX 516-576-2374) (Co-sponsors: American Chemical Society; U.S. National Institute for Standards and Technology)
—BLDSC (5035.705000); CASDDS.

THE JOURNAL OF PHYSICS AND CHEMISTRY OF SOLIDS. see *PHYSICS*

540 UK ISSN 1088-4246
▼ **JOURNAL OF PORPHYRINS AND PHTHALOCYANINES.** 1997. bi-m. $195 (foreign $195) (effective 1998). John Wiley & Sons Ltd., Journals, Baffins Ln., Chichester, W. Sussex PO19 1UD, England. TEL 44-1243-779777. FAX 44-1243-775878. E-mail: info-assets@wiley.co.uk. (Subscr. in the Americas to: John Wiley & Sons, Inc., 605 Third Ave., New York, NY 10158. TEL 212-850-6645. FAX 212-850-6021) Ed. Hari Singh Nalwa. adv.: B&W page £595, color page £1495; trim 297 x 210; adv. contact: Bob Kern. **Document type:** academic/scholarly publication.
—BLDSC (5041.146800).
Refereed Serial

540 US CODEN: RACUDO
TP156.C8
JOURNAL OF RADIATION CURING. 1974. q. $98 (foreign $113). Technology Marketing Corporation, One Technology Plaza, Norwalk, CT 06854. TEL 203-852-6800. FAX 203-853-2845. Ed. Nadji Tehrani; Pub. Ray Tompkins. adv. contact: Mark Hoag. bk.rev.; bibl.; charts; illus.; pat.; index. (back issues avail.) **Indexed:** Alloys Ind., Chem.Abstr., Eng.Mat.Abstr., INIS Atomind., Int.Packag.Abstr., Met.Abstr., Met.Abstr.Ind., Nonfer.Met.Alert, PCC Alert, Print.Abstr., Steels Alert, World Alum.Abstr. **Document type:** trade publication.
—BLDSC (5043.790000); CASDDS; Ei; KR SourceOne; Linda Hall; SWETS.
Former titles (until 1993): Journal of Radiation Curing - Radiation Curing (ISSN 1057-5715); (until Fall 1990): Journal of Radiation Curing (ISSN 0361-6428); Incorporates (1974-1990): Radiation Curing (ISSN 0146-4604)
Refereed Serial

541.2 US ISSN 0022-4766
QD1 CODEN: JSTCAM
JOURNAL OF STRUCTURAL CHEMISTRY. English translation of: Zhurnal Strukturnoi Khimii (RU ISSN 0136-7463) 1960. bi-m. $1595 (foreign $1865) (effective 1998). (Russian Academy of Sciences, RU) Plenum Publishing Corp., Consultants Bureau, 233 Spring St., New York, NY 10013-1578. TEL 212-620-8468. FAX 212-463-0742. TELEX 23-421139. Ed. L.N. Mazalov. (also avail. in microfilm from UMI; back issues avail.) **Indexed:** Alloys Ind., ASCA, Chem.Cit.Ind., Chem.Titles, Curr.Adv.Ecol.Sci., Curr.Cont., Energy Res.Abstr., Eng.Mat.Abstr., Ind.Sci.Rev., INIS Atomind., INSPEC (1972-), Mass Spectr.Bull., Mat.Sci.Cit.Ind., Met.Abstr., Met.Abstr.Ind., Nonfer.Met.Alert, PCC Alert, Sci.Cit.Ind., Steels Alert, World Alum.Abstr. **Document type:** academic/scholarly publication.
—BLDSC (0415.360000); AskIEEE; CISTI; Ei; Genuine Article; KR SourceOne; SWETS; UMI; UnCover. **CCC.**
Refereed Serial

JOURNAL OF SYNTHETIC LUBRICATION; research, development and application of synthetic lubricants and functional fluids. see *PETROLEUM AND GAS*

540 US ISSN 0163-4526
CODEN: JWBCDV
JOURNAL OF WATER BORNE COATINGS; magazine and buyer's guide. 1978-1989; resumed 1992. s-a. $99 (foreign $112). Technology Marketing Corporation, One Technology Plaza, Norwalk, CT 06854. TEL 203-852-6800. FAX 203-853-2845. Ed. Nadji Tehrani; Pub. Tay Tompkins. adv. contact: Mark Hoag. **Indexed:** Chem.Abstr. **Document type:** trade publication.
—BLDSC (5072.536000); CASDDS; CISTI; Ei; Linda Hall; SWETS.
Incorporates: Journal of Water Borne Coatings Buyer's Guide.

540 US ISSN 0277-3813
TS932 CODEN: JWCTDJ
JOURNAL OF WOOD CHEMISTRY AND TECHNOLOGY. 1981. q. $695 (foreign $710) (effective 1998). Marcel Dekker Journals, 270 Madison Ave., New York, NY 10016. TEL 212-696-9000. FAX 212-685-4540. TELEX 421419 MARDEEK. (Subscr. to: Box 5017, Monticello, NY 12701) Eds D.C. Johnson, L.R. Schroeder. (also avail. in microform from RPI) **Indexed:** Abstr.Bull.Inst.Pap.Chem., ASCA, Chem.Abstr., Chem.Cit.Ind., Curr.Cont., Forest.Abstr., Forest Prod.Abstr., Mat.Sci.Cit.Ind., Paper & Bd.Abstr., Sci.Cit.Ind. **Document type:** academic/scholarly publication.
—BLDSC (5072.635500); CASDDS; CISTI; Ei; Genuine Article; Linda Hall; SWETS; UMI; UnCover. **CCC.**
Refereed Serial

JUGOSLAVENSKA MEDICINSKA BIOKEMIJA. see *BIOLOGY — Physiology*

540   UK
K R ONDISC CHEMICAL BUSINESS NEWSBASE. 1993. base vol. (plus m. updates). $2495. The Royal Society of Chemistry, Thomas Graham House, Science Park, Milton Rd., Cambridge CB4 4WF, England. TEL 44-1223-420066. FAX 44-1223-423623. E-mail: sales@rsc.org; URL: http://chemistry.rsc.org/rsc/. (Subscr. to: Knight-Ridder Information Services, CD-ROM Division, 2440 El Camino Real, Mountain View, CA 94040, USA. TEL 415-254-7000. FAX 415-254-8486) **Document type:** trade publication.
●Available only on CD-ROM.
     Formerly: Dialog OnDisc Chemical Business NewsBase.
     Description: Features chemical business news on the chemical industry and all its allied sectors.

540   JA   ISSN 0451-1964
TP1   CODEN: KAKYAU
KAGAKU (KYOTO)/CHEMISTRY. (Supplement avail.: Kagaku, Zokan (ISSN 0368-5470)) (Text in Japanese) 1946. m. 800 Yen per no. Kagaku Dojin Publishing Co., Inc., Gojo-agaru, Tominokoji-dori, Shimogyo-ku, Kyoto 600, Japan. TEL 81-75-352-3373. FAX 81-75-351-8301. Ed. Yuko Taira; Pub. Hiroyuki Shiota. R&P contact: Hisashi Hirabayashi. adv. contact: Ryosuke Sone. **Indexed:** Chem.Abstr., INIS Atomind., Jap.Per.Ind. **Document type:** academic/scholarly publication.
—CASDDS; CISTI; Linda Hall.

540   JA   ISSN 0368-5470
                                CODEN: KGZKA3
KAGAKU. ZOKAN/CHEMISTRY, EXTRA NUMBER. (Text in Japanese) 1956. irreg. 3800 Yen per no. Kagaku Dojin Publishing Co., Inc., Gojo-agaru, Tominokoji-dori, Shimogyo-ku, Kyoto 600, Japan. TEL 81-75-352-3373. Ed. Yuko Taira; Pub. Hiroyuki Shiota. R&P contact: Hisashi Hirabayashi. adv. contact: Ryosuke Sone. **Indexed:** Chem.Abstr., Jap.Per.Ind. **Document type:** academic/scholarly publication.
—CASDDS; CISTI.

KAGAKU KOENKAI KOEN YOSHI. see *PHYSICS*

660   JA
KAGAKU KOGYO NIPPO/CHEMICAL DAILY. (Text in Japanese) 1937. d. Chemical Daily Co. Ltd., International Affairs, 3-16-8 Nihonbashi Hama-cho, Chuo-ku, Tokyo 103, Japan. TEL 81-3-3663-7932. FAX 81-3-3663-7275. TELEX 2422362 NIPPO J. E-mail: chemnews@tky.threewebnet.or.hp; URL: http://www.chemnews-japan.com. Ed. Isao Imanaka. adv. circ. 130,000. **Indexed:** Chem.Abstr.

660 540   JA   ISSN 0022-7684
                              CODEN: KAKTAF
KAGAKU TO KOGYO (TOKYO)/CHEMISTRY AND CHEMICAL INDUSTRY. (Text in Japanese) 1948. m. $111 to members; non-members $276 (effective 1994). Chemical Society of Japan - Nippon Kagakukai, 5, 1-chome, Kanda-Surugadai, Chiyoda-ku, Tokyo 101, Japan. Ed. Akira Morikawa. bibl. circ. 35,000. (reprint service avail. from UMI) **Indexed:** Chem.Abstr., JTA.
—CASDDS; CISTI; Linda Hall; UMI. **CCC.**

540 370   JA   ISSN 0386-2151
                             CODEN: KAKYEY
KAGAKU TO KYOIKU/CHEMICAL EDUCATION. (Text in Japanese) 1952. m. $114 to non-members; members $54. Chemical Society of Japan - Nippon Kagakkai, 1-5, Kanda Surugadai, Chiyoda-ku, Tokyo 101, Japan. Ed. Yoshito Takeuchi. circ. 5,300. **Indexed:** Chem.Abstr.
—CASDDS.

540   JA   ISSN 0386-9512
QD11   CODEN: KAKEE8
KAGAKUSHU KENKYU (TOKYO, 1974)/JAPANESE SOCIETY FOR THE HISTORY OF CHEMISTRY. JOURNAL. (Text in Japanese; summaries in English) 1974. 4/yr. 2000 Yen per no. Kagakushi Gakkai - Japanese Society for the History of Chemistry, Chiba Kogyo Daigaku, 2-17, Tsudanuma 2-chome, Narashino-shi, Chiba-ken 275, Japan. **Indexed:** Chem.Abstr., Jap.Per.Ind.
—CASDDS.

KAIYO KAGAKU KENKYU/RESEARCH INSTITUTE OF OCEANOCHEMISTRY. TRANSACTIONS. see *EARTH SCIENCES — Oceanography*

540   JA   ISSN 0917-2408
                              CODEN: KKAGEY
KANKYO KAGAKU/JOURNAL OF ENVIRONMENTAL CHEMISTRY. (Text in English, Japanese) 1991. q. 4000 Yen per no. Kankyo Kagaku Kenkyukai - Japan Society for Environmental Chemistry, Kokuritsu Kankyo Kenkyujo Kaggaku Kankyobu, 16-2, Onogawa, Tsukuba-shi, Ibaraki-ken 305, Japan. **Indexed:** Food Sci.& Tech.Abstr.
—BLDSC (4979.359500); CASDDS.

540   JA
KAO INSTITUTE FOR FUNDAMENTAL RESEARCH. BULLETIN. (Text in English) 1985. a. Kao Corporation, Kao Institute for Fundamental Research, 2606, Akabane, Ichikai-machi, Haga-gun, Tochigi-ken 321-34, Japan. **Document type:** bulletin.

540   KR   ISSN 0453-3585
                              CODEN: KAKAAQ
KATALIZ I KATALIZATORY; respublikanskii mezhvedomstvennyi sbornik nauchnykh trudov. (Text in Russian) 1965. a. (Akademiya Nauk Ukrainy, Institut Fizicheskoi Khimii im. L.V. Pisarzhevskogo) Izdatel'stvo Naukova Dumka, c/o Yu.A. Khramov, Dir, Ul. Repina, 3, Kiev 252 601, Ukraine. (Subscr. to: Mezhdunarodnaya Kniga, Moscow, G-200, Russia) Ed. V.M. Vlasenko. **Indexed:** Chem.Abstr.
—CASDDS; CISTI; Linda Hall.

338.4 660   FI   ISSN 0355-1628
TP1   CODEN: KMKMAA
KEMIA - KEMI/FINNISH CHEMISTRY. (Text in Finnish and Swedish, summaries in English) 1974. m. FIM 600 (effective 1997). (Suomen Kemian Seura - Association of Finnish Chemical Societies) Kemian Kustannus Oy, Mariankatu 26 B9, FIN-00170 Helsinki, Finland. TEL 358-9-6220930. FAX 358-9-62209337. (Co-sponsor: Chemical Industry Federation of Finland) Ed. Marjatta Kivimaki-Majanen. adv. contact: Irja Marttila. bk.rev.; abstr.; charts; illus.; mkt.; pat.; stat.; tr.lit.; tr.mk.; index. circ. 5,600. (reprint service avail. from UMI,ISI) **Indexed:** Chem.Abstr., Chem.Eng.Abstr., Curr.Biotech.Abstr., Dairy Sci.Abstr., Food Sci.& Tech.Abstr., INIS Atomind., Paper & Bd.Abstr., Soils & Fert., T.C.E.A. **Document type:** trade publication.
—BLDSC (5089.263500); CASDDS; CISTI; Ei; Linda Hall.
     Formed by the merger of: Kemian Teollisuus (ISSN 0022-9822) & Suomen Kemistilehti A (ISSN 0371-4098) & Finska Kemistsamfundet. Meddelanden (ISSN 0015-2498)

660   CI   ISSN 0022-9830
TP1   CODEN: KJUIAR
KEMIJA U INDUSTRIJI; casopis kemicara i tehnologa Jugoslavije. (Text in Croatian; summaries in English) 1952. m. $80. Savez Kemicara i Tehnologa Hrvatske, Berislaviceva 6-1, P.O. Box 697, 41001 Zagreb, Croatia. Ed. Ivan Butula. adv.; bk.rev.; charts; illus. circ. 2,000. **Indexed:** Chem.Abstr., Chem.Eng.Abstr., Chem.Infd., INIS Atomind., Nutr.Abstr., Ref.Zh., T.C.E.A.
—BLDSC (5089.300000); CASDDS; CISTI; Ei.

540   SW
KEMIKALIER. 1976. biennial. SEK 160 (effective 1997). Plast- och Kemibranscherna - Plastics and Chemicals Federation, P.O. Box 105, S-101 22 Stockholm, Sweden. FAX 46-8-411-45-26.

540   SW   ISSN 1104-2788
QD1   CODEN: KETIAL
KEMISK TIDSKRIFT, KEMIVAERLDEN. 1889. 12/yr. SEK 933 (effective 1998). (Svenska Kemistsamfundet) Arbor Publishing AB, P.O. Box 26212, S-100 41 Stockholm, Sweden. TEL 46-8-611-60-30. FAX 46-8-679-90-50. (Co-sponsors: Svenska Kemiingenjoerers Riksfoering; Sveriges Kemiska Industrikontor) Ed. Andres Forstroem. adv. contact: Stephan Martins. bk.rev.; abstr.; bibl.; charts; illus.; stat.; index. circ. 10,500. **Indexed:** Biol.Abstr., C.I.S.Abstr., Chem.Abstr., Chem.Infd., Curr.Cont., Dairy Sci.Abstr., Food Sci.& Tech.Abstr., GeoRef., INIS Atomind., Paper & Bd.Abstr., Risk Abstr. **Document type:** trade publication.
—BLDSC (5089.355000); CASDDS; CISTI; Ei; KNAW; Linda Hall; UMI.
     Formed by the 1993 merger of: Kemivaerlden (ISSN 1102-6650) & Kemisk Tidskrift (ISSN 0039-6605); Formed by the 1969 merger of: Svensk Kemisk Tidskrift; Kemiteknik.

540   FI   ISSN 0022-9865
KEMISTI/KEMISTEN. (Text in Finnish and Swedish) bi-m. FIM 250. Suomen Kemistiliitto - Finnish Union of Chemists, Rautatielaisenkatu 6, 00520 Helsinki 52, Finland. FAX 90-142208. Ed. Kirsti Janhunen. adv. contact: Raili Pimia. charts. circ. 5,000.
     Description: Focuses on professional and social questions concerning chemists, the chemical industry and trade.

540   FI   ISSN 0356-7818
KEMISTIN KALENTERI. (Text in Finnish and Swedish) 1947. a. Suomen Kemistiliitto - Finnish Union of Chemists, Rautatielaisenkatu 6, 00520 Helsinki 52, Finland. Ed. Irmeli Puntari. adv. contact: Irmeli Puntari. circ. 3,500.

660   UK
KEY NOTE MARKET REVIEW: U K CHEMICAL INDUSTRY. Variant title: U K Chemical Industry. irreg., no.2, 1993. £410. Key Note Ltd., Field House, 72 Oldfield Rd., Hampton, Middlesex TW12 2HQ, England. TEL 44-181-783-0755. FAX 44-181-783-0049. **Document type:** trade publication.
●Also available online.
Also available on CD-ROM.

540   LV   ISSN 0201-7474
TS920   CODEN: KHDRDQ
KHIMIYA DREVESINY. (Text in Russian) 1974. bi-m. $109 (effective 1996). (Latvijas Zinatnu Akademijas - Latvian Academy of Sciences) Izdevejs Zinatne, Turgeneva iela, 19, Riga LV-1530, Latvia. TEL 371-2-212797. Ed. V. Viesturs. bk.rev.; illus.; index. circ. 77,251. **Indexed:** Abstr.Bull.Inst.Pap.Chem., Art & Archaeol.Tech.Abstr., Chem.Abstr., Crop Physiol.Abstr., Forest.Abstr., Forest Prod.Abstr., INIS Atomind., Paper & Bd.Abstr. **Document type:** academic/scholarly publication.
—CASDDS; CISTI; Linda Hall. **CCC.**

660   KR   ISSN 0204-3556
TD204   CODEN: KTVODL
KHIMIYA I TEKHNOLOGIYA VODY; nauchno-teoreticheskii zhurnal. English translation: Journal of Water Chemistry and Technology (US ISSN 1063-455X) (Text in Russian; summaries in English and Russian) 1979. m. $155 (effective 1998). Akademiya Nauk Ukrainy, Institut Koloinoi Khimii ta Khimii Vodu, Bul'v. Akad. Vernads'kogo, 42, 252680 Kief, Ukraine. TEL 38-44-4443126. (Dist. by: Mezhdunarodnaya Kniga, B. Yakimanka 39, 117049 Moscow, Russia. TEL 7-095-2384967. FAX 7-095-2384634) Ed. A.T. Pilipenko. **Indexed:** Chem.Abstr., Djerelo, Sugar Ind.Abstr., W.R.C.Inf. **Document type:** academic/scholarly publication.
—BLDSC (0393.846500); CASDDS; CISTI; Linda Hall. **CCC.**

540   RU   ISSN 0130-5972
                              CODEN: KHZHAZ
KHIMIYA I ZHIZN'. 1965. m. $150 (effective 1998). (Rossiiskaya Akademiya Nauk) Izdatel'stvo Nauka, 90 Profsoyuznaya ul., 117864 Moscow, Russia. (Dist. by: Mezhdunarodnaya Kniga, B. Yakimanka 39, 117049 Moscow, Russia. TEL 7-095-2384967. FAX 7-095-2384634) circ. 150,000. **Indexed:** Chem.Abstr., Int.Aerosp.Abstr.
—CASDDS; CISTI; Linda Hall.

KHIMIYA TVERDOGO TOPLIVA. see *ENGINEERING — Chemical Engineering*

CHEMISTRY

540   RU   ISSN 0869-8538
TP1   CODEN: KIURFI
KHIMIYA V INTERESAKH USTOICHEVOGO RAZVITIYA.
English edition: Chemistry for Sustainable Development (ISSN 0869-8546) (Text in Russian; summaries in English) 1963. 6/yr. 360000 Rub.($138) (effective 1998). Rossiiskaya Akademiya Nauk, Sibirskoe Otdelenie, Morskoi pr. 2, 630090 Novosibirsk, Russia. TEL 7-3832-350570. FAX 7-3832-356002. (Dist. by: Mezhdunarodnaya Kniga, B. Yakimanka 39, 117049 Moscow, Russia. TEL 7-095-2384967. FAX 7-095-2384634) Ed. V.A. Koptiuk. bk.rev.; illus.; index. circ. 1,400. **Indexed:** Alloys Ind., Cadscan, Chem.Abstr., Chem.Cit.Ind., Chem.Titles, Eng.Mat.Abstr., INIS Atomind., Lead Abstr., Mass Spectr.Bull., Mat.Sci.Cit.Ind., Met.Abstr., Met.Abstr.Ind., Nonfer.Met.Alert, PCC Alert, Sci.Cit.Ind., Steels Alert, Sugar Ind.Abstr., World Alum.Abstr., Zincscan. **Document type:** academic/scholarly publication.
—BLDSC (0394.220000); CASDDS; CISTI; Linda Hall. **CCC.**
    Former titles (until 1993): Sibirskii Khimicheskii Zhurnal; (until 1990): Akademiya Nauk S.S.S.R. Sibirskoe Otdelenie. Izvestiya. Seriya Khimicheskikh Nauk (ISSN 0002-3426)

KHIMIYA V SEL'SKOM KHOZYAISTVE. see *AGRICULTURE*

540   JA
KIKAN KAGAKU SOSETSU/SURVEY OF CHEMISTRY. QUARTERLY. (Text in Japanese; summaries in English, Japanese) 1973. q. 4800 Yen. (Nippon Kagakkai - Chemical Society of Japan) Gakkai Shuppan Senta - Japan Scientific Societies Press, 2-10, Hongo 6-chome, Bunkyo-ku, Tokyo 113, Japan. **Indexed:** Chem.Abstr., Jap.Per.Ind.

540   MY   ISSN 0126-9070
QD1   CODEN: KMIADZ
KIMIA.* 1970. a. free to qualified personnel. Malaysian Institute of Chemistry, c/o Rubber Research Institute of Malaysia, 260 Jalan Ampang, 50450 Kuala Lumpur, Malaysia. adv.; illus. circ. 1,500. **Indexed:** Chem.Abstr., INIS Atomind.
—CASDDS.

540   PH   ISSN 0115-2130
    CODEN: KIMIDH
KIMIKA. (Text in English) 1961. a. P.100 (foreign $15). Kapisanan ng mga Kimiko sa Pilipinas - Chemical Society of the Philippines, PFC Office, NSRI Bldg., U.P. Diliman, Quezon City, Philippines. TEL 632-97-57-74. FAX 632-928-68-68. E-mail: nsri@nicole.upd.edu.ph; URL: http://luff.latrobe.edu.au/~chejs/chemistry/kkp.html. Ed. Fortunato Sevilla III. adv.; B&W page P.3000; adv. contact: Florian Del Mundo. bk.rev.; charts; illus. circ. 750. (processed) **Indexed:** Chem.Abstr.
—BLDSC (5095.330000); CASDDS.
    Formerly: Chemists' Quarterly (ISSN 0045-6527)
    Description: Publishes original papers on chemical researches and chemical education, preliminary communications and reviews.
    Refereed Serial

540   JA   ISSN 0916-4367
KISO KAGAKU KENKYUJO KOENKAI KOENSHU/PROCEEDINGS FOR THE I F C SYMPOSIUM. (Text in English, Japanese) 1985. a. Kiso Kagaku Kenkyujo - Institute for Fundamental Chemistry, 3-4, Takano Nishibiraki-cho, Sakyo-ku, Kyoto 606, Japan. **Document type:** proceedings.

540 620   NO   ISSN 0023-1983
QD1   CODEN: KJEMAR
KJEMI. 1913. m. (10/yr.). NOK 295 in Nordic countries; rest of Europe NOK 400; elsewhere NOK 450 (effective 1996 & 1997). (Norsk Kjemisk Selskap - Norwegian Chemical Society) Kjemi AS, Storgata 14, P.O. Box 151 Sentrum, 0102 Oslo 1, Norway. TEL 47-22-17-20-60. FAX 47-22-17-12-79. E-mail: kjemi@online.no. Ed. Lars Ole Oerjasaeter. R&P contact: Lars Ole Oerjasaeter. adv. contact: Sveinung Paulsen. bk.rev.; bibl.; illus.; pat.; stat.; tr.lit.; index. circ. 7,663. (also avail. in microform from UMI; reprint service avail. from UMI) **Indexed:** Alloys Ind., Chem.Abstr., Chem.Infd., Eng.Ind., Eng.Mat.Abstr., INIS Atomind., Met.Abstr., Met.Abstr.Ind., PCC Alert, Steels Alert, World Alum.Abstr. **Document type:** academic/scholarly publication.
—BLDSC (5098.430000); CASDDS; CISTI; Linda Hall; UMI.
    Former titles (until 1968): Tidsskrift for Kjemi, Bergvesen og Metallurgi (ISSN 0040-7097); (until 1941): Tidsskrift for Kjemi og Bergvesen (ISSN 0371-8697)

KLEBEN & DICHTEN; Klebstoffe, Dichtstoffe, Geraete- und Anlagentechnik, Anwendungen. see *PLASTICS*

540   JA   ISSN 0389-0279
QD1   CODEN: KDRKDD
KOCHI UNIVERSITY. FACULTY OF SCIENCE. MEMOIRS. SERIES C, CHEMISTRY/KOCHI DAIGAKU RIGAKUBU KIYO. KAGAKU. (Text in English) 1980. a. Kochi University, Faculty of Science - Kochi Daigaku Rigakubu, 5-1, Akebonocho 2-chome, Kochi-shi, Kochi-ken 780, Japan. **Indexed:** Chem.Abstr.
—BLDSC (5597.834000); CISTI.

KOLORISZTIKAI ERTESITO/COLORISTICAL REVIEW. see *ENGINEERING — Chemical Engineering*

KOMPASS CHEMICAL, PLASTIC AND RUBBER PRODUCTS. see *BUSINESS AND ECONOMICS — Trade And Industrial Directories*

KOMPASS PROFESSIONNEL. CHIMIE, PLASTIQUES, CAOUTCHOUC, PRODUITS MINERAUX. see *BUSINESS AND ECONOMICS — Trade And Industrial Directories*

660.025489   DK   ISSN 0106-1119
KOMPASS SELECT EXPORT. CHEMICAL INDUSTRY. Cover title: Euro Kompass Denmark. Chemicals. (Text in Danish, English, French, German and Spanish) 1980. a. DKK 300 (listed companies DKK 100). Forlaget Kompass Danmark, Oeveroedvej 5, DK-2840 Holte, Denmark. TEL 45-45-41-21-00. FAX 45-45-41-21-00. illus. **Document type:** directory.
● Also available on CD-ROM.
    Formerly: Kompass Select Denmark. Chemicals.

540   BE   ISSN 0770-1926
    CODEN: VCTIDT
KONINKLIJKE VLAAMSE CHEMISCHE VERENIGING. TIJDINGEN. (Text in Dutch) 1939. m. Koninklijke Vlaams Chemische Vereniging, 168 Coupure Rechts, 9000 Ghent, Belgium. adv.; bk.rev.; index. **Indexed:** Chem.Abstr., Curr.Cont. **Document type:** bulletin.
—CASDDS.
    Former titles (until 1973): Vlaamse Chemische Vereniging. Mededelingen (ISSN 0369-2787); (until 1941): Vlaamse Chemische Vereniging. Huishoudelijke Mededelingen (ISSN 0772-3822)

KORROZIOS FIGYELO/CORROSION OBSERVER. see *PAINTS AND PROTECTIVE COATINGS*

KUMAMOTO JOURNAL OF MATHEMATICS. see *MATHEMATICS*

540   KN
KWAHAKGWA KWAHAKGONEOP. (Text in Korean) bi-m. Korean Academy of Sciences, Hamhung Branch, Pyongyang, N. Korea.

KYUSHU DAIGAKU CHUO BUNSEKI SENTA HOKOKU/KYUSHU UNIVERSITY. CENTER OF ADVANCED INSTRUMENTAL ANALYSIS. REPORT. see *INSTRUMENTS*

KYUSHU DAIGAKU CHUO BUNSEKI SENTA NYUSU/KYUSHU UNIVERSITY. CENTER OF ADVANCED INSTRUMENTAL ANALYSIS. NEWS. see *INSTRUMENTS*

540   JA   ISSN 0085-2635
QD1   CODEN: MFKCAL
KYUSHU UNIVERSITY. FACULTY OF SCIENCE. MEMOIRS. SERIES C: CHEMISTRY/KYUSHU DAIGAKU RIGAKUBU KIYO C. KAGAKU. (Text in English) 1948. a. exchange basis. Kyushu University, Faculty of Science, Department of Chemistry - Kyushu Daigaku Rigakubu Kagaku Kyoshitsu, 6-10-1 Hakozaki, Higashi-ku, Fukuoka 812, Japan. circ. 650. **Indexed:** Alloys Ind., Chem.Abstr., Eng.Mat.Abstr., INIS Atomind., INSPEC, JCT, JTA, Mass Spectr.Bull., Met.Abstr., Met.Abstr.Ind., Nonfer.Met.Alert, PCC Alert, Steels Alert, World Alum.Abstr.
—BLDSC (5600.000000); AskIEEE; CASDDS; CISTI; KR SourceOne; Linda Hall; UnCover.

540   US
LABORATORY DIGEST (WASHINGTON). 1982. s-a. free. American Chemical Society, 1155 16th St., N.W., Washington, DC 20036. TEL 202-872-4363. FAX 202-872-4615. Ed. Lisa Stenza. adv. circ. 75,000. **Document type:** academic/scholarly publication.

540 531   AG   ISSN 0327-0793
    CODEN: LAARE8
LATIN AMERICAN APPLIED RESEARCH. (Text in English) 1988. q. $100 (effective 1996). Asociacion de Investigadores en Ciencias de Ingenieria Quimica y Quimica Aplicada, Plapiqui (UNS - Conicet), C.C. 717, 8000 Bahia Blanca, Argentina. TEL 54-091-552541. FAX 54-091-565764. TELEX 81758 PPINQ. E-mail: dtpretel@criba.edu.ar. (Co-sponsors: Comite Argentino de Transferencia de Calor y Materia; Centro Latinoamericano de Transferencia de Calor y Materia; Asociacion Agentina de Mecanica Computacional) Ed. Dr. Esteban A. Brignole. bk.rev. **Document type:** academic/scholarly publication.
—CASDDS; CISTI; Linda Hall; SWETS; UnCover.

540   LV   ISSN 0868-8249
QD1   CODEN: LKZUE8
LATVIJAS KIMIJAS ZURNALS. 1961. bi-m. $37 (effective 1998). (Latvijas Zinatnu Akademijas) Izdevejs Zinatne, Turgeneva iela, 19, Riga LV-1530, Latvia. TEL 371-2-212797. (Dist. by: Mezhdunarodnaya Kniga, B. Yakimanka 39, 117049 Moscow, Russia. TEL 7-095-2384967. FAX 7-095-2384634) Ed. T. Millers. index. **Indexed:** Abstr.Bull.Inst.Pap.Chem., Alloys Ind., Chem.Abstr., Eng.Mat.Abstr., Mass Spectr.Bull., Met.Abstr.Ind., Met.Abstr., Nonfer.Met.Alert, PCC Alert, Steels Alert, World Alum.Abstr.
—BLDSC (0095.410000); CASDDS; CISTI; KNAW; Linda Hall. **CCC.**
    Formerly (until 1991): Akademiya Nauk Latviisko S.S.R. Izvestiya. Seriya Khimicheskaya (ISSN 0002-3248)

540   IT   ISSN 1122-4967
LEADER FOR CHEMIST. 1990. 10/yr. Via Olmetto 5, 20123 Milan, Italy. TEL 2-87-83-97. FAX 2-86-65-76. Ed. Genina Jacoboni. adv.

LEBENSMITTEL- UND BIOTECHNOLOGIE. see *FOOD AND FOOD INDUSTRIES*

LEBENSMITTELCHEMIE. see *FOOD AND FOOD INDUSTRIES*

540   US   ISSN 0342-4901
    CODEN: LNCHDA
LECTURE NOTES IN CHEMISTRY. 1976. irreg., vol.64, 1995. price varies. Springer-Verlag, 175 Fifth Ave., New York, NY 10010. TEL 212-460-1500. FAX 212-473-6272. (Also: Berlin, Heidelberg, Tokyo and Vienna) Ed.Bd. (reprint service avail. from ISI) **Indexed:** Chem.Abstr., INSPEC. **Document type:** monographic series.
—BLDSC (5180.184600); CASDDS; CISTI. **CCC.**

540   SI
LECTURES AND COURSE NOTES IN CHEMISTRY. (Text English) 1991. irreg., vol.5, 1991. price varies. World Scientific Publishing Co. Pte. Ltd., Farrer Rd., P.O. Box 128, Singapore 9128, Singapore. TEL 65-3825663. FAX 54-3825919. TELEX RS 28561 WSPC. (UK addr.: 57 Shelton St., Covent Garden, London WC2H 9HE, England. TEL 44-171-836-0888; US addr.: 1060 Main St., River Edge, NJ 07661. TEL 800-227-7562) **Document type:** academic/scholarly publication.

660 GW ISSN 0024-2845
TP1101 CODEN: LIBOAM
LICHTBOGEN; Hauszeitschrift der Huels-Gesellschaften. 1951. s-a. free. Huels AG, 45764 Marl, Germany. Ed. Georg Heinze. **Indexed:** Chem.Abstr., INSPEC. **Document type:** trade publication.
—AskIEEE; CASDDS; KR SourceOne.

540 GW ISSN 0947-3440
QD241 CODEN: LANAEM
LIEBIGS ANNALEN; organic and bioorganic chemistry. (Text in English) 1832. m. DM.2175 (foreign DM.2235) (effective 1997). (Gesellschaft Deutscher Chemiker) Wiley - V C H, Postfach 101161, 69451 Weinheim, Germany. TEL 49-6201-606147. FAX 49-6201-606117. TELEX 465516-VCHWH-D. E-mail: liebigsann@vchgroup.de; URL: http://www.vchgroup.de. (Subscr. in the Americas to: John Wiley & Sons, Inc., 605 Third Ave., New York, NY 10185. TEL 212-850-6645. FAX 212-580-6021) Ed. Robert Temme. adv. contact: R. Roth. circ. 1,500. (also avail. in microfilm from VCI; reprint service avail. from ISI; back issues avail.) **Indexed:** Apic.Abstr., ASCA, Biol.Abstr., Biotech.Abstr., Cadscan, Chem.Abstr., Chem.Cit.Ind., Curr.Adv.Ecol.Sci., Curr.Chem.React., Curr.Cont., Excerp.Med., Ind.Chem., Ind.Sci.Rev., INIS Atomind., Lead Abstr., Met.Abstr., Nutr.Abstr., Sci.Cit.Ind., Zincscan. **Document type:** academic/scholarly publication.
●Also available online.
—BLDSC (5208.516000); CASDDS; CISTI; Ei; Genuine Article; Linda Hall; SWETS; UnCover. **CCC.**
Former titles: Liebigs Annalen der Chemie (ISSN 0170-2041); Justus Liebigs Annalen der Chemie (ISSN 0075-4617)
Description: Publishes original papers in the areas of experimental organic chemistry, bioorganic chemistry, and the chemistry of natural products.

540 NE ISSN 0278-6281
QP501 CODEN: LCHRDM
LIFE CHEMISTRY REPORTS. (Supplement series avail.) 2/yr. $196 (effective 1998). Gordon and Breach - Harwood Academic, Amsteldisk 166, 1st Fl., 1079 LH Amsterdam, Netherlands. (Subscr. to: International Publisher Distributor, Box 32160, Newark, NJ 07102. TEL 800-545-8398. FAX 215-750-6343) Eds. D. Cocco, J.V. Bannister. (also avail. in microform) **Indexed:** Chem.Abstr. **Document type:** monographic series.
—BLDSC (5208.921250); CASDDS; CISTI; UnCover. **CCC.**
Refereed Serial

540 CC ISSN 1001-5493
CODEN: LJYXE5
LIZI JIAOHUAN YU XIFU. (Text in Chinese) bi-m. Nankai Daxue, Gaofenzi Huaxue Yanjiusuo - Nankai University, Polymer Chemistry Institute, Balitai, Nankai-qu, Tianjin 300071, People's Republic of China. TEL 345084. Ed. He Binglin.
—BLDSC (4564.320000); CASDDS.

540 US
CCUTCHEON'S EMULSIFIERS AND DETERGENTS - INTERNATIONAL EDITION. a. $72 (effective 1997). M C Publishing Company, Inc., McCutcheon Division, 175 Rock Rd., Glen Rock, NJ 07452. TEL 201-652-2655. FAX 201-652-3419. Ed. Michael Allured. **Document type:** directory.
Formerly (until 1981): McCutcheon's Detergents and Emulsifiers - International Edition (ISSN 0734-0567)

540 US ISSN 0145-7055
TP992.5
CCUTCHEON'S EMULSIFIERS AND DETERGENTS - NORTH AMERICAN EDITION. 1949. a. $72 (effective 1997). M C Publishing Company, Inc., McCutcheon Division, 175 Rock Rd., Glen Rock, NJ 07452. TEL 201-652-2655. FAX 201-652-3419. Ed. Michael Allured. adv. circ. 5,300. **Document type:** directory.
Description: List of over 4,000 surfactant materials for users and purchasers, categorized by trade name, identity, manufacturer, concentration, type, HLB index, CAS number, and application.

540 HU ISSN 0025-0155
QD1 CODEN: MGKFA3
MAGYAR KEMIAI FOLYOIRAT/HUNGARIAN JOURNAL OF CHEMISTRY. (Text in Hungarian; summaries in another language) 1895. m. $80. Magyar Kemikusok Egyesulete - Hungarian Chemical Society, Fo u. 68, 1027 Budapest, Hungary. TEL 36-1-2016883. Ed. E. Pungor. adv.; bk.rev.; charts; illus.; index. circ. 1,400. **Indexed:** Anal.Abstr., ASCA, Biol.Abstr., Chem.Abstr., Chem.Cit.Ind., Chem.Infd., Curr.Chem.React., Curr.Cont., GeoRef., Ind.Chem., Ind.Sci.Rev., INIS Atomind., Mass Spectr.Bull., Mat.Sci.Cit.Ind., Met.Abstr., Ref.Zh., Sci.Cit.Ind., Soils & Fert., World Alum.Abstr. **Document type:** bulletin.
—BLDSC (5342.000000); CASDDS; CISTI; Ei; Genuine Article.

540 HU ISSN 0025-0163
QD1 CODEN: MGKLAL
MAGYAR KEMIKUSOK LAPJA. 1946. m. $43. Magyar Kemikusok Egyesulete - Hungarian Chemical Society, Fo u. 68, 1027 Budapest, Hungary. TEL 36-1-2016883. Ed. Gabor Szekeres. adv.; bk.rev. **Indexed:** Anal.Abstr., Art & Archaeol.Tech.Abstr., Chem.Abstr., Chem.Infd., INIS Atomind. **Document type:** bulletin.
—BLDSC (5343.000000); CASDDS; CISTI; Linda Hall.

546 NE ISSN 1024-1221
CODEN: MGCHE7
▼MAIN GROUP CHEMISTRY. 1995. 4/yr. $103 (effective 1998). Gordon and Breach - Harwood Academic, Amsteldisk 166, 1st Fl., 1079 LH Amsterdam, Netherlands. (Subscr. to: International Publishers Distributor, Box 32160, Newark, NJ 07102. TEL 800-545-8398. FAX 215-750-6343) Ed. David Atwood. **Indexed:** Chem.Cit.Ind. **Document type:** academic/scholarly publication.
—CASDDS.

546 NE ISSN 1068-3119
CODEN: MGCNEP
MAIN GROUP CHEMISTRY NEWS. Short title: M G C N. 1993. 4/yr. $50 (effective 1998). Gordon and Breach - Harwood Academic, Amsteldisk 166, 1st Fl., 1079 LH Amsterdam, Netherlands. (Subscr. to: International Publishers Distributor, Box 32160, Newark, NJ 07102. TEL 800-545-8398. FAX 215-750-6343) (back issues avail.) **Document type:** academic/scholarly publication.
—BLDSC (5351.845000); CASDDS; CISTI.

MAIN GROUP METAL CHEMISTRY. see METALLURGY

540 IR ISSN 1015-2849
MAJALLAH-I SHIMI/IRANIAN JOURNAL OF CHEMISTRY. (Text in Persian) 1988. 3/yr. IRI.6000 (Middle East £18; Europe £20; elsewhere £25). Markaz-i Nashr-i Danishgahi - Iran University Press, 85 Park Ave., Dr. Bihishti Ave., P.O. Box 15875-4748, Tehran, Iran. TEL 98-21-8713232. FAX 98-21-8861749. TELEX 213636-8-D5300. Ed. Ali Pourjavady. circ. 4,000. **Document type:** academic/scholarly publication.
Description: Publishes news and articles on chemistry, including philosophical and historical aspects.

MAJOR CHEMICAL AND PETROCHEMICAL COMPANIES OF EUROPE. see PETROLEUM AND GAS

540 JA
MAKU SHINPOJUMU/MEMBRANE SYMPOSIUM. (Text in English, Japanese) 1989. a. Nihon Maku Gakkai - Membrane Society of Japan, 3-1, Hongo 4-chome, Bunkyo-ku, Tokyo 113, Japan.

MARINE CHEMISTRY; an international journal for studies of all chemical aspects of the marine environment. see EARTH SCIENCES

540 UN ISSN 0255-5131
MARKET TRENDS & PROSPECTS FOR CHEMICAL PRODUCTS. quinquennial. price varies. Economic Commission for Europe (ECE), Palais des Nations, 1211 Geneva 10, Switzerland. TEL 022-917-2893. FAX 022-917-0036. (Or: United Nations Publications, Rm. DC2-853, New York, NY 10017. TEL 212-963-8302. FAX 212-963-3489) (also avail. in microfiche) **Document type:** government publication.

540 XR
MASARYK UNIVERSITY. FACULTY OF SCIENCES. SCRIPTA CHEMIA/SCRIPTA FACULTATIS SCIENTIARUM NATURALIUM UNIVERSITATIS MASARYKIANAE BRUNENSIS. CHEMIA. (Text in English, French and Russian) a. price varies. Masarykova Universita, Prirodovedecka Fakulta - Masaryk University, Faculty of Sciences, Kotlarska 2, 611 37 Brno, Czech Republic. Ed. Jiri Hala. illus. **Indexed:** Forest.Abstr. **Document type:** academic/scholarly publication.
Formerly: Scripta Facultatis Scientiarum Naturalium Universitatis Purkynianae Brunensis. Chemia (ISSN 0231-5971); Supersedes in part (in 1970): Universita J.E. Purkyne. Prirodovedecka Fakulta. Spisy.

543 UK ISSN 0305-9987
QD95 CODEN: MSSYBF
MASS SPECTROMETRY. 1971. irreg., vol.10, 1989. price varies. The Royal Society of Chemistry, Thomas Graham House, Science Park, Milton Rd., Cambridge CB4 4WF, England. TEL 44-1223-420066. FAX 44-1223-423623. E-mail: sales@rsc.org; URL: http://chemistry.rsc.org/rsc/. (Subscr. to: Turpin Distribution Services Ltd., Blackhorse Rd., Letchworth, Herts. SG6 1HN, England. TEL 44-1462-672555. FAX 44-1462-480947) Ed. M.E. Rose. charts; illus. (back issues avail.) **Indexed:** Chem.Abstr., Chem.Cit.Ind. **Document type:** academic/scholarly publication.
—BLDSC (5388.100000); CASDDS; CISTI; Ei; Linda Hall. **CCC.**
Description: Covers all aspects of mass spectrometry.

540 510 GW ISSN 0340-6253
QD39.3.M3 CODEN: MATCDY
MATCH; communications in mathematical and computer chemistry. (Text mostly in English; occasionally in French and German) 1975. 2/yr. DM.180 for 4 issues. Universitaet Bayreuth, Lehrstuhl II fuer Mathematik, 95540 Bayreuth, Germany. TEL 49-921-553387. FAX 49-921-553385. E-mail: kerber@btm2x2.mat.uni-bayreuth.de; URL: http://www.mathe2.uni-bayreuth.de/match. Ed. A. Kerber. R&P contact: A. Kerber. bk.rev.; abstr.; bibl.; charts; index. circ. 150. **Indexed:** Chem.Abstr., Chem.Cit.Ind., Math.R., Zent.Math. **Document type:** academic/scholarly publication.
●Also available online.
—CASDDS; CISTI; Linda Hall; UnCover. **CCC.**
Refereed Serial

MATERIALS CHEMISTRY AND PHYSICS; the international journal which unites the chemical and physical fields of research in materials science. see ENGINEERING — Engineering Mechanics And Materials

MATERIALS RESEARCH SOCIETY SYMPOSIUM PROCEEDINGS. see PHYSICS

540 510 NE ISSN 1049-2801
CODEN: MCHEET
MATHEMATICAL CHEMISTRY. irreg., latest vol.4. price varies. Gordon and Breach - Harwood Academic, Amsteldisk 166, 1079 LH Amsterdam, Netherlands. (Subscr. to: International Publishers Distributor, Box 32160, Newark, NJ 07102. TEL 800-545-8398. FAX 215-750-6343) Eds. D. Bonchev, D.H. Rouvray. (also avail. in microform) **Indexed:** Zent.Math. **Document type:** monographic series.
—BLDSC (5401.850000); CASDDS; CISTI. **CCC.**

MEDICINAL CHEMISTRY RESEARCH; an international journal for rapid communications on design and mechanisms of action of biologically active agents. see MEDICAL SCIENCES

MEISEI DAIGAKU KENKYU KIYO. RIKOGAKUBU/MEISEI UNIVERSITY. RESEARCH BULLETIN. PHYSICAL SCIENCES AND ENGINEERING. see ENGINEERING

540 US
MEMBRANE PLANNING CONFERENCE (YEAR). 1983. a. $350. Business Communications Co., Inc. (Norwalk), 25 Van Zant St., Norwalk, CT 06855. TEL 203-853-4266. FAX 203-853-0348. **Document type:** proceedings.

1760 CHEMISTRY

661   UK   ISSN 0958-2118
MEMBRANE TECHNOLOGY; an international newsletter. 1991. m. fl.969($557) (effective 1998). Elsevier Science Ltd., P.O. Box 800, Kidlington, Oxford OX5 1DX, England. TEL 44-1865-843000. FAX 44-1865-843010. E-mail: nlinfo-f@elsevier.nl; usinfo-f@elsevier.com; forinfo-kyf04035@niftyserve.or.jp; URL: http://www.elsevier.nl/. (Subscr. to: Elsevier Science, Regional Sales Office, P.O. Box 211, 1000 AE Amsterdam, Netherlands. TEL 31-20-4853757. FAX 31-20-4853432; Subscr. in the Americas to: Elsevier Science, Regional Sales Office, Box 945, New York, NY 10159-0945. TEL 212-633-3730. FAX 212-633-3680; Subscr. in Australasia and the Far East to: Elsevier Science (Singapore) Pte Ltd, No.1 Temasek Ave., No.17-01 Millenia Tower, Singapore 039192, Singapore. TEL 65-434-3727. FAX 65-337-2230) Ed. S. Atkinson. adv. (also avail. in microform from UMI) **Document type:** academic/scholarly publication, newsletter.
—BLDSC (5548.026600); EMDOCS; KR SourceOne; SWETS. **CCC.**
Description: Covers developments in membrane separation and purification technology, research and applications in a wide variety of industries, including pharmaceuticals, food and beverages, electronics, biotechnology and chemicals.

540   US   ISSN 0025-925X
QD1
MENDELEEV CHEMISTRY JOURNAL. English translation of: Rossiiskii Khimicheskii Zhurnal. 1966. bi-m. $1055 (effective 1998). (Rossiiskoe Khimicheskoe Obshchestvo im. D.I. Mendeleeva, RU - Mendeleev Chemical Society) Allerton Press, Inc., 150 Fifth Ave., New York, NY 10011. TEL 212-924-3950. FAX 212-463-9684. Ed. G.V. Lisichkin. bk.rev.; abstr.; charts; illus.; index. **Indexed:** Excerp.Med., Soils & Fert. **Document type:** academic/scholarly publication.
—BLDSC (0415.892000); CISTI; UnCover. **CCC.**
Description: Covers organic, inorganic and physical chemistry. Each issue is devoted to a specific topic.

540   RU   ISSN 0959-9436
QD1   CODEN: MENCEX
MENDELEEV COMMUNICATIONS. Online edition (UK ISSN 1364-551X) (Text in English) 1991. bi-m. £110 (U.S. $180) to individuals; institutions £385 (U.S. 620) (effective 1998). (The Royal Society of Chemistry, UK) Turpion - Moscow Ltd., 47 Leninsky prospekt, 117913 Moscow, Russia. TEL 7-95-1356417. FAX 7-95-1358860. E-mail: turpion@cacr.ioc.ac.ru; URL: http://turpion.ioc.ac.ru. (Dist. by: Turpin Distribution Services Ltd., Blackhorse Rd., Letchworth, Herts. SG6 1HN, England. TEL 44-1462-672555. FAX 44-1462-480947) (Co-sponsor: Russian Academy of Science) Ed. O.M. Nefedov. (also avail. in microform from UMI) **Indexed:** ASCA, Chem.Cit.Ind., Curr.Cont., Mat.Sci.Cit.Ind., Sci.Cit.Ind. **Document type:** academic/scholarly publication.
●Also available online.
Also available on CD-ROM.
—BLDSC (5678.442050); CASDDS; CISTI; Ei; Genuine Article; SWETS; UMI; UnCover. **CCC.**
Description: Provides access in English to Russian chemical research.
Refereed Serial

MICROCHEMICAL JOURNAL; devoted to the application of microtechniques in all branches of chemistry. see BIOLOGY — Microscopy

540   US   ISSN 0026-5411
MINNESOTA CHEMIST. 1942. 8/yr. $6. American Chemical Society, Minnesota Section, c/o Peter Howell, Ed., 1896 Yorkshire Ave., St. Paul, MN 55116. TEL 612-698-4507. FAX 612-696-6432. R&P contact: Peter Howell. adv. contact: Rodney L. Olsen. bk.rev. circ. 2,200. **Document type:** academic/scholarly publication, newsletter.

540   US   ISSN 0146-0420
                     CODEN: MTCHDT
MODERN THEORETICAL CHEMISTRY. 1976. irreg., latest vol.4. price varies. Plenum Publishing Corp., 233 Spring St., New York, NY 10013-1578. TEL 212-620-8000. FAX 212-463-0742. TELEX 23-421139. E-mail: books@plenum.com. (back issues avail.) **Document type:** monographic series.
—CASDDS; CISTI.
Refereed Serial

MOESSBAUER EFFECT REFERENCE AND DATA JOURNAL. see PHYSICS — Optics

MOLECULAR AND CELLULAR PROBES; the location, diagnosis, and monitoring of disease by nucleic acid techniques. see MEDICAL SCIENCES — Experimental Medicine, Laboratory Technique

540   NE   ISSN 0892-7022
QC167.5   CODEN: MOSIEA
MOLECULAR SIMULATION. 18/yr. (in 3 vols., 6 nos./vol.). $118 (effective 1998). Gordon and Breach - Harwood Academic, Amsteldisk 166, 1st Fl., 1079 LH Amsterdam, Netherlands. URL: http://www.gbhap.com/Molecular__Simulation/. (Subscr. to: International Publishers Distributor, Box 32160, Newark, NJ 07102. TEL 800-545-8398. FAX 215-750-6343) Ed. Nick Quirke. (also avail. in microform) **Indexed:** ASCA, Chem.Cit.Ind., Curr.Cont., Ind.Sci.Rev., Intl.Polym.Sci.& Tech., Mat.Sci.Cit.Ind., RAPRA, Sci.Cit.Ind. **Document type:** academic/scholarly publication.
●Also available online.
Also available on CD-ROM.
—BLDSC (5900.833000); CASDDS; CISTI; SWETS; UnCover. **CCC.**
Refereed Serial

540   AU   ISSN 0026-9247
                     CODEN: MOCMB7
MONATSHEFTE FUER CHEMIE/CHEMICAL MONTHLY. (Text in English, German) 1880. m. DM.1614 (effective 1998). Springer-Verlag, Sachsenplatz 4-6, P.O. Box 89, A-1201 Vienna, Austria. TEL 43-1-330-2415. FAX 43-1-330-2426. E-mail: springer@springer.co.at. (N. American subscr. to: Springer-Verlag New York Inc., 175 Fifth Ave., New York, NY 10010. TEL 212-460-1500. FAX 212-473-6272) Ed. K. Schloegl. adv.; charts; illus.; index. (also avail. in microform from UMI; reprint service avail. from UMI) **Indexed:** Alloys Ind., Biol.Abstr., Biotech.Abstr., Bull.Thermodyn.& Thermochem., Chem.Abstr., Chem.Cit.Ind., Chem.Infd., Curr.Adv.Ecol.Sci., Curr.Chem.React., Curr.Cont., Eng.Mat.Abstr., Ind.Chem., Ind.Med., Ind.Sci.Rev., Mass Spectr.Bull., Met.Abstr., Met.Abstr.Ind., Nonfer.Met.Alert, PCC Alert, Sci.Cit.Ind., Steels Alert, World Alum.Abstr. **Document type:** academic/scholarly publication.
—BLDSC (5904.000000); ADONIS; CASDDS; CISTI; Ei; Genuine Article; KNAW; Linda Hall; SWETS; UMI; UnCover. **CCC.**
Description: Features recent research results in inorganic, structural, physical, and organic chemistry and biochemistry.

MONOGRAPHS ON THE PHYSICS AND CHEMISTRY OF MATERIALS. see PHYSICS

540   US   ISSN 0027-1314
QD1
MOSCOW UNIVERSITY CHEMISTRY BULLETIN. English translation of: Moskovskii Universitet. Vestnik. Seriya 2: Khimiya (RU ISSN 0579-9384) 1966. bi-m. $1005 (effective 1998). (Moskovskii Universitet, RU) Allerton Press, Inc., 150 Fifth Ave., New York, NY 10011. TEL 212-924-3950. FAX 212-463-9684. Ed. Yu.Ya. Kuzyakov. bk.rev.; charts; illus.; index. **Indexed:** Anal.Abstr., Bull.Thermodyn.& Thermochem. **Document type:** academic/scholarly publication.
—BLDSC (0416.238000); CISTI; UnCover. **CCC.**
Description: Covers general, radiation, analytical, organic, petroleum chemistry and electrochemistry.

540   RU   ISSN 0579-9384
                     CODEN: VMUKA5
MOSKOVSKII UNIVERSITET. VESTNIK. SERIYA 2: KHIMIYA. English translation: Moscow University Chemistry Bulletin (US ISSN 0027-1314) (Contents page in English) bi-m. $85 (effective 1998). Moskovskii Universitet, Ul. Gertsena 5-7, 103009 Moscow, Russia. bk.rev.; bibl.; index. **Indexed:** Alloys Ind., ASCA, Chem.Abstr., Eng.Mat.Abstr., Int.Aerosp.Abstr., Met.Abstr., Met.Abstr., Met.Abstr.Ind., Nonfer.Met.Alert, PCC Alert, Steels Alert, World Alum.Abstr. **Document type:** academic/scholarly publication.
—BLDSC (0032.350000); CASDDS; CISTI; Genuine Article; Linda Hall.
Supersedes in part (in 1960): Moskovskii Universitet. Vestnik. Seriya Matematiki, Mekhaniki, Astronomii, Fiziki, Khimii (ISSN 0579-9376)

660   GW   ISSN 0341-5163
QD1   CODEN: NCTLDI
NACHRICHTEN AUS CHEMIE, TECHNIK UND LABORATORIUM. 1953. m. DM.405 (effective 1997). (Gesellschaft Deutscher Chemiker) V C H Verlagsgesellschaft mbH, Postfach 101161, 69451 Weinheim, Germany. TEL 49-6201-606-147. FAX 49-6201-606117. TELEX 465516-VCHWH-D. (US addr.: V C H Publishers Inc., 220 E. 23rd St., New York, NY 10010-4606. TEL 212-683-8333) adv. contact: R. Roth. bk.rev.; index. circ. 28,500. (also avail. in microform from VCI; reprint service avail. from ISI) **Indexed:** ASCA, Chem.Abstr., Chem.Cit.Ind., Chem.Infd., Excerp.Med., Mat.Sci.Cit.Ind., SSCI. **Document type:** academic/scholarly publication.
—BLDSC (6006.410000); CASDDS; CISTI; Ei; Genuine Article; Linda Hall; SWETS. **CCC.**
Formerly (until 1977): Nachrichten aus Chemie und Technik (ISSN 0027-738X)

NATIONAL FISHERIES UNIVERSITY OF PUSAN. INSTITUTE OF MARINE SCIENCES. CONTRIBUTIONS. see BIOLOGY

540   JA   ISSN 0919-7087
TP1   CODEN: BKGHE2
NATIONAL INSTITUTE OF MATERIALS AND CHEMICAL RESEARCH. JOURNAL/BUSSHITSU KOUGAKU KOUGYOUGIJUTSU KENKYUJO HOKOKU. (Text in English or Japanese; abstracts in English) 1993. bi-m. free to academic institutions. National Institute of Materials and Chemical Research, Ibaraki 305, Japan. TEL 81-298-54-4410. FAX 81-298-54-4422. Ed. Masanori Tachiya; Pub. Seiichi Yamaguchi. R&P contact: Kazuhiro Fujita. adv. contact: Kazuhiro Fujita. bibl.; illus.; circ. 2,700 (controlled). **Indexed:** Abstr.Bull.Inst.Pap.Chem., INIS Atomind. **Document type:** academic/scholarly publication.
—BLDSC (4831.020000); CASDDS; CISTI; Linda Hall.
Formed by the 1993 merger of: Research Institute for Polymers and Textiles. Bulletin - Sen'i Kobunshi Zairyo Kenkyu Hokoku (ISSN 0371-0807); Which was formerly (until 1969): Textile Research Institute Bulletin - Sen'i Kogyo Shikensho Hokoku (ISSN 0371-0734); And: National Chemical Laboratory for Industry. Journal - Kagaku Gijutsu Kenkyujo Hokoku (ISSN 0388-3213); Which was formerly (until 1979): Japan. Government Chemical Industrial Research Institute, Tokyo. Reports - Tokyo Kogyo Shikensho Hokoku (ISSN 0371-8808); And: Industrial Products Research Institute. Bulletin - Seihinkagaku Kenkyujo Hokoku (ISSN 0389-9659)
Description: Covers chemistry, polymer science and materials science.
Refereed Serial

NATIONAL INSTITUTE OF STANDARDS AND TECHNOLOGY. JOURNAL OF RESEARCH. see METROLOGY AND STANDARDIZATION

NATIONAL TECHNICAL REPORT. see ENGINEERING — Electrical Engineering

540 574.192   NE   ISSN 1057-5634
QD415.A1   CODEN: NPLEEF
NATURAL PRODUCT LETTERS. 1992. 4/yr. $86 (effective 1998). Gordon and Breach - Harwood Academic, Amsteldisk 166, 1st Fl., 1079 LH Amsterdam, Netherlands. URL: http://www.gbhap.com/Natural__Product__Letters/. (Subscr. to: International Publishers Distributor, Box 32160, Newark, NJ 07102. TEL 800-545-8398. FAX 215-750-6343) Eds. Ernest Wenkert, Atta-ur-Rahman. (also avail. in microform) **Indexed:** ASCA, Chem.Cit.Ind., Excerp.Med. (1994-). **Document type:** academic/scholarly publication.
●Also available online.
Also available on CD-ROM.
—BLDSC (6040.737700); CASDDS; CISTI; EMDOCS; SWETS. **CCC.**
Description: Covers all aspects of research in the chemistry and biochemistry of naturally occurring compounds.

NATURE BIOTECHNOLOGY. see BIOLOGY — Biotechnology

CHEMISTRY

570 610   US   ISSN 0195-7198
          CODEN: PSSBDF
NAUKOVE TOVARYSTVO IMENI SHEVCHENKA. PROCEEDINGS OF THE SECTION OF CHEMISTRY, BIOLOGY AND MEDICINE. (Text in English and Ukrainian) vol.7, 1973. irreg. price varies. Shevchenko Scientific Society, 63 Fourth Ave., New York, NY 10003. TEL 212-254-5130. **Document type:** proceedings.
   Supersedes in part: Naukove Tovarystvo Imeni Shevchenka. Proceedings of the Section of Mathematics, Natural Sciences and Medicine (ISSN 0470-5017)

540   NE   ISSN 1380-3689
          CODEN: NTKCFX
NEDERLANDS TIJDSCHRIFT VOOR KLINISCHE CHEMIE. 1976. bi-m. fl.140. Nederlandse Vereniging voor Klinische Chemie, Vredenburg 134, 2nd Fl., 3511 BG Utrecht, Netherlands. TEL 31-30-2328623. FAX 31-30-2311178. adv.; bk.rev.; index. circ. 800. (back issues avail.) **Indexed:** Excerp.Med. **Document type:** academic/scholarly publication.
   —BLDSC (6071.950000); CASDDS; CISTI; KNAW; SWETS.
   Formerly: Nederlandse Vereniging voor Klinische Chemie. Tijdschrift (ISSN 0168-8472)

546   RU   ISSN 0869-5784
          CODEN: IVNMAW
NEORGANICHESKIE MATERIALY. English translation: Inorganic Materials (US ISSN 0020-1685) 1965. m. $346 (effective 1998). (Rossiiskaya Akademiya Nauk) Neorganicheskie Materialy, Leninskii pr. 31, Komn. 71, 117907 Moscow, Russia. TEL 7-095-9543397. (Dist. by: Mezhdunarodnaya Kniga, B. Yakimanka 39, 114079 Moscow, Russia) Ed. G.G. Devyatykh. bk.rev.; abstr.; charts; illus.; index. **Indexed:** Alloys Ind., Bull.Thermodyn.& Thermochem., Chem.Abstr., Eng.Mat.Abstr., INIS Atomind., INSPEC, Met.Abstr., Met.Abstr.Ind., Nonfer.Met.Alert, PCC Alert, Phys.Ber., Steels Alert, World Alum.Abstr. **Document type:** academic/scholarly publication.
   —BLDSC (0124.160000); CASDDS; CISTI; KNAW; Linda Hall. **CCC.**
   Formerly: Akademiya Nauk S.S.S.R. Izvestiya. Seriya Neorganicheskie Materialy (ISSN 0002-337X)

NEUROCHEMISTRY INTERNATIONAL; the international journal for the rapid publication of critical reviews, original and rapid research communications in neurochemistry. see *MEDICAL SCIENCES — Psychiatry And Neurology*

540   FR   ISSN 1144-0546
QD1   CODEN: NJCHE5
NEW JOURNAL OF CHEMISTRY. (Text in English) 1977. 11/yr. 1150 F. to individuals (foreign 1500 F.); institutions 2900 F. (foreign 3500 F.) (effective 1997). (Centre National de la Recherche Scientifique) Gauthier-Villars, 15 rue Gossin, 92543 Montrouge Cedex, France. TEL 33-1-40926500. FAX 33-1-40466201. TELEX 634 916 F. E-mail: gauthier.villars.publisher@mail.sgip.fr; URL: http://www.gauthier-villars.fr. (Subscr. to: Societe de Periodiques Specialises, B.P. 22-F, 41354 Vineuil Cedex, France. TEL 33-2-54504612. FAX 33-2-54504611) Ed. O. Eisenstein. circ. 1,000. **Indexed:** ASCA, Biwk.Pap.Rad.Chem.& Photochem., Cadscan, Chem.Abstr., Chem.Cit.Ind., Compumath, Curr.Adv.Ecol.Sci., Curr.Chem.React., Curr.Cont., Ind.Chem., Ind.Sci.Rev., INSPEC (1978-), Lead Abstr., Mass Spectr.Bull., Mat.Sci.Cit.Ind., Sci.Cit.Ind., Zincscan. **Document type:** academic/scholarly publication.
   —BLDSC (6084.319900); AskIEEE; CASDDS; CISTI; Ei; Genuine Article; KR SourceOne; Linda Hall; SWETS; UnCover. **CCC.**
   Formerly (until 1987): Nouveau Journal de Chimie (ISSN 0398-9836)

540   UN   ISSN 0077-8885
NEW TRENDS IN CHEMISTRY TEACHING SERIES. (Text in English and French) 1967. irreg., vol.6, 1992. UNESCO Publishing, 7 Place de Fontenoy, 75352 Paris 07 SP, France. TEL 33-1-45684300. FAX 33-1-45685741. URL: http://www.unesco.org/publications. (Dist. in U.S. by: Bernan Associates, 4611-F Assembly Dr., Lanham, MD 20706-4391. TEL 800-274-4888. FAX 800-865-3450) Ed. P. Farago.

540   JA
NIHON BUNSEKI SENTA KOHO/JAPAN CHEMICAL ANALYSIS CENTER. REPORT. (Text in Japanese) 1979. s-a. Nihon Bunseki Senta - Japan Chemical Analysis Center, 295-3, Sannocho, Inage-ku, Chiba-shi, Chiba-ken 263, Japan. Ed. Yoh Katayama. **Document type:** bulletin.

540   JA
NIHON BUNSEKI SENTA NYUSU/JAPAN CHEMICAL ANALYSIS CENTER NEWS. (Text in Japanese) 1985. bi-m. Nihon Bunseki Senta - Japan Chemical Analysis Center, 295-3, Sannocho, Inage-ku, Chiba-shi, Chiba-ken 263, Japan. Ed. Yoh Katayama. **Document type:** newsletter.

540   JA   ISSN 0915-860X
          CODEN: NKOGEZ
NIHON ION KOKAN GAKKAISHI/JAPAN ASSOCIATION OF ION EXCHANGE. JOURNAL. (Text in English, Japanese; summaries in English) 1990. s-a. Nihon Ion Kokan Gakkai - Japan Association of Ion Exchange, Tokyo Kogyo Daigaku Rigakubu Kagakka Abe Kenkyushitsu, 12-1, Ookayama 2-chome, Meguro-ku, Tokyo 152, Japan. **Document type:** academic/scholarly publication.
   —BLDSC (4804.560000); CASDDS.

NIHON RIKAGAKU KYOKAI. KENKYU KIYO. see *PHYSICS*

NIIGATA RIKAGAKU/JOURNAL OF PHYSICS AND CHEMISTRY OF NIIGATA. see *PHYSICS*

540   JA   ISSN 0369-4356
NIIGATA UNIVERSITY. FACULTY OF SCIENCE. SCIENCE REPORTS. SERIES C: CHEMISTRY. (Text in European languages) 1964. irreg. exchange basis. Niigata Daigaku, Rigakubu - Niigata University, Faculty of Science, 8050 Igarashi Nino-cho, Niigata-shi 950-21, Japan.

540   JA   ISSN 0285-7626
NIPPON KAGAKKAI KOEN YOKOSHU/CHEMICAL SOCIETY OF JAPAN. PREPRINTS OF THE CONFERENCE. (Text in Japanese) s-a. Chemical Society of Japan - Nippon Kagakkai, 1-5, Kanda Surugadai, Chiyoda-ku, Tokyo 101, Japan.
   —BLDSC (6112.702000).

660.2 540   JA   ISSN 0369-4577
QD1   CODEN: NKAKB8
NIPPON KAGAKU KAISHI/CHEMICAL SOCIETY OF JAPAN. CHEMISTRY AND INDUSTRIAL CHEMISTRY. JOURNAL. (Text in Japanese; summaries in English) 1972. m. $75 to members; non-members $276 (effective 1994). Chemical Society of Japan - Nippon Kagakukai, 5, 1-chome, Kanda-Surugadai, Chiyoda-ku, Tokyo 101, Japan. Ed. Shinsaku Shiraishi. circ. 3,600. (also avail. in microfiche from BHP; reprint service avail. from UMI) **Indexed:** Alloys Ind., Anal.Abstr., API Abstr., API Catal., API Hlth.& Environ., API Oil., API Pet.Subst., API Transport., ASCA, Cadscan, Ceram.Abstr., Chem.Abstr., Chem.Cit.Ind., Chem.Infd., Curr.Chem.React., Curr.Cont., Deep Sea Res.& Oceanogr.Abstr., Eng.Mat.Abstr., Ind.Chem., JTA, Lead Abstr., Mass Spectr.Bull., Mat.Sci.Cit.Ind., Met.Abstr., Met.Abstr.Ind., Nonfer.Met.Alert, PCC Alert, Sci.Cit.Ind., Steels Alert, Text.Tech.Dig., World Alum.Abstr., Zincscan. **Document type:** academic/scholarly publication.
   —BLDSC (6113.284000); CASDDS; CISTI; Ei; Genuine Article; Linda Hall; SWETS; UMI. **CCC.**
   Formed by the merger of: Kogyo Kagaku Zasshi (ISSN 0023-2734); Nippon Kagaku Zasshi (ISSN 0369-5387)

NIPPON KAYAKU. ANNUAL REPORT. see *PHARMACY AND PHARMACOLOGY*

540   SP
NOTICIAS PARA QUIMICOS. 11/yr. Avda. Puerta del Angel 24, 1o, 08002 Barcelona, Spain. TEL 3-179-249. FAX 3-179-299. Ed. Antonio P. Gasco. circ. 4,200.

540   IT
NOTIZIE DOW. 1967. bi-m. free. Dow Italia, Via Murat 23, Milan, Italy. FAX 02-27772710. adv. circ. 2,500. (tabloid format; back issues avail.)
   Formerly: Dow in Italia.

NUCLEUS. see *ENERGY — Nuclear Energy*

540   US   ISSN 0362-0026
          CODEN: NCLUA2
THE NUCLEUS (HARVARD). 1922. m. (except June and Aug.) $10. American Chemical Society, Northeastern Section, 19 Mill Rd., Harvard, MA 01451. TEL 508-456-8622. Ed. Arno Heyn. R&P contact: Aron Heyn. adv. contact: Vincent J. Gale. circ. 5,000 (controlled). (back issues avail.) **Document type:** newsletter.
   Description: Announces section meetings, section and member news, and articles of general interest to members.

O P D CHEMICAL BUYERS DIRECTORY. see *BUSINESS AND ECONOMICS — Trade And Industrial Directories*

540   US   ISSN 0029-8271
THE OCTAGON. 1918. m. 8/yr. $1 to non-members. American Chemical Society, Lehigh Valley Section, 744 N. Broad St., Allentown, PA 18104. TEL 610-770-7348. FAX 610-770-7348. E-mail: gbcmars@enter.net. Ed. Gail Marsella. adv.; bk.rev.; circ. 1,000 (controlled). (also avail. in microform from UMI; reprint service avail. from UMI) **Document type:** newsletter.
   Description: Contains organization news.

540   AU   ISSN 0379-5314
          CODEN: OCMZAX
OESTERREICHISCHE CHEMIE ZEITSCHRIFT. 1947. bi-m. S.776 (effective 1997). Verlag Lorenz, Ebendorferstr. 10, A-1010 Vienna, Austria. TEL 43-1-4056695. FAX 43-1-4068693. Ed. Sepp Fischer. adv.: B&W page S.24500, color page S.40100. bk.rev.; illus.; tr.lit. circ. 5,600. **Indexed:** Chem.Abstr., Chem.Infd. **Document type:** trade publication.
   —BLDSC (6305.700000); CASDDS; CISTI; KNAW.
   Formerly (until 1974): Oesterreichische Chemiker-Zeitung (ISSN 0258-4336)

OIL & CHEMICAL WORKER. see *LABOR UNIONS*

660   NE
ONDERNEMINGSANALYSES CHEMIE. a. fl.89.50. Delwel Uitgeverij B.V., Postbus 19110, 2500 CC The Hague, Netherlands. TEL 31-70-3624800. FAX 31-70-3605606.
   Description: Financial and economic information on the chemical industry and related industries in the Netherlands.

540   US   ISSN 0553-0377
ORGANIZATION OF AMERICAN STATES. DEPARTMENT OF SCIENTIFIC AFFAIRS. SERIE DE QUIMICA: MONOGRAFIAS. 1965. irreg., no.21, 1979. $3.50. Organization of American States, Department of Publications, 1889 F St., N.W., Washington, DC 20006. TEL 703-941-1617. circ. 3,000. **Document type:** monographic series.

660   US
ORGANIZED ASSEMBLIES IN CHEMICAL ANALYSIS. 1994. irreg., vol.2, 1997. $109.50. J A I Press Inc., 55 Old Post Rd., No.2, Box 1678, Greenwich, CT 06830-1678. TEL 203-661-7602. FAX 203-661-0792. E-mail: jai@jaipress.com. (In Europe: JAI Press Ltd., 38 Tavistock St., Covent Garden, London WC2E 7PB, England. TEL 44-171-379-8834. FAX 44-171-379-8835) Ed. Willie Hinze. **Document type:** academic/scholarly publication, monographic series.

ORIGINS OF LIFE AND EVOLUTION OF THE BIOSPHERE. see *BIOLOGY*

540   UK
OXFORD CHEMISTRY PRIMERS. vol.11, 1993. irreg., vol.33, 1995. price varies. Oxford University Press, Walton St., Oxford OX2 6DP, England. TEL 44-1865-56767. FAX 44-1865-56646. (Subscr. in U.S. to: Oxford University Press Inc., 2001 Evans Rd., Cary, NC 27513. TEL 919-677-0977. FAX 919-677-1714) **Document type:** monographic series.

540   UK   ISSN 0302-4199
OXFORD CHEMISTRY SERIES. irreg. price varies. Oxford University Press, Walton St., Oxford OX2 6DP, England. TEL 44-1865-56767. FAX 44-1865-56646. (Subscr. in US to: Oxford University Press Inc., 2001 Evans Rd., Cary, NC 27513. TEL 919-677-0977. FAX 919-677-1714) **Document type:** monographic series.
   —CISTI.

PACKAGING, TECHNOLOGY AND SCIENCE. see *PACKAGING*

540   330   UK   ISSN 0950-3870
PERFORMANCE CHEMICALS. 1986. m. £76 in Europe; elsewhere £81. Reed Business Information (Subsidiary of: Reed Elsevier group), Quadrant House, The Quadrant, Sutton, Surrey SM2 5AS, England. TEL 44-181-652-8146. FAX 44-181-652-8918. (Subscr. to: Stuart House, Perrymount Rd., Haywards Heath, Sussex RH16 3BN, England. TEL 44-1444-445355) Ed. Geoff Hadwick; Pub. Les Edwards. adv. contact: John Wright. charts; illus.; stat. circ. 6,582. (back issues avail.) **Indexed:** Intl.Polym.Sci.& Tech., RAPRA, World Surf.Coat. **Document type:** trade publication.
—CISTI; SWETS. **CCC.**
  Description: Covers commercially oriented research development work in pharmaceuticals, pesticides, and electronic chemicals.

PERFUMER & FLAVORIST. see *BEAUTY CULTURE — Perfumes And Cosmetics*

THE PESTICIDE MANUAL. see *AGRICULTURE*

PHARMACEUTICAL CHEMISTRY JOURNAL. see *PHARMACY AND PHARMACOLOGY*

PHARMACOCHEMISTRY LIBRARY. see *PHARMACY AND PHARMACOLOGY*

540   US
PHI LAMBDA UPSILON. REGISTER. 1925. s-a. $3. Phi Lambda Upsilon, Honorary Chemical Society, c/o John Zimmerman, Ed., Department of Chemistry, Wabash College, Crawfordsville, IN 47933. circ. 3,500. **Indexed:** Chem.Abstr.

540   570   US   ISSN 0363-499X
QH515   CODEN: PPHRDL
PHOTOCHEMICAL & PHOTOBIOLOGICAL REVIEWS. 1976. irreg., vol.7, 1983. Plenum Publishing Corp., 233 Spring St., New York, NY 10013-1578. TEL 212-620-8000. FAX 212-463-0742. TELEX 23-421139. E-mail: books@plenum.com. Ed. K.C. Smith. (back issues avail.) **Document type:** monographic series.
—CASDDS; CISTI; Linda Hall. **CCC.**
  Refereed Serial

540   UK   ISSN 0556-3860
QD601.A1   CODEN: PHCYAQ
PHOTOCHEMISTRY (CAMBRIDGE). (In five parts: Part I (Physical Aspects of Photochemistry), Part II (Photochemistry of Inorganic and Organometallic Compounds), Part III (Organic Aspects of Photochemistry), Part IV (Polymer Photochemistry), Part V (Photochemical Aspects of Solar Energy)) 1968. a. price varies. The Royal Society of Chemistry, Thomas Graham House, Science Park, Milton Rd., Cambridge CB4 4WF, England. TEL 44-1223-420066. FAX 44-1223-423623. E-mail: sales@rsc.org; URL: http://chemistry.rsc.org/rsc/. (Subscr. to: Turpin Distribution Services Ltd., Blackhorse Rd., Letchworth, Herts. SG6 1HN, England. TEL 44-1462-672555. FAX 44-1462-480947; Subscr. in N. America to: ACS, 1155 Sixteenth St., N.W., Washington, DC 22036, USA. TEL 202-776-8100. FAX 202-872-6067) Eds. D. Bryce-Smith, A. Gilbert. charts; index. (back issues avail.) **Indexed:** Chem.Abstr. **Document type:** academic/scholarly publication.
—BLDSC (6465.983000); CASDDS; CISTI; Ei; Linda Hall; UnCover. **CCC.**

541.35   US   ISSN 0031-8655
QD601.A1   CODEN: PHCBAP
PHOTOCHEMISTRY AND PHOTOBIOLOGY. 1962. 12/yr. (in 2 vols.) $575 (effective 1997). American Society for Photobiology, BioTech Park, Ste. 9, 1021 15th St., Augusta, GA 30901. TEL 706-721-2601. FAX 706-721-3048. E-mail: photochem@helix.mgh.harvard.edu; URL: http://www.humc.edu/POL/PAPHome. (Subscr. to: Allen Press, Inc., Box 1897, Lawrence, KS 66044-8897. TEL 913-843-1234. FAX 913-843-1274) Ed. Irene E. Kochevar. adv. contact: Sarah A. Stephens. bk.rev.; bibl.; charts; illus. circ. 2,100. (also avail. in microfilm from UMI; back issues avail.) **Indexed:** ASCA, Bibl.Agri., Biol.Abstr., Biwk.Pap.Rad.Chem.& Photochem., Chem.Abstr., Chem.Cit.Ind., Curr.Adv.Biochem., Curr.Adv.Cancer Res., Curr.Adv.Ecol.Sci., Curr.Adv.Genetics & Molec.Biol., Curr.Cont., Dairy Sci.Abstr., Deep Sea Res.& Oceanogr.Abstr., Excerp.Med., Field Crop Abstr., Herb.Abstr., Ind.Med., Ind.Sci.Rev., Int.Aerosp.Abstr., Mass Spectr.Bull., Med.& Surg.Dermat., Neurosci.Cit.Ind., Nutr.Abstr., Sci.Cit.Ind. **Document type:** academic/scholarly publication.
—BLDSC (6465.985000); CASDDS; CISTI; Ei; EMDOCS; Linda Hall; SWETS; UMI; UnCover. **CCC.**
  Description: Publishes original reports and reviews on current topics in photobiology and in photobiologically relevant photochemistry.
  Refereed Serial

540   530   US   ISSN 0079-1938
QC801   CODEN: PCSPDD
PHYSICS AND CHEMISTRY IN SPACE. 1970. irreg., vol.24, 1993. price varies. Springer-Verlag, 175 Fifth Ave., New York, NY 10010. TEL 212-460-1500. FAX 212-473-6272. (Also: Berlin, Heidelberg, Tokyo and Vienna) Ed. F. Roederes. (reprint service avail. from ISI) **Indexed:** INSPEC. **Document type:** monographic series.
—CISTI.

PHYSICS AND CHEMISTRY OF MATERIALS TREATMENT. see *ENGINEERING — Engineering Mechanics And Materials*

PHYSICS AND CHEMISTRY OF MATERIALS WITH LOW-DIMENSIONAL STRUCTURES. see *PHYSICS — Mechanics*

PLASMA CHEMISTRY & PLASMA PROCESSING. see *ENGINEERING — Chemical Engineering*

PLATINUM METALS REVIEW. see *METALLURGY*

540   PL   ISSN 0239-7285
QD1   CODEN: BPACEQ
POLISH ACADEMY OF SCIENCES. BULLETIN. CHEMISTRY. (Text in English, French, German) 1953. q. $100. Polska Akademia Nauk, Centrum Upowszechniania Nauki, Palac Kultury i Nauki, Pietro XXIII, pok.23-10, 00-901 Warsaw, Poland. (Dist. by: Ars Polona-Ruch, Krakowskie Przedmiescie 7, 00-068 Warsaw, Poland) Ed. H. Ratajczak. R&P contact: Ewa Bartkowiak. adv. contact: Irmina Grodzka-Autoszkiewicz. bibl.; charts; illus. circ. 170. **Indexed:** Alloys Ind., Anal.Abstr., ASCA, Cadscan, Chem.Abstr., Chem.Cit.Ind., Curr.Cont., Eng.Mat.Abstr., Geo.Abstr.P.G., INIS Atomind., Lead Abstr., Mass Spectr.Bull., Met.Abstr., Met.Abstr.Ind., Nonfer.Met.Alert, PCC Alert, Steels Alert, World Alum.Abstr., Zincscan. **Document type:** academic/scholarly publication, bulletin.
—CASDDS; CISTI; Genuine Article; Linda Hall.
  Formerly (until 1983): Academie Polonaise des Sciences. Bulletin. Serie des Sciences Chimiques (ISSN 0001-4095)
  Refereed Serial

660   PL   ISSN 0867-8928
TP1   CODEN: PJACE2
POLISH JOURNAL OF APPLIED CHEMISTRY. (Text in English) 1957. q. $90. (Polska Akademia Nauk, Komitet Nauk Chemicznych) Wydawnictwo Naukowe P W N, Ul. Miodowa 10, 00-251 Warsaw, Poland. TEL 48-22-312738. FAX 48-22-6954288. (Dist. by: Ars Polona, Krakowskie Przedmiescie 7, 00-068 Warsaw, Poland) Ed. Zbigniew Jedlinski. abstr.; charts; illus.; index. circ. 700. **Indexed:** Chem.Abstr., INIS Atomind. **Document type:** academic/scholarly publication.
—BLDSC (6543.666000); CASDDS; CISTI; Linda Hall; UnCover.
  Former titles: Chemia Stosowana (ISSN 0376-0898); Chemia Stosowana. Seria A: Zagadnienia Technologii Chemicznej (ISSN 0009-2231)

540   PL   ISSN 0137-5083
QD1   CODEN: PJCHDQ
POLISH JOURNAL OF CHEMISTRY. (Text in English) 1921. m. $300. Polskie Towarzystwo Chemiczne - Polish Chemical Society, Ul. Freta 16, 00-227 Warsaw, Poland. TEL 48-22-6320749. Ed. Bogdan Baranovski. bk.rev.; charts; index. circ. 730. **Indexed:** ASCA, Cadscan, Chem.Abstr., Chem.Cit.Ind., Chem.Infd., Curr.Cont., Ind.Chem., Ind.Sci.Rev., Lead Abstr., Mass Spectr.Bull., Mat.Sci.Cit.Ind., Met.Abstr., Sci.Cit.Ind., Zincscan. **Document type:** academic/scholarly publication.
—BLDSC (6543.667000); CASDDS; CISTI; Ei; Genuine Article; Linda Hall; SWETS; UnCover. **CCC.**
  Formerly (until 1978): Roczniki Chemii (ISSN 0035-7677)

540   PL   ISSN 0416-7341
    CODEN: ZNGCAU
POLITECHNIKA GDANSKA. ZESZYTY NAUKOWE. CHEMIA. (Text in English, Polish; summaries in Russian and one West-European language) 1955. irreg. price varies. Politechnika Gdanska, Ul. G. Narutowicza 11-12, 80-952 Gdansk 6, Poland. (Dist. by: Osrodek Rozpowszechniania Wydawnictw Naukowych PAN, Palac Kultury i Nauki, 00-901 Warsaw, Poland) abstr.; bibl.; charts. **Indexed:** Chem.Abstr. **Document type:** academic/scholarly publication.
—CASDDS; Linda Hall.
  Description: Deals with organic, analytic and physical chemistry: corrosion protection technology, drugs, fats, food and fish technology.

540
POLITECHNIKA KRAKOWSKA. MONOGRAFIE. SERIA: INZYNIERIA I TECHNOLOGIA CHEMICZNA. (Subseries of: Politechnika Krakowska. Monografie (ISSN 0860-097X)) (Text in Polish; summaries in English, French, German, Russian) 1985. irreg. price varies. Politechnika Krakowska, Ul. Warszawska 24, 31-155 Krakow, Poland. TEL 48-12-374289. FAX 48-12-335773. TELEX 322468 PK PL. E-mail: marcinek@biblos.pk.edu.pl. bibl.; charts; illus. circ. 200. **Document type:** academic/scholarly publication, monographic series.

540   PL   ISSN 0867-7735
    CODEN: ZNPCB8
POLITECHNIKA KRAKOWSKA. ZESZYTY NAUKOWE. INZYNIERIA I TECHNOLOGIA CHEMICZNA. (Text in Polish; summaries in English, French, German, Russian) 1968. irreg. price varies. Politechnika Krakowska, Warszawska 24, 31-155 Krakow, Poland. TEL 48-12-374289. FAX 48-12-335773. TELEX 322468 PK PL. E-mail: Marcinek@biblos.pk.edu.pl. bibl.; charts; illus. circ. 200. **Indexed:** Chem.Abstr. **Document type:** academic/scholarly publication, monographic series.
—BLDSC (9512.305200); CASDDS; CISTI.
  Formerly: Politechnika Krakowska. Zeszyty Naukowe. Chemia (ISSN 0075-7055)

540   PL   ISSN 0458-1555
QD1   CODEN: ZNPLAY
POLITECHNIKA LODZKA. ZESZYTY NAUKOWE. CHEMIA. (Text in Polish; summaries in English and Russian) 1954. irreg. price varies. Wydawnictwo Politechniki Lodzkiej, Ul. Wolczanska 223, 93-005 Lodz, Poland. (Dist. by: Ars Polona-Ruch, Krakowskie Przedmiesci 7, Warsaw, Poland) Ed. Andrzej Cyganski. circ. 206. **Indexed:** Chem.Abstr. **Document type:** academic/scholarly publication.
—CASDDS; CISTI; Linda Hall.
  Description: Articles on analytical chemistry, organic chemistry, inorganic chemistry, polymer chemistry and radiation chemistry.

540   660   PL   ISSN 0372-9494
QD1   CODEN: ZNSCAM
POLITECHNIKA SLASKA. ZESZYTY NAUKOWE. CHEMIA. (Text in Polish; summaries in English, German, Russian) 1957. irreg. price varies. Politechnika Slaska, Katowicka 7, 44-100 Gliwice, Poland. FAX 371655. TELEX 036304. (Dist. by Ars Polona, Krakowskie Przedmiescie 7, 00-068 Warsaw, Poland) Ed. Genowefa Bienkiewicz. circ. 205. **Indexed:** Chem.Abstr., Met.Abstr. **Document type:** academic/scholarly publication.
—BLDSC (9512.325700); CASDDS; Linda Hall.

540   PL   ISSN 0137-2300
CODEN: PNPWBQ
POLITECHNIKA WARSZAWSKA. PRACE NAUKOWE. CHEMIA. 1954. irreg., no.60, 1995. Politechnika Warszawska, c/o Biblioteka Glowna, Pl. Politechniki 1, 00-661 Warsaw, Poland. E-mail: bgpw@pg.pw.edu.pl. **Document type:** academic/scholarly publication.
—BLDSC (6590.790000); CASDDS; Linda Hall.
     Formerly (until 1968): Politechnika Warszawska. Zeszyty Naukowe. Chemia (ISSN 0372-9478)

540   GW   ISSN 0170-0839
QD380   CODEN: POBUDR
POLYMER BULLETIN. (Text in English) 1978. m. DM.1732.80 (foreign DM.1743.60) (effective 1998). Springer-Verlag, Heidelberger Platz 3, 14197 Berlin, Germany. TEL 49-30-82787-0. FAX 49-30-82787448. E-mail: subscriptions@springer.de. (Subscr. in N. America to: Springer-Verlag New York, Inc., 333 Meadowlands Pkwy., Secaucus, NJ 07094. TEL 212-460-1500. FAX 212-473-6272) Ed.Bd. (also avail. in microfiche from UMI; reprint service avail. from ISI) **Indexed:** Abstr.Bull.Inst.Pap.Chem., Alloys Ind., Cadscan, Chem.Cit.Ind., Curr.Cont., Eng.Ind., Eng.Mat.Abstr., INSPEC, Intl.Polym.Sci.& Tech., Lead Abstr., Mat.Sci.Cit.Ind., Met.Abstr.Ind., Met.Abstr., Nonfer.Met.Alert, PCC Alert, Phys.Ber., RAPRA, Sci.Cit.Ind., Steels Alert, Sugar Ind.Abstr., World Alum.Abstr., Zincscan. **Document type:** academic/scholarly publication.
—BLDSC (6547.702500); CASDDS; CISTI; Ei; Genuine Article; Linda Hall; SWETS; UMI; UnCover. **CCC.**
     Description: Offers results in advances in polymer science, including biopolymers polymer engineering.

540   NE   ISSN 0926-9118
CODEN: PSLIF3
POLYMER SCIENCE LIBRARY. (Text in English) 1979. irreg., vol.9, 1990. price varies. Elsevier Science B.V., Books Division, P.O. Box 211, 1000 AE Amsterdam, Netherlands. TEL 31-20-4853911. FAX 31-20-4853705. TELEX 18582 ESPA NL. E-mail: nlinfo-f@elsevier.nl; usinfo-f@elsevier.com; forinfo-kyf04035@niftyserve.or.jp; URL: http://www.elsevier.nl/. (Subscr. in the Americas to: Elsevier Science, Regional Sales Office, Box 945, New York, NY 10159-0945. TEL 212-633-3730. FAX 212-633-3680; Subscr. in Australasia and the Far East to: Elsevier Science (Singapore) Pte Ltd, No.1 Temasek Ave., No.17-01 Millenia Tower, Singapore 039192, Singapore. TEL 65-434-3727. FAX 65-337-2230; Subscr. in Japan to: Elsevier Science Japan, 9-15 Higashi-Azabu 1-chome, Minato-ku, Tokyo 106, Japan. TEL 81-3-5561-5033. FAX 81-3-5561-5047) Ed. A.D. Jenkins. **Document type:** monographic series.
—BLDSC (6547.738400); CASDDS.
Refereed Serial

540   NE   ISSN 0738-1743
QD380   CODEN: POYEFS
POLYMER YEARBOOK. 1984. a. price varies. Gordon and Breach - Harwood Academic, Amsteldisk 166, 1st Fl., 1079 LH Amsterdam, Netherlands. (Subscr. to: International Publishers Distributor, Box 32160, Newark, NJ 07102. TEL 800-545-8398. FAX 215-750-6343) Ed. R.A. Pethrick. (also avail. in microform) **Document type:** monographic series.
—BLDSC (6547.740700); CASDDS; CISTI; Linda Hall; UnCover.
Refereed Serial

POLYMERS FOR ADVANCED TECHNOLOGIES. see *PLASTICS*

540 660   RM   CODEN: SICSEI
POLYTECHNICAL UNIVERSITY OF BUCHAREST. SCIENTIFIC BULLETIN. SERIES B: CHEMISTRY AND MATERIALS SCIENCE. (Text in English, French, German or Spanish; summaries in Rumanian and English) 1929. q. $100. Universitatea Politehnica Bucuresti, Biblioteca Centrala, Splaiul Independentei 313, 77206 Bucharest 16, Rumania. FAX 401-3120188. (Subscr. to: Rodipet, Piata presei Libere 1, Bucharest, Rumania. FAX 401-2226439) Ed. C. Berbente. bk.rev.; abstr.; bibl.; charts. circ. 1,000. **Document type:** academic/scholarly publication, bulletin.
—BLDSC (8177.820000); AskIEEE; CASDDS; CISTI; Ei; KR SourceOne; Linda Hall.
     Former titles: Universitatea Politehnica Bucuresti. Buletin Stiintific. Chimie si Stiinta Materialelor; Institutul Politehnic Bucuresti. Buletin Stiintific. Chimie, Metalurgie si Stiinta Materialelor (ISSN 1220-305X); Formed by the 1990 merger of: Institutul Politehnic Bucuresti. Buletin. Seria Chimie (ISSN 1012-3229); Institutul Politehnic Bucuresti. Buletin. Seria Metalurgia (ISSN 1012-3210); Seria Metalurgie was formerly (until 1983); Institutul Politehnic Gheorghe Gheorghiu-Dej Bucuresti. Buletin. Seria Metalurgia (ISSN 0256-4580); Seria Chimie was formerly (until 1983): Institutul Politehnic Gheorghe Gheorghiu-Dej Bucuresti. Buletin. Seria Chimie (ISSN 0257-7798); Which both superseded in part (in 1982): Institutul Politehnic Gheorghe Gheorghiu-Dej Bucuresti. Buletin. Seria Chimie - Metalurgie (ISSN 0378-9616); Which had former titles (until 1976): Institutul Politehnic Gheorghe Gheorghiu-Dej Bucuresti. Buletin (ISSN 0366-0419); (until 1965): Institutul Politehnic Bucuresti. Buletin (ISSN 0020-4242); Poltitehnicei din Bucuresti. Buletin.

540 370   GW   ISSN 0177-9516
CODEN: PXNCAP
PRAXIS DER NATURWISSENSCHAFTEN. CHEMIE. 1951. 8/yr. DM.112 (foreign DM.128) (effective 1997). Aulis-Verlag Deubner und Co. KG, Antwerpener Str. 6-12, 50672 Cologne, Germany. TEL 49-221-951454-0. FAX 49-221-518443. Ed.Bd. R&P contact: Wolfgang Deubner. adv. contact: Ulrike Lennertz. bk.rev.; abstr.; bibl.; illus.; index. **Indexed:** Chem.Abstr. **Document type:** academic/scholarly publication.
—BLDSC (6603.175800); CASDDS; CISTI. **CCC.**
     Former titles (until 1980): Praxis der Naturwissenschaften. Chemie im Unterricht der Schulen (ISSN 0342-8745); (until 1973): Praxis der Naturwissenschaften. Teil 3, Chemie (ISSN 0342-8737)

540   JA   ISSN 0915-1699
CODEN: PJPCE9
PROCEEDINGS OF JAPANESE SYMPOSIUM OF PLASMA CHEMISTRY. (Text in English) 1988. a. Organizing Committee of Japanese Symposium of Plasma Chemistry - Purazuma Kagaku Godo Shinpojumu Soshiki Iinkai, Kyoto Daigaku Kogakubu Denshi Kogakka, Yoshida Honmachi, Sakyo-ku, Kyoto-shi, Kyoto 606, Japan. **Indexed:** Chem.Abstr. **Document type:** proceedings.
—BLDSC (6847.143340); CASDDS.

540   NE   ISSN 0167-6938
TP156.F5   CODEN: PFSEDZ
PROGRESS IN FILTRATION AND SEPARATION. 1979. irreg., vol.4, 1986. price varies. Elsevier Science B.V., Books Division, P.O. Box 211, 1000 AE Amsterdam, Netherlands. TEL 31-20-4853911. FAX 31-20-4853705. TELEX 18582 ESPA NL. E-mail: nlinfo-f@elsevier.nl; usinfo-f@elsevier.com; forinfo-kyf04035@niftyserve.or.jp; URL: http://www.elsevier.nl/. (Subscr. in the Americas to: Elsevier Science, Regional Sales Office, Box 945, New York, NY 10159-0945. TEL 212-633-3730. FAX 212-633-3680; Subscr. in Australasia and the Far East to: Elsevier Science (Singapore) Pte Ltd, No.1 Temasek Ave., No.17-01 Millenia Tower, Singapore 039192, Singapore. TEL 65-434-3727. FAX 65-337-2230; Subscr. in Japan to: Elsevier Science Japan, 9-15 Higashi-Azabu 1-chome, Minato-ku, Tokyo 106, Japan. TEL 81-3-5561-5033. FAX 81-3-5561-5047) Ed. R.J. Wakeman. **Indexed:** AESIS, Chem.Abstr., I.M.M.Abstr. **Document type:** monographic series.
—CASDDS; CISTI.
Refereed Serial

CHEMISTRY   1763

540 510   NE   ISSN 0079-6468
RM30   CODEN: PMDCAY
PROGRESS IN MEDICINAL CHEMISTRY. 1961. irreg., vol.31, 1994. price varies. Elsevier Science B.V., Books Division, P.O. Box 211, 1000 AE Amsterdam, Netherlands. TEL 31-20-4853911. FAX 31-20-4853705. TELEX 18582 ESPA NL. E-mail: nlinfo-f@elsevier.nl; usinfo-f@elsevier.com; forinfo-kyf04035@niftyserve.or.jp; URL: http://www.elsevier.nl/. (Subscr. in the Americas to: Elsevier Science, Regional Sales Office, Box 945, New York, NY 10159-0945. TEL 212-633-3730. FAX 212-633-3680; Subscr. in Australasia and the Far East to: Elsevier Science (Singapore) Pte Ltd, No.1 Temasek Ave., No.17-01 Millenia Tower, Singapore 039192, Singapore. TEL 65-434-3727. FAX 65-337-2230; Subscr. in Japan to: Elsevier Science Japan, 9-15 Higashi-Azabu 1-chome, Minato-ku, Tokyo 106, Japan. TEL 81-3-5561-5033. FAX 81-3-5561-5047) Eds. G.P. Ellis, D.K. Luscombe. (back issues avail.) **Indexed:** Biol.Abstr., Biotech.Abstr., Chem.Abstr., Ind.Med., Ind.Sci.Rev. **Document type:** monographic series.
—BLDSC (6868.970000); CASDDS; CISTI; KNAW; Linda Hall; SWETS; UnCover. **CCC.**
Refereed Serial

PROTECTION OF ATMOSPHERE AGAINST POLLUTION; determination of atmospheric background pollution in South Prebaltic. see *ENVIRONMENTAL STUDIES — Pollution*

540   SP
PROYECTOS QUIMICOS. 1976. w. 38900 ptas. (foreign 49900 ptas.) (effective 1997). Tecnipublicaciones, S.A., C. Albacete 5, 28027 Madrid, Spain. TEL 34-1-3261440. FAX 36-1-3262407. stat.; circ. 3,000 (controlled). (processed)
     Description: Covers chemistry, drugs, plastics and paper.

660   PL   ISSN 0033-2496
TP1   CODEN: PRCHAB
PRZEMYSL CHEMICZNY. (Text in Polish; summaries in English, Polish and Russian; contents page in English, French, Polish, Russian) 1917. m. $102. (Ministerstwo Przemyslu Chemicznego) Wydawnictwo Czasopism i Ksiazek Technicznych SIGMA - NOT, Ul. Ratuszowa 11, P.O. Box 1004, 00-950 Warsaw, Poland. TEL 48-22-180918. FAX 48-22-192187. TELEX 814550 SIGMA PL. (Dist. by: SIGMA NOT Ltd., Ul. Bartycka 20, 00-716 Warsaw, Poland) (Co-sponsor: Stowarzyszenie Inzynierow i Technikow Przemyslu Chemicznego) Ed. Tadeusz Brzozowski. adv.; bk.rev.; abstr.; bibl.; charts; illus.; index. circ. 1,250. **Indexed:** ASCA, Cadscan, Ceram.Abstr., Chem.Abstr., Chem.Cit.Ind., Chem.Eng.Abstr., Chem.Infd., Curr.Chem.React., Curr.Cont., Ind.Chem., Lead Abstr., Mat.Sci.Cit.Ind., Risk Abstr., Soils & Fert., SSCI, T.C.E.A., Text.Tech.Dig., World Surf.Coat., Zincscan.
—BLDSC (6945.050000); CASDDS; CISTI; Ei; Genuine Article; SWETS.

CHEMISTRY

540 660 QD1 — UK — ISSN 0033-4545 — CODEN: PACHAS
PURE AND APPLIED CHEMISTRY. 1960. m. £720($1090) (foreign £788) (effective 1998). (International Union of Pure and Applied Chemistry) Blackwell Science Ltd., Osney Mead, Oxford OX2 0EL, England. TEL 44-1865-206206. FAX 44-1865-721205. E-mail: journals.cs@blacksci.co.uk; URL: http://www.black.co.uk. Ed. P.D. Gujral; Pub. Allen Stevens. R&P contact: Sarah Pollard. adv. contact: Martine Cariou-Keen. bk.rev.; abstr.; illus.; stat.; index. circ. 950. (also avail. in microform from UMI; back issues avail.) **Indexed:** Alloys Ind., Anal.Abstr., Apic.Abstr., Art & Archaeol.Tech.Abstr., ASCA, Biol.Abstr., Bull.Thermodyn.& Therm.Chem., Cadscan, Chem.Abstr., Chem.Cit.Ind., Chem.Infd., Curr.Cont., Dairy Sci.Abstr., Deep Sea Res.& Oceanogr.Abstr., Eng.Mat.Abstr., Excerp.Med., Food Sci.& Tech.Abstr., GeoRef., Ind.Med., Ind.Sci.Rev., INSPEC, Intl.Polym.Sci.& Tech., Lead Abstr., Mat.Sci.Cit.Ind., Met.Abstr., Met.Abstr.Ind., Nonfer.Met.Alert, PCC Alert, RAPRA, Rice Abstr., Sci.Cit.Ind., Steels Alert, World Alum.Abstr., Zincscan. **Document type:** academic/scholarly publication.
—BLDSC (7161.300000); ADONIS; CASDDS; CISTI; Ei; Genuine Article; Linda Hall; SWETS; UMI; UnCover. **CCC.**
Formerly: International Congress of Pure and Applied Chemistry. Lectures (ISSN 0074-3925)
Description: Publishes the text of lectures delivered by scientists at IUPAC symposia and specially commissioned review articles on important topics within the field.

PYROTECHNICA; occasional papers in pyrotechnics. see ENGINEERING — Chemical Engineering

540 — PO — CODEN: BSPQES
QUIMICA. 1977. q. Esc.5000 (foreign Esc.6000) to non-members. Sociedade Portuguesa de Quimica, Avda. da Republica 37, 4o, 1000 Lisbon, Portugal. Ed. Carlos Pessoa. circ. 3,800. **Document type:** newsletter.
—CASDDS; CISTI.
Formerly (until 1992): Sociedade Portuguesa de Quimica. Boletim (ISSN 0870-1180)

540 — BL — ISSN 0481-4118
QUIMICA E DERIVADOS. 1965. m. $70 (foreign $200) (effective 1997 & 1998). Editora Quimica e Derivados Ltda., Rua Conselheiro Brotero, 589, Cj.11 - 1o. Andar, 01154-001 Sao Paulo SP, Brazil. TEL 55-11-8266899. FAX 55-11-8258192. E-mail: edqd@embratel.net.br; URL: http://www.qd.com.br. Ed. Emanuel Fairbanks. adv.: B&W page $3950, color page $6350. charts; illus.; tr.lit. circ. 15,000.
Description: Deals with the chemical-petrochemical industry. Covers marketing development, researches, chemical and petrochemical sales in Brazil.

540 — SP — ISSN 0213-7828
QUIMICA HOY. 11/yr. $100 in Europe; elsewhere $115 (effective 1994). Saber Hoy S.A., Santiago de Compostela 64, 28034 Madrid, Spain. TEL 730-5801. FAX 1-738-72-66. Ed. Basilio Ballestin. adv. contact: Pepa de los Pinos. circ. 7,500.

540 — SP — ISSN 0213-4152
QUIMICA 2000. 6/yr. $73 in Europe; America $88 (effective 1997). Ediciones Tecnicas Izaro S.A., Mazustegui 21, 2a. y 4a. Planta, 48006 Bilbao, Spain. TEL 34-4-4159022. FAX 34-4-4162743. Ed. Ramon Urizar. circ. 4,000.

540 — AG
QUIMINOTICIAS. 1971. w. $300. Editorial Tecnica Siglo XXI, S.A., Talcahuano 342 PB 4, 1013 Buenos Aires, Argentina. TEL 54-1-3754458. bk.rev.; abstr.; bibl.; stat. circ. 500.
Formerly: Noticiero Quimico (ISSN 0048-0908)
Description: Covers chemical and petrochemical products, statistics, market analysis, news and technology reports.

R T E C S. (Registry of Toxic Effects of Chemical Substances) see OCCUPATIONAL HEALTH AND SAFETY

540 530 — JA — ISSN 0286-6722 — CODEN: HOKAER
RADIATION CHEMISTRY/HOSHASEN KAGAKU. (Text in Japanese) 1966. s-a. 3000 Yen. Japanese Society of Radiation Chemistry - Nihon Hoshasen Kagakkai, Nihon Genshiryoku Kenkyujo Takasaki Kenkyujo, 1233, Watanukicho, Takasaki-shi 370-12, Japan. Ed. S. Takamuku. circ. 600. **Indexed:** Chem.Abstr. —CASDDS.

RADIATION PHYSICS AND CHEMISTRY. see PHYSICS — Nuclear Physics

541.3884 R895.A1 — JA — ISSN 0033-8303 — CODEN: RAISAB
RADIOISOTOPES. (Text in English, Japanese; summaries in English) 1952. m. 15000 Yen. Japan Radioisotope Association - Nihon Aisotope Kyokai, 28-45 Hon-Komagome 2-chome, Bunkyo-ku, Tokyo 113, Japan. TEL 81-3-3946-7110. FAX 81-3-3946-2640. Ed. Tatsuyi Hamada. adv.; abstr.; bibl.; charts; illus.; index. circ. 5,000. **Indexed:** Art & Archaeol.Tech.Abstr., Biol.Abstr., Chem.Abstr., Dairy Sci.Abstr., Dent.Ind., Excerp.Med., Food Sci.& Tech.Abstr., Ind.Med., INIS Atomind., INSPEC, JTA, Nucl.Sci.Abstr. **Document type:** academic/scholarly publication.
—BLDSC (7237.300000); AskIEEE; CASDDS; CISTI; KR SourceOne; Linda Hall.

660 — US — ISSN 1056-0793 — CODEN: RARPEH
RADTECH REPORT. 1988. bi-m. $60 (foreign $95). RadTech International North America, 60 Revere Dr., Ste. 500, Northbrook, IL 60062. TEL 847-480-9576. FAX 847-480-9282. E-mail: uveb@radtech.com; URL: http://www.radtech.com. Ed. Angelo Artemakis. adv. circ. 1,038. **Indexed:** Intl.Polym.Sci.& Tech., RAPRA. **Document type:** trade publication.
—BLDSC (7242.275000); CASDDS.
Description: Covers research, development, marketing and end-use of UV-EB cured inks, coatings and adhesives.

RECENT ADVANCES IN PHYTOCHEMISTRY. see BIOLOGY — Botany

RESEARCH. see PHARMACY AND PHARMACOLOGY

540 QD501 — NE — ISSN 0922-6168 — CODEN: RCINEE
RESEARCH ON CHEMICAL INTERMEDIATES; an international journal. 1972. 9/yr. DM.980 (effective 1997). V S P, P.O. Box 346, 3700 AH Zeist, Netherlands. TEL 31-30-6925790. FAX 31-30-6932081. E-mail: 100341.2372@compuserve.com. Ed.Bd. adv. (back issues avail) **Indexed:** ASCA, Chem.Abstr., Chem.Cit.Ind., Curr.Chem.React., Curr.Cont., Ind.Chem., Ind.Sci.Rev., Sci.Cit.Ind. **Document type:** academic/scholarly publication.
—BLDSC (7734.775000); CASDDS; CISTI; Ei; Linda Hall; SWETS; UnCover. **CCC.**
Former titles (until 1988): Reviews of Chemical Intermediates (ISSN 0162-7546); (until 1977): Reviews on Reactive Species in Chemical Reactions (ISSN 0048-7562)
Description: Publishes current research and reviews on the properties, structures and reactivities of intermediate species in all the various domains of chemistry and related disciplines.
Refereed Serial

540 574.192 TP194.J3 — JA — ISSN 0919-9179 — CODEN: AGSHEN
RESEARCHES ASSISTED BY THE ASAHI GLASS FOUNDATION. REPORTS. (Text in Japanese; abstracts in English) 1934. a. exchange basis. Asahi Glass Foundation, 1-4-2, Marunouchi, Chiyoda-ku, Tokyo 100, Japan. TEL 83-3-3285-0591. FAX 83-3-3285-0592. Ed. Osamu Shiragami. **Indexed:** Alloys Ind., Eng.Mat.Abstr., Met.Abstr.Ind., Met.Abstr., Nonfer.Met.Alert, PCC Alert, Steels Alert, World Alum.Abstr. **Document type:** academic/scholarly publication.
—BLDSC (7666.945000); CASDDS; CISTI.
Description: Publishes results of researches assisted by the Asahi Glass Foundation.

REVIEWS IN CHEMICAL ENGINEERING. see ENGINEERING — Chemical Engineering

542 QD39.3.E46 — US — ISSN 1069-3599 — CODEN: RCCHEY
REVIEWS IN COMPUTATIONAL CHEMISTRY. 1990. a. V C H Publishers, Inc., c/o John Wiley, 605 3rd Ave., New York, NY 10158-0180. E-mail: order@vch.com. (Subscr. to: 303 N.W. 12th Ave., Deerfield Beach, FL 33442-1788. TEL 800-367-8249) Eds. K.B. Lipkowitz, D.B. Boyd. (back issues avail.) **Indexed:** Chem.Cit.Ind. **Document type:** monographic series.
—BLDSC (7789.077000); CASDDS; CISTI. **CCC.**
Description: Brings together renowned experts in the field of computer-aided research.

541 — US
REVIEWS OF PLASMA CHEMISTRY. 1991. irreg., vol.3, 1995. price varies. Plenum Publishing Corp., Consultants Bureau, 233 Spring St., New York, NY 10013-1578. TEL 212-620-8000. FAX 212-463-0742. Ed. B.M. Smirnov. (back issues avail.) **Document type:** monographic series.
Description: English translations of works originally published in Russian.

540 — JA — ISSN 0915-6151 — CODEN: RHCHEZ
REVIEWS ON HETEROATOM CHEMISTRY. (Text in English) 1988. 2/yr. 28000 Yen. M Y U, Scientific Publishing Division, 2-32-3 Sendagi, Bunkyo-ku, Tokyo 113, Japan. TEL 81-3-3821-2930. FAX 81-3-3827-8547. Ed. Shigeru Oae. **Indexed:** ASCA, Chem.Cit.Ind. **Document type:** academic/scholarly publication.
—BLDSC (7790.768800); CASDDS; CISTI; KNAW.
Description: Covers physical inorganic and organic chemistry, and physical as well as synthetic organic chemistry of sulfur, phosphorous, selenium, boron, and many other elements.
Refereed Serial

540 QD1 — CU — ISSN 1015-8553 — CODEN: RCCQER
REVISTA C E N I C. CIENCIAS QUIMICAS. (Text and summaries in English, Spanish) 1969. 3/yr. $60 in N. America and S. America; elsewhere $90 (effective 1997). (Ministerio de Educacion Superior) Centro Nacional de Investigaciones Cientificas, Ave. 25 y 158, Apdo. 6880 y 6990, Havana 10600, Cuba. TEL 537-219045. FAX 537-330497. TELEX 51-1582 CNIC CU. E-mail: cnic@reduniv.edu.cu. Ed. Juan J. Meitin Casas. bibl.; charts. circ. 750. (back issues avail.) **Indexed:** Alloys Ind., Chem.Abstr., Eng.Mat.Abstr., Met.Abstr., Met.Abstr.Ind., Nonfer.Met.Alert, PCC Alert, Steels Alert, Sugar Ind.Abstr., World Alum.Abstr.
—BLDSC (7804.765000); CASDDS; CISTI.
Formerly (until 1986): Revista de Ciencias Fisicas (ISSN 0254-0525)
Description: Presents national and international articles in the chemical sciences; covers organic, inorganic, physical and analytical chemistry.

REVISTA COLOMBIANA DE CIENCIAS QUIMICO FARMACEUTICAS. see PHARMACY AND PHARMACOLOGY

540 — CU — ISSN 0258-5995 — CODEN: RCQUE7
REVISTA CUBANA DE QUIMICA. (Summaries in English, Spanish) 1985? q. $25 in N. America; S. America $26; Europe $28. (Ministerio de Educacion Superior) Ediciones Cubanas, Obispo No. 527, Apdo 605, Havana, Cuba. TEL 32-5556-60.
—CASDDS; CISTI.

660 — RM — ISSN 0034-7752 — CODEN: RCBAUU
REVISTA DE CHIMIE. (Text in Rumanian; summaries in English, French, German, Russian) 1949. m. $144. Chiminform Data S.A., Calea Plevnei 139, 77131 Bucharest, Rumania. FAX 3-1231-60. TELEX 1030 CHINF. Ed. Nelia Mihaila. adv. contact: Nelia Mihaila. bk.rev.; abstr.; bibl.; illus.; pat.; index. circ. 1,600. **Indexed:** Anal.Abstr., ASCA, C.I.S. Abstr., Chem.Abstr., Chem.Cit.Ind., Chem.Eng.Abstr., Curr.Cont., Mass Spectr.Bull., Mat.Sci.Cit.Ind., SSCI, T.C.E.A. **Document type:** academic/scholarly publication.
—BLDSC (7849.500000); CASDDS; CISTI; Ei; Genuine Article; Linda Hall; UMI.

REVISTA DE FIZICA SI CHIMIE. see PHYSICS

| 540 | | PE | ISSN 1012-3946 |

REVISTA DE QUIMICA. 1987. s-a. $28. Pontificia Universidad Catolica del Peru, Fondo Editorial, Apdo. 1761, Lima 32, Peru. TEL 51-14-626390. FAX 5114-611785. E-mail: editorial@pucp.edu.pe; URL: http://www.pucp.edu.co. Ed. Olga Lock de Ugaz. bk.rev. **Document type:** academic/scholarly publication.
Refereed Serial

| 540 | | MX | ISSN 0370-5943 |
| QD1 | | | CODEN: RLAQA8 |

REVISTA LATINOAMERICANA DE QUIMICA. (Text in English or Spanish, with some abstracts in English) 1970. q. $55 (effective 1994). Federacion Latinoamericana de Quimica, Instituto Tecnologico y de Estudios Superiores de Monterrey, Apdo. Postal 4606, Sucursal de Correos "J", 64849 Monterrey, NL, Mexico. TEL 8-363-49-26. FAX 8-345-76-28. (Co-sponsor: Sociedad Fitoquimica de Mexico) Ed. Julia Verde. adv.; bk.rev.; illus. circ. 3,000. **Indexed:** Biol.Abstr., Chem.Abstr., Curr.Cont., Food Sci.& Tech.Abstr. **Document type:** academic/scholarly publication.
—BLDSC (7863.514500); CASDDS; CISTI; Ei; KNAW; Linda Hall; UMI.
Description: Contains original papers and reviews on organic chemistry, natural products, and phytochemistry.

| 540 | | PO | ISSN 0035-0419 |
| | | | CODEN: RPTQAT |

REVISTA PORTUGUESA DE QUIMICA. (Text and summaries in English, French, Portuguese) 1905. q. Esc.4500($18) Sociedade Portuguesa de Quimica, Av. da Republica 37-4o, 1000 Lisbon, Portugal. TEL 351-1-7934637. FAX 351-1-7952349. TELEX 28109 FCUP P. Ed. Manuel A. V. Ribeiro da Silva. adv.; bibl.; charts; illus.; index. circ. 4,000. **Indexed:** Biol.Abstr., Chem.Abstr., Curr.Cont.
—CASDDS; CISTI.

| 540 | | CU | |

REVISTA TECNOLOGIA: QUIMICA. q. $25 in N. America; S. America $26; Europe $28. (Ministerio de la Industria Basica) Ediciones Cubanas, Obispo No. 527, Apdo. 605, Havana, Cuba. TEL 32-5556-60.

REVUE DES COMPOSITES ET DES MATERIAUX AVANCES. *see* ENGINEERING — Engineering Mechanics And Materials

REVUE EUROPEENNE DES ELEMENTS FINIS. *see* ENGINEERING — Engineering Mechanics And Materials

| 540 | | RM | ISSN 0035-3930 |
| QD1 | | | CODEN: RRCHAX |

REVUE ROUMAINE DE CHIMIE. (Text in English, French, German, Russian, Spanish) 1956. 10/yr. (Academia Romana) Editura Academiei Romane, Calea 13 Septembrie 13, 76117 Bucharest, Rumania. (Dist. by: Rodipet SA, Piata Presei Libere 1, Sec. 1, P.O. Box 33-57, Bucharest, Rumania. TEL 401-6185103. FAX 401-2226407) Ed. A.T. Balaban. bk.rev.; bibl.; charts; illus.; index. circ. 3,000. **Indexed:** Abstr.Bull.Inst.Pap.Chem., Anal.Abstr., ASCA, Biol.Abstr., Cadscan, Ceram.Abstr., Chem.Abstr., Chem.Cit.Ind., Chem.Eng.Abstr., Chem.Infd., Curr.Chem.React., Curr.Cont., Ind.Chem., Ind.Sci.Rev., Lead Abstr., Mass Spectr.Bull., Mat.Sci.Cit.Ind., Met.Abstr., Sci.Cit.Ind., World Surf.Coat., Zincscan. **Document type:** academic/scholarly publication.
—BLDSC (7946.200000); CASDDS; CISTI; Genuine Article; KNAW; Linda Hall; SWETS; UnCover.

| 540 | | IT | |

RICH-MAC MAGAZINE. 1988. 6/yr. L.50000. Editrice B.I.A.S. s.a.s., Viale Premuda 2, 20129 Milan, Italy. TEL 39-2-55181842. FAX 39-2-5400481. TELEX 352110 BIAS I. Ed. Mario Gargantini. adv.: B&W page L.1600000, color page L.2500000. circ. 14,000.

| 540 | | JA | ISSN 0913-302X |

RIGAKU DENKI JANARU/RIGAKU DENKI JOURNAL. (Text in Japanese; summaries in English) 1959. s-a. Rigaku Denki K.K. - Rigaku Corp., 3-9-12 Matsubara-cho, Akishima-shi, Tokyo 196, Japan. TEL 0425-45-8139. FAX 0425-46-7090. Ed. Tomoya Arai; Hikaru Shimura. **Indexed:** Chem.Abstr. **Document type:** academic/scholarly publication.
—BLDSC (7970.680450).

RIKAGAKKAISHI/JOURNAL OF PHYSICS, CHEMISTRY AND EARTH SCIENCE. *see* SCIENCES: COMPREHENSIVE WORKS

RIKAGAKU KENKYUJO HOKOKU/INSTITUTE OF PHYSICAL AND CHEMICAL RESEARCH. REPORTS. *see* PHYSICS

| 540 | | US | |

ROCHESTER CHEMUNICATIONS. 1949. bi-m. $6. American Chemical Society, Rochester Section, Inc., Box 15571, Rochester, NY 14615-0571. TEL 716-338-3995. FAX 716-588-7611. Ed. Susan Mattes. adv. contact: Susan Mattes. charts; illus.; tr.lit. circ. 1,500. (back issues avail.) **Document type:** newsletter.
Formerly: Genesee Valley Chemunications (ISSN 0016-6642)

ROPA A UHLIE. *see* PETROLEUM AND GAS

| 540 660 | | RU | |
| AS262 | | | CODEN: IASKA6 |

ROSSIISKAYA AKADEMIYA NAUK. IZVESTIYA. SERIYA KHIMICHESKAYA. English translation: Russian Chemical Bulletin. (Text in Russian) 1936. m. 84 Rub. Izdatel'stvo Nauka, 90 Profsoyuznaya ul., 117864 Moscow, Russia. (Dist. by: Mezhdunarodnaya Kniga, B. Yakimanka 39, 117049 Moscow, Russia) Ed. M.M. Dubinin. charts; illus.; index. circ. 2,750. **Indexed:** Alloys Ind., Anal.Abstr., Chem.Abstr., Eng.Mat.Abstr., INIS Atomind., Met.Abstr., Met.Abstr.Ind., Nonfer.Met.Alert, PCC Alert, Steels Alert, World Alum.Abstr., World Surf.Coat. **Document type:** academic/scholarly publication.
—CASDDS; CISTI; KNAW; Linda Hall. **CCC.**
Formerly (until no.2, 1992): Akademiya Nauk S.S.S.R. Izvestiya. Seriya Khimicheskaya (ISSN 0002-3353)

| 540 | | RU | |
| TP1.V82 | | | CODEN: ZVKOA6 |

ROSSIISKII KHIMICHESKII ZHURNAL. English translation: Mendeleev Chemistry Journal (US ISSN 0025-925X) 1960. bi-m. Rossiiskoe Khimicheskoe Obshchestvo im. D.I. Mendeleeva, Krivokolennyi per., 12, 101000 Moscow, Russia. TEL 7-95-9219810. **Indexed:** Food Sci.& Tech.Abstr.
—CASDDS; CISTI; KNAW; Linda Hall. **CCC.**
Formerly (until 1994): Vsesoyuznoe Khimicheskoe Obshchestvo im. D.I. Mendeleeva. Zhurnal (ISSN 0373-0247)

| 540 | | RM | ISSN 1221-5260 |
| | | | CODEN: RCQREW |

ROUMANIAN CHEMICAL QUARTERLY REVIEWS. (Text in English) 1993. q. (Academia Romana) Editura Academiei Romane, Calea 13 Septembrie 13, 76117 Bucharest, Rumania. (Dist. by: Rodpiet SA, Piata presei Libere 1, Sec. 1, PO Box 33-57, Bucharest, Rumania. TEL 401-6185103. FAX 401-2226407) Ed. Alexandru Balaban.
—BLDSC (8025.759500); CASDDS; CISTI.
Supersedes (1953-1974): Studii si Cercetari de Chimie (ISSN 0039-3908)

| 540 | | UK | ISSN 0306-0012 |
| QD1 | | | CODEN: CSRVBR |

ROYAL SOCIETY OF CHEMISTRY. REVIEWS. Short title: Chemical Society Reviews. 1972. bi-m. £130 to institutions (US $234) (effective 1997). The Royal Society of Chemistry, Thomas Graham House, Science Park, Milton Rd., Cambridge CB4 4WF, England. TEL 44-1223-420066. FAX 44-1223-423429. E-mail: sales@rsc.org; URL: http://chemistry.rsc.org/rsc/. (Subscr. to: Turpin Distribution Services Ltd., Blackhorse Rd., Letchworth, Herts. SG6 1HN, England. TEL 44-1462-672555. FAX 44-1462-480947) bibl.; charts; index, cum.index. (also avail. in microfilm from PMC) **Indexed:** Anal.Abstr., Appl.Mech.Rev., ASCA, Biol.Abstr., Biotech.Abstr., Br.Ceram.Abstr., Bull.Thermodyn.& Thermochem., Cadscan, Chem.Abstr., Chem.Cit.Ind., Chem.Infd., Curr.Adv.Ecol.Sci., Curr.Chem.React., Curr.Cont., Curr.Leather Lit., Dairy Sci.Abstr., Deep Sea Res.& Oceanogr.Abstr., Food Sci.& Tech.Abstr., Ind.Chem., Ind.Sci.Rev., INIS Atomind., Lead Abstr., Mat.Sci.Cit.Ind., Risk Abstr., Sci.Cit.Ind., World Surf.Coat., World Text.Abstr., Zincscan. **Document type:** academic/scholarly publication.
—BLDSC (3151.550000); CASDDS; CISTI; Ei; Genuine Article; Linda Hall; SWETS; UMI; UnCover. **CCC.**
Superseded: Chemical Society, London. Quarterly Reviews (ISSN 0009-2681); Royal Institute of Chemistry Reviews (ISSN 0035-8940)
Description: Provides in-depth coverage of the state-of-the-art of subject under review, and introductory reviews of new topics. Also contains texts of the lectures given by the society's named lecturers.

| 540 660 | | US | ISSN 1066-5285 |
| QD1 | | | CODEN: RCBUEY |

RUSSIAN CHEMICAL BULLETIN. English translation of: Rossiiskaya Akademiya Nauk. Izvestiya. Seriya Khimicheskaya. 1936. m. $1855 (foreign $2170) (effective 1998). (Rossiiskaya Akademiya Nauk, RU) Plenum Publishing Corp., Consultants Bureau, 233 Spring St., New York, NY 10013-1578. TEL 212-620-8468. FAX 212-463-0742. TELEX 23-421139. Ed. O.M. Nefedov. (also avail. in microfilm from UMI; back issues avail.) **Indexed:** Alloys Ind., ASCA, Cadscan, Chem.Cit.Ind., Chem.Titles, Curr.Cont., Energy Res.Abstr., Eng.Mat.Abstr., Ind.Sci.Rev., INIS Atomind., Lead Abstr., Mass Spectr.Bull., Met.Abstr., Met.Abstr.Ind., Nonfer.Met.Alert, PCC Alert, Sci.Cit.Ind., Steels Alert, World Alum.Abstr., Zincscan. **Document type:** academic/scholarly publication.
—BLDSC (0420.754200); CASDDS; CISTI; Genuine Article; Linda Hall; SWETS; UMI; UnCover. **CCC.**
Former titles (until 1994): Russian Academy of Sciences. Division of Chemical Sciences. Bulletin (ISSN 1063-5211); (until 1992): Academy of Sciences of the U S S R. Division of Chemical Sciences. Bulletin (ISSN 0568-5230)
Refereed Serial

| 660 | | US | ISSN 1068-3704 |
| TP1 | | | |

RUSSIAN CHEMICAL INDUSTRY. English translation of: Khimicheskaya Promyshlennost' (RU ISSN 0023-110X) 1969. m. $1025 (effective 1998). (Ministry of the Chemical Industry, RU) Allerton Press, Inc., 150 Fifth Ave., New York, NY 10011. TEL 212-924-3950. FAX 212-463-9684. Ed. M.G. Slin'ko. charts; illus.; stat.; index. (back issues avail.) **Indexed:** Chem.Eng.Abstr., Excerp.Med., Fuel & Energy Abstr., Soils & Fert., T.C.E.A., Text.Tech.Dig. **Document type:** academic/scholarly publication.
—BLDSC (0420.754500); CISTI; SWETS; UnCover. **CCC.**
Formerly: Soviet Chemical Industry (ISSN 0038-5344)
Description: Covers industrial chemistry research and development in Russia, including organic and inorganic chemistry, and technology.

CHEMISTRY

540   RU   ISSN 0036-021X
QD1   CODEN: RCRVAB
RUSSIAN CHEMICAL REVIEWS. English translation of: Uspekhi Khimii (RU ISSN 0042-1308) (Text in English) 1960. m. £790 (US $1250) (effective 1998). (The Royal Society of Chemistry, UK) Turpion - Moscow Ltd., 47 Leninsky prospekt, 117913 Moscow, Russia. TEL 7-95-1356417. FAX 7-95-1358860. E-mail: turpion@cacr.ioc.ac.ru; URL: http://turpion.ioc.ac.ru. (Dist. by: Turpin Distribution Services Ltd., Blackhorse Rd., Letchworth, Herts. SB6 1HN, England. TEL 44-1462-672555. FAX 44-1462-480947) (Co-sponsor: Russian Academy of Sciences) Ed.Bd. bibl.; charts. **Indexed:** Alloys Ind., Eng.Mat.Abstr., Excerp.Med., GeoRef., Mass Spectr.Bull., Met.Abstr.Ind., Met.Abstr., Nonfer.Met.Alert, PCC Alert, Steels Alert, W.R.C.Inf., World Alum.Abstr., World Text.Abstr. **Document type:** academic/scholarly publication.
●Also available online.
Also available on CD-ROM.
—BLDSC (0420.755000); CISTI; Ei; Linda Hall; SWETS; UnCover.
Description: Serves to set Russian chemical research in an international context.
Refereed Serial

541.224   RU   ISSN 1070-3284
QD474   CODEN: RJCCEY
RUSSIAN JOURNAL OF COORDINATION CHEMISTRY. English translation of: Koordinatsionnaya Khimiya (RU ISSN 0132-344X) 1975. m. $1235 in US; elsewhere $1445 (effective 1998). (Russian Academy of Sciences) Maik Nauka - Interperiodica, Mezhdunarodnyi Otdel, Ul. Profsoyuznaya, 90, 117864 Moscow, Russia. TEL 7-095-3360066. FAX 7-095-3360666. (Dist. by: Plenum Publishing Corp., 233 Spring St., New York, NY 10013-1578. TEL 212-620-8468. FAX 212-463-0742) Ed. N.T. Kuznetsov. (also avail. in microfilm from UMI; back issues avail.) **Indexed:** Chem.Abstr., Chem.Titles, Mass Spectr.Bull. **Document type:** academic/scholarly publication.
—BLDSC (0420.760850); CASDDS; CISTI; UMI; UnCover. CCC.
Formerly (until 1994): Soviet Journal of Coordination Chemistry (ISSN 0364-4626)
Refereed Serial

540   RU   ISSN 1070-3632
QD1   CODEN: RJGCEK
RUSSIAN JOURNAL OF GENERAL CHEMISTRY. English translation of: Zhurnal Obshchei Khimii (RU ISSN 0044-460X) 1949. m. $1875 in US; elsewhere $2195 (effective 1998). (Russian Academy of Sciences) Maik Nauka - Interperiodica, Mezhdunarodnyi Otdel, Ul. Profsoyuznaya, 90, 17864 Moscow, Russia. TEL 7-095-3360066. FAX 7-095-3360666. Ed. Anatolii I. Rusanov. (also avail. in microfilm from UMI; back issues avail.) **Indexed:** Chem.Titles, Energy Res.Abstr., INIS Atomind., Mass Spectr.Bull., Met.Abstr., Sugar Ind.Abstr. **Document type:** academic/scholarly publication.
—BLDSC (0420.760950); CASDDS; CISTI; Linda Hall; SWETS; UMI; UnCover. CCC.
Former titles (until 1994): Journal of General Chemistry; (until 1993): Journal of General Chemistry of the U S S R (ISSN 0022-1279)
Refereed Serial

540   US   ISSN 1061-8309
TA417.2   CODEN: RJNTE4
RUSSIAN JOURNAL OF NONDESTRUCTIVE TESTING. English translation of: Defektoskopiya (RU ISSN 0130-3082) 1964. m. $1845 (foreign $2160) (effective 1998). (Russian Academy of Sciences, RU) Plenum Publishing Corp., Consultants Bureau, 233 Spring St., New York, NY 10013-1578. TEL 212-620-8468. FAX 212-463-0742. TELEX 23-421139. Ed. V.E. Shcherbinin. charts; illus. (also avail. in microfilm from UMI; back issues avail.) **Indexed:** Appl.Mech.Rev., ASCA, Curr.Cont., Electron.& Communic.Abstr.J., Energy Res.Abstr., Eng.Ind., Eng.Mat.Abstr., INSPEC (1992-), ISMEC, Mat.Sci.Cit.Ind., Met.Abstr.Ind., Met.Abstr., Nonfer.Met.Alert, PCC Alert, Solid.St.Abstr., Steels Alert, World Alum.Abstr. **Document type:** academic/scholarly publication.
—BLDSC (0420.762000); AskIEEE; CASDDS; CISTI; Genuine Article; KR SourceOne; Linda Hall; SWETS; UMI; UnCover. CCC.
Former titles (until 1992): Soviet Journal of Nondestructive Testing (ISSN 0038-5492); (until 1968): Defectoscopy (ISSN 0418-4947)
Refereed Serial

540   US
S A C I SLANTS. 1952. 3/yr. membership. Sales Association of the Chemical Industry, Inc., 66 Morris Ave., Ste. 2A, Springfield, NJ 07081-1450. TEL 201-379-1100. FAX 201-379-6507. adv. contact: Dle Nieves. bk.rev. circ. 3,000. **Document type:** newsletter.

540   US   ISSN 0044-7595
S C A L A C S. (Southern California Section of American Chemical Society) 1945. 7/yr. $10. American Chemical Society, Southern California Section, 14934 S. Figueroa St., Gardena, CA 90248. TEL 310-327-1216. FAX 310-538-9709. Ed. Heather Kinney. R&P contact: Rita Boggs. adv. contact: Charles Wallace. bk.rev. circ. 2,500. **Indexed:** Art & Archaeol.Tech.Abstr., Excerp.Med. **Document type:** newsletter.

660 547   US
S O C M A NEWSLETTER. 1966. fortn. membership. Synthetic Organic Chemical Manufacturers Association, 1100 New York Ave., Ste. 1090, Washington, DC 20007. TEL 202-414-4100. FAX 202-289-8584. Ed. Amy L. Clapper. circ. 1,400. (processed; reprint service avail.) **Document type:** newsletter.
●Also available online.
Description: Covers the latest developments affecting the chemical industry; reviews membership activities, including seminars and workshops.

SAITAMA MATHEMATICAL JOURNAL. see *MATHEMATICS*

SANKT-PETERBURGSKII UNIVERSITET. VESTNIK. SERIYA FIZIKA I KHIMIYA. see *PHYSICS*

660   JA   ISSN 0036-4649
CODEN: SAKNBI
SANYO KASEI NEWS. (Text in Japanese) 1949. bi-m. free. Sanyo Chemical Industries Ltd., 11-1 Ikkyo Nomoto-cho, Higashiyama-ku, Kyoto 605, Japan. Ed. Yoshizo Takayanagi. bk.rev.; charts; illus.; circ. 6,000 (controlled).
—CASDDS.

660.029   US
THE SCHNELL RED BOOK OF CHEMICAL SERVICES. (Companion vol. to O P D Chemical Buyers Directory (ISSN 0276-539X)) 1990. a. (issued in Dec.). Schnell Publishing Co. Inc., 80 Broad St., New York, NY 10004-2203. TEL 212-248-4177. FAX 212-248-4903. Pub. James Hannan. adv. **Document type:** directory, trade publication.
Description: Lists chemical distributors, manufacturers, and services. Also identifies environmental services, consultants, and chemical associations.

540   UK   ISSN 0792-1233
CODEN: SCMAE6
SCIENCE AND ENGINEERING OF COMPOSITE MATERIALS. (Text in English) 1986. q. $250 (effective 1997). Freund Publishing House Ltd., Ste. 500, Chesham House, 150 Regent St., London W1R 5FA, England. (And: P.O. Box 35010, Tel Aviv, Israel. TEL 972-3-5628540. FAX 972-3-5628538) Eds. S.V. Hoa, M. Sako. adv. circ. 1,000. (back issues avail.) **Indexed:** Alloys Ind., ASCA, Eng.Mat.Abstr., Mat.Sci.Cit.Ind., Met.Abstr.Ind., Met.Abstr., Nonfer.Met.Alert, PCC Alert, Steels Alert, World Alum.Abstr. **Document type:** academic/scholarly publication.
—BLDSC (8133.023000); CASDDS; CISTI; SWETS.
Formerly (until 1992): Composite Materials Science (ISSN 0334-181X)

540   NE   ISSN 1006-9291
CODEN: SCBCFQ
SCIENCE IN CHINA. SERIES B: CHEMISTRY. (Text in English) 1952. 12/yr. $250 (effective 1998). (Chinese Academy of Sciences) Gordon and Breach - Harwood Academic, Amsteldisk 166, 1st Fl., 1079 LH Amsterdam, Netherlands. (Subscr. to: International Publishers Distributor, Box 32160, Newark, NJ 07102. TEL 800-545-8398. FAX 215-750-6343) Ed. Dongsheng Yan. adv.; index. circ. 10,000. (also avail. in microform; back issues avail.; reprint service avail. from KTO) **Indexed:** ASCA, Cadscan, Chem.Cit.Ind., Curr.Cont., Curr.Ref.Fish Res., Ecol.Abstr., Geo.Abstr.H.G., Geol.Abstr., Lead Abstr., Mat.Sci.Cit.Ind., Meteor.& Geoastrophys.Abstr., Sci.Cit.Ind., SSCI, World Surf.Coat., Zincscan. **Document type:** academic/scholarly publication.
—BLDSC (8141.669500); CASDDS; CISTI; Ei; Genuine Article; Linda Hall; SWETS; UMI; UnCover.
Supersedes in part (in 1996): Science in China. Series B: Chemistry, Life Sciences and Earth Sciences (ISSN 1001-652X); Which was formerly (until 1989): Scientia Sinica. Series B: Chemistry, Life Sciences and Earth Sciences (ISSN 0253-5823); Which superseded in part: Scientia Sinica.
Description: Contains academic papers on scientific work in the field of chemistry.
Refereed Serial

540   YU   ISSN 0352-5139
QD1   CODEN: JSCSEN
SERBIAN CHEMICAL SOCIETY. JOURNAL. (Subseries of: Documenta Chemica Yugoslavica) (Text in English; abstracts in Serbo-Croatian) 1930. 12/yr. $70. Srpsko Hemijsko Drustvo - Serbian Chemical Society, Karnegijeva 4, Box 462, 11001 Belgrade, Yugoslavia. TEL 011-328-583. (Subscr. to: Jugoslavenska Knjiga, Export-Import, Trg Republike 5, 11000 Belgrade, Yugoslavia) Ed. Dragutin Drazic. adv.; bk.rev.; charts; illus.; index. circ. 1,300. **Indexed:** Alloys Ind., Anal.Abstr., Biol.Abstr., Chem.Abstr., Corros.Abstr., Curr.Cont., Eng.Mat.Abstr., Food Sci.& Tech.Abstr., INIS Atomind., Mass Spectr.Bull., Met.Abstr.Ind., Met.Abstr., Nonfer.Met.Alert, PCC Alert, Steels Alert, Sugar Ind.Abstr., World Alum.Abstr. **Document type:** academic/scholarly publication.
—BLDSC (4874.638000); CASDDS; CISTI; Ei; Linda Hall; UnCover.
Formerly: Glasnik Hemijskog Drustva-Societe Chimique, Belgrade. Bulletin (ISSN 0017-0941)

SEVERO-KAVKAZSKII NAUCHNYI TSENTR VYSSHEI SHKOLY. ESTESTVENNYE NAUKI. IZVESTIYA/NORTH-CAUCASUS SCIENTIFIC CENTER OF HIGH SCHOOL. NATURAL SCIENCES. NEWS. see *MATHEMATICS*

SHIKISAI KOGAKU KONFARENSU RONBUNSHU/PROCEEDINGS OF JOINT CONFERENCE ON COLOR TECHNOLOGY. see *PHYSICS — Optics*

SHIYOU HUAGONG/PETROCHEMICAL TECHNOLOGY. see *PETROLEUM AND GAS*

540   SI   ISSN 0129-5772
CODEN: SNIBDV
SINGAPORE NATIONAL INSTITUTE OF CHEMISTRY. BULLETIN. Cover title: S N I C Bulletin. (Text in English) 1972. a. S.$30 (foreign $20). Singapore National Institute of Chemistry, c/o Department of Chemistry, National University of Singapore, Kent Ridge, Singapore 0511, Singapore. TEL 65-772-2914. FAX 65-779-1691. TELEX UNISPO-RS33943. E-mail: chmlaiyh@leonis.nus.sg. Ed. Yee-Hing Lai. adv.; charts. circ. 1,000. **Indexed:** Chem.Abstr. **Document type:** academic/scholarly publication, bulletin.
—BLDSC (2720.298000); CASDDS.
Refereed Serial

CHEMISTRY 1767

540   XO   ISSN 0366-6352
                                    CODEN: CHPAEG
SLOVENSKA CHEMICKA SPOLOCNOST. CHEMICKE ZVESTI/CHEMICAL PAPERS. (Text in English, French, German or Russian; summaries in English and Russian) 1947. bi-m. $120 in US (effective 1996). Vydavatel'stvo S A P, s.r.o., Faculty of Chemical Technology - Slovak Academic Press Ltd., P.O. Box 57, Nam. Slobody 6, 810 05 Bratislava, Slovakia. TEL 42-7-211728. (Co-sponsor: Slovak Technical University, Faculty of Chemical Technology) Ed. M. Zikmund. bk.rev.; charts; illus.; index. **Indexed:** Abstr.Bull.Inst.Pap.Chem., Anal.Abstr., ASCA, Biol.Abstr., C.I.S. Abstr., Cadscan, Chem.Abstr., Chem.Cit.Ind., Chem.Eng.Abstr., Curr.Cont., Ind.Sci.Rev., INIS Atomind., Lead Abstr., Mass Spectr.Bull., Mat.Sci.Cit.Ind., RAPRA, Sci.Cit.Ind., T.C.E.A., World Surf.Coat., Zincscan. **Document type:** academic/scholarly publication.
—CASDDS; CISTI; Genuine Article; Linda Hall. **CCC.**
   Description: Publishes original works from physical, organic, macromolecular and analytical chemistry, biochemistry, chemical engineering, from inorganic and organic technology as well as from technology of wood, cellulose and chemical fibres.

540   CL   ISSN 0366-1644
                                    CODEN: BOCQAX
SOCIEDAD CHILENA DE QUIMICA. BOLETIN/CHILEAN CHEMICAL SOCIETY. BULLETIN. (Text and summaries in English, Spanish) 1949. q. $80 to non-members. Sociedad Chilena de Quimica, Casilla 2613, Concepcion, Chile. TEL (0056)-41-235819. Dir. Mario Silva. adv.; bk.rev.; bibl.; charts; illus.; cum.index. circ. 600. (also avail. in microfilm) **Indexed:** ASCA, Biol.Abstr., Chem.Abstr., Curr.Cont., Ref.Zh. **Document type:** bulletin.
—BLDSC (2190.250000); CASDDS; CISTI; Genuine Article.

SOCIEDAD COLOMBIANA DE QUIMICOS FARMACEUTICOS. BOLETIN. see *PHARMACY AND PHARMACOLOGY*

540   SP   ISSN 0213-8514
                                    CODEN: RSQCEV
SOCIEDAD ESPANOLA DE QUIMICA CLINICA. REVISTA. (Text in Spanish; summaries in English) 1982. 5/yr. Ediciones Mayo, S.A., Muntaner, 374-376, 4o, 08006 Barcelona, Spain. TEL 34-3-2090255. FAX 34-3-2020643. (Subscr. to: S.E.Q.C., Llanca, 51 baixos 3a, 08015 Barcelona, Spain. TEL 34-3-2269827) Ed. Jordi Hugnet. adv. contact: Jose Mayoral. bk.rev.; bibl.; charts; illus.; index. **Indexed:** Chem.Abstr., Curr.Adv.Clin.Chem., Excerp.Med. **Document type:** academic/scholarly publication.
—CASDDS; EMDOCS.
   Description: Contains original articles on research in clinical chemistry.
   Refereed Serial

540   MX   ISSN 0583-7693
QD1   CODEN: RSQMAN
SOCIEDAD QUIMICA DE MEXICO. REVISTA. 1957. bi-m. $55 (effective 1997). Sociedad Quimica de Mexico, Mar del Norte 5, Col. San Alvaro, Deleg. Azcapotzalco, 02090 Mexico, D.F., Mexico. TEL 52-5-3860255. FAX 52-5-3862905. Eds. Federico Garcia Jimenez, Guillermo Delgado Lamas; Pub. Claudia S. Lopez Cruz. adv. contact: Rosa Jaime C. circ. 3,500. **Indexed:** Biol.Abstr., Chem.Abstr. **Document type:** academic/scholarly publication.
—CASDDS; Linda Hall.
   Refereed Serial

540   PE   ISSN 0037-8623
                                    CODEN: BSQPAQ
SOCIEDAD QUIMICA DEL PERU. BOLETIN. 1934. q. $50 (effective 1996). Sociedad Quimica del Peru, Comision de Publicaciones, Presidente, Apdo. 14-0576, Av. Nicolas de Aranibar 696, Santa Beatriz, Lima 100, Peru. TEL 51-14-4723925. Ed. Juan de Dios Guevara. R&P contact: Juan de Dios Guevara. adv.; bk.rev.; abstr.; bibl. circ. 1,500. **Indexed:** Biol.Abstr., Chem.Abstr., INIS Atomind. **Document type:** bulletin.
—BLDSC (2196.000000); CASDDS; CISTI; Linda Hall.

540   AE   ISSN 1111-4797
                                    CODEN: JSACEX
SOCIETE ALGERIENNE DE CHIMIE. JOURNAL/ALGERIAN CHEMICAL SOCIETY. JOURNAL. Short title: J S A C. (Text in Arabic, English, French) q.? Societe Algerienne de Chimie, B.P. 109, El Alia, 16111 Bab Ezzouar, Alger, Algeria. Ed. B.Y. Meklati.
—BLDSC (4876.680000); CASDDS.
   Description: Publishes research done in all areas of chemistry.
   Refereed Serial

540   FR   ISSN 0037-8968
QD1   CODEN: BSCFAS
SOCIETE CHIMIQUE DE FRANCE. BULLETIN. (Text and summaries in English, French) 1858. 11/yr. 3800 F. to institutions (US $727; outside the Americas 4710 F) (effective 1998). Editions Scientifiques et Medicales Elsevier, 141 rue de Javel, 75747 Paris, France. TEL 33-1-45589022. FAX 33-1-45589421. URL: http://www.elsevier.nl/. (Subscr. in N. America to: Elsevier Science Inc., Box 945, Madison Sq. Sta., New York, NY 10159-0945. TEL 212-633-3730. FAX 212-633-3680) Ed. J.Y. Lallemand. adv.; bk.rev.; bibl.; charts. circ. 3,000. (also avail. in microfilm from UMI,PMC; reprint service avail. from ISI) **Indexed:** API Abstr., API Catal., API Hlth.& Environ., API Pet.Ref., API Pet.Subst., API Transport., ASCA, Biol.Abstr., Cadscan, Chem.Abstr., Chem.Cit.Ind., Curr.Adv.Ecol.Sci., Curr.Chem.React., Curr.Cont., Dairy Sci.Abstr., Excerp.Med., GeoRef., Ind.Chem., Ind.Sci.Rev., INIS Atomind., Lead Abstr., Mass Spectr.Bull., Met.Abstr., Sci.Cit.Ind., Sugar Ind.Abstr., World Alum.Abstr., Zincscan. **Document type:** academic/scholarly publication, bulletin.
—BLDSC (2733.000000); ADONIS; CASDDS; CISTI; Ei; Genuine Article; Linda Hall; SWETS; UMI. **CCC.**
   Description: Devoted to electrochemistry; catalysis and chemical engineering; analytic, organic, metallo-organic and biological organic chemistry.
   Refereed Serial

540   FR   ISSN 0996-8083
SOCIETE FRANCAISE DE CHIMIE. ANNUAIRE. 1956. biennial. Societe Francaise de Chimie, 250 rue St. Jacques, 75005 Paris, France. TEL 33-1-40467160. FAX 33-1-40467161. **Document type:** directory.
   Formerly (until 1983): Societe Chimique de France. Annuaire (ISSN 0996-8091)
   Refereed Serial

SOCIETE NATIONALE DES SCIENCES NATURELLES ET MATHEMATIQUES DE CHERBOURG. MEMOIRES. see *SCIENCES: COMPREHENSIVE WORKS*

540   JA
SOCIETY FOR CHROMATOGRAPHIC SCIENCES. CONFERENCE ON LIQUID CHROMATOGRAPHY. PROCEEDINGS/EKITAI KUROMATOGURAFI TORONKAI KOEN YOSHISHU. Variant title: Conference on Liquid Chromatography. (Text in English, Japanese; summaries in English) 1980. a. Society for Chromatographic Sciences - Kuromatogurafi, Tokyo Toritsu Daigaku, Rigakubu Kagaku Kyoshitsu, 1-1, Minamiosawa, Hachioji-shi, Tokyo 192-03, Japan. **Document type:** proceedings.

SOCIETY OF DYERS AND COLOURISTS. JOURNAL. see *CLEANING AND DYEING*

SOCIETY OF LEATHER TECHNOLOGISTS AND CHEMISTS. JOURNAL. see *LEATHER AND FUR INDUSTRIES*

540   BU
SOFIISKI UNIVERSITET. KHIMICHESKI FAKULTET. GODISNIK. (Text in Bulgarian; summaries in English) irreg., vol.71, 1976. price varies. (Sofiiski Universitet, Khimicheski Fakultet) Publishing House of the Bulgarian Academy of Sciences, Acad. G. Bonchev St., Bldg. 6, 1113 Sofia, Bulgaria. Ed.Bd. circ. 550. (reprint service avail. from IRC) **Indexed:** Chem.Abstr.

SOLID FUEL CHEMISTRY. see *ENGINEERING — Chemical Engineering*

540   UK   ISSN 0191-5622
QD543   CODEN: SDSEDK
SOLUBILITY DATA SERIES. Variant title: I U P A C Solubility Data Series. 1979. q. £310($475) (effective 1997). (International Union of Pure and Applied Chemistry) Oxford University Press, Oxford Journals, Walton St., Oxford OX2 6DB, England. TEL 44-1865-56767. FAX 44-1865-267985. (U.S. subscr. to: Oxford University Press Inc., 2001 Evans Rd., Cary, NC 27513. TEL 919-677-0977) (also avail. in microfilm from UMI; back issues avail.) **Indexed:** Chem.Abstr. **Document type:** academic/scholarly publication.
—BLDSC (8327.750000); CASDDS; CISTI; SWETS. **CCC.**
   Refereed Serial

540   SA   ISSN 0379-4350
QD1   CODEN: SAJCDG
SOUTH AFRICAN JOURNAL OF CHEMISTRY/SUID-AFRIKAANSE TYDSKRIF VIR CHEMIE. (Text and summaries in English) 1948. q. R.162 to individuals; institutions R.182 (foreign $60) (effective 1997). (South African Chemical Institute) Foundation for Education, Science & Technology, P.O. Box 1758, Pretoria 0001, South Africa. TEL 27-12-3226404. FAX 27-12-3207803. E-mail: buro@shuttle.up.ac.za. Ed. A.T. Hutton. adv. contact: A.T. Hutton. charts; illus.; index. circ. 2,000. (also avail. in microform from UMI) **Indexed:** ASCA, Chem.Abstr., Chem.Cit.Ind., Chem.Titles, Curr.Cont., GeoRef., Ind.S.A.Per., INIS Atomind., Mass Spectr.Bull., Sci.Cit.Ind. **Document type:** academic/scholarly publication.
—BLDSC (8338.800000); CASDDS; CISTI; Ei; Genuine Article; Linda Hall; SWETS; UMI; UnCover. **CCC.**
   Incorporates: South African Chemical Institute. Journal (ISSN 0038-2078)
   Description: Publishes original work in all branches of chemistry.
   Refereed Serial

540   NE   ISSN 0275-780X
SOVIET SCIENTIFIC REVIEWS SUPPLEMENT SERIES. SECTION B: CHEMISTRY. irreg., latest vol.4. price varies. Gordon and Breach - Harwood Academic, Amsteldisk 166, 1st Fl., 1079 LH Amsterdam, Netherlands. (Subscr. to: International Publishers Distributor, Box 32160, Newark, NJ 07102. TEL 800-545-8398. FAX 215-750-6343) Ed. M.E. Vol'pin. (also avail. in microform) **Document type:** monographic series.
—CISTI.

540   UK   ISSN 0584-8555
QD95   CODEN: SPIOAD
SPECTROSCOPIC PROPERTIES OF INORGANIC & ORGANOMETALLIC COMPOUNDS. 1968. a. price varies. The Royal Society of Chemistry, Thomas Graham House, Science Park, Milton Rd., Cambridge CB4 4WF, England. TEL 44-1223-420066. FAX 44-1223-423623. E-mail: sales@rsc.org; URL: http://chemistry.rsc.org/rsc/. (Subscr. to: Turpin Distribution Services Ltd., Blackhorse Rd., Letchworth, Herts. SG6 1HN, England. TEL 44-1462-672555. FAX 44-1462-480947; Subscr. in N. America to: ACS, 1155 Sixteenth St., N.W., Washington, DC 20036, USA. TEL 202-776-8100. FAX 202-872-6067) Eds. E.A.V. Ebsworth, D.M. Adams. charts; illus.; index. (back issues avail.) **Indexed:** Chem.Abstr. **Document type:** academic/scholarly publication.
—BLDSC (8411.110000); CASDDS; CISTI; Linda Hall; SWETS. **CCC.**
   Description: Reviews the literature in the field.

SPECTROSCOPY; an international journal. see *BIOLOGY — Biological Chemistry*

540   US   ISSN 0172-6323
SPRINGER ADVANCED TEXTS IN CHEMISTRY. irreg. price varies. Springer-Verlag, 175 Fifth Ave., New York, NY 10010. TEL 212-460-1500. FAX 212-473-6272. (Also: Berlin, Heidelberg, Tokyo and Vienna) Ed. C. Cantor. **Document type:** monographic series.

CHEMISTRY

540　　　　　　GW　　ISSN 0945-2737
STANDORT CHEMIE; das Journal fuer Chemie, Wirtschaft und Politik. 1994. 24/yr. DM.108 (students DM.82) (effective 1997). (Arbeitsgemeinschaft Chemiepublizistik e.V.) V C H Verlagsgesellschaft mbH, Postfach 101161, 69451 Weinheim, Germany. TEL 49-6201-606-0. FAX 49-6201-606117. (U.S. addr.: V C H Publishers Inc., 220 E. 23rd St., New York, NY 10010-4606. TEL 212-683-8333) Ed. Ewald Schlueter. **Document type:** newspaper.
—SWETS.
   Description: Short reports on current events in chemistry and the chemical industry, including economic and political developments.

540　　　　　　US　　ISSN 1040-0400
QD471　　　　　　　CODEN: STCHES
STRUCTURAL CHEMISTRY; an international journal concerned with energy, structure and their relationships to chemical, physical, and biological properties. 1990. bi-m. $425 (foreign $495) (effective 1998). Plenum Publishing Corp., 233 Spring St., New York, NY 10013-1578. FAX 212-463-0742. TELEX 23-421139. Eds. Arthur Greenberg, Istvan Hargittai. bk.rev. **Indexed:** ASCA, Chem.Cit.Ind., Curr.Cont., Ind.Sci.Rev., INSPEC (1991-), Sci.Cit.Ind. **Document type:** academic/scholarly publication.
—BLDSC (8476.380000); AskIEEE; CASDDS; CISTI; Ei; Genuine Article; KR SourceOne; SWETS; UnCover. **CCC.**
   Refereed Serial

541　　　　　　US　　ISSN 0081-5993
QD461　　　　　　　CODEN: STBGAG
STRUCTURE AND BONDING. (Text in English) 1966. irreg., vol.84, 1995. price varies. Springer-Verlag, 175 Fifth Ave., New York, NY 10010. TEL 212-460-1500. (Also: Berlin, Heidelberg, Tokyo and Vienna) circ. 1,500. (reprint service avail. from ISI) **Indexed:** ASCA, Biol.Abstr., Chem.Cit.Ind., Ind.Sci.Rev., Mat.Sci.Cit.Ind., Sci.Cit.Ind. **Document type:** monographic series.
—BLDSC (8478.700000); CASDDS; CISTI; Genuine Article; Linda Hall; SWETS; UnCover. **CCC.**

STRUCTURE AND DYNAMICS OF MOLECULAR SYSTEMS. see *PHYSICS*

540　　　　　　SP　　ISSN 0370-923X
　　　　　　　　　　CODEN: SCUSAS
STUDIA CHEMICA. (Text in English, Spanish) 1965. a. 1500 ptas. (effective 1995). Ediciones Universidad de Salamanca, Apdo. 325, 37080 Salamanca, Spain. TEL 34-23-294598. Dir. Julio Casado. **Indexed:** Ind.SST. **Document type:** academic/scholarly publication.
—BLDSC (8482.376300); CASDDS. **CCC.**

540　　　　　　RM　　ISSN 1224-7154
QD1　　　　　　　　CODEN: SUBCAB
STUDIA UNIVERSITATIS "BABES-BOLYAI". CHEMIA. (Text in English, French, German, Rumanian) 1958. s-a. exchange basis. Universitatea "Babes-Bolyai", Biblioteca Centrala Universitara, Str. Clinicilor Nr. 2, Cluj-Napoca 3400, Rumania. TEL 40-64-197092. FAX 40-64-197633. Ed. A. Marga. abstr.; charts; illus.; index. **Indexed:** Anal.Abstr., Chem.Abstr., Psychol.Abstr. **Document type:** academic/scholarly publication.

STUDIES IN INTERFACE SCIENCE. see *PHYSICS*

540　　　　　　NE
STUDIES IN NATURAL PRODUCTS CHEMISTRY. (Text in English) 1988. irreg., vol.14, 1994. price varies. Elsevier Science B.V., Books Division, P.O. Box 211, 1000 AE Amsterdam, Netherlands. TEL 31-20-4853911. FAX 31-20-4853705. TELEX 18582 ESPA NL. E-mail: nlinfo-f@elsevier.nl; usinfo-f@elsevier.com; forinfo-kyf04035@niftyserve.or.jp; URL: http://www.elsevier.nl/. (Subscr. in the Americas to: Elsevier Science, Regional Sales Office, Box 945, New York, NY 10159-0945. TEL 212-633-3730. FAX 212-633-3680; Subscr. in Australasia and the Far East to: Elsevier Science (Singapore) Pte Ltd, No.1 Temasek Ave., No.17-01 Millenia Tower, Singapore 039192, Singapore. TEL 65-434-3727. FAX 65-337-2230; Subscr. in Japan to: Elsevier Science Japan, 9-15 Higashi-Azabu 1-chome, Minato-ku, Tokyo 106, Japan. TEL 81-3-5561-5033. FAX 81-3-5561-5047) Ed. Prof. Atta-ur-Rahman. (back issues avail.) **Indexed:** Chem.Cit.Ind., Curr.Cont. (1988-). **Document type:** monographic series.
   Refereed Serial

668.42　　　　　　NE　　ISSN 0922-5579
　　　　　　　　　　CODEN: SPLSEA
STUDIES IN POLYMER SCIENCE. (Text in English) 1988. irreg., vol.10, 1993. price varies. Elsevier Science B.V., Books Division, P.O. Box 211, 1000 AE Amsterdam, Netherlands. TEL 31-20-4853911. FAX 31-20-4853705. TELEX 18582 ESPA NL. E-mail: nlinfo-f@elsevier.nl; usinfo-f@elsevier.com; forinfo-kyf04035@niftyserve.or.jp; URL: http://www.elsevier.nl/. (Subscr. in the Americas to: Elsevier Science, Regional Sales Office, Box 945, New York, NY 10159-0945. TEL 212-633-3730. FAX 212-633-3680; Subscr. in Australasia and the Far East to: Elsevier Science (Singapore) Pte Ltd, No.1 Temasek Ave., No.17-01 Millenia Tower, Singapore 039192, Singapore. TEL 65-434-3727. FAX 65-337-2230; Subscr. in Japan to: Elsevier Science Japan, 9-15 Higashi-Azabu 1-chome, Minato-ku, Tokyo 106, Japan. TEL 81-3-5561-5033. FAX 81-3-5561-5047) (back issues avail.) **Document type:** monographic series.
—BLDSC (8491.224300); CASDDS. **CCC.**
   Refereed Serial

STUDIES OF COLOR/SHIKISAI KENKYU. see *PHYSICS — Optics*

540　　　　　　NE　　ISSN 0278-6117
QD181.S1　　　　　　CODEN: SULED2
SULFUR LETTERS. 1984. 6/yr. $183 (effective 1998). Gordon and Breach - Harwood Academic, Amsteldisk 166, 1st Fl., 1079 LH Amsterdam, Netherlands. URL: http://www.gbhap.com/Sulfur__Letters/. (Subscr. to: International Publishers Distributor, Box 32160, Newark, NJ 07102. TEL 800-545-8398. FAX 215-750-6343) Ed. Alexander Senning. index. (also avail. in microform; back issues avail.) **Indexed:** Mass Spectr.Bull.
●Also available online.
Also available on CD-ROM.
—BLDSC (8516.500000); CASDDS; CISTI; Ei. **CCC.**
   Refereed Serial

546.723　　　　　　NE　　ISSN 0196-1772
QD181.S1　　　　　　CODEN: SUREDW
SULFUR REPORTS. 1980. 2/yr. $263 (effective 1998). Gordon and Breach - Harwood Academic, Amsteldisk 166, 1st Fl., 1079 LH Amsterdam, Netherlands. URL: http://www.gbhap.com/Sulfur__Reports?. (Subscr. to: International Publishers Distributor, Box 32160, Newark, NJ 07102. TEL 800-545-8398. FAX 215-750-6343) Ed. Alexander Senning. (also avail. in microform) **Indexed:** Chem.Abstr. **Document type:** monographic series.
●Also available online.
Also available on CD-ROM.
—BLDSC (8516.550000); CASDDS; CISTI; SWETS. **CCC.**
   Refereed Serial

540　　　　　　JA　　ISSN 0370-8047
TP215　　　　　　　CODEN: RYUSAZ
SULPHURIC ACID AND INDUSTRY. (Text in Japanese) 1948. m. 7200 Yen. Sulphuric Acid Association of Japan, 21-1, 2-chome, Shinbashi, Minato-ku, Tokyo 105, Japan. TEL 81-3-3572-5498. FAX 81-3-3572-5490. Ed. Haruo Yamaguchi. adv.; bk.rev.; index. circ. 1,300. (back issues avail.) **Document type:** bulletin.
—CASDDS; CISTI.
   Refereed Serial

SUPERCONDUCTOR SCIENCE & TECHNOLOGY. see *PHYSICS*

540 530　　　　　　UK　　ISSN 0749-6036
QC611.8.S86　　　　　CODEN: SUMIEK
SUPERLATTICES AND MICROSTRUCTURES. 1985. 8/yr. £105($167) to individuals; institutions £395 (effective 1998). Academic Press Ltd. (Subsidiary of: Harcourt Brace & Company Ltd.), 24-28 Oval Rd., London NW1 7DX, England. TEL 44-171-267-4466. FAX 44-171-482-2293. TELEX 25775 ACPRES G. E-mail: apsubs@acad.com; URL: http://www.hbuk.co.uk/ap/superlattices; http://www.europe.idealibrary.com/. (Subscr. to: Harcourt Brace & Company Ltd., Foots Cray High St., Sidcup, England. TEL 44-181-300-3322. FAX 44-181-309-0807) Ed. John D. Dow. R&P contact: Catherine John. adv. contact: Nik Screen. (reprint service avail. from SWZ) **Indexed:** Alloys Ind., ASCA, Curr.Cont., Eng.Mat.Abstr., INSPEC (1985-), Mat.Sci.Cit.Ind., Met.Abstr., Met.Abstr.Ind., Nonfer.Met.Alert, PCC Alert, Sci.Cit.Ind., Steels Alert, World Alum.Abstr. **Document type:** academic/scholarly publication.
—BLDSC (8547.076700); AskIEEE; CASDDS; CISTI; Ei; Genuine Article; KR SourceOne; Linda Hall; SWETS; UnCover. **CCC.**
   Description: Devoted to the physics, chemistry, materials science, and electrical engineering aspects of submicron structures and the materials from which such structures will be fabricated.

540　　　　　　NE　　ISSN 1061-0278
QD380　　　　　　　CODEN: SCHEER
SUPRAMOLECULAR CHEMISTRY. 1992. 8/yr. (in 2 vols., 4 nos./vol.) $135 (effective 1998). Gordon and Breach - Harwood Academic, Amsteldisk 166, 1st Fl., 1079 LH Amsterdam, Netherlands. URL: http://www.gbhap.com/Supramolecular_Chemistry/. (Subscr. to: International Publishers Distributor, Box 32160, Newark, NJ 07102. TEL 800-545-8398. FAX 215-750-6343) Eds. Jerry Atwood, George W. Gokel. (also avail. in microform) **Indexed:** ASCA, Chem.Cit.Ind., Curr.Cont. **Document type:** academic/scholarly publication.
●Also available online.
Also available on CD-ROM.
—BLDSC (8547.638685); CASDDS; CISTI; SWETS. **CCC.**
   Description: Publishes research in the many facets of supramolecular chemistry including: analytical, inorganic, organic and physical chemistry.
   Refereed Serial

SURFACE INVESTIGATION: X-RAY, SYNCHROTRON AND NEUTRON TECHNIQUES. see *ENGINEERING — Mechanical Engineering*

570　　　　　　US　　ISSN 0081-9603
　　　　　　　　　　CODEN: SFSSA5
SURFACTANT SCIENCE SERIES. 1966. irreg., vol.69, 1997. price varies. Marcel Dekker, Inc., 270 Madison Ave., New York, NY 10016. TEL 212-696-9000. FAX 212-685-4540. TELEX 421419. Eds. M.J. Schick, F.M. Fowkes; Pub. Graham Garratt. R&P contact: Julia Mulligan. **Indexed:** Biol.Abstr., Chem.Abstr. **Document type:** monographic series.
—BLDSC (8548.100000); CASDDS; CISTI. **CCC.**
   Refereed Serial

TAKEDA RESEARCH LABORATORIES. JOURNAL. see *BIOLOGY*

TECHNIQUE (SAN DIEGO). see *BIOLOGY*

540　　　　　　US　　ISSN 0082-2531
QD61　　　　　　　CODEN: TQCMAT
TECHNIQUES OF CHEMISTRY. 1971. irreg., vol.22, 1992. price varies. John Wiley & Sons, Inc., 605 Third Ave., New York, NY 10158. TEL 212-850-6000. FAX 212-850-6088. TELEX 12-7063. Ed. A. Weissberger. **Indexed:** Chem.Abstr. **Document type:** monographic series.
—BLDSC (8743.870000); CASDDS; CISTI. **CCC.**
   Incorporates: Technique of Inorganic Chemistry; Technique of Organic Chemistry (ISSN 0082-240X)
   Refereed Serial

660　　　　　　CU　　ISSN 0253-9276
　　　　　　　　　　CODEN: TEQUD8
TECNOLOGIA QUIMICA. 1980. 3/yr. $15. (Universidad de Oriente) Ediciones Cubanas, Obispo No. 527, Apdo. 605, Havana, Cuba. TEL 32-5556. (Co-sponsor: Sociedad Cubana de Quimica) Ed. Maria Luz Garcia Ferrada. charts; illus. circ. 1,000. **Indexed:** Chem.Abstr., Chem.Eng.Abstr., Food Sci.& Tech.Abstr., T.C.E.A.
—CASDDS.

540 IT
TECNORAMA CHIMICA. 2/yr. Pubblicita Edizioni Associate s.r.l., Via Simone d'Orsenigo 22, 20135 Milan, Italy. TEL 2-551-18-42. FAX 2-551-85-263. Ed. Ugo Carutti. circ. 6,600.

540 KR ISSN 0497-2627
CODEN: TEKHA4
TEORETICHESKAYA I EKSPERIMENTAL'NAYA KHIMIYA; nauchno-teoretichekii zhurnal. English translation: Theoretical and Experimental Chemistry (US ISSN 0040-5760) (Text in Russian) 1965. bi-m. $115 (effective 1998). Akademiya Nauk Ukrainy, Institut Fizichnoi Khimi im. L.V. Pisarzhevskogo, Prosp. Nauki, 31, 252650 Kiev, Ukraine. TEL 38-44-2656209. (Subscr. to: Mezhdunarodnaya Kniga, Moscow, G-200, Russia) Ed. K.B. Yatsimirskiy. **Indexed:** ASCA, Chem.Abstr., Chem.Cit.Ind., Djerelo, INSPEC, Math.R., Sci.Cit.Ind. **Document type:** academic/scholarly publication.
—BLDSC (0177.700000); AskIEEE; CASDDS; CISTI; Genuine Article; KR SourceOne; Linda Hall. **CCC.**

660 RU ISSN 0040-3571
CODEN: TOKTA8
TEORETICHESKIE OSNOVY KHIMICHESKOI TEKHNOLOGII. English translation: Theoretical Foundation of Chemical Engineering (US ISSN 0040-5795) 1967. bi-m. $158 (effective 1998). (Rossiiskaya Akademiya Nauk) Izdatel'stvo Nauka, 90 Profsoyuznaya ul., 117864 Moscow, Russia. **Indexed:** Chem.Abstr. **Document type:** academic/scholarly publication.
—BLDSC (0177.900000); CASDDS; CISTI; KNAW; Linda Hall. **CCC.**

540 UK ISSN 1359-8570
▼**TETRAHEDRON ALERT.** 1996. w. Elsevier Science Ltd., Pergamon, P.O. Box 800, Kidlington, Oxford OX5 1DX, England. TEL 44-1865-843000. FAX 44-1865-843100. E-mail: j.macmillan@elsevier.nl; URL: http://www.elsevier.nl/. (Subscr. to: Elsevier Science, Regional Sales Office, P.O. Box 211, 1000 AE Amsterdam, Netherlands. TEL 31-20-4853757. FAX 31-20-4853432; Subscr. in the Americas to: Elsevier Science, Regional Sales Office, Box 945, New York, NY 10159-0945. TEL 212-633-3730. FAX 212-633-3680; Subscr. in Australasia and the Far East to: Elsevier Science (Singapore) Pte Ltd, No.1 Temasek Ave., No.17-01 Millenia Tower, Singapore 039192, Singapore. TEL 65-434-3727. FAX 65-337-2230) **Document type:** bulletin.
●Available only online.
Description: Provides pre-publication information and abstracts of current and forthcoming issues of the 5 Tetrahedron journals.

542 NE
THEORETICAL AND COMPUTATIONAL CHEMISTRY. (Text in English) 1994. irreg. price varies. Elsevier Science B.V., Books Division, P.O. Box 211, 1000 AE Amsterdam, Netherlands. TEL 31-20-4853911. FAX 31-20-4853705. URL: http://www.elsevier.nl/. (Subscr. in the Americas to: Elsevier Science, Regional Sales Office, Box 945, New York, NY 10159-0945. TEL 212-633-3730. FAX 212-633-3680; Subscr. in Australasia and the Far East to: Elsevier Science (Singapore) Pte Ltd, No.1 Temasek Ave., No.17-01 Millenia Tower, Singapore 039192, Singapore. TEL 65-434-3727. FAX 65-337-2230; Subscr. in Japan to: Elsevier Science Japan, 9-15 Higashi-Azabu 1-chome, Minato-ku, Tokyo 106, Japan. TEL 81-3-5561-5033. FAX 81-3-5561-5047) **Document type:** monographic series.

541 US ISSN 0040-5760
QD1 CODEN: TEXCAK
THEORETICAL AND EXPERIMENTAL CHEMISTRY. English translation of: Teoreticheskaya i Eksperimental'naya Khimiya (KR ISSN 0497-2627) 1965. bi-m. $1455 (foreign $1700) (effective 1998). (Ukrainian Academy of Sciences, KR) Plenum Publishing Corp., Consultants Bureau, 233 Spring St., New York, NY 10013-1578. TEL 212-620-8468. FAX 212-463-0742. TELEX 23-421139. Ed. V.D. Pokhodenko. (also avail. in microfilm from UMI; back issues avail.) **Indexed:** Chem.Titles, INSPEC. **Document type:** academic/scholarly publication.
—BLDSC (0426.200000); AskIEEE; CISTI; KR SourceOne; UMI; UnCover. **CCC.**
Refereed Serial

541 US ISSN 0082-3961
THEORETICAL CHEMISTRY; a series of monographs. 1965. irreg., vol.9, 1984. Academic Press, Inc., 525 B St., Ste. 1900, San Diego, CA 92101-4495. TEL 619-231-0926. FAX 619-699-6715. (Subscr. to: Order Dept., 6277 Sea Harbor Dr., 4th Fl., Orlando, FL 32887. TEL 800-321-5068) Eds. D.P. Craig, R. McWeeny. **Indexed:** Chem.Abstr. **Document type:** monographic series.
Refereed Serial

541.2 GW ISSN 1432-881X
QD1 CODEN: TCHAAM
THEORETICAL CHEMISTRY ACCOUNTS; theory, computation and modeling. Online edition (GW ISSN 1432-2234) (Text in English) 1962. 12/yr. DM.2032.80 (foreign DM.2043.60) (effective 1998). Springer-Verlag, Heidelberger Platz 3, 14197 Berlin, Germany. TEL 49-30-82787-0. FAX 49-30-82787448. E-mail: subscriptions@springer.de; URL: http://link.springer.de. (Subscr. in N. America to: Springer-Verlag New York, Inc., 333 Meadowlands Pkwy., Secaucus, NJ 07094. TEL 212-460-1500. FAX 212-473-6272) Ed. K. Ruedenberg. adv.; bk.rev.; charts; illus. (also avail. in microform from UMI; back issues avail.; reprint service avail. from ISI) **Indexed:** ASCA, Chem.Abstr., Chem.Cit.Ind., Compumath, Curr.Adv.Ecol.Sci., Curr.Cont., Ind.Sci.Rev., INSPEC (1972-), Mass Spectr.Bull., Phys.Ber., Sci.Cit.Ind. **Document type:** academic/scholarly publication.
●Also available online.
—BLDSC (8814.550000); AskIEEE; CASDDS; CISTI; Ei; Genuine Article; KR SourceOne; Linda Hall; SWETS; UMI; UnCover. **CCC.**
Formerly (until 1997): Theoretica Chimica Acta (ISSN 0040-5744)
Description: Covers theoretical chemistry, chemical physics, quantum chemistry, gas phase dynamics, structure and dynamics of condensed phases, statistical mechanics.

THIN FILMS SCIENCE AND TECHNOLOGY. see *PHYSICS*

540 CC ISSN 1001-6880
CODEN: TCYKE5
TIANRAN CHANWU YANJIU YU KAIFA/NATURAL PRODUCT RESEARCH AND DEVELOPMENT. (Text in Chinese; abstracts in English) 1989. q. $100 (effective 1997). Zhongguo Kexueyuan, Chengdu Fenyuan - Chinese Academy of Sciences, Chengdu Branch, 9 Renmin Nanlu 4 Duan, Chengdu, Sichuan 610015, People's Republic of China. TEL 86-28-521-0304. FAX 86-28-558-0439. TELEX 28-600321 SICD CN. E-mail: clcas@rose.cnc.ac.cn. (Co-sponsor: Chengdu Library of the Chinese Academy of Sciences) Ed. Bogang Li. R&P contact: Yan Wang. adv. contact: Yan Wang. circ. 2,000 (paid). (reprint service avail.) **Indexed:** Chem.Abstr. **Document type:** academic/scholarly publication.
—BLDSC (6040.738100); CASDDS.

540 US ISSN 1062-094X
QD1 CODEN: TCWOE7
TODAY'S CHEMIST AT WORK. 1988. 9/yr. $95 to institutional non-members; members $17 (effective 1997). American Chemical Society, 1155 16th St., N.W., Washington, DC 20036. TEL 800-227-5558. FAX 202-872-4615. Ed. Patrick P. McCurdy. adv.: B&W page $5200, color page $7400; trim 8 x 10 7/8. circ. 100,000. **Indexed:** Ind.Hyg.Dig. **Document type:** academic/scholarly publication.
—BLDSC (8859.727750); CISTI; UnCover. **CCC.**
Formerly (until 1992): Today's Chemist (ISSN 0896-7067)

TODAY'S CHEMIST AT WORK. COMPUTERS IN CHEMISTRY BUYERS GUIDE. see *COMPUTERS — Computer Industry Directories*

TOHOKU JOURNAL OF AGRICULTURAL RESEARCH. see *AGRICULTURE — Crop Production And Soil*

TOHOKU UNIVERSITY. SCIENCE REPORTS OF THE RESEARCH INSTITUTES. SERIES A: PHYSICS, CHEMISTRY, AND METALLURGY/TOHOKU DAIGAKU KENKYUJO HOKOKU. A-SHU: BUTSURIGAKU, KAGAKU, YAKINGAKU. see *PHYSICS*

TOHOKU UNIVERSITY. SCIENCE REPORTS. SERIES 8: PHYSICS AND ASTRONOMY. see *PHYSICS*

TOKYO DAIGAKU RIGAKUBU CHIKAKU KAGAKU JIKKEN SHISETSU IHO/LABORATORY FOR EARTHQUAKE CHEMISTRY. BULLETIN. see *EARTH SCIENCES*

540 660 NE ISSN 1022-5528
CODEN: TOCAFI
TOPICS IN CATALYSIS. (Text in English) 1994. 4/yr. 376 SFr. (effective 1998). Baltzer Science Publishers B.V., P.O. Box 221, 1400 AE Bussum, Netherlands. TEL 31-20-6370061. FAX 31-20-6323651. E-mail: subscribe@baltzer.nl; URL: http://www.baltzer.nl. (Subscr. in N. America to: Baltzer Science Publishers, Box 8577, Red Bank, NJ 07701-8577) Eds. Gabor Somorjai, John Thomas. (back issues avail.) **Indexed:** ASCA, Curr.Cont. **Document type:** academic/scholarly publication.
—BLDSC (8867.432100); CASDDS; CISTI; Genuine Article. **CCC.**
Refereed Serial

540 US ISSN 0340-1022
QD1 CODEN: TPCCAQ
TOPICS IN CURRENT CHEMISTRY. 1965. irreg., vol.177, 1996. price varies. Springer-Verlag, 175 Fifth Ave., New York, NY 10010. TEL 212-460-1500. FAX 212-473-6272. (Also: Berlin, Heidelberg, Tokyo and Vienna) Ed. F.L. Boschke. (reprint service avail. from ISI) **Indexed:** ASCA, Biol.Abstr., Chem.Abstr., Chem.Cit.Ind., Chem.Infd., Curr.Chem.React., Deep Sea Res.& Oceanogr.Abstr., GeoRef., Ind.Chem., Ind.Sci.Rev., INIS Atomind., Sci.Cit.Ind. **Document type:** monographic series.
—BLDSC (8867.435000); CASDDS; CISTI; Linda Hall; SWETS; UnCover. **CCC.**
Formerly: Fortschritte der Chemischen Forschung (ISSN 0071-7894)

TOPICS IN INORGANIC AND GENERAL CHEMISTRY. see *CHEMISTRY — Inorganic Chemistry*

541.223 US ISSN 0082-500X
QD481 CODEN: TOSTBF
TOPICS IN STEREOCHEMISTRY. 1967. irreg., vol.20, 1991. price varies. John Wiley & Sons, Inc., 605 Third Ave., New York, NY 10158. TEL 212-850-6000. FAX 212-850-6088. TELEX 12-7063. Eds. N.L. Allinger, E.L. Eliel. **Indexed:** ASCA, Chem.Abstr. **Document type:** monographic series.
—BLDSC (8867.490000); CASDDS; CISTI; Linda Hall; SWETS; UnCover.
Refereed Serial

TOXICOLOGICAL AND ENVIRONMENTAL CHEMISTRY. see *ENVIRONMENTAL STUDIES — Toxicology And Environmental Safety*

TOYODA KENKYU HOKOKU/TOYODA PHYSICAL AND CHEMICAL RESEARCH INSTITUTE. REPORTS. see *PHYSICS*

540 530 NE ISSN 0169-3913
QC173.4.P67 CODEN: TPMEEI
TRANSPORT IN POROUS MEDIA. 1986. m. fl.1840 to institutions; $944 to institutions in U.S. (effective 1998). Kluwer Academic Publishers, Postbus 17, 3300 AA Dordrecht, Netherlands. TEL 31-78-6392392. FAX 31-78-6392254. TELEX 29245 KAPG NL. E-mail: services@wkap.nl; URL: http://www.wkap.nl. (Dist. by: Kluwer Academic Publishers Group, P.O. Box 322, 3300 AH Dordrecht, Netherlands. TEL 31-78-6392392. FAX 31-78-6546474; N. America dist. addr.: Box 358, Accord Sta., Hingham, MA 02018-0358. TEL 617-871-6600. FAX 617-871-6528) Ed. Jacob Bear. adv.; bk.rev.; illus.; index. (also avail. in microform from UMI; back issues avail.; reprint service avail. from SWZ) **Indexed:** Abstr.Bull.Inst.Pap.Chem., Appl.Mech.Rev., ASCA, Bull.Signal., Chem.Cit.Ind., Curr.Cont., Eng.Ind., Geo.Abstr.H.G., Geol.Abstr., Geotech.Abstr., Irr.& Drain.Abstr., Mat.Sci.Cit.Ind., Petrol.Abstr., Sel.Water Res.Abstr., Soils & Fert., T.C.E.A. **Document type:** academic/scholarly publication.
—BLDSC (9025.871000); CASDDS; CISTI; Ei; EMDOCS; Genuine Article; KR SourceOne; Linda Hall; PADDS; SWETS; UMI; UnCover. **CCC.**
Description: Presents original basic and applied research work on the physical and chemical aspects of transport phenomena in a porous medium, including microscopic and large-scale processes, mathematical and numerical models, in such diverse fields as petroleum engineering and biomedicine.
Refereed Serial

CHEMISTRY

540   TU   ISSN 1300-0527
CODEN: TJCHE3
TURKISH JOURNAL OF CHEMISTRY. (Text in English) 1976. 4/yr. $200 (effective 1996 & 1997). Scientific and Technical Research Council of Turkey - TUBITAK - Turkiye Bilimsel ve Teknik Arastirma Kurumu, Ataturk Bulvari, No. 221, Kavaklidere, 06100 Ankara, Turkey. TEL 90-312-4685300. FAX 90-312-4271336. TELEX 43186 BTAK TR. E-mail: bdym@tubitak.gov.tr. Ed. Bahattin Baysal. **Indexed:** ASCA, Bio-Contr.News & Info., Biol.Abstr., Chem.Abstr., Chem.Cit.Ind., Food Sci.& Tech.Abstr., INIS Atomind., INSPEC (1984-1985), Mat.Sci.Cit.Ind., Soils & Fert. **Document type:** academic/scholarly publication.
—BLDSC (9072.468300); CASDDS; CISTI; Genuine Article; Linda Hall.
Formerly (until 1994): Doga Turkish Journal of Chemistry (ISSN 1010-7614); Supersedes in part (in 1986): Doga Bilim Dergisi. Serie A: Basic Sciences.
Refereed Serial

UIT EUROPOORTKRINGEN; euregionaal management magazine voor het bedrijfsleven van Amsterdam tot en met Vlanderen. see *TRANSPORTATION — Ships And Shipping*

540   US   ISSN 1063-4568
QD1
UKRAINIAN CHEMISTRY JOURNAL. English translation of: Ukrainskii Khimicheskii Zhurnal (KR ISSN 0041-6045) 1966. m. $1175 (effective 1998). (Ukrainian Academy of Sciences, Institute of General and Inorganic Chemistry, KR) Allerton Press, Inc., 150 Fifth Ave., New York, NY 10011. TEL 212-924-3950. FAX 212-463-9684. Eds. S.V. Volkov, O.G. Zarubitskii. bk.rev.; abstr.; charts; illus.; index. **Indexed:** Alloys Ind., Eng.Mat.Abstr., Met.Abstr., Met.Abstr.Ind., Nonfer.Met.Alert, PCC Alert, Soils & Fert., Steels Alert, Steels Alert, World Alum.Abstr. **Document type:** academic/scholarly publication.
—BLDSC (0428.300000); CISTI; Linda Hall; SWETS; UnCover. **CCC.**
Formerly: Soviet Progress in Chemistry (ISSN 0038-5743)
Description: Covers inorganic and physical chemistry, electrochemistry, organic chemistry, analytical chemistry, high-molecular compounds and catalytic reactions.

540   KR   ISSN 0041-6045
QD1   CODEN: UKZHAU
UKRAINSKII KHIMICHESKII ZHURNAL; nauchnyi zhurnal. Ukrainian edition: Ukrains'kyi Khimichnyi Zhurnal (ISSN 0372-4204) English translation: Ukrainian Chemistry Journal (US ISSN 1063-4568) (Text in Russian) 1925. m. 14.40 Rub.($25.20) Akademiya Nauk Ukrainy, Institut Obshchei i Neorganicheskoi Khimii, Prosp. Akad. Pallabina, 32-31, 252680 Kiev, Ukraine. TEL 38-44-4440322. Ed. A.V. Gorodyskii. bk.rev.; tr.lit.; index. circ. 1,624. **Indexed:** Abstr.Bull.Inst.Pap.Chem., Alloys Ind., Anal.Abstr., Chem.Abstr., Chem.Cit.Ind., Chem.Infd., Djerelo, Eng.Mat.Abstr., Mass Spectr.Bull., Mat.Sci.Cit.Ind., Met.Abstr., Met.Abstr.Ind., Nonfer.Met.Alert, Nutr.Abstr., PCC Alert, Potato Abstr., Sci.Cit.Ind., Steels Alert, Weed Abstr., World Alum.Abstr.
—BLDSC (0384.720000); CASDDS; CISTI; Ei; Genuine Article; KNAW; Linda Hall. **CCC.**

540   NE   ISSN 0924-6223
CODEN: UCREEV
UNDERSTANDING CHEMICAL REACTIVITY. (Text in English) 1986. irreg., vol.7, 1994. price varies. Kluwer Academic Publishers, Postbus 17, 3300 AA Dordrecht, Netherlands. TEL 31-78-6392392. FAX 31-78-6392254. TELEX 29245 KAPG NL. E-mail: services@wkap.nl; URL: http://www.wkap.nl. (Dist. by: Kluwer Academic Publishers Group, P.O. Box 322, 3300 AH Dordrecht, Netherlands. TEL 31-78-6392392. FAX 31-78-6546474; N. America dist. addr.: Box 358, Accord Sta., Hingham, MA 02018-0358. TEL 617-871-6600. FAX 617-871-6528) **Document type:** monographic series.
—BLDSC (9090.004250); CISTI.
Refereed Serial

UNIVERSITATEA DIN TIMISOARA. ANALELE. STIINTE FIZICE. see *PHYSICS*

540   PL   ISSN 0554-8241
CODEN: SCUCDH
UNIWERSYTET IM. ADAMA MICKIEWICZA. CHEMIA. (Text in Polish; summaries in English) 1960. irreg., no.64, 1995. Adam Mickiewicz University Press, Nowowiejskiego 55, 61-734 Poznan, Poland. TEL 48-61-527380. FAX 48-61-527701. TELEX 413260 UAMPL. Pub. Maria Jankowska. R&P contact: Malgorzata Bis. circ. 280. **Document type:** academic/scholarly publication, monographic series.
—BLDSC (9120.450000); CASDDS; CISTI; Linda Hall.
Formerly (until 1971): Uniwersytet im. Adama Mickiewicza w Poznaniu. Wydzial Matematyki, Fizyki i Chemii. Prace. Seria Chemia (ISSN 1230-0063)
Description: Contains current research results of the university's scholars, their Ph.D. works and monographs. Each volume contains the work of one author.

540   PL   ISSN 0083-4319
QD1   CODEN: UIACEG
UNIWERSYTET JAGIELLONSKI. ZESZYTY NAUKOWE. PRACE CHEMICZNE. (Text in English, Polish; summaries in English, Polish, Russian) no.5, 1959. irreg., vol.28, 1983. price varies. Uniwersytet Jagiellonski, Ul. Golebia 24, 31-007 Krakow, Poland. (Dist. by: Ars Polona, Krakowskie Przedmiescie 7, 00-068 Warsaw, Poland) bibl.; illus. **Indexed:** Chem.Abstr.
—CASDDS; CISTI; Linda Hall.

540   PL
QD1   CODEN: ZWSCDK
UNIWERSYTET OPOLSKI. ZESZYTY NAUKOWE SERIA A. CHEMIA. (Text in Polish; summaries in English) 1974. irreg., vol.17, 1994. price varies, avail. on exchange basis. Uniwersytet Opolski, Sienkiewicza 33, 45-037 Opole, Poland. TEL 48-77-538376. E-mail: rektorat@opole.pl. Ed. Witold Waclawek. **Indexed:** Chem.Abstr. **Document type:** academic/scholarly publication.
—CASDDS.
Formerly (until 1994): Wyzsza Szkola Pedagogiczna, Opole. Zeszyty Naukowe. Seria A. Chemia (ISSN 0324-9034)

540   GW
CODEN: NUCHFF
UNTERRICHT CHEMIE. 6/yr. DM.103 (foreign DM.109). Erhard Friedrich Verlag GmbH, Im Brande 17, 30926 Seelze, Germany. TEL 49-511-40004-0. FAX 49-511-40004170. (Subscr. to: Postfach 100150, 30917 Seelze, Germany) **Document type:** academic/scholarly publication.
—CASDDS. **CCC.**
Formerly: Naturwissenschaften im Unterricht Chemie (ISSN 0946-2139)

540   RU   ISSN 0042-1308
QD1   CODEN: USKHAB
USPEKHI KHIMII. English translation: Russian Chemical Reviews (UK ISSN 0036-021X) 1932. m. $194 (effective 1998). (Rossiiskaya Akademiya Nauk) Izdatel'stvo Nauka, 90 Profsoyuznaya ul., 117864 Moscow, Russia. Ed. N.M. Emanuel. bibl.; charts; illus.; index. circ. 4,225. **Indexed:** Alloys Ind., ASCA, Biol.Abstr., Chem.Abstr., Chem.Cit.Ind., Curr.Cont., Eng.Mat.Abstr., GeoRef., Ind.Sci.Rev., Mat.Sci.Cit.Ind., Met.Abstr., Met.Abstr.Ind., Nonfer.Met.Alert, PCC Alert, Sci.Cit.Ind., Steels Alert, World Alum.Abstr.
—BLDSC (0388.000000); CASDDS; CISTI; Ei; Genuine Article; KNAW; Linda Hall. **CCC.**

540   UZ   ISSN 0042-1707
QD1   CODEN: UZKZAC
UZBEKSKII KHIMICHESKII ZHURNAL. (Text in Russian) 1957. bi-m. 11.10 Rub. (Akademiya Nauk Uzbekistana) Izdatel'stvo Fan, Ul. Gogolya 70, k. 105, 700000 Tashkent, Uzbekistan. charts; index. **Indexed:** Abstr.Bull.Inst.Pap.Chem., Biol.Abstr., Chem.Abstr., GeoRef.
—BLDSC (0384.100000); CASDDS; CISTI; Linda Hall.

V W D - CHEMIE: KAUTSCHUK. (Vereinigte Wirtschaftsdienste GmbH) see *BUSINESS AND ECONOMICS — Investments*

VEGYIPARI SZAKIRODALMI TAJEKOZTATO/CHEMICAL ENGINEERING ABSTRACTS. see *CHEMISTRY — Abstracting, Bibliographies, Statistics*

540   NE   ISSN 0924-2031
QD96.I5   CODEN: VISPEK
VIBRATIONAL SPECTROSCOPY; an international journal devoted to applications of infrared and Raman spectroscopy. (Section of: Analytica Chimica Acta (ISSN 0003-2670)) 1990. bi-m. fl.1800($1034) to institutions (effective 1998). Elsevier Science B.V., P.O. Box 211, 1000 AE Amsterdam, Netherlands. TEL 31-20-4853911. FAX 31-20-4853598. TELEX 18582 ESPA NL. E-mail: nlinfo-f@elsevier.nl; usinfo-f@elsevier.com; forinfo-kyf04035@niftyserve.or.jp; URL: http://www.elsevier.nl/. (Subscr. in the Americas to: Elsevier Science, Regional Sales Office, Box 945, New York, NY 10159-0945. TEL 212-633-3730. FAX 212-633-3680; Subscr. in Australasia and the Far East to: Elsevier Science (Singapore) Pte Ltd, No.1 Temasek Ave., No.17-01 Millenia Tower, Singapore 039192, Singapore. TEL 65-434-3727. FAX 65-337-2230; Subscr. in Japan to: Elsevier Science Japan, 9-15 Higashi-Azabu 1-chome, Minato-ku, Tokyo 106, Japan. TEL 81-3-5561-5033. FAX 81-3-5561-5047) Eds. J.G. Grasselli, J.H. van der Maas. bk.rev.; illus.; index. circ. 30,000. (also avail. in microform from UMI; back issues avail.) **Indexed:** Abstr.Bull.Inst.Pap.Chem., Alloys Ind., Anal.Abstr., ASCA, Biol.Abstr., Chem.Abstr., Chem.Cit.Ind., Curr.Cont., Eng.Mat.Abstr., Excerp.Med., Ind.Med., INSPEC (1991-), Mass Spectr.Bull., Mat.Sci.Cit.Ind., Met.Abstr., Met.Abstr.Ind., Nonfer.Met.Alert, PCC Alert, Sci.Cit.Ind., Steels Alert, World Alum.Abstr., World Surf.Coat. **Document type:** academic/scholarly publication.
—BLDSC (9232.252100); ADONIS; AskIEEE; CASDDS; CISTI; Ei; EMDOCS; Genuine Article; KR SourceOne; Linda Hall; SWETS; UnCover. **CCC.**
Description: Publishes original research and short communications in vibrational spectroscopy, review articles, and news dealing with theory, applications, techniques and instrumentation in infrared, near infared and Raman spectroscopy.
Refereed Serial

VOM WASSER; ein Fachbuch fuer Wasserchemie und Wasserreinigungstechnik. see *WATER RESOURCES*

540   US   ISSN 0506-1083
CODEN: VRTXA6
VORTEX. 1939. m. $10 (effective 1996). American Chemical Society, California Section, 2140 Shattuck Ave., Rm. 1101, Berkeley, CA 94704. TEL 415-848-0512. Ed. Lou Rigali. adv. contact: Pam Rabaino. bk.rev.; circ. 3,500 (controlled). (back issues avail.) **Document type:** academic/scholarly publication, newsletter.
Description: News of interest to chemists in Northern California.

WASTE MANAGEMENT; industrial - radioactive - hazardous. see *ENVIRONMENTAL STUDIES — Waste Management*

340   US
WASTE MANAGEMENT GUIDE; an advisory bulletin on industry practices, regulatory impact, and control techniques. (Subseries of: B N A Policy and Practice Series; Environment, Safety, and Health Series) 1980. bi-w. $680 (effective July 1995). The Bureau of National Affairs, Inc., 1231 25th St., N.W., Washington, DC 20037. TEL 202-452-4200. FAX 202-822-8092. TELEX 285656 BNAI WSH. URL: http://www.bna.com/. (Subscr. to: 9435 Key West Ave., Rockville, MD 20850. TEL 800-372-1033) Ed. Randy Kubetin. index. (looseleaf format; back issues avail.)
• Also available online. Vendor(s): Human Resources Information Network (CDD, HDD).
—**CCC.**
Formerly (until 1996): Chemical Substances Control (ISSN 0271-1478)
Description: Reference and advisory service on the management of chemicals from premanufacture through use and disposal.
Refereed Serial

WELLA AKTIENGESELLSCHAFT. REPORT; Mitarbeitermagazin fuer Mitarbeiter und Pensionaer der weltweiten Wella-Unternehmen. see *BUSINESS AND ECONOMICS*

540   GW
WERK & WIRKEN. (Text in English, German) 1970. m. Wacker-Chemie GmbH, Prinzregentenstr. 22, 80538 Munich, Germany. circ. 18,000.

WEST AFRICAN JOURNAL OF BIOLOGICAL AND APPLIED CHEMISTRY. see *BIOLOGY — Biological Chemistry*

CHEMISTRY — ABSTRACTING, BIBLIOGRAPHIES, STATISTICS

WHERE TO BUY: CHEMICALS & CHEMICAL PLANT (YEAR). see BUSINESS AND ECONOMICS — Marketing And Purchasing

540   PL   ISSN 0043-5104
CODEN: WICHAP
WIADOMOSCI CHEMICZNE. (Text in Polish; summaries in English) 1947. bi-m. $20. (Polskie Towarzystwo Chemiczne - Polish Chemical Society) Wydawnictwo Uniwersytetu Wroclawskiego, Spolka z o.o., Pl. Uniwersytecki 9-13, 50-137 Wroclaw, Poland. TEL 48-71-441006. FAX 48-71-402735. (Subscr. to: Redakcja Wiadomosci Chemicznych, ul. F. Joliot-Curie 14, 50-383 Wroclaw, Poland. TEL 48-71-204389. FAX 48-71-221406) Ed. Jozef Ziolkowski. bk.rev.; abstr.; illus.; index. circ. 600. **Indexed:** Chem.Abstr. **Document type:** academic/scholarly publication.
—CASDDS; CISTI; Linda Hall.
Description: Research reports on theoretical chemistry and practical applications of experimental results.

WONDERSCIENCE. see CHILDREN AND YOUTH — For

540   US
WORLD AROMATICS AND DERIVATIVES. 1973. a. (S R I International, World Petrochemicals Program) S R I Consulting, World Petrochemicals Program, Chemical Business Research Center, Menlo Park, CA 94025. TEL 415-859-5211. FAX 415-859-2182. E-mail: eric_linak@qm.sri.com; URL: http://www-cmrc.sri.com. Ed. E.J. Linak. charts; stat. **Document type:** trade publication.
● Also available on CD-ROM.
Formerly: Benzene-Toluene-Xylenes and Derivatives.

540   US
WORLD C4 HYDROCARBONS AND DERIVATIVES. 1974. a. S R I Consulting, World Petrochemicals Program, Chemical Business Research Center, Menlo Park, CA 94025. TEL 415-859-5211. FAX 415-859-2182. E-mail: eric_linak@qm.sri.com; URL: http://www-cmrc.sri.com. Ed. E.J. Linak. charts; stat. **Document type:** trade publication.
● Also available on CD-ROM.
Formerly: C4 Hydrocarbons and Derivatives.

540   US
WORLD ETHYLENE AND DERIVATIVES. 1973. a. S R I Consulting, World Petrochemicals Program, Chemical Business Research Center, Menlo Park, CA 94025. TEL 415-859-5211. FAX 415-859-2182. E-mail: eric_linak@qm.sri.com; URL: http://www-cmrc.sri.com. Ed. E.J. Linak. charts; stat. **Document type:** trade publication.
● Also available on CD-ROM.
Formerly: Ethylene and Derivatives.

660   US
WORLD FEEDSTOCKS. 1984. a. (S R I International) S R I Consulting, World Petrochemicals Program, Chemical Business Research Center, Menlo Park, CA 94025. TEL 415-859-5211. FAX 415-859-2182. E-mail: eric_linak@qm.sri.com; URL: http://www-cmrc.sri.com. Ed. E.J. Linak. charts; stat. **Document type:** trade publication.
● Also available on CD-ROM.

540   US
WORLD METHANOL AND DERIVATIVES. 1981. a. S R I Consulting, World Petrochemicals Program, Chemical Business Research Center, Menlo Park, CA 94025. TEL 415-859-5211. FAX 415-859-2182. E-mail: eric_linak@qm.sri.com; URL: http://www-cmrc.sri.com. Ed. E.J. Linak. charts; stat. **Document type:** trade publication.
● Also available on CD-ROM.

540   US
WORLD PROPYLENE AND DERIVATIVES. 1973. a. S R I Consulting, World Petrochemicals Program, Chemical Business Research Center, Menlo Park, CA 94025. TEL 415-859-5211. FAX 415-859-2182. E-mail: eric_linak@qm.sri.com; URL: http://www-cmrc.sri.com. Ed. E.J. Linak. charts; stat. **Document type:** trade publication.
● Also available on CD-ROM.
Formerly: Propylene and Derivatives.

WORLD SCIENTIFIC SERIES IN CONTEMPORARY CHEMICAL PHYSICS. see PHYSICS

660   US
YOUR CONSULTANT. 1928. q. $25 (foreign $70). Association of Consulting Chemists and Chemical Engineers, Inc., 40 W. 45th St., New York, NY 10036. TEL 212-983-3160. FAX 212-983-3161. adv.; bk.rev. circ. 2,000. **Document type:** newsletter.

YUKAGAKU. see ENGINEERING — Chemical Engineering

ZAOZHI HUAXUE PIN/PAPER CHEMICALS. see PAPER AND PULP

540   GW   ISSN 0044-2313
CODEN: ZAACAB
ZEITSCHRIFT FUER ANORGANISCHE UND ALLGEMEINE CHEMIE. (Text in English, German) 1892. m. DM.1242 (foreign $768) (effective 1997). Huethig GmbH, Postfach 102869, 69018 Heidelberg, Germany. TEL 49-6221-489261. FAX 49-6221-489623. Ed.Bd. adv.: B&W page DM.1200; trim 178 x 236; adv. contact: Michael Loebach. illus.; index. circ. 1,100. (also avail. in microform from PMC) **Indexed:** Alloys Ind., Anal.Abstr., ASCA, Br.Ceram.Abstr., Bull.Thermodyn.& Thermochem., Chem.Abstr., Chem.Cit.Ind., Curr.Adv.Ecol.Sci., Curr.Cont., Eng.Mat.Abstr., GeoRef., Ind.Sci.Rev., Mass Spectr.Bull., Met.Abstr., Met.Abstr., Met.Abstr.Ind., Nonfer.Met.Alert, PCC Alert, Sci.Cit.Ind., Steels Alert, World Alum.Abstr. **Document type:** academic/scholarly publication.
—BLDSC (9452.000000); AskIEEE; CASDDS; CISTI; Ei; Genuine Article; KR SourceOne; Linda Hall; SWETS; UnCover. **CCC.**
Description: Covers all areas of inorganic chemistry, including solid-state, coordination, molecular and inorganic element.

540 373   CC   ISSN 1001-2958
ZHONGXUE HUAXUE JIAOXUE/SECONDARY SCHOOL CHEMISTRY EDUCATION. (Subseries of: Fuyin Baokan Ziliao) (Text in Chinese) 1980. bi-m. $18.79. Zhongguo Renmin Daxue, Shubao Ziliao Zhongxin - China People's University, Book & Newspaper Information Center, 3 Zhang Zizhong Rd., P.O. Box 1122, Beijing 100007, People's Republic of China. TEL 86-10-4015080. (Dist. in US by: China Publications Service, Box 49614, Chicago, IL 60649. TEL 312-288-3291. FAX 312-288-8570) pp./issue: 56.
Description: Covers secondary school chemistry education, teaching methods and curriculum.

ZHONGXUESHENG SHU-LI-HUA (GAOZHONG BAN). see EDUCATION — Teaching Methods And Curriculum

540   RU   ISSN 0044-460X
CODEN: ZOKHA4
ZHURNAL OBSHCHEI KHIMII. English translation: Russian Journal of General Chemistry (US ISSN 1070-3632) 1931. m. 18 Rub. (Rossiiskaya Akademiya Nauk) Izdatel'stvo Nauka, 90 Profsoyuznaya ul., 117864 Moscow, Russia. TEL 234-05-84. Ed. V.D. Gidaspov. bibl.; charts; index. circ. 3,335. **Indexed:** Abstr.Bull.Inst.Pap.Chem., Anal.Abstr., ASCA, Biotech.Abstr., Chem.Abstr., Chem.Cit.Ind., Chem.Infd., Curr.Chem.React., Curr.Cont., Excerp.Med., Ind.Chem., Ind.Sci.Rev., Mat.Sci.Cit.Ind., Sci.Cit.Ind., World Text.Abstr. **Document type:** academic/scholarly publication.
—BLDSC (0064.000000); CASDDS; CISTI; Ei; Genuine Article; KNAW; Linda Hall. **CCC.**

ZHURNAL PRIKLADNOI KHIMII. see ENGINEERING — Chemical Engineering

CHEMISTRY — Abstracting, Bibliographies, Statistics

540   JA
ABSTRACTS OF SYMPOSIUM ON MOLECULAR SIMULATION, JAPAN/BUNSHI SHIMYURESHON TORONKAI KOEN YOSHISHU. (Text in English, Japanese) a. 2000 Yen($1987) Symposium Organizing Committee for Molecular Simulation, Japan - Bunshi Shimyureshon Toronkai Jikko Iinkai, c/o Dr. Katsuyuki Kawamura, Tokyo Institute of Technology, Ookayama-Meguro-ku, Tokyo 152, Japan. R&P contact: Katsuyuki Kawamura. adv. contact: Katsuyuki Kawamura. **Document type:** abstracting/indexing.

547   JA
ABSTRACTS OF THE SYMPOSIUM ON ORGANOMETALLIC CHEMISTRY, JAPAN/YUKI KINZOKU KAGAKU TORONKAI KOEN YOSHISHU. (Text in English) a. Kinki Chemical Society - Kinki Kagaku Kyokai, 8-4, Utsubohon-machi 1-chome, Nishi-ku, Osaka 550, Japan. **Document type:** abstracting/indexing.

544   JA
ABSTRACTS OF THE TOKYO CONFERENCE ON INSTRUMENTAL ANALYSIS AND ANALYTIC SYSTEMS/BUNSEKI KIKI TO KAISEKI SHISUTEMU NI KANSURU TOKYO TORONKAI KOEN YOSHISHU. (Text in Japanese) a. Japan Society for Analytical Chemistry - Nihon Bunseki Kagakkai, 26-2, Nishigotanda 1-chome, Shinagawa-ku, Tokyo 141, Japan. **Document type:** abstracting/indexing.

544   JA
ABSTRACTS ON THE SYMPOSIUM ON MOLECULAR STRUCTURE/BUNSHI KOZO SOGO TORONKAI KOEN YOSHISHU. (Text in Japanese) 1973. a. Chemical Society of Japan - Nippon Kagakkai, 1-5, Kanda Surugadai, Chiyoda-ku, Tokyo 101, Japan. **Document type:** abstracting/indexing.

540   UK   ISSN 0891-7760
TP967
ADHESIVES ABSTRACTS. 1988. m. £240 (foreign £260) (effective 1998). Rapra Technology Ltd., Shawbury, Shrewsbury, Shrops. SY4 4NR, England. TEL 44-1939-250383. FAX 44-1939-251118. E-mail: info@rapra.net; URL: http://www.rapra.net. **Indexed:** Intl.Polym.Sci.& Tech., RAPRA. **Document type:** abstracting/indexing.
● Also available online. Vendor(s): Data-Star, Knight-Ridder Information, Inc., Questel Orbit Inc., STN International.
Also available on CD-ROM.
—UMI.
Description: Provides references to bibliographic information on all types of adhesives, sealants, bonding agents and technologies.

540 011   US
ADVANCE A C S ABSTRACTS. 1993. 26/yr. $260 to institutional non-members; members $29 (effective 1997). American Chemical Society, 1155 16th St., N.W., Washington, DC 20036. TEL 800-333-9511. FAX 614-447-3671. (Subscr. to: Membership and Subscription Services, Box 3337, Columbus, OH 43210. TEL 614-447-3776) **Document type:** abstracting/indexing.
Description: For researchers to scan and preview the latest work in nearly two dozen chemistry disciplines. Features the author abstracts of papers accepted for publication.

540   US   ISSN 1085-7915
TA455.P58
▼**ADVANCED POLYMERS ABSTRACTS.** 1996. m. A S M International, Materials Information, Materials Park, OH 44073-0002. TEL 216-338-4634. FAX 216-338-4634. E-mail: mi@po.asm-intl.org; URL: http://www.asm-intl.org/mi. (U.K. addr.: Institute of Materials, Materials Information, 1 Carlton House Terr., London SW1Y 5DB, England. TEL 44-171-839-4071. FAX 44-171-839-2289) Ed. Mark Furneaux. **Document type:** abstracting/indexing.

016.540   US   ISSN 0065-7727
CODEN: ACSRAL
AMERICAN CHEMICAL SOCIETY. ABSTRACTS OF PAPERS (AT THE NATIONAL MEETING). 1937. s-a. $40 to non-members; ACS members $30; division members $28. American Chemical Society, National Meetings Office, 1155 16th St., N.W., Washington, DC 20036. TEL 800-227-5558. FAX 202-872-4615. circ. 13,000. (processed) **Indexed:** API Abstr., ASCA, Biol.Abstr., Chem.Cit.Ind., Dairy Sci.Abstr., Food Sci.& Tech.Abstr., Mass Spectr.Bull., Mat.Sci.Cit.Ind., Neurosci.Cit.Ind., Text.Tech.Dig., World Surf.Coat. **Document type:** academic/scholarly publication, proceedings.
—BLDSC (0566.000000); CASDDS; CISTI; Genuine Article; KNAW; Linda Hall; SWETS.

CHEMISTRY — ABSTRACTING, BIBLIOGRAPHIES, STATISTICS

543 016   UK   ISSN 0003-2689
QD71   CODEN: AABSAR
ANALYTICAL ABSTRACTS. 1954. m. £656 (US $1174) (effective 1997). The Royal Society of Chemistry, Thomas Graham House, Science Park, Milton Rd., Cambridge CB4 4WF, England. TEL 44-1223-420066. FAX 44-1223-423429. E-mail: sales@rsc.org; URL: http://chemistry.rsc.org/rsc/. (Subscr. to: Turpin Distribution Services Ltd., Blackhorse Rd., Letchworth, Herts. SG6 1HN, England. TEL 44-1462-672555. FAX 44-1462-480947; Subscr. in N. America to: ACS, 1155 Sixteenth St., N.W., Washington, DC 22036, USA. TEL 202-776-8100. FAX 202-872-6067) Ed. Lynn Hatley. adv.; abstr.; index. (also avail. in microform from UMI,PMC) **Indexed:** Abstr.Bull.Inst.Pap.Chem., AESIS, Br.Ceram.Abstr., Chem.Abstr., Dairy Sci.Abstr., Field Crop.Abstr., Hort.Abstr., Ind.Vet., RAPRA, Vet.Bull., Weed Abstr., World Surf.Coat., World Text.Abstr. **Document type:** abstracting/indexing.
●Also available online. Vendor(s): Data-Star (ANAB), Knight-Ridder Information, Inc. (File no.305), Questel Orbit Inc. (ANAB), STN International (ANABSTR). Also available on CD-ROM. Producer(s): SilverPlatter Information, Inc.
—BLDSC (0896.000000); CISTI; Linda Hall; UMI. CCC.
    Description: Provides abstracts of papers and books considered to be of importance and interest to analytical chemists.

540 015   PL   ISSN 0137-5040
BIBLIOTEKA CHEMII. 1977. irreg., vol.11, 1987. Wydawnictwo Naukowe P W N - Polish Scientific Publishers P W N Ltd., Ul. Miodowa 10, 00-251 Warsaw, Poland. TEL 48-22-267163. FAX 48-22-6954288. (Dist. by: Ars Polona, Krakowskie Przedmiescie 7, 00-068 Warsaw, Poland)

540 016   YU   ISSN 0351-756X
BILTEN DOKUMENTACIJE. SERIJA D1. HEMIJA I HEMIJSKA INDUSTRIJA/BULLETIN OF DOCUMENTATION. SERIES D1. CHEMISTRY AND CHEMICAL INDUSTRY. (Text in Serbo-Croatian) 1950. bi-m. $264. Jugoslovenski Centar za Tehnicku i Naucnu Dokumentaciju - Yugoslav Center for Technical and Scientific Documentation (YCTSD), Sl. Penezica-Krcuna 29-31, Box 724, 11000 Belgrade, Yugoslavia. Ed. Ljiljana Kojic-Bogdanovic.

543 016   YU   ISSN 0352-633X
BILTEN DOKUMENTACIJE. SERIJA D6. ANALITICKA HEMIJA/BULLETIN OF DOCUMENTATION. SERIES D6. ANALYTICAL CHEMISTRY. 1971. bi-m. $198. Jugoslovenski Centar za Tehnicku i Naucnu Dokumentaciju, Sl. Penezica-Krcuna 29-31, Box 724, 11000 Belgrade, Yugoslavia. Ed. Ljiljana Kojic-Bogdanovic.
    Former titles (until 1985): Bilten Dokumentacje. Serija D6, 1. Analiticka Hemija (ISSN 0351-5915); (until 1980): Bilten Dokumentacije. Serija D6. Analiticka Hemija (ISSN 0350-0101)

C A S BIOTECH UPDATES. AGRICULTURE. (Chemical Abstracts Service) see *AGRICULTURE — Abstracting, Bibliographies, Statistics*

540 610   US   ISSN 0895-6499
    CODEN: CBUCE5
C A S BIOTECH UPDATES. ANTIBODY CONJUGATES. s-w. $240 (effective 1998). Chemical Abstracts Service (Subsidiary of: American Chemical Society), 2540 Olentangy River Rd., Box 3012, Columbus, OH 43210-0012. TEL 614-447-3600. FAX 614-447-3713. TELEX 6842086. **Document type:** abstracting/indexing.
    Description: Covers preparation and uses of antibody conjugates, including disease diagnosis and therapy; immunochemical techniques and antibody immobilization studies.

540 612.015   US   ISSN 0895-6626
    CODEN: CBUREG
C A S BIOTECH UPDATES. BIOCHEMICAL IMMOBILIZATION & BIOCATALYTIC REACTORS. s-w. $240 (effective 1998). Chemical Abstracts Service (Subsidiary of: American Chemical Society), 2540 Olentangy River Rd., Box 3012, Columbus, OH 43210-0012. TEL 614-447-3600. FAX 614-447-3713. TELEX 6842086. **Document type:** abstracting/indexing.
    Description: Preparation and use of biological reactors and of immobilized microorganisms, plant and animal cells, enzymes, and other biological molecules; fermentors, biological electrodes, affinity chromatography, and enzyme immunoassay.

C A S BIOTECH UPDATES. BIOSENSORS. see *BIOLOGY — Abstracting, Bibliographies, Statistics*

540 612.015   US   ISSN 1045-8565
    CODEN: CBUFEE
C A S BIOTECH UPDATES. COMMERCIAL FERMENTATION. s-w. $240 (effective 1998). Chemical Abstracts Service (Subsidiary of: American Chemical Society), 2540 Olentangy River Rd., Box 3012, Columbus, OH 43210-0012. TEL 614-447-3600. FAX 614-447-3713. TELEX 6842086. **Document type:** abstracting/indexing.
    Description: Covers processes, products, and equipment of industry-scale production using microorganisms or enzymes; organism strain selection, culturing, fermentation, culture enhancement, immobilization, assays, and product recovery.

C A S BIOTECH UPDATES. D N A & R N A PROBES. see *BIOLOGY — Abstracting, Bibliographies, Statistics*

C A S BIOTECH UPDATES. ENVIRONMENTAL BIOTECHNOLOGY. see *ENVIRONMENTAL STUDIES — Abstracting, Bibliographies, Statistics*

C A S BIOTECH UPDATES. ENZYMES IN BIOTECHNOLOGY. see *BIOLOGY — Abstracting, Bibliographies, Statistics*

540   US   ISSN 0884-7487
    CODEN: CBUAEX
C A S BIOTECH UPDATES. PHARMACEUTICAL APPLICATIONS. s-w. $240 (effective 1998). Chemical Abstracts Service (Subsidiary of: American Chemical Society), 2540 Olentangy River Rd., Box 3012, Columbus, OH 43210-0012. TEL 614-447-3600. FAX 614-447-3713. TELEX 6842086. **Document type:** abstracting/indexing. —CISTI.
    Description: Covers the production of pharmaceuticals by microorganisms and nonmicrobial tissue cultures, bioreactors and enzymes, and genetic engineering; antibiotics, hormones, immunological substances (interferon, antibodies), vaccines, blood factors and related products, and other pharmaceuticals.

540 011   US   ISSN 1040-7103
    CODEN: CUPSEP
C A S BIOTECH UPDATES. PRODUCT PURIFICATION & SEPARATION. s-w. $240 (effective 1998). Chemical Abstracts Service (Subsidiary of: American Chemical Society), 2540 Olentangy River Rd., Box 3012, Columbus, OH 43210-0012. TEL 614-447-3600. FAX 614-447-3713. TELEX 6842086. **Document type:** abstracting/indexing.
    Description: Covers methods and apparatus for the purification and separation of products of such processes as chemical and enzymic syntheses, fermentation, and genetic engineering; including purification and natural sources.

540 016   US
C A SELECTS. (Separate publications on 250 areas of chemistry) 1976. s-w. $240 per section to non-members; members $70 (effective 1998). Chemical Abstracts Service (Subsidiary of: American Chemical Society), 2540 Olentangy River Rd., Box 3012, Columbus, OH 43210-0012. TEL 614-447-3600; 800-333-9511. FAX 614-447-3713. TELEX 6842086. Ed. David W. Weisgerber. **Document type:** abstracting/indexing.

540 011   US   ISSN 1045-8514
    CODEN: CAACEY
C A SELECTS. ACTIVATED CARBON. s-w. $240 to non-members; members $70 (effective 1998). Chemical Abstracts Service (Subsidiary of: American Chemical Society), 2540 Olentangy River Rd., Box 3012, Columbus, OH 43210-0012. TEL 614-447-3600. FAX 614-447-3713. TELEX 6842086. **Document type:** abstracting/indexing.
    Description: Covers manufacture, properties, and uses of activated carbon including sorption of volatile solvents, purification of aqueous solutions in the refining of sugar and alcohols, water purification, wastewater treatment, immobile phase in gas chromatography, and vacuum technology.

540 011   US   ISSN 1045-8506
    CODEN: CSADER
C A SELECTS. ADSORPTION. s-w. $240 to non-members; members $70 (effective 1998). Chemical Abstracts Service (Subsidiary of: American Chemical Society), 2540 Olentangy River Rd., Box 3012, Columbus, OH 43210-0012. TEL 614-447-3600. FAX 614-447-3713. TELEX 6842086. **Document type:** abstracting/indexing.
    Description: Covers the phenomena of adsorption as well as the properties of adsorbed substances.

C A SELECTS. AIR POLLUTION (BOOKS & REVIEWS). see *ENVIRONMENTAL STUDIES — Abstracting, Bibliographies, Statistics*

540 574   US   ISSN 1051-3884
    CODEN: CAAOE2
C A SELECTS. ALKOXYLATED OLEOCHEMICALS. 1990. s-w. $240 to non-members; members $70 (effective 1998). Chemical Abstracts Service (Subsidiary of: American Chemical Society), 2540 Olentangy River Rd., Box 3012, Columbus, OH 43210-0012. TEL 614-447-3600. FAX 614-447-3713. TELEX 6842086. **Document type:** abstracting/indexing.
    Description: Covers analysis, preparation, properties, reactions, and uses of ethoxylated and - or propoxylated alcohols.

540   US   ISSN 0895-5964
    CODEN: CSACEO
C A SELECTS. ALKYLATION & CATALYSTS. 1988. s-w. $240 to non-members; members $70 (effective 1998). Chemical Abstracts Service (Subsidiary of: American Chemical Society), 2540 Olentangy River Rd., Box 3012, Columbus, OH 43210-0012. TEL 614-447-3600. FAX 614-447-3713. TELEX 6842086. **Document type:** abstracting/indexing.
    Description: Covers alkylation of such compounds as alkanes, alkenes, benzenes, and amines with agents such as alcohols and olefins; catalysts used to effect alkylations.

540 011   US   ISSN 1066-1166
    CODEN: CSLCEB
C A SELECTS. ALUMINUM - LITHIUM AND ALUMINUM - CERIUM ALLOYS. 1993. s-w. $240 to non-members; members $70 (effective 1998). Chemical Abstracts Service (Subsidiary of: American Chemical Society), 2540 Olentangy River Rd., Box 3012, Columbus, OH 43210-0012. TEL 614-447-3600. FAX 614-447-3713. TELEX 6842086. **Document type:** abstracting/indexing.
    Description: Covers the manufacture, characterization, properties, and applications of the title alloys.

541.37   US   ISSN 0160-8959
    CODEN: CSAEDT
C A SELECTS. ANALYTICAL ELECTROCHEMISTRY. s-w. $240 to non-members; members $70 (effective 1998). Chemical Abstracts Service (Subsidiary of: American Chemical Society), 2540 Olentangy River Rd., Box 3012, Columbus, OH 43210-0012. TEL 614-447-3600; 800-333-9511. FAX 614-447-3713. TELEX 6842086. **Document type:** abstracting/indexing.
    Description: Covers analytical electrochemistry involving organic and inorganic compounds; amperometric, conductometric, coulometric, and potentiometric titrations; stripping voltammetry, polarographic analysis; and electroanalysis using ion-specific electrodes.

540   US   ISSN 0890-1848
                CODEN: CSDAEX
C A SELECTS. ANTIBACTERIAL AGENTS. s-w. $240 to non-members; members $70 (effective 1998). Chemical Abstracts Service (Subsidiary of: American Chemical Society), 2540 Olentangy River Rd., Box 3012, Columbus, OH 43210-0012. TEL 614-447-3600. FAX 614-447-3713. TELEX 6842086. **Document type:** abstracting/indexing.
Formerly (until 1989): C A Selects. Bactericides, Disinfectants and Antiseptics.
Description: Covers design, synthesis, therapeutic use, mode of action, and structure-activity relationships of antibacterial agents.

540   US   ISSN 0275-7028
                CODEN: CAAODZ
C A SELECTS. ANTIOXIDANTS. s-w. $240 to non-members; members $70 (effective 1998). Chemical Abstracts Service (Subsidiary of: American Chemical Society), 2540 Olentangy River Rd., Box 3012, Columbus, OH 43210-0012. TEL 614-447-3600. FAX 614-447-3713. TELEX 6842086. **Document type:** abstracting/indexing.
Description: Covers chemistry of oxidation prevention; and manufacture and new uses of antioxidants.

540   US   ISSN 0740-0683
                CODEN: CSAAEI
C A SELECTS. AUTOMATED CHEMICAL ANALYSIS. s-w. $240 to non-members; members $70 (effective 1998). Chemical Abstracts Service (Subsidiary of: American Chemical Society), 2540 Olentangy River Rd., Box 3012, Columbus, OH 43210. TEL 614-447-3600. FAX 614-447-3713. TELEX 6842086. **Document type:** abstracting/indexing.
Description: Covers chemical analysis automated by computer control or mechanical means; automatic sampling analysis procedures.

540 011   US   ISSN 1061-5342
                CODEN: CABCE5
C A SELECTS. BISMUTH CHEMISTRY. 1992. s-w. $240 to non-members; members $70 (effective 1998). Chemical Abstracts Service (Subsidiary of: American Chemical Society), 2540 Olentangy River Rd., Box 3012, Columbus, OH 43210-0012. TEL 614-447-3600. FAX 614-447-3713. TELEX 6842086. **Document type:** abstracting/indexing.
Description: Covers all aspects of the chemistry of bismuth.

547   US   ISSN 0734-8851
                CODEN: CASPER
C A SELECTS. BLOCK & GRAFT POLYMERS. s-w. $240 to non-members; members $70 (effective 1998). Chemical Abstracts Service (Subsidiary of: American Chemical Society), 2540 Olentangy River Rd., Box 3012, Columbus, OH 43210-0012. TEL 614-447-3600. FAX 614-447-3713. TELEX 6842086. **Document type:** abstracting/indexing.
Description: Covers preparation, properties, uses of block or segmented polymers; compositional block copolymers and stereoblock polymers (additional and, or condensation); synthesis of graft copolymers: catalytic, mechanistic, kinetic aspects.

540   US   ISSN 1051-3906
                CODEN: CASBEJ
C A SELECTS. CALCIUM CHANNEL BLOCKERS. 1990. s-w. $240 to non-members; members $70 (effective 1998). Chemical Abstracts Service (Subsidiary of: American Chemical Society), 2540 Olentangy River Rd., Box 3012, Columbus, OH 43210-0012. TEL 614-447-3600. FAX 614-447-3713. TELEX 6842086. **Document type:** abstracting/indexing.
Description: Covers agents that act as calcium antagonists; biochemical and pharmacological effects, mechanisms of action, synthesis, physicochemical properties, modeling, QSAR, and structure-activity studies.

547   US   ISSN 0890-1856
                CODEN: CSCFE9
C A SELECTS. CARBON & GRAPHITE FIBERS. s-w. $240 to non-members; members $70 (effective 1998). Chemical Abstracts Service (Subsidiary of: American Chemical Society), 2540 Olentangy River Rd., Box 3012, Columbus, OH 43210-0012. TEL 614-447-3600. FAX 614-447-3713. TELEX 6842086. **Document type:** abstracting/indexing.
Description: Covers preparation, properties, and uses of carbon fibers; includes highly carbonized fibers called graphite fibers.

540   US   ISSN 0895-5956
                CODEN: CSCCEY
C A SELECTS. CARBON FIBER COMPOSITES. 1988. s-w. $240 to non-members; members $70 (effective 1998). Chemical Abstracts Service (Subsidiary of: American Chemical Society), 2540 Olentangy River Rd., Box 3012, Columbus, OH 43210-0012. TEL 614-447-3600. FAX 614-447-3713. TELEX 6842086. **Document type:** abstracting/indexing.
Description: Covers the chemistry, production, and use of carbon fiber-reinforced composites with ceramic, metallic, and polymeric matrixes.

540   US   ISSN 0734-8800
                CODEN: CASREX
C A SELECTS. CATALYST REGENERATION. s-w. $240 to non-members; members $70 (effective 1998). Chemical Abstracts Service (Subsidiary of: American Chemical Society), 2540 Olentangy River Rd., Box 3012, Columbus, OH 43210-0012. TEL 614-447-3600. FAX 614-447-3713. TELEX 6842086. **Document type:** abstracting/indexing.
Description: Covers regeneration and reactivation of catalysts in laboratory process and industrial applications; reclamation and recovery of active components; and reprocessing of used catalysts.

540   US   ISSN 0890-1864
                CODEN: CSKAEY
C A SELECTS. CATALYTIC & KINETIC ANALYSIS. 1987. s-w. $240 to non-members; members $70 (effective 1998). Chemical Abstracts Service (Subsidiary of: American Chemical Society), 2540 Olentangy River Rd., Box 3012, Columbus, OH 43210-0012. TEL 614-447-3600. FAX 614-447-3713. TELEX 6842086. **Document type:** abstracting/indexing.
Description: Covers analytic methods involving kinetic and catalytic procedures; catalytic thermometric titration, reaction rate titration, and analysis involving Landolt reactions.

C A SELECTS. CERAMIC MATERIALS (JOURNALS). see CERAMICS, GLASS AND POTTERY — Abstracting, Bibliographies, Statistics

540   US   ISSN 0734-8797
                CODEN: CASAEG
C A SELECTS. CHELATING AGENTS. s-w. $240 to non-members; members $70 (effective 1998). Chemical Abstracts Service (Subsidiary of: American Chemical Society), 2540 Olentangy River Rd., Box 3012, Columbus, OH 43210-0012. TEL 614-447-3600. FAX 614-447-3713. TELEX 6842086. **Document type:** abstracting/indexing.
Description: Covers chelating agents and complexing agents in analytical procedures, separation processes, isolation of metals, and industrial processes.

540   US   ISSN 1040-712X
                CODEN: CASOEO
C A SELECTS. CHEMICAL ENGINEERING OPERATIONS. 1989. s-w. $240 to non-members; members $70 (effective 1998). Chemical Abstracts Service (Subsidiary of: American Chemical Society), 2540 Olentangy River Rd., Box 3012, Columbus, OH 43210-0012. TEL 614-447-3600. FAX 614-447-3713. TELEX 6842086. **Document type:** abstracting/indexing.
Description: Covers the theory and technology of unit operations including flow, heat transfer, mass transfer, material handling, size modification, and mixing; separation by absorption, adsorption, crystallization, drying, evaporation, and sedimentation.

C A SELECTS. CHEMICAL INSTRUMENTATION. see INSTRUMENTS — Abstracting, Bibliographies, Statistics

540   US   ISSN 0885-0119
                CODEN: CSCDE3
C A SELECTS. CHEMICAL VAPOR DEPOSITION. s-w. $240 to non-members; members $70 (effective 1998). Chemical Abstracts Service (Subsidiary of: American Chemical Society), 2540 Olentangy River Rd., Box 3012, Columbus, OH 43210-0012. TEL 614-447-3600. FAX 614-447-3713. TELEX 6842086. **Document type:** abstracting/indexing.
Description: Covers CVD processes, with emphasis on device fabrications; epitaxial growth of semiconductors; and deposition of thin film for recording and memory devices.

540   US   ISSN 1040-7138
                CODEN: CSCHEF
C A SELECTS. CHEMILUMINESCENCE. 1989. s-w. $240 to non-members; members $70 (effective 1998). Chemical Abstracts Service (Subsidiary of: American Chemical Society), 2540 Olentangy River Rd., Box 3012, Columbus, OH 43210-0012. TEL 614-447-3600. FAX 614-447-3713. TELEX 6842086. **Document type:** abstracting/indexing.
Description: Covers the phenomenon of chemiluminescence and the chemistry of compounds showing chemiluminescence.

540   US   ISSN 1040-7146
                CODEN: CSIRE7
C A SELECTS. CHEMISTRY OF IR, OS, RH, & RU. 1989. s-w. $240 to non-members; members $70 (effective 1998). Chemical Abstracts Service (Subsidiary of: American Chemical Society), 2540 Olentangy River Rd., Box 3012, Columbus, OH 43210-0012. TEL 614-447-3600. FAX 614-447-3713. TELEX 6842086. **Document type:** abstracting/indexing.
Description: Covers the preparation, properties, uses, and characterization of compounds containing iridium, osmium, rhodium, and ruthenium.

549   US   ISSN 0146-4426
                CODEN: CSCCDX
C A SELECTS. COAL SCIENCE AND PROCESS CHEMISTRY. s-w. $240 to non-members; members $70 (effective 1998). Chemical Abstracts Service (Subsidiary of: American Chemical Society), 2540 Olentangy River Rd., Box 3012, Columbus, OH 43210-0012. TEL 614-447-3600. FAX 614-447-3713. TELEX 6842086. **Document type:** abstracting/indexing.
Description: Covers coal liquefaction, gasification, coal combustion, and coal mine gases.

540   US   ISSN 0160-8967
                CODEN: CSCADR
C A SELECTS. COLLOIDS (APPLIED ASPECTS). s-w. $240 to non-members; members $70 (effective 1998). Chemical Abstracts Service (Subsidiary of: American Chemical Society), 2540 Olentangy River Rd., Box 3012, Columbus, OH 43210-0012. TEL 614-447-3600. FAX 614-447-3713. TELEX 6842086. **Document type:** abstracting/indexing.
Description: Covers emulsions, gels, latexes, micellar solutions, sols, and other forms of colloidal dispersions; uses of these materials in cosmetics, foods, fuels, metals, and other products.

540   US   ISSN 0190-9444
                CODEN: CCMADX
C A SELECTS. COLLOIDS (MACROMOLECULAR ASPECTS). s-w. $240 to non-members; members $70 (effective 1997). Chemical Abstracts Service (Subsidiary of: American Chemical Society), 2540 Olentangy River Rd., Box 3012, Columbus, OH 43210-0012. TEL 614-447-3600. FAX 614-447-3713. TELEX 6842086. **Document type:** abstracting/indexing.
Description: Covers macromolecular emulsions, gels, latexes, micellar solutions, sols, and other forms of colloidal dispersions; uses in coatings, elastomers, plastics, textiles, and other industries.

540   US   ISSN 0160-8975
                CODEN: CCPADE
C A SELECTS. COLLOIDS (PHYSICOCHEMICAL ASPECTS). s-w. $240 to non-members; members $70 (effective 1998). Chemical Abstracts Service (Subsidiary of: American Chemical Society), 2540 Olentangy River Rd., Box 3012, Columbus, OH 43210-0012. TEL 614-447-3600. FAX 614-447-3713. TELEX 6842086. **Document type:** abstracting/indexing.
Description: Covers the physical chemistry of colloids, suspensions, and dispersions.

540   US   ISSN 0885-0127
                CODEN: CSCSEE
C A SELECTS. COLOR SCIENCE. s-w. $240 to non-members; members $70 (effective 1998). Chemical Abstracts Service (Subsidiary of: American Chemical Society), 2540 Olentangy River Rd., Box 3012, Columbus, OH 43210-0012. TEL 614-447-3600. FAX 614-447-3713. TELEX 6842086. **Document type:** abstracting/indexing.
Description: Covers photochromic materials, phosphors, and light-emitting substances with respect to color.

CHEMISTRY — ABSTRACTING, BIBLIOGRAPHIES, STATISTICS

540 011   US   ISSN 1066-1158
CODEN: CSCEE6
C A SELECTS. COMPOSITE MATERIALS (CERAMIC). 1993. s-w. $240 to non-members; members $70 (effective 1998). Chemical Abstracts Service (Subsidiary of: American Chemical Society), 2540 Olentangy River Rd., Box 3012, Columbus, OH 43210-0012. TEL 614-447-3600. FAX 614-447-3713. TELEX 6842086. **Document type:** abstracting/indexing.
Description: Covers the chemistry, phase composition, mechanical and physical properties, fabrication, and use of the material. Both oxide and nonoxide ceramic matrixes are included.

540 011   US   ISSN 1066-114X
CODEN: CSMPEL
C A SELECTS. COMPOSITE MATERIALS (METALLIC). 1993. s-w. $240 to non-members; members $70 (effective 1998). Chemical Abstracts Service (Subsidiary of: American Chemical Society), 2540 Olentangy River Rd., Box 3012, Columbus, OH 43210-0012. TEL 614-447-3600. FAX 614-447-3713. TELEX 6842086. **Document type:** abstracting/indexing.
Description: Covers the chemistry, phase composition, mechanical and physical properties, fabrication, and use of the materials.

540   US   ISSN 1040-7154
CODEN: CAMTE9
C A SELECTS. COMPOSITE MATERIALS (POLYMERIC). 1989. s-w. $240 to non-members; members $70 (effective 1998). Chemical Abstracts Service (Subsidiary of: American Chemical Society), 2540 Olentangy River Rd., Box 3012, Columbus, OH 43210-0012. TEL 614-447-3600. FAX 614-447-3713. TELEX 6842086. **Document type:** abstracting/indexing.
Description: Covers the chemistry, manufacture, and use of composites with plastic (polymeric) matrixes and fibrous, granular, or spherical fillers.

540   US   ISSN 0160-9025
CODEN: CCOCDF
C A SELECTS. COMPUTERS IN CHEMISTRY. s-w. $240 to non-members; members $70 (effective 1998). Chemical Abstracts Service (Subsidiary of: American Chemical Society), 2540 Olentangy River Rd., Box 3012, Columbus, OH 43210-0012. TEL 614-447-3600. FAX 614-447-3713. TELEX 6842086. **Document type:** abstracting/indexing.
Description: Covers the online and offline uses of computers in chemistry; data processing, information retrieval; process control, programmed calculations, computer simulation models.

540   US   ISSN 0885-0135
CODEN: CACPEF
C A SELECTS. CONDUCTIVE POLYMERS. s-w. $240 to non-members; members $70 (effective 1998). Chemical Abstracts Service (Subsidiary of: American Chemical Society), 2540 Olentangy River Rd., Box 3012, Columbus, OH 43210-0012. TEL 614-447-3600. FAX 614-447-3713. TELEX 68420866. **Document type:** abstracting/indexing.
Description: Covers the preparation, properties, and uses of conductive polymers.

540   US   ISSN 0146-4434
CODEN: CSCODZ
C A SELECTS. CORROSION. s-w. $240 to non-members; members $70 (effective 1998). Chemical Abstracts Service (Subsidiary of: American Chemical Society), 2540 Olentangy River Rd., Box 3012, Columbus, OH 43210-0012. TEL 614-447-3600. FAX 614-447-3713. TELEX 6842086. **Document type:** abstracting/indexing.
Description: Covers the corrosion, rusting, tarnishing of metals and alloys.

540   US   ISSN 0740-0721
CODEN: CSCREB
C A SELECTS. CROSSLINKING REACTIONS. s-w. $240 to non-members; members $70 (effective 1998). Chemical Abstracts Service (Subsidiary of: American Chemical Society), 2540 Olentangy River Rd., Box 3012, Columbus, OH 43210-0012. TEL 614-447-3600. FAX 614-447-3713. TELEX 6842086. **Document type:** abstracting/indexing.
Description: Covers the formulation of three-dimensional polymer networks by various means, e.g., polymerization of monomers with functionally greater than two, reaction of functional linear polymers with multifunctional agents, irradiation of linear polymers to generate free radicals.

548   US   ISSN 0162-7740
CODEN: CSCGDB
C A SELECTS. CRYSTAL GROWTH. s-w. $240 to non-members; members $70 (effective 1998). Chemical Abstracts Service (Subsidiary of: American Chemistry Society), 2540 Olentangy River Rd., Box 3012, Columbus, OH 43210-0012. TEL 614-447-3600. FAX 614-447-3713. TELEX 6842086. **Document type:** abstracting/indexing.
Description: Covers the growth of crystals, dendrites, whiskers, and crystallites.

540   US   ISSN 0275-7052
CODEN: CDITD9
C A SELECTS. DISTILLATION TECHNOLOGY. s-w. $240 to non-members; members $70 (effective 1998). Chemical Abstracts Service (Subsidiary of: American Chemical Society), 2540 Olentangy River Rd., Box 3012, Columbus, OH 43210-0012. TEL 614-447-3600. FAX 614-447-3713. TELEX 6842086. **Document type:** abstracting/indexing.
Description: Covers distillation as a unit process; design of distillation equipment; extractive and molecular distillation; applications of distillation technology.

540 011   US   ISSN 1045-8557
CODEN: CSELE3
C A SELECTS. ELASTOMERS. s-w. $240 to non-members; members $70 (effective 1998). Chemical Abstracts Service (Subsidiary of: American Chemical Society), 2540 Olentangy River Rd., Box 3012, Columbus, OH 43210-0012. TEL 614-447-3600. FAX 614-337-3713. TELEX 6842086. **Document type:** abstracting/indexing.
Description: Covers preparation, properties, reactions, and uses of elastomers.

541.37   US   ISSN 0885-0143
CODEN: CSEOEC
C A SELECTS. ELECTRICALLY CONDUCTIVE ORGANICS. s-w. $240 to non-members; members $70 (effective 1998). Chemical Abstracts Service (Subsidiary of: American Chemical Society), 2540 Olentangy River Rd., Box 3012, Columbus, OH 43210-0012. TEL 614-447-3600. FAX 614-447-3713. TELEX 6842086. **Document type:** abstracting/indexing.
Description: Covers electrical conductors and superconductors based on organic compounds.

547   US   ISSN 0734-8770
CODEN: CAESEY
C A SELECTS. ELECTROCHEMICAL ORGANIC SYNTHESIS. s-w. $240 to non-members; members $70 (effective 1998). Chemical Abstracts Service (Subsidiary of: American Chemical Society), 2540 Olentangy River Rd., Box 3012, Columbus, OH 43210-0012. TEL 614-447-3600. FAX 614-447-3713. TELEX 6842086. **Document type:** abstracting/indexing.
Description: Covers organic synthesis in which the starting material, one or more intermediates, or the final product is prepared by a specific electrochemical process.

541.37   US   ISSN 0146-4442
CODEN: CSERDK
C A SELECTS. ELECTROCHEMICAL REACTIONS. s-w. $240 to non-members; members $70 (effective 1998). Chemical Abstracts Service (Subsidiary of: American Chemical Society), 2540 Olentangy River Rd., Box 3012, Columbus, OH 43210-0012. TEL 614-447-3600. FAX 614-447-3713. TELEX 6842086. **Document type:** abstracting/indexing.
Description: Covers electrolysis, electrooxidation, electroreduction, polarography; electrochemical reactions in biochemistry, organic, macromolecular, applied, and inorganic chemistry.

541.37   US   ISSN 0162-7783
CODEN: CSELD2
C A SELECTS. ELECTRODEPOSITION. s-w. $240 to non-members; members $70 (effective 1998). Chemical Abstracts Service (Subsidiary of: American Chemical Society), 2540 Olentangy River Rd., Box 3012, Columbus, OH 43210-0012. TEL 614-447-3600. FAX 614-447-3713. TELEX 6842086. **Document type:** abstracting/indexing.
Description: Covers electroplating and electroforming.

541.37   US   ISSN 0146-4469
CODEN: CSEAD3
C A SELECTS. ELECTRON SPIN RESONANCE (CHEMICAL ASPECTS). s-w. $240 to non-members; members $70 (effective 1998). Chemical Abstracts Service (Subsidiary of: American Chemical Society), 2540 Olentangy River Rd., Box 3012, Columbus, OH 43210-0012. TEL 614-447-3600. FAX 614-447-3713. TELEX 6842086. **Document type:** abstracting/indexing.
Description: Includes information on electron nuclear double resonance and electron paramagnetic resonance.

541.37   US   ISSN 0885-0151
CODEN: CSEME6
C A SELECTS. ELECTRONIC CHEMICALS & MATERIALS. s-w. $240 to non-members; members $70 (effective 1998). Chemical Abstracts Service (Subsidiary of: American Chemical Society), 2540 Olentangy River Rd., Box 3012, Columbus, OH 43210-0012. TEL 614-447-3600. FAX 614-447-3713. TELEX 6842086. **Document type:** abstracting/indexing.
Description: Covers specialty chemicals, materials, and processes involved in the fabrication of solid-state electronic devices.

540   US   ISSN 0734-8754
CODEN: CAEDEN
C A SELECTS. EMULSIFIERS AND DEMULSIFIERS. s-w. $240 to non-members; members $70 (effective 1998). Chemical Abstracts Service (Subsidiary of: American Chemical Society), 2540 Olentangy River Rd., Box 3012, Columbus, OH 43210-0012. TEL 614-447-3600. FAX 614-447-3713. TELEX 6842086. **Document type:** abstracting/indexing.
Description: Preparation, properties, uses of surface-active agents in formation, stabilization, or destabilization of emulsions.

660.284   US   ISSN 0195-4970
CODEN: CEPOD2
C A SELECTS. EMULSION POLYMERIZATION. s-w. $240 to non-members; members $70 (effective 1998). Chemical Abstracts Service (Subsidiary of: American Chemical Society), 2540 Olentangy River Rd., Box 3012, Columbus, OH 43210-0012. TEL 614-447-3600. FAX 614-447-3713. TELEX 6842086. **Document type:** abstracting/indexing.
Description: Covers polymerizations carried out in emulsion to produce plastics, elastomers, coating materials.

540   US   ISSN 0895-5808
CODEN: CSEAE4
C A SELECTS. ENZYME ASSAYS. 1988. s-w. $240 to non-members; members $70 (effective 1998). Chemical Abstracts Service (Subsidiary of: American Chemical Society), 2540 Olentangy River Rd., Box 3012, Columbus, OH 43210-0012. TEL 614-447-3600. FAX 614-447-3713. TELEX 6842086. **Document type:** abstracting/indexing.
Description: Covers quantitative and qualitative methods (e.g., spectrophotometric, radiometric, immunochemical, histochemical, cytochemical) for the determination of enzymes and for the use of enzymes in laboratory or clinical analysis.

540   US   ISSN 0275-7060
CODEN: CEPRDB
C A SELECTS. EPOXY RESINS. s-w. $240 to non-members; members $70 (effective 1998). Chemical Abstracts Service (Subsidiary of: American Chemical Society), 2540 Olentangy River Rd., Box 3012, Columbus, OH 43210-0012. TEL 614-447-3600. FAX 614-447-3713. TELEX 6842086. **Document type:** abstracting/indexing.
Description: Covers synthesis, curing, properties, uses of macromolecular compounds containing multiple epoxide rings; application as thermosetting resin, coatings, adhesives.

665   US   ISSN 0275-7079
CODEN: CSFODG
C A SELECTS. FATS & OILS. s-w. $240 to non-member members $70 (effective 1998). Chemical Abstract Service (Subsidiary of: American Chemical Society), 2540 Olentangy River Rd., Box 3012, Columbus, OH 43210-0012. TEL 614-447-3600. FAX 614-447-3713. TELEX 6842086. **Document type:** abstracting/indexing.
Description: Covers extraction, analysis, properties, uses, synthesis and manufacture of analogs.

CHEMISTRY — ABSTRACTING, BIBLIOGRAPHIES, STATISTICS

540   US   ISSN 0740-0713   CODEN: CSFCEF
C A SELECTS. FERMENTATION CHEMICALS. s-w. $240 to non-members; members $70 (effective 1998). Chemical Abstracts Service (Subsidiary of: American Chemical Society), 2540 Olentangy River Rd., Box 3012, Columbus, OH 43210-0012. TEL 614-447-3600. FAX 614-447-3713. TELEX 6842086. **Document type:** abstracting/indexing.
Description: Covers compounds prepared by fermentation processes; compounds routinely used in fermentation processes.

540   US   ISSN 0162-7805   CODEN: CSFLD7
C A SELECTS. FLAMMABILITY. s-w. $240 to non-members; members $70 (effective 1998). Chemical Abstracts Service (Subsidiary of: American Chemical Society), 2540 Olentangy River Rd., Box 3012, Columbus, OH 43210-0012. TEL 614-447-3600. FAX 614-447-3713. TELEX 6842086. **Document type:** abstracting/indexing.
Description: Covers flammability of materials and test methods for determining it; relationship of chemical structure to flammability; enhancing flammability of combustibles; reducing flammability of materials; synthesis and use of flame retardants and fireproofing agents.

540   US   ISSN 0195-4989   CODEN: CFSTD5
C A SELECTS. FLUIDIZED SOLIDS TECHNOLOGY. s-w. $240 to non-members; members $70 (effective 1998). Chemical Abstracts Service (Subsidiary of: American Chemical Society), 2540 Olentangy River Rd., Box 3012, Columbus, OH 43210-0012. TEL 614-447-3600. FAX 614-447-3713. TELEX 6842086. **Document type:** abstracting/indexing.
Description: Covers apparatus design and engineering; fluidized combustion for energy production and waste disposal.

540   US   ISSN 0895-5921   CODEN: CASFEV
C A SELECTS. FLUOROPOLYMERS. 1988. s-w. $240 to non-members; members $70 (effective 1998). Chemical Abstracts Service (Subsidiary of: American Chemical Society), 2540 Olentangy River Rd., Box 3012, Columbus, OH 43210-0012. TEL 614-447-3600. FAX 614-447-3713. TELEX 6842086. **Document type:** abstracting/indexing.
Description: Covers preparation, properties, and use of organic polymeric substances with a substantial fluorine content.

C A SELECTS. FOOD & FEED ANALYSIS. see FOOD AND FOOD INDUSTRIES — Abstracting, Bibliographies, Statistics

664 615.9   US   ISSN 0162-7813   CODEN: CSFTDV
C A SELECTS. FOOD TOXICITY. s-w. $240 to non-members; members $70 (effective 1998). Chemical Abstracts Service (Subsidiary of: American Chemical Society), 2540 Olentangy River Rd., Box 3012, Columbus, OH 43210-0012. TEL 614-447-3600. FAX 614-447-3713. TELEX 6842086. **Document type:** abstracting/indexing.
Description: Covers mutagenicity, teratogenicity, carcinogenicity, toxic side effects, and health hazards of foods and additives; contamination of foods by agrochemicals, nitroso compounds, heavy metals, aromatic hydrocarbons, and other toxicants.

540   US   ISSN 0890-1880   CODEN: CAFCEP
C A SELECTS. FORMULATION CHEMISTRY. 1987. s-w. $240 to non-members; members $70 (effective 1998). Chemical Abstracts Service (Subsidiary of: American Chemical Society), 2540 Olentangy River Rd., Box 3012, Columbus, OH 43210-0012. TEL 614-447-3600. FAX 614-447-3713. TELEX 6842086. **Document type:** abstracting/indexing.
Description: Covers materials used as fillers and inactive agents in processed materials; drugs, cleaning agents, paints, and cosmetics.

540   US   ISSN 0895-5905   CODEN: CAFRE2
C A SELECTS. FREE RADICALS (BIOCHEMICAL ASPECTS). 1988. s-w. $240 to non-members; members $70 (effective 1998). Chemical Abstracts Service (Subsidiary of: American Chemical Society), 2540 Olentangy River Rd., Box 3012, Columbus, OH 43210-0012. TEL 614-447-3600. FAX 614-447-3713. TELEX 6842086. **Document type:** abstracting/indexing.
Description: Covers reactions and interactions of free radicals, including activated oxygen species in biological systems; formation, metabolic aspects, and toxicity of free radicals in intact organisms, isolated organs, tissues, cells, and subcellular systems, as well as in model biological systems.

540   US   ISSN 0895-5972   CODEN: CFRAEC
C A SELECTS. FREE RADICALS (ORGANIC ASPECTS). 1987. s-w. $240 to non-members; members $70 (effective 1998). Chemical Abstracts Service (Subsidiary of: American Chemical Society), 2540 Olentangy River Rd., Box 3012, Columbus, OH 43210-0012. TEL 614-447-3600. FAX 614-447-3713. TELEX 6842086. **Document type:** abstracting/indexing.
Description: Covers formation, chemical reactions, and reactivities of organic free radicals.

540   US   ISSN 0195-4997   CODEN: CSFAD8
C A SELECTS. FUEL & LUBRICANT ADDITIVES. s-w. $240 to non-members; members $70 (effective 1998). Chemical Abstracts Service (Subsidiary of: American Chemical Society), 2540 Olentangy River Rd., Box 3012, Columbus, OH 43210-0012. TEL 614-447-3600. FAX 614-447-3713. TELEX 6842086. **Document type:** abstracting/indexing.
Description: Covers manufacture, development, and use of additives for fuels and lubricants; petroleum-based and non-petroleum-based products.

430   US
C A SELECTS. FUNGICIDES. s-w. $240 to non-members; members $70 (effective 1998). Chemical Abstracts Service (Subsidiary of: American Chemical Society), 2540 Olentangy River Rd., Box 3012, Columbus, OH 43210-0012. TEL 614-447-3600. FAX 614-447-3713. TELEX 6842086. **Document type:** abstracting/indexing.
Description: Covers preparation, mechanism of action, and effects of antifungal agents.

540   US   ISSN 0160-9076   CODEN: CSGTD2
C A SELECTS. GASEOUS WASTE TREATMENT. s-w. $240 to non-members; members $70 (effective 1998). Chemical Abstracts Service (Subsidiary of: American Chemical Society), 2540 Olentangy River Rd., Box 3012, Columbus, OH 43210-0012. TEL 614-447-3600. FAX 614-447-3713. TELEX 6842086. **Document type:** abstracting/indexing.
Description: Covers treatment and control of gaseous waste products from stationary sources, primarily industrial.

540 011   US   ISSN 1066-5730   CODEN: CSGEEQ
C A SELECTS. GEOCHEMISTRY. 1993. s-w. $240 to non-members; members $70 (effective 1998). Chemical Abstracts Service (Subsidiary of: American Chemical Society), 2540 Olentangy River Rd., Box 3012, Columbus, OH 43210-0012. TEL 614-447-3600. FAX 614-447-3713. TELEX 6842086. **Document type:** abstracting/indexing.
Description: Provides information on mineralogy, soils, geochemistry, geochronology, economic geology, paleoenvironment reconstruction, and extraterrestrial geochemistry.

660.284   US   ISSN 0162-7821   CODEN: CSHPDT
C A SELECTS. HEAT-RESISTANT AND ABLATIVE POLYMERS. s-w. $240 to non-members; members $70 (effective 1998). Chemical Abstracts Service (Subsidiary of: American Chemical Society), 2540 Olentangy River Rd., Box 3012, Columbus, OH 43210-0012. TEL 614-447-3600. FAX 614-447-3713. TELEX 6842086. **Document type:** abstracting/indexing.
Description: Covers polymers which are stable at high temperatures, e.g., plastic, fibers, rubbers, coatings; polymeric ablative materials; means of increasing thermal stability of polymers, e.g., heat-stabilizer additives.

540   US
C A SELECTS. HERBICIDES. s-w. $240 to non-members; members $70 (effective 1998). Chemical Abstracts Service (Subsidiary of: American Chemical Society), 2540 Olentangy River Rd., Box 3012, Columbus, OH 43210-0012. TEL 614-447-3600. FAX 614-447-3713. TELEX 6842086. **Document type:** abstracting/indexing.
Description: Covers preparation, mechanism of action, and effects of herbicides.

540   US   ISSN 0895-5891   CODEN: CSHAEJ
C A SELECTS. HOT-MELT ADHESIVES. 1988. s-w. $240 to non-members; members $70 (effective 1998). Chemical Abstracts Service (Subsidiary of: American Chemical Society), 2540 Olentangy River Rd., Box 3012, Columbus, OH 43210-0012. TEL 614-447-3600. FAX 614-447-3713. TELEX 6842086. **Document type:** abstracting/indexing.
Description: Covers preparation, composition, properties, and uses of hot-melt adhesives and sealants.

535   US   ISSN 0190-9428   CODEN: CSIADN
C A SELECTS. INFRARED SPECTROSCOPY (ORGANIC ASPECTS). s-w. $240 to non-members; members $70 (effective 1998). Chemical Abstracts Service (Subsidiary of: American Chemical Society), 2540 Olentangy River Rd., Box 3012, Columbus, OH 43210-0012. TEL 614-337-3600. FAX 614-447-3713. TELEX 6842086. **Document type:** abstracting/indexing.
Description: Covers organic, macromolecular, and biochemical aspects of infrared spectroscopy; spectroscopic characterization of substances.

660.284   US   ISSN 0734-8843   CODEN: CAIPEB
C A SELECTS. INITIATION OF POLYMERIZATION. s-w. $240 to non-members; members $70 (effective 1998). Chemical Abstracts Service (Subsidiary of: American Chemical Society), 2540 Olentangy River Rd., Box 3012, Columbus, OH 43210-0012. TEL 614-447-3600. FAX 614-447-3713. TELEX 6842086. **Document type:** abstracting/indexing.
Description: Covers preparation of polymerization catalysts or initiators, characterization and use in polymerization; kinetic and mechanistic aspects.

643 546   US   ISSN 0275-7087   CODEN: CSACDN
C A SELECTS. INORGANIC ANALYTICAL CHEMISTRY. s-w. $240 to non-members; members $70 (effective 1998). Chemical Abstracts Service (Subsidiary of: American Chemical Society), 2540 Olentangy River Rd., Box 3012, Columbus, OH 43210-0012. TEL 614-447-3600. FAX 614-447-3713. TELEX 6842086. **Document type:** abstracting/indexing.
Description: Covers methods and reagents for detection and determination of elements, radicals, and compounds in inorganic materials; analysis of inorganic coordination compounds; analytical apparatus and techniques; analysis of nuclear materials, water, sewage, wastes, agrochemicals, soils, cement, concrete products.

546   US   ISSN 0195-5012   CODEN: CIOMDJ
C A SELECTS. INORGANIC & ORGANOMETALLIC REACTION SYSTEMS. s-w. $240 to non-members; members $70 (effective 1998). Chemical Abstracts Service (Subsidiary of: American Chemical Society), 2540 Olentangy River Rd., Box 3012, Columbus, OH 43210-0012. TEL 614-447-3600. FAX 614-447-3713. TELEX 6842086. **Document type:** abstracting/indexing.
Description: Covers mechanistic and kinetic aspects of reactions of inorganic, organometallic and organometalloidal compounds.

546   US   ISSN 0275-7095   CODEN: CIRCD4
C A SELECTS. INORGANIC CHEMICALS & REACTIONS. s-w. $240 to non-members; members $70 (effective 1998). Chemical Abstracts Service (Subsidiary of: American Chemical Society), 2540 Olentangy River Rd., Box 3012, Columbus, OH 43210-0012. TEL 614-447-3600. FAX 614-447-3713. TELEX 6842086. **Document type:** abstracting/indexing.
Description: Covers synthesis, chemical properties, reactions, nonindustrial preparation and applications of inorganic compounds; properties of metal carbonyls, cyanides, carbides, cyanates, and carbonates.

CHEMISTRY — ABSTRACTING, BIBLIOGRAPHIES, STATISTICS

540   US   ISSN 0890-1899
CODEN: CSICEU
C A SELECTS. ION CHROMATOGRAPHY. 1987. s-w. $240 to non-members; members $70 (effective 1998). Chemical Abstracts Service (Subsidiary of: American Chemical Society), 2540 Olentangy River Rd., Box 3012, Columbus, OH 43210-0012. TEL 614-447-3600. FAX 614-447-3713. TELEX 6842086. **Document type:** abstracting/indexing.
    Description: Covers the principle and application of ion chromatography in analytical procedures.

540   US   ISSN 0195-5020
CODEN: CSIPDY
C A SELECTS. ION-CONTAINING POLYMERS. s-w. $240 to non-members; members $70 (effective 1998). Chemical Abstracts Service (Subsidiary of: American Chemical Society), 2540 Olentangy River Rd., Box 3012, Columbus, OH 43210-0012. TEL 614-447-3600. FAX 614-447-3713. TELEX 6842086. **Document type:** abstracting/indexing.
    Description: Covers theoretical and practical aspects; polyelectrolytes.

430   US   ISSN 0146-4493
CODEN: CSIODV
C A SELECTS. ION EXCHANGE. s-w. $240 to non-members; members $70 (effective 1998). Chemical Abstracts Service (Subsidiary of: American Chemical Society), 2540 Olentangy River Rd., Box 3012, Columbus, OH 43210-0012. TEL 614-447-3600. FAX 614-447-3713. TELEX 6842086. **Document type:** abstracting/indexing.
    Description: Covers theory and applications including material and equipment for ion exchange.

540   US   ISSN 0895-5883
CODEN: CAICE6
C A SELECTS. ISOMERIZATION & CATALYSTS. 1988. s-w. $240 to non-members; members $70 (effective 1998). Chemical Abstracts Service (Subsidiary of: American Chemical Society), 2540 Olentangy River Rd., Box 3012, Columbus, OH 43210-0012. TEL 614-447-3600. FAX 614-447-3713. TELEX 6842086. **Document type:** abstracting/indexing.
    Description: Covers organic isomerizations (as distinct from rearrangements) and the agents used for effecting them.

535.58   US   ISSN 0195-5039
CODEN: CLAPDD
C A SELECTS. LASER APPLICATIONS. s-w. $240 to non-members; members $70 (effective 1998). Chemical Abstracts Service (Subsidiary of: American Chemical Society), 2540 Olentangy River Rd., Box 3012, Columbus, OH 43210-0012. TEL 614-447-3600. FAX 614-447-3713. TELEX 6842086. **Document type:** abstracting/indexing.
    Description: Covers interactions of laser radiation with materials; physicochemical and biochemical effects of laser radiation; applications of lasers and laser radiation.

540   US   ISSN 0885-0178
CODEN: CSLREM
C A SELECTS. LASER-INDUCED CHEMICAL REACTIONS. s-w. $240 to non-members; members $70 (effective 1998). Chemical Abstracts Service (Subsidiary of: American Chemical Society), 2540 Olentangy River Rd., Box 3012, Columbus, OH 43210-0012. TEL 614-447-3600. FAX 614-447-3713. TELEX 6842086. **Document type:** abstracting/indexing.
    Description: Covers laser-induced processes; photochemical reactions initiated by laser radiation; thermal reactions induced by laser heating.

610 011   US   ISSN 1047-8086
CODEN: CSLEEH
C A SELECTS. LEUKOTRIENES. 1985. s-w. $240 to non-members; members $70 (effective 1998). Chemical Abstracts Service (Subsidiary of: American Chemical Society), 2540 Olentangy River Rd., Box 3012, Columbus, OH 43210-0012. TEL 614-447-3600. FAX 614-447-3713. TELEX 6842086. **Document type:** abstracting/indexing.
    Formerly (until 1989): BIOSIS CAS Selects: Leukotrienes and Slow-Reacting Substances.
    Description: Covers the synthesis, chemistry, biochemistry, physiology and pathology, and pharmacology, including pharmaceutical formulation of leukotrienes and slow-reacting substances of anaphylaxis.

548   US   ISSN 0148-2351
CODEN: CSLCDA
C A SELECTS. LIQUID CRYSTALS. s-w. $240 to non-members; members $70 (effective 1998). Chemical Abstracts Service (Subsidiary of: American Chemical Society), 2540 Olentangy River Rd., Box 3012, Columbus, OH 43210-0012. TEL 614-447-3600. FAX 614-447-3713. TELEX 6842086. **Document type:** abstracting/indexing.
    Description: Covers application, preparation, properties, and structure of liquid crystals.

540 665   US   ISSN 0734-8738
CODEN: CASLEF
C A SELECTS. LUBRICANTS, GREASES, & LUBRICATION. s-w. $240 to non-members; members $70 (effective 1998). Chemical Abstracts Service (Subsidiary of: American Chemical Society), 2540 Olentangy River Rd., Box 3012, Columbus, OH 43210-0012. TEL 614-447-3600. FAX 614-447-3713. TELEX 6842086. **Document type:** abstracting/indexing.
    Description: Covers manufacture, properties, and use of lubricants; oils, emulsions, greases, solid lubricants; additives for lubricants.

540   US   ISSN 1040-7197
CODEN: CAMSE6
C A SELECTS. MEMBRANE SEPARATION. 1989. s-w. $240 to non-members; members $70 (effective 1998). Chemical Abstracts Service (Subsidiary of: American Chemical Society), 2540 Olentangy River Rd., Box 3012, Columbus, OH 43210-0012. TEL 614-447-3600. FAX 614-447-3713. TELEX 6842086. **Document type:** abstracting/indexing.
    Description: Covers theory and technology of dialysis, electrodialysis, electroosmosis, gas separation by membrane permeation and pervaporation.

661   US   ISSN 0890-1821
CODEN: CSMMEC
C A SELECTS. MEMORY & RECORDING DEVICES & MATERIALS. 1987. s-w. $240 to non-members; members $70 (effective 1998). Chemical Abstracts Service (Subsidiary of: American Chemical Society), 2540 Olentangy River Rd., Box 3012, Columbus, OH 43210-0012. TEL 614-447-3600. FAX 614-447-3713. TELEX 6842086. **Document type:** abstracting/indexing.
    Description: Covers materials used for information storage; recording tapes and disks, optical disks, and computer memories.

669   US   ISSN 1062-8681
C A SELECTS. METALLIC GLASSES. 1992. s-w. $240 to non-members; members $70 (effective 1998). Chemical Abstracts Service (Subsidiary of: American Chemical Society), 2540 Olentangy River Rd., Box 3012, Columbus, OH 43210-0012. TEL 614-447-3600. FAX 614-447-3713. TELEX 6842086. **Document type:** abstracting/indexing.
    Description: Covers preparation, such as rapid solidification; mechanical alloying; and deposition.

669   US   ISSN 0160-9114
CODEN: CSMCDF
C A SELECTS. METALLO ENZYMES & METALLO COENZYMES. s-w. $240 to non-members; members $70 (effective 1998). Chemical Abstracts Service (Subsidiary of: American Chemical Society), 2540 Olentangy River Rd., Box 3012, Columbus, OH 43210-0012. TEL 614-447-3600. FAX 614-447-3713. TELEX 6842086. **Document type:** abstracting/indexing.
    Description: Covers preparation, analysis, and biochemical effects of enzymes and coenzymes that contain metals (cobalt, copper, iron, zinc, and molybdenum); metalloproteins, metal-containing vitamins; mechanisms by which metals are bound to enzymes.

540 011   US   ISSN 1059-2784
CODEN: CAMMEM
C A SELECTS. MOLECULAR MODELING (BIOCHEMICAL ASPECTS). 1992. s-w. $240 to non-members; members $70 (effective 1998). Chemical Abstracts Service (Subsidiary of: American Chemical Society), 2540 Olentangy River Rd., Box 3012, Columbus, OH 43210-0012. TEL 614-447-3600. FAX 614-447-3713. TELEX 6842086. **Document type:** abstracting/indexing.
    Description: Covers the design of pharmaceuticals, agrochemicals, and other bioactive agents; modeling studies on structures of macromolecules; pharmacophores; and quantitative structure-activity relationships.

540   US   ISSN 0740-0691
CODEN: CSNSEZ
C A SELECTS. NATURAL PRODUCT SYNTHESIS. s-w. $240 to non-members; members $70 (effective 1998). Chemical Abstracts Service (Subsidiary of: American Chemical Society), 2540 Olentangy River Rd., Box 3012, Columbus, OH 43210-0012. TEL 614-447-3600. FAX 614-447-3713. TELEX 6842086. **Document type:** abstracting/indexing.
    Description: Covers laboratory synthesis of known natural products; partial and total synthesis, unsuccessful attempts at synthesis.

540   US   ISSN 0148-2416
CODEN: CSBCDS
C A SELECTS. NEW BOOKS IN CHEMISTRY. s-w. $240 to non-members; members $70 (effective 1998). Chemical Abstracts Service (Subsidiary of: American Chemical Society), 2540 Olentangy River Rd., Box 3012, Columbus, OH 43210. TEL 614-447-3600. FAX 614-447-3713. TELEX 6842086. **Document type:** abstracting/indexing.
    Description: Covers all new books in chemistry and chemical engineering cited in CA; includes monographs, series publications, and conference proceedings.

540 011   US   ISSN 1047-8108
CODEN: CSNFEU
C A SELECTS. NITROGEN FIXATION. 1987. s-w. $240 to non-members; members $70 (effective 1998). Chemical Abstracts Service (Subsidiary of: American Chemical Society), 2540 Olentangy River Rd., Box 3012, Columbus, OH 43210-0012. TEL 614-447-3600. FAX 614-447-3713. TELEX 6842086. **Document type:** abstracting/indexing.
    Formerly (until 1989): BIOSIS CAS Selects: Nitrogen Fixation.
    Description: Covers nitrogen fixation in bacteria and plants. Includes genetic engineering as well as biochemical, physiological, and ecological aspects.

016.57   US   ISSN 0734-872X
CODEN: CAPREI
C A SELECTS. NOVEL NATURAL PRODUCTS. s-w. $240 to non-members; members $70 (effective 1998). Chemical Abstracts Service (Subsidiary of: American Chemical Society), 2540 Olentangy River Rd., Box 3012, Columbus, OH 43210-0012. TEL 614-447-3600. FAX 614-447-3713. TELEX 6842086. **Document type:** abstracting/indexing. —CISTI.
    Description: Covers new natural products; isolation, detection, or discovery of previously unknown natural products; and synthesis of new derivatives or compounds of new or known natural products.

C A SELECTS. NOVEL POLYMERS FROM PATENTS. see PATENTS, TRADEMARKS AND COPYRIGHTS — Abstracting, Bibliographies, Statistics

540 011   US   ISSN 0275-7109
CODEN: CSNHDZ
C A SELECTS. NOVEL SULFUR HETEROCYCLES. 1981. s-w. $240 to non-members; members $70 (effective 1998). Chemical Abstracts Service (Subsidiary of: American Chemical Society), 2540 Olentangy River Rd., Box 3012, Columbus, OH 43210-0012. TEL 614-447-3600. FAX 614-447-3713. TELEX 6842086. **Document type:** abstracting/indexing.
    Description: Covers the synthesis of new sulfur-containing ring systems and new compounds containing known sulfur heterocycles.

540   US   ISSN 1052-1976
CODEN: CSOOES
C A SELECTS. OLEOCHEMICALS CONTAINING NITROGEN. 1990. s-w. $240 to non-members; members $70 (effective 1998). Chemical Abstracts Service (Subsidiary of: American Chemical Society), 2540 Olentangy River Rd., Box 3012, Columbus, OH 43210-0012. TEL 614-447-3600. FAX 614-447-3713. TELEX 6842086. **Document type:** abstracting/indexing.
    Description: Covers analysis, preparation, properties, reactions, and uses of amides, amines, betaines, imidazoles, imidazolines, nitriles, and quaternary ammonium compounds derived from fats and oils.

540 574   US   ISSN 1052-1984
CODEN: CSONEP
C A SELECTS. OMEGA-3 FATTY ACIDS & FISH OIL. 1990. s-w. $240 to non-members; members $70 (effective 1998). Chemical Abstracts Service (Subsidiary of: American Chemical Society), 2540 Olentangy River Rd., Box 3012, Columbus, OH 43210-0012. TEL 614-447-3600. FAX 614-447-3713. TELEX 6842086. **Document type:** abstracting/indexing.
Description: Covers all aspects of the chemistry of omega-3 fatty acids, freshwater and marine fish oils, and oils from other marine animals.

C A SELECTS. OPTICAL AND PHOTOSENSITIVE MATERIALS. see PHYSICS — Abstracting, Bibliographies, Statistics

540   US   ISSN 0195-5071
CODEN: COORD8
C A SELECTS. OPTIMIZATION OF ORGANIC REACTIONS. s-w. $240 to non-members; members $70 (effective 1998). Chemical Abstracts Service (Subsidiary of: American Chemical Society), 2540 Olentangy River Rd., Box 3012, Columbus, OH 43210-0012. TEL 614-447-3600. FAX 614-447-3713. TELEX 6842086. **Document type:** abstracting/indexing.
Description: Covers parameters and variables that affect reaction selectivity, product yield, and product quality; includes computer-based and other simulation models.

547.3   US   ISSN 0275-7117
CODEN: COACDT
C A SELECTS. ORGANIC ANALYTICAL CHEMISTRY. s-w. $240 to non-members; members $70 (effective 1998). Chemical Abstracts Service (Subsidiary of: American Chemical Society), 2540 Olentangy River Rd., Box 3012, Columbus, OH 43210-0012. TEL 614-447-3600. FAX 614-447-3713. TELEX 6842086. **Document type:** abstracting/indexing.
Description: Covers methods, reagents, apparatus; detection and determination of elements, radicals, and compounds in organic materials; and analysis of organometallic compounds.

540   US   ISSN 0885-0186
CODEN: CSOMEM
C A SELECTS. ORGANIC OPTICAL MATERIALS. s-w. $240 to non-members; members $70 (effective 1998). Chemical Abstracts Service (Subsidiary of: American Chemical Society), 2540 Olentangy River Rd., Box 3012, Columbus, OH 43210-0012. TEL 614-447-3600. FAX 614-447-3713. TELEX 6842086. **Document type:** abstracting/indexing.
Description: Covers optical materials based on organic compounds.

540   US   ISSN 0162-7848
CODEN: CSOMDL
C A SELECTS. ORGANIC REACTION MECHANISMS. s-w. $240 to non-members; members $70 (effective 1998). Chemical Abstracts Service (Subsidiary of: American Chemical Society), 2540 Olentangy River Rd., Box 3012, Columbus, OH 43210-0012. TEL 614-447-3600. FAX 614-447-3713. TELEX 6842086. **Document type:** abstracting/indexing.
Description: Covers organic reaction pathways; organic reaction intermediates.

540   US   ISSN 0195-508X
CODEN: CORSDQ
C A SELECTS. ORGANIC STEREOCHEMISTRY. s-w. $240 to non-members; members $70 (effective 1998). Chemical Abstracts Service (Subsidiary of: American Chemical Society), 2540 Olentangy River Rd., Box 3012, Columbus, OH 43210-0012. TEL 614-447-3600. FAX 614-447-3713. TELEX 6842086. **Document type:** abstracting/indexing.
Description: Covers conformational and configurational analysis; steric factors in organic reactions and properties of organic compounds; asymmetric synthesis, preparation of specific stereoisomers, and stereoselectivity of organic reactions.

540   US   ISSN 0160-9130
C A SELECTS. ORGANO-TRANSITION METAL COMPLEXES. s-w. $240 to non-members; members $70 (effective 1998). Chemical Abstracts Service (Subsidiary of: American Chemical Society), 2540 Olentangy River Rd., Box 3012, Columbus, OH 43210-0012. TEL 614-447-3600. FAX 614-447-3713. TELEX 6842086. **Document type:** abstracting/indexing.
Description: Covers organic complexes of copper, silver, gold, titanium, zirconium, hafnium, vanadium, niobium, tantalum, chromium, manganese, molybdenum, tungsten, technetium, rhenium, iron, cobalt, nickel, ruthenium, platinum, palladium, osmium, and iridium; compounds with a bond between a transition metal and carbon; complexes with bonds between metals and compounds such as phosphines.

540   US   ISSN 0160-905X
CODEN: CORCDC
C A SELECTS. ORGANOFLUORINE CHEMISTRY. s-w. $240 to non-members; members $70 (effective 1998). Chemical Abstracts Service (Subsidiary of: American Chemical Society), 2540 Olentangy River Rd., Box 3012, Columbus, OH 43210-0012. TEL 614-447-3600. FAX 614-447-3713. TELEX 6842086. **Document type:** abstracting/indexing.
Description: Covers synthesis and manufacture of organofluorine compounds; includes properties, reactions, and use of compounds containing a carbon-fluorine bond.

540   US   ISSN 0895-5859
CODEN: COOSEC
C A SELECTS. ORGANOMETALLICS IN ORGANIC SYNTHESIS. 1988. s-w. $240 to non-members; members $70 (effective 1998). Chemical Abstracts Service (Subsidiary of: American Chemical Society), 2540 Olentangy River Rd., Box 3012, Columbus, OH 43210-0012. TEL 614-447-3600. FAX 614-447-3713. TELEX 6842086. **Document type:** abstracting/indexing.
Description: Covers uses of organometallic compounds and complexes in the synthesis of organic compounds, generally those containing no carbon-metal bonds.

540   US   ISSN 0162-783X
CODEN: CAOCDZ
C A SELECTS. ORGANOPHOSPHORUS CHEMISTRY. s-w. $240 to non-members; members $70 (effective 1998). Chemical Abstracts Service (Subsidiary of: American Chemical Society), 2540 Olentangy River Rd., Box 3012, Columbus, OH 43210-0012. TEL 614-447-3600. FAX 614-447-3713. TELEX 6842086. **Document type:** abstracting/indexing.
Description: Covers preparation, reactions and applications of organophosphorus compounds.

540   US   ISSN 1040-7189
CODEN: CAOCE2
C A SELECTS. ORGANOSULFUR CHEMISTRY (JOURNALS). 1989. s-w. $240 to non-members; members $70 (effective 1998). Chemical Abstracts Service (Subsidiary of: American Chemical Society), 2540 Olentangy River Rd., Box 3012, Columbus, OH 43210-0012. TEL 614-447-3600. FAX 614-447-3713. TELEX 6842086. **Document type:** abstracting/indexing.
Description: Journal literature on the chemistry of organic compounds containing sulfur.

540   US   ISSN 0195-5101
CODEN: COGCDP
C A SELECTS. ORGANOTIN CHEMISTRY. s-w. $240 to non-members; members $70 (effective 1998). Chemical Abstracts Service (Subsidiary of: American Chemical Society), 2540 Olentangy River Rd., Box 3012, Columbus, OH 43210-0012. TEL 614-447-3600. FAX 614-447-3713. TELEX 6842086. **Document type:** abstracting/indexing.
Description: Covers preparation, properties, chemical behavior, and use of compounds containing one or more carbon-tin bonds.

540   US   ISSN 1040-7170
CODEN: COXCE9
C A SELECTS. OXIDATION CATALYSTS. 1989. s-w. $240 to non-members; members $70 (effective 1998). Chemical Abstracts Service (Subsidiary of: American Chemical Society), 2540 Olentangy River Rd., Box 3012, Columbus, OH 43210-0012. TEL 614-447-3600. FAX 614-447-3713. TELEX 6842086. **Document type:** abstracting/indexing.
Description: Covers new catalysts for known oxidation processes as well as catalysts for new oxidations.

540   US   ISSN 1040-7219
CODEN: CAOSEG
C A SELECTS. OXIDE SUPERCONDUCTORS. 1989. s-w. $240 to non-members; members $70 (effective 1998). Chemical Abstracts Service (Subsidiary of: American Chemical Society), 2540 Olentangy River Rd., Box 3012, Columbus, OH 43210-0012. TEL 614-447-3600. FAX 614-447-3713. TELEX 6842086. **Document type:** abstracting/indexing.
Description: Covers oxides that are used as or suitable for superconductors.

540   US   ISSN 0146-4515
CODEN: CSPCDU
C A SELECTS. PAPER & THIN-LAYER CHROMATOGRAPHY. s-w. $240 to non-members; members $70 (effective 1998). Chemical Abstracts Service (Subsidiary of: American Chemical Society), 2540 Olentangy River Rd., Box 3012, Columbus, OH 43210-0012. TEL 614-447-3600. FAX 614-447-3713. TELEX 6842086. **Document type:** abstracting/indexing.
Description: Covers theory and applications; equipment and materials; paper, plate and thin-layer chromatography.

540   US   ISSN 1040-7200
CODEN: CPCME9
C A SELECTS. PAPER CHEMISTRY. 1989. s-w. $240 to non-members; members $70 (effective 1998). Chemical Abstracts Service (Subsidiary of: American Chemical Society), 2540 Olentangy River Rd., Box 3012, Columbus, OH 43210-0012. TEL 714-447-3600. FAX 714-447-3713. TELEX 6842086. **Document type:** abstracting/indexing.
Description: Covers chemical aspects of paper manufacture; includes stock preparation, various additives, sizing, and coating.

540   US   ISSN 0885-0194
CODEN: CSPCEV
C A SELECTS. PHASE TRANSFER CATALYSIS. s-w. $240 to non-members; members $70 (effective 1998). Chemical Abstracts Service (Subsidiary of: American Chemical Society), 2540 Olentangy River Rd., Box 3012, Columbus, OH 43210-0012. TEL 614-447-3600. FAX 614-447-3713. TELEX 6842086. **Document type:** abstracting/indexing.
Description: Covers reactions deliberately carried out in systems containing two or more phases, in the presence of agents that promote contact of materials in the phases.

C A SELECTS. PHOSPHOLIPIDS (CHEMICAL ASPECTS). see BIOLOGY — Abstracting, Bibliographies, Statistics

016.572   US   ISSN 0148-2335
CODEN: CSPHDB
C A SELECTS. PHOTOBIOCHEMISTRY. s-w. $240 to non-members; members $70 (effective 1998). Chemical Abstracts Service (Subsidiary of: American Chemical Society), 2540 Olentangy River Rd., Box 3012, Columbus, OH 43210-0012. TEL 614-447-3600. FAX 614-447-3713. TELEX 6842086. **Document type:** abstracting/indexing.
Description: Covers photochemistry of biological materials, their constituents, and molecules of biological interest.

540 011   US   ISSN 1051-3949
CODEN: CPHOE6
C A SELECTS. PHOTOCATALYSTS. 1990. s-w. $240 to non-members; members $70 (effective 1998). Chemical Abstracts Service (Subsidiary of: American Chemical Society), 2540 Olentangy River Rd., Box 3012, Columbus, OH 43210-0012. TEL 614-447-3600. FAX 614-447-3713. TELEX 6842086. **Document type:** abstracting/indexing.
Description: Covers preparation and usage of photocatalysts; photocatalyzed reactions.

CHEMISTRY — ABSTRACTING, BIBLIOGRAPHIES, STATISTICS

547 US ISSN 0885-0208
CODEN: CSPSEB
C A SELECTS. PHOTOCHEMICAL ORGANIC SYNTHESIS. s-w. $240 to non-members; members $70 (effective 1998). Chemical Abstracts Service (Subsidiary of: American Chemical Society), 2540 Olentangy River Rd., Box 3012, Columbus, OH 43210-0012. TEL 614-447-3600. FAX 614-447-3713. TELEX 6842086. **Document type:** abstracting/indexing.
Description: Covers preparation and reactions of organic compounds under ultraviolet or other irradiation.

540 US ISSN 0885-0216
CODEN: CSPHEC
C A SELECTS. PHOTORESISTS. s-w. $240 to non-members; members $70 (effective 1998). Chemical Abstracts Service (Subsidiary of: American Chemical Society), 2540 Olentangy River Rd., Box 3012, Columbus, OH 43210-0012. TEL 614-447-3600. FAX 614-447-3713. TELEX 6842086. **Document type:** abstracting/indexing.
Description: Covers materials and technology for fabricating and developing photoresists; photoresists used in photolithography, printing, microelectronics.

540 US ISSN 0749-7326
CODEN: CSPPE2
C A SELECTS. PHOTOSENSITIVE POLYMERS. s-w. $240 to non-members; members $70 (effective 1998). Chemical Abstracts Service (Subsidiary of: American Chemical Society), 2540 Olentangy River Rd., Box 3012, Columbus, OH 43210-0012. TEL 614-447-3600. FAX 614-447-3713. TELEX 6842086. **Document type:** abstracting/indexing.
Description: Covers preparation, properties, and uses of light-sensitive polymers; photocurable coatings and sheet material.

540 US ISSN 0749-7334
CODEN: CSPEE3
C A SELECTS. PLASMA & REACTIVE ION ETCHING. s-w. $240 to non-members; members $70 (effective 1998). Chemical Abstracts Service (Subsidiary of: American Chemical Society), 2540 Olentangy Rd., Box 3012, Columbus, OH 43210-0012. TEL 614-447-3600. FAX 614-447-3713. TELEX 6842086. **Document type:** abstracting/indexing.
Description: Covers etching processes used in fabricating semiconductors and integrated circuits; laser etching in the fabrication of electronic devices.

540 US ISSN 0890-1937
CODEN: CPCHES
C A SELECTS. PLATINUM AND PALLADIUM CHEMISTRY. s-w. $240 to non-members; members $70 (effective 1998). Chemical Abstracts Service (Subsidiary of: American Chemical Society), 2540 Olentangy River Rd., Box 3012, Columbus, OH 43210-0012. TEL 614-447-3600. FAX 614-447-3713. TELEX 6842086. **Document type:** abstracting/indexing.
Description: Covers preparation, properties, reactions, uses, and characterization of compounds that contain platinum or palladium.

540 US ISSN 0890-1945
CODEN: CSPJEI
C A SELECTS. POLYACRYLATES (JOURNALS). s-w. $240 to non-members; members $70 (effective 1998). Chemical Abstracts Service (Subsidiary of: American Chemical Society), 2540 Olentangy River Rd., Box 3012, Columbus, OH 43210-0012. TEL 614-447-3600. FAX 614-447-3713. TELEX 6842086. **Document type:** abstracting/indexing.
Description: Covers polymers prepared from acrylic and or methacrylic acid esters.

540 US ISSN 1045-8549
CODEN: CAPLEY
C A SELECTS. POLYACRYLATES (PATENTS). s-w. $240 to non-members; members $70 (effective 1998). Chemical Abstracts Service (Subsidiary of: American Chemical Society), 2540 Olentangy River Rd., Box 3012, Columbus, OH 43210-0012. TEL 614-447-3600. FAX 614-447-3713. TELEX 6842086. **Document type:** abstracting/indexing.
Description: Includes patent literature dealing with preparation, properties, and uses of polymers and copolymers from acrylic acid and - or methacrylic acid esters.

540 011 US ISSN 0734-8703
CODEN: CAPOE9
C A SELECTS. POLYESTERS. s-w. $240 to non-members; members $70 (effective 1998). Chemical Abstracts Service (Subsidiary of: American Chemical Society), 2540 Olentangy River Rd., Box 3012, Columbus, OH 43210-0012. TEL 614-447-3600. FAX 614-447-3713. TELEX 6842086. **Document type:** abstracting/indexing.
Description: Covers the chemistry of polyesters: preparation, properties, formulation, and use.

540 US ISSN 0895-5840
CODEN: CSEPEF
C A SELECTS. POLYIMIDES. 1988. s-w. $240 to non-members; members $70 (effective 1998). Chemical Abstracts Service (Subsidiary of: American Chemical Society), 2540 Olentangy River Rd., Box 3012, Columbus, OH 43210-0012. TEL 614-447-3600. FAX 614-447-3713. TELEX 6842086. **Document type:** abstracting/indexing.
Description: Covers preparation, properties, and uses of polymers that contain imide linkages in the main chain.

541.3 US ISSN 0734-8827
CODEN: CAPBE4
C A SELECTS. POLYMER BLENDS. s-w. $240 to non-members; members $70 (effective 1998). Chemical Abstracts Service (Subsidiary of: American Chemical Society), 2540 Olentangy River Rd., Box 3012, Columbus, OH 43210-0012. TEL 614-447-3600. FAX 614-447-3713. TELEX 6842086. **Document type:** abstracting/indexing.
Description: Covers morphology and physical and mechanical properties of mixtures of polymers.

541.3 US ISSN 0734-8835
CODEN: CAPDEA
C A SELECTS. POLYMER DEGRADATION. s-w. $240 to non-members; members $70 (effective 1998). Chemical Abstracts Service (Subsidiary of: American Chemical Society), 2540 Olentangy River Rd., Box 3012, Columbus, OH 43210-0012. TEL 614-447-3600. FAX 614-447-3713. TELEX 6842086. **Document type:** abstracting/indexing.
Description: Covers chemical, photochemical, radiochemical, mechanical, thermal, and oxidative degradation of polymers; kinetics and mechanisms of degradative reactions.

541.3 US ISSN 0195-5128
CODEN: CAPMD2
C A SELECTS. POLYMER MORPHOLOGY. s-w. $240 to non-members; members $70 (effective 1998). Chemical Abstracts Service (Subsidiary of: American Chemical Society), 2540 Olentangy River Rd., Box 3012, Columbus, OH 43210-0012. TEL 614-447-3600. FAX 614-447-3713. TELEX 6842086. **Document type:** abstracting/indexing.
Description: Covers crystallinity and noncrystalline ordering on a supramolecular level in polymeric materials and their effect on physical and chemical properties of natural and synthetic polymers.

541.3 US ISSN 0885-0224
CODEN: CPKCEJ
C A SELECTS. POLYMERIZATION KINETICS & PROCESS CONTROL. s-w. $240 to non-members; members $70 (effective 1998). Chemical Abstracts Service (Subsidiary of: American Chemical Society), 2540 Olentangy River Rd., Box 3012, Columbus, OH 43210-0012. TEL 614-447-3600. FAX 614-447-3713. TELEX 6842086. **Document type:** abstracting/indexing.
Description: Covers kinetic studies on addition, condensation, and other types of polymerization.

540 US ISSN 0195-5136
CODEN: CLPODH
C A SELECTS. PORPHYRINS. s-w. $240 to non-members; members $70 (effective 1998). Chemical Abstracts Service (Subsidiary of: American Chemical Society), 2540 Olentangy River Rd., Box 3012, Columbus, OH 43210-0012. TEL 614-447-3600. FAX 614-447-3713. TELEX 6842086. **Document type:** abstracting/indexing.
Description: Covers chemical and biochemical aspects of porphyrins.

540 US ISSN 0148-2343
CODEN: CSEPDE
C A SELECTS. PROSTAGLANDINS. s-w. $240 to non-members; members $70 (effective 1998). Chemical Abstracts Service (Subsidiary of: American Chemical Society), 2540 Olentangy River Rd., Box 3012, Columbus, OH 43210-0012. TEL 614-447-3600. FAX 614-447-3713. TELEX 6842086. **Document type:** abstracting/indexing.
Description: Covers the chemistry of prostaglandins, prostacyclins, thromboxanes, leukotrienes; enzymes of prostaglandin metabolism.

540 US ISSN 0190-941X
CODEN: CPMRD5
C A SELECTS. PROTON MAGNETIC RESONANCE. s-w. $240 to non-members; members $70 (effective 1998). Chemical Abstracts Service (Subsidiary of: American Chemical Society), 2540 Olentangy River Rd., Box 3012, Columbus, OH 43210-0012. TEL 614-447-3600. FAX 614-447-3713. TELEX 6842086. **Document type:** abstracting/indexing.
Description: Covers the chemical aspects of nuclear magnetic resonance (NMR) of hydrogen, deuterium, and tritium.

C A SELECTS. PSYCHOBIOCHEMISTRY. see *BIOLOGY — Abstracting, Bibliographies, Statistics*

540 US ISSN 0890-1953
CODEN: CSQPE7
C A SELECTS. QUATERNARY AMMONIUM COMPOUNDS. 1987. s-w. $240 to non-members; members $70 (effective 1998). Chemical Abstracts Service (Subsidiary of: American Chemical Society), 2540 Olentangy River Rd., Box 3012, Columbus, OH 43210-0012. TEL 614-447-3600. FAX 614-447-3713. TELEX 6842086. **Document type:** abstracting/indexing.
Description: Covers preparation, properties, reactions, and uses of compounds that contain at least one nitrogen atom covalently bonded to four non-hydrogen atoms.

540 US ISSN 0146-4523
CODEN: CSRCD6
C A SELECTS. RADIATION CHEMISTRY. s-w. $240 to non-members; members $70 (effective 1998). Chemical Abstracts Service (Subsidiary of: American Chemical Society), 2540 Olentangy River Rd., Box 3012, Columbus, OH 43210-0012. TEL 614-477-3600. FAX 614-447-3713. TELEX 6842086. **Document type:** abstracting/indexing.
Description: Covers radiation chemistry and biochemistry; radiation chemistry in aqueous and non-aqueous systems; energy transfer and ionic reactions.

540 US ISSN 0749-7342
CODEN: CSRCE7
C A SELECTS. RADIATION CURING. s-w. $240 to non-members; members $70 (effective 1998). Chemical Abstracts Service (Subsidiary of: American Chemical Society), 2540 Olentangy River Rd., Box 3012, Columbus, OH 43210-0012. TEL 614-447-3600. FAX 614-447-3713. TELEX 6842086. **Document type:** abstracting/indexing.
Description: Covers treatment of polymers with electron beams, gamma rays, and other forms of ionizing radiation.

544.92 US ISSN 0148-2432
CODEN: CARSDU
C A SELECTS. RAMAN SPECTROSCOPY. s-w. $240 to non-members; members $70 (effective 1998). Chemical Abstracts Service (Subsidiary of: American Chemical Society), 2540 Olentangy River Rd., Box 3012, Columbus, OH 43210-0012. TEL 614-447-3600. FAX 614-447-3713. TELEX 6842086. **Document type:** abstracting/indexing.
Description: Covers all aspects of Raman spectroscopy; includes methodology, apparatus, experimental results, and theoretical treatments.

540 011 US ISSN 1062-869X
CODEN: CSSLE5
C A SELECTS. SHAPE MEMORY ALLOYS. 1992. s-w. $240 to non-members; members $70 (effective 1998). Chemical Abstracts Service (Subsidiary of: American Chemical Society), 2540 Olentangy River Rd., Box 3012, Columbus, OH 43210-0012. TEL 614-447-3600. FAX 614-447-3713. TELEX 6842086. **Document type:** abstracting/indexing.
Description: Covers fabrication, testing, properties applications, and fundamental studies, including phase transformations, crystallography, and modeling of the title alloys.

CHEMISTRY — ABSTRACTING, BIBLIOGRAPHIES, STATISTICS

540 US ISSN 0890-1961
CODEN: CSSSEQ
C A SELECTS. SILICAS & SILICATES. 1987. s-w. $240 to non-members; members $70 (effective 1998). Chemical Abstracts Service (Subsidiary of: American Chemical Society), 2540 Olentangy River Rd., Box 3012, Columbus, OH 43210-0012. TEL 614-447-3600. FAX 614-447-3713. TELEX 6842086. **Document type:** abstracting/indexing.
Description: Covers preparation, properties, reaction, and uses of synthetic and naturally occurring inorganic compounds that contain silicon tetrahedrally bonded to oxygen.

540 US ISSN 0895-5832
CODEN: CSISEA
C A SELECTS. SILOXANES & SILICONES. 1988. s-w. $240 to non-members; members $70 (effective 1998). Chemical Abstracts Service (Subsidiary of: American Chemical Society), 2540 Olentangy River Rd., Box 3012, Columbus, OH 43210-0012. TEL 614-447-3600. FAX 614-447-3713. TELEX 6842086. **Document type:** abstracting/indexing.
Description: Covers preparation, properties, reactions, and uses of monomeric, oligomeric, and polymeric compounds, the basic structure of which consists of alternating silicon and oxygen atoms.

540 US ISSN 0895-5824
CODEN: CSSNEB
C A SELECTS. SOLID STATE N M R. (Nuclear Magnetic Resonance) 1988. s-w. $240 to non-members; members $70 (effective 1998). Chemical Abstracts Service (Subsidiary of: American Chemical Society), 2540 Olentangy River Rd., Box 3012, Columbus, OH 43210-0012. TEL 614-447-3600. FAX 614-447-3713. TELEX 6842086. **Document type:** abstracting/indexing.
Description: Covers methodology and apparatus for solid-state NMR studies.

540 US ISSN 0146-4531
CODEN: CSSEDH
C A SELECTS. SOLVENT EXTRACTION. s-w. $240 to non-members; members $70 (effective 1998). Chemical Abstracts Service (Subsidiary of: American Chemical Society), 2540 Olentangy River Rd., Box 3012, Columbus, OH 43210-0012. TEL 614-447-3600. FAX 614-447-3713. TELEX 6842086. **Document type:** abstracting/indexing.
Description: Covers chemical applications of solvent extraction; solvent properties, solvent recovery, fuel processing.

540 US ISSN 0885-0232
CODEN: CSANEN
C A SELECTS. SPECTROCHEMICAL ANALYSIS. s-w. $240 to non-members; members $70 (effective 1998). Chemical Abstracts Service (Subsidiary of: American Chemical Society), 2540 Olentangy River Rd., Box 3012, Columbus, OH 43210-0012. TEL 614-447-3600. FAX 614-447-3713. TELEX 6842086. **Document type:** abstracting/indexing.
Description: Covers spectroscopic techniques used in chemical analysis.

615 US ISSN 0160-9181
CODEN: CSASD3
C A SELECTS. STEROIDS (CHEMICAL ASPECTS). s-w. $240 to non-members; members $70 (effective 1998). Chemical Abstracts Service (Subsidiary of: American Chemical Society), 2540 Olentangy River Rd., Box 3012, Columbus, OH 43210-0012. TEL 614-447-3600. FAX 614-447-3713. TELEX 6842086. **Document type:** abstracting/indexing.
Description: Covers isolation and synthesis of steroids and their chemical reactions and transformations.

540 011 US ISSN 1066-1174
CODEN: CSSTET
C A SELECTS. STRESS CORROSION - METALS. 1993. s-w. $240 to non-members; members $70 (effective 1998). Chemical Abstracts Service (Subsidiary of: American Chemical Society), 2540 Olentangy River Rd., Box 3012, Columbus, OH 43210. TEL 614-447-3600. FAX 614-447-3713. TELEX 6842086. **Document type:** abstracting/indexing.
Description: Provides information on such topics as corrosion mechanisms, hydrogen embrittlement, and hydrogen sulfide cracking of structural metal and alloys.

540 US ISSN 0895-5816
CODEN: CSSREN
C A SELECTS. STRUCTURE-ACTIVITY RELATIONSHIPS. 1988. s-w. $240 to non-members; members $70 (effective 1998). Chemical Abstracts Service (Subsidiary of: American Chemical Society), 2540 Olentangy River Rd., Box 3012, Columbus, OH 43210-0012. TEL 614-447-3600. FAX 614-447-3713. TELEX 6842086. **Document type:** abstracting/indexing.
Description: Covers structure-activity relationships of therapeutic agents and compounds that have potential therapeutic uses.

540 US ISSN 0195-5152
CODEN: CSUADF
C A SELECTS. SURFACE ANALYSIS. s-w. $240 to non-members; members $70 (effective 1998). Chemical Abstracts Service (Subsidiary of: American Chemical Society), 2540 Olentangy River Rd., Box 3012, Columbus, OH 43210-0012. TEL 614-447-3600. FAX 614-447-3713. TELEX 6842086. **Document type:** abstracting/indexing.
Description: Covers the analytical chemistry of surface technology.

540 US ISSN 0146-454X
CODEN: CSSAD5
C A SELECTS. SURFACE CHEMISTRY (PHYSICOCHEMICAL ASPECTS). s-w. $240 to non-members; members $70 (effective 1998). Chemical Abstracts Service (Subsidiary of: American Chemical Society), 2540 Olentangy River Rd., Box 3012, Columbus, OH 43210-0012. TEL 614-447-3600. FAX 614-447-3713. TELEX 6842086. **Document type:** abstracting/indexing.
Description: Covers the physical chemistry and properties of solid surface.

540 US ISSN 0195-5160
CODEN: CSSYD9
C A SELECTS. SYNFUELS. s-w. $240 to non-members; members $70 (effective 1998). Chemical Abstracts Service (Subsidiary of: American Chemical Society), 2540 Olentangy River Rd., Box 3012, Columbus, OH 43210-0012. TEL 614-447-3600. FAX 614-447-3713. TELEX 6842086. **Document type:** abstracting/indexing.
Description: Covers production of fuel from new sources.

541.3 US ISSN 0275-7168
CODEN: CSYPDC
C A SELECTS. SYNTHETIC HIGH POLYMERS. s-w. $240 to non-members; members $70 (effective 1998). Chemical Abstracts Service (Subsidiary of: American Chemical Society), 2540 Olentangy River Rd., Box 3012, Columbus, OH 43210-0012. TEL 614-447-3600. FAX 614-447-3713. TELEX 6842086. **Document type:** abstracting/indexing.
Description: Covers the organic and physical chemistry of linear and branched synthetic organic and inorganic polymers.

540 US ISSN 0195-5179
CODEN: CSCPD4
C A SELECTS. SYNTHETIC MACROCYCLIC COMPOUNDS. s-w. $240 to non-members; members $70 (effective 1998). Chemical Abstracts Service (Subsidiary of: American Chemical Society), 2540 Olentangy River Rd., Box 3012, Columbus, OH 43210-0012. TEL 614-447-3600. FAX 614-447-3713. TELEX 6842086. **Document type:** abstracting/indexing.
Description: Covers synthesis and applications of macrocyclic compounds and ligands, e.g. crown ethers, macrocyclic tetramines.

540 US
C A SELECTS. TECHNICAL CERAMICS. s-w. $240 to non-members; members $70 (effective 1998). Chemical Abstracts Service (Subsidiary of: American Chemical Society), 2540 Olentangy River Rd., Box 3012, Columbus, OH 43210-0012. TEL 614-447-3600. FAX 614-447-3713. TELEX 6842086. **Document type:** abstracting/indexing.
Description: Covers advanced and high temperature ceramics, fracture toughness and strength, engineering ceramics, nitride and carbide ceramics, and ceramic composites.

536 US ISSN 0195-5187
CODEN: CSANDM
C A SELECTS. THERMAL ANALYSIS. s-w. $240 to non-members; members $70 (effective 1998). Chemical Abstracts Service (Subsidiary of: American Chemical Society), 2540 Olentangy River Rd., Box 3012, Columbus, OH 43210-0012. TEL 614-447-3600. FAX 614-447-3713. TELEX 6842086. **Document type:** abstracting/indexing.
Description: Covers DTA, thermogravimetry, differential scanning calorimetry; evolved-gas analysis, thermodilatometry, thermoelectrometry, thermomagnetometry, thermosonimetry.

536 US ISSN 0162-7864
CODEN: CSTHDV
C A SELECTS. THERMOCHEMISTRY. s-w. $240 to non-members; members $70 (effective 1998). Chemical Abstracts Service (Subsidiary of: American Chemical Society), 2540 Olentangy River Rd., Box 3012, Columbus, OH 43210-0012. TEL 614-447-3600. FAX 614-447-3713. TELEX 6842086. **Document type:** abstracting/indexing.
Description: Covers chemical thermodynamics: heat capacities and thermodynamic functions such as enthalpies, free energies, and entropies for physicochemical and biochemical processes.

540 US ISSN 0160-919X
CODEN: CSTADA
C A SELECTS. TRACE ELEMENT ANALYSIS. s-w. $240 to non-members; members $70 (effective 1998). Chemical Abstracts Service (Subsidiary of: American Chemical Society), 2540 Olentangy River Rd., Box 3012, Columbus, OH 43210-0012. TEL 614-447-3600. FAX 614-447-3713. TELEX 6842086. **Document type:** abstracting/indexing.
Description: Covers detection and determination of trace elements found in solid, liquid, or gaseous environments (food, rocks, soils, petroleum products, sewage).

535 US ISSN 0195-5209
CODEN: CUVSDK
C A SELECTS. ULTRAVIOLET & VISIBLE SPECTROSCOPY. s-w. $240 to non-members; members $70 (effective 1998). Chemical Abstracts Service (Subsidiary of: American Chemical Society), 2540 Olentangy River Rd., Box 3012, Columbus, OH 43210-0012. TEL 614-447-3600. FAX 614-447-3713. TELEX 6842086. **Document type:** abstracting/indexing.
Description: Covers methodology and experimental measurement of absorption and emission spectroscopy for UV and visible regions.

C A SELECTS. X-RAY ANALYSIS & SPECTROSCOPY. see PHYSICS — Abstracting, Bibliographies, Statistics

540 US ISSN 1083-2726
CODEN: CSPEF4
C A SELECTS PLUS. ADHESIVES. s-w. $250 to non-members; members $75 (effective 1998). Chemical Abstracts Service (Subsidiary of: American Chemical Society), 2540 Olentangy River Rd., Box 3012, Columbus, OH 43210-0012. TEL 614-447-3600; 800-333-9511. FAX 614-447-3713. TELEX 6842086. **Document type:** abstracting/indexing.
Formerly: C A Selects. Adhesives (ISSN 0162-7686)
Description: Covers adhesives, binders, glues, caulks, sealants, mastics, grouts.

540 US ISSN 1084-2306
CODEN: CAPIFQ
C A SELECTS PLUS. ASYMMETRIC SYNTHESIS & INDUCTION. s-w. $250 to non-members; members $75 (effective 1998). Chemical Abstracts Service (Subsidiary of: American Chemical Society), 2540 Olentangy River Rd., Box 3012, Columbus, OH 43210-0012. TEL 614-447-3600. FAX 614-447-3713. TELEX 6842086. **Document type:** abstracting/indexing.
Formerly: C A Selects. Asymmetric Synthesis and Induction (ISSN 0890-183X)
Description: Covers synthetic methods for enantiomeric enrichment of compounds that contain one or more asymmetric centers.

CHEMISTRY — ABSTRACTING, BIBLIOGRAPHIES, STATISTICS

541.37   US   ISSN 1083-267X
CODEN: CSPBFT
C A SELECTS PLUS. BATTERIES & FUEL CELLS. s-w. $250 to non-members; members $75 (effective 1998). Chemical Abstracts Service (Subsidiary of: American Chemical Society), 2540 Olentangy River Rd., Box 3012, Columbus, OH 43210-0012. TEL 614-447-3600. FAX 614-447-3713. TELEX 6842086. **Document type:** abstracting/indexing.
Formerly: C A Selects. Batteries and Fuel Cells (ISSN 0162-7708)
Description: Covers design, manufacture, properties, and use of primary and secondary batteries; materials-related and electrochemical aspects; reclamation of materials from spent batteries; and electrodes for batteries and fuel cells.

547   US   ISSN 1084-2314
CODEN: CPCCFE
C A SELECTS PLUS. CARBOHYDRATES (CHEMICAL ASPECTS). s-w. $250 to non-members; members $75 (effective 1998). Chemical Abstracts Service (Subsidiary of: American Chemical Society), 2540 Olentangy River Rd., Box 3012, Columbus, OH 43210-0012. TEL 614-447-3600. FAX 614-447-3713. TELEX 6842086. **Document type:** abstracting/indexing.
Formerly: C A Selects. Carbohydrates (Chemical Aspects) (ISSN 0740-0756)
Description: Characterization, reactions, structure analysis, and nonindustrial synthesis of carbohydrates and their derivatives and polymers.

547   US   ISSN 1083-2793
CODEN: CSPCFW
C A SELECTS PLUS. CARBON & HETEROATOM N M R. s-w. $250 to non-members; members $75 (effective 1998). Chemical Abstracts Service (Subsidiary of: American Chemical Society), 2540 Olentangy River Rd., Box 3012, Columbus, OH 43210-0012. TEL 614-447-3600. FAX 614-447-3713. TELEX 6842086. **Document type:** abstracting/indexing.
Formerly: C A Selects. Carbon and Heteroatom N M R (ISSN 0190-9401)
Description: Covers the chemical aspects of nuclear magnetic resonance (NMR) of carbon, fluorine, phosphorus, and other heteroatoms; and chemically-induced dynamic nuclear polarization.

540   US   ISSN 1083-2777
CODEN: CSPAFQ
C A SELECTS PLUS. CATALYSIS (APPLIED & PHYSICAL ASPECTS). s-w. $250 to non-members; members $75 (effective 1998). Chemical Abstracts Service (Subsidiary of: American Chemical Society), 2540 Olentangy River Rd., Box 3012, Columbus, OH 43210-0012. TEL 614-447-3600. FAX 614-447-3713. TELEX 6842086. **Document type:** abstracting/indexing.
Formerly: C A Selects. Catalysis (Applied and Physical Aspects) (ISSN 0146-440X)
Description: Covers the theory and applications of heterogeneous and homogeneous catalysis and catalysts; and effect of catalysts on reaction kinetics.

547   US   ISSN 1083-2785
CODEN: CSPYFU
C A SELECTS PLUS. CATALYSIS (ORGANIC REACTIONS). s-w. $250 to non-members; members $75 (effective 1998). Chemical Abstracts Service (Subsidiary of: American Chemical Society), 2540 Olentangy River Rd., Box 3012, Columbus, OH 43210-0012. TEL 614-447-3600. FAX 614-447-3713. TELEX 6842086. **Document type:** abstracting/indexing.
Formerly: C A Selects. Catalysis (Organic Reactions) (ISSN 0146-4396)
Description: Covers the theory and applications of heterogeneous and homogeneous catalysis and catalysts in organic chemistry.

540   US   ISSN 1084-2330
CODEN: CPCTFV
C A SELECTS PLUS. CONTROLLED RELEASE TECHNOLOGY. s-w. $250 to non-members; members $75 (effective 1998). Chemical Abstracts Service (Subsidiary of: American Chemical Society), 2540 Olentangy River Rd., Box 3012, Columbus, OH 43210-0012. TEL 614-447-3600. FAX 614-447-3713. TELEX 6842086. **Document type:** abstracting/indexing.
Formerly: C A Selects. Controlled Release Technology (ISSN 0740-0748)
Description: Covers the science and technology of controlled release of biologically active materials (drugs, agrochemicals).

540   US   ISSN 1083-2807
CODEN: CSPDF2
C A SELECTS PLUS. DETERGENTS, SOAPS, & SURFACTANTS. s-w. $250 to non-members; members $75 (effective 1998). Chemical Abstracts Service (Subsidiary of: American Chemical Society), 2540 Olentangy River Rd., Box 3012, Columbus, OH 43210-0012. TEL 614-447-3600. FAX 614-447-3713. TELEX 6842086. **Document type:** abstracting/indexing.
Formerly: C A Selects. Detergents, Soaps, and Surfactants (ISSN 0162-7767)
Description: Covers preparation, properties, and uses of soaps and synthetic detergents; formulation; dry-cleaning solvents.

541.37   US   ISSN 1084-0036
CODEN: CPELFH
C A SELECTS PLUS. ELECTROPHORESIS. s-w. $250 to non-members; members $75 (effective 1998). Chemical Abstracts Service (Subsidiary of: American Chemical Society), 2540 Olentangy River Rd., Box 3012, Columbus, OH 43210-0012. TEL 614-447-3600. FAX 614-447-3713. TELEX 6842086. **Document type:** abstracting/indexing.
Formerly: C A Selects. Electrophoresis (ISSN 0195-4962)
Description: Covers techniques of electrophoretic processes; cataphoresis, ionophoresis, isoelectric focusing.

540   US   ISSN 1084-2357
CODEN: CSEAF5
C A SELECTS PLUS. ENZYME APPLICATIONS. 1988. s-w. $250 to non-members; members $75 (effective 1998). Chemical Abstracts Service (Subsidiary of: American Chemical Society), 2540 Olentangy River Rd., Box 3012, Columbus, OH 43210-0012. TEL 614-447-3600. FAX 614-447-3713. TELEX 6842086. **Document type:** abstracting/indexing.
Formerly: C A Selects. Enzyme Applications (ISSN 0895-593X)
Description: Covers studies in which enzymes are used as catalytic agents for the synthesis of organic compounds; synthetic or artificial enzymes (synzymes, e.g., cyclodextrins, cyclophanes, polyethylenimines, crown ethers) and semisynthetic enzymes (e.g., flavopapains).

540   US   ISSN 1083-2688
CODEN: CSPFF7
C A SELECTS PLUS. FLAVORS & FRAGRANCES. s-w. $250 to non-members; members $75 (effective 1998). Chemical Abstracts Service (Subsidiary of: American Chemical Society), 2540 Olentangy River Rd., Box 3012, Columbus, OH 43210-0012. TEL 614-447-3600. FAX 614-447-3713. TELEX 6842086. **Document type:** abstracting/indexing.
Formerly: C A Selects. Flavors and Fragrances (ISSN 0148-2327)
Description: Covers substances affecting senses of smell and taste; aromas, odorants, deodorants, perfumes, essential oils, flavoring materials, artificial sweeteners, acidulants, taste-modifying compounds; and synthetic methods for these compounds.

614.19   US   ISSN 1084-2365
CODEN: CSFCFG
C A SELECTS PLUS. FORENSIC CHEMISTRY. s-w. $250 to non-members; members $75 (effective 1998). Chemical Abstracts Service (Subsidiary of: American Chemical Society), 2540 Olentangy River Rd., Box 3012, Columbus, OH 43210-0012. TEL 614-447-3600. FAX 614-447-3713. TELEX 6842086. **Document type:** abstracting/indexing.
Formerly: C A Selects. Forensic Chemistry (ISSN 0362-9880)
Description: Covers the chemistry of investigative science.

430   US   ISSN 1084-0052
CODEN: CSFUF2
C A SELECTS PLUS. FUNGICIDES. s-w. $250 to non-members; members $75 (effective 1998). Chemical Abstracts Service (Subsidiary of: American Chemical Society), 2540 Olentangy River Rd., Box 3012, Columbus, OH 43210-0012. TEL 614-447-3600. FAX 614-447-3713. TELEX 6842086. **Document type:** abstracting/indexing.
Formerly: C A Selects. Fungicides (ISSN 0160-9068)
Description: Covers preparation, mechanism of action, and effects of antifungal agents.

544.92   US   ISSN 1083-2734
CODEN: CSPGFA
C A SELECTS PLUS. GAS CHROMATOGRAPHY. s-w. $250 to non-members; members $75 (effective 1998). Chemical Abstracts Service (Subsidiary of: American Chemical Society), 2540 Olentangy River Rd., Box 3012, Columbus, OH 43210-0012. TEL 614-447-3600. FAX 614-447-3713. TELEX 6842086. **Document type:** abstracting/indexing.
Formerly: C A Selects. Gas Chromatography (ISSN 0146-4477)
Description: Covers gas chromatography in chemical analysis; gas-liquid and vapor phase chromatography; and instrumentation and apparatus for gas chromatography.

544.92   US   ISSN 1084-290X
CODEN: CSGCFL
C A SELECTS PLUS. GEL PERMEATION CHROMATOGRAPHY. s-w. $250 to non-members; members $75 (effective 1998). Chemical Abstracts Service (Subsidiary of: American Chemical Society), 2540 Olentangy River Rd., Box 3012, Columbus, OH 43210-0012. TEL 614-447-3600. FAX 614-447-3713. TELEX 6842086. **Document type:** abstracting/indexing.
Formerly: C A Selects. Gel Permeation Chromatography (ISSN 0146-4485)
Description: Covers theory and application of gel permeation chromatography; high-speed gel chromatography; size exclusion chromatographic techniques; affinity chromatography.

540   US   ISSN 1084-0060
CODEN: CSHEFW
C A SELECTS PLUS. HERBICIDES. s-w. $250 to non-members; members $75 (effective 1998). Chemical Abstracts Service (Subsidiary of: American Chemical Society), 2540 Olentangy River Rd., Box 3012, Columbus, OH 43210-0012. TEL 614-447-3600. FAX 614-447-3713. TELEX 6842086. **Document type:** abstracting/indexing.
Formerly: C A Selects. Herbicides (ISSN 0160-9084)
Description: Covers preparation, mechanism of action, and effects of herbicides; plant growth inhibitors and defoliants.

540   US   ISSN 1083-2815
CODEN: CSPHFD
C A SELECTS PLUS. HIGH PERFORMANCE LIQUID CHROMATOGRAPHY. s-w. $250 to non-members; members $75 (effective 1998). Chemical Abstracts Service (Subsidiary of: American Chemical Society), 2540 Olentangy River Rd., Box 3012, Columbus, OH 43210-0012. TEL 614-447-3600. FAX 614-447-3713. TELEX 6842086. **Document type:** abstracting/indexing.
Formerly: C A Selects. High Performance Liquid Chromatography (ISSN 0195-5217)
Description: Covers high speed, high pressure, high performance, and high resolution liquid chromatography.

C A SELECTS PLUS. INSECTICIDES. see *BIOLOGY — Abstracting, Bibliographies, Statistics*

438   US
CODEN: CSLTFT
C A SELECTS PLUS. LIQUID WASTE TREATMENT. s-w. $250 to non-members; members $75 (effective 1998). Chemical Abstracts Service (Subsidiary of: American Chemical Society), 2540 Olentangy River Rd., Box 3012, Columbus, OH 43210-0012. TEL 614-447-3600. FAX 614-447-3713. TELEX 6842096. **Document type:** abstracting/indexing.
Formerly: C A Selects. Liquid Waste Treatment (ISSN 0160-9106)
Description: Covers treatment and disposal by physical, chemical, and biological methods; domestic and industrial sewage and wastewater; sludge that results from liquid waste treatment.

CHEMISTRY — ABSTRACTING, BIBLIOGRAPHIES, STATISTICS

535   US   ISSN 1083-2742
CODEN: CSPMFS
C A SELECTS PLUS. MASS SPECTROMETRY. s-w. $250 to non-members; members $75 (effective 1998). Chemical Abstracts Service (Subsidiary of: American Chemical Society), 2540 Olentangy River Rd., Box 3012, Columbus, OH 43210-0012. TEL 614-447-3600. FAX 614-447-3713. TELEX 6842086. **Document type:** abstracting/indexing.
Formerly: C A Selects. Mass Spectrometry (ISSN 0362-9872)
Description: Covers methodology, apparatus, and experimental results obtained by various spectrometric techniques; structure, thermochemistry, energetics, reaction kinetics and mechanisms, analytical applications.

540   US   ISSN 1083-2653
CODEN: CSPOFY
C A SELECTS PLUS. ORGANOSILICON CHEMISTRY. s-w. $250 to non-members; members $75 (effective 1998). Chemical Abstracts Service (Subsidiary of: American Chemical Society), 2540 Olentangy River Rd., Box 3012, Columbus, OH 43210-0012. TEL 614-447-3600. FAX 614-447-3713. TELEX 6842086. **Document type:** abstracting/indexing.
Formerly: C A Selects. Organosilicon Chemistry (ISSN 0362-9899)
Description: Covers compounds containing a silicon-carbon bond, silanes, siloxanes, silocarbonates.

547   US   ISSN 1083-270X
CODEN: CSPTFF
C A SELECTS PLUS. PHOTOCHEMISTRY. s-w. $250 to non-members; members $75 (effective 1998). Chemical Abstracts Service (Subsidiary of: American Chemical Society), 2540 Olentangy River Rd., Box 3012, Columbus, OH 43210-0012. TEL 614-447-3600. FAX 614-447-3713. TELEX 6842086. **Document type:** abstracting/indexing.
Formerly: C A Selects. Photochemistry (ISSN 0362-9856)
Description: Covers fluorescence, luminescence, phosphorescence, photochromism, phosphors, light-induced excited state interactions, photochemical mechanisms.

540   US   ISSN 1083-2696
CODEN: CSPCFP
C A SELECTS PLUS. POLYURETHANES. s-w. $250 to non-members; members $75 (effective 1998). Chemical Abstracts Service (Subsidiary of: American Chemical Society), 2540 Olentangy River Rd., Box 3012, Columbus, OH 43210-0012. TEL 614-447-3600. FAX 614-447-3713. TELEX 6842086. **Document type:** abstracting/indexing.
Formerly: C A Selects. Polyurethanes (ISSN 0740-0705)
Description: Covers preparation, properties, reaction, uses of urethane polymers, i.e. derived from polyisocyanates and polyols.

540   US   ISSN 1084-0087
CODEN: CSPWFO
C A SELECTS PLUS. RECOVERY & RECYCLING OF WASTES. s-w. $250 to non-members; members $75 (effective 1998). Chemical Abstracts Service (Subsidiary of: American Chemical Society), 2540 Olentangy River Rd., Box 3012, Columbus, OH 43210-0012. TEL 614-447-3600. FAX 614-447-3713. TELEX 6842086. **Document type:** abstracting/indexing.
Formerly: C A Selects. Recovery and Recycling of Wastes (ISSN 0160-9157)
Description: Covers processes and equipment used for recycling or recovery of all types of waste materials; inorganic and organic wastes, plastics, oils, industrial effluents, sewage, steel and other metals, ashes, slags; conversion and utilization of waste material.

540   US   ISSN 1084-0095
CODEN: CSSTFU
C A SELECTS PLUS. SOLID & RADIOACTIVE WASTE TREATMENT. s-w. $250 to non-members; members $75 (effective 1998). Chemical Abstracts Service (Subsidiary of: American Chemical Society), 2540 Olentangy River Rd., Box 3012, Columbus, OH 43210-0012. TEL 614-447-2086. TELEX 6842086. **Document type:** abstracting/indexing.
Formerly: C A Selects. Solid and Radioactive Waste Treatment (ISSN 0160-9165)
Description: Covers the chemical and chemical engineering aspects of treatment and disposal.

540   US   ISSN 1084-0117
CODEN: CSPUFI
C A SELECTS PLUS. ULTRAFILTRATION. s-w. $250 to non-members; members $75 (effective 1998). Chemical Abstracts Service (Subsidiary of: American Chemical Society), 2540 Olentangy River Rd., Box 3012, Columbus, OH 43210-0012. TEL 614-447-3600. FAX 614-447-3713. TELEX 6842086. **Document type:** abstracting/indexing.
Formerly: C A Selects. Ultrafiltration (ISSN 0195-5195)
Description: Covers technology and use of hyperfiltration and ultrafiltration; reverse osmosis (biochemical, medical, food technology, water purification, waste treatment).

540   US   ISSN 1084-0109
CODEN: CSWTFG
C A SELECTS PLUS. WATER TREATMENT. s-w. $250 to non-members; members $75 (effective 1998). Chemical Abstracts Service (Subsidiary of: American Chemical Society), 2540 Olentangy River Rd., Box 3012, Columbus, OH 43210-0012. TEL 614-447-3600. FAX 614-447-3713. TELEX 6842086. **Document type:** abstracting/indexing.
Formerly: C A Selects. Water Treatment (ISSN 0740-073X)
Description: Covers chemical and physical purification of water for home and industrial use; water softening.

540   US   ISSN 1083-2718
CODEN: CSPZFX
C A SELECTS PLUS. ZEOLITES. s-w. $250 to non-members; members $75 (effective 1998). Chemical Abstracts Service (Subsidiary of: American Chemical Society), 2540 Olentangy River Rd., Box 3012, Columbus, OH 43210-0012. TEL 614-447-3600. FAX 614-447-3713. TELEX 6842086. **Document type:** abstracting/indexing.
Formerly: C A Selects. Zeolites (ISSN 0190-4949)
Description: Covers preparation of synthetic zeolites; use of synthetic and natural zeolites and molecular sieves in adsorption and drying, catalysis, ion exchange, separation by molecular size.

723 541.3   NE   ISSN 1025-9309
C S T COMMUNICATIONS. (Combustion Science and Technology) bi-m. $50 (effective 1998). Gordon and Breach - Harwood Academic, Amsteldisk 166, 1st Fl., 1079 LH Amsterdam, Netherlands. URL: http://www.gbhap.com/CST_Communications/. (Subscr. to: International Publishers Distributor, Box 32160, Newark, NJ 07102. TEL 800-545-8398. FAX 215-750-6343) **Document type:** abstracting/indexing.
●Also available online.
Description: Provides abstracts of the latest submissions to the journal Combustion Science and Technology.

540   US   ISSN 0009-2258
QD1   CODEN: CHABA8
CHEMICAL ABSTRACTS. 1907. w. $19800 (effective 1998). Chemical Abstracts Service (Subsidiary of: American Chemical Society), 2540 Olentangy River Rd., Box 3012, Columbus, OH 43210-0012. TEL 614-447-3600. FAX 614-447-3713. TELEX 6842086. (also avail. in microfiche from IDC; microform) **Document type:** abstracting/indexing.
●Also available online. Vendor(s): STN International. Also available on CD-ROM.
—BLDSC (3134.000000); CISTI; Linda Hall.
Description: Provides summaries and indexes of disclosures in recently published scientific documents. Approximately 9,000 journals, technical reports, dissertations, conference proceedings, and new books, in any of 50 languages, are monitored yearly, as are patent specifications from 27 countries and two international organizations.

540 016   US   ISSN 0090-8363
CODEN: CAAEA2
CHEMICAL ABSTRACTS - APPLIED CHEMISTRY AND CHEMICAL ENGINEERING SECTIONS. 1963. s-w. $2210 to CA subscribers; others $2450; members $490 (effective 1998). Chemical Abstracts Service (Subsidiary of: American Chemical Society), 2540 Olentangy River Rd., Box 3012, Columbus, OH 43210-0012. TEL 614-447-3663. FAX 614-447-3713. TELEX 6842086. Ed. David W. Weisgerber. charts; pat.; stat.; index. **Document type:** abstracting/indexing.
●Also available online. Vendor(s): STN International (CA).
Supersedes: Chemical Abstracts - Applied Chemistry Sections (ISSN 0009-2266)

540 574.192 016   US   ISSN 0009-2304
CODEN: CABSBG
CHEMICAL ABSTRACTS - BIOCHEMISTRY SECTIONS. Abbreviated title: C A B S. 1963. s-w. $2210 to CA subscribers; others $2450; members $490 (effective 1998). Chemical Abstracts Service (Subsidiary of: American Chemical Society), 2540 Olentangy River Rd., Box 3012, Columbus, OH 43210-0012. TEL 614-447-3600. FAX 614-447-3713. TELEX 6842086. Ed. Dr. David W. Weisgerber. charts; pat.; stat.; index. **Indexed:** Dairy Sci.Abstr., VITIS. **Document type:** abstracting/indexing.
●Also available online. Vendor(s): STN International (CA).

547.7 016   US   ISSN 0009-2274
CODEN: CAMLAF
CHEMICAL ABSTRACTS - MACROMOLECULAR SECTIONS. 1963. s-w. $2210 to CA subscribers; others $2450; members $490 (effective 1998). Chemical Abstracts Service (Subsidiary of: American Chemical Society), 2540 Olentangy River Rd., Box 3012, Columbus, OH 43210-0012. TEL 614-447-3600. FAX 614-447-3713. TELEX 6842086. Ed. David W. Weisgerber. abstr.; charts; pat.; stat.; index. **Indexed:** World Text.Abstr. **Document type:** abstracting/indexing.
●Also available online. Vendor(s): STN International (CA).

547 016   US   ISSN 0009-2282
CODEN: CAOCAW
CHEMICAL ABSTRACTS - ORGANIC CHEMISTRY SECTIONS. 1963. s-w. $2210 to CA subscribers; others $2450; members $490 (effective 1998). Chemical Abstracts Service (Subsidiary of: American Chemical Society), 2540 Olentangy River Rd., Box 3012, Columbus, OH 43210-0012. TEL 614-447-3600. FAX 614-447-3713. TELEX 6842086. Ed. David W. Weisgerber. abstr.; charts; pat.; stat.; index. **Document type:** abstracting/indexing.
●Also available online. Vendor(s): STN International (CA).

543 016 547   US   ISSN 0278-1832
CODEN: CAISDJ
CHEMICAL ABSTRACTS - PHYSICAL, INORGANIC AND ANALYTICAL CHEMISTRY SECTIONS. 1963. s-w. $2210 to CA subscribers; others $2450; members $490 (effective 1998). Chemical Abstracts Service (Subsidiary of: American Chemical Society), 2540 Olentangy River Rd., Box 3012, Columbus, OH 43210-0012. TEL 614-447-3600. FAX 614-447-3713. TELEX 6842086. Ed. David W. Weisgerber. abstr.; charts; pat.; stat.; index. **Document type:** abstracting/indexing.
●Also available online. Vendor(s): STN International (CA).
Supersedes: Chemical Abstracts - Physical and Analytical Chemistry Sections (ISSN 0009-2290)

540 016   US   ISSN 0001-0634
Z5523   CODEN: CASSI6
CHEMICAL ABSTRACTS SERVICE SOURCE INDEX. Abbreviated title: C A S S I. 1969. base vol. (covers 1907-1994) plus q. supplements. $1195 for base vol. (CD-ROM $1790); q. supplements $255 (CD-ROM $395) (effective Jan. 1996). Chemical Abstracts Service (Subsidiary of: American Chemical Society), 2540 Olentangy River Rd., Columbus, OH 43210-0012. TEL 614-447-3600. FAX 614-447-3713. TELEX 6842086. Ed. David W. Weisgerber. **Document type:** abstracting/indexing.
●Also available online.
—CISTI; Linda Hall. **CCC.**

540 660 016   US   ISSN 0045-639X
CODEN: CINTAW
CHEMICAL INDUSTRY NOTES. Short title: C I N. 1971. w. $995 (effective 1998). Chemical Abstracts Service (Subsidiary of: American Chemical Society), 2540 Olentangy River Rd., Box 3012, Columbus, OH 43210-0012. TEL 614-447-3600. FAX 614-447-3713. TELEX 6842086. Ed. David W. Weisgerber. index. **Document type:** abstracting/indexing.
●Also available online.
—CCC.
Description: Contains citations to worldwide chemical business news related to production, pricing, sales facilities, products and processes, corporate activities and people in the news.

CHEMISTRY — ABSTRACTING, BIBLIOGRAPHIES, STATISTICS

540 016   US   ISSN 0009-2711
CODEN: CHTIAM
CHEMICAL TITLES. 1961. bi-w. $585 to non-members; members $235; small colleges $160 (effective 1998). Chemical Abstracts Service (Subsidiary of: American Chemical Society), 2540 Olentangy River Rd., Columbus, OH 43210-0012. TEL 614-447-3600. FAX 614-447-3713. TELEX 6842086. Ed. David W. Weisgerber. index. **Document type:** abstracting/indexing.
●Also available online.
—Linda Hall. **CCC**.

540 016   GW   ISSN 0931-7597
QD1   CODEN: CINFES
CHEMINFORM. CD-ROM edition (GW ISSN 1431-5890) 1970. 52/yr. DM.4250 (foreign DM.4510) (CD-ROM DM.3590 (foreign DM.3618); combined DM.5180 (foreign DM.5465)) (effective 1997). (Gesellschaft Deutscher Chemiker) Wiley - V C H, Postfach 101161, 69451 Weinheim, Germany. TEL 49-6201-606147. FAX 49-6201-606117. TELEX 465516-VCHWH-D. E-mail: sales-journal@vchgroup.de; URL: http://www.vchgroup.de. (Subscr. in the Americas to: John Wiley & Sons, Inc., 605 Third Ave., New York, NY 10158. TEL 212-850-6645. FAX 212-850-6021) (Co-sponsor: Fachinformationszentrum Chemie und Bayer AG) Ed.Bd. index. circ. 1,250. (also avail. in microfilm from VCI; reprint service avail. from ISI) **Indexed:** Chem.Abstr. **Document type:** abstracting/indexing.
●Also available on CD-ROM.
—CASDDS. **CCC**.
Formerly: Chemisches Informationsdienst (ISSN 0009-2975); Supersedes: Chemisches Zentralblatt.

540   US   ISSN 1057-6088
CHEMISTRY CITATION INDEX. bi-m. $2320. Institute for Scientific Information, 3501 Market St., Philadelphia, PA 19104. TEL 215-386-0100. FAX 215-386-2911. (U.K. addr.: Brunel Science Park, Brunel University, Uxbridge UB6 3PQ, England) (also avail. in magnetic tape) **Document type:** academic/scholarly publication, bibliography.
●Also available on CD-ROM.
Description: Provides bibliographic data, cited references, related records and English-language author abstracts from international scholarly research journals and conference proceedings.

540 016   US   ISSN 0300-1261
QP455
CHEMORECEPTION ABSTRACTS; chemical senses & applied techniques. 1973. q. $455 (foreign $520). (European Chemoreception Research Organization) Cambridge Scientific Abstracts, 7200 Wisconsin Ave., 6th Fl., Bethesda, MD 20814. TEL 301-961-6750. FAX 301-961-6720. E-mail: market@csa.com; URL: http://www.csa.com. Ed. Fred Spangler; Pub. Ted Caris. adv.; bk.rev.; abstr.; index. (also avail. in magnetic tape; back issues avail.) **Indexed:** Cal.Tiss.Abstr., Chemorec.Abstr., Comput.& Info.Sys., Oncol.Abstr., Pollut.Abstr. **Document type:** abstracting/indexing.
●Also available online. Vendor(s): Knight-Ridder Information, Inc. (File no.76/LIFE SCIENCES COLLECTION), STN International (LIFESCI).
Also available on CD-ROM. Producer(s): SilverPlatter Information, Inc.
—BLDSC (3172.270000).
Description: Covers research into taste, smell, internal chemoreception, chemotaxis, and practical applications.

547 011   US   ISSN 1431-9268
QD241   CODEN: CHEMFW
CHEMTRACTS. 1997. 14/yr. $441 to institutions (effective 1998). Springer-Verlag, Life Science Journals, 175 Fifth Ave., New York, NY 10160. TEL 212-460-1500; 800-777-4643. FAX 212-473-6272. E-mail: orders@springer-ny.com; URL: http://www.springer-ny.com. (N. American subscr. to: Journal Fulfillment Services, 333 Meadowlands Pkwy., Secaucus, NJ 07094. FAX 49-30-82787448; Elsewhere: Heidelberger Platz 3, 14197, Berlin, Germany. TEL 49-30-82787-0) (Co-publisher: Data Trace Publishing Company) Ed. F. Basolo. adv. **Document type:** abstracting/indexing.
—BLDSC (3172.325700); CASDDS; CISTI; UnCover. **CCC**.
Formed by the merger of (1988-1997): Chemtracts: Organic Chemistry (ISSN 0895-4445); (1991-1997): Chemtracts: Biochemistry and Molecular Biology (ISSN 1045-2680); (1990-1997): Chemtracts: Inorganic Chemistry (ISSN 1051-7227); Which was formerly: Chemtracts: Analytical, Physical and Inorganic Chemistry (ISSN 1048-7840); (1989-1990): Chemtracts: Analytical and Physical Chemistry (ISSN 0899-7810).
Description: Publishes reviews, condensations, and commentaries that give scientists efficient access to the latest and most significant research in chemistry. Issues are devoted to organic chemistry, inorganic chemistry, and biochemistry and molecular biology.

544.92 016   UK   ISSN 0268-6287
QD117.C5
CHROMATOGRAPHY ABSTRACTS. 1958. m. £549($988) (effective 1997). The Royal Society of Chemistry, Thomas Graham House, Science Park, Milton Rd., Cambridge CB4 4WF, England. TEL 44-1223-420066. FAX 44-1223-423429. E-mail: sales@rsc.org; URL: http://chemistry.rsc.org/rsc/. (Subscr. to: Turpin Distribution Services Ltd., Blackhorse Rd., Letchworth, Herts. SG6 1HN, England. TEL 44-1462-672555. FAX 44-1462-480947) (Co-sponsor: Chromatographic Society) Ed.Bd. adv.; index. (also avail. in microform from UMI; back issues avail.) **Document type:** abstracting/indexing.
—CISTI; Linda Hall. **CCC**.
Former titles (until 1986): Gas and Liquid Chromatography Abstracts (ISSN 0301-388X); (until 1973): Gas Chromatography Abstracts (ISSN 0016-4887)
Description: Provides a rapid update on the latest literature in chromatography and separation science.
Refereed Serial

547   JA
CONGRESS OF HETEROCYCLIC CHEMISTRY. BOOK OF ABSTRACTS/FUKUSOKAN KAGAKU TORONKAI KOEN YOSHISHU. (Text in English, Japanese) a. Society of Synthetic Organic Chemistry, Japan - Yuki Gosei Kagaku Kyokai, 1-5, Kanda Surugadai, Chiyoda-ku, Tokyo 101, Japan. **Document type:** abstracting/indexing.

540   UK   ISSN 0885-1980
CURRENT ADVANCES IN CLINICAL CHEMISTRY. 1974. m. fl.1530($879) (effective 1998). (Association of Clinical Biochemists) Elsevier Science B.V., P.O. Box 211, 1000 AE Amsterdam, Netherlands. TEL 31-20-4853911. FAX 31-20-48535988. TELEX 18582 ESPA NL. E-mail: nlinfo-f@elsevier.nl; usinfo-f@elsevier.com; forinfo-kyf04035@niftyserve.or.jp; URL: http://www.elsevier.nl/. (Subscr. in the Americas to: Elsevier Science, Regional Sales Office, Box 945, New York, NY 10159-0945. TEL 212-633-3730. FAX 212-633-3680; Subscr. in Australasia and the Far East to: Elsevier Science (Singapore) Pte Ltd, No.1 Temask Ave., No.17-01 Millenia Tower, Singapore 039192, Singapore. TEL 65-434-3727. FAX 65-337-2230; Subscr. in Japan to: Elsevier Science Japan, 9-15 Higashi-Azabu 1-chome, Minato-ku, Minato-ku, Tokyo 106, Japan. TEL 81-3-5561-5033. FAX 81-3-5561-5047) adv.; bk.rev. circ. 2,400. (also avail. in diskette format; microform from UMI) **Document type:** abstracting/indexing.
●Also available online. Vendor(s): Ovid Technologies, Inc. (CABS).
—BLDSC (3494.062500); UMI. **CCC**.
Formerly: Current Clinical Chemistry (ISSN 0305-0165)
Description: Provides a current awareness service for clinical chemists, research workers, teachers and students in the field of clinical chemistry. Lists titles of papers published throughout the world classified into 29 main areas and provides a comprehensive listing of review articles.

016 540   KO
CURRENT BIBLIOGRAPHIES ON SCIENCE AND TECHNOLOGY: CHEMISTRY AND CHEMICAL INDUSTRY. 1962. m. $114. Korea Institute for Economics and Technology, P.O. Box 205, 206-9 Cheongryangri-Dong, Dongdaimun-Ku, Seoul, S. Korea. circ. 450. (reprint service avail. from UMI) **Document type:** bibliography.
Formerly: Current Index to Journals in Science and Technology: Chemistry and Chemical Industry; Supersedes in part: Current Bibliography on Sciences and Technology.

540 660 016   JA   ISSN 0011-3271
CODEN: KGBHDD
CURRENT BIBLIOGRAPHY ON SCIENCE AND TECHNOLOGY: CHEMISTRY AND CHEMICAL ENGINEERING (FOREIGN)/KAGAKU GIJUTSU BUNKEN SOKUHO. KAGAKU, KAGAKU KOGYO-HEN (GAIKOKU-HEN). (Text in Japanese) 1958. 3/m. $2580. Japan Science and Technology Corporation, Information Center for Science and Technology - Kagaku Gijutsu Shinko Jigyodan, 5-3 Yonbancho, Chiyoda-ku, Tokyo 102, Japan. TEL 81-3-3214-8413. FAX 81-3-5214-8410. index. circ. 900. **Document type:** bibliography.
●Also available online. Vendor(s): JICST.
Also available on CD-ROM.

540 660 016   JA   ISSN 0385-6003
CURRENT BIBLIOGRAPHY ON SCIENCE AND TECHNOLOGY: CHEMISTRY AND CHEMICAL ENGINEERING (JAPANESE)/KAGAKU GIJUTSU BUNKEN SOKUHO KAGAKU. KAGAKU KOGYO-HEN (KOKUNAI-HEN). (Text in Japanese) 1958. m. $1020. Japan Science and Technology Corporation, Information Center for Science and Technology - Kagaku Gijutsu Shinko Jigyodan, 5-3 Yonbancho, Chiyoda-ku, Tokyo 102, Japan. TEL 81-3-5214-8413. FAX 81-3-5214-8410. index. circ. 1,200. **Document type:** bibliography.
●Also available online. Vendor(s): JICST.
Also available on CD-ROM.

540 016   US   ISSN 0163-6278
CODEN: CCHRDP
CURRENT CHEMICAL REACTIONS. Short Title: C C R. 1979. m. $1325. Institute for Scientific Information 3501 Market St., Philadelphia, PA 19104. TEL 215-386-0100. FAX 215-386-2911. (And: Brunel Science Park, Brunel University, Uxbridge UB8 3PQ, England) **Document type:** academic/scholarly publication, bibliography.
—BLDSC (3496.005000); CASDDS.
Description: Indexes new or modified reactions or syntheses reported on in chemistry and pharmaceutical journals.

CHEMISTRY — ABSTRACTING, BIBLIOGRAPHIES, STATISTICS

011 US
CURRENT CHEMICAL REACTIONS DATABASE. Short title: C C R Database. 1986. a. $35000 primary site fee for initial CPU-CPU cluster; additional site fee $12500. Institute for Scientific Information, 3501 Market St., Philadelphia, PA 19104. TEL 215-386-0100. FAX 215-386-2991. (And: Brunel Science Park, Brunel University, Uxbridge UB8 3PQ, England) **Document type:** academic/scholarly publication, bibliography.
 Formerly: Current Chemical Reactions Inhouse Database for R E A C C S.
 Description: Indexes new or modified reactions or syntheses reported in chemistry and pharmaceutical journals.

530 540 016 US ISSN 0163-2574
Z7143 CODEN: CPCSDQ
CURRENT CONTENTS: PHYSICAL, CHEMICAL & EARTH SCIENCES. Short title: C C: P C & E S. (Includes Author Index and Address Directory. Current Book Contents and Title Word Index) 1961. w. $730. Institute for Scientific Information, 3501 Market St., Philadelphia, PA 19104. TEL 215-386-0100. FAX 215-386-2211. (And: Brunel Science Park, Brunel University, Uxbridge UB8 3PQ, England) (also avail. in magnetic tape; diskette format) **Indexed:** Abstr.Bull.Inst.Pap.Chem., AESIS, Compumath, Ind.Sci.Rev., Sci.Cit.Ind., SSCI. **Document type:** abstracting/indexing.
 •Also available online. Vendor(s): Knight-Ridder Information, Inc. (File no.440), Ovid Technologies, Inc. (CTOC,CBIB,PHYS).
 Also available on CD-ROM.
 —BLDSC (3496.206300); CASDDS; KNAW.
 Formerly: Current Contents, Physical and Chemical Sciences (ISSN 0011-3417); Which was formed by the merger of: Current Contents, Physical Sciences; Current Contents, Chemical Sciences.
 Description: Tables of contents of important publications covering physical, chemical and earth sciences.

660 016 II ISSN 0300-4376
CURRENT TITLES IN ELECTROCHEMISTRY. (Text in English) 1969. m. Rs.100($65) to individuals; institutions Rs.150($135). Society for Advancement of Electrochemical Science and Technology, Karaikudi 623 006, Tamil Nadu, India. TEL 91-4565-22368. FAX 91-4565-22088. TELEX 0443-211 ECRI IN. E-mail: cecrik@cscecri.ren.nic.in. Ed. Dr. S. Krishnamurthy. adv.; index. circ. 1,000. **Indexed:** Chem.Abstr. **Document type:** abstracting/indexing.
 Incorporates: Electrochemical News.
 Description: Bibliographic listing of classified titles in electrochemistry.

543 US ISSN 1049-1260
C2C ABSTRACTS: JAPAN - ANALYTICAL CHEMISTRY. 1990. m. $200. Scan C2C, 1001 Pennsylvania Ave., N.W., No. 1300, Washington, DC 20024-2505. TEL 800-525-3865. FAX 202-863-3855. **Document type:** abstracting/indexing.
 •Also available online. Vendor(s): Data-Star (JPTC), European Space Agency (File no.241), Knight-Ridder Information, Inc. (File no.582), Questel Orbit Inc. (JTEC).
 Also available on CD-ROM. Producer(s): Knight-Ridder, Inc.
 Description: Contains abstracts of articles from Japanese scientific, business, and technical journals. Each entry lists title, author, author affiliation, journal title, volume and number, page numbers, date, abstract, number of bibliographic references, and language (if not Japanese).

2C ABSTRACTS: JAPAN - CERAMICS. see CERAMICS, GLASS AND POTTERY — Abstracting, Bibliographies, Statistics

2C ABSTRACTS: JAPAN - CHEMICAL ENGINEERING. see ENGINEERING — Abstracting, Bibliographies, Statistics

548 US ISSN 1049-1287
C2C ABSTRACTS: JAPAN - CRYSTALLOGRAPHY. 1990. m. $200. Scan C2C, 1001 Pennsylvania Ave., N.W., No. 1300, Washington, DC 20024-2505. TEL 800-525-3865. FAX 202-863-3855. **Document type:** abstracting/indexing.
 •Also available online. Vendor(s): Data-Star (JPTC), European Space Agency (File no.241), Knight-Ridder Information, Inc. (File no.582), Questel Orbit Inc. (JTEC).
 Also available on CD-ROM. Producer(s): Knight-Ridder, Inc.
 Description: Contains abstracts of articles from Japanese scientific, business, and technical journals. Each entry lists title, author, author affiliation, journal title, volume and number, date, page numbers, abstract, number of bibliographic references, and language (if not Japanese).

547 661.81 US ISSN 1049-1295
C2C ABSTRACTS: JAPAN - HYDROCARBONS. 1990. m. $200. Scan C2C, 1001 Pennsylvania Ave., N.W., No. 1300, Washington, DC 20024-2505. TEL 800-525-3865. FAX 202-863-3855. **Document type:** abstracting/indexing.
 •Also available online. Vendor(s): Data-Star (JPTC), European Space Agency (File no.241), Knight-Ridder Information, Inc. (File no.582), Questel Orbit Inc. (JTEC).
 Also available on CD-ROM. Producer(s): Knight-Ridder, Inc.
 Description: Contains abstracts of articles from Japanese scientific, business, and technical journals. Each entry lists title, author, author affiliation, journal title, volume and number, page numbers, abstract, number of bibliographic references, and language (if not Japanese).

546 US ISSN 1049-1309
C2C ABSTRACTS: JAPAN - INORGANIC CHEMISTRY. 1990. m. $200. Scan C2C, 1001 Pennsylvania Ave., N.W., No. 1300, Washington, DC 20024-2505. TEL 800-525-3865. FAX 202-863-3855. **Document type:** abstracting/indexing.
 •Also available online. Vendor(s): Data-Star (JPTC), European Space Agency (File no.241), Knight-Ridder Information, Inc. (File no.582), Questel Orbit Inc. (JTEC).
 Also available on CD-ROM. Producer(s): Knight-Ridder, Inc.
 Description: Contains abstracts of articles from Japanese scientific, business, and technical journals. Each entry lists title, author, author affiliation, journal title, volume and number, page numbers, date, abstract, number of bibliographic references, and language (if not Japanese).

C2C ABSTRACTS: JAPAN - MATERIALS SCIENCE. see ENGINEERING — Abstracting, Bibliographies, Statistics

C2C ABSTRACTS: JAPAN - METALS. see METALLURGY — Abstracting, Bibliographies, Statistics

547 US ISSN 1049-1325
C2C ABSTRACTS: JAPAN - ORGANIC CHEMISTRY. 1990. m. $200. Scan C2C, 1001 Pennsylvania Ave., N.W., No. 1300, Washington, DC 20024-2505. TEL 800-525-3865. FAX 202-863-3855. **Document type:** abstracting/indexing.
 •Also available online. Vendor(s): Data-Star (JPTC), European Space Agency (File no.241), Knight-Ridder Information, Inc. (File no.582), Questel Orbit Inc. (JTEC).
 Also available on CD-ROM. Producer(s): Knight-Ridder, Inc.
 Description: Contains abstracts of articles from the leading 500 Japanese scientific, business, and technical journals. Each entry lists title, author, author affiliation, journal title, volume and number, date, page numbers, abstract, number of bibliographic references, and language (if not Japanese).

541.3 US ISSN 1049-1333
C2C ABSTRACTS: JAPAN - PHYSICAL CHEMISTRY. 1990. m. $200. Scan C2C, 1001 Pennsylvania Ave., N.W., No. 1300, Washington, DC 20024-2505. TEL 800-525-3865. FAX 202-863-3855. **Document type:** abstracting/indexing.
 •Also available online. Vendor(s): Data-Star (JPTC), European Space Agency (File no.241), Knight-Ridder Information, Inc. (File no.582), Questel Orbit Inc. (JTEC).
 Also available on CD-ROM. Producer(s): Knight-Ridder, Inc.
 Description: Contains abstracts of articles from Japanese scientific, business, and technical journals. Each entry lists title, author, author affiliation, journal title, volume and number, date, page numbers, abstract, number of bibliographic references, and language (if not Japanese).

C2C ABSTRACTS: JAPAN - PLASTICS. see PLASTICS — Abstracting, Bibliographies, Statistics

547 US ISSN 1049-135X
C2C ABSTRACTS: JAPAN - POLYMER CHEMISTRY. 1990. m. $200. Scan C2C, 1001 Pennsylvania Ave., N.W., No. 1300, Washington, DC 20024-2505. TEL 800-525-3865. FAX 202-863-3855. **Document type:** abstracting/indexing.
 •Also available online. Vendor(s): Data-Star (JPTC), European Space Agency (File no.241), Knight-Ridder Information, Inc. (File no.582), Questel Orbit Inc. (JTEC).
 Also available on CD-ROM. Producer(s): Knight-Ridder, Inc.
 Description: Contains abstracts from Japanese scientific, business, and technical journals. Each entry lists title, author, author affiliation, journal title, volume and number, date, page numbers, abstract, number of bibliographic references, and language (if not Japanese). Covers polymer chemistry, elastomers, semisynthetics, thermoplastics, and thermosetting.

541.345 US ISSN 1049-1368
C2C ABSTRACTS: JAPAN - SURFACE CHEMISTRY. 1990. m. $200. Scan C2C, 1001 Pennsylvania Ave., N.W., No. 1300, Washington, DC 20024-2505. TEL 800-525-3865. FAX 202-863-3855. **Document type:** abstracting/indexing.
 •Also available online. Vendor(s): Data-Star (JPTC), European Space Agency (File no.241), Knight-Ridder Information, Inc. (File no.582), Questel Orbit Inc. (JTEC).
 Also available on CD-ROM. Producer(s): Knight-Ridder, Inc.
 Description: Contains abstracts of articles from Japanese scientific, business, and technical journals. Each entry lists title, author, author affiliation, journal title, volume and number, date, page numbers, abstract, number of bibliographic references, and language (if not Japanese).

C2C ABSTRACTS: JAPAN - TEXTILES. see TEXTILE INDUSTRIES AND FABRICS — Abstracting, Bibliographies, Statistics

540 US ISSN 1049-1228
C2C CURRENTS: JAPAN - CHEMISTRY. 1989. m. $100. Scan C2C, 1001 Pennsylvania Ave., N.W., No. 1300, Washington, DC 20024-2025. TEL 800-525-3865. FAX 202-863-3855. **Document type:** abstracting/indexing.
 •Also available online. Vendor(s): Data-Star (JPTC), European Space Agency (File no.241), Knight-Ridder Information, Inc. (File no.582), Questel Orbit Inc. (JTEC).
 Also available on CD-ROM. Producer(s): Knight-Ridder, Inc.
 Description: Provides a summary of the contents of leading scientific and business journals in Japan. Contains a table of contents for selected journals. Lists title, author, date of publication, number of pages, and source journal.

C2C CURRENTS: JAPAN - MATERIALS. see ENGINEERING — Abstracting, Bibliographies, Statistics

541.37 JA
DENKI KAGAKU KYOKAI TAIKAI KOEN YOSHISHU/ELECTROCHEMICAL SOCIETY OF JAPAN. ABSTRACTS OF ANNUAL MEETING. (Text in Japanese) a. 7000 Yen. Denki Kagaku Kyokai - Electrochemical Society of Japan, 12-1, Yurakucho 1-chome, Chiyoda-ku, Tokyo 100, Japan. Ed. Masahiro Watanabe. **Document type:** abstracting/indexing.

CHEMISTRY — ABSTRACTING, BIBLIOGRAPHIES, STATISTICS

547 016 RU ISSN 0131-047X
EKSPRESS-INFORMATSIYA. SINTETICHESKIE VYSOKOPOLIMERNYE MATERIALY. 1958. 48/yr. 99 Rub. Vsesoyuznyi Institut Nauchno-Tekhnicheskoi Informatsii (VINITI), Baltiiskaya ul., 14, Moscow A-219, Russia. (Subscr. to: Mezhdunarodnaya Kniga, Dimitrova ul. 39, 113095 Moscow, Russia)

540 660 GW ISSN 0930-276X
F I Z CHEMIE AKTUELL. (Fachinformationszentrum) 1986. q. free. Fachinformationszentrum Chemie, Franklinstr. 11, 10587 Berlin, Germany. TEL 49-30-39977111. FAX 49-30-39977134. E-mail: info@fiz-chemie.de; URL: http://www.fiz-chemie.de. Ed. Raymond Saenger. circ. 2,200. (back issues avail.) **Document type:** newsletter.

540 GW ISSN 0949-9342
FACHBUCHVERZEICHNIS MATHEMATIK - PHYSIK - CHEMIE. 1900. a. DM.6. Rossipaul Kommunikation GmbH, Menzingerstr. 37, 80638 Munich, Germany. TEL 49-89-179106-0. FAX 49-89-17910622. Ed. Angela Sendlinger. circ. 30,000. **Document type:** trade publication.
  Formed by the merger of: Fachbuchverzeichnis Chemie (ISSN 0343-6438) & Fachbuchverzeichnis Mathematik - Physik (ISSN 0343-639X)

540 FR
FRANCE. SERVICE D'ETUDE DES STRATEGIES ET DES STATISTIQUES INDUSTRIELLES. RESULTATS MENSUELS DES ENQUETES DE BRANCHE. INDUSTRIE CHIMIQUE DE BASE. m. 260 F. (foreign 310 F.) (effective 1991). Service d'Etude des Strategies et des Statistiques Industrielles (SESSI), 85 Bd. du Montparnasse, 75270 Paris Cedex 06, France. TEL 45-56-42-34. FAX 45-56-40-71. stat. **Document type:** government publication.
  Description: Follows developments in the chemical industry through the performance of selected indicators.

540 FR
FRANCE. SERVICE D'ETUDE DES STRATEGIES ET DES STATISTIQUES INDUSTRIELLES. RESULTATS MENSUELS DES ENQUETES DE BRANCHE. PARACHIMIE. m. 260 F. (foreign 310 F.) (effective 1991). Service d'Etude des Strategies et des Statistiques Industrielles (SESSI), 85 Bd. du Montparnasse, 75270 Paris Cedex 06, France. TEL 45-56-42-34. FAX 45-56-40-71. stat. **Document type:** government publication.
  Description: Follows industry developments through the performance of selected indicators.

540 FR
FRANCE. SERVICE D'ETUDE DES STRATEGIES ET DES STATISTIQUES INDUSTRIELLES. RESULTATS TRIMESTRIELS DES ENQUETES DE BRANCHE. INDUSTRIE CHIMIQUE DE BASE. q. 180 F. (foreign 210 F.) (effective 1991). Service d'Etude des Strategies et des Statistiques Industrielles (SESSI), 85 Bd. du Montparnasse, 75270 Paris Cedex 06, France. TEL 45-56-42-34. FAX 45-56-40-71. **Document type:** government publication.
  Description: Provides detailed industry-wide performance statistics for comparative evaluations.

540 FR
FRANCE. SERVICE D'ETUDE DES STRATEGIES ET DES STATISTIQUES INDUSTRIELLES. RESULTATS TRIMESTRIELS DES ENQUETES DE BRANCHE. PARACHIMIE. q. 180 F. (foreign 210 F.) (effective 1991). Service d'Etude des Strategies et des Statistiques Industrielles (SESSI), 85 Bd. du Montparnasse, 75270 Paris Cedex 06, France. TEL 45-56-42-34. FAX 45-56-40-71. **Document type:** government publication.
  Description: Provides detailed industry-wide performance statistics for comparative evaluations.

643 JA
FURO INJEKUSHON BUNSEKI KOENKAI KOEN YOSHISHU/ABSTRACTS OF MEETING ON FLOW INJECTION ANALYSIS. (Text in Japanese) 1984. s-a. 3000 Yen (effective 1997). Nihon Bunseki Kagakkai, Furo Injekushon Bunseki Kenkyu Kondankai - Japan Society for Analytical Chemistry, Division of Flow Injection Analysis, Okayama University, Faculty of Science, Dept. of Chemistry, 3-1-1 Tsushimanaka, Okayama 700, Japan. FAX 8-86-2548376. E-mail: motomizu@cc.okayama-u.ac.jp. **Document type:** abstracting/indexing.

544.92 016 US ISSN 1059-3160
QD79.C45
GAS & LIQUID CHROMATOGRAPHY LITERATURE - ABSTRACTS & INDEX. 1992. bi-m. $595 (effective 1995). Preston Publications, Inc., Box 48312, Niles, IL 60714. TEL 847-965-0566. FAX 847-965-7639. Pub. S. Tinsley Preston. R&P contact: Larry Hooper. bk.rev.; index. circ. 100. (back issues avail.) Indexed: VITIS. **Document type:** abstracting/indexing.
  ●Also available on CD-ROM.
  —BLDSC (4076.850000). CCC.
  Formed by merger of (1972-1991): Liquid Chromatography Literature - Abstracts and Index (ISSN 0147-328X); (1958-1991): Gas Chromatography Literature - Abstracts and Index (ISSN 0016-4895); Which was formerly: Gas Chromatography Abstracts Service.

540 UK ISSN 0261-4707
HIGH PERFORMANCE LIQUID CHROMATOGRAPHY. 1982. s-m. (diskette m.). £115 (diskette £120; both £180) (effective 1997). S U B I S, Mansion House, 19 Kingfield Rd., Sheffield S11 9AS, England. TEL 44-114-2554433. FAX 44-114-2554626. E-mail: subis@sheffac.demon.co.uk; URL: http://www.shef.ac.uk/uni/companies/shap. (also avail. in diskette format) **Document type:** abstracting/indexing.
  —CISTI. CCC.
  Description: Current awareness service for researchers focusing on pharmacological substances.

540 UK ISSN 0142-8128
IMMUNOASSAY. 1970. s-m. (diskette m.). £160 (diskette £120; both £180) (effective 1997). S U B I S, Mansion House, 19 Kingfield Rd., Sheffield S11 9AS, England. TEL 44-114-2554433. FAX 44-114-2554626. E-mail: subis@sheffac.demon.co.uk; URL: http://www.shef.ac.uk/uni/companies/shap. abstr. (also avail. in diskette format; looseleaf format) **Document type:** abstracting/indexing.
  —CCC.
  Description: Current awareness service for researchers. Covers radioimmunoassay, fluorescence immunoassay and enzyme immunoassay.

540 016 US ISSN 0891-6055
INDEX CHEMICUS. Short title: I C. 1960. w. $7400 for CD-ROM. Institute for Scientific Information, 3501 Market St., Philadelphia, PA 19104. TEL 215-386-0100. FAX 215-386-2911. (And: Brunel Science Park, Brunel University, Uxbridge UB8 3PQ, England) q. and a. index. **Document type:** abstracting/indexing.
  ●Also available on CD-ROM.
  —CISTI.
  Former titles: Current Abstracts of Chemistry and Index Chemicus (ISSN 0011-3158); Index.
  Description: Abstract reports on the synthesis, isolation and identification of new organic compounds as reported in journals worldwide.

540 US
INDEX TO CHEMICAL REGULATIONS. (Subseries of: Chemical Regulation Reporter (ISSN 0148-7973)) 1980. m. $737. The Bureau of National Affairs, Inc., 1231 25th St., N.W., Washington, DC 20037. TEL 202-452-4200. FAX 202-822-8092. TELEX 285656 BNAI WSH. URL: http://www.bna.com/. (Subscr. to: 9435 Key West Ave., Rockville, MD 20850. TEL 800-372-1033) Ed. Inara Z. Apinis. (looseleaf format; back issues avail.) **Document type:** abstracting/indexing.
  —CCC.
  Formerly: Index to Government Regulation (ISSN 0195-9492)
  Description: Contains more than 80,000 citations by chemical name to the Code of Federal Regulations and the Federal Register.

661 SP
INDUSTRIA QUIMICA EN CIFRAS. a. Federacion Empresarial de la Industria Quimica Espanola, Hermosilla, 31, 28001 Madrid, Spain. TEL 4317964. FAX 576-33-81.

JAPANESE PATENTS ABSTRACTS. EXAMINED. see PATENTS, TRADEMARKS AND COPYRIGHTS — Abstracting, Bibliographies, Statistics

016.540 JA ISSN 0915-0447
JAPANESE SYMPOSIUM ON PLASMA CHEMISTRY. ABSTRACT PAPERS/PURAZUMA KAGAKU GODO SHINPOJUMU ABUSUTORAK UTOSHU. (Text in English, Japanese) 1988. a. Organizing Committee of Japanese Symposium on Plasma Chemistry - Purazuma Kagaku Godo Shinpojumu Soshiki Iinkai, Kyoto Daigaku Kogakubu Denshi Kogakka, Yoshida Honmachi, Sakyo-ku, Kyoto-shi, Kyoto 606, Japan. **Document type:** abstracting/indexing.

548 JA
JINKO KESSHO KOGAKKAI TOKUBETSU KOENKAI KOEN YOSHISHU/ASSOCIATION OF SYNTHETIC CRYSTAL SCIENCE AND TECHNOLOGY. ABSTRACTS OF THE SPECIAL MEETING. (Text in Japanese) 1983. a. Jinko Kessho Kogakkai - Association of Synthetic Crystal Science and Technology, Nagoya Daigaku Kogakubu Oyo Kagakka Dai 1 Koza, Furocho, Chikusa-ku, Nagoya-shi, Aichi-ken 462, Japan. **Document type:** abstracting/indexing.

540 JA
KAGAKU HANNO TORNKAI KOEN YOSHISHU/ABSTRACTS OF THE MEETING ON CHEMICAL REACTION. (Text in Japanese) 1984. a. Chemical Society of Japan - Nippin Kagakkai, 1-5, Kanda Surugadai, Chiyoda-ku, Tokyo 101, Japan. **Document type:** abstracting/indexing.

540 016 JA ISSN 0386-2143
CODEN: KASHDM
KAGAKU SHOHO/CHEMICAL ABSTRACTS. (Text mostly in English) 1973. fortn. 42000 Yen (effective 1997). Japan Association for International Chemical Information - Kagaku Joho Kyokai, 6-25-4 Honkomagome, Bunkyo-ku, Tokyo 113, Japan. TEL 81-3-5978-3631. FAX 81-3-5978-3600. (Dist. overseas by: Japan Publications Trading Co., Ltd., Box 5030, Tokyo International, Tokyo 100-31, Japan) Ed. Yumi Ishizaka. adv.; bk.rev. circ. 50. Indexed: Abstr.Bull.Inst.Pap.Chem. **Document type:** abstracting/indexing.

541.3 JA
KOKAGAKU TORONKAI KOEN YOSHISHU/ABSTRACTS OF SYMPOSIUM ON PHOTOCHEMISTRY. (Text in Japanese) 1953. a. Chemical Society of Japan - Nippon Kagakkai, 1-5, Kanda Surugadai, Chiyoda-ku, Tokyo 101, Japan.

540 JA
KOTAI NO HANNOSEI TORONKAI KOEN YOKOSHU/ABSTRACTS OF THE MEETING ON SOLID REACTIVITY. (Text in Japanese; summaries in English) 1990. a. Chemical Society of Japan - Nippon Kagakkai, 1-5, Kanda Surugadai, Chiyoda-ku, Tokyo 101, Japan. **Document type:** abstracting/indexing.

540 JA
KYUCHAKU SHINPOJUMU ABUSUTORAKUTOSHU/ABSTRACTS FROM SYMPOSIUM ON ADSORPTION. (Text in Japanese) a. Nihon Kyuchaku Gakkai - Japan Society on Adsorption, Tokyo Daigaku, Seisan Gijutsu Kenkyujo 6-22-1, Roppongi, Minato-ku, Tokyo 106, Japan.

548 NE ISSN 1025-9252
M C L C COMMUNICATIONS. (Molecular Crystals, Liquid Crystals) bi-m. $50 (effective 1998). Gordon and Breach - Harwood Academic, Amsteldisk 166, 1st Fl., 1079 LH Amsterdam, Netherlands. URL: http://www.gbhap.com/MCLC__Communications/. (Subscr to: International Publishers Distributor, Box 32160, Newark, NJ 07102. TEL 800-545-8398. FAX 215-750-6343)
  ●Also available online.
  Description: Provides abstracts of the latest submissions to the journal Molecular Crystals, Liquid Crystals.

CHEMISTRY — ABSTRACTING, BIBLIOGRAPHIES, STATISTICS

540 NE ISSN 1025-9295
MAIN GROUP CHEMISTRY NEWS COMMUNICATIONS.
bi-m. $50 (effective 1998). Gordon and Breach - Harwood Academic, Amsteldisk 166, 1st Fl., 1079 LH Amsterdam, Netherlands. URL: http://www.gbhap.com/Main_Group_Chemistry_News_Communications/. (Subscr. to: International Publishers Distributor, Box 32160, Newark, NJ 07102. TEL 800-545-8398. FAX 215-750-6343)
●Also available online.
—SWETS.
   Description: Provides abstracts of the latest submissions to the journals: Phosphorous, Sulfur and Silicon and the Related Elements; Supramolecular Chemistry; Main Group Chemistry.

540 016 UK ISSN 0025-4738
QC451   CODEN: MSPBBX
MASS SPECTROMETRY BULLETIN. 1966. m. £596($1090) (effective 1997). The Royal Society of Chemistry, Thomas Graham House, Science Park, Milton Rd., Cambridge CB4 4WF, England. TEL 44-1223-420066. FAX 44-1223-423429. E-mail: sales@rsc.org; URL: http://chemistry.rsc.org/rsc/. (Subscr. to: Turpin Distribution Services Ltd., Blackhorse Rd., Letchworth, Herts. SG6 1HN, England. TEL 44-1462-672555. FAX 44-1462-480947) Ed. Lynn Hatley. adv.; bk.rev.; bibl.; index, cum.index. circ. 500. (magnetic tape) **Document type:** academic/scholarly publication, bulletin.
—BLDSC (5388.200000); CISTI; Linda Hall.
   Description: Contains titles and bibliographic details of recently published documents dealing with mass spectrometry.

540 016 US
N T I S ALERTS: CHEMISTRY. w. $125 (foreign $175). U.S. National Technical Information Service, 5285 Port Royal Rd., Springfield, VA 22161. TEL 703-487-4630. FAX 703-321-8547. TELEX 64617. index. (back issues avail.) **Document type:** abstracting/indexing.
   Former titles: Abstract Newsletter: Chemistry (ISSN 0163-1519); Weekly Abstract Newsletter; Chemistry; Weekly Government Abstracts. Chemistry.

540 JA
NIHON BUNSEKI KAGAKKAI KOEN YOSHISHU/JAPAN SOCIETY FOR ANALYTICAL CHEMISTRY. ABSTRACTS OF THE ANNUAL MEETING. (Text in Japanese) a. Nihon Bunseki Kagakkai - Japan Society for Analytical Chemistry, 26-2, Nishigotanda 1-chome, Shinagawa-ku, Tokyo 141, Japan. **Document type:** abstracting/indexing.

548 JA
NIHON KESSHO GAKKAI NENKAI KOEN YOSHISHU/CRYSTALLOGRAPHIC SOCIETY OF JAPAN. ABSTRACTS OF ANNUAL MEETING. (Text in English, Japanese) a. Nihon Kessho Gakkai, Cosmos Hongo Bldg., 8F, 4-1-4 Hongo, Bunkyo-ku, Tokyo 113, Japan. **Document type:** abstracting/indexing.

540 JA
NIHON KYUCHAKU GAKKAI KENKYU HAPPYOKAI KOEN YOSHISHU/JAPAN SOCIETY ON ADSORPTION. ABSTRACTS OF THE MEETING. (Text in English, Japanese) 1987. a. Nihon Kyuchaku Gakkai, Tokyo Daigaku, Seisan Gijutsu Kenkyujo, 6-22-1, Roppongi, Minato-ku, Tokyo 106, Japan. TEL 03-3408-1483. **Document type:** abstracting/indexing.

540 JA
NIHON MAKU GAKKAI NENKAI KOEN YOSHISHU/MEMBRANE SOCIETY OF JAPAN. ABSTRACTS OF ANNUAL MEETING. (Text in English, Japanese) a. Nihon Maku Gakkai, 14-9, Hongo 4-chome, Bunkyo-ku, Tokyo 113, Japan. **Document type:** abstracting/indexing.

547.05 016 UK ISSN 0030-5138
ORGANOMETALLIC COMPOUNDS; abstracts of literature and patents relating to compounds which contain at least metal, carbon and hydrogen atoms. 1961. fortn. $940 (effective 1996). R.H. Chandler Ltd., 21 The Avenue, Braintree, Essex CM7 6HY, England. TEL 01376-553033. Ed. R.H. Chandler. bk.rev.; bibl.; pat ; index. circ. 260. (processed; also avail. from UMI; reprint service avail. from UMI) **Document type:** abstracting/indexing.
—UMI. **CCC.**

548 016 FR ISSN 1146-5336
P A S C A L E 13: STRUCTURE DES LIQUIDES ET DES SOLIDES - CRISTALLOGRAPHIE. (Printed format ceased Jan. 1995) (Text in French, English) 1984. 10/yr. Centre National de la Recherche Scientifique, Institut de l'Information Scientifique et Technique, 2 allee du Parc de Brabois, 54514 Vandoeuvre-Les-Nancy Cedex, France. TEL 83-50-46-00. FAX 83-50-46-50. adv. contact: Veronique Guinvarc'h. abstr.; index, cum.index. (also avail. in microfiche) **Document type:** bibliography.
●Also available online. Vendor(s): European Space Agency (File no.14), Knight-Ridder Information, Inc. (File no.144), Telesystemes - Questel.
Also available on CD-ROM.
   Former titles: P A S C A L Explore. E 13: Structure des Liquides et des Solides. Cristallographie (ISSN 0761-1978); P A S C A L Explore. Part 13: Structure des Liquides et des Solides. Cristallographie; Supersedes: Bulletin Signaletique. Part 161: Structure de l'Etat Condense. Cristallographie (ISSN 0304-1298); Bulletin Signaletique. Part 161. Cristallographie (ISSN 0301-3340); Which supersedes in part: Bulletin Signaletique. Part 161. Structure de la Matiere II (ISSN 0007-5388).

544 FR ISSN 1146-5344
P A S C A L E 18: CHROMATOGRAPHIE. (Printed format ceased Jan. 1995) (Text in English, French) 1984. 10/yr. Centre National de la Recherche Scientifique, Institut de l'Information Scientifique et Technique, 2 allee du Parc de Brabois, 54514 Vandoeuvre-les-Nancy Cedex, France. TEL 83-50-46-00. FAX 83-50-46-50. adv. contact: Veronique Guinvarc'h. (also avail. in microfiche) **Document type:** bibliography.
●Also available online. Vendor(s): European Space Agency (File no.14), Knight-Ridder Information, Inc. (File no.144), Telesystemes - Questel.
Also available on CD-ROM.
   Formerly (until 1989): P A S C A L Explore. E 18: Chromatographie (ISSN 0246-1307)

543 FR ISSN 1146-5115
P A S C A L. F 16: CHIMIE ANALYTIQUE, MINERALE ET ORGANIQUE. (Printed format ceased Jan. 1995) (Text in English, French) 1984. 10/yr. Centre National de l'Information Scientifique et Technique, Institut de l'Information Scientifique et Technique, 2 allee du Parc de Brabois, 54514 Vandoeuvre-Les-Nancy Cedex, France. TEL 83-50-46-00. FAX 83-50-46-50. Ed. Claude Patou. adv. contact: Veronique Guinvarc'h. abstr.; bibl.; stat.; index, cum.index. (also avail. in microfiche) **Document type:** bibliography.
●Also available online. Vendor(s): European Space Agency (File no.14), Knight-Ridder Information, Inc. (File no.144), Telesystemes - Questel.
Also available on CD-ROM.
—Linda Hall.
   Former titles: P A S C A L Folio. F 16: Chimie Analytique Minerale et Organique (ISSN 0761-1749); P A S C A L Folio. Part 16: Chimie Analytique Minerale et Organique; Supersedes (1982-1984): Bulletin Signaletique. Part 172: Chimie Analytique (ISSN 0240-8473)

540 016 FR ISSN 1146-5123
P A S C A L. F 17: CHIMIE GENERALE, MINERALE ET ORGANIQUE. (Printed format ceased Jan. 1995) (Text in English, French) 1984. 10/yr. Centre National de la Recherche Scientifique, Institut de l'Information Scientifique et Technique, 2 allee du Parc de Brabois, 54514 Vandoeuvre-Les-Nancy Cedex, France. TEL 83-50-46-00. FAX 83-50-46-50. adv. contact: Veronique Guinvarc'h. abstr.; index, cum.index. (also avail. in microfiche) **Document type:** bibliography.
●Also available online. Vendor(s): European Space Agency (File no.14), Knight-Ridder Information, Inc. (File no.144), Telesystemes - Questel.
Also available on CD-ROM.
—Linda Hall.
   Formerly: P A S C A L Folio. F 17: Chimie Generale, Minerale et Organique (ISSN 0761-1757); Superseded (in 1984): Bulletin Signaletique. Part 173: Chimie Minerale et Organique (ISSN 0240-8481); Bulletin Signaletique. Part 171: Chimie Generale et Chimie Physique; Formerly: P A S C A L Folio. Part 17: Chimie Generale, Minerale et Organique.

540 016 FR ISSN 1146-514X
P A S C A L. F 23: GENIE CHIMIQUE. INDUSTRIES CHIMIQUE ET PARACHIMIQUE. (Printed format ceased Jan. 1995) (Text in English, French) 1984. 10/yr. Centre National de la Recherche Scientifique, Institut de l'Information Scientifique et Technique, 2 allee du Parc de Brabois, 54514 Vandoeuvre-Les-Nancy Cedex, France. TEL 83-50-46-00. FAX 83-50-46-50. (Co-sponsor: Centre d'Etude des Matieres Plastiques) adv. contact: Veronique Guinvarc'h. index, cum.index. (also avail. in microform) **Document type:** bibliography.
●Also available online. Vendor(s): European Space Agency (File no.14), Knight-Ridder Information, Inc. (File no.144), Telesystemes - Questel.
Also available on CD-ROM.
—Linda Hall.
   Former titles: P A S C A L Folio. F 23: Genie Chimique. Industries Chimique et Parachimique (ISSN 0761-1781); P A S C A L Folio. Part 23: Genie Chimique. Industries Chimique et Parachimique; Which superseded (1961-1984): Bulletin Signaletique. Part 880: Genie Chimique. Industries Chimique et Parachimique (ISSN 0007-568X)

668.4 016 FR ISSN 1146-5158
P A S C A L F 24: POLYMERES - PEINTURES - BOIS. (Printed format ceased Jan. 1995) (Text in English, French) 1984. 10/yr. Centre National de la Recherche Scientifique, Institut de l'Information Scientifique et Technique, 2 allee du Parc de Brabois, 54514 Vandoeuvre-Les-Nancy Cedex, France. TEL 83-50-46-00. FAX 83-50-46-50. adv. contact: Veronique Guinvarc'h. abstr.; index, cum.index. (also avail. in microform) **Document type:** bibliography.
●Also available online. Vendor(s): European Space Agency (File no.14), Knight-Ridder Information, Inc. (File no.144), Telesystemes - Questel.
Also available on CD-ROM.
   Former titles: P A S C A L Folio. F 24: Polymeres. Peintures. Bois (ISSN 0761-179X); P A S C A L Folio. Part 24: Polymeres. Peintures. Bois; Which supersedes: Bulletin Signaletique. Part 780: Polymeres. Peintures. Bois. Cuirs; Bulletin Signaletique. Part 780. Polymeres (ISSN 0007-5671)

541.3 US ISSN 0893-6684
POLYMER BLENDS, ALLOYS AND INTERPENETRATING POLYMER NETWORKS ABSTRACTS. 1987. m. $395 (foreign $425) (effective 1997); $425 (foreign $455) (effective 1998). Technomic Publishing Co., Inc., 851 New Holland Ave., Box 3535, Lancaster, PA 17604. TEL 717-291-5609. FAX 717-295-4538. TELEX 230 753565 (TECHNOIC UD). E-mail: marketing@techpub.com; URL: http://www.techpub.com. Ed. John W. DeGroot, Jr. circ. 100. (back issues avail.) **Document type:** academic/scholarly publication.
—UMI. **CCC.**
   Description: Covers polymer science and product development.
   Refereed Serial

POLYMER CONTENTS; international current awareness publication for polymer science and engineering. see ENGINEERING — *Abstracting, Bibliographies, Statistics*

PREDICASTS OVERVIEW OF MARKETS AND TECHNOLOGY. see ENGINEERING — *Abstracting, Bibliographies, Statistics*

540 016 RU ISSN 0486-2325
QD1   CODEN: RZKHAR
REFERATIVNYI ZHURNAL. KHIMIYA. 1953. 24/yr. $11109 (effective 1998). Vsesoyuznyi Institut Nauchno-Tekhnicheskoi Informatsii (VINITI), Baltiiskaya ul., 14, Moscow A-219, Russia. (Subscr. to: Mezhdunarodnaya Kniga, Dimitrova ul. 39, 113095 Moscow, Russia) Indexed: Anal.Abstr., Chem.Abstr. **Document type:** abstracting/indexing.
—BLDSC (0151.000000); CASDDS.

RIKAGAKU KENKYUJO KENKYU HAPPYO RONBUN MOKUROKU/INSTITUTE OF PHYSICAL AND CHEMICAL RESEARCH. LIST OF PAPERS. see PHYSICS — *Abstracting, Bibliographies, Statistics*

RIKAGAKU KENKYUJO KENKYU NENPO/I P C R. ANNUAL REPORTS OF RESEARCH ACTIVITIES. see PHYSICS — *Abstracting, Bibliographies, Statistics*

CHEMISTRY — ANALYTICAL CHEMISTRY

RIKAGAKU KENKYUJO NYUSU/RIKEN NEWS. see PHYSICS — Abstracting, Bibliographies, Statistics

543 016 RU ISSN 0234-9744
SIGNAL'NAYA INFORMATSIYA. ANALITICHESKAYA KHIMIYA. 1970. s-m. 34.60 Rub. Vsesoyuznyi Institut Nauchno-Tekhnicheskoi Informatsii (VINITI), Baltiiskaya ul. 14, Moscow A-219, Russia. **Document type:** abstracting/indexing.
Formerly (until 1987): Signal'naya Informatsiya. Analiticheskaya Khimiya-Oborudovanie Laboratorii (ISSN 0202-8565)

540 011 RU ISSN 0234-9736
SIGNAL'NAYA INFORMATSIYA. KATALIZ I KATALIZATORY. 1987. s-m. 54.20 Rub. Vsesoyuznyi Institut Nauchno-Tekhnicheskoi Informatsii (VINITI), Baltiiskaya ul. 14, A-219 Moscow, Russia. **Document type:** abstracting/indexing.

540 016 RU ISSN 0202-8948
SIGNAL'NAYA INFORMATSIYA. KHIMIYA VODY. 1971. s-m. 24.20 Rub. Vsesoyuznyi Institut Nauchno-Tekhnicheskoi Informatsii (VINITI), Baltiiskaya ul. 14, Moscow A-219, Russia. (Subscr. to: Mezhdunarodnaya Kniga, Dimitrova ul. 39, 113095 Moscow, Russia) **Document type:** abstracting/indexing.

540 011 RU ISSN 0234-968X
SIGNAL'NAYA INFORMATSIYA. KHIMIYA VYSOKIKH ENERGII. 1987. s-m. 17.60 Rub. Vsesoyuznyi Institut Nauchno-Tekhnicheskoi Informatsii (VINITI), Baltiiskaya ul. 14, A-219 moscow, Russia. **Document type:** abstracting/indexing.

540 011 RU ISSN 0234-971X
SIGNAL'NAYA INFORMATSIYA. NAPOLNENNYE I ARMIROVANNYE PLASTIKI. 1987. s-m. 6.80 Rub. Vsesoyuznyi Institut Nauchno-Tekhnicheskoi Informatsii (VINITI), Baltiiskaya ul. 14, A-219 Moscow, Russia. **Document type:** abstracting/indexing.

540 011 RU ISSN 0234-9701
SIGNAL'NAYA INFORMATSIYA. OCHISTKA I UTILIZATSIYA OTKHODOV KHIMICHESKIKH PROIZVODSTV. 1987. s-m. 21.20 Rub. Vsesoyuznyi Institut Nauchno-Tekhnicheskoi Informatsii (VINITI), Baltiiskaya ul. 14, A-219 Moscow, Russia. **Document type:** abstracting/indexing.

540 011 RU ISSN 0234-9698
SIGNAL'NAYA INFORMATSIYA. SORBENTY. POVERKHNOSTNO-AKTIVNYE VESHCHESTVA. 1987. s-m. 10.20 Rub. Vsesoyuznyi Institut Nauchno-Tekhnicheskoi Informatsii (VINITI), Baltiiskaya ul. 14, A-219 Moscow, Russia. **Document type:** abstracting/indexing.

541.3 JA
SOCIETY OF PROPERTY OF PHYSICAL CHEMISTRY. ABSTRACTS OF MEETING/BUSSEI BUTSURI KAGAKU KENKYUKAI KOEN YOSHISHU. (Text in Japanese) 1983. a. Society of Property of Physical Chemistry - Bussei Butsuri Kagaku Kenkyukai, Kyoto Daigaku Yakugakubu, Yoshida Shimoadachi-cho, Sakyo-ku, Kyoto 606, Japan. **Document type:** abstracting/indexing.

540 005 US ISSN 1040-1229
Z699.5.S3 CODEN: STNWEQ
STNEWS. Variant title: S T N News. 1985. m. free to users. Chemical Abstracts Service, 240 Olentangy River Rd., Box 3012, Columbus, OH 43210-0012. TEL 614-447-3600. FAX 614-447-3713. TELEX 6842086. Ed. Cynthia McClung. circ. controlled. **Document type:** newsletter.
Description: Informs and educates online users about content, changes, efficient ways to search the more than 200 databases on STN International - chemistry, engineering, health and safety, materials and numeric data, and more.

016.5413 JA
SYMPOSIUM ON RADIOCHEMISTRY. ABSTRACTS OF PAPERS/HOSHA KAGAKU TORONKAI KOEN YOKOSHU. (Text in Japanese; summaries in English) 1957. a. Chemical Society of Japan - Nippon Kagakkai, 1-5, Kanda Surugadai, Chiyoda-ku, Tokyo 101, Japan. **Document type:** abstracting/indexing.

540 665.5 US
CODEN: TCZEFR
TECHNICAL LITERATURE ABSTRACTS: CATALYSTS - ZEOLITES. 1985. w. $270 to non-subscribers; subscribers $135. American Petroleum Institute, EnCompass, 275 Seventh Ave., New York, NY 10001-6708. TEL 212-366-4040. FAX 212-366-4298. E-mail: info@apienncompass.org; URL: http://www.api.org. **Document type:** abstracting/indexing.
●Also available online. Vendor(s): Knight-Ridder Information, Inc., Questel Orbit Inc. (APILIT), STN International, Telesystemes - Questel.
Former titles: Literature Abstracts: Catalysts - Zeolites (ISSN 1074-6870); (until 1994): Literature Abstracts: Catalysts and Catalysis (ISSN 1065-0539); (until 1992): A P I Abstracts - Catalysts and Catalysis.
Description: Reports scientific and technical developments, and general news concerning catalysts and zeolites used in the petroleum, energy, and petrochemical industries, including pollution-control catalysts. The information is drawn from trade magazines and scientific journals published world-wide, as well as conference papers.

540 665.5 US
CODEN: TFREF8
TECHNICAL LITERATURE ABSTRACTS: FUEL REFORMULATION. 1994. m. $270 to non-subscribers; subscribers $135. American Petroleum Institute, EnCompass, 275 Seventh Ave., New York, NY 10001-6708. TEL 212-366-4040. FAX 212-366-4298. E-mail: info@apienncompass.org; URL: http://www.api.org. **Document type:** abstracting/indexing.
●Also available online. Vendor(s): Knight-Ridder Information, Inc., Questel Orbit Inc. (APILIT), STN International (APILIT), Telesystemes - Questel.
Formerly: Literature Abstracts: Fuel Reformulation (ISSN 1074-6854)
Description: Reports on composition, properties, regulations, blending, preparations of compounds for use in reformulated fules, and related topics.

540 665.5 US
TECHNICAL LITERATURE ABSTRACTS: TRIBOLOGY. 1994. m. $270 to non-subscribers; subscribers $135. American Petroleum Institute, EnCompass, 275 Seventh Ave., New York, NY 10001-6708. TEL 212-366-4040. FAX 212-366-4298. E-mail: info@apienncompass.org; URL: http://www.api.org. **Document type:** abstracting/indexing.
●Also available online. Vendor(s): Knight-Ridder Information, Inc., Questel Orbit Inc. (APILIT), STN International (APILIT), Telesystemes - Questel.
Formerly: Literature Abstracts: Tribology (ISSN 1074-6889)
Description: Reports on the tribology of both petroleum-based and synthetic lubricants and industrial oils, including tribology, friction, lubrication and wear.

540 JA
TOSHITSU SHINPOJUMU KOEN YOSHISHU/ABSTRACTS OF JAPANESE CARBOHYDRATE SYMPOSIUM. (Text in Japanese; summaries in English) 1978. a. 4000 Yen. Nihon Toshitsu Gakkai - Japanese Society for Carbohydrate Research, Tokyo Yakka Daigaku Daiichi Yakkagaku Kyoshitsu, 1432-1, Horinouchi, Hachioji-shi, Tokyo 192-03, Japan. **Document type:** abstracting/indexing.

540 US ISSN 1061-9143
HD9651.1
U S CHEMICAL INDUSTRY STATISTICAL HANDBOOK. 1990. a. Chemical Manufacturers Association, 1300 Wilson Blvd., Arlington, VA 22209. TEL 703-741-5000. FAX 703-741-6000. R&P contact: Carolyn Dillingham. TEL 703-741-5929. **Indexed:** SRI. **Document type:** corporate report.

540 016 660 HU ISSN 0231-0775
VEGYIPARI SZAKIRODALMI TAJEKOZTATO/CHEMICAL ENGINEERING ABSTRACTS. 1949. m. 9900 Ft. Orszagos Muszaki Informacios Kozpont es Konyvtar (O.M.I.K.K.) - National Technical Information Centre and Library, Muzeum u. 17, P.O. Box 12, 1428 Budapest, Hungary. (Subscr. to: Kultura, Box 149, 1389 Budapest, Hungary) Ed. Eszter Molnar. index. circ. 520. **Document type:** abstracting/indexing.
Supersedes (as from 1982): Muszaki Lapszemle. Kemia Vegyipar - Technical Abstracts. Chemistry, Chemical Industry (ISSN 0027-5026)

643 JA
X SEN BUNSEKI TORONKAI KOEN YOSHISHU/ABSTRACTS OF ANNUAL CONFERENCE ON X-RAY CHEMICAL ANALYSIS. (Text in Japanese) 1964. a. membership. Nihon Bunseki Kagakkai - Japan Society for Analytical Chemistry, 26-2, Nishigotanda 1-chome, Shinagawa-ku, Tokyo 141, Japan. **Document type:** abstracting/indexing.

547 JA
YUKI HANNO KAGAKU TORONKAI KOEN YOKOSHU/ABSTRACTS OF SYMPOSIUM ON ORGANIC REACTIONS. (Text in Japanese; summaries in English) a. Chemical Society of Japan - Nippon Kagakkai, 1-5, Kanka Surugadai, Chiyoda-ku, Tokyo 101, Japan.

643 546 CC
ZHONGGUO WUJI FENXI HUAXUE WENZHAI/CHINESE INORGANIC ANALYTICAL CHEMISTRY ABSTRACTS. (Text in Chinese) bi-m. Yejin Gongye Chubanshe, 39 Gaozhuyuan Beixiang, Shatan, Beijing 100009, People's Republic of China. TEL 4015599. Ed. Xu Junduo. **Document type:** abstracting/indexing.

CHEMISTRY — Analytical Chemistry

543 US ISSN 1060-3271
S583 CODEN: JAINEE
A O A C INTERNATIONAL. JOURNAL. 1915. bi-m. $242 to non-members; members $176; institutions $262 in N. America; elsewhere $291 to non-members; members $225; institutions $311. A O A C International, 481 N. Frederick Ave., Ste. 500, Gaithersburg, MD 20877-2417. TEL 301-924-7077. FAX 301-924-7089. Ed. James Tanner. R&P contact: Krystyna McIver. adv. contact: Randy McClure. abstr.; charts; illus.; pat.; stat.; index. circ. 4,200. (also avail. in microform from PMC; back issues avail.) **Indexed:** Abstr.Bull.Inst.Pap.Chem., AESIS, Anal.Abstr., Apic.Abstr., ASCA, Biol.Abstr., Biol.& Agr.Ind., Biotech.Abstr., Cadscan, Chem.Abstr., Chem.Cit.Ind., Curr.Adv.Ecol.Sci., Curr.Cont., Dairy Sci.Abstr., Environ.Abstr., Excerp.Med., Food Sci.& Tech.Abstr., GeoRef., Helminthol.Abstr., Herb.Abstr., Hort.Abstr., I.P.A., Ind.Med., Ind.Vet., INIS Atomind., Int.Packag.Abstr., Lab.Haz.Bull., Lead Abstr., Maize Abstr., Mass Spectr.Bull., Nutr.Abstr., Ocean.Abstr., Packag.Sci.Tech., Pig News & Info., Plant Breed.Abstr., Pollut.Abstr., Potato Abstr., Poult.Abstr., Protozool.Abstr., Rev.Appl.Entomol., Rev.Med.& Vet.Mycol., Seed Abstr., Sel.Water Res.Abstr., So.Pac.Per.Ind., Soils & Fert., Soyabean Abstr., Sugar Ind.Abstr., Telegen, Triticale Abstr., Vet.Bull., VITIS, W.R.C.Inf., Weed Abstr., Zincscan. **Document type:** academic/scholarly publication.
●Also available online. Vendor(s): STN International (CJAOAC).
—BLDSC (4698.400000); CASDDS; CIS; CISTI; Genuine Article; KR SourceOne; Linda Hall; SWETS; UnCover. **CCC.**
Former titles: Association of Official Analytical Chemists. Journal (ISSN 0004-5756); Association of Official Agricultural Chemists. Journal.
Description: Papers on chemical analytical methodology pertaining to food, agriculture, drugs, forensics, industrial chemicals and the environment. *Refereed Serial*

543 US ISSN 0066-961X
S587
A O A C INTERNATIONAL. OFFICIAL METHODS OF ANALYSIS. 1920. quinquennial (plus 5 a. updates). $359 in N. America (single-user CD-ROM $575); elsewhere $399 (CD-ROM $595). A O A C International, 481 N. Frederick Ave., Ste. 500, Gaithersburg, MD 20877-2417. TEL 301-924-7077. FAX 301-924-7089. Ed. Patricia Cunniff. R&P contact: Krystyna McIver. index. circ. 20,000. (looseleaf format) **Indexed:** Chem.Abstr.
●Also available on CD-ROM.
—CISTI. **CCC.**
Former titles (until 1970): Association of Official Analytical Chemists. Official Methods of Analysis (ISSN 0884-0474); (until 1965): Association of Official Analytical Chemists. Official and Tentative Methods of Analysis (ISSN 0884-0466)
Description: Tested and officially adopted chemical and biological methods pertaining to food, agriculture, pharmaceuticals, and the environment.

ABSTRACTS OF THE TOKYO CONFERENCE ON INSTRUMENTAL ANALYSIS AND ANALYTIC SYSTEMS/BUNSEKI KIKI TO KAISEKI SHISUTEMU NI KANSURU TOKYO TORONKAI KOEN YOSHISHU. see CHEMISTRY — Abstracting, Bibliographies, Statistics

ABSTRACTS ON THE SYMPOSIUM ON MOLECULAR STRUCTURE/BUNSHI KOZO SOGO TORONKAI KOEN YOSHISHU. see CHEMISTRY — Abstracting, Bibliographies, Statistics

544 GW ISSN 0949-1775
CODEN: AQASF3
▼ACCREDITATION AND QUALITY ASSURANCE; journal for quality, comparability and reliability in chemical measurements. Online edition (GW ISSN 1432-0517) (Text in English) 1996. 8/yr. DM.232.80 (foreign DM.243.60) (effective 1998). Springer-Verlag, Heidelberger Platz 3, 14197 Berlin, Germany. TEL 49-30-82787-0. FAX 49-30-82787448. E-mail: subscriptions@springer.de; URL: http://link.springer.de. (Subscr. in N. America to: Springer-Verlag New York, Inc., 333 Meadowlands Pkwy., Secaucus, NJ 07094. TEL 212-460-1500. FAX 212-473-6272) Document type: academic/scholarly publication.
●Also available online.
—BLDSC (0573.743000); CASDDS. CCC.

545.3 US ISSN 0896-422X
ADVANCED COATINGS & SURFACE TECHNOLOGY. 1985. m. $590 (foreign $650). Technical Insights (Subsidiary of: John Wiley & Sons, Inc.), 32 N. Dean St., Englewood, NJ 07631-2807. TEL 201-568-4744. FAX 201-568-8247. E-mail: actinfo@insights.com; URL: http://www.insights.com. Ed. Peter Katz; Pub. Peter Katz. Indexed: Paper & Bd.Abstr., Print.Abstr. Document type: newsletter.
—BLDSC (0696.837000). CCC.
Description: Reports and puts into perspective significant developments in coatings and surface modification across a broad range of industry lines.

544 US
▼ADVANCES IN ASYMMETRIC SYNTHESIS. 1995. irreg., vol.2, 1997. $128.50. J A I Press Inc., 55 Old Post Rd., No.2, Box 1678, Greenwich, CT 06830-1678. TEL 203-661-7602. FAX 203-661-0792. E-mail: jai@jaipress.com. (In Europe: JAI Press Ltd., 38 Tavistock St., Covent Garden, London WC2E 7PB, England. TEL 44-171-379-8834. FAX 44-171-379-8835) Ed. Alfred Hassner. Document type: academic/scholarly publication, monographic series.

535.84 US ISSN 1068-5561
CODEN: AATSEJ
ADVANCES IN ATOMIC SPECTROSCOPY. 1992. irreg., vol.3, 1997. $109.50 per vol. (effective 1997). J A I Press Inc., 55 Old Post Rd., No. 2, Greenwich, CT 06830-1678. TEL 203-661-7602. FAX 203-661-0792. E-mail: jai@jaipress.com. (Addr. in Europe: J A I Press Ltd., 38 Tavistock St., Covent Garden, London WC2E 7PB, England. TEL 44-171-379-8834. FAX 44-171-379-8835) Ed. Joseph Sneddon. (back issues avail.) Document type: academic/scholarly publication.
—BLDSC (0699.820000); CASDDS.
Description: Publishes papers on recent developments in the research and application of atomic spectroscopy.

544.92 US ISSN 0065-2415
QD271 CODEN: ADCYA3
▼ADVANCES IN CHROMATOGRAPHY. 1966. irreg., vol.37, 1997. price varies. Marcel Dekker, Inc., 270 Madison Ave., New York, NY 10016. TEL 212-696-9000. FAX 212-685-4540. TELEX 421419. Ed. Russell Dekker; Pub. Graham Garratt. R&P contact: Julia Mulligan. adv. contact: Lourdes Barroso. Indexed: ASCA, Biol.Abstr., Chem.Abstr., Chem.Cit.Ind., Curr.Adv.Ecol.Sci., Dairy Sci.Abstr., Dent.Ind., Food Sci.& Tech.Abstr., GeoRef., Ind.Med., Ind.Sci.Rev., Sci.Cit.Ind. Document type: monographic series.
—BLDSC (0703.850000); CASDDS; CISTI; Genuine Article; KNAW; Linda Hall; SWETS; UnCover. CCC.
Refereed Serial

544 US
ADVANCES IN DENDRITIC MACROMOLECULES. 1994. irreg., vol.3, 1996. $109.50. J A I Press Inc., 55 Old Post Rd., No.2, Box 1678, Greenwich, CT 06830-1678. TEL 203-661-7602. FAX 203-661-0792. E-mail: jai@jaipress.com. (In Europe: JAI Press Ltd., 38 Tavistock St., Covent Garden, London WC2E 7PB, England. TEL 44-171-379-8834. FAX 44-171-379-8835) Ed. George Newkome. Document type: academic/scholarly publication, monographic series.

542.1 US ISSN 0044-7749
Q184 CODEN: ALBYBL
AMERICAN LABORATORY. (Includes annual Buyers' Guide) 1968. m. $195. International Scientific Communications, Inc., 30 Controls Dr., Box 870, Shelton, CT 06484-0870. TEL 203-926-9300. FAX 203-926-9310. (U.K. subscr. to: I.S.C. House, Progress Business Centre, 5 Whittle Pkwy., Slough SL1 6DQ, England. TEL 44-1628-668881. FAX 44-1628-669199) Ed. Brian Howard. adv.: B&W page $7530, color page $9610; adv. contact: Julie DeMaio. bk.rev.; charts; illus.; stat; tr.lit.; index; circ. 135,000 (controlled). (also avail. in microfiche; back issues avail.) Indexed: Abstr.Bull.Inst.Pap.Chem., ASCA, Biol.Abstr., CAD CAM Abstr., Ceram.Abstr., Chem.Abstr., Chem.Cit.Ind., CINAHL, Curr.Cont., Curr.Pack.Abstr., Energy Ind., Energy Info.Abstr., Environ.Abstr., Excerp.Med., Food Sci.& Tech.Abstr., Ind.Hyg.Dig., Ind.Sci.Rev., INSPEC (1974-1992), Nutr.Abstr., Oper.Res.Manage.Sci., Qual.Contr.Appl.Stat., Risk Abstr., Sci.Cit.Ind., Tel.Abstr., Telegen, W.R.C.Inf. Document type: trade publication.
—BLDSC (0840.300000); AskIEEE; CASDDS; CISTI; Ei; Genuine Article; KR SourceOne; Linda Hall; SWETS; UnCover.
Description: Dedicated to chemists and biologists interested in all aspects of laboratory practice and basic research.

643 US ISSN 0893-8830
CODEN: ALANEK
AMERICAN LABORATORY NEWS. 1987. bi-m. International Scientific Communications, Inc., 30 Controls Dr., Box 870, Shelton, CT 06484-0870. TEL 203-926-9300. FAX 203-926-9310. (U.K. subscr. to: I.S.C. House, Progress Business Centre, 5 Whittle Pkwy., Slough, Berks. SL1 6DQ, England. TEL 44-1628-668881. FAX 44-1628-669199) Ed. Brian Howard. circ. 130,321. (tabloid format) Document type: newsletter.

AMERICAN SOCIETY FOR MASS SPECTROMETRY. JOURNAL. see PHYSICS — Optics

543 FR ISSN 0365-4877
QD71 CODEN: ANLSCY
ANALUSIS; le journal de la physico-chimie analytique et de l'analyse industrielle. (Text and summaries in English, French) 1896. 10/yr. 3036 F. (institutions in the Americas $580; elsewhere 3700F.) (effective 1998). (Societe Francaise de Chimie) Editions Scientifiques et Medicales Elsevier, 141 rue de Javel, 75747 Paris, France. TEL 33-1-45589022. FAX 33-1-45589421. URL: http://www.elsevier.nl/. (Subscr. in U.S. and Canada to: Elsevier Science Inc., Box 945, Madison Sq. Sta., New York, NY 10159-0945. TEL 212-633-3730. FAX 212-633-3680) (Co-sponsor: Societe de Chimie Industrielle) Ed. P. Arpino. adv.; bk.rev.; abstr.; charts; illus.; pat.; tr.lit. circ. 3,000. (back issues avail.; reprint service avail. from ISI) Indexed: Alloys Ind., Anal.Abstr., ASCA, Biol.Abstr., Chem.Abstr., Chem.Cit.Ind., Curr.Cont., Dairy Sci.Abstr., Deep Sea Res.& Oceanogr.Abstr., Eng.Mat.Abstr., Excerp.Med., Food Sci.& Tech.Abstr., GeoRef., Ind.Sci.Rev., INIS Atomind., Mass Spectr.Bull., Mat.Sci.Cit.Ind., Met.Abstr., Met.Abstr.Ind., Nonfer.Met.Alert, Numis.Lit., PCC Alert, Sci.Cit.Ind., Steels Alert, World Alum.Abstr. Document type: academic/scholarly publication, trade publication.
—BLDSC (0890.800000); CASDDS; CISTI; Ei; Genuine Article; Linda Hall; SWETS; UnCover. CCC.
Formed by the merger of: Chimie Analytique (ISSN 0009-4331) & Methodes Physiques d'Analyse.
Description: Divided into two sections. The first section publishes only refereed original manuscripts. The second section provides professional information: company news, meetings, application of techniques, new instruments and equipment, catalogues and brochures, a full coverage of all new products and a dossier on a special subject.
Refereed Serial

ANALYSES OF HAZARDOUS SUBSTANCES IN BIOLOGICAL MATERIALS. see ENVIRONMENTAL STUDIES — Toxicology And Environmental Safety

543 UK ISSN 0003-2654
QD71 CODEN: ANALAO
THE ANALYST. Online edition (UK ISSN 1364-5528) 1876. m. £535 to institutions (US $963) (effective 1997). The Royal Society of Chemistry, Thomas Graham House, Science Park, Milton Rd., Cambridge CB4 4WF, England. TEL 44-1223-420066. FAX 44-1223-423429. E-mail: sales@rsc.org; URL: http://chemistry.rsc.org/rsc/. (Subscr. to: Turpin Distribution Services Ltd., Blackhorse Rd., Letchworth, Herts. SG6 1HN, England. TEL 44-1462-672555. FAX 44-1462-480947) Ed. Harpal Minhas. adv.; bk.rev.; abstr.; charts; illus.; index, cum.index every 10 yrs. (1876-1965). (also avail. in microform from UMI) Indexed: Abstr.Bull.Inst.Pap.Chem., AESIS, Alloys Ind., Anal.Abstr., Art & Archaeol.Tech.Abstr., Biol.Abstr., Br.Tech.Ind., C.I.S. Abstr., Chem.Abstr., Curr.Adv.Biochem., Curr.Adv.Ecol.Sci., Deep Sea Res.& Oceanogr.Abstr., Dent.Ind., Eng.Mat.Abstr., Excerp.Med., Food Sci.& Tech.Abstr., Geo.Abstr., GeoRef., Hort.Abstr., I.P.A., Ind.Med., Ind.Sci.Rev., Ind.Vet., Int.Packag.Abstr., Intl.Polym.Sci.& Tech., Mass Spectr.Bull., Met.Abstr., Met.Abstr.Ind., Nonfer.Met.Alert, Nutr.Abstr., Paper & Bd.Abstr., PCC Alert, Protozool.Abstr., RAPRA, Soils & Fert., Steels Alert, Vet.Bull., W.R.C.Inf, Weed Abstr., World Alum.Abstr., World Surf.Coat. Document type: academic/scholarly publication.
●Also available online. Vendor(s): STN International (CJRSC).
—BLDSC (0893.000000); CASDDS; CISTI; EMDOCS; Genuine Article; Linda Hall; SWETS; UMI; UnCover. CCC.
Description: Contains original research papers on the theory and practice of all aspects of analytical chemistry.
Refereed Serial

544 669 SA ISSN 1022-1123
ANALYTICA. (Former name of issuing body: South African Institute of Assayers and Analysts - Suid-Afrikaanse Instituut van Essaieurs en Analitici) (Text in Afrikaans and English) 1958; N.S. 1993. q. membership. South African Chemical Institute, Analytical Division - Suid-Afrikaanse Chemiese Instituut, Analitiese Divisie, P.O. Box 93480, Yeoville 2143, South Africa. adv.; illus. Indexed: Ind.S.A.Per. Document type: bulletin.
Former titles (until Sep. 1993): South African Institute of Assayers and Analysts. Bulletin (ISSN 0254-1831); (until 1968): Suid-Afrikaanse Instituut van Essaieurs en Analitici. Joernaal (ISSN 0038-2213).

CHEMISTRY — ANALYTICAL CHEMISTRY

543   NE   ISSN 0003-2670
QD71   CODEN: ACACAM
ANALYTICA CHIMICA ACTA; international journal devoted to all branches of analytical chemistry. (Section avail.: Vibrational Spectroscopy (ISSN 0924-2031)) (Text in English, French and German; summaries in English) 1947. 66/yr. fl.9900($5690) (effective 1998). Elsevier Science B.V., P.O. Box 211, 1000 AE Amsterdam, Netherlands. TEL 31-20-4853911. FAX 31-20-4853598. TELEX 18582 ESPA NL. E-mail: nlinfo-f@elsevier.nl; usinfo-f@elsevier.nl; forinfo-kyf04035@niftyserve.or.jp; URL: http://www.elsevier.nl/. (Subscr. in the Americas to: Elsevier Science, Regional Sales Office, Box 945, New York, NY 10159-0945. TEL 212-633-3730. FAX 212-633-3680; Subscr. in Australasia and the Far East to: Elsevier Science (Singapore) Pte Ltd, No.1 Temasek Ave., No.17-01 Millenia Tower, Singapore 039192, Singapore. TEL 65-434-3727. FAX 65-337-2230; Subscr. in Japan to: Elsevier Science Japan, 9-15 Higashi-Azabu 1-chome, Minato-ku, Tokyo 106, Japan. TEL 212-989-5800. FAX 212-633-3990) Ed.Bd. adv.; bk.rev.; charts; illus.; index, cum.index. (also avail. in microform from UMI) **Indexed:** Abstr.Bull.Inst.Pap.Chem., AESIS, Alloys Ind., Anal.Abstr., ASCA, Biol.Abstr., Biotech.Abstr., Br.Ceram.Abstr., Cadscan, Ceram.Abstr., Chem.Abstr., Chem.Cit.Ind., Compumath, Curr.Adv.Ecol.Sci., Curr.Biotech.Abstr., Curr.Cont., Dairy Sci.Abstr., Deep Sea Res.& Oceanogr.Abstr., Eng.Mat.Abstr., Excerp.Med., Food Sci.& Tech.Abstr., Helminthol.Abstr., Hort.Abstr., Ind.Med., Ind.Sci.Rev., Ind.Vet., INIS Atomind., Lead Abstr., Mass Spectr.Bull., Mat.Sci.Cit.Ind., Met.Abstr., Met.Abstr.Ind., Nonfer.Met.Alert, Nutr.Abstr., PCC Alert, Pollut.Abstr., Potato Abstr., Rev.Med.& Vet.Mycol., Sci.Cit.Ind., Sel.Water Res.Abstr., Soils & Fert., Steels Alert, Sugar Ind.Abstr., Triticale Abstr., Vet.Bull., W.R.C.Inf., Weed Abstr., World Alum.Abstr., Zincscan. **Document type:** academic/scholarly publication.
●Also available online. Vendor(s): STN International.
—BLDSC (0895.000000); ADONIS; CASDDS; CISTI; Ei; EMDOCS; Genuine Article; Linda Hall; SWETS; UnCover. **CCC.**
  Incorporates: Analytica Chimica Acta - Computer Technique and Optimization (ISSN 0378-4304)
  Description: Publishes research papers, reviews and short communications covering all aspects of analytical science.
Refereed Serial

543   US   ISSN 0003-2700
TP1   CODEN: ANCHAM
ANALYTICAL CHEMISTRY. 1929. s-m. plus Review Issue and Labguide. $105 to individual non-members; institutional non-members $740; members $54 (effective 1997). American Chemical Society, 1155 16th St., N.W., Washington, DC 20036. TEL 800-333-9511. FAX 614-447-3671. (Subscr. to: Membership and Subscription Services, Box 3337, Columbus, OH 43210. TEL 614-447-3776) Ed. Royce W. Murray. adv.; bk.rev.; abstr.; bibl.; charts; illus.; tr.lit.; index. circ. 27,017. (also avail. in microform from PMC,UMI; reprint service avail. from ISI) **Indexed:** A.I.Abstr., A.S.& T.Ind., Abstr.Bull.Inst.Pap.Chem., Acid Rain Abstr., Acid Rain Ind., AESIS, Alloys Ind., Anal.Abstr., API Abstr., API Catal., API Hlth.& Environ., API Oil., API Pet.Ref., API Pet.Subst., API Transport., Apic.Abstr., ASCA, B.C.I.R.A., Biol.Abstr., Biotech.Abstr., Br.Ceram.Abstr., C.I.J.E., C.I.S. Abstr., Ceram.Abstr., Chem.Abstr., Chem.Cit.Ind., CJPI, Comput.Abstr., Curr.Adv.Biochem., Curr.Adv.Ecol.Sci., Curr.Cont., Curr.Leather Lit., Dairy Sci.Abstr., Deep Sea Res.& Oceanogr.Abstr., Dent.Ind., E&P Hlth. (1993-), Energy Info.Abstr., Eng.Ind., Eng.Mat.Abstr., Environ.Abstr., Excerp.Med., Food Sci.& Tech.Abstr., Fuel & Energy Abstr., Gas Abstr., Gas Process.& Ppl. (1993-), Gen.Sci.Ind., Hort.Abstr., I.P.A., Ind.Hyg.Dig., Ind.Med., Ind.Sci.Rev., INIS Atomind., INSPEC (1968-), Intl.Polym.Sci.& Tech., Lead Abstr., Mass Spectr.Bull., Mat.Sci.Cit.Ind., Met.Abstr., Met.Abstr.Ind., Mineral.Abstr., Neurosci.Cit.Ind., Nonfer.Met.Alert, Nutr.Abstr., Ocean.Abstr., Off.Tech. (1993-), Paper & Bd.Abstr., PCC Alert, Petrol.Abstr. (1961-), Pollut.Abstr., RAPRA, Repindex, Risk Abstr., Sci.Cit.Ind., Sel.Water Res.Abstr., Soils & Fert., SSCI, Steels Alert, Sugar Ind.Abstr., Telegen, Text.Tech.Dig., THA, W.R.C.Inf., Weed Abstr., World Alum.Abstr., World Alum.Abstr., World Surf.Coat., World Text.Abstr., Zincscan. **Document type:** academic/scholarly larly publication.
●Also available online. Vendor(s): STN International (CJACS).
—BLDSC (0897.000000); AskIEEE; CASDDS; CISTI; Ei; EMDOCS; Genuine Article; KNAW; KR SourceOne; Linda Hall; SWETS; UMI; UnCover. **CCC.**
  Formerly (until 1946): Industrial and Analytical Chemistry. Analytical Edition (ISSN 0096-4484)
  Description: Contains scientific articles on both theoretical and applied aspects of analysis, as well as correspondence and laboratory aids.

544   JA   ISSN 0386-2178
CODEN: BUNSD3
ANALYTICAL CHEMISTRY/BUNSEKI. (Text in Japanese) 1975. m. 1000 Yen per no. Japan Society for Analytical Chemistry - Nihon Bunseki Kagakkai, 26-2, Nishigotanda 1-chome, Shinagawa-ku, Tokyo 141, Japan. **Indexed:** Apic.Abstr., Chem.Abstr., INIS Atomind., Jap.Per.Ind.
—CASDDS; CISTI. **CCC.**

643   US
ANALYTICAL CHEMISTRY. LABGUIDE (YEAR). (Special issue of Analytical Chemistry) 1955. a. $50 (free to qualified personnel). American Chemical Society, 1155 16th St., N.W., Washington, DC 20036. TEL 800-227-5558. FAX 614-447-3671. (Subscr. to: Membership and Subscription Services, Box 3337, Columbus, OH 43210. TEL 614-447-3776) Ed. Royce Murray. adv.; bk.rev. circ. 75,000. **Document type:** academic/scholarly publication, directory.
  Former titles: Lab Guide; Laboratory Guide to Instruments, Equipment and Chemicals (ISSN 0458-595X); A C S Laboratory Guide (ISSN 0065-7700); Analytical Chemistry Buyers Guide.
  Description: Comprehensive directory of instruments, equipment, supplies, and services.

547.7 664.9   US
ANALYTICAL CHEMISTRY LABORATORY GUIDEBOOK. RESIDUE CHEMISTRY. irreg. $39 per no. (foreign $48.75). U.S. Department of Agriculture, Office of Public Affairs, Administration Bldg., Rm. 201A, Independence Ave., between 12th and 14th Sts., S.W., Washington, DC 20250. (Orders to: Superintendent of Documents, U.S. Government Printing Office, Box 371954, Pittsburgh, PA 15250-7954. TEL 202-512-1800. FAX 202-512-2250) **Document type:** government publication.
  Description: Provides persons involved with analyzing meat and poultry products for U.S.D.A. regulation compliance with a compendium of analytical methods to ensure quality results in laboratory practice and training.

544.92   NE   ISSN 0167-6350
CODEN: ACSSDR
ANALYTICAL CHEMISTRY SYMPOSIA SERIES. 1979. irreg., vol.25, 1986. price varies. Elsevier Science B.V., Books Division, P.O. Box 211, 1000 AE Amsterdam, Netherlands. TEL 31-20-4853911. FAX 31-20-4853705. TELEX 18582 ESPA NL. E-mail: nlinfo-f@elsevier.nl; usinfo-f@elsevier.com; forinfo-kyf04035@niftyserve.or.jp; URL: http://www.elsevier.nl/. (Subscr. in the Americas to: Elsevier Science, Regional Sales Office, Box 945, New York, NY 10159-0945. TEL 212-633-3730. FAX 212-633-3680; Subscr. in Australasia and the Far East to: Elsevier Science (Singapore) Pte Ltd, No.1 Temasek Ave., No.17-01 Millenia Tower, Singapore 039192, Singapore. TEL 65-434-3727. FAX 65-337-2230; Subscr. in Japan to: Elsevier Science Japan, 9-15 Higashi-Azabu 1-chome, Minato-ku, Tokyo 106, Japan. TEL 81-3-5561-5033. FAX 81-3-5561-5047) **Indexed:** Biol.Abstr., Chem.Abstr. **Document type:** monographic series, proceedings.
—CASDDS; KNAW. **CCC.**
  Formerly: Chromatography Symposia Series (ISSN 0166-2732)
Refereed Serial

543   UK   ISSN 1359-7337
QD71   CODEN: ANCOFE
ANALYTICAL COMMUNICATIONS. 1964. m. £210 (US $378) (effective 1997). The Royal Society of Chemistry, Thomas Graham House, Science Park, Milton Rd., Cambridge CB4 4WF, England. TEL 44-1223-420066. FAX 44-1223-423429. E-mail: sales@rsc.rg; URL: http://chemistry.rsc.org/rsc/. (Subscr. to: Turpin Distribution Services Ltd., Blackhorse Rd., Letchworth, Herts. SG6 1HN, England. TEL 44-1462-672555. FAX 44-1462-480947) Ed. R.A. Young. bibl.; charts; illus.; index. (also avail. in microfilm from UMI; reprint service avail. from UMI) **Indexed:** Abstr.Bull.Inst.Pap.Chem., AESIS, Agri.Eng.Abstr., Alloys Ind., Anal.Abstr., Apic.Abstr., ASCA, Biodet.Abstr., Biol.Abstr., Biotech.Abstr., Br.Ceram.Abstr., C.I.S. Abstr., Cadscan, Chem.Abstr., Chem.Cit.Ind., Dairy Sci.Abstr., Eng.Mat.Abstr., Excerp.Med., Food Sci.& Tech.Abstr., Geo.Abstr., GeoRef., Ind.Vet., INIS Atomind., Lab.Haz.Bull., Lead Abstr., Mass Spectr.Bull., Mat.Sci.Cit.Ind., Met.Abstr., Met.Abstr.Ind., Nonfer.Met.Alert, PCC Alert, Soils & Fert., Steels Alert, Vet.Bull., W.R.C.Inf., Weed Abstr., World Alum.Abstr., World Surf.Coat., Zincscan. **Document type:** academic/scholarly publication.
●Also available online.
—BLDSC (0897.030200); CASDDS; CISTI; Genuine Article; Linda Hall; SWETS; UMI; UnCover. **CCC.**
  Formerly (until 1996): Analytical Proceedings (ISSN 0144-557X); Which superseded (in Jan. 1981): Chemical Society. Analytical Division. Proceedings (ISSN 0306-1396); Which was formerly: Society for Analytical Chemistry. Proceedings (ISSN 0037-9697)
Refereed Serial

ANALYTICAL INSTRUMENT INDUSTRY REPORT. see INSTRUMENTS

543   US   ISSN 0003-2719
CODEN: ANALBP
ANALYTICAL LETTERS. 1967. 15/yr. $1995 (foreign $2051.25) (effective 1998). Marcel Dekker Journals, 270 Madison Ave., New York, NY 10016. TEL 212-696-9000. FAX 212-685-4540. TELEX 421419. (Subscr. to: Box 5017, Monticello, NY 12701) Ed. G.G. Guilbault. R&P contact: Julia Mulligan. adv.: B&W page $610, color page $1335 adv. contact: Lourdes Barroso. abstr. (also avail. in microform from RPI) **Indexed:** Alloys Ind., Alloys Ind. Anal.Abstr., Apic.Abstr., ASCA, Biol.Abstr., Cadscan, Chem.Abstr., Chem.Cit.Ind., Curr.Adv.Ecol.Sci., Curr.Cont., Dairy Sci.Abstr., Deep Sea Res.& Oceanogr.Abstr., Eng.Mat.Abstr., Excerp.Med., Food Sci.& Tech.Abstr., GeoRef., INIS Atomind., Lead Abstr., Mass Spectr.Bull., Mat.Sci.Cit.Ind., Met.Abstr.Ind., Met.Abstr., Nonfer.Met.Alert, Nutr.Abstr., PCC Alert, Rev.Med.& Vet.Mycol., Sci.Cit.Ind., Sel.Water Res.Abstr., Steels Alert, W.R.C.Inf., Weed Abstr., World Alum.Abstr., Zincscan. **Document type:** academic/scholarly publication.
—BLDSC (0897.100000); CASDDS; CISTI; Ei; Genuine Article; Linda Hall; SWETS; UMI; UnCover. **CCC.**
  Supersedes in part: Analytical Letters.
Refereed Serial

543 NE ISSN 0926-4345
CODEN: ASLIE7
ANALYTICAL SPECTROSCOPY LIBRARY. (Text in English) 1987. irreg., vol.5, 1991. Elsevier Science B.V., Books Division, P.O. Box 211, 1000 AE Amsterdam, Netherlands. TEL 31-20-4853911.
FAX 31-20-4853705. TELEX 18582 ESPA NL.
E-mail: nlinfo-f@elsevier.nl; usinfo-f@elsevier.com; forinfo-kyf04035@niftyserve.or.jp; URL: http://www.elsevier.nl/. (Subscr. in the Americas to: Elsevier Science, Regional Sales Office, Box 945, New York, NY 10159-0945; Subscr. in Australasia and the Far East to: Elsevier Science (Singapore) Pte Ltd, No.1 Temasek Ave., No.17-01 Millenia Tower, Singapore 039192, Singapore; Subscr. in Japan to: Elsevier Science Japan, 9-15 Higashi-Azabu 1-chome, Minato-ku, Tokyo 106, Japan. TEL 212-989-5800) Ed.Bd. (back issues avail.) **Document type:** monographic series.
—BLDSC (0897.143700); CASDDS; KNAW. **CCC.**
Refereed Serial

ANNALES DE BIOCHIMIE CLINIQUE DU QUEBEC. see *MEDICAL SCIENCES — Experimental Medicine, Laboratory Technique*

ANNUAL BOOK OF A S T M STANDARDS. VOLUME 03.05. CHEMICAL ANALYSIS OF METALS; METAL BEARING ORES. see *ENGINEERING — Engineering Mechanics And Materials*

ANNUAL BOOK OF A S T M STANDARDS. VOLUME 14.01. ANALYTICAL METHODS - SPECTROSCOPY; CHROMATOGRAPHY; TEMPERATURE MEASUREMENT; COMPUTERIZED SYSTEMS. see *ENGINEERING — Engineering Mechanics And Materials*

643 US ISSN 0195-5373
QC454.A8 CODEN: ASPND7
ATOMIC SPECTROSCOPY. 1962. bi-m. $45 (effective 1997). Perkin - Elmer Corp., 761 Main Ave., Norwalk, CT 06859-0219. TEL 203-761-2532.
FAX 203-761-2892. (Subscr. to: Box 557, Florham Park, NJ 07932. Fax 201-822-9162) Ed. Anneliese Lust. R&P contact: Anneliese Lust. charts; illus.; index. circ. 3,500. (also avail. in microfilm from UMI; back issues avail.; reprint service avail. from UMI) **Indexed:** Abstr.Bull.Inst.Pap.Chem., AESIS, Alloys Ind., Anal.Abstr., ASCA, Br.Ceram.Abstr., Cadscan, Chem.Abstr., Chem.Cit.Ind., Curr.Cont., Dairy Sci.Abstr., Energy Info.Abstr., Eng.Mat.Abstr., Environ.Abstr., Excerp.Med., INSPEC (1980-), Lead Abstr., Mass Spectr.Bull., Met.Abstr., Met.Abstr.Ind., Nonfer.Met.Alert, Ocean.Abstr., PCC Alert, Pollut.Abstr., Sci.Cit.Ind., Sel.Water Res.Abstr., Steels Alert, W.R.C.Inf., World Alum.Abstr., World Surf.Coat., Zincscan. **Document type:** trade publication, academic/scholarly publication.
—BLDSC (1771.080000); AskIEEE; CASDDS; CISTI; Ei; Genuine Article; KR SourceOne; Linda Hall; SWETS; UMI; UnCover.
Supersedes (in 1980): Atomic Absorption Newsletter (ISSN 0044-9954)
Description: Disseminates information, new applications and analytical data in atomic absorption spectrophotometry and related disciplines.
Refereed Serial

547.3 574.191 US ISSN 1075-4261
QP519.9.S6 CODEN: BIOSFS
BIOSPECTROSCOPY; an international interdisciplinary journal. 1995. 7/yr. $225 (foreign $347.5) (effective 1998). John Wiley & Sons, Inc., Journals, 605 Third Ave., New York, NY 10158.
TEL 212-850-6645. FAX 212-850-6021. TELEX 12-7063. E-mail: subinfo@jwiley.com; URL: http://www.wiley.co.uk. (Overseas subscr. to: John Wiley & Sons Ltd., Baffins Ln., Chichester, W. Sussex PO19 1UD, England. TEL 44-1243-779777. FAX 44-1243-776128) Ed. Laurence A. Nafie. adv.: B&W page £640, color page £1515; trim 279 x 216; adv. contact: Roberta Frederick. circ. 850. (also avail. in microform from UMI; back issues avail.; reprint service avail.) **Indexed:** ASCA, Curr.Cont. **Document type:** academic/scholarly publication.
—BLDSC (2089.616700); CASDDS; CISTI; Genuine Article. **CCC.**
Description: Provides a forum for molecular spectroscopists and researchers. Emphasizes the benefits of applying molecular spectroscopy to biomolecular problems.
Refereed Serial

543 JA ISSN 0525-1931
QD71 CODEN: BNSKAK
BUNSEKI KAGAKU. (Text in Japanese; summaries in English) 1952. m. $229. Japan Society for Analytical Chemistry - Nihon Bunseki Kagaku Kai, Gotanda Sanhaitsu, 26-2, Nishigotanda 1-chome, Shinagawa-ku, Tokyo 141, Japan.
TEL 81-3-3490-3351. FAX 81-3-3490-3572. (Dist. by: Japan Publications Trading Co., 2-1, Saruguku-cho 1-chome, Chiyoda-ku, Tokyo, Japan) Ed. Yoshimasa Nihei. adv. circ. 4,400. (also avail. in microfiche; back issues avail.) **Indexed:** Anal.Abstr., Anal.Abstr., Art & Archaeol.Tech.Abstr., Arts & Hum.Cit.Ind., ASCA, Cadscan, Chem.Abstr., Chem.Cit.Ind., Curr.Cont., Food Sci.& Tech.Abstr., Ind.Sci.Rev., INIS Atomind., JTA, Lead Abstr., Mass Spectr.Bull., Mat.Sci.Cit.Ind., Nutr.Abstr., Sci.Cit.Ind., Soils & Fert., Sugar Ind.Abstr., Weed Abstr., Zincscan. **Document type:** academic/scholarly publication.
—BLDSC (2930.600000); CASDDS; CISTI; Ei; Genuine Article; Linda Hall; SWETS. **CCC.**

544 JA
CODEN: CACFEJ
C A C S FORUM. (Text in Japanese) 1981. a. Saitama University, Chemical Analysis Center - Saitama Daigaku Bunseki Senta, 255, Shimookubo, Urawa-shi, Saitama-ken 338, Japan. **Indexed:** Chem.Abstr.

358 US ISSN 0899-7047
C M L ARMY CHEMICAL REVIEW. 1985. s-a. $5 (foreign $6.25) (effective Summer 1997). U.S. Army, Chemical Corps, U.S. Army Chemical School, Ft. McClellan, AL 36205. TEL 205-848-5725.
FAX 205-848-5058. E-mail: helmg@mcclellan-cmls.army.mil. (Subscr. to: Superintendent of Documents, U.S. Government Printing Office, Box 371954, Pittsburgh, PA 15250-7954. TEL 202-512-1800. FAX 202-512-2250) Ed. Gloria Helm. circ. 8,600. **Document type:** government publication.

543 US
C P A C MONITOR. 1983. 2/yr. Center for Process Analytical Chemistry, Box 351700, University of Washington, Seattle, WA 98195-1700.
TEL 206-685-2326. FAX 206-543-6506. URL: http://www.cpac.washington.edu. Ed. Betsy McGrath. pat.; tr.lit.; circ. 1,800 (controlled). (tabloid format; back issues avail.) **Document type:** newsletter.
Description: Covers general research topics currently pursued at the center; upcoming conferences; science articles highlighting new technology advances.

CANADIAN JOURNAL OF ANALYTICAL SCIENCES AND SPECTROSCOPY. see *PHYSICS — Optics*

CERAMICS. see *CHEMISTRY — Physical Chemistry*

543 PL ISSN 0009-2223
CODEN: CANWAJE
CHEMIA ANALITYCZNA. (Text in English; summaries in English and Polish) 1956. bi-m. 180 Zl. (foreign $108) (effective 1998). (Polska Akademia Nauk, Komitet Chemii Analitycznej - Polish Academy of Sciences, Committee on Analytical Chemistry) Instytut Chemii Fizycznej - Institute of Physical Chemistry, Ul. Kasprzaka 44-52, 01-224 Warsaw, Poland. TEL 48-22-222393. FAX 48-22-225996.
E-mail: Ahulan@chem.uw.edu.pl. Ed. Adam Hulanicki. R&P contact: Adam Hulanicki. adv. contact: Alicja Jedlewska. bk.rev.; bibl.; charts; illus.; index. circ. 300. **Indexed:** Anal.Abstr., ASCA, Cadscan, Chem.Abstr., Chem.Cit.Ind., Curr.Cont., Dairy Sci.Abstr., Food Sci.& Tech.Abstr., Fuel & Energy Abstr., Ind.Sci.Rev., INIS Atomind., Lead Abstr., Mass Spectr.Bull., Nutr.Abstr., Sci.Cit.Ind, Zincscan. **Document type:** academic/scholarly publication.
—BLDSC (3133.700000); CASDDS; CISTI; Ei; Genuine Article; Linda Hall.
Description: Publishes original research papers, short communications, laboratory notes, reviews.
Refereed Serial

543 US ISSN 0069-2883
CODEN: CAMCBN
CHEMICAL ANALYSIS; a series of monographs on analytical chemistry and its applications. 1953. irreg. price varies. John Wiley & Sons, Inc., 605 Third Ave., New York, NY 10158-0012.
TEL 212-850-6000. FAX 212-850-6088. TELEX 12-7063. Eds. P.J. Elving, J.D. Winefordner. index. **Indexed:** Biol.Abstr., Chem.Abstr., GeoRef. **Document type:** monographic series.
—BLDSC (3137.500000); CASDDS; CISTI; Ei; SWETS.
Refereed Serial

542 US ISSN 1049-1015
CHEMICAL MONITOR. 1985. m. $95 (foreign $110). Desktop Publishing, Box 314, Lindenhurst, NY 11757-0314. TEL 516-669-8147. Ed. Angelo Tulumello. (tabloid format; back issues avail.) **Document type:** newsletter.
●Also available online. Vendor(s): Data-Star, Information Access Co., Knight-Ridder Information, Inc., NewsNet (CH15).
Description: Covers developments that influence changes in the field of chemical instrumentation.

643 GW
CODEN: CHLBAT
CHEMIE IN LABOR UND BIOTECHNIK. (Includes supplement: C L B Memory (ISSN 0179-9389)) 1949. m. DM.132.60 (students DM.108.72) (effective 1997). Umschau Zeitschriftenverlag Breidenstein GmbH, Stuttgarter Str. 18-24, 60329 Frankfurt a.M., Germany. TEL 49-69-2600-0.
FAX 49-69-2600609. Ed. E. Guggolz. adv.: B&W page DM.5285, color page DM.8420; trim 176 x 257; adv. contact: Eckard von der Luehe. bk.rev.; abstr.; charts; illus.; stat.; index. circ. 5,863. **Indexed:** C.I.S. Abstr., Chem.Abstr., Excerp.Med., INIS Atomind. **Document type:** academic/scholarly publication.
—BLDSC (3157.160000); CASDDS; CISTI; SWETS. **CCC.**
Former titles: C L B Chemie fuer Labor und Betrieb (ISSN 0722-6764); (until 1982): Chemie fuer Labor und Betrieb (ISSN 0009-2835)

CHEMOMETRICS AND INTELLIGENT LABORATORY SYSTEMS. see *CHEMISTRY — Computer Applications*

544.92 UK ISSN 0009-5893
CODEN: CHRGB7
CHROMATOGRAPHIA; an international journal for rapid communication in chromatography and associated techniques. (Text in English; summaries in English, French and German) 1968. 25/yr. fl.1660($954) (effective 1998). Elsevier Science Ltd., Pergamon, P.O. Box 800, Kidlington, Oxford OX5 1DX, Germany. TEL 44-1865-843000.
FAX 44-1865-843010. E-mail: nlinfo@elsevier.nl; usinf-f@elsevier.com; URL: http://www.elsevier.nl/. (Subscr. to: Elsevier Science, Regional Sales Office, P.O. Box 211, 1000 AE Amsterdam, Netherlands. TEL 31-20-4853757. FAX 31-20-4853432; Subscr. in the Americas to: Elsevier Science, Regional Sales Office, Box 945, New York, NY 10159-0945. TEL 212-633-3730. FAX 212-633-3680; Subscr. in Australasia and the Far East to: Elsevier Science (Singapore) Pte Ltd, No.1 Temasek Ave., No.17-01 Millenia Tower, Singapore 039192, Singapore. TEL 65-434-3727. FAX 65-337-2230) (Co-publisher: Friedr. Vieweg und Sohn Verlagsgesellschaft mbH, GW) Ed.Bd. adv.; bk.rev.; charts; illus.; index. circ. 2,000. (also avail. in microfilm from UMI) **Indexed:** Anal.Abstr., ASCA, Biodet.Abstr., Biol.Abstr., C.I.S. Abstr., Cadscan, Chem.Abstr., Chem.Cit.Ind., Curr.Cont., Dairy Sci.Abstr., Deep Sea Res.& Oceanogr.Abstr., Excerp.Med., Food Sci.& Tech.Abstr., GeoRef., Ind.Sci.Rev., Ind.Vet., INIS Atomind., Lead Abstr., Mass Spectr.Bull., Mat.Sci.Cit.Ind., Rev.Med.& Vet.Mycol., Sci.Cit.Ind., Sel.Water Res.Abstr., Sugar Ind.Abstr., Vet.Bull., VITIS, W.R.C.Inf., Weed Abstr., Zincscan. **Document type:** academic/scholarly publication.
—BLDSC (3182.450000); ADONIS; CASDDS; CISTI; EMDOCS; Genuine Article; Linda Hall; SWETS; UnCover. **CCC.**
Refereed Serial

CHEMISTRY — ANALYTICAL CHEMISTRY

543 US ISSN 0069-3936
CODEN: CHGSAL
CHROMATOGRAPHIC SCIENCE SERIES. 1965. irreg., vol.74, 1996. price varies. Marcel Dekker, Inc., 270 Madison Ave., New York, NY 10016. TEL 212-696-9000. FAX 212-685-4540. TELEX 421419. Ed. J.C. Giddings; Pub. Graham Garratt. R&P contact: Julia Mulligan. **Indexed:** Chem.Abstr. **Document type:** monographic series.
—CASDDS; CISTI; KNAW. **CCC.**
Refereed Serial

543 NE ISSN 0166-526X
COMPREHENSIVE ANALYTICAL CHEMISTRY. 1959. irreg., vol.27, 1992. price varies. Elsevier Science B.V., Books Division, P.O. Box 211, 1000 AE Amsterdam, Netherlands. TEL 31-20-4853911. FAX 31-20-4853705. TELEX 18582 ESPA NL. E-mail: nlinfo-f@elsevier.nl; usinfo-f@elsevier.com; forinfo-kyf04035@niftyserve.or.jp; URL: http://www.elsevier.nl/. (Subscr. in the Americas to: Elsevier Science, Regional Sales Office, Box 945, New York, NY 10159-0945. TEL 212-633-3730. FAX 212-633-3680; Subscr. in Australasia and the Far East to: Elsevier Science (Singapore) Pte Ltd, No.1 Temasek Ave., No.17-01 Millenia Tower, Singapore 039192, Singapore. TEL 65-434-3727. FAX 65-337-2230; Subscr. in Japan to: Elsevier Science Japan, 9-15 Higashi-Azabu 1-chome, Minato-ku, Tokyo 106, Japan. TEL 81-3-5561-5033. FAX 81-3-5561-5047) Ed. G. Svehla. (back issues avail.) **Document type:** monographic series.
—BLDSC (3366.240000); CISTI; SWETS.
Formerly: Wilson and Wilson's Comprehensive Analytical Chemistry (ISSN 0069-8024)
Refereed Serial

543 US ISSN 1040-8347
QD71 CODEN: CCACBB
CRITICAL REVIEWS IN ANALYTICAL CHEMISTRY. 1970. q. $375 (effective 1998). C R C Press, Inc., 2000 Corporate Blvd., N.W., Boca Raton, FL 33431. TEL 561-994-0555; 800-272-7737. FAX 561-998-9784. TELEX 568689-CRC PRESS. E-mail: clochmul@chem.duke.edu; URL: http://www.crcpress.com/jour/crac/crac.htm. Ed. Charles H. Lochmueller. bibl.; charts; illus. circ. 590. (back issues avail.) **Indexed:** Anal.Abstr., ASCA, Biol.Abstr., Chem.Abstr., Chem.Cit.Ind., Curr.Cont., Ind.Sci.Rev., Mass Spectr.Bull., Sci.Cit.Ind., Soils & Fert. **Document type:** academic/scholarly publication.
●Also available online.
—BLDSC (3487.470000); CASDDS; CISTI; Ei; Genuine Article; Linda Hall; SWETS; UnCover. **CCC.**
Formerly: C R C Critical Reviews in Analytical Chemistry (ISSN 0007-8980)
Description: Provides scholarly reviews of topics within the vast discipline of analytical chemistry.
Refereed Serial

542 GW ISSN 0070-315X
CODEN: DMDGAG
DECHEMA MONOGRAPHIEN. irreg., vol.121, 1990. price varies. (Deutsche Gesellschaft fuer Chemisches Apparatewesen e.V. - DECHEMA) V C H Verlagsgesellschaft mbH, Postfach 101161, 69451 Weinheim, Germany. TEL 06201-606-0. FAX 06201-606328. TELEX 465516-VCHWH-D. (U.S. addr.: V C H Publishers Inc., 220 E. 23rd St., New York, NY, 10010-4606. TEL 212-683-8333) index. (reprint service avail. from ISI) **Indexed:** Chem.Abstr., Dairy Sci.Abstr., Food Sci.& Tech.Abstr. **Document type:** monographic series.
—BLDSC (3535.995000); CASDDS; CISTI; Linda Hall. **CCC.**

643 MX
DICCIONARIO DE ESPECIALIDADES EN ANALISIS CLINICOS. 1985. a. Ediciones P L M, S.A. de C.V., San Bernadino 17, Col. del Valle, 03100 Mexico, D.F., Mexico. TEL 687-1766. FAX 536-5027. Ed. Patricia Calderon. circ. 5,000.

643 615.19 JA ISSN 0385-1516
CODEN: DONED9
DOJIN NYUSU/DOJIN NEWS. (Text in Japanese; summaries and captions in English) 1976. 6/yr. free. Dojindo Laboratories, Kumamoto Techno Research Park, Tabaru 2025-5, Mashiki-machi, Kamimashiki-gun, Kumamoto-ken 861-22, Japan. TEL 81-96-286-1515. FAX 81-96-286-1525. E-mail: info@dojindo.co.jp; order@dojindo.co.jp; URL: http://www.dojindo.co.jp. **Indexed:** Biol.Abstr., Chem.Abstr. **Document type:** newsletter.
—CASDDS.
Description: Covers topics in chemistry and their applications in pharmacology.

643 615.19 JA ISSN 0919-9322
DONJINDO NEWSLETTER. (Text in English) 1992. 3/yr. free. Dojindo Laboratories, Kumamoto Techno Research Park, Tabaru 2025-5, Mashiki-machi, Kamimashiki-gun, Kumamoto-ken 861-22, Japan. TEL 096-286-1515. FAX 096-286-1525. E-mail: info@dojindo.co.jp; order@dojindo.co.jp; URL: http://www.dojindo.co.jp. Ed. Meiko Sato. R&P contact: Mikihiko Saito. adv. contact: Ken'yu Kina. **Document type:** newsletter.
Description: Covers topics in chemistry and their application in pharmacology.

DRUG AND ALCOHOL TESTING; advising the employer. see *LAW*

643 GW ISSN 1040-0397
QD115 CODEN: ELANEU
ELECTROANALYSIS. (Text in English) 1989. 18/yr. DM.295 (foreign DM.331) to individuals; institutions DM.1395 (foreign DM.1485) (effective 1997). Wiley - V C H, Postfach 101161, 69451 Weinheim, Germany. TEL 49-6201-606147. FAX 49-6201-606-117. TELEX 465516-VCHWH-D. E-mail: cs-journals@vchgroup.de; URL: http://www.vchgroup.de. (Subscr. in the Americas to: John Wiley & Sons, Inc., 605 Third Ave., New York, NY 10158. TEL 212-850-6645. FAX 212-850-6021) Ed. J. Wang. adv. contact: R. Roth. (also avail. in microfilm from VCI) **Indexed:** ASCA, Chem.Cit.Ind., Curr.Cont., Ind.Sci.Rev., Mat.Sci.Cit.Ind. **Document type:** academic/scholarly publication.
—BLDSC (3698.789000); CASDDS; CISTI; Ei; Genuine Article; Linda Hall; SWETS; UnCover. **CCC.**
Description: Covers all branches of electroanalytical chemistry.

543 US ISSN 0070-9778
QD115 CODEN: ELCHAI
ELECTROANALYTICAL CHEMISTRY: A SERIES OF ADVANCES. (Subseries of Monographs in Electroanalytical Chemistry and Electrochemistry) 1966. irreg., vol.19, 1996. price varies. Marcel Dekker, Inc., 270 Madison Ave., New York, NY 10016. TEL 212-696-9000. FAX 212-685-4540. TELEX 421419. Ed. A.J. Bard; Pub. Graham Garratt. R&P contact: Julia Mulligan. **Indexed:** ASCA, Ind.Sci.Rev., Sci.Cit.Ind. **Document type:** monographic series.
—BLDSC (3698.795000); CASDDS; CISTI; Linda Hall. **CCC.**
Refereed Serial

544 UK ISSN 1082-4928
CODEN: EJTCFB
▼**ELECTRONIC JOURNAL OF THEORETICAL CHEMISTRY.** (Not avail. in printed format) 1996. irreg. (1 vol./yr.) $300 includes CD-ROM cumulation (effective 1997). John Wiley & Sons Ltd., Journals, Baffins Ln., Chichester, W. Sussex PO19 1UD, England. TEL 44-1243-779777. FAX 44-1243-843232. E-mail: cs-journals@wiley.co.uk; URL: http://www.wiley.co.uk. (Subscr. in the Americas to: John Wiley & Sons, Inc., 605 Third Ave., New York, NY 10158. TEL 212-850-6645. FAX 212-850-6021) Ed. Alan Hinchliffe. **Document type:** academic/scholarly publication.
●Also available online.
Also available on CD-ROM.
—**CCC.**
Description: Publishes theoretical studies of large molecular systems and their interactions. Publishes on an article by article basis.

545 539 UK ISSN 1356-1049
CODEN: EMSPFW
▼**EUROPEAN MASS SPECTROSCOPY;** the international journal in molecular science. 1995. bi-m. £270 to Europe; rest of world $485 (effective 1997). I M Publications, 6 Charlton Mill, Charlton, Chichester, W. Sussex PO18 OHY, England. TEL 44-1243-811334. FAX 44-1243-811711. E-mail: 100136.1577@compuserve.com; ian-michael@impub.demon.co.uk. Ed. P.J. Derrick. **Indexed:** Curr.Cont. **Document type:** academic/scholarly publication.
—BLDSC (3829.760310); CASDDS; CISTI; Genuine Article; SWETS.
Description: Disseminates original research concerned with the mass spectrometry of atomic and molecular species.
Refereed Serial

EXPERIMENTAL AND MOLECULAR PATHOLOGY. see *MEDICAL SCIENCES*

643 CC ISSN 0253-3820
QD71 CODEN: FHHHDT
FENXI HUAXUE/CHINESE JOURNAL OF ANALYTICAL CHEMISTRY. (Text in Chinese; abstracts in English) 1972. m. Y108($84) (effective 1997). Zhongguo Kexueyuan, Changchun Yingyong Huaxue Yanjiusuo - Chinese Academy of Sciences, Changchun Institute of Applied Chemistry, 159 Renmin Street, Changchun, Jilin 130022, People's Republic of China. TEL 86-431-5682801. FAX 86-431-5685653. TELEX 83063 CHIAC CN. (Dist. outside China by: China International Book Trading Corp., P.O. Box 399, Beijing, P.R.C.. TEL 86-10-8413063) (Co-sponsor: Chinese Chemical Society) Ed. Er-Kang Wang. adv.: page $750; adv. contact: Bao-Ning Wang. circ. 4,000. **Indexed:** Alloys Ind., Anal.Abstr., Chem.Abstr., Eng.Mat.Abstr., INIS Atomind., Met.Abstr., Met.Abstr.Ind., Nonfer.Met.Alert, PCC Alert, Steels Alert, World Alum.Abstr. **Document type:** academic/scholarly publication.
—BLDSC (3180.290800); CASDDS; Linda Hall.
Description: Provides the latest research results concerning all branches of analytical chemistry.

543 614.7 US ISSN 1086-900X
CODEN: FACTFR
▼**FIELD ANALYTICAL CHEMISTRY AND TECHNOLOGY.** 1996. bi-m. $224 (foreign $260) (effective 1998). John Wiley & Sons, Inc., 605 Third Ave., New York, NY 10158. TEL 212-850-6645. FAX 212-850-6021. (Subscr. outside the Americas to: John Wiley & Sons Ltd., Baffins Ln., Chichester, W. Sussex PO19 1UD, England. TEL 44-1243-779777. FAX 44-1243-775878) Ed. Henk Meuzelaar. adv.: B&W page £640, color page £1515. **Document type:** academic/scholarly publication.
—CASDDS.
Description: Dedicated to the publication of research and development work concerned with the application of analytical chemistry outside the conventional, fixed-site laboratory.

543 688.55 US ISSN 0887-736X
QD415.A1 CODEN: FCINEI
FOR FORMULATION CHEMISTS ONLY. Abbreviated title: 2 C O. 1989. a. $285. C I T A International (USA), Industrial Journals Division, 3464 W. Earll Dr., Ste. E-F, Phoenix, AZ 85017-5260. TEL 602-447-0480. FAX 602-447-0305. Ed. E.M. Morsy. adv.; bibl.; charts; illus.; index, cum.index. circ. 2,000. (back issues avail.) **Document type:** trade publication.
—CCC.
Incorporates (1988-1991): Acta Industria Chimic (ISSN 1042-2013); (1989-1991): Applied Esthetiques (ISSN 0896-5056); (1989-1991): C I T A Exam Reviews (ISSN 1042-8933); (1989-1991): Cosmetech (ISSN 0895-8718); (1988-1991): Health and Beauty Formulary (ISSN 0892-4643); And (1989-1991): Technitrivia (ISSN 0892-4651); (1982-1985): Erde Novus; Which was formerly: Erde International (ISSN 0735-2840)
Description: Covers applied research, raw materials, chemical and formulation technology for technicians in the chemical specialty and consumer product industries.

CHEMISTRY — ANALYTICAL CHEMISTRY

643   GW   ISSN 0937-0633
QD71   CODEN: FJACES
FRESENIUS' JOURNAL OF ANALYTICAL CHEMISTRY.
Online edition (GW ISSN 1432-1130) (Text in English or German) 1862. 24/yr. DM.3387 (foreign DM.3445.80) (effective 1998). (Gesellschaft Deutscher Chemiker, Fachgruppe Analytische Chemie) Springer-Verlag, Heidelberger Platz 3, 14197 Berlin, Germany. TEL 49-30-82787-0. FAX 49-30-82787448. E-mail: subscriptions@springer.de; URL: http://link.springer.de. (Subscr. in N. America to: Springer-Verlag New York, Inc., 333 Meadowlands Pkwy., Secaucus, NJ 07094. TEL 212-460-1500. FAX 212-473-6272) Eds. W. Fresenius, I. Luederwald. adv.; bk.rev.; abstr.; bibl.; charts; index, cum.index. (also avail. in microform from UMI,PMC; back issues avail.; reprint service avail. from ISI) **Indexed:** Alloys Ind., Anal.Abstr., Apic.Abstr., Art & Archaeol.Tech.Abstr., ASCA, Biotech.Abstr., Chem.Cit.Ind., Compumath, Curr.Adv.Ecol.Sci., Curr.Cont., Eng.Mat.Abstr., Excerp.Med., Field Crop Abstr., Food Sci.& Tech.Abstr., Hort.Abstr., I.M.M.Abstr., Ind.Sci.Rev., INIS Atomind., Mass Spectr.Bull., Mat.Sci.Cit.Ind., Met.Abstr.Ind., Met.Abstr., Nonfer.Met.Alert, Nutr.Abstr., Ocean.Abstr., PCC Alert, Pollut.Abstr., Sci.Cit.Ind., Sel.Water Res.Abstr., Soils & Fert., SSCI, Steels Alert, Sugar Ind.Abstr., Triticale Abstr., VITIS, W.R.C.Inf., Weed Abstr., World Alum.Abstr. **Document type:** academic/scholarly publication.
●Also available online.
—BLDSC (4036.380000); ADONIS; AskIEEE; CASDDS; CISTI; Ei; Genuine Article; KR SourceOne; Linda Hall; SWETS; UMI; UnCover. **CCC.**
Formerly: Fresenius' Zeitschrift fuer Analytische Chemie (ISSN 0016-1152)
Description: Original articles and short communications on new results from all fields of analytical chemistry.

FURO INJEKUSHON BUNSEKI KOENKAI KOEN YOSHISHU/ABSTRACTS OF MEETING ON FLOW INJECTION ANALYSIS. see CHEMISTRY — Abstracting, Bibliographies, Statistics

544.92   GW
G I T SPEZIAL CHROMOTAGRAPHIE. 2/yr. DM.38 (effective 1996). G I T Verlag GmbH, Roesslerstr. 90, 64293 Darmstadt, Germany. TEL 49-6151-8090-0. FAX 49-6151-8090144. E-mail: gitverlag@t-online.de; URL: http://www.gitverlag.com. Ed. Ernst Giebeler. adv.: B&W page DM.9230, color page DM.12545; trim 185 x 260; adv. contact: Walter Depner. circ. 25,000. **Document type:** trade publication.

544.92   US   ISSN 1046-039X
HIGH TECH SEPARATIONS NEWS. 1988. m. $375. Business Communications Co., Inc. (Norwalk), 25 Van Zant St., Ste. 13, Norwalk, CT 06855. TEL 203-853-4266. FAX 203-853-0348. TELEX 6502934929 WUI. Ed. Anna Crull.
●Also available online. Vendor(s): Data-Star, Information Access Co., Knight-Ridder Information, Inc., NewsNet (BT04).
Description: Covers the fields of high-technology organic separations and biomolecular separations, including benchtop supercritical fluid chromatography, large-scale commercial gel chromatography, affinity technologies, and biosensors.

544   US
I U P A C HANDBOOK (YEAR). irreg. (International Union of Pure and Applied Chemistry) C R C Press, Inc., 2000 Corporate Blvd., N.W., Boca Raton, FL 33431. TEL 561-994-0555; 800-272-7737. FAX 561-998-9784. TELEX 568689-CRC PRESS. **Document type:** academic/scholarly publication.

543   US   ISSN 1073-9149
QD53   CODEN: ISCTEF
INSTRUMENTATION SCIENCE & TECHNOLOGY. 1968. q. $595 (foreign $613.75) (effective 1998). Marcel Dekker Journals, 270 Madison Ave., New York, NY 10016. TEL 212-696-9000. FAX 212-685-4540. TELEX 421419. (Subscr. to: Marcel Dekker Journals, Box 5017, Monticello, NY 12701) Ed. Jack Cazes. adv. contact: Eridania Perez. bk.rev.; bibl.; charts; illus. (also avail. in microform from RPI) **Indexed:** Abstr.Bull.Inst.Pap.Chem., Anal.Abstr., ASCA, Biol.Abstr., Chem.Abstr., Chem.Cit.Ind., Curr.Cont., Excerp.Med., INIS Atomind., INSPEC (1984-), Int.Sci.Rev., Mass Spectr.Bull., Sci.Cit.Ind. **Document type:** academic/scholarly publication.
—BLDSC (4529.043800); AskIEEE; CASDDS; CISTI; Ei; Genuine Article; KR SourceOne; Linda Hall; SWETS; UMI; UnCover. **CCC.**
Former titles (until 1994): Analytical Instrumentation (ISSN 0743-5797); (until 1984): Chemical, Biomedical and Environmental Instrumentation (ISSN 0190-4094); Chemical Instrumentation (ISSN 0009-2592)
Refereed Serial

544   NE   ISSN 1068-0659
CODEN: IJOBEQ
INTERNATIONAL JOURNAL OF BIOCHROMATOGRAPHY. 1994. 4/yr. $117 (effective 1998). Gordon and Breach - Harwood Academic, Amsteldisk 166, 1st Fl., 1079 LH Amsterdam, Netherlands. (Subscr. to: International Publishers Distributor, Box 32160, Newark, NJ 07102. TEL 800-545-8398. FAX 215-750-6343) Ed. Jean-Pierre Dandeu. (back issues avail.) **Indexed:** Excerp.med. (1996-), Food Sci.& Tech.Abstr. **Document type:** academic/scholarly publication.
—BLDSC (4542.140000); CASDDS; EMDOCS.
Description: Provides an international forum on research and applications concerning the separation and purification of biomolecules to better know their structure.

543 614.7   NE   ISSN 0306-7319
QD71   CODEN: IJEAA3
INTERNATIONAL JOURNAL OF ENVIRONMENTAL ANALYTICAL CHEMISTRY. 1972. 16/yr. (in 4 vols., 4 nos./vol.). $386 (effective 1998). Gordon and Breach - Harwood Academic, Amsteldisk 166, 1st Fl., 1079 LH Amsterdam, Netherlands. URL: http://www.gbhap.com/Environmental__Analytical__Chemistry/. (Subscr. to: International Publishers Distributor, Box 32160, Newark, NJ 07102. TEL 800-545-8398. FAX 215-750-6343) Ed. J. Albaiges. adv.; bk.rev.; bibl.; charts; index. (also avail. in microform) **Indexed:** Acid Rain Abstr., Anal.Abstr., Apic.Abstr., ASCA, Biol.Abstr., Cadscan, Chem.Abstr., Chem.Cit.Ind., Crop Physiol.Abstr., Curr.Adv.Ecol.Sci., Curr.Cont., Dairy Sci.Abstr., Dok.Arbeitsmed., Energy Ind., Energy Info.Abstr., Environ.Abstr., Environ.Per.Bibl. (1991-), Excerp.Med., Field Crop Abstr., Food Sci.& Tech.Abstr., Forest.Abstr., Forest Prod.Abstr., Geo.Abstr., Hort.Abstr., Ind.Med., Ind.Sci.Rev., Irr.& Drain.Abstr., Lab.Haz.Bull., Lead Abstr., Mass Spectr.Bull., Ocean.Abstr., Pollut.Abstr., Risk Abstr., Sci.Cit.Ind., Sel.Water Res.Abstr., Soils & Fert., Soyabean Abstr., W.R.C.Inf., Weed Abstr., Zincscan. **Document type:** academic/scholarly publication.
●Also available online.
Also available on CD-ROM.
—BLDSC (4542.241000); CASDDS; CISTI; EMDOCS; SWETS; UnCover. **CCC.**
Refereed Serial

INTERNATIONAL JOURNAL OF P I X E. see PHYSICS — Nuclear Physics

INTERNATIONAL JOURNAL OF POLYMER ANALYSIS & CHARACTERIZATION. see ENGINEERING — Chemical Engineering

643   US   ISSN 0010-2164
CODEN: ILBYA6
INTERNATIONAL LABORATORY. (Buyers Guide avail.) 1971. 9/yr. £150 (outside Europe £165). International Scientific Communications, Inc., 30 Controls Dr., Box 870, Shelton, CT 06484-0870. TEL 203-926-9300. FAX 203-926-9310. (U.K. subscr. to: I.S.C. House, Progress Business Centre, 5 Whittle Pkwy., Slough, Berks. SL1 60Q, England. TEL 55-1628-668881. FAX 44-1628-669199) Ed. Brian Howard. adv.; bk.rev.; charts; illus.; stat.; tr.lit.; circ. 52,503 (controlled). **Indexed:** Biol.Abstr., C.I.S.Abstr., Chem.Abstr., Curr.Cont., Excerp.Med., Intl.Polym.Sci.& Tech., Lab.Haz.Bull., Mass Spectr.Bull., Met.Abstr., RAPRA, World Surf.Coat., World Text.Abstr. **Document type:** trade publication.
—BLDSC (4542.705000); CASDDS; SWETS.

643   US
INTERNATIONAL LABORATORY. PACIFIC RIM EDITION. q. International Scientific Communications, Inc., 30 Controls Dr., Box 870, Shelton, CT 06484-0870. TEL 203-926-9300. (U.K. subscr. to: I.S.C. House, Progress Business Centre, 5 Whittle Pkwy., Slough, SL1 6DQ, England. TEL 44-1628-668881. FAX 44-1628-669199) **Document type:** trade publication.
Formerly: International Laboratory. Asian - Australian Edition (ISSN 0894-1661)

INTERNATIONAL LABORATORY BUYERS' GUIDE. see BIOLOGY — Biotechnology

543   US   ISSN 1027-3085
INTERNATIONAL SYMPOSIUM ON CAPILLARY CHROMATOGRAPHY AND ELECTROPHORESIS. PROCEEDINGS. 5th, 1968. irreg. Butterworth - Heinemann (Subsidiary of: Reed International PLC), 80 Montvale Ave., Stoneham, MA 02180. TEL 800-366-2665. FAX 617-438-1479.
Formerly: International Symposium on Chromatography and Electrophoresis. Proceedings (ISSN 0074-8781)

INTERNATIONAL SYMPOSIUM ON RAREFIED GAS DYNAMICS. PROCEEDINGS. see PHYSICS

643   NE   ISSN 1065-6081
QD272.C4   CODEN: IOPUEL
ISOLATION AND PURIFICATION. 1988. 4/yr. (in 1 vol.; 4 nos./vol.) $124 (effective 1998). Gordon and Breach - Harwood Academic, Amsteldisk 166, 1st Fl., 1079 LH Amsterdam, Netherlands. URL: http://www.gbhap.com/Isolation__Purification/. (Subscr. to: International Publishers Distributor, Box 32160, Newark, NJ 07102. TEL 800-545-8398. FAX 215-750-6343) Ed. Satinder Ahuja. (also avail. in microform) **Indexed:** Food Sci.& Tech.Abstr. **Document type:** academic/scholarly publication.
●Also available online.
Also available on CD-ROM.
—BLDSC (4583.290000); CASDDS; CISTI. **CCC.**
Formerly (until vol.2): Preparative Chromatography (ISSN 0890-9075)
Refereed Serial

CHEMISTRY — ANALYTICAL CHEMISTRY

643 UK ISSN 0267-9477
QD96.A8 CODEN: JASPE2
JOURNAL OF ANALYTICAL ATOMIC SPECTROMETRY. Online edition (UK ISSN 1364-5544) 1986. m. £657 (US $1183); diskette edition £108 (US $194); backfile (1986-1995) £308 (US $550) (effective 1997). The Royal Society of Chemistry, Thomas Graham House, Science Park, Milton Rd., Cambridge CB4 4WF, England. TEL 44-1223-420066. FAX 44 1223 423429. E-mail: sales@rsc.org; URL: http://chemistry.rsc.org/rsc/. (Dist. by: Turpin Distribution Services Ltd., Blackhorse Rd., Letchworth, Herts. SG6 1HN, England. TEL 44-1462-672555. FAX 44-1462-480947) adv.; bk.rev. **Indexed:** Alloys Ind., Arts & Hum.Cit.Ind., ASCA, Chem.Cit.Ind., Curr.Cont., Deep Sea Res.& Oceanogr.Abstr., Eng.Mat.Abstr., Excerp.Med., Food Sci.& Tech.Abstr., Forest.Abstr., Ind.Sci.Rev., INIS Atomind., Mat.Sci.Cit.Ind., Met.Abstr., Met.Abstr.Ind., Mineral.Abstr., Nonfer.Met.Alert, PCC Alert, Soils & Fert., Steels Alert, W.R.C.Inf., World Alum.Abstr. **Document type:** academic/scholarly publication.
●Also available online. Vendor(s): STN International (CJRSC).
—BLDSC (4928.200000); CASDDS; CISTI; Ei; Genuine Article; Linda Hall; SWETS; UMI; UnCover. **CCC.**
Incorporated (in 1985): Annual Reports on Analytical Atomic Spectroscopy (ISSN 0306-1353)
Description: Contains original research papers, short papers, communications and letters concerned with the development and analytical application of atomic spectrometric techniques.
Refereed Serial

543 RU ISSN 1061-9348
QD71 CODEN: JACTE2
JOURNAL OF ANALYTICAL CHEMISTRY. English translation of: Zhurnal Analiticheskoi Khimii (RU ISSN 0044-4502) 1952. m. $1765 in US; elsewhere $2065 (effective 1998). (Russian Academy of Sciences) Maik Nauka - Interperiodica, Mezhdunarodnyi Otdel, Ul. Profsoyuznaya, 90, 117864 Moscow, Russia. TEL 7-095-33600664. FAX 7-095-3360666. (Dist. by: Plenum Publishing Corp., 233 Spring St., New York, NY 10013-1578, U.S.A.) TEL 212-620-8468. FAX 212-463-0742) Ed. Yu.A. Zolotov. (also avail. in microfilm from UMI; back issues avail.) **Indexed:** ASCA, Cadscan, Chem.Abstr., Chem.Cit.Ind., Chem.Titles, Curr.Cont., Excerp.Med., Ind.Sci.Rev., INIS Atomind., Lead Abstr., Mass Spectr.Bull., Mat.Sci.Cit.Ind., Rev.Med.& Vet.Mycol., Soils & Fert., W.R.C.Inf., Weed Abstr., Zincscan. **Document type:** academic/scholarly publication.
—BLDSC (0412.990000); CASDDS; CISTI; Genuine Article; Linda Hall; SWETS; UMI; UnCover. **CCC.**
Formerly (until 1993): Journal of Analytical Chemistry of the U S S R (ISSN 0021-8766)
Refereed Serial

JOURNAL OF APPLIED SPECTROSCOPY. see *PHYSICS — Optics*

JOURNAL OF BIOLUMINESCENCE AND CHEMILUMINESCENCE. see *CHEMISTRY — Physical Chemistry*

543 UK ISSN 0886-9383
QD39.3.M3 CODEN: JOCHEU
JOURNAL OF CHEMOMETRICS. 1987. bi-m. $745 (foreign $745) (effective 1998). John Wiley & Sons Ltd., Journals, Baffins Ln., Chichester, W. Sussex PO19 1UD, England. TEL 44-1243-779777. FAX 44-1243-775878. E-mail: info-assets@wiley.co.uk; URL: http://www.wiley.co.uk. (Subscr. to the Americas to: John Wiley & Sons, Inc., 605 Third Ave., New York, NY 10158. TEL 212-850-6645. FAX 212-850-6021) Ed. S.D. Brown. adv.: B&W page £595, color page £1495; trim 260 x 200; adv. contact: Bob Kern. bk.rev. circ. 312. (also avail. in microform from UMI; back issues avail.; reprint service avail. from SWZ) **Indexed:** ASCA, Chem.Abstr., Chem.Cit.Ind., Curr.Cont., Food Sci.& Tech.Abstr., Ind.Sci.Rev., INSPEC, Mass Spectr.Bull., Stat.Theor.Meth.Abstr. **Document type:** academic/scholarly publication.
—BLDSC (4957.380000); ADONIS; CASDDS; CISTI; Ei; EMDOCS; Genuine Article; Linda Hall; SWETS; UMI; UnCover. **CCC.**
Description: Contains papers on fundamental and applied aspects of chemometrics and provides a forum for the exchange of information on meetings, and such for the international chemometrics research community.
Refereed Serial

544.92 US ISSN 0021-9665
QD271 CODEN: JCHSBZ
JOURNAL OF CHROMATOGRAPHIC SCIENCE. Includes annual: International Chromatography Guide. 1963. m. $200. Preston Publications, Inc., 7800 Merrimac Ave., Box 48312, Niles, IL 60714. TEL 847-965-0566. FAX 847-965-7639. Eds. B.M. Gordon, J.Q. Walker; Pub. S. Tinsley Preston. R&P contact: Larry Hooper. adv.; bk.rev.; charts; illus.; index. circ. 2,775. (also avail. in microfilm from MML; microfiche; back issues avail.) **Indexed:** Abstr.Bull.Inst.Pap.Chem., Abstr.Hyg., AESIS, Anal.Abstr., API Abstr., API Catal., API Hlth.& Environ., API Oil., API Pet.Ref., API Pet.Subst., API Transport., ASCA, Biol.Abstr., Biotech.Abstr., Chem.Abstr., Chem.Cit.Ind., Curr.Cont., Dairy Sci.Abstr., Deep Sea Res.& Oceanogr.Abstr., Excerp.Med. (until 1993), Food Sci.& Tech.Abstr., Fuel & Energy Abstr., Gas Abstr., GeoRef., Hort.Abstr., Ind.Med., Ind.Sci.Rev., Ind.Vet., INIS Atomind., Mass Spectr.Bull., Nutr.Abstr., Rev.Med.& Vet.Mycol., Sci.Cit.Ind., Sel.Water Res.Abstr., Soils & Fert., Trop.Dis.Bull., Vet.Bull., W.R.C.Inf., Weed Abstr., World Surf.Coat. **Document type:** academic/scholarly publication.
—BLDSC (4958.300000); CASDDS; CISTI; Ei; Genuine Article; KNAW; Linda Hall; SWETS; UnCover. **CCC.**
Formerly: Journal of Gas Chromatography (ISSN 0096-2686)

544.92 NE ISSN 0021-9673
QD271 CODEN: JOCRAM
JOURNAL OF CHROMATOGRAPHY; international journal on chromatography, electrophoresis and related methods. Variant title: Journal of Chromatography A. (Text in English, French, German; summaries in English) 1958. 72/yr. fl.14615($8399) (effective 1998). Elsevier Science B.V., P.O. Box 211, 1000 AE Amsterdam, Netherlands. TEL 31-20-4853911. FAX 31-20-4853598. TELEX 18582 ESPA NL. E-mail: nlinfo@elsevier.nl; usinfo-f@elsevier.com; forinfo-kyf04035@niftyserve.or.jp; URL: http://www.elsevier.nl/. (Subscr. in the Americas to: Elsevier Science, Regional Sales Office, Box 945, New York, NY 10159-0945. TEL 212-633-3730. FAX 212-633-3680; Subscr. in Australasia and the Far East to: Elsevier Science (Singapore) Pte Ltd, No.1 Temasek Ave., No.17-01 Millenia Tower, Singapore 039192, Singapore. TEL 65-434-3727. FAX 65-337-2230; Subscr. in Japan to: Elsevier Science Japan, 9-15 Higashi-Azabu 1-chome, Minato-ku, Tokyo 106, Japan. TEL 81-3-5561-5033. FAX 81-3-5561-5047) Ed.Bd. adv.; bk.rev.; bibl.; charts; illus.; index, cum.index. circ. 3,693. (also avail. in microform from UMI) **Indexed:** Abstr.Bull.Inst.Pap.Chem., Agroforest.Abstr., Anal.Abstr., Anal.Abstr., Anim.Breed.Abstr., Apic.Abstr., ASCA, Bibl.Agri., Biodet.Abstr., Biol.Abstr., Biotech.Abstr., Cadscan, Chem.Abstr., Chem.Cit.Ind., Chem.Titles, Curr.Leather Lit., Dairy Sci.Abstr., Deep Sea Res.& Oceanogr.Abstr., Dent.Ind., Environ.Per.Bibl, Excerp.Med., Fababean Abstr., Field Crop Abstr., Food Sci.& Tech.Abstr., Forest.Abstr., GeoRef., Herb.Abstr., Hort.Abstr., Ind.Med., Ind.Sci.Rev., Ind.Vet., Lead Abstr., Maize Abstr., Mass Spectr.Bull., Mat.Sci.Cit.Ind., Neurosci.Cit.Ind., Nutr.Abstr., Packag.Sci.Tech., Paper & Bd.Abstr., Pig News & Info., Plant Grow.Reg.Abstr., Potato Abstr., Poult.Abstr., Protozool.Abstr., Ref.Zh., Rev.Med.& Vet.Mycol., Rev.Plant Path., Sci.Cit.Ind., Seed Abstr., Sel.Water Res.Abstr., Soils & Fert., Soyabean Abstr., SSCI, SSCI, Sugar Ind.Abstr., THA, Triticale Abstr., Trop.Oil Seeds Abstr., Vet.Bull., VITIS, W.R.C.Inf., Weed Abstr., Zincscan. **Document type:** academic/scholarly publication.
—BLDSC (4958.350200); ADONIS; CASDDS; CISTI; Genuine Article; Linda Hall; SWETS; UnCover. **CCC.**
Incorporates: Chromatographic Reviews (ISSN 0009-5907); Supersedes (1956-1957): Chromatographic Methods (ISSN 0412-3425)
Description: Covers all aspects of chromatography, electrophoresis and related methods.
Refereed Serial

544.92 NE ISSN 0301-4770
QD271 CODEN: JCLIDR
JOURNAL OF CHROMATOGRAPHY LIBRARY. (Text in English) 1973. irreg., vol.55, 1993. price varies. Elsevier Science B.V., Books Division, P.O. Box 211, 1000 AE Amsterdam, Netherlands. TEL 31-20-4853911. FAX 31-20-4853705. TELEX 18582 ESPA NL. E-mail: nlinfo-f@elsevier.nl; usinfo-f@elsevier.com; forinfo kyf04035@niftyserve.or.jp; URL: http://www.elsevier.nl/. (Subscr. in the Americas to: Elsevier Science, Regional Sales Office, Box 945, New York, NY 10159-0945. TEL 212-633-3730. FAX 212-633-3680; Subscr. in Australasia and the Far East to: Elsevier Science (Singapore) Pte Ltd, No.1 Temasek Ave., No.17-01 Millenia Tower, Singapore 039192, Singapore. TEL 65-434-3727. FAX 65-337-2230; Subscr. in Japan to: Elsevier Science Japan, 9-15 Higashi-Azabu 1-chome, Minato-ku, Tokyo 106, Japan. TEL 81-3-5561-5033. FAX 81-3-5561-5047) **Indexed:** Biol.Abstr., Chem.Abstr. **Document type:** monographic series.
—BLDSC (4958.351000); CASDDS; CISTI; KNAW. **CCC.**
Refereed Serial

545.3 SZ CODEN: JECHES
QD551
JOURNAL OF ELECTROANALYTICAL CHEMISTRY; an international journal devoted to all aspects of electrode kinetics, interfacial structure, properties of electrolytes, colloid and biological electrochemistry. (Text in English) 1959. 40/yr. (in 20 vols.; 2 nos./vol.) fl.11772($6765) (effective 1998). Elsevier Science S.A., P.O. Box 564, CH-1001 Lausanne 1, Switzerland. TEL 41-21-3207381. FAX 41-21-3235444. TELEX 450620-ELSA-CH. (Subscr. to: Elsevier Science, Regional Sales Office, P.O. Box 211, 1000 AE Amsterdam, Netherlands. TEL 31-20-4853757. FAX 31-20-4853432; Subscr. in the Americas to: Elsevier Science, Regional Sales Office, Box 945, New York, NY 10159-0945. TEL 212-633-3730. FAX 212-633-3680; Subscr. in Australasia to: Elsevier Science (Singapore) Pte. Ltd., No. 1 Temasek Ave., No. 17-01 Millenia Tower, Singapore 039192, Singapore. TEL 65-434-3727. FAX 65-337-2230) Eds. R. Parsons, W.R. Fawcett. adv.; illus.; index. (also avail. in microform from UMI; back issues avail.) **Indexed:** Alloys Ind., Anal.Abstr., ASCA, Cadscan, Chem.Abstr., Chem.Cit.Ind., Curr.Cont., Eng.Ind., Eng.Mat.Abstr., Excerp.Med., Fuel & Energy Abstr., Ind.Sci.Rev., INSPEC, Int.Aerosp.Abstr., Lead Abstr., Mat.Sci.Cit.Ind., Met.Abstr.Ind., Met.Abstr., Nonfer.Met.Alert, PCC Alert, Risk Abstr., Sci.Cit.Ind., Steels Alert, World Alum.Abstr., Zincscan. **Document type:** academic/scholarly publication.
—BLDSC (4974.700000); ADONIS; AskIEEE; CASDDS; CISTI; Genuine Article; KR SourceOne; Linda Hall; SWETS; UnCover. **CCC.**
Former titles (until 1992): Journal of Electroanalytical Chemistry and Interfacial Electrochemistry (ISSN 0022-0728); (until 1966): Journal of Electroanalytical Chemistry (ISSN 0368-1874)
Refereed Serial

643 JA ISSN 0911-775X
CODEN: JFIAEA
JOURNAL OF FLOW INJECTION ANALYSIS/F I A KENKYU KONDANKAI KAISHI. (Text in Japanese; summaries English) 1984. s-a. 3000 Yen (effective 1998). Nihon Bunseki Kagakkai, Furo Injekushon Bunseki Kenkyu Kondankai - Japan Society of Analytical Chemistry, Division of Flow Injection Analysis, Okayama University, Faculty of Science, Dept. of Chemistry, 3-1-1 Tsushimanaka, Okayama 700, Japan. TEL 8-86-251-7846. FAX 8-86-254-8376. E-mail: motomizu@cc.okayama-u.ac.jp. Ed. Takuji Kawashima. **Document type:** academic/scholarly publication.
—BLDSC (4984.430000).

547 016 UK ISSN 0362-4803
QD466   CODEN: JLCRD4
JOURNAL OF LABELLED COMPOUNDS AND RADIOPHARMACEUTICALS. (Text in English, French and German) 1964. m. $1725 (foreign $1725) (effective 1998). (International Isotope Society) John Wiley & Sons Ltd., Journals, Baffins Ln., Chichester, W. Sussex PO19 1UD, England. TEL 44-1243-779777. FAX 44-1243-775878. E-mail: info-assets@wiley.co.uk; URL: http://www.wiley.co.uk. (Subscr. in the Americas to: John Wiley & Sons, Inc., Baffins Ln., Chichester, W. Sussex PO19 1UD, England. TEL 212-850-6645. FAX 212-850-6021) Ed.Bd. adv.: B&W page £595, color page £1495; trim 248 x 165; adv. contact: Bob Kern. bk.rev.; bibl.; charts; illus.; index. (also avail. in microform from UMI; back issues avail.; reprint service avail. from ISI,SWZ,UMI) **Indexed:** Anal.Abstr., ASCA, Biol.Abstr., Biotech.Abstr., Chem.Abstr., Chem.Cit.Ind., Curr.Adv.Biochem., Curr.Adv.Ecol.Sci., Curr.Chem.React., Curr.Cont., Dairy Sci.Abstr., Ind.Chem., Ind.Sci.Rev., INIS Atomind., Mass Spectr.Bull., Neurosci.Cit.Ind., Rev.Med.& Vet.Mycol., Sci.Cit.Ind., Telegen. **Document type:** academic/scholarly publication.
—BLDSC (5009.910000); ADONIS; CASDDS; CISTI; Ei; EMDOCS; Genuine Article; KNAW; Linda Hall; SWETS; UMI; UnCover. **CCC.**
Formerly: Journal of Labelled Compounds (ISSN 0022-2135).
Description: Publishes original scientific manuscripts dealing with all aspects of research and development leading to and resulting in labelled compound preparation.
Refereed Serial

547 UK ISSN 1076-5174
QD272.S6 CODEN: JMSPFJ
JOURNAL OF MASS SPECTROMETRY. 1968. m. $2850 (foreign $2850) (effective 1998). John Wiley & Sons Ltd., Journals, Baffins Ln., Chichester, W. Sussex PO19 1UD, England. TEL 44-1243-779777. FAX 44-1243-775878. E-mail: info-assets@wiley.co.uk; URL: http://www.wiley.co.uk. (Subscr. in the Americas to: John Wiley & Sons, Inc., 605 Third Ave., New York, NY 10158. TEL 212-850-6645. FAX 212-850-6021) Ed. Richard Caprioli. adv.: B&W page £595, color page £1495; trim 297 x 210; adv. contact: Bob Kern. bk.rev.; index, cum.index. circ. 1,200. (also avail. in microform from UMI; back issues avail.; reprint service avail. from SWZ) **Indexed:** ASCA, Chem.Abstr., Chem.Cit.Ind., Curr.Chem.React., Curr.Cont., Environ.Per.Bibl. (1992-1994), Excerp.Med., Ind.Chem., Ind.Sci.Rev., Mass Spectr.Bull., Sci.Cit.Ind. **Document type:** academic/scholarly publication.
—BLDSC (5012.179500); ADONIS; CASDDS; CISTI; Ei; EMDOCS; Genuine Article; KR SourceOne; Linda Hall; SWETS; UMI; UnCover. **CCC.**
Formerly: O M S - Organic Mass Spectrometry (ISSN 0030-493X); Which incorporates: Biological Mass Spectrometry (ISSN 1052-9306); Which was formerly (until 1991): Biomedical and Environmental Mass Spectrometry (ISSN 0887-6134); (1974-1986): B M S - Biomedical Mass Spectrometry (ISSN 0306-042X)
Description: Concerned with promoting mass spectrometry as an international and multidisciplinary field of scientific enquiry.
Refereed Serial

544.92 US ISSN 1040-7685
CODEN: JMSEEJ
JOURNAL OF MICROCOLUMN SEPARATIONS. 1989. 8/yr. $497 (foreign $637) (effective 1998). John Wiley & Sons, Inc., Journals, 605 Third Ave., New York, NY 10158-0012. TEL 212-850-6645. FAX 212-850-6021. (Subscr. outside the Americas to: John Wiley & Sons. Ltd., Baffins Ln., Chichester, W. Sussex PO19 1UD, England. TEL 44-1243-779777. FAX 44-1243-776128) Eds. Milton L. Lee, Pat Sandra. adv.: B&W page £640, color page £1515; trim 279 x 210. circ. 855. **Indexed:** ASCA, Chem.Cit.Ind., Curr.Cont., Ind.Sci.Rev. **Document type:** academic/scholarly publication.
—BLDSC (5019.450000); CASDDS; CISTI; Ei; Genuine Article; KNAW; Linda Hall; SWETS; UnCover. **CCC.**
Description: Dedicated to the advancement of all aspects of microcolumn separation methods, including microcolumn supercritical fluid chromatography and capillary gas chromatography.
Refereed Serial

OURNAL OF MOLECULAR SPECTROSCOPY. see PHYSICS — Optics

544 UK ISSN 0967-0335
CODEN: JNISEI
JOURNAL OF NEAR INFRARED SPECTROSCOPY. q. £120 in Europe; rest of world $235 (effective 1998). N I R Publications, 6 Charlton Mill, Charlton, Chichester, W. Sussex PO18 0HY, England. TEL 44-1243-811334. FAX 44-1243-811711. E-mail: subs@impub.demon.co.uk. Ed. A.M.C. Davies. R&P contact: Jill Stockford. adv.: B&W page £330, color page £530; trim 260 x 190; adv. contact: Ian Michael. bk.rev. **Indexed:** Food Sci.& Tech.Abstr., Text.Tech.Dig. **Document type:** academic/scholarly publication.
—BLDSC (5021.393500); CASDDS; CISTI. **CCC.**
Description: Covers research and applications of near-infrared spectroscopy.
Refereed Serial

544.92 HU ISSN 0933-4173
QD79.C8 CODEN: JPCTE5
JOURNAL OF PLANAR CHROMATOGRAPHY - MODERN T L C. (Text in English) 1987. bi-m. $258 (effective 1998). Research Institute for Medicinal Plants, Lupaszigeti st. 4, P.O. Box 11, 2011 Budakalasz, Hungary. TEL 36-1-1688042. FAX 36-26-340426. (Dist. by: Springer Hungarica, Csanyi L. ut 36, 1043 Budapest, Hungary. TEL 36-1-3909074. FAX 36-1-3909075; Subscr. in N. America to: Springer-Verlag New York, Inc., 44 Hartz Way, Secaucus, NJ 07096-2491. TEL 201-348-4033. FAX 201-348-4505) Ed. Szabolcs Nyiredy. adv. contact: J. Tutschek. bk.rev.; index; circ. 1,450 (paid); 220 (controlled). (back issues avail.) **Indexed:** ASCA, Chem.Cit.Ind., Excerp.Med. (1995-), Sugar Ind.Abstr. **Document type:** academic/scholarly publication.
—BLDSC (5073.675000); CASDDS; CISTI; Ei; Genuine Article; Linda Hall; SWETS. **CCC.**
Description: Publishes papers on analytical and preparative planar chromatography in the pharmaceutical and chemical industries.

543.088 HU
CODEN: JRNCDM
JOURNAL OF RADIOANALYTICAL AND NUCLEAR CHEMISTRY. ARTICLES; an international journal dealing with all aspects and applications of nuclear chemistry. (Text in English) 1984. 24/yr. 7921 Ft. (includes Letters section) (effective 1998). Akademiai Kiado Rt., P.O. Box 245, H-1519 Budapest, Hungary. TEL 36-1-2043976. FAX 36-1-2043973. (Subscr. to: Elsevier Science, P.O. Box 330, 1000 AH Amsterdam, The Netherlands. TEL 31-20-4853642. FAX 31-20-4853598) Eds. Tibor Braun. adv.: bk.rev.; bibl.; charts; illus.; index. (also avail. in microform from UMI) **Indexed:** Alloys Ind., Anal.Abstr., Apic.Abstr., Art & Archaeol.Tech.Abstr., Arts & Hum.Cit.Ind., ASCA, Biol.Abstr., Biwk.Pap.Rad.Chem.& Photochem., Chem.Abstr., Chem.Cit.Ind., Curr.Cont., Dairy Sci.Abstr., Eng.Mat.Abstr., Excerp.Med., Food Sci.& Tech.Abstr., GeoRef, Ind.Sci.Rev., INIS Atomind., INSPEC, Mass Spectr.Bull., Mat.Sci.Cit.Ind., Met.Abstr., Met.Abstr.Ind., Nonfer.Met.Alert, Nutr.Abstr., PCC Alert, Phys.Ber., Sci.Cit.Ind., Soils & Fert., SSCI, Steels Alert, Sugar Ind.Abstr., W.R.C.Inf., World Alum.Abstr. **Document type:** academic/scholarly publication.
—BLDSC (5043.890000); AskIEEE; CASDDS; CISTI; Ei; EMDOCS; Genuine Article; KR SourceOne; Linda Hall; SWETS; UnCover. **CCC.**
Supersedes in part: Journal of Radioanalytical and Nuclear Chemistry (ISSN 0236-5731); Which was formed by the merger of (1968-1983): Journal of Radioanalytical Chemistry (ISSN 0134-0719); (1969-1983): Radiochemical and Radioanalytical Letters (ISSN 0079-9483)
Description: Publishes original papers, review papers, and short communications.
Refereed Serial

543.088 HU
CODEN: JRNCDM
JOURNAL OF RADIOANALYTICAL AND NUCLEAR CHEMISTRY. LETTERS; an international journal for rapid communication on all aspects and applications of nuclear chemistry. (Text in English) 1968. 16/yr. 7921 Ft. (includes Articles section) (effective 1998). Akademiai Kiado Rt., P.O. Box 245, H-1519 Budapest, Hungary. TEL 36-1-2043976. FAX 36-1-2043973. (Subscr. to: Elsevier Science, P.O. Box 330, 1000 AH Amsterdam, The Netherlands. TEL 31-20-4853642. FAX 31-20-4853598) Ed. Tibor Braun. (also avail. in microform from UMI) **Indexed:** Alloys Ind., Apic.Abstr., Arts & Hum.Cit.Ind., ASCA, Biol.Abstr., Cadscan, Chem.Abstr., Chem.Cit.Ind., Curr.Cont., Dairy Sci.Abstr., Deep Sea Res.& Oceanogr.Abstr., Eng.Mat.Abstr., INIS Atomind., INSPEC (1975-), Lead Abstr., Mass Spectr.Bull., Mat.Sci.Cit.Ind., Met.Abstr.Ind., Met.Abstr., Nonfer.Met.Alert, PCC Alert, Ref.Zh., Risk Abstr., Sci.Cit.Ind., Soils & Fert., Steels Alert, Sugar Ind.Abstr., W.R.C.Inf., World Alum.Abstr., Zincscan. **Document type:** academic/scholarly publication.
—BLDSC (5043.890000); AskIEEE; CASDDS; CISTI; Ei; EMDOCS; Genuine Article; KR SourceOne; Linda Hall; SWETS; UnCover. **CCC.**
Supersedes in part: Journal of Radioanalytical and Nuclear Chemistry (ISSN 0236-5731); Which was formed by the merger of (1968-1983): Journal of Radioanalytical Chemistry (ISSN 0134-0719); (1969-1983): Radiochemical and Radioanalytical Letters (ISSN 0079-9483)
Description: Publishes original papers and short communications on nuclear chemistry and radiochemistry.
Refereed Serial

540 UK ISSN 0377-0486
QC454.R36 CODEN: JRSPAF
JOURNAL OF RAMAN SPECTROSCOPY. Short title: J R S. (Text in English, French and German) 1973. m. $2695 (foreign $2695) (effective 1998). John Wiley & Sons Ltd., Journals, Baffins Ln., Chichester, W. Sussex PO19 1UD, England. TEL 44-1243-779777. FAX 44-1243-775878. E-mail: info-assets@wiley.co.uk; URL: http://www.wiley.co.uk. (Subscr. in the Americas to: John Wiley & Sons, Inc., 605 Third Ave., New York, NY 10158. TEL 212-850-6645. FAX 212-850-6021) Ed. D.A. Long. adv.: B&W page £595, color page £1495; trim 297 x 210; adv. contact: Bob Kern. bk.rev.; index. (also avail. in microform from UMI; back issues avail.; reprint service avail. from SWZ) **Indexed:** Abstr.Bull.Inst.Pap.Chem., Alloys Ind., ASCA, Chem.Abstr., Chem.Cit.Ind., Curr.Cont., Eng.Mat.Abstr., Ind.Sci.Rev., INIS Atomind., INSPEC, Mat.Sci.Cit.Ind., Met.Abstr.Ind., Met.Abstr., Nonfer.Met.Alert, PCC Alert, Sci.Cit.Ind., Steels Alert, World Alum.Abstr. **Document type:** academic/scholarly publication.
—BLDSC (5045.600000); AskIEEE; CASDDS; CISTI; Ei; Genuine Article; KR SourceOne; Linda Hall; SWETS; UMI; UnCover. **CCC.**
Description: Provides readers with original work in all aspects of Ramam spectroscopy, including higher-order processes and Brillouin and Rayleigh scattering.
Refereed Serial

CHEMISTRY — ANALYTICAL CHEMISTRY

544   NE   ISSN 0896-8446
TP156.E8   CODEN: JSFLEH
JOURNAL OF SUPERCRITICAL FLUIDS. 1988. q. fl.1144($657) (effective 1998). Elsevier Science B.V., P.O. Box 211, 1000 AE Amsterdam, Netherlands. TEL 31-20-4853911. FAX 31-20-4853598. E-mail: nlinfo-f@elsevier.nl; usinfo-f@elsevier.com; forinfo-kyf04035@niftyserve.or.jp; URL: http://www.elsevier.nl/. (Subscr. in the Americas to: Elsevier Science, Regional Sales Office, Box 945, New York, NY 10159-0945. TEL 212-633-3730. FAX 212-633-3680; Subscr. in Australasia and the Far East to: Elsevier Science (Singapore) Pte Ltd, No.1 Temasek Ave., No.17-01, Millenia Tower, Singapore 039192, Singapore. TEL 65-434-3727. FAX 65-337-2230; Subscr. in Japan to: Elsevier Science Japan, 9-15 Higashi-Azabu, 1-chome, Minato-ku, Tokyo 106, Japan. TEL 81-3-5561-5033. FAX 81-3-5561-5047) Ed. Erdogan Kiran. adv.; bk.rev. circ. 250. (back issues avail.) **Indexed:** Alloys Ind., ASCA, Chem.Cit.Ind., Curr.Cont., Eng.Mat.Abstr., Food Sci.& Tech.Abstr., Met.Abstr., Met.Abstr.Ind., Nonfer.Met.Alert, PCC Alert, Sci.Cit.Ind., Steels Alert, World Alum.Abstr. **Document type:** academic/scholarly publication.
—BLDSC (5067.119000); CASDDS; CISTI; Ei; Genuine Article; Linda Hall; SWETS; UMI; UnCover. **CCC.**
Refereed Serial

643   US   ISSN 0733-4680
QD139.T7   CODEN: JTMTDE
JOURNAL OF TRACE AND MICROPROBE TECHNIQUES. 1982. q. $545 (foreign $560) (effective 1998). Marcel Dekker Journals, 270 Madison Ave., New York, NY 10016. TEL 212-696-9000. FAX 212-685-4540. TELEX 421419 MARDEEK. (Subscr. to: Box 5017, Monticello, NY 12701) Ed. E.A. Schweikert. illus.; index. (also avail. in microform from RPI) **Indexed:** Anal.Abstr., ASCA, Biol.Abstr., Chem.Abstr., Curr.Adv.Ecol.Sci., Curr.Cont., Excerp.Med., Mass Spectr.Bull., W.R.C.Inf. **Document type:** academic/scholarly publication.
—BLDSC (5069.744000); CASDDS; CISTI; Ei; Genuine Article; KR SourceOne; SWETS; UMI; UnCover. **CCC.**
Refereed Serial

643   JA   ISSN 0917-3048
    CODEN: KUROE9
KUROMATOGURAFI/CHROMATOGRAPHY. (Text in English, Japanese) 1989. bi-m. Kuromatogurafi Kagakkai - Society for Chromatographic Sciences, Tokyo Toritsu Daigaku Rigakubu Kagaku Kyoshitsu, 1-1, Minamiosawa, Hachioji-shi, Tokyo 192-03, Japan.
—CASDDS.

544.92   US   ISSN 0888-9090
QD79.C454   CODEN: LCGCE7
L C - G C. (Liquid and Gas Chromatography); the magazine of separation science. European edition: L C - G C International (ISSN 0895-5441) 1983. m. $64 (foreign $124) (effective 1996). Advanstar Communications, Inc., 7500 Old Oak Blvd., Cleveland, OH 44130. TEL 216-826-2839. FAX 216-891-2726. (Subscr. to: 1 E. First St., Duluth, MN 55082. TEL 800-346-0085; Addr. in the U.K.: Advanstar House, Park West, Sealand Rd., Chester CH1 4RN, England. TEL 44-244-378888. FAX 44-244-370011) Ed. Jeff Schier. adv. circ. 58,000. (also avail. in microform from UMI; back issues avail.) **Indexed:** Chem.Abstr., Chem.Cit.Ind., Telegen. **Document type:** trade publication.
—BLDSC (5162.246000); CASDDS; CISTI; Ei; Genuine Article; KNAW; Linda Hall; SWETS; UMI; UnCover. **CCC.**
Formerly: L C - Liquid Chromatography and H P L C Magazine (ISSN 0746-0252)
Description: Devoted exclusively to the needs of chromatographers in industry and academia. Highlights concise research papers that examine a wide variety of new or improved applications of liquid, gas, and supercritical chromatography.

544.92   US   ISSN 0895-5441
L C - G C INTERNATIONAL. (Liquid and Gas Chromatography); the magazine of separation science. 1988. m. $102 (effective 1996). Advanstar Communications, Inc., 7500 Old Oak Blvd., Cleveland, OH 44130. TEL 216-826-2839. FAX 216-891-2726. (Subscr. to: 1 E. First St., Duluth, MN 55082. TEL 800-346-0085) Ed. Sarah Evans. adv. contact: Carol Chinn. circ. 32,000. (back issues avail.) **Indexed:** Food Sci.& Tech.Abstr., World Surf.Coat. **Document type:** trade publication.
—BLDSC (5162.246200); Ei; SWETS; UMI. **CCC.**
Description: Targets users and specifiers of chromatographic equipment in Western Europe.

544   IT   ISSN 1120-8376
LABORATORIO 2000; rivista del ricercatore chimico e biologico. 1987. 9/yr. L.100000 (foreign L.180000) (effective 1996). Morgan Edizioni Tecniche s.r.l., Via Ercole Oldofredi, 39, 20124 Milan, Italy. TEL 39-2-69001227. FAX 39-2-69001229. E-mail: iuppiter@mbox.vol.it; URL: http://www.lab2000.com. Ed. Enrico Boeri. R&P contact: Enrico Boeri. adv.: B&W page L.1950000, color page L.2900000; adv. contact: Monica Marchesi. bk.rev. circ. 10,000. **Document type:** newsletter.
—BLDSC (5137.955000).

643 610   GW   ISSN 0172-908X
    CODEN: MABUDW
MAGNESIUM BULLETIN. (Text in German; summaries in English) q. DM.74 (students DM.57). (Gesellschaft fuer Magnesiumforschung e.V.) Karl F. Haug Verlag GmbH, Fritz-Frey-Str. 21, 69121 Heidelberg, Germany. TEL 49-6221-4062-0. Eds. Joachim Helbig, Kai Paschen. **Indexed:** ASCA, Chem.Abstr., Curr.Adv.Ecol.Sci., Curr.Cont., Ind.Sci.Rev., Sci.Cit.Ind. **Document type:** academic/scholarly publication.
—BLDSC (5334.890000); CASDDS; CISTI; Ei; Genuine Article. **CCC.**

620.1   GW   ISSN 0025-5270
TA418.74   CODEN: MTOGAF
MATERIAL UND ORGANISMEN/MATERIALS AND ORGANISMS/MATERIAU ET ORGANISMES. (Supplements avail.) (Text in English, French and German; summaries in English, French, German and Spanish) 1965. q. price varies. Duncker and Humblot GmbH, Postfach 410329, 12113 Berlin, Germany. TEL 49-30-7900060. FAX 49-30-79000631. E-mail: duh-werbung@t-online.de. Ed. J.N.R. Ruddick. adv.; bk.rev.; charts; illus.; index. circ. 500. **Indexed:** ASCA, Biol.Abstr., Chem.Abstr., Curr.Adv.Ecol.Sci., Curr.Cont, Forest.Abstr., Forest Prod.Abstr., Helminthol.Abstr., INIS Atomind., Mat.Sci.Cit.Ind., Rev.Plant Path., Soils & Fert. **Document type:** academic/scholarly publication.
—BLDSC (5393.600000); CASDDS; CISTI; Ei; Genuine Article; Linda Hall; SWETS. **CCC.**

544 615   UK   ISSN 0793-0291
    CODEN: MBADEI
METAL-BASED DRUGS. 1994. bi-m. $310 (effective 1997). Freund Publishing House Ltd., Ste. 500, Chesham House, 150 Regent St., London W1R 5FA, England. (And: P.O. Box 35010, Tel Aviv, Israel. TEL 972-3-5625840. FAX 972-3-5625838) Ed. M. Gielen. **Document type:** academic/scholarly publication.
—BLDSC (5683.686000); CASDDS; EMDOCS; KNAW.

METALURGIJA. see METALLURGY

543   AU   ISSN 0026-3672
QD71   CODEN: MIACAQ
MIKROCHIMICA ACTA; micro and trace analysis. 1923. m. DM.1896 (effective 1998). Springer-Verlag, Sachsenplatz 4-6, P.O. Box 89, A-1201 Vienna, Austria. TEL 43-1-330-2415. FAX 43-1-330-2426. E-mail: springer@springer.co.at. (Subscr. in N. America to: Springer-Verlag New York, Inc., 175 Fifth Ave., New York, NY 10010. TEL 212-460-1500. FAX 212-473-6272) Ed. W. Wegscheider. adv.; charts; illus.; index. (also avail. in microform from UMI; reprint service avail. from ISI) **Indexed:** Alloys Ind., Anal.Abstr., ASCA, Biol.Abstr., Cadscan, Chem.Abstr., Chem.Cit.Ind., Compumath, Curr.Cont., Dairy Sci.Abstr., Deep Sea Res.& Oceanogr.Abstr., Eng.Mat.Abstr., Excerp.Med., Food Sci.& Tech.Abstr., GeoRef., Ind.Sci.Rev., Lead Abstr., Mass Spectr.Bull., Met.Abstr.Ind., Met.Abstr., Mineral.Abstr., Nonfer.Met.Alert, Numis.Lit., Nutr.Abstr., PCC Alert, Sci.Cit.Ind., Sel.Water Res.Abstr., SSCI, Steels Alert, W.R.C.Inf., World Alum.Abstr., Zincscan. **Document type:** academic/scholarly publication.
—BLDSC (5762.000000); CASDDS; CISTI; Genuine Article; Linda Hall; SWETS; UMI; UnCover. **CCC.**
Formerly: Mikrochimica et Ichnoanalytica Acta.
Description: Presents latest results from all areas of analytical chemistry.

543   US   ISSN 0076-8642
    CODEN: MKASAK
MIKROCHIMICA ACTA. SUPPLEMENT. 1966. irreg. price varies. Springer-Verlag, 175 Fifth Ave., New York, NY 10010. TEL 212-460-1500. FAX 212-473-6272. (N. American subscr. to: Journal Fulfillment Services, Box 2483, Secaucus, NJ 07096. TEL 800-777-4643; Subscr. outside N. America to: Springer-Verlag, Heidelberger Platz 3, 14197 Berlin, Germany. TEL 030-8207-0. FAX 030-8214091) (also avail. in microform from UMI; reprint service avail. from ISI) **Indexed:** Chem.Abstr. **Document type:** academic/scholarly publication.
—BLDSC (5762.010000); CASDDS; CISTI; Linda Hall; UMI. **CCC.**

543   US
MODERN ANALYTICAL CHEMISTRY. irreg., latest 1995. price varies. Plenum Publishing Corp., 233 Spring St., New York, NY 10013-1578. TEL 212-620-8000. FAX 212-463-0742. TELEX 23-421139. E-mail: books@plenum.com. Ed. David Hercules. **Document type:** monographic series.
Refereed Serial

643   US
MODERN MONOGRAPHS IN ANALYTICAL CHEMISTRY. 1981. irreg., vol.3, 1991. price varies. Marcel Dekker, Inc., 270 Madison Ave., New York, NY 10016. TEL 212-696-9000. FAX 212-658-4540. TELEX 421419. Ed. George G. Guilbault; Pub. Graham Garratt. R&P contact: Julia Mulligan. **Document type:** monographic series.
Refereed Serial

MONOGRAPHS IN ELECTROANALYTICAL CHEMISTRY AND ELECTROCHEMISTRY SERIES. see CHEMISTRY — Electrochemistry

544   UK   ISSN 0960-3360
N I R NEWS. bi-m. £70 to Europe; rest of world $135 (effective 1998). N I R Publications, 6 Charlton Mil Charlton, Chichester, W. Sussex PO18 0HY, England. TEL 44-1243-811334. FAX 44-1243-811711. E-mail: subs@impub.demon.co.uk. Ed. A.M.C. Davies. adv.: B&W page £330, color page £530; trim 297 x 210; adv. contact: Ian Michael. bk.rev. **Indexed:** Text.Tech.Dig. **Document type:** newsletter.
—BLDSC (6113.568400); SWETS.

N K I REPORT. (Nathan S. Kline Institute for Psychiatri Research) see MEDICAL SCIENCES — Psychiatry And Neurology

CHEMISTRY — ANALYTICAL CHEMISTRY

544 615.9   **US**   **ISSN 1056-9014**
QP631   CODEN: NATOEE
NATURAL TOXINS. 1992. bi-m. $395 (foreign $500) (effective 1998). John Wiley & Sons, Inc., Journals, 605 Third Ave., New York, NY 10158. TEL 212-692-6645. FAX 212-850-6021. TELEX 12-7063. E-mail: SUBINFO@JWILEY.COM; URL: http://www.wiley.co.uk. (Subscr. outside the Americas to: John Wiley & Sons Ltd., Baffins Ln., Chichester, W. Sussex PO19 1UD, England. TEL 44-1243-779777. FAX 44-1243-776128) Eds. John A. Simon, J. David Miller. adv.: B&W page £640, color page £1515; trim 279 x 210. bk.rev. circ. 400. (also avail. in microform from UMI; back issues avail.) **Indexed:** Environ.Per.Bibl., Excerp.Med. (1993-), Food Sci.& Tech.Abstr., Ind.Med. (1994-), Zoo.Rec. **Document type:** academic/scholarly publication.
—BLDSC (6041.515000); CASDDS; CISTI; EMDOCS; KNAW; SWETS. **CCC**.
Description: Provides a forum for original research on the occurrence, isolation, identification, and characterization of natural products with toxic activities.
Refereed Serial

NIGERIAN STORED PRODUCTS RESEARCH INSTITUTE. ANNUAL REPORT. see AGRICULTURE — Agricultural Equipment

643   **JA**
NIHON BUNSEKI KAGAKKAI GAKUJUTSU KOENKAI/PROCEEDINGS OF THE LECTURE MEETING ON ANALYTICAL CHEMISTRY. (Text in Japanese) a. Japan Society for Analytical Chemistry - Nihon Bunseki Kagakkai, 26-2, Nishigotanda 1-chome, Shinagawa-ku, Tokyo 141, Japan. **Document type:** proceedings.

543 547   **US**   **ISSN 0078-6136**
QC437
ORGANIC ELECTRONIC SPECTRAL DATA. 1960. irreg., vol.28, 1992. price varies. (Organic Electronic Spectral Data, Inc.) John Wiley & Sons, Inc., 605 Third Ave., New York, NY 10158. TEL 212-850-6000. FAX 212-850-6088. TELEX 12-7063. Ed.Bd. **Document type:** monographic series.
—BLDSC (6287.400000); CISTI; Linda Hall.
Refereed Serial

P A S C A L. F 16: CHIMIE ANALYTIQUE, MINERALE ET ORGANIQUE. see CHEMISTRY — Abstracting, Bibliographies, Statistics

PHOTONICS SPECTRA. see PHYSICS — Optics

544.66   **US**   **ISSN 0092-0509**
QC482.D5
POWDER DIFFRACTION FILE SEARCH MANUAL. ALPHABETICAL LISTING. INORGANIC. a. $300 (includes supplement). Joint Committee on Powder Diffraction Standards, International Centre for Diffraction Data, 12 Campus Blvd., Newtown Square, PA 19073. TEL 610-325-9814. FAX 610-325-9823. index.

544.66   **US**   **ISSN 0092-1319**
QC482.D5
POWDER DIFFRACTION FILE SEARCH MANUAL. HANAWALT METHOD. INORGANIC.* (Subseries of the Committee's Publication SMH) a. $225. Joint Committee on Powder Diffraction Standards, International Centre for Diffraction Data, Newton Sq. Corp. Camp, 12, Newton Square, PA 19073. TEL 215-328-9400. FAX 215-328-2503. TELEX 847170. index. (also avail. in microfiche; magnetic tape)
●Also available on CD-ROM.
—CISTI.

547.3   **US**   **ISSN 0148-9054**
   CODEN: PSPED9
PRACTICAL SPECTROSCOPY SERIES. 1976. irreg., vol.22, 1996. price varies. Marcel Dekker, Inc., 270 Madison Ave., New York, NY 10016. TEL 212-696-9000. FAX 212-685-4540. TELEX 421419. Pub. Graham Garratt. R&P contact: Julia Mulligan. **Indexed:** Biol.Abstr. **Document type:** monographic series.
—BLDSC (6595.850000); CASDDS; CISTI. **CCC**.
Refereed Serial

544   **NE**   **ISSN 0920-9832**
   CODEN: PRHPEU
PROGRESS IN H P L C. (High Performance Liquid Chromatography) (Text in English) 1985. irreg., vol.6, 1997. price varies. V S P, P.O. Box 346, 3700 AH Zeist, Netherlands. TEL 31-30-6925790. FAX 31-30-6932081. E-mail: 100341.2372@compuserve.com. (Dist. in U.S. and Canada by: Books International Inc., Box 605, Herndon, VA 22070. TEL 703-661-1500. FAX 703-661-1501) (back issues avail.) **Document type:** monographic series.
—CASDDS; CISTI.

544.6   **NE**   **ISSN 0079-6565**
QC762   CODEN: PNMRAT
PROGRESS IN NUCLEAR MAGNETIC RESONANCE SPECTROSCOPY. (Text in English) 1966. 8/yr. fl.1300($747) (effective 1998). Elsevier Science B.V., P.O. Box 211, 1000 AE Amsterdam, Netherlands. TEL 31-20-4853911. FAX 31-20-4853598. E-mail: nlinfo-f@elsevier.nl; usinfo-f@elsevier.com; forinfo-kyf04035@niftyserve.or.jp; URL: http://www.elsevier.nl/. (Subscr. in the Americas to: Elsevier Science, Regional Sales Office, Box 945, New York, NY 10159-0945. TEL 212-633-3730. FAX 212-633-3680; Subscr. in Australasia and the Far East to: Elsevier Science (Singapore) Pte Ltd, No.1 Temasek Ave., No.17-01 Millenia Tower, Singapore 039192, Singapore. TEL 65-434-3727. FAX 65-337-2230; Subscr. in Japan to: Elsevier Science Japan, 9-15 Higashi-Azabu 1-chome, Minato-ku, Tokyo 106, Japan. TEL 81-3-5561-5033. FAX 81-3-5561-5047) Ed.Bd. index. (also avail. in microfilm from UMI) **Indexed:** ASCA, Chem.Abstr., Chem.Cit.Ind., Curr.Cont., Ind.Sci.Rev., INSPEC, Met.Abstr., Sci.Cit.Ind., World Alum.Abstr. **Document type:** academic/scholarly publication.
—BLDSC (6870.750000); ADONIS; AskIEEE; CASDDS; CISTI; Ei; Genuine Article; KR SourceOne; Linda Hall; SWETS; UMI; UnCover. **CCC**.
Description: Publishes review articles covering applications of NMR in chemistry, biochemistry and biological science, as well as fundamental theory and instrumental developments.
Refereed Serial

PTERIDINES. see BIOLOGY — Biological Chemistry

R & D DIGEST. (Research & Development) see ENERGY

543   **IT**   **ISSN 0033-9334**
TP1   CODEN: RACHAG
RASSEGNA CHIMICA. 1949. bi-m. $125 (effective 1996). Societa Editoriale Farmaceutica s.r.l., Via Ausonio 12, 20123 Milan, Italy. TEL 39-2-89404545. FAX 39-2-89401168. Ed. Elena Ragno. adv.; bk.rev.; bibl.; charts; tr.lit.; index. circ. 2,000. **Indexed:** Art & Archaeol.Tech.Abstr., Chem.Abstr., Dairy Sci.Abstr., Food Sci.& Tech.Abstr., Rural Recreat.Tour.Abstr., World Agri.Econ.& Rural Sociol.Abstr.
—CASDDS; CISTI; Linda Hall.

543   **US**
REAGENT CHEMICALS. irreg. (approx. every 5 yrs.). price varies. American Chemical Society, Committee on Analytical Reagents, 1155 16th St., N.W., Washington, DC 20036. TEL 800-227-5558. FAX 202-872-4615. **Document type:** academic/scholarly publication.

543   **US**   **ISSN 0896-7695**
REFEREE (GAITHERSBURG). m. $75 to non-members. A O A C International, 481 N. Frederick Ave., Ste. 500, Gaithersburg, MD 20877-2417. TEL 301-924-7077. FAX 301-924-7089. **Document type:** newsletter.
—CCC.
Description: Subjects covered include methods program developments and concerns, collaborative studies, symposia, sections, publications, employment needs and opportunities and details on meetings.

545.32   **JA**   **ISSN 0034-6691**
QD116.P64
REVIEW OF POLAROGRAPHY/PORAROGURAFI. (Text in Japanese or Western languages) 1953. bi-m. 4000 Yen. Polarographic Society of Japan - Nihon Porarogurafu Gakkai, Department of Agricultural Chemistry, Kyoto University, Kyoto 606, Japan. (Order from: Japan Publications Trading Co., Ltd., Box 5030, Tokyo International, Tokyo 100-31, Japan; or 1255 Howard St., San Francisco, CA 94103) Ed. Masanori Sato. adv. contact: Masanori Sato. bk.rev.; charts; illus.; index. circ. 650. **Indexed:** Chem.Abstr., Electroanal.Abstr. **Document type:** academic/scholarly publication.
—BLDSC (7794.100000); CISTI.

543   **UK**   **ISSN 0048-752X**
QD71   CODEN: RACYAX
REVIEWS IN ANALYTICAL CHEMISTRY. (Text in English) 1971. q. $250 (effective 1997). Freund Publishing House Ltd., Ste. 500, Chesham House, 150 Regent St., London W1R 5FA, England. (And: P.O. Box 35010, Tel Aviv, Israel. TEL 972-3-5628540. FAX 972-3-5628538) Ed. M. Zangen. adv.; bk.rev.; index. circ. 1,000. (back issues avail.) **Indexed:** Alloys Ind., Anal.Abstr., ASCA, Chem.Abstr., Eng.Mat.Abstr., Excerp.Med., GeoRef., Mass Spectr.Bull., Met.Abstr., Met.Abstr.Ind., Nonfer.Met.Alert, Nucl.Sci.Abstr., PCC Alert, Steels Alert, World Alum.Abstr. **Document type:** academic/scholarly publication.
—BLDSC (7786.930000); CASDDS; CISTI; Linda Hall; UnCover.

S I A - SURFACE AND INTERFACE ANALYSIS. see ENGINEERING — Chemical Engineering

544   **US**
SELECTED TOPICS IN MASS SPECTROMETRY. 1994. irreg. price varies. Plenum Publishing Corp., 233 Spring St., New York, NY 10013-1578. TEL 212-620-8000. FAX 212-463-0742. E-mail: books@plenum.com. Ed. David H. Russell. **Document type:** monographic series.
Refereed Serial

543   **US**   **ISSN 0360-2540**
TP156.S45   CODEN: SPMHBD
SEPARATION AND PURIFICATION METHODS. 1972. s-a. $450 (foreign $457.50) (effective 1998). Marcel Dekker Journals, 270 Madison Ave., New York, NY 10016. TEL 212-696-9000. FAX 212-685-4540. TELEX 421419 MARDEEK. (Subscr. to: Box 5017, Monticello, NY 12701) Ed.Bd. adv.; charts; illus. (also avail. in microform from RPI) **Indexed:** Alloys Ind., Anal.Abstr., ASCA, Biol.Abstr., Chem.Abstr., Chem.Cit.Ind., Chem.Eng.Abstr., Curr.Cont., Eng.Mat.Abstr., Excerp.Med., Met.Abstr., Met.Abstr.Ind., Nonfer.Met.Alert, PCC Alert, Sci.Cit.Ind., Steels Alert, T.C.E.A., W.R.C.Inf., World Alum.Abstr. **Document type:** academic/scholarly publication.
—BLDSC (8242.230000); CASDDS; CISTI; Genuine Article; SWETS; UMI; UnCover. **CCC**.
Refereed Serial

543   **US**   **ISSN 0149-6395**
TP156.S45   CODEN: SSTEDS
SEPARATION SCIENCE AND TECHNOLOGY. 1966. 16/yr. $1895 (foreign $1955) (effective 1998). Marcel Dekker Journals, 270 Madison Ave., New York, NY 10016. TEL 212-696-9000. FAX 212-685-4540. TELEX 421419 MARDEEK. (Subscr. to: Box 5017, Monticello, NY 12701) Ed. J. Calvin Giddings. adv.; charts; illus.; stat. (also avail. in microform from RPI) **Indexed:** Abstr.Bull.Inst.Pap.Chem., Alloys Ind., Anal.Abstr., ASCA, Biol.Abstr., Chem.Abstr., Chem.Cit.Ind., Chem.Eng.Abstr., Curr.Adv.Ecol.Sci., Curr.Cont., Dairy Sci.Abstr., Eng.Mat.Abstr., Excerp.Med., Fluidex, GeoRef., Ind.Sci.Rev., INIS Atomind., Mat.Sci.Cit.Ind., Met.Abstr., Met.Abstr.Ind., Nonfer.Met.Alert, PCC Alert, Sci.Cit.Ind., Sci.Cit.Ind., Sel.Water Res.Abstr., Soils & Fert., Steels Alert, T.C.E.A., W.R.C.Inf., World Alum.Abstr. **Document type:** academic/scholarly publication.
—BLDSC (8242.255000); CASDDS; CISTI; Ei; Genuine Article; Linda Hall; SWETS; UMI; UnCover. **CCC**.
Formerly (until vol.13, 1978): Separation Science (ISSN 0037-2366)
Refereed Serial

CHEMISTRY — ANALYTICAL CHEMISTRY

643 JA ISSN 0542-8645
CODEN: SHIBAK
SHITSURYO BUNSEKI/MASS SPECTROSCOPY. (Text in English, Japanese; summaries in English) 1953. bi-m. Nihon Shitsuryo Bunseki Gakkai - Mass Spectroscopy Society of Japan, Nihon Gakkai Jimu Senta, 16-9, Honkomagome 5-chome, Bunkyo-ku, Tokyo 113, Japan. **Indexed:** Chem.Abstr., Curr.Cont., INIS Atomind., INSPEC (1993-), Jap.Per.Ind.
—AskIEEE; CASDDS; CISTI; KR SourceOne; Linda Hall. **CCC.**

643 JA
SHITSURYO BUNSEKI RENGO TORONKAI KOEN YOSHISHU/PROCEEDINGS OF THE FORUM ON THE MASS SPECTROSCOPY. (Text in English, Japanese) a. Nihon Shitsuryo Bunseki Gakkai - Mass Spectroscopy Society of Japan, Nihon Gakkai Jimu Senta, 6-9, Honkomagome 5-chome, Bunkyo-ku, Tokyo 113, Japan.

543 616.075 NE ISSN 0926-2040
QC762 CODEN: SSNRE4
SOLID STATE NUCLEAR MAGNETIC RESONANCE; an international journal. Abbreviated title: S S N M R. (Text in English) 1992. 16/yr. fl.2600($1494) (effective 1998). Elsevier Science B.V., P.O. Box 211, 1000 AE Amsterdam, Netherlands. TEL 31-20-4853911. FAX 31-20-4853598. TELEX 18582 ESPA NL. E-mail: nlinfo-f@elsevier.nl; usinfo-f@elsevier.com; forinfo-kyf04035@niftyserve.or.jp; URL: http://www.elsevier.nl/. (Subscr. in the Americas to: Elsevier Science, Regional Sales Office, Box 945, New York, NY 10159-0945. TEL 212-633-3730. FAX 212-633-3680; Subscr. in Australasia and the Far East to: Elsevier Science (Singapore) Pte Ltd, No.1 Temasek Ave., No.17-01 Millenia Tower, Singapore 039192, Singapore. TEL 65-434-3727. FAX 65-337-2230; Subscr. in Japan to: Elsevier Science Japan, 9-15 Higashi-Azabu 1-chome, Minato-ku, Tokyo 106, Japan. TEL 81-3-5561-5033. FAX 81-3-5561-5047) Ed. J. Klinowksi. (also avail. in microform from UMI; back issues avail.) **Indexed:** Alloys Ind., ASCA, Chem.Abstr., Chem.Cit.Ind., Curr.Cont., Eng.Ind., Eng.Mat.Abstr., Ind.Med. (1994-), Ind.Sci.Rev., INSPEC (1992-), Met.Abstr., Met.Abstr.Ind., Nonfer.Met.Alert, PCC Alert, Sci.Cit.Ind., Steels Alert, World Alum.Abstr. **Document type:** academic/scholarly publication.
—BLDSC (8327.391000); AskIEEE; CASDDS; CISTI; Ei; Genuine Article; KR SourceOne; SWETS. **CCC.**
Description: Covers experimental and theoretical aspects of solid state NMR, including advances in instrumentation, techniques and methodology, simulation and applications.
Refereed Serial

643 US ISSN 0736-6299
QD63.E88 CODEN: SEIEDB
SOLVENT EXTRACTION AND ION EXCHANGE. (A companion journal to Separation Science and Technology) 1983. bi-m. $925 (foreign $947.50) (effective 1998). Marcel Dekker Journals, 270 Madison Ave., New York, NY 10016. TEL 212-696-9000. FAX 212-685-4540. TELEX 421419 MARDEEK. (Subscr. to: Box 5017, Monticello, NY 12701) Eds. Kenneth L. Nash, Renato Chiarizia. bibl.; illus.; charts; index. (also avail. in microform from RPI) **Indexed:** Alloys Ind., Anal.Abstr., ASCA, Chem.Abstr., Chem.Cit.Ind., Chem.Eng.Abstr., Curr.Cont., Eng.Mat.Abstr., I.M.M.Abstr., Ind.Sci.Rev., Met.Abstr.Ind., Met.Abstr., Sci.Cit.Ind., Soils & Fert., Steels Alert, T.C.E.A., World Alum.Abstr. **Document type:** academic/scholarly publication.
—BLDSC (8327.806500); CASDDS; CISTI; Ei; Genuine Article; SWETS; UMI; UnCover. **CCC.**
Refereed Serial

543 FR ISSN 1255-2909
CODEN: SPDMDJ
SPECTRA ANALYSE; la revue scientifique d'actualite sur les techniques et l'instrumentation d'analyse destinee aux laboratoires industriels a la recherche et a l'enseignement. (Text in French; summaries in English, French) 1972. bi-m. 350 F. (foreign 527 F.). P C I, 24 rue de Dunkerque, 75010 Paris, France. TEL 33-1-45267865. FAX 33-1-42806436. Ed. Monique Chevalier. adv. contact: Frederic Reux. bk.rev./; bibl.; illus. circ. 4,000. **Indexed:** Anal.Abstr., Mass Spectr.Bull. **Document type:** academic/scholarly publication.
—BLDSC (8408.820100); CASDDS; CISTI; KNAW; SWETS.
Formerly: Spectra 2000 (ISSN 0399-1172)
Description: Covers physico-chemistry, physics, optics and biology used in university and research labs, as well as quality control labs.

535.84 NE ISSN 1386-1425
QD95 CODEN: SAMCAS
SPECTROCHIMICA ACTA. PART A: MOLECULAR AND BIOMOLECULAR SPECTROSCOPY. (Text in English, French and German) 1939. 14/yr. fl.4125($2371) (effective 1998). Elsevier Science B.V., P.O. Box 211, 1000 AE Amsterdam, Netherlands. TEL 31-20-4853911. FAX 31-20-4853598. E-mail: nlinfo-f@elsevier.nl; usinfo-f@elsevier.com; forinfo-kyf04035@niftyserve.or.jp; URL: http://www.elsevier.nl/. (Subscr. in the Americas to: Elsevier Science, Regional Sales Office, Box 945, New York, NY 10159-0945. TEL 212-633-3730. FAX 212-633-3680; Subscr. in Australasia and the Far East to: Elsevier Science (Singapore) Pte Ltd, No.1 Temasek Ave., No.17-01 Millenia Tower, Singapore 039192, Singapore. TEL 65-434-3727. FAX 65-337-2230; Subscr. in Japan to: Elsevier Science Japan, 9-15 Higashi-Azabu 1-chome, Minato-ku, Tokyo 106, Japan. TEL 81-3-5561-5033. FAX 81-3-5561-5047) Eds. S.F.A. Kettle, J. Steinfeld. adv.; bk.rev./; charts; illus. circ. 1,800. (also avail. in microfiche from MIM; microfilm from UMI; back issues avail.) **Indexed:** Abstr.Bull.Inst.Pap.Chem., Anal.Abstr., ASCA, Biol.Abstr., Br.Ceram.Abstr., Bull.Thermodyn.& Thermochem., Chem.Abstr., Chem.Cit.Ind., Curr.Adv.Biochem., Curr.Cont., Deep Sea Res.& Oceanogr.Abstr., Ind.Sci.Rev., INSPEC, Mass Spectr.Bull., Mat.Sci.Cit.Ind., Sci.Cit.Ind., W.R.C.Inf. **Document type:** academic/scholarly publication.
—BLDSC (8410.010000); ADONIS; AskIEEE; CASDDS; CISTI; Ei; EMDOCS; Genuine Article; KR SourceOne; SWETS; UMI; UnCover. **CCC.**
Formerly: Spectrochimica Acta. Part A: Molecular Spectroscopy (ISSN 0584-8539)
Description: Rapid publication journal for original work in molecular spectroscopy and its applications in chemical problems.
Refereed Serial

535.84 NE ISSN 0584-8547
QD95 CODEN: SAASBH
SPECTROCHIMICA ACTA. PART B: ATOMIC SPECTROSCOPY. (Text in English, French and German) 1939. 14/yr. fl.4200($2414) (effective 1998). Elsevier Science B.V., P.O. Box 211, 1000 AE Amsterdam, Netherlands. TEL 31-20-4853911. FAX 31-20-4853598. E-mail: nlinfo-f@elsevier.nl; usinfo-f@elsevier.com; forinfo-kyf04035@niftyserve.or.jp; URL: http://www.elsevier.nl/. (Subscr. in the Americas to: Elsevier Science, Regional Sales Office, Box 945, New York, NY 10159-0945. TEL 212-633-3730. FAX 212-633-3680; Subscr. in Australasia and the Far East to: Elsevier Science (Singapore) Pte Ltd, No.1 Temasek Ave., No.17-01 Millenia Tower, Singapore 039192, Singapore. TEL 65-434-3727. FAX 65-337-2230; Subscr. in Japan to: Elsevier Science Japan, 9-15 Higashi-Azabu 1-chome, Minato-ku, Tokyo 106, Japan. TEL 81-3-5561-5033. FAX 81-3-5561-5047) Eds. P.W.J.M. Boumans, W. Slavin. adv.: B&W page $550, color page $1350. bk.rev./; charts; illus./; index. circ. 1,600. (also avail. in microfiche from MIM; microfilm from UMI; back issues avail.) **Indexed:** Alloys Ind., Anal.Abstr., ASCA, B.C.I.R.A., Biol.Abstr., Chem.Abstr., Chem.Cit.Ind., Curr.Cont., Deep Sea Res.& Oceanogr.Abstr., Eng.Mat.Abstr., Excerp.Med., Fuel & Energy Abstr., Ind.Sci.Rev., INSPEC, Mass Spectr.Bull., Mat.Sci.Cit.Ind., Met.Abstr., Met.Abstr.Ind., Nonfer.Met.Alert, PCC Alert, Phys.Ber., Sci.Cit.Ind., Steels Alert, W.R.C.Inf., World Alum.Abstr. **Document type:** academic/scholarly publication.
—BLDSC (8410.020000); ADONIS; AskIEEE; CASDDS; CISTI; Ei; EMDOCS; Genuine Article; KR SourceOne; SWETS; UMI; UnCover. **CCC.**
Description: Addresses theory and fundamentals, methodology, development, instrumentation and applications in atomic spectroscopy, and mass spectroscopy for inorganic analysis.
Refereed Serial

SPECTROSCOPY. see PHYSICS — Optics

544 UK ISSN 0966-0941
QC450 CODEN: SPEUEF
SPECTROSCOPY EUROPE. bi-m. DM.170 (Germany DM.140) (effective 1997). (Association of British Spectroscopists) I M Publications, 6 Charlton Mill, Charlton, Chichester, W. Sussex PO18 0HY, England. TEL 49-1243-811334. FAX 49-1243-811711. E-mail: 100136,1577@compuserve.com. (Subscr. in the Americas to: John Wiley & Sons, Inc., 605 Third Ave., New York, NY 10158. TEL 212-850-6645. FAX 212-850-6021) (Co-publisher: Wiley - V C H) Ed. Jenny Cossham; Pub. Ian Michael. adv.: B&W page DM.6680, color page DM.9180; trim 297 x 210. circ. 21,000. **Indexed:** Food Sci.& Tech.Abstr., INSPEC (1993-), World Surf.Coat. **Document type:** academic/scholarly publication.
—BLDSC (8411.115300); AskIEEE; CASDDS; CISTI KR SourceOne. **CCC.**
Formed by the 1992 merger of: Spectroscopy World (ISSN 0956-9820); Spectroscopy International (ISSN 1040-7669)

544 NE ISSN 0924-3984
QD481 CODEN: SOICE8
STEREOCHEMISTRY OF ORGANOMETALLIC AND INORGANIC COMPOUNDS. (Text in English) 1986. irreg., vol.5, 1994. price varies. Elsevier Science B.V., Books Division, P.O. Box 211, 1000 AE Amsterdam, Netherlands. TEL 31-20-4853911. FAX 31-20-4853705. E-mail: nlinfo@elsevier.nl; usinfo@elsevier.com; forinfo-kyf04035@niftyserv or.jp; URL: http://www.elsevier.nl/. (Subscr. in the Americas to: Elsevier Science, Regional Sales Office Box 945, New York, NY 10159-0945. TEL 212-633-3730. FAX 212-633-3680; Subscr. in Australasia and the Far East to: Elsevier Science (Singapore) Pte Ltd, No.1 Temasek Ave., No.17-01 Millenia Tower, Singapore 039192, Singapore. TEL 65-434-3727. FAX 65-337-2230; Subscr. in Japa to: Elsevier Science Japan, 9-15 Higashi-Azabu 1-chome, Minato-ku, Tokyo 106, Japan. TEL 81-3-5561-5033. FAX 81-3-5561-5047)
Document type: monographic series.
—CASDDS; CISTI.
Refereed Serial

CHEMISTRY — ANALYTICAL CHEMISTRY

643   NE   ISSN 0168-6461
STUDIES IN ANALYTICAL CHEMISTRY. (Text in English) 1981. irreg., vol.8, 1989. price varies. Elsevier Science B.V., Books Division, P.O. Box 211, 1000 AE Amsterdam, Netherlands. TEL 31-20-4853911. FAX 31-20-4853705. TELEX 18582 ESPA NL. E-mail: nlinfo-f@elsevier.nl; usinfo-f@elsevier.com; forinfo-kyf04035@niftyserve.or.jp; URL: http://www.elsevier.nl/. (Subscr. in the Americas to: Elsevier Science, Regional Sales Office, Box 945, New York, NY 10159-0945. TEL 212-633-3730. FAX 212-633-3680; Subscr. in Australasia and the Far East to: Elsevier Science (Singapore) Pte Ltd, No.1 Temasek Ave., No.17-01 Millenia Tower, Singapore 039192, Singapore. TEL 65-434-3727. FAX 65-337-2230; Subscr. in Japan to: Elsevier Science Japan, 9-15 Higashi-Azabu 1-chome, Minato-ku, Tokyo 106, Japan. TEL 81-3-5561-5033. FAX 81-3-5561-5047) **Indexed:** INSPEC. **Document type:** monographic series.
Refereed Serial

545.3   SZ   ISSN 0257-8972
TS670.A1   CODEN: SCTEEJ
SURFACE AND COATINGS TECHNOLOGY; an international journal devoted to the science and application of advanced surface treatments for improvement of material properties. (Text in English, French, German) 1972. 33/yr. fl.7906($4544) (effective 1998). Elsevier Science S.A., P.O. Box 564, CH-1001 Lausanne 1, Switzerland. TEL 41-21-3207381. FAX 41-21-3235444. TELEX 450620-ELSA-CH. (Subscr. to: Elsevier Science, Regional Sales Office, P.O. Box 211, 1000 AE Amsterdam, Netherlands. TEL 31-20-4853757. FAX 31-20-4853432; Subscr. in the Americas to: Elsevier Science, Regional Sales Office, Box 945, New York, NY 10159-0945. TEL 212-633-3730. FAX 212-337-2230; Subscr. in Australasia to: Elsevier Science (Singapore) Pte. Ltd., No. 1 Temasek Ave., No. 17-01 Millenia Tower, Singapore 039192, Singapore. TEL 65-434-3727. FAX 65-434-2230) Eds. A. Matthews, B.D. Sartwell. adv.: bk.rev.; illus.; index. (also avail. in microform from UMI; back issues avail.) **Indexed:** Abstr.Bull.Inst.Pap.Chem., Alloys Ind., ASCA, Chem.Abstr., Chem.Cit.Ind., Copper Abstr., Curr.Cont., Eng.Ind., Eng.Mat.Abstr., Excerp.Med., Ind.Sci.Rev., INSPEC (1972-), Int.Aerosp.Abstr., Mass Spectr.Bull., Mat.Sci.Cit.Ind., Met.Abstr., Met.Abstr.Ind., Met.Finish.Abstr., Nonfer.Met.Alert, PCC Alert, Phys.Ber., Sci.Cit.Ind., Steels Alert, World Alum.Abstr. **Document type:** academic/scholarly publication.
—BLDSC (8547.720000); AskIEEE; CASDDS; CISTI; Ei; EMDOCS; Genuine Article; KR SourceOne; Linda Hall; SWETS; UnCover. **CCC.**
Former titles (until 1986): Surface Technology (ISSN 0376-4583); (until 1976): Electrodeposition and Surface Treatment (ISSN 0300-9416)
Description: Forum for the exchange of information on the science, technology and applications of thin and thick coatings and modified surfaces which alter the properties of materials.
Refereed Serial

545.3 698   UK   ISSN 1351-0525
SURFACE WORLD. 1994. bi-m. £52 (foreign £78). Hill Media Ltd., Castle Chambers, 85 High St., Berkhamsted, Herts HP4 2DF, England. TEL 44-1442-878787. FAX 44-1442-870888. Ed. Stephen Godson. adv.: B&W page £800, color page £1200; trim 297 x 210; adv. contact: Nigel Bean. circ. 10,500. (back issues avail.) **Document type:** trade publication.

544.63   US
T R C SPECTRAL DATA - INFRARED. 1943. biennial. $600. Thermodynamics Research Center, Texas Engineering Experiment Station, Texas A & M University System, College Station, TX 77843-3111. TEL 409-845-4940. FAX 409-847-8590. E-mail: info@trchpl.tamu.edu; URL: http://trcweb.tamu.edu. Ed. Kenneth N. Marsh; Pub. Kenneth N. Marsh. R&P contact: Kenneth N. Marsh. circ. 238. (looseleaf format) **Document type:** academic/scholarly publication.
Former titles: Thermodynamics Research Center. Hydrocarbon Project. Selected Values of Properties of Hydrocarbons and Related Compounds. Category B: Selected Infrared Spectral Data; A P I Research Project 44. Selected Values of Properties of Hydrocarbons and Related Compounds. Category B: Selected Infrared Spectral Data (ISSN 0065-9649)
Description: Data sheets include the structure, empirical formula, CAS registry number, Wiswesser line notation, instrumental parameters, and analytical data for each sample.
Refereed Serial

547.3 543.085   US
T R C SPECTRAL DATA - MASS. 1947. biennial. $600. Thermodynamics Research Center, Texas Engineering Experiment Station, Texas A & M University System, College Station, TX 77843-3111. TEL 409-845-4940. FAX 409-847-8590. E-mail: info@trchpl.tamu.edu; URL: http://trcweb.tamu.edu. Ed. Kenneth N. Marsh; Pub. Kenneth N. Marsh. R&P contact: Kenneth N. Marsh. circ. 283. (looseleaf format) **Document type:** academic/scholarly publication.
Former titles: Thermodynamics Research Center. Hydrocarbon Project. Selected Values of Properties of Hydrocarbons and Related Compounds. Category E: Selected Mass Spectral Data; A P I Research Project 44. Selected Values of Properties of Hydrocarbons and Related Compounds. Category E: Selected Mass Spectral Data (ISSN 0065-9673); Incorporates: Thermodynamics Research Center. Data Project. Selected Values of Properties of Chemical Compounds. Category E. Selected Mass Spectral Data.

547.3 543.085   US
T R C SPECTRAL DATA - RAMAN. 1948. bi-a. $600 per supplement. Thermodynamics Research Center, Texas Engineering Experiment Station, Texas A & M University System, College Station, TX 77843-3111. TEL 409-845-4940. FAX 409-847-8590. E-mail: info@trchpl.tamu.edu; URL: http://trcweb.tamu.edu. Ed. Kenneth N. Marsh; Pub. Kenneth N. Marsh. R&P contact: Kenneth N. Marsh. circ. 159. **Document type:** academic/scholarly publication.
Former titles: Thermodynamics Research Center. Hydrocarbon Project. Selected Values of Properties of Hydrocarbons and Related Compounds. Category D: Selected Raman Spectral Data; A P I Research Project 44. Selected Values of Properties of Hydrocarbons and Related Compounds. Category D: Selected Raman Spectral Data (ISSN 0065-9665); Incorporates: Thermodynamics Research Center. Data Project. Selected Values of Properties of Chemical Compounds. Category D. Selected Raman Spectral Data (ISSN 0082-4038)

547.3 543.085   US
T R C SPECTRAL DATA - ULTRAVIOLET. 1945. bi-a. $600. Thermodynamics Research Center, Texas Engineering Experiment Station, Texas A & M University System, College Station, TX 77843-3111. TEL 409-845-4940. FAX 409-847-8590. E-mail: info@trchpl.tamu.edu; URL: http://trcweb.tamu.edu. Ed. Kenneth N. Marsh; Pub. Kenneth N. Marsh. R&P contact: Kenneth N. Marsh. circ. 227. (looseleaf format) **Document type:** academic/scholarly publication.
Former titles: Thermodynamics Research Center. Hydrocarbon Project. Selected Values of Properties of Hydrocarbons and Related Compounds. Category C: Selected Ultraviolet Spectral Data; A P I Research Project 44. Selected Values of Properties of Hydrocarbons and Related Compounds. Category C: Selected Ultraviolet Spectral Data (ISSN 0065-9657); Incorporating: Thermodynamics Research Center. Data Project. Selected Values of Properties of Chemical Compounds. Category C. Selected Ultraviolet Spectral Data.
Description: Data sheets include the structure, empirical formula, CAS registry number, Wiswesser line notation, instrumental parameters and analytical data for each sample.
Refereed Serial

547.3   US
T R C SPECTRAL DATA - 1 H NUCLEAR MAGNETIC RESONANCE. 1959. biennial. $600. Thermodynamics Research Center, Texas Engineering Experiment Station, Texas A & M University System, College Station, TX 77843-3111. TEL 409-845-4940. FAX 409-847-8590. E-mail: info@trchpl.tamu.edu; URL: http://trcweb.tamu.edu. Ed. Kenneth N. Marsh; Pub. Kenneth N. Marsh. R&P contact: Kenneth N. Marsh. circ. 146. (looseleaf format) **Document type:** academic/scholarly publication.
Former titles: Thermodynamics Research Center. Hydrocarbon Project. Selected Values of Properties of Hydrocarbons and Related Compounds. Category F: Selected Nuclear Magnetic Resonance Data; A P I Research Project 44. Selected Values of Properties of Hydrocarbons and Related Compounds. Category F: Selected Nuclear Magnetic Resonance Data (ISSN 0065-9681)

547.3 543.085   US
T R C SPECTRAL DATA - 13 C NUCLEAR MAGNETIC RESONANCE. 1975. s-a. $550. Thermodynamics Research Center, Texas Engineering Experiment Station, Texas A & M University System, College Station, TX 77843-3111. TEL 409-845-4940. FAX 409-847-8590. E-mail: info@trchpl.tamu.edu; URL: http://trcweb.tamu.edu. Ed. Kenneth N. Marsh; Pub. Kenneth N. Marsh. R&P contact: Kenneth N. Marsh. circ. 140. **Document type:** academic/scholarly publication.
Former titles: Thermodynamics Research Center. Hydrocarbon Project. Selected Values of Properties of Hydrocarbons and Related Compounds. Category G: Selected 13-C Nuclear Magnetic Resonance Spectral Data; A P I Research Project 44. Selected Values of Properties of Hydrocarbons and Related Compounds. Category G: Selected 13 C Nuclear Magnetic Resonance Spectral Data.
Refereed Serial

541.36 541.3   US
T R C THERMODYNAMIC TABLES - NON-HYDROCARBONS. 1955. biennial. $1200. Thermodynamics Research Center, Texas Engineering Experiment Station, Texas A & M University System, College Station, TX 77843-3111. TEL 409-845-4940. FAX 409-847-8590. E-mail: info@trchpl.tamu.edu; URL: http://trcweb.tamu.edu. Ed. Kenneth N. Marsh; Pub. Kenneth N. Marsh. R&P contact: Kenneth N. Marsh. circ. 230. (looseleaf format) **Document type:** academic/scholarly publication.
—**CCC.**
Formerly: Thermodynamics Research Center. Data Project. Selected Values of Properties of Chemical Compounds. Category A. Tables of Selected Values of Physical and Thermodynamic Properties of Chemical Compounds (ISSN 0082-4046)
Refereed Serial

CHEMISTRY — ANALYTICAL CHEMISTRY

543 NE ISSN 0039-9140
QD71 CODEN: TLNTA2
TALANTA; international journal of pure and applied analytical chemistry. (Text in English) 1958. m. fl.3500($2011) (effective 1998). Elsevier Science B.V., P.O. Box 211, 1000 AE Amsterdam, Netherlands. TEL 31-20-4853911. FAX 31-20-4853598. E-mail: nlinfo-f@elsevier.nl; usinfo-f@elsevier.com; forinfo-kyf04035@niftyserve.or.jp; URL: http://www.elsevier.nl/. (Subscr. in the Americas to: Elsevier Science, Regional Sales Office, Box 945, New York, NY 10159-0945. TEL 212-633-3730. FAX 212-633-3680; Subscr. in Australasia and the Far East to: Elsevier Science (Singapore) Pte Ltd, No.1 Temasek Ave., No.17-01 Millenia Tower, Singapore 039192, Singapore. TEL 65-434-3727. FAX 65-337-2230; Subscr. in Japan to: Elsevier Science Japan, 9-15 Higashi-Azabu 1-chome, Minato-ku, Tokyo 106, Japan. TEL 81-3-5561-5033. FAX 81-3-5561-5047) Eds. G.D. Christian, E.H. Hansen. adv.; bk.rev.; charts; illus.; index. circ. 2,100. (also avail. in microfiche from MIM; microfilm from UMI) Indexed: Alloys Ind., ASCA, Biol.Abstr., Chem.Abstr., Chem.Cit.Ind., Curr.Cont., Deep Sea Res.& Oceanogr.Abstr., Eng.Mat.Abstr., Excerp.Med., Food Sci.& Tech.Abstr., GeoRef., Ind.Sci.Rev., Mass Spectr.Bull., Mat.Sci.Cit.Ind., Met.Abstr., Met.Abstr.Ind., Nonfer.Met.Alert, PCC Alert, Sci.Cit.Ind., Steels Alert, W.R.C.Inf., World Alum.Abstr. **Document type:** academic/scholarly publication.
—BLDSC (8601.100000); CASDDS; CISTI; EMDOCS; Genuine Article; Linda Hall; SWETS; UMI; UnCover. **CCC**.
Description: Publishes papers, reviews, and communications in all branches of pure and applied analytical chemistry, including relevant advances in the study of chemical sensors.
Refereed Serial

543 NE ISSN 0167-9244
CODEN: TIACD4
TECHNIQUES AND INSTRUMENTATION IN ANALYTICAL CHEMISTRY. (Text in English) 1978. irreg., vol.13, 1993. price varies. Elsevier Science B.V., Books Division, P.O. Box 211, 1000 AE Amsterdam, Netherlands. TEL 31-20-4853911. FAX 31-20-4853705. TELEX 18582 ESPA NL. E-mail: nlinfo-f@elsevier.nl; usinfo-f@elsevier.com; forinfo-kyf04035@niftyserve.or.jp; URL: http://www.elsevier.nl/. (Subscr. in the Americas to: Elsevier Science, Regional Sales Office, Box 945, New York, NY 10159-0945. TEL 212-633-3730. FAX 212-633-3680; Subscr. in Australasia and the Far East to: Elsevier Science (Singapore) Pte Ltd, No.1 Temasek Ave., No.17-01 Millenia Tower, Singapore 039192, Singapore. TEL 65-434-3727. FAX 65-337-2230; Subscr. in Japan to: Elsevier Science Japan, 9-15 Higashi-Azabu 1-chome, Minato-ku, Tokyo 106, Japan. TEL 81-3-5561-5033. FAX 81-3-5561-5047) Indexed: Chem.Abstr. **Document type:** monographic series.
—BLDSC (8743.280000); CASDDS; CISTI; KNAW. **CCC**.
Refereed Serial

544 535 UK ISSN 0262-8716
CODEN: TVUSD5
TECHNIQUES IN VISIBLE AND ULTRAVIOLET SPECTROMETRY. 1981. irreg., no.4, 1993. (U V Spectrometry Group) Chapman & Hall, 2-6 Boundary Row, London SE1 8HN, England. TEL 44-171-8650066. FAX 44-171-5229623. TELEX 290164 CHAPMA G. E-mail: chsub@itps.co.uk. (Orders to: International Thomson Publishing Services Ltd., Cheriton House, N. Way, Andover, Hants. SP10 5BE, England. TEL 44-1264-342713. FAX 44-1264-342807; N. America: Chapman & Hall, 115 Fifth Ave., New York, NY 10003. TEL 212-780-6235. FAX 212-260-1363) Ed.Bd. **Document type:** monographic series.
—BLDSC (8745.410000); CASDDS.

543.0858 US
TOPICS IN FLUORESCENCE SPECTROSCOPY. 1991. irreg., vol.5, 1997. price varies. Plenum Publishing Corp., 233 Spring St., New York, NY 10013-1578. TEL 212-620-8000. FAX 212-463-0742. TELEX 23-421139. Ed. Joseph R. Lakowicz. (back issues avail.) **Document type:** monographic series.

543 NE ISSN 0165-9936
QD71 CODEN: TTAEDJ
TRENDS IN ANALYTICAL CHEMISTRY; a magazine publishing short, critical reviews and news on trends and developments in analytical chemistry. Key Title: TrAC - Trends in Analytical Chemistry. Reference edition (ISSN 0167-2940) (Supplement avail.) (Text in English) 1981. 10/yr. (plus a. cumulation). fl.1248($761) includes library Compendium (effective 1996). Elsevier Science B.V., P.O. Box 211, 1000 AE Amsterdam, Netherlands. TEL 31-20-4853911. FAX 31-20-4853598. TELEX 18582 ESPA NL. E-mail: nlinfo-f@elsevier.nl; usinfo-f@elsevier.com; forinfo-kyf04035@niftyserve.or.jp; URL: http://www.elsevier.nl/. (Subscr. in the Americas to: Elsevier Science, Regional Sales Office, Box 945, New York, NY 10159-0945. TEL 212-633-3730. FAX 212-633-3680; Subscr. in Australasia and the Far East to: Elsevier Science (Singapore) Pte Ltd, No.1 Temasek Ave., No.17-01 Millenia Tower, Singapore 039192, Singapore. TEL 65-434-3727. FAX 65-337-2230; Subscr. in Japan to: Elsevier Science Japan, 9-15 Higashi-Azabu 1-chome, Minato-ku, Tokyo 106, Japan. TEL 81-3-5561-5033. FAX 81-3-5561-5047) Ed. D. Coleman. adv.; bk.rev. circ. 5,000. (also avail. in microfiche from UMI; back issues avail.) Indexed: AESIS, Anal.Abstr., ASCA, Biol.Abstr., Br.Ceram.Abstr., Chem.Abstr., Chem.Cit.Ind., Curr.Biotech.Abstr., Curr.Cont., Dairy Sci.Abstr., Eng.Ind., Excerp.Med., Food Sci.& Tech.Abstr., I.P.A., Ind.Sci.Rev., INSPEC (1981-), Mass Spectr.Bull., Met.Abstr., Nutr.Abstr., Sci.Cit.Ind., Soils & Fert., W.R.C.Inf., World Alum.Abstr. **Document type:** academic/scholarly publication.
—BLDSC (9049.529000); ADONIS; AskIEEE; CASDDS; CISTI; Ei; Genuine Article; KR SourceOne; SWETS; UnCover. **CCC**.
Description: Covers analytical chemistry, biotechnology, clinical chemistry, environmental chemistry, pharmaceutical chemistry, toxicology, industrial chemistry, process analytical chemistry, food chemistry and geochemistry.
Refereed Serial

543 NE
TRENDS IN ANALYTICAL CHEMISTRY. SUPPLEMENT. Running title: TrAC Supplement. (Text in English) vol.2, 1994. price varies. Elsevier Science B.V., Books Division, P.O. Box 211, 1000 AE Amsterdam, Netherlands. TEL 31-20-4853911. FAX 31-20-4853705. E-mail: nlinfo-f@elsevier.nl; usinfo-f@elsevier.com; forinfo-kyf04035@niftyserve.or.jp; URL: http://www.elsevier.nl/. (Subscr. in the Americas to: Elsevier Science, Regional Sales Office, Box 945, New York, NY 10159-0945. TEL 212-633-3730. FAX 212-633-3680; Subscr. in Australasia and the Far East to: Elsevier Science (Singapore) Pte Ltd, No.1 Temasek Ave., No.17-01 Millenia Tower, Singapore 039192, Singapore. TEL 65-434-3727. FAX 65-337-2230; Subscr. in Japan to: Elsevier Science Japan, 9-15 Higashi-Azabu 1-chome, Minato-ku, Tokyo 106, Japan. TEL 81-3-5561-5033. FAX 81-3-5561-5047)

544 NE ISSN 0167-2940
QD71
TRENDS IN ANALYTICAL CHEMISTRY: REFERENCE EDITION. Key Title: TrAC - Trends in Analytical Chemistry (Reference Edition). Variant title: TrAC Compendium Series. (Text in English) 1981. 10/yr. fl.1407($869) (effective 1997). Elsevier Science B.V., Books Division, P.O. Box 211, 1000 AE Amsterdam, Netherlands. TEL 31-20-4853911. FAX 31-20-4853705. TELEX 18582 ESPA NL. E-mail: nlinfo-f@elsevier.nl; usinfo-f@elsevier.com; forinfo-kyf04035@niftyserve.or.jp; URL: http://www.elsevier.nl/. (Subscr. in the Americas to: Elsevier Science, Regional Sales Office, Box 945, New York, NY 10159-0945. TEL 212-633-3730. FAX 212-633-3680; Subscr. in Australasia and the Far East to: Elsevier Science (Singapore) Pte Ltd, No.1 Temasek Ave., No.17-01 Millenia Tower, Singapore 039192, Singapore. TEL 65-434-3727. FAX 65-337-2230; Subscr. in Japan to: Elsevier Science Japan, 9-15 Higashi-Azabu 1-chome, Minato-ku, Tokyo 106, Japan. TEL 81-3-5561-5033. FAX 81-3-5561-5047) Ed. D. Coleman. (back issues avail.) Indexed: Anal.Abstr., Biol.Abstr., Chem.Abstr., Chem.Cit.Ind., Curr.Cont., Dairy Sci.Abstr., Eng.Ind., Food Sci.& Tech.Abstr., I.P.A., Mass Spectr.Bull., Met.Abstr., Sci.Cit.Ind., World Alum.Abstr. **Document type:** monographic series.
—CISTI; Linda Hall. **CCC**.
Description: Collects archival material from Trends in Analytical Chemistry.
Refereed Serial

544 UK ISSN 0965-6758
V G MONOGRAPHS IN MASS SPECTROMETRY. irreg., no. 3. V G Instruments Ltd., Tudor Rd., Altrincham, Manchester WA14 5RZ, England. TEL 0161-929-9666. Ed. R.A.W. Johnstone. **Document type:** monographic series, academic/scholarly publication.
—BLDSC (9231.555000).

643 US
VARIAN SAMPLE PREPARATION PRODUCTS. ANNUAL INTERNATIONAL SYMPOSIUM. PROCEEDINGS. a. Varian Sample Preparation Products, 24201 Frampton Ave., Harbor City, CA 90710. R&P contact: Nigel Simpson. **Document type:** proceedings.
Formerly: Analytichem International. Annual International Symposium. Proceedings.
Description: Brings together scientists who use bonded silica extraction techniques in their sample preparation methodologies.

543.085 JA ISSN 0911-7806
CODEN: XBNSDA
X SEN BUNSEKI NO SHINPO/ADVANCES IN X-RAY CHEMICAL ANALYSIS. (Text in Japanese; summaries in English, Japanese) 1970. a. 4500 Yen. (Nihon Bunseki Kagakkai - Japan Society for Analytical Chemistry) Agune Gijutsu Senta, 1-25, Minamiaoyama 5-chome, Minato-ku, Tokyo 107, Japan. Indexed: Chem.Abstr., INIS Atomind.
—BLDSC (0712.205000); CASDDS. **CCC**.

X SEN BUNSEKI TORONKAI KOEN YOSHISHU/ABSTRACTS OF ANNUAL CONFERENCE ON X-RAY CHEMICAL ANALYSIS. see CHEMISTRY — Abstracting, Bibliographies, Statistics

543 541 660 RU ISSN 0321-4265
TA401 CODEN: ZVDLAU
ZAVODSKAYA LABORATORIYA; zhurnal po analiticheskoi khimii, fizicheskim, matematicheskim i mekhanicheskim metodam issledovaniya materialov. English translation: Industrial Laboratory (US ISSN 0019-8447) (Text in Russian) 1932. m. $246 (effective 1998). Izdatel'stvo Metallurgiya, 2-i Obydenskii per., 14, 119857 Moscow, Russia. TEL 095-202-5756. (Dist. by: Mezhdunarodnaya Kniga, B. Yakimanka 39, 117049 Moscow, Russia) Ed. N.P. Lyakishev. adv.: page $300. bk.rev.; bibl.; charts; illus.; index, cum.index: 1932-1968 (in 3 vols.). circ. 11,500. Indexed: Alloys Ind., Anal.Abstr., Biol.Abstr., Chem.Abstr., Eng.Ind., Eng.Mat.Abstr., INSPEC (1969-), Met.Abstr., Met.Abstr.Ind., Met.Abstr., Nonfer.Met.Alert, PCC Alert, Steels Alert, World Alum.Abstr. **Document type:** academic/scholarly publication.
—BLDSC (0069.000000); AskIEEE; CASDDS; CISTI; Ei; KR SourceOne. **CCC**.

543.089 US ISSN 0144-2449
TP159.M6 CODEN: ZEOLD3
ZEOLITES; the international journal of molecular sieves. 1981. m. fl.2250($1293) to institutions (effective 1998). Elsevier Science Inc., Box 945, New York, NY 10159-0945. TEL 212-633-3730. FAX 212-633-3680. E-mail: usinfo-f@elsevier.com; URL: http://www.elsevier.nl/. (Subscr. outside the Americas to: Elsevier Science, Regional Sales Office, P.O. Box 211, 1000 AE Amsterdam, Netherlands. TEL 31-20-4853757. FAX 31-20-4853432; Subscr. in Australasia and the Far East to: Elsevier Science (Singapore) Pte Ltd, No.1 Temasek Ave., No.17-01 Millenia Tower, Singapore 039192, Singapore. TEL 65-434-3727. FAX 65-337-2230; Subscr. in Japan to: Elsevier Science Japan, 9-15 Higashi-Azabu 1-chome, Minato-ku, Tokyo 106, Japan. TEL 81-3-5561-5033. FAX 81-3-5561-5047) Eds. R. von Ballmoos, L.V.C. Rees. adv.; bk.rev.; abstr.; illus.; index. (also avail. in microform from UMI; back issues avail.) Indexed: AF Abstr., API Catal., API Hlth.& Environ., API Oil., API Pet.Ref., API Pet.Subst., API Transport., ASCA, Chem.Abstr., Chem.Cit.Ind., Curr.Cont., Mat.Sci.Cit.Ind., Sci.Cit.Ind., Telegen. **Document type:** academic/scholarly publication.
—BLDSC (9512.114300); CASDDS; CISTI; Ei; Genuine Article; Linda Hall; SWETS; UMI; UnCover. **CCC**.
Description: Includes information on structure, properties and applications of natural and synthetic zeolites and other molecules.
Refereed Serial

543   **RU**   **ISSN 0044-4502**
QD71   **CODEN: ZAKHA8**
ZHURNAL ANALITICHESKOI KHIMII. English translation: Journal of Analytical Chemistry (US ISSN 1061-9348) (Text in Russian; contents page and summaries in English) 1946. m. $299 (effective 1998). (Rossiiskaya Akademiya Nauk) Izdatel'stvo Nauka, 90 Profsoyuznaya ul., 117864 Moscow, Russia. TEL 234-05-84. Ed. Yu.A. Zolotov. adv.; bk.rev.; charts; index. circ. 4,050. **Indexed:** Abstr.Bull.Inst.Pap.Chem., Anal.Abstr., Chem.Abstr., Deep Sea Res.& Oceanogr.Abstr., Food Sci.& Tech.Abstr., GeoRef., Met.Abstr., W.R.C.Inf., Weed Abstr. **Document type:** academic/scholarly publication.
—BLDSC (0060.600000); CASDDS; CISTI; KNAW; Linda Hall; SWETS. **CCC.**

CHEMISTRY — Computer Applications

C A SELECTS. COMPUTERS IN CHEMISTRY. see CHEMISTRY — Abstracting, Bibliographies, Statistics

542.85 006   **US**
TP184
C E P SOFTWARE DIRECTORY. 1984. a. price varies. American Institute of Chemical Engineers, 345 E. 47th St., New York, NY 10017. TEL 212-705-8100; 800-242-4363. FAX 212-705-8400. R&P contact: Karen Simpson. TEL 212-705-7337. adv. contact: Jerry Moss. index. **Document type:** directory.
—CISTI.
Formerly: A.I.Ch.E. Applications Software Survey of Personal Computers (ISSN 0743-0183)
Description: Provides information on currently available software for use in chemical engineering applications, including artificial intelligence, equipment design, environmental control, and reaction kinetics.

542.85 613.1   **US**
C I S NEWS. 1984. bi-m. Chemical Information Systems, Inc., 810 Glen Eagles Ct., Ste. 300, Baltimore, MD 21286-2203. TEL 410-321-8440. FAX 410-296-0712. TELEX 9103801738. Ed. Bill Earle. circ. 2,500 (controlled). **Document type:** newsletter.
Refereed Serial

542.85 006   **UK**   **ISSN 0364-5916**
QD503   **CODEN: CCCTD6**
ALPHAD. (Computer Coupling of Phase Diagrams and Thermochemistry); the international research journal for calculation of phase diagrams. 1977. q. fl.1505($865) (effective 1998). Elsevier Science Ltd., Pergamon, P.O. Box 800, Kidlington, Oxford OX5 1DX, England. TEL 44-1865-843000. FAX 44-1865-843010. E-mail: nlinfo-f@elsevier.nl; usinfo-f@elsevier.com; forinfo-kyf04035@niftyserve.or.jp/; URL: http://www.elsevier.nl/. (Subscr. to: Elsevier Science, Regional Sales Office, P.O. Box 211, 1000 AE Amsterdam, Netherlands. TEL 31-20-4853757. FAX 31-20-4853432; Subscr. in the Americas to: Elsevier Science, Regional Sales Office, Box 945, New York, NY 10159-0945. TEL 212-633-3730. FAX 212-633-3680; Subscr. in Australasia and the Far East to: Elsevier Science (Singapore) Pte Ltd, No.1 Temasek Ave., No.17-01 Millenia Tower, Singapore 039192, Singapore. TEL 65-434-3727. FAX 65-337-2230) Ed. Larry Kaufman. adv.; software rev. circ. 1,025. (also avail. in microfilm from UMI) **Indexed:** Alloys Ind., ASCA, Biol.Abstr., Chem.Abstr., Chem.Cit.Ind., Comput.Cont., Curr.Cont., Eng.Mat.Abstr., Ind.Sci.Rev., INIS Atomind., INSPEC (1977-), Mat.Sci.Cit.Ind., Met.Abstr., Metal.Abstr.Ind., Nonfer.Met.Alert, PCC Alert, Sci.Cit.Ind., Steels Alert, World Alum.Abstr. **Document type:** academic/scholarly publication.
—BLDSC (3015.540000); AskIEEE; CASDDS; CISTI; Ei; Genuine Article; KR SourceOne; Linda Hall; SWETS; UMI. **CCC.**
Description: Covers all aspects of calculating and using phase diagrams in thermochemistry and studies of phase equilibrium, including applications in industrial processes.
Refereed Serial

542.85   **NE**   **ISSN 0169-7439**
                                  CODEN: CILSEN
CHEMOMETRICS AND INTELLIGENT LABORATORY SYSTEMS. (Text in English) 1986. 10/yr. fl.2800($1609) (effective 1998). (Chemometrics Society) Elsevier Science B.V., P.O. Box 211, 1000 AE Amsterdam, Netherlands. TEL 31-20-4853911. FAX 31-20-4853598. TELEX 18582 ESPA NL. E-mail: nlinfo-f@elsevier.nl; usinfo-f@elsevier.com; forinfo-kyf04035@niftyserve.or.jp; URL: http://www.elsevier.nl/. (Subscr. in the Americas to: Elsevier Science, Regional Sales Office, Box 945, New York, NY 10159-0945. TEL 212-633-3730. FAX 212-633-3680; Subscr. in Australasia and the Far East to: Elsevier Science (Singapore) Pte Ltd, No.1 Temasek Ave., No.17-01 Millenia Tower, Singapore 039192, Singapore. TEL 65-434-3727. FAX 65-337-2230; Subscr. in Japan to: Elsevier Science Japan, 9-15 Higashi-Azabu 1-chome, Minato-ku, Tokyo 106, Japan. TEL 81-3-5561-5033. FAX 81-3-5561-5047) Ed. D.L. Massart. adv.; bk.rev.; illus.; stat.; index, cum.index. (also avail. in microform from UMI; back issues avail.) **Indexed:** Anal.Abstr., Chem.Abstr., Chem.Cit.Ind., Compumath, Curr.Cont., Curr.Ind.Stat., Excerp.Med., Food Sci.& Tech.Abstr., Ind.Sci.Rev., INSPEC (1986-), Sugar Ind.Abstr. **Document type:** academic/scholarly publication.
—BLDSC (3172.264000); AskIEEE; CASDDS; CISTI; Ei; EMDOCS; Genuine Article; KR SourceOne; Linda Hall; SWETS. **CCC.**
Description: Publishes articles about new developments on laboratory techniques in chemistry and related disciplines which are characterized by the application of statistical and computer methods.
Refereed Serial

542.85   **NE**   **ISSN 1386-7857**
▼**CLUSTER COMPUTING.** Announced for publication in 1998. q. 376 SFr. (effective 1998). Baltzer Science Publishers B.V., P.O. Box 221, 1400 AE Bussum, Netherlands. TEL 31-20-6370061. FAX 31-20-6323651. E-mail: subscribe@baltzer; URL: http://www.baltzer.nl. **Document type:** academic/scholarly publication.

COMPUTER-AIDED CHEMICAL ENGINEERING. see ENGINEERING — Computer Applications

542.85   **CC**
COMPUTER CHEMISTRY MONOGRAPH SERIES. (Text in English) 1992. irreg., no.3, 1993. Science Press, Marketing and Sales Department, 16 Donghuangchenggen North St., Beijing 100717, People's Republic of China. TEL 4010642. FAX 4019810. Ed. Jianrong Zhang. **Document type:** monographic series.

660.285 006   **UK**   **ISSN 0098-1354**
TP149   **CODEN: CCENDW**
COMPUTERS & CHEMICAL ENGINEERING; an international journal of computer applications in chemical engineering. 1977. 13/yr. fl.2905($1670) (effective 1998). Elsevier Science Ltd., Pergamon, P.O. Box 800, Kidlington, Oxford OX5 1DX, England. TEL 44-1865-843000. FAX 44-1865-843010. E-mail: nlinfo-f@elsevier.nl; usinfo-f@elsevier.com; forinfo-kyf04035@niftyserve.or.jp; URL: http://www.elsevier.nl:80/inca/publications/store/3/4/9/349.pub.shtml. (Subscr. to: Elsevier Science, Regional Sales Office, P.O. Box 211, 1000 AE Amsterdam, Netherlands. TEL 31-20-4853757. FAX 31-20-4853432; Subscr. in the Americas to: Elsevier Science, Regional Sales Office, Box 945, New York, NY 10159-0945. TEL 212-633-3730. FAX 212-633-3680; Subscr. in Australasia and the Far East to: Elsevier Science (Singapore) Pte Ltd, No.1 Temasek Ave., No.17-01 Millenia Tower, Singapore 039192, Singapore. TEL 914-524-9200. FAX 914-333-2444) Eds. G.V. Reklaitis, David W.T. Rippin. adv.; bk.rev. circ. 1,000. (also avail. in microfilm from UMI) **Indexed:** A.I.Abstr., A.S.& T.Ind., Abstr.Bull.Inst.Pap.Chem., API Abstr., API Catal., API Hlth.& Environ., API Oil., API Pet.Ref., API Pet.Subst., API Transport, ASCA, CAD CAM Abstr., Chem.Abstr., Chem.Cit.Ind., Chem.Eng.Abstr., Compumath, Comput.Abstr., Comput.Cont., Curr.Cont., Eng.Ind., Excerp.Med., Ind.Sci.Rev., INSPEC, Sci.Cit.Ind., Soft.Abstr.Eng., SSCI, T.C.E.A., W.R.C.Inf. **Document type:** academic/scholarly publication.
—BLDSC (3394.664000); AskIEEE; CASDDS; CISTI; Ei; EMDOCS; Genuine Article; KR SourceOne; SWETS; UMI; UnCover. **CCC.**
Description: Presents information on developments in computer applications used to solve chemical engineering problems.
Refereed Serial

542.85   **UK**
COMPUTERS AND CHEMICAL STRUCTURE INFORMATION SERIES. irreg., no.4, 1993. £60. Research Studies Press Ltd., 24 Belvedere Rd., Taunton, Somerset TA1 1HD, England. TEL 44-1823-336197. FAX 44-1823-253252. E-mail: vaw@rspltd.demon.co.uk. (Dist. by: John Wiley & Sons Ltd., Baffins Ln., Chichester, W. Sussex PO19 1UD, England. TEL 44-1243-779777. FAX 44-1243-775878) Ed. D. Bawden. **Document type:** monographic series.

542.85   **UK**   **ISSN 0097-8485**
QD39.3.E46   **CODEN: COCHDK**
COMPUTERS & CHEMISTRY. 1976. bi-m. fl.1852($1064) (effective 1998). Elsevier Science Ltd., Pergamon, P.O. Box 800, Kidlington, Oxford OX5 1DX, England. TEL 44-1865-843000. FAX 44-1865-843010. E-mail: nlinfo-f@elsevier.nl; usinfo-f@elsevier.com; forinfo-kyf04035@niftyserve.or.jp; URL: http://www.elsevier.nl/. (Subscr. to: Elsevier Science, Regional Sales Office, P.O. Box 211, 1000 AE Amsterdam, Netherlands. TEL 31-20-4853757. FAX 31-20-4853432; Subscr. in the Americas to: Elsevier Science, Regional Sales Office, Box 945, New York, NY 10159-0945. TEL 212-633-3730. FAX 212-633-3680; Subscr. in Australasia and the Far East to: Elsevier Science (Singapore) Pte Ltd, No.1 Temasek Ave., No.17-01 Millenia Tower, Singapore 039192, Singapore. TEL 65-434-3727. FAX 65-337-2230) Ed. David Edelson. adv.; bk.rev. circ. 1,000. (also avail. in microfilm from UMI) **Indexed:** Abstr.Bull.Inst.Pap.Chem., ASCA, Biol.Abstr., Cadscan, Chem.Abstr., Chem.Cit.Ind., Chem.Eng.Abstr., Compumath, Comput.Abstr., Comput.Cont., Comput.Rev., Curr.Cont., Ind.Med. (1994-), Ind.Sci.Rev., INSPEC (1976-), Lead Abstr., Mass Spectr.Bull., Sci.Cit.Ind., Zent.Math., Zincscan. **Document type:** academic/scholarly publication.
—BLDSC (3394.667000); ADONIS; AskIEEE; CASDDS; CISTI; Ei; Genuine Article; KR SourceOne; Linda Hall; SWETS; UMI; UnCover. **CCC.**
Description: Publishes papers on applications of computer techniques to chemistry and biochemistry.
Refereed Serial

CHEMISTRY — CRYSTALLOGRAPHY

542.85   CC   ISSN 1001-4160
QA75.5   CODEN: JYYHE6
JISUANJI YU YINGYONG HUAXUE/COMPUTERS AND APPLIED CHEMISTRY. (Text in Chinese) 1984. q. $52.80. (Chinese Academy of Sciences, East China Institute of Metallurgy) Science Press, Marketing and Sales Department, 16 Donghuangchenggen North St., Beijing 100717, People's Republic of China. TEL 4010642. FAX 4019810. (Co-sponsor: Chinese University of Science and Technology) adv. circ. 4,000. **Document type:** academic/scholarly publication.
—BLDSC (3394.647000); CASDDS.
   Description: Covers applied chemistry, chemical mathematics, computer advances in chemometrics, process simulation, control, artificial intelligence, optimization and graphics in chemistry, molecular modeling, structure-property correlation and data processing. Emphasis is on computational chemistry.
Refereed Serial

542.85 006   US   ISSN 0095-2338
QD1   CODEN: JCISD8
JOURNAL OF CHEMICAL INFORMATION AND COMPUTER SCIENCES. 1960. bi-m. $298 to institutional non-members; members $27 (effective 1997). American Chemical Society, 1155 16th St. N.W., Washington, DC 20036. TEL 800-333-9511. FAX 614-447-3671. (Subscr. to: Membership and Subscription Services, Box 3337, Columbus, OH 43210. TEL 614-447-3776) Ed. George W.A. Milne. adv.; bk.rev.; charts; index. circ. 2,606. (also avail. in microfilm; microfiche; back issues avail.) **Indexed:** Abstr.Bull.Inst.Pap.Chem., Alloys Ind., ASCA, Bibl.Agri., Biol.Abstr., Chem.Abstr., Chem.Cit.Ind., Chem.Eng.Abstr., Compumath, Comput.Abstr., Comput.Cont., Curr.Cont., Deep Sea Res.& Oceanogr.Abstr., Eng.Ind., Eng.Mat.Abstr., Excerp.Med., GeoRef., Ind.Med., Ind.Sci.Rev., INSPEC, Intl.Civil Eng.Abstr., LISA, Met.Abstr.Ind., Met.Abstr., Nonfer.Met.Alert, PCC Alert, PROMT, Risk Abstr., Sci.Cit.Ind., Soft.Abstr.Eng., SSCI, Steels Alert, T.C.E.A., World Alum.Abstr. **Document type:** academic/scholarly publication.
●Also available online. Vendor(s): STN International (CJACS).
—BLDSC (4956.800000); AskIEEE; CASDDS; CISTI; Ei; Genuine Article; KR SourceOne; Linda Hall; SWETS; UMI; UnCover. **CCC.**
   Formerly (until 1975): Journal of Chemical Documentation (ISSN 0021-9576).
   Description: Publishes research papers in all areas of information and computer science relevant to chemistry and chemical technology.
Refereed Serial

542.85   JA   ISSN 0918-0761
   CODEN: CHSFEC
JOURNAL OF CHEMICAL SOFTWARE. (Text in English or Japanese) 1992. q. Kagaku Sofutowea Gakkai - Chemical Software Society of Japan, Fukui Kogyo Koto Senmon Gakko, Geshicho, Sabae-shi, Fukui-ken 916, Japan. TEL 048-853-2417. Ed. Haruo Hosoya.
—**CCC.**

542.85 006   NE   ISSN 0928-1045
   CODEN: JCODES
JOURNAL OF COMPUTER - AIDED MATERIALS DESIGN. (Text in English) 1993. 3/yr. fl.645 to institutions; $331 to institutions in U.S. (effective 1998). E S C O M Science Publishers BV, P.O. Box 214, 2300 AE Leiden, Netherlands. TEL 31-71-127052. FAX 31-71-121772. Ed.Bd. **Indexed:** Chem.Cit.Ind. **Document type:** academic/scholarly publication.
—BLDSC (4963.570000); CASDDS; SWETS. **CCC.**
   Description: Publishes original contributions dealing with recent advances in materials design with special emphasis on the role of computations in these developments. Covers theoretical and computational approaches to materials design and applications in chemistry, biochemistry, biotechnology, catalysis, superconductors and electronics.
Refereed Serial

542.85 006   NE   ISSN 0920-654X
QD480   CODEN: JCADEQ
JOURNAL OF COMPUTER - AIDED MOLECULAR DESIGN. 1987. bi-m. fl.1930 to institutions (effective 1998). E S C O M Science Publishers BV, P.O. Box 214, 2300 AE Leiden, Netherlands. TEL 31-71-127052. FAX 31-71-121772. E-mail: jcamd@wucmd.wustl.edu; URL: http://wucmd.wustl.edu/jcamd/jcamd.html. Ed.Bd. charts; illus.; stat. (also avail. in diskette format) **Indexed:** ASCA, Chem.Cit.Ind., Curr.Cont., Food Sci.& Tech.Abstr. **Document type:** academic/scholarly publication.
●Also available online.
—BLDSC (4963.580000); CASDDS; CISTI; Genuine Article; Linda Hall; SWETS; UnCover. **CCC.**
   Description: Disseminates information on both the theory and application of computer-based methods in the analysis and design of molecules. Includes molecular modelling studies in pharmaceutical, polymer, materials, and surface sciences, as well as other molecular based disciplines.

542.85   JA   ISSN 0919-3391
KAGAKU SOFUTOWEA GAKKAI KENKYU TORONKAI KOEN YOSHISHU. (Text in Japanese) 1986. a. Kagaku Sofutowea Gakkai - Chemical Software Society of Japan, Fukui Kogyo Koto Senmon Gakko, Geshicho, Sabae-shi, Fukui-ken 916, Japan. TEL 0778062-1111. FAX 0778-62-1108.

542.85   JA   ISSN 0918-0869
   CODEN: KASOEA
KAGAKU TO SOFUTOWEA/CHEMISTRY AND SOFTWARE. (Text in Japanese; summaries in English) q. membership. Kagaku Sofutowea Gakkai - Chemical Software Society of Japan, Fukui Kogyo Koto Senmon Gakko, Geshi-cho, Sabae-shi, Fukui-ken 916, Japan. TEL 0778-62-1111. FAX 0778-62-1108. **Indexed:** Chem.Abstr.
—BLDSC (3170.150000).

542.85   US   ISSN 1059-7530
   CODEN: MCCHED
METHODS IN COMPUTATIONAL CHEMISTRY. 1987. irreg., vol.5, 1992. price varies. Plenum Publishing Corp., 233 Spring St., New York, NY 10013-1578. TEL 212-620-8000. FAX 212-463-0742. TELEX 23-421139. E-mail: books@plenum.com. Ed. Stephen Wilson. (back issues avail.) **Indexed:** Chem.Cit.Ind. **Document type:** monographic series.
—BLDSC (5747.480000); CASDDS; KNAW.
   Description: Computer methods applicable to chemical problems.
Refereed Serial

542.85   JA   ISSN 0919-4894
SAISHIN KAGAKU SOFUTOWEASHU/ANNUAL REPORT OF CHEMICAL SOFTWARES. (Text in English, Japanese) 1985. a. Kagaku Sofutowea Gakkai - Chemical Software Society of Japan, Fukui Kogyo Koto Senmon Gakko, Geshicho, Sabae-shi, Fukui-ken 916, Japan. TEL 0778-62-1111. FAX 0778-62-1108.

THEORETICAL AND COMPUTATIONAL CHEMISTRY. see *CHEMISTRY*

720   UK   ISSN 0966-9086
WINDOW ON CHEMOMETRICS. 1993. m. £120($211) (effective 1997). The Royal Society of Chemistry, Thomas Graham House, Science Park, Milton Rd., Cambridge CB4 4WF, England. TEL 44-1223-420066. FAX 44-1223-423429. E-mail: sales@rsc.org; URL: http://chemistry.rsc.org/rsc/. (Dist. by: Turpin Distribution Services, Blackhorse Rd., Letchworth, Herts. SG6 1HN, England. TEL 44-1462-672555. FAX 44-1462-480947) Ed. Lynn Hatley. **Document type:** abstracting/indexing.
   Description: Summarizes articles on the computer processing of analytical data.

CHEMISTRY — Crystallography

548   DK   ISSN 0108-7673
QD901   CODEN: ACACEQ
ACTA CRYSTALLOGRAPHICA. SECTION A: FOUNDATIONS OF CRYSTALLOGRAPHY. (Text in English, French, German, Russian) 1948. bi-m. DKK 2230 in Europe (US, Canada and Japan DKK 2325); sections A, B, C & D combined DKK 11660 (US, Canada and Japan DKK 12180); A, B & C combined DKK 9360 (US, Canada and Japan DKK 9785) (effective 1997). (International Union of Crystallography) Munksgaard International Publishers Ltd., 35 Noerre Soegade, P.O. Box 2148, DK-1016 Copenhagen K, Denmark. TEL 45-33-127030. FAX 45-33-129387. E-mail: fsub@mail.munksgaard.dk. (In N. America: Commerce Place, 350 Main St., Malden, MA 02148-5018. TEL 617-388-8273. FAX 617-388-8274) Ed. C.E. Bugg. adv.; bk.rev. circ. 1,500. (also avail. in microfilm from PMC; reprint service avail. from ISI) **Indexed:** ASCA, Biol.Abstr., Br.Ceram.Abstr., Cadscan, Chem.Abstr., Chem.Cit.Ind., Curr.Cont., GeoRef., Ind.Sci.Rev., INSPEC (1983-), Lead Abstr., Mat.Sci.Cit.Ind., Math.R., Met.Abstr., Sci.Cit.Ind., Soils & Fert., World Alum.Abstr., Zincscan. **Document type:** academic/scholarly publication.
—BLDSC (0612.015000); AskIEEE; CASDDS; CISTI; Ei; Genuine Article; KR SourceOne; Linda Hall; SWETS; UnCover. **CCC.**
   Formerly: Acta Crystallographica. Section A: Crystal Physics, Diffraction, Theoretical and General Crystallography (ISSN 0567-7394); Which superseded in part: Acta Crystallographica (ISSN 0001-5520).
Refereed Serial

548   DK   ISSN 0108-7681
QD901   CODEN: ASBSDK
ACTA CRYSTALLOGRAPHICA. SECTION B: STRUCTURAL SCIENCE. (Text in English, French, German, Russian) bi-m. DKK 2230 in Europe (US, Canada and Japan DKK 2325); sections A, B, C & D combined DKK 11660 (US, Canada and Japan DKK 12180); A, B & C combined DKK 9360 (US, Canada and Japan DKK 9785) (effective 1997). (International Union of Crystallography) Munksgaard International Publishers Ltd., 35 Noerre Soegade, P.O. Box 2148, DK-1016 Copenhagen K, Denmark. TEL 45-33-127030. FAX 45-33-129387. E-mail: fsub@mail.munksgaard.dk. (In N. America: Commerce Place, 350 Main St., Malden, MA 02148-5018. TEL 617-388-8273. FAX 617-388-8274) Ed. C.E. Bugg. adv.; bk.rev. circ. 1,400. (also avail. in microfilm from PMC; reprint service avail. from ISI) **Indexed:** Abstr.Bull.Inst.Pap.Chem., ASCA, Biol.Abstr., Cadscan, Chem.Abstr., Chem.Cit.Ind., Curr.Cont., Ind.Sci.Rev., INSPEC (1983-), Lead Abstr., Mat.Sci.Cit.Ind., Math.R., Met.Abstr., Sci.Cit.Ind., Soils & Fert., World Alum.Abstr., Zincscan. **Document type:** academic/scholarly publication.
—BLDSC (0612.020500); AskIEEE; CASDDS; CIS; Ei; Genuine Article; KR SourceOne; Linda Hall; SWETS; UnCover. **CCC.**
   Formerly: Acta Crystallographica. Section B: Structural Crystallography and Crystal Chemistry (ISSN 0567-7408); Which superseded in part: Acta Crystallographica (ISSN 0001-5520).
Refereed Serial

548   DK   ISSN 0108-2701
QD901   CODEN: ACSCEE
ACTA CRYSTALLOGRAPHICA. SECTION C: CRYSTAL STRUCTURE COMMUNICATIONS. (Text in English, French, German, Russian) m. DKK 5390 in Europe (US, Canada and Japan DKK 5625); sections A, B, C & D combined DKK 11660 (US, Canada and Japan DKK 12180); A, B, & C combined DKK 9360 (US, Canada and Japan DKK 9785) (effective 1997). (International Union of Crystallography) Munksgaard International Publishers Ltd., 35 Noerre Soegade, P.O. Box 2148, DK-1016 Copenhagen K, Denmark. TEL 45-33-127030. FAX 45-33-129387. E-mail: fsub@mail.munksgaard.dk. (In N. America: Commerce Place, 350 Main St., Malden, MA 02148-5018. TEL 617-388-8273. FAX 617-388-8274) Ed. C.E. Bugg. adv.; bk.rev. circ. 1,400. (also avail. in microfilm from PMC; reprint service avail. from ISI) **Indexed:** ASCA, Chem.Abstr., Chem.Cit.Ind., Curr.Cont., Ind.Sci.Rev., INSPEC (1983-), Mat.Sci.Cit.Ind., Sci.Cit.Ind., Soils & Fert. **Document type:** academic/scholarly publication.
—BLDSC (0612.021000); AskIEEE; CASDDS; CISTI; Ei; Genuine Article; KR SourceOne; Linda Hall; SWETS; UnCover. **CCC.**
    Incorporates (1972-1982): Crystal Structure Communications (ISSN 0302-1742); Supersedes in part: Acta Crystallographica (ISSN 0001-5520)
    Refereed Serial

548   DK   ISSN 0907-4449
QP519.9.X72   CODEN: ABCRE6
ACTA CRYSTALLOGRAPHICA. SECTION D: BIOLOGICAL CRYSTALLOGRAPHY. 1993. bi-m. DKK 2420 in Europe (US, Canada and Japan DKK 2515); sections A, B, C & D combined DKK 11660 (US, Canada and Japan DKK 12180) (effective 1997). (International Union of Crystallography) Munksgaard International Publishers Ltd., 35 Noerre Soegade, P.O. Box 2148, DK-1016 Copenhagen K, Denmark. TEL 45-33-127030. FAX 45-33-129387. E-mail: fsub@mail.munksgaard.dk. (In N. America: Commerce Place, 350 Main St., Malden, MA 02148-5018. TEL 617-388-8273. FAX 617-388-8274) Ed. C.E. Bugg. adv.; bk.rev. circ. 1,400. **Indexed:** ASCA, Biol.Abstr., Chem.Cit.Ind., Curr.Cont., Food Sci.& Tech.Abstr., Ind.Sci.Rev., INSPEC (1993-), Sci.Cit.Ind. **Document type:** academic/scholarly publication.
—BLDSC (0612.022000); ADONIS; AskIEEE; CASDDS; EMDOCS; Genuine Article; KR SourceOne; Linda Hall; SWETS; UnCover. **CCC.**
    Refereed Serial

548 666   US   ISSN 0896-1654
AMERICAN ASSOCIATION FOR CRYSTAL GROWTH NEWSLETTER. 1970. 3/yr. membership. American Association for Crystal Growth, Box 3233, Thousand Oaks, CA 91359-0233. TEL 805-492-7047. FAX 805-492-4062. E-mail: ba643@lafn.org; URL: http://www.aml.arizona.edu/aacg/aacghome.html. Ed. Patricia A. Morris Hotsenpiller. R&P contact: Anthony L. Gentile. adv. contact: John DeCosta. bk.rev.; bibl.; charts; illus. circ. 1,000. (back issues avail.) **Document type:** newsletter.

548   US   ISSN 0514-8863
AMERICAN CRYSTALLOGRAPHIC ASSOCIATION. MONOGRAPHS. 1944. irreg., no.8, 1979. price varies. American Crystallographic Association, Box 96, Ellicott Sta., Buffalo, NY 14205-0096. TEL 716-856-9600. FAX 716-852-4846. (Dist. by: Polycrystal Book Service, Box 3439, Dayton, OH 45401) Ed. S.C. Abrahams. circ. 1,250. **Indexed:** Bull.Signal, Chem.Abstr., INSPEC. **Document type:** monographic series.

548   US   ISSN 0569-4221
QD901   CODEN: ACRABY
AMERICAN CRYSTALLOGRAPHIC ASSOCIATION. PROGRAM & ABSTRACTS. 1950. a. $10. American Crystallographic Association, Box 96, Ellicott Sta., Buffalo, NY 14205-0096. TEL 716-856-9600. FAX 716-852-4846. (Distr. by: Polycrystal Book Service, Box 3439, Dayton, OH 45401) Ed. S.C. Abrahams. circ. 2,500. **Indexed:** Bull.Signal, Chem.Abstr., GeoRef., INSPEC. **Document type:** proceedings.
—BLDSC (6864.405000).

548   US   ISSN 0065-8006
QD901   CODEN: TACAAH
AMERICAN CRYSTALLOGRAPHIC ASSOCIATION. TRANSACTIONS. 1965. a. $25. American Crystallographic Association, Box 96, Ellicott Sta., Buffalo, NY 14205-0096. TEL 716-856-9600. FAX 716-852-4846. (Dist. by: Polycrystal Book Service, Box 3439, Dayton, OH 45401) circ. 2,500. (back issues avail.) **Indexed:** Chem.Abstr., GeoRef. **Document type:** proceedings.
—CASDDS; CISTI; Ei; Linda Hall.

AMERICAN MINERALOGIST. see *MINES AND MINING INDUSTRY*

548   GW   ISSN 0948-1907
                                 CODEN: CVDEFX
▼**CHEMICAL VAPOR DEPOSITION.** (Supplement to: Advanced Materials (ISSN 0935-9648)) (Text in English) 1995. bi-m. (effective 1998). V C H Verlagsgesellschaft mbH, Postfach 101161, 69451 Weinheim, Germany. TEL 49-6201-606147. FAX 49-6201-606117. (US addr.: VCH Publishers Inc., 220 E. 23rd St., New York, NY 10010-4606. TEL 212-683-8333) Eds. M. Hitchman, P. Gregory. —AskIEEE; CASDDS; Genuine Article; KR SourceOne. **CCC.**
    Description: Publishes reviews, short communications and full papers on all aspects of chemical vapor disposition and related technologies.
    Refereed Serial

548   US   ISSN 1067-6147
QC173.45
CONDENSED MATTER AND MATERIALS COMMUNICATIONS. 1993. q. $295 (effective 1996). Nova Science Publishers, Inc., 6080 Jericho Tpke., Ste. 207, Commack, NY 11725-2808. TEL 516-499-3103. E-mail: novasci1@aol.com. Ed. A.V. Narlikar. **Document type:** academic/scholarly publication.
—CISTI.
    Description: Provides information on crystal growth, thin film processing, amorphous and disordered systems, magnetism, superfluidity, surfaces, and phase transitions.

CONDENSED MATTER THEORIES. see *PHYSICS*

548 660   GW   ISSN 0232-1300
QD901   CODEN: CRTEDF
CRYSTAL RESEARCH AND TECHNOLOGY. journal of experimental and industrial crystallography. (Text in English) 1966. 8/yr. DM.195 (foreign DM.211) to individuals; institutions DM.1095 (foreign DM.1135) (effective 1997). Akademie Verlag GmbH, Muehlenstr. 33-34, 13187 Berlin, Germany. TEL 49-30-47889348. FAX 49-30-47889357. E-mail: info@akademie-verlag.de. (Subscr. in the Americas to: John Wiley & Sons, Inc., 605 Third Ave., New York, NY 10158. TEL 212-850-6645. FAX 212-850-6021) Ed. W. Neumann. bk.rev.; charts; illus.; index. **Indexed:** Alloys Ind., ASCA, Cadscan, Chem.Abstr., Chem.Cit.Ind., Curr.Cont., Eng.Mat.Abstr., Ind.Sci.Rev., INIS Atomind., INSPEC, Lead Abstr., Mat.Sci.Cit.Ind., Met.Abstr.Ind., Met.Abstr., Nonfer.Met.Alert, PCC Alert, Phys.Ber., Sci.Cit.Ind., Soils & Fert., Steels Alert, World Alum.Abstr., Zincscan. **Document type:** academic/scholarly publication.
—BLDSC (3490.157500); AskIEEE; CASDDS; CISTI; Ei; Genuine Article; KR SourceOne; Linda Hall; SWETS; UnCover. **CCC.**
    Formerly (until 1981): Kristall und Technik (ISSN 0023-4753)

548   RU   ISSN 1063-7745
QD901   CODEN: CYSTE3
CRYSTALLOGRAPHY REPORTS. English translation of: Kristalografiya (RU ISSN 0023-4761) 1957. bi-m. $1410 to institutions (effective 1997). (Rossiiskaya Akademiya Nauk) Maik Nauka - Interperiodica, Mezhdunarodnyi Otdel, Ul. Profsoyuznaya, 90, 117864 Moscow, Russia. (Subscr. to: American Institute of Physics, Member and Subscriber Services, 500 Sunnyside Blvd., Woodbury, NY 11797-2999, U.S.A. TEL 516-576-2270. FAX 516-349-9704) Ed. B.K. Vainshtein. bibl.; charts; illus.; index. (also avail. in microform from AIP; back issues avail.) **Indexed:** Alloys Ind., C.P.I., Eng.Mat.Abstr., Gen.Phys.Adv.Abstr., GeoRef., INSPEC, Math.R., Met.Abstr., Met.Abstr.Ind., Nonfer.Met.Alert, PCC Alert, Phys.Ber., Steels Alert, World Alum.Abstr., Zent.Math. **Document type:** academic/scholarly publication.
—BLDSC (0411.083000); AskIEEE; CISTI; KR SourceOne; Linda Hall; SWETS; UnCover. **CCC.**
    Formerly: Soviet Physics - Crystallography (ISSN 0038-5638)

548   NE   ISSN 0889-311X
QD901   CODEN: CRRVEN
CRYSTALLOGRAPHY REVIEWS. a. $131 (effective 1998). Gordon and Breach - Harwood Academic, Amsteldisk 166, 1st Fl., 1079 LH Amsterdam, Netherlands. (Subscr. to: International Publishers Distributor, Box 32160, Newark, NJ 07102. TEL 800-545-8398. FAX 215-750-6343) Eds. Moreton Moore, John J. Stezowski. (also avail. in microform) —BLDSC (3490.162000); CASDDS; CISTI; SWETS. **CCC.**
    Refereed Serial

548   US   ISSN 0172-5076
QD921   CODEN: CGPAD8
CRYSTALS: GROWTH, PROPERTIES AND APPLICATIONS. 1978. irreg., vol.13, 1991. price varies. Springer-Verlag, 175 Fifth Ave., New York, NY 10010. TEL 212-460-1500. FAX 212-473-6272. (Also: Berlin, Heidelberg, Tokyo and Vienna) (reprint service avail. from ISI) **Indexed:** Chem.Abstr., INSPEC. **Document type:** monographic series.
—CASDDS; CISTI. **CCC.**

553.82 622.382   SZ   ISSN 0925-9635
                                 CODEN: DRMTE3
DIAMOND AND RELATED MATERIALS. (Text in English) 1991. m. fl.2437($1400) (effective 1998). Elsevier Science S.A., P.O. Box 564, CH-1001 Lausanne 1, Switzerland. TEL 41-21-3207381. FAX 41-21-3235444. TELEX 450620-ELSA-CH. (Subscr. to: Elsevier Science, Regional Sales Office, P.O. Box 211, 1000 AE Amsterdam, Netherlands. TEL 31-20-4853757. FAX 31-20-4853432; Subscr. in the Americas to: Elsevier Science, Regional Sales Office, Box 945, New York, NY 10159-0945. TEL 212-633-3730. FAX 212-633-3680; Subscr. in Australasia to: Elsevier Science (Singapore) Pte. Ltd., No. 1 Temasek Ave., No. 17-01 Millenia Tower, Singapore 039192, Singapore. TEL 65-434-3727. FAX 65-434-3680) Ed. R. Messier. (also avail. in microform from UMI; back issues avail.) **Indexed:** Alloys Ind., ASCA, Chem.Cit.Ind., Curr.Cont., Eng.Mat.Abstr., Ind.Sci.Rev., INSPEC (1990-), Mat.Sci.Cit.Ind., Met.Abstr., Met.Abstr.Ind., Nonfer.Met.Alert, PCC Alert, Sci.Cit.Ind., Steels Alert. **Document type:** academic/scholarly publication.
—BLDSC (3579.835200); AskIEEE; CASDDS; CISTI; EMDOCS; Genuine Article; KR SourceOne; SWETS. **CCC.**
    Description: Covers basic and applied research on diamond materials and related substances, including high-temperature high-pressure synthetic materials.
    Refereed Serial

DISLOCATIONS IN SOLIDS. see *PHYSICS*

548   JA
EKISHO DISUPUREI SANGYO NENKAN/ANNUAL OF LIQUID CRYSTAL DISPLAY INDUSTRIES. (Text in Japanese) 1992. a. 56650 Yen. C M C Co., Ltd., 5-4, Uchikanda 1-chome, Chiyoda-ku, Tokyo 101, Japan.

548   JA
EKISHO TORONKAI KEON YOKOSHU/PREPRINTS OF SYMPOSIUM ON LIQUID CRYSTALS. (Text in Japanese) 1975. a. Chemical Society of Japan - Nippon Kagakkai, 1-5, Kanda Surugadai, Chiyoda-ku, Tokyo 101, Japan.

CHEMISTRY — CRYSTALLOGRAPHY

GEMS & GEMOLOGY. see *JEWELRY, CLOCKS AND WATCHES*

548 DK ISSN 0074-9389
INTERNATIONAL UNION OF CRYSTALLOGRAPHY. ABSTRACTS OF THE TRIENNIAL CONGRESS. (Supplement to: Acta Crystallographica. Section A) (Text in English, French or German) 1960. triennial; 1990, 15th General Assembly. (International Union of Crystallography) Munksgaard International Publishers Ltd., 35 Noerre Soegade, P.O. Box 2148, DK-1016 Copenhagen K, Denmark. TEL 45-33-127030. FAX 45-33-129387. TELEX 19431-MUNKS-DK. E-mail: fsub@mail.munksgaard.dk. (In N. America: Commerce Place, 350 Main St., Malden, MA 02148-5018. TEL 617-388-8273. FAX 617-388-8274) (reprint service avail. from ISI) **Document type:** proceedings.

548 UK
INTERNATIONAL UNION OF CRYSTALLOGRAPHY. TEXTS ON CRYSTALLOGRAPHY. irreg., vol.2, 1992. Oxford University Press, Walton St., Oxford OX2 6DP, England. TEL 01865-56767. FAX 01865-56646. TELEX 837330-OXPRES-G. Ed. C. Giacovazzo. **Document type:** monographic series.

548 RU ISSN 0202-7984
CODEN: INKKBO
ITOGI NAUKI I TEKHNIKI: KRISTALLOKHIMIYA. irreg., latest vol.23, 1989. price varies. Vsesoyuznyi Institut Nauchno-Tekhnicheskoi Informatsii (VINITI), Ul. Baltiiskaya 14, Moscow A-219, Russia. **Indexed:** Chem.Abstr. **Document type:** monographic series. —CASDDS.

JINKO KESSHO KOGAKKAI TOKUBETSU KOENKAI KOEN YOSHISHU/ASSOCIATION OF SYNTHETIC CRYSTAL SCIENCE AND TECHNOLOGY. ABSTRACTS OF THE SPECIAL MEETING. see *CHEMISTRY — Abstracting, Bibliographies, Statistics*

548 DK ISSN 0021-8898
QD901 CODEN: JACGAR
JOURNAL OF APPLIED CRYSTALLOGRAPHY. 1968. bi-m. DKK 2080 in Europe (US, Canada and Japan DKK 2175); with Journal of Synchrotron Radiation DKK 3625 (US, Canada and Japan DKK 3815) (effective 1997). (International Union of Crystallography) Munksgaard International Publishers Ltd., 35 Noerre Soegade, P.O. Box 2148, DK-1016 Copenhagen K, Denmark. TEL 45-33-127030. FAX 45-33-129387. E-mail: fsub@mail.munksgaard.dk. (In N. America: Commerce Place, 350 Main St., Malden, MA 02148-5018. TEL 617-388-8273. FAX 617-388-8274) Ed. A.M. Glazer. adv.; bk.rev.; charts; illus.; stat. circ. 1,250. (reprint service avail. from ISI) **Indexed:** Abstr.Bull.Inst.Pap.Chem., Alloys Ind., Apic.Abstr., Art & Archaeol.Tech.Abstr., ASCA, Br.Ceram.Abstr., Cadscan, Chem.Abstr., Chem.Cit.Ind., Curr.Cont., Deep Sea Res.& Oceanogr.Abstr., Eng.Mat.Abstr., GeoRef., Ind.Sci.Rev., INSPEC, Lead Abstr., Mat.Sci.Cit.Ind., Met.Abstr.Ind., Met.Abstr., Nonfer.Met.Alert, PCC Alert, Phys.Ber., Sci.Cit.Ind., Steels Alert, World Alum.Abstr., World Text.Abstr., Zincscan. **Document type:** academic/scholarly publication.
—BLDSC (4942.400000); AskIEEE; CASDDS; CISTI; Ei; Genuine Article; KR SourceOne; Linda Hall; SWETS; UnCover. **CCC.**
Refereed Serial

548 US ISSN 1074-1542
QD901 CODEN: JCCYEV
JOURNAL OF CHEMICAL CRYSTALLOGRAPHY. 1971. m. $575 (foreign $675) (effective 1997). Plenum Publishing Corp., 233 Spring St., New York, NY 10013-1578. TEL 212-620-8000. FAX 212-463-0742. TELEX 23-421139. Eds. J.L. Atwood, R.D. Rogers. adv.; index. (back issues avail.) **Indexed:** ASCA, Chem.Abstr., Chem.Cit.Ind., Curr.Cont., Ind.Sci.Rev., INIS Atomind., INSPEC, Mass Spectr.Bull., Phys.Ber., Sci.Cit.Ind. **Document type:** academic/scholarly publication.
—BLDSC (4955.840000); AskIEEE; CASDDS; CISTI; Genuine Article; KR SourceOne; Linda Hall; SWETS; UMI; UnCover. **CCC.**
Former titles (until vol.24, no.1, 1994): Journal of Crystallographic and Spectroscopic Research (ISSN 0277-8068); Journal of Crystal and Molecular Structure (ISSN 0308-4086)
Description: Publishes research results in the general area of crystallography and its relation to problems of molecular structure.
Refereed Serial

548 US ISSN 1056-7860
TS695 CODEN: JCVDET
JOURNAL OF CHEMICAL VAPOR DEPOSITION. 1992. q. $215 (foreign $253) (effective 1997); $245 (foreign $300) (effective 1998). Technomic Publishing Co., Inc., 851 New Holland Ave., Box 3535, Lancaster, PA 17604. TEL 717-291-5609. FAX 717-295-4538. TELEX 230-753565 (TECHNOMIC UD). E-mail: marketing@techpub.com; URL: http://www.techpub.com. Ed. Shojiro Komatsu. circ. 115. **Indexed:** Alloys Ind., Eng.Mat.Abstr., INSPEC (1992-), Intl.Polym.Sci.& Tech., Met.Abstr.Ind., Met.Abstr., Nonfer.Met.Alert, PCC Alert, RAPRA, Steels Alert, World Alum.Abstr. **Document type:** academic/scholarly publication.
—BLDSC (4957.150000); AskIEEE; CASDDS; CISTI; KR SourceOne; SWETS; UMI. **CCC.**
Description: Publishes original research studies on the experimental, theoretical, and applied science aspects of vapor deposition phenomena.
Refereed Serial

548 NE ISSN 0022-0248
QD921 CODEN: JCRGAE
JOURNAL OF CRYSTAL GROWTH. 1967. 48/yr. fl.13236($7607) (effective 1998). North-Holland (Subsidiary of: Elsevier Science B.V.), P.O. Box 211, 1000 AE Amsterdam, Netherlands. TEL 31-20-4853911. FAX 31-20-4853598. TELEX 18582 ESPA NL. (Subscr. in the Americas to: Elsevier Science, Regional Sales Office, Box 945, New York, NY 10159-0945. TEL 212-633-3730. FAX 212-633-3680; Subscr. in Australasia and the Far East to: Elsevier Science (Singapore) Pte Ltd, No.1 Temasek Ave., No.17-01 Millenia Tower, Singapore 039192, Singapore. TEL 65-434-3727. FAX 65-337-2230; Subscr. in Japan to: Elsevier Science Japan, 9-15 Higashi-Azabu 1-chome, Minato-ku, Tokyo 106, Japan. TEL 81-3-5561-5033. FAX 81-3-5561-5047) Ed. M. Schieber. adv.; bk.rev.; index. (also avail. in microform from UMI; back issues avail.; reprint service avail. from SWZ) **Indexed:** Alloys Ind., ASCA, Cadscan, Chem.Abstr., Chem.Cit.Ind., Chem.Eng.Abstr., Curr.Cont., Eng.Mat.Abstr., GeoRef., Ind.Sci.Rev., INSPEC, Int.Aerosp.Abstr., Lead Abstr., Mat.Sci.Cit.Ind., Met.Abstr., Met.Abstr.Ind., Mineral.Abstr., Nonfer.Met.Alert, PCC Alert, Phys.Ber., Sci.Cit.Ind., Soils & Fert., Steels Alert, T.C.E.A., World Alum.Abstr., Zincscan. **Document type:** academic/scholarly publication.
—BLDSC (4965.800000); AskIEEE; CASDDS; CISTI; Ei; Genuine Article; KR SourceOne; Linda Hall; SWETS; UnCover. **CCC.**
Formerly: International Journal for Crystal Growth.
Description: Offers a common reference and publication source for workers engaged in research on the experimental and theoretical aspects of crystal growth and its applications.
Refereed Serial

JOURNAL OF SUPERHARD MATERIALS. see *PHYSICS*

548 JA
KEIKOTAI DOGAKKAI KOEN YOKO/PHOSPHOR RESEARCH SOCIETY. PREPRINTS OF MEETING. (Text in Japanese) bi-m. Keikotai Dogakkai, Denki Kagaku Kyokai, 12-1, Yurakucho 1-chome, Chiyoda-ku, Tokyo 100, Japan.

548 RU ISSN 0023-4761
QD901 CODEN: KRISAJ
KRISTALLOGRAFIYA. English translation: Crystallography Reports (US ISSN 1063-7745) 1956. bi-m. $252 (effective 1998). (Rossiiskaya Akademiya Nauk) Izdatel'stvo Nauka, 90 Profsoyuznaya ul., 117864 Moscow, Russia. Ed A.V. Shubnikov. (tabloid format) **Indexed:** Alloys Ind., ASCA, Biol.Abstr., Cadscan, Chem.Abstr., Chem.Cit.Ind., Curr.Cont., Eng.Mat.Abstr., GeoRef., Ind.Sci.Rev., INIS Atomind., INSPEC, Lead Abstr., Mat.Sci.Cit.Ind., Met.Abstr., Met.Abstr.Ind., Nonfer.Met.Alert, PCC Alert, Sci.Cit.Ind., Steels Alert, World Alum.Abstr., Zent.Math., Zincscan. **Document type:** academic/scholarly publication.
—BLDSC (0093.000000); AskIEEE; CASDDS; CISTI; Ei; Genuine Article; KR SourceOne; Linda Hall. **CCC.**

LANDOLT-BOERNSTEIN, ZAHLENWERTE UND FUNKTIONEN AUS NATURWISSENSCHAFTEN UND TECHNIK. NEUE SERIE. GROUP 3: CRYSTAL PHYSICS. see *PHYSICS*

548 UK ISSN 0267-8292
QD923 CODEN: LICRE6
LIQUID CRYSTALS; an international journal in the field of anisotropic fluids. Online edition (UK ISSN 1366-5855) 1986. m. £1327($2189) to institutions (£1592($2627) with online ed.) (effective 1998). Taylor & Francis Ltd., 1 Gunpowder Sq., London EC4A 3DE, England. TEL 44-171-583-0490. FAX 44-171-583-0585. E-mail: info@tandf.co.uk; URL: http://www.tandf.co.uk/. (Subscr. in N. America to: Taylor & Francis Inc., 1900 Frost Rd., Ste. 101, Bristol, PA 19007-1598. TEL 215-785-5800. FAX 215-785-5515) Ed. G.W. Gray. index. (back issues avail.) **Indexed:** Alloys Ind., ASCA, Chem.Cit.Ind., Curr.Cont., Eng.Mat.Abstr., Mat.Sci.Cit.Ind., Met.Abstr., Met.Abstr.Ind., Nonfer.Met.Alert, PCC Alert, Sci.Cit.Ind., Steels Alert, World Alum.Abstr. **Document type:** academic/scholarly publication.
●Also available online.
—BLDSC (5221.923000); AskIEEE; CASDDS; CISTI; Ei; Genuine Article; KR SourceOne; Linda Hall; SWETS; UnCover. **CCC.**
Description: Presents reports of original research of an experimental or a theoretical nature on all liquid-crystalline materials, their synthesis and their applications.
Refereed Serial

548 US ISSN 1358-314X
LIQUID CRYSTALS TODAY. 1990. q. £65($108) to institutions (effective 1998). Taylor & Francis Inc., 1900 Frost Rd., Ste. 101, Bristol, PA 19007-1598. TEL 215-785-5800; 800-821-8312. FAX 215-785-5515. E-mail: info@tandf.co.uk; URL: http://www.tandf.co.uk/. (Subscr. in Europe to: Taylor & Francis Ltd., Rankine Rd., Basingstoke, Hants. RG24 8PR, England. TEL 44-1256-840366. FAX 44-1256-479438) Ed. D.A. Dunmur. **Document type:** academic/scholarly publication.
—BLDSC (5221.931000); CISTI; SWETS.
Description: Provides a link between liquid crystal technology and the more fundamental aspects of liquid crystal science.
Refereed Serial

M C L C COMMUNICATIONS. (Molecular Crystals, Liquid Crystals) see *CHEMISTRY — Abstracting, Bibliographies, Statistics*

548 UK ISSN 0025-5408
TA404.2 CODEN: MRBUAC
MATERIALS RESEARCH BULLETIN. (Text in English, French, German and Russian; summaries in English) 1966. m. fl.2315($1330) (effective 1998). Elsevier Science Ltd., Pergamon, P.O. Box 800, Kidlington, Oxford OX5 1DX, England. TEL 44-1865-843000. FAX 44-1865-843010. E-mail: nlinfo-f@elsevier.nl; usinfo-f@elsevier.com; forinfo-kyf04035@niftyserve.or.jp; URL: http://www.elsevier.nl/. (Subscr. to: Elsevier Science, Regional Sales Office, P.O. Box 211, 1000 AE Amsterdam, Netherlands. TEL 31-20-4853757. FAX 31-20-4853432; Subscr. in the Americas to: Elsevier Science, Regional Sales Office, Box 945, New York, NY 10159-0945. TEL 212-633-3730. FAX 212-633-3680; Subscr. in Australasia and the Far East to: Elsevier Science (Singapore) Pte Ltd, No.1 Temasek Ave., No.17-01 Millenia Tower, Singapore 039192, Singapore. TEL 65-434-3727. FAX 65-337-2230) Ed. Heinz K. Henisch. adv.; bk.rev.; charts; illus. circ. 1,400. (also avail. in microfilm from UMI; back issues avail.) **Indexed:** Alloys Ind., Appl.Mech.Rev., ASCA, Cadscan, Ceram.Abstr., Chem.Abstr., Chem.Cit.Ind., Curr.Cont., Eng.Ind., Eng.Mat.Abstr., GeoRef., Ind.Sci.Rev., INIS Atomind., INSPEC, Int.Aerosp.Abstr., Lead Abstr., Mat.Sci.Cit.Ind., Met.Abstr., Met.Abstr.Ind., Nonfer.Met.Alert, PCC Alert, Phys.Ber., Sci.Cit.Ind., Steels Alert, World Alum.Abstr., Zincscan. **Document type:** academic/scholarly publication, bulletin.
—BLDSC (5396.410000); AskIEEE; CASDDS; CIST Ei; Genuine Article; KR SourceOne; Linda Hall; SWETS; UMI; UnCover. **CCC.**
Description: Publishes research on crystal growth, materials preparation and characterization, and the structure and properties of electronically, optically mechanically interesting solids.
Refereed Serial

MICROSCOPE. see *BIOLOGY — Microscopy*

548 NE ISSN 1058-725X
QD901 CODEN: MCLCE9
MOLECULAR CRYSTALS AND LIQUID CRYSTALS SCIENCE AND TECHNOLOGY. SECTION A: MOLECULAR CRYSTALS AND LIQUID CRYSTALS. 1966. 56/yr. (in 14 vols., 4 nos./vol.). $386 (effective 1998). Gordon and Breach - Harwood Academic, Amsteldisk 166, 1st Fl., 1079 LH Amsterdam, Netherlands. URL: http://www.gbhap.com/Molecular__Crystals__Liquid__Crystals/. (Subscr. to: International Publishers Distributor, Box 32160, Newark, NJ 07102. TEL 800-545-8398. FAX 215-750-6343) Ed. M.M. Labes. adv.; bk.rev.; charts; illus. (also avail. in microform) Indexed: Appl.Mech.Rev., ASCA, Biol.Abstr., Biwk.Pap.Rad.Chem.& Photochem., Cadscan, Chem.Abstr., Chem.Cit.Ind., Curr.Cont., Eng.Ind., Ind.Sci.Rev., INSPEC, Intl.Polym.Sci.& Tech., Lead Abstr., RAPRA, Zincscan. Document type: academic/scholarly publication.
●Also available online.
Also available on CD-ROM.
—BLDSC (5900.817000); AskIEEE; CASDDS; CISTI; KR SourceOne; Linda Hall; SWETS. CCC.
 Supersedes in part (in 1991): Molecular Crystals and Liquid Crystals Incorporating Nonlinear Optics (ISSN 1044-1859); Which was formerly (until 1987): Molecular Crystals and Liquid Crystals (ISSN 0026-8941); Incorporates (in 1982): Nonlinear Optics; Formerly (until 1969): Molecular Crystals (ISSN 0369-1152)
Refereed Serial

548 NE ISSN 1058-7276
QD901 CODEN: MOMAEO
MOLECULAR CRYSTALS AND LIQUID CRYSTALS SCIENCE AND TECHNOLOGY. SECTION C: MOLECULAR MATERIALS. 1992. 8/yr. (in 2 vols., 4 nos./vol.). $112 (effective 1998). Gordon and Breach - Harwood Academic, Amsteldisk 166, 1st Fl., 1079 LH Amsterdam, Netherlands. URL: http://www.gbhap.com/Molecular__Materials/. (Subscr. to: International Publishers Distributor, Box 32160, Newark, NJ 07102. TEL 800-545-8398. FAX 215-750-6343) Ed. L.M. Blinov. (also avail. in microform) Indexed: ASCA, Chem.Cit.Ind., Mat.Sci.Cit.Ind. Document type: academic/scholarly publication.
●Also available online.
Also available on CD-ROM.
—BLDSC (5900.817860); AskIEEE; CASDDS; CISTI; KR SourceOne. CCC.
 Description: Focuses on current industrial and academic research, both theoretical and experimental, on the design, investigation and application of various molecular organic materials.
Refereed Serial

548 NE ISSN 0377-2012
MOLECULAR STRUCTURES AND DIMENSIONS. 1970. irreg. price varies. Kluwer Academic Publishers, Postbus 17, 3300 AA Dordrecht, Netherlands. TEL 31-78-6392392. FAX 31-78-6392254. TELEX 29245 KAPG NL. E-mail: services@wkap.nl; URL: http://www.wkap.nl. (Dist. by: Kluwer Academic Publishers Group, P.O. Box 322, 3300 AH Dordrecht. TEL 31-78-6392392. FAX 31-78-6546474; N. America dist. addr.: Box 358, Accord Sta., Hingham, MA 02018-0358. TEL 617-871-6600) Ed. Olga Kennard. Document type: monographic series.
—CISTI.
Refereed Serial

548 JA
NEW DIAMOND. Japanese edition: Nyu Daiyamondo. (Text in English) 1988. biennial. (Nyu Daiyamondo Foramu - Japan New Diamond Forum) Ohm-sha, 3-1, Kanda Nishiki-cho, Chiyoda-ku, Tokyo 113, Japan.

NIHON KESSHO GAKKAI NENKAI KOEN YOSHISHU/CRYSTALLOGRAPHIC SOCIETY OF JAPAN. ABSTRACTS OF ANNUAL MEETING. see CHEMISTRY — Abstracting, Bibliographies, Statistics

548 JA ISSN 0369-4585
 CODEN: NKEGAF
NIHON KESSHO GAKKAISHI/CRYSTALLOGRAPHIC SOCIETY OF JAPAN. JOURNAL. (Text in Japanese; summaries in English) 1959. bi-m. Nihon Kessho Gakkai, Cosmos Hongo Bldg., 8F, 4-1-4 Hongo, Bunkyo-ku, Tokyo 113, Japan. Indexed: Chem.Abstr., INIS Atomind., INSPEC (1983-), Jap.Per.Ind.
—BLDSC (4732.560000); AskIEEE; CASDDS; CISTI; KR SourceOne; Linda Hall.

548 JA ISSN 0385-6275
QD921 CODEN: NKSGDK
NIHON KESSHO SEICHO GAKKAISHI/JAPANESE ASSOCIATION OF CRYSTAL GROWTH. JOURNAL. (Text in Japanese; summaries in English) 1974. 3/yr. Nihon Kessho Seicho Gakkai - Japanese Association of Crystal Growth, Nihon Gakkai Jumu Senta, 16-9, Honkomagome 5-chome, Bunkyo-ku, Tokyo 113, Japan. Indexed: Chem.Abstr., Jap.Per.Ind., Mineral.Abstr.
—CASDDS.

548 JA
NYU DAIYAMONDO. English edition: New Diamond. (Text in Japanese) 1985. q. 1550 Yen per no. (Nyu Daiyamondo Foramu - Japan New Diamond Forum) Ohm-sha, 3-1, Kanda Nishiki-cho, Chiyoda-ku, Tokyo 101, Japan.

PERIODICO DI MINERALOGIA. see MINES AND MINING INDUSTRY

548 UK ISSN 0960-8974
QD921 CODEN: PCGMED
PROGRESS IN CRYSTAL GROWTH AND CHARACTERIZATION OF MATERIALS; an international review journal. 1978. 8/yr. fl.3272($1881) (effective 1998). Elsevier Science Ltd., Pergamon, P.O. Box 800, Kidlington, Oxford OX5 1DX, England. TEL 44-1865-843000. FAX 44-1865-843010. E-mail: nlinfo-f@elsevier.nl; usinfo-f@elsevier.com; forinfo-kyf04035@niftyserve.or.jp; URL: http://www.elsevier.nl/. (Subscr. to: Elsevier Science, Regional Sales Office, P.O. Box 211, 1000 AE Amsterdam, Netherlands. TEL 31-20-4853757. FAX 31-20-4853432; Subscr. in the Americas to: Elsevier Science, Regional Sales Office, Box 945, New York, NY 10159-0945. TEL 212-633-3730. FAX 212-633-3680; Subscr. in Australasia and the Far East to: Elsevier Science (Singapore) Pte Ltd, No.1 Temasek Ave., No.17-01 Millenia Tower, Singapore 039192, Singapore. TEL 65-434-3727. FAX 65-337-2230) Ed. J.B Mullin. (also avail. in microfilm from UMI) Indexed: Alloys Ind., ASCA, Chem.Abstr., Chem.Cit.Ind., Curr.Cont., Eng.Mat.Abstr., GeoRef., Ind.Sci.Rev., Ind.Sci.Rev., INSPEC, Mat.Sci.Cit.Ind., Met.Abstr.Ind., Met.Abstr., Nonfer.Met.Alert, PCC Alert, Phys.Ber., Steels Alert, World Alum.Abstr. Document type: academic/scholarly publication.
—BLDSC (6868.085000); AskIEEE; CASDDS; CISTI; Ei; Genuine Article; KR SourceOne; SWETS; UMI; UnCover. CCC.
 Formerly (until 1992): Progress in Crystal Growth and Characterization (ISSN 0146-3535)
 Description: Covers all aspects of crystal growth and characterization, including crystals of semiconductors and electronic materials, oxides, synthetic minerals, magnetic and optical crystals, organic crystals, metals and thin films.
Refereed Serial

RARE EARTH BULLETIN. see METALLURGY

548 NE ISSN 0166-6983
STRUCTURE REPORTS. SECTION A: METALS AND INORGANIC COMPOUNDS. 1940. irreg., vol.58A, 1993. (International Union of Crystallography) Kluwer Academic Publishers, Postbus 17, 3300 AA Dordrecht, Netherlands. TEL 31-78-6392392. FAX 31-78-6392254. TELEX 29245 KAPG NL. E-mail: services@wkap.nl; URL: http://www.wkap.nl. (Dist. by: Kluwer Academic Publishers Group, P.O. Box 322, 3300 AH Dordrecht, Netherlands. TEL 31-78-6392392. FAX 31-78-6546474; N. America dist. addr.: Box 358, Accord Sta., Hingham, MA 02018-0358. TEL 617-871-6600. FAX 617-871-6528) Ed. G. Ferguson. Document type: monographic series.
—CISTI; Linda Hall.
 Supersedes in part (in 1965): Structure Reports (Utrecht) (ISSN 0373-8264); Which was formerly: International Union of Crystallography. Structure Reports (ISSN 0074-9397)
Refereed Serial

548 NE ISSN 0166-7033
STRUCTURE REPORTS. SECTION B: ORGANIC COMPOUNDS. 1940. a. price varies. (International Union of Crystallography) Kluwer Academic Publishers, Postbus 17, 3300 AA Dordrecht, Netherlands. TEL 31-78-6392392. FAX 31-78-6392254. TELEX 29245 KAPG NL. E-mail: services@wkap.nl; URL: http://www.wkap.nl. (Dist. by: Kluwer Academic Publishers Group, P.O. Box 322, 3300 AH Dordrecht, Netherlands. TEL 31-78-6392392. FAX 31-78-6546474; N. America dist. addr.: Box 358, Accord Sta., Hingham, MA 02018-0358. TEL 617-871-6600. FAX 617-871-6528) Ed. G. Ferguson. index, cum.index: 1940-1950 in vol.14, 1951-1960 in vol.25. Document type: monographic series.
—CISTI; Linda Hall.
 Supersedes in part (in 1965): Structure Reports (Utrecht) (ISSN 0373-8264); Which was formerly: International Union of Crystallography. Structure Reports (ISSN 0074-9397)

548 UK
U.K. HIGH PRESSURE CRYSTALLOGRAPHY GROUP NEWSLETTER. 1990. q. Science & Engineering Research Council, Daresbury Laboratory, Warrington, Ches. WA4 4AD, England. TEL 44-1925-603123. FAX 44-1925-603174. Ed. S.M. Clark. Document type: newsletter.

548 GW ISSN 0044-2968
QD901 CODEN: ZKKKAJ
ZEITSCHRIFT FUER KRISTALLOGRAPHIE; international journal for structural, physical, and chemical aspects of crystalline materials. (Supplement avail.: Zeitschrift fuer Kristallographie. Supplement Issues (ISSN 0930-486X)) (Text and summaries in English, French and German) 1877. 12/yr. DM.1877 (effective 1997). R. Oldenbourg Verlag GmbH, Rosenheimerstr. 145, 81671 Munich, Germany. TEL 49-89-45051-0. FAX 49-89-45051207. (Subscr. to: Postfach 801360, 81613 Munich, Germany) Ed.Bd. bibl.; charts; illus.; index. (also avail. in microform from PMC; back issues avail.) Indexed: ASCA, Br.Ceram.Abstr., Chem.Abstr., Chem.Cit.Ind., Curr.Cont., GeoRef., Ind.Sci.Rev., INSPEC, Mat.Sci.Cit.Ind., Math.R., Met.Abstr., Mineral.Abstr., Phys.Ber., Sci.Cit.Ind., Soils & Fert., Zent.Math. Document type: academic/scholarly publication.
—BLDSC (9468.000000); AskIEEE; CASDDS; CISTI; Ei; Genuine Article; KR SourceOne; Linda Hall; SWETS; UnCover. CCC.
 Description: International coverage of structural, physical, and chemical aspects of crystalline materials.

548 GW ISSN 0930-486X
ZEITSCHRIFT FUER KRISTALLOGRAPHIE. SUPPLEMENT ISSUES. (Supplement to: Zeitschrift fuer Kristallographie (ISSN 0044-2968)) (Text in English) 1984. irreg. price varies. R. Oldenbourg Verlag GmbH, Rosenheimerstr. 145, 81671 Munich, Germany. TEL 49-89-45051-0. FAX 49-89-45051207. (Subscr. to: Postfach 801360, 81613 Munich, Germany) Document type: academic/scholarly publication.
—BLDSC (9468.050000); CISTI.

CHEMISTRY — Electrochemistry

541.37 535   UK   ISSN 1057-9257
TK7874.8   CODEN: AMELE7
ADVANCED MATERIALS FOR OPTICS AND ELECTRONICS. 1992. bi-m. £785 (foreign $785) (effective 1998). John Wiley & Sons Ltd., Journals, Baffins Ln., Chichester, W. Sussex PO19 1UD, England. TEL 44-1243-779777. FAX 44-1243-843232. E-mail: cs-journals@wiley.co.uk; URL: http://www.wiley.co.uk. (Subscr. in the Americas to: John Wiley & Sons, Inc., 605 Third Ave., New York, NY 10158. TEL 212-850-6645. FAX 212-850-6021) Ed. D.J. Cole-Hamilton. adv.: B&W page £595, color page £1495; trim 260 x 200; adv. contact: Bob Kern. bk.rev.; index. circ. 450. (also avail. in microform from UMI; back issues avail.; reprint service avail. from SWZ) **Indexed:** ASCA, Chem.Abstr., Chem.Cit.Ind., Curr.Cont., Eng.Ind., INSPEC (1992-), Intl.Polym.Sci.& Tech., Mat.Sci.Cit.Ind. **Document type:** academic/scholarly publication.
—BLDSC (0696.898700); AskIEEE; CASDDS; CISTI; Ei; Genuine Article; KR SourceOne; Linda Hall; SWETS; UMI; UnCover. **CCC.**
 Formed by the merger of (1986-1991): Chemtronics (ISSN 0267-5900); (1985-1991): Journal of Molecular Electronics (ISSN 0748-7991)
 Description: Provides a forum for the exchange of knowledge of those materials - inorganic, organic, polymeric and biological - whose focus of interest is the emerging discipline of information technology.
 Refereed Serial

ADVANCES IN ELECTROCHEMICAL SCIENCE AND ENGINEERING. see ENGINEERING — Chemical Engineering

541.37   US
ADVANCES IN GAS PHASE ION CHEMISTRY. 1992. irreg., vol.3, 1997. $109.50. J A I Press Inc., 55 Old Post Rd., No.2, Box 1678, Greenwich, CT 06830-1678. TEL 203-661-7602. FAX 203-661-0792. E-mail: jai@jaipress.com. (In Europe: JAI Press Ltd., 38 Tavistock St., Covent Garden, London WC2E 7PB, England. TEL 44-171-379-8834. FAX 44-171-379-8835) Eds. Nigel Adams, Lucia Babcock. **Indexed:** Chem.Cit.Ind. **Document type:** monographic series, academic/scholarly publication.

APPLIED SURFACE SCIENCE; a journal devoted to the properties of interfaces in relation to the synthesis and behaviour of materials. see METALLURGY

541.37   AT
                             CODEN: COAUDF
AUSTRALASIAN CORROSION ASSOCIATION. ANNUAL CONFERENCE PROCEEDINGS. 1960. a. Aus.$130. Australasian Corrosion Association, c/o Australasian Secretariat, P.O. Box 5142, Clayton, Vic. 3168, Australia. TEL 61-3-544-0066. FAX 61-3-543-5905. bk.rev. circ. 350. **Indexed:** Chem.Abstr. **Document type:** proceedings.

541.37   II   ISSN 0256-1654
                             CODEN: BUELE6
BULLETIN OF ELECTROCHEMISTRY. 1985. m. Rs.600($300) (effective 1997). Central Electrochemical Research Institute, c/o Scientific Distribution Service, 5-A, Bhagat-kj-kothi Box No. 33, Jodhpur, Rajasthan 342 001, India. FAX 91-291-49093. E-mail: comcomp.sewa@ascess.net.in. Ed. S.K Rangarajan. adv.; bk.rev. circ. 300. (back issues avail.) **Indexed:** Alloys Ind., ASCA, Biodet.Abstr., Chem.Abstr., Chem.Cit.Ind., Corros.Abstr., Eng.Mat.Abstr., Gas Abstr., INIS Atomind., INSPEC, Mat.Sci.Cit.Ind., Met.Abstr.Ind., Met.Abstr., Nonfer.Met.Alert, PCC Alert, Steels Alert, World Alum.Abstr., World Surf.Coat. **Document type:** academic/scholarly publication.
—BLDSC (2850.500000); CASDDS; CISTI; Ei; Genuine Article; Linda Hall; SWETS. **CCC.**
 Incorporates: Electrometallurgy Bulletin.
 Description: Comprehensive journal on electrochemistry.
 Refereed Serial

BUSINESS RATIO REPORT: PRINTED CIRCUIT MANUFACTURERS; an industry sector analysis. see ELECTRONICS

541.37   JA
CHEMICAL SENSORS/KAGAKU SENSA. (Text in Japanese; summaries in English) 1985. 4/yr. Electrochemical Society of Japan, Japan Association of Chemical Sensors - Denki Kagaku Kyokai Kagaku Sensa Kenkyukai, c/o Mr. Shimizu, Kyushu Daigaku Daigakuin Sogo Rikogaku Kenkyuka, 6-1, Kasuga Koen, Kasuga-shi, Fukuoka-ken 550, Japan.

541.37   AT
                             CODEN: COAUDF
CORROSION AND MATERIALS. 1976. 6/yr. Aus.$42. Australasian Corrosion Association, c/o Australasian Secretariat, P.O. Box 5142, Clayton, Vic. 3168, Australia. TEL 61-3-544-0066. FAX 61-3-543-5905. (Co-sponsor: Asian Pacific Materials and Corrosion Association) **Indexed:** Alloys Ind., Eng.Mat.Abstr., Met.Abstr., Met.Abstr.Ind., Nonfer.Met.Alert, PCC Alert, Steels Alert, World Surf.Coat. **Document type:** academic/scholarly publication.
—CASDDS; CISTI; Linda Hall; UnCover.
 Formerly: Corrosion Australasia (ISSN 0155-6002)

CORROSION ENGINEERING. see METALLURGY

DENKI KAGAKU KYOKAI TAIKAI KOEN YOSHISHU/ELECTROCHEMICAL SOCIETY OF JAPAN. ABSTRACTS OF ANNUAL MEETING. see CHEMISTRY — Abstracting, Bibliographies, Statistics

541.37   CC   ISSN 1006-3471
▼**DIAN HUAXUE/ELECTROCHEMISTRY.** (Text in Chinese; abstracts in English) 1994. q. $30 (effective 1997). Chinese Chemical Society - Zhongguo Huaxuehui, P.O. Box 2709, Beijing 100080, People's Republic of China. TEL 86-10-62568157. FAX 86-10-62568157. E-mail: xiaodh@xmu.ecu.cn; URL: http://www.xmu.edu.cn/library.html. (Alt. addr.: c/o Xiamen University Library, International Exchange Section, Xiamen, Fujian 361005, P.R. China. TEL 86-592-2186144. FAX 86-592-2186127) (Co-sponsor: Xiamen University, School of Chemistry & Chemical Engineering) Ed. Zhaowu Tian. **Document type:** academic/scholarly publication.
●Also available online.
 Refereed Serial

541.37   CC   ISSN 1001-3849
DIANDU YU JINGSHI/PLATING AND FINISHING. (Text in Chinese) 1973. bi-m. $10 (effective 1992). Tianjin Diandu Gongcheng Xuehui - Tianjin Electroplating Engineering Society, Hebei Zhigong Dexue, Xingfu Dao, Wangchuanchang, Hebei Qu, Tianjin 300150, People's Republic of China. TEL 661431. Ed. Liang Qimin. adv.; bk.rev. circ. 5,000.
—Ei.

541.37   CC   ISSN 1004-227X
                             CODEN: DYTUEM
DIANDU YU TUSHI/ELECTROPLATING & FINISHING. (Text in Chinese) 1982. q. $20. Guangdong Qinggong Diandu Xuehui - Electroplaters Society of Guangdong Light Industry, No.1, En-long Bei, Zhongshan Rd. 7, Guangzhou, Guangdong 510170, People's Republic of China. TEL 8172-6886. FAX 8170-1214. Ed. Xie Suling. R&P contact: Xie Suling. adv. contact: Xie Suling. circ. 10,000. **Indexed:** Chem.Abstr. **Document type:** trade publication.
—BLDSC (3706.950000); CASDDS.

541.37   US
E C S MONOGRAPH SERIES. irreg. Electrochemical Society, Inc., 10 S. Main St., Pennington, NJ 08534-2896. TEL 609-737-1902. R&P contact: Mary E. Yess. **Document type:** monographic series.
 Description: Provides authoritative accounts of specific topics in electrochemistry, solid state science and related disciplines.

547   UK   ISSN 0963-5637
                             CODEN: ESTPEA
ELECTROCHEMICAL SCIENCE AND TECHNOLOGY OF POLYMERS. 1987. irreg., vol.2, 1990. price varies. Elsevier Science Ltd., Books Division, P.O. Box 800, Kidlington, Oxford OX5 1DX, England. TEL 44-1865-843000. FAX 44-1865-843010. E-mail: nlinfo-f@elsevier.nl; usinfo-f@elsevier.com; forinfo-kyf04035@niftyserve.or.jp; URL: http://www.elsevier.nl/. (Subscr. to: Elsevier Science, Regional Sales Office, P.O. Box 211, 1000 AE Amsterdam, Netherlands. TEL 31-20-4853757. FAX 31-20-4853432; Subscr. in the Americas to: Elsevier Science, Regional Sales Office, Box 945, New York, NY 10159-0945. TEL 212-633-3730. FAX 212-633-3680; Subscr. in Australasia and the Far East to: Elsevier Science (Singapore) Pte Ltd, No.1 Temasek Ave., No.17-01 Millenia Tower, Singapore 039192, Singapore. TEL 65-434-3727. FAX 65-337-2230) Ed. R.G. Linford. (back issues avail.) **Document type:** monographic series.
—CASDDS.
 Refereed Serial

541.37   US   ISSN 0013-4651
TP250   CODEN: JESOAN
ELECTROCHEMICAL SOCIETY. JOURNAL. 1902. m. $425 (foreign $450). Electrochemical Society, Inc., 10 S. Main St., Pennington, NJ 08534-2896. TEL 609-737-1902. FAX 609-737-2743. Ed. Paul A. Kohl. charts; illus.; index. circ. 8,600. (also avail. in microfilm from UMI,PMC; reprint service avail. from UMI) **Indexed:** A.S.& T.Ind., Abstr.Bull.Inst.Pap.Chem., Alloys Ind., Anal.Abstr., Appl.Mech.Rev., Art & Archaeol.Tech.Abstr., Br.Ceram.Abstr., Bull.Thermodyn.& Thermochem., Cadscan, Chem.Abstr., Chem.Cit.Ind., Chem.Infd., Compumath, Copper Abstr., Corros.Abstr., Curr.Cont., Eng.Ind., Eng.Mat.Abstr., Fuel & Energy Abstr., INIS Atomind., INSPEC (1968-), Int.Aerosp.Abstr., Lead Abstr., Met.Abstr.Ind., Met.Abstr., Nonfer.Met.Alert, PCC Alert, Photo.Abstr. Soils & Fert., Steels Alert, World Alum.Abstr., Zincscan. **Document type:** academic/scholarly publication.
—BLDSC (4737.000000); AskIEEE; CASDDS; CISTI; Ei; Genuine Article; KR SourceOne; Linda Hall; SWETS; UMI; UnCover. **CCC.**
 Description: Contains technical papers covering basic researches in electrochemical science and technology and solid state science and technology.

541.37   US   ISSN 1091-8213
QD551
ELECTROCHEMICAL SOCIETY. MEETING ABSTRACTS. s-a. $170 (Canada $180; elsewhere $200). Electrochemical Society, Inc., 10 S. Main St., Pennington, NJ 08534-2896. TEL 609-737-1902. **Indexed:** INSPEC. **Document type:** abstracting/indexing.
—BLDSC (5536.222420); CISTI; Linda Hall; UMI. **CCC.**
 Formerly (until 1996): Electrochemical Society. Extended Abstracts (ISSN 0160-4619)
 Description: Contains abstracts of technical papers presented at the society Spring and Fall meetings.

541.37   US   ISSN 0161-6374
                             CODEN: PESODO
ELECTROCHEMICAL SOCIETY. PROCEEDINGS. Key Title: Proceedings - Electrochemical Society. 1967. irreg. 20-40/yr. Electrochemical Society, Inc., 10 S. Main St., Pennington, NJ 08534-2896. TEL 609-737-1902. FAX 609-737-2743. R&P contact: Mary E. Yess. (also avail. in microform from UMI; back issues avail.) **Document type:** proceedings.
—BLDSC (6695.400000); CASDDS; CISTI; Ei. **CCC.**
 Description: Publishes proceedings of symposia and international conferences sponsored by the society in such fields as electrodeposition, batteries, corrosion, dielectric science and technology, electronics, compound semiconductors, high temperature materials, physical electrochemistry, industrial electrolysis and electrochemical engineering.

CHEMISTRY — ELECTROCHEMISTRY

541.37   **US**   ISSN 1064-8208
TP250   CODEN: ELSIE3
ELECTROCHEMICAL SOCIETY INTERFACE. 1992. q. $40. Electrochemical Society, Inc., 10 S. Main St., Pennington, NJ 08534-2896. TEL 609-737-1902. FAX 609-737-2743. Ed. Jan B. Talbot. R&P contact: Mary E. Yess. adv.: B&W page $873, color page $1590; trim 8 1/8 x 10 7/8; adv. contact: Paul Cooper. circ. 8,600. **Indexed:** Corros.Abstr., INSPEC (1993-). **Document type:** academic/scholarly publication.
—BLDSC (4533.447500); AskIEEE; CASDDS; CISTI; Ei; KR SourceOne; Linda Hall; SWETS; UnCover. **CCC.**
  Description: Contains news, reviews, and articles on technical matters of general interest to Electrochemical Society members.

541.37   **II**   ISSN 0013-466X
TP250   CODEN: JESIA5
ELECTROCHEMICAL SOCIETY OF INDIA. JOURNAL. (Text in English) 1952. q. Rs.300 (foreign $70). Electrochemical Society of India, c/o Indian Institute of Science, Bangalore 560 012, India. TEL 91-80-3340977. FAX 91-80-3341683. TELEX 0846-8349 BG ECSI. Ed. S.K. Vijayalakshamma. adv.; bk.rev.; abstr.; illus.; index. circ. 600. **Indexed:** Alloys Ind., Cadscan, Chem.Abstr., Curr.Cont., Curr.Tit.Electrochem., Eng.Ind., Eng.Mat.Abstr., Indian Sci.Abstr., INSPEC (1971-), Lead Abstr., Met.Abstr., Met.Abstr.Ind., Nonfer.Met.Alert, PCC Alert, Steels Alert, World Alum.Abstr., Zincscan. **Document type:** academic/scholarly publication.
—BLDSC (4737.500000); AskIEEE; CASDDS; CISTI; Ei; KR SourceOne; Linda Hall. **CCC.**
  Description: Publishes papers on all aspects of the science, technology and engineering of electrochemistry and related subjects.

541.37   **US**   ISSN 0275-0171
ELECTROCHEMICAL SOCIETY SERIES. 1948. irreg., latest 1992. price varies. (Electrochemical Society, Inc.) John Wiley & Sons, Inc., 605 Third Ave., New York, NY 10158. TEL 212-850-2000. FAX 212-850-6088. **Indexed:** INSPEC. **Document type:** monographic series.

541.37   **JA**   ISSN 0366-9297
QD551   CODEN: DNKKA2
ELECTROCHEMISTRY AND INDUSTRIAL PHYSICAL CHEMISTRY/DENKI KAGAKU OYOBI KOGYO BUTSURI KAGAKU. (Text mainly in English) 1933. m. 24000 Yen to non-members. Electrochemical Society of Japan - Denki Kagaku Kai, Shin-yurakucho Bldg., 1-12-1 Yuraku-cho, Chiyoda-ku, Tokyo 100, Japan. TEL 81-3-3214-6001. FAX 81-3-3287-0037. Ed. Tsutomu Nonaka. adv.; bk.rev.; abstr.; charts; illus.; stat.; index; circ. 2,500 (controlled). (reprint service avail.) **Indexed:** Chem.Abstr., Curr.Cont., Ind.Sci.Rev., INIS Atomind., INSPEC, JCT, JTA, Met.Abstr., Sci.Cit.Ind. **Document type:** academic/scholarly publication.
—BLDSC (3550.900000); AskIEEE; CASDDS; CISTI; Genuine Article; KR SourceOne; Linda Hall; SWETS. **CCC.**
  Incorporates: Electrochemical Society of Japan. Journal - Denki Kagaku (ISSN 0013-4678); Denki Kagaku Newsletter (ISSN 0418-6303)

541.37   **UK**   ISSN 0013-4686
TP250   CODEN: ELCAAV
ELECTROCHIMICA ACTA. (Text in English, French, German) 1959. s-m. fl.4922($2829) (effective 1998). (International Society of Electrochemistry) Elsevier Science Ltd., Pergamon, P.O. Box 800, Kidlington, Oxford OX5 1DX, England. TEL 44-1865-843000. FAX 44-1865-843010. E-mail: nlinfo-f@elsevier.nl; usinfo-f@elsevier.com; forinfo-kyf04035@niftyserve.or.jp; URL: http://www.elsevier.nl/. (Subscr. to: Elsevier Science, Regional Sales Office, P.O. Box 211, 1000 AE Amsterdam, Netherlands. TEL 31-20-4853757. FAX 31-20-4853432; Subscr. in the Americas to: Elsevier Science, Regional Sales Office, Box 945, New York, NY 10159-0945. TEL 212-633-3730. FAX 212-633-3680; Subscr. in Australasia and the Far East to: Elsevier Science (Singapore) Pte Ltd, No.1 Temasek Ave., No.17-01 Millenia Tower, Singapore 039192, Singapore. TEL 65-434-3727. FAX 65-337-2230) Ed. R. Armstrong. adv.; bk.rev.; charts; illus.; index. circ. 1,900. (also avail. in microfilm from UMI; reprint service avail. from UMI) **Indexed:** Alloys Ind., Anal.Abstr., Cadscan, Chem.Abstr., Chem.Cit.Ind., Chem.Eng.Abstr., Chem.Infd., Curr.Cont., Eng.Ind., Eng.Mat.Abstr., Excerp.Med., Ind.Sci.Rev., INIS Atomind., INSPEC, Lead Abstr., Mat.Sci.Cit.Ind., Met.Abstr., Met.Abstr.Ind., Nonfer.Met.Alert, PCC Alert, Sci.Cit.Ind., Steels Alert, T.C.E.A., World Alum.Abstr., World Alum.Abstr., Zincscan. **Document type:** academic/scholarly publication.
—BLDSC (3698.950000); CASDDS; CISTI; Ei; Genuine Article; SWETS; UMI; UnCover. **CCC.**
  Description: Publishes original papers and critical reviews in pure and applied electrochemistry.
Refereed Serial

HOKKAIDO UNIVERSITY. CATALYSIS RESEARCH CENTER. ANNUAL REPORT (YEAR)/HOKKAIDO DAIGAKU SHOKUBAI KAGAKU KENKYU CENTER NENPO. see *CHEMISTRY — Physical Chemistry*

669   **JA**   ISSN 0915-1869
     CODEN: HYGIEX
HYOMEN GIJUTSU. (Text in English) 1950. s-a. 10000 Yen. Surface Finishing Society of Japan - Hyomen Gijutsu Kyokai, 2 Kanda-Iwamoto-cho, Chiyoda-ku, Tokyo 101, Japan. TEL 03-3252-3286. FAX 03-3252-3288. Ed. Tetsuya Osaka. adv.; bk.rev.; charts; illus.; index. circ. 5,000. **Indexed:** Alloys Ind., Chem.Abstr., Eng.Mat.Abstr., INIS Atomind., Met.Abstr.Ind., Met.Abstr., Nonfer.Met.Alert, PCC Alert, Steels Alert, World Alum.Abstr.
—BLDSC (4904.472000); CASDDS; CISTI; Ei; Linda Hall. **CCC.**
  Former titles (until Jan. 1989): Jitsumu Hyomen Gijutsu (ISSN 0368-2358); Kinzoku Hyomen Gijutsu (ISSN 0026-0614)

541.37   **US**   ISSN 0741-1413
INTERNATIONAL ELECTROCHEMICAL PROGRESS.* 1972. m. $360 (foreign $450). International Electrochemical Institute, 189 Parsonage Hill Rd., Short Hills, NJ 07078-1523. TEL 201-273-1088. Ed. J.A. LeDuc. bk.rev.; abstr.; bibl.; pat.; stat. (back issues avail.) **Indexed:** Chem.Abstr.

541.37   **RU**   ISSN 0202-8093
QD551   CODEN: ITEKB2
ITOGI NAUKI I TEKHNIKI: ELEKTROKHIMIYA. irreg., vols.29-30, 1989. 12 Rub. Vsesoyuznyi Institut Nauchno-Tekhnicheskoi Informatsii (VINITI), Ul. Baltiiskaya 14, Moscow A-219, Russia. (Subscr. to: Mezhdunarodnaya Kniga, Dimitrova ul. 39, 113095 Moscow, Russia) **Indexed:** Chem.Abstr., INSPEC (1971-), Met.Abstr.
—AskIEEE; CASDDS; KR SourceOne.

541.37   **UK**   ISSN 0021-891X
TP250   CODEN: JAELBJ
JOURNAL OF APPLIED ELECTROCHEMISTRY. 1971. m. £825 (foreign $1370) (effective 1998). (International Society of Electrochemistry) Thomson Science (Subsidiary of: International Thomson Publishing Group), 2-6 Boundary Row, London SE1 8HN, England. TEL 44-171-8650066. FAX 44-171-5229623. E-mail: journal@rapidcom.co.uk; URL: http://www.thomsonscience.com. (Dist. by: International Thomson Publishing Services Ltd., Cheriton House, North Way, Andover, Hants. SP10 5BE, England. TEL 44-1264-342713. FAX 44-1264-342807; Subscr. in US & Canada to: 400 Market St., Philadelphia, PA 19106. TEL 800-552-5866) Ed. A.A. Wragg. adv. (reprint service avail. from ISI, UMI) **Indexed:** A.S.& T.Ind., Alloys Ind., ASCA, Cadscan, Chem.Abstr., Chem.Cit.Ind., Curr.Cont., Eng.Ind., Eng.Mat.Abstr., Excerp.Med., Ind.Sci.Rev., INIS Atomind., INSPEC, Lead Abstr., Mat.Sci.Cit.Ind., Met.Abstr., Met.Abstr.Ind., Nonfer.Met.Alert, PCC Alert, Sci.Cit.Ind., Steels Alert, W.R.C.Inf., World Alum.Abstr., Zincscan. **Document type:** academic/scholarly publication.
●Also available online.
—BLDSC (4942.600000); AskIEEE; CASDDS; CISTI; Ei; Genuine Article; KR SourceOne; Linda Hall; SWETS; UMI; UnCover. **CCC.**
  Description: Reviews technological advancements in electrochemistry.
Refereed Serial

541.37   **GW**   ISSN 1432-8488
▼**JOURNAL OF SOLID STATE ELECTROCHEMISTRY.** (Text in English) 1997. 6/yr. DM.381.50 (foreign DM.384.95) (effective 1998). Springer-Verlag, Heidelberger Platz 3, 14197 Berlin, Germany. TEL 49-30-82787-0. FAX 49-30-82787448. E-mail: subscriptions@springer.de; URL: http://link.springer.de. (Subscr. in N. America to: Springer-Verlag New York, Inc., 333 Meadowlands Pkwy., Secaucus, NJ 07094. TEL 212-460-1500. FAX 212-473-6272) Ed. F. Scholz. **Document type:** academic/scholarly publication.
●Also available online.
  Description: Devoted to all aspects of solid-state chemistry and solid-state physics in electrochemistry.

541.3   **JA**
     CODEN: KAGSEU
KAGAKU SENSA KENKYU HAPPYOKAI/DIGEST OF THE CHEMICAL SENSOR SYMPOSIUM. (Text in Japanese) 1981. s-a. 5000 Yen. Denki Kagaku Kyokai, Kagaku Sensa Kenkyukai - Electrochemical Society of Japan, Japan Association of Chemical Sensors, Kyushu Daigaku Daigakuin, Sogo Rikogaku Kenkyuka, 6-1, Kasuga Koen, Kasuga-shi, Fukuoka-ken 816, Japan. TEL 81-92-583-7537. FAX 81-92-583-7539. E-mail: yamazigz@mbox.nc.kyushu-u.ac.jp; URL: http://chemsens.mase.nagasaki-v.ac.jp. Ed. Noboru Yamazoe. adv. contact: Noboru Yamazoe. **Document type:** proceedings.

KEY ABSTRACTS - HIGH-TEMPERATURE SUPERCONDUCTORS. see *PHYSICS — Abstracting, Bibliographies, Statistics*

541.37   **JA**
KYOKAI RYOIKI NI OKERU DENKI KAGAKU SEMINA/SEMINAR ON ELECTROCHEMISTRY IN BOUNDARY REGION. PROCEEDINGS. (Text in Japanese) s-a. Denki Kagaku Kyokai, Kanto Shibu - Electrochemical Society of Japan, Kanto Branch, Yamanashi Daigaku Kogakubu, Muki Gosei Kenkyu Shisetsu, 3-11, Takeda 4-chome, Kofu-shi, Yamanashi-ken 400, Japan. **Document type:** proceedings.

541.37   **CN**
LE LINGOT. (Text in French) 1943. s-m. Societe d'Electrolyse et de Chimie Alcan Ltee., P.O. Box 1370, Jonquiere, Que. G7S 4K9, Canada. Ed. Vital Munger. circ. 16,000.

CHEMISTRY — INORGANIC CHEMISTRY

641 668 US ISSN 1068-7440
CODEN: MPFAEU
METALLIZED PLASTICS; fundamental and applied aspects. 1989. irreg., vol.3, 1992. price varies. (Electrochemical Society, Inc.) Plenum Publishing Corp., 233 Spring St., New York, NY 10013-1578. TEL 212-620-8000. FAX 212-863-0742. TELEX 23-421139. E-mail: books@plenum.com. Ed. K.L. Mittal. (back issues avail.) **Indexed:** Mat.Sci.Cit.Ind. **Document type:** proceedings.
—CASDDS. **CCC**.
Refereed Serial

540 US ISSN 1063-8814
CODEN: MSUCEU
METHODS OF SURFACE CHARACTERIZATION. 1987. irreg., vol.3, 1995. price varies. Plenum Publishing Corp., 233 Spring St., New York, NY 10013-1578. TEL 212-620-8000. FAX 212-463-0742. TELEX 23-421139. E-mail: books@plenum.com. Ed.Bd. (back issues avail.) **Document type:** monographic series.
—BLDSC (5748.207500); CASDDS.
Refereed Serial

541.37 US ISSN 0076-9924
QD552 CODEN: MAECAO
MODERN ASPECTS OF ELECTROCHEMISTRY. 1964. irreg., no.30, 1997. price varies. Plenum Publishing Corp., 233 Spring St., New York, NY 10013-1578. TEL 212-620-8000. FAX 212-463-0742. TELEX 23-421139. E-mail: books@plenum.com. Eds. B.E. Conway, J. Bockris. **Indexed:** Chem.Abstr., Chem.Cit.Ind. **Document type:** monographic series.
—BLDSC (5883.670000); CASDDS; CISTI; KNAW; UnCover. **CCC**.
Refereed Serial

543 541.37 US ISSN 0077-0833
MONOGRAPHS IN ELECTROANALYTICAL CHEMISTRY AND ELECTROCHEMISTRY SERIES. 1969. irreg., vol.7, 1995. price varies. Marcel Dekker, Inc., 270 Madison Ave., New York, NY 10016. TEL 212-696-9000. FAX 212-658-4540. TELEX 421419. Ed. A.J. Bard; Pub. Graham Garratt. R&P contact: Julia Mulligan. **Document type:** monographic series.
Refereed Serial

NIHON KAISUI GAKKAISHI/SOCIETY OF SEA WATER SCIENCE, JAPAN. BULLETIN. see EARTH SCIENCES — Oceanography

660 NO ISSN 0801-9606
OVERFLATE TEKNIKK. 1958. q. NOK 200. Norsk Galvanoteknisk Landsforening, P.B. 2608, St. Hanshaugen, 0131 Oslo 1, Norway. TEL 02-865139. Ed. Erik Bang. circ. 3,700. **Indexed:** C.I.S. Abstr., Met.Abstr., World Alum.Abstr. *Former titles:* Galvano Teknisk Tidsskrift (ISSN 0046-5372); Norsk Galvano Teknisk Tidsskrift.

541.37 JA
P E D KENKYUKAI/RESEARCH GROUP OF PASSIVE ELECTROCHEMICAL DEVICES. PROCEEDINGS. (Text in Japanese) 1988. s-a. P E D Research Group, Promising Surface Science Laboratory, 5-9-2-102 Minamiosawa, Hachioji-shi, Tokyo 192-03, Japan. **Document type:** proceedings.

PRINTED CIRCUIT FABRICATION. see ELECTRONICS

PRINTED CIRCUIT FABRICATION ASIA. see ELECTRONICS

REVIEW OF POLAROGRAPHY/PORAROGURAFI. see CHEMISTRY — Analytical Chemistry

541.37 RU ISSN 1023-1935
QD551 CODEN: RUELEC
RUSSIAN JOURNAL OF ELECTROCHEMISTRY. English translation of: Elektrokhimiya (RU ISSN 0424-8570) 1965. m. $1765 in US; elsewhere $2065 (effective 1998). (Russian Academy of Sciences) Maik Nauka - Interperiodica, Mezhdunarodnyi Otdel, Ul. Profsoyuznaya, 90, 117864 Moscow, Russia. TEL 7-095-3360066. FAX 7-095-3360066. (Dist. by: Plenum Publishing Corp., 233 Spring St., New York, NY 10013-1578, U.S.A. TEL 212-620-8468. FAX 212-463-0742) Ed. V.E. Kozarinov. (also avail. in microfilm from UMI; back issues avail.) **Indexed:** Alloys Ind., ASCA, Chem.Cit.Ind., Chem.Titles, Curr.Cont., Eng.Ind., Eng.Mat.Abstr., Ind.Sci.Rev., Mat.Sci.Cit.Ind., Met.Abstr., Met.Abstr.Ind., Nonfer.Met.Alert, PCC Alert, Sci.Cit.Ind., SSCI, Steels Alert, World Alum.Abstr. **Document type:** academic/scholarly publication.
—CISTI; Genuine Article; Linda Hall; UMI; UnCover. **CCC**.
Former titles (until 1994): Russian Electrochemistry (ISSN 1070-3276); (until 1993): Soviet Electrochemistry (ISSN 0038-5387)
Refereed Serial

541.37 SZ ISSN 0925-4005
TK7881.2 CODEN: SABCEB
SENSORS AND ACTUATORS: B CHEMICAL; international journal devoted to research and development of physical and chemical transducers. (Text in English) 1990. 24/yr. fl.4320($2483) (effective 1998). Elsevier Science S.A., P.O. Box 564, CH-1001 Lausanne 1, Switzerland. TEL 41-21-3207381. FAX 41-21-3235444. TELEX 450620-ELSA-CH. (Subscr. to: Elsevier Science, Regional Sales Office, P.O. Box 211, 1000 AE Amsterdam, Netherlands. TEL 31-20-4853757. FAX 31-20-4853432; Subscr. in the Americas to: Elsevier Science, Regional Sales Office, Box 945, New York, NY 10159-0945. TEL 212-633-3730. FAX 212-633-3680; Subscr. in Australasia to: Elsevier Science (Singapore) Pte. Ltd., No. 1 Temasek Ave., No. 17-01 Millenia Tower, Singapore 039192, Singapore. TEL 65-434-3727. FAX 65-337-2230) Ed. S. Middelhoek, K. Camman. (also avail. in microform from UMI; back issues avail.) **Indexed:** Alloys Ind., Chem.Abstr., Chem.Cit.Ind., Compumath, Curr.Cont., Eng.Ind., Eng.Mat.Abstr., Eng.Mat.Abstr., Ind.Sci.Rev., INSPEC (1990-), Mat.Sci.Cit.Ind., Met.Abstr.Ind., Met.Abstr., Nonfer.Met.Alert, PCC Alert, Phys.Ber., Sci.Cit.Ind., Sci.Cit.Ind., Steels Alert, World Alum.Abstr. **Document type:** academic/scholarly publication.
—BLDSC (8241.785220); AskIEEE; CASDDS; CISTI; Ei; Genuine Article; KR SourceOne; Linda Hall; SWETS; UnCover. **CCC**.
Supersedes in part (in 1990): Sensors and Actuators (ISSN 0250-6874)
Description: Covers all aspects of research and development of sensor elements transforming and transducing chemical signals into information about the chemical composition of the sample analyzed.
Refereed Serial

STUDIES IN SURFACE SCIENCE AND CATALYSIS. see PHYSICS — Mechanics

541.37 536 US ISSN 1050-3943
CODEN: STSUEB
STUDIES OF HIGH TEMPERATURE SUPERCONDUCTORS. 1989. irreg., vol.11, 1993. price varies. Nova Science Publishers, Inc., 6080 Jericho Tpke., Ste. 207, Commack, NY 11725-2808. TEL 516-499-3103. Ed. A.V. Narlikar. **Document type:** monographic series.
—BLDSC (8490.632500); CASDDS; CISTI; Linda Hall; UnCover.

SURFACE ENGINEERING AND APPLIED ELECTROCHEMISTRY. see ENGINEERING — Mechanical Engineering

541.37 II ISSN 0036-0678
CODEN: TSETA6
TRANSACTIONS S A E S T. (Text in English) 1966. q. Rs.100($25) to non-members. Society for Advancement of Electrochemical Science and Technology, Karaikudi 623 006, Tamil Nadu, India. TEL 91-4565-22088. FAX 91-4565-22088. TELEX 0443-211 ECRI IN. E-mail: cecrik@cscecri.ren.nic.in. Ed. S. Krishnamurthy. adv.; bk.rev.; bibl.; charts; illus. circ. 1,800. (processed) **Indexed:** Chem.Abstr., INSPEC, Met.Abstr., World Alum.Abstr.
—BLDSC (9005.200000); CASDDS; CISTI; Ei; Linda Hall. **CCC**.

ZAIRYO TO KANKYO. see METALLURGY

CHEMISTRY — Inorganic Chemistry

ACTA CHEMICA SCANDINAVICA. see CHEMISTRY — Physical Chemistry

546 IS
ADVANCES IN BIOINORGANIC CHEMISTRY. (Text in English) a. $40. Freund Publishing House Ltd., P.O. Box 35010, 61 Nachmani St., Tel Aviv 61350, Israel. TEL 972-3-615335. FAX 972-3-5605335. (And: Chesham House, Ste. 500, 150 Regent St., London W1R 5FA, England) Ed. Z. Dori. **Document type:** academic/scholarly publication.

546 NE ISSN 0190-0218
CODEN: AIBIDM
ADVANCES IN INORGANIC BIOCHEMISTRY. 1979. irreg., latest 1996. price varies. Elsevier Science B.V., Books Division, P.O. Box 211, 1000 AE Amsterdam, Netherlands. TEL 31-20-4853911. FAX 31-20-4853705. TELEX 18582 ESPA NL. E-mail: nlinfo-f@elsevier.nl; usinfo-f@elsevier.com; forinfo-kyf04035@niftyserve.or.jp; URL: http://www.elsevier.nl/. (Subscr. in the Americas to: Elsevier Science, Regional Sales Office, Box 945, New York, NY 10159-0945. TEL 212-633-3730. FAX 212-633-3680; Subscr. in Australasia and the Far East to: Elsevier Science (Singapore) Pte Ltd, No.1 Temasek Ave., No.17-01 Millenia Tower, Singapore 039192, Singapore. TEL 65-434-3727. FAX 65-337-2230; Subscr. in Japan to: Elsevier Science Japan, 9-15 Higashi-Azabu 1-chome, Minato-ku, Tokyo 106, Japan. TEL 81-3-5561-5033. FAX 81-3-5561-5047) **Indexed:** ASCA, Ind.Sci.Rev. **Document type:** monographic series.
—BLDSC (0709.180000); CASDDS; CISTI; KNAW. **CCC**.
Description: Publishes studies and research in the area of inorganic biochemistry.
Refereed Serial

546 541.38 US ISSN 0898-8838
QD151 CODEN: AICHEP
ADVANCES IN INORGANIC CHEMISTRY. 1959. irreg., vol.44, 1996. Academic Press, Inc., 525 B St., Ste. 1900, San Diego, CA 92101-4495. TEL 619-231-0926. FAX 619-699-6715. (Subscr. to: Order Dept., 6277 Sea Harbor Dr., 4th Fl., Orlando, FL 32887. TEL 800-321-5068) Eds. H.J. Emeleus, A.G. Sharpe. index. (reprint service avail. from ISI) **Indexed:** ASCA, Chem.Abstr., Chem.Cit.Ind. Chem.Infd., Ind.Sci.Rev., Sci.Cit.Ind. **Document type:** monographic series.
—BLDSC (0709.197000); CASDDS; CISTI; Linda Hall; SWETS; UnCover. **CCC**.
Formerly (until 1987): Advances in Inorganic Chemistry and Radiochemistry (ISSN 0065-2792)
Refereed Serial

546.34 NE ISSN 0065-2954
QD189 CODEN: AMSCCE
ADVANCES IN MOLTEN SALT CHEMISTRY. 1971. irreg. vol.6, 1987. price varies. Elsevier Science B.V., Books Division, P.O. Box 211, 1000 AE Amsterdam, Netherlands. TEL 31-20-4853911. FAX 31-20-4853705. TELEX 18582 ESPA NL. E-mail: nlinfo-f@elsevier.nl; usinfo-f@elsevier.com; forinfo-kyf04035@niftyserve.or.jp; URL: http://www.elsevier.nl/. (Subscr. in the Americas to: Elsevier Science, Regional Sales Office, Box 945, New York, NY 10159-0945. TEL 212-633-3730. FAX 212-633-3680; Subscr. in Australasia and the Far East to: Elsevier Science (Singapore) Pte Ltd, No.1 Temasek Ave., No.17-01 Millenia Tower, Singapore 039192, Singapore. TEL 65-434-3727. FAX 65-337-2230; Subscr. in Japan to: Elsevier Science Japan, 9-15 Higashi-Azabu 1-chome, Minato-ku, Tokyo 106, Japan. TEL 81-3-5561-5033. FAX 81-3-5561-5047) Eds. G. Mamantov, C.B. Mamantov. **Indexed:** Chem.Abstr., INSPEC. **Document type:** monographic series.
—CASDDS; CISTI; Linda Hall. **CCC**.
Refereed Serial

546 US ISSN 1059-4256
QD181.S6 CODEN: ADSDEO
ADVANCES IN SILICON CHEMISTRY; a research annual. irreg., vol.3, 1996. $109.50. J A I Press Inc., 55 Old Post Rd., Box 1678, Greenwich, CT 06830-1678. TEL 203-661-7602. FAX 203-661-0792. E-mail: jai@jaipress.com. (In Europe: J A I Press Ltd., 38 Tavistock St., Covent Garden, London WC2E 7PB, England. TEL 44-171-379-8834. FAX 44-171-379-8835) Ed. Gerald L. Larson. Document type: academic/scholarly publication.
—CASDDS.
Description: Covers new research in the field.

AGROW; world crop protection news. see AGRICULTURE

BEIKOKU TOKKYO SHOROKU. MUKI KAGAKU, KINZOKU, BUKI DAN'YAKU HEN/U.S. PATENT ABSTRACTS. INORGANIC CHEMISTRY, METALS, ARMAMENT AND AMMUNITION. see PATENTS, TRADEMARKS AND COPYRIGHTS — Abstracting, Bibliographies, Statistics

CARBON. see CHEMISTRY — Organic Chemistry

546 NE ISSN 0260-3594
QD146 CODEN: COICDZ
COMMENTS ON INORGANIC CHEMISTRY. 6/yr. $230 (effective 1998). Gordon and Breach - Harwood Academic, Amsteldisk 166, 1st Fl., 1079 LH Amsterdam, Netherlands. (Subscr. to: International Publishers Distributor, Box 32160, Newark, NJ 07102. TEL 800-545-8398. FAX 215-750-6343) Ed. Fred Basolo. bk.rev. (also avail. in microform) Indexed: ASCA, Chem.Abstr., Curr.Cont. Document type: academic/scholarly publication.
—BLDSC (3336.028500); CASDDS; CISTI; SWETS; UnCover. **CCC.**

546 CC ISSN 0253-9837
QD505 CODEN: THHPD3
CUIHUA XUEBAO/CHINESE JOURNAL OF CATALYSIS. (Text in Chinese; summaries in English) 1979. bi-m. $85.70. (Chinese Academy of Sciences, Dalian Institute of Chemical Physics) Science Press, Marketing and Sales Department, 16 Donghuangchenggen North St., Beijing 100717, People's Republic of China. TEL 4010642. FAX 4019810. adv. circ. 6,000. Document type: academic/scholarly publication.
—CASDDS; CISTI; Linda Hall.
Description: Covers heterogeneous and homogeneous catalysis, surface chemistry, catalytic kinetics, and biocatalysis. Occasionally presents special review articles.
Refereed Serial

546 UK ISSN 0300-9246
QD1 CODEN: JCDTBI
DALTON TRANSACTIONS; a journal of inorganic chemistry. Online edition (UK ISSN 1364-5447) 1972. s-m. £1070 to institutions (US $1926) (effective 1997). The Royal Society of Chemistry, Thomas Graham House, Science Park, Milton Rd., Cambridge CB4 4WF, England. TEL 44-1223-420066. FAX 44-1223-423623. E-mail: sales@rsc.org; URL: http://chemistry.rsc.org/rsc/. (Dist. by: Turpin Distribution Services Ltd., Blackhorse Rd., Letchworth, Herts. SG6 1HN, England. TEL 44-1462-672555. FAX 44-1462-480947) adv.; charts; illus.; index. (also avail. in microform from UMI; microfilm from KTO,PMC) Indexed: A.S.& T.Ind., Abstr.Bull.Inst.Pap.Chem., ASCA, Biol.Abstr., Br.Ceram.Abstr., Bull.Thermodyn.& Thermochem., Cadscan, Chem.Abstr., Chem.Cit.Ind., Chem.Infd., Chem.Titles, Curr.Cont., Ind.Chem., INIS Atomind., Lead Abstr., Mass Spectr.Bull., Ref.Zh., Zincscan. Document type: academic/scholarly publication.
●Also available online. Vendor(s): STN International (CJRSC).
—BLDSC (4727.200000); CASDDS; CISTI; Ei; Genuine Article; KR SourceOne; Linda Hall; SWETS; UMI; UnCover. **CCC.**
Supersedes in part: Chemical Society, London. Journal. Section A: Inorganic, Physical and Theoretical Chemistry (ISSN 0022-4944)
Description: Contains papers on all aspects of the chemistry of inorganic and organometallic compounds, including bio-inorganic and solid-state inorganic chemistry.
Refereed Serial

546 FR ISSN 0992-4361
QD1 CODEN: EJSCE5
EUROPEAN JOURNAL OF SOLID STATE AND INORGANIC CHEMISTRY. 1964. 11/yr. 1879 F. to institutions (foreign 2365 F.) (effective 1998). Gauthier-Villars, 5 rue Laromiguiere, 75005 Paris, France. TEL 33-1-40466201. FAX 33-1-40466201. TELEX 634 916 F. E-mail: gauthier.villars.publisher@mail.sgip.fr; URL: http://www.gauthier-villars.fr. (Subscr. to: Societe de Periodiques Specialises, B.P. 22-F, 41354 Vineuil Cedex, France. TEL 33-2-54504612. FAX 33-2-54504611) Ed. P. Hagenmuller. (also avail. in microform from UMI) Indexed: ASCA, Cadscan, Chem.Abstr., Chem.Cit.Ind., Chem.Infd., Curr.Cont., GeoRef., INSPEC, Lead Abstr., Mat.Sci.Cit.Ind., Sci.Cit.Ind., Zincscan. Document type: academic/scholarly publication.
—BLDSC (3829.742000); AskIEEE; CASDDS; CISTI; Ei; Genuine Article; KR SourceOne; Linda Hall; SWETS; UnCover. **CCC.**
Formerly (until 1988): Revue de Chimie Minerale - Inorganic Chemistry Review - Revue fuer Anorganische Chemie (ISSN 0035-1032)
Description: Covers all fields of solid state and inorganic chemistry.

546 CC ISSN 1001-1625
QE389.62 CODEN: GUTOE9
GUISUANYAN TONGBAO/CHINESE SILICATE SOCIETY. BULLETIN. (Text in Chinese) bi-m. Y1 per no. Tianjin Guisuanyan Xuehui - Tianjin Silicate Society, 26 Qudian Jie, Hongqiao-qu, Tianjin 300230, People's Republic of China. TEL 250852.
—CASDDS.

546 CC ISSN 0454-5648
TP785 CODEN: KSYHA5
GUISUANYAN XUEBAO/CHINESE CERAMIC SOCIETY. JOURNAL. (Former name of issuing body: Chinese Silicate Society) (Text in Chinese; abstracts and tables in English) 1957. bi-m. $60. Chinese Ceramic Society, Guojia Jiancaiju Nei (Inside National Bureau of Bldg. Materials), Baiwanzhuang, Beijing 100831, People's Republic of China. TEL 861-8311144. FAX 861-8313364. TELEX 22076 SABM CN. Ed. Fuxi Gan. R&P contact: Keshun Shi. adv.: B&W page $300, color page $900; adv. contact: Keshun Shi. Indexed: Art & Archaeol.Tech.Abstr., Chem.Abstr. Document type: academic/scholarly publication.
—BLDSC (4729.240000); CASDDS; CISTI; Linda Hall.
Description: Covers the latest development in research, production and design of cement, glass, ceramics, refractory, artificial crystal and nonmetal mine.
Refereed Serial

HANDBOOK OF BINARY PHASE DIAGRAMS. see ENGINEERING — Mechanical Engineering

546 US ISSN 1042-7163
QD399 CODEN: HETCE8
HETEROATOM CHEMISTRY. 1990. 7/yr. $692 (foreign $814.5) (effective 1998). John Wiley & Sons, Inc., Journals, 605 Third Ave., New York, NY 10158-0012. TEL 212-850-6645. FAX 212-850-6021. TELEX 12-7063. E-mail: subinfo@jwiley.com; URL: http://www.wiley.co.uk. (Subscr. outside the Americas to: John Wiley & Sons Ltd., Baffins Ln., Chichester, W. Sussex PO19 1UD, England. TEL 44-1243-779777. FAX 44-1243-776128) Ed. W.E. McEwen. adv.: B&W page £640, color page £1515; trim 279 x 210. circ. 855. (also avail. in microfilm) Indexed: ASCA, Chem.Cit.Ind., Curr.Cont. Document type: academic/scholarly publication.
—BLDSC (4301.230000); CASDDS; CISTI; Ei; Genuine Article; SWETS; UnCover. **CCC.**

546 US ISSN 0020-1669
QD1 CODEN: INOCAJ
INORGANIC CHEMISTRY. 1962. s-m. $1395 to institutional non-members; members $103 (effective 1997). American Chemical Society, 1155 16th St., N.W., Washington, DC 20036. TEL 800-333-9511. FAX 614-447-3671. (Subscr. to: Membership and Subscription Services, Box 3337, Columbus, OH 43210. TEL 614-447-3776) Ed. Dr. M. Frederick Hawthorne. adv.; bk.rev.; index. circ. 4,000. (also avail. in microform) Indexed: ASCA, Biwk.Pap.Rad.Chem.& Photochem., Br.Ceram.Abstr., Bull.Thermodyn.& Thermochem., Cadscan, Chem.Abstr., Chem.Cit.Ind., Chem.Infd., Curr.Cont., Eng.Ind., Excerp.Med., Gen.Sci.Ind., Ind.Chem., Ind.Sci.Rev., INIS Atomind., Lead Abstr., Mass Spectr.Bull., Mat.Sci.Cit.Ind., Soils & Fert., Zincscan. Document type: academic/scholarly publication.
●Also available online. Vendor(s): STN International (CJACS).
—BLDSC (4515.870000); CASDDS; CISTI; Ei; Genuine Article; KR SourceOne; Linda Hall; SWETS; UMI; UnCover. **CCC.**
Description: Publishes fundamental studies, both experimental and theoretical, in all phases of inorganic chemistry.

546 US ISSN 0172-7966
INORGANIC CHEMISTRY CONCEPTS. 1977; N.S 1986. irreg., vol.13, 1990. price varies. Springer-Verlag, 175 Fifth Ave., New York, NY 10010. TEL 212-460-1500. FAX 212-473-6272. (Also: Berlin, Heidelberg, Tokyo and Vienna) Ed.Bd. (reprint service avail. from ISI) Document type: monographic series.
—BLDSC (4515.871000).
Supersedes (1949-1969): Anorganische und Allgemeine Chemie in Einzeldarstellungen (ISSN 0066-4553)

546 660 RU ISSN 0020-1685
TN4 CODEN: INOMAF
INORGANIC MATERIALS. English translation of: Neorganicheskie Materialy. 1965. m. $1875 in US; elsewhere $2195 (effective 1998). (Russian Academy of Sciences) Maik Nauk - Interperiodica, Mezhdunarodnyi Otdel, Ul. Profsoyuznaya, 90, 117864 Moscow, Russia. TEL 7-095-3360066. FAX 7-095-3360666. (Dist. by: Plenum Publishing Corp., 233 Spring St., New York, NY 10013-1578, U.S.A.. TEL 212-620-8468. FAX 212-463-0742) Ed. G.G. Devyatykh. charts; illus.; index. (also avail. in microfilm from UMI; back issues avail.) Indexed: Alloys Ind., Cadscan, Chem.Cit.Ind., Chem.Titles, Curr.Cont., Energy Res.Abstr., Eng.Mat.Abstr., Ind.Sci.Rev., INIS Atomind., INSPEC (1971-), Lead Abstr., Mass Spectr.Bull., Mat.Sci.Cit.Ind., Met.Abstr., Met.Abstr.Ind., Nonfer.Met.Alert, PCC Alert, Solid St.Abstr., Steels Alert, World Alum.Abstr., Zincscan. Document type: academic/scholarly publication.
—BLDSC (0412.620000); AskIEEE; CASDDS; CISTI; Ei; Genuine Article; KR SourceOne; SWETS; UMI; UnCover. **CCC.**
Refereed Serial

CHEMISTRY — INORGANIC CHEMISTRY

546   SZ   ISSN 0020-1693
QD146   CODEN: ICHAA3
INORGANICA CHIMICA ACTA; the international inorganic chemistry journal. (Text in English) 1967. 26/yr. fl.9639($5540) (effective 1998). Elsevier Science S.A., P.O. Box 564, CH-1001 Lausanne 1, Switzerland. TEL 41-21-3207381. FAX 41-21-3235444. TELEX 450620-ELSA-CH. (Subscr. to: Elsevier Science, Regional Sales Office, P.O. Box 211, 1000 AE Amsterdam, Netherlands. TEL 31-20-4853757. FAX 31-20-4853432; Subscr. in the Americas to: Elsevier Science, Regional Sales Office, Box 945, New York, NY 10159-0945. FAX 212-633-3680; Subscr. in Australasia to: Elsevier Science (Singapore) Pte. Ltd., No. 1 Temasek Ave., No. 17-01 Millenia Tower, Singapore 039192, Singapore. TEL 65-434-3727. FAX 65-337-2230) Ed. U. Belluco. adv.; bk.rev.; bibl.; stat.; index. (also avail. in microform from UMI) **Indexed:** Acoust.Abstr., ASCA, Biwk.Pap.Rad.Chem.& Photochem., Chem.Abstr., Chem.Cit.Ind., Chem.Infd., Curr.Adv.Ecol.Sci., Curr.Cont., Excerp.Med., Ind.Chem., Ind.Sci.Rev., INIS Atomind., Mass Spectr.Bull., Mat.Sci.Cit.Ind., Sci.Cit.Ind., Soils & Fert. **Document type:** academic/scholarly publication.
—BLDSC (4515.910000); ADONIS; CASDDS; CISTI; Ei; Genuine Article; Linda Hall; SWETS; UnCover. **CCC.**
Incorporates: Chimica Acta Reviews (ISSN 0073-8085)
Description: Covers various aspects of inorganic chemistry. For inorganic chemists and organometallic chemists.
Refereed Serial

INTERNATIONAL FIBER JOURNAL. see *TEXTILE INDUSTRIES AND FABRICS*

546   KR   ISSN 0234-4483
QD189   CODEN: IRTEEE
IONNYE RASPLAVY I TVERDYE ELEKTROLITY; respublikanskii mezhvedomstvennyi sbornik nauchnykh trudov. 1985. a. (Akademiya Nauk Ukrainy, Institut Obshchei i Neorganicheskoi Khimii Izdatel'stvo Naukova Dumka, c/o Yu.A. Khramov, Dir., Ul. Repina 3, Kiev 252601, Ukraine. Ed. Yu.K. Delimarskii.
—CASDDS; Linda Hall.

ISSLEDOVANIYA V OBLASTI KHIMII REDKOZEMEL'NYKH ELEMENTOV. see *EARTH SCIENCES*

JOURNAL OF BIOLOGICAL INORGANIC CHEMISTRY. see *BIOLOGY — Biological Chemistry*

546 549.125   US   ISSN 1053-0509
QC477   CODEN: JOFLEN
JOURNAL OF FLUORESCENCE. 1991. q. $345 (foreign $405) (effective 1998). Plenum Publishing Corp., 233 Spring St., New York, NY 10013-1578. TEL 212-620-8000. FAX 212-463-0742. TELEX 23-421139. Ed. Joseph R. Lakowicz. adv. (back issues avail.) **Document type:** academic/scholarly publication.
—BLDSC (4984.525000); CASDDS; CISTI; Ei; Linda Hall; SWETS; UnCover. **CCC.**
Refereed Serial

546 661   SZ   ISSN 0022-1139
QD181.F1   CODEN: JFLCAR
JOURNAL OF FLUORINE CHEMISTRY. (Text in English, French and German) 1971. m. fl.4358($2504) (effective 1998). Elsevier Science S.A., P.O. Box 564, CH-1001 Lausanne 1, Switzerland. TEL 41-21-3207381. FAX 41-21-3235444. TELEX 450620-ELSA-CH. (Subscr. to: Elsevier Science, Regional Sales Office, P.O. Box 211, 1000 AE Amsterdam, Netherlands; Subscr. in the Americas to: Elsevier Science, Regional Sales Office, Box 945, New York, NY 10159-0945. TEL 212-633-3730. FAX 212-633-3680; Subscr. in Australasia to: Elsevier Science (Singapore) Pte. Ltd., No. 1 Temasek Ave., No. 17-01 Millenia Tower, Singapore 039192, Singapore. TEL 65-434-3727. FAX 65-337-2230) Eds. D.W.A. Sharp, J.C. Tatlow. adv.; bk.rev. (also avail. in microform from UMI) **Indexed:** ASCA, Chem.Abstr., Chem.Cit.Ind., Chem.Infd., Curr.Chem.React., Curr.Cont., Ind.Chem., Ind.Sci.Rev., Mass Spectr.Bull., Mat.Sci.Cit.Ind., Phys.Ber., Sci.Cit.Ind. **Document type:** academic/scholarly publication.
—BLDSC (4984.530000); ADONIS; CASDDS; CISTI; Ei; Genuine Article; Linda Hall; SWETS; UnCover. **CCC.**
Description: Contains research data on the chemistry of fluorine and of compounds where halogen is a dominant element. Deals with the fundamental and industrial aspects of fluorine and its components. Serves both pure and applied research in this field.
Refereed Serial

JOURNAL OF INORGANIC AND ORGANOMETALLIC POLYMERS. see *CHEMISTRY — Organic Chemistry*

JOURNAL OF INORGANIC BIOCHEMISTRY; an interdisciplinary journal. see *BIOLOGY — Biological Chemistry*

M I R L REPORTS. (Mineral Industry Research Laboratory) see *MINES AND MINING INDUSTRY*

MACROMOLECULAR THEORY AND SIMULATIONS. see *CHEMISTRY — Organic Chemistry*

546   US   ISSN 0740-8900
QD501   CODEN: MIORD8
MECHANISMS OF INORGANIC AND ORGANOMETALLIC REACTIONS. 1983. irreg., vol.8, 1994. Plenum Publishing Corp., 233 Spring St., New York, NY 10013-1578. TEL 212-620-8000. FAX 212-463-0742. TELEX 23-421139. E-mail: books@plenum.com. Ed. M.V. Twigg. **Indexed:** Chem.Abstr. **Document type:** monographic series.
—BLDSC (5424.571600); CASDDS; CISTI; KNAW. **CCC.**
Refereed Serial

546   US   ISSN 0161-5149
QP532   CODEN: MIBSCD
METAL IONS IN BIOLOGICAL SYSTEMS. 1974. irreg., vol.34, 1997. price varies. Marcel Dekker, Inc., 270 Madison Ave., New York, NY 10016. TEL 212-696-9000. FAX 212-658-4540. TELEX 421419. Ed. Helmut Siegel; Pub. Graham Garratt. R&P contact: Julia Mulligan. **Indexed:** ASCA, Chem.Abstr., Chem.Cit.Ind., Ind.Med. (1995-), Ind.Sci.Rev., Sci.Cit.Ind. **Document type:** monographic series.
—BLDSC (5687.100000); CASDDS; CISTI; Genuine Article; KNAW; UnCover. **CCC.**
Refereed Serial

546   US   ISSN 0271-2911
CODEN: MIOBDS
METAL IONS IN BIOLOGY. 1980. irreg., vol.7. John Wiley & Sons, Inc., 605 Third Ave., New York, NY 10158. TEL 212-850-6645. FAX 212-850-6021. (Subscr. ouside the Americas to: John Wiley & Sons Ltd., Baffins Ln., Chichester, W. Sussex PO19 1UD, England. TEL 44-1243-779777. FAX 44-1243-776128) **Document type:** monographic series.
—CASDDS.

546   US   ISSN 0891-4540
MODERN INORGANIC CHEMISTRY. irreg., latest 1990. price varies. Plenum Publishing Corp., 233 Spring St., New York, NY 10013-1578. TEL 212-620-8000. FAX 212-463-0742. TELEX 23-421139. E-mail: books@plenum.com. Ed. John P. Fackler, Jr. (back issues avail.) **Indexed:** INSPEC. **Document type:** monographic series.
Refereed Serial

MOLTEN SALT FORUM. see *ENGINEERING — Chemical Engineering*

547 550   JA   ISSN 1340-7899
CODEN: MUMAFX
MUKI MATERIARU/INORGANIC MATERIALS. (Text in Japanese) 1953. bi-m. Society of Gypsum & Lime, No. 12 Sankyo Bldg., 13-5, Nishi-Shinjuku 7-chome, Shinjuku-ku, Tokyo 160, Japan. **Indexed:** Alloys Ind., Curr.Cont., Eng.Mat.Abstr., Met.Abstr.Ind., PCC Alert, Steels Alert, World Alum.Abstr.
—BLDSC (4515.881000); CASDDS; CISTI.
Former titles (until 1994): Sekko to Sekkai - Gypsum and Lime (ISSN 0559-331X); (until 1953): Sekko - Gypsum (ISSN 0370-954X)

NEWSLETTER GOLD, SILVER AND URANIUM FROM SEAS AND OCEANS PROGRESS UPDATE. see *ENGINEERING — Chemical Engineering*

NH3 NEWS. see *HEATING, PLUMBING AND REFRIGERATION*

546.536   JA   ISSN 0388-0664
CODEN: NTRED4
NIPPON TUNGSTEN REVIEW. (Text in English) 1968. a. free. Nippon Tungsten Co., Ltd., NT Bldg., 2-8, Minosima 1-chome, Hakata-ku, Fukuaka 812, Japan. TEL 81-942-81-7710. Ed. T. Koumura. **Indexed:** Alloys Ind., Chem.Abstr., Eng.Mat.Abstr., Met.Abstr.Ind., Met.Abstr., Nonfer.Met.Alert, PCC Alert, Steels Alert, World Alum.Abstr. **Document type:** bulletin.
—BLDSC (6113.563000); CASDDS.

546   US
NOMENCLATURE SERIES. Variant title: I U P A C Nomenclature Series. irreg., 1990. (International Union of Pure and Applied Chemistry) C R C Press, Inc., 2000 Corporate Blvd., N.W., Boca Raton, FL 33431. TEL 561-998-9784; 800-272-7737. FAX 561-994-0555. TELEX 568689-CRC PRESS. **Document type:** monographic series.

546   US   ISSN 1062-239X
QP550   CODEN: PBICEK
PERSPECTIVES ON BIOINORGANIC CHEMISTRY. 1991. irreg., vol.3, 1996. J A I Press Inc., 55 Old Post Rd. No.2, Box 1678, Greenwich, CT 06830-1678. TEL 203-661-7602. FAX 203-661-0792. E-mail: jai@jaipress.com. (In Europe: JAI Press Ltd., 38 Tavistock St., Covent Garden, London WC2E 7PB, England. TEL 44-171-379-8834. FAX 44-171-379-8835) Ed.Bd. **Document type:** monographic series, academic/scholarly publication.
—BLDSC (6428.138150); CASDDS; CISTI.

546   JA   ISSN 0917-9976
PHOSPHORUS LETTER. (Text in Japanese) 1986. s-a. Nihon Muki Rin Kagakkai - Japanese Association of Inorganic Phosphorus Chemistry, c/o Umegaki Kenkyushitsu, Tokyo Toritsu Daigaku Kogakubu Kogyo Kagakka, 1-1, Minamiosawa, Hachioji-shi, Tokyo 192-03, Japan.
—**CCC.**

CHEMISTRY — INORGANIC CHEMISTRY

546.7   NE   ISSN 1042-6507
QD181.S1   CODEN: PSSLEC
PHOSPHORUS, SULPHUR AND SILICON AND THE RELATED ELEMENTS. 1976. 48/yr. (in 12 monthly vols.; 4 nos./vol.) $415 (effective 1998). Gordon and Breach - Harwood Academic, Amsteldisk 166, 1st Fl., 1079 LH Amsterdam, Netherlands. URL: http://www.gbhap.com/Phosporus_Sulfur_Silicon/. (Subscr. to: International Publishers Distributor, Box 32160, Newark, NJ 07102. TEL 800-545-8398. FAX 215-750-6343) Ed. Robert Holmes. adv.; bk.rev.; index. (also avail. in microform; back issues avail.) **Indexed:** ASCA, Biol.Abstr., Cadscan, Chem.Abstr., Chem.Cit.Ind., Curr.Adv.Ecol.Sci., Curr.Chem.React., Curr.Cont., Ind.Chem., Lead Abstr., Mass Spectr.Bull., Mat.Sci.Cit.Ind., Sci.Cit.Ind., Soils & Fert., Zincscan. **Document type:** academic/scholarly publication.
● Also available online.
Also available on CD-ROM.
—BLDSC (6465.312000); CASDDS; CISTI; Ei; Linda Hall; SWETS; UnCover. **CCC.**
    Formerly: Phosphorous and Sulfur and the Related Elements (ISSN 0308-664X); Formed by the merger of: International Journal of Sulfur Chemistry. Part A. Original Articles, Notes and Communications (ISSN 0094-9337); International Journal of Sulfur Chemistry. Part B. Quarterly Reports (ISSN 0094-9345); International Journal of Sulfur Chemistry. Part C. Mechanisms of Reactions of Sulfur Compound (ISSN 0094-9353)
    Description: Covers the organic, inorganic and biochemistry of phosphorus (including arsenic, antimony and bismuth), sulfur (including selenium, tellurium), and silicon (including germanium, tin).
Refereed Serial

546   PL   ISSN 0324-9832
POLITECHNIKA WROCLAWSKA. INSTYTUT CHEMII NIEORGANICZNEJ I METALURGII PIERWIASTKOW RZADKICH. PRACE NAUKOWE. KONFERENCJE. (Text in Polish; summaries in English and Russian) 1973. irreg., no.15, 1990. price varies. Oficyna Wydawnicza Politechniki Wroclawskiej, Wybrzeze Wyspianskiego 27, 50-370 Wroclaw, Poland. TEL 47-71-222940. FAX 48-71-223664. TELEX 712559 PWRPL. (Dist. by: Ars Polona, Krakowskie Przedmiescie 7, Warsaw, Poland) R&P contact: Halina Dudek. adv. **Indexed:** Alloys Ind., Chem.Abstr., Eng.Mat.Abstr., Met.Abstr.Ind., Met.Abstr., PCC Alert, Steels Alert, World Alum.Abstr.

546   PL   ISSN 0324-9840
QD1   CODEN: PNCNB2
POLITECHNIKA WROCLAWSKA. INSTYTUT CHEMII NIEORGANICZNEJ I METALURGII PIERWIASTKOW RZADKICH. PRACE NAUKOWE. MONOGRAFIE. (Text in Polish; summaries in English and Russian) 1970. irreg., no.33, 1997. price varies. Oficyna Wydawnicza Politechniki Wroclawskiej, Wybrzeze Wyspianskiego 27, 50-370 Wroclaw, Poland. TEL 48-71-222940. FAX 48-71-223664. TELEX 712254 PWRPL. (Dist. by: Ars Polona, Krakowskie Przedmiescie 7, Warsaw, Poland) Ed. Wladyslawa Mulak. R&P contact: Halina Dudek. adv. **Indexed:** Alloys Ind., Eng.Mat.Abstr., Met.Abstr., Met.Abstr., Nonfer.Met.Alert, PCC Alert, Steels Alert, World Alum.Abstr. **Document type:** monographic series.
—CASDDS.
    Description: Halina/Dudek

546   PL   ISSN 0370-0755
POLITECHNIKA WROCLAWSKA. INSTYTUT CHEMII NIEORGANICZNEJ I METALURGII PIERWIASTKOW RZADKICH. PRACE NAUKOWE. STUDIA I MATERIALY. (Text in Polish; summaries in English and Russian) 1970. irreg., no.18, 1981. price varies. Oficyna Wydawnicza Politechniki Wroclawskiej, Wybrzeze Wyspianskiego 27, 50-370 Wroclaw, Poland. TEL 48-71-222940. FAX 48-71-223664. TELEX 712554 PWRPL. (Dist. by: Ars Polona, Krakowskie Przedmiescie 7, Warsaw, Poland) Ed. Wladyslaw Mulak. R&P contact: Halina Dudek. adv. **Indexed:** Alloys Ind., Eng.Mat.Abstr., Met.Abstr., Met.Abstr., Nonfer.Met.Alert, PCC Alert, Steels Alert, World Alum.Abstr. **Document type:** academic/scholarly publication.

546   UK   ISSN 0277-5387
QD1   CODEN: PLYHDE
POLYHEDRON; international journal for inorganic and organometallic chemistry. 1982. 26/yr. fl.7384($4244) (effective 1998). Elsevier Science Ltd., Pergamon, P.O. Box 800, Kidlington, Oxford OX5 1DX, England. TEL 44-1865-843000. FAX 44-1865-843010. E-mail: nlinfo-f@elsevier.nl; usinfo-f@elsevier.com; forinfo-kyf04035@niftyserve.or.jp; URL: http://www.elsevier.nl/. (Subscr. to: Elsevier Science, Regional Sales Office, P.O. Box 211, 1000 AE Amsterdam, Netherlands. TEL 31-20-4853757. FAX 31-20-4853432; Subscr. in the Americas to: Elsevier Science, Regional Sales Office, Box 945, New York, NY 10159-0945. TEL 212-633-3730. FAX 212-633-3680; Subscr. in Australasia and the Far East to: Elsevier Science (Singapore) Pte Ltd, No.1 Temasek Ave., No.17-01 Millenia Tower, Singapore 039192, Singapore. TEL 65-434-3727. FAX 65-337-2230) Ed. Geoffrey Wilkinson. (also avail. in microfiche from MIM; microfilm from UMI; reprint service avail. from UMI) **Indexed:** ASCA, Biol.Abstr., Bull.Thermodyn.& Thermochem., Cadscan, Chem.Abstr., Chem.Cit.Ind., Curr.Chem.React., Curr.Cont., GeoRef., Ind.Chem., Ind.Sci.Rev., INSPEC, Lead Abstr., Mat.Sci.Cit.Ind., Sci.Cit.Ind., Zincscan. **Document type:** academic/scholarly publication.
—BLDSC (6547.690000); CASDDS; CISTI; Ei; Genuine Article; Linda Hall; SWETS; UMI; UnCover. **CCC.**
    Incorporated: Journal of Inorganic and Nuclear Chemistry (ISSN 0022-1902); Inorganic and Nuclear Chemistry Letters (ISSN 0020-1650)
    Description: Publishes original, fundamental, experimental and theoretical research in major areas of inorganic and organometallic chemistry, as well as review articles and collections of research papers on selected topics.
Refereed Serial

POWDER DIFFRACTION FILE SEARCH MANUAL. ALPHABETICAL LISTING. INORGANIC. see *CHEMISTRY — Analytical Chemistry*

POWDER DIFFRACTION FILE SEARCH MANUAL. HANAWALT METHOD. INORGANIC. see *CHEMISTRY — Analytical Chemistry*

PREVISIONS GLISSANTES DETAILLEES EN PERSPECTIVES SECTORIELLES (VOL.20): CHIMIE MINERALE. see *BUSINESS AND ECONOMICS — Economic Situation And Conditions*

PROBLEMY PROJEKTOWE PRZEMYSLU I BUDOWNICTWA/PROJECT DESIGN PROBLEMS OF THE INDUSTRY AND BUILDING ENGINEERING; czasopismo naukowo-techniczne. see *METALLURGY*

546   JA
PROCEEDINGS OF SYMPOSIUM ON HETEROATOM CHEMISTRY/HETERO GENSHI KAGAKU TORONKAI KOEN YOSHISHU. (Text in Japanese; summaries in English) a. Chemical Society of Japan - Nippon Kagakkai, 1-5, Kanda Surugadai, Chiyoda-ku, Tokyo 101, Japan. **Document type:** proceedings.

546   US   ISSN 0079-6379
QD151   CODEN: PIOCAR
PROGRESS IN INORGANIC CHEMISTRY. 1959. irreg., vol.41, 1993. price varies. John Wiley & Sons, Inc., 605 Third Ave., New York, NY 10158. TEL 212-850-6000. FAX 212-850-6088. TELEX 12-7063. Ed. S.J. Lippard. **Indexed:** ASCA, Ind.Sci.Rev. **Document type:** monographic series.
—BLDSC (6868.600000); CASDDS; CISTI; Linda Hall; SWETS; UnCover.
Refereed Serial

REGARDS SUR L'ETAIN. see *METALLURGY*

546   UK   ISSN 0193-4929
    CODEN: RICHD7
REVIEWS IN INORGANIC CHEMISTRY. (Text in English) q. $270 (effective 1997). Freund Publishing House Ltd., Ste. 500, Chesham House, 150 Regent St., London W1R 5FA, England. (And: P.O. Box 35010, Tel Aviv, Israel. TEL 972-3-5628540. FAX 972-3-5628538) Ed. M. Zangen. adv.; bk.rev.; index. (back issues avail.) **Indexed:** ASCA, Chem.Abstr. **Document type:** academic/scholarly publication.
—BLDSC (7790.796000); CASDDS; CISTI; Linda Hall; SWETS; UnCover.

541.3 546   UK   ISSN 0260-1818
QD1   CODEN: APCCDO
ROYAL SOCIETY OF CHEMISTRY. ANNUAL REPORTS ON THE PROGRESS OF CHEMISTRY. SECTION A: INORGANIC CHEMISTRY. 1904. a. £122 (US $220); all 3 sections £324 (US $583) (effective 1997). The Royal Society of Chemistry, Thomas Graham House, Science Park, Milton Rd., Cambridge CB4 4WF, England. TEL 44-1223-420066. FAX 44-1223-423623. E-mail: sales@rsc.org; URL: http://chemistry.rsc.org/rsc/. (Subscr. to: Turpin Distribution Services Ltd., Blackhorse Rd., Letchworth, Herts. SG6 1HN, England. TEL 44-1462-672555. FAX 44-1462-480947) Ed. J. Donaldson. index, cum.index: vols.1-46. circ. 2,000. (also avail. in microfilm from PMC) **Indexed:** INIS Atomind. **Document type:** academic/scholarly publication.
—BLDSC (1513.807000); CASDDS; CISTI; Linda Hall. **CCC.**
    Supersedes: Chemical Society. Annual Reports on the Progress of Chemistry. Section A: Physical and Inorganic Chemistry (ISSN 0308-6003); Which was formerly: Chemical Society, London. Annual Reports on the Progress of Chemistry. Section A: General, Physical and Inorganic Chemistry (ISSN 0069-3022)
    Description: Provides critical coverage of the significant advances in inorganic chemistry for the general reader.

546   RU   ISSN 0036-0236
QD1   CODEN: RJICAQ
RUSSIAN JOURNAL OF INORGANIC CHEMISTRY. Russian edition: Zhurnal Neorganicheskoi Khimii (ISSN 0044-457X) 1959. m. $1779 in U.S. & Canada (elsewhere $1938) (effective 1995). Maik Nauka - Interperiodica, Mezhdunarodnyi Otdel, Ul. Profsoyuznaya 90, Moscow 117864, Russia. TEL 7-095-3360066. FAX 7-095-3360066. (Subscr. to: Maik Nauka - Interperiodica, Subscription Office, Box 1831, Birmingham, AL 35201-1831, U.S.A.. TEL 205-995-1567. FAX 205-995-1588) bk.rev.; bibl.; charts; index. (also avail. in microform from PMC) **Indexed:** Alloys Ind., Eng.Mat.Abstr., Excerpt.Med., GeoRef., Mass Spectr.Bull., Met.Abstr.Ind., Met.Abstr., Nonfer.Met.Alert, PCC Alert, Soils & Fert., Steels Alert, World Alum.Abstr. **Document type:** academic/scholarly publication.
—BLDSC (0420.761000); AskIEEE; CISTI; KR SourceOne; Linda Hall; SWETS; UnCover.

666 669   IT   ISSN 1124-4003
TS700   CODEN: NCIPD9
SMALTO PORCELLANATO; tecnologia e mercati. (Text in Italian; summaries in English) 1964. 3/yr. free. Centro Italiano Smalti Porcellanati, Via Olona n.41, 20016 Pero (MI), Italy. TEL 39-2-38103333. FAX 39-2-38103288. Ed. Maria De Carli. adv. contact: Mariella Dell'Anna. bk.rev.; charts; illus.; stat.; cum.index every 3 yrs. circ. 2,600. **Indexed:** Alloys Ind., Eng.Mat.Abstr., Met.Abstr., Met.Abstr.Ind., Nonfer.Met.Alert, PCC Alert, Steels Alert, World Alum.Abstr. **Document type:** academic/scholarly publication.
—BLDSC (8310.190530); CASDDS.
    Formerly (until 1994): Smalto e Smaltatura; Supersedes (1964-1987): Notiziario Informativo (ISSN 0392-6648)
    Description: Covers the field of enamelling, includes research, experiments and the new initiatives taken in this field.

546   NE   ISSN 0169-3158
    CODEN: SICHEJ
STUDIES IN INORGANIC CHEMISTRY. (Text in English) 1978. irreg., vol.18, 1993. price varies. Elsevier Science B.V., Books Division, P.O. Box 211, 1000 AE Amsterdam, Netherlands. TEL 31-20-4853911. FAX 31-20-4853705. TELEX 18582 ESPA NL. E-mail: nlinfo-f@elsevier.nl; usinfo-f@elsevier.com; forinfo-kyf04035@niftyserve.or.jp; URL: http://www.elsevier.nl/. (Subscr. in the Americas to: Elsevier Science, Regional Sales Office, Box 945, New York, NY 10159-0945. TEL 212-633-3730. FAX 212-633-3680; Subscr. in Australasia and the Far East to: Elsevier Science (Singapore) Pte Ltd, No.1 Temasek Ave., No.17-01 Millenia Tower, Singapore 039192, Singapore. TEL 65-434-3727. FAX 65-337-2230; Subscr. in Japan to: Elsevier Science Japan, 9-15 Higashi-Azabu 1-chome, Minato-ku, Tokyo 106, Japan. TEL 81-3-5561-5033. FAX 81-3-5561-5047) **Indexed:** Chem.Abstr., INSPEC. **Document type:** monographic series.
—BLDSC (8490.739000); CASDDS. **CCC.**
Refereed Serial

CHEMISTRY — ORGANIC CHEMISTRY

546   KR   ISSN 0203-3119
TA418.26   CODEN: SVMAD2
SVERKHTVERDYE MATERIALY; nauchno-teoreticheskii zhurnal. English translation: Journal of Superhard Materials (US ISSN 1063-4576) (Text in Russian; summaries in English and Russian) 1979. bi-m. $57 (effective 1998). Akademiya Nauk Ukrainy, Institut Nadtverdikh Materialiv im. V.M. Bakulya, Vul. Avtozavods'ka, 3, 254153 Kiev 153, Ukraine. TEL 38-44-4303441. (Dist. by: Mezhdunarodnaya Kniga, B. Yakimanka 39, 117049 Moscow, Russia. TEL 7-095-2384967. FAX 7-095-2384634) (Co-sponsor: Rossiiskaya Akademiya Nauk, Otdelenie Fizikokhimii i Tekhnologii Neorganicheskikh Materialov) Ed. N.V. Novikov. **Indexed:** Djerelo.
—BLDSC (0160.897000); CASDDS; CISTI; Linda Hall.
Formerly: Sinteticheskie Almazy (ISSN 0586-4534)

TETRAHEDRON: ASYMMETRY; international journal for rapid publication on all aspects of asymmetry in organic, inorganic, organometallic, physical and bio-organic chemistry. see *CHEMISTRY — Organic Chemistry*

546   NE   ISSN 0924-6142
                   CODEN: TELCEW
TOPICS IN F-ELEMENT CHEMISTRY. (Text in English) 1985. irreg., vol.3, 1995. price varies. Kluwer Academic Publishers, Postbus 17, 3300 AA Dordrecht, Netherlands. TEL 31-78-6392392. FAX 31-78-6392254. TELEX 29245 KAPG NL. E-mail: services@wkap.nl; URL: http://www.wkap.nl. (Dist. by: Kluwer Academic Publishers Group, P.O. Box 322, 3300 AH Dordrecht, Netherlands. TEL 31-78-6392392. FAX 31-78-6546474; N. America dist. addr.: Box 358, Accord Sta., Hingham, MA 02018-0358. TEL 617-871-6600) **Document type:** monographic series.
—CASDDS; CISTI.
Refereed Serial

546 540   NE   ISSN 0082-495X
TOPICS IN INORGANIC AND GENERAL CHEMISTRY. (Text in English) 1964. irreg., vol.23, 1990. price varies. Elsevier Science B.V., Books Division, P.O. Box 211, 1000 AE Amsterdam, Netherlands. TEL 31-20-4853911. FAX 31-20-4853705. TELEX 18582 ESPA NL. E-mail: nlinfo-f@elsevier.nl; usinfo-f@elsevier.com; forinfo-kyf04035@niftyserve.or.jp; URL: http://www.elsevier.nl/. (Subscr. in the Americas to: Elsevier Science, Regional Sales Office, Box 945, New York, NY 10159-0945. TEL 212-633-3730. FAX 212-633-3680; Subscr. in Australasia and the Far East to: Elsevier Science (Singapore) Pte Ltd, No.1 Temasek Ave., No.17-01 Millenia Tower, Singapore 039192, Singapore. TEL 65-434-3727. FAX 65-337-2230; Subscr. in Japan to: Elsevier Science Japan, 9-15 Higashi-Azabu 1-chome, Minato-ku, Tokyo 106, Japan. TEL 81-3-5561-5033. FAX 81-3-5561-5047) Eds. P.L. Robinson, R.J.H. Clark. **Document type:** monographic series.
—KNAW.
Refereed Serial

546   NO
UNIVERSITETET I TRONDHEIM. NORGES TEKNISKE HOEGSKOLE. INSTITUTT FOR UORGANISK KJEMI. AVHANDLING. 1976. irreg., no.53, 1988. NOK 300. Universitetet i Trondheim, Norges Tekniske Hoegskole. Instituut for Uorganisk Kjemi, 7034 Trondheim-NTH, Norway. FAX 47-7-593992. TELEX 5563NTHAD.N. circ. 250.

UNIVERSITY OF ALASKA. MINERAL INDUSTRY RESEARCH LABORATORY. ANNUAL REPORT OF RESEARCH PROGRESS. see *MINES AND MINING INDUSTRY*

546   CC   ISSN 1000-324X
TP785   CODEN: WCXUET
WUJI CAILIAO XUEBAO/JOURNAL OF INORGANIC MATERIALS. (Text in Chinese; summaries in English) 1986. q. $63. (Chinese Academy of Sciences, Shanghai Institute of Silica) Science Press, Marketing and Sales Department, 16 Donghuangchenggen North St., Beijing 100717, People's Republic of China. TEL 4010642. FAX 4019810. adv. circ. 8,000. **Document type:** academic/scholarly publication.
—BLDSC (5007.300000); CASDDS.
Description: Covers research on man-made crystals, special glass and ceramics, amorphous semiconductors, inorganic coating materials, and inorganic composites.
Refereed Serial

546   CC   ISSN 1001-4861
                   CODEN: WHUXEO
WUJI HUAXUE XUEBAO/JOURNAL OF INORGANIC CHEMISTRY. (Text in Chinese or English) 1985. q. $39 (effective 1997). Chinese Chemical Society - Zhongguo Huaxuehui, P.O. Box 2709, Beijing 100080, People's Republic of China. TEL 86-10-6256-8157. FAX 86-10-6256-8157.
—BLDSC (5007.220000); CASDDS; CISTI.

546.34   JA
YOYUEN KAGAKU TORONKAI YOSHISHU/SYMPOSIUM ON MOLTEN SALT CHEMISTRY. (Text in English, Japanese; summaries in English) 1967. a. Denki Kagaku Kyokai, Yoyuen linkai - Electrochemical Society of Japan, Molten Salt Committee, c/o Osaka Daigaku Kogakubu Zairyo Kaihatsu Kogakka, 2-1, Yamadaoka, Suita-shi, Osaka 565, Japan.

546.34   JA   ISSN 0916-1589
                  CODEN: YKKAEG
YOYUEN OYOBI KOON KAGAKU/MOLTEN SALTS. (Text in Japanese; summaries in English) 1989. 3/yr. Denki Kagaku Kyokai, Yoyuen linkai - Electrochemical Society of Japan, Molten Salt Committee, c/o Osaka Daigaku Kogakubu Zairyo Kaihatsu Kogakka, 2-1, Yamadaoka, Suita-shi, Osaka 565, Japan. **Indexed:** Chem.Abstr.
—CASDDS.

546 547   GW   ISSN 0932-0776
QD1   CODEN: ZNBSEN
ZEITSCHRIFT FUER NATURFORSCHUNG. SECTION B: A JOURNAL OF CHEMICAL SCIENCES. (Text in English and German) 1947. m. DM.967 (effective 1998). Verlag der Zeitschrift fuer Naturforschung, Postfach 2645, 72016 Tuebingen, Germany. TEL 49-7071-31555. FAX 49-7071-360571. Ed. Dr. Voelter. R&P contact: Tamina Greifeld. adv. contact: Anneliese Eipper. bk.rev.; charts; illus.; index. circ. 600. **Indexed:** ASCA, Biol.Abstr., Biotech.Abstr., Bull.Thermodyn.& Thermochem., Chem.Abstr., Chem.Cit.Ind., Chem.Infd., Curr.Adv.Ecol.Sci., Curr.Chem.React., Curr.Cont., Deep Sea Res.& Oceanogr.Abstr., Excerp.Med., Helminthol.Abstr., Hort.Abstr., Ind.Chem, Ind.Sci.Rev., Mass Spectr.Bull., Mat.Sci.Cit.Ind., Met.Abstr., Rev.Med.& Vet.Mycol., Sci.Cit.Ind., Weed Abstr. **Document type:** academic/scholarly publication.
—BLDSC (9475.000000); AskIEEE; CASDDS; CISTI; Genuine Article; KR SourceOne; Linda Hall; SWETS; UnCover. **CCC**.
Former titles: Zeitschrift fuer Naturforschung. Section B: Inorganic and Organic Chemistry (ISSN 0340-5087); Zeitschrift fuer Naturforschung. Ausgabe B. (ISSN 0044-3174)
Refereed Serial

ZHONGGUO WUJI FENXI HUAXUE WENZHAI/CHINESE INORGANIC ANALYTICAL CHEMISTRY ABSTRACTS. see *CHEMISTRY — Abstracting, Bibliographies, Statistics*

546   RU   ISSN 0044-457X
                   CODEN: ZNOKAQ
ZHURNAL NEORGANICHESKOI KHIMII. English edition: Russian Journal of Inorganic Chemistry (ISSN 0036-0236) 1956. m. 118.80 Rub. (Rossiiskaya Akademiya Nauk, Institut Obshchei i Neorganicheskoi Khimii im. N.S. Kurnakova) Maik Nauka, Ul. Profsoyuznaya 90, Moscow 117864, Russia. TEL 7-095-3360066.
FAX 7-095-3360066. Ed. V.I Spitjin. adv.; bk.rev.; bibl.; charts; illus.; index. circ. 2,825. **Indexed:** Alloys Ind., ASCA, Bull.Thermodyn.& Thermochem., Chem.Abstr., Chem.Cit.Ind., Chem.Infd., Curr.Chem.React., Curr.Cont., Eng.Mat.Abstr., Ind.Chem., Ind.Sci.Rev., Mat.Sci.Cit.Ind., Met.Abstr.Ind., Met.Abstr., Met.Abstr., Nonfer.Met.Alert, PCC Alert, Ref.Zh., Sci.Cit.Ind., Steels Alert, World Alum.Abstr.
—BLDSC (0062.000000); AskIEEE; CASDDS; CISTI; Genuine Article; KNAW; KR SourceOne; Linda Hall. **CCC**.

CHEMISTRY — Organic Chemistry

ABSTRACTS OF THE SYMPOSIUM ON ORGANOMETALLIC CHEMISTRY, JAPAN/YUKI KINZOKU KAGAKU TORONKAI KOEN YOSHISHU. see *CHEMISTRY — Abstracting, Bibliographies, Statistics*

ADDITIVES FOR POLYMERS; an international newsletter. see *PLASTICS*

ADVANCED COMPOSITES MANUFACTURING CENTRE NEWSLETTER. see *PLASTICS*

547.3   US   ISSN 1068-7394
ADVANCES IN CARBANION CHEMISTRY. 1992. irreg., vol.2, 1996. $109.50. J A I Press Inc., 55 Old Post Rd., No.2, Box 1678, Greenwich, CT 06830-1678. TEL 203-661-7602. FAX 203-661-0792. E-mail: jai@jaipress.com. (In Europe: JAI Press Ltd., 38 Tavistock St., Covent Garden, London WC2E 7PB, England. TEL 44-171-379-8834. FAX 44-171-379-8835) Ed. Victor Snieckus. **Document type:** academic/scholarly publication, monographic series.
Description: Aims to provides a series which lends itself to pedagogic and resource use by beginning and experienced investigators, graduate students, and professionals.

547.3   US   ISSN 1079-350X
ADVANCES IN CARBENE CHEMISTRY. 1994. irreg., vol.2, 1997. $109.50. J A I Press Inc., 55 Old Post Rd., No.2, Box 1678, Greenwich, CT 06830-1678. TEL 203-661-7602. FAX 203-661-0792. E-mail: jai@jaipress.com. (In Europe: JAI Press Ltd., 38 Tavistock St., Covent Garden, London WC2E 7PB, England. TEL 44-171-379-8834. FAX 44-171-379-8835) Ed. Udo Brinker. **Document type:** academic/scholarly publication, monographic series.
Description: Provides authoritative and timely contributions addressing a wide range of topics associated with carbene chemistry.

547.3   US   ISSN 1047-3645
ADVANCES IN CARBOCATION CHEMISTRY. 1989. irreg., vol.3, 1997. $109.50. J A I Press Inc., 55 Old Post Rd., No.2, Box 1678, Greenwich, CT 06830-1678. TEL 203-661-7602. FAX 203-661-0792. E-mail: jai@jaipress.com. (In Europe: JAI Press Ltd., 38 Tavistock St., Covent Garden, London WC2E 7PB, England. TEL 44-171-379-8834. FAX 44-171-379-8835) Ed. James Coxon. **Document type:** academic/scholarly publication, monographic series.
Description: Provides a detailed account of some of the recent work in the carbocation area.

547.78 574.192   US   ISSN 0065-2318
QD321   CODEN: ACBYAP
ADVANCES IN CARBOHYDRATE CHEMISTRY AND BIOCHEMISTRY. 1945. irreg., vol.52, 1997. Academic Press, Inc., 525 B St, Ste. 1900, San Diego, CA 92101-4495. TEL 619-231-0926. FAX 619-699-6715. (Subscr. to: Order Dept., 6277 Sea Harbor Dr., 4th Fl., Orlando, FL 32887. TEL 800-321-5068) Eds. Melville L. Wolfrom, R. Stuart Tipson. (reprint service avail. from ISI) **Indexed:** Abstr.Bull.Inst.Pap.Chem., ASCA, Biol.Abstr., Chem.Abstr., Chem.Cit.Ind., Chem.Infd., Curr.Adv.Ecol.Sci., Curr.Chem.React., Excerp.Med., Food Sci.& Tech.Abstr., Ind.Chem, Ind.Med., Ind.Sci.Rev., Nutr.Abstr., Trop.Dis.Bull. **Document type:** monographic series.
—BLDSC (0702.100000); CASDDS; CISTI; EMDOCS; KNAW; Linda Hall; SWETS; UnCover. **CCC**.
Formerly (until 1968): Advances in Carbohydrate Chemistry (ISSN 0096-5332)
Refereed Serial

547   US   ISSN 1052-2077
ADVANCES IN CYCLOADDITION. 1988. irreg., vol.4, 1997. $109.50. J A I Press Inc., 55 Old Post Rd., No.2, Box 1678, Greenwich, CT 06830-1678. TEL 203-661-7602. FAX 203-661-0792. E-mail: jai@jaipress.com. (In Europe: JAI Press Ltd., 38 Tavistock St., Covent Garden, London WC2E 7PB, England. TEL 44-171-379-8834. FAX 44-171-379-8835) Ed. Dennis Curran. **Document type:** academic/scholarly publication, monographic series.

547.1   US   ISSN 1061-8937
ADVANCES IN ELECTRON TRANSFER CHEMISTRY. 199 irreg., vol.6, 1997. $109.50. J A I Press Inc., 55 Old Post Rd., No.2, Box 1678, Greenwich, CT 06830-1678. TEL 203-661-7602. FAX 203-661-0792. E-mail: jai@jaipress.com. (In Europe: JAI Press Ltd., 38 Tavistock St., Covent Garden, London WC2E 7PB, England. TEL 44-171-379-8834. FAX 44-171-379-8835) Ed. Patrick Mariano. **Document type:** academic/scholarly publication, monographic series.
Description: Focuses on chemical and biochemical aspects of electron transfer chemistry.

CHEMISTRY — ORGANIC CHEMISTRY

547.59   US   ISSN 0065-2725
QD400   CODEN: AHTCAG
ADVANCES IN HETEROCYCLIC CHEMISTRY. (Supplement avail.: Advances in Heterocyclic Chemistry. Supplement (ISSN 0191-2887)) 1963. irreg., no.69, 1997. Academic Press, Inc., 525 B St., Ste. 1900, San Diego, CA 92101-4495. TEL 619-231-0926. FAX 619-699-6715. (Subscr. to: Order Dept., 6277 Sea Harbor Dr., 4th Fl., Orlando, FL 32887. TEL 800-321-5068) Ed. A.R. Katritzky. index. (reprint service avail. from ISI) **Indexed:** ASCA, Chem.Cit.Ind., Chem.Infd., Curr.Chem.React., Ind.Chem., Ind.Sci.Rev., Sci.Cit.Ind. **Document type:** monographic series.
—BLDSC (0709.020000); CASDDS; CISTI; Linda Hall; SWETS; UnCover. **CCC.**
Refereed Serial

547   US   ISSN 1067-571X
ADVANCES IN HETEROCYCLIC NATURAL PRODUCT SYNTHESIS. 1991. irreg., vol.4, 1997. $109.50. J A I Press Inc., 55 Old Post Rd., No.2, Box 1678, Greenwich, CT 06830-1678. TEL 203-661-7602. FAX 203-661-0792. E-mail: jai@jaipress.com. (In Europe: JAI Press Ltd., 38 Tavistock St., Covent Garden, London WC2E 7PB, England. TEL 44-171-379-8834. FAX 44-171-379-8835) Ed. William Pearson. **Document type:** academic/scholarly publication, monographic series.
—Linda Hall.
Description: Focuses on recent progress in various aspects of heterocycle synthesis as applied to natural compounds.

547   NE
ADVANCES IN INCLUSION SCIENCE. 1983. irreg. price varies. Kluwer Academic Publishers, Postbus 17, 3300 AA Dordrecht, Netherlands. TEL 31-78-6392392. FAX 31-78-6392254. TELEX 29245 KAPG NL. E-mail: services@wkap.nl; URL: http://www.wkap.nl. (Dist. by: Kluwer Academic Publishers Group, P.O. Box 322, 3300 AH Dordrecht, Netherlands. TEL 31-78-6392392. FAX 31-78-6546474; N. America dist. addr.: Box 358, Accord Sta., Hingham, MA 02018-0358. TEL 617-871-6600) **Document type:** monographic series.
Refereed Serial

547   US   ISSN 1045-0688
QD410   CODEN: ADMCEP
ADVANCES IN METAL-ORGANIC CHEMISTRY. irreg., vol.6, 1997. $109.50. J A I Press Inc., 55 Old Post Rd., No. 2, Box 1678, Greenwich, CT 06830-1678. TEL 203-661-7602. FAX 203-661-0792. E-mail: jai@jaipress.com. (Addr. in the U.K. and Europe: J A I Press Ltd., 38 Tavistock St., Covent Garden, London WC2E 7PB, England. TEL 44-171-379-8834. FAX 44-171-379-8835) **Document type:** monographic series.
—CASDDS; CISTI.

547.7   US
▼**ADVANCES IN MOLECULAR SIMILARITY.** 1996. irreg., vol.2, 1997. $112.50. J A I Press Inc., 55 Old Post Rd., No.2, Box 1678, Greenwich, CT 06830-1678. TEL 203-661-7602. FAX 203-661-0792. E-mail: jai@jaipress.com. (In Europe: JAI Press Ltd., 38 Tavistock St., Covent Garden, London WC2E 7PB, England. TEL 44-171-379-8834. FAX 44-171-379-8835) Eds. Ramon Carbo-Dorca, P.G. Mezey. **Document type:** academic/scholarly publication, monographic series.

547.7   US   ISSN 1087-3295
▼**ADVANCES IN MOLECULAR STRUCTURE RESEARCH.** 1995. irreg., vol.3, 1997. $109.50. J A I Press Inc., 55 Old Post Rd., No.2, Box 1678, Greenwich, CT 06830-1678. TEL 203-661-7602. FAX 203-661-0792. E-mail: jai@jaipress.com. (In Europe: JAI Press Ltd., 38 Tavistock St., Covent Garden, London WC2E 7PB, England. TEL 44-171-379-8834. FAX 44-171-379-8835) Eds. Magdolna Hargittai, Istvan Hargittai. **Document type:** academic/scholarly publication, monographic series.
Description: Reports on progress in structural studies, both methodological and interpretational.

547.59   US
ADVANCES IN NITROGEN HETEROCYCLES. 1994. irreg., vol.3, 1997. $109.50. J A I Press Inc., 55 Old Post Rd., No.2, Box 1678, Greenwich, CT 06830-1678. TEL 203-661-7602. FAX 203-661-0792. E-mail: jai@jaipress.com. (In Europe: JAI Press Ltd., 38 Tavistock St., Covent Garden, London WC2E 7PB, England. TEL 44-171-379-8834. FAX 44-171-379-8835) Ed. Christopher Moody. **Document type:** academic/scholarly publication, monographic series.

547.05   US   ISSN 0065-3055
QD411   CODEN: AOMCAU
ADVANCES IN ORGANOMETALLIC CHEMISTRY. 1964. irreg., vol.41, 1997. Academic Press, Inc., 525 B St., Ste. 1900, San Diego, CA 92101-4495. TEL 619-231-0926. FAX 619-699-6715. (Subscr. to: Order Dept., 6277 Sea Harbor Dr., 4th Fl., Orlando, FL 32887. TEL 800-321-5068) Eds. F.G.A. Stone, Robert West. index. (reprint service avail. from ISI) **Indexed:** ASCA, Chem.Abstr., Chem.Cit.Ind., Chem.Infd., Curr.Chem.React., Ind.Chem., Ind.Sci.Rev., Mass Spectr.Bull., Sci.Cit.Ind. **Document type:** monographic series.
—BLDSC (0709.561000); CASDDS; CISTI; KNAW; Linda Hall; SWETS; UnCover. **CCC.**
Refereed Serial

547.1   US   ISSN 1044-4696
ADVANCES IN OXYGENATED PROCESSES. 1988. irreg., vol.5, 1997. $109.50. J A I Press Inc., 55 Old Post Rd., No.2, Box 1678, Greenwich, CT 06830-1678. TEL 203-661-7602. E-mail: jai@jaipress.com. (In Europe: JAI Press Ltd., 38 Tavistock St., Covent Garden, London WC2E 7PB, England. TEL 44-171-379-8834. FAX 44-171-379-8835) Ed. Alfons Baumstark. **Document type:** academic/scholarly publication, monographic series.
Description: Deals with important aspects of oxygen-chemistry in the organic, bio-organic and biochemical areas.

547   US   ISSN 0065-3195
QD281.P6   CODEN: APSIDK
ADVANCES IN POLYMER SCIENCE/FORTSCHRITTE DER HOCHPOLYMEREN-FORSCHUNG. (Text in English, French, German) 1958. irreg., vol.124, 1995. price varies. Springer-Verlag, 175 Fifth Ave., New York, NY 10010. TEL 212-460-1500. FAX 212-473-6272. (Also: Berlin, Heidelberg, Tokyo and Vienna) (reprint service avail. from ISI) **Indexed:** ASCA, Biol.Abstr., Chem.Abstr., Chem.Cit.Ind., Ind.Sci.Rev., INSPEC, Intl.Polym.Sci. & Tech., Mat.Sci.Cit.Ind., RAPRA, Sci.Cit.Ind, World Text.Abstr. **Document type:** monographic series.
—BLDSC (0710.600000); CASDDS; CISTI; Ei; Genuine Article; Linda Hall; SWETS; UnCover. **CCC.**

547   US   ISSN 1061-8902
QD461   CODEN: AOCEEO
ADVANCES IN STRAIN IN ORGANIC CHEMISTRY. 1991. irreg., vol.6, 1997. $109.50. J A I Press Inc., 55 Old Post Rd., No.2, Box 1678, Greenwich, CT 06830-1678. TEL 203-661-7602. FAX 203-661-0792. E-mail: jai@jaipress.com. (In Europe: J A I Press Ltd., 38 Tavistock St., Covent Garden, London WC2E 7PB, England. TEL 44-171-379-8834. FAX 44-171-379-8835) Ed. Brian Halton. **Indexed:** Chem.Cit.Ind. **Document type:** monographic series, academic/scholarly publication.
—BLDSC (0711.583500); CISTI. **CCC.**

547   US   ISSN 1075-2099
ADVANCES IN THE USE OF SYNTHONS IN ORGANIC CHEMISTRY. 1993. irreg., vol.3, 1997. $109.50. J A I Press Inc., 55 Old Post Rd., No.2, Box 1678, Greenwich, CT 06830-1678. TEL 203-661-7602. FAX 203-661-0792. E-mail: jai@jaipress.com. (In Europe: JAI Press Ltd., 38 Tavistock St., Covent Garden, London WC2E 7PB, England. TEL 44-171-379-8834. FAX 44-171-379-8835) Ed. Alessandro Dondoni. **Document type:** academic/scholarly publication, monographic series.

547   660.284 668.4   US   ISSN 0044-6378
TP1180.P8   CODEN: AUSTCJ
ADVANCES IN URETHANE SCIENCE AND TECHNOLOGY. 1971. irreg., vol.13, 1996. price varies. Technomic Publishing Co., Inc., 851 New Holland Ave., Box 3535, Lancaster, PA 17604. TEL 717-291-5609. FAX 717-295-4538. TELEX 230-753565 (TECHNOMIC UD). E-mail: marketing@techpub.com. Eds. Kurt C. Frisch, Sidney L. Reegen. charts; illus.; stat.; index. **Indexed:** Chem.Abstr., Eng.Ind., Ind.Sci.Rev., Sci.Cit.Ind. **Document type:** monographic series.
—BLDSC (0711.680000); CASDDS; CISTI; Linda Hall; UnCover. **CCC.**
Description: Explores polymers and polymerization.
Refereed Serial

630   US
AGRICULTURAL CHEMICAL NEWSLETTER. 1979. m. $80 (foreign $100). Thomson Publications, Box 9335, Fresno, CA 93791. TEL 209-435-2163. FAX 209-435-8319. Ed. W.T. Thomson. R&P contact: W.T. Thomson. circ. 575. (back issues avail.) **Document type:** newsletter.
Description: Presents new developments with agricultural chemicals. Features new registrations, use patterns, experimental permits on insecticides, herbicides, fungicides and miscellaneous pesticides used in the U.S.

630   US
AGRICULTURAL SPRAY ADJUVANTS. a. $17.50. Thomson Publications, Box 9335, Fresno, CA 93791. TEL 209-435-2163. FAX 209-435-8319. Ed. W.T. Thomson. R&P contact: Lori Thomson Harvey. TEL 209-323-1533. **Document type:** trade publication.

547   US   ISSN 0002-5100
QD1   CODEN: ALACBI
ALDRICHIMICA ACTA. 1967. q. free. Aldrich Chemical Company, Inc., 1001 W. St. Paul Ave., Milwaukee, WI 53233. TEL 414-298-7907. FAX 414-273-4979. E-mail: aldrich@sial.com; URL: http://www.sigma.sial.com/aldrich/acta29__2/content.htm. Ed. Alfonse/Runquist. R&P contact: Alfonse Runquist. adv.; charts; illus.; mkt.; pat.; stat.; tr.lit.; tr.mk.; circ. 200,000. (looseleaf format) **Indexed:** ASCA, Chem.Abstr., Chem.Infd., Ind.Chem., Lab.Haz.Bull. **Document type:** academic/scholarly publication, newsletter.
●Also available online.
—BLDSC (0786.810000); CASDDS; CISTI; Linda Hall.
Formerly: Kardinex Sheets.

547   615.7   US   ISSN 0099-9598
QD421.A1   CODEN: ALKAAR
THE ALKALOIDS; chemistry and pharmacology. 1950. irreg., vol.50, 1997. Academic Press, Inc., 525 B St., Ste. 1900, San Diego, CA 92101-4495. TEL 619-231-0926. FAX 619-699-6715. (Subscr. to: Order Dept., 6277 Sea Harbor Dr., 4th Fl., Orlando, FL 32887. TEL 800-321-5068) (reprint service avail. from ISI) **Indexed:** Chem.Abstr. **Document type:** monographic series.
—BLDSC (0788.529000); CASDDS; CISTI; SWETS. **CCC.**
Refereed Serial

CHEMISTRY — ORGANIC CHEMISTRY

665 547.8 US ISSN 0003-021X
TP1 CODEN: JAOCA7
AMERICAN OIL CHEMISTS' SOCIETY. JOURNAL. 1917. m. $145 to individuals (foreign $160); institutions $195 (foreign $210). (American Oil Chemists' Society) A O C S Press, 1608 Broadmoor Dr., Box 3489, Champaign, IL 61821-0489. TEL 217-359-2344. FAX 217-351-8091. E-mail: publications@aocs.org; URL: http://www.aocs.org. Ed. L.H. Princen. R&P contact: Connie Winslow. TEL 217-359-5401. bibl.; charts; illus.; stat.; index. circ. 4,000. (also avail. in microfilm from UMI,PMC; reprint service avail. from UMI; back issues avail.) **Indexed:** A.S.& T.Ind., Abstr.Bull.Inst.Pap.Chem., Anal.Abstr., Art & Archaeol.Tech.Abstr., ASCA, Bibl.Agri., Biol.Abstr., Biotech.Abstr., Cadscan, Chem.Abstr., Chem.Cit.Ind., Chem.Eng.Abstr., Chem.Infd., Cott.& Trop.Fibr.Abstr., Curr.Adv.Biochem., Curr.Adv.Ecol.Sci., Curr.Cont., Dairy Sci.Abstr., Deep Sea Res.& Oceanogr.Abstr., Excerp.Med., Field Crop Abstr., Food Sci.& Tech.Abstr., Herb Abstr., Ind.Sci.Rev., INIS Atomind., Lead Abstr., Maize Abstr., Mass Spectr.Bull., Nutr.Abstr., Pig News & Info., Rev.Plant Path., Seed Abstr., Soyabean Abstr., T.C.E.A., Text.Tech.Dig., Trop.Oil Seeds Abstr., World Surf.Coat., World Text.Abstr., Zincscan. **Document type:** academic/scholarly publication.
—BLDSC (4689.300000); CASDDS; CISTI; Ei; Genuine Article; KR SourceOne; Linda Hall; SWETS; UMI; UnCover. **CCC**.
Refereed Serial

547 660.284 SZ ISSN 0003-3146
TP1101 CODEN: ANMCBO
ANGEWANDTE MAKROMOLEKULARE CHEMIE; an international journal of applied macromolecular chemistry and physics. (Text in English, French, German) 1967. 10/yr. 1370 SFr. (DM.1690) (effective 1997). Huethig & Wepf Verlag, Neugasse 29, CH-6301 Zug, Switzerland. TEL 41-41-7102494. FAX 41-41-7118360. E-mail: 100755.154@compuserve.com. Ed. Dietrich Braun. charts; illus.; cum.index every 50 vols. **Indexed:** Alloys Ind., Anal.Abstr., Art & Archaeol.Tech.Abstr., ASCA, Cadscan, Chem.Abstr., Chem.Cit.Ind., Curr.Chem.React., Curr.Cont., Eng.Mat.Abstr., Excerp.Med., Ind.Chem., Ind.Sci.Rev., Intl.Polym.Sci.& Tech., Lead Abstr., Mat.Sci.Cit.Ind., Met.Abstr., Met.Bull.Abstr., Nonfer.Met.Alert, PCC Alert, RAPRA, Sci.Cit.Ind., Steels Alert, Text.Tech.Dig., World Alum.Abstr., World Surf.Coat., World Text.Abstr., Zincscan. **Document type:** academic/scholarly publication.
—BLDSC (0902.260000); CASDDS; CISTI; Ei; Genuine Article; Linda Hall; SWETS; UnCover. **CCC**.

547 NE
ASPECTS OF HOMOGENEOUS CATALYSIS: A SERIES OF ADVANCES. (Text in English) 1970. irreg., vol.7, 1990. price varies. Kluwer Academic Publishers, Postbus 17, 3300 AA Dordrecht, Netherlands. TEL 31-78-6392392. FAX 31-78-6392254. TELEX 29245 KAPG NL. E-mail: services@wkap.nl; URL: http://www.wkap.nl. (Dist. by: Kluwer Academic Publishers Group, P.O. Box 322, 3300 AH Dordrecht, Netherlands. TEL 31-78-6392392. FAX 31-78-6546474; N. America dist. addr.: Box 358, Accord Sta., Hingham, MA 02018-0358. TEL 617-871-6600) Ed. Renato Ugo. (back issues avail.) **Document type:** monographic series.
Refereed Serial

BEIKOKU TOKKYO SHOROKU. OYO YUKI KAGAKU, NOSUISAN, IJUTSU HEN/U.S. PATENT ABSTRACTS. APPLIED ORGANIC CHEMISTRY, AGRICULTURE AND FISHERY, MEDICINE. see *PATENTS, TRADEMARKS AND COPYRIGHTS — Abstracting, Bibliographies, Statistics*

BEIKOKU TOKKYO SHOROKU. YUKI KAGAKU HEN/U.S. PATENT ABSTRACTS. ORGANIC CHEMISTRY. see *PATENTS, TRADEMARKS AND COPYRIGHTS — Abstracting, Bibliographies, Statistics*

547 US ISSN 0067-4915
BEILSTEINS HANDBUCH DER ORGANISCHEN CHEMIE. SUPPLEMENT. (The main work was published: 1918-1937; First Supplement: 1928-1938; Second Supplement: 1941-1957; Third Supplement: 1930-1949; Fourth Supplement: 1950-1959; Fifth Supplement: 1960-1979) 1972. irreg., latest 1987. price varies. Springer-Verlag, 175 Fifth Ave., New York, NY 10010. TEL 212-460-1500. FAX 212-473-6272. (Also: Berlin, Heidelberg, Tokyo and Vienna) (reprint service avail. from ISI) **Document type:** academic/scholarly publication.
●Also available online. Vendor(s): Knight-Ridder Information, Inc. (File no.390).
—Linda Hall.

BIOCHEMICAL PHARMACOLOGY. see *PHARMACY AND PHARMACOLOGY*

547 610 UK ISSN 0968-0896
QP550 CODEN: BMECEP
BIOORGANIC & MEDICINAL CHEMISTRY. 1993. m. fl.2153($1237) (effective 1998). Elsevier Science Ltd., Pergamon, P.O. Box 800, Kidlington, Oxford OX5 1DX, England. TEL 44-1865-843000. FAX 44-1865-843010. E-mail: nlinfo-f@elsevier.nl; usinfo-f@elsevier.com; forinfo-kyf04035@niftyserve.or.jp; URL: http://www.elsevier.nl/. (Subscr. to: Elsevier Science, Regional Sales Office, P.O. Box 211, 1000 AE Amsterdam, Netherlands. TEL 31-20-4853757. FAX 31-20-4853432; Subscr. in the Americas to: Elsevier Science, Regional Sales Office, Box 945, New York, NY 10159-0945. TEL 212-633-3730. FAX 212-633-3680; Subscr. in Australasia and the Far East to: Elsevier Science (Singapore) Pte Ltd, No.1 Temasek Ave., No.17-01 Millenia Tower, Singapore 039192, Singapore. TEL 65-434-3727. FAX 65-337-2230) Ed. Chi-Huey Wong. (also avail. in microfilm from UMI; back issues avail.) **Indexed:** ASCA, Chem.Cit.Ind., Excerp.Med. (1995-), Ind.Med. (1994-). **Document type:** academic/scholarly publication.
●Also available online.
—BLDSC (2089.325000); CASDDS; CISTI; EMDOCS; Genuine Article; KNAW; SWETS. **CCC**.
Description: Publishes full original research papers and critical reviews on biomolecular chemistry, medicinal chemistry and related disciplines.

547 610 UK ISSN 0960-894X
QP501 CODEN: BMCLE8
BIOORGANIC & MEDICINAL CHEMISTRY LETTERS; for rapid dissemination of preliminary communications on all aspects of bioorganic chemistry, medicinal chemistry and related disciplines. 1991. s-m. fl.2752($1582) to institutions; with Tetrahedron Letters fl.15930 ($9155) (effective 1998). Elsevier Science Ltd., Pergamon, P.O. Box 800, Kidlington, Oxford OX5 1DX, England. TEL 44-1865-843000. FAX 44-1865-843010. E-mail: nlinfo-f@elsevier.nl; usinfo-f@elsevier.com; forinfo-kyf04035@niftyserve.or.jp; URL: http://www.elsevier.nl/. (Subscr. to: Elsevier Science, Regional Sales Office, P.O. Box 211, 1000 AE Amsterdam, Netherlands. TEL 31-20-4853757. FAX 31-20-4853432; Subscr. in the Americas to: Elsevier Science, Regional Sales Office, Box 945, New York, NY 10159-0945. TEL 212-633-3730. FAX 212-633-3680; Subscr. in Australasia and the Far East to: Elsevier Science (Singapore) Pte Ltd, No.1 Temasek Ave., No.17-01 Millenia Tower, Singapore 039192, Singapore. TEL 65-434-3727. FAX 65-337-2230) Ed. D.L. Boger. (also avail. in microfilm from UMI; back issues avail.) **Indexed:** ASCA, Curr.Cont., Excerp.Med. (1992-), Ind.Sci.Rev., Neurosci.Cit.Ind., Sci.Cit.Ind. **Document type:** academic/scholarly publication.
●Also available online.
—BLDSC (2089.330000); ADONIS; CASDDS; CISTI; EMDOCS; Genuine Article; KNAW; Linda Hall; SWETS; UMI; UnCover. **CCC**.
Description: Publishes preliminary communications and theoretical research results in bioorganic and medicinal chemistry.
Refereed Serial

547 US ISSN 0045-2068
QP501 CODEN: BOCMBM
BIOORGANIC CHEMISTRY; an international journal. 1971. bi-m. $250 (foreign $295) (effective 1997). Academic Press, Inc., Journal Division, 525 B St., Ste. 1900, San Diego, CA 92101-4495. TEL 619-230-1840. FAX 619-699-6800. E-mail: apsubs@acad.com; URL: http://www.apnet.com/ www/journal/bh.htm; http://www.idealibrary.com/. (Subscr. to: Box 861213, Orlando, FL 32886-1213. TEL 407-347-4040. FAX 407-363-9661) Ed. Gordon A. Hamilton. adv.; bk.rev.; charts; illus.; stat.; index. (back issues avail.) **Indexed:** Abstr.Bull.Inst.Pap.Chem., ASCA, Bibl.Agri., Biol.Abstr., Biotech.Abstr., Chem.Abstr., Chem.Cit.Ind., Curr.Adv.Ecol.Sci., Curr.Cont., Excerp.Med. (1993-), Ind.Sci.Rev., Mass Spectr.Bull., Nutr.Abstr., Sci.Cit.Ind. **Document type:** academic/scholarly publication.
●Also available online.
—BLDSC (2089.350000); ADONIS; CASDDS; CISTI; EMDOCS; Genuine Article; SWETS; UnCover. **CCC**.
Description: Presents articles in which the principles and techniques of organic and physical organic chemistry are used to solve problems of relevance to biology or to chemical studies inspired by biology.
Refereed Serial

547 574.192 RU ISSN 0132-3423
QD415.A1 CODEN: BIKHD7
BIOORGANICHESKAYA KHIMIYA. English translation: Russian Journal of Bioorganic Chemistry (US ISSN 1068-1620) (Text in Russian; summaries in English) 1975. m. $336 (effective 1998). (Rossiiskaya Akademiya Nauk) Izdatel'stvo Nauka, 90 Profsoyuznaya ul., 117864 Moscow, Russia. TEL 234-05-71. (Dist. by: Mezhdunarodnaya Kniga, ul. Dimitrova D.39, 113095 Moscow, Russia) Ed. Yu.A. Ovchinnikov. illus. **Indexed:** ASCA, Biol.Abstr., Biotech.Abstr., Chem.Abstr., Chem.Cit.Ind., Curr.Adv.Ecol.Sci., Curr.Cont., Dairy Sci.Abstr., Excerp.Med., Ind.Med., Ind.Sci.Rev., Ind.Vet., INIS Atomind., Mass Spectr.Bull., Nutr.Abstr. **Document type:** academic/scholarly publication.
—BLDSC (0017.993000); CASDDS; CISTI; Genuine Article; KNAW; Linda Hall. **CCC**.

547 US ISSN 0006-3525
QP801.P64 CODEN: BIPMAA
BIOPOLYMERS; original research on biological molecules and assemblies. 1961. 24/yr. $4295 (foreign $4715) (effective 1998). John Wiley & Sons, Inc., Journals, 605 Third Ave., New York, NY 10158. TEL 212-692-6645. FAX 212-850-6021. TELEX 12-7063. URL: http://www.wiley.co.uk. (Subscr. outside the Americas to: John Wiley & Sons Ltd., Baffins Ln., Chichester, W. Sussex PO19 1UD, England. TEL 44-1243-779777. FAX 44-1243-776128) Ed. Murray Goodman. adv.: B&W page £640, color page £1515; trim 279 x 210. index. circ. 1,000. (also avail. in microfilm from UMI; back issues avail.; reprint service avail. from UMI) **Indexed:** A.A.P.P.Abstr., Abstr.Bull.Inst.Pap.Chem., Appl.Mech.Rev., ASCA, Biol.Abstr., Chem.Abstr., Chem.Cit.Ind., Curr.Adv.Biochem., Curr.Adv.Cell & Devel.Biol., Curr.Adv.Ecol.Sci., Curr.Adv.Genetics & Molec.Biol., Curr.Cont., Dairy Sci.Abstr., Excerp.Med., Food Sci.& Tech.Abstr., Ind.Med., Ind.Sci.Rev., INIS Atomind., Mat.Sci.Cit.Ind., Sci.Cit.Ind. **Document type:** academic/scholarly publication.
●Also available online. Vendor(s): STN International (CJWILEY).
—BLDSC (2089.470000); CASDDS; CISTI; Ei; EMDOCS; Genuine Article; Linda Hall; SWETS; UMI; UnCover. **CCC**.
Description: Covers organic and physical chemistry, experimental and theoretical research, static and dynamic aspects of structure. Includes an examination of the broad aspects of biospectroscopy.
Refereed Serial

CHEMISTRY — ORGANIC CHEMISTRY

547   UK   ISSN 0951-8428
CODEN: CBHCA4
CARBOHYDRATE CHEMISTRY. PART 1: MONOSACCHARIDES, DISACCHARIDES, AND SPECIFIC OLIGOSACCHARIDES. 1967. a. price varies. The Royal Society of Chemistry, Thomas Graham House, Science Park, Milton Rd., Cambridge CB4 4WF, England. TEL 44-1223-420066. FAX 44-1223-423429. E-mail: sales@rsc.org; URL: http://chemistry.rsc.org/rsc/. (Subscr. to: Turpin Distribution Services Ltd., Blackhorse Rd., Letchworth, Herts. SG6 1HN, England. TEL 44-1462-672555. FAX 44-1462-480947; Subscr. in N. America to: ACS, 1155 Sixteenth St., N.W., Washington, DC 22036. TEL 202-776-8100. FAX 202-872-6067) Ed. Neil R. Williams. charts; illus.; index. (back issues avail.) Indexed: Chem.Abstr., Sugar Ind.Abstr. Document type: academic/scholarly publication.
—BLDSC (3050.980000); CASDDS; CISTI; Linda Hall. **CCC**.
   Formerly (until 1986): Carbohydrate Chemistry. Part 1: Mono-Di-Tri-saccharides and Their Derivatives (ISSN 0951-8401); Supersedes in part: Carbohydrate Chemistry (ISSN 0576-7172)

547.782   UK   ISSN 0144-8617
QD320
CARBOHYDRATE POLYMERS; scientific and technological aspects of industrially important polysaccharides. 1981. m. fl.2780($1598) (effective 1998). Elsevier Science Ltd., P.O. Box 800, Kidlington, Oxford OX5 1DX, England. TEL 44-1865-843000. FAX 44-1865-843010. E-mail: nlinfo-f@elsevier.nl; usinfo-f@elsevier.com; forinfo-kyf04035@niftyserve.or.jp; URL: http://www.elsevier.nl/. (Subscr. to: Elsevier Science, Regional Sales Office, P.O. Box 211, 1000 AE Amsterdam, Netherlands. TEL 31-20-4853757. FAX 31-20-4853432; Subscr. in the Americas to: Elsevier Science, Regional Sales Office, Box 945, New York, NY 10159-0945. TEL 212-633-3730. FAX 212-633-3680; Subscr. in Australasia and the Far East to: Elsevier Science (Singapore) Pte Ltd, No.1 Temasek Ave., No.17-01 Millenia Tower, Singapore 039192, Singapore. TEL 65-434-3727. FAX 65-337-2230) Ed.Bd. adv.; bk.rev.; charts; illus. (also avail. in microform from UMI; back issues avail.) Indexed: Abstr.Bull.Inst.Pap.Chem., ASCA, Biol.Abstr., Chem.Abstr., Chem.Cit.Ind., Curr.Adv.Ecol.Sci., Curr.Cont, Eng.Ind., Food Sci.& Tech.Abstr., Ind.Sci.Rev., Mat.Sci.Cit.Ind., Paper & Bd.Abstr., Sci.Cit.Ind. Document type: academic/scholarly publication.
—BLDSC (3050.990480); CASDDS; CISTI; Ei; Genuine Article; Linda Hall; SWETS; UnCover. **CCC**.
   Description: Covers the study and exploitation of the industrial PTO applications of carbohydrate polymers in areas such as food, textiles, papers, wood, oil field applications and industrial chemistry.
Refereed Serial

547   UK   ISSN 0008-6215
QD321   CODEN: CRBRAT
CARBOHYDRATE RESEARCH; an international journal. (Text in English, French and German) 1965. 36/yr. fl.9278($5332) (effective 1998). Elsevier Science Ltd., P.O. Box 800, Kidlington, Oxford OX5 1DX, England. TEL 44-1865-843000. FAX 44-1865-843010. E-mail: nlinfo-f@elsevier.nl; usinfo-f@elsevier.com; forinfo-kyf04035@niftyserve.or.jp; URL: http://www.elsevier.nl/. (Subscr. to: Elsevier Science, Regional Sales Office, P.O. Box 211, 1000 AE Amsterdam, Netherlands. TEL 31-20-4853757. FAX 31-20-4853432; Subscr. in the Americas to: Elsevier Science, Regional Sales Office, Box 945, New York, NY 10159-0945. TEL 212-633-3730. FAX 212-633-3680; Subscr. in Australasia and the Far East to: Elsevier Science (Singapore) Pte Ltd, No.1 Temasek Ave., No.17-01 Millenia Tower, Singapore 039192, Singapore. TEL 914-524-9200. FAX 914-333-2444) Ed.Bd. adv.; bk.rev.; charts; illus.; index. (also avail. in microform from UMI; back issues avail.) Indexed: Abstr.Bull.Inst.Pap.Chem., ASCA, Bibl.Agri., Biol.Abstr., Biotech.Abstr., Chem.Abstr., Chem.Cit.Ind., Chem.Infd., Curr.Adv.Biochem., Curr.Adv.Ecol.Sci., Curr.Chem.React., Curr.Cont., Dairy Sci.Abstr., Excerp.Med., Field Crop Abstr., Food Sci.& Tech.Abstr., Ind.Chem., Ind.Med., Ind.Sci.Rev., Mass Spectr.Bull., Mat.Sci.Cit.Ind., Nutr.Abstr., Paper & Bd.Abstr., Rev.Med.& Vet.Mycol., Rev.Plant Path., Sci.Cit.Ind., Soils & Fert., Sugar Ind.Abstr. Document type: academic/scholarly publication.
●Also available online. Vendor(s): STN International.
—BLDSC (3050.990500); ADONIS; CASDDS; CISTI; Ei; EMDOCS; Genuine Article; Linda Hall; SWETS; UnCover. **CCC**.
   Description: Includes all aspects of carbohydrate chemistry and biochemistry. Covers sugars and their derivatives (also cyclitols, and model compounds for carbohydrate reactions), oligo- and polysaccharides, nucleosides, nucleotides, and glycoconjugates.
Refereed Serial

547   UK   ISSN 0008-6223
QD181.C1   CODEN: CRBNAH
CARBON. (Text in English, French and German) 1963. m. fl.3096($1779) (effective 1998). (American Carbon Society, US) Elsevier Science Ltd., Pergamon, P.O. Box 800, Kidlington, Oxford OX5 1DX, England. TEL 44-1865-843000. FAX 44-1865-843010. E-mail: nlinfo-f@elsevier.nl; usinfo-f@elsevier.com; forinfo-kyf04035@niftyserve.or.jp; URL: http://www.elsevier.nl/. (Subscr. to: Elsevier Science, Regional Sales Office, P.O. Box 211, 1000 AE Amsterdam, Netherlands. TEL 31-20-4853757. FAX 31-20-4853432; Subscr. in the Americas to: Elsevier Science, Regional Sales Office, Box 945, New York, NY 10159-0945. TEL 212-633-3730. FAX 212-633-3680; Subscr. in Australasia and the Far East to: Elsevier Science (Singapore) Pte Ltd, No.1 Temasek Ave., No.17-01 Millenia Tower, Singapore 039192, Singapore. TEL 65-434-3727. FAX 65-337-2230) Ed. Peter Thrower. adv.; bk.rev.; abstr.; charts; illus.; index. circ. 1,600. (also avail. in microfilm from UMI; back issues avail.) Indexed: Alloys Ind., ASCA, Chem.Abstr., Chem.Cit.Ind., Chem.Eng.Abstr., Curr.Adv.Ecol.Sci., Curr.Cont., Eng.Ind., Eng.Mat.Abstr., Excerp.Med., Fuel & Energy Abstr., Ind.Sci.Rev., INIS Atomind., INSPEC (1968-), Mass Spectr.Bull., Mat.Sci.Cit.Ind., Met.Abstr., Met.Abstr.Ind., Nonfer.Met.Alert, PCC Alert, Sci.Cit.Ind., Steels Alert, World Alum.Abstr. Document type: academic/scholarly publication.
—BLDSC (3050.991000); AskIEEE; CASDDS; CISTI; Ei; Genuine Article; KR SourceOne; Linda Hall; SWETS; UMI; UnCover. **CCC**.
   Description: Covers topics in the physics and chemistry of substances related to aromatic or tetrahedrally bonded carbonaceous solids, and compounds transformed into them by heat treatment and other means.
Refereed Serial

547   NE   ISSN 0920-4652
CODEN: CMCOES
CATALYSIS BY METAL COMPLEXES. 1976. irreg., vol.17, 1994. price varies. Kluwer Academic Publishers, Postbus 17, 3300 AA Dordrecht, Netherlands. TEL 31-78-6392392. FAX 31-78-6392254. TELEX 29245 KAPG NL. E-mail: services@wkap.nl; URL: http://www.wkap.nl. (Dist. by: Kluwer Academic Publishers Group, P.O. Box 322, 3300 AH Dordrecht, Netherlands. TEL 31-78-6392392. FAX 31-78-6546474; N. America dist. addr.: Box 358, Accord Sta., Hingham, MA 02018-0358. TEL 617-871-6600. FAX 617-871-6528) Eds. Renato Ugo, B.R. James. Indexed: Biol.Abstr., Chem.Abstr. Document type: monographic series.
—BLDSC (3090.910000); CASDDS; CISTI
   Formerly (until 1980): Homogeneous Catalysis in Organic and Inorganic Chemistry (ISSN 0920-4393)
Refereed Serial

CELLULAR POLYMERS. see *PLASTICS*

547   RM   ISSN 0576-9787
TS920   CODEN: CECTAH
CELLULOSE CHEMISTRY AND TECHNOLOGY; international journal for physics, chemistry and technology of cellulose and lignin. (Text and summaries in English, French, German, Russian) 1967. 6/yr. Editura Academiei Romane, Calea 13 Septembrie 13, 76117 Bucharest, Rumania. (Dist. by: Rodipet SA, Piata Presei Libere 1, Sec. 1, PO Box 33-57, Bucharest, Rumania. TEL 401-6185103. FAX 401-2226407) Ed. Cristofor I. Simionescu. bk.rev. Indexed: Abstr.Bull.Inst.Pap.Chem., ASCA, Chem.Abstr., Chem.Cit.Ind., Curr.Cont., Excerp.Med., Mat.Sci.Cit.Ind., Nonwov.Abstr., Paper & Bd.Abstr., Sci.Cit.Ind., Text.Tech.Dig.
—BLDSC (3098.090000); CASDDS; CISTI; Ei; Genuine Article; KNAW; Linda Hall; SWETS.

547   UK
CHEM-FACTS: ETHYLENE & PROPYLENE. 1990. irreg., latest 1991. £75. Chem-Intell, Reed Information Services (Subsidiary of: Reed Telepublishing Ltd.), Windsor Ct., East Grinstead House, E. Ginstead, W. Sussex RH19 1XA, England. TEL 44-1342-335831. FAX 44-1342-335612. TELEX 95127 INFSER G.
●Also available online. Vendor(s): Data-Star, Knight-Ridder Information, Inc.
   Description: Presents a survey of ethylene and propylene production and trade, covering 87 countries.

547 668.4   UK
CHEM-FACTS: P V C. 1992. irreg. £100. Chem-Intell, Reed Information Services (Subsidiary of: Reed Telepublishing Ltd.), Windsor Ct., East Grinstead House, E. Grinstead, W. Sussex RH19 1XA, England. TEL 44-1342-335831. FAX 44-1342-335612. TELEX 95127 INFSER G. Document type: directory.
●Also available online. Vendor(s): Data-Star, Knight-Ridder Information, Inc.
   Description: Surveys the worldwide trade and manufacture of polyvinyl chloride, profiling more than 100 chemical firms.

547 668.4   UK
CHEM-FACTS: POLYETHYLENE. 1987. irreg. £100. Chem-Intell, Reed Information Services (Subsidiary of: Reed Telepublishing Ltd.), Windsor Ct., East Grinstead House, E. Grinstead, W. Sussex RH19 1XA, England. TEL 44-1342-335831. FAX 44-1342-335612. TELEX 95127 INFSER G. Document type: directory.
●Also available online. Vendor(s): Data-Star, Questel Orbit Inc.
   Description: Presents the findings of a detailed survey of worldwide polyethylene manufacture and trade, covering high-density, low-density, and linear low-density types (HPDE, LDPE and LLDPE).

547 668.4   UK
CHEM-FACTS: POLYPROPYLENE. 1988. irreg. £225. Chem-Intell, Reed Information Services (Subsidiary of: Reed Telepublishing Ltd.), Windsor Ct., East Grinstead House, E. Grinstead, W. Sussex RH19 1XA, England. TEL 44-1342-335831. FAX 44-1342-335612. TELEX 95127 INFSER G. Document type: directory.
●Also available online. Vendor(s): Data-Star, Knight-Ridder Information, Inc., Questel Orbit Inc.
   Description: Presents the findings of a detailed survey of worldwide polypropylene manufacture and trade, covering homopolymers and copolymers (impact and random).

CHEMISTRY — ORGANIC CHEMISTRY

547 668.4   UK
CHEM-FACTS: STYRENICS. 1991. irreg. £75. Chem-Intell, Reed Information Services (Subsidiary of: Reed Telepublishing Ltd.), Windsor Ct., East Grinstead House, E. Grinstead, W. Sussex RH19 1XA, England. TEL 44-1342-335831. FAX 44-1342-335612. TELEX 95127 INFSER G. **Document type:** directory.
●Also available online. Vendor(s): Data-Star, Knight-Ridder Information, Inc.
Description: Provides a detailed survey of worldwide polystyrene and ABS and SAN resins manufacture and trade. More than 150 companies are profiled.

547   US   ISSN 0009-255X
CHEMICAL HIGHLIGHTS. 1969. 6/yr. $60 to individuals; institutions $135; students $45. Columbia University, Department of Chemistry, 3000 Broadway, MC 3117, New York, NY 10027-6948. TEL 212-854-2172. FAX 212-854-5429. E-mail: jqh@still3.chem.columbia.edu. adv. contact: Joan Horgan. circ. 400. (processed) **Document type:** academic/scholarly publication.

CHEMISTRY & BIOLOGY. see *BIOLOGY — Biotechnology*

547   US   ISSN 0069-3138
QD181.C1   CODEN: CPHCAY
CHEMISTRY AND PHYSICS OF CARBON: A SERIES OF ADVANCES. 1966. irreg., vol.25, 1996. price varies. Marcel Dekker, Inc., 270 Madison Ave., New York, NY 10016. TEL 212-696-9000. FAX 212-685-4540. TELEX 421419. Ed. Russell Dekker; Pub. Graham Garratt. R&P contact: Julia Mulligan. **Indexed:** ASCA, Chem.Abstr., GeoRef., Ind.Sci.Rev., Sci.Cit.Ind. **Document type:** monographic series.
—BLDSC (3170.050000); CASDDS; CISTI; Genuine Article; Linda Hall; SWETS; UnCover. **CCC.**
Refereed Serial

547.59   US   ISSN 0069-3154
CODEN: CHECAV
CHEMISTRY OF HETEROCYCLIC COMPOUNDS (NEW YORK, 1951); a series of monographs. 1951. irreg., vol.52, 1993. John Wiley & Sons, Inc., 605 Third Ave., New York, NY 10158. TEL 212-850-6000. FAX 212-850-6088. TELEX 12-7063. Eds. Arnold Weissburger, Edward C. Taylor. index. (also avail. in microfilm from UMI) **Document type:** monographic series. **Indexed:** Chem.Abstr., INIS Atomind.
—BLDSC (3171.300000); CASDDS; CISTI.
Refereed Serial

547   US   ISSN 0009-3122
QD400   CODEN: CHCCAL
CHEMISTRY OF HETEROCYCLIC COMPOUNDS (NEW YORK, 1965). English translation of: Khimiya Geterotsiklicheskikh Soedinenii (LV ISSN 0132-6244) 1965. m. $1685 (foreign $1970) (effective 1998). (Latvian Academy of Sciences, LV) Plenum Publishing Corp., Consultants Bureau, 233 Spring St., New York, NY 10013-1578. TEL 212-620-8468. FAX 212-463-0742. TELEX 23-421139. Ed. E.Ya. Lukevits. (also avail. in microfilm from UMI; back issues avail.) **Indexed:** Chem.Titles. **Document type:** academic/scholarly publication.
—BLDSC (0410.600000); CASDDS; CISTI; Ei; SWETS; UMI; UnCover. **CCC.**
Refereed Serial

547   US   ISSN 0009-3130
QD415.A1   CODEN: CHNCA8
CHEMISTRY OF NATURAL COMPOUNDS. English translation of: Khimiya Prirodnykh Soedinenii (UZ ISSN 0023-1150) 1965. bi-m. $1455 (foreign $1700) (effective 1998). (Uzbek Academy of Sciences, UZ) Plenum Publishing Corp., Consultants Bureau, 233 Spring St., New York, NY 10013-1578. TEL 212-620-8468. FAX 212-463-0742. TELEX 23-421139. Ed. Kh.N. Aripov. (also avail. in microfilm from UMI; back issues avail.) **Indexed:** Biol.Abstr., Chem.Titles, Excerp.Med., INIS Atomind., Mass Spectr.Bull., Sugar Ind.Abstr. **Document type:** academic/scholarly publication.
—BLDSC (0410.650000); CISTI; SWETS; UMI; UnCover. **CCC.**
Refereed Serial

547   US   ISSN 0069-3162
CHEMISTRY OF NATURAL PRODUCTS. (Subseries of: I U P A C Chemical Data Series (ISSN 0275-0910)) (Text in English; occasionally in French or German) 1961. irreg., no.10, Ottawa, 1979. price varies. (International Union of Pure and Applied Chemistry) C R C Press, Ltd., 2000 Corporate Blvd., N.W., Boca Raton, FL 33431. TEL 561-994-0555; 800-272-7737. FAX 561-998-9784. TELEX 568689-CRC PRESS. **Document type:** proceedings.

CHEMTRACTS. see *CHEMISTRY — Abstracting, Bibliographies, Statistics*

660.284   CC   ISSN 0256-7679
QD380   CODEN: CJPSEG
CHINESE JOURNAL OF POLYMER SCIENCE. Chinese edition: Gaofenzi Xuebao (ISSN 1000-3304) (Text in English) 1983. q. DM.440($236) (effective 1997). Science Press, Marketing and Sales Department, 16 Donghuangchenggen North St., Beijing 100717, People's Republic of China. TEL 86-10-4010642. FAX 86-10-4019810. (Dist. in Europe. by: V S P, P.O. Box 346, 3700 AH Zeist, Netherlands. TEL 31-30-6925790. FAX 31-30-6932081; Dist. in N. America by: Science Press New York, Ltd., 80-04 58th Ave., Elmhurst, NY 11373. TEL 718-476-0238) (Co-publisher: V S P) adv. circ. 6,000. pp./issue: 96. (back issues avail.) **Indexed:** Alloys Ind., ASCA, Chem.Cit.Ind., Eng.Mat.Abstr., Intl.Polym.Sci.& Tech., Met.Abstr., Met.Abstr.Ind., Nonfer.Met.Alert, PCC Alert, RAPRA, Steels Alert, World Alum.Abstr. **Document type:** academic/scholarly publication.
—BLDSC (3180.559000); CASDDS; CISTI; Ei; Genuine Article; Linda Hall; SWETS; UnCover.
Description: Studies polymer synthesis, polymer physics, polymer chemistry, specialty polymers.
Refereed Serial

547   GW   ISSN 0303-402X
QD549   CODEN: CPMSB6
COLLOID AND POLYMER SCIENCE. (Supplement avail.: Progress in Colloid and Polymer Sciences) (Text in English) 1906. m. DM.2460 (foreign DM.2489.40) (effective 1998). Dr. Dietrich Steinkopff Verlag, Saalbaustr. 12, 64283 Darmstadt, Germany. TEL 49-6151-1745-0. FAX 49-6151-174510. E-mail: maubach.stk@springer.de. (Subscr. to: Steinkopff Verlag, c/o Springer-Verlag, Postfach 311340, 10643 Berlin, Germany. FAX 49-30-82787448; Subscr. in Austria to: Springer-Verlag Wien, Sachsenplatz 4-6, A-1201 Vienna, Austria; subscr. in N. America to: Springer-Verlag, Journals, 175 Fifth Ave., New York, NY 10010) Eds. F. Kremer, G. Lagaly. adv.; bk.rev.; abstr.; bibl.; charts; illus.; index. circ. 2,000. (also avail. in microform from PMC,UMI) **Indexed:** Abstr.Bull.Inst.Pap.Chem., Appl.Mech.Rev., Art & Archaeol.Tech.Abstr., ASCA, Biol.Abstr., Biwk.Pap.Rad.Chem.& Photochem., Chem.Abstr., Chem.Cit.Ind., Curr.Cont., Dairy Sci.Abstr., Deep Sea Res.& Oceanogr.Abstr., E&P Hlth. (1993-), Eng.Ind., Excerp.Med. (1996-), Gas Process.& Ppl. (1993-), GeoRef., Ind.Sci.Rev., INSPEC (1988-), Intl.Polym.Sci.& Tech., Mat.Sci.Cit.Ind., Paper & Bd.Abstr., Petrol.Abstr. (1975-), Photo.Abstr., RAPRA, Sci.Cit.Ind., Soils & Fert., World Surf.Coat. **Document type:** academic/scholarly publication.
—BLDSC (3313.350000); AskIEEE; CASDDS; CISTI; Ei; EMDOCS; Genuine Article; KNAW; KR SourceOne; Linda Hall; SWETS; UMI; UnCover. **CCC.**

547   US   ISSN 0149-9378
COMPENDIUM OF ORGANIC SYNTHETIC METHODS. 1971. irreg. John Wiley & Sons, Inc., 605 Third Ave., New York, NY 10158. TEL 212-850-6645. FAX 212-850-6021. E-mail: subinfo@jwiley.com. (Subscr. outside the Americas to: John Wiley & Sons Ltd., Baffins Ln., Chichester, W. Sussex PO19 1UD, England. TEL 44-1243-779777. FAX 44-1243-776128) **Document type:** monographic series.
—BLDSC (3363.969000); CISTI.

CONDENSED MATTER AND MATERIALS COMMUNICATIONS. see *CHEMISTRY — Crystallography*

CONGRESS OF HETEROCYCLIC CHEMISTRY. BOOK OF ABSTRACTS/FUKUSOKAN KAGAKU TORONKAI KOEN YOSHISHU. see *CHEMISTRY — Abstracting, Bibliographies, Statistics*

547   UK   ISSN 1350-4894
CODEN: COGSE6
CONTEMPORARY ORGANIC SYNTHESIS. 1994. bi-m. £199 (U.S. $358) (effective 1997). The Royal Society of Chemistry, Thomas Graham House, Science Park, Milton Rd., Cambridge CB4 4WF, England. TEL 44-1223-420066. FAX 44-1223-423429. E-mail: sales@rsc.org; URL: http://chemistry.rsc.org/rsc/. (Dist. by: Turpin Distribution Services Ltd., Blackhorse Rd., Letchworth, Herts. SG6 1HN, England. TEL 44-1462-672555. FAX 44-1462-480947) Ed.Bd. **Document type:** academic/scholarly publication.
—BLDSC (3425.197550); CASDDS; CISTI; Genuine Article; SWETS. **CCC.**
Description: Assesses reactions, reagents, strategies and designs, and provides up-to-date information in all areas of organic synthesis.

547 011   US
CONTROLLED RELEASE NEWSLETTER. 1982. irreg. (2-3/yr.) $65 membership. Controlled Release Society, Inc., 1020 Milwaukee Ave., Ste. 235, Deerfield, IL 60015-3500. TEL 847-808-7071. Ed. T.J. Roseman. bk.rev. circ. 3,000. **Document type:** newsletter.

547 615   NE   ISSN 0921-3759
CODEN: CRSEEB
CONTROLLED RELEASE SERIES. (Text in English) 1986. irreg., vol.4, 1990. price varies. Elsevier Science B.V., Books Division, P.O. Box 211, 1000 AE Amsterdam, Netherlands. TEL 31-20-4853911. FAX 31-20-4853705. E-mail: nlinfo-f@elsevier.nl; usinfo-f@elsevier.com; forinfo-kyf04035@niftyserve.or.jp; URL: http://www.elsevier.nl/. (Subscr. in the Americas to: Elsevier Science, Regional Sales Office, Box 945, New York, NY 10159-0945. TEL 212-633-3730. FAX 212-633-3680; Subscr. in Australasia and the Far East to: Elsevier Science (Singapore) Pte Ltd, No.1 Temasek Ave., No.17-01, Millenia Tower, Singapore 039192, Singapore. TEL 65-434-3727. FAX 65-337-2230; Subscr. in Japan to: Elsevier Science Japan, 9-15 Higashi-Azabu 1-chome, Minato-ku, Tokyo 106, Japan. TEL 81-3-5561-5033. FAX 81-3-5561-5047) **Document type:** monographic series.
Refereed Serial

547   US   ISSN 1022-0178
RS201.C64   CODEN: PCRMEY
CONTROLLED RELEASE SOCIETY. INTERNATIONAL SYMPOSIUM ON CONTROLLED RELEASE OF BIOACTIVE MATERIALS. PROCEEDINGS. 1973. a. $80 membership. Controlled Release Society, Inc., 1020 Milwaukee Ave., Ste. 235, Deerfield, IL 60015-3500. TEL 847-808-7071. Ed.Bd. circ. 3,000. (back issues avail.) **Indexed:** Excerp.Med. (1993-). **Document type:** proceedings.
—BLDSC (6846.782860); CASDDS; KNAW.

547   US   ISSN 1385-2728
▼**CURRENT ORGANIC CHEMISTRY.** (Text in English) 1997. 6/yr. fl.319 to individuals (outside Europe $145); institutions fl.869 (outside Europe $395) (effective 1998). Bentham Science Publishers, 7436 S.W. 117 Ave., Box 130, Miami, FL 33183. FAX 305-596-5120. adv. contact: T. Lucas. **Document type:** academic/scholarly publication.
Description: Publishes reviews on the current progress in the fields of asymmetric synthesis, organo-metallic chemistry, bioorganic chemistry, heterocyclic chemistry, natural product chemistry, and analytic methods in organic chemistry.
Refereed Serial

665   JA   ISSN 0011-5355
CODEN: DKSSAB
DAIICHI KOGYO SEIYAKU SHAHO. (Text in Japanese) 1931. bi-m. free. Daiichi Kogyo Seiyaku Co. Ltd., Shiokozidori-Karasuma, Nishiiru, Shimogyo-ku, Kyoto 600, Japan. TEL 075-343-1835. FAX 075-343-1421. Ed. Syoichi Haatori. adv.; bk.rev.; charts; illus. circ. 4,000. **Document type:** trade publication.
—CASDDS.

CHEMISTRY — ORGANIC CHEMISTRY

664   NE   ISSN 0167-4501
CODEN: DFSCDX
DEVELOPMENTS IN FOOD SCIENCE. (Text in English) 1978. irreg., vol.35, 1994. price varies. Elsevier Science B.V., Books Division, P.O. Box 211, 1000 AE Amsterdam, Netherlands. TEL 31-20-4853911. FAX 31-20-4853705. TELEX 18582 ESPA NL. E-mail: nlinfo-f@elsevier.nl; usinfo-f@elsevier.com; forinfo-kyf04035@niftyserve.or.jp; URL: http://www.elsevier.nl/. (Subscr. in the Americas to: Elsevier Science, Regional Sales Office, Box 945, New York, NY 10159-0945. TEL 212-633-3730. FAX 212-633-3680; Subscr. in Australasia and the Far East to: Elsevier Science (Singapore) Pte Ltd, No.1 Temasek Ave., No.17-01 Millenia Tower, Singapore 039192, Singapore. TEL 65-434-3727. FAX 65-337-2230; Subscr. in Japan to: Elsevier Science Japan, 9-15 Higashi-Azabu 1-chome, Minato-ku, Tokyo 106, Japan. TEL 81-3-5561-5033. FAX 81-3-5561-5047) (back issues avail.) **Indexed:** Chem.Abstr., Food Sci.& Tech.Abstr. **Document type:** monographic series.
—BLDSC (3579.071800); CASDDS; CISTI. **CCC.**
Refereed Serial

547.84   UK   ISSN 0264-3022
QD380   CODEN: DOPODF
DEVELOPMENTS IN ORIENTED POLYMERS. 1982. irreg., vol.2, 1987. price varies. Elsevier Science Ltd., Books Division, P.O. Box 800, Kidlington, Oxford OX5 1DX, England. TEL 44-1865-843000. FAX 44-1865-843010. E-mail: nlinfo-f@elsevier.nl; usinfo-f@elsevier.com; forinfo-kyf04035@niftyserve.or.jp; URL: http://www.elsevier.nl/. (Subscr. to: Elsevier Science, Regional Sales Office, P.O. Box 211, 1000 AE Amsterdam, Netherlands. TEL 31-20-4853757. FAX 31-20-4853432; Subscr. in the Americas to: Elsevier Science, Regional Sales Office, Box 945, New York, NY 10159-0945. TEL 212-633-3730. FAX 212-633-3680; Subscr. in Australasia and the Far East to: Elsevier Science (Singapore) Pte Ltd, No.1 Temasek Ave., No.17-01 Millenia Tower, Singapore 039192, Singapore. TEL 65-434-3727. FAX 65-337-2230) Ed. I.M. Ward. (back issues avail.) **Document type:** monographic series.
—CASDDS; CISTI. **CCC.**
Refereed Serial

547 660   US
CODEN: KLCBDZ
EASTMAN FINE CHEMICALS NEWS. 1927. 3/yr. free to qualified personnel. Eastman Kodak Co., Laboratory and Research Products, 343 State St., Rochester, NY 14650. TEL 716-724-2207. FAX 716-722-3179. TELEX 68-54148. Ed. Deborah Nippon. adv. circ. 90,000. (looseleaf format; also avail. in microform from UMI; reprint service avail. from UMI) **Indexed:** Chem.Abstr.
—CASDDS; CISTI; Linda Hall.
Former titles: Kodak Laboratory Chemicals News; (until 1987): Kodak Laboratory Chemicals Bulletin (ISSN 0270-4986); (until 1980): Eastman Organic Chemical Bulletin (ISSN 0096-221X); Organic Chemical Bulletin (ISSN 0012-897X)

ELECTROCHEMICAL SCIENCE AND TECHNOLOGY OF POLYMERS. see CHEMISTRY — Electrochemistry

547   UK
QD95   CODEN: ESRNBP
ELECTRON SPIN RESONANCE. PART A. 1973. biennial. price varies. The Royal Society of Chemistry, Thomas Graham House, Science Park, Milton Rd., Cambridge CB4 4WF, England. TEL 44-1223-420066. FAX 44-1223-423429. E-mail: sales@rsc.org; URL: http://chemistry.rsc.org/rsc/. (Subscr. to: Turpin Distribution Services Ltd., Blackhorse Rd., Letchworth, Herts. SG6 1HN, England. TEL 44-1462-672555. FAX 44-1462-480947) Ed. P.B. Ayscough. charts; illus.; index. (back issues avail.) **Indexed:** Chem.Abstr., Sci.Cit.Ind. **Document type:** academic/scholarly publication.
—BLDSC (3699.763000); CASDDS; UnCover. **CCC.**
Superseded in part: Electron Spin Resonance (ISSN 0305-9758)
Description: Reviews electron spin resonance literature to mid 1994.

660.284 547   JA   ISSN 0013-8460
ENBI TO PORIMA/VINYLS AND POLYMERS. (Text in Japanese; summaries in English) 1961. m. 16000 Yen. Institute of Polymer Industry, Inc. - Porima Kogyo Kenkyujo, C.P.O. Box 1176, Tokyo 100-91, Japan. URL: http://www.rapra.net. Ed. Fumio Miyamoto. adv.; bk.rev.; abstr.; charts; illus.; stat.; index. circ. 16,000. (processed; reprint service avail. from UMI) **Indexed:** ASCA, JTA.
●Also available online.

665   IT   ISSN 0014-0902
CODEN: EDAGAH
ESSENZE-DERIVATI AGRUMARI. 1930. q. L.32000($13) Stazione Sperimentale per l'Industria delle Essenze e dei Derivati Agrumari, Corso Vittorio Emanuele 131, 89100 Reggio Calabria, Italy. Ed. Angelo Di Giacomo. adv.; bk.rev.; abstr.; bibl.; charts; stat.; index. circ. 500. (also avail. in microform) **Indexed:** Anal.Abstr., Chem.Abstr., Food Sci.& Tech.Abstr., Hort.Abstr., Weed Abstr.
—CASDDS.

EUROPEAN JOURNAL OF MEDICINAL CHEMISTRY. see BIOLOGY — Biological Chemistry

547   UK   ISSN 0014-3057
QD281.P6   CODEN: EUPJAG
EUROPEAN POLYMER JOURNAL. (Text in English, French, German and Italian) 1965. m. fl.3664($2106) (effective 1998). Elsevier Science Ltd., Pergamon, P.O. Box 800, Kidlington, Oxford OX5 1DX, England. TEL 44-1865-843000. FAX 44-1865-843010. E-mail: nlinfo-f@elsevier.nl; usinfo-f@elsevier.com; forinfo-kyf04035@niftyserve.or.jp; URL: http://www.elsevier.nl/. (Subscr. to: Elsevier Science, Regional Sales Office, P.O. Box 211, 1000 AE Amsterdam, Netherlands. TEL 31-20-4853757. FAX 31-20-4853432; Subscr. in the Americas to: Elsevier Science, Regional Sales Office, Box 945, New York, NY 10159-0945. TEL 212-633-3730. FAX 212-633-3680; Subscr. in Australasia and the Far East to: Elsevier Science (Singapore) Pte Ltd, No.1 Temasek Ave., No.17-01 Millenia Tower, Singapore 039192, Singapore. TEL 65-434-3727. FAX 65-337-2230) Eds. John C. Bevington, J.V. Dawkins. adv.; bk.rev.; abstr.; charts; illus. circ. 1,400. (also avail. in microfilm from UMI; back issues avail.) **Indexed:** Alloys Ind., Anal.Abstr., ASCA, Chem.Abstr., Chem.Cit.Ind., Curr.Cont., Dairy Sci.Abstr., Eng.Mat.Abstr., Excerp.Med., Ind.Sci.Rev., INSPEC, Int.Aerosp.Abstr., Intl.Polym.Sci.& Tech., Mass Spectr.Bull., Mat.Sci.Cit.Ind., Met.Abstr.Ind., Met.Abstr., Nonfer.Met.Alert, PCC Alert, RAPRA, Sci.Cit.Ind., Steels Alert, Text.Tech.Dig., World Alum.Abstr., World Surf.Coat. **Document type:** academic/scholarly publication.
—BLDSC (3829.791000); CASDDS; CISTI; Ei; Genuine Article; Linda Hall; SWETS; UMI; UnCover. **CCC.**
Description: Publishes results bearing on the physics and chemistry of natural and synthetic macronuclear substances, and review articles covering advances in polymer technology.
Refereed Serial

547   US   ISSN 0271-616X
CODEN: FFRSEV
FIESER AND FIESER'S REAGENTS FOR ORGANIC SYNTHESIS. 1967. irreg. John Wiley & Sons, Inc., 605 Third Ave., New York, NY 10158. TEL 212-850-6645. FAX 212-850-6021. (Subscr. outside the Americas to: John Wiley & Sons Ltd., Baffins Ln., Chichester, W. Sussex PO19 1UD, England. TEL 44-1243-779777. FAX 44-1243-776128) **Document type:** monographic series.
—BLDSC (3925.430800); CASDDS; CISTI.
Formerly (until 1980): Reagents for Organic Synthesis (ISSN 0271-6747)

FITOTERAPIA; rivista di studi ed applicazioni delle piante medicinali. see BIOLOGY — Botany

547 664   UK   ISSN 0882-5734
CODEN: FFJOED
FLAVOUR & FRAGRANCE JOURNAL. 1986. bi-m. $695 (foreign $695) (effective 1998). John Wiley & Sons Ltd., Journals, Baffins Ln., Chichester, W. Sussex PO19 1UD, England. TEL 44-1243-779777. FAX 44-1243-775878. E-mail: info-assets@wiley.co.uk; URL: http://www.wiley.co.uk. (Subscr. in the Americas to: John Wiley & Sons, Inc., 605 Third Ave., New York, NY 10158. TEL 212-850-6645. FAX 212-850-6021) Ed. A.J. Taylor. adv.: B&W page £595, color page £1495; trim 260 x 200; adv. contact: Bob Kern. bk.rev. circ. 326. (back issues avail.; reprint service avail. from SWZ) **Indexed:** Anal.Abstr., Chem.Abstr., Excerp.Med., Food Sci.& Tech.Abstr., Forest.Abstr., Forest Prod.Abstr., Hort.Abstr., Plant Grow.Reg.Abstr., Weed Abstr. **Document type:** trade publication.
—BLDSC (3950.047000); CASDDS; CISTI; Ei; EMDOCS; SWETS; UMI. **CCC.**
Description: Devoted to the rapid publication of scientific and technical papers on essential oils and related products.

665   UK   ISSN 1351-4202
FOCUS ON SOLVENTS. 1994. m. £245($450) (effective 1997). The Royal Society of Chemistry, Thomas Graham House, Science Park, Milton Rd., Cambridge CB4 4WF, England. TEL 44-1223-420066. FAX 44-1223-423429. E-mail: sales@rsc.org; URL: http://chemistry.rsc.org/rsc/. (Subscr. to: Turpin Distribution Services Ltd., Blackhorse Rd., Letchworth, Herts. SG6 1HN, England. TEL 44-1462-672555. FAX 44-1462-480947) Ed. Bob Gladding. **Document type:** newsletter.
Description: Covers commercial and technical issues for suppliers and users of solvents.

547   US   ISSN 0071-7886
QD241   CODEN: FCONAA
FORTSCHRITTE DER CHEMIE ORGANISCHER NATURSTOFFE/PROGRESS IN THE CHEMISTRY OF ORGANIC NATURAL PRODUCTS. 1938. irreg., vol.66, 1996. price varies. Springer-Verlag, 175 Fifth Ave., New York, NY 10010. TEL 212-460-1500. FAX 212-473-6272. (Also: Berlin, Heidelberg, Tokyo and Vienna) cum.index: vols.1-20 (1938-1962). (reprint service avail. from ISI) **Indexed:** Biol.Abstr., Biotech.Abstr., Chem.Abstr., Chem.Cit.Ind., Chem.Infd., Excerp.Med., Ind.Med., VITIS. **Document type:** monographic series.
—BLDSC (6867.200000); CASDDS; CISTI; Linda Hall; SWETS; UnCover. **CCC.**

660   US   ISSN 1058-9937
CODEN: MMIEE2
FUNCTIONAL MATERIALS - INTERNATIONAL EDITION. 1985. a. $61 (effective 1997). M C Publishing Co., Inc., 175 Rock Rd., Glen Rock, NJ 07452. TEL 201-652-2655. E-mail: MCPUB@AOL.COM. **Document type:** directory.
—BLDSC (5413.423800).
Description: Comprehensive formulator's guide to over 4000 products used in conjunction with surface active agents which are categorized by trade name identity, physical characteristics and product applications.

547   SP   ISSN 0017-3495
CODEN: GRACAN
GRASAS Y ACEITES. (Text and summaries in English, Spanish) 1950. bi-m. 16100 ptas. (Latin America 17100 ptas.; elsewhere 18700 ptas.) (effective 1997). Instituto de la Grasa, Avda. Padre Garcia Tejero, 4, 41012 Seville, Spain. TEL 34-5-4611550. FAX 34-5-4616790. adv.; bk.rev.; abstr.; bibl.; charts; illus.; pat.; stat.; index. circ. 1,000. **Indexed:** Apic.Abstr., ASCA, Biol.Abstr., Chem.Abstr., Curr.Adv.Ecol.Sci., Curr.Cont., Curr.Leather Lit., Dairy Sci.Abstr., Field Crop Abstr., Food Sci.& Tech.Abstr., Herb.Abstr., Ind.Sci.Rev., Ind.SST, Nutr.Abstr., Sci.Cit.Ind.
—BLDSC (4213.000000); CASDDS; Genuine Article; UMI. **CCC.**
Description: Includes articles on seed oil products, proteins, vegetable products, detergents and surfactants, by-products and vegetation water treatment.

CHEMISTRY — ORGANIC CHEMISTRY

547 — US — ISSN 0163-9102
QP751 — CODEN: HLREDI
HANDBOOK OF LIPID RESEARCH. 1978. irreg., vol.8, 1996. price varies. Plenum Publishing Corp., 233 Spring St., New York, NY 10013-1578. TEL 212-620-8000. FAX 212-463-0742. TELEX 23-421139. E-mail: books@plenum.com. Ed. Fred Snyder. (back issues avail.) **Document type:** monographic series.
 —BLDSC (4250.850000); CASDDS; CISTI; KNAW.
Refereed Serial

547 — CC — ISSN 1005-1511
CODEN: HEHUE2
HECHENG HUAXUE/CHINESE JOURNAL OF SYNTHETIC CHEMISTRY. (Text in Chinese or English) 1993. q. Y7.50 (foreign $17) (effective 1996 & 1997). Sichuang Sheng Huaxue Huagong Xuehui, Chengdu Youji Huaxue Yanjiusuo, No. 9, Renmin Nanlu 4 Duan, Chengdu, Sichuan 610041, People's Republic of China. TEL 86-28-5581317. FAX 86-28-5583978. E-mail: yjk@ntr.cdb.ac.cn. (Dist. overseas by: China International Book Trading Corp., P.O. Box 399, Beijing 100044, P.R. China) (Co-sponsor: Chengdu Youji Huaxue Yanjiusuo) Ed. Yaozhong Jiang. bk.rev. circ. 1,000. pp./issue: 96. **Document type:** academic/scholarly publication.
 —BLDSC (3180.680200); CASDDS.

547.59 — JA — ISSN 0385-5414
QD399 — CODEN: HTCYAM
HETEROCYCLES; international journal for reviews and communications in heterocyclic chemistry. (Text in English) 1973. 3/yr. fl.4919($2827) (effective 1998). Japan Institute of Heterocyclic Chemistry, 1-1-7-804 Motoakasaka, Minato-ku, Tokyo 107, Japan. TEL 81-3-3404-5019. FAX 81-3-3497-9370. E-mail: be3k-kmtn@asahi-net.ov.jp. (Dist. outside Japan by: Elsevier Science Customer Service Dept., P.O. Box 211, 1001 AE Amsterdam, Netherlands. TEL 31-20-485-3757. FAX 31-20-485-3432; Subscr. in U.S. and Canada to: Elsevier Science Customer Support Dept., Box 945, New York, NY 10010) Ed. Keiichiro Fukumoto; Pub. Koichi Kametani. R&P contact: Koichi Kametani. bk.rev.; index. circ. 1,100. (also avail. in microform from UMI; reprint service avail. from UMI) **Indexed:** ASCA, Chem.Abstr., Chem.Cit.Ind., Chem.Infd., Curr.Chem.React., Curr.Cont., Ind.Chem., Ind.Sci.Rev., Mass Spectr.Bull., Sci.Cit.Ind., SSCI. **Document type:** academic/scholarly publication.
 —BLDSC (4301.250000); CASDDS; CISTI; Genuine Article; Linda Hall; SWETS; UMI; UnCover. **CCC.**
 Description: Publishes accounts of research on the organic chemistry of heterocyclic compounds and natural products having the heterocyclic system.
Refereed Serial

660.284 547 — UK — ISSN 0954-0083
TA455.P58 — CODEN: HPPOEX
HIGH PERFORMANCE POLYMERS. 1989. q. £182($370) to institutions (microfiche edition £137) (effective 1997). (Institute of Physics) I O P Publishing Ltd., Dirac House, Temple Back, Bristol BS1 6BE, England. TEL 44-117-929-7481. FAX 44-117-929-4318. E-mail: custserv@ioppublishing.co.uk; URL: http://www.iop.org. (US subscr. to: American Institute of Physics, Member and Subscriber Services, 500 Sunnyside Blvd., Woodbury, NY 11797-2900. TEL 516-349-7800) Ed. D. Wilson. index. circ. 141. **Indexed:** Alloys Ind., Eng.Mat.Abstr., INSPEC (1989-), Intl.Polym.Sci.& Tech., Met.Abstr., Met.Abstr.Ind., Nonfer.Met.Alert, PCC Alert, RAPRA, Steels Alert, World Alum.Abstr. **Document type:** academic/scholarly publication.
 ●Also available online.
 —BLDSC (4307.338660); AskIEEE; CASDDS; CISTI; Ei; Genuine Article; KR SourceOne; Linda Hall; SWETS; UnCover. **CCC.**
 Description: Publishes research papers on polymer chemistry. Covers molecular modeling and polymer design, as well as the testing and performance of polymers.

INDIAN JOURNAL OF HEREDITY. see *BIOLOGY — Genetics*

547 662.6 — US — ISSN 1056-7194
TP360 — CODEN: INBOES
INDUSTRIAL BIOPROCESSING; a monthly intelligence service. 1979. m. $595 (foreign $655). Technical Insights (Subsidiary of: John Wiley & Sons, Inc.), 32 N. Dean St., Englewood, NJ 07631-2807. TEL 201-568-4744. FAX 201-568-8247. E-mail: ibinfo@insights.com; URL: http://www.insights.com. Ed. Peter Savage; Pub. Peter Katz. abstr.; bibl.; charts; pat.; stat.; tr.lit. (back issues avail.) **Indexed:** Abstr.Bull.Inst.Pap.Chem., Curr.Biotech.Abstr. **Document type:** newsletter.
 —CISTI. **CCC.**
 Former titles (until 1991): Bioprocessing Technology (ISSN 0885-5625); (until 1985): Biomass Digest (ISSN 0163-6766)
 Description: Focuses on industrial processes involving biological routes to produce chemicals and energy; reflects the growing interest in bioproducts and the marketplace.

INTERNATIONAL DATA SERIES. SELECTED DATA ON MIXTURES. SERIES A. THERMODYNAMIC PROPERTIES OF NON-REACTING BINARY SYSTEMS OF ORGANIC SUBSTANCES. see *CHEMISTRY — Physical Chemistry*

547 600 — US — ISSN 1073-2136
 — CODEN: IFSSEZ
INTERNATIONAL FIBER SCIENCE AND TECHNOLOGY SERIES. 1983. irreg., vol.14, 1996. Marcel Dekker, Inc., 270 Madison Ave., New York, NY 10016. TEL 212-696-9000. FAX 212-685-4540. TELEX 421419. Ed. Russell Dekker; Pub. Graham Garratt. R&P contact: Julia Mulligan. **Document type:** monographic series.
 —BLDSC (4540.186650); CASDDS. **CCC.**
Refereed Serial

INTERNATIONAL JOURNAL OF POLYMERIC MATERIALS. see *ENGINEERING — Chemical Engineering*

547 — NE
ISOTOPES IN ORGANIC CHEMISTRY. 1975. irreg., vol.8, 1992. price varies. Elsevier Science B.V., Books Division, P.O. Box 211, 1000 AE Amsterdam, Netherlands. TEL 31-20-4853911. FAX 31-20-4853705. TELEX 18582 ESPA NL. E-mail: nlinfo-f@elsevier.nl; usinfo-f@elsevier.com; forinfo-kyf04035@niftyserve.or.jp; URL: http://www.elsevier.nl/. (Subscr. in the Americas to: Elsevier Science, Regional Sales Office, Box 945, New York, NY 10159-0945. TEL 212-633-3730. FAX 212-633-3680; Subscr. in Australasia and the Far East to: Elsevier Science (Singapore) Pte Ltd, No.1 Temasek Ave., No.17-01 Millenia Tower, Singapore 039192, Singapore. TEL 65-434-3727. FAX 65-337-2230; Subscr. in Japan to: Elsevier Science Japan, 9-15 Higashi-Azabu 1-chome, Minato-ku, Tokyo 106, Japan. TEL 81-3-5561-5033. FAX 81-3-5561-5047) Eds. E. Buncel, C.C. Lee. **Indexed:** Chem.Abstr. **Document type:** monographic series.
Refereed Serial

547 — RU — ISSN 0137-0251
QD245 — CODEN: ITOKDK
ITOGI NAUKI I TEKHNIKI: ORGANICHESKAYA KHIMIYA. irreg., vols.10-12, 1989. price varies. Vsesoyuznyi Institut Nauchno-Tekhnicheskoi Informatsii (VINITI), Ul. Baltiiskaya 14, Moscow A-219, Russia. (Subscr. to: Mezhdunarodnaya Kniga, Dimitrova ul. 39, 113095 Moscow, Russia) **Indexed:** Chem.Abstr.
 —CASDDS; Linda Hall.

540 547 — JA — ISSN 0075-2010
ITSUU LABORATORY, TOKYO. ANNUAL REPORT/ITSUU KENKYUJO NENPO. (Text in English and German; summaries in Japanese) 1950. irreg. (a. or biennial). exchange basis. Itsuu Laboratory - Itsuu Kenkyujo, 28-10 Tamagawa 2-chome, Setagaya-ku, Tokyo 173, Japan. Ed. M. Natsume.
 ●Also available on CD-ROM.
 —CISTI.

547.8 — JA
J A S E COMMUNICATIONS. (Text in English, Japanese) 1982. q. Japanese Association of Solvent Extraction - Nihon Yobai Chushutsu Gakkai, Dept. of Chemical Science & Technology, Kyushu University, Fukuoka 812-81, Japan. Ed. Masahiro Goto. R&P contact: Masahiro Goto. adv. contact: Masahiro Goto. **Document type:** proceedings.

JOURNAL OF BIOMATERIALS SCIENCE. POLYMER EDITION. see *BIOLOGY — Biotechnology*

547 — US — ISSN 0022-152X
QD400 — CODEN: JHTCAD
JOURNAL OF HETEROCYCLIC CHEMISTRY; international journal. 1964. 6/yr. $530 (foreign $590) (effective 1998). HeteroCorporation, Box 993, Odessa, FL 33556-0993. Ed. Raymond N. Castle; Pub. Raymond Castle. R&P contact: Raymond Castle. adv.; bk.rev.; bibl.; charts; illus.; index; circ. 1,600 (paid). **Indexed:** ASCA, Biol.Abstr., Biotech.Abstr., Chem.Abstr., Chem.Cit.Ind., Chem.Infd., Curr.Chem.React., Curr.Cont., Excerp.Med., Helminthol.Abstr., Ind.Chem., Ind.Sci.Rev., Ind.Vet., Mass Spectr.Bull., Sci.Cit.Ind. **Document type:** academic/scholarly publication.
 —BLDSC (4998.200000); CASDDS; CISTI; Ei; Genuine Article; Linda Hall; SWETS; UnCover. **CCC.**
 Incorporates: Lectures in Heterocyclic Chemistry (ISSN 0090-2268)
Refereed Serial

660.284 546 — US — ISSN 1053-0495
QD196 — CODEN: JIOPE4
JOURNAL OF INORGANIC AND ORGANOMETALLIC POLYMERS. 1991. q. $345 (foreign $405) (effective 1998). Plenum Publishing Corp., 233 Spring St., New York, NY 10013-1578. TEL 212-620-8000. FAX 212-463-0742. TELEX 23-421139. Ed. Martel Zeldin. adv. (back issues avail.) **Indexed:** ASCA, Chem.Cit.Ind., Curr.Cont., Intl.Polym.Sci.& Tech., Mat.Sci.Cit.Ind., RAPRA. **Document type:** academic/scholarly publication.
 —BLDSC (5007.100000); CASDDS; CISTI; Ei; Genuine Article; Linda Hall; SWETS. **CCC.**
 Description: Addresses the synthesis, characterization, evaluation, and phenomena of inorganic and organometallic polymers.
Refereed Serial

547 — US — ISSN 1060-1325
QD380 — CODEN: JSPCE6
JOURNAL OF MACROMOLECULAR SCIENCE: PART A - PURE AND APPLIED CHEMISTRY. (Supplement avail.: Macromolecular Reports) 1967. 8/yr. $2795 (foreign $2840) (effective 1998). Marcel Dekker Journals, 270 Madison Ave., New York, NY 10016. TEL 212-696-9000. FAX 212-685-4540. TELEX 421419 MARDEEK. (Subscr. to: Box 5017, Monticello, NY 12701) Ed. Russell A. Gaudiana. adv. contact: Lourdes Barroso. (also avail. in microform from RPI) **Indexed:** Alloys Ind., ASCA, Biol.Abstr., Chem.Abstr., Chem.Cit.Ind., Curr.Adv.Ecol.Sci., Curr.Cont., Curr.Leather Lit., Eng.Mat.Abstr., Ind.Sci.Rev., Intl.Polym.Sci.& Tech., Mass Spectr.Bull., Mat.Sci.Cit.Ind., Met.Abstr.Ind., Met.Abstr., Nonfer.Met.Alert, PCC Alert, RAPRA, Sci.Cit.Ind., Steels Alert, World Alum.Abstr., World Surf.Coat. **Document type:** academic/scholarly publication.
 —BLDSC (5010.762000); ADONIS; CASDDS; CISTI; Ei; Genuine Article; Linda Hall; SWETS; UMI; UnCover. **CCC.**
 Formerly (until 1992): Journal of Macromolecular Science: Part A - Chemistry (ISSN 0022-233X); Supersedes in part: Journal of Macromolecular Chemistry (ISSN 0449-2730)
Refereed Serial

JOURNAL OF MACROMOLECULAR SCIENCE: PART B - PHYSICS. see *PHYSICS*

547 — US — ISSN 0736-6574
QD380 — CODEN: JMSPDH
JOURNAL OF MACROMOLECULAR SCIENCE: PART C - REVIEWS IN MACROMOLECULAR CHEMISTRY AND PHYSICS. 1967. q. $825 (foreign $840) (effective 1998). Marcel Dekker Journals, 270 Madison Ave., New York, NY 10016. TEL 212-696-9000. FAX 212-685-4540. TELEX 421419 MARDEEK. (Subscr. to: Box 5017, Monticello, NY 12701) Ed.Bd. adv. contact: Lourdes Barroso. (also avail. in microform from RPI) **Indexed:** ASCA, Chem.Abstr., Chem.Cit.Ind., Curr.Chem.React., Curr.Cont., Ind.Chem., Ind.Sci.Rev., Intl.Polym.Sci.& Tech., Mat.Sci.Cit.Ind., RAPRA, Sci.Cit.Ind. **Document type:** academic/scholarly publication.
 —BLDSC (5010.781000); AskIEEE; CASDDS; CIST; Ei; Genuine Article; KR SourceOne; Linda Hall; SWETS; UMI; UnCover. **CCC.**
 Former titles: Journal of Macromolecular Science. Part C. Reviews in Macromolecular Chemistry (ISSN 0022-2356); Reviews in Macromolecular Chemistry
Refereed Serial

JOURNAL OF NATURAL GAS CHEMISTRY. see *PETROLEUM AND GAS*

CHEMISTRY — ORGANIC CHEMISTRY 1817

547   US   ISSN 0022-3263
QD241   CODEN: JOCEAH
JOURNAL OF ORGANIC CHEMISTRY (WASHINGTON). 1936. 24/yr. $1895 (foreign $2215) (effective 1998). American Chemical Society, 1155 16th St., N.W., Washington, DC 20036. TEL 800-333-9511; 800-333-9511. FAX 614-447-3671. (Subscr. to: Membership and Subscription Services, Box 3337, Columbus, OH 43210. TEL 614-447-3776) Ed. Clayton H. Heathcock. adv.; charts; illus.; index. circ. 9,800. (also avail. in microform; back issues avail.) **Indexed:** Abstr.Bull.Inst.Pap.Chem., Alloys Ind., Biol.Abstr., Biotech.Abstr., Cadscan, Chem.Abstr., Chem.Cit.Ind., Chem.Infd., Curr.Adv.Biochem., Curr.Adv.Ecol.Sci., Curr.Chem.React., Curr.Cont., Dairy Sci.Abstr., Deep Sea Res.& Oceanogr.Abstr., Eng.Mat.Abstr., Excerp.Med., Food Sci.& Tech.Abstr., Gen.Sci.Ind., Ind.Chem., Ind.Med., Ind.Sci.Rev., INIS Atomind., Lead Abstr., Mass Spectr.Bull., Met.Abstr.Ind., Met.Abstr., Nutr.Abstr., Ocean.Abstr., PCC Alert, RAPRA, Rev.Med.& Vet.Mycol., Steels Alert, World Alum.Abstr., Zincscan. **Document type:** academic/scholarly publication.
●Also available online. Vendor(s): STN International (CJACS).
—BLDSC (5027.000000); CASDDS; CISTI; Ei; Genuine Article; KR SourceOne; Linda Hall; SWETS; UMI; UnCover. **CCC.**
Description: Offers the organic chemist critical accounts of original work in a given field, and interpretative reviews of existing data that present new viewpoints.
Refereed Serial

547.05 669   SZ   ISSN 0022-328X
QD411   CODEN: JORCAI
JOURNAL OF ORGANOMETALLIC CHEMISTRY. (Text in English, French and German; summaries in English) 1963. 44/yr. fl.13246($7613) (effective 1998). Elsevier Science S.A., P.O. Box 564, CH-1001 Lausanne 1, Switzerland. TEL 41-21-3207381. FAX 41-21-3235444. TELEX 450620-ELSA-CH. (Subscr. to: Elsevier Science, Regional Sales Office, P.O. Box 211, 1000 AE Amsterdam, Netherlands. TEL 31-20-4853757. FAX 31-20-4853432; Subscr. in the Americas to: Elsevier Science, Regional Sales Office, Box 945, New York, NY 10159-0945. TEL 212-633-3730. FAX 212-633-3680; Subscr. in Australasia to: Elsevier Science (Singapore) Pte. Ltd., No. 1 Temasek Ave., No. 17-01 Millenia Tower, Singapore 039192, Singapore. TEL 65-434-3727. FAX 65-337-2230) Ed.Bd. adv.; bk.rev.; illus.; index. (also avail. in microform from UMI) **Indexed:** ASCA, Biwk.Pap.Rad.Chem.& Photochem., Chem.Abstr., Chem.Cit.Ind., Chem.Infd., Curr.Chem.React., Curr.Cont., Ind.Chem., Ind.Sci.Rev., Mass Spectr.Bull., Mat.Sci.Cit.Ind., Sci.Cit.Ind. **Document type:** academic/scholarly publication.
●Also available online. Vendor(s): STN International.
—BLDSC (5027.100000); CASDDS; CISTI; Ei; Genuine Article; Linda Hall; SWETS; UMI; UnCover. **CCC.**
Incorporates: Organometallic Chemistry Reviews. Section A: Subject Reviews (ISSN 0030-5111); Organometallic Chemistry Reviews. Section B: Annual Surveys (ISSN 0030-512X)
Description: Deals with theoretical aspects, structural chemistry, synthesis, physical and chemical properties including reaction mechanisms, and practical applications of organo-elements compounds in a sense corresponding essentially to Section 29 of Chemical Abstracts.
Refereed Serial

OURNAL OF PHYSICAL ORGANIC CHEMISTRY. see CHEMISTRY — Physical Chemistry

660.284   II   ISSN 0970-0838
QD380   CODEN: JOPME8
JOURNAL OF POLYMER MATERIALS. 1984. q. fl.195($125) (effective 1997). Oxford & I.B.H. Publishing Co. Pvt. Ltd., 66 Janpath, New Delhi 110 001, India. FAX 91-11-3322639. (Co-published and distributed outside India by: A.A. Balkema, P.O. Box 1675, 3000 BR Rotterdam, Netherlands. TEL 31-10-4145822. FAX 31-10-435947) Ed. Sukumar Maiti. adv.; bk.rev.; illus. **Indexed:** Alloys Ind., ASCA, Chem.Abstr., Curr.Leather Lit., Eng.Mat.Abstr., Excerp.Med., INIS Atomind., Intl.Polym.Sci.& Tech., Met.Abstr.Ind., Met.Abstr., Nonfer.Met.Alert, PCC Alert, RAPRA, Steels Alert, World Alum.Abstr.
—BLDSC (5040.998000); CASDDS; CISTI; Ei; Genuine Article; Linda Hall; SWETS; UnCover. **CCC.**
Description: Publishes original laboratory findings and research relevant to the field of polymer science and technology, including synthesis, morphology, structure, new analytical techniques, processing and fabrication.
Refereed Serial

547   US   ISSN 0887-624X
QD471   CODEN: JPACEC
JOURNAL OF POLYMER SCIENCE. PART A: POLYMER CHEMISTRY. (Text in English, French, German) 1962. 34/yr. $6500 (foreign $7095) (effective 1998). John Wiley & Sons, Inc., Journals, 605 Third Ave., New York, NY 10158. TEL 212-850-6645. FAX 212-850-6021. TELEX 12-7063. E-mail: SUBINFO@JWILEY.COM; URL: http://www.wiley.co.uk. (Subscr. outside the Americas to: John Wiley & Sons Ltd., Baffins Ln., Chichester, W. Sussex PO19 1UD, England. TEL 44-1243-779777. FAX 44-1243-776128) Eds. David Tirrell, Eli Pearce. adv.: B&W page £640, color page £1515; trim 279 x 216. bk.rev.; bibl.; charts; illus.; index. circ. 1,850. (also avail. in microform from UMI; back issues avail.; reprint service avail. from UMI) **Indexed:** Abstr.Bull.Inst.Pap.Chem., Alloys Ind., Anal.Abstr., Appl.Mech.Rev., ASCA, Biwk.Pap.Rad.Chem.& Photochem., Chem.Abstr., Chem.Cit.Ind., Chem.Titles, Curr.Cont., Curr.Leather Lit., Eng.Mat.Abstr., Ind.Sci.Rev., INSPEC, Intl.Polym.Sci.& Tech., Mat.Sci.Cit.Ind., Met.Abstr.Ind., Met.Abstr., Nonfer.Met.Alert, Paper & Bd.Abstr., PCC Alert, RAPRA, Sci.Cit.Ind., Steels Alert, Text.Tech.Dig., World Alum.Abstr., World Surf.Coat., World Text.Abstr. **Document type:** academic/scholarly publication.
●Also available online. Vendor(s): STN International (CJWILEY).
—BLDSC (5041.002050); AskIEEE; CASDDS; CISTI; Ei; Genuine Article; KR SourceOne; Linda Hall; SWETS; UMI; UnCover. **CCC.**
Former titles: Journal of Polymer Science. Polymer Chemistry Edition (ISSN 0360-6376); Journal of Polymer Science. Part A-1: Polymer Chemistry; Incorporates in part (in 1991): Journal of Polymer Science. Part C: Polymer Letters (ISSN 0887-6258); Which was formerly (until 1986): Journal of Polymer Science. Polymer Letters Edition (ISSN 0360-6384); (1963-1972): Journal of Polymer Science. Part B: Polymer Letters (ISSN 0449-2986).
Refereed Serial

547   US   ISSN 0887-6266
QD471   CODEN: JPBPEM
JOURNAL OF POLYMER SCIENCE. PART B: POLYMER PHYSICS. (Text in English, French and German) 1962. 17/yr. $5494 (Canada and Mexico $5834; elsewhere $6055) (subscr. includes Part A: Polymer Chemistry & Symposia) (effective 1997). John Wiley & Sons, Inc., Journals, 605 Third Ave., New York, NY 10158. TEL 212-850-6645. FAX 212-850-6021. TELEX 12-7063. E-mail: SUBINFO@JWILEY.COM; URL: http://www.wiley.co.uk. (Subscr. outside the Americas to: John Wiley & Sons Ltd., Baffins Ln., Chichester, W. Sussex PO19 1UD, England. TEL 44-1243-779777. FAX 44-1243-776128) adv.: B&W page £640, color page £1515; trim 279 x 216. bibl.; charts; illus.; index. circ. 1,850. (also avail. in microform from UMI; back issues avail.) **Indexed:** Abstr.Bull.Inst.Pap.Chem., Alloys Ind., Appl.Mech.Rev., ASCA, Biwk.Pap.Rad.Chem.& Photochem., Chem.Abstr., Chem.Cit.Ind., Chem.Titles, Curr.Cont., Curr.Cont., Curr.Leather Lit., Eng.Ind., Eng.Mat.Abstr., Ind.Sci.Rev., INSPEC, Int.Aerosp.Abstr., Intl.Polym.Sci.& Tech., Mat.Sci.Cit.Ind., Met.Abstr., Met.Abstr.Ind., Nonfer.Met.Alert, Paper & Bd.Abstr., PCC Alert, Phys.Ber., RAPRA, Sci.Cit.Ind., Steels Alert, Text.Tech.Dig., World Alum.Abstr., World Surf.Coat., World Text.Abstr. **Document type:** proceedings.
●Also available online. Vendor(s): STN International (CJWILEY).
—BLDSC (5041.005000); AskIEEE; CASDDS; CISTI; Ei; Genuine Article; KR SourceOne; Linda Hall; SWETS; UMI; UnCover. **CCC.**
Former titles: Journal of Polymer Science. Polymer Physics Edition (ISSN 0098-1273); Journal of Polymer Science. Part A-2: Polymer Physics; Incorporates in part (in 1991): Journal of Polymer Science. Part C: Polymer Letters (ISSN 0887-6258); Which was formerly (until 1986): Journal of Polymer Science. Polymer Letters Edition (ISSN 0360-6384); (1963-1972): Journal of Polymer Science. Part B: Polymer Letters (ISSN 0449-2986).
Refereed Serial

547.84   US   ISSN 0360-8905
QD471   CODEN: JPYCAQ
JOURNAL OF POLYMER SCIENCE. SYMPOSIA PROCEEDINGS. 1963. irreg., no.74, 1986. (subscr. includes Part A: Polymer Chemistry & Part B: Polymer Physics). John Wiley & Sons, Inc., Journals, 605 Third Ave., New York, NY 10158-0012. TEL 212-850-6000. FAX 212-850-6088. illus. (also avail. in microform from UMI; back issues avail. from UMI) **Indexed:** Abstr.Bull.Inst.Pap.Chem., Alloys Ind., Chem.Abstr., Curr.Cont., Eng.Mat.Abstr., Field Crop Abstr., Ind.Sci.Rev., INSPEC, Met.Abstr.Ind., Met.Abstr., Nonfer.Met.Alert, PCC Alert, Steels Alert, World Alum.Abstr., World Surf.Coat., World Text.Abstr. **Document type:** proceedings.
●Also available online. Vendor(s): STN International.
—BLDSC (5041.030000); AskIEEE; CASDDS; CISTI; KR SourceOne; Linda Hall; SWETS; UMI; UnCover. **CCC.**
Supersedes: Journal of Polymer Science. Part C - Polymer Symposia (ISSN 0449-2994)
Refereed Serial

547 574.192   US   ISSN 0277-8033
QP551   CODEN: JPCHD2
JOURNAL OF PROTEIN CHEMISTRY. 1982. 8/yr. $525 (foreign $615) (effective 1998). Plenum Publishing Corp., 233 Spring St., New York, NY 10013-1578. TEL 212-620-8000. FAX 212-463-0742. TELEX 23-421139. Ed. M. Zouhair Atassi. adv. (also avail. in microfilm from UMI; back issues avail.) **Indexed:** ASCA, Chem.Cit.Ind., Curr.Adv.Biochem., Curr.Adv.Cell & Devel.Biol., Curr.Cont., Ind.Sci.Rev., Sci.Cit.Ind. **Document type:** academic/scholarly publication.
—BLDSC (5042.950000); CASDDS; CISTI; Ei; EMDOCS; Genuine Article; KNAW; Linda Hall; SWETS; UMI; UnCover. **CCC.**
Refereed Serial

CHEMISTRY — ORGANIC CHEMISTRY

547   JA   ISSN 0037-9980
CODEN: YGKKAE
JOURNAL OF SYNTHETIC ORGANIC CHEMISTRY/YUKI GOSEI KAGAKU KYOKAISHI. (Text in Japanese; summaries in English) 1943. m. 1500 Yen per no. Society of Synthetic Organic Chemistry, Japan - Yuki Gosei Kagaku Kyokai, 1-5, Kanda Surugadai, Chiyoda-ku, Tokyo 101, Japan. adv.; abstr.; bibl.; charts. **Indexed:** ASCA, Chem.Abstr., Chem.Cit.Ind., Chem.Infd., Curr.Chem.React., Curr.Cont., Eng.Ind., Ind.Chem., Ind.Sci.Rev., Jap.Per.Ind., JTA, Mass Spectr.Bull., Mat.Sci.Cit.Ind., Sci.Cit.Ind.
—BLDSC (5068.050000); CASDDS; CISTI; Ei; Genuine Article; SWETS. **CCC.**

547   UZ   ISSN 0023-1150
CODEN: KPSUAR
KHIMIYA PRIRODNYKH SOEDINENII. English translation: Chemistry of Natural Compounds (US ISSN 0009-3130) (Text in Russian) 1965. bi-m. $94 (effective 1998). (Akademiya Nauk Uzbekistana) Izdatel'stvo Fan, Ul. Gogolya 70, k. 105, 700000 Tashkent, Uzbekistan. index. circ. 816. (tabloid format) **Indexed:** Abstr.Bull.Inst.Pap.Chem., Apic.Abstr., ASCA, Biol.Abstr., Chem.Abstr., Chem.Cit.Ind., Curr.Adv.Ecol.Sci., Curr.Cont., Dairy Sci.Abstr., Forest.Abstr., Forest Prod.Abstr., Hort.Abstr., Ind.Chem., Ind.Sci.Rev., Plant Grow.Reg.Abstr., Sci.Cit.Ind., Seed Abstr., Soils & Fert.
—BLDSC (0394.300000); CASDDS; CISTI; Ei; Genuine Article; Linda Hall. **CCC.**

660.284   JA   ISSN 0454-1138
CODEN: KOBUA3
KOBUNSHI/HIGH POLYMERS, JAPAN. (Text in Japanese) 1952. m. 28000 Yen. Nihon Kobunshi Gakkai - Society of Polymer Science, Japan, Tsukiji Daisan Nagaoka Bldg., 2-4-2 Tsukiji, Chuo-ku, Tokyo 104, Japan. TEL 81-3-3543-3771. FAX 81-3-3545-8560. Ed. Shiro Kobayashi. adv. circ. 14,000. **Indexed:** INIS Atomind. **Document type:** academic/scholarly publication.
—BLDSC (5100.615000); CASDDS; CISTI; Linda Hall.

547 660.284   JA   ISSN 0386-2186
TP1080   CODEN: KBRBA3
KOBUNSHI RONBUNSHU. (Text in Japanese; summaries in English) 1944. m. 30000 Yen. Society of Polymer Science, Japan - Nihon Kobunshi Gakkai, Nagaoka Bldg., 2-4-2, Tsukiji, Chuo-ku, Tokyo 104, Japan. TEL 03-3543-3771. Ed. Takukei Nose. index. circ. 2,000. **Indexed:** Alloys Ind., Art & Archaeol.Tech.Abstr., ASCA, Chem.Abstr., Chem.Cit.Ind., Curr.Cont., Eng.Mat.Abstr., Ind.Sci.Rev., INIS Atomind., Intl.Polym.Sci.& Tech., Mat.Sci.Cit.Ind., Met.Abstr., Nonfer.Met.Alert, PCC Alert, RAPRA, SSCI, Steels Alert, Text.Tech.Dig., World Alum.Abstr. **Document type:** academic/scholarly publication.
—CASDDS; CISTI; Ei; EMDOCS; Genuine Article; KR SourceOne; Linda Hall; SWETS. **CCC.**
Formerly: Kobunshi Kagaku (ISSN 0023-2556)
Description: An international journal containing original papers, notes and short communications on all aspects of polymers, such as polymer chemistry, physics, and biopolymers.

547 669   RU   ISSN 0023-2815
TP1   CODEN: KOKKAI
KOKS I KHIMIYA. English translation: Coke and Chemistry (US ISSN 1068-364X) 1931. m. $120 (effective 1998). (Nauchno-tekhnicheskoe Obshchestvo Chernoi Metallurgii) Izdatel'stvo Metallurgiya, 2-i Obydenskii per., 14, 119587 Moscow, Russia. TEL 095-202-5532. FAX 095-230-6610. (Dist. by: Mezhdunarodnaya Kniga, B. Yakimanka 39, 117049 Moscow, Russia) (Co-sponsor: Ministerstvo Chernoi Metallurgii) Ed. N.V. Braun. adv.; bk.rev.; abstr.; bibl.; charts; stat.; index. circ. 7,650. **Indexed:** Alloys Ind., Chem.Abstr., Eng.Mat.Abstr., Fuel & Energy Abstr., Met.Abstr., Met.Abstr., Nonfer.Met.Alert, PCC Alert, Steels Alert, World Alum.Abstr.
—BLDSC (0090.000000); CASDDS; CISTI; Linda Hall. **CCC.**

668.9   KO
KOREA POLYMER JOURNAL. (Text in English) 1993. s-a. Polymer Society of Korea, Rm. 601, Hatchon Bldg., 831 Yeoksam-dong, Kangnam-ku, Seoul 135-792, S. Korea. TEL 02-561-5203. FAX 02-553-6938. Ed. Iwhan Cho. **Indexed:** ASCA. **Description:** Contains original researches on all aspects of polymer science, engineering, and technology.

547   US   ISSN 0937-3055
CODEN: LNBCEP
LECTURE NOTES IN BIO-ORGANIC CHEMISTRY. 1986. irreg. price varies. Springer-Verlag, 175 Fifth Ave., New York, NY 10010. TEL 212-460-1500. FAX 212-473-6272. (Also: Berlin, Heidelberg, Tokyo, Vienna) (reprint service avail. from ISI) **Document type:** monographic series.
—CISTI.

665.4   GW   ISSN 0076-891X
M W V JAHRESBERICHT; Mineraloel-zahlen. 1950. a. DM.8. Mineraloelwirtschafts Verband e.V., Steindamm 55, 20099 Hamburg, Germany. TEL 49-40-24849-0. FAX 49-40-24849253. circ. 4,500. **Document type:** bulletin.
Formerly: M W V - A E V Jahresbericht.

547   US   ISSN 0734-0559
TP202   CODEN: MMNEER
MCCUTCHEON'S FUNCTIONAL MATERIALS - NORTH AMERICAN EDITION. a. $72 (effective 1997). M C Publishing Company, Inc., McCutcheon Division, 175 Rock Rd., Glen Rock, NJ 07452. TEL 201-652-2655. FAX 201-652-3419. Ed. Michael Allured. **Document type:** directory.
—BLDSC (5413.424000); CASDDS.
Description: Comprehensive formulator's guide to over 4000 products used in conjunction with surface active agents which are categorized by trade name, identity, physical characteristics and product application.

547   US   ISSN 0076-2075
CODEN: MMCEB3
MACROMOLECULAR CHEMISTRY. (Subseries of: I U P A C Chemical Data Series (ISSN 0275-0910)) (Text in English; occasionally in French or German) 1962; latest 1972. irreg. price varies. (International Union of Pure and Applied Chemistry) C R C Press, Inc., 2000 Corporate Blvd., N.W., Boca Raton. TEL 561-994-0555; 800-272-7737. FAX 561-998-9784. TELEX 568689-CRC PRESS. **Document type:** monographic series.
—CASDDS.

547   SZ   ISSN 1022-1352
QD471   CODEN: MCHPES
MACROMOLECULAR CHEMISTRY AND PHYSICS. (Text in English) 1947. m. 3130 SFr. (DM.3860) (effective 1997). Huethig & Wepf Verlag, Neugasse 29, CH-6301 Zug, Switzerland. TEL 41-41-7102494. FAX 41-41-7118360. E-mail: 100755.154@compuserve.com. (German addr.: Huethig GmbH, Im Weiher 10, 69121 Heidelberg, Germany) Ed. Prof. Dr. H. Hoecker. charts; illus.; index. **Indexed:** Alloys Ind., ASCA, Biol.Abstr., Chem.Abstr., Chem.Cit.Ind., Curr.Cont., Eng.Mat.Abstr., Ind.Chem., Intl.Polym.Sci.& Tech., Mat.Sci.Cit.Ind., Met.Abstr.Ind., Met.Abstr., Nonfer.Met.Alert, PCC Alert, RAPRA, Sci.Cit.Ind., Steels Alert, World Alum.Abstr., World Surf.Coat. **Document type:** academic/scholarly publication.
—BLDSC (5330.398000); CASDDS; CISTI; Ei; Genuine Article; Linda Hall; SWETS; UnCover. **CCC.**
Formerly (until 1993): Makromolekulare Chemie (ISSN 0025-116X)

547   SZ   ISSN 1022-1336
QD380   CODEN: MRCOE3
MACROMOLECULAR RAPID COMMUNICATIONS. m. 310 SFr. (DM.380) (effective 1997). Huethig & Wepf Verlag, Neugasse 29, CH-6301 Zug, Switzerland. TEL 41-41-7102494. FAX 41-41-7118860. E-mail: 100755.154@compuserve.com. Ed. Prof. Dr. Hartwig Hoecker. index. **Indexed:** ASCA, Chem.Abstr., Chem.Cit.Ind., Curr.Chem.React., Curr.Cont., Ind.Chem., Ind.Sci.Rev., Intl.Polym.Sci.& Tech., Mat.Sci.Cit.Ind., RAPRA, Sci.Cit.Ind., World Surf.Coat. **Document type:** academic/scholarly publication.
—BLDSC (5330.400000); CASDDS; CISTI; Genuine Article; Linda Hall; SWETS; UnCover. **CCC.**
Former Titles (until 1993): Makromolekulare Chemie. Rapid Communications (ISSN 0173-2803); Makromolekulare Chemie. Short Communications.

547   US   ISSN 1060-278X
QD380   CODEN: MREPEG
MACROMOLECULAR REPORTS. (Supplement to: Journal of Macromolecular Science. Part A: Pure and Applied Chemistry) 1991. 8/yr. $295. Marcel Dekker Journals, 270 Madison Ave., New York, NY 10016. TEL 212-696-9000. FAX 212-685-4540. (Subscr. to: Box 5017, Monticello, NY 12701) Ed.Bd. **Indexed:** Intl.Polym.Sci.& Tech., RAPRA, World Surf.Coat. **Document type:** academic/scholarly publication.
—CASDDS; CISTI; Ei; UMI; UnCover. **CCC.**

547   SZ   ISSN 1022-1360
QD380   CODEN: MSYMEC
MACROMOLECULAR SYMPOSIA. 1986. 12/yr. 1050 SFr. (DM.1300) (effective 1997). Huethig & Wepf Verlag, Neugasse 29, CH-6301 Zug, Switzerland. TEL 41-41-7102494. FAX 41-41-7118360. E-mail: 100755.154@compuserve.com. (German addr.: Huethig GmbH, Im Weiher 10, 69121 Heidelberg, Germany) Ed. Prof. Dr. H. Hoecker. charts; illus.; index. **Indexed:** Alloys Ind., ASCA, Chem.Abstr., Curr.Cont., Eng.Mat.Abstr., Intl.Polym.Sci.& Tech., Mat.Sci.Cit.Ind., Met.Abstr., Met.Abstr.Ind., Nonfer.Met.Alert, PCC Alert, RAPRA, Steels Alert, World Alum.Abstr., World Surf.Coat. **Document type:** academic/scholarly publication.
—BLDSC (5330.416400); CASDDS; CISTI; Genuine Article; Linda Hall; SWETS; UnCover. **CCC.**
Formerly (until 1993): Makromolekulare Chemie. Macromolecular Symposia (ISSN 0258-0322)

547 546   SZ   ISSN 1022-1344
QD380   CODEN: MTHSEK
MACROMOLECULAR THEORY AND SIMULATIONS. (Text in English) 1975. 6/yr. 325 SFr. (DM.400) (effective 1997). Huethig & Wepf Verlag, Neugasse 29, CH-6301 Zug, Switzerland. TEL 41-41-7102494. FAX 41-41-7118360. E-mail: 100755.154@compuserve.com. Ed. Dr. Hartwig Hoecker. adv. **Indexed:** ASCA, Chem.Abstr., Chem.Cit.Ind., Curr.Cont., Ind.Sci.Rev., INSPEC (1994-), Mat.Sci.Cit.Ind., World Surf.Coat. **Document type:** academic/scholarly publication.
—BLDSC (5330.418000); AskIEEE; CASDDS; CISTI; Genuine Article; KR SourceOne; Linda Hall; SWETS; UnCover.
Formerly (until 1993): Makromolekulare Chemie. Supplement (ISSN 0253-5904)

547   US   ISSN 0024-9297
QD380   CODEN: MAMOBX
MACROMOLECULES. 1968. bi-w. $1400 to institutional non-members; members $104 (effective 1997). American Chemical Society, 1155 16th St., N.W., Washington, DC 20036. TEL 800-333-9511. FAX 614-447-3671. (Subscr. to: Membership and Subscription Services, Box 3337, Columbus, OH 43210. TEL 614-447-3776) Ed. Dr. Field H. Winslow. adv.; charts; index. circ. 2,800. (also avail. in microform; back issues avail.) **Indexed:** Abstr.Bull.Inst.Pap.Chem., Alloys Ind., ASCA, Biwk.Pap.Rad.Chem.& Photochem., Chem.Abstr., Chem.Cit.Ind., Compumath, Curr.Cont., Eng.Mat.Abstr., Food Sci.& Tech.Abstr., Ind.Sci.Rev., INIS Atomind., Intl.Aerosp.Abstr., Intl.Polym.Sci.& Tech., Mass Spectr.Bull., Mat.Sci.Cit.Ind., Met.Abstr.Ind., Met.Abstr., Nonfer.Met.Alert, Paper & Bd.Abstr., PCC Alert, RAPRA, RAPRA, Sci.Cit.Ind., Steels Alert, Text.Tech.Dig., World Alum.Abstr., World Surf.Coat., World Text.Abstr. **Document type:** academic/scholarly publication.
●Also available online. Vendor(s): STN International (CJACS).
—BLDSC (5330.420000); CASDDS; CISTI; Ei; Genuine Article; Linda Hall; SWETS; UMI; UnCover. **CCC.**
Description: Areas covered include synthesis, polymerization mechanisms and kinetics, chemical reactions, solution characteristics, spectroscopy, and bulk properties of organic, inorganic, and biopolymers.
Refereed Serial

CHEMISTRY — ORGANIC CHEMISTRY

547   UK   ISSN 0265-4245
CODEN: MOSYDN
METHODS IN ORGANIC SYNTHESIS. m. £270($472) (effective 1997). The Royal Society of Chemistry, Thomas Graham House, Science Park, Milton Rd., Cambridge CB4 4WF, England. TEL 44-1223-420066. FAX 44-1223-423623. E-mail: sales@rsc.org; URL: http://chemistry.rsc.org/rsc/. (Subscr. to: Turpin Distribution Services Ltd., Blackhorse Rd., Letchworth, Herts. SG6 1HN, England. TEL 44-1462-672555. FAX 44-1462-480947) Ed. Mike Corkill. cum.index. **Document type:** academic/scholarly publication.
—BLDSC (5748.203300). **CCC.**
Description: Aimed at synthetic organic chemists. Each issue contains about 200 items, including titles, bibliographic details and schematic reaction diagrams. Text is included where necessary to clarify reaction schemes.

547   US   ISSN 0176-7615
QD262   CODEN: MSMEDT
MODERN SYNTHETIC METHODS. 1976. triennial. price varies. (Association of Swiss Chemists, SZ) Springer-Verlag, 175 Fifth Ave., New York, NY 10010. TEL 212-460-1500. FAX 212-473-6272. Ed. R. Scheffold. (back issues avail.) **Indexed:** Chem.Cit.Ind., Chem.Infd. **Document type:** academic/scholarly publication.
—CASDDS; CISTI. **CCC.**
Description: Contains reviews in organic synthesis, including unpublished experimental details.

547   GW
▼**MOLECULES;** journal of synthetic organic and natural product chemistry. Online edition (GW ISSN 1420-3049) 1996. m. (with a cumulation in print or on CD-ROM). Springer-Verlag, Heidelberger Platz 3, 14197 Berlin, Germany. TEL 49-30-82787-0. FAX 49-30-82787448. E-mail: subscriptions@springer.de; URL: http://science.springer.de/molec/molecule.htm. (Subscr. in N. America to: Springer-Verlag New York, Inc., 333 Meadowlands Pkwy., Secaucus, NJ 07094. TEL 212-460-1500. FAX 212-473-6272) Ed. Shu-Kun Lin. abstr. **Document type:** academic/scholarly publication.
●Also available online.
Also available on CD-ROM.
Description: Covers small- and medium-sized molecules and their preparation (synthesis, biosynthesis, extraction), structural elucidation, properties and applications.

547   UK   ISSN 0265-0568
QD415.A1   CODEN: NPRRDF
NATURAL PRODUCT REPORTS. 1984. bi-m. £355 to institutions (US $640) (effective 1997). The Royal Society of Chemistry, Thomas Graham House, Science Park, Milton Rd., Cambridge CB4 4WF, England. TEL 44-1223-420066. FAX 44-1223-423623. E-mail: sales@rsc.org; URL: http://chemistry.rsc.org/rsc/. (Subscr. to: Turpin Distribution Services Ltd., Blackhorse Rd., Letchworth, Herts SG6 1HN, England. TEL 44-1462-672555. FAX 44-1462-480947) index. **Indexed:** ASCA, Bibl.Agri., Chem.Cit.Ind., Curr.Adv.Ecol.Sci., Curr.Cont., Ind.Sci.Rev., Sci.Cit.Ind. **Document type:** academic/scholarly publication.
—BLDSC (6040.738000); CASDDS; CISTI; EMDOCS; Genuine Article; Linda Hall; SWETS; UMI; UnCover. **CCC.**
Description: Contains critical and comprehensive reviews of papers published on general and natural product chemistry.

547   UK   ISSN 0950-1711
CODEN: NPUPEP
NATURAL PRODUCT UPDATES. m. £295($510) (effective 1997). The Royal Society of Chemistry, Thomas Graham House, Science Park, Milton Rd., Cambridge CB4 4WF, England. TEL 44-1223-420066. FAX 44-1223-423623. E-mail: sales@rsc.org; URL: http://chemistry.rsc.org/rsc/. (Dist. by: Turpin Distribution Services Ltd., Blackhorse Rd., Letchworth, Herts. SG6 1HN, England. TEL 44-1462-672555. FAX 44-1462-480947) Ed. Mike Hannant. **Document type:** academic/scholarly publication.
Description: Includes isolation studies (e.g., new compounds and known compounds from new sources), structure determinations, new properties, total and biosyntheses. Contains six indexes, author plus five subject indexes (source, taxonomic names, biological activity, trivial names, and compound class).

NEW CONCEPTS IN POLYMER SCIENCE. see ENGINEERING — Chemical Engineering

660.284   NE   ISSN 0169-6424
CODEN: MVLGDH
NEW POLYMERIC MATERIALS. (Text in English) 1987. q. DM.330 (effective 1997). V S P, P.O. Box 346, 3700 AH Zeist, Netherlands. TEL 31-30-6925790. FAX 31-30-6932081. E-mail: 100341.2372@compuserve.com. Ed. F.E. Karasz. **Indexed:** Alloys Ind., ASCA, Chem.Cit.Ind., Curr.Cont., Eng.Mat.Abstr., Intl.Polym.Sci.& Tech., Met.Abstr.Ind., Met.Abstr., Nonfer.Met.Alert, PCC Alert, RAPRA, Steels Alert, World Alum.Abstr. **Document type:** academic/scholarly publication.
—BLDSC (6085.821000); CASDDS; Ei; Linda Hall; SWETS; UnCover.
Description: Examines research on the chemistry, physics and biochemistry of macromolecules and oligomers.

NORWICH RESEARCH PARK NEWSLETTER. see BIOLOGY — Genetics

547   FR   ISSN 1258-8210
CODEN: RFCGAE
O C L. (Oleagineux Corps gras Lipides) 1954; N.S. 1994. m. 980 F. (foreign 1250 F.) (effective 1997). John Libbey Eurotext, 127 av. de la Republique, 92120 Montrouge, France. TEL 33-1-46730660. FAX 33-1-40840999. E-mail: marketing@jle.com. (Subscr. to: A T E I, 3 av. Pierre Kerautret, 93230 Romainville, France. TEL 33-1-48408686. FAX 33-1-48400731) Ed. Jean-Claude Icart. adv.; bk.rev.; bibl.; charts; pat.; index. (also avail. in microform from PMC) **Indexed:** Arts & Hum.Cit.Ind., ASCA, Bull.Signal., C.I.S. Abstr., Chem.Abstr., Curr.Adv.Ecol.Sci., Curr.Cont., Dairy Sci.Abstr., Excerp.Med., Field Crop Abstr., Food Sci.& Tech.Abstr., Herb.Abstr., Nutr.Abstr., SSCI. **Document type:** academic/scholarly publication.
—BLDSC (6235.135900); CASDDS; CISTI; Ei; Genuine Article; Linda Hall; SWETS.
Supersedes (in 1994): Revue Francaise des Corps Gras (ISSN 0035-3000)
Description: For scientists, industrialists, producers and advisors in the oilseeds industries.
Refereed Serial

665.4   AU
OE M V - MIX. 1958. 10/yr. free. Oe M V Aktiengesellschaft, Otto-Wagner-Platz 5, A-1090 Vienna, Austria. TEL 43-1-40440-0. FAX 43-1-40440999. URL: http://www.omv.co.at/omv. Ed. Dr. Hermann Michelitsch. bk.rev.; illus.; stat. circ. 16,400. **Document type:** consumer publication.
Former titles (until 1987): Oe M V - Magazin; Oe M V - Zeitschrift (ISSN 0029-7194); (until 1968): O M V - Werkzeitung.
Description: Covers refineries, technological research, production, transportation, economics, events and industry of the entire Oe M V group.

665   UK   ISSN 0267-8853
CODEN: OFINE2
OILS & FATS INTERNATIONAL. 1985. 5/yr. £75 (overseas £87) (effective 1997). Argus Business Media Ltd. (Subsidiary of: D M G Exhibitions Group Ltd.), Queensway House, 2 Queensway, Redhill, Surrey RH1 1QS, England. TEL 44-1737-768611. FAX 44-1737-761989. Ed. W. Lavers. adv.; illus. circ. 4,200. **Indexed:** Food Sci.& Tech.Abstr., Sugar Ind.Abstr. **Document type:** trade publication.
—BLDSC (6252.298100).

382 665   UK   ISSN 0265-6477
OILS AND FATS INTERNATIONAL DIRECTORY. 1984. a. £107 (overseas £115) (effective 1997). Argus Business Media Ltd. (Subsidiary of: D M G Exhibitions Group Ltd.), Queensway House, 2 Queensway, Redhill, Surrey RH1 1QS, England. TEL 44-1737-768611. FAX 44-1737-761989. **Document type:** directory.

665   SP   ISSN 0472-8807
OLEO; revista semanal de aceites y grasas. 1961. w. (48/yr.). 27500 ptas. (foreign 36000 ptas.) (effective 1997). Tecnipublicaciones, S.A., C. Albacete 5, 28028 Madrid, Spain. TEL 34-1-3261440. FAX 34-2-3264707. adv.: page 65000 ptas.; trim 190 x 265; adv. contact: Maximiliano Munoz. bk.rev.; stat. circ. 8,000. **Document type:** trade publication.
Description: Covers oils and greases of animal or vegetable origin for the food and mechanical industries.

665   SP
OLEO: ANUARIO ESPANOL DE ACEITES Y GRASAS E INDUSTRIAS AUXILIARES. 1961. 2/yr. 4900 ptas. (foreign 6700 ptas.) (effective 1997). Tecnipublicaciones, S.A., C. Albacete 5, 28027 Madrid, Spain. TEL 34-1-3261440. FAX 34-1-3262407. adv.; stat. circ. 3,000.

ORGANIC AND ORGANOMETALLIC CRYSTAL STRUCTURES; BIBLIOGRAPHY. see BIBLIOGRAPHIES

547   US   ISSN 0078-611X
CODEN: OCSMBP
ORGANIC CHEMISTRY; a series of monographs. 1964. irreg., vol.48, 1987. Academic Press, Inc., 525 B St., Ste. 1900, San Diego, CA 92101-4495. TEL 619-231-0926. FAX 619-699-6715. (Subscr. to: Order Dept., 6277 Sea Harbor Dr., 4th Fl., Orlando, FL 32887. TEL 800-321-5068) Ed. Harry W. Wasserman. (reprint service avail. from ISI) **Indexed:** Curr.Adv.Ecol.Sci. **Document type:** monographic series.
—CASDDS; CISTI.
Refereed Serial

ORGANIC ELECTRONIC SPECTRAL DATA. see CHEMISTRY — Analytical Chemistry

560 551.9   UK   ISSN 0146-6380
QE516.5   CODEN: ORGEDE
ORGANIC GEOCHEMISTRY. 1978. 20/yr. fl.3419($1965) (effective 1998). (European Association of Organic Geochemists) Elsevier Science Ltd., Pergamon, P.O. Box 800, Kidlington, Oxford OX5 1DX, England. TEL 44-1865-843000. FAX 44-1865-843010. E-mail: nlinfo-f@elsevier.nl; usinfo-f@elsevier.com; forinfo-kyf04035@niftyserve.or.jp; URL: http://www.elsevier.nl/. (Subscr. to: Elsevier Science, Regional Sales Office, P.O. Box 211, 1000 AE Amsterdam, Netherlands. TEL 31-20-4853757. FAX 31-20-4853432; Subscr. in the Americas to: Elsevier Science, Regional Sales Office, Box 945, New York, NY 10159-0945. TEL 212-633-3730. FAX 212-633-3680; Subscr. in Australasia and the Far East to: Elsevier Science (Singapore) Pte Ltd, No.1 Temasek Ave., No.17-01 Millenia Tower, Singapore 039192, Singapore. TEL 65-434-3727. FAX 65-337-2230) Eds. Earl W. Baker, A.G. Douglas. adv.; bk.rev.; index. circ. 1,100. (also avail. in microform from UMI) **Indexed:** AESIS, ASCA, Chem.Abstr., Chem.Cit.Ind., Curr.Adv.Ecol.Sci., Curr.Cont., Deep Sea Res.& Oceanogr.Abstr., Ecol.Abstr., Excerp.Med., Geo.Abstr.H.G., Geol.Abstr., GeoRef., I.M.M.Abstr., Ind.Sci.Rev., Mass Spectr.Bull., Petrol.Abstr., Sci.Cit.Ind., Soils & Fert., W.R.C.Inf. **Document type:** academic/scholarly publication.
—BLDSC (6288.200000); CASDDS; CISTI; Ei; EMDOCS; Genuine Article; KR SourceOne; Linda Hall; PADDS; SWETS; UMI; UnCover. **CCC.**
Description: Covers subjects, including organic chemistry, geology, mineralogy, biogeochemistry, oceanography and hydrology.
Refereed Serial

547 541.35   US   ISSN 0078-6152
QD601.A1   CODEN: ORPHAV
ORGANIC PHOTOCHEMISTRY: A SERIES OF ADVANCES. 1967. irreg., vol.11, 1991. price varies. Marcel Dekker, Inc., 270 Madison Ave., New York, NY 10016. TEL 212-696-9000. FAX 212-685-4540. TELEX 421419. Ed. O.L. Chapman; Pub. Graham Garratt. R&P contact: Julia Mulligan. **Indexed:** Chem.Abstr.
—BLDSC (6288.850000); CASDDS; CISTI; Linda Hall. **CCC.**
Refereed Serial

547 541.39   US   ISSN 0030-4948
QD262   CODEN: OPPIAK
ORGANIC PREPARATIONS AND PROCEDURES INTERNATIONAL; the new journal for organic synthesis. 1971. bi-m. $110 to individuals; institutions $235 (effective 1996). Organic Preparations and Procedures, Inc., Box 9, Newton Highlands, MA 02161. Ed. J.P. Anselme. adv.; bk.rev.; index. circ. 600. (back issues avail.) **Indexed:** ASCA, Chem.Abstr., Chem.Cit.Ind., Chem.Titles, Curr.Chem.React, Curr.Cont., Ind.Chem., Ind.Sci.Rev., Sci.Cit.Ind., SSCI. **Document type:** academic/scholarly publication.
—BLDSC (6288.875000); CASDDS; CISTI; Genuine Article; Linda Hall; SWETS; UnCover.
Refereed Serial

CHEMISTRY — ORGANIC CHEMISTRY

547 UK
▼**ORGANIC PROCESS RESEARCH AND DEVELOPMENT.** 1997. bi-m. £264($380) The Royal Society of Chemistry, Thomas Graham House, Science Park, Milton Rd., Cambridge CB4 4WF, England. TEL 44-1223-420066. FAX 44-1223-423429. E-mail: sales@rsc.org; URL: http://chemistry.rsc.org/rsc/. (Subscr. to: American Chemical Society, 1155 Sixteenth St., N.W., Washington, DC 20036. TEL 202-776-8100. FAX 202-872-6067) **Document type:** academic/scholarly publication.
Description: Contains original research reports on developments relating to batch and semi-batch chemical process industries.

547 541.39 US ISSN 0078-6160
ORGANIC REACTION MECHANISMS. ANNUAL SURVEY. 1966. irreg., latest 1991. price varies. John Wiley & Sons, Inc., 605 Third Ave., New York, NY 10158. TEL 212-850-6000. FAX 212-850-6088. TELEX 12-7063. Ed.Bd. **Indexed:** Chem.Abstr.
Refereed Serial

547 541.39 US ISSN 0078-6179
QD251 CODEN: ORREAW
ORGANIC REACTIONS. 1942. irreg., vol.43, 1993. price varies. John Wiley & Sons, Inc., 605 Third Ave., New York, NY 10158. TEL 212-850-6000. FAX 212-850-6088. Ed. W.G. Dauben. **Indexed:** Biol.Abstr., Chem.Abstr., Chem.Cit.Ind., Curr.Cont., Ind.Sci.Rev., Nutr.Abstr. **Document type:** monographic series.
—BLDSC (6288.910000); CASDDS; CISTI; Linda Hall; SWETS.
Refereed Serial

547 541.39 US ISSN 0078-6209
QD262 CODEN: ORSYAT
ORGANIC SYNTHESES. (Vols. 1-69 avail. in: Organic Syntheses - Collective Volumes) vol.71, 1993. a. price varies. John Wiley & Sons, Inc., 605 Third Ave., New York, NY 10158. TEL 212-850-6000. FAX 212-850-6088. (also avail. in microform from PMC) **Indexed:** Abstr.Bull.Inst.Pap.Chem., ASCA, Chem.Abstr. **Document type:** monographic series.
—BLDSC (6288.950000); CASDDS; CISTI; SWETS; UnCover.
Refereed Serial

547 541.39 US ISSN 0078-6217
QD262
ORGANIC SYNTHESES - COLLECTIVE VOLUMES. 1941. irreg., vol.8, nos.1-69, 1993. price varies. John Wiley & Sons, Inc., 605 Third Ave., New York, NY 10158. TEL 212-850-6000. FAX 212-850-6088. **Document type:** monographic series.
—CISTI; Linda Hall; SWETS. CCC.

547 US ISSN 1047-773X
ORGANIC SYNTHESIS; theory and applications. 1989. irreg., vol.3, 1996. $109.50. J A I Press Inc., 55 Old Post Rd., No.2, Box 1678, Greenwich, CT 06830-1678. TEL 203-661-7602. FAX 203-661-0792. E-mail: jai@jaipress.com. (In Europe: JAI Press Ltd., 38 Tavistock St., Covent Garden, London WC2E 7PB, England. TEL 44-171-379-8834. FAX 44-171-379-8835) Ed. Tomas Hudlicky. **Document type:** academic/scholarly publication, monographic series.
—CCC.
Description: Covers areas of organic synthesis ranging from the latest developments in enantioselective methodologies to reviews of updated chemical methods.

547 US ISSN 0078-6225
ORGANISCHE CHEMIE IN EINZELDARSTELLUNGEN. 1950. irreg. price varies. Springer-Verlag, 175 Fifth Ave., New York, NY 10010. TEL 212-460-1500. FAX 212-473-6272. (Also: Berlin, Heidelberg, Tokyo and Vienna) (reprint service avail. from ISI) **Document type:** academic/scholarly publication.

547 615.9 GW
ORGANOHALOGEN COMPOUNDS. (Text in English) irreg., vol.30. DM.200. (Verein zur Foerderung der Umweltforschung, -Erziehung und Oeffentlichkeitsarbeit e.V.) Eco-Informa Press, Jean-Paul-Str. 30, 95444 Bayreuth, Germany. TEL 49-921-552156. FAX 49-921-54626. Ed. Dr. O. Hutzinger. **Document type:** academic/scholarly publication.

547.05 UK ISSN 0301-0074
QD410 CODEN: OGMCAQ
ORGANOMETALLIC CHEMISTRY. 1971. a. price varies. The Royal Society of Chemistry, Thomas Graham House, Science Park, Milton Rd., Cambridge CB4 4WF, England. TEL 44-1223-420066. FAX 44-1223-423623. E-mail: sales@rsc.org; URL: http://chemistry.rsc.org/rsc/. (Subscr. to: Turpin Distribution Services Ltd., Blackhorse Road, Letchworth, Herts. SG6 1HN, England. TEL 44-1462-672555. FAX 44-1462-480947; Subscr. in N. America to: ACS, 1155 Sixteenth St., N.W., Washington, DC 22036, USA. TEL 202-776-8100. FAX 202-872-6067) Eds E.W. Abel, F.G. Stone. charts; illus.; index. (back issues avail.) **Indexed:** Chem.Abstr. **Document type:** academic/scholarly publication.
—BLDSC (6291.080000); CASDDS; CISTI; Ei; Linda Hall; UnCover. CCC.
Description: Includes extensive references.

547.5 RU ISSN 0955-8586
QD410
ORGANOMETALLIC CHEMISTRY IN THE U S S R. English translation of: Metalloorganicheskaya Khimiya. bi-m. Maik Nauka - Interperiodica, Mezhdunarodnyi Otdel, Ul. Profsoyuznaya, 90, 117864 Moscow, Russia. (Subscr. to: Maik Nauka - Interperiodica, Subscription Office, Box 1831, Birmingham, AL 35201-1831, U.S.A. TEL 205-995-1567. FAX 205-995-1588) **Indexed:** Chem.Cit.Ind. **Document type:** academic/scholarly publication.
—CISTI; Genuine Article.

ORGANOMETALLIC COMPOUNDS; abstracts of literature and patents relating to compounds which contain at least metal, carbon and hydrogen atoms. see CHEMISTRY – *Abstracting, Bibliographies, Statistics*

547 JA ISSN 0917-1274
ORGANOMETALLIC NEWS. (Text in Japanese) q. Kinki Chemical Society, Division of Organometallic Chemistry - Kinki Kagaku Kyokai Yuki Kinzoku Bukai, 8-4, Utsubohonmachi 1-chome, Nishi-ku, Osaka 550, Japan. TEL 06-441-5531. FAX 06-443-6685.
—BLDSC (6291.100700).

547 US ISSN 0276-7333
QD410 CODEN: ORGND7
ORGANOMETALLICS. 1982. m. $1340 to institutional non-members; members $98 (effective 1997). American Chemical Society, 1155 16th St., N.W., Washington, DC 20036. TEL 800-333-9511. FAX 614-447-3671. (Subscr. to: Membership and Subscription Services, Box 3337, Columbus, OH 43210. TEL 614-447-3776) Ed. Dr. Dietmar Seyferth. adv.; charts; index. circ. 2,800. (also avail. in microform; microfiche; back issues avail.) **Indexed:** ASCA, Cadscan, Chem.Abstr., Chem.Cit.Ind., Chem.Infd., Curr.Cont., Ind.Chem., Ind.Sci.Rev., Lead Abstr., Mass Spectr.Bull., Mat.Sci.Cit.Ind., Sci.Cit.Ind., Zincscan. **Document type:** academic/scholarly publication.
●Also available online. Vendor(s): STN International (CJACS).
—BLDSC (6291.102500); CASDDS; CISTI; Ei; Genuine Article; Linda Hall; SWETS; UMI; UnCover. CCC.
Refereed Serial

547 UK ISSN 0306-0713
QD412.P1 CODEN: OPCMAZ
ORGANOPHOSPHORUS CHEMISTRY. 1968. a. price varies. The Royal Society of Chemistry, Thomas Graham House, Science Park, Milton Rd., Cambridge CB4 4WF, England. TEL 44-1223-420066. FAX 44-1223-423623. E-mail: sales@rsc.org; URL: http://chemistry.rsc.org/rsc/. (Subscr. to: Turpin Distribution Services Ltd., Blackhorse Rd. Letchworth, Herts. SG6 1HN, England. TEL 44-1462-672555. FAX 44-1223-480947; Subscr. in N. America to: ACS, 1155 Sixteenth St., N.W., Washington, DC 22036, USA. TEL 202-776-8100. FAX 202-872-6067) Eds. B.J. Walker, D.W. Allen. charts; illus.; index. (back issues avail.) **Indexed:** Chem.Abstr. **Document type:** academic/scholarly publication.
—BLDSC (6291.110000); CASDDS; CISTI; Linda Hall. CCC.

547 BU ISSN 0209-4541
QD281.09 CODEN: OXCODW
OXIDATION COMMUNICATIONS. (Text in English) 1977. q. $285 in Europe; elsewhere $295 (effective 1998). SciBulCom, Ltd., 7, Nezabravka Str., P.O. Box 249, 1113 Sofia, Bulgaria. TEL 359-79934211. FAX 3592-517025. TELEX 25427. E-mail: margi@bgearn.bitnet. Ed. Slavi K. Ivanov. adv. contact: Zh. Kalitchin. bk.rev. **Indexed:** ASCA, Chem.Abstr., Chem.Cit.Ind., Curr.Cont. **Document type:** academic/scholarly publication.
—BLDSC (6321.035000); CASDDS; CISTI; Genuine Article. **CCC.**
Description: Devoted to the global oxy-reduction interactions in nature with an international focus on new fundamental and technological research.

660 US ISSN 1084-0184
QA381.8 CODEN: PLPOFQ
▼**PLASMAS AND POLYMERS.** 1996. q. $175 (foreign $204.75) (effective 1998). Plenum Publishing Corp., 233 Spring St., New York, NY 10013-1578. TEL 212-620-8000. FAX 212-463-0742. TELEX 23-421139. Eds. R. D'Agostino, B. Ratner. adv.; bk.rev. (also avail. in microfilm from UMI) **Document type:** academic/scholarly publication.
—BLDSC (6528.789000); AskIEEE; CASDDS; CISTI; KR SourceOne.
Description: Presents research on the synthesis, characterization, physical properties and technological possibilities of plasmas used in depositing or treating organic or polymeric substances.
Refereed Serial

547 PL ISSN 0032-2725
CODEN: POLIA4
POLIMERY/POLYMERS; macromolecular materials, chemistry and technology of polymers. Variant title: Polimery Tworzywa Wieloczasteczkowe. (Text in English, Polish; summaries in English, Polish, Russian) 1956. m. $126 (effective 1994). Instytut Chemii Przemyslowej - Industrial Chemistry Research Institute, Ul. Rydgiera 8, 01-793 Warsaw, Poland. TEL 48-22-633-9804. FAX 48-22-633-8295. TELEX 813586 PL. Ed. Barbara Witowska-Mocek. adv.; bk.rev.; bibl.; pat. **Indexed:** Abstr.Bull.Inst.Pap.Chem., Alloys Ind., ASCA, Chem.Abstr., Eng.Ind., Eng.Mat.Abstr., Intl.Polym.Sci.& Tech., Met.Abstr., Met.Abstr.Ind., Nonfer.Met.Alert, PCC Alert, RAPRA, Ref.Zh., Steels Alert, Text.Tech.Dig., W.R.C.Inf., World Alum.Abstr., World Surf.Coat. **Document type:** academic/scholarly publication, newsletter.
—CASDDS; CISTI; Genuine Article; Linda Hall; SWETS.
Former titles (until 1961): Tworzywa Wieloczasteczkowe (ISSN 0372-3364); (until 1960): Towarzywa, Guma, Lakiery (ISSN 0372-3313); (until 1958): Tworzywa.
Description: Covers such topics as: synthesis, analysis and properties of polymers, technology of plastics, rubbers, synthetic fibers and lacquers, manufacturing processes and apparatuses, processing machinery.

668.9 610 PL ISSN 0370-0747
CODEN: PMYMAX
POLIMERY W MEDYCYNIE. 1965. 4/yr. 8 Zl.($58) (effective 1998). Akademia Medyczna we Wroclawiu, Zaklad Chirurgii Eksperymentalnej i Badania Biomaterialow, Ul. Poniatowskiego 2, 50-326 Wroclaw, Poland. TEL 48-71-226310. FAX 48-71-215729. (Dist. by: Mezhdunarodnaya Kniga, B. Yakimanka 39, 117049 Moscow, Russia. TEL 7-095-2384967. FAX 7-095-2384634) Ed. Roman Rutowski. R&P contact: Urszula Tomczyk. adv. contact: Roman Rutowski. bk.rev.; circ. 800 (paid); 200 (controlled). **Document type:** academic/scholarly publication.
—BLDSC (6547.742600); CASDDS; CISTI.
Formerly (until 1971): Tworzywa Sztuczne w Medycynie (ISSN 0372-3356)
Refereed Serial

541 547 PL ISSN 0324-9824
POLITECHNIKA WROCLAWSKA. INSTYTUT CHEMII ORGANICZNEJ I FIZYCZNEJ. PRACE NAUKOWE. KONFERENCJE. (Text in Polish and English) 1974. irreg., no.8, 1988. price varies. Oficyna Wydawnicza Politechniki Wroclawskiej, Wybrzeze Wyspianskiego 27, 50-370 Wroclaw, Poland. TEL 48-71-222940. FAX 48-71-223664. TELEX 712550 PWRPL. (Dist. by: Ars Polona, Krakowskie Przedmiescie 7, Warsaw Poland) R&P contact: Halina Dudek. adv. circ. 325. **Document type:** proceedings.
—CISTI.

CHEMISTRY — ORGANIC CHEMISTRY

541 547   PL   ISSN 0324-9816
POLITECHNIKA WROCLAWSKA. INSTYTUT CHEMII ORGANICZNEJ I FIZYCZNEJ. PRACE NAUKOWE. MONOGRAFIE. (Text in Polish; summaries in English and Russian) 1969. irreg., no.21, 1990. price varies. Oficyna Wydawnicza Politechniki Wroclawskiej, Wybrzeze Wyspianskiego 27, 50-370 Wroclaw, Poland. TEL 48-71-222940. FAX 48-71-223664. TELEX 71-25-50 PWRPL. (Dist. by: Ars Polona, Krakowskie Przedmiescie 7, Warsaw, Poland) R&P contact: Halina Dudek. adv. **Document type:** monographic series.

541 547   PL   ISSN 0370-081X
CODEN: PNICBX
POLITECHNIKA WROCLAWSKA. INSTYTUT CHEMII ORGANICZNEJ I FIZYCZNEJ. PRACE NAUKOWE. STUDIA I MATERIALY. (Text in Polish; summaries in English and Russian) 1970. irreg., no.8, 1978. price varies. Oficyna Wydawnicza Politechniki Wroclawskiej, Wybrzeze Wyspianskiego 27, 50-370 Wroclaw, Poland. TEL 48-71-222940. FAX 48-71-223664. TELEX 712559 PWRPL. (Dist. by: Ars Polona, Krakowskie Przedmiescie 7, Warsaw, Poland) R&P contact: Halina Dudek. adv. **Indexed:** Chem.Abstr. **Document type:** academic/scholarly publication.
—CASDDS.

547   NE   ISSN 1040-6638
QD335   CODEN: PARCEO
POLYCYCLIC AROMATIC COMPOUNDS. 1990. q. $255 (effective 1998). Gordon and Breach - Harwood Academic, Amsteldisk 166, 1st Fl., 1079 LH Amsterdam, Netherlands. URL: http://www.gbhap.com/Polycyclic_Aromatic_Compounds/. (Subscr. to: International Publishers Distributor, Box 32160, Newark, NJ 07102. TEL 800-545-8398. FAX 215-750-6343) Ed. Maximilian Zander. (also avail. in microform) **Indexed:** ASCA, Chem.Cit.Ind., Food Sci.& Tech.Abstr., Intl.Polym.Sci.& Tech., RAPRA. **Document type:** academic/scholarly publication.
●Also available online.
Also available on CD-ROM.
—BLDSC (6547.558000); CASDDS; CISTI; SWETS. **CCC.**
Refereed Serial

547 660.284   UK   ISSN 0032-3861
TP156.P6   CODEN: POLMAG
POLYMER. 1960. 26/yr. fl.6518($3746) (effective 1998). Elsevier Science Ltd., Part of the Reed Elsevier group, Langford Ln., Kidlington, Oxford OX5 3DR, England. TEL 44-1865-843000. FAX 44-1865-843010. TELEX 83111 BHPOXF G. E-mail: nlinfo-f@elsevier.com; usinfo-f@elsevier.com; forinfo-kyf04035@niftyserve.or.jp; URL: http://www.elsevier.nl/. (Subscr. to: Elsevier Science, Regional Sales Office, P.O. Box 211, 1000 AE Amsterdam, Netherlands. TEL 31-20-4853757. FAX 31-20-4853432; Subscr. in the Americas to: Elsevier Science, Regional Sales Office, Box 945, New York, NY 10159-0945. TEL 212-633-3730. FAX 212-633-3680; Subscr. in Australasia and the Far East to: Elsevier Science (Singapore) Pte Ltd, No.1 Temasek Ave., No.17-01 Millenia Tower, Singapore 039192, Singapore. TEL 65-434-3727. FAX 65-337-2230) Ed.Bd. adv. contact: Paul Titcombe. bk.rev.; abstr.; bibl.; charts; index; circ. 2,000 (paid). (also avail. in microfilm from UMI; back issues avail.) **Indexed:** Abstr.Bull.Inst.Pap.Chem., Alloys Ind., ASCA, Chem.Abstr., Chem.Cit.Ind., Curr.Cont., Curr.Pack.Abstr., Eng.Mat.Abstr., Ind.Sci.Rev., INSPEC (1971-), Mat.Sci.Cit.Ind., Met.Abstr., Met.Abstr.Ind., PCC Alert, RAPRA, Sci.Cit.Ind., Steels Alert, Text.Tech.Dig., World Alum.Abstr., World Surf.Coat., World Text.Abstr. **Document type:** academic/scholarly publication.
—BLDSC (6547.700000); AskIEEE; CASDDS; CISTI; Ei; EMDOCS; Genuine Article; KR SourceOne; Linda Hall; SWETS; UMI; UnCover. **CCC.**
Incorporates (in 1991): Polymer Communications (ISSN 0263-6476)
Description: Provides international coverage of the science and technology of polymers.
Refereed Serial

660.284 668.4   UK   ISSN 0141-3910
QD380   CODEN: PDSTDW
POLYMER DEGRADATION AND STABILITY. 1979. m. fl.4260($2448) (effective 1997). Elsevier Science Ltd., P.O. Box 800, Kidlington, Oxford OX5 1DX, England. TEL 44-1865-843000. FAX 44-1865-843010. E-mail: nlinfo-f@elsevier.nl; usinfo-f@elsevier.com; forinfo-kyf04035@niftyserve.or.jp; URL: http://www.elsevier.nl/. (Subscr. to: Elsevier Science, Regional Sales Office, P.O. Box 211, 1000 AE Amsterdam, Netherlands. TEL 31-20-4853757. FAX 31-20-4853432; Subscr. in the Americas to: Elsevier Science, Regional Sales Office, Box 945, New York, NY 10159-0945. TEL 212-633-3730. FAX 212-633-3680; Subscr. in Australasia and the Far East to: Elsevier Science (Singapore) Pte Ltd, No.1 Temasek Ave., No.17-01 Millenia Tower, Singapore 039192, Singapore. TEL 65-434-3727. FAX 65-337-2230) Eds. N. Grassie, J.C.W. Chen. adv.; bk.rev.; charts; illus.; index. (also avail. in microform from UMI; back issues avail.) **Indexed:** Alloys Ind., ASCA, Chem.Abstr., Chem.Cit.Ind., Curr.Cont., Eng.Ind., Eng.Mat.Abstr., Excerp.Med., Ind.Sci.Rev., Intl.Polym.Sci.& Tech., Mat.Sci.Cit.Ind., Met.Abstr., Met.Abstr.Ind., Nonfer.Met.Alert, PCC Alert, RAPRA, Sci.Cit.Ind., Steels Alert, World Alum.Abstr., World Surf.Coat. **Document type:** academic/scholarly publication.
—BLDSC (6547.704700); CASDDS; CISTI; Ei; Genuine Article; KR SourceOne; Linda Hall; SWETS; UnCover. **CCC.**
Incorporates: Polymer Photochemistry (ISSN 0144-2880)
Description: Deals with the degradation reactions and their control which are a major preoccupation of practitioners of the many and diverse aspects of modern polymer technology.
Refereed Serial

POLYMER ENGINEERING AND SCIENCE. see *ENGINEERING — Chemical Engineering*

POLYMER GELS AND NETWORKS. see *ENGINEERING — Chemical Engineering*

547   JA   ISSN 0032-3896
QD380   CODEN: POLJB8
POLYMER JOURNAL. (Text in English) 1970. m. 47000 Yen. Society of Polymer Science, Japan - Nihon Kobunshi Gakkai, Tsukiji Daisan Nagaoka Bldg., 2-4-2 Tsukiji, Chuo-ku, Tokyo 104, Japan. TEL 03-3543-3772. FAX 03-3545-8560. Ed. Akihiro Abe. index. circ. 2,000. **Indexed:** Abstr.Bull.Inst.Pap.Chem., Alloys Ind., ASCA, Chem.Abstr., Chem.Cit.Ind., Curr.Cont., Eng.Mat.Abstr., Intl.Polym.Sci.& Tech., JCT, JTA, Mat.Sci.Cit.Ind., Met.Abstr., Met.Abstr.Ind., Nonfer.Met.Alert, PCC Alert, RAPRA, Sci.Cit.Ind., Steels Alert, Text.Tech.Dig., World Alum.Abstr. **Document type:** academic/scholarly publication.
—BLDSC (6547.707000); CASDDS; CISTI; Ei; Genuine Article; Linda Hall; SWETS; UnCover. **CCC.**
Description: International coverage of every field of polymers such as polymer chemistry, physics and biopolymers.

541.393   NE   ISSN 0275-5777
POLYMER MONOGRAPHS. 1968. irreg., latest vol.11. price varies. Gordon and Breach - Harwood Academic, Amsteldisk 166, 1st Fl., 1079 LH Amsterdam, Netherlands. (Subscr. to: International Publishers Distributor, Box 32160, Newark, NJ 07102. TEL 800-545-8398. FAX 215-750-6343) Ed. M. Huglin. **Indexed:** INSPEC. **Document type:** monographic series.
—BLDSC (6547.712500); CISTI.
Refereed Serial

660.284 547   NE   ISSN 0032-3918
TP1101   CODEN: PLYNBU
POLYMER NEWS. 1970. m. $293 (effective 1998). Gordon and Breach - Harwood Academic, Amsteldisk 166, 1st Fl., 1079 LH Amsterdam, Netherlands. (Subscr. to: International Publishers Distributor, Box 32160, Newark, NJ 07102. TEL 800-545-8398. FAX 215-750-6343) Ed. G.S. Kirshenbaum. adv.; bk.rev.; illus.; pat.; tr.lit.; index. (also avail. in microform) **Indexed:** Chem.Abstr., INSPEC, Intl.Polym.Sci. & Tech., PROMT, RAPRA. **Document type:** trade publication.
—BLDSC (6547.713000); CASDDS; CISTI; SWETS. **CCC.**
Refereed Serial

547 660.084   US   ISSN 0360-2559
CODEN: PPTEC7
POLYMER-PLASTICS TECHNOLOGY AND ENGINEERING. Hardcover edition (ISSN 0092-5012) 1970. q. $995 (foreign $1010) (effective 1998). Marcel Dekker Journals, 270 Madison Ave., New York, NY 10016. TEL 212-696-9000. FAX 212-685-4540. TELEX 421419 MARDEEK. (Subscr. to: Box 5017, Monticello, NY 12701) Ed. Nicholas P. Cheremisinoff. adv. (also avail. in microform from RPI) **Indexed:** Alloys Ind., ASCA, Chem.Abstr., Chem.Cit.Ind., Curr.Cont., Eng.Mat.Abstr., Excerpt.Med., INSPEC (1989-), Intl.Polym.Sci.& Tech., Mat.Sci.Cit.Ind., Met.Abstr., Met.Abstr.Ind., Nonfer.Met.Alert, PCC Alert, RAPRA, SSCI, Steels Alert, W.R.C.Inf., World Alum.Abstr., World Surf.Coat. **Document type:** academic/scholarly publication.
—BLDSC (6547.714500); AskIEEE; CASDDS; CISTI; Ei; EMDOCS; Genuine Article; KR SourceOne; Linda Hall; SWETS; UMI; UnCover. **CCC.**
Formerly (until 1972): Journal of Macromolecular Science: Part D - Reviews in Polymer Processing and Technology (ISSN 0022-2321); **Incorporates** (1982-1990): Polymer-Plastics Manufacturing Journal; Which was formerly: Polymer Process Engineering (ISSN 0735-7931)
Refereed Serial

547   US   ISSN 0032-3934
CODEN: ACPPAY
POLYMER PREPRINTS. 1960. s-a. $100. American Chemical Society, Division of Polymer Chemistry, Inc., College of Dentistry, Ohio State University, 305 W. 12th Ave., Columbus, OH 43210. FAX 614-292-9422. E-mail: culbertson.4@oso.edu. Ed. Bill M. Culbertson. R&P contact: Bill M. Culbertson. adv. contact: Bill M. Culbertson. circ. 9,000. (back issues avail.) **Indexed:** Alloys Ind., Chem.Abstr., Eng.Mat.Abstr., Met.Abstr.Ind., Met.Abstr., Nonfer.Met.Alert, PCC Alert, RAPRA, Steels Alert, Text.Tech.Dig., World Alum.Abstr. **Document type:** academic/scholarly publication.
—BLDSC (6547.715000); CASDDS; CISTI; Ei; SWETS.

547   RU   ISSN 0965-545X
QD471   CODEN: PSSAFE
POLYMER SCIENCE. Russian edition: Vysokomokelularnye Soedineniya. Seriya A i B (ISSN 1023-3091) (In 2 Series: A & B) 1960. m. $2164 in U.S. & Canada (elsewhere $2382) (effective 1995). Maik Nauka - Interperiodica, Mezhdunarodnyi Otdel, Ul. Profsoyuznaya, 90, 117864 Moscow, Russia. TEL 7-095-3360066. FAX 7-095-3360666. (Subscr. to: Maik Nauka - Interperiodica, Subscription Office, Box 1831, Birmingham, AL 35201-1831, U.S.A. TEL 205-995-1567. FAX 205-995-1588) adv.; abstr.; charts; illus.; index. circ. 1,000. (also avail. in microfilm from UMI; reprint service avail. from UMI) **Indexed:** Alloys Ind., Appl.Mech.Rev., Art & Archaeol.Tech.Abstr., Eng.Mat.Abstr., INSPEC, Intl.Polym.Sci.& Tech., Met.Abstr.Ind., Met.Abstr., Nonfer.Met.Alert, PCC Alert, RAPRA, Steels Alert, World Alum.Abstr. **Document type:** academic/scholarly publication.
—BLDSC (0416.904000); CISTI; Linda Hall; SWETS; UMI; UnCover. **CCC.**
Formerly (until Jan. 1992): Polymer Science U.S.S.R. (ISSN 0032-3950)
Description: Offers a comprehensive view of all multidisciplinary aspects of theoretical and experimental polymer research and application.
Refereed Serial

660.284   US   ISSN 0093-6286
CODEN: POSTB5
POLYMER SCIENCE AND TECHNOLOGY. 1973. irreg., vol.38, 1988. price varies. Plenum Publishing Corp., 233 Spring St., New York, NY 10013-1578. TEL 212-620-8000. FAX 212-463-0742. TELEX 23-421139. E-mail: books@plenum.com. (back issues avail.) **Indexed:** INSPEC, Sugar Ind.Abstr. **Document type:** monographic series.
—CASDDS; CISTI. **CCC.**
Refereed Serial

POLYMER TESTING. see *PLASTICS*

CHEMISTRY — ORGANIC CHEMISTRY

660.284 US ISSN 0743-0515
TP935 CODEN: PMSEDG
POLYMERIC MATERIALS SCIENCE AND ENGINEERING. s-a. $30. American Chemical Society, Division of Polymeric Materials Science & Engineering, 1155 16th St., N.W., Washington, DC 20036. circ. 4,200. (back issues avail.) **Indexed:** Alloys Ind., Chem.Abstr., Eng.Mat.Abstr., Int.Packag.Abstr., Met.Abstr.Ind., Met.Abstr., Nonfer.Met.Alert, Nonwov.Abstr., Paper & Bd.Abstr., PCC Alert, Steels Alert, Text.Tech.Dig., World Alum.Abstr. **Document type:** academic/scholarly publication.
—BLDSC (6547.741400); CASDDS; CISTI; Ei; Linda Hall; SWETS.
Incorporates: Organic Coatings and Plastics Chemistry Preprints; Which was formerly titled: Coatings and Plastics Preprints.
Refereed Serial

547.3466 US ISSN 0092-0576
QC482.D5
POWDER DIFFRACTION FILE SEARCH MANUAL. ORGANIC. Cover title: Powder Diffraction File Search Manual (Numerical, Alphabetical, Formulae) Organic Compounds. (Subseries of the Committee's Publication SMO) a. $300. Joint Committee on Powder Diffraction Standards, International Centre for Diffraction Data, 12 Campus Blvd., Newtown Square, PA 19073. TEL 610-325-9814. FAX 610-325-9823. TELEX 847170. index. (also avail. in microfiche; magnetic tape)
●Also available on CD-ROM.

PREVISIONS GLISSANTES DETAILLEES EN PERSPECTIVES SECTORIELLES (VOL.21): CHIMIE ORGANIQUE. see *BUSINESS AND ECONOMICS — Economic Situation And Conditions*

PROBLEMY PROJEKTOWE PRZEMYSLU I BUDOWNICTWA/PROJECT DESIGN PROBLEMS OF THE INDUSTRY AND BUILDING ENGINEERING; czasopismo naukowo-techniczne. see *METALLURGY*

PROGRESS IN COLLOID AND POLYMER SCIENCE. see *CHEMISTRY — Physical Chemistry*

547 UK ISSN 0163-7827
QD301 CODEN: PLIRDW
PROGRESS IN LIPID RESEARCH. 1952. q. fl.1494($858) (effective 1998). Elsevier Science Ltd., Pergamon, P.O. Box 800, Kidlington, Oxford OX5 1DX, England. TEL 44-1865-843000. FAX 44-1865-843010. E-mail: nlinfo-f@elsevier.nl; usinfo-f@elsevier.com; forinfo-kyf04035@niftyserve.or.jp; URL: http://www.elsevier.nl/. (Subscr. to: Elsevier Science, Regional Sales Office, P.O. Box 211, 1000 AE Amsterdam, Netherlands. TEL 31-20-4853757. FAX 31-20-4853432; Subscr. in the Americas to: Elsevier Science, Regional Sales Office, Box 945, New York, NY 10159-0945. TEL 212-633-3730. FAX 212-633-3680; Subscr. in Australasia and the Far East to: Elsevier Science (Singapore) Pte Ltd, No.1 Temasek Ave., No.17-01 Millenia Tower, Singapore 039192, Singapore. TEL 65-434-3727. FAX 65-337-2230) Eds. John L. Harwood, Howard Sprecher. (also avail. in microfilm from UMI) **Indexed:** ASCA, Biol.Abstr., Chem.Abstr., Curr.Adv.Biochem., Curr.Adv.Cell & Devel.Biol., Curr.Adv.Ecol.Sci., Curr.Cont., Dairy Sci.Abstr., Food Sci. & Tech.Abstr., Ind.Med., Ind.Sci.Rev., Nutr.Abstr., Sci.Cit.Ind. **Document type:** academic/scholarly publication.
—BLDSC (6868.450000); CASDDS; CISTI; Ei; Genuine Article; KNAW; Linda Hall; SWETS; UMI; UnCover. CCC.
Formerly: Progress in the Chemistry of Fats and Other Lipids (ISSN 0079-6832)
Description: Includes topics on analysis, properties, chemistry, metabolism, medicine, nutrition, molecular biology, food science and technology related to lipid chemistry.
Refereed Serial

PROGRESS IN ORGANIC COATINGS; an international review journal. see *PAINTS AND PROTECTIVE COATINGS*

PROGRESS IN PHYSICAL ORGANIC CHEMISTRY. see *CHEMISTRY — Physical Chemistry*

547 660.284 UK ISSN 0079-6700
QD281.P6 CODEN: PRPSB8
PROGRESS IN POLYMER SCIENCE; an international review journal. 1967. 8/yr. fl.2428($1396) (effective 1998). Elsevier Science Ltd., Pergamon, P.O. Box 800, Kidlington, Oxford OX5 1DX, England. TEL 44-1865-843000. FAX 44-1865-843010. E-mail: nlinfo-f@elsevier.nl; usinfo-f@elsevier.com; forinfo-kyf04035@niftyserve.or.jp; URL: http://www.elsevier.nl/. (Subscr. to: Elsevier Science, Regional Sales Office, P.O. Box 211, 1000 AE Amsterdam, Netherlands. TEL 31-20-4853757. FAX 31-20-4853432; Subscr. in the Americas to: Elsevier Science, Regional Sales Office, Box 945, New York, NY 10159-0945. TEL 212-633-3730. FAX 212-633-3680; Subscr. in Australasia and the Far East to: Elsevier Science (Singapore) Pte Ltd, No.1 Temasek Ave., No.17-01 Millenia Tower, Singapore 039192, Singapore. TEL 65-434-3727. FAX 65-337-2230) Ed. O. Vogl. index. (also avail. in microfilm from UMI) **Indexed:** Alloys Ind., ASCA, Chem.Abstr., Chem.Cit.Ind., Curr.Cont., Eng.Mat.Abstr., HRIS, Ind.Sci.Rev., INSPEC, Intl.Polym.Sci.& Tech., Mat.Sci.Cit.Ind., Met.Abstr., Met.Abstr.Ind., Nonfer.Met.Alert, PCC Alert, RAPRA, Sci.Cit.Ind., Steels Alert, World Alum.Abstr. **Document type:** academic/scholarly publication.
—BLDSC (6873.570000); CASDDS; CISTI; Ei; Genuine Article; Linda Hall; SWETS; UMI; UnCover. CCC.
Description: Covers developments in polymers in the fields of chemistry, engineering and physics, as well as emerging disciplines such as the study of functional and specialty polymers.
Refereed Serial

547 NE ISSN 0165-2362
CODEN: PTOCD5
PROGRESS IN THEORETICAL ORGANIC CHEMISTRY. 1976. irreg., vol.3, 1982. price varies. Elsevier Science B.V., Books Division, P.O. Box 211, 1000 AE Amsterdam, Netherlands. TEL 31-20-4853911. FAX 31-20-4853705. TELEX 18582 ESPA NL. E-mail: nlinfo-f@elsevier.nl; usinfo-f@elsevier.com; forinfo-kyf04035@niftyserve.or.jp; URL: http://www.elsevier.nl/. (Subscr. in the Americas to: Elsevier Science, Regional Sales Office, Box 945, New York, NY 10159-0945. TEL 212-633-3730. FAX 212-633-3680; Subscr. in Australasia and the Far East to: Elsevier Science (Singapore) Pte Ltd, No.1 Temasek Ave., No.17-01 Millenia Tower, Singapore 039192, Singapore. TEL 65-434-3727. FAX 65-337-2230; Subscr. in Japan to: Elsevier Science Japan, 9-15 Higashi-Azabu 1-chome, Minato-ku, Tokyo 106, Japan. TEL 81-3-5561-5033. FAX 81-3-5561-5047) **Indexed:** Chem.Abstr., INSPEC. **Document type:** monographic series.
—CASDDS; CISTI.
Refereed Serial

547 RU ISSN 0079-6883
PROGRESS POLIMERNOI KHIMII. 1965. irreg. (Akademiya Nauk S.S.S.R., Institut Elementoorganicheskikh Soedinenii) Izdatel'stvo Nauka, 90 Profsoyuznaya ul., 117864 Moscow, Russia. TEL 234-05-84.

547 US ISSN 0341-2377
CODEN: RSCCDS
REACTIVITY AND STRUCTURE: CONCEPTS OF ORGANIC CHEMISTRY. 1975. irreg., vol.31, 1994. price varies. Springer-Verlag, 175 Fifth Ave., New York, NY 10010. TEL 212-460-1500. FAX 212-473-6272. (Also: Berlin, Heidelberg, Tokyo and Vienna) Ed.Bd. (reprint service avail. from ISI) **Document type:** academic/scholarly publication.
—BLDSC (7300.283000); CASDDS.
Refereed Serial

547 574.192 NE ISSN 0167-0115
CODEN: REPPDY
REGULATORY PEPTIDES. 1980. 21/yr. fl.3803($2186) (effective 1998). Elsevier Science B.V., P.O. Box 211, 1000 AE Amsterdam, Netherlands. TEL 31-20-4853911. FAX 31-20-4853598. TELEX 18582 ESPA NL. E-mail: nlinfo-f@elsevier.nl; usinfo-f@elsevier.com; forinfo-kyf04035@niftyserve.or.jp; URL: http://www.elsevier.nl/. (Subscr. in the Americas to: Elsevier Science, Regional Sales Office, Box 945, New York, NY 10159-0945. TEL 212-633-3730. FAX 212-633-3680; Subscr. in Australasia and the Far East to: Elsevier Science (Singapore) Pte Ltd, No.1 Temasek Ave., No.17-01 Millenia Tower, Singapore 039192, Singapore. TEL 65-434-3727. FAX 65-337-2230; Subscr. in Japan to: Elsevier Science Japan, 9-15 Higashi-Azabu 1-chome, Minato-ku, Tokyo 106, Japan. TEL 81-3-5561-5033. FAX 81-3-5561-5047) Eds. M.I. Phillips, R. Hakanson. (also avail. in microform from UMI; reprint service avail. from ISI,SWZ) **Indexed:** ASCA, Biol.Abstr., Chem.Abstr., Curr.Adv.Cell & Devel.Biol., Curr.Adv.Ecol.Sci., Curr.Cont., Dairy Sci.Abstr., Excerp.Med., Ind.Med., Ind.Sci.Rev., Neurosci.Cit.Ind., Sci.Cit.Ind. **Document type:** academic/scholarly publication.
—BLDSC (7350.030000); ADONIS; CASDDS; CISTI; Genuine Article; KNAW; SWETS; UnCover. CCC.
Description: Provides a medium for the rapid publication of interdisciplinary studies on the physiology and pathology of peptides of the gut, endocrine and nervous systems which regulate cell or tissue function.
Refereed Serial

REPORTS ON PROGRESS IN POLYMER PHYSICS IN JAPAN. see *PHYSICS*

547 US ISSN 0742-5996
QD390 CODEN: RSHAEE
RING SYSTEMS HANDBOOK. 1960. irreg. (every 4-5 yrs., latest 1993); 3 base vols. plus s-a. cum. supplements. $585 (supplements $370; combined $755) (effective 1998). Chemical Abstracts Service (Subsidiary of: American Chemical Society), 2540 Olentangy River Rd., Box 3012, Columbus, OH 43210-0012. TEL 614-447-3600; 800-333-9511. FAX 614-447-3713. TELEX 6842086. **Indexed:** Chem.Abstr. **Document type:** abstracting/indexing.
—BLDSC (7971.490400); CISTI.
Former titles: Parent Compound Handbook; Ring Index: A List of Ring Systems Used in Organic Chemistry. Supplement (ISSN 0080-309X)

664 IT ISSN 0035-6808
TP670.A1 CODEN: RISGAD
RIVISTA ITALIANA DELLE SOSTANZE GRASSE. 1924. m. L.180000 (foreign L.300000) (effective 1997). Stazione Sperimentale per le Industrie degli Oli e Grassi, Via Giuseppe Colombo 79, 20133 Milan, Italy. TEL 39-2-2361051. FAX 39-2-2363953. TELEX 340129 SSOG I. Ed. Enzo Fedeli. R&P contact: Fedeli Enzo. adv.: B&W page L.600000; trim 180 x 260; adv. contact: Lionello Cariboni. bk.rev.; abstr.; charts; illus.; stat.; index. circ. 4,000. (reprint service avail.) **Indexed:** Apic.Abstr., Biol.Abstr., Chem.Abstr., Dairy Sci.Abstr., Food Sci.& Tech.Abstr., Nutr.Abstr., Trop.Oil Seeds Abstr.
—BLDSC (7987.650000); CASDDS; Linda Hall; SWETS.
Description: Publishes original works concerning chemistry, analysis, technology, and problems relating to pollution in fields connected with fats and oils and derivatives.

CHEMISTRY — ORGANIC CHEMISTRY

547 NE ISSN 0080-3758
RODD'S CHEMISTRY OF CARBON COMPOUNDS. (2nd edition) (Supplement avail.). 1964. irreg., latest 1990. price varies. Elsevier Science B.V., Books Division, P.O. Box 211, 1000 AE Amsterdam, Netherlands. TEL 31-20-4853911. FAX 31-20-4853705. TELEX 18582 ESPA NL. E-mail: nlinfo-f@elsevier.nl; usinfo-f@elsevier.com; forinfo-kyf04035@niftyserve.or.jp; URL: http://www.elsevier.nl/. (Subscr. in the Americas to: Elsevier Science, Regional Sales Office, Box 945, New York, NY 10159-0945. TEL 212-633-3730. FAX 212-633-3680; Subscr. in Australasia and the Far East to: Elsevier Science (Singapore) Pte Ltd, No.1 Temasek Ave., No.17-01 Millenia Tower, Singapore 039192, Singapore. TEL 65-434-3727. FAX 65-337-2230; Subscr. in Japan to: Elsevier Science Japan, 9-15 Higashi-Azabu 1-chome, Minato-ku, Tokyo 106, Japan. TEL 81-3-5561-5033. FAX 81-3-5561-5047) Eds. S. Coffey, M.F. Ansell. **Document type:** monographic series.
Refereed Serial

547 NE
RODD'S CHEMISTRY OF CARBON COMPOUNDS. SUPPLEMENTS TO THE SECOND EDITION. (Text in English) 1973. irreg., latest 1995. price varies. Elsevier Science B.V., Books Division, P.O. Box 211, 1000 AE Amsterdam, Netherlands. TEL 31-20-4853911. FAX 31-20-4853705. TELEX 18582 ESPA NL. E-mail: nlinfo-f@elsevier.nl; usinfo-f@elsevier.com; forinfo-kyf04035@niftyserve.or.jp; URL: http://www.elsevier.nl/. (Subscr. in the Americas to: Elsevier Science, Regional Sales Office, Box 945, New York, NY 10159-0945. TEL 212-633-3730. FAX 212-633-3680; Subscr. in Australasia and the Far East to: Elsevier Science (Singapore) Pte Ltd, No.1 Temasek Ave., No.17-01 Millenia Tower, Singapore 039192, Singapore. TEL 65-434-3727. FAX 65-337-2230; Subscr. in Japan to: Elsevier Science Japan, 9-15 Higashi-Azabu 1-chome, Minato-ku, Tokyo 106, Japan. TEL 81-3-5561-5033. FAX 81-3-5561-5047) Ed. M. Sainsbury. (back issues avail.) **Document type:** monographic series.
Refereed Serial

547 UK ISSN 0069-3030
QD1 CODEN: CACBB4
ROYAL SOCIETY OF CHEMISTRY. ANNUAL REPORTS ON THE PROGRESS OF CHEMISTRY. SECTION B: ORGANIC CHEMISTRY. 1904. a. £116 (US $210); all 3 sections £324 (US $583) (effective 1997). The Royal Society of Chemistry, Thomas Graham House, Science Park, Milton Rd., Cambridge CB4 4WF, England. TEL 44-1223-420066. FAX 44-1223-423623. E-mail: sales@rsc.org; URL: http://chemistry.rsc.org/rsc/. (Subscr. to: Turpin Distribution Services Ltd., Blackhorse Rd., Letchworth, Herts. SG6 1HN, England. TEL 44-1462-672555. FAX 44-1462-480947) Eds. A.G. Davies, P.G. Garrett. index, cum.index: vols.1-46. circ. 3,500. (back issues avail.) **Indexed:** INIS Atomind. **Document type:** academic/scholarly publication.
—BLDSC (1513.820000); CASDDS; CISTI; Linda Hall. **CCC.**
Description: Provides for the general reader critical coverage of the important advances in organic chemistry.

547 574.192 UK ISSN 0300-922X
QD241 CODEN: JCPRB4
ROYAL SOCIETY OF CHEMISTRY. JOURNAL: PERKIN TRANSACTIONS 1; a journal of organic and bio-organic chemistry. Key Title: Perkin Transactions 1. Online edition (UK ISSN 1364-5463) 1972. fortn. £860 to institutions (US $1548) (effective 1997). The Royal Society of Chemistry, Thomas Graham House, Science Park, Milton Rd., Cambridge CB4 4WF, England. TEL 44-1223-420066. FAX 44-1223-423429. E-mail: sales@rsc.org; URL: http://chemistry.rsc.org/rsc/. (Subscr. to: Turpin Distribution Services Ltd., Blackhorse Rd., Letchworth, Herts. SG6 1HN, England. TEL 44-1462-672555. FAX 44-1462-480947) adv.; charts; illus.; index. (also avail. in microform from UMI,PMC) **Indexed:** Abstr.Bull.Inst.Pap.Chem., Art & Archaeol.Tech.Abstr., ASCA, Biol.Abstr., Biotech.Abstr., Cadscan, Chem.Abstr., Chem.Cit.Ind., Chem.Titles, Curr.Adv.Biochem., Curr.Adv.Ecol.Sci., Curr.Chem.React., Curr.Cont., Hort.Abstr., Ind.Chem., Ind.Med., INIS Atomind., Lead Abstr., Mass Spectr.Bull., Ref.Zh., Rev.Plant Path., Soils & Fert., Sugar Ind.Abstr., Zincscan. **Document type:** academic/scholarly publication.
•Also available online. Vendor(s): STN International (CJRSC).
—BLDSC (4729.100000); ADONIS; CASDDS; CISTI; Ei; Genuine Article; Linda Hall; SWETS; UMI; UnCover. **CCC.**
Formerly: Chemical Society, London. Journal. Section C: Organic Chemistry (ISSN 0022-4952)
Description: Contains papers on all aspects of organic and bio-organic chemistry.
Refereed Serial

547 574.192 RU ISSN 1068-1620
QD415.A1 CODEN: RJBCET
RUSSIAN JOURNAL OF BIOORGANIC CHEMISTRY. English translation of: Bioorganicheskaya Khimiya (RU ISSN 0132-3423) 1975. m. $1245 in US; elsewhere $1445 (effective 1998). (Russian Academy of Sciences) Maik Nauka - Interperiodica, Mezhdunarodnyi Otdel, Ul. Profsoyuznaya, 90, 117864 Moscow, Russia. TEL 7-095-3360066. FAX 7-095-3360066. (Dist. by: Plenum Publishing Corp., 233 Spring St., New York, NY 10013-1578, U.S.A. TEL 212-620-8468. FAX 212-463-0742) Ed. V.T. Ivanov. (also avail. in microfilm from UMI; back issues avail.) **Indexed:** Biol.Abstr., Chem.Titles, Mass Spectr.Bull. **Document type:** academic/scholarly publication.
—BLDSC (0420.760700); CISTI; UMI; UnCover. **CCC.**
Formerly (until 1993): Soviet Journal of Bioorganic Chemistry (ISSN 0360-4497)
Refereed Serial

547 RU ISSN 1070-4280
QD241 CODEN: RJOCEQ
RUSSIAN JOURNAL OF ORGANIC CHEMISTRY. English translation of: Zhurnal Organicheskoi Khimii (RU ISSN 0514-7492) 1965. s-m. $1895 in US; elsewhere $2215 (effective 1998). (Russian Academy of Sciences) Maik Nauka - Interperiodica, Mezhdunarodnyi Otdel, Ul. Profsoyuznaya, 90, 117864 Moscow, Russia. TEL 7-095-3360066. FAX 7-095-3360066. (Dist. by: Plenum Publishing Corp., 233 Spring St., New York, NY 10013-1578. TEL 212-620-8468. FAX 212-463-0742) Ed. I.P. Beletskaya. (also avail. in microfilm from UMI; back issues avail.) **Indexed:** Apic.Abstr., Chem.Cit.Ind., Chem.Titles, Ind.Sci.Rev., INIS Atomind., Mass Spectr.Bull., Mat.Sci.Cit.Ind., Sci.Cit.Ind. **Document type:** academic/scholarly publication.
—BLDSC (0420.762500); CASDDS; CISTI; SWETS; UMI; UnCover. **CCC.**
Former titles (until 1994): Journal of Organic Chemistry (New York); (until 1993): Journal of Organic Chemistry of the U S S R (ISSN 0022-3271); Soviet Journal of Organic Chemistry.
Refereed Serial

SENJO NI KANSURU SHINPOJUMU/SYMPOSIUM OF CLEANING. see *ENGINEERING — Chemical Engineering*

547.8 JA ISSN 1341-7215
CODEN: SERDEK
SOLVENT EXTRACTION RESEARCH AND DEVELOPMENT, JAPAN. (Text in English) 1994. a. 5000 Yen($45) Japan Association of Solvent Extraction, Dept. of Chemical Science & Technology, Kyushu University, Fukuoka 812-81, Japan. TEL 81-952-288671. FAX 81-952-288591. E-mail: inoue@ccs.ce.saga-u.ac.jp. Ed. Katsutoshi Inoue. circ. 200. **Indexed:** Anal.Abstr., Chem.Abstr. **Document type:** academic/scholarly publication.
—CASDDS.
Description: Covers pure chemistry and technology related to solvent extraction such as coordination chemistry, analytical chemistry, chemical engineering, metallurgy and pharmaceutics.
Refereed Serial

664.2 547 GW ISSN 0038-9056
TP248.S7 CODEN: STARDD
STARCH/STAERKE; international journal for the investigation, processing and use of carbohydrates and their derivatives. (Text in English, German) 1949. m. DM.795 (foreign DM.855) (effective 1997). Wiley - V C H, Postfach 101161, 69451 Weinheim, Germany. TEL 49-6201-606147. FAX 49-6201-606117. TELEX 465516-VCHWH-D. E-mail: subservice@vchgroup.de; URL: http://www.vchgroup.de. (Subscr. in the Americas to: John Wiley & Sons, Inc., 605 Third Ave., New York, NY 10158. TEL 212-850-6645. FAX 212-850-6021) Ed. G. Tegge. adv.; bk.rev.; abstr.; bibl.; charts; illus.; stat.; index. circ. 1,000. (also avail. in microfilm from VCl; reprint service avail. from ISI) **Indexed:** Abstr.Bull.Inst.Pap.Chem., ASCA, Biol.Abstr., Biotech.Abstr., Chem.Abstr., Chem.Cit.Ind., Curr.Adv.Ecol.Sci., Curr.Cont., Excerp.Med., Field Crop Abstr., Food Sci.& Tech.Abstr., Herb.Abstr., Ind.Sci.Rev., Maize Abstr., Mat.Sci.Cit.Ind., Nutr.Abstr., Sci.Cit.Ind., Triticale Abstr., World Text.Abstr. **Document type:** academic/scholarly publication.
—BLDSC (8434.735000); CASDDS; CISTI; Genuine Article; SWETS; UnCover. **CCC.**

547 NE ISSN 0165-3253
CODEN: SOCHDQ
STUDIES IN ORGANIC CHEMISTRY. (Text in English) 1979. irreg., vol.50, 1994. price varies. Elsevier Science B.V., Books Division, P.O. Box 211, 1000 AE Amsterdam, Netherlands. TEL 31-20-4853911. FAX 31-20-4853705. TELEX 18582 ESPA NL. E-mail: nlinfo-f@elsevier.nl; usinfo-f@elsevier.com; forinfo-kyf04035@niftyserve.or.jp; URL: http://www.elsevier.nl/. (Subscr. in the Americas to: Elsevier Science, Regional Sales Office, Box 945, New York, NY 10159-0945. TEL 212-633-3730. FAX 212-633-3680; Subscr. in Australasia and the Far East to: Elsevier Science (Singapore) Pte Ltd, No.1 Temasek Ave., No.17-01 Millenia Tower, Singapore 039192, Singapore. TEL 65-434-3727. FAX 65-337-2230; Subscr. in Japan to: Elsevier Science Japan, 9-15 Higashi-Azabu 1-chome, Minato-ku, Tokyo 106, Japan. TEL 81-3-5561-5033. FAX 81-3-5561-5047) (back issues avail.) **Indexed:** Curr.Cont. **Document type:** monographic series, proceedings.
—BLDSC (8491.185000); CASDDS; CISTI; KNAW; SWETS. **CCC.**
Description: Scholarly monographs and proceedings on topics in organic chemistry.
Refereed Serial

SULFUR REPORTS. see *CHEMISTRY*

547 JA
SYMPOSIUM ON SOLVENT EXTRACTION. PROCEEDINGS. (Text in English) 1981. a. 5000 Yen. Japanese Association of Solvent Extraction - Nihon Yobai Chushutsu Gakkai, Dept. of Chemical Science & Technology, Kyushu University, Fukuoka 812-81, Japan. FAX 81-92-642-3575. Ed. Masahiro Goto. R&P contact: Masahiro Goto. adv. contact: Masahiro Goto. **Indexed:** Chem.Abstr. **Document type:** proceedings.

CHEMISTRY — ORGANIC CHEMISTRY

547 541.39 GW ISSN 0936-5214
QD262 CODEN: SYNLES
SYNLETT. 1989. m. DM.444. Georg Thieme Verlag, Ruedigerstr. 14, 70469 Stuttgart, Germany. TEL 0711-8931-0. FAX 0711-8931298. (Subscr. to: Postfach 104853, 70042 Stuttgart, Germany) Ed. K. Vollhardt. circ. 2,200. **Indexed:** Abstr.Bull.Inst.Pap.Chem., ASCA, Curr.Cont., Ind.Chem., Ind.Sci.Rev., Sci.Cit.Ind. **Document type:** academic/scholarly publication.
—BLDSC (8585.970000); ADONIS; CASDDS; CISTI; Ei; Genuine Article; Linda Hall; SWETS; UMI; UnCover. **CCC.**
Description: Covers modern synthetic methodology as applied to both traditional and new areas of organic research.

547 541.39 GW ISSN 0039-7881
QD262 CODEN: SYNTBF
SYNTHESIS; journal of synthetic organic chemistry. (Text in English) 1969. m. DM.636. Georg Thieme Verlag, Ruedigerstr. 14, 70469 Stuttgart, Germany. TEL 0711-8931-0. FAX 0711-8931298. (Subscr. to: Postfach 104853, 70042 Stuttgart, Germany) Ed.Ed. adv.; bk.rev.; abstr.; bibl.; charts; illus.; stat.; index. circ. 3,300. (also avail. in microform from UMI; reprint service avail. from UMI) **Indexed:** Abstr.Bull.Inst.Pap.Chem., ASCA, Curr.Cont., Excerp.Med., Ind.Sci.Rev. **Document type:** academic/scholarly publication.
—BLDSC (8586.785000); ADONIS; CASDDS; CISTI; Ei; Genuine Article; Linda Hall; SWETS; UMI; UnCover. **CCC.**

547 US ISSN 0039-7911
QD262 CODEN: SYNCAV
SYNTHETIC COMMUNICATIONS; an international journal for rapid communication of synthetic organic chemistry. 1971. 24/yr. $1650 (foreign $1740) (effective 1998). Marcel Dekker Journals, 270 Madison Ave., New York, NY 10016. TEL 212-696-9000. FAX 212-685-4540. TELEX 421419 MARDEEK. (Subscr. to: Box 5017, Monticello, NY 12701) Ed. M. Kolb. R&P contact: Julia Mulligan. adv. contact: Lourdes Barroso. (also avail. in microform from RPI) **Indexed:** ASCA, Biol.Abstr., Biotech.Abstr., Chem.Abstr., Chem.Cit.Ind., Chem.Infd., Curr.Chem.React, Curr.Cont., Excerp.Med. (1992-), Ind.Chem., Sci.Cit.Ind. **Document type:** academic/scholarly publication.
—BLDSC (8586.830000); ADONIS; CASDDS; CISTI; Ei; Genuine Article; Linda Hall; SWETS; UMI; UnCover. **CCC.**
Supersedes: Organic Preparations and Procedures.
Refereed Serial

547 541.39 SZ ISSN 0253-200X
QD262
SYNTHETIC METHODS OF ORGANIC CHEMISTRY. Cover title: Theilheimer's Synthetic Methods of Organic Chemistry. (Text in English) 1946. s-a. price varies. S. Karger AG, Allschwilerstr. 10, P.O. Box, CH-4009 Basel, Switzerland. TEL 41-61-3061111. FAX 41-61-3061234. E-mail: karger@karger.ch; URL: http://www.karger.ch. Ed. A.F. Finch. **Indexed:** ASCA, Biol.Abstr., Chem.Abstr., Curr.Cont., Ind.Med. **Document type:** academic/scholarly publication.
●Also available online. Vendor(s): Questel Orbit Inc.
—CISTI; KNAW; Linda Hall. **CCC.**
Refereed Serial

547 US
TECHNIQUES IN PROTEIN CHEMISTRY. 1990. a. (Protein Society) Academic Press, Inc., 525 B St., Ste. 1900, San Diego, CA 92101-4495. TEL 619-231-0926. FAX 619-699-6715. **Document type:** academic/scholarly publication.

547 664 II ISSN 0040-2818
TELHAN PATRIKA/OILSEEDS JOURNAL. (Text in English and Hindi) 1969. q. Rs.43.50. Directorate of Oilseeds Development, Telhan Bhavan, Himayatnagar, Hyderabad 500029, India. Ed. Dr. G.V. Ramana Murthy. adv.; bk.rev.; charts; illus.; stat. circ. 300. **Indexed:** Field Crop Abstr., Herb.Abstr., Ind.S.A.Per.
—CISTI.

547 JA
TENNEN YUKI KAGOBUTSU TORONKAI KOEN YOSHISHU/SYMPOSIUM ON THE CHEMISTRY OF NATURAL PRODUCTS. SYMPOSIUM PAPERS. (Text in Japanese) 1957. a. Chemical Society of Japan - Nippon Kagakkai, 1-5, Kanda Surugadai, Chiyoda-ku, Tokyo 101, Japan. **Indexed:** Chem.Abstr.

547 UK ISSN 0040-4020
QD241 CODEN: TETRAB
TETRAHEDRON; international journal for the rapid publication of critical reviews and original research in organic chemistry and related disciplines, including bio-organic chemistry. (Text in English, French and German) 1957. m. fl.13780($8506) includes Tetrahedron: Asymmetry (effective 1995). Elsevier Science Ltd., Pergamon, P.O. Box 800, Kidlington, Oxford OX5 1DX, England. TEL 44-1865-843000. FAX 44-1865-843010. E-mail: nlinfo-f@elsevier.nl; usinfo-f@elsevier.com; forinfo-kyf04035@niftyserve.or.jp; URL: http://www.elsevier.nl/. (Subscr. to: Elsevier Science, Regional Sales Office, P.O. Box 211, 1000 AE Amsterdam, Netherlands. TEL 31-20-4853757. FAX 31-20-4853432; Subscr. in the Americas to: Elsevier Science, Regional Sales Office, Box 945, New York, NY 10159-0945. TEL 212-633-3730. FAX 212-633-3680; Subscr. in Australasia and the Far East to: Elsevier Science (Singapore) Pte Ltd, No.1 Temasek Ave., No.17-01 Millenia Tower, Singapore 039192, Singapore. TEL 65-434-3727. FAX 65-337-2230) Ed. Derek Barton. adv.; bk.rev.; illus.; index. circ. 3,000. (also avail. in microfiche from MIM; microfilm from UMI) **Indexed:** Abstr.Bull.Inst.Pap.Chem., Agroforest.Abstr., Apic.Abstr., Biol.Abstr., Biotech.Abstr., Chem.Abstr., Chem.Cit.Ind., Chem.Infd., Crop Physiol.Abstr., Curr.Adv.Biochem., Curr.Adv.Ecol.Sci., Curr.Chem.React., Curr.Cont., Dairy Sci.Abstr., Deep Sea Res.& Oceanogr.Abstr., Excerp.Med., Forest.Abstr., Forest Prod.Abstr., Hort.Abstr., Ind.Chem., Ind.Sci.Rev., Int.Aerosp.Abstr., Mass Spectr.Bull., Mat.Sci.Cit.Ind., Rev.Plant Path., Sci.Cit.Ind., Seed Abstr. **Document type:** academic/scholarly publication.
—BLDSC (8796.850000); ADONIS; CASDDS; CISTI; Ei; Genuine Article; SWETS; UMI; UnCover. **CCC.**
Description: Topics covered include organic synthesis, natural products chemistry, studies of reaction mechanisms, and various aspects of spectroscopy.
Refereed Serial

547 546 UK ISSN 0957-4166
QD481 CODEN: TASYE3
TETRAHEDRON: ASYMMETRY; international journal for rapid publication on all aspects of asymmetry in organic, inorganic, organometallic, physical and bio-organic chemistry. 1990. 24/yr. fl.2752($1582) (effective 1998). Elsevier Science Ltd., Pergamon, P.O. Box 800, Kidlington, Oxford OX5 1DX, England. TEL 44-1865-843000. FAX 44-1865-843010. E-mail: nlinfo-f@elsevier.nl; usinfo-f@elsevier.com; forinfo-kyf04035@niftyserve.or.jp; URL: http://www.elsevier.nl. (Subscr. to: Elsevier Science, Regional Sales Office, P.O. Box 211, 1000 AE Amsterdam, Netherlands. TEL 31-20-4853757. FAX 31-20-4853432; Subscr. in the Americas to: Elsevier Science, Regional Sales Office, Box 945, New York, NY 10159-0945. TEL 212-633-3730. FAX 212-633-3680; Subscr. in Australasia and the Far East to: Elsevier Science (Singapore) Pte Ltd, No.1 Temasek Ave., No.17-01 Millenia Tower, Singapore 039192, Singapore. TEL 65-434-3727. FAX 65-337-2230) Ed. S.G. Davies. abstr. (also avail. in microfiche from MIM; microfilm from UMI; back issues avail.) **Indexed:** ASCA, Chem.Cit.Ind., Curr.Cont., Ind.Chem., Ind.Sci.Rev., Sci.Cit.Ind. **Document type:** academic/scholarly publication.
—BLDSC (8796.852000); ADONIS; CASDDS; CISTI; Ei; EMDOCS; Genuine Article; Linda Hall; SWETS; UMI; UnCover. **CCC.**
Description: Presents experimental or theoretical research results on asymmetry in various chemical compounds.
Refereed Serial

547 UK ISSN 0040-4039
QD241 CODEN: TELEAY
TETRAHEDRON LETTERS; international journal for the rapid publication of preliminary communications in organic chemistry. (Text in English, French and German) 1959. 52/yr. fl.13808($7936) (fl.12389($7647) with Tetrahedron Letters Online) (effective 1998). Elsevier Science Ltd., Pergamon, P.O. Box 800, Kidlington, Oxford OX5 1DX, England. TEL 44-1865-843000. FAX 44-1865-843010. E-mail: nlinfo-f@elsevier.nl; usinfo-f@elsevier.com; forinfo-kyf04035@niftyserve.or.jp; URL: http://www.elsevier.nl/. (Subscr. to: Elsevier Science, Regional Sales Office, P.O. Box 211, 1000 AE Amsterdam, Netherlands. TEL 31-20-4853757. FAX 31-20-4853432; Subscr. in the Americas to: Elsevier Science, Regional Sales Office, Box 945, New York, NY 10159-0945. TEL 212-633-3730. FAX 212-633-3680; Subscr. in Australasia and the Far East to: Elsevier Science (Singapore) Pte Ltd, No.1 Temasek Ave., No.17-01 Millenia Tower, Singapore 039192, Singapore. TEL 65-434-3727. FAX 65-337-2230) Ed. Derek Barton. adv. circ. 3,380. (also avail. in microfiche from MIM; microfilm from UMI) **Indexed:** Agroforest.Abstr., Apic.Abstr., ASCA, Bibl.Agri., Biol.Abstr., Chem.Abstr., Chem.Cit.Ind., Chem.Infd., Compumath, Crop Physiol.Abstr., Curr.Adv.Biochem., Curr.Adv.Cancer Res., Curr.Adv.Ecol.Sci., Curr.Chem.React., Curr.Cont., Dairy Sci.Abstr., Deep Sea Res.& Oceanogr.Abstr., Excerp.Med., Forest.Abstr., Hort.Abstr., Ind.Chem., Ind.Sci.Rev., Mass Spectr.Bull., Mat.Sci.Cit.Ind., Plant Grow.Reg.Abstr., Rev.Med.& Vet.Mycol., Rev.Plant Path., Sci.Cit.Ind., Seed Abstr. **Document type:** academic/scholarly publication.
●Also available online.
—BLDSC (8796.860000); ADONIS; CASDDS; CISTI; Ei; Genuine Article; Linda Hall; SWETS; UMI; UnCover. **CCC.**
Description: Covers developments in techniques, structures, methods and conclusions in experimental and theoretical organic chemistry.
Refereed Serial

547 660 NE ISSN 0923-6732
CODEN: TISCER
TOPICS IN INCLUSION SCIENCE. (Text in English) 1988. irreg., vol.5, 1994. price varies. Kluwer Academic Publishers, Postbus 17, 3300 AA Dordrecht, Netherlands. TEL 31-78-6392392. FAX 31-78-6392254. TELEX 29245 KAPG NL. E-mail: services@wkap.nl; URL: http://www.wkap.nl. (Dist. by: Kluwer Academic Publishers Group, P.O. Box 322, 3300 AH Dordrecht, Netherlands. TEL 31-78-6392392. FAX 31-78-6546474; N. America dist. addr.: Box 358, Accord Sta., Hingham, MA 02018-0358. TEL 617-871-6600. FAX 617-871-6528) **Document type:** monographic series.
—BLDSC (8867.448000); CASDDS.
Refereed Serial

547 JA ISSN 0915-7352
CODEN: TGGLEE
TRENDS IN GLYCOSCIENCE AND GLYCOTECHNOLOGY. (Text in English, Japanese) 1989. bi-m. 7000 Yen to individuals; institutions 22000 Yen. F C C A, 3-10-1 Koufudai, Fujishiro-cho, Kitasoma-gun, Ibaraki-ken 300-15, Japan. TEL 81-297-837635. FAX 81-297-837645. **Indexed:** ASCA.
—BLDSC (9049.610000); CASDDS; CISTI; Genuine Article.
Refereed Serial

TRENDS IN POLYMER SCIENCE. see ENGINEERING — Chemical Engineering

TRENDS IN POLYMER SCIENCE (REFERENCE EDITION). see ENGINEERING — Chemical Engineering

TRIBOLOGIE UND SCHMIERUNGSTECHNIK. see ENGINEERING — Chemical Engineering

547 660 631 UK
WORLD DIRECTORY OF AGROBIOLOGICALS. 1990. a. £95. C P L Scientific Ltd., 43 Kingfisher Ct., Harbridge Rd., Newbury, Berks. RG14 5SJ, England. TEL 01635-524064. FAX 01635-529322. Eds. S.G. Lisansky, J. Coombs. (back issues avail.) **Document type:** trade publication.
Description: Lists more than 1,000 biological and other nonsynthetic chemical products for use in agriculture, horticulture, forestry, and garden.

CHEMISTRY — PHYSICAL CHEMISTRY

547　　　　　　CC　　ISSN 0253-2786
QD241　　　　　　CODEN: YCHHDX
YOUJI HUAXUE/ORGANIC CHEMISTRY. (Text in Chinese; summaries in English) 1972. bi-m. $108 (effective 1997). (Shanghai Institute of Organic Chemistry) Science Press, Marketing and Sales Department, 16 Donghuangchenggen North St., Beijing 100717, People's Republic of China. TEL 4010642. FAX 4019810. adv. circ. 12,000. **Document type:** academic/scholarly publication.
—CASDDS; Linda Hall.
Description: Publishes research papers, communications and reviews of developments both in China and abroad.
Refereed Serial

YUKAGAKU SANKA SEMINA/SEMINAR ON OXIDATION. see *ENGINEERING — Chemical Engineering*

YUKI HANNO KAGAKU TORONKAI KOEN YOKOSHU/ABSTRACTS OF SYMPOSIUM ON ORGANIC REACTIONS. see *CHEMISTRY — Abstracting, Bibliographies, Statistics*

ZEITSCHRIFT FUER NATURFORSCHUNG. SECTION B: A JOURNAL OF CHEMICAL SCIENCES. see *CHEMISTRY — Inorganic Chemistry*

CHEMISTRY — Physical Chemistry

541.3　546　　DK　　ISSN 0904-213X
　　　　　　　　　　CODEN: ACHSE7
ACTA CHEMICA SCANDINAVICA. (Text in English) 1947. m. DKK 3235 in Europe (US, Canada and Japan DKK 3295 (effective 1997). (Chemical Societies of Denmark, Finland, Norway and Sweden) Munksgaard International Publishers Ltd., 35 Noerre Soegade, P.O. Box 2148, DK-1016 Copenhagen K, Denmark. TEL 45-33-127030. FAX 45-33-129387. E-mail: fsub@mail.munksgaard.dk. (In N. America: Commerce Place, 350 Main St., Malden, MA 02148-5018. TEL 617-388-8273. FAX 617-388-8274) Ed. Christian Roemming. adv.; bibl.; charts; illus.; index. circ. 1,300. (reprint service avail. from ISI) **Indexed:** Abstr.Bull.Inst.Pap.Chem., Alloys Ind., ASCA, Biol.Abstr., Bull.Thermodyn.& Thermochem., C.I.S. Abstr., Cadscan, Chem.Abstr., Chem.Cit.Ind., Chem.Infd., Curr.Cont., Deep Sea Res.& Oceanogr.Abstr., Excerp.Med., Ind.Sci.Rev., INIS Atomind., INSPEC, Lead Abstr., Mass Spectr.Bull., Met.Abstr., Met.Abstr.Ind., Mineral.Abstr., Nonfer.Met.Alert, Nutr.Abstr., Paper & Bd.Abstr., PCC Alert, Sci.Cit.Ind., Soils & Fert., Steels Alert, World Alum.Abstr., Zincscan. **Document type:** academic/scholarly publication.
—BLDSC (0609.000000); ADONIS; CASDDS; CISTI; Ei; Genuine Article; Linda Hall; SWETS; UnCover. **CCC.**
Formed by 1989 merger of: Acta Chemica Scandinavica. Series A: Physical and Inorganic Chemistry (ISSN 0302-4377); Acta Chemica Scandinavica. Series B: Organic Chemistry and Biochemistry (ISSN 0302-4369); Which superseded: Acta Chemica Scandinavica (ISSN 0001-5393)
Refereed Serial

541.3 574.192　US　　ISSN 1057-8943
QH345　　　　　　CODEN: ABCHEA
ADVANCES IN BIOPHYSICAL CHEMISTRY. 1990. irreg., vol.6, 1997. $112.50. J A I Press Inc., 55 Old Post Rd., No. 2, Box 1678, Greenwich, CT 06830-1678. TEL 203-661-7602. FAX 203-661-0792. E-mail: jai@jaipress.com. Ed. C. Allen Bush. **Indexed:** Chem.Cit.Ind. **Document type:** monographic series.
—BLDSC (0700.258000); CASDDS; CISTI.

541.395　　　US　　ISSN 0360-0564
QD501　　　　　　CODEN: ADCAAX
ADVANCES IN CATALYSIS. 1948. irreg., no.41, 1996. Academic Press, Inc., 525 B St., Ste. 1900, San Diego, CA 92101-4495. TEL 619-231-0926. FAX 619-699-6715. (Subscr. to: Order Dept., 6277 Sea Harbor Dr., 4th Fl., Orlando, FL 32887. TEL 800-321-5068) Ed.Bd. (reprint service avail. from ISI) **Indexed:** ASCA, Biol.Abstr., Chem.Abstr., Chem.Cit.Ind., Chem.Infd., Curr.Chem.React, Ind.Chem., Ind.Sci.Rev., Sci.Cit.Ind.
—BLDSC (0702.990000); CASDDS; CISTI; Linda Hall; SWETS; UnCover. **CCC.**
Formerly: Advances in Catalysis and Related Subjects (ISSN 0065-2342)
Refereed Serial

541.3　　　　US
QD461
ADVANCES IN CATALYTIC PROCESSES. 1995. irreg., vol.2, 1997. $109.50. J A I Press Inc., 55 Old Post Rd., No.2, Box 1678, Greenwich, CT 06830-1678. TEL 203-661-7602. FAX 203-661-0792. E-mail: jai@jaipress.com. (Addr. in Europe: J A I Press Ltd., 38 Tavistock St., Covent Garden, London WCE 7 PB, England. TEL 44-171-379-8834. FAX 44-171-379-8835) Ed. Michael Doyle. **Document type:** academic/scholarly publication, monographic series.

ADVANCES IN CHEMICAL PHYSICS. see *PHYSICS*

541　　　　　　NE　　ISSN 0001-8686
QD506　　　　　　CODEN: ACISB9
ADVANCES IN COLLOID AND INTERFACE SCIENCE; an international journal devoted to experimental and theoretical developments in interfacial and colloidal phenomena and their implications in biology, chemistry, physics and technology. (Text in English, French & German) 1967. m. fl.2320($1333) (effective 1998). Elsevier Science B.V., P.O. Box 211, 1000 AE Amsterdam, Netherlands. TEL 31-20-4853911. FAX 31-20-4853598. TELEX 18582 ESPA NL. E-mail: nlinfo-f@elsevier.nl; usinfo-f@elsevier.com; forinfo-kyf04035@niftyserve.or.jp; URL: http://www.elsevier.nl/. (Subscr. in the Americas to: Elsevier Science, Regional Sales Office, Box 945, New York, NY 10159-0945. TEL 212-633-3730. FAX 212-633-3680; Subscr. in Australasia and the Far East to: Elsevier Science (Singapore) Pte Ltd, No.1 Temasek Ave., No.17-01 Millenia Tower, Singapore 039192, Singapore. TEL 65-434-3727. FAX 65-337-2230; Subscr. in Japan to: Elsevier Science Japan, 9-15 Higashi-Azabu 1-chome, Minato-ku, Tokyo 106, Japan. TEL 81-3-5561-5033. FAX 81-3-5561-5047) Ed. T.F. Tadros. adv.; bk.rev.; charts. (also avail. in microform from UMI; reprint service avail.) SWZ) **Indexed:** Abstr.Bull.Inst.Pap.Chem., Acoust.Abstr., ASCA, Chem.Abstr., Chem.Cit.Ind., Curr.Cont., Dairy Sci.Abstr., Ind.Sci.Rev., INSPEC (1979-1983), Mat.Sci.Cit.Ind., Photo.Abstr., Phys.Ber., Sci.Cit.Ind., World Surf.Coat. **Document type:** academic/scholarly publication.
—BLDSC (0703.950000); CASDDS; CISTI; Ei; Genuine Article; Linda Hall; SWETS; UnCover. **CCC.**
Refereed Serial

541.2　　　　US　　ISSN 1054-0954
QD461　　　　　　CODEN: AMMOEM
ADVANCES IN MOLECULAR MODELING. 1988. irreg., vol.4, 1997. $109.50. J A I Press Inc., 55 Old Post Rd., No. 2, Box 1678, CT 06830-1678. TEL 203-661-7602. FAX 203-661-0792. E-mail: jai@jaipress.com. (Subscr. in UK and Europe to: JAI Press Ltd., 38 Tavistock St., Covent Garden, London WC2E 7PB, England. TEL 44-171-379-8834. FAX 44-171-379-8835) Ed. Dennis Liotta. **Document type:** monographic series.
—CASDDS; CISTI.

541.3　　　　US　　ISSN 1063-5467
　　　　　　　　　　CODEN: AMUDEY
ADVANCES IN MOLECULAR VIBRATIONS AND COLLISION DYNAMICS. 1991. irreg., vol.3, 1997. $109.50. J A I Press Inc., 55 Old Post Rd., No. 2, Greenwich, CT 06830-1678. TEL 203-661-7602. FAX 203-661-0792. E-mail: jai@jaipress.com. (Addr. in Europe: J A I Press Ltd., 38 Tavistock St., Covent Garden, London WC2E 7PB, England. TEL 44-171-379-8834. FAX 44-171-379-8835) Ed. Joel M. Bowman. (back issues avail.) **Document type:** academic/scholarly publication.
—BLDSC (0709.443000); CASDDS; CISTI.

ADVANCES IN MOLTEN SALT CHEMISTRY. see *CHEMISTRY — Inorganic Chemistry*

543 541.35　　US　　ISSN 0065-3152
QD601.A1　　　　CODEN: ADPCA2
ADVANCES IN PHOTOCHEMISTRY. 1963. irreg., vol.18, 1993. price varies. John Wiley & Sons, Inc., 605 Third Ave., New York, NY 10158-0012. TEL 212-850-6645. Ed. A. Noyes. index. **Indexed:** Chem.Infd. **Document type:** monographic series.
—BLDSC (0709.780000); CASDDS; CISTI; Linda Hall. **CCC.**
Refereed Serial

547.1　　　　US　　ISSN 0065-3160
QD476　　　　　　CODEN: APORAO
ADVANCES IN PHYSICAL ORGANIC CHEMISTRY. 1963. irreg., vol.30, 1995. Academic Press, Inc., 525 B St., Ste. 1900, San Diego, CA 92101-4495. TEL 619-231-0926. FAX 619-699-6715. (Subscr. to: Order Dept., 6277 Sea Harbor St., 4th Fl., Orlando, FL 32887. TEL 800-321-5068) Ed. V. Gold. (reprint service avail. from ISI) **Indexed:** ASCA, Chem.Abstr., Chem.Cit.Ind., Chem.Infd., Ind.Sci.Rev., Sci.Cit.Ind.
—BLDSC (0709.800000); CASDDS; CISTI; Linda Hall; SWETS; UnCover. **CCC.**
Refereed Serial

541.3　　　　US
▼**ADVANCES IN QUANTITATIVE STRUCTURE-PROPERTY RELATIONSHIPS.** 1996. irreg., vol.2, 1997. $109.50. J A I Press Inc., 55 Old Post Rd., No.2, Box 1678, Greenwich, CT 06830-1678. TEL 203-661-7602. FAX 203-661-0792. E-mail: jai@jaipress.com. (In Europe: JAI Press Ltd., 38 Tavistock St., Covent Garden, London WC2E 7PB, England. TEL 44-171-379-8834. FAX 44-171-379-8835) Ed. Marvin Charton. **Document type:** academic/scholarly publication, monographic series.

ADVANCES IN SOLID STATE TECHNOLOGY. see *PHYSICS*

541.3　　　　US
ADVANCES IN SONOCHEMISTRY. 1990. irreg., vol.4, 1996. $109.50. J A I Press Inc., 55 Old Post Rd., No.2, Box 1678, Greenwich, CT 06830-1678. TEL 203-661-7602. FAX 203-661-0792. E-mail: jai@jaipress.com. (In Europe: J A I Press Ltd., 38 Tavistock St., Covent Garden, London WC2E 7PB, England. TEL 44-171-379-8834. FAX 44-171-379-8835) Ed. Timothy Mason. **Indexed:** Chem.Cit.Ind. **Document type:** monographic series, academic/scholarly publication.

541.3　　　　UK　　ISSN 0961-5415
　　　　　　　　　　CODEN: ASRTE2
ADVANCES IN THE SYNTHESIS AND REACTIVITY OF SOLIDS. 1990. irreg. $90.25. J A I Press Ltd., The Courtyard, 28 High St., Hampton Hill, Mddx. TW12 1PD, England. TEL 44-181-943-9296. FAX 44-181-943-9317. E-mail: jai@cix.compulink.co.uk. (Addr. in the US: J A I Press Inc., 55 Old Post Rd., No. 2, Greenwich, CT 06836. TEL 203-661-7602. FAX 203-661-0792) Ed. Thomas Mallouk. **Document type:** monographic series, academic/scholarly publication.
—CASDDS.

541.3　　　　UK
AEROFILL NEWS. 1980. s-a. Aerofill Ltd., Clayton Rd., Hayes, Mddx. UB3 1RU, England. FAX 44-181-561-3308. Ed. C.M. Nimmo. circ. 5,000.

AMERICAN MINERALOGIST. see *MINES AND MINING INDUSTRY*

547.1 541.39　US　　ISSN 0066-409X
QD262　　　　　　CODEN: ARSYEF
ANNUAL REPORTS IN ORGANIC SYNTHESIS. 1971. irreg., vol.26, 1996. Academic Press, Inc., 525 B St., Ste. 1900, San Diego, CA 92101-4495. TEL 619-231-0926. FAX 619-699-6715. (Subscr. to: Order Dept., 6277 Sea Harbor Dr., 4th Fl., Orlando, FL 32887. TEL 800-321-5068) (reprint service avail. from ISI)
—BLDSC (1513.600000); CISTI; Linda Hall. **CCC.**
Refereed Serial

CHEMISTRY — PHYSICAL CHEMISTRY

541.3 US ISSN 0066-426X
QD1 CODEN: ARPLAP
ANNUAL REVIEW OF PHYSICAL CHEMISTRY. 1950. a. $64 to individuals (foreign $69); institutions $128 (foreign $138) (effective 1998). Annual Reviews Inc., 4139 El Camino Way, Box 10139, Palo Alto, CA 94303-0139. TEL 650-493-4400; 800-523-8635. FAX 650-424-0910. E-mail: service@annurev.org; URL: http://www.annurev.org. Ed. Herbert L. Strauss. R&P contact: Jeanne Kunz. bibl.; index, cum.index. (also avail. in microfilm from UMI; back issues avail., reprint service avail.) **Indexed:** Abstr.Bull.Inst.Pap.Chem., ASCA, Cadscan., Chem.Abstr., Chem.Cit.Ind., Compumath, Curr.Cont., Deep Sea Res.& Oceanogr.Abstr., Fuel & Energy Abstr., Ind.Sci.Rev., INSPEC, Lead Abstr., M.M.R.I., Nucl.Sci.Abstr., Sci.Cit.Ind., World Surf.Coat., Zincscan. **Document type:** academic/scholarly publication.
—BLDSC (1526.000000); CASDDS; CISTI; Ei; Genuine Article; KNAW; Linda Hall; SWETS; UMI; UnCover. **CCC**.
Description: Original critical reviews of the significant primary literature and current developments in physical chemistry.

ARCHIVES OF THERMODYNAMICS. see PHYSICS — Heat

331.88 541.3 NO ISSN 0801-6828
BIOINGENIOEREN; the medical laboratory technologist. 1965. m. NOK 384 (foreign NOK 444) (effective 1996). Norsk Bioingenioerenforbund - Norwegian Association of Medical Laboratory Technologists, P.O. Box 9057 Groenland, N-0133 Oslo, Norway. TEL 47-22-17-52-00. FAX 47-22-17-52-04. Ed. Patricia Ann Melsom. adv.: B&W page NOK 6200, color page NOK 10100; trim 185 x 260; adv. contact: Hanne Huseby Aune. bk.rev.; illus.; stat.; tr.lit.; index. circ. 4,551. **Indexed:** INIS Atomind. **Document type:** academic/scholarly publication.
—**CCC**.
Formerly (until 1987): Fysiokjemikeren (ISSN 0333-0796)

541.36 US ISSN 0572-6921
BRIGHAM YOUNG UNIVERSITY. CENTER FOR THERMOCHEMICAL STUDIES. CONTRIBUTIONS.* irreg., no.66, 1975. price varies. Brigham Young University, Center for Thermochemical Studies, Provo, UT 84602.

541.3 GW ISSN 0005-9021
TP250 CODEN: BBPCAX
BUNSENGESELLSCHAFT FUER PHYSIKALISCHE CHEMIE. BERICHTE; physical chemistry, chemical physics. (Text in English) 1897. m. DM.1395 (foreign DM.1455) (effective 1997). (Bunsengesellschaft fuer Physikalische Chemie) Wiley - V C H, Postfach 101161, 69451 Weinheim, Germany. TEL 49-6201-606-147. FAX 49-6201-606117. TELEX 465516-VCHWH-D. E-mail: subservice@vchgroup.de; URL: http://www.vchgroup.de. (Subscr. in the Americas to: John Wiley & Sons, Inc., 605 Third Ave., New York, NY 10158. TEL 212-850-6645. FAX 212-850-6021) Ed.Bd. adv. contact: R. Roth. bk.rev.; charts; illus.; tr.lit.; index, cum.index: vols.1-10, 11-30. circ. 2,450. (also avail. in microfilm from VCI; reprint service avail. from ISI; back issues avail.) **Indexed:** Alloys Ind., API Catal., API Hlth.& Environ., API Oil., API Pet.Ref., API Pet.Subst., API Transport., Biol.Abstr., Chem.Abstr., Eng.Mat.Abstr., INIS Atomind., INSPEC, Mass Spectr.Bull., Met.Abstr., Met.Abstr.Ind., Nonfer.Met.Alert, PCC Alert, Phys.Ber., Steels Alert, World Alum.Abstr. **Document type:** academic/scholarly publication.
—AskIEEE; CISTI; Ei; Genuine Article; KR SourceOne; Linda Hall; SWETS; UnCover. **CCC**.
Description: Publishes original papers and communications which report on the results of experimental and theoretical investigations in all fields of pure and applied chemistry.

C A SELECTS. LASER APPLICATIONS. see CHEMISTRY — Abstracting, Bibliographies, Statistics

541.3 UK
CAMBRIDGE MONOGRAPHS ON ATOMIC, MOLECULAR AND CHEMICAL PHYSICS. irreg., no.2, 1993. price varies. Cambridge University Press, The Pitt Bldg., Trumpington St., Cambridge CB2 1RP, England. TEL 44-1223-312393. FAX 44-1223-315052. E-mail: information@cup.cam.ac.uk; URL: http://www.cup.cam.ac.uk. (U.S. addr.: 40 W. 20th St., New York, NY 10011-4211) R&P contact: Linda Nicol. **Document type:** monographic series.

541.3 UK ISSN 0140-0568
QD505 CODEN: CATADK
CATALYSIS. 1976. irreg., vol.12, 1996. price varies. The Royal Society of Chemistry, Thomas Graham House, Science Park, Milton Rd., Cambridge CB4 4WF, England. TEL 44-1223-420066. FAX 44-1223-423623. E-mail: sales@rsc.org; URL: http://chemistry.rsc.org/rsc/. (Dist. by: Turpin Distribution Services Ltd., Blackhorse Rd., Letchworth, Herts. SG6 1HN, England. TEL 44-1462-672555. FAX 44-1462-480947; Subscr. in N. America to: ACS, 1155 Sixteenth St., N.W., Washington, DC 22036. TEL 202-776-8100. FAX 202-872-6067) **Indexed:** Chem.Cit.Ind. **Document type:** academic/scholarly publication.
—BLDSC (3090.880000); CASDDS; CISTI; Linda Hall. **CCC**.

660.299 541.395 US ISSN 0161-4940
QD501 CODEN: CRSEC9
CATALYSIS REVIEWS: SCIENCE AND ENGINEERING. 1967. q. $650 (foreign $665) (effective 1998). Marcel Dekker Journals, 270 Madison Ave., New York, NY 10016. TEL 212-696-9000. FAX 212-685-4540. TELEX 421419. (Subscr. to: Box 5017, Monticello, NY 12701) Eds. A.T. Bell, K. Klier. adv. contact: Eridania Perez. (also avail. in microform from RPI) **Indexed:** Alloys Ind., API Abstr., API Catal., API Hlth.& Environ., API Oil., API Pet.Ref., API Pet.Subst., API Transport., ASCA, Chem.Abstr., Chem.Cit.Ind., Chem.Eng.Abstr., Chem.Infd., Curr.Chem.React., Curr.Cont., Eng.Mat.Abstr., Gas Abstr., Ind.Chem., Ind.Sci.Rev., INIS Atomind., Met.Abstr., Met.Abstr.Ind., Nonfer.Met.Alert, PCC Alert, Steels Alert, T.C.E.A., World Alum.Abstr. **Document type:** academic/scholarly publication.
—CASDDS; CISTI; Ei; Genuine Article; SWETS; UMI; UnCover. **CCC**.
Formerly: Catalysis Reviews (ISSN 0008-7645)
Refereed Serial

660.299 541.395 NE ISSN 1384-6574
▼**CATALYSIS SURVEYS FROM JAPAN.** 1997. s-a. 410 SFr. (effective 1998). Baltzer Science Publishers B.V., P.O. Box 221, 1400 AE Bussum, Netherlands. TEL 31-20-6370061. FAX 31-20-6323651. E-mail: subscribe@baltzer.nl; URL: http://www.baltzer.nl. **Document type:** academic/scholarly publication.

541.3 JA
CODEN: SHKUAJ
CATALYSTS & CATALYSIS. (Text in English) 1959. 8/yr. 2000 Yen per no. Shokubai Gakkai - Catalysis Society of Japan, 21-13-302, Higashigotanda 5-chome, Shinagawa-ku, Tokyo 141, Japan. **Indexed:** Chem.Abstr., INIS Atomind., Jap.Per.Ind. **Document type:** academic/scholarly publication.
—CASDDS; CISTI; Linda Hall. **CCC**.
Formerly: Shokubai - Catalyst (ISSN 0559-8958)

541.395 UK ISSN 0309-5770
CODEN: CACHDO
CATALYSTS IN CHEMISTRY. 1977. m. $720 (effective 1996). R.H. Chandler Ltd., 21 The Avenue, Braintree, Essex CM7 6HY, England. TEL 01376-553033. Ed. R.H. Chandler. pat. (reprint service avail. from UMI) **Document type:** abstracting/indexing.
—**CCC**.

549.6 XR ISSN 0862-5468
TA585.S46 CODEN: CERSEP
CERAMICS. (Text in Czech or English; summaries in Czech, English, Russian) 1957. q. DM.136. (Vysoka Skola Chemicko Technologicka v Praze) S K Press, v.o.s., Masarykovo nam. 35, 251 01 Ricany, Czech Republic. (Dist. in Western countries by: Kubon & Sagner, Postfach 340108, 8000 Munich 34, Germany) bk.rev.; charts; illus.; index. circ. 1,350. **Indexed:** ASCA, Br.Ceram.Abstr., Ceram.Abstr., Chem.Abstr., Curr.Cont., GeoRef., INSPEC (1990-1992), Sci.Cit.Ind.
—BLDSC (3119.058000); AskIEEE; CASDDS; CISTI; Ei; Genuine Article; KR SourceOne; Linda Hall.
Formerly (until 1990): Silikaty (ISSN 0037-5241)
Description: Original articles covering all branches of silicate research, including chemistry, physical chemistry and engineering.

541.3 530 NE ISSN 0301-0104
QD450 CODEN: CMPHC2
CHEMICAL PHYSICS; a journal devoted to the experimental and theoretical research involving problems of both a chemical and a physical nature. (Text in English) 1973. 39/yr. fl.8580($4931) (effective 1998). North-Holland (Subsidiary of: Elsevier Science B.V.), P.O. Box 211, 1000 AE Amsterdam, Netherlands. TEL 31-20-4853911. FAX 31-20-4853598. TELEX 18582 ESPA NL. (Subscr. in the Americas to: Elsevier Science, Regional Sales Office, Box 945, New York, NY 10159-0945. TEL 212-633-3730. FAX 212-633-3680; Subscr. in Australasia and the Far East to: Elsevier Science (Singapore) Pte Ltd, No.1 Temasek Ave., No.17-01 Millenia Tower, Singapore 039192, Singapore. TEL 65-434-3727. FAX 65-337-2230; Subscr. in Japan to: Elsevier Science Japan, 9-15 Higashi-Azabu 1-chome, Minato-ku, Tokyo 106, Japan. TEL 81-3-5561-5033. FAX 81-3-5561-5047) Eds. R.M. Hochstrasser, G.L. Hofacker. index. (also avail. in microform from UMI; back issues avail.) **Indexed:** Apic.Abstr., ASCA, Biwk.Pap.Rad.Chem.& Photochem., Cadscan., Chem.Abstr., Chem.Cit.Ind., Curr.Cont., Ind.Sci.Rev., INIS Atomind., INSPEC (1973-), Lead Abstr., Mass Spectr.Bull., Mat.Sci.Cit.Ind., Math.R., Phys.Ber., Sci.Cit.Ind., Zincscan. **Document type:** academic/scholarly publication.
—BLDSC (3148.820000); AskIEEE; CASDDS; CISTI; Genuine Article; KR SourceOne; Linda Hall; SWETS; UnCover. **CCC**.
Description: Publishes experimental and theoretical papers on all aspects of chemical physics.
Refereed Serial

541.3 NE ISSN 0009-2614
CODEN: CHPLBC
CHEMICAL PHYSICS LETTERS. 1967. 102/yr. fl.14025($8060) (effective 1998). North-Holland (Subsidiary of: Elsevier Science B.V.), P.O. Box 211, 1000 AE Amsterdam, Netherlands. TEL 31-20-4853911. FAX 31-20-4853598. TELEX 18582 ESPA NL. (Subscr. in the Americas to: Elsevier Science, Regional Sales Office, Box 945, New York, NY 10159-0945. TEL 212-633-3730. FAX 212-633-3680; Subscr. in Australasia and the Far East to: Elsevier Science (Singapore) Pte Ltd, No.1 Temasek Ave., No.17-01 Millenia Tower, Singapore 039192, Singapore. TEL 65-434-3727. FAX 65-337-2230; Subscr. in Japan to: Elsevier Science Japan, 9-15 Higashi-Azabu 1-chome, Minato-ku, Tokyo 106, Japan. TEL 81-3-5561-5033. FAX 81-3-5561-5047) Ed. A.D. Buckingham. adv.; illus.; index, cum.index. (also avail. in microfilm from UMI; back issues avail.) **Indexed:** ASCA, Biwk.Pap.Rad.Chem.& Photochem., Bull.Thermodyn.& Thermochem., Cadscan., Chem.Abstr., Chem.Cit.Ind., Curr.Cont., Ind.Sci.Rev., INIS Atomind., INSPEC (1968-), Int.Aerosp.Abstr., Lead Abstr., Mass Spectr.Bull., Mat.Sci.Cit.Ind., Math.R., Phys.Ber., Sci.Cit.Ind., Zincscan. **Document type:** academic/scholarly publication.
—BLDSC (3148.830000); AskIEEE; CASDDS; CISTI; Ei; Genuine Article; KR SourceOne; Linda Hall; SWETS; UnCover. **CCC**.
Description: Devoted to the analysis of phenomena in the domain of chemical physics.
Refereed Serial

541.3 NE
CHEMICAL PHYSICS OF SOLID SURFACES. (Text in English) 1981. irreg., vol.6, 1993. price varies. Elsevier Science B.V., Books Division, P.O. Box 211, 1000 AE Amsterdam, Netherlands. TEL 31-20-4853911. FAX 31-20-4853705. E-mail: nlinfo-f@elsevier.nl; usinfo-f@elsevier.com; forinfo-kyf04035@niftyserve.or.jp; URL: http://www.elsevier.nl/. (Subscr. in the Americas to: Elsevier Science, Regional Sales Office, Box 945, New York, NY 10159-0945. TEL 212-633-3730. FAX 212-633-3680; Subscr. in Australasia and the Far East to: Elsevier Science (Singapore) Pte Ltd, No.1 Temasek Ave., No.17-01 Millenia Tower, Singapore 039192, Singapore. TEL 65-434-3727. FAX 65-337-2230; Subscr. in Japan to: Elsevier Science Japan, 9-15 Higashi-Azabu 1-chome, Minato-ku, Tokyo 106, Japan. TEL 81-3-5561-5033. FAX 81-3-5561-5047) (back issues avail.) **Document type:** monographic series.
Refereed Serial

CHEMICAL PHYSICS REPORTS. see PHYSICS

CHEMISTRY — PHYSICAL CHEMISTRY

541.3   NE
CHEMICAL SENSOR TECHNOLOGY. (Text in English) 1988. a., vol.4, 1992. price varies. Elsevier Science B.V., Books Division, P.O. Box 211, 1000 AE Amsterdam, Netherlands. TEL 31-20-4853911. FAX 31-20-4853705. E-mail: nlinfo-f@elsevier.nl; usinfo-f@elsevier.com; forinfo-kyf04035@niftyserve.or.jp; URL: http://www.elsevier.nl/. (Subscr. in the Americas to: Elsevier Science, Regional Sales Office, Box 945, New York, NY 10159-0945. TEL 212-633-3730. FAX 212-633-3680; Subscr. in Australasia and the Far East to: Elsevier Science (Singapore) Pte Ltd, No.1 Temasek Ave., No.17-01 Millenia Tower, Singapore 039192, Singapore. TEL 65-434-3727. FAX 65-337-2230; Subscr. in Japan to: Elsevier Science Japan, 9-15 Higashi-Azabu 1-chome, Minato-ku, Tokyo 106, Japan. TEL 81-3-5561-5033. FAX 81-3-5561-5047) (back issues avail.) Document type: monographic series.

541.3   NE   ISSN 0884-948X
CODEN: CMOSEW
CHEMICALLY MODIFIED SURFACES. 1980. irreg., latest vol.3. Gordon and Breach - Harwood Academic, Amsteldisk 166, 1st Fl., 1079 LH Amsterdam, Netherlands. (Subscr. to: International Publishers Distributor, Box 32160, Newark, NJ 07102. TEL 800-545-8398. FAX 215-750-6343) Ed. D.E. Leyden. Document type: monographic series.
—BLDSC (3153.150000); CASDDS; CISTI. **CCC**.
Refereed Serial

COLLOID AND POLYMER SCIENCE. see CHEMISTRY — Organic Chemistry

541.3   NE   ISSN 0927-7757
QD549   CODEN: CPEAEH
COLLOIDS AND SURFACES A: PHYSICOCHEMICAL AND ENGINEERING ASPECTS; an international journal devoted to the applications and principles of colloid and interface science. (Text in English) 1980. 39/yr. fl.7228($4154) (effective 1998). Elsevier Science B.V., P.O. Box 211, 1000 AE Amsterdam, Netherlands. TEL 31-20-4853911. FAX 31-20-4853598. TELEX 18582 ESPA NL. E-mail: nlinfo-f@elsevier.nl; usinfo-f@elsevier.com; forinfo-kyf04035@niftyserve.or.jp; URL: http://www.elsevier.nl/. (Subscr. in the Americas to: Elsevier Science, Regional Sales Office, Box 945, New York, NY 10159-0945. TEL 212-633-3730. FAX 212-633-3680; Subscr. in Australasia and the Far East to: Elsevier Science (Singapore) Pte Ltd, No.1 Temasek Ave., No.17-01 Millenia Tower, Singapore 039192, Singapore. TEL 65-434-3727. FAX 65-337-2230; Subscr. in Japan to: Elsevier Science Japan, 9-15 Higashi-Azabu 1-chome, Minato-ku, Tokyo 106, Japan. TEL 81-3-5561-5033. FAX 81-3-5561-5047) Ed. P. Somasundaran. adv.; bk.rev. (also avail. in microform from UMI; back issues avail.) **Indexed:** Abstr.Bull.Inst.Pap.Chem., ASCA, Biol.Abstr., Br.Ceram.Abstr., Chem.Abstr., Chem.Cit.Ind., Curr.Cont., Dairy Sci.Abstr., Excerp.Med., Fluidex, Ind.Sci.Rev., INIS Atomind., INSPEC (1980-), Intl.Polym.Sci.& Tech., Mat.Sci.Cit.Ind., Met.Abstr., Photo.Abstr., RAPRA, Sci.Cit.Ind., SSCI, Sugar Ind.Abstr., World Alum.Abstr., World Surf.Coat. Document type: academic/scholarly publication.
—BLDSC (3313.552010); AskIEEE; CASDDS; CISTI; Ei; EMDOCS; Genuine Article; KR SourceOne; Linda Hall; SWETS; UnCover. **CCC**.
Supersedes in part (in 1993): Colloids and Surfaces (ISSN 0166-6622)
Description: Publishes original papers on basic colloid and surface science and, in particular, its application in engineering and applied science.
Refereed Serial

541.3   NE   ISSN 0927-7765
QP517.S87   CODEN: CSBBEQ
COLLOIDS AND SURFACES B: BIOINTERFACES. (Text in English) 1980. 18/yr. fl.1701($978) (effective 1998). Elsevier Science B.V., P.O. Box 211, 1000 AE Amsterdam, Netherlands. TEL 31-20-4853911. FAX 31-20-4853598. TELEX 18582 ESPA NL. E-mail: nlinfo-f@elsevier.nl; usinfo-f@elsevier.com; forinfo-kyf04035@niftyserve.or.jp; URL: http://www.elsevier.nl/. (Subscr. in the Americas to: Elsevier Science, Regional Sales Office, Box 945, New York, NY 10159-0945. TEL 212-633-3730. FAX 212-633-3680; Subscr. in Australasia and the Far East to: Elsevier Science (Singapore) Pte Ltd, No.1 Temasek Ave., No.17-01 Millenia Tower, Singapore 039192, Singapore. TEL 65-434-3727. FAX 65-337-2230; Subscr. in Japan to: Elsevier Science Japan, 9-15 Higashi-Azabu 1-chome, Minato-ku, Tokyo 106, Japan. TEL 81-3-5561-5033. FAX 81-3-5561-5047) Ed.Bd. (also avail. in microform from UMI; back issues avail.) **Indexed:** ASCA, Chem.Cit.Ind., Intl.Polym.Sci.& Tech., Mat.Sci.Cit.Ind., Paper & Bd.Abstr., Photo.Abstr., RAPRA, SSCI. Document type: academic/scholarly publication.
—BLDSC (3313.552020); AskIEEE; CASDDS; CISTI; Ei; EMDOCS; Genuine Article; KR SourceOne; Linda Hall; SWETS; UnCover. **CCC**.
Supersedes in part (in 1993): Colloids and Surfaces (ISSN 0166-6622)
Description: Provides an international forum for fundamental and applied research on colloids and interfacial phenomena in relation to systems of biological origin, with particular attention to the medical, pharmaceutical, biotechnology, food and cosmetics fields.
Refereed Serial

COMBUSTION INSTITUTE. WESTERN STATES SECTION. PAPERS. see ENGINEERING — Chemical Engineering

662 541   NE   ISSN 0010-2202
QD516   CODEN: CBSTB9
COMBUSTION SCIENCE AND TECHNOLOGY. 1969. 48/yr. (in 8 vols., 6 nos./vol.). $242 (effective 1998). Gordon and Breach - Harwood Academic, Amsteldisk 166, 1st Fl., 1079 LH Amsterdam, Netherlands. E-mail: glassman@princeton.edu; URL: http://www.gbhap.com/Combustion___Science___Technology/. (Subscr. to: International Publishers Distributor, Box 32160, Newark, NJ 07102. TEL 800-545-8398. FAX 215-750-6343) Ed. Irvin Glassman. adv.; charts; illus.; index. (also avail. in microform) **Indexed:** A.S.& T.Ind., Appl.Mech.Rev., ASCA, Chem.Abstr., Chem.Cit.Ind., Chem.Eng.Abstr., Curr.Cont., Eng.Ind., Environ.Per.Bibl., Excerp.Med., Fuel & Energy Abstr., Gas Abstr., Ind.Sci.Rev., INSPEC, Int.Aerosp.Abstr., Mat.Sci.Cit.Ind., Sci.Cit.Ind. Document type: academic/scholarly publication.
●Also available online.
Also available on CD-ROM.
—BLDSC (3330.205000); CASDDS; CISTI; KR SourceOne; SWETS; UnCover. **CCC**.
Incorporates (in 1975): Pyrodynamics.
Refereed Serial

541.3   NE   ISSN 0069-8040
COMPREHENSIVE CHEMICAL KINETICS. (Text in English) 1969. irreg., vol.33, 1992. price varies. Elsevier Science B.V., Books Division, P.O. Box 211, 1000 AE Amsterdam, Netherlands. TEL 31-20-4853911. FAX 31-20-4853705. TELEX 18582 ESPA NL. E-mail: nlinfo-f@elsevier.nl; usinfo-f@elsevier.com; forinfo-kyf04035@niftyserve.or.jp; URL: http://www.elsevier.nl/. (Subscr. in the Americas to: Elsevier Science, Regional Sales Office, Box 945, New York, NY 10159-0945. TEL 212-633-3730. FAX 212-633-3680; Subscr. in Australasia and the Far East to: Elsevier Science (Singapore) Pte Ltd, No.1 Temasek Ave., No.17-01 Millenia Tower, Singapore 039192, Singapore. TEL 65-434-3727. FAX 65-337-2230; Subscr. in Japan to: Elsevier Science Japan, 9-15 Higashi-Azabu 1-chome, Minato-ku, Tokyo 106, Japan. TEL 81-3-5561-5033. FAX 81-3-5561-5047) Ed.Bd. (back issues avail.) Document type: monographic series.
—BLDSC (3366.300000); CISTI; Ei.
Refereed Serial

CONCEPTS IN MAGNETIC RESONANCE; an educational quarterly. see MEDICAL SCIENCES — Radiology And Nuclear Medicine

537   BW   ISSN 0573-3022
CONFERENCE INTERNATIONALE SUR LES PHENOMENES D'IONISATION DANS LES GAZ. COMPTES RENDUS.* irreg. Akademiya Navuk Belarusi, Institut Fiziki, Prospekt Skoriny, 70, 220602 Minsk, Belarus. TEL 39-47-55.

541.3   US   ISSN 1049-9407
QD506.A1   CODEN: CRCYEP
CRITICAL REVIEWS IN SURFACE CHEMISTRY. 1990. q. $98.50 to individuals; institutions $306 (effective 1997). Begell House Inc., 79 Madison Ave., Ste. 1205, New York, NY 10016-7892. TEL 212-725-1999. FAX 212-213-8368. E-mail: begellhouse@worldnet.att.net. Ed. Peter M.A. Sherwood; Pub. William Begell. R&P contact: Jim Kelly. adv. contact: Jim Kellyan. **Indexed:** Alloys Ind., ASCA, Chem.Cit.Ind., Mat.Sci.Cit.Ind., Met.Abstr.Ind., Met.Abstr., Nonfer.Met.Alert, PCC Alert, Steels Alert, World Alum.Abstr. Document type: academic/scholarly publication.
—BLDSC (3487.483200); CASDDS; CISTI; Ei; Genuine Article; SWETS; UnCover. **CCC**.
Description: Provides critical evaluations of new research and developments in surface chemistry.

541.345   US   ISSN 1359-0294
▼**CURRENT OPINION IN COLLOID & INTERFACE SCIENCE.** 1996. bi-m. Current Science, 400 Market St., Ste. 700, Philadelphia, PA 19106. TEL 215-274-2210; 800-552-5860. FAX 215-574-3533. (And: Current Science Ltd., 34-42 Cleveland St., London W1P 6LB, England. TEL 0171-323-0323. FAX 0171-636-6911) Eds. Eric W. Kaler, Brian H. Robinson.
—BLDSC (3500.773540); CISTI; Genuine Article; SWETS. **CCC**.

541.3   RU   ISSN 0012-5016
QD1   CODEN: DKPCAG
DOKLADY PHYSICAL CHEMISTRY. English translation of: Rossiiskaya Akademiya Nauk. Doklady. 1957. m. $1795 in US; elsewhere $2100 (effective 1998). (Russian Academy of Sciences, Physical Chemistry Section) Maik Nauka - Interperiodica, Mezhdunarodnyi Otdel, Ul. Profsoyuznaya, 90, 117864 Moscow, Russia. TEL 7-095-3360066. FAX 7-095-3360666. (Dist. by: Plenum Publishing Corp., 233 Spring St., New York, NY 10013-1578, U.S.A. TEL 212-620-8468. FAX 212-463-0742) Ed. V.A. Kabanov. (also avail. in microform from UMI; back issues avail.) **Indexed:** Alloys Ind., Chem.Titles, Energy Res.Abstr., Eng.Mat.Abstr., INIS Atomind., Mass Spectr.Bull., Met.Abstr.Ind., Met.Abstr., Nonfer.Met.Alert, PCC Alert, Steels Alert, World Alum.Abstr. Document type: academic/scholarly publication.
—BLDSC (0411.350000); CISTI; Ei; SWETS; UMI; UnCover. **CCC**.
Refereed Serial

541.3   US   ISSN 0737-3937
TP363   CODEN: DRTEDQ
DRYING TECHNOLOGY; an international journal. 1983. 10/yr. $1095 (foreign $1132.50) (effective 1998). Marcel Dekker Journals, 270 Madison Ave., New York, NY 10016. TEL 212-696-9000. FAX 212-685-4540. TELEX 421419. (Subscr. to: Box 5017, Monticello, NY 12701) Ed. A. Mujumdar. R&P contact: Julia Mulligan. adv. contact: Lourdes Barroso. bk.rev.; charts. (also avail. in microform from RPI) **Indexed:** Abstr.Bull.Inst.Pap.Chem., ASCA, Chem.Eng.Abstr., Curr.Adv.Ecol.Sci., Curr.Cont., Excerp.Med., Food Sci & Tech.Abstr., Forest Prod.Abstr., Maize Abstr., Mat.Sci.Cit.Ind., T.C.E.A.
—BLDSC (3630.226500); CASDDS; CISTI; Ei; Genuine Article; Linda Hall; SWETS; UMI. **CCC**.
Refereed Serial

541.35   GW   ISSN 1011-4246
CODEN: EPNWDD
E P A NEWSLETTER. (Text in English) 1978. q. 30 SFr. European Photochemistry Association, Stiftstr. 34-36, 45470 Muelheim, Germany. TEL 49-208-30643672. FAX 49-208-30643951. E-mail: kuhn@mpi-muelheim.mpg.de; URL: http://cric.chemres.hu. Ed. Hans Jochen Kuhn. adv. contact: Hans Jochen Kuhn. bk.rev. circ. 1,200. **Indexed:** Chem.Abstr. Document type: newsletter.
—BLDSC (3793.301830); CASDDS.
Description: Contains research articles, technical reports, local and national photochemistry reports, historical articles, travel reports, association news, reports and announcements of events, abstracts of theses, titles of new photochemistry books and review papers, and positions available.
Refereed Serial

CHEMISTRY — PHYSICAL CHEMISTRY

ELECTROCHEMICAL SOCIETY OF INDIA. JOURNAL. see CHEMISTRY — *Electrochemistry*

ENSANIAN PHYSICOCHEMICAL INSTITUTE. JOURNAL. see *PHYSICS*

541.3   US
EXPERIMENTAL THERMODYNAMICS SERIES. Variant title: I U P A C Experimental Thermodynamics Series. (Subseries of: I U P A C Chemical Data Series) irreg, vol.4, 1994. (International Union of Pure and Applied Chemistry, Commission on Thermodynamics) C R C Press, Inc., 2000 Corporate Blvd., N.W., Boca Raton, FL 33431. TEL 561-994-0555; 800-272-7737. FAX 561-998-9784. TELEX 568689-CRC PRESS. **Document type:** monographic series.

620.11217 541.361   UK   ISSN 0308-0501
TH1092   CODEN: FMATDV
F A M - FIRE AND MATERIALS; an international journal. 1976. bi-m. $925 (foreign $925) (effective 1998). John Wiley & Sons Ltd., Journals, Baffins Ln., Chichester, W. Sussex PO19 1UD, England. TEL 44-1243-779777. FAX 44-1243-775878. E-mail: info-assets@wiley.co.uk; URL: http://www.wiley.co.uk. (Subscr. in the Americas to: John Wiley & Sons, Inc., 605 Third Ave., New York, NY 10158. TEL 212-850-6645. FAX 212-850-6021) Ed. J.P. Redfern. adv.: B&W page £595, color page £1495; trim 297 x 210; adv. contact: Bob Kern. bk.rev.; charts; stat.; index. circ. 241. (also avail. in microform from UMI; back issues avail.; reprint service avail. from SWZ) Ed. J.P. Redfern. **Indexed:** Chem.Abstr., Curr.Cont., Eng.Ind. **Document type:** academic/scholarly publication.
—BLDSC (3930.250000); CASDDS; CISTI; Ei; Linda Hall; SWETS; UMI; UnCover. **CCC.**
Description: Contains scientific and technological communications directed at the fire properties of materials and the products into which they are made.
Refereed Serial

541   UK   ISSN 0301-7249
QD1   CODEN: FDISE6
FARADAY DISCUSSIONS. Key Title: Faraday Discussions of the Chemical Society. Online edition (UK ISSN 1364-5498) 1946. s-a. £250 to institutions (US $450) (effective 1997). The Royal Society of Chemistry, Thomas Graham House, Science Park, Milton Rd., Cambridge CB4 4WF, England. TEL 44-1223-420066. FAX 44-1223-423429. E-mail: sales@rc.org; URL: http://chemistry.rsc.org/rsc/. (Subscr. to: Turpin Distribution Services Ltd., Blackhorse Rd., Letchworth, Herts. SG6 1HN, England. TEL 44-1462-672555. FAX 44-1462-480947) index. (also avail. in microfilm from UMI,PMC) **Indexed:** ASCA, Biol.Abstr., Biwk.Pap.Rad.Chem.& Photochem., Br.Ceram.Abstr., Cadscan., Chem.Abstr., Chem.Cit.Ind., Curr.Cont., Eng.Ind., Ind.Med., Ind.Sci.Rev., INSPEC, Lead Abstr., Mass Spectr.Bull., Mat.Sci.Cit.Ind., Math.R., Met.Abstr., RAPRA, Sci.Cit.Ind., Zincscan. **Document type:** academic/scholarly publication.
●Also available online. Vendor(s): STN International (CJRSC).
—BLDSC (3866.900000); AskIEEE; CASDDS; CISTI; Genuine Article; KR SourceOne; Linda Hall; SWETS; UMI. **CCC.**
Formerly: Faraday Society. Discussions (ISSN 0014-7664)
Description: Designed to cover the broad aspects of physicochemical topics to encourage scientists of various disciplines to contribute their varied viewpoints to a common theme.
Refereed Serial

541.3   UK   ISSN 0956-5000
QD450   CODEN: JCFTEV
FARADAY TRANSACTIONS; a journal of physical chemistry and chemical physics. Online edition (UK ISSN 1364-5455) 1972. s-m. £1018 to institutions (US $1832) (effective 1997). The Royal Society of Chemistry, Thomas Graham House, Science Park, Milton Rd., Cambridge CB4 4WF, England. TEL 44-1223-420066. FAX 44-1223-423623. E-mail: sales@rsc.org; URL: http://chemistry.rsc.org/rsc/. (Subscr. to: Turpin Distribution Services Ltd., Blackhorse Rd., Letchworth, Herts. SG6 1HN, England. TEL 44-1462-672555. FAX 44-1462-480947) bk.rev.; charts; illus.; index. (also avail. in microform from UMI,PMC) **Indexed:** Alloys Ind., API Catal., API Hlth.& Environ., API Oil., API Pet.Ref., API Pet.Subst., API Transport., ASCA, Biol.Abstr., Biwk.Pap.Rad.Chem.& Photochem., Cadscan., Chem.Abstr., Chem.Cit.Ind., Chem.Eng.Abstr., Curr.Cont., Eng.Mat.Abstr., Ind.Chem., INIS Atomind., INSPEC (1990-), Lead Abstr., Mass Spectr.Bull., Met.Abstr., Met.Abstr.Ind., Nonfer.Met.Alert, PCC Alert, Ref.Zh., Soils & Fert., Steels Alert, Sugar Ind.Abstr., World Alum.Abstr., Zincscan. **Document type:** academic/scholarly publication.
●Also available online. Vendor(s): STN International (CJRSC).
—BLDSC (4727.290000); AskIEEE; CASDDS; CISTI; Genuine Article; KR SourceOne; Linda Hall; SWETS; UMI; UnCover. **CCC.**
Incorporates (in 1990): Royal Society of Chemistry. Journal: Faraday Transactions 1 (ISSN 0300-9599); Royal Society of Chemistry. Journal: Faraday Transactions 2 (ISSN 0300-9238); Which superseded: Faraday Society. Transactions (ISSN 0014-7672)
Description: Provides coverage of work on topics such as colloid and interface science, surface science, physisorption and chromatographic science, chemisorption and heterogeneous catalysis, zeolites and ion-exchange phenomena, as well as molecular and chemical physics.
Refereed Serial

541   BU   ISSN 0204-5958
TA405   CODEN: FKMEDW
FIZIKO-KHIMICHESKA MEKHANIKA/PHYSICO-CHEMICAL MECHANICS. (Text in Bulgarian, German, Russian; summaries in English, Russian) 1975. irreg. 1.15 lv. per no. (Bulgarska Akademiia na Naukite) Publishing House of the Bulgarian Academy of Sciences, Acad. G. Bonchev St., Bldg. 6, 1113 Sofia, Bulgaria. (Dist. by: Hemus, 6, Rouski Blvd., 1000 Sofia, Bulgaria) illus. circ. 480. (reprint service avail. from IRC) **Indexed:** BSL Math., Chem.Abstr.
—BLDSC (0390.007000); CASDDS; CISTI; Linda Hall.

541.3   KR   ISSN 0367-2409
Z5524.C7   CODEN: FKMLAG
FIZIKO-KHIMICHESKAYA MEKHANIKA I LIOFILNOST' DISPERSNYKH SISTEM; respublikanskii mezhvedomstvennyi sbornik nauchnykh trudov. (Text in Russian) 1968. a. (Akademiya Nauk Ukrainy, Institut Kolloidnoi Khimii i Khimii Vody, Otdelenie Prirodnykh Dispersnykh Sistem) Vidavnitstvo Naukova Dumka, Vul. Tereshchenivska 3, 252601 Kiev, Ukraine. TEL 044-224-4068. FAX 044-224-7060. (Dist. by: Mezhdunarodnaya Kniga, B. Yakimanka 39, 117049 Moscow, Russia) Ed. F.D. Ovcharenko. **Indexed:** Chem.Abstr.
—CASDDS; CISTI; Linda Hall.

541.3   KR   ISSN 0430-6252
CODEN: FKMMAJ
FIZIKO-KHIMICHESKAYA MEKHANIKA MATERIALOV/FIZYKO-KHIMICHNA MEKHANIKA MATERIALIV; nauchno-tekhnicheskii zhurnal. English translation: Materials Sciences. (Text in English, Russian, Ukrainian) 1965. bi-m. $260 (effective 1998). Fyzyko-Mekhanichnyi Instytut im. G.V. Karpenko, Vul. Naukova 5, 290601 Lviv, Ukraine. TEL 38-322-637374. FAX 38-322-649427. E-mail: panasiuk@kvant.lviv.ua. (Dist. by: Mezhdunarodnaya Kniga, B. Yakimanka 39, 117049 Moscow, Russia) Ed. V.V. Panasiuk. adv. contact: R.R. Kokot. circ. 300. **Indexed:** Alloys Ind., Chem.Abstr., Djerelo, Eng.Mat.Abstr., INIS Atomind., INSPEC (1970-), Int.Aerosp.Abstr., Met.Abstr., Met.Abstr.Ind., Nonfer.Met.Alert, PCC Alert, Steels Alert, World Alum.Abstr. **Document type:** academic/scholarly publication.
—BLDSC (0390.010000); AskIEEE; CASDDS; CISTI; KNAW; KR SourceOne; Linda Hall. **CCC.**

541.392   NE   ISSN 0378-3812
QD504   CODEN: FPEQDT
FLUID PHASE EQUILIBRIA. (Text in English) 1978. 26/yr. fl.6776($3894) (effective 1998). Elsevier Science B.V., P.O. Box 211, 1000 AE Amsterdam, Netherlands. TEL 31-20-4853911. FAX 31-20-4853598. TELEX 18582 ESPA NL. E-mail: nlinfo-f@elsevier.nl; usinfo-f@elsevier.com; forinfo-kyf04035@niftyserve.or.jp; URL: http://www.elsevier.nl/. (Subscr. in the Americas to: Elsevier Science, Regional Sales Office, Box 945, New York, NY 10159-0945. TEL 212-633-3730. FAX 212-633-3680; Subscr. in Australasia and the Far East to: Elsevier Science (Singapore) Pte Ltd, No.1 Temasek Ave., No.17-01 Millenia Tower, Singapore 039192, Singapore. TEL 65-434-3727. FAX 65-337-2230; Subscr. in Japan to: Elsevier Science Japan, 9-15 Higashi-Azabu 1-chome, Minato-ku, Tokyo 106, Japan. TEL 81-3-5561-5033. FAX 81-3-5561-5047) Ed. H. Renon. adv.; bk.rev.; charts; illus.; index. (also avail. in microform from UMI; reprint service avail. from SWZ) **Indexed:** ASCA, Chem.Abstr., Chem.Cit.Ind., Chem.Eng.Abstr., Curr.Cont., E&P Hlth. (1993-), Eng.Ind., Gas Abstr., Gas Process.& Ppl. (1993-), Geo.Abstr.P.G., Ind.Sci.Rev., INSPEC, INSPEC, Mat.Sci.Cit.Ind., Off.Tech. (1993-), Petrol.Abstr. (1981-), Sci.Cit.Ind., T.C.E.A. **Document type:** academic/scholarly publication.
—BLDSC (3962.170000); CASDDS; CISTI; Ei; EMDOCS; Genuine Article; KR SourceOne; Linda Hall; PADDS; SWETS; UnCover. **CCC.**
Description: For researchers and applied scientists, particularly those in chemical and metallurgical engineering, concerned with the properties or applications of fluid-phase equilibria.
Refereed Serial

541.3   JA
FULLERENE INFORMATION. (Text in Japanese) q. 150000 Yen. Daiya Risachi - Dia Research Institute, 1-30, Shiba 2-chome, Minato-ku, Tokyo 105, Japan. TEL 81-3-3798-2611. FAX 81-3-3798-1224.
Description: Contains latest information of advanced science, technology and application in the field of fullerene.

500 541.3   US   ISSN 1064-122X
QD181.C1   CODEN: FTECEG
FULLERENE SCIENCE AND TECHNOLOGY. 1992. bi-m. $695 (foreign $717.50) (effective 1998). Marcel Dekker, Inc., 270 Madison Ave., New York, NY 10016. TEL 212-696-9000. FAX 212-685-4540. TELEX 421419. (Subscr. to: Box 5017, Monticello, NY 12701) Ed. T. Braun; Pub. Graham Garratt. R&P contact: Julia Mulligan. adv.; bibl.; charts; illus. (also avail. in microfilm from RPI) **Indexed:** Alloys Ind., ASCA, Curr.Cont., Eng.Mat.Abstr., INSPEC (1993-), Intl.Polym.Sci.& Tech., Met.Abstr.Ind., Met.Abstr., Nonfer.Met.Alert, PCC Alert, RAPRA, Steels Alert, World Alum.Abstr. **Document type:** academic/scholarly publication.
—BLDSC (4055.559950); AskIEEE; CASDDS; CISTI; Ei; Genuine Article; KR SourceOne; UMI. **CCC.**
Refereed Serial

541.393   CC   ISSN 1000-3304
QD380   CODEN: GAXUE9
GAOFENZI XUEBAO. English edition: Chinese Journal of Polymer Science (ISSN 0256-7679) (Text in Chinese; summaries in English) 1957. bi-m. $135 (effective 1997). (Chinese Chemical Society) Science Press, Marketing and Sales Department, 16 Donghuangchenggen North St., Beijing 100717, People's Republic of China. TEL 4010642. FAX 4019810. adv. circ. 6,000. **Document type:** academic/scholarly publication.
—BLDSC (0660.800000); CASDDS; Linda Hall.
Formerly (until 1986): Gaofenzi Tongxun (ISSN 0453-2880)
Description: Includes polymer synthesis, polymer chemistry, polymer physics, and physical chemistry, as well as applied polymer science.
Refereed Serial

CHEMISTRY — PHYSICAL CHEMISTRY

541.3 JA ISSN 0910-6774
HANDAI KAGAKU NETSUGAKU REPOTO/OSAKA UNIVERSITY. MICROCALORIMETRY RESEARCH CENTER. ANNUAL REPORT. (Text in English, Japanese; summaries in English) 1984. a. Osaka Daigaku, Rigakubu, Fuzoku Mikuro Netsu Kenkyu Senta - Osaka University, Faculty of Science, Microcalorimetry Research Center, 1-1, Machikaneyamacho, Toyonaka-shi, Osaka 560, Japan. TEL 81-6-850-5523. FAX 81-6-850-5526. E-mail: sorai@chem.Sci.osaka-u.ac.jp. Ed. Michio Sorai. R&P contact: Michio Sorai. circ. 900. **Document type:** academic/scholarly publication.
Refereed Serial

541.3 NE ISSN 0169-2909
HANDBOOK OF COMPOSITES. 1985. irreg., vol.4, 1988. price varies. Elsevier Science B.V., Books Division, P.O. Box 211, 1000 AE Amsterdam, Netherlands. TEL 31-20-4853911. FAX 31-20-4853705. TELEX 18582 ESPA NL. E-mail: nlinfo-f@elsevier.nl; usinfo-f@elsevier.com; forinfo-kyf04035@niftyserve.or.jp; URL: http://www.elsevier.nl/. (Subscr. in the Americas to: Elsevier Science, Regional Sales Office, Box 945, New York, NY 10159-0945. TEL 212-633-3730. FAX 212-633-3680; Subscr. in Australasia and the Far East to: Elsevier Science (Singapore) Pte Ltd, No.1 Temasek Ave., No.17-01 Millenia Tower, Singapore 039192, Singapore. TEL 65-434-3727. FAX 65-337-2230; Subscr. in Japan to: Elsevier Science Japan, 9-15 Higashi-Azabu 1-chome, Minato-ku, Tokyo 106, Japan. TEL 81-3-5561-5033. FAX 81-3-5561-5047) **Indexed:** INSPEC, Zent.Math. **Document type:** monographic series.
Refereed Serial

541.3 RU ISSN 0018-1439
QD601.A1 CODEN: HIECAP
HIGH ENERGY CHEMISTRY. English translation of: Khimiya Vysokikh Energii (RU ISSN 0023-1193) 1967. bi-m. $1595 in US; elsewhere $1865 (effective 1998). (Russian Academy of Sciences) Maik Nauka - Interperiodica, Mezhdunarodnyi Otdel, Ul. Prosoyuznaya, 90, 117864 Moscow, Russia. TEL 7-095-3360066. FAX 7-095-3360666. (Dist. by: Plenum Publishing Corp., 233 Spring St., New York, NY 10013-1578, U.S.A.) Ed. A.K. Pikaev. adv.; bk.rev.; illus. (also avail. in microfilm from UMI; back issues avail.) **Indexed:** Cadscan., Chem.Titles, Curr.Cont., Energy Res.Abstr., Ind.Sci.Rev., INIS Atomind., Lead Abstr., Zincscan. **Document type:** academic/scholarly publication.
—BLDSC (0412.086500); CASDDS; CISTI; Genuine Article; UMI; UnCover. **CCC.**
Refereed Serial

541.39 US
QC276 CODEN: HTMSFP
HIGH TEMPERATURE AND MATERIALS SCIENCE. 1969. bi-m. $395 (foreign $420) (effective 1998). (High Temperature Society) Humana Press Inc., 999 Riverview Dr., Ste. 208, Totowa, NJ 07512. TEL 973-256-1699. FAX 973-256-8341. E-mail: humana@mindspring.com; URL: http://www.humanapress.com. (Dist. in Japan by: Maruzen Co. Ltd., Journals Division, P.O. Box 5050, Tokyo 100-31, Japan. TEL 03-3275-8591. FAX 03-3275-8591) Ed. John Margrave. R&P contact: Richard Hruska. adv. contact: Thomas B. Lanigan. bk.rev.; bibl.; charts; illus. **Indexed:** Alloys Ind., ASCA, Br.Ceram.Abstr., Bull.Thermodyn.& Thermochem., Cadscan, Chem.Abstr., Chem.Cit.Ind., Curr.Cont., Eng.Mat.Abstr., Ind.Sci.Rev., INIS Atomind., INSPEC, Lead Abstr., Mass Spectr.Bull., Mat.Sci.Cit.Ind., Met.Abstr., Met.Abstr.Ind., Nonfer.Met.Alert, PCC Alert, Phys.Ber., Sci.Cit.Ind., Steels Alert, World Alum.Abstr. **Document type:** academic/scholarly publication.
—BLDSC (4307.365600); AskIEEE; CASDDS; CISTI; Ei; Genuine Article; KR SourceOne; Linda Hall; SWETS; UnCover. **CCC.**
Former titles: High Temperature Materials Science (ISSN 1080-1278); (until 1995): High Temperature Science and Material (ISSN 0018-1536); Journal of High Temperature Science (ISSN 0022-1538)
Description: Publishes articles in high temperature science, chemistry, ceramics, material science, spectroscopy, metallurgy, energy technology, physics, and the engineering aspects of these fields.
Refereed Serial

HIGH TEMPERATURES - HIGH PRESSURES. see PHYSICS — Heat

541.37 JA ISSN 0915-8170
HOKKAIDO UNIVERSITY. CATALYSIS RESEARCH CENTER. ANNUAL REPORT (YEAR)/HOKKAIDO DAIGAKU SHOKUBAI KAGAKU KENKYU CENTER NENPO. (Text in English, Japanese) 1989. a. free. Hokkaido University, Catalysis Research Center, Kita-11, Nishi-10, Kita-ku, Sapporo 060, Japan. TEL 011-716-2111. FAX 011-709-4748. Ed. Matsushima Tatsuo. circ. 1,000. **Indexed:** Alloys Ind., Eng.Mat.Abstr., Mel.Abstr., Met.Abstr.Ind., Nonfer.Met.Alert, PCC Alert, Steels Alert, World Alum.Abstr.
—BLDSC (1140.870000); Linda Hall.
Formerly (until 1989): Hokkaido University. Catalysis Research Center. Annual Report (ISSN 0911-6664)
Description: Provides information concerning activities of the institute.

541.3 JA
HOSHASEN KAGAKU TORONKAI KOEN YOSHISHU/PROCEEDINGS OF SYMPOSIUM ON RADIATION CHEMISTRY. (Text in English, Japanese) 1957. a. Nihon Hoshasen Kagakkai - Japanese Society of Radiation Chemistry, Nihon Genshiryoku Kenkyujo Takasaki Kenkyujo, 1233, Watanukicho, Takasaki-shi 370-12, Japan. **Document type:** proceedings.

660.299 541.395 NE ISSN 1386-4556
▼**INDUSTRIAL CATALYSIS NEWS.** Announced for publication in 1998. m. 1374 SFr. (effective 1998). Baltzer Science Publishers B.V., P.O. Box 221, 1400 AE Bussum, Netherlands. TEL 31-20-6370061. FAX 31-20-6323651. E-mail: subscribe@baltzer.nl; URL: http://www.baltzer.nl. **Document type:** academic/scholarly publication.

547.1 541.39 US ISSN 0073-8077
QD156 CODEN: INSYA3
INORGANIC SYNTHESES SERIES. 1939. irreg., vol.30, 1995. (American Chemical Society) John Wiley & Sons, Inc., Journals, 605 Third Ave., New York, NY 10158-0012. TEL 212-850-6645. adv.; bk.rev.; index, cum.index: vols.1-10 in vol.10. **Indexed:** ASCA, Chem.Abstr., Ind.Sci.Rev., Sci.Cit.Ind. **Document type:** monographic series.
—BLDSC (4515.900000); CASDDS; CISTI; SWETS.
Refereed Serial

541.3 530 US ISSN 0927-7056
QD506.A1 CODEN: INSCE9
INTERFACE SCIENCE. 1993. q. fl.595 to institutions; $305.50 to institutions in U.S. (effective 1998). Kluwer Academic Publishers Boston, Box 358, Accord Sta., Hingham, MA 02018-0358. TEL 617-871-6600. FAX 617-871-6528. TELEX 200190. E-mail: services@wkap.nl; URL: http://www.wkap.nl. (Dist. outside N. America by: Kluwer Academic Publishers Group, P.O. Box 322, 3300 AH Dordrecht, Netherlands. TEL 31-78-6392392. FAX 31-78-6546474) Ed. David J. Srolovitz. (back issues avail.; reprint service avail. from SWZ) **Indexed:** Alloys Ind., ASCA, Eng.Mat.Abstr., INSPEC, Met.Abstr., Met.Abstr.Ind., Nonfer.Met.Alert, PCC Alert, Steels Alert, World Alum.Abstr. **Document type:** academic/scholarly publication.
—BLDSC (4533.460000); CASDDS; CISTI; Ei; Genuine Article; KR SourceOne; SWETS. **CCC.**
Description: Concentrates on the structure and properties of the internal interfaces in solids.
Refereed Serial

541.3 547.1 US
CODEN: ISDMAT
INTERNATIONAL DATA SERIES. SELECTED DATA ON MIXTURES. SERIES A. THERMODYNAMIC PROPERTIES OF NON-REACTING BINARY SYSTEMS OF ORGANIC SUBSTANCES. 1973. q. $1200. Thermodynamics Research Center, Texas Engineering Experiment Station, Texas A & M University System, College Station, TX 77843-3111. TEL 409-845-4940. FAX 409-847-8590. E-mail: info@trchpl.tamu.edu; URL: http://trcweb.tamu.edu. Ed. Kenneth N. Marsh; Pub. Kenneth N. Marsh. R&P contact: Kenneth N. Marsh. adv. contact: Kenneth N. Marsh. circ. 128. **Indexed:** Chem.Abstr. **Document type:** academic/scholarly publication.
—BLDSC (4539.503000); CASDDS; CISTI. **CCC.**
Formerly: Thermodynamics Research Center. International Data Series. Selected Data on Mixtures. Series A. Thermodynamic Properties on Non-reacting Binary Systems of Organic Substances (ISSN 0147-1503)
Description: Data on the thermodynamic properties of organic substances.

541.3 US ISSN 0538-8066
QD501 CODEN: IJCKBO
INTERNATIONAL JOURNAL OF CHEMICAL KINETICS. 1968. m. $1789 (foreign $1999) (effective 1998). John Wiley & Sons, Inc., Journals, 605 Third Ave., New York, NY 10158. TEL 212-850-6645. FAX 212-850-6021. TELEX 12-7063. E-mail: SUBINFO@JWILEY.COM; URL: http://www.wiley.co.uk. (Subscr. outside the Americas to: John Wiley & Sons Ltd., Baffins Ln., Chichester, W. Sussex PO19 1UD, England. TEL 44-1243-779777. FAX 44-1243-776128) Ed. David M. Golden. adv.: B&W page £640, color page £1515; trim 279 x 210. bk.rev.; index. circ. 650. (also avail. in microform from UMI; back issues avail.; reprint service avail. from UMI) **Indexed:** ASCA, Biol.Abstr., Biwk.Pap.Rad.Chem.& Photochem., Chem.Abstr., Chem.Cit.Ind., Chem.Infd., Curr.Adv.Ecol.Sci., Curr.Cont., Excerp.Med., Ind.Sci.Rev., Mass Spectr.Bull., Sci.Cit.Ind. **Document type:** academic/scholarly publication.
—BLDSC (4542.165000); CASDDS; CISTI; Ei; Genuine Article; Linda Hall; SWETS; UMI; UnCover. **CCC.**
Description: Covers quantitative relationships between molecular structure and chemical activity, organic and inorganic chemistry, biochemical kinetics, reaction mechanisms, and surface kinetics.
Refereed Serial

541.3 UK ISSN 0144-235X
QD450 CODEN: IRPCDL
INTERNATIONAL REVIEWS IN PHYSICAL CHEMISTRY. Online edition (UK ISSN 1366-591X) 1981-1984; resumed 1985. q. £361($595) to institutions (£433($714) with online ed.) (effective 1998). Taylor & Francis Ltd., 1 Gunpowder Sq., London EC4A 3DE, England. TEL 44-171-583-0490. FAX 44-171-583-0585. E-mail: info@tandf.co.uk; URL: http://www.tandf.co.uk/. (Subscr. in N. America to: Taylor & Francis Inc., 1900 Frost Rd., Ste. 101, Bristol, PA 19007-1598. TEL 800-821-8312. FAX 215-785-5515) Ed. D.C. Clary. adv.; bk.rev.; bibl.; charts; illus.; index. (back issues avail.) **Indexed:** Alloys Ind., ASCA, Chem.Abstr., Chem.Cit.Ind., Curr.Cont., Eng.Mat.Abstr., Ind.Sci.Rev., INIS Atomind., Met.Abstr.Ind., Met.Abstr., Nonfer.Met.Alert, Sci.Cit.Ind., Steels Alert, World Alum.Abstr. **Document type:** academic/scholarly publication.
●Also available online.
—BLDSC (4547.440000); CASDDS; CISTI; Ei; Genuine Article; Linda Hall; UnCover. **CCC.**
Description: Presents scholarly and critical reviews on important and developing aspects of modern physical chemistry and chemical physics. Provides a means by which to assist specialists and generalists in research, industry and teaching so they can keep abreast of advances in expanding subjects.
Refereed Serial

541.3 US
INTERNATIONAL THERMODYNAMIC TABLES OF THE FLUID STATE. Variant title: I U P A C International Thermodynamic Tables of the Fluid State. irreg., vol.12, 1993. (International Union of Pure and Applied Chemistry) C R C Press, Inc., 2000 Corporate Blvd., N.W., Boca Raton, FL 33431. TEL 561-994-0555; 800-272-7737. FAX 561-998-9784. TELEX 568689-CRC PRESS. **Document type:** monographic series.

541.372 US ISSN 0092-0193
QD561 CODEN: IESEBH
ION EXCHANGE AND SOLVENT EXTRACTION; a series of advances. 1966. irreg., vol.13, 1997. Marcel Dekker, Inc., 270 Madison Ave., New York, NY 10016. TEL 212-696-9000. FAX 212-685-4540. TELEX 421419. Eds. J.A. Marinsky, Y. Marcus; Pub. Graham Garratt. R&P contact: Julia Mulligan. illus. (also avail. in microform from RPI) **Indexed:** Chem.Abstr., Chem.Cit.Ind. **Document type:** monographic series.
—BLDSC (4564.390000); CASDDS; CISTI; Linda Hall; UnCover.
Formed by the 1973 merger of: Ion Exchange: A Series of Advances (ISSN 0075-0328); Solvent Extraction Reviews.
Refereed Serial

CHEMISTRY — PHYSICAL CHEMISTRY

541.36   RU   ISSN 0202-8050
ITOGI NAUKI I TEKHNIKI: KHIMICHESKAYA TERMODINAMIKA I RAVNOVESIYA. irreg., vol.7, 1991. price varies. Vsesoyuznyi Institut Nauchno-Tekhnicheskoi Informatsii (VINITI), Ul. Baltiiskaya 14, Moscow A-219, Russia. (Subscr. to: Mezhdunarodnaya Kniga, Moscow A-219, Russia) **Indexed:** Chem.Abstr.

541.3   RU   ISSN 0202-7968
QD502   CODEN: ITKKDY
ITOGI NAUKI I TEKHNIKI: KINETIKA. KATALIZ. irreg., vol.19, 1989. 11.40 Rub. Vsesoyuznyi Institut Nauchno-Tekhnicheskoi Informatsii (VINITI), Ul. Baltiiskaya 14, Moscow A-219, Russia. (Subscr. to: Mezhdunarodnaya Kniga, Dimitrova ul. 39, 113095 Moscow, Russia) **Indexed:** Chem.Abstr.
—CASDDS; Linda Hall.

541.3   NE   ISSN 0075-3696
                        CODEN: JSQCA7
JERUSALEM SYMPOSIA ON QUANTUM CHEMISTRY AND BIOCHEMISTRY. 1969. irreg., vol.27, 1995. price varies. (Israel Academy of Sciences and Humanities, Section on Sciences, IS) Kluwer Academic Publishers, Postbus 17, 3300 AA Dordrecht, Netherlands. TEL 31-78-6392392. FAX 31-78-6392254. TELEX 29245 KAPG NL. E-mail: services@wkap.nl; URL: http://www.wkap.nl. (Dist. by: Kluwer Academic Publishers Group, P.O. Box 322, 3300 AH Dordrecht, Netherlands. TEL 31-78-6392392. FAX 31-78-6546474; N. America dist. addr.: Box 358, Accord Sta., Hingham, MA 02018-0358. TEL 617-871-6600) Ed. B. Pullman. **Indexed:** Biol.Abstr., Chem.Abstr. **Document type:** proceedings.
—CASDDS; CISTI.
Refereed Serial

541   FR   ISSN 0021-7689
QD1   CODEN: JCPBAN
JOURNAL DE CHIMIE PHYSIQUE ET DE PHYSICO-CHIMIE BIOLOGIQUE; an international journal of physical chemistry, chemical physics and biophysics. (Text and summaries in English, French) 1903. 10/yr. 3516 F.($672) 4450 F. to institutions in Europe (effective 1998). (Societe Francaise de Chimie, Division de Chimie Physique) Editions Scientifiques et Medicales Elsevier, 141 rue de Javel, 75747 Paris, France. TEL 33-1-45589022. FAX 33-1-45589421. URL: http://www.elsevier.nl/. (Subscr. in U.S. and Canada to: Elsevier Science Inc., Box 945, Madison Sq. Sta., New York, 10159-0945. TEL 212-633-3730. FAX 212-633-3680) Ed. R. Marx. adv.; bk.rev.; charts; index. circ. 2,000. (also avail. in microfilm from UMI,PMC) **Indexed:** Anal.Abstr., ASCA, Cadscan, Chem.Abstr., Chem.Cit.Ind., Curr.Cont., GeoRef., Ind.Sci.Rev., INIS Atomind., INSPEC, Lead Abstr., Mass Spectr.Bull., Mat.Sci.Cit.Ind., Met.Abstr., Sci.Cit.Ind., Zincscan. **Document type:** academic/scholarly publication.
—BLDSC (4958.000000); CASDDS; CISTI; Ei; Genuine Article; Linda Hall; SWETS. **CCC.**
Formerly (until 1931): Revue Generale des Colloides (ISSN 0370-5048)
Description: Covers all fields of physical chemistry and chemical physics, including biophysics, quantum and theoretical chemistry, physical chemistry or polymers, computer science in physical chemistry.
Refereed Serial

JOURNAL OF ADHESION. see *PHYSICS*

541.3   CN   ISSN 1203-8407
▼**JOURNAL OF ADVANCED OXIDATION TECHNOLOGIES.** 1996. bi-m. $500. Science & Technology Integration, Inc., University of Western Ontario Research Park, 100 Collip Circle, Ste. 110, London, ON N6G 4X8, Canada. TEL 519-858-5055. FAX 519-858-5056. E-mail: sti.ekabi@info.london.on.ca. **Document type:** academic/scholarly publication.
—BLDSC (4918.947200).
Description: Provides an international forum that accepts papers describing basic research and practical applications of advanced oxidation technologies.

540   UK   ISSN 0884-3996
QH641   CODEN: JBCHE7
JOURNAL OF BIOLUMINESCENCE AND CHEMILUMINESCENCE. 1987. bi-m. £695 (foreign $695) (effective 1997). John Wiley & Sons Ltd., Journals, Baffins Ln., Chichester, W. Sussex PO19 1UD, England. TEL 44-1243-779777. FAX 44-1243-775878. E-mail: info-assets@wiley.co.uk; URL: http://www.wiley.co.uk. (Subscr. in N. America to: John Wiley & Sons, Inc., 605 Third Ave., New York, NY 10158. TEL 212-850-6645. FAX 212-850-6021) Ed. L.J. Kricka. adv.; B&W page £595, color page £1495; trim 260 x 200; adv. contact: Bob Kern. (also avail. in microform from UMI; back issues avail.; reprint service avail. from SWZ) **Indexed:** ASCA, Chem.Abstr., Curr.Biotech.Abstr., Curr.Cont., INSPEC (1988-), Sci.Cit.Ind., Telegen. **Document type:** academic/scholarly publication.
—BLDSC (4953.510000); AskIEEE; CASDDS; CISTI; Ei; Genuine Article; KR SourceOne; Linda Hall; SWETS; UMI; UnCover. **CCC.**
Description: Devoted to fundamental and applied aspects of chemiluminescence and bioluminescence, including their uses as research tools in such diverse fields as chemistry, clinical sciences, environmental monitoring and microbiology.

JOURNAL OF BIOMOLECULAR NMR. see *BIOLOGY — Biological Chemistry*

541.395 660   US   ISSN 0021-9517
QD501   CODEN: JCTLA5
JOURNAL OF CATALYSIS. 1962. 16/yr. $1999 (foreign $2239) (effective 1997). Academic Press, Inc., Journal Division, 525 B St., Ste. 1900, San Diego, CA 92101-4495. TEL 619-230-1840. FAX 619-699-6800. E-mail: apsubs@acad.com; URL: http://www.apnet.com/www/journal.ca.htm; http://www.idealibrary.com/. (Subscr. to: Box 861213, Orlando, FL 32886-12123. TEL 407-347-4040. FAX 407-363-9661) Eds. W. Nicholas Delgass, Roel Prins. adv.; bibl.; charts; illus.; index. (back issues avail.) **Indexed:** A.S.& T.Ind., API Abstr., API Catal., API Hlth.& Environ., API Oil., API Pet.Ref., API Pet.Subst., API Transport., ASCA, Biol.Abstr., Chem.Abstr., Chem.Cit.Ind., Chem.Eng.Abstr., Chem.Infd., Curr.Cont., Eng.Ind., Excerp.Med., Gas Abstr., Ind.Sci.Rev., INIS Atomind., Mass Spectr.Bull., Mat.Sci.Cit.Ind., Sci.Cit.Ind., T.C.E.A. **Document type:** academic/scholarly publication.
●Also available online.
—BLDSC (4954.890000); CASDDS; CISTI; Ei; Genuine Article; KR SourceOne; Linda Hall; SWETS; UnCover. **CCC.**
Description: Publishes original studies in heterogeneous and homogeneous catalysis as well as studies relating catalytic properties with chemical processes at surface, studies of the chemistry of surfaces, and engineering studies related to catalysis.
Refereed Serial

JOURNAL OF CHEMICAL PHYSICS. see *PHYSICS*

541.36   UK   ISSN 0021-9614
QD501   CODEN: JCTDAF
JOURNAL OF CHEMICAL THERMODYNAMICS. 1969. m. £519 (effective 1998). Academic Press Ltd. (Subsidiary of: Harcourt Brace & Company Ltd.), 24-28 Oval Rd., London NW1 7DX, England. TEL 44-171-267-4466. FAX 44-171-482-2293. TELEX 25775 ACPRES G. E-mail: apsubs@acad.com; URL: http://www.hbuk.co.uk/ap/jct; http://www.europe.idealibrary.com/. (Subscr. to: Harcourt Brace & Company Ltd., Foots Cray High St., Sidcup, Kent DA14 5HP, England. TEL 44-181-300-3322. FAX 44-181-309-0807) Ed.Bd. R&P contact: Catherine John. adv. contact: Nik Screen. (reprint service avail. from SWZ) **Indexed:** ASCA, Bull.Thermodyn.& Thermochem., Cadscan, Chem.Abstr., Chem.Cit.Ind., Chem.Infd., Curr.Cont., Gas Abstr., Ind.Sci.Rev., INIS Atomind., INSPEC, Lead Abstr., Mass Spectr.Bull., Met.Abstr., Sci.Cit.Ind., Soils & Fert., World Alum.Abstr., Zincscan. **Document type:** academic/scholarly publication.
●Also available online.
—BLDSC (4957.100000); AskIEEE; CASDDS; CISTI; Ei; Genuine Article; KR SourceOne; Linda Hall; SWETS; UnCover. **CCC.**
Description: Reports the results of significant new measurements of thermodynamical and equilibrium quantities for chemical reactions and of thermodynamic properties of pure substances and of mixtures, using calorimetric, (P, V, T), spectroscopic, and other methods.

541.3   UK
JOURNAL OF COLLECTIVE CHEMISTRY AND PHYSICS. * 1952. s-a. (in double nos.). 150s.($21) Drs. L. Zakarias & J. Zakarias, 7 Downside Rd., Clifton, Bristol BS8 2XE, England. adv.; abstr.; bibl.; charts; illus.; pat.
Formerly: Journal of Detergents and Collective Chemistry and Physics (ISSN 0022-0361)

541.345   US   ISSN 0021-9797
QD549   CODEN: JCISA5
JOURNAL OF COLLOID AND INTERFACE SCIENCE. 1946. 24/yr. $2100 (foreign $2352) (effective 1997). Academic Press, Inc., Journal Division, 525 B St., Ste. 1900, San Diego, CA 92101-4495. TEL 619-230-1840. FAX 619-699-6800. E-mail: apsubs@acad.com; URL: http://www.apnet.com/www/journal.cs.htm; http://www.idealibrary.com/. (Subscr. to: Box 861213, Orlando, FL 32886-1213. TEL 407-347-4040. FAX 407-363-9661) Ed. Darsh Wasan. adv.; bk.rev.; illus.; index. (back issues avail.) **Indexed:** A.S.& T.Ind., Abstr.Bull.Inst.Pap.Chem., API Abstr., API Catal., API Hlth.& Environ., API Oil., API Pet.Ref., API Pet.Subst., API Transport., Appl.Mech.Rev., ASCA, Bibl.Agri., Biol.Abstr., Br.Ceram.Abstr., Chem.Abstr., Chem.Cit.Ind., Chem.Eng.Abstr., Curr.Cont., Dairy Sci.Abstr., Deep Sea Res.& Oceanogr.Abstr., E&P Hlth. (1993-), Energy Info.Abstr., Excerp.Med., Food Sci.& Tech.Abstr., Gas Process.& Ppl. (1993-), GeoRef., Ind.Sci.Rev., INIS Atomind., INSPEC, Int.Aerosp.Abstr., Mat.Sci.Cit.Ind., Met.Abstr., Off.Tech. (1993-), Paper & Bd.Abstr., Petrol.Abstr. (1961-), Photo.Abstr., Phys.Ber., RAPRA, Sci.Cit.Ind., Sel Water Res.Abstr., Soils & Fert., T.C.E.A., World Surf.Coat. **Document type:** academic/scholarly publication.
●Also available online.
—BLDSC (4958.900000); ADONIS; CASDDS; CISTI; Ei; EMDOCS; Genuine Article; KR SourceOne; Linda Hall; PADDS; SWETS; UnCover. **CCC.**
Formerly: Journal of Colloid Science (ISSN 0095-8522)
Description: Publishes original research on fundamental principles and their applications.
Refereed Serial

541.3   US   ISSN 0193-2691
QD549   CODEN: JDTEDS
JOURNAL OF DISPERSION SCIENCE AND TECHNOLOGY. 1980. 7/yr. $715 (foreign $741.25) (effective 1998). Marcel Dekker Journals, 270 Madison Ave., New York, NY 10016. TEL 212-696-9000. FAX 212-685-4540. TELEX 421419. (Subscr. to: Box 5017, Monticello, NY 12701) Eds. Stig Friberg, Paul Becher. (also avail. in microform from RPI) **Indexed:** API Abstr., API Oil., ASCA, Biol.Abstr., Chem.Abstr., Chem.Cit.Ind., Chem.Eng.Abstr., Curr.Cont., Dairy Sci.Abstr., Food Sci.& Tech.Abstr., I.P.A., Ind.Sci.Rev., Mat.Sci.Cit.Ind., Photo.Abstr., Sci.Cit.Ind., T.C.E.A., World Surf.Coat. **Document type:** academic/scholarly publication.
—BLDSC (4969.820000); CASDDS; CISTI; Ei; Genuine Article; Linda Hall; SWETS; UMI. **CCC.**
Refereed Serial

541.3   NE   ISSN 0923-0750
QD471   CODEN: JIMCEN
JOURNAL OF INCLUSION PHENOMENA AND MOLECULAR RECOGNITION IN CHEMISTRY. (Text in English) 1983. m. fl.1395 to institutions; $715.50 to institutions in U.S. (effective 1998). Kluwer Academic Publishers, Postbus 17, 3300 AA Dordrecht, Netherlands. TEL 31-78-6392392. FAX 31-78-6392254. TELEX 29245 KAPG NL. E-mail: services@wkap.nl; URL: http://www.wkap.nl. (Dist. by: Kluwer Academic Publishers Group, P.O. Box 322, 3300 AH Dordrecht, Netherlands. TEL 31-78-6392392. FAX 31-78-6546474; N. America dist. addr.: Box 358, Accord Sta., Hingham, MA 02018-0358. TEL 617-871-6600) Eds. Jerry L. Atwood, J. Eric D. Davies. adv.; bk.rev.; illus.; index. (also avail. in microform from UMI; reprint service avail. from SWZ) **Indexed:** ASCA, Chem.Abstr., Chem.Cit.Ind., Chem.Titles, Curr.Adv.Ecol.Sci., Curr.Cont., IBR, IBZ, Ind.Chem., Ind.Sci.Rev., Int.Abstr.Biol.Sci., Mat.Sci.Cit.Ind., Sci.Cit.Ind. **Document type:** academic/scholarly publication.
—BLDSC (5005.104000); CASDDS; CISTI; Ei; Genuine Article; Linda Hall; SWETS; UMI; UnCover. **CCC.**
Formerly: Journal of Inclusion Phenomena (ISSN 0167-7861)
Description: Reports original research into all aspects of host-guest systems.
Refereed Serial

CHEMISTRY — PHYSICAL CHEMISTRY

541.3　　　　　　　NE　　ISSN 0376-7388
TP159.M4　　　　　　　　CODEN: JMESDO
JOURNAL OF MEMBRANE SCIENCE. 1977. 26/yr. fl.7798($4482) (effective 1998). Elsevier Science B.V., P.O. Box 211, 1000 AE Amsterdam, Netherlands. TEL 31-20-4853911. FAX 31-20-4853598. TELEX 18582 ESPA NL. E-mail: nlinfo-f@elsevier.nl; usinfo-f@elsevier.com; forinfo kyf04035@niftyserve.or.jp; URL: http://www.elsevier.nl:80/inca/publications/store/5/0/2/6/9/2/502692.pub.shtml. (Subscr. in the Americas to: Elsevier Science, Regional Sales Office, Box 945, New York, NY 10159-0945. TEL 212-633-3730. FAX 212-633-3680; Subscr. in Australasia and the Far East to: Elsevier Science (Singapore) Pte Ltd, No.1 Temasek Ave., No.17-01 Millenia Tower, Singapore 039192, Singapore. TEL 65-434-3727. FAX 65-337-2230; Subscr. in Japan to: Elsevier Science Japan, 9-15 Higashi-Azabu 1-chome, Minato-ku, Tokyo 106, Japan. TEL 81-3-5561-5033. FAX 81-3-5561-5047) Ed. H.K. Lonsdale. (also avail. in microform from UMI; reprint service avail. form SWZ) **Indexed:** ASCA, Biol.Abstr., Chem.Abstr., Chem.Cit.Ind., Curr.Cont., Dairy Sci.Abstr., Eng.Ind., Excerp.Med., Food Sci.& Tech.Abstr., Ind.Sci.Rev., INSPEC, ISMEC, Mat.Sci.Cit.Ind., Nonwov.Abstr., Sci.Cit.Ind., Sel.Water Res.Abstr., Solid St.Abstr., Sugar Ind.Abstr., W.R.C.Inf. **Document type:** academic/scholarly publication.
—BLDSC (5017.620000); AskIEEE; CASDDS; CISTI; Ei; EMDOCS; Genuine Article; KR SourceOne; Linda Hall; SWETS; UnCover. **CCC.**
　Description: Research on the structure and functions of non-biological membranes, with relevant papers on aspects of biological membranes.
　Refereed Serial

541.395　　　　　　NE　　ISSN 1381-1169
QD505　　　　　　　　　CODEN: JMCCF2
JOURNAL OF MOLECULAR CATALYSIS A: CHEMICAL. (Text in English, French, German) 1975. 30/yr. fl.5900($3391) (effective 1998). Elsevier Science B.V., P.O. Box 211, 1000 AE Amsterdam, Netherlands. TEL 31-20-4853911. FAX 31-20-4853598. TELEX 18582 ESPA NL. E-mail: nlinfo-f@elsevier.nl; usinfo-f@elsevier.com; forinfo kyf04035@niftyserve.or.jp; URL: http://www.elsevier.nl/. (Subscr. in the Americas to: Elsevier Science, Regional Sales Office, Box 945, New York, NY 10159-0945. TEL 212-633-3730. FAX 212-633-3680; Subscr. in Australasia and the Far East to: Elsevier Science (Singapore) Pte Ltd, No.1 Temasek Ave., No.17-01 Millenia Tower, Singapore 039192, Singapore. TEL 65-434-3727. FAX 65-337-2230; Subscr. in Japan to: Elsevier Science Japan, 9-15 Higashi-Azabu 1-chome, Minato-ku, Tokyo 106, Japan. TEL 81-3-5561-5033. FAX 81-3-5561-5047) Ed.Bd. bk.rev. (also avail. in microform from UMI) **Indexed:** ASCA, Biol.Abstr., Chem.Abstr., Chem.Cit.Ind., Curr.Cont., Dairy Sci.Abstr., Excerp.Med., Ind.Sci.Rev., Mat.Sci.Cit.Ind., Sci.Cit.Ind. **Document type:** academic/scholarly publication.
—BLDSC (5020.705050); CASDDS; CISTI; Ei; EMDOCS; Genuine Article; Linda Hall; SWETS; UnCover. **CCC.**
　Supersedes in part (in 1995): Journal of Molecular Catalysis (ISSN 0304-5102)
　Description: Covers new research in molecular activation in chemical and metal complex catalysis, heterogenous catalysis, and biochemical catalysis.
　Refereed Serial

541.395 660　　　　　NE　　ISSN 1381-1177
QD505　　　　　　　　　CODEN: JMCEF8
JOURNAL OF MOLECULAR CATALYSIS B: ENZYMATIC. (Text in English) 1975; N.S. 1995. bi-m. fl.584($336) (effective 1998). Elsevier Science B.V., P.O. Box 211, 1000 AE Amsterdam, Netherlands. TEL 31-20-4853911. FAX 31-20-4853598. TELEX 18582 ESPA NL. E-mail: nlinfo-f@elsevier.nl; usinfo-f@elsevier.com; forinfo kyf04035@niftyserve.or.jp; URL: http://www.elsevier.nl/. (Subscr. in the Americas to: Elsevier Science, Regional Sales Office, Box 945, New York, NY 10159-0945. TEL 212-633-3730. FAX 212-633-3680; Subscr. in Australasia and the Far East to: Elsevier Science (Singapore) Pte Ltd, No.1 Temasek Ave., No.17-01 Millenia Tower, Singapore 039192, Singapore. TEL 65-434-3727. FAX 65-337-2230; Subscr. in Japan to: Elsevier Science Japan, 9-15 Higashi-Azabu 1-chome, Minato-ku, Tokyo 106, Japan. TEL 81-3-5561-5033. FAX 81-3-5561-5047) adv. (also avail. in microform from UMI) **Indexed:** ASCA, Chem.Cit.Ind., Curr.Cont. **Document type:** academic/scholarly publication.
—BLDSC (5020.705060); CASDDS; CISTI; Genuine Article; Linda Hall; SWETS; UnCover. **CCC.**
　Supersedes in part (in 1995): Journal of Molecular Catalysis (ISSN 0304-5102)
　Refereed Serial

541.3　　　　　　　NE　　ISSN 0167-7322
QC173　　　　　　　　　CODEN: JMLIDT
JOURNAL OF MOLECULAR LIQUIDS. (Text in English, French and German) 1969. m. fl.2520($1448) (effective 1998). Elsevier Science B.V., P.O. Box 211, 1000 AE Amsterdam, Netherlands. TEL 31-20-4853911. FAX 31-20-4853598. TELEX 18582 ESPA NL. E-mail: nlinfo-f@elsevier.nl; usinfo-f@elsevier.com; forinfo kyf04035@niftyserve.or.jp; URL: http://www.elsevier.nl/. (Subscr. in the Americas to: Elsevier Science, Regional Sales Office, Box 945, New York, NY 10159-0945. TEL 212-633-3730. FAX 212-633-3680; Subscr. in Australasia and the Far East to: Elsevier Science (Singapore) Pte Ltd, No.1 Temasek Ave., No.17-01 Millenia Tower, Singapore 039192, Singapore. TEL 65-434-3727. FAX 65-337-2230; Subscr. in Japan to: Elsevier Science Japan, 9-15 Higashi-Azabu 1-chome, Minato-ku, Tokyo 106, Japan. TEL 81-3-5561-5033. FAX 81-3-5561-5047) Eds. W.J. Orville-Thomas, H. Ratajczak. adv.; bk.rev.; illus. (also avail. in microform from UMI) **Indexed:** ASCA, Biol.Abstr., Chem.Abstr., Chem.Cit.Ind., Curr.Cont., Ind.Sci.Rev., INSPEC (1973-), Mat.Sci.Cit.Ind., Phys.Ber., Sci.Cit.Ind. **Document type:** academic/scholarly publication.
—BLDSC (5020.714000); AskIEEE; CASDDS; CISTI; Ei; Genuine Article; KR SourceOne; Linda Hall; SWETS; UnCover. **CCC.**
　Former titles (until vol.24, 1982): Advances in Molecular Relaxation and Interaction Processes (ISSN 0378-4487); Advances in Molecular Relaxation Processes (ISSN 0001-8716)
　Description: Publishes both primary papers and authoritative review articles covering all aspects of molecular liquid processes based on the increasing variety of experimental and theoretical methods now available.
　Refereed Serial

541.2　　　　　　　GW　　ISSN 0948-5023
　　　　　　　　　　　　　CODEN: JMMOFK
▼**JOURNAL OF MOLECULAR MODELING.** 1996. m. DM.125 to individuals; libraries DM.396 (effective 1997). (Friedrich-Alexander-Universitaet Erlangen-Nuernberg, Institut fuer Organische Chemie) Springer-Verlag, Heidelberger Platz 3, 14197 Berlin, Germany. TEL 49-30-82787-0. FAX 49-30-82787448. E-mail: subscriptions@springer.de; URL: http://link.springer.de. Ed. Tim Clark. **Document type:** academic/scholarly publication.
●Available only online.
—CASDDS; Genuine Article.
　Description: Publishes papers from all areas of molecular modeling, both applications and method development.

541.35　　　　　　SZ　　ISSN 1010-6030
QD701　　　　　　　　　CODEN: JPPCEJ
JOURNAL OF PHOTOCHEMISTRY AND PHOTOBIOLOGY, A: CHEMISTRY; an international journal devoted to the study of the quantitative and qualitative aspects of photochemistry and energy transfer. (Text in English) 1972. 30/yr. fl.5805($3336) (effective 1998). Elsevier Science S.A., P.O. Box 564, CH-1001 Lausanne 1, Switzerland. TEL 41-21-3207381. FAX 41-21-3235444. TELEX 450620-ELSA-CH. (Subscr. to: Elsevier Science, Regional Sales Office, P.O. Box 211, 1000 AE Amsterdam, Netherlands. TEL 31-20-4853757. FAX 31-20-4853432; Subscr. in the Americas to: Elsevier Science, Regional Sales Office, Box 945, New York, NY 10159-0945. TEL 212-633-3730. FAX 212-633-3680; Subscr. in Australasia to: Elsevier Science Pte. Ltd., No. 1 Temasek Ave., No. 17-01 Millenia Tower, Singapore 039192, Singapore. TEL 65-434-3727. FAX 65-337-2230) Ed. R.P. Wayne. adv.; bk.rev.; illus.; index. (also avail. in microform from UMI) **Indexed:** ASCA, Biwk.Pap.Rad.Chem.& Photochem., Chem.Abstr., Chem.Cit.Ind., Curr.Cont., Eng.Ind., Excerp.Med., Ind.Sci.Rev., Mat.Sci.Cit.Ind., Met.Abstr., Photo.Abstr., Phys.Ber., Sci.Cit.Ind. **Document type:** academic/scholarly publication.
—BLDSC (5034.840000); CASDDS; CISTI; Ei; Genuine Article; Linda Hall; SWETS; UnCover. **CCC.**
　Formerly: Journal of Photochemistry (ISSN 0047-2670)
　Description: Concerned with either quantitative or qualitative aspects of photochemistry. Includes papers on applied photochemistry which entails photoinitiation of polymerization, photo cross-linking, photodegradation or photostabilization of polymers, photohalogenation, chemical aspects of photography and the design of photoreactors.
　Refereed Serial

541.3　　　　　　　US　　ISSN 0022-3654
QD1　　　　　　　　　　CODEN: JPCHAX
JOURNAL OF PHYSICAL CHEMISTRY. (In 2 parts) 1896. w. $1955 to institutional non-members; members $140 (effective 1997). American Chemical Society, 1155 16th St., N.W., Washington, DC 20036. TEL 800-333-9511. FAX 614-447-3671. E-mail: jphyschm@chemistry.gatech.edu; URL: http://acsinfo.acs.org/plweb/jrpublic/jpchax/. (Subscr. to: Membership and Subscription Services, Box 3337, Columbus, OH 43210. TEL 614-447-3376) Ed. Dr. Mostafa A. El-Sayed. adv.; charts; index. circ. 4,400. (also avail. in microform from PMC) **Indexed:** A.S.& T.Ind., Abstr.Bull.Inst.Pap.Chem., Alloys Ind., API Abstr., API Catal., API Hlth.& Environ., API Oil., API Pet.Ref., API Pet.Subst., API Transport., ASCA, Biwk.Pap.Rad.Chem.& Photochem., Br.Ceram.Abstr., Cadscan., Chem.Abstr., Chem.Cit.Ind., Chem.Eng.Abstr., Compumath, Curr.Cont., Dairy Sci.Abstr., E&P Hlth. (1993-), Eng.Ind., Eng.Mat.Abstr., Gas Process.& Ppl. (1993-), Ind.Med., Ind.Sci.Rev., INIS Atomind., INSPEC, Int.Aerosp.Abstr., Lead Abstr., Mass Spectr.Bull., Mat.Sci.Cit.Ind., Met.Abstr., Met.Abstr.Ind., Nonfer.Met.Alert, Off.Tech. (1993-), PCC Alert, Petrol.Abstr. (1961-), Phys.Ber., RAPRA, Sci.Cit.Ind., Soils & Fert., Steels Alert, T.C.E.A., World Alum.Abstr., Zincscan. **Document type:** academic/scholarly publication.
●Also available online. Vendor(s): STN International (CJACS).
—AskIEEE; CASDDS; CISTI; Ei; Genuine Article; KR SourceOne; Linda Hall; PADDS; SWETS; UMI; UnCover. **CCC.**
　Formerly (until 1952): Journal of Physical and Colloid Chemistry (ISSN 0092-7023)
　Description: Reports new experimental and theoretical research dealing with fundamental aspects of physical chemistry and chemical physics.
　Refereed Serial

CHEMISTRY — PHYSICAL CHEMISTRY

541.3 547   UK   ISSN 0894-3230
QD476   CODEN: JPOCEE
JOURNAL OF PHYSICAL ORGANIC CHEMISTRY. 1988. m. $1045 (foreign $1045) (effective 1998). John Wiley & Sons Ltd., Journals, Baffins Ln., Chichester, W. Sussex PO19 1UD, England.
TEL 44-1243-779777. FAX 44-1243-775878.
E-mail: info-assets@wiley.co.uk; URL: http://www.wiley.co.uk. (Subscr. in the Americas to: John Wiley & Sons, Inc., 605 Third Ave., New York, NY 10158. TEL 212-850-6645. FAX 212-850-6021) Ed. Joseph B. Lambert. adv.: B&W page £595, color page £1495; trim 260 x 200; adv. contact: Bob Kern. circ. 500. (also avail. in microform from UMI; back issues avail.; reprint service avail. from SWZ). **Indexed:** ASCA, Chem.Cit.Ind., Curr.Cont., Ind.Sci.Rev., INSPEC (1988-), Mass Spectr.Bull., Sci.Cit.Ind. **Document type:** academic/scholarly publication.
—BLDSC (5036.211000); AskIEEE; CASDDS; CISTI; Ei; Genuine Article; KR SourceOne; SWETS; UMI; UnCover. **CCC.**
   Description: Provides an international forum for the rapid publication of original scientific papers dealing with physical organic chemistry in its broadest sense.
   Refereed Serial

JOURNAL OF PLANAR CHROMATOGRAPHY - MODERN T L C. see *CHEMISTRY — Analytical Chemistry*

541 531   US   ISSN 0022-4596
QD901   CODEN: JSSCBI
JOURNAL OF SOLID STATE CHEMISTRY. (Text in English, French, German) 1969. 16/yr. $1844 (foreign $2066) (effective 1997). Academic Press, Inc., Journal Division, 525 B St., Ste. 1900, San Diego, CA 92101-4495. TEL 619-230-1840.
FAX 619-699-6800. E-mail: apsubs@acad.com; URL: http://www.apnet.com/journal/sc.htm; http://www.idealibrary.com/. (Subscr. to: Box 861213, Orlando, FL 32886-1213. TEL 407-347-4040. FAX 507-363-9661) Ed. J.M. Honig. adv.; bk.rev.; abstr.; bibl.; charts; index. (back issues avail.) **Indexed:** Alloys Ind., ASCA, Cadscan., Chem.Abstr., Chem.Cit.Ind., Curr.Cont., Eng.Ind., Eng.Mat.Abstr., GeoRef., Ind.Sci.Rev., INIS Atomind., INSPEC, Lead Abstr., Mat.Sci.Cit.Ind., Met.Abstr., Met.Abstr.Ind., Nonfer.Met.Alert, PCC Alert, Sci.Cit.Ind., SSCI, Steels Alert, World Alum.Abstr., Zincscan. **Document type:** academic/scholarly publication.
●Also available online.
—BLDSC (5065.400000); AskIEEE; CASDDS; CISTI; Ei; Genuine Article; KR SourceOne; Linda Hall; SWETS; UnCover. **CCC.**
   Description: Covers developments in the field of solid state chemistry and related areas such as ceramics and amorphous materials. Features studies of chemical, structural, thermodynamic, electronic, magnetic, and optical processes in solids.
   Refereed Serial

541.34   US   ISSN 0095-9782
QD541   CODEN: JSLCAG
JOURNAL OF SOLUTION CHEMISTRY. 1972. m. $745 (foreign $870) (effective 1998). Plenum Publishing Corp., 233 Spring St., New York, NY 10013-1578. TEL 212-620-8000. FAX 212-463-0742. TELEX 23-421139. Ed. Robert L. Kay. adv.; index. (also avail. in microfilm from UMI; back issues avail.) **Indexed:** ASCA, Biol.Abstr., Cadscan., Chem.Abstr., Chem.Cit.Ind., Curr.Cont., GeoRef., Ind.Sci.Rev., INIS Atomind., Lead Abstr., Phys.Ber., Sci.Cit.Ind., Soils & Fert., Zincscan. **Document type:** academic/scholarly publication.
—BLDSC (5065.600000); CASDDS; CISTI; Ei; Genuine Article; Linda Hall; SWETS; UMI; UnCover. **CCC.**
   Refereed Serial

541.36   HU   ISSN 0368-4466
QD515   CODEN: JTHEA9
JOURNAL OF THERMAL ANALYSIS; an international forum for thermal studies. (Text in English, French, German) 1969. 15/yr. $2895 (effective 1997). Akademiai Kiado Rt., P.O. Box 245, H-1519 Budapest, Hungary. TEL 36-1-2043976. FAX 36-1-2045600. (Dist. Kluwer Academic Publishers, P.O. Box 17, 3300 AA Dordrecht, Netherlands. TEL 31-78-6392120. FAX 31-78-6392254) Ed. Judit Simon. adv.: B&W page £595, color page £1495; trim 240 x 169; adv. contact: Bob Kern. bk.rev.; abstr.; bibl.; index. (also avail. in microform from UMI; back issues avail.; reprint service avail.) **Indexed:** Alloys Ind., ASCA, Bull.Thermodyn.& Thermochem., Cadscan, Chem.Abstr., Chem.Cit.Ind., Curr.Cont., Eng.Ind., Eng.Mat.Abstr., Food Sci.& Tech.Abstr., INIS Atomind., INSPEC, Lead Abstr., Mass Spectr.Bull., Mat.Sci.Cit.Ind., Met.Abstr., Met.Abstr.Ind., Nonfer.Met.Alert, PCC Alert, Sci.Cit.Ind., Soils & Fert., Steels Alert, Therm.Abstr., World Alum.Abstr., Zincscan. **Document type:** academic/scholarly publication.
—BLDSC (5069.090000); CASDDS; CISTI; Ei; Genuine Article; SWETS; UMI; UnCover. **CCC.**
   Description: International forum for communications on thermal investigations. Includes thermogravimetry, differential thermal analysis, dilatometry, thermometry, evolved gas detection and analysis, techniques and instrumentation.
   Refereed Serial

541.3   RU   ISSN 0023-1584
QD501   CODEN: KICAA8
KINETICS AND CATALYSIS. English translation of: Kinetika i Kataliz (RU ISSN 0453-8811) 1960. bi-m. $1735 in US; elsewhere $2030 (effective 1998). (Russian Academy of Sciences) Maik Nauka - Interperiodica, Mezhdunarodnyi Otdel, Ul. Profsoyuznaya, 90, 117864 Moscow, Russia. TEL 7-095-3360066. FAX 7-095-3360066. (Dist. by: Plenum Publishing Corp., 233 Spring St., New York, NY 10013-1578, U.S.A.. TEL 212-260-8468. FAX 212-463-0742) Ed. V.B. Kazanskii. (also avail. in microfilm from UMI; back issues avail.) **Indexed:** ASCA, Chem.Cit.Ind., Chem.Eng.Abstr., Chem.Titles, Curr.Cont., Energy Res.Abstr., Eng.Ind., Ind.Sci.Rev., INIS Atomind., Mass Spectr.Bull., Mat.Sci.Cit.Ind., Sci.Cit.Ind., T.C.E.A. **Document type:** academic/scholarly publication.
—BLDSC (0415.410000); CASDDS; CISTI; Ei; Genuine Article; Linda Hall; SWETS; UMI; UnCover. **CCC.**
   Refereed Serial

541.3   JA   ISSN 0913-4689
KOKAGAKU/PHOTOCHEMISTRY. (Text in Japanese; summaries in English) 1977. a. Kokagaku Kyokai, c/o Obi Kenkyushitsu, Tokyo Kogyo Daigaku Rigakubu, 12-1, Ookayama 2-chome, Meguro-ku, Tokyo 162, Japan. **Indexed:** Chem.Abstr.
—BLDSC (6465.984500).

KOKAGAKU TORONKAI KOEN YOSHISHU/ABSTRACTS OF SYMPOSIUM ON PHOTOCHEMISTRY. see *CHEMISTRY — Abstracting, Bibliographies, Statistics*

541.345   RU   ISSN 0023-2912
QD549   CODEN: KOZHAG
KOLLOIDNYI ZHURNAL; journal of physico-chemistry of surface phenomenon and dispersed systems. English translation: Russian Academy of Sciences. Colloid Journal (US ISSN 1061-933X) (Text in Russian; contents page and summaries in English) 1935. bi-m. $222 (effective 1998). (Rossiiskaya Academiya Nauk) Izdatel'stvo Nauka, 90 Profsoyuznaya ul., 117864 Moscow, Russia. charts; illus.; index, cum.index vols. 1-10. circ. 2,290. **Indexed:** Abstr.Bull.Inst.Pap.Chem., Chem.Abstr., GeoRef., Geotech.Abstr., INIS Atomind., INSPEC, Phys.Ber., RAPRA.
—BLDSC (0091.000000); CASDDS; CISTI; KNAW; Linda Hall; SWETS.

541.393   KR   ISSN 0203-3275
TA418.9.C6   CODEN: KPMAD8
KOMPOSITSIONNYE POLIMERNYE MATERIALY; respublikanskii mezhvedomstvennyi sbornik nauchnykh trudov. (Text in Russian) 1979. 4/yr. (Akademiya Nauk Ukrainy, Institut Khimii Vysokomolekulyarnykh Soedinenii) Vydavnitstvo Naukova Dumka, Vul. Tereshchenkivska 3, 252601 Kiev, Ukraine. (Dist. by: Mezhdunarodnaya Kniga, B. Yakimanka 39, 117049 Moscow, Russia) Ed. E.V. Lebedev. **Indexed:** Alloys Ind., Chem.Abstr, Eng.Mat.Abstr., Met.Abstr., Met.Abstr.Ind., Nonfer.Met.Alert, PCC Alert, Steels Alert, World Alum.Abstr.
—BLDSC (0091.797800); CASDDS; CISTI; Linda Hall. **CCC.**

541.3   US   ISSN 0743-7463
QD506.A1   CODEN: LANGD5
LANGMUIR; the A C S journal of surfaces and colloids. 1985. m. $1191 to institutional non-members; members $90 (effective 1997). American Chemical Society, 1155 16th St., N.W., Washington, DC 20036. TEL 800-333-9511. FAX 614-447-3671. (Subscr. to: Membership and Subscription Services, Box 3337, Columbus, OH 43210. TEL 614-447-3776) Ed. William A. Steele. adv.; bk.rev. circ. 1,300. (also avail. in microfiche) **Indexed:** Abstr.Bull.Inst.Pap.Chem., API Catal., API Hlth.& Environ., API Oil., API Pet.Ref., API Pet.Subst., API Transport., ASCA, Chem.Cit.Ind., Curr.Cont., Mat.Sci.Cit.Ind., Paper & Bd.Abstr., Sci.Cit.Ind., World Surf.Coat. **Document type:** academic/scholarly publication.
●Also available online. Vendor(s): STN International (CJACS).
—BLDSC (5155.686000); CASDDS; CISTI; Ei; Genuine Article; Linda Hall; SWETS; UMI; UnCover. **CCC.**
   Description: Offers broad coverage of all areas of fundamental surface and colloid science.

LASER FOCUS WORLD BUYERS' GUIDE. see *PHYSICS — Optics*

547.1   UK   ISSN 0749-1581
QD476   CODEN: MRCHEG
MAGNETIC RESONANCE IN CHEMISTRY. 1969. 13/yr. $2850 (foreign $2850) (effective 1998). John Wiley & Sons Ltd., Journals, Baffins Ln., Chichester, W. Sussex PO19 1UD, England.
TEL 44-1243-779777. FAX 44-1243-775878.
E-mail: info-assets@wiley.co.uk; URL: http://www.wiley.co.uk. (Subscr. in the Americas to: John Wiley & Sons, Inc., 605 Third Ave., New York, NY 10158. TEL 212-850-6645. FAX 212-850-6021) Ed. H. Guenther. adv.: B&W page £595, color page £1495; trim 297 x 210; adv. contact: Bob Kern. bk.rev.; charts; index, cum.index. circ. 900. (also avail. in microform from UMI; back issues avail.; reprint service avail. from SWZ) **Indexed:** ASCA, Chem.Abstr., Chem.Cit.Ind., Curr.Chem.React., Curr.Cont., Excerp.Med., Ind.Chem., Mass Spectr.Bull., Mat.Sci.Cit.Ind., Sci.Cit.Ind. **Document type:** academic/scholarly publication.
—BLDSC (5337.790000); ADONIS; CASDDS; CISTI; Ei; EMDOCS; Genuine Article; Linda Hall; SWETS; UMI; UnCover. **CCC.**
   Formerly: O M R - Organic Magnetic Resonance (ISSN 0030-4921)
   Description: Designed to provide comprehensive coverage of magnetic resonance in all branches of chemistry.
   Refereed Serial

MATERIALS CHARACTERIZATION; an international journal on materials structure and behavior. see *METALLURGY*

MATERIALS SCIENCE FORUM. see *PHYSICS*

CHEMISTRY — PHYSICAL CHEMISTRY

541.7 620.1   NE   ISSN 0927-6513
                   CODEN: MCMTEV
MICROPOROUS MATERIALS; an international journal devoted to their applications and science. (Text in English) 1993. 20/yr. fl.2755($1701) (effective 1997). Elsevier Science B.V., P.O. Box 211, 1000 AE Amsterdam, Netherlands. TEL 31-20-4853911. FAX 31-20-4853598. TELEX 18582 ESPA NL. E-mail: nlinfo-f@elsevier.nl; usinfo-f@elsevier.com; forinfo-kyf04035@niftyserve.or.jp; URL: http://www.elsevier.nl/. (Subscr. in the Americas to: Elsevier Science, Regional Sales Office, Box 945, New York, NY 10159-0945. TEL 212-633-3730. FAX 212-633-3680; Subscr. in Australasia and the Far East to: Elsevier Science (Singapore) Pte Ltd, No.1 Temasek Ave., No.17-01 Millenia Tower, Singapore 039192, Singapore. TEL 65-434-3727. FAX 65-337-2230; Subscr. in Japan to: Elsevier Science Japan, 9-15 Higashi-Azabu 1-chome, Minato-ku, Tokyo 106, Japan. TEL 81-3-5561-5033. FAX 81-3-5561-5047) Eds. J. Weitkamp, P.A. Jacobs. pat. (also avail. in microform from UMI; back issues avail.) **Indexed**: ASCA, Chem.Cit.Ind., Curr.Cont., Mat.Sci.Cit.Ind. **Document type**: academic/scholarly publication.
—BLDSC (5759.731500); CASDDS; CISTI; Ei; Genuine Article; SWETS. **CCC**.
     Description: Publishes research on all aspects of crystalline and amorphous solids such as zeolites, carbon molecular sieves, pillared clays, microporous metal oxides and other related microporous solids, including practical applications of such materials in environmental protection or electronics related processes.
     Refereed Serial

MOCAXUE XUEBAO/TRIBOLOGY. see *PHYSICS — Mechanics*

541.3   UK   ISSN 0026-8976
QC173   CODEN: MOPHAM
MOLECULAR PHYSICS. Online edition (UK ISSN 1362-3028) (Text in English, French, German) 1958. 18/yr. £1452($2395) to institutions (£1742($2874) with online ed.) (effective 1998). Taylor & Francis Ltd., 1 Gunpowder Sq., London EC4A 3DE, England. TEL 44-171-583-0490. FAX 44-171-583-0585. E-mail: info@tandf.co.uk; URL: http://www.tandf.co.uk/. (Subscr. in N. America to: Taylor & Francis Inc., 1900 Frost Rd., Ste. 101, Bristol, PA 19007-1598. TEL 800-821-8312. FAX 215-785-5515) Ed.Bd. adv.; bk.rev.; bibl.; charts. (also avail. in microform) **Indexed**: ASCA, Biwk.Pap.Rad.Chem.& Photochem., Chem.Abstr., Chem.Cit.Ind., Curr.Cont., Ind.Sci.Rev., INSPEC, Int.Aerosp.Abstr., Mass Spectr.Bull., Mat.Sci.Cit.Ind., Math.R., Phys.Ber., Sci.Cit.Ind., SSCI. **Document type**: academic/scholarly publication.
●Also available online.
—BLDSC (5900.820000); AskIEEE; CASDDS; CISTI; Ei; Genuine Article; KR SourceOne; Linda Hall; SWETS; UnCover. **CCC**.
     Description: Contains original research papers on chemical physics, including all aspects of the physics and biophysics of molecules and, particularly, on molecular structure, properties, dynamics and collisions and on the equilibrium, transport and relaxation properties of molecular assemblies.
     Refereed Serial

541.3   JA   ISSN 0918-5712
                 CODEN: NNKGF3.
NENSHO NO KAGAKU TO GIJUTSU/COMBUSTION SCIENCE AND TECHNOLOGY; official publication for the Association of Combustion and Environmental Sciences. (Text in Japanese) 1992. q. 35700 Yen (foreign 38000 Yen). (Association of Combustion and Environment Science of Japan) Saiensu Komyunikeshonzu Intanashonaru - Science Communications International, 3-14-9 Okubo, Shinjuku-ku, Tokyo 169, Japan. TEL 81-3-3208-2325. FAX 81-3-3204-7303. E-mail: gbtokyo@twics.com. Ed. Toshisuke Hirano. circ. 2,000 (paid). **Document type**: academic/scholarly publication.
—BLDSC (3330.205100); CASDDS.
     Description: Provides a forum for open discussion and prompt publication of new results, discoveries and developments in the various disciplines which constitute the field of combustion.
     Refereed Serial

541.3   UK   ISSN 0305-9804
QC762   CODEN: NMRNBE
NUCLEAR MAGNETIC RESONANCE. 1972. a. price varies. The Royal Society of Chemistry, Thomas Graham House, Science Park, Milton Rd., Cambridge CB4 4WF, England. TEL 44-1223-420066. FAX 44-1223-423623. E-mail: sales@rsc.org; URL: http://chemistry.rsc.org/rsc/. (Subscr. to: Turpin Distribution Services Ltd., Blackhorse Road, Letchworth, Herts. SG6 1HN, England. TEL 44-1462-672555. FAX 44-1462-480947; Subscr. in N. America to: ACS, 1155 Sixteenth St., N.W., Washington, DC 22036, USA. TEL 202-776-8100. FAX 202-872-6067) Ed. G.A. Webb. charts; illus.; index. (back issues avail.) **Indexed**: Chem.Abstr., GeoRef. **Document type**: academic/scholarly publication.
—BLDSC (6180.902000); CASDDS; CISTI; Ei; Linda Hall; UnCover. **CCC**.

541.3   JA   ISSN 0078-429X
QD506
OKAYAMA UNIVERSITY. FACULTY OF SCIENCE. RESEARCH LABORATORY FOR SURFACE SCIENCE. REPORTS/OKAYAMA DAIGAKU RIGAKUBU KAIMEN KAGAKU KENKYU SHISETSU HOKOKU. (Text in English) 1954. a. free or exchange basis. Okayama University, Faculty of Science, Research Laboratory for Surface Science, 1-1, Tsushima Naka 3-chome, Okayama-shi, Okayama-ken 700, Japan. TEL 0862-52-1111. FAX 0862-52-6601. Dir. M. Iwami. circ. 350.
—BLDSC (7592.500000); AskIEEE; KR SourceOne.

ORGANIC PHOTOCHEMISTRY: A SERIES OF ADVANCES. see *CHEMISTRY — Organic Chemistry*

ORGANIC PREPARATIONS AND PROCEDURES INTERNATIONAL; the new journal for organic synthesis. see *CHEMISTRY — Organic Chemistry*

ORGANIC REACTION MECHANISMS. ANNUAL SURVEY. see *CHEMISTRY — Organic Chemistry*

ORGANIC REACTIONS. see *CHEMISTRY — Organic Chemistry*

ORGANIC SYNTHESES. see *CHEMISTRY — Organic Chemistry*

ORGANIC SYNTHESES - COLLECTIVE VOLUMES. see *CHEMISTRY — Organic Chemistry*

541.3   US   ISSN 0030-770X
QD171   CODEN: OXMEAF
OXIDATION OF METALS; an international journal of the science of gas-solid reactions. 1969. m. $845 (foreign $990) (effective 1998). Plenum Publishing Corp., 233 Spring St., New York, NY 10013-1578. TEL 212-620-8000. FAX 212-463-0742. TELEX 23-421139. Ed. D.L. Douglass. adv. (also avail. in microfilm from UMI; back issues avail.) **Indexed**: Alloys Ind., ASCA, Chem.Abstr., Chem.Cit.Ind., Corros.Abstr., Curr.Cont., Eng.Ind., Eng.Mat.Abstr., Fuel & Energy Abstr., GeoRef., Ind.Sci.Rev., INSPEC, Int.Aerosp.Abstr., Mass Spectr.Bull., Mat.Sci.Cit.Ind., Met.Abstr., Met.Abstr., Met.Abstr.Ind., Nonfer.Met.Alert, Nucl.Sci.Abstr., PCC Alert, Sci.Cit.Ind., Steels Alert, World Alum.Abstr. **Document type**: academic/scholarly publication.
●Also available online.
—BLDSC (6321.040000); AskIEEE; CASDDS; CISTI; Ei; Genuine Article; KR SourceOne; Linda Hall; SWETS; UMI; UnCover. **CCC**.
     Refereed Serial

541.38   JA
OYO HOSHASEN KAGAKU SHINPOJUMU KOEN YOSHISHU/PROCEEDINGS OF APPLIED RADIATION CHEMISTRY SYMPOSIUM. (Text in Japanese) a. Nihon Koshasen Kagakkai - Japanese Society of Radiation Chemistry, Nihon Genshiryoku Kenkyujo Takasaki Kenkyujo, 1233 Watanukicho, Takasaki-shi 370-12, Japan. **Document type**: proceedings.

541.35   US   ISSN 0079-1806
PHOTOCHEMISTRY. (Subseries of: I U P A C Chemical Data Series (ISSN 0275-0910)) (Text in English; occasionally in French or German) 1964. irregr. price varies. (International Union of Pure and Applied Chemistry) C R C Press, Inc., 2000 N.W. Corporate Blvd., Boca Raton, FL 33431. TEL 561-994-0555; 800-272-7737. FAX 561-998-9784. TELEX 568689-CRC PRESS. **Document type**: monographic series.
     Refereed Serial

PHYSICS AND CHEMISTRY OF LIQUIDS. see *PHYSICS — Mechanics*

PLASTICHEM. see *ENGINEERING — Chemical Engineering*

POLITECHNIKA WROCLAWSKA. INSTYTUT CHEMII ORGANICZNEJ I FIZYCZNEJ. PRACE NAUKOWE. KONFERENCJE. see *CHEMISTRY — Organic Chemistry*

POLITECHNIKA WROCLAWSKA. INSTYTUT CHEMII ORGANICZNEJ I FIZYCZNEJ. PRACE NAUKOWE. MONOGRAFIE. see *CHEMISTRY — Organic Chemistry*

POLITECHNIKA WROCLAWSKA. INSTYTUT CHEMII ORGANICZNEJ I FIZYCZNEJ. PRACE NAUKOWE. STUDIA I MATERIALY. see *CHEMISTRY — Organic Chemistry*

541.3 547   US   ISSN 0340-255X
QD549   CODEN: PCPSD7
PROGRESS IN COLLOID AND POLYMER SCIENCE. (Supplement to: Colloid and Polymer Science (ISSN 0303-402X)) 1909. irreg., vol.98, 1995. price varies. Springer-Verlag, 175 Fifth Ave., New York, NY 10160. TEL 212-460-1500. FAX 212-473-6272. (Dist. in Germany by: Dr. Dietrich Steinkopff Verlag, Postfach 111442, 64293 Darmstadt, Germany) Eds. H.G. Kilian, G. Lacey. adv. circ. 2,000. (reprint service avail. from ISI) **Indexed**: Apic.Abstr., Chem.Abstr., Curr.Cont., INSPEC, Intl.Polym.Sci.& Tech., Paper & Bd.Abstr., RAPRA, World Surf.Coat., World Text.Abstr. **Document type**: monographic series.
—BLDSC (6867.750000); CASDDS; CISTI; Ei; KNAW; Linda Hall; SWETS; UnCover. **CCC**.

547.1   US   ISSN 0079-6662
QD476   CODEN: PPOCA8
PROGRESS IN PHYSICAL ORGANIC CHEMISTRY. 1963. irreg., vol.20, 1993. price varies. John Wiley & Sons, Inc., 605 Third Ave., New York, NY 10158. TEL 212-850-6000. FAX 212-850-6088. TELEX 12-7063. Eds. A. Streitwieser, Jr., R.W. Taft. **Indexed**: Chem.Abstr., Chem.Infd., Ind.Sci.Rev. **Document type**: monographic series.
—BLDSC (6873.400000); CASDDS; CISTI; Linda Hall; SWETS.
     Refereed Serial

541.39   UK   ISSN 0079-6743
QD501   CODEN: PRKNAZ
PROGRESS IN REACTION KINETICS. (Annual bound vol. avail.) 1961. q. fl.627($387) (effective 1997). Elsevier Science Ltd., Pergamon, P.O. Box 800, Kidlington, Oxford OX5 1DX, England. TEL 44-1865-843000. FAX 44-1865-843010. E-mail: usinfo-f@elsevier.nl; usinfo-f@elsevier.com; forinfo-kyf04035@niftyserve.or.jp; URL: http://www.elsevier.nl/. (Subscr. to: Elsevier Science, Regional Sales Office, P.O. Box 211, 1000 AE Amsterdam, Netherlands. TEL 31-20-4853757. FAX 31-20-4853432; Subscr. in the Americas to: Elsevier Science, Regional Sales Office, Box 945, New York, NY 10159-0945. TEL 212-633-3730. FAX 212-633-3680; Subscr. in Australasia and the Far East to: Elsevier Science (Singapore) Pte Ltd, No.1 Temasek Ave., No.17-01 Millenia Tower, Singapore 039192, Singapore. TEL 65-434-3727. FAX 65-337-2230) Ed.Bd. index. (also avail. in microfilm from UMI) **Indexed**: ASCA, Biol.Abstr., Chem.Abstr., Chem.Cit.Ind., Chem.Infd., Curr.Adv.Ecol.Sci., Curr.Cont. **Document type**: academic/scholarly publication.
—BLDSC (6873.750000); CASDDS; CISTI; Ei; Genuine Article; Linda Hall; SWETS; UMI; UnCover. **CCC**.
     Description: Publishes authoritative review articles on all aspects of chemical kinetics, with particular emphasis on quantitative aspects.
     Refereed Serial

CHEMISTRY — PHYSICAL CHEMISTRY

541   UK   ISSN 0079-6786
QD473   CODEN: PSSTAW
PROGRESS IN SOLID STATE CHEMISTRY. 1964. q. fl.937($539) (effective 1998). Elsevier Science Ltd., Pergamon, P.O. Box 800, Kidlington, Oxford OX5 1DX, England. TEL 44-1865-843000. FAX 44-1865-843010. E-mail: nlinfo-f@elsevier.nl; usinfo-f@elsevier.com; forinfo-kyf04035@niftyserve.or.jp; URL: http://www.elsevier.nl/. (Subscr. to: Elsevier Science, Regional Sales Office, P.O. Box 211, 1000 AE Amsterdam, Netherlands. TEL 31-20-4853757. FAX 31-20-4853432; Subscr. in the Americas to: Elsevier Science, Regional Sales Office, Box 945, New York, NY 10159-0945. TEL 212-633-3730. FAX 212-633-3680; Subscr. in Australasia and the Far East to: Elsevier Science (Singapore) Pte Ltd, No.1 Temasek Ave., No.17-01 Millenia Tower, Singapore 039192, Singapore. TEL 65-434-3727. FAX 65-337-2230) Eds. Gerd M. Rosenblatt, Wayne L. Worrell. index. (also avail. in microfilm from UMI) **Indexed:** Alloys Ind., ASCA, Chem.Abstr., Chem.Cit.Ind., Eng.Mat.Abstr., Ind.Sci.Rev., INSPEC, Mass Spectr.Bull., Mat.Sci.Cit.Ind., Met.Abstr., Met.Abstr.Ind., Nonfer.Met.Alert, PCC Alert, Sci.Cit.Ind., Steels Alert, World Alum.Abstr. **Document type:** academic/scholarly publication.
—BLDSC (6924.565000); AskIEEE; CASDDS; CISTI; Ei; Genuine Article; KR SourceOne; Linda Hall; SWETS; UMI; UnCover. **CCC.**
    Description: Reviews recent advances, with an emphasis on physical properties and structural chemistry.
    Refereed Serial

543.0858   US
R L B L NEWSLETTER. 1977. 2/yr. free. Regional Laser & Biotechnology Laboratories, Dept. of Chemistry, Univ. of Pennsylvania, 231 S. 34th St., Philadelphia, PA 19104-6323. TEL 215-898-3605. FAX 215-898-0590. E-mail: phillips@a.chem.upen.edu; URL: http://rlbl.chem.upenn.edu. Ed. Charles M. Phillips. circ. 2,000. (looseleaf format) **Document type:** newsletter.
    Description: Covers ultrafast laser spectroscopy.

541.38   US   ISSN 1045-845X
QD601.A1   CODEN: RARAE6
RADIOACTIVITY & RADIOCHEMISTRY; a journal of applied measurements. 1990. q. $58 to individuals (foreign $98); institutions $118 (foreign $158). Caretaker Technology, Inc., 1380 Seaboard Industrial Blvd., Atlanta, GA 30318. TEL 404-352-4620. FAX 404-352-0515. (Subscr. to: Box 19656, Atlanta, GA 30325) Ed. Thetis S. McFarland. R&P contact: Thetis S. McFarland. adv. contact: Michele Johnson. circ. 1,200. (back issues avail.) **Document type:** academic/scholarly publication.
—BLDSC (7234.229700); CASDDS; CISTI; Ei; SWETS; UnCover.
    Description: Provides practical information for those working in the field of radioactivity measurements.

541   JA   ISSN 0441-2516
RADIOACTIVITY SURVEY DATA IN JAPAN. (Includes 2 vols.: Environmental Materials; Dietary Materials) (Text in English) 1963. s-a. free. national Institute of Radiological Sciences - Hoshasen Igaku Sogo Kenkyujo, 4-9-1 Anagawa, Chiba 260, Japan. TEL 043-251-2111. FAX 047-256-9616. Ed. S. Sakurai. circ. 1,300. **Document type:** government publication.
—BLDSC (7234.240000).

541.38   RU   ISSN 1066-3622
QD601.A1   CODEN: RDIOEO
RADIOCHEMISTRY. English translation of: Radiokhimiya (RU ISSN 0033-8311) 1962. bi-m. $1595 in US; elsewhere $1865 (effective 1998). (Russian Academy of Sciences) Maik Nauka - Interperiodica, Mezhdunarodnyi Otdel, Ul. Profsoyuznaya, 90, 117864 Moscow, Russia. TEL 7-095-3360066. FAX 7-095-3360066. (Dist. by: Plenum Publishing Corp., 233 Spring St., New York, NY 10013-1578, U.S.A. TEL 212-620-8468. FAX 212-463-0742) Ed. B.F. Myasoedov. (also avail. in microfilm from UMI; back issues avail.) **Indexed:** Chem.Cit.Ind., Chem.Titles, Curr.Cont., Ind.Sci.Rev., Mass Spectr.Bull., Pollut.Abstr., Sci.Cit.Ind. **Document type:** academic/scholarly publication.
—BLDSC (0420.716000); CASDDS; CISTI; Ei; Genuine Article; SWETS; UMI. **CCC.**
    Formerly (until 1993): Soviet Radiochemistry (ISSN 0038-576X)
    Refereed Serial

541.38   GW   ISSN 0033-8230
QD601.A1   CODEN: RAACAP
RADIOCHIMICA ACTA; international journal for chemical aspects of nuclear science and technology. (Text in English) 1962. 16/yr. (in 4 vols., 4 nos./vol.). DM.1495 (effective 1997). R. Oldenbourg Verlag GmbH, Rosenheimerstr. 145, 81671 Munich, Germany. TEL 49-89-45051-0. FAX 49-89-45051207. Ed.Bd. adv.; bibl.; charts. circ. 1,000. (back issues avail.) **Indexed:** ASCA, Biol.Abstr., Chem.Abstr., Chem.Cit.Ind., Curr.Cont., GeoRef, Ind.Sci.Rev., Mat.Sci.Cit.Ind., Sci.Cit.Ind. **Document type:** academic/scholarly publication.
—BLDSC (7234.495000); AskIEEE; CASDDS; CISTI; Ei; Genuine Article; KR SourceOne; Linda Hall; SWETS; UnCover. **CCC.**

541.3 615.842   RU   ISSN 0033-8311
    CODEN: RADKAU
RADIOKHIMIYA. English translation: Radiochemistry (US ISSN 1066-3622) 1959. bi-m. $191 (effective 1998). (Rossiiskaya Akademiya Nauk) Izdatel'stvo Nauka, 90 Profsoyuznaya ul., 117864 Moscow, Russia. Ed. V.M. Vdovenko. index. (tabloid format) **Indexed:** Chem.Abstr., Fuel & Energy Abstr., Ocean.Abstr. **Document type:** academic/scholarly publication.
—BLDSC (0139.500000); CASDDS; CISTI; Linda Hall.

RANLIAO HUAXUE XUEBAO/JOURNAL OF FUEL CHEMISTRY AND TECHNOLOGY. see
ENGINEERING — *Chemical Engineering*

541.3   HU   ISSN 0133-1736
QD502   CODEN: RKCLAU
REACTION KINETICS AND CATALYSIS LETTERS. (Text in English) 1974. bi-m. fl.2500($1437) (effective 1998). (Hungarian Academy of Sciences, HU) Akademiai Kiado Rt., P.O. Box 245, H-1519 Budapest, Hundary. TEL 36-1-20439761. FAX 36-1-2043973. (Subscr. to: Elsevier Science, P.O. Box 330, 1000 AH Amstrerdam, The Netherlands. TEL 31-20-4853642. FAX 31-20-4853598) Ed. L.I. Simandi. (also avail. in microfilm from UMI) **Indexed:** ASCA, Chem.Abstr., Chem.Cit.Ind., Curr.Cont., Mat.Sci.Cit.Ind. **Document type:** academic/scholarly publication.
—BLDSC (7300.268000); Ei; Genuine Article; SWETS; UnCover. **CCC.**
    Description: Covers kinetics of homogeneous reactions in gas, liquid and solid phase; homogeneous catalysis; heterogeneous catalysis; adsorption in heterogeneous catalysis; transport processes related to reaction kinetics and catalysis; preparation and study of catalysts; reactors and apparatus.
    Refereed Serial

541.3   NE
RESEARCH IN CHEMICAL KINETICS. (Text in English) 1993. irreg., vol.2, 1994. price varies. Elsevier Science B.V., Books Division, P.O. Box 211, 1000 AE Amsterdam, Netherlands. TEL 31-20-4853911. FAX 31-20-4853705. TELEX 18582 ESPA NL. E-mail: nlinfo-f@elsevier.nl; usinfo-f@elsevier.com; forinfo-kyf04035@niftyserve.or.jp; URL: http://www.elsevier.nl/. (Subscr. in the Americas to: Elsevier Science, Regional Sales Office, Box 945, New York, NY 10159-0945. TEL 212-633-3730. FAX 212-633-3680; Subscr. in Australasia and the Far East to: Elsevier Science (Singapore) Pte Ltd, No.1 Temasek Ave., No.17-01 Millenia Tower, Singapore 039192, Singapore. TEL 65-434-3727. FAX 65-337-2230; Subscr. in Japan to: Elsevier Science Japan, 9-15 Higashi-Azabu 1-chome, Minato-ku, Tokyo 106, Japan. TEL 81-3-5561-5033. FAX 81-3-5561-5047) Eds. R.G. Compton, G. Hancock. (back issues avail.) **Document type:** monographic series.

REVIEW OF POLAROGRAPHY/PORAROGURAFI. see
CHEMISTRY — *Analytical Chemistry*

541.3   UK   ISSN 0260-1826
QD1   CODEN: ACPCDW
ROYAL SOCIETY OF CHEMISTRY. ANNUAL REPORTS ON THE PROGRESS OF CHEMISTRY. SECTION C: PHYSICAL CHEMISTRY. a. £122 (US $220); all 3 sections £324 ($583) (effective 1997). The Royal Society of Chemistry, Thomas Graham House, Science Park, Milton Rd., Cambridge CB4 4WF, England. TEL 44-1223-420066. FAX 44-1223-423623. E-mail: sales@rsc.org; URL: http://chemistry.rsc.org. (Subscr. to: Turpin Distribution Services Ltd., Blackhorse Rd., Letchworth, Herts. SG6 1HN, England. TEL 44-1462-372555. FAX 44-1462-480947) Ed. M.C.R. Symons. circ. 2,000. (back issues avail.) **Indexed:** INIS Atomind. **Document type:** academic/scholarly publication.
—BLDSC (1513.850000); CASDDS; CISTI; Linda Hall. **CCC.**
    Supersedes in part: Royal Society of Chemistry. Annual Reports on the Progress of Chemistry. Section A: Physical and Inorganic Chemistry.
    Description: Provides critical coverage for the general reader of the important advances in physical chemistry.

541.3   UK   ISSN 0300-9580
QD476   CODEN: JCPKBH
ROYAL SOCIETY OF CHEMISTRY. JOURNAL: PERKIN TRANSACTIONS 2; a journal of physical organic chemistry. Key Title: Perkin Transactions 2. Online edition (UK ISSN 1364-5471) 1972. m. £715 to institutions (US $1287) (effective 1997). The Royal Society of Chemistry, Thomas Graham House, Science Park, Milton Rd., Cambridge CB4 4WF, England. TEL 44-1223-420066. FAX 44-1223-423429. E-mail: sales@rsc.org; URL: http://chemistry.rsc.org/rsc/. (Subscr. to: Turpin Distribution Services Ltd., Blackhorse Rd., Letchworth, Herts. SG6 1HN, England. TEL 44-1462-672555. FAX 44-1462-480947) adv.; charts; illus.; index. (also avail. in microform from UMI,PMC) **Indexed:** Abstr.Bull.Inst.Pap.Chem., Anal.Abstr., Appl.Mech.Rev., ASCA, Biotech.Abstr., Biwk.Pap.Rad.Chem.& Photochem., Bull.Thermodyn.& Thermochem., Cadscan., Chem.Abstr., Chem.Cit.Ind., Chem.Titles, Curr.Adv.Ecol.Sci., Curr.Chem.React., Food Sci.& Tech.Abstr., Ind.Chem., INIS Atomind., Lead Abstr., Mass Spectr.Bull., Ref.Zh., Zincscan. **Document type:** academic/scholarly publication.
●Also available online. Vendor(s): STN International (CJRSC).
—BLDSC (4729.110000); CASDDS; CISTI; Genuine Article; Linda Hall; SWETS; UMI; UnCover. **CCC.**
    Formerly: Chemical Society, London. Journal. Section B: Physical Organic Chemistry (ISSN 0045-6470)
    Description: Covers physicochemical aspects of organic, organometallic, bio-organic chemistry and supramolecular chemistry including kinetic, mechanistics, structural, spectroscopic and theoretical studies.
    Refereed Serial

541.345   RU   ISSN 1061-933X
QD549   CODEN: CJRSEQ
RUSSIAN ACADEMY OF SCIENCES. COLLOID JOURNAL. Key Title: Colloid Journal of the Russian Academy of Sciences. English translation of: Kolloidnyi Zhurnal (RU ISSN 0023-2912) 1952. bi-m. $1575 in US; elsewhere $1845 (effective 1998). (Russian Academy of Sciences) Maik Nauka - Interperiodica, Mezhdunarodnyi Otdel, Ul. Profsoyuznaya, 90, 117864 Moscow, Russia. TEL 7-095-3360066. FAX 7-095-3360066. (Dist. by: Plenum Publishing Corp., 233 Spring St., New York, NY 10013-1578, U.S.A. TEL 212-620-8468. FAX 212-463-0742) Ed. I.V. Petryanov-Sokolov. (back issues avail.) **Indexed:** Chem.Cit.Ind., Chem.Titles, Curr.Cont., Eng.Ind., Geotech.Abstr., Ind.Sci.Rev., INIS Atomind., Mat.Sci.Cit.Ind. **Document type:** academic/scholarly publication.
—BLDSC (0410.950000); CISTI; Ei; Genuine Article; Linda Hall; SWETS; UMI; UnCover. **CCC.**
    Former titles (until 1992): Colloid Journal of the U S S R (ISSN 0010-1303); (until 1963): Colloid Journal (New York) (ISSN 0190-4337)
    Refereed Serial

541   RU   ISSN 0036-0244
QD1   CODEN: RJPCAR
RUSSIAN JOURNAL OF PHYSICAL CHEMISTRY. Russian edition: Zhurnal Fizicheskoi Khimii (ISSN 0044-4537) 1959. m. $1779 in U.S. and Canada (elsewhere $1938) (effective 1995). Maik Nauka - Interperiodica, Mezhdunarodnyi Otdel, Ul. Profsoyuznaya, 90, 117864 Moscow, Russia. TEL 7-095-3360066. FAX 7-095-3360666. (Subscr. to: Maik Nauka - Interperiodica, Subscription Office, Box 1831, Birmingham, AL 35201-1831, U.S.A. TEL 205-995-1567. FAX 205-995-1588) Ed. R.P. Bell. bibl.; charts; illus. (also avail. in microform from PMC) **Indexed:** Alloys Ind., Chem.Eng.Abstr., Eng.Mat.Abstr., INSPEC (1987-), Mass Spectr.Bull., Met.Abstr., Met.Abstr.Ind., Nonfer.Met.Alert, PCC Alert, Phys.Ber., Soils & Fert., Steels Alert, T.C.E.A., World Alum.Abstr. **Document type:** academic/scholarly publication.
—BLDSC (0420.763000); AskIEEE; CISTI; KR SourceOne; Linda Hall; SWETS; UnCover.

541.3   JA
SEKIGAI RAMAN BUNKENSHU/INFRARED AND RAMAN SPECTROSCOPY. (Text in English) 1978. bi-m. 5000 Yen to individuals; institutions 32000Yen. Sekigai Raman Kenkyukai - Raman and Infrared Analysis Committee, c/o Tokyo Daigaku Rigakubu, Kagaku Kyoshitsu Tasumi Kenyushitsu, 3-1, Hongo 7-chome, Bunkyo-ku, Tokyo 113, Japan. circ. 200. **Document type:** academic/scholarly publication.

541.3   JA   ISSN 0919-6064
SHOKUBAI KENKYU HAPPYOKAI KOEN YOKOSHU/CATALYSIS SOCIETY OF JAPAN. PREPRINTS OF MEETING. (Text in Japanese) a. 3500 Yen. Shokubai Gakkai - Catalysis Society of Japan, 21-13-302, Higashigotanda 5-chome, Shinagawa-ku, Tokyo 141, Japan.

541.3   JA
SHOKUBAI KENKYU KONDANKAI/KANSAI CATALYSIS RESEARCH GROUP. REPORT OF THE MEETING. (Text in Japanese) a. membership. Shokubai Gakkai, Kansai Chiku - Catalysis Society of Japan, Kansai Branch, Osaka Kagaku Gijutsu Senta, 8-4, Utsubohon-machi 1-chome, Nishi-ku, Osaka 550, Japan.

541.3   JA
SHOKUBAI NENSHO NI KANSURU SHINPOJUMU/SYMPOSIUM ON CATALYTIC COMBUSTION. (Text in Japanese) 1986. s-a. Shokubai Gakkai - Catalysis Society of Japan, 21-13-302, Higashigotanda 5-chome, Shinagawa-ku, Tokyo 141, Japan. **Document type:** proceedings.

541.3   JA
SHOKUBAI TORONKAI A KOEN YOKOSHU/PREPRINTS OF THE COLLOQUIA ON CATALYSTS. (Text in Japanese) 1972. s-a. 3500 Yen. Shokubai Gakkai - Catalysis Society of Japan, 5-21-1 Higashi-gatanda, Shinagawa-ku, Tokyo 141, Japan. **Document type:** proceedings.

SOCIETY OF PROPERTY OF PHYSICAL CHEMISTRY. ABSTRACTS OF MEETING/BUSSEI BUTSURI KAGAKU KENKYUKAI KOEN YOSHISHU. see *CHEMISTRY — Abstracting, Bibliographies, Statistics*

SOLID STATE COMMUNICATIONS; an international journal. see *PHYSICS*

SPRINGER SERIES IN CHEMICAL PHYSICS. see *PHYSICS*

541.36   NE   ISSN 0166-6061
                        CODEN: SMTHDT
STUDIES IN MODERN THERMODYNAMICS. 1979. irreg., vol.12, 1991. price varies. Elsevier Science B.V., Books Division, P.O. Box 211, 1000 AE Amsterdam, Netherlands. TEL 31-20-4853911. FAX 31-20-4853705. TELEX 18582 ESPA NL. E-mail: nlinfo-f@elsevier.nl; usinfo-f@elsevier.com; forinfo-kyf04035@niftyserve.or.jp; URL: http://www.elsevier.nl/. (Subscr. in the Americas to: Elsevier Science, Regional Sales Office, Box 945, New York, NY 10159-0945. TEL 212-633-3730. FAX 212-633-3680; Subscr. in Australasia and the Far East to: Elsevier Science (Singapore) Pte Ltd, No.1 Temasek Ave., No.17-01 Millenia Tower, Singapore 039192, Singapore. TEL 65-434-3727. FAX 65-337-2230; Subscr. in Japan to: Elsevier Science Japan, 9-15 Higashi-Azabu 1-chome, Minato-ku, Tokyo 106, Japan. TEL 81-3-5561-5033. FAX 81-3-5561-5047) **Indexed:** Chem.Abstr., INSPEC. **Document type:** monographic series.
—BLDSC (8491.124700); CASDDS; CISTI.
Refereed Serial

541.3   NE   ISSN 0167-6881
                        CODEN: SPTCDZ
STUDIES IN PHYSICAL AND THEORETICAL CHEMISTRY. 1978. irreg., vol.82, 1994. price varies. Elsevier Science B.V., Books Division, P.O. Box 211, 1000 AE Amsterdam, Netherlands. TEL 31-20-4853911. FAX 31-20-4853705. TELEX 18582 ESPA NL. E-mail: nlinfo-f@elsevier.nl; usinfo-f@elsevier.com; forinfo-kyf04035@niftyserve.or.jp; URL: http://www.elsevier.nl/. (Subscr. in the Americas to: Elsevier Science, Regional Sales Office, Box 945, New York, NY 10159-0945. TEL 212-633-3730. FAX 212-633-3680; Subscr. in Australasia and the Far East to: Elsevier Science (Singapore) Pte Ltd, No.1 Temasek Ave., No.17-01 Millenia Tower, Singapore 039192, Singapore. TEL 65-434-3727. FAX 65-337-2230; Subscr. in Japan to: Elsevier Science Japan, 9-15 Higashi-Azabu 1-chome, Minato-ku, Tokyo 106, Japan. TEL 81-3-5561-5033. FAX 81-3-5561-5047) **Indexed:** Biol.Abstr., Chem.Abstr., INSPEC. **Document type:** monographic series.
—BLDSC (8491.222400); CASDDS; CISTI; KNAW. **CCC.**
Refereed Serial

SULZER TECHNICAL REVIEW. see *ENGINEERING*

541.3   US   ISSN 0081-9573
QD506.A1   CODEN: SCOSBX
SURFACE AND COLLOID SCIENCE. 1969. irreg., vol.15, 1993. price varies. Plenum Publishing Corp., 233 Spring St., New York, NY 10013-1578. TEL 212-620-8000. FAX 212-463-0742. TELEX 23-421139. E-mail: books@plenum.com. Ed. E. Matijevic. **Indexed:** Appl.Mech.Rev., Chem.Abstr., Chem.Cit.Ind. **Document type:** monographic series.
—BLDSC (8547.730000); CASDDS; CISTI; KNAW; Linda Hall; SWETS; UnCover.
Refereed Serial

SURFACE SCIENCE; a journal devoted to the physics and chemistry of interfaces. see *PHYSICS*

541.36 536   US   ISSN 0082-0784
QD516   CODEN: SYMCAQ
SYMPOSIUM (INTERNATIONAL) ON COMBUSTION. Variant title: International Symposium on Combustion. Proceedings. (Research papers) biennial, 25th, 1994. $225. Combustion Institute, 5001 Baum Blvd., Pittsburgh, PA 15213. TEL 412-387-1366. FAX 412-687-0340. cum.index in 10th and 20th issues. circ. 3,500. **Indexed:** Chem.Abstr. **Document type:** proceedings.
—BLDSC (8585.300000); CASDDS; Ei.
Description: Agenda of symposium and lists of session participants on applied and theoretical research activities in the industry.
Refereed Serial

SYMPOSIUM ON RADIOCHEMISTRY. ABSTRACTS OF PAPERS/HOSHA KAGAKU TORONKAI KOEN YOKOSHU. see *CHEMISTRY — Abstracting, Bibliographies, Statistics*

SYNLETT. see *CHEMISTRY — Organic Chemistry*

SYNTHESIS; journal of synthetic organic chemistry. see *CHEMISTRY — Organic Chemistry*

541.39 546.1   US   ISSN 0094-5714
QD156   CODEN: SRIMCN
SYNTHESIS AND REACTIVITY IN INORGANIC AND METALORGANIC CHEMISTRY. 1971. 10/yr. $1125 (foreign $1162.50) (effective 1998). Marcel Dekker Journals, 270 Madison Ave., New York, NY 10016. TEL 212-696-9000. FAX 212-685-4540. TELEX 421419 MARDEEK. (Subscr. to: Box 5017, Monticello, NY 12701) Ed. Kurt Moedritzer. R&P contact: Julia Mulligan. adv. contact: Lourdes Barroso. (also avail. in microform from RPI) **Indexed:** ASCA, Chem.Abstr., Chem.Cit.Ind., Curr.Cont., Ind.Chem., Sci.Cit.Ind. **Document type:** academic/scholarly publication.
—BLDSC (8586.787000); CASDDS; CISTI; Genuine Article; Linda Hall; SWETS; UMI; UnCover. **CCC.**
Formerly: Synthesis in Inorganic and Metalorganic Chemistry (ISSN 0039-789X)
Refereed Serial

SYNTHETIC METHODS OF ORGANIC CHEMISTRY. see *CHEMISTRY — Organic Chemistry*

547.1   US
T R C THERMODYNAMIC TABLES - HYDROCARBONS. 1942. biennial. $1200. Thermodynamics Research Center, Texas Engineering Experiment Station, Texas A & M University System, College Station, TX 77843-3111. TEL 409-845-4940. FAX 409-847-8590. E-mail: info@trchpl.tamu.edu; URL: http://trcweb.tamu.edu. Ed. Kenneth N. Marsh; Pub. Kenneth N. Marsh. R&P contact: Kenneth N. Marsh. charts; stat. circ. 319. (looseleaf format) **Document type:** academic/scholarly publication.
—CCC.
Former titles: Thermodynamics Research Center. Hydrocarbons Project. Selected Values of Properties of Hydrocarbons and Related Compounds. Category A: Tables of Selected Values of Physical and Thermodynamic Properties of Hydrocarbons; A P I Research Project 44. Selected Values of Properties of Hydrocarbons and Related Compounds. Category A: Tables of Selected Values of Physical and Thermodynamic Properties of Hydrocarbons (ISSN 0065-9630)
Description: Includes properties of hydrocarbons and sulfur compounds related to petroleum.
Refereed Serial

T R C THERMODYNAMIC TABLES - NON-HYDROCARBONS. see *CHEMISTRY — Analytical Chemistry*

668   GW   ISSN 0932-3414
                       CODEN: TSDEES
TENSIDE SURFACTANTS DETERGENTS; journal for theory, technology & application of surfactants. (Text in English or German) 1964. bi-m. DM.458.40. (Gesellschaft Deutscher Chemiker) Carl Hanser Verlag, Kolbergerstr. 22, 81679 Munich, Germany. TEL 49-89-998300. FAX 49-89-984809. (Subscr. to: Postfach 860420, 81631 Munich, Germany) (Deutscher Ausschuss fuer Grenzflaechenaktive Stoffe) Ed. B. Fell. adv.; bk.rev.; charts; illus.; pat.; index. circ. 1,850. **Indexed:** ASCA, Chem.Abstr., Chem.Infd., Curr.Cont., Excerp.Med., PROMT. **Document type:** trade publication.
—BLDSC (8790.932000); CASDDS; CISTI; Ei; Genuine Article; Linda Hall; SWETS. **CCC.**
Former titles: Tenside - Detergents (ISSN 0040-3490); Tenside.

CHEMISTRY — PHYSICAL CHEMISTRY

541.36 NE ISSN 0040-6031
QD510 CODEN: THACAS
THERMOCHIMICA ACTA; an international journal concerned with the broader aspects of thermochemistry and its applications to chemical problems. 1970. 42/yr. fl.11760($6759) (effective 1998). Elsevier Science B.V., P.O. Box 211, 1000 AE Amsterdam, Netherlands. TEL 31-20-4853911. FAX 31-20-4853598. TELEX 18582 ESPA NL. E-mail: nlinfo-f@elsevier.nl; usinfo-f@elsevier.com; forinfo-kyf04035@niftyserve.or.jp; URL: http://www.elsevier.nl/. (Subscr. in the Americas to: Elsevier Science, Regional Sales Office, Box 945, New York, NY 10159-0945. TEL 212-633-3730. FAX 212-633-3680; Subscr. in Australasia and the Far East to: Elsevier Science (Singapore) Pte Ltd, No.1 Temasek Ave., No.17-01 Millenia Tower, Singapore 039192, Singapore. TEL 65-434-3727. FAX 65-337-2230; Subscr. in Japan to: Elsevier Science Japan, 9-15 Higashi-Azabu 1-chome, Minato-ku, Tokyo 106, Japan. TEL 81-3-5561-5033. FAX 81-3-5561-5047) Ed. W.W. Wendlandt. adv.; bk.rev. (also avail. in microform from UMI) **Indexed**: Alloys Ind., Art & Archaeol.Tech.Abstr., ASCA, Bull.Thermodyn.& Thermochem., Ceram.Abstr., Chem.Abstr., Chem.Cit.Ind., Chem.Infd., Curr.Cont., Eng.Mat.Abstr., Excerp.Med., GeoRef., Ind.Sci.Rev., Mass Spectr.Bull., Mat.Sci.Cit.Ind., Met.Abstr.Ind., Met.Abstr., Nonfer.Met.Alert, PCC Alert, Sci.Cit.Ind., Soils & Fert., Steels Alert, Sugar Ind.Abstr., World Alum.Abstr. **Document type**: academic/scholarly publication.
—BLDSC (8814.820000); CASDDS; CISTI; Ei; Genuine Article; Linda Hall; SWETS; UnCover. **CCC.**
Description: Covers thermal analysis, thermochemistry, and chemical thermodynamics.
Refereed Serial

541.36 536.7 US
THERMODYNAMICS AT TEXAS A & M. 1973. s.a. free. Thermodynamics Research Center, Texas Engineering Experiment Station, Texas A & M University System, College Station, TX 77843. TEL 409-845-4940. FAX 409-847-8590. E-mail: info@trchpl.tamu.edu; URL: http://trcweb.tamu.edu. (Co-sponsor: Chemical Engineering Department) Pub. Kenneth N. Marsh. R&P contact: Kenneth N. Marsh. **Document type**: academic/scholarly publication.
Formerly: T R C Current Data News.
Description: Describes activities, publications and projects at the Thermodynamics Research Center and the Chemical Engineering Department at Texas A & M University.
Refereed Serial

541.38 JA ISSN 0289-6893
CODEN: TASHEK
TOKYO TORITSU AISOTOPU SOGO KENKYUJO KENKYU HOKOKU/TOKYO METROPOLITAN ISOTOPE RESEARCH CENTER. BULLETIN. (Text in Japanese; summaries in English, Japanese) 198 a. Tokyo Toritsu Aisotopu Sogo Kenkyujo, 11-1, Fukazawa 2-chome, Setagaya-ku, Tokyo 158, Japan. **Indexed**: Chem.Abstr. **Document type**: bulletin.
—CASDDS.

541.3 GW ISSN 0941-2646
CODEN: TPCHFC
TOPICS IN PHYSICAL CHEMISTRY. (Text in English) irreg. (Deutsche Bunsen Gesellschaft fuer Physikalische Chemie) Dr. Dietrich Steinkopff Verlag, Saalbaustr. 12, 64283 Darmstadt, Germany. TEL 49-6151-1745-0. FAX 49-6151-174510. (Subscr. to: Postfach 111442, 64229 Darmstadt, Germany) Ed.Bd. **Document type**: monographic series.
—BLDSC (8867.485200); CASDDS; CISTI.

547.1 UK
TOPICS IN PHYSICAL ORGANOMETALLIC CHEMISTRY. 1985. a. $80 for vol. 4; $60 each for vols. 1-3. Freund Publishing House, Ltd., Ste. 500, Chesham House, 150 Regent St., London W1R 5FA, England. (And: P.O. Box 35010, Tel Aviv, Israel. TEL 972-3-5628540. FAX 972-3-5628538) Ed. Marcel Gielen. adv. **Document type**: academic/scholarly publication.

541.38 JA ISSN 0916-8486
CODEN: KTSSEJ
TOYAMA DAIGAKU SUISO DOITAI KINO KENKYU SENTA KENKYU HOKOKU/TOYAMA UNIVERSITY. HYDROGEN ISOTOPE RESEARCH CENTER. ANNUAL REPORT. (Text in English, Japanese; summaries in English) 1981. a. free. Toyama Daigaku, Suiso Doitai Kino Kenkyu Senta, 3190, Gofu-ke, Toyama-shi, Toyama-ken 930, Japan.
—BLDSC (1471.919270); CASDDS.

ULTRASONICS SONOCHEMISTRY. see *PHYSICS — Sound*

530 NE ISSN 0090-1911
QC454.V5 CODEN: VBSSBB
VIBRATIONAL SPECTRA AND STRUCTURE. 1972. irreg., vol.20, 1993. price varies. Elsevier Science B.V., Books Division, P.O. Box 211, 1000 AE Amsterdam, Netherlands. TEL 31-20-4853911. FAX 31-20-4853705. TELEX 18582 ESPA NL. E-mail: nlinfo-f@elsevier.nl; usinfo-f@elsevier.com; forinfo-kyf04035@niftyserve.or.jp; URL: http://www.elsevier.nl/. (Subscr. in the Americas to: Elsevier Science, Regional Sales Office, Box 945, New York, NY 10159-0945. TEL 212-633-3730. FAX 212-633-3680; Subscr. in Australasia and the Far East to: Elsevier Science (Singapore) Pte Ltd, No.1 Temasek Ave., No.17-01 Millenia Tower, Singapore 039192, Singapore. TEL 65-434-3727. FAX 65-337-2230; Subscr. in Japan to: Elsevier Science Japan, 9-15 Higashi-Azabu 1-chome, Minato-ku, Tokyo 106, Japan. TEL 81-3-5561-5033. FAX 81-3-5561-5047) Ed. J.R. Durig. charts; illus.; index. (back issues avail.; reprint service avail. from ISI) **Indexed**: Chem.Abstr., INSPEC. **Document type**: monographic series.
—BLDSC (9232.252000); CASDDS; CISTI; Linda Hall.
Refereed Serial

541 KR ISSN 0321-4095
CODEN: VKKCAJ
VOPROSY KHIMII I KHIMICHESKOI TEKHNOLOGII. 1965. 3/yr. 1.40 Rub. per no. (Dnepropetrovskii Khimiko-Tekhnologicheskii Institut) Izdatel'stvo Vysshaya Shkola, Khar'kovskoe Otdelenie, Ul. Universitetskaya 16, Khar'kov 310003, Ukraine. Ed. J. Bely. abstr.; bibl.; charts; illus. circ. 700. **Indexed**: Chem.Abstr.
—CASDDS; CISTI.

541 RU
VYSOKOMOLEKULYARNYE SOEDINENIYA. KRATKIE SOOBSHCHENIYA. (Text in Russian; summaries in English) 1959. m. Rossiiskaya Akademiya Nauk, Otdelenie Obshchei i Tekhnicheskoi Khimii, Leninskii prospekt, 14, Moscow V-71, Russia. Ed. V.A. Kargin. charts; illus.; index. (tabloid format) **Indexed**: Alloys Ind., Chem.Abstr., Eng.Mat.Abstr., Intl.Polym.Sci.& Tech., Met.Abstr., Met.Abstr.Ind., Nonfer.Met.Alert, PCC Alert, World Alum.Abstr.

541 RU ISSN 1023-3091
CODEN: VYSBAI
VYSOKOMOLEKULYARNYE SOEDINENIYA. SERIYA A I B. English edition: Polymer Science (ISSN 0965-545X) (Text in Russian; summaries in English) 1959. m. $312. (Rossiiskaya Akademiya Nauk, Institut Neftekhimichskogo Sinteza im. A.V. Tonchieva) Maik Nauka, Profsoyuznaya 90, 117864 Moscow, Russia. TEL 7-095-3360066. FAX 7-095-3360666. (Dist. in U.S. by: Victor Kamkin Inc., 4956 Boiling Brook Pkwy., Rockville, MD 20852. TEL 301-881-5973. FAX 301-881-1637) Ed. N.A. Plate. charts; illus.; index. (tabloid format) **Indexed**: Abstr.Bull.Inst.Pap.Chem., ASCA, Chem.Abstr., Chem.Cit.Ind., Curr.Cont., Ind.Sci.Rev., Intl.Polym.Sci.& Tech., Mat.Sci.Cit.Ind., RAPRA, Sci.Cit.Ind., World Text.Abstr.
—CASDDS; CISTI; EMDOCS; Genuine Article; KR SourceOne; Linda Hall; SWETS. **CCC.**
Formed by the 1993 merger of: Vysokomolekylyarnye Soedineniya. Seriya A (ISSN 0507-5475) & Vysokomolekylyarnye Soedineniya. Seriya B (ISSN 0507-5483)

541.3 CC ISSN 1000-6818
CODEN: WHXUEU
WULI HUAXUE XUEBAO/ACTA PHYSICO - CHIMICA SINICA. (Text in Chinese or English) 1985. m. $126 (effective 1997). (Zhongguo Huaxuehui - Chinese Chemical Society) Beijing Daxue Chubanshe - Beijing University Press, Haidian-qu, Beijing 100871. TEL 86-10-2182998. FAX 86-10-2181051.
—BLDSC (0650.655000); AskIEEE; CASDDS; KR SourceOne.

541.34 JA
YOEKI KAGAKU SHINPOJUMU KOEN YOSHISHU/SYMPOSIUM ON SOLUTION CHEMISTRY OF JAPAN. (Text in Japanese) 1978. a. Yoeki Kagaku Kenkyukai - Association of Japanese Solution Chemists, c/o Prof. M. Nakahara, Institute for Chemical Research, Kyoto University, Uji, Kyoto 611, Japan. TEL 81-774-38-3076. FAX 81-774-38-3076. E-mail: yoeki@nmr.kuicr.kyoto-u.ac.jp. Ed. Masaru Nakahara. **Document type**: proceedings.
Refereed Serial

YOYUEN KAGAKU TORONKAI YOSHISHU/SYMPOSIUM ON MOLTEN SALT CHEMISTRY. see *CHEMISTRY — Inorganic Chemistry*

YOYUEN OYOBI KOON KAGAKU/MOLTEN SALTS. see *CHEMISTRY — Inorganic Chemistry*

ZEITSCHRIFT FUER NATURFORSCHUNG. SECTION A: A JOURNAL OF PHYSICAL SCIENCES. see *PHYSICS*

541.3 GW ISSN 0044-3336
QD1 CODEN: ZPCFAX
ZEITSCHRIFT FUER PHYSIKALISCHE CHEMIE; international journal of research in physical chemistry and chemical physics. (Text in English, French and German) 1887. 10/yr. (in 5 vols., 2 nos./vol.). DM.1538 (effective 1997). R. Oldenbourg Verlag GmbH, Rosenheimerstr. 145, 81671 Munich, Germany. TEL 49-89-45051-0. FAX 49-89-45051207. (Subscr. to: Postfach 801360, 81613 Munich, Germany) Ed.Bd. adv.; bk.rev.; charts; illus.; index. circ. 1,700. (also avail. in microform from PMC) **Indexed**: A.S.& T.Ind., API Abstr., API Catal., API Hlth.& Environ., API Oil., API Pet.Ref., API Pet.Subst., API Transport., Appl.Mech.Rev., ASCA, Biol.Abstr., Bull.Thermodyn.& Thermochem., Chem.Abstr., Chem.Cit.Ind., Chem.Infd., Curr.Cont., GeoRef., Ind.Sci.Rev., INSPEC, Mass Spectr.Bull., Mat.Sci.Cit.Ind., Met.Abstr., Sci.Cit.Ind. **Document type**: academic/scholarly publication.
—BLDSC (9481.800000); CASDDS; CISTI; Ei; Linda Hall; UnCover. **CCC.**
Description: Contains research articles and short communications.

541 RU ISSN 0044-4537
QD1 CODEN: ZFKHA9
ZHURNAL FIZICHESKOI KHIMII. English edition: Russian Journal of Physical Chemistry (ISSN 0036-0244) 1930. m. $554 (effective 1998). Rossiiskaya Akademiya Nauk, Ul. Profsoyuznaya 90, Moscow 117864, Russia. TEL 7-095-3361600. FAX 7-095-3360666. Ed. V.M. Gryaznov. bk.rev.; bibl.; charts; illus.; index. circ. 3,185. **Indexed**: ASCA, Bull.Thermodyn.& Thermochem., Chem.Abstr., Chem.Cit.Ind., Chem.Infd., Curr.Cont., Eng.Mat.Abstr., Gas Abstr., Ind.Sci.Rev., INSPEC (1987-), Mat.Sci.Cit.Ind., Met.Abstr., Met.Abstr.Ind., Nonfer.Met.Alert, PCC Alert, RAPRA, Sci.Cit.Ind., Steels Alert, World Alum.Abstr.
—BLDSC (0067.000000); AskIEEE; CASDDS; CISTI; Genuine Article; KR SourceOne; Linda Hall. **CCC.**

541 RU ISSN 0136-7463
QD1 CODEN: ZSTKAI
ZHURNAL STRUKTURNOI KHIMII. (Text in Russian; summaries in English, Russina) 1960. bi-m. $229 (effective 1998). Rossiiskaya Akademiya Nauk, Sibirskoe Otdelenie, Institut Neorganicheskoy Khimii, Pr. Akademika Lavrenteva 3, 630090 Novosibirsk, Russia. TEL 3832-351066. E-mail: lm@che.nsk.su. (Subscr. to: Rossiiskaya Akademiya Nauk, Sibirskoe Otdelenie, Morskoy pr. 2, 630090 Novosibirsk, Russia. TEL 3832-350570. FAX 3832-356002) Ed. L.N. Mazalov. bibl.; index. circ. 450. (tabloid format) **Indexed**: Alloys Ind., Chem.Abstr., Eng.Mat.Abstr., INSPEC, Met.Abstr., Met.Abstr.Ind., Nonfer.Met.Alert, RAPRA, Steels Alert, World Alum.Abstr. **Document type**: academic/scholarly publication.
—BLDSC (0065.500000); CASDDS; CISTI.
Description: Covers theory of molecular structure and chemical bonding; study of the structure of molecules by physical methods; structure of liquids and solutions; crystal chemistry; questions of methodology; brief communications.

CHILDREN AND YOUTH — About

see also Education; Medical Sciences–Pediatrics

A A C E BONUS BRIEFS; connecting careers, education, and work. (American Association for Career Education) see OCCUPATIONS AND CAREERS

A A C E CAREERS UPDATE; connecting careers, education and work. (American Association for Career Education) see OCCUPATIONS AND CAREERS

A A C E DISTINGUISHED MEMBER SERIES; connecting careers, education, and work. (American Association for Career Education) see OCCUPATIONS AND CAREERS

A A T E NEWSLETTER. (American Alliance for Theatre & Education) see THEATER

362.7   US   ISSN 0887-896X
KF479.A59
A B A JUVENILE AND CHILD WELFARE LAW REPORTER. 1982. m. $169 to individuals; institutions $199 (effective 1997). American Bar Association, Center on Children and the Law, 740 15th St., N.W., Washington, DC 20005-1009. TEL 202-662-1739. URL: http://www.abanet.org. Ed. Jane Nusbaum Feller. bk.rev. circ. 800. (back issues avail.) **Indexed:** Viol.& Abuse Abstr. **Document type:** newsletter.
  Formerly: National Juvenile Law Reporter.
  Description: Keeps lawyers, judges and other professionals abreast of case law and legislative developments, particularly in the areas of child maltreatment, adoption, termination of parental rights, civil rights, juvenile justice, school law, day care, and tort actions involving children and families.

A C T A C NEWSLETTER. (Australian Children's Television Action Committee) see COMMUNICATIONS — Television And Cable

155.4 371.3 371.2   AT   ISSN 1320-2170
A E C A RESOURCE BOOK SERIES. 1978. q. Aus.$30 (effective 1996). Australian Early Childhood Association, P.O. Box 105, Knox St., Watson, A.C.T. 2602, Australia. TEL 61-2-416900. FAX 61-2-2415547. Ed. Jane Smyth. R&P contact: Kevin Hoare. bibl.; charts; illus. circ. 2,500. (back issues avail.) **Indexed:** Aus.Educ.Ind. **Document type:** monographic series.
  Formerly: Australian Early Childhood Resource Booklets (ISSN 0156-0999)
  Description: Contains practical information to workers in all early childhood settings.

A L S C NEWSLETTER. (Association for Library Service to Children) see LIBRARY AND INFORMATION SCIENCES

649 367   AT   ISSN 0815-1652
A M B A NEWS. 1984. 5/yr. Aus.$7.50 to members; non-members Aus.$15; foreign Aus.$20. Australian Multiple Birth Association Inc., P.O. Box 105, Coogee, N.S.W. 2034, Australia. TEL 49-468030. bk.rev. circ. 1,800. **Document type:** newsletter.
  Description: Articles relevant to multiple births: personal experiences, research, information.

A TO ZOO; subject access to children's picture books. see BIBLIOGRAPHIES

ACCENT (BIRMINGHAM). see RELIGIONS AND THEOLOGY — Protestant

ACTA MEDICA AUXOLOGICA. see MEDICAL SCIENCES — Endocrinology

155.4   US   ISSN 0737-5166
ACTA PAEDOLOGICA; an international journal of child development. 1984. q. Eterna International, Inc., Box 5731, Hauppauge, NY 11788-0154. Ed. Howard M. Bahr. adv.; bk.rev.; charts; illus.; index. **Indexed:** Psychol.Abstr.

ACTEENS ACCESSORIES. see RELIGIONS AND THEOLOGY — Protestant

ADOLESCENCE. see MEDICAL SCIENCES — Psychiatry And Neurology

155.5   US   ISSN 0001-8449
HQ793   CODEN: ADOLAO
ADOLESCENCE (SAN DIEGO); an international quarterly devoted to the physiological, psychological, psychiatric, sociological, and educational aspects of the second decade of human life. 1966. q. $71 to individuals; institutions $97 (effective 1997). Libra Publishers, Inc., 3089C Clairemont Dr., Ste. 383, San Diego, CA 92117. TEL 619-571-1414. Ed. William Kroll. adv. contact: Betty Kroll. bk.rev.; bibl.; charts; illus.; stat.; index, cum.index. circ. 3,000. (also avail. in microform from UMI; back issues avail.; reprint service avail. from ISI,UMI) **Indexed:** Abstr.Anthropol., Abstr.Crim.& Pen., Adol.Ment.Hlth.Abstr., ASCA, ASSIA, Bibl.Agri., Biol.Abstr., C.I.J.E., Child.Lit.Abstr., CINAHL, Crim.Just.Abstr., Curr.Cont., Curr.Lit.Fam.Plan., Educ.Ind., Except.Child.Educ.Abstr., Excerp.Med., High.Educ.Abstr., IBR, IMFL, Ind.Med., INIS Atomind., Lang.& Lang.Behav.Abstr., Mid.East: Abstr.& Ind., Mult.Ed.Abstr., Psychol.Abstr. (1966-), Psycscan D.P., Sage Fam.Stud.Abstr., Soc.Sci.Ind., Soc.Work Res.& Abstr., Sociol.Educ.Abstr., Sp.Ed.Needs Abstr., SSCI, Stud.Wom.Abstr., Tech.Educ.Abstr., THA, Viol.& Abuse Abstr. **Document type:** academic/scholarly publication.
  ●Also available online. Vendor(s): Information Access Co., UMI.
  Also available on CD-ROM.
  —BLDSC (0696.581000); Genuine Article; KR SourceOne; SWETS; UMI; UnCover. **CCC.**
  Description: Articles cover a variety of viewpoints on topics relating to adolescence.

362.7   RM
▼**ADOLESCENTA.** 1995. m. 5000 lei($250) Grupul Salor Industrial Tractorul, Str. Turnului Nr. 3, 2200 Brasov, Rumania. TEL 139311. (Subscr. to: Prof. Laura Tobescu, Str. Cometei Nr. 9, Sc. B, Ap. 2, 1068 Brasov, Rumania. TEL 313250) Ed. Georgeta Blendea. illus.

362.7   IT   ISSN 1120-3714
ADOLESCENZA. 1990. 3/yr. L.125000 (effective 1997). (Associazione per lo Studio e la Ricerca nell'Adolescenza) Pensiero Scientifico Editore s.r.l., Via Bradano 3-C, 00199 Rome, Italy. TEL 06-86207158. FAX 06-86207160. E-mail: pensiero@pensiero.it; URL: http://www.pensiero.it. adv. contact: Barbara Vella. circ. 800.

ADOPTALK. see SOCIAL SERVICES AND WELFARE

649   US   ISSN 0745-3167
ADOPTED CHILD. 1981. m. $22 (foreign $34) (effective 1997). Lois R. Melina, Ed. & Pub., Box 9362, Moscow, ID 83843. TEL 208-882-1794. FAX 208-883-8035. E-mail: LMELINA@moscow.com. bk.rev.; index. circ. 3,500. (looseleaf format; back issues avail.) **Document type:** newsletter.
  —CCC.
  Description: Newsletter of articles of advice and information for adoptive families, social workers, and therapists.

362.7   CN   ISSN 1181-845X
ADOPTION HELPER; devoted to helping people adopt. 1990. q. Can.$32 (foreign $32) (effective 1997). Helper Publishing, 36 Norwood Rd., Toronto, ON M4E 2S2, Canada. TEL 416-690-9593. FAX 416-690-9593. E-mail: helper@helping.com; URL: http://www.helping.com/family. Ed. Mr. Robin Hilborn; Pub. Mr. Robin Hilborn. adv.; bk.rev.; bibl.; illus.; circ. 700 (paid). (back issues avail.) **Document type:** consumer publication.
  Description: Covers adoption news, adoption processes, domestic and international adoptions, adoption for singles and special needs adoptions.

649   US   ISSN 1076-1020
ADOPTIVE FAMILIES.* 1967. bi-m. $24.95 (foreign $57) (effective July 1996). Adoptive Families of America, 2309 Como Ave., St. Paul, MN 55108-1723. TEL 612-535-4829; 800-372-3300. FAX 612-535-7808. Ed. Linda Lynch. R&P contact: Linda Lynch. adv. contact: Sue Slominski. bk.rev.; index. circ. 25,000.
  Formerly (until 1994): Ours (Minneapolis) (ISSN 0899-9333)
  Description: Information and support on educational, media, legislation, social, medical and adjustment issues in adoptive families.

ADVANCES IN LEARNING AND BEHAVIORAL DISABILITIES. see EDUCATION — Special Education And Rehabilitation

ADVANCES IN MOTOR DEVELOPMENT RESEARCH. see PHYSICAL FITNESS AND HYGIENE

ADVENTURE EDUCATION AND OUTDOOR LEADERSHIP. see SPORTS AND GAMES — Outdoor Life

AETAS NOSTRA. see CHILDREN AND YOUTH — For

369.4   BG   ISSN 0002-1040
AGRADOOT. (Text in Bengali) 1950. m. Tk.12. Bangladesh Scout Samity, National Headquarters, 67-A Purana Paltan, Dhaka 2, Bangladesh. Ed. Abdul Wahab. adv.; bk.rev.; illus.; index. circ. 2,000.
  Formerly: East Bengal Scout.

AKCENTY. see RELIGIONS AND THEOLOGY — Protestant

362.7 157.61   GW   ISSN 0720-3551
AKTION JUGENDSCHUTZ. INFORMATIONEN. Short title: A J S Informationen. 1965. bi-m. DM.6($5) Aktion Jugendschutz Landesarbeitsstelle Baden-Wuerttemberg, Stafflenbergstr. 44, 70184 Stuttgart, Germany. TEL 49-711-2373730. FAX 49-711-2373730. Ed. Birgit Ebbert. adv.; bk.rev.; bibl.; charts; illus.; stat. circ. 20,000. (back issues avail.) **Document type:** government publication.

649   US
ALL ABOUT KIDS. 1988. m. $15. All About Kids, 1077 Celestial St., Ste. 101, Cincinnati, OH 45202. TEL 513-684-0501. FAX 513-684-0507. E-mail: Ebadger@aak.com; URL: http://www.aak.com. Ed. Tricia Miller; Pub. arladeen Badger. adv.; bk.rev.; circ. 50,000 (controlled). **Document type:** consumer publication.

AMBULATORY CHILD HEALTH. see MEDICAL SCIENCES — Pediatrics

AMERICAN ACADEMY OF CHILD AND ADOLESCENT PSYCHIATRY. JOURNAL. see MEDICAL SCIENCES — Psychiatry And Neurology

649   US   ISSN 0044-7544
HQ750.A2
AMERICAN BABY; for expectant and new parents. 1938. m. single copies free. K-III Communications Corp., 745 Fifth Ave., New York, NY 10151. TEL 212-745-0100. (Subscr. to: Neodata Services, Box 2971, Boulder, CO 80329. TEL 303-447-9330) Pub. Sharon Summer. adv.: B&W page $50600; adv. contact: Sharon Summer. bk.rev.; illus. circ. 1,650,000. **Indexed:** CHNI, Hlth.Ind., Mag.Ind. **Document type:** consumer publication.
  —UMI; UnCover.
  Formerly: Mothers-to-Be - American Baby (ISSN 0027-156X)
  Description: Covers the basics of baby care, maternal health, early learning and prenursery education. Includes new products and services, such as toys and fashions.

AMERICAN JOURNAL OF ORTHOPSYCHIATRY. see PSYCHOLOGY

267 282   US
ANGELIC WARFARE DISPATCH. 1982. irreg. free. Catholics United for Life Youth Crusaders, Star Rt., Box 42, New Hope, KY 40052. TEL 502-325-3829. Eds. Joseph Stearns, Tamar Cesare. bk.rev. circ. 4,500. (back issues avail.)
  Description: Education of young people on morality in modern day life.

370 649.1   FR   ISSN 0245-2030
ANNUAIRE DES COMMUNAUTES D'ENFANTS. 1954. a. 15 F. Association Nationale des Communautes Educatives, 145 bd. Magenta, 75010 Paris, France. TEL 33-1-44635115. FAX 33-1-42855614.

ANTENNE AKTUELL. see EDUCATION

ANTI-CENSORSHIP NEWSLETTER. see SOCIOLOGY

APPRAISAL; science books for young people. see PUBLISHING AND BOOK TRADE

APPRENTISSAGE ET SOCIALISATION. see EDUCATION — Special Education And Rehabilitation

THE ARC TODAY. see SOCIAL SERVICES AND WELFARE

CHILDREN AND YOUTH — ABOUT

649 618.082 US
ARIZONA PARENTING FROM A TO Z. 1989. m. $12. Arizona Parenting, Box 63922, Phoenix, AZ 85082-3922. TEL 602-840-6650. FAX 602-840-6592. Ed. Greg Stiles. circ. 60,000. **Document type:** newspaper.
  Description: Covers parenting topics relating to raising children ages 0 - 12.

369.4 PH
ASIA - PACIFIC SCOUTING. 1974. bi-m. $4. World Scout Bureau, Asia - Pacific Region, Box 7369, Airmail Distribution Center, M.I.A. Rd., Metro Manila, Philippines. Ed. J. Plaridel Silvestre. circ. 600.
  Supersedes: Far East Scouting Bulletin (ISSN 0430-0610); Far East Scouting Newsletter; Asia-Pacific Scouting Newsletter.

367 UY
ASOCIACION. 1959-1978; resumed 1979. q. free. Confederacion Latinoamericana de Asociaciones Cristianas de Jovenes - Latin American Confederation of YMCAs, Colonia 1884, p.1, Montevideo, Uruguay. Ed. Edgardo G. Crovetto.
  Formerly: Confederacion Sudamericana de Asociaciones Cristianas de Jovenes. Noticias (ISSN 0010-5503)

155.4 616.8 US ISSN 1077-0305
ASSOCIATION FOR CHILD PSYCHOANALYSIS. NEWSLETTER. 1980. q. free. Association for Child Psychoanalysis, Inc., Box 253, Ramsey, NJ 07446. TEL 201-825-3138. FAX 201-825-3138. E-mail: 76422.3352@compuserve.com. Ed. Paul Brinich. bk.rev.; abstr.; bibl. circ. 700. (tabloid format; back issues avail.) **Document type:** newsletter.
  Description: Publishes abstracts of scientific meetings and reports on the activities of the members of the association

647 US
ATLANTA BABY. 1992. 6/yr. 4330 Georgetown Sq. II, No. 506, Atlanta, GA 30338-6217. TEL 770-454-7599. FAX 770-454-7699. Ed. Liz White; Pub. Liz White. R&P contact: Peggy Middendorf. adv.: B&W page $1356; trim 7 1/2 x 9 3/4; adv. contact: Nancy McDanie. circ. 30,000 (controlled). **Document type:** consumer publication.
  Description: Designed for expectant parents as well as new parents of children up to 18 months old. Covers resources, hospitals, maternity, and new baby issues.

647 US
ATLANTA PARENT. 1983. m. $12. Atlanta Parent, Inc., 4330 Georgetown Sq., Ste. 506, Atlanta, GA 30338. TEL 770-454-7599. FAX 770-454-7699. E-mail: http://family.com/ Ed. Liz White. adv.: B&W page $2198; trim 9 3/4 x 13. bk.rev.; circ. 70,000 (controlled). (tabloid format) **Document type:** consumer publication.
  Description: Covers family life, child care, adolescence, motherhood, schools, drugs, crafts and activities.

ATT ADOPTERA. see SOCIAL SERVICES AND WELFARE

AUSTRALIAN CHILDREN'S FOLKLORE NEWSLETTER. see FOLKLORE

AUSTRALIAN EARLY CHILDHOOD ASSOCIATION. VICTORIAN BRANCH. JOURNAL. see EDUCATION

362.7 AT ISSN 1030-0236
AUSTRALIAN EARLY CHILDHOOD NEWSLETTER. Short title: A E C A Newsletter. 1984. 4/yr. Aus.$23 (effective 1996). Australian Early Childhood Association, P.O. Box 105, Watson, A.C.T. 2602, Australia. TEL 61-2-416900. FAX 61-2-415547. Ed. Pamela Cahir. R&P contact: Kevin Heare. circ. 1,000. (looseleaf format) **Document type:** newsletter.
  Description: Features publications and conferences on early childhood.

640 052 AT
THE AUSTRALIAN FAMILY. 1980. q. Aus.$25. Australian Family Association, 582 Queensberry, N. Melbourne, Vic. 3051, Australia. TEL 61-3-329-8663. FAX 61-3-328-2877. Ed. Mary Helen Woods. bk.rev. circ. 2,500. (back issues avail.) **Document type:** bulletin.
  —UnCover.
  Formerly: Australian Family Bulletin (ISSN 0811-3661)
  Description: "Pro-family" view of social, economic, educational and moral issues.

649 AT ISSN 1036-0921
AUSTRALIA'S PARENTS. 1981. bi-m. Aus.$20. Magazine House Pty. Ltd., P.O. Box 1067, Crows Nest, N.S.W. 2065, Australia. TEL 61-2-94382399. FAX 61-2-94363014. E-mail: parents@ozemail.com.au. Ed. Carol Fallows. adv.: B&W page Aus.$3600, color page Aus.$4900; adv. contact: Lee Vecchiet. bk.rev.; charts; illus. circ. 40,440. (back issues avail.) **Document type:** consumer publication.
  —UnCover.
  Former titles (until 1991): Parents and Children Magazine (ISSN 0725-8186); Australian Parents and Children Magazine; Australian Parents Magazine.

AWARE. see RELIGIONS AND THEOLOGY — Protestant

B F H I NEWS. (Baby-Friendly Hospital Initiative) see SOCIAL SERVICES AND WELFARE

362.7 800 GW ISSN 0943-5638
B P J S AKTUELL. 1993. q. DM.56.50 (effective 1996). (Bundespruefstelle fuer Jugendgefaehrdende Schriften) Forum Verlag Godesberg GmbH, Parkstr. 55, 41061 Moenchengladbach, Germany. TEL 49-2161-206669. FAX 49-2161-209183. adv.: B&W page DM.1111; trim 262 x 185. circ. 4,200. **Document type:** government publication.

649 613.7 JA
BABY AGE. (Text in Japanese) 1969. m. 7560 Yen. Fujin Seikatsu Sha, 19-5, 2-chome, Yushima, Bunkyo-ku, Tokyo, Japan. Ed. Chioho Toui.

618 US ISSN 0894-3990
BABY CONNECTION NEWS JOURNAL; for new and expectant parents and their children 0-5 years. 1986. q. $4.75. Parent Education Center for Infant Development, Drawer 3350, San Antonio, TX 78265-3350. Ed. G. Morris Boyd; Pub. Kim Everett. R&P contact: G. Morris Boyd. adv. contact: Ed Boyd. bk.rev. circ. 45,000. (tabloid format) **Document type:** newspaper.
  Description: Provides articles on infant sensory stimulation, fetal development, pregnancy. Includes inspirational support for parents and advice on positive family lifestyles.
  Refereed Serial

BABY MAGAZINE INFANT CARE GUIDE. see MEDICAL SCIENCES — Pediatrics

BABY ON THE WAY: BASICS. see MEDICAL SCIENCES — Obstetrics And Gynecology

649.1 US ISSN 0749-971X
BABY TALK MAGAZINE. 1935. 10/yr. $19.95. Time Inc. Ventures, Baby Talk, 1325 Sixth Ave., 27th Fl., New York, NY 10019. TEL 212-522-8989. Eds. Trisha Thompson, Fred Levine. adv. contact: Lori Fromm. bk.rev.; charts; illus.; tr.lit. circ. 1,100,000. **Document type:** consumer publication.
  Former titles (until 1977): New Baby Talk (ISSN 0364-1554); (until 1976): Baby Talk (ISSN 0005-3589)
  Description: Discusses pregnancy, birth, and parenting from prenatal to age 2. Focuses on heath issues, personal stories, and newborn care.

BABYFIRST. see MEDICAL SCIENCES — Pediatrics

790.019 JA
BALLOON. (Text in Japanese) 1986. m. 11800 Yen. Shufunotomo Co., Ltd., 2-9 Kanda Surugadai, Chiyoda-ku, Tokyo 101, Japan. TEL 03-3294-1137. FAX 03-3291-5093. TELEX 26925. Ed. Mariko Hosoda. circ. 250,000. **Document type:** consumer publication.

649 US
BALTIMORE'S CHILD. 1984. m. $21. 11 Dutton Ct., Baltimore, MD 21228. TEL 410-367-5883. FAX 410-719-9342. E-mail: baltochild@aol.com; URL: http://family.com. Ed. Sharon Keech; Pubs. Sharon Keech, Joanne Giza. adv.: B&W page $2111; trim 11 1/2 x 14 1/2. bk.rev.; circ. 70,000. circ. 70,000 (controlled). **Document type:** consumer publication.
  ●Also available online.

362.7 IT ISSN 0393-4209
BAMBINI; una societa che cambia. 1984. m. L.65000 (foreign L.80000) (effective 1997). Edizioni Junior s.r.l., Via Pescaria 32, 24128 Bergamo, Italy. TEL 39-35-235361. FAX 39-35-236322. Ed. Ferruccio Cremaschi. adv.: page L.1400000. bk.rev. **Document type:** academic/scholarly publication.

649 IT
BAMBINISANI. 1992. q. Eurotrend S.p.A., Via Nino Bixio 6, 20129 Milan, Italy. TEL 39-2-29405653. FAX 39-2-29404868. Ed. Cesi Alessi. adv.: B&W or color page Lit.35300000. circ. 283,000. **Document type:** consumer publication.

362.7 UK
BARNARDO'S TODAY. 1987. bi-a. free. Tanner Ln., Barkingside, Ilford, Essex 1G6 1QG, England. TEL 44-181-550-8822. FAX 44-181-550-0429. Ed. Ali Worthy. circ. 40,000. **Document type:** newsletter.
  Description: Addresses the changing needs and problems of today's British children.

808.068 SW ISSN 0347-772X
BARNBOKEN. 1978. s-a. SEK 100 (effective 1997). Svenska barnboksinstitutet, (SBI) - Swedish Institute for Children's Books, Odengatan 61, S-113 22 Stockholm, Sweden. TEL 46-8-33-23-23. FAX 46-8-33-24-23. E-mail: sv.barnboksinstitutet@sbbi.se. Ed. Cecilia Oestlund. circ. 1,000. **Indexed:** Child.Lit.Abstr.
  Description: Articles and essays on children's literature by specialists; information on research in the field.

BAUSTEINE KINDERGARTEN. see EDUCATION — Teaching Methods And Curriculum

649 US
BAY AREA BABY; pregnancy & new parent resource magazine. 1986. s-a. Bay Area Publishing Group Inc., 401 Alberto Way, Ste. A, Los Gatos, CA 95032-5404. TEL 408-358-1414. FAX 408-356-4903. Ed. Lynn Berardo. adv.: B&W page $1675, color page $2185; bleed 8 5/16 x 10 1/2. circ. 60,000(controlled). **Document type:** consumer publication.

649 US
BAY AREA PARENT. m. $12. Bay Area Publishing Group Inc., 401 Alberto Way, Ste. A, Los Gatos, CA 95032-5404. TEL 408-358-1414. FAX 408-356-4903. Ed. Lynn Berardo; Pub. Sandy Moeckel. adv.: B&W page $2120, color page $2770; trim 9 1/2 x 12 5/8; adv. contact: Dale Ganzow. circ. 75,000. **Document type:** newspaper.

369.4 GW ISSN 0174-2175
BAYERISCHE LANDJUGEND. 1951. m. DM.20. Bayerische Jungbauernschaft e.V., Aubinger Weg 5, 82110 Germering, Germany. TEL 49-89-894414-0. Ed. Harald Fehde. adv.; bk.rev.; abstr.; illus. circ. 1,800. **Document type:** newsletter.

BEGINNING (NASHVILLE). see RELIGIONS AND THEOLOGY — Protestant

028.5 US
BEST BOOKS FOR CHILDREN; preschool through grade 6. (Part of Bowker's Best Books Series) irreg., 5th ed., 1994. $65. R.R. Bowker, A Division of Reed Elsevier Inc., 121 Chanlon Rd., New Providence, NJ 07974. TEL 908-464-6800. FAX 908-665-6688. TELEX 138 755. E-mail: info@bowker.com; URL: http://www.bowker.com. (Subscr. to: Order Dept., Box 31, New Providence, NJ 07974-9903. TEL 800-521-8110) Eds. John T. Gillespie, Corinne J. Naden. **Document type:** bibliography.
  ●Also available on CD-ROM. Producer(s): Bowker Electronic Publishing.
  Description: Provides an evaluative listing of 15,647 titles that have been recommended by at least two review sources.

CHILDREN AND YOUTH — ABOUT

649 US
THE BEST TOYS, BOOKS & VIDEOS FOR KIDS (YEAR). a. $13. Harper Collins Publishers, 10 E. 53rd St., New York, NY 10022. (Orders to: Order Department, 1000 Keystone Industrial Park, Scranton, PA 18512-4621. TEL 800-242-7737. FAX 800-822-4090; Orders in Canada to: HarperCollins Canada Ltd., 1995 Markham Rd., Scarborough, ON M1B 5M8, Canada. TEL 416-321-2241. FAX 416-321-3033) Eds. Joanne & Stephanie Oppenheim. **Document type:** consumer publication.
Description: Helps parents find the best-designed, most educational, and most entertaining toys, games, books, recordings, videos, and software programs for their children.

649 CN ISSN 0005-965X
BEST WISHES. 1949. s-a. free to new mothers. Family Communications, Inc., 37 Hanna Ave., Toronto, ON M6K 1X1, Canada. adv.; illus.; circ. 170,000 (controlled). **Document type:** consumer publication.

BIBLIOTHEQUE DE TRAVAIL JUNIOR. see *EDUCATION*

790.019 US
BIG APPLE PARENTS' PAPER. 1985. m. $28. Family Communications, 36 E. 12th St., 4th Fl., New York, NY 10003-4604. TEL 212-533-2277. FAX 212-475-6186. Ed. Helen Freedman. adv. contact: Steve Bauman. bk.rev.; circ. 62,000 (controlled). **Document type:** newspaper.
Formerly: Big Apple Parent.

649 IT
BIMBISANI E BELLI. 1993. m. L.25000 (foreign L.62000). Tre D Editoriale s.r.l., Viale Regina Giovanna 37, 20129 Milan, Italy. TEL 39-2-29528330. FAX 39-2-29528448. Ed. Gabriele Zappa. adv.; page L.30600000. circ. 205,000. **Document type:** consumer publication.

362.7 US
BIRTH TO THREE PARENTING NEWSLETTER. 1978. bi-m. $15. Birth to Three, 3875 Kincaid St., Ste. 15, Eugene, OR 97405-4554. TEL 503-484-5316. FAX 503-484-1449. Ed. Sylvia Lee Hanley. R&P contact: Sylvia Lee Hanley. adv.; bk.rev. circ. 12,000. (looseleaf format) **Document type:** newsletter.
Former titles: Birth to Three & Birth to Three and Beyond; Birth to Three Newsletter (ISSN 0895-6669)
Description: For parents of children under age 3. Includes articles about parenting issues and a list of events for children and parents.

369.4 FR ISSN 0980-2371
BIVOUAC. 1954. 6/yr. 50 F. Federation des Eclaireuses et Eclaireurs Unionistes de France, 15 rue Klock, 92110 Clichy, France. TEL 42-70-52-20. FAX 16-1-47-30-40-30. Ed. David Honegger. adv.; bk.rev. circ. 5,000.
Formerly: A.E.I.O.U.

362.7 US
BLACK CHILD ADVOCATE. 1971. 4/yr. $12.50 to non-members. National Black Child Development Institute, 1023 15th St., N.W., 6th Fl., Washington, DC 20005. TEL 202-387-1281. FAX 202-234-1738. Ed. Carla Taylor. R&P contact: Sherry C. Deane. bk.rev. circ. 3,500. **Indexed:** Viol.& Abuse Abstr. **Document type:** newsletter.
Description: For those interested in issues affecting the lives of Black children, youth and families. Includes public policy information, and updates of the activities of NBCDI's volunteer affiliate network.

BOERNE- OG UNGDOMSTANDPLEJEN I DANMARK. see *MEDICAL SCIENCES — Dentistry*

BOERNS HVERDAG; tidsskrift for foraeldre, paedagoger og bestyrelsesmedlemmer. see *EDUCATION*

028.5 US ISSN 1055-4742
Z1037
BOOK LINKS; connecting books, libraries, and classrooms. 1991. bi-m. $18.95 (Canada & Mexico $20; elsewhere $25). American Library Association, 50 E. Huron St., Chicago, IL 60611. TEL 312-955-6780; 800-545-2433. FAX 312-440-9374. URL: http://www.ala.org/70/00/alagophiv/alaperiodicals.txt. (Subscr. to: A L A, Subscription Dept., S&S Computer Services, Inc., 434 W. Downer Pl., Aurora, IL 60506-9936. TEL 630-892-7465. FAX 630-892-7466) Ed. Barbara Elleman. adv.; bk.rev.; bibl. circ. 30,000. **Document type:** bibliography.
—BLDSC (2248.120000); KR SourceOne; UnCover. CCC.
Description: Designed for teachers, librarians, library media specialists, booksellers, parents, and other adults interested in introducing children to books.

028.5 371.3 US
BOOK MARK; children's literature in review with related activities for preschoolers through young adults. 1977. 2/yr. $10. c/o Jane Bingham, Oakland University, School of Human and Educational Services, Rochester, MI 48063. TEL 313-370-3015. Eds. Jane Bingham, Gloria Blatt. bk.rev. circ. 1,000. **Indexed:** Bk.Rev.Ind. (1980-1982); Child.Bk.Rev.Ind. (1980-1982).
Former titles (until 1982): In Review: Books for Children and Young People with Related Activities; Children's Literature in Review.

649 US ISSN 1059-1710
BOSTON PARENTS' PAPER. 1984. m. $15. Parents' Plus, Inc., 670 Centre St., Jamaica Plain, MA 02130. TEL 617-522-1515. FAX 617-522-1694. E-mail: tbpp@aol.com. Ed. William Lindsay; Pub. Betsy Weaver. R&P contact: William Lindsay. adv. contact: Douglas Solomon. bk.rev.; video rev. circ. 75,000. **Document type:** newspaper.
Description: Provides practical parenting information.

BOY SCOUTS OF AMERICA. ANNUAL REPORT TO THE NATION. see *CLUBS*

369.4 US
BOYS & GIRLS CLUBS OF AMERICA BULLETIN.* (Former name of issuing body: Boys Clubs of America) 1965. 4/yr. free. Boys & Girls Clubs of America, 3 W. 35th St., 9th Fl., New York, NY 10001-2204. TEL 212-351-5900. Ed. Glen Slattery. bk.rev.; charts; illus. circ. 25,000. (reprint service avail. from UMI)
Formerly (until 1991): Boys Club Bulletin (ISSN 0006-8586)

370 GW ISSN 0006-9949
BRIEF AUS WAHLWIES; Mitteilungen aus dem Pestalozzi Kinder- und Jugenddorf. 1962. q. free. Pestalozzi Kinder- und Jugenddorf Wahlwies, 78333 Stockach, Germany. TEL 49-7771-8003-0. FAX 49-7771-800320. Ed. R. Beringer. adv.; bk.rev.; illus. circ. 5,000. **Document type:** newsletter.

053.932 BE
BRIEVEN AAN JONGE OUDERS. (Published in 4 editions: For Expecting Parents, 1st Year of Life, 2nd Year of Life, Infants) 1979. a. free. Publicarto N.V., Langestraat 170, B-1150 Brussels 15, Belgium. TEL 32-2-7790000. FAX 32-2-7791616. Ed. Jef Berghmans. adv. contact: Catherine Doolaege. bk.rev.; illus. circ. 91,579. **Document type:** consumer publication.
Former titles: Brieven aan Gezinnen; Brieven aan Jonge Gezinnen.
Description: For parents who are expecting a baby, or who have young children from 0 to 3 years old.

305.23 UK ISSN 1360-4430
▼**BRITISH INTERDISCIPLINARY JOURNAL OF CHILDHOOD.** 1996-1997. s-a. £40 in Europe; N. America $65; elsewhere £45 (effective 1996). Whiting & Birch Ltd., P.O. Box 872, Forest Hill, London SE23 3HL, England. TEL 44-181-244-2421. FAX 44-181-244-2448. Ed. Rupert Hughes. **Document type:** academic/scholarly publication.

362.7 US ISSN 1058-1073
HQ767.8
BROWN UNIVERSITY CHILD AND ADOLESCENT BEHAVIOR LETTER; monthly reports on the problems of children and adolescents growing up. 1984. m. $167 (Canada $177; elsewhere $187) (effective 1997). Manisses Communications Group, Inc., Box 9758, Providence, RI 02940-9758. TEL 401-831-6020; 800-333-7771. FAX 401-861-6370. E-mail: manissesCS@manisses.com; URL: http://www.manisses.com. Ed. Lewis P. Lippsitt; Pub. Fraser A. Lang. bk.rev.; abstr.; bibl.; stat. **Document type:** newsletter.
●Also available online. Vendor(s): Information Access Co.
—CCC.
Incorporates (in 1992): Children and Teens Today (ISSN 0882-942X); Which was formerly (until 1985): Children and Teens in Crisis (ISSN 0732-7420); Formerly (until 1991): Brown University Child Behavior and Development Letter (ISSN 0898-2562)
Description: Practical counseling techniques and authoritative summaries of research on development and behavior of children and adolescents.

369.4 CN ISSN 0045-334X
BUFFALO. 1946. 6/yr. Can.$15 (effective 1997). Girl Guides of Canada, Manitoba Council, 872 St. James St., Winnipeg, MB R3G 3J7, Canada. TEL 204-774-1939. FAX 204-774-9271. E-mail: info@manitoba.girlguides.ca. circ. 1,474. **Document type:** newsletter.

BULLETIN JUGEND UND LITERATUR. see *LIBRARY AND INFORMATION SCIENCES*

C B C FEATURES; containing news of the children's book world. (Children's Book Council, Inc.) see *PUBLISHING AND BOOK TRADE*

C C B D NEWSLETTER. (Council for Children with Behavioral Disorders) see *EDUCATION — Special Education And Rehabilitation*

369.4 DK ISSN 0109-2979
C C ORIENTERING. 1983. q. free. Coordination Committee for Polish-Jewish Youth in Denmark, Box 77, 1000 Copenhagen K, Denmark. illus.

362.7 US ISSN 0276-6531
HV741
C D F REPORTS. m. $29.95. Children's Defense Fund, 25 E St., N.W., Washington, DC 20001. TEL 202-628-8787. FAX 202-662-3530. circ. 8,000. (back issues avail.)
Description: Covers a range of issues concerning child welfare, including poverty, maternal and child health, education, employment, housing and more.

649 US
C F CHILD CARE BULLETIN. 1978. 6/yr. $20 to individuals; agencies $30. Children's Foundation, 725 15th St., N.W., Ste. 505, Washington, DC 20005. TEL 202-347-3300. Ed. Kay Hollestelle. bk.rev. circ. 2,000. **Document type:** newsletter.
Former titles: C F Child & Family Day Care Bulletin; Family Day Care Food Bulletin.

362.7 US
C H I L D NEWSLETTER. 1984. q. $25 includes membership. (Children's Healthcare Is a Legal Duty) C H I L D, Inc., Box 2604, Sioux City, IA 51106. TEL 712-948-3500. FAX 712-948-3500. E-mail: childink@netins.net; URL: http://members.aol.com/childink. Ed. Dr. Rita Swan. R&P contact: Rita Swan. bk.rev.; circ. 440 (controlled). **Document type:** newsletter.
Description: Seeks to end the child abuse and neglect associated with the practices of certain religious groups.

C S L I PUBLICATION. (Center for the Study of Language and Information) see *LINGUISTICS*

649 FR ISSN 0007-9820
CAHIERS DE LA PUERICULTRICE.* q. 70 F. Editions de Medecine Pratique, 4 rue Louis-Armand, 92600 Asnieres, France. Ed. F. Alison.
—CISTI.

CAMARADERIE. see *CLUBS*

CHILDREN AND YOUTH — ABOUT

790.019   US   ISSN 0740-4131
SK601.A1
CAMPING MAGAZINE. 1926. bi-m. $24.95 (effective July 1995). American Camping Association, Inc., 5000 State Rd. 67 N., Martinsville, IN 46151-7902. TEL 317-342-8456. Ed. Karen M. Pavlicin. R&P contact: Christy Phillips. adv. contact: Bill Willems. charts; illus.; stat.; tr.lit.; index. circ. 8,000. (also avail. in microform from UMI; back issues avail.; reprint service avail. from UMI) Indexed: C.I.J.E., Mag.Ind., R.G., Rehabil.Lit., Sports.Per.Ind., Sportsearch. Document type: consumer publication.
● Also available online. Vendor(s): Information Access Co.
—SWETS; UMI; UnCover.

362.7 796   CN   ISSN 0300-435X
CANADIAN GUIDER. 1932. 5/yr. Can.$9($12.50) (effective 1997); newsstand price: Can.$2. Girl Guides of Canada, National Council - Guides du Canada, 50 Merton St., Toronto, ON M4S 1A3, Canada. TEL 416-487-5281. FAX 416-487-7024. URL: http://www.girlguides.ca. Ed. Sharon Pruner. R&P contact: Barbara Crocker. adv.: page Can.$2200; trim 8 1/8 x 10 7/8; adv. contact: Barbara Crocker. bk.rev. circ. 55,000.
Description: Includes leadership tips and program activities for guide leaders.

CANADIAN INTRAMURAL RECREATION ASSOCIATION. BULLETIN; the voice of intramurals in Canada. see PHYSICAL FITNESS AND HYGIENE

369.4   CN   ISSN 0711-5377
CANADIAN LEADER. 1923. 10/yr. Can.$10.70 (foreign Can.$18) (effective 1997). (Scouts Canada) Canyouth Publications Ltd., Box 5112, Station F, Ottawa, ON K2C 3H4, Canada. TEL 613-224-5131. FAX 613-224-5982. Ed. Allen Macartney; Pub. Garth Johnson. R&P contact: Garth Johnson. adv. contact: Laureen Duquette. bk.rev.; illus.; tr.lit.; index. circ. 47,000.
Supersedes (in 1970): Scout Leader.
Refereed Serial

CANDLELIGHTERS CHILDHOOD CANCER FOUNDATION YOUTH NEWSLETTER. see MEDICAL SCIENCES — Oncology

362.7   US
CARING FOR THE LITTLE ONES; creating a network of people who work with infants and toddlers. m. Box 97, Cowdrey, CO 80434-0097.
TEL 303-723-4708.
Description: Provides information on how to teach and take care of infants and toddlers.

CARNEGIE-MELLON SYMPOSIA ON COGNITION SERIES. see PSYCHOLOGY

CATHOLIC EDUCATION CIRCULAR. see EDUCATION — Teaching Methods And Curriculum

362.7 282   US   ISSN 1069-4862
CATHOLIC PARENT. 1993. bi-m. $18 (foreign $24). Our Sunday Visitor, Inc., 200 Noll Plaza, Huntington, IN 46750. TEL 219-356-8400.
FAX 219-356-8472. Ed. Woodeen Koenig-Bricker. adv.: B&W page $1000, color page $1250; trim 8 3/8 x 10 7/8. circ. 32,000. Document type: consumer publication.

CENTER FOR CHILDREN'S BOOKS. BULLETIN. see BIBLIOGRAPHIES

649   US
CENTRAL FLORIDA FAMILY JOURNAL.* 1985. m. Family Journal Publications, Inc., Box 1100, Orlando, FL 32802-1100. TEL 407-774-9863.
FAX 407-788-2099. Ed. Patrick McGuffin. adv.: B&W page $1850; trim 14 x 16. circ. 56,312 (controlled). Document type: consumer publication.

362.7   FR
CENTRE INTERNATIONAL DE L'ENFANCE. PROGRAMME OF ACTIVITIES. a. Centre International de l'Enfance - International Children's Center, Chateau de Longchamp, Bois de Boulogne, 75016 Paris, France. TEL 33-1-44302062. FAX 33-1-44302065. E-mail: 100631,1101@compuserve.com.
Description: Directed toward planning and long-term action for the benefit of mothers and children.

649   CN   ISSN 0705-3215
C'EST POUR QUAND. 1978. s-a. Family Communications, Inc. - Communications Famille Inc., 37 Hanna Ave., Toronto, ON M6K 1X1, Canada. Ed. Manon Leymone. adv.; circ. 52,000. Document type: consumer publication.

267   US   ISSN 0009-1723
CHARITY AND CHILDREN; the voice of child care in North Carolina. 1887. 12/yr. free. Baptist Children's Homes of North Carolina, Inc., Box 338, Thomasville, NC 27361-0338. TEL 910-474-1211. FAX 910-472-3802. Ed. Norman Jameson; Pub. Michael C. Blackwell. adv.; bk.rev. circ. 53,000. (tabloid format) Document type: newspaper.
Description: Provides information to friends and supporters about services.

CHEROKEE BOYS CLUB NEWSLETTER. see ETHNIC INTERESTS

649   US
CHICAGO PARENT MAGAZINE. 1985. m. $6.95. Wednesday Journal Inc., 141 S. Oak Park Ave., Oak Park, IL 60302-2901. TEL 708-386-5555.
FAX 708-524-0447. Ed. Sharon Bloyd-Peshkin; Pub. Dan Haley. adv. contact: Kit Olah. bk.rev.; circ. 85,000 (controlled). Document type: consumer publication.

CHIEF ADJUDICATION OFFICER. ANNUAL REPORT. see SOCIAL SERVICES AND WELFARE

649 371.3   US   ISSN 0894-7988
CHILD. 1986. 10/yr. $7.97. Gruner & Jahr U.S.A. Publishing, 110 Fifth Ave., New York, NY 10011. TEL 212-499-2000. FAX 212-463-1383. Ed. Pamela Abrams. adv. contact: Jyll Holzmann. circ. 775,000. Document type: consumer publication.
Formerly: For Today's Children.
Description: Offers information on child rearing and includes articles on child development, behavior, health, nutrition, fitness, and education. Covers new products and services for children and their parents, as well as travel, fashion, food and beauty topics.

362.7 301   UK   ISSN 0145-2134
HV713   CODEN: CABND3
CHILD ABUSE & NEGLECT; the international journal. 1977. m. fl.1715($986) (effective 1998). (International Society for Prevention of Child Abuse and Neglect) Elsevier Science Ltd., Pergamon, P.O. Box 800, Kidlington, Oxford OX5 1DX, England. TEL 44-1865-843000. FAX 44-1865-843010. E-mail: nlinfo-f@elsevier.nl; usinfo-f@elsevier.com; forinfo-kyf04035@niftyserve.or.jp; URL: http://www/elsevier.nl/. (Subscr. to: Elsevier Science, Regional Sales Office, P.O. Box 211, 1000 AE Amsterdam, Netherlands. TEL 31-20-4853757. FAX 31-20-4853432; Subscr. in the Americas to: Elsevier Science, Regional Sales Office, Box 945, New York, NY 10159-0945. TEL 212-633-3730. FAX 212-633-3680; Subscr. in Australasia and the Far East to: Elsevier Science (Singapore) Pte Ltd, No.1 Temasek Ave., No.17-01 Millenia Tower, Singapore 039192, Singapore. TEL 65-434-3727. FAX 65-337-2230) Ed. Richard D. Krugman. adv.; bk.rev.; index. circ. 1,500. (also avail. in microfilm from UMI; back issues avail.) Indexed: Abstr.Crim.& Pen., Adol.Ment.Hlth.Abstr., ASCA, ASSIA, Bibl.Dev.Med.& Child Neur., Br.Educ.Ind., C.I.J.E., Child Devel.Abstr., Crim.Just.Abstr., Curr.Cont., Educ.Ind., Except.Child.Educ.Abstr., Excerp.Med., Fam.Ind., Ind.Med., Ind.Per.Art.Relat.Law, Ind.U.S.Gov.Per., Psychol.Abstr. (1980-), Risk Abstr., Soc.Sci.Ind. (1994-), Soc.Work Res.& Abstr., SSCI, Viol.& Abuse Abstr. Document type: academic/scholarly publication.
● Also available online.
—BLDSC (3172.912500); EMDOCS; Genuine Article; KNAW; KR SourceOne; SWETS; UMI; UnCover. CCC.
Formerly: International Journal on Child Abuse and Neglect.
Description: Provides an international multidisciplinary forum on all aspects of child abuse and neglect, including sexual abuse, with emphasis on prevention and treatment.
Refereed Serial

362.7   US   ISSN 1078-6651
HV713
CHILD ABUSE & NEGLECT C D - R O M. 1993. s-a. free to institutions and libraries. (National Clearinghouse on Child Abuse & Neglect Information) National Information Services Corporation (NISC), 3100 St. Paul St., Ste. 806, Baltimore, MD 21218.
TEL 410-243-0797. FAX 410-243-0982. (Subscr. to: National Clearinghouse on Child Abuse & Neglect Information, Box 1182, Washington, DC 20013-1182) Document type: abstracting/indexing.
● Available only on CD-ROM. Producer(s): NISC.
Description: Provides access to information on child abuse: documents, legal statutes, public awareness materials, audiovisual resources and local, state, federal and international programs.

CHILD AND ADOLESCENT SOCIAL WORK JOURNAL. see SOCIOLOGY

649   US   ISSN 0009-3882
                     CODEN: CHFMB
CHILD AND FAMILY. 1962. q. $12 (foreign $16). National Commission on Human Life, Reproduction and Rhythm, Box 508, Oak Park, IL 60303.
TEL 708-383-8766. Ed. Dr. Herbert Ratner. bk.rev. index. circ. 1,000. (back issues avail.; reprint service avail. from KTO) Indexed: ASSIA, Child Devel.Abstr., Mid.East: Abstr.& Ind. Document type: academic/scholarly publication.
—BLDSC (3172.915000); UnCover.
Description: Presents supportive articles on the family, on children, and on nature; has editorial comments.

CHILD AND FAMILY LAW QUARTERLY. see LAW — Family And Matrimonial Law

CHILD & FAMILY SOCIAL WORK. see SOCIAL SERVICES AND WELFARE

155.4   US   ISSN 1053-1890
HV701   CODEN: CYCFEH
CHILD AND YOUTH CARE FORUM; an independent journal of day and residential child and youth care practice. 1971. bi-m. $295 (foreign $345) (effective 1997). Human Sciences Press, Inc. (Subsidiary of: Plenum Publishing Corp.), 233 Spring St., New York, NY 10013-1578.
TEL 212-620-8000. FAX 212-463-0742. TELEX 23-421139. Ed. Jerome Beker. adv.; bk.rev.; bibl.; index. (also avail. in microform from UMI; back issues avail.; reprint service avail. from ISI,UMI) Indexed: Abstr.Crim.& Pen., Abstr.Soc.Work., Adol.Ment.Hlth.Abstr., ASCA, ASSIA, Bibl.Agri., C.I.J.E., Child Devel.Abstr., Community Ment.Health.Rev., Curr.Cont., Educ.Ind., Except.Child.Educ.Abstr., IMFL, Mid.East: Abstr.& Ind., Mult.Ed.Abstr., Psychol.Abstr. (1965-), Psycscan D.P., Sage Fam.Stud.Abstr., Sage Urb.Stud.Abstr., Soc.Work Res.& Abstr., Sociol.Educ.Abstr., SOMA, Sp.Ed.Needs Abstr., SSCI. Document type: academic/scholarly publication.
—BLDSC (3172.915800); Genuine Article; KR SourceOne; SWETS; UMI; UnCover. CCC.
Former titles (until 1990): Child and Youth Care Quarterly (ISSN 0893-0848); (until 1987): Child Care Quarterly (ISSN 0045-6632)
Description: Covers the training of personnel and psychological testing.
Refereed Serial

CHILD & YOUTH SERVICES. see SOCIAL SERVICES AND WELFARE

155.4   US   ISSN 1055-0518
CHILD ASSESSMENT NEWS. 1991. 6/yr. $75 (foreign $83.50) to individuals; institutions $95 (foreign $103.50) (effective 1997). Guilford Publications, Inc., 72 Spring St., 4th Fl., New York, NY 10012.
TEL 212-431-9800; 800-365-7006.
FAX 212-966-6708. E-mail: info@guilford.com. Ed. Randy Kamphaus; Pub. Robert Matloff. R&P contact: Kathy Kuehl. Document type: newsletter.

362.7   US
CHILD CARE ACTION NEWS. 1983. bi-m. $25 includes membership. Child Care Action Campaign, 330 Seventh Ave., 17th Fl., New York, NY 10001.
FAX 212-268-6515. Ed. Barbara Reisman. bk.rev.; tr.lit. circ. 5,000. (back issues avail.) Document type: newsletter.

CHILDREN AND YOUTH — ABOUT

649 373   CN   ISSN 0847-3234
CHILD CARE FOCUS. 1976. q. Can.$35. Manitoba Child Care Association, 364 McGregor St., Winnipeg, MB R2W 4X3, Canada. TEL 204-586-8587. FAX 204-589-5613. Ed. Debra Mayer. R&P contact: Debra Mayer. adv. contact: Claire Funk. bk.rev. circ. 2,600. **Document type:** newsletter.
   Description: A regular update of the association's work towards quality care and of issues and developments affecting children, child care programs and early childhood educators in centres and family day care homes.
Refereed Serial

649 155.4   US   ISSN 0009-3920
HQ750.A1   CODEN: CHDEAW
CHILD DEVELOPMENT. 1930. bi-m. $156 (Canada $179.92; elsewhere $169) (effective 1997). (Society for Research in Child Development) University of Chicago Press, Journals Division, Box 37005, Chicago, IL 60637. TEL 773-753-3347. FAX 773-753-0811. E-mail: subscriptions@journals.uchicago.edu; URL: http://www.journals.uchicago.edu/CD. Ed. Marc H. Bornstein. adv.: page $410; trim 8 1/2 x 11. bk.rev.; index. circ. 8,600. (also avail. in microform from UMI; reprint service avail. from ISI,KTO,UMI) **Indexed:** Abstr.Anthropol., Abstr.Crim.& Pen., Acad.Ind., Adol.Ment.Hlth.Abstr., ASCA, ASSIA, Behav.Med.Abstr., Bibl.Agri., Bibl.Dev.Med.& Child Neur., Biol.Abstr., Bk.Rev.Ind. (1977-1980), C.I.J.E., Child.Bk.Rev.Ind. (1977-1980), Cont.Pg.Educ., Crim.Just.Abstr., Curr.Adv.Ecol.Sci., Curr.Cont., Dent.Ind., DSH Abstr., Educ.Ind., Fam.Ind., Hlth.Ind., IBR, IMFL, Ind.Med., Lang.& Lang.Behav.Abstr., Ling.Abstr., M.L.A., Mid.East: Abstr.& Ind., MLA Intl.Bibl., Mult.Ed.Abstr., Neurosci.Cit.Ind., Nutr.Abstr., Psychol.Abstr. (1930-), Psycscan D.P., Sage Fam.Stud.Abstr., Soc.Sci.Ind., Sociol.Abstr., Sociol.Educ.Abstr., SOMA, Sp.Ed.Needs Abstr., SSCI, Stud.Wom.Abstr., Yrbk.Assoc.Educ.& Rehab.Blind. **Document type:** academic/scholarly publication.
  —BLDSC (3172.940000); CISTI; Genuine Article; KNAW; KR SourceOne; SWETS; UMI; UnCover. **CCC.**
   Description: Publishes original articles on all aspects of child development, from the prenatal period through adolescence.
Refereed Serial

362.7   US
CHILD HEALTH TALK. 1987. q. $10 to non-members. National Black Child Development Institute, 1023 15th St., N.W., 6th Fl., Washington, DC 20005. TEL 202-387-1281. FAX 202-234-1738. Ed. Marlene A. Vassall. R&P contact: Sherry C. Deanne. circ. 5,000. **Document type:** newsletter.
   Description: Provides practical guidance and advice to parents on health issues facing Black children. Covers topics such as nutrition, safety, exercise, and common childhood illnesses.

331.31 363.1
346.01   US   ISSN 1060-6661
HD6228
CHILD LABOR MONITOR. 1991. q. $15. National Consumers League, Inc., 1701 K. St., N.W., Ste. 1200, Washington, DC 20006. TEL 202-835-3323. FAX 202-835-0747. E-mail: nclncl@aol.com; URL: http://www.essential.org/clc. Eds. Cleo, Manuel, Kim Michalski. R&P contact: Cleo A. Manuel. (looseleaf format; back issues avail.) **Document type:** newsletter.
   Description: Focuses on state, national, and international efforts to end child labor exploitation, and to ensure the health, education and well being of working minors.

649   US
CHILD MAGAZINE'S GUIDE TO BABY PRODUCTS; the resource for new parents. 1992. a. newsstand price: $4.95. New York Times Company, Magazine Group, 110 Fifth Ave., New York, NY 10011. TEL 212-463-1600. FAX 212-463-1383. Pub. Rebecca McPheters. adv.: B&W page $14025, color page $16900; trim 8 x 10 1/2; adv. contact: Pam Sigal. circ. 600,000 (controlled). **Document type:** consumer publication.

649   US   ISSN 1049-2402
CHILD MAGAZINE'S GUIDE TO HAVING A BABY. 1990. a. (Nurses Association for the American College of Obstetricians and Gynecology (NAACOG) New York Times Company, Magazine Group, 110 Fifth Ave., New York, NY 10011. TEL 212-463-1600. FAX 212-463-1553. Ed. Laura Manske. adv.; circ. 1,200,000 (controlled).
   Description: Information for expectant parents.

362.7   US   ISSN 1077-5595
RC569.5.C55   CODEN: CMALFA
▼**CHILD MALTREATMENT.** 1996. q. $155 to institutions (effective Sept. 1996). (American Professional Society on the Abuse of Children) Sage Publications, Inc., 2455 Teller Rd., Thousand Oaks, CA 91320. TEL 805-499-0721. FAX 805-499-0871. E-mail: libraries@sagepub.com; URL: http://www.sagepub.com. (Overseas subscr. to: Sage Publications Ltd., 6 Bonhill St., London EC2A 4PU, England; Sage Publications India Pvt. Ltd., P.O. Box 4215, New Delhi 110 048, India) Ed. Mark Chaffin. adv. contact: Margaret Travers. **Indexed:** Crim.Just.Abstr. **Document type:** academic/scholarly publication.
  —BLDSC (3172.944770). **CCC.**
   Description: Reports the latest scientific information and technical innovations relating to child abuse.
Refereed Serial

CHILD NEUROPSYCHOLOGY; a journal on normal and abnormal development in childhood and adolescence. see *PSYCHOLOGY*

362.7   US   ISSN 0738-4726
CHILD NURTURANCE. 1982. irreg., vol.4, 1984. Plenum Publishing Corp., 233 Spring St., New York, NY 10013-1578. TEL 212-620-8000. FAX 212-463-0742. TELEX 23-421139. E-mail: books@plenum.com. Eds. M.J. Kostelnik, H.E. Fitzgerald. (back issues avail.) **Document type:** monographic series.
Refereed Serial

362.7   US   ISSN 0147-1260
CHILD PROTECTION REPORT; the independent newsletter for professionals covering the funding and politics of national child-youth health, welfare and juvenile justice service programs. 1975. bi-w. $208 (effective Sep. 1992). Business Publishers, Inc., 951 Pershing Dr., Silver Spring, MD 20910-4432. TEL 301-587-6300. FAX 301-585-9075. Ed. Linda Roeder. bk.rev.; charts; stat.; index. (looseleaf format; back issues avail.) **Indexed:** Viol.& Abuse Abstr. **Document type:** newsletter.
  ●Also available online. Vendor(s): NewsNet.
  —**CCC.**
   Description: Advice and funding information for managers of child-assistance programs.

362.7   UK   ISSN 0957-4107
CHILD SAFETY REVIEW. 1989. q. £17.50 (overseas £26.25). Child Accident Prevention Trust, Clerks Ct., 4th Fl., 18-20 Farringdon Ln., London EC1R 3AU, England. TEL 44-171-636-3828. E-mail: safe@capt.demon.co.uk. Ed. Susan Pinckney. R&P contact: Susan Pinckney. bk.rev.; circ. 500 (controlled). **Document type:** newsletter.
   Description: Covers news and developments in child accident prevention at the trust and throughout the United Kingdom. Includes briefings on conferences, new publications, and reports.

CHILD STUDY JOURNAL. see *EDUCATION*

362.7   US
CHILD SUPPORT BULLETIN. q. $12. Children's Foundation, 725 15th St., N.W., Ste. 505, Washington, DC 20005. TEL 202-347-3300. Ed. Carole Hobbes. **Document type:** newsletter.
   Description: Resource for advocates, agencies, and grassroots groups.

CHILD SUPPORT PROSECUTORS' BULLETIN. see *LAW — Family And Matrimonial Law*

CHILD WELFARE; journal of policy, practice and program. see *SOCIAL SERVICES AND WELFARE*

305.23   UK   ISSN 0907-5682
HQ767.8   CODEN: CHILFF
CHILDHOOD; a global journal of child research. 1993. q. £36($58) to individuals; institutions £130($208) (effective 1998). (Norwegian Centre for Child Research) Sage Publications Ltd., 6 Bonhill St., London EC2A 4PU, England. TEL 44-171-374-0645. FAX 44-171-374-8741. E-mail: market@sagepub.co.uk; URL: http://www.sagepub.co.uk/. Ed.Bd. adv. contact: Bernie Folan. bk.rev.; charts; illus. (reprint service avail.) **Indexed:** ASSIA, C.I.J.E., Curr.Cont., Psychol.Abstr., Sociol.Abstr., SSCI. **Document type:** academic/scholarly publication.
  —BLDSC (3172.951500); Genuine Article; SWETS. **CCC.**
   Description: Interdisciplinary forum for research relating to children in contemporary global society that spans divisions between geographical regions, disciplines, social and cultural contexts, and applied and basic research.
Refereed Serial

CHILDHOOD EDUCATION; a journal for teachers, teachers-in-training, teacher educators, parents, day care workers, librarians, pediatricians and other child caregivers. see *EDUCATION*

362.7   PH
CHILDHOPE ASIA NEWSLETTER. (Text in English) 1991. q. $20. Childhope Asia Philippines, 1210 Penafrancia, Paco, Manila 1007, Philippines. TEL 632-583537. FAX 632-5217225. E-mail: igc:chsea. Ed. Teresita L. Silva. circ. 2,000. **Document type:** newsletter.
   Description: Aims to raise awareness and knowledge about the situation of street children in Asia through publication of research findings on street children issues.

CHILDLIFE. see *RELIGIONS AND THEOLOGY — Protestant*

362.7   UK
CHILDMINDING. 1990. q. membership. Scottish Childminding Association, Rm. 7, Stirling Business Centre, Wellgreen, Stirling FK8 2DZ, Scotland. TEL 44-1786-445377. FAX 44-1786-449062. Ed. Sandra Currie. R&P contact: Sandra Currie. adv. contact: Karine Lee. bk.rev. circ. 6,250. **Document type:** newsletter.
   Formerly: Scottish Childminding Association Magazine (ISSN 0959-0145)
   Description: Deals with all aspects of childminding and child care.
Refereed Serial

362.7   UK
K1
CHILDREN AND FAMILIES. 1982. irreg. $88. Jessica Kingsley Publishers, 116 Pentonville Rd., London N1 9JB, England. TEL 44-171-883-2307. FAX 44-171-837-2917. E-mail: post@jkp.com; URL: http://www.jkp.com. (Dist. in U.S. by: Taylor & Francis, 1900 Frost Rd., Ste. 101, Bristol, PA 19007-1598. TEL 215-785-5800. FAX 215-785-5515) Eds. Sandra Garcia, Robert Batey. **Indexed:** Psychol.Abstr. **Document type:** monographic series.
  —BLDSC (0709.256200).
   Formerly (until 1991): Advances in Law and Child Development (ISSN 0732-3565)

362.7   UK   ISSN 0960-8699
CHILDREN AND PARLIAMENT. 1982. fortn. £75. National Children's Bureau, 8 Wakley St., London EC1V 7QE, England. TEL 071-278-9441. FAX 071-278-9512. Ed. Lisa Payne. circ. 200. **Document type:** bulletin.

CHILDREN AND YOUTH — ABOUT

649   UK   ISSN 0951-0605
HQ767.8
CHILDREN & SOCIETY. 1987. 5/yr. $185 (foreign $185) (effective 1998). (National Children's Bureau of the U.K.) John Wiley & Sons Ltd., Journals, Baffins Ln., Chichester, W. Sussex PO19 1UD, England. TEL 44-1243-779777. FAX 44-1243-775878. E-mail: info-assets@wiley.co.uk; URL: http://www.wiley.co.uk. (Subscr. in the Americas to: John Wiley & Sons, Inc., 605 Third Ave., New York, NY 10158. TEL 212-850-6645. FAX 212-850-6021) Eds. Gillian Pugh, Nigel Parton. adv.: B&W page £595, color page £1495; trim 260 x 200; adv. contact: Bob Kern. bk.rev.; index. circ. 700. (back issues avail.) **Indexed:** Abstr.Crim.& Pen., ASSIA, Br.Educ.Ind., C.I.J.E., Cont.Pg.Educ., IBR, Mult.Ed.Abstr., Psychol.Abstr. (1987-), Soc.Work Res.& Abstr., Sociol.Abstr., Sociol.Educ.Abstr., Sp.Ed.Needs Abstr. **Document type:** academic/scholarly publication.
—BLDSC (3172.961300). **CCC.**
Description: Covers all aspects of child health, education, care and development.

340 028.5   US
KF479.A15
CHILDREN AND THE LAW. 1986. s-a. $8. American Bar Association, Young Lawyers Division, 750 N. Lake Shore Dr., Chicago, IL 60611. TEL 312-988-5555. FAX 312-988-6281. **Indexed:** Viol.& Abuse Abstr. **Document type:** newsletter.
Formerly: Child Advocacy and Protection Newsletter.
Description: Articles on children's rights, information on current services and resources.

649   UK   ISSN 0956-3113
CHILDREN AND WAR NEWSLETTER; a newsletter for adults. 1988. a. £5. Peace Pledge Union, 6 Endsleigh St., London WC1H 0DX, England. TEL 44-171-387-5501. Ed. Jan Melichar. illus. circ. 400. (back issues avail.) **Document type:** newsletter.
Description: Critiques the militarization of children who play with war toys.

362.7   UK   ISSN 0190-7409
HV701
CHILDREN AND YOUTH SERVICES REVIEW; an international multidisciplinary review of the welfare of young people. 1979. 10/yr. fl.1074($617) (effective 1998). Elsevier Science Ltd., Pergamon, P.O. Box 800, Kidlington, Oxford OX5 1DX, England. TEL 44-1865-843000. FAX 44-1865-843010. E-mail: nlinfo-f@elsevier.nl; usinfo-f@elsevier.com; forinfo-kyf04035@niftyserve.or.jp; URL: http://www.elsevier.nl/. (Subscr. to: Elsevier Science, Regional Sales Office, P.O. Box 211, 1000 AE Amsterdam, Netherlands. TEL 31-20-4853757. FAX 31-20-4853432; Subscr. in the Americas to: Elsevier Science, Regional Sales Office, Box 945, New York, NY 10159-0945. TEL 212-633-3730. FAX 212-633-3680; Subscr. in Australasia and the Far East to: Elsevier Science (Singapore) Pte Ltd, No.1 Temasek Ave., No.17-01 Millenia Tower, Singapore 039192, Singapore. TEL 65-434-3727. FAX 65-337-2230) Ed. Dr. Duncan Lindsey. circ. 1,200. (also avail. in microfilm from UMI) **Indexed:** Abstr.Crim.& Pen., Adol.Ment.Hlth.Abstr., ASCA, ASSIA, C.I.J.E., Chic.Per.Ind., Child Devel.Abstr., Crim.Just.Abstr., Curr.Cont., Except.Child.Educ.Abstr., Excerp.Med., Fam.Ind., Lang.& Lang.Behav.Abstr., PSI, Psychol.Abstr. (1979-), Risk Abstr., Sage Fam.Stud.Abstr., Sage Pub.Admin.Abstr., Soc.Work Res.& Abstr., Sociol.Abstr., Sp.Ed.Needs Abstr., SSCI. **Document type:** academic/scholarly publication.
—BLDSC (3172.962000); Genuine Article; SWETS; UMI; UnCover. **CCC.**
Description: Provides a forum for the critical analysis and assessment of social service programs designed to serve young people throughout the world, including in-depth coverage of child welfare, foster care, adoptions, child abuse and neglect, income support, mental health services, and social policy.
Refereed Serial

CHILDREN BEFORE THE COURT; reflections on legal issues affecting minors. see *LAW — Judicial Systems*

CHILDREN FIRST! see *SOCIAL SERVICES AND WELFARE*

364.36   US   ISSN 0147-9881
HV9103
CHILDREN IN CUSTODY; a report on public juvenile detention and correctional facility census. 1971. biennial. free. U.S. Department of Justice, Office of Juvenile Justice and Delinquency Prevention, 633 Indiana Ave. N.W., Washington, DC 20531. TEL 202-307-5929. FAX 202-514-6384. (Subscr. to: Box 6000, Rockville, MD 20850) circ. 10,000.
Supersedes: U.S. Department of Health, Education and Welfare. Statistics on Public Institutions for Delinquent Children (ISSN 0082-9935)

CHILDREN IN FINLAND. see *SOCIAL SERVICES AND WELFARE*

CHILDREN IN FOCUS. see *SOCIAL SERVICES AND WELFARE*

649   FR   ISSN 0379-2269
RJ103.T76
CHILDREN IN THE TROPICS. French edition: Enfant en Milieu Tropical (ISSN 0013-7561) (Editions in English, French, Spanish) 1969. 5/yr. (includes one double issue). 280 F.($35) (effective 1997). Centre International de l'Enfance - International Children's Center, Chateau de Longchamp, Bois de Boulogne, 75016 Paris, France. TEL 33-1-44302062. FAX 33-1-44302065. adv.; bk.rev.; charts; illus.; stat. circ. 10,000. (back issues avail.) **Indexed:** Abstr.Hyg., Biol.Abstr., Trop.Dis.Bull.
Description: Offers information to update skills in the fields of health, education, diet and development as well as planning, programme administration and methods for research and action.

CHILDREN - MUSICIANS. see *MUSIC*

362.7   US   ISSN 0361-4336
HV741   CODEN: CHTDA
CHILDREN TODAY; an interdisciplinary journal for the professions serving children. 1954. q. $8 (foreign $10). U.S. Department of Health and Human Services, Administration for Children and Families, Office of Public Affairs, 370 L'Enfant Promenade, S.W., 7th Fl., Washington, DC 20447. TEL 202-401-9215. (Subscr. to: Superintendent of Documents, U.S. Government Printing Office, Box 371954, Pittsburgh, PA 15250-7954. TEL 202-512-1800. FAX 202-512-2250) bk.rev.; bibl.; illus.; index. circ. 10,000. (also avail. in microform from MIM,UMI; back issues avail.) **Indexed:** Acad.Ind., Adol.Ment.Hlth.Abstr., ASSIA, Bk.Rev.Ind. (1972-), C.I.J.E., C.I.N.L., Child.Bk.Rev.Ind. (1972-), Consum.Ind., Curr.Lit.Fam.Plan., Educ.Ind., Except.Child Educ.Abstr., Excerp.Med., Fam.Ind., G.Soc.Sci&Rel.Per.Lit., Hlth.Ind., Hosp.Lit.Ind., Ind.Med., Ind.U.S.Gov.Per., Int.Nurs.Ind., Mag.Ind., MEDOC, Mid.East: Abstr.& Ind., PMR, R.G.Abstr., R.G., Rehabil.Lit., Sage Fam.Stud.Abstr., Sage Fam.Stud.Abstr., Soc.Work Res.& Abstr. **Document type:** government publication.
● Also available online. Vendor(s): Information Access Co., Knight-Ridder Information, Inc., UMI.
—BLDSC (3172.975000); KNAW; KR SourceOne; SWETS; UMI; UnCover.
Formerly: Children (ISSN 0009-4064)

362   UK
CHILDREN U K. q. membership. National Children's Bureau, 8 Wakley St., London EC1V 7QE, England. TEL 071-278-9441. FAX 071-278-9512. Ed. Alison Love. **Indexed:** Br.Educ.Ind. **Document type:** bulletin.
Formerly (until 1994): Concern (ISSN 0591-017X)
Description: For professionals in the children's sector. Covers children's rights, education, health and welfare. Reviews relevant publications.

362.7   US   ISSN 0739-425X
CHILDREN'S ADVOCATE. (Text mainly in English; occasionally in Spanish) 1973. bi-m. $18 (effective 1997). Action Alliance for Children, 1201 Martin Luther King, Jr. Way, Oakland, CA 94612. TEL 510-444-7136. E-mail: hn5887@handsnet.org. Ed. Jean Tepperman. adv.: page $490; adv. contact: Joy Shioshita. bk.rev. circ. 10,000. **Document type:** newspaper.
Description: Covers California, national, and international policy issues affecting children and families. Written for children's service providers, parents, policy makers, and educators.

CHILDREN'S AID SOCIETY. ANNUAL REPORT. see *SOCIAL SERVICES AND WELFARE*

CHILDREN'S AID SOCIETY NEWS. see *SOCIAL SERVICES AND WELFARE*

CHILDREN'S BOOKWATCH. see *CHILDREN AND YOUTH — Abstracting, Bibliographies, Statistics*

CHILDREN'S BUSINESS. see *CLOTHING TRADE — Fashions*

CHILDREN'S CLOTHING INTERNATIONAL. see *CLOTHING TRADE*

CHILDREN'S COURT OF NEW SOUTH WALES INFORMATION BULLETIN. see *LAW — Criminal Law*

CHILDREN'S ENTERTAINMENT BUSINESS. see *COMMUNICATIONS — Television And Cable*

CHILDREN'S ENVIRONMENTS; theory, research, policy and applications. see *PSYCHOLOGY*

028.5 398   US   ISSN 0739-5558
GR43.C4
CHILDREN'S FOLKLORE REVIEW. 1979. s-a. $10. East Carolina University, Department of English, Greenville, NC 27858-4353. TEL 919-757-6660. FAX 919-757-4889. Ed. C.W. Sullivan, III. bk.rev.; cum.index: 1978-1988. circ. 150. (back issues avail.) **Indexed:** Child.Lit.Abstr., MLA Intl.Bibl. **Document type:** academic/scholarly publication.

372   US
CHILDREN'S HOUSE - CHILDREN'S WORLD; a magazine for parents, teachers and professionals about today's children. 1966. bi-m. $10.50 (effective Jan. 1991). (Montessori-Piaget for Health) Children's House, Inc., Box 111, Caldwell, NJ 07006. TEL 973-239-3442. FAX 973-483-1234. Ed. Kenneth Edelson; Pub. Avi Ben Edelson. R&P contact: Kenneth Edelson. adv. contact: Bob Hanson. bk.rev.; abstr.; charts; illus.; stat. circ. 50,000. (also avail. in diskette format) **Indexed:** Educ.Ind, Except.Child Educ.Abstr., Rehabil.Lit. **Document type:** consumer publication, trade publication.
—UnCover.
Formerly (until 1978): Children's House Magazine (ISSN 0009-4137)
Description: Discusses education and development of children from ages 3-16.

CHILDREN'S LAW NEWS. see *LAW — Family And Matrimonial Law*

CHILDREN'S LEGAL RIGHTS JOURNAL. see *LAW — Family And Matrimonial Law*

CHILDREN'S LITERATURE ASSOCIATION QUARTERLY. see *LIBRARY AND INFORMATION SCIENCES*

028.5 370   US   ISSN 0045-6713
Z1037.A1   CODEN: CLEDEW
CHILDREN'S LITERATURE IN EDUCATION; an international quarterly. 1970. q. $185 (foreign $215) (effective 1998). Human Sciences Press, Inc. (Subsidiary of: Plenum Publishing Corp.), 233 Spring St., New York, NY 10013. TEL 212-620-8000. FAX 212-463-0742. TELEX 23-421139. Eds. Margaret Mackey, Geoff Fox. adv.; bk.rev.; index. (also avail. in microform from UMI; reprint service avail. from UMI) **Indexed:** Abstr.Engl.Stud., Arts & Hum.Cit.Ind., ASCA, Bibl.Engl.Lang.& Lit., Bk.Rev.Ind. (1986-), Br.Educ.Ind., C.I.J.E., Child.Bk.Rev.Ind. (1986-), Child.Lit.Abstr., Cont.Pg.Educ., Curr.Cont., Educ.Ind., MLA Intl.Bibl. **Document type:** academic/scholarly publication.
—BLDSC (3172.991000); Genuine Article; KR SourceOne; SWETS; UMI; UnCover. **CCC.**
Description: Intended for librarians, teachers, teachers-in-training, writers and interested parents. Seeks to promote lively discussion of writing for young people.
Refereed Serial

CHILDREN'S MENTAL HEALTH SERVICES. see *PSYCHOLOGY*

CHILDREN AND YOUTH — ABOUT

369.4 200 US ISSN 1054-1144
CHILDREN'S MINISTRY. 1991. 6/yr. $24.95 (effective 1997 & 1998). Group Publishing, Inc., 1515 Cascade Ave., Loveland, CO 80538-3274. TEL 970-669-3836. FAX 970-669-1994. (Subscr. to: Box 469081, Escondido, CA 92046-9081) Ed. Christine Yount; Pub. Tim Gilmour. R&P contact: Laurie Copley. adv. contact: Kami Simianer. circ. 60,000. Document type: trade publication.
Description: Provides practical help for Christian adults who work with children from birth to sixth grade.

CHILDREN'S MONITOR. see LAW — Family And Matrimonial Law

362.7 US
CHILDREN'S NEWS.* 1973. bi-m. $10. Children's Council of San Francisco, 1 Second St., 4th fl., San Francisco, CA 94105-3407. TEL 415-864-1881. Ed. Linda Revel. adv.; bk.rev. circ. 20,000. (tabloid format; back issues avail.)

CHILDREN'S SOFTWARE REVUE. see COMPUTERS — Software

362.7 SA
CHILDREN'S VOICE; a forum for our children. (Text in Afrikaans, English) 1994. s-a. S A B C Group Communications Division, Private Bag X1, Aucklandpark 2006, South Africa. illus.

362.7 UK ISSN 0265-1459
KD735.A13
CHILDRIGHT. 1983. 10/yr. £27 to individuals; institutions £38; students and youth £18. Children's Legal Centre Ltd., University of Essex, Wivenhoe Park, Colchester, Essex CO4 3SQ. TEL 44-1206-872477. FAX 44-1206-873428. Eds. Carolyn Hamilton, Bob Watt. bk.rev.; circ. 2,500 (paid). Indexed: Euro.LJI, HR Rep., LJI. Document type: bulletin.
—BLDSC (3172.992700).
Description: Explains enacted and proposed legislation affecting children and provides news coverage of policy developments.
Refereed Serial

155.4 US
CHILD'S PLAY. 1984. q. $50 membership. U S A Toy Library Association, 2530 Cawford Ave., Ste. 111, Evanston, IL 60201. TEL 708-864-3330. FAX 708-864-3331. Ed. Judith Iacuzzi; Pub. Judith Q. Iacuzzi. adv.; bk.rev. circ. 700. (back issues avail.) Document type: newsletter.
Description: Covers toy libraries, toys, play and programs advantageous to the healthy development of children. Also provides a network among professionals who work with children in play settings.

267 258 US ISSN 1064-2781
CHILDWORLD. 1976. q. free. Christian Children's Fund, Inc., Development Office, Box 85066, Richmond, VA 23286-8912. TEL 800-776-6767. FAX 804-756-2718. Ed. Cheri Dahl. illus.; abstr. circ. 300,000. Document type: newsletter.
Formerly (until Aug. 1978): C C F World News.

028.5 US ISSN 1089-8018
CHOICES FOR YOUNG READERS. 1997. biennial. $89.50. John Gordon Burke Publisher, Inc., Box 1492, Evanston, IL 60204-1492. TEL 847-866-8625. FAX 847-866-6639.
●Also available on CD-ROM.
Description: Provides reading recommendations for second-sixth graders and is designed for use by teachers, librarians, and reading specialists.

649 377.8 US ISSN 0009-5389
CHRISTIAN HOME & SCHOOL. 6/yr. $11.95. Christian Schools International, 3350 E. Paris Ave., S.E., Grand Rapids, MI 49512. TEL 616-957-1070. Ed. Gordon L. Bordewyk. adv. contact: Lori Feenstra. bk.rev. circ. 61,000.
Description: Aimed at contemporary Christian families. Focuses on family life and educational and parenting issues.

649 266 US ISSN 1065-7215
CHRISTIAN PARENTING TODAY. 1988. 6/yr. $16.97 (foreign $22.37) (effective Jan. 1992). Good Family Magazines, 4050 Lee Vance View, Colorado Springs, CO 80918-7102. TEL 719-531-7776. FAX 719-535-0172. Ed. Erin Healy; Pub. Jay Griffin. R&P contact: Sherry Dixon-Leonard. adv.: B&W page $4256, color page $5100; trim 7 7/8 x 10 1/2; adv. contact: Debbie Mitchell. bk.rev. circ. 150,000. Indexed: Chr.Per.Ind. Document type: consumer publication.
Formerly: Christian Parenting (ISSN 1040-8088)
Description: Encourages and informs parents of children 0-12 who want to build strong families from a positive Christian perspective.

CHUAN DAO TIAN DI. see RELIGIONS AND THEOLOGY — Protestant

200 369.4 UK ISSN 0045-2831
CHURCH LADS' AND CHURCH GIRLS' BRIGADE. ANNUAL REPORT. 1891. a. free. Church Lads' and Church Girls' Brigade, 2 Barnsley Rd., Wath upon Dearne, Rotherham, S. Yorks. S63 6PY, England. TEL 44-1709-876535. FAX 44-1709-878089. Ed. J.S. Cresswell. R&P contact: J.S. Cresswell. bk.rev. circ. 1,200. Document type: corporate report.
Formerly: Brigade.

CLARKE HALL & MORRISON ON CHILDREN. see LAW

649 US
CLEVELAND - AKRON FAMILY. 1989. m. $35. Hearth Publications, Inc., 13110 Shaker Square, Cleveland, OH 44120-2313. TEL 216-752-3700. FAX 216-752-3860. Ed. Ann V. Billingsley; Pub. Ann V. Billingsley. R&P contact: Ann V. Billingsley. adv.: page $1220; adv. contact: Gina F. Sidari. bk.rev. circ. 45,000. (tabloid format; back issues avail.) Document type: newspaper.
Formerly: Family Times of Cleveland (ISSN 1043-836X)
Description: For parents in the Cleveland-Akron area. Features topics of concern to parents including health, family finances, movies, safety, and a calendar of events.

CLIK; jeune et franco-ontarien. see CHILDREN AND YOUTH — For

616.8 362 UK ISSN 1359-1045
RJ499.A1 CODEN: CCPPFR
▼**CLINICAL CHILD PSYCHOLOGY & PSYCHIATRY.** 1996. q. £47($75) to individuals; institutions £160 ($256) (effective 1998). Sage Publications Ltd., 6 Bonhill St., London EC2A 4PU, England. TEL 44-171-374-0645. FAX 44-171-374-8741. E-mail: market@sagepub.co.uk; URL: http://www.sagepub.co.uk/. Ed. Bryan Lask. adv. contact: Bernie Folan. bk.rev. Indexed: ASSIA, Excerp.Med.
—BLDSC (3286.268400).
Description: Publishes papers that focus on clinical and therapeutic aspects of child and adolescent psychology and psychiatry.

CLUB CONNECTION. see RELIGIONS AND THEOLOGY — Other Denominations And Sects

649 US
COLORADO PARENT MAGAZINE. m. free. American Parent Communications, 2430 S. University Blvd., Ste. 205, Denver, CO 80210. TEL 303-320-1000. Ed. Kerry Arquette; Pub. Jill Hess. adv.: page $1925; trim 10 x 13. bk.rev.; film rev.; music rev.; software rev.; video rev. circ. 100,000. Document type: consumer publication.
Description: Contains parenting articles and a calendar of events and activities to inform families and children.

THE COMPLEAT MOTHER; the magazine of pregnancy, birth and breastfeeding. see MEDICAL SCIENCES — Obstetrics And Gynecology

COMUNITA SPORTIVA; settimanale di informazione e orientamento delle attivita CSI. see CHILDREN AND YOUTH — For

649 US ISSN 1053-0126
CONNECTICUT FAMILY; the magazine just for the Fairfield County parent. 1990. 11/yr. $22. Family Publishing Group, Inc., 141 Halstead Ave., Ste. 3D, Mamaroneck, NY 10543-2652. TEL 914-381-7474. Ed. Susan Ross; Pubs. Susan Ross, Felice Shapiro. adv.; bk.rev.; circ. 35,000 (controlled). Document type: consumer publication.

649 US
CONNECTICUT PARENT. 1984. m. $24. Choice Media, Inc., 315 Peck St., Box 580, New Haven, CT 06513-0580. TEL 203-782-1420. FAX 203-782-3793. E-mail: ctfamily@family.com; URL: http://family.com. Ed. Joel MacClaren; Pub. Joel MacClaren. R&P contact: Karen Donnelly. adv. contact: Karen Brown. bk.rev. circ. 45,000. (tabloid format; back issues avail.) Document type: newspaper.
Description: Focuses on independent education, healthcare, birthing, family travel, camps and summer programs and more relating to parents who are planning to have children, or who have children - newborn through twelve.

155.4 US ISSN 0147-1082
CONTEMPORARY PROBLEMS OF CHILDHOOD; a bibliographic series. 1977. irreg. price varies. Greenwood Press, Inc. (Subsidiary of: Greenwood Publishing Group Inc.), 88 Post Rd. W., Box 5007, Westport, CT 06881-5007. TEL 203-226-3571. FAX 203-222-1502. Ed. Carol Ann Winchell.

CONTRIBUTIONS TO RESIDENTIAL TREATMENT. see PSYCHOLOGY

155 US ISSN 0273-124X
CONTRIBUTIONS TO THE STUDY OF CHILDHOOD AND YOUTH. 1982. irreg. price varies. Greenwood Press, Inc. (Subsidiary of: Greenwood Publishing Group Inc.), 88 Post Rd. W., Box 5007, Westport, CT 06881-5007. TEL 203-226-3571. FAX 203-222-1502.

362.7 US
COUNCIL FOR EARLY CHILDHOOD PROFESSIONAL RECOGNITION. COUNCIL NEWS & VIEWS. 1983. 3/yr. free. Council for Early Childhood Professional Recognition, 1341 G. St., N.W., Ste. 400, Washington, DC 20005. TEL 202-265-9090. FAX 202-265-9161. Ed. Patricia Brown. circ. 10,000. Document type: newsletter.
Formerly (until Aug. 1996): Competence.
Description: Informs the CDA community about the activities occurring nationwide regarding the Child Development Associate credential.

COUNSELING AND HUMAN DEVELOPMENT. see EDUCATION

CREATIONS. see ART

790.019 370.15 US ISSN 0098-7565
CREATIVE CHILD AND ADULT QUARTERLY. 1976. q. $55 (foreign $65). National Association for Creative Children and Adults, 8080 Springvalley Dr., Cincinnati, OH 45236-1395. TEL 513-631-1777. Ed. Ann F. Isaacs. adv.; bk.rev.; abstr.; bibl.; charts; illus.; tr.lit. circ. 6,000. (also avail. in microform from UMI; reprint service avail. from UMI) Indexed: C.I.J.E., Child Devel.Abstr., Curr.Cont., Educ.Ind., Except.Child.Educ.Abstr., Psychol.Abstr.
—UMI; UnCover.
Description: Includes research studies, reviews, reports on programs and in-depth career guidance interviews with functioning creative individuals.

649.4 US
THE CREATIVE CHILD - INTERACTIVE PARENTING NEWSLETTER. m. E-mail: tereson@net-connect.net; URL: http://www.the-creative-child.com/newsletter. Document type: newsletter.
●Available only online.
Description: Encourages parents to spend more quality time with their children through time saving techniques and creative play.

362.7 SP
CRECER FELIZ. 1988. m. 4200 ptas. Hachette Filipacchi Revistas, Cardenal Herrera Oria 3, 28034 Madrid, Spain. TEL 34-1-358-1122. FAX 34-1-358-2059. (Subscr. to: Santa Engracia 23, 28010 Madrid, Spain. TEL 34-1-447-2238). Ed. Margie Igoa. adv.; circ. 76,481 (paid). (back issues avail.) Document type: consumer publication.
●Also available online.
Description: For new parents, covers pregnancy, delivery, health, development and education of children 0-5.

1844 CHILDREN AND YOUTH — ABOUT

028.5 378 GW
CRISS CROSS. 1975. s-a. DM.1.50. Schuelerzeitung Criss Cross, Mozartstr. 15, 78604 Rietheim-Weilheim, Germany. TEL 07461-71307. FAX 07424-501273. Ed. Wencke Hauser. adv.: B&W page DM.180; adv. contact: Karin Merkt. bk.rev.; illus. circ. 600. (back issues avail.) **Document type:** bulletin.

CRUSADER (MEMPHIS). see RELIGIONS AND THEOLOGY — Protestant

D E C COMMUNICATOR. (Division for Early Childhood) see EDUCATION — Special Education And Rehabilitation

155.5 GW ISSN 0930-7842
D J I - BULLETIN. (Editions in English, French, German and Spanish) 1986. q. (English, French and Spanish editions: a.). free. Deutsches Jugendinstitut e.V. - German Youth Institute, Nockherstr. 2, 81541 Munich, Germany. TEL 49-89-623060. FAX 49-89-62306265. Ed. Richard Rathgeber. circ. 8,000. **Document type:** bulletin.

649.1 US
D P F NEWSLETTER. 1981. bi-m. $30. Diaper Pail Friends, 38 Miller Ave., Ste. 127, Mill Valley, CA 94941. Ed. Thomas E. Siegel. circ. 1,500. (back issues avail.) **Document type:** newsletter.
Description: For people interested in the adult baby games.

649 US
DALLAS CHILD. 1986. m. Lauren Publications, 4125 Keller Springs Rd., Ste. 146, Dallas, TX 75244-2035. TEL 214-447-9188. FAX 214-447-0633. E-mail: dchild@pic.net. Ed. Elizabeth Robbins; Pub. Joylyn Niebes. adv. contact: Claudia Burus. circ. 75,000. **Document type:** consumer publication.

369.4 FR ISSN 0751-5812
DEMAIN. 1920. m. (7/yr.). 90 F. Editions Scouts de France, 54 av. Jean Jaures, 75019 Paris, France. TEL 44-52-37-37. FAX 42-38-09-87. Ed. Philippe Da Costa. bk.rev.; film rev.; abstr.; charts; illus.; stat. circ. 40,000.
Formerly: Chef.

028.5 RU ISSN 0130-3104
PN1009.R8
DETSKAYA LITERATURA. (Text in Russian; summaries in English, French and German) 1966. bi-m. $39 (effective 1998). Izdatel'stvo Khudozhestvennaya Literatura, Novo-Basmannaya ul., 19, Moscow B-66, Russia. Ed. S.P. Alekseev. bk.rev.; bibl. Indexed: Child Lit.Abstr.
Description: Contains children's fiction.

649 GW ISSN 0012-0332
DEUTSCHE JUGEND; Zeitschrift fuer die Jugendarbeit. 1953. m. (11/yr.). DM.95 (foreign DM.105) (effective 1998). Juventa Verlag GmbH, Ehretstr. 3, 69469 Weinheim, Germany. TEL 49-6201-61035. FAX 49-6201-13135. E-mail: juventa@t-online.de; URL: http://www.juventa-t-online.de. Ed. Gerd Brenner. adv.; bk.rev.; film rev.; index. circ. 4,000. **Document type:** consumer publication.
—SWETS. **CCC.**

DIMENSION (BIRMINGHAM). see RELIGIONS AND THEOLOGY — Protestant

371.3 US
HQ767.8
DIMENSIONS OF EARLY CHILDHOOD. 1972. q. $15 to non-members. Southern Early Childhood Association, Box 55930, Little Rock, AR 72215-5930. TEL 501-663-0353. FAX 501-663-2114. E-mail: secal@aristotle.net; URL: http://www.seca.org. Ed. Jan Brown McCracken; Pub. Clarissa Willis. R&P contact: Tanya Poole. adv. contact: Clarissa Willis. bk.rev.; index. circ. 20,000. (back issues avail.) Indexed: C.I.J.E., IMFL. **Document type:** academic/scholarly publication.
Formerly: Dimensions (Little Rock) (ISSN 0160-6425)
Description: Focuses on issues concerning people working in early childhood education and care including theory, practice, and public policy. Aims to provide useful articles for teachers.
Refereed Serial

DIRECTORY OF AMERICAN YOUTH ORGANIZATIONS (YEAR); a guide to 500 clubs, groups, troops, teams, societies, lodges, and more for young people. see CHILDREN AND YOUTH — For

362.7 028.5
DIRECTORY OF FAMILY CHILD CARE ASSOCIATIONS, SUPPORT AGENCIES, & SUPPORT GROUPS. 1984. a. $20. Children's Foundation, 725 15th St., N.W., Ste. 505, Washington, DC 20005. TEL 202-347-3300. Ed. Sandra Gellert. **Document type:** directory.
Former titles: Directory of Family Child Care Associations and Support Groups & Directory of Family Day Care Associations and Support Groups.

DISCOVERY (BIRMINGHAM). see RELIGIONS AND THEOLOGY — Protestant

DISCOVERY (NEW YORK). see CHILDREN AND YOUTH — For

DISCOVERY Y M C A. see SOCIAL SERVICES AND WELFARE

362.7 370 IT
DOCUMENTI DELLA SCUOLA. m. Documenti della Scuola, Viale Isonzo 60, 20135 Milan, Italy. TEL 02-5454313. Ed. Giovanni Girgenti.

155 US ISSN 0889-8804
DOUBLE TALK (AMELIA); newsletter for parents of multiples. 1981. q. $8 (Canada $10). Double Talk, Dept. 15, Box 412, Amelia, OH 45102. TEL 513-231-8946. FAX 513-231-1855. Ed. Karen Kerkhoff Gromada. adv.; bk.rev. circ. 2,000.

649 US
THE DOULA;* mothering the mother. 1986. q. $15; newsstand price: $3.95. Democratic Management Services, Box 5174, Dover, NH 03821-5174. TEL 408-464-9488. FAX 408-464-9488. E-mail: thedoula@aol.com. Ed. Michele Winkler; Pub. Michele Winkler. adv.: page $450; trim 8 1/2 x 11. bk.rev. circ. 3,000. (back issues avail.) **Document type:** consumer publication.
Description: Provides information and support to mothers and fathers who practice responsive parenting, with a special emphasis on supporting full-time mothers.

DYNAMITE WRITE CHILDREN'S NEWSPAPER. see CHILDREN AND YOUTH — For

E R I C - C U E TRENDS AND ISSUES. (Educational Resource Information Center, Clearinghouse on Urban Education) see EDUCATION

E R I C CLEARINGHOUSE ON URBAN EDUCATION. DIGEST. (Educational Resources Information Center) see EDUCATION

362.7 NE ISSN 0300-4430
HQ767.8 CODEN: ECDCAD
EARLY CHILD DEVELOPMENT AND CARE. 1971. 12/yr. (in 12 vols., 1 no./vol.). $113 (effective 1998). Gordon and Breach - Harwood Academic, Amsteldisk 166, 1st Fl., 1079 LH Amsterdam, Netherlands. (Subscr. to: International Publishers Distributor, Box 32160, Newark, NJ 07102. TEL 800-545-8398. FAX 215-750-6343) Ed. Roy Evans. adv.; bk.rev.; abstr.; charts; illus.; index. (also avail. in microform) Indexed: ASSIA, Biol.Abstr., Br.Educ.Ind., C.I.J.E., Child Devel.Abstr., Cont.Pg.Educ., Educ.Ind., Excerp.Med., Indian Psychol.Abstr., Mult.Ed.Abstr., Psychol.Abstr. (1973-). **Document type:** academic/scholarly publication.
—BLDSC (3642.950000); CISTI; KR SourceOne; SWETS; UnCover. **CCC.**
Refereed Serial

EARLY CHILDHOOD EDUCATION JOURNAL. see EDUCATION

362.7 649 US ISSN 1080-3564
EARLY CHILDHOOD NEWS. 1989. bi-m. $30 (effective 1995-96). Peter Li, Inc., 330 Progress Rd., Dayton, OH 45449-1597. TEL 573-847-5900. FAX 513-847-5910. Ed. Tim Bete. bk.rev. circ. 36,500. Indexed: C.I.J.E.
Description: For owners, directors, principals and administrators of child-care programs serving children from six weeks old to third grade. Provides news, articles and analysis of trends in child care, and product reviews.

EARLY INTERVENTION. see EDUCATION — Special Education And Rehabilitation

EARNSHAW'S INFANTS, GIRLS AND BOYS WEAR REVIEW. see CLOTHING TRADE

155.649 US ISSN 1065-2655
EASTSIDE PARENT. 1986. m. $15. Northwest Parent Publishing, Inc., 2107 Elliott Ave., Ste. 303, Seattle, WA 98121. TEL 206-441-0191. FAX 206-441-4919. adv. contact: Alayne Sulkin. bk.rev.; play rev. circ. 20,000. (tabloid format) **Document type:** consumer publication.
Description: Guide for parents, educators and child-care providers. Features include a calendar of events, plays, movies, and ideas for outings and restaurants.

370 IT ISSN 0012-9453
ECO DEGLI ORATORI E DEI CIRCOLI GIOVANILI. 1907. m. L.50000. Fondazione Oratori Milanesi, Via S. Antonio 5, 20122 Milan, Italy. TEL 02-58304383. FAX 02-58304003. Ed. Sergio Gianelli. bk.rev.; film rev.; bibl.; index; circ. 1,100 (controlled).

ECOLE DES PARENTS. see EDUCATION — Adult Education

362.7 CN ISSN 0840-4445
THE EDGE. 1989. 10/yr. Can.$11 (foreign $14). Salvation Army, 2 Overlea Blvd., Toronto ON M4H 1P4, Canada. TEL 416-424-6114. FAX 416-424-6120. Ed. Major Sharon Stinka. R&P contact: Major Sharon Stinka. circ. 5,000. **Document type:** consumer publication.
Description: Official youth publication of the Salvation Army in Canada. Includes contemporary social and moral issues, Christian lifestyle and contemporary Christian music.

362.7 372 GW
EINHARD INTERN; Schulzeitschrift des staedtischen Einhard-Gymnasiums Aachen. 1978. s-a. DM.9. Staedtisches Einhard-Gymnasium, Robert-Schuman-Str. 4, 52066 Aachen, Germany. TEL 0241-67017. adv.; bk.rev.; circ. 1,000. (back issues avail.) **Document type:** academic/scholarly publication.

649 370 GW ISSN 0046-1849
ELTERN. 1966. m. DM.56.40 (effective 1997); newsstand price: DM.4.70. Gruner und Jahr AG & Co. (Munich), Neherstr. 9, 81675 Munich, Germany. TEL 49-89-4152-0. FAX 49-89-4152651. (Subscr. to: P M S GmbH, Postfach 290180, 47261 Duisburg, Germany. TEL 49-203-76908-0. FAX 49-203-7690830) Ed. Norbert Hinze. circ. 663,000. **Document type:** consumer publication.

649 GW
ELTERN SONDERHEFT MEIN BABY. a. DM.9.50. Gruner und Jahr AG & Co. (Munich), Neherstr. 9, 81675 Munich, Germany. TEL 49-89-4152-0. FAX 49-89-4152665. circ. 170,000. (back issues avail.) **Document type:** consumer publication.

155.4 GW
ELTERN UNSER KIND. 1980. q. free. Gruner und Jahr AG & Co. (Munich), Neherstr. 9, 81675 Munich, Germany. TEL 49-89-4152-0. FAX 49-89-4152665. circ. 303,000. **Document type:** consumer publication.
Formerly: Eltern das Gesunde Kind.

ELTERNFORUM; Zeitschrift fuer Eltern und alle, die an Erziehung und Schule interressiert sind. see EDUCATION

362.7 CN ISSN 0825-7531
EMPATHIC PARENTING. (Text in English; editorial in English, French) 1978. q. Can.$10 membership. Canadian Society for the Prevention of Cruelty to Children, 356 First St., Box 700, Midland, ON L4R 4P4, Canada. TEL 705-526-5647. FAX 705-526-0214. Ed. Dr. E.T. Barker. bk.rev. circ. 2,000. (also avail. in microform) Indexed: Can.B.P.I., Can.Per.Ind., CMI. **Document type:** newsletter.
Former titles: Canadian Society for the Prevention of Cruelty to Children. Journal (ISSN 0705-6591); Empathic Parenting.
Description: Reprint journal that focuses on the long-term emotional consequences of child abuse and neglect, and discusses nurturing alternatives to chauvinism and consumerism in parenting.

CHILDREN AND YOUTH — ABOUT

155.4 618.92   FR   ISSN 0013-7545
HQ768
ENFANCE; psychologie, pedagogie, neuro-psychiatrie, sociologie. 1948. q. 370 F. to individuals (foreign 430 F.); agencies 333 F. (foreign 387 F.) (effective 1998). Presses Universitaires de France, Departement des Revues, 14 av. du Bois-de-l'Epine, 91003 Evry Cedex, France. TEL 33-1-60778205. FAX 33-1-60792045. TELEX PUF 600 474 F. Ed. Helene Gratiot-Alphandery. adv.; bk.rev.; index. circ. 2,000. **Indexed:** IBR, Psychol.Abstr. (1948-).
—BLDSC (3747.869000); SWETS.
Description: Publishes the works of well-known developmental psychologists.

649   FR   ISSN 0013-7561
ENFANT EN MILIEU TROPICAL. English edition: Children in the Tropics (ISSN 0379-2269) (Editions in English, French, Spanish) 1961. 5/yr. (includes one double issue). 280 F.($35) (effective 1997). Centre International de l'Enfance - International Children's Center, Chateau de Longchamp, Bois de Boulogne, 75016 Paris, France. TEL 33-1-44302062. FAX 33-1-44302065. adv.; bk.rev.; charts; illus.; stat. circ. 5,000. (back issues avail.) **Indexed:** Diar.Dis.Res.

649 362.7   FR   ISSN 0397-4820
ENFANT MAGAZINE. 1967. m. 180 F. (outside EU 240 F.). Bayard Presse, 3 rue Bayard, 75393 Paris Cedex 08, France. TEL 33-1-44356060. FAX 33-1-44356091. TELEX 648 094 F. (Subscr. to: Bayard Presse International, B.P. 12, 99505 Paris Entreprises, France. TEL 33-1-44216000. FAX 33-3-20274192) Ed. Elisabeth Lefebvre; Pub. Catherine Gourlat. adv.; illus. circ. 202,299.
Description: Offers important information to help young parents with the early stages of their child's life.

ENFANTS. see WOMEN'S INTERESTS

ENFANTS DU MONDE. see SOCIAL SERVICES AND WELFARE

362.7 300   GW   ISSN 1432-0258
ERZIEHUNG, SCHULE, GESELLSCHAFT. 1994. irreg., vol.12, 1996. Ergon Verlag, Grombuehlstr. 7, 97080 Wuerzburg, Germany. TEL 49-931-280084. FAX 49-931-282872. E-mail: ergon-verlag@t-online.de. Ed.Bd. **Document type:** academic/scholarly publication.

ESPERANTO - U S A; news of the language problem and Esperanto as a solution. see LINGUISTICS

ETABLISSEMENTS MEDICAUX POUR ENFANTS. see HOSPITALS

362.7   GW
▼**EUROPEAN YEARBOOK ON YOUTH POLICY AND RESEARCH**. (Text in English) 1996. biennial. DM.112. (Circle for Youth Research Cooperation in Europe) Walter de Gruyter und Co., Genthiner Str. 13, 10785 Berlin, Germany. TEL 49-30-26005-0. FAX 49-30-26005251. E-mail: wdg-info@degruyter.de; URL: http://www.degruyter.de. **Document type:** academic/scholarly publication.
Description: Provides a forum for transnational networking in European youth policy, research and practice.

EVANGELISCHE JUGEND IN BAYERN. NACHRICHTEN. see RELIGIONS AND THEOLOGY — Protestant

EVANGELIZING TODAY'S CHILD. see RELIGIONS AND THEOLOGY — Protestant

155.4   US   ISSN 0014-4029
                CODEN: EXCCAJ
EXCEPTIONAL CHILDREN. 1934. q. $58 (foreign $66). Council for Exceptional Children, 1920 Association Dr., Reston, VA 22091. TEL 703-620-3660. FAX 703-264-9494. Eds. Bob Algozzine, Martha Thurlow. R&P contact: Virginia Miller. adv. contact: Victo Erickson. bibl.; index. circ. 58,000. (also avail. in microfilm from UMI; reprint service avail. from UMI) **Indexed:** Acad.Ind., Adol.Ment.Hlth.Abstr., ASCA, ASSIA, Bibl.Dev.Med.& Child Neur., C.I.J.E., Cont.Pg.Educ., Curr.Cont., Educ.Admin.Abstr., Educ.Ind., Educ.Tech.Abstr., Except.Child.Educ.Abstr., Excerp.Med., Fam.Ind., IBR, IMFL, Ind.Med., Lang.& Lang.Behav.Abstr., Mult.Ed.Abstr., Psychol.Abstr. (1935-), Psycscan D.P., Rehabil.Lit., Soc.Work Res.& Abstr., Sociol.Educ.Abstr., SOMA, Sp.Ed.Needs Abstr., SSCI, Tech.Educ.Abstr. **Document type:** academic/scholarly publication.
●Also available online. Vendor(s): Information Access Co., UMI.
—BLDSC (3835.300000); Genuine Article; KR SourceOne; SWETS; UMI; UnCover.
Description: Contains current articles on critical and controversial issues in special education, as well as credible articles on research and developments in the field.
Refereed Serial

371.9 362.4   US   ISSN 0046-9157
EXCEPTIONAL PARENT.★ 1971. m. $24. Psy-Ed. Corp., 555 Kinderkamack Rd., Oradell, NJ 07649-1517. TEL 201-489-0871. FAX 201-489-1240. E-mail: epmag12@aol.com; URL: http://families.com. (Subscr. to: Dept. EP, Box 3000, Denville, NJ 07834. TEL 800-561-1973) Ed. Stanley D. Klein; Pub. Joseph M. Valenzano. R&P contact: Bridget M. Lyne. adv.; bk.rev.; circ. 65,000 (paid); 33,000 (controlled). (also avail. in microfilm from UMI; reprint service avail. from UMI) **Indexed:** C.I.J.E., Educ.Ind., Except.Child Educ.Abstr., Fam.Ind., Hlth.Ind., IMFL, Ind.Med., Ment.Retard.Abstr., Psychol.Abstr., Rehabil.Lit., Sp.Ed.Needs Abstr., Yrbk.Assoc.Educ.& Rehab.Blind. **Document type:** consumer publication.
●Also available online. Vendor(s): Information Access Co., UMI.
—BLDSC (3835.500000); KR SourceOne; UMI; UnCover. CCC.
Description: Soruce of help and guidance for the parents of children and young adults with disabilities and special health needs and the professionals who serve them.

649   CN   ISSN 0827-6366
EXPECTING. s-a. Family Communications, Inc., 37 Hanna Ave., Toronto, ON M6K 1X1, Canada. TEL 416-537-2604. FAX 416-538-1794. circ. 145,000.

EXTRATOUR. see TRAVEL AND TOURISM

362.7 362.41   UK   ISSN 0967-8719
EYE CONTACT. 1991. 3/yr. £9 (effective 1997 & 1998). Royal National Institute for the Blind, Education, Training and Employment Division, 224 Great Portland St., London W1N 6AA, England. TEL 44-171-388-1266. FAX 44-171-383-4921. E-mail: kporter@rnib.org.uk. Ed. Karen Porter. adv. contact: Karen Porter. bk.rev.; circ. 1,000 (paid). **Document type:** bulletin.
—BLDSC (3854.590000).
Description: Information about visually impaired children with additional needs.

362.732   DK   ISSN 0108-2418
F I C E INFORMATION. 1977. q. DKK 200 (effective 1997). Federation Internationale des Communautes d'Enfants - Denmark, Sekretariatet, Limosegyden 6, DK-5580 Nr. Aaby, Denmark. TEL 45-64-42-16-16. FAX 45-64-42-16-12. Ed. Fanni Vibeke Lasson. bk.rev. circ. 300. **Document type:** bulletin.

FAIR LADY JUNIOR. see WOMEN'S INTERESTS

649   AU
FAMILIENMAGAZIN.★ 1910. 10/yr. S.180. Jugend und Volk Verlagsgesellschaft, Universitaetstr. 11, A-1010 Vienna, Austria. Ed. Hubert Hladej. adv.; bk.rev.; illus. circ. 65,000. **Document type:** consumer publication.
Formerly: Elternblatt (ISSN 0013-6441)

362.7   GW   ISSN 0944-6982
FAMILY. 1992. q. 29 SFr. (effective 1997). Bundes Verlag GmbH, Bodenborn 43, 58452 Witten, Germany. TEL 49-2302-9309320. FAX 49-2302-9309310. E-mail: bv.witten@t-online.de; URL: http://www.jesus-online.de/bv/bv__home.htm. Ed. Ulrich Eggers. adv.: B&W page DM.3800, color page DM.5000; trim 188 x 258. circ. 100,000 (paid). (back issues avail.) **Document type:** bulletin.

051   US
FAMILY FUN. 1991. 10/yr. $12.95 (Canada and overseas $22.95) (effective 1995). Disney Magazine Publishing, Inc., 114 Fifth Ave., New York, NY 10011. TEL 212-807-5400. (Subscr. to: Box 10159, Des Moines, IA 50347-0159) Ed. Jake Winebaum. adv. circ. 400,000. **Document type:** consumer publication.
Description: Family-oriented publication directed to parents with children ages 3-12.

362.7 028.5   US
FAMILY GUIDE FOR PARENTS AND KIDS. 1987. a. $4. Gail Eagle Associates Custom Publishing, 3 Rosemary Rd., E. Brunswick, NJ 08816. TEL 908-390-1273. FAX 908-390-2058. (Subscr. to: Box 265, E. Brunswick, NJ 08816) Ed. Sandra G. King. adv. contact: Judith Weinberg. circ. 50,000. (back issues avail.) **Document type:** consumer publication.
Description: Listings of schools, activities, events and health care information in central New Jersey.

051   US
FAMILY LIFE. 1993. 10/yr. $19.94 (effective through 1998). Hachette Filipacchi Magazines, Inc. (Subsidiary of: Hachette Filipacchi Press), 1633 Broadway, 41st Fl., New York, NY 10019. TEL 212-767-6000. FAX 212-767-5631. Ed. Peter Herbst; Pub. Joan Sheridan LaBarge. adv. contact: James Docherty. music rev.; illus. **Indexed:** Access(1994-). **Document type:** consumer publication.
Description: For families with children ages 3 to 12.

FAMILY SERVICE PERSPECTIVES; useful information for the workplace and home. see SOCIOLOGY

FAMILY SPIRIT; dedicated to the spiritual well-being of parent and child. see RELIGIONS AND THEOLOGY

FAMILY TIMES (EAU CLAIRE); the newspaper for Chippewa Valley parents. see HOME ECONOMICS

362.7   US
FAMILY TIMES (WILMINGTON). 1990. m. $18 (effective 1997). Family Times, Inc., 1900 Superfine Ln., No. 6, Wilmington, DE 19802. TEL 302-575-0935. FAX 302-575-0933. E-mail: family@family.com. Ed. Denise Yearian; Pub. James Tomey. adv.: B&W page $1495; trim 10 x 12 3/8; adv. contact: Joseph Nudge. bk.rev.; circ. 35,000 (controlled). **Document type:** newsletter.
Description: For parents and caregivers of children, newborn to 14 years.

FAMILY WAYS; education resources for pregnancy to parenthood. see MEDICAL SCIENCES — Obstetrics And Gynecology

649 306.874   US   ISSN 1091-5516
▼**FATHERING MAGAZINE**. 1995. m. Box 3284, Galveston, TX 77552. E-mail: sheldon@fathermag.com; URL: http://www.fathermag.com/. Ed. Alexander Sheldon.
●Available only online.
Description: Publishes news and articles related to fathering.

FEDERATION OF CATHOLIC PARENT-TEACHER ASSOCIATIONS OF ONTARIO. NEWSLETTER. see EDUCATION

FIRST CALL FOR CHILDREN. see SOCIAL SERVICES AND WELFARE

FIRST LANGUAGE. see LINGUISTICS

FIRST STEPS IN MISSIONS. see RELIGIONS AND THEOLOGY — Protestant

FIRST TEACHER; for people who care for young children. see EDUCATION

CHILDREN AND YOUTH — ABOUT

649   **US**
FIRST-TIME PARENTS. 1989. a. included in American Baby. (Playskool) K-III Communications Corp., 745 Fifth Ave., New York, NY 10151. TEL 212-745-0100. (Dist. by: Neodata Services, Box 2971, Boulder, CO 80329) Pub. Sharon Summer. circ. 500,000 (controlled). **Document type:** consumer publication.
    Description: Provides information pertinent to the first three months after delivery, through the first year.

348   **US**
FIRST YEAR OF LIFE; a guide to your baby's growth and development month by month. 1977. a. single copies free. K-III Communications Corp., 745 Fifth Ave., New York, NY 10151. TEL 212-745-0100. adv. circ. 3,200,000. **Document type:** consumer publication.
    Description: Details physical, emotional and social growth of the baby during monthly stages.

028.5 371.3   **US**   **ISSN 0892-6735**
FIVE OWLS; a publication for readers, personally and professionally involved in children's literature. 1986. bi-m. (except July-Aug.). $20 (Canada $26; elsewhere $36) (effective 1997). Hawline Univ. Crossroads Ctr. MS-C1924, 1536 Hewitt Ave., St. Paul, MN 55104. TEL 612-644-7377. FAX 612-641-2956. E-mail: fiveowls@seq.hamline.edu; URL: http://www.hamline.edu/depts/gradprog/5owls. Ed. Susan Stan. R&P contact: Susan Stan. adv. contact: Christine Anning. bk.rev.; bibl.; index; circ. 4,000 (paid). (back issues avail.) **Indexed:** Bk.Rev.Ind. (1988-), Child.Bk.Rev.Ind. (1988-), Child.Lit.Abstr. **Document type:** academic/scholarly publication.
    Description: Each issue contains articles about trends and issues in the field of children's literature, an interview with an author or illustrator, and 15-20 book reviews.

FOCUS (BURLINGTON). see RELIGIONS AND THEOLOGY — Protestant

FOCUS ON EXCEPTIONAL CHILDREN. see EDUCATION — Special Education And Rehabilitation

649   **US**
FOCUS ON THE FAMILY PLUGGED IN. 1990. m. $20 donation. Focus on the Family, Inc., 8605 Explorer Dr., Colorado Springs, CO 80920. TEL 719-531-3400. Ed. Bob Smithouser. R&P contact: Lianne Belote. circ. 24,000. **Document type:** newsletter.
    Formerly: Focus on the Family Parental Guidance.
    Description: Informs adults of popular culture, specifically as it relates to media messages being consumed by children and teens.

FOEDSEL & FOERAELDRASKAP. see MEDICAL SCIENCES — Obstetrics And Gynecology

THE FOREIGN-BORN PARENT NETWORK; an interactive and multicultural forum for patners in education and parents of bilingual smart kids. see LINGUISTICS

649   **NO**   **ISSN 0332-513X**
FORELDRE OG BARN. 1977. fortn. NOK 230. Hjemmet Mortensens Forlag AS, Soerkedalsveien 10 A, N-0369 Oslo, Norway. TEL 47-2-961-500. FAX 47-2-961-382. Ed. Edda Espeland. adv.: B&W page NOK 11900, color page NOK 19800. circ. 62,000.

FORUM JUGENDHILFE. see SOCIAL SERVICES AND WELFARE

362.7   **UK**   **ISSN 0262-8120**
FOSTER CARE. 1975. q. £8. National Foster Care Association, Leonard House, 5-7 Marshalsea Rd., London SE1 1EP, England. TEL 44-171-828-6266. FAX 44-171-357-6668. E-mail: 106144.167@compuserve.com; URL: http://ourworld.compuserve.com/homepages/fostering. Ed. Gillian Davies. R&P contact: Gillian Davies. adv. contact: Gillian Davies. bk.rev. circ. 23,000. (back issues avail.) **Indexed:** ASSIA. **Document type:** newsletter.
    —BLDSC (4024.385000).
    Description: News items and informational articles on the legislative, health care, parenting, and child care issues pertaining to fostering, with advertisements of children to be placed, and announcements of courses and conferences.

FRIA TIDER. see LEISURE AND RECREATION

649   **CC**   **ISSN 1000-727X**
FUMU BIDU/PARENTS MONTHLY. (Text in Chinese) m. $36.80. Beijing Chubanshe - Beijing Publishing House, 6 Beisanhuan Zhonglu, Beijing 100011, People's Republic of China. TEL 2016699. (Dist. in US by: China Books & Periodicals, Inc., 2929 24th St., San Francisco, CA 94110. TEL 415-282-2994) Ed. Tao Xincheng.

028.5   **GW**   **ISSN 0176-2753**
FUNDEVOGEL; kritisches Kinder-Medien-Magazin. 1984. q. DM.60 (effective 1996). Dipa-Verlag, Nassauer Str. 1-3, 60439 Frankfurt a.M., Germany. TEL 49-69-95732044. FAX 49-69-576128. circ. 1,200. (back issues avail.) **Indexed:** Child.Lit.Abstr. **Document type:** consumer publication.

362.7   **US**   **ISSN 1054-8289**
HV741   **CODEN: FCHIEW**
THE FUTURE OF CHILDREN. 1991. 3/yr. free. David and Lucile Packard Foundation, Center for the Future of Children, 300 Second St., Ste. 102, Los Altos, CA 94022. TEL 415-948-3696. FAX 415-948-6498. URL: http://www.futureofchildren.org. Ed. Richard E. Behrman. R&P contact: Dona M. LeyVa. circ. 50,000. **Indexed:** ASCA, C.I.J.E., Curr.Cont., Fam.Ind., IMFL, Ind.Med. (1994-). **Document type:** academic/scholarly publication.
    ●Also available online.
    —BLDSC (4060.523000); Genuine Article; KR SourceOne; UnCover.
    Description: Covers child health, education, and welfare public policy issues.

GAY YOUTH COMMUNITY NEWS. see HOMOSEXUALITY

371.95 649.155   **US**   **ISSN 0016-9862**
LC3991   **CODEN: GICQAC**
GIFTED CHILD QUARTERLY. 1957. q. $50 membership (foreign $60). National Association for Gifted Children, 1707 L St., N.W., Ste. 550, Washington, DC 20036-4201. TEL 202-785-4268. Ed. Ann Robinson. R&P contact: Peter D. Rosenstein. adv.: B&W page $700; trim 8 1/2 x 11; adv. contact: Peter D. Rosenstein. bk.rev.; circ. 6,500 (paid). (also avail. in microfilm from UMI; back issues avail.) **Indexed:** Acad.Ind., Arts & Hum.Cit.Ind., ASCA, ASSIA, C.I.J.E., Child Devel.Abstr., Cont.Pg.Educ., Curr.Cont., Educ.Ind., Except.Child.Educ.Abstr., Fam.Ind., IMFL, Psychol.Abstr. (1958-), SSCI, SSCI. **Document type:** academic/scholarly publication.
    —BLDSC (4175.300000); KR SourceOne; SWETS; UMI; UnCover.
    Description: For educational researchers, administrators, teachers and parents of gifted children. Publishes research and theoretical papers on the nature and needs of high-ability children.
    Refereed Serial

790.019 371.95   **US**   **ISSN 1076-2175**
LC3991
GIFTED CHILD TODAY MAGAZINE. 1978. bi-m. $29.95 (foreign $36). Prufrock Press, Box 8813, Waco, TX 76714-8813. TEL 800-998-2208. FAX 800-240-0333. Ed. Stephanie Stout; Pub. Joel McIntosh. adv.: page $850. bk.rev.; bibl.; illus. circ. 20,000. (back issues avail.; reprint service avail. from UMI) **Indexed:** C.I.J.E., Educ.Ind., ERIC, Except.Child.Educ.Abstr. **Document type:** consumer publication.
    —BLDSC (4175.306000); KR SourceOne; UMI; UnCover.
    Former titles (until 1993): Gifted Child Today (ISSN 0892-9580); G C T (Gifted, Creative, Talented Children) (ISSN 0164-9728)
    Description: Designed to meet the needs of parents and teachers of gifted, creative and talented youngsters.

GIFTED EDUCATION PRESS QUARTERLY. see EDUCATION — Special Education And Rehabilitation

GIFTED UNLIMITED. see EDUCATION — Special Education And Rehabilitation

155.5   **JA**   **ISSN 0915-4965**
GIFU SHISHUNKI KENKYU/GIFU SOCIETY OF ADOLESCENTOLOGY. JOURNAL. (Text in Japanese) 1985. a. (Gifu Shishunki Kenkyukai) Gifuken Seishin Hoken Senta - Gifu Prefectural Mental Health Center, 8-1, Shimonara 2-chome, Gifu-shi, Gifu-ken 500, Japan. Ed. Akihiko Shibata. adv. contact: Hiroyuki Koide. **Document type:** bulletin.

649   **IT**
GIORNALE DELL'INFANZIA. 3/yr. Eurotrend S.p.A., Via Nino Bixio 6, 20129 Milan, Italy. TEL 39-2-29405653. FAX 39-2-29525624. Ed. Guido Colonna. adv.: page L.4000000. circ. 7,000.

028.5
GIRAFFE NEWS. 1982. s-a. $35. Giraffe Project, 197 Second St., Box 759, Langley, WA 98260. TEL 360-221-7989. FAX 360-2217817. E-mail: office@giraffe.org; URL: http://www.giraffe.org/giraffe/. Ed. Ann Medloch. circ. 2,000 (paid).
    Formerly: Giraffe Gazette.
    Description: Presents stories about people and news about Giraffe Project.

369.4   **US**   **ISSN 0017-0577**
GIRL SCOUT LEADER; for adults in girl scouting. 1923. 4/yr. $5 (foreign $7.50) (effective 1997 & 1998). Girl Scouts of the U.S.A., 420 Fifth Ave., New York, NY 10018-2798. TEL 212-852-8000. FAX 212-852-6511. Ed. Carolyn Caggine. R&P contact: Colleen Floyd. TEL 212-852-8133. circ. 800,000 (controlled). **Document type:** consumer publication.
    Description: Contains news and features concerning the national Girl Scout movement for all adults in girl scouting.

649   **US**
GOOD HOUSEKEEPING'S NINE MONTHS. 1989. s-a. $1.95. Hearst Corporation, 959 Eigth Ave. Ave., New York, NY 10019. TEL 212-649-2200. FAX 212-265-3307. adv. circ. 400,000.
    Description: For the contemporary career woman faced with balancing the demands and rewards of impending motherhood.

649   **US**   **ISSN 1055-5153**
GRAND RAPIDS PARENT. 1989. m. $12. Gemini Publications, 549 Ottawa Ave., N.W., Grand Rapids, MI 49503-1444. TEL 616-459-4545. FAX 616-459-4800. Ed. Carole Valade. adv. contact: Randy Prichard. circ. 15,000. **Document type:** consumer publication.
    Description: Covers finance, psychology, humor, child development, dining, education, food, new products, healthcare, events and recipes for parents.

GRANTS FOR WOMEN AND GIRLS. see WOMEN'S STUDIES

369.4 200   **US**   **ISSN 0163-8971**
GROUP (LOVELAND); the youth ministry magazine. 1974. 6/yr. $25.95 (effective 1997 & 1998). Group Publishing, Inc., 1515 Cascade Ave., Loveland, CO 80538-3274. TEL 970-669-3836. FAX 970-669-3269. (Subscr. to: Box 469080, Escondida, CA 92046-9080) Ed. Rick Lawrence; Pub. Tim Gilmour. adv. contact: Larry Bonjour. bk.rev.; film rev.; index. circ. 55,000. (back issues avail.) **Indexed:** Biol.Abstr., CCR, Curr.Cont., SSCI. **Document type:** trade publication.
    —UMI.
    Description: Contains practical help for Christian adults who work with youth.

649 155.4
GROWING CHILD. (Separate editions for different age groups; supplement avail.: Growing Parent) 1971. m. $20. Dunn & Hargitt, Inc., 22 N. Second St., Box 620, Lafayette, IN 47902. TEL 317-423-2624. Ed. Nancy Kleckner. adv.; bk.rev. circ. 120,000. (looseleaf format; back issues avail.) **Document type:** newsletter.
    Description: For parents of children up to age 6.

649   **US**   **ISSN 0193-8037**
GROWING PARENT NEWSLETTER. (Supplement to: Growing Child) 1975. m. (included with subscr. to Growing Child). Dunn & Hargitt, Inc., 22 N. Second St., Box 620, Lafayette, IN 47902. TEL 317-423-2624. Ed. Nancy Kleckner. circ. 120,000. (back issues avail.) **Document type:** newsletter.

155.4   **US**
GROWING TOGETHER. 1985. m. $30. Dunn & Hargitt, Inc., 22 N. Second St., Box 620, Lafayette, IN 47902. TEL 317-423-2624. Ed. Nancy Kleckner. circ. 2,500.
    Description: For use by daycare and preschool facilities.

GROWING WITHOUT SCHOOLING. see EDUCATION

649 IT
GUIDA DI IO E IL MIO BAMBINO. 1989. s-a. Eurotrend s.r.l., Via Nino Bixio 6, 20129 Milan, Italy. TEL 39-2-29405653. FAX 39-2-29404868. Ed. Cesi Alessi. adv.: page L.35300000. circ. 439,968. **Document type:** consumer publication.

369.4 UK ISSN 0265-2706
GUIDING. (Former name of issuing body: Girl Guides Association) 1914. m. £15. Guide Association, 17-19 Buckingham Palace Rd., London SW1, England. E-mail: CHQ@guides.org.uk; URL: http://www.guides.org.uk. Ed. Nora Warner; Pub. Sara Swan. R&P contact: Nora Warner. adv. contact: Nicky Hoy. bk.rev.; charts; illus.; index. circ. 27,500. **Document type:** newsletter.
Formerly (until Jan. 1983): Guider (ISSN 0017-534X)

GUIDING IN AUSTRALIA. see CHILDREN AND YOUTH — For

GUILFORD SCHOOL PRACTITIONER SERIES. see PSYCHOLOGY

HAANDBOGEN DAG- OG DOEGNINSTITUTIONER. see SOCIAL SERVICES AND WELFARE

790.019 CC ISSN 1002-4069
HAIZI TIANDI/CHILDREN'S WORLD. (Text in Chinese) 1989. bi-m. Zhongguo Heping Chubanshe - China Peace Publishing House, c/o Songqingling Foundation, No. 21 Andeli North St., Beijing 100011, People's Republic of China. TEL 6744507. Ed. Nie Dapeng.

HAWAII. DEPARTMENT OF HEALTH. MENTAL HEALTH SERVICES FOR CHILDREN AND YOUTH; children's MH services branch. see SOCIAL SERVICES AND WELFARE

649 US ISSN 1076-1764
HEALTHY KIDS. 1989. bi-m. single issues free. (American Academy of Pediatrics) K-III Communications Corp., 745 Fifth Ave., New York, NY 10151. TEL 212-463-6578. FAX 212-463-6410. (Dist. by: Neodata Services, Box 2971, Boulder, CO 80329. TEL 303-447-9330) Ed. Laura Broadwell; Pub. Sharon Summer. adv.: B&W page $50200, color page $69500; trim 7 7/8 x 10 3/4. illus. circ. 1,500,000. **Document type:** consumer publication.
Formed by the merger of (1990-1994): Healthy Kids: 4-10 Years. (ISSN 1062-4236); Which was formerly: American Baby's Healthy Kids: 4-10 Years; (1989-1994): Healthy Kids: Birth - 3 (ISSN 1063-0945); Which was formerly: American Baby's Healthy Kids: Birth - 3; (until 1990) American Baby's Healthy Kids.
Description: For parents of children from birth to age ten, with information about children's physical and emotional well-being.

HIGH - SCOPE BUYER'S GUIDE TO CHILDREN'S SOFTWARE; survey of computer programs for children ages 3 to 7. see COMPUTERS — Software

HIP MAMA; the parenting zine. see LITERARY AND POLITICAL REVIEWS

HISPANIC AMERICAN FAMILY MAGAZINE. see SOCIOLOGY

HOFKLATSCH; Magazin fuer Schueler. see EDUCATION — Higher Education

HORN BOOK GUIDE TO CHILDREN'S AND YOUNG ADULT BOOKS. see PUBLISHING AND BOOK TRADE

HORN BOOK MAGAZINE; recommending books for children and young adults. see PUBLISHING AND BOOK TRADE

HOT 100; a quick guide to federal programs and services for youth. see SOCIAL SERVICES AND WELFARE

HOTLINE (STONY BROOK); news service on the missing children field. see CRIMINOLOGY AND LAW ENFORCEMENT

HUMAN STRESS: CURRENT SELECTED RESEARCH. see PSYCHOLOGY

HUNYIN YU JIATING/MARRIAGE & FAMILY. see MATRIMONY

I C A N COMMUNICATE. (Invalid Children's Aid Nationwide) see EDUCATION — Special Education And Rehabilitation

I C C W JOURNAL. (Indian Council for Child Welfare) see SOCIAL SERVICES AND WELFARE

649.4 US
I LOVE MY NANNY NEWS. m. free. I Love My Nanny, Inc., E-mail: nannies-request@parentsplace.com; NannyLuvsU@aol.com; URL: http://www.ilovemynanny.com/. **Document type:** newsletter.
●Available only online.
Description: For parents who are interested in hiring nannies, women interested in finding employment in the nanny field, and professionals who work with children and families.

649 PH
I M C H NEWSLETTER. (Text in English) 1969. m. P.10($1.50) Institute of Maternal and Child Health, National Training Center for Maternal Health Services, 11 Banawe St., Quezon City, Philippines. TEL 712-01-49. FAX 712-10-13. Dir. Jose O. Obordo. abstr.; charts; illus. circ. 4,000. **Document type:** newsletter.

THE I S I S MAGAZINE. (Independent Schools Information Service) see EDUCATION — Guides To Schools And Colleges

IMPACT (WESTPORT). see SOCIAL SERVICES AND WELFARE

370 UK ISSN 0962-3507
IN COMMON. 1974. 3/yr. free. Commonwealth Youth Programme, Commonwealth Secretariat, Marlborough House, Pall Mall, London, England. TEL 44-171-839-3411. FAX 44-171-930-1647. Ed. Jacqui Kissai. bk.rev. circ. 4,000. **Document type:** newsletter.
Former titles (until 1989): C Y P News Service; Commonwealth Youth News.

267 US
INCONTACT. 1984. q. free. Pioneer Clubs, Box 788, Wheaton, IL 60189-0788. TEL 630-293-1600. FAX 630-293-3053. Ed. Gary L. Wall. circ. 6,000. **Document type:** newsletter.
Description: Primarily for donors to club and camp ministry for children; covers issues affecting children and youth, stories of children and adult volunteers involved in the program.

649 US ISSN 1072-2084
INDY'S CHILD.* 1984. m. $18. Indy's Child, Inc., 6502 E. Westfield Blvd., Indianapolis, IN 46220-1110. TEL 317-843-1494. FAX 317-574-3233. Ed. Pamela Fettig; Pub. Greg Wynne. R&P contact: Pamela Fetting. adv.: B&W page $1400, color page $1800; trim 11 1/4 x 13 1/2; adv. contact: Anne-Marie Damler. bk.rev.; charts. circ. 70,000. **Document type:** consumer publication.
Description: Covers education, women's issues, camps, enrichement, teen issues, computer hardware and software and gives parenting advice.

362.7 PE ISSN 1024-6363
INFANCIA Y SOCIEDAD. 1994. irreg., no.5, 1996. price varies. (Instituto de Estudios Peruanos) I E P Ediciones, Horacio Urteaga 694, Lima 11, Peru. TEL 51-14-323070. FAX 51-14-324981. E-mail: libreria@iep.org.pe. **Document type:** academic/scholarly publication.

INFANTS AND YOUNG CHILDREN; an interdisciplinary journal of special care practices. see MEDICAL SCIENCES — Pediatrics

155.4 IT ISSN 0390-2420
INFANZIA. 1973. m. L.55000 (foreign L.65000) (effective 1995-96). Nuova Italia Editrice S.p.a., Via Ernesto Codignola, 50018 Scandicci (FI), Italy. Ed. Pietro Bertolini. adv.; bk.rev.

267 NE ISSN 0041-2562
INKLUSIEF. 1971. 4/yr. fl.22.50. Y M C A Nederland, Postbus 115, 3970 AC Driebergen, Netherlands. Eds. H. Dekker, A.A. Dekker. adv.; bk.rev. circ. 6,000. **Document type:** bulletin, newsletter.

155.4 US ISSN 1065-1039
INSIDE - OUTSIDE; a guide to positive parenting. 1991. q. $35 for 15 copies; membership. Institute for Women and Children, 4680 Lake Underhill Rd., Orlando, FL 32807. TEL 407-277-1942. FAX 407-381-0907. Ed. Judy Peterson. adv.; bk.rev.; charts. circ. 7,000.
Description: Covers positive parenting issues, self esteem issues, positive interaction and bonding-nurturing with children, and health and safety articles.

362.7 US ISSN 0020-4056
HV703
INSTITUTO INTERAMERICANO DEL NINO. BOLETIN. (Text in English, French, Portuguese and Spanish) 1927. s-a. $26. Organization of American States, Instituto Interamericano del Nino - Organizacion de Estados Americanos, 1889 F St., N.W., Washington, DC 20006-4499. TEL 202-458-3527. FAX 202-458-3534. (Dist. by: Center for Promotion and Distribution of Publications, Box 66398, Washington DC 20035) bk.rev.; abstr.; charts; illus.; stat. circ. 2,400. **Indexed:** P.A.I.S.For.Lang.Ind.

649 610.73 US
INTENSIVE CARING UNLIMITED.* 1983. q. $8. Intensive Caring Unlimited (ICU), 571 Creek Rd., Ivyland, PA 18974. TEL 215-629-0449. Ed. Lenette S. Moses. adv.; bk.rev.; circ. 3,000 (controlled). (back issues avail.)
Description: Support and information for parents of infants with medical and developmental problems, high-risk pregnancy and bereavement.

268.6 649.7 NE ISSN 1383-9632
INTERMEZZO; nieuws- en informatieblad over jeugd- en jongerenwerk in en rond de sow-kerken. 1958; N.S. 1995. bi-m. donation. Samen op Weg Jeugdwerk, Postbus 99, 3970 AB Driebergen, Netherlands. TEL 31-343-523222. FAX 31-343-523250. Ed. Ineke van der Vegt. bk.rev. circ. 5,000.
Formerly (until Sep. 1995): Bijblijven (Driebergen) (ISSN 0006-226X)
Description: Features youth projects sponsored by Reformed churches in the Netherlands.

INTERNATIONAL CHILDREN'S CENTRE. PARIS. REPORT OF THE DIRECTOR-GENERAL TO THE EXECUTIVE BOARD. see SOCIOLOGY

INTERNATIONAL CHILDREN'S RIGHTS MONITOR. see POLITICAL SCIENCE — Civil Rights

362.7 155.4 UK ISSN 0267-3843
INTERNATIONAL JOURNAL OF ADOLESCENCE AND YOUTH. 1987. q. £79($159) A B Academic Publishers, P.O. Box 42, Bicester, Oxon. OX6 7NW, England. TEL 44-1869-320949. Ed. Roy Evans. **Indexed:** ASSIA, Br.Educ.Ind., Cont.Pg.Educ., Fam.Ind., Mult.Ed.Abstr., Psychol.Abstr. (1987-), Sociol.Educ.Abstr., Sp.Ed.Needs Abstr. **Document type:** academic/scholarly publication.
—BLDSC (4541.562000).
Description: Covers psychological growth and development, health and medical care, social policy, education, employment, unemployment, leisure, sex education, family relationships, and homelessness.
Refereed Serial

155.4 CN ISSN 1206-8330
▼**INTERNATIONAL JOURNAL OF CHILDREN & ADOLESCENTS.** (Text in Arabic, English) 1997. q. Can.$400. P.O. Box 98029, S. Common Post, 2150 Burnhamthorpe Rd., Mississagua, ON L5L 3A0, Canada. FAX 416-277-2875. (And: Box 38552, Abdulla Al-Salem, Kuwait City 72256, Kuwait. FAX 965-489-1179) Ed. M.I. Ismail.
Description: Designed for concise, cooperative publication of simple accelerated and safe creative ideas.
Refereed Serial

THE INTERNATIONAL JOURNAL OF CHILDREN'S RIGHTS. see POLITICAL SCIENCE — Civil Rights

CHILDREN AND YOUTH — ABOUT

372.21 US ISSN 0020-7187
INTERNATIONAL JOURNAL OF EARLY CHILDHOOD.* (Text in English, French and Spanish) 1969. 2/yr. membership. World Organization for Early Childhood Education - Organisation Mondiale pour l'Education Prescolaire (OMEP), c/o Dr. Margaret Devine, 81 Irving Pl., Apt.16, New York, NY 10003. Ed. Anne McKenna. adv.; bk.rev. circ. 1,650. (also avail. in microform from UMI; reprint service avail. from UMI) **Indexed:** ASSIA, Br.Educ.Ind., C.I.J.E., Child Devel.Abstr., Cont.Pg.Educ., Educ.Ind., ERIC, Mult.Ed.Abstr., Soc.Sci.Ind.
—BLDSC (4542.190000); KR SourceOne; SWETS; UMI; UnCover.

649 IT
IO E IL MIO BAMBINO. 1984. m. L.1500 per no. Eurotrend S.p.A., Via Nino Bixio 6, 20129 Milan, Italy. TEL 39-2-29405643. FAX 39-2-29404868. Ed. Cesi Alessi. adv.: page L.35300000. circ. 200,996.

649 IT
IO E MIO FIGLIO. 1978. m. Publibaby S.r.l., Via Enrico Fermi 18, 20090 Cusago (MI), Italy. TEL 39-2-90119700. FAX 39-2-90390464. Ed. Emilio Terzagli. adv.: color page L.21750000. circ. 185,000.

649 US
IOWA PARENT.* m. Iowa Parent Magazine, 740 42nd St., West Des Moines, IA 50265-3808. TEL 515-981-0282. Ed. Jan R. Walker. circ. 40,000.

363.2 616.89 US ISSN 1043-8823
HV8079.C48 CODEN: ICCAEG
ISSUES IN CHILD ABUSE ACCUSATIONS. 1989. q. $50 (foreign $70). Institute for Psychological Therapies, 13200 Cannon City Blvd., Northfield, MN 55057. TEL 507-645-8881. FAX 507-645-8883. E-mail: under006@gold.tc.umn.edu. Ed. Hollida Wakefield. bk.rev.; circ. 200 (paid). (back issues avail.) **Indexed:** Sociol.Abstr. **Document type:** academic/scholarly publication.
—BLDSC (4584.145000); UnCover.
Description: Provides a multidisciplinary forum on all aspects of child abuse, with special emphasis on research and commentary that questions the methods and conventional wisdom of the child abuse establishment.
Refereed Serial

362.7 US
ISSUES IN CHILDREN'S AND FAMILIES' LIVES SERIES. (Subseries of: The John & Kelly Hartman Series) irreg., vol.2, 1995. price varies. Sage Publications, Inc., 2455 Teller Rd., Thousand Oaks, CA 91320. TEL 805-499-0721. FAX 805-499-0871. (Overseas addr.: Sage Publications Ltd., 6 Bonhill St., London EC2A 4PU, England; And: Sage Publications India Pvt. Ltd., P.O. Box 4125, New Delhi 110 048, India) **Document type:** monographic series.

362.7 380 AU
J U M - JUGEND UND MEDIEN; Lehrerzeitung des Buchklubs. 1990. 4/yr. membership. Oesterreichischer Buchklub der Jugend, Mayerhofgasse 6, A-1041 Vienna, Austria. TEL 43-1-5051754-0. FAX 43-1-505175450. **Document type:** bulletin.

649 296.7 649 US ISSN 1071-8826
THE JEWISH PARENT CONNECTION. 8/yr. $10. Torah Umesorah - National Society for Hebrew Day Schools (Manhattan), Parent Enrichment Program, 160 Broadway, 4th Fl., New York, NY 10038. TEL 212-227-1000. FAX 212-406-6934. Ed. Joyce Lempel; Pub. Rabbi Joshua Fishman. R&P contact: Joyce Lempel. adv. contact: Rachel Wolff. bk.rev. circ. 22,600. (back issues avail.) **Indexed:** Ind.Jew.Per. **Document type:** newsletter, consumer publication.
Description: Deals with topics and issues of interest to Jewish parents.

JIATING/FAMILY. see *HOME ECONOMICS*

THE JOURNAL FOR TRUANCY AND DROPOUT PREVENTION. see *EDUCATION*

155.5 UK ISSN 0140-1971
RJ499.A1
JOURNAL OF ADOLESCENCE. 1978. bi-m. £198 (effective 1998). Academic Press Ltd. (Subsidiary of: Harcourt Brace & Company Ltd.), 24-28 Oval Rd., London NW1 7DX, England. TEL 44-171-267-4466. FAX 44-171-482-2293. TELEX 25775 ACPRES G. E-mail: apsubs@acad.com; URL: http://www.hbuk.co.uk/ap/adolescence; http://www.europe.idealibrary.com/. (Subscr. to: Harcourt Brace & Company Ltd., Foots Cray High St., Sidcup, Kent DA14 5HP, England. TEL 44-181-300-3322. FAX 44-181-309-0807) Ed. John Coleman. R&P contact: Catherine John. adv. contact: Nik Screen. bk.rev.; index. (reprint service avail. from SWZ) **Indexed:** Abstr.Crim.& Pen., Amer.Hist.& Life (1986-), ASCA, ASSIA, Bibl.Agri., Br.Educ.Ind., C.I.J.E., Crim.Just.Abstr., Curr.Cont., Excerp.Med., Fam.Ind., Hist.Abstr. (1986-), Ind.Med., Psychol.Abstr. (1980-), Soc.Sci.Ind., Sociol.Educ.Abstr., SOMA, SSCI, Stud.Wom.Abstr., Tech.Educ.Abstr. **Document type:** academic/scholarly publication.
●Also available online.
—BLDSC (4918.942000); Genuine Article; KNAW; KR SourceOne; SWETS; UnCover. **CCC.**
Description: International, broadly based, cross-disciplinary journal that addresses itself to issues of professional and academic importance.

JOURNAL OF ADOLESCENT HEALTH. see *MEDICAL SCIENCES*

155.5 370.15 US ISSN 0743-5584
HQ796
JOURNAL OF ADOLESCENT RESEARCH. 1986. q. $150 to institutions (effective Sep. 1996). Sage Publications, Inc., 2455 Teller Rd., Thousand Oaks, CA 91320. TEL 805-499-0721. FAX 805-499-0871. E-mail: libraries@sagepub.com; URL: http://www.sagepub.com. (Overseas subscr. to: Sage Publications, Ltd., 6 Bonhill St., London EC2A 4PU, England; Sage Publications India Pvt. Ltd., P.O. Box 4215, New Delhi 110 048, India) Ed. E. Ellen Thornburg. adv. contact: Margaret Travers. circ. 1,000. (also avail. in microform; back issues avail.; reprint service avail.) **Indexed:** ASCA, Bibl.Agri., C.I.J.E., Crim.Just.Abstr., Curr.Cont., Educ.Ind., Fam.Ind., IMFL, Psychol.Abstr. (1986-), Soc.Work Res.& Abstr., Sociol.Abstr., THA, Viol.& Abuse Abstr. **Document type:** academic/scholarly publication.
—BLDSC (4918.943500); Genuine Article; SWETS; UMI. **CCC.**
Description: Takes an interdisciplinary perspective in providing professionals and practitioners with current and relevant information on many aspects of individuals 10-20 years old.
Refereed Serial

362.7 896 US ISSN 0795-4506
JOURNAL OF AFRICAN CHILDREN'S AND YOUTH LITERATURE. Variant title: J A C Y L. 1989. a. $12 to individuals; libraries $25 (effective 1997). Department of English and Foreign Languages, Mississippi Valley State University, Itta Bena, MS 38941. TEL 601-254-3453. FAX 601-254-3452. E-mail: oosa@fielding.mvsu.edu. Ed. Osayimwense Osa. adv.; bk.rev. **Document type:** academic/scholarly publication.
Description: Provides a forum in which scholars working in the field of children's literature and youth literature can address a cross section of those who work with children and books.

JOURNAL OF CHILD AND ADOLESCENT GROUP THERAPY. see *MEDICAL SCIENCES — Psychiatry And Neurology*

JOURNAL OF CHILD AND ADOLESCENT PSYCHIATRIC NURSING. see *MEDICAL SCIENCES — Nurses And Nursing*

JOURNAL OF CHILD & ADOLESCENT SUBSTANCE ABUSE. see *DRUG ABUSE AND ALCOHOLISM*

649 CN ISSN 0840-982X
JOURNAL OF CHILD AND YOUTH CARE. (Supplement avail.) 1982. q. Can.$38.50($49.50) to qualified personnel; individuals Can.$49.50; institutions Can.$71.50 (effective 1996). Malaspina University College, Dept. of Human Services, 900 Fifth St., Nanaimo, BC V9R 5S5, Canada. Ed. Gerry Fewster. adv.: page Can.$100. circ. 450. (back issues avail.) **Indexed:** Psychol.Abstr. (1982-), Soc.Work Res.& Abstr. **Document type:** trade publication.
—BLDSC (4957.427000); UnCover. **CCC.**
Formerly (until 1989): Journal of Child Care (ISSN 0715-5883)
Description: Covers all areas of child and youth care with emphasis on the field of social services and welfare.

155.4 UK ISSN 0305-0009
P118
JOURNAL OF CHILD LANGUAGE. 1974. 3/yr. £97($163) (effective 1998). Cambridge University Press, Edinburgh Bldg., Shaftesbury Rd., Cambridge CB2 2RU, England. TEL 44-1223-312393. FAX 44-1223-315052. TELEX 851817256. E-mail: information@cup.cam.ac.uk; URL: http://www.cup.cam.ac.uk. (N. American addr.: Cambridge University Press, Journals Dept., 40 W. 20th St., New York, NY 10011. TEL 212-924-3900. FAX 212-691-3239) Ed. Elena Lieven. R&P contact: Linda Nicol. adv. contact: Rebecca Symons. bk.rev. (also avail. in microform from UMI; back issues avail.; reprint service avail. from SWZ,UMI) **Indexed:** Abstr.Anthropol., Arts & Hum.Cit.Ind., ASCA, ASSIA, Bibl.Dev.Med.& Child Neur., Bibl.Ling., Br.Educ.Ind., C.I.J.E., Child Devel.Abstr., Child.Lit.Abstr., Commun.Abstr., Cont.Pg.Educ., Curr.Cont., Educ.Ind., Fam.Ind., Lang.& Lang.Behav.Abstr. (1974-), Lang.Teach.& Ling.Abstr., Ling.Abstr., M.L.A., Mid.East: Abstr.& Ind., MLA Intl.Bibl., Mult.Ed.Abstr., Psychol.Abstr. (1974-), Psycscan D.P., Sage Fam.Stud.Abstr., Sociol.Abstr., SSCI, Stud.Wom.Abstr., Yrbk.Assoc.Educ.& Rehab.Blind. **Document type:** academic/scholarly publication.
—BLDSC (4957.600000); Genuine Article; KR SourceOne; SWETS; UMI; UnCover. **CCC.**
Description: Covers all aspects of the scientific study of language behavior in children and the underlying principles, including normal and pathological development of both monolingual and bilingual children.

JOURNAL OF CHILDREN & POVERTY. see *SOCIAL SERVICES AND WELFARE*

JOURNAL OF CHILDREN'S COMMUNICATION DEVELOPMENT. see *EDUCATION — Special Education And Rehabilitation*

028.5 070.5 US
JOURNAL OF CHILDREN'S LITERATURE. s-a. $20 in U.S., Canada $22; Students $10 (foreign $30) (effective 1997). Children's Literature Assembly, c/o Marjorie R. Hancock, 2037 Plymouth Rd., Manhattan, KS 66503. TEL 913-532-5917. Eds. Evelyn Freeman, Barbara Lehman, Patrick Scharer. adv. contact: Carole Rhodes. bk.rev.; bibl. circ. 550. **Document type:** academic/scholarly publication.
Formerly (until 1994): Children's Literature Assembly Bulletin.
Description: Serves those with a personal and professional interest in children's literature. Includes scholarly and practical articles and booklists.
Refereed Serial

JOURNAL OF CLINICAL CHILD PSYCHOLOGY. see *PSYCHOLOGY*

JOURNAL OF COMPUTING IN CHILDHOOD EDUCATION. an international journal of research and application on using computer technologies in the education of children. see *EDUCATION — Computer Applications*

155 US ISSN 0272-4316
HQ796
JOURNAL OF EARLY ADOLESCENCE. 1981. q. $152 to institutions (effective Sept. 1996). Sage Publications, Inc., 2455 Teller Rd., Thousand Oaks, CA 91320. TEL 805-499-0721. FAX 805-499-0871. E-mail: libraries@sagepub.com; URL: http://www.sagepub.com. (Overseas subscr. to: Sage Publications Ltd., 6 Bonhill St., London EC2A 4PU, England; Sage Publications India Pvt. Ltd., P.O. Box 4215, New Delhi 110 048, India) Ed. E. Ellen Thornburg. adv. contact: Margaret Travers. bk.rev.; film rev. circ. 1,200. (also avail. in microform; back issues avail.; reprint service avail. from UMI.) **Indexed:** Adol.Ment.Hlth.Abstr., ASCA, C.I.J.E., Child Devel.Abstr., Crim.Just.Abstr., Curr.Cont., Curr.Lit.Fam.Plan., Educ.Ind., ERIC, Fam.Ind., IMFL, Mult.Ed.Abstr., Psychol.Abstr. (1981-), Soc.Sci.Ind., Soc.Work Res.& Abstr., Sociol.Abstr., Viol.& Abuse Abstr. **Document type:** academic/scholarly publication.
—BLDSC (4970.701000); Genuine Article; UMI; UnCover. **CCC.**
Description: Takes an interdisciplinary approach through research studies, reviews, and theoretical papers the need for focus on the characteristics of persons 10-14 years old.
Refereed Serial

JOURNAL OF EARLY INTERVENTION. see *EDUCATION — Special Education And Rehabilitation*

JOURNAL OF EXPERIMENTAL CHILD PSYCHOLOGY. see *PSYCHOLOGY*

JOURNAL OF HIV - AIDS PREVENTION & EDUCATION FOR ADOLESCENTS & CHILDREN. see *MEDICAL SCIENCES — Communicable Diseases*

JOURNAL OF PRACTICAL APPROACHES TO DEVELOPMENTAL HANDICAP. see *EDUCATION — Special Education And Rehabilitation*

JOURNAL OF RESEARCH IN CHILDHOOD EDUCATION; an international journal of research on the education of children. see *EDUCATION*

155.4 US ISSN 1050-8392
HQ796 CODEN: JRADET
JOURNAL OF RESEARCH ON ADOLESCENCE. 1991. q. $39 to individuals (foreign $69); institutions $205 (foreign $235) (effective 1997). (Society for Research on Adolescence) Lawrence Erlbaum Associates, Inc., 10 Industrial Dr., Mahwah, NJ 07430-2262. TEL 201-236-9500; 800-926-6579. FAX 201-236-0072. E-mail: orders@erlbaum.com; URL: http://www.erlbaum.com. Ed. Diane Scott-Jones. adv.: page $375; 5 x 8. **Indexed:** ASCA, C.I.J.E., Curr.Cont., Fam.Ind., Mult.Ed.Abstr., Psychol.Abstr. (1991-), Sociol.Educ.Abstr., THA. **Document type:** academic/scholarly publication.
—BLDSC (5051.920000); SWETS; UnCover. **CCC.**
Description: Publishes original researches pertinent to the development patterns inherent throughout adolescence.
Refereed Serial

JOURNAL OF SOCIAL WORK PRACTICE. see *SOCIAL SERVICES AND WELFARE*

155.4 US ISSN 0047-2891
HQ796 CODEN: JYADA
JOURNAL OF YOUTH AND ADOLESCENCE; a multidisciplinary research publication. 1972. bi-m. $425 (foreign $495) (effective 1998). Plenum Publishing Corp., 233 Spring St., New York, NY 10013-1578. TEL 212-620-8000. FAX 212-463-0742. TELEX 23-421139. Ed. Daniel Offer. adv.; bibl.; charts. (also avail. in microfilm from UMI; back issues avail.) **Indexed:** Abstr.Crim.& Pen., Adol.Ment.Hlth.Abstr., ASCA, ASSIA, Bibl.Agri., C.I.J.E., CERDIC, Child Devel.Abstr., Commun.Abstr., Crim.Just.Abstr., Curr.Cont., Curr.Lit.Fam.Plan., Educ.Ind., Excerp.Med., Fam.Ind., High.Educ.Abstr., IMFL, Lang.& Lang.Behav.Abstr., Mid.East: Abstr.& Ind., Mult.Ed.Abstr., Psychol.Abstr. (1972-), Psycscan D.P., Sage Urb.Stud.Abstr., Soc.Sci.Ind., Sociol.Abstr., Sociol.Educ.Abstr., SOMA, Sp.Ed.Needs Abstr., SSCI, Stud.Wom.Abstr., THA. **Document type:** academic/scholarly publication.
●Also available online. Vendor(s): Information Access Co., UMI.
—BLDSC (5072.720000); Genuine Article; KNAW; KR SourceOne; SWETS; UMI; UnCover. **CCC.**
Refereed Serial

369.4 200 US ISSN 1055-1409
JR. HIGH MINISTRY MAGAZINE. 1985. 5/yr. $19.95. Group Publishing, Inc., 1515 Cascade Ave., Loveland, CO 80538-3274. TEL 970-669-3836. FAX 970-669-1994. (Subscr. to: Box 469082, Escondido, CA 92046-9082) Ed. Janice Long; Pub. Tim Gilmour. adv. contact: Larry Bonjour. circ. 25,000. **Document type:** trade publication.
Formerly: Group's Jr. High Ministry Magazine (ISSN 0884-0504)
Description: Contains practical help for Christian adults who work with junior-high age youth.

028.5 UK
JUDY AND TRACY. 1960. w. £16. D.C. Thomson & Co. Ltd., 2 Albert Sq., Dundee DD1 9QJ, Scotland.
Formed by the merger of: Tracy & Judy (ISSN 0022-5851)

362.7 GW ISSN 0342-0175
JUGEND BERUF GESELLSCHAFT; Journal for professionals in youth social service. 1949. q. DM.22. Bundesarbeitsgemeinschaft Jugendsozialarbeit, Kennedyallee 105-107, 53175 Bonn, Germany. TEL 49-228-959680. FAX 49-228-9596830. E-mail: 0228959680-001@t-online.de. Ed. Paul Fuelbier; Pub. Henrik von Bothmer. R&P contact: Paul Fuelbier. bk.rev.; index. circ. 1,500. **Document type:** academic/scholarly publication.

155.5 GW ISSN 0943-058X
JUGEND - MEDIEN - SCHUTZ - REPORT. 6/yr. DM.76.80 (foreign DM.88.80) (effective 1996). Nomos Verlagsgesellschaft mbH und Co. KG, Waldseestr. 3-5, 76530 Baden-Baden, Germany. TEL 49-7221-21040. FAX 49-7221-210427. (Subscr. to: Postfach 610, 76484 Baden-Baden, Germany) **Document type:** bulletin.
—CCC.
Former titles (until 1992): J M S - Report (ISSN 0941-732X); (until 1991): B P S - Report (ISSN 0170-5067)

362.7 GW ISSN 0177-4247
JUGENDBUCHMAGAZIN. 1950. a. DM.50.06. Arbeitskreis das Gute Jugendbuch e.V., Hahnenacker 21, 47533 Kleve, Germany. TEL 02821-98964. adv. circ. 1,500. **Indexed:** Child.Lit.Abstr. **Document type:** bulletin.
Formerly (until 1979): Gute Jugendbuch.

JUGENDHILFE. see *SOCIAL SERVICES AND WELFARE*

028.5 027.62 SZ ISSN 0256-6532
JUGENDLITERATUR. (Text in German) 1975. 4/yr. 25 SFr. Schweizerischer Bund fuer Jugendliteratur, Zentralsekretariat, Gewerbestr. 8, CH-6330 Cham, Switzerland. adv.; bk.rev. circ. 5,000. **Indexed:** Child.Lit.Abstr. **Document type:** bulletin.
Formerly: Schweizerischer Bund fuer Jugendliteratur. Nachrichten.
Description: News and information concerning children's literature. Covers writers, reports of events, honor list, choice of books on various subjects. Includes list of events.

JUGENDNACHRICHTEN. see *EDUCATION — International Education Programs*

JUGENDWOHL; Zeitschrift fuer Kinder- und Jugendhilfe. see *SOCIAL SERVICES AND WELFARE*

JUNGE FAMILIE. see *MEDICAL SCIENCES — Pediatrics*

362.7 US
JUNIOR CITIZEN. 1910. s-a. free to qualified personnel. Connecticut Junior Republic Association Inc., Box 161, Goshen Rd., Litchfield, CT 06759. TEL 203-567-9423. Ed. Hedy L. Barton. circ. 11,000. (tabloid format) **Document type:** newsletter.

JUVENILE AND FAMILY COURT JOURNAL. see *LAW — Family And Matrimonial Law*

JUVENILE AND FAMILY JUSTICE TODAY. see *LAW — Family And Matrimonial Law*

JUVENILE AND FAMILY LAW DIGEST. see *LAW — Family And Matrimonial Law*

369.4 020 US
JUVENILE MISCELLANY. 1970. 2/yr. free. University of Southern Mississippi, McCain Library, De Grummond Children's Literature Research Collection, Box 5148, Hattiesburg, MS 39406-5148. TEL 601-266-4349. Ed. Dee Jones. circ. 1,400. **Indexed:** Child.Lit.Abstr.

362.7 CU
JUVENTUD REBELDE. d. $25 in Central America; S. America $30; Europe $35; U.S., Canada, Asia, and Africa $40; Japan and Australia $45. (Union de Jovenes Comunistas) Ediciones Cubanas, Obispo No. 527, Apdo. 605, Havana, Cuba. TEL 32-5556-60.

362.7 GW ISSN 0946-4824
K I D - KINDERINFORMATIONSDIENST. 1991. q. DM.30. K I D Verlag, Samansstr. 4, 53227 Bonn, Germany. TEL 49-228-443195. FAX 49-228-443195. E-mail: hanswein@t-online.de. Ed. Hans Weingartz; Pub. Hans Weingartz. adv.; bk.rev. **Document type:** academic/scholarly publication.

K J R BURG INFO; Jugendpolitik und Jugendarbeit im Landkreis Muenchen. (Kreisjugendring Muenchen-Land) see *SOCIAL SERVICES AND WELFARE*

KAKS PLUS. see *GENERAL INTEREST PERIODICALS — Finland*

796.1 910.4 GW
DIE KAKTUSBLUETE. 1973. 3/yr. DM.5. Geschwister-Scholl-Schule, Kapellenstr. 38, 58099 Hagen, Germany. TEL 49-2331-61060. FAX 49-2331-82631. Pub. Friedhelm Kuhl. adv.: page DM.120. bk.rev.; film rev. circ. 1,500. (back issues avail.) **Document type:** bulletin.

KEEPING POSTED WITH N C S Y. see *RELIGIONS AND THEOLOGY — Judaic*

362.7 UK
KEY NOTE MARKET REPORT: BABY PRODUCTS. Variant title: Baby Products. irreg., no.8, 1994. £205. Key Note Ltd., Field House, 72 Oldfield Rd., Hampton, Middlesex TW12 2HQ, England. TEL 44-181-783-0755. FAX 44-181-783-0049. **Document type:** trade publication.
●Also available online.
Also available on CD-ROM.
Formerly: Key Note Report: Baby Products.

649 391 US
KID NEWS; children's bargain guide. 1990. bi-m. $26.95 (effective 1997). Kid News, Box 797, Forest Hills, NY 11375. TEL 718-520-8829. Ed. Susan Robinson. adv. contact: Lori Frank. bk.rev. circ. 20,000. (looseleaf format; back issues avail.) **Document type:** newsletter, consumer publication.

KID'N AROUND. see *CHILDREN AND YOUTH — For*

362.7 US
KIDS LIB NEWS; natural family resources. 1985. q. $12. Oness Press, Box 1064, Kurtistown, HI 96760. Ed. Mycall Sunanda. adv.; bk.rev. circ. 1,000.
Description: Covers holistic parenting instincts and children's rights, with articles on home-birth and midwifery, circumcision, sex education, kiddie porno paranoia, underwater homebirthing, TV violence and advertising.

649 CN ISSN 0847-3935
KIDS TRIBUTE. q. Can.$12 (US Can.$18; elsewhere Can.$24) (effective 1997). Tribute Publishing, Inc., 71 Barber Greene Rd., Don Mills, ON M3C 2A2, Canada. TEL 416-445-0544. FAX 416-445-2894. Ed. Kim Green; Pub. Sandra I. Stewart. R&P contact: Sandra Stewart. adv. contact: Donnalyn Coyne. circ. 305,000. **Document type:** consumer publication.
Description: Film and general interest magazine for children.

362.7 AT
KIDSAFE. 1979. q. Aus.$15 (effective 1995). Child Accident Prevention Foundation of Australia, 123 Queen St., 10th Fl., Melbourne, Vic. 3000, Australia. TEL 61-3-6701319. FAX 61-3-6707616. Ed. Carol Taylor. adv. contact: Jannie O'Longhlan. circ. 3,000. **Document type:** consumer publication.
Former titles (until Autumn 1994): Safeguard (ISSN 1038-3409); Safe Guard (ISSN 0818-0474); (until 1986): Child Accident Prevention Foundation of Australia. Quarterly Journal (ISSN 0725-9573); (until 1981): Child Accident Prevention Foundation of Australia. Journal (ISSN 0728-8778)
Description: Information on prevention of Children's injuries.
Refereed Serial

C

CHILDREN AND YOUTH — ABOUT

649 US
KIDSTODAY; the magazine for New Jersey parents. 10/yr. $25 for 20 nos. Kidstoday Inc., 540 Rt. 10 W., Ste. 322, Randolph, NJ 07869. TEL 201-586-2373. Pub. Elaine Ferguson. adv. contact: Denise Lyons. bk.rev. **Document type:** consumer publication.

649 US
KIDZ MAGAZINE.* 1988. m. $12. Kids Production, Inc., 700 W. Center Rd., Ste. 110, Omaha, NE 68126-2717. TEL 402-391-0441. Ed. Melanie Morrissey Clark. adv.; bk.rev.; film rev. circ. 50,000.
   Formerly: Kids, Kids, Kidz.
   Description: For parents, doctors and teachers who are involved with children. Includes a calendar of events and medical reviews.

155.4 GW ISSN 0945-5582
DAS KIND. 1987. s-a. DM.24. Deutsche Montessori Gesellschaft e.V., Postfach 5461, 97004 Wuerzburg, Germany. TEL 0931-8885560. Ed. Waltraud Harth-Peter. bk.rev. circ. 500. (back issues avail.) **Document type:** newsletter.

KIND EN ADOLESCENT. see *MEDICAL SCIENCES — Pediatrics*

362.7 GW ISSN 0939-4354
KIND - JUGEND - GESELLSCHAFT. 1956. q. DM.48. (Bundesarbeitsgemeinschaft Kinder- und Jugendschutz e.V.) Luchterhand Verlag, Heddesdorferstr. 31, 56564 Neuwied, Germany. TEL 49-2631-801-0. FAX 49-2631-801204. Ed. Ingrid Hillebrandt. adv. contact: Gabriele Pannwitz. **Document type:** academic/scholarly publication.
   Formerly (until 1991): Jugendschutz (ISSN 0342-6394)

362.7 305.31 GW ISSN 0176-8115
KIND UND VATER. 1984. irreg. DM.20. Eltern fuer Aktive Vaterschaft e.V., Friedrich-August-Platz 2, 26121 Oldenburg, Germany. TEL 49-441-81134. FAX 49-441-81165. E-mail: efav__e.v@t-online.de. Ed. Klaus Anders. bk.rev.; circ. 1,800 (paid). (back issues avail.) **Document type:** bulletin.

618 688.72 649
362.7 GW
KINDER; das Journal des Kindergartens. 1971. 8/yr. DM.16. Junior-Verlag GmbH und Co. KG, Fehlandtstr. 41, 20354 Hamburg, Germany. TEL 49-40-344434. FAX 49-40-352540. Ed. Dagmar von Schweinitz; Pub. Manfred Zedler. R&P contact: Birgit Koenig. adv. contact: Birgit Koenig. circ. 270,000. **Document type:** consumer publication.

362.7 053.1 GW
▼**KINDER- UND JUGENDLITERATURFORSCHUNG.** 1995. a. (Arbeitsgemeinschaft Kinder- und Jugendliteraturforschung) Verlag J.B. Metzler, Postfach 103241, 70028 Stuttgart, Germany. TEL 49-711-2194102. FAX 49-711-2194119. Eds. Gina Weinkauff, Hans-Heino Ewers. **Document type:** academic/scholarly publication.

KINDERANALYSE. see *PSYCHOLOGY*

286.7 SA
KINDERGARTEN. (Text in English) 1994. q. Southern Africa Union Conference of Seventh-Day Adventists - Suider-Afrika Uniekonferensie van Sewendedag-Adventiste, P.O. Box 468, Bloemfontein 9300, South Africa. illus.

362.7 GW ISSN 0344-3949
KINDERGARTEN HEUTE. 1970. 10/yr. DM.48.50. Verlag Herder GmbH und Co. KG, Hermann-Herder-Str. 4, 79104 Freiburg, Germany. TEL 49-761-2717-208. FAX 49-761-2717210. adv.: color page DM.14090; adv. contact: Bettina Wegmann. circ. 55,000. **Document type:** academic/scholarly publication.

267 GW
KINDERGARTEN UND MISSION; Religionspaedagogischer Arbeitshilfen. 1982. s-a. DM.14. Kindermissionswerk, Stephanstr. 35, 52064 Aachen, Germany. TEL 49-241-4461-0. FAX 49-241-446140. Ed. Arnold Poll. circ. 10,000. **Document type:** academic/scholarly publication.

KINDERMODE. see *CLOTHING TRADE — Fashions*

286.7 SA
KINDERTUIN. (Text in Afrikaans) q. Southern Africa Union Conference of Seventh-Day Adventists - Suider-Afrika Uniekonferensie van Sewendedag-Adventiste, P.O. Box 468, Bloemfontein 9300, South Africa. illus.
   Formerly (until 1994): Primkin-maatjie Kindertuin.

649 NE
KINDERVERZORGING/JEUGDVERZORGING.* 1960. 5/yr. fl.17.50 for members. K & O-Vereniging voor Jeugdwelzijnswerk, Gr. de Combinatie, Jonker Fransstraat 43, 3031 AM Rotterdam, Netherlands. Ed.Bd. circ. 6,500.

362.7 GW ISSN 0936-4463
KINDESWOHL; Fachzeitschrift fuer Pflegekinder- und Adoptionswesen. 1979. q. DM.30. (Bundesverband der Pflege- und Adoptiveltern e.V.) Schulz - Kirchner Verlag GmbH, Itzbachweg 2, 65510 Idstein, Germany. TEL 49-6126-93200. FAX 49-6126-52179. adv.: page DM.1500; trim 180 x 260. bk.rev.; circ. 4,500 (paid). (back issues avail.) **Document type:** academic/scholarly publication.
   Former titles (until 1989): Bundesverband der Pflege- und Adoptiveltern. Info (ISSN 0721-8648); (until 1981): Bundesverband der Pflege- und Adoptiveltern. Informationen (ISSN 0721-863X)

369.4 AU
KIRCHBERGER PFADFINDER JAHRBUCH. 1982. a. free. Pfadfindergruppe Kirchberg am Wechsel, Alte Schule, Postfach 11, A-2880 Kirchberg am Wechsel, Austria. Ed. Bruno Bauer; Pub. Bruno Bauer. circ. 250. **Document type:** bulletin.
   Formerly: Kirchberger Pfadfinderzeitung.

KIRKUS REVIEWS; adult, young adult and children's book reviews. see *PUBLISHING AND BOOK TRADE*

KLINGE. see *SOCIAL SERVICES AND WELFARE*

KLOEVERBLADET. see *CHILDREN AND YOUTH — For*

KNIPPIE. see *CLOTHING TRADE — Fashions*

KNIPPIE'S BABY. see *CLOTHING TRADE — Fashions*

THE KOBRIN LETTER; concerning children's books about real people, places and things. see *LITERATURE*

KONTRAPUNKTE. see *CHILDREN AND YOUTH — For*

369.4 KN ISSN 0454-420X
HQ799.K6
KOREAN YOUTH AND STUDENTS. (Editions in English, French) bi-m. Pyongyang, N. Korea.

KUTTIKALUDE DEEPIKA; children's fortnightly. see *CHILDREN AND YOUTH — For*

KVINNER I BEVEGELSE. see *WOMEN'S INTERESTS*

155.4 649 US ISSN 0740-3437
L A PARENT; magazine for Southern California families. 1981. m. $12. Wingate Enterprises, Ltd., 443 E. Irving Dr., Box 3204, Burbank, CA 91504. TEL 818-846-0400. FAX 818-841-4380. Ed. Jack Bierman. adv. circ. 220,000.
   Description: City magazine for informed parents.

LANDSCHAFTSVERBAND WESTFALEN-LIPPE. MITTEILUNGEN DES LANDESJUGENDAMTES; Beitraege zur Jugendhilfe. see *SOCIAL SERVICES AND WELFARE*

LAPSEN MAILMA/CHILD'S WORLD. see *SOCIAL SERVICES AND WELFARE*

649 US
LAS VEGAS KIDZ MAGAZINE. 1989. m. $20 (effective 1997). 9208 Siena Vista Dr., Las Vegas, NV 89117-7031. TEL 702-233-8388. FAX 702-233-8399. Ed. Mya Collins. adv. contact: Ana Basa. bk.rev. circ. 40,000. **Document type:** bulletin.

369.4 IE
THE LEADER. 1961. bi-m. I£6.50. Catholic Boy Scouts of Ireland, 19 Herbert Pl., Dublin 2, Ireland. TEL 353-1-6761598. FAX 353-1-6768059. Eds. Cathy Walsh, Eric Henry. adv. contact: Pat Hollingsworth. bk.rev. circ. 8,500. (tabloid format; also avail. in microfilm) **Document type:** newsletter.
   Formerly (until 1991): Scout Leader (ISSN 0048-9816)

LEADER (STOCKPORT). see *RELIGIONS AND THEOLOGY*

362.7 US
LEADER MAGAZINE; the magazine of video-based parent, loss and self-esteem education and teacher training. 1985. q. free. Active Parenting Publishers, 810 Franklin Court, Ste. B, Marietta, GA 30067-8943. TEL 770-429-0565. FAX 770-429-0334. E-mail: cservice@activeparenting.com; URL: http://www.activeparenting. com/~info/. Ed. Karen Gray. R&P contact: Deb Pruitt. adv. contact: Karen Gray. bk.rev.; circ. 55,000 (controlled). **Document type:** trade publication.
   Formerly: Active Parenting Leader.
   Refereed Serial

LEARNING DISABILITIES RESEARCH AND PRACTICE. see *EDUCATION — Special Education And Rehabilitation*

LEARNING EDGE; home based education program news. see *EDUCATION — Teaching Methods And Curriculum*

649 US ISSN 8750-2011
LEAVEN (FRANKLIN PARK). bi-m. $12 (effective 1996). La Leche League International, Inc., 1400 N. Meacham Rd., P.O. Box 4079, Schaumburg, IL 60168-4079. TEL 708-455-7730. FAX 708-455-0125. Ed. Judy Torgus. adv.: Color page $1300; trim 7 1/2 x 10; adv. contact: Maureen Schumar. circ. 7,500.
   Description: Articles on breastfeeding and organizational matters.

649 GW ISSN 0047-4274
LEBEN UND ERZIEHEN. 1952. m. DM.45.60. Weltbild Verlag GmbH, Frauentorstr. 5, 86152 Augsburg, Germany. TEL 49-821-3257-0. FAX 49-821-3257201. Ed. Marilis Kurz. adv. contact: Kurt Telschig. bk.rev.; illus. circ. 124,009. **Document type:** consumer publication.

305.23 369.4 SW ISSN 0345-7052
LEDARKONTAKT; tidskrift foer barn- och ungdomsledare. 1956. q. SEK 75 (effective 1994). Helgelsefoerbundet, P.O. Box 67, S-692 22 Kumla, Sweden. TEL 46-19-58-14-00. FAX 46-19-58-14-50. Ed. Susanne Olofsson. adv.: B&W page SEK 2000; adv. contact: Nils Norburg. circ. 1,200. **Document type:** trade publication.

LEDARTIPS; Oe M Us tidskrift foer foeraeldrar, barn- och ungdomsledare. see *SOCIAL SERVICES AND WELFARE*

369.4 NO
LEDERFORUM. 5/yr. Norges K F U M-Speidere, P.O. Box 6810, St. Olavs Pl., N-0130 Oslo, Norway. TEL 47-2-11-50-32. FAX 47-2-20-47-59. adv. circ. 2,600.

LEESGOED; wat en hoe kinderen (leren) lezen. see *EDUCATION*

LIBERIA. MINISTRY OF LABOUR, YOUTH & SPORTS. ANNUAL REPORT. see *SOCIAL SERVICES AND WELFARE*

362.7 FR ISSN 0767-0303
HQ767.8
LIEUX DE L'ENFANCE. 1984. q. 200 F. Editions Eschel, 23 rue Saint-Ferdinand, 75017 Paris, France. (Subscr. to: Centrale des Revues (CDR), 11 rue Gossin, 92543 Montrouge Cedex, France) Ed. Pierre Ferrari.

THE LION AND THE UNICORN; a critical journal of children's literature. see *LITERATURE*

649 US ISSN 1069-6202
THE LITTLE TIMES. 1992. 10/yr. $24.95. Meigher Communications, L.P., 100 Avenue of the Americas, New York, NY 10013. Ed. Lori Bernstein.

649 268 US ISSN 0162-4261
LIVING WITH TEENAGERS. m. $18.95. Southern Baptist Convention, Sunday School Board, 127 Ninth Ave., N., Nashville, TN 37234. TEL 800-458-2772. FAX 615-251-5933. E-mail: customerservice@bss com.
   Description: Deals with issues of parenting teenagers from a Protestant perspective.

CHILDREN AND YOUTH — ABOUT

371 155.4 SW ISSN 1100-3197
LOCUS. 1989. q. SEK 135 (effective 1996). Laerarhoegskolan i Stockholm, Centrum foer Barn- och Ungdomsvetenskap, Box 47308, S-100 74 Stockholm, Sweden. TEL 46-8-737-55-85. FAX 46-8-737-56-94. E-mail: hls-forlag@hls.se. (Subscr. to: H L S Foerlag, Box 34103, S-100 26 Stockholm, Sweden. TEL 46-8-737-56-62. FAX 46-8-656-11-53)
Incorporates (in 1992): Kunskap om Barn (ISSN 0283-8516); Formerly: Kunskap om Barn i Barnomsorg och Skola (ISSN 0281-1782)

LOLLIPOPS; the magazine for preschool and early childhood educators. see EDUCATION — Teaching Methods And Curriculum

649 US
LONG ISLAND PARENTING NEWS. 1989. m. $25. R D M Publishing Corporation, Box 214, Island Park, NY 11558. TEL 516-889-5510. FAX 516-889-5513. Ed. Pat Simms-Elias. R&P contact: Andrew Elias. adv.; bk.rev.; circ. 55,000 (controlled). (tabloid format) **Document type:** newspaper.
Description: Provides local news, features and a calendar of family events.

LOOK AND LISTEN. see RELIGIONS AND THEOLOGY — Protestant

M A K. (Mladosc, Aktivnosc, Kreativnocs) see CHILDREN AND YOUTH — For

M R D D EXPRESS. (Mental Retardation and Developmental Disabilities) see EDUCATION — Special Education And Rehabilitation

362.7 CN ISSN 1187-435X
MAGAZINE ENFANTS QUEBEC. 1988. 10/yr. $18. Mensuel Enfants, 300 Arran St., St-Lambert, PQ J4R 1K5, Canada. TEL 514-672-7027. FAX 514-672-5442. Ed. Mireille Leduc. adv.: B&W page $1840, color page $2400; adv. contact: Carole Martin. circ. 45,000. (tabloid format) **Document type:** newspaper.
Formerly (until 1991): Mensuel Enfants (ISSN 0835-5223)
Description: Offers practical information for parents in the Greater Montreal region concerning children's health, leisure activities, and education.

028.5 800 AT ISSN 0817-0088
MAGPIES; talking about books for children. 1986. 5/yr. Aus.$32 (New Zealand Aus.$39.50; elsewhere Aus.$49.50). Magpies Magazine Pty. Ltd., P.O. Box 563, Hamilton, Qld. 4007, Australia. TEL 61-7-2560064. FAX 61-7-2560922. Ed. Rayma Turton. R&P contact: James Turton. adv. contact: James Turton. bk.rev. circ. 4,500. (back issues avail.) Indexed: Bk.Rev.Ind. (1991-), Child.Bk.Rev.Ind. (1991-), Child.Lit.Abstr. **Document type:** academic/scholarly publication.
—BLDSC (5340.215700); UnCover.
Description: Articles and reviews on children's literature for teachers, librarians and parents.

362.7 GW ISSN 0943-3546
MEIN KIND UND ICH. 1992. m. DM.45.60 (effective 1996). Gruner und Jahr AG & Co. (Munich), Neherstr. 9, 81675 Munich, Germany. TEL 49-89-4152-0. FAX 49-89-4152665. Ed. Norbert Hinze. circ. 186,000. **Document type:** consumer publication.

MERRILL - PALMER QUARTERLY. see PSYCHOLOGY

362.7 618.92 FR ISSN 1258-780X
METIERS DE LA PETITE ENFANCE. 1994. 10/yr. 220 Fr. (foreign 340 F.) (effective 1997). Expansion Scientifique Francaise, 31 bd. de la Tour Maubourg, 75343 Paris Cedex 07, France. TEL 33-1-40626400. FAX 33-1-45556920. (Subscr. to: 15 rue Saint-Benoit, 75278 Paris Cedex 06, France. TEL 33-1-45484260. FAX 33-1-45448155) circ. 10,000.
Description: Includes articles and research, professional news coverage, medical issues and practical mementos.

649 US
METRO PARENT. 1986. 12/yr. $15.95. Thomson Newspapers, Box 13323, Wauwatosa, WI 53213-0323. TEL 414-259-1884. Ed. Kathy Mangold; Ed. Todd koharek. adv. contact: Kathryn Jensen. bk.rev. circ. 45,000. **Document type:** consumer publication.

362.7 US
METRO PARENT MAGAZINE.* 1985. m. $20. 24567 Northwestern Highway, Ste. 150, Southfield, MI 48075-2412. TEL 313-352-0990. Ed. Jody Densmore; Pub. Alyssa Martina. adv. contact: Ruth Robbins. circ. 80,000.
Formerly: All Kids Considered.

028.5 US
METROKIDS. 1989. m. $18. KidStuff Publication, Inc., 1080 N. Delaware Ave., Ste. 702, Philadelphia, PA 19125-4330. TEL 215-551-3200. FAX 215-551-3203. E-mail: metrokid@family.com. Ed. Nancy Lisagor. adv.: B&W page $1950; adv. contact: Carol Valaitis. bk.rev.; video rev.; circ. 75,000 (controlled). **Document type:** consumer publication.
Description: Serves as a resource publication for families who live in the greater metropolitan Philadelphia area.

649 US ISSN 1075-8305
MINNESOTA PARENT. 1987. m. $25. Padres Publishing, 401 N. Third St., Ste. 550, Minneapolis, MN 55401. TEL 612-375-1203. FAX 612-372-3782. Ed. Gail Rosenblum. adv.; bk.rev.; film rev.; video rev. circ. 65,000.
Description: Covers health, education, sports and recreation, travel, the home, shopping and older children for parents.

649 IT ISSN 0026-5756
MIO BEBE. 1966. s-a. L.12000($14) Edizioni Moderne Internazionali, Via Burlamacchi, 11, 20135 Milan, Italy. TEL 39-2-55189297. FAX 39-2-5465954. Ed. Luigi Emilio Lodigiani. adv.: B&W page L.2100000. circ. 64,000.

362.7 051 US
MISS MOM - MISTER MOM.* 1986. bi-m. $15. P.O. Box 1468, Moab, UT 84532-1468. TEL 801-259-5090. Ed. Tina L. Lopez. adv. circ. 7,000.
Description: For single parents.

MISSIONS MOSAIC. see RELIGIONS AND THEOLOGY — Protestant

MITTENDRIN. see TRAVEL AND TOURISM

369.4 XO ISSN 0862-1853
MLADE ROZLETY. 1987. w. Smena Publishing House, Prazska 11, 812 84 Bratislava, Slovakia. (Subscr. to: P N S, Gottwaldovo nam. 6, 813 81 Bratislava, Slovakia) Ed. Lubomir Stancel. bk.rev. circ. 117,000.

649 CN ISSN 0384-0816
MON BEBE. 1951. s-a. Family Communications, Inc. - Communications Famille Inc., 37 Hanna Ave., Toronto, ON M6K 1X1, Canada. Ed. Manon Leymone. adv.; illus. circ. 51,000. **Document type:** consumer publication.

MONTESSORI EDUCATION; the international Montessori journal. see EDUCATION — Teaching Methods And Curriculum

MONTESSORI LIFE. see EDUCATION — Teaching Methods And Curriculum

649 US
MORRIS COUNTY FAMILY. 1994. 8/yr. $18 (effective 1997). Kids Monthly Publications, Inc., Box 159, Westfield, NJ 07091. TEL 908-232-2913. Ed. Farn Dupre; Pub. Cindy Mironovich. R&P contact: Farn Dupre. adv. contact: Cindy Mironovich. circ. 110,000. cols./p.: 4; pp./issue: 40. (tabloid format) **Document type:** consumer publication, newspaper.
Description: Contains articles on effective child rearing, health, education, child care, and other topics of importance and interest to New Jersey parents, particularly those in Morris County.
Refereed Serial

MOTDRAG; Accent. see DRUG ABUSE AND ALCOHOLISM

649 UK ISSN 0047-8172
MOTHER & BABY. 1956. m. £16.20 (foreign £27.30) (effective 1996). E M A P - Elan, 20 Orange St., London WC2H 7ED, England. TEL 44-171-957-8383. FAX 44-171-930-5728. (Subscr. to: Tower Publishing Services Ltd., Tower House, Sovereign Park, Lathkill St., Market Harborough, Leics. LE16 9EF, England. TEL 44-1858-468811. FAX 44-1858-432164) adv.; bk.rev. circ. 110,000. **Document type:** consumer publication.

MOTHER AND CHILD. see WOMEN'S INTERESTS

649 UK ISSN 1353-7059
MOTHER & CHILD HEALTH.* 1986. a. Nexus Business Communications Ltd., Warwick House, Azalea Dr., Swanley, Kent BR8 8HY, England. Ed. Jackie Marsh; Pub. Lynn Pearce. adv.: B&W page £2667, color page £4200; trim 184 x 130; adv. contact: Ruth Dickinson. circ. 300,000. **Document type:** consumer publication.
Formerly: Pregnancy and Babycare.
Description: Offers practical advice and health care for the pregnant woman and the new baby or toddler through school age.

306.874 US
MOTHER-TO-MOTHER.* 1980. bi-m. $25 to individuals; institutions $35. Mothers Without Custody, 609 North Ave., Crystal Lake, IL 60014-4981. TEL 800-457-6962. Ed. Jennifer Isham. **Document type:** newsletter.
Description: Discusses issues affecting non-custodial mothers.

MOTHERING; the magazine of natural family living. see WOMEN'S HEALTH

MOUNTAIN SPIRIT. see SOCIAL SERVICES AND WELFARE

MUCHACHA. see CHILDREN AND YOUTH — For

649 GW ISSN 0047-8482
MUTTER UND KIND. 1928. 3/yr. DM.6. Dr. Curt Haefner Verlag, Bachstr. 14-16, 69121 Heidelberg, Germany. TEL 49-6221-6446-0. FAX 49-6221-644640. (Subscr. to: Postfach 106060, 69050 Heidelberg, Germany) adv.; illus. circ. 900,000. **Document type:** consumer publication. —CCC.

649 640 AT ISSN 0813-4626
MY BABY. 1983. a. Aus.$5.95 (foreign Aus.$9.50). Magazine House Pty. Ltd., P.O. Box 1067, Crows Nest, N.S.W. 2065, Australia. TEL 61-2-94382399. FAX 61-2-94363014. Ed. Carol Fallows. adv.; bk.rev. circ. 40,000. **Document type:** consumer publication.

MY FRIEND; a Catholic magazine for kids. see RELIGIONS AND THEOLOGY — Roman Catholic

362.7 364.6 UK
N A C R O YOUTH CRIME SECTION. q. £10 to non-members; members £5 (effective 1996). National Association for the Care and Resettlement of Offenders, 169 Clapham Rd., London SW9 0PU, England. TEL 44-171-582-6500. FAX 44-171-735-4666. **Document type:** bulletin.
Description: Essential information for practitioners and others interested in youth crime and young offenders.

N A Y S I RESOURCE LIST. (North American Youth Sport Institute) see SPORTS AND GAMES

362.7 360 UK
N C H ACTION FOR CHILDREN FACTFILE. a. N C H Action for Children, 85 Highbury Park, London N5 1UD, England. TEL 0171-226-2033. **Document type:** bulletin.
Formerly (until 1994): N C H Factfile.

301 UK
N C O P F ANNUAL REPORT. a. £5.25. National Council for One Parent Families, 255 Kentish Town Rd., London NW5 2LX, England. TEL 44-171-267-1361. FAX 44-171-482-4851. **Document type:** corporate report.

CHILDREN AND YOUTH — ABOUT

028.5 II
NANDAN. (Text in Hindi) 1964. m. Rs.65 (foreign Rs.375). Hindustan Times, Ltd., 18-20 Kasturba Gandhi Marg, New Delhi 110 001, India. TEL 91-11-331-8201. FAX 91-11-332-1189. TELEX TIMES IN 66310. Ed. Jai Prakash Bharti. adv.; bk.rev. circ. 220,000.

NATIONAL ADVOCATE. see SOCIAL SERVICES AND WELFARE

NATIONAL CENTER FOR JUVENILE JUSTICE. ANNUAL REPORT. see CRIMINOLOGY AND LAW ENFORCEMENT

362 UK ISSN 0302-1998
NATIONAL CHILDREN'S BUREAU. ANNUAL REVIEW. a. National Children's Bureau, 8 Wakley St., London EC1V 7QE, England. TEL 071-278-9441. FAX 071-278-9512. (back issues avail.) **Document type:** corporate report.
Description: Informs members of the year's developments in social policy and the Bureau's response to them. Outlines the year's expenditure and income.

NATIONAL DEAF CHILDREN'S SOCIETY. ANNUAL REPORT. see HANDICAPPED — Hearing Impaired

369.4 374 AT ISSN 0158-9539
NETWORK NEWS. 1975. q. Aus.$40 (effective 1995 & 1996). Network of Community Activities, 66 Albion St., Surry Hills, Sydney, N.S.W. 2010, Australia. TEL 61-2-212-3244. FAX 61-2-281-9645. Ed. Judy Finlason. R&P contact: J. Finlason. adv. contact: Jone Lunsmann. bk.rev.; index. circ. 1,000. (tabloid format) **Document type:** newspaper.

THE NEW ADVOCATE. see LITERATURE

392.1 649 US ISSN 8756-9981
NEW BEGINNINGS (FRANKLIN PARK); every baby is a new beginning. 1958. bi-m. $18 to non-members (foreign $22); membership $30 (effective 1996). La Leche League International, Inc, 1400 N. Meacham Rd., P.O. Box 4079, Schaumburg, IL 60168-4079. TEL 708-445-7730; 847-519-7730. FAX 708-455-0125. Ed. Judy Torgus. adv.; Color page $1620; trim 7 1/8 x 9 3/8; adv. contact: Maureen Schumar. bk.rev.; illus.; index. circ. 40,000. (also avail. in microfilm from UMI)
Formerly (until 1985): La Leche League News.
Description: Includes stories, poems, and research materials for parents of breastfed infants.
Refereed Serial

THE NEW GOOD APPLE NEWSPAPER. see EDUCATION — Teaching Methods And Curriculum

NEW JERSEY FAMILY; a news magazine for parents and kids. see CHILDREN AND YOUTH — For

649 US
NEW MOON NETWORK; for adults who care about girls. (Supplement to: New Moon (ISSN 1069-238X)) 1993. bi-m. $25 (Canada $30; elsewhere $37) (with New Moon $49; Canada $54; elsewhere $64) (effective 1998). New Moon Publishing, Box 3587, Duluth, MN 55803-3587. TEL 218-728-5507. FAX 218-728-0314. E-mail: newmoon@computerpro.com; URL: http://www.newmoon.org. Ed. Joe Kelly; Pubs. Nancy Gruver, Joe Kelly. R&P contact: Joe Kelly. adv. contact: Joe Kelly. circ. 3,500 (paid). (also avail. in looseleaf format; back issues avail.) **Document type:** consumer publication, newsletter.
Formerly: New Moon Parenting (ISSN 1070-1451)
Description: For parents, teachers, counselors and others working to broaden horizons for girls.

618 649 CN ISSN 1193-9397
NEW MOTHER. French edition: Mere Nouvelle (ISSN 1193-9389) 1979. s-a. free. (Today's Parent Group) Professional Publishing Associates, 269 Richmond St. W., Toronto, ON M5V 1X1, Canada. TEL 416-596-8680. FAX 416-596-1991. Ed. Holly Bennett. adv.; circ. 160,000 (controlled).
Formerly (until 1992): Chatelaine's New Mother (ISSN 0708-5303)
Description: Provides articles on parenting the newborn, feeding, development and daily care issues.

NEW YORK (STATE). ASSEMBLY. STANDING COMMITTEE ON CHILDREN AND FAMILIES. ANNUAL REPORT. see SOCIAL SERVICES AND WELFARE

790.019 US ISSN 0896-7199
NEW YORK FAMILY; the magazine just for the N Y parent. 1986. 11/yr. $22. Family Publishing Group, Inc., 141 Halstead Ave., Ste. 3D, Mamaroneck, NY 10543-2652. TEL 914-381-7474. Eds. Susan Ross, Felice Shapiro; Pubs. Susan Ross, Felice Shapiro. adv.; bk.rev. circ. 60,000. (back issues avail.) **Document type:** consumer publication.

NEW YORK FAMILY LAW UPDATE. see LAW — Family And Matrimonial Law

028.5 340 NZ ISSN 0114-166X
NEW ZEALAND CHILDCARE ASSOCIATION. REPORT TO ANNUAL CONFERENCE. (Text in English, Maori) 1963. a. New Zealand Childcare Association, P.O. Box 11-863, Wellington, New Zealand. Ed. Rose Cole. circ. 800 (controlled). (also avail. in diskette format; record; back issues avail.) **Document type:** corporate report.

NO. see WOMEN'S INTERESTS

371.8 YU
NON; list mladih srbije. 1973. w. 12000 din.($30) Savez Socijalisticke Omladine Srbije, Republicka Konferencija, Ho Si Minova 27, 11070 Novi Beograd, Yugoslavia. TEL 011 135804. Ed. Zoran Miljatovic. bk.rev.; film rev.; play rev.; abstr.; illus. circ. 25,000.
Formerly (until 1984): Omladinske Novine.

649 US
▼**NORTHWEST FAMILY MAGAZINE.** 1995. m. $18; newsstand price: free. Family Publishing, 1014 12th St., Bellingham, WA 98225. TEL 360-734-3025. FAX 360-734-1550. E-mail: nwfamily@family.com; URL: http://www.nwfamily.com. Ed. Colleen Rupp; Pub. Kevin Rupp. adv.: page $1650; trim 10 1/2 x 13. bk.rev.; film rev.; software rev.; tele.rev.; video rev. circ. 33,000. (tabloid format; back issues avail.) **Document type:** consumer publication.
Description: Parenting resource for families living between Seattle and Vancouver, Canada. Covers local family events and activities, health, education, and entertainment.

369.4 LS
NOUM LAO/LAO YOUTH. (Text in Lao) 1979. fortn. Lao People's Revolutionary Youth Union, Vientiane, Laos. Ed. Douangdy Inthavong. circ. 6,000.

NUESTRA TAREA. see RELIGIONS AND THEOLOGY — Protestant

649 UK ISSN 0029-6422
NURSERY WORLD. devoted to professional, child care and pre-school education. 1925. w. £45. Nursery World Ltd., 5th Fl., Lector Ct., 151-153 Farringdon Rd., London EC1R 3AD, England. TEL 44-171-837-7224. FAX 44-171-278-3896. Ed. Ruth Beattie; Pub. Jane Smith. adv. contact: Tracey Davies. bk.rev. circ. 25,000. **Document type:** academic/scholarly publication.
—BLDSC (6187.029500).

649.1 US ISSN 1084-9041
THE NURTURING PARENT. vol.3, 1995. q. $18.50 (foreign $28.50). 3213 W. Main St., Ste. 153, Rapid City, SD 57702-2314. TEL 605-399-2990. FAX 605-399-3224. E-mail: tnparent@aol.com. Ed. Jacquelyn deLaveaga. adv.; bk.rev.; circ. 2,000 (paid). **Document type:** newsletter.
Description: Encourages attachment-continuum parenting practices.

362.7 US
NURTURING THE CHILD AS ARTIST OCCASIONAL PAPERS. irreg., latest no.27, 1994. $2.50 to non-members; members, schools, libraries free. Vermont Academy of Arts & Sciences, 2 Buxton Ave., Middletown Springs, VT 05757. TEL 802-235-2302. Ed.Bd. **Document type:** monographic series.

301 UK ISSN 0143-0211
O P T: ONE PARENT TIMES. 1979. irreg. £0.80 per no. National Council for One Parent Families, 255 Kentish Town Rd., London NW5 2LX, England. TEL 44-171-267-1361. FAX 44-171-482-4851. bk.rev.; illus. circ. 2,500. **Document type:** newsletter.
Formerly: One Parent Families.
Description: News of Council activities and campaigns.

362.7 US
▼**OBLIVION.** 1995. q. 120 State Ave., N.E., Ste. 76, Olympia, WA 98501-8212. E-mail: oblivion@oblivion.net; URL: http://www.oblivion.net.
●Also available online.

OFFSPRING - BOING. see CHILDREN AND YOUTH — For

370 CY ISSN 0253-0910
OIKOGENEIA KAI SKOLEIO/FAMILY AND SCHOOL; dimenaio pedagogiko periodiko. (Text in Greek) 1970. bi-m. £C15 (foreign $12) (effective 1997). Pancyprian School for Parents, 18 Archbishop Makarios III Ave., Flat 8, 5th Fl., Nicosia, Cyprus. TEL 357-2-454466. Ed. A.D. Christodoulides. adv.; bk.rev. circ. 7,000.
Description: Discusses the theoretical and practical aspects of child development, parent-child relationships, and other relevant problems for parents and teachers.

OMVAARDAREN. see SOCIAL SERVICES AND WELFARE

ONCE UPON A TIME. see PUBLISHING AND BOOK TRADE

306.874 362.7 US ISSN 1078-0831
OPEN ADOPTION BIRTHPARENT. 1994. q. $16 (effective 1996). R-Squared Press, 2113 Arborview Blvd., Ann Arbor, MI 48103. TEL 313-930-6564. (Subscr. to: 721 Hawthorne St., Royal Oak, MI 48067. TEL 810-543-0997) Ed. Brenda Romanchik; Pub. Daniel M. Romanchik. R&P contact: Brenda Romanchik. bk.rev.; circ. 500 (paid). (back issues avail.) **Document type:** newsletter.
Description: Helps birthparents make the most of their open adoption relationship.

649 UK
OPEN HOUSE. 1894. 3/yr. free. Spurgeon's Child Care, 74 Welling Borough Rd., Rushden, Northants NN10 9TY, England. TEL 44-1933-412412. FAX 44-1933-412010. Ed. Marilyn Willis. bk.rev. circ. 17,000. **Document type:** newsletter.
Formerly (until 1984, vol.24, no.10): Within Our Gates (ISSN 0043-6992)

OPSIS KALOPSIS; om barn- och ungdomskultur. see CHILDREN AND YOUTH — For

649 NE ISSN 0165-6414
OUDERS VAN NU. 1967. m. fl.72; newsstand price: fl.9.50. Uitgeverij Spaarnestad B.V., Postbus 1, 2000 MA Haarlem, Netherlands. TEL 31-23-304304. FAX 31-23-361624. adv.; illus.; circ. 145,295 (paid). **Document type:** consumer publication.

649 UK ISSN 1355-8269
OUR BABY. 1994. m. £19.20 (foreign £25.50) (effective 1996). I P C Magazines, Specialist Magazine Group (Subsidiary of: Reed Elsevier group), King's Reach Tower, Stamford St., London SE1 9LS, England. TEL 44-171-261-5000. FAX 44-1444-445599. **Document type:** consumer publication.

790.019 370.15 US ISSN 1055-1336
OUR GIFTED CHILDREN. 1991. m. $30. Royal Fireworks Press, Box 399, Unionville, NY 10988. TEL 914-726-4444. FAX 914-726-3824. E-mail: rfpress@frontiercomm.net. Ed. Michael Clay Thompson; Pub. T.M. Kemnitz. R&P contact: Myrna Kaye. bk.rev. **Document type:** trade publication.
Description: Directed to those concerned with gifted children and covers psychology, schooling, work force, and leadership.

649 US
OUR KIDS HOUSTON. 1988. m. Branford Publishing, 8400 Blanco Rd., Ste. 201, San Antonio, TX 78216-3055. TEL 713-781-7535. FAX 713-781-0405. Ed. Gail B. Goodwin; Pub. Robert Stanley. R&P contact: Nancy Diehl. adv. contact: Mary Chatoney. circ. 75,000.
Description: Lists activities and resources for children and their parents.

CHILDREN AND YOUTH — ABOUT

649 US
OUR KIDS SAN ANTONIO. 1985. m. Branford Publishing, 8400 Blanco Rd., Ste. 201, San Antonio, TX 78216-3055. TEL 210-349-6667. FAX 210-349-5618. Ed. Nancy S. Diehl; Pub. Robert Stanley. adv.: B&W page $1430, color page $2030; adv. contact: Pat Ranotowski. circ. 42,000.
   Description: Lists activities and resources for children and their parents.

OUR MISSIONS WORLD. see *RELIGIONS AND THEOLOGY — Protestant*

OUR WAY. see *RELIGIONS AND THEOLOGY — Judaic*

649 028.5 CN
OWL CANADIAN FAMILY. 6/yr. Can.$24 (foreign $20) (effective 1997). Multi-Vision Publishing, 655 Bay St., Ste. 1100, Toronto, ON M5G 2K4, Canada. TEL 800-387-4378. FAX 416-971-5294. (Subscr. in US to: 25 Boxwood Lane, Buffalo, NY 14225) Ed. Kristin Jenkins.
   Description: Contains short, informative articles, family entertainment reviews, news and reader advice.

370.193 362.7 US
P T A COMMUNICATOR. 1922. 9/yr. $8. Texas Congress of Parents and Teachers, 408 W. 11th St., Austin, TX 78701-2199. TEL 512-476-6769. FAX 512-476-8152. E-mail: txpta@onr.com; URL: http://www.onr.com/tpta.html. Ed. Linda Jackson. bk.rev. circ. 5,000. **Document type:** newsletter.
   Former titles: Texas P T A Communicator; Texas P T A; Texas Parent-Teacher (ISSN 0040-4578)
   Description: Contains organization news, advocates for children, and informs parents.

649 MX ISSN 0188-0667
PADRES E HIJOS. 1980. m. Editorial Samra, S.A. de C.V., Lucio Blanco 435, Azcapotzalco, 02400 Mexico D.F., Mexico. TEL 5-352-6444. Ed. Pilar S. Hoyos. circ. 105,000.

649 US ISSN 0737-5158
PAEDONOSON;* an international journal of chronic illness and disability in childhood. 1984. q. Eterna International, Inc., Box 5731, Hauppauge, NY 11788-0154. Ed. Stephen B. Parrish. adv.; bk.rev.; abstr.; charts; illus.; index.

PAEDOVITA; an international journal of child-life. see *SOCIAL SERVICES AND WELFARE*

649 PO
PAIS & FILHOS. 1991. m. newsstand price: Esc. 500. Motorpress Lisboa, Rua Sacadura Cabral 26, 3oD, 1495 Dafundo, Portugal. TEL 351-1-4149900. FAX 351-1-4140327. Ed. Laurinda Alves; Pub. Luis Penha e Costa. adv. contact: Cecilia Prata. circ. 19,196. **Document type:** consumer publication.

649 618.2 BL ISSN 0030-9567
PAIS E FILHOS; revista mensal da familia moderna. 1968. m. $42. Bloch Editores S.A., Rua do Russel 766-804, 22210-000 Rio de Janeiro, RJ, Brazil. TEL 021-5554000. FAX 021-2059998. TELEX 2121525 BLOC. Ed. Silvia Leal. adv.; bk.rev.; film rev.; charts; illus. circ. 120,000. **Document type:** consumer publication.
   Description: Contains information about pregnancy and children from birth to 12 years.

369.4 PK ISSN 0030-9605
THE PAK-SCOUT. (Editions in English and Urdu) 1948. m. Rs.35($3) Pakistan Boy Scouts Association, Sumabl Park Aabpara, Muree Link Road, Islambad, Pakistan. Ed. Mohammad Rafiq Aslam. adv.; bk.rev.; charts; illus. circ. 1,000. **Document type:** bulletin.

155 US ISSN 0887-0365
PARENT AND PRESCHOOLER NEWSLETTER; a monthly exploration of early childhood topics. (Bilingual English - Spanish edition avail.) 1986. m. $30 (foreign $42; bilingual edition $40; foreign $52). North Shore Child & Family Guidance Center, Lindner Early Childhood Training Institute, 480 Old Westbury Rd., Roslyn Heights, NY 11577-2215. TEL 516-626-1971; 800-595-9053. FAX 516-626-8043. Ed. Neala Schwartzburg. bk.rev.; illus.; index; circ. 3,800 (paid). (back issues avail.) **Document type:** newsletter.
   Description: Explores child development, birth to 6, and family life issues for librarians, educators, and other professionals. Includes theory, practical activities, and children's health information. Lists resources for children and adults.

155.4 362.7 CN ISSN 1191-002X
PARENT - TO - PARENT. 1987. bi-m. Can.$18. Parent-to-Parent, P.O. Box 85324, Burlington, ON L7R 4K5, Canada. TEL 416-335-3549. FAX 416-336-0761. Ed. Angela Greenway; Pub. B. Burrows. adv. contact: Dee Gonsalves. bk.rev. circ. 60,000. (back issues avail.) **Document type:** newsletter.
   Description: Offers information to help adults understand both child and adult behavior and motivation from a psychological perspective.

649 US ISSN 0896-1468
PARENTGUIDE NEWS. 1984. m. $11.90. Parents Guide Network, Corp., 419 Park Ave. S., 13th Fl., New York, NY 10016. TEL 212-213-8840. Ed. Leslie Elgort; Pub. Steve Elgort. adv. circ. 200,000. (tabloid format) **Document type:** newspaper.
   Description: Parenting newspaper for New York and New Jersey parents of children under 12 years of age.

649 US ISSN 0890-247X
PARENTING. 1987. m. (10/yr.) $18 (foreign $26). Health Publishing Group (Subsidiary of: Time Warner Inc.), 301 Howard St., 17th Fl., San Francisco, CA 94105-2252. TEL 415-546-7575. FAX 415-546-0578. (Subscr. to: P.O. Box 56861, Boulder, CO 80323) Ed. Anne Cougar. adv.; film rev.; index. circ. 1,100,000. (also avail. in Braille; back issues avail.) **Document type:** consumer publication.
   —UMI.
   Description: For parents of children of 0 to 10 years old.

649.4 II
PARENTING. (Text in English) 1992. m. newsstand price: Rs.35. First City Publications P. Ltd., A 602 Som Vihar, New Delhi 110 022, India. TEL 91-11-6169111. FAX 91-11-6103740. Ed. Bharat Kapur; Pub. Bharat Kapur. adv.: B&W page Rs.35000, color page Rs.45000; trim 178 x 242. **Document type:** consumer publication.

649.155 US
▼**PARENTING FOR HIGH POTENTIAL.** 1996. q. $50 (foreign $60). National Association for Gifted Children, 1707 L St., N.W., Ste. 550, Washington, DC 20036-4201. TEL 202-785-4268. Ed. James Alvino. R&P contact: Peter D. Rosenstein. adv. contact: Peter D. Rosenstein. **Document type:** consumer publication.
   Description: For parents and teachers who want to help develop the gifts and talents that will enable all children to reach their full potential.

PARENTING FOR PEACE & JUSTICE NETWORK NEWSLETTER. see *EDUCATION — Adult Education*

155.4 649 US
PARENTING MAGAZINE OF ORANGE COUNTY. 1981. m. $12. Wingate Enterprises, Ltd., 443 E. Irving Dr., Box 3204, Burbank, CA 91504. TEL 818-846-0400. FAX 818-841-4380. Ed. Jack Bierman. adv.

PARENTING'S HEALTHY PREGNANCY. see *MEDICAL SCIENCES — Obstetrics And Gynecology*

649 648 US ISSN 1074-326X
PARENTLIFE. m. $19.95. (Southern Baptist Convention, Sunday School Board) LifeWay Press, 127 Ninth Ave., N., Nashville, TN 37234-0140. TEL 800-458-2772.
   Formed by the merger of: Living with Children (ISSN 0456-3271) & Living with Preschoolers (ISSN 0162-4350)
   Description: Deals with issues of parenting children from a Protestant perspective.

649 US ISSN 0195-0967
HQ768
PARENTS; on rearing children from crib to college. 1926. m. $12.75; newsstand price: $2.50. Gruner & Jahr U.S.A. Publishing, 110 Fifth Ave., New York, NY 10011. TEL 212-499-2000. (Subscr. to: Box 3042, Harlan, IA 51537. TEL 800-727-3682) Ed. Ann Pleshette Murphy. adv.; bk.rev.; index. circ. 1,737,000. (also avail. in microform from UMI; reprint service avail. from UMI) **Indexed:** Abr.R.G., Acad.Ind., Biog.Ind., Bk.Rev.Ind. (1965-), Child.Bk.Rev.Ind. (1965-), CHNI, Consum.Ind., Educ.Ind., Hlth.Ind., Ind.How To Do It (1978-1981), Mag.Ind., PMR, Pt.de Rep., R.G., R.G.Abstr., TOM. **Document type:** consumer publication.
   ●Also available online. Vendor(s): Information Access Co.
   Also available on CD-ROM. Producer(s): UMI.
   —KR SourceOne; UnCover.
   Former titles: Parents' Magazine (ISSN 0161-4193); Parents' Magazine and Better Homemaking; Parents' Magazine and Better Family Living (ISSN 0031-191X); Incorporates (1976-1981): Parents Home (ISSN 0278-1409); Which incorporated (in Apr. 1981): Handy Andy Magazine (ISSN 0162-6663)
   Description: Emphasizes family formation and growth. Focuses on the needs and concerns of today's woman.

649 FR ISSN 0553-2159
HQ768
PARENTS. 1969. m. 140 F. (foreign 250 F.). Filipacchi Medias, 151 rue Anatole France, 92598 Levallois Perret Cedex, France. TEL 33-1-41347330. FAX 33-1-41347503. (Subscr. to: 5 rue Naracci, 59884 Lille Cedex 9, France. TEL 33-1-20121110. FAX 33-1-20121111) Ed. Roger Coral. circ. 700,000. **Indexed:** Consum.Ind., Curr.Lit.Fam.Plan., Pt.de Rep. (1979-), R.G.Abstr. **Document type:** consumer publication.

649 UK
PARENTS. 1976. m. £18 (foreign £30) (effective 1996). E M A P - Elan, 20 Orange St., London WC2H 7ED, England. TEL 44-171-957-8383. FAX 44-171-930-5728. (Subscr. to: Tower Publishing Services Ltd., Tower House, Sovereign Park, Lathkill St., Market Harborough, Leics. LE16 9EF, England. TEL 44-1858-468811. FAX 44-1858-432164) Ed. S. Kilby. adv. contact: Julie Hughes. **Indexed:** R.G.Abstr. **Document type:** consumer publication.

PARENTS AND CHILDREN TOGETHER ONLINE. see *CHILDREN AND YOUTH — For*

796.1 649 US
PARENTS AND KIDS DIRECTORY. 1985. q. $18.95. Marquee Communications, Inc., Box 1257, Peter Cooper Station, New York, NY 10276. (Subscr. to: Box 1717, Dover, NJ 07802-1717. TEL 201-328-0204) Ed. W.G. Weber. adv.; bk.rev.; play rev. circ. 20,000. (back issues avail.)
   Description: Guide to opportunities in family health, education and entertainment in the New York metropolitan area.

649 US
PARENTS BABY CARE. (Avail. in 7 age-specific editions.) 1986. a. free to new parents. Gruner & Jahr U.S.A. Publishing, 110 Fifth Ave., New York, NY 10011. TEL 212-463-1636. circ. 2,500,000. **Document type:** consumer publication.
   Description: Offers articles selected from Parents magazine.

649 US
PARENTS' CHOICE (WABAN); a review of children's media. 1978. q. $20. Parents' Choice Foundation, Box 185, Waban, MA 02168. TEL 617-965-5913. FAX 617-965-4516. E-mail: dianahg@erols.com. Ed. Diana Huss Green. R&P contact: Maggie Russell. adv. contact: Ann Brathwaite. bk.rev.; film rev.; software rev.; video rev. circ. 25,000. (tabloid format; back issues avail.) **Document type:** consumer publication.
   Formerly (until 1979): It's the Parents' Choice (ISSN 0161-8164)
   Description: Provides parents with information to help their children learn in and out of school, including reviews of children's books, videos, toys, games, computer products, TV and more.

CHILDREN AND YOUTH — ABOUT

790.019 CC ISSN 1003-2983
PARENTS' DIGEST/FUMU WENZHAI. (Text in Chinese) 1985. bi-m. Y15($48) Zhongguo Ertong Fazhan Zhongxin - Chinese Child Development Center, Guanyuan, Beijing 100035, People's Republic of China. TEL 603-1897. FAX 602-4579. Ed. Li Shushen. adv.; bk.rev. **Document type:** abstracting/indexing.
  Formerly (until Jan. 1994): Chinese Child Development - Zhongguo Ertong Fazhan.

371 US ISSN 1046-0446
PARENTS MAKE THE DIFFERENCE; practical ideas for parents to help their children. 1989. m. (Sep.-May). $79. Parent Institute, Box 7474, Fairfax Station, VA 22039-7474. TEL 703-323-9170; 800-756-5525. FAX 703-323-9173. Ed. John H. Wherry. (looseleaf format; back issues avail.) **Document type:** newsletter.
  Description: Contains practical ideas for parents to help their children do better in school.

362.7 UK ISSN 1362-5551
PARENTS NEWS. 1993. 11/yr. £12 (foreign £20) (effective 1997). 10 The Manor Dr., Worcester Park, Surrey KT4 7LG, England. TEL 44-181-337-6337. FAX 44-181-715-2842. E-mail: editor@parents-news.co.uk; URL: http://www.businessweb.co.uk/parentnews/index.html; http://www.users.dircon.co.uk/~parentsn. Eds. Fergus McCarthy, Penny McCarthy. adv.: page £1514; trim 270 x 370; adv. contact: Fergus McCarthy. bk.rev.; circ. 83,000. (tabloid format) **Document type:** newsletter.

649 US
PARENTS' PLUS FAMILY TRAVEL & LEISURE. 1993. q. $8 (effective 1995). Parents' Plus, Inc., 670 Centre St., Jamaica Plain, MA 02130. TEL 617-522-1515. FAX 617-522-1694. E-mail: tbpp@aol.com. Pub. Betsy Weaver. adv.: B&W page $2300; trim 8 1/4 x 10 3/4; adv. contact: Dena O'Shaughnessy. bk.rev. (back issues avail.)
  Formerly: Our Times.
  Description: Travel and leisure guide for families with children 0-12. Regional to New England and New York and includes calendar listings of family-friendly attractions and events.

649 US ISSN 0889-8863
PARENTS' PRESS. 1980. m. 1454 Sixth St., Berkeley, CA 94710-1431. TEL 415-524-1602. FAX 415-524-0912. Ed. Dixie M. Jordan. circ. 75,000.

371 US ISSN 1071-5118
PARENTS STILL MAKE THE DIFFERENCE; practical ideas for parents to help their children. 1993. m. (Sep.-May). $79. Parent Institute, Box 7474, Fairfax Station, VA 22039-7474. TEL 703-323-9170; 800-756-5525. FAX 703-323-9173. Ed. John H. Wherry. bk.rev. (looseleaf format; back issues avail.) **Document type:** newsletter.
  Description: Ideas for parents of children in grades 7-12, to help their children do better in school.

PARIYAL KALYAN. see SOCIAL SERVICES AND WELFARE

369.4 FI ISSN 0085-4794
PARTIOJOHTAJA/SCOUTLEDAREN. 1970. 6/yr. FIM 130. Suomen Partiolaiset - Guides and Scouts of Finland, Kylaenvanhimmantie 2n, FIN-00640 Helsinki, Finland. TEL 0-728-2811. FAX 0-7522-681. E-mail: Hanne.Partanen@SP.Partio.Fi. Ed. Hanne Partanen. adv. circ. 16,000.

PARTNERS. see RELIGIONS AND THEOLOGY — Protestant

362.7 613.9 US ISSN 1071-3158
PASSAGES. Key Title: Passages (Washington, D.C.). (Text in English, French, Spanish) 1978. 3/yr. $15. Advocates for Youth, 1025 Vermont Ave., N.W., Ste. 200, Washington, DC 20005. TEL 202-347-5700. FAX 202-347-2263. TELEX 425900 SWIFT UI ATT CFP. Ed. Cate Lane. bk.rev.; film rev.; charts; illus.; stat. (back issues avail.) **Document type:** newsletter.
  Description: Includes summaries of projects on adolescent reproductive health.

PEDIATRICS FOR PARENTS; the monthly newsletter for caring adults. see MEDICAL SCIENCES — Pediatrics

362.7 US
PENN STATE SERIES ON CHILD AND ADOLESCENT DEVELOPMENT. irreg. Lawrence Erlbaum Associates, Inc., 10 Industrial Ave., Mahwah, NJ 07430-2262. TEL 201-236-9500; 800-926-6579. FAX 201-236-0072. E-mail: jamsel@erlbaum.com; URL: http://www.erlbaum.com. Eds. David Palermo, Richard Lerner. **Document type:** monographic series.

268 282 FR ISSN 1164-9526
PERLIN. (Supplement avail.: Parents) 1956. w. 372 F. (foreign 684 F.) (effective 1997). Fleurus Presse, 21 rue du Faubourg St-Antoine, 75550 Paris Cedex 11, France. TEL 33-1-40026300. (Subscr. to: B.P. 72, 77932 Perthes Cedex, France. TEL 33-1-64380389) Ed. Valerie Fert. circ. 150,000.
  Former titles (until 1992): Perlin et Pinpin (ISSN 1153-0308); (until 1990): Perlin (ISSN 0244-9811); (until 1980): Perlin et Pinpin (ISSN 0031-546X)
  Description: For children 5-8 years old, to develop their reading, memory and observational skills.

PHILOSOPHY FOR CHILDREN NEWSLETTER. see PHILOSOPHY

PIED PIPER. see LAW — Family And Matrimonial Law

155.649 US ISSN 1065-2671
PIERCE COUNTY PARENT; a monthly guide for parents. 1985. m. $15. Northwest Parent Publishing, Inc., 2107 Elliott Ave., Ste. 303, Seattle, WA 98121. TEL 206-272-0775. FAX 206-441-4919. Ed. Susan Garrett. adv. contact: Alayne Sulkin. bk.rev.; film rev. circ. 15,000. (tabloid format) **Document type:** consumer publication.
  Formerly: Parent Connection.
  Description: For parents, educators, and child-care providers. Provides information on what to do and where to go with children.

362.7 US
PITTSBURGH'S CHILD. Pittsburgh's preference for parenting news. 1988. 12/yr. $25. Honey Hill Publishing, Inc., Winwood Bldg., 3611 Bakerstown Rd., Box 374, Bakerstown, PA 15007. TEL 412-443-1891. FAX 412-443-1877. Ed. Patricia Poshard; Pub. Marilyn Honeywill. adv.: B&W page $1600; trim 10 x 12 3/8; adv. contact: Debbie Iszauk. bk.rev.; video rev. circ. 48,000. (tabloid format) **Document type:** newspaper.
  Description: Covers health, education, the arts and activities pertaining to parents and children.

362.7 BL
PIXOTE; revista sobre meninos e meninas. 1993. Cr.$100 per no. Centro de Articulacao de Populacoes Marginalizadas, Nucleo de Comunicacao, Rua da Lapa 200-809, Centro, 20021 Rio de Janeiro RJ, Brazil. TEL 55-21-2246771. FAX 55-21-2326249. circ. 3,000.

790.019 US ISSN 1062-6956
PLAY. 1992. bi-m. $12; newsstand price: $3.95. M.E.G., Inc., 3620 N.W. 43rd St., Ste. D, Gainesville, FL 32606. TEL 904-375-3705. FAX 904-375-7268. Ed. Roy Parkhurst. adv.: B&W page $3500, color page $4500; trim 8 3/8 x 11 x 1/8; adv. contact: Lori B. Fagien. circ. 100,000. **Document type:** consumer publication.
  Description: Brings together a vast array of information and entertainment for today's parent; bridges the gap of learning and playing.

649 362.7 CN ISSN 0835-4014
PLAY AND PARENTING CONNECTIONS. 1978. q. $25. Canada Association of Toy Libraries and Parent Resource Centres, 205-120 Holland Ave., Ottawa, Ont. K1Y 0X6, Canada. TEL 613-728-3307. FAX 613-729-5421. adv.; bk.rev. circ. 500. (back issues avail.)
  Description: For and about family resource programs and toy libraries across Canada.

649 790 AT
PLAYGROUPER MAGAZINE. 1974. q. Aus.$16; newsstand price: Aus.$4. Victorian Playgroup Association Inc., 346 Albert St., Brunswick, Vic. 3056, Australia. TEL 61-3-93973499. FAX 61-3-93973047. Ed. Helen Schwab. R&P contact: Helen Schwab. adv.: B&W page Aus.$495; 290 x 205; adv. contact: Helen Schwab. bk.rev. circ. 30,000. (back issues avail.) **Document type:** consumer publication.
  Description: Covers parenting, play ideas, community group interests, health and safety issues.

649 790 AT
PLAYGROUPER NEWSLETTER. 1989. q. Victorian Playgroup Association Inc., 346 Albert St., Brunswick, Vic. 3056, Australia. TEL 61-3-93973499. FAX 61-3-93973047. Ed. Helen Schwab. R&P contact: Helen Schwab. adv. contact: Helen Schwab. **Document type:** newsletter.
  Description: Covers parenting, play ideas, community group interests, health and safety issues. Alternates with Playgrouper Magazine.

790.019 UK
PLAYRIGHTS/DROITS AU JEU/SPIEL RECHTE/DERECHO A JUGAR. (Text in English, French, Portuguese, Spanish) 1977. q. £25 to non-members. (International Association for the Child's Right to Play) I P A Resources, c/o National Play Information Centre, 359-361 Euston Rd., London NW1 3AL, England. TEL 44-71-3835455. FAX 44-71-3873152. (Edit. addr.: Box 12907, Raleigh, NC 27605-2907. TEL 919-515-2204. FAX 919-821-4913) Ed. Robin C. Moore. adv.; bk.rev. circ. 1,500.
  Formerly: I P A Newsletter.
  Description: Deals with children's playright opportunities, and the barriers against them.

790.019 AT ISSN 1038-2852
PLAYTIMES. 1992. bi-m. Aus.$10. Playgroup Association of Queensland, 396 Milton Rd., Auchenflower, Qld. 4066, Australia. TEL 61-7-3718253. FAX 61-7-8700569. Ed. Vivian Dray. R&P contact: Fiona Pearce. adv. contact: Fiona Pearce. circ. 18,000 (controlled). (back issues avail.) **Document type:** newspaper.
  Formerly (until Apr. 1992): Playgroup (ISSN 0312-3898)
  Description: Helps members run their playgroup, to inform parents about children and child rearing, discuss issues of concern to families of young children.
  Refereed Serial

POD WIATR; sami o sobie - czasopismo mlodziezowe. see CHILDREN AND YOUTH — For

POLYTECHNI OIKOGENEIA. see RELIGIONS AND THEOLOGY — Eastern Orthodox

PONY BASEBALL - SOFTBALL EXPRESS. see SPORTS AND GAMES — Ball Games

649 BN ISSN 0032-4787
PORODICA I DIJETE. (Text in Serbo-Croatian) 1953. m. 50 din. Savez Organizacija za Socijalisticko Vaspitanje i Brigu o Djeci Bosne i Hercegovine, JNA 28-I, Sarajevo, Bosnia Hercegovina. Eds. Adila Kreso, Mladen Arapovic. adv.; bk.rev. circ. 15,000.

649 US ISSN 1065-2663
PORTLAND PARENT. 1991. m. $15. Northwest Parent Publishing, Inc. (Portland), Box 80040, Portland, OR 97280. TEL 503-245-8036. FAX 503-246-6860. Ed. Ann Bergman. adv.: B&W page $1395. bk.rev. circ. 30,000. (tabloid format) **Document type:** newspaper.
  Description: Provides a reliable source of information about activities of interest to parents in the Portland area.

362.7 CN ISSN 1206-7989
▼**POST-ADOPTION HELPER**; support for parents, after the adoption. 1997. q. Can.$24 (US $24; elsewhere $35) (effective 1997-98). Helper Publishing, 36 Norwood Rd., Toronto, ON M4E 2S2, Canada. TEL 416-690-9593. FAX 416-690-9593. E-mail: helper@helping.com; URL: http://www.helping.com/family/pa/pa.html. Ed. Jennifer Smart. Pub. Mr. Robin Hilborn. adv.; bk.rev.; bibl.; illus.; circ. 500 (paid). (back issues avail.) **Document type:** consumer publication.
  ●Also available online.
  Description: Presents medical issues, behaviour management, family and society, culture and heritage, search and reunion and provides resources.

649 US ISSN 0883-9905
POTOMAC CHILDREN. 1984. 10/yr. $17.85. Potomac Children, Box 151544, Bethesda, MD 20825-1544. TEL 301-656-2133. FAX 301-656-2133. Ed. Margaret W. Hut. adv.: B&W page $1150; trim 11 3/8 x 15; adv. contact: Margaret W. Hut. circ. 34,000. **Document type:** newspaper.
  Description: Covers crafts, cooking, parenting, summer programs and preschools.

CHILDREN AND YOUTH — ABOUT

649   UK   ISSN 0954-9846
PRACTICAL PARENTING. 1987. m. £21 (foreign £26) (effective 1996). I P C Magazines, Southbank Publishing Group (Subsidiary of: Reed Elsevier group), King's Reach Tower, Stamford St., London SE1 9LS, England. TEL 44-171-261-5000. FAX 44-1444-445599. TELEX 892084 REEDBP G. (Dist. by: Quadrant Subscription Services, Oakfield House, Perrymount Rd., Haywards Heath, W. Sussex RH16 3DH, England. TEL 44-1444-445555) adv. contact: Sue Valentine. **Document type:** consumer publication.
—BLDSC (6595.315000).
   Description: Provides interactive practical information, value for money, reader appeal, and in-depth coverage of all parenting issues.

PRACTITIONERS' CHILD LAW BULLETIN. see LAW — Family And Matrimonial Law

PRAXIS DER PSYCHOMOTORIK. see PHYSICAL FITNESS AND HYGIENE

PRAXIS SPIEL UND GRUPPE. see EDUCATION

649 268   US   ISSN 1048-5260
PRESCHOOLERS AT CHURCH AND HOME. 1991. q. $7.24. Southern Baptist Convention, Sunday School Board, 127 Ninth Ave., N., Nashville, TN 37234. TEL 800-458-2772. FAX 615-251-5933. E-mail: customerservice@bssb.com.
   Description: Consists of leaflets with Bible learning activities for parents of preschoolers.

362.7   GW
▼**PREVENTION AND INTERVENTION IN CHILDHOOD AND ADOLESCENCE.** (Text in English) 1995. irreg., vol.20, 1996. price varies. Walter de Gruyter und Co., Genthiner Str. 13, 10785 Berlin, Germany. TEL 49-30-26005-0. FAX 49-30-26005251. E-mail: wdg-info@degruyter.de; URL: http://www.degruyter.de. (In US and Canada: Walter de Gruyter, Inc., 200 Saw Mill River Rd., Hawthorne, NY 10532. TEL 914-747-0110) (back issues avail.) **Document type:** monographic series.
   Formerly: International Studies on Childhood and Adolescence.

649   US
PRIORITY PARENTING.* 1987. m. $14. Priority Parenting Plus, 830 S. Union St., Warsaw, IN 46580-4701. TEL 219-268-1415. Ed. Tamra Orr. adv.; bk.rev.; circ. 200 (paid). **Document type:** newsletter.
   Description: Encourages parents to raise their children by following basic human nature and instinct.

790.019   CE
PRIYAVI. (Text in Sinhala) 1976. w. 5 Gunasena Mawatha, Colombo 12, Sri Lanka. TEL 1-23882. Ed. W. Waturegama. circ. 37,000.
   Description: Covers teenage pop scene.

THE PROGRESS OF NATIONS; the nations of the world ranked according to their achievements in health, nutrition, education, family planning, and progress for women. see SOCIAL SERVICES AND WELFARE

PROTECTING CHILDREN. see SOCIAL SERVICES AND WELFARE

PUERICULTURA MARKET; revista profesional de los productos para bebes y la infancia. see INTERIOR DESIGN AND DECORATION — Furniture And House Furnishings

369.4   CC   ISSN 1004-3780
QINGNIAN TANSUO/YOUTH STUDIES. (Text in Chinese) 1983. bi-m. newsstand price: Y3.50. Guangzhou Shi Gongqingtuan Tuanxiao, Shibei Gangding, Guangzhou, Guangdong 510360, People's Republic of China. TEL 86-20-8551-6234. FAX 86-20-8551-6817. Ed. Ang Liu. circ. 5,000.
   Description: Covers youth culture, youth studies, youth counselling, youth and society, university students and more.

RAINER FOUNDATION. ANNUAL REPORT. see CRIMINOLOGY AND LAW ENFORCEMENT

RALLY LEADERS BULLETIN. see CHILDREN AND YOUTH — For

649 362.7   GW   ISSN 0034-1312
K18
RECHT DER JUGEND UND DES BILDUNGSWESENS; Zeitschrift fuer Schule, Berufsbildung und Jugenderziehung. 1953. q. DM.188. Luchterhand Verlag, Heddesdorfstr. 31, 56564 Neuwied, Germany. TEL 49-2631-801-0. FAX 49-2631-801204. TELEX 867853-HLVN-D. Ed. Karsten Fuchs. adv. contact: Gabriele Pannwitz. bk.rev.; abstr.; bibl.; index. circ. 1,200. (reprint service avail. from SCH) **Indexed:** Abstr.Crim.& Pen., IBR. **Document type:** bulletin.
—BLDSC (7309.350000). CCC.
   Formerly: Recht der Jugend (ISSN 0481-9306)

649   SP   ISSN 0211-1799
RECIEN NACIDO; guia de los papas. 1970. s-m. free. Av. del Jordan s-n, Edificio B-2, Barcelona 16, Spain. Ed. Joaquin Motger. adv. circ. 240,000.

RECLAIMING CHILDREN AND YOUTH; the journal of emotional and behavioral problems. see PSYCHOLOGY

362.7 370   US   ISSN 1041-5246
REPORT ON SCHOOL-AGE CHILD CARE. 1988. m. $168. Business Publishers, Inc., 951 Pershing Dr., Silver Spring, MD 20910-4464. TEL 301-587-6300. FAX 301-585-9075. Ed. Mary Crowley; Pub. Lawrence Fishbein. (looseleaf format; back issues avail.) **Document type:** newsletter.
● Also available online. Vendor(s): NewsNet.
—CCC.
   Formerly: School Child Care Report.
   Description: Provides education tips and covers sources of funding for program administrators in preschool and elementary school programs.

REPRESENTING CHILDREN; a quarterly journal for all professionals concerned with the rights and welfare of children. see SOCIAL SERVICES AND WELFARE

647 610   JA   ISSN 0386-8435
HQ767.8
RESEARCH AND CLINICAL CENTER FOR CHILD DEVELOPMENT. ANNUAL REPORT. (Text and summaries in English) 1978. a. free. Hokkaido University, Research and Clinical Center for Child Development, Nishi 7-chome, Kita 11-jo, Kita-ku, Sapporo-shi 060, Japan. TEL 81-11-706-2607. FAX 81-11-706-4946. Ed. Shing-Jen Chen; Pub. Takashi Morotomi. cum.index. circ. 500. (back issues avail.) **Indexed:** Psychol.Abstr. **Document type:** academic/scholarly publication.
—BLDSC (1289.661000).
   Refereed Serial

362.7   US
RESEARCH MONOGRAPHS IN ADOLESCENCE. irreg. Lawrence Erlbaum Associates, Inc., 10 Industrial Ave., Mahwah, NJ 07430-2262. TEL 201-236-9500; 800-926-6579. FAX 201-236-0072. E-mail: orders@erlbaum.com; URL: http://www.erlbaum.com. Eds. Nancy Galambos, Nancy Busch-Rossnagel. **Document type:** monographic series.

362.7   US   ISSN 0886-571X
HV59   CODEN: RTCYEY
RESIDENTIAL TREATMENT FOR CHILDREN & YOUTH; a journal of professional practice. 1979. q. $45 to individuals (Canada $58.50; elsewhere $63); institutions $120 (Canada $156; elsewhere $168); libraries $225 (Canada $292.50; elsewhere $315) (effective 1996-1997). Haworth Press, Inc., 10 Alice St., Binghamton, NY 13904. TEL 607-722-5857; 800-342-9676. FAX 607-722-6362. TELEX 4932599. E-mail: getinfo@haworth.com; URL: http://www.haworth.com. Ed. Gordon Northrup; Pub. Bill Cohen. R&P contact: Ruthann Heath. adv.: B&W page $300; trim 4 3/8 x 7 1/8; adv. contact: Jackie Blakeslee. bk.rev. circ. 642. (also avail. in microfiche from UMI; microform from HAW; back issues avail.; reprint service avail. from HAW) **Indexed:** Abstr.Crim.& Pen., Adol.Ment.Hlth.Abstr., Behav.Abstr., Biol.Abstr., Bull.Signal., C J P I, Chicago Psychoanal.Lit.Ind., Child Devel.Abstr., Crim.Just.Abstr., Except.Child.Educ.Abstr., Excerp.Med., Human Resour.Abstr., IMFL, Lang.& Lang.Behav.Abstr., Past.Care & Couns.Abstr., Psychol.Abstr. (1982-), Rehabil.Lit., Sage Fam.Stud.Abstr., Soc.Work Res.& Abstr., Sociol.Abstr., Sociol.Educ.Abstr., Sp.Ed.Needs Abstr. **Document type:** academic/scholarly publication.
—BLDSC (7777.247000); Haworth; SWETS; UnCover.
   Former titles (until 1986): Residential Group Care and Treatment (ISSN 0731-7123); (until 1981): Residential and Community Child Care Administration (ISSN 0162-1408)
   Description: Provides a forum for persons engaged in the interdisciplinary task of the residential group care of children and youth. Provides a national exchange of scientific views, innovative practices and perspectives on current issues and developments in the field.
   Refereed Serial

RESIDENTIAL TREATMENT NEWS. see PSYCHOLOGY

649   US
RHODE ISLAND PARENTS' PAPER. 1989. m. $15. Parents' Plus, Inc., 670 Centre St., Jamaica Plain, MA 02130. TEL 617-522-1515. FAX 617-522-1694. E-mail: tbpp@aol.com. Ed. William Lindsay. adv.; bk.rev.; video rev. circ. 30,000. **Document type:** newspaper.
   Description: Provides practical parenting information.

RIGHT START. see CHILDREN AND YOUTH — For

369.4   GW
RING JUNGER BUENDE. MITTEILUNGEN. 1964. q. free. Ring Junger Buende, An der Neckarspitze 6, 69115 Heidelberg, Germany. TEL 49-6221-20263. Ed. Waldemar Wagner. bk.rev. circ. 2,200. **Document type:** newsletter.

362.7   US
THE ROAD HOME. s-a. free. Vanished Children's Alliance, 2095 Park Ave., San Jose, CA 95126. TEL 408-296-1113. FAX 408-296-1117. circ. 23,000. **Document type:** newsletter.
   Formerly: Vanished Children's Alliance Newsletter.
   Description: Contains news and views from the VCA, which is dedicated to the prevention, location, and recovery of missing and abducted children. Lists missing children and advises parents what to do if their child is abducted.

S C B W I BULLETIN. (Society of Children's Book Writers & Illustrators) see PUBLISHING AND BOOK TRADE

S M Y A L NEWS. (Sexual Minority Youth Assistance League, Inc.) see HOMOSEXUALITY

S O S KINDERDORF INTERNATIONAL. see SOCIAL SERVICES AND WELFARE

S O S KINDERDORFBOTE. see SOCIAL SERVICES AND WELFARE

S O S S I JOURNAL. (Scouts on Stamps Society International, Inc.) see PHILATELY

CHILDREN AND YOUTH — ABOUT

649 **US**
SAN DIEGO FAMILY MAGAZINE. 1982. m. $12. Sharon Bay, Ed. & Pub., Box 23960, San Diego, CA 92193. TEL 619-685-6970. URL: http://www.sandiegofamily.com. R&P contact: Sharon Bay. adv. circ. 76,000. **Document type:** consumer publication.
Formerly: San Diego Family Press.
Description: Provides a country-wide calendar of family events and classes for both parents and children. Includes educational and informative tips for parents, and many San Diego resources.

155.4 649 **US**
SAN DIEGO PARENT. 1981. m. $12. Wingate Enterprises, Ltd., 443 E. Irving Dr., Box 3204, Burbank, CA 91504. TEL 818-846-0400. FAX 818-841-4380. Ed. Jack Bierman.

155.6 **US**
SAN FRANCISCO PENINSULA PARENT. 1984. m. $15. Peninsula Parent Newspaper Inc., 1480 Rollins Rd., Burlingame, CA 94010-2307. TEL 415-342-9203. FAX 415-342-9276. E-mail: sfpp@aol.com. Ed. Lisa Rosenthal; Pub. Marlene Douglas. R&P contact: Lisa Rosenthal. adv. contact: Marlene Douglas. bk.rev.; circ. 60,000 (controlled). (tabloid format) **Document type:** newspaper.
Description: Resource guide for local events and information geared to parents.

362.7 649 **FR** **ISSN 0036-5041**
SAUVEGARDE DE L'ENFANCE. 1946. 5/yr. 500 F. (foreign 580 F.) (effective 1997). (Association Francaise pour la Sauvegarde de l'Enfance et de l'Adolescence) Expansion Scientifique Francaise, 31 Bd. de la Tour Maubourg, 75343 Paris Cedex 07, France. TEL 33-1-40626400. FAX 33-1-45556920. (Subscr. to: 15 rue St-Benoit, 75278 Paris Cedex 06, France. TEL 33-1-45484260. FAX 33-1-45448155) Ed. Prof. D.J. Duche. bk.rev.; bibl.; charts; illus.; stat. circ. 3,000. **Indexed:** Abstr.Crim.& Pen.
—SWETS.

SAVE THE CHILDREN. ANNUAL REPORT. see *SOCIAL SERVICES AND WELFARE*

362.7 **UK** **ISSN 0966-6982**
SAVE THE CHILDREN DEVELOPMENT MANUALS. 1991. irreg. Save the Children Fund, Mary Datchelor House, 17 Grove Ln., London SE5 8RD, England. TEL 44-171-703-5400. FAX 44-171-703-2278. URL: http://www.oneworld.org/scf/. **Document type:** monographic series.
Description: Short practical guides for field staff in particular areas of field work.

362.7 **UK** **ISSN 0966-6931**
SAVE THE CHILDREN OVERSEAS DEPARTMENT WORKING PAPER. 1992. irreg., no.17, 1997. £2.95. Save the Children Fund, Mary Datchelor House, 17 Grove Ln., London SE5 8RD, England. TEL 44-171-703-5400. FAX 44-171-703-2278. URL: http://www.oneworld.org/scf/. **Document type:** monographic series.
—BLDSC (8077.245000).
Description: Disseminates research and project experience to a wider audience, particularly targeting development practitioners, researchers and policy makers throughout the world.

369.4 **IT** **ISSN 0036-5696**
SCAUTISMO; rivista di divulgazione del metodo scout. 1959. m. membership. Corpo Nazionale Giovani Esploratori ed Esploratrici Italiani, Via Ennio Quirino Visconti 8, 00193 Rome, Italy. Ed. Sergio Guida. adv.; bibl. circ. 13,500.
Description: Educational publication from the Italian boy scouts organization.

369.4 **IT**
SCAUTISMO VENETO. 1985. bi-m. L.20000. Cooperativa Veneta Scout, Via R. Fowst, 9, 35135 Padova, Italy. TEL 39-49-8644003. FAX 39-49-8643605. circ. 4,000. **Document type:** bulletin.
Description: For leaders of scout and guide units.

SCHNELLER-MAGAZIN. see *RELIGIONS AND THEOLOGY — Protestant*

362.7 **US** **ISSN 0278-3126**
SCHOOL AGE NOTES; the newsletter for school-age care professionals. 1980. m. $24.95 (Canada $27.95; elsewhere $29.95) (effective 1996). Box 40205, Nashville, TN 37204. TEL 615-242-8464. Pub. Richard T. Scofield. bk.rev.; cum.index: 1980-1985; circ. 5,300 (paid). **Document type:** newsletter.
Description: Covers administrative and curriculum issues in after-school programs.

362.7 157.63 **US** **ISSN 0894-5152**
SCHOOL INTERVENTION REPORT. Abbreviated title: S I R. 1987. q. $22 to non-members (foreign $30). Safe Schools Coalition, Inc., 5351 Gulf Dr., Holmes Beach, FL 35217-1338. TEL 813-778-9140. FAX 813-778-6818. (Subscr. to: Box 1326, Holmes Beach, FL 34218-1326) Ed. Alan W. McEvoy. R&P contact: Edsel Erickson. bk.rev.; cum.index 1987-1990. circ. 3,000. (back issues avail.) **Document type:** newsletter.
Description: Covers students at risk from drugs, alcohol, dropping out, physical violence, and adolescent pregnancy.

SCHOOL PSYCHOLOGY QUARTERLY. see *PSYCHOLOGY*

SCHOOL SOCIAL WORK JOURNAL. see *EDUCATION — Special Education And Rehabilitation*

028.5 **GW**
SCHWARTE. 1978. s-a. DM.0.50 per no. Willibald-Gluck-Gymnasium, Dr.-Grundler-Str. 7, 92318 Neumarkt, Germany. (back issues avail.)

362.7 **UK** **ISSN 0950-4176**
SCOTTISH CHILD. 1988. bi-m. £15 to individuals; institutions £20. Scottish Child Ltd., 35 Avenuepark St., Marthill, Glasgow G20 9TS, Scotland. Ed. Rosemary Milne. adv. contact: Aileen Bruce. bk.rev. circ. 4,000. (back issues avail.) **Document type:** consumer publication.

369.4 **UK**
SCOTTISH SCOUT NEWS. 1977. 5/yr. £5. Scottish Council of The Scout Association, Fordell Firs, Hillend, Dunfermline, Fife KY11 5HQ, Scotland. TEL 44-1383-419073. FAX 44-1383-414892. Ed. David Shelmerdine. adv. contact: bk.rev. circ. 8,500. (back issues avail.) **Document type:** newsletter.

369.4 **SW** **ISSN 0346-0827**
SCOUT. Variant title: Scout med Ledarbladet. (Supplement avail.: Ledarbladet) 1965. 6/yr. SEK 105 (effective 1993). Svenska Scoutfoerbundet, P.O. Box 49005, 100 28 Stockholm, Sweden. TEL 08-6520980. FAX 08-6537497. adv.; B&W page SEK 6800, color page SEK 1100; trim 185 x 263. circ. 60,000.

369.4 **CN** **ISSN 0380-8696**
SCOUT EXECUTIVE. 1969. 6/yr. Boy Scouts of Canada, National Council, Box 5151, Sta. F, Ottawa, Ont. K2C 3G7, Canada. TEL 613-224-5131. Ed. Garth Johnson. bk.rev.; illus. circ. 200.
Formerly: Canadian Scout Executive (ISSN 0380-8688)

369.4 **AT** **ISSN 0815-4627**
SCOUT MAGAZINE. 1912. 11/yr. Aus.$17.50. Scout Association of Australia, Victoria Branch, P.O. Box 190, Carlton, Vic. 3053, Australia. Ed. Andrew Taylor. adv. circ. 22,000. **Document type:** bulletin.
Formerly: Victorian Scout (ISSN 0159-897X)
Description: Discusses program ideas, reports, training and inspirational information.

369.4 **US** **ISSN 0890-8206**
SCOUTER'S DIGEST; condensed scouting news for busy Boy Scout leaders. 1986. bi-m. $18 (foreign $25). Box 1052, Marinette, WI 54143-6052. TEL 906-863-3863. FAX 906-863-3863. E-mail: paul_ferris@cybrzn.com. Ed. Paul Ferris; Pub. Paul Ferris. R&P contact: Paul Ferris. adv. contact: Paul Ferris. bk.rev.; index. (back issues avail.) **Document type:** newsletter.
Description: Digests scouting publications and literature for adult Boy Scout leaders.

SCOUTING ABOUT. see *CLUBS*

369.4 HS3313.B7 **US** **ISSN 0036-9500**
SCOUTING MAGAZINE. 1913. bi-m. $15 to non-members (foreign $24); members $2 (effective 1998). Boy Scouts of America, Box 152079, Irving, TX 75015-2079. TEL 972-580-2367. FAX 972-580-2079. Ed. Jon C. Halter; Pub. J. Warren Young. R&P contact: Jon C. Halter. adv.: B&W page $10540, color page $15060; adv. contact: Lisa Hott. bk.rev.; film rev.; illus.; index. circ. 900,000. (also avail. in microform from UMI; reprint service avail. from UMI) **Indexed:** Mag.Ind. **Document type:** consumer publication.
—UMI.

369.4 **SW** **ISSN 0036-9519**
SCOUTLEDAREN. 1943. 6/yr. SEK 100 (effective 1997). Nykterhetsroerelsens Scoutfoerbund (NSF) - Temperance Guide and Scout Association (NSF), P.O. Box 1747, S-111 87 Stockholm, Sweden. TEL 46-8-7894940. FAX 46-8-24-90-03. E-mail: nying@nsf.scout.se; scoutledaren@nsf.scout:se. Ed. Bodil Hansen. adv.; illus. circ. 3,000.

SCOUTS ON STAMPS OF THE WORLD. see *PHILATELY*

362.7 360 **IT** **ISSN 0036-9802**
SCUGNIZZO. (English supplement: Casa dello Scugnizzo News) 1951. q. donation. Foundation Casa dello Scugnizzo, Piazza S. Gennaro a Materdei 3, Casella Postale 378, Naples, Italy. TEL 39-81-5641419. FAX 39-81-5642279. Ed. Mario Borrelli. circ. 10,000. (tabloid format) **Document type:** newsletter.
Description: Covers the needs and problems of children, women and the elderly.

155.649 **US**
SEATTLE'S CHILD. 1979. m. $15. Northwest Parent Publishing, Inc., 2107 Elliott Ave., Ste. 303, Seattle, WA 98121. TEL 206-441-0191. FAX 206-441-4919. Ed. Ann Bergman. adv. contact: Alayne Sulkin. bk.rev. circ. 30,000. (tabloid format) **Document type:** consumer publication.
Description: Guide for parents, educators and child-care providers. Features include a calendar of events, plays, movies, and ideas for outings and restaurants.

362.7 371.2 **SZ**
SEKTOR ERZIEHUNG. 1974. q. 20 SFr. Gewerkschaft Erziehung Basel, Rebgasse 1, Postfach, CH-4005 Basel, Switzerland. TEL 061-6921400. Ed. Martin Stohler. bk.rev.; circ. 1,250. (back issues avail.) **Document type:** newsletter.

SER PADRES/BEING PARENTS. see *WOMEN'S INTERESTS*

649 **SP**
SER PADRES HOY. 1974. m. 4200 ptas. (Europe 7670 ptas.; elsewhere 10470 ptas.) (effective 1997). G y J Espana Ediciones, S.L., Marques de Villamagna 4, 28001 Madrid, Spain. TEL 34-1-4369898. FAX 34-1-5752617. Ed. Javier Garcia. adv. contact: Elena Sanchez Fabres. circ. 105,000. **Document type:** consumer publication.

SERVANT LEADER. see *RELIGIONS AND THEOLOGY — Protestant*

SERVICES FOR CHILDREN. see *SOCIAL SERVICES AND WELFARE*

369.4 **CC**
SHANDONG QINGNIAN/SHANDONG YOUTH. (Text in Chinese) m. Shandong Gongqingtuan Shengwei, No 4, Yingxiongshan Lu, Jinan, Shandong 250002, People's Republic of China. TEL 25829. Ed. Zhou Jianqing.

155.5 **CC** **ISSN 1002-9915**
SHAONIAN ERTONG YANJIU/ADOLESCENT STUDIES. (Text in Chinese) bi-m. Zhongguo Qingnian Zhengzhi Xueyuan, Qingshaonian Yanjiusuo, 25, Xisanhuan Beilu, Beijing 100081, People's Republic of China. TEL 8021144. **Document type:** academic/scholarly publication.

SHARING SPACE. see *EDUCATION*

028.5 **CC**
SHIJIE ERTONG/WORLD CHILDREN. (Text in Chinese, English) q. Sichuan Waiyu Xueyuan, Shijie Ertong Bianjibu, Chongqing, Sichuan 630031, People's Republic of China. TEL 661737. Ed. Zheng Huizhong.

CHILDREN AND YOUTH — ABOUT

SHMUESSEN MIT KINDER UN YUGENT. see *RELIGIONS AND THEOLOGY* — Judaic

649 610   JA   ISSN 0385-2792
                                               CODEN: JOCMC
SHONI NO HOKEN/OSAKA CHILDREN'S MEDICAL CENTER. JOURNAL. (Text in Japanese; summaries in English) 1966. a. free. Osaka Shiritsu Shoni Hoken Senta, 5-30, Higashinakamoto 2-chome, Higashinari-ku, Osaka 547, Japan. TEL 06-976-0071. FAX 06-976-1849. Ed. Masashi Takesada. adv.; bk.rev. circ. 1,000. (back issues avail.)
    Description: Contains papers covering medical problems and related subjects affecting children from newborn to adolescent.

362.7   US
SIBLING INFORMATION NETWORK NEWSLETTER. 1981. q. $8.50 to individuals; institutions $15. A.J. Pappanikou Center, 249 Glenbrook Rd., Storrs, CT 06269-2064. TEL 860-486-4985. Ed. Lisa Glidden. bk.rev. circ. 1,500. (back issues avail.) **Document type:** newsletter.

027.62 028.5   UK   ISSN 0037-4954
PN1009.A1
SIGNAL; approaches to children's books. 1970. 3/yr. £12.75 (foreign £15($27) (effective 1998). Thimble Press, Lockwood, Station Rd., South Woodchester, Stroud, Glos. GL5 5EQ, England. TEL 44-1453-873716. FAX 44-1453-878599. Ed. Nancy Chambers; Pub. Aidan Chambers. R&P contact: Nancy Chambers. bk.rev. **Indexed:** Abstr.Engl.Stud., Child.Lit.Abstr. **Document type:** academic/scholarly publication.
    —BLDSC (8275.900000); UnCover.
    Description: Articles on writing, illustrating, publishing, criticism, educational theory and practice.

267 284   US   ISSN 0893-0880
SIGNAL (STREAMWOOD). 1962. q. $2.50. Awana Clubs International, 1 E. Bode Rd., Streamwood, IL 60107. TEL 708-213-2000. FAX 708-213-9704. Ed. Beecher Bailey. R&P contact: Sue Hickey. bk.rev. circ. 100,000. **Indexed:** Tel.Abstr.
    Description: For leaders and supporters of Awana Clubs; contains mostly news about the Awana ministry, leadership aids and inspirational material.

649   US   ISSN 1077-4092
SINGLE-PARENT FAMILY. 1994. m. $12 donation. Focus on the Family, Inc., 8605 Explorer Dr., Colorado Springs, CO 80920. TEL 719-531-3400. Ed. Lynda Hunter. R&P contact: Lianne Belote. adv. circ. 70,000.
    Description: Encourages and equips single parents to do the best job they can at creating stable, godly homes for themselves and their children.

SINGLEMOTHER; a support group in your hands. see *WOMEN'S INTERESTS*

SMART DADS. see *SOCIOLOGY*

SOCIAL SERVICES RESEARCH. see *SOCIAL SERVICES AND WELFARE*

155.4   US   ISSN 0037-976X
LB1103   CODEN: MSCDA7
SOCIETY FOR RESEARCH IN CHILD DEVELOPMENT. MONOGRAPHS. 1935. irreg. (2-3/yr.), vol.62, 1997. $75 (Canada $88.25; elsewhere $82) (effective 1997). (Society for Research in Child Development) University of Chicago Press, Journals Division, 7520 S. Woodlawn Ave., Chicago, IL 60637. TEL 773-702-7600. FAX 773-702-0172. TELEX 25-4603. E-mail: subscriptions@journals.uchicago.edu; URL: http://www.journals.uchicago.edu/CDM/. (Subscr. to: Box 37005, Chicago, IL 60637. TEL 773-753-3347. FAX 773-753-0811) Ed. Rachel K. Clifton. (also avail. in microform from UMI; reprint service avail. from UMI,ISI,KTO) **Indexed:** Adol.Ment.Hlth.Abstr., ASCA, Bibl.Dev.Med.& Child Neur., Biol.Abstr., C.I.J.E., Child Devel.Abstr., Crim.Just.Abstr., Curr.Cont., Educ.Ind., IBR, IMFL, Ind.Med., Lang.& Lang.Behav.Abstr., Mid.East: Abstr.& Ind., Psychol.Abstr., Psycscan D.P., Sci.Cit.Ind., Sociol.Abstr., SSCI. **Document type:** monographic series.
    —BLDSC (5914.820000); CISTI; KR SourceOne; SWETS; UMI; UnCover. **CCC.**
    Description: Presents in-depth research studies and findings in child development and related disciplines.
    Refereed Serial

362.7 300   US   ISSN 1080-0778
SOCIOLOGICAL STUDIES OF CHILDREN. 1986. irreg., vol.8, 1997. $73.25. J A I Press Inc., 55 Old Post Rd., No. 2, Box 1678, Greenwich, CT 06830-1678. TEL 203-661-7602. FAX 203-661-0792. E-mail: jai@jaipress.com. (Subscr. in the UK and Europe to: JAI Press Ltd., 38 Tavistock St., Covent Garden, London WC2E 7PB, England. TEL 44-171-379-8834. FAX 44-171-379-8835) Ed. Nancy Mandell. **Document type:** academic/scholarly publication, monographic series.
    —BLDSC (8319.649250). **CCC.**
    Formerly (until 1993): Sociological Studies of Child Development (ISSN 1058-8930)

362.7   CU
SOMOS JOVENES. 1977. m. $34 in S. America; N. America $36; elsewhere $42. (Editorial Abril) Ediciones Cubanas, Obispo No. 527, Apdo. 605, Havana, Cuba. TEL 7-32-4571. Dir. Guillermo Cabrera. circ. 200,000.

790.019 646   US
SOUTH FLORIDA PARENTING.* 1990. m. $21. Ken Roberts, Ed. & Pub., 8323 N.W. 12th St., Ste. 212, Miami, FL 33126-1840. TEL 305-448-6003. FAX 305-448-6290. adv.; bk.rev.; illus.; circ. 100,000 (controlled).
    Description: Focuses on concerns of parents, includes feature articles and activities listings.

SPECIAL CHILDREN. see *EDUCATION* — Special Education And Rehabilitation

028.5 371.9   US
▼**SPECIALKIDS.** 1996. a. $18. Kidfstuff Publications, Inc., 1080 N. Delaware Ave., Ste. 702, Philadelphia, PA 19125-4330. TEL 215-551-3200. FAX 215-551-3203. Ed. Nancy Lisagor. circ. 40,000. **Document type:** consumer publication.

028.5
SPECTRUM NEWSLETTER (ALBANY). 1979. q. free. Parsons Child and Family Center, 60 Academy Rd., Albany, NY 11203-3198. TEL 518-426-2600. Ed. B.A. Unser. circ. 25,000. (looseleaf format) **Document type:** newsletter.

SPIELEN UND LERNEN. see *EDUCATION*

SPOOFING. see *FOLKLORE*

SPORT SCENE; focus on youth programs. see *SPORTS AND GAMES*

SPOTLIGHT ON YOUTH SPORTS. see *SPORTS AND GAMES*

649   US
SPRINGFIELD PARENT. 1987. m. $15. Box 4732, Springfield, MO 65808. TEL 417-869-9800. FAX 417-831-5478. (Subscr. to: 313 Park Central W., Springfield, MO 65806. TEL 417-831-3238) Ed. Dianne Elizabeth; Pub. Dianne Elizabeth. R&P contact: Dianne Elizabeth. adv. contact: Stanley E. Coffman. bk.rev. circ. 28,000. **Document type:** newspaper, consumer publication.
    Description: Discusses families parenting and pediatric care, psychology, and education.
    Refereed Serial

START (BIRMINGHAM). see *RELIGIONS AND THEOLOGY* — Protestant

STARTING LINE. see *SPORTS AND GAMES*

STATE OF AMERICA'S CHILDREN YEARBOOK; an analysis of our nation's investment in children. see *SOCIAL SERVICES AND WELFARE*

THE STATE OF THE WORLD'S CHILDREN. see *SOCIAL SERVICES AND WELFARE*

361   US
STEP-UP; America's first independent newsletter about remarriage for stepparents and professionals. 1980. bi-m. $19.95 (effective 1997). Listening Inc., 8716 Pine Ave., Gary, IN 46403. TEL 219-938-6962. FAX 219-938-7435. Ed. Patricia Work Bennett; Pub. Richard C. Bennett. bk.rev. (back issues avail.) **Document type:** newsletter.
    Former titles: Stepfamilies and Beyond; Stepparent News (ISSN 0271-3225)
    Description: Articles, announcements, and forum for families of remarriages, with a special children's page.

649   GW   ISSN 0938-0914
STEPPKE; Zeitschrift von und fuer Eltern. 1990. m. DM.20($40) Doterner GmbH, Westfalenstr. 98, 45136 Essen, Germany. TEL 0201-85111-1. FAX 0201-8511155. Eds. Bodo and Petra Schmischke. adv.; bk.rev. circ. 10,000. **Document type:** consumer publication.
    Description: Provides information for and about young parents.

STUDENT ASSISTANCE JOURNAL. see *DRUG ABUSE AND ALCOHOLISM*

028.5 808.68   SW   ISSN 0347-5387
SVENSKA BARNBOKSINSTITUTET. SKRIFTER/SWEDISH INSTITUTE FOR CHILDREN'S BOOKS. STUDIES. 1971. irreg., no.60, 1996. Svenska Barnboksinstitutet - Swedish Institute for Children's Books, Odengatan 61, S-113 22 Stockholm, Sweden. TEL 46-8-332323. FAX 46-8-332423. Ed. Sonja Svensson. **Document type:** monographic series.

369.4   XV   ISSN 0492-1127
TABOR. (Text in Slovenian) 1951. m. $24. Zveza Tabornikov Slovenije, Parmova 33, 61000 Ljubljana, Slovenia. TEL 38-61-313180. FAX 38-61-1321107. Ed. Igor Drakulic. adv.: B&W page DM.400, color page DM.500; adv. contact: Frank Merela. bk.rev.; cum.index. circ. 4,000. (back issues avail.) **Document type:** newspaper.
    Description: Covers scouting, mountaineering, bicycling, ecology.

TALKING SENSE. see *SOCIAL SERVICES AND WELFARE*

649   US
TAMPA BAY FAMILY JOURNAL. 1985. m. free. Family Journal Publications, Inc., Box 1100, Orlando, FL 32802-1100. TEL 813-289-4060. FAX 813-289-4585. Ed. Patrick McGuffin. adv.: B&W page $1350, color page $1750; trim 14 x 16. circ. 25,000 (controlled).

TANDLAEGERNES NYE TIDSSKRIFT. see *MEDICAL SCIENCES* — Dentistry

TE TARI PUNA ORA O AOTEAROA. ITIREAREA/NEW ZEALAND CHILDCARE ASSOCIATION. NEWSLETTER. see *CHILDREN AND YOUTH* — For

TEACHING SECONDARY PHYSICAL EDUCATION; the independent voice of secondary physical educators. see *EDUCATION* — Teaching Methods And Curriculum

600   YU
TEHNICKE NOVINE. 1948. m. Tehnicka Knjiga, Vojvode Stepe 89, 11000 Belgrade, Yugoslavia. Ed. Sasa Imperl. adv.; bk.rev.; charts; illus. circ. 50,000.

TENNESSEE COMPILATION OF SELECTED LAWS ON CHILDREN, YOUTH AND FAMILIES. see *LAW* — Family And Matrimonial Law

649   US   ISSN 1049-9466
HQ768
TEXAS CHILD CARE; the quarterly journal for caregivers everywhere. 1977. q. $10.83 to Texas residents; non-residents $10; foreign $14 (subscr. includes newsletter). Texas Workforce Commission, Box 162881, 101 E.. 15th St., Rm. 416T, Austin, TX 78716-2881. TEL 512-441-6633. FAX 512-441-6522. E-mail: 57222.2621@compuserve.com. Ed. Louise Parks. R&P contact: Louise Parks. bk.rev. circ. 30,000. **Indexed:** C.I.J.E. **Document type:** consumer publication, government publication.
    Formerly: Texas Child Care Quarterly (ISSN 0192-6756)
    Description: Features development theory and professional development advice, as well as child-building articles that provide hands-on activities for children. Includes product reviews, child-care news events, and regulatory information.
    Refereed Serial

CHILDREN AND YOUTH — ABOUT

649   US
THAT'S MY BABY; the magazine for moms. 1990. m. $12.95. That's My Baby, Inc., Box 1156, Lake Oswego, OR 97035. TEL 503-620-9132. FAX 503-620-3800. Ed. Pamila Kesterson; Pub. Dan L. Kesterson. adv. contact: Dan L. Kesterson. bk.rev.; circ. 500,000 (controlled). **Document type:** consumer publication.
●Also available online.
    Description: Covers prenatal through kindergarten topics for expectant and new parents in the Northwest U.S. Covers women's issues, provides product reviews, and contains a Big Kids section.

THEIR WORLD. see *EDUCATION — Special Education And Rehabilitation*

649 268   GW   ISSN 0342-7145
THEORIE UND PRAXIS DER SOZIALPAEDAGOGIK. 1949. bi-m. DM.49.60. (Evangelische Bundesarbeitsgemeinschaft fuer Sozialpaedagogik im Kindersalter e.V. (EBASKA)) Kallmeyer'sche Verlagsbuchhandlung GmbH, Im Brande 19, 30926 Seelze, Germany. TEL 49-511-40004175. FAX 49-511-40004176. Ed. Inge Pape. adv.; bk.rev. circ. 6,100. **Document type:** academic/scholarly publication.
    Formerly: Evangelische Kinderpflege fuer Kindergarten, Hort, Heim und Familie (ISSN 0014-3421)

649   US   ISSN 1081-2334
TIDEWATER PARENT. 1990. m. $15. Windmill Publishing, Inc., 2753 Atwoodtown Rd., Virginia Beach, VA 23456. TEL 757-426-2595. FAX 757-426-5299. E-mail: tidewatr@family.wm. Ed. Peggy Sijswerda; Pub. Peter Sijswerda. R&P contact: Peggy Sijswerda. adv.: B&W page $1710; trim 11 3/8 x 14; adv. contact: Peter Sijswerda. bk.rev.; illus.; circ. 40,000 (controlled). cols./p.: 4; pp./issue: 36. (tabloid format; back issues avail.) **Document type:** consumer publication, newspaper.
    Description: Advises parents of children of all ages on issues in health, education, travel and recreation, and development.

649 910.03   US
TODAY'S BLACK FATHER.* q. Renaissance Magazine Inc., 4457 E. 154th St., Cleveland, OH 44128-2908. TEL 216-491-8900. Ed. Dibri Beavers. circ. 250,000.

TODAY'S DELINQUENT. see *CRIMINOLOGY AND LAW ENFORCEMENT*

649   CN   ISSN 0823-9258
TODAY'S PARENT. 1984. bi-m. Can.$14.95($20.95) (effective 1997). (Today's Parent Group) Professional Publishing Associates, 269 Richmond St. W., Toronto, ON M5V 1X1, Canada. TEL 416-596-8680. FAX 416-596-1991. URL: http://www.todaysparent.com. Ed. Fran Fearnley. adv.; bk.rev.; circ. 110,000 (paid); 50,000 (controlled). (back issues avail.) Indexed: Can.B.P.I. **Document type:** consumer publication.
●Also available online.
—CCC.
    Description: Key topics such as health, education, cooking, social, emotional and physical development are covered through regular departments.

TODAY'S YOUTH: AMERICA'S FUTURE; a periodic information brief. see *CRIMINOLOGY AND LAW ENFORCEMENT*

649   US
TOLEDO AREA PARENT NEWS. 1992. m. $20. 1120 Adams St., Toledo, OH 43624-1509. Ed. Veronica Hughes; Pubs. Collette Jacobs, Becky Harris. R&P contact: Veronica Hughes. TEL 419-244-9859. adv.: B&W page $1350; trim 10 x 13; adv. contact: Becky Harris. circ. 50,000. pp./issue: 60. (tabloid format) **Document type:** newspaper.
    Description: Contains articles on education, early childhood development, and health and safety tips for parents in northwestern Ohio, and alerts them to product recalls and other safety issues.

TOPICS IN EARLY CHILDHOOD SPECIAL EDUCATION. see *EDUCATION — Special Education And Rehabilitation*

790.019   US
TOTLINE NEWSLETTER. 1979. bi-m. $24 (includes rights to make copies for internal distribution). Totline Publications (Subsidiary of: Frank /Schaffer Publications, Inc.), Box 37267, Boone, IA 50037-0267. TEL 800-609-1724. Ed. Susan Hodges; Pub. Jean Warren. R&P contact: Susan Sexton. bk.rev.; illus. circ. 13,000. (back issues avail.) **Document type:** newsletter.
    Formerly: Totline (Everett) (ISSN 0734-4473)
    Description: Provides parents and teachers with activities and songs for children 3-5 years old.

362.7   US
TRANSITIONS. 1980. q. $15. (Advocates for Youth) Center for Population Options, 1025 Vermont Ave., N.W., Ste. 200, Washington, DC 20005. TEL 202-347-5700. FAX 202-347-2263. Ed. Robin Hatziyannis. bk.rev.; circ. 5,000. (back issues avail.) **Document type:** newsletter.
    Formerly: Options (ISSN 1073-7022);
Incorporates: Issues - Action; Population Options.

369.4   DK   ISSN 0109-0003
TREKLANGEN; hjem, hjemstavn, faedreland. Variant title: Treklang. 1951. m. DKK 40. Dansk Ungdomssekretariat, Moltkesgade 20 A, 2390 Flensborg, Denmark. Ed. Ingolf Julius. adv.; bk.rev.; illus. circ. 6,500.

369.4   CN
THE TRUMPET. 1962. 3/yr. Can.$14 (effective 1997). Girl Guides of Canada, Quebec Council - Guides du Canada, 1939 De Maisonneuve Blvd. W., Montreal, PQ H3H 1K3, Canada. TEL 514-933-5839. FAX 514-933-7591. circ. 1,300. **Document type:** newsletter.
    Description: Covers training and program ideas, camp applications, activities of the Guides for adult members.

649 305.4   US
TUCSON PARENT. 1989. m. $15. Tucson Parent Publications, Box 40356, Tucson, AZ 85717. TEL 520-544-0101. FAX 520-544-0202. Ed. Robert Kemper. adv. contact: Robert Kemper. bk.rev. circ. 26,000. (tabloid format; back issues avail.) **Document type:** consumer publication.
    Description: Covers all areas of interest to women and men in their roles as parents.

TUCSON TEEN. see *CHILDREN AND YOUTH — For*

649   US   ISSN 0895-0784
TWIN SERVICES REPORTER. 1983. bi-a. free to donors. Box 10066, Berkeley, CA 94709. TEL 510-524-0863. FAX 510-524-0894. Ed. Patricia Malmstrom. adv.; bk.rev.; index. circ. 850. (looseleaf format; back issues avail.) **Document type:** newsletter.
    Formerly: Twinline Reporter.
    Description: Provides information about multiple births.

649 301.412   US   ISSN 0890-3077
TWINS. 1984. bi-m. $23.95. Twins Magazine, Inc., 6740 Antioch, Ste.155, Merriam, KS 66204. TEL 913-722-1090. FAX 913-722-1767. E-mail: mhussey@sound.net; URL: http://www.twinsmagazine.com. Ed. Jean Cesne; Pub. Robert Unell. R&P contact: Matthew Hussey. adv. contact: Brenda Schifman. bk.rev.; circ. 34,000 (paid); 17,000. **Document type:** consumer publication.
    Description: For parents of twins, triplets or more. Covers subjects from birth through the teenage years.

TWOJE DZIECKO. see *WOMEN'S INTERESTS*

TY I SZKOLA; gazeta rodzinna. see *EDUCATION*

U N I C E F POLICY REVIEW SERIES. (United Nations Children's Fund) see *SOCIAL SERVICES AND WELFARE*

U S Y S A NETWORK. (United States Youth Soccer Association, Inc.) see *SPORTS AND GAMES — Ball Games*

790.019   CI   ISSN 0503-1575
UMJETNOST I DIJETE. 1956. bi-m. Skolske Novine, Brace Kavurica 40, P.O. Box 785, 41000 Zagreb, Croatia. TEL 041-433-415. Ed. Danica Nola. (also avail. in microfiche)

UNDER FIVE CONTACT. see *EDUCATION*

305.230   DK   ISSN 0906-1592
UNDER PARAPLYEN. 1941. 4/yr. DKK 50($6) Dansk Ungdoms Faellesraad - Danish Youth Council, Scherfigsvej 5, DK-2100 Copenhagen, Denmark. TEL 45-39-29-88-88. FAX 45-39-29-83-82. Ed. Erling Boettcher. adv.; bk.rev.; film rev. circ. 10,000.
    Formerly: Du-Bladet (ISSN 0109-8608)

649   US
UNION COUNTY FAMILY. 1991. 8/yr. $18 (effective 1997). Kids Monthly Publications, Inc., Box 159, Westfield, NJ 07091. TEL 908-232-2913. Ed. Farn Dupre; Pub. Cindy Mironovich. R&P contact: Farn Dupre. adv. contact: Cindy Mironovich. circ. 110,000. cols./p.: 4; pp./issue: 44. (tabloid format) **Document type:** consumer publication, newspaper.
    Description: Provides New Jersey parents in Union County with tips on child rearing, health, education, child care, and other issues of importance.

028.5   YU
UNION OF YUGOSLAV YOUTH. NEWSLETTER. (Text in English) 1971. m. free. Union of Yugoslav Youth, Bulevar Lenjina 6, 11070 Belgrade, Yugoslavia. Ed. Nebojsa Dimitrijevic. bk.rev.; film rev.; charts; illus. circ. 4,000. **Document type:** newsletter.
    Supersedes: Youth Life (ISSN 0044-1244)

UNITED NATIONS CHILDREN'S FUND. ANNUAL REPORT. see *SOCIAL SERVICES AND WELFARE*

UNITED NATIONS CHILDREN'S FUND. PROGRAMME DIVISION. STAFF WORKING PAPERS SERIES. see *SOCIAL SERVICES AND WELFARE*

UNSCHOOLERS NETWORK. see *EDUCATION — Teaching Methods And Curriculum*

790.019   GW
UNSER ARBEITSBRIEF; Materialien fuer Jugendgruppenleiter. 1965. m. DM.15. D J O - Deutsche Jugend in Europa Land Baden-Wuerttemberg e.V., Schlossstr. 92, 70176 Stuttgart, Germany. TEL 0711-625138.

155.4   GW   ISSN 0342-5258
UNSERE JUGEND. 1949. m. DM.68 (students DM.54.40) (effective 1997). Ernst Reinhardt Verlag Kemnatenstr. 46, 80639 Munich, Germany. TEL 49-89-1780160. FAX 49-89-17801630. Ed. Marika Meyer. adv.; bk.rev. circ. 2,200. Indexed: IBR **Document type:** academic/scholarly publication.
—CCC.

URI UI SON' GYO SEGYE. see *RELIGIONS AND THEOLOGY — Protestant*

UTAH. JUVENILE COURT. ANNUAL REPORT. see *LAW — Judicial Systems*

649   US
VALLEY PARENT. m. Bay Area Publishing Group, Inc., 401 Alberto Way, Ste. A, Los Gatos, CA 95032-5404. TEL 408-358-1414. FAX 408-356-4903. Ed. Lynn Berardo; Pub. Sandy Moeckel. adv.: B&W page $1375, color page $2025; trim 9 1/2 x 12 5/8; adv. contact: Dale Ganzow. circ. 55,000 (paid). **Document type:** newspaper.
    Description: Serves communities along the Route 680 corridor of Contra Costa and Alameda counties

649   US
VALLEYKIDS PARENT NEWS. 1991. 10/yr. $15. 227 N. Second St., Geneva, IL 60134-1436. TEL 708-208-7221. FAX 708-208-7257. Ed. Vivi J. Nimmo; Pub. Mary J. Brown. R&P contact: Mary Brown. adv.: B&W page $1040; trim 11 3/8 x 14 adv. contact: Susan Reetz. bk.rev.; circ. 60,000 (controlled). **Document type:** consumer publication, newspaper.
    Formerly: Valleykids Newsmagazine for West Suburban Parents.

649   FI   ISSN 0789-9238
VAUVA. 1992. bi-m. FIM 280. Helsinki Media Magazines, P.O. Box 100, FIN-00040 Helsinki Media, Finland. TEL 358-9-1201. FAX 358-9-1205428. Ed. Pirkko Vuorio. adv.: B& page FIM 13620, color page FIM 18900; 194 x 248. circ. 34,717 (paid). **Document type:** consumer publication.

CHILDREN AND YOUTH — ABOUT

649 US
VERMONT PARENT AND CHILD MAGAZINE. 1990. bi-m. $10. Box 545, Montpelier, VT 05601-0545. TEL 802-425-3835. Ed. Susan Yougwood. adv.: Abby/Rehkugler. bk.rev.; circ. 25,000 (controlled). **Document type:** consumer publication.

VESELKA. see CHILDREN AND YOUTH — For

649 SW ISSN 0346-4245
VI FOERAELDRAR. 1968. m. SEK 390 (effective 1994). Bonniers Specialtidningar, P.O. Box 70452, S-107 26 Stockholm, Sweden. TEL 46-8-736-53-00. FAX 46-8-341138. Ed. Maria Hoernfeldt. adv. contact: Lars Knutas. circ. 85,523.

VILLAGE NEWS. see SOCIAL SERVICES AND WELFARE

VMESTE/TOGETHER. see CHILDREN AND YOUTH — For

VOGUE BAMBINI. see CLOTHING TRADE — Fashions

362.7 US ISSN 0160-4201
Z718.5
VOICE OF YOUTH ADVOCATES. Short title: V O Y A. 1978. bi-m. $38.50. Scarecrow Press, Inc., 4720 Boston Way, Ste. A, Lanham, MD 20706-4310. TEL 800-460-6420. Ed. Cathi Dunn MacRaeick. adv.; bk.rev.; film rev.; bibl.; charts; illus.; index. circ. 4,000. (also avail. in microform from UMI) Indexed: Bk.Rev.Dig., Bk.Rev.Ind. (1981-), C.I.J.E., Child.Bk.Rev.Ind. (1981-), Child.Lit.Abstr., LHTN, Lib.Lit. **Document type:** academic/scholarly publication.
—BLDSC (9258.701500); KR SourceOne; UMI; UnCover. **CCC.**
Description: Contains articles, bibliographies, and media reviews of materials for or about adolescents.

VOICES FROM THE MIDDLE. see EDUCATION — Teaching Methods And Curriculum

267 GW
VON B BIS Y; Materialhefte fuer Gemeindejugendarbeit. 1977. q. DM.20.80. Oncken Verlag GmbH, Muendener Str. 13, 34123 Kassel, Germany. TEL 49-561-52005-0. Ed. Olaf Kormannshaus. bk.rev. circ. 1,600. **Document type:** bulletin.
Description: Details Bible study, teacher training, lesson plans for group meetings, biographies, games, retreats and book discussions.

649 FR
VOS ENFANTS. 1971. bi-m. 1 ter rue Chotard, 30100 Ales, France. Ed. J.C. Manzano. adv.; illus.

WACKENBERGER ECHO. see HOUSING AND URBAN PLANNING

649 JA
WATASHI NO AKACHAN/MY BABY. (Text in Japanese) 1973. m. 16440 Yen. Shufunotomo Co. Ltd., 2-9 Kanda Surugadai, Chiyoda-ku, Tokyo 101, Japan. Ed. Shizuko Aiba. circ. 260,000. **Document type:** consumer publication.

649 CC ISSN 1000-4319
WEILE HAIZI/FOR THE CHILDREN. (Text in Chinese) 1982. m. $26. (Shanghai Funu Lianhehui - Shanghai Women's Association) Weile Haizi Zazhishe, 7, 101 Lane, Songshan Lu, Shanghai 200021, People's Republic of China. TEL 3264961. (Dist. in US by: China Books & Periodicals, Inc., 2929 24th St., San Francisco, CA 94110. TEL 415-282-2994)

WELCOME HOME; a publication for support and encouragement as you nurture your children. see WOMEN'S INTERESTS

WELT DES KINDES; Zeitschrift fuer Kleinkindpaedagogik und ausserschulische Erziehung. see RELIGIONS AND THEOLOGY — Roman Catholic

WENXUE SHAONIAN/ADOLESCENT LITERATURE. see LITERATURE

WEST SIDE STORY. see EDUCATION

649 US ISSN 1043-6774
WESTCHESTER FAMILY; the magazine just for the Westchester County parent. 1989. 11/yr. $22. Family Publishing Group, Inc., 141 Halstead Ave., Ste. 3D, Mamaroneck, NY 10543-2652. TEL 914-381-7474. Ed. Susan Ross; Pubs. Felice Shapiro, Susan Ross. circ. 60,000 (controlled). **Document type:** consumer publication.

WHAT'S WORKING IN PARENT INVOLVEMENT. see EDUCATION

WHO'S WHO AMONG AMERICAN HIGH SCHOOL STUDENTS. see EDUCATION — Abstracting, Bibliographies, Statistics

790 NE ISSN 0039-9736
WIJK EN SPEELTUINVERENIGING TARWEWIJK. MEDEDELINGENBLAD. 1948. bi-m. fl.15. (Wijk en Speeltuinvereniging Tarwewijk) S.V. Tarwewijk, Mijnkintstraat 5, 3081 XB Rotterdam, Netherlands. TEL 31-10-3858394. Ed. A. Wyers deJonge. adv. circ. 550. (processed)
Formerly: Tarwewijk.

WILSON ON CHILDREN AND THE LAW. see POLITICAL SCIENCE — Civil Rights

362.7 UK ISSN 0267-3142
WINNICOTT STUDIES. 1985. irreg., vol.9, 1994. (Squiggle Foundation) Karnac Books, 58 Gloucester Rd., London SW7 4QY, England. Ed. Laurence Spurling. **Document type:** monographic series.
—BLDSC (9319.418080).

649 US
WORKING MOMS AND DADS. 1989. m. free. Corporate Marketing and Publishing Inc., Box 12217, Tucson, AZ 85732-2217. TEL 520-790-4044. Ed. Roberta R. McGuire. R&P contact: Roberta R. McGuire. adv.: B&W page $1360, color page $1855; trim 13 x 14; adv. contact: Patrick McGuire. bk.rev.; circ. 10,000 (controlled).
Description: Directed to working professionals interested in education, health care, child care, changing employment market and camp activities.
Refereed Serial

362.7 360 UK
WORKING TOGETHER FOR CHILDREN IN NEED. CONFERENCE REPORT. irreg., no.11, 1996. Michael Sieff Foundation, 74 Cadogan Pl., London SW1X 9RP, England. TEL 44-171-565-0163. FAX 44-171-565-0163. Ed. Jonathan Cooley. **Document type:** monographic series.
Formerly: Working Together for Children's Welfare. Conference Report (ISSN 1343-5833)
Description: Aims to foster innovation and development in the care of abused and neglected children.

WORLD ALLIANCE OF Y M C A'S DIRECTORY. see CLUBS

369.43 SZ
WORLD SCOUT ORGANIZATION REPORT. 1922. triennial. 15 Fr. (World Organization of the Scout Movement - Organisation Mondiale du Mouvement Scout) World Scout Bureau, Case Postale 241, CH-1211 Geneva 4, Switzerland. TEL 022-204233. FAX 022-7812053. TELEX 428139-WSB-CH.
Former titles: World Scout Bureau Report & Boy Scouts World Bureau.

369.4 SZ
WORLD SCOUTING NEWS/BULLETIN DU SCOUTISME MONDIAL. (Text in English and French) 1969. m. 42 Fr.($32) (World Organization of the Scout Movement - Organisation Mondiale du Mouvement Scout) World Scout Bureau, Case Postale 241, CH-1211 Geneva 4, Switzerland. TEL 022-204233. FAX 022-7812053. TELEX 428139-WSB-CH. Ed. Mark Clayton. bk.rev. circ. 3,00. (looseleaf format)
Formerly: World Scouting Newsletter (ISSN 0043-9002)

WORLD VISION. see RELIGIONS AND THEOLOGY — Protestant

362.7 UK ISSN 0043-9290
WORLD'S CHILDREN. 1920. q. donation. Save the Children Fund, Mary Datchelor House, 17 Grove Ln., London SE5 8RD, England. TEL 44-171-703-5400. FAX 44-171-703-2278. URL: http://www.oneworld.org/scf/. Ed. Lotte Hughes. illus.; circ. 200,000 (controlled). **Document type:** bulletin.
Description: International journal of Save the Children's development and relief work overseas.

XIANDAI JIATING/MODERN FAMILY. see HOME ECONOMICS

369.4 CC
XIAO XUESHENG/ELEMENTARY SCHOOL PUPILS. (Text in Chinese) m. Shanxi Qingshaonian Baokan She, 43, Xinnan 4 Tiao, Qingnian Lu, Taiyuan, Shanxi 030001, People's Republic of China. TEL 222501. Ed. Duan Zhanxiang.

369.4 CC
XIN QINGNIAN/NEW YOUTH. (Text in Chinese) 1978. m. Y2.50 per no. Gongqingtuan Heilongjiang Shengwei, 11, Ashihe Jie, Nangang-qu, Harbin, Heilongjiang 150001, People's Republic of China. TEL 0451-3642171. (Dist. overseas by: China International Book Trading Corp., P.O. Box 399, Beijing, P.R. China) Ed. Yuan Qingguo. adv. contact: Wu Shengshan. **Document type:** consumer publication.

790.019 CC ISSN 1003-2975
XUE YU WAN/STUDY AND PLAY. (Text in Chinese) 1983. m. Y18($60) (effective 1994). Zhongguo Ertong Shaonian Huodong Zhongxin - Chinese Children Recreational Activities Center, Guanyuan, Beijing 100035, People's Republic of China. TEL 6024589. Ed. Ma Guangfu. adv.: page Y9000; adv. contact: Han Jianxin.
Description: Contains writings and drawings for teenagers.

362.7 AT ISSN 1324-4795
Y A C V BITS. bi-m. Youth Affairs Council of Victoria, 259 Gore St., Ste. 1, Fitzroy, Vic. 3065, Australia. TEL 61-3-9419-9122. FAX 61-3-9416-0450. Ed. Merryl Key. adv. contact: Merryl Key. abstr.; charts; illus. circ. 500. (back issues avail.) **Document type:** newsletter.
Description: Current issues and debate of interest to the youth sector and workers with young people, including resources, policy and research.

060 363 367 SZ
Y M C A WORLD. (Young Men's Christian Association) (Text in English) 1947. q. 25 SFr. World Alliance of Young Men's Christian Associations, 12 Clos-Belmont, CH-1208 Geneva, Switzerland. TEL 41-22-8495100. FAX 41-22-8495110. Ed. Ranjan Solomon. R&P contact: Ranjan Solomon. circ. 5,000. Indexed: HR Rep., Refug.Abstr. **Document type:** bulletin.
Former titles (until 1992): World Communique; Y M C A World Communique; (until 1979): World Alliance of Young Men's Christian Associations. World Communique.

YINGER HUABAO/INFANT PICTORIAL. see CHILDREN AND YOUTH — For

155.4 CC
YOU'ER ZHILI SHIJIE/TODDLERS' INTELLIGENCE WORLD. (Text in Chinese) 1986. m. Y1.10 per no. Zhejiang Shaonian Ertong Chubanshe - Zhejiang Children's Publishing House, 125 Wulin Lu, Hangzhou, Zhejiang 310006, People's Republic of China. TEL 86-571-5170300. Ed. Shen Hugen. circ. 450,000. **Document type:** consumer publication.

305.235 373 SW ISSN 1103-3088
▼**YOUNG;** Nordic journal of youth research. 1993. q. SEK 290 to individuals (foreign $40); institutions SEK 425 (foreign $55) (effective 1997). Tidskriftsfoereningen - Young, c/o Monica Rudberg, Ed., Institute of Educational Research, University of Oslo, Box 1092 Blindern, NO-0317 Oslo, Norway. TEL 47-22-85-53-69. FAX 47-22-85-42-50. E-mail: monica.rudberg@ped.uio.no; URL: http://www.sub.su.se/sam/nyri/young.htm. (Subscr. to: Swedish Science Press, Box 18, S-751 04, Uppsala, Sweden. TEL 46-18-36-55-66. FAX 46-18-36-52-77) adv.; bk.rev. circ. 350.
—BLDSC (9421.384550).
Description: Interdisciplinary journal of youth research, aimed at researchers, students and all who are interested in youth research.
Refereed Serial

362.7 028.5 US ISSN 1075-6523
YOUNG AMERICAN PRESS, bi-m. Young American Press, Inc., 2650 E. 26th St., Brooklyn, NY 11235. TEL 718-332-7062. Ed. Jay Kwasnicki.

YOUNG CHILDREN. see EDUCATION — Teaching Methods And Curriculum

1860 CHILDREN AND YOUTH — ABOUT

051 US
YOUNG HORIZONS INDIGO. 1990. m. $15. Box 371595, Decatur, GA 30037-1595. TEL 404-241-5003. FAX 404-241-2668. Ed. Terry Williams; Pub. William Stery. adv. contact: Terry Williams. bk.rev. (tabloid format) **Document type:** consumer publication, newspaper.
Description: News and features relating to African American history, holidays and genealogy for parents and teachers. Includes discussions of new books, lesson plans and teaching materials relating to black history, parenting tips and noteworthy products.

790.019 US
YOUNG IDEAS. 1966. s-a. $25. Vanguard Productions, 160 Aptos Ave., San Francisco, CA 94127-2521. TEL 415-337-1617. Ed. Keith St. Clare; Pub. Keith St. Clare. adv. contact: Robert Oliver. bk.rev.; illus.; index. circ. 12,800. (processed) **Indexed:** RILA. **Document type:** consumer publication.
Formerly: Vanguard (San Francisco) (ISSN 0042-255X)
Description: Reviews children's books, video tapes, cassette tapes and computer software.

YOUNG MINDS MAGAZINE. see *MEDICAL SCIENCES — Psychiatry And Neurology*

YOUNG OFFENDERS SERVICE. see *LAW*

649 SI
YOUNG PARENTS. (Text in English) 1986. m. S.$48; newsstand price: S.$5. Times Periodicals Pte. Ltd., 422 Thomson Rd., Singapore 298131, Singapore. TEL 65-255-0011. FAX 65-256-8016. Ed. Angeline Thier. adv.: B&W page S.$1600, color page S.$2200; 275 x 205; adv. contact: David Tay. illus. circ. 15,000. cols./p.: 3; pp./issue: 120. **Document type:** consumer publication.
Description: For parents with growing children. Covers pregnancy, babyhood, the toddler years, and also children up to 13 years.

THE YOUNGSTER; the illustrated magazine. see *CHILDREN AND YOUTH — For*

649.1 FR ISSN 1188-2360
YOUR BABY. French edition: Mon Enfant (ISSN 1188-2379) 1991. 3/yr. (Today's Parent Group) Professional Publishing Associates, 269 Richmond St. W., Toronto, ON M5V 1X1, Canada. TEL 416-596-8680. FAX 416-596-1991. Ed. Holly Bennett. circ. 190,000. (controlled).
Description: Published for parents of babies and toddlers from birth to 24 months.

YOUR PROM. see *CHILDREN AND YOUTH — For*

362.7 US ISSN 0273-2610
HQ796
YOUTH (BOCA RATON). (Subseries of: S I R S Social Issues (ISSN 0740-3127)) 1976. a. price varies; a. supplement $19. Social Issues Resources Series, Box 2348, Boca Raton, FL 33427-2348. TEL 561-994-0079; 800-232-SIRS. FAX 561-994-4704. E-mail: custserve@sirs.com; URL: http://www.sirs.com. Ed. Trudy Collins; Pub. Eleanor Goldstein. R&P contact: Bonnie Milnes. (back issues avail.) **Document type:** academic/scholarly publication.
Description: Reprints articles that probe what youth means and the prospects for young people today.

YOUTH ALIYAH REVIEW. see *ETHNIC INTERESTS*

362.7 UK ISSN 0262-9798
CODEN: YOPOFA
YOUTH AND POLICY. 1982. q. £25 to individuals; institutions £43 (effective 1996). Youth and Policy, 10 Lady Beatrice Terrace, New Herrington, Tyne & Wear DH4 4NE, England. Ed. C. Parkin. R&P contact: C. Parkin. adv. contact: J. Cocker. bk.rev. circ. 1,500. (back issues avail.) **Indexed:** Sociol.Educ.Abstr., Tech.Educ.Abstr. **Document type:** academic/scholarly publication.
—BLDSC (9421.509000).

649 US ISSN 0044-118X
HQ793
YOUTH & SOCIETY. 1969. q. $198 to institutions (effective Sep. 1996). Sage Publications, Inc., 2455 Teller Rd., Thousand Oaks, CA 91320. TEL 805-499-0721. FAX 805-499-0871. E-mail: libraries@sagepub.com; URL: http://www.sagepub.com. (Overseas subscr. to: Sage Publications Ltd., 6 Bonhill St., London EC2A 4PU, England; Sage Publications India Pvt. Ltd., P.O. Box 4215, New Delhi 110 048, India) Ed. Kathryn G. Herr. adv. contact: Margaret Travers. bk.rev.; index. circ. 1,250. (also avail. in microfilm from UMI; back issues avail.; reprint service avail.) **Indexed:** Abstr.Crim.& Pen., Abstr.Soc.Work, Adol.Ment.Hlth.Abstr., Amer.Hist.& Life (1970-1991), ASCA, ASSIA, C.I.J.E., Commun.Abstr., Cont.Pg.Educ., Crim.Just.Abstr., Curr.Cont., Fam.Ind., High.Educ.Abstr., High.Educ.Curr.Aware.Bull., Hist.Abstr. (1970-1991), Int.Polit.Sci.Abstr., Lang.& Lang.Behav.Abstr., Mid.East: Abstr.& Ind., Psychol.Abstr. (1990-), Sage Fam.Stud.Abstr., Sage Urb.Stud.Abstr., Soc.Sci.Ind., Soc.Work Res.& Abstr., Sociol.Abstr., Sociol.Educ.Abstr., Sociol.Educ.Abstr., SSCI, Stud.Wom.Abstr., Tech.Educ.Abstr., Viol.& Abuse Abstr. **Document type:** academic/scholarly publication.
—BLDSC (9421.510000); Genuine Article; KR SourceOne; SWETS; UMI; UnCover. **CCC.**
Description: Covers the broad social and political implications of youth culture and development, focusing on middle adolescents to young adults.

369.4 UK ISSN 0309-7315
YOUTH CLUBS. 1911. bi-m. £10. Youth Clubs UK, 11 St. Bride St., London EC4A 4AS, England. TEL 0171-353-2366. FAX 0171-353-2369. Ed. Alan Rogers. adv. contact: Carola Adams. bk.rev. circ. 7,500. **Document type:** consumer publication.
Formerly (until 1977): N A Y C News.

362.7 AT ISSN 0817-5586
YOUTH ISSUES FORUM. s-a. Youth Affairs Council of Victoria, 250 Gore St., Ste. 1, Fitzroy, Vic. 3065, Australia. TEL 61-3-9419-9122. FAX 61-3-9416-0450. abstr.; charts; illus. (back issues avail.)
Description: Issues about and for workers with young people, including latest research, resources, policy and issues of debate facing the youth sector.

YOUTH LAW NEWS. see *LAW*

YOUTH MINISTRY QUARTERLY (NEW HAMPTON). see *RELIGIONS AND THEOLOGY*

350 US ISSN 8756-0909
YOUTH POLICY. 1978. irreg., approx. 12/yr. $127 includes Youth Record. Youth Policy Institute, 1333 Green Court, N.W., Washington, DC 20005. TEL 202-638-2144. FAX 202-638-2325. E-mail: corpsnet@mnsinc.com. Ed. David Hackett. bk.rev.; index. circ. 4,500. (back issues avail.)
—UnCover.
Incorporates (1977-199?): American Family (Washington) (ISSN 0161-1178)
Description: Policy forum for a broad, comprehensive discussion of issues and presentation of proposed solutions and their status.

350 US ISSN 1047-7144
HV1431
YOUTH RECORD; the semi-monthly report on federal youth-related policy. s-m. $97 (foreign $237) includes Youth Policy. Youth Policy Institute, 1333 Green Court, N.W., Washington, DC 20005. TEL 202-638-2144. FAX 202-638-2325. E-mail: corpsnet@mnsinc.com. Ed. David Hackett.
Description: Covers current news of federal legislative and executive actions, and the private sector. Presents viewpoints, solution options and outlook on youth-related policy in areas of housing, health, social services and more.

YOUTH RESEARCH NEWS. see *CHILDREN AND YOUTH — For*

362.7 AT ISSN 1038-2569
YOUTH STUDIES AUSTRALIA. 1982. q. Aus.$50($60) National Clearinghouse for Youth Studies, G.P.O. Box 252-64, Hobart, Tas. 7001, Australia. TEL 61-3-62262591. FAX 61-2-3-62262578. URL: http://www.educ.utas.edu.au/ncys/. Ed. Sheila Allison; Pub. Sheila Allison. R&P contact: Sheila Allison. adv.: page Aus.$300; trim 260 x 210; adv. contact: Cate Lowry. bk.rev.; abstr.; bibl.; cum.index; circ. 1,500 (paid). (back issues avail.) **Document type:** academic/scholarly publication.
Description: For youth workers, policy makers, health and community workers. Includes feature articles, research date, media monitoring and information sources.

155.4 320 GW ISSN 0177-9419
ZEITUNGS - DOKUMENTATION BILDUNGSWESEN. 1978. fortn. DM.136 (effective 1998). (Deutsches Institut fuer Internationale Paedagogische Forschung) V W B - Verlag fuer Wissenschaft und Bildung, Markgrafenstr. 67, 10969 Berlin, Germany. TEL 49-30-2510415. FAX 49-30-2510412. E-mail: 100615.1565@compuserve.com. (Co-sponsor: Zentralstelle fuer Paedagogische Information und Dokumentation) index. circ. 200. (back issues avail.) **Document type:** abstracting/indexing.
Description: Contains systematically arranged index of current magazine and newspaper articles on education, including research, politics, schools, teachers, and vocational education.

155.4 362.7 US ISSN 0736-8038
ZERO TO THREE. 1980. 6/yr. $37. Zero to Three - National Center for Infants, Toddlers and Families, 734 15th St., N.W., Ste. 1000, Washington, DC 20005-1013. TEL 800-899-4301. FAX 202-638-0851. URL: http://www.zerotothree.org. Ed. Emily Fenichel. R&P contact: Joan Melner. bk.rev. circ. 7,500. (also avail. in microfiche) **Indexed:** ERIC, Fam.Ind., Psychol.Abstr. **Document type:** bulletin.
—BLDSC (9512.114970).
Description: Research and service programs for children 0-3 and their families. Includes case reports, conferences, information on new publications, and training and funding opportunities.

ZHONGGUO ERTONG/CHINESE CHILDREN. see *CHILDREN AND YOUTH — For*

369.4 CC ISSN 1002-9931
ZHONGGUO QINGNIAN YANJIU/CHINA YOUTH STUDY. (Text in Chinese) bi-m. $18. Zhongguo Qingnian Yanjiu Zazhishe, No. 25, Xisanhuan Beilu, Beijing 100081, People's Republic of China. TEL 86-10-8421144. FAX 86-10-8426270. Ed. Huang Zhijian. circ. 10,000. **Document type:** academic/scholarly publication.

369.4 CC
ZHONGWAI SHAONIAN. (Text in Chinese) bi-m. Guangxi Renmin Chubanshe, Qikan Bu - Guangxi People's Publishing House, 14 Heti Lu, Nanning, Guangxi 530021, People's Republic of China. TEL 24571. Ed. Li Yuanjun.

155.5 AG
ZONA ROJA. 1991. bi-m. Arg.$20000 per no. Comite Nacional de la Juventud Radical, Alsino 1786, 4o piso, Buenos Aires C.F., Argentina. TEL 01-318-6828. Ed. Sergio Pardo.

649 BE
12 MAANDEN. French edition: 12 Mois. (Text in Dutch) 1987. a. free. C & B s.a., Chemin des 2 Maison 61-5, B-1200 Brussels, Belgium. TEL 32-2-7624139. FAX 32-2-7706429. Ed. Philippe Derecque. adv. circ. 120,000 (62,400 Dutch ed.; 57,600 French ed.). (back issues avail.) **Document type:** consumer publication.
Formerly (until 1995): Eerste 12 Maanden (ISSN 0778-1881)
Description: Covers the first year of a baby's life for young mothers.

CHILDREN AND YOUTH — Abstracting, Bibliographies, Statistics

362.7 011   CN   ISSN 1198-3906
ADOPTION NEWSLETTER DIRECTORY. 1992. a. Can.$18 (foreign $18) (effective 1997). Helper Publishing, 36 Norwood Rd., Toronto, ON M4E 2S2, Canada. TEL 416-690-9593. FAX 416-690-9593. E-mail: helper@helping.com; URL: http://www.helping.com/family. Ed. Robin Hilborn. circ. 100. **Document type:** consumer publication, bibliography, directory.
   Description: Lists adoption newsletters and magazines worldwide. Includes title, address, contact, frequency, circulation, pages, cost, ISSN. Covers adoption, infertility, attachment disorder and searching for a birth parent or adopted child.

649   FR   ISSN 1016-8834
B I R D. (Base d'Information Robert-Debre) (Not avail. in printed format) (Text in English, French, Spanish) a. $600 for CD-Rom (effective 1997). Centre International de l'Enfance - International Children's Center, Chateau de Longchamp, Bois de Boulogne, 75016 Paris, France. TEL 33-1-44302062. FAX 33-1-44302065. E-mail: 100631,1101@compuserve.com. (Co-sponsor: French Ministry of Research (D.I.S.T.)) **Document type:** bibliography.
●Also available online.
Also available on CD-ROM.
   Description: Database of 100,000 bibliographic references and CIE products, a catalog of ICC publications, periodicals and a bibliographic synthesis on AIDS.

028 016   GW
BEITRAEGE JUGENDLITERATUR UND MEDIEN. 1893; N.S. 1949. q. DM.57 (foreign DM.69) (effective 1998). (Gewerkschaft Erziehung und Wissenschaft, Arbeitsgemeinschaft Jugendliteratur und Medien) Juventa Verlag GmbH, Ehretstr. 3, 69469 Weinheim, Germany. TEL 49-6201-61035. FAX 49-6201-13135. E-mail: juventa@t-online.de; URL: http://www.juventa@t-online.de. Ed. M. Dahrendorf, H. Heidtmann. bk.rev.; bibl. circ. 1,900. **Document type:** abstracting/indexing.
—CCC.
   Former titles (until 1993): Informationen Jugendliteratur und Medien (ISSN 0937-6755); (until 1989): Information Jugendliteratur und Medien - Jugendschriften - Warte (ISSN 0340-7756)

BERLIN. SENATSVERWALTUNG FUER FRAUEN, JUGEND UND FAMILIE. STATISTISCHER DIENST. see *SOCIAL SERVICES AND WELFARE — Abstracting, Bibliographies, Statistics*

028.5 010   US   ISSN 0067-9070
BLACK EXPERIENCE IN CHILDREN'S BOOKS. 1946. quinquennial, latest 1994. $6. New York Public Library, Office of Branch Libraries, 455 Fifth Ave., New York, NY 10016. TEL 212-340-0892. FAX 212-689-3193. index.
   Formerly: Books About Negro Life for Children.

011.6209489   DK   ISSN 0109-193X
BOERNEBIBLIOTEKSKATALOG. LYDBOEGER, BOG & BAAND. (Not avail. in printed format) 1983. a. DKK 675 (effective 1996). Dansk BiblioteksCenter as, Tempovej 7-11, DK-2750 Ballerup, Denmark. TEL 45-44-867777. FAX 45-44-867892. TELEX 35370. E-mail: dbc@dan.bib.dk.
●Also available online.
Also available on CD-ROM.
   Formerly: Boernebibliotekskatalog. Lydboeger.

BREASTFEEDING ABSTRACTS. see *MEDICAL SCIENCES — Abstracting, Bibliographies, Statistics*

028.5 011   CN
CANADIAN BOOKS FOR YOUNG PEOPLE/LIVRES CANADIENS POUR LA JEUNESSE. (Text in English and French) 1976. irreg. Can.$19.95. University of Toronto Press, Directories Departement, 10 St. Mary St., Ste. 700, Toronto, ON M4Y 2W8, Canada. TEL 416-978-2239. FAX 416-978-4738. E-mail: utpbooks@gpu.utcc.utoronto.ca. (U.S. Address: 340 Nagel Dr., Cheektowaga, NY 14225) circ. 1,500. **Document type:** bibliography.

CANDLELIGHTERS CHILDHOOD CANCER FOUNDATION BIBLIOGRAPHY AND RESOURCE GUIDE. see *MEDICAL SCIENCES — Abstracting, Bibliographies, Statistics*

016.61892 155.4   US   ISSN 0009-3939
HQ750.A1
CHILD DEVELOPMENT ABSTRACTS AND BIBLIOGRAPHY. 1927. 3/yr. $75 to individuals (Canada $87.25; elsewhere $82) (effective 1997). (Society for Research in Child Development) University of Chicago Press, Journals Division, 5720 S. Woodlawn Ave., Chicago, IL 60637. TEL 773-753-3347. FAX 773-753-0811. E-mail: subscriptions@journals.uchicago.edu; URL: http://www.journals.uchicago.eud/CDAB/journal/. (Subscr. to: Box 37005, Chicago, IL 60637) Ed. Neil Joseph Salkind. bk.rev.; index. circ. 5,700. index. avail. in microform from UMI; reprint service avail. from UMI,ISI,KTO) **Indexed:** C.I.J.E., Except.Child.Educ.Abstr. **Document type:** abstracting/indexing.
●Also available online.
   Description: Contains abstracts and reviews research literature in journals, technical reports, and books related to the growth and development of children. Classified by major subject headings, with author index.
   Refereed Serial

362.7 360   UK   ISSN 0968-4050
CHILDREN LOOKED AFTER BY LOCAL AUTHORITIES IN WALES. 1982. a. £5. Welsh Office, Statistical Directorate, Publication Unit, Cathays Park, Cardiff CF1 3NQ, Wales. TEL 44-1222-825054. FAX 44-1222-825350. E-mail: statswales@gtnet.gov.uk. **Document type:** government publication.
—BLDSC (3172.963000).
   Formerly (until 1993): Children in Care or Under Supervision Orders in Wales (ISSN 0263-2667)

028.1   US   ISSN 0147-5681
Z1037.A1
CHILDREN'S BOOK REVIEW INDEX. 1976. a. $103 (effective 1993). Gale Research, 835 Penobscot Bldg., 645 Griswold St., Detroit, MI 48226-4094. TEL 313-961-2242; 800-877-4253. FAX 800-414-5043. E-mail: daniel_snyder@gale.com. Eds. Neil E. Walker, Beverly Baer. **Document type:** abstracting/indexing.
   Description: Index of book reviews of children's books.

028.5   US
CHILDREN'S BOOKWATCH. 1991. m. $12 (effective 1997). Midwest Book Review, 12424 Mill St., Petaluma, CA 94952. TEL 415-437-5731. Ed. Diane C. Donovan. **Indexed:** Bk.Rev.Ind. (1991-), Child.Bk.Rev.Ind. (1991-). **Document type:** bibliography.
   Description: Capsule reviews of children's literature for librarians and teachers.

016   US
CHILDREN'S CATALOG. (In 3 parts) 1909. quinquennial (with a. supplements). price varies. H.W. Wilson Co., 950 University Ave., Bronx, NY 10452. TEL 718-588-8400; 800-367-6770. FAX 718-590-1617. TELEX 4990003HWILSON. Ed. Juliette Yaakov. bk.rev. **Document type:** bibliography, catalog.
   Description: Classified list of books recommended for children from pre-school through sixth grade, with separate sections for fiction, story collections, and easy books. Includes author, title, subject, and analytical index.

011.62 028.5   UK   ISSN 1350-4347
CHILDREN'S FICTION ON FICHE. 1992. q. £140 (effective 1997). British Library, National Bibliographic Service, Boston Spa, Wetherby, W. Yorks. LS23 7BQ, England. TEL 44-1937-546585. FAX 44-1937-546586. URL: http://portico.bl.uk. (Subscr. to: Turpin Distribution Services, Blackhorse Rd., Letchworth, Herts. SG6 1HN, England. TEL 44-1462-672555. FAX 44-1462-480947) (microfiche) **Document type:** bibliography.
   Description: Lists, by author of novels and short-story collections for children published worldwide in English, Gaelic, Welsh, and Irish since 1950.

028.5 016   US   ISSN 0306-2015
Z1037
CHILDREN'S LITERATURE ABSTRACTS. 1973. q. $32 (Canada & Mexico $33; elsewhere $35) (effective 1997). International Federation of Library Associations, Children's Libraries Section, 5906 Fairlane Dr., Austin, TX 78757-4417. TEL 512-454-1799. E-mail: clabs@bga.com; URL: http://www.nlc-bnc.ca/ifla/. Ed. Gillian Adams. R&P contact: Gilliam Adams. bk.rev.; index. circ. 500. (also avail. in microform) **Document type:** abstracting/indexing, bibliography.
—BLDSC (3172.990700).
   Description: Contains an international guide to periodical articles and books on children's literature and allied topics. Abstracts are prepared with international cooperation, giving access to articles in Great Britain, U.S., French, German, Scandinavian, Dutch, Australian and other journals, specialized and general.

028.5 011   US   ISSN 0743-9873
AI3
CHILDREN'S MAGAZINE GUIDE; subject index to children's magazines. 1948. 9/yr. (plus a. cumulation). $55. R.R. Bowker, A Division of Reed Elsevier Inc., 121 Chanlon Rd., New Providence, NJ 07974. TEL 908-771-7753. FAX 908-771-8784. TELEX 138 755. E-mail: info@bowker.com; URL: http://www.bowker.com. (Subscr. to: Order Dept., Box 31, New Providence, NJ 07974-9903. TEL 800-521-8110) Ed. Patrick Gibbons. circ. 13,000. **Indexed:** Ind.Child.Mag. **Document type:** consumer publication, bibliography.
—CCC.
   Formerly: Subject Index to Children's Magazines (ISSN 0039-4351)
   Description: Indexes 48 of the most popular kids' magazines. Points children, ages 8-12, to recent articles on science, sports, current events, popular culture, and more. Every citation includes the name of the article, author, magazine, issue date and number of pages. Also indexes 14 professional magazines for teachers and librarians; multimedia supplement indexes reviews of software, audios, videos, and CD-ROMs in 8 professional magazines.

EXCEPTIONAL CHILD EDUCATION RESOURCES. see *EDUCATION — Abstracting, Bibliographies, Statistics*

GERMANY. STATISTISCHES BUNDESAMT. FACHSERIE 13, SOZIALLEISTUNGEN, REIHE 6: JUGENDHILFE. see *SOCIAL SERVICES AND WELFARE — Abstracting, Bibliographies, Statistics*

INTERNATIONAL DIRECTORY OF CHILDREN'S LITERATURE. see *PUBLISHING AND BOOK TRADE — Abstracting, Bibliographies, Statistics*

KINDEX; an index to legal periodical literature concerning children. see *LAW — Abstracting, Bibliographies, Statistics*

015.489062 028.5   DK   ISSN 0107-4636
LAES OM; emne- og genredelt katalog for de 9-13 aarige. 1981. biennial. DKK 262.60 (effective 1996). Dansk BiblioteksCenter as, Tempovej 7-11, DK-2750 Ballerup, Denmark. TEL 45-44-867777. FAX 45-44-867892. E-mail: dbc@dan.bib.dk. illus. **Document type:** catalog.

362.7   PY   ISSN 1017-2807
MENORES. 1989. q. $10. Centro de Estudios Humanitarios, Azara 3267, Asuncion, Paraguay. Ed. Esther Prieto. circ. 500.

NOTABLE CHILDREN'S TRADE BOOKS IN THE FIELD OF SOCIAL STUDIES. see *SOCIAL SCIENCES: COMPREHENSIVE WORKS — Abstracting, Bibliographies, Statistics*

OHIO. DEPARTMENT OF HUMAN SERVICES. CHILD WELFARE STATISTICS. see *SOCIAL SERVICES AND WELFARE — Abstracting, Bibliographies, Statistics*

CHILDREN AND YOUTH — FOR

028.5 800 US ISSN 1052-3472
Z1037
OLDERR'S YOUNG ADULT FICTION INDEX FOR (YEAR). a. $58. Gale Research, 835 Penobscot Bldg., 645 Griswold St., Detroit, MI 48226-4094. TEL 313-961-2242; 800-877-4253. FAX 800-414-5043. E-mail: daniel__snyder@gale.com. Ed. Stephen Olderr. bk.rev. **Document type:** abstracting/indexing.
Description: Lists and categorizes 1,000 young adult fiction books per issue. Each entry includes author, title, series, publication information, 1-4 star rating. Contains subject, title and character indexes.

800 011 500 US
OUTSTANDING SCIENCE TRADE BOOKS FOR CHILDREN. 1971. a. $2. (National Science Teachers Association, Joint Committee Project) Children's Book Council, Inc., 568 Broadway, New York, NY 10012-3225. TEL 212-966-1990. FAX 212-966-2073. E-mail: Staff@CBCBooks.org; URL: http://www.CBCBooks.org. Ed. Gitta Raffelsbauer. **Document type:** bibliography.
Description: Annotated, committee-selected bibliography of the year's most outstanding science trade books for children.

PARAPARA SELECCION DE LIBROS PARA NINOS Y JOVENES. see *PUBLISHING AND BOOK TRADE*

362.7 US ISSN 1075-5063
STATISTICAL RECORD OF CHILDREN. 1994. biennial. Gale Research, 835 Penobscot Bldg., 645 Griswold St., Detroit, MI 48226-4094. TEL 313-961-2242; 800-877-4253. FAX 800-414-5043. E-mail: daniel__snyder@gale.com. Ed. Linda Schmittroth.

028.5 US
STORIES: A LIST OF STORIES TO TELL AND TO READ ALOUD. irreg., no.8, 1990. $6. New York Public Library, Office of Branch Libraries, 455 Fifth Ave., New York, NY 10016. TEL 212-340-0892. FAX 212-689-3193. Ed. Marilyn Berg Iarusso. **Document type:** bibliography.

016.808 028.5 DK ISSN 0108-6952
UNGE LAESER OM; emne- og genredelt katalog. 1983. a. DKK 186.40 (effective 1994). Dansk BiblioteksCenter as, Tempovej 7-11, DK-2750 Ballerup, Denmark. TEL 45-44-867777. FAX 45-44-867892. E-mail: dbc@dan.bib.dk.

369.4 790.1 ZA
ZAMBIA. MINISTRY OF YOUTH AND SPORT. DEPARTMENT OF YOUTH DEVELOPMENT. ANNUAL REPORT. (Text in English) 1982. a. Zambia Government Printing Department, P.O. Box 30136, Lusaka, Zambia. circ. 810. **Document type:** government publication.
Description: Annual report of affairs in Zambia's Ministry of Youth and Sport and the Department of Youth Development.

ZENTRALBLATT FUER JUGENDRECHT; Jugend und Familie - Jugendhilfe - Jugendgerichtshilfe. see *LAW — Abstracting, Bibliographies, Statistics*

CHILDREN AND YOUTH — For

A B C PINPIN DUDU HUABAO/A B C SPELLING AND READING PICTORIAL. see *EDUCATION*

028.5 FR ISSN 0994-2653
ABRICOT. m. 240 F. (foreign 324 F.) (effective 1997). Fleurus Presse, 21 rue de Faubourg St. Antoine, 75550 Paris Cedex 11, France. TEL 33-1-40026300. (Subscr. to: B.P. 72, 77932 Perthes Cedex, France. TEL 33-1-64380389) Ed. Pascal Teulade. illus.
Description: Presents stories to be read to children 18 months to 3 years old.

028.5 370 GW
ACADEMIA. 1888. bi-m. Cartellverband der Katholischen Deutschen Studentenverbindungen, Truderingerstr. 9, 81677 Munich, Germany. TEL 49-89-4702823. FAX 49-89-4706599. Ed. Johannes Leclercup. adv.: B&W page DM.2400, color page DM.3300; trim 185 x 255; adv. contact: Johannes Leclercup. circ. 35,000. **Document type:** academic/scholarly publication.

028.5 370 US
ACORN EARLY YEARS STORYTELLER. 1978. q. $14.95. Bur Oak Press, Inc., 8717 Mockingbird Rd., Platteville, WI 53818. TEL 608-348-8662. Ed. Susan Pagnucci; Pub. Susan Pagnucci. R&P contact: Susan Pagnucci. adv. contact: Susan Pagnucci. bk.rev.; circ. 1,000 (paid). **Document type:** consumer publication.
Former titles: Acorn Storyteller; Acorn (ISSN 0274-8762)
Description: Contains read-aloud folk tales and stories for the pre-K to grade 3 children's librarian or elementary teacher to use, along with flannel patterns, story props, masks, bulletin board characters, name tags and bookmarks; on such themes as dinosaurs, the Wild West, circus, jungle, insects, and pirates.

ADULESCENS. see *LINGUISTICS*

028.5 286 US ISSN 0001-8783
ADVENTURE (NASHVILLE). m. (plus regular w. nos.) $20.04. Southern Baptist Convention, Sunday School Board, 127 Ninth Ave., N., Nashville, TN 37234. TEL 800-458-2772. FAX 615-251-5933. E-mail: customerservice@bssb.com. **Document type:** bulletin.
Description: Serves as a devotional magazine for children grades 3-4.

028.5 JA
ADVENTURE KING/BOKEN-O. (Text in Japanese) 1949. m. 4560 Yen. Akita Shoten Publishing Co., Ltd., 10-8, 2-chome, Iidabashi, Chiyoda-ku, Tokyo 102, Japan. Ed. Kiyomi Narita.

028.5 574.192 550 US
ADVENTURES WITH SCIENCE. 1985. irreg. $89.75. Enslow Publishers, Inc., 44 Fadem Rd., Box 699, Springfield, NJ 07081-0699. TEL 201-379-8890. FAX 201-379-7940. E-mail: annette@enslow.com; URL: http://www.enslow.com. Ed. Brian D. Enslow; Pub. Annette Noce. R&P contact: Annette Noce. **Document type:** academic/scholarly publication.
Description: Book series of biology, chemistry and geology experiments that can be done at home or in the classroom using easily found and inexpensive materials. Each book includes step-by-step instructions for 30 experiments that show the effectiveness of the scientific method. Each book contains a list of materials used in the experiments and an index.

028.5 IC ISSN 1021-7258
AESKAN. 1897. 9/yr. ISK 3960. Storstuka Islands I O G T, Eiriksgata 5, IS-101 Reykjavik, Iceland. TEL 354-551-0248. FAX 354-551-0248. Ed. Karl Helgason. adv. circ. 6,100.

369.4 YU
▼**AETAS NOSTRA.** 1995. m.? Druga Kragujevacka Gimnazija, Kragujevac, Yugoslavia. Ed. Mila Stefanovic.

028.5 920 US
▼**AFRICAN-AMERICAN BIOGRAPHIES.** 1996. irreg. $246.35. Enslow Publishers, Inc., 44 Fadem Rd., Box 699, Springfield, NJ 07081-0699. TEL 201-379-8890. FAX 201-379-7940. E-mail: annette@enslow.com; URL: http://www.enslow.com. Ed. Brian D. Enslow; Pub. Annette Noce. R&P contact: Annette Noce.
Description: Book series for the middle school and high school level reader. Focuses on inspirational African Americans of the nineteenth and twentieth centuries. Explores both the personal and professional lives of these exemplary men and women. Each book contains chapter notes, a chronology, a further reading list and in index.

358.4 028.5 UK
AIR CADET; the journal for air minded youth. 1970. bi-m. £3.50. Headquarters Air Cadets, R.A.F. Cranwell, Sleaford, Lincolnshire NG34 8HB, England. TEL 44-1400-261201. FAX 44-1400-261201. Ed. Denise Housby; Pub. Stuart Hardy. R&P contact: Denise Housby. adv. contact: Barnes James. bk.rev.; illus.; circ. 38,000 (controlled). **Document type:** newsletter.
Former titles: Air Cadet Review (ISSN 0964-0207); (until Dec. 1991): Air Cadet (ISSN 0964-6302); (until Feb. 1983): Air Cadet News (ISSN 0002-2209)
Description: Publishes articles of interest to cadets in the Air Training Corps of Great Britain.

028.5 LI
AITVARAS. 1989. w. A. Smetonos 2, Vilnius 2600, Lithuania. TEL 370-2-223244. FAX 370-2-223538. Ed. Jonas Krisciusan. circ. 8,000. **Document type:** newspaper.

AKCENTY. see *RELIGIONS AND THEOLOGY — Protestant*

AKTION; Zeitung junger Arbeiter. see *RELIGIONS AND THEOLOGY*

028.5 US ISSN 1054-1411
ALATEEN TALK. 1964. q. $2.50. (Al-Anon Family Group Headquarters, Inc.) A F G, Inc., 1600 Corporate Landing Pkwy., Virginia Beach, VA 23454-5617. TEL 757-563-1600. FAX 757-563-1655. (Braille and large print editions avail. from: Volunteer Braille Services, Inc., Box 12238, Eugene, OR 97440-4438. TEL 503-683-3032) Ed.Bd. illus. circ. 4,500. (looseleaf format; also avail. in Braille; large print edition in 24 pt.) **Document type:** newsletter.
Description: Alateen members, young people whose lives have been affected by someone else's drinking, share their experiences through articles of interest to young people and professionals working with adolescents.

028.5 US
ALBUM & STICKER COLLECTIONS. q. newsstand price: $0.79. Diamond Publishing, 6401 Gross Point Rd., Niles, IL 60714. TEL 708-647-1375. FAX 708-647-0633. **Document type:** consumer publication.

028.5 GR ISSN 1106-1391
ALMANAKO. 1990. m. $45 (effective 1997). Terzopoulos Publishing Ltd., 7 Frakoklisias St., 151 25 Marousi, Greece. TEL 30-1-689-6366. FAX 30-1-680-6631. E-mail: gea@compulink.gr. Ed. Stelios Nicolaou. adv. contact: Angela Daramara. illus. circ. 22,000. **Document type:** consumer publication.
Description: Contains adventure stories and comics. Reviews video games.

059.927 LY
AL-AMAL. w. Press Service, P.O. Box 4845, Tripoli, Libya.

028.5 II
AMBULI AMMAVAN. (Text in Malayalam) 1970. m. 188 N.S.K. Salai, Chandamama Bldgs., Vadapalani, Madras 600 026, India. Ed. Nagi Reddi. circ. 15,000.

028.5 US ISSN 1062-7812
AMERICAN GIRL. 1992. bi-m. $19.95 (overseas $24); newsstand price: $3.95. Pleasant Company, 8400 Fairway Pl., Madison, WI 53562. TEL 608-836-4848. FAX 608-831-7089. Ed. Bryan Freney; Pub. Margo Clark. illus.; circ. 700,000 (paid). **Document type:** consumer publication. —KR SourceOne.
Description: Features articles on American girls, past and present, stories by noted children's authors, paper dolls and cut-out clothes, games and entertainment. For girls ages 8-12.

028.5 324 US
▼**AMERICAN GOVERNMENT IN ACTION.** 1996. irreg. $113.70. Enslow Publishers, Inc., 44 Fadem Rd., Box 699, Springfield, NJ 07081-0699. TEL 201-379-8890. FAX 201-379-7940. E-mail: annette@enslow.com; URL: http://www.enslow.com. Ed. Brian D. Enslow; Pub. Annette Noce. R&P contact: Annette Noce.
Description: For young readers to understand the various branches and workings of American government and the key documents upon which our government is based. Each book contains chapter notes, a further reading list, a glossary and an index.

028.5 970 US
AMERICAN WAR SERIES. 1994. irreg. $151.60. Enslow Publishers, Inc., 44 Fadem Rd., Box 699, Springfield, NJ 07081-0699. TEL 201-379-8890. FAX 201-379-7940. E-mail: annette@enslow.com; URL: http://www.enslow.com. **Document type:** academic/scholarly publication.
Description: Book series designed to give students an objective historical view of American wars. Useful for book reports, research and casual reading. Each book contains a chronology, chapter notes, a further reading list, maps and an index.

028.5 II
ANANDAMELA. (Text in Bengali) 1975. m. newsstand price: Rs.10. Ananda Bazar Patrika Ltd., 6 Prafulla Sarkar St., Calcutta 700 001, India. TEL 33-376000. TELEX 215468. Ed. Debashish Bandhopadhayay. adv.: B&W page Rs.15000, color page Rs.30000; trim 16 x 23.5; adv. contact: S.N. Roychoudhury. circ. 54,000.

808.836 DK ISSN 0900-4556
ANDERS AND CO. 1949. w. Serieforlaget AS, Vognmagergade 11, 1148 Copenhagen K, Denmark. adv. circ. 163,553.
Description: Contains cartoons and caricatures.

028.5 DK ISSN 0900-0097
ANDERS AND EKSTRA. Key Title: Walt Disney's Anders And Ekstra. 1970. m. Serieforlaget AS, Vognmagergade 11, 1148 Copenhagen K, Denmark. adv. circ. 135,000.
Formerly (until 1977): Ekstra Haefte (ISSN 0900-0089)

ANNALS OF CHILD DEVELOPMENT. see PSYCHOLOGY

028.5 282 XR ISSN 0862-6952
ANNO DOMINI; magazine pro mlade. 1990. m. 216 Kc. Portal, Klapkova 2, 182 00 Prague 8, Czech Republic. TEL 420-2-6885216. Ed. Josef Beranek. R&P contact: Jindrich Sirovatka. adv.; circ. 12,000 (paid). Document type: consumer publication.
Description: Youth magazine written from Christian point of view.

028.5 NR ISSN 0331-6289
APOLLO; magazine for young Nigerians. 1973. q. £N1.20. Modern Publications Co. Ltd., P.O. Box 2583, Marina, Lagos, Nigeria. Ed. Toun Onabanto. circ. 35,000. (back issues avail.) Indexed: Avery Ind.Archit.Per.

028.5 500 SA ISSN 0003-8385
ARCHIMEDES; natural science magazine for the whole family. (Editions in Afrikaans, English) 1959. q. R.24 (effective 1994). Foundation for Education, Science and Technology, P.O. Box 1758, Pretoria 0001, South Africa. TEL 27-12-322-6404. FAX 27-12-320-7803. Ed. G.W.B. Stoop. adv.; abstr.; charts; illus.; cum.index. circ. 30,000. Indexed: Ind.S.A.Per., INIS Atomind.

ARKEO JUNIOR. see ARCHAEOLOGY

ARMONIA DI VOCI. see MUSIC

028.5 840 SZ ISSN 1421-0908
AS TU LU? (Supplement to: Parole (ISSN 1421-0851)) (Text in French) 1983. 3/yr. Association Romande de Litterature pour l'Enfance et la Jeunesse, Case postale, CH-1000 Lausanne 4, Swizterland. TEL 41-21-3202328. Document type: newsletter.

028.5 FR ISSN 0220-1186
ASTRAPI. 1978. 22/yr. 559 F. (EU 689 F.; elsewhere 789 F.) (effective 1997). Bayard Presse, 3 rue Bayard, 75393 Paris Cedex 08, France. TEL 33-1-44356060. FAX 33-1-44356091. TELEX 648 094 F. (Subscr. to: Bayard Presse International, B.P. 12, 99505 Paris Entreprises, France. TEL 33-1-44216000. FAX 33-3-20274192) Eds. Catherine Peugeot, Serge Bloch. circ. 71,957.
Description: Helps children 7 and over to develop autonomy, creativity and curiosity.

ASTRO-NEWS. see AERONAUTICS AND SPACE FLIGHT

028.5 570 CN ISSN 0843-7777
ATELIERS. 1989. irreg. (1-4/yr.) Can.$1.50 per no. Les Cercles des Jeunes Naturalistes, 4101 rue Sherbrooke Est, Montreal, Que. H1X 2B2, Canada. TEL 514-252-3023. illus.
Description: Suggests games and activities on natural sciences for young people.

028.5 CM
AU LARGE/GO AHEAD; magazine of young Cameroonian students. vol.15, 1974. m. 350 Fr. B.P. 504, Yaounde, Cameroon. Ed. Mam Dieudonne. adv.; bk.rev.; illus.

AUBERGE DE LA JEUNESSE. see TRAVEL AND TOURISM

808.87 AT ISSN 0726-1810
AUSTRALIAN MAD MAGAZINE. 1979. 8/yr. Aus.$26.50 (effective Dec. 1994); newsstand price: Aus.$3.40. Horwitz Publications Pty. Ltd., 55 Chandos St., St. Leonards, N.S.W. 2065, Australia. TEL 61-2-99016100. FAX 61-2-99016166. Ed. Steve Lopes; Pub. Susan Horwitz. R&P contact: Steve Lopes. adv.: page Aus.$3000; adv. contact: Howard Jenkis. film rev.; tele.rev.; illus.; cum.indexs. circ. 60,000. Document type: consumer publication.
Description: Covers adolescent humor aimed at 10-17 year olds.

AUSTRALIA'S ECONOMIC OBJECTIVES AND MANAGEMENT. see BUSINESS AND ECONOMICS — Economic Situation And Conditions

AUSTRALIA'S ECONOMIC STATISTICS; a student guide to recent Australian experience. see BUSINESS AND ECONOMICS — Abstracting, Bibliographies, Statistics

028.5 US ISSN 1040-5682
PS490
AUTHORS & ARTISTS FOR YOUNG ADULTS. (In 7 vols.) s-a. $75 per vol. (effective 1997). Gale Research, 835 Penobscot Bldg., 645 Griswold St., Detroit, MI 48226-4094. TEL 313-961-2242; 800-877-4253. FAX 800-414-5043. E-mail: daniel__snyder@gale.com. Eds. Agnes Garrett, Helga P. McCue. illus.

AUTUMN SCHOOL OF STUDIES ON ALCOHOL & DRUGS. PROCEEDINGS OF SEMINARS. see DRUG ABUSE AND ALCOHOLISM

028.5 CY ISSN 0256-8209
AVGERINOS. 1985. bi-m. £C3($10) New Generation, 18 Makarios Ave., Flat 8, 2nd Fl., P.O. Box 5105, Nicosia, Cyprus. TEL 357-2-454466. FAX 357-2-454466. Ed. A.D. Christoulides. circ. 4,000 (paid). (back issues avail.) Document type: consumer publication.
Description: Aims to educate and entertain children 7-14 years old.

AWARD-WINNING BOOKS FOR CHILDREN AND YOUNG ADULTS. see BIBLIOGRAPHIES

AZZURRO; il mensile per il tuo italiano. see LINGUISTICS

028.5 780 US
B B. 1987. m. newsstand price: $3.50. Laufer Publishing Co., 12711 Ventura Blvd., Ste. 220, Studio City, CA 91604-2431. TEL 818-508-2010. FAX 818-508-2030. Ed. Cathee Sandstrom. R&P contact: Bob Finnan. Document type: consumer publication.
Formerly: Big Bopper (ISSN 1053-9212)
Description: Contains photos and stories about the latest male teen stars for girls 10-16.

268 GW ISSN 0948-0188
B D K J JOURNAL. 1952. m. DM.30. Bund der Deutschen Katholischen Jugend, Carl-Mosterts-Platz 1, 40477 Duesseldorf, Germany. TEL 49-211-4693155. FAX 49-211-4693120. E-mail: ml@project.fido.de. (Co-sponsor: Jugendhaus Duesseldorf eV.) Ed. Markus Lahrmann. R&P contact: Markus Lahrmann. adv.; bk.rev.; stat. circ. 4,000. (back issues avail.) Document type: newsletter.
Formerly (until 1992): Bund der Deutschen Katholischen Jugend. Informationsdienst (ISSN 0007-5833)

B U M. (Boerne og Ungdoms-Litteratur Magasinet) see LITERATURE

028.5 IS
BAAMLEH. 1926. m. Rehov Kibbutz Galuot 120, Tel Aviv, Israel. TEL 972-3-834248. Ed. Oded Bar-Meir. Document type: newspaper.

028.5 FR ISSN 1163-6262
BABAR; un journal de roi pour tous les enfants. 1991. 10/yr. 199 F. (EU 269 F.; elsewhere 319 F.) (effective 1997). Bayard Presse, 3 rue Bayard, 75393 Paris Cedex 08, France. TEL 33-1-44356060. FAX 33-1-44356091. TELEX 648 094 F. (Subscr. to: Bayard Presse International, B.P. 12, 99505 Paris Entreprises, France. TEL 33-1-44216000. FAX 33-3-20274192) Ed. Stephanie Janicot.
Description: Follows the adventures of Babar the elephant king, for children 3 and older.

808.89 US ISSN 1077-1131
BABYBUG. 1994. 9/yr. $32.97 (Canada Can.$42.97; overseas $41.97). Carus Corporation, 315 Fifth St., Box 300, Peru, IL 61354. TEL 815-224-6656. FAX 815-224-6615. (Subscr. to: Box 7437, Red Oak, IA 51591-2437. TEL 800-827-0227) Ed. Paula Morrow; Pub. Bob Harper. illus. circ. 45,000. Document type: consumer publication.
Description: Features simple stories, rhymes, and word introductions for infants and toddlers 6 months to 2 years old.

028.5 II ISSN 0005-4194
BAL BHARATI. (Text in Hindi) 1948. m. Rs.7($2.70) Ministry of Information & Broadcasting, Publications Division, Patiala House, Tilak Marg, New Delhi 110001, India. (Subscr. in U.S. to: M-S Inter Culture Associates, Thompson, CT 06277) Ed. Shiv Kumar. adv. contact: Baij Nath Rajbhar. bk.rev.; illus. circ. 30,000. (tabloid format) Document type: government publication.
Description: Contains stories and informative articles for children aged 8-14.

028.5 II ISSN 0005-4208
BAL SANDESH. (Text and summaries in Punjabi) 1942. m. Rs.20. Preet Lari Publishers, c/o S. Darshan Singh, Preet Nagar, Amritsar, Punjab, India. Ed. Hirday Paul Singh. adv.; bk.rev.; illus. circ. 6,231. (tabloid format)

028.5 II
BALARAMA; children's fortnightly. (Text in Malayalam) 1972. fortn. Rs.120; newsstand price: Rs.5. M.M. Publications Limited, P.O. Box 226, Erayilkadavu, Kottayam 686 001, India. TEL 91-481-563721. FAX 91-481-564393. TELEX 0888-201 MNR IN. Ed. N.M. Mohanan; Pub. K.I. George. adv.: B&W page Rs.6000, color page Rs. 12000; trim 125 x 178. bk.rev. circ. 291,921.
Description: Stories, poems, cartoons, and essays for children up to the age of fifteen.

028.5 II
BALARAMA AMAR CHITHRAKATHA; children's fortnightly. (Text in Malayalam) 1990. fortn. Rs.72; newsstand price: Rs.3. M.M. Publications Limited, P.O. Box 226, Erayilkadavu, Kottayam 686 001, India. TEL 91-481-563721. FAX 91-481-564393. TELEX 0888-201 MNR IN. Ed. Ammu Mathew. adv.: B&W page Rs.3600, color page Rs.7200. circ. 43,373.

028.5 II
BALHANS. (Text in Hindi) 1986. fortn. newsstand price: Rs.4. Rajasthan Patrika Ltd., J.L.N. Marg, Jaipur 302004, India. TEL 91-141-561582. FAX 91-141-566011. TELEX 365 2435 NEWSIN. Ed. Anant Kushwaha; Pub. Milap Kothari. adv.: B&W page Rs.2500, color page Rs.5000; trim 240 x 170. circ. 54,349 (paid).

028.5 II ISSN 0005-4291
BALJIVAN. (Text in Gujarati) 1920. m. Rs.5($1.) L.M. Patel, Ed. & Pub., Wadi, Vayada Pole, Baroda 1, India.

028.5 IS
BAMAALEH. 1926. m. Tenuat Hanoar Haoved Vehalomed, 120 Kibbutz Galuyot St., Tel Aviv 66877, Israel. TEL 972-3-814488. FAX 972-3-816852. Ed. Oded Bar-Meir. Document type: newspaper.

028.5 FR ISSN 0996-5777
BAMBI. m. 229 F. (outside E.C. 313 F.) (effective 1997). Disney Hachette Presse, 10 rue Thierry le Luron, 92592 Levallois Perret Cedex, France. TEL 33-1-41348500. FAX 33-1-41348989. (Subscr. to: 90 rue de Flandre, 75947 Paris Cedex 19, France. TEL 33-1-44894484) Ed. Gilles Heylen. circ. 55,700. Document type: consumer publication.
Description: Stories about Bambi and his friends, for children 1 to 3 years old.

028.5 YU ISSN 0354-5490
BAMBI. 1990. fortn. Popovic i Synovi, P.O. Box 66, Kostolac, Yugoslavia. Ed. Miodrag Popovic.

THE BANNER OF SOVEREIGN GRACE TRUTH. see RELIGIONS AND THEOLOGY

CHILDREN AND YOUTH — FOR

028.5 US ISSN 0743-4898
BARBIE;* the magazine for girls. 1983. 6/yr. $10.30. Marvel Entertainment Group, 387 Park Ave. S. Fl. 9, New York, NY 10016-8810. TEL 212-687-0680. FAX 212-986-5849. **Document type:** consumer publication.
  Description: Fashion and beauty tips for young girls and owners of Barbie dolls.

808.068 MX
BARBIE. 1985. m. Editorial Armonia, S.A., Magdalena 135, Col. del Valle, 03100 Mexico D.F., Mexico. TEL 525-687-2666. FAX 525-543-2073. TELEX 1764640 KENAME. Ed. Liliana Moreno G. adv. circ. 92,371. **Document type:** consumer publication.

BARNARDO NEWS. see *SOCIAL SERVICES AND WELFARE*

028.5 UK ISSN 1319-0849
BASEM. (Text in Arabic) 1987. w. £70 (effective 1997). Saudi Research and Marketing, Arab Press House, 184 High Holborn, London WC1V 7AP, England. TEL 44-171-831-8181. FAX 44-171-831-2310. TELEX 889272. (And: P.O. Box 4556, Jeddah 21441, Saudi Arabia. TEL 966-2-6691888. FAX 966-2-6671650; Subscr. in U.S. to: Attache International, 3050 Broadway, Ste. 300, Boulder, CO 80304-3154. TEL 303-442-8900. FAX 303-442-7979) Ed. Jamal Inayat. adv.: B&W page $1333, color page $2333; trim 220 x 285. illus.; circ. 40,809 (paid). (also avail. in microfilm; back issues avail.) **Document type:** consumer publication.
  Description: A magazine for children ages 6 to 15, including educational matters, competitions and informative pieces.

028.5 DK
BASSERNE.* bi-m. DKK 162.25 for 6 mos. Interpresse A-S, Roennegade 1-5, DK-2100 Copenhagen Oe, Denmark. TEL 45-33-33-75-35. FAX 45-33-33-75-05. adv. circ. 70,000.

BATNUA. see *POLITICAL SCIENCE*

028.5 GW ISSN 0005-6790
BAUSTEIN; evangelische Jugendzeitschrift. 1946. m. DM.19.80. C V J M Gesamtverband in Deutschland e.V., C V J M- Westbund, Bundeshoehe 6, 5600 Wuppertal 2, Germany. Ed. Friedhelm Ringelband. bk.rev.; film rev.; illus. circ. 17,000.
  Description: Helps adolescents aged 14 to 18 live their daily lives as Christians.

374 GW
BAYREUTHER PAUKE; Schuelerzeitung des Gymnasiums, Bayreutherstr. 1956. q. DM.4($3) Staedtisches Gymnasium, Wuppertal, Bayreuther Str. 35, 5600 Wuppertal 1, Germany. Ed. Joerg Gerald Jagdberg. adv.; bk.rev.; play rev.; abstr.; bibl.; illus. circ. 600. (back issues avail.)

BE'EMMET; a miscellany of studies, teaching and research in children's literature. see *LITERATURE*

BEENBREEK; Natuur 2000. see *CONSERVATION*

BEGEGNUNG UND AUSTAUSCH MIT FRANZOSEN. see *POLITICAL SCIENCE — International Relations*

028.5 FR
LES BELLES HISTOIRES. 1972. m. 385 F. (EU 459 F.; elsewhere 509 F.) (effective 1997). Bayard Presse, 3 rue Bayard, 75393 Paris Cedex 08, France. TEL 33-1-44356060. FAX 33-1-44356091. TELEX 648 094 F. (Subscr. to: Bayard Presse International, B.P. 12, 99505 Paris Entreprises, France. TEL 33-1-44216000. FAX 33-3-20274192) Ed. Marie-Agnes Gaudrat. circ. 67,494.
  Formerly: Belles Histoires de Pomme d'Api (ISSN 0991-8787)
  Description: Promotes the development of the senses, the imagination and sense of humor in children 3 to 7 years old through stories and pictures.

028.1 200 GW ISSN 0863-2863
BENJAMIN; evangelische Monatszeitschrift fuer Maedchen und Jungen. m. DM.36. Wartburg Verlag GmbH, Marienstr. 14, 99423 Weimar, Germany. TEL 49-3643-246111. FAX 49-3643-246112. Ed. Dietlind Steinhoefel. adv. contact: Christian Machalet. circ. 8,000. **Document type:** bulletin.

028.5 GW ISSN 0177-2589
BENNI. 1984. m. DM.46.80. Weltbild Verlag GmbH, Frauentorstr. 5, 86152 Augsburg, Germany. TEL 49-821-3257-0. FAX 49-821-3257201. Ed. Marilis Kurz. adv. contact: Kurt Telschig. circ. 65,166. **Document type:** consumer publication.

028.5 US
BERGEN COUNTY KIDS MAGAZINE. 1990. bi-w. $30. Park Avenue Publishing, 701 Broadway, Westwood, NJ 07675. TEL 201-722-0100. FAX 201-722-0505. Ed. Janet Dengel. adv.; bk.rev.; film rev. circ. 30,000. **Document type:** consumer publication.
  Description: Includes places to go, things to do, child and youth information for parent, features, etc.

028.5 900 US
BEST HOLIDAY BOOKS. 1990. irreg. $359. Enslow Publishers, Inc., 44 Fadem Rd., Box 699, Springfield, NJ 07081-0699. TEL 201-379-7890. FAX 201-379-7940. E-mail: annette@enslow.com; URL: http://www.enslow.com. Ed. Brian D. Enslow; Pub. Annette Noce. R&P contact: Annette Noce. **Document type:** academic/scholarly publication.
  Description: Book series that introduces young readers to the origins of holidays important to children and families of many ethnicities and describes how those holidays are celebrated.

028.5 UK ISSN 0956-1951
THE BEST OF 2000 A D MONTHLY. 1985. m. newsstand price: £1.25. Fleetway Edition Ltd., 25-31 Tavistock Pl., Bloomsbury, London WC1H 9SU, England. TEL 0171-344-6400. FAX 0171-388-4020. (Dist. by: Comag, Tavistock Rd., W. Drayton, Mddx. UB7 7QE, England. TEL 01895-444055; Subscr. to: Aim, P.O. Box 10, Pallion Industrial Estate, Sunderland SR4 6SN, England. TEL 0191-510-0201) Ed. Tharg the Mighty. adv.; illus.; circ. 30,000 (paid). (back issues avail.) **Document type:** consumer publication.
  Description: Provides science-fiction stories geared toward teenage males.

028.5 JA
BEST ONE. (Text in Japanese) 1979. m. 4560 Yen. Gakken Co. Ltd., 40-5, 4-chome, Kamiikedai, Ohta-ku, Tokyo 145, Japan. Ed. Hojun Kigidera.

BETREFF; Magazin fuer junge Leute im oeffentlichen Dienst. see *PUBLIC ADMINISTRATION*

028.5 628 US
BETTER EARTH SERIES. 1993. irreg. $113.70. Enslow Publishers, Inc., 44 Fadem Rd., Box 699, Springfield, NJ 07081-0699. TEL 201-379-7890. FAX 201-379-7940. E-mail: annette@enslow.com; URL: http://www.enslow.com. Ed. Brian D. Enslow; Pub. Annette Noce. R&P contact: Annette Noce. **Document type:** academic/scholarly publication.
  Description: Book series for teenagers to explore the actions taken by individuals and groups to help save the environment.

BIBLE DISCOVERERS. see *RELIGIONS AND THEOLOGY — Protestant*

BIBLE EXPRESS. see *RELIGIONS AND THEOLOGY — Protestant*

028.5 US ISSN 0039-5250
BIBLE-IN-LIFE PIX. 1948. w. $3.25. David C. Cook Publishing Co., 850 N. Grove Ave., Elgin, IL 60120. TEL 312-741-2400. Ed. Iva S. Hoth. illus.
  Formerly: Sunday Pix.

BIBLE LEARNERS. see *RELIGIONS AND THEOLOGY — Protestant*

028.5 FR ISSN 0005-335X
BIBLIOTHEQUE DE TRAVAIL. Short title: B T. 10/yr. 252 F. Ecole Moderne Francaise - Pedagogie Freinet, B.P. 109, 06322 Cannes - La Bocca Cedex, France. adv.; illus.

028.5 AG ISSN 0006-2553
BILLIKEN. 1919. w. Editorial Atlantida, S.A., Azopardo 579, 1307 Buenos Aires, Argentina. TEL 1-30-7040. TELEX 21163. Ed. Carlos Silveyra. adv.; illus. circ. 240,000.

BIMBO; der kleine Tierfreund. see *BIOLOGY — Zoology*

BIOGRAPHY FOR BEGINNERS. see *BIOGRAPHY*

BIOGRAPHY TODAY; profiles of people of interest to young readers. see *BIOGRAPHY*

BIRD LIFE. see *BIOLOGY — Ornithology*

028.5 780.42
305.896 US ISSN 0745-8649
ML3478
BLACK BEAT. m. $21.95 (foreign $26.95). Sterling - Macfadden Partnership, 335 Wilbur St., Lynbrook, NY 11563. TEL 516-593-1220. FAX 516-593-0065. **Document type:** consumer publication.

028.5 305.896073 US
BLACK EXCELLENCE. 1987. 5/yr. $19. N A F E O Excellence, Lovejoy Bldg., 400 12th St., N.E., Washington, DC 20002. TEL 202-543-9111. Ed. Michelle E. Lewis; Pub. Henry Ponder. R&P contact: Henry Ponder. adv. contact: Roy Watson. illus.; circ. 60,000 (paid). **Document type:** proceedings, trade publication.
  Refereed Serial

028.5 FR ISSN 0982-8648
BLAIREAU. 11/yr. 295 F. (foreign 416 F.) (effective 1997). Fleurus Presse, 21 rue du Faubourg St-Antoine, 75550 Paris Cedex 11, France. TEL 33-1-40026300. (Subscr. to: B.P. 72, 77932 Perthes Cedex, France. TEL 33-1-64380389) illus.
  Description: Aims to instill the pleasures of reading, creating and observing in children 3 years and older.

028.5 UK
BLUE JEANS. 1977. w. D.C. Thomson & Co. Ltd., Albert Square, Dundee DD1 9QJ, Scotland.

028.5 649.7 PO
BOA SEMENTE. m. Casa Publicadora das Assembleias de Deus, Av. Alm. Gago Coutinho 158, 1700 Lisboa, Portugal. Ed. Fernando Martinez da Silva. circ. 4,200.

028.5 IO
BOBO. 1973. w. P T Gramedia, Jalan Kebahagiaan 4-14, Jakarta 11140, Indonesia. TEL 021-6297809. FAX 021-6390080. TELEX 41216. Ed. Tineke Latumeten. circ. 240,000.

028.5 SW ISSN 1100-780X
BOECKER, BILDER OCH SAANT; tidskrift foer barnens kultur. 1988. q. SEK 275 (effective 1997). Boecker Bilder & Saant, P.O. Box 19, S-161 26 Bromma, Sweden. TEL 46-8-29-70-09. FAX 46-8-26-27-36.

028.5 NE ISSN 0926-3985
BOEKIE BOEKIE. 1992. 4/yr. fl.25($20) Autoped, Postbus 26072, 3002 EB Rotterdam, Netherlands. TEL 31-10-4767381. FAX 31-4768647. Ed. Jet Manrho. adv.: B&W page fl.5000. bk.rev. (tabloid format; back issues avail.)
  Description: Art, literature and science for children including book previews, short stories, poems, activities and science experiments.

BOERN & UNGE. see *EDUCATION*

BOERNEBLADET. see *RELIGIONS AND THEOLOGY — Protestant*

016.80883 DK ISSN 0106-8199
BOERNEBOGSSERIER TEGNESERIER. (Supplement avail 1976. a. DKK 164.51 (with supplement DKK 169.60) (effective 1996). Dansk BiblioteksCenter as, Tempovej 7-11, DK-2750 Ballerup, Denmark. TEL 45-44-867777. FAX 45-44-867892. E-mail: dbc@dan.bib.dk.
  Formerly: Boernebogsserier.

011.08 778.5 DK
BOERNEFILM & VIDEO. 1976. a. DKK 141.20 (effective 1996). (Danske Filminstitut) Dansk BiblioteksCenter as, Tempovej 7-11, DK-2750 Ballerup, Denmark. TEL 45-44-867777. FAX 45-44-867892. E-mail: dbc@dan.bib.dk. (Co-sponsor: Statens Filmcentral) illus.
  Formerly(until 1992): Boernefilmkataloget (ISSN 0105-1377)

028.5 JA
BOMB. (Text in Japanese) 1981. m. 3600 Yen. Gakken Co. Ltd., 40-5, 4-chome, Kamiikedai, Ohta-ku, Tokyo 145, Japan. Ed. Kazuo Kinoshita.

CHILDREN AND YOUTH — FOR   1865

028.5   BE   ISSN 0773-0306
BONJOUR! (Text in French) 1960. w. 1450 BEF (in Europe 2080 BEF; elsewhere 2320 BEF) (effective 1997-98). Editions G.P. Averbode, B.P. 54, B-3271 Averbode, Belgium. TEL 32-13-780111. FAX 32-13-776837. Ed. Christiane Thiry.
   Description: Aims to develop the full range of early language and mathematics skills, with activities suited for 6-8 year olds.

028.5   GW
BONNVUE: TIPS FUER SCHULABGAENGER; Schulerzeitung fuer Bonn. 1984. bi-m. DM.1. Bonnvue-Verlag, Im Eichholz 12, 53127 Bonn, Germany. TEL 0228-384267. Eds. Michael Rolland, Rainer Emmerich.

BOODLE. see EDUCATION

028.5   US   ISSN 0006-7377
PN1009.A1
BOOKBIRD; world of children's books. 1963. q. $40 to individuals (Canada $45; elsewhere $48); institutions $50 (Canada $55; elsewhere $58) (effective 1998). Box 807, Highland Park, IL 60035-0807. TEL 317-494-0400. FAX 317-496-1700. E-mail: meenakh@aol.com. Ed. Meena Khorana. R&P contact: Meena Khorana. adv. contact: Dennis Butler-Klinghammer. bk.rev.; bibl.; illus. circ. 1,700. (also avail. in microform from UMI; reprint service avail. from UMI) **Indexed:** Child.Lit.Abstr., Lib.Lit. **Document type:** academic/scholarly publication.
   —KR SourceOne; SWETS; UMI; UnCover.
   Description: Special topics in international children's books, plus news, events, prizes worldwide.
   Refereed Serial

028.5   US
BOOKS FOR GROWING MINDS. a. Baker & Taylor, Inc., Information and Entertainment Services, Box 734, Somerville, NJ 08876. TEL 908-218-0400; 800-775-1800. FAX 908-218-3980. **Document type:** catalog.
   Description: Annual listing of children's book titles.

028.5   US   ISSN 1052-1682
▼**BOOMERANG!;** the children's audiomagazine about big ideas. 1990. m. $43.95. (Listen and Learn Home Education) Boomerang! Media Inc., Box 261, La Honda, CA 94020-0261. TEL 800-333-7858. FAX 415-747-0754. E-mail: boomkids@aol.com. Eds. David Strohm, Annie Breed. adv. contact: Tony Cacciotti. bk.rev. circ. 34,000. (audio cassette; 70 minutes) **Document type:** consumer publication, newspaper.
   Description: Children's audiomagazine featuring stories on current events, economics, history, geography, mysteries and jokes. Geared toward children 6-12 years old.

780   US   ISSN 8750-7242
BOP. m. newsstand price: $3.50. Laufer Publishing Co., 12711 Ventura Blvd., Ste. 220, Studio City, CA 91604-2431. TEL 818-508-2010. FAX 818-508-2030. Ed. Cathee Sandstrom. R&P contact: Bob Finnan. circ. 360,000. **Document type:** consumer publication.
   Formerly (until 1983): Tiger Beat (Burbank).
   Description: Teen-age entertainment: news about pop music and young actors.

028.5   UK   ISSN 0006-7709
BORE DA. 1965. m. (Sept.-June). £7. Urdd Gobaith Cymru, Llanbadarn Rd., Aberystwyth, Wales. Ed. Sian Eleri Davies. illus. circ. 6,100. **Document type:** academic/scholarly publication.
   Description: For children up to age 11 learning Welsh as a second language. Follows key stages 1 and 2 of the national curriculum.

301.58   UK   ISSN 0068-0605
BOYS' BRIGADE. ANNUAL REPORT. 1883. a. £9.50. Boys' Brigade, Inc., Felden Lodge, Felden, Hemel Hempstead, Herts. HP3 OBL, England. TEL 44-1442-231681. FAX 44-1442-235391. Ed. Sydney Jones. circ. 10,000. **Document type:** corporate report.

369.4   UK   ISSN 0006-8578
BOYS BRIGADE GAZETTE. 1886. bi-m. £9.50. Boys' Brigade, Inc., Felden Lodge, Felden, Hemel Hempstead, Herts. HP3 OBL, England. TEL 44-1442-231681. FAX 44-1442-235391. Ed. Sydney Jones. adv. circ. 7,000. **Document type:** newsletter.
   Description: Promotes Christian behavior among boys by helping them practice obedience, reverence, discipline, and self-respect.

BOYS' LIFE (BRAILLE EDITION). see HANDICAPPED — Visually Impaired

369.4   US   ISSN 0006-8608
AP201
BOYS' LIFE (INKPRINT EDITION). 1911. m. $9 to Boy Scouts; others $18 (foreign 27) (effective 1998). Boy Scouts of America, Box 152079, Irving, TX 75015-2079. TEL 972-580-2366. FAX 972-580-2079. Ed. J.D. Owen; Pub. J. Warren Young. R&P contact: B.L. Peters. adv.; B&W page $21240; adv. contact: Nick Noyes. bk.rev.; film rev.; rec.rev.; illus.; tr.lit.; index. circ. 1,300,000. (also avail. in microfiche from NBI,UMI; Braille; back issues avail.; reprint service avail. from UMI) **Indexed:** Access (1975-), Hlth.Ind., Ind.Child.Mag., Ind.How To Do It (1963-), Jun.High.Mag.Abstr., Mag.Ind., PMR, TOM. **Document type:** consumer publication.
   ●Also available online. Vendor(s): Information Access Co.
   Also available on CD-ROM.
   —KR SourceOne; UMI; UnCover.
   Description: Covers Scouting, sports, science, hobbies, careers, health, history, video games and more.

028.5   US   ISSN 1078-9006
▼**BOYS' QUEST.** 1995. bi-m. $15 (effective 1997); newsstand price: $3.95. Bluffton News Publishing and Printing Co., Box 227, 103 N. Main St., Bluffton, OH 45817-0164. TEL 419-358-4610; 800-358-4732. FAX 419-358-5027. Ed. Marilyn Edwards; Pub. Tom Edwards. circ. 5,000 (paid). (back issues avail.) **Document type:** consumer publication.
   Description: Aims to inspire reading among young boys. Offers wholesome, innocent childhood interests.

028.5   GW   ISSN 0939-8511
BRAVO GIRL! 1988. fortn. Heinrich Bauer Verlag (Munich), Charles-de-Gaulle-Str. 8, 81737 Munich, Germany. TEL 49-89-678600. FAX 49-89-6374404. (Dist. in U.S. by: GLP International, Inc., 153 S. Dean St., Englewood, NJ 07631-3513. TEL 201-871-1010. FAX 201-871-0870) Ed. Gerald Buechelmaier. adv.; B&W page DM.22944, color page DM.35042. circ. 1,006,866. **Document type:** consumer publication.

BRAVO SPORT. see SPORTS AND GAMES

028.5   US   ISSN 1048-2881
BREAKAWAY. 1990. m. $15 donation. Focus on the Family, Inc., 8605 Explorer Dr., Colorado Springs, CO 80920. TEL 719-531-3400. Ed. Michael Ross. R&P contact: Lianne Belote. adv. circ. 99,000.
   Description: For teen boys, ages 12-16. Designed to creatively teach, entertain, inspire, and challenge the emerging teenager.

028.5   GW
BRIGITTE YOUNG MISS. 12/yr. DM.42. Gruner und Jahr AG & Co., Am Baumwall 11, 20459 Hamburg, Germany. TEL 49-40-3703-0. FAX 49-40-37035617. Ed. Ulrike Fischer. adv. contact: Rolf-Ruediger Nausch. circ. 211,424. **Document type:** consumer publication.

028.5   US   ISSN 0884-3635
BRILLIANT STAR. 1969. bi-m. $18. National Spiritual Assembly of the Baha'is of the United States, 536 Sheridan Rd., Wilmette, IL 60091. TEL 847-869-9039. FAX 847-869-0247. Ed. Pepper Oldziey. R&P contact: Larisa Smith-Cortes. TEL 847-251-1854. bk.rev.; index. circ. 2,100. (back issues avail.)
   Formerly (until Mar. 1983): Child's Way.

028.5   US   ISSN 1048-2873
BRIO. 1990. m. $15. Focus on the Family, Inc., 8605 Explorer Dr., Colorado Springs, CO 80920. TEL 719-531-3400. Ed. Susie Shellenberger. R&P contact: Lianne Belote. circ. 166,000.
   Description: For teen girls, ages 12-16. Designed to teach creatively, to entertain, and to challenge girls towards healthy self-concepts and a closer relationship with Jesus Christ.

028.5   AG
BRONCA. 1981. m. Sarmiento 2210 1ro. A, Buenos Aires, Argentina. Ed. Mauricio Clansig.

369.4   UK   ISSN 0007-2524
BROWNIE. (Former name of issuing body: Girl Guides Association) 1962. m. £17.52. Guide Association, 17-19 Buckingham Palace Rd., London SW1, England. E-mail: CHQ@guides.org.uk; URL: http://www.guides.org.uk. Ed. Marion Thompson; Pub. Sara Swan. R&P contact: Marion Thompson. adv. contact: Nicky Hoy. bk.rev.; charts; illus. circ. 26,500.

BRUSHSTROKES. see ART

BUDGET ACCOMMODATION. see TRAVEL AND TOURISM

028.5   GW   ISSN 0323-8954
BUMMI. 1957. m. DM.32.40. Verlagsunion Pabel Moewig KG, Karlsruherstr. 31, 76437 Rastatt, Germany. TEL 07222-13-0. FAX 07222-13218. Ed. Sabine Drachsel. adv.; color page DM.9100; trim 210 x 280; adv. contact: Rainer Gross. circ. 200,000. **Document type:** consumer publication.

369.4   GW
BUNDESINFO - IMPULSE. 1977. 4/yr. DM.18. Pfadfinderinnenschaft St. Georg, Unstrutstr. 10, 51371 Leverkusen, Germany. TEL 0214-23015. Ed. Edith Sachs. adv. circ. 3,000. **Document type:** newsletter.
   Formerly: Impulse.

028.5   GW   ISSN 0721-183X
DER BUNTE HUND; Magazin fuer Kinder in den besten Jahren. 1981. 3/yr. DM.30. Verlag Julius Beltz GmbH, Werderstr. 10, 69469 Weinheim, Germany. TEL 49-6201-60070. FAX 49-6201-600738. Ed. Barbara Gelberg. R&P contact: Anette Riley. bk.rev. circ. 15,000. **Document type:** consumer publication.
   Description: Full color children's magazine with stories, pictures, puzzles, comics by a wide range of artists.

028.5   UK   ISSN 0262-2475
BUNTY. 1958. w. D.C. Thomson & Co., Ltd., Albert Square, Dundee DD1 9QJ, Scotland. adv.

BURBUJAS. see HANDICAPPED — Visually Impaired

028.5   GW
BURGGEIST; Cochemer Realschulblaetter. 1970. s-a. DM.1.50. Realschule Cochem, 56812 Cochem, Germany. TEL 02671-3051. adv.; bk.rev. circ. 2,500.

028.5   US   ISSN 1043-0806
BURIED TREASURE. 1988. m. $15. Learning Exchange, 25935 Detroit Rd., Ste. 331, Westlake, OH 44145. TEL 216-331-8494. Ed. Virginia Spencer. bk.rev. (back issues avail.)
   Description: Covers activities created to develop a positive self-concept, good relationships with others and improvement in scholastic progress. Includes treasure maps, pirate stories and high-seas adventure.

BUSINESSDATE. see BUSINESS AND ECONOMICS — Management

028.5   UK   ISSN 0262-5326
BUTTONS.* 1981. w. London Editions Magazine Ltd., Egmont House, P.O. Box 111, Great Ducic St., Manchester 3BL, England. circ. 80,000.

028.5   BW   ISSN 0007-7429
BYAROZKA. 1924. m. $4.20. Leninsky pr. 79, 220041 Minsk, Belarus. TEL 0172-329466. Ed. V.V. Adamchik. bk.rev.; illus.; index.

796.5   NO   ISSN 0333-1997
BYGDEUNGDOMMEN. bi-m. NOK 25. Norges Bygdeungdomslag, Schweigaards Gate 34, Boks 3737 Gamlebyen, Oslo 1, Norway. FAX 02-173668. adv.; bk.rev. circ. 16,000.
   Formerly (until 1981): N B U Nytt (ISSN 0333-2047)

CHILDREN AND YOUTH — FOR

C C L/LITTERATURE CANADIENNE POUR LA JEUNESSE. (Canadian Children's Literature) see *PUBLISHING AND BOOK TRADE*

028.5 BE
C J P MAGAZINE. 1974. 8/yr. 350 BEF membership. Cultureel Jeugd Paspoort - C J P v.z.w, P/a Lunatheater, Sainctelettesquare 19, 1000 Brussels, Belgium. TEL 32-2-2030200. FAX 32-2-2010929. Ed. Peter Ploegaerts. adv. contact: Veerle Moens. circ. 20,000. **Document type:** consumer publication. **Former titles** (until 1994): Snippers (ISSN 0774-8124); Former titles (until 1986): Rimboe (ISSN 0773-3739); (until 1984): C J P Magazine (ISSN 0773-3720)
Description: News of culture and youth activities.

C M MAGAZINE. see *PUBLISHING AND BOOK TRADE*

028.5 GW
C P M; Stadt Jugend Magazin. 1987. q. free. C P M Stadt Jugend Magazin, Winkelriede 7, 30627 Hannover, Germany. TEL 0511-579811. Ed. Thorsten Luedtke. bibl.; charts; film rev.; illus.; play rev.; stat. circ. 4,500. (back issues avail.)
Formerly: Comic Paper Magazin.
Description: Contains journalism and features for and about youth, as well as literary and political reviews and music reports.

054 FR ISSN 0335-6469
CALAO; journal bimestriel des jeunes. 1974. bi-m. 42 F. Societe d'Editions Generales et de Documentation (SEGEDO), 6 Villa Bosquet, 75007 Paris, France. Ed. Pierre Rostini. adv. circ. 180,000.

028.5 US ISSN 0197-7547
CALIFORNIA WEEKLY EXPLORER. 1979. w. (from Sep. to Jun.). $30 (effective 1998). California Weekly Explorer, Inc., 285 E. Main St., Ste. 3, Tustin, CA 92780. TEL 714-730-5991. FAX 714-730-3548. Ed. R. Don Oliver; Pub. Don Oliver. bk.rev.; charts; illus.; index. circ. 30,000. (tabloid format) **Document type:** newsletter.
• Available only on CD-ROM.
Description: Contains California history for elementary school children.

CALLIOPE (PETERBOROUGH); world history for young people. see *HISTORY*

CAMERA CANADA. see *PHOTOGRAPHY*

028.5 FR
CAMPUS LE MAG; les annees etudiantes. 1993. m. free. Rayonnement 5, 4 rue Barthelemy, 92120 Montrouge, France. TEL 33-1-42537875. Ed. Patrick Bancarel; Pub. Serge Zagdanski. R&P contact: Serge Zagdanski. adv. contact: Serge Zagdanski. bk.rev.; circ. 150,000 (controlled). (tabloid format) **Document type:** newspaper.
Formerly: Campus le Mensuel (ISSN 1248-914X)

CANADIAN BUSINESS. see *BUSINESS AND ECONOMICS*

CANDLELIGHTERS CHILDHOOD CANCER FOUNDATION PROGRESS REPORTS. see *MEDICAL SCIENCES — Oncology*

369.5 028.5 FR ISSN 0750-4160
CAP LEVANT. 1967. q. 105 F. (foreign 130 F.). Guides de France, 65 rue de la Glaciere, 75013 Paris, France. TEL 47-07-85-59. FAX 43-37-77-69. Ed. Marie-Therese Chotard.
Description: For girls 14-16.

028.5 BL
CARICIA. (Bi-monthly supplement avail.) 1975. m. $34.80. Editora Azul, S.A., Av. Nacoes Unidas, 5777, 05479-900 Sao Paulo, SP, Brazil. TELEX 55-11-8673000. FAX 55-11-8673311. TELEX 55-11-83178-EDAZ. E-mail: benjamin.goncalvez@email.abril.com. Ed. Lana Nowikow. R&P contact: Benjamin Goncalvez. TEL 55-11-8673304. adv. color page $9700; 134 x 190; adv. contact: Enio Vergeiro. bk.rev.; music rev.; charts; illus.; circ. 240,675 (paid). **Document type:** consumer publication.
Description: For young girls.

028.5 051 UK
CAROUSEL. 1995. 3/yr. £8 (Europe £10; elsewhere £12). 7 Carrs Ln., Birmingham B4 7TG, England. TEL 44-121-643-6411. FAX 44-121-643-3152. Ed. David Blanch; Pubs. David & Jenny Blanch. adv.; bk.rev.; software rev, video rev. circ. 10,000. **Document type:** bulletin.
Description: Varied and in-depth articles that inform, educate and stimulate, and prove that the world of children's books can be fun and rewarding.

CELEBRATE CHORAL MUSIC. see *MUSIC*

C'EST FACILE!; le mensuel pour ton francais. see *LINGUISTICS*

028.5 UK ISSN 0009-1006
CHALLENGE (LONDON, 1960). 1960. q. £6. National Association of Boys' Clubs, 369 Kennington Lane, London SE11 5QY, England. FAX 01-820-9815. Ed. Annette Carson. adv.; bk.rev.; play rev.; illus. circ. 6,000. (tabloid format) **Indexed:** Acad.Ind., CERDIC.
Description: Aimed at young people.

CHALLENGE (MEMPHIS); missions magazines for the high school Baptist young men. see *RELIGIONS AND THEOLOGY — Protestant*

028.5 II ISSN 0009-1332
CHAMPAK. Key Title: Campaka (New Delhi). English edition (ISSN 0971-1651) (Text in Hindi; Gujarati, Marathi editions also avail.) 1968. fortn. Rs.340($10) for Hindi ed.; Marathi ed. or Gujarati ed. Rs.238($7); Kannada ed. Rs.136($4). Delhi Press Patra Prakashan Ltd., Delhi Press Bldg., E-3 Jhandewala, New Delhi 110 055, India. TEL 91-11-526311. FAX 91-11-7525020. TELEX 31-63053 DEPR IN. Ed. Vishwa Nath. circ. 170,000.
Description: Colorful magazine for children from five to ten years old.

028.5 II
CHANDAMAMA. (Editions in Assamese, Bengali, English, Gujarati, Hindi, Kannada, Telugu) 1947. m. Rs.72 (foreign Rs.276); newsstand price: Rs.4. Chandamama Publications, 188 N.S.K. Salai, Vadapalani, Madras 600 026, India. TEL 91-44-4838787. FAX 91-44-4838333. Ed. Nagi Reddi. adv.: Full page Rs.3250, color page Rs.6500; trim 17.8 x 12.8. circ. 420,000.

CHANTE ET RIS. see *MUSIC*

028.5 UY
CHARONA. 1968. fortn. Gutierrez Ruiz 1276, Esc. 201, Montevideo, Uruguay. TEL 2-986665. Ed. Sergio Boffano. circ. 25,000.

028.5 GR ISSN 1106-1405
CHAROUMENES ISTORIES. Key Title: Charoumenes Istories Ntisney. 1989. m. $53 (effective October 1997). Terzopoulos Publishing Ltd., 7 Fragoklisias St., 151 25 Marousi, Greece. TEL 30-1-689-6366. FAX 30-1-680-6631. E-mail: tpc@terz.hol.gr. Ed. Stelios Nicolaou. adv. contact: Angela Daramara. illus. circ. 17,000. **Document type:** consumer publication.
Description: Contains selected Disney stories for young readers and preschool children.

CHECK IT OUT! see *LIBRARY AND INFORMATION SCIENCES*

CHEERING WORDS. see *RELIGIONS AND THEOLOGY — Protestant*

CHEM MATTERS. see *CHEMISTRY*

028.5 CN ISSN 0707-4611
CHICKADEE. 1979. 9/yr. Can.$24 (foreign $20) (effective 1997). Owl Communications (Subsidiary of: Combined Media), Box 53, 370 King St. W., Ste. 300, Toronto, ON M5V 1J9, Canada. TEL 800-387-4378. FAX 416-971-5294. E-mail: owl@combinedmedia.com. (Subscr. in US to: 25 Boxwood Lane, Buffalo, NY 14225) Ed. Nyla Ahmad; Pub. Diane Davy. R&P contact: Ekaterina Gitlin. adv. contact: Susan Thornburrow. bk.rev.; illus. circ. 170,000. **Indexed:** Can.B.P.I., Can.Per.Ind., CMI, Ind.Child.Mag. **Document type:** consumer publication.
Description: An award-wiining magazine for children between the ages of 5 and 8. A "hands-on" magazine for children to learn about the world around them, featuring animals, experiments, puzzles, crafts and a read-to-me section.

CHICOS; tu revista en espanol. see *LINGUISTICS*

915.3 SU
CHILD. 1976. w. Okaz Organization for Press and Publication, P.O. Box 1508, Jeddah 21412, Saudi Arabia. TEL 02-672-2630. circ. 5,000. **Indexed:** RILM.

CHILD AND FAMILY MAGAZINE. see *CONSUMER EDUCATION AND PROTECTION*

028.5 US ISSN 0009-3971
AP201
CHILD LIFE. 1921. 8/yr. $16.95 (foreign $26.95). (Benjamin Franklin Literary and Medical Society, Inc.) Children's Better Health Institute, 1100 Waterway Blvd., Box 567, Indianapolis, IN 46202. TEL 317-636-8881. FAX 317-684-8094. (Subscr. to: Box 420235, Palm Coast, FL 32142. TEL 904-447-0818) Ed. Dr. Cory ServVaas; Pub. Greg Joray. R&P contact: Danny Lee. adv.: page $1071; trim 7 5/8 x 10 1/8; adv. contact: Todd Seifferlein. bk.rev.; software rev.; illus.; index. circ. 54,000. (also avail. in microform from UMI; back issues avail.) **Indexed:** Ind.Child.Mag. **Document type:** consumer publication.
—UMI; UnCover.
Incorporates: Young World (ISSN 0162-3664); Which was formerly: Golden Magazine (ISSN 0017-159X)
Description: Contains stories, articles, and activities for children ages 9-11.

800 US
PN1009.A1
CHILDREN'S BOOK AND PLAY REVIEW. 1980. bi-m. $15 (Canada $22; elsewhere $30) (effective 1996 & 1997). Brigham Young University, Harold B. Lee Library, 5042-J HBLL, Provo, UT 84602. TEL 801-378-6685. FAX 801-378-6708. Ed. Marsha D. Broadway. R&P contact: Marsha D. Broadway. index. **Document type:** trade publication.
Formerly (until 1995): Children's Book Review (ISSN 0890-5746)
Description: Reviews fiction, non-fiction and plays written for young people. Includes 40-50 book reviews, 10-15 play reviews, and feature articles on children's literature and picture book illustrators.
Refereed Serial

CHILDREN'S BOOK INSIDER; your monthly guide to children's writing success. see *PUBLISHING AND BOOK TRADE*

CHILDREN'S BOOK NEWS. see *PUBLISHING AND BOOK TRADE*

028.5 370 070.5 US
CHILDREN'S BOOKS OF THE YEAR. 1916. a. $5. Child Study, Children's Book Committee at Bank Street, 610 W. 112th St., New York, NY 10025. TEL 212-875-4400. Ed.Bd. bk.rev. circ. 3,500. (back issues avail.)
Description: Includes approximately 600 titles selected from over 4500 new books published each year for children from preschool to 14 years. Annotated and arranged according to age and interest. Includes tips for parents.

THE CHILDREN'S CHOIR. see *MUSIC*

028.5 II ISSN 0009-4080
CHILDREN'S DIGEST. (Text in English) 1967. m. $36. 87 Wodehouse Rd., Colaba, Bombay 5, India. TEL 91-22-2185679. Ed. Nadir Kamal. adv.: B&W page $100. bk.rev. circ. 24,570.

CHILDREN AND YOUTH — FOR 1867

028.5   US   ISSN 0272-7145
CHILDREN'S DIGEST. 1950. 8/yr. $16.95 (foreign $23.95). (Benjamin Franklin Literary & Medical Society, Inc.) Children's Better Health Institute, Box 567, 1100 Waterway Blvd., Indianapolis, IN 46202. TEL 317-636-8881. FAX 317-684-8094. (Subscr. to: Box 420235, Palm Coast, FL 32142. TEL 904-447-0818.) Ed. Dr. Cory SerVaas; Pub. Greg Joray. R&P contact: Danny Lee. adv. contact: Todd Seifferlein. bk.rev.; software rev.; video rev.; illus.; index. circ. 120,000. (also avail. in microform from UMI; Braille) **Indexed:** Ind.Child.Mag. **Document type:** consumer publication.
—KR SourceOne; UMI.
  Former titles (Mar.-Nov. 1980): Children's Digest and Children's Playcraft (ISSN 0273-7582); (Until 1980): Children's Digest (1950) (ISSN 0009-4099)
  Description: Offers preteen children articles, stories, puzzles, and recipes reflecting a healthy lifestyle.

CHILDREN'S LITERATURE REVIEW. see *LITERATURE*

CHILDREN'S LITERATURE SERIES. see *LITERATURE*

028.5   JM   ISSN 0009-4153
CHILDREN'S OWN. 1951. w. (during school term). J.$1.50 per no. Gleaner Company Ltd., 7 North St., P.O. Box 40, Kingston, Jamaica, W.I. TEL 809-922-3400. FAX 809-922-6223. TELEX 2319 GLEANER JA. Ed. Miss Wyvolyn Gager. adv. contact: Moveta Munroe. illus. circ. 118,000. **Document type:** newspaper.

028.5   US   ISSN 0009-4161
CHILDREN'S PLAYMATE. 1929. 8/yr. $16.95 (foreign $23.95). (Benjamin Franklin Literary and Medical Society, Inc.) Children's Better Health Institute, Box 567, 1100 Waterway Blvd., Indianapolis, IN 46202. TEL 904-447-0818. FAX 317-684-8094. (Subscr. to: Box 420235, Palm Coast, FL 32142) Ed. Dr. Cory SerVaas; Pub. Greg Joray. R&P contact: Terry Harshman. adv. contact: Todd Seifferlein. bk.rev.; illus. circ. 114,000. (also avail. in microfilm from UMI; back issues avail.) **Indexed:** Ind.Child.Mag. **Document type:** consumer publication.
—KR SourceOne; UMI.
  Description: Contains stories, articles, activities, recipes, and crafts for children ages 6-8 with an emphasis on health and safety.

CHILDREN'S VIDEO REPORT. see *COMMUNICATIONS — Video*

CHILDREN'S VIDEO REVIEW NEWSLETTER. see *COMMUNICATIONS — Video*

028.5 179.3   US
CHILDREN'S WHALEWATCH. q. $17 membership. International Wildlife Coalition, 70 E. Falmouth Hwy., East Falmouth, MA 02536. TEL 508-548-8328. Ed. James Kinney. adv. contact: James Kinney. circ. 200,000. (back issues avail.) **Document type:** newsletter.
  Description: Designed to educate children about whales and the marine environment.

028.5   II   ISSN 0009-420X
CHILDREN'S WORLD. Short title: C W. 1968. m. $12. Children's Book Trust, Nehru House, 4, Bahadur Shah Zafar Marg, New Delhi 110002, India. TEL 91-11-3316970. FAX 91-11-3721090. Ed. Vaijayanti Tonpe. R&P contact: Mrs. Vaijayanti Tonpe. adv.: B&W page Rs.1500, color page Rs.3000; trim 205 x 150; adv. contact: C.P. Ravindran. bk.rev. circ. 25,000. **Document type:** consumer publication.

CHILDREN'S WRITER'S AND ILLUSTRATOR'S MARKET. see *PUBLISHING AND BOOK TRADE*

028.5   CN   ISSN 1206-4580
CHIRP. 1992. 9/yr. Can.$24 (foreign $20) (effective 1997). Owl Communications (Subsidiary of: Combined Media), Box 53, 370 King St. W., Ste. 300, Toronto, ON M5V 1J9, Canada. TEL 416-971-5275; 800-387-4378. FAX 416-971-5294. E-mail: owl@combinedmedia.com; URL: http://www.owlkids.com. (Subscr. in US to: 25 Boxwood Lane, Buffalo, NY 14225) Ed. Nyla Ahmad. circ. 189,279. **Indexed:** Can.B.P.I.
  Formerly: Tree House.
  Description: A discovery magazine for pre-schoolers. Each issue will entertain and teach pre-schoolers about animals, nature, and letters.

028.5   US   ISSN 0735-6358
Z1039.S5
CHOICES: A CORE COLLECTION FOR YOUNG RELUCTANT READERS. 1983. triennial. $45. John Gordon Burke Publisher, Inc., Box 1492, Evanston, IL 60204-1492. TEL 847-866-8625. FAX 847-866-6639. URL: http://www.nlightn.com.
●Also available online.
  Description: Provides reading recommendations for second - sixth graders and is designed for use by teachers, librarians, reading specialists and parents.

THE CHORISTER. see *MUSIC*

028.5 367 791.43   CN
CHRISTIAN BALE FAN CLUB. NEWSLETTER. 1989. q. Can.$15($10) (foreign $20). Christian Bale Fan Club, P.O. Box 66534, 685 McCowan Rd., Toronto, ON M1J 3N8, Canada. FAX 416-289-7609. E-mail: cbale@asgo.net; URL: http://www.asga.net/~cbale.htm. Ed. Harrison Cheung. R&P contact: David Bale. adv.; bk.rev. **Document type:** newsletter.
  Formerly: Banner.
  Description: Contains studio information about the past, present and future film projects of actor Christian Bale.

028.5 280   US
CHRISTIAN PATHWAY. 1962. w. $6.50 (effective 1993). Rod and Staff Publishers, Inc., State Rte. 172, Crockett, KY 41413. TEL 606-522-4348. FAX 606-522-4896. Ed. Kenneth Mast, Robert Zimmerman. circ. 4,075.
  Description: Publishes stories promoting Biblical values for children.

CHRISTLICH-PAEDAGOGISCHE BLAETTER; Zeitschrift fuer den katechetischen Dienst. see *RELIGIONS AND THEOLOGY*

CHUZHONGSHENG SHUXUE FUDAO/MATHEMATICS TUTORING FOR JUNIOR HIGH SCHOOL STUDENTS. see *MATHEMATICS*

CIAO ITALIA; il mensile per il tuo italiano. see *LINGUISTICS*

028.5 780   IT
CIAO 2001. 1969. fortn. L.90000. (Europa 2001 Coop) Edizioni L.E.T.I. s.r.l., Viale E.Q. Visconti, 20, 00198 Rome, Italy. TEL 39-6-3207101. Ed. Francesco Puzzo. adv.: B&W page L.5610000, color page L.10200000. circ. 72,000.
  Description: Covers various topics in music.

CINEMA. see *MOTION PICTURES*

028.5   IT
CIOE. 1980. w. newsstand price: Lit.3000. Edizioni Internazionale Cioe s.r.l., Via G. Fabroni, 24, 00191 Rome, Italy. TEL 39-6-3287309. Ed. Fabio Piscopo. adv.: page Lit.25000000. circ. 320,704.

028.5   IT
CIOE GIRL. 1989. m. Edizioni Internazionale Cioe s.r.l., Via G. Fabbroni, 24, 00191 Rome, Italy. TEL 39-6-3287309. FAX 39-6-3274576. Ed. Fabio Piscopo. adv.: page L.9000000. circ. 67,687.

028.5   UK   ISSN 1350-8547
CIP. 1963. m. (Sep.-Jun.). £8. Urdd Gobaith Cymru, Llanbadarn Rd., Aberystwyth, Wales. Ed. Sian Eleri Davies. illus. circ. 5,000. **Document type:** academic/scholarly publication.
  Incorporates: Cymric Plant; Formerly (until 1987): Deryn (ISSN 0011-9148)
  Description: For children ages 7-11.

028.5   UK   ISSN 0267-4548
CIRCLE. 1956. s-a. donation. International Friendship Circle, 30A Wellington Parade, Blackfen Rd., Sidcup, Kent DA15 9NF, England. Ed. T.L. Simmons.

028.5   PL   ISSN 1231-1677
CIUCHCIA; miesiecznik nie tylko dla grzecznych dzieci. 1994. m. 26.40 Zl. (US $10); newsstand price: 2.20 Zl. Telewizja Polska S.A., Biuro Handlu i Promocji, Ul. Jana Pawla Woronicza 17, 00-999 Warsaw, Poland. TEL 48-22-6476907. FAX 48-22-6476907. (Dist. by: Ruch S.A., ul. Towarowa 28, Warsaw, Poland. TEL 48-22-6201271) Ed. Andrzej Grabowski. adv.: page 4000 Zl. ($1500). bk.rev.; film rev.; illus. circ. 200,000.
  Description: Aims to educate and entertain children 5-10 years of age. Includes adventures of the main characters from the popular TV series for children.

028.5   CN   ISSN 1191-8845
CLASS MONITOR. 1991. q. Kansulin Press, P.O. Box 720, Sta. Q, Toronto, ON M4T 2N5, Canada. TEL 416-932-1771. FAX 416-480-9435. Ed. Shelley Robertson. adv.: B&W and color, B&W page Can.$10000; trim 10 1/4 x 15. circ. 188,250. (tabloid format) **Document type:** newspaper.
  Formerly (until 1993): Monitor (ISSN 1183-9473)

028.5   IT
CLEO. 1986. bi-m. newsstand price: L.3000. Edizioni Internazionale Cioe s.r.l., Via G. Fabroni 24, 00191 Rome, Italy. TEL 39-6-3287309. Ed. Lamberto Antonelli. adv.: page L.6000000. circ. 60,000.

028.5   GW
CLEVER & SMART. bi-m. newsstand price: DM.6.30. ConPart Verlag GmbH und Co. Zeitschriften KG, Karlsruherstr. 31, 76437 Rastatt, Germany. TEL 49-7222-13403. FAX 49-7222-13404. **Document type:** consumer publication.

028.5   CN   ISSN 0835-3565
CLIK; jeune et franco-ontarien. 1987. 6/yr. Can.$14 (foreign Can.$28). Clik, 20 Lower Spadina Ave., Toronto, ON M5V 2Z1, Canada. TEL 416-367-2545. FAX 416-367-0382. Ed. Brigitte Hebert. adv.; bk.rev.; film rev.; illus.; stat.; circ. 2,500 (controlled). (back issues avail.)

028.5   US   ISSN 1084-9343
▼**CLUB Z!;** it's the place to be. 1995. bi-m. $14.95. Club Z!, Inc., 10045 Adamo Dr., Ste. 3, Tampa, FL 33619. TEL 813-661-3379; 800-434-2582. FAX 813-661-5703. E-mail: zfun@club-z.com; URL: http://www.club-z.com. Ed. Aimee Sottilaro; Pubs. Mark Lucas, James Murphy. R&P contact: James Murphy. illus. (back issues avail.) **Document type:** consumer publication.
  Description: Offers activities, jokes and educational articles for elementary school children.

028.5 284   US   ISSN 1071-4073
CLUBHOUSE. 1951. 12/yr. $5. Your Story Hour, Inc., 464 W. Ferry, Box 15, Berrien Springs, MI 49103. TEL 616-471-9009. FAX 616-471-4661. Ed. Krista Phillips-Hainey. circ. 500. **Document type:** consumer publication.
  Description: For children 9-15 years old. Adventure, true and historical stories, puzzles, advice column. Contains religious overtones.

028.5 973   US   ISSN 0199-5197
E169.1
COBBLESTONE; the history magazine for young people. 1980. 9/yr. $26.95 (foreign $34.95). Cobblestone Publishing, 7 School St., Peterborough, NH 03458. TEL 603-924-7209. FAX 603-924-7380. Ed. Meg Chorlian; Pub. Malcolm Jensen. R&P contact: Pat Sylvestro. bk.rev.; film rev.; charts; illus.; cum.index: 1980-1996. circ. 34,000. (back issues avail.) **Indexed:** Ind.Child.Mag., Jun.High.Mag.Abstr.
—KR SourceOne; UncOver.
  Description: Explores themes in American history through lively articles, puzzles, games, and recipes. For children ages 8-14. Each issue is devoted to a single theme.

028.5   GW   ISSN 0942-4997
COCKTAIL (FRANKFURT). 1988. q. Deutsche Jungsozialisten (JUSOS), Fischerfeldstr. 7-11, 60311 Frankfurt, Germany. TEL 069-291096. adv.; bk.rev.

028.5 920   US
COLLECTIVE BIOGRAPHIES. 1994. irreg. $227.40. Enslow Publishers, Inc., 44 Fadem Rd., Box 699, Springfield, NJ 07081-0699. TEL 201-379-8890. FAX 201-379-7940. E-mail: annette@enslow.com; URL: http://www.enslow.com. Ed. Brian D. Enslow; Pub. Annette Noce. R&P contact: Annette Noce.
  Description: Book series on biographies of important people. Books are organized around interesting themes and include women and minorities.

028.5   UY
COLORIN COLORADO. 1980. m. Dalmiro Costa 4482, Montevideo, Uruguay. Dir. Sara Minster de Murninkas. circ. 3,000.

C

CHILDREN AND YOUTH — FOR

808.836   US   ISSN 1053-0398
COMICS SCENE. 1981-1983; resumed 1987. 8/yr. $29.99 (foreign $36.99). Starlog Group, Inc., 475 Park Ave. S., New York, NY 10016. TEL 212-689-2830. FAX 212-889-7933. Ed. David McDonnell. adv. **Document type:** consumer publication.
 Formerly: Starlog Presents Comics Scene (ISSN 0732-5622)
 Description: Devoted to comic books and strips, the writers, artists and talents who create them, and film and TV adaptations of them, as well as animated projects.

028.5 267   IT   ISSN 0393-7984
COMUNITA SPORTIVA; settimanale di informazione e orientamento delle attivita CSI. 1975. w. L25000. Centro Sportivo Italiano (CSI), Via S. Antonio 5, 20122 Milan, Italy. TEL 02-58304279. FAX 02-58307612. circ. 3,000.

028.5 780   GW
CONCERT. 10/yr. Spezial Zeitschriftenverlagsgesellschaft mbH, Edisonstr. 8, 85718 Unterschleisshei, Germany. TEL 49-89-321422-0. FAX 49-89-32142259. Ed. Andreas Kraatz. adv. contact: Inge Jansen. circ. 46,613. **Document type:** consumer publication.

THE CONCORD REVIEW. see *HISTORY*

CONTEMPORARY PRAISE. see *MUSIC*

028.5 305.4 920   US
CONTEMPORARY WOMEN. 1988. irreg. $208.45. Enslow Publishers, Inc., 44 Fadem Rd., Box 699, Springfield, NJ 07081-0699. TEL 201-379-8890. FAX 201-379-7940. E-mail: annette@enslow.com; URL: http://www.enslow.com. Ed. Brian D. Enslow; Pub. Annette Noce. R&P contact: Annette Noce.
 Description: Book series of biographies of famous contemporary women, who provide positive role models for today's teenagers.

028.5   US
CONTESTS FOR STUDENTS. 1990. biennial. $29.95. Gale Research, 835 Penobscot Bldg., 645 Griswold St., Detroit, MI 48226-4094. TEL 313-961-2242; 800-877-4253. FAX 800-414-5043. E-mail: daniel_snyder@gale.com. Ed. Mary Ellen Snodrass.
 Description: Describes over 600 national and regional competitions designed to challenge students of all ages - at the elementary, junior high, and high school levels.

028.5 284   GW   ISSN 0343-3935
CONTRAPUNKT; christliche Zweimonatszeitschrift fuer junge Leute. 1925. bi-m. DM.24. M B K Verlag, Hermann-Loens-Str. 14, 32105 Bad Salzuflen, Germany. TEL 49-5222-180540. FAX 49-5222-180559. Ed. Antje Borchers. adv. circ. 6,000. (back issues avail.) **Document type:** bulletin.

028.5   IT   ISSN 0010-9185
CORRIERE DEI PICCOLI. 1908. w. L.67600($12.50) Rizzoli Editore-Corriere della Sera, Via A. Rizzoli 2, 20132 Milan, Italy. Ed. M. Minerbi. adv.; charts; illus.

028.5   CN   ISSN 0822-7098
COULICOU. 1984. 9/yr. Can.$20.95 (foreign Can.$30.95) (effective 1997). Les Editions Heritage Inc., 300 Avenue Arran, Saint-Lambert, PQ J4R 1K5, Canada. TEL 514-875-0327. Ed. Claire Chabot; Pub. Sylvie Payette. R&P contact: Sylvie Payette. circ. 20,000. (back issues avail.) **Indexed:** Can.Per.Ind., Pt.de Rep. **Document type:** academic/scholarly publication.

248.82   US   ISSN 0885-0283
COUNSELOR (WHEATON).* 1941. q. $9.95. Scripture Press Publications, Inc., 4050 Lee Vance View, Colorado Springs, CO 80918-7102. Ed. Janice K. Burton. illus. **Document type:** newspaper.
 Formerly: My Counselor (ISSN 0011-0019)
 Description: Sunday school take-home paper, for ages 8-11.

▼**COUNTDOWN TO SPACE.** 1995. irreg. $101.70. Enslow Publishers, Inc., 44 Fadem Rd., Box 699, Springfield, NJ 07081-0699. TEL 201-379-8890. FAX 201-379-7940. E-mail: annette@enslow.com; URL: http://www.enslow.com. Ed. Brian D. Enslow; Pub. Annette Noce. R&P contact: Annette Noce.
 Description: Book series that recaps the most exciting manned spaceflights, the successes as well as failures.

028.5 629.1   US

CRACKING THE SYSTEM: THE S A T & P S A T. see *EDUCATION — Guides To Schools And Colleges*

028.5   US   ISSN 1074-1348
CRAYOLA KIDS. 1994. bi-m. $19.97 (Canada $25.97). Meredith Custom Publishing, 1716 Locust St., Des Moines, IA 50309-9708. TEL 515-284-2007. FAX 515-284-2064. Ed. Mary Heaton; Pub. Deborah Barrow. R&P contact: Mary Heaton. adv. contact: Andrew Schultz. bk.rev.; illus.; circ. 250,000 (paid). **Document type:** consumer publication.
 Description: Provides young readers with educational and entertaining games and activities.

541.3   US   ISSN 0892-9599
CREATIVE KIDS. 1980. q. $19.95 (foreign $29.95). Prufrock Press, Box 8813, Waco, TX 76714-8813. TEL 800-998-2208. FAX 800-240-0333. Ed. Libby Lindsey; Pub. Joel McIntosh. circ. 35,000. **Document type:** consumer publication.
 Formerly: Chart Your Course (ISSN 0744-3420)
 Description: Stories, poems, art, music, and more, all submitted by children for all children to enjoy. Motivates and encourages creative production.

808.89   US   ISSN 0090-6034
AP201
CRICKET. 1973. m. $32.97 (Canada Can.$42.97; overseas $41.97). Carus Corporation, 315 Fifth St., Box 300, Peru, IL 61354. TEL 815-224-6656. FAX 815-224-6615. (Subscr. to: Box 7433, Red Oak, IA 51591-2433. TEL 800-827-0227) Ed. Deborah Vetter; Pub. Bob Harper. bk.rev. circ. 77,000. (also avail. in microfilm from UMI; reprint service avail. from UMI) **Indexed:** A.I.P.P., Ind.Child.Mag., Jun.High.Mag.Abstr. **Document type:** consumer publication.
 —KR SourceOne; UMI.
 Description: Publishes fiction, nonfiction, poetry, and folklore for children ages 9 to 14.

CRISS CROSS. see *CHILDREN AND YOUTH — About*

CRUSADER (MEMPHIS). see *RELIGIONS AND THEOLOGY — Protestant*

028.5 284   US
CRUSADER MAGAZINE (GRAND RAPIDS). 1958. 7/yr. $9.50 (effective Mar. 1997). Calvinist Cadet Corps, 1333 Alger St., Box 7259, Grand Rapids, MI 49510. TEL 616-241-5616. FAX 616-241-5558. E-mail: cadets@aol.com; URL: http://ww.gospelcom.net/cadets/. Ed. G. Richard Broene. R&P contact: G. Richard Broene. adv. contact: Kathy Door. circ. 13,000 (paid).
 Description: For boys 9-14. Helps them see how God is at work in their lives and in the world around them.

268   PO   ISSN 0011-2194
CRUZADA EUCARISTICA. 1930. m. Esc.250($7) L. das Teresinhas 5, Braga, Portugal. Ed. Fernando Leite. circ. 120,000.

028.5   II
CUB MAGAZINE. (Text in English) 1984. bi-m. newsstand price: Rs.7. Advertising Concessionaires Pvt. Ltd., 602 Maker Chamber V, Nariman Point, Bombay 400 021, India. TEL 2830061. Ed. Bittu Sahgal; Pub. Shashi Kumar. adv.: B&W page Rs.3000, color page Rs. 5500; trim 168 x 232; adv. contact: Shashi Kumar.

808.068   CR
CUENTA QUETE CUENTO. revista latinoamericana de literatura infantil. 1992. q. Col.1300 (America $16; Europe $18). Fundacion Educativa San Judas Tadeo, P.O. Box 1248, 1007 Centro Colon San Jose, Costa Rica. TEL 506-2215948. FAX 506-2333973. Ed. Helia Betancourt de Sanchez. circ. 900. **Document type:** consumer publication.

028.5 371.3   US   ISSN 0011-3492
CURRENT EVENTS.* 1902. w. (during school year). $29.95 for single subscr. (effective 1997-1998). Weekly Reader Corporation, Box 120023, Stamford, CT 06912-0023. TEL 800-446-3355. FAX 609-786-3360. (Subscr. to: 3000 Cindel Dr., Delran, NJ 08075; Large Print and Braille editions avail. from: American Printing House for the Blind Inc., 1839 Frankfort Ave., Box 6389, Louisville, KY 40206-0085. TEL 502-895-2405) Ed. Sandra Maccarone; Pub. Richard J. Le Brasseur. R&P contact: Shirley Peterson. circ. 251,378 (paid). (also avail. in microfilm from UMI; Braille; large print edition in 14 pt.; reprint service avail. from UMI) **Indexed:** Ind.Child.Mag., Jun.High.Mag.Abstr. **Document type:** newspaper.
 —UMI.
 Description: Contains educational articles on national and foreign events for students in grades 6-10. Includes separate teacher's guide.

CURRENT ISSUES SOURCEFILE. see *SOCIAL SCIENCES: COMPREHENSIVE WORKS*

028.5 500   US   ISSN 0011-3905
CURRENT SCIENCE.* 1927. 18/yr. $29.95 for single subscr. (effective 1997-1998). Weekly Reader Corporation, Box 120023, Stamford, CT 06912-0023. TEL 800-446-3355. FAX 609-786-3360. (Subscr. to: 300 Cindel Dr., Delran, NJ 08075; Large Print and Braille editions avail. from: American Printing House for the Blind, Inc., 1839 Frankfort Ave., Box 6389, Louisville, KY 40206-0085. TEL 502-895-2405) Ed. Sandra Maccarone; Pub. Richard J. Le Brasseur. R&P contact: Shirley Peterson. circ. 316,975 (paid). (also avail. in microfilm from UMI; Braille; large print edition in 14 pt.; reprint service avail. from UMI) **Indexed:** Anal.Abstr., Biodet.Abstr., Biotech.Abstr., Cadscan, Chem.Abstr., Chem.Cit.Ind., Curr.Adv.Genetics & Molec.Biol., Curr.Cont., Curr.Leather Lit., Deep Sea Res.& Oceanogr.Abstr., Food Sci.& Tech.Abstr., Geo.Abstr.H.G., Geo.Abstr.P.G., Ind.Child.Mag., Ind.Vet., Jun.High.Mag.Abstr., Lead Abstr., Nutr.Abstr., Protozool.Abstr., Rev.Appl.Entomol., Sci.Cit.Ind., SSCI, Sugar Ind.Abstr., Vet.Bull., Zincscan.
 —KR SourceOne; SWETS; UMI.
 Description: Reports the latest news in all areas of science, health, and technology for junior and senior high school students. Includes separate teacher's guide.

028.5   CC
DA HUILANG HUABAO. (Text in Chinese) bi-m. 21 Shiji Chubanshe - 21st Century Publishing, No.5, Xinwei Lu, Nanchang, Jiangxi 330002, People's Republic of China. TEL 333749. Ed. Zheng Yuanjie.

266   IT
DAFUR; Monatszeitschrift der Jugend Sudtirols. (Text in German) 1921. m. L.34000 (effective 1995). Verlagsanstalt Athesia, Weinbergweg 7, 39100 Bozen, Italy. TEL 39-471-925111. FAX 39-471-925569. Ed. Uli Mair. adv. contact: Ilse Egger. bk.rev.; film rev.; illus. circ. 1,860. **Document type:** consumer publication.
 Formerly: Jugendwacht (ISSN 0022-5967)

DAILY POWER; daily Bible reading notes for young people for the whole year. see *RELIGIONS AND THEOLOGY*

DANISH CHILDREN'S LITERATURE. see *LITERATURE*

028.5   BE   ISSN 0773-0292
DAUPHIN. (Text in French) 1978. w. 1450 BEF (in Europe 2080 BEF; elsewhere 2320 BEF) (effective 1997-98). Editions G.P. Averbode, B.P. 54, B-3271 Averbode, Belgium. TEL 32-13-780111. FAX 32-13-776837. Ed. Jan Lembrechts.
 Description: Helps children discover the world in time and space, to look at things from a different angle and have fun with reading. For ages 8-10.

DAVAI. see *LINGUISTICS*

059.927   TS
DAWHAT AL-MUTANABBI'. (Text in Arabic) 1987. a. exchange basis. Al- Mutanabbi' Secondary School, P.O. Box 46071, Abu Dhabi, United Arab Emirates. TEL 478374. Ed. Ghazi Salim. circ. 300.
 Description: Student publication covering literary, cultural and social activities in the school community.

CHILDREN AND YOUTH — FOR 1869

DAYBREAK STAR INDIAN READER. see *ETHNIC INTERESTS*

DEAF BLIND NEWS SUMMARY. see *HANDICAPPED — Visually Impaired*

028.5 IT
DEBBY PIU. 1985. m. Edizioni Internazionale Cioe s.r.l., Via G. Fabroni, 24, 00191 Rome, Italy. TEL 39-6-3287309. Ed. Lamberto Antonelli. adv.: page L.6000000. circ. 60,000.

028.5 CN ISSN 1187-8681
LES DEBROUILLARDS. (Text in French) 1982. m. (10/yr.). Can.$29.57 (effective 1997). Publications BLD, 3995 rue Sainte-Catherine Est, Montreal, PQ H1W 2G7, Canada. TEL 514-522-1304. FAX 514-522-1761. (Subscr. to: Service des Abonnements, 2924 bvd. Taschereau, Bureau 201, Greenfield Park, PQ J4V 3P1, Canada) Ed. Sarah Perreault; Pub. Felix Maltais. R&P contact: Felix Maltais. adv.: B&W page Can.$1600, color page Can.$2400; trim 7 1/4 x 9 3/4; adv. contact: Nathalie Forget. bk.rev.; index. circ. 29,000. **Indexed:** Pt.de Rep. (1991-). **Document type:** consumer publication.
● Also available on CD-ROM.
   Formerly: Je Me Petit Debrouille (ISSN 0714-4067)
   Description: Science magazine for children ages 9-14.

DELTA RESEARCH MONOGRAPH. see *EDUCATION*

028.5 BL
DEMAIS! 1992. m. $33. Bloch Editores S.A., Rua do Russel 766-804, 22210-000 Rio de Janeiro, RJ, Brazil. TEL 021-5554000. FAX 021-2059998. TELEX 2121525 BLOC. Ed. Janir Hollanda. circ. 80,000. **Document type:** consumer publication.
   Description: Presents a forum for teenagers.

028.5 MY ISSN 0417-3910
DEWAN PELAJAR. 1967. m. Dewan Bahasa dan Pustaka, Jalan Wisma Putra, P.O. Box 10803, 50926 Kuala Lumpur, Malaysia. TEL 03-2481011. Ed. Zaleha Hashim. circ. 71,000.

028.5 MY
DEWAN PERINTIS. (Text in English and Malay; summaries in English) 1960. m. M.$7.20. National Language and Literary Agency of Malaysia, Cawangan Sarawak - Dewan Bahasa dan Pustaka Ma Aysia, Box 1390, Kuching, Sarawak, Malaysia. Eds. Hamzah Hamdoni, Yeop Johari Yaakob. adv.; bk.rev.; illus. circ. 6,000.
   Former titles (until Jan. 1978): Dewan Pemadah; Perintis; Pelita Pelalar; Dolphin (ISSN 0012-5253)
   Description: Aimed at children aged 9-12.

028.5 IT ISSN 0391-5468
DIMENSIONI NUOVE. 1962. m. (9/yr.). L.34000 (foreign L.50000) (effective 1998). (Centro Catechistico Salesiano) Editrice Elle Di Ci, Corso Francia 214, 10096 Leumann (TO), Italy. TEL 39-11-9552111. FAX 39-11-9572900. Ed. Giuseppe Pelizza. adv.: color page L.3500000. circ. 19,000.
   Description: Review of current events and culture for young students.

560 US
DINO TIMES. 1992. m. $19.95 (includes membership). Dinosaur Society, 200 Carleton Ave., East Islip, NY 11730. TEL 516-277-7855. FAX 516-277-1479. E-mail: dsociety@aol.com; URL: http://www.dinosociety.org. **Document type:** newspaper.
   Description: News about dinosaurs and how they lived, recent excavations, and other news of interest to children.

028.5 US
DINOSAURS! * bi-w. newsstand price: $3.50. Atlas Editions, 4343 Equity Dr., Columbus, OH 43228-3842. TEL 203-549-1014. FAX 203-349-8896. **Document type:** consumer publication.

282 GW
DIRECT. 1971. q. DM.21.40($20) Katholische Studierende Jugend, Gabelsbergerstr. 19, 50674 Cologne, Germany. TEL 49-221-9420180. FAX 49-221-94201822. E-mail: ksj-deutschland@t-online.de; URL: http://www.ksj.in-trier.de. Ed. Eva-Marie Schnurr. adv. contact: Olaf Roettig. bk.rev.; film rev.; play rev. circ. 4,000. (back issues avail.) **Document type:** newsletter.
   Description: Periodical for members of KSJ, a secondary school student's youth group.

658.048 US ISSN 1044-4440
HS3260.U5
DIRECTORY OF AMERICAN YOUTH ORGANIZATIONS (YEAR); a guide to 500 clubs, groups, troops, teams, societies, lodges, and more for young people. 1988. biennial. $21.95 (effective 1996). Free Spirit Publishing, Inc., 400 First Ave. N., Ste. 616, Minneapolis, MN 55401-1730. TEL 800-735-7323. FAX 612-337-5050. E-mail: help4kids@freespirit.com. Ed. Judith B. Erickson; Pub. Judy Galbraith. R&P contact: Elizabeth Verdick. circ. 4,000. **Document type:** directory.
   Description: Lists groups by hobby and special interest, sport, school subject, religion and more.

DIRECTORY OF FAMILY CHILD CARE ASSOCIATIONS, SUPPORT AGENCIES, & SUPPORT GROUPS. see *CHILDREN AND YOUTH — About*

371.91 028.5 US
DISCOVERY (NEW YORK). 1935. q. free. John Milton Society for the Blind, Rm. 455, 475 Riverside Dr., New York, NY 10115. TEL 212-870-3335. FAX 212-870-3229. Ed. Darcy Quigley. circ. 2,000. (Braille) **Indexed:** Biol.Dig., PMR, South.Bap.Per.Ind.
   Description: Contains Braille reprints of Christian and educational stories, pen pals, quizzes, and historical, inspirational and geographical articles for readers ages 8 to 18.

028.5 US
DISCOVERY CREW SCIENCE CLUB NEWS. 1987. m. $29 membership. Discovery Crew, c/o Knickerbocker Publishing, Box 113, Fiskdale, MA 01518. Ed. Michael Glaser.
   Description: For children approximately 6-11 years old.

028.5 614 US
DISEASES AND PEOPLE. 1994. irreg. $189.50. Enslow Publishers, Inc., 44 Fadem Rd., Box 699, Springfield, NJ 07081-0699. TEL 201-379-8890. FAX 201-379-7940. E-mail: annette@enslow.com; URL: http://www.enslow.com. Ed. Brian D. Enslow; Pub. Annette Noce. R&P contact: Annette Noce. bibl. **Document type:** monographic series.
   Description: Discusses diagnosis, treatment, prevention and possible cures of diseases. Each book contains case studies, as well as questions and answers, a timeline, a further reading list, chapter notes, a glossary, and more.

028.5 371 GW ISSN 0012-3730
DISKUS; Frankfurter Studentenzeitung. 1950. 6/yr. DM.16. (Studentenschaft der Johann Wolfgang Goethe-Universitaet Frankfurt) Diskus-Verlag, Juegelstr. 1, 60325 Frankfurt a.M., Germany. Ed.Bd. adv.; bk.rev.; film rev.; play rev.; abstr.; illus. circ. 10,000.

028.5 US ISSN 1050-2491
DISNEY ADVENTURES. 1990. m. $19.95 (Canada $29.95); newsstand price: $2.95. Walt Disney Consumer Products, Walt Disney Publishing, 114 Fifth Ave., 16th Fl., New York, NY 10011. TEL 212-633-4400; 800-829-5146. Ed. Phillis Ehrlich. adv.; bk.rev. circ. 846,276. **Document type:** consumer publication.
   Description: Covers entertainment, science and technology, travel, the environment, and sports for ages 7-14. Contains comics featuring Disney characters.

DO DO. see *BIOLOGY*

301 AT ISSN 0811-7179
DOLLY. 1970. m. Aus.$42. A C P Publishing Pty. Ltd., 54-58 Park St., Sydney, N.S.W. 2000, Australia. TEL 02-282-8437. FAX 02-267-4911. Ed. Susie Pitts; Pub. Richard Walsh. adv. contact: Nick Cham. circ. 165,008. **Document type:** consumer publication.

028.5 IT
DOLLY. 1978. w. L.113400. Arnoldo Mondadori Editore S.p.A., Casella Postale 1833, 20101 Milan, Italy. Ed. Patrizia Avoledo. adv. circ. 198,417.

028.5 614.7 333.7 US ISSN 8756-6362
DOLPHIN LOG. bi-m. $15 (overseas $25). Cousteau Society, Inc., 870 Greenbrier Cir., Ste. 402, Chesapeake, VA 23320. TEL 804-523-9335. FAX 804-523-2747. Ed. Elizabeth Foley. circ. 80,000. **Indexed:** Ind.Child.Mag.
   —KR SourceOne; UMI; UnCover.
   Description: For children ages 7-13 years, covers marine animals, the oceans, science, natural history, and the arts as they relate to the global water system.

028.5 XO ISSN 1210-2245
DOMINO. 1970. 12/yr. $124 (effective 1998). Smena Publishing House, Prazska 11, 812 84 Bratislava, Slovakia. (Dist. by: Mezhdunarodnaya Kniga, B. Yakimanka 39, 117049 Moscow, Russia. TEL 7-095-2384967. FAX 7-095-2384634)
   Formerly (until 1990): Pionier (ISSN 1210-227X)

028.5 PL ISSN 1231-0174
DOMOWE PRZEDSZKOLE. 1993. 10/yr. Wydawnictwa Szkolne i Pedagogiczne, Pl. Dabrowskiego 8, 00-950 Warsaw, Poland. TEL 48-22-265451. FAX 48-22-268971. (Dist. by: Ars Polona, Krakowskie Przedmiescie 7, 00-068 Warsaw, Poland) Ed. Hanna Ratynska. illus. circ. 75,000.
   Description: For children 4-6 years old. Includes poems, fairy tales, stories, crossword puzzles, quizzes, lyrics and songs.

028.5 NO
DONALD DUCK & CO. 1948. w. NOK 468. A-S Hjemmet, Kristian IV. Gt. 13, N-0107 Oslo, Norway. Ed. Svein Erik Soeland. adv. circ. 225,000.

028.5 BE ISSN 0778-0265
DOPIDO. Dutch edition (ISSN 0778-0273) (Supplements avail.: Dopido Kerst (ISSN 0778-6425); Dopido Noel (ISSN 0778-6433)) (Text in French) 1991. 12/yr. 1000 BEF (in Europe 1360 BEF; elsewhere 1450 BEF) (effective 1997-98). Editions G.P. Averbode, B.P. 54, B-3271 Averbode, Belgium. TEL 32-13-780111. FAX 32-13-776837. Ed. Christiane Thiry. **Document type:** consumer publication.
   Description: Filled with things to make and do for children 2-3 years old.

028.5 NE ISSN 0928-6799
DOPIDO. 1991. 10/yr. Kok Tijdschriften, Postbus 5018, 8260 GA Kampen, Netherlands. illus. **Document type:** consumer publication.
   Description: For children ages 2-4.

028.5 AU
DOPPELKLICK; die neue Edition Buchklub. 1987. a. membership. Oesterreichischer Buchklub der Jugend, Mayerhofgasse 6, A-1041 Vienna, Austria. TEL 43-1-5051754-0. FAX 43-1-505175450. **Document type:** bulletin.
   Formerly (until 1995): Edition Buchklub.

649 BE ISSN 0773-0179
DOREMI. Dutch Edition: Doremi (ISSN 0772-7453) (Text in French) 1965. bi-m. 1000 BEF (in Europe 1360 BEF; elsewhere 1450 BEF) (effective 1997-98). Editions G.P. Averbode, B.P. 54, B-3281 Averbode, Belgium. TEL 32-13-780111. FAX 32-13-776837. Ed. Christiane Thiry. illus.
   Description: Packed with things to make and do for children.

028.5 NE ISSN 0165-5019
DOREMI. 1977. 10/yr. Kok Tijdschriften, Postbus 5018, 8260 GA Kampen, Netherlands. illus. **Document type:** consumer publication.
   Description: For children ages 4-6.

028.5 II
DOST AUR DOSTI. 1988. m. Rs.55($35) Shama Distributors Private Ltd., 13-14 Asaf Ali Road, New Delhi 110 002, India. TEL 91-11-732666. TELEX 3161601 SHMA IN. Ed.Bd. circ. 50,000.

1870 CHILDREN AND YOUTH — FOR

028.5 **GW** ISSN 0946-5081
DRAN. 9/yr. 58.30 SFr. (effective 1997). Bundes Verlag GmbH, Bodenborn 43, 58452 Witten, Germany. TEL 49-2302-9309320. FAX 49-2302-9309310. E-mail: bv.witten@t-online.de; URL: http://www.jesus-online.de/bv/bv__home.htm. Ed. Martin Gundlach. adv.: B&W page DM.1600, color page DM.1890; trim 188 x 258. circ. 20,000 (paid). (back issues avail.) **Document type:** bulletin.
  Former titles (until 1993): Punkt (ISSN 0721-7145); (until 1978): Pflueger (ISSN 0342-8605)

028.5 780.6 791.4 **US**
DREAM GUYS.* 1986. 9/yr. Dream Guys, Inc., Box 7042, New York, NY 10128-0010. Ed. Roseonn Hirsch. circ. 200,000.
  Description: For teenagers. Covers the gamut of the entertainment industry (music, film, television), with a focus on younger male stars.

028.5 **US**
THE DRUG LIBRARY. 1994. irreg. $322.15. Enslow Publishers, Inc., 44 Fadem Rd., Box 699, Springfield, NJ 07081-0699. TEL 201-379-8890. FAX 201-379-7940. E-mail: annette@enslow.com; URL: http://www.enslow.com. Ed. Brian D. Enslow; Pub. Annette Noce. R&P contact: Annette Noce.
  Description: Book series designed for teen readers. Offers current information on frequently abused drugs. Each book takes an in-depth look at individual drugs or a class of drugs, including the history of its use and physical aspects such as the drug's effects on the body and the emotional impact of substance abuse.

028.5 **XN** ISSN 0012-6632
DRUGARCE. (Text in Macedonian) 1950. fortn. $2.50. Nova Makedonija, Mito Hadzivasilev Jasmin bb, 91000 Skopje, Macedonia. Ed. Gligor Popovski. illus. circ. 25,000.

028.5 **RU** ISSN 0320-1031
PG3227
DRUZHBA. 1977. bi-m. 15 Rub.($30) Izdatel'stvo Molodaya Gvardiya, Suchchevskaya ul., 21, 103030 Moscow, Russia. TEL 285-1935. (Dist. by: Mezhdunarodnaya Kniga, ul. Dimitrova D.39, 113095 Moscow, Russia) Ed. V.I. Firosov. adv.; bk.rev.; illus. circ. 80,000.

028.5 **IS**
DUBBON. (Text in Hebrew) 1970. fortn. $60. Etzb'oni Publishing House, P.O. Box 28110, Tel Aviv 61280, Israel. FAX 972-3-5373906. Ed. Michael Shir. circ. 27,000.

028.5 **RM** ISSN 1224-3957
▼**DUELUL MINTII.** 1996. m. Trustul de Presa Agenda, Str. 1 Mai Nr. 2, 1900 Timisoara, Timis, Rumania. TEL 40-56-190835. FAX 40-56-190839. Ed. Zoltan Kovacs. circ. 10,000. **Document type:** consumer publication.
  Description: Contains puzzles, brainteasers and features for children and teens.

028.5 **GW**
▼**DUERER!** 1995. bi-m. newsstand price: DM.0.35. Albrecht-Duerer-Oberschule, Emserstr. 137, 12051 Berlin, Germany. TEL 49-30-68092421. (Subscr. to: Bjoern Wilde, Suderoderstr. 48b, 12347 Berlin, Germany. TEL 49-30-6257927) Ed. Christian Doganer. adv. circ. 250. **Document type:** newspaper.

028.5 **GW**
DUMBO; Lernen mit Spass. 1987. m. DM.50.40; newsstand price: DM.4.20. Ehapa Verlag GmbH, Im Riedenberg 54, 70771 Leinfelden-Echterdingen, Germany. TEL 0711-79711. FAX 0711-7971239. (Subscr. to: Vertriebsservice Ehapa Verlag, Postfach 810640, 70523 Stuttgart, Germany. TEL 0711-7252235) Ed. Peter Sonnhuetter. adv. contact: Olaf Hansen. circ. 120,000. **Document type:** consumer publication.

028.5 510 **US** ISSN 0732-7773
DYNAMATH. 1982. 8/yr. $25. Scholastic Inc., 555 Broadway, New York, NY 10012-3999. TEL 212-343-6100. Ed. Jackie Glasthal. (reprint service avail. from UMI)
—UMI.
  Description: Helps solve computation word problems and enhances test-taking math skills for grades 5-6. Seeks to make math enjoyable.

DYNAMIC. see *POLITICAL SCIENCE*

028.5 **US** ISSN 0163-3562
DYNAMITE. 1974. irreg. (approx. 12/yr.) $1.95 per no. Scholastic Inc., Books Division, 555 Broadway, New York, NY 10012-3999. TEL 212-343-6100. Ed. Sonia Black. illus.; index. circ. 150,000. (also avail. in microform from UMI; reprint service avail. from UMI) **Indexed:** Ind.Child.Mag. **Document type:** monographic series.
  Description: Contains general-interest material for children and youth.

808.068 **CN** ISSN 0843-1639
DYNAMITE WRITE CHILDREN'S NEWSPAPER. 1986. q. Canadian Trade and Business Opportunities Inc., 2185 Victoria Park Ave., Scarborough, ON M1R 1V5, Canada. TEL 416-449-1931. Ed. Israelin Shockness. circ. 20,000.

E C. (Essential Connection) see *RELIGIONS AND THEOLOGY — Protestant*

028.5 550 **US**
EARTH PROCESSES. 1989. irreg. $76.75. Enslow Publishers, Inc., 44 Fadem Rd., Box 699, Springfield, NJ 07081-0699. TEL 201-379-8890. FAX 201-379-7940. E-mail: annette@enslow.com; URL: http://www.enslow.com. Ed. Brian D. Enslow; Pub. Annette Noce. R&P contact: Annette Noce.
  Description: Book series for teens, describing the natural forces that shape our earth.

ECODATE. see *BUSINESS AND ECONOMICS*

THE EDGE. see *CHILDREN AND YOUTH — About*

028.5 **IS** ISSN 0793-1891
AP221
EINAYIM. (Text in Hebrew) 1994. q. IS.60. (Israel Museum, Ruth Youth Wing) Einayim Publishers, P.O. Box 3211, Jerusalem 91031, Israel. TEL 972-2-433485. adv.; illus. **Document type:** consumer publication.
  Description: Publishes feature articles on art, history and other topics of interest to children, stories, activities and cartoons.

028.5 **II** ISSN 0013-2926
EKALABYA. (Text in Marathi) 1970. m. Rs.12($2.) V.M. Book Co., c/o A.J. Prabhu, Ed., 1334 Shukrawar Peth, Poona 2, India. circ. 6,000.

028.5 **JA**
EKUBO. (Text in Japanese) 1962. m. Kodansha Ltd., 12-21 Otowa 2-chome, Bunkyo-ku, Tokyo 112, Japan. TEL 03-5395-3492. FAX 03-3942-7705. TELEX J34509 KODANSHA. Ed. Yuzuru Utagawa. circ. 200,000. **Document type:** consumer publication.
  Formerly (until 1989): Shukan Shojo Friend.

808 **US** ISSN 1081-5201
ELEMENTARY SCHOOL WRITER. 1995. m. (Sep.-May). $69.95 for 25 copies (effective Jan. 1998). Writer Publications, Box 718, Grand Rapids, MN 55744. TEL 218-326-8025. Ed. Roxanne Kain; Pub. Donald Kain. R&P contact: Donald Kain. circ. 18,000 (paid).

372 500
ELEMENTARY SCIENCE THIS MONTH. 1994. m. Mankato State University, College of Education, Box 8400, Mankato, MN 56002-8400. E-mail: drlit@vax1.mankato.msus.edu; URL: http://www.lme.mankato.msus.edu/ci/elem.sci.html. Ed. Karl A. Matz.
  ●Available only online.
  Description: For elementary school-aged children and the adults who teach them.

ELEVFORUM. see *EDUCATION*

028.5 791.43 **CN** ISSN 1191-2286
EN PRIMEUR JEUNESSE. (Text in French) 1991. q. Can.$12 (US Can.$18). Tribute Publishing Inc., 900A Don Mills Rd., Ste. 1000, Don Mills, ON M3C 1V6, Canada. TEL 416-445-0544. FAX 416-445-2894. E-mail: 104362.1210@compuserve.com. Ed. Alain Tittley; Pub. Geoffrey Dawe. R&P contact: Alain Tittley. adv.: trim 7 7/8 x 10 7/8; adv. contact: Donnalyn Coyne. film rev.; music rev.; tele.rev.; illus. circ. 50,000. **Document type:** consumer publication.
  Description: Entertainment for kids 6 to 13, covering movies, TV, music, fashion, puzzles and games.

028.5 **FR** ISSN 0750-8158
ENFANTS S'AMUSENT. bi-m. 91 F. Publications Guy-Hachette, La Petite Motte Senille, 86100 Chatellerault, France. **Document type:** consumer publication.
—CCC.

ENSEMBLE; le mensuel pour ton francais. see *LINGUISTICS*

028.5 333.7 **US**
ENVIRONMENT REFERENCE. 1990. irreg. $96.75. Enslow Publishers, Inc., 44 Fadem Rd., Box 699, Springfield, NJ 07081-0699. TEL 201-379-8890. FAX 201-379-7940. E-mail: annette@enslow.com; URL: http://www.enslow.com. Ed. Brian D. Enslow; Pub. Annette Noce. R&P contact: Annette Noce.
  Description: Reference book series on environmental subjects for young readers.

028.5 333.7 **US**
ENVIRONMENTAL ISSUES. 1990. irreg. $63.80. Enslow Publishers, Inc., 44 Fadem Rd., Box 699, Springfield, NJ 07081-0699. TEL 201-379-8890. FAX 201-379-7940. E-mail: annette@enslow.com; URL: http://www.enslow.com. Ed. Brian D. Enslow; Pub. Annette Noce. R&P contact: Annette Noce.
  Description: Book series for teens focusing on key issues and threats to our environment.

ERTONG CHUANGZHAO/CHILDREN'S CREATION. see *EDUCATION*

028.5 **CC** ISSN 1003-4692
ERTONG DASHIJIE/CHILDREN'S BIG WORLD. (Text in Chinese) 1985. m. Hebei Shaonian Ertong Chubanshe, 45 Beima Lu, Shijiazhuang, Hebei 050071, People's Republic of China. TEL 741616. Ed. Du Fushan.

028.5 **CC** ISSN 1002-0330
ERTONG GUSHI HUABAO/CHILDREN'S STORY PICTORIAL (Text in Chinese) 1985. m. Jiangsu Shaonian Ertong Chubanshe, 56 Gaoyunling, Nanjing, Jiangsu 210009, People's Republic of China. TEL 638808. Ed. Yan Xuzhi.

028.5 **CC** ISSN 1005-7153
ERTONG HUABAO/CHILDREN'S PICTORIAL. (Text in Chinese) m. $12.70. Tianjin Renmin Meishu Chubanshe - Tianjin People's Fine Art Publishing House, 150 Machang Dao, Heping Qu, Tianjin 300050, People's Republic of China. TEL 86-2-3313358. (Dist. overseas by: China International Book Trading Corp., P.O. Box 399, Beijing, P.R. China; Dist. in US by: China Books & Periodicals, Inc., 2929 24th St., San Francisco, CA 94110. TEL 415-282-2994) Ed. Du Ziling. illus.

028.5 **CC** ISSN 0423-3174
ERTONG SHIDAI/CHILDREN'S EPOCH. (Text in Chinese) m. $36.80. (Zhongguo Fulihui - China Welfare Institute) Ertong Shidai She, 157 Changshu Lu, Shanghai 200031, People's Republic of China. TEL 86-21-6433-5806. (Dist. in US by: China Books & Periodicals, Inc., 2929 24th St., San Francisco, CA 94110. TEL 415-282-2994) Ed. Qiou Shilongg.

028.5 **CC** ISSN 0257-6562
ERTONG WENXUE/CHILDREN'S LITERATURE. (Text in Chinese) m. $36.80. Zhongguo Shaonian Ertong Chubanshe, 21 Dongsi 12 Tiao, Beijing 100708, People's Republic of China. TEL 444761. (Dist. in US by: China Books & Periodicals, Inc., 2929 24th St., San Francisco, CA 94110. TEL 415-282-2994) Ed. Wang Yidi. **Indexed:** IBR, MLA Intl.Bibl.

028.5 **CC**
ERTONG WENXUE XUANKAN/SELECTIONS OF CHILDREN'S LITERATURE. (Text in Chinese) 1981. bi-m. $16.80. Shaonian Ertong Chubanshe - Juvenile & Children Publishing House, 1538 Yan'an Xilu, Shanghai 200052, People's Republic of China. TEL 86-21-6282-3025. FAX 86-21-6282-1726. (Dist. in US by: China Books & Periodicals, Inc., 2929 24th St., San Francisco, CA 94110. TEL 415-282-2994) Ed. Zhou Xiao.

028.5 800 CC ISSN 1005-4839
ERTONG XIAOSHUO/SHORT STORIES FOR CHILDREN. (Text in Chinese) 1985. bi-m. $6. Tianjin Zuojia Xiehui - Writer's Association of Tianjin, 237 Xinhua Lu, Heping Qu, Tianjin 300040, People's Republic of China. TEL 2330-4152. Ed. Zhan Dai'er. circ. 80,000.
Description: Serves children from elementary schools to secondary schools.

ERTONG YINYUE/CHILDREN'S MUSIC. see *MUSIC*

028.5 GW ISSN 0178-0905
ESELSOHR; die Fachzeitschrift fuer Kinder- und Jugendmedien. 1982. m. Rheinallee 9, 55118 Mainz, Germany. TEL 06131-676868. FAX 06131-604015. **Document type:** bulletin.

ESTUDIOS BIBLICOS PARA NINOS. ALUMNOS. see *RELIGIONS AND THEOLOGY — Protestant*

028.5 367 US
ETCH A SKETCH CLUB. NEWSLETTER. 3/yr. $4 for 3 yr. membership (foreign $5). Ohio Art Company, Etch a Sketch Club, 1 Toy St., Box 111, Bryan, OH 43506. TEL 419-636-3141. FAX 419-636-7614. E-mail: segul@bright.net; URL: http://world-of-toys.com/; http://etch-a-sketch.com. Ed. Kelby McRobbie. R&P contact: Diana Hoffman. **Document type:** newsletter.
Description: Offers news and articles of interest to aficionados of the popular toy.
Refereed Serial

028.5 371.8 FR ISSN 0766-6330
L'ETUDIANT. 1975. m. 320 F. Editions Generation, 27 rue du Chemin-Vert, 75543 Paris Cedex 11, France. TEL 48-07-41-41. FAX 47-00-79-80. Ed. Philippe Nanday; Pub. Benoit Prot. adv. contact: Elisabeth Levy. bk.rev. circ. 100,000.
Formerly: Dossiers de l'Etudiant (ISSN 0181-513X)

028.5 IS
ETZB'ONI. (Text in Hebrew) 1953. fortn. $60. Etzb'oni Publishing House, P.O. Box 28110, Tel Aviv 61280, Israel. FAX 31-3-5373906. Ed. Michael Shir. circ. 30,000.

EXPECTATIONS. see *HANDICAPPED — Visually Impaired*

028.5 US ISSN 0014-5033
EXPLORING (IRVING). 1971. q. $8 to non-members (foreign $17); members $1.50 (effective 1998). Boy Scouts of America, Box 152079, Irving, TX 75015-2079. TEL 972-580-2367. FAX 972-580-2079. Ed. Jon C. Halter; Pub. J. Warren Young. R&P contact: Jon C. Halter. adv.: B&W page $7425, color page $9900; trim 8 x 10 3/4; adv. contact: Lisa Hott. bk.rev.; charts; illus. circ. 230,000. **Document type:** consumer publication.
Description: Covers Boy Scouts of America exploring programs; focuses on careers, hobbies, camping, canoeing and music.

EXPLORING (SAN FRANCISCO). see *SCIENCES: COMPREHENSIVE WORKS*

EXPLORING FOR OLDER CHILDREN. see *RELIGIONS AND THEOLOGY — Protestant*

EXPLORING FOR YOUNGER CHILDREN. see *RELIGIONS AND THEOLOGY — Protestant*

028.5 133 US
EXPLORING THE UNKNOWN. 1993. irreg. $74.75. Enslow Publishers, Inc., 44 Fadem Rd., Box 699, Springfield, NJ 07081-0699. TEL 201-379-8890. FAX 201-379-7940. E-mail: annette@enslow.com; URL: http://www.enslow.com. Ed. Brian D. Enslow; Pub. Annette Noce. R&P contact: Annette Noce.
Description: Book series for children, investigating puzzling events for which neither scientists or skeptics can offer any explanations.

028.5 GW ISSN 0014-5386
EXTEMPORALE. 1958. q. DM.2. Albrecht-Altdorfer-Gymnasium, Regensburg, Minoritenweg 33, 93047 Regensburg, Germany. Ed. Andreas Kapphan. adv.; bk.rev.; film rev.; play rev.; illus.; mkt.; stat. circ. 1,000.

THE FACE. see *MUSIC*

028.5 572 US ISSN 0749-1387 GN301
FACES; the magazine about people. 1984. 9/yr. $26.95 (foreign $34.95). Cobblestone Publishing, 7 School St., Peterborough, NH 03458. TEL 603-924-7209. FAX 603-924-7380. Ed. Lynn Sloeneker; Pub. Malcolm Jensen. R&P contact: Pat Sylvestro. bk.rev.; film rev.; charts; illus. circ. 13,000. (back issues avail.) **Indexed:** Ind.Child.Mag. —KR SourceOne; UnCover.
Description: Youth publication about world cultures. Includes authoritative articles, legends, games, and recipes. Each issue features a theme or country.

FAMILY BIBLE SERIES. POWER & PAGES. see *RELIGIONS AND THEOLOGY — Protestant*

FAMILY BIBLE SERIES. POWER PAGES. see *RELIGIONS AND THEOLOGY — Protestant*

FAMILY BIBLE SERIES: PRESCHOOL BIBLE FUN. see *RELIGIONS AND THEOLOGY — Protestant*

FAMILY BIBLE SERIES: YOUTH. see *RELIGIONS AND THEOLOGY — Protestant*

FAMILY GUIDE FOR PARENTS AND KIDS. see *CHILDREN AND YOUTH — About*

FAMILY WALK. see *RELIGIONS AND THEOLOGY — Protestant*

784.61 NE ISSN 1383-9683
FANCY. 1945. m. fl.43.20. Geillustreerde Pers B.V., Haaksbergweg 75, 1101 BR Amsterdam, Netherlands. TEL 31-30-4300300. FAX 31-30-4300316. Ed. Riek Tawfik. adv.; bk.rev.; illus. circ. 78,000. **Document type:** consumer publication.
Former titles (until Sep. 1995): Popfoto (ISSN 0032-4345); (until 1967): Pop-Foto-Tuney-Tunes.

FANTASTIC FLYER MAGAZINE. see *TRAVEL AND TOURISM — Airline Inflight And Hotel Inroom*

028.5 DK
FANTOMET. m. Interpresse A-S, Roennegade 1-5, DK-2100 Copenhagen Oe, Denmark. TEL 45-33-33-75-35. FAX 45-33-33-75-05. adv. circ. 15,000.

THE FARNATCHI SERIES. see *EDUCATION — Teaching Methods And Curriculum*

028.5 US
FAST TIMES. 1984. 5/yr. Fast Times, Inc., 810 Los Vallecitos Blvd., Ste. 201, San Marcos, CA 92069-1449. TEL 619-591-9433. adv. circ. 580,570.
Description: Provides news and accompanying homework assignments for high-school students. Includes celebrity interviews and record, movie and fashion notes.

028.5 AA
FATOSI/VAILLANT. 1959. fortn. $11.30. Bashkimi i Rinise se Punes te Shqiperise, Rr. Punetoret e Rilindjes, Tirana, Albania. TEL 355-42-23024. Ed. Xhevat Beqaraj. circ. 21,200.
Description: Literary and artistic magazine for children.

051 US
FAVES. m. $2.75 per no. Howard Weiss Publications, Box 24497, Los Angeles, CA 90024. TEL 213-477-0441.

FERTIG... LOS!; Jugendmagazin in deutscher Sprache. see *LINGUISTICS*

500.9 028.5 CN ISSN 0827-1356
FEUILLETS DU NATURALISTE. 1970. irreg. (10-12/yr.). Can.$0.50. Cercles des Jeunes Naturalistes, 4101 rue Sherbrooke Est, Ste 124, Montreal, PQ H1X 2B2, Canada. TEL 514-252-3023. adv.; bk.rev. **Document type:** consumer publication.
Former titles: Cercles des Jeunes Naturalistes. Feuillets du Club (ISSN 0045-6179); Feuillets du Naturaliste.
Description: Deals with a variety of science subjects written in a manner appealing to young people.

FICTION FACUS. see *LITERATURE*

028.5 GW
FILIA UND FILIUS. 1956. irreg. Leibniz Gymnasium, Klagenfurter Str. 75, 70469 Stuttgart, Germany. adv.; bk.rev.; film rev.; play rev.; bibl.; charts; illus. circ. 800.

028.5 PL ISSN 0426-1216
FILIPINKA. 1957. fortn. 1.85 Zl.($1) per no. (effective 1996). Ul. Chlodna 35-37, 00-867 Warsaw, Poland. TEL 48-22-447823. FAX 48-22-247004. Ed. Hanna Jaworowska-Blonska; Pub. Danuta Bierzanska. adv.; bk.rev.; play rev. circ. 152,600. **Document type:** consumer publication.
Description: For girls and young women aged 15 - 20.

028.5 XR ISSN 1210-6801
FILIPS; film - literatura - pisnicky - sport. 1953. m. 24 Kc.($11) Mlada Fronta, Radlicka 61, 150 02 Prague 5, Czech Republic. (Dist. by: Artia, Ve Smeckach 30, 111 27 Prague 1, Czech Republic) Ed. Vladimir Klevis. circ. 135,000.
Former titles (until 1993): Filip (ISSN 0862-6464); (until 1991): Pionyr (ISSN 0042-4919); Vetrnik.

028.5 CN ISSN 0227-0315
FILLES D'AUJOURD'HUI. 1980. m. Can.$25. Publicor Inc., 7 chemin Bates, Outremont, PQ H2V 1A6, Canada. TEL 514-270-1100. FAX 514-270-7079. Ed. Chrisitane Gauthier. circ. 60,000. **Indexed:** Pt.de Rep. (1991-).
Description: Edited for young women ages 12-24. Dedicated to fashion, beauty, careers and health with articles on nutrition and make-up hints, career hints and hair care.

FILM AUSTRALIA EDUCATION CATALOGUE. see *MOTION PICTURES*

FILM FAN SAT. see *MOTION PICTURES*

FILMJOURNALEN; pop topp. see *MOTION PICTURES*

928.5 069 US
FINGERPRINTS. 6/yr. $20. Children's Museum, 311 Main St., Utica, NY 13501. TEL 315-724-6129. circ. 2,000. **Document type:** newsletter.

028.5 799.1 JA
FISHING MAGAZINE FOR YOUNG BOY. (Text in Japanese) 1981. m. 4800 Yen. Gakken Co. Ltd., 40-5, 4-chome, Kamiikedai, Ohta-ku, Tokyo 145, Japan. Ed. Yasuo Nakama.

028.5 282 GW
FIT DURCH TIP. 1969. 5/yr. DM.10. Kolpingwerk Dioezesanverband Muenster, Gerlever Weg 1, 48653 Coesfeld, Germany. TEL 02541-803464. Ed. Raimund Weber. adv. contact: Raimund Weber. circ. 1,000. **Document type:** bulletin.

028.5 GW
FIX UND FOXI. w. DM.135.20 (foreign DM.197.60). Verlagsunion Pabel Moewig KG, Karlsruherstr. 31, 76437 Rastatt, Germany. TEL 07222-13-0. FAX 07222-13218. Ed. Hans-Juergen Weller. adv. contact: Rainer Gross. circ. 54,469. **Document type:** consumer publication.

FIZBIN MAGIC MAGAZINE. see *HOBBIES*

028.5 GW
FLOH. 1975. bi-w. DM.114. (Bayerischer Lehrer- und Lehrerinnenverband) Domino Verlag, Hubertusstr. 22, 80639 Munich, Germany. TEL 089-179130. **Document type:** bulletin.

028.5 GW
FLOHKISTE. 1979. bi-w. DM.114. (Bayerischer Lehrer- und Lehrerinnenverband) Domino Verlag, Hubertusstr. 22, 80639 Munich, Germany. TEL 089-179130. **Document type:** bulletin.

028.5 US ISSN 1065-4631
FLY! 1992. bi-m. newsstand price: $3.50. Glendi Publications, Inc., 7002 W. Butler Pike, Ambler, PA 19002. TEL 215-643-6385. FAX 215-540-0146. adv. contact: Joe Pomaco. **Document type:** consumer publication.
Description: Contains material of interest to teens.

CHILDREN AND YOUTH — FOR

028.5 US ISSN 0895-1136
FOCUS ON THE FAMILY CLUBHOUSE. 1988. m. $12 donation. Focus on the Family, Inc., 8605 Explorer Dr., Colorado Springs, CO 80920. TEL 719-531-3400. R&P contact: Lianne Belote. adv. circ. 110,000.
  Description: For ages 8-12. Provides fresh, exciting material that promotes biblical thinking, values and behavior in every area of life.

028.5 US
FOCUS ON THE FAMILY CLUBHOUSE JR. 1988. m. $12 donation. Focus on the Family, Inc., 8605 Explorer Dr., Colorado Springs, CO 80920. TEL 719-531-3400. R&P contact: Lianne Belote. adv. circ. 86,000.
  Description: For ages 4-8. Provides fresh, exciting material that promotes biblical thinking, values and behavior in every area of life.

FOOTY STARS. see *SPORTS AND GAMES — Ball Games*

THE FOUNTAIN; popular, educational and scientific magazine. see *SCIENCES: COMPREHENSIVE WORKS*

028.5 US ISSN 0015-9077
FOUR AND FIVE. 1918. w. $11.99. Standard Publishing, 8121 Hamilton Ave., Cincinnati, OH 45231. TEL 513-931-4050. FAX 513-931-0904. Ed. Wendy McKain; Pub. Mark A. Taylor. R&P contact: Bob Nealeigh. illus. circ. 134,000.

362.7 GW
FRAGEZEICHEN. 1949. bi-m. DM.16. Pfadfinderinnenschaft St. Georg, Unstrutstr. 10, 51371 Leverkusen, Germany. TEL 0214-23015. Ed. Barbara Runkel. bk.rev.; play rev.; bibl.; illus. circ. 8,500. **Document type**: newsletter.
  Former titles: Fragechen; Fragezeider; Unser Kleeblatt (ISSN 0049-5581)

028.5 305.896073 US
FRESH! 1985. m. $20. Ashley Communications, Box 91878, Los Angeles, CA 90009. Eds. Debi Fee, Ralph Benner. circ. 100,000. **Document type**: consumer publication.

FREUNDE; Jugendmagazin in deutscher Sprache. see *LINGUISTICS*

028.5 790.1 SI
FRIDAY WEEKLY. (Supplement avail.: Ad-hoc) (Text in Chinese) 1991. w. S.$26; newsstand price: S.$0.50. Singapore Press Holdings Ltd., Corporate Relations Department, 82 Genting Lane, News Centre, Singapore 349567, Singapore. TEL 740-1081. Ed. Chew Keng Juea. adv. contact: Lawrence Loh. bk.rev.; film rev.; music rev.; play rev.; circ. 42,963 (paid). cols./p.: 6; pp./issue: 241. (tabloid format; also avail. in microfilm; back issues avail.) **Document type**: newspaper.
  Description: Focuses on social issues, sports and recreational activities for teenagers.

FRIEND. see *RELIGIONS AND THEOLOGY — Other Denominations And Sects*

FRIEND INTERNATIONAL. see *HOBBIES*

FRIENDLY COMPANION. see *RELIGIONS AND THEOLOGY*

028.5 179 US
FRIENDS IN DANGER. 1993. irreg. $79.75. Enslow Publishers, Inc., 44 Fadem Rd., Box 699, Springfield, NJ 07081-0699. TEL 201-379-8890. FAX 201-379-7940. E-mail: annette@enslow.com; URL: http://www.enslow.com. Ed. Brian D. Enslow; Pub. Annette Noce. R&P contact: Annette Noce. illus. **Document type**: monographic series.
  Description: Book series of easy-reading, nonfiction titles focuses on endangered North American animals. Each book uses color photographs and large readable type to introduce these animals and to instill beginning readers with a sense of environmental awareness.

FROM PAGE TO SCREEN. see *MOTION PICTURES*

028.5 CC
FUJIAN QINGNIAN/FUJIAN YOUTH. (Text in Chinese) m. Y11.40. Fujian Qingnian Zazhishe, No. 5, Jinjishan, Fuzhou, Fujian 350001, People's Republic of China. TEL 551944. (Dist. overseas by: Jiangsu Publications Import & Export Corp., 56 Gao Yun Ling, Nanjing, Jiangsu, P.R.C.) Ed. Lin Yunqing.
  Description: Aimed at college students and young people.

028.5 UK ISSN 1352-1942
FUN TO LEARN - PETER RABBIT AND FRIENDS. 1994. m. £11.90; newsstand price: £0.99. The Redan Company Ltd., Appleton House, 139 King St., London W6 9JG, England. TEL 0181-563-1563. FAX 0181-563-1478. (Dist. by: MMC, Octagon House, White Hart Meadows, Ripley, Woking, Surrey GU23 6HR, England. TEL 01483-211222. FAX 01483-211731; Subscr. to: P.O. Box 430, Woking, Surrey GU21 1ZF, England. TEL 01483-747008. FAX 01483-776573) Ed. Diana Barton. adv.: page £960; trim 300 x 220. circ. 140,000 (paid). (back issues avail.) **Document type**: consumer publication.
  Description: Educational activity based magazine aimed at children 3-7 years of age.

FUNDACAO NACIONAL DO LIVRO INFANTIL E JUVENIL. NOTICIAS. see *PUBLISHING AND BOOK TRADE*

FUTURE REFLECTIONS. see *HANDICAPPED — Visually Impaired*

G A WORLD. (Girls in Action) see *RELIGIONS AND THEOLOGY — Protestant*

369.463 US ISSN 1071-1309
G.I.R.L. MAGAZINE. (Girl Scout edition also avail.) 1994. bi-m. $15. (Girl Scouts of the U.S.A.) Scholastic Inc., 555 Broadway, New York, NY 10012-3999. TEL 212-343-6100. (Alt. addr.: Scholastic Inc., 2931 E. McCarty St., Box 3710, Jefferson City, MO 65102-3710) Ed. Patricia Levi. adv.: page $10588; adv. contact: Jean Isobe. film rev.; music rev.; video rev.; illus.; circ. 100,000 (paid). (back issues avail.) **Document type**: consumer publication.
  Description: Provides girls ages 8-15 from diverse backgrounds with activities and articles promoting role models.

028.5 614.7 IT
GABBIANI NEWS. 1991. m. L.22000. Publi Rid s.r.l., Via Martiri della Liberazione 79-3, 16043 Chiavari GE, Italy. TEL 0185-308606. FAX 0185-309171.
  Description: Covers ecology for children ages 8-14.

GAY YOUTH COMMUNITY NEWS. see *HOMOSEXUALITY*

028.5 PL ISSN 1233-2615
GAZETA DZIECI. 1994. bi-m. 15 Zl. (foreign 45 Zl.) (effective 1997); 20 Zl. (foreign 60 Zl.) (effective 1998); newsstand price: 1.50 Zl. (Narodowy Fundusz Ochrony Srodowiska) Izba Wydawnicza Swiatowit, Ul. Legnicka 84-4, 54-206 Wroclaw, Poland. TEL 48-71-517334. FAX 48-71-517334. Ed. Stanislaw Srokowski. R&P contact: Stanislaw Srokowski. adv.: page 1500 Zl.; adv. contact: Lukasz Srokowski. bk.rev.; cum.index. circ. 8,000. **Document type**: newspaper.
  Description: Aims to educate children. Covers arts, literature, music, film, science.

028.5 GW ISSN 0936-1111
GEMEINSCHAFTS- UND SOZIALKUNDE; Kurzausgabe der Arbeitsmappe Sozial- und Wirtschaftskunde. 1964. q. DM.96. Erich Schmidt Verlag GmbH & Co. (Berlin), Genthiner Str. 30G, 10785 Berlin, Germany. TEL 49-30-50085-0. FAX 49-30-25008521. Ed. Gerhard Huck. charts; index. (looseleaf format; back issues avail.) **Document type**: academic/scholarly publication.

028.5 LI ISSN 0132-649X
GENYS. 1940. m. 96 Lt.($24) Lietuvos Rytas, Gedimino av. 12a, 2001 Vilnius, Lithuania. TEL 370-2-616334. FAX 370-2-227656. Ed. Gintare Adomaityte. adv. circ. 11,000.

GEODATE. see *GEOGRAPHY*

GEOGRAPHIE HEUTE. see *GEOGRAPHY*

028.5 500 US
▼**GETTING STARTED IN SCIENCE**. 1995. irreg. $75.80. Enslow Publishers, Inc., 44 Fadem Rd., Box 699, Springfield, NJ 07081-0699. TEL 201-379-8890. FAX 201-379-7940. E-mail: annette@enslow.com; URL: http://www.enslow.com. Ed. Brian D. Enslow; Pub. Annette Noce. R&P contact: Annette Noce.
  Description: Book series for students in the elementary to middle school grades. Contains simple experiments using easily-obtainable materials.

028.5 GW ISSN 0016-9668
GIB ACHT; Taschenbuch (Year). 1949. a. DM.6. (Arbeitsgemeinschaft Jugend und Bildung) Universum Verlagsanstalt GmbH KG, Langenbeckstr. 9, 65189 Wiesbaden, Germany. TEL 49-611-9030-0. FAX 49-611-9030382. E-mail: uv@universum.de; URL: http://www.universum.de. Ed. Jutta Filzek. adv. contact: Jochen Hillesheim. circ. 250,000. **Document type**: academic/scholarly publication.
  Description: General publication for children in the higher grades. Subject coverage includes astronomy, biology, geography, history, and music.

028.5 IT
GIORNALINO; settimanale dei ragazzi. 1924. w. Lit.250000 (Europe Lit.280000; Africa Lit.352000; Asia and The Americas Lit.372000; Oceania Lit.444000) (effective 1997-1998). Periodici San Paolo S.r.l., Via Liberazione 4, 12051 Alba (CN), Italy. TEL 39-173-296292. FAX 39-173-296431. Ed. Tommaso Mastrandrea. adv.: page Lit.15000000; adv. contact: Corrado Minnella. bk.rev. circ. 173,229.

028.5 IT ISSN 1120-2564
GIOVANI AMICI. 1966. m. L.28000($19) Universita Cattolica del Sacro Cuore, Largo Gemelli 1, 20123 Milan, Italy. TEL 39-2-72342817. FAX 39-2-72342855. Ed. Roberta Maria Rosa Grazzani. adv.: color page L.4400000. circ. 45,000. **Document type**: consumer publication.

028.5 UK
GIRLTALK. fortn. £24 (Europe & Ireland £32; rest of world £45) (effective 1996). B B C Worldwide Publishing, Broadcasting House, Whiteladies Rd., Bristol GS8 2LR, England. TEL 44-181-576-2000. FAX 44-181-576-2931. (Subscr. to: P.O. Box 425, Woking, Surrey GU21 1GP, England. TEL 44-1483-733716. FAX 44-1483-756792) **Document type**: consumer publication.

028.5 NE
GITTA. m. fl.42. Holco Publications B.V., Postbus 267, 1800 AE Alkmaar, Netherlands. adv.

028.5 YU ISSN 0017-0798
GLAS OMLADINE; list mladih. vol.14, 1966. bi-w. 0.50 din. Narodne Novine, Nis, Balkanska 2, Nis, Yugoslavia. Ed. Ljubisa Igic.

028.5 CI
GLASILO D P M; organizacijski list Drustev in Zvez Prijateljev Mladine. (Text in Slovenian) 1959. bi-m. Zveza Prijateljev Mladine Slovenije, Miklosiceva 16, 61000 Ljubljana, Slovenia. TEL 061-316 760. circ. 2,600.

028.5 GW
DIE GLOCKE (SACHSENHEIM). m. DM.69.20. Burg Verlag GmbH, Vaihingerstr. 41, 74343 Sachsenheim, Germany. TEL 49-7147-6091. FAX 49-7147-12447. Ed. Guenter Irmler. R&P contact: Guenter Einenkel. adv. contact: Gisela Stenzel. circ. 30,000. **Document type**: consumer publication.

808.068 915.4 II
GLORY; a Baha'i youth deepening magazine. (Text in English) 1973. q. $15 for 6 nos. Lucky Bldg., Main Rd., Panchgani 412 805, India. Ed. Marzia S. Rowhani. bk.rev. circ. 1,000.

028.5 370 GW
GOLD-BAERCHI. 1992. bi-m. newsstand price: DM.4. ConPart Verlag GmbH und Co. Zeitschriften KG, Karlsruherstr. 31, 76437 Rastatt, Germany. TEL 49-7222-13403. FAX 49-7222-13404. Ed. Wolfgang Biehler. adv. circ. 100,000. **Document type**: consumer publication.
  Description: Contains stories, pictures, puzzles, songs and other forms of entertainment for 3-8 year old children.

CHILDREN AND YOUTH — FOR

028.5 GW ISSN 0017-1646
DER GOLDENE PFENNIG; Zeitschrift fuer junge Sparer. 1964. q. DM.26.10. (Deutscher Raiffeisenverband e.V.) Deutscher Genossenschafts-Verlag GmbH, Postfach 2140, 65011 Wiesbaden, Germany. Ed. K. Vollath.

028.5 SA
GOOD COMPANY. (Text in English) 1982. q. R.15 (effective 1997). Girl Guide Association of South Africa - Dogtergidsvereniging van Suid-Afrika, c/o Mrs. P. Kirkland, P.O. Box 3343, Honeydew 2040, South Africa. TEL 27-11-795-3741. FAX 27-11-7941091. Ed. Mrs. P. Kirkland. circ. 3,000. (back issues avail.)
 Description: For girl guides ages 10-14. Covers camping, conservation, cooking, and ideas for individual and group activities.

GOOD-NEWS-LETTER (WASHINGTON, 1990). see NUTRITION AND DIETETICS

GOSPEL STANDARD. see RELIGIONS AND THEOLOGY

028.5 282 FR ISSN 0993-0787
GRAIN DE SOLEIL; le journal des enfants curieux de Dieu. 1988. 11/yr. 299 F. (EU 369 F.; elsewhere 419 F.) (effective 1997). Bayard Presse, 3 rue Bayard, 75393 Paris Cedex 08, France. TEL 33-1-44356060. FAX 33-1-44356091. TELEX 648 094 F. (Subscr. to: Bayard Presse International, B.P. 12, 99505 Paris Entreprises, France. TEL 33-1-44216000. FAX 33-3-20274192) Ed. Emmanuelle Dalyac. circ. 62,684.
 Description: Provides an introduction to religion for youngsters in the hope they will continue their studies.

028.5 IS
GRASHUEPFER. (Text in German) 1979. m. Etzb'oni Publishing House, P.O. Box 28110, Tel Aviv 61280, Israel. FAX 972-3-5373906. Ed. Michael Shir. circ. 78,000.

028.5 910.03 920 US
GREAT AFRICAN AMERICANS. 1991. irreg. $233.10. Enslow Publishers, Inc., 44 Fadem Rd., Box 699, Springfield, NJ 07081-0699. TEL 201-379-8890. FAX 201-379-7940. E-mail: annette@enslow.com; URL: http://www.enslow.com. Ed. Brian D. Enslow; Pub. Annette Noce. R&P contact: Annette Noce.
 Description: Book series of biographies of African-American leaders.

028.5 920 US
GREAT MINDS OF SCIENCE. 1994. irreg. $247.35. Enslow Publishers, Inc., 44 Fadem Rd., Box 699, Springfield, NJ 07081-0699. TEL 201-379-8890. FAX 201-379-7940. E-mail: annette@enslow.com; URL: http://www.enslow.com. Ed. Brian D. Enslow; Pub. Annette Noce. R&P contact: Annette Noce.
 Description: Book series that chronicles the lives and important contributions of great scientists from around the world. Each book includes several hands-on activities that give young readers an understanding of the scientist's work.

GROWING (NASHVILLE). see RELIGIONS AND THEOLOGY — Protestant

028.5 UK ISSN 0961-981X
GROWN UPS MAGAZINE. 1991. s-a. £1.95 per no. Custom Publishing Company Ltd. (Subsidiary of: Glendower Holdings Ltd.), 45 Station Rd., Redhill, Surrey RH1 1QH, England. TEL 44-1737-767213. FAX 44-1737-771662. Ed. David Hoppit. adv.: B&W page 1,050; color page £1,500; adv. contact: John Bailey. circ. 75,000 (paid). **Document type:** consumer publication.
 Formerly: Grown Ups Annual (ISSN 0965-2736)
 Description: Aimed at an affluent 50-plus readership.

GRRR!; the zine that bites back. see ANIMAL WELFARE

GUIDE (HAGERSTOWN). see RELIGIONS AND THEOLOGY — Other Denominations And Sects

369.5 028.5 FR ISSN 0750-4152
GUIDE DE FRANCE. 1927. q. 105 F. (foreign 130 F.). Guides de France, 65, rue de la Glaciere, 75013 Paris, France. TEL 47-07-85-59. FAX 43-37-77-69. Ed. Marie-Therese Chotard.
 Description: Directed to girls 12-14.

028.5 US
GUIDE TO FEDERAL FUNDING FOR CHILD CARE & EARLY CHILDHOOD DEVELOPMENT. 1992. a. (in 2 vols.). $169. Government Information Services, 4301 N. Fairfax Dr., Ste. 875, Arlington, VA 22203-1627. TEL 703-528-1000. FAX 703-528-6060. Ed. Heather C. Bodell. (looseleaf format)
 Description: Describes more than 60 federal grant, loan and tax credit programs to assist child care and early child development programs.

028.5 200 US
GUIDEPOSTS FOR KIDS. bi-m. $15.95. Guideposts Associates, Inc., 39 Seminary Hill Rd., Carmel, NY 10512. TEL 914-225-3681. Ed. Mary Lou Carney. **Document type:** consumer publication.
 Formerly (until 1994): Faith 'n' Stuff (ISSN 1068-9869)

028.5 AT ISSN 0159-0340
GUIDING IN AUSTRALIA. 1980. m. Aus.$26.80. Girl Guide Association of Australia, 59 Buckingham St., Surry Hills, N.S.W. 2010, Australia. Ed. Veronica Kells. R&P contact: Nadine Cattell. adv. contact: Nadine Cattell. bk.rev. circ. 7,500. **Document type:** newsletter.

GURL. see WOMEN'S INTERESTS

GUSHI DAWANG/KING OF STORY TELLERS. see LITERATURE

028.5 CC
GUSHI DAWANG HUABAO/ACE STORY - TELLER PICTORIAL. (Text in Chinese) m. $36. Shaonian Ertong Chubanshe - Juvenile & Children Publishing House, 1538 Yan'an Xilu, Shanghai 200052, People's Republic of China. TEL 86-21-6282-3025. FAX 86-21-6282-1726. Ed. Han Shuo. illus.
 Formerly: Wanhuatong Lianhuan Huabao - Kaleidoscope.

028.5 GW
GYMNASE. 1956. 6/yr. DM.10($20) c/o Mulle Harbort, Ed., Mitscherlichstr. 1, 34346 Muenden, Germany. TEL 05541-4048. adv.; bk.rev. circ. 1,000.
 Former titles (until 1990): Welt von A bis Z; (until 1987): Gymnase.

H S SPORTS. (High School) see SPORTS AND GAMES

028.5 FR ISSN 0153-4165
HAGA. 1972-1986. q. Club de la Bande Dessinee et de l'Illustration (CBDI), 63 rue Croix Verte, 81000 Albi, France. Ed. Denis Privat.

028.5 CC
HAHA HUABAO/HAHA PICTORIAL. (Text in Chinese) m. $36.80 (effective 1998). (Zhongguo Fulihui - China Welfare Institute) Ertong Shidai She, 157 Changshu Lu, Shanghai 200031, People's Republic of China. TEL 86-21-6433-5806. Ed. Wang Guojii.

028.5 IO
HAI. 1973. w. Jalan Palmerah Selatan 22, Jakarta 10270, Indonesia. TEL 021-5483008. FAX 021-6390080. TELEX 41216. Ed. Arswendo Atmowiloto.
 Description: Youth magazine.

028.5 IT
HALLO! m. (Coop Athena 2001) Edizioni L.E.T.I. s.r.l., Via E.Q. Visconti, 20, 00193 Rome, Italy. TEL 39-6-3207101. adv.: B&W page L.4945000, color page L.8915000. circ. 47,000.

028.5 332 AU
HALLO SPAREFROH; Freund der Sparjugend. 1955. 7/yr. free. (Hauptverband der Oesterreichischen Sparkassen) Sparkassenverlag GmbH, Grimmelshausengasse 1, A-1030 Vienna, Austria. TEL 43-1-71170-0. FAX 43-1-71170310. Ed. Franz Josef Barta. illus. circ. 150,000. **Document type:** bulletin.
 Formerly: Sparefroh (ISSN 0038-6510)

028.5 CC
HAO ERTONG/GOOD CHILDREN. (Text in Chinese) m. $21.50. (Shanghai Shi Jiaoyu-ju - Shanghai Bureau of Education) Hao Ertong Bianjibu, 500 Shaanxi Beilu, Shanghai 200041, People's Republic of China. TEL 2532973. (Dist. in US by: China Books & Periodicals, Inc., 2929 24th St., San Francisco, CA 94110. TEL 415-282-2994) Ed. Zhang Qiusheng.

HEARTS AFLAME; Catholic youth magazine. see RELIGIONS AND THEOLOGY — Roman Catholic

028.5 268 FR
HEBDO DES JUNIORS. 1993. w. 372 F. (foreign 767 F.) (effective 1997). Fleurus Presse, 21 rue Faubourg St-Antoine, 75550 Paris Cedex 11, France. TEL 33-1-40026300. (Subscr. to: B.P. 72, 77932 Perthes Cedex, France. TEL 33-1-64380389) Ed. Armelle Breton. circ. 250,000. **Document type:** consumer publication.
 Formerly: Infos Junior (ISSN 1240-4454); Which was formed by the 1993 merger of: Fripounet (ISSN 0016-1446); Which was formerly (until 1969): Fripounet et Marisette (ISSN 0992-7891); (1945-194?): Massage aux Coeurs Vaillants (ISSN 0992-7883); And: Triolo (ISSN 0292-2614); Which was formed by the 1981 merger of: Djin (ISSN 0335-1866); Which was formerly (until 1974): J 2 Magazine (ISSN 0994-8392); (1937-1963): Ames Vaillantes (ISSN 0994-8384); And: Formule 1 (ISSN 0994-8422); Which was formerly (until 1970): J 2 Jeunes (ISSN 0994-8414); (1928-1963): Coeurs Vaillants (ISSN (0944-8406).
 Description: Stresses Christian values for children.

028.5 GW ISSN 0018-1099
HESSISCHE JUGEND. 1949. 4/yr. DM.12. Hessischer Jugendring e.V., Bismarckring 23, 65183 Wiesbaden, Germany. TEL 0611-990830. FAX 0611-9908360. Ed. Benno Hafenegger. bk.rev. **Document type:** consumer publication.

028.5 CN ISSN 0709-9177
HIBOU; Canada's french-language discovery magazine for kids 240. 1980. 9/yr. Can.$20.95 (foreign Can.$30.95) (effective 1997). Les Editions Heritage Inc., 300 Avenue Arran, Saint-Lambert, PQ J4R 1K5, Canada. TEL 514-875-0327. Ed. Claire Chabot; Pub. Sylvie Payette. R&P contact: Sylvie Payette. circ. 20,000. (back issues avail.) **Indexed:** Can.Per.Ind., Pt.de Rep. (1984-). **Document type:** academic/scholarly publication.

028.5 FR
HIBOU. m. (11/yr.). 240 F. (foreign 300 F.) (effective 1997). Publicat, 17 Bd. Poissonniere, 75002 Paris, France. TEL 33-1-40391313. FAX 33-1-40391454. (Subscr. to: B.P. 72, 77932 Perthes Cedex, France. TEL 33-1-64380389) Ed. Hedwige Pasquet. illus.
 Description: Shows children 8 and older the great adventures of nature.

028.5 289.9 US ISSN 0190-3802
HIGH ADVENTURE; a Royal Rangers magazine for boys. 1971. q. $9.95 for leader edition. (General Council of the Assemblies of God) Gospel Publishing House, 1445 Boonville Ave., Springfield, MO 65802-1894. TEL 417-862-2781. Ed. Marshall Bruner. circ. 88,000.
 Description: Features religious and inspirational subjects for boys.

808 US ISSN 1048-3373
HIGH SCHOOL WRITER. (In 2 editions: Senior High, Junior High) 1985. m. (Sep.-May). $69.95 for 25 copies (effective Jan. 1998). Writer Publications, Box 718, Grand Rapids, MN 55744. TEL 218-326-8025. Ed. Roxanne Kain; Pub. Donald Kain. R&P contact: Donald Kain. circ. 38,000 (paid). **Document type:** academic/scholarly publication.
 Former titles: High School Writer of the Midwest (ISSN 1040-760X); (until 1988): High School Writer of Minnesota (ISSN 0894-5608)

028.5 US ISSN 0018-165X
AP201
HIGHLIGHTS FOR CHILDREN. 1946. 12/yr. $26.04 (Canada $32.86; overseas $36.04) (effective 1996). Highlights for Children, Inc., Box 269, Columbus, OH 43216-0269. TEL 614-486-0631. FAX 614-486-0762. Ed. Kent L. Brown, Jr. bk.rev.; index; circ. 2,800,000 (paid). (also avail. in microform from UMI; back issues avail.) **Indexed:** Ind.Child.Mag., Jun.High.Mag.Abstr. **Document type:** consumer publication.
 —KR SourceOne; UMI.
 Incorporates: Children's Activities.
 Description: Contains fiction; articles on crafts, science, history, and biography; activities; puzzles; children's submissions.

HIP MAGAZINE. see HANDICAPPED — Hearing Impaired

CHILDREN AND YOUTH — FOR

028.5 920 305.86 US
▼HISPANIC BIOGRAPHIES. 1996. irreg. $151.60. Enslow Publishers, Inc., 44 Fadem Rd., Box 699, Springfield, NJ 07081-0699. TEL 201-379-8890. FAX 201-379-7940. E-mail: annette@enslow.com; URL: http://www.enslow.com. Ed. Brian D. Enslow; Pub. Annette Noce. R&P contact: Annette Noce.
Description: Features biographies about Hispanic individuals who have become well-known due to their contributions to society.

HISTORIAS BIBLICAS PARA PREESCOLARES. ALUMNOS. see *RELIGIONS AND THEOLOGY — Protestant*

028.5 RW
HOBE. (Text in Kinyarwanda) 1955. m. B.P. 761, Kigali, Rwanda. Ed. Andre Sibomana. circ. 95,000.

028.5 780 RU
HOLIDAYS AT THE KINDERGARTEN. 4/yr. 7.70 Rub. Izdatel'stvo Muzyka, Ul. Neglinnaya 14, Moscow 103031, Russia. TEL 924-81-63. FAX 921-83-53.

028.5 US ISSN 1065-9269
HOLLYWOOD TEEN PARTY. 6/yr. newsstand price: $3.50. Glendi Publications, Inc., 7002 W. Butler Pike, Ambler, PA 19002. TEL 215-643-6385. FAX 215-540-0146. **Document type:** consumer publication.

028.5 US ISSN 1044-0488
HOPSCOTCH; for girls. 1989. bi-m. $15 (foreign $21). Bluffton News Printing and Publishing Co., Box 164, 103 N. Main St., Bluffton, OH 45817-0164. TEL 419-358-4610. FAX 419-358-5027. Ed. Marilyn Edwards; Pub. Thomas M. Edwards. R&P contact: Becky Jackson. adv.; bk.rev.; circ. 10,000 (paid). **Document type:** consumer publication.
●Also available on CD-ROM.
—KR SourceOne.
Description: Contains activities and stories for girls 6 to 12. Promotes reading, creativity, and self-esteem.
Refereed Serial

HORIZONTI. see *SCIENCES: COMPREHENSIVE WORKS*

028.5 US
HOT DOG. 1979. irreg. (approx. 12/yr.). $1.95 per no. Scholastic Inc., Books Division, 555 Broadway, New York, NY 10012-3999. TEL 212-343-6100. Ed. Nancy Krulik. (reprint service avail. from UMI).
Document type: monographic series.
Description: Aimed at children aged 7-8.

HOW ON EARTH!; youth supporting compassionate, ecologically sound living. see *NUTRITION AND DIETETICS*

HUAXI; qingnian wenxue yuekan. see *LITERATURE*

028.5 US ISSN 0273-7590
AP201
HUMPTY DUMPTY'S MAGAZINE. 1952. 8/yr. $16.95 (foreign $23.95). (Benjamin Franklin Literary & Medical Society, Inc.) Children's Better Health Institute, Box 567, 1100 Waterway Blvd., Indianapolis, IN 46202. TEL 317-636-8881. FAX 317-684-8094. (Subscr. to: Box 420235, Palm Coast, FL 32142. TEL 904-447-0818) Ed. Dr. Cory SerVaas; Pub. Greg Joray. R&P contact: Sandy Grieshop. adv. contact: Todd Seifferlein. bk.rev.; software rev.; illus.; index. circ. 200,000. (also avail. in microfilm from UMI; reprint service avail. from UMI) **Indexed:** Ind.Child.Mag. **Document type:** consumer publication.
—UMI.
Formerly (until 1979): Humpty Dumpty's Magazine for Little Children (ISSN 0018-7666)
Description: Contains simple puzzles, crafts, and stories to teach children ages 4 to 6 good health habits.

HYOGO KENRITSU KODOMO BYOIN NENPO/HYOGO PREFECTURAL KOBE CHILDREN'S HOSPITAL. ANNUAL REPORT. see *HOSPITALS*

HYPE HAIR; for Black teens. see *BEAUTY CULTURE*

I J B - REPORT. (Internationale Jugendbibliothek) see *LITERATURE*

028.5 420 375.4 FR
I LOVE ENGLISH. (Annual supplement avail.: I Love English Junior) (Text in English) 1987. 10/yr. 244 F. (EU 339 F.; elsewhere 379 F.) (effective 1997). Bayard Presse, 3 rue Bayard, 75393 Paris Cedex 08, France. TEL 33-1-44356060. FAX 33-1-44356091. TELEX 648 094 F. (Subscr. to: Bayard Presse International, B.P. 12, 99505 Paris Entreprises, France. TEL 33-1-44216000. FAX 33-3-20274192) Ed. Nathalie Becht. circ. 53,884.
Description: Helps children 10 to 15 years old to learn English.

028.5 UK ISSN 1359-7396
IAW. 1965. m. (Sep.-Jun.). £10. Urdd Gobaith Cymru, Llanbadarn Rd., Aberystwyth, Wales. Ed. Sian Eleri Davies. illus. circ. 3,000. **Document type:** academic/scholarly publication.
Formerly (until 1995): Mynd (ISSN 0026-4431)
Description: For children from age 11 up to the GCSE examination stage. Follows key stages 3 and 4 of the national curriculum.

282 GW
IDEENREICH. 1990. 2/yr. DM.8.56. Katholische Studierende Jugend, Gabelsbergerstr. 19, 50674 Cologne, Germany. TEL 49-221-9420180. FAX 49-221-94201822. E-mail: ksj-deutschland@t-online.de; URL: http://www.ksj.in-trier.de. Ed. Insa Mueller. R&P contact: Olaf Roettig. adv. contact: Olaf Roettig. **Document type:** academic/scholarly publication.

808 891 YU ISSN 0350-6339
IDEJE; jugoslovenski studentski casopis. 1970. bi-m. 50 din.($10) (Savez Socijalisticke Omladine Jugoslavije) Mladost, Marsala Tita 2, Belgrade, Yugoslavia. Ed. Milutin Stanisavac.

ILLINOIS HISTORY; a magazine for young people. see *HISTORY — History Of North And South America*

028.5 FR ISSN 0995-1121
IMAGES DOC. 1989. m. 330 F. (EU 399 F.; elsewhere 449 F.) (effective 1997). Bayard Presse, 3 rue Bayard, 75393 Paris Cedex 08, France. TEL 33-1-44356060. FAX 33-1-44356091. TELEX 648 094 F. (Subscr. to: Bayard Presse International, B.P. 12, 99505 Paris Entreprises, France. TEL 33-1-44216000. FAX 33-3-20274192) Ed. Francoise Recamier. circ. 81,943.
Description: Stimulates the desire for knowledge in 8 to 12 year olds through the use of photos.

IMAGINE (BALTIMORE); opportunities and resources for academically talented youth. see *EDUCATION — Abstracting, Bibliographies, Statistics*

028.5 970 US
▼IN AMERICAN HISTORY. 1996. irreg. $170.55. Enslow Publishers, Inc., 44 Fadem Rd., Box 699, Springfield, NJ 07081-0699. TEL 201-379-8890. FAX 201-379-7940. E-mail: annette@enslow.com; URL: http://www.enslow.com. Ed. Brian D. Enslow; Pub. Annette Noce. R&P contact: Annette Noce.
Description: Offers in-depth coverage of events in American history.

IN FOCUS (NEW YORK). see *HANDICAPPED — Visually Impaired*

028.5 800 US
IN SEARCH OF A SONG. 1981. s-a. $3 per no. Ten Penny Players, Inc., 393 St. Pauls Ave., Staten Island, NY 10304-2127. TEL 718-442-7429. FAX 718-442-4978. Ed. Barbara Fisher; Pub. Richard Spiegel. illus. circ. 200. (back issues avail.)
Description: Comprises a series of miniature chapbooks including fiction, poetry, and drawings by New York City public school children and at risk young adults.

INDIAN COUNCIL FOR CHILD WELFARE. ANNUAL REPORT. see *SOCIAL SERVICES AND WELFARE*

INFOPOST. see *MILITARY*

028.5 AU
INITIATIVE. 1966. irreg. (4-6/yr.). membership. Junge Generation in der Volkspartei, Jugendklub Innere Stadt, Wollzeile 24, 1010 Vienna, Austria. Ed. Guenter Zillich. adv.; illus. circ. 1,000.
Formerly (until 1972): Magazin Vier und Zwanzig (ISSN 0024-9785)

028.5 SP ISSN 1130-4618
INJUVE. 1990. bi-m. free to institutions only. Instituto de la Juventud, Ortega y Gasset, 71, 28006 Madrid, Spain. TEL 347-76-90. FAX 402-21-94. bk.rev.; film rev. circ. 15,000. **Document type:** government publication.
Description: Provides information to young people to promote communication between them and participation in society.

028.5 II ISSN 0046-9599
INQUISITOR; a student's magazine. (Text in English) 1971. m. Rs.5. Sudhir Sharma, Ed. & Pub., 2165 Sector 21-C, Chandigarh, India. adv.; bk.rev.; film rev. (also avail. in microfilm from UMI; reprint service avail. from UMI)

INSIGHT (HAGERSTOWN); a magazine of Christian understanding for young Adventists. see *RELIGIONS AND THEOLOGY — Protestant*

028.5 286 US ISSN 1060-5614
INSIGHT - OUT. m. $9.47 (effective 1997). Review and Herald Publishing Association, 55 W. Oak Ridge Dr., Hagerstown, MD 21740. TEL 301-791-7000.
Description: Missionary magazine for teenagers.

INTEEN. see *RELIGIONS AND THEOLOGY — Protestant*

INTERAMERICAN CHILDREN'S INSTITUTE. REPORT OF THE GENERAL DIRECTOR. see *SOCIAL SERVICES AND WELFARE*

028.5 283 UK
INTO VIEW. q. Youth for Christ, P.O. Box 5254, Halesowen, W. Midlands B63 3DG, England. TEL 44-121-550-8055. FAX 44-121-550-9979. E-mail: 100434.3535@compuserve.com. Ed. Wendy Beech. bk.rev.; circ. 6,000. **Document type:** newsletter.

268 IS ISSN 0334-7397
INYAN-CHADDASH. (Text in Hebrew) 1984. w. $90. Etzb'oni Publishing House, P.O. Box 28110, Tel Aviv 61280, Israel. FAX 972-3-5373906. Ed. Talila Rosenboim. circ. 35,000.
Description: For children ages 8-12.

059.927 TS
IQRA/READ. (Text in Arabic) 1984. a. exchange basis. Mintaqat Dubai al-Ta'limiyyah - Dubai Educational Region, P.O. Box 8353, Dubai, United Arab Emirates. TEL 691405. Ed. Hamad Ahmed al-Shaibani. circ. 3,000.
Description: Student publication covering literary and cultural activities in the school community.

028.5 808 RU ISSN 0130-6634
PN6071.S33
ISKATEL. (Supplement to: Vokrug Sveta (ISSN 0321-0669)) (Text in Russian) 1961. m. $86 (effective 1998). Izdatel'stvo Vokrug Sveta, Novodmitrovskaya ul., 5a, kom. 1607, 125015 Moscow, Russia. TEL 7-095-2858058. FAX 7-095-2850930. (Dist. by: Mezhdunarodnaya Kniga, B. Yakimanka 39, 117049 Moscow, Russia. TEL 7-095-2384967. FAX 7-095-2384634; Dist. in U.S. by: Victor Kamkin Inc., 4956 Boiling Brook Pkwy., Rockville, MD 20852. TEL 301-881-5973) Ed. A.A. Poleshchuk. adv.

ISLAND PARENT MAGAZINE. see *CONSUMER EDUCATION AND PROTECTION*

028.5 301 US
ISSUES IN FOCUS. 1989. irreg. $986.40. Enslow Publishers, Inc., 44 Fadem Rd., Box 699, Springfield, NJ 07081-0699. TEL 201-379-8890. FAX 201-379-7940. E-mail: annette@enslow.com; URL: http://www.enslow.com. Ed. Brian D. Enslow; Pub. Annette Noce. R&P contact: Annette Noce.
Description: Book series for teens, presenting the facts and analyzing the most controversial topics in today's news. Offers excellent and up-to-date information for reports or debates. Helps teenagers developing critical thinking skills.

266 028.5 IT ISSN 0021-2806
ITALIA MISSIONARIA. Cover title: I M. 1919. m. L.30000. Pontificio Istituto Missioni Estere, Via Mos Bianchi 94, 20149 Milan, Italy. TEL 39-2-48009191. FAX 39-2-4695193. Ed. P. Massimo Casaro. adv.: page L.400000. bk.rev.; bibl.; illus. circ. 13,000.
Description: Discusses mission work in third world countries.

268 US
IT'S OUR WORLD; mission news from the Holy Childhood Association. (In 2 editions: Grades K-4, 5-8) vol.74, 1974. 3/yr. $1. (Pontifical Association of the Holy Childhood) Holy Childhood Association, National Office-U.S., 1720 Massachusetts Ave., N.W., Washington, DC 20036. TEL 202-775-8637. FAX 202-429-2987. Ed. Mary Connors. illus. circ. 200,000. **Document type:** newspaper.
 Formerly: Annals of the Holy Childhood (ISSN 0003-4940)
 Description: Seeks to help Catholic children cultivate an awareness and appreciation of children of other cultures.

IUVENIS. see *LINGUISTICS*

790 FI ISSN 0781-7177
J P; paper for boys and girls. 1938. m. (10/yr.). FIM 145. Suomen Poikien ja Tyttoejen Keskus-PTK ry, Partaharjuntie 361, FIN-76280, Finland. FAX 358-58-420108. Ed. Pirjo Huttunen. adv.; bk.rev. circ. 21,000.
 Former titles: J P Joka Poika (ISSN 0355-4201) & Joka Poika (ISSN 0047-2050)

028.5 GW
J P I - JUGEND PRESSE INFORMATIONEN. 1978. 8/yr. free. Stiftung Politische Christliche Jugendbildung e.V., Kottenforststr. 20, 53340 Meckenheim, Germany. TEL 02225-13213. FAX 02225-10688. adv.; bk.rev. circ. 6,000. (back issues avail.) **Document type:** bulletin.
 Description: Provides information and ideas concerning various current topics to editors of school magazines.

JACK AND JILL (BRAILLE EDITION). see *HANDICAPPED — Visually Impaired*

028.5 US ISSN 0021-3829
JACK AND JILL (INKPRINT EDITION). 1938. 8/yr. $16.95 (foreign $23.95). (Benjamin Franklin Literary and Medical Society, Inc.) Children's Better Health Institute, Box 567, 1100 Waterway Blvd., Indianapolis, IN 46202. TEL 317-636-8881. FAX 317-684-8094. (Subscr. to: Box 420235, Palm Coast, FL 32142. TEL 904-447-0818) Ed. Dr. Cory ServVaas; Pub. Greg Joray. R&P contact: Danny Lee. adv. contact: Todd Seifferlein. bk.rev.; software rev, charts; illus.; maps. circ. 327,000. (also avail. in Braille; microform from UMI; reprint service avail. from UMI) Indexed: Ind.Child.Mag. **Document type:** consumer publication.
 —KR SourceOne; UMI.
 Description: Offers children ages 7-10 articles, stories, puzzles, and recipes promoting health and safety.

028.5 UK ISSN 0262-0286
JACKIE. 1964. w. D.C. Thomson & Co. Ltd., Albert Square, Dundee DD1 9QJ, Scotland.

028.5 II
JAHANAMAMU. (Text in Oriya) 1972. m. newsstand price: Rs.4. Chandamama Publications, Chandamama Bldgs., Vadapalani, Madras 600 026, India. Ed. B. Nagi Reddi. adv.; B&W page Rs.4250, color page Rs.8500; trim 198 x 160.

028.5 II
JAHNAMAMU (ORIYA). (Text in Indian languages) 1972. m. 188 N.S.K. Salai, Vadapalani, Madras 600 026, India. Ed. Nagi Reddi. circ. 110,000.

028.5 FR ISSN 0399-4600
J'AIME LIRE. 1977. m. 330 F. (EU 429 F.; elsewhere 479 F.) (effective 1997). Bayard Presse, 3 rue Bayard, 75393 Paris Cedex 08, France. TEL 33-1-44356060. FAX 33-1-44356091. TELEX 648 094 F. (Subscr. to: Bayard Presse International, B.P. 12, 99505 Paris Entreprises, France. TEL 33-1-44216000. FAX 33-3-20274192) Eds. Martine Lamy, Martin Berthommier. circ. 162,314.
 Description: Promotes the love of reading in children 7 years and older.

028.5 CN ISSN 0835-7714
J'AIME LIRE. (Text in French) 1987. 10/yr. Can.$29.95($39.95) (effective Sep. 1994). Bayard Presse Canada Inc., 3995 Ste. Catherine E., Montreal, PQ H1W 2G7, Canada. TEL 514-522-3936. FAX 514-522-1761. Pub. Suzanne Spino. adv.: color page Can.$800; trim 6 1/8 x 7 1/2; adv. contact: Nathalie Forget. bk.rev/; circ. 16,000 (paid). (back issues avail.) **Document type:** consumer publication.
 Description: Contains a complete short-story, games around a theme and a comic strip. Intended for first readers.

028.5 LI ISSN 0132-6562
JAUNIMO GRETOS; independent Lithuanian popular youth magazine. (Text in Lithuanian) 1944. m. $84. Bernardinu St. 8, 232600 Vilnius, Lithuania. Ed. Kazys Zilenas. circ. 106,000.
 Description: General interest magazine for 18-26 year old readers.

059.915 IR
JAVANAN EMROOZ. 1966. w. £148 in Middle East & Pakistan; £192 in Europe & Japan; £256 in N. America & Australia (effective 1996). Ettela'at Publications, P.O. Box 11365-9365, Khayyam Ave., Tehran 11144, Iran. TEL 98-21-328203. FAX 98-21-3111223. TELEX 212336. Ed. Mohammad Javad Rafi. **Document type:** consumer publication.
 Formerly (until 1983): Javanan.

028.5 FR ISSN 0756-564X
JE BOUQUINE. 1984. m. 466 F. (EU 559 F.; elsewhere 619 F.) (effective 1997). Bayard Presse, 3 rue Bayard, 75393 Paris Cedex 08, France. TEL 33-1-44356060. FAX 33-1-44356091. TELEX 648 094 F. (Subscr. to: Bayard Presse International, B.P. 12, 99505 Paris Entreprises, France. TEL 33-1-44216000. FAX 33-3-20274192) Ed. Beatrice Valentin. circ. 58,644.
 Description: Inspires the desire to read in children 10 and older.

028.5 FR ISSN 0995-5038
JE LIS DEJA. 1989. m. (11/yr.). 270 F. (foreign 354 F.) (effective 1997). Fleurus Presse, 21 rue du Faubourg St-Antoine, 75550 Paris Cedex 11, France. TEL 33-1-40026300. (Subscr. to: B.P. 72, Perthes Cedex, France. TEL 33-1-64380389) Ed. Beatrice Guthart. illus.
 Description: Helps children to read on their own, with emphasis on vocabulary retention and comprehension of difficult vocabulary through illustrations.

658.048 FR ISSN 0750-3806
JEANNETTE. 1946. 5/yr. 105 F. (foreign 130 F.). Guides de France, 65 rue de la Glaciere, 75013 Paris, France. TEL 47-07-85-59. FAX 43-37-77-69. Ed. Marie-Therese Chotard.
 Description: Of interest to girls 8-11.

268 SP
JESUS MAESTRO. 1872. m. 800 ptas.($17) Compania de Santa Teresa de Jesus, Ganduxer 85, Barcelona-22, Spain. Ed. Maria Victoria Molins. bk.rev.; cum.index every 5 yrs. circ. 14,000.

025.8 FR ISSN 0984-760X
JEUNE ET JOLIE. 1987. m. 125 F. (foreign 189 F.) (effective 1997). Filipacchi Medias, 151 rue Anatole France, 92598 Levallois Perret Cedex, France. TEL 33-1-41347330. FAX 33-1-41347503. (Subscr. to: 5 rue Naracci, 59884 Lille Cedex 9, France. TEL 33-1-20121110. FAX 33-1-20121111; Subscr. in. N. America to: Express Magazine, 4011 Blvd. Robert, Montreal, PQ H1Z 4H6, Canada. TEL 514-374-9661) **Document type:** consumer publication.

JEUNES. see *SPORTS AND GAMES*

JEUNES; le mensuel pour ton francais. see *LINGUISTICS*

028.5 FR ISSN 0021-6143
JEUNES ANNEES.* (In two editions: for ages 3-8 and 9-14) 1947. 8/yr. 50 F. for 2 yrs. (3-8 ed.), 54 F for 2 yrs. (9-14 ed.). Federation des Francs et Franches Camarades, 10-14 rue Tolian, 75020 Paris, France. illus.

JEUNES EN MOUVEMENT. see *RELIGIONS AND THEOLOGY — Roman Catholic*

028.5 FR ISSN 0396-7360
JEUNESSE DU QUART MONDE. 1974. m. 20 F. (Alternatives 114 - Jeunesse Quart Monde) Voix de l'Ain, 29 rue du Stade, Champeaux, 77720 Normande, France. Ed. Jean Claude Ferrand. (back issues avail.) **Document type:** newspaper.

JEWISH CURRENT EVENTS. see *ETHNIC INTERESTS*

JIANKANG SHAONIAN HUABAO/HEALTHY CHILDREN'S PICTORIAL. see *PHYSICAL FITNESS AND HYGIENE*

028.5 780 US
▼ **JITTER.** 1996. m. Columbia House, 600 108th Ave. N.E., Ste. 120, Bellevue, WA 98004. E-mail: piper@jitter.com; URL: http://www.jitter.com. Ed. Piper Carr.
 ●Available only online.
 Description: Targets teenagers, featuring music reviews, articles, interviews, celebrity chat, and more.

028.5 BE ISSN 1370-2114
JOEPIE T V - PLUS. (Text in Dutch) vol.20, 1992. w. 2300 BEF (foreign 3900 BEF). N.V. Sparta, Brandekensweg 2, B-2627 Schelle, Belgium. TEL 32-3-8446261. FAX 32-3-8446152. Eds. Peter Van Dyck, Serge Vanhellemont. adv.; illus. **Document type:** consumer publication.
 Formerly (until 1994): Joepie (ISSN 1370-2106)
 Description: Covers music, popular culture and other items of interest to young people.

JONGE KERK. see *RELIGIONS AND THEOLOGY*

028.5 FR ISSN 0767-8088
JOURNAL DE MICKEY. 1934. w. 409 F. (outside E.C. 669 F.) (effective 1997). Disney Hachette Presse, 10 rue Thierry le Luron, 92592 Levallois Perret Cedex, France. TEL 33-1-41348500. FAX 33-1-41348599. (Subscr. to: 90 rue de Flandre, 75947 Paris Cedex 19, France. TEL 33-1-44894484) Ed. Gilles Heylen. circ. 212,000. **Document type:** consumer publication.
 Description: Features comics of various Disney characters as well as spotlights on celebrities, and news.

028.5 282 FR
▼ **LE JOURNAL EXPERIMENTAL DE PHOSPHORE.** 1996. 5/yr. 150 F. (EU 209 F.; elsewhere 219 F.) (effective 1997). Bayard Presse, 3 rue Bayard, 75393 Paris Cedex 08, France. TEL 33-1-44356846. FAX 33-1-44356078. (Subscr. to: Bayard Presse International, B.P. 12, 99505 Paris Entreprises, France) Ed. Etienne Seguier; Pub. Anne-Marie de Besombes. circ. 10,000.

JOVENES AGRICULTORES. see *AGRICULTURE*

028.5 MX
JOVENES SONORENSES. 1994. m. E R A Comunicacion, S.A. de C.V., Heriberto Aja 155, Hermosillo, Sonora, Mexico. Ed. Ramon Martinez Esquer. circ. 1,000.

JR. HIGH MINISTRY MAGAZINE. see *CHILDREN AND YOUTH — About*

028.5 AU
JUGEND IN WIEN. 1983. 10/yr. free. Verein Wiener Jugendkreis, Friedrich-Schmidt-Platz 5, A-1082 Vienna, Austria. FAX 0222-487000. Ed. Ali Foeger. adv. **Document type:** newsletter.
 Description: Listing of leisure activities for young people.

028.5 943 GW
JUGENDBUECHER ZUM THEMA; Drittes Reich. 1986. s.a. Stiftung Lesen, Fischtorplatz 23, 55116 Mainz, Germany. TEL 06131-288900. FAX 06131-230333. **Document type:** bibliography.

028.5 070 GW
JUGENDPRESSEREPORT; Magazin fuer engagierte Schueler und Nachwuchsjournalisten. 1986. q. DM.8. Freie Jugendpresse Baden - Wuerttemberg e.V., Reichenhallerstr. 10, 70372 Stuttgart, Germany. TEL 0711-562279. Ed. Frank Peter Unterreined. circ. 4,000.

CHILDREN AND YOUTH — FOR

028.5 GW
JUGENDROTKREUZ. 1986. m. DM.33.60. (Deutsches Rotes Kreuz, Referat Jugendrotkreuz) D R K Werbung GmbH, Friedrich-Ebert-Allee 71, 53113 Bonn, Germany. TEL 49-228-541278. FAX 49-228-541450. Ed. Hildegard Witteler.
  Document type: bulletin.
  Formerly: Bernie.
  Description: Health information from the Red Cross, geared toward young children.

200 DK ISSN 0905-9466
JUL I FAMILIEN. 1982. a. (Kirkelig Forening for den Indre Mission) Lohses Forlag, Korskaervej 25, 7000 Fredericia, Denmark. FAX 0045-75926146. illus.
  Former titles (until 1990): Alle Boerns Jul (ISSN 0109-050X) & Boernebladets Jul (ISSN 0105-709X)
  Description: Contains Christmas readings and Christmas time activities for families.

DER JUNGE ELEKTRO-TECHNIKER. see EDUCATION — Teaching Methods And Curriculum

JUNGE GEMEINDE. see RELIGIONS AND THEOLOGY

JUNGE SAMMLER; Zeitschrift fuer junge Briefmarkenfreunde. see PHILATELY

JUNGSCHARHELFER; Mitarbeiterhilfe fuer Jungen- und Maedchenarbeit. see RELIGIONS AND THEOLOGY

028.5 SZ ISSN 0022-6475
JUNIOR; jugend-zeitschrift. (Text in German) 1950. m. 0.55 SFr. per no. Hug-Verlag AG, Hohenrainweg 1, CH-8802 Kilchberg, Switzerland. TEL 41-1-7154928. FAX 41-1-7154192. Ed. Daniela Hug. adv. contact: Yvonne Keufer. illus. circ. 1,400,000. **Document type:** consumer publication.

028.5 CN
JUNIOR.* (Text in French) 1991. q. Can.$22 (foreign Can.$40). Editions Multi Concept Inc., 1600 Henri-Bourissa West Ste. 425, Montreal PQ H3M 3E2, Canada. TEL 514-331-0661. Ed. Ronald Lapierre. adv.: B&W page Can.$3465, color page Can.$3850; trim 8 1/8 x 10 7/8. circ. 48,500. **Document type:** consumer publication.

JUNIOR CLUBHOUSE. see RELIGIONS AND THEOLOGY — Protestant

028.5 JA
JUNIOR LAND. (Text in Japanese) 1978. m. 3000 Yen. Sekai Bunka Publishing Inc., 2-29, 4-chome, Kudan-Kita, Chiyoda-ku, Tokyo 102, Japan.
  Description: Aimed at pre-schoolers.

373 371.3 US ISSN 0022-6688
AP201
JUNIOR SCHOLASTIC. (Includes Junior Review) 1937. 18/yr. (Sep.-May). $11. Scholastic Inc., 555 Broadway, New York, NY 10012-3999. TEL 212-343-6100; 800-325-6149. Ed. Lee Baier. bibl.; charts; illus.; index. circ. 825,000. (also avail. in microfilm from UMI; reprint service avail. from UMI) **Indexed:** Ind.Child.Mag.
  —SWETS; UMI.
  Description: Covers U.S. and world events for children in grades 6-8.

028.5 500 US
JUNIOR SCIENCE/KODOMO NO KAGAKU. (Text in Japanese) 1924. m. 12900 Yen. Seibundo Shinkosha Publishing Co. Ltd., 1-13-7 Yayoi-cho, Nakano-ku, Tokyo 164, Japan. Ed. Yoshiaki Kato. circ. 78,000.

028.5 US
JUNIOR STATEMENT. 1934. 4/yr. membership. Junior Statesmen of America, 60 E. Third Ave., Ste. 320, San Mateo, CA 94401. TEL 415-347-1600. FAX 415-347-7200. Ed. Richard Prosser; Pub. Richard Prosser. bk.rev.; illus.; circ. 20,000 (controlled).
  Former titles: Junior State Report; Junior Statesman (ISSN 0022-6696); Youth News Report.
  Description: Directed to high-school students interested in politics and government.

JUNIOR TRAILS. see RELIGIONS AND THEOLOGY — Other Denominations And Sects

JUPRECU. see RELIGIONS AND THEOLOGY — Protestant

JUREN/GIANT. see LITERATURE

028.5 GW
JUROPE;* Magazin fuer junge Leute. 1963. q. Verlag Ruprecht Kertscher, Am Schlag 1, 82223 Eichenau, Germany. circ. 10,000.

028.5 305.4 UK ISSN 0266-8173
JUST SEVENTEEN. 1983. w. £50 (foreign £62) (effective 1996). E M A P - New Woman, 20 Orange St., London WC2H 7ED, England. TEL 44-171-957-8383. FAX 44-171-930-5728. (Subscr. to: Tower Publishing Services Ltd., Tower House, Sovereign Park, Lathkill St., Market Harborough, Leics. LE16 9EF, England. TEL 44-1858-468811. FAX 44-1858-432164) Ed. Sarah Bailey; Pub. Louise Matthews. adv. contact: Paula Cain. circ. 269.581. **Document type:** consumer publication.
  Description: Contains articles for girls ages 12-18.

028.5 920 340 US
▼**JUSTICES OF THE SUPREME COURT.** 1995. irreg. $113.70. Enslow Publishers, Inc., 44 Fadem Rd., Box 699, Springfield, NJ 07081-0699. TEL 201-379-8890. FAX 201-379-7940. E-mail: annette@enslow.com; URL: http://www.enslow.com. Ed. Brian D. Enslow; Pub. Annette Noce. R&P contact: Annette Noce.
  Description: Book series for teens. Analyzes some very important U.S. Chief Justices and their influential decisions. Also includes anecdotes and the personal and legal opinions of some famous public figures.

JUVENILE MERCHANDISING. see INTERIOR DESIGN AND DECORATION — Furniture And House Furnishings

028.5 JA
KAGAKU LAND. (Text in Japanese) 1975. m. 3000 Yen. Sekai Bunka Publishing Inc., 2-29, 4-chome, Kudan-Kita, Chiyoda-ku, Tokyo 102, Japan. Ed. Zenki Egawa. (also avail. in microform from UMI)
  Formerly: Science Land - Kagaku Land.
  Description: Aimed at pre-schoolers.

028.5 II
KALIKKUDUKKA. (Text in Malalayalam) 1994. fortn. Rs.168; newsstand price: Rs.7. M.M. Publications Limited, P.O. Box 226, Erayilkadavu, Kottayam 686 001, India. TEL 91-481-563721. FAX 91-481-564393. TELEX 0888-201 MNR IN. Ed. Bina Mathew. adv.: B&W page Rs.8000, color page Rs.16000. circ. 95,219.

028.5 SW ISSN 0345-6048
KALLE ANKA & CO. Variant title: Walt Disney's Kalle Anka & Co. 1948. w. SEK 575. Hemmets Journal AB, S-212 05 Malmoe, Sweden. adv. circ. 209,300.

028.5 XO
KAMARAT. 1950. 52/yr. Vydavatel'stvo King, P.O. Box 73, 820 14 Bratislava, Slovakia. Ed. Vladimir Topercer. circ. 60,000.

770 SW ISSN 0022-8273
KAMRATPOSTEN. Abbreviated title: K P. 1892. 17/yr. SEK 379 (effective 1995). Bonniers Specialtidningar, P.O. Box 70452, S-107 26 Stockholm, Sweden. TEL 46-8-736-37-00. FAX 46-8-736-38-42. Ed. Mona Johansson. bk.rev.; film rev.; play rev. circ. 65,000.
  Formerly (until 1950): Folkskolans Barntidning.
  Description: Presents news and current affairs articles for children ages 8-15.

KANSAS 4-H JOURNAL. see AGRICULTURE

028.5 CC ISSN 1006-1614
KANTU SHUOHUA/PICTURE TALK. (Text in Chinese) m. (foreign Y250). Shanghai Jiaoyu Chubanshe - Shanghai Educational Publishing House, 123 Yongfu Road, Shanghai 200031, People's Republic of China. TEL 4377165. (Dist. in US by: China Books & Periodicals, Inc., 2929 24th St., San Francisco, CA 94110. TEL 415-282-2994) Ed. Dai Keqi. illus. circ. 200,000.
  Description: For preschool children.

028.5 IR ISSN 1023-182X
KAYHAN-E BACHEHA/CHILDREN'S WORLD. (Text in Persian) 1956. w. $164 airmail to N. America; Europe $101 (effective 1996). Kayhan Publications, Ferdowsi Ave., P.O. Box 11365-9631, Tehran, Iran. TEL 98-21-3110251. FAX 98-21-314228. TELEX 212467. Ed. Amir Hossan Fardi. adv. circ. 150,000. **Document type:** consumer publication.

KID; your English monthly. see LINGUISTICS

808.068 US ISSN 0899-4293
KID CITY. 1974. 10/yr. $19.70 (foreign $22.97) (effective 1997). Children's Television Workshop, One Lincoln Plaza, New York, NY 10023. TEL 800-678-0613. (Subscr. to: Box 53349, Boulder, CO 80322) Ed. Maureen Hunter-Bone. illus. circ. 250,000. **Indexed:** Ind.Child.Mag.
  —KR SourceOne.
  Formerly: Electric Company Magazine (ISSN 0197-0062)
  Description: Educates and entertains children through stories, puzzles, word games, and projects.

028.5 793 US
▼**KID CROSSWORDS AND OTHER PUZZLES.** 1996. m. E-mail: kidcross@aol.com; URL: http://members.aol.com/kidcross. Ed. Brian R. Goss.
  ●Available only online.
  Description: Magazine of original and challenging puzzles on academic subjects taught by K-12 teachers.

028.5 362.5 US
▼**KID'N AROUND.** 1996. m. 17205 Vashon Hwy. S.W., Vashon, WA 98070. E-mail: bluesnow@halcyon.com; URL: http://www.kidnaround.com. Ed. Kaj Berry.
  ●Also available online.
  Description: Educational publication for children ages 6 to 12.

028.5 US ISSN 1054-2868
KIDS DISCOVER. 1991. 10/yr. $19.95 (foreign $27.95) (effective 1998). 170 Fifth Ave., New York, NY 10010. TEL 212-242-5133. FAX 212-242-5628. (Subscr. to: Box 54205, Boulder, CO 80322-4205. TEL 800-284-8276) Ed. Stella Sands. circ. 430,000. **Document type:** consumer publication.
  —KR SourceOne.
  Description: For children ages 5-12; each issue explores a different topic.

028.5 US ISSN 1051-421X
KID'S KORNER! m. Box 413, Joaquin, TX 75954.

028.5 US ISSN 0738-7431
KIDS RHYME NEWSLETTER; stories, games and more. 1991. a. $6. Story Time Stories That Rhyme, Box 416, Denver, CO 80201-0416. TEL 303-575-5676. Ed. A. Doyle. R&P contact: A. Doyle. illus. circ. 1,500. (looseleaf format) **Document type:** newsletter.
  Description: Provides parents with educational stories in rhyming verse to read to their children.

028.5 US
KID'S WORLD. 1993. 4/yr. $3. 1300 Kicker Rd., Tuscaloosa, AL 35404. TEL 205-553-2284. Ed. Morgan Kopaska-Merkel; Pub. David Kopaska-Merkel. R&P contact: Morgan Kopaska-Merkel. circ. 100. **Document type:** consumer publication.

028.5 CN
KIDS WORLD MAGAZINE. 1992. 5/yr. Can.$16.99. M2 Communications, 93 Lombard Ave., Ste. 108, Winnipeg, MB R3B 3B1, Canada. TEL 204-985-8160. FAX 204-943-8991. Ed. Stuart Slayen; Pub. Nancy Moore. R&P contact: Nancy Moore. adv.: trim 7 7/8 x 10 3/4; adv. contact: Michael Sheasgreen. circ. 225,000 (controlled). **Document type:** consumer publication.
  Description: Educational magazine distributed to elementary schools across Canada.
  Refereed Serial

028.5 020 US ISSN 0278-632X
KIDSTUFF. 1981. m. $24. Guidelines Press, 1307 S. Killian Dr., Lake Park, FL 33403. Ed. Sheila Debs.
  Description: Contains complete story hour programs, fingerplays, songs, crafts, flannelboard stories and patterns.

CHILDREN AND YOUTH — FOR 1877

028.5 US
KIDSVILLE NEWS; the triangle's fun family newspaper. 1993. m. free. Box 3009, Cary, NC 27519. TEL 919-469-8855. Pub. Michael Whelan. adv.; bk.rev.; illus. **Document type:** consumer publication.
Description: For preteens and their families.

028.5 US
KIDSVILLE NEWS. 1995. m. $35. Hearth Publications, Inc., 13110 Shaker Square, Cleveland, OH 44120-2313. TEL 216-752-3700. Ed. Ann V. Billingsley; Pub. Ann V. Billingsley. R&P contact: Ann V. Billingsley. adv.: page $1050; adv. contact: Gina F. Sidari. **Document type:** newspaper.

028.5 HU ISSN 0133-3755
KINCSKERESO. 1974. 9/yr. $5 (effective 1993). (Muvelodesi Ministerium Osvat Erno Alapitvanya es Szeged Megyei Jogu Varos Polgarmesteri Hivatala) Kultura, P.O. Box 149, 1389 Budapest 62, Hungary. TEL 361-250-01-94. FAX 361-250-02-33. TELEX 20-2855 KULT H. Ed. Laszlo Deme. bk.rev.; illus.

KIND NEWS JR. see ANIMAL WELFARE

KIND NEWS PRIMARY. see ANIMAL WELFARE

KIND NEWS SR. see ANIMAL WELFARE

KINDER; Judgendmagazin in deutscher Sprache. see LINGUISTICS

028.5 778.534 GW ISSN 0721-8486
KINDER JUGEND FILM KORRESPONDENZ. 1980. q. DM.30 to individuals; institutions DM.40 (effective 1997). Kinderkino Muenchen e.V., Werner-Friedmann-Bogen 18, 80993 Munich, Germany. TEL 49-89-1491453. FAX 49-89-1494836. Ed. Hans Strobel. adv. contact: Christel Strobel. bk.rev.; illus.; film rev. circ. 1,000. **Document type:** bulletin.

028.5 GW
KINDER- UND JUGENDBUECHER. a. DM.2.20. K.F. Koehler Verlag GmbH, Am Wallgraben 110, 70565 Stuttgart, Germany. FAX 49-711-7892-132. **Document type:** bibliography.

KINDEREN VOORRANG! see TRANSPORTATION

808.8 TZ ISSN 0856-1982
KIPEPEO. (Text in English, Swahili) 1969-1988; resumed 1994. q. $20. Tanzania Library Services Board, P.O. Box 9283, Dar es Salaam, Tanzania. TEL 255-51-150047. TELEX TANLIS. Ed. Elizabeth M. Dalotta. bk.rev.; illus. circ. 250. **Document type:** consumer publication, newsletter.
Former titles: Mapinduzi Katika Uandishi (ISSN 0856-0498); Gazeti la Watoto.

028.5 XO
KIS EPITO. 24/yr. Smena Publishing House, Prazska 11, 812 84 Bratislava, Slovakia.

305.235 PO ISSN 0873-7037
KISS ME! m. Esc.2400 (foreign Esc.4740) (effective 1997). Impala Sociedade Editorial, S.A., Av. Miguel Bombarda, 33, 2745 Queluz, Portugal. TEL 351-4364401. FAX 351-4365001. (Distr. by: Electroliber, Rua Vasco de Gama, 4-A, Portugal. TEL 531-9425407) Ed. Luis Peniche. adv. contact: Lucilia Simoes.

028.5 NE ISSN 0922-2715
KIVIVE. 1980. 10/yr. fl.35. Stichting Gereformeerd Jongerenblad, Zwanenkamp 1048, 3607 NJ Maarssenbroek, Netherlands. TEL 31-4365-74909. Ed. Dhr. van Dooren. adv.; illus. circ. 7,500.

028.5 UG ISSN 0023-1975
KIZITO; a children's magazine. (Text in Luganda) 1957. 3/yr. Sh.500 per no. Kampala Archdiocese, c/o Sr. Olivia Nakiganda, Ed., P.O. Box 14, Kisubi, Kampala, Uganda. Ed. M.O. Nakiganda. **Document type:** academic/scholarly publication.
Description: Promotes Catholic principles while educating children from all walks of life.

028.5 GW
▼**KLAEX.** 1996. q. 26 SFr. (effective 1997). Bundes Verlag GmbH, Bodenborn 43, 58452 Witten, Germany. TEL 49-2302-9309320. FAX 49-2302-9309310. E-mail: bv.witten@t-online.de; URL: http://www.jesus-online.de/bv/bv__home.htm. Ed. Martin Gundlach. adv.: B&W page DM.2150, color page DM.2500; trim 188 x 258. circ. 20,000 (paid). (back issues avail.) **Document type:** bulletin.

028.5 GW ISSN 0938-3026
KLICK; Zeitschrift fuer Durchblick. 1985. s-m. DM.34($15) Verl. Die Tollkirsche, Friesenstr. 90, 28203 Bremen, Germany. TEL 0421-72993. FAX 0421-700555. Ed. Erwin Bienewald.
Description: For young people ages 9 - 14.

369.4 630 SW ISSN 0281-1278
KLOEVERBLADET. 1921. q. SEK 50 ($10) Riksfoerbundet Sveriges 4H - Swedish Association of 4H Clubs, P.O. Box 2012, S-641 02 Katrineholm, Sweden. TEL 0150-50380. FAX 0150-53599. Ed. Pernilla Hjelm. adv.; bk.rev.; illus. circ. 27,500. **Document type:** bulletin.
Former titles (until 1983): 4H - Journalen; (until 1963): Jord och Ungdom; (until 1949): J.U.F. Bladet; (until 1923): Jordbrukareungdomens Foereningsblad (ISSN 0016-335X)

028.5 II ISSN 0254-6205
KNANAYAMITHRAM; a Christian magazine for children. (Text in English, Malayalam) 1982. m. Rs.20($10) Jaffe Publishing Management Service, Kunnuparambil Bldgs., Kurichy, Kottayam 686 549, India. TEL 04826-470. Ed. Nicy K. Punnoose. circ. 5,000. (back issues avail.)

028.5 US ISSN 0163-4844
KNOW YOUR WORLD EXTRA.* 1967. 14/yr. $29.95 for single subscr. (effective 1997-1998). Weekly Reader Corporation, Box 120023, Stamford, CT 06912-0023. TEL 800-446-3355. FAX 609-786-3360. (Subscr. to: 3000 Cindel Dr., Delran, NJ 08075; Large Print and Braille editions avail. from: American Printing House for the Blind Inc., 1839 Frankfort Ave., Box 6389, Louisville, KY 40206-0085. TEL 502-895-2405) Ed. Sandra Maccarone; Pub. Richard J. Le Brasseur. R&P contact: Shirley Peterson. circ. 145,584 (paid). (also avail. in microfilm from UMI; Braille; large print edition in 14 pt.; reprint service avail. from UMI) **Indexed:** Ind.Child.Mag. **Document type:** newspaper. —UMI.
Formerly (until 1977): Know Your World (ISSN 0023-2483)
Description: Builds reading success for remedial reading students in grade 5 and up. Includes separate teacher's guide and a bound set of reproducible skills extenders.

028.5 AF ISSN 0023-2572
KOCHNIANO ANEES/ANEES FOR CHILDREN.* (Text in Dari, Pashto) 1970. w. $13. Anees Publishing Co., Ansari Ave., Kabul, Afghanistan. Ed. Mohammed Taher Paknihad. adv.; abstr.; charts; illus.; stat. circ. 30,000.

KOL HATNUAH. see ETHNIC INTERESTS

KOLEINU. see RELIGIONS AND THEOLOGY — Judaic

028.5 II ISSN 0023-2963
KOMAL PATRA. (Text in Bengali) 1969. q. Rs.1($0.30) 153 Sarat Chandra Chatterjee Rd., Shibpur, Howrah 2, India. Ed. Sanjit K. Mukherjee. adv.; bk.rev. circ. 600.

028.5 NE ISSN 0166-3119
KOMBY; aktiviteiten voor jeugd en jongeren. vol.4, 1982; N.S. 1984. 6/yr. fl.37.50. Y M C A Nederland, Postbus 115, 3970 AC Driebergen, Netherlands. Ed. Ms. J.J.E. Keiluhu. illus. **Document type:** bulletin.

839.7 808.8068 SW ISSN 0283-6335
KOMETEN. 1978. q. SEK 60 (effective 1995). Skrivarklubben i Blekinge, c/o A-C Nilsson, Urmakaregraend 3, S-371 33 Karlskrona, Sweden. TEL 46-455-813-68.

028.5 GR ISSN 1105-1469
KOMIX. 1988. m. $60 (effective 1997). Terzopoulos Publishing Ltd., 7 Fragoklisias St., 151 25 Marousi, Greece. TEL 30-1-689-6366. FAX 30-1-680-6631. Ed. Stelios Nicolaou. adv. contact: Angela Daramara. illus. circ. 18,000. **Document type:** consumer publication.
Description: Contains Walt Disney stories and comics for children and adult collectors.

028.5 GW
KOMPOST. 1980. m. DM.20($7) J Z Alte Post, Denkmalplatz 1, 90579 Langenzenn, Germany. Ed.Bd. circ. 5,000.

268 AU
KONTAKT; K J in Wien. 1968. m. S.250. Katholische Jugend, Erzdioezese Wien, Stephansplatz 6-6-62, A-1010 Vienna, Austria. TEL 0222-51552380. FAX 0222-51552366. bk.rev. (looseleaf format; also avail. in cards)
Former titles: Kontakt und Reflexionen (ISSN 0034-3013); Studpress auf Reflexionen.

028.5 NE ISSN 0023-3692
KONTAKTO. (Text in Esperanto) 1963. bi-m. fl.41($22) (Tutmonda Esperantista Junulara Organizo - World Organization of Young Esperantists) Universala Esperanto-Asocio, Nieuwe Binnenweg 176, 3015 BJ Rotterdam, Netherlands. TEL 31-10-4361044. FAX 31-10-4361751. E-mail: uea@inter.nl.net. Ed. Francisco L. Veuthey. adv.: B&W page fl.780; adv. contact: Osmo Buller. illus. circ. 2,200. (back issues avail.)

028.5 GW
KONTRAPUNKTE. 1953. s-a. free. Kontrapunkte Schuelerzeitung, Zinzendorfgymnasium, Moenchweilerstr. 7, 78126 Koenigsfeld, Germany. Ed. Peter Vogt. adv.; bk.rev.; film rev.; play rev.; illus. circ. 600. (back issues avail.)

028.5 GW
KORRESPONDENZ. 1978. 3/yr. free. Landesjugendring Niedersachsen e.V., Maschstr. 24, 30169 Hannover, Germany. TEL 0511-805055. FAX 0511-805057. Eds. Beate Frey, Hans Schwab. circ. 7,000. **Document type:** academic/scholarly publication.

028.5 RU ISSN 0130-2574
KOSTER. 1936. m. $54 (effective 1998). Mitninskaya ul. 1-20, 193024 St. Petersburg, Russia. TEL (812) 274-15-72. Ed. O.W. Tsakunov.

054 FR ISSN 0765-1376
KOUAKOU. 1966. bi-m. 30 F. Societe d'Editions Generales et de Documentation (SEGEDO), 6 Villa Bosquet, 75007 Paris, France. Ed. Pierre Rostini. adv. circ. 425,000.

028.5 372 FI ISSN 0357-2714
KOULULAINEN. (Text in Finnish) 1944. m. FIM 240. Yhtyneet Kuvalehdet Oy, Maistraatinportti 1, FIN-00240 Helsinki, Finland. TEL 358-0-156-6524. FAX 358-0-156-6505. TELEX 121364. Ed. Sirkku Kuusava. adv.: B&W page FIM 7500, color page FIM 11000. illus. circ. 47,054. **Document type:** consumer publication.
Description: For school children aged 7 to 13.

028.5 GR ISSN 0023-4664
KRIKOS TON VATHMOFORON. 1948. m. included with subscription to Proscopos. Boy Scouts of Greece - Soma Hellinon Proscopon, 1 Ptolemeon St., Athens 516, Greece. Ed. Demetrius Marinopoulos. circ. 7,500.

028.5 IS ISSN 0334-648X
KULANU. 1985. 26/yr. IS.156. Z.Z. Printing & Productions, Derech Ben-Zvi 84, Tel Aviv 68104, Israel. TEL 972-3-5180820. FAX 972-3-820401. Ed. Oren Zivlin. adv.; bk.rev. circ. 40,000.
Formed by the merger of (1936-1985): Davar (ISSN 0333-5860); (1945-1985): Mishmar (ISSN 0333-5364)
Description: For children ages 8-14.

028.5 IS ISSN 0792-8149
KULANU - PILON; semi-monthly magazine for children. 1976. 26/yr. IS.156. Z.Z. Printing & Productions, Derech Ben-Zvi 84, Tel Aviv 68104, Israel. TEL 972-3-5180820. FAX 972-3-820401. Ed. Nurit Yuval. adv.; bk.rev. circ. 12,000.
Formerly (until 1992): Pilon (ISSN 0333-5410)
Description: For children ages 6-8.

CHILDREN AND YOUTH — FOR

KUMAR. see *ART*

028.5 155.4 II
KUTTIKALUDE DEEPIKA; children's fortnightly. (Text in Malayalam) s-m. Rs.190 for 2 yrs.; newsstand price: Rs.5. Rashtra Deepika Ltd., Deepika Bldg., C.M.S. College Rd., P.B. No. 7, Kottayam 686 001, India. TEL 91-481-566706. FAX 91-481-567947. TELEX 0888-203 DPKA IN. adv.: page Rs.5000; 160 x 110. circ. 50,000.

KVANT. see *SCIENCES: COMPREHENSIVE WORKS*

028.5 US
L.A. YOUTH; the newspaper by and about Los Angeles teens. (Text in English, Spanish) 1987. bi-m. $12. Youth News Service, L.A. Bureau, 6030 Wilshire Blvd., Ste. 201, Los Angeles, CA 90036. TEL 213-938-9194. FAX 213-938-0940. E-mail: layouth@worldsite.net; URL: http://www.layouth.com/. Ed.Bd.; Pub. Elizabeth Hartigan. R&P contact: Donna C. Myrow. illus.; film rev.; music rev. circ. 100,000. **Document type:** newspaper.
Description: Addresses topics of concern to teens, such as racism, dysfunctional relationships, abuse, school dress codes, and earthquake preparedness.

L.G. ARGOMENTI. (Letteratura Giovanile) see *LITERARY AND POLITICAL REVIEWS*

LAD. see *RELIGIONS AND THEOLOGY — Protestant*

808.89 US ISSN 1051-4961
AP201
LADYBUG; the magazine for young children. 1990. m. $32.97 (Canada Can.$42.97; overseas $41.97) (effective 1996). Carus Corporation, 315 Fifth St., Box 300, Peru, IL 61354. TEL 815-224-6656. FAX 815-224-6615. (Subscr. to: Box 7436, Red Oak, IA 51591-2436. TEL 800-827-0227) Ed. Paula Morrow; Pub. Bob Harper. illus. circ. 139,000. **Document type:** consumer publication.
Description: For children ages 2-6. Includes picture stories, songs, poems, rhymes, and read-aloud stories.

028.5 AU ISSN 0023-7957
LANDJUGEND; Magazin fuer junge Leute. 1956. m. S.280 (foreign S.370). (Bundesministerium fuer Land- und Forstwirtschaft) Oesterreichischer Agrarverlag GmbH, Inkustr. 1-7, A-3400 Klosterneuburg, Austria. TEL 02243-333006. FAX 02243-3330056. Eds. Renate Gailer, Franz Kamleitner. adv.; bk.rev. circ. 40,000.

028.5 340 US
LANDMARK SUPREME COURT CASES. 1994. irreg. $284.25. Enslow Publishers, Inc., 44 Fadem Rd., Box 699, Springfield, NJ 07081-0699. TEL 201-379-8890. FAX 201-379-7940. E-mail: annette@enslow.com; URL: http://www.enslow.com. Ed. Brian D. Enslow; Pub. Annette Noce. R&P contact: Annette Noce.
Description: Book series for teens. Contains some of the most important United States Supreme Court cases. Each book examines the issues leading up to a case, the case itself, and the present-day effects of the court's decision.

LEARNING EDGE; home based education program news. see *EDUCATION — Teaching Methods And Curriculum*

028.5 UK
LEARNING IS FUN. m. £24 (Europe & Ireland £30; rest of world £50) (effective 1996). B B C Worldwide Publishing, Broadcasting House, Whiteladies Rd., Bristol GS8 2LR, England. TEL 44-181-576-2000. FAX 44-181-576-2931. (Subscr. to: P.O. Box 425, Woking, Surrey GU21 1GP, England. TEL 44-1483-733716. FAX 44-1483-756792) **Document type:** consumer publication.

373.1 US ISSN 1075-8852
LEBANON LIGHT. 1919. 8/yr. (Aug.-June). $18 (foreign $25) (effective 1997). Lebanon High School, Journalism Class, c/o Wayne L. Dunn, Advisor, 160 Miller Rd., Lebanon, OH 45036-1299. TEL 513-933-2150. FAX 513-933-2150. E-mail: leblight@your-net.com. Ed. Jeff Weisenborn. R&P contact: Wayne Dunn. adv.; B&W page $120; adv. contact: Zach Dilgard. bk.rev.; illus. circ. 1,500. pp./issue: 16. (tabloid format) **Document type:** newspaper.
Description: Reports on school activities and news of the city of Lebanon, OH.

LEFT. see *POLITICAL SCIENCE*

LEGALDATE. see *LAW*

028.5 920 US
▼**LEGENDARY HEROES OF THE WILD WEST.** 1996. irreg. $179.40. Enslow Publishers, Inc., 44 Fadem Rd., Box 699, Springfield, NJ 07081-0699. TEL 201-379-8890. FAX 201-379-7940. E-mail: annette@enslow.com; URL: http://www.enslow.com. Ed. Brian D. Enslow; Pub. Annette Noce. R&P contact: Annette Noce.
Description: Examines the adventure of the explorers, frontiersmen, pioneers, and westerners of the West and Southwest.

028.5 IT
LEGGO LEGGO. 1992. m. (10/yr.). L.75000($50) (effective 1997). Zanfi Editori s.r.l., Via Emilia Ovest 954, 41100 Modena, Italy. TEL 39-59-891700. FAX 39-59-891701. E-mail: zanfi.editori@mo.nettuno.it. adv.: B&W page L.2000000, color page L.3000000. **Document type:** consumer publication.
Description: For children ages 7 to 10. Designed to make reading pleasurable.

370 US ISSN 0024-1261
LET's FIND OUT. 1966. 32/yr. $4.95. Scholastic Inc., 555 Broadway, New York, NY 10012-3999. TEL 212-343-6100. Ed. Mary Reid. illus. circ. 500,000. (reprint service avail. from UMI)
—UMI.
Description: Aimed at children in kindergarten.

808.068 IT
LETTERATURA PER RAGAZZI IN ITALIA. a. Edizioni Piemme S.p.A., Via del Carmine 5, 15033 Casale Monferrato (AL), Italy. TEL 39-142-3361. FAX 39-142-74223.

028.5 FR ISSN 0760-9191
LA LETTRE DE TAPORI. (Text in Dutch, English, French, German, Spanish) 1969. m. 80 F. (effective 1997). (Mouvement International A T D Quart Monde - International Movement A T D Fourth World) Editions Quart Monde, 15 rue Maitre Albert, 75005 Paris, France. TEL 33-1-46334977. FAX 33-1-43296448. Ed. Noldi Christen. (back issues avail.) **Document type:** newsletter.
Formerly (until 1984): Tapori (ISSN 0754-362X)
Description: Connects groups of children in France and around the world who react against injustice and poverty.
Refereed Serial

L I B E R. (Libri per Bambini e Ragazzi) see *PUBLISHING AND BOOK TRADE*

028.5 CC ISSN 1002-1922
LIAONING QINGNIAN/LIAONING YOUTH. (Text in Chinese) 1972. s-m. Gongqingtuan Liaoning Shengwei, 21, Wujing Jie, Heping-qu, Shenyang, Liaoning 110003, People's Republic of China. TEL 23684. Ed. Li Yingmin.

THE LINK. see *RELIGIONS AND THEOLOGY — Roman Catholic*

LISSY; ein Herz fuer Pferde. see *SPORTS AND GAMES — Horses And Horsemanship*

LISTO. see *LINGUISTICS*

028.5 US ISSN 0024-4511
AP2
LITERARY CAVALCADE. 1948. 8/yr. $12 for student ed.; teacher's ed. $31.80 (effective 1997). Scholastic Inc., 555 Broadway, New York, NY 10012-3999. TEL 212-343-6100; 800-325-6149. URL: http://www.scholastic.com. Ed. Katherine Robinson. illus.; index. circ. 280,405. (also avail. in microfiche from UMI,MIM; reprint service avail. from UMI)
—UMI.
Description: Features contemporary and modern classic literature; dramatic scripts, stories, essays, poetry and writing lessons.

028.5 820 AT ISSN 1034-6244
THE LITERATURE BASE. 1990. q. Aus.$39.95 (New Zealand Aus.$37.95; elsewhere Aus.$49.95). Literature Base, P.O. Box 563, Hamilton, Qld. 4007, Australia. TEL 61-7-2560064. FAX 61-7-2560922. Ed. Margaret Phillips. R&P contact: James Turton. adv. contact: James Turton. circ. 3,500. (back issues avail.) **Indexed:** Child.Lit.Abstr. **Document type:** academic/scholarly publication.
—UnCover.
Description: Contains practical ideas for using literature with children in schools.

028.5 370 RU ISSN 0203-5847
LITERATURNAYA UCHEBA. 1930. bi-m. $55 (effective 1998). T, Novodmitrovskaya ul. 5A, 125015 Moscow, Russia. TEL 7-095-02858903. FAX 7-095-2856298. (Dist. by: Mezhdunarodnaya Kniga, B. Yakimanka 39, 117049 Moscow, Russia. TEL 7-095-2384967. FAX 7-095-2384634; Dist. in U.S. by: Victor Kamkin Inc., 4956 Boiling Brook Pkwy, Rockville, MD 20852. TEL 301-881-5973) Ed. V.A. Malutin. adv.; bk.rev.; illus.

028.5 CC
LITTLE FROG. (Text in Chinese) 1985. bi-w. $21.60. Shaonian Ertong Chubanshe - Juvenile & Children Publishing House, 1538 Yan'an Xilu, Shanghai 200052, People's Republic of China. TEL 86-21-6282-3025. FAX 86-21-6282-1726. Ed. Shunpei Zhou. **Document type:** newspaper.
Formerly: You'er Wenxue Bao - Literature for Preschool Children.
Description: Carries Chinese and foreign fairy tales, poems, children songs, proses and dramas.

808.068 CN
LITTLE THINGS WORD LOOM. 1981. irreg. Word Loom, Box 20, 242 Montrose, Winnipeg, MB, Canada. Ed. Ronan Reinart. circ. 100.

028.5 UK ISSN 1351-3397
LIVE AND KICKING. 1993. m. £20 (Europe & Ireland £25; rest of world £37) (effective 1996). B B C Worldwide Publishing, Broadcasting House, Whiteladies Rd., Bristol GS8 2LR, England. TEL 44-181-576-2000. FAX 44-181-576-2931. (Subscr. to: P.O. Box 425, Woking, Surrey GU21 1GP, England. TEL 44-1483-733716. FAX 44-1483-756792) **Document type:** consumer publication.

028.5 283 UK
LOOK!; the juniors' magazine of the Baptist Missionary Society. 1845. m. £1.50. Baptist Missionary Society, P.O. Box 49, Baptist House, 129 Broadway, Didcot, Oxon. OX11 8XA, England. TEL 01235-512044. FAX 01235-511265. Ed. Rev. D.E. Pountain. circ. 8,000.

LOOK IN TELEVISION ANNUAL; for children. see *COMMUNICATIONS — Television And Cable*

369.4 FR ISSN 0751-5685
LOUVETEAU. 1924. bi-m. 70 F. Editions Scouts de France, 54 av. Jean Jaures, 75019 Paris, France. TEL 42-52-37-37. FAX 42-38-09-87. Ed. Philippe Da Costa. adv.
Formerly: Scouts Louveteau.
Description: For scouts ages 10-12.

028.5 AT ISSN 0158-099X
LOWDOWN; youth performing arts in Australia. 1978. bi-m. Aus.$36 (foreign Aus.$52). Carclew Youth Performing Arts Centre, Inc., 11 Jeffcott St., North Adelaide, S.A. 5006, Australia. TEL 08-267-5111. FAX 08-239-0689. (Co-sponsor: Youth Performing Arts Council of South Australia) Ed. Belinda MacQueen. adv. contact: Leigh Mangin. bk.rev.; play rev.; abstr. circ. 4,000. (back issues avail.) **Indexed:** Child.Lit.Abstr. **Document type:** directory, trade publication.

028.5 372.21 AT ISSN 0816-3642
LUCKY; the magazine for young readers. 1986. 7/yr. Aus.$28.50 (foreign Aus.$42). Scholastic Pty. Ltd., Railway Crescent, Lisarow, N.S.W. 2250, Australia. TEL 043-28-3555. FAX 043-23-3827. (Subscr. to: P.O. Box 579, Gosford, N.S.W. 2250, Australia. TEL 02-4164000) Ed. Sharon Dalgleish. circ. 50,000. (back issues avail.)

028.5 SP
LUNA DE MADRID. 1983. m. Ediciones el Jueves, S.A., Pintor Noreno Carbonero 18, 28028 Madrid, Spain. TEL 91-2550505. Dir. Jorge Gines. circ. 150,000.

028.5 369.4 YU ISSN 0350-8080
M A K. (Mladosc, Aktivnosc, Kreativnocs) 1972. m. 3000 din.($21) N I U "Ruske Slovo", Bul. 23, Oktobra 31, 21000 Novi Sad, Vojvodina, Yugoslavia. TEL 621-433. bk.rev.; film rev.; play rev.; illus.; tr.lit. (back issues avail.)

028.5 NE ISSN 0166-3917
M.3. 1952. 8/yr. fl.37.50. Landelyre Hervormde Jeugdraad, Postbus 114, 3970 AC Driebergen, Netherlands. TEL 03438-23144. FAX 03438-23250. Ed. Bep Smits. bk.rev.; film rev.; play rev.; illus. circ. 2,000.
 Formerly: Materiaal, Metodiek, Mededelingen (ISSN 0025-5254)

MA'AGALAI KERI'A. see *LITERATURE*

028.5 US
THE MCGUFFEY WRITER & ILLUSTRATOR. 1977. 3/yr. $10 to individuals; institutions $40 (effective 1997); newsstand price: $4. McGuffey Foundation School, 5128 Westgate Dr., Oxford, OH 45056. TEL 513-523-7742. FAX 513-523-5565. E-mail: jchurch@tlcnet.muchio.edu. Ed. Susan Kammeraad-Campbell. bk.rev. circ. 500. **Document type:** consumer publication.
 Formerly: McGuffey Writer (ISSN 0891-1673)
 Description: Devoted to the creative writing and illustrative art work (black and white) of K through 12 students from across the United States and Canada.
 Refereed Serial

MAD. see *LITERARY AND POLITICAL REVIEWS*

028.5 SZ
MAEDCHEN. fortn. DM.75.40 (foreign DM.83.20) (effective 1997). Z A G Zeitschriften Verlag, Baarerstr. 22, CH-6300 Zug, Switzerland. TEL 41-41-7102020. FAX 41-41-7115268. Ed. Isabella Flohr. adv.: B&W page DM.16700, color page DM.26000; 205 x 285; adv. contact: Ingrid Krafft. circ. 421,598 (paid). **Document type:** consumer publication.

028.5 GW ISSN 1430-9467
MAGAZIN JUNGER MEDIENMACHER. 1982. 5/yr. $10. Verband der Niedersaechsischen Jugendredakteure, Ziegelstr. 24, 49074 Osnabrueck, Germany. TEL 49-541-27209. FAX 49-541-29414. E-mail: d.freytag@netlive.sub.de. Ed. Dirk Freytag. bk.rev. circ. 10,000. **Document type:** newsletter.
 Former titles: Jugendpressedienst des V N J; Krake.

028.5 CN ISSN 1189-9069
MAGAZINE JEUNESSE. (Text in French) 1990. 4/yr. Productions Tel-Art, 7383 rue de la Roche, Montreal, PQ H2R 2T4, Canada. TEL 514-274-6124. FAX 514-272-5939. Ed. Jean-Yves Daigle. adv.: B&W page Can.$3000, color page Can.$4300; trim 8 1/4 x 10 7/8; adv. contact: Diane Charest. circ. 59,000. **Document type:** consumer publication.
 Formerly (until 1992): Magazine (ISSN 1189-9050)

MAGAZINES FOR YOUNG PEOPLE; a Children's Magazine Guide companion volume. see *BIBLIOGRAPHIES*

MAGYAR CSERKESZ/HUNGARIAN SCOUT MAGAZINE. see *CLUBS*

059.927 TS
MAJID. (Text in Arabic) 1979. w. 300DH. (Europe 420DH.; elsewhere 500DH.). Al- Ittihad Press, Publishing and Distribution Corp., Majallat Majid, P.O. Box 3558, Abu Dhabi, United Arab Emirates. TEL 971-2-451804. FAX 971-2-451455. TELEX 22984 ITPRESS EM. Ed. Ahmed Omar. adv. circ. 170,000. **Document type:** consumer publication.
 Description: For children 4-16 years old.

028.5 500 UK ISSN 1355-8560
MAKING SENSE OF SCIENCE. 1995. irreg. £6.99($11.90) Portland Press Ltd., 59 Portland Pl., London W1N 3AJ, England. TEL 44-171-580-5530. FAX 44-171-323-1136. E-mail: sales@portlandpress.co.uk; URL: http://www.portlandpress.co.uk. (Subscr. to: Commerce Way, P.O. Box 32, Colchester, Essex CO2 8HP, England) Ed. F. Balkwill. R&P contact: Adam Marshall. **Document type:** consumer publication.
 Refereed Serial

028.5 SZ
MAKY/RATAPLAN. (Editions in French and German) 1949. m. 21 SFr. Editions Maky - Rataplan, 18 rue Camille-Martin, CH-1203 Geneva, Switzerland. TEL 022-7962552. FAX 022-7961583. adv.: B&W page 2540 SFr., color page 3350 SFr.; trim 132 x 190. bk.rev. circ. 82,949. **Document type:** consumer publication.
 Formerly: Tim (ISSN 0040-7704)

MALADOSTS'. see *LITERARY AND POLITICAL REVIEWS*

301.43 MW
MALAWI YOUTH NEWS. 1972. q. Malawi Young Pioneers, Youth News Magazine, P.O. Box 5694, Limbe, Malawi.

028.5 GW ISSN 0945-2400
MAMAMIA. 1980. 10/yr. DM.35. Randersackererstr. 81, 97074 Nuernberg, Germany. TEL 49-931-15729. FAX 49-931-3552512. Ed. Barbara Pohl-Hildemann. circ. 10,000. **Document type:** newsletter.

028.5 UK ISSN 0262-2440
MANDY. w. D.C. Thomson & Co. Ltd., Albert Square, Dundee DD1 9QJ, Scotland. adv.

059.927 TS
AL-MANHAL/FOUNTAIN. (Text in Arabic, English) 1982. 2/yr. Abu Dhabi Secondary School for Boys, P.O. Box 2616, Abu Dhabi, United Arab Emirates. TEL 662874. Ed. Gumaa Eid M. Al-Muhairi. circ. 300.
 Description: Student publication covering school activities.

MARIEMOU; revue de la jeune fille et de la femme Mauritaniennes. see *WOMEN'S INTERESTS*

MARTHA'S KIDLIT NEWSLETTER. see *LITERATURE*

808.836 US ISSN 8750-4367
MARVEL AGE. 1983. m. Marvel Comics Ltd., 387 Park Ave. S., New York, NY 10016. Ed. Tom DeFalco. illus.

059.927 QA
AL-MASHA'IL. (Text in Arabic) 1987. m. Qatar Establishment for Journalism, Printing and Publication, P.O. Box 1838, Doha, Qatar. TEL 448282. FAX 446723. Ed. Ahmed Abdul-Rahman al-Syid. circ. 22,000.

028.5 XR ISSN 0025-5440
MATERIDOUSKA; literarni mesicnik pro nejmensi ctenare. 1945. m. 18 Kc.($10.60) Mlada Fronta, Radlicka 61, 150 02 Prague 5, Czech Republic. (Dist. by: Artia, Ve Smeckach 30, 111 27 Prague 1, Czech Republic) Ed. Josef Brukner. illus.

028.5 CY ISSN 0025-5904
MATHITIKI ESTIA. (Text in English, French, Greek) 1950. a. free. Ministry of Education and Culture, Pagkyprion Gymnasium, P.O. Box 1034, 1500 Nicosia, Cyprus. TEL 357-2-430670. FAX 357-2-430915. Ed. Stylianos Papantoniou. bk.rev.; film rev.; play rev.; bibl.; charts; illus.; circ. 1,000 (controlled). (processed)
 Description: Contains essays, poems, articles, interviews, and other materials written by students.

028.5 282 XV
MAVRICA/RAINBOW. m. Slovenske Rimskokatoliske Skofije, Cankarejevo Nabrezje 3, 61001 Ljubljana, Slovenia. TEL 061-329-793. Ed. Joze Bertoncelj. circ. 50,000.

028.5 FI ISSN 0785-3416
ME KAKSI. 1987. m. FIM 220. Ten Point Press Oy (Subsidiary of: Helsinki Media Magazines), P.O. Box 501, 90101 Oulu, Finland. TEL 358-81-373-770. Ed. Peppina Matila. adv.: B&W page FIM 9250, color page FIM 12850; 194 x 248. circ. 24,484 (paid). **Document type:** consumer publication.

MEDIEN & ERZIEHUNG; Zweimonatsschrift fuer audiovisuelle Kommunikation. see *COMMUNICATIONS — Television And Cable*

028.5 GW
MEGAPHON. (Text in English, German) 1984. bi-m. DM.10($15) Schuelerzeitung Megaphon, Philipp-Reis-Schule, Hoher Weg 29, 61381 Friedrichsdorf, Germany. Ed.Bd. adv.; bk.rev.; film rev.; play rev.; charts. circ. 2,000.

MEHR FREUDE MAGAZIN. see *RELIGIONS AND THEOLOGY*

028.5 GW
MEIN KLEINES PONY. m. Ehapa Verlag GmbH, Im Riedenberg 54, 70771 Leinfelden-Echterdingen, Germany. TEL 0711-79711. FAX 0711-7971202. Ed. Elvira Braendle. adv. contact: Olaf Hansen. circ. 80,000. **Document type:** consumer publication.

369.4 NZ
MEMBERS MAG E.B.R. E.G.R. Variant title: New Zealand Rally Council. Members Magazine. q. NZ.$5.25. Every Boy's and Every Girl's Rally Council N.Z. Inc., P.O. Box 1903, Palmerston North, New Zealand. TEL 64-6-3593735. Ed. Lee Taylor. circ. 3,100 (paid). **Document type:** bulletin.
 Description: Contains articles, news, poetry and puzzles for children.

028.5 PK ISSN 0025-9144
MEMON ALAM. (Text in English, Gujratti) 1958. m. Rs.5($1.) Memon Youths Organisation, O.T. 9-145, Kagazi Bazar, Box 5097, Karachi 2, Pakistan. Ed. Umer A. Rehman. adv.; bk.rev. circ. 5,000.

810 028.5 US ISSN 0882-2050
MERLYN'S PEN; the national magazines of student writing. (Avail. in two eds.: Intermediate (grades 6-9) and Senior (grades 9-12)) 1985. a. $29 (foreign $32) (effective 1997). Merlyn's Pen, Inc., Dept. UPD, Box 1058, E. Greenwich, RI 02818. TEL 401-885-5175; 800-247-2027. FAX 401-885-5222. E-mail: Merlynspen@aol.com. Ed. R. James Stahl. adv.: B&W page $1450, color page $1950; trim 8 1/8 x 10 7/8; adv. contact: Kate Leach. bk.rev.; film rev.; play rev.; illus. circ. 50,000. (back issues avail.) **Document type:** consumer publication, trade publication.
 Description: Fiction and non-fiction writing (plays, short stories, essays, poetry) by students in grades 6-12.

028.5 IT ISSN 0026-0304
MESSAGGERO DEI RAGAZZI. 1922. s-m. Lit.37000 (foreign Lit.57000) (effective 1997). Editrice Grafiche Messaggero Sant' Antonio, Basilica del Santo, 35123 Padua, Italy. TEL 39-49-8225000. FAX 39-49-8225650. Ed. Giacomo Pantechini. adv.: page Lit.6000000. illus. circ. 60,000. **Document type:** consumer publication.

METAL EDGE. see *MUSIC*

METAL MANIACS. see *MUSIC*

028.5 CI ISSN 0026-1939
MI MLADI. 1956. q. Savez Omaldine Gimnazije, "Vladimir Vitasovic", Kuslanova 52, Zagreb, Croatia.

028.5 BL
MICKEY. 1952. m. Editora Abril Jovem, S.A., Rua Bela Cintra 299, 01415-000 Sao Paulo, Brazil. TEL 011-257-0999. TELEX 011-22115. Ed. Elizabeth De Fiore. adv. circ. 55,000. (back issues avail.) **Document type:** consumer publication.

028.5 FR ISSN 0242-9217
MICKEY PARADE. m. 149 F. (outside E.C. 214 F.) (effective 1997). Disney Hachette Presse, 10 rue Thierry le Luron, 92592 Levallois Perret Cedex, France. TEL 33-1-41348500. FAX 33-1-41348989. (Subscr. to: 90 rue de Flandre, 75947 Paris Cedex 19, France. TEL 33-1-44894484) Ed. Gilles Heylen. circ. 178,000. **Document type:** consumer publication.

028.5 CE
MIHIRA. (Text in Sinhala) 1964. w. newsstand price: Rs.4.50. Associated Newspapers of Ceylon Ltd., Lake House, D.R. Wijewardena Mawatha, Colombo 10, Sri Lanka. TEL 94-1-421181. FAX 94-1-449069. TELEX 22262 CE. Ed. M. Newton Pinto. circ. 145,000.

CHILDREN AND YOUTH — FOR

028.5   **CC**
MIMI HUABAO/MIMI PICTORIAL. (Text in Chinese) bi-m. Y.3.90. Fujian Shaonian Ertong Chubanshe, 27 Degui Xiang, Fuzhou, Fujian 350001, People's Republic of China. TEL 537301. (Dist. overseas by: Jiangsu Publications Import & Export Corp., 56 Gao Yun Ling, Nanjing, Jiangsu, P.R.C.) Ed. Xu Daojing.
    Description: For children 3-7 years of age.

028.5 798   **DK**
MIN HEST.* m. Interpresse A-S, Roennegade 1-5, DK-2100 Copenhagen Oe, Denmark. TEL 45-33-33-75-35. FAX 45-33-33-75-05. adv. circ. 15,000.

028.5   **IT**
MINI. 1976. bi-m. newsstand price: L.3000. Edizioni Internazionali Cioe s.r.l., Via G. Fabbroni 24, 00191 Rome, Italy. TEL 39-6-3287609. Ed. Lamberto Antonelli. adv.: page L.6000000. circ. 60,000.
    Document type: consumer publication.

028.1   **SA**   ISSN 1022-3053
MINIMAG; the magazine for kids. (Text in English) 1994. m. R.50. Elken Publishing, P.O. Box 72738, Lynnwood Ridge 0040, South Africa.

028.5   **IS**
MISHBETZET. (Text in Hebrew) 1958. m. $26. Etzb'oni Publishing House, P.O. Box 28110, Tel Aviv 61280, Israel. FAX 972-3-5373906. Ed. Michael Shir. circ. 20,000.

MISHKAFAYIM. see *ART*

MISSIONARIES OF THE SACRED HEART. ANNALS AUSTRALIA; journal of Catholic culture. see *RELIGIONS AND THEOLOGY — Roman Catholic*

028.5   **YU**   ISSN 0026-7031
MLADOST. 1955. w. 80 din. (Savez Socijalisticke Omladine Jugoslavije) Mladost, Marsala Tita 2, Belgrade, Yugoslavia. Ed. Aleksandar Dukanovic. (also avail. in microfilm from NRP)

028.5   **GW**   ISSN 0942-7147
MOBILE; Zeitschrift fuer junge Eltern. 1992. bi-m. DM.6 (effective 1997). Verlag Herder GmbH und Co. KG, Hermann-Herder-Str. 4, 79104 Freiburg, Germany. TEL 49-761-2717-438. FAX 49-761-2717426. Ed. Renate Ferrari. adv.; color page DM.30320; adv. contact: Bettina Wegmann. circ. 320,000. (back issues avail.) **Document type:** consumer publication.

028.5   **RU**   ISSN 0131-2243
MODELIST - KONSTRUKTOR. 1962. m. $86 (effective 1998). Redaktsiya Modelist - Konstruktor, Novodmitrovskaya ul. 5A, 103030 Moscow, Russia. TEL 7-095-2851704. (Dist. by: Mezhdunarodnaya Kniga, B. Yakimanka 39, 117049 Moscow, Russia. TEL 7-095-2384067. FAX 7-095-2384634; Dist. in U.S. by: Victor Kamkin Inc., 4956 Boiling Brook Pkwy, Rockville, MD 20852. TEL 301-881-5973) Ed. A.S. Raguzin. adv.; bk.rev.; illus. circ. 60,000.

028.5   **CN**   ISSN 0026-9042
MOLODA UKRAINA/YOUNG UKRAINE; zhurnal ukrayiniskoyi demokratychnoyi. 1951. m. Can.$25. (Ob'yednannya Demokratychnoyi Ukrayins'koyi Molodi. Tzentral'nyi Komitet) The Moloda Ukraina Publishers, Postal Station M, Box 40, Toronto, ON M6S 4T2, Canada. TEL 416-763-3422. Ed. L. Lishchyna. adv.; bk.rev.; bibl.; illus.; play rev.; index. circ. 1,050.

028.5 780.42   **RU**   ISSN 0132-8816
PG3201
MOLODEZHNAYA ESTRADA. (Former name of issuing body: Vsesoyuznyi Leninski Kommunisticheskii Soyuz Molodezhi, Tsentral'nyi Komitet) 1943. q. $52 (effective 1998). Izdatel'stvo Molodaya Gvardiya, Sushchevskaya ul., 21, 103030 Moscow, Russia. TEL 7-095-9720546. FAX 7-095-9720582. TELEX 411261 FAKEL. (Dist. by: Mezhdunarodnaya Kniga, B. Yakimanka 39, 117049 Moscow, Russia. TEL 7-095-2384067. FAX 7-095-2384634; Dist. in U.S. by: Victor Kamkin Inc., 4956 Boiling Brook Pkwy, Rockville, MD 20852. TEL 301-881-5973) Ed. N. Schantarenkov. adv.; bk.rev. circ. 185,000.
    Description: Presents a collection of popular and modern songs and plays.

MOME; le mensuel pour ton francais. see *LINGUISTICS*

028.5   **IT**   ISSN 0391-5484
MONDO ERRE. 1975. fortn. (16/yr.) L.35000 (foreign L.56000) (effective 1998). (Centro Catechistico Salesiano) Editrice Elle Di Ci, Corso Francia 214, 10096 Leumann (Turin), Italy. TEL 39-11-9552111. FAX 39-11-9572900. Ed. Valerio Bocci. adv.: B&W page L.2700000, color page L.4500000. circ. 30,000.
    Description: Review of current events for boys and girls.

028.5   **US**
MONKEYSHINES ON AMERICA. 1986. 5/yr. (during school yr.). $28. North Carolina Learning Institute for Fitness and Education, Box 10245, Greensboro, NC 27404. TEL 919-292-6999. URL: http://www.Monkeyshinespublishers.com. Ed. Phyllis Goldman. (back issues avail.)
    Description: Covers American history and geography for elementary, middle and high school students and their teachers.

028.5   **US**
MONKEYSHINES ON HEALTH AND SCIENCE. 1987. 2/yr. $25. North Carolina Learning Institute for Fitness and Education, Box 10245, Greensboro, NC 27404. TEL 919-292-6999. URL: http://www.Monkeyshinespublishers.com. (back issues avail.)
    Description: For elementary, middle and high school students and their teachers.

028.5   **JA**
MONTHLY BOY'S CHAMPION/GEKKAN SHONEN-CHAMPION. (Text in Japanese) 1970. m. 30000 Yen. Akita Shoten Publishing Co. Ltd., 10-8,2-chome, Iidabashi, Chiyoda-ku, Tokyo 102, Japan. Ed. Taizo Kabemura.

MORE. see *RELIGIONS AND THEOLOGY — Protestant*

028.5   **GW**   ISSN 0323-8857
MOSAIK (BERLIN); die unglaubliche Reise der Abrafaxe. 1955. m. DM.37.20 (effective 1996). Mosaik Steinchen fuer Steinchen Verlag GmbH, Lindenallee 5, 14050 Berlin, Germany. TEL 030-3017084. FAX 030-3012194. Ed. Joerg Reuter; Pubs. Anne Hauser-Thiele, Klaus Schleiter. adv.: B&W page DM.6o00, color page DM.11600; adv. contact: Reinhard Fischer. bk.rev.; circ. 104,151 (paid).
    Document type: consumer publication.

MOSHIACH TIMES. see *RELIGIONS AND THEOLOGY — Judaic*

310.412   **CU**   ISSN 0864-0327
HQ1104
MUCHACHA. 1980. m. C.$19.20($21) in N. America; S. America $27; Europe $30; elsewhere $42. Federacion de Mujeres Cubanas, Editora de la Mujer, Galiano 264 esq. Neptuno, Apdo. 2545, Havana 2, Cuba. TEL 7-61-5919. (Dist. by: Ediciones Cubanas, Obispo No. 527, Apdo. 605, Havana, Cuba) Dir. Silvia Martinez. circ. 120,000.

MUCHACHOS. see *LINGUISTICS*

028.5   **GW**   ISSN 0930-7818
MUECKE; die Kinder-Zeitschrift fuer Schule und Freizeit. 1960. m. DM.49.80 (foreign DM.57) (effective 1997). Universum Verlagsanstalt GmbH KG, Langenbeckstr. 9, 65189 Wiesbaden, Germany. TEL 49-611-9030-0. FAX 49-611-9030382. E-mail: uv@universum.de; URL: http://www.universum.de. Eds. Sonja Student, Jutta Filzek. adv. contact: Jochen Hillesheim. **Document type:** academic/scholarly publication.
    Description: Magazine for children in the higher grades. Aims to be educational and informative through the use of stories, pictures, puzzles, games and crafts.

028.5   **GW**   ISSN 0940-8495
MUECKI UND MAX; die Kinder-Zeitschrift fuer Schule und Freizeit. 1987. m. DM.49.80 (foreign DM.57) (effective 1997). Universum Verlagsanstalt GmbH KG, Langenbeckstr. 9, 65189 Wiesbaden, Germany. TEL 49-611-9030-0. FAX 49-611-9030382. E-mail: uv@universum.de; URL: http://www.universum.de. Ed. Jutta Filzek. adv. contact: Jochen Hillesheim. **Document type:** academic/scholarly publication.
    Formerly (until 1991): Muecki (ISSN 0932-4755)
    Description: Magazine for children in the lower grades. Aims to be educational and informative through the use of stories, pictures, puzzles, games and crafts.

028.5   **II**
MULTICULTURAL CHILDREN'S LITERATURE. 1979. 4/yr. Rs.495($102) K.K. Roy (Private) Ltd., 55 Gariahat Rd., P.O. Box 10210, Calcutta 700 019, India. Ed. Dr. K.K. Roy. adv.; abstr.; bibl.; index. circ. 1,900.
    Indexed: Child.Lit.Abstr.

028.5 301   **US**
▼**MULTICULTURAL ISSUES.** 1995. irreg. $113.70. Enslow Publishers, Inc., 44 Fadem Rd., Box 699, Springfield, NJ 07081-0699. TEL 201-379-8890. FAX 201-379-7940. E-mail: annette@enslow.com; URL: http://www.enslow.com. Ed. Brian D. Enslow; Pub. Annette Noce. R&P contact: Annette Noce.
    Description: Book series for teens. Discusses the challenges and problems of being a multicultural society in the U.S.

028.5 920   **US**
▼**MULTICULTURAL JUNIOR BIOGRAPHIES.** 1995. irreg. $94.75. Enslow Publishers, Inc., 44 Fadem Rd., Box 699, Springfield, NJ 07081-0699. TEL 201-379-8890. FAX 201-379-7940. E-mail: annette@enslow.com; URL: http://www.enslow.com. Ed. Brian D. Enslow; Pub. Annette Noce. R&P contact: Annette Noce.
    Description: Each biography in this book series for young readers portrays an inspirational individual who faced many challenges and became a success in their particular culture.

305.232   **SP**   ISSN 1132-7731
MUNDO DE TU BEBE. 1993. m. 4200 ptas. (effective 1997); newsstand price: 350 ptas. H Y M S A, Muntaner 40-42, 08011 Barcelona, Spain. TEL 34-3-4541004. FAX 34-3-4545949. adv. contact: Margarita Masip. (back issues avail.)
    Document type: consumer publication.

028.5 370   **RU**   ISSN 0132-1943
MURZILKA. 1924. m. $43 (effective 1998). Murzilka, Novodmitrovskaya ul. 5A, 125015 Moscow, Russia. TEL 7-095-2851881. FAX 7-095-2851881. (Dist. by: Mezhdunarodnaya Kniga, B. Yakimanka 39, 117049 Moscow, Russia. TEL 7-095-2384967. FAX 7-095-2384634; Dist. in U.S. by: Victor Kamkin Inc., 4956 Boiling Brook Pkwy., Rockville, MD 20852. TEL 301-881-5973) Ed. Tat'yana Androsenko. adv.; bk.rev.; illus. circ. 500,000.

028.5   **US**
▼**MUSE (PERU).** 1996. bi-m. $22. (Smithsonian Institution) Carus Corporation, 315 Fifth St., Box 300, Peru, IL 61354. TEL 312-939-1500. FAX 312-939-8150. Ed. Andre Carus. illus.
    Document type: consumer publication.
    Description: Articles and activities on historical subjects, for ages 6 to 14.

MUSIC AT THE KINDERGARTEN. see *MUSIC*

THE MUSIC LEADER. see *MUSIC*

MUSIC MAKERS (NASHVILLE). see *MUSIC*

028.5   **CG**
MWANA SHABA JUNIOR; magazine des jeunes de la Gecamines. 1964. m. Generale des Carrieres et des Mines, Division des Relations Publiques, B.P. 450, Lubumbashi, Democratic Republic of the Congo.

MY DEVOTIONS. see *RELIGIONS AND THEOLOGY — Protestant*

MY DEVOTIONS (LARGE PRINT EDITION). see *RELIGION AND THEOLOGY — Protestant*

028.5 371   **US**   ISSN 1057-1558
MY FIRST MAGAZINE. 24/yr. (Sep.-May). Scholastic Inc 555 Broadway, New York, NY 10012-3999. Ed. Helen Benham.

MY FRIEND; a Catholic magazine for kids. see *RELIGIONS AND THEOLOGY — Roman Catholic*

028.5   **GW**
N O W SCHUELERZEITUNG DER STAATLICHEN REALSCHULE SPEYER. 1970. a. Realschule im Georg-Friedrich-Kolb-Schulzentrum, 67346 Speyer, Germany. circ. 400.

N S T A REPORTS. (National Science Teachers Association) see *EDUCATION*

051　　　　　US　　ISSN 0737-285X
N Y C. (New Youth Connections); the magazine written by and for New York youth. 1980. 8/yr. $10. Youth Communication - New York Center, Inc., 144 W. 27th St., Ste. 8R, New York, NY 10001-6214. TEL 212-243-3270. Ed. Philip Kay. adv.; bk.rev.; index. circ. 76,000.

371.83　　　　　US
NATIONAL BETA CLUB JOURNAL. 1934. 6/yr. membership. National Beta Club, 151 W. Lee St., Spartanburg, SC 29306-3012. TEL 864-583-4553. Ed. Marggi Roldan. illus. circ. 300,000. **Document type:** newsletter.
   Description: For honor student members of the club.

NATIONAL GEOGRAPHIC. see *GEOGRAPHY*

NATIONAL GEOGRAPHIC WORLD. see *GEOGRAPHY*

028.5 790.1　　　US
NATIONAL P A L UPDATE. q. National Police Athletic League, 200 Castlewood Dr., N. Palm Beach, FL 33408. TEL 407-844-1823. FAX 407-863-6120. Ed. Sally S. Cunningham. circ. 171,311. **Document type:** newspaper.

028.5 920 970.1　　US
NATIVE AMERICAN LEADERS OF THE WILD WEST. 1994. irreg. $104.65. Enslow Publishers, Inc., 44 Fadem Rd., Box 699, Springfield, NJ 07081-0699. TEL 201-379-8890. FAX 201-379-7940. E-mail: annette@enslow.com; URL: http://www.enslow.com. Ed. Brian D. Enslow; Pub. Annette Noce. R&P contact: Annette Noce.
   Description: Book series of biographies on Native Americans for young readers.

NATIVE MONTHLY READER; a scholastic newspaper for young adults. see *ETHNIC INTERESTS*

028.5 591　　　GW
NATUR UND TIERSCHUTZ KALENDER DES DEUTSCHEN TIERSCHUTZBUNDES. 1896. a. DM.4. Johann Michael Sailer Verlag GmbH, Aeusserer-Laufer-Platz 22, 90403 Nuernberg, Germany. TEL 49-911-53961. Ed. Wilfried Beuerle. circ. 230,000. **Document type:** bulletin.

028.5　　　　GW
NATURFREUNDE - KINDERPOST. 1948. bi-m. DM.25 membership. (Naturfreundejugend Deutschlands) Verlag Naturfreunde Freizeit und Wandern GmbH, c/o Jutta Roewer, Ed., Goldkampstr. 59, 49086 Osnabrueck, Germany. TEL 49-541-78999. FAX 49-541-78998. circ. 12,500. **Document type:** newsletter.

359 028.5　　　UK
NAVY NEWS. SEA CADET EDITION. 1954. m. £14. (Sea Cadet Association) Navy News, H.M.S. Nelson, Portsmouth, Hants PO1 3HH, England. TEL 44-1705-826040. FAX 44-1705-830149. Ed. Jim Allaway. R&P contact: Anne Driver. adv. contact: Anne Driver. bk.rev.; charts; illus. circ. 7,500. (tabloid format) **Document type:** newsletter.
   Formerly: Sea Cadet (ISSN 0036-9985)
   Description: Aimed at youths aged 12-18.

028.5 792　　　AA
NE SKENEN E FEMIJEVE. m. Ministry of Culture, Youth and Sport, Tirana, Albania.

NEMLI. see *RELIGIONS AND THEOLOGY — Protestant*

028.5　　　　LI　　ISSN 0134-3149
NEMUNAS. 1967. m. $40. Lithuanian Writers' Union, Gedimino 45, 3000 Kaunas, Lithuania. TEL 0127-223-066. Ed. Algimantas Mikuta. bk.rev. circ. 5,000.

NEUE MUSIKZEITUNG. see *MUSIC*

028.5　　　　AU　　ISSN 0028-3444
NEUE WEGE; Kulturzeitschrift junger Menschen. 1947. irreg. (7-8/yr.). S.60. Theater der Jugend, Neubaugasse 38, A-1070 Vienna, Austria. Ed. Herman Mayer. bk.rev.; play rev.; illus.; index. circ. 7,000. (tabloid format)

028.5　　　　US
NEW EXPRESSION. 1977. 10/yr. $25. Youth Communication - Chicago Center, 70 E. Lake St., Ste. 815, Chicago, IL 60601-5907. TEL 312-663-0543. Ed. Dennis Sylees. adv. contact: Greg McClain. bk.rev. circ. 72,000.

028.5 649　　　US
NEW JERSEY FAMILY; a news magazine for parents and kids. 1993. m. $15. 104 LaBarre Ave., Trenton, NJ 08618. TEL 609-695-5646. URL: http://family.com. Ed. Barbara M. Gaeta; Pub. Barbara M. Gaeta. R&P contact: Barbara M. Gaeta. adv. contact: Rebecca Schaeffer. bk.rev.; film rev.; illus.; circ. 30,000 (controlled). (tabloid format) **Document type:** consumer publication.
   Description: Advises parents on how to best provide for their children through articles on health, education, and well-being; reviews new products and lists a calendar of local events.

028.5　　　　US　　ISSN 1069-238X
HQ1101
NEW MOON; the magazine for girls and their dreams. 1993. bi-m. $29 (Canada $34; elsewhere $41) (with New Moon Network $49; Canada $54; elsewhere $64) (effective 1998); newsstand price: $5.50. New Moon Publishing, Box 3587, Duluth, MN 55803-3587. TEL 218-728-5507. FAX 218-728-0314. E-mail: newmoon@computerpro.com; URL: http://www.newmoon.org. Ed. Barbara Stretchberry; Pub. Nancy Gruver. R&P contact: Barbara Stretchberry. illus.; circ. 22,000 (paid). (back issues avail.) **Document type:** consumer publication.
   —KR SourceOne.
   Description: By and for girls ages 8-14. Focuses on personal history, inventing, creativity, relationships, and mothers and daughters, with the goal of helping girls ease into adolescence and womanhood with self-confidence.

THE NEW REVIEW OF CHILDREN'S LITERATURE AND LIBRARIANSHIP. see *LITERATURE*

NEW YORK (CITY). DEPARTMENT OF JUVENILE JUSTICE. ANNUAL REPORT. see *LAW — Family And Matrimonial Law*

372　　　　　NZ　　ISSN 0111-6355
NEW ZEALAND SCHOOL JOURNAL. (In four graded parts) 1907. q. NZ.$97 (effective 1997). Learning Media, P.O. Box 3293, Wellington, New Zealand. TEL 64-4-4725522. FAX 64-4-4726444. Eds. D. Noonan, T. Glensor. adv. contact: Angie Herman. circ. 70,000. **Document type:** government publication.
   —CCC.
   Description: Aimed at children aged 7-13.

028.5　　　　US　　ISSN 1058-8795
NEWS FOR KIDS. 1991. m. $18.95. D M Publications, 812 W. Southern Ave., Orange, CA 92665-3224. TEL 714-526-6634. Ed. Fran Mulvania. circ. 328,000.
   Description: Provides kids, ages seven to 12, with news on sports, world politics, environment, fashion and entertainment.

NICKI - JESUS LIEBT KINDER. see *RELIGIONS AND THEOLOGY — Protestant*

028.5　　　　UK　　ISSN 0029-0556
NINETEEN. 1968-1975; resumed. m. £18 (foreign £28.80) (effective 1996). I P C Magazines, Southbank Publishing Group (Subsidiary of: Reed Elsevier group); King's Reach Tower, Stamford St., London SE1 9LS, England. TEL 44-171-261-5000. FAX 44-1444-445599. TELEX 892084 REEDBP G. (Dist. by: Quadrant Subscription Services, Oakfield House, Perrymount Rd., Haywards Heath, W. Sussex RH16 3DH, England. TEL 44-1444-445555) Ed. April Joyce. adv. contact: Nicole Marks. illus. circ. 168,668. **Document type:** consumer publication.
   —CCC.
   Incorporates (1960-1986): Honey (ISSN 0018-4551); Vanity Fair (ISSN 0042-2584)
   Description: Covers fashion, beauty, careers and film for young women.

028.5 296　　　US　　ISSN 0892-4945
NOAH'S ARK; a newspaper for Jewish children. 1978. m. (Sep.-Jun.). $8.50. Noah's Ark Publishing Co., 7726 Portal Dr., Houston, TX 77071-1831. TEL 713-771-7143. Eds. Linda Freedman Block, Debbie Israel Dubin. circ. 445,000. **Document type:** newspaper.
   Description: Presents Jewish culture, history, holidays, and events in creative ways in order to make learning fun for Jewish children, ages 6-12.

028.5　　　　UK
NODDY. m. £15 (Europe £25; rest of world £30) (effective 1996). B B C Worldwide Publishing, Broadcasting House, Whiteladies Rd., Bristol GS8 2LR, England. TEL 44-181-576-2000. FAX 44-181-576-2931. (Subscr. to: P.O. Box 425, Woking, Surrey GU21 1GP, England. TEL 44-1483-733716. FAX 44-1483-756792) **Document type:** consumer publication.

890 630　　　CC　　ISSN 0469-2225
NONGCUN QINGNIAN/COUNTRY YOUTH. (Text in Chinese) 1946. m. Y12. (Communist Youth League, Central Committee - Gong Qing Tuan Zhongyang Weiyuanhui) Zhongguo Qingnian Zazhishe, Chinese Youth Magazine House, A5 Dongsanhuan Nanlu, Shuang Jing, Chaoyang Qu, Beijing 100021, People's Republic of China. TEL 7111516. Ed. Yuan Jianmin. adv.; illus. circ. 250,000. (back issues avail.)
   Description: Aims to help young people in rural areas of China to pursue wealth both materially and spiritually. Introduces ways and methods through a wide range of subject areas. Contains stories, articles, questions and answers on legal issues, and suggestions for agricultural techniques.

028.5　　　　ER　　ISSN 0134-2304
NOORUS. (Text in Estonian) 1946. m. $84 (effective 1998). Parnu mnt. 67a, 0007 Tallinn, Estonia. TEL 681-307. (Dist. by: Mezhdunarodnaya Kniga, B. Yakimanka 39, 117049 Moscow, Russia. TEL 7-095-2384967. FAX 7-095-2384634) Ed. Linda Jarve. circ. 25,000.

NORTHWEST INDIANA CATHOLIC. see *RELIGIONS AND THEOLOGY — Roman Catholic*

NOTABLE CHILDREN'S TRADE BOOKS IN THE FIELD OF SOCIAL STUDIES. see *SOCIAL SCIENCES: COMPREHENSIVE WORKS — Abstracting, Bibliographies, Statistics*

NOTES FROM THE WINDOWSILL. see *PUBLISHING AND BOOK TRADE*

NU PA VEJ; en bibelnoegle for juniorer. see *RELIGIONS AND THEOLOGY*

NUTRIDATE. see *NUTRITION AND DIETETICS*

267.6 200　　　NO　　ISSN 0804-1997
NY DAG. 1880. s-m. NOK 150. Norges K F U K - K F U M - Norwegian Christian Youth Organization, St. Olavsplass, Box 6814, N-0130 Oslo, Norway. Eds. Oernolf Elseth, Gunnar Mathiesen. adv. circ. 15,000.
   Formerly (until 1946): Unges Ven (ISSN 0804-2195)

369.4 796　　　SW　　ISSN 0280-6436
NYING. 1981. 6/yr. SEK 100 membership (effective 1997). Nykterhetsroerelsens Scoutfoerbund (NSF) - Temperance Guide and Scout Association, P.O. Box 1747, S-111 87 Stockholm, Sweden. Ed. Ove Ernstroem. circ. 9,000.

NYT FRA D U K. (Danmarks Unge Katolikker) see *RELIGIONS AND THEOLOGY — Roman Catholic*

O LITERATURE DLYA DETEI. see *LITERATURE*

O M S OUTREACH; official publication of O M S International. see *RELIGIONS AND THEOLOGY — Protestant*

OCTOPUS. see *EDUCATION*

520　　　　　US　　ISSN 0163-0946
QB46
ODYSSEY (PETERBOROUGH); the young people's magazine of astronomy and outer space. 1979. 9/yr. $26.95 (foreign $34.95). Cobblestone Publishing, 7 School St., Peterborough, NH 03458. TEL 603-924-7209. FAX 603-924-7380. Ed. Elizabeth Lindstrom; Pub. Malcolm Jensen. R&P contact: Pat Sylvestro. adv.; bk.rev.; film rev.; charts; illus. circ. 26,000. **Indexed:** Ind.Child.Mag., Jun.High.Mag.Abstr.
   —KR SourceOne; UnCover.
   Description: Describes basic principles and concepts of astronomy and space exploration while introducing young readers (ages 8 to 14) to basic concepts in the physical sciences.

OESTERREICHISCHES JUGENDROTKREUZ. ARBEITSBLAETTER. see *SOCIAL SERVICES AND WELFARE*

CHILDREN AND YOUTH — FOR

028.5 AU ISSN 0029-9928
OESTERREICHISCHES KOLPINGBLATT. 1933. bi-m. free. Oesterreichisches Kolpingwerk, Paulanergasse 11, A-1040 Vienna 5, Austria. TEL 0222-58735420. Ed. Ludwig Zack. adv.; bk.rev. circ. 16,000. **Document type:** bulletin.

028.5 370 US
OFFSPRING - BOING. 1978. bi-m. $9.50. Children's Museum of Denver, 2121 Crescent Dr., Denver, CO 80211. TEL 303-433-7444. Ed. D. Todd Clough. adv.; bk.rev. circ. 100,000. (tabloid format)
Formed by the merger of: Offspring & Boing.

OGGITALIA; panorama della stampa italiana. see *LINGUISTICS*.

028.5 XR ISSN 0030-1272
OHNICEK; zabava do kapsy. 1950. fortn. 12 Kc.($15.80) Mlada Fronta, Radlicka 61, 150 02 Prague 5, Czech Republic. TEL 42-2-544941. (Subscr. to: Artia, Ve Smeckach 30, 111 27 Prague 1, Czech Republic) Ed. Eva Vondraskova. circ. 100,000.

028.5 XO ISSN 0139-8911
OHNIK. 1948. fortn. Smena Publishing House, Prazska 11, 812 84 Bratislava, Slovakia. Ed. Magdalena Gocnikova. circ. 130,000.

028.5 FR ISSN 0751-6002
OKAPI. 1971. bi-m. 545 F. (EU 689 F.; elsewhere 789 F.) (effective 1997). Bayard Presse, 3 rue Bayard, 75393 Paris Cedex 08, France. TEL 33-1-44356060. FAX 33-1-44356091. TELEX 648 094 F. (Subscr. to: Bayard Presse International, B.P. 12, 99505 Paris Entreprises, France. TEL 33-1-44216000. FAX 33-3-20274192) Ed. Martine de Sauto. adv.; bk.rev.; film rev.; play rev.; illus. circ. 87,226.
Description: For boys and girls 10 to 15 years old.

028.5 284 GW
OKAY, Schuelerkalender und taegliche Bibellese. 1898. a. DM.9.95. (Deutscher E C - Verband) Born-Verlag, Leuschnerstr. 72-74, 34134 Kassel, Germany. TEL 49-561-40950. FAX 49-561-4095112. circ. 16,000. **Document type:** bulletin.

028.5 NE ISSN 0030-1612
OKKI. 1920. fortn. fl.2 per no. L.C.G. Malmberg B.V., Leeghwaterlaan 16, 5223 BA 's-Hertogenbosch, Netherlands. TEL 31-73-210512. Ed. M. Heemelaar. circ. 115,000. **Document type:** consumer publication.
Description: For children aged 6-7 years.

892 296.7 US ISSN 0472-8637
OLAM HADASH. (Text in Hebrew) 1961. 9/yr. $12. Hebrew Publications for Children, Inc., 110 E. 59th St., 4th Fl., New York, NY 10022. TEL 212-339-6022. FAX 212-826-8959. Ed. Bina Ofek. adv. contact: Sam E. Bloch. bk.rev.; charts; illus. circ. 8,000. **Document type:** newspaper.
Description: Offers short stories, poems, news features in beginner's Hebrew for children and youth.

OLDERR'S YOUNG ADULT FICTION INDEX FOR (YEAR). see *CHILDREN AND YOUTH — Abstracting, Bibliographies, Statistics*

OLOMEINU/OUR WORLD. see *RELIGIONS AND THEOLOGY — Judaic*

268 US ISSN 0043-7999
ON THE LINE (SCOTTDALE). 1971. m. $18.85. Mennonite Publishing House, 616 Walnut Ave., Scottdale, PA 15683-1999. TEL 412-887-8500. FAX 412-887-3111. (Co-publisher: Faith and Life Press) Ed. Mary Clemens Meyer. illus. circ. 6,000.
Formerly: Words of Cheer.
Description: Aimed at adolescents aged 9-14.

028.5 NE ISSN 0165-8905
ONZE EIGEN KRANT; jeugdmagazine. 1946. 7/yr. fl.16.75. Kok Tijdschriften, Postbus 5018, 8260 GA Kampen, Netherlands. Ed. Henk Keijzer; Pub. Rien Ipenbrug. illus. **Document type:** consumer publication.

028.5 IT
OP LA. m. $54 (effective Jan. 1997). Zanfi Editori s.r.l., Via Emilia Ovest 954, 41100 Modena, Italy. TEL 39-59-891700. FAX 39-59-891701. E-mail: zanfi.editori@mo.nettuno.it. **Document type:** consumer publication.
Description: For children ages 3-7.

028.5 SW ISSN 0283-653X
OPSIS KALOPSIS; om barn- och ungdomskultur. 1986. q. SEK 300 in Sweden; Nordic and Baltic countries SEK 340; elsewhere SEK 350 (effective 1997). Opsis Kalopsis AB, St. Paulsgatan 13, S-118 46 Stockholm, Sweden. TEL 46-8-640-01-22. FAX 46-8-641-16-68. (Subscr. to: PROGEK, P.O. Box 31003, S-400 32 Goeteborg, Sweden. TEL 46-31-24-34-25. FAX 46-31-24-38-10) **Indexed:** Child.Lit.Abstr.

ORANA; journal for school and children's librarians. see *LIBRARY AND INFORMATION SCIENCES*

028.5 ZA
ORBIT "EDUCATION FOR ALL" MAGAZINE. (Text in English) 1971. 4/yr. kip 15 per no. (effective Sep. 1992). Ministry of Education, Curriculum Development Centre, P.O. Box 50092, Lusaka, Zambia. FAX 254848. (Subscr. to: Private Bag RW18X, Lusaka, Zambia) Ed. Mrs. Elidah Banda Chisha. adv.; bk.rev.; charts; illus. circ. 65,000. **Document type:** consumer publication.
Formerly (until 1991): Orbit.
Description: For schools and literacy classes. Includes articles on agriculture, health, sports, music, profiles of women, the environment and more.

970 US
OUTLAWS AND LAWMEN OF THE WILD WEST. 1992. irreg. $149.50. Enslow Publishers, Inc., 44 Fadem Rd., Box 699, Springfield, NJ 07081-0699. TEL 201-379-8890. FAX 201-379-7940. E-mail: annette@enslow.com; URL: http://www.enslow.com. Ed. Brian D. Enslow; Pub. Annette Noce. R&P contact: Annette Noce.
Description: Book series introduces young readers to the lives and deeds of famous and infamous men and women of the western frontier.

028.5 US ISSN 1069-420X
OUTSIDE KIDS. 1993. q. newsstand price: $1.95. Mariah Media Inc., Outside Plaza, 400 Market St., Santa Fe, NM 87501. TEL 505-989-7100. FAX 505-989-4700. **Document type:** consumer publication.

OUTYOUTH; for and by lesbian, bisexual, gay and transgender young people. see *HOMOSEXUALITY*

028.5 GW
OVERBACHER BRUECKE. 1980. s-a. Gymnasium Haus Overbach in Juelich, Haus Overbach, 52428 Juelich, Germany. TEL 02461-4016. (back issues avail.)

500.9 CN ISSN 0382-6627
OWL. 1976. 9/yr. Can.$24 (foreign $20) (effective 1997). Owl Communications (Subsidiary of: Combined Media), Box 53, 370 King St.W. Ste. 300, Toronto, ON M5V 1J9, Canada. TEL 800-387-4378. FAX 416-971-5294. E-mail: owl@combinedmedia.com; URL: http://www.owlkids.com. (U.S. subscr. to: 25 Boxwood Lane, Buffalo, NY 14225) Ed. Nyla Ahmad. bk.rev.; illus. circ. 170,000. **Indexed:** Can.B.P.I., Can.Per.Ind., CMI, Ind.Child.Mag.
—KR SourceOne; UnCover.
Description: An award-winning magazine for kids between the ages of 8 and 12. A fun and funky way to discover art, science, nature and the environment through interactive activities, puzzles and experiments.

OWL CANADIAN FAMILY. see *CHILDREN AND YOUTH — About*

028.5 530 IS ISSN 0333-6948
P-H'ATOM; popular physics magazine. (Text in Hebrew) 1981. 3/yr. IS.95. Weizmann Institute of Science, Youth Activities Section, P.O. Box 26, Rehovot 76100, Israel. TEL 972-8-9343959. FAX 972-9344130. E-mail: hamish@weizmann.weizmann.ac.il; URL: http://www.weizman.ac.il/youthact/publications.html. (Co-sponsor: Faculty of Physics) Ed. H. Shmueli. adv.; bk.rev. circ. 1,000.

P I P COLLEGE "H E L P S" NEWSLETTER; college - handicapped and exceptional learners programs and services. (Partners in Publishing) see *EDUCATION — Special Education And Rehabilitation*

PACIFIC HOSTELLER. see *TRAVEL AND TOURISM*

028.5 CY ISSN 1022-9582
PAEDIKI HARA. 8/yr. £C3($20) (Greece C£6; foreign C£10). Cyprus Greek Teachers Organization, Makarios III Ave., 18, Nicosia, Cyprus. TEL 357-2-442638. FAX 257-2-360410. circ. 13,000. (back issues avail.) **Document type:** consumer publication.
Description: Teaches children 7-12 about their nation's history. Also chronicles school life in Cyprus and describes myths, books, school curricula, and hobbies.

PAGINE GIOVANI. see *PUBLISHING AND BOOK TRADE*

PAPERS: EXPLORATIONS INTO CHILDREN'S LITERATURE. see *LITERATURE*

028.5 II ISSN 0031-1642
PARAG. (Text in Hindi) 1958. m. $12. 10 Daryaganj, Delhi 110 002, India. TEL 11-277360. (U.S. subscr. to: Ms. Kalpana, 42-75 Main St., Flushing, NY 11355) Ed. Hari Krishna Devsare. bk.rev.; film rev.; play rev.; illus. circ. 60,000.

PARAPARA BOLETIN INFORMATIVO. see *PUBLISHING AND BOOK TRADE*

028.5 649 US
PARENTS AND CHILDREN TOGETHER ONLINE. (Print version ceased in 1995.) 1990. s-a. (Distance Education) Edinfo Press, 2805 E. 10th St., Ste. 150, Bloomington, IN 47408. TEL 812-855-5847; 800-759-4723. E-mail: disted@indiana.edu; URL: http://www.indiana.edu/~eric_rec/fl/pcto/menu.html. Ed. Christopher Essex.
●Available only online.
Description: Features original stories, poems and articles for children, and articles on parenting topics for adults.

PARENTS EXPRESS; the newspaper for Philadelphia area parents. see *EDUCATION — Teaching Methods And Curriculum*

PARENTWISE. see *RELIGIONS AND THEOLOGY — Protestant*

028.5 840 SZ ISSN 1421-0851
PAROLE. (Text in French) 1985. 3/yr. 35 SFr. (foreign 45 SFr.) (effective 1996). Association Romande de Litterature pour l'Enfance et la Jeunesse, Case postale, CH-1000 Lausanne 4, Switzerland. TEL 41-21-3202328. Ed. Ulrike Blatter. bk.rev. circ. 750. (back issues avail.) **Document type:** newsletter.

028.5 FI ISSN 0556-3488
PARTIO. 1919. 7/yr. FIM 145. Suomen Partiolaiset - Guides and Scouts of Finland, Kylaenvanhimmantie 29, FIN-00640 Helsinki, Finland. FAX 0-7522-681. E-mail: Hanne.Partanen@SP.Partio.Fi. Ed. Hanne Partanen. adv. circ. 55,000.
Description: Covers scouting.

028.5 IS ISSN 0334-3022
PASHOSH. m. $39.50. Society for the Protection of Nature in Israel, 4 Hashefela St., Tel Aviv 66183, Israel. TEL 972-3-375063. Ed. A. Bar.
Description: Articles on nature intended for small children.

028.5 178 GW ISSN 0724-6404
PATIENTENPOST. 1983. q. free. Aerztliche Pressestelle Niedersachsen, Postfach 326, 30003 Hanover, Germany. Ed. Wolfgang Koch. circ. 27,000. (back issues avail.)

028.5 BL ISSN 0104-2092
PATO DONALD. 1950. fortn. Editora Abril Jovem, S.A., Rua Bela Cintra 299, 01415-000 Sao Paulo, Brazil. TEL 011-257-0999. TELEX 011-22115. Ed. Elizabeth De. Fiore. adv. circ. 60,000. (back issues avail.) **Document type:** consumer publication.

028.5 US
PEANUT BUTTER. 1981. irreg. (approx. 12/yr.). $1.95 per no. Scholastic Inc., Books Division, 555 Broadway, New York, NY 10012-3999. TEL 212-343-6100. Ed. Nancy Krulik. (reprint service avail. from UMI) **Document type:** monographic series.
Description: Aimed at children ages 4-7.

PEARS JUNIOR ENCYCLOPAEDIA. see *ENCYCLOPEDIAS AND GENERAL ALMANACS*

CHILDREN AND YOUTH — FOR

028.5 US
PEN PAL POST; friendship through understanding. 1950. a. $3 for each pen pal request (membership only). Afro-Asian Center, World Pen Pals, Box 337, Saugerties, NY 12477-0337. TEL 914-246-7828. FAX 914-246-7828. (Co-sponsor: United Way) Ed. Robert Carroll. circ. 16,000. **Document type:** newspaper.
  Former titles: Write in There; Silver Lining.
  Description: Helps children 10-20 explore other cultures through letter writing.

028.5 920 US
PEOPLE TO KNOW. 1992. irreg. $606.40. Enslow Publishers, Inc., 44 Fadem Rd., Box 699, Springfield, NJ 07081-0699. TEL 201-379-8890. FAX 201-379-7940. E-mail: annette@enslow.com; URL: http://www.enslow.com. Ed. Brian D. Enslow; Pub. Annette Noce. R&P contact: Annette Noce.
  Description: Book series for teen readers. Describes the lives and achievements of influential twentieth century Americans.

028.5 AU
PERPLEX ZEITUNG. 1978. q. S.130. Perplex Verlag, Hans-Sachs-Gasse 14-III, Postfach 752, A-8010 Graz, Austria. TEL 43-316-837203. FAX 43-316-837203. Ed. Franz Kirnbauer. adv.: B&W page S.9000. circ. 3,500. **Document type:** newspaper.

028.5 FR
PETIT LEONARD. m. (11/yr). 260 F. (foreign 310 F.) (effective 1997). Editions Faton S.A., 25 rue Berbisey, 21000 Dijon, France. TEL 33-1-80404104. (Subscr. to: 1 rue des Artisans, B.P. 90, 21803 Quetigny Cedex, France. TEL 33-3-80489848. FAX 33-3-80489846)

054.1 IT ISSN 1120-270X
PETIT RAPPORTEUR; journal des branches du francais. (Text in French) 1988. 8/yr. L.33000 (foreign L.43000) (effective Sep. 1995). Reporter Publishing, Via Manzoni 31, 50018 Scandicci, Italy. TEL 39-55-2578346. FAX 39-55-250868. E-mail: mc7386@mclink.it; URL: http://www.mclink.it/com/reporter. Ed. Robin Poppelsdorff. adv.: page $1000. bk.rev. circ. 15,000. cols./p.: 6; pp./issue: 12. (tabloid format) **Document type:** newspaper.
  Description: Contains graded reading articles in newspaper format for students of French. Subjects vary from film and music to literature and politics.

028.5 053.5 SZ
PFIFF. m. 28 SFr. (foreign 36 SFr.). Buery Verlag AG, Hugostr. 2, Postfach 8392, CH-8050 Zurich, Switzerland. TEL 01-3126475. FAX 01-3126511. adv. contact: Ariane Demieville. circ. 12,500. **Document type:** consumer publication.

028.5 AU
PHILIPP LESEHEFTE. 1949. 6/yr. membership. Oesterreichischer Buchklub der Jugend, Mayerhofgasse 6, A-1041 Vienna, Austria. TEL 43-1-5051754-0. FAX 43-1-505175450. **Document type:** bulletin.
  Formerly (until 1990): Oesterreichischer Buchklub der Jugend. Jahrbuch (ISSN 0078-3560)

028.5 059.914 PK
PHOOL. (Text in Urdu) 1990. m. $30 to U.S. Nawa-i-Waqt, Lahore, NIPCO House, 4 Sharae Fatima Jinnah, Lahore, Pakistan. TEL 92-42-6367551. FAX 92-42-6367005. Ed. Majid Nizami; Pub. Majid/Nizami. adv. contact: M.A. Latif. bk.rev.; illus.; circ. 47,000 (paid). (tabloid format; back issues avail.) **Document type:** consumer publication.
  Description: News and information of broad appeal.

028.5 FR ISSN 0249-8138
PHOSPHORE. 1981. m. 398 F. (EU 479 F.; elsewhere 519 F.) (effective 1997). Bayard Presse, 5 rue Bayard, 75393 Paris Cedex 08, France. TEL 33-1-44356060. FAX 33-1-44356091. TELEX 648 094 F. (Subscr. to: Bayard Presse International, B.P. 12, 99505 Paris Entreprises, France. TEL 33-1-44216000. FAX 33-3-20274192) Ed. Jean-Jacques Fresko. adv.; bk.rev.; film rev.; illus. circ. 96,894.
  Formerly: Record - Dossier (ISSN 0048-6957)
  Description: Covers news and culture for high-schoolers.

028.5 UK
PICK OF THE YEAR; a selection of 50 recommended books, chosen for families, tried and tested by children, and voted the best of (year). a. Federation of Children's Book Groups, The Old Malt House, Aldbourne, Marlborough, Wiltshire SN8 2DW, England. TEL 44-1672-540629. Ed. Marianne Adey. R&P contact: Marianne Adey. adv. contact: Marianne Adey. illus. circ. 10,000. **Document type:** bibliography.
  Former titles: About Books for Children (ISSN 0144-574X); Federation for Children's Book Groups. Yearbook (ISSN 0307-6091)

PICO; illustrierte Kinderzeitschrift ab 7 Jahre. see RELIGIONS AND THEOLOGY

028.5 FR ISSN 0767-807X
PICSOU. 1972. m. 159 F. (effective 1997). Disney Hachette Presse, 10 rue Thierry le Luron, 92592 Levallois Perret Cedex, France. TEL 33-1-41348500. FAX 33-1-41348989. (Subscr. to: 90 rue de Flandre, 75947 Paris Cedex 19, France. TEL 33-1-44894484) Ed. Gilles Heylen. circ. 250,000. **Document type:** consumer publication.
  Description: Leisure magazine for teenagers.

028.5 UK ISSN 1351-0304
PINGU. 1993. m. £15 (Europe & Ireland £25; rest of world £30) (effective 1996). B B C Worldwide Publishing, Broadcasting House, Whiteladies Rd., Bristol GS8 2LR, England. TEL 44-181-576-2000. FAX 44-181-576-2931. (Subscr. to: P.O. Box 425, Woking, Surrey GU21 1GP, England. TEL 44-1483-733716. FAX 44-1483-756792) **Document type:** consumer publication.

028.5 RU ISSN 0130-8009
PIONER. 1924. m. $52 (effective 1998). Bumazhnyi proezd 14, 101459 Moscow, Russia. TEL 7-095-2573427. (Dist. by: Mezhdunarodnaya Kniga, B. Yakimanka 39, 117049 Moscow, Russia. TEL 7-095-2384967. FAX 7-095-2384634; Dist. in U.S. by: Victor Kamkin Inc., 4956 Boiling Brook Pkwy., MD 20852. TEL 301-881-5973) Ed. A.S. Moroz. bk.rev.; illus.; index. circ. 32,400.

028.5 KR ISSN 0032-0102
PIONERIYA. (Editions in Russian and Ukrainian) 1967. m. $13. (Soyuz Molodezhnikh Organizatsii Ukrainy) Vydavnitstvo Molod, Vul. Degtyarivska 38-44, 252119 Kiev, Ukraine. TEL 380-44-2131160. FAX 380-44-2256356. Ed. S. Chyrkov. index.

028.5 RU ISSN 0032-0048
PIONERSKAYA PRAVDA; gazeta dlya detei i podrostkov. (Includes supplements: Yunaya Moskva (2/m.); Privet Devchonki i Mal'chishki (2/m.); Olimpionik (m.)) 1925. 4/m. 35450 Rub.($86) for 6 mos. (effective 1998). Redaktsiya Pionerskaya Pravda, Sushchevskaya ul. 21, 101502 Moscow, Russia. TEL 7-095-9722238. FAX 7-095-9721028. (Dist. by: Mezhdunarodnaya Kniga, B. Yakimanka 39, 117049 Moscow, Russia. TEL 7-095-2384967. FAX 7-095-2384634; Dist. in U.S. by: Victor Kamkin Inc., 4956 Boiling Brook Pkwy., Rockville, MD 20852. TEL 301-881-5973) Ed. O.I. Grekova. adv.; bk.rev.; illus. circ. 1,550,000. (tabloid format; also avail. in microform from UMI) Indexed: Curr.Dig.Sov.Press. **Document type:** newspaper.

028.5 AA
PIONIERI. fortn. $11.30. Union de la Jeunesse du Travail d'Albanie, Tirana, Albania.

028.5 YU ISSN 0032-0099
PIONIR-KEKEC;* jugoslovenski pionirski list. w. 44 din. Borba, Trg Marksa i Engelsa 9/1, Belgrade, Yugoslavia. Ed. Jela Petrovic-Vukojevic.

369.4 FR ISSN 0751-5723
PIONNIER. 1924. bi-m. 90 F. Editions Scouts de France, 54 Av. Jean Jaures, 75019 Paris, France. TEL 44-52-37-37. FAX 42-38-09-87. Ed. Philippe Da Costa. adv.; charts; illus.
  Formerly: Scout Pionnier (ISSN 0036-9470)
  Description: For scouts ages 15-17.

028.5 362.7 FR ISSN 1254-874X
PLANETE JEUNES. 1993. 6/yr. 94 F. (foreign 120 F.) (effective 1997). Bayard Presse, 3 rue Bayard, 75393 Paris Cedex 08, France. TEL 33-1-44356060. FAX 33-1-44356091. (Subscr. to: Bayard Presse International, B.P. 12, 99505 Paris Entreprises, France. TEL 33-1-44216000. FAX 33-3-20274192) Ed. Simon P. Njami. **Document type:** consumer publication.
  Description: For young people, 12 to 18, who are open-minded about the rest of the world and interested in speaking or learning French.

PLATTFORM. see RELIGIONS AND THEOLOGY — Protestant

028.5 UK ISSN 0960-0272
PLAYDAYS. 1990. fortn. £25 (Europe & Ireland £38; rest of world £52) (effective 1996). B B C Worldwide Publishing, Broadcasting House, Whiteladies Rd., Bristol GS8 2LR, England. TEL 44-181-576-2000. FAX 44-181-576-2931. (Subscr. to: P.O. Box 425, Woking, Surrey GU21 1GP, England. TEL 44-1483-733716. FAX 44-1483-756792) Ed. Alison Boyle. circ. 58,381. **Document type:** consumer publication.
  Description: Presents educational material compatible with the national curriculum and covers reading, writing, numerical skills, nature studies, language and science in an entertaining and interactive format.

PLAYS; the drama magazine for young people. see THEATER

028.5 GW ISSN 0032-1605
PLOMJO. Lower-Sorbian edition: Plomje (ISSN 0138-2594) (Text in Upper-Sorbian) 1952. m. DM.0.50 per no. Domowina Verlag GmbH, Tuchmacherstr. 27, 02625 Bautzen, Germany. illus. **Document type:** bulletin.

028.5 UK
PLUS. 1967. bi-m. £3.06 (effective 1997); £5.60 (effective Jan. 1998). Challenge Publishing, P.O. Box 300, Kingstown Broadway, Carlisle, Cumbria CA3 0QS, England. TEL 44-1228-512512. FAX 44-1228-512512. Ed. Andrew Wooding. circ. 6,818. **Document type:** newspaper.

POCKETS. see RELIGIONS AND THEOLOGY — Protestant

305.23 PL ISSN 1231-0875
POD WIATR; sami o sobie - czasopismo mlodziezowe. 1993. m. 10 Zl.($18) (effective 1997). Agencja Wydawniczo-Reklamowa M T, Ul. Zmudzka 5-29, 85-028 Bydgoszcz, Poland. TEL 48-52-421546. FAX 48-52-421546. E-mail: wiatr@byd.ternet.pl. Ed. Miroslaw Twarog; Pub. Miroslaw Twarog. R&P contact: Miroslaw Twarog. adv. contact: Miroslaw Twarog. bk.rev.; film rev.; play rev.; music rev.; illus.; circ. 400 (paid). (back issues avail.)
  Description: Aims to allow young people to talk about their own problems, to promote individuals who have a talent for journalism, literature, photography and art, and to support youngsters in their aspirations to realize their intellectual potential. *Refereed Serial*

371.8 YU ISSN 0354-0375
POKRET. 1975. m. 30 din. Savez Socijalisticke Omladine Crne Gore, Novaka Milosova 12, Titograd, Montenegro, Yugoslavia.
  Formerly (until 1991): Omladinski Pokret (ISSN 0351-8930)

028.5 CN ISSN 1204-4571
POMME D'API. (Text in French) 1991. m. (10/yr.). Can.$29.95($49.95) (effective Sep. 1996). Bayard Presse Canada Inc., 3995 Ste. Catherine E., Montreal, PQ H1W 2G7, Canada. TEL 514-522-3936. FAX 514-522-1761. Ed. Suzanne Spino; Pub. Suzanne Spino. adv.: color page Can.$800; trim 6 1/2 x 8 7/16; adv. contact: Nathalie Forget. bk.rev.; circ. 8,500 (paid). (back issues avail.) **Document type:** consumer publication.
  Formerly (until 1994): Pomme d'Api Quebec (ISSN 1188-1585)
  Description: For children aged 3 to 7. Includes games, comics, educational tips, and stories to read.

CHILDREN AND YOUTH — FOR

028.5   SZ
POP - ROCKY. w. DM.98.80 (foreign DM.119.20) (effective 1997). Z A G Zeitschriften Verlag, Baarerstr. 22, CH-6300 Zug, Switzerland. TEL 41-41-7102020. FAX 41-41-7115268. Ed. Peter Franz. adv.: B&W page DM.20900, color page DM.20900; 205 x 285; adv. contact: Ingrid Krafft. circ. 314,028 (paid). **Document type:** consumer publication.

028.5 780   SZ
POPCORN. m. DM.48 (foreign DM.52.80) (effective 1997). Z A G Zeitschriften Verlag, Baarerstr. 22, CH-6300 Zug, Switzerland. TEL 41-41-7102020. FAX 41-41-7115268. Ed. Uli Weissbrod. adv.: B&W page DM.13700, color page DM.20900; 205 x 285; adv. contact: Ingrid Krafft. circ. 390,384 (paid). **Document type:** consumer publication.

028.5   FR   ISSN 0299-3147
POPI. 1986. m. 285 F. (EU 369 F.; elsewhere 419 F.) (effective 1997). Bayard Presse, 3 rue Bayard, 75393 Paris Cedex 08, France. TEL 33-1-44356060. FAX 33-1-44356091. TELEX 648 094 F. (Subscr. to: Bayard Presse International, B.P. 12, 99505 Paris Entreprises, France. TEL 33-1-44216000. FAX 33-3-20274192) Ed. Marie-Agnes Gaudrat.
Description: Responds to the curiosity of babies 15 months and older through pictures and games.

028.5   UK   ISSN 0955-0321
POSTMAN PAT PICTURE PAPER.* 1986. w. London Editions Magazine Ltd., Egmont House, P.O. Box 111, Great Ducic St., Manchester, Lancs 3BL, England. TEL 01-482-3202. circ. 95,000.

PRESSE - PAPIERS; extraits de la presse francais. see LINGUISTICS

028.5   IT   ISSN 0032-8340
PRIMAVERA; mondo giovane. 1950. s-m. L.46200 (foreign L.59000). Istituto Maria Mazzarello, Via Laura Vicuna 1, 20092 Ciniselo Balsamo (MI), Italy. TEL 39-2-66048229. FAX 39-2-6128337. Ed. Graziella Boscato. adv.: B&W page L.6000000, color page L.11000000. bk.rev.; film rev.; bibl.; charts; illus.; tr.lit. circ. 130,000. **Indexed:** Amer.Hum.Ind.

PRIONS EN EGLISE JUNIOR. see RELIGIONS AND THEOLOGY — Roman Catholic

028.5   GR   ISSN 0033-1465
PROSCOPOS. 1946. m. Dr.100($4) includes Krikos Ton Vathmoforon. Boy Scouts of Greece - Soma Hellinon Proscopon, 1 Ptolemeon St., Athens 516, Greece. Ed. Demetrios Marinopoulos. illus. circ. 10,000.

028.5   FR   ISSN 0997-3745
P'TIT LOUP. m. 229 F. (outside E.C. 289 F.) (effective 1997). Disney Hachette Presse, 10 rue Thierry le Luron, 92592 Levallois Perret Cedex, France. TEL 33-1-41348500. FAX 33-1-41378989. (Subscr. to: 90 rue de Flandre, 75947 Paris Cedex 19, France. TEL 33-1-44894484) Ed. Gilles Heylen. circ. 77,000. **Document type:** consumer publication.
Description: Fifty questions and answers on subjects of interest to kids between 7 and 10 years old.

028.5   US   ISSN 1073-8320
PUDDLER. bi-m. Ducks Unlimited, Inc., 1 Waterfowl Way, Memphis, TN 38120-2351. TEL 901-758-3825. Ed. Lee Salber.

PULP; fashion, not fiction. see CLOTHING TRADE — Fashions

028.5   RU   ISSN 0868-5401
HQ799.R9
PUL'S. (Former name of issuing body: Vsesoyuznyi Leninskii Kommunisticheskii Soyuz Molodezhi, Tsentral'nkyi Komitet) 1920. m. $52 (effective 1998). Novodmitrovskaya ul. 5A, 125015 Moscow, Russia. TEL 7-095-2850741. (Dist. by: Mezhdunarodnaya Kniga, Ul. B. Yakimanka 39, 117049 Moscow, Russia. TEL 7-095-2384967. FAX 7-095-2384634; Dist. in U.S by: Victor Kamkin Inc., 4956 Boiling Brook Pkwy., Rockville, MD 20852. TEL 301-881-5973) Ed. I.I. Shestopalov. bk.rev.; illus. circ. 920,000.
Formerly (until 1990): Komsomol'skaya Zhizn' (ISSN 0130-2469)

028.5   II   ISSN 0033-4227
PULSE OF YOUTH. (Text in English) 1968. q. Rs.3. c/o Kamlendra Kanwar, 86 Hindu College Hostel, New Delhi, India. adv.

028.5 364.4   IT
PUNGOLO; periodico dei giovani. (Text in English, Italian) 1982. m. L.40000($25) (effective Jan. 1996); newsstand price: L.4000. Centro Internazionale di Studi per i Giovani, Via Col. Romej 7, 91100 Trapani, Italy. TEL 39-923-546700. Ed. Pietro Vento. adv.: page L.5000000($3000); adv. contact: Sabrina Titone. bk.rev.; software rev.; tele.rev.; abstr.; bibl.; illus.; maps; stat.; index. circ. 12,000. (also avail. in diskette format) **Document type:** newspaper.
● Also available on CD-ROM.
Description: Informs young people in Italy who are against the Mafia's power and all forms of corruption.

028.5   IT
PUPA. 1986. m. newsstand price: L.3000. Edizioni Internazionale Cioe s.r.l., Via G. Fabroni, 24, 00191 Rome, Italy. TEL 39-6-3287309. Ed. Lamberto Antonelli. adv.: page L.6000000. circ. 60,000.

028.5   CC
QINGCHUN SUIYUE/YOUTHFUL YEARS. (Text in Chinese) 1982. m. Y1.85 per no. Gong Qing Tuan Hebei Sheng Weiyuanhui, 244 Nanma Lu, Shijiazhuang, Hebei 050051, People's Republic of China. TEL 86-311-7027226. Ed. Zhang Hongde. adv. contact: Li Wushen. bk.rev.; circ. 120,000 (paid).

028.5   CC
QINGNIAN BOLAN. (Text in Chinese) m. Y12. Fujian Qingnian Zazhishe, No. 5, Jinjishan, Fuzhou, Fujian 350001, People's Republic of China. TEL 551944. (Dist. overseas by: Jiangsu Publications Import & Export Corp., 56 Gao Yun Ling, Nanjing, Jiangsu, P.R.C.) Ed. Lin Yunqing.
Description: Publishes selected articles from other publications, featuring local and international events of general interest.

028.5   CC
QINGNIAN SHEJIAO/SOCIAL AFFAIRS FOR YOUTH. (Text in Chinese) Tuan de Gongqingtuan Shanghai Shiwei, 17 Donghu Lu, Shanghai 200031, People's Republic of China. TEL 4311925. Ed. Li Zhiping.

028.5   CC   ISSN 1003-0565
QINGNIAN WENZHAI. (Text in Chinese) m. Zhongguo Qingnian Chubanshe, Qikan Bu - China Youth Press, 21, Dongsi 12 Tiao, Beijing 100708, People's Republic of China. TEL 442125. Ed. Hu Shouwen.

059.951   CC   ISSN 1000-4807
QINGNIAN YIDAI/YOUNG GENERATION. (Text in Chinese) m. Y26.40. Shanghai Renmin Chubanshe, Qikan Bu - Shanghai People's Publishing House, 54 Shaoxing Road, Shanghai 200020, People's Republic of China. (Dist. outside China by: China International Book Trading Corp., P.O. Box 399, Beijing, P.R.C.) Ed. Zhang Baoni. adv. **Document type:** consumer publication.

028.5   CC
QINGNIAN YUEKAN/YOUTH MONTHLY. (Text in Chinese) m. Gongqingtuan Jilin Shengwei, 49, Stalin Street, Changchun, Jilin 130051, People's Republic of China. TEL 823744. Ed. Yang Dejun.

QINGNIAN ZUOJIA/YOUNG WRITERS; wenxue shuang yuekan. see LITERATURE

028.5   CC   ISSN 1004-1079
QINGSHAONIAN RIJI/YOUTHS DIARY. (Text in Chinese) 1984. m. Y0.66 per no. Shanxi Ribao She - Shanxi Daily Publishing Company, 24 Shuangtasi Jie, Taiyuan, Shanxi 030012, People's Republic of China. TEL 446561. Ed. Guo Huarong.
Description: Discusses how to keep a diary.

QUANGUO ZHONGXUE YOUXIU ZUOWEN XUAN/SELECTED EXCELLENT COMPOSITIONS FROM NATION-WIDE MIDDLE SCHOOLS. see LINGUISTICS

QUANTUM (NEW YORK); the magazine of math and science. see SCIENCES: COMPREHENSIVE WORKS

028.5   IT
QUIGIOVANI.* d. Editrice Pentapolis s.r.l., Via Aurelia 641, 00165 Rome, Italy. TEL 6-68-08-809. FAX 6-6808-044. Ed. Salvatore Puzzo.

RAADGIVEREN; boerne og juniorlederen. see RELIGIONS AND THEOLOGY — Protestant

RACING FOR KIDS. see SPORTS AND GAMES

028.5   US   ISSN 0162-5217
RADAR. Key Title: R-A-D-A-R. 1886. w. $11.99. Standard Publishing, 8121 Hamilton Ave., Cincinnati, OH 45231. TEL 513-931-4050. FAX 513-931-0904. Ed. Elaina Meyers; Pub. Mark A. Taylor. R&P contact: Bob Nealeigh. illus. circ. 112,000.
Former titles: Jet Cadet (ISSN 0022-6645); Junior Life.
Description: For children 8-10 years old.

RAGAZZI; il mensile per il tuo italiano. see LINGUISTICS

RAINBOW (LONDON). see RELIGIONS AND THEOLOGY — Protestant

028.5   XR
RAINBOW & RAINDROPS. Short title: R & R. (Text in English) 1949. 10/yr. 80 Kc. Publishing House R & R, Preslickova 2886, 106 00 Prague, Czech Republic. Ed. Vlasta Herinkova. adv. circ. 50,000.
Formerly (until 1989): Ogoniok (ISSN 0030-073X)
Description: Aimed at children aged 9-13.

369.4 790.019   NZ
RALLY LEADERS BULLETIN. q. NZ.$10.50. Every Boy's and Every Girl's Rally Council N.Z. Inc., P.O. Box 1903, Palmerston North, New Zealand. TEL 64-6-3593735. Ed. D. McClunie. circ. 700 (paid). **Document type:** bulletin.
Description: Brings ideas, information, games, hobbies and encouragement to rally leaders.

RAN; ein politisches Jugendmagazin. see POLITICAL SCIENCE

028.5   US   ISSN 0738-6656
QH48
RANGER RICK. 1967. m. $15 junior membership (foreign $26) (effective 1997). National Wildlife Federation, 8925 Leesburg Pike, Vienna, VA 22184-0001. TEL 703-790-4000; 800-588-1650. FAX 703-790-4075. E-mail: pubs@nwf.org; URL: http://www.nwf.org. Ed. Bob Strohm. R&P contact: Gerry Bishop. TEL 703-790-4283. adv. contact: Thuy Senser. bk.rev.; illus.; index. circ. 850,000. (also avail. in microfiche from NBI,UMI; reprint service avail. from UMI) **Indexed:** Can.B.P.I., Ind.Child.Mag., Jun.High.Mag.Abstr. **Document type:** consumer publication.
— KR SourceOne; UnCover.
Formerly (until 1983): Ranger Rick's Nature Magazine (ISSN 0033-9229)
Description: Contains articles for children with full-color photos about wildlife and children in the outdoors. Advocates the wise use of natural resources.

028 331.8   GW   ISSN 0936-871X
RASANT; Zeitschrift der D A G-Jugend. 1948. 6/yr. DM.55. Deutsche Angestellten-Gewerkschaft, Johannes-Brahms-Platz 1, 20355 Hamburg, Germany. TEL 49-40-34915-1. FAX 49-40-34915400. Ed. Peter Stueber. adv.; bk.rev.; index. circ. 25,000. **Document type:** bulletin.
Formerly: Jugendpost (ISSN 0933-6265)

028.5
RASHTRA DEEPIKA CHILDREN'S DIGEST. m.? Rs.100; newsstand price: Rs.10. Rashtra Deepika Ltd., Deepika Bldg., C.M.S. College Rd., P.B. No. 7, Kottayam 686 001, India. TEL 91-481-566706. FAX 91-481-567947. TELEX 0888-203 DPKA IN. Ed. James K. Joseph; Pub. James K. Joseph. adv.: B&W page Rs.5000, color page Rs.10000; 160 x 110. circ. 25,000.

CHILDREN AND YOUTH — FOR 1885

028.5   US   ISSN 0034-0359
READ MAGAZINE.* 1951. 18/yr. $29.95 for single subscr. (effective 1997-1998). Weekly Reader Corporation, Box 120023, Stamford, CT 06912-0023. TEL 203-638-2400; 800-446-3355. FAX 203-346-5826. (Subscr. to: 300 Cindel Dr., Delran, NJ 08075) Ed. Sandra Maccarone; Pub. Richard J. Le Brasseur. R&P contact: Shirley Peterson. illus.; circ. 363,970 (paid). (also avail. in microfilm from UMI; reprint service avail. from UMI) Indexed: Ind.Child.Mag., So.Pac.Per.Ind.
—UMI.
   Description: Language arts magazine for junior and senior high school students. Includes separate teacher's guide.

READING AND WRITING QUARTERLY: OVERCOMING LEARNING DIFFICULTIES. see *EDUCATION — Special Education And Rehabilitation*

READY FOR ENGLISH. see *LINGUISTICS*

028.5   US   ISSN 1043-3945
THE REAL GHOSTBUSTERS MAGAZINE.* q. $1.95 per no. Webb Publishing Group, 387 Park Ave. S., Fl. 9, New York, NY 10016-8810. TEL 212-687-0680. FAX 212-986-1849.

028.5 371.42   US
▼**REAL LIFE.** 1996. 16/yr. $495. Career Solutions Training Group, 13 E. Central Ave., Paoli, PA 19301. TEL 610-993-8292. FAX 610-993-8249. E-mail: cstg@bellatlantic.com. Ed. Doris Humphrey; Pub. Doris Humphrey. R&P contact: Friede Borst. circ. 200 (paid). **Document type:** monographic series.
   Description: Addresses workplace ethics and employment skills through an evolving story about 5 teenage friends who are employed part time. Each story ends in a dilemma students are asked to solve.

028.5 371.0025   US
REAL TALK. (Text in English, Spanish) 1977. m. $12. Boces Geneseo Migrant Center, Migrant Dropout Reconnection Program, 210 Holcomb Bldg., Geneseo, NY 14454. TEL 716-245-5681. FAX 716-245-5680. Ed. Mary A. Fink. charts; illus. circ. 2,000. (looseleaf format; back issues avail.)
   Description: For migrant farmworker youth. Discusses careers, health and role models.

THE RECREATION AND SPORTS MINISTRY NEWSLETTER. see *RELIGIONS AND THEOLOGY — Protestant*

028.5 604.6   US
RECYCLING STORIES THAT RHYME. 1991. a. $5 per no. Prosperity & Profits Unlimited Distribution Services, Box 416, Denver, CO 80201-0416. TEL 303-575-5676. Ed. A. Doyle. circ. 1,500 (paid). (looseleaf format) **Document type:** newsletter.
   Description: Publishes stories that give children ideas on recycling.

REFLECTIONS (DUNCAN FALLS); the national student poetry magazine for grades K-12. see *LITERATURE — Poetry*

REGENBOGEN; Zeitung fuer Maedchen und Buben. see *RELIGIONS AND THEOLOGY*

028.5   CC   ISSN 1002-5677
RENSHENG ZIXUN/LIFE CONSULTATION. (Text in Chinese) bi-m. Beijing Shi Guanxin Qingshannian Jiaoyu Xiehui, 20, Guangheli Baxiang, Guangqumenwai, Beijing 100021, People's Republic of China. TEL 785142. Ed. Ke Yan.

052   IT   ISSN 0394-848X
REPORTER; articles and entertainment for students of the English language. (Text in English) 1984. 8/yr. L.39000 in Europe; US L.50000) (effective Sep. 1995). Reporter Publishing, Via Manzoni 31, 70018 Scandicci, Italy. TEL 39-55-2578346. FAX 39-55-250868. E-mail: mc7386@mclink.it. Ed. Robin Poppelsdorff. adv.: page $1000. bk.rev. circ. 30,000. cols./p.: 6; pp./issue: 20. (tabloid format) **Document type:** newspaper.
   Description: Contains graded reading articles in newspaper format for students of English. Subjects include film, music, literature and politics.

REPORTS TO THE NATION ON OUR CHANGING PLANET. see *ENVIRONMENTAL STUDIES*

028.5   CN   ISSN 1201-7647
▼**RESOURCE LINKS.** Variant title: Connecting Classrooms, Libraries and Canadian Learning Resources. 1995. bi-m. $49. (Council for Canadian Learning Resources) Rockland Press, 810 W. Broadway, Ste. 604, Vancouver, BC V5Z 4C9, Canada.
   Description: Strives to focus greater attention on young adult and children's materials set in Canada and written by Canadian authors.

028.5   CN
THE REZ. q. Can.$16 (foreign Can.$25). All Right Production Ltd., 443 W. Third St., N. Vancouver, BC V7M 1G9, Canada.

RIGHT ON! see *ETHNIC INTERESTS*

028.5   UK   ISSN 0957-3704
RIGHT START. 1989. 6/yr. £13.80. Needmarsh Publishing Ltd., 71 Newcomen St., London SE1 1YT, England. TEL 44-171-403-0840. FAX 44-171-378-6883. Ed. Anita Bevan. R&P contact: Anita Bevan. adv.: color page £2650; adv. contact: Sarah Warden. bk.rev. **Document type:** consumer publication.
   Description: For parents of 1-6 year olds with a special interest in education, health and development.

AL-RIYADAH WAL-SHABAB. see *SPORTS AND GAMES*

028.5   BE   ISSN 0771-8128
ROBBEDOES. French edition: Spirou (ISSN 0771-8071) (Text in Dutch) 1938. w. Editions Dupuis, S.A., 52 rue Destree, B-6001 Marcinelle, Belgium. TEL 32-71-600500. FAX 32-71-600599. circ. 32,000. (back issues avail.)

THE ROCK (ELGIN). see *RELIGIONS AND THEOLOGY*

028.5 781.57   IT
ROCKSTAR; numero uno. 1980. m. L.30000; newsstand price: L.6000. Ediversale s.r.l., Largo Luigi Antonelli 27, 00145 Rome, Italy. TEL 39-6-5417100. FAX 39-6-5433504. Ed. Giuseppe Videtti. adv.: color page L.10078750. circ. 180,000.

ROLF KAUKAS BUSSI BAER. see *EDUCATION*

028.5   NO   ISSN 0035-8142
ROMANTIKK. 1937. w. NOK 754($93) Bladkompaniet A-S, P.O. Box 148, Kalbakken, N-0902 Oslo, Norway. TEL 47-22-25-71-90. FAX 47-22-16-50-59. Ed. Gustav M. Galaasen. adv.: B&W page NOK 3700, color page NOK 8500. illus. circ. 50,000. cols./p.: 2; pp./issue: 90.
—CCC.

ROUNDABOUT. see *HANDICAPPED — Visually Impaired*

028.5   RU   ISSN 0131-5994
ROVESNIK. 1962. m. $71 (effective 1998). Rovesnik, Novodmitrovskaya ul. 5A, 125015 Moscow, Russia. TEL 7-095-285-8920. FAX 7-095-285-0627. (Dist. by: Mezhdunarodnaya Kniga, B. Yakimanka 39, 117049 Moscow, Russia. TEL 7-095-2384967. FAX 7-095-2384634; Dist. in U.S. by: Victor Kamkin Inc., 4956 Boiling Brook Pkwy, Rockville, MD 20852. TEL 301-881-5973) Ed. I.A. Chernyshkov. adv.; bk.rev.; illus. circ. 120,000.

ROYAL AMBASSADOR LEADERSHIP. see *RELIGIONS AND THEOLOGY — Protestant*

028.5 375   US
SAFETY NET NEWSLETTER. m. E-mail: matink@eagle.ca; URL: http://www.eagle.ca/~matink/. Ed. Carolyn Bierworth. **Document type:** newsletter.
●Available only online.
   Description: Includes more than 50 sites categorized as curriculum, kids, parents and teachers, and reference.

028.5   US   ISSN 0896-8276
ST. PAUL'S FAMILY MAGAZINE. 1984. q. $25. St. Paul's Publishing Co., Inc., 14780 W. 159th St., Olathe, KS 66062. TEL 913-780-0405. Ed. James R. Leek. adv.; bk.rev.; illus. circ. 600. (back issues avail.)
   Description: Includes classic children's literature, poetry, art, and music as well as cooking, crafts, and puzzle projects.

028.5 613.7   CR
SALUD PARA TODOS. 1977. a. free. Asociacion Demografica Costarricense, Apdo. Postal 10203, 1000 San Jose, Costa Rica. TEL 31-4211. (Co-sponsor: Ministerio de Salud) Ed. Lia Barth. illus.; charts. circ. 125,000.

028.5   FR
SALUT. 1962. bi-w. 136 F. (foreign 242 F.). Edipresse, 13 rue de la Cerisaie, 75004 Paris, France. adv.; bk.rev.; bibl.; illus.; stat. circ. 26,000. (tabloid format)
   Formerly (until 1978): Salut les Copains (ISSN 0036-3650)

028.5 327 362.7   US
SAMANTHA SMITH FOUNDATION NEWSLETTER. 1987. q. $25 (effective 1995). Samantha Smith Foundation, 9 Union St., Hallowell, ME 04347. TEL 207-626-3415. FAX 207-626-3417. Ed. Donna Brunstad. circ. 5,000. (back issues avail.) **Document type:** newsletter.
   Description: Profiles program participants and programs to promote better understanding between Americans and Russians. Also publishes pen-pal letters and contains grant information. Named in honor of the Maine girl who sought a peaceful understanding between the U.S. and the then Soviet Union before she was killed in a plane crash.

SAPPORO-SHI SEISHONEN KAGAKUKAN KIYO. see *SCIENCES: COMPREHENSIVE WORKS*

SCHOLAR'S MATE. see *SPORTS AND GAMES*

028.5   US   ISSN 0883-475X
TX1
SCHOLASTIC CHOICES; personal development & living skills. 1956. m. (Sep.-May). $11.50. Scholastic Inc., 555 Broadway, New York, NY 10012-3999. TEL 212-343-6100. Ed. Lauren Tarshis. adv.; index. circ. 180,000. (also avail. in microfilm from UMI; reprint service avail. from UMI) Indexed: Educ.Ind., Ind.Child.Mag., Mag.Ind.
●Also available online. Vendor(s): Knight-Ridder Information, Inc.
—KR SourceOne; UMI; UnCover.
   Incorporates (in 1991): Forecast for the Home Economist (ISSN 0890-9849); Which was formerly titled (until 1986): Forecast for Home Economics (ISSN 0015-7090); (1963-1966): Practical Forecast for Home Economics (ISSN 0742-8693); Supersedes (in 1984): Co-Ed (ISSN 0009-9724)
   Description: Aimed at adolescents.

028.5   US   ISSN 0736-0614
AP201
SCHOLASTIC NEWS (CITIZEN EDITION). 1941. w. (26/yr.: Sep.-May). $3.25. Scholastic Inc., 555 Broadway, New York, NY 10012-3999. TEL 212-343-6100; 800-325-6149. Ed. Alexandra Harding. illus.; maps; index. (also avail. in microfilm from UMI; reprint service avail. from UMI) Indexed: Ind.Child.Mag.
—UMI.
   Former titles (until 1982): Scholastic News Citizen (ISSN 0091-2484); (until 1973): Young Citizen (ISSN 0044-0744)
   Description: For students in the fifth grade.

028.5   US   ISSN 1070-1206
SCHOLASTIC NEWS (EDITION 6). 1952. w. (26/yr.: Sep.-May). $3.25. Scholastic Inc., 555 Broadway, New York, NY 10012-3999. TEL 212-343-6100; 800-325-6149. Ed. Alexandra Tarding. illus.; index. (also avail. in microfilm from UMI; reprint service avail. from UMI) Indexed: Ind.Child.Mag.
—UMI.
   Former titles (until 1993): Scholastic Newstime (ISSN 1058-1537); (until 1989): Scholastic News (Newstime Edition) (ISSN 0736-0622); (until 1982): Scholastic Newstime (ISSN 0028-9590)
   Description: For students in the sixth grade.

028.5   US   ISSN 0736-0592
SCHOLASTIC NEWS (EXPLORER EDITION). 1957. w. (26/yr.: Sep.-May). $2.95. Scholastic Inc., 555 Broadway, New York, NY 10012-3999. TEL 212-343-6100; 800-325-6149. Ed. J. Safro. illus.; index. (also avail. in microfilm from UMI; reprint service avail. from UMI) Indexed: Ind.Child.Mag. **Document type:** newsletter.
—UMI.
   Formerly (until 1982): News Explorer (ISSN 0028-9019)
   Description: For students in the fourth grade.

CHILDREN AND YOUTH — FOR

371.3 US ISSN 0736-0533
SCHOLASTIC NEWS (PILOT EDITION). (Spanish-language edition avail. (ISSN 1070-5880) 1960. 8/yr. $2.65. Scholastic Inc., 555 Broadway, New York, NY 10012-3999. TEL 212-343-6100; 800-325-6149. Ed. Shelly Bedik. illus.; index. (also avail. in microform from UMI; reprint service avail. from UMI) **Document type:** newsletter.
—UMI.
Formerly (until 1982): Scholastic News Pilot (ISSN 0028-9329)
Description: Geared toward students in the first grade.

371.3 US ISSN 0736-055X
SCHOLASTIC NEWS (RANGER EDITION). (Spanish-language edition avail. (ISSN 1070-1176)) 1960. 8/yr. $2.65. Scholastic Inc., 555 Broadway, New York, NY 10012-3999. TEL 212-343-6100. Ed. Shelly Bedik. illus.; index. (also avail. in microform from UMI; reprint service avail. from UMI)
—UMI.
Formerly (until 1982): Scholastic News Ranger (ISSN 0036-6404)
Description: For students in the second grade.

028.5 US ISSN 0736-0576
SCHOLASTIC NEWS (TRAILS EDITION). (Editions in English, Spanish) 1960. w. (26/yr.: Sep.-May). $2.95. Scholastic Inc., Scholastic Magazines, 555 Broadway, New York, NY 10012-3999. TEL 212-343-6100; 800-325-6149. (Subscr. to: Scholastic Classroom Magazines, 2931 E. McCarthy St., P.O. Box 3710, Jefferson City, MO 65102-3710. TEL 800-325-6149) Eds. Alexandra Hanson-Harding, Tracey West. bibl.; charts; illus.; stat.; index. circ. 3,500,000. (tabloid format; also avail. in microform from UMI; reprint service avail. from UMI) **Indexed:** Ind.Child.Mag.
—UMI.
Formerly (until 1982): Scholastic News Trails (ISSN 0028-9361)
Description: For students in the third grade.

371.3 US ISSN 0745-7065
SCHOLASTIC UPDATE. 1983. 14/yr. $11.45 for student ed.; teacher and student ed. $24 (effective 1997). Scholastic Inc., 555 Broadway, New York, NY 10012-3999. TEL 212-343-6100; 800-325-6149. E-mail: updatemag@aol.com; URL: http://www.scholastic.com. (Subscr. to: 2931 E. McCarty St., Box 3710, Jefferson City, MO 65102. TEL 800-631-1586. FAX 314-635-8937; Addr. in Canada: Scholastic-TAB Publications Ltd., Richmond Hill, ON L4C 3GS, Canada) Ed. Steven Manning; Pub. Hugh Roome. adv.; bk.rev.; film rev.; charts; illus.; index. circ. 288,000. (also avail. in microfiche from UMI; microfilm from UMI; back issues avail.; reprint service avail. from UMI) **Indexed:** Abr.R.G., Ind.Child.Mag., Jun.High.Mag.Abstr., Mag.Ind., PMR, PSI, R.G., R.G.Abstr., TOM. **Document type:** academic/scholarly publication.
●Also available online. Vendor(s): Information Access Co., Knight-Ridder Information, Inc., UMI.
Also available on CD-ROM. Producer(s): UMI.
—KR SourceOne; UMI; UnCover.
Formed by the merger of (1972-1983): Scholastic Search (ISSN 0163-3597); (1920-1983): Senior Scholastic (ISSN 0037-2242); Which incorporated: American Observer (ISSN 0003-0201); World Week (ISSN 0043-9231)
Description: Each issue focuses on a single topic in the news and presents in-depth facts and opinions aimed at helping teenagers shape their views on the issue.

028.5 AT ISSN 0155-1108
SCHOOL MAGAZINE. (In 4 parts: Countdown, Blast Off, Orbit, Touchdown) 1916. m. Aus.$7 per no. (effective 1997). Department of Education, P.O. Box 1928, Macquarie Centre, N.S.W. 2113, Australia. TEL 61-2-9889-0044. FAX 61-2-9889-0040. E-mail: schmag@geko.net; URL: http://www.geko.net.au/~schmag. Ed. Jonathan Shaw. bk.rev.; illus.; index. circ. 180,000. (back issues avail.)
Description: Literary magazine for elementary school children (8 to 11 years old).

SCHOOL MATES. see SPORTS AND GAMES

028.5 UK ISSN 0036-6862
SCHOOL YARN MAGAZINE.* 1946. bi-m. School Yarn Publications, Ltd., 93 Brownspring Drive, New Eltham, London, S.E.9, England.

028.5 UK ISSN 0036-6897
SCHOOLGIRL STORY MAGAZINE.* 1947. fortn. School Yarn Publications, Ltd., 93 Brownspring Drive, New Eltham, London S.E.9, England.

028.5 373 GW
DER SCHWAMM. 1955. irreg. (3-4/yr.). free. Gottlieb-Daimler-Gymnasium, Kattowitzer Str. 8, 70374 Stuttgart, Germany. Ed. Franziska Kellner. R&P contact: Jochen Schorn. adv.: page DM.130; adv. contact: Lars Oberg. circ. 350. (back issues avail.) **Document type:** newsletter.

SCHWARTE. see CHILDREN AND YOUTH — About

028.5 SZ
SCHWEIZERISCHER BUND FUER JUGENDLITERATUR. JAHRESBERICHT/LIGUE SUISSE DE LITTERATURE POUR LA JEUNESSE. RAPPORT ANNUEL. 1954. a. 30 SFr. membership. Schweizerischer Bund fuer Jugendliteratur, Zentralsekretariat, Gewerbestr. 8, CH-6330 Cham, Switzerland. **Document type:** bulletin.
Description: Details the financial situation, activities and important news of the youth union during the last year.

SCIENCE ET VIE JUNIOR. see SCIENCES: COMPREHENSIVE WORKS

028.5 500 US
SCIENCE EXPERIMENTS FOR YOUNG PEOPLE. 1993. irreg. $53.85. Enslow Publishers, Inc., 44 Fadem Rd., Box 699, Springfield, NJ 07081-0699. TEL 201-379-8890. FAX 201-379-7940. E-mail: annette@enslow.com. Ed. Brian D. Enslow; Pub. Annette Noce. R&P contact: Annette Noce.
Description: Book series contains fun environmental experiments for teen readers.

028.5 500 US
SCIENCE PROJECTS. 1993. irreg. $113.70. Enslow Publishers, Inc., 44 Fadem Rd., Box 699, Springfield, NJ 07081-0699. TEL 201-379-8890. FAX 201-379-7940. E-mail: annette@enslow.com; URL: http://www.enslow.com. Ed. Brian D. Enslow; Pub. Annette Noce. R&P contact: Annette Noce.
Description: Book series on experiments explaining interesting areas of science to teen readers. Provides science project ideas. Each book contains careful drawings and safety tips.

028.5 500 US
SCIENCE WEEKLY. (Available in Levels Pre-A through F (K-8): Level Pre-A (Kdg.)(ISSN 0890-0388); Level A (1st grade)(ISSN 0748-8904); Level B (2nd grade)(ISSN 8756-176X); Level C (3rd grade)(ISSN 8756-1778); Level D (4th grade)(ISSN 8756-1786); Level E (5th & 6th Grade)(ISSN 8756-1794); Level F (7th & 8th grade)(ISSN 1043-0997)) 1984. 16/yr. (during school yr.). $4.95 for subscr. of 20 or more; for less than 20 $9.95. 2141 Industrial Pkwy., No. 202, Silver Spring, MD 20904. TEL 301-680-8804; 800-4WE-EKLY. FAX 301-680-9240. E-mail: sciencew@erols.com; URL: http://www.scienceweekly.com. Ed. Deborah Lazar; Pub. Claude Mayberry. illus. (back issues avail.) **Document type:** academic/scholarly publication.
Description: Classroom tool for students K-8 designed to stimulate their interest in science, mathematics, and technology. Each issue is developed at 7 different reading levels and emphasizes "hands-on" labs and challenging activities.

SCIENCE WORLD. see SCIENCES: COMPREHENSIVE WORKS

507 028.5 US ISSN 0147-3654
SCIENCELAND; to nurture scientific thinking. 1977. q. $36 (foreign $41) (effective 1997). Komat Inc., 501 Fifth Ave., Ste. 2108, New York, NY 10017. TEL 212-490-2180. FAX 212-490-2187. Ed. A.H. Matano. R&P contact: A.H. Matano. bk.rev.; illus.; index. circ. 16,000. (back issues avail.) **Indexed:** Ind.Child.Mag. **Document type:** consumer publication.
—KR SourceOne; UMI; UnCover.
Refereed Serial

028.5 UK ISSN 0262-4206
SCOOP SPORT ANNUAL. 1980. a. £1.65. D.C. Thomson & Co. Ltd., Albert Sq., Dundee DD1 9QJ, Scotland. illus.

028.5 IT
SCOPERTE/DISCOVER. m. (10/yr.). $50 (effective Jan. 1997). Zanfi Editori s.r.l., Via Emilia Ovest 954, 41100 Modena, Italy. TEL 39-59-891700. FAX 39-59-891701. E-mail: zanfi.editori@mo.nettuno.it. **Document type:** consumer publication.
Description: For children ages 8-13.

SCOTTISH YOUTH HOSTELS ASSOCIATION HANDBOOK. see HOTELS AND RESTAURANTS

369.4 FR ISSN 0751-5731
SCOUT. 1924. bi-m. 90 F. Editions Scouts de France, 54 av. Jean Jaures, 75019 Paris, France. TEL 44-52-37-37. FAX 42-38-09-87. Ed. Philippe Da Costa. illus.
Formerly: Ranger (ISSN 0033-9237)
Description: For scouts ages 12-14.

SCOUT. see CHILDREN AND YOUTH — About

369.4 FR ISSN 0249-2644
SCOUT - AVENIR. 1924. bi-m. 90 F. Editions Scouts de France, 54 av. Jean Jaures, 75019 Paris, France. TEL 44-52-37-37. FAX 42-38-09-87. Ed. Philippe Da Costa. illus.

028.5 IT
SCOUT D'EUROPA; famiglia felice, carnet d'Marcia, Azimuth. 1977. m. L.50000. Associazione Italiana Guide e Scouts d'Europa Cattolici, Via Anicia 10, 00152 Rome, Italy. TEL 39-6-5884430. FAX 39-6-5885229. (back issues avail.) **Document type:** corporate report.

SCOUT MEMORABILIA. see HOBBIES

369.4 UK ISSN 0036-9489
SCOUTING; the national magazine of the Scout Association. 1909. m. £25. Scout Association, Baden-Powell House, Queen's Gate, London SW7 5JS, England. TEL 44-171-584-7030613scoutingmag@enterprise.net. FAX 44-171-590-5124. URL: http://www.enterprise.net/scoutingmagazine/. Ed. David Easton. adv.; bk.rev.; illus.; index. circ. 30,000. **Indexed:** Mag.Ind., Rehabil.Lit. **Document type:** consumer publication.
●Also available online. Vendor(s): Knight-Ridder Information, Inc.

028.5 FI
SCOUTPOSTEN. (Text in Swedish) 1918. 6/yr. FIM 60. Finlands Svenska Scouter, By Aeldstevaegen 29, 00640 Helsinki, Finland. TEL 358-0-728-2811. FAX 358-0-752-2681. Eds. Carita Francke-Mattsson, Lisbeth Rosenback. adv. circ. 5,700.

THE SCREAM. see LITERATURE — Science Fiction, Fantasy, Horror

SE VUOI. see RELIGIONS AND THEOLOGY

268 UK
SEARCH (LONDON, 1924). 1924. m. free. Scripture Gi Mission, Radstock House, 3 Eccleston St., London SW1W 9LZ, England. circ. 5,000. **Indexed:** Br.Archaeol.Abstr., CERDIC, So.Pac.Per.Ind.
Former titles: Y S L Magazine; Young Sower (ISSN 0044-0914)
Description: For ages 9-15.

028.5 RU ISSN 0203-3569
HQ799.R9
SEL'SKAYA MOLODEZH. (Former name of issuing body Vsesoyuznyi Leninskii Kommunisticheskii Soyuz Molodezhi, Tsentral'nyi Komitet) 1925. m. $85 (effective 1998). Novodmitrovskaya ul. 5A, 12501 Moscow, Russia. TEL 7-095-2850830. (Dist. by: Mezhdunarodnaya Kniga, B. Yakimanka 39, 117049 Mowcow, Russia. TEL 7-095-2384967. FAX 7-095-2384634; Dist. in U.S. by: Victor Kamkin Inc., 4956 Boiling Brook Pkwy., Rockville, MD 20852. TEL 301-881-5973) Ed. A. Shelevel. adv.; bk.rev.; bibl.; illus. circ. 26,000.
Formerly: Sputnik Sel'skoi Molodezhi.

369.4 IT ISSN 0037-2765
SERVIRE; rivista scout per educatori. 1946. bi-m. L.30000 (effective Jan. 1997). Cooperativa Servir s.r.l., Via Olona 25, 20123 Milan, Italy. TEL 39-2-8394301. Ed. Dr. Vittorio Ghetti. illus. circ. 1,500. (processed) **Document type:** monographic series.

CHILDREN AND YOUTH — FOR 1887

028.5 US ISSN 0049-0253
SESAME STREET. (Includes: Sesame Street Parent's Guide) (Text in English and Spanish) 1971. 10/yr. $19.90 (foreign $29.90) (effective 1997). Children's Television Workshop, One Lincoln Plaza, New York, NY 10023. TEL 212-595-3456; 800-678-0613. Ed. Rebecca Herman. circ. 1,104,697. **Indexed:** Ind.Child.Mag. **Document type:** consumer publication.
 Description: Uses Sesame Street TV Muppets to help teach young children. Includes a 36-page child's book and a separate 36-page Parents' Guide.

SFOGLIALIBRO; la biblioteca dei ragazzi. see *PUBLISHING AND BOOK TRADE*

SHALOM INFANTIL. see *ETHNIC INTERESTS*

028.5 CC ISSN 1001-5590
SHAO NU/YOUNG GIRL. (Text in Chinese) m. Y18. Shanghai Renmin Chubanshe, Qikan Bu - Shanghai People's Publishing House, 54 Shaoxing Road, Shanghai 200020, People's Republic of China. TEL 4315882. Ed. Zhang Baoni.

028.5 CC
SHAONIAN BAO/JUVENILE PRESS. (Text in Chinese) 1967. w. Y43.20 (effective 1997). (Shanghai Education Bureau) Shaonian Bao She - Juvenile Press Agency, 61 Zhejiang Beilu, Shanghai 200085, People's Republic of China. TEL 86-21-6306-6161. FAX 86-21-6306-9036. Ed. Renxiao Li. R&P contact: Renxiao Li. adv. contact: Peisheng Li. lit. circ. 500,000. (tabloid format; also avail. in microfiche) **Document type:** newspaper.

SHAONIAN JIYOU/JUVENILE PHILATELY. see *PHILATELY*

500 CC
SHAONIAN KEXUE/JUVENILE SCIENCE. (Text in Chinese) 1976. m. $26.40. Shaonian Ertong Chubanshe - Juvenile & Children Publishing House, 1538 Yan'an Xilu, Shanghai 200052, People's Republic of China. TEL 86-21-6282-3025. FAX 86-21-6282-1726. (Dist. in US by: China Books & Periodicals, Inc., 2929 24th St., San Francisco, CA 94110. TEL 415-282-2994)
 Description: Introduces new developments in science and technology for young readers.

500 CC ISSN 1000-7776
SHAONIAN KEXUE HUABAO/JUVENILE SCIENTIFIC PICTORIAL. (Text in Chinese) 1979. m. $32.30. Beijing Chubanshe - Beijing Publishing House, 6 Beisanhuan Zhonglu, Beijing 100011, People's Republic of China. TEL 2016699. (Dist. in US by: China Books & Periodicals, Inc., 2929 24th St., San Francisco, CA 94110. TEL 415-282-2994) Ed. Zhao Meng. illus.

808.068 700 CC ISSN 0559-7412
SHAONIAN WENYI/JUVENILE LITERATURE. (Text in Chinese) 1953. m. $36. Shaonian Ertong Chubanshe - Juvenile & Children Publishing House, 1538 Yan'an Xilu, Shanghai 200052, People's Republic of China. TEL 86-21-6282-3025. FAX 86-21-6282-1726. (Dist. in US by: China Books & Periodicals, Inc., 2929 24th St., San Francisco, CA 94110. TEL 415-282-2994) Ed. Zhou Jiting. **Document type:** consumer publication.
 Description: Contains fictions, poems, proses, fairy tales, and translated foreign stories for teenagers.

SHARING SPACE. see *EDUCATION*

028.5 284 US ISSN 0884-5514
SHINING STAR MAGAZINE.* 1986. q. $16.95 (effective 1992). Good Apple, P.O. Box 2649, Columbus, OH 43216-2649. TEL 217-357-3981. FAX 217-357-3987. Ed. Becky Daniel. adv.: B&W page $600, color page $1000. bk.rev. circ. 16,000. (back issues avail.)

028.5 BG
SHISHU. (Text in Bengali) 1977. m. Bangladesh Shishu Academy, Old High Court Compound, Dhaka 1000, Bangladesh. TEL 2-238871. Ed. Golam Kibria. circ. 9,000.

SHKOL'NYI VESTNIK; zhurnal dlya slepykh detei. see *HANDICAPPED — Visually Impaired*

296.7 028.5 US ISSN 0748-9706
SHOFAR (MELVILLE). 1984. 10/yr. $14.95. 43 Northcote Dr., Melville, NY 11747. TEL 516-643-4598. (Subscr. to: Box 852, Wheatley Heights, NY 11798) Ed. Kerry Olitzky; Pub. Gerald H. Grayson. R&P contact: Gerald H. Grayson. adv.: B&W page $2300, color page $2800; adv. contact: Gerald H. Grayson. circ. 16,000. **Indexed:** Ind.Jew.Per. **Document type:** consumer publication.
 Description: Presents a forum intended to enhance the Jewish child's identity by featuring profiles of high-profile Jewish celebrities.

028.5 US
SHOOFLY; an audiomagazine for children. 1994. 4/yr. $33.90. Shoofly, Box 1237, Carrboro, NC 27510. TEL 919-968-7846; 800-919-9989. circ. 500. (audio cassette)
 Description: Features original and traditional stories, poems, and songs for children ages 3 to 7.

028.5 BR
SHWE THWE. (Text in Burmese, English) w. Sarpay Beikman Management Board, 529 Merchant St., Yangon, Union of Myanmar. circ. 100,000.

028.5 LS
SIANG KHONG GNAOVASON SONG THANVA/VOICE OF THE 2ND DECEMBER YOUTHS. m. Vientiane, Laos.

028.5 IS ISSN 0334-276X
SIFRUT YELADIM VANOAR; journal for children's and youth literature. (Text in Hebrew) 1974. q. IS.16($8) Ministry of Education and Culture, 8 King David Street, Jerusalem, Israel. Ed. Devora Hanevia. bk.rev.; index. circ. 1,500. **Indexed:** Ind.Heb.Per.
 Description: Presents literature for children and teenagers. Includes study, research and personalities sections.

SIGLO XXI CIENCIA AND TECNOLOGIA. see *SCIENCES: COMPREHENSIVE WORKS*

028.5
SINDBAD. (Text in Arabic) 1969. 7/yr. $10. (Histadrut) Arabic Publishing House, P.O. Box 28049, Tel Aviv 61280, Israel. TEL 972-3-371438. Ed. Walid Hussein. circ. 8,500.

SKI CANADA. see *SPORTS AND GAMES — Outdoor Life*

SKIPPER. see *ENVIRONMENTAL STUDIES*

028.5 US ISSN 0899-529X
SKIPPING STONES; a multicultural children's magazine. 1988. 5/yr. $25 to individuals; institutions $35 (foreign $40) (effective 1997). Box 3939, Eugene, OR 97403-0939. TEL 541-342-4956. Ed. Arun N. Toke; Pub. Arun N. Toke. R&P contact: Arun N. Toke. bk.rev. circ. 2,500. (back issues avail.) **Document type:** consumer publication.
 Description: Provides a multilingual, multicultural forum for communication among children from various lands and backgrounds. Publishes stories, nonfiction, pictures, games, and poems written by children for children and adults around the world. Each issue contains a parent/teacher guide and sections on international penpals and Noteworthy News. Winner of the 1995 EdPress Golden Shoestring Award and the 1996 EEA Golden Apple Award.
 Refereed Serial

SKOTAVILLE AFRICAN CLASSICS SERIES. see *LITERATURE*

SKOTAVILLE CHILDREN'S BOOK SERIES. see *LITERATURE*

SLAP. see *SPORTS AND GAMES*

SLINGERVEL. see *RELIGIONS AND THEOLOGY — Protestant*

028.5 XR ISSN 0231-7222
SLUNICKO; mesicnik pro nejmensi. 1967. m. 24 Kc.($7.90) Mlada Fronta, Radlicka 61, 150 02 Prague 5, Czech Republic. TEL 42-2-544941. (Dist. by: Artia, Ve Smeckach 30, 111 27 Prague 1, Czech Republic) Ed. Jan Kruta.

028.5 RU ISSN 0131-6656
SMENA. 1924. m. $102 (effective 1998). Bumazhnyi pr., 14, 101457 Moscow A-15, Russia. TEL 7-095-2121507. FAX 7-095-2505928. (Dist. by: Mezhdunarodnaya Kniga, B. Yakimanka 39, 117049 Moscow, Russia. TEL 7-095-2384967. FAX 7-095-2384634; Dist. in U.S. by: Victor Kamkin Inc., 4956 Boiling Brook Pkwy, Rockville, MD 20852. TEL 301-881-5973) Ed. Mikhail Kizilov. bk.rev.; film rev.; abstr.; bibl.; illus. circ. 65,000.

028.5 US
SMILE MAKERS. a. Smile Makers, Box 2543, Spartanburg, SC 29304. FAX 803-585-3958.
 Description: Covers stickers, balloons, buttons, costume jewelry, fancy shaped erasers, colored pencils and other items suitable for children's prizes at fairs or as incentives.

SOCCER JR.; the soccer magazine for kids. see *SPORTS AND GAMES — Ball Games*

SOENDAGSKOLEKONTAKT. see *RELIGIONS AND THEOLOGY — Protestant*

SOFUS' LILLEBROR. see *SPORTS AND GAMES*

SOMETHING ABOUT THE AUTHOR. see *LITERATURE*

028.5 KO
SONYON DONG-A. 1964. d. Dong-A Ilbo, 139 Sejongno, Chongno-gu, Seoul, S. Korea. TEL 02-721-7114. Ed. Kwon O-Kie. circ. 381,150.

SOUTH CAROLINA Y F AND F F A. (South Carolina Young Farmers and Future Farmers) see *AGRICULTURE*

SPANISH LANGUAGE BOOKS FOR CHILDREN. see *PUBLISHING AND BOOK TRADE*

028.5 KE
SPARKLE MAGAZINE; a magazine for young children. (Text in English) 1983. m. KShs.580 (rest of Africa $52; Europe and the Middle East $60; Australia and the Far East $68) (effective 1997). Space Sellers Ltd., Chepkorio Rd., P.O. Box 47186, Nairobi, Kenya. TEL 254-2-555811. FAX 254-2-557813. Ed. Serah Mwangi; Pub. Sylvia King. R&P contact: Sylvia King. TEL 254-2-530598. adv. contact: Serah Mwangi. circ. 12,000.
 Formerly (until Feb. 1990): Watoto Magazine.
 Description: Written for primary school children with educational and entertaining material.

028.5 US
▼**SPEEDMETER.** 1996. irreg. 4532 Bryant, Maples, MN 55409-1755. E-mail: speedmeter@frodo.com; URL: http://www.pressenter.com/~emo123/speedmeter/. Ed. Erik Moe.
 ●Available only online.
 Description: Covers youth culture, pop culture, independent or underground culture.

028.5 369.4 NO ISSN 0800-0646
SPEIDEREN. 1978. q. NOK 150. Norges Speiderforbund, Oevre Vollgate 9, N-0158 Oslo, Norway. TEL 47-22-42-26-60. FAX 47-22-42-07-04. Eds. Jens Doevik, Karen Johanne Stroemstad. adv.; bk.rev.; circ. 40,000 (controlled).
 —CCC.

369.4 267 NO
SPEIDING. 4/yr. Norges K F U M-Speidere, P.O. Box 6810, St. Olavs Pl., N-0130 Oslo, Norway. TEL 47-2-11-50-32. FAX 47-2-20-47-59. adv. circ. 9,000.

369.4 DK ISSN 0108-7967
SPEJD. 1971. 8/yr. DKK 100. Danske Spejderkorps, Lundsgade 6, DK-2100 Copenhagen OE, Denmark. Ed. Inge Lavallee. adv. circ. 42,500.
 Description: For scouts ages 8-15.

028.5 GW
SPEKTRUM (GELNHAUSEN). 1949. 3/yr. DM.11. Grimmelshausen Gymnasium, In der Aue 3, 63571 Gelnhausen, Germany. TEL 06051-17008. Eds. Soeren Kroh, Oliver Klein. adv.; bk.rev.; illus. circ. 1,500. (back issues avail.) **Document type:** consumer publication.

SPES NOSTRA - OUR HOPE; a marian missionary magazine for youth and families. see *RELIGIONS AND THEOLOGY — Roman Catholic*

SPEX. see *GENERAL INTEREST PERIODICALS — Germany*

SPHINX; the student magazine for Liverpool. see *LITERARY AND POLITICAL REVIEWS*

028.5　　　　GW
SPHINX. 1975. q. DM.1.20. Sphinx Schuelerzeitung, Helmholtz Gymnasium, 4300 Essen 1, Germany. TEL 0201-714175. Ed. Joerg Bolender. adv. circ. 1,000.

SPICE (NEW YORK). see *ETHNIC INTERESTS*

808.89　　　US　　ISSN 1070-2911
SPIDER. 1993. m. $32.97 (Canada Can.$42.97; overseas $41.97). Carus Corporation, 315 Fifth St., Box 300, Peru, IL 61354. TEL 815-224-6656. FAX 815-224-6615. (Subscr. to: Box 7435, Red Oak, IA 51591-2435. TEL 800-827-0227) Ed. Christine Walske; Pub. Bob Harper. illus. circ. 92,000. **Document type:** consumer publication.
  Description: Contains stories, poems, and informational articles geared toward independent readers ages 6-9.

028.5 808.836　　BE　　ISSN 0771-8071
SPIROU. Dutch edition: Robbedoes (ISSN 0771-8128) (Text in French) 1938. w. 2630 BEF($44) Editions Dupuis, S.A., 52 rue Destree, B-6001 Marcinelle, Belgium. TEL 32-71-600500. FAX 32-71-600599. (Subscr. in Belgium to: Spirou-Service Abonnements, BP 41, 1050 Brussels, Belgium; Subscr. in other countries to: Spirou-Service Abonnements, B 250, F-60720 Sainte-Genvieve, France) Ed. Jean Denemostier. R&P contact: Cecile Hisette. adv. circ. 120,000. (back issues avail.)

051　　　US　　ISSN 0892-5089
SPLICE;* for teens. 1986. bi-m. $11.70. Jannis Communications, Box 267, Brookfield, CT 06804. TEL 203-740-2606. FAX 203-740-2602. Ed. Bob W. Woods. circ. 200,000.

028.5 790.1　　US
SPORTS GREAT BOOKS. 1990. irreg. $653.95. Enslow Publishers, Inc., 44 Fadem Rd., Box 699, Springfield, NJ 07081-0699. TEL 201-379-8890. FAX 201-379-7940. E-mail: annette@enslow.com; URL: http://www.enslow.com. Ed. Brian D. Enslow; Pub. Annette Noce. R&P contact: Annette Noce.
  Description: Book series for teen readers. Contains easy-reading stories about star athletes.

028.5 790.1　　US　　ISSN 1042-394X
SPORTS ILLUSTRATED FOR KIDS. 1989. m. $27.95 (overseas $49) (effective 1997). Time Inc. (Subsidiary of: Time Warner, Inc.), Time & Life Bldg., Rockefeller Center, New York, NY 10020-1393. TEL 212-522-1212. (Subscr. to: Box 830609, Birmingham, AL 35283-0609. TEL 800-992-0196) Ed. Neil Cohen; Pub. Cleary Simpson. R&P contact: Marlene Zeddies. adv. contact: Gail oleman Healy. circ. 950,000 (paid). **Indexed:** Ind.Child.Mag. **Document type:** consumer publication.
  —KR SourceOne; UMI; UnCover.

028.5 790.1　　US
SPORTS REPORTS. 1994. irreg. $379. Enslow Publishers, Inc., 44 Fadem Rd., Box 699, Springfield, NJ 07081-0699. TEL 201-379-8890. FAX 201-379-7940. E-mail: annette@enslow.com; URL: http://www.enslow.com. Ed. Brian D. Enslow; Pub. Annette Noce. R&P contact: Annette Noce.
  Description: Book series of sports biographies for young readers. Each title gives an in-depth look at one of the most exciting sports figures today.

028.5 790.1　　US
SPORTS TOP 10. 1994. irreg. $305.15. Enslow Publishers, Inc., 44 Fadem Rd., Box 699, Springfield, NJ 07081-0699. TEL 201-379-8890. FAX 201-379-7940. E-mail: annette@enslow.com; URL: http://www.enslow.com. Ed. Brian D. Enslow; Pub. Annette Noce. R&P contact: Annette Noce.
  Description: Each book of the series describes ten of the greatest athletes ever to play a particular sport or certain position.

SPORTSTALK; the Women's Sports Foundation newsletter for young female athletes. see *SPORTS AND GAMES*

028.5　　　　UK　　ISSN 1354-9308
SPOT. 1994. m. £15 (Europe & Ireland £25; rest of world £30) (effective 1996). B B C Worldwide Publishing, Broadcasting House, Whiteladies Rd., Bristol GS8 2LR, England. TEL 44-181-576-2000. FAX 44-181-576-2931. (Subscr. to: P.O. Box 425, Woking, Surrey GU21 1GP, England. TEL 44-1483-733716. FAX 44-1483-756792) **Document type:** consumer publication.

SQUIRES NEWSLETTER. see *CLUBS*

028.5　　　　GW　　ISSN 0174-5832
STAFETTE. 1946. m. DM.45.60. Johann Michael Sailer Verlag GmbH, Aeusserer-Laufer-Platz 22, 90403 Nuernberg, Germany. TEL 49-911-53961. Ed. Eduard W. Laenger. adv.; bk.rev.; film rev.; illus. circ. 115,000. (back issues avail.) **Document type:** bulletin.
  Formerly: Neue Stafette.
  Description: Information and entertainment for children ages 8-15.

STATION TO STATION. see *GENERAL INTEREST PERIODICALS — Germany*

028.5 796　　XR　　ISSN 0862-6553
STEZKA; mesicnik pro sport, turistiku, brannost. 1970. m. 48 Kc.($18.50) Mlada Fronta, Radlicka 61, 150 02 Prague 5, Czech Republic. (Dist. by: Artia, Ve Smeckach 30, 111 27 Prague 1, Czech Republic) Ed. J. Prchal. circ. 105,000.
  Formerly (until 1990): Pionyrska Stezka (ISSN 0231-5521)

028.5 011　　GW
STIFTUNG LESEN. LESE-EMPFEHLUNGEN. 1978. bi-m. DM.3. Stiftung Lesen, Fischtorplatz 23, 55116 Mainz, Germany. TEL 06131-288900. FAX 06131-230333. Ed.Bd. bk.rev. circ. 55,000. (back issues avail.) **Document type:** bibliography.
  Former titles: Stiftung Lesen. Buchempfehlungen; Deutsche Lesegesellschaft. Buchempfehlungen.

028.5　　　　GW
STIPENDIEN FUER SPRACHKURSE. 1974. a. Deutsch-Franzoesisches Jugendwerk, Rhoendorferstr. 23, 53604 Bad Honnef, Germany. TEL 49-2224-1808-0. FAX 49-2224-1808-52. URL: http://www.dfjw.org. circ. 5,000. **Document type:** bulletin.

028.5　　　US　　ISSN 0094-579X
PS508.C5
STONE SOUP; the magazine by young writers and artists. 1973. 5/yr. $26 (Canada $31; elsewhere $36). Children's Art Foundation, Box 83, Santa Cruz, CA 95063. TEL 408-426-5557. FAX 408-426-1161. E-mail: editor@stonesoup.com; URL: http://www.stonesoup.com. Eds. Gerry Mandel, William Rubel. R&P contact: Gerry Mandel. adv. contact: William Rubel. bk.rev.; illus.; circ. 20,000 (paid). **Document type:** consumer publication.
  —UnCover.
  Description: Publishes fiction and poetry by children ages 6 through 13. Emphasizes topics relevant to children's lives.

268　　　US　　ISSN 0039-2006
STORY FRIENDS. 1905. w. $14.80. Mennonite Publishing House, 616 Walnut Ave., Scottdale, PA 15683. TEL 412-887-8500. FAX 412-887-3111. Ed. Rose Mary Stutzman. bk.rev.; illus. circ. 6,100.
  Description: For students ages 4-9.

028.5　　　US
STORY RHYME NEWSLETTER FOR SCHOOLS. 1992. irreg. $2 (Canada $3; elsewhere $4). Story Time Stories That Rhyme, Box 416, Denver, CO 80201-0416. TEL 303-575-5676. Ed. A. Doyle. R&P contact: A. Doyle. illus. **Document type:** newsletter.
  Description: Contains stories that rhyme for children ages 9-16.

028.5　　　US　　ISSN 1045-5515
STORY TIME STORIES THAT RHYME NEWSLETTER. 1990. q. $20. Story Time Stories That Rhyme, Box 416, Denver, CO 80201-0416. TEL 303-575-5676. Ed. A. Doyle. R&P contact: A. Doyle. TEL 305-575-5676. (looseleaf format; back issues avail.) **Document type:** newsletter.

373　　　US　　ISSN 1068-0292
STORYWORKS. 1993. 6/yr. (during school yr.) $3.95. Scholastic Inc., 555 Broadway, New York, NY 10012-3999. TEL 212-343-6100. Ed. Tamara Hanneman.
  Description: Literature magazine for third to fifth grade students.

051　　　　　　ISSN 1062-0095
STRAIGHT TALK (PLEASANTVILLE); a magazine for teens. (Consists of 4 topical issues: HIV - AIDS and Other STDs; Self-Esteem; Substance Abuse; Teen Relationships and Choices) 1991. irreg. $16.80 to individuals; institutions $14.30. (National Education Association, Health Information Network) Learning Partnership, Box 199, Pleasantville, NY 10570. TEL 914-769-0055. circ. 300,000.
  Formerly (until 1992): Rodale's Straight Talk.
  Description: Covers topics such as drugs, relationships, self-esteem, and sexually transmitted diseases for teenagers, grades seven through 12.

STREAMS. see *LITERATURE*

028.5 340 360　　AT　　ISSN 0815-0486
STREETWIZE COMICS; youth rights comics. 1984. irreg. Aus.$20. Streetwize Comics Ltd., 2-111 Moore St., Leichhardt, N.S.W. 2040, Australia. TEL 61-2-95603244. FAX 61-2-95603170. E-mail: stwize@ozemail.com.au. Ed. Renata Jones. R&P contact: Jeremy Campbell. circ. 100,000. **Document type:** consumer publication.
  Description: Provides health, legal and survival information, passed on to young disadvantaged people in an entertaining format.

028.5　　　　RU　　ISSN 0321-3803
STUDENCHESKII MERIDIAN/STUDENT MERIDIAN. Abbreviated title: St M. 1924. m. $102 (effective 1998). Studencheskii Meridian - Student Meridian, Novodmitrovskaya ul. 5A, 125015 Moscow, Russia. TEL 095-285-8071. FAX 095-972-0582. TELEX 411261 FAKEL. (Dist. by: Mezhdunarodnaya Kniga, ul. Dimitrova D. 39, 113095 Moscow, Russia; Dist. in U.S. by: Victor Kamkin Inc., 4956 Boiling Brook Pkwy, Rockville, MD 20852. TEL 301-881-5973) Ed. Y.A. Rostovtsev. adv.; bk.rev.; illus. circ. 1,110,000.
  Description: Aimed at high school and college students, as well as young professionals. Covers current affairs, the arts, popular culture, education, history, and more.

STUDENT'S MESSAGE/RISALAT AL-TALIB. see *EDUCATION*

028.5　　　　GW
STUFE; Jugendzeitschrift der Albvereinsjugend. 1972. q. Schwaebischer Albverein e.V., Hospitalstr. 21B, 70174 Stuttgart, Germany. TEL 49-711-2258574. Ed. Hans-Peter Wolf. bk.rev. (tabloid format) **Document type:** newsletter.

028.5　　　　RU　　ISSN 0869-0022
HS3325.R8
STUPENI. 1924. m. 13.20 Rub.($27) Izdatel'stvo Molodaya Gvardiya, Sushchevskaya ul., 21, 103030 Moscow, Russia. TEL 285-8856. (Dist. by: Mezhdunarodnaya Kniga, B. Yakimanka 39, 117049 Moscow, Russia) Ed. S.V. Tupichenkov. adv.; bk.rev.; illus.; index. circ. 200,000.
  Formerly: Vozhatyi (ISSN 0321-0642)

028.5　　　　II
SUKTARA. (Text in Bengali) 1948. m. 11 Jhamapooke Ln., Calcutta 700 009, India. TEL 33-355294. Ed. M. Majumdar. circ. 61,300.

028.5　　　　II
SUMAN SAURABH. (Text in Hindi) 1983. m. Rs.238($7) Delhi Press Patra Prakashan Ltd., Delhi Press Bldg., E-3, JHandewalan Estate, Rani Jhansi Rd., New Delhi 110 055, India. TEL 91-11-52631 FAX 91-11-7525020. TELEX 31-63053 DEPR IN. Ed. Vishwa Nath. adv.: B&W page Rs.21000, color page Rs.35000; 175 x 240. circ. 57,561.
  Description: Includes fiction, informative articles and regular columns of interest to children from 11-16 years old.

CHILDREN AND YOUTH — FOR 1889

028.5 **FI** **ISSN 0355-4260**
SUOSIKKI. m. FIM 237. Yhtyneet Kuvalehdet Oy, Maistraatinportti 1, FIN-00240 Helsinki, Finland. TEL 358-0-156-6524. FAX 358-0-156-6505. TELEX 121364. Ed. Jyrki Hamalainen. adv.: B&W page FIM 17200, color page FIM 25300. circ. 77,445. **Document type:** consumer publication.
  Description: Covers popular media and music for a youth audience (ages 12-20).

028.5 **IT**
SUPER MATTISSIMO. 1985. m. newsstand price: L.5000. Edizioni Internazionale Cioe s.r.l., Via G. Fabroni 24, 00191 Rome, Italy. TEL 39-6-3287309. Ed. Lamberto Antonelli. adv.: page L.8000000. circ. 46,065. **Document type:** consumer publication.

028.5 **SP**
SUPER POP. 1976. fortn. Publicaciones Ekdosis, S.A., Gran Via Carlos III, 124, 08034 Barcelona, Spain. TEL 34-3-2800088. FAX 34-3-2800837. Dir. Carmen Grasa. adv. contact: Merce Cano. circ. 206,524.
  Description: Covers music and cinema for young people (14-19 years old).

028.5 500 **US** **ISSN 1040-144X**
SUPER SCIENCE BLUE. 8/yr. $15. Scholastic Inc., 555 Broadway, New York, NY 10012-3999. TEL 212-343-6100; 800-325-6149. Ed. Kathy Burkett.
  —KR SourceOne; UMI.
  Description: Contains science and technology news and describes science experiments. Geared toward readers 9-12.

028.5 500 **US** **ISSN 1040-1431**
SUPER SCIENCE RED. 1990. 8/yr. $15. Scholastic Inc., 555 Broadway, New York, NY 10012-3999. TEL 212-343-6100; 800-325-6149. Ed. Fran Nankin.
  —UMI.
  Description: Contains science and technology news and discusses science experiments. Geared toward readers ages 5-8.

028.5 **US**
SUPERTEEN. 1977. bi-m. $11.95 (foreign $16.95). Sterling - Macfadden Partnership, 35 Wilbur St., Lynbrook, NY 14563. TEL 516-593-1220. FAX 516-593-0065. adv. **Document type:** consumer publication.
  Description: Provides news and gossip on stars in television, movies, and music. Includes contests, fashion, and service features and an advice column.

028.5 **US**
SUPERTEEN'S LOUDMOUTH.* 1975. m. $19. Sterling - Macfadden Partnership, 35 Wilbur St., Lynbrook, NY 11563. TEL 516-593-1220. adv. **Document type:** consumer publication.
  Description: Provides the teenage audience with news and gossip of music, movie and television stars. Includes advice columns, contests, fashion and service features.

SURE!; the English monthly magazine for you. see LINGUISTICS

028.5 **US** **ISSN 0890-3573**
SURPRISES; activities for today's kids & parents. 1985. bi-m. $14.95. The Publishing Group, Inc., 1200 N. 7th St., Minneapolis, MN 55411-4000. TEL 612-522-1200. FAX 612-522-1182. Ed. Helen Yarmoska. adv. contact: Helen Yarmoska. circ. 105,000. **Document type:** consumer publication.

SVARTVITT. see EDUCATION — Special Education And Rehabilitation

028.5 **AT** **ISSN 0727-4327**
SYDNEY FOR KIDS. 1982. biennial. Aus.$6.95. Universal Magazines Pty. Ltd., 64 Talavera Rd., Macquarie Park, N.S.W. 2113, Australia. TEL 02-805-0399. FAX 02-805-0714.
  —CCC.

499.992 **NE**
E J O - TUTMONDE. (Text in Esperanto) 1983. q. fl.20($11) (Tutmonda Esperantista Junulara Organizo) Universala Esperanto-Asocio, Nieuwe Binnenweg 176, 3015 BJ Rotterdam, Netherlands. TEL 31-10-4361044. FAX 31-10-4361751. E-mail: uea@inter.nl.net. Ed. Kalle Kniivila. bk.rev. circ. 1,000.

028.5 **CN** **ISSN 0843-4557**
T G - VOICES OF TODAY'S GENERATION. (Text in English, French) 1940. 6/yr. Can.$12($20) (effective 1994). Teen Generation Inc., 202 Cleveland St., Toronto, ON M4S 2W6, Canada. TEL 416-487-3204. Ed. Donna Douglas. adv.; bk.rev.; index. circ. 165,000. (also avail. in microfiche; back issues avail.) **Indexed:** Can.B.P.I., Can.Per.Ind., CMI.
  Former titles: Teen Generation; (until Dec.-Jan. 1977): Todays Generation (ISSN 0384-1405); Canadian High News (ISSN 0008-3747)
  Description: Covers music, fashion, careers, emotional growth issues, advice and empowerment.

028.5 **XV** **ISSN 0040-7712**
T I M; revija za tehnicno in znanstveno dejavnost mladine. (Text in Slovenian) 1963. m. 70 din. Tehniska Zalozba Slovenije, Lepi Pot 6, Ljubljana, Slovenia. Ed. Bozidar Grabnar.

028.5 375 **US**
T O W S. (The Online Write Stuff) 3/yr. E-mail: jpost@santacruz.k12.ca.us; URL: http://www.santacruz.k12.ca.us/~jpost/projects/tows/tows.html. Ed. Jory Post. **Document type:** newsletter.
  ●Available only online.

T V M S TIGER BEAT. see MOTION PICTURES

T V MAGAZINE. see COMMUNICATIONS — Television And Cable

028.5 **XO**
TABORTUZ. (Text in Hungarian) 24/yr. Smena Publishing House, Prazska 11, 812 84 Bratislava, Slovakia.

028.5 **ER** **ISSN 0134-2266**
TAHEKE. (Text in Estonian) 1960. m. Publishing House of the Tallinn, Parnu mnt. 67a, 200106 Tallinn, Estonia. TEL 681-495. (Subscr. to: Ajakirjanduslevi, Kreutzwaldi 12, 200100 Tallinn, Estonia) Ed. Elju Mardi. illus. circ. 20,000.
  Description: For children 3-10 years old.

028.5 **PK** **ISSN 0039-9175**
TALIM-O-TARBIAT. (Text in Urdu) 1941. m. Rs.515 in S. Asia & Middle East; Europe Rs.715; US & Canada Rs.735. Ferozsons Ltd., 60-Shara-e-Quaid-e-Azam, Lahore, Pakistan. FAX 92-42-305504. Ed. A. Salam; Pub. Zaheer Salam. bk.rev.; bibl. circ. 45,000.

TALKS AND TALES. see RELIGIONS AND THEOLOGY

028 **JA**
TANOSHII YOCHIEN. 1947. m. Kodansha Ltd., 12-21, Otowa, 2-chome, Bunkyo-ku, Tokyo 112, Japan. Ed. Yukio Shindo. illus. circ. 400,000.

028.5 **US** **ISSN 0882-5424**
TAPORI. 1974. bi-m. $10. Fourth World Movement, 7600 Willow Hill Dr., Landover, MD 20785-4658. TEL 301-336-9489. FAX 301-336-0092. E-mail: fourworl@his.com. Ed. Susan M. Devins. R&P contact: Susan M. Devins. illus. circ. 1,600. **Document type:** newsletter.
  Description: Brings together children from different backgrounds and allows them to show their concern for and solidarity with children who live in poverty.

028.5 **NE** **ISSN 0039-9604**
TAPTOE. 1920. fortn. fl.2 per no. L.C.G. Malmberg B.V., Leeghwaterlaan 16, 5223 BA 's-Hertogenbosch, Netherlands. FAX 31-73-210512. Ed. A. Bon. illus. circ. 120,000. **Document type:** consumer publication.
  Description: For ages 8-12.

028.5 **II**
TARGET. (Text in English) 1979. fortn. newsstand price: Rs.12. Living Media India Ltd., F-14-15 Competent House, Connaught Circus, New Delhi, 110001, India. TEL 91-11-3315801. FAX 91-11-3316180. TELEX 031-62634 INTO IN. Ed. Ameena Jayal. adv.: B&W page Rs.16000, color page Rs.32000; trim 191 x 273.

028.5 **AT**
TAS TOTS. 1988. 3/yr. Aus.$3 plus postage. Playgroup Association of Tasmania, 82 Hampden Rd., Battery Point, Tas. 7004, Australia. TEL 02-234814. adv.; bk.rev. circ. 1,100. (back issues avail.)
  Description: Covers child care, playgroups, and activities for children.

028.5 370 **NZ**
TE TARI PUNA ORA O AOTEAROA. ITIREAREA/NEW ZEALAND CHILDCARE ASSOCIATION. NEWSLETTER. (Text in English, Maori) 1990. bi-m. NZ.$60. New Zealand Childcare Association, P.O. Box 11-863, Wellington, New Zealand. Ed. Rose Cole. circ. 800. (also avail. in diskette format; back issues avail.) **Document type:** newsletter.

TEAM OF ADVOCATES FOR SPECIAL KIDS NEWSLETTER. see HANDICAPPED

028.5 600 372 **US**
▼**TECHNOLOGY AND CHILDREN.** 1996. 4/yr. $40 to non-members (foreign $50); members $20 (effective 1997). International Technology Education Association, 1914 Association Dr., Reston, VA 20191. TEL 703-860-2100. FAX 703-860-0353. E-mail: itea@iris.org; URL: http://www.iteawww.org. Ed. Kathleen Sheehan; Pub. Kendall Starkweather. adv. contact: Rich Smith.
  Description: Practical and innovative articles and activities to teach children about technology.

028.5 600 **US** **ISSN 1066-3428**
TECHNOSCENE. 1992. s-a. Technology Student Association, 1914 Association Dr., Reston, VA 22091. TEL 703-860-9000. FAX 703-620-4483. **Document type:** newsletter.
  Description: Covers technology for elementary school readers (grades K-2 and 3-5) in activity-based articles for use in the classroom.

028.5 **US** **ISSN 0040-2001**
TEEN. 1957. m. $13.95 (effective 1996). Petersen Publishing Co., 6420 Wilshire Blvd., Los Angeles, CA 90048. TEL 213-782-2000. Ed. Roxie Camron. adv.: B&W page $23865, color page $35800. bk.rev.; illus.; circ. 1,360,411 (paid). (also avail. in microform from UMI.) **Indexed:** Access, Jun.High.Mag.Abstr., Mag.Ind., PMR, PSI, R.G.Abstr., R.G., TOM. **Document type:** consumer publication.
  ●Also available online. Vendor(s): Information Access Co., Knight-Ridder Information, Inc.
  —KR SourceOne; UMI; UnCover.
  Description: For girls ages 13-18.

TEEN; your English monthly. see LINGUISTICS

052 **NR** **ISSN 0331-4502**
TEEN AND TWENTY; Africa's youth magazine. (Text in English) 1968. m. £N2. Teen Topics Publications, P.O. Box 14, Ikeja, Lagos State, Nigeria. Ed. Adeyola David. adv.; charts; illus. **Document type:** consumer publication.

780.42 **US** **ISSN 1056-0505**
TEEN BEAT ALLSTARS. bi-m. $14.95 (foreign $19.95). Sterling - Macfadden Partnership, 35 Wilbur St., Lynbrook, NY 11563. TEL 516-593-1220. FAX 516-593-0065. adv. **Document type:** consumer publication.

028.5 **US** **ISSN 0884-1675**
TEEN IDOL MANIA. 1985. 8/yr. $1.95 per no. Marvel Entertainment Group, 387 Park Ave. S., New York, NY 10016. **Document type:** consumer publication.

TEEN LIFE. see RELIGIONS AND THEOLOGY — Other Denominations And Sects

028.5 **US** **ISSN 0747-4695**
TEEN MACHINE. q. newsstand price: $2.95. Sterling - Macfadden Partnership, 233 Park Ave. S., New York, NY 10017. TEL 212-780-3500. FAX 212-780-3555. adv. **Document type:** consumer publication.
  Description: Provides news and gossip on music, movie and television personalities. Includes advice columns, contests, fashion and service features.

200 **US**
TEEN POWER;* a powerline paper. 1966. q. $9.95. Scripture Press Publications, Inc., 4050 Lee Vance View, Colorado Springs, CO 80918-7102. Ed. Amy J. Cox. (looseleaf format) **Document type:** newspaper.
  Former titles: Connect; Teen Power; Young Teen Power (ISSN 0044-0922).
  Description: Sunday school take-home paper for young readers ages 12-16.

028.5 **US**
TEEN SCENE. 1990. q. $24. Davis Lott, Ed. & Pub., Box 710, Santa Monica, CA 90406-0710. TEL 310-397-4217. adv.; bk.rev. circ. 10,000. **Document type:** consumer publication.

CHILDREN AND YOUTH — FOR

790 US
TEEN STAR ZINE; a newsletter for 10-18 year olds who love the performing arts. 1993. m. $5. 5863 Chevy Chase Pkwy., Box 22, Washington, DC 20015. Ed. Gina G. Young. R&P contact: Gina G. Young. adv.; illus.; music rev.; play rev. (also avail. in looseleaf format; back issues avail.) **Document type:** newsletter.

028.5087 US
TEEN TIME (LARGE PRINT EDITION). 8/yr. free. Lutheran Library for the Blind, 1333 S. Kirkwood Rd., St. Louis, MO 63122. TEL 800-433-3954. (also avail. in Braille; large print in 22 pt.)
Description: Inspirational articles and pen pal letters for young adults.

640 US ISSN 0735-6986
TEEN TIMES. 1945. q. $7 to non-members. Future Homemakers of America, Inc., 1910 Association Dr., Reston, VA 20191. TEL 703-476-4900. FAX 703-860-2713. URL: http://www.fhahero.org. Ed. Patti Frattarola; Pub. Alan T. Rains. adv. contact: Patti Frattarola. circ. 250,000 (paid). **Document type:** trade publication.
Description: Helps prepare students with skills they can use in everyday life. Articles cover issues such as peer pressure, nutrition and fitness, parenting, family relationships and career options.

TEEN VOICES. see *WOMEN'S INTERESTS*

051 US ISSN 1049-0183
TEENAGE MUTANT NINJA TURTLES MAGAZINE.* 1990. q. $7.80. Mirage Publishers, PO Box 486, Northhampton, MA 01061-0486.
Ed. Adam Philips. circ. 100,000.
Description: A forum for the superheros to defend and protect against the evil shredder and his clan.

200 US ISSN 0890-4006
TEENQUEST. Variant title: T Q Magazine. 1946. 10/yr. $16.50 (Canada $22) (effective 1996). Shepherd Ministries, 2221 Walnut Hill Ln., Irving, TX 75038-4410. TEL 214-580-8000. FAX 214-580-1329. E-mail: teenquest@aol.com. Ed. Christopher Lyon; Pub. Al Macdonald. R&P contact: Christopher Lyon. adv. contact: Barabara Macdonald. illus. circ. 35,000. **Document type:** consumer publication.
Formerly: Young Ambassador (ISSN 0044-071X)
Description: For Bible-believing Christian students seeking Christian fiction; articles on teen issues, and the latest in Christian music.

028.5 US
TEENS TODAY (KANSAS CITY, 1988).* 1988. 10/yr. Elbert Harris, Ed. & Pub., 4747 Troost Ave., Kansas City, MO 64110. TEL 816-931-8336. FAX 816-931-1096. adv. circ. 20,000.
Description: For, by and about teens. Covers education, health, sports, fashion, art, environment and psychology.

028.5 284 GW
TEENSMAG; Trends, Glaube, Action, Tiefgang. 1985. bi-m. 26 SFr. (effective 1997). Bundes Verlag GmbH, Bodenborn 43, 58452 Witten, Germany. TEL 49-2302-9309320. FAX 49-2302-9309310. E-mail: bv.witten@t-online.de; URL: http://www.jesus-online.de/bv/bv_home.htm. adv.; B&W page DM.1300, color page DM.2000; trim 188 x 258. circ. 20,000. (back issues avail.) **Document type:** bulletin.

TEKHNIKA MOLODEZHI. see *TECHNOLOGY: COMPREHENSIVE WORKS*

028.5 AT ISSN 1030-8768
TELL; the journal of the "breakthru generation". 1961. q. Aus.$10; newsstand price: Aus.$2.50. Fusion Australia Ltd., 688 Parramatta Rd., Croydon, N.S.W. 2132, Australia. TEL 61-2-716-8277. FAX 61-2-716-8237. E-mail: fusion@vision.net.au; URL: http://www.vision.net.au/~fusion.tell.htm. Ed. Mal Garvin. R&P contact: Dave Mitchell. TEL 61-3-63978280. adv. contact: Dave Mitchell. circ. 10,000. (back issues avail.)
Description: Examines current issues, music, films, and personalities from a Christian perspective.

028.5 US ISSN 1074-4606
TELL (NEW YORK). 1993. q. $1.95 per no. (N B C - T V) Hachette Filipacchi Magazines, Inc., 1633 Broadway, New York, NY 10009. TEL 212-767-6000. FAX 212-767-5619. adv.; illus. circ. 500,000. **Document type:** consumer publication.
Description: For teenagers. Ties in with TNBC programming schedule.

028.5 FR ISSN 0492-7958
TERRES LOINTAINES. 1955. 11/yr. 195 F. Enfance Missionnaire, 21-23 av. Aristide Briand, 92170 Vanves, France. TEL 41-10-21-60. FAX 49-09-00-03. circ. 75,000. (back issues avail.)
Description: For children ages 10-15, with news about different countries and people.

TEXAS F F A MAGAZINE. see *AGRICULTURE*

028.5 BR
TEZA. (Text in Burmese, English) 1965. m. Myawaddy Press, 181-3 Sule Pagoda Rd., Yangon, Union of Myanmar. circ. 29,500.
Description: Pictorial publication for children.

THEATRE ENFANCE ET JEUNESSE. see *THEATER*

028.5 VN
THIEU NIEN TIEN PHONG/YOUNG PIONEERS. w. 15 Ho Xuan Huong, Hanoi, Socialist Republic of Vietnam. TEL 64031. Ed. Le Tran. circ. 80,000.

811 US ISSN 0197-9302
THIS AND THAT. (Text in English, Russian) 1980. s-a. $8. (Gnosis Charitable Trust) Gnosis Press, Box 42, Prince St. Sta., New York, NY 10012. TEL 212-505-7190. Ed. Victoria Andreyeva. adv. circ. 1,000.

THRASHER. see *SPORTS AND GAMES*

028.5 VN
TIEN PHONG/VANGUARD. 1953. w. $110 (effective 1992). Ho Chi Minh Communist Youth Union, 15 Ho Xuan Huong, Hanoi, Socialist Republic of Vietnam. TEL 64031. Ed. Duong Xuan Nam. circ. 110,000.

028.5 VN
TIEN PHONG CHU NHAT/SUNDAY VANGUARD. 1988. w. Ho Chi Minh Communist Youth Union, 15 Ho Xuan Huong, Hanoi, Socialist Republic of Vietnam. TEL 64031. Ed. Duong Xuan Nam.

028.5 VN
TIEN PHONG CUOI THANG/MONTHLY VANGUARD. 1991. m. Ho Chi Minh Communist Youth Union, 15 Ho Xuan Huong, Hanoi, Socialist Republic of Vietnam. TEL 64031. Ed. Duong Xuan Nam.

028.5 GW ISSN 0342-3018
TIERFREUND; die Jugendzeitschrift fuer Tier-, Natur- und Umweltschutz. 1947. m. DM.42. Johann Michael Sailer Verlag GmbH, Auesserer-Laufer-Platz 22, 90403 Nuernberg, Germany. TEL 49-911-53961. Ed. Andrea Hoesel. bk.rev. circ. 180,000. (back issues avail.) **Document type:** bulletin.
Description: Information about nature, animals and environmental protection for children ages 9-15.

028.5 GW
TIGERMAEDCHEN; Geschichten und Gedichte von Maedchen. (Text in English, German and Turkish) 1984. q. DM.10. Bund Demokratische Pfadfinderinnen, Lasiuszeile 2, 13585 Berlin, Germany. TEL 030-3358393. Ed. Anje Tuckermann. adv.; bk.rev. circ. 600.

028.5 NE ISSN 0165-0890
TIKKER; literatuurmagazine voor het onderwijs. 1978. 3/yr. fl.33.75. WoltersgroepGroningen b.v. (Subsidiary of: Wolters Kluwer N.V.), Postbus 58, 9700 MB Groningen, Netherlands. TEL 31-50-5226524. FAX 31-50-5264866. illus.

028.5 US ISSN 1084-0168
▼**TIME FOR KIDS**. Short title: T F K. 1995. w. $3.95. Time Inc. (Subsidiary of: Time Warner, Inc.), Time & Life Bldg., Rockefeller Center, 1271 Ave. of the Americas, New York, NY 10020-1393. TEL 212-522-8743. FAX 212-522-4799. E-mail: tfk@time.com. Ed. Claudia Wallis; Pub. Lisa Quiroz. R&P contact: Marion Powers. TEL 212-522-2587. **Document type:** consumer publication.

900 028.5 US ISSN 1087-6847 E178.3
▼**TIME MACHINE**; the American history magazine for kids. 1996. bi-m. $24 (foreign $32) (effective 1997); newsstand price: $3. (Smithsonian Institution, National Museum of American History) American Historical Publications, 29 W. 38th St., New York, NY 10018. TEL 212-398-1550. FAX 212-840-6790. E-mail: tmachine@inx.net. (Subscr. to: Box 2879, Clifton, NJ 07015-9611. TEL 800-742-5401) Ed. Tamara Glenny; Pub. Byron Hollinshead. R&P contact: Helena deChappe. illus. **Document type:** consumer publication.
Description: Covers history and historical subjects for readers aged 9 to 14.

808.836 II
TINKLE. (Editions in Assamese, English) 1980. fortn. Rs.725. India Book House Ltd., Fleet Bldg., 1st Fl., M V Rd., Marol Naa, Andheri (E), Mumbai 400 059, India. TEL 91-22-2610216. FAX 91-22-8500645. TELEX 011-86297 DANI IN. Ed. Anant Pai. adv.: B&W page Rs.14000, color page Rs.17000; adv. contact: Richardo Furtado. circ. 82,500. (also avail. in microfilm) **Document type:** consumer publication.
Description: Entertains and educates using the comics medium.

028.5 053.5 SZ
TOASTER. 1971. m. 30 SFr. Postfach 2050, CH-8035 Zurich, Switzerland. TEL 43-1-3636678. FAX 43-1-3635354. E-mail: toaster@music.ch; URL: http://www.music.ch/toaster. Eds. Esther Banz, Didi Mueller. adv.; bk.rev. circ. 13,000. (back issues avail.) **Document type:** consumer publication.

028.5 UK ISSN 0040-8360
TODAY (KENT).* 1966. q. 25p. Pollyhaugh Press Ltd., Nealhampton House, Speldhurst, Tunbridge Wells, Kent, England. Ed. Jonathan Michael Barker. bk.rev.; abstr.; bibl.; illus. circ. 15,000.
Formerly: Today's Topic.

TODAY (LAWSON); family magazine. see *RELIGIONS AND THEOLOGY — Protestant*

028.5 420 375.4 FR ISSN 1154-5992
TODAY IN ENGLISH. 1991. 11/yr. 378 F. includes four tapes (EU 459 F.; elsewhere 499 F.) (effective 1997). Bayard Presse, 3 rue Bayard, 75393 Paris Cedex 08, France. TEL 33-1-44356060. FAX 33-1-44356091. TELEX 648 094 F. (Subscr. to: Bayard Presse International, B.P. 12, 99505 Paris Entreprises, France. TEL 33-1-44216000. FAX 33-3-20274192) Ed. Nathalie Becht. circ. 50,852.
Description: Helps students 15 and older to improve their English.

028.5 372.21 AT
TODDLERS & PRESCHOOLERS. 1992. a. Aus.$5.95 (foreign Aus.$9.50). Magazine House Pty. Ltd., P.O Box 1067, Crows Nest, N.S.W. 2065, Australia. TEL 61-2-94382399. FAX 61-2-94363014. Ed. Carol Fallows. **Document type:** consumer publication.
Formerly: My Preschooler.

TOKTOKKIE. see *CONSERVATION*

808.836 FI ISSN 0357-6493
TOM & JERRY. 1980. m. FIM 99. Yhtyneet Kuvalehdet Oy - United Magazines Ltd., Maistraatinportti 1, FIN-00240 Helsinki, Finland. TEL 358-0-156-6524. FAX 358-0-156-6505. Ed. Hannele Willberg. adv.: B&W page FIM 1950, color page FIM 5300; trim 170 x 260; adv. contact: Eeva Siukosaari. circ. 10,230. **Document type:** consumer publication.

268 IS ISSN 0040-912X
TOM THUMB; a magazine for the young Jewish child. (Text in English) 1960. m. $26. Etzb'oni Publishing House, P.O. Box 28110, Tel Aviv 61280, Israel. FAX 972-5-5373906. Ed. Michael Shir. adv.; bk.rev.; illus. circ. 35,000.

CHILDREN AND YOUTH — FOR

028.5   IT
▼**TOMORROW PEOPLE NEWS**; European magazine for young people. (Text in English, Italian) 1995. bi-m. L.30000($20) (effective Jan. 1996). European Network for Information and International Cooperation, Via Col. Romej 7, 91100 Trapani, Italy. TEL 39-923-546700. Eds. Pietro Vento, Maria Sabrina Titone. adv.: page L.5000000; adv. contact: Maria Sabrina Titone. film rev., software rev.; illus.; stat.; index. circ. 10,000. (also avail. in diskette format; back issues avail.) Document type: newspaper.
●Also available on CD-ROM.
    Description: Presents information on European topics of interest to young people.

051   US   ISSN 1068-865X
TOMORROW'S MORNING; news stories for kids. (Supplement avail.: Tomorrow's Morning Classroom Edition (ISSN 1085-0821)) 1992. w. Tomorrow's Morning, Inc., 160 N. Thurston Ave., Los Angeles, CA 90049. TEL 310-440-2778; 800-607-4410. FAX 310-476-6406. E-mail: tomorrow@morning.com; URL: http://morning.com. (Subscr. to: Box 388, Vandalia, OH 45377; Alt. addr.: 200 Hudson St., N.Y., NY 10013. TEL 212-966-3200. FAX 212-966-3001) Ed. Adam Linter; Pub. Adam Linter. bk.rev.; film rev.; play rev.; video rev.; music rev.; illus. (tabloid format; back issues avail.) Document type: newspaper.
●Also available online. Vendor(s): CompuServe, Inc.
    Description: Contains news stories written for childrent ages 6 to 12. Includes articles about the arts, science, society, and sports as well as national and international news.

051 375   US   ISSN 1085-0821
TOMORROW'S MORNING CLASSROOM EDITION; born to read. (Supplement to: Tomorrow's Morning (ISSN 1068-865X)) 1996. bi-w. (Oct.-Apr.), m. (Sept.-May). $16.17 ($6.95 for 10 or more subs.) (effective 1996). Tomorrow's Morning, Inc., 160 N. Thurston Ave., Los Angeles, CA 90049. TEL 310-440-2778; 800-607-4410. FAX 610-476-6406. E-mail: tomorrow@morning.com; URL: http://morning.com. (Subscr. to: Box 388, Vandalia, OH 45377; Alt addr.: 200 Hudson St., N.Y., NY 10013. TEL 212-966-3200. FAX 212-966-3001) Ed. Adam Linter; Pub. Adam Linter. bk.rev.; film rev.; play rev.; video rev.; music rev.; illus.; circ. 10,000 (paid). (tabloid format; back issues avail.) Document type: newspaper.
●Also available online. Vendor(s): CompuServe, Inc.
    Description: Contains news and stories written for elementary school students. Aims to educate children and help teachers put current events into the curriculum.

028.5   CC
ONGHUA YU CHUANSHUO/FAIRY TALES AND LEGENDS. (Text in Chinese) bi-m. Y2 per no. Zhongguo Minjian Wenyijia Xiehui, Shanxi Fenhui - China Folk Artists' Association, Shanxi Chapter, 62 Yingze Dajie, Taiyuan, Shanxi 030001, People's Republic of China. TEL 4048712. Ed. Li Weijia.

028.5 790.13   GW
OP (BENNINGEN). 1980. q. free. Publikum Verlag GmbH, Otto-Hahn-Str. 10, 71726 Benningen, Germany. TEL 07144-18002. circ. 5,000. (back issues avail.)
    Formerly: Schooltime.

OP GEAR; discipleship studies for youth. see RELIGIONS AND THEOLOGY — Protestant

028.5   AU
OPIC; das junge Magazin. 1988. m. S.170 (foreign S.280). (Austrian Youth Red Cross) Kinderzeitung Zeitschriften Verlagsgesellschaft mbH, Hohenstaufengasse 5, A-1010 Vienna, Austria. TEL 43-1-535-5783. FAX 43-1-535-578375. E-mail: topic@netway.at. (Subscr. to: Oesterreichischer Buchklub der Jugend, Mayerhofgasse 6, A-1040 Vienna, Austria) Ed. Thomas Aistleitner. adv.; bk.rev. circ. 120,000. Document type: bulletin.
    Formerly: Klex - Das Junge Magazin.

808.836   IT   ISSN 1120-611X
OPOLINO. 1949. w. L.95680. Arnoldo Mondadori Editore S.p.A., Casella Postale 1833, 20101 Milan, Italy. Ed. Gaudenzio Capelli. adv.: color page L.22000000. circ. 471,971.

RTOISE; the conservation magazine. see ENVIRONMENTAL STUDIES

331.8   NE   ISSN 0929-0214
TOT & MET. 1947. 10/yr. fl.22.50. Christelijk Nationaal Vakverbond (C.N.V.), Postbus 2475, 3500 GL Utrecht, Netherlands. TEL 31-30-2913715. FAX 31-30-2964907. Ed. K. Rijlaarsdam. adv.; bk.rev.; illus. circ. 2,000. (tabloid format)
    Former titles (until 1992): Splinter (ISSN 0169-3921); (until 1985): Warempel (ISSN 0166-5391); Jonge Handen (ISSN 0021-7379)
    Description: Provides information on sports, cultural events, studies, labor, and the environment. Includes interviews for young people.

A TOT OF ENGLISH; your English monthly. see LINGUISTICS

TOUCH. see RELIGIONS AND THEOLOGY — Protestant

028.5 910.09   IT
TOURING GIOVANI. 7/yr. membership. (Touring Club Italiano) Touring Periodici s.r.l., Corso Italia 10, Milan, Italy. TEL 02-852673. FAX 02-58300315. TELEX 312476 TCIADM. Ed. Giuseppe Bozzini. adv. circ. 55,000.

028.5   UK   ISSN 0968-6940
TOYBOX. 1993. m. £15 (Europe & Ireland £25; elsewhere £30) (effective 1996). B B C Worldwide Publishing, Broadcasting House, Whiteladies Rd., Bristol GS8 2LR, England. TEL 44-181-576-2000. FAX 44-181-576-2931. (Subscr. to: P.O. Box 425, Woking, Surrey GU21 1GP, England. TEL 44-1483-733716. FAX 44-1483-756792) Document type: consumer publication.

028.5 910   US
▼**TRAILBLAZERS OF THE WILD WEST**. 1995. irreg. $89.70. Enslow Publishers, Inc., 44 Fadem Rd., Box 699, Springfield, NJ 07081-0699. TEL 201-379-8890. FAX 201-379-7940. E-mail: annette@enslow.com; URL: http://www.enslow.com. Ed. Brian D. Enslow; Pub. Annette Noce. R&P contact: Annette Noce.
    Description: Book series for young readers. Each book captures the experiences of one group who helped tame the frontier in American history.

028.5   GW   ISSN 0177-4719
TREFF - SCHUELERMAGAZIN. 1974. m. DM.53.40 (foreign DM.60). Velber Verlag GmbH, Im Brande 15c, 30926 Seelze, Germany. TEL 0511-40003-0. FAX 0511-4000370. Ed. Detlef Kersten. adv. contact: Bernd Sandvoss. circ. 190,516. Document type: academic/scholarly publication, consumer publication.

TREFFPUNKT JUGENDPRESSE. see JOURNALISM

028.5   SZ
TREFLE/KIM. (Text in French and German) 1920. 9/yr. 28 SFr.($20) Pfadibewegung Schweiz - Mouvement Scout de Suisse, P.O. Box, CH-3000 Bern 7, Switzerland. TEL 031-3110545. FAX 031-3119828. adv.; bk.rev.; charts; illus.; index. circ. 6,000.
    Former titles (until 1986): Kim; Kim - Trefle (ISSN 0023-141X)

649   BE   ISSN 0041-2279
TREMPLIN. (Text in French) 1960. w. 1450 BEF (in Europe 2080 BEF; elsewhere 2320 BEF) (effective 1997-98). Editions G.P. Averbode, B.P. 54, B-3271 Averbode, Belgium. TEL 32-13-780111. FAX 32-13-776837. Ed. Jan Lembrechts.
    Description: For young people, ages 10-12.

TREND DISCOTEC. see MUSIC

028.5   SP
TRETZEVENTS; l'infantil. (Text in Catalan) 1963. s-m. 4200 ptas. (Europe 6400 ptas.; elsewhere $70) (effective 1994). Publicacions de l' Abadia de Montserrat, Ausias March 92-98, Apdo. 244, 08013 Barcelona, Spain. Ed. Miguel Sayrach. illus. circ. 6,000.
    Formerly (until 1973): Infantil.

TRIANGLE. see TRAVEL AND TOURISM

370   VE   ISSN 0041-2902
TRICOLOR;* revista Venezolana para los ninos. 1950. 9/yr. free. Ministerio de Educacion, Ministerio de Relaciones Exteriores, Direccion de Relaciones Culturales, Caracas, Venezuela. Ed. Jose Quiaragua. illus.; index. circ. 150,000.

TRY IT YOURSELF HAIR; for Black teens. see BEAUTY CULTURE

028.5 790.1 780   US   ISSN 1044-954X
TUCSON TEEN. Variant title: Teen On-Line. (Print edition ceased 1994.) 1977. fortn. Southwest Alternatives Institute, Inc., Box 3355, Tucson, AZ 85722-3355. TEL 520-623-3733. FAX 520-623-3733. E-mail: teens@emol.org; URL: http://emol.org/emol/tucsonteen/. Pub. Robert E. Zucker. adv.: page $399; adv. contact: Robert Laver. bk.rev.; film rev.; music rev.; software rev.; tele.rev.; illus.; mkt.; index. circ. 5,000. (back issues avail.) Document type: consumer publication.
●Available only online.
    Description: Provides information, listings of events and internet connections for teenagers.

028.5   US   ISSN 0191-3654
TURTLE; magazine for preschool kids. 1979. 8/yr. $16.95 (foreign $23.95). (Benjamin Franklin Literary and Medical Society, Inc.) Children's Better Health Institute, Box 567, 1100 Waterway Blvd., Indianapolis, IN 46202. TEL 317-636-8881. FAX 317-684-8094. (Subscr. to: Box 420235, Palm Coast, FL 32142. TEL 904-447-0818) Ed. Dr. Cory ServVaas; Pub. Greg Joray. R&P contact: Sandy Grieshop. adv.: color page $7000; trim 7 5/8 x 10 1/8; adv. contact: Todd Seifferlein. bk.rev.; video rev. circ. 370,000. (back issues avail.) Document type: consumer publication.
    Description: For children ages 2-5 with an emphasis on health and safety.

028.5   MX
TUS ROLLOS. 1993. m. Mex.$6 per no. Editorial Jakan, S.A. de C.V., Patricio Sanz 1445, Col. Del Valle 03100 Mexico DF, Mexico. TEL 575-90-09. (Co-publisher: Magno Central de Publicaciones, S.A. de C.V.) Dir. Jorge Planella Gil. adv.; bk.rev. Document type: consumer publication.
    Description: Covers music, video games, health and beauty, food, toys and crafts, current events and social issues, and celebrities.

028.5   US   ISSN 1056-2567
TUTTI FRUTTI. 9/yr. $19. Jimmijack Publishing Co., Box 1308, West Babylon, NY 11704. TEL 516-586-4587. FAX 516-516-4587. Ed. Bonnie Geraldi. illus.
    Description: For the typical teen fan magazine reader.

TUTTI INSIEME; il mensile per il tuo italiano. see LINGUISTICS

TUTTO DISCOTECA DANCE. see MUSIC

028.5 296   US   ISSN 1062-8711
TZIVOS HASHEM CHILDREN'S NEWSLETTER. 1981. 5/yr. $5 to non-members. Tzivos Hashem, 332 Kingston Ave., Brooklyn, NY 11213. TEL 718-467-6630. FAX 718-467-8527. E-mail: tzivos-h@chl.chabad.org; URL: http://www.tzivos-hashem.org. Ed. David S. Pape. bk.rev. circ. 130,000. Document type: newsletter.
    Description: Contains stories, contests and activities that teach about Jewish holidays and good behavior. Children submit pictures of themselves and write about their interests and family.

028.5   US   ISSN 0895-9471
U S KIDS. 1987. 8/yr. $21.95 (foreign $27.95). (Benjamin Franklin Literary and Medical Society, Inc.) Children's Better Health Institute, 1100 Waterway Blvd., Box 567, Indianapolis, IN 46202. TEL 317-636-8881. FAX 317-684-8094. (Subscr. to: Box 420235, Palm Coast, FL 32142. TEL 904-447-0818) Ed. Dr. Cory ServVaas; Pub. Greg Joray. R&P contact: Jeff Ayers. adv.: color page $5950; trim 8 x 10 7/8; adv. contact: Todd Seifferlein. circ. 250,000. (back issues avail.) Indexed: Ind.Child.Mag. Document type: consumer publication.
—KR SourceOne.
    Description: Publishes true-life stories and articles promoting sports, health and safety for children ages 5-10.

U S Y S A NATIONAL DIRECTORY. (United States Youth Soccer Association, Inc.) see SPORTS AND GAMES — Ball Games

U S Y S A NETWORK. (United States Youth Soccer Association, Inc.) see SPORTS AND GAMES — Ball Games

CHILDREN AND YOUTH — FOR

028.5 370. 371.3   YU   ISSN 0352-2253
UCITELJ/TEACHER. (Text in Serbian) 1983. q. 250 din.($15) to individuals; institutions 500 din.($30). Savez Ucitelja Srbije - Association of Teacher's in Serbia, Mose Pijade 6-III, Postanski Fah 628, 11000 Belgrade, Yugoslavia. TEL 011 683-675. adv.; bk.rev. circ. 4,000.

028.5   XO
UJ IFJUSAG. (Text in Hungarian) w. Smena Publishing House, Prazska 11, 812 84 Bratislava, Slovakia.

331.702   DK   ISSN 0107-7783
UNGDOMSKALENDER; ideer til aaret skolen. 1983. a. DKK 162.50 (effective 1997). Ole Camaae, Ed. & Pub., Lerbjergstien 18, DK-3460 Birkeroed, Denmark. TEL 45-48-17-62-82. FAX 45-48-17-78-80. adv.; bk.rev.; illus. circ. 2,300.

369.4   GW
UNTERWEGS (LEVERKUSEN). 1948. q. DM.16. Pfadfinderinnenschaft St. Georg, Unstrutstr. 10, 51371 Leverkusen, Germany. TEL 0214-23015. Ed. Cornelia Inkmann. bk.rev.; bibl. circ. 9,500.
Document type: newsletter.
Former titles: Doch; Dienen und Fuehren (ISSN 0012-2564)

028.5   SA   ISSN 0257-8697
UPBEAT; the youth magazine for all. 1981. 11/yr. R.22 (overseas R.65). S A C H E D, Allied Building, 236 Bree St., Johannesburg 2001, South Africa. TEL 011-333-9746. FAX 011-333-2297. (Subscr. to: P.O. Box 11350, Johannesburg 2000, South Africa) Ed. Harriet Perlman. adv. contact: Barbara Shaffer. illus. circ. 63,000. (back issues avail.)
Document type: consumer publication.
Description: Educational magazine for youth and teachers in South Africa. Main purpose is to upgrade English skills and encourage reading.

VAMOS; tu revista en espanol. see *LINGUISTICS*

VANCOUVER MAGAZINE. see *LEISURE AND RECREATION*

028.5   GW   ISSN 0934-8786
VANESSAS ZEITGEIST. 1987. q. DM.5($5) Oldenburger Str. 13a, 46149 Oberhausen, Germany. TEL 0208-669872. Ed. Marc Mulia. adv.; bk.rev. circ. 5,000. (back issues avail.)

028.5   XO
VCIELKA. 24/yr. Smena Publishing House, Prazska 11, 812 84 Bratislava, Slovakia.

028.5   XR   ISSN 1210-0897
VEDA, TECHNIKA A MY/SCIENCE, TECHNOLOGY AND WE. 1946. 12/yr. 156 Kc. Mlada Fronta, Radlicka 61, 150 02 Prague 5, Czech Republic. TEL 54-49-41. FAX 54-51-82. TELEX 123302. (Dist. by: PNS, Kafkova 19, 160000 Prague 6, Czech Republic) Ed. Z. Bares. adv.; bk.rev. circ. 35,700.
Former titles (until 1990): Veda a Tachnika Mlodezi (ISSN 0322-9017); (until 1954): Mlady Technik.
Description: Tells its readers about the latest trends of development in science and technology, popularizes leading experts in these spheres, inspires creative thinking, deepens young people's self-education and helps them to choose their field of study and profession.

011.62   NO   ISSN 0802-1147
VEILEDENDE LISTE FOR BARNE- OG UNGDOMSLITTERATUR; utvalg av boeker utkommet i (year). 1967. a. free. Statens Bibliotekstilsyn - Norwegian Directorate for Public Libraries, P.O. Box 8145 DEP, N-0033 Oslo, Norway. TEL 47-22-83-25-85. FAX 47-22-83-15-52. E-mail: sb@bibtils.no. Ed. Elin Thomsen. bk.rev. circ. 7,000. (back issues avail.) **Document type:** abstracting/indexing, academic/scholarly publication.
Former titles (until 1985): Barne- og Ungdomslitteratur (ISSN 0800-5923); (until 1983): Utvalg for Skolebibliotekar av Boeker Utkommet i (Year) (ISSN 0302-8968); (until 1973): Boeker for Skoleboksamlinger (ISSN 0332-7922)
Description: Presents an annotated booklist of recommended literature for children and young adults.

VERDETA; le grande moda dei bambini. see *CLOTHING TRADE*

028.5 369.4   XO
VESELKA. 24/yr. Smena Publishing House, Prazska 11, 812 84 Bratislava, Slovakia.

028.5   RU   ISSN 0320-8044
VESELYE KARTINKI; detskii yumoristicheskii zhurnal. 1956. m. $36 (effective 1998). Novodmitrovskaya ul. 5A, 125015 Moscow, Russia. TEL 7-095-2858894. FAX 7-095-2857274. (Dist. by: Mezhdunarodnaya Kniga, B. Yakimanka 39, 117049 Moscow, Russia. TEL 7-095-2384967. FAX 7-095-2384634; Dist. in U.S. by: Victor Kamkin Inc., 4956 Boiling Brook Pkwy, Rockville, MD 20852. TEL 301-881-5973) Ed. R.A. Varshamov. adv.; bk.rev.; illus. circ. 500,000.

028.5   AU
VETO - OESTERREICHS JUGENDMAGAZIN. 1983. bi-m. S.40. Taubstummengasse 5-16, A-1040 Vienna, Austria. TEL 01-4065840. FAX 01-4065833. Ed. Michael Schinogel. adv.; bk.rev. (back issues avail.)
Document type: bulletin.
Formerly (until 1994): Oesterreichisches Schuelerblatt.

VEZETOK LAPJA/BULLETIN OF HUNGARIAN SCOUT LEADERS AND PARENTS. see *CLUBS*

028.5   BL
VIDA INFANTIL. m. Carlos Goncalves Fidalgo, Ed. & Pub., Rua Riachuelo 414, Rio de Janeiro GB, Brazil.

028.5   BL
VIDA JUVENIL. m. Carlos Goncalves Fidalgo, Ed. & Pub., Rua Riachuelo 414, Rio de Janeiro GB, Brazil.

028.5 059.959   VN   ISSN 0049-6375
VIETNAM YOUTH. French edition: Jeunesse du Vietnam. irreg. (Vietnam Youth Federation) Vietnam National Union of Students, 64 Ba Trieu St., Hanoi, Socialist Republic of Vietnam. illus.

028.5   JA
VIEWS. (Text in Japanese) 1982. s-m. Kodansha Ltd., 12-21 Otowa 2-chome, Bunkyo-ku, Tokyo 112, Japan. TEL 03-5395-3443. FAX 03-3943-7815. TELEX J34509 KODANSHA. Ed. Makoto Sugawa. circ. 150,000. **Document type:** consumer publication.
Formerly (until 1992): Scholar.
Description: Variety magazine for young men.

371.3   II
VIJAYAVEEDHI. (Text in Malayalam) 1994. w. newsstand price: Rs.3. Malayala Manorama Co. Ltd., P.O. Box 26, Kottayam 686 001, Kerala, India. TEL 91-481-563646. FAX 91-481-562479. TELEX 0888-201-MNR IN. Ed. K.M. Mathew; Pub. Jacob Mathew. adv.; B&W page Rs.6000. circ. 63,000.

VITA DELL'INFANZIA. see *EDUCATION*

VITA E SALUTE JUNIOR; rivista mensile per ragazzi che vogliono crescere e capire. see *PHYSICAL FITNESS AND HYGIENE*

028.5   BE   ISSN 0773-1027
VLAAMSE FILMPJES. (Text in Dutch) 1930. w. 1540 BEF (in Europe 2170 BEF; elsewhere 2380 BEF) (effective 1997-98). Uitgeverij G.P. Averbode, P.B. 54, B-3271 Averbode, Belgium. TEL 32-13-780111. FAX 32-13-776837. Ed. Theo Lenaerts.
Description: For ages 10-14.

370.19   RU   ISSN 0869-1169
VMESTE/TOGETHER. (Text in English and Russian) bi-m. 18000 Rub. Ostuzheva ul., 16-2, 103001 Moscow, Russia. TEL 7-095-2023573. FAX 7-095-2996732. E-mail: cnit@mirea.ac.ru. (Subscr. addr.: Mashala Zhukova ul., 4, 122837 Moscow, Russia. TEL 7-095-1952275) Ed. Ludmila Annenkova. adv.; page $615. (back issues avail.)
Description: Written by teenages about themselves and the world.

028.5   US   ISSN 0042-8256
E148.S65
VOICE OF YOUTH. (Text in English and Slovenian) 1922. m. membership. Slovene National Benefit Society, 247 W. Allegheny Rd., Imperial, PA 15126-9774. TEL 412-695-1100; 800-445-2693. FAX 412-695-1555. Ed. Jay Sedmak. R&P contact: Jay Sedmak. bk.rev.; bibl. circ. 4,000.

VOILA LE FRANCAIS. see *LINGUISTICS*

028.5   RU   ISSN 0321-0669
G1
VOKRUG SVETA. (Supplement avail.: Iskatel (ISSN 0130-6634))) 1861. m. $66 (effective 1998). Izdatel'stvo Vokrug Sveta, Novodmitrovskaya ul. 5A, kom. 1607, 125015 Moscow, Russia. TEL 7-095-2858058. FAX 7-095-2850930. (Dist. by: Mezhdunarodnaya Kniga, B. Yakimanka 39, 117049 Moscow, Russia. TEL 7-095-2384967. FAX 7-095-2384634; Dist. in U.S. by: Kamkin Inc., 4956 Bioling Brook Pkwy, Rockville, MD 20852. TEL 301-881-5973) Ed. A.A. Poleshchuk. adv.; bk.rev.; illus.; index. circ. 210,000.

028.5   GW   ISSN 0936-9686
VORHANG AUF; Zeitschrift fuer Kinder und Eltern. 1989. q. DM.43 (effective 1997). Waldow Verlag, Rotkreuzstr. 2, 87488 Betzigau, Germany. TEL 49-831-770209. FAX 49-831-770390. Ed. Eckehard Waldow. adv.: page DM.1800. (back issues avail.) **Document type:** consumer publication.

VRIEND. see *HANDICAPPED — Hearing Impaired*

369.4   DK   ISSN 0049-8033
W A Y FORUM. (Text in English) 1953. q. $30. World Assembly of Youth, Ved Bella Hoej 4, DK-2700 Broenshoej, Denmark. TEL 45-38-60-77-70. FAX 45-38-60-57-97. Ed. Datuk Ali Rustam. R&P contact: Datuk Ali Rustam. adv. contact: Ali Rustam. bk.rev.; illus. circ. 20,000. **Document type:** newsletter.
Description: Highlights youth-related issues from all over the world.

369.4 320.5   HU   ISSN 0049-8076
W F D Y NEWS. (Editions in English and Spanish) 1972. bi-m. $4. World Federation of Democratic Youth, XIII, Frangepan u. 16, P.O. Box 147, 1389 Budapest, Hungary. TEL 36-1-3443830. Ed. Mun Chol. adv. contact: Halim Awad. circ. 2,000.

059.927 028.5   TS
AL-WA'I. 1983. m. exchange basis. Daba Sports Club, Cultural Group - Nadi Daba al-Riyadi, Al-Lajnah al-Thiqafiyyah, P.O. Box 12002, Fujairah, United Arab Emirates. TEL 44216. Ed. Abdullah Said Rashid. circ. 500.
Description: Covers cultural and Islamic topics of interest to young people in the U.A.E.

333.7 028.5   FR   ISSN 0998-2221
WAKOU; pour les petits curieux de nature. m. 300 F. Milan Presse, B.P. 82, 31150 Fenouillet, France. TEL 61-76-64-11. FAX 61-76-65-67.
Description: For children 3 to 7 years old who are interested in nature.

028.5   GW
WALT DISNEY'S DONALD DUCK. 1974. m. Ehapa Verlag GmbH, Im Riedenberg 54, 70771 Leinfelden-Echterdingen, Germany. Ed. Peter Schlecht. illus. circ. 180,000. (back issues avail.)
Document type: consumer publication.

028.5   GW
WALT DISNEY'S LUSTIGES TASCHENBUCH. 1967. 12/yr. DM.81.60 (effective 1997). Ehapa Verlag GmbH, Im Riedenberg 54, 70771 Stetten, Germany. TEL 49-711-79711. FAX 49-711-7971239. Ed. Harald Faalbach. illus. circ. 250,000. (back issues avail.) **Document type:** consumer publication.

028.5   GW
WALT DISNEY'S MICKY MAUS. 1951. w. (Thu.). DM.156; newsstand price: DM.3. Egmont Ehapa Verlag GmbH, Im Riedenberg 54, 70771 Leinfelden-Echterdingen, Germany. TEL 49-711-79711. FAX 49-711-7971239. (Subscr. to: Vertriebsservice Egmont Ehapa Verlag, Postfach 810640, 70523 Stuttgart, Germany. TE 49-711-7252225. FAX 49-7252333) Ed. Susan Pohlmann. adv.: page DM.38200; adv. contact: Ol Hansen. illus.; film rev. circ. 1,039,955. (back issues avail.) **Document type:** consumer publication.

028.5   CC   ISSN 1003-4013
WANPI WAWA/NAUGHTY BABY. (Text in Chinese) 198 m. Y1.50 per no. Sichuan Shaonian Ertong Chubanshe, 3, Yandao Jie, Chengdu, Sichuan 610016, People's Republic of China. TEL 660232 FAX 028-660320. TELEX 600324 SJCPH CN. Ed Wang Jitong.

333.7 028.5   FR
WAPITI; un oeil fute sur la nature. m. 300 F. Milan Press, B.P. 82, 31150 Fenoiullet, France. TEL 61-76-64-11. FAX 61-76-65-67.
   Description: For children 7 to 13 years old who are interested in nature.

028.5   UK   ISSN 0307-3459
WARLORD. 1974. w. D.C. Thomson & Co. Ltd., Albert Square, Dundee DD1 9QJ, Scotland.

WARP; the surf - skate - snow experience. see SPORTS AND GAMES — Outdoor Life

028.5   CN
WATCH MAGAZINE. 1992. m. Can.$29.95. Watch Magazines Inc., 245-401 Richmond St. W., Toronto, ON M5V 1X3, Canada. TEL 416-595-1313. FAX 416-595-1312. Ed. Paul Andersen; Pub. Doug Stewart. R&P contact: Paul Andersen. adv.: B&W page Can.$2475, color page Can.$2975; trim 10 1/2 x 11; adv. contact: Doug Stewart. bk.rev.; music rev, software rev.; circ. 75,000 (controlled). (tabloid format) Document type: consumer publication.
   Description: For youth ages 13-19.
   Refereed Serial

WATERWAYS; poetry in the mainstream. see LITERATURE — Poetry

028.5   CC
WAWA HUABAO/ILLUSTRATED PERIODICAL FOR KINDERGARTENERS. (Text in Chinese) 1981. m. $24. Shaonian Ertong Chubanshe - Juvenile & Children Publishing House, 1538 Yan'an Xilu, Shanghai 200052, People's Republic of China. TEL 86-21-6282-3025. FAX 86-21-6282-1726. (Dist. in US by: China Books & Periodicals, Inc., 2929 24th St., San Francisco, CA 94110. TEL 415-282-2994) Ed. Hong Zunian. illus. Document type: consumer publication.
   Description: Contains stories, fairy tales, and poems for children under five years old.

028.5   GW
WE ARE ONE WORLD. Abbreviated title: W A O W. 1991. a. free. Kindernothilfe e.V., Duesseldorfer Landstr. 180, 47249 Duisburg, Germany. TEL 49-203-7789-0. FAX 49-203-7789118. circ. 14,000. Document type: academic/scholarly publication.

028.5   US   ISSN 1088-985X
▼**WEBINK**. 1996. bi-m. $19.95. Internet Public Library, 4029 SEB, 610 E. University, University of Michigan, Ann Arbor, MI 48109-1259. E-mail: subscriptions@ipl.org; URL: http://www.ipl.org/weblink. adv.; illus.
   Description: Includes timely articles related to the Internet on topics of interest to children ages 7 to 13.

028.5   GW
WECKER (HAMBURG); Schuelerzeitung der Hansaschule. 1955. s-a. $3. Hermann-Distel-Str. 25, 21029 Hamburg, Germany. TEL 040-72550-0. adv.; bk.rev. circ. 1,200. (back issues avail.)

WEE LAMBS. see RELIGIONS AND THEOLOGY

WEEKLY BIBLE READER. see RELIGIONS AND THEOLOGY

028.5   US   ISSN 0890-3166
WEEKLY READER, EDITION K.* 1959. w. (28/yr. during school yr.). $24.95 for single subscr. (effective 1997-1998). Weekly Reader Corporation, Box 120023, Stamford, CT 06912-0023. TEL 800-446-3355. FAX 609-786-3360. (Subscr. to: 3000 Cindel Dr., Delran, NJ 08075) Ed. Sandra Maccarone; Pub. Richard J. Le Brasseur. R&P contact: Shirley Peterson. illus.; circ. 997,435 (paid). (also avail. in microfilm from UMI; reprint service avail. from UMI) Document type: newspaper.
   Formerly: Weekly Reader Surprise (ISSN 0163-4887)
   Description: Provides kindergarten students with news stories, photos, and articles. Includes separate teacher's guide.

028.5   US   ISSN 0890-3220
WEEKLY READER, EDITION 1.* 1928. w. (26/yr. during school yr.). $24.95 for single subscr. (effective 1997-1998). Weekly Reader Corporation, Box 120023, Stamford, CT 06912-0023. TEL 800-446-3360. FAX 609-786-3360. (Subscr. to: 3000 Cindel Dr., Delran, NJ 08075) Ed. Sandra Maccarone; Pub. Richard J. Le Brasseur. R&P contact: Shirley Peterson. circ. 1,152,740 (paid) (also avail. in microfilm from UMI; reprint service avail. from UMI) Document type: newspaper.
   Former titles: Buddy's Weekly Reader (ISSN 0163-4895); My Weekly Reader 1.
   Description: Provides first-grade students with news stories, photos, and articles. Includes separate teacher's guide.

028.5   US   ISSN 0890-3212
WEEKLY READER, EDITION 2. 1929. w. (during school yr.). $24.95 for single subscr. (effective 1997-1998). Weekly Reader Corporation, Box 120023, Stamford, CT 06912-0023. TEL 800-446-3355. FAX 609-786-3360. (Subscr. to: 3000 Cindel Dr., Delran, NJ 08075; Large Print and Braille editions avail. from: American Printing House for the Blind, Inc., 1839 Frankfort Ave., Box 6389, Louisville, KY 40206-0085. TEL 502-895-2405) Ed. Sandra Maccarone; Pub. Richard J. Le Brasseur. R&P contact: Shirley Peterson. circ. 1,272,621 (paid). (also avail. in microfilm from UMI; Braille; large print edition in 14 pt.; reprint service avail. from UMI) Document type: newspaper. —UMI.
   Former titles: Weekly Reader News Hunt (ISSN 0163-4909); (until 1976): My Weekly Reader 2.
   Description: Provides second-grade students with news stories, photos, and articles. Includes separate teacher's guide.

028.5   US   ISSN 0890-3204
WEEKLY READER, EDITION 3.* 1930. w. (26/yr. during school yr.). $24.95 for single subscr. (effective 1997-1998). Weekly Reader Corporation, Box 120023, Stamford, CT 06912-0023. TEL 800-446-3355. FAX 609-786-3360. (Subscr. to: 3000 Cindel Dr., Delran, NJ 08075; Large Print and Braille editions avail. from: American Printing House for the Blind, Inc., 1839 Frankfort Ave., Box 6389, Louisville, KY 40206-0085. TEL 502-895-2405) Ed. Sandra Maccarone; Pub. Richard J. Le Brasseur. R&P contact: Shirley Peterson. circ. 1,176,534 (paid). (also avail. in microfilm from UMI; Braille; large print edition in 14 pt.; reprint service avail. from UMI) Document type: newspaper.
   Former titles: Weekly Reader News Patrol (ISSN 0163-4879); (until 1978): Weekly Reader Whiz; (until 1976): My Weekly Reader 3.
   Description: Provides third-grade students with news stories, photos, maps, graphs, and charts. Includes separate teacher's guide.

028.5   US   ISSN 0890-3190
WEEKLY READER, EDITION 4.* 1934. w. (26/yr. during school yr.). $24.95 for single subscr. (effective 1997-1998). Weekly Reader Corporation, Box 120023, Stamford, CT 06921-0023. TEL 800-446-3355. FAX 609-786-3360. (Subscr. to: 3000 Cindel Dr., Delran, NJ 08075; Large Print and Braille editions avail. from: American Printing House for the Blind, Inc., 1839 Frankfort Ave., Box 6389, Louisville, KY 40206-0085. TEL 502-895-2405) Ed. Sandra Maccarone; Pub. Richard J. Le Brasseur. R&P contact: Shirley Peterson. circ. 964, 461 (paid). (also avail. in microfilm from UMI; Braille; large print edition in 14 pt.; reprint service avail. from UMI) Indexed: Ind.Child.Mag. Document type: newspaper. —UMI.
   Former titles: Weekly Reader News Parade (ISSN 0163-4860); (until 1976): My Weekly Reader News Parade Edition 4.
   Description: Provides fourth-grade students with news stories, photos, maps, graphs, and charts. Includes separate teacher's guide.

028.5   US   ISSN 0890-3182
WEEKLY READER, EDITION 5.* 1954. w. (26/yr. during school yr.). $24.95 for single subscr. (effective 1997-1998). Weekly Reader Corporation, Box 120023, Stamford, CT 06912-0023. TEL 800-446-3355. FAX 609-786-3360. (Subscr. to: 3000 Cindel Dr., Delran, NJ 08075; Large Print and Braille editions avail. from: American Printing House for the Blind Inc., 1839 Frankfort Ave., Box 6389, Louisville, KY 40206-0085. TEL 502-895-2405) Ed. Sandra Maccarone; Pub. Richard J. Le Brasseur. circ. 674,354 (paid). (also avail. in microfilm from UMI; Braille; large print edition in 14 pt.; reprint service avail. from UMI) Indexed: Ind.Child.Mag. Document type: newspaper.
   Former titles: Weekly Reader Eye (ISSN 0163-4828); (until 1976): My Weekly Reader Eye 5; (until 1973): My Weekly Reader 5.
   Description: Presents fifth-grade students with news stories, photos, maps, graphs, and charts. Includes separate teacher's guide.

028.5   US   ISSN 0890-3174
WEEKLY READER, PRE-K EDITION.* 1980. w. (28/yr. during school yr.). $24.95 for single subscr. (effective 1997-1998). Weekly Reader Corporation, Box 120023, Stamford, CT 06912-0023. TEL 800-446-3355. FAX 609-786-3360. (Subscr. to: 3000 Cindel Dr., Delran, NJ 08075-9291) Ed. Sandra Maccarone; Pub. Richard J. Le Brasseur. R&P contact: Shirley Peterson. circ. 558,363 (paid). (also avail. in microfilm from UMI) Document type: newspaper.
   Formerly: Weekly Reader Funday (ISSN 0271-1443)
   Description: Supports nursery school and pre-kindergarten language arts curricula.

028.5   US   ISSN 0890-3239
WEEKLY READER, SENIOR EDITION.* 1947. w. (26/yr. during school yr.). $24.95 for single subscr. (effective 1997-1998). Weekly Reader Corporation, Box 120023, Stamford, CT 06912-0023. TEL 800-446-3355. FAX 609-786-3360. (Subscr. to: 3000 Cindel Dr., Delran, NJ 08075; Large Print ed. avail. from: American Printing House for the Blind, Inc., 1839 Frankfort Ave., Box 6389, Louisville, KY 40206-0085. TEL 502-895-2405) Ed. Sandra Maccarone; Pub. Richard J. Le Brasseur. R&P contact: Shirley Peterson. illus.; circ. 360,489 (paid). (also avail. in microfilm from UMI; large print edition in 14 pt.; reprint service avail. from UMI) Indexed: Ind.Child.Mag. Document type: newspaper. —UMI.
   Formerly: Senior Weekly Reader (ISSN 0163-4852)
   Description: Provides sixth-grade students with news stories, photos, maps, graphs, and charts. Includes separate teacher's guide.

500   US
▼**WEIRD AND WACKY SCIENCE**. 1996. irreg. $107.70. Enslow Publishers, Inc., 44 Fadem Rd., Box 699, Springfield, NJ 07081-0699. TEL 201-379-8890. FAX 201-379-7940. E-mail: annette@enslow.com; URL: http://www.enslow.com. Ed. Brian D. Enslow; Pub. Annette Noce. R&P contact: Annette Noce.
   Description: Investigates the fascinating world of scientific phenomena. Reports today's findings on high-interest science topics.

WEITE WELT; illustrierte Kinderzeitschrift ab 10 Jahre. see RELIGIONS AND THEOLOGY

028.5   GW
WENDELIN; liberales Magazin fuer junge Leute. 1987. irreg. (2-3/yr.) DM.10($15) Postfach 10 16 04, 5600 Wuppertal 1, Germany. TEL 0202-712454. Ed. H. Cremer. adv.; bk.rev.; play rev.; illus.; pat.; stat. circ. 4,000. (back issues avail.)

028.5   US
WE'RE NEXT; for us, by us. 1992. 10/yr. Box GG, Jal, NM 88252. TEL 505-395-2053. Ed. John Cox. circ. 200,000 (controlled).
   Description: To stimulate teenagers' reading, writing and creativity.

DE WERELD VAN HET JONGE KIND. see EDUCATION

1894 CHILDREN AND YOUTH — FOR

028.5
HN90.V64	US	ISSN 1070-7255
WHO CARES; a journal of service and action. 1993. q. $15 to individuals; institutions $20; newsstand price: 3.95. 1511 K St., N.W., Ste. 1042, Washington, DC 20005. TEL 202-628-1691. FAX 202-628-2063. E-mail: info@whocares.org. (Subscr. to: Who Cares, Subscriptions, Box 3000, Denville, NJ 07834. TEL 800-628-1692) Ed. Leslie Crutchfield; Pub. Cheryl Cole-Dodwell. adv. circ. 13,000. **Document type:** consumer publication.
Description: Informs readers through incisive, nonpartisan coverage of service-related issues and inspires them with profiles of activists, volunteers, and entrepreneurs who are making a difference. Challenges young people to consider new ways of fixing old problems.

028.5 333.7	US	ISSN 1092-0331
WILD OUTDOOR WORLD (W.O.W.). 1993. bi-m. $14.95 (Canada & Mexico $25.95; elsewhere $44.95) (effective 1997). Rocky Mountain Elk Foundation, Box 1249, Helena, MT 59624. TEL 406-449-1335. FAX 406-449-9197. E-mail: wowmag@mt.net. Ed. Kay Morton Ellerhoff. R&P contact: Carolyn Cunningham. bk.rev.; index; circ. 120,000 (paid). **Document type:** consumer publication.
Former titles: Falcon for Kids (ISSN 1085-4126); (until 1996): Falcon Magazine for Kids (ISSN 1085-4126)
Description: Covers North American wildlife, wildlife habitat conservation, outdoor recreation for 8-12 year olds.
Refereed Serial

028.5	FR	ISSN 0296-8576
WINNIE. m. 229 F. (outside E.C. 289 F.) (effective 1997). Disney Hachette Presse, 10 rue Thierry le Luron, 92592 Levallois Perret Cedex, France. TEL 33-1-41378500. FAX 33-1-41348989. (Subscr. to: 90 rue de Flandre, 75947 Paris Cedex 19, France. TEL 33-1-44894484) Ed. Gilles Heylen. circ. 95,000. **Document type:** consumer publication.
Description: Educational magazine for children 3 to 7 years old.

028.5	GW
WIR (MINDEN). 1959. 3/yr. DM.3. Wir am Besselgymnasium, Hahlerstr. 134, 32427 Minden, Germany. TEL 49-571-22869. Ed. Nadine Meier. adv.: page DM.150. bk.rev. circ. 700. (looseleaf format; back issues avail.) **Document type:** newsletter.

028.5	AU
WIR LEHRLINGE. 1955. m. S.204. Oesterreichischer Wirtschaftsverlag, Nikolsdorfergasse 7-11, A-1051 Vienna, Austria. TEL 0222-555585. TELEX 1-11669. Ed. Ingeborg Reisner. adv.; bk.rev.; bibl.; film rev.; illus.; tr.lit. circ. 142,000.
Formerly: Wir und Unsere Welt (ISSN 0043-5988)
Description: Aimed at young people ages 15-18.

500	CC	ISSN 0510-7148
WOMEN AI KEXUE/WE LOVE SCIENCE. (Text in Chinese) m. $31.40. Zhongguo Shaonian Ertong Chubanshe, 21 Dongsi 12 Tiao, Beijing 100708, People's Republic of China. TEL 444761. (Dist. in US by: China Books & Periodicals, Inc., 2929 24th St., San Francisco, CA 94110. TEL 415-282-2994) Ed. Xu Junxiong.

028.5 284	US
WONDER TIME. w. $6.75. Word Action Publishing Company, 6401 The Paseo, Kansas City, MO 64131. TEL 816-333-7000. Ed. Lois Perrigo. circ. 37,000.
Description: Aimed at first- and second-grade Sunday school students.

028.5 540	US
WONDERSCIENCE. m. (Oct.-May). American Chemical Society, 1155 16th St., N.W., Washington, DC 20036. TEL 202-452-2113. FAX 202-872-6336. Ed. James Kessler. circ. 15,000. **Document type:** newspaper.

WORD UP! (PARAMUS). see *MUSIC*

028.5	US	ISSN 1071-6602
WORDDANCE. 1991. q. $18 (foreign $23). Playful Productions, Inc., Box 10804, Wilmington, DE 19850-0804. TEL 302-322-6699. E-mail: Haikustu@aol.com. Ed. Steuart Ungar; Pub. Stuart Ungar.
Description: For and by school children, grades K-8

028.5	US
WORLD ALMANAC FOR KIDS. a. $8.95 (effective 1997). World Almanac Books, 1 International Blvd., Mahwah, NJ 07495. TEL 201-529-6900. FAX 201-529-6901. Ed. Judy Levey. **Document type:** consumer publication, directory.
Formerly (until 1996): Kid's World Almanac of Records and Facts.

WORLD ISSUES. see *SOCIAL SERVICES AND WELFARE*

028.5	HU	ISSN 0043-9274
WORLD YOUTH/JEUNESSE DU MONDE/JUVENTUD DEL MUNDO; international youth magazine. (Editions in English, French, Spanish) 1952. s-a. $10. World Federation of Democratic Youth, XIII, Frangepan u. 16, P.O. Box 147, 1389 Budapest, Hungary. TEL 36-1-3443830. (Subscr. to: Kultura, Box 147, H-1389 Budapest, Hungary) Ed. Mun Chol. adv. contact: Halim Awad. illus.; tr.lit.; index. circ. 5,000. (tabloid format)

266	CN	ISSN 0707-2279
WORLDWIND. 1978. a. Can.$2.50 (effective 1997). United Church of Canada, 3250 Bloor St. W., Etobicoke, ON M8X 2Y4, Canada. TEL 416-231-5931. FAX 416-232-6004. Ed. Rebekah Chevalier. illus. **Document type:** consumer publication.
Description: Focuses on mission education for children ages 6-11.

WRITES OF PASSAGE; the literary journal for teenagers. see *LITERARY AND POLITICAL REVIEWS*

028.5	GW
WURZEL; regionale Kinderzeitung fuer den Stadt- und Landkreis Karlsruhe. 1987. 8/yr. Paedagogischer Hochschule Karlsruhe, Didaktische Werkstatt, Bismarckstr. 10, 76133 Karlsruhe, Germany. TEL 0721-23991. FAX 0721-28150. Ed. Rolf Siller.

028.5	GW
X-MAG. m. DM.36. Weltbild Verlag GmbH, Frauentorstr. 5, 86152 Augsburg, Germany. TEL 49-821-3257190. FAX 49-821-3257157. Ed. Andre Lorenz. adv. contact: Kurt Telschig. circ. 46,800. **Document type:** consumer publication.
Formerly: Junge Zeit (ISSN 0170-5857)

028.5	CC
XIAO HUOJU/LITTLE TORCHES. (Text in Chinese) m. Y5.04. (Fujian Sheng Shaoxiandui Gongzuo Weiyuanhui) Fujian Shaonian Ertong Chubanshe, 27 Degui Xiang, Fuzhou, Fujian 350001, People's Republic of China. TEL 537301. (Dist. overseas by: Jiangsu Publications Import & Export Corp., 56 Gao Yun Ling, Nanjing, Jiangsu, P.R.C.) Ed. Lu Dasheng.
Description: Aims to make science and other knowledge interesting to children.

028.5	CC	ISSN 1005-9881
XIAO MIHOU/LITTLE MACAQUE; intelligence pictorial. (Text in Chinese) 1980. bi-m. Y24. Jiangxi Fine Arts Publishing House, No.5, Xinwei Rd., Nanchang, Jiangxi 330002, People's Republic of China. TEL 86-791-850-2724. FAX 86-791-851-2107. Ed.Bd.

028.5	CC
XIAO PENGYOU/LITTLE FRIENDS. (Text in Chinese) 1922. m. $26.40. Shaonian Ertong Chubanshe - Juvenile & Children Publishing House, 1538 Yan'an Xilu, Shanghai 200052, People's Republic of China. TEL 86-21-6282-3025. FAX 86-21-6262-1726. (Dist. in US by: China Books & Periodicals, Inc., 2929 24th St., San Francisco, CA 94110. TEL 415-282-2994) Ed. Hong Zunian. **Document type:** consumer publication.
Description: Contains fairy tales, poems, science stories, games, and exercises in composition.

028.5	CC
XIAO XINGXING/LITTLE STAR. (Text in Chinese) m. 21 Shiji Chubanshe - 21st Century Publishing, No.5, Xinwei Lu, Nanchang, Jiangxi 330002, People's Republic of China. TEL 333749. Ed. Wan Wangming.

028.5	CC
XIAO XUEHUA. (Text in Chinese) 1992. m.? Y1 per no. Gongqingtuan Heilongjiang Shengwei, 11, Ashihe Jie, Nangang-qu, Harbin, Heilongjiang 150001, People's Republic of China. TEL 0451-3642171. Ed. Yuan Qingguo. adv.: page Y5000; adv. contact: Wu Shengshan. circ. 350,000. **Document type:** consumer publication.

XIAOXUE KEJI/ELEMENTARY SCHOOL SCIENCE AND TECHNOLOGY. see *SCIENCES: COMPREHENSIVE WORKS*

028.5	CC
XIAOXUE SHIDAI/ELEMENTARY SCHOOL YEARS. (Text in Chinese) m. Beifang Funu Ertong Chubanshe - Northern Women and Children's Publishers, 102, Stalin Street, Changchun, Jilin 130021, People's Republic of China. TEL 884811. Ed. Wu Fei.

XIAOXUESHENG YUWEN XUEXI/CHINESE STUDIES FOR PUPILS. see *LINGUISTICS*

Y A B A FRAMEWORK. (Young American Bowling Alliance) see *SPORTS AND GAMES — Ball Games*

028.5	US
Y E S MAGAZINE. (Youth Excited about Success) 1992. m. (Sep.-May). $15. Y E S Communications Company, Inc., 144 North Ave., Plainfield, NJ 07060. TEL 908-754-4466. FAX 908-753-1036. Ed. Jan M. Edgenton-Johnson; Pub. Henry C. Johnson. R&P contact: Jill Johnson. adv. contact: Jill L. Johnson. film rev.; music rev.; software rev.; video rev. circ. 100,000. (back issues avail.) **Document type:** consumer publication.
Description: Provides valuable resource information on scholarships, resume writing, and study tips for students age 12 to 18. Helps students develop positive self-esteem.

028.5	US	ISSN 0888-5842
AP201
Y M. (Young and Modern) (Supplement avail.: Y M Special) 1953. m. (10/yr.) $13.97; newsstand price: $2.50. Gruner & Jahr U.S.A. Publishing, 685 Third Ave., New York, NY 10017. TEL 212-878-8700. FAX 212-286-0935. Ed. Christina Ferrari; Pub. Victoria Lasdon Rose. adv.: B&W page $43630, color page $68100; trim 7 7/8 x 10 7/8; adv. contact: Stephanie Smith. bk.rev.; film rev.; circ. 1,829,515 (paid). (also avail. in microform from UMI) Indexed: Ind.Child.Mag. **Document type:** consumer publication.
—KR SourceOne.
Former titles: Young Miss (ISSN 0044-0833); Calling All Girls.
Description: For young women between the ages of 14 and 20. Covers relationships, self discovery, entertainment, fitness and careers, with emphasis on beauty and fashion.

028.5	US
Y M SPECIAL. (Published in 3 thematic issues: Prom; Love; Find the Real You) 3/yr. (no subscr. avail.); newsstand price: $2.50. Gruner & Jahr U.S.A. Publishing, 110 Fifth Ave., New York, NY 10017. TEL 212-499-2000. Ed. Sally Lee; Pub. Victoria Lasdon Rose. adv.; illus. **Document type:** consumer publication.
Description: Each issue focuses on a single topic of interest to young women, ages 14-20.

028.5	US
Y O! (YOUTH OUTLOOK). 1991. bi-m. $25 (students $12; free to schools). Pacific News Service, 450 Mission St., Rm. 204, San Francisco, CA 94105. TEL 415-243-4304. E-mail: yo@pacificnews.com; URL: http://www.pacificnews.com/yo/. Ed. Nell Bernstein. illus. circ. 46,000. (back issues avail.)
● Also available online.

028.5 780	US	ISSN 1056-6198
E185.5
Y S B.* (Young Sisters & Brothers) 1991. m. Paige Publications, 1900 W. Pl., N.E., Washington, DC 20018-1230. Ed. Frank Dexter Brown. adv.; illus. **Document type:** consumer publication.
Description: Covers music, movies and other news for a teenage African-American audience.

028.5 808.8	US
YELLOW TURTLE. irreg. (2-4/yr.). Spring Rain Press, Box 277, Port Townsend, WA 98368. Ed. Karen Gates; Pub. Karen Gates.
Description: Publishes children's literature.

770	CC
YINGER HUABAO/INFANT PICTORIAL. (Text in Chinese) m. $25.10. Zhongguo Shaonian Ertong Chubanshe, 21 Dongsi 12 Tiao, Beijing 100708, People's Republic of China. TEL 444761. (Dist. in US by: China Books & Periodicals, Inc., 2929 24th St., San Francisco, CA 94110. TEL 415-282-2994) Ed. H Jianzhong. illus.

028.5   AA
YLLKAT/ETOILES. m. Instittutit te Studimeve Pedagogjike, Rruga Naim Frasheri No. 37, Tirana, Albania. TEL 355-42-23860. FAX 355-42-23860.

YO! MAGAZINE. see *MUSIC*

028.5   US   ISSN 0897-7704
YO-YO TIMES; a world of fun on a string for children of all ages. 1988. 4/yr. $12 (foreign $18). Creative Communications Inc. (Herndon), Box 1519-ULR, Herndon, VA 20172-1519. TEL 703-742-9696. Ed. Stuart F. Crump Jr. adv. **Document type:** consumer publication.

028.5 282   US   ISSN 1064-8682
YOU!. 1987. 10/yr. $19.95 (foreign $29.95) (effective 1997). Veritas Communications Inc., 31194 La Baya Dr., Ste. 200, Westlake Village, CA 91362-4022. TEL 818-991-1813. FAX 818-991-2024. E-mail: youmag@earthlink.net; URL: http://www.youmagazine.com. Ed. Juliette Buerkle; Pub. Paul Lauer. R&P contact: Juliette Buerkle. adv.: B&W page $1420, color page $2483; trim 10 x 12; adv. contact: Derrick Kunz. bk.rev.; film rev.; tele.rev.; circ. 30,000 (paid). **Document type:** consumer publication.
Description: Covers entertainment, news, sports, celebrities, athletes, and youth living their Catholic faith.
Refereed Serial

028.5   CC   ISSN 1003-0220
YOU'ER HUABAO/TODDLERS' PICTORIAL. (Text in Chinese) m. $24.20. Zhongguo Shaonian Ertong Chubanshe, 21 Dongsi 12 Tiao, Beijing 100708, People's Republic of China. TEL 444761. Ed. Hu Jianzhong. illus.

028.5   US   ISSN 1075-3656
YOUNG ADULT PRESS. 1991. 10/yr. $18. Box 21, Mound, MN 55364. TEL 612-472-0809. FAX 612-472-0842. Ed. Tamara Crea; Pub. Beverly Smith. adv.: B&W page $995; trim 23 x 16. bk.rev. circ. 30,000. **Document type:** newspaper.
Formerly (until Mar. 1994): Midwest Teen Scene.
Description: Written by and for teens on issues of importance to them such as violence in the schools, relationships, health, religion, money and sex.

YOUNG AMERICAN PRESS. see *CHILDREN AND YOUTH — About*

YOUNG & ALIVE (LARGE PRINT EDITION). see *HANDICAPPED — Visually Impaired*

808.068   US   ISSN 0741-7594
YOUNG AUTHORS MAGAZINE. Abbreviated title: Y A M. 1984. 10/yr. $29.95. Regulus Communications, Inc., 140 N. 8th St., Ste. 201, Lincoln, NE 68508-1353. TEL 402-435-2111. FAX 402-435-2552. Ed. Jane A. Austin. bk.rev. circ. 33,144.
Description: Creative writing by children and youths.

028.5   SI   ISSN 0129-6639
YOUNG GENERATION. (Text in Chinese, English) 1974. m. S.$30. E P B Publishers Pte. Ltd., 162 Bukit Merah Central 04-3545, Singapore 150162, Singapore. TEL 278-0881. FAX 276-6970. TELEX RS 56289 EPB. Ed.Bd. adv. circ. 80,000.
Formerly (until 1981): Young Singaporean.
Description: For primary to lower secondary students. Includes riddles, stories, cartoons, contests, and poems. Focuses on science, geography, history, wildlife, and famous people and stories for kids.

YOUNG JUDAEAN. see *ETHNIC INTERESTS*

YOUNG MUSICIANS. see *MUSIC*

YOUNG SALVATIONIST. see *RELIGIONS AND THEOLOGY — Other Denominations And Sects*

268   UK   ISSN 0044-0906
YOUNG SOLDIER. 1881. w. £23.54. Salvation Army, 101 Queen Victoria St., London EC4P 4EP, England. TEL 0171-236-5222. FAX 0171-236-3491. Ed. Philippa Smale. adv. contact: Len Dorman. bk.rev.; rec.rev.; illus. circ. 50,000. **Document type:** bulletin.

YOUNG SOLDIER. see *RELIGIONS AND THEOLOGY — Other Denominations And Sects*

028.5   UK
YOUNG TELEGRAPH. 1990. w. Two-Can Publishing, 346 Old St., London EC1V 9NQ, England. TEL 44-171-684-4000. FAX 44-171-613-3372. Ed. Damian Kelleher. adv. contact: Philippa Perry. bk.rev.; circ. 1,300,000. (back issues avail.) **Document type:** newspaper.

028.5 362.7   PH   ISSN 0116-1091
THE YOUNGSTER; the illustrated magazine. (Text in English) 1956. m. (Jun.-Mar.). P.150 (foreign P.500). Society of St. Paul, Inc., MCPO Box 1722, 1299 Makati City, Metro Manila, Philippines. Ed. Hansel B. Mapayo. circ. 90,000.
Description: Dedicated to the youth. Contains sections on teen problems and topics aimed at deepening Christian values.
Refereed Serial

028.5   FR
YOUPI; le petit curieux. 1988. m. 350 F. (EU 399 F.; elsewhere 449 F.) (effective 1997). Bayard Presse, 3 rue Bayard, 75393 Paris Cedex 08, France. TEL 33-1-44356060. FAX 33-1-44356091. TELEX 648 094 F. (Subscr. to: Bayard Presse International, B.P. 12, 99505 Paris Entreprises, France. TEL 33-1-44216000. FAX 33-3-20274192) Ed. Marie-Agnes Gaudrat. circ. 41,586.
Formerly: Youpi Decouvertes.
Description: Provides a companion for 3 year olds to understand the world, gain knowledge and start to act independently.

YOUR BIG BACKYARD. see *ENVIRONMENTAL STUDIES*

028.5   US   ISSN 1067-005X
YOUR PROM. 1990. a. newsstand price: $2.95. Modern Bride (Subsidiary of: K-III Communications Corp.), 249 W. 17th St., New York, NY 10011. TEL 212-462-3400. Ed. Cele Lalli; Pub. Nina Lawrence. adv. contact: Steven Ritterman. circ. 650,000. **Document type:** consumer publication.
Description: Targeted to teenagers. Provides "how-to" advice on preparing for the prom and reflections on this rite of passage in the life of teenagers.

028.5   ZA
YOUTH. vol.2, 1976. fortn. United National Independence Party, Youth League, Box 302, Lusaka, Zambia. Ed. P.J. Njeleka. adv.; bk.rev.; illus. circ. 15,000.

028.5   US   ISSN 0279-6651
YOUTH (YEAR). 1981. bi-m. $14.95 (Canada Can.$19.95; elsewhere $24.95) (effective 1997); newsstand price: $2.50. House of White Birches, 306 E. Parr Rd., Berne, IN 46711. TEL 219-589-8741. FAX 219-589-8093. E-mail: youth97@aol.com; URL: http://www.whitebirches.com. Ed. vivian Rothe; Pub. Karen Muselman Thomas. adv. contact: Ellie Trumbull. bk.rev.; circ. 45,000 (paid). **Document type:** consumer publication.
—UnCover.
Description: Focuses on teen concerns like relationships, family, college, and career planning. Examines moral principles, as they relate to teenagers, from a Christian perspective.

THE YOUTH DISCIPLE. see *RELIGIONS AND THEOLOGY — Protestant*

YOUTH DISCIPLE LEADER'S PACKET. see *RELIGIONS AND THEOLOGY — Protestant*

YOUTH EXPLORE THE BIBLE SERIES. STUDENT. see *RELIGIONS AND THEOLOGY — Protestant*

YOUTH IN ACTION. see *RELIGIONS AND THEOLOGY — Protestant*

YOUTH IN DISCOVERY. see *RELIGIONS AND THEOLOGY — Protestant*

028.5   II
YOUTH LIFE. (Text in English) 1973. fortn. All India Youth Federation, 4-7 Asaf Ali Rd., New Delhi 110001, India. Ed. K.C. Chandrappan. adv.; illus.

YOUTH MINISTRY UPDATE. see *RELIGIONS AND THEOLOGY — Protestant*

028.5   AT
YOUTH RESEARCH NEWS. 1991. irreg., approx. q. Aus.$20 to individuals (foreign Aus.$30); institutions Aus.$30 (foreign Aus.$40). Youth Research Centre, Faculty of Education, University of Melbourne, Parkville, Vic. 3052, Australia. TEL 61-3-93448251. FAX 61-3-93448256. E-mail: r.holdsworth@edfac.unimelb.edu.au; URL: http://yarn.insted.univelb.edu.au/yarn/yrc-home.html. Ed. Roger Holdsworth. circ. 500. (back issues avail.) **Document type:** newsletter.
●Also available online.
Description: Provides information about projects, publications and seminars.

YOUTH THEATRE JOURNAL. see *THEATER*

028.5   NL   ISSN 0294-7579
YOUTHLINK. French edition: Interjeunes (ISSN 1021-0024) (Text in English) 1979. irreg. South Pacific Commission, B.P. D5, 98848 Noumea Cedex, New Caledonia. TEL 687-262000. FAX 687-263818. E-mail: spc@spc.org.nc. **Document type:** newsletter.

YOUTHWALK. see *RELIGIONS AND THEOLOGY*

YOUTHWORK; ideas, resources & guidance for youth ministry. see *RELIGIONS AND THEOLOGY — Protestant*

028.5   CE
YOVUN JANATHA. (Text in Sinhala) 1964. w. newsstand price: Rs.4.50. Associated Newspapers of Ceylon Ltd., Lake House, D.R. Wijewardena Mawatha, Colombo 10, Sri Lanka. TEL 94-1-421181. FAX 94-1-449069. Ed. M. Newton Pinto. adv. circ. 115,000. **Document type:** newspaper.

028.5   GW
YPS. 1975. w. DM.148.80. Gruner und Jahr AG & Co. (Munich), Neherstr. 9, 81675 Munich, Germany. TEL 49-89-4152-0. FAX 49-89-4152665. circ. 130,000. **Document type:** consumer publication.

028.5   CN   ISSN 0044-1384
YUNAK/YOUTH. (Text in Ukrainian) 1963. bi-m. Can.$30. Plast-Ukrainian Youth Organization, 2199 Bloor St. West, Toronto, ON M6S 1N2, Canada. TEL 416-763-2186. FAX 416-763-0185. Ed. O. Zakydalsky. R&P contact: O. Zakydalsky. adv. contact: G. Senkiw. illus. circ. 1,000. **Document type:** newsletter.
Description: For ages 12-17.

028.5 700   RU   ISSN 0205-5791
YUNYI KHUDOZHNIK. 1936. m. $120 (effective 1998). (Rossiiskaya Akademiya Khudozhestv) Izdatel'stvo Molodaya Gvardiya, Sushchevskaya ul., 21, 103030 Moscow, Russia. TEL 7-095-2858901. (Dist. by: Mezhdunarodnaya Kniga, B. Yakimanka 39, 117049 Moscow, Russia. TEL 7-095-2384967. FAX 7-095-2384634) (Co-sponsor: Soyuz Khudozhnikov Rossii) adv.; bk.rev.; illus.

028.5 570   RU   ISSN 0205-5767
YUNYI NATURALIST. (Text in Russian) 1928. m. $71 (effective 1998). Novodmitrovskaya ul. 5A, 125015 Moscow, Russia. TEL 7-095-2851906. FAX 7-095-2851906. (Dist. by: Mezhdunarodnaya Kniga, B. Yakimanka 39, 117049 Moscow, Russia. TEL 7-095-2384967. FAX 7-095-2384634; Dist. in U.S. by: Victor Kamkin Inc., 4956 Boiling Brook Pkwy., Rockville, MD 20852. TEL 301-881-5973) Ed. Boris A. Chashcharin. adv.; bk.rev.; illus.; index. circ. 69,000.
Description: For children in 4th - 10th grades who are interested in biology.

028.5 600   RU   ISSN 0131-1417
T4
YUNYI TEKHNIK. 1956. m. $64 (effective 1998). Novodmitrovskaya ul. 5A, 125015 Moscow, Russia. TEL 7-095-2851205. FAX 7-095-2851809. (Dist. by: Mezhdunarodnaya Kniga, B. Yakimanka 39, 117049 Moscow, Russia. TEL 7-095-2384967. FAX 7-095-2384634; Dist. in U.S. by: Victor Kamkin Inc., 4956 Boiling Brook Pkwy, Rockville, MD 20852. TEL 301-881-5973) Ed. Boris Cheremisinov. adv.; bk.rev.; bibl.; illus. circ. 50,700.

028.5   820   II   ISSN 0302-6981
YUVA BHARATI; voice of youth. (Text in English) 1973. q. $25. Vivekananda Kendra Prakashan, 3 Singarachari St., Triplicane, Madras 600005, India. (Co-sponsor: Swami Vivekananda Centenary Celebration) Ed. P. Parameswaram; Pub. N. Viswanath. adv.; bk.rev.
Description: Examines Indian culture for youth.

028.5   LU   ISSN 1016-2399
ZACK; Letzebuerger Kannerzeitung. (Text in French, German) 1946. s-m. 450 Fr. (effective 1997). Editions Saint Paul, S.A., 2 rue Christophe Plantin, L-2988 Luxembourg, Luxembourg. TEL 49-93-258. FAX 48-58-386.
Description: Covers daily life, sports, tourism and geography, politics, stories, comic strips, guessing games, coloring and posters.

028.5   II
ZAGMAG. (Text in Gujarati) 1952. w. Gujarat Samachar Bhavan, Khanpur, Ahmedabad 380 001, India. TEL 272-22821. TELEX 1216642. Ed. Bahubali S. Shah. circ. 38,000.

028.5   BE   ISSN 0778-2322
ZAP. (Text in Dutch) 1983. q. 200 BEF (effective 1992). Mutualistische Jongeren Aktie - M J A, Sint Jansstraat 32, B-1000 Brussels, Belgium. TEL 32-2-5150251. FAX 32-2-5150207. adv.; bk.rev. circ. 10,000. (also avail. in diskette format; back issues avail.) **Document type:** consumer publication.
Formerly (until 1991): Inforclub (ISSN 0775-8340)
Description: For young people age 14-18.

268   IS   ISSN 0792-9307
ZAV-ZAV. (Text in Hebrew) 1989. m. $35. Select Publishing House, P.O. Box 28110, Tel Aviv 61280, Israel. FAX 972-3-5373906. Ed. Rami Shir. circ. 15,000.
Description: For children ages 3-6.

028.5   BL   ISSN 0104-3404
ZE CARIOCA. 1961. fortn. Editora Abril Jovem, S.A., Rua Bela Cintra 299, 01415-000 Sao Paulo SP, Brazil. TEL 011-257-0999. TELEX 011-22115. Ed. Elizabeth De Fiore. adv. circ. 60,000. **Document type:** consumer publication.

248.83   US
ZELOS.* 1973. q. Scripture Press Publications, Inc., 4050 Lee Vance View, Colorado Springs, CO 80918-7102. Ed. Amy J. Cox.
Former titles (until 1995): Freeway; Youth Illustrated; Power Life (ISSN 0032-6046)
Description: Christian life notebook aimed at teenagers, ages 16 to 19.

028.5   AA
ZERI I RINISE/VOIX DE LA JEUNESSE. (Text in Albanian) s-w. $175 in Europe; $247 in US. Union de la Jeunesse du Travail d'Albanie, Tirana, Albania. (Dist. by: Agjencia Quendrore e Tregtimit, Te Librit Artistik e Shkencor, Rruga e Kavajes, Nr.42, Tirana, Albania. FAX 355-42-27246)

028.5   CC   ISSN 0412-4154
PZ10.831
ZHONGGUO ERTONG/CHINESE CHILDREN. (Text in Chinese) m. $25.10. Zhongguo Shaonian Ertong Chubanshe, 21 Dongsi 12 Tiao, Beijing 100700, People's Republic of China. TEL 444761-225. TELEX 4357. (Dist. in US by: China Books & Periodicals, Inc., 2929 24th St., San Francisco, CA 94110. TEL 415-282-2994)
Description: Illustrated journal for elementary school pupils.

059.951 890   CC
ZHONGGUO QINGNIAN/CHINESE YOUTH. (Text in Chinese) 1923. m. Zhongguo Qingnian Zazhishe, Jia-22 Yuqiang Hutong, Guanyuan, Xicheng, Beijing 100034, People's Republic of China. TEL 86-10-6018167. FAX 86-10-6068918. (Dist. overseas by: China International Book Trading Corp., P.O. Box 399, Beijing 100044, P.R. China; Dist. in US by: China Books & Periodicals, Inc., 2929 24th St., San Francisco, CA 94110. TEL 415-282-2994) Ed. Shi Guoxiong. circ. 1,000,000. pp./issue: 64.

895.1   CC
ZHONGGUO QINGNIAN BAO/CHINESE YOUTH DAILY. (Text in Chinese) 1951. d. $557.90. 2, Haiyun Cang, Beijing 100702, People's Republic of China. TEL 44-6581. FAX 861-4015084. (Dist. in US by: China Books & Periodicals, Inc., 2929 24th St., San Francisco, CA 94110. TEL 415-282-2994) Ed. Xu Zhuqing. adv.; bk.rev. circ. 1,000,000. (reprint service avail. from China Book & Periodicals, Inc.) **Document type:** newspaper.

028.5   US
ZHONGGUO SHAONIAN BAO/CHINA YOUNGSTER NEWS. (Text in Chinese) w. $43.50. China Books & Periodicals, Inc., 2929 24th St., San Francisco, CA 94110. TEL 415-282-2994. FAX 415-282-0994.
Document type: newspaper.

028.5   CC
ZHONGWAI TONGHUA HUAKAN/CHINESE AND FOREIGN FAIRY TALES PICTORIAL. (Text in Chinese) m. Nei Menggu Zizhiqu Funu Lianhehui - Inner Mongolian Autonomous Region Women's Association, 9 Zhongshan Donglu, Huhhot, Nei Menggu 010020, People's Republic of China. TEL 662584. Ed. Xi Xingfang.

ZHONGXUESHENG SHUXUE/MATHEMATICS FOR MIDDLE SCHOOL STUDENTS. see *MATHEMATICS*

640.73   US   ISSN 1050-8163
TX336   CODEN: ZILLEH
ZILLIONS. 1980. bi-m. $16 (foreign $20). Consumers Union of the United States, Inc., 101 Truman Ave., Yonkers, NY 10703-1057. TEL 914-378-2000. (Subscr. to: Box 51777, Boulder, CO 80321. TEL 800-234-1645) Ed. Charlotte Baecher. illus. circ. 260,000. (also avail. in microfiche from NBI,UMI) **Indexed:** Ind.Child.Mag., Jun.High.Mag.Abstr.
Document type: consumer publication.
—KR SourceOne; UnCover.
Formerly (until Sep. 1990): Penny Power (ISSN 0190-1966)
Description: Offers product-rating and consumer advice for young people ages 10 to 14.

028.5   CN   ISSN 0832-8242
ZIP: LE MAGAZINE DES JEUNES. 1986. m. $20 to individuals; institutions $18. Publications Audiovisuelles, 415 80 rue ouest, Charlesbourg, PQ G1H 4M9, Canada. TEL 418-622-3491. Ed. Pierre Coulombe. circ. 87,000.

028.5   800   XR   ISSN 0044-4871
PG5019.5
ZLATY MAJ; casopis o detske literature a umeni. (Text in Czech or Slovak; summaries in English, German and Russian) 1956. m. (10/yr.) 30 Kc.($27) (I B B Y, Ceska Sekce) Albatros, Havelska 20, 110 01 Prague, Czech Republic. TELEX 121604 ALBA C. (Subscr. to: Artia, Ve Smeckach 30, 111 27 Prague 1, Czech Republic) Ed. Jiri Lapacek. bk.rev.; bibl.; illus. circ. 3,500.

028.5   BE   ISSN 0772-7402
ZONNEKIND. (Text in Dutch) 1958. w. 1450 BEF (in Europe 2080 BEF; elsewhere 2320 BEF) (effective 1997-98). Uitgeverij G.P. Averbode, P.B. 54, B-3271 Averbode, Belgium. TEL 32-13-780111. FAX 32-13-776837. Ed. Christiane Thiry. illus.
Description: Aims to develop early language and mathematics skills for ages 6-8. Includes relevant activities.

028.5   BE   ISSN 0049-8750
ZONNELAND. (Text in Dutch) 1920. w. 1779 BEF. Uitgeverij G.P. Avebode, P.B. 54, B-3271 Averbode, Belgium. TEL 32-13-780111. FAX 32-13-776837. Ed. Jan Lembrechts. adv.; illus.

028.5   BE   ISSN 0772-9898
ZONNESTRAAL. (Text in Dutch) 1966. w. 1450 BEF (in Europe 2080 BEF; elsewhere 2320 BEF) (effective 1997-98). Uitgeverij G.P. Averbode, P.B. 54, B-3271 Averbode, Belgium. TEL 32-13-780111. FAX 32-13-776837. Ed. Jan Lembrechts.
Description: Helps children ages 8-10 discover the world in time and space, showing them new ways of looking at things from different angles. Presents reading as fun.

ZOOBOOKS. see *BIOLOGY — Zoology*

616.86   FI   ISSN 0783-5469
ZOOM. (Text in Swedish) 1985. bi-m. FIM 70; newsstand price: FIM 15. Finlands Svenska Nykterhetsfoerbund rf, Fredsgatan 8 B, FIN-65100 Vasa, Finland. TEL 358-61-317-26-04. FAX 358-61-317-28-31. Ed. Tomas Lundquvist. adv.; B&W page FIM 4000; adv. contact: Ralf Nordman. circ. 7,000. (tabloid format; back issues avail.)

028.5   XO   ISSN 0139-8962
ZORNICKA. 1948. 24/yr. Smena Publishing House, Prazska 11, 812 84 Bratislava, Slovakia.

028.5   IS
ZRAIM. bi-m. free. Bnei Akiva, P.O. Box 40027, Tel Aviv 61 400, Israel. TEL 972-3-6917145. Ed. Uri Orbach.

028.5   CU
ZUN ZUN; revista infantil. m. $34 in S. America; N. America $36; elsewhere $42. (Editorial Abril) Ediciones Cubanas, Obispo No. 527, Apdo. 605, Havana, Cuba.

028.5   GW   ISSN 0721-4626
ZUSAMMEN. 10/yr. DM.85 (foreign DM.95). Erhard Friedrich Verlag GmbH, Im Brande 17, 30926 Seelze, Germany. TEL 49-511-40004-0. FAX 49-511-40004170. (Subscr. to: Postfach 100150, 30917 Seelze, Germany) illus. **Indexed:** IBR. **Document type:** consumer publication.

ZUSAMMEN; Jugendmagazin in deutscher Sprache. see *LINGUISTICS*

028.5   500   US   ISSN 0195-4105
3-2-1 CONTACT. 1979. 10/yr. $19.90 (foreign $29.90) (effective 1997); newsstand price: $2. Children's Television Workshop, One Lincoln Plaza, New York, NY 10023. TEL 212-595-3456. FAX 212-595-3650. Ed. Jonathan Rosenbloom; Pub. Nina B. Link. circ. 300,000. **Indexed:** Ind.Child.Mag., Jun.High.Mag.Abstr. **Document type:** consumer publication.
—KR SourceOne; UnCover.
Description: For ages 8-14. Packed with puzzles, projects and challenging "Square One" TV math pages. Designed to help children learn while having fun.

369.4   NO   ISSN 0800-6032
4 H - KLUBBEN. 1949. m. NOK 60. Norske 4H, Postboks 113, 2013 Skjetten, Norway. Ed. Lars H. Alstadseter. adv. circ. 22,900.
—CCC.
Formerly (until 1956): Klubben Vaar (ISSN 0800-6725)

028.5   IT
16 ANNI. 1990. m. newsstand price: L.3000. Edizioni Internazionale Cioe s.r.l., Via G. Fabbroni 24, 0019 Rome, Italy. TEL 39-6-3287309. Ed. Umberto Mazzarini. adv.: page L.6000000. circ. 60,000. **Document type:** consumer publication.

028.5   US   ISSN 0270-899X
16 MAGAZINE. 1957. m. $19.95 (foreign $25.95) (effective 1997). Sterling - Macfadden Partnership, 233 Park Ave. S., 6th Fl., New York, NY 10003. TEL 212-780-3500. (Subscr. to: 35 Wilbur St., Lynbrook, NY 11563. TEL 516-593-1220. FAX 516-593-0065) Ed. Ellen Jurcsak. adv.; bk.rev.; illus. circ. 400,000. **Document type:** consumer publication.

028.5   US   ISSN 1044-0836
16 SUPERSTARS. bi-m. newsstand price: $2.95. Sterling - Macfadden Partnership, 233 Park Ave. S. New York, NY 10003. TEL 212-780-3500. FAX 212-780-3555. adv. **Document type:** consumer publication.
Description: Contains articles on celebrities geared toward teenagers.

17; illustrierte Monatszeitschrift fuer junge Christen. see *RELIGIONS AND THEOLOGY*

028.5   UK   ISSN 1357-1028
95 PER CENT. 1993. q. £8; newsstand price: £2. (Youth Clubs UK) B C Publications, 16C Market Pl Diss, Norfolk IP22 3AB, England. TEL 44-1379-644200. FAX 44-1379-650480. E Richard Ings. adv.: page £320; trim 297 x 190; adv. contact: Alison Mann. circ. 1,500. (back issue avail.) **Document type:** consumer publication.

100 BEST BOOKS (YEAR). see PUBLISHING AND BOOK TRADE

305.235 PO ISSN 0873-4801
▼ **100 POR CENTO JOVEM;** para elas. 1996. s-m. Esc.3240 (foreign Esc.7260) (effective 1997). Impala Sociedade Editorial, S.A., Cont. no. 501 405 127, C.S. 750000c., Av. Miguel Bombarda, 332745 Queluz, Portugal. TEL 351-4364401. FAX 351-4365001. (Dist. by: Electroliber, Rua Vascoi da Gama, 4-A. TEL 351-9425394) Ed. Dr. Luis Peniche.

028.5 301 US ISSN 1077-3878
360 DEGREES: THE MAGAZINE WITH EVERY ANGLE. 1993. q. $10 to individuals; free to high school students. 360 Degree Exchange, Inc., Box 25356, Washington, DC 20007. TEL 202-628-1836. FAX 202-628-1843. E-mail: mag360@aol.com; URL: http://www.360.org. Pub. Parker Stanzione. adv.; bk.rev.; film rev.; music rev.; software rev.; tele.rev.; video rev. circ. 40,000. (back issues avail.)
●Also available online.
Description: Provides a forum for the nation's youth to discuss social issues. The publication is written entirely by and for high school students.

028.5 UK ISSN 0262-284X
2000 A D; featuring Judge Dredd. 1977. w. newsstand price: £0.80. Fleetway Editions Ltd., 25-31 Tavistock Pl., Bloomsbury, London WC1 9SU, England. TEL 0171-344-6400. FAX 0171-388-4020. (Dist. by: Comag, Tavistock Rd., W. Drayton, Mddx. UB7 7QE, England. TEL 0191-510-0201; Subscr. to: Aim, P.O. Box 10, Pallion Industrial Estate, Sunderland SR4 6SN, England) Ed. Tharg the Mighty. adv.; film rev.; software rev.; music rev.; illus.; circ. 75,000 (paid). (back issues avail.) **Document type:** consumer publication.
Description: Provides illustrated science fiction stories for teenage males.

CHIROPRACTIC, HOMEOPATHY, OSTEOPATHY

see Medical Sciences–Chiropractic, Homeopathy, Osteopathy

CIRCUITS

see Computers–Circuits

CIVIL DEFENSE

see also Military

350.755 363.6
614.85 UN
P E L L NEWSLETTER. (Awareness and Preparedness for Emergencies at Local Level) (Supplement to: Industry and Environment) 2/yr. United Nations Environment Programme, Industry and Environment Programme Activity Centre - Programme des Nations Unies pour l'Environnement, 39-43 quai Andre Citroen, 73739 Paris Cedex 15, France. TEL 33-1-44371437. FAX 33-1-44371474. TELEX 204 997 F. E-mail: unepie@unep.fr. Ed. J. Stevens. **Document type:** newsletter.
Description: Seeks to minimize the occurrence and impact of industrial accidents. Keeps readers informed of APELL-related news, including information on programs in progress around the world.

363.3 NE ISSN 0920-3168
UA929.N2
ALERT; maandblad voor rampenbestrijding en crisisbeheersing. 1984. m. fl.97.50 (foreign fl.125) (effective 1996). Vuga Uitgeverij B.V., Postbus 16400, 2500 BK The Hague, Netherlands. TEL 31-70-6131500. FAX 31-70-6131503. Ed. Marcel Bayer. R&P contact: M. Fruin. adv. contact: Christine Peelen. bk.rev.; abstr.; illus.; tr.lit. circ. 2,334. Indexed: C.I.S.Abstr., Excerp.Med. **Document type:** trade publication.
—SWETS.
Incorporates (1954-1984): Paladijn (ISSN 0031-0166); (1957-1984): Netherlands. Ministerie van Binnenlandse Zaken. Inspectie voor het Brandweerwezen. Maandelijkse Mededelingen (ISSN 0020-2045); (in 1984): Noodzaak (ISSN 0165-1471); Which was formerly (1952-1973): Civiele Verdediging (ISSN 0009-7802)
Description: Covers all aspects of disaster planning and relief, crisis management and related public safety topics.

363 US ISSN 8750-5878
AMERICAN SURVIVAL GUIDE. 1982. m. $15. McMullen & Yee Publishing, 774 S. Placentia Ave., Placentia, CA 92670-6846. TEL 714-572-2255. FAX 714-572-1864. Ed. Jim Benson. adv. circ. 90,000.
Formerly (until 1985): Survival Guide (ISSN 0745-1113)

350.755 IT
AZIONE NONVIOLENTA. 1964. m. L.35000 (foreign L.50000). Azione Nonviolenta, Coop, Via Spagna 8, 37123 Verona, Italy. TEL 045-8009803. FAX 045-8009212. E-mail: azionenonviolenta@sis.it. Ed. Massimo Valpiana. R&P contact: Stefano Guffanti. adv. contact: Stefano Giuffanti. bk.rev. circ. 5,000. (tabloid format; back issues avail.) **Document type:** newsletter.

363.3509489 DK ISSN 0908-9594
UA926.A1
BEREDSKAB. 1950. bi-m. DKK 120. Beredskabs-Forbundet, Noerre Brogade 66 D, 3. sal, DK-2200 Copenhagen N, Denmark. adv. circ. 18,787.
Former titles (until 1994): Civilforsvar (ISSN 0107-0665); (until 1979): Civilforsvarsbladet (ISSN 0009-8116)

363.35 GW ISSN 0940-7154
UA926.A1
BEVOELKERUNGSSCHUTZ-MAGAZIN; Zeitschrift fuer Zivilschutz, Katastrophenschutz und Selbstschutz. 1971. q. DM.14. Bundesverband fuer Zivilschutz, Deutschherrenstr. 93-95, 53177 Bonn, Germany. FAX 49-228-9401424. Ed. Peter Eykmann. bk.rev. circ. 60,000. (back issues avail.) **Document type:** trade publication.
—BLDSC (1947.281500). **CCC.**
Former titles (until 1989): Zivilschutz-Magazin (ISSN 0173-7872); Z B - Ziviler Bevoelkerungsschutz; Helferbrief (ISSN 0017-9930)

363.35 SW ISSN 1102-0180
CIVIL; civila foersvarstidningen; foer foersvar av maenniskovaerde och en humanistisk samhaellssyn. 1937. 9/yr. SEK 195 (effective 1991). Sveriges Civilfoersvarsfoerbund, P.O. Box 2034, S-171 02 Solna, Sweden.
Incorporates (in 1991): Civila Foersvarsbulletinen; (until 1991): Civila Foersvarstidningen; (until 1983): Civilt Foersvar; (until 1963): Tidskrift foer Sveriges Civilfoersvar; (until vol.11, 1945): Flyglarm.

CIVIL AIR PATROL NEWS. see AERONAUTICS AND SPACE FLIGHT

350.755 UK ISSN 0961-2564
CIVIL PROTECTION. 1986. q. Home Office, 50 Queen Anne's Gate, London SW1H 9AT, England. TEL 071-273-3378. Ed. Benard Snyth. circ. 50,000. (back issues avail.) **Document type:** government publication.
—BLDSC (3273.823500).

363.3 IT
CORPO NAZIONALE SOCCORSO ALPINO E SPELEOLOGICO. NOTIZIE. (Text in English, French, Italian) q. membership. Corpo Nazionale Soccorso Alpino e Speleologico, Via E. Fonseca Pimentel 7, 20127 Milan, Italy. TEL 39-2-26141375. FAX 39-2-2888010. Ed. Alessio Fabbricatore. R&P contact: Alessio Fabbricatore. TEL 39-481-531514. adv. contact: Alessio Fabbricatore. bk.rev.; illus, maps, stat. circ. 8,000. (tabloid format) **Document type:** bulletin, proceedings, newsletter.
Formerly (until 1990): Speleo Soccorso.
Description: Covers national and international meetings on rescue issues as well as laws regarding alpine and speleological rescues.

D R C BOOK & MONOGRAPH SERIES. (Disaster Research Center) see PUBLIC HEALTH AND SAFETY

350.755 AT ISSN 0811-6407
DEFENDER; information and comment on defence matters. 1979. q. Aus.$15. (Australia Defence Association) Janbar Publishing Co., P.O. Box 351, Cronulla, N.S.W. 2230, Australia. TEL 612-527-4980. FAX 612-527-4950. circ. 1,100.
Formerly: A.D.A. Journal (ISSN 0157-4310)

DEFENSE TRANSPORTATION JOURNAL; magazine of international defense transportation and logistics. see TRANSPORTATION

DENMARK. FORSVARSMINISTERIET. AARLIGE REDEGOERELSE. see MILITARY

DOCTORS FOR DISASTER PREPAREDNESS NEWSLETTER. see MEDICAL SCIENCES

363.35 UK
EASINGWOLD PAPERS. 1990. irreg., no.8, 1994. price varies. Home Office Emergency Planning College, Easingwold, York YO6 3EG, England. TEL 44-1347-822877. FAX 44-1347-822575. **Document type:** monographic series, government publication.
Description: Discusses topics of current importance in emergency planning. Fosters a practical method of understanding developments in emergency planning in both the public and private sectors.

363.35 CN ISSN 0837-5771
UA926.A1 CODEN: EPDIEO
EMERGENCY PREPAREDNESS DIGEST/REVUE PROTECTION CIVILE. 1974. q. Can.$20 (foreign Can.$26). (Emergency Preparedness Canada) Canada Communications Group, 45 Sacre-Coeur Blvd., Rm. A2411E, Hull, PQ K1A 0S9, Canada. TEL 819-956-5365. FAX 819-956-5134. (Dist. by: Canada Communication Group, 45 Sacre-Coeur Blvd., Rm. A2411 E Hull, PQ K1A 0S9, Canada) Ed. Anne-Marie Demers. adv.: B&W page Can.$550, color page Can.$1650; 7 x 9 1/2; adv. contact: Neil Patterson. bk.rev.; stat.; index. circ. 2,700. (also avail. in microform from UMI; reprint service avail. from UMI) Indexed: Abstr.J.Earthq.Eng., Can.B.P.I., INIS Atomind., Mid.East: Abstr.& Ind., Repindex. **Document type:** government publication.
—UMI.
Formerly (until 1986): Emergency Planning Digest (ISSN 0317-3518); Supersedes: E M O National Digest (ISSN 0012-7787)
Description: Provides current information and reference material on a broad range of subjects involving emergency preparedness.

363 US ISSN 0275-3782
EMERGENCY PREPAREDNESS NEWS; contingency planning, crisis management, disaster relief. 1977. bi-w. $286. Business Publishers, Inc., 951 Pershing Dr., Silver Spring, MD 20910-4464. TEL 301-587-6300. FAX 301-585-9075. Ed. Bonita Becker. (looseleaf format; back issues avail.) **Document type:** newsletter.
●Also available online. Vendor(s): NewsNet (GT34).
—CCC.
Description: For public officials, business executives and nonprofit-sector managers charged with the task of preparing for natural and man-made disasters, protecting the public when they occur, and relieving the suffering that inevitably follows.

CIVIL DEFENSE

363.35   SZ   ISSN 0015-0428
FEUILLE OFFICIELLE DE LA PROTECTION CIVILE/MITTEILUNGSBLATT DES ZIVILSCHUTZES/FOGLIO D'INFORMAZIONE DELLA PROTEZIONE CIVILE. (Text in French, German, Italian) 1964. s-a. 10 SFr. Bundesamt fuer Zivilschutz - Federal Office of Civil Defense, Case Postale 3003, Berne, Switzerland. adv.; charts; illus. circ. 19,000.

FOLK OCH FOERSVAR. see *MILITARY*

363.35 355   SW   ISSN 0349-9715
FRITT MILITAERT FORUM. 1940. 4/yr. SEK 150 membership (effective 1995). (Foersvarsfremjandet) Fritt Militaert Forum, Teaterg. 3, S-111 48 Stockholm, Sweden.
Former titles: (until 1981): Fritt Militaert Forum, Folkfoersvaret (ISSN 0345-0287); (until 1972): Folkfoersvaret (ISSN 0015-5853)

GAKEKUZURE SAIGAI NO JITTAI/RESEARCH DATA OF LANDSLIDE DISASTERS. see *EARTH SCIENCES — Geology*

GREENPEACE MAGAZIN. see *ENVIRONMENTAL STUDIES*

350.755 363.35   US
HAZARD TECHNOLOGY. 1980. q. free. Emergency Information System, International, 1401 Rockville Pike, Ste. 500, Rockville, MD 20852. TEL 301-738-6900; 800-999-5009. FAX 301-738-1026. E-mail: info@eisint.com; URL: http://www.eisintl.com. Ed. K.C. Chartrand; Pub. James W. Morentz. adv. circ. 55,000. (tabloid format) **Document type:** newspaper.
●Also available online.
Formerly: Hazard Monthly (ISSN 0742-6410); **Incorporates:** Corporate Emergency Management.
Description: Covers the use of technology in the field of emergency and environmental management.

INSTITUTE FOR DEFENCE STUDIES AND ANALYSES. STRATEGIC ANALYSIS. see *POLITICAL SCIENCE — International Relations*

355   II   ISSN 0970-017X
UA840
INSTITUTE FOR DEFENCE STUDIES AND ANALYSES. STRATEGIC DIGEST. (Text in English) 1971. m. Rs.120. Institute for Defence Studies and Analyses, Sapru House, Barakhamba Rd., New Delhi 110 001, India. Ed. Jasjit Singh. circ. 2,000. **Indexed:** Int.Polit.Sci.Abstr., Pub.Admin.Abstr. **Document type:** academic/scholarly publication.
Incorporates: Defence and Disarmament Review.

363.35   SZ   ISSN 1022-3908
INTERNATIONAL CIVIL DEFENCE JOURNAL/REVUE INTERNATIONALE DE PROTECTION CIVILE/REVISTA INTERNACIONAL DE PROTECCION CIVIL. (Text in Arabic, English, French, Spanish) 1952. q. 50 SFr. (foreign 70 SFr.). International Civil Defence Organization - Organisation Internationale de Protection Civile, Information Service, 10-12 Chemin de Surville, CH-1213 Petit-Lancy - Geneva, Switzerland. TEL 022-7934433. FAX 022-7934428. TELEX 423786-CH. adv.; bk.rev.; stat. circ. 3,000. **Document type:** bulletin.
Formerly: International Civil Defence (ISSN 0020-6369)
Description: Includes information on civil defense, disaster prevention, as well as related laws and directives from an international perspective.

ITALIA NOSTRA. SEZIONE DI TRENTO. BOLLETTINO. see *ENVIRONMENTAL STUDIES*

JISHIN YOCHI RENRAKUKAI KAIHO/COORDINATING COMMITTEE FOR EARTHQUAKE PREDICTION. REPORT. see *EARTH SCIENCES — Geophysics*

363.35   US   ISSN 0740-5537
UA926.A1
JOURNAL OF CIVIL DEFENSE. 1968. q. $18. The American Civil Defense Association, Box 1057, Starke, FL 32091. TEL 904-964-5397. FAX 904-964-9641. Ed. Walter Murphey. adv. contact: Kathy Eiland. bk.rev.; charts; illus.; index. circ. 1,000. (also avail. in microform; reprint service avail. from UMI) **Indexed:** Abstr.Mil.Bibl., DM& T, PROMT. **Document type:** academic/scholarly publication.
—UMI.
Formerly (until Jan. 1976): Survive (ISSN 0039-6354)
Description: Covers subjects in the fields of civil and strategic defense strategies.

363.35   JA   ISSN 0286-7745
KOZUI/FLOODS. (Text in Japanese) 1961. a. Tonegawa Arakawa Kozui Yoho Renrakukai - Tonegawa and Arakawa River Communication Association for Flood Forecasting, Kensetsusho Kanto Chiho Kensetsukyoku Kasen Kanrika, 3-1, Ote-machi 1-chome, Chiyoda-ku, Tokyo 100, Japan.

350.755   FR   ISSN 0290-9464
LIEN DES FOURNISSEURS DE LA DEFENSE NATIONALE. 1981. 4/yr. Gepo 19, Villa Croix-Nivert, 75015 Paris, France. Ed. Jacques Vuvan.

363.35   JA   ISSN 0285-7502
MINATO NO BOSAI/JOURNAL OF DISASTER PREVENTION OF HARBOURS. (Text in Japanese) q. Kowan Kaigan Bosai Kyogikai - Disaster Prevention Association for Harbours and Coasts, Nihon Kowan Kyokai, 2-8, Toranomon 1-chome, Minato-ku, Tokyo 105, Japan.

363   US   ISSN 0197-6672
MISSOURI. EMERGENCY MANAGEMENT AGENCY. NEWSLETTER. vol.22, 1975. q. free. State Emergency Management Agency, Box 116, Jefferson City, MO 65102. TEL 573-526-9136. FAX 573-634-7966. E-mail: mosema@mail.state.mo.us; URL: http://www.state.mo.us/sema/semapage.htm. Ed. Carolyn Stonner. bk.rev.; charts; illus. circ. 1,200. **Document type:** newsletter.
Former titles: Missouri. Disaster Operations Office. Newsletter (ISSN 0364-0337); Missouri Disaster Planning and Operations Newsletter (ISSN 0026-6531)
Description: News and announcements of emergency-preparedness activities for natural and man-made disasters at the local level in Missouri.

MIZU SHIGEN KENKYU SENTA KENKYU HOKOKU/WATER RESOURCES CENTER. RESEARCH REPORT. see *WATER RESOURCES*

363.35   GW
UA926.A1
NOTFALLVORSORGE; Zeitschrift fuer Katastrophenvorbeugung und Gefahrenabwehr. 1970. q. DM.49.90 (effective 1997 & 1998). Osang Verlag GmbH, Am Roemerlager 2, 53117 Bonn, Germany. TEL 49-228-678383. FAX 49-228-679631. E-mail: osang@osang.de; URL: http://www.osang.de. Ed. Guenther Wollmer. adv.; bk.rev.; abstr.; charts; illus.; pat.; tr.lit. circ. 6,000. **Indexed:** C.I.S. Abstr. **Document type:** consumer publication.
Former titles: Notfallvorsorge und Zivile Verteidigung (ISSN 0938-7390); Zivilverteidigung (ISSN 0044-4839)

363.35   YU   ISSN 0029-8344
ODBRANA I ZASTITA. (Text in Albanian, Macedonian, Serbo-Croatian, Slovenian) 1965. bi-m. 180 din. Savezni Sekretarijat za Narodnu Odbranu, Kneza Milosa 37, 11002 Belgrade, Serbia, Yugoslavia. Ed. Radko Kovacic. adv.; bibl.; illus.; index.

350.755   IT
PROTEZIONE CIVILE ITALIANA. 4/yr. Edizioni Nazionali s.r.l., Viale Faenza 26-5, 20142 Milan, Italy. TEL 2-81-36-669. FAX 2-81-34-925. Ed. Luigi Rigo. circ. 15,000.

363.1   SP   ISSN 0214-8102
REVISTA DE PROTECCION CIVIL. 1984. bi-m. Direccion General de Proteccion Civil, C. Quintiliano 21, 28071 Madrid, Spain. TEL 34-1-5373125.
Formerly (until 1988): Cuadernos de Proteccion Civil (ISSN 0214-8099)

363.35   FR   ISSN 0222-559X
SECURITE CIVILE ET INDUSTRIELLE. 1953. q. 580 F. France-Selection, 9-13 rue de la Nouvelle France, B.P. 118, 93303 Aubervilliers Cedex, France. TEL 33-1-48331818. FAX 33-1-48332160. Ed. Jean Rue. adv. contact: Frederique Fardeau. bk.rev.; bibl.; charts; illus.; cum.index. circ. 8,000. **Indexed:** C.I.S. Abstr. **Document type:** trade publication.
Formerly: Protection Civile et Securite Industrielle (ISSN 0033-1724)

363.3481 616.025   SW   ISSN 0283-9865
SIRENEN; Raeddningsverkets tidning. 1986. q. free. Statens Raeddningsverk (SRV), Rum M 420 Karolinen, S-651 80 Karlstad, Sweden.

363.35   NO   ISSN 0332-902X
UA929.N7
SIVILT BEREDSKAP. 1958. q. NOK 10. Direktoratet for Sivilt Beredskap - Directorate for Civil Defence and Emergency Planning, Postboks 8136, Oslo Dep., Oslo 1, Norway. (Co-sponsor: Norges Sivilforsvarsforbund) Ed. Rolf Thue. bk.rev.; charts; illus. circ. 65,000.
Formerly (until 1970): Sivilforvarsblad (ISSN 0800-2665)

STRATEGIC AND DEFENCE STUDIES CENTRE. WORKING PAPERS. see *MILITARY*

363   US   ISSN 1057-364X
SURVIVALIST S I G NEWSLETTER. 1990. q. $5 in N. America; overseas $7. Survivalist Special Interest Group, Box 20188, Cleveland, OH 44120-0188. Ed. Richard Hershbain. adv.; bk.rev.; index; circ. 250 (paid). (back issues avail.) **Document type:** newsletter.
Description: Deals with the issues of surviving man-made and natural disasters through preparedness, self-sufficiency, and self-reliance.

350.755   US
T A C D A ALERT. 1978. 8/yr. $50 includes membership. The American Civil Defense Association, Box 1057, Starke, FL 32091. TEL 904-964-5397. FAX 904-964-9641. Ed. Walter Murphey. R&P contact: Katy Eiland. circ. 1,000. (looseleaf format; back issues avail.; reprint service avail. from UMI) **Document type:** newsletter.
Formerly: T A C D A Update (ISSN 0740-0179)
Description: Covers current events pertaining to the strategic defense initiative and civil defense.

TSUNAMI KOGAKU KENKYU HOKOKU/TSUNAMI ENGINEERING TECHNICAL REPORT. see *ENGINEERING — Civil Engineering*

UNIVERSITY OF DELAWARE. DISASTER RESEARCH CENTER. DISSERTATIONS. see *PUBLIC HEALTH AND SAFETY*

UNIVERSITY OF DELAWARE. DISASTER RESEARCH CENTER. FINAL PROJECT REPORTS. see *PUBLIC HEALTH AND SAFETY*

UNIVERSITY OF DELAWARE. DISASTER RESEARCH CENTER. MISCELLANEOUS REPORTS. see *PUBLIC HEALTH AND SAFETY*

UNIVERSITY OF DELAWARE. DISASTER RESEARCH CENTER. PRELIMINARY PAPERS. see *PUBLIC HEALTH AND SAFETY*

UNIVERSITY OF DELAWARE. DISASTER RESEARCH CENTER. REPORT SERIES. see *PUBLIC HEALTH AND SAFETY*

363.35   FR
V I P. 10/yr. Imprimerie de Bussac, 2 cours Sablon, 63100 Clermont-Ferrand, France. TEL 42-93-06-45. FAX 42-94-28-79. Ed. J.-F. Pillebout. circ. 9,500.

363.35   DK   ISSN 0109-0100
VAERNSKONTAKT. 1983. q. free. Forsvarskommandoen, Presse- og Informationstjeneste, P.O. Box 202, 2950 Vedbaek Denmark. illus.

ZASTITA OD POZARA/FIREFIGHTING PROTECTION. see *FIRE PREVENTION*

363.35   SZ
ZIVILSCHUTZ. 1954. 9/yr. 49 SFr. (foreign 60 SFr.). (Schweizerischer Zivilschutzverband) Vogt-Schild AG Zuchwilerstr. 21, CH-4501 Solothurn, Switzerland. TEL 065-247247. FAX 065-247235. Ed. Hans Juerg Muenger. adv.: B&W page 2350 SFr., color page 3450 SFr.; trim 185 x 270; adv. contact: Hansruedi Spiri. circ. 21,066. **Document type:** bulletin.

350.755   AU
ZIVILSCHUTZ AKTUELL. 1987. q. S.248. (Oesterreichischer Zivilschutzverband) Bohmann Druck und Verlag GmbH & Co. KG, Leberstr. 122, A-1110 Vienna, Austria. TEL 43-1-74095-0. FAX 43-1-74095-183. TELEX 132312. circ. 41,000. **Document type:** bulletin.

CIVIL DEFENSE — Abstracting, Bibliographies, Statistics

353 011   US   ISSN 1050-4850
Z1361.D4
CURRENT WORLD AFFAIRS; a quarterly bibliography. 1975. q. $170 (foreign $180). George A. Daoust, Ed. & Pub., 1336 Kingston Ave., Alexandria, VA 22302. TEL 703-759-2085. FAX 703-759-6291. bk.rev. circ. 200. **Document type:** bibliography.
    Formerly (until 1989): Quarterly Strategic Bibliography (ISSN 0198-9006); Supersedes (in 1977): Current Bibliographic Survey of National Defense (ISSN 0364-3352)
    Description: Bibliographic compilation of articles, editorials, books and government documents pertaining to current international affairs.

363.35 355 016   SW   ISSN 0016-1543
FOERSVARSFORSKNINGSREFERAT/DEFENCE RESEARCH ABSTRACTS. UNCLASSIFIED; oeppen del. Short title: F R O E. (Text in English, Swedish) 1966. q. Foersvarets Forskningsanstalt (FOA) - National Defence Research Establishment, Central Administration, Centralkansliet, 172 90 Sundbyberg, Sweden. Ed. Eva B. Bjoerck. index; circ. 950 (controlled). **Document type:** abstracting/indexing.
    Description: Contains unclassified reports published by the Swedish Defence Research Establishment, The Swedish Board of Psychological Defence and a selection of reports from the Royal Swedish Fortification Administration.

CIVIL ENGINEERING

see Engineering–Civil Engineering

CIVIL LAW

see Law–Civil Law

CIVIL RIGHTS

see Political Science–Civil Rights

CLASSICAL STUDIES

see also Archaeology; History; Linguistics; Literature; Museums and Art Galleries

880 830   US
M S ANCIENT AND CLASSICAL STUDIES. 1993. irreg. (Abrahams Magazine Service) A M S Press, Inc., 56 E. 13th St., New York, NY 10003. TEL 212-777-4700. FAX 212-995-5413. **Document type:** academic/scholarly publication, monographic series.

870 470   HU   ISSN 0044-5975
CC1   CODEN: AAASAM
ACADEMIAE SCIENTIARUM HUNGARICAE. ACTA ANTIQUA. (Text in English, French, German, Latin, Russian) 1951. a. $144 (effective 1998). (Magyar Tudomanyos Akademia) Akademiai Kiado Rt., P.O. Box 245, H-1519 Budapest, Hungary. TEL 36-1-2043976. FAX 36-1-2043973. Ed. Zsigmond Ritook. adv.; bk.rev. **Indexed:** Arts & Hum.Cit.Ind., Bibl.Ling., Curr.Cont., IBR, M.L.A., Numis.Lit. **Document type:** academic/scholarly publication.
   —BLDSC (0595.900000). **CCC.**
    Description: Publishes original articles on classical philology. Covers history, literature, philology and material culture of the Ancient East, the Classical Antiquity and Byzantium.

800   SA   ISSN 0065-1141
PA25
ACTA CLASSICA. (Text mainly in English; occasionally in Afrikaans, French or German) 1958. a. $50 (effective 1994). Classical Association of South Africa, P.O. Box 392, Pretoria 0001, South Africa. TEL 27-12-429-6501. FAX 27-12-429-3221. TELEX 350068. E-mail: bothmh@alpha.unisa.ac.za. Ed. U.R.D. Vogel-Weidemann. bk.rev. circ. 500. **Indexed:** Bibl.Ling., IBR, Ind.S.A.Per. **Document type:** academic/scholarly publication, proceedings.
   —CCC.
    Refereed Serial

ACTA HYPERBOREA. see *ARCHAEOLOGY*

930 913   HU   ISSN 0567-7246
ACTA UNIVERSITATIS DE ATTILA JOZSEF NOMINATAE. ACTA ANTIQUA ET ARCHAEOLOGICA. (Text in German, Greek or Latin; notes in French or German; supplement in Hungarian) 1958. a. exchange basis. Attila Jozsef University, c/o E. Szabo, Exchange Librarian, Dugonics ter 13, P.O. Box 393, 6701 Szeged, Hungary. (Subscr. to: Kultura, Box 149, 1389 Budapest, Hungary) Eds. Samu Szadeczky-Kardoss, Egon Maroti. circ. 600.
    Incorporates: Opuscula Byzantina (ISSN 0139-2751)
    Description: Journal of classical and Byzantine studies and archaeology.

937 745.1   PL   ISSN 0524-4463
D51
ACTA UNIVERSITATIS WRATISLAVIENSIS. ANTIQUITAS. (Text in Polish; summaries in English or French) 1963. irreg. price varies. (Uniwersytet Wroclawski) Wydawnictwo Uniwersytetu Wroclawskiego, Spolka z o.o., Pl. Uniwersytecki 9-13, 50-137 Wroclaw, Poland. TEL 48-71-441006. FAX 48-71-402735. Ed. Eugeniusz Konik. circ. 300. **Document type:** academic/scholarly publication.

937   PL   ISSN 0578-4387
PA9
ACTA UNIVERSITATIS WRATISLAVIENSIS. CLASSICA WRATISLAVIENSIA. (Text in German or Polish; summaries in English, French or German) 1961. irreg. price varies. (Uniwersytet Wroclawski) Wydawnictwo Uniwersytetu Wroclawskiego, Spolka z o.o., Pl. Uniwersytecki 9-13, 50-137 Wroclaw, Poland. TEL 48-71-441006. FAX 48-71-402735. Ed. Alicja Szastynska-Siemion. circ. 300. **Document type:** academic/scholarly publication.

ADULESCENS. see *LINGUISTICS*

937   IT   ISSN 1121-8932
AEVUM ANTIQUUM. 1988. a. Lit.42000 (foreign Lit.69000($50)) (effective 1997). (Universita Cattolica del S. Cuore) Vita e Pensiero, Largo A. Gemelli, 1, 20123 Milan, Italy. TEL 39-2-72342370. FAX 39-2-72342974. Ed. Giovanni Tarditi. circ. 900. **Document type:** academic/scholarly publication.
    Description: Features a critical article on a cultural aspect, literary genre or an author of the classical era. Includes analyses of historical-philological or archaeological-antiquarian character.

800   SA   ISSN 0303-1896
AKROTERION. (Text in Afrikaans and English) 1956. q. R.25 ($15 or £10) (effective 1995). University of Stellenbosch, Department of Classics, Private Bag X1, Matielands, Stellenbosch 7602, South Africa. TEL 27-21-8083136. FAX 27-21-8084336. E-mail: grieks@maties.sun.ac.za; URL: http://www.sun.ac.za/local/academic/greek/akroteri.html. (Co-sponsor: Classical Association of South Africa) Ed. P.J. Conradie. adv.; bk.rev.; abstr. circ. 475. (processed) **Indexed:** Ind.S.A.Per. **Document type:** academic/scholarly publication.
    Formerly: Klassieke Nuusbrief (ISSN 0023-2033)

400   GW   ISSN 0179-387X
DIE ALTEN SPRACHEN IM UNTERRICHT. 1953. q. DM.23. (Altphilologische Fachgruppe im Bayerischen Philologenverband) C.C. Buchners Verlag, Laubanger 8, 96052 Bamberg, Germany. TEL 49-951-96501-0. FAX 49-951-61774. adv.; bk.rev. circ. 1,300. **Document type:** academic/scholarly publication.

571 930   NE   ISSN 0002-6646
DE1
DAS ALTERTUM. 1955. q. $43 (effective 1998). (Akademie der Wissenschaften der DDR, Zentralinstitut fuer Alte Geschichte und Archaeologie) Gordon and Breach - Harwood Academic, Amsteldisk 166, 1st Fl., 1079 LH Amsterdam, Netherlands. (Subscr. to: International Publishers Distributor, Box 32160, Newark, NJ 07102. TEL 800-545-8398. FAX 215-750-6343) Ed.Bd. adv.; bibl.; charts; illus.; index. **Indexed:** Bibl.Ling., IBR.
   —SWETS. **CCC.**

700   IT   ISSN 0065-681X
AMERICAN ACADEMY IN ROME. PAPERS AND MONOGRAPHS. 1919. irreg. price varies. American Academy in Rome, Via Angelo Masina 5 C, 00153 Rome, Italy. TEL 39-6-58461. **Document type:** monographic series.

480 880   US   ISSN 0044-7633
Z7016
AMERICAN CLASSICAL REVIEW. 1971. bi-m. $5 to individuals; institutions $7.50. City University of New York, Queens College, American Classical Review, Flushing, NY 11367. TEL 718-520-7000. Eds. Ursula Schoenheim, Ethyle R. Wolfe. bk.rev.; bibl.; index. circ. 1,400. (back issues avail)

AMERICAN JOURNAL OF PHILOLOGY. see *LINGUISTICS*

AMERICAN PHILOLOGICAL ASSOCIATION. NEWSLETTER. see *LITERATURE*

AMERICAN PHILOLOGICAL ASSOCIATION. SPECIAL PUBLICATIONS. see *LINGUISTICS*

800   US   ISSN 0741-9309
AMERICAN UNIVERSITY STUDIES. SERIES 17. CLASSICAL LANGUAGE AND LITERATURE. 1986. irreg. Peter Lang Publishing, Inc., 275 Seventh Ave., 28th Fl., New York, NY 10001. TEL 212-647-7700; 800-770-5264. FAX 212-647-7707. E-mail: customerservice@plang.com; URL: http://www.peterlang.com. Ed. Christopher Myers. **Indexed:** Bibl.Ling. **Document type:** academic/scholarly publication, monographic series.
    Description: Takes an in-depth look at the literature of classical Greece and Rome.

870 937   NE   ISSN 0928-2130
AMSTERDAM CLASSICAL MONOGRAPHS. (Text in English) 1992. irreg., latest 1995. price varies. J.C. Gieben, Nieuwe Herengracht 35, 1011 RM Amsterdam, Netherlands. TEL 31-20-6275170. FAX 31-20-6275170. (Dist. in N. America by: John Benjamins Publishing Co., Box 27519, Philadelphia, PA 19118-0519. TEL 215-836-1200. FAX 215-836-1204) **Document type:** academic/scholarly publication.

ANCIENT CIVILIZATIONS FROM SCYTHIA TO SIBERIA; an international journal of comparative studies in history and archaeology. see *HISTORY — History Of Asia*

ANCIENT HISTORY BULLETIN. see *HISTORY*

ANCIENT NEAR EAST: HISTORY AND PHILOLOGY. see *ORIENTAL STUDIES*

ANCIENT SOCIETY; journal of ancient history of the Greek, Hellenistic and Roman world. see *HISTORY*

ANCIENT WORLD; a scholarly journal for the study of antiquity. see *HISTORY*

880   AT   ISSN 0066-4774
ANTICHTHON. 1967. a. Aus.$25 to individuals; institutions & libraries Aus.$30 (effective through 1996). Australian Society for Classical Studies, c/o Prof. G.R. Stanton, Ed., Dept. of Classics and Ancient History, University of New England, Armidale, N.S.W. 2351, Australia. FAX 61-67-73-3122. Eds. N. O'Sullivan, G.R. Stanton. adv.; circ. 400 (paid). **Indexed:** Aus.P.A.I.S., Bibl.Ling., IBR, Numis.Lit. **Document type:** academic/scholarly publication.
   —BLDSC (1547.320000); UnCover.
    Refereed Serial

CLASSICAL STUDIES

930 571   HU   ISSN 0003-567X
ANTIK TANULMANYOK/STUDIA ANTIQUA. (Text in Hungarian) 1954. s-a. $34 (effective 1998). (Magyar Tudomanyos Akademia) Akademiai Kiado Rt., P.O. Box 245, H-1519 Budapest, Hungary. TEL 36-1-2043976. FAX 36-1-2043973. Ed. Istvan Borzsak. adv.; bk.rev.; illus.; index. **Document type:** academic/scholarly publication.

930   GW   ISSN 0003-5696
PA3
ANTIKE UND ABENDLAND; Beitraege zum Verstaendnis der Griechen und Roemer und ihres Nachlebens. 1945. a. DM.236 (effective 1998). Walter de Gruyter und Co., Genthiner Str. 13, 10785 Berlin, Germany. TEL 49-30-26005-0. FAX 49-30-26005251. E-mail: wdg-info@degruyter.de; URL: http://www.degruyter.de (U.S. addr.: Walter de Gruyter, Inc., 200 Saw Mill River Rd., Hawthorne, NY 10532. TEL 914-747-0110) Ed.Bd. adv.; bk.rev.; illus. **Indexed:** Arts & Hum.Cit.Ind., ASCA, Can.Rev.Comp.Lit, Curr.Cont., IBR. **Document type:** academic/scholarly publication.
—Genuine Article; SWETS. **CCC.**

930 800   AU   ISSN 0003-6293
CC5
ANZEIGER FUER DIE ALTERTUMSWISSENSCHAFT. 1948. q. S.580. (Oesterreichische Humanistische Gesellschaft) Universitaetsverlag Wagner, Andreas-Hofer-Str. 13, Postfach 165, A-6010 Innsbruck, Austria. TEL 43-512-587721. FAX 43-512-582209. Ed. Gottfried Grasl; Pub. Gottfried Grasl. R&P contact: Gottfried Grasl. bk.rev.; abstr.; bibl.; index. (also avail. in microform from SWZ; back issues avail.) **Indexed:** Amer.Hist.& Life, Bibl.Ling., Hist.Abstr., IBR. **Document type:** academic/scholarly publication.
—SWETS.

APEIRON; a journal of ancient philosophy and science. see *PHILOSOPHY*

ARBEITEN ZUR GESCHICHTE DES ANTIKEN JUDENTUMS UND DES URCHRISTENTUMS. see *RELIGIONS AND THEOLOGY — Judaic*

ARBEITEN ZUR LITERATUR UND GESCHICHTE DES HELLENISTISCHEN JUDENTUMS. see *RELIGIONS AND THEOLOGY — Judaic*

870   UK   ISSN 0309-5541
ARCA; classical and medieval texts, papers and monographs. 1976. irreg. (1-5/yr.). price varies. Francis Cairns (Publications) Ltd., c/o The University, Leeds LS2 9JT, England. Ed.Bd. (back issues avail.) **Document type:** monographic series.
—BLDSC (1594.460000).

ARCHAEOLOGICAL NEWS. see *ARCHAEOLOGY*

ARCHAIA HELLAS; monographs on ancient Greek History and archaeology. see *ARCHAEOLOGY*

ARCHAIOLOGIA. see *ARCHAEOLOGY*

ARCHEOLOGIA CLASSICA. see *ARCHAEOLOGY*

800 930   PL   ISSN 0066-6866
ARCHIWUM FILOLOGICZNE. (Vols. are not issued in chronological order) (Text in French, German, Latin and Polish; summaries in French) 1958. irreg., vol.49, 1994. price varies. (Polska Akademia Nauk, Komitet Nauk o Kulturze Antycznej) Ossolineum, Publishing House of the Polish Academy of Sciences, Pl. Solny 14a, 50-062 Wroclaw, Poland. TEL 48-71-343-6961. FAX 48-71-448-103. TELEX 0712771 OSS PL. Ed. J. Wolski. circ. 750. **Document type:** monographic series.
  Description: Dissertations and monographical papers on literature, history, archaeology and culture in ancient world.

489   FI   ISSN 0570-734X
ARCTOS; ACTA PHILOLOGICA FENNICA. (Supplement avail.) (Text in English, French, German and Italian) 1954. a. FIM 250($60) (effective 1997). Klassillis - Filologinen Yhdistys, PL 4, Vuorikatu 3 A, 00014 University of Helsinki, Finland. TEL 358-9-19122681. FAX 358-9-19122161. (Dist. by: Bookstore Tiedekirja, Kirkkokatu 14, FIN-00170 Helsinki 17, Finland) Ed. Jaakko Froesen. adv. contact: Raija Sarasti-Wilenius. bk.rev. circ. 50. **Indexed:** Bibl.Ling., IBR. **Document type:** academic/scholarly publication.

489   FI   ISSN 0066-6998
ARCTOS; ACTA PHILOLOGICA FENNICA. SUPPLEMENTUM. 1968. irreg. Klassillis - Filologinen Yhdistys, PL 4, Vuorikatu 3 A, 00014 University of Helsinki, Finland. TEL 358-9-19122681. FAX 358-9-19122161. (Dist. by: Bookstore Tiedekirja, Kikkokatu 14, FIN-00170 Helsinki 17, Finland) Ed. Jaakko Froesen. adv. contact: Raija Sarasti-Wilenius. **Document type:** academic/scholarly publication.
—BLDSC (1663.210000).

930.1   US   ISSN 0004-0975
PA1   **CODEN: AETHEE**
ARETHUSA. Online edition (US ISSN 1080-6504) 1968. 3/yr. $25 to individuals; institutions $49 (effective 1997). Johns Hopkins University Press, Journals Publishing Division, 2715 N. Charles St., Baltimore, MD 21218-4319. TEL 410-516-6987. FAX 410-516-6968. URL: http://muse.jhu.edu. Ed. Martha Malamud. adv. contact: Stasia Macsherry. bk.rev. circ. 608. (also avail. in microform from UMI; reprint service avail. from UMI) **Indexed:** Amer.Hum.Ind., ASCA, ASCA, Curr.Cont., IBR, IBR, IBZ. **Document type:** academic/scholarly publication.
●Also available online.
—Genuine Article; KR SourceOne; SWETS; UMI; UnCover. **CCC.**
  Description: Publishes literary and cultural studies that represent new approaches to the study of classics.

800   AG   ISSN 0325-4194
ARGOS. 1977. a. $20 (effective 1993). Asociacion Argentina de Estudios Clasicos, Beruti 3199, 1425 Buenos Aires, Argentina. Ed. R. Buzon. adv.; bk.rev. circ. 300.

870   US   ISSN 0095-5809
PA1
ARION; a journal of humanities and the classics. 1962-1972; N.S. 1974-1976; N.S. 1990. 3/yr. $19 to individuals (foreign $22); institutions $35 (foreign $38); students $12 (foreign $15) (effective 1996). Boston University, 10 Lenox St., Brookline, MA 02146. TEL 617-353-6480. FAX 617-353-5905. E-mail: arion@acs.bu.edu. (Subscr. to: Boston University, Scholarly Publications, 985 Commonwealth Ave., Boston, MA 02215) Ed. Herbert Golder. R&P contact: David Banchs. adv. contact: Julie Seeger. bk.rev.; illus.; index; circ. 800 (controlled). (also avail. in microform from UMI) **Indexed:** Amer.Hum.Ind., Arts & Hum.Cit.Ind., Arts & Hum.Cit.Ind., ASCA, Curr.Cont., Hum.Ind., Ind.Amer.Per.Verse, Phil.Ind. **Document type:** academic/scholarly publication.
—BLDSC (1668.423000); UMI; UnCover.
  Description: Takes an interdisciplinary approach to the classics.

ART AND ARCHAEOLOGY NEWSLETTER. see *ARCHAEOLOGY*

ASSOCIATION OF ANCIENT HISTORIANS. PUBLICATIONS. see *HISTORY — History Of Europe*

930 800 400   IT   ISSN 0004-6493
ATENE E ROMA. 1898. q. L.26000 (foreign L.45000($35)) (effective 1994). (Associazione Italiana di Cultura Classica) Editoriale e Finanziaria Le Monnier, S.p.a., Via. A. Meucci 2, Casella Postale 202, 50100 Florence, Italy. TEL 39-55-6813801. FAX 39-55-643983. Ed.Bd. bk.rev. (reprint service avail. from SWZ) **Indexed:** Arts & Hum.Cit.Ind., ASCA, Bibl.Ling., Curr.Cont., IBR, SSCI.
—BLDSC (1765.859000); Genuine Article; KR SourceOne; SWETS.
  Description: Studies the classics, with an emphasis on Greek and Roman history.

470 410   GR   ISSN 1011-1557
AS202
ATHENA. (Text in English, French, Greek) 1889. a. Dr.5000. Athenais Epistemonike Hetaireia - Scientific Society of Athens, 74 Eressou St., 106 83 Athens, Greece. TEL 30-1-3834-069. (Dist. by: Institute of Books, M. Kardamitsa, 8 Ippokratous St., 106 80 Athens, Greece) Ed. Nicolaos Livadaras. bk.rev.; bibl. **Indexed:** Amer.Hist.& Life, Bibl.Ling., Hist.Abstr. **Document type:** academic/scholarly publication.

800 930   IT   ISSN 0004-6574
PA1.A1
ATHENAEUM; studi periodici di letteratura e storia dell'antichita. (Text in English, French, German, Italian) 1913. s-a. $80. Universita degli Studi di Pavia, Facolta di Lettere, 27100 Pavia, Italy. Dir. Prof. Emilio Gabba. adv. contact: Emilio Gabba. bk.rev.; index. circ. 600. **Indexed:** Arts & Hum.Cit.Ind., ASCA, Bibl.Ling., Curr.Cont., IBR, M.L.A., Numis.Lit. **Document type:** academic/scholarly publication.
—BLDSC (1765.868700); SWETS.

BERLINER BYZANTINISTISCHE ARBEITEN. see *HISTORY — History Of Europe*

800   SP
BIBLIOTECA CLASICA GREDOS. 1976. irreg. Editorial Gredos, S.A., Sanchez Pacheco 81, 28002 Madrid, Spain. FAX.341-5192033.

800 950   IT
BIBLIOTECA DEGLI STUDI CLASSICI E ORIENTALI. 1974. irreg., no.19, 1989. price varies. Giardini Editori e Stampatori, Via Santa Bibbiana 28, 56100 Pisa, Italy. TEL 050 502531.

800 870   IT
BIBLIOTECA DI STUDI ANTICHI. (Text in Greek, Italian, Latin) 1974. q. Giardini Editori e Stampatori, Via Santa Bibbiana 28, 56100 Pisa, Italy. Eds. Graziano Arrighetti, Emilio Gabba. (back issues avail.)

800   SZ   ISSN 0067-7965
BIBLIOTHECA HELVETICA ROMANA. (Text in French) 1954. irreg., no.26, 1994. (Institut Suisse de Rome, IT) Librairie Droz S.A., 11, rue Massot, CH-1211 Geneva 12, Switzerland. TEL 41-22-3466666. FAX 41-22-3472391. E-mail: drozsa@dial.eunet.ch; URL: http://www.eunet.ch/customers/droz. **Document type:** academic/scholarly publication.
—CCC.
  Description: Ancient, classical and medieval studies.

400   MX
BIBLIOTHECA HUMANISTICA MEXICANA. 1987. irreg., no.6, 1991. Universidad Nacional Autonoma de Mexico, Centro de Estudios Clasicos, Ciudad Universitaria, 04510 Mexico D.F., Mexico. TEL 525-6227488. FAX 525-6657874.

937 938   MX
BIBLIOTHECA SCRIPTORUM GRAECORUM ET ROMANORUM MEXICANA. 1944. irreg., no.92, 1989. Universidad Nacional Autonoma de Mexico, Centro de Estudios Clasicos, Ciudad Universitaria, 04510 Mexico D.F., Mexico. TEL 525-6227488. FAX 525-6657874.

880   GW   ISSN 0340-7853
BIBLIOTHEK DER GRIECHISCHEN LITERATUR. Abbreviated title: B G L. 1971. irreg., vol.43, 1997 price varies. Anton Hiersemann Verlag, Rosenbergstr. 113, 70193 Stuttgart, Germany. TEL 49-711-638265. FAX 49-711-6369010. (Subscr. to: Postfach 140155, 70071 Stuttgart, Germany) Eds. P. Wirth, W. Gessel. **Document type:** monographic series.

800   IT   ISSN 0391-8270
BOLLETTINO DEI CLASSICI. (Text in English, French, German, Greek, Italian, Latin and Spanish) 1940. a. L.30000. Academia Nazionale dei Lincei, Via della Lungara 10, 00165 Rome, Italy. TEL (06) 650.831. Ed. Cesare Franco Golisano. **Indexed:** Bibl.Ling.

870   IT   ISSN 0006-6583
PA2004
BOLLETTINO DI STUDI LATINI; rassegna semestrale di bibliographia e saggistica della letteratura latina. 1971. s-a. L.90000 (foreign L.110000) (effective 1996). Loffredo Editore S.p.A., Via Consalvo, 99 H 80126 Naples, Italy. TEL 081-5937073. FAX 081-5936953. Ed. Fabio Cupaiuolo. adv.; bk.rev.; index. circ. 500. **Indexed:** Bibl.Ling.
—KR SourceOne; SWETS.

BRITISH SCHOOL AT ATHENS. ANNUAL. see *ARCHAEOLOGY*

CLASSICAL STUDIES

930 US ISSN 1055-7660
PA1
BRYN MAWR CLASSICAL REVIEW. Online edition: B M C R (US ISSN 1063-2948) 1990. 8/yr. $20 (free in electronic format). Bryn Mawr Commentaries, Inc., Bryn Mawr College, Thomas Library, Bryn Mawr, PA 19010. TEL 610-526-5384. FAX 610-526-7475. E-mail: bmr@ccat.sas.upenn.edu; URL: gopher://gopher.lib.Virginia.EDU:70/11/alpha/bmcr/. Ed. Richard Hamilton. bk.rev. circ. 2,700. **Document type:** academic/scholarly publication.
●Also available online.
Also available on CD-ROM.
Refereed Serial

BRYN MAWR REVIEWS. see HISTORY — History Of Europe

BULLETIN ANTIEKE BESCHAVING; annual papers on classical archaeology. see ARCHAEOLOGY

880 FR ISSN 0007-4217
DF10
BULLETIN DE CORRESPONDANCE HELLENIQUE. 1877. a. (in 2 vols.). price varies. (Ecole Francaise d'Athenes, GR) De Boccard Edition, 11 rue de Medicis, 75006 Paris, France. charts; illus. (also avail. in microform from BHP; microfiche from IDC; reprint service avail. from KTO) **Indexed:** Arts & Hum.Cit.Ind., ASCA, Bibl.Ling., Curr.Cont., IBR, M.L.A., MLA Intl.Bibl., Numis.Lit. **Document type:** academic/scholarly publication, bulletin.
—Genuine Article; SWETS.

880 GR
BYZANTINA. (Text and summaries in English, French and Greek) 1969. a. $40. University of Thessaloniki, Byzantine Research Center, 71 Solonos St., 10679 Athens, Greece. Ed. Kas M. Grigori. **Indexed:** CERDIC, Numis.Lit.

BYZANTINISCHE FORSCHUNGEN. see HISTORY — History Of Europe

BYZANTINOSLAVICA; revue internationale des etudes byzantines. see ORIENTAL STUDIES

N I PUBLICATIONS. (Carsten Niebuhr Institute) see HISTORY — History Of The Near East

ALABRIA LIBRI; panorama bibliografico e di vita culturale. see BIBLIOGRAPHIES

ALLIOPE (PETERBOROUGH); world history for young people. see HISTORY

870 UK
AMBRIDGE CLASSICAL STUDIES. irreg., latest 1993. price varies. Cambridge University Press, Edinburgh Bldg., Shaftesbury Rd., Cambridge CB2 2RU, England. TEL 44-1223-312393. FAX 44-1223-315052. TELEX 851817256. E-mail: information@cup.cam.ac.uk; URL: http://www.cup.cam.ac.uk. (N. American addr.: Cambridge University Press, Journals Dept., 40 W. 20th St., New York, NY 10011. TEL 212-924-3900. FAX 212-691-3239) Ed.Bd. R&P contact: Linda Nicol. **Document type:** monographic series.

880 870 UK ISSN 0068-6638
AMBRIDGE CLASSICAL TEXTS AND COMMENTARIES. 1965. irreg., no.27, 1985. price varies. Cambridge University Press, Edinburgh Bldg., Shaftesbury Rd., Cambridge CB2 2RU, England. TEL 44-1223-312393. FAX 44-1223-315052. TELEX 851817256. E-mail: information@cup.cam.ac.uk; URL: http://www.cup.cam.ac.uk. (N. American addr.: Cambridge University Press, Journals Dept., 40 W. 20th St., New York, NY 10011. TEL 212-924-3900. FAX 212-691-3239) Ed.Bd. R&P contact: Linda Nicol. index. **Document type:** academic/scholarly publication.

400 UK ISSN 0068-6735
P11
CAMBRIDGE PHILOLOGICAL SOCIETY. PROCEEDINGS. (Supplements avail.) 1882; N.S. 1950. a. £15($36) to libraries; members £12 ($18) (effective 1995, 1996 & 1997). Cambridge Philological Society, c/o Dr. C. Austin, Trinity Hall, Cambridge CB2 1TJ, England. Eds. P.R. Hardie, S. Oakley. circ. 700. (also avail. in microform from UMI; microfiche from IDC; back issues avail.) **Indexed:** Arts & Hum.Cit.Ind., ASCA, Bibl.Ling., Curr.Cont., Numis.Lit., SSCI. **Document type:** proceedings.
—BLDSC (6671.900000); Genuine Article; SWETS.
Description: Covers a wide variety of issues pertaining to the history, culture, literature, and archaeology of the ancient Greek and Roman worlds.

400 UK ISSN 0068-6743
CAMBRIDGE PHILOLOGICAL SOCIETY. PROCEEDINGS. SUPPLEMENT. 1965. irreg., vol.18, 1994. £15($36) per vol. to non-members; members £12.50 ($30) (effective 997). Cambridge Philological Society, c/o Dr. C. Austin, Trinity Hall, Cambridge CB2 1TJ, England. Eds. P.R. Hardie, S. Oakley. (back issues avail.) **Document type:** proceedings.
Description: Covers a variety of topics pertaining to the history, archaeology, literature, and culture of ancient Greece and Rome.

400 MX
CENTRO DE ESTUDIOS CLASICOS. SERIE DIDACTICA. 1977. irreg., no.15, 1990. Universidad Nacional Autonoma de Mexico, Centro de Estudios Clasicos, Ciudad Universitaria, 04510 Mexico D.F., Mexico.

930 IT
CENTRO RICERCHE E DOCUMENTAZIONE SULL'ANTICHITA CLASSICA. MONOGRAFIE. irreg., no.16. price varies. L'Erma di Bretschneider, Via Cassiodoro 19, 00193 Rome, Italy. TEL 39-6-6874127. FAX 39-6-687-4129.

800 NE ISSN 0169-7692
CINCINNATI CLASSICAL STUDIES. NEW SERIES. 1977. irreg., vol.7, 1990. price varies. E.J. Brill, P.O. Box 9000, 2300 PA Leiden, Netherlands. TEL 31-71-5353500. FAX 31-71-5317532. TELEX 39296 BRILL NL. E-mail: ejbrill@brill.nl. (In N. America: E.J. Brill, 24 Hudson St., Kinderhook, NY 12106. TEL 800-962-4406. FAX 518-758-1959) R&P contact: Elizabeth Vennekamp. (back issues avail.) **Document type:** monographic series.
Refereed Serial

800 PO ISSN 0870-0141
PA2009
CLASSICA; boletim de pedagogia e cultura. 1977. irreg. price varies. Universidade de Lisboa, Departamento de Estudos Classicos, Cidade Universitaria, 1699 Lisbon Codex, Portugal. TEL 351-1-7965162. FAX 351-1-7960063. Ed. Victor Jaboville. bk.rev. circ. 1,000. **Document type:** academic/scholarly publication.

905 DK ISSN 0106-5815
CLASSICA ET MEDIAEVALIA; revue Danoise de philologie et d'histoire. (Supplement avail.: Classica et Mediaevalia Dissertationes) (Text in English, French, German) 1968. a. DKK 395 (effective 1997). (Dansk Selskab for Oldtids og Middelalderforskning) Museum Tusculanum Press, University of Copenhagen, Njalsgade 92, DK-2300 Copenhagen S, Denmark. TEL 45-35-32-91-09. FAX 45-35-32-91-13. (Dist. in U.S. and Canada by: Paul & Co., c/o P C S Data Processing, Inc., 360 W. 31st St., New York, NY 10001. TEL 212-564-3730. FAX 212-971-7200) Ed.Bd. (reprint service avail. from KTO) **Indexed:** Bibl.Engl.Lang.& Lit., Bibl.Ling., IBR. **Document type:** academic/scholarly publication.
●Also available on CD-ROM.
—SWETS; UnCover.
Description: Devoted to philology, history, philosophy Graeco-Roman antiquity and the Middle Ages.

880 930.1 SP ISSN 1381-2955
CLASSICAL AND BYZANTINE MONOGRAPHS. (Text in various languages) 1973. vol.35, 1996. price varies. A.M. Hakkert, C. Parroco Fr. Rodriguez Rodriguez 26, 35010 Las Palmas de Gran Canaria, Spain. TEL 34-28-277350. FAX 34-28-761619. E-mail: willem@dial.ecunet.es. (Dist. in N. America by: John Benjamins Publishing Co., Box 27519, Philadelphia, PA 19118-0519. TEL 215-836-1200. FAX 215-836-1204) **Document type:** monographic series.

480 880 US ISSN 0278-6656
DE1
CLASSICAL ANTIQUITY. US 1067-8344. 1968. s-a. $34 to individuals (foreign $38); institutions $75 (foreign $79); $79 with domain electronic access ($59 domain access only) (effective 1997). University of California Press, Journals Division, 2120 Berkeley Way, No. 5812, Berkeley, CA 94720-5812. TEL 510-643-7154. FAX 510-642-9917. E-mail: journal@ucop.edu; URL: http://sunsite.berkeley.edu:8080/scan. Ed.Bd. adv.: B&W page $275; adv. contact: Marge Dean. index; circ. 650 (paid). (also avail. in microform from UMI; back issues avail.) **Indexed:** Acad.Ind., Arts & Hum.Cit.Ind., ASCA, Bibl.Ling., Curr.Cont., Hum.Ind., Hum.Ind., SSCI. **Document type:** academic/scholarly publication.
●Also available online. Vendor(s): Information Access Co.
—BLDSC (3274.534500); Genuine Article; KR SourceOne; SWETS; UMI; UnCover. **CCC.**
Formerly (until 1982): California Studies in Classical Antiquity (ISSN 0068-5895)
Description: Features interdisciplinary research and discussion of major issues in the field of classics.
Refereed Serial

800 US
CLASSICAL ASSOCIATION OF NEW ENGLAND. ANNUAL BULLETIN. 1906. a. membership only. Classical Association of New England (Exeter), Phillips Exeter Academy, Exeter, NH 03833. TEL 603-772-4311 ext. 3258. FAX 603-778-9563. E-mail: a_wooley@mentor.unh.edu. Ed. Allan Wooley. bibl.; illus. circ. 900. **Document type:** bulletin.
Description: Presents the minutes of executive committee's meetings. Includes meetings, reports of officers, abstracts of papers delivered at the annual meeting, and a membership list.

150 US
CLASSICAL ASSOCIATION OF THE PACIFIC NORTHWEST. BULLETIN. 1971. s-a. $9. Classical Association of the Pacific Northwest, Univ. of Washington, Dept. of Classics, Box 353110, Seattle, WA 98195. TEL 206-543-2266. FAX 206-543-2267. Ed. Alain M. Gowing. R&P contact: Alain M. Gowing. adv.; bibl. circ. 150. **Document type:** bulletin.

800 976 US ISSN 0009-8337
PA1
CLASSICAL BULLETIN. 1925. s-a. $25 to individuals (Canada $30; elsewhere $35); institutions $40 (effective 1998). Bolchazy - Carducci Publishers, Inc., 1000 Brown St., Unit 101, Wauconda, IL 60084. TEL 847-526-4344. FAX 847-526-2867. E-mail: bolchazy@aol.com. Eds. Ladislaus Bolchazy, Martin Miller; Pub. Ladislaus Bolchazy. R&P contact: Ladislaus Bolchazy. bk.rev.; index. circ. 600. (also avail. in microform from UMI; back issues avail.; reprint service avail. from UMI) **Indexed:** Arts & Hum.Cit.Ind., ASCA, Bibl.Engl.Lang.& Lit., Curr.Cont., SSCI. **Document type:** academic/scholarly publication.
—UMI; UnCover.
Description: Specializes in publishing scholarship from abroad and the history of scholarship.
Refereed Serial

CLASSICAL STUDIES

938 US ISSN 0009-8353
PA1
CLASSICAL JOURNAL. (Includes bound almanac) 1905. bi-m. $30. Classical Association of the Middle West and South, Inc., c/o John F. Miller, Ed., University of Virginia, Dept. of Classics, 146 New Cabell Hall, Charlottesville, VA 22903. TEL 804-924-6538. FAX 804-982-2002. (Subscr. to: c/o Gregory N. Daugherty, Dept. of Classics, Box 5005, Randolph-Macon College, Ashland, VA 23005-5005) adv.; bk.rev.; abstr.; bibl.; charts; illus.; index, cum.index every 25 yrs.: vols.26-50 (1931-1955). circ. 3,500. (also avail. in microform from PMC,UMI; reprint service avail. from SCH) **Indexed:** Arts & Hum.Cit.Ind., Bibl.Ling., Bk.Rev.Ind. (1965-), Child.Bk.Rev.Ind. (1965-), Curr.Cont., Educ.Ind., Hum.Ind., Ind.Bk.Rev.Hum., M.L.A., MLA Intl.Bibl., New Test.Abstr., Numis.Lit. **Document type:** academic/scholarly publication.
—BLDSC (3274.550000); Genuine Article; KR SourceOne; SWETS; UMI; UnCover.

880 016 489 US ISSN 0009-8361
CLASSICAL OUTLOOK. (Text in English, Greek, Latin) 1923. q. $35. American Classical League, Miami University, Oxford, OH 45056. TEL 513-529-7741. FAX 513-529-7742. Ed. Richard La Fleur. adv.; bk.rev.; index. circ. 4,000. (also avail. in microform from UMI) **Indexed:** Bibl.Ling., Bk.Rev.Ind. (1981-), C.I.J.E., Child.Bk.Rev.Ind. (1981-). **Document type:** academic/scholarly publication.
—BLDSC (3274.560000); UMI; UnCover.
Description: Specifically for teachers. Offers articles, reports, instructional materials, and reviews of immediate interest and use to active classroom teachers of Latin, Greek, and classical humanities in elementary, middle, secondary schools, and in the colleges and universities.

930 800 400 US ISSN 0009-837X
PA1
CLASSICAL PHILOLOGY; devoted to research in the languages, literatures, history and life of classical antiquity. 1906. q. $42 to individuals (Canada $49.94; elsewhere $47); institutions $113 (Canada $125.91; elsewhere $118) (effective 1998). University of Chicago Press, Journals Division, Box 37005, Chicago, IL 60637. TEL 773-753-3347. FAX 773-753-0811. TELEX 25-4603. E-mail: subscriptions@journals.uchicago.edu; URL: http://www.journals.uchicago.edu/CP/. Ed. Elizabeth Asmis. adv.: $355; trim 6 x 9. bk.rev.; bibl.; index. circ. 1,300. (also avail. in microform from UMI,PMC; microfiche from IDC; reprint service avail. from UMI,ISI,SCH) **Indexed:** Arts & Hum.Cit.Ind., ASCA, Bibl.Ling., Curr.Cont., Hum.Ind., IBR, Ind.Bk.Rev.Hum., New Test.Abstr., Numis.Lit., SSCI. **Document type:** academic/scholarly publication.
—Genuine Article; KR SourceOne; SWETS; UMI; UnCover. **CCC**.
Description: Studies the life, languages, and thought of classical antiquity.
Refereed Serial

800 400 UK ISSN 0009-8388
PA1
THE CLASSICAL QUARTERLY. (Text in English; occasionally in other languages) 1906; N.S. 1951. s-a. £46 (foreign $82) (effective 1998). (Classical Association) Oxford University Press, Academic Division, Great Clarendon St., Oxford OX2 6DP, England. TEL 44-1865-267907. TELEX 837330-OXPRES-G. E-mail: jnl.info@oup.co.uk; URL: http://www.oup.co.uk/journals. (U.S. subscr. to: Oxford University Press Inc., 2001 Evans Rd., Cary, NC 27513. TEL 800-852-7323. FAX 919-677-1714) Eds. P. Millett, S.J. Heyworth; Pub. Nina Curtis. R&P contact: Joolz Longley. adv. contact: Jane Parker. index. circ. 1,650. (also avail. in microform from UMI) **Indexed:** Arts & Hum.Cit.Ind., ASCA, Bibl.Ling., Br.Archaeol.Abstr., Br.Hum.Ind., Curr.Cont., Hum.Ind., IBR, Int.G.Class.Stud., M.L.A., MLA Intl.Bibl., New Test.Abstr., Phil.Ind., SSCI. **Document type:** academic/scholarly publication.
●Also available online. Vendor(s): Information Access Co.
—BLDSC (3274.580000); Genuine Article; KR SourceOne; SWETS; UMI; UnCover. **CCC**.
Description: Covers Greco-Roman antiquity in the English-speaking world. Includes research papers and short notes in the fields of language, literature, history and philosophy.

930 800 UK ISSN 0009-840X
PA1
THE CLASSICAL REVIEW. 1886. s-a. £46 (foreign $82) (effective 1998). (Classical Association) Oxford University Press, Academic Division, Great Clarendon St., Oxford OX2 6DP, England. TEL 44-1865-267907. FAX 44-1865-267485. TELEX 837330-OXPRES-G. E-mail: jnl.info@oup.co.uk; URL: http://www.oup.co.uk/journals. (U.S. subscr. to: Oxford University Press Inc., 2001 Evans Rd., Cary, NC 27513. TEL 800-852-7323. FAX 919-677-1714) Eds. C. Carey, R.G. Mayer; Pub. Nina Curtis. R&P contact: Joolz Longley. adv. contact: Jane Parker. bk.rev.; index. circ. 1,650. (also avail. in microform from PMC,UMI; reprint service avail. from SCH) **Indexed:** Arts & Hum.Cit.Ind., ASCA, Bibl.Ling., Bk.Rev.Dig., Bk.Rev.Ind. (1990-), Br.Hum.Ind., Child.Bk.Rev.Ind. (1990-), Curr.Cont., Hum.Ind., IBR, Ind.Bk.Rev.Hum., Int.G.Class.Stud., M.L.A., Mid.East: Abstr.& Ind., Numis.Lit., SSCI. **Document type:** academic/scholarly publication.
—Genuine Article; KR SourceOne; SWETS; UMI. **CCC**.
Description: Critical reviews in the field of Graeco-Roman antiquity from all countries.

930 US ISSN 0009-8418
CLASSICAL WORLD. 1907. 6/yr. $22. Duquesne University, Department of Classics, Pittsburgh, PA 15282-1704. TEL 412-396-6450. FAX 412-396-5197. Ed. Matthew S. Santurocco. adv. contact: Lawrence E. Gaichas. bk.rev.; abstr.; bibl.; index. circ. 3,000. (also avail. in microform from MIM,UMI; reprint service avail. from KTO) **Indexed:** Arts & Hum.Cit.Ind., ASCA, Bk.Rev.Dig., Bk.Rev.Ind. (1965-), Child.Bk.Rev.Ind. (1965-), Curr.Cont., IBR, Ind.Bk.Rev.Hum., Mid.East: Abstr.& Ind., New Test.Abstr., Numis.Lit., SSCI.
—BLDSC (3274.590000); KR SourceOne; SWETS; UMI; UnCover.
Description: Covers all aspects of Greek and Roma literature, history and society, or classical tradition.
Refereed Serial

THE CLASSICIST. see *ARCHITECTURE*

800 410 AT ISSN 0155-0659
CLASSICUM. 1975. s-a. Aus.$15 to non-members (foreign $20) (effective 1997). Classical Association of New South Wales, c/o H. Tarrant, Ed., Dept. of Classics, University of Newcastle, N.S.W. 2308, Australia. FAX 61-49-21-6947. E-mail: clhast@cc.newcastle.edu.au. (Co-sponsor: Classical Languages Teachers Association Inc.) adv.; bk.rev.; circ. 300 (controlled). (back issues avail.) **Document type:** academic/scholarly publication.
Refereed Serial

CODICES MANUSCRIPTI; Zeitschrift fuer Handschriftenkunde. see *LIBRARY AND INFORMATION SCIENCES*

870 UK ISSN 0951-7405
COLLECTED CLASSICAL PAPERS. 1987. irreg., vol. 2, 1991. price varies. Francis Cairns (Publications) Ltd., c/o The University, Leeds LS2 9JT, England. illus. **Document type:** monographic series.

800 NE ISSN 0166-1302
COLUMBIA STUDIES IN THE CLASSICAL TRADITION. 1976. irreg., vol.22, 1995. price varies. E.J. Brill, P.O. Box 9000, 2300 PA Leiden, Netherlands. TEL 31-71-5353500. FAX 31-71-5317532. TELEX 39296 BRILL NL. E-mail: ejbrill@brill.nl. (In N. America: E.J. Brill, 24 Hudson St., Kinderhook, NY 12106. TEL 800-962-4406. FAX 518-758-1959) R&P contact: Elizabeth Vennekamp. (back issues avail.) **Document type:** monographic series.
Description: Publishes scholarly discussions of literary, historical and cultural issues from European classical antiquity and studies of classical ideas in medieval and Renaissance Europe.
Refereed Serial

470 IT ISSN 1121-306X
CONVIVIUM; rassegna trimestrale di studi tradizionali. 1990. q. L.30000 (foreign L.50000). S.E.A.R. Edizioni, Piazza L. Spallanzani 9, 42019 Scandiano R.E., Italy. Ed. Amaini Danilo.

870 880 IT ISSN 1122-0872
CORPUS DEI PAPIRI FILOSOFICI GRECI E LATINI. STUDI E TESTI. 1985. irreg., no.7, 1996. price varies. (Accademia Toscana de Scienze e Lettere La Colombaria) Casa Editrice Leo S. Olschki, Casella Postale 66, 50100 Florence, Italy. TEL 39-55-6530684. FAX 39-55-6530214. E-mail: celso@olschki.it. **Document type:** monographic series.

745 091 GW
CORPUS DER BYZANTINISCHEN MINIATURENHANDSCHRIFTEN (C B M). 1977. irreg., vol.5, 1997. price varies. (Oesterreichische Akademie der Wissenschaften, Kommission fuer Byzantinistik, AU) Anton Hiersemann Verlag, Rosenbergstr. 113, 70193 Stuttgart, Germany. TEL 49-711-638265. FAX 49-711-6369010. (Subscr. to: Postfach 140155, 70071 Stuttgart, Germany) Ed. Irmgard Hutter. **Document type:** academic/scholarly publication.

CORPUS VASORUM ANTIQUORUM (NETHERLANDS). see *MUSEUMS AND ART GALLERIES*

CUADERNOS DE FILOLOGIA CLASICA. ESTUDIOS GRIEGOS E INDOEUROPEOS. see *LINGUISTICS*

CUADERNOS DE FILOLOGIA CLASICA. ESTUDIOS LATINOS. see *LINGUISTICS*

CYPRUS. DEPARTMENT OF ANTIQUITIES. ANNUAL REPORT. see *ARCHAEOLOGY*

CYPRUS. DEPARTMENT OF ANTIQUITIES. REPORT. see *ARCHAEOLOGY*

DANISH HUMANIST TEXTS AND STUDIES. see *LITERATURE*

400 GW ISSN 0011-9830
DEUTSCHER ALTPHILOLOGEN-VERBAND. MITTEILUNGSBLATT. 1957. q. DM.25. C.C. Buchners Verlag, Laubanger 8, 96052 Bamberg, Germany. TEL 49-951-96501-0. FAX 49-951-61774. Ed. Andreas Fritsch. adv.; bk.rev. circ. 7,200. **Document type:** academic/scholarly publication.

480 938 800 UK ISSN 1351-0355
PA1
DIALOGOS; Hellenic studies review. 1994. a. £25($45 to individuals; institutions £45($60) (effective 1998). (King's College London, Centre for Hellenic Studies) Frank Cass, Newbury House, 890-900 Eastern Ave., Newbury Park, Ilford, Essex IG2 7HH England. TEL 44-181-599-8866. FAX 44-181-599-0984. E-mail: jnlsubs@frankcass.com; URL: http://www.frankcass.com. (Dist. in US by: ISBS, 5804 N.E. Hassalo St., Portland, OR 97213-3644. TEL 800-944-6190. FAX 503-280-8832) Eds. Michael Silk, David Ricks. adv. B&W page £195 ($275); adv. contact: Anne Kidson. bk.rev.; index. **Indexed:** Amer.Hist.& Life, Hist.Abstr. **Document type:** academic/scholarly publication.
—BLDSC (3579.737500).
Description: Seeks to foster a critical awareness and informed debate about the ideas, events, and achievements of ancient and modern Greek language and literature, Greek history, and classical archaeology.
Refereed Serial

489 BE ISSN 0070-4792
DIDACTICA CLASSICA GANDENSIA. 1962. a. 300 BEF. Rijksuniversiteit te Gent, Blandijnberg 2, B-9000 Ghent, Belgium. (Subscr. to: Mrs. Verbeken-De Pau Baertsoenkaai 3, B-9000 Ghent, Belgium) Eds. J. Veremans, F. Decreus.

480 792 AT ISSN 1321-4853
PN2131
DIDASKALIA; ancient theater today. 1994. bi-m. free. University of Tasmania, Department of Classics, Hobart, Tasmania 7001, Australia. TEL 61-02-202-294. FAX 61-02-202-288. E-mail: didaskalia-editor@classics.utas.edu.au. Eds. Ian Worthington, Sallie Goetsch. **Document type:** academic/scholarly publication.
●Available only online.

DIOTIMA; epitheoresis philosophikes erevnes - revue recherche philosophique - review of philosophical research. see *PHILOSOPHY*

DUTCH MONOGRAPHS ON ANCIENT HISTORY AND ARCHAEOLOGY. see *ARCHAEOLOGY*

CLASSICAL STUDIES

930 930.1   CN   ISSN 0012-9356
ECHOS DU MONDE CLASSIQUE/CLASSICAL VIEWS. (Text in English or French) 1956. 3/yr. Can.$20 to individuals; institutions Can.$35 (effective 1997). (Classical Association of Canada) University of Calgary Press, 2500 University Dr. N.W., Calgary, AB T2N 1N4, Canada. TEL 403-220-7578. FAX 403-282-0085. E-mail: 470513@ucdasvm1. admin.ucalgary.ca; URL: http://www.ucalgary.ca/ucpress. Ed. Mark Joyal. R&P contact: Mark Joyal. TEL 709-737-8593. adv.; bk.rev. circ. 750. **Indexed:** IBR. **Document type:** academic/scholarly publication.
—BLDSC (3274.589000); UnCover.
Description: Reports on the activities of Canadian classical archaeologists. Includes articles on various archaeological subjects, as well as classical history and literature.
Refereed Serial

880   US
EIDOS: STUDIES IN CLASSICAL KINDS. 1982. irreg., vol.3, 1991. price varies. University of California Press, 2120 Berkeley Way, Berkeley, CA 94720. TEL 510-642-4247. FAX 510-643-7127. (Orders to: California-Princeton Fulfillment Services, 1445 Lower Ferry Rd., Ewing, NJ 08618. TEL 800-777-4726. FAX 800-999-1958) Ed. Thomas G. Rosenmeyer. (back issues avail.) **Document type:** monographic series.
Description: Discusses the history and literature of ancient Greece and Rome.
Refereed Serial

480 930.1   NE   ISSN 0046-1628
EIRENE; studia graeca et latina. (Not published in 1979 and 1991) (Text in English, French, German, Latin and Russian) 1960. a. fl.174 (effective 1998). (Czech Academy of Sciences, Institute for Greek, Latin and Roman Studies, XR) John Benjamins Publishing Co., Amsteldijk 44, P.O. Box 75577, 1070 AN Amsterdam, Netherlands. TEL 31-20-6738156. FAX 31-20-6792956. URL: http://www.benjamins.nl. (In N. America: Box 27519, Philadelphia, PA 19118-0519. TEL 215-836-1200. FAX 215-836-1204) Ed. Jan Bazant. (back issues avail.) **Indexed:** Bibl.Ling., Bull.Signal. **Document type:** academic/scholarly publication.
Description: Provides a source of information on Greek and Latin studies published in Eastern European countries.
Refereed Serial

880   AT   ISSN 1320-3606
PA1
ELECTRONIC ANTIQUITY; communicating the classics. 1993. m. University of Tasmania, Department of Classics, Hobart, Tasmania 7001, Australia. TEL 61-02-202-294. FAX 61-02-202-288. E-mail: antiquity-editor@classics.utas.edu.au. Ed. Ian Worthington. **Document type:** academic/scholarly publication, newsletter.
●Available only online.
Refereed Serial

880 930   GR   ISSN 0013-6336
PA1005
ELLINIKA; philological, historical and folkloric review. (Text in English, French, German, Greek, Italian; summaries in English, Greek) 1928. s-a. Dr.5000($40) (effective 1997). Society for Macedonian Studies, Ethnikis Amymis 4, 546 21 Thessaloniki, Greece. TEL 30-31-268710. FAX 30-31-271501. Ed.Bd. bk.rev.; bibl. circ. 1,000. (back issues avail.) **Indexed:** Amer.Hist.& Life, Hist.Abstr. **Document type:** academic/scholarly publication.
Description: Contains articles that promote research in archaeology, classical studies, folklore, history, linguistics, and Greek literature (ancient, Byzantine, and modern).

EMERITA; revista de linguistica y filologia clasica. see LINGUISTICS

800   SZ   ISSN 0071-0822
ENTRETIENS SUR L'ANTIQUITE CLASSIQUE. no.3, 1958. a., vol.41, 1996. price varies. (Fondation Hardt pour l'Etude de l'Antiquite Classique) Librairie Droz S.A., 11, rue Massot, CH-1211 Geneva 12, Switzerland. TEL 41-22-3466666. FAX 41-22-3472391. E-mail: drozsa@dial.eunet.ch; URL: http://www.eunet.ch/customers/droz. Ed. O. Reverdin. **Indexed:** Rel.Ind.Two. **Document type:** monographic series.
—CCC.
Description: Focuses on ancient classical studies.

ERANOS; acta philologica Suecana. see LINGUISTICS

930   SP   ISSN 0014-1453
ESTUDIOS CLASICOS.* 1950. 3/yr. 450 ptas.($7.75) Consejo Superior de Investigaciones Cientificas (C.S.I.C.), Instituto "Antonio de Nebrija", Duque de Medinaceli 6, 28006 Madrid, Spain. (Co-sponsor: Sociedad Espanola de Estudios Clasicos) bk.rev.; bibl.; index. circ. 1,400. **Indexed:** Arts & Hum.Cit.Ind., ASCA, Bibl.Ling., Curr.Cont., SSCI.
—CINDOC; Genuine Article.

937   US   ISSN 1080-1960
DG222.5   CODEN: ETSTFP
ETRUSCAN STUDIES. 1994. a. $25 per vol. (effective 1997). (Etruscan Foundation) Wayne State University Press, 4809 Woodward Ave., Detroit, MI 48201-1309. TEL 313-577-6120. FAX 313-577-6131. Ed. Jane Whitehead. R&P contact: Mary Garcia. (back issues avail.) **Document type:** academic/scholarly publication.
Description: Publishes scholarly articles and reports of archaeological investigations relating to the Etruscan civilization.
Refereed Serial

930 870   BE   ISSN 0014-200X
AS241
LES ETUDES CLASSIQUES. (Supplement avail.) (Text in French) 1932. q. 1400 BEF (students 500 BEF). Facultes Notre-Dame de la Paix, Faculte de Philosophie et Lettres, Rue de Bruxelles, 61, B-5000 Namur, Belgium. TEL 32-81-724189. FAX 32-81-724203. Ed. L. Isebaert. adv.; bk.rev.; abstr.; charts; illus.; index, cum.index every 10 yrs. circ. 1,000. **Indexed:** Arts & Hum.Cit.Ind., ASCA, Curr.Cont., IBR, M.L.A., MLA Intl.Bibl., Numis.Lit., RILM, SSCI. **Document type:** academic/scholarly publication.
—BLDSC (3817.050000); SWETS.
Description: Publishes contributions on classical culture and it connections with the various modern European literatures.
Refereed Serial

937   SZ   ISSN 0721-3433
EUROPEAN UNIVERSITY STUDIES. SERIES 15: CLASSICS. (Text in English) irreg., vol.71, 1997. 68 SFr.($54.95) Verlag Peter Lang AG, Jupiterstr. 15, CH-3000 Bern 15, Switzerland. TEL 41-31-9402121. FAX 41-31-9402131. E-mail: 101630.1473@compuserve.com; URL: http://www.peterlang.ch. (Dist. in US by: Peter Lang, Inc., 275 Seventh Ave., 28th Fl., New York, NY 10001-6708. TEL 800-770-5264. FAX 212-647-7707) **Document type:** academic/scholarly publication, monographic series.

930   UK
EXCERITUS; bulletin for practical research into the Roman army. 1980. s-a. £7($20) Ermine Street Guard, Oaklands Farm, Dog Ln., Crickley Hill, Witcombe, Glos. GL3 4UG, England. TEL 045-286-2235. Eds. Bill Mayes, Chris Hayes. bk.rev. circ. 300. **Document type:** bulletin.

937   US
EXPLORING THE ROMAN WORLD. 1987. irreg., vol.4, 1993. price varies. University of California Press, 2120 Berkeley Way, Berkeley, CA 94720. TEL 510-642-4247. FAX 510-643-7127. (Orders to: California-Princeton Fulfillment Services, 1445 Lower Ferry Rd., Ewing, NJ 08618. TEL 800-777-4726. FAX 800-999-1958) (back issues avail.) **Document type:** monographic series.
Description: Covers the history and archaeology of the Roman provinces.
Refereed Serial

800   US   ISSN 1047-0204
FAVONIUS; a journal devoted to the classics and the classical tradition. 1987. a. $10. Department of Classics, University of California, Los Angeles, CA 90024. adv.; bk.rev. circ. 600.
Description: A forum for graduate students and recent graduates in classical studies; contains articles on broad themes of interest to specialists.

938   SP   ISSN 1131-8848
DE1   CODEN: FLILF8
FLORENTIA ILIBERRITANA; revista de estudios de antiguedad clasica. 1990. a. Universidad de Granada, Servicio de Publicaciones, Antiguo Colegio Maximo, Campus de Cartuja, 18071 Granada, Spain.
—CINDOC.

FONDATION DE RECHERCHE ET D'EDITIONS DE PHILOSOPHIE NEOHELLENIQUE. SERIE RECHERCHES. see PHILOSOPHY

400   GW   ISSN 0017-1298
PA3
GLOTTA; Zeitschrift fuer griechische und lateinische Sprache. (Text partly in English and French; occasionally in Italian) 1909. 2/yr. DM.98 (effective 1997). Vandenhoeck und Ruprecht, Robert-Bosch-Breite 6, 37079 Goettingen, Germany. TEL 49-551-6959-26. FAX 49-551-695917. (Subscr. to: 37070 Goettingen, Germany) Ed.Bd. adv.; index. (reprint service avail. from SCH) **Indexed:** Arts & Hum.Cit.Ind., ASCA, Bibl.Ling., Curr.Cont., IBR, Lang.& Lang.Behav.Abstr. (1986-), M.L.A., MLA Intl.Bibl. **Document type:** academic/scholarly publication.
—BLDSC (4195.850000); Genuine Article; SWETS; UnCover. CCC.

800   GW   ISSN 0017-1417
PA3
GNOMON; kritische Zeitschrift fuer die gesamte klassische Altertumswissenschaft. CD-ROM edition: Gnomon Bibliographische Datenbank (GW ISSN 0945-9790) (Text in several languages) 1924. 8/yr. DM.298 (CD-ROM edition DM.598) (effective 1997). Verlag C.H. Beck, 80791 Munich, Germany. TEL 49-89-38189-338. FAX 49-89-38189-398. URL: http://www.beck.de/gw/i_gnomon.htm. Eds. Ernst Vogt, H.-W. Noerenberg. adv.; bk.rev. circ. 1,400. (back issues avail.) **Indexed:** Arts & Hum.Cit.Ind., ASCA, Bibl.Ling., Curr.Cont., M.L.A., MLA Intl.Bibl., Numis.Lit., RILM. **Document type:** academic/scholarly publication.
●Also available on CD-ROM.
—Genuine Article; SWETS. CCC.

GRAEZER BEITRAEGE; Zeitschrift fuer klassische Altertumswissenschaft. see ARCHAEOLOGY

930   UK   ISSN 0017-3835
DE1
GREECE AND ROME. (Supplement avail.: New Surveys in the Classics (ISSN 0533-2451)) 1931. s-a. £41 (foreign $76) (effective 1998). (Classical Association) Oxford University Press, Academic Division, Great Clarendon St., Oxford OX2 6DP, England. TEL 44-1865-267907. FAX 44-1865-267485. TELEX 837330 OXPRESS G. E-mail: jnl.info@oup.co.uk; URL: http://www.oup.co.uk/journals. (U.S. subscr. to: Oxford University Press Inc., 2001 Evans Rd., Cary, NC 27513. TEL 800-852-7323. FAX 919-677-1714) Eds. Ian McAuslan, P. Walcot; Pub. Nina Curtis. R&P contact: Joolz Longley. adv. contact: Jane Parker. bk.rev.; abstr.; bibl.; illus.; index. circ. 1,600. (also avail. in microform from UMI; reprint service avail. from SCH) **Indexed:** Arts & Hum.Cit.Ind., ASCA, Br.Archaeol.Abstr., Br.Hum.Ind., Curr.Cont., Hum.Ind., IBR, Int.G.Class.Stud. **Document type:** academic/scholarly publication.
●Also available online. Vendor(s): Information Access Co.
—BLDSC (4214.830000); Genuine Article; KR SourceOne; SWETS; UMI; UnCover. CCC.
Description: Literary evaluation of the major Greek and Roman authors, and articles on ancient history, art, archaeology, the classical tradition, and the teaching of the classics at the tertiary level.

930 940   US   ISSN 0072-7474
GREEK, ROMAN AND BYZANTINE MONOGRAPHS. 1959. irreg., no.11, 1994. price varies. Duke University, Department of Classical Studies, Box 90199, Durham, NC 27708-0199. TEL 919-684-6456. Ed. Keith Stanley. **Indexed:** New Test.Abstr., Numis.Lit. **Document type:** monographic series.
—BLDSC (4214.909000).

930   US   ISSN 0017-3916
DE1
GREEK, ROMAN AND BYZANTINE STUDIES. 1958. q. $30. Duke University, Department of Classical Studies, Box 90199, Durham, NC 27708-0199. TEL 919-684-6456. Ed. Keith Stanley. charts; illus.; index. circ. 850. (also avail. in microform from UMI; reprint service avail. from UMI) **Indexed:** Arts & Hum.Cit.Ind., ASCA, Bibl.Ling., Curr.Cont., Hum.Ind., IBR, New Test.Abstr., Numis.Lit., Rel.Ind.One, RILA.
●Also available online. Vendor(s): UMI.
—KR SourceOne; SWETS; UMI; UnCover.
Description: Research articles on all aspects of the Greek world, from the prehistoric through the Hellenic, Hellenistic, Roman and Byzantine periods.

CLASSICAL STUDIES

930 940   US   ISSN 0072-7482
GREEK, ROMAN, AND BYZANTINE STUDIES. SCHOLARLY AIDS. (Supplement to: Greek, Roman and Byzantine Studies) 1961. irreg. price varies. Duke University, Department of Classical Studies, Box 90199, Durham, NC 27708-0199. TEL 919-684-6456. Ed. Keith Stanley. R&P contact: Keith Stanley. **Indexed:** Curr.Cont. **Document type:** monographic series.

930   NE   ISSN 0169-8206
GRIEKSE EN LATIJNSE SCHRIJVERS. irreg. price varies. E.J. Brill, P.O. Box 9000, 2300 PA Leiden, Netherlands. TEL 31-71-5353500. FAX 31-71-5317532. TELEX 39296 BRILL NL. E-mail: ejbrill@brill.nl. (In N. America: E.J. Brill, 24 Hudson St., Kinderhook, NY 12106. TEL 800-962-4406. FAX 518-758-1959) R&P contact: Elizabeth Vennekamp. **Document type:** monographic series.

930 800   GW   ISSN 0342-5231
GYMNASIUM; Zeitschrift fuer Kultur der Antike und Humanistische Bildung. 1931. 6/yr. DM.150 (students DM.110) (effective 1997). Universitaetsverlag C. Winter Heidelberg GmbH, Hans-Bunte-Str. 18, 69123 Heidelberg, Germany. TEL 49-6221-770260. FAX 49-6221-770269. Ed.Bd. adv.; bk.rev.; index. (reprint service avail. from SCH) **Indexed:** Arts & Hum.Cit.Ind., ASCA, Bibl.Ling., Curr.Cont., IBR, M.L.A., MLA Intl.Bibl. **Document type:** academic/scholarly publication.
—Genuine Article.

HARVARD STUDIES IN CLASSICAL PHILOLOGY. see *LINGUISTICS*

800   US   ISSN 0073-0718
HARVARD STUDIES IN ROMANCE LANGUAGES. irreg., no.42, 1987. price varies. Harvard University, Department of Romance Languages and Literature, Cambridge, MA 02138. (reprint service avail. from KTO) **Indexed:** M.L.A, MLA Intl.Bibl.

930 410   SZ   ISSN 0073-0939
HAUTES ETUDES DU MONDE GRECO-ROMAIN. 1964. irreg., no.22, 1996. price varies. (Ecole Pratique des Hautes Etudes, Centre de Recherches d'Histoire et de Philologie, FR) Librairie Droz S.A., 11, rue Massot, CH-1211 Geneva 12, Switzerland. TEL 41-22-3466666. FAX 41-22-3472391. E-mail: drozsa@dial.eunet.ch; URL: http://www.eunet.ch/customers/droz. circ. 600. **Document type:** monographic series.
—CCC.

480   IT   ISSN 0017-9981
HELIKON; rivista di tradizione e cultura classica. 1961. a. $120. (Universita degli Studi di Messina) Herder Editrice e Libreria s.r.l., Piazza Montecitorio, 120, 00186 Rome, Italy. TEL 67-94-628. FAX 678-47-51. Eds. Antonio Mazzarino, J. irmscher. circ. 450. **Indexed:** IBR. **Document type:** academic/scholarly publication.

949.5 938 480   SW   ISSN 0348-0100
HELLENIKA. 1977. q. SEK 150 (effective 1996). Foereningen Svenska Atheninstitutets Vanner, P.O. Box 14124, S-104 41 Stockholm, Sweden. TEL 46-8-663-21-02. Ed. Eric Mattsson. adv. circ. 2,200. **Indexed:** MLA Intl.Bibl. **Document type:** academic/scholarly publication.
   Refereed Serial

938   US   ISSN 1054-0857
HELLENISTIC CULTURE & SOCIETY. 1987. irreg., vol.21, 1996. price varies. University of California Press, 2120 Berkeley Way, Berkeley, CA 94720. TEL 510-642-4247. FAX 510-643-7127. (Orders to: California-Princeton Fulfillment Services, 1445 Lower Ferry Rd., Ewing, NJ 08618. TEL 800-777-4726. FAX 800-999-1958) Ed.Bd. (back issues avail.) **Document type:** monographic series.
—BLDSC (4285.490000).
   Description: Discusses the cultural legacy of the ancient Greeks from the reign of Alexander the Great to the Roman conquest.
   Refereed Serial

HERMES; Zeitschrift fuer klassische Philologie. see *LINGUISTICS*

870   US   ISSN 0741-1286
HERMES AMERICANUS. (Text in Latin) 1983. q. $25 to individuals; libraries $40. Academia Latina Danburiensis, 45 Dodgingtown Rd., Box 322, Bethel, CT 06801-0322. TEL 203-778-1778. Ed. Alvin P. Dobsevage. adv.; bk.rev. circ. 500. (back issues avail.) **Document type:** academic/scholarly publication.

HERMES - EINZELSCHRIFTEN. see *LINGUISTICS*

HESPERIA. see *ARCHAEOLOGY*

930   IT
HESPERIA. 1990. irreg., vol.8, 1996. price varies. (Universita di Venezia, Dipartimento di Antichita e Tradizione Classica) L'Erma di Bretschneider, Via Cassiodoro 19, 00193 Rome, Italy. TEL 39-6-6874127. FAX 39-6-6874129. Dir. Lorenzo Braccesi. **Indexed:** Art Ind., Curr.Cont.

HETHITICA. see *ORIENTAL STUDIES*

HISTORY OF POLITICAL THOUGHT; controversies in science & the humanities. see *POLITICAL SCIENCE*

930   BE   ISSN 0774-2908
HUMANISTICA LOVANIENSIA; journal of Neo-Latin studies. (Supplement avail.) 1928. a. 3200 BEF (effective 1994). (Katholieke Universiteit Leuven, Seminarium Philologiae Humanisticae) Leuven University Press, Blijde Inkomststraat 5, 3000 Leuven, Belgium. TEL 32-16-325345. FAX 32-16-325352. E-mail: university.press@upers.kuleuven.ac.be; URL: http://www.kuleuven.ac.be/upers. Ed.Bd. bk.rev. circ. 750. (back issues avail.; reprint service avail. from KTO) **Indexed:** IBR, M.L.A., MLA Intl.Bibl. **Document type:** academic/scholarly publication.
—KNAW; KR SourceOne.

930   BE
HUMANISTICA LOVANIENSIA. SUPPLEMENTA. 1978. irreg., vol.9, 1996. Leuven University Press, Blijde Inkomststraat, 3000 Leuven, Belgium. TEL 32-16-325345. FAX 32-16-325352. E-mail: university.press@upers.kuleuven.ac.be; URL: http://www.kuleuven.ac.be/upers. Ed.Bd. (back issues avail.) **Document type:** academic/scholarly publication.

937   GW
HYPERBOREUS. 1994. s-a. DM.68 (effective 1997). (Bibliotheka Classica Petropolitana, RU) Verlag C.H. Beck, 80791 Munich, Germany. TEL 49-89-38189338. FAX 49-89-38189398. Ed. Dmitri Panchenko. **Document type:** academic/scholarly publication.

480 880   GW   ISSN 0085-1671
HYPOMNEMATA; Untersuchungen zur Antike und zu ihrem Nachleben. 1962. irreg., vol.114, 1997. price varies. Vandenhoeck und Ruprecht, Robert-Bosch-Breite 6, 37079 Goettingen, Germany. TEL 49-551-6959-0. FAX 49-551-695917. (Subscr. to: 37070 Goettingen, Germany) **Document type:** monographic series.

800   US   ISSN 0363-1923
PA1
ILLINOIS CLASSICAL STUDIES. 1976. a. $30 (foreign $35) (effective 1998). (University of Illinois, Department of Classics) Scholars Press, Box 15399, Atlanta, GA 30333-0399. TEL 404-727-2320; 888-747-2354. FAX 404-727-2348. E-mail: scholars@emory.edu. Ed. David Sansone. R&P contact: Dennis Ford. circ. 250. (back issues avail.) **Indexed:** Bibl.Ling. **Document type:** academic/scholarly publication.
—BLDSC (4365.113000); SWETS; UnCover.
   Description: Publishes academic papers on classical literature and ancient civilizations.

870 200   BE   ISSN 0771-5463
INSTRUMENTA LEXICOLOGIA LATINA. Key Title: Corpus Christianorum. Instrumenta Lexicologia Latina. (In 2 Series: A - Formae; B - Lemmata) 1982. irreg. (approx. 10/yr.). (Cetedoc) N.V. Brepols, Steenweg op Tielen 68, 2300 Turnhout, Belgium. TEL 32-14-402500. FAX 32-14-428919. (back issues avail.) **Document type:** monographic series.
   Description: Provides lexicographical materials relating to the writing of the Latin Fathers of the Christian Church, and works of the Middle Ages.

INTERNATIONAL ASSOCIATION FOR CLASSICAL ARCHAEOLOGY. PROCEEDINGS OF CONGRESS. see *ARCHAEOLOGY*

930 880   US   ISSN 1073-0508
PN883
INTERNATIONAL JOURNAL OF THE CLASSICAL TRADITION. (Includes: Analytical Bibliography of the Classical Tradition) (Text in English, French, German, Italian, Spanish) 1994. q. $52 to individuals (foreign $84); institutions $108 (foreign $140) (effective 1997). (International Society for the Classical Tradition, NE) Transaction Publishers, Transaction Periodicals Consortium, Department 3092, Rutgers University, New Brunswick, NJ 08903. TEL 908-445-2280. FAX 908-445-3138. (Dist. in Europe by: Swets Publishing Service, Heereweg 347, 2161 CA Lisse, Netherlands. TEL 31-2521-35111. FAX 31-2521-15888) Eds. Meyer Reinhold, Wolfgang Haase; Pub. Mary Curtis. adv.: page $300; 5 1/4 x 8 1/2. bk.rev.; abstr.; bibl. circ. 800. **Document type:** academic/scholarly publication.
—BLDSC (4542.167500).
   Description: Publishes scholarly studies on the influence of Greek and Roman antiquity on other cultures, from the ancient world up to the present. Focuses on the reception and use and transformation of the Graeco-Roman heritage in other regions and periods in literature, the arts, philosophy, sciences and the law.
   Refereed Serial

INTERPRETING THE PAST. see *ARCHAEOLOGY*

870 880   AT
IRIS. 1973. s-a. Aus.$20. Classical Association of Victoria, c/o Dept. of Classical Studies, University of Melbourne, Parkville, Vic. 3052, Australia. FAX 03-344-4161. Ed. P.J. Connor. bk.rev. circ. 200.
   Formerly: Iris and Res Novissimae (ISSN 0310-9186)

950   IT
ISTITUTO UNIVERSITARIO ORIENTALE DI NAPOLI. SEMINARIO DI STUDI DEL MONDO CLASSICO. ANNALI SEZIONE LINGUISTICA. 1978. irreg. $50. Herder Editrice e Libreria s.r.l., Piazza Montecitorio 117-121, 00186 Rome, Italy. TEL 6794628. FAX 678-47-51. TELEX 621427 NATEL. Ed. Domenico Silvestri. **Indexed:** Bibl.Ling. **Document type:** academic/scholarly publication.

938   IT   ISSN 1122-553X
ITALOHELLENIKA; rivista di cultura greco-moderna. 1988. a. Istituto Universitario Orientale di Napoli, Dipartimento di Studi dell'Europa Orientale, Piazza San Giovanni Maggiore 30, 80134 Naples, Italy. **Document type:** academic/scholarly publication.

IUVENIS. see *LINGUISTICS*

800 370   UK   ISSN 0268-0181
J A C T REVIEW. 1963. 2/yr. $30 membership. Joint Association of Classical Teachers, 31-34 Gordon Sq., London WC1H OPY, England. TEL 44-171-387-0348. (Subscr. in US to: Rick LaFleur, Department of Classics, Park Hall, University of Georgia, Athens, GA 30602) Eds. J. Affleck, J. Stone. adv.; bk.rev. circ. 2,200. **Indexed:** Cont.Pg.Educ. **Document type:** academic/scholarly publication.
   Incorporates (in 1987): Latin Teaching (ISSN 0023-8821); **Former titles** (until 1984): Hesperian (until 1978): Didaskalos.
   Description: Articles and book reviews covering all aspects of the classical world.

J R A - THE SUPPLEMENTARY SERIES. (Journal of Roman Archaeology) see *ARCHAEOLOGY*

800   UK   ISSN 0267-8349
JOINT ASSOCIATION OF CLASSICAL TEACHERS. BULLETIN. 1963. 3/yr. $30 membership. Joint Association of Classical Teachers, 31-34 Gordon Sq., London WC1H OPY, England. TEL 44-171-387-0348. (Subscr. in US to: Rick LaFleur, Department of Classics, Park Hall, University of Georgia, Athens, GA 30602) Ed. R.W. Shone. bibl. circ. 2,200. **Document type:** bulletin.
   Description: News and information broadsheet fo classics teachers.

JOURNAL FOR THE STUDY OF JUDAISM IN THE PERSIA HELLENISTIC AND ROMAN PERIOD. see *RELIGIONS AND THEOLOGY* — Judaic

CLASSICAL STUDIES

880 UK ISSN 0075-4269
DF10
JOURNAL OF HELLENIC STUDIES. Issued with: Archaeological Reports (ISSN 0570-6084) 1880. a. £40 (foreign £41($90)) (effective 1998). Society for the Promotion of Hellenic Studies, Senate House, London WC1E 7HU, England. TEL 44-171-232-9590. FAX 44-171-232-9591. E-mail: hellenic@sas.ac.uk. Ed. Richard Hunter. R&P contact: Jane Fisher. adv. contact: Jane Fisher. bk.rev. circ. 3,000. (also avail. in microfilm from UMI; back issues avail.; reprint service avail. from KTO,UMI) **Indexed:** A.I.C.P., Art Ind., Arts & Hum.Cit.Ind., ASCA, Avery Ind.Archit.Per., Bibl.Ling., Br.Hum.Ind, Curr.Cont., Hum.Ind., IBR, Ind.Bk.Rev.Hum., M.L.A., MLA Intl.Bibl., New Test.Abstr., Numis.Lit., Phil.Ind., SSCI. **Document type:** academic/scholarly publication.
—BLDSC (4996.950000); KR SourceOne; SWETS; UnCover.
Description: Covers Greek language, literature, history and art in the ancient and Byzantine periods.
Refereed Serial

JOURNAL OF PREHISTORIC RELIGION. see *ARCHAEOLOGY*

JOURNAL OF ROMAN ARCHAEOLOGY. see *ARCHAEOLOGY*

870 UK ISSN 0075-4358
DG11
JOURNAL OF ROMAN STUDIES. (Text in English, French, German, Greek and Latin) 1911. a. £25($50) to individuals; institutions £30($60) (effective 1997 & 1998). Society for the Promotion of Roman Studies, Senate House, Malet St., London WC1E 7HU, England. TEL 44-171-323-9583. FAX 44-171-323-9584. E-mail: romansoc@sas.ac.uk. Ed. Simon Price. adv.; bk.rev.; cum.index: vols.21-60. circ. 2,800. (back issues avail.; reprint service avail.) **Indexed:** Arts & Hum.Cit.Ind., ASCA, Bibl.Ling., Br.Archaeol.Abstr., Br.Hum.Ind., Curr.Cont., Hum.Ind., IBR, Ind.Bk.Rev.Hum., Mid.East: Abstr.& Ind., New Test.Abstr., Numis.Lit., SSCI. **Document type:** academic/scholarly publication.
—BLDSC (5052.120000); KR SourceOne; SWETS; UnCover.
Description: Articles on the history, archeology, literature and art of Rome, Italy and the Roman Empire to 700 A.D.

870 UK ISSN 0951-6549
JOURNAL OF ROMAN STUDIES MONOGRAPH SERIES. 1982. irreg., no.8, 1997. Society for the Promotion of Roman Studies, Senate House, Malet St., London WC1E 7HU, England. TEL 44-171-323-9583. FAX 44-171-323-9584. E-mail: romansoc@sas.ac.uk. **Document type:** monographic series.
—BLDSC (5052.120100).
Description: Studies on the history, archaeology, literature and art of Rome, Italy and the Roman empire to 700 A.D.

930 CY ISSN 0071-0954
DS54.A2
KENTRON EPISTEMONIKON EREUNON. EPETERIS/CYPRUS RESEARCH CENTRE. ANNUAL. (Text in English, French, German, Greek) 1968. a. £C12. Ministry of Education, Cyprus Research Centre, P.O. Box 1952, Nicosia 1515, Cyprus. FAX 357-2-445021. Ed. Constantinos Yiangoullis. bk.rev.; bibl.; charts; illus. circ. 500. (back issues avail.) **Indexed:** M.L.A. **Document type:** government publication, academic/scholarly publication.

880 SW ISSN 1104-3180
KLASSIKER. 1991. a. price varies. Paul Aastroems Foerlag, William Gibsons Vaeg 11, S-43376 Jonsered, Sweden. TEL 46-31-795-6600. Ed. Paul Aastroem. circ. 1,250. (back issues avail.)
Description: Publishes classical Greek and Roman literature in Swedish translation.

930 IT
KLEIO. 1977. irreg., no.4, 1990. price varies. L'Erma di Bretschneider, Via Cassiodoro 19, 00193 Rome, Italy. TEL 39-6-6874127. FAX 39-6-6874127. Ed. S. Calderone.

930 GW ISSN 0075-6334
D51
KLIO; Beitraege zur Alten Geschichte. (Text in English, French, German) 1897. 2/yr. DM.95 (foreign DM.99) to individuals; institutions DM.375 (foreign DM.385) (effective 1997). Akademie Verlag GmbH, Muehlenstr. 33-34, 13187 Berlin, Germany. TEL 49-30-47889348. FAX 49-30-47889357. E-mail: info@akademie-verlag.de. (Subscr. in the Americas to: John Wiley & Sons, Inc., 605 Third Ave., New York, NY 10058. TEL 212-850-6645. FAX 212-850-6021) (also avail. in microfiche from IDC; reprint service avail. from KTO) **Indexed:** Bibl.Ling., Br.Archaeol.Abstr., IBR, Numis.Lit. **Document type:** academic/scholarly publication.
—SWETS.
Description: Contains contributions on the history of ancient Greece and Rome.

KTEMA; civilisations de l'Orient, de la Grece et de Rome Antiques. see *HISTORY — History Of Asia*

LALIES. see *LINGUISTICS*

800 US ISSN 0891-4087
LANG CLASSICAL STUDIES. (Text in English and other West European languages.) 1988. irreg., vol.8, 1996. price varies. Peter Lang Publishing, Inc., 275 Seventh Ave., 28th Fl., New York, NY 10001. TEL 212-647-7700; 800-770-5264. FAX 212-647-7707. E-mail: customerservice@plang.com; URL: http://www.peterlang.com. Ed. Daniel Garrison. (back issues avail.) **Document type:** academic/scholarly publication, monographic series.
Description: Monograph series on the history and literature of the Greek and Roman world, embracing all subjects relevant to Classical humanities.

480 375 GW ISSN 0723-6050
LATEIN UND GRIECHISCH IN BERLIN. 1954. q. (Deutschen Altphilologenverband (DAV), Landesverband Berlin) C.C. Buchners Verlag, Laubanger 8, 96052 Bamberg, Germany. TEL 49-951-96501-0. FAX 49-951-61774. Ed.Bd. circ. 300. **Document type:** academic/scholarly publication.

870 UK ISSN 0951-7391
LATIN AND GREEK TEXTS; classical and medieval. 1980. irreg., latest vol.6, 1990. £7.50($13.50) Francis Cairns (Publications) Ltd., c/o The University, Leeds LS2 9JT, England. (back issues avail.) **Document type:** academic/scholarly publication.
—BLDSC (5160.223500).
Formerly: Liverpool Latin Texts (ISSN 0144-9451)

LATINITAS; commentarii linguae latinae excolendae. see *LINGUISTICS*

470 BE ISSN 0023-8856
PA2002
LATOMUS; revue d'etudes latines. (Text in English, French, German, Italian, Latin, Spanish) 1937. q. 3200 BEF (effective 1997). Societe d'Etudes Latines de Bruxelles, 6 rue du Palais St. Jacques, 7500 Tournai, Belgium. Ed. C. Deroux. R&P contact: Mrs. J. Dumortier-Bibauw. adv. contact: J. Dumortier. bk.rev.; bibl.; illus.; index, cum.index. circ. 1,000. (reprint service avail. from SCH) **Indexed:** Arts & Hum.Cit.Ind., ASCA, Br.Archaeol.Abstr., Curr.Cont., IBR, M.L.A., MLA Intl.Bibl., Numis.Lit., SSCI. **Document type:** academic/scholarly publication.
—SWETS; UnCover.

800 GW
LAVERNA. 1990. a. DM.46. Scripta Mercaturae Verlag, Am Roten Berg 5-9, 55595 St. Katharinen, Germany. TEL 49-6706-8800. Eds. H.J. Drexhage, J. Suenskes Thompson. **Document type:** academic/scholarly publication.

480 880 SA ISSN 1021-2981
LEWENDE WOORDE. (Text in Afrikaans) 1993. q. Rand Afrikaans Universiteit, Departement Klassieke Tale, P.O. Box 524, Auckland Park 2006, South Africa. **Document type:** academic/scholarly publication.

800 UK ISSN 0309-3700
LIVERPOOL CLASSICAL MONTHLY. 1976; N.S. 1996. m. (except Aug. & Sep.). £19.50($40) Blackburns' Building, Great Newton St., University of Liverpool, Liverpool L69 3BX, England. TEL 44-151-794-5316. FAX 44-151-794-5317. E-mail: 100115.642@compuserve.com. Ed. Helena V. Hurt Pinsent. bk.rev.; illus. circ. 450. (looseleaf format; back issues avail.) **Indexed:** Bibl.Ling. **Document type:** bulletin.
—BLDSC (5281.130500).

480 880 GW ISSN 0024-7421
LUSTRUM; Internationale Forschungsberichte aus dem Bereich des Klassischen Altertums. 1956. irreg., vol.28, 1994. DM.136. Vandenhoeck und Ruprecht, Robert-Bosch-Breite 6, 37079 Goettingen, Germany. TEL 49-551-6959-0. FAX 49-551-695917. (Subscr. to: 37070 Goettingen, Germany) Eds. Hans Gaertner, Hubert Petersmann. adv. circ. 1,000. **Indexed:** IBR. **Document type:** monographic series.
—BLDSC (5307.600000). CCC.

MCGILL UNIVERSITY MONOGRAPHS IN CLASSICAL ARCHAEOLOGY AND HISTORY. see *ARCHAEOLOGY*

800 IT ISSN 0025-0538
PA9
MAIA; rivista di letterature classiche. 1948. 3/yr. L.60000($60) Nuova Casa Editrice Licinio Cappelli di G.E.M. s.r.l., Via Farini,14, 40126 Bologna, Italy. TEL 39-51-239060. FAX 39-51-239268. Eds. F. della Corte, A. la Penna. adv.; bk.rev.; index. circ. 2,000. **Indexed:** Arts & Hum.Cit.Ind., ASCA, Bibl.Ling., Curr.Cont., IBR.
—Genuine Article; SWETS.

870 880 US ISSN 0076-471X
PA25
MARTIN CLASSICAL LECTURES. (A series of lectures delivered annually at Oberlin College) 1931. irreg., vol.30, 1986. price varies. (Oberlin College) Princeton University Press, 41 William St., Princeton, NJ 08540. TEL 609-258-4900. FAX 609-258-6305. URL: http://pup.princeton.edu. **Document type:** monographic series.
Refereed Serial

480 XR ISSN 1211-6335
MASARYKOVA UNIVERZITA. FILOZOFICKA FAKULTA. SBORNIK PRACI. N: RADA KLASICKA. (Text in Czech; summaries in various languages) 1956. a. price varies. Masarykova Univerzita, Filozoficka Fakulta, A. Novaka 1, 660 88 Brno, Czech Republic. TEL 420-5-41121102. FAX 420-5-41121406. E-mail: exchange@phil.muni.cz. R&P contact: Ivan Seidl. TEL 420-5-41121337. bk.rev. **Document type:** academic/scholarly publication.
Supersedes in part (in 1996): Masarykova Univerzita. Filozoficka Fakulta. Sbornik Praci. E: Rada Archeologicko - Klasicka; Which was formerly: Univerzita J.E. Purkyne. Filozoficka Fakulta. Sbornik Praci. E: Rada Archeologico - Klasicka (ISSN 0231-7915)

800 IT ISSN 0392-6338
MATERIALI E DISCUSSIONI PER L'ANALISI DEI TESTI CLASSICI. 1978. s-a. L.45000. Giardini Editori e Stampatori, Via Santa Bibbiana 28, 56100 Pisa, Italy. TEL 050 502531. Ed. Gian Biagio Conte. **Indexed:** Bibl.Ling.

MAVORS. ROMAN ARMY RESEARCHES. see *HISTORY*

800 PL ISSN 0025-6285
DE71
MEANDER; miesiecznik poswiecony kulturze swiata starozytnego. (Text in Polish; summaries in Latin) 1946. m. $66. (Polska Akademia Nauk, Komitet Nauk o Kulturze Antycznej) Wydawnictwo Naukowe P W N, Ul. Miodowa 10, 00-251 Warsaw, Poland. TEL 48-22-312738. FAX 48-22-6954288. Ed. Anna M. Komornicka. bibl.; illus.; index. circ. 1,100. **Indexed:** M.L.A.
Description: Focuses on the ancient world.

MINERVA: REVISTA DE FILOLOGIA CLASICA. see *LINGUISTICS*

CLASSICAL STUDIES

800 930 NE ISSN 0026-7074
PA9
MNEMOSYNE; bibliotheca classica batava. (Supplement avail. (ISSN 0169-8958)) (Text in English, French, German or Latin) 1852. 6/yr. fl.228($134) to individuals; institutions fl.361($212) (effective 1998). E.J. Brill, P.O. Box 9000, 2300 PA Leiden, Netherlands. TEL 31-71-5353500. FAX 31-71-5317532. TELEX 39296 BRILL NL. E-mail: cs@brill.nl. (In N. America: E.J. Brill, 24 Hudson St., Kinderhook, NY 12106. TEL 800-962-4406. FAX 518-758-1959) Ed.Bd. R&P contact: Elizabeth Vennekamp. bk.rev.; bibl. (also avail. in microform from SWZ; reprint service avail. from SWZ) **Indexed:** Arts & Hum.Cit.Ind., Bibl.Ling., Curr.Cont., Hum.Ind., IBR, Ind.Bk.Rev.Hum., MLA Intl.Bibl. **Document type:** academic/scholarly publication.
—Genuine Article; KR SourceOne; SWETS; UnCover. CCC.
Description: Focuses on the ancient world, including inscriptions, papyri, language, religion and philosophy.
Refereed Serial

800 NE ISSN 0169-8958
MNEMOSYNE. SUPPLEMENTS; bibliotheca classica batava. (Supplement to: Mnemosyne (ISSN 0026-7074)) 1938. irreg., vol.162, 1996. price varies. E.J. Brill, P.O. Box 9000, 2300 PA Leiden, Netherlands. TEL 31-71-5353500. FAX 31-71-5317532. TELEX 39296 BRILL NL. E-mail: ejbrill@brill.nl. (In N. America: E.J. Brill, 24 Hudson St., Kinderhook, NY 12106. TEL 800-962-4406. FAX 518-758-1959) R&P contact: Elizabeth Vennekamp. illus. (back issues avail.) **Document type:** monographic series.
—BLDSC (5879.821000).
Description: Scholarly monographs and bibliographical works on historical, literary, linguistic, cultural, political and economic aspects of classical Greek and Roman civilizations.
Refereed Serial

MONUMENTA GRAECA ET ROMANA. see *ARCHITECTURE*

930 GW ISSN 0722-4532
MUENSTERSCHE BEITRAEGE ZUR ANTIKEN HANDELSGESCHICHTE. 1982. s-a. DM.46. Scripta Mercaturae Verlag, Am Roten Berg 5-9, 55595 St. Katharinen, Germany. TEL 49-6706-8800. Ed. H.J. Drexhage. **Document type:** academic/scholarly publication.

MUSEION 2000; glaube, wissen, kunst in geschichte und gegenwart. see *HISTORY — History Of Europe*

930 SZ ISSN 0027-4054
PA3
MUSEUM HELVETICUM; Schweizerische Zeitschrift fuer klassische Altertumswissenschaft. (Text in English, French, German and Italian) 1944. q. 96 SFr. (effective 1997). (Schweizerische Vereinigung fuer Altertumswissenschaft) Schwabe and Co. AG, Steinentorstr. 13, CH-4010 Basel, Switzerland. TEL 41-61-2789565. FAX 41-61-2789566. E-mail: verlag@schwabe.ch. Ed.Bd. adv.; bk.rev.; charts; illus.; index. circ. 1,000. (also avail. in microform from SWZ; back issues avail.; reprint service avail. from SWZ) **Indexed:** Bibl.Ling., IBR, M.L.A., MLA Intl.Bibl. **Document type:** academic/scholarly publication.
—SWETS. CCC.
Description: Examines classical archeology from an international perspective.

930 AU
MYKENISCHE STUDIEN. (Subseries of: Oesterreichische Akademie der Wissenschaften. Philosophisch-Historische Klasse. Sitzungsberichte) 1972. irreg. price varies. (Oesterreichische Akademie der Wissenschaften, Kommission fuer Mykenische Forschung) Verlag der Oesterreichischen Akademie der Wissenschaften, Dr. Ignaz-Seipel-Platz 2, A-1010 Vienna, Austria. TEL 43-1-51581401. FAX 43-1-51581400. E-mail: verlag@oeaw.ac.at; URL: http://www.oeaw.ac.at/einheiten/verlag. **Document type:** monographic series.

MYRTIA: REVISTA DE FILOLOGIA CLASICA. see *LINGUISTICS*

800 US
NEW ENGLAND CLASSICAL NEWSLETTER & JOURNAL. 1972. q. $15. Classical Association of New England, Greek and Roman Studies, Fairfield University, Fairfield, CT 06430. TEL 203-254-4000. E-mail: necnj@fair1.fairfield.edu; URL: http://www.circe.unh.edu/classics/necn. Ed. Vincent J. Rosivach. R&P contact: Vincent J. Rosivach. bk.rev.; bibl. circ. 800. (processed)
Former titles: New England Classical Newsletter (ISSN 0739-1188); Bay State Classical Newsletter.
Description: Articles and news of interest to Latin and Greek teachers and classics professors.
Refereed Serial

800 US
NEW JERSEY CLASSICAL ASSOCIATION. BULLETIN.* 1930. s-a. membership; or free to Latin teachers in New Jersey. New Jersey Classical Association, c/o N. McKee, 19 Donna Lynn Ln., Lawrenceville, NJ 08648-2823. bk.rev.; bibl. circ. 500. (processed)

800 UK ISSN 0533-2451
NEW SURVEYS IN THE CLASSICS. (Supplement to: Greece and Rome (ISSN 0017-3835)) 1966. a. price varies. (Classical Association) Oxford University Press, Academic Division, Great Clarendon St., Oxford OX2 6DP, England. TEL 44-1865-267907. FAX 44-1865-267485. TELEX 837330-OXPRES-G. E-mail: jnl.info@oup.co.uk; URL: http://www.oup.co.uk/journals. (U.S. subscr. to: Oxford University Press Inc., 2001 Evans Rd., Cary, NC 27513. TEL 800-852-7323. FAX 919-677-1714) Ed.Bd.; Pub. Nina Curtis. R&P contact: Joolz Longley. bibl. **Document type:** academic/scholarly publication.
—BLDSC (6088.784000).

NOVA TELLUS. see *HUMANITIES: COMPREHENSIVE WORKS*

937 938 DK ISSN 0107-1378
ODENSE UNIVERSITY CLASSICAL STUDIES. (Text in English, French) 1971. irreg. price varies. Odense University Press, Campusvej 55, DK-5230 Odense M, Denmark. TEL 66-157999. FAX 66-158126. E-mail: press@forlag.ou.dk. (back issues avail.)

938 US
OKLAHOMA SERIES IN CLASSICAL CULTURE. 1989. irreg. price varies. University of Oklahoma Press, 1005 Asp Ave., Norman, OK 73019. TEL 405-325-5111. FAX 405-325-4000. **Document type:** academic/scholarly publication, monographic series.

OLYMPISCHE FORSCHUNGEN. see *ARCHAEOLOGY*

870 UK ISSN 0261-507X
OMNIBUS (LONDON). 1981. 2/yr. $10. Joint Association of Classical Teachers, 31-34 Gordon Sq., London WC1H 0PY, England. TEL 44-171-387-0348. (Subscr. in US to: Rick LaFleur, Department of Classics, Park Hall, University of Georgia, Athens, GA 30602) Ed. G. Fallows. circ. 10,000. **Document type:** bulletin.

938 SW ISSN 0078-5520
DE3
OPUSCULA ATHENIENSIA. (Supplement to: Svenska Institutet i Athen. Skrifter (ISSN 0586-0539)) (Text in English, French, German) 1953. irreg. SEK 400. Svenska Institutet i Athen, c/o P. Aastroem, William Gibsons vaeg 11, S-433 76 Jonsered, Sweden. Ed. B. Alroth. bk.rev. circ. 500. **Indexed:** Numis.Lit. **Document type:** academic/scholarly publication.

930 DK ISSN 0107-8089
OPUSCULA GRAECOLATINA. (Text in Danish, English) 1975. irreg. price varies. Museum Tusculanum Press, University of Copenhagen, Njalsgade 92, DK-2300 Copenhagen S, Denmark. TEL 45-33-32-91-09. FAX 45-35-32-91-13. (Dist. in U.S. and Canada by: Paul & Co., c/o P C S Data Processing, Inc., 360 W. 31st St., New York, NY 10001. TEL 212-564-3730. FAX 212-971-7200) Ed. Ivan Boserup. **Document type:** academic/scholarly publication.
Description: Publishes smaller monographs on Greek and Latin subjects.

930 GW ISSN 0078-5555
ORBIS ANTIQUUS. 1950. irreg. price varies. Aschendorffsche Verlagsbuchhandlung, Soesterstr. 13, 48155 Muenster, Germany. TEL 49-251-690-0. FAX 49-251-690143. Ed. Max Wegner. R&P contact: Georg Backhaus. **Document type:** monographic series.
—BLDSC (6277.855500).

937 IT
ORIENS GRAECOLATINUS. 1994. irreg., no.2, 1994. price varies. Istituto Ellenico di Studi Bizantini e Post-Bizantini, Castello 3412, 30122 Venice, Italy. FAX 39-41-5238248. Ed. Nikolaos M. Panayotakis. **Document type:** monographic series.

ORPHEUS; rivista di umanita classica e cristiana. see *LITERATURE*

937 IT ISSN 1122-259X
OSTRAKA; rivista di antichita. 1992. s-a. L.75000 (foreign L.96000) (effective 1996). Loffredo Editore S.p.A., Via Consalvo, 99 H, 80126 Naples, Italy. TEL 081-5937073. FAX 081-5936953. Ed. Mario Torelli.

930 UK
OXFORD CLASSICAL AND PHILOSOPHICAL MONOGRAPHS. irreg. price varies. Oxford University Press, Walton St., Oxford OX2 6DP, England. TEL 44-1865-56767. FAX 44-1865-56646. (Subscr. in US to: Oxford University Press Inc., 2001 Evans Rd., Cary, NC 27513. TEL 919-677-0977. FAX 919-677-1714) **Document type:** monographic series.

OXFORD MONOGRAPHS ON CLASSICAL ARCHAEOLOGY. see *ARCHAEOLOGY*

OXFORD STUDIES IN ANCIENT PHILOSOPHY. see *PHILOSOPHY*

800 GW ISSN 0552-9638
PALINGENESIA; Monographien und Texte zur klassischen Altertumswissenschaft. (Text in English and German) irreg., vol.63, 1997. price varies. Franz Steiner Verlag Wiesbaden GmbH, Birkenwaldstr. 44, 70191 Stuttgart, Germany. TEL 49-711-2582-0. FAX 49-711-2582390. (Subscr. to: Postfach 101061, 70009 Stuttgart, Germany) Eds. P. Steinmetz, O. Lendle. R&P contact: Sabine Koerner. **Document type:** monographic series.

937 480 FR ISSN 0031-0387
PALLAS; revue d'etudes antiques. 1953. s-a. 220 F. (foreign 230 F.) (effective 1997). (Universite de Toulouse II (le Mirail)) Presses Universitaires du Mirail, 56 rue du Taur, 31000 Toulouse, France. TEL 33-5-61225831. FAX 33-5-61218420. (Co-sponsors: Universites d'Aix, Limoges, Montpellier, Pau, Perpignan) Ed. H. Guiraud. illus. (back issues avail.) **Indexed:** Bibl.Ling. **Document type:** academic/scholarly publication.
Description: Publishes articles on the literature, linguistics, history and archeology of the Greek and Roman periods.

001.2 880 SW ISSN 1105-4204
PAPERS FROM THE NORWEGIAN INSTITUTE AT ATHENS. (Text in English) 1991. irreg., no.3, 1995. price varies. Paul Aastroem Foerlag, William Gibsons vaeg 11, S-433 76 Jonsered, Sweden. TEL 46-31-795-6600. FAX 46-31-795-6710.

PHILOLOGICAL MONOGRAPHS. see *LINGUISTICS*

PHILOLOGICAL QUARTERLY; devoted to scholarly investigation of the classical and modern languages and literatures. see *LINGUISTICS*

880 100 GR
PHILOLOGOS/SCHOLAR. 1964. q. Dr.3000($40) Syllogos Apophoiton tes Philosophikes Scholes tou Panepistemiou Thessalonikes - Graduate Society of the School of Philosophy for the University of Thessaloniki, P.O. Box 10836, 541 10 Thessaloniki, Greece. TEL 30-31-272-735. Ed. Christos L. Tsolakis. adv.; bk.rev.; bibl. circ. 2,500. **Document type:** academic/scholarly publication.

400　　　　　　GW　　　ISSN 0031-7985
PA3
PHILOLOGUS; Zeitschrift fuer klassische Philologie. (Text in English, French, German) 1846. s-a. DM.95 (foreign DM.99) to individuals; institutions DM.345 (foreign DM.355) (effective 1997). Akademie Verlag GmbH, Muehlenstr. 33-34, 13187 Berlin, Germany. TEL 49-30-47889348. FAX 49-30-47889357. E-mail: info@akademie-verlag.de. (Subscr. in the Americas to: John Wiley & Sons, Inc., 605 Third Ave., New York, NY 10158. TEL 212-850-6645. FAX 212-850-6021) Ed.Bd. charts; illus.; index. (also avail. in microfiche from IDC,BHP; reprint service avail. from SCH) **Indexed:** Arts & Hum.Cit.Ind., ASCA, Bibl.Ling., Curr.Cont., IBR, M.L.A., MLA Intl.Bibl. **Document type:** academic/scholarly publication.
—Genuine Article; SWETS; UnCover.
　Description: Contributes to reconstructing and understanding ancient intellectual culture and its lasting influence on European civilization.

PHILOSOPHIA ANTIQUA. see *PHILOSOPHY*

800　　　　　　CN　　　ISSN 0079-1784
PHOENIX. SUPPLEMENTARY VOLUMES. 1952. irreg. price varies. (Classical Association of Canada) University of Toronto Press, Directories Departement, 10 St. Mary St., Ste. 700, Toronto, ON M4Y 2W8, Canada. TEL 416-978-2239. FAX 416-978-4738. E-mail: utpbooks@gpu.utcc.utoronto.ca. (U.S. address: 340 Nagel Dr., Cheektowaga, NY 14225) Ed. Catherine Rubincan. **Document type:** academic/scholarly publication.
—BLDSC (6465.120020).

800　　　　　　CN　　　ISSN 0031-8299
PA1
PHOENIX (TORONTO, 1946). (Text in English and French) 1946. q. Can.$50 to individuals; institutions Can.$55. Classical Association of Canada, Trinity College, University of Toronto, Toronto, ON M5S 1H8, Canada. TEL 416-978-3037. FAX 416-978-4949. Ed. C.I. Rubincam. adv.; bk.rev.; charts; illus.; index. circ. 1,142. **Indexed:** Curr.Cont., IBR, Ind.Bk.Rev.Hum., Lang.& Lang.Behav.Abstr., Numis.Lit. **Document type:** academic/scholarly publication.
—BLDSC (6465.120000); SWETS; UnCover. **CCC.**

880　410.5　　　GR　　　ISSN 1105-073X
PLATON. (Text in English, French, German, Greek, and Italian) 1949. a. $50. Hetaireia Hellenon Philologon, Platon, P.O. Box 3373, Athens 102 10, Greece. TEL 30-1-3213-363. (Subscr. to: Demetrios N. Papadimas, 8, Ippokratous str., Athens 10679, Greece. TEL 30-1-362-7318. FAX 30-1-361-0271) Ed. Georgia Xanthaxis-Kamanos. bk.rev.; bibl. circ. 2,000. **Document type:** bulletin.

800　　　　　　US　　　ISSN 0258-655X
PLOUTARKHOS. (Text mainly in English; occasionally in other European languages) 1984. s-a. $10 to individuals (foreign $15); institutions $20; students $5 (effective 1997). International Plutarch Society, c/o Frances B. Titchener, Ed., Dept. of History, Utah State Univ., Logan, UT 84322-0710. TEL 801-797-1298. FAX 801-797-3899. Ed. Frances B. Titchener; Pub. Frances B. Titchener. R&P contact: Frances B. Titchener. adv. contact: Frances B. Titchener. bk.rev. circ. 650. (back issues avail.) **Document type:** academic/scholarly publication.

POSITIONS FOR CLASSICISTS & ARCHAEOLOGISTS. see *OCCUPATIONS AND CAREERS*

937　　　　　　IT　　　ISSN 0079-5682
PROBLEMI E RICERCHE DI STORIA ANTICA. 1951. irreg., vol.18, 1996. price varies. L'Erma di Bretschneider, Via Cassiodoro 19, 00193 Rome, Italy. TEL 39-6-6874127. FAX 39-6-6874129.

880　　　　　　IT　　　ISSN 0391-2698
PROMETHEUS (FLORENCE). 1975. 3/yr. $20. Associazione Culturale Filologi, Amici di Prometheus, Universita degli Studi di Firenze, Cattedra di Letteratura Greca, Via Alfani 31, 50121 Florence, Italy. (Subscr. to: Prometheus, via C. Pisacane 11-4, 50134 Florence, Italy) Ed. Adelmo Barigazzi. bk.rev.
—SWETS.

480　　　　　　IT　　　ISSN 0390-1068
QUADERNI DI STORIA. 1975. s-a. Lit.40000 (foreign Lit.60000) (effective 1997). Edizioni Dedalo s.r.l., Casella Postale 362, 70100 Bari, Italy. TEL 39-80-5311413. FAX 39-80-5311414. (Edit. addr.: Casella Postale 200, 70100 Bari, Italy) Ed. Claudia Coga; Pub. Claudia Coga. R&P contact: Claudia Coga. adv. contact: Claudia Coga. circ. 4,000. **Document type:** academic/scholarly publication.
　Description: Joins historians from different areas and experiences. Links ancient times and the modern world.

870　　　　　　GW　　　ISSN 0721-6203
QUELLEN UND UNTERSUCHUNGEN ZUR LATEINISCHEN PHILOLOGIE DES MITTELALTERS. 1981. irreg., vol.11, 1995. price varies. Anton Hiersemann Verlag, Rosenbergstr. 113, 70193 Stuttgart, Germany. TEL 49-711-6386265. FAX 49-711-6369010. (Subscr. to: Postfach 140155, 70071 Stuttgart, Germany) Ed. W. Berschin. **Document type:** academic/scholarly publication, monographic series.

480　470　　　AT　　　ISSN 0048-671X
PA1
RAMUS; critical studies in Greek and Roman literature. 1972. s-a. Aus.$27.70 to individuals; institutions Aus.$39.50 (effective 1997). Aureal Publications, P.O. Box 49, Bendigo North, Vic. 3550, Australia. FAX 61-3-54447970. E-mail: j.penwill@bendigo.latrobe.edu.au. Eds. A.J. Boyle, J.L. Penwill; Pub. J.L. Penwill. R&P contact: J.L. Penwill. adv. contact: J.L. Penwill. bk.rev.; bibl. circ. 300. (reprint service avail. from ISI) **Indexed:** Arts & Hum.Cit.Ind, ASCA, Aus.P.A.I.S., Curr.Cont., IBR. **Document type:** academic/scholarly publication.
—BLDSC (7254.250000); Genuine Article; UnCover. **CCC.**
　Refereed Serial

800　　　　　　SP　　　ISSN 0210-7694
REVISTA HABIS. (Text in English, French, German, Spanish) 1970. a. price varies. Universidad de Sevilla, Departamentos de Arqueologia, Filologia Clasica, Historia Antigua, Servicio de Publicaciones, Calle Porvenir 27, 41013 Seville, Spain. TEL 34-4-4231958. FAX 34-5-4232245. charts, illus.
—CINDOC.

800　　　　　　FR　　　ISSN 0035-2004
PA12
REVUE DES ETUDES ANCIENNES. 1899. 2/yr. 500 F. (effective 1997). Universite de Bordeaux III, Esplanade des Antilles, 33405 Talence Cedex, France. TEL 33-5-56845171. FAX 33-5-56845167. bk.rev.; abstr.; bibl.; charts; illus.; index. (back issues avail.; reprint service avail. from SWZ) **Indexed:** Bibl.Ling., Br.Archaeol.Abstr., M.L.A., MLA Intl.Bibl., Numis.Lit. **Document type:** academic/scholarly publication.
—SWETS.

880　480　　　FR　　　ISSN 0035-2039
DF10
REVUE DES ETUDES GRECQUES. 1888. 1/yr. (in 2 nos.). 617 F. (Societe des Etudes Grecques) Societe d'Edition les Belles Lettres, 95 bd. Raspail, 75006 Paris, France. TEL 1-45485826. FAX 1-45485860. bk.rev.; abstr.; bibl.; illus.; index. circ. 2,000. (also avail. in microfilm from BHP; reprint service avail. from SCH) **Indexed:** Bibl.Ling., IBR, M.L.A., MLA Intl.Bibl., Numis.Lit. **Document type:** academic/scholarly publication.
—KR SourceOne; SWETS.

930　400　　　FR　　　ISSN 0373-5737
PA2002
REVUE DES ETUDES LATINES. 1928. a. 357 F. (Societe des Etudes Latines) Societe d'Edition les Belles Lettres, 95 bd. Raspail, 75006 Paris, France. TEL 1-45485826. FAX 1-45485860. Ed. P. Grimal. bk.rev.; bibl.; cum.index every 5 yrs. circ. 2,000. (reprint service avail. from SCH) **Indexed:** Arts & Hum.Cit.Ind., ASCA, Bibl.Ling., Br.Archaeol.Abstr., Curr.Cont., IBR, M.L.A., MLA Intl.Bibl., SSCI.
—BLDSC (7900.166500); Genuine Article; SWETS.

REVUE DES LANGUES ROMANES. see *LINGUISTICS*

RHEINISCHES MUSEUM FUER PHILOLOGIE. see *LINGUISTICS*

RIVISTA DI FILOLOGIA E DI ISTRUZIONE CLASSICA. see *LINGUISTICS*

470　480　　　IT　　　ISSN 0035-6581
RIVISTA DI STUDI CLASSICI. (Text in English, French, Italian) 1952. 3/yr. L.7000. Vittorio d' Agostino, Ed. & Pub., Via S. Pio V 16, 10125 Turin, Italy. bk.rev.; bibl.; illus.; index. **Indexed:** Bibl.Ling., M.L.A.

ROEMISCHE HISTORISCHE MITTEILUNGEN. see *HISTORY — History Of Europe*

870　930　　　IT　　　ISSN 0391-285X
ROMANOBARBARICA; contributi allo studio dei rapporti culturali tra mondo latino e mondo barbarico. 1976. a. L.100000. (Universita degli Studi di Roma La Sapienza) Herder Editrice e Libreria s.r.l., Piazza Montecitorio 120, 00186 Rome, Italy. TEL 67-94-628. FAX 678-47-51. TELEX 621427 NATEL. Ed. Bruno Luiselli, Manlio Simonetti. **Indexed:** IBR, Numis.Lit. **Document type:** academic/scholarly publication.

930　　　　　　US　　　ISSN 0732-9814
RUTGERS UNIVERSITY STUDIES IN CLASSICAL HUMANITIES. 1982. biennial. $49.95 cloth. Transaction Publishers, Transaction Periodicals Consortium, Department 3092, Rutgers University, New Brunswick, NJ 08903. TEL 908-445-2280. FAX 908-445-3138. Ed. William W. Fortenbaugh. **Document type:** academic/scholarly publication, monographic series.
—**CCC.**
　Description: Publishes research and analysis in the classics. Each volume has a particular focus (e.g., Arius Didymus, Theophrastus, Cicero).

800　400　　　IT　　　ISSN 0392-5099
SANDALION. 1978. a. L.80000. (Universita degli Studi di Sassari) Herder Editrice e Libreria s.r.l., Piazza Montecitorio 120, 00186 Rome, Italy. TEL 6794628. FAX 67-84-751. TELEX 621422 NATEL. Ed.Bd. **Indexed:** Bibl.Ling., IBR. **Document type:** academic/scholarly publication.

800　　　　　　US　　　ISSN 0080-6684
SATHER CLASSICAL LECTURES. 1924. irreg., vol.59, 1995. price varies. University of California Press, 2120 Berkeley Way, Berkeley, CA 94720. TEL 510-642-4247. FAX 510-643-7127. (Orders to: California-Princeton Fulfillment Services, 1445 Lower Ferry Rd., Ewing, NJ 08618. TEL 800-777-4726. FAX 800-999-1958) (back issues avail.) **Document type:** monographic series.
—BLDSC (8076.575000).
　Description: Discusses ancient Greek and Roman art, literature, religion, philosophy, economics, and politics.
　Refereed Serial

930　880　　　SA　　　ISSN 1018-9017
PA1
SCHOLIA; Natal studies in classical antiquity. (Text mainly in English, occasionally in Afrikaans, French, German, Italian, Spanish) 1987; N.S. 1992. a. R.22.80 in RSA; Africa R.20; elsewhere $20(£13) (effective 1997 & 1998). University of Natal (Durban), Department of Classics, Durban 4041, South Africa. TEL 27-31-2602312. FAX 27-31-2602698. TELEX 621231 SA. E-mail: dominik@classics.und.ac.za; URL: http://www.und.ac.za/und/classics. Ed. William J. Dominik. R&P contact: William J. Dominik. adv. contact: William J. Dominik. bk.rev.; abstr.; illus. circ. 300. (back issues avail.) **Indexed:** Ind.S.A.Per. **Document type:** academic/scholarly publication.
—UnCover.
　Description: Offers critical and pedagogical articles dealing with classical antiquity, including relevant studies from the late antique and medieval periods, book reviews, information about programs and activities in African universities, and news about classical museums and artifacts.
　Refereed Serial

870　　　　　　IT
SCRIPTORUM ROMANORUM QUAE EXTANT OMNIA. s-m? L.180000 for 12 nos. Giardini Editori e Stampatori, Via Santa Bibbiana 28, 56100 Pisa, Italy. TEL 050 502531. Ed. Francesco Semi.

800　　　　　　IT　　　ISSN 0392-1697
SCRITTURA E CIVILTA. 1977. a. Lit.95000 (foreign Lit.115000($72)) (effective 1998). (Universita degli Studi di Roma, Istituto di Paleografia) Casa Editrice Leo S. Olschki, Casella Postale 66, 50100 Florence, Italy. TEL 39-55-6530684. FAX 39-55-6530214. E-mail: celso@olschki.it; URL: http://www.olschki.it. Ed. Armando Petrucci. adv.; bk.rev. circ. 500.

CLASSICAL STUDIES

930 880   JA   ISSN 0582-4524
SEIYO KOTENGAKU KENKYU/JOURNAL OF CLASSICAL STUDIES. (Text in Japanese; summaries in English) 1928. a. (Classical Society of Japan - Nihon Koten Gakkai) Iwanami Shoten Publishers, 2-5-5 Hitotsubashi, Chiyoda-ku, Tokyo 101-02, Japan. FAX 03-239-9618. (Dist. overseas by: Japan Publications Trading Co., Ltd., Box 5030, Tokyo International, Tokyo 100-31, Japan; Or in US: 1255 Howard St., San Francisco, CA 94103)

937   IT   ISSN 1123-6477
DE1
▼**SIMBOLOS**; scritti di storia antica. 1995. irreg. (Universita degli Studi di Bologna, Dipartimento di Storia Antica) Cooperativa Libraria Universitaria Editrice Bologna, Via Marsala 24, 40126 Bologna, Italy. TEL 39-51-220736. FAX 39-51-237758. Ed.Bd. **Document type:** academic/scholarly publication.

937 410   GW   ISSN 0584-9705
SPUDASMATA; Studien zur Klassischen Philologie und ihren Grenzgebieten. irreg., vol.60, 1995. Georg Olms Verlag, Hagentorwall 7, 31134 Hildesheim, Germany. TEL 49-5121-1501-0. FAX 49-5121-150150. (U.S. subscr. to: 350 Fifth Ave., Ste. 3304, New York, NY 10118-0069. TEL 800-920-9334) Eds. Gottfried Kiefner, Ulrich Koepf. **Document type:** monographic series.

930 950   IT   ISSN 0081-6124
STUDI CLASSICI E ORIENTALI. 1951. irreg. L.90000($100) (Universita degli Studi di Pisa, Istituto per le Scienze dell'Antichita) Giardini Editori e Stampatori, Istituti per le Scienze dell'Antichita, 56100 Pisa, Italy. TEL 050 502531. Ed. Graziano Arrighetti. **Indexed:** Bibl.Ling.
—BLDSC (8481.538000).

STUDI ITALIANI DI FILOLOGIA CLASSICA. see *LINGUISTICS*

480 470   SW   ISSN 0081-6450
STUDIA GRAECA ET LATINA GOTHOBURGENSIA. (Subseries of Acta Universitatis Gothoburgensis.) (Text in various languages) 1955. irreg., no.62, 1996. price varies; also exchange basis. Acta Universitatis Gothoburgensis, P.O. Box 5096, S-402 22 Goeteborg, Sweden. TEL 46-31-7731733. FAX 46-31-163797. Ed. Tore Jansson. **Document type:** monographic series.

880   SW   ISSN 1100-7931
STUDIA GRAECA ET LATINA LUNDENSIA. (Text in English) 1989. irreg. price varies. Lund University Press, P.O. Box 141, S-221 00 Lund, Sweden. TEL 46-46-31-20-00. FAX 46-46-30-53-38. E-mail: order@studli.se. Eds. B. Bergh, J. Blomqvist. **Document type:** academic/scholarly publication.

880 930   BE   ISSN 0779-3448
STUDIA HELLENISTICA. 1942. irreg., vol.32, 1996. price varies. Editions Peeters s.p.r.l., Bondgenotenlaan 153, 3000 Leuven, Belgium. URL: http://www.peeters-leuven.be. (back issues avail.) **Document type:** monographic series, proceedings.
—KNAW.
Description: Publishes studies on the history and literature of Egypt and the eastern Mediterranean during the Hellenistic period.

932   GW   ISSN 0340-2215
DT61
STUDIEN ZUR ALTAEGYPTISCHEN KULTUR. 1974. irreg., no.23. price varies. Helmut Buske Verlag GmbH, Richardstr. 47, 22081 Hamburg, Germany. TEL 49-40-299958-0. FAX 49-40-2993614. Ed. Hartwig Altenmueller. **Indexed:** Bibl.Ling. **Document type:** monographic series.
—CCC.

962   GW   ISSN 0934-7879
STUDIEN ZUR ALTAEGYPTISCHEN KULTUR. BEIHEFTE. 1988. irreg. Helmut Buske Verlag GmbH, Richardstr. 47, 22081 Hamburg, Germany. TEL 49-40-299958-0. FAX 49-40-2993614. Ed. H. Altenmueller. **Document type:** monographic series.

938 930.1   GW   ISSN 1432-7228
▼**STUDIEN ZUR GESCHICHTE NORDWEST-GRIECHENLANDS.** 1996. irreg., vol.2, 1997. (Oberhummer Gesellschaft e.V.) Ergon Verlag, Grombuehlstr. 7, 97080 Wuerzburg, Germany. TEL 49-931-280084. FAX 49-931-282872. E-mail: ergon-verlag@t-online.de. **Document type:** academic/scholarly publication, monographic series.

930   DK   ISSN 0107-9212
STUDIER FRA SPROG- OG OLDTIDSFORSKNING. 1891. s-a. price varies. (Filologisk-Samfund) Museum Tusculanum Press, University of Copenhagen, Njalsgade 92, DK-2300, Copenhagen S, Denmark. TEL 45-35-32-91-09. FAX 45-35-32-91-13. (Dist. in U.S. and Canada by: Paul & Co., c/o P C S Data Processing, Inc., 360 W. 31st St., New York, NY 10001. TEL 212-564-3730. FAX 212-971-7200) Ed.Bd. **Indexed:** MLA Intl.Bibl. **Document type:** academic/scholarly publication.
Description: Treats subjects from the fields of literature, philosophy, history and philology with an emphasis on ancient Greek and Latin topics.

STUDIES IN GREEK AND ROMAN RELIGION. see *RELIGIONS AND THEOLOGY*

STUDIES IN MEDITERRANEAN ARCHAEOLOGY. MONOGRAPH SERIES. see *ARCHAEOLOGY*

STUDIES IN MEDITERRANEAN ARCHAEOLOGY. POCKET-BOOK SERIES. see *ARCHAEOLOGY*

STUDIES IN THE HISTORY OF THE ANCIENT NEAR EAST. see *HISTORY — History Of The Near East*

489 890   RM   ISSN 0081-8844
STUDII CLASICE. (Text in English, French, German, Italian, Rumanian and Russian) 1959. a. (Societatea de Studii Clasice din Romania) Editura Academiei Romane, Calea 13 Septembrie 13, 76117 Bucharest, Rumania. (Subscr. to: Rodipet SA, Piata Presei Libere 1, Sec. 1, P.O. Box 33-57, Bucharest, Rumania. TEL 401-6185103. FAX 401-226407) Eds. Zoe Petre, I. Fischer. bk.rev. circ. 900. **Indexed:** Bibl.Ling., Numis.Lit.
—KNAW.

880 938   NE   ISSN 0920-8399
SUPPLEMENTUM EPIGRAPHICUM GRAECUM. 1923. a., vol.41, 1994 (for the year 1991). fl.195 (effective 1994). J.C. Gieben, Nieuwe Herengracht 35, 1011 RM Amsterdam, Netherlands. TEL 31-20-6275170. FAX 31-20-6275170. (Dist. in N. America by: John Benjamins Publishing Co., Box 27519, Philadelphia, PA 19118-0519. TEL 215-836-1200. FAX 215-836-1204) Eds. H.W. Pleket, R.S. Stroud. cum.index: vols.11-20, 26-35. (back issues avail.) **Document type:** academic/scholarly publication.
Description: Reviews the progress of research on Greek inscriptions, presents commentary on new research on previously published documents; publishes the complete text of recently discovered inscriptions with full bibliographic citations.

SVENSKA INSTITUTET I ATHEN. SKRIFTER. see *ARCHAEOLOGY*

938   SW   ISSN 0586-0539
SVENSKA INSTITUTET I ATHEN. SKRIFTER; series prima in 4 J. (Supplement avail.: Opuscula Atheniensia (ISSN 0078-5520)) (Text in various languages) 1951. irreg. Svenska Institutet i Athen, c/o P. Aastroem, William Gibsons vaeg 11, S-433 76 Jonsered, Sweden. Ed. B. Alroth. **Document type:** academic/scholarly publication.

SVENSKA INSTITUTET I ROM. SKRIFTER. ACTA SERIES PRIMA. see *ARCHAEOLOGY*

480   NO   ISSN 0039-7679
PA19
SYMBOLAE OSLOENSES; covering all branches of classical research. (Text mainly in English; occasionally in French or German) 1922. a. NOK 320 in Nordic countries; elsewhere $62 (effective 1997). Scandinavian University Press, P.O. Box 2959 Toeyen, N-0608 Oslo, Norway. TEL 47-22-57-54-00. FAX 47-22-57-53-53. E-mail: mail@scup.no; URL: http://www.scup.no. (US addr.: 875 Massachusetts Ave., Ste. 84, Cambridge, MA 02139. TEL 617-497-6515. FAX 617-354-6875) Ed. Egil Kraggerud. illus.; cum.index: vols.1-35. circ. 350. (back issues avail.) **Indexed:** Bibl.Ling., IBR, M.L.A., MLA Intl.Bibl. **Document type:** academic/scholarly publication.
—BLDSC (8582.050000).
Formerly (until 1926): Symbolae Arctoae.
Description: Covers all branches of classical research.

480 880   PL   ISSN 0302-7384
PA25
SYMBOLAE PHILOLOGORUM POSNANIENSIUM. (Text in English, Latin and Polish; summaries in Latin) 1973. irreg., vol.11, 1997. price varies. (Uniwersytet im. Adama Mickiewicza) Adam Mickiewicz University Press, Nowowiejskiego 55, 61-734 Poznan, Poland. TEL 48-61-527380. FAX 48-61-527701. TELEX 413260 UAMPL. Ed. Georgius Danielewicz; Pub. Maria Jankowska. R&P contact: Malgorzata Bis. **Indexed:** Bibl.Ling. **Document type:** academic/scholarly publication, monographic series.
—BLDSC (8582.070000).
Description: Papers devoted to the history of Latin studies; Latin literatures, linguistics and methods of teaching.

880   CN   ISSN 0381-9361
TEIRESIAS; a review and continuing bibliography of Boiotian studies. 1971. a. McGill University, Department of History, 855 Sherbrooke St. W., Montreal, PQ H3A 2T7, Canada. TEL 514-398-1797. E-mail: czas@musica.mcgill.ca. Ed. A. Schachter. bibl.; illus. circ. 300. **Indexed:** Can.Per.Ind. **Document type:** bibliography.
●Also available online.

TIRYNS. see *ARCHAEOLOGY*

470 870   US   ISSN 0493-5284
TORCH: U.S. 1951. 4/yr. membership. National Junior Classical League, American Classical League, Miami University, Oxford, OH 45056. TEL 513-529-7741. stat. circ. 1,400. (processed) **Document type:** academic/scholarly publication, newsletter.

930   US
TRANSFORMATION OF THE CLASSICAL HERITAGE. 1981. irreg., vol.25, 1996. price varies. University of California Press, 2120 Berkeley Way, Berkeley, CA 94720. TEL 510-642-4247. FAX 510-613-7127. (Orders to: California-Princeton Fulfillment Services, 1445 Lower Ferry Rd., Ewing, NJ 08618. TEL 800-777-4726. FAX 800-999-1958) (back issues avail.) **Document type:** monographic series.
Description: Explores the cultural, religious, and philosophical traditions of classical Greece and Rome, late antiquity, and the Byzantine Empire.
Refereed Serial

930   MX
UNIVERSIDAD NACIONAL AUTONOMA DE MEXICO. CENTRO DE ESTUDIOS CLASICOS. CUADERNOS. 1975. irreg., no.32, 1991. price varies. Universidad Nacional Autonoma de Mexico, Centro de Estudios Clasicos, Ciudad Universitaria, 04510 Mexico D.F., Mexico. FAX 6657874. bk.rev.

UNIVERSITA DEGLI STUDI DI GENOVA. ISTITUTO DI ARCHEOLOGIA E FILOLOGIA CLASSICA "F. DELLA CORTE". PUBBLICAZIONI. see *LINGUISTICS*

UNIVERSITA DEGLI STUDI DI MACERATA. FACOLTA DI LETTERE E FILOSOFIA. ANNALI. see *ARCHAEOLOGY*

937   NE   ISSN 0167-7551
UNIVERSITE DES SCIENCES HUMAINES DE STRASBOURG. CENTRE DE RECHERCHE SUR LE PROCHE ORIENT ET LA GRECE ANTIQUES. TRAVAUX. Represents: Actes du Colloque de Strasbourg. 1973. irreg., approx. biennial, vol.12, 1992. price varies. E.J. Brill, P.O. Box 9000, 2300 PA Leiden, Netherlands. TEL 31-71-5353500. FAX 31-71-5317532. TELEX 39296 BRILL NL. E-mail: ejbrill@brill.nl. (In N. America: E.J. Brill, 24 Hudson St., Kinderhook, NY 12106. TEL 800-962-4406. FAX 518-758-1959) R&P contact: Elizabeth Vennekamp. illus.; maps. (back issues avail.) **Document type:** monographic series, proceedings.
Refereed Serial

880 937   US   ISSN 0068-6344
UNIVERSITY OF CALIFORNIA PUBLICATIONS. CLASSICAL STUDIES. 1965. irreg., vol.35, 1993. price varies. University of California Press, 2120 Berkeley Way, Berkeley, CA 94720. TEL 510-642-4247. FAX 510-643-7127. (Orders to: California-Princeton Fulfillment Services, 1445 Lower Ferry Rd., Ewing, NJ 08618. TEL 800-777-4726. FAX 800-999-1958) Ed.Bd. **Document type:** monographic series.
Description: Delves into classical Greek and Latin literature and archaeology.
Refereed Serial

489   UK   ISSN 0076-0730
PA25
UNIVERSITY OF LONDON. INSTITUTE OF CLASSICAL STUDIES. BULLETIN. (Supplement avail.) 1954. a. £28. University of London, Institute of Classical Studies, 31-34 Gordon Square, London WC1H OPY, England. TEL 44-171-380-7498.
FAX 44-171-383-4807. **Indexed:** Arts & Hum.Cit.Ind., Bibl.Ling., Curr.Cont., Numis.Lit.
Document type: bulletin.

489   UK   ISSN 0076-0749
UNIVERSITY OF LONDON. INSTITUTE OF CLASSICAL STUDIES. BULLETIN SUPPLEMENT. 1955. irreg., no.66, 1995. price varies. University of London, Institute of Classical Studies, 31-34 Gordon Sq., London WC1H OPY, England.
TEL 44-171-380-7498. FAX 44-171-383-4807.
Document type: bulletin.

930 913 480 880   XO   ISSN 0083-4114
UNIVERZITA KOMENSKEHO. FILOZOFICKA FAKULTA. ZBORNIK: GRAECOLATINA ET ORIENTALIA. (Text in English, French, German) 1968. irreg. exchange basis. Univerzita Komenskeho, Filozoficka Fakulta, c/o Ustredna Kniznica Filozofickej Fakulty, Gondova 2, 818 01 Bratislava, Slovakia. circ. 500. **Document type:** academic/scholarly publication.

UNIWERSYTET IM. ADAMA MICKIEWICZA. FILOLOGIA KLASYCZNA. see *LINGUISTICS*

VERBA SENIORUM; collana di testi e studi patristici. see *RELIGIONS AND THEOLOGY*

809 016   US   ISSN 0506-7294
PA6825.A2
VERGILIUS. Variant title (1956-58): Vergilian Digest. 1956. a. $20 to non-members. Vergilian Society of America, Box 817, Oxford, OH 45056.
TEL 803-777-2765. FAX 803-777-0454. Ed. Ward Briggs, Jr. adv. contact: Richard A. LaFleur. bk.rev. circ. 1,400. **Document type:** academic/scholarly publication.
—BLDSC (9156.025000); UMI.
Description: Discusses the life and work of the Roman poet Publius Vergilius Maro (70-19 B.C.).
Refereed Serial

VESTNIK DREVNEI ISTORII/JOURNAL OF ANCIENT HISTORY. see *HISTORY*

VETERA CHRISTIANORUM. see *ARCHAEOLOGY*

880   UK   ISSN 0083-629X
VIRGIL SOCIETY. PROCEEDINGS. 1961. irreg., vol.22, 1996. £12. Virgil Society, c/o M.M. Willcock, Dept. of Latin, University College, Gower St., London WC1E, England. TEL 44-181-761-5615. Ed. J.C.B. Foster. bk.rev. circ. 200. **Document type:** proceedings.

WIENER STUDIEN. ZEITSCHRIFT FUER KLASSISCHE PHILOLOGIE UND PATRISTIK. see *LINGUISTICS*

800   UK   ISSN 0084-330X
PA25
YALE CLASSICAL STUDIES. irreg., no.28, 1982. price varies. (Yale University, Department of Classics, US) Cambridge University Press, Edinburgh Bldg., Shaftesbury Rd., Cambridge CB2 2RU, England. TEL 44-1223-312393. FAX 44-1223-315052. TELEX 851817256. E-mail: information@cup.cam. ac.uk; URL: http://www.cup.cam.ac.uk. (N. American addr.: Cambridge University Press, Journals Dept., 40 W. 20th St., New York, NY 10011. TEL 212-924-3900. FAX 212-691-3239) R&P contact: Linda Nicol. **Indexed:** IBR. **Document type:** academic/scholarly publication.
—BLDSC (9369.920000).

CLASSICAL STUDIES — Abstracting, Bibliographies, Statistics

880 016   FR   ISSN 0184-6949
L'ANNEE PHILOLOGIQUE; bibliographie critique et analytique de l'antiquite greco-latine. (Text in Occidental languages; summaries in English, French and German) 1924; N.S. 1928. a. 850 F. Societe International de Bibliographie Classique - Internationale Society of Classical Bibliography, c/o Pierre-Paul Corsetti, Ed., Tour Chephren, 7 square Dunois, 75646 Paris Cedex 13, France. (Dist. by: Societe d'Edition les Belles Lettres, 95 bd. Raspail, 75006 Paris, France. TEL 33-1-45487055. FAX 33-1-45449288) bk.rev. circ. 2,000. (also avail. in microfilm from BHP) **Indexed:** Br.Archaeol.Abstr., SSCI. **Document type:** bibliography.

NESTOR. see *ARCHAEOLOGY — Abstracting, Bibliographies, Statistics*

CLEANING AND DYEING

see also Textile Industries and Fabrics

667 658.8   UK
AIR FRESHENERS AND INSECTICIDES: THE INTERNATIONAL MARKET. (Subseries of: Market Direction reports) a. £1595($3190) (effective 1997). Euromonitor, 60-61 Britton St., London EC1M 5NA, England. TEL 44-171-251-8024. FAX 44-171-608-3149. E-mail: info@euromonitor. com; URL: http://www.euromonitor.com. (Addr. in N. America: Euromonitor International, 122 S. Michigan Ave., Ste. 1200, Chicago, IL 60603. TEL 800-577-3876. FAX 312-922-1157) (looseleaf format) **Document type:** trade publication.
●Also available online. Vendor(s): Data-Star, Knight-Ridder Information, Inc.
Description: Analyzes the markets for air fresheners and insecticides for France, Germany, Italy, Spain, the U.K., the U.S., and Japan.

667.1 658.9   US   ISSN 0092-2811
HD9999.L38
AMERICAN COIN-OP; the magazine for coin-operated laundry and drycleaning businessmen. 1959. m. $35. Crain Associated Enterprises, 500 N. Dearborn St., Chicago, IL 60610. TEL 312-337-7700. Ed. Paul Partyka. adv.; charts; illus.; tr.lit. circ. 20,000. (also avail. in microform from UMI; reprint service avail. from UMI)
—UMI.
Formerly: Coin-Op (ISSN 0010-0404)

667.12   US   ISSN 0002-8258
HD9999.C48
AMERICAN DRYCLEANER. 1934. m. $35. Crain Associated Enterprises, 500 N. Dearborn St., Chicago, IL 60610. TEL 312-337-7700. Ed. Earl Fischer. adv.; illus.; tr.lit. circ. 24,000. (also avail. in microform from UMI; reprint service avail. from UMI) **Indexed:** Art & Archaeol.Tech.Abstr., Chem.Abstr., Text.Tech.Dig.
—BLDSC (0812.950000); Linda Hall; UMI. CCC.

667.3 677   US   ISSN 0002-8266
TP890   CODEN: ADREAI
AMERICAN DYESTUFF REPORTER; devoted to textile wet-processing, dyeing, finishing, bleaching, etc., new product information, news of the industry. 1917. m. $40 in N. America; elsewhere $60. S A F International Publications, Promenade A, Ste. 2, Harmon Cove Towers, Secaucus, NJ 07094. TEL 201-867-9230. FAX 201-867-0545. Ed. Edward Fox; Pub. Herbert A. Stauderman. adv. contact: John Nestor. bk.rev.; abstr.; bibl.; charts; illus.; pat.; tr.lit.; index. circ. 12,000. (also avail. in microform from PMC,UMI; reprint service avail. from UMI) **Indexed:** A.S.& T.Ind., Abstr.Bull.Inst.Pap.Chem., Art & Archaeol.Tech.Abstr., Biol.Abstr., Chem.Abstr., Curr.Cont., Eng.Ind, Excerp.Med., PROMT, Text.Tech.Dig., World Text.Abstr. **Document type:** trade publication.
—BLDSC (0813.000000); CASDDS; CISTI; Ei;. EMDOCS; KR SourceOne; Linda Hall; SWETS; UMI; UnCover.
Formerly: Textile Colorist and Converter (ISSN 0096-591X)

667.12   AT
AUSTRALIAN NATIONAL DRYCLEANER & LAUNDERER.* 1950. m. Aus.$78. National Drycleaner & Launderer Pty. Ltd., P.O. Box 12177, Taren Point, N.S.W. 2229, Australia. TEL 61-2-525-2277. FAX 61-2-525-8532. Ed. Shirley Naylor. adv.; bk.rev. circ. 1,100.
Formerly: Australian National Drycleaner (ISSN 0045-074X)

667   UK   ISSN 1358-5185
BUSINESS RATIO PLUS: CONTRACT CLEANERS. 1981. a. £195. I C C Business Publications (Subsidiary of: I C C Information Group), Field House, 72 Oldfield Rd., Hampton, Mddx. TW12 2HQ, England.
TEL 44-181-783-0922. FAX 44-181-783-1940. charts; stat. **Document type:** trade publication.
Formerly (until 1995): Business Ratio Report: Contract Cleaners (ISSN 0261-7765)

667 658.8   UK   ISSN 0261-7846
BUSINESS RATIO REPORT: DYERS & FINISHERS; an industry sector analysis. 1975. a. I C C Business Ratios Ltd., Freepost, Field House, Hampton, Mddx. TW12 1BR, England. TEL 081-783-0977.
FAX 081-783-1940. charts; stat. **Document type:** trade publication.

667 658.8   UK
BUSINESS RATIO REPORT: LAUNDERERS, DRY CLEANERS AND TEXTILE RENTAL; an industry sector analysis. 1986. a. I C C Business Ratios Ltd., Freepost, Field House, Hampton, Mddx. TW12 1BR, England. TEL 081-783-0977. FAX 081-783-1940. charts; stat. **Document type:** trade publication.
Formerly (until 1990): Business Ratio Report: Launderers and Dry Cleaners (ISSN 0269-087X)

667 330   US   ISSN 1042-6442
CLEANFAX MAGAZINE. 1986. 9/yr. $19 (Canada $29; elsewhere $38) (effective 1997). National Trade Publications, Inc., 13 Century Hill, Latham, NY 12110-1386. TEL 518-783-1281.
FAX 518-783-1386. Ed. John Downey, IV; Pub. Alice Savino. R&P contact: Steve Kane. adv. contact: Jim Gardner. circ. 29,000. **Document type:** trade publication.
Description: Contains information on business management, marketing, technical skills and new products and services for professional carpet, upholstery and house cleaning firms.

667.1 677   US   ISSN 0886-9901
CLEANING & RESTORATION. 1963. m. $27 to non-members; members $20; foreign $36. (Association of Specialists in Cleaning and Restoration) A S C R International, 10830 Annapolis Junction Rd., Ste. 312, Annapolis Junction, MD 20701-1120. TEL 301-604-4411.
FAX 301-604-4713. E-mail: info@ascr.org; URL: http://www.ascr.org. Ed. Patricia Harmanrd; Pub. Claudia L. Ramirez. R&P contact: Susan Rimland. adv. contact: Kerrie Bartlett. bk.rev.; charts; illus.; index; circ. 2,500 (paid). **Indexed:** Art & Archaeol.Tech.Abstr. **Document type:** trade publication.
—CISTI.
Former titles (until 1985): Voice (Falls Church); A I D S International Voice; National Institute of Rug Cleaning Voice (ISSN 0042-806X)
Description: Covers cleaning and restoration of textile interior furnishings (carpets, draperies, rugs and upholstery) and restoration of fire, water, smoke and otherwise damaged contents and stuctures.

COLOUR INDEX. see *TEXTILE INDUSTRIES AND FABRICS*

667.3   II   ISSN 0010-1826
TP890   CODEN: COLOBG
COLOURAGE. (Text in English) 1955. m. Rs.350($100) Colour Publications Pvt. Ltd., 126-A Dhuruwadi, Off Dr. Nariman Rd., Bombay 400 025, India. TEL 22-430-9318. TELEX 71242 CEPE IN. Ed. R.V. Raghavan. adv.; bk.rev.; abstr.; bibl.; charts; illus.; mkt.stat.; index, cum.index. circ. 7,400. **Indexed:** Art & Archaeol.Tech.Abstr., Chem.Abstr., Curr.Cont., PROMT, Risk Abstr., Text.Tech.Dig., World Text.Abstr.
—BLDSC (3322.400000); CASDDS; CISTI; Ei; EMDOCS; Genuine Article; KR SourceOne; UMI.

667   SA
COMING CLEAN. (Text in English) 1993. irreg. Carpet and Upholstery Cleaners Association of South Africa, P.O. Box 19139, Fisher's Hill 1408, South Africa. illus. **Document type:** newsletter.

1910 CLEANING AND DYEING

667 IT ISSN 1120-6942
DETERGO; la rivista italiana di lavanderia pulitura a secco tintoria. 1952. m. (11/yr.). Lit.100000($82) (effective 1997). (Unione Italiana Manutenzione dei Tessili e Affini) Auxilia s.r.l., Via Petitti 16, 20149 Milan, Italy. TEL 39-2-32673332. FAX 39-2-33003819. E-mail: union.manut.tessili@agora.stm.it; URL: http://dbweb.agora.stm.it/market/uimta. Ed. Emilia Pecorara; Pub. Umberto Maltagliati. adv.: B&W page Lit.1250000; color page Lit.1550000; trim 210 x 297; adv. contact: Rosanna d'Isabella. charts; illus. circ. 15,000. (back issues avail.) **Document type:** trade publication.
Former titles: Detergo L P T; L P T Lavanderia; Tintoria, Lavanderia e Pulitura a Secco.
Description: Covers laundry, dry-cleaning and dyeing.

667.12 US ISSN 0012-6802
DRYCLEANERS NEWS. m. $36. Zackin Publications, Inc., Box 2180, Waterbury, CT 06722. TEL 203-755-0158. Ed. Dave Johnston; Pub. David Zackin. R&P contact: John Florian. adv. contact: Linda Zackin. circ. 10,500. **Document type:** trade publication.
Description: Aimed at owners and managers of drycleaning plants in the Northeastern US.

667.13 US ISSN 1084-6778
FABRICARE. 1972. m. $65. International Fabricare Institute, 12251 Tech Rd., Silver Spring, MD 20904. TEL 301-622-1900; 800-638-2627. FAX 301-236-9350. URL: http://www.ifi.org. Ed. Jillian Handman; Pub. William E. Fisher. R&P contact: Coleen Sallot. adv. contact: Jillian Handman. illus.; stat.; index; circ. 10,000 (paid). **Indexed:** Text.Tech.Dig. **Document type:** trade publication.
Former titles: Fabricare News (ISSN 0161-8040); Monthly Mailer (ISSN 0027-0466)

667.12 FR
FEDERATION DES ENTREPRENEURS DE NETTOYAGE DE FRANCE. ANNUAIRE OFFICIEL. a. 300 F. (Federation des Entrepreneurs de Nettoyage de France) Heral, 44 rue Jules Ferry, 94400 Vitry, France. adv.

FINANCIAL SURVEY. TEXTILE RENTAL, LAUNDERERS AND DRY CLEANERS. see *BUSINESS AND ECONOMICS — Trade And Industrial Directories*

667.1 FR ISSN 1251-3865
HEBDO-TEX. BLANCHISSERIE.* 1960. w. 380 F. Editions Henri Belouze, B.P. 5, 7 rue Cacheux, 92100 Boulogne-Billancourt, France. TEL 46-38-20-00. FAX 46-38-87-74. adv.
Supersedes in part (in 1993): Hebdo-Tex (ISSN 0989-4985); Which was formed by the merger of: Hebdo de la Blanchisserie - Teinturerie (ISSN 0046-7154); Tex (ISSN 0247-8447)

667.1 FR ISSN 1251-3873
HEBDO-TEX. PRESSING, LAVERIE, LIBRE-SERVICE.* 1960. m. Editions Henri Belouze, B.P. 5, 7 rue Cacheux, 92100 Boulogne-Billancourt, France. TEL 46-38-20-00. FAX 46-38-87-74.
Supersedes in part (in 1993): Hebdo-Tex (ISSN 0989-4985); Which was formed by the merger of: Hebdo de la Blanchisserie - Teinturerie (ISSN 0046-7154); Tex (ISSN 0247-8447)

667 658.8 UK
HOUSEHOLD CLEANING AGENTS: THE INTERNATIONAL MARKET. (Subseries of: Market Direction reports) a. £1595($3190) (effective 1997). Euromonitor, 60-61 Britton St., London EC1M 5QU, England. TEL 44-171-251-8024. FAX 44-171-608-3149. E-mail: info@euromonitor.com; URL: http://www.euromonitor.com. (Addr. in N. America: Euromonitor International, 122 S. Michigan Ave., Ste. 1200, Chicago, IL 60603. TEL 800-577-3876. FAX 312-922-1157) (looseleaf format) **Document type:** trade publication.
●Also available online. Vendor(s): Data-Star, Knight-Ridder Information, Inc.
Description: Analyzes the household cleaning products market for France, Germany, Italy, Spain, the U.K., the U.S., and Japan.

667 AT
INCLEAN; Australasia's cleaning industry magazine. 1987. m. Aus.$60 (foreign Aus.$90) (effective 1997). Hardcastle Media, P.O. Box 180, Thirroul, N.S.W. 2515, Australia. TEL 61-42-673566. FAX 61-42-681469. E-mail: sibbay@ozemail.com.au; URL: http://www.buynet.com.au. Ed. Angela Hardcastle. R&P contact: Alan Hardcastle. adv.: B&W page Aus.$1450, color page AUS.$1950; trim 297 x 210; adv. contact: Alan Hardcastle. circ. 5,000. (back issues avail.) **Document type:** trade publication.
Description: Provides information on new products technology, industry issues and distribution of products.

667.13 US ISSN 0046-9211
INDUSTRIAL LAUNDERER. 1950. m. $50 (effective 1993). Institute of Industrial Launderers, 1300 North 17th. St., Ste. 750, Arlington, VA 22209. TEL 703-247-2600. FAX 703-841-4750. Ed. Joan Leotta; Pub. Ken Koepper. adv. contact: Ken Koepper. bk.rev.; index; circ. 4,000 (paid). **Indexed:** Text.Tech.Dig. **Document type:** trade publication.
—BLDSC (4457.532000).
Description: Provides management information for commercial and retail laundering.

INSTALLATION & CLEANING SPECIALIST. see *INTERIOR DESIGN AND DECORATION — Furniture And House Furnishings*

INTERNATIONAL DYER. see *TEXTILE INDUSTRIES AND FABRICS*

INTERNATIONAL TEXTILE BULLETIN: DYEING - PRINTING - FINISHING EDITION. see *TEXTILE INDUSTRIES AND FABRICS*

JOURNAL FOR WEAVERS, SPINNERS & DYERS. see *TEXTILE INDUSTRIES AND FABRICS*

667 US ISSN 1062-8088
JOURNAL OF THE COIN LAUNDRY AND DRYCLEANING INDUSTRY. 1990. cum.index. $18. Coin Laundry Association, 1315 Butterfield Rd., Ste. 212, Downers Grove, IL 60515. TEL 708-963-5547. FAX 708-963-5864. Ed. Maureen McLynn. adv. contact: Maureen McLynn. charts; illus.; stat. circ. 26,000. (back issues avail.) **Document type:** trade publication.
Incorporates (1972-1990): C L A News.
Description: Includes industry news, educational material, legislative alerts, managing tips and guidelines for the coin laundry and dry cleaning industry.

667 UK
KEY NOTE MARKET REPORT: CONTRACT CLEANING. Variant title: Contract Cleaning. irreg., no.10, 1995. £205. Key Note Ltd., Field House, 72 Oldfield Rd., Hampton, Middlesex TW12 2HQ, England. TEL 44-181-783-0755. FAX 44-181-783-0049. **Document type:** trade publication.
●Also available online.
Also available on CD-ROM.
Formerly (until 1995): Key Note Report: Contract Cleaning (ISSN 0956-201X)

668 658.8 UK
KEY NOTE MARKET REPORT: SOAPS & DETERGENTS. Variant title: Soaps & Detergents. irreg., no.10, 1994. £205. Key Note Ltd., Field House, 72 Oldfield Rd., Hampton, Middlesex TW12 2HQ, England. TEL 44-181-783-0755. FAX 44-181-783-0049. Ed. Andrew Beatt. charts; stat. **Document type:** trade publication.
●Also available online.
Also available on CD-ROM.
Formerly: Key Note Report: Soaps and Detergents.

667 677 NE ISSN 0023-4958
KRUL'S MAANDBLAD VOOR STOOM- EN CHEMISCHE WASSERIJEN, VERVERIJEN EN WASSALONS. 1899. m. fl.37.50. P.O. Box 1332, Rotterdam, Netherlands. TEL 31-10-4736111. FAX 31-10-4730393. Ed. W. Graveland; Pub. A. Schuddebeurs. R&P contact: A. Schuddebeurs. adv. contact: W. Graveland. charts; circ. 90 (paid). **Document type:** trade publication.

667.1 SP
L & E. 4/yr. Mora di Ebre 55, 08023 Barcelona, Spain. TEL 3-213-41-96. FAX 3-210-28-66.

667.1 UK ISSN 0142-9442
LAUNDRY AND CLEANING NEWS. 1885. bi-m. £45 (Europe £65; N. America £110; rest of world £81). Reed Business Publishing Group (Subsidiary of: Reed Elsevier group), Quadrant House, The Quadrant, Sutton, Surrey SM2 5AS, England. TEL 44-181-652-3500. FAX 44-181-652-8909. (Subscr. to: Oakfield House, Perrymount Rd., Haywards Heath, W. Sussex RH16 3DH, England) Ed. Nicholas Marshall. adv. contact: Christopher Shepherd. bk.rev.; charts; illus.; mkt.; tr.lit. circ. 4,894. (back issues avail.) **Indexed:** Text.Tech.Dig. **Document type:** trade publication.
Formerly: Laundry and Cleaning (ISSN 0023-8961)
Description: Covers professional laundries, dry cleaning, textile rental and launderette operations.

667.1 UK ISSN 0261-4421
LAUNDRY & CLEANING NEWS INTERNATIONAL; the world-wide publication for the fabric care industry. 1885. bi-m. £45 (Europe £65; N. America £110; rest of world £81). Reed Business Publishing Group (Subsidiary of: Reed Elsevier group), Quadrant House, The Quadrant, Sutton, Surrey SM2 5AS, England. TEL 44-181-652-3500. FAX 44-181-652-8909. (Subscr. to: Oakfield House, Perrymount Rd., Haywards Heath, W. Sussex RH16 3DH, England) Ed. Nicholas Marshall. adv. contact: Christopher Shepherd. bk.rev.; charts; illus.; circ. 9,316. (back issues avail.) **Document type:** trade publication.
—EMDOCS; KR SourceOne.
Formerly: Laundry and Cleaning International (ISSN 0023-897X)

647 US ISSN 0164-5765
LAUNDRY NEWS.* 1974. m. $24 (free to qualified personnel). Mill Hollow Publications, 100 Avenue of the Americas, 6th Fl., New York, NY 10013-1689. TEL 212-741-2095. Ed. Sylvia Levine. adv.; bk.rev. circ. 15,723. (also avail. in microform from UMI)

667 IT ISSN 0393-4365
LAVAGGIO INDUSTRIALE. 1981. q. L.40000 (foreign L.80000). Rivista del Colore s.r.l., Via degli Imbriani, 10, 20158 Milan, Italy. Ed. Danilo O. Malavolti. adv.; bk.rev.; abstr.; tr.lit.; index. circ. 10,000. **Indexed:** World Surf.Coat.

667 SP
LIMPIEZA INFORM; revista tecnica limpieras generales. 1972. m. 7450 ptas.($76) Ediciones Revitec, Pla de les Vives, Edifici ITEL, Apartat de Correus 93, 08295 Sant Vicenc de Castellet (Barcelona), Spain. TEL 93-8333030. FAX 93-8333474. Ed. Valenti Casas. adv.; bk.rev.; abstr.; illus.; pat.; stat.; tr.lit. circ. 20,500.
Formerly: Revitec 2.

667 352.7 US
M L A NEWS (RALEIGH). 1981. bi-m. membership. Multi-Housing Laundry Association, 4101 Lake Boone Trail, Ste., 201, Raleigh, NC 27607. TEL 919-787-5181. FAX 919-787-4916. Ed. Banner Huggins. adv.; charts. circ. 300. **Document type:** newsletter.
Description: Information on professional laundry services for multi-family housing units.

667 SP
MUNDO T & L; tintoreria, lavanderia, limpieza. 1989. bi-m. 7000 ptas. Tecnipress, S.L., C. Paris 73, Entresuelo 2a, 08029 Barcelona, Spain. TEL 34-3-3225357. FAX 34-3-4051802. Ed. Gonzalo Amoros. R&P contact: Eliana Solsona. adv.: page 100000 ptas.; trim 210 x 297; adv. contact: Eliana Solsona. circ. 5,000. (back issues avail.) **Document type:** trade publication.
Description: For professionals in the cleaning and laundering industry and services and user of these services.

667.13 US
N A I L M BULLETIN; of practical answers to practical questions. no. 389, 1976. m. National Association of Institutional Linen Management, 2130 Lexington Rd., Ste. H, Richmond, KY 40475. Ed. Connie B. Parker. **Document type:** bulletin.

667.13 658.9 US ISSN 0027-5875
N A I L M NEWS. Also known as: Nailm News. 1937. m. $30 to non-members. National Association of Institutional Linen Management, 2130 Lexington Rd., Ste. H, Richmond, KY 40475. Ed. Connie B. Parker. circ. 2,400.

CLEANING AND DYEING 1911

667 US ISSN 0744-6306
NATIONAL CLOTHESLINE. 1961. m. free. B P S Communications, Box 340, Willow Grove, PA 19090-0340. TEL 215-830-8467. FAX 215-830-8490. Ed. Hal Horning; Pubs. Carol & Scott Memberg. R&P contact: Carol Memberg. adv. contact: Scott Segal. illus.; circ. 38,000 (controlled). **Document type:** newspaper.
  Former titles: Clothesline-Laundryline; Clothesline (ISSN 0009-9473)

667.1 US ISSN 1068-7076
NEW ERA MAGAZINE. 1959. m. $30 (foreign $75); newsstand price: $5. New Era Magazine, 22031 Bushard St., Huntington Beach, CA 92646-8490. TEL 714-962-1351. FAX 714-962-1354. Ed. Judith E. Frye; Pub. Judith E. Frye. adv.; bk.rev.; circ. 19,615 (controlled). **Document type:** trade publication.
  Formerly: New Era Laundry and Cleaning Lines (ISSN 0028-5056)
  Description: Independent magazine for the laundry and drycleaning trade.

667 GW ISSN 0034-3625
TP932
REINIGER UND WAESCHER; Fachblatt fuer die gesamte Textilpflege. 1947. m. DM.96 (foreign DM.104). (Textilreinigungsverband e.V.) Verlag Neuer Merkur GmbH, Ingolstaedter Str. 63a, 80939 Munich, Germany. TEL 089-318905-0. FAX 089-31890553. Ed. Juergen Tross. adv.; bk.rev.; pat.; stat.; tr.lit.; index. circ. 6,600. (tabloid format) **Indexed:** Art & Archaeol.Tech.Abstr., C.I.S. Abstr., Excerp.Med., Text.Tech.Dig. **Document type:** trade publication.
  Formed by the merger of: Waescherei-Technik und -Chemie; Reiniger - Revue; Faerber-Zeitung.

667 GW ISSN 0724-603X
REINIGUNG & SERVICE; Zeitschrift fuer Versorgungstechnik. 1975. 10/yr. DM.89. Verlag Moderne Industrie, Justus-von-Liebig-Str. 1, 86899 Landsberg, Germany. TEL 49-8191-125-0. FAX 49-8191-125483. Ed.Bd. adv.: B&W page DM.5600; trim 190 x 270. circ. 16,000. (back issues avail.) **Document type:** trade publication.

667.1 DK
RENS OG VASK. 1888. 10/yr. DKK 520 in Scandinavia; elsewhere in Europe DKK 390. Visholm Media AS, Sydvestvej 49, P.O. Box 221, DK-2600 Glostrup, Denmark. Ed. Benno Arndt. adv.; illus.; circ. 3,000 (controlled). **Document type:** trade publication.
  Formerly: Nordisk Tidsskrift for Rensning og Vask (ISSN 0105-6611)
  Description: Directed to individuals in the cleaning and laundry industry, as well as institutes and organizations such as hospitals and sanatoriums.

667 SW ISSN 0282-1168
RENT/CLEAN; Scandinavian laundry and dry cleaning journal. (Text in Danish, Norwegian, Swedish) 1956. 6/yr. SEK 500 (foreign SEK 582) (effective 1998). (Sveriges Tvaetteriföerbund) Mentor Communications ab, P.O. Box 27817, S-115 93 Stockholm, Sweden. TEL 46-8-6704128. FAX 46-8-6616455. adv.; illus. circ. 8,500. **Indexed:** Chem.Abstr. **Document type:** trade publication.
  Formed by the merger of (1969-1982): Staednytt (ISSN 0346-198X); (1972-1982): Tvaettnytt (ISSN 0049-4887); Which was formed by the merger of (1960-1971): Tvaettbranschen (ISSN 0022-1664); (1961-1971): Tvaettindustrin (ISSN 0041-4557)

667 SP ISSN 0214-7394
REVITEC; revista tecnica tintoreria y lavanderia. 1963. m. 6450 ptas.($66) Ediciones Revitec, Pla de les Vives, Edifici ITEL, Apartat de Correus 93, 08295 Sant Vicenc de Castellet (Barcelona), Spain. TEL 93-8333030. FAX 93-8333474. Ed. Valenti Casas. adv.; bk.rev.; abstr.; illus.; pat.; stat.; tr.lit. circ. 20,500.
  Formerly (until 1967): Tintoreria y Lavanderia (ISSN 0214-7408)

667 SA
S A CLEANING REVIEW. (South Africa) (Text in English) 1956. bi-m. R.64.98 (R.76 in Africa; elsewhere R.96) (effective 1997). George Warman Publications (Pty.) Ltd., P.O. Box 704, Cape Town 8000, South Africa. TEL 27-21-245320. FAX 27-21-261332. Ed. John Kencls. adv.; bk.rev.; circ. 1,417 (controlled). (tabloid format; back issues avail.) **Indexed:** Text.Tech.Dig. **Document type:** trade publication.
  Incorporates: South African Laundry and Cleaning Review (ISSN 0250-1325); Coming Clean.
  Description: Covers the laundry, dry cleaning and industrial cleaning industry in South Africa.

S OE F W JOURNAL. see *BEAUTY CULTURE — Perfumes And Cosmetics*

SEN'I KAKO/DYEING & FINISHING. see *TEXTILE INDUSTRIES AND FABRICS*

667.12 FR ISSN 0398-8716
SERVICE 2000. 1972. q. 450 F. Heral, 44 rue Jules Ferry, 94400 Vitry, France. TEL 42-66-15-26. FAX 47-42-44-66. Ed.Bd. adv. circ. 8,560. **Indexed:** C.I.S. Abstr.

SHUTTLE, SPINDLE & DYEPOT. see *TEXTILE INDUSTRIES AND FABRICS*

667.2 UK ISSN 0037-9859
TP890 CODEN: JSDCAA
SOCIETY OF DYERS AND COLOURISTS. JOURNAL. 1884. 10/yr. £135 to non-members (includes Review of Progress in Coloration and Related Topics) (effective 1996). Society of Dyers and Colourists, Box 244, Perkin House, Grattan Rd., Bradford, Yorkshire BD1 2JB, England. TEL 44-1274-725138. FAX 44-1274-392888. Ed. Paul Dinsdale. adv.; bk.rev.; abstr.; bibl.; charts; illus.; stat.; index. circ. 3,500. (also avail. in microform from UMI) **Indexed:** A.S.& T.Ind., Anal.Abstr., Art & Archaeol.Tech.Abstr., ASCA, Br.Tech.Ind., Chem.Abstr., Chem.Cit.Ind., Chem.Eng.Abstr., Curr.Cont., Curr.Leather Lit., Excerp.Med., Photo.Abstr., Text.Tech.Dig., W.R.C.Inf., World Surf.Coat., World Text.Abstr. **Document type:** trade publication.
  —BLDSC (4886.000000); CASDDS; CISTI; Ei; EMDOCS; KR SourceOne; Linda Hall; SWETS; UnCover.
  Description: Research and practical papers on coloration.

667.1 AU
T W F. (Oesterreichische Textilreiniger-, Waescher- und Faerberzeitschrift) 1948. m. S.492 (foreign S.684) (effective 1996). (Bundesinnung der Chemischreiniger, Waescher und Faerber) Bastei Verlags- und Anzeigengesellschaft mbH, Nikolsdorfergasse 7-11, A-1051 Vienna, Austria. TEL 43-1-5452359. FAX 43-1-54664330. adv.: B&W page S.15300, color page S.24360; trim 184 x 125; adv. contact: Ingeborg Eisenkolb. charts. circ. 2,100. **Document type:** trade publication.
  Formerly: C W F (ISSN 0029-9367)

667.1 IT
TECNO CLEAN. 11/yr. C I D A Editrice Stampa Periodica, Viale Certosa 238, 20156 Milan, Italy. TEL 2-30-85-141. FAX 2-30-88-503. Ed. Franco Pigozzi.

667 NE ISSN 0929-2012
TEXTIEL BEHEER. 1964. bi-m. fl.100. Stichting Vakblad Textielreiniging, Postbus 10, 4060 GA Ophmert, Netherlands. FAX 31-34-4651525. E-mail: menp@pi.net. Ed. P.N.M. Wennekes. adv.; bk.rev.; illus.; mkt.; pat.; tr.mk.; circ. 1,000 (controlled). **Indexed:** Excerp.Med., Key to Econ.Sci. **Document type:** trade publication.
  —BLDSC (8800.649500).
  Former titles (until 1990): Textielverzorging (ISSN 0169-5584); (until 1984): Vakblad voor Textielreiniging (ISSN 0042-224X)
  Refereed Serial

667 658.8 UK
TEXTILE AND FABRIC WASHING PRODUCTS: THE INTERNATIONAL MARKET. (Subseries of: Market Direction reports) a. £1595($3190) (effective 1997). Euromonitor, 60-61 Britton St., London EC1M 5NA, England. TEL 44-171-251-8024. FAX 44-171-608-3149. E-mail: info@euromonitor.com; URL: http://www.euromonitor.com. (Addr. in N. America: Euromonitor International, 122 S. Michigan Ave., Ste. 1200, Chicago, IL 60603. TEL 800-577-3876. FAX 312-922-1157) (looseleaf format) **Document type:** trade publication.
  ●Also available online. Vendor(s): Data-Star, Knight-Ridder Information, Inc.
  Description: Analyzes the fabric detergent market for France, Germany, Italy, Spain, the U.K., the U.S., and Japan.

TEXTILE CHEMIST AND COLORIST. see *TEXTILE INDUSTRIES AND FABRICS*

TEXTILE RENTAL. see *CLOTHING TRADE*

667 SZ
TEXTILPFLEGE SCHWEIZ. 1905. m. 225 SFr. (effective 1997 & 1998). Schweizerischer Waescherei Verband, Postfach 6922, CH-3001 Bern, Switzerland. TEL 41-31-3822322. FAX 41-31-3822670. (Co-sponsors: Verband Textilreiniger Schweiz; Schweizerische Fachvereinigung der Waeschereileiter) Ed. Markus Kamber. adv.: B&W page 1020 SFr., color page 2220 SFr.; 171 x 248. bk.rev. circ. 1,100. **Document type:** trade publication.
  Former titles: Fachschrift Textilpflege (ISSN 1421-0223); (until 1987): Fachschrift fuer Textilreinigung (ISSN 1421-2307)

TINCTORIA (MILAN). see *TEXTILE INDUSTRIES AND FABRICS*

667.3 UK
UNIVERSITY OF LEEDS. DEPARTMENT OF COLOUR CHEMISTRY AND DYEING. REPORT. irreg. University of Leeds, Department of Colour Chemistry and Dyeing, Leeds LS2 9JT, England. **Document type:** bulletin.
  Formerly (until 1994): University of Leeds. Committee on the Departments of Textile Industries and Colour Chemistry and Dyeing. Report.

667.1 GW ISSN 0042-9937
CODEN: WREID2
WAESCHEREI- UND REINIGUNGS-PRAXIS. 1952. m. DM.108 (foreign DM.120) (effective 1997). (Gesamtverband Neuzeitliche Textilpflege-Betriebe Deutschlands e.V.) Panorama Verlags- und Werbegesellschaft mbH, Sudbrackstr. 14-18, 33611 Bielefeld, Germany. TEL 49-521-585540. FAX 49-521-585371. Ed. Gabriele Wehmeyer. charts; illus. circ. 6,000. **Document type:** trade publication.
  —CCC.
  Description: Trade journal for the whole range of cleaning and dyeing.

WER UND WAS IN DER DEUTSCHEN KOERPERPFLEGE-, WASCH- UND REINIGUNGSMITTEL-INDUSTRIE. see *BEAUTY CULTURE — Perfumes And Cosmetics*

667 US ISSN 0049-741X
WESTERN CLEANER AND LAUNDERER. 1959. m. $60 (foreign $80) (effective 1997 & 1998). Wakefield Publishing Co., 3236 Estado St., Pasadena, CA 91107-2916. TEL 818-793-2911. FAX 818-793-5540. Ed. Randy Wente; Pub. Albane Wente. adv.: B&W page $750, color page $1260; trim 11 1/4 x 15; adv. contact: Albane Wente. bk.rev.; circ. 15,000 (controlled). (tabloid format; reprint service avail.) **Document type:** trade publication.

667 US ISSN 1073-1709
HD9999.C483
WOLGAN SET'AKIN.* 1993. m. Korean Cleaners Monthly Co., P.O. Box 318, Fort Lee, NJ 07024-0318.

CLEANING AND DYEING —
Abstracting, Bibliographies, Statistics

667   US   ISSN 0734-8789
CODEN: CASDEP
C A SELECTS. COLORANTS AND DYES. s-w. $240 to non-members; members $70 (effective 1998). Chemical Abstracts Service (Subsidiary of: American Chemical Society), 2540 Olentangy River Rd., Box 3012, Columbus, OH 43210-0012. TEL 614-447-3600. FAX 614-447-3713. TELEX 6842086. **Document type:** abstracting/indexing.
   Description: Covers the isolation, identification, processing, use of natural dyes and pigments; and the synthesis, manufacture, properties, use of synthetic dyes and pigments.

667 316.8   SA
SOUTH AFRICA. CENTRAL STATISTICAL SERVICE. CENSUS OF SOCIAL, RECREATIONAL AND PERSONAL SERVICES - LAUNDRY, CLEANING AND DYEING SERVICES. (Report No. 95-04-01) irreg., latest 1988. R.4.40 (foreign R.4.80). Central Statistical Service - Sentrale Statistiekdiens, Private Bag X44, Pretoria 0001, South Africa. TEL 27-12-310-8911. FAX 27-12-310-8500. (Orders to: Government Printing Works, Private Bag X85, Pretoria 0001, South Africa) **Document type:** government publication.

CLOTHING TRADE

see also Clothing Trade–Fashions; Leather and Fur Industries; Shoes and Boots; Textile Industries and Fabrics

330.9 658   US
A A C A NEWS. m. membership only. American Apparel Contractors Association, 140 Maryeanna Dr., Atlanta, GA 30342. TEL 404-843-3171. FAX 404-256-5380. Ed. Sue C. Strickland. adv. circ. 3,000. **Document type:** newsletter.
   Formerly: Ragtime.

687   US
A A M A COMMITTEE MANUAL. a. free. American Apparel Manufacturers Association, 2500 Wilson Blvd., Ste. 301, Arlington, VA 22201. TEL 703-524-1864. FAX 703-522-6741. **Document type:** trade publication.
   Description: Covers A A M A's 26 Committees, Divisions and Councils.

687.19   US   ISSN 8750-2453
ACCESSORIES. 1908. m. $35. Business Journals, 50 Day St., Box 5550, Norwalk, CT 06856. TEL 203-853-6015. Ed. Karen Alberg Grossman. adv.; bk.rev.; charts; illus.; mkt.; stat. circ. 22,000. **Document type:** trade publication.
   Former titles (until 1984): Fashion Accessories (East Norwalk) (ISSN 0193-0915); (until 1976): Handbags and Accessories (ISSN 0017-7172)

687   US
ACCESSORIES RESOURCES DIRECTORY. a. $15. Business Journals, 50 Day St., Box 5550, Norwalk, CT 06856. TEL 203-853-6015. adv. circ. 11,645. **Document type:** directory.
   Formerly: Accessories Directory.

687.3
TT679   US
AMERICAN SPORTSWEAR & KNITTING TIMES. 1933. m. $40 includes Buyers' Guide. National Knitwear and Sportswear Association, 386 Park Ave. S., New York, NY 10016. TEL 212-683-7520. FAX 212-532-0766. TELEX 239801 KNIT UR. Ed. David Gross. adv.: B&W page $2145, color page $3880; trim 8 1/8 x 10 7/8. bk.rev.; charts; illus.; mkt.; pat.; tr.lit. circ. 7,500. (also avail. in microform from UMI; back issues avail.) **Indexed:** Art & Archaeol.Tech.Abstr., Text.Tech.Dig., World Text.Abstr. **Document type:** trade publication.
   —EMDOCS; KR SourceOne; UMI.
   Formerly: Knitting Times (ISSN 0023-2300); Incorporates (1980-198?): Apparel World (ISSN 0277-9609); *Formerly:* Knitted Outerwear Times.
   Description: For garment manufacturers, contractors, and knitters working in the US.

687   FR
ANNUAIRE DE LA MERCERIE, NOUVEAUTES, BONNETERIE, LINGERIE, CONFECTIONS. 1923. a. 150 F. Editions Duc, 10 rue de Lancry, 75010 Paris, France. TEL 42-06-03-31. FAX 42-38-92-08. adv.: B&W page 6500 F., color page 13800 F.; trim 210 x 297. illus.

687   CH
APPAREL ACCESSORIES. (Text in English) a. $30 for 2 yrs. Taiwan Trade Pages Corp., P.O. Box 72-50, Taipei, Taiwan, Republic of China. TEL 02-3050759. FAX 886-2-3071000. TELEX 24838 TRADEPAG. **Document type:** directory.
   Description: Trade directory focusing on garment accessories, yarns, machines for garment accessories.

687   US   ISSN 1041-5181
HD9940.U3   CODEN: AIDIFY
APPAREL IMPORT DIGEST. a. free. American Apparel Manufacturers Association, 2500 Wilson Blvd., Ste. 301, Arlington, VA 22201. TEL 703-524-1864. FAX 703-522-6741. **Document type:** trade publication.
   Description: Covers statistical information on apparel imports for the previous year.

687 677   AT   ISSN 1039-8694
APPAREL INDUSTRY. 1926. bi-m. Aus.$37 (foreign Aus.$102) (effective Aug. 1996). Yaffa Publishing Group, 17-21 Bellevue St., Surry Hills, N.S.W. 2010, Australia. TEL 61-2-92812333. FAX 61-2-92812750. E-mail: yaffa@yaffa.com.au. Ed. D. Adams; Pub. Michael Merrick. adv.: B&W page Aus.$1960, color page Aus.$2680; trim 297 x 210; adv. contact: Paul Tout. bk.rev.; bibl.; charts; illus.; pat.; stat.; circ. 3,367. **Indexed:** Chem.Abstr., Text.Tech.Dig., World Text.Abstr. **Document type:** trade publication.
   —Linda Hall.
   Former titles: Australian Apparel Manufacturer (ISSN 0816-3588) & Textile and Apparel Manufacturer (ISSN 0810-574X); Textile Journal of Australia (ISSN 0040-5019)
   Description: For key executives in every sector of the Australian apparel manufacturing industry.

687   US   ISSN 0192-1878
HD9940.U3
APPAREL INDUSTRY MAGAZINE. 1939. m. $59. Shore-Varrone, Inc., 6255 Barfield Rd. N.E., Ste. 200, Atlanta, GA 30328-4300. TEL 404-252-8831. FAX 404-252-4436. E-mail: Andree_Conrad@svi.ccmail.compuserve.com; URL: http://www.svi-atl.com. Ed. Andree Conrad; Pub. Sean McGinnis. R&P contact: Susan Hasty. adv. contact: Sean McGinnis. bk.rev.; charts; illus.; index; circ. 18,600 (controlled). (also avail. in microform from UMI) **Indexed:** Text.Tech.Dig., World Text.Abstr. **Document type:** trade publication.
   ●Also available online. Vendor/s: Information Access Co., Knight-Ridder Information, Inc., UMI.
   —BLDSC (1569.940000); EMDOCS; KR SourceOne; UMI; UnCover. **CCC.**
   Supersedes in part (in 1946): Western Apparel Industry (ISSN 0043-3470)
   Description: Discusses apparel manufacturing nationwide, including Canada and Latin America. Covers issues such as management, technology, merchandising and quality.

687   US
APPAREL INDUSTRY TRENDS. bi-m. free. American Apparel Manufacturers Association, 2500 Wilson Blvd., Ste. 301, Arlington, VA 22201. TEL 703-524-1864. FAX 703-522-6741. circ. 900. **Document type:** trade publication.
   Description: Economic reports on apparel industry covering current domestic apparel production, employment, imports and retail sales.

687 685.31   UK   ISSN 0263-1008
APPAREL INTERNATIONAL.* (Former name of issuing body: Textile Institute) 1952. m. membership. (C F I International - Institute for Apparel and Fashion Worldwide) Cowise International Publishing Group, 60 High St., Potters Bar, Hertfordshire EN6 5AB, England. adv.; bk.rev.; charts; illus.; tr.lit. circ. 4,500. **Indexed:** Br.Tech.Ind., Text.Tech.Dig., World Text.Abstr. **Document type:** trade publication.
   —UnCover.
   Formerly: Clothing and Footwear Journal (ISSN 0142-0534); Which was formed by the merger of: Clothing Institute Journal (ISSN 0578-5294); British Boot and Shoe Institution. Journal (ISSN 0007-0351)

687   US
APPAREL: LATIN AMERICAN INDUSTRIAL REPORT. (Avail. for each of 22 Latin American countries) 1985. a. $435 per country report. Aquino Productions, Box 125, Rochester, VT 05767. Ed. Andres C. Aquino.

687   US   ISSN 0746-889X
HD9940.U3
APPAREL MERCHANDISING. (Issued with: Discount Store News) 1982. 8/yr. Lebhar-Friedman, Inc., 425 Park Ave., New York, NY 10022. TEL 212-756-5269. Ed. Jeffrey ArlEn. adv.; tr.lit. circ. 31,000. (also avail. in microfiche from CIS) **Indexed:** B.P.I., SRI.
   —KR SourceOne; UMI. **CCC.**

APPAREL PLANT WAGES SURVEY. *see TEXTILE INDUSTRIES AND FABRICS*

687 659.1   JA   ISSN 0914-7594
APPAREL PRODUCTION NEWS. (Text in English) 1953. m. 9600 Yen. New Japan Sewing Machine News, Ltd., 2nd Kosumo Bldg., 8-5, Sugamo 1-chome, Toshima-ku, Tokyo 170, Japan. TEL 81-3-3942-2574. FAX 81-3-3942-1827. Ed. Makoto Nakajima; Pub. Makoto Nakajima. adv. contact: Tammie Imai. circ. 9,000. **Document type:** trade publication.
   Formerly (until 1987): New Japan Sewing Machine News (ISSN 0545-1914)

687   US
APPAREL RESEARCH NOTES. irreg. free. American Apparel Manufacturers Association, 2500 Wilson Blvd., Ste. 301, Arlington, VA 22201. TEL 703-524-1864. FAX 703-522-6741. circ. 4,500. **Document type:** trade publication.
   Description: Covers apparel technology and current manufacturing systems.

687   US   ISSN 0731-3802
HF5439.7
APPAREL SALES - MARKETING COMPENSATION SURVEY.* a. $60 to non-members; members $25. (American Apparel Manufacturers Association) Systems Publications, Box 351, Dunkirk, MD 20754-0351. TEL 301-773-1616. FAX 703-522-6741. (And: 2500 Wilson Blvd., Arlington, VA 22201. TEL 703-524-1864) Ed. Joar McNeal. charts; stat. circ. 700.
   Formerly: A A M A Apparel Sales Compensation Survey (ISSN 0270-2681)
   Description: Covers sales structure of apparel manufacturers, compensation programs, benefits and marketing.

687 796.5   US   ISSN 0160-7278
ARMY - NAVY STORE & OUTDOOR MERCHANDISER. 1953. m. $25. P T N Publishing Corp., 445 Broad Hollow Rd., Melville, NY 11747. TEL 516-845-2700. FAX 516-845-2707. Ed. Paul Bubny; Pub. Howard Wasserman. adv.; bk.rev. circ. 12,000. **Document type:** trade publication.
   Formerly: Army - Navy Store.
   Description: Reaches retailers of military surplus, sporting goods, camping and closeout items; soft goods such as apparel, not hard goods.

687   GW   ISSN 0005-3554
BABY & JUNIOR; international trade magazine for children's and youth fashions and supplies. (Text in English, French, German) 1959. 12/yr. DM.117 (foreign DM.123) (effective 1997). (Verband der Korbwaren-, Korbmoebel- und Kinderwagen-Industrie) Meisenbach GmbH, Hainstr. 18, 96047 Bamberg, Germany. TEL 49-951-861135. FAX 49-951-861158. (Subscr. to: Postfach 2069, 96011 Bamberg, Germany) (Co-sponsors: Modekreis Kind und Jugend; Bundesverband Spielwaren im Hauptverbar des Deutschen Einzelhandels) Ed. Hedda Mikuta. adv.: B&W page DM.3425, color page DM.5685.50 trim 260 x 184; adv. contact: Angelika Zeiss. illus.; stat.; index. circ. 6,037. **Document type:** trade publication.

CLOTHING TRADE

687.1 UK ISSN 0266-5794
BEACHWEAR FORECAST INTERNATIONAL. (Text in English, French, German, Italian, Spanish) s-a. £30 (outside Europe £40 ($72)) (effective 1997). Benjamin Dent & Co. Ltd. (Subsidiary of: I T B D Publications), 23 Bloomsbury Sq., London WC1A 2PJ, England. TEL 44-171-637-2211. FAX 44-171-637-2248. TELEX 8954884 BENDEN G. (N. American subscr. to: Box 1897, Lawrence, KS 66044-8897) **Document type:** trade publication.
Description: Covers the professional needs of swim- and beachwear buyers and producers worlwide.

687 677 GW ISSN 0722-8929
BEKLEIDUNGS-INDUSTRIE (YEAR). JAHRBUCH. 1970. a. DM.68. Fachverlag Schiele und Schoen GmbH, Markgrafenstr. 11, 10969 Berlin, Germany. TEL 49-30-253752-0. FAX 49-30-2517248. E-mail: 0302537520-0001@t-online.de. Ed. W. Schierbaum. adv.; charts; illus.; stat. circ. 3,000. **Document type:** trade publication.
Formerly (until 1983): Taschenbuch fuer die Bekleidungs-Industrie (ISSN 0341-9703)

687 GW
DIE BEKLEIDUNGS- UND WAESCHE-INDUSTRIE UND IHRE HELFER/CLOTHING AND LINGERIE INDUSTRIES AND THEIR SUPPLIERS. 1952. a. $51. Industrieschau-Verlagsgesellschaft mbH, Postfach 100262, 64202 Darmstadt, Germany. TEL 49-6151-38920. FAX 49-6151-33164. (U.S. subscr. to: Western Hemisphere Publishing Corp., Box 847, Hillsboro, OR 97123-0847. TEL 503-640-3736. FAX 503-640-2748) Ed. Margit Selka. R&P contact: Margit Selka. circ. 3,000. **Document type:** directory.
●Also available online.
Also available on CD-ROM.

687.19 US
BELT LINE. * m. Belt Association, 145 W. 45th St., Ste. 800, New York, NY 10036-4008. TEL 212-564-2500.

687 US ISSN 0896-3991
TT490
BOBBIN. 1958. m. free to qualified. Bobbin Publishing, Inc., 1110 Shop Rd., Box 1986, Columbia, SC 29202. TEL 803-771-7500. FAX 803-799-1461. URL: http://www.bobbin.com. Ed. Susan Black; Pub. Manuel Gaetan. R&P contact: Jackie Ellen. bk.rev.; charts; illus.; index; circ. 18,752 (controlled). (also avail. in microform from UMI) **Indexed:** ABI Inform., Art & Archaeol.Tech.Abstr., B.P.I., Text.Tech.Dig., World Text.Abstr. **Document type:** trade publication.
●Also available online. Vendor(s): Information Access Co., UMI.
—BLDSC (2116.720000); CISTI; EMDOCS; KR SourceOne; UMI; UnCover.
Incorporates (1989-1991): Apparel Manufacturer; Former titles (until 1987): Bobbin Magazine (ISSN 0894-8259); (until 1985): Bobbin (ISSN 0006-5412)
Description: For management in the sewn products industry; covers problem solving, technology, legislation and trade, new products, and manufacturing.

687 US
LA BOBINA. (Text in Spanish) 1968. m. 70. Bobbin Publishing, Inc., 1110 Shop Rd., Box 1986, Columbia, SC 29202. TEL 803-771-7500. FAX 803-799-1461. URL: http://www.bobbin.com. Ed. Amy Gabriel; Pub. Manuel Gaetan. R&P contact: Amy Gabriel. adv. contact: Jackie Ellen. illus.; circ. 13,345 (controlled). **Document type:** trade publication.
—CCC.
Formerly: Bobina - Notivest; Which was formed by the 1991 merger of: Bobina (ISSN 0194-7249) & Notivest (ISSN 0195-0827)
Description: Serves executives in the Latin-American apparel-sewn products industry. Contains industry news; features on trends, merchandising, manufacturing, labor, and marketing.

687.2 US ISSN 0360-3520
TT490
BODY FASHIONS - INTIMATE APPAREL. 1913. m. $35 (effective 1996). Advanstar Communications, Inc., 7500 Old Oak Blvd., Cleveland, OH 44130. TEL 216-826-2839. FAX 216-891-2726. (Subscr. to: 131 W. First St., Duluth, MN 55802. TEL 800-346-0085) Ed. Linda Harris. adv.; tr.lit.; tr.mk. circ. 8,010. (tabloid format; also avail. in microform from UMI) **Indexed:** Bus.Ind., Text.Tech.Dig., Tr.& Indus.Ind. **Document type:** trade publication.
—UMI. CCC.
Formed by the merger of: Market Maker Body Fashions - Intimate Apparel & Hosiery and Underwear (ISSN 0018-5396) & Intimate Apparel (ISSN 0020-9791) & Body Fashions (ISSN 0010-941X); Which was formerly: Corset and Underwear Review; Market Maker.
Description: For retail executives in department stores and women's specialty stores and chains, variety stores, drug and mail order chains and mass merchandisers selling lingerie, foundation garments, brassieres, bodywear, daywear, sleepwear, loungewear, leisurewear, swimwear and postmastectomy garments; covers management, advertising, sales training and fashion trends.

687.2 US ISSN 0362-2452
TT495
BODY FASHIONS - INTIMATE APPAREL DIRECTORY. 1913. a. $20 (effective 1996). Advanstar Communications, Inc., 7500 Old Oak Blvd., Cleveland, OH 44130. TEL 216-826-2839. FAX 216-891-2726. (Subscr. to: 131 W. First St., Duluth, MN 55802. TEL 800-346-0085) Ed. Linda Harris. adv.; index. **Indexed:** Tr.& Indus.Ind., World Text.Abstr. **Document type:** directory, trade publication.
Former titles: Body Fashions Directory and Source of Supply; Corset and Underwear Review Directory.
Description: Directory of merchandisers and retail executives in the body fashions and intimate apparel industry.

687.2 UK ISSN 1359-1479
BODY STYLE; the UK trade magazine for lingerie, corsetry, nightwear, swimwear and hosiery. 1986. q. £16 (Europe £20; elsewhere £30) (effective 1996). William Hook Associates, 549 Crow Rd., Glasgow G13 1NY, Scotland. TEL 44-141-954-0249. FAX 44-141-954-0249. (U.K. subscr. to: Franks Ltd., Kent House, Market Place, Oxford Circus, London W1N 8EJ; U.S. & Canada to: Mr. Lawrence Schneider, 811 N. Longfellow Ave., Tucson, AZ 85711) Ed. Bill Hook. adv.; bk.rev. circ. 7,000. (back issues avail.) **Document type:** trade publication.
Description: Serves professionals in the ladies' undergarment and intimate apparel industries.

687 SP
BOLETIN TECNICO SARTORIAL. (Includes s-a. supplement) q. 2500 ptas.($20) (Academia ROCOSA) D. Emilio Oromi, Ed. & Pub., Ronda Universidad 31, 4o, 08008 Barcelona, Spain. TEL 3-317-12-37. circ. 18,000.

338 FR ISSN 0291-0764
BOUTIQUES DE FRANCE INTERNATIONAL. 1953. m. (plus supplement). 580 F. (in EU 640 F., elsewhere 750 F.). 19 rue Froment, 75011 Paris, France. TEL 40-21-13-40. FAX 42-46-25-91. Ed. Francois Gattegno; Pub. Maurice Gattegno. adv. contact: Marie Jeanne Manlhiot. circ. 13,913.
Formerly: Boutiques de France.
Description: Covers the trends of fashion and the economical and commercial problems of the apparel industry.

BRITAIN'S CLOTHING AND FOOTWEAR INDUSTRY. see BUSINESS AND ECONOMICS — Trade And Industrial Directories

687 UK ISSN 0141-1470
THE BRITISH CLOTHING INDUSTRY YEARBOOK. 1974. a. £50. (British Knitting and Clothing Export Council) Kemps Publishing Ltd., 11 The Swan Courtyard, Charles Edward Rd., Birmingham B26 1BU, England. TEL 44-121-765-4144. FAX 44-121-706-6210. adv.; bk.rev. **Document type:** trade publication.
—BLDSC (2296.090000).
Formerly (until 1978): Clothing Export Council of Great Britain. Directory for the Clothing Industry.

687 UK ISSN 0963-9438
BRITISH STYLE. 1988. q. £40($71) Beacon Enterprises Ltd., 2 Beacon Hill, London N7 9LY, England. TEL 44-171-609-5100. FAX 44-171-700-4368. Ed. John Taylor; Pub. Marie Scott. R&P contact: John Taylor. adv. contact: Evelyn Bainsfair. bk.rev.; cum. issues avail.; index, vols.1-9 (1988-1995). circ. 10,000. (back issues avail.) **Document type:** trade publication.
Description: Covers British merchandise, services, and culture especially regarding clothing, giftware, jewelry, and food and drink.

658 GW ISSN 0937-356X
BURDA INTERNATIONAL. 1953. q. Verlag Aenne Burda, Am Kestendamm 2, 77652 Offenburg, Germany. TEL 0781-843348. FAX 0781-843487. TELEX 752804-BUMOD-D. Ed. Eva Maria Schick; Pub. Aenne Burda. adv. contact: Peter Hampel. circ. 86,528. (back issues avail.) **Document type:** consumer publication.

BURDA MODEN (ARABIC EDITION). see BEAUTY CULTURE

687 US ISSN 0747-4598
BUREAU NEWS. 1946. m. $10. Bureau of Wholesale Sales Representatives, 1819 Peachtree Rd., N.E., Ste. 210, Atlanta, GA 30309-1854. TEL 404-351-7355. FAX 404-352-5298. Ed. Mike Blackman. adv.; bk.rev.; charts; illus. circ. 16,250. **Document type:** newsletter, proceedings.
Formerly: Bureau of Wholesale Sales Representatives News (ISSN 0745-5704); Which was formed by the 1980 merger of: N A W C A S Guild News (National Association of Women & Children's Apparel Salesmen); N A M B A C News (National Association Men's & Boys' Apparel Clubs).

687.3 UK ISSN 1357-6844
BUSINESS RATIO PLUS: HOSIERY AND KNITWEAR MANUFACTURERS. 1975. a. £195. I C C Business Publications (Subsidiary of: I C C Information Group), Field House, 72 Oldfield Rd., Hampton, Mddx. TW12 2HQ, England. TEL 44-181-783-0922. FAX 44-181-783-1940. charts; stat. **Document type:** trade publication.
Former titles (until 1994): Business Ratio Report: Hosiery and Knitwear Industry; (until 1992): Business Ratio Report: Hosiery and Knitwear (ISSN 0261-8419)

687 658.8 UK ISSN 0950-2297
BUSINESS RATIO REPORT: CLOTHING MANUFACTURERS. INTERMEDIATE; an industry sector analysis. 1974. a. I C C Business Ratios Ltd., Freepost, Field House, Hampton, Mddx. TW12 1BR, England. TEL 081-783-0977. FAX 081-783-1940. charts; stat. **Document type:** trade publication.
Supersedes in part (in 1986): Business Ratio Report: Clothing Manufacturers (ISSN 0261-7595)

687 658.8 UK ISSN 0950-2300
BUSINESS RATIO REPORT: CLOTHING MANUFACTURERS. MAJOR; an industry sector analysis. 1974. a. I C C Business Ratios Ltd., Freepost, Field House, Hampton, Mddx. TW12 1BR, England. TEL 081-783-0977. FAX 081-783-1940. charts; stat. **Document type:** trade publication.
Supersedes in part (in 1986): Business Ratio Report: Clothing Manufacturers (ISSN 0261-7595)

687 658.8 UK ISSN 0261-7617
BUSINESS RATIO REPORT: CLOTHING RETAILERS; an industry sector analysis. 1979. a. I C C Business Ratios Ltd., Freepost, Field House, Hampton, Mddx. TW12 1BR, England. TEL 081-783-0977. FAX 081-783-1940. charts; stat. **Document type:** trade publication.

687 658.8 UK ISSN 0950-0871
BUSINESS RATIO REPORT: CLOTHING WHOLESALERS; an industry sector analysis. 1986. a. I C C Business Ratios Ltd., Freepost, Field House, Hampton, Mddx. TW12 1BR, England. TEL 081-783-0977. FAX 081-783-1940. charts; stat. **Document type:** trade publication.

687 GW ISSN 0341-521X
BUTONIA. (Text in English, French, German, Italian) 1891. bi-m. DM.94.90. Butonia Verlag, Bahnhofstr. 5a, 56130 Bad Ems, Germany. TEL 49-2603-2675. FAX 49-2603-2625. Ed. Kurt Schmidt. adv. circ. 1,200. **Document type:** academic/scholarly publication.

1914 CLOTHING TRADE

658 747   US
C A U S COLOR FORECASTS. (Includes s-a. Forecast for Fashion and a. Forecasts for Interiors) 1917. 2/yr. Color Association of the United States, 409 W. 44th St., New York, NY 10036-4402. TEL 212-582-6884. FAX 212-757-4557. Ed. Margaret Walch. adv. contact: Davin McKenna.
Description: Forecasts women's, men's, children's clothing colors; interiors and environmental colors.

658 747   US
C A U S NEWS; color, design, fashion, marketing. 1980. 8/yr. membership only. Color Association of the United States, 409 W. 44th St., 2nd Fl., New York, NY 10036. TEL 212-582-6884. FAX 212-757-4557. Ed. Margaret Walch. adv. contact: Davin McKenna. bk.rev. circ. 6,000. (also avail. in microform) **Document type:** newsletter.
Formerly: C A U S Newsletter.
Description: News and articles on developments in the fashion and decorating industries, with announcements pertaining to the association's activities.

687 685.31   UK
C F I INTERNATIONAL DIRECTORY. 1956. a. £30. (C F I International - Institute for Apparel and Fashion Worldwide) McMillan Group PLC, Charles Roe House, Chestergate, Macclesfield, Cheshire SK11 6DZ, England. TEL 01625-6130006. FAX 01625-511446. (Alt. addr.: C F I International, Butlers Wharf Business Centre, Ste. 105-106, 45 Curlew St., London SE1 2ND, England. TEL 0171-403-9926. FAX 0171-403-9927) adv. circ. 3,000. **Indexed:** ASCA. **Document type:** directory.
Former titles (until 1993): Clothing and Footwear Institute. Year Book and Membership Register (ISSN 0261-2690); (until 1980): Clothing Institute. Year Book and Membership Register (ISSN 0307-8515); (until 1973): Clothing Institute. Year Book.

687   IT
C T M NEWS. (Commercio Tessuti Moda) 1987. 6/yr. Editrice La Martesana s.r.l., Via Luini 3, 20063 Cernusco s-n (MI), Italy. TEL 39-2-9249905. FAX 39-2-9232054. Ed. Saverio Collio. adv.: B&W page L.1700000, color page L.2800000; adv. contact: Cario Collio. circ. 23,000. **Document type:** trade publication.

646   SP
C Y L MODA INTIMA. (Corseteria y Lenceria) 1965. q. $80 $100 to Europe; $130 to America & Africa; $165 elsewhere (effective 1997); newsstand price: 1500Ptas. Indice, S.L., C. Caspe 118, 5o, 08013 Barcelona, Spain. TEL 265-04-41. FAX 34-3-2321361. URL: http://www.networkdessous.it. Ed. Eugenio Rodriguez Fernandez. adv. contact: Laura Ugalde. circ. 7,000.

687   US   ISSN 0008-0896
CALIFORNIA APPAREL NEWS. 1945. w. $58 (foreign $165). Apparel News Group, 110 E. 9th St., Ste. A-777, Los Angeles, CA 90079-1929. TEL 213-627-3737. E-mail: we.master@apparelnews.net; URL: http://www.apparelnews.com. (Subscr. to: Box 18449, Anaheim, CA 92817-8449) Ed. Anne Harnagel; Pub. Martin Wernicke. R&P contact: Molly Rhodes. adv. contact: Jack Marquette. charts; illus.; stat.; tr.lit. circ. 19,480. (tabloid format; back issues avail.) **Document type:** trade publication.
Description: For apparel retailers and manufacturers in the U.S. and the Pacific Rim.

687   CN   ISSN 0705-3010
CANADIAN APPAREL MANUFACTURE. (Text in English, French) 1977. bi-m. Can.$50. Canadian Textile Journal Pub. Co., 1 rue Pacifique, Ste. Anne De Bellevue, PQ H9X 1C5, Canada. TEL 514-457-2347. FAX 514-457-2147. Ed. L. Fillion. adv. contact: Lumina Fillion. bk.rev. circ. 4,200. **Indexed:** Art & Archaeol.Tech.Abstr., Can.B.P.I., Text.Tech.Dig., World Text.Abstr. **Document type:** trade publication.
—CISTI. **CCC.**

CATALOG CONNECTION. see *GIFTWARE AND TOYS*

687   IT
CHARME MODA. 1986. 6/yr. Lit.60000 (Europe Lit.100000; elsewhere Lit.150000) (effective 1997). I G O s.r.l., Via Cappuccini 14-16, 20122 Milan, Italy. TEL 39-2-781368. FAX 39-2-76020487. Ed. Andrea Gobbo. R&P contact: Claudia Manini. TEL 39-2-781381. adv. contact: Claudia Manini. circ. 25,000. **Document type:** trade publication.
Description: Covers the clothing trade: underwear, nightwear, seawear and hosiery for children, women and men.

687.13 362.7   UK   ISSN 0261-6025
CHILDREN'S CLOTHING INTERNATIONAL. 1981. q. £15. Children's Clothing International Magazine Ltd., 83 High St., Waltham Cross, Herts. EN8 7AF, England. TEL 44-1992-715600. FAX 44-1992-715200. Ed. Tamsin Kingswell; Pub. Selina Rankin. R&P contact: Bryan Green. adv.: B&W page £1125, color page £1545; trim 285 x 210; adv. contact: Selina Rankin. illus.; charts. circ. 4,500.

687.13   US
CHILDRENSWEAR MANUFACTURERS ASSOCIATION. NEWSLETTER. q. membership only. Childrenswear Manufacturers Association, 236 Rt. 38 W., Ste. 100, Moorestown, NJ 08057. TEL 609-231-8500. FAX 609-231-4664. **Document type:** newsletter.
Description: Covers trends and developments in the children's apparel industry.

CHINA TEXTILE & APPAREL. see *TEXTILE INDUSTRIES AND FABRICS*

CLEO EN LA MODA. see *LEATHER AND FUR INDUSTRIES*

687 677   US   ISSN 0887-302X   CODEN: CTRJEZ
CLOTHING & TEXTILES RESEARCH JOURNAL. 1982. q. $55 (Canada $62; elsewhere $75). International Textile and Apparel Association, Box 1360, Monument, CO 80132. TEL 719-488-3716. Ed. Joan Laughlin. circ. 1,200. (back issues avail.) **Indexed:** Amer.Hist.& Life (1989-), Fam.Ind., Hist.Abstr. (1989-), Psychol.Abstr., Text.Tech.Dig. **Document type:** academic/scholarly publication.
—BLDSC (3286.820000); Ei; SWETS; UnCover.
Description: Presents latest research on all areas of clothing and textiles.
Refereed Serial

CLOTHING MACHINERY TIMES. see *MACHINERY*

687   US
CLOTHING MANUFACTURERS ASSOCIATION OF THE U S A. MEMBERS NEWS BULLETIN. w. membership. Clothing Manufacturers Association of the U S A, 730 Broadway, 9th Fl., New York, NY 10003-9511. TEL 212-529-0823. Ed. Robert A. Kaplan. **Document type:** bulletin.

687   UK   ISSN 0267-3622
CLOTHING WORLD. 1984. 10/yr. £45 (Europe £65; elsewhere £75) (effective 1997). Company Clothing Information Services Ltd., Parkgate House, 356 W. Barnes Lane, Motspur Park, Surrey KT3 6NB. TEL 44-181-942-7800. FAX 44-181-949-7033. Ed. Leonie Barrie; Pub. Malcolm Gill. adv. contact: Nigel Smith. circ. 5,938. (back issues avail.) **Document type:** trade publication.
Description: Contains technical articles, management articles, news, interviews and fabric information of interest to clothing manufacturers.

687   SP   ISSN 0211-3708
CONFECCION INDUSTRIAL. 1963. bi-m. 6500 ptas. (effective 1997). Prensa Tecnica, S.A., Caspe 118-120, 6o, 08013 Barcelona, Spain. TEL 3-245-51-90. FAX 3-232-27-73. TELEX 93457 PRTC E. Ed. F. Canet Tomas. adv.; abstr.; bibl.; charts; illus.; stat.; index. circ. 3,000. **Indexed:** World Text.Abstr. **Document type:** trade publication.

687   FR
CONFECTION 2000. 11/yr. 14 rue des Reculettes, 75013 Paris, France. TEL 45-35-24-01. FAX 43-31-71-01. TELEX 270 019. Ed. Virginie Transon. circ. 5,000.

687   IT   ISSN 0393-4888
CONFEZIONE; mensile per l'abbigliamento e maglieria. 1985. m. (9/yr.) L.70000 (Europe L.135000; elsewhere L.180000) (effective 1997). Tecniche Nuove s.p.a., Via Menotti 14, 20129 Milan, Italy. TEL 39-2-75701. FAX 39-2-7610351. E-mail: abbonamenti@tecnet.it; URL: http://www.tecnet.it. adv.: B&W page L.1960000, color page L.3136000; trim 210 x 297. circ. 7,000.
Description: Presents fashion trends, work optimization methods, design automation, market trends, new technology, and cost evaluation and calculation.

687.2   US   ISSN 1047-8701
CONTOURS; the US intimate apparel, body fashion, hosiery and swimwear magazine. 1988. q. $45. Communications, Conferences and Exhibitions Ltd., 197 N. Main St., Boonton, NJ 07005. TEL 212-802-4646. FAX 201-316-5781. Ed. Kim Rawlings; Pub. Ben Yedder. adv.: B&W page $3350, color page $4770: trim 9 1/2 x 12 1/4; adv. contact: Brenda Smith. circ. 8,000. (back issues avail.) **Document type:** trade publication.
Description: Reports on fashion and styling trends in the intimate apparel, hosiery, body fashion and swimwear industries. For buyers and executives.

687.22   FR   ISSN 0336-7266
CREATIONS LINGERIE. 1970. q. 280 F. (Europe 350 F.; elsewhere 580 F.) (effective 1996). Groupe Creations, 40 rue de Chabrol, 75010 Paris, France. TEL 42-46-44-73. FAX 42-46-14-38. Ed. Philippe Maillot. adv. circ. 8,500.
Description: Examines the liaison between the production and sales of lingerie

687.1   US   ISSN 0011-412X
CUSTOM TAILOR.* 1912. 3/yr. $50. Custom Tailors and Designers Association of America, Inc., Box 53052, Washington, DC 20009-9052. TEL 212-661-1960. (Co-Sponsor: Merchant Tailors & Designers Association of America, Inc.) Ed. Irma B Lipkin. adv.; charts; illus.; circ. 1,000 (controlled). **Document type:** trade publication.

CUSTOM TAILORS AND DESIGNERS ASSOCIATION OF AMERICA. MAGAZINE. see *CLOTHING TRADE — Fashions*

687.2   FR   ISSN 0981-1842
DESSOUS MODE INTERNATIONAL. 1945. s-a. 650 F. Mereau, 175 bd. Anatole France, 93208 Saint-Denis, France. TEL 48-13-38-58. FAX 48-13-09-08. adv.; illus. circ. 38,000.
Formerly: Corset de France (ISSN 0010-9436); Incorporates (in 1978): Votre Ligne les Dessous Elegants; Dessous Elegants (ISSN 0011-9539)
Description: Focuses on foundation garments.

DIRECTORY OF APPAREL SPECIALITY STORES (YEAR); includes: family wear, sporting goods, and activewear retailers. see *BUSINESS AND ECONOMICS — Trade And Industrial Directories*

687   PH
DIRECTORY OF PHILIPPINE GARMENT & TEXTILE EXPORTERS. 1984. biennial. P.300. Garments and Textile Export Board, Market Development Division, P.O. Box 1771 MCC - New Solid Bldg., 357 Gil J. Puyat Ave. Ext., Makati, Metro Manila, Philippines. TEL 632-8904651. FAX 632-8904653. Ed. Fidelit L. de Guzman. adv.; stat. circ. 3,000. **Document type:** directory.
Description: Lists over 1,000 garment exporting companies as well as associations.
Refereed Serial

DRAPERS RECORD. see *CLOTHING TRADE — Fashions*

683.13   US   ISSN 0161-2786
TT635
EARNSHAW'S INFANTS, GIRLS AND BOYS WEAR REVIEW 1917. m. $24. Earnshaw Publications, Inc., 225 W 34th St., Ste. 1212, New York, NY 10001. TEL 212-563-2742. Ed. Thomas W. Hudson. adv.; bk.rev.; illus.; mkt. circ. 11,500.
Former titles: Earnshaw's Infants' and Children's Review (ISSN 0012-8198); Infants' and Children's Review.

EAST EUROPEAN CLOTHING INDUSTRY DIRECTORY. see *BUSINESS AND ECONOMICS — Trade And Industr. Directories*

ECHO. see *HOME ECONOMICS*

CLOTHING TRADE 1915

FAIRCHILD'S TEXTILE & APPAREL FINANCIAL DIRECTORY. see *TEXTILE INDUSTRIES AND FABRICS*

687.3 746.92   US
FASHION COLOR FORECAST.* s-a. Woolknit Associates, Inc., c/o Kairalla Agency, 27 Raymond St., Manchester, MA 01944-1614. TEL 212-683-6422.
  Description: Directed to wool growers as well as top makers, designers, spinners, dyers, knitters, and dealers in knitted wool apparel and accessories for women, men, and children.

687.1   UK   ISSN 0952-701X
FASHION FORECAST INTERNATIONAL. (Text in English, French, German) 1946. s-a. £30 (outside Europe £40 ($72)) (effective 1997). Benjamin Dent & Co. Ltd. (Subsidiary of: I T B D Publications), 23 Bloomsbury Sq., London WC1A 2PJ, England. TEL 44-171-637-2211. FAX 44-171-637-2248. TELEX 8954884 BENDEN G. (N. American subscr. to: Box 1897, Lawrence, KS 66044-8897) Ed. Stephen Higginson; Pub. Ken Manel. adv. contact: Brian Fox. circ. 11,000. **Document type:** trade publication.
  Formerly (until 1988): Fashion Forecast for International Buyers (ISSN 0014-8679); Which incorporates: Fashion Buyers Diary (ISSN 0264-357X)
  Description: Predicts the serious style directions to watch for in a wide range of apparel.

FASHION MARKET DIRECTORY. see *BUSINESS AND ECONOMICS — Trade And Industrial Directories*

658   US   ISSN 0014-9918
FEMME-LINES. 1957. bi-m. $8. Earl Barron Publications, Inc., 225 E. 36th St., New York, NY 10016. TEL 212-683-6593. Ed. Earl Barron. adv.; bk.rev.; illus.; stat. circ. 11,000. **Indexed:** Text.Tech.Dig.

658   PH
FIESTA BOUTIQUE; Philippine Airlines' inflight duty free shop. (Text in English) 1989. q. (Philippine Airlines) Eastgate Publishing Corporation, Rms. 603-604, Emerald Bldg., Emerald Ave., Pasig, 1600 Metro Manila, Philippines. TEL 63-2-6312921. FAX 63-2-6312992. Ed. Cecile G. Mauricio. adv. contact: Gina Dimayuga. circ. 300,000. **Document type:** catalog.
  Description: Introduces every product to PAL's inflight potential buyers.

FINANCIAL SURVEY. TEXTILE RENTAL, LAUNDERERS AND DRY CLEANERS. see *BUSINESS AND ECONOMICS — Trade And Industrial Directories*

687   US   ISSN 0749-8357
HD9940.U3
FOCUS: AN ECONOMIC PROFILE OF THE APPAREL INDUSTRY. a. $75 to non-members; members $25. American Apparel Manufacturers Association, 2500 Wilson Blvd., Ste. 301, Arlington, VA 22201. TEL 703-524-1864. FAX 703-522-6741. **Indexed:** SRI. **Document type:** trade publication.
  Description: Traces economic trends of the American apparel industry and discusses its place in American commerce.

687   TR
FOCUS ON THE GARMENT INDUSTRY. 1983. bi-m. free. Management Development Centre, Library, Salvatori Bldg., P.O. Box 1301, Port-of-Spain, Trinidad & Tobago, W.I. Ed. Sheila John. circ. 1,000.

687   US   ISSN 0888-2053
FOOTWEAR NEWS MAGAZINE. (Supplement to: Footwear News) m. Fairchild Fashion & Merchandising Group, 7 W. 34th St., 3rd Fl., New York, NY 10001. TEL 212-630-4199. FAX 212-630-4201. Ed. Dick Silverman. adv. circ. 23,000.

687   FR   ISSN 0993-3042
FRANCE TEXTILE. 1986. 6/yr. S E M A C, 54 rue Saint-Alban, 42380 Roanne, France. TEL 16-77-72-66-66. FAX 16-77-71-15-57. Ed. Meyer Bitter. circ. 12,000.
  Formerly (until 1989): Info Service (ISSN 0981-0080)

687   US   ISSN 1065-1330
GARMENT MANUFACTURER'S INDEX. 1938. a. $60 (effective 1997). Klevens Publications, Inc., 7600 Ave. V, Littlerock, CA 93543. TEL 805-944-4111. FAX 805-944-1800. Ed. H.B. Schwartz. adv.; tr.lit. circ. 18,684.
  Description: Provides sources to purchase any materials such as fabric, trimmings, supplies, and equipment used in the manufacturing of men's, women's, children's apparel. Also includes an international list of sewing contractors.

GARMENT WORKER. see *LABOR UNIONS*

697   CN
GARMENTS IMPORTS AMERICA DIRECTORY. 1994. a. $110. Global Traders Association, P.O. Box 797, Sta. A, Scarborough, ON M1K 5C8, Canada. TEL 416-650-9309. FAX 416-650-9280. Ed. K. Bhattacharyya. bk.rev.; charts; illus.; stat. **Document type:** directory.

687   IT   ISSN 0394-2481
GUIDA ALL'ABBIGLIAMENTO ITALIANO. 1978. a. Lit.100000 (effective 1997). (Associazione Italiana Industriali Abbigliamento - Italian Association of Clothing Producers) Gesto s.r.l., Via Cesare Battisti 21, 20122 Milan, Italy. TEL 39-2-55187581. FAX 39-2-5465310. adv.: color page Lit.3900000. circ. 15,000. **Document type:** directory.
  Description: Directory of Italian clothing industry and its suppliers.

330.1   US
GUIDE TO SOURCING AMERICAN MADE APPAREL. a. $97.50 to non-members. American Apparel Contractors Association, 140 Maryeanna Dr., Atlanta, GA 30342. TEL 404-843-3171. FAX 404-256-5380. Ed. Sue C. Strickland. **Document type:** directory.

H K P C TEXTILE AND CLOTHING BULLETIN. (Hong Kong Productivity Council) see *TEXTILE INDUSTRIES AND FABRICS*

687   SW   ISSN 0283-572X
HABIT BUTIK. 1985. q. SEK 250 (effective 1994); newsstand price: SEK 79. Mentor Communications AB, P.O. Box 27817, S-115 93 Stockholm, Sweden. TEL 46-8-670-41-28. FAX 46-8-661-64-55. Ed. Nils Ellstroem. adv.: B&W page SEK 18200, color page SEK 23600; trim 205 x 280. circ. 7,900. cols./p.: 4. **Document type:** consumer publication.

687.4   US   ISSN 1066-4122
HD9948.U6
HAT LIFE DIRECTORY; directory of men's hat and cap industry. 1872. a. $19 (foreign $21) (effective May, 1997). 66 York St., Jersey City, NJ 07302. TEL 201-434-8322. FAX 201-434-8277. Ed. Peter Annunziata. R&P contact: Peter Annunziata. adv. circ. 7,000. **Document type:** directory, trade publication.
  Former titles: Hat Life Yearbook and Directory; American Hatter (ISSN 0073-0904)
  Description: Contains information regarding where to and how to find supplies, headwear, plus selling manual, sales ideas.

687.11   UK   ISSN 0961-1266
HE LINES. 1991. q. £25 (foreign £50). Streamline Fashion Publishing Ltd., 6-8 Vestry St., 2nd Fl., London N1 7RE, England. TEL 0171-490-0745. FAX 0171-490-0709. Ed. Pamela Scott; Pub. Andrew Sharp. adv.: B&W page £1350, color page £2350; adv. contact: Sue Hall. circ. 10,000. (back issues avail.) **Document type:** trade publication.

687.4   US
HEADPIECE.* s-a. Bridal Marketing Association of America, 2956 S.W. 30th Ave., Hallandale, FL 33009-5105. TEL 305-463-1773. FAX 305-463-8732. Ed. Phil Youtie. circ. 10,000.

687.4   US
HEADWEAR INSTITUTE OF AMERICA. NEWSLETTER. irreg. Headwear Institute of America, One W. 64th St., Ste. 3G, New York, NY 10023. TEL 212-724-0888. **Document type:** newsletter.

HENNE. see *CLOTHING TRADE — Fashions*

687 659.152   CC   ISSN 1021-8939
HONG KONG APPAREL. (Text in English) 1969. s-a. $54 for 2 yrs. in Asia; elsewhere $72. Hong Kong Trade Development Council, 36-39th Fl., Office Tower, Convention Plaza, 1 Harbour Rd., Wanchai, Hong Kong, People's Republic of China. TEL 584-4333. FAX 824-0249. Ed. Mimi Yeung. adv.; illus.; stat.; circ. 30,000 (controlled). **Indexed:** HongKongiana, Text.Tech.Dig. **Document type:** trade publication.
  Formerly: Apparel.
  Description: For buyers, wholesalers, importers and exporters, traders of Hong Kong garments and ready-to-wear fashion.

HONG KONG ENTERPRISE. see *GIFTWARE AND TOYS*

687.3   II   ISSN 0018-5388
HOSIERY AND TEXTILE JOURNAL; monthly review for manufacturers and merchants. (Text in English) 1932. m. Rs.20. Journal's Publication, Samrala Rd., Ludhiana 141008, India. Ed. Narinder Mahan. **Indexed:** World Text.Abstr.

687.3   US   ISSN 0742-8065
HD9969.H6
HOSIERY NEWS. 1924. m. membership. National Association of Hosiery Manufacturers, 200 N. Sharon Amity Rd., Charlotte, NC 28211. TEL 704-365-0913. FAX 704-362-0566. Ed. Cathy Snyder. R&P contact: Cathy Snyder. adv.; mkt.; stat. circ. 2,700. **Indexed:** Text.Tech.Dig., World Text.Abstr.
  —BLDSC (4331.925000).
  Formerly: Hosiery Newsletter (ISSN 0018-540X)
  Description: Provides information on the hosiery industry, including production, foreign trade, retail sales, marketing, financial and personnel news, legislative issues, and Association activities.

687.4 685.5   AU   ISSN 0018-8050
HUTMACHER-, MODISTEN- UND SCHIRMMACHER- ZEITUNG. m. S.219. Steiger-Werbung Verlags- und Werbegesellschaft mbH, Hermanngasse 25, A-1070 Vienna, Austria. adv.; illus. circ. 1,100.

687   US
I T A A MONOGRAPHS. (Former name of issuing body: Association of College Professors of Textiles and Clothing) irreg. International Textile and Apparel Association, Box 1360, Monument, CO 80132-1360. TEL 719-488-3716. **Document type:** monographic series.
  Former titles: I T A A Special Publications; A C P T C Special Publications.

687   US
I T A A NEWSLETTER. (Former name of issuing body: Association of College Professors of Textiles and Clothing) 1975. 6/yr. free to qualified personnel. International Textile and Apparel Association, Box 1360, Monument, CO 80132. TEL 719-488-3716. Ed. Sandra S. Hutton. adv.; bk.rev.; bibl. circ. 1,200. (tabloid format; back issues avail.) **Document type:** newsletter.
  Formerly: A C P T C Newsletter.
  Description: Geared toward scholars of textile and apparel.

687.1   US
IMPRINTING BUSINESS. 1979. m. $30. W F C, Inc., 3000 Hadley St., S. Plainfield, NJ 07080. TEL 908-769-1160. FAX 908-769-1171. Ed. Bruce Sachenski. adv. contact: Chris Pucci. circ. 24,000. **Document type:** trade publication.
  Formerly (until 1992): T-Shirt Retailer and Screen Printer.
  Description: Contains information for the imprinted garment industry.

687.12 658.7   US
INDEPENDENT WOMEN'S SPECIALTY STORES & BOUTIQUES. a. $179.95. Salesman's Guide, A Division of Reed Elsevier Inc., 121 Chanlon Rd., New Providence, NJ 07974. TEL 908-464-6800. FAX 908-665-2895. TELEX 138 755. E-mail: info@reedref.com; URL: http://www.reedref.com. (Subscr. to: Salesman's Guide, Order Dept., Box 1009, Summit, NJ 07902. TEL 800-521-8110) Ed. Elizabeth Kizar; Pub. Peter Simon. (also avail. in magnetic tape; diskette format)
  Description: Lists about 11,000 independent women's specialty stores and boutiques throughout the United States.

CLOTHING TRADE

687 II
INDIAN HOSIERY DIRECTORY. (Text in English) 1950. a. Rs.20. Journal's Publication, Samrala Rd., Ludhiana 141008, India. Ed. Narinder Mohan. **Document type:** directory.

687 658.7 US ISSN 0019-9559
INFANTS TO TEENS WEAR BUYERS; metropolitan NYC area. 1951. a. $50. Salesman's Guide, A Division of Reed Elsevier Inc., 121 Chanlon Rd., New Providence, NJ 07974. TEL 908-464-6800. FAX 908-665-2894. TELEX 138 755. E-mail: info@reedref.com; URL: http://www.reedref.com. (Subscr. to: Salesman's Guide, Order Dept., Box 1009, Summit, NJ 07902. TEL 800-521-8110) Ed. Elizabeth Kizar; Pub. Peter Simon. adv. **Document type:** directory, trade publication.
Formerly: Infants and Teens Wear.

687 IT
INFORMATORE TESSILE. Short title: I T. 1978. 9/yr. free to qualified personnel. Beta Editoriale s.a.s., Via Duomo 305, 80133 Naples, Italy. TEL 39-81-207166. FAX 39-81-268943. Ed. Mimmo Tartaglia. adv.: B&W page L.2000000, color page L.3000000. circ. 30,000.

687 UK ISSN 0955-6222
TS1300 CODEN: ICSTEH
INTERNATIONAL JOURNAL OF CLOTHING SCIENCE AND TECHNOLOGY. 1989. bi-m. £1349($1999) (foreign Aus.$2629) (effective 1998). M C B University Press Ltd., 60-62 Toller Ln., Bradford, W. Yorks BD8 9BY, England. TEL 44-1274-777700. FAX 44-1274-785200. TELEX 51317-MCBUNI-G. URL: http://www.mcb.co.uk. Ed. George Stylios. (reprint service avail. from SWZ) Indexed: Text.Tech.Dig. **Document type:** academic/scholarly publication.
—BLDSC (4542.172170); CISTI; Ei; UMI. **CCC.**
Description: Aimed at all academics working in the field of clothing science and technology as well as industrialists involved in either research or production in the clothing and allied industries.

687.2 US ISSN 1061-5792
INTIMATE FASHION NEWS. 1895. 24/yr. $30 includes Fashion Merchandiser (effective 1997). Mackay Publishing Corp., 307 Fifth Ave., New York, NY 10016. TEL 212-679-6677. Ed. Milton J. Kristt. adv. contact: Ron Wieder. illus.; mkt.; tr.lit. circ. 8,000. **Document type:** trade publication, newspaper.
Formerly: Corset, Bra and Lingerie Magazine (ISSN 0010-9428)
Description: Features current trade happenings, new products, opinions, personnel changes, industry functions, merchandising and retailing techniques and experiences, new developments in production and styles, forecasts and general product information.

JEANSFLASH. see *TEXTILE INDUSTRIES AND FABRICS*

687 NE ISSN 0927-4367
JEANSWEAR; vakblad voor de jeansmarkt. 1992. 4/yr. fl.121.50. Misset (Subsidiary of: Reed Elsevier plc), Postbus 4, 7000 BA Doetinchem, Netherlands. TEL 31-8340-49911. FAX 31-8340-63638. Eds. Steffen van Beek, Hanneke van der Linden. adv.: B&W page fl.2975, color page fl.4750; trim 240 x 340; adv. contact: Cor van Nek. circ. 3,900. **Document type:** trade publication.
Description: Supplies information about trends in in jeans fashion, consumers, and management concerns for persons involved in the sale of jeans.

687 SP
JOBWEAR. 3/yr. 3000 ptas. (effective 1997). Prensa Tecnica, S.A., Caspe 118-120, 6o, 08013 Barcelona, Spain. TEL 34-3-2455190. FAX 34-3-2322773.

JOURNAL DU TEXTILE. see *TEXTILE INDUSTRIES AND FABRICS*

JUSTICE. see *LABOR UNIONS*

JUSTICIA. see *LABOR UNIONS*

687.12 306.8 UK
KEY NOTE MARKET REPORT: BRIDALWEAR. Variant title: Bridalwear. irreg. £205. Key Note Ltd., Field House, 72 Oldfield Rd., Hampton, Middlesex TW12 2HQ, England. TEL 44-181-783-0755. FAX 44-181-783-0049. **Document type:** trade publication.

687.083 UK
KEY NOTE MARKET REPORT: CHILDRENSWEAR. 1994. irreg. £205. Key Note Ltd., Field House, 72 Oldfield Rd., Hampton, Middlesex TW12 2HQ, England. TEL 44-181-783-0755. FAX 44-181-783-0049. Ed. Samantha Miller. **Document type:** bulletin.
●Also available online.
Also available on CD-ROM.
Formerly: Key Note Report: Childrenswear.

687 UK
KEY NOTE MARKET REPORT: CLOTHING MANUFACTURING. Variant title: Clothing Manufacturers. irreg., no.9, 1993. £205. Key Note Ltd., Field House, 72 Oldfield Rd., Hampton, Middlesex TW12 2HQ, England. TEL 44-181-783-0755. FAX 44-181-783-0049. **Document type:** trade publication.
●Also available online.
Also available on CD-ROM.
Formerly: Key Note Report: Clothing Manufacturers (ISSN 0954-4534)

687 UK
KEY NOTE MARKET REPORT: CLOTHING RETAILING. Variant title: Clothing Retailing. 1994. irreg. £205. Key Note Ltd., Field House, 72 Oldfield Rd., Hampton, Middlesex TW12 2HQ, England. TEL 44-181-783-0755. FAX 44-181-783-0049. Ed. Samantha Miller. **Document type:** trade publication.
●Also available online.
Also available on CD-ROM.
Formerly: Key Note Report: Clothing Retailing (ISSN 1354-2133)

687.2 UK
KEY NOTE MARKET REPORT: LINGERIE. Variant title: Lingerie. 1989. irreg., no.2, 1994. £205. Key Note Ltd., Field House, 72 Oldfield Rd., Hampton, Middlesex TW12 2HQ, England. TEL 44-181-783-0755. FAX 44-181-783-0049. **Document type:** trade publication.
●Also available online.
Also available on CD-ROM.
Formerly: Key Note Report: Lingerie (ISSN 0959-552X)

687 UK
KEY NOTE MARKET REPORT: SPORTS CLOTHING AND FOOTWEAR. Variant title: Sports Clothing and Footwear. irreg., no.7, 1995. £205. Key Note Ltd., Field House, 72 Oldfield Rd., Hampton, Middlesex TW12 2HQ, England. TEL 44-181-783-0755. FAX 44-181-783-0049. **Document type:** trade publication.
●Also available online.
Also available on CD-ROM.
Formerly: Key Note Report: Sports Clothing and Footwear.

687 UK ISSN 1356-6121
KEY NOTE MARKET REVIEW: U K CLOTHING & FOOTWEAR. Variant title: U K Clothing & Footwear. 1990. irreg., no.6, 1996. £410. Key Note Ltd., Field House, 72 Oldfield Rd., Hampton, Middlesex TW12 2HQ, England. TEL 44-181-783-0755. FAX 44-181-783-0049. **Document type:** trade publication.
●Also available online.
Also available on CD-ROM.

658 UK ISSN 0953-0703
KEY NOTE REPORT: MEN'S CLOTHING RETAILERS. Variant title: Men's Clothing Retailers. 1987. a. £155 per no. Key Note Publications Ltd., Field House, 72 Oldfield Rd., Hampton, Middlesex TW12 2HQ, England. TEL 0181-783-0977. FAX 0181-783-1940. charts; stat. **Document type:** trade publication.
Description: Industry overview of men's clothing retailers in the U.K. Includes industry structure, market size and trends, major company profiles, developments and prospects.

658.8 CN ISSN 1202-7588
KIDS CREATIONS. (Text in English, French) 1959. q. Can.$35($50) (effective 1997). Children's Apparel Manufacturers' Association, 6900 Decarie Blvd., Ste. 3110, Montreal, PQ, H3X 2T8, Canada. TEL 514-731-7774. FAX 514-731-7459. Ed. Lisa Peters. R&P contact: Lisa Peters. adv. contact: Della Druick. circ. 5,500. **Document type:** directory, trade publication.
Former titles: Kids Parade (ISSN 1183-4501); (until 1991): C A M A Parade (ISSN 1182-3429); (until 1989): C A M A Parade of Children's Fashion (ISSN 0847-0847); (until 1988): Children's Apparel Merchandising Aids.

KOMPASS PROFESSIONNEL. TEXTILE, HABILLEMENT, CUIRS ET PEAUX. see *BUSINESS AND ECONOMICS — Trade And Industrial Directories*

687 TU ISSN 1300-9974
KONFEKSIYON & TEKNIK; specialist clothing magazine. (Text in Turkish; summaries in English) 1994. m. $100 (effective 1997 & 1998). Bab-i Ali Cad No.23, 34410 Cagaloglu - Istanbul, Turkey. TEL 90-212-5138720. FAX 90-212-5140650. Ed. Dervis Turasan. R&P contact: Muhsin Yilmaz. adv. contact: Namik Ozer Erdogan. illus. **Document type:** trade publication.
Description: Serves as a link between apparel importers and Turkish designers, manufacturers and exporters.

687.22 IT ISSN 0394-8048
LINEA INTIMA. (Text in English and Italian) 1958. bi-m. L.45000($90) ($210 outside Europe). Publitype S.A.S., Viale Watt 27-1, 20143 Milan, Italy. FAX 39-2-89122288. TELEX 332181 PBT. (U.S. subscr. to: Charles W. Baw, 811 N. Longfellow Ave., Tucson, AZ 85711) Ed. Vito Pisani. adv.: B&W or color page L.4200000. circ. 18,000. (back issues avail.)
Formerly (until 1959): Boutique Intima (ISSN 0394-8056)

687.2 IT ISSN 1120-5644
LINEA INTIMA FRANCE. 1990. 4/yr. Publitype S.A.S., Viale Watt 27-1, 20143 Milan, Italy. TEL 39-2-89122288. TELEX 353437 PBT I. Ed. Marco B. Pisani. circ. 10,000.

687.2 UK
LINGERIE BUYER. 7/yr. £20 (U.S. £25); newsstand price: £2.50. R A S Publishing Ltd., The Old Hall, Lewisham Rd., Slaithwaite, Huddersfield HD7 5AL, England. TEL 01484-846069. FAX 01484-846069. Ed. Anita Saunders; Pub. Colette Mahon. adv. contact: Anne Jones. bk.rev.; tr.lit. (tabloid format; back issues avail.) **Document type:** trade publication.
Description: Contains news and trends reports on lingerie, hosiery and swimwear.

688.2 US ISSN 1049-6726
M R (NORWALK). (Menswear Retailing) 1990. 8/yr. $24. Business Journals, 50 Day St., Box 5550, Norwalk, CT 06856. TEL 203-853-6015. adv. circ. 20,276. **Document type:** trade publication.
Description: Directed to retailers of men's furnishings, accessories and sportswear featuring individual product categories and interviews and what affects the menswear business.

MACHINE KNIT TODAY. see *BUSINESS AND ECONOMICS — Small Business*

MACHINE KNITTING NEWS. see *NEEDLEWORK*

687 IT
MADE IN BIELLA. 2/yr. Via Italia 50, 13051 Biella (VC), Italy. TEL 39-15-31665. FAX 39-15-31726. Ed. Ezio Greggio; Pub. David B. Dondena. adv.: B&W page L.2830000, color page L.4030000; trim 210 x 297; adv. contact: Gianfranco Ferrari. circ. 15,000. **Document type:** trade publication.

687 US
MADE TO MEASURE. 1930. s-a. Halper Publishing Company, 600 Central Ave., Ste. 226, Highland Park, IL 60035. TEL 847-433-1114. Pub. William Halper. adv. contact: Rick Levine. circ. 24,227. **Document type:** trade publication.

CLOTHING TRADE

687.3   IT
MAGLIERIA ITALIANA. (Text in English, Italian) q. L.32000. Editoriale Moda, Via Giardini 476, Scala N, 41100 Modena, Italy. TEL 39-59-342-001. FAX 39-59-351-290. Ed. Ettore Zanfi. adv.: B&W page L.3200000, color page L.3800000. circ. 18,000. **Indexed:** DAAI. **Document type:** trade publication.

687.3   FR   ISSN 1146-5735
MAILLE ET TECHNIQUE. 1990. 6/yr. 430 F. (foreign 480 F.) (effective 1995). (Editions Vauclair) Editions Vauclair, 41 Bd du General Martial Valin, 75015 Paris, France. TEL 45-57-60-60. FAX 45-57-60-61. Ed. Alain Raye. circ. 6,000 (paid). **Document type:** newspaper.
—EMDOCS; KR SourceOne.

687   CC
▼**MANUFACTURING SUPPLIES & FABRICS.** (Text in English) 1995. m. $55. Asian Sources Media Group, G.P.O. Box 12367, Hong Kong, People's Republic of China. TEL 852-2555-4777. E-mail: asmgroup@singnet.com.sg. (Subscr. to: Wordright Enterprises Inc., Box 3062, Evanston, IL 60204-3062. TEL 708-475-1900) Ed. Michael Hay. **Document type:** trade publication.
●Also available on CD-ROM.
Description: Covers the clothing manufacturing industry, including materials, supplies and machinery.

687.1 658.7   US   ISSN 1045-4071
HD9940.U3
MEN'S AND BOYS' WEAR BUYERS. Variant title: Metro New York Men's and Boys' Wear Buyers. 1951. a. $199.95. Salesman's Guide, A Division of Reed Elsevier Inc., 121 Chanlon Rd., New Providence, NJ 07974. TEL 908-464-6800. FAX 908-665-2894. TELEX 138 755. E-mail: infp@reedref.com; URL: http://www.reedref.com. (Subscr. to: Salesman's Guide, Order Dept., Box 1009, Summit, NJ 07902. TEL 800-521-8110) Ed. Elizabeth Kizar; Pub. Peter Simon. adv. **Document type:** trade publication, directory.
Formerly: Men's and Boy's Wear.

687.11   SP
MERCERIA ACTUALIDAD. q. 4400 ptas. (effective 1997). Prensa Tecnica, S.A., Caspe 118-120, 6o, 08013 Barcelona, Spain. TEL 3-2455190. FAX 34-3-2322773.

687.12   US
METRO NEW YORK READY-TO-WEAR. 1951. a. $50. Salesman's Guide, A Division of Reed Elsevier Inc., 121 Chanlon Rd., New Providence, NJ 07974. TEL 908-464-6800. FAX 908-665-2894. TELEX 138 755. E-mail: info@reedref.com; URL: http://www.reedref.com. (Subscr. to: Salesman's Guide, Order Dept., Box 1009, Summit, NJ 07902. TEL 800-521-8110) Ed. Elizabeth Kizar; Pub. Peter Simon. index. **Document type:** trade publication, directory.
Former titles: Women's, Misses and Jr. Coats and Suits Buyers Directory - New York Metropolitan Area; Women's Coats and Suits Directory - New York Metropolitan Area (ISSN 0084-1064)
Description: Lists major stores and buyers in the New York metropolitan area.

687.13   IT   ISSN 0026-7252
MODA DEI BIMBI. 1963. s-a. L.12000($12) Edizioni Moderne Internazionali, Via Burlamacchi 11, 20135 Milan, Italy. TEL 39-2-55189297. FAX 39-2-5465954. Ed. A. Maria Pietraccini. adv.: B&W page L.2100000. circ. 90,000.

687   JA
MODE ET MODE. 4/yr. $18. Intercontinental Marketing Corp., I.P.O. Box 5056, Tokyo 100-31, Japan. TEL 81-3-3661-7458. FAX 81-3-3667-9646.

687   IT
MODITALIA. 1965. q. L.4500. Via Aretina 167, 50136 Florence, Italy. TEL 055-672-441. Ed. Mario Lepri. adv. circ. 20,000.

687   SP
MUESTRAS Y MOTIVOS. 2/yr. M Y M S.A., C. Julian Camarillo 27, 28037 Madrid, Spain. TEL 1-408-62-40. TELEX 44972 EMYME. Ed. Manuel Arroyo.

687   US
N A M D T NEWSLETTER. m. National Association of Milliners, Dressmakers and Tailors, c/o Harlem Institute of Fashion, 157 W. 126th St., New York, NY 10027. TEL 212-666-1320. **Document type:** newsletter.

687.11   US
N A M S B NEWS. m. membership. National Association of Men's Sportswear Buyers, Inc., 500 Fifth Ave., Ste. 1425, New York, NY 10110. TEL 212-391-8580. FAX 212-827-0166. Ed. Jack Herschlag. circ. 1,200. (back issues avail.) **Document type:** newsletter.

687   US
N A U M D NEWS.* 3/yr. National Association of Uniform Manufacturers and Distributors, 1156 Ave. of the Americas, New York, NY 10036. TEL 212-869-0670. circ. 650.

687   US
N A U M D OFFICE REPORTS.* bi-m. National Association of Uniform Manufacturers and Distributors, 1156 Ave. of the Americas, New York, NY 10036. TEL 212-869-0670.

687   US
N A U M D POSTAL UPDATE.* m. National Association of Uniform Manufacturers and Distributors, 115 Ave. of the Americas, New York, NY 10036. TEL 212-869-0670.

687.19   US
N F A A BULLETIN. s-w. National Fashion Accessories Association, 330 Fifth Ave., New York, NY 10001. TEL 212-947-3424. **Document type:** bulletin.

687.19   US
N F A A NEWSLETTER. m. National Fashion Accessories Association, 330 Fifth Ave., New York, NY 10001. TEL 212-947-3424. **Document type:** newsletter.

687.11   US
N O S A PRODUCTION BULLETIN. m. National Outerwear and Sportswear Association, c/o A A M A, 2500 Wilson Blvd., Arlington, VA 22201.
Description: For manufacturers of men's and boys' outerwear and sportswear.

687.11   US
N O S A FASHION BULLETIN. irreg. National Outerwear and Sportswear Association, c/o A A M A, 2500 Wilson Blvd, Arlington, VA 22201.
Description: For manufacturers of men's and boys' sportswear and outerwear.

687.11   US
N O S A NEWS. irreg. National Outerwear and Sportswear Association, c/o A A M A, 2500 Wilson Blvd., Arlington, VA 22201. **Document type:** newsletter.
Description: For manufacturers of men's and boys' sportswear and outerwear.

687.19   US
NATIONAL ASSOCIATION OF FASHION AND ACCESSORY DESIGNERS. NEWSLETTER. s-a. National Association of Fashion and Accessory Designers, 2180 E. 93rd St., Cleveland, OH 44106. TEL 216-231-0375.

687   US   ISSN 0077-5983
NATIONWIDE DIRECTORY OF MEN'S AND BOYS' WEAR BUYERS (EXCLUSIVE OF NEW YORK METROPOLITAN AREA). 1965. a. $210. Salesman's Guide, A Division of Reed Elsevier Inc., 121 Chanlon Rd., New Providence, NJ 07974. TEL 908-464-6800. FAX 908-665-2894. TELEX 138 755. E-mail: info@reedref.com; URL: http://www.reedref.com. (Subscr. to: Salesman's Guide, Order Dept., Box 1009, Summit, NJ 07902. TEL 800-521-8110) Ed. Elizabeth Kizar; Pub. Peter Simon. index. (also avail. in magnetic tape) **Document type:** directory, trade publication.
Description: Lists 11,300 buyers and executives for 6,500 retail stores carrying men's and boys' wear.

658.8 687   US   ISSN 0077-5991
NATIONWIDE DIRECTORY OF WOMEN'S AND CHILDREN'S WEAR BUYERS (EXCLUSIVE OF NEW YORK METROPOLITAN AREA). 1963. a. $210. Salesman's Guide, A Division of Reed Elsevier Inc., 121 Chanlon Rd., New Providence, NJ 07974. TEL 908-464-6800. FAX 908-665-2894. TELEX 138 755. E-mail: info@reedref.com; URL: http://www.reedref.com. (Subscr. to: Salesman's Guide, Order Dept., Box 1009, Summit, NJ 07902. TEL 800-521-8110) Ed. Elizabeth Kizar; Pub. Peter Simon. **Document type:** directory, trade publication.
Description: Lists 17,000 buyers and executives of women's and children's apparel for 8,500 retailers.

658.8   US   ISSN 0077-6009
NATIONWIDE MAJOR MASS MARKET MERCHANDISERS (EXCLUSIVE OF NEW YORK METROPOLITAN AREA). 1964. a. $169.95. Salesman's Guide, A Division of Reed Elsevier Inc., 121 Chanlon Rd., New Providence, NJ 07974. TEL 908-464-6800. FAX 908-665-2894. TELEX 138 755. E-mail: info@reedref.com; URL: http://www.reedref.com. (Subscr. to: Salesman's Guide, Order Dept., Box 1009, Summit, NJ 07902. TEL 800-521-8110) Ed. Elizabeth Kizar; Pub. Peter Simon. index. circ. 1,500. (reprint service avail. from UMI) **Document type:** directory, trade publication.
Description: Lists 5,000 buyers of men's, women's, children's apparel for over 2,800 discount and chain store operators.

687   US
NECKWEAR INDUSTRY DIRECTORY. biennial. $20. Neckwear Association of America, 151 Lexington Ave., New York, NY 10016. TEL 212-683-8454. Ed. Gerald Andersen. circ. 25,000. **Document type:** directory.

687   US   ISSN 0028-2359
TJ1501
NEEDLE'S EYE. 1930. q. free. Union Special Corp., 1 Union Special Plaza, Huntley, IL 60142. TEL 847-669-4334. FAX 847-669-3534. Ed. David Kiesa. R&P contact: David Kiesa. adv. contact: Daniel Kennedy. charts; illus.; tr.lit.; circ. 26,300 (controlled). **Indexed:** Text.Tech.Dig., World Text.Abstr. **Document type:** trade publication.
—Linda Hall.
Description: Provides news and information on developments in the needle trades, including new products, technical articles, and profiles of garment and other sewn product manufacturers.
Refereed Serial

NEW BODIES. see *CLOTHING TRADE — Fashions*

687.12   US
NEW YORK SKIRT AND SPORTSWEAR ASSOCIATION. BULLETIN. irreg. New York Skirt and Sportswear Association, 225 W. 34th St., Rm. 1416, New York, NY 10122. TEL 212-564-0040. **Document type:** bulletin.

687   SZ
NEWS BY SPORTSWEAR. 18/yr. Sportswear International Verlag, Innere Gueterstr. 4, Postfach 4029, CH-6304 Zug, Switzerland. TEL 042-217563. FAX 042-224171. Ed. Hugo Kaufmann. circ. 5,500.

NYKYTEKSTIILI. see *TEXTILE INDUSTRIES AND FABRICS*

687   PL   ISSN 0471-0320
ODZIEZ. 1950. m. $51. (Stowarzyszenie Wlokiennikow Polskich) Wydawnictwo Czasopism i Ksiazek Technicznych SIGMA - NOT, Ul. Ratuszowa 11, Box 1004, 00-950 Warsaw, Poland. TEL 48-22-180918. FAX 48-22-192187. TELEX 814550 SIGMA PL. (Dist. by: SIGMA NOT Ltd., Ul. Bartycka 20, 00-716 Warsaw, Poland) circ. 900. **Indexed:** World Text.Abstr.

OFFICIEL DES TEXTILES (HABILLEMENT). see *TEXTILE INDUSTRIES AND FABRICS*

687   SZ   ISSN 0030-4867
ORELLA; Schweizer Zeitschrift fuer die kreative Frau. m. 95 SFr. (effective 1997). Habegger Verlag Zuerich, Morgartenstr. 6-10, Postfach 9230, CH-8036 Zurich, Switzerland. TEL 41-1-2981220. FAX 41-1-2981277. adv. circ. 128,000. **Document type:** trade publication.

OUR LOCAL SIXTY SIX. see *LABOR UNIONS*

1918 CLOTHING TRADE

687.1   US   ISSN 1066-3991
OUTERWEAR. 1992. m. $80 (effective 1997). Creative Marketing Plus, 19 W. 21st St., Ste. 403, New York, NY 10010. TEL 212-727-1210. Ed. Richard S. Harrow; Pub. Richard S. Harrow. adv.; circ. 16,000 (controlled). **Document type:** trade publication.

OUTLET REPORT. see BUSINESS AND ECONOMICS — Trade And Industrial Directories

687   GW
PFAFF INFORMATION; fuer die Naehende Industrie. (Editions in English, French, German, Italian, Spanish) 1953. 3/yr. Pfaff AG, Koenigstr. 154, 67655 Kaiserslautern, Germany. TEL 49-631-2000. FAX 49-631-17202. Ed. Karin Geib. circ. 30,000. **Document type:** trade publication.

687   US
PLEATERS, STITCHERS AND EMBROIDERERS ASSOCIATION. NEWSLETTER.* irreg. Pleaters, Stitchers and Embroiderers Association, 145 W. 45th St., Ste. 800, New York, NY 10036-4008. TEL 212-564-2500.

687   IT
PLUS. 1994. bi-m. L.60000 (foreign L.150000). Leader Interservice s.r.l., Piazza Piemonte 8, 20145 Milan, Italy. TEL 39-2-463462. FAX 39-2-4980526. Ed. Margherita Gertolotti. adv.: color page L.4000000. circ. 15,000. **Document type:** trade publication.

688.76   US   ISSN 0744-3161
PRESS MAGAZINE. m. $25. Entertec Publishing, Inc., 7009 S. Potomac St., Englewood, CO 80112. TEL 303-397-7600. FAX 303-397-7619. Ed. Craig Howson. adv. circ. 27,500. **Document type:** trade publication.
—CCC.
Description: Presents a forum on apparel screenprinting and other kinds of custom apparel retailing.

687   US
PRIDE (NEW YORK). s-a. National Association of Milliners, Dressmakers and Tailors, c/o Harlem Institute of Fashion, 157 W. 126th St., New York, NY 10027. TEL 212-666-1320.

687   US   ISSN 0898-3313
PRINTWEAR MAGAZINE. 1987. m. $26. National Business Media, Inc., Box 1416, Broomfield, CO 80020. TEL 303-469-0424. FAX 303-469-5730. Ed. Mark Buchannan. adv.: B&W page $1725; trim 8 1/8 x 10 7/8. circ. 25,000. **Indexed:** Abstr.Bull.Inst.Pap.Chem. **Document type:** trade publication.
Description: Covers garment screen printing.

867.3   IT
R M 1 MAGLIERIA IN ITALIA/R M 1 ITALIAN KNITWEAR. (Text in English and Italian) 1965. s-a. L.30000. Publitype S.A.S., Viale G. Watt 27-1, 20143 Milan, Italy. TEL 2-89122288. FAX 02-89127095. (U.S. subscr. to: Charles W. Baw, 811 N. Longfellow Ave., Tucson, AZ 85711) Ed. Vito Pisani. adv. circ. 15,000.
Formerly: Maglieria in Italia (ISSN 0394-8064)

687   AT
RAGTRADER; Australia's clothing fashion. 1972. s-m. Aus.$173($326) (effective 1997). Reed Business Publishing Pty. Ltd. (Subsidiary of: Reed International PLC), P.O. Box 5487, W. Chatswood, N.S.W. 2056, Australia. TEL 61-2-699-2411. FAX 61-2-319-7926. Ed. Sarah Stowe. circ. 5,500. **Incorporates:** Menswear.
Description: Covers women's, men's and children's clothing industry in Australia.

687   GW   ISSN 0935-6452
READYWEAR. (Text in English) 1972. 2/yr. DM.75 (foreign DM.80.50). S N Verlag Michael Steinert, An der Alster 21, 20099 Hamburg, Germany. TEL 040-240852. FAX 040-2803788.

687.3   SP
REVISTA TECNICA DE LA INDUSTRIA DE GENEROS DE PUNTO. Variant titles: Revista de la Promocion Tecnica de la Industria de Generos de Punto. Tecnica del Punto. 1956. bi-m. 6500 ptas. (effective 1997). Prensa Tecnica, S.A., Caspe, 118-120, 6o, 08013 Barcelona, Spain. TEL 3-245-51-90. FAX 3-232-27-73. TELEX 93457 PRTC E. Ed. F. Canet Tomas. adv.; charts; illus.; stat.; tr.lit. circ. 3,000. **Indexed:** World Text.Abstr.

687   FR
REVUE DE LA MERCERIE, NOUVEAUTES, BONNETERIE, LINGERIE, CONFECTIONS. 5/yr. 175 F. (foreign 250 F.). Editions Duc, 10 rue de Lancry, 75010 Paris, France. TEL 42-06-03-31. FAX 42-38-92-08. Ed. Paulette Chevassus. adv.: B&W page 10700 F., color page 18700 F.; trim 210 x 297. illus.

ROUND BOBBIN. see NEEDLEWORK

646 687   GW   ISSN 0722-2866
RUNDSCHAU FUER INTERNATIONALE HERRENMODE; Fachzeitschrift fuer Mode und Schnitttechnik. 1882. m. DM.193.92. Rundschau-Verlag Otto G. Koeniger GmbH und Co., Karlstr. 41, 89075 Ulm, Germany. TEL 49-731-1520187. FAX 49-731-1520188. adv.; bk.rev.; index. circ. 3,000. **Document type:** consumer publication.

687   US   ISSN 1045-6996
THE S & B REPORT. (Sales and Bargains) m. $59 (effective Sep. 1997). Lazar Media Group, Inc., 108 E. 38th St., Ste. 2000, New York, NY 10016. TEL 212-683-7612. FAX 212-683-7704. Ed. Ann Rizzo. **Document type:** newsletter.
Description: Lists between 50 to 250 different New York City designer showroom sales, including addresses, sale dates and a description of merchandise.

687   IT   ISSN 0036-4460
SANNIO ELEGANTE.* 1953. q. L.2000. Luigi Cantone, Ed. & Pub., Via Lucia 10, Benevento, Italy. illus. circ. 2,000.

687   SZ
SCHWEIZER STICKEREIFACHBLATT. 6/yr. Verband Schweizerische Stickerfabrikant, Waldmannstr. 6, CH-9014 St. Gallen, Switzerland. TEL 071-272233. circ. 440.

687 658   GW
SEASON - MODE IM VERKAUF. 2/yr. Deutscher Fachverlag GmbH, Mainzer Landstr. 251, 60326 Frankfurt a.M., Germany. TEL 49-69-759501. FAX 49-69-75952999. (Subscr. to: Postfach 100606, 60006 Frankfurt a.M., Germany) adv.: B&W page DM.8901, color page DM.12776; trim 208 x 294. illus. circ. 80,000. **Document type:** publication.
Formerly: Mode im Verkauf (ISSN 0342-3689)

687.19   SP
SELECCIONES DE FORNITURAS; y complementos para la confeccion y merceria. 1974. q. 3000 ptas. (foreign 5000 ptas.) (effective 1995). Ser-Graf, C. Vilamari 81, 08015 Barcelona, Spain. TEL 34-3-2260424. FAX 34-3-2263298. Ed. A. Palazon Serrano; Pub. Pep Blanes. adv.: color page 92000 ptas.; 275 x 185; adv. contact: Javier Palazon Barriuso. circ. 5,000. **Document type:** consumer publication.

687   UK
SHUTTLE PLUS. 1979. q. £21 (foreign £24). Sewing Machine Trade Association, 24 Fairlawn Grove, Chiswick, London W4 5EH, England. TEL 44-181-995-0411. FAX 44-181-742-2396. Ed. Arthur Spencer-Bolland. adv.: B&W page £470, color page £550. circ. 3,200. **Document type:** trade publication.
Description: Represents industrial and domestic sewing and clothing machine dealers and distributors, and those selling haberdashery products.

687   RU   ISSN 0132-0955
SHVEINAYA PROMYSHLENNOST.* 1959. bi-m. $111 (effective 1998). Izdatel'stvo Legkaya Promyshlennosti i Bytovoe Obsluzhivanie, 12, 1st Kardashevskii pereulok, Moscow 113184, Russia. (Dist. by: Mezhdunarodnaya Kniga, Moscow, G-200, Russia) index. **Indexed:** C.I.S. Abstr., Text.Tech.Dig., World Text.Abstr.
—BLDSC (0397.360000).
Description: Covers the garment industry.

687   SW   ISSN 0346-1386
SKRAEDDERI;* Skraeddarmaestaren - Svensk Skraedderitidning. 1938. bi-m. SEK 205. Sveriges Skraedderiidkarefoerbund, P.O. Box 1011, 100 55 Stockholm, Sweden. Ed. Ragnar Bjoerkman. adv. circ. 1,400.
Formerly: Skraeddarmaestaren (ISSN 0037-6590)

687.2   IT
SOLOINTIMO INTERNATIONAL. (Includes a. Solomare International; Supplements avail.: World of Solointimo International) (Text in English, French, German, Spanish) 1987. 2/yr. L.40000 (foreign L.90000) (effective 1993). Editrice Acalifa s.r.l., Via San Rocco, 17, 20135 Milan, Italy. TEL 02-5831-5800. FAX 02-5831-6313. Ed. Silvano Marzenta. adv. contact: Eva Sabbatini. circ. 31,000.
Formerly: Modasport Intimo.

SPORTSHOP; international trade magazine for the sporting goods trade. see SPORTS AND GAMES

SPORTSTYLE. see SPORTS AND GAMES

687   US
SPORTSWEAR INTERNATIONAL. 1982. 7/yr. $60. Opal Publishing, 29 W. 38th St., 15th fl., New York, NY 10018. TEL 212-768-8450. Ed. Michael Belluomo. adv.; tr.lit. circ. 18,664. (reprint service avail.)
Formerly: Sportswear Jeans International.

687   GW   ISSN 1021-0989
SPORTSWEAR INTERNATIONAL. (Supplement avail.: Sportswear International News (ISSN 1021-0970)) (Editions in English, German) bi-m. DM.220 (E.U. DM.250.10; elsewhere DM.262.10) (effective 1996). Deutscher Fachverlag GmbH, Mainzer Landstr. 251, 60326 Frankfurt a.M., Germany. TEL 49-69-759501. FAX 49-69-75952999. adv.: B&W page DM.13880, color page DM.18980; trim 223 x 290. **Document type:** trade publication.

687   GW   ISSN 1021-0970
SPORTSWEAR INTERNATIONAL NEWS. (Supplement to: Sportswear International (ISSN 1021-0989)) 18/yr. DM.111.50 (E.U. DM.128.15; elsewhere DM.137.15) (effective 1996). Deutscher Fachverlag GmbH, Mainzer Landstr. 251, 60326 Frankfurt a.M., Germany. TEL 49-69-759501. FAX 49-69-75952999. adv.: B&W page DM.4390, color page DM.7150; trim 190 x 270. circ. 7,600. **Document type:** trade publication.

687.12   US   ISSN 0899-5893
TS1783
STITCHES. 1987. m. $28 (foreign $50). Entertec Publishing, Inc., 7009 S. Potomac St., Englewood, CO 80112. TEL 303-397-7600. FAX 303-397-7619. Ed. Melissa J. Thompson Maher. adv.; bk.rev. circ. 15,000. **Document type:** trade publication.
—CCC.
Description: Aimed at the North American commercial monogramming and embroidery industry, both retail and wholesale.

STYLE FORECAST. see CLOTHING TRADE — Fashions

687.19   US
SUNGLASS ASSOCIATION OF AMERICA. NEWSLETTER. m. membership only. Sunglass Association of America, 49 East Ave., Norwalk, CT 06851. TEL 203-845-9015. FAX 203-847-1304. **Document type:** trade publication.
Description: Association and industry news with updates on new members and address corrections.

687.3   US
SWIM FASHION QUARTERLY.* q. Virgo Publishing, Inc., 3300 N. Central Ave., Ste. 2500, Phoenix, AZ 85012. Ed. Tracy Benson. circ. 13,123.

SWIMWEAR U S A. see CLOTHING TRADE — Fashions

687 747   CY   ISSN 1015-3004
SYNTHESIS/COMPOSITION. 1988. bi-m. £C10. P.O. Box 3539, 5 V. Michaelides St., Limassol, Cyprus. TEL 357-5-344154. FAX 357-5-357122. Ed. Yiannis Kouzarides. circ. 5,500. **Document type:** consumer publication.
Description: Features Greek-Cypriot interior design

TAIWAN SPORTS GOODS BUYER'S GUIDE. see SPORTS AND GAMES

CLOTHING TRADE — ABSTRACTING, BIBLIOGRAPHIES, STATISTICS

687   IT   ISSN 0392-8136
TECNICA DELLA CONFEZIONE E DELLA MAGLIERIA. 1963. bi-m. L.70000 (foreign L.130000). Ed. Elio Clemente; Pub. Aurelio Canevari. adv.: B&W page L.1600000, color page L.2785000; 185 x 248; adv. contact: Elio Clemente. bk.rev.; abstr.; charts; illus.; stat.; tr.lit. circ. 5,600. **Indexed:** World Text.Abstr. **Document type:** trade publication.
 Formerly: Tecnica della Confezione (ISSN 0040-1749)
 Description: Informs technical managers, production managers, stylists, pattern makers, managing directors and company owners about the development of the industry.

687   MX
TEXTIL VESTIDO. 1952. m. Mex.$200. Melchor Ocampo 156, Mexico 4, D.F., Mexico. Ed. Ramon Marinello. adv. circ. 5,000.

687 677   XR
TEXTIL ZURNAL. 1992. bi-m. Ceske a Slovenske Odborne Nakladatelstvi (Subsidiary of: Deutscher Fachverlag GmbH), Na Prikope 27, 11349 Prague 1, Czech Republic. TEL 02-268964. FAX 02-262893. circ. 3,000. **Document type:** trade publication.
 Description: Reports on the latest in fashion and on the fashion markets.

667.13 658.8   US   ISSN 0195-0118
TEXTILE RENTAL. 1917. m. $110. Textile Rental Services Association of America, Box 1283, Hallandale, FL 33008. TEL 954-457-7555. FAX 954-457-3890. E-mail: SRBiller@aol.com. Ed. Christine Seaman. R&P contact: Steven Biller. adv. contact: Steve Feldman. bk.rev.; illus.; index; circ. 6,000 (paid). **Indexed:** PROMT, Text.Tech.Dig. **Document type:** trade publication.
 ●Also available online.
 —BLDSC (8808.700000).
 Formerly: Linen Supply News (ISSN 0024-3825)
 Description: Contains management information for uniform and linen rental executives.

687.19   US
TIE LINES. irreg. Neckwear Association of America, 151 Lexington Ave., New York, NY 10016. TEL 212-683-8454.

330.9   US
TRADE WINDS. irreg. membership. Apparel Guild, 2655 Park Cir., East Meadow, NY 11554-3525. TEL 516-735-1595. Ed. Leon Newman. **Document type:** newsletter.
 Formerly: Apparel Guild. Journal.
 Description: Provides a forum for exchange in industry relations, and exchange of well-being of members.

687.1   US
UNIFORM MANUFACTURERS EXCHANGE. NEWSLETTER. irreg. Uniform Manufacturers Exchange, 1156 Ave. of the Americas, New York, NY 10036. TEL 212-869-0670. **Document type:** newsletter.

687.3   US
UNITED KNITWEAR MANUFACTURERS LEAGUE. BULLETIN.* irreg. United Knitwear Manufacturers League, 500 Seventh Ave., New York, NY 10018. TEL 212-819-1011. **Document type:** bulletin.

687.13 028.5   IT
VERDETA; le grande moda dei bambini. s-m. L.10000. Herisson S.r.l., Via Appia Nuova 716A, 00179 Rome, Italy. TEL 06-79-45420. FAX 06-79-45420.

687   PO
VESTIR. 4/yr. Rua Palma 219 2o, Lisbon, Portugal.

687.11   US
W E R A BROCHURE. a. membership only. Western English Retailers Association, 451 E. 58th Ave., Box 087, Denver, CO 80216. TEL 303-298-7882. FAX 303-292-3468. circ. 1,000 (controlled).

687.11   US
W E R A SPECIAL NEWSLETTER. q. membership only. Western English Retailers Association, 451 E. 58th Ave., Box 087, Denver, CO 80216. TEL 303-298-7882. FAX 303-292-3468. circ. 300 (controlled). **Document type:** newsletter.

687   US   ISSN 1067-6236
W W D BUYER'S GUIDE. (Women's Wear Daily); women's apparel & accessories manufacturers. a. Fairchild Fashion & Merchandising Group (Subsidiary of: Capital Cities - A B C, Inc.), 7 W. 34th St., New York, NY 10001. TEL 212-630-3880; 800-247-6622. FAX 212-630-3868.

W W D SUPPLIER'S GUIDE; women's apparel and accessories manufacturers. (Women's Wear Daily) see BUSINESS AND ECONOMICS — Trade And Industrial Directories

677   PL   ISSN 0137-8120
WIADOMOSCI PRODUKCYJNE: WLOKNO, ODZIEZ, SKORA. 1972. m. $71. (Stowarzyszenie Wlokiennikow Polskich) Wydawnictwo Czasopism i Ksiazek Technicznych SIGMA - NOT, Ul. Ratuszowa 11, P.O. Box 1004, 00-950 Warsaw, Poland. TEL 48-22-180918. FAX 48-22-192187. TELEX 814550 SIGMA PL. (Dist. by: SIGMA NOT Ltd., Ul. Bartycka 20, 00-716 Warsaw, Poland) Ed. Zdzislaw Marzec. circ. 1,150.
 Description: News for workers and master craftsmen.

687.2 658.7   US   ISSN 0043-7549
WOMEN'S INTIMATE APPAREL BUYERS. 1951. a. $50. Salesman's Guide, A Division of Reed Elsevier Inc., 121 Chanlon Rd., New Providence, NJ 07974. TEL 908-464-6800. FAX 908-665-2894. TELEX 138 755. E-mail: info@reedref.com; URL: http://www.reedref.com. (Subscr. to: Salesman's Guide, Order Dept., Box 1009, Summit, NJ 07902. TEL 800-521-8110) adv.; index. circ. 2,000. **Document type:** directory, trade publication.
 Formerly: Women's Intimate Apparel.
 Description: Lists intimate apparel buyers for top stores in New York.

687.12 658.7   US   ISSN 0043-7549
WOMEN'S, MISSES & JR. SPORTSWEAR BUYERS. 1951. a. $50. Salesman's Guide, A Division of Reed Elsevier Inc., 121 Chanlon Rd., New Providence, NJ 07974. TEL 908-464-6800. FAX 908-665-2894. TELEX 138 755. E-mail: info@reedref.com; URL: http://www.reedref.com. (Subscr. to: Salesman's Guide, Order Dept., Box 1009, Summit, NJ 07902. TEL 800-521-8110) Ed. Elizabeth Kizar; Pub. Peter Simon. adv.; index. circ. 1,500. **Document type:** directory, trade publication.
 Former titles: Women's Sportswear Buyers (ISSN 0043-7565); Women's Sportswear.
 Description: Lists ladies sportswear buyers for top stores in New York.

687   US
WOMEN'S WEAR DAILY; the retailer's daily newspaper. 1892. d. (Mon.-Fri.). $75 to educational institutions; retailers $95; manufacturers $135; other institutions $260 (effective 1996). Fairchild Publications, Fashion & Merchandising Group (Subsidiary of: Capital Cities - A B C, Inc.), 7 W. 34th St., New York, NY 10001. TEL 212-630-4000. FAX 212-630-3566. Ed. Edward Nardoza. adv.; play rev.; illus.; mkt. circ. 55,162. (tabloid format; also avail. in microfilm from KTO,FCM) **Indexed:** Bus.Ind., Text.Tech.Dig., Tr.& Indus.Ind. **Document type:** trade publication, newspaper.
 ●Also available online. Vendor(s): Information Access Co., Knight-Ridder Information, Inc., Lexis-Nexis.
 —CCC.
 Former titles: W W D (ISSN 0149-5380); Women's Wear Daily (ISSN 0043-7581)
 Description: Covers news of the fashion industry, trends, designers, and events in the social world.

687.1   UK   ISSN 1350-6773
WORLD CLOTHING MANUFACTURER; essential reading for the clothing industry worldwide. 10/yr. £70 (outside Europe £100 ($190)) (effective 1997). Benjamin Dent & Co. Ltd. (Subsidiary of: I T B D Publications), 23 Bloombury Sq., London WC1A 2PJ, England. TEL 44-171-637-2211. FAX 44-171-637-2248. TELEX 8954884 BENDEN G. (N. American subscr. to: Box 1897, Lawrence, KS 66044-8897) Ed. Leonie Barrie. adv. contact: Keith Collins. bk.rev.; illus.; pat.; tr.lit.; tr.mk.; index. (back issues avail.) **Indexed:** Text.Tech.Dig., World Text.Abstr. **Document type:** trade publication.
 —BLDSC (9353.234000).
 Former titles (until 1993): Manufacturing Clothier (ISSN 0025-2565); (until 1946): Tailor and Cutter and Women's Wear.
 Description: Covers the clothing manufacturing industry worldwide, including new manufacturing techniques, marketing, finance, and management.

330.9   UK   ISSN 1356-644X
▼**WORLD SPORTS ACTIVEWEAR.** 1995. q. £40($65) (effective 1997). World Trades Publishing, P.O. Box 6, Liverpool L22 0QN, England. **Document type:** trade publication.
 —BLDSC (9360.041030).

CLOTHING TRADE — Abstracting, Bibliographies, Statistics

687.11   US
ANNUAL STATISTICAL REPORT ON PROFIT, SALES & PRODUCTION TRENDS FOR THE MEN'S & BOY'S TAILORED CLOTHING INDUSTRY. 1982. a. $25. Clothing Manufacturers Association of the U S A, 730 Broadway, Fl. 9, New York, NY 10003-9511. TEL 212-529-0823. Ed. Robert A. Kaplan. bk.rev. circ. 350. (back issues avail.)
 Former titles: Annual Statistical Report on Profit, Sales and Marketing Trends for the Men's and Boy's Tailored Clothing Industry; Special Report on Financial and Economic Data for the Men's and Boy's Clothing Industry.
 Description: Current trends in U.S. production, dollar volume, imports and exports.

338.4   CN   ISSN 0835-006X
HD9940.C18
CANADA. STATISTICS CANADA. CLOTHING INDUSTRIES/INDUSTRIES DE L'HABILLEMENT. (Text in English and French) 1918. a. Can.$40 (foreign $40) (effective 1998). Statistics Canada, Operations and Integration Division, Circulation Management, Jean Talon Bldg., 2-C12, Tunney's Pasture, Ottawa, ON K1A 0T6, Canada. TEL 613-951-7277; 800-267-6677. FAX 613-951-1584. URL: http://www.statcan.ca. (also avail. in microform from MML) **Document type:** government publication.
 Incorporates: Women's and Children's Clothing Industries (ISSN 0384-4498); Canada. Statistics Canada. Men's Clothing Industries (ISSN 0527-5679); Miscellaneous Clothing Industries.

687   US   ISSN 0887-2937
TT507
CLOTHING AND TEXTILE ARTS INDEX. 1970. a. $75. Box 1300, Monument, CO 80132. TEL 719-488-3716. Ed. Sandra S. Hutton. bk.rev. circ. 200. (back issues avail.) **Document type:** abstracting/indexing.
 ●Also available on CD-ROM.
 Description: Covers social, historic and behavioral aspects of clothing, costumes and textile art.

687 011   US
COSTUME SOCIETY OF AMERICA. SYMPOSIA ABSTRACTS. 1/yr. membership. Costume Society of America, 55 Edgewater Dr., Box 73, Earleville, MD 21919. TEL 410-275-2329; 800-CSA-9447. FAX 410-275-8936. (back issues avail.)

687 011   US
COSTUME SOCIETY OF AMERICA BIBLIOGRAPHY. irreg. (approx. quadrennial). membership. Costume Society of America, 55 Edgewater Dr., Box 73, Earleville, MD 21919. TEL 410-275-2329; 800-CSA-9447. FAX 410-275-8936. Ed. Polly Willman. bibl. (back issues avail.) **Document type:** bibliography.
 Description: Lists recent reprints and publications relating to fashion and costume.

EXTRAKTE: TEXTILIEN UND BEKLEIDUNG. see TEXTILE INDUSTRIES AND FABRICS — Abstracting, Bibliographies, Statistics

CLOTHING TRADE — FASHIONS

687   FR
FRANCE. SERVICE D'ETUDE DES STRATEGIES ET DES STATISTIQUES INDUSTRIELLES. RESULTATS TRIMESTRIELS DES ENQUETES DE BRANCHE. INDUSTRIE DE L'HABILLEMENT. q. 180 F. (foreign 210 F.)(effective 1991). Service d'Etude des Strategies et des Statistiques Industrielles (SESSI), 85 Bd. du Montparnasse, 75270 Paris Cedex 06, France. TEL 45-56-42-34. FAX 45-56-40-71. stat.
   Description: Provides detailed industry-wide performance statistics for comparative evaluations.

687.3   US
HOSIERY STATISTICS. 1934. a. $50. National Association of Hosiery Manufacturers, 200 N. Sharon Amity Rd., Charlotte, NC 28211. TEL 704-365-0913. FAX 704-362-2056. Ed. Mary Ann Blansett. R&P contact: Mary Ann Blansett. charts; stat.; circ. 1,000 (controlled). (back issues avail.)
   Description: Provides data on annual production, shipments and stocks of various hosiery categories, per capita consumption and imports and exports.

687   US   ISSN 1067-2850
TS1300
I T A A PROCEEDINGS. (Former name of issuing body: Association of College Professors of Textiles and Clothing) 1944. a. $22 (foreign $25). International Textile and Apparel Association, Box 1360, Monument, CO 80132. TEL 719-488-3716. Ed. Sandra S. Hutton. abstr. circ. 1,100. **Document type:** proceedings.
   Formerly: A C P T C Proceedings (ISSN 1051-1466)
   Description: Presents abstracts of papers introduced at the meeting.

N S G A TEAM LICENSED & SPORTS CLOTHING DIARY. (National Sporting Goods Association) see SPORTS AND GAMES — Abstracting, Bibliographies, Statistics

CLOTHING TRADE — Fashions

687.19   IT   ISSN 1120-1991
ACCESSORI COLLEZIONI. (Text in English, Italian) s-a. $140 (effective Jan. 1997). Zanfi Editori s.r.l., Via Emilia Ovest 954, 41100 Modena, Italy. TEL 39-59-891700. FAX 39-59-891701. E-mail: zanfi.editori@mo.nettuno.it. illus. (back issues avail.) **Document type:** trade publication.
   Description: Covers all accessories for women's fashion: costume jewelry, jewels, hats, scarves, belts, shoes, gloves.

ACCESSORIES. see CLOTHING TRADE

ALLURE. see PHYSICAL FITNESS AND HYGIENE

659.152   JA
AN-AN. (Text in Japanese) 1970. w. newsstand price: 340Yen. Magazine House, 3-13-10 Ginza, Chuo-ku, Tokyo 104-03, Japan. TEL 81-3-3545-7050. FAX 81-3-3545-6346. Ed. Miyoko Yodogawa. circ. 650,000. **Document type:** consumer publication.

746.92   US   ISSN 1089-4322
APPAREL INDUSTRY INTERNACIONAL. 1991. m. $47. Shore-Varrone, Inc., 6255 Barfield Rd. N.E., Ste. 200, Atlanta, GA 30328-4300. TEL 404-252-8831. FAX 404-252-4436. E-mail: Mercedes_Cortazar@svi.ccmail.compuserve.com; URL: http://www.svi-atl.com. Ed. Mercedes Cortazar; Pub. Sean McGinnis. R&P contact: Karen Schaffner. adv. contact: Sean McGinnis. circ. 13,500. **Document type:** trade publication.
   Description: Covers factory management for apparel companies in Latin America, including technology, personnel, and quality issues.

AREA MAGAZINE. see ART

ARIADNE. see INTERIOR DESIGN AND DECORATION

746.92   US   ISSN 0742-034X
ARIZONA TRENDS. 1982. m. (Sep.-June). $18. Dandick Company, Box 8508, Scottsdale, AZ 85252. TEL 602-948-1799. FAX 602-994-9284. Ed. Penny Johnson; Pub. Danny Medina. adv. contact: Renee Cohen. bk.rev. circ. 32,000. (tabloid format; back issues avail.) **Document type:** newspaper.

ARPEL FUR; fashion review on Italian and international furs and leather garments. see LEATHER AND FUR INDUSTRIES

ARS SUTORIA; cultural fashion review on Italian and international footwear. see SHOES AND BOOTS

659.152   CC   ISSN 0254-1130
ASIAN SOURCES FASHION ACCESSORIES. 1978. m. $60. Asian Sources Media Group, 22-F Vita Tower, 29 Wong Chuk Hang Rd., Aberdeen, Hong Kong, People's Republic of China. TEL 852-2555-4777. FAX 852-2873-0488. (People's Republic of China; Subscr. to: G.P.O. Box 12367, Hong Kong; US subscr. to: Wordright Enterprises Inc., Box 3062, Evanston, IL 60204-3062. TEL 708-475-1900) Ed. Michael Hay. adv. circ. 20,900. **Indexed:** HongKongiana. **Document type:** trade publication.
   Formerly: Asian Sources Garment Accessories.
   Description: Covers clothing trade, fashions, and fashion accessories.

AUSTIN HOMES & GARDENS. see INTERIOR DESIGN AND DECORATION

AUSTRALASIAN TEXTILES & FASHION. see TEXTILE INDUSTRIES AND FABRICS

746   US   ISSN 0192-5938
B B W: BIG BEAUTIFUL WOMAN MAGAZINE.* 1979. bi-m. $9.95 (foreign $19.95). Larry Flynt Publications, Inc., 8484 Wilshire Blvd., Ste. 900, Beverly Hills, CA 90211-3227. TEL 310-858-7100. FAX 310-274-7985. Ed. Linda Arroz. adv.; bk.rev. **Document type:** consumer publication.
   —CCC.
   Description: Fashion magazine for the large-size woman.

B INTERNATIONAL. see GENERAL INTEREST PERIODICALS — Hong Kong

687.13   IT   ISSN 1120-1983
BAMBINI COLLEZIONI. (Text in English, Italian) s-a. $67 (effective Jan. 1997). Zanfi Editori s.r.l., Via Emilia Ovest 954, 41100 Modena, Italy. TEL 39-59-891700. FAX 39-59-891701. E-mail: zanfi.editori@mo.nettuno.it. adv.: B&W page L.2750000, color page L.3600000. (back issues avail.) **Document type:** trade publication.
   Description: Covers children's fashion from age 4 to 14.

BELLEZA Y MODA. see BEAUTY CULTURE

746.9   IT   ISSN 1121-175X
BENISSIMO. 1982. m. L.48000. Fabbri Rizzoli Edizioni Periodiche srl, Via Mecenate 87-6, 20138 Milan, Italy. TEL 39-2-580801. FAX 39-2-5062865. Ed. Mara Santini. adv.: color page L.19200000. (back issues avail.)

746.92 646.7   FR   ISSN 0221-7996
BIBA.* 1978. m. 16 F. per no. Groupe Media S.A., 5 rue des Morillons, 75740 Paris Cedex 15, France. Ed. Willy Stricker. adv.: B&W page 61500 F., color page 98200 F.; trim 215 x 282. circ. 202,348. **Document type:** consumer publication.

BIKINI. see MEN'S INTERESTS

746.96   GW
BILD DER FRAU. 1983. w. (Mon.). newsstand price: DM.1.20. Axel Springer Verlag AG, Axel-Springer-Platz 1, 20355 Hamburg, Germany. TEL 49-40-3470-0. FAX 49-40-34722064. (Subscr. to: DSB Abo-Betreuung, 74168 Neckarsulm, Germany. TEL 49-7132-9590. FAX 49-7132-959216) Ed. Andrea Zangemeister. adv.: B&W page DM.47152, color page DM.70728; adv. contact: Angelika Breske. circ. 2,108,309 (paid). **Document type:** consumer publication.

746.92 791.43   SZ
BOLERO; mode beaute cinema travel. (Text in German) 11/yr. 71.40 SFr. (Europe 85 SFr.; elsewhere 89 SFr.) (effective 1996). Bolero Zeitschriftenverlag AG, Giesshuebelstr. 62i, CH-8021 Zurich, Switzerland. TEL 41-1-4548282. FAX 41-1-4548272. Ed. Sithara Atasoy; Pub. Susanne Bruengger. adv.: B&W page 6000 SFr., color page 9000 SFr.; trim 186 x 246; adv. contact: Nicole Nussbaumer. **Document type:** consumer publication.

746.92   BL
BRASIL VOGUE. 1975. m. $170. Carta Editorial Ltda., Ave Brazil 1456, CEP 01430 Jardim America, Sao Paulo, Brazil. TEL 883-3366. FAX 853-7331. TELEX 1138516 CTED BR. Ed. Luiz Carta. adv.; bk.rev. circ. 30,500.

659.152 392.5   US
BRIDAL APPAREL NEWS.* 1980. s-a. $10. MnM Publishing Corp., 110 E. 9th St., A777, Los Angeles, CA 90079-1929. TEL 213-627-3737. (Subscr. to: 5615 W. Cermak Rd., Cicero, IL, 60650) Ed. Anne Harnagel. adv.; charts; illus.; stat.; tr.lit. circ. 10,100. (back issues avail.)
   Description: For bridal and formal wear retailers and manufacturers throughout the world.

BRIDE TO BE. see MATRIMONY

BRIDE'S. see MATRIMONY

BRIDES OF BERKSHIRE. see MATRIMONY

BRIDES OF BRISTOL, BATH & AVON. see MATRIMONY

BRIDES OF BRITAIN SERIES. see MATRIMONY

BRIDES OF DEVON & CORNWALL. see MATRIMONY

BRIDES OF EAST ANGLIA. see MATRIMONY

BRIDES OF HERTS, BUCKS & BEDS. see MATRIMONY

BRIDES OF NORTH EAST ENGLAND. see MATRIMONY

BRIDES OF SCOTLAND. see MATRIMONY

BRIDES OF SOMERSET. see MATRIMONY

746.96   AU
BRIGITTE (AUSTRIA). 1971. 26/yr. Gruner and Jahr, Parkring 12, A-1011 Vienna, Austria. circ. 80,000.

659.152 746.92   SZ
BURDA. (Text in Arabic) 1985. m. DM.84. I P M Press and Marketing S.A., 2 Cours de Rive, CH-1204 Geneva, Switzerland. Ed. Ingrid Kuederle. adv.; illus. circ. 77,000. **Document type:** trade publication.

746.92   SA   ISSN 1022-2405
BURDA; a world of fashion. (Text in English) 1993. m. R.93. Burda South Africa, P.O. Box 642, Irene 1675, South Africa. adv.; illus. **Document type:** consumer publication.

646.3   GW
BURDA BLUSEN, ROECKE, HOSEN. s-a. Verlag Aenne Burda, Am Kestendamm 2, 77652 Offenburg, Germany. TEL 0781-8402. Ed. Anna Tiganeli. circ. 130,000.

646.3   GW
BURDA BRAUTMODE. biennial. Verlag Aenne Burda, Am Kestendamm 2, 77652 Offenburg, Germany. TEL 0781-8402. circ. 150,000.

BURDA INTERNATIONAL. see CLOTHING TRADE

646.3   GW
BURDA KLEINKINDERMODE. s-a. Verlag Aenne Burda, Am Kestendamm 2, 77652 Offenburg, Germany. TEL 0781-8402. Ed. Astrid Hauser. circ. 195,000.

646.3   GW
BURDA MISS B TRENDS. a. Verlag Aenne Burda, Am Kestendamm 2, 77652 Offenburg, Germany. TEL 0781-8402. circ. 160,000.

646.3   GW
BURDA MODE FUER MAEDCHEN UND JUNGEN. s-a. Verlag Aenne Burda, Am Kestendamm 2, 77652 Offenburg, Germany. TEL 0781-8402. Ed. Astrid Hauser. circ. 125,000.

746.96   GW
BURDA MODEN (AUSTRIAN EDITION). 1950. m. S.504. Verlag Aenne Burda, Am Kestendamm 2, 77652 Offenburg, Germany. Ed. Aenne Burda. circ. 90,000.

687   ISSN 0007-6031
BURDA MODEN (GERMAN EDITION). 1950. m. DM.88.80 (effective 1997); newsstand price: DM.7.40. Burda Verlag GmbH, Postfach 1230, 77602 Offenburg, Germany. TEL 49-89-9250-0. FAX 49-89-92503519. (Subscr. to: Burda Medien Abo-Service, Postfach 1351, 88131 Lindau, Germany) Ed. Susanne Stein; Pub. Aenne Burda. adv. contact: Volker Wrobel. charts; illus.; tr.lit. circ. 502,000. **Document type:** consumer publication.
   —CCC.

CLOTHING TRADE — FASHIONS

659.152   GR
BURDA MODEN (GREEK EDITION);* fashion for everyone. (Text in Greek) 1983. m. Dr.8400($80) H A Samouhos Publications, Ltd., 3Stiron St., Zografou, Greece. FAX 770-4475. TELEX 215578-ABNA-GR. Ed. Chris Samouhos. adv.; bk.rev. circ. 90,000. (back issues avail.)

646.3   GW
BURDA TRACHTENMODE. biennial. Verlag Aenne Burda, Am Kestendamm 2, 77652 Offenburg, Germany. TEL 0781-8402. circ. 170,000.

646.3   GW
BURDA TRACHTENSTRICKMODE. biennial. Verlag Aenne Burda, Am Kestendamm 2, 77652 Offenburg, Germany. TEL 0781-8402. circ. 220,000.

646.3   GW
BURDA UMSTANDSMODE. biennial. Verlag Aenne Burda, Am Kestendamm 2, 77652 Offenburg, Germany. TEL 0781-8402. Ed. Beate Mannes. circ. 150,000.

646.3   GW
BURDA UNSER BABY. s-a. Verlag Aenne Burda, Am Kestendamm 2, 77652 Offenburg, Germany. TEL 0781-8402. Ed. Anna Tiganeli. circ. 160,000.

646.4   US   ISSN 0895-6871
BUTTERICK HOME CATALOG. 1959. q. $9.95 (effective 1997 & 1998). Butterick Co., Inc., 161 Ave. of the Americas, New York, NY 10013. TEL 212-620-2500. (Subscr. to: 2900 Beale Ave., Altoona, PA 16603. TEL 800-766-3619) Ed. Mary Fotherby. adv.; illus. circ. 312,000. **Document type:** catalog.

659.152   US
C S A NEWS. 1975. 4/yr. $60 for individual membership; libraries $35; institutions $95; corporate $350. Costume Society of America, 55 Edgewater Dr., Box 73, Earleville, MD 21919. TEL 410-275-2329; 800-CSA-9447. FAX 410-275-8936. Ed. Kristina Harris. bk.rev. circ. 1,500. (tabloid format; back issues avail.) **Document type:** newsletter.
   Formerly: Costume Society of America Newsletter.
   Description: Covers membership activities and regional events.

659.152   GW   ISSN 0175-9477
CARINA. 1977. m. F M C Magazin Verlag GmbH, Ararellastr. 23, 81975 Munich, Germany. TEL 089-92500. FAX 089-92502654. Ed. Eberhard Henschel; Pub. Aenne Burda. adv. contact: Wolfgang Plate. charts; illus. circ. 301,835. **Document type:** consumer publication.
   Formerly: Carina Burda.

659.152   IT
CARNET DE MODE.* (Text in English, French, German, Italian) 1971. s-a. L.10000 per no. Societa Creazioni Moda per Azioni, Corso Giulio Cesare 31, 10152 Turin, Italy. TEL 39-11-287933. Ed. Giovanni Robazza. adv. circ. 46,000.

746.92   JA
CHECKMATE. (Text in Japanese) 1974. m. Kodansha Ltd., 12-21, Otowa 2-chome, Bunkyo-ku, Tokyo 112, Japan. TEL 81-3-5395-3476. FAX 81-3-3943-8587. TELEX J34509 KODANSHA. Ed. Minoru Takeuch. circ. 270,000.

646   IT   ISSN 0009-3203
CHERIE MODA/CHERIE MODE. 1955. q. L.18000($20) Edizioni Moderne Internazionali, Via Burlamacchi 11, 20135 Milan, Italy. TEL 39-2-55189297. FAX 39-2-5465954. adv.: B&W page L.2400000. circ. 125,000.

746.92 649   US   ISSN 0884-2280
CHILDREN'S BUSINESS. 1985. m. $39 (Canada $49; elsewhere $60) (effective 1995). Fairchild Fashion & Merchandising Group (Subsidiary of: Capital Cities - A B C, Inc.), 7 W. 34th St., New York, NY 10001. TEL 212-630-4199. FAX 212-630-4201. adv. circ. 20,000. (also avail. in microfilm from FCM) **Document type:** trade publication.
   ●Also available online. Vendor(s): Information Access Co.
   —CCC.

687.13   JA   ISSN 0009-417X
CHILDREN'S STYLES. (Text in Japanese) q. 6300 Yen. Kamakura-Shobo Publishing Co., Ltd., 21 Ichigaya-Sanai-cho, Shinjuku-ku, Tokyo 162, Japan. FAX 03-3268-1133. Ed. K. Ichiba. illus. **Document type:** consumer publication.
   Description: Highlights clothing trends.

646.3 646.7   CN
CLIN D'OEIL. (Text in French) 1980. m. $26.95. Quebecor Inc., 7 Chemin Bates, Outrement, PQ H2V 1A6, Canada. TEL 514-270-1100. FAX 514-270-6900. Ed. Danielle Paquin. adv. circ. 67,000.

746.92   UK   ISSN 0953-6353
CLOTHES SHOW. 1988. q. £20.40 (Europe & Ireland £38.90; rest of world £56.05) (effective 1996). B B C Worldwide Publishing, Broadcasting House, Whiteladies Rd., Bristol GS8 2LR, England. TEL 44-181-576-2000. FAX 44-181-576-2931. (Subscr. to: P.O. Box 425, Woking, Surrey GU21 1GP, England. TEL 44-1483-733716. FAX 44-1483-756792) **Document type:** consumer publication.

659.152 778.53   US
CLUB MODELE. 1991. bi-m. Aquino Productions, Box 125, Rochester, VT 05767. Ed. Elaine Hallgren. adv.: B&W page $1400, color page $2800. circ. 114,000.
   Formerly: Model and Performer.
   Description: For performers, models, photographers, production companies, agencies and night clubs.

COLLECTIONS INCLUDING VEILS AND HEADPIECES. see MATRIMONY

COLLECTOR. see ADVERTISING AND PUBLIC RELATIONS

659.152   IT
COLLEZIONI DONNA. (Text in English, French, Italian) 6/yr. $260 (effective Jan. 1997). Zanfi Editori s.r.l., Via Emilia Ovest 954, 41100 Modena, Italy. TEL 39-59-891700. FAX 39-59-891701. E-mail: zanfi.editori@mo.nettuno.it. adv.: B&W page L.4600000, color page L.6600000. illus. (back issues avail.) **Document type:** trade publication.
   Description: Covers the best of the fashion shows worldwide. Four issues cover pret-a-porter, two cover high fashion.

CONFEZIONE; mensile per l'abbigliamento e maglieria. see CLOTHING TRADE

COSMOPOLITAN. see WOMEN'S INTERESTS

COSMOPOLITAN. see WOMEN'S INTERESTS

COSMOPOLITAN. see WOMEN'S INTERESTS

746.92   UK   ISSN 0590-8876
COSTUME. 1967. a. £18 to individuals (foreign £20); institutions £23 (foreign £25); students £8 (foreign £10) (effective 1997-98). Costume Society, c/o National Museums of Scotland, Chambers St., Edinburgh EH1 1JF, Scotland. TEL 44-131-247-4292. FAX 44-131-220-4819. E-mail: nt@nms.ac.uk. (Subscr. to: Pat Poppy, 56 Wareham Rd., Lytchett, Matravers, Poole, Dorset BH16 6DS, England) Ed. Ann Saunders. bk.rev.; bibl.; charts; illus. circ. 1,100. Indexed: Artbibl.Mod., Br.Archaeol.Abstr., Br.Hum.Ind., DAAI, RILA, World Text.Abstr. **Document type:** academic/scholarly publication.
   —BLDSC (3477.300000); EMDOCS; KR SourceOne; UnCover.
   Description: Promotes the study and preservation of historic and contemporary costume.

746.92 390   CN
COSTUME JOURNAL. 1971. 3/yr. Can.$25 membership; institutions $20 (effective 1997). Costume Society of Ontario, Box 981, Station F, Toronto, ON M4Y 2N9, Canada. TEL 416-977-4280. Ed. Mary Humphries. bk.rev. circ. 400. **Document type:** consumer publication.
   Formerly: Costume Society of Ontario. Newsletter (ISSN 0834-2520)

659.152   CC
COUTOURE. (Text in Chinese, English) 1988. 2/yr. HK.$99. Communication Management Ltd., 1811 Hong Kong Plaza, 188 Connaught Rd. W., Hong Kong, People's Republic of China. TEL 852-2547-7117. FAX 852-2858-2671. TELEX 61758 TATCO HX. Ed. Lina Ross; Pub. M. Mohindar. adv. contact: Michelle Lee. circ. 29,500. **Document type:** consumer publication.
   Description: Forecasts the Spring/Summer and Autumn/Winter women's collections from around the world.

746.92 687   US
CUSTOM TAILORS AND DESIGNERS ASSOCIATION OF AMERICA. MAGAZINE.* bi-m. $25. Custom Tailors and Designers Association of America, Box 53052, Washington, DC 20009-9052. TEL 212-661-1960. Ed. Irma B. Lipkin. adv. contact: Irma B. Lipkin. circ. 1,000. **Document type:** trade publication.

DAMERNAS VAERLD. see GENERAL INTEREST PERIODICALS — Sweden

687.11   SP   ISSN 0011-6068
DANDY; men's fashions. (Text in English, French, Portuguese, Spanish) s-a. $20. D. Emilio Oromi, Ed. & Pub., Ronda Universidad 31, Barcelona 7, Spain. adv.; illus.

DETOUR. see WOMEN'S INTERESTS

746.92   GW
DEUTSCHE MODE-INSTITUT. TENDENZFARBENKARTE. Cover title: Tendenzfarbenkarte D M I. s-a. DM.108.50 (E.U. DM.114.50; elsewhere DM.122.50) (effective 1996). Deutscher Fachverlag GmbH, Mainzer Landstr. 251, 60326 Frankfurt a.M., Germany. TEL 49-69-75951984. FAX 49-69-75951980. **Document type:** trade publication.

746.92   GW
DEUTSCHES INSTITUT FUER HERRENMODE. TENDENZFARBENKARTE. Cover title: Tendenzfarbenkarte D I H. s-a. DM.94 (E.U. DM.100.95; elsewhere DM.108) per no. (effective 1996). Deutscher Fachverlag GmbH, Mainzer Landstr. 251, 60326 Frankfurt a.M., Germany. TEL 49-69-75951984. FAX 49-69-75951980. **Document type:** trade publication.

668.54 668.55 301.412   UK
DIARY. 1969. m. £165. Courtyard Studio, 27 Harcourt St., London W1H 1DT, England. TEL 0171-724-7770. FAX 0171-724-7357. Ed. Emma Garton; Pub. Gail Raymonde. adv.; bk.rev. circ. 1,500. (back issues avail.) **Document type:** trade publication.

DOMINA SPOSA. see MATRIMONY

959.152 301.412   IT
DONNA; international fashion magazine. 1979. m. L.64000 (foreign L.120000). Edimoda, Viale Sarca 235, 20126 Milan, Italy. TEL 39-2-66191. Ed. Giorgio Valle. adv.: page L.20000000. circ. 38,725. **Document type:** consumer publication.

260   UK   ISSN 0967-3776
DRAPERS RECORD. 1887. w. £68 (rest of Europe £95). E M A P Maclaren Ltd., Maclaren House, 19 Scarbrook Rd., Croydon, Surrey CR9 1QH, England. TEL 0181-688-7788. FAX 0181-688-9300. Ed. Juliet Warkentin. adv.: B&W page £1098, color page £1995; trim 275 x 205. illus.; mkt.; rev. circ. 19,568. Indexed: DAAI, World Text.Abstr. **Document type:** trade publication.
   —BLDSC (3623.200000).
   Former tiles (until 1992): D R: The Fashion Business (ISSN 0955-2499); (until 1988): Drapers' Record (ISSN 0012-6020); Incorporates: Career & Workwear News; D R - The Fashion Business.

CLOTHING TRADE — FASHIONS

391 900   **US**   **ISSN 0361-2112**
GT605
DRESS. 1975. a. $60 individual membership; libraries $35; institutions $95; corporate $350. Costume Society of America, 55 Edgewater Dr., Box 73, Earlville, MD 21919. TEL 410-275-2329; 800-CSA-9447. FAX 410-275-8936. Ed. Patricia Cunningham. bk.rev.; illus. circ. 1,500. (back issues avail.) **Indexed:** Amer.Hist.& Life (1993-), Artbibl.Mod., DAAI, Hist.Abstr. (1993-), RILA.—BLDSC (3623.435000); UnCover.
   Description: Covers all areas of study of dress, with scholarly emphasis on history and preservation.

659.152   **JA**
DRESSMAKING & MADAM'S STYLE BOOK. m. 15400 Yen. Kamakura-Shobo Publishing Co., Ltd., 21 Ichigaya-Sanaicho, Shinjuku-ku, Tokyo 162, Japan. Ed. K. Maekawa. **Document type:** consumer publication.

DUNIA. see *WOMEN'S INTERESTS*

746.92   **JA**
EDGE. (Text in Japanese) 1983. q. 3120 Yen. Gakken Co., Ltd., 40-5, 4-chome, Kamiikedai, Ohta-ku, Tokyo 145, Japan. Ed. Jun Usami.

746.92   **CN**   **ISSN 0315-3037**
EGO;* Canada's men's fashion magazine. (Text in English, French) 1971. q. Can.$20. Harrison Fashion Publishing Ltd., 254 Brighton Dr., Beaconsfield, PQ H9W 2L4, Canada. TEL 514-426-1446. FAX 514-426-1448. Ed. Tina Richman. adv. circ. 5,811.

746.92   **CN**   **ISSN 1194-5540**
EGO SPORT; Canada's sports fashion magazine. (Text in English, French) 1991. 2/yr. Can.$12 (foreign Can.$20). Harrison Fashion Publishing Ltd., 254 Brighton Dr., Beaconsfield, PQ H9W 2L4, Canada. TEL 514-426-1446. FAX 514-426-1448. Ed. Tina Richman. adv. circ. 7,500.

ELEGANCE. see *WOMEN'S INTERESTS*

646.4   **IT**
L'ELEGANTE UOMO SUD. 1980. m. L.12000. Mario Stefanelli Editore, Universita Sartor, Via Polare, 5, 71100 Foggia, Italy. TEL 0881-720-176.

659.152 646.7   **IT**   **ISSN 1121-8312**
ELEGANTISSIMA. 1945. q. L.8360. IBI s.r.l., Via Finocchiaro Aprile 5, 20124 Milan, Italy. adv.

ELLE. see *WOMEN'S INTERESTS*

ELLE. see *WOMEN'S INTERESTS*

ELLE, CHINA. see *WOMEN'S INTERESTS*

646.4 641.5   **MX**
ESPECIALES TEENAGER INTERNACIONAL. 3/yr. Consorcio Sayrols, Mier y Pesado 126, Col. del Valle, 03100 Mexico D.F., Mexico. TEL 52-5-6874699. FAX 52-5-5237045. E-mail: beatrizc@spin.com.mx; URL: http://www.sayrols.com. mx. Ed. Patricia Olvera. R&P contact: Roberto Davo. TEL 52-5-5236714. adv.: B&W page $3370, color page $4312; 210 x 275; adv. contact: Beatriz Coria. circ. 45,000. **Document type:** consumer publication.
   Description: Each issue focuses on a topic in sewing, cooking, clothing, knitting and Christmas decoration.

659.152 646.724   **XO**   **ISSN 0139-8717**
EVA. 1970. m. $59 (effective 1998); newsstand price: 25 Sk. Euroskop, Inc., Pribinova 25, 819 37 Bratislava, Slovakia. TEL 421-7-2103340. FAX 421-7-2104128. (Distr. by: Mezhdunarodnaya Kniga, B. Yakimanka 39, 117049 Moscow, Russia. TEL 7-095-2384967. FAX 7-095-2384634) Ed. Gita Pechova. adv.: B&W page 50000, color page 72000; trim 175 x 260; adv. contact: Jana Sokolova. circ. 160,000. **Document type:** consumer publication.
   Description: Covers fashion, hair and beauty, health, travel, leisure time.

746.92   **US**
FABRIC AND FASHION. 1992. m. $30. Box 237, Murray Hill Sta., New York, NY 10156-0237. TEL 212-683-7886. Ed. Virginia Stiles. adv. contact: Jeanne Coogan. bk.rev. circ. 2,400. **Document type:** newsletter.
   Description: For designers, manufacturers and retailers.

746.96   **LE**   **ISSN 1017-7760**
FAIRUZ. (Text in Arabic) 1981. m. $150. Dar Assayad S.A.L., P.O. Box 1038, Hazmieh, Beirut, Lebanon. FAX 961-1-456373. (UK addr.: c/o Contact PR & Mgt. (UK) Ltd., 3 Park Pl., 12 Lawn Ln., London SW8, England. TEL 071-582-2220) Ed. Elham Freiha. adv. contact: Salim Zreik. circ. 84,207.

FANS. see *SPORTS AND GAMES*

746.92   **US**   **ISSN 1091-031X**
▼**FASHION ALMANAC.** 1997. q. $9.95 (effective 1997); newsstand price: $3.50; Canada $4.95. Fashion Almanac Publishing, 350 Fifth Ave., Ste. 5516, New York, NY 10118. TEL 212-564-0005. FAX 212-290-8120. (Distr. by: Kable News Company,) Ed. Amedeo Angiolillo; Pub. Amedeo Angiolillo. adv.; illus. **Document type:** consumer publication.

659.152   **US**   **ISSN 0014-8660**
FASHION CALENDAR. 1941. bi-m. $365. Fashion Calendar International, 153 E. 87th St., New York, NY 10128. TEL 212-289-0420. FAX 212-289-5917. Pub. Ruth Finley. (processed) **Document type:** trade publication.
   Description: Targeted to buyers, designers, manufacturers, retailers, and the media regarding national and international fashion events and collection openings.

FASHION COLOR FORECAST. see *CLOTHING TRADE*

746.92   **SA**   **ISSN 1023-1803**
FASHION ENSEMBLE. 1994. q. R.9.69. Fashion Ensemble Publications, P.O. Box 1711, Parklands 2121, South Africa. adv.; illus. **Document type:** consumer publication.

746.92   **UK**   **ISSN 0264-8555**
FASHION EXTRAS. 1916. m. £29 (Europe £45; elsewhere £59) (effective 1997). Reflex Publishing Ltd., 177A High St., Tonbridge, Kent TN9 1BX, England. TEL 44-1732-362445. FAX 44-1732-362447. Ed. Bridget Gill; Pub. Adrian Watkins. adv.; bk.rev.; stat.; tr.lit. circ. 3,750. (back issues avail.) **Indexed:** Key to Econ.Sci. **Document type:** trade publication.
   Incorporates: Leathergoods (ISSN 0023-9798)

746.92   **US**
FASHION INTERNATIONAL. 1972. m. $100. Fashion Calendar International, 153 E. 87th St., New York, NY 10128. TEL 212-289-0420. Ed. Deborah Brumfield; Pub. Ruth Finley. **Document type:** trade publication, newsletter.
   Description: Provides manufacturers and retailers with trends and forecasting information; evaluations of new creations, price ranges, trends in fabric and color; and special reports on current developments in the industry.

391 659.152   **US**
THE FASHION MANUSCRIPT. (Text in Chinese, English) 1994. m. $29; newsstand price: $3. Jeff Mann Ed. & Pub., 1440 Broadway, New York, NY 10018. TEL 212-840-1549. FAX 212-840-1954. adv.: page $1475; 10 x 7. **Document type:** consumer publication.
   Description: Gets the reader inside the fashion business with important apparel manufacturers and major textile mills; also gives legal and financial money saving tips, marketing insights and fashion dates.

659.152   **UK**
FASHION MONITOR. 1954. m. £498. Profile Systems Ltd., 32-38 Saffron Hill, London EC1N 8FH, England. TEL 44-171-405-4455. FAX 44-171-430-1089. Ed. Louise Stocks. adv.; bk.rev. circ. 1,000. **Document type:** trade publication.
   Formerly: Fashion Calendar.

746.92   **US**
FASHION NETWORK REPORT. 1982. m. $95. Fashion Network Inc., 220 E. 57th St., New York, NY 10022-2805. TEL 212-752-5611. FAX 212-888-0181. Ed. Alan G. Millstein. circ. 2,000 (paid). **Document type:** newsletter.

746.92   **US**   **ISSN 0300-7111**
FASHION NEWSLETTER; an international forecast of incoming fashion influences. 1963. m. (11/yr.). $179 (foreign $219). Newsletter Services, Inc., 9700 Philadelphia Ct., Lanham, MD 20706-4405. TEL 301-731-5200; 800-345-2611. FAX 301-731-5201. Ed. Alice Meyer. bk.rev. **Document type:** newsletter.
   Incorporates (1978-1991): Specialty Store Service Bulletin.
   Description: Contains news about international fashion trends, for designers, manufacturers, and store buyers.

746.92   **US**
▼**FASHION REPORTER.** 1996. m. 300 Park Ave. S., 3rd Fl., New York, NY 10011. TEL 212-477-2343. FAX 212-614-3018. E-mail: fashion101@aol.com. stat.; circ. 25,000 (paid). **Document type:** trade publication.
   Description: Features news of people and business in the fashion industry.

746.92   **UK**
▼**FASHION U K.** 1995. m. Portland House, 164 New Cavendish St., London W1M 7FJ, England. E-mail: fuk@sunshyne.demon.co.uk; URL: http://www.widemedia.com/fashionuk/. Ed. Marian Buckley.
● Available only online.
   Description: Covers the UK street fashion scene and delivers up to the minute information to style fans across the planet.

659.152   **UK**   **ISSN 0265-1084**
FASHION UPDATE; Paris, London, Milan & New York. 1983. q. £199($302) Emmett Publishing, 21 West St., Haslemere, Surrey GU27 2AB, England. TEL 01428-654443. FAX 01428-661582. E-mail: jim@emmetpub.demon.co.uk. index. (also avail. in microfiche from EMP; not avail. in printed format; back issues avail.) **Document type:** academic/scholarly publication.
   Description: Promotes particular collections of new talent each season.

746.92   **US**
FASHION UPDATE. 1987. q. $70 (effective 1997). Fashion Update, Inc., 1274 49th St., No. 209, Brooklyn, NY 11219. TEL 718-377-8873. FAX 718-258-9091. E-mail: fashionupdate@juno.com. Ed. Sarah Gardner.

746 659   **US**   **ISSN 1044-3568**
FASHION WATCH. m. $299 (effective 1994). Retail Reporting Bureau, 302 Fifth Ave., New York, NY 10001. TEL 212-279-7000; 800-251-4545. FAX 212-279-7014. **Document type:** trade publication.

646.4   **UK**   **ISSN 0957-6630**
FASHION WEEKLY. 1910. w. £60. E M A P Maclaren Ltd., Maclaren House, 19 Scarbrook Rd., Croydon, Surrey CR9 1QH, England. TEL 0181-688-7788. FAX 0181-688-9300. Ed. Martin Raymond; Pub. Paul Keenan. adv.: B&W page £1550, color page £2170; trim 290 x 400. circ. 8,500. (tabloid format) **Indexed:** DAAI. **Document type:** trade publication, newspaper.
   Formerly: Drapery and Fashion Weekly.

391   **US**
FASHIONSTANCE. 1976. m. $12 via e-mail. E-mail: jelaine@fashionstance.com; URL: http://www.fashionstance.com; http://www.users.wineasy.se/bjornt/fshead.html. Ed. J. Elaine Spear.
● Available only online.
   Description: Written by consumers for consumers all over the world, offering information on beauty and fashion.

746.9   **CN**   **ISSN 0318-871X**
FEM EGO.* (Text in English and French) 1975. q. Can.$10. Harrison Fashion Publishing Ltd., 254 Brighton Dr., Beaconsfield, PQ H9W 2L4, Canada. TEL 514-426-1446. FAX 514-426-1448. illus.

FEMINA. see *WOMEN'S INTERESTS*

FEMINA. see *WOMEN'S INTERESTS*

CLOTHING TRADE — FASHIONS

FEMINA MAANADENS MAGASIN/FEMINA MONTHLY MAGAZINE. see *WOMEN'S INTERESTS*

746.96   MY
FEMININE. 1978. m. Voice Publications Sdn. Bhd., 2A Jalan 19-1, Petaling Jaya, Selangor, Malaysia. Ed. Yap Choy Hong.

646   FR   ISSN 0010-0773
FEMME CHIC. (Text in French, German, Spanish) 1953. q. $22. Editions Rusconi, 8 rue Halevy, 75009 Paris, France. Ed. Giuseppe Marzulli. adv.; illus. circ. 45,000.

659.152   SP
FEMME ELEGANTE. bi-m. 250 ptas.($7.20) Publicaciones Mundial, Cjo. de Ciento 201, Barcelona 11, Spain. circ. 18,000.

FILM MIRROR. see *MOTION PICTURES*

640   CN   ISSN 0708-4927
FLARE; fashion beauty and lifestyle magazine for working women. 1964. m. Can.$17.70 (foreign Can.$39.70) (effective 1998). Maclean-Hunter Publishing Ltd., Magazine Division, Maclean-Hunter Bldg., 777 Bay St., Toronto, ON M5W 1A7, Canada. TEL 416-596-5462. FAX 416-596-5799. TELEX 062-19547. E-mail: editors@flare.com; URL: http://www.flare.com. (Subscr. to: Box 1600, Postage Station A, Toronto, ON M5W 2B8, Canada) Ed. Suzanne Boyd; Pub. David Hamilton. R&P contact: Liza Finlay. TEL 416-596-5456. adv. contact: Orietta Minatel. circ. 201,000 (paid). **Indexed:** Can.B.P.I., CMI. **Document type:** consumer publication.
   Formerly: Miss Chatelaine (ISSN 0026-5918)
   Description: Features emerging trends from international and Canadian centres and covers prominent and new designers from Canada and abroad.

FOR THE BRIDE BY DEMETRIOS. see *MATRIMONY*

659.152   US
FORMALWORDS. 1987. bi-m. membership. International Formalwear Association, 401 N. Michigan Ave., Chicago, IL 60611. FAX 312-321-6869. Ed. Annette Claussen. adv. circ. 450. **Document type:** newsletter.

746.96   AU
FRAU UND FREIZEIT. 1975. m. S.180. Lisey Gmbh, Walfischgasse 11, A-1010 Vienna, Austria. TEL 513-13-95. Eds. Harry & Hedy Gruber. adv.; bk.rev. circ. 85,000.

746.92   JA
FUSION PLANNING. (Text in Japanese) 1985. bi-m. 10800 Yen. Gakken Co., Ltd., 40-5, 4-chome, Kamiikedai, Ohta-ku, Tokyo 145, Japan. Ed. Shun'Ichiro Aikawa.

646   303.5   US   ISSN 0016-6979
TT570
G Q. (Gentlemen's Quarterly) 1957. m. $20 (Canada $37, elsewhere $38); libraries $12.50. Conde Nast Publications Inc., G Q Magazine, 350 Madison Ave., New York, NY 10017. TEL 212-880-8800. FAX 212-880-8757. (Subscr. to: Box 53816, Boulder, CO 80322. TEL 800-289-9330) Ed. Arthur Cooper; Pub. Richard Beckman. adv. contact: Giulio Capua. bk.rev.; illus.; mkt. circ. 650,000. (also avail. in microform from UMI; reprint service avail. from UMI) **Indexed:** Access (1986-1988), DAAI, Mag.Ind., R.G. (1989-), R.G.Abstr. **Document type:** consumer publication.
   —KR SourceOne; UMI; UnCover.
   Description: Covers men's fashion; includes interviews, economic advice, health issues, food, and travel.

646.3   303.5   UK   ISSN 0954-8750
TT570
G Q. (Gentlemen's Quarterly) 1988. m. £27 (Europe and N. America £48; elsewhere £54). Conde Nast Publications Ltd., Vogue House, Hanover Sq., London W1R 0AD, England. TEL 44-171-499-9080. FAX 44-171-193-1345. URL: http://www.condenast.co.uk/. (Subscr. to: Quadrant Subscription Services, Oakfield House, Perrymount Rd., Haywards Heath, W. Sussex RH16 3DH, England. TEL 44-1444-445432) Ed. Angus MacKinnon; Pub. Peter Stuart. adv. circ. 126,227. **Indexed:** DAAI. **Document type:** consumer publication.

746.92   SP
GALICIA MODA. 2/yr. Gran Via 181, 36210 Vigo, Spain. TEL 86-42-36-99. FAX 86-41-52-96. Ed. Luis Carballo Taboada.

746.96   GW   ISSN 0176-6104
GERMAN VOGUE. (Text in German) 1979. m. DM.114($96) Conde Nast Verlag Gmbh, Ainmillerstr. 8, 80801 Munich, Germany. TEL 089-381040. FAX 089-38104230. Ed. Angelica Blechschmidt; Pub. Wolf Hoffmann. adv. contact: Dagmar Huber. circ. 115,334. **Indexed:** DAAI. **Document type:** consumer publication.
   Description: Beauty, fashion and lifestyle in Germany.

746.92   II
GLAD RAGS. (Text in English) 1987. bi-m. Rs.900. Business Press, Transmission House, Compartment No. 82, Plot No. 6-19, Marol Co-op Industrial Estate, M.V. Rd., Andheri East, Mumbai 400 059, India. TEL 91-22-850-9100. FAX 91-22-850-2070. TELEX 011-78455 BPPL IN. Ed. Samson D'Silva. adv.; bk.rev.; abstr.; charts; illus. circ. 40,000. **Document type:** academic/scholarly publication.
   Description: Covers latest fashion, designs, models and interviews.

640   US   ISSN 0017-0747
TT500
GLAMOUR. 1939. m. $15 (Canada $31, elsewhere $34). Conde Nast Publications Inc., Glamour Magazine, 350 Madison Ave., New York, NY 10017. TEL 212-880-8800. E-mail: GlamourMag@aol.com. (Subscr. to: Box 53716, Boulder, CO 80322. TEL 800-274-7410) Ed. Ruth Whitney; Pub. Charles H. Townsend. adv.: B&W page $75050, color page $83000; adv. contact: Deborah Fine. bk.rev.; illus. circ. 2,081,212. (also avail. in microform from UMI; reprint service avail. from UMI) **Indexed:** Access, Consum.Ind., Hlth.Ind., Mag.Ind., Media Rev.Dig., PMR, R.G., R.G.Abstr., TOM.
   —KR SourceOne; UMI; UnCover.
   Incorporates Charm.
   Description: Provides information and how-to tips on beauty, health, fashion, and travel.

GLAMOUR. see *WOMEN'S INTERESTS*

GOLF TENNIS POLO; magazine for sports, journeys, pastime, society and fashion. see *SPORTS AND GAMES*

GRAPHIS T - SHIRT DESIGN. see *ART*

GYNAIKA/WOMAN. see *WOMEN'S INTERESTS*

687   SW   ISSN 0017-6362
HABIT; Sveriges modefacktidning. (Includes Skor & Accessorarer; Textil Nyhetsmagazine) 1961. 12/yr. SEK 1087 (foreign SEK 1210) (effective 1998). Mentor Communications ab, P.O. Box 27817, S-115 93 Stockholm, Sweden. TEL 46-8-6704128. FAX 46-8-6616455. Ed. Olav Rebane. adv.; abstr.; charts; illus.; mkt.; stat.; circ. 8,049 (controlled). **Document type:** consumer publication.
   Incorporates (in 1991): Textil Magazine; (in 1970): Herr- och Dammodebranschen.

HAIRTELL. see *BEAUTY CULTURE*

646.3   535   CN
HAKIM FASHION EYEWEAR MAGAZINE. q. Hakim Optical, 1913 Weston Rd., Toronto, ON M9N 1W7, Canada. Ed. Elizabeth Hakim.
   Description: Presents eyewear fashions, products, and technology.

640   US   ISSN 0017-7873
TT500
HARPER'S BAZAAR. 1867. m. $8.97 (Canada $31; elsewhere $28.97). Hearst Corporation, Harper's Bazaar, 1700 Broadway, New York, NY 10019. TEL 212-903-5464. E-mail: bazaar@hearst.com; URL: http://www.hearstcorp.com. (Subscr. to: C.D.S., 1901 Bell Ave., Des Moines, IA 50315. TEL 800-888-3045) Ed. Liz Tilberis; Pub. Jeannette Chung. adv.; illus. circ. 736,095. (also avail. in microfiche from NBI,PMC,UMI; reprint service avail. from UMI) **Indexed:** Biog.Ind., DAAI, Hlth.Ind., Mag.Ind., PMR, PSI, R.G., R.G.Abstr. **Document type:** consumer publication.
   ●Also available online. Vendor(s): Information Access Co.
   —KR SourceOne; UnCover.
   Description: Contains news of fashion; features by well-known authors and beauty advice.

746.92   US   ISSN 0890-9598
HARPER'S BAZAAR EN ESPANOL. (Editions avail. for Central America, Chile, Colombia, Ecuador, Mexico, Puerto Rico, U.S., Venezuela) (Text in Spanish) 12/yr. $24.95 (foreign $42.95). Editorial Televisa, Vanidades Continental Bldg., 6355 N.W. 36th St., Virginia Gardens, FL 33166. TEL 305-871-6400. FAX 305-871-7146. E-mail: subscriptions@editorialtelevisa.com. Ed. Carols Mendez. circ. 52,000.

640   IT
HARPER'S BAZAAR FRANCE AND ITALY.* (Text in French, Italian) 1983. m. 525 F. Dellaschiava Editore Srl, Viale Stelvio 57, 20159 Milan, Italy. TEL 45-53-05-55. FAX 45-53-94-27. film rev.; play rev.; illus. circ. 50,000. (back issues avail.)
   Formerly: Harper's Bazaar France.
   Description: Provides coverage of fashion, trends, beauty tips, and feature articles.

659.152   IT   ISSN 1121-7375
HARPER'S BAZAAR ITALIA. 1970. 8/yr. L.81000; newsstand price: L.8000. Edizioni S Y D S Italia s.r.l., Viale Stelvio, 57, 20159 Milan, Italy. TEL 39-2-6988. FAX 39-2-6988337. (Dist. for foreign subscr. by: A I E, Corso Italia 13, Milan, Italy) Ed. Giuseppe Della Schiava. adv.: page L.10500000. circ. 56,000.

659.152   IT   ISSN 1121-7251
HARPER'S BAZAAR ITALIA UOMO; bimestrale moda uomo. 1979. bi-m. L.30000. Edizioni S Y D S Italia s.r.l., Viale Stelvio 57, 20159 Milan, Italy. TEL 39-2-6988. FAX 39-2-6988337. Ed. Giuseppe Della Schiava. adv.: page L.10500000. circ. 75,000. **Document type:** consumer publication.
   Former titles (until 1992): Uomo Harper's Bazaar (ISSN 1121-5496); (until 1984): Men's Bazaar Italia (ISSN 1121-550X)

HEADWEAR INSTITUTE OF AMERICA. NEWSLETTER. see *CLOTHING TRADE*

746.92   646.4   NO   ISSN 0804-7464
▼**HENNE.** 1994. m. Se og Hoer Forlaget A-S, P.O. Box 250, Oekern, N-0510 Oslo, Norway. TEL 47-22-63-60-00. FAX 47-22-63-60-36. Ed. Ellen Arnstad. adv.: B&W page 32600; trim 286 x 212; adv. contact: Elizabeth Melson. circ. 57,169. **Document type:** consumer publication.

746.92   JA
HIGH FASHION. (Text in Japanese) 1960. bi-m. 11820 Yen. Bunka Publishing Bureau, 22-1, 3-chome, Yoyogi, Shibuya-ku, Tokyo, Japan. Ed. Shoko Hisada.

HONG KONG APPAREL. see *CLOTHING TRADE*

746.92   UK   ISSN 0262-3579
I - D. 1980. m. £27 (Europe £36; rest of world £58). Levelprint Ltd., Universal House, 251-255 Tottenham Court Rd., London W1P OAE, England. TEL 071-813-6170. Ed. Avril Mair; Pubs. Terry Jones, Tony Elliott. adv. contact: Jo Peters. bk.rev.; film rev.; illus. circ. 35,000. (back issues avail.) **Indexed:** DAAI. **Document type:** consumer publication.
   Description: Covers fashion, youth culture, music and film.

659.152   US   ISSN 1045-0629
I F M T MAGAZINE. (International Fashion Model & Talent) 1989. m. $20. Aquino Productions, Box 125, Rochester, VT 05767. Ed. Andres Aquino. adv.; bk.rev.; index, cum.index. circ. 90,000. (also avail. in microfiche; back issues avail.)
   Description: Covers up and coming fashion designers, photographers, fashion models and entertainers.

CLOTHING TRADE — FASHIONS

746.92 US ISSN 1043-6839
IMPRESSIONS (DALLAS); the magazine for the imprinted sportswear industry. 1977. 15/yr. $36 in the U.S.; Canada & Mexico $75; elsewhere $100 (effective 1997). Miller Freeman Inc. (Dallas) (Subsidiary of: United News and edia Co.), 13760 Noel Rd., Ste. 500, Dallas, TX 75240. TEL 214-239-3060. FAX 214-419-7825. E-mail: dsexton@mfi.com; URL: http://www.impressionsmag.com. (Subscr. to: Impressions, Box 1265, Skokie, IL 60076. TEL 800-447-0138. FAX 847-647-5972) Ed. Deborah Sexton; Pub. Laurie Gonz. adv. contact: Michelle Campbell. circ. 40,000. **Document type:** trade publication.
   Description: Contains news, trends, how-to information for those involved in decorating and selling imprinted sportswear.
   Refereed Serial

746.92 CN
INFLUENCE. 1992. 3/yr. Can.$3.25 per no. Groupe Magazines S.A. Inc., 275 rue des Braves, Ste. 300, Terrebonne, PQ J6W 3H6, Canada. TEL 514-964-7590. FAX 514-964-2327. Ed. Sophie Bertrand. adv.: B&W page Can.$3995; adv. contact: Denis Clermont. circ. 80,000. **Document type:** consumer publication.

746.92 US
INTERNATIONAL ASSOCIATION OF CLOTHING DESIGNERS. BULLETIN.* irreg. International Association of Clothing Designers, 475 Park Ave. S., 17th Fl., New York, NY 10016-6901. TEL 212-685-6602.
   Description: For designers of men's and boys' clothing.

746.92 US
INTERNATIONAL ASSOCIATION OF CLOTHING DESIGNERS. CONVENTION YEARBOOK.* a. International Association of Clothing Designers, 475 Park Ave. S., 17th Fl., New York, NY 10016-6901. TEL 212-685-6602.
   Description: Directed to designers of men's and boys' clothing.

746.92 US
INTERNATIONAL ASSOCIATION OF CLOTHING DESIGNERS. INDUSTRY RESOURCES BOOK.* irreg. International Association of Clothing Designers, 475 Park Ave. S., 17th Fl., New York, NY 10016-6901. TEL 212-685-6602.
   Description: For men's and boys' clothing designers.

746.92 US
INTERNATIONAL ASSOCIATION OF CLOTHING DESIGNERS. TECHNOLOGY AND PRODUCTIVITY RESOURCES DIRECTORY.* a. International Association of Clothing Designers, 475 Park Ave. S., 17th Fl., New York, NY 10016-6901. TEL 212-685-6602.

646 UK ISSN 0952-0708
INTERNATIONAL COLOUR AUTHORITY. (Consists of: Womenswear, Menswear, and Interior Colours (Interior Textile, Carpets, Paints and Decorative Effects)) (Text in English, French, German) a, s-a. £500 for compendium edition (outside Europe £525) (effective 1997); sections can also be purchased separately. Benjamin Dent & Co. Ltd. (Subsidiary of: I T B D Publications), 23 Bloomury Sq., London WC1A 2PJ, England. TEL 44-171-637-2211. FAX 44-171-637-2248. TELEX 8954884 BENDEN G. (N. American subscr. to: Box 1897, Lawrence, KS 66044-8897) charts. **Document type:** trade publication.
   Description: Forecasts the colors in fashion over the following 21 months; includes palettes.

646 747 UK
INTERNATIONAL COLOUR AUTHORITY. COLOUR FORECAST FOR CARPETS. 1994. a. £170 (outside Europe) £180 ($320)); all 3 Colour Forecasts £480 (outside Europe £504 ($896)). Benjamin Dent & Co. Ltd. (Subsidiary of: I T B D Publications), 23 Bloomury Sq., London WC1A 2PJ, England. TEL 44-171-637-2211. FAX 44-171-637-2248. TELEX 8954884 BENDEN G. (N. American subscr. to: Box 1897, Lawrence, KS 66044-8897) **Document type:** trade publication.
   Description: Forecasts the colors for residential and commercial carpeting and provides color samples for analysis and inspiration.

646 747 UK
INTERNATIONAL COLOUR AUTHORITY. COLOUR FORECAST FOR INTERIOR TEXTILES. 1994. a. £170 ($320) (outside Europe £180); all 3 Colour Forecasts £504 (outside Europe £504 ($896)) (effective 1995). Benjamin Dent & Co. Ltd. (Subsidiary of: I T B D Publications), 23 Bloomury Sq., London WC1A 2PJ, England. TEL 44-171-637-2211. FAX 44-171-637-2248. TELEX 8954884 BENDEN G. (N. American subscr. to: Box 1897, Lawrence, KS 66044-8897) **Document type:** trade publication.
   Description: Forecasts the colors that will be in fashion for interior textiles. Includes color samples.

646 747 UK
INTERNATIONAL COLOUR AUTHORITY. PAINTS AND DECORATIVE EFFECTS. FORECASTS FOR CONTRACT & RESIDENTIAL COLOURS (YEAR). 1994. a. £260 ($480) (outside Europe £270); all 3 Colour Forecasts £480 (outside Europe £504 ($896)) (effective 1995). Benjamin Dent & Co. Ltd. (Subsidiary of: I T B D Publications), 23 Bloomury Sq., London WC1A 2PJ, England. TEL 0171-637-2211. FAX 0171-637-2248. TELEX 8954884 BENDEN G. (N. American subscr. to: Box 1897, Lawrence, KS 66044-8897) **Document type:** trade publication.
   Description: Forecasts paint colors and patterns for the coming year. Includes color palette.

746.92 US
INTERNATIONAL DESIGNER.* q. International Association of Clothing Designers, 475 Park Ave. S., 17th Fl., New York, NY 10016-6901. TEL 212-685-6602.

646.3 US
INTERNATIONAL FASHION GROUP. ANNUAL REPORT.* a. for members only. International Fashion Group, 597 5th Ave., 8th Fl., New York, NY 10017-0120. TEL 212-247-3940.
   Description: Directed to women executives in the fashion industry.

646.3 US
INTERNATIONAL FASHION GROUP. BULLETIN.* q. for members only. International Fashion Group, 597 5th Ave., 8th Fl., New York, NY 10017-1020. TEL 212-247-3940.
   Description: For women executives in fashion and related industries.

646.3 US
INTERNATIONAL FASHION GROUP. NEWSLETTER.* 10/yr. for members only. International Fashion Group, 957 5th Ave., 8th Fl., New York, NY 10017-1020. TEL 212-247-3940. **Document type:** newsletter.
   Description: For women executives in fashion and related industries.

746.92 NE
INTERNATIONAL JEANS CULT; street corner bulletin. (Text in Dutch) 1990. 8/yr. fl.89($150) Uitgeverij Product Promotion bv, Spaarne 59, 2011 CE Haarlem, Netherlands. TEL 31-23-5336726. FAX 31-23-5332554. (Subscr. to: Postbus 45, 5710 AC Someren, Netherlands) Ed. Esther van Maurik. adv.: B&W page fl.4025, color page fl.5300; trim 297 x 420. bk.rev.; illus. (tabloid format) **Document type:** trade publication.
   Description: News and information for the casual clothing trade in the Netherlands and Belgium.

INTERNATIONAL SADDLERY AND APPAREL JOURNAL.
see *SPORTS AND GAMES — Horses And Horsemanship*

INTERNATIONAL TEXTILES; information and inspiration.
see *TEXTILE INDUSTRIES AND FABRICS*

687.2 SP
INTIMA. 1969. 3/yr. 10000 ptas.($100) Ediciones Esfer, Bruch 71, 4o 2a, 08009 Barcelona, Spain. TEL 34-3-4881820. FAX 34-3-4881820. URL: http://www.ed.es/buscapress/modaintima. Ed. Esteban Ferrer. adv.: B&W page 115000 ptas., color page 140000 ptas.; 210 x 290; adv. contact: Eduardo Ferrer. circ. 4,000. **Document type:** trade publication.
   Formerly: Catalogo Moda Intima Femenina (ISSN 1136-3622)
   Description: Specializes in corsetry, lingerie and swimwear designing.

659.152 US
INTIMATE FASHION NEWS DIRECTORY. 1955. a. $27.50 (effective 1997). Mackay Publishing Corp., 307 Fifth Ave., New York, NY 10016. TEL 212-679-6677. Ed. Milton J. Kristt. adv. contact: Ron Wieder. **Document type:** directory.

746.92 IT
INTIMO PIU MARE. (Text in English, Italian) 6/yr. L.48000. Editoriale Moda, Via Giardini 476, Torre F Scala N, 41100 Modena, Italy. TEL 59-342-001. FAX 59-351-290. Ed. Ettore Zanfi. adv.: B&W page L.3200000, color page L.3800000. circ. 20,000. **Document type:** trade publication.
   Description: Covers intimate apparel and swimwear.

659.152 IT
ITALIAN FASHION REPORT. 1977. m. L.15000. Editore I.F.R. s.r.l., Via Borgo Tegolaio 5, c/o Il Fauno, 50125 Florence, Italy. adv. circ. 2,500.

659.152 FR ISSN 0021-5457
JARDIN DES MODES. 1922. 4/yr. 110 F. Vercingetorix International Publications, 3 rue Clement Marot, 75008 Paris, France. TEL 33-1-44439977. FAX 33-1-47239481. (Subscr. to: 64 bis av. de New York, 75016 Paris, France) Ed. Alice Morgaine; Pub. Alice Morgaine. R&P contact: Alice Morgaine. adv.; bk.rev.; illus. circ. 20,000. **Document type:** consumer publication.
   Description: Covers all fields of fashion, beauty, design, architecture, photography, cinema and the visual arts.

659.152 MY ISSN 0126-6594
AP95.M24
JELITA. 1973. m. Berita Publishing, 22 Jalan Liku, 59100 Kuala Lumpur, Malaysia. TEL 03-2744322. FAX 03-2740605. Ed. Rohani Pa'Wan Chik. circ. 65,000.

746.92 SU
AL-JOHRAH FASHION. q. $12 per no. P.O. Box 755, Jeddah 21421, Saudi Arabia. TEL 643-9911. FAX 643-1293. TELEX 601-863-KINDI-SJ.
   Description: Information on hand embroidered wedding dresses, hand embroidered party dresses, evening dresses, maternity dresses and children's dresses.

746.92 SU
JOHRATH AL-ARAIES. s-a. $15 per no. Al-Johrah Fashion, P.O. Box 755, Jeddah 21421, Saudi Arabia. TEL 6439911. FAX 6431293. TELEX 601863 KINDI SJ.
   Description: Focuses on hand embroidered wedding dresses.

746.92 SU
JOHRATH AL-KHALIG. q. $10 per no. Al-Johrah Fashion, P.O. Box 755, Jeddah 21421, Saudi Arabia. TEL 6439911. FAX 643-1293. TELEX 601863 KINDI SJ.
   Description: Information on hand embroidered wedding dresses, hand embroidered party dresses, evening dresses, maternity dresses and children's dresses.

746.96 GW ISSN 0178-7284
JOURNAL FUER DIE FRAU. 1978. fortn. DM.104 (effective 1997); newsstand price: DM.4. Axel Springer Verlag AG, Axel-Springer-Platz 1, 20350 Hamburg, Germany. TEL 49-40-3470-0. FAX 49-40-345811. URL: http://www.asv.de. (Subscr. to: P M S GmbH, Postfach 290180, 47261 Duisburg, Germany. TEL 49-203-76908-0. FAX 49-203-7690830) Ed. Stefan Lewerenz. adv.: B&W page DM.15640, color page DM.27680; trim 176 x 246; adv. contact: Michael Bayer. circ. 517,300 (paid). (back issues avail.) **Document type:** consumer publication.

JOURNAL OF FASHION MARKETING AND MANAGEMENT.
see *BUSINESS AND ECONOMICS — Marketing And Purchasing*

JUST YOU NOW. see *BEAUTY CULTURE*

746.9 UK
KEY NOTE MARKET REPORT: WOMEN'S FASHIONS.
Variant title: Women's Fashions. irreg., no.6, 1991. £185. Key Note Ltd., Field House, 72 Oldfield Rd., Hampton, Middlesex TW12 2HQ, England. TEL 44-181-783-0755. FAX 44-181-783-1940. **Document type:** trade publication.

CLOTHING TRADE — FASHIONS

KEY NOTE REPORT: MEN'S CLOTHING RETAILERS. see *CLOTHING TRADE*

746.92 NE
KINDERMODE. 3/yr. newsstand price: fl.8.95. Uitgeverij Spaarnestad B.V., Postbus 1, 2000 MA Haarlem, Netherlands. TEL 31-23-304289. FAX 31-23-332071. Pub. K. van der Pas. adv.; illus. **Document type:** consumer publication.

659.152 IT
KING. m. L.48000 (foreign L.84000). E R I Edizioni R A I, Via Arsenale, 41, 10121 Turin, Italy. TEL 011-8800. FAX 011-534732. adv.: page L.33000000.

746.92 NE ISSN 0926-759X
KNIP MODE. 1969. m. fl.69. Uitgeverij Spaarnestad B.V., Postbus 1, 2000 MA Haarlem, Netherlands. TEL 31-23-304289. FAX 31-23-332071. Ed. J. Martens. adv.; circ. 248,600 (paid). **Document type:** consumer publication.
   Incorporates (1948-1993): Marion (ISSN 0025-3383); **Formerly** (until 1991): Knip (ISSN 0023-2289).

746.92 NE ISSN 0921-2744
KNIPPIE. 1977. 3/yr. newsstand price: fl.8.95. Uitgeverij Spaarnestad B.V., Postbus 1, 2000 MA Haarlem, Netherlands. TEL 31-23-304289. FAX 31-23-332071. Ed. T. Jorgensen; Pub. K. van der Pas. adv.; circ. 111,960 (paid). **Document type:** consumer publication.
   Description: Fashion patterns and ideas for children's clothing.

746.92 NE
KNIPPIE'S BABY. 1991. 2/yr. newsstand price: fl.8.95. Uitgeverij Spaarnestad B.V., Postbus 1, 2000 MA Haarlem, Netherlands. TEL 31-23-304289. FAX 32-23-332071. Ed. T. Jorgensen. adv.; circ. 120,000 (paid). **Document type:** consumer publication.
   Formerly: Baby en Peuter (ISSN 0927-1368)
   Description: Patterns and ideas for children's fashions, toys and decorations.

391 646 BU
LADA. (Editions in Bulgarian, German, Russian) 1959. m. 12 lv.($12) Ministerstvo na Vutreshnita Turgoviia i Uslugite, Sofia, Bulgaria. (Dist. by: Hemus, 6, Rouski Blvd., 1000 Sofia, Bulgaria) Ed. N. Gancheva. illus. circ. 31,000.

746.96 US
LADIES MAGAZINE/SHIH NU TSA CHIH. (Text in Chinese) m. $120. World Journal Bookstore, 141-07 20th Ave., Whitestone, NY 11357. TEL 718-746-8889. Pub. Bobby Chou. **Document type:** consumer publication.

659.152 IT ISSN 1120-1959
LADY MODA. (Text in English, Italian) q. $55 (effective Jan. 1997). Zanfi Editori s.r.l., Via Emilia Ovest 954, P.O. Box 70, 41100 Modena, Italy. TEL 39-59-222292. FAX 39-59-225719. E-mail: zanfi.editori@mo.nettuno.it. adv.: color page L.3600000. (back issues avail.) **Document type:** consumer publication.
   Description: Classic elegance in ladies' outerwear.

LEDERWAREN-REPORT. see *LEATHER AND FUR INDUSTRIES*

746.9 US
LILLY. m. E-mail: lillymag@io-online.com; URL: http://members.aol.com/lillymag2.
●Available only online.
   Description: Contains articles covering fashion trends, model of the month, and other regular colums.

687.12 GW ISSN 0344-5224
DIE LINIE (COLOGNE). 1950. bi-m. DM.235. Rudolf Heber Verlag GmbH, Stadtwaldgurtel 46, 50931 Cologne, Germany. TEL 49-221-940533-0. FAX 49-221-94053316. TELEX 8882249. Ed. Robert Loy. adv. contact: Marlis Seger. bk.rev. circ. 5,000. **Document type:** trade publication.

746.92 CC
LIUXING SE/COLOUR IN FASHION. (Text in Chinese) q. $12. Zhongguo Liuxing Se Xiehui, 35 Yongjia Lu, Shanghai 200000, People's Republic of China. TEL 4710214. Ed. Cai Zuoyi.

746.92 646.7 US
▼**LUMIERE.** 1995. m. E-mail: email@lumiere.com; URL: http://www.lumiere.com/.
●Available only online.
   Description: International online fashion and style magazine.

659 303.5 US ISSN 0887-5219
M G F.* (Men's Guide to Fashion) 1985. m. $24. M G F Publications, 6 W. 18th St., Frnt. 2, New York, NY 10011-4608. TEL 212-685-5050. Ed. Gerald Rothberg. adv.; bk.rev. circ. 200,000. **Document type:** consumer publication.
   Description: Geared to men, ages 18-29, with information and articles on fitness, fashion, grooming, and life-style.

MCCALL'S. see *WOMEN'S INTERESTS*

640 JA ISSN 0024-9343
MADAM. (Text in Japanese) m. and q. editions. 14800 Yen. Kamakura-Shobo Publishing Co., Ltd., 21 Ichigaya-Sanaicho, Shinjuku-ku, Tokyo 162, Japan. Ed. H. Miura. illus. **Document type:** consumer publication.

MADAME. see *WOMEN'S INTERESTS*

746.96 FR ISSN 0246-5205
MADAME FIGARO. w. Figaro Publiprint, 25 av. Matignon, 75008 Paris, France. TEL 33-1-44555708. circ. 710,000. **Document type:** newspaper.

MADEMOISELLE. see *WOMEN'S INTERESTS*

746.92 303.5 GW ISSN 0177-7246
MAENNER VOGUE. 1984. m. DM.72.40($94) Conde Nast Verlag GmbH, Ainmillerstr. 8, 80801 Munich, Germany. TEL 089-381040. FAX 089-38194260. Ed. Leo Pesch; Pub. Wolf Hoffmann. adv. contact: Dagmar Huber. film rev. circ. 68,193. **Document type:** consumer publication.
   Description: Lifestyle and fashion magazine for men.

646 746 641.5 BL ISSN 0025-2077
MANEQUIM. (Supplements avail.: Moldes Manequim, Atelie Manequim) 1959. m. $115. Editora Abril, S.A., R. Geraldo Flausino Gomes, 61, 04573-900 Sao Paulo SP, Brazil. TEL 55-11-534-5598. FAX 55-11-534-5779. (Subscr. to: Rua do Curtume, 769, 05063-900 Sao Paulo SP, Brazil. TEL 55-11-823-9100) Ed. Anna Maria Iughetti. adv.; charts; illus. circ. 383,000. **Document type:** consumer publication.
   Description: Covers fashion, including new styles from major designers, styles for everyday and evening wear, beauty, cooking, crocheting, crafts and sewing.

646 NE ISSN 0168-7883
MANNENMODE. (Text in Dutch) 1963. 6/yr. fl.63 (Belgium 1145 BEF; elsewhere fl.105). Blauw Media Uitgeverij B.V., Postbus 1043, 3600 BA Maarssen, Netherlands. TEL 31-346-574040. FAX 31-346-576056. adv.; bk.rev.; illus.; tr.lit. circ. 2,500. **Document type:** trade publication.
   Former titles (until 1984): Spectrum der Herenmode (ISSN 0038-7096); Spectrum Mannenmode.

MARIAGES. see *MATRIMONY*

640 FR ISSN 0025-3049
MARIE CLAIRE. 1954. m. 165 F. (foreign 333 F.) Marie-Claire-Album, 10 bd des Freres Voisin, 92792 Issy-les-Moulineaux Cedex 9, France. TEL 33-1-41468888. FAX 33-1-41468686. Ed. Martine Scaravelli; Pub. Marie Paule Laval. R&P contact: Christine Lecomte. adv.: B&W page $54700 F., color page 87200 F.; trim 227 x 293; adv. contact: Monique Mathrowicz. illus.; circ. 180,000 (paid). **Indexed:** DAAI.

659.152 IT ISSN 1120-4435
MAX. 1985. m. L.57600. Rizzoli Editore-Corriere della Sera, Via A. Rizzoli, 2, 20132 Milan, Italy. TEL 02-2588. Ed. Carlo Dansi. adv.: page L.36300000; adv. contact: Flavio Biondi. circ. 149,739.

746.92 GW ISSN 0938-8737
MAX. 1991. m. DM.66 (Europe DM.87.60; elsewhere DM.164.40); newsstand price: DM.6. Gruner und Jahr AG & Co., Am Baumwall 11, 20459 Hamburg, Germany. TEL 49-40-3703-0. FAX 49-40-37035617. (Co-publisher: Max Verlag) circ. 201,011. **Document type:** consumer publication.

659.152 CC
MENMODE. (Text in Chinese, English) 1991. s-a. HK.$99. Communication Management Ltd., 1811 Hong Kong Plaza, 188 Connaught Rd. W., Hong Kong, People's Republic of China. TEL 852-2547-7117. FAX 852-2858-2671. TELEX 61758 TATCO HX. Ed. Lina Ross; Pub. M. Mohindar. adv. contact: Michelle Lee. circ. 20,248. **Document type:** consumer publication.
   Description: Presents the international men's fashion collections: Spring-Summer and Autumn-Winter.

746.92 790.13 JA
MEN'S CLUB. (Text in Japanese) 1954. m. 6600 Yen. Fujin Gaho Sha, 9-1, 2-chome, Nishi-Shimbashi, Minato-ku, Tokyo, Japan. Ed. Keiji Kokuboda.

746.92 GW ISSN 0936-1863
MEN'S FASHION. (Text in English, French and German) 1983. 2/yr. DM.38 (foreign DM.42) (effective 1996). Deutscher Fachverlag GmbH, Mainzer Landstr. 251, 60326 Frankfurt a.M., Germany. TEL 49-69-7595-01. FAX 49-69-75952999. Ed. Peter Alex Pohl. adv.: B&W page DM.7068, color page DM.11272; trim 208 x 300; adv. contact: Peter Alex Pohl. circ. 11,000. **Document type:** trade publication.
   Formerly (until 1988): German Men's Fashion (ISSN 0178-2673)

687.11 UK ISSN 0025-9519
MEN'S WEAR. w. £30 (overseas £45). E M A P Maclaren Ltd., Maclaren House, 19 Scarbrook Rd., Croydon, Surrey CR9 1QH, England. TEL 0181-688-7788. FAX 0181-688-9300. Ed. Chris Scott-Gray; Pub. Eric Fuller. adv.: B&W page £825; color page £1780; adv. contact: David McConnell. illus. circ. 10,500. **Indexed:** Key to Econ.Sci., Text.Tech.Dig. **Document type:** trade publication.

746.92 MX
MEXICO VOGUE. m. Carta Editorial de Mexico, Av. Morelos 16, Planta Baja, Mexico 1, D.F., Mexico.

646 SZ ISSN 0026-1866
MEYERS MODEBLATT. 1924. w. 105.80 Fr. Verlag Meyer & Co., Klausstr. 33, CH-8008 Zurich, Switzerland. Ed. Rolf C. Mueller. adv.; bk.rev.; film rev.; illus. circ. 209,358.

646.4 IT ISSN 1121-1741
MIA BOUTIQUE. idee da cucire. 1986. m. L.52800. Fabbri Rizzoli Edizioni Periodiche srl, Via Mecenate 87-6, 20138 Milan, Italy. TEL 39-2-580801. FAX 39-2-5062865. Ed. Bice Invernizzi. adv.: page L.13200000. circ. 111,097. (back issues avail.)

659.182 301.412 IT
MINERVA. 1983. m. L.50000 (Europe L.100000; elsewhere L.150000). Minerva s.c. a r.l., Via Pierluigi de Palestrina 48, 00193 Rome, Italy. TEL 39-6-3211638. FAX 39-6-3211968. Ed. Anna Maria Mammoliti. adv. contact: Beatrice Mancini. **Indexed:** Curr.Cont. **Document type:** trade publication.

MIRABELLA. see *WOMEN'S INTERESTS*

659.152 IT
MODA. m. L.48000 (foreign L.84000). E R I Edizioni R A I, Via Arsenale, 41, 10121 Turin, Italy. TEL 011-8800. FAX 011-534732.

659.152 PO
MODA E MODA. 5/yr. Rua Braamcamp 12, r-c Dto., 12000 Lisbon, Portugal. TEL 01-562426. Dir. Marionela Gusmao. circ. 20,000.

746.92 SP ISSN 1132-0931
MODA EN ESPANA. 12/yr. Ruiz Perello 15, 28028 Madrid, Spain. TEL 1-255-27-43. Ed. Pilar de Abi.

746.92 SP ISSN 1133-6463
MODA EN LAS CALLES. 2/yr. M E P S A, Abtao 11, 2o C, 28007 Madrid, Spain. TEL 1-551-91-97. FAX 1-552-73-43. Ed. A. Ferrer Rosello.

1926 CLOTHING TRADE — FASHIONS

659.152　　　　IT　　ISSN 1120-1967
MODA IN COLLEZIONI. q. $55 (effective 1997). Zanfi Editori s.r.l., Via Emilia Ovest 954, 41100 Modena, Italy. TEL 39-59-891700. FAX 39-59-891701. E-mail: zanfi.editori@mo.nettuno.it. adv.: B&W page L.3100000, color page L.4100000. (back issues avail.)
   Description: Presents trendy fashions for young women from international shows.

746.92
MODA ITALIA. m. L.48000. Via Stilicone 16, 20145 Milan, Italy. TEL 39-2-331281. FAX 39-2-33103060. Ed. Willy Molco. adv.: page L.35000000. circ. 116,580. **Document type:** consumer publication.

746.92　　　　　　IT
MODA MARKETING. (Text in Italian; international issues in English, Italian) 1977. m. (10/yr.). L.70000 (Europe L.130000; elsewhere L.180000) (effective 1997). (Federazione Nazionale Dettaglianti T.A.) Editoriale Alfa s.r.l., Viale Marelli 19, 20099 Sesto S. Giovanni (MI), Italy. TEL 39-2-2423566. FAX 39-2-22476521. URL: http://www.sirtec.it/itw/riv/moda/moda.htm. Ed. Milvia Maida. adv.: B&W page L.4000000, color page L.5000000; trim 230 x 335; adv. contact: Milvia Maida. circ. 20,000.
   Formerly (until 1994): Panorama Moda Abbigliamento.
   Description: Four international issues are mainly photographic, the other 6 supply economic and marketing news and information.

MODA MOLDES. see *NEEDLEWORK*

746　　　　　　FI　　ISSN 1238-5646
▼**MODA MUOTIKAAVAT.** 1995. q. Yhtyneet Kuvalehdet Oy, Maistraatinportti 1, FIN-00240 Helsinki, Finland. TEL 358-0-156-6524. FAX 358-0-156-6505. Ed. Heidi Peltonen. adv.: B&W page FIM 7800, color page FIM 11500. illus. circ. 40,000. **Document type:** consumer publication.

746.9 646.7　　　PL　　ISSN 1230-042X
MODA TOP. 1992. q. $54 (effective 1998). Warsaw Voice S.A., Ksiecia Janusza 64, 01-452 Warsaw, Poland. TEL 48-22-366377. FAX 48-22-371995. (Dist. by: Mezhdunarodnaya Kniga, B. Yakimanka 39, 117049 Moscow, Russia. TEL 7-095-2384967. FAX 7-095-2384634) Ed. Jadwiga Komorowska. **Document type:** consumer publication.
   Description: Contains a presentation of the newest ideas from top fashion designers, advice on creating a personal style, interviews with top models, beauty secrets, focusing on the art of makeup and personal care, descriptions of the newest interior designs.

659.152　　　　　IT
MODASPORT VACANZE INTERNATIONAL. (Supplement avail.: Modasport Vacanze Collection) (Text in English, French, German, Italian, Spanish) 1973. 4/yr. L.65000 (foreign L.135000) (effective 1993). Acalifa s.r.l., Via San Rocco, 17, 20135 Milan, Italy. TEL 39-2-58315800. FAX 39-2-58316313. Ed. Silvano Marzenta. adv.: B&W page L.5000000, color page L.7100000; adv. contact: Eva Sabbatini. circ. 46,000. **Document type:** trade publication.
   Formerly: Modasport Vacanze.

687.19　　　　　　IT
MODAVIVA. 1985. m. L.35000($136) Renoma Editrice S.P.A., Via IV Novembre 54, 20019 Seguro di Settimo Milanese (MI), Italy. TEL 39-2-33500337. FAX 39-2-33501391. Ed. Silvana Gallo. adv.: B&W page L.4700000, color page L.7600000. circ. 60,000.

746.96 301.412　　AT　　ISSN 0155-4611
MODE AUSTRALIA. 1977. bi-m. plus s-a. extra issues. Aus.$47.20 (New Zealand NZ.$68; elsewhere Aus.$103.50). A C P Publishing Pty. Ltd., 54-58 Park Rd., Sydney, N.S.W. 2000, Australia. TEL 61-2-2828701. FAX 61-2-2674456. Ed. Karin Upton-Baker; Pub. Richard Walsh. adv. contact: Patricia Connolly. circ. 38,000. **Document type:** consumer publication.

MODE BRIDES. see *MATRIMONY*

746.92　　　　GW　　ISSN 0947-5974
MODE SPECIAL. q. DM.6.80 per no. Ivy Stoll Verlag, Ridlerstr. 36, 80339 Munich, Germany. TEL 089-509545. FAX 089-503189. Ed. Ivy Stoll. circ. 70,000. **Document type:** trade publication.

MODEL CALL. see *OCCUPATIONS AND CAREERS*

659.152　　　　RU　　ISSN 0132-0793
MODELI SEZONA. (Supplement to: Zhurnal Mod (ISSN 0321-1576)) 1957. 4/yr. 20000 Rub. Joint-stock Company Fashion Journal, Kuznetskii Most 7-9, 103031 Moscow, Russia. TEL 7-95-9217393. FAX 7-95-9287793. Ed. N.A. Kasatkina. circ. 50,000. **Document type:** catalog.
   Description: Covers modern fashion styles for different ages and sizes, fashion trends; provides knitting instructions and patterns.

746.92　　　　GW　　ISSN 0723-7839
DER MODELLHUT. 1948. m. DM.102 (foreign DM.120) (effective 1997). Verlag Neuer Merkur, Ingolstaedter Str. 63A, 80939 Munich, Germany. TEL 49-89-318905-0. FAX 49-89-31890553. Ed. Dr. Joerg Lingenberg. R&P contact: Joerg Lingenberg. adv. contact: Gabriele Meier. charts; illus. **Document type:** trade publication.
   Former titles (until 1975): Modellhut und Accessoires (ISSN 0723-788X); (until 1973): Modellhut (ISSN 0723-7898)

659.152　　　　IT　　ISSN 1121-8290
MODELLINA. 1946. q. L.7220. IBI s.r.l., Via Finocchiaro Aprile 5, 20124 Milan, Italy. Ed. Silvana Mattei. adv.

640　　　　　　　FR　　ISSN 0026-8739
MODES ET TRAVAUX. 1919. m. 135 F. (foreign 236 F.). Editions Edouard Boucherit S.A., 10 rue de la Pepiniere, 75380 Paris Cedex 08, France. TEL 45-22-78-05. FAX 45-22-85-99. TELEX 280 286. Ed. Catherine Gourlat. adv.; illus. circ. 1,500,000.

MODUS. see *HOME ECONOMICS*

659.152　　　　　IT
MONDO UOMO. (Text in English and Italian) 1980. 6/yr. L.43200 (foreign L.85000). Edimoda S.p.A., Viale Sarca 235, 20126 Milan, Italy. TEL 39-2-66491. Ed. Giorgio Valle. adv.: page L.17000000. circ. 27,508.

640　　　　　　　FI　　ISSN 0355-192X
MUOTI & KAUNEUS. 1944. 6/yr. FIM 159. Yhtyneet Kuvalehdet Oy, Maistraatinportti 1, 00240 Helsinki, Finland. TEL 0-15661. FAX 0-156-6505. TELEX 121364. Ed. Anja Schone. adv.: B&W page FIM 15500, color page FIM 22700. charts; illus. circ. 54,790. **Document type:** consumer publication.
   Formerly: Muotisorja (ISSN 0027-3635)

DAS NEUE. see *GENERAL INTEREST PERIODICALS — Germany*

659.152　　　　　US
NEW BODIES. m. newsstand price: $2.95. G C R Publishing Group, Inc., 1700 Broadway, 34th Fl., New York, NY 10019. TEL 212-541-7100. FAX 212-245-1241. Pub. Jason Goodman.

746.92　　　　SP　　ISSN 1136-3630
NINSMODA; revista de moda infantil. 1971. 4/yr. 10000 ptas.($150) Ediciones Esfer, Bruch 71, 4o 2a, 08009 Barcelona, Spain. TEL 34-3-4881820. FAX 34-3-4881820. URL: http://www.ed.es/buscapress.ninsmoda. Ed. Esteban Ferrer. adv.: B&W page 120000 ptas., color page 150000 ptas.; 210 x 290; adv. contact: Eduardo Ferrer. circ. 4,000. **Document type:** trade publication.
   Formerly (until 1991): Nins (ISSN 1136-3681)
   Description: Specializes in the designing of infants', children's and youth's apparel.

746　　　　　　　JA
NON-NO. (Text in Japanese) 1971. s-m. 400 Yen per no. Shueisha Inc., 1-5-14 Sarugaku, Chiyoda-ku, Tokyo 101-50, Japan. TEL 81-3-3230-6379. Ed. Hiroshi Otsuka. circ. 1,500,000.
   Description: Covers clothing trade, fashions for young women.

746.92　　　　　CU
NUEVA LINEA. s-a. $20 in S. America; N. America $22; elsewhere $24. Ediciones Cubanas, Obispo No. 527, Apdo. 605, Havana, Cuba.

NYTT LIF; fashion magazine. see *WOMEN'S INTERESTS*

659.152　　　　　IT
OBIETTIVO MODA. 1978. s-a. L.130000. Associazione Stilisti, Via B. Franceschini 5, 50142 Florence, Italy. TEL 39-55-7398754. FAX 39-55-700478. TELEX 572290 CENTRO I. Ed. Forconi Fulvio. adv.: B&W page L.1600000, color page L.2400000. circ. 15,000.

OFFICIEL DU PRET-A-PORTER. see *TEXTILE INDUSTRIES AND FABRICS*

746.92 646.7　　US　　ISSN 1075-3133
PAGEANTRY; the magazine for the pageant, talent, and fashion industry. 1980. q. $16 (Canada $24; elsewhere $28). (World Pageant Association) Pageantry, Talent & Entertainment Services, Inc., 1855 W. State Rd. 434, Ste. 254, Longwood, FL 32750. TEL 407-260-2262. FAX 407-260-5131. E-mail: pageantmag@aol.com. Ed. Brian Chambers; Pub. Charles Dunn. R&P contact: Charles Dunn. adv. contact: Charles Dunn. illus. circ. 50,000. **Document type:** consumer publication, trade publication.
   Description: News, interviews and information on the people and fashions of the talent and dance competition, beauty pageant and prom industries.

PAGINAS. see *WOMEN'S INTERESTS*

PANACHE. see *WOMEN'S INTERESTS*

PANORAMA - DE POST. see *GENERAL INTEREST PERIODICALS — Belgium*

306 746.92 781.64　US　ISSN 1092-6305
PAPER (NEW YORK). m. $19.97 (effective 1997); newsstand price: $3.50. Paper Publishing Co., Inc., 529 Broadway, New York, NY 10012. TEL 212-226-4405. FAX 212-226-1091. E-mail: edit@papermag.com. (Subscr. to: Box 47, Canal St. Sta., New York, NY 10013) Eds. Kim Hastreiter, David Hershkovits; Pubs. Kim Hastreiter, David Hershkovits. adv. contact: Michael Neumann. **Document type:** consumer publication.
   Former titles (until 1996): Paper Magazine (ISSN 1073-9122); (until 1993): Paper (ISSN 0892-3809)

PHELON'S WOMEN'S APPAREL AND ACCESSORY SHOPS. see *BUSINESS AND ECONOMICS — Trade And Industrial Directories*

PICTURE PERFECT. see *PHOTOGRAPHY*

PINKER MODA. see *TEXTILE INDUSTRIES AND FABRICS*

PLAYBOY FASHION. see *MEN'S INTERESTS*

PLAYBOY'S BOOK OF LINGERIE. see *MEN'S INTERESTS*

746.92　　　　　CN
POINT OF VIEW. French edition: Point du Vue. 1987. s-a. membership. Holt Renfrew & Co., Limited, 50 Bloor St., W., Toronto, Ont. M4W 1A1, Canada. TEL 416-922-2333. FAX 416-922-3240. Ed. Nancy Moore. adv.: color page Can.$13000; trim 9 x 10 7/8; adv. contact: John Duncan. circ. 150,000 (controlled). **Document type:** catalog.

659.152　　　　　JA
POPEYE. (Text in Japanese) 1976. bi-w. newsstand price: 380Yen. Magazine House, 3-13-10, Ginza, Chuo-ku, Tokyo 104, Japan. TEL 81-3-3545-7160. FAX 81-3-3545-9026. Ed. Shiro Mizokawa. circ. 352,000. **Document type:** consumer publication.

PREVISIONS GLISSANTES DETAILLEES EN PERSPECTIVES SECTORIELLES (VOL.3): TEXTILE - HABILLEMENT - CUIR. see *BUSINESS AND ECONOMICS — Economic Situation And Conditions*

746.96　　　　FR　　ISSN 0293-2407
PRIMA. 1982. m. 106 F.($120) Prisma Presse, 6 rue Daru, 75008 Paris, France. TEL 33-1-44966700. FAX 33-1-44966721. Ed. Fabienne Azire. adv.; bk.rev. circ. 1,171,460.
   Description: Covers fashion, beauty, crafts, home decoration, cooking, health, the law and education.

PROFESSIONAL MODEL NEWSLETTER. see *WOMEN'S INTERESTS*

CLOTHING TRADE — FASHIONS

746.92 **NZ**
PULP; fashion, not fiction. q. free. Apparel Publishing Ltd., P.O. Box 56071, Dominion Rd., Auckland 3, New Zealand. TEL 64-9-6315685. FAX 64-9-6303706. E-mail: apparel@iprolink.co.nz. Ed. Daya Willis. adv.: B&W page NZ.$1120, color page NZ.$1900; trim 230 x 290. circ. 20,000. **Document type:** trade publication.
Description: Offers news, trends and information for young consumers.

746.92 **SA**
PURSUIT; the journal for the apparel industry. 1989. bi-m. R.195 (foreign R.300) includes Index. Pursuit Holdings, P.O. Box 15793, Vlaberg, Cape Town, South Africa. TEL 27-21-242154. FAX 27-21-242212. E-mail: pursuit@aztec.co.za. Ed. Joanna Broughton. adv.: B&W page R.6360, color page R.6955; illus. circ. 6,000. **Document type:** trade publication. adv. contact: Yasmeen Braaf.

746.92 **SA**
PURSUIT: THE FASHION INDEX. 1989. a. Pursuit Publishing, P.O. Box 15793, Vlaeberg, Capetown, South Africa. TEL 27-21-2421540. FAX 27-21-2422422. Ed. Joanna Broughton; Pub. Joanna Broughton. R&P contact: Joanna.Broughton. adv.; illus. circ. 6,000. **Document type:** trade publication.
Description: Covers the fashion textile industry in Suth Africa.

746.92 **US** ISSN 0887-3003
HD9940.U4
R T W REVIEW. Variant title: Retailing in Today's World Review. 1985. bi-m. $149 (Canada & Mexico $169; elsewhere $199). Danielle Consultants, 8314 S. Tuckaway Shores, Franklin, WI 53132. TEL 414-425-5503. FAX 414-425-2501. E-mail: rtwrev@aol.com. (Subscr. to: P.O. Box 27688, Milwaukee, WI 53227) Ed. Lauren Daniel-Falk. R&P contact: Lauren Daniel-Falk. adv. contact: Kelly Smith. bk.rev. circ. 5,000. (tabloid format; back issues avail.) **Document type:** trade publication.
Description: Trade publication for the retail industry featuring alternative retail formats for the new millennium, comprehensive retail coverage, merchandising strategies and emerging industry trends.

659.152 **IT**
RENEL.* (Text in English, French, German, Italian, Spanish) 1969. s-a. L.12000 per no. S I M Arbiter, Via Walter Tobagi 19, 20090 Vimodrone (MI), Italy. TEL 39-2-253001. Ed. Francesco DiCarlo. adv. circ. 8,000.

659.152 **UK** ISSN 0144-7416
RITZ NEWSPAPER. 1977. m. £12. Litchfield Productions Ltd., 35 Brittania Row, London N1 8QH, England. TEL 01-359 7486. Ed. David Litchfield. film rev.; play rev. circ. 15,000. (tabloid format) **Document type:** newspaper.
Description: Includes features and photos about contemporary, cosmopolitan fashion, social and cultural events; dining and entertainment section; interviews, profiles, and critical reviews.

746.92 **SZ**
ROBES COUTURE. (Text in English, French and German) s-a. 46 SFr. (foreign 50 SFr.) (combined subscr. with Robes Manteaux 84 SFr.(foreign 93 SFr.)) (effective 1997). Editions C. Weder Ltd., Rennweg 64, CH-4052 Basel, Switzerland. TEL 41-61-3126263. FAX 41-61-3126266. TELEX 965920-WEDER-CH. Ed. Walter Beyeler. **Document type:** trade publication.

746.92 **SZ**
ROBES MANTEAUX. (Text in English, French and German) s-a. 46 SFr. (foreign 50 SFr.) (combined subscr. with Robes Couture 84 SFr.(foreign 93 SFr.)) (effective 1997). Editions C. Weder Ltd., Rennweg 64, CH-4052 Basel, Switzerland. TEL 41-61-3126263. FAX 41-61-3126266. TELEX 965920-WEDER-CH. Ed. Walter Beyeler. **Document type:** trade publication.

687 **GW** ISSN 0035-9912
RUNDSCHAU FUER INTERNATIONALE DAMENMODE; Fachzeitschrift fuer Mode und Schnittechnik. 1928. m. DM.191.20. Rundschau-Verlag Otto G. Koeniger GmbH und Co., Karlstr. 41, 89073 Ulm, Germany. TEL 49-731-1520187. FAX 49-731-1520188. adv.; charts; illus. **Document type:** consumer publication.
Formerly: Rundschau fuer die Deutsche Damenschneiderei.

RUSE MAGAZINE. see *ART*

SAN ANTONIO HOMES & GARDENS. see *INTERIOR DESIGN AND DECORATION*

746.92 **JA**
SAN SUN. (Text in Japanese) 1983. m. 4800 Yen. Gakken Co., Ltd., 40-5, 4 chome, Kamiikedai, Ohta-ku, Tokyo 145, Japan. Ed. Hiroshi Tsunematsu.

646.4 **IT**
SCUOLA DI TAGLIO E CUCITO.* m. L.30000. Curcio Periodici S.p.A., Via IV Novembre 149, 00187 Rome, Italy. Ed. Rosanna Falconi. adv. circ. 110,000.

SEASON - MODE IM VERKAUF. see *CLOTHING TRADE*

746.92 **JA**
SESAMI. (Text in Japanese) 1975. q. 4020 Yen. Fujin Seikatsu Sha, 19-5, 2-chome, Yushima, Bunkyo-ku, Tokyo, Japan. Ed. Mizue Hotta.

SEW BEAUTIFUL. see *NEEDLEWORK*

746 646.4 **US** ISSN 0273-8120
SEW NEWS; the newspaper for people who sew. 1980. m. $23.98. P J S Publications, Inc., 2 News Plaza, Box 1790, Peoria, IL 64656. TEL 309-682-6626. FAX 309-682-7394. Ed. Linda Turner Griepentrog. adv.; bk.rev. circ. 191,672. **Document type:** newspaper, consumer publication.

746.9 **IT**
SHAHRAZAD. (Text in Arabic) s-a. $25 (effective Jan. 1997). Zanfi Editori s.r.l., Via Emilia Ovest 954, 41100 Modena, Italy. TEL 39-59-891700. FAX 39-59-891701. E-mail: zanfi.editori@mo.nettuno.it.
Description: Offers women's fashions, bridal gowns, evening gowns, children's clothing, jewelry, perfumes, interior furnishings and cookery.

746.92 **CC** ISSN 1000-8888
SHANGHAI FUSHI. (Text in Chinese) q. Shanghai Scientific and Technical Publishers, Journal Department, 450 Ruijin 2 Lu, Shanghai 200020, People's Republic of China. TEL 4370160. Ed. Gong Gang.

746.92 **CC** ISSN 1002-4158
SHIZHUANG/FASHIONABLE CLOTHES. (Text in Chinese) 1980. bi-m. $23.70. China Silk Import and Export General Corporation - Zhongguo Sichou Jinchukou Zonggongsi, 82 Dong'anmen Dajie, Beijing 100744, People's Republic of China. TEL 86-10-6512-038. FAX 86-10-6512-0378. (Dist. in US by: China Books & Periodicals, Inc., 2929 24th St., San Francisco, CA 94110. TEL 415-282-2994) Ed. Rui Wang.

659.152 **US**
SHOW BIZ NEWS AND MODEL NEWS. 1970. m. $18 (foreign $32) (effective 1997); newsstand price: $1.50. John King, Ed. & Pub., 244 Madison Ave., Ste. 393, New York, NY 10016. TEL 212-969-8715. FAX 212-969-8715. adv.: page $3,000; trim 10 x 16; adv. contact: Joe Thomas. bk.rev.; dance rev.; film rev.; music rev.; play rev.; software rev.; video rev. circ. 288,000. (tabloid format; also avail. in microfiche) **Document type:** newspaper, consumer publication, trade publication.
Formerly: Model News and Talent; Which was formed by the merger of: Model News & Model and Talent.
Description: Covers the entertainment world. Aimed at show people, models, producers, agents, and directors.

SIMAC - PRESELEZIONE ITALIANA MODA. see *SHOES AND BOOTS*

687 **CC**
SINGAPORE EVE MODE. (Text in English) 1988. s-a. S.$9.90 per no. Communication Management Ltd., 1811 Hong Kong Plaza, 188 Connaught Rd. W., Hong Kong, People's Republic of China. TEL 852-2547-7117. FAX 852-2858-2671. TELEX 61758 TATCO HX. Ed. Lina Ross; Pub. M. Mohinder. adv. contact: Desmond Teo. circ. 17,000. **Document type:** consumer publication.
Formerly (until 1990): Singapore Eve.

659.152 **CC**
SINGAPORE MENMODE. (Text in English) 1993. s-a. S.$9.90. Communication Management Ltd., 1811 Hong Kong Plaza, 188 Connaught Rd. W., Hong Kong, People's Republic of China. TEL 852-2547-7117. FAX 852-2858-2671. TELEX 61758 TATCO HX. Ed. Lina Ross; Pub. M. Mohinder. adv. contact: Desmond Teo. circ. 14,300. **Document type:** consumer publication.
Description: Presents the international men's fashion collections: Spring/Summer and Autumn/Winter.

746.92 640 **JA**
SO-EN. (Text in Japanese) 1936. m. 14220 Yen. Bunka Publishing Bureau, 3-22-1, Yoyogi, Shibuya-ku, Tokyo 151, Japan. TEL 03-3370-3111. TELEX 32475. Ed. Tamae Ejima.
Formerly: Fashion Garden.

746.9 **IT**
SPORT & STREET COLLEZIONI. (Text in English, Italian) s-a. newsstand price: L.50000. Zanfi Editori s.r.l., Via Emilia Ovest 954, 41100 Modena, Italy. TEL 39-59-891700. FAX 39-59-891701. E-mail: zanfi.editori@mo.nettuno.it. (Dist. by: Mode Information GmbH, Pilgerstr. 20, 51491 Overath, Germany. TEL 49-2206-60070. FAX 49-2206-600717)
Description: Presents sportswear, jeanswear, casualwear, and activewear.

SPORTSHOP; international trade magazine for the sporting goods trade. see *SPORTS AND GAMES*

SPOSA. see *MATRIMONY*

STAR & STYLE. see *MOTION PICTURES*

646.3 **AT** ISSN 0816-939X
STUDIO BAMBINI. s-a. Aus.$86. Studio Magazines Pty. Ltd., Level 3, 101-111 William St., Sydney, N.S.W. 2011, Australia. TEL 61-2-3601422. FAX 61-2-3609550. **Document type:** consumer publication.

746.92 **AT**
STUDIO COLLECTION; Australia's fashion magazine. 1984. 4/yr. Aus.$86. Studio Magazines Pty. Ltd., Level 3, 101-111 William St., Sydney, N.S.W. 2011, Australia. TEL 61-2-3601422. FAX 61-2-3609550. **Document type:** consumer publication.
Former titles: Australian Collections Quarterly (ISSN 1037-7735); (until 1992): Studio Collections (ISSN 0813-4634)

STUDIO FOR BRIDES. see *MATRIMONY*

646.3 **AT** ISSN 1031-735X
STUDIO FOR MEN. s-a. Aus.$86. Studio Magazines Pty. Ltd., Level 3, 101-111 William St., Sydney, N.S.W. 2011, Australia. TEL 61-2-3601422. FAX 61-2-3609550. **Document type:** consumer publication.

687 **CN** ISSN 0039-4246
STYLE; Canada's womenswear fashion news. (Buyers Guide avail. (ISSN 0227-4272)) 1888. 15/yr. Can.$42 (US Can.$60; foreign Can.$84). Style Communications Inc., 1448 Lawrence Ave. E., Ste. 302, Toronto, ON M4A 4V6, Canada. TEL 416-755-5199. FAX 416-755-9123. E-mail: stylcom@cycor.ca. Ed. Doris Montanera; Pub. Pat McLean. adv.: B&W page Can.$3960, color page Can.$4680; trim 10 3/16 x 13 3/4; adv. contact: Sharon Payne. illus.; stat.; index. circ. 10,000. (tabloid format; also avail. in microform from UMI; reprint service avail. from UMI) **Indexed:** Abstr.Engl.Stud., Arts & Hum.Cit.Ind., Curr.Cont., Ind.Bk.Rev.Hum., M.L.A. **Document type:** trade publication.
—Genuine Article; UMI.

746.92 687 **US**
STYLE FORECAST.* s-a. International Association of Clothing Designers, 475 Park Ave. S., 17th fl., New York, NY 10016-6091. TEL 212-685-6602.

746.92 780 **US**
▼**SWEATER**. 1997. bi-m. free. Raygun Publishing, 2812 Santa Monica Blvd., Ste. 204, Santa Monica, CA 90404. TEL 310-828-0522. FAX 310-452-8076. (Co-publisher: K B A Marketing) Ed. Jim Greer. **Document type:** consumer publication.
Description: Nightclub magazine aimed at the 21- to 34-year-old consumer.

CLOTHING TRADE — FASHIONS

659.152 US ISSN 0894-4075
SWIMWEAR U S A. 1987? m. newsstand price: $2.95. G C R Publishing Group, Inc., 1700 Broadway, 34th Fl., New York, NY 10019. TEL 212-541-7100. FAX 212-245-1241. Pub. Jason Goodman. **Document type:** trade publication.

646.4 MX
TEENAGER INTERNACIONAL. (Text in Spanish) q. Consorcio Sayrols, Mier y Pesado 126, Col. del Valle, 03100 Mexico D.F., Mexico. TEL 52-5-6874699. FAX 52-5-5237045. E-mail: beatrizc@spin.com.mx; URL: http://www.sayrols.com.mx. Ed. Patricia Olvera; Pub. Patricia Olivera. R&P contact: Roberto Davo. TEL 52-5-5236714. adv.: B&W page $3370, color page $4312; 210 x 275; adv. contact: Beatriz Coria. circ. 100,000. **Document type:** consumer publication.
Description: Includes sewing patterns and instructions for young women.

TEKSI; the Finnish trade magazine for fashion. see *TEXTILE INDUSTRIES AND FABRICS*

TEKSTILFORUM MED PARFYMERIET. see *TEXTILE INDUSTRIES AND FABRICS*

759.152 IT
TEMI - TENDENZE MODA ITALIA. 1984. bi-m. L.40000. Temi, Via Lamarmora 22, 20122 Milan, Italy. TEL 39-2-55192002. FAX 39-2-55015325. Ed. Simonetti Edoardo. adv.: B&W page L.2500000, color page L.5000000.

TEXBEL (EDITION FRANCAISE). see *TEXTILE INDUSTRIES AND FABRICS*

TEXBEL (NEDERLANDSE EDITIE). see *TEXTILE INDUSTRIES AND FABRICS*

746.92 GW ISSN 1430-7774
▼**TEXDECOR.** 1996. q. DM.120 (foreign DM.136) (effective 1997). Meisenbach GmbH, Hainstr. 18, 96047 Bamberg, Germany. TEL 49-951-861135. FAX 49-951-861158. **Document type:** trade publication.

746.92 370 GW ISSN 0342-7358
TEXTILARBEIT UND UNTERRICHT. q. DM.76 (students DM.60.80) (effective 1998). Schneider Verlag Hohengehren GmbH, Wilhelmstr. 13, 73666 Baltmannsweiler, Germany. TEL 49-7153-41206. FAX 49-7153-48761. **Document type:** academic/scholarly publication.
—CCC.

380.145687 DK
TOEJ - FASHION & BUSINESS TRENDS. 1979. m. DKK 552 (effective 1997). P.e.j. Gruppen ApS, Hybenvej 4-6, Hammerum, DK-7400 Herning, Denmark. TEL 45-97-11-89-00. FAX 45-97-11-85-11. Ed. Helle Mathiesen. adv.: B&W page DKK 12500, color page DKK 14700; trim 210 x 297; adv. contact: Morten Dybro. bk.rev. circ. 5,000. **Document type:** trade publication.
Formerly: Toej - Scandinavian Fashion (ISSN 0107-0290)
Description: Provides a running commentary on all relevant Dansih and international trade fairs.

746.92 TT500 US ISSN 1079-171X
TOP MODEL. Key Title: Elle TopModel. 1994. bi-m. Elle Publishing (Subsidiary of: Hachette Filipacchi Magazines), 1633 Broadway, New York, NY 10019. TEL 212-787-5800. Ed. Martine Sicard; Pub. Richard Rabinowitz. adv. contact: Robea Panorella. illus. **Document type:** consumer publication.

746.92 CN ISSN 0821-7955
TORONTO LIFE FASHION. (Supplement to: Toronto Life (ISSN 0049-4194)) 1977. 8/yr. Toronto Life Publishing Co. Ltd., 59 Front St. E., 3rd Fl., Toronto, ON M5E 1B3, Canada. TEL 416-364-3334. Ed. Joan Harting-Barham; Pub. Shelagh Tarleton. adv. contact: Shelagh Tarleton. illus. circ. 130,437. **Indexed:** Can.B.P.I., CMI. **Document type:** consumer publication.
Formerly: (until 1979): Toronto Life Fashion Magazine (ISSN 0705-2715)

TREND-BOUTIQUE; vakblad voor de eigentijdse ondernemer in lederwaren, bijoux en modeaccessoires. see *BUSINESS AND ECONOMICS — Marketing And Purchasing*

TRICOT PRESTIGE. see *NEEDLEWORK*

TRICOTS CHICS; layette, adults. see *NEEDLEWORK*

659.152 SI
TUNE MONTHLY MAGAZINE. (Text in Chinese) 1988. m. Block 203A Henderson Industrial Park, Henderson Rd. 0604, Singapore 0315, Singapore. TEL 2733000. FAX 2749538. Ed. Chan Eng. circ. 25,000.

646.3 646.7 PL ISSN 0867-1826
TWOJ STYL. 1990. m. newsstand price: 5. Twoj Styl, Spolka z o.o., Ul. Swietojerska 5-7, 00-236 Warsaw, Poland. TEL 48-2-6359533. FAX 48-22-311541. (Dist. in U.S. & Canada by: Andrew Artistic Distribution Inc., c/o Janusz Czuj, 417 Manhattan Ave., Brooklyn, NY 11222. TEL 718-384-6050. FAX 718-387-0484) Ed. Krystyna Kaszuba. adv. contact: Malgorzata Skrobiszewska. illus.

746.92 781.64 US
▼**UHF.** 1995. s-m. $14.95 (effective 1997); newsstand price: $3. Supersonic Media Inc., 1522-B Cloverfield Blvd., Santa Monica, CA 90404. TEL 310-449-0120. FAX 310-449-1153. Ed. Jason Fine; Pub. Scott Becker. R&P contact: Scott Becker. adv.: page $1900; trim 8 3/8 x 10 7/8; adv. contact: Wendy Thompson. dance rev.; music rev.; tr.lit. circ. 42,000. (back issues avail.) **Document type:** consumer publication.
Description: Covers alternative music and fashion.

646 MX ISSN 0041-6223
ULTIMA MODA. 1966. fortn. Mex.$110($10) Publicaciones Herrerias, S.A., Balderas 87, 2o, 06040 Mexico D.F., Mexico. TEL 5-518-5481. Ed. Jose Pichel. adv.; charts; illus. circ. 230,000.

687.11 IT
UOMO COLLEZIONI. (Text in English, Italian) s-a. $150 (effective Jan. 1997). Zanfi Editori s.r.l., Via Emilia Ovest 954, 41100 Modena, Italy. TEL 059-891700. FAX 059-891701. E-mail: zanfi.editori@mo.nettuno.it. illus. (back issues avail.) **Document type:** trade publication.
Description: Covers the best of men's fashion shows throughout the world: pret-a-porter, knitwear, accessories, casualwear and more.

646 IT ISSN 1120-7760
UOMO VOGUE. m. (10/yr.) L.72000 (foreign L.126500). Edizioni Conde Nast S.p.A., Piazza Castello 27, 20121 Milan, Italy. TEL 39-2-85611. FAX 39-2-8055716. Ed. A. Premoli. adv.: page L.14000000. circ. 35,638. **Indexed:** DAAI. **Document type:** consumer publication.

746.92 JA
UTSUKUSHII-KIMONO/BEAUTIFUL KIMONO. (Text in Japanese) 1953. q. 3600 Yen. Fujin Gaho Sha, 9-1, 1-chome, Nishi-Shimbashi, Minato-ku, Tokyo, Japan. Ed. Yoshihiko Fukuchi.

746.4 646 SP ISSN 0212-2995
VESTIDAL; moda y patrones. 1978. bi-m. 6819 ptas. (effective 1997). Editorial America Iberica, C. Miguel Yuste 26, 28037 Madrid, Spain. (Dist. in Mexico by: Distribuidora Intermex, S.A. de C.V., Lucio Blanco 435, Azcapotzalco, C.P. 02400 Mexico DF (Mexico) Dir. Begona Gutierrez. adv. **Document type:** consumer publication.
Description: Presents clothing styles for women and men that are available as patterns. Includes articles on beauty, interior decoration, and food.

687 IT
VESTIRE UOMO;* rivista di alta moda maschile, di tessuti, di abbigliamento. (Text in English and Italian) 1960. s-a. $14. Societa Creazioni Moda per Azioni, Corso Giulio Cesare 31, 10152 Turin, Italy. TEL 39-11-287933. Ed. Franco Bosco. adv.; bk.rev.; illus. circ. 30,000.
Formerly: Vestire (ISSN 0042-4579)

659.152 384.554 US
VIDEOFASHION; news, men, specials. w. $795. Videofashion, Inc., One W. 37th St., New York, NY 10018. TEL 212-869-4666. FAX 212-869-8208. E-mail: videofashion@videofashion.com. Ed. Nicolas H. Charney; Pub. Nicolas H. Charney. R&P contact: Anne V. Adami. (video cassette) **Document type:** trade publication.
Description: Devoted to men's and women's wear and the fashion industry.

746.92 CN ISSN 1191-226X
VISION MODE. 1991. 3/yr. Can.$2.95 per no. Groupe Magazines S.A. Inc., 275 rue des Braves, Ste. 300, Terrebonne, PQ J6W 3H6, Canada. TEL 514-964-7590. FAX 514-964-2327. Pub. Denis Clermont. R&P contact: Denis Clermont. adv.: B&W page Can.$3995; trim 8 1/4 x 10 7/8; adv. contact: Katie Tremblay. circ. 95,000. **Document type:** consumer publication.

640 TT500 US ISSN 0042-8000
VOGUE. (American, Australian, Brazilian, British, French, German, Italian and Spanish editions avail.) 1892. m. $28 (foreign $50); libraries $20. Conde Nast Publications Inc., Vogue Magazine, 350 Madison Ave., New York, NY 10017. TEL 212-880-8800. FAX 212-880-8169. (Subscr. to: Box 55980, Boulder, CO 80322. TEL 800-234-2347) Ed. Anna Wintour. adv.; bk.rev.; illus. circ. 1,219,958. (also avail. in microform from UMI; microfilm from KTO; reprint service avail. from UMI) **Indexed:** Acad.Ind., Biog.Ind., Consum.Ind., DAAI, Mag.Ind., Media Rev.Dig., PMR, PSI, R.G., R.G.Abstr., TOM. **Document type:** consumer publication.
—BLDSC (9251.415000); KR SourceOne; SWETS; UMI; UnCover.
Description: Features current trends in haute couture; advance information on the international fashion scene.

640 UK ISSN 0262-2130
VOGUE. 1916. m. £33 (rest of Europe and N. America £54; elsewhere £60). Conde Nast Publications Ltd., Vogue House, Hanover Sq., London W1R OAD, England. TEL 44-171-499-9080. FAX 44-171-493-1345. E-mail: pluard@condenast.co.uk; URL: http://www.condenast.co.uk/vogue. (Subscr. to: Quadrant Subscription Services, Oakfield House, Perrymount Rd., Haywards Heath, W. Sussex RH16 3DH, England. TEL 44-1444-445432) Ed. Alexandra Shulman; Pub. Stephen Quinn. adv.; bk.rev.; illus. circ. 188,669. **Indexed:** DAAI, GdIns. **Document type:** consumer publication.
●Also available online.

640 AT ISSN 0042-8019
VOGUE AUSTRALIA. 1959. 12/yr. Aus.$60 (foreign Aus.$110) (effective 1996). Conde Nast Publications Pty. Ltd., 170 Pacific Highway, Greenwich, N.S.W. 2065, Australia. TEL 61-2-99643888. FAX 61-2-99605938. Ed. Nancy Pilcher; Pub. Lesley Wild. R&P contact: Patricia Watson. adv. contact: Jane Purves. bk.rev. circ. 70,660. **Indexed:** GdIns. **Document type:** consumer publication.

646 IT ISSN 1120-7787
VOGUE BAMBINI. bi-m. L.43200 (foreign L.75900). Edizioni Conde Nast S.p.A., Piazza Castello 27, 20121 Milan, Italy. TEL 39-2-85611. FAX 39-2-8055716. Ed. G. Parabiago. adv.: page L.9200000. circ. 18,000. **Indexed:** DAAI. **Document type:** consumer publication.

640 TT500 IT ISSN 0042-8027
VOGUE ITALIA. 1950. m. L.80000 (foreign L.146800). Edizioni Conde Nast S.p.A., Piazza Castello 27, 20121 Milan, Italy. TEL 39-2-85611. FAX 39-2-8055716. TELEX 313454. Ed. Franca Sozzani. adv.: page L.25000000. illus. circ. 73,773. **Document type:** consumer publication.
—SWETS.

646.4 TT500 US ISSN 0095-2788
VOGUE PATTERNS. British edition (ISSN 0142-338X) 1915. bi-m. $12.95 (effective 1997-1998). Butterick Co., Inc., 161 Ave. of the Americas, New York, NY 10013. TEL 212-620-2500. (Subscr. to: 2900 Beale Ave., Altoona, PA 16603. TEL 800-766-3619) Ed. Jan Watkins. adv.; illus. circ. 225,000. **Document type:** consumer publication.
Formerly: (until 1972): Vogue Pattern Book International (ISSN 0042-8043)

746.92 685.2 IT ISSN 1120-7795
VOGUE PELLE. 2/yr. L.19200 (foreign L.31300). Edizioni Conde Nast S.p.A., Piazza Castello 27, 20121 Milan, Italy. TEL 39-2-85611. FAX 39-2-8055716. Ed. A. Premoli. adv.: page L.9200000. circ. 13,000. **Document type:** consumer publication.

VOGUE SPOSA. see *MATRIMONY*

746.92   US   ISSN 0162-9115
TT500
W. European edition: W. Europe. 1971. m. $29.90 (European ed. $45) (effective 1996). Fairchild Publications, Fashion & Merchandising Group (Subsidiary of: Capital Cities - A B C, Inc.), 7 W. 34th St., New York, NY 10001. TEL 212-630-4230. FAX 212-630-4000. Ed. Michael F. Coady. adv.; bk.rev.; illus.; index. circ. 226,321. (also avail. in microfilm from FCM) **Indexed:** Access (1975-). **Document type:** trade publication.
  Incorporates (1987-1988): Scene (New York).

746.92   MY   ISSN 0126-544X
WANITA. m. M.2.50. Utusan Melayu (Malaysia) Berhad, 46 M Jalan Chan Sow Lin, Kuala Lumpur, Malaysia. Ed.Bd. adv.; charts; illus.

746.96   AU
WELT DER FRAU.* m. Verlag Welt der Frau, Spiegelgasse 3-11, A-1010 Vienna, Austria. Ed. Baerbl Glaeser. circ. 79,500.

659.152   KO
WOLGAN MOT. 1984. m. Dong-A Ilbo, 139 Sejongno, Chongno-gu, Seoul, S. Korea. TEL 02-721-7114. Ed. Kwon O-Kie. circ. 120,000.

646.4   JA
WOMAN BOUTIQUE. (Text in Japanese) 1979. bi-m. Kodansha Ltd., 12-21 Otowa 2-chome, Bunkyo-ku, Tokyo 112, Japan. TEL 03-5395-3445. FAX 03-3945-4821. TELEX J34509 KODANSHA. Ed. Takashi Sasagawa. circ. 150,000. **Document type:** consumer publication.
  Description: Fashion and sewing magazine for women.

746.92   CC   ISSN 1002-7920
XIANDAI FUZHUANG/MODERN CLOTHES. (Text in Chinese) bi-m. Qinggongye Chubanshe, 25 Nanhebin Lu, Guang'anmen, Beijing 100055, People's Republic of China. TEL 366773. Ed. Wang Zhao.

XPRESS. see ART

YGIA KAI OMORPHIA/HEALTH AND BEAUTY. see PHYSICAL FITNESS AND HYGIENE

ZEITSPIEGEL FRAU. see WOMEN'S INTERESTS

746.92   US
ZHONGGUO FUZHUANG/CHINA GARMENTS. (Text in Chinese) q. $21.90. China Books & Periodicals, Inc., 2929 24th St., San Francisco, CA 94110. TEL 415-282-2994. FAX 415-282-0994.

746.92   US
ZHONGGUO SHIZHUANG/FASHION IN CHINA. (Text in Chinese) bi-m. Zhongguo Shizhuang Zazhishe, 82 Dong'anmen Dajie, Beijing 100747, People's Republic of China. TEL 5125588. Ed. Ma Jun.

746.92   CC
ZHONGWAI FUZHUANG/CHINESE & FOREIGN GARMENTS. (Text in Chinese) q. $19.50. Dalian Fuzhuang Yanjiusuo - Dalian Garment Design Institute, 889 Changjiand Lu, Dalian, Liaoning 116021, People's Republic of China. TEL 443638. (Dist. in US by: China Books & Periodicals, Inc., 2929 24th St., San Francisco, CA 94110. TEL 415-282-2994)

646   RU   ISSN 0321-1576
ZHURNAL MOD. (Supplement avail.: Modeli Sezona (ISSN 0132-0793) 1945. 4/yr. 26000 Rub. Joint-stock Company Fashion Journal, Kuznetskii Most, 7-9, 103031 Moscow, Russia. TEL 7-95-9217393. FAX 7-95-9287793. Ed. N.A. Kasatkina. adv.; illus.; pat.; index. circ. 100,000.
  Description: Covers modern fashion styles for different ages and sizes; fashion trends. Provides knitting instructions and patterns.

687.13   IT
3 BABY COLLEZIONI. s-a. $67 (effective Jan. 1997). Zanfi Editori s.r.l., Via Emilia Ovest 954, 41100 Modena, Italy. TEL 39-59-891700. FAX 39-59-891701. E-mail: zanfi.editori@mo.nettuno.it. (back issues avail.)
  Description: Presents fashions for babies up to 3 years old.

0 ANS. see WOMEN'S INTERESTS

2029 MAGAZIN. see PHOTOGRAPHY

CLUBS

see also College and Alumni

327   IS
A B C MAGAZINE INTERNATIONAL. (Text in English) 1971. m. $12. International Free-Lancers' Organization, c/o Uri Paz, Ed., 45 Palmach St., Rishon-le-Zion, Israel. (Subscr. to: Box 26424, Tel Aviv, Israel) adv.; bk.rev. circ. 35,000.

A H E P A N. (American Hellenic Educational Progressive Association) see ETHNIC INTERESTS

A L A WORLDWIDE DIRECTORY AND FACT BOOK. (American Logistics Association) see MILITARY

A M B A NEWS. (Australian Multiple Birth Association Inc.) see CHILDREN AND YOUTH — About

367   US
A M B U C S. (American Business Clubs) 1923. q. $8 (effective 1997). A M B U C S, Box 5127, High Point, NC 27262. TEL 910-869-2166. FAX 910-887-8451. E-mail: ambucs@hte.infi.net; URL: http://www.ambucs.com. Ed. J. Joseph Copeland. adv.; B&W page $600. circ. 6,500.
  Description: News and information for officers and members. Dedicated to creating independence and opportunities for people with disabilities.

A V A CHECKPOINT. (American Volkssport Association) see PHYSICAL FITNESS AND HYGIENE

367   US
ACRON. a. Lambda Kappa Mu, c/o Mrs. Marie Leatheman, 503 Trowbridge, Detroit, MI 48202-1341.

ADCLUBBER. see ADVERTISING AND PUBLIC RELATIONS

AGRADOOT. see CHILDREN AND YOUTH — About

790.1   TS
AL-AHLY. (Text in Arabic) 1972. m. membership. Al-Ahly Club, P.O. Box 1551, Dubai, United Arab Emirates. TEL 660528. Ed. Abdullah al-Ewais. circ. 500.
  Description: Covers sports and club activities.

371.83   US
ALBRICIAS. 1957. q. free. Sociedad Honoraria Hispanica, c/o Frederick N. Raile, William Workman High School, 16303 E. Temple Ave., City of Industry, CA 91744. TEL 818-867-1166. (Orders to: Dr. Frank M. Figueroa, Collegium of Comparative Cultures, Eckerd College, St. Petersburg, FL 33733) circ. 700. (tabloid format)

367 790.1   GR
ALLELOGRAPHIA WORLDWIDE; publication for international correspondence-hobby exchange personal acquaintance. (Text mainly in English; occasionally in French, Greek) 1967. q. $6. P.O. Box 80.200, GR-185 10, Piraeus, Greece. (Or: Box 70, Coburg 3058, Australia) Ed. Stavros Varonakis. adv. circ. 5,000.

658.048   US
ALTERNATIVE AMERICA. 1974. s-a. $29.95. Box 1067, St. Harvard Sq. Sta., Cambridge, MA 02238-1067. TEL 617-623-3795. FAX 617-876-8186. Ed. Richard Gardner. bk.rev. circ. 1,500. (reprint service avail.)
  Formerly: Resources (Cambridge).

AMERICAN FANCY RAT AND MOUSE ASSOCIATION YEARBOOK. see PETS

369.1   US   ISSN 1062-4244
AMERICAN LEGION AUXILIARY. NATIONAL NEWS. 1921. bi-m. $7 to non-members. American Legion Auxiliary, 777 N. Meridian St., 3rd Fl., Indianapolis, IN 46204. TEL 317-635-6291. FAX 317-636-5590. Ed. Lauralyn T. Mohr. R&P contact: Lauralyn T. Mohr. adv.: B&W page $9763, color page $13860; trim 8 1/8 x 10 7/8; adv. contact: Thomas Bowman. circ. 857,000. **Document type:** trade publication.

355.1   US   ISSN 0002-9734
D570.A1
AMERICAN LEGION MAGAZINE. 1919. m. $15 to non-members; members $3. Box 1055, Indianapolis, IN 46206. TEL 317-630-1200. FAX 317-630-1280. Eds. Joe Stuteville, Diane Andretti; Pub. Steve Salerno. R&P contact: Joan Berzins. adv.; charts; illus. circ. 2,800,000. (also avail. in microfilm from UMI; reprint service avail. from UMI) **Indexed:** HRIS, Mag.Ind., P.A.I.S., PSI. **Document type:** consumer publication.
●Also available online. Vendor(s): UMI.

AMERICAN LEGION PRESS ASSOCIATION NEWS-LETTER. see JOURNALISM

THE AMERICAN WANDERER. see PHYSICAL FITNESS AND HYGIENE

371.85   US
ANCHORA. 1884. q. membership. Delta Gamma Fraternity, 3250 Riverside Dr., Columbus, OH 43221. TEL 614-481-8169. FAX 614-481-0133. Ed. Laurie Watson. circ. 95,000.

ANNEE SPORTIVE U.S.M.T.. see SPORTS AND GAMES

367   US
ARCHON. 1945. s-a. $6. Zeta Phi Beta, 1734 New Hampshire Ave. N.W., Washington, DC 20009-1595. TEL 202-387-3103. Ed. Sharon Hardin. circ. 10,000.
  Description: Serves as the official magazine of Zeta Phi Beta Sorority Inc.

367 917.306   US
ARKANSAS LEGIONNAIRE. 1921. q. $0.80. Arkansas Legionnaire, Box 3280, 702 Victory St., AR 72203. TEL 501-375-1104. FAX 501-375-4236. Ed. R.A. Stewart. adv. circ. 30,000. **Document type:** newspaper.

366.1   UK   ISSN 0066-7900
ARS QUATUOR CORONATORUM; transaction of the Quatuor Coronati Lodge of Research. 1888. a. $30 membership. Q.C. Correspondence Circle Ltd., 60 Great Queen St., London WC2B 5BA, England. TEL 44-171-405-7340. FAX 44-171-404-8131. Ed. R.A. Gilbert. R&P contact: C.J. Carter. bk.rev.; index. circ. 15,000. **Document type:** academic/scholarly publication.

AURORA. see GEOGRAPHY

369.5   AT
AUSTRALIAN JUNIOR CHAMBER. vol.3, 1973. 4/yr. Aus.$4. Australian Junior Chamber, 6 Thesiger Court, Deakin, A.C.T. 2600, Australia. TEL 61-6-281-1066. FAX 61-6-281-4709. Ed. Judith Eadon. adv.; circ. 3,000 (controlled). (tabloid format) **Document type:** newsletter.
  Former titles: Australian Jaycee (ISSN 0725-3133); Enterprise (Deakin).
  Description: Lists events and membership information.

658   AT
AUSTRALIAN JUNIOR CHAMBER NATIONAL DIRECTORY. 1970. a. Aus.$2. Australian Junior Chamber, 6 Thesiger Court, Deakin A.C.T. 2600, Australia. TEL 61-6-281-1066. FAX 61-6-281-4709. **Document type:** directory.
  Formerly: Australian Jaycees National Directory.

AUTO UND VERKEHR. see TRANSPORTATION — Automobiles

367   US
AUTUMN LEAVES. q. $5. National Federation of Grandmother Clubs of America, Box 786, Wauconda, IL 60084-0786. TEL 847-526-4811. **Document type:** newsletter.

367   GW   ISSN 0724-1631
BAGATELLE; Mind- und Mensa-Magazin. 1979. bi-m. DM.32 membership. Kapuzinerstr. 7, 94032 Passau, Germany. TEL 0851-2510. Ed. Hans D. Lippmann. adv.; bk.rev. circ. 2,800. **Document type:** bulletin.

1930 CLUBS

658.048 US
BARBARA EDEN'S OFFICIAL FAN CLUB NEWSLETTER. 1977. irreg. $15. Barbara Eden Official Fan Club, Box 5556, Sherman Oaks, CA 91403. Ed. Kathy Bartels. circ. 320. (looseleaf format) **Document type:** newsletter.
Formerly: Barbara Eden International Fan Club Newsletter.
Description: Follows career of actress Barbara Eden through her film, television and theater reviews.

BEATLES: GOOD DAY SUNSHINE. see *MUSIC*

BENNIES. see *MILITARY*

367 GW ISSN 0005-9269
BERLINER BAER. 1956. 4/yr. DM.18. Bund der Berliner und Freunde Berlins e.V., Augustinergasse 2, 52064 Aachen, Germany. TEL 49-241-35973. FAX 49-241-27165. Ed. Heilwig Mulot. bk.rev.; abstr. circ. 5,000. **Document type:** bulletin.

BILLIE JO WILLIAMS INTERNATIONAL FAN CLUB. see *MUSIC*

BLAETTER - REVUE - RIVISTA. see *EDUCATION — Teaching Methods And Curriculum*

BORUSSEN-ECHO; Monatsblatt mit freier Meinungsaeusserung. see *COLLEGE AND ALUMNI*

367 US ISSN 0006-8306
BOUMI TEMPLE NEWS. 1936. m. $5. Boumi Temple A.A.O.N.M.S., Oasis of Baltimore, 4900 Charles St., Baltimore, MD 21210. TEL 410-435-1600. FAX 410-433-2995. Ed. William F. Wells. adv. circ. 8,100. **Document type:** newsletter.

369.4 US
BOY SCOUTS OF AMERICA. ANNUAL REPORT TO THE NATION. 1917. a. free. Boy Scouts of America, Box 152079, Irving, TX 75015-2079. TEL 972-580-2000. FAX 972-580-2079. Ed. Ray Sleater; Pub. J. Warren Young. circ. 4,000. **Document type:** consumer publication.
Formerly: Boy Scouts of America. Annual Report to Congress.

BOYS' LIFE (BRAILLE EDITION). see *HANDICAPPED — Visually Impaired*

BOYS' LIFE (INKPRINT EDITION). see *CHILDREN AND YOUTH — For*

BRIEFLY SPEAKING. see *LAW*

367 SP
BROTS DE COLLCEROLA. (Text in Catalan) 1970. irreg., no.62, 1994. C.E.A. Aliga de Vallvidrera, Mont d'Orsa 17, 08017 Barcelona, Spain. Ed. Josep Morero. play rev.; abstr.; illus.; pat.; circ. 150 (controlled).

BUFFALO. see *CHILDREN AND YOUTH — About*

367 US
BUGLE CALL. bi-m. Ladies of the Grand Army of the Republic, 17 Trail Ridge Rd. 3305 W., Kiva Ct., E8, Edmond, OK 73034. TEL 309-685-9462.

366 FR
BULLETIN DES ANYSETIERS. bi-m. Ordre International des Anysetiers, 76-78 Champs Elysees, 75008 Paris, France. TEL 1-42-25-30-68. FAX 1-45-62-11-51.

367 US ISSN 0747-1866
C A C JOURNAL. 1908. 12/yr. 1118 Euclid Ave., Cleveland, OH 44115-1603. TEL 216-621-8900. FAX 216-621-3864. Ed. Robert W. Gibb. adv. circ. 1,500.

267.242 US ISSN 0007-8530
C K OF A JOURNAL. 1897. m. $4.20 (effective 1996). Catholic Knights of America, 1850 Dalton Ave., Cincinnati, OH 45214. TEL 513-721-0781. FAX 513-721-0783. Ed. Richard J. Berning; Pub. Richard J. Berning. circ. 9,600 (controlled). **Document type:** bulletin.

367 US
CALIFORNIA CLUBWOMAN.* 1909. s-m. $1. California Federation of Women's Clubs, 837 Glenn Ave., N., Fresno, CA 93728. TEL 209-264-3690. Ed. Fred H. Ellis. adv. circ. 20,000.

366 US
CALIFORNIA ODD FELLOW AND REBEKAH. 1949. bi-m. $4 in U.S. and Canada; elsewhere $6 (effective 1996). (Independent Order of Odd Fellows, California Lodge) Linden Publications, Box 129, Linden, CA 95236. TEL 209-887-3829. FAX 209-887-3829. E-mail: dons@inreach.com. Ed. Don R. Smith. circ. 9,649 (paid). (back issues avail.) **Document type:** newsletter.
Description: Fraternal publication serving Odd Fellows and Rebekahs in California.

CALLIGRAPHER. see *HOBBIES*

369.4 FR ISSN 0397-5266
CAMARADERIE.* 1945. 6/yr. 15 F. Federation des Francs et Franches Camarades, 10-14 rue Tolian, 75020 Paris, France. TEL 43-67-40-00. FAX 43-67-28-29. Ed. Claude Goecckle. bk.rev.; play rev.; illus. circ. 35,000.

CE MOIS-CI A L'ALLIANCE. see *EDUCATION*

369.5 IT
CENTOOTTO A. bi-m. (Lions International, Distretto 108-A) Gruppo Editoriale Faenza Editrice S.p.A., Via Pier. de Crescenzi 44, 48018 Faenza RA, Italy. TEL 39-546-663688. FAX 39-546-660440. E-mail: gefe.vendita@uno.dinamica.it; gefe.info@uno.dinamica.it. adv.: B&W page Lit.1080000. circ. 4,000 (controlled).

658.048 US
CHERRY DIAMOND. 1907. m. $23. Missouri Athletic Club, 405 Washington Ave., St. Louis, MO 63102. TEL 314-231-7220. FAX 314-231-2327. Eds. Daniel A. Kimack, Brian Gravette. adv. circ. 4,800.

CHORMAGAZIN. see *MUSIC*

CHRISTIAN BALE FAN CLUB. NEWSLETTER. see *CHILDREN AND YOUTH — For*

CHRISTIAN COURIER. see *RELIGIONS AND THEOLOGY — Protestant*

366 FR
CHRONIQUE DES ANYSETIERS. no.63, 1981. m. membership. Ordre International des Anysetiers, 76-78 Champs Elysees, 75008 Paris, France. TEL 1-42-25-30-68. FAX 1-45-62-11-51. illus.
Formerly: Ordre International des Anysetiers. Chronique.

366.1 FR ISSN 0240-7418
CHRONIQUES D'HISTOIRE MACONNIQUE. (Supplement to: Humanisme) (Text in French) 1980. a. 125 F. (Francs-Macons du Grand Orient, Institut d'Etudes et de Recherches Maconniques) Editions Maconniques de France, 16 rue Cadet, 75009 Paris, France. TEL 47-70-27-15. Ed. Roger Viry-Babal. bk.rev. circ. 1,500. **Document type:** academic/scholarly publication.

371.85 US
CIRCUMFERENCE. 1937. q. free. Phi Epsilon Phi Sorority, Box 4096, Burlingame, CA 94011-4096. TEL 415-347-1765. Ed. Barbara Mehan. adv. circ. 500. (looseleaf format; back issues avail.) **Document type:** newsletter.

367 US ISSN 0194-5785
CIVITAN MAGAZINE. 1920. 6/yr. $6. Civitan International, Box 130744, Birmingham, AL 35213-0744. TEL 205-591-8910. FAX 205-592-6307. Ed. Dorothy Wellborn. adv.; bk.rev.; illus.; circ. 37,000 (controlled).

367 UK ISSN 0009-952X
CLUB AND INSTITUTE JOURNAL. m. 96p. Working Men's Club and Institute Union Ltd., Progress House, 418 Chester Rd., Manchester M16 9HP, England. Ed. Frank Morris. adv. circ. 50,166.

367 UK ISSN 0009-9538
CLUB COMMITTEE & NORTHERN FREE TRADE NEWS.* 1967. m. 55s. Provincial Trade Press Ltd., 320 Higher Lane, Lymm, Cheshire, England. adv.; abstr.; illus.
Formerly: Northern Club Trade News.

367 US ISSN 1050-8600
CLUB DIRECTOR. 1962. 6/yr. $15. National Club Association, One Lafayette Center, 1120 20th St., N.W., Ste. 725, Washington, DC 20036. TEL 202-822-9822. FAX 202-822-9808. Ed. Mary Barnes Embody. R&P contact: Mary Barnes Embody. adv. contact: Bruce Hambro. bk.rev.; circ. 8,500 (controlled). **Document type:** trade publication.
Description: Covers strategic planning, policies and procedures, taxation and capital improvements, industry trends, and financial and personnel management for officers, directors and managers of private clubs.

658.048 GW
CLUB-ILLUSTRIERTE. 1949. a. membership. Tennisclub Weissenhof e.V., Parlerstr. 102-110, 70192 Stuttgart, Germany. TEL 0711-1654321. FAX 0711-2572933. Ed. Walter Schweiker. adv. circ. 4,000. **Document type:** newsletter.

CLUB LIVING. see *SPORTS AND GAMES*

367 US ISSN 0009-9589
CLUB MANAGEMENT; the resource for successful club operations. 1922. bi-m. $21.95 (foreign $45) (effective 1997). (Club Managers Association of America) Finan Publishing, 8730 Big Bend Blvd., St. Louis, MO 63119. TEL 314-961-6644. FAX 314-961-4809. E-mail: tgowran@finan.com; URL: http://www.club-mgmt.com. Ed. Teri Gowran; Pub. Thomas J. Finan. adv. contact: Dee Kaplan. illus.; tr.lit. circ. 16,600. (also avail. in microform from UMI) **Indexed:** Account.Ind. (1974-), Hospit.Ind., Lod.Restr.& Tour.Ind. **Document type:** trade publication.
●Also available online. Vendor(s): UMI.
—UMI.
Description: Designed to provide information and ideas to the managers of all types of private clubs.

CLUB MANAGEMENT IN AUSTRALIA. see *BUSINESS AND ECONOMICS — Management*

367 UK ISSN 0045-7213
CLUB MIRROR; the national trade newspaper. 1968. m. £32. Quantam Publishing Ltd., 29-31 Lower Coombe St., Croydon CR9 0LX, England. TEL 0181-681-2099. FAX 0181-681-2389. Ed. Dominic Roskrow; Pub. Sarah Jones. adv. contact: Lorraine Wood. bk.rev.; illus.; stat.; circ. 25,855 (controlled). (tabloid format) **Document type:** trade publication.
—CCC.
Description: Advises owners and managers about how to operate clubs.

367 UK ISSN 0009-9635
CLUB SECRETARY. 1953. m. £18($85) United Trade Press Ltd., U.T.P. House, 33-35 Bowling Green Lane, London EC1R 0DA, England. TEL 01-837 1212. Ed. Sharon Gailer. adv.; bk.rev.; illus.; tr.lit.; index. circ. 8,408.

367 200 US
CLUBS & ORGANIZATIONS. 1989. m. $25. Creative Consultants, 150 S. 38th St., Box 31097, Omaha, NE 68131. TEL 402-554-1800. adv.: B&W page $960. **Document type:** newspaper.
Description: Covers the past & upcoming organizational & community events. Provides comprehensive calendar of events.

367 US
CO-ETTE MAGAZINE. 1955. a. $10. Co-Ette Club, Inc., 2020 W. Chicago Blvd., Detroit, MI 48206. TEL 313-867-0880. Ed. Mary Agnes Mill Davis. adv. circ. 500.
Description: Reports on the annual program of the organization and highlights the accomplishments of people associated with the club.

367 US ISSN 1059-132X
COLUMBIAN (INDIANAPOLIS). 1906. 10/yr. $36. Columbia Club, 121 Monument Circle, Indianapolis, IN 46204. TEL 317-635-1361. FAX 317-638-3137. Ed. Rachel Daeger. adv. circ. 3,000.

CLUBS

367 615   US   ISSN 0746-3979
COMMUNICATOR. 1889. q. $10. Phi Delta Chi Pharmacy Fraternity, Box 6565, Athens, GA 30604-6565. TEL 706-613-0100. FAX 706-613-0200. E-mail: phidexnatl@aol.com; URL: http://www.umich.edu/~jbonnsso/pdcnew/home.htm. Ed. David Karls. R&P contact: Anthony D. Chaffee△; adv. contact: David Karls. circ. 4,500. (back issues avail.) **Document type:** trade publication.

CORRESPONDENT (APPLETON). see *INSURANCE*

CROSS; national Catholic magazine. see *RELIGIONS AND THEOLOGY — Roman Catholic*

CUBE. see *LITERATURE — Science Fiction, Fantasy, Horror*

796   US   ISSN 0011-4707
D A C NEWS. 1916. 9/yr. $36. Detroit Athletic Club, 241 Madison Ave., Detroit, MI 48226. TEL 313-963-5993. FAX 313-963-8891. Ed. John A. Bluth; Pub. John A. Bluth. adv.: B&W page $705, color page $1365; trim 8 5/8 x 11 1/4; adv. contact: Albert C. Cochrane. circ. 4,000.
    Description: Features news about social and athletic events, entertainment, membership approvals, membership listing and club activities.

371.85   GW   ISSN 0011-5193
D W V - MITTEILUNGEN. 1951. q. DM.1.50 to non-members per no. Deutscher Wissenschaftler Verband, Hoehlenweg 31, 38642 Goslar, Germany. Ed. Hans Heinz Vogel. circ. 1,700.

367   US
DAEDALUS FLYER. 1959. q. membership. Daedalian Foundation, Box 249, Randolph A F B, TX 78148-0249. TEL 210-945-2113. Ed. Clem E. Bellion. R&P contact: Clem E. Bellion. circ. 17,000. **Document type:** academic/scholarly publication.
    Description: Contains historical articles, features, and membership news.

DANISH SISTERHOOD NEWS. see *ETHNIC INTERESTS*

DATA EXTRACT. see *COMMUNICATIONS — Television And Cable*

367   US   ISSN 0164-8314
DEKE QUARTERLY. 1883. q. membership. Delta Kappa Epsilon Fraternity, Inc., 35 McKinley Place, Grosse Pte Farms, MI 48236. TEL 313-886-2400. FAX 313-8862227. Ed. David K. Easlick, Jr. adv.; bk.rev.; circ. 25,000 (controlled).
    Description: News and feature articles concerning the activities and members of Delta Kappa Epsilon fraternity.

367   GW
DEUTSCHES DISCOTHEKEN JAHRBUCH. 1993. a. DM.48 (foreign DM.56). Verlag Disco Post GmbH, Oststr. 2, 56424 Staudt, Germany. TEL 49-2602-70044. FAX 49-2602-69939. Ed. Karl-Heinz Busch. R&P contact: Karl-Heinz Busch. adv.: B&W page DM.1250, color page DM.1875; trim 120 x 180; adv. contact: Karin Ostrowski. circ. 10,000. (back issues avail.) **Document type:** directory.

367   US
DICKIN' AROUND. 1986. q. membership. (Dicks of America) Sunsponges Publishing, Box 600782, San Diego, CA 92160. TEL 619-582-5783. FAX 619-582-1750. Ed. Dick Monaco. circ. 5,500. **Document type:** newsletter.
    Description: Contains messages from the founders of this club catering to persons named Richard or any of its variations, as well as special product offerings.

DIRECTORY OF AMERICAN YOUTH ORGANIZATIONS (YEAR); a guide to 500 clubs, groups, troops, teams, societies, lodges, and more for young people. see *CHILDREN AND YOUTH — For*

DIRECTORY OF PROFESSIONAL ASSOCIATION AND LEARNED SOCIETIES IN HONG KONG. see *BUSINESS AND ECONOMICS — Trade And Industrial Directories*

367   GW   ISSN 0179-3020
DISCO POST. 1981. m. DM.48 (U.S. DM.120). Verlag Disco Post GmbH, Oststr. 2, 56424 Staudt, Germany. TEL 49-2602-70044. FAX 49-2602-69939. Ed. Karl-Heinz Busch. R&P contact: Karl-Heinz Busch. adv.: B&W page DM.2550, color page DM.3825; trim 190 x 255; adv. contact: Karin Ostrowski. circ. 20,000. (back issues avail.) **Document type:** trade publication.

DOMINANT NEWSLETTER. see *PSYCHOLOGY*

796   US   ISSN 0046-0656
DOWNTOWN ATHLETIC CLUB JOURNAL. 1932. m. $20. Downtown Athletic Club of New York, Inc., 19 West St., New York, NY 10004. TEL 212-425-7000. Ed. Margaret B. Koenig. adv.; charts; illus. circ. 3,500.

371.85   US
TO DRAGMA. 1897. q. $30. Alpha Omicron Pi Fraternity, Inc., 9025 Overlook Blvd., Brentwood, TN 37027. TEL 615-370-0920. Ed. Mariellen Sasseen. circ. 70,000.
    Description: Provides news in the fraternity and Greek world in general

367   US
DRY CREEK VALLEY NEWS. irreg. (4-6/yr). Dry Creek Valley Association, Box 1221, Healdsburg, CA 95448. TEL 707-433-1120. adv.
    Description: Covers community news and activities.

367   SA   ISSN 0012-7221
DURBAN HIGH SCHOOL OLD BOYS' CLUB. BULLETIN. 1945. bi-m. Durban High School Old Boys' Club, 20 Gainsborough Dr., Box 20092, Durban North 4016, South Africa. Ed. R.E. Ronaldson. adv.; abstr.; illus.; stat. circ. 2,000. **Document type:** bulletin.

DYNAMITE INTERNATIONAL. see *MUSIC*

366   US
EAGLE LEADER. m. membership only. (Fraternal Order of Eagles) F O E Publications, Box 25916, Milwaukee, WI 53225-0916. TEL 414-781-7585. FAX 414-781-5046. (Street addr.: 12660 W. Capitol Dr., Brookfield, WI 53005-2427) Ed. Robert W. Hansen.

366   US   ISSN 0012-8090
EAGLE MAGAZINE. 1913. q. $1 membership only. Fraternal Order of Eagles, Box 25916, Milwaukee, WI 53225-0916. TEL 414-781-7585. FAX 414-781-5046. Ed. Peter N. Ehrman. circ. 971,000. **Document type:** newsletter.
    Description: Covers news, events and activities of the Fraternal Order of Eagles.

366   US   ISSN 0046-1067
ECHO (SKOKIE). 1878. q. membership only. United Order True Sisters, Inc., c/o Mrs. Joanne F. Caldara, Ed., 212 Fifth Ave., New York, NY 10016. TEL 212-679-6790. charts; illus.; circ. 12,000 (controlled). **Indexed:** GeoRef.

ED: ONE CLUB, ONE HORSE, ONE WORLD. see *COMMUNICATIONS — Television And Cable*

EDSELETTER. see *TRANSPORTATION — Automobiles*

301.4157   US
EDUCATIONAL T V CHANNEL NEWSLETTER. 1982. bi-m. $20 membership. (Educational T V Channel) E T V C, Box 426486, San Francisco, CA 94142. TEL 510-549-2665. adv.; bk.rev.; circ. 650. (back issues avail.) **Document type:** newsletter.
    Description: Membership newsletter of a social and support group of and for transvestites, transsexuals, transgenderists, their spouses and friends.

EL PASO ARCHAEOLOGY. see *ARCHAEOLOGY*

366.5   US   ISSN 0013-6263
HS1510.E4
ELKS MAGAZINE. 1922. 10/yr. $5 to non-members. Benevolent and Protective Order of Elks of the United States of America, 425 W. Diversey Pkwy., Chicago, IL 60614. TEL 713-528-4500. FAX 713-528-0433. Ed. Fred D. Oakes. adv.; illus. circ. 1,250,975.
    Description: Contains general-interest feature articles and news of the Elks fraternity. Covers health, business, retirement, and travel.

367 780   US
ELVIS NOW FAN CLUB. 1973. q. $11 (foreign $15). Box 6581, San Jose, CA 95150. TEL 408-745-7077. Ed. Sue McCasland. adv.; bk.rev. circ. 356. (back issues avail.) **Document type:** newsletter.

ELVIS WORLD. see *MUSIC*

366.1   US   ISSN 0013-6794
EMPIRE STATE MASON. 1923. q. $6 (foreign $15). Grand Lodge Free and Accepted Masons of the State of New York, Committee on Publications, 37 Oliver St., Lockport, NY 14094-4615. TEL 716-434-4946. FAX 716-434-4946. Ed. Ronald Bower. adv.; bk.rev.; circ. 120,000 (controlled).
    Formerly (until 1952): Masonic Outlook.
    Refereed Serial

367   VE
ENCUENTROS. 1987. q. $16 (effective 1997). Asociacion Cultural Humboldt, Goethe-Institute, Av. J. Washington, c. Av. J. German Roscio, San Bernardino, Caracas, Venezuela. TEL 58-2-526445. FAX 58-2-525621. Ed. Henning Schroedter-Albers. R&P contact: Sandra Vetter-Ward. circ. 1,000. **Document type:** academic/scholarly publication.
    Description: Covers general social, cultural issues.

ETCH A SKETCH CLUB. NEWSLETTER. see *CHILDREN AND YOUTH — For*

EUROPHIL NEWS. see *PHILATELY*

367   US
EXCHANGE TODAY; an educational publication for Exchange Club members. 1921. bi-m. $6. National Exchange Club, 3050 Central Ave., Toledo, OH 43606. TEL 419-535-3232. FAX 419-535-1989. E-mail: nechq@aol.com; URL: http://rtpnet.org/~nec/. Ed. James R. Lazette; Pub. David R. Nershi. R&P contact: James R. Lazette. adv. contact: Ellie Williams. illus. circ. 35,000.
    Formerly (until 1997): Exchangite (ISSN 0014-4487)

658.048   US   ISSN 1081-1788
FAN CLUB DIRECTORY. a. $12 (foreign $17) (effective 1997). National Association of Fan Clubs, Box 7487, Burbank, CA 91510-7487. TEL 818-763-3280. FAX 818-752-4848. E-mail: lknafc@aol.com. Ed. Linda Kay. **Document type:** directory.
    Former titles: Fan Club Information Booklet Guide; Fan Club Spotlight.
    Description: Lists fan clubs from all over the world.

658.048   US   ISSN 1081-5538
THE FAN CLUB MONITOR. q. $10 membership (foreign $15). National Association of Fan Clubs, Box 7487, Burbank, CA 91510-7487. TEL 818-763-3280. FAX 818-752-4848. E-mail: lknafc@aol.com. Ed. Linda Kay. adv.: B&W page $80; 7 1/2 x 9 1/2. **Document type:** newsletter.
    Description: Provides a forum through which members can share information relating to fan club operation, and works to improve fan club standards.

369.5   IT
FIRMA. 1961. m. (10/yr.). (Diners Club d'Italia) S.E.E.S. s.r.l., Piazza San Lorenzo in Lucina, 40, 00186 Rome, Italy. TEL 06-6876549. FAX 06-6878737. TELEX 06-611344. Ed. Claudio Caporaso. adv.: B&W page L.10500000, color page L.15000000. bk.rev. circ. 220,000.

366 070.5   US
FOOTPRINTS (TEMPE). fortn. $100 to non-members. Evangelical Christian Publishers Association, 1969 E. Broadway Rd., Ste. 2, Tempe, AZ 85282-1731. TEL 602-966-3998. FAX 602-966-1944. E-mail: jmeegan@ecpa.org; URL: http://www.ecpa.org. Ed. Doug Ross. circ. 600. **Document type:** newsletter.
    Description: Association newsletter geared to publishing executives.

366   UK   ISSN 0015-7511
FORESTERS MISCELLANY. 1836. m. £5. Ancient Order of Foresters Friendly Society, College Pl., Southampton SO9 1FP, England. Ed. K.W. Anthony. adv.; bk.rev.; illus. circ. 6,000.

FRATERNAL LAW. see *LAW*

1932 CLUBS

658.048 US
FREE SONS REPORTER. 1912. s.-a. membership. Free Sons of Israel, 250 Fifth Ave., 2nd Fl., New York, NY 10001-6405. TEL 212-725-3690. FAX 212-725-5874. Ed. Leo Hoenig. adv. contact: Rudolph Gordon. circ. 5,000 (paid). **Document type:** newspaper.
Formerly: Free Son.
Description: Provides news of the fraternal benefit order's national bodies and subordinate lodges, as well as features about members, news on anti-semitism and Jewish interests.

369.5 US
FREE STATE WARRIOR. 1966. bi-m. $1.50. American Legion, Department of Maryland, Inc., The War Memorial, 101 N. Gay St., Baltimore, MD 21202. TEL 301-752-3104. FAX 301-752-3822. Ed. Paul F. Moran; Pub. Tom Davis. R&P contact: Tom Davis. TEL 410-752-1405. stat. circ. 90,000. (tabloid format)

FRIENDS OF JULIO INTERNATIONAL NEWSLETTER. see MUSIC

367 UK
FRIENDSHIP NEWS. 1931. 3/yr. £7 (effective 1997). International Friendship League (British Section), 3 Creswick Rd., Acton, London W3 9HE, England. TEL 0181-894-0664. Ed. M. Hewett. adv.: B&W page £100. bk.rev. circ. 1,100. **Document type:** newsletter.
Former titles: International Friendship League. Newsletter (ISSN 0020-6806); Friendship News.
Description: Contains news of events in Britain and overseas, along with news of society branches, including information on the I.F.L. Residential Centre, Peace Haven, service work, branch and membership news, and future events.

366 US
FRONTIERSMAN. 1948. q. membership. Frontiers International, 6301 Crittenden St., Philadelphia, PA 19188-1081. TEL 215-549-4550. Ed. Chas H. Clarke, Jr. circ. 1,200. (back issues avail.) **Document type:** newsletter.

367 US ISSN 0745-2209
HQ1871
G F W C CLUBWOMAN. 1897. bi-m. $6 (foreign $12). General Federation of Women's Clubs, 1734 N St., N.W., Washington, DC 20036. TEL 202-347-3168. Ed. Ellen Kranick. adv.; illus. circ. 20,000. **Document type:** trade publication.
Former titles (until 1978): Clubwoman News; (until 1976): General Federation Clubwoman (ISSN 0016-6537)
Description: Contains stories on projects and programs dealing with education, public affairs, conservation, home life, international affairs, and the arts.

367 US
G F W C OF MINNESOTA NEWS. 1912. 4/yr. membership. General Federation of Women's Clubs of Minnesota, Inc., 5701 Normandale Rd., Ste. 345, Minneapolis, MN 55424. TEL 612-920-2057. Ed. Jackie Barrett. R&P contact: Jackie Barrett. TEL 507-535-7883. adv.; circ. 3,900 (controlled). (back issues avail.) **Document type:** newsletter.
Formerly: Minnesota Clubwoman.
Refereed Serial

GAY AIRLINE & TRAVEL CLUB NEWSLETTER. see HOMOSEXUALITY

367 UK
GLOBE (LONDON). 1946. bi-m. £12($18) Globetrotters Club, BCM-Roving, London WC1N 3XX, England. Ed. Patti Taylor. R&P contact: Patti Taylor. adv. contact: Patti Taylor. bk.rev. circ. 1,500. (looseleaf format; back issues avail.) **Document type:** newsletter.
Description: Directed to those who swap travel information; advertising for travel companions for budget travel.

366 UK ISSN 0801-2547
THE GLOBE (ST. IVES). 1853. q. £7 (effective 1997). (International Assembly) International Organization of Good Templars (I.O.G.T.), Elmgren House, 1 The Quay, St. Ives, Cambs. PE1 4AR, England. TEL 44-1480-466766. E-mail: theglobe@ias.org.uk; URL: http://www.ias.org.uk/theglobe. (Globe Subscriptions, Institute of Alcohol Studies, Alliance House, 12 Caxton St., London SW1H OQS. TEL 44-171-222-4001. FAX 44-171-799-2510) Ed. Derek Rutherford. R&P contact: Derek Rutherford. bk.rev.; charts; illus.; index. circ. 2,200. **Indexed:** LISA.
Formerly (until 1974): International Organization of Good Templars Journal (ISSN 0020-8175)

GLOS POLEK/POLISH WOMENS' VOICE. see ETHNIC INTERESTS

371.85 CN
THE GOLDEN LINKS. 1962. 5/yr. Can.$7.50. Independent Order of Odd Fellows, 381 Parkway Blvd., Flin Flon, MB R8A 0K5, Canada. TEL 204-687-6120. Ed. Joyce C. Henderson. circ. 450. **Document type:** bulletin, newsletter.
Formerly: Golden Links Bulletin.

658.048 US
GRAND NEST BULLETIN. 1907. s.-a. free. Honorable Order of the Blue Goose International, 12940 Walnut Rd., Elm Grove, WI 53122. TEL 414-782-7608. Ed. T.M. Maloney. adv. circ. 10,000. (back issues avail.) **Document type:** bulletin.

GRANGE ADVOCATE. see AGRICULTURE

658.048 384.554 US
GUARDIAN ENGEL. 1971. m. $10 (foreign $15). Engel's Angels in Humperdinck Heaven Fan Club, 3024 Fourth Ave., Carney, Baltimore, MD 21234-3208. TEL 410-665-0744. Ed. Jean R. Marshalek. R&P contact: Jean Marshalek. circ. 95. (looseleaf format) **Document type:** newsletter.
Description: Established for the fans of Engelbert Humperdinck regarding his concerts, records, and club activities.

366 FR ISSN 1164-1975
GUIDE ANNUAIRE DES FONDATIONS ET DES ASSOCIATIONS.* Short title: G A F A. 1981. a. Editions S A 2, 94 rue Saint-Lazare, 75009 Paris, France. Ed. Bernard Descours.
Formerly: Guide Annuaire des Associations (ISSN 0759-4364)

658.048 US ISSN 0279-6694
GYROSCOPE. 1917. 4/yr. $2. Gyro International, 1096 Mentor Ave., Box 489, Painesville, OH 44077. FAX 216-352-3882. Ed. Leonard D. Cary. circ. 5,400.
Description: Contains news, information, and announcements about the Gyro International Friendship Fraternity (a male-oriented organization promoting friendship through constructive, coherent fellowship based on tolerance, good will, and helpfulness).

HADASSAH MAGAZINE. see ETHNIC INTERESTS

658.048 US
HELLO AGAIN. 1970. bi-m. $15. Jay Hickerson, Ed.& Pub., Box 4321, Hamden, CT 06514-0321. TEL 203-248-2887. FAX 203-281-1322. E-mail: jayhick@aol.com. adv.; bk.rev. circ. 400. (back issues avail.) **Document type:** newsletter.

790.1 US ISSN 1082-7536
HILL VALLEY TELEGRAPH. 1992. q. $20 membership (foreign $25) (effective 1997 &1998). (Back to the Future... The Fan Club) To Be Continued..., Box 880, Athens, AL 35612-0880. TEL 205-230-6288. FAX 205-230-6288. E-mail: time@traveller.com; URL: http://www.bttf.com/. Ed. Stephen M. Clark; Pub. Stephen M. Clark. R&P contact: Stephen M. Clark. adv. contact: Stephen M. Clark. bk.rev.; illus.; film rev.; software rev.; video rev. circ. 500. (back issues avail.) **Document type:** newsletter.
Description: Contains up-to-date news and information on the Back to the Future film series, featuring interviews with the cast and crew, and scientific studies and theories on time travel.

366 HO
HONDURAS ROTARIA. 1943. m. $10 (free in Honduras). Club Rotario de Tequcigalpa, Apdo. Postal 2240, Tegucigalpa, DC, Honduras. TEL 32-7505. FAX 33-1812. Ed. Rafael O. Castillo. adv.: B&W page $200, color page $300. bk.rev.; charts; illus. circ. 600.
Description: Covers topics of interest to Rotarians, and literary, historic, economic and social themes.

THE HOOK. see MILITARY

HOOSIER LEGIONNAIRE. see MILITARY

HOPPY TALK. see MOTION PICTURES

HORISONT. see LITERATURE

658.048 020 069 HU ISSN 0139-1380
HORIZONT; veszprem megyei kozmuvelodesi tajekoztato. 1973. q. 28 Ft.($1) Veszprem Megyei Tanacs V.B. Muvelodesi Osztaly, Lenin Ter. 5, 8201 Veszprem, Hungary. TEL 80 12-700. Ed. Toth Dezso. bk.rev.; index, cum.index. circ. 600. (back issues avail.)
Description: Provides information about methods in public culture in Veszprem country. Includes studies on new methods, events, reviews of cultural traditions.

366.1 FR ISSN 0018-7364
HUMANISME. (Supplement avail.: Chroniques d'Histoire Maconique) 1956. bi-m. 132 F. (Francs-Macons du Grand Orient de France, Institut des Etudes et Recherches Maconniques) Editions Maconniques de France, 16 rue Cadet, 75009 Paris, France. TEL 47-70-27-15. Ed. Roger Viry-Babal; Dir. P. Kessel. adv.; bk.rev.; play rev.; abstr. circ. 33,000. **Document type:** academic/scholarly publication.
Formerly: Bulletin du Centre de Documentation du Grand Orient de France.

I F C O CLUB HOUSE. see MUSIC

I F C O JOURNAL. (International Fan Club Organization) see MUSIC

367 NE ISSN 0018-9707
I F L NIEUWS. 1936. bi-m. fl.35 membership. International Friendship League, Nederlandlaan 1, 6414 HA Heerlen, Netherlands. Ed. H.M. v.d. Wijst-Koning; Pub. H.M. v.d. Wijst-Koning. R&P contact: H.M. v.d. Wijst-Koning. adv. circ. 300. **Document type:** newsletter.

367 US ISSN 0019-3569
I N D A C MAGAZINE. Key Title: Indac. 1921. bi-m. $20. Indianapolis Athletic Club, 350 North Meridian St., Indianapolis, IN 46204. TEL 317-634-4331. FAX 317-686-4155. Ed. Aimee Helton. adv.; illus.; circ. 3,500 (controlled).
Description: Informs the club's members of events and programs and promotes communication with the community.

780.42 US
IDOL OF MY HEART ELVIS PRESLEY FAN CLUB NEWSLETTER. 1973. m. $5. Idol of My Heart Elvis Presley Fan Club, c/o Genie Rasmussen, Pres., 3307 W. Marshall Ave., Phoenix, AZ 85017. TEL 602-841-9219. **Document type:** newsletter.

366.1 US ISSN 0019-6622
INDIANA FREEMASON. 1923. m. $8. Grand Lodge Free and Accepted Masons of Indiana, Box 38, Franklin, IN 46131. Ed. Dwight L. Smith. adv. circ. 8,500.

INTERFACE. see EDUCATION — Teaching Methods An Curriculum

366 US
INTERNATIONAL ODD FELLOW AND REBEKAH. 1892. bi-m. $4 in U.S. and Canada; elsewhere $6 (effective 1996). (Independent Order of Odd Fellows Sovereign Grand Lodge) Linden Publications, Box 129, Linden, CA 95236. TEL 209-887-3829. FAX 209-887-3829. E-mail: dons@inreach.com. (Co-sponsor: International Association of Rebekah) Ed. Don R. Smith. adv.; circ. 22,423 (paid). (back issues avail.) **Document type:** newsletter.
Formerly: International Rebekah News.
Description: Serves a family fraternity which sponsors youth activities, educational scholarships, retirement facilities and nursing homes.

CLUBS

658.048 780 US
INTERNATIONAL SINATRA SOCIETY NEWSLETTER. 1979. bi-m. $20 (foreign $25). International Sinatra Society, Box 7176, Lakeland, FL 33807-7176. TEL 813-646-7650. Ed. Dustin Doctor. adv.; bk.rev.; film rev. (back issues avail.) **Document type:** newsletter.
Description: Provides information on Frank Sinatra, including concert dates, records and CD's, reviews and articles.

500 UK
INTERNATIONAL SOROPTIMIST. 1973. q. £2.50($4) Soroptimist International, 87 Glisson Rd., Cambridge CB1 2HG, England. TEL 44-1223-311833. FAX 44-1223-467951. E-mail: sorophq@dial.pipex.com. Ed. Betty Loughhead-Turland. circ. 38,500. **Document type:** newsletter.
Description: Serves the 95,000 members of the Soroptimist Clubs in 112 countries; news of projects and work with the United Nations.

INTERSERVICE. see MILITARY

355.15 ISSN 0021-0560
IOWA LEGIONNAIRE. 1924. bi-m. $2 to non-members. American Legion, Department of Iowa, 720 Lyon, Des Moines, IA 50309. TEL 515-282-5068. Ed. James E. Demarest. adv. circ. 82,000. (tabloid format)

658.048 US
IOWA SIERRAN.* bi-m. $5 to non-members. Sierra Club, Iowa Chapter, R.R. 1 Box 38, Gilbert, IA 50105-9712. TEL 319-273-2761. Ed. Leigh Rigby-Adcock. adv.
Description: Provides information about club activities.

650 US
J C I NEWS. (Editions in Chinese, English, Finnish, French, German, Icelandic, Japanese, Korean, Spanish) 1962. q. Jaycees International, Junior Chamber International, 400 University Dr., Box 140577, Coral Gables, FL 33114-0577. TEL 305-446-7608. FAX 305-442-0041. Ed. Peggy Fisher; Pub. Benny Ellerbe. adv.; bk.rev.; charts; illus. circ. 300,000. **Document type:** trade publication.
—UMI.
Former titles: Leader (Coral Gables); J C I World (ISSN 0021-3578)

367 384.55 US
JACK BENNY TIMES.* 1982. 3/yr. Can.$6.39($6.39) (effective 1990). International Jack Benny Fan Club, 9461 Skyline Blvd., Oakland, CA 94611-1738. TEL 510-933-3879. FAX 510-210-3699. Ed. Laura Lee. adv. contact: Laura Lee. circ. 150 (paid). (back issues avail.) **Document type:** newsletter.
Description: Information and articles pertaining to Jack Benny and his associates; purpose to further the comedy of Jack Benny and provide a channel for its acquisition.

369.5 US ISSN 0893-0031
JAYCEES MAGAZINE. 1938. q. $10 to non-members. United States Jaycees, 4 W. 21st St., Box 7, Tulsa, OK 74102-0007. TEL 918-584-2481. FAX 918-584-4422. TELEX 293292 USJC UR. URL: http://www.usjaycees.org. Ed. Rebecca Currington; Pub. John Shiroma. R&P contact: John Shiroma. adv. contact: Beverly Molyneux. bk.rev.; illus.; index; circ. 140,000 (controlled). (also avail. in microfiche from UMI; microfilm from UMI; reprint service avail. from UMI) **Indexed:** Int.Aerosp.Abstr.
—UMI; UnCover.
Formerly (until Feb. 1987): Future (ISSN 0016-3260)
Description: Promotes the purposes and objectives of the United States Junior Chambers of Commerce, which is devoted to the development of the individual for the betterment of the community.

JAZZ INTERACTIONS. see MUSIC

658.048 US
JONATHAN. 1930. m. $20 membership. Jonathan Club, 545 S. Figueroa St., Los Angeles, CA 90071. TEL 213-624-0881. FAX 213-488-1425. Ed. Wanda White. adv.; bk.rev. circ. 4,000. (back issues avail.) **Document type:** newsletter.

366 360 US ISSN 0744-3943
JONQUIL. 1930. q. $9.50. Epsilon Sigma Alpha International, 363 W. Drake Rd., Ft. Collins, CO 80526. TEL 970-223-2824. FAX 970-223-4456. Ed. Laurie Steele; Pub. Michael Burns. circ. 13,500. **Document type:** newsletter.
—UnCover.
Description: Provides information and subjects of interest to members, covers fund raising, education, social activities, and leadership.

JOURNAL FUER U F O - FORSCHUNG. see AERONAUTICS AND SPACE FLIGHT

366 641 US
K D A COMMUNICATOR. 1946. 6/yr. $25 (foreign $75) (effective 1997). Kansas Dietetic Association, c/o Department of Hotel, Restaurant, Institution Management and Dietetics, Justin Hall 104, Kansas State University, Manhattan, KS 66103. TEL 913-532-5521. FAX 913-532-5504. E-mail: cws@ksuvm.edu. Ed. Karen A. Miller. bk.rev. circ. 750. **Document type:** newsletter.
Formerly: Sunflower (ISSN 0039-5382)
Description: Covers professional and educational activities of the association's members.

367 US
K J Z T NEWS. (Text occasionally in Czech) 1955. m. membership. Catholic Women's Fraternal of Texas, Box 1884, Austin, TX 78767. Ed. Benita Pavlu.

KANSAS 4-H JOURNAL. see AGRICULTURE

642.5 DK ISSN 0022-8885
KANTINEN. 1960. m. DKK 200. Kantineledernes Landsklub, Kolleruplund 63, 2665 Vallensbaek Strand, Denmark. FAX 45-43-54-34-52. Ed. Benno Arndt. adv.; circ. 4,347 (controlled).

366 US
KAPPA ALPHA PSI JOURNAL. 1914. q. $10. (Kappa Alpha Psi) McQuiddy Publishing Co., 2320 N. Broad St., Philadelphia, PA 19132. TEL 215-228-7184. Ed. Mel L. Davis. adv.; circ. 16,000 (controlled).

THE KAPPA PROFILE. see EDUCATION

369.43 TS
KASHSHAFAT AL-IMARAT/EMIRATES BOY SCOUTS. (Text in Arabic) 1989. q. Mu'assasat al- Fajr, P.O. Box 2004, Abu Dhabi, United Arab Emirates. TEL 446562. FAX 448228. TELEX 3516 MABANE EM. Ed. Ubaid Bukhait al-Mazrawi. circ. 3,000.
Description: News of scouting activities in the U.A.E. and the Arab world.

366 US
KEY OF KAPPA KAPPA GAMMA. 1882. q. Kappa Kappa Gamma Fraternity, 530 E. Town St., Box 2079, Columbus, OH 43215-4820. TEL 614-228-6515. Ed. William Lanford. adv.; B&W page $3000, color page $3950; trim 8 1/2 X 11. circ. 109,000.
Description: Covers career opportunities, member activities, rehabilitation fields served by philanthropy.

369.5 US
KEYNOTER. 1950. m. (except summer). $4 to non-members. Key Club International, 3636 Woodview Trace, Indianapolis, IN 46268. (Affiliate: Kiwanis International) Ed. Julie A. Carson. adv. contact: Patrick Hatcher. circ. 180,000.

366 CN ISSN 0023-1436
KIN. (Text in English and French) 1921. 5/yr. Can.$3. Association of Kinsmen Clubs, P.O. Box KIN, Cambridge, ON N3H 5C6, Canada. TEL 519-653-1920. FAX 519-650-1091. Ed. J.D. Booth. adv.; bk.rev.

369.5 US ISSN 0162-5276
HF5001
KIWANIS MAGAZINE; published for community leaders. 1917. 10/yr. $7.50 (effective 1997). Kiwanis International, 3636 Woodview Trace, Indianapolis, IN 46268. TEL 317-875-8755. FAX 317-879-0204. E-mail: kiwanismail@kiwanis.org; URL: http://www.kiwanis.org. Ed. Chuck Jouak. adv. contact: Patrick Hatcher. illus. circ. 276,524. (also avail. in microform from UMI) **Indexed:** Ind.Free Per., Rehabil.Lit.
—UMI.

366 282 US
KOLPING BANNER. 1929. m. $10. Cath. Kolping Society of America, Box 46252, Chicago, IL 60646. TEL 312-763-5511. Ed. Matthew J. Boyle. R&P contact: Matthew J. Boyle. circ. 2,000. **Document type:** newsletter.
Description: Serves as a religious, fraternal, and social service magazine.

KRIKOS TON VATHMOFORON. see CHILDREN AND YOUTH — For

367 US
LAST MONTH'S NEWSLETTER. 1968. irreg. membership only. Procrastinators' Club of America, Box 712, Bryn Athyn, PA 19009. FAX 215-947-7007. Ed.Bd. circ. 16,000. **Document type:** newsletter.

367 612 US
LEFTHANDER. 1975. bi-m. $15 (foreign $33). Lefthanders International, 3600 N.E. Sardov Bldg. 2, Box 8249, Topeka, KS 66608. TEL 913-234-2177. Ed. Kim Kipers. adv. contact: Carol Riddle. bk.rev. circ. 25,000. (back issues avail.)
Former titles: Lefthander Magazine; Lefty Magazine.
Description: Publishes interviews with left-handed celebrities, research on left-handedness, superstitions and facts about left-handedness and parenting skills; includes catalog product section.

658.048 US
LEGEND OF JENNIE LEE. 1986. a. $10. Exotic World, Exotic Dancers League of North America, 29053 Wild Rd., Helendale, CA 92342. TEL 619-243-5261. Ed. Greg Johnston. bibl. circ. 5,000. (back issues avail.)

389.1 UK ISSN 0144-6533
LEGION. 1921. bi-m. £3. Royal British Legion, 48 Pall Mall, London SW1Y 5JY, England. Ed. W.J. Kingdon. adv. contact: Sarah Frisby. circ. 620,000. **Document type:** bulletin.

305.851 US ISSN 0024-0958
IL LEONE; giornale ufficiale della grande loggia di California dell'Ordine Figli d'Italia in America. (Text mainly in English; occasionally in Italian) 1929. m. $5. Order of the Sons of Italy in America, Grand Lodge of California, 5051 Mission St., San Francisco, CA 94112. TEL 415-285-2933. FAX 415-586-4780. Ed. Lou Cavecche. adv.; illus. circ. 14,250. **Document type:** newspaper.

369.1 IT
LION. 1953. m. (10/yr.). L.2400. (Lions International) Magalini Editrice, Via Gramsci 5, 25086 Rezzato (BS), Italy. TEL 030-2792968. FAX 030-2592291. Ed. Carlo Martinenghi. adv.; B&W page L.5000000, color page L.7000000. circ. 42,500.

367 CN
LION. bi-m. $10. Lions International, 71 Morton Ave., Sharon, Ont. LOG 1V0, Canada. TEL 416-491-9905. Ed. Ellerby Farr. circ. 23,500.

369.5 IC
LION. bi-m. membership. Lionsumdaemid a Islandi, Sigtuni 9, 105-Reykjavik, Iceland. TEL 354-561-3122. FAX 354-561-5122. circ. 3,300.

369.5 US ISSN 0024-4163
HS2705.L5
THE LION; an international magazine for service-minded individuals. (Editions in 20 languages) 1918. 10/yr. $6 to non-members (outside N. America $12) (effective 1997). International Association of Lions Clubs, 300 22nd St., Oak Brook, IL 60523-8842. TEL 630-571-5466. FAX 630-571-8890. Ed. Robert Kleinfelder. adv.; B&W page $4660. illus. circ. 575,000.

366 US ISSN 0024-4171
THE LION EN ESPANOL. (Text in Spanish) 1944. bi-m. $5.50 (foreign $10) (effective 1997). International Association of Lions Clubs, 300 22nd St., Oak Brook, IL 60523-8842. TEL 630-571-5466. FAX 630-571-8890. Ed. Fernando Fernandez. circ. 86,000.

371.85 US ISSN 1041-6935
LION OF ALPHA EPSILON PI. 1920. q. $7.50. Alpha Epsilon Pi Fraternity, 8815 Wesleyan Rd., Indianapolis, IN 46268-1171. TEL 317-876-1913. E-mail: aepihq@indy.net; URL: http://www.aepihq.org. Ed. Sidney N. Dunn. adv. contact: April E. Clark. bk.rev.; illus. circ. 24,485.

369.5 IT
LIONISMO. 1974. bi-m. free. Lions International, Distretto 108L, Via Montalbano, 15, Quarrata (PT), Italy. Ed. D.G. Dario Pinti. adv.: B&W page L.2600000.

271.83 SW ISSN 0345-7338
LUNDAGAARD. 1920. 10/yr. SEK 170; newsstand price: SEK 20. Lunds Studentkaar, Sandgatan 2, S-223 50 Lund, Sweden. TEL 46-46-14-40-20. FAX 46-211-46-56. E-mail: lundagard@af.lu.se. Ed. Yens Wahlgren; Pub. Doc Stig Tejning. adv. contact: Ivar Berge. circ. 28,000. cols./p.: 5; pp./issue: 32.

367 CN ISSN 0820-4217
M C C MENSA CANADA COMMUNICATIONS. (Text in English, French) 1967. 10/yr. Can.$25 (US Can.$30; elsewhere Can.$40). Mensa Canada, 329 March Rd., Ste. 232, Box 11, Kanata, ON K2K 2E1, Canada. TEL 416-497-7070. FAX 416-497-6134. adv.: B&W page Can.$255; trim 8 3/8 x 10 7/8; adv. contact: Ian Buyers. circ. 2,945. **Document type:** bulletin.
  Former titles (until 1981): Mensa Canada Communications (ISSN 0229-5342); (until 1978): M C 2 (ISSN 0380-5344)

791.43 US
M 3. 1985. bi-m. $7 (effective 1997). Michele Lee Fan Club, 114 Magnolia Dr., Levittown, PA 19054-2004. circ. 100. (back issues avail.) **Document type:** newsletter.
  Formerly: Michele's Magic Moments.
  Description: Notifies fans of Michele Lee's acting career and her personal life.

305.8911 US ISSN 0024-9009
MACEDONIAN TRIBUNE. (Text in Bulgarian, English, Macedonian) 1927. bi-w. $20 (foreign $28) (effective 1997). Macedonian Patriotic Organization of the U S and Canada, 124 W. Wayne, Fort Wayne, IN 46802-2505. TEL 219-422-5900. FAX 219-422-1348. E-mail: mtfw@serv2.fwi.com. Ed.Bd. adv.; bk.rev.; charts; illus. circ. 11,000. (also avail. in microfilm from LPC) **Document type:** newspaper.
  Refereed Serial

658.048 028.5 US ISSN 0865-1167
MAGYAR CSERKESZ/HUNGARIAN SCOUT MAGAZINE. s-a. $5. Hungarian Scout Association, Box 68, Garfield, NJ 07026. TEL 201-772-8810. FAX 201-772-5145. Ed. Julius Pap. circ. 1,500. (back issues avail.)
  Description: Contains articles of Hungarian ethnic, cultural, and religious interest for members of Hungarian Scout Troops.

367 780 GW
MANNHEIMER LIEDERTAFEL. MITTEILUNGEN. 1920. bi-m. membership. Mannheimer Liedertafel e.V., Nibelungenstr. 2, 68782 Bruehl, Germany. TEL 49-6202-77997. Ed. Karin Rose. R&P contact: Karin Rose. adv. contact: Barbara Beyer. circ. 350. **Document type:** newsletter.
  Description: Reports about the club's events and concerts.

366.1 UK ISSN 0306-6088
MASONIC SQUARE. 1975. q. £10($25) Ian Allen Regalia, Coomblands House, Coombelands Ln., Addlestone, Surrey KT15 1HY, England. TEL 01932-820552. FAX 01932-821258. E-mail: 101455.3575@compuserve.com. Ed. Leo Zanelli. adv. contact: Ena Langmead. bk.rev. circ. 9,000. (back issues avail.) **Document type:** consumer publication.
  Description: Presents a general forum for freemasons.

366.1 US
MASONIC WORLD. 1934. m. (except Aug.). $7.50 (foreign $8.50). Publishers, Inc., 500 Temple Ave., Detroit, MI 48201. TEL 313-831-6250. Ed. S.J. Penberthy, Jr. adv.: B&W page $1100. circ. 12,000. (controlled).
  Description: Contains Masonic fraternal news.

367 US ISSN 0025-9543
AS36.A4868
MENSA BULLETIN. 1962. 10/yr. $12 to non-members. American Mensa Ltd. (Fort Worth), 201 Main St., Ste. 1101, Fort Worth, TX 76102-3115. TEL 817-332-2600. Ed. Marjorie Mandelblatt. R&P contact: Marjorie Mandelblatt. adv. contact: Marjorie Mandelblatt. bk.rev.; illus.; circ. 49,000 (controlled). **Document type:** bulletin.
  —UnCover.
  Formerly: Interim; Incorporates: Mensa Journal; Intelligence.
  Description: Serves as a forum for the exchange of ideas among Mensa members, including provocative views which may challenge the perceptions, opinions, values and taste of the members.

367 UK ISSN 0958-0638
MENSA MAGAZINE. 1972. m. membership. British Mensa Ltd., Mensa House, St. Johns Square, Wolverhampton WV2 4AH, England. TEL 0902-772771. FAX 0902-22327. Ed. Simon Clark. adv. circ. 33,000.
  Former titles: Mensa (ISSN 0958-062X); British Mensa; British Mensa Newsletter (ISSN 0306-5065)

367 US ISSN 0025-9969
MERCURY (LOS ANGELES). 1911. m. $12. (Los Angeles Athletic Club) L A A C O, Ltd., 431 W. Seventh St., Los Angeles, CA 90014. TEL 213-625-2211. FAX 213-689-1194. Ed. Linda Reid. adv.; bk.rev. circ. 6,000.

MESEMB STUDY BULLETIN. see *BIOLOGY — Botany*

MILITARY AND POLICE UNIFORM ASSOCIATION NEWSLETTER. see *HOMOSEXUALITY*

355.15 US ISSN 0026-6299
MISSISSIPPI LEGION-AIRE. vol.43, 1970. m. $7. (American Legion, Department of Mississippi) Rankin County News, Box 107, Brandon, MS 39043. TEL 601-825-8333. FAX 601-825-8334. Pub. Marcus Bowers. circ. 16,000. **Document type:** newspaper.

367 US ISSN 0279-8670
HS1510.W7
MODERN WOODMEN. q. membership (free to libraries by request). Modern Woodmen of America, 1701 First Ave., Rock Island, IL 61204-2005. TEL 309-786-6481. Ed. Gloria Bergh. circ. 400,000. **Document type:** trade publication.

658.048 780 US ISSN 1092-1125
MONKEES, BOYCE & HART PHOTO FAN CLUB; the photo club. 1969. bi-m. $9.50 in the U.S. & Canada; elsewhere $14 (effective 1997). Box 411, Watertown, SD 57201-0411. TEL 603-886-3017. FAX 605-882-5891. E-mail: seagal@daknet.com. Eds. Jodi Hammrich, Shan S. Cain. R&P contact: Shan S. Cain. adv.; bk.rev. circ. 11,000. (looseleaf format; back issues avail.) **Document type:** newsletter.
  Description: Presents current news and information on the Monkees, Boyce and Hart.

355.15 US ISSN 0026-9999
MONTANA LEGIONNAIRE. 1919. m. $5. American Legion, Department of Montana, Box 6075, Helena, MT 59604. TEL 406-442-5260. Ed. Odelta Thomsen. adv. circ. 20,000. (tabloid format) **Document type:** newsletter.

366 US ISSN 0027-0954
MOOSE MAGAZINE. 1910. bi-m. $2 to members. Moose International, Inc., Supreme Lodge Bldg., Mooseheart, IL 60539-1174. TEL 708-859-2000. FAX 630-859-6620. Ed. Kurt N. Wehrmeister; Pub. Frank A. Sarnecki. R&P contact: Kurt N. Wehrmeister. circ. 1,200,000.

366 US ISSN 0889-4760
MRS. EAGLE. 1948. q. $4 membership. Fraternal Order of Eagles, Box 25916, Milwaukee, WI 53225-0916. TEL 414-781-7585. FAX 414-781-5046. Ed. Fran Ehrman. circ. 350,000 (controlled).
  Description: Reports on Mrs. Eagle programs and activities at local and national levels.

658.048 US
N M A BULLETIN BOARD. 1986. 4/yr. membership only. Nonprofit Management Association, 315 W. Ninth St., Ste. 1100, Los Angeles, CA 90015. bk.rev. **Document type:** newsletter.

366 US
N S C A R MAGAZINE. a. National Society of the Children of the American Revolution, 1776 D St., N.W., Washington, DC 20006-5303.

366.1 AT ISSN 1039-6977
N.S.W. FREEMASON.* 1966. q. Aus.$20. (United Grand Lodge of New South Wales) Associated Business Publications Pty. Ltd., P.O. Box 440, Broadway, N.S.W. 2007, Australia. TEL 02-212-2780. FAX 61-2-2812594. (Subscr. to: P.O. Box 440, Broadway 2007, Australia) Ed. Ron Maguire. adv.; bk.rev. circ. 37,000. **Document type:** bulletin.

790.1 TS
NADI ABU DHABI AL-SIYAHI/ABU DHABI TOURIST CLUB. (Text in Arabic, English) 1978. m. membership. Nadi Abu Dhabi al-Siyahi - Abu Dhabi Tourist Club, P.O. Box 28, Abu Dhabi, United Arab Emirates. TEL 724954. circ. 1,000 (controlled).
  Formerly (until 1985): Al-Faridah.
  Description: Covers club news and activities.

369 790.1 TS
NADI AL-WASL. (Text in Arabic) 1970. m. membership. Nadi al-Wasl - Al-Wasl Club, P.O. Box 3888, Dubai, United Arab Emirates. TEL 374487. circ. 500 (controlled).
  Formerly (until 1974): Al-Zamalek.
  Description: News of sporting and cultural activities.

NAROD POLSKI. see *ETHNIC INTERESTS*

369 790.1 TS
AL-NASR. (Text in Arabic) 1978. m. free. Nadi Al-Nasr, Al-Lajnah al-Thiqafiyyah - Al-Nadi Club, Cultural Committee, P.O. Box 2226, Dubai, United Arab Emirates. TEL 472220. Ed. Abdullah Ibrahim. circ. 500.
  Description: Covers club sporting and social activities.

NATIONAL AMVET. see *MILITARY*

NATIONAL BETA CLUB JOURNAL. see *CHILDREN AND YOUTH — For*

366 US
NATIONAL FRATERNAL CLUBS NEWS.* 1885. m. $12. National Fraternal Clubs News, Inc., 205 N. Michigan Ave., Ste. 1900, Chicago, IL 60601-5916. TEL 312-527-0580. adv. circ. 5,060. **Document type:** newsletter.
  Description: Contains news and editorials regarding service clubs and volunteer social groups.

NATIONAL PRESS CLUB RECORD. see *JOURNALISM*

366 US
NATIONAL SON. m. Sons of Spanish American War Veterans, 646 Scott St., Redwood City, CA 94063-2937. **Document type:** newspaper.

NAVY NEWS. SEA CADET EDITION. see *CHILDREN AND YOUTH — For*

355.15 US ISSN 0028-1875
NEBRASKA LEGIONNAIRE. 1922. m. $4. American Legion, Department of Nebraska, Box 5205, Lincoln, NE 68505. TEL 402-464-6338. FAX 402-464-6330. Pub. Robert Craig. R&P contact: John R. Petelle. circ. 57,000. (tabloid format) **Document type:** newspaper.
  Description: Covers national, state and local American Legion activities and veterans issues.

367 629.1 US
NEGRO AIRMEN INTERNATIONAL NEWSLETTER. 1967. q. free. Negro Airmen International, Inc., 8891 Airport Rd., N.E., Blaine, MN 55449-7250. TEL 205-727-0721. Ed. Solomon P. Hamilton. adv. circ. 1,000. (back issues avail.) **Document type:** newsletter.

658.048 SZ ISSN 0257-3830
NEUE HELVETISCHE GESELLSCHAFT. MITTEILUNGEN. 1913. 4/yr. membership. (Neue Helvetische Gesellschaft) Sauerlaender AG, Laurenzenvorstadt 89, CH-5001 Aarau, Switzerland. TEL 064-268626. FAX 064-245780. TELEX 981196-SAG-CH. Ed.Bd. adv.: B&W page 431 SFr.; trim 117 x 175. **Document type:** bulletin.
  —CCC.

CLUBS

366   US   ISSN 0028-5021
NEW ERA (ELY)/NOVA DOBA. (Text in English & Slovenian) vol.68, 1973. m. $1.50. American Fraternal Union, 111 S. 4th Ave. E., Ely, MN 55731. TEL 218-365-3143. Ed. Julia F. Pirc.

658.048   US
NONPROFIT MAILERS FEDERATION. NEWS UPDATE. m. National Federation of Nonprofits, 815 15th St., N.W., Ste. 822, Washington, DC 20005-2201.
    Description: Promotes non-profit groups and monitors relevant legislation.

366 355   US
NORTH CAROLINA AMERICAN LEGION NEWS. 1950. bi-m. North Carolina Department of American Legion, Box 26657, Raleigh, NC 27611. TEL 919-832-7506. Ed. William Patterson. circ. 45,000. **Document type:** newspaper.
    Description: Covers programs sponsored and conducted by the American Legion and news of legion events.

366.1   US   ISSN 1088-4416
NORTHERN LIGHT. 1970. q. $10 non-members (foreign $20). Supreme Council Ancient Accepted Scottish Rite, Northern Masonic Jurisdiction, U.S.A., Box 519, Lexington, MA 02173. TEL 617-862-4410. FAX 617-863-1833. E-mail: dcurtis@world.std.com; URL: http://world.std.com/~sysmgr. Ed. Richard H. Curtis. bk.rev.; cum.index every 5 yrs. circ. 340,000. **Document type:** consumer publication.
    Description: Contains articles on Freemasonry.

NUORTEN SARKA. see *AGRICULTURE*

366   UK   ISSN 0048-1408
ODD FELLOW. 1830. m. £5.30. Independent Order of Odd Fellows, Manchester Unity Friendly Society, 40 Fountain St, Manchester M2 2AB, England. TEL 061-832-9361. FAX 061-832-3750. Ed. R.J. Bell. adv.; bk.rev. circ. 7,000. (processed)

367   AT
ODDFELLOW. 1953. q. Aus.$0.05 per no. Grand United Order of Oddfellows, Box 1507 G.P.O., Sydney, N.S.W. 2001, Australia. Ed.Bd. adv. circ. 20,000.

366 355   US
OKLAHOMA LEGIONNAIRE. q. $5. American Legion of Oklahoma, Box 53201, Oklahoma City, OK 73152. TEL 405-525-3511. FAX 405-521-0178. Ed. Jerry Askins. R&P contact: Jerry Askins. adv. circ. 41,300. **Document type:** newspaper.
    Description: Presents national and state American Legion news, with emphasis on local post news.

366.1   US   ISSN 0030-1779
OKLAHOMA MASON. 1934. m. $2. Grand Lodge of Ancient, Free and Accepted Masons of the State of Oklahoma, Box 1019, Guthrie, OK 73044. TEL 405-282-3212. Ed. Thomas K. Wright. adv.; bk.rev. circ. 49,000.
    Description: Contains news, information, photographs, and announcements on the members and activities of the Grand Lodge of Ancient, Free, and Accepted Masons in the state.

366   US   ISSN 0030-1809
OKLAHOMA ODD FELLOW. 1893. 6/yr. $3. Independent Order of Odd Fellows, Sovereign Grand Lodge, 1610 N.W. Columbia, Lawton, OK 73507. Ed. Esther Stringer. circ. 4,000. (tabloid format)

366   US   ISSN 1085-5017
THE OPTIMIST (ST. LOUIS). 1919. bi-m. membership. Optimist International, 4494 Lindell Blvd., St. Louis, MO 63108. TEL 314-371-6000; 800-OPT-8389. FAX 314-371-6006. E-mail: orders@ruh.com; URL: http://optimist.org. Ed. Dennis R. Osterwisch; Pub. Dawn M. Blair. adv.; illus. circ. 155,000. **Document type:** consumer publication.
    Formerly: Optimist Magazine (ISSN 0744-4672)
    Description: Promotes optimism, patriotism, and a respect for law.

ORDER OF ONTARIO/ORDRE DE L'ONTARIO. see *GENEALOGY AND HERALDRY*

810 366   US
OZIANA.* 1971. a. $3. International Wizard of Oz Club, Inc., P.O. Box 10117, Berkeley, CA 94709-5117. Ed. Robin Olderman. circ. 800.
    Description: Contains stories, artwork and quizzes about the Land of Oz.

367   US
P F A TODAY. bi-m. Professional Fraternity Association, Box 90264, Indianapolis, IN 46290. TEL 317-257-5235. FAX 317-253-5067.

P M C C MEMBERSHIP ROSTER. (Post Mark Collectors Club) see *PHILATELY*

366   US
PACIFIC ECHO.* 1907. q. $1. Neighbors of Woodcraft, Box 769, Oregon City, OR 97045-0052. TEL 503-224-3525. FAX 503-223-5140. Ed. Keith Yates. circ. 10,000. (controlled).

THE PAK-SCOUT. see *CHILDREN AND YOUTH — About*

366   CN   ISSN 0820-2605
PAPYRUS. 1976. bi-m. free. Rameses Temple A.A.O.N.M.S., 3100 Keele St., Downsview, ON M3M 2H4, Canada. TEL 416-633-6317. FAX 416-633-6345. Ed. Otto Yoworski. R&P contact: Otto Yoworsky. adv. contact: Otto Yoworski. circ. 7,300. **Document type:** newsletter.

PARADE OF ROYALTY (YEAR). see *PETS*

658.048   AT
PENFRIEND & ETHNIC LINKUP INDEX. irreg. $1 with self-addressed return envelope. Penfriend Linkup Index, Box 70, Coburg, Vic. 3058, Australia. Ed. Bill Helem.

366   US
PENNSYLVANIA CLUBWOMAN.* 1912. q. $1. Penn Harris Inn, 1150 Camp Hill Bypass, Camp Hill, PA 17011-3734. circ. 20,000.

PERSPECTIVES (BLOOMINGTON). see *BUSINESS AND ECONOMICS — Management*

366   US   ISSN 0149-8754
PHI ALPHA DELTA REPORTER. q. membership. Phi Alpha Delta, 10722 White Oak Ave., Granda Hills, CA 91344-4698. TEL 818-360-1941. FAX 818-363-5851. E-mail: PADOffice@aol.com. Ed. Maree Wiggins Blackston. adv.; circ. 95,000. (controlled). **Document type:** newspaper.
    Description: Covers association activities.

366   US
PHILALETHES. 1946. bi-m. $15. Philalethes Society, Drawer 70, 110 Quince Ave., Highland Springs, VA 23075. TEL 804-737-4498. Ed. Jerry Marsengill. circ. 4,800 (controlled).
    Description: Publishes articles of Masonic interest.

PHILATELIC EXHIBITOR. see *PHILATELY*

THE PHILATELIC FREEMASON. see *PHILATELY*

366   PH
PHILIPPINE ROTARY. (Text in English) m. P.180 (foreign $30). Philippines College of Rotary Governors, 2nd Fl., PNR Bldg., Plaza Dilao, P.O. Box 3199, Manila, Philippines. TEL 805-955-607401. Ed. Jose M. Barredo.
    Description: Aims to advance high standards, understanding and good will in business and professions.

PHOTO STAR. see *AGRICULTURE*

367   US   ISSN 1045-179X
THE PILOT LOG. 1922. 6/yr. $10 to non-members (foreign $15); members free. Pilot International, 244 College Street, Macon, GA 31201. TEL 912-743-7403. FAX 912-743-2173. Ed. Jan Brown. circ. 17,500 (controlled).
    Description: Provides articles of interest for members of an international classified service club for executives and professionals.

PIONNIER. see *CHILDREN AND YOUTH — For*

366   US   ISSN 0032-163X
PLUMB LINE. 1970. m. $1. (M. W. Prince Hall, Grand Lodge Free & Accepted Masons of Louisiana) Fraternal Press, Box 2974, Baton Rouge, LA 70821. Ed. Samuel P. Jenkins. illus. circ. 2,800.

PODIUM. see *COMMUNICATIONS*

PORTSEA BOOMER. see *SPORTS AND GAMES*

POWER STROKE. see *SPORTS AND GAMES — Boats And Boating*

367   US   ISSN 0887-8420
PRIVATE CLUBS; the magazine for members of city, country, and athletic clubs. 1986. bi-m. $12. Associate Clubs Publications, Inc., 3030 LBJ Freeway, Ste. 600, Dallas, TX 75234-7703. TEL 214-888-7547. FAX 214-888-7338. E-mail: PrivClubs@aol.com. Ed. Julie Bain; Pub. Georg Gretser. adv. contact: Bunny Pool. circ. 216,000 (paid). **Document type:** consumer publication.
    Description: Informs and entertains club members with articles on travel, health and fitness, business and finance, food and wine, and golf and tennis.

369.5   CN
PROGRESSION. 1971. q. Canadian Progress Club, 2395 Bayview Ave., North York, ON M2L 1A2, Canada. TEL 416-446-1830. Ed. Roy Urbach. circ. 1,300. **Document type:** newsletter.

PROSCOPOS. see *CHILDREN AND YOUTH — For*

367 370   US   ISSN 0734-3612
PURPLE AND GOLD. 1884. q. membership. Chi Psi Educational Trust, 20180 Governors Hwy., Ste. 303, Olympia Fields, IL 60461-1066. Ed. William J. Green. circ. 17,000. circ. 17,000 (controlled). **Document type:** academic/scholarly publication.
    Description: Educational journal of the Chi Psi Educational Trust.

366   CN
PYTHIAN RECORD. 1946. 3/yr. membership. Grand Lodge Knights of Pythias of British Columbia, 447 Penticton Ave., Penticton, BC V2A 2M5, Canada. TEL 250-492-6520. FAX 250-492-6520. Ed. Marv Wilson. circ. 2,000. **Document type:** newsletter.

322.4   IT   ISSN 1123-9700
Q C R. (Quaderni del Circolo Rosselli) 1981. q. Lit.64000 (foreign Lit.75000) (effective 1997). Giunti Gruppo Editoriale S.p.A., Via Bolognese 165, 50139 Florence, Italy. TEL 39-55-6679267. FAX 39-55-6679298. URL: http://www.giunti.it. Ed. Valdo Spini.
    Formerly (until 1995): Circolo Rosselli. Quaderni (ISSN 0392-6656)

367 790.1   SA   ISSN 0033-6661
QUONDAM MAGAZINE. 1944. s-a. membership. Jeppe High Schools' Quondam Club, c/o Mrs. M.D. Sparke, P.O. Box 24, Bedfordview 2008, Transvaal, South Africa. TEL 011-53-8720. Ed. Dave Herald. adv.; bk.rev.; illus. circ. 1,800.
    Description: Covers sports and related activities of the club.

367   US   ISSN 0747-2072
QUOTARIAN. 1919. q. $5. Quota International, 1420 21st St., N.W., Washington, DC 20036. TEL 202-331-9694. Ed. Kathleen Thomas. circ. 14,000.
    Description: Covers quota service related information and news of club activities.

367   CN   ISSN 0033-6734
R A NEWS. 1942. 4/yr. Can.$15. Recreation Association of the Public Service of Canada, 2451 Riverside Dr., Ottawa, ON K1H 7X7, Canada. TEL 613-733-5100. FAX 613-733-3310. Ed. Jane Proudfoot. R&P contact: Jane Proudfoot. adv. contact: Jane Proudfoot. bk.rev.; illus.; circ. 100 (paid); 40,000 (controlled).
    Description: Wellbeing magazine, aims to inform members and recruit potential members.

367 780   US
REBA MCENTIRE INTERNATIONAL FAN CLUB NEWSLETTER. 1979. bi-m. $12 (foreign $15). Reba McEntire International Fan Club, Box 121996, Nashville, TN 37212-1996. TEL 615-259-3311. FAX 615-742-5160. Ed. Mary Dawson. R&P contact: Mary Dawson. circ. 45,000 (paid). **Document type:** newsletter.

366   US
RED MEN MAGAZINE. 1970. s-a. membership. Improved Order of Red Men, Box 683, Waco, TX 76703. TEL 817-756-1221. FAX 817-756-4828. Ed. Robert E. Davis. adv.; circ. 27,000 (controlled).

CLUBS

367 610.73　　US　　ISSN 0885-8144
REFLECTIONS (INDIANAPOLIS). q. $18 (foreign $28). Sigma Theta Tau International Honor Society of Nursing, 550 W. North St., Indianapolis, IN 46202. TEL 317-634-8171. FAX 317-634-8188. Ed. Julie Goldsmith. R&P contact: Julie Goldsmith. adv. contact: Kathy Bennison. (back issues avail.) **Document type:** newsletter.
  Description: Highlights the meetings, conferences, seminars, and national and international events of the organization.

790　　US
ROBIN RIGHT FAN CLUB. NEWSLETTER. 1980. m. $8. Robin Right Fan Club, Box 676, Concord, MA 01742-0676. TEL 617-259-8759. Ed. Donna Sheppard. circ. 1,000. **Document type:** newsletter.

ROLLING STONE. see *MUSIC*

ROMANSK FILMKLUB. see *MOTION PICTURES*

369.5　　US　　ISSN 0035-838X
HF5001
THE ROTARIAN. 1911. m. $12. Rotary International, 1560 Sherman Ave., Evanston, IL 60201. TEL 708-866-3000. FAX 708-866-9732. E-mail: 75457.3577@compuserve.com; URL: http://www.rotary.org. Ed. Willmon L. White. R&P contact: Judith Lee. TEL 847-866-3194. adv. contact: Edward A. Schimmelpfennig. bk.rev.; illus.; index; circ. 521,111 (paid). (also avail. in microfilm from UMI; reprint service avail. from UMI) **Indexed:** Ind.Free Per., Mag.Ind.
  —UMI; UnCover.
  Description: International service organization membership magazine.

369.5　　IT
ROTARY. 1924. m. L.18000 donation. Istituto Culturale Rotariano, Via Morozzo della Rocca 9, 20123 Milan, Italy. TEL 02-4818683. FAX 02-4819130. Ed. Alessandro Ubertone. adv.: B&W page L.4400000, color page L.6900000. circ. 33,000.

366　　AT　　ISSN 0048-8631
ROTARY DOWN UNDER. 1965. m. Aus.$12.50 for six mos. Rotary Down Under Incorporated, P.O. Box 779, Parramatta, N.S.W. 2124, Australia. TEL 61-2-6334888. FAX 61-2-8915984. Ed. Robert Aitken. R&P contact: Joy Gillett. adv. contact: Warwick Heath. bk.rev.; circ. 50,752 (paid). **Indexed:** So.Pac.Per.Ind. **Document type:** bulletin, newsletter.
  Description: Provides information for Rotarians and their families in Australia, New Zealand and South Pacific.

369.5　　SA
ROTARY IN AFRICA. (Text in Afrikaans and English) 1926. m. R.4. Rotary in Africa, Ltd., P.O. Box 2586, Durban 4000, South Africa. Ed. Peter Wrinch-Schulz. adv.; charts; illus. circ. 7,000.

369.5　　UK
ROTARY MAGAZINE. 1915. bi-m. £6($20) (effective 1997). Rotary International in Great Britain and Ireland, Kinwarton Rd., Alcester, Warwickshire B49 6BP, England. TEL 44-1789-765411. FAX 44-1789-765570. Ed. Mike Redfern. adv.: B&W page £455, color page £687; trim 272 x 185; adv. contact: Cara Key. bk.rev.; illus.; index. circ. 63,960. **Document type:** bulletin.
  Former titles: Rotary (ISSN 0035-8401); Rotary Service.
  Description: Information about the organization and its activities, particularly in Great Britain and Ireland.

366.1　　US　　ISSN 0035-8649
ROYAL ARCH MASON. 1943. q. $1.75. (Royal Arch Masons, General Grand Chapter) York Rite Publishing Co., Box 529, 305 W. 12th St., Trenton, MO 64683. TEL 816-359-6008. Ed. William R. Denslow. bk.rev.; illus.; index every 3 yrs. circ. 115,000.

367　　US　　ISSN 0035-905X
HS1510.R895
ROYAL NEIGHBOR; a home magazine. 1900. bi-m. membership. Royal Neighbors of America, 230 16th St., Rock Island, IL 61201. TEL 309-788-4561. FAX 309-788-9234. Ed. Kathleen J. Wheeler. circ. 195,000. (back issues avail.)

ROYAL SCOTTISH AUTOMOBILE CLUB OFFICIAL HANDBOOK. see *SPORTS AND GAMES*

367　　US　　ISSN 0036-0147
RURITAN. 1932. q. $8. Ruritan National, Inc., Box 487, Dublin, VA 24084. TEL 540-674-5431. FAX 540-674-2304. E-mail: ruritan@swva.net. Ed. Richard N. Ely. R&P contact: Michael Chrisley. adv. contact: Michael Chrisley. bk.rev.; illus.; circ. 36,000 (paid).
  Formerly: Ruritan National.
  Description: Promotes fellowship, goodwill and community service, and provides news of membership activities.

366　　MM
RUSSIAN GRAND PRIORY OF MALTA. BULLETIN. 1964. q. donation. Russian Grand Priory of Malta, 223 St. Paul St., Valletta, Malta. bk.rev. circ. 1,300. **Indexed:** Hist.Abstr. **Document type:** bulletin.
  Former titles: Order of St. John. Bulletin; Knights of Malta. Bulletin.

S R A T E JOURNAL. (Southeastern Regional Association of Teacher Educators) see *EDUCATION*

S W L. (Shortwave Listener) see *COMMUNICATIONS — Radio*

367　　SW　　ISSN 0036-3790
SAMLARNYTT. 1947. 10/yr. SEK 90 membership. Samlarfoerbundet Nordstjaernan, Tideliusgatan 59, S-116 69 Stockholm, Sweden. Eds. Birgitta, Rolf Rundstroem. adv.; bk.rev.; illus.; cum.index: 1946-1966. circ. 6,000.
  Supersedes: Kaepphaesten.

658.85　　US　　ISSN 0036-3898
HF5441
SAMPLE CASE. 1891. q. $3. Order of United Commercial Travelers of America, 632 N. Park St., Columbus, OH 43215. TEL 614-228-3276. FAX 614-228-1898. Ed. Megan Woitovich; Pub. Megan Woitovich. R&P contact: Megan Woitovich. adv. contact: Megan Woitovich. circ. 160,000 (controlled).
  Description: Focuses on seniors, travel, finances, retirement planning, health, etc.

SAMSOM SPORTSECRETARIS. see *SPORTS AND GAMES*

THE SAND PAPER. see *HOBBIES*

SCAUTISMO; rivista di divulgazione del metodo scout. see *CHILDREN AND YOUTH — About*

SCAUTISMO VENETO. see *CHILDREN AND YOUTH — About*

366.1　　US　　ISSN 1076-8572
THE SCOTTISH RITE JOURNAL. 1904. m. $4. The Supreme Council, 33 Degrees, Ancient & Accepted Rite of Freemasonry, Southern Jurisdiction, 1715 16th St., N.W., Washington, DC 20009-3103. TEL 202-232-3579. FAX 202-387-1843. Ed. John W. Boettjer. adv.; bk.rev.; index. circ. 460,000. (back issues avail.)
  Formerly (until 1989): New Age (Washington).

SCOUT. see *CHILDREN AND YOUTH — For*

369.4　　AT　　ISSN 0312-5203
SCOUT ASSOCIATION OF AUSTRALIA. ANNUAL REPORT.* 1971. a. free. Scout Association of Australia, National Headquarters, P.O. Box 115, Habetfield, N.S.W. 2045, Australia. FAX 61-62-574594. Ed. R.J. Perryman. circ. 3,650. **Document type:** proceedings.
  Formerly: Scout Association of Australia. Review of Progress (ISSN 0310-818X)

SCOUT MEMORABILIA. see *HOBBIES*

SCOUTER'S DIGEST; condensed scouting news for busy Boy Scout leaders. see *CHILDREN AND YOUTH — About*

369.4　　SA　　ISSN 1021-3562
SCOUTING ABOUT. (Text in English) 1993. q. R.15. South African Scout Association, P.O. Box 2434, Clareinch 7740, South Africa. TEL 27-21-6833910. FAX 27-21-6833716. URL: http://www.web.co.za/scouts. Ed. Jay Heale. adv. contact: John Hunneyball. bk.rev. circ. 800. **Document type:** newsletter.
  Description: Contains news items on international scouting, national scouting within South Africa, and practical ideas for Scout and Cub leaders.

SCOUTING MAGAZINE. see *CHILDREN AND YOUTH — About*

THE SCREAM. see *LITERATURE — Science Fiction, Fantasy, Horror*

658.048 362.6　　CN　　ISSN 1180-8063
SENIORS CHOICE.* 1989. m. Can.$16. Egress Enterprises Inc., RR 2, Cite 5, Kelowna, BC V1Y 7R1, Canada. TEL 604-765-6065. FAX 604-765-7346. Ed. Darlene Rickard. adv. circ. 10,000. (tabloid format)

366　　CN　　ISSN 0049-0202
SENTINEL (WILLOWDALE). 1875. 6/yr. Can.$12($14) (effective 1998). (Loyal Orange Association) British America Publishing Co. Ltd., Canadian Orange Hdqs., 94 Sheppard Ave. W., Willowdale, ON M2N 1M5, Canada. TEL 416-223-1690; 800-565-6248. FAX 416-223-1324. Ed. Norman R. Ritchie. R&P contact: Norman R. Ritchie. adv.: page Can.$150; adv. contact: Norman R. Ritchie. bk.rev.; circ. 2,426 (paid). (also avail. in microfilm) **Document type:** directory, newsletter.

366 973　　US
SEVENTEENTH CENTURY REVIEW. 1976. 12/yr? National Society Colonial Dames XVII Century, 1300 New Hampshire Ave. N.W., Washington, DC 20036. TEL 202-293-1700. Ed. William Briggs. adv. circ. 13,000.
  Description: Features the history, education, especially the heraldry and genealogy pertaining to the 17th century.

296　　US　　ISSN 0745-9327
SHOFAR (WASHINGTON); the high school Jewish newspaper. 1925. 4/yr. membership. B'nai B'rith Youth Organization, 1640 Rhode Island Ave., N.W., Washington, DC 20036. TEL 202-857-1099. Ed. Lisa A. Witkin. circ. 30,000. (tabloid format)
  Indexed: Ind.Jew.Per., Rel.& Theol.Abstr. (1990-).

367 630　　US　　ISSN 8750-6866
SICKLE & SHEAF. 1910. q. Alpha Gamma Rho Fraternity, 1001 N. Executive Hills Blvd., Kansas City, MO 64153. TEL 816-891-9200. FAX 816-891-9401. E-mail: agrho@aol.com; URL: http//www.agrs.org. Ed. Ken Root. R&P contact: Katie Thomas. bk.rev. circ. 40,000.
  Description: Publishes fraternal activities and agricultural articles.

SILVER CIRCLE. see *GENERAL INTEREST PERIODICALS — United States*

367 153　　US
SINISTRALIAN. 1977. q. $5.75. Sinistral SIG, 200 Emmett Ave., Derby, CT 06418. TEL 203-735-1759. Ed. Sharlene McEvoy. bk.rev. circ. 100. (back issues avail.)
  Description: Provides information on the recent developments in left-handedness studies for Mensans.

367　　US
SKULL. s-a. Psi Sigma Alpha, 703 W. Washington Dr., San Angelo, TX 76903-6717.

305.89185　　US　　ISSN 0038-0822
SOKOL POLSKI/POLISH FALCON. (Text in English and Polish) 1896. m. membership only. Polish Falcons of America, 615 Iron City Dr., Pittsburgh, PA 15205-4397. TEL 412-922-2244. FAX 412-922-5029. Ed. Timothy L. Kuzma. adv.; bk.rev.; illus.; circ. 15,300 (controlled). (tabloid format; also avail. in microform) **Document type:** newspaper.

366　　US　　ISSN 0745-0095
SOKOL TIMES. 1905. m. $7. Sokol U S A, 276 Prospect St., East Orange, NJ 07019. TEL 201-676-0280. Ed. Ellen Kovac. bk.rev. **Document type:** newspaper.
  Description: Promotes this fraternal organization and their interest in physical activities and Slovak heritage.

367　　US　　ISSN 0038-1446
SONS OF ITALY NEWS. 1931. m. free. Order of the Sons of Italy in America, Grand Lodge of Massachusetts, 93 Concord Ave., Belmont, MA 02178-4042. Ed. Dorothy Berlandi. adv.; bk.rev.; circ. 17,500 (controlled).
  Formerly: Sons of Italy Magazine.

SONS OF ITALY TIMES. see *ETHNIC INTERESTS*

367 US
SOUTH CAROLINA CLUBWOMAN. 1945. q. $5. General Federation of Women's Clubs of South Carolina, 1511 Laurel St., Columbia, SC 29201. TEL 803-781-4442. FAX 803-366-9666. Ed. Marian St.Clair; Pub. June Troyan. R&P contact: Marian St.Clair. adv. circ. 2,400.
   Description: Covers club activities, and news of interest to women's organizations.

369.1 US ISSN 0745-5801
SOUTH DAKOTA LEGION NEWS. 1932. bi-m. membership. American Legion, Department of South Dakota, Box 67, Watertown, SD 57201. TEL 605-886-3604. FAX 605-886-2870. Ed. Denny Warrick; Pub. A.W. Anderson. adv. circ. 28,400. (tabloid format) **Document type:** newspaper.

SPORTHANDBUCH NIEDERSACHSEN; fuer alle Verbaende, Vereine und Sportinteressierte. see SPORTS AND GAMES

366 US
SQUIRES NEWSLETTER. 1929. m. $1. Knights of Columbus, Columbus Plaza, Drawer 1670, New Haven, CT 06507. TEL 203-772-2130. Ed. William O'Brien. bk.rev.; illus. circ. 25,000. **Document type:** newsletter.
   Formerly: Squires (ISSN 0010-2032)
   Description: For teenage boys.

658.048 US
STATE OF THE UNION. 1925. bi-m. membership. Union League Club of Chicago, 65 W. Jackson Blvd., Chicago, IL 60604. TEL 312-427-7800. Ed. Betsy Buckley. bk.rev.; circ. 4,800 (controlled).
   Formerly: Men and Events.

367 336.2 GW ISSN 0948-4248
STEUER-BRIEF FUER PERSONENGESELLSCHAFTEN. m. DM.9.85 per no. (effective 1997). Verlag Peter Deubner GmbH, Wolfgang-Mueller-Str. 14, 50968 Cologne, Germany. TEL 49-221-9370180. FAX 49-221-93701890. **Document type:** bulletin.

367 336.2 GW ISSN 0947-5303
STEUER-BRIEF FUER VEREINE. m. DM.9.85 per no. (effective 1997). Verlag Peter Deubner GmbH, Wolfgang-Mueller-Str. 14, 50968 Cologne, Germany. TEL 49-221-9370180. FAX 49-221-93701890. **Document type:** bulletin.

367 GW
SUEDDEUTSCHE GEMEINSCHAFTSVERBAND. NACHRICHTEN. 1914. m. DM.12.50. Sueddeutsche Gemeinschaftsverband, Kreuznacherstr. 43c, 70372 Stuttgart, Germany. TEL 0711-560068. FAX 0711-569264. **Document type:** newsletter.

367 US ISSN 0728-909X
SUNSHINE BULLETIN. 1896. q. $1. International Sunshine Society, 503 N. Bradford St., Seaford, DE 19973-2405. TEL 302-764-1405. Ed. Mildred Whitham. circ. 1,000. (back issues avail.)

SUZI DEVERAUX INTERNATIONAL FAN CLUB. see MUSIC

T U S VEREINSNACHRICHTEN. (Turn- und Sportvereinigung Gaarden von 1875 e.V.) see SPORTS AND GAMES

367 US
TALENT MAGAZINE. 1831. q. membership. International Platform Association, Box 250, Winnetka, IL 60093. TEL 847-446-4321. adv. circ. 16,000. **Document type:** newsletter.

746.92
THE TANYA ROBERTS TIMES. 1987. $5. (National Association of Fan Clubs) Tanya Roberts Fan Club, 63 Eastgate Dr., Daly City, CA 94015-3069. TEL 415-755-7762. FAX 415-992-4455. Ed. Chuck Meagher. adv. circ. 150. (looseleaf format; back issues avail.) **Document type:** newsletter.
   Description: Keeps club members current on Tanya Roberts' career with the opportunity to acquire pen pals and related movie memorabilia.

366.1 TU ISSN 1301-2754
ESVIYE. 1991. bi-w. $3 members only. Hur ve Kabul Edilmis Masonlar Locasi, Nuru Ziya Sokak 21, 80050 Beyoglu, Istanbul, Turkey. TEL 90-22-2497294. FAX 90-212-2494753. E-mail: mason@yore.com.tr. Ed. Celil Layiktez. circ. 5,000. (back issues avail.) **Document type:** proceedings.
   Description: Research studies on Masonic subjects.

369.1 US
TEXAS LEGION TIMES.* 1923. m. $2 to non-members; members $0.80. (American Legion, Department of Texas) Adcraft Agency, Box 337, Jacksboro, TX 76458-0337. TEL 817-567-6622. FAX 817-567-6372. Ed. Missy Costello Matthews. adv.; bk.rev.; circ. 100,500 (controlled).
   Formerly: Texas Legion News.

367 US
TEXAS MASON. 1989. q. $6. Grand Lodge of Texas, A.F. & A.M., 715 Columbus, Box 607, Waco, TX 76703. TEL 817-753-7395. Ed. John Rasco. circ. 185,000.
   Formerly: Texas Free Mason.
   Description: Devoted to matters of interest to Texas Masons.

THUNDER FROM HEAVEN. see MILITARY

TOGETHER WE CAN. see EDUCATION — Adult Education

367 US ISSN 0040-9448
TORCH (CHICAGO). 1928. 3/yr. $20 to non-members; libraries $7.50; foreign $25. International Association of Torch Clubs, c/o R. Patrtick Deans, Ed., Strickland & Jones, PC, 749 Boush St., Norfolk, VA 23510-1517. TEL 757-627-7672. FAX 757-623-9740. Ed. Patrick Deans. bk.rev.; index; circ. 2,850 (controlled). **Document type:** academic/scholarly publication.

369.5 IT
TOSCANA LIONS. 1972. m. Lions International, Distretto 108, Via Valdelsa 23, 53011 Castellina in Chianti, Italy. TEL 39-577-740374. circ. 3,500 (controlled). **Document type:** bulletin.

367 UK ISSN 0266-8491
TOWNSWOMAN. 1933. m. £6.05. E C N Special Publications, 69 Thorpe Rd., Norwich, Norfolk. NR1 1TB, England. FAX 01603-615973. Ed. Maria Eagling. adv.; bk.rev.; charts; illus. circ. 42,000.

658.048
TRACES (JACKSON). bi-m. $8 to non-members. Sierra Club, Mississippi Chapter, 921 N. Congress St., Jackson, MS 39202. TEL 601-352-1026. Ed. Harry Seeley. adv. circ. 550.
   Description: Provides information on club events, and on local legal developments related to the environment.

THE TRUTH (PHILADELPHIA). see INSURANCE

TUCKER TOPICS. see TRANSPORTATION — Automobiles

L'UNION. see RELIGIONS AND THEOLOGY — Roman Catholic

366 973 US ISSN 1070-9487
UNITED DAUGHTERS OF THE CONFEDERACY MAGAZINE.* 1933. m. $10. (United Daughters of the Confederacy) Acron Publishing, Inc., 1306 Gaskins Rd., Richmond, VA 23233-4919. TEL 804-762-8608. FAX 804-762-8610. (Subscr. to: UDC, 328 N. Boulevard, Richmond, VA 34330-4057. TEL 804-355-1636. FAX 804-353-1396) Ed. Dorothy Edgar. adv.: page $1100. index; circ. 9,300 (paid). (back issues avail.)
   Description: Focuses on Civil War and related topics.

369.11 355.115 US ISSN 0199-865X
V F W AUXILIARY. 1939. m. (8/yr.). membership only. Veterans of Foreign Wars of the United States, Ladies Auxiliary, 406 W. 34th St., Kansas City, MO 64111. TEL 816-561-8655. FAX 816-931-4753. Ed. Marilyn Ebersole; Pub. Rosemary Mazer. R&P contact: Marilyn Ebersole. TEL 816-561-7663. adv. contact: Al Cohen. bk.rev.; circ. 775,000 (controlled). **Document type:** bulletin.
   Formerly: Veterans of Foreign Wars. Ladies Auxiliary. National Bulletin.

367 GW
VERBAND DER DEUTSCHER-AMERIKANISCHEN CLUBS E.V. GAZETTE. 1954. q. DM.12. Verband der Deutsch-Amerikanischen Clubs e.V., Taubenweg 1, 35619 Braunfels, Germany. TEL 06442-8590. Ed. Hans Kubatz. circ. 8,700.

367 GW ISSN 0934-9022
VERBANDS-HANDBUCH. 1988. irreg. DM.128. Erich Schmidt Verlag GmbH & Co. (Berlin), Genthiner Str. 30G, 10785 Berlin, Germany. TEL 49-30-250085-0. FAX 49-30-25008521. (looseleaf format) **Document type:** bulletin.

367 658 GW ISSN 0937-4574
DER VEREIN. 1989. bi-m. DM.78. Verlag Wirtschaft Recht und Steuern, Fraunhoferstr. 5, 82152 Planegg, Germany. TEL 49-89-89517-0. FAX 49-89-89517250. (Subscr. to: Postfach 1363, 82142 Planegg, Germany) (looseleaf format) **Document type:** bulletin.

658.048 GW
VEREINS PRAXIS; Arbeitshilfen fuer Fuehrungskraefte und Organisationsleiter. 1981. m. DM.38.50 (effective 1996). (Deutscher Sportbund) Limpert Verlag GmbH, Postfach 4027, 65030 Wiesbaden, Germany. TEL 49-611-373072. FAX 49-611-373060. Ed. Karl Hoffmann. (looseleaf format; back issues avail.) **Document type:** bulletin.

366 355 US
VETERANS' BULLETIN. 1954. q. Georgia Department of Veterans Service, Floyd Veterans Bldg., 970 East, Atlanta, GA 30334. TEL 404-656-5933. FAX 404-656-5934. Ed. Charles Willey. circ. 2,400 (controlled). **Document type:** bulletin.
   Description: Contains all matters pertaining to veterans' affairs.

658.048 028.5 US ISSN 0865-3623
VEZETOK LAPJA/BULLETIN OF HUNGARIAN SCOUT LEADERS AND PARENTS. 1952. s-a. $5. Hungarian Scout Association, Box 68, Garfield, NJ 07026. TEL 201-772-8810. FAX 201-772-5145. Ed. Rev. John Adam. circ. 1,500. (back issues avail.) **Document type:** bulletin.
   Description: Articles of Hungarian ethnic cultural and religious interest and on techniques of passing on such values through scouting and through the family.

VIOLA D'AMORE SOCIETY OF AMERICA. NEWSLETTER. see MUSIC

369.2 US
VIRGINIA LEGIONNAIRE. vol.49, 1975. m. $1.50. American Legion, Department of Virginia, 1805 Chantilly St., Richmond, VA 23230. TEL 804-353-6606. FAX 804-358-1940. Ed. Cornelius T. O'Neill. R&P contact: Cornelius T. O'Neill. bk.rev. circ. 55,000. **Document type:** newspaper.

369.5 IT
VITA LIONS. bi-m. (7/yr.). (Lions International della Lombardia e della Provincia di Piacenza) Editrice Magalini, Via Gramsci 5, Rezzato (BS), Italy. TEL 030-2792968. FAX 030-2592291. TELEX 323088 PEGMOS I. Ed. Sirio Marciano. adv.: B&W page L.1012000. circ. 10,000.

367 CN ISSN 1201-6179
VOYAGEUR (WOODBRIDGE). 1990. m. Can.$30 membership (effective 1997). (U.S.S. Hudson Bay) Infinite Diversity International Corporation, c/o Lynda Ciaschini, 7050 Weston Rd., Ste. 301, Woodbridge, ON L4L 8G7, Canada. TEL 905-850-6080. FAX 905-850-6082. E-mail: l.ciaschini@genie.com. Ed. Sharon Lowachee; Pub. Peter Johnson. R&P contact: Lynda Ciaschini. adv.: page Can.$25; adv. contact: Sharon Lowachee. bk.rev. circ. 200. **Document type:** newsletter.
   Description: Covers Star Trek and other media news, puzzles, creative articles.

366 US ISSN 0042-9384
HS2008.L49
VYTIS/KNIGHT.* (Text in English and Lithuanian) 1915. 10/yr. $8. Knights of Lithuania, 6591 McEwen Rd., Centerville, OH 45459. TEL 513-433-2702. Ed. Aldona Ryan. adv.; bk.rev. circ. 3,000. (also avail. in microfilm)

AL-WA'I. see CHILDREN AND YOUTH — For

367 US
WESTCHESTER COUNTRY CLUB NEWS. 1933. 7/yr. $20. Westchester Country Club, Rye, NY 10580. TEL 914-967-6000. Ed. Cathy McCabe. adv.

COLLEGE AND ALUMNI

658 808.838 US
WESTWIND (SEATTLE). 1977. m. $15 (foreign $18). Northwest Science Fiction Society, Box 24207, Seattle, WA 98124-0207. TEL 206-248-2010. Ed.Bd. adv.; bk.rev.; film rev. circ. 300. (back issues avail.)
 Formerly: Northwest Science Fiction Society. Newsletter.
 Description: Publishes fiction, non-fiction, artwork, editorials, reviews and event listings.

WHOOP 'N' HOLLER. see *SPORTS AND GAMES — Outdoor Life*

WHO'S WHO IN ASSOCIATION PUBLISHING. see *PUBLISHING AND BOOK TRADE*

367 US ISSN 0043-5864
WINGED HEAD. 1911. m. $18. Pittsburgh Athletic Association, 4215 Fifth Ave., Pittsburgh, PA 15213. TEL 412-621-2400. FAX 412-321-4541. Ed. Kevin J. Gordon. adv.; circ. 3,500 (controlled).

366.1 368 US
WOMAN'S LIFE. 1894. q. membership. Woman's Life Insurance Society, Box 5020, Port Huron, MI 48061-5020. TEL 810-985-5191; 800-521-9292. FAX 810-985-6881. Ed. Patricia J. Samar. R&P contact: Patricia J. Samar. illus. circ. 36,000.
 Former titles: N A B A Review (ISSN 0027-5689); W B A Review.
 Description: Publishes articles on careers and employment, fitness, parenting and other issues relevant to women 25 to 44.

WOMEN'S CLUBS MAGAZINE. see *WOMEN'S INTERESTS*

658.048 US
WORKING CLASS HERO. 1968. 3/yr. $10 (foreign $15). Working Class Hero Club, 3311 Niagara St., Pittsburgh, PA 15213-4223. Ed. Barb Whatmough; Pub. Maxwell Cameron. R&P contact: Charles Koelmel. adv. contact: Sue Link. bk.rev. circ. 500. (looseleaf format) **Document type:** newsletter.
 Description: Covers news, pictures, and contributions of the Beatles.

369.4 SZ ISSN 0513-6032
WORLD ALLIANCE OF Y M C A'S DIRECTORY. 1920. biennial. 9 SFr. World Alliance of Young Men's Christian Associations, 12 Clos-Belmont, CH-1208 Geneva, Switzerland. TEL 41-22-8495100. FAX 41-22-8495110. Ed. Ranjan Solomon. R&P contact: Ranjan Solomon. adv. contact: Monika Rudiger. circ. 5,000. **Document type:** directory.

367 US
Y W C A INTERCHANGE. 1974. 2/yr. Young Women's Christian Association of the United States of America, 726 Broadway, New York, NY 10003. TEL 212-614-2700. FAX 212-677-9716. URL: http://www.ywca.org. Ed. Cindy Sutliff. bk.rev.; illus. circ. 35,000. (tabloid format) **Document type:** newsletter.

658.048 917.306 US
YE OLDE DUTCH MILL. 1957. q. $25. Holland America Club of the Pacific Northwest, Inc., 17122 25th Ave., N.E., Lake Forest Park, WA 98155-6134. TEL 206-363-2772. (Subscr. to: Albert Nijenhuis, 13727 41st Ave. N.E., Seattle, WA 98125) Ed. Albert Nijenhuis. adv. contact: George Klungel. bk.rev.; circ. 350 (paid). **Document type:** newsletter.

369.5 US
YOUNG WOMEN'S CHRISTIAN ASSOCIATION OF THE UNITED STATES OF AMERICA. NATIONAL BOARD. ANNUAL REPORT. a. Young Women's Christian Association of the United States of America, 726 Broadway, New York, NY 10003. TEL 212-614-2700. FAX 212-677-9716. URL: http://www.ywca.org. Ed. Cindy Sutliff. **Document type:** corporate report.

367 US
THE 170 NEWS. 1969. q. $25 (effective 1997). International Cessna 170 Association Inc., Box 1667, Lebanon, MO 65536-1667. TEL 417-532-4847. FAX 417-532-4847. E-mail: c170hq@mail.llion.org. Ed. Velvet Fackeldey. adv.; circ. 1,550 (controlled). (back issues avail.)

COLLEGE AND ALUMNI

see also *Literary and Political Reviews; Literature*

378.1 US
A A U W NEW YORKER. Variant title: A A U W New York Division Reports. vol.25, 1976. q. membership. American Association of University Women, New York State Division, c/o Barbara P. Carier, Ed., 295 Lakewood Pkwy., Snyder, NY 14226. illus. circ. 9,000.
 Formerly (until 1977): A A U W New York Division. Newsletter (ISSN 0001-0286)

378 910.03 US
A & T REGISTER. (Agricultural & Technical) 1892. w. $12. North Carolina Agricultural and Technical University, Box E25, Greensboro, NC 27411. TEL 919-334-7700. Ed. Esther Woods. adv. **Document type:** newspaper.
 Description: Oriented toward the collegiate black-American.

378 US
A C CURRENT. s-a. Amarillo College, Box 447, Amarillo, TX 79178. TEL 806-371-5290. **Document type:** consumer publication.

378 500 AT ISSN 0727-386X
A N U REPORTER. 1970. s-m. Aus.$30 to non-members. Australian National University, I Block, Canberra, A.C.T. 0200, Australia. TEL 61-6-2494171. FAX 61-6-2495568. E-mail: editor.anu.reporter@anu.edu.au; URL: http://online.anu.edu.au/pad/theanureporter.html. Ed. Liz Tynan. adv. contact: Christine Callen. bk.rev. circ. 10,000. **Document type:** academic/scholarly publication.
 Description: Covers research and science discoveries at ANU. Publishes new academic papers on theories involving ANU.

378.198 US ISSN 0895-5433
A P U LIFE. q. Azusa Pacific University, 901 E. Alosta Ave., Box 7000, Azusa, CA 91702-7000. TEL 818-815-5339. FAX 818-815-5415. Ed. Cynndie Hoff. circ. 55,000. (back issues avail.) **Document type:** academic/scholarly publication.
 Description: News of the university for parents, donors, alumni and friends.

371.83 US
A T O PALM.* 1880. 2/yr. $4. Alpha Tau Omega Fraternity, Inc., 141 E. Washington St., Ste. 300, Indianapolis, IN 46204-3614. TEL 217-351-1865. FAX 217-355-0910. Ed. Wynn Smuey. circ. 100,000.
 Description: News of interest to Fraternity members - alumni in particular.

378 IS
HA-ACADAMAI. bi-m. free. Union of Graduates in the Social Sciences and Humanities, 93 Arlozorov St., Tel Aviv, Israel. TEL 972-3-6919239. FAX 972-3-5441285. Ed. Uzi Berlinski. circ. 30,000.

378.1 CN ISSN 0044-5843
ACADIA BULLETIN. 1912. 3/yr. free. Acadia University, Associated Alumni, Box 520, Wolfville, NS B0P 1X0, Canada. TEL 902-585-1626. FAX 902-585-1058. E-mail: alumni.office@acadian.ca; URL: http://acadian.ca/alumni/alumni.html. Ed. Linda Cann; Pub. Steven Pound. adv.; bk.rev. circ. 20,000. **Document type:** bulletin.

378 US
ACKNOWLEDGE. 1962. q. Austin College, 900 N. Grand Ave., Ste. 6H, Sherman, TX 75090-4440. TEL 903-813-2386. FAX 903-813-2415. adv.; illus. circ. 13,500 (controlled). **Document type:** academic/scholarly publication, newsletter.

378.1 NE ISSN 0001-8139
ADELAAR. 1948. irreg. (3-4/yr.). free. Sint Janscollege, c/o Editor, Colijnplein 9, 2555 HA The Hague, Netherlands. Ed. B.W. Dijkmans. bk.rev.; film rev.; play rev.; rec.rev.; illus. circ. 850. (tabloid format)

378 US
ADVANCE - TITAN. 1894. w. $5. (University of Wisconsin at Oshkosh) Advance - Titan, 800 Algoma Blvd., Oshkosh, WI 54901. TEL 414-424-3048. FAX 414-424-0866. E-mail: atitan@vaxa.cis.uwosh.edu. Ed. Gerald L. Rhoden. R&P contact: Gerald L. Rhoden. adv. contact: Diana Bagley. bk.rev.; film rev.; play rev.; illus.; circ. 9,000 (controlled). (broadsheet format) **Document type:** newspaper.
 Formerly: Oshkosh Advance - Titan (ISSN 0300-676X)
 Refereed Serial

378.1 US
ADVOCATE (JOHNSTOWN). 1929. 24/yr. $6. University of Pittsburgh at Johnstown, Johnstown, PA 15904. TEL 814-269-7470. adv.; bk.rev.; film rev.; bibl. circ. 2,800. (tabloid format; also avail. in microform)
 Formerly (until vol.46, 1973): Panther (ISSN 0031-1006)

378.198 US
ADVOCATE (KANSAS CITY). 1969. 15/yr. $5. Kansas City Community College, 7250 State Ave., Kansas City, KS 66112. TEL 913-334-1100. FAX 913-596-9606. adv.; bk.rev. circ. 3,000. (back issues avail.)

378 US
THE ADVOCATE (SAN PABLO). 1950. w. free. Contra Costa College, 2600 Mission Bell Dr., San Pablo, CA 94806. TEL 510-235-7800. FAX 510-236-6768. Ed. Corey Pride. R&P contact: Paul DeBolt. adv. contact: Diana Christian. circ. 2,500. (also avail. in microfilm from LIB) **Document type:** newspaper.
 Description: Covers news and issues about Contra Costa College.

378 352.9 US
AGENDA (NEW BRUNSWICK). q. $25 donation. Rutgers University, Edward J. Bloustein School of Planning and Public Policy, New Brunswick, NJ 08903. Ed. Henry F. de Mena. illus. **Document type:** newsletter.

378 US ISSN 1070-1745
AGGIE PANORAMA; for alumni and friends of NMSU. 1951. q. free. New Mexico State University, Box 3K, Las Cruces, NM 88003-8001. TEL 505-646-3221. FAX 505-646-2099. URL: http://www.nmsu.edu/-ncomm/Panorama/Panoramatoc.html. Ed. Catherine Lazorko. circ. 60,000. (tabloid format; back issues avail.) **Document type:** newsletter.
 ●Also available online.
 Description: Includes alumni and university news.

378 US
AGNES SCOTT ALUMNAE MAGAZINE. 1923. 2/yr. free to qualified personnel. Agnes Scott College, 141 E. College Ave., Decatur, GA 30030. TEL 404-638-6315. FAX 404-638-6177. bk.rev. circ. 16,000.

378.18 CN ISSN 0828-5225
AGORA. 1968. m. Lakehead University, Student Union, Thunder Bay, ON P7B 5E1, Canada. TEL 807-343-8193. FAX 807-343-8192. TELEX 073-4594. Ed. Frances Harding. adv.; bk.rev.; circ. 2,000 (controlled). (back issues avail.) **Document type:** newsletter.
 Former titles (until 1985): Alias L U Week 2 (ISSN 0828-5217); (until 1984): L U Week 2 (ISSN 0828-5209); (until 1974): L U Week (ISSN 0827-9616)

378 GW ISSN 0177-9265
AGORA. 1984. q. Katholische Universitaet Eichstaett, Ostenstr. 26, 85072 Eichstaett, Germany. TEL 08421-20246. adv.; illus. circ. 5,000. **Document type:** bulletin.

AGRI-NATURALIST. see *AGRICULTURE*

AKADEMISCHE MONATSBLAETTER. see *RELIGIONS AND THEOLOGY — Roman Catholic*

378.198 US
AKRON; the magazine of the University of Akron. 1986. 4/yr. free. University of Akron, Office of the Alumni Association, Akron, OH 44325-2602. TEL 216-972-7270. FAX 216-972-5335. E-mail: editor@uakron.edu. Ed. Jennifer Lavy. adv.: B&W page $2000, color page $2750; trim 8 3/8 x 10 7/8; adv. contact: Jennifer Lavy. circ. 85,000 (controlled). (back issues avail.)
  Formerly: Akron Magazine.
  Description: Contains news and features about the University of Akron for employees, friends and alumni.

378 US
ALABAMA ALUMNI MAGAZINE. bi-m. membership. (University of Alabama, National Alumni Association) University of Alabama, Office of Alumni Affairs, Box 1928, Tuscaloosa, AL 35486. Ed. Kelly Saxton; Pub. Pat Whetstone. adv. contact: Pam Lyons. circ. 33,000.
  Supersedes: Alabama Alumni Bulletin; Incorporates: Alabama Alumni News.
  Description: Features news of alumni and of events on campus.

378 US
THE ALABAMIAN. 1922. fortn. $7. (University of Montevallo) Selma Times Press, Sta. 6230, Montevallo, AL 35115. TEL 205-665-6230. FAX 205-665-6224. Ed. Alan Jefferson. adv.; bk.rev. circ. 2,500. (also avail. in microfilm) **Document type:** newspaper.

378.198 US
ALBRIGHTIAN. s-m. $25. Albright College, Albrightian, Box 15234, Reading, PA 19612-5234. Ed. Rebecca Ann York. adv.; film rev.; play rev.; illus.; tr.lit.; circ. 1,600 (controlled). (tabloid format; back issues avail.)

378 US
ALESTLE. 1957. s-w. $36. Southern Illinois University at Edwardsville, Campus Box 1167, Edwardsville, IL 62025. TEL 618-692-3528. FAX 618-692-3528. adv. circ. 5,000. (tabloid format) **Document type:** newspaper.

378 CN
ALGONQUIN TIMES. 1986. bi-m. Algonquin College, 1385 Woodroffe Ave., Nepean, ON K2G 1V8, Canada. FAX 613-727-7684. Ed. Steve Forster. R&P contact: Steve Forster. TEL 613-727-4723. adv.; film rev. circ. 5,000. **Document type:** newspaper.
  Formerly: Impact (Nepean).

378 US
ALL STATE. w. (Sep.-May). $12. Austin Peay State University, Box 8334, Clarksville, TN 37044-8334. TEL 615-648-7376.

378 US
ALLIANCE (CHARLESTON). 1985. a. $15 membership (effective 1997). Medical University of South Carolina, College of Health Related Professions, Alumni Association, 171 Ashley Ave., Charleston, SC 29425. Ed. Wanda Hancock. circ. 3,200. **Document type:** newsletter.
  Description: News, information, and announcements for the alumni of the Medical University of South Carolina, College of Health-Related Professions.

371.85 US ISSN 0162-5918
ALPHA; the magazine for campus Greeks. 1979. m. (during academic year). $8. Alpha Publications Inc., 3235 Glen Logan Rd., Memphis, TN 38134. adv. circ. 500,000.

ALPHA DIGEST. see *GENERAL INTEREST PERIODICALS — India*

378 US
ALPHA KAPPA PSI. DIARY.* 1908. q. $10. Alpha Kappa Psi National Business Fraternity, 9595 Angola Ct., Indianapolis, IN 46268. TEL 317-872-1553. Ed. Frank J. Brye. adv. circ. 25,000.
  Description: Provides articles on achieving executive success in business, college education for business, news of chapters and prominent members.

ALPHA PSI OMEGA: PLAYBILL. see *THEATER*

378.1 US ISSN 0892-7839
ALUMNEWS. 1967. 4/yr. free to alumni and donors. Creighton University, University Relations Division, 2500 California, Omaha, NE 68178. TEL 402-280-2700. Ed. Pamela A. Vaughn. bk.rev. circ. 41,500. (tabloid format)
  Formerly: P.S.: Postscript to Education (ISSN 0030-8315)

378.198 US
ALUMNI COLUMNS. 1975. 4/yr. Augusta College, 2500 Walton Way, Augusta, GA 30910. TEL 404-737-1759.

378.1 US
ALUMNI COMPANION. 1985. 3/yr. free to alumni. University of New Hampshire, Alumni Association, Elliott Alumni Center, 9 Edgewood Rd., Durham, NH 03824. TEL 603-862-2040. FAX 603-862-4126. Ed. Kimberly Swick Slover. R&P contact: Kimberly Swick Slover. adv. contact: Kimberly Swick Slover. bk.rev.; circ. 75,000 (controlled). **Document type:** newspaper.
  Formerly (until 1991): New Hampshire Alumnus (ISSN 0028-5196)
  Description: Articles of general interest for alumni(ae), donors and other friends of the University.
  Refereed Serial

378 US
ALUMNI NEWS (GREENSBORO). 1912. 3/yr. free to members. University of North Carolina at Greensboro, Alumni Association, Greensboro, NC 27412-5001. TEL 910-334-5921. FAX 910-334-4055. Ed. Miriam C. Barkley. bk.rev.; circ. 4,000 (controlled). (back issues avail.) **Document type:** bulletin.
  Formerly: Alumnae News.
  Description: Communicates to the members of the Alumni Association.

378 US
ALUMNI NEWS (ST. LOUIS). 1982. s-a. free to alumni. School of the Art Institute of Chicago, 37 S. Wabash, Chicago, IL 60603. FAX 312-263-0141. E-mail: KPAPAICD@ARTIC.EDU. Ed. Rita Price. R&P contact: Rita Price. bk.rev.; circ. 12,000 (controlled). **Document type:** newsletter.
  Formerly: Visions (St. Louis).

378.198 US
ALUMNI RELATIONS NEWS - CARSON-NEWMAN COLLEGE. 3/yr. Carson - Newman College, Office of Alumni Relations, S. Russell Ave., Jefferson City, TN 37760.

378.1 CN ISSN 0041-4999
ALUMNI U B C CHRONICLE. 1941. 3/yr. Can.$10 ($15) University of British Columbia, Alumni Association, Cecil Green Park, 6251 Cecil Green Park Rd., Vancouver, BC V6T 1Z1, Canada. TEL 604-882-3313. FAX 604-822-8928. E-mail: cpetty@alumni.ubc.ca; alumni@alumni.ubc.ca; URL: http://www.alumi.ubc.ca. Ed. Chris Petty. R&P contact: Oiyce Kwan. adv.: B&W page $1600, color page $2100; 7 1/2 x 9 3/4; adv. contact: Mangot Dear. bk.rev.; illus.; circ. 120,000 (controlled). (back issues avail.) Indexed: Can.Educ.Ind., Can.Per.Ind. **Document type:** academic/scholarly publication.
  Formerly: U B C Alumni Chronicle.

ALUMNUS (NEW YORK). see *MEDICAL SCIENCES — Orthopedics And Traumatology*

378.1 US ISSN 1056-6295
ALUMNUS - THE CITY COLLEGE OF NEW YORK. 1904. 4/yr. membership. City College of New York, Alumni Association, Box 177, New York, NY 10027. TEL 212-234-3000. FAX 212-368-6576. Ed. Marlene Charnizon. bk.rev.; illus. circ. 20,000.
  Former titles (until 1993): City College Alumnus (ISSN 0045-6993); (until 1926): City College Quarterly.
  Description: Articles profiling prominent alumni; their endeavors; programs; faculty or students of the City College.
  Refereed Serial

378 US
ALVERNO TODAY. 1968. 3/yr. free. Alverno College, 3401 S. 39th St., Box 343922, Milwaukee, WI 53234-3922. TEL 414-382-6166. FAX 414-382-6167. Ed. Kathleen A. Mulvey. R&P contact: Kathleen A. Mulvey. circ. 17,000. **Document type:** newsletter.
  Description: Carries news of Alverno alumnae, students, and faculty.

378 CN
THE AMBASSADOR. 1979. bi-w. free. University of Windsor, 484 Sunset Ave., Windsor, ON N9B 3P4, Canada. TEL 519-253-4232. E-mail: ambassad@uwindsor.ca. Ed. Jennifer Barone. R&P contact: Jennifer Barone. adv. circ. 2,100. **Document type:** newspaper.
  Formerly (until 1995): University of Windsor. Newsline 0709-4132)

378 US
AMERICAN. 1977. q. free. American University, Office of University Publications, Washington, DC 20016-8121. TEL 202-885-5970. FAX 202-885-5949. Ed. Mary Jo Binker. circ. 65,000 (controlled).
  Supersedes: American University Report (ISSN 0300-7421)
  Description: News and updates about The American University sent to alumni and other constituents of the university community.

378 US
AMERICAN SCENE (WASHINGTON). vol.2, 1984. bi-w. American University, Office of University Relations, Letts Hall, Lower Level, University Publications and Printing Office, 4400 Mass. Ave. N.W., Washington, DC 20016. Ed. Marion Martin. illus. circ. 7,100.

378.1 US
AMHERST. 1949. q. free to alumni. Amherst College, Alumni Council, Public Affairs Office, Box 2202, Amherst, MA 01002. TEL 413-542-2313. FAX 413-542-2042. Ed. Douglas C. Wilson. bk.rev. circ. 21,000. **Document type:** bulletin.
  Formerly: Amherst Alumni News (ISSN 0003-1690)

378 US
AMHERST STUDENT. 1868. w. (Sep.-Dec. & Feb.-May). $50. Box 1816, Amherst College, Amherst, MA 01002-5000. TEL 413-542-2304. FAX 413-542-2305. E-mail: student@amhest.edu. Ed. Jefferson Decker; Pub. Jason Eugene Heindel. R&P contact: Jason Eugene Heindel. adv. contact: Jay Rho. bk.rev. circ. 2,500. (tabloid format) **Document type:** newspaper.

AMUDIM. see *ETHNIC INTERESTS*

378.1 NE ISSN 0003-3669
ANIMO. (Supplement) 1928. bi-m. membership. Baarnsch Lyceum, Torenlaan 77, Baarn, Netherlands. Ed.Bd. adv.; charts; illus. circ. 900.

378.18 US
ANNANDALE CAMPUS PEASHOOTER. 1984. s-m. $12 to non-members. North Virginia Community College, Student Activities, 8333 Little River Tpk., Annandale, VA 22003. TEL 703-323-3147. FAX 703-323-3437. adv.; bk.rev.; film rev.; play rev. circ. 5,000. (back issues avail.)
  Formerly: Parthian Shot.

ANTHEON. see *LITERATURE*

378 US
THE APPALACHIAN. 1934. s-w. free. Appalachian State University, W.H. Plemmons Student Union, ASU Drawer 9025, Boone, NC 28608. TEL 704-262-3104. Ed. Darin Glass. R&P contact: Darin Glass. TEL 704-262-6149. adv. contact: John O'Brien. bk.rev. circ. 7,000. **Document type:** newspaper.

378 CN
AQUINIAN. 1935. bi-w (during school year). Can.$26 (free in Fredericton). Saint Thomas University, Student Union Bldg., Rm. 32, Fredericton, NB E3B 5G3, Canada, Canada. TEL 506-460-0300. FAX 506-453-4538. E-mail: aquinian@stthomasu.ca. Ed. Adam Jarris. adv. contact: Ryan Carr. bk.rev.; circ. 4,400 (controlled). (tabloid format) **Document type:** academic/scholarly publication.
  Description: Student-run publication covering topics of interest at the University.
  Refereed Serial

378 US
THE ARBITER. 1955. w. free. Boise State University, 1910 University Dr., Boise, ID 83725. TEL 208-345-8204. FAX 208-385-3198. Ed. Adam Rush. adv. contact: Jeff Thompson. circ. 15,000. **Document type:** newspaper.

378
THE ARCHWAY (SMITHFIELD); Bryant College student newspaper. 1905. w. $25. Bryant College, Box 7, 1150 Douglas Pike, Smithfield, RI 02917-1284. TEL 401-232-6028. FAX 401-232-6319. Ed. Julia M. Arovchon. adv. circ. 3,500. **Document type:** newspaper.
●Also available online.
Formerly (until 1946): Bryant & Stratton News.

378 SA
ARENA. 1994. a. R.7.50 per issue (free to alumni). University of the Witwatersrand, Office of Alumni Affairs, P.O. Box 98034, Sloane Park 2152, South Africa. adv.; illus.

378.1 CN ISSN 0044-8818
ARGOSY WEEKLY. 1875. w. Can.$25 (students Can.$18). (Mount Allison University) Argosy Publications Inc., Rm. 302, University Centre, Sackville, NB E0A 3C0, Canada. TEL 506-364-2235. FAX 506-536-4230. Ed. Marty Patriguin. adv. contact: Deanna Christie. bk.rev. circ. 2,200. **Document type:** newspaper.
Description: Independent journal of news, opinion and the arts, written, edited and published by students of Mount Allison University.

378.1 US ISSN 0004-1181
ARGUS (BLOOMINGTON). 1894. w. $23 (effective 1997-98). Illinois Wesleyan University, Box 2900, Bloomington, IL 61702. TEL 309-556-3036. E-mail: theargus@sun.iwv.edu; URL: http://www.iwv.edu/~theargus. Ed. Ethan Schrum. adv.: page $295; adv. contact: Matt O Connor. bk.rev.; play rev.; film rev.; illus. circ. 3,000. (broadsheet format; also avail. in microfiche from UMI) **Document type:** newspaper.
Refereed Serial

371.85 CN ISSN 0004-1165
THE ARGUS (THUNDER BAY); the student newspaper of Lakehead University. 1966. w. Can.$4.50 (foreign Can.$7) (effective 1997). Lakehead University, Student Union, 955 Oliver Rd., Thunder Bay, ON P7B 5E1, Canada. TEL 807-344-6911. FAX 807-343-8598. E-mail: argus@sky.lakeheadu.ca. Ed. Graig Kent. R&P contact: Graig Kent. adv. contact: Anna DeZan. bk.rev.; film rev.; play rev. circ. 5,000. (tabloid format) Indexed: Lib.Lit., Pt.de Rep. **Document type:** newspaper.

378.1 US ISSN 0004-1394
ARIZONA ALUMNUS. 1923. s-a. free. University of Arizona, Alumni Association, 1111 N. Cherry Ave., Tucson, AZ 85721. TEL 602-621-3791. FAX 602-621-9030. E-mail: rochlin@al.arizona.edu. Ed. Jay Rochlin. adv.; bk.rev.; illus. circ. 150,000.

378 US
ARIZONA DAILY WILDCAT. 1915. d. (Mon.- Fri.). $75. University of Arizona, Board of Publications, Students Union Bldg., Rm. 5, Tucson, AZ 85721. TEL 602-621-3408. FAX 602-621-3409. E-mail: wildcat@u.arizona.edu; URL: http://wildcat.arizona.edu/~wildcat. Ed. Christine Verges; Pub. Mark Woodhams. adv. contact: Anna Martinez-Ross. bk.rev. circ. 22,500. (tabloid format) **Document type:** newspaper.

378.1 US ISSN 0004-1882
ARKA-TECH. 1925. w. $5. Arkansas Tech University, Russellville, AR 72801. TEL 501-968-0284. adv.; bk.rev. circ. 2,500. (tabloid format)

378 US
ARKANSAS TRAVELER. 1907. 2/w. $20. University of Arkansas, Board of Publications, 747 W. Dixon St., Ste. 5, Fayetteville, AR 72701. TEL 501-575-3406. FAX 501-575-3306. Ed. Candace K. Meierdiercks. R&P contact: Patsy Watkins. TEL 501-575-3601. circ. 8,000. (tabloid format) **Document type:** newspaper.

378 051
AROUND & ABOUT K S U. 1983. bi-w. Kentucky State University, Office of Publicity Relations, Hume Hall, Frankfort, KY 40601. TEL 502-227-6688. circ. 450. **Document type:** newsletter.
Description: Acts as a faculty newsletter

378.1 CN ISSN 0044-9091
ARTHUR. 1966. w. Can.$24. Trent University, Peterborough, ON K9J 7B8, Canada. TEL 705-748-1786. Eds. Naomi Petersen, Sharon Charke. adv.; bk.rev. circ. 3,000. (tabloid format)
Formerly: Sword.

378 CN
L'ASSETU. m. free. Publi-PEQ, 3575 bd. St. Laurent, Ste. 232, Montreal, PQ H2X 2T7, Canada. TEL 514-845-8628. circ. 2,000. (tabloid format)

378 US
ASSOCIATION OF COLLEGE HONOR SOCIETIES, BOOKLET OF INFORMATION. 1945. triennial. latest 1995. free. Association of College Honor Societies, c/o Dorothy I. Mitstifer, Sec.-Treas., 4990 Northwind Dr., Ste. 140, East Lansing, MI 48823-5031. TEL 517-351-8335. FAX 517-351-8336. E-mail: dmitstifer@achsnatl.org; URL: http://www.achsnatl.org. R&P contact: Dorothy Mitstifer. circ. 15,000. **Document type:** directory.

ASSOCIATION OF COLLEGE UNIONS - INTERNATIONAL. BULLETIN. see *EDUCATION*

ASSOCIATION OF M B AS ADDRESS BOOK. see *BUSINESS AND ECONOMICS — Management*

378.1 US ISSN 0004-6434
AT COOPER UNION. 1964. irreg. (3-4/yr.). free. Cooper Union for the Advancement of Science and Art, 41 Cooper Sq., New York, NY 10003. TEL 212-353-4155. FAX 212-353-4327. Ed. Todd Brewster. circ. 15,500.
Description: News, articles, announcements, book market, and alumni notes of interest to the students, faculty, and alumni administrators of this science and art institution.

378 CN ISSN 0004-6566
ATHENAEUM. 1874. w. free. (Acadia University, Students' Union) Athenaeum Publications, P.O. Box 698, Wolfville, NS B0P 1X0, Canada. TEL 902-585-2147. FAX 902-542-3901. E-mail: ath@admin.acadiau.ca. Ed. Cherri Greeno. R&P contact: Craig Kennedy. adv. contact: Sujata Dey. bk.rev. circ. 3,000. (tabloid format) **Document type:** newspaper.

378.1 CN
ATKINSONIAN. (Text mainly in English; occasionally in French) 1968. 15/yr. free. Atkinson College Students' Association, Atkinson College, 4700 Keel St., Rm. 105, Downsview, Ont. M3J 1P3, Canada. TEL 416-736-2100. Ed. Edmund Abaka. adv.; bk.rev. circ. 6,000.
Former titles: Atkinson Balloon; Balloon (ISSN 0045-1355).

378 US
ATLANTA UNIVERSITY BULLETIN. 1934. s-a. Atlanta University, 223 James P. Brawley Dr., S.W., Atlanta, GA 30314. TEL 404-653-8400. Ed. Gwen Calleway. circ. 8,500. **Document type:** bulletin.

378 US ISSN 1077-8640
AUBURN MAGAZINE. 1946. q. $30 membership. Auburn University Alumni Association, 317 S. College St., Auburn, AL 36849-5150. TEL 334-844-1149. FAX 334-844-3716. E-mail: abumag@alumni.auburn.edu. Ed. Michael Jernigan. adv. contact: Mary Ellen Hendrix. bk.rev. circ. 41,000. (back issues avail.)
Formerly (until Jan. 1994): Auburn Alumnews.

378 US ISSN 1071-1279
AUBURN PLAINSMAN. 1893. w. $15. Auburn University, Board of Student Communications, B-100 Foy Union Bldg., Auburn, AL 36849-3501. TEL 205-844-4130. Ed. Greg Klein. adv. circ. 18,000. (also avail. in microform)

610 US
AUCTUS; the alumni and development bulletin. 1942. s-a. membership. Medical University of South Carolina, Office of Development, 171 Ashley Ave., Charleston, SC 29425. TEL 803-792-4275. Ed. Bonnie Jerdan Sayles. charts; illus.; circ. 20,000 (controlled). (tabloid format)
Former titles (until 1985): Auctus Alumni Bulletin; (until 1978): Medical University of South Carolina. Bulletin (ISSN 0049-1497); 1952-1969: Medical College of South Carolina Bulletin (ISSN 0098-5805)
Description: Articles, news, and photographs on the activities of and the issues affecting the alumni of the Medical University of South Carolina.

378 GW
AUDIMAX; die Hochschulzeitschrift. 1988. m. DM.20 to students. Audimax Verlag GmbH, Postfach 120240, 90109 Nuernberg, Germany. TEL 49-911-209099. FAX 49-911-204939. Ed. Barbara Martin. adv.: color page DM.35000; adv. contact: Marc Huebner. (back issues avail.) **Document type:** academic/scholarly publication.

378 US ISSN 0300-6964
AUGSBURG COLLEGE NOW. vol.36, 1973. 3/yr. free. Augsburg College, 2211 Riverside Ave., Minneapolis, MN 55454. TEL 612-330-1181. Ed. Betsey Norgard. illus. circ. 18,000. **Document type:** academic/scholarly publication.

378.1 US ISSN 0004-7945
AUGSBURG ECHO. 1891. 22/yr. $35. Augsburg College, 2211 Riverside Ave., Minneapolis, MN 55454. TEL 612-330-1102. adv.; bk.rev.; play rev. circ. 3,000. (tabloid format; back issues avail.) **Document type:** newspaper.

378 US ISSN 0746-1704
AUGUSTANA COLLEGE MAGAZINE. 1935. 2/yr. Augustana College, Office of Publications, Rock Island, IL 61201. TEL 309-794-7721. Ed. Debbie Blaylock. circ. 26,000.

378 UK ISSN 0950-7167
AVENUE; the magazine for graduates and friends of the University of Glasgow. 1987. s-a. free. University of Glasgow, Publicity Services, Glasgow G12 8QQ, Scotland. TEL 44-141-339-8855. FAX 44-141-330-5643. URL: http://www.gla.ac.uk. Ed. Mike Brown. adv.; bk.rev. circ. 75,000. (back issues avail.)
Description: Feature articles on people, research and events in the University of Glasgow.

378 US
AZTEC PRESS. 1973. w. Pima County Community College, 2202 W. Anklam Rd., Tucson, AZ 85709. TEL 602-884-6800. FAX 602-884-6215. adv. circ. 9,000.

810 US
B C C EVENING REPORTER. vol.17, 1975. q. free to B.C.C. students. Bronx Community College, Evening Student Association, University Ave. & W. 181st St., New York, NY 10458. TEL 212-220-6487. Ed. Joe Sanders. illus.

378.198 US
B G NEWS. 1920. 5/w. $108.50. Bowling Green State University, University Board of Student Publications, 214 W. Hall, Bowling Green, OH 43403. TEL 419-372-2601. FAX 419-372-0202. Ed. Scott Brown. adv. contact: Todd Wise. circ. 11,200. (also avail. in microfiche) **Document type:** newspaper.

378.1 IS
B G U NOW. (Text in English) 1975; N.S. 1995. s-a. free. Ben Gurion University, Department of Public Affairs, P.O. Box 653, Beersheva 84105, Israel. TEL 972-7-239943. FAX 972-7-472937. E-mail: prpub@bgumail.ac.il. Eds. Etti Naven, Angie Zamir. circ. 11,000.
Supersedes: Negev (ISSN 0334-374X) & Ben Gurion University. Bulletin (ISSN 0334-3790)

378.1 US
BABSON BULLETIN. 1933. 3/yr. free. Babson College, Babson Park, MA 02157-0310. TEL 617-239-5256. FAX 617-239-5989. E-mail: alumnews@babson.edu; URL: http://www.babson.edu/alumni. Ed. Melinda Lamb Theodore. R&P contact: Melinda Lamb Theodore. illus.; circ. 31,000 (controlled). **Document type:** bulletin.
Formerly: Babson Alumni Bulletin (ISSN 0005-3538)

378 UK
BACUS. 1972. 8/yr. University of the West of England, Students' Union, Frenchay Campus, Bristol BS16 1QY, England. TEL 0117-965-6261. FAX 0117-976-3909. Ed. Mike Lock. adv.: page £320; adv. contact: Mike Lock. bk.rev. circ. 8,000. **Document type:** bulletin.

378.1 US ISSN 0045-1304
BADGER HERALD. 1969. d. $160. Badger Herald, Inc., 550 State St., Madison, WI 53703. TEL 608-257-4712. FAX 608-257-6899. Ed. Eric Dunn; Pub. Eric Hartung. adv. contact: Robert LeGrand. bk.rev.; film rev.; play rev.; illus. circ. 20,000. **Document type:** newspaper.

371.8 PH
▼**BALINGHAD**; an institutional publication of the Notre Dame University. (Text in English) 1996. 2/yr. Notre Dame University, 9600 Cotabato City, Philippines. TEL 63-64-21-4312. FAX 63-64-21-4312.
Description: Covers university news and activities.

378 US
BALL STATE DAILY NEWS. (Annual supplement avail.: Homecoming Issue) 1922. d. (Mon.-Fri.). $30. Ball State University, W. Quad., Rm. 212, Muncie, IN 47306. TEL 317-285-8218. FAX 317-285-8248. URL: http://www.dailynews.bsu.edu. Ed. Bill Webster. R&P contact: David Knott. adv. contact: Kelly Ratliff. bk.rev. circ. 14,000. **Document type:** newspaper.

378 CN
BANDERSNATCH. 1971. bi-w. free. John Abbott College, Student Activities Committee, P.O. Box 2000, St. Anne de Bellvue, PQ H9X 3L9, Canada. TEL 514-457-6610. FAX 514-457-4730. adv.: B&W page Can.$220; adv. contact: Tara Morrison. bk.rev.; film rev. circ. 2,200. (tabloid format) **Document type:** newspaper.
Description: Review of campus news and the entertainment scene.

378 US
BARD OBSERVER. 1961. w. $20. Observer Press, Inc., Bard College, Annandale, NY 12504. TEL 914-758-0772. Ed. Kristan Hutchison. adv.; bk.rev.; film rev.; play rev.; illus. circ. 2,000.

378 US ISSN 0749-1263
LH1.B23
BARNARD ALUMNAE.* 1912. q. free. Barnard College, 111 Milbank, 3009 Broadway, New York. TEL 212-854-2006. FAX 212-749-6531. Ed. Kate Walbert. bk.rev. circ. 23,000. (back issues avail.) **Document type:** bulletin.
Description: Includes articles about Barnard College and about issues of interest to educated women of all ages.

378.1 US ISSN 0005-6014
BARNARD BULLETIN. 1901. w. $12. Barnard College, 3009 Broadway, New York, NY 10027-6598. TEL 212-854-2005. FAX 212-749-6531. Eds. Gretchen Crary, Ali Stone. adv.; bk.rev.; film rev.; play rev. circ. 5,000. (also avail. in microform) **Document type:** bulletin.
Description: Articles on campus news and features on the arts and entertainment.

378.1 CN ISSN 0845-2660
BARON. 1966. bi-w. free. (University of New Brunswick, Students' Representative Council) Tucker Park Press, P.O. Box 5050, Saint John, NB E2L 4L5, Canada. TEL 506-648-5676. FAX 506-648-5541. Ed. Lindy MacNeill. R&P contact: Lindy MacNeill. adv.; bk.rev.; film rev. circ. 1,500. (tabloid format) **Indexed:** Can.Per.Ind. **Document type:** newspaper.
Former titles (until 1988): Tucker Park Press (ISSN 0845-2652); (until 1984): Saint John Viewpoint (ISSN 0046-2381); Equinox.

378 US
BARTON SCOPE. 1956. s-a. free. Barton College, Box 5000, College Station, Wilson, NC 27893. TEL 919-399-6529. FAX 919-399-0893. E-mail: wdaughet@barton.edu; URL: http://www.barton.edu. Ed. Kathy Daughety; Pub. James B. Hemry, Jr. circ. 17,500. (controlled).
Description: Provides alumni and campus news for alumni and friends of Barton College.

378.198 US
BARUCH TODAY. 1953. a. free to qualified personnel. City University of New York, Baruch College, 17 Lexington Ave., Box 516, New York, NY 10010. TEL 212-387-1130. stat. circ. 41,000.
Description: For the faculty, staff and alumni of Baruch College.

378.198 US
BATES; the alumni magazine. 1921. 3/yr. free to qualified personnel. Bates College, 141 Nichols St., Lewiston, ME 04240. TEL 207-786-6330. FAX 207-786-8241. URL: http://www.bates.edu/pubs/mag/. Ed. Betsy Kimball. bk.rev. circ. 19,000.

378.198 US
THE BATES STUDENT. 1873. w. $18. Trustees of Bates College, 309 Bates College, Lewiston, ME 04240. TEL 207-795-7494. Ed. Laura Mytels. adv.; bk.rev. circ. 2,500. (tabloid format; back issues avail.) **Document type:** newspaper.
Description: Informs students and alumni of campus events.

378.1 US ISSN 1055-4726
THE BATTALION. Variant title: Texas A & M Battalion. 1893. d. (Mon.-Fri.). $50 (students free). Texas A & M University, Student Publications, Department of Journalism, 015 Reed McDonald Bldg., College Station, TX 77843-1111. TEL 409-845-2611. FAX 409-845-2678. E-mail: batt@tamvm1.tamu.edu; URL: http://bat-web.tamu.edu. adv. circ. 22,000. (also avail. in microfilm) **Document type:** newspaper.

378 US
BATTLER COLUMNS. m. Alderson-Broaddus College, Philippi, WV 26416. TEL 304-457-1700. FAX 304-457-1700. adv.; circ. 1,200 (controlled). (tabloid format)

378 US
BAYLOR LARIAT. 1900. d. (Tue.-Fri.). $40. Baylor University, Lariat, Box 97353, Waco, TX 76798. TEL 817-755-1711. FAX 817-755-1714. E-mail: lariat@baylor.edu; URL: http://www.baylor.edu/student_orgs/lariat/. R&P contact: Jason Ranton. adv.: color page $350; adv. contact: Jason Ranton. bk.rev. circ. 7,500. **Document type:** newspaper.
Refereed Serial

378.198 US
BAYOU BENGAL. 1967. m. free on campus. Louisiana State University at Eunice, Box 1129, Eunice, LA 70535. TEL 318-457-7311. FAX 318-546-6620. Ed. Sherryl Guillory. adv. contact: David Simpson. circ. 1,000 (controlled). **Document type:** newspaper.
Description: College student newspaper.

378.1 UK ISSN 0005-7525
BEAVER. 1959. w. free. London School of Economics and Political Science, Students' Union, CO23, St. Clements Bldg., Houghton St., London WC2A 2AE, England. TEL 0171-955-6705. FAX 0171-955-7717. E-mail: beaver@lse.ac.uk. Ed. Rachel Cuthbert. adv.: B&W page £250; trim 256 x 393; adv. contact: Scott Wayne. bk.rev.; film rev.; illus. circ. 2,500. (tabloid format) **Indexed:** Amer.Hist.& Life (1955-), Hist.Abstr., Ind.Child.Mag. **Document type:** newspaper.

378.198 US
BELMONT VISION. 1951. bi-m. $10. Belmont University, Belmont Blvd., Box B-16, Nashville, TN 37212. TEL 615-385-6433. FAX 615-386-4532. Ed. Cree Lawson. adv.; bk.rev.; film rev. circ. 3,000. (tabloid format; also avail. in microfilm; back issues avail.) **Document type:** newspaper.

378.198 US
BELOIT MAGAZINE. 1909. q. Beloit College, 700 College St., Beloit, WI 53511. TEL 608-363-2828. FAX 608-363-2870. URL: http://www.beloit.edu. Ed. Peter T. Maiken. circ. 20,000 (controlled).
Description: News of college and alumni.

378 US
BENEDICT TIGER. 1924. m. $12. Benedict College, Harden & Blanding Sts., Columbia, SC 29204. TEL 803-253-5297. Ed. Samuel Cousar. adv.; bk.rev. circ. 2,500. **Document type:** newspaper.
Description: Covers the Benedict College campus: students, faculty and staff, alumni, and organizations.

378 US
BENGAL. 1910. w. $15. Idaho State University, Box 8009, Pocatello, ID 83209. TEL 208-236-3990. FAX 208-236-4600. Ed. Janet Howard. adv. contact: Maureen Van Horn. bk.rev. circ. 5,000. (tabloid format) **Document type:** newspaper.

371.85 US ISSN 0005-884X
BENT OF TAU BETA PI. 1906. q. $10. Tau Beta Pi Association, Inc., Box 2697, Knoxville, TN 37901-2697. TEL 423-546-4578. URL: http://www.tbp.org. Ed. James D. Froula. R&P contact: James D. Froula. adv. contact: Calvin Hart. bk.rev.; illus.; circ. 92,000 (paid).
—UnCover.
Description: Articles on leadership and general items of interest to members of the National Engineering Honor Society and other engineers.

378.198 US
BENTLEY OBSERVER. q. free. Bentley College, Public Affairs Office, 175 Forest St., Waltham, MA 02154-4705. TEL 617-891-2241. FAX 617-891-3418. URL: http://www.bentley.edu. Ed. Susan Simpson. R&P contact: Susan Simpson. (tabloid format)
Description: News and feature stories about Bentley College people, programs, and events.

378.1 US ISSN 0005-8874
LH1.B35
BEREA ALUMNUS. 1931. q. free. Berea College Alumni Association, CPO 2316, Berea, KY 40404. TEL 606-986-9341. FAX 606-986-4506. adv.; bk.rev.; illus. circ. 45,000.

BERKLEE TODAY; a forum for contemporary music and musicians. see *MUSIC*

378 917.306 US
BETA THETA PI. 1872. q. Beta Theta Pi Fraternity, Box 6277, Oxford, OH 45056-6277. TEL 513-523-7591. FAX 513-523-2381. Ed. Erv Johnson. adv. contact: Erv Johnson. circ. 93,000 (controlled).
Description: Supplies news about activities of the 136 chapters of the organization and its members, and feature articles on outstanding alumni in all fields.

378 US
BETHANY MAGAZINE. 1907. q. Bethany College, 421 N. First, Lindsborg, KS 67456-1897. TEL 913-227-3311. Ed. Harold L. Rothgeb. R&P contact: Harold L. Rothgeb. circ. 7,500 (controlled). **Document type:** academic/scholarly publication.

378.1 US ISSN 0005-982X
BETHEL COLLEGE BULLETIN. 1914. 4/yr. Bethel College, 300 E. 27th St., N. Newton, KS 67117. TEL 316-283-2500. circ. 11,500. **Document type:** bulletin.
Description: Features Bethel College events and personalities.

378.198 US
BETHEL FOCUS. 1948. q. free. Bethel College (St. Paul), 3900 Bethel Dr., St. Paul, MN 55112. TEL 612-638-6083. FAX 612-638-6003. Ed. Patricia J. Bower. circ. 35,000 (controlled). **Document type:** academic/scholarly publication.
Description: For alumni of Bethel College; reports on college life and campus news.

378 IS
BEZALEL IN BRIEF. (Text in Hebrew) 1979. a. Bezalel Academy of Art and Design, Department of Public Information, P.O. Box 24046, Jerusalem 91240, Israel. FAX 972-2-5823094. URL: http://www.bezalel.ac.il. Ed. Ran Sapoznik. bk.rev.

378 GW ISSN 0939-4648
BIELEFELDER UNIVERSITAETSZEITUNG. 1970. q. Universitaet Bielefeld, Informations- und Pressestelle, Postfach 100131, 33501 Bielefeld, Germany. TEL 49-521-1064146. FAX 49-521-1062964. TELEX 932362-UNIBI. E-mail: gerhard.trott@post.uni-bielefeld.de; URL: http://www.uni-bielefeld.de. Ed. Gerhard Trott. adv. circ. 7,000. **Document type:** bulletin.

COLLEGE AND ALUMNI

378.1 US
BILLBOARD (CHAMBERSBURG). 1929. m. $8. (Wilson College Government Association) Wilson College, Chambersburg, PA 17201. TEL 717-264-4141. Ed. Samantha Ainuddin. adv.; bk.rev.; illus. circ. 1,000. (tabloid format) **Indexed:** B.P.I. **Document type:** newspaper.
   Formerly: Wilson Billboard.

378.1 NE ISSN 0006-2812
BINDEN EN BOUWEN. 1933. bi-m. fl.5.($1.50) Sint-Bernardinuscollege, Akerstraat 95, Heerlen, Netherlands. Ed. Marcel Gussenhouen. adv.; bk.rev.; illus.; circ. 2,000 (controlled).

378 UK
BIRMINGHAM SUN. 1948. fortn. Aston Students' Guild, Aston University, The Triangle, Birmingham B4 7ES, England. TEL 0121-359-6531. FAX 0121-333-4218. Ed. Simon Hindle. adv.; film rev.; music rev.; play rev. circ. 3,500. cols./p.: 6; pp./issue: 16. (tabloid format) **Document type:** newspaper.
   Description: Informs and entertains Aston University students, covering a wide variety of subjects and interests.

378.198 US
BLACK AND MAGENTA. 1885. w. $25. Muskingum College, New Concord, OH 43762. TEL 614-826-8296. Ed. Jennifer Hoke. adv. contact: Gaurav Agarwal. play rev.; illus. circ. 1,500. **Document type:** newspaper.

378.1 US ISSN 0192-3757
LC2781
THE BLACK COLLEGIAN; the career and self-development magazine for African-American. 1970. bi-m. (during school yr.). $12. 140 Carondelet St., New Orleans, LA 70130-2526. TEL 504-523-0154. FAX 504-523-0271. E-mail: scott@black-collegian.com; URL: http://www.black-collegian.com/. Ed. Kuumba Kazi. adv.; bk.rev. circ. 106,000. (also avail. in microform from UMI; reprint service avail. from UMI) **Indexed:** Acad.Ind., Ind.Per.Blacks. **Document type:** consumer publication. ●Also available online. **Vendor(s):** Information Access Co., UMI.
   —UMI; UnCover.
   Incorporates: Expressions, a National Review of the Black Arts.

378 US
BLACK HILLS STATE UNIVERSITY TODAY. 1902. w. $10. Black Hills State University, 1200 University Ave., USB 9003, Spearfish, SD 57799-9003. TEL 605-642-6389. FAX 605-642-6762. adv.: page $337.50. bk.rev.; film rev.; play rev.; illus. circ. 2,500. (tabloid format) **Document type:** newspaper.
   Former titles: Black Hills State College Today; Black Hills Anemone (ISSN 0006-4173).

378.198 US
BLOOMSBURG LITERARY JOURNAL. s-a. Community Government Association, Community Activities Office, 400 E. Second St., Bloomsburg, PA 17815. TEL 717-389-4461. FAX 717-389-2095. R&P contact: Terrance Riley. play rev. circ. 1,500.
   Formerly (until 1989): Bloom Magazine.

378.198 US
BLUE BANNER. 1982. w. $12. University of North Carolina at Asheville, One University Heights, Asheville, NC 28804. TEL 704-251-6586. adv.; bk.rev.; film rev.; play rev.; charts; illus. circ. 2,700. (tabloid format; back issues avail.)
   Formerly: Kaleidoscope (Asheville).

378 US
BLUEFIELDIAN. 1921. s-a. Bluefield State College, 219 Rock St., Bluefield, WV 24701. TEL 304-327-4159. FAX 304-325-7747. adv. contact: Jack Yates. circ. 1,000. (tabloid format; back issues avail.) **Document type:** newspaper.
   Description: Includes editorials, feature pages, school news, Greek news, organizational news, entertainment news.

378 US
THE BONA VENTURE. w. $12 (effective 1997-98). St. Bonaventure University, Drawer X, St. Bonaventure, NY 14778. TEL 716-375-2128. FAX 716-375-2252. E-mail: bonavent@sbu.edu. Ed. Rachael Astrachan; Pub. Robert Wickenheiser. R&P contact: Rachael Astrachan. TEL 716-375-2128. adv. contact: Corrie Spike. bk.rev.; index. circ. 3,200. (also avail. in microform; back issues avail.) **Document type:** newspaper.

378 US
BONHOMIE. 1901. a. $15. Furman University, Board of Student Communications, 3300 Poinsett Hwy., Greenville, SC 29613-0639. TEL 864-294-2096. FAX 864-294-3001. Ed. Sarah Thomas. circ. 2,200.
   Description: Pictorial review of year's events and personnel directory.

378.1 AU ISSN 0006-7865
BORUSSEN-ECHO; Monatsblatt mit freier Meinungsaeusserung. 1953. m. free. Katholische Oesterreichische Studentenverbindung "Borussia" im MKV, Bandgasse 31-8, A-1070 Vienna 7, Austria. TEL 43-1-5239090. Ed. Gottfried Fanninger. adv.; bk.rev.; abstr. circ. 550. (processed) **Document type:** bulletin.

378 US ISSN 0885-2049
BOSTON COLLEGE MAGAZINE. 1978. q. free. Trustees of Boston College, Publications & Print Marketing, Lawrence House, 122 College Rd., Chestnut Hill, MA 02167. Ed. Ben Birnbaum. adv.; bk.rev. circ. 117,000.
   Description: Focuses on the arts, education, culture and religion for graduates and friends of Boston College.

378.198 US ISSN 0895-2604
BOWDOIN. 1927. 3/yr. free. Bowdoin College, Office of Communications, Brunswick, ME 04011. TEL 207-725-3253. FAX 207-725-3003. E-mail: dodsm@henry.bowdoin.edu. Ed. Alison M. Dodson. R&P contact: Lucie G. Teegarden. adv. circ. 21,000. (back issues avail.) **Document type:** academic/scholarly publication.
   Formerly (until 1987): Bowdoin Alumni Magazine (ISSN 0746-3332)
   Description: Articles cover Bowdoin College or its alumni.

378.1 US ISSN 0006-8667
BRACKETY - ACK. 1915. w. $25. Roanoke College, Salem, VA 24153. TEL 703-375-2327. FAX 703-375-2404. Ed. Valerie Lambros. adv. contact: Michael Edwards. circ. 1,000. **Document type:** newspaper.

378.1 UK ISSN 0006-8675
BRADFIELD COLLEGE CHRONICLE. 1860. s-a. £3 per no. Bradfield College, Bradfield, Berks. RG7 6AU, England. TEL 44-1189-744208. FAX 44-1734-744195. Ed. James Nairne. adv.; bk.rev.; illus. circ. 2,500.

378.198 US
BRANDEIS REVIEW. 1980. 4/yr. $15. Brandeis University, 415 South St., Waltham, MA 02254. TEL 617-736-4220. FAX 617-736-4227. Ed. Cliff Hauptman. bk.rev. circ. 30,000. (back issues avail.) **Document type:** academic/scholarly publication.
   Formerly: Brandeis Quarterly (ISSN 0273-7175)

378 US
BREEZE (HARRISONBURG). 4/w. $30. James Madison University, Anthony-Seeger Hall, Harrisonburg, VA 22807. TEL 703-568-6127. FAX 703-568-6736. Ed. Nicole Motley. adv. contact: Jonathan Rhudy. bk.rev. circ. 13,500. **Document type:** newspaper.
   Description: Maintains communications within the university community and the spirit of intellectual growth and free inquiry.

378 US
THE BREEZE (MATHISTON). 5/yr. free. Wood Junior College, Box 289, Mathiston, MO 39752. Ed. Keith Chadwick. adv.; bk.rev.; film rev.; music rev.; circ. 1,200 (controlled). (tabloid format; back issues avail.) **Document type:** newspaper.

378 CN
BRICKLAYER. 1972. bi-w. free. Bricklayer Publishing Society, P.O. Box 5005, Red Deer, AB T4N 5H5, Canada. TEL 403-346-2400. FAX 403-347-8510. E-mail: bricklayer@rdc.ab.ca. Ed. Brenda Cosens; Pub. Jennifer Nelson. R&P contact: Jennifer Nelson. adv. contact: Jennifer Nelson. bk.rev.; film rev, rec.rev. circ. 3,000. **Document type:** newspaper.
   Description: Contains campus news, reviews of music, movies and restaurants, upcoming events information, health issues and on-campus sporting events.

378.198 US
BRIDGEWATER ALUMNI MAGAZINE. 1949. q. free to qualified personnel. Bridgewater College, Box 33, Bridgewater, VA 22812. TEL 540-828-5452. FAX 540-828-5480. E-mail: alumnews@bridgewater.edu; URL: http://www.bridgewater.edu. Ed. Ellen K. Layman. circ. 16,400. (back issues avail.) **Document type:** newsletter.
   Formerly: Bridgewater.
   Description: Provides news for alumni and friends.

378 UK
BRIG. 1971. m. (during school term). free. Stirling University Students' Association, Stirling FK9 4LA, Scotland. TEL 44-1786-467166. FAX 44-1786-467190. Ed. Suzanne Bush. adv.: B&W page £300; trim 280 x 400; adv. contact: Suzanne Bush. bk.rev. circ. 3,000. **Document type:** newspaper.
   Description: Provides news, features, sports and opinion on the latest campus, national and international issues.
   Refereed Serial

378.198 US
BRIGADIER. 1909. 20/yr. $27. The Citadel - The Military College of South Carolina, Charleston, SC 29409. TEL 803-792-5111. FAX 803-792-7084. Ed. Cadet Caldwell Warley. adv.: page $280; 10 x 13.75; adv. contact: Paryn A. Wallace. circ. 3,500. (tabloid format) **Document type:** newspaper.

378 US
BRIGHAM YOUNG MAGAZINE. 1946. 4/yr. $15 (free to qualified personnel). Brigham Young University, C-366 ASB, Provo, UT 84602. TEL 801-378-4900. (Subscr. to: Record Department, Alumni House, Provo, UT 84602. TEL 801-378-6740) Ed. James P. Bell. adv. circ. 135,000. (back issues avail.)
   Formerly: B Y U Today.
   Description: Includes research activities, news and issues relating to the university.

378.198 US
BROADSIDE (BEND). 1935. bi-w. free. Central Oregon Community College, College Way, Bend, OR 97701. TEL 503-382-2743. FAX 503-385-5978. Ed. Todd Pittman. adv.; bk.rev. circ. 2,000.

378 US
BROADSIDE (FAIRFAX); student newspaper. 1963. bi-w. free. George Mason University, Mailstop 2C5, 4400 University, Fairfax, VA 22030. TEL 703-993-2945. FAX 703-993-2948. adv.; bk.rev.; film rev. circ. 15,000. (tabloid format) **Document type:** newspaper.
   Description: Covers campus events, and general educational events.

BROADSIDE (WASHINGTON). see POLITICAL SCIENCE

378 CN
THE BROCK PRESS; writing stuff 'till our brains go gooey. (Includes s-a supplement: Brock Crass) 1963. w. free. Brock University Student Union Inc., 500 Glenridge Ave., St. Catherines, Ont. L2S 4A1, Canada. TEL 416-688-5550. FAX 416-641-7581. Ed. Tricia Bunnett. adv. contact: Paula Woodward. film rev.; play rev.; illus. circ. 5,000. (tabloid format) **Document type:** newspaper.

378 US ISSN 0007-2478
LH1.B8
BROWN ALUMNI MONTHLY. 1900. m. (9/yr.). $30. Brown University, Box 1854, Providence, RI 02912 TEL 401-863-2873. FAX 401-751-9255. Ed. Anne Diffily. adv.; bk.rev.; illus. circ. 70,000.

COLLEGE AND ALUMNI

378 US
BROWN DAILY HERALD. 1891. d. (5/w.). $55. Box 2538, Providence, RI 02906. TEL 401-351-3260. FAX 401-351-9297. E-mail: herald@netscape.org; URL: http://www.netscape.org/herald/. Ed. Tom Benson. R&P contact: Jonathan Kohler. adv. contact: Lawrie Prime. bk.rev. circ. 5,000. (tabloid format) **Document type:** newspaper.

378.1 CN ISSN 0007-2699
BRUNSWICKAN. 1867. w. Can.$26.50. University of New Brunswick, Student Union, P.O. Box 4400, Fredericton, NB E3B 5A3, Canada. TEL 506-453-4983. FAX 506-458-4958. TELEX BRUNS@UNB.CA. Ed. Mark Morgan. adv.: page Can.$375. bk.rev.; illus.; circ. 10,000 (controlled). (also avail. in microfilm)
Refereed Serial

378 US
BRYN MAWR ALUMNAE BULLETIN. 1921. q. free to qualified personnel. Bryn Mawr Alumnae Association, Wyndham, 101 N. Merion Ave., Bryn Mawr, PA 19010-2899. TEL 215-526-5224. FAX 215-526-5228. Ed. Jan T. Trembley. bk.rev. circ. 17,000.

378 US
BRYN MAWR - HAVERFORD COLLEGE NEWS. 1968. w. $27. (Haverford College) Students of Haverford and Bryn Mawr Colleges, Haverford, PA 19041. TEL 215-527-8995. Ed. Ruth Polk. adv.; bk.rev.; film rev.; play rev.; illus. circ. 3,800. (tabloid format)

378 US ISSN 1044-7563
BUCKNELL WORLD. 1914. 6/yr. free. Bucknell University, Division of University Relations, Lewisburg, PA 17837. TEL 717-524-3260. FAX 717-524-3683. E-mail: bworld@bucknell.edu; URL: http://www.bucknell.edu; Ed. Sally Atwood. adv.; bk.rev. circ. 42,500. **Document type:** academic/scholarly publication, newsletter. **Description:** Covers Bucknell alumni and issues in higher education as related to Bucknell.

378 US
BUENA VISTA TODAY. 1895. q. free to qualified personnel. Buena Vista University, 610 W. Fourth St., Storm Lake, IA 50588. TEL 712-749-2120. FAX 712-749-1459. E-mail: bvtoday@bvu.edu. Ed. Tim Seydel. R&P contact: Tim Seydel. circ. 18,000. **Document type:** bulletin.
Formerly: View.
Description: Provides information of interest to alumni, parents of students, and friends.
Refereed Serial

378.1 US
BULLDOG WEEKLY. 1909. w. (during school yr.). $30. University of Redlands, Redlands, CA 92373. TEL 904-335-5137. Ed. Greg Huntoon. adv.: B&W page $280; 10 1/2 x 13; adv. contact: Richard Carney. bk.rev.; film rev.; music rev. circ. 2,000. (tabloid format)
Formerly: Redlands Bulldog (ISSN 0034-2130)
Description: Covers material relating to the student body including: sports coverage, relevant political and social news, entertainment, editorials and calendar of events.

378 US
BULLET (FREDERICKSBURG). w. Mary Washington College, Campus Center, Fredericksburg, VA 22401. TEL 703-899-4393.

371.8 US ISSN 0007-7100
BUSINESS TODAY (PRINCETON). 1968. 3/yr. $9. Foundation for Student Communication, Inc., 305 Aaron Burr Hall, Princeton University, Princeton, NJ 08540. TEL 609-258-1111. FAX 609-258-1222. E-mail: FSCINT@phoenix.princeton.edu; URL: http://www.princeton.edu/~fscint. Ed. Alison Badgett; Pub. Neetu Bhat. adv. contact: Emma Penick. bk.rev.; charts; illus.; stat. circ. 200,000. (also avail. in microform from UMI,MIM; reprint service avail. from UMI)
—UMI; UnCover.
Description: Promotes communication between college students and the business community.

378.198 US
BUTLER ALUMNI QUARTERLY. 1989. q. Butler University, 4600 Sunset Ave., Indianapolis, IN 46208. TEL 317-283-9426. Ed. Nancy L. Alexander. circ. 24,000 (controlled). (tabloid format)
Description: Covers issues in higher education, alumni profiles, campus news, class notes, and faculty information.

378 US
BUTLER COLLEGIAN. 1886. w. $40. Butler University, Journalism Department, 4600 Sunset Blvd., Indianapolis, IN 46208-3485. TEL 317-283-9358. FAX 317-283-9930. adv. contact: Kevin Foltz. bk.rev.; film rev.; play rev.; circ. 3,000 (controlled). (tabloid format; back issues avail.) **Document type:** newspaper.
Description: Informs students and faculty of school and national news.

378.1 US ISSN 0045-3919
C C A C REVIEW. 1970. 4/yr. free. California College of Arts and Crafts, Office of Alumni Affairs, 5212 Broadway, Oakland, CA 94618. TEL 415-653-8118. Ed. Sandra Meber. illus.; stat. circ. 8,000.

378 374.8 UK
C E D E P EUROPEAN CENTRE FOR CONTINUING EDUCATION ADDRESS BOOK. 1982. a. £95 to non-members. A P Information Services, Roman House, 296 Golders Green Rd., London NW11 9PZ, England. TEL 44-181-455-4550. FAX 44-181-455-6381. Ed. Alan Philipp. circ. 9,200. (also avail. in diskette format) **Document type:** directory.
Description: Lists all alumni from CEDEP according to member company and geographical location.

378 CN
C E G E P PLUS. (Text in French) bi-m. College d'Enseignement Generale et Professionnel de Valleyfield, 169 rue Champlain, Valleyfield, Que. J6T 1X6, Canada. adv. circ. 2,000.

378 US
▼**C M.** (College Magazine) 1995. bi-m. Sara Fiedelholtz, Ed. & Pub., 23 E. 10th St., No. 706, New York, NY 10003. TEL 212-529-1515. FAX 212-979-8772. adv.: B&W page $10450; color page $12320; adv. contact: Nancy Rosenberg. (back issues avail.)
●Also available online.
Description: Covers college lifestyles and topics of interest to college students.

378.1 US
C M A NEWSLETTER. 1955. bi-m. $60. College Media Advisers, c/o Department of Journalism, University of Memphis, Memphis, TN 38152. TEL 901-678-2403. E-mail: rspelbrgr@cc.memphis.edu; URL: http://www.spub.ksu.edu/ncma. Ed. Ken Rosenauer. bk.rev.; film rev.; abstr.; bibl.; stat.; tr.lit. circ. 625. (processed) **Document type:** newsletter.
Formerly: N C C P A Newsletter (ISSN 0027-6251)

378.198 US
C U A MAGAZINE. 1973. 3/yr. $15 to non-alumni; alumni free. Catholic University of America, Office of Public Affairs, 620 Michigan Ave., N.E., McMahon Hall, Rm. 311, Washington, DC 20064. TEL 202-319-5600. FAX 202-635-4440. Ed. Anne Smith; Pub. Dennis J. Mahon. bk.rev. circ. 46,000. (back issues avail.)
Formerly (until 1989): Envoy (Washington) (ISSN 0896-288X)
Description: General interest magazine circulated to alumni and friends of the university.

378 US ISSN 1042-9220
C W R U: THE MAGAZINE OF CASE WESTERN RESERVE UNIVERSITY. 1979. 4/yr. free to qualified personnel. Case Western Reserve University, 10900 Euclid Ave., Cleveland, OH 44106. TEL 216-368-6265. FAX 216-368-4835. Ed. Ken Kesegich. R&P contact: Ken Kesegich. adv. contact: Roberta Hubbard. circ. 92,000 (controlled). **Document type:** academic/scholarly publication.
Former titles (until vol.3, no.4, 1988): C W R U Today; Case Reserve Today; (until 1984): Insight (Cleveland); (until 1983): Campus News; Images.

378.198 US
THE CABLE. 1932. w. $15. College of St. Scholastica, 1200 Kenwood Ave., Duluth, MN 55811. TEL 218-723-6187. FAX 218-723-6290. Ed. Jessica McDonald. adv.: B&W page $270, color page $370; 9 1/2 x 15; adv. contact: Dana Burkovich. film rev.; music rev.; play rev. circ. 1,500. (tabloid format)

378 CN ISSN 0226-3467
CADUCEE. (Text in French) 1920. 4/yr. Association des Diplomes de l'Ecole des Hautes Etudes Commercials de Montreal, 3000 Ch. de la Cote St. Catherine, RJ-210, Montreal, PQ H3T 2A7, Canada. TEL 514-340-6025. FAX 514-340-6508. Ed. Isabelle Gagne. adv.: B&W page Can.$1800, color page Can.$2250; trim 8 1/8 x 10 7/8; adv. contact: Nathalie Leonard. bk.rev. circ. 30,000. **Document type:** consumer publication.

378 US
CALIFORNIA AGGIE. (Supplements avail.: Praxis, Arena) 1915. d. (5/w.). $35. University of California at Davis, 25 Lower Freeborn Hall, Davis, CA 95616. TEL 916-752-0365. FAX 916-752-0355. Ed. Matthias Gafni. adv. circ. 13,000. (also avail. in microfilm from LIB) **Document type:** newspaper.

378.1 US ISSN 0008-1302
CALIFORNIA MONTHLY. 1909. 6/yr. $40. California Alumni Association, Alumni House, Berkeley, CA 94720. TEL 510-642-5781. Ed. Russell Schoch. adv.; bk.rev. circ. 99,048. (also avail. in microfilm from LIB)

378.1 US ISSN 0008-1582
CALIFORNIA TECH. 1913. w. $11 (effective Sep. 1994). (Associated Students of the California Institute of Technology) A S C I T, Inc., 40-58 SAC, California Institute of Technology, 1201 E. California Blvd., Pasadena, CA 91125. TEL 818-395-6153. adv.; bk.rev.; film rev.; play rev.; illus. circ. 3,500. **Document type:** newspaper.

378 IT
CAMPUS; il giornale dell'universita della ricerca e della formazione. 1988. m. (10/yr.) L.28000 (effective 1995). Campus Editori s.r.l., Via Burigozzo 5, 20122 Milan, Italy. TEL 39-2-582191. FAX 39-2-58317438. Ed. Alessandro Giuoli; Pub. Paolo Panerai. adv.: B&W page L.15000000, color page L.21000000. circ. 70,000. **Document type:** consumer publication.
Description: Gives information on universities, post-graduate courses, professions, and the academic world.

378.198 US
CAMPUS ACTIVITIES TODAY. 1992. 8/yr. $18 (Canada $24; elsewhere $36). Cameo Publishing Group, 134 S. Main St., Box 509, Prosperity, SC 29127. TEL 800-728-2950. FAX 803-364-1013. URL: http://www.cameopub.com. Ed. Jennifer Lester; Pub. W.C. Kirby. adv.: B&W page $1025 color page $1680; trim 8 3/8 x 10 7/8; adv. contact: Dean Kirby. circ. 4,874. **Document type:** trade publication.
Description: Provides information on entertainment, films, music and special events for student activities directors.

378 US
CAMPUS CAMERA; the student newspaper of Eastern Nazarene College. 1936. s-m. $20 (free to students). Eastern Nazarene College, 23 E. Elm St., Wollaston, MA 02170. TEL 617-745-3577. Ed. Catherine Walchle. R&P contact: Catherine Walchle. adv.: page $260; 16 x 10; adv. contact: Vlad Samarin. bk.rev.; play rev.; bibl. (back issues avail.) **Document type:** newspaper.
Description: Covers world, local and campus news and events.

378 CN ISSN 0829-3309
CAMPUS CANADA. 1983. q. Can.$12. Canadian Controlled Media Communications, 287 MacPherson Ave., Toronto, ON M4V 1A4, Canada. TEL 416-928-2909. FAX 416-966-1181. Ed. Sarah Moore. adv. contact: Harvey Wolfe. circ. 125,000. **Indexed:** Can.B.P.I. **Document type:** consumer publication.
Description: University related topics: entertainment, careers, health, travel, money, sports, campus issues.

COLLEGE AND ALUMNI

378.18 US
CAMPUS CARRIER. 1913. w. $20. Berry College, Box 520, Mt. Berry, GA 30149-0520. TEL 706-236-2294. FAX 706-236-2248. Ed. Richard Quartarone; Pub. Kevin Kleine. adv. contact: Julie Yamamoto. film rev.; music rev.; play rev. circ. 2,000. (tabloid format) **Document type:** newspaper.

CAMPUS LEADER. see EDUCATION

378.198 US ISSN 0008-2538
BV3750
CAMPUS LIFE. 1942. 10/yr. $19.95. Christianity Today, Inc., 465 Gundersen Dr., Carol Stream, IL 60188. TEL 630-260-6200. FAX 630-260-0114. E-mail: cledit@aol.com; URL: http://www.christianity.net/campuslife. (Subscr. to: CDS Box 37060, Boone, IA 50037-0060. TEL 800-678-6083) Ed. Chris Lutes. R&P contact: Marilyn Roe. adv.: B&W page $3826; adv. contact: Linda Schambach. bk.rev.; illus. circ. 104,013. (also avail. in microform from UMI; reprint service avail. from UMI) **Indexed:** CCR, Chr.Per.Ind. **Document type:** consumer publication.
●Also available online.
—UMI.
Description: Communicates to high school and early college students the value and impact of a Christ-centered faith.

378 US
CAMPUS TIMES (LA VERNE). 1919. w. free. University of La Verne, Communications Department, 1950 Third St., La Verne, CA 91750. TEL 909-392-2712. FAX 909-392-2706. E-mail: ctimes@ulvacs.laverne.edu. Ed. Raechel Fittante. R&P contact: Eric Borer. adv. contact: Chester Tadeja. circ. 2,000. **Document type:** newspaper.
Description: Reports campus news for the University of La Verne, located in southern California.

378 US
CAMPUS TIMES (ROCHESTER). 1873. w. $18.75 (effective 1995-1996). University of Rochester, Students Association, Wilson Commons 102, CPU 277060, Rochester, NY 14627-7086. TEL 716-275-5943. FAX 716-256-3664. E-mail: ct_editor@cc.rochester.edu; URL: http://www.ctrochester.edu. Ed. David I. Leavitt. adv.: page $448; 10 x 16; adv. contact: Linda J. Goodwin. bk.rev. circ. 6,000. (tabloid format) **Document type:** newspaper.
Refereed Serial

378.1 US
CAMPUS VOICE (BLOOMSBURG).* 1920. w. free. Bloomsburg University, Campus Voice, 400 E. Second St., Bloomsburg, PA 17815. TEL 717-389-4557. Ed. Mike Lester. adv. contact: Kimberly Jackson. bk.rev.; illus. circ. 4,500. (tabloid format) **Document type:** newspaper.

378.198 US
CAMPUS WEEKLY. vol.7, 1986. w. free. New Hampshire College, 2500 N. River Rd., Manchester, NH 03106. TEL 603-645-9635. circ. 1,500. **Document type:** newsletter.
Formerly: Campus News (Manchester).

378 BE ISSN 0779-0821
CAMPUSKRANT; tijdschrift van de K.U.Leuven. (Includes supplement (8/yr.): Alumnibijlage) (Text in Dutch) 1990. bi-w. (except July-Aug.). 300 BEF (foreign 600 BEF). Katholieke Universiteit Leuven, Dienst Communicatie, Oude Markt 13, B-3000 Louvain, Belgium. TEL 32-16-324013. FAX 32-16-324014. E-mail: mirella.kimpen@dcom.kuleuven.ac.be. Ed. Mirella Kimpen. R&P contact: Mirella Kimpen. adv.: B&W page 39500 BEF, color page 72500 BEF; 360 x 260; adv. contact: Mirella Kimpen. bk.rev. circ. 17,000 (40,000 Alumni ed.). (tabloid format; back issues avail.) **Document type:** newspaper.
Supersedes: Academische Tijdingen.
Description: Contains news of university policy, science, cultural activities and sports for staff, faculty, students and alumni.

378 US
CANDOR. w. free. Illinois Benedictine College, 5700 College Rd., Lisle, IL 60532-0900. TEL 708-960-1500. FAX 708-960-1126. E-mail: candor@eagle.ibc.edu. Ed. Joseph Ursitti. adv.: B&W page $400; adv. contact: Krissy Miller. bk.rev.; film rev.; play rev.; charts; illus.; index. circ. 1,750. (tabloid format; back issues avail.) **Document type:** newspaper.
Description: Aimed at traditional college students. Includes campus activities and issues, world issues and entertainment venues.

378 266 US
CANNON. 6/yr. Christian Brothers College, Memphis, TN 38104-5581. TEL 901-278-0100.

378 CN
CAPER TIMES. vol.4, 1984. bi-w. Can.$23. College of Cape Breton, Student's Union, P.O. Box 5300, Sydney, NS B1P 6L2, Canada. TEL 902-562-8857. E-mail: kk911239@caper1.uccb.ns.ca. Ed. Rob Gildert. adv. contact: Jamie Whitty. bk.rev.; film rev. circ. 2,000. **Document type:** newspaper.

378 CN
CAPILANO COURIER. 1968. bi-w. Can.$10. Capilano College, Courier Publishing Society, 2055 Purcell Way, North Vancouver, BC V7J 3H5, Canada. TEL 604-984-4949. FAX 604-984-4985. Ed. Keirr Wills; Pub. Dennis LeDoc. adv. contact: Jason Fischer. bk.rev.; film rev. circ. 3,500. (tabloid format) **Document type:** newspaper.
Description: Includes student news, opinion and letters.

378.1 371.42 US
CAREER VISION.* 1989. 6/yr. $2.95 per no. Michael Tannen Publishers, 153 E. 53rd St., Ste. 5500, New York, NY 10022-4666. TEL 212-475-8200. Ed. Marian Salzman. circ. 28,000.
Description: Covers the lifestyles and careers of college students, with the students as target readers.

378.1 CN ISSN 0008-6576
CARILLON (REGINA). 1962. w. Can.$40. University of Regina, Students' Union, Students' Union Bldg., Rm. 113, Regina, SK S4S 0A2, Canada. TEL 306-586-8867. FAX 306-586-8812. E-mail: carillon@ursu.cc.uregina.ca; URL: http://ursu.uregina.ca/~carillon. Ed. Alexis Roman. R&P contact: Craig Saunders. adv. contact: Wade McKim. bk.rev.; film rev.; play rev.; abstr.; illus. circ. 4,000. (tabloid format) **Document type:** newspaper.
Description: Covers news, sports, arts. Also accepts editorials, opinions, letters and analysis pieces.

371.805 US
THE CARLETONIAN. 1877. w. $38. Carleton College, 1 N. College St., Northfield, MN 55057. TEL 507-646-4158. FAX 507-646-4146. E-mail: carletonian@carleton.edu; URL: http://www.carletonian.carleton.edu. adv.; bk.rev.; dance rev.; film rev.; music rev.; play rev.; charts; illus. circ. 3,100. cols./p.: 6; pp./issue: 12. (back issues avail.) **Document type:** newspaper.
Description: Includes news, viewpoint, features, movie page, calendar, and humor sections.

378 US ISSN 0747-0835
CAROLINA ALUMNI REVIEW. 1912. bi-m. $30 (effective 1996). University of North Carolina, General Alumni Association, Box 660, Chapel Hill, NC 27514. TEL 919-962-1208. FAX 919-962-0010. Ed. Regina Oliver. adv.: B&W page $1350, color page $2365. circ. 55,000.
Incorporates (as of Jan. 1995): University Alumni Report; Which was formerly (until 1989): University Report.
Description: Provides alumni and University news, photography & editorial features on subjects of interest to University of N. Carolina and members of the General Alumni Association.

378 US
CARROLL ALUMNI JOURNAL. 1960. q. free to qualified personnel. John Carroll University, Department of Public Affairs, University Heights, Cleveland, OH 44118. TEL 216-397-1687. FAX 216-397-3028. Ed. Jerome Pockar. circ. 28,000. **Document type:** newsletter.

378.1 UK ISSN 0008-7033
CARTHUSIAN. 1873. 3/yr. £2. Charterhouse School, Godalming, Surrey, England. adv.; bk.rev.; film rev.; play rev.; illus. circ. 1,000.

378.198 US
CASE ALUMNUS. 1921. q. free. Case Western Reserve University, Case Alumni Association, Crawford Hall 107, 10900 Euclid Ave., Cleveland, OH 44106-7073. TEL 216-231-4567. FAX 216-368-4714. E-mail: casealum@po.cwra.edu. Ed. Madelyn Lefkowitz. R&P contact: Madelyn Lefkowitz. circ. 16,000 (controlled). (back issues avail.) **Document type:** academic/scholarly publication.
Description: Articles by, for and about alumni of Case School of Engineering.

378 AT
CATALYST (MELBOURNE). 1945. fortn. free. Royal Melbourne Institute of Technology, Student Union, P.O. Box 12387, A'Beckett St., Melbourne, Vic. 8006, Australia. TEL 61-3-96602884. FAX 61-3-96603705. Ed. Adam Gardiner. R&P contact: Janine Wurfel. adv. contact: Emma Maroney. bk.rev.; film rev.; play rev.; charts; illus.; circ. 10,000 (controlled). **Indexed:** E.I.
●Also available online.
Description: Includes arts section, cinema section, music section, poetry, short stories, real estate, politics, philosophy, environmental issues, garden design, industrial designs.
Refereed Serial

378 US
CAULDRON. bi-w. free. University of St. Thomas (Houston), 3800 Montrose, Houston, TX 77006. TEL 713-522-7911. FAX 713-522-9920. adv.; bk.rev. circ. 2,100.
Description: News, features, sports, and opinions for college students, faculty and alumni.

378.1 US ISSN 0008-8609
THE CAVALIER DAILY. 1890. d. (5/w.). $44.95. (University of Virginia) Cavalier Daily, Inc., Newcomb Hall, Charlottesville, VA 22903. TEL 804-924-1086. FAX 804-924-7290. URL: http://www.virginia.edu/~cavdaily. Ed. Kate Kofteci. R&P contact: Kate Kofteci. adv. contact: Lyndsey McCabe. bk.rev. circ. 10,000. **Document type:** newspaper.
●Also available online.

378.198 US
CAVEAT. m. free. Golden Gate University, School of Law, 536 Mission St., San Francisco, CA 94105. TEL 415-442-6698. Ed. Tod Manning. film rev.; play rev.; abstr.; charts; illus.; stat. circ. 1,000. **Document type:** newspaper, academic/scholarly publication.

378 US
CEDAR DIGEST. s-a. Tall Cedars of Lebanon of North American, 2609 N. Front St., Harrisburg, PA 17110. TEL 703-549-3622. Ed. James Wood. adv. circ. 32,000.
Description: Covers fraternal information and public relations.

378 266 US ISSN 1093-4618
CEDARVILLE TORCH. 1978. 3/yr. free. Cedarville College, Box 601, Cedarville, OH 45314. TEL 937-766-7808. FAX 937-766-2760. Ed. Dr. Martin Clark. R&P contact: Roscoe Smith. circ. 60,000 (controlled). (back issues avail.) **Description:** Features Bible-based articles that challenge and encourage evangelical Christians. Audience is adult Christians and alumni and friends of the college.

378.1 US ISSN 0008-9001
CENTENARY COLLEGE CONGLOMERATE. 1922. bi-w. $10. Centenary College of Louisiana, Student Government Association, Shreveport, LA 71134-0188. TEL 318-869-5269. Ed. Erica Johnson. adv.; bk.rev.; play rev. circ. 1,000.

378.1 US ISSN 0008-9141
CENTO. 1863. w. $15 (effective 1994-95). Centre College, Box 745, Danville, KY 40422. TEL 606-238-5533. FAX 606-236-7925. Ed. Robert Alford. adv. contact: Barcley Houston. bk.rev.; film rev.; play rev.; illus. circ. 1,500. (tabloid format) **Document type:** newspaper.
Refereed Serial

COLLEGE AND ALUMNI

371.805 US
CENTRAL FLORIDA FUTURE.* 1968. s-w. $50 free. Campbell Communications, 94 E. Mitchell Hammock Rd., Oviedo, FL 32765-9783. TEL 407-823-8054. FAX 407-823-9495. E-mail: cffuture@gdi.net. Ed. Sean Perry; Pub. Stephen Norris. circ. 10,000.
Document type: newspaper.
Description: Covers the University of Central Florida.

378.1 US ISSN 0008-9451
CENTRAL MICHIGAN LIFE; the official campus newspaper. 1919. 3/w. $65. Central Michigan University, 8 Anspach, Mt. Pleasant, MI 48859. TEL 517-774-3493. FAX 517-774-7805. Ed. Jennifer Ackerman. R&P contact: Jim Wojcik. adv. contact: Cynthia Sedlak. bk.rev.; play rev.; charts; illus. circ. 13,500. (also avail. in microform from UMI; reprint service avail. from UMI) Document type: newspaper.

378.198 US
CENTRALIGHT. s-a. Central Michigan University, Alumni House, Mt. Pleasant, MI 48859. TEL 517-774-3312. Ed. Mike Silverthorn. adv.; B&W page $1200. circ. 40,000. (tabloid format) Document type: newspaper.
Description: News and features about alumni and the university.

378.599 PH
CENTRALITE. 1921. irreg. $4.50. Central Philippine University, Box 231, Iloilo City 5000, Philippines. FAX 63-33-73470. illus.

378.198 US
CENTREPIECE. 1959. 4/yr. free to qualified personnel. Centre College, Alumni House, Danville, KY 40422. TEL 606-238-5500. FAX 606-238-5507. Ed. Diane Fisher Johnson. bk.rev. circ. 13,000. (tabloid format)

378 US
CHAMINADE NEWSLETTER. 1955. q. free. Chaminade University, 3140 Walalae Ave., Honolulu, HI 96816. TEL 808-735-4711. FAX 808-735-4870. Ed. Dennis R. Boutista. bk.rev.; illus. circ. 9,000.
Document type: newsletter.
Former titles: Chaminade University Newsletter; Chaminade College Newsletter (ISSN 0009-1286); Kaminaka.

378 CN
CHAMPLAIN BUGLE. 1973. bi-m. Editions Portes Ouvertes, Rm. F-144, 900 Riverside Dr., St. Lambert, Que. J4P 3P2, Canada. adv.; bk.rev.; film rev. circ. 2,500. (tabloid format)

378 GW ISSN 0945-2133
CHANCE; das bundesweite Schuelermagazin. 1990. bi-m. DM.20. Unicum Verlag GmbH, Willy-Brandt-Platz 5-7, 44787 Bochum, Germany. TEL 49-234-96151-0. FAX 49-234-60256. URL: http://www.chance.de. Ed. Thomas Friedenberger; Pub. Manfred Baldschus. adv.; B&W page DM.16800; trim 210 x 295; adv. contact: Norbert Neuhaus. bk.rev.; film rev.; music rev.; circ. 333,000. cols./p.: 4; pp./issue: 32. Document type: consumer publication.
Description: Nationwide magazine for high school students.

378.1 US
THE CHANTICLEER. 1934. w. $10 (effective 1997). Jacksonville State University, Communications Board, Jacksonville, AL 36265. TEL 205-782-5701. FAX 205-782-5445. Ed. Mai Martinez. adv. contact: Emily Wester. bk.rev.; circ. 7,000 (controlled). Document type: newspaper.
Former titles: Collegian; (until 1967): Collegian; Teacola.

378.1 CN ISSN 0315-1859
THE CHARLATAN. 1945. w. Can.$42 to individuals; institutions Can.$52. Charlatan Publications Inc., Rm. 531 Unicentre, Ottawa, ON K1S 5B6. TEL 613-520-8680. FAX 613-520-4051. E-mail: charlatan@carleton.ca. Ed. Dave Ebner. adv. contact: Jennifer Lalonde. bk.rev.; film rev.; illus.; play rev. circ. 12,000. (tabloid format; back issues avail.) Document type: newspaper.
Formerly: Carleton (ISSN 0008-6630).

378 UK
CHELTENHAM LADIES COLLEGE MAGAZINE. 1880. a. £5.75 (effective 1992). Cheltenham Ladies' College, Bayshill Rd., Cheltenham, Glos. GL50 3EP, England. TEL 0242-520691. FAX 0242-227882. bk.rev. circ. 2,000.

CHEMICAL ENGINEERING PROGRESS - STUDENT EDITION. see ENGINEERING — Chemical Engineering

378 UK ISSN 0308-731X
CHERWELL; the Oxford University newspaper. 1920. 24/yr. free. Oxford Student Publications Ltd., 7 St. Aldates, Oxford OX1 1BS, England. TEL 44-1865-246461. FAX 44-1865-200341. Ed. David Black; Pub. Jeni Palmer. R&P contact: Jeni Palmer. adv. contact: Jeni Palmer. bk.rev.; film rev.; play rev.; illus. circ. 17,000. Document type: newspaper.

CHICAGO CHRONICLE. see EDUCATION — Higher Education

378.1 US ISSN 0009-3610
CHICAGO MAROON. 1892. s-w. $70. University of Chicago, Chicago Maroon, 1212 E. 59th St., No. 305, Chicago, IL 60637. TEL 312-702-9555. FAX 312-702-3032. Ed. David Rodnitzky. adv.; bk.rev.; film rev.; play rev.; charts; illus. circ. 11,500. (tabloid format; also avail. in microform) Document type: newspaper.

378.198 US
CHIEFTAIN. 1970. w. free. Black Hawk College, Quad Cities Campus, 6600 34th Ave., Moline, IL 61265. FAX 309-792-5976. Ed. Carrie L. Browning. adv. contact: Mario Hernandez. film rev.; play rev.; circ. 3,000 (controlled). (back issues avail.) Document type: newspaper.
Refereed Serial

378 US
THE CHIMES (LA MIRADA). 1938. w. $20. Biola University, 13800 Biola Ave., La Mirada, CA 90639. TEL 310-903-4879. Ed. Jennifer Bunch. adv.; bk.rev.; circ. 2,000 (controlled). (also avail. in microfilm from LIB) Document type: newspaper.
Description: Student newspaper serving over 2,000 students, faculty and staff at Biola University.

CHIMES (NOTRE DAME). see LITERATURE

378 US
THE CHINOOK. 1945. s-w. $8. Casper College, 125 College Dr., Casper, WY 82601. TEL 307-268-2236. FAX 307-268-2682. adv. circ. 2,000. Document type: newspaper.

378 US
CHIPS-O-WOOD. 3/yr. free. Wood Junior College, Alumni Development, Box 289, Mathiston, MS 39752. TEL 601-263-5352. play rev.; circ. 7,000 (controlled). (tabloid format; back issues avail.)
Description: Includes alumni and development news.

CHRISTIAN MEDICAL COLLEGE VELLORE ALUMNI JOURNAL. see MEDICAL SCIENCES

378 US
CHRONICLE (DURHAM).* (Supplements avail.: R & R, Sportswrap) 1905. d. (Mon.-Fri.). free. Duke Student Publishing Company, Inc., Box 90858, Durham, NC 27708. TEL 919-684-3811. Ed. Brian Harris. adv. contact: Sue Newsome. bk.rev. circ. 15,000. (tabloid format) Document type: newspaper.

378.198 US
CHRONICLE (GRAYSLAKE). 1969. bi-w. free to students. College of Lake County, 19351 W. Washington, Grayslake, IL 60030. TEL 708-223-3634. FAX 708-223-9371. Ed. Charles Jurgaitis. adv.; B&W page $350; adv. contact: Diane Summers. bk.rev.; circ. 3,750 (controlled). Document type: newspaper.

378.18 US
CHRONICLE (HAMDEN). 1967. w. Quinnipiac College, Box 10, Hamden, CT 06518-0569. TEL 203-288-5251. FAX 203-288-8098. Ed. Sharon P. Moore. adv.; bk.rev. circ. 2,000. (back issues avail.) Document type: newspaper.

378.1 US
CHRONICLE (HEMPSTEAD). 1935. w. (Sep.-May). $25 per semester. Hofstra University, 203 Student Center, Hempstead, NY 11550. TEL 516-463-6965. adv.; bk.rev.; film rev.; play rev.; circ. 11,000 (controlled). (tabloid format; also avail. in microfiche; back issues avail.)
Formerly: Hofstra Chronicle (ISSN 0018-3172).

378 UK
CHRONICLE (ST. ANDREWS). 1984. fortn. £0.30 per issue. Chronicle Board, Students' Union, Students Association Building, St. Mary's Pl., St. Andrews, Fife KY16 9U2, Scotland. TEL 0334-77755. FAX 0334-77761. Ed. John Edward. adv.; bk.rev. circ. 3,500. Document type: newspaper.
Formerly: Alien.
Description: Independent student newspaper featuring sports, arts, music and book reviews, science reports and interviews.

THE CHRONICLE OF HIGHER EDUCATION. see EDUCATION — Higher Education

THE CHRONICLE OF HIGHER EDUCATION ALMANAC. see EDUCATION — Higher Education

378.1 KO ISSN 0009-6253
CHUNG-ANG HERALD. 1957. m. free. Chung-Ang University, 221 Heuksuk-dong, Dongjak-ku, Seoul, S. Korea. TEL 815-5031. Ed.Bd. bk.rev.; charts; illus.; stat. circ. 20,000. (tabloid format)
Description: Presents university, local, national and international news with an emphasis on the youth democratic movement within the country.

378.1 CC ISSN 0009-6261
CHUNG CHI BULLETIN. (Text in Chinese and English) 1951. a. Chinese University of Hong Kong, Chung Chi College, Shatin, New Territories, Hong Kong, People's Republic of China. TEL 852-2609-6450. Ed. Angeline Kwok. bibl.; charts; illus. circ. 3,800. Document type: bulletin.
Formerly: Chung Chi College Bulletin.

378.1 US ISSN 0745-1962
CIRCLE K. 1956. 5/yr. $6. Circle K International, 3636 Woodview Trace, Indianapolis, IN 46268. TEL 317-875-8755. FAX 317-879-0204. Ed. Nicholas K. Drake. adv. circ. 15,000. Document type: academic/scholarly publication, consumer publication, trade publication.
Formerly: Circle K Magazine (ISSN 0578-3097).
Description: Contains information on the latest trends affecting college students worldwide and activities of the international collegiate service organization, committed to community service and leadership development.

378 UK
CITY REFLECTIONS. 1969. w. free. City of London Polytechnic, Students' Union, Fairholt House, 102-105 Whitechapel High St., London E1 7RA, England. Ed. Dermot Bolger. adv.; bk.rev.; film rev.; play rev. circ. 2,000. (back issues avail.)
Former titles: Graffiti; (until 1984): Pepys.

378.1 UK
CITYSCAPE. 1947. 8/yr. free. City University Union Society, Northampton Sq., London EC1V 0HB, England. Ed. Andrew Baird. adv.; bk.rev.; illus. circ. 3,000.
Formerly (until 1988): Beacon (ISSN 0005-7320).
Description: Publication of the Student Union. Includes relevant political and social issues, social and sporting events, art reviews and more from a student point of view.

378 CN
CITYSIDE. 1980. m. $10. University of Regina, School of Journalism and Communications, Regina, SK S4S 0A2, Canada. TEL 306-584-5051. FAX 306-585-4867. E-mail: bryan.olney@uregina.ca. Ed. Bryan Olney. adv. contact: Bryan Olney. bk.rev.; circ. 1,000 (controlled). (tabloid format) Document type: newspaper.

378 CN
CLAN MACDONALD ANNUAL. a. McGill University, Macdonald College, Box 202, Ste. Anne de Bellevue, PQ H9X 1C0, Canada. TEL 514-392-4311. Ed. Elizabeth Koessler. adv.

COLLEGE AND ALUMNI

378.198 US
CLARION ALUMNI NEWS. 1867. q. Clarion University, 974 E. Wood St., Clarion, PA 16214. TEL 814-226-2334. Ed. Ron Wilshire. R&P contact: R. Wilshire. circ. 27,000 (controlled). (back issues avail.) **Document type:** newsletter.
Former titles: Clarion Magazine; Clarion University Alumni Magazine.
Description: Provides articles on Clarion University, faculty, and alumni.

CLARION SCIENCE FICTION AND FANTASY WRITERS' WORKSHOP NEWSLETTER. see *LITERATURE — Science Fiction, Fantasy, Horror*

378 US
CLARK UNIVERSITY NEWS. 1978. 4/yr. free to qualified personnel. Clark University, 950 Main St., Worcester, MA 01610. TEL 508-793-7441. FAX 508-794-7565. Ed. Jillian Peterson. circ. 25,000 (controlled). (tabloid format) **Document type:** newspaper.
Description: University tabloid featuring news of campus events, faculty research, alumni news and profiles of students, faculty and alumni.

378 US
CLARKE COLLEGE COURIER. 1930. w. Clarke College, Dubuque, IA 52001. TEL 319-588-6306. FAX 319-588-6789. circ. 1,000. **Document type:** newspaper.

378 US
CLEMSON WORLD. 1956. q. free. Clemson University, Office of Publication & Marketing Services, 103 Fike, Clemson, SC 29634-5608. TEL 864-656-2467. FAX 864-656-5004. URL: http://pubnet.clemson.edu/cwonline/cwmag.html. Ed. Liz Newall. R&P contact: Dave Dryden. adv. contact: Liz Newall. bk.rev.; circ. 75,000 (controlled).

378 US
CLIFF NEWS. 1946. 15/yr. $6. Briar Cliff College, 3303 Rebecca St., Sioux City, IA 51104. Ed. Neal Recker. circ. 1,000.

378.1 US ISSN 0009-9430
CLOCKTOWER. 1927. w. $12. Union College (Lincoln), Associated Student Body, 3800 S. 48th St., Lincoln, NE 68506. TEL 402-488-2331. Ed. Leland Krum. adv.; bk.rev.; play rev. circ. 1,500. (tabloid format)

378 US
CLOSEUP. vol.22, 1990. s-a. free. Queens College, 1900 Selwyn Ave., Charlotte, NC 28274. TEL 704-337-2252. FAX 704-337-2503. Ed. Anthony T. Hoppa. circ. 15,000. (tabloid format; also avail. in microfilm from KTO) **Document type:** newspaper.
Description: Provides news of the college and its alumni, for alumni and supporters.

378.198 US
COLBY MAGAZINE. 1911. 5/yr. Colby College, Mayflower Hill, Waterville, ME 04901. TEL 207-872-3549. circ. 22,000.
Formerly: Colby Alumnus.

378 MX ISSN 0188-7408
COLEGIO DE SONORA. REVISTA. 1990. s-a. Colegio de Sonora, Av. Obregon 54, Centro, 83000 Hemosillo, Sonora, Mexico. TEL 12-65-51. FAX 12-00-15. **Document type:** academic/scholarly publication.

378.1 UK ISSN 0010-0676
COLFEIAN. 1900. a. £1. Old Colfeians Association, Horn Park, Eltham Rd., London S.E. 12, England. Ed.Bd. adv.; illus. circ. 1,750.

378.1 US
COLGATE SCENE. 1972. 6/yr. free. Colgate University, Communications Office, Administration Bldg., Hamilton, NY 13346. TEL 315-824-1000. FAX 315-824-7798. E-mail: scene@center.colgate.edu; URL: http://www2.colgate.edu/scene/. Ed. James Leach. bk.rev.; illus. circ. 35,000. (tabloid format)
Formed by the merger of: What's New at Colgate (ISSN 0043-454X); Colgate (ISSN 0010-0684)
Description: News of Colgate University, its alumni, faculty and students.

278 US
COLLAGE (CLAREMONT). 1966. 21/yr. $40 (foreign $80). Claremont Colleges, 175 E. 8th St., Claremont, CA 91711. TEL 909-624-1887. Ed. Kacey Crtig; Pub. John Duke. R&P contact: Tappan Zee. adv. contact: Tappan Zee. circ. 6,000 (controlled). **Document type:** newspaper.

378 CN
COLLECTIF (MONTREAL).* s-m. free. Publi-PEQ, 3575 bd. St. Laurent, Ste. 232, Montreal, PQ H2X 2T7, Canada. TEL 514-845-8628. circ. 4,000. (tabloid format)

378.1 CN ISSN 0228-734X
LE COLLECTIF (SHERBROOKE). (Text in French) 1955. w. Can.$15 (effective Aug. 1995). Journal le Collectif Inc., Local 107, Universite de Sherbrooke, Centre Social, Cite Universitaire, Sherbrooke, PQ J1K 2R1, Canada. TEL 819-821-7641. FAX 819-562-2324. Ed. Beatrice Farand. adv.: page Can.$600; adv. contact: Eric Fournier. bk.rev. circ. 4,000. (tabloid format) **Document type:** academic/scholarly publication.
Formerly (until 1976): Campus Estrien (ISSN 0008-2511)

378 355 US ISSN 1046-7602
LH1
COLLEGE ALUMNI AND MILITARY PUBLICATIONS. 1980. a. $75. C A P Communications Associates, Ltd., 35-20 Broadway, Astoria, NY 11106. TEL 718-315-8250. Ed. Bob Madison.
Formerly: College Alumni Publications.

378 US
COLLEGE HEIGHTS HERALD. (Supplement avail. monthly magazine) 1925. s-w. (Tues., Thurs.). $25. Western Kentucky University, 109 Garrett Center, Bowling Green, KY 42101. TEL 502-745-2653. FAX 502-745-2697. E-mail: HERALD@msc.wku.edu; URL: http://www.msc.edu/info/herald. Ed. Lori Becker; Pub. Robert R. Adams. R&P contact: Jo Ann Thompson. adv. contact: Jo Ann Thompson. circ. 12,000. (tabloid format) **Document type:** newspaper.
●Also available online.

COLLEGE MEDIA REVIEW. see *JOURNALISM*

378.198 US
COLLEGE OF ST. SCHOLASTICA TIMES MAGAZINE. 1971. q. free. College of St. Scholastica, Office of Public Relations, 1200 Kenwood Ave., Duluth, MN 55811. TEL 218-723-6074. FAX 218-723-6290. circ. 15,000.

378 US ISSN 0888-210X
LB2341
COLLEGE STUDENT AFFAIRS JOURNAL. 1978. s-a. $25. Southern Association for College Student Affairs, c/o Diane L. Cooper, Ed., University of Georgia, 402 Aderhold Hall, GA 30602-7142. TEL 706-542-1812. FAX 706-542-4130. R&P contact: Diane L. Cooper. adv.; bk.rev. circ. 1,200. (also avail. in microform from UMI; back issues avail.) Indexed: C.I.J.E., Coll.Stud.Pers.Abstr., High.Educ.Abstr. **Document type:** academic/scholarly publication.
Formerly: Southern College Personnel Association Journal.
Description: Focuses on concepts, practices, and research that have implications and applicability for practitioners involved in college student affairs work.
Refereed Serial

378.83 US ISSN 0887-431X
COLLEGE UNION & ON-CAMPUS HOSPITALITY. 1979. bi-m. $18. Executive Business Media, Inc., 825 Old Country Rd., Box 1500, Westbury, NY 11590. TEL 516-334-3030. Ed. Cathy Orobona. adv.; circ. 11,000 (controlled).
Formerly (until 1986): College Union (ISSN 0192-3307)

378.1 US
COLLEGE VOICE (STATEN ISLAND). vol.21, 1973. every 3 wks. $4. (City University of New York, College of Staten Island, Student Government) Staten Island Register, 2100 Clove Rd., Staten Island, NY 10305. TEL 718-442-4813. Ed. Toby R. Greenzang. adv.; bk.rev.; illus. circ. 5,000. (also avail. in microfilm)
Formed by the 1980 merger of: Student Voice; College Times; Which was formed by the June 1975 merger of: Richmond Times; S I C C Dolphin (ISSN 0046-0516)

378 UK ISSN 0305-1064
THE COLLEGIAN. 1974. a. £4.86. Daniel Stewart's and Melville College, Queensferry Rd., Edinburgh EH4 3EZ, Scotland. TEL 0131-332-7925. Ed. Eileen Elder. illus. circ. 2,400. (back issues avail.)
Description: Covers various college affairs, as well as art and literature.

378.1 US
COLLEGIAN (BROOKINGS). 1894. w. $12. South Dakota State University, Student Publications, USU 069, Box 2815, Brookings, SD 57007. TEL 605-688-6164. FAX 605-688-4974. Ed. Michael Ridgeway. film rev.; play rev.; charts; illus. circ. 6,900. **Document type:** newspaper.

378.1 US ISSN 0010-1206
COLLEGIAN (ELYRIA). 1965. 4/yr. free. Lorain County Community College, Student Activities Office, 1005 N. Abbe Rd., Elyria, OH 44035. TEL 216-365-5122. Ed. Karen Huerner. adv.; B&W page $210; adv. contact: Deanna White. bk.rev.; circ. controlled. **Document type:** newspaper, academic/scholarly publication.

378 US
THE COLLEGIAN (FAYETTE). 1883. w. free. Upper Iowa University, Box 1857, Fayette, IA 52142. TEL 319-425-5273. FAX 319-425-5271. circ. 500. **Document type:** newspaper.

378 US
COLLEGIAN (TOLEDO). 1922. d. (Mon.-Thu.). $30. University of Toledo, 3504 Student Union, 2801 W. Bancroft, Toledo, OH 43606. TEL 419-537-4203. FAX 419-537-2108. adv. contact: Jim McLean. circ. 11,500. **Document type:** newspaper.

378.198 US
COLLEGIAN (TULSA). 1912. w. $8. University of Tulsa, 600 S. College, Tulsa, OK 74104. TEL 918-631-3817. adv. circ. 4,000. (tabloid format)

378.1 US ISSN 0010-1249
COLLEGIO. 1910. w. $15. Pittsburg State University, Pittsburg, KS 66762. TEL 316-231-7000. Ed. Mike Vore. adv.; play rev. circ. 7,500. **Document type:** newspaper.

378 US
COLONNADE. 1924. w. free. Georgia College & State University, Box 2442, Milledgeville, GA 31061. TEL 912-453-4511. FAX 912-454-1472. E-mail: colonnade@mail.gac.peachnet.edu; URL: http://acs5.gac.peachnet.edu/~colonnade. Pub. Mary Jean Land. adv.: page $425. bk.rev.; dance rev.; film rev.; music rev.; play rev.; software rev.; video rev. circ. 2,500. cols./p.: 6; pp./issue: 12. (broadsheet format) **Document type:** newspaper.
●Also available online.
Description: Covers news and life on campus, arts and entertainment, previews, local entertainment, and sports.

378.198 US
COLORADO COLLEGE BULLETIN. 1955. q. Colorado College, College Relations, 14 E. Cache La Poudre, Colorado Springs, CO 80903-3294. TEL 719-389-6646. FAX 719-389-6256. Ed. Jane Koerner. circ. 25,000. **Document type:** bulletin.
Description: For college alumni, staff and parents of current students.

378 US
COLORADO DAILY. 1892. d. (Mon.-Fri.). $125. Front Range Publishing, Inc., Box 1719, Boulder, CO 80306. TEL 303-443-6272. FAX 303-443-9357. Ed. Clint Talbott. adv.; bk.rev. circ. 22,000. (tabloid format) **Document type:** newspaper.

378 US ISSN 0162-3893
LD1237.5
COLUMBIA (NEW YORK). q. $5. Columbia University, Trustees of Columbia University, 310 Uris Hall, New York, NY 10027. TEL 212-854-3431. circ. 50,000. Indexed: Rehabil.Lit. **Document type:** academic/scholarly publication.
Formerly: Columbia Today (ISSN 0146-423X)

COLLEGE AND ALUMNI

378 US ISSN 0572-7820
COLUMBIA COLLEGE TODAY. 1954. 3/yr. $15. Columbia University, Columbia College, Office of Alumni Affairs, 475 Riverside Dr., Rm. 917, New York, NY 10115. TEL 212-870-2752. FAX 212-870-2747. E-mail: cct@columbia.edu; URL: http://www.columbia.edu/cu/college/alumni/CCT/. Ed. James C. Katz; Pub. James C. Katz. R&P contact: Thomas Vinciguerra. adv. contact: Donna Satow. bk.rev.; circ. 46,000 (controlled). (back issues avail.)
●Also available online.
Description: Feature articles and news about the college and its alumni.

378.198 US ISSN 0010-1915
COLUMBIA JESTER. 1900. s-a. $20. Columbia University, Jester of Columbia, 206 Ferris Booth Hall, New York, NY 10027. TEL 212-854-3611. adv.; illus. circ. 10,000.
Description: Humorous prose, poetry, satire, cartoons.

378 340 US
COLUMBIA LAW SCHOOL NEWS. 1901. 8/yr. Columbia Law School, News Association, 435 W. 116th St., Box A-27, New York, NY 10027. TEL 212-854-2640.

378.198 US ISSN 0747-4504
COLUMBIA UNIVERSITY RECORD. 1975. s-m. $20. Columbia University, Office of Public Affairs, 304 Low Library, 535 W. 116th St., MC 4321, New York, NY 10027. TEL 212-854-3282. FAX 212-678-4817. Ed. Roger J. Hackett. bk.rev. circ. 16,000. **Document type:** newspaper.

378.1 US ISSN 0010-2091
THE COLUMNS (FAIRMONT). 1923. w. free to qualified personnel. Fairmont State College, Office of Publications, 121 Library Bldg., Locust Ave., Fairmont, WV 26554. Ed. Lynn Williams. R&P contact: Patricia Whiting. adv. contact: Patricia Whiting. film rev.; play rev.; illus. circ. 2,000. (tabloid format) **Document type:** newspaper.
Description: Covers educational and social activities and events of interest to the student body and faculty of Fairmont State College, West Virginia.

378.198 US ISSN 1047-8604
COLUMNS (SEATTLE); the University of Washington alumni magazine. 1909. q. membership. University of Washington Alumni Association, 1415 N.E. 45th St., Seattle, WA 98105. TEL 206-543-0540. FAX 206-685-0611. E-mail: telnet://uwin.u. washington.edu. Ed. Tom Griffin; Pub. Jon K. Rider. adv.; bk.rev.; circ. 170,000 (controlled). **Document type:** consumer publication.
Formerly (until Dec. 1989): Washington Alumnus.

378.1 296 US ISSN 0010-2652
COMMENTATOR. 1935. bi-w. (Sep.-Jun.) Yeshiva College Student Council, Student Information Center, 500 W. 185th St., New York, NY 10033. TEL 212-740-2155. Ed. Joshua Feldman. adv.; bk.rev.; film rev.; play rev.; illus. circ. 5,000. (also avail. in microfilm from AJP; back issues avail.) **Document type:** newspaper.

378 US
COMMONWEALTH TIMES. (Supplements avail.) 1969. 3/wk. free. Virginia Commonwealth University, 901 W. Main St., Richmond, VA 23284-2010. TEL 804-828-1058. FAX 804-828-9201. Ed. Melanie Irvin. adv. contact: John Battema. bk.rev. circ. 9,000. (tabloid format) **Document type:** newspaper.

378 610 US
COMMUNIQUE (ITHACA). 1978. 4/yr. free. Cornell University, Office of University Development, 55 Brown Rd., Ithaca, NY 14850-1266. TEL 607-254-7111. FAX 607-254-7167. Ed. Caissa Willmer. circ. 17,000 (controlled). **Document type:** newsletter.
Description: Published as a leadership report to alumni and friends of Cornell University.

378 US
HE COMMUNIQUE (PITTSBURGH, 1984). 1984. s-m. $12. Chatham College, Woodland Rd., Box 596, Pittsburgh, PA 15232. TEL 412-365-1561. Ed. Julie Saunders. adv.; B&W page $125; adv. contact: Amy Huseman. circ. 800. (back issues avail.) **Document type:** newspaper.
Formerly: First Edition.

COMPANY; a magazine of the American Jesuits. see RELIGIONS AND THEOLOGY — Roman Catholic

378.198 UK ISSN 0140-315X
CONCETTO; newspaper of Chelsea College students. 1960. fortn. free. Chelsea College, Students Union, Manresa Rd., London SW3 6LX, England. Ed. Pete Sawyer. adv.; bk.rev.; film rev.; play rev. circ. 1,000. **Document type:** newspaper.

378 US
CONCORDIA ALUMNI NEWS. 1961. 3/yr. Concordia College, 901 S. Eighth St., Moorhead, MN 56562. TEL 218-299-4000. FAX 218-299-3646. Ed. Maureen Zimmerman. circ. 34,000 (controlled). (back issues avail.) **Document type:** newsletter.
Description: Covers news and features for alumni and friends of the college.

378 UK
CONCOURSE. N.S. 1978. 3/yr. (during school term). University of Keele, Keele University Students' Union, Keele, Staffs ST5 5BJ, England. TEL 0782-711411. FAX 0782-712671. Eds. Clare Alverson, Rick Crownshaw. adv.; bk.rev. circ. 1,000. (tabloid format)

CONFRONTATION; a literary journal of Long Island University. see LITERATURE

378 US
CONNECTOR (LOWELL). w. free. Connector - UMass Lowell, 1 University Ave., Lowell, MA 01854. TEL 508-934-5009. FAX 508-934-3031. Ed. David W. Pearson, Jr. adv. contact: Danielle Woods. bk.rev. circ. 4,000. (tabloid format) **Document type:** newspaper.
Description: Contains on-campus news and news from other colleges and universities. Includes art, entertainment and sports news.

378.198 US ISSN 0888-7586
CONTRABAND (LAKE CHARLES). 1939. w. $30. McNeese State University, Box 91375, Lake Charles, LA 70609-1375. TEL 318-437-5645. adv.; film rev.; play rev.; illus. circ. 4,500.

378 CN
THE CORD. 1926. w. $15. Wilfrid Laurier University, Student Publications, 75 University Ave. W., Waterloo, ON N2L 3C5, Canada. TEL 519-884-2990. FAX 519-884-7723. E-mail: 22cord@mach1.wlv.ca. Ed. Katherine M. Harding. R&P contact: Kevin MacDonald. adv. contact: Lars Parstrik. bk.rev.; film rev. circ. 5,000. (tabloid format) **Document type:** newspaper.
Formerly: Cord Weekly.

378 US
CORNELL DAILY SUN. 1880. d. (5/w.) $55. Cornell Daily Sun, Inc., 119 S. Cayuga St., Ithaca, NY 14850. TEL 607-273-3606. FAX 607-273-0746. E-mail: sun-mailbox@cornellsun.com; URL: http://www.cornellsun.com. bk.rev.; film rev.; play rev.; illus. circ. 5,000. (tabloid format; also avail. in microfiche; back issues avail.) **Document type:** newspaper.
Refereed Serial

378 US ISSN 1070-2733
LH1.C8
CORNELL MAGAZINE. 1899. bi-m. $29. Cornell Alumni Federation, 55 Brown Rd., Ithaca, NY 14850. FAX 607-257-1782. E-mail: cornell_magazine@cornell.edu. Ed. David J. Gibson. adv.; bk.rev. circ. 40,000. **Document type:** academic/scholarly publication.
●Also available online.
Formerly (until 1993): Cornell Alumni News (ISSN 1058-3467)

CORNELL MEDICINE. see MEDICAL SCIENCES

635 581 900 US ISSN 0010-8863
CORNELL PLANTATIONS. 1944. s-a. $35 includes membership. Cornell University, Cornell Plantations, One Plantations Rd., Ithaca, NY 14850. TEL 607-255-3020. FAX 607-255-2404. E-mail: ew28@cornell.edu; URL: http://www.img.cornell.edu/plantations. Ed. Elissa Wolfson. R&P contact: Elissa Wolfson. bk.rev.; illus. circ. 3,600. (also avail. in microform from UMI) Indexed: Biol.Abstr., Forest.Abstr., Forest Prod.Abstr., Sci.Cit.Ind. **Document type:** academic/scholarly publication. —UMI.
Description: Articles about Cornell Plantations and on topics related to horticulture, ecology, conservation, gardening tips, landscape design, and plant and natural sciences.

371.85 GW ISSN 0947-3297
DER CORPSSTUDENT; Nachrichten fuer Weinheimer Corpsstudenten. 1953. q. DM.12. (Weinheimer Verband Alter Corpsstudenten) Verlag Ernst Voegel GmbH, Postfach 1000, 93491 Stamsried, Germany. TEL 49-9466-94000. FAX 49-9466-1276. adv.; bk.rev. circ. 10,000. **Document type:** newsletter.
Formed by the merger of (1953-1993): Wachenburg (ISSN 0935-0659); Deutsche Corpszeitung (ISSN 0931-0215)

378 UK
THE COURIER. 1947. w. (during school term). Union Society, King's Walk, Newcastle-upon-Tyne NE1 8QB, England. TEL 44-191-232-4050. FAX 44-191-222-1876. URL: http://www.ncl.ac.uk/~ncourier/. Ed. Alistair Thomson. R&P contact: Miles Starforth. adv. contact: Monica Doughty. bk.rev.; circ. 3,000. (tabloid format) Indexed: P.A.I.S. **Document type:** newspaper.
●Also available online.

378 US
COURIER (FARMERS BRANCH). 1978. bi-w. newsstand price: free. Brookhaven College, 3939 Valley View Lane, Farmers Branch, TX 75244-4497. TEL 214-860-4787. FAX 214-620-4675. Ed. Shane Goins. adv. contact: Becky Chapman. circ. 2,500. **Document type:** newspaper.

378 US
COURIER (MEQUON). q. free. Concordia University Wisconsin, Mequon, WI 53092-9652. TEL 414-243-5700. FAX 414-243-4351. Ed. Jeffrey Bandurski. circ. 80,000.

378 US
COURIER (SOUTH HOLLAND). 1927. m. free. South Suburban College, 15800 S. State St., South Holland, IL 60473-1270. TEL 708-596-2000. FAX 708-210-5758. Ed. Susan Sebok. adv.; bk.rev.; charts; film rev.; illus.; play rev. (tabloid format) **Document type:** newspaper.
Description: Discusses all matters of concern to college students.

378 US
THE COWL. w. $8. Providence College, Box 2981, Friaar Sta., Providence, RI 02918. TEL 401-865-2214.

378 US
COYOTE. 1909. 6/yr. free to students. Albertson College, Associated Students, 2112 Cleveland Blvd., Caldwell, ID 83605. TEL 208-459-5508. FAX 208-454-2077. circ. 1,000. (tabloid format) **Document type:** newspaper.

378 UK ISSN 0308-048X
CRANFIELD SCHOOL OF MANAGEMENT ADDRESS BOOK. 1975. a. A P Information Services, Roman House, 296 Golders Green Rd., London NW11 9PZ, England. TEL 44-181-455-4550. FAX 44-181-455-6381. adv.; page £600; 210 x 150. circ. 4,800. (also avail. in diskette format) **Document type:** directory.
Description: Lists all graduates of Cranfield School of Management in alphabetical, chronological, geographical, and professional order.

378 US
CRESCENT. 1915. q. $15. Phi Beta Sigma Fraternity, Inc., 145 Kennedy St., N.W., Washington, DC 20011. TEL 202-726-5434. FAX 202-881-1681. **Document type:** newsletter.
Description: Contains information for and about the members of the fraternity.

COLLEGE AND ALUMNI

378.198 US
CREST. 1939. w. $10. Teikyo Maycrest University, 1607 W. 12th St., Davenport, IA 52804. TEL 319-327-9610. FAX 319-325-9250. Ed. Jennifer Holbo. adv. contact: Tina Burgmeier. bk.rev. circ. 1,200. (broadsheet format; back issues avail.) **Document type:** newspaper.

378 US
CRIMSON - WHITE.* 1894. 4/w. University of Alabama, Media Planning Board, 923 University Blvd., Box 2389, Tuscaloosa, AL 35403. TEL 205-348-8036. FAX 205-348-8036. Ed.Bd. adv. circ. 15,000. **Document type:** newspaper.
Formerly: Crimson News.

378 CN
LA CRISE.* m. free. Publi-PEQ, 3575 bd. St- Laurent, Ste. 232, Montreal, PQ H2X 2T7, Canada. TEL 514-845-8628. circ. 2,000. (tabloid format)

CRISS CROSS. see *CHILDREN AND YOUTH — About*

070 378 US
CRITERION (RIVERSIDE).* 1939. bi-m. $15. (Associated Students of Loma Linda University) Riverside County Publishing Co., 7190 Jurupa Ave., Riverside, CA 92504-1016. Ed. Peter Thornburgh. adv.; bk.rev.; circ. 2,000 (controlled). **Indexed:** CERDIC, Rel.& Theol.Abstr., Rel.Ind.One.

378.198 US
THE CRUSADER (LANCASTER). 1936. w. free. Antelope Valley College, 3041 W. Ave. K, Lancaster, CA 93536. TEL 805-943-3241. FAX 805-943-5573. Ed. Catherine Dodson. adv. contact: Sandy Rowley. bk.rev. circ. 1,850. (tabloid format)
Formerly: Marauder Times.

371.8 US
THE CRUSADER (NAMPA). 1942. w. $20. Associated Students of Northwest Nazarene College, Northwest Nazarene College, Box C, Nampa, ID 83686. TEL 208-467-8656. FAX 208-467-8468. E-mail: crusader@science.nnc.edu; URL: http://www.nne.edu. Ed. D. Andrew Zirschky. adv.: page $200; adv. contact: David Roemhildt. bk.rev.; film rev.; music rev.; software rev.; tele.rev.; video rev.; charts; illus.; maps; stat. circ. 1,500. (tabloid format; back issues avail.) **Document type:** newspaper.
Description: Contains news, opinion, and features from a Christian standpoint.

378 US ISSN 1082-0523
CRUSADER (SELINSGROVE). 1956. w. (Sep.-Apr.). $21.25 (effective 1997 & 1998). Susquehanna University, Campus Activities, Box 22, Selinsgrove, PA 17870. TEL 717-372-4298. FAX 717-372-2757. E-mail: crusader@susqu.edu. Ed. Brett Marcy. R&P contact: Catherine Hastings. TEL 717-372-9359. adv. contact: Christy Walter. bk.rev.; film rev.; play rev. circ. 1,800. (broadsheet format) **Document type:** newspaper.
Description: Covers campus events, student life, college sports, and national issues of interest to students, faculty, staff, and parents.
Refereed Serial

378 UK
CUB T N G. (The Next Generation) 1947. m. free. Queen Mary & Westfield College, Students' Union, 432 Bancroft Rd., London E1 4DH, England. TEL 0171-975-5390. FAX 0181-981-0802. Ed. Samuel Welbeck. adv.; bk.rev. circ. 3,000. **Document type:** newspaper.
Formerly: Cub (ISSN 0964-8070)

378 UK
CULFORDIAN. 1895. a. £3($6) Culford School, Bury St. Edmunds, Suffolk IP28 6TX, England. TEL 44-284-728619. FAX 44-284-728631. Ed. John Humphries. adv.; bk.rev. circ. 2,250. (back issues avail.) **Document type:** newsletter.

378 US
CUMBERLAND LAWYER. a. $10. Samford University, Cumberland School of Law, 800 Lakeshore Dr., Birmingham, AL 35229. TEL 205-870-2444. FAX 205-870-2673. Ed. Elaine D. Chambless. circ. 7,000. **Document type:** academic/scholarly publication, corporate report.
Description: Published for alumni and friends of Cumberland School of Law, Samford University. Includes scholarly activities, school and international program news, and alumni updates.

378 AT
CURIO. 1970. fortn. free. University of Canberra Students' Association, Students' Association, Box 1, Belconnen, A.C.T. 2616, Australia. TEL 61-6-2012063. FAX 61-6-2514248. E-mail: curio@student.canberra.edu.au. Ed.Bd. R&P contact: Darren Langlands. adv. contact: Carol Battle. bk.rev. circ. 2,000. **Document type:** newspaper.
Former titles: Caesarian (ISSN 0311-1229); Yarruga.

371.83 US
CURRENT (KENOSHA); student voice of Carthage College. 1892. w. free. Carthage College, Kenosha, WI 53141. TEL 414-551-6150. E-mail: current%student%carthage@cns.carthage.edu; URL: http://www.carthage.edu/current. Ed. Kim Bednarczyk. R&P contact: Kim Bednarczyk. adv. contact: Nicole Phelps. bk.rev.; film rev.; play rev.; illus. circ. 2,000. (tabloid format) **Document type:** newspaper.
Former titles: Arrow (ISSN 0001-3056); Crimson Arrow.
Description: News, features, sports and opinions pertaining to student activities at the college.
Refereed Serial

378 071 US
CURRENT SAUCE. 1914. w. $20. Northwestern State University of Louisiana, Student Publications, NSU Box 5306, Natchitoches, LA 71497. TEL 318-357-5213. FAX 318-357-6564. Ed. Andrew Martin. R&P contact: Steve Hunt. adv. contact: Adrienne Weldon. illus.; circ. 3,500 (controlled). cols./p.: 6; pp./issue: 8. (broadsheet format) **Document type:** newspaper.

D U Z. see *EDUCATION — Higher Education*

378.1 US ISSN 0011-5371
THE DAILY ATHENAEUM. (Summer edition: Summer Athenaeum) 1887. d. (Aug.-May); w. (June-Aug.). $35. West Virginia University, 284 Prospect St., Morgantown, WV 26506. TEL 304-293-4141. FAX 304-293-6857. Ed. Eric Lawrence; Pub. Alan R. Waters. adv. contact: Alan R. Waters. bk.rev.; film rev.; play rev. circ. 15,000. **Document type:** newspaper.

378.1 US
DAILY BAROMETER. 1895. d. (Mon.-Fri.). $36. Oregon State University, University Student Media, Memorial Union E. 117, Corvallis, OR 97331. TEL 503-737-6373. FAX 503-737-4999. Ed. John Lovdokken. adv. circ. 10,000. (tabloid format) **Document type:** newspaper.

378.198 US ISSN 1050-2300
DAILY CALIFORNIAN. 1871. 5/w. $65 (effective 1997). Independent Berkeley Student Publishing Co., 600 Eshleman St., UC, Berkeley, CA 94704. TEL 510-548-8300. FAX 510-849-2803. URL: http://www.dailycal.org. Ed. Ryan Tate. R&P contact: Bita Rahebi. adv. contact: Hubert Brucher. bk.rev.; film rev.; play rev.; charts; illus. circ. 23,000. (tabloid format; also avail. in microfilm from LIB) **Document type:** newspaper.
Description: Serves the University of California and the city of Berkeley.

378 US
DAILY CAMPUS (DALLAS). 1915. 4/w. $110. Student Media Company, Inc., 3140 Dyer St., Dallas, TX 75275. TEL 214-768-4555. FAX 214-768-4573. E-mail: rlytle@post.smu.edu; URL: http://www.sde.htrigg.smv.edu. Ed. Ann Gonzalez; Pub. Richard C. Lytle. adv. contact: Paula Streiff. bk.rev.; circ. 4,500 (controlled). **Document type:** newspaper.
●Also available online.

378 US
DAILY CAMPUS (STORRS MANSFIELD). 1896. d. $40. University of Connecticut Board of Trustees, 11 Dog Ln., Storrs Mansfield, CT 06268. TEL 203-486-3407. FAX 203-486-4388. Ed. Rachel Oischan. adv.; bk.rev. circ. 10,000. (tabloid format) **Document type:** newspaper.

051 US ISSN 0011-5398
DAILY CARDINAL. 1892. d. (exc. w. during Summer). $95. Daily Cardinal Newspaper Corporation, 821 University Ave., Madison, WI 53706. TEL 608-262-5857. Ed. James R. Norton. adv.; bk.rev.; film rev.; play rev. circ. 20,000. (tabloid format) **Document type:** newspaper.

378 US
DAILY COLLEGIAN (FRESNO). (Includes supplements) 1921. 4/w. (Mon.-Thur., academic year). $17.50 per semester. California State University, Fresno, Keats Campus Bldg., Fresno, CA 93740. TEL 209-294-2266. Ed. Chris Branam. adv. contact: Lance Jackson. bk.rev. circ. 3,500. (tabloid format; also avail. in microfilm from LIB) **Document type:** newspaper.

378.198 US
DAILY COLLEGIAN (UNIVERSITY PARK). 1887. d. $84. Collegian Inc., James Bldg., 123 S. Burrowes St., University Park, PA 16801-3882. TEL 814-865-2531. FAX 814-865-3848. Ed. Rachel A. Hogan. circ. 19,000. (back issues avail.) **Document type:** newspaper.
Description: Independent student newspaper serving the University Park campus of Penn State University.

378 US
DAILY COUGAR. (Supplement avail.: Transitions) 1934. 5/w. $70. University of Houston, Student Publications Department, Houston, TX 77204-4071. TEL 713-743-5350. FAX 713-743-5384. E-mail: LCasares@wh.edu; URL: http://www.wh.edu/campus/cougar. Ed. Scott Williams. R&P contact: Dick Cigle. TEL 213-743-5353. adv. contact: Loida Casares. circ. 13,000. (tabloid format) **Document type:** newspaper.

378.1 US ISSN 0894-1599
DAILY EASTERN NEWS. 1915. N. (Mon.-Fri.). $60. Eastern Illinois University, Student Publications, Charleston, IL 61920. TEL 217-581-2812. Ed. Travis Spencer. adv.; film rev.; play rev.; index. circ. 8,900. (tabloid format; also avail. in microfilm) **Document type:** newspaper.
Formerly: Eastern News (ISSN 0012-8864)

378 US
DAILY EGYPTIAN. 1921. d. (Mon.-Fri.). $55. Southern Illinois University at Carbondale, Communications Bldg., SIU-C, Carbondale, IL 62901. TEL 618-533-3311. FAX 618-453-1992. Ed. Lloyd Goodman. circ. 23,000. **Document type:** newspaper.

378 US
DAILY FORTY-NINER. 1949. d. $54 per semester. California State University, Long Beach, 1250 Bellflower Blvd., Long Beach, CA 90840. TEL 310-985-8000. Ed. Virginia McCrum; Pub. William Mulligan. R&P contact: William Mulligan. adv. contact: Jamie Eggleston. circ. 10,000. **Document type:** newspaper.

378.198 US
DAILY FREE PRESS. 1970. d. (Mon.-Fri.). $85. Back Bay Publishing Co., 842 Commonwealth Ave., Boston, MA 02215. TEL 617-232-6841. FAX 617-232-0592. E-mail: letters@dfpress.com; editor@dfpress.com; URL: http://www.dfpress.com. Ed. Chris Walker. R&P contact: Chris Walker. adv. contact: Taylor Knight. bk.rev.; film rev.; play rev.; charts; illus.; stat. circ. 12,000. (tabloid format; back issues avail.) **Document type:** newspaper.

378 US
THE DAILY IOWAN. 1868. 5/w. $75. Students Publications, Inc., 111 Communications Center, Iowa City, IA 52242. TEL 319-335-5786. Ed. Annette Segreto. adv. contact: James Leonard. circ. 20,000. **Document type:** newspaper.

378.1 US ISSN 0011-5444
DAILY KENT STATER. 1926. 4/w. $40. Kent State University, Student Media Policy Committee, Taylor Hall, Rm. 101, Kent, OH 44242. TEL 216-672-2586. adv.; bk.rev.; illus. circ. 14,000. (also avail. in microform from UMI) **Document type:** newspaper.

378 US
DAILY MISSISSIPPIAN. 1912. d. (Mon.-Fri.). $50 (effective 1997). Farley Hall, University, MS 3867 TEL 601-232-7118. FAX 601-232-5703. E-mail: dmnews@olemiss.edu; URL: http://www.lemiss.edu/news/dm. Ed. Jenny Dodson; Pub. S. Gale Denley. R&P contact: Jenny Dodson. adv. contact: Melanie Wadkins. bk.rev. circ. 11,500. (tabloid format) **Document type:** newspaper.
Refereed Serial

COLLEGE AND ALUMNI

378.198 US
LY NEBRASKAN. 1900. d. $55. University of Nebraska at Lincoln, 34 Nebraska Union, 1400 R St., Lincoln, NE 68588-0448. TEL 402-472-2588. AX 402-472-1761. URL: http://www.unl.edu/ dailyneb/. Ed. Paula Lavigne. adv. contact: Amy Struthers. bk.rev.; film rev.; play rev.; charts; illus. circ. 16,000. (tabloid format) **Document type:** newspaper.

378 US
DAILY NORTHWESTERN. (Supplements avail.) 1881. d. (Mon.-Fri.). $45. Northwestern University, Students Publishing Co., 1999 Sheridan Rd., Evanston, IL 60208. TEL 708-491-7206. AX 708-491-9905. E-mail: daily@merle.acns.nwu. edu. Ed. Christina Headrick; Pub. Stacia Campbell. adv.: B&W page $396. bk.rev. circ. 8,500. (tabloid format) **Document type:** newspaper.

378 US
LY O'COLLEGIAN. 1926. 5/w. $131. O'Collegian Publishing Co., 109 Paul Miller Journalism Bldg., Stillwater, OK 74078. TEL 405-744-6362. AX 405-744-7936. Ed. Carol Brorsen. adv. contact: Don Forbes. circ. 11,000. **Document type:** newspaper.

378.198 US
LY ORANGE. 1903. d. $110. Daily Orange Corp., Syracuse University, 744 Ostrom Ave., Syracuse, NY 13210. TEL 315-443-2315. FAX 315-443-3686. Ed. Erin Banning. R&P contact: Erin Banning. adv. contact: David Jack. film rev.; play rev. circ. 10,000. (tabloid format) **Document type:** newspaper.

378.198 US
LY OTHER. 1976. 5/w. free. MacMurray College, Journalism Program, Jacksonville, IL 62650. TEL 217-479-7049. adv.; bk.rev.; circ. 700.

378 US
LY PENNSYLVANIAN. 1885. d. (Mon.-Fri. fr. Sep. to Apr.) $200 (effective 1993). Daily Pennsylvanian, Inc., 4015 Walnut St., Philadelphia, PA 19104. TEL 215-898-6581. FAX 215-898-2050. Ed. Stephen Glass. adv.; bk.rev.; film rev.; play rev. circ. 14,000. (back issues avail.) **Document type:** newspaper.
 Description: Daily newspaper covering news, sports and opinion at University of Pennsylvania and surrounding Philadelphia community.

378.1 US ISSN 0885-7601
LH1.P8
THE DAILY PRINCETONIAN. 1876. d. (Mon.-Fri., Sep.-May). $55. (Princeton University) Daily Princetonian, Inc., Box 469, Princeton, NJ 08542. TEL 609-924-7570. FAX 609-924-4039. Ed. Buster Kantrow. adv. contact: Aisha Nawaz. illus. circ. 4,000. (tabloid format) **Document type:** newspaper.

378 US
LY REVEILLE. 1898. d. (Tue.-Fri.). $50. Louisiana State University, 39 Hodges, L.S.U., Baton Rouge, LA 70803. TEL 504-388-1697. FAX 504-388-1698. Ed. Jon E. Fisher. circ. 19,000. (tabloid format) **Document type:** newspaper.

378 US
LY SUNDIAL. 1957. d. (Mon.-Thu.). free. California State University, Northridge, 18111 Nordhoff St., Northridge, CA 91330. TEL 818-885-2998. FAX 818-885-3638. Ed. Chris Reed; Pub. Henrietta E. Charles. adv. contact: Elizabeth Whirledge. circ. 10,000. (also avail. in microfilm from LIB) **Document type:** newspaper.

378 US
LY TAR HEEL. 1893. 5/w. $90. University of North Carolina, CB 5210, Carolina Union No. 49, Chapel Hill, NC 27514. TEL 919-962-1163. Ed. Jennifer Wing. adv. circ. 20,000. **Document type:** newspaper.

378.198 US
LY TARGUM. 1869. d. (Mon.-Fri.). $49. Rutgers University, 126 College Ave., Ste. 431, New Brunswick, NJ 08903. TEL 201-932-7051. Ed. Josh Rotnick. adv. contact: Michele Albert. bk.rev. circ. 17,000. (tabloid format) **Document type:** newspaper.

378.1 US
DAILY TEXAN. 1900. d. (5/w., when classes are in session). $75. Texas Student Publications, Box D, Austin, TX 78713-9804. TEL 512-471-4591. FAX 512-471-1576. Ed. Robert Rogers. R&P contact: Robert Rogers. adv. contact: Evelyn Gardner. bk.rev.; film rev.; play rev.; illus. circ. 30,000. (also avail. in microfilm) **Document type:** newspaper.
 ● Also available online.
 Incorporates: Summer Texan (ISSN 0039-5021)

378 US
DAILY TITAN. 1962. d. (Tues.-Fri.) (during the academic year). $65. California State University, Fullerton, 800 N. State College Blvd., Humanities Rm. H213, Fullerton, CA 92634. TEL 714-773-2128. FAX 714-773-2702. Ed. Marie Loggia. adv. contact: Suzie Fung. bk.rev. circ. 6,000. (also avail. in microfilm from LIB) **Document type:** newspaper.

378 US
DAILY TROJAN. d. (Mon.-Fri.). $140. University of Southern California, Student Union 404, Univ. Park, Los Angeles, CA 90089-0895. TEL 213-740-2707. FAX 213-740-5701. Ed. Jennifer Hamm. circ. 10,000. (tabloid format) **Document type:** newspaper.

378 US
DAILY UNIVERSE. 1902. 5/w. $38. Brigham Young University, 538 Wilkinson Center, Box 27917, Provo, UT 84602-7917. TEL 801-378-2957. Ed. JoLynne VanValkenburg. circ. 19,000. **Document type:** newspaper.

378.198 US
DAILY UNIVERSITY STAR. 1911. 4/w. $35. Southwest Texas State University, Department of Journalism, 102 Old Main, San Marcos, TX 78666-4616. TEL 512-245-3487. FAX 512-245-3708. adv.; bk.rev. circ. 12,000. (also avail. in microfilm) **Document type:** newspaper.
 Formerly: University Star.

378 US
DAILY UTAH CHRONICLE. 1850. d. (Mon.-Fri.). University of Utah, 240 Union Bldg., Salt Lake City, UT 84103. TEL 801-581-7041. FAX 801-581-3299. circ. 18,000. (tabloid format) **Document type:** newspaper.

378 US
DAILY VIDETTE. 1888. d. (Mon.-Fri.). $25 off-campus. Illinois State University, Vidette Publications Board, Edwards Annex, Normal, IL 61761. TEL 309-438-7685. FAX 309-438-5211. Ed. Jennifer Johnson. adv.; bk.rev. circ. 16,000. (tabloid format) **Document type:** newspaper.

378.1 CN ISSN 0011-5819
DALHOUSIE GAZETTE; Canada's oldest college newspaper. 1867. w. Can.$25. Dalhousie Gazette Publications Society, Dalhousie University, Halifax, N.S. B3H 4J2, Canada. TEL 902-424-2507. adv.; bk.rev.; film rev.; play rev. circ. 10,000. (tabloid format)

378.198 CN ISSN 1185-4014
DALHOUSIE MAGAZINE; the alumni magazine. 1983. 3/yr. free. Dalhousie Alumni Affairs, Dalhousie University, Macdonald Bldg., Halifax, NS B3H 3J5, Canada. TEL 902-494-2071. FAX 902-494-1141. URL: jdavidso@kilcom1.ucis.dal.ca. Ed. June Davidson. R&P contact: June Davidson. circ. 45,000. (back issues avail.) **Document type:** bulletin.
 Description: Provides alumni and campus news.

378 US
DANA REVIEW. 1944. 4/yr. free. Dana College, Blair, NE 68008. TEL 402-426-7781. FAX 402-426-7386. E-mail: ann@fs1.dana.edu. Ed. Ann George. R&P contact: Ann George. circ. 12,000. **Document type:** newsletter.

DANGXIAO LUNTAN/C C P PARTY SCHOOL MAGAZINE.
 see POLITICAL SCIENCE

378 US ISSN 0199-9931
THE DARTMOUTH. 1799. d. (Mon.-Fri.). $56. Dartmouth College, 6175 Robinson Hall, Hanover, NH 03755. TEL 603-646-2600. Ed.Bd. adv.; bk.rev. circ. 2,500. (tabloid format) **Document type:** newspaper.

378 US
DARTMOUTH ALUMNI MAGAZINE. 1908. 9/yr. $21.50. Dartmouth College, 38 N. Main St., Hanover, NH 03755. TEL 603-646-2256. FAX 603-646-1209. Ed. Jay Heinrichs. adv.; bk.rev. circ. 45,000.

DARTMOUTH MEDICINE. see MEDICAL SCIENCES

378.1 US ISSN 1074-083X
DARTMOUTH REVIEW. 1980. w. $30. Hanover Review, Inc., Box 343, Hanover, NH 03755. TEL 603-643-4370. FAX 603-643-3070. Ed. Doris Brewer. adv. contact: Mark Kelly. bk.rev. circ. 12,300. **Document type:** newspaper.
 Description: Covers campus news for Dartmouth College, as well as national news.

378 UK
DARTS. 1947. fortn. Sheffield University Students Union, Western Bank, Sheffield S10 2TG, England. Ed. Justin Springham. adv.: page £500. film rev.; music rev. circ. 6,000. cols./p.: 5; pp./issue: 20. (tabloid format) **Document type:** newspaper.

378 AT
DEAKIN UNIVERSITY, OFF-CAMPUS GUIDE. 1978. a. Deakin University, Victoria 3217, Australia. TEL 052-442777. FAX 052-472020. circ. 30,000.
 Formerly: Deakin University. Guide to Off-Campus Studies.

378 CN
LE DECLIN. (Text in French) 6/yr. College d'Enseignement Generale et Professionel de l'Abitibi - Tesmiscaminque, 425 boul. du College, C.P. 1500, Rouyn, Que. J9X 5E5, Canada. TEL 819-762-1894. adv. circ. 700.
 Formerly (until 1987): Bof.

378.1 US ISSN 0011-7501
DEFENDER (DEFIANCE). vol.10, 1970. w. free to students. Defiance College, 701 N. Clinton St., Defiance, OH 43512. TEL 419-784-4010. Ed. Pat Olsen. adv.; film rev.; play rev.; illus. circ. 800. (also avail. in microform from UMI; reprint service avail. from UMI)
 —UMI.

378 CN
DEFI-SCIENCES. (Text in French) s-m. free. Publi-PEQ, 3575 bd. St. Laurent, Ste. 232, Montreal, PQ H2X 2T7, Canada. TEL 514-845-8628. circ. 3,500. (tabloid format)

378.1 CN
DEFISCIENCE; journal des etudiants en sciences et genie de l'univers-cite laval. (Text in French) 1977. 8/yr. Can.$14. Universite Laval, Sainte-Foy, Association des Etudiants en Sciences et Genie, Pavillon Vachon, Ste. 0060, Cite Universitaire, Quebec, PQ G1K 7P4, Canada. TEL 418-656-2131. FAX 418-656-3082. E-mail: vpcom@aesgul.ulaval. ca. Ed. Jean Paul Vermette. adv.: page Can.$325. bk.rev. circ. 3,000. (tabloid format) **Document type:** academic/scholarly publication.
 Former titles: Eprouvette (ISSN 0046-2373); Carabin.
 Description: Humoristic student publication addressing science and engineering majors.

378 UK
DEGREES NORTH (LEEDS). 1992. s-a. University of Leeds, Alumni Office, 18 Blenheim Terrace, Leeds LS2 9HD, England. TEL 44-113-233-6109. FAX 44-113-233-4029. E-mail: degreesnorth@ alumni.leeds.ac.uk; URL: http://www.leeds.ac.uk/. Ed. Jayne Glennon. R&P contact: Jayne Glennon. adv. contact: Jayne Glennon. circ. 55,000. (back issues avail.) **Document type:** newsletter.
 Description: Keeps alumni of the University of Leeds in touch, informed and involved with their university and each other.

378.1 UK
DEGREES NORTH (SUNDERLAND). 1959. 12/yr. free. University of Sunderland, Students Union, Wearmouth Hall, Chester Rd., Sunderland SR1 3SD, England. TEL 44-191-5145512. Ed. Alex Dippie. R&P contact: Joe Williams. adv. contact: Allen Humes. bk.rev.; film rev.; play rev. circ. 5,000. **Document type:** newspaper.
 Former titles (until 1996): Monopoly; (until 1981): Dais (ISSN 0011-5754)

COLLEGE AND ALUMNI

378.1 — NE — ISSN 0011-782X
DELFTS BOUWKUNDIG STUDENTEN GEZELSCHAP STYLES. MEDEDELINGEN.* 1961. w. (Sep.-Jun.). free. Delfts Bouwkundig Studenten Gezelschap Stylos, Berlageweg 1, Delft, Netherlands. charts; stat. circ. 2,500.

378 — CN
LE DELIRE. (Text in French) 1984. fortn. Publi-PEQ, 3575 bd. St. Laurent, Ste. 232, Montreal, PQ H2X 2T7, Canada. TEL 514-845-8628. adv. circ. 700.

378 — US
DELTA (LEXINGTON). 1883. q. $10. Sigma Nu Fraternity, Inc., Box 1869, Lexington, VA 24450. TEL 540-463-2164. FAX 540-463-1669. E-mail: sigmanuhq@aol.com. Ed. M.E. Littlefield. R&P contact: M.E. Littlefield. TEL 540-463-1869. circ. 100,000. **Document type:** consumer publication.
Description: Provides news from the fraternity's college chapters and alumni and features on Sigma Nu's past and present. Reports on issues affecting the fraternity community and its relationship to higher education.

378 — US
DELTA CHI QUARTERLY.* 1903. q. $1. Delta Chi Fraternity, Box 1817, Iowa City, IA 52244-1817. TEL 319-337-4811. Ed. Raymond Galbreth. adv. circ. 36,000.
Description: Devoted exclusively to programs, events and news for undergraduate members.

371.85 — US — ISSN 0745-0958
LJ75
DELTA EPSILON SIGMA JOURNAL. 1947. 3/yr. membership. Delta Epsilon Sigma National Scholastic Honor Society, c/o George Herndl, Ed., Belmont Abbey College, Belmont, NC 28012. TEL 704-825-5026. FAX 305-899-3026. R&P contact: George Herndle. index; circ. 20,000 (controlled). **Indexed:** Cath.Ind. **Document type:** academic/scholarly publication.
Formerly: Delta Epsilon Sigma Bulletin (ISSN 0011-8028)
Description: Publishes articles on a wide range of subjects, as well as fiction and poetry.

378 — US
DELTAN (NEW YORK).* 1914. q. free to members only. Zeta Beta Tau Fraternity, Inc., 3905 Vincennes Rd., Ste. 101, Indianapolis, IN 46268-3025. TEL 212-629-0888. FAX 212-643-0717. Ed. Howard A. Siegel. circ. 55,000.
Description: Provides reports on the state of the Fraternity, Chapter news, alumni awards and donors.

669 — RU
DENNITSA. 1966. w. Magnitogorskii Gorno-Metallurgicheskii Institut im. G.I. Nosova, Pr. Lenina 38, auditoriya 248, 455000 Magnitogorsk, Russia. TEL 2-85-36. Ed. A.Yu. Shemetova. circ. 1,067. **Document type:** newspaper.
Formerly (until Dec. 1990): Za Kadry.

DENTAL IMAGES. see *MEDICAL SCIENCES — Dentistry*

378 — US
DEPAUW. 1852. 2/w. $35. DePauw University, Student Publication Board, Center for Contemporary Media, 609 S. Locust, Greencastle, IN 46135-0512. TEL 317-658-5972. FAX 317-658-5991. Ed. Jon Jenkins. circ. 2,600 (paid). (tabloid format) **Document type:** newspaper.
Description: Contains local news, commentary, sports and features covering the DePauw University campus.

378 — UK
DEUCE. 1992. every 3 wks. free. University of Central England, Students' Union, Perry Barr, Birmingham B42 2SU, England. TEL 44-121-356-8164. FAX 44-121-344-3670. Ed. Sam Bennett. adv.: page £315; adv. contact: Jill Drinkwater. bk.rev.; circ. 4,000. (back issues avail.) **Document type:** newsletter.

378 — PR
DIALOGO. 1987? newsstand price: $1. Universidad de Puerto Rico, Apdo. 364984, San Juan, PR 00936-4984. TEL 787-763-1015. FAX 787-250-8729. Ed. Luis Fernando Coss Ponton. (tabloid format) **Document type:** newspaper.

378 — US
DIAMOND (SIOUX CENTER). 1957. 12/yr. $10. Dordt College, 498 Fourth Ave. N.E., Sioux Center, IA 51250. TEL 712-722-3771. Ed. Lorna Van Gilst. R&P contact: Lorna Van Gilst. circ. 1,000. **Document type:** newspaper.
Description: Covers news and events of interest to college students.

378 — US
DIAMONDBACK. 1908. 5/w. $55. (University of Maryland) Maryland Media, Inc., S. Campus Dining Hall, Rm. 3150, College Park, MD 20742. TEL 301-314-8200. FAX 301-314-8358. adv. circ. 21,000. **Document type:** newspaper.

378 — RW
DIAPASON. 1966. q. Universite Nationale du Rwanda, B.P. 117, Butare, Rwanda. TEL 30272. TELEX 605. Ed. Pierre Turatsinze. circ. 300.

378 — US
DIORAMA. 1948. a. $15. University of North Alabama, 330 Keller Hall, Florence, AL 35430. TEL 205-760-4363. FAX 205-760-4296. Ed. Paul Maxwell III. adv.: page $200; adv. contact: Julie Steele. circ. 3,500. (back issues avail.) **Document type:** consumer publication.
Description: Covers events of the previous academic year.

378.198 — CN — ISSN 0228-9636
LES DIPLOMES. (Text in French) vol.14, 1973. 3/yr. Can.$6($8) Les Diplomes de l'Universite de Montreal, 3744 rue Jean-Brillant, Ste. 410, Montreal, PQ H3C 3J7, Canada. TEL 514-343-6230. FAX 514-343-5798. URL: http://www.umontreal.ca. Ed. Michel Saint-Laurent. adv.: B&W page Can.$2000, color page Can.$2700; trim 19 x 24. bk.rev.; illus. circ. 95,000. **Document type:** academic/scholarly publication.
Former titles (until Sep. 1980): Interdit (ISSN 0300-3965); Inter.
Description: Each issues presents a particular topic of interest to University graduates and the general public.

378.198 — US
DIRECTIONS (EDGERTON). 1981. a. Directions Publishing, Inc., 21 N. Henry St., Edgerton, WI 53534. TEL 608-884-3367. FAX 608-884-8187. Ed. Diane Everson. adv.; bk.rev. circ. controlled.

378 — US
DOLPHIN. 1946. w. (during academic yr.). $6. Loyola Hall, LeMoyne College, Syracuse, NY 13214-1399. TEL 315-445-4542. Ed. Rob Weston. adv. circ. 2,500. **Document type:** newspaper.

378.1 — UK — ISSN 0012-5695
DOUAI MAGAZINE. 1894. a. £3.50. Douai Abbey, Woolhampton, Near Reading, Berkshire, England. FAX 0737-713896. Ed. O. Holt. adv.; bk.rev.; illus. circ. 1,300.

378.198 — UK
DOUBLE TAKE. 1981. w. free. University College of Swansea, Students Union, Mandela House, Singleton Park, Swansea SA2 8PP, Wales. Ed. Steven Bird. circ. 2,250.

378 — US
DOUGLASS ALUMNAE MAGAZINE. 1922. q. $10. Douglass College, Associate Alumnae, 80 Clifton Ave., New Brunswick, NJ 08901-1599. TEL 908-247-0700. FAX 908-247-1974. Ed. Beth DeMavro. circ. 13,000.
Formerly: Douglass Alumnae Bulletin.

378.198 — US
DRAKE UPDATE. 1987. 3/yr. free to qualified personnel. Drake University, Office of Marketing and Communications, 316 Old Main, Des Moines, IA 50311. TEL 515-271-2169. FAX 515-271-3798. E-mail: alumninews@acad.drake.edu. Ed. Barbara Dietrich Boose. R&P contact: Barbara Dietrich Boose. circ. 44,000. **Document type:** newspaper.
Description: Contains alumni and campus news and features.

DROEMMEN OM ELIN. see *BUSINESS AND ECONOMICS*

378.198 — US
DRURY MIRROR.* 1885. w. $20. Drury College, 900 N. Benton, Springfield, MO 65802. TEL 417-865-8731. FAX 416-865-3138. adv.; bk.rev.; film rev.; play rev.; charts; illus.; circ. 1,000 (controlled). (tabloid format; back issues avail.) **Document type:** newspaper.
Description: Campus newspaper for students, alumni, and others interested in the college.

378 — GW — ISSN 0937-3780
DUESSELDORFER UNI-ZEITUNG. 1972. 6/yr. Heinrich-Heine-Universitaet Duesseldorf, Pressestelle, Universitaetsstr. 1, 40225 Duesseldorf, Germany. FAX 49-211-8115279. TELEX 8587384-UNI-D. Ed. Rolf Willhardt. adv.; bk.rev. circ. 7,500. **Document type:** corporate report.

378 — US
DUSTER. bi-w. Lubbock Christian College, 5601 W. 19th, Lubbock, TX 79407-2099. TEL 806-792-3221.

378 — US
THE DYNAMO. 1889. w. $18. (Mount Union College) Dix Communications, 1972 Clark Ave., Alliance, OH 44601. TEL 216-823-2884. Ed. Joann Hentsch. adv. circ. 1,000. (tabloid format) **Document type:** newspaper.
Description: Covers campus events, sports, state and national news, art and leisure for students and faculty.

378 — US
E T S U SPECIAL. (East Texas State University) irreg. (2-4/yr.) Texas A & M - Commerce, Student Publications Business Office, Journalism & Printing Dept., Box 4104, ET Sta., Commerce, TX 75427. TEL 903-886-5985. FAX 903-886-5230. E-mail: busm@boisdarc.etsu.edu. Ed. Michael Tribble. R&P contact: Annette Black. adv.: page $100; trim 8 1/2 x 11. circ. 3,000. **Document type:** newspaper.

378 — US
EAGLE (PRICE). 1937. bi-m. $12. College of Eastern Utah, 451 E. 4th North, Price, UT 84501. TEL 801-637-2120 ext. 5250. FAX 801-637-4102. E-mail: spolster@ac.ceu.edu. Ed. Miranda Oldendahl. R&P contact: Susan Polster. adv. contact: Sarah Nielson. bk.rev.; film rev.; play rev.; charts; illus.; tr.lit. circ. 1,500. (tabloid format; back issues avail.; reprint service avail.) **Document type:** newsletter.

378.1 — US — ISSN 0012-8082
EAGLE (WASHINGTON). 1925. w. $50. American University, 277 Mary Graydon Center, Massachusetts & Nebraska Aves., N.W., Washington DC 20016-8028. TEL 202-885-1414. Ed. Erik Diehn. adv.; bk.rev.; film rev.; play rev.; charts; illus. circ. 10,000. (also avail. in microfiche) **Document type:** newspaper.

378 — US
EAGLE EYE. 1924. w. free. Lock Haven University, Parsons Union Bldg., Lock Haven, PA 17745. TEL 717-893-2334. circ. 3,600. (tabloid format) **Document type:** newspaper.

378 — US
EAST CAROLINIAN. 1925. 2/w. $110. East Carolina University, Student Publications Bldg. - ECU, Greenville, NC 27858-4353. TEL 919-328-6366. FAX 919-328-6558. circ. 12,000 (controlled). **Document type:** newspaper.

378.198 — US
EAST TENNESSEAN. 1926. s-w. $10. East Tennessee State University, Box 23140A, Johnson City, TN 37614. TEL 615-929-4387. circ. 4,000.

378 — US
EAST TEXAN. w. $10 per semester. Texas A & M - Commerce, Student Publications Business Office, Journalism & Printing Dept., Box 4104, ET Sta., Commerce, TX 75427. TEL 903-886-5985. FAX 903-886-5230. E-mail: busm@boisdarc.etsu.edu. Ed. Michael Tribble. R&P contact: Annette Black. adv. contact: Annette Black. circ. 4,500. (tabloid format) **Document type:** newspaper.

378.1 — UK — ISSN 0012-8643
EASTBOURNIAN. 1870. a. £1.50. Eastbourne College, Eastbourne, Sussex, England. Ed. N.L. Wheeler. ad. illus.; circ. 1,200 (controlled).

378 US
EASTERN ECHO. 1881. 3/wk. $65. c/o Eastern Michigan University, 121 Goodison Hall, Ypsilanti, MI 48197. TEL 313-487-1010. FAX 313-487-1241. Ed. Tonja Wilson; Pub. Paul Heaton. R&P contact: Paul Heaton. adv. contact: Joe Miko. bk.rev. circ. 10,000. **Document type:** newspaper.

THE EASTERN PROGRESS. see *EDUCATION — Higher Education*

378 US
EASTERN TODAY.* 1987. 3/yr. free. Eastern Kentucky University, Division of Public Information, 7A Coates Bldg., 521 Lancaster Ave., Richmond, KY 40475-3101. TEL 606-622-2301. FAX 606-622-1595. Ed. Ron Harrell. circ. 45,000. **Document type:** newsletter.

378 CN ISSN 0849-9748
ECLOSION.* 3/yr. Access Media, 1124 Marie Anne Rd., East, Montreal, PQ H2J 1Z4, Canada. TEL 514-524-1182. FAX 514-524-7771. circ. 2,000.
 Formerly (until 1989): Moucheurs du Montreal Metropolitain (ISSN 0849-973X)

378 SA
EDGE. 1993. irreg. Technikon of Southern Africa, Private Bag X6, Florida 1710, South Africa.

378 US
EDGEWOOD COLLEGE TODAY. 1981. 3/yr. Edgewood College, 855 Woodrow St., Madison, WI 53711. TEL 608-257-4861. Ed. David E. Smith. circ. 6,500. **Document type:** newsletter.

378 UK
THE EDINBURGH STUDENT. 1887. 12/yr. Student Newspaper Society, 60 Pleasance, Edinburgh EH8 9TJ, Scotland. TEL 44-131-650-2363. FAX 44-131-650-2358. URL: http://www.ed.ac.uk/~eusn. Ed.Bd. adv.: page £500; 365 x 268; adv. contact: Dan Baring. bk.rev. circ. 5,000. **Document type:** newspaper.
 Formerly (until 1997): Student.
 Description: Provides news, services, advertising, reviews and communication between students and staff in Edinburgh.

378 UK
EDIT. 1992. s-a. University of Edinburgh, Old College, South Bridge, Edinburgh EH8 9YL, Scotland. TEL 44-131-650-2252. FAX 44-131-650-2253. URL: http://www.ed.ac.uk/pub/edit/edit_menu.html. Ed. Anne McKelvie. adv.; bk.rev.; illus. circ. 75,000. (back issues avail.) **Document type:** bulletin.

378
EDWARDIAN. m. St. Edward's University, 30010 S. Congress, Box 714, Austin, TX 78704. TEL 512-448-8426.

378 GW ISSN 0930-8253
EINBLICKE; Forschungsmagazin der Carl-von-Ossietzky Universitaet Oldenburg. (Text in German; summaries in English) 1985. 2/yr. DM.5. Carl von Ossietzky Universitaet Oldenburg, Ammerlaender Heerstr. 114, 26111 Oldenburg, Germany. TEL 49-441-7982417. FAX 49-441-7982435. E-mail: presse@admin.uni-oldenburg.de; URL: http://www.admin.uni-oldenburg.de/presse/einblick/. adv.: page DM.1850. illus. circ. 3,000. **Document type:** academic/scholarly publication.

378.198 US ISSN 0897-2303
ELMHURST COLLEGE MAGAZINE. 1967. q. Elmhurst College, 190 Prospect Ave., Elmhurst, IL 60126. TEL 630-617-3033. FAX 630-617-3282. Ed. Kristin Whitehurst. R&P contact: Kristin Whitehurst. circ. 30,000 (controlled).
 Description: For alumni, donors, parents and friends.

378.1 US ISSN 0013-6727
EMORY MAGAZINE. 1924. q. free to qualified personnel. Emory University, Office of University Periodicals, 1655 N. Decatur Rd., Atlanta, GA 30322. TEL 404-727-7872. FAX 404-727-0169. Ed. Andrew W.M. Beierle. R&P contact: Andrew W.M. Beierle. bk.rev.; illus.; circ. 78,000. (controlled).

378.198 US
EMORY WHEEL. 1918. s-w. (Tue.& Fri.). $65. Emory University, Drawer W, Atlanta, GA 30322. TEL 404-727-6175. FAX 404-727-3613. Ed. Kimberly L. Freeman. R&P contact: Richard Daigle. adv. contact: Shyam Reddy. circ. 7,500. **Document type:** newspaper.
 Description: Student newspaper that covers Atlanta and the university community.

378 CN ISSN 0822-8531
EN TETE. 1983. w. Can.$20 (effective 1997). Universite du Quebec a Trois-Rivieres, Service de l'Information, C.P. 500, Trois-Rivieres, PQ G9A 5H7, Canada. TEL 819-376-5151. FAX 819-376-5200. Ed. Guy Godin. adv. contact: Sylvie Gervais. bk.rev. circ. 6,000. **Document type:** academic/scholarly publication.
 Formerly: Trouvez un Nom (ISSN 0822-8523)

378 AT
ENCOUNTER. 2/yr. free. Flinders University of South Australia, Public Relations and Information Office, G.P.O. Box 2100, Adelaide, S.A. 5001, Australia. TEL 61-8-82013707. FAX 61-8-82013027. Ed. Nick Carne. circ. 20,000. (back issues avail.) **Document type:** newsletter.
 Formerly: Convocation News.

378.198 US
ENCOUNTER (JOLIET). 1976. fortn. free. College of St. Francis, Journalism - Communications Department, 500 N. Wilcox, Joliet, IL 60435. TEL 815-740-3461. FAX 815-740-4285. Ed. Rita Travis. adv.; bk.rev.; film rev.; circ. 1,200 (controlled). (tabloid format) **Document type:** newspaper.
 Description: Informs, entertains, educates and provides a forum for public debate. Also functions as a laboratory newspaper for students majoring in journalism - communications.

378 CN
ENTREMETTEUR.* s-m. free. Publi-PEQ, 3575 bd. St. Laurent, Ste. 232, Montreal, PQ H2X 2T7, Canada. TEL 514-845-8628. circ. 3,000. (tabloid format)

ENTUSIASMEN. see *EDUCATION — Higher Education*

378.1 US
ENVOY (SAN DIEGO). 1955. bi-w. free. United States International University, 10455 Pomerado Rd., San Diego, CA 92131. TEL 619-693-4842. FAX 619-693-8562. Ed. Aretha Brown. adv.; bk.rev. circ. 2,000. (tabloid format)
 Former titles (until 1991): U S I U News; (until 1986): U S I U International News; Western Tide (ISSN 0008-1647)
 Description: Aimed at students, staff, and friends of the university.

378 SW ISSN 0345-2875
ERGO. 1924. 15/yr. SEK 150. Uppsala Studentkaar, Oevre Slottsg. 7, S-753 10 Uppsala, Sweden. TEL 46-18-10-90-29. FAX 46-18-12-07-90. E-mail: red.ergo@us.uu.se. Ed. Gert Helgesson. adv.; bk.rev. circ. 30,000.

051 US ISSN 1074-2174
ETHOS (AMES). 1953. bi-m. $18 (effective 1997). Iowa Scientist Incorporated, Student Publications, Ames, IA 50011. TEL 515-294-9388. FAX 515-294-5108. (Subscr. to: 16D Hamilton Hall, Ames, IA 50011) Ed. Anne Rosso; Pub. Marcia Prior-Miller. adv.: B&W page $389, color page $564; 9 x 6 7/8. bk.rev. circ. 5,600. (back issues avail.) **Indexed:** Mid.East: Abstr.& Ind. **Document type:** consumer publication.
 Incorporates (in July 1993): Outlook (Ames).
 Description: Examines academic issues and trends related to today's college student.

378.1 CN ISSN 0014-3987
EXCALIBUR. 1966. w. Can.$40. Excalibur Publications Inc., 4700 Keele St., Downsview, ON M3J 1P3, Canada. TEL 416-736-5239. FAX 416-736-5841. adv.; bk.rev.; film rev.; illus.; circ. 17,000 (controlled). (tabloid format) **Document type:** newspaper.

378 UK
EXEPOSE. 1988. w. £50. (Exeter University Guild of Students) Third Degree, Devonshire House, Stocker Rd., Exeter EX4 4PZ, England. TEL 44-1392-263540. FAX 44-1392-263531. URL: http://www.gosu.ex.ac.uk/campusmedia. Ed. Charles Offer. adv.: B&W page £600; 360 x 255. bk.rev. circ. 3,000. **Document type:** newspaper.
 Former titles: Third Degree; Signature.
 Description: University students' magazine covers news, arts, film and music.

373 US
LD7501.E9
EXETER BULLETIN. 1905. 4/yr. Phillips Exeter Academy, 20 Main St., Exeter, NH 03833-2460. TEL 603-778-3450. FAX 603-778-4397. E-mail: bulletin@exeter.edu; URL: http://www.exeter.edu. Ed. Stephanie Casale. R&P contact: Stephanie Casale. bk.rev.; charts; illus.; circ. 26,500 (controlled). **Document type:** academic/scholarly publication.
 Former titles: Exeter (ISSN 0195-0207); Philips Exeter Bulletin (ISSN 0031-7942)
 Description: Publishes articles of interest to alumni, class news, events schedules.

378 US
EXPERTS CONTACT DIRECTORY. 1993. a. $89. Gale Research, 835 Penobscot Bldg., 645 Griswold St., Detroit, MI 48226-4094. TEL 313-961-2242; 800-877-4253. FAX 800-41-50433. E-mail: daniel_snyder@gale.com. Ed. Nora Paul. (also avail. in diskette format) **Document type:** directory.
 ●Also available online.
 Also available on CD-ROM.
 Description: Compiles lists of experts from over 250 U.S. colleges and universities and specialists from government agencies.

378.1 US ISSN 0014-5076
EXPONENT; Montana's premier student newspaper. Variant title: M S U Exponent. 1895. s-w. $19.95 (free distribution on campus). Montana State University, Associated Students, Rm. 305, Strand Union, Bozeman, MT 59717. TEL 406-994-2611. FAX 406-994-2253. adv.; bk.rev. circ. 7,500. (tabloid format) **Indexed:** PROMT. **Document type:** newspaper.

378 CK ISSN 0121-6279
K5
EXTERNADISTA. 1992. s-a. Col.10000 per no. (effective 1997). Universidad Externado de Colombia, Departamento de Publicaciones, Calle 12 No. 0-46 Este, Apdo. Aereo 034141, Bogota, Colombia. TEL 341-2610. FAX 2843769. Ed. Camilo Calderon.

378.1 CN ISSN 0014-5513
EYEOPENER. 1967. w. (during academic yr.). Can.$10. Rye Eye Publishing Inc, 380 Victoria, Rm. A-54, Toronto, ON M5B 1W7, Canada. TEL 416-595-1490. FAX 416-595-1374. E-mail: eyeopenr@acs.ryerson.ca. Ed. Matthew Sheperd. adv. contact: Ryad Ali. bk.rev.; film rev.; play rev.; illus. circ. 8,000. (tabloid format) **Indexed:** Can.B.P.I. **Document type:** newspaper.
 Description: Campus and community news, entertainment, sports and features.
 Refereed Serial

378.1 US
F A U FREE PRESS. 1966. w. $10. Florida Atlantic University, Boca Raton, FL 33431. TEL 407-363-2393. Ed. Ross A. Levy. adv. contact: Bryan Bates. bk.rev.; film rev.; play rev.; illus. circ. 17,000. (tabloid format) **Document type:** newspaper.
 Formerly: Atlantic Sun (ISSN 0004-685X)

378 GW ISSN 0944-0585
F U: NACHRICHTEN. m. DM.30. Freie Universitaet Berlin, Kaiserswertherstr. 16-18, 14195 Berlin, Germany. TEL 030-83873180. FAX 030-83873187. E-mail: fupresse@zedat.fu-berlin.de. Ed. Christian Walther. adv.: page DM.1900; adv. contact: Gabriela Gast-Anhuth. film rev.; play rev.; circ. 20,000. **Document type:** bulletin.
 Former titles (until 1992): F U Info (ISSN 0173-4105); (until 1979): F U Berlin. Info (ISSN 0302-2161)

1952 COLLEGE AND ALUMNI

378   **UK**   ISSN 0141-4704
FALMER. 1983. 2/yr. free. University of Sussex Society, Alumni Office, Sussex House, Falmer, Brighton BN1 9RH, England. TEL 44-1273-678258. FAX 44-1273-678335. E-mail: alumni@sussex.ac.uk; URL: http://www.sussex.ac.uk/usis/alumni/default.html. Ed. Sara Dyer. R&P contact: Sara Dyer. adv.; bk.rev. circ. 28,000. (tabloid format; back issues avail.) **Document type:** newsletter.
  Formerly: Falmer News.
  Description: Newsletter for alumni of University of Sussex.
Refereed Serial

378.198   **AT**   ISSN 0159-2920
FARRAGO. 1920. every 3 wks. (during school yr.). free in Australia. Melbourne University, Students Union, 1st Fl., Union Bldg., Parkville, Vic. 3052, Australia. TEL 61-3-9344-6957. FAX 61-3-9347-9453. URL: http://www.union.unimelb.edu.au/farrago. Ed.Bd.; Pub. Elizabeth Humphrys. adv.; bk.rev.; film rev.; play rev.; illus. circ. 11,000. (tabloid format; back issues avail.) **Document type:** newspaper.
  Description: Focuses on music, the arts, politics and "university-inner city coffee culture."

378.198   **US**
FEDERALIST PAPER; a student newspaper in the tradition of Columbians Hamilton and Jay. vol.3, 1988. q. Columbia University, Federalist, 206 Ferris Booth Hall, New York, NY 10027. **Document type:** newspaper.

378   **UK**   ISSN 0140-0711
FELIX; the student's newspaper at imperial college. 1949. w. (every Fri. during college term). Imperial College Union Publications Board, Belt Quad, Prince Consort Rd., London SW7 2BB, England. TEL 44-171-594-8072. FAX 44-171-594-8072. E-mail: felix@ic.ac.uk; URL: http://www.su.ic.ac.uk/Felix. Ed. Jeremy Thomson. R&P contact: Jeremy Thomson. adv. contact: David Roberts. bk.rev. circ. 4,500. **Document type:** newspaper.

378   **US**
FERRUM MAGAZINE. q. free. Ferrum College, Ferrum, VA 24088. TEL 540-365-4216. FAX 540-365-4203. Eds. Tom Rickard, Wes Astin. R&P contact: Wes Astin. circ. 14,000 (controlled). **Document type:** academic/scholarly publication.
  Formerly: Ferrum Bulletin.
  Description: Contains alumni news and information about activities at Ferrum.

378.1   **UK**   ISSN 0046-3701
FETTESIAN. 1878. a. £4.50. Fettes College, Edinburgh, Scotland. Ed. A.F. Reeves. adv. circ. 1,200.

378   **GW**   ISSN 0179-6607
FH-BO-JOURNAL. 1982. 2/yr. Fachhochschule Bochum, Universitaetsstr. 150, 44801 Bochum, Germany. TEL 0231-7007800. FAX 0234-7094312. TELEX 825860-RUB-D. Ed. Detlef Bremkens. circ. 2,000. **Document type:** academic/scholarly publication.

378   **NE**
FISS. 1977. bi-m. fl.12.50. Kandinsky College, Malderburchstraat 11, 6535 ND Nijmegen, Netherlands. TEL 31-24-3561454. FAX 31-24-3567378. adv.: page fl.200. bk.rev. circ. 1,600. **Document type:** academic/scholarly publication.
  Formerly: Fizz.
  Description: High school paper with news for its pupils.

378   **AT**
FLINDERS JOURNAL. no.277, 1988. fortn. Flinders University of South Australia, Public Relations and Information Office, G.P.O. Box 2100, Adelaide, S.A. 5001, Australia. TEL 61-8-82012916. FAX 61-8-82013027. Ed. Charles Gent. circ. 3,000. **Document type:** newspaper.
  Formerly (until 1990): Flindersweek.

378   **US**
FLOR-ALA. 1931. w. $12. University of North Alabama, Box 5300, Florence, AL 35632-0001. TEL 205-760-4364. FAX 205-760-4644. Ed. Shannon Heupel. adv.; bk.rev.; film rev.; music rev.; play rev. 4,500. **Document type:** consumer publication.

378   **US**
FLORIDA FLAMBEAU. 1913. d. $115 (effective 1996 & 1997). Florida Flambeau Foundation, Inc., Box 20287, Tallahassee, FL 32316. TEL 904-681-6692. FAX 904-681-3577. Ed. Che Odom. adv. contact: Josh Kasper. circ. 21,000. (tabloid format; back issues avail.) **Document type:** newspaper.
  Description: Covers events at Florida State University.

378.198   **US**   ISSN 0898-4387
FLORIDA LEADER. (In 2 editions: College & High School) 1983. 3/yr. $35. Oxendine Publishing, Inc., Box 14081, Gainesville, FL 32604-2081. TEL 352-373-6907. FAX 352-373-8120. E-mail: 75143.2043@compuserve.com. Ed. W.H. Oxendine, Jr.; Pub. W.H. Oxendine, Jr. adv. contact: W.H. Oxendine, Jr. bk.rev. circ. 45,000 (College ed. 20,000; High School ed. 25,000). (back issues avail.) **Document type:** academic/scholarly publication, consumer publication.
•Also available online.
  Description: Covers education issues, employment and entertainment for and about Florida students.

378   **UK**
FLY MAGAZINE; the official student publication of the University of Plymouth. 1972. w. free. University of Plymouth, Student Union, Drake Circus, Plymouth, Devon OL4 8AA, England. TEL 44-1752-663337. FAX 44-1752-251669. E-mail: fly@plym.ac.uk. Ed. Pete Everett. adv.: page £220; adv. contact: Pete Everett. charts; illus.; film rev.; music rev.; play rev.; video rev. circ. 2,000. (back issues avail.) **Document type:** newspaper.
•Also available online.
  Description: Covers anything remotely connected to student life.

378   **US**
FLYER NEWS. 1953. s-w. $15. University of Dayton, 300 College Park, Dayton, OH 45469. TEL 513-229-3226. FAX 513-229-4000. Ed. Lisa Morawski; Pub. Lisa Morawski. R&P contact: Larry Lain. TEL 937-229-2742. adv. contact: Tom Stanton. bk.rev. circ. 5,000. (tabloid format) **Document type:** newspaper.

378.1   **GH**   ISSN 0046-4260
FOCUS. 1969. bi-m. $0.50. University of Science and Technology, Students' Representative Council, Kumasi, Ghana. Ed. E. Kwabena Ansah. adv.; illus.; stat. circ. 1,500. (tabloid format)

378   **SA**
FOCUS. 1990. q. R.48 (SADC countries R.60; elsewhere £40($60)). University of Natal, Pietermaritzburg, Communication & Publicity Division, Private Bag X01, Scottsville 3209, South Africa. TEL 27-331-2605011. FAX 27-331-62210. E-mail: vadyvaloo@pro.unp.ac.za; URL: http://www.unp.ac.za. Ed. George Parker. adv.; illus. **Document type:** academic/scholarly publication.
  Formerly (until 1993): N U Focus (ISSN 1016-3425)

378   **US**
FOCUS (WESTFIELD). 1974. q. free. Westfield State College, Public Affairs Office, Western Ave., Westfield, MA 01086. TEL 413-572-5208. FAX 413-572-4843. E-mail: wisdom.wsc.mass.edu. Ed. Jeanne M. Julian. R&P contact: J. Julian. circ. 22,000 (controlled). (reprint service avail.) **Document type:** newsletter.
  Formerly (until 1992): Westfield State College. Alumni Chronicle.
  Description: Contains news and features pertaining to the college and its alumni.
Refereed Serial

(YEAR) FOOTBALL MEDIA GUIDE. see *SPORTS AND GAMES — Ball Games*

378   **CN**   ISSN 0824-6017
FOOTPRINT.* Key Title: Zhu Ji. (Text mainly in Chinese; some in English) vol.2, 1982. bi-m. free. University of Toronto, John Robbart Library, Serial Dept., 130 St. George St., Toronto, Ont. M5S 1A5, Canada. TEL 416 978 7694. Ed. Lester Wong. adv.; bk.rev. circ. 5,000. (tabloid format)

378   **US**
FOOTPRINTS (PLAINVIEW). 1953. q. free to alumni. Wayland Baptist University, 1900 W. 7th St., Plainview, TX 79072. TEL 806-296-4844. FAX 806-296-4580. Ed. Joe L. Provence. circ. 12,000 (controlled). **Document type:** consumer publication.
  Description: Covers topics of interest to alumni of Wayland Baptist University.

378.198   **US**
THE FORESTER. 1956. q. Concordia University, 7400 Augusta, River Forest, IL 60305-1499. TEL 708-209-3110. FAX 708-209-3176. Ed. Kristin Aasmundstad Walsh. circ. 45,000. (tabloid format) **Document type:** newspaper.
  Description: Contains university news, features, alumni news, and development news.

FORSCHUNG AN DER UNIVERSITAET BIELEFELD. see *SCIENCES: COMPREHENSIVE WORKS*

378   **US**
THE FORUM (SOUTH ROYALTON). 1976. fortn. $12. Vermont Law School, South Royalton, VT 05068. TEL 802-763-8303. adv.; bk.rev. circ. 1,000.

FORUM (WASHINGTON, 1970). see *LIBRARY AND INFORMATION SCIENCES*

378   **US**
THE FORWARD (ELKINS). 4/yr. free. Davis and Elkins College, Box 10, Elkins, WV 26241. TEL 304-636-1900. Ed. Mary McMahon.

378.198   **US**   ISSN 0279-3016
FOUNDERS HALL. 1979. 6/yr. free. St. Michael's College, Winooski Park, Colchester, VT 05439. TEL 802-654-2535. FAX 802-654-2592. E-mail: BLINDAU@SMCVAX.SMCVT.edu. Ed. Buff Lindau. R&P contact: Buff Lindau. bk.rev.; circ. 200,000. (back issues avail.) **Document type:** newsletter.
  Description: For alumni, parents and friends of the College.

378   **US**
FRANKLIN AND MARSHALL. q. Franklin & Marshall College, College Ave., Lancaster, PA 17604. Ed. Linda Whipple.
  Formerly: F and M Today.

378   **US**
FRANKLIN AND MARSHALL COLLEGE REPORTER. 1881 w. $30. Franklin and Marshall College, Box 3003, Lancaster, PA 17604. TEL 717-291-4095. FAX 717-291-4088. Ed. Steve Goldstein. adv.: page $400. circ. 3,000. (tabloid format) **Document type:** newspaper.

378   **GW**   ISSN 0941-0155
FREIE UNIVERSITAET BERLIN. ZENTRALEINRICHTUNG STUDIENBERATUNG UND PSYCHOLOGISCHE BERATUNG. STUDIENHANDBUCH. 1978. a. DM.20. Freie Universitaet Berlin, Zentraleinrichtung Studienberatung und Psychologische Beratung, Bruemmerstr. 50, 14195 Berlin, Germany. TEL 49-30-8285236. FAX 49-30-8383913. adv. **Document type:** directory.

378   **IT**
FRIULI UNIVERSITARIO. 1966. m. free to qualified personnel. C.U.F., Casella Postale 183, Udine, Italy. TEL 39-432-233006. Ed. Paolo Zucconi. adv.: B&W page L.800000, color page L.1200000. circ. 20,000. **Document type:** academic/scholarly publication, newspaper.

378   **CN**
LE FRONT. (Text in French) vol.21, 1984. w. Federation des Etudiants de l'Universite de Moncton, Moncton, N.B., Canada.

378   **UK**
FRONT PAGE. 1982. m. free. Anglia Polytechnic Cambridge, Students Union Office, Collier Rd., Cambridge CB1 2AH, England. FAX 01223-460008. Ed. C. Ledwith. adv.; bk.rev. circ. 2,000.

378   **US**
FRONTLINES. 1990. m. free. Northern Virginia Community College, 8333 Little River Tpk., Annandale, VA 22003. TEL 703-323-3579. FAX 703-323-3399. Ed. Joseph Wink. adv.: page $190; 13 1/2 x 10 1/4. bk.rev.; film rev.; play rev. circ. 3,000. (tabloid format) **Document type:** newspaper.

378.1 II ISSN 0046-5259
FULBRIGHT NEWSLETTER. 1953. q. free. United States Educational Foundation in India, Fulbright House, 12 Hailey Rd., New Delhi 110001, India. Ed. P.D. Sayal. circ. 6,500. **Indexed:** Numis.Lit. **Document type:** newsletter.

378.1 CN ISSN 0016-2604
FULCRUM. French edition: Rotonde. 1927. w. Can.$10($25) University of Ottawa Students' Federation, 85 Hastey St., Rm. 07, Ottawa, ON K1N 6N5, Canada. TEL 613-562-5260. Ed. Laurel Fortin. adv. contact: Dan Cummins. bk.rev.; abstr.; film rev.; play rev.; illus. circ. 13,000. (tabloid format; also avail. in microfilm; back issues avail.) **Document type:** newspaper.

378
FURMAN MAGAZINE. 1951. a. free. Furman University, University Relations, 3300 Poinsett Hwy., Greenville, SC 29613-0691. TEL 864-294-2185. FAX 864-294-3023. Ed. Marguerite J. Hays. circ. 26,000.
Description: Contains articles on Furman-related issues, events and individuals.

378 US
FURMAN REPORTS. 1968. q. free. Furman University, University Relations, 3300 Poinsett Hwy., Greenville, SC 29613-0691. TEL 864-294-2185. FAX 864-294-3023. Ed. James T. Stewart. circ. 30,000. **Document type:** newsletter.
Description: Review of campus events, faculty research and alumni news.

G L A S OF (YEAR). (Gay and Lesbian Alliance at Stanford) see HOMOSEXUALITY

378.198 US
G M I ALUMNI NEWS. 1970. q. free. G M I Engineering & Management Institute, 1700 W. Third Ave., Flint, MI 48504-4898. TEL 810-762-9824. FAX 810-762-7435. E-mail: lallen@elite.gmi.edu. Ed. Lisa J. Allen. circ. 21,000 (controlled). **Document type:** consumer publication.
Description: Informs alumni of current activities and events.

G S B CHICAGO. (Graduate School of Business) see BUSINESS AND ECONOMICS

378.198 US
G S M CHRONICLE. 1974. q. free. University of Dallas. Graduate School of Management, Department of Communications, 1845 E. Northgate Dr., Irving, TX 75062-4799. TEL 214-721-5199. FAX 214-721-5017. circ. 6,500. (tabloid format) **Document type:** newsletter.

378.1 US
G W HATCHET. 1904. s-w. (Sep.-May). $50. George Washington University, 800 21 St., N.W., Washington, DC 20052. FAX 202-994-1309. Ed.Bd. adv.; bk.rev.; film rev.; play rev.; illus. circ. 10,000. (tabloid format; also avail. in microfilm)
Formerly: Hatchet (ISSN 0017-8357)
Description: News, opinions, editorials, arts, music, and sports coverage, announcements, and classifieds pertaining to faculty, students, and activities at the George Washington University, Washington, D.C.

378.1 US
G W MAGAZINE. 1972. 6/yr. free to qualified personnel. George Washington University, University Relations, 512 Rice Hall, Washington, DC 20052. TEL 202-994-6460. FAX 202-994-9025. E-mail: magazine@gwisz.circ.gwu.edu. Ed. Robert Guldin; Pub. Sandy Holland. R&P contact: Robert Guldin. TEL 202-994-6462. adv. contact: Dan Feller. bk.rev.; illus. circ. 120,000. **Document type:** consumer publication.
Former titles (until 1990): G W Times (ISSN 0279-2435); G W: George Washington University Magazine (ISSN 0016-366X)
Description: Focuses on news and features related to the university and its alumni.

378 GW
GAESDONCKER BLAETTER. 1949. a. DM.20. Collegium Augustinianum Gaesdonck, Gaesdoncker Str. 220, 47574 Goch, Germany. TEL 02823-961-0. FAX 02823-961100. Ed. Karl-Heinz Mengedodt. circ. 2,000. **Document type:** academic/scholarly publication.

378 US
GARNET LETTER. 1979. s-a. free. Swarthmore College, Swarthmore, PA 19081-1397. TEL 610-328-8009. FAX 610-328-7796. Ed. Susan Hodge. circ. 23,200.

378 US
GATES.* 1991. bi-m. $10.95. Gates Publishing & Design Group Inc., 1500 Huguenot Rd., Ste. 104, Midlothian, VA 23113-2478. TEL 804-355-0999. Ed. Brian T. Ford. adv.: B&W page $6240, color page $7800; trim 8 1/4 x 10 7/8. circ. 50,000.
Indexed: Per.Islam. (1994-).
Description: Contains news, personalities and trends for college students.

378.1 CN ISSN 0016-5190
GATEWAY. 1910. s-w. Can.$40. University of Alberta, Students Union, Students' Union Building, Edmonton, AB T6G 2J7, Canada. TEL 403-492-5168. FAX 403-492-4643. E-mail: gateway@pybus.su.ualberta.ca; URL: http://www.su.ualberta.ca/gateway. Ed. Rose Yewchuk. adv. contact: Sandra Horrigan. bk.rev.; film rev.; play rev.; illus.; circ. 12,000 (controlled). (tabloid format) **Document type:** newspaper.
Description: Covers news, opinion, entertainment and sports.

378.1 SW ISSN 0016-5247
GAUDEAMUS. 1924. m. SEK 75. Stockholms Universitets Studentkaar, Box 50006, S-104 05 Stockholm, Sweden. Ed. Magnus Lindvall. adv.; bk.rev.; film rev.; play rev.; illus. circ. 33,000.

378 UK
GAUDIE. 1934. w. free. (University of Aberdeen) S.R.C. Publications Department, 50-52 College Bounds, Old Aberdeen AB2 3DS, Scotland. FAX 01224-272977. TELEX 73458 UNIABN G. Ed. Matthew Grant. adv. contact: Gillian Taylor. bk.rev.; film rev.; play rev. circ. 4,500. (tabloid format; back issues avail.) **Document type:** newspaper.

378 CN
GAUNTLET. 1960. w. Can.$35. University of Calgary, Gauntlet Publications Society, Rm. 310, MacEwan Hall, 2920-24th Ave., N.W., Calgary, AB T2N 1N4, Canada. TEL 403-220-7755. FAX 403-282-3218. adv.: B&W page Can.$840; adv. contact: Wayne Cropper. bk.rev.; film rev.; play rev. circ. 13,000. (tabloid format)

371.83 IE
THE GAZETTE (CORK). 1980. w. free. University College, Cork, Student's Union, 4 Carrigside, College Rd., Cork, Ireland. TEL 021-276871. FAX 021-272065. adv.; bk.rev.; illus.
Formerly: Sage (Cork).

378 CN
GEM. vol.2, 1984. w. Can.$24. University of Prince Edward Island, Charlottetown, PE C1A 4P3, Canada. TEL 902-566-0629. FAX 902-566-0729. E-mail: x-press@upei.ca. Eds. Kent Driscoll, Jennifer Caseley. adv. contact: Finley Martin. bk.rev.; film rev. circ. 1,300. **Document type:** newspaper.
Former titles (until Mar. 1995): U P E I X-Press (ISSN 1193-3984); (until 1990): X-Press (ISSN 1193-3976); (until 1990): Gem (ISSN 0839-2625); (until 1986): Netted Gem (ISSN 0839-2617)

378.198 US
GENERAL STUDIES NEWSLETTER. q. Columbia University, School of General Studies, 411 Lewisohn Hall, New York, NY 10027. **Document type:** newsletter.

378.198 US
GENESIS (GARDEN CITY). 1969. a. free. Nassau Community College, State University of New York, Department of English, Garden City, NY 11530. TEL 516-222-7185. circ. 3,000. **Indexed:** Alloys Ind., Eng.Mat.Abstr., Met.Abstr.Ind., Met.Abstr., Nonfer.Met.Alert, PCC Alert, Steels Alert, World Alum.Abstr.
Formerly: Taking Shape.
Description: Includes poetry and prose for college and university faculties and libraries.

378.198 US
GEODE. 1925. 2/yr. $7. University of Wisconsin-Platteville, Engineering Chapter of the Alumni Association, College of Engineering, 100 Ottensman Hall, One University Plaza, Platteville, WI 53818. circ. 1,500. (back issues avail.)

378 US
GEORGE - ANNE. 1927. s-w. $18 (effective July 1995). (Georgia Southern University) George-Anne, Rm. 111, Williams Ctr., Box 8068, Georgia Southern Univ., Statesboro, GA 30460. TEL 912-681-5246. FAX 912-681-0863. E-mail: stud__pub@gsaix2.gasou.edu. Ed. Chris Cole. adv. contact: Brooks Clemente. bk.rev.; film rev.; play rev.; charts; illus. circ. 7,000. (broadsheet format; back issues avail.) **Document type:** newspaper.
Description: Campus paper covering issues of interest to campus community.

378 US ISSN 0745-9009
LH1.G5
GEORGETOWN MAGAZINE. 4/yr. free. Georgetown University, Office of Alumni and University Relations, 37th & O Sts., N.W., Washington, DC 20057. TEL 202-687-4317. FAX 202-687-1670. Ed. Nancy Robertson. R&P contact: Nancy Robertson. bk.rev. circ. 110,000. **Document type:** academic/scholarly publication.

378 US ISSN 0435-5253
GEORGIA ADVOCATE. 1970. s-a. free to qualified persons. University of Georgia Law School Association, University of Georgia School of Law, Athens, GA 30602. TEL 706-542-5172. FAX 706-542-5556. E-mail: pharr@jd.lawsch.uga.edu. Ed. Kathy R. Pharr. circ. 7,500 (controlled). **Document type:** newsletter.
Formerly: Georgia Advocate Advance Sheet.

378.1 US ISSN 0016-8130
LH1.U47
GEORGIA ALUMNI RECORD. 1920. 4/yr. $25. University of Georgia Alumni Society, Alumni House, Athens, GA 30602-4370. TEL 706-542-3354. FAX 706-542-9492. Ed. Kent Hannon. adv.; bk.rev.; circ. 25,000 (controlled).

378.198 US
GEORGIA COLLEGE ALUMNI NEWS QUARTERLY. 1920. q. free to qualified personnel. Georgia College Alumni Association, Campus Box 98, Milledgeville, GA 31061. TEL 912-453-5400. FAX 912-453-6795. adv. circ. 20,000. (tabloid format)

378.1 US ISSN 0016-8424
GEORGIA STATE UNIVERSITY SIGNAL. 1933. w. $48. Georgia State University, Box 1862, University Plaza, Atlanta, GA 30303. TEL 404-651-2242. FAX 404-651-1045. Ed. Derrick Peavy. adv. contact: Lee Miller. bk.rev.; film rev.; play rev.; circ. 15,000 (controlled). (tabloid format; reprint service avail.)

378.198 US ISSN 1061-9747
GEORGIA TECH ALUMNI MAGAZINE. 1923. q. $10. Georgia Tech Alumni Association, Alumni-Faculty House, Atlanta, GA 30332-0175. TEL 404-894-2391. FAX 404-894-5113. URL: http://www.gatech.edu/alumni/alumni.html. Ed. John Dunn. adv. contact: Robb Stanek. circ. 30,000.
Supersedes: Georgia Tech Alumnus (ISSN 0016-8440)
Description: Contains articles relating to technology or the management of technology.

278 US
GILA MONSTER. 1921. m. free. Eastern Arizona College, Thatcher, AZ 85552-0769. TEL 520-428-8321. FAX 520-428-8462. Ed. Paul Phelps. R&P contact: Paul Phelps. circ. 1,000. **Document type:** newspaper.

378.1 UK ISSN 0017-0917
GLASGOW UNIVERSITY GUARDIAN. 1954. fortn. free. University of Glasgow, Students' Representative Council, John McIntyre Bldg., Glasgow G12 8QQ, Scotland. TEL 44-141-339-8541. FAX 44-141-337-3557. E-mail: guardian@src.gla.ac.uk; URL: http://www.src.gla.ac.uk/publications/guardian. Ed. Ed Grenby. R&P contact: Ed Grenby. adv. contact: Ken Hardy-Smith. bk.rev.; film rev.; rec.rev.; dance rev.; abstr.; bibl.; charts; illus. circ. 7,000. (tabloid format) **Document type:** newspaper. —CCC.

COLLEGE AND ALUMNI

378.1 US ISSN 0017-1131
THE GLEANER (CAMDEN). 1951. w. (Wed.) during academic yr. $48. (Rutgers University, Camden) The Gleaner, Camden Campus Center, Rm. 310, Camden, NJ 08102. TEL 609-225-6304. FAX 225-6579. Ed. Matthew Appleton. adv. contact: Ray Lopez. bk.rev.; film rev.; play rev.; charts; illus. circ. 4,000. (tabloid format) **Document type:** newspaper.

378 CN ISSN 0712-337X
GLOBULE ROUGE.* m. free. Publi-PEQ, 3575 bd. St. Laurent, Ste. 232, Montreal, PQ H2X 2T7, Canada. TEL 514-845-8628. circ. 600. (tabloid format)

378 US
GOLD AND BLUE. 1961. q. free. Atlanta Christian College, 2605 Ben Hill Rd., E. Point, GA 30344. TEL 404-761-8861. Ed. Charles F. Turner. circ. 12,500. **Document type:** newsletter.

378.198 US
GOLD TORCH. 1950. s-m. Central State University, Wilberforce, OH 45384. TEL 513-376-6103. FAX 513-376-6530. adv.; bk.rev. circ. 2,400. (tabloid format) **Document type:** newspaper.

070 US
GOLDEN GATER. 1931. s-w. $30. San Francisco State University, 1600 Holloway Ave., San Francisco, CA 94132. TEL 415-338-3123. FAX 415-338-3111. Ed. Douglas Allen; Pub. Douglas Allen. bk.rev.; film rev.; play rev.; circ. 10,000 (controlled). (broadsheet format) **Document type:** newspaper.
  Description: Contains news for students and alumni.

378 CN
GOLDEN WORDS. 1967. w. Can.$28 (foreign Can.$40) (effective 1997). Queen's University, Engineering Society, Clark Hall, Kingston, ON K7L 3N6, Canada. TEL 613-545-6000. FAX 613-545-6678. Eds. Peter Lynn, Jess Aldred. adv. contact: Becky Pearce. (tabloid format) **Document type:** newspaper.

378 US
GOOD 5-CENT CIGAR. 1971. 4/wk. $30. (University of Rhode Island, Student Senate) Narragansett Litho, Inc., Memorial Union, Rm. 139, Kingston, RI 02881. TEL 401-792-2914. FAX 401-789-4475. Ed. Gina Imperato. adv. contact: Martin Berube. bk.rev.; film rev.; play rev.; charts; illus. circ. 6,500. (tabloid format) **Document type:** newspaper.

378.1 US ISSN 0017-2308
GOSHEN COLLEGE BULLETIN. vol.70, 1985. 4/yr. free. Goshen College, 1700 S. Main St., Goshen, IN 46526. TEL 219-535-7569. FAX 219-535-7660. bk.rev.; illus. circ. 27,000. **Document type:** bulletin.
  Description: News of alumni and college events.

378 US
GOUCHER COLLEGE. PRESIDENT'S LETTER. suspended. 3/yr. Goucher College, Baltimore, MD 21204. TEL 410-337-6116. **Document type:** newsletter.
  Former titles: Goucher College News; Goucher College Bulletin.
  Description: Timely news of interest to alumni and friends of the school.

378 US ISSN 0739-5795
LH1
GOUCHER QUARTERLY. Key Title: Goucher. q. $3. Goucher College, Baltimore, MD 21204. TEL 410-337-6180. Ed. Susan Gossling. circ. 15,000.
  Former titles: Goucher Quarterly (ISSN 0274-5046); Goucher College Quarterly.
  Description: News, notes, articles, features, and announcements on issues affecting the alumni, faculty, students, and educational activities of this coeducational college in Baltimore.

378.1 UK ISSN 0017-2693
GOWN. 1954. 6/yr. (during academic yr.). free. Gown Publications, Students' Union, University Rd., Belfast 7 1NN, N. Ireland. TEL 324803. E-mail: gown@queens-belfast.ac.uk. Ed. Colin Blackstock. adv. contact: Gillian Duffy. bk.rev. circ. 3,000. (tabloid format) **Document type:** newspaper.

378.198 200 US
GRACE TIDINGS. 1943. q. Grace University, Ninth & William, Omaha, NE 68108-3600. TEL 402-449-2800. FAX 402-341-9587. E-mail: graceu@aol.com. Ed. Leo Thomas. circ. 19,000 (controlled).
  Description: Informs alumni and friends of the activities of the college.

378 CN
GRAFFITI.* s-m. free. Publi-PEQ, 3575 bd. St. Laurent, Ste. 232, Montreal, PQ H2X 2T7, Canada. TEL 514-845-8628. circ. 2,500. (tabloid format)

378.1 CN ISSN 0017-3924
GREEN AND WHITE. 1939. 2/yr. free to alumi of the U. of S. University of Saskatchewan, Development and Alumni Affairs, 232-117 Science Pl., Saskatoon, SK S7N 5C8, Canada. TEL 306-966-5186. FAX 306-966-5571. E-mail: rossnagel@admin.usask.ca; URL: http://www.usask.ca/alumni/. Ed. Paul Martin; Pub. Murray Osborn. R&P contact: Laurel Rossnagel. adv. contact: Marsha Martin. bk.rev. circ. 70,000. **Document type:** newspaper.
  Description: Helps to maintain bonds among the alumni and carries a variety of material presenting the U of S and its alumni.

378.1 US ISSN 0017-3991
GREEN RIVER CURRENT. 1965. w. free. Green River Community College, Associated Student Body, 12401 S.E. 320th St., Auburn, WA 98002. TEL 206-833-9111. FAX 206-288-3457. Ed. Stephanie Jacobson. adv.: B&W page $110; trim 7.5 X 10; adv. contact: Amanda Kleinert. film rev.; play rev.; illus. circ. 1,000. **Document type:** newspaper.
  Description: Aims to bring forth and objectively report issues and events for students, faculty and staff at Green River Community College, offers a valuable learning experience and supplies a forum by which the voice of the college may be heard.

378 CN ISSN 0384-5907
LA GREFFE.* m. free. Publi-PEQ, 3575 bd. St. Laurent, Ste. 232, Montreal, PQ H2X 2T7, Canada. TEL 514-845-8628. circ. 1,500. (tabloid format)

378.198 US ISSN 0276-1947
GRIFFIN. 1933. 22/yr. $12. Canisius College, 2001 Main St., Buffalo, NY 14028-1098. TEL 716-888-2195. FAX 716-888-2525. E-mail: griffin@gort.canisius.edu; URL: http://www.canisius.edu. adv.: page $420; trim 10 x 16. circ. 3,500. **Indexed:** Paper & Bd.Abstr. **Document type:** newspaper.
●Also available online.

378.198 US
GRIZZLY. 1978. w. $10. (Ursinus College) Evening Phoenix, Phoenixville, PA 19460. TEL 215-489-4111. Eds. Lora L. Hart, Jean Marie Kiss. adv.; film rev.; play rev.; stat. circ. 1,800. (tabloid format; back issues avail.)

378 US
GROVE CITY COLLEGE ALUMNI BULLETIN. 1912. q. free. Grove City College, Public Relations Office, Grove City, PA 16127. TEL 412-458-3100. FAX 412-458-3334. Ed. Lee Wishing. circ. 18,500. **Document type:** bulletin.

378.198 US
GROWL. 1930. m. $10 (effective through 1999). Holmes Community College, Box 367, Goodman, MS 39079. TEL 601-472-2312. FAX 601-472-2566. R&P contact: Jim Williams. adv.; bk.rev. circ. 6,031. (tabloid format) **Document type:** newspaper.

378 US
THE GUARDIAN (DAYTON). 1965. w. $15 per quarter. Wright State University, WO16C Student Union, Dayton, OH 45435. TEL 937-775-5537. FAX 937-775-5535. Ed. Alexis Larsen. adv. contact: Shawn Rubel. circ. 6,000. **Indexed:** Child.Lit.Abstr. **Document type:** newspaper.

378.18 US
THE GUARDSMAN. 1935. bi-w. City College of San Francisco, Journalism Department, 50 Phelan Ave., San Francisco, CA 94112. TEL 415-239-3446. FAX 415-239-3884. Ed. Eugene Bronstein. R&P contact: Juan Gonzales. adv. contact: Kerri Hillman. bk.rev. circ. 10,000. (also avail. in microfilm from LIB; back issues avail.) **Document type:** newspaper.
  Description: Campus news and local arts and entertainment news, with a calendar and free classified section for students and faculty.

378 CN ISSN 0830-3630
GUELPH ALUMNUS. 1968. 3/yr. University of Guelph, Communications and Public Affairs, Guelph, ON N1G 2W1, Canada. TEL 519-824-4120. FAX 519-824-7962. E-mail: mdickies@exec.admin.uoguelph.ca; URL: http://www.uoguelph.ca. Ed. Mary Dickieson. R&P contact: Mary Dickieson. adv.: color page Can.$2000; trim 8 1/4 x 10 3/4; adv. contact: John Rolfe. circ. 70,000. **Document type:** bulletin.
  Description: Contains research and features pertaining to the university campus, profiles of graduates, personal news items, and obits from graduates.
Refereed Serial

378.1 UK
GUILD AND CITY GAZETTE. 1936. every 3 wks. free. University of Liverpool, Guild of Undergraduates, N. Liverpool L7 7BD, England. TEL 051-709-4147. Ed. Kate Sandilands. adv.; bk.rev.; illus. circ. 5,000.
  Formerly: Guild Gazette (ISSN 0017-5374)

378 US
GWYNMERCIAN. 1948. m. free. Gwynedd Mercy College, Gwynedd Valley, PA 19437. TEL 717-646-7300. Ed. Donna Speers. adv.; bk.rev.; film rev.; play rev.; charts; illus. circ. 900. **Document type:** newspaper.
  Description: Covers campus news, world events, and student and faculty profiles.

378.1 US ISSN 0017-6249
H S U BRAND. 1915. w. (Sep.-May). Hardin - Simmons University, Drawer P, H-SU Sta., Abilene, TX 79698. TEL 915-670-1438. adv. circ. 1,200. **Document type:** newspaper.

378 UK
HAILEYBURIAN. 1868. 2/yr. £10. Haileybury College, Haileybury, Hertford SG13 7NU, England. TEL 0992-462507. FAX 0992-467603. Ed. R.G.F. Miles. adv.; bk.rev. circ. 2,500. (back issues avail.)

378 GW
HAMBURGER UNIZEITUNG. 1990. 6/yr. Universitaet Hamburg, Studierendenparlament, Von-Melle-Park 5, 20146 Hamburg, Germany. TEL 49-40-440943. FAX 49-40-440943. E-mail: huz@rrz.uni-hamburg.de. adv.: B&W page DM.1200; trim 193 x 280; adv. contact: Michael Loose. bk.rev. circ. 7,000. (back issues avail.) **Document type:** newspaper.

378.1 US ISSN 0017-7067
HAMILTON ALUMNI REVIEW. 1935. 4/yr. free. Hamilton College, Trustees of Hamilton College, 198 College Hill Rd., Anderson-Connell Alumni Center, Clinton, NY 13323. TEL 315-859-4680. FAX 315-859-4035. Ed. Frank K. Lorenz. illus.; circ. 19,000 (controlled). **Document type:** academic/scholarly publication.
  Description: Provides news about the college, the alumni, faculty and administrators.

378 US
HAMPDEN-SYDNEY TIGER. a. $5 per no. (effective 1997). Hampden-Sydney College, Box 126, Hampden-Sydney, VA 23943. TEL 804-223-4348.

378 US
HAMPTON SCRIPT. 1939. s-m. $10. Hampton Institute, Hampton University, Hampton, VA 23668. TEL 757-727-5385. FAX 757-727-5085. Ed. Judith Malveaux. adv.: page $936; trim 12 x 19.5. bk.rev.; play rev. circ. 4,500. **Document type:** newspaper.

COLLEGE AND ALUMNI

378.198   US   ISSN 0749-4882
HARBUS NEWS. 1936. w. $67. (Harvard Business School) Harbus News Corp., Gallatin Hall, Boston, MA 02163. TEL 617-495-6528. FAX 617-495-8619. Ed. Ann Pao. adv.; bk.rev. circ. 4,000. (tabloid format; back issues avail.) **Document type:** academic/scholarly publication, newspaper.
  Description: Includes news, opinions, humor and entertainment.

378.198   US
HARTFORD COLLEGE FOR WOMEN. CHRONICLE. 1979. s-a. free. Hartford College for Women, 1265 Asylum Ave., Hartford, CT 06105. TEL 203-768-5653. Ed. Kathleen P. Teso. adv.; bk.rev. circ. 3,000.

378   UK   ISSN 0308-0463
HARVARD BUSINESS SCHOOL CLUB OF LONDON ADDRESS BOOK. 1974. a. free to members. A P Information Services, Roman House, 296 Golders Green Rd., London NW11 9PZ, England. TEL 44-181-455-4550. FAX 44-181-455-6381. Ed. Alan Phillipp. adv.: page £600; 150 x 105. circ. 13,500. (also avail. in diskette format) **Document type:** directory.
  Description: Lists members of the Harvard Business School.

378.1   US   ISSN 0017-8098
HARVARD LAMPOON. 1876. 5/yr. $15. Harvard Lampoon, Inc., 44 Bow St., Cambridge, MA 02138. TEL 617-495-7801. Ed. Jon D. Beckerman. adv.; bk.rev.; illus. circ. 25,000. (also avail. in microform from UMI; reprint service avail. from UMI)
  Description: Humor magazine from Harvard University.

378.198 340   US   ISSN 1053-8186
KF292.H34
HARVARD LAW BULLETIN. 1948. 3/yr. for qualified personnel only. Harvard University, Law School, Communications Department, Holmes Hall, Cambridge, MA 02138. TEL 617-495-3118. Ed. Deborah Little. R&P contact: Lillian Gagliardi. adv.; bk.rev.; charts; illus.; stat. circ. 32,000. **Indexed:** Abstr.Bk.Rev.Curr.Leg.Per., Leg.Per.
—BLDSC (4267.490000).
  Formerly (until 1986): Harvard Law School Bulletin (ISSN 0017-8128)
  Description: News for Harvard Law School alumni.

378 610   US   ISSN 0191-7757
R747
HARVARD MEDICAL ALUMNI BULLETIN. 1891. q. free. Harvard Medical School Alumni Association, 25 Shattuck St., Boston, MA 02115. FAX 617-432-0013. E-mail: bulletin@warren.med.harvard.edu. Ed. William Ira Bennett. adv. contact: Sarah Jane Nelson. bk.rev.; illus.; index. circ. 15,000. **Document type:** academic/scholarly publication.
—BLDSC (4268.230000).

HARVARD UNIVERSITY. GRADUATE SCHOOL OF EDUCATION. BULLETIN. see EDUCATION

378   US   ISSN 0364-7692
LH1.H3
HARVARD UNIVERSITY GAZETTE. 1890. w. (except s-m. Jul.-Aug.; m. Dec., Jun.) $25 (foreign $32). Harvard University, Holyoke Center 1060, 1350 Massachusetts Ave., Cambridge, MA 02138. TEL 617-495-1585. FAX 617-495-0754. URL: http://www.news.harvard.edu/. Ed. John Lenger. R&P contact: John Lenger. circ. 31,000.

378   US
HASTINGS COLLEGE COLLEGIAN. 1898. w. $10. Hastings College, 7th & Turner, Box 269, Hastings, NE 68902-0269. TEL 402-461-7399. FAX 402-461-7442. E-mail: collegian@hastings.edu; URL: http://www.hastings.edu. Ed. Josh Awtry. R&P contact: Kathryn Stofer. adv.: page $425; trim 11 1/4 x 13 3/4; adv. contact: Jon Mires. film rev, music rev, tele.rev, video rev, charts, illus.; circ. 1,000 (paid). (tabloid format; back issues avail.) **Document type:** newspaper.
  Description: Covers news of interest to Hastings College community.

378   US
HAWK REPORTER. m. Howard College, 1001 Birdwell Ln., Big Spring, TX 78720. TEL 915-267-6311.

378   US
HAWKEYE (LA PLATA). 197? bi-w. free. Charles County Community College, Box 910, Mitchell Rd., La Plata, MD 20646-0910. TEL 301-934-2251. FAX 301-934-7698. Ed. Theresa Chaney. R&P contact: Mike Shields. circ. 1,000. **Document type:** newspaper.
● Also available on CD-ROM.

378   US
HEALTH PROFESSIONS NEWS AND NOTES. 1986. irreg. $24. (University of Maine, Houlton Center) Medi-Search of Maine, Box 323, Houlton, ME 04730-0323. TEL 207-532-4771. FAX 207-532-4039. Ed. Lloyd R. Chase. adv. contact: Paul Romanelli. bk.rev. circ. 350. **Document type:** newsletter.
  Formerly: Mobile Graduate News and Notes (ISSN 0887-3887)

378.1   US   ISSN 0017-9175
HEAR THIS; Kings Points monthly newspaper. 1946. m. $10. United States Merchant Marine Academy, Kings Point, NY 11024. TEL 516-482-8416. bk.rev. circ. 3,000. **Document type:** newspaper.

378   IS
LG341.J4
HEBREW UNIVERSITY NEWS. 1953. q. free. Hebrew University of Jerusalem, Division for Development and Public Relations, Mount Scopus, Jerusalem 91905, Israel. TEL 972-2-882811. FAX 972-2-811264. Ed. D. Avihai-Kremer. bk.rev.; bibl.; illus. circ. 27,500. (back issues avail.) **Document type:** newsletter.
  Formerly: Hebrew University of Jerusalem. News (ISSN 0334-2581)

378.1   US   ISSN 0017-9590
THE HEIGHTS. 1919. w. (Sep.-May). $45 (free to Boston College community). The Heights Inc., Boston College, McElroy 113, Chestnut Hill, MA 02167. TEL 617-552-2221. FAX 617-552-4823. adv.: page $600. bk.rev.; film rev.; play rev.; abstr.; illus. circ. 10,000. (tabloid format; back issues avail.) **Document type:** newspaper.

300   US   ISSN 0734-4031
HENRY GEORGE NEWSLETTER. 1937. m. $10. Henry George School of Social Science, 121 E. 30th St., New York, NY 10016. TEL 212-889-8020. Ed. Mark A. Sullivan. bk.rev. circ. 1,000.
  Formerly: Henry George News (ISSN 0018-0424)
  Description: Reports on the activities of the school and its affiliates.

378.198   US
THE HIGHLANDER. 1958. fortn. (during school yr.). $5. Highland Community College, Journalism Department, Box 68, Highland, KS 66035. TEL 913-442-3236. adv. circ. 2,000. (tabloid format) **Document type:** newspaper.

378.198   US
HILLSDALE MAGAZINE. vol.63, 1988. q. free. Hillsdale College, 38 E. College St., Hillsdale, MI 49242. TEL 517-437-7341. FAX 517-437-0160. Ed. Joseph McNamara. circ. 24,000 (controlled). (back issues avail.)
  Description: Coverage of Hillsdale College programs, activities, students, faculty, and on- and off-campus public policy seminars.

278   US   ISSN 1068-1566
HILLTOP. 1924. w. $40. Howard University, 2251 Sherman Ave., N.W., Washington, DC 20059. TEL 202-806-6866. Ed. Georges Daniels. adv.: page $1150. bk.rev.; film rev.; play rev.; circ. 10,000 (controlled).

HOCHSCHULSPORT. see SPORTS AND GAMES

HOLZAUGE. see LITERARY AND POLITICAL REVIEWS

378.1   AT   ISSN 1325-6734
HONI SOIT. 1929. w. Aus.$30 (foreign Aus.$60); free to Syndey University campuses. Students Representative Council, University of Sydney, N.S.W. 2006, Australia. TEL 61-2-96605222. FAX 61-2-96604260. Ed.Bd. R&P contact: Mark West. adv. contact: Mark West. bk.rev.; film rev.; play rev.; illus. circ. 6,000. **Document type:** newspaper.
  Description: Covers social, political and cultural issues, and student issues.

378   US
HOOD TODAY. 1986. irreg. (every 2-3 wks.). $15. Hood College, 401 Rosemount Ave., Frederick, MD 21701. TEL 301-696-3641. FAX 301-696-3727. film rev.; play rev.; charts. circ. 1,500. (tabloid format) **Document type:** newspaper.

378.198   US
HOPKINS NEWS-LETTER. 1897. w. $40. Johns Hopkins University, Shriver 6, 3400 N. Charles St., Baltimore, MD 21218. TEL 410-516-6000. FAX 410-516-6565. E-mail: News.Letter@jhu.edu; URL: http://www.jhu.edu/~newslett. Eds. Gianna Abruzzo, Douglas Steinke. R&P contact: Douglas Steinke. adv.: B&W page $750; trim 12 2/3 x 21 1/2; adv. contact: Reni John. bk.rev.; film rev.; play rev. circ. 7,000. cols./p.: 6; pp./issue: 26. **Document type:** newspaper.

378   US
HORIZON (SALT LAKE CITY). 1949. w. $15. S L C C S A - Salt Lake Community College, 4600 S. Redwood Rd., Box 30808, Salt Lake City, UT 84130-0808. TEL 801-967-4019; 801-967-4522. adv. circ. 5,000.
  Formerly: Points West.

371.8   US
HORIZONS (KINGSTON). 3/yr. free to qualified personnel. U R I Foundation, 10 Lippitt Rd., Kingston, RI 02881-2011. TEL 401-874-5836. Ed. Janet Heffernan; Pub. Bob Coleman. R&P contact: Bob Coleman. circ. 19,000. **Document type:** newsletter.
  Description: For alumni, faculty members, donors, foundations, corporations and friends of the University of Rhode Island.

378.1   US   ISSN 0018-5086
HORNET. 1923. w. free to qualified personnel. Fullerton College, 321 E. Chapman Ave., Fullerton, CA 92634. TEL 714-871-8000. adv.; bk.rev.; film rev.; play rev.; illus. circ. 5,000.

378.198   US
HOUGHTON STAR. 1908. w. $15. Houghton College, Box 378, Houghton, NY 14744. TEL 716-567-2211. Ed. Patricia Uleskey. adv.; bk.rev. circ. 1,250.

378   US   ISSN 0888-4013
HOUSTONIAN. 1984. s-m. $15. Sam Houston State University, Box 2178, Huntsville, TX 77341. TEL 409-294-1495. Ed. Jenna Jackson. adv. contact: Kerri Tuma. circ. 6,000.
  Formerly (until 1986): Houston Style (ISSN 8750-7013)

378   US
HOWARD UNIVERSITY ALUMNI NEWS. 1969. q. free. Howard University, Office of the Vice President for Development and University Relations, Department of Alumni Affairs, 2400 Sixth St., N.W., Ste. 310, Washington, DC 20059. TEL 202-686-6693. FAX 202-966-0701. Ed. Keith D. Miles. adv.; bk.rev. circ. 36,000.

378.198   US   ISSN 0742-2075
F127.H8
HUDSON VALLEY REGIONAL REVIEW; a journal of regional studies. 1984. s-a. $8 to individuals; institutions $10; students $6. Bard College, Tewksbury Rm. 200, Box 180, Annandale, NY 12504. TEL 914-758-6971. Eds. Richard C. Wiles, William Wilson. bk.rev. circ. 350. (back issues avail.) **Indexed:** Amer.Hist.& Life (1987-), Hist.Abstr. (1987-). **Document type:** academic/scholarly publication.

378   UK
HULLFIRE. 1974. fortn. (during school term). free. Hull University, Students' Union, University House, Cottingham Rd., Hull, North Humberside HU6 7RX, England. TEL 44-1482-466269. FAX 44-1482-466280. Ed. Simon Williams. adv. contact: Duncan Exley. bk.rev.; circ. 8,000 (controlled). **Document type:** newspaper.
  Description: Student newspaper of Hull University Union.

HUMAN ECOLOGY FORUM. see SOCIAL SCIENCES: COMPREHENSIVE WORKS

COLLEGE AND ALUMNI

370 CN
HUMBER ETC.... 1967. w. Can.$50. Humber College of Applied Arts and Technology, Journalism Department, School of Media Studies, Box 1900, Rexdale, Ont. M9W 5L7, Canada. TEL 416-675-3111. adv.; bk.rev. circ. 4,000. **Document type:** newspaper.
Formerly: Coven (ISSN 1184-3071)

378 US
HUMPHREYS COLLEGE QUARTERLY NEWS BULLETIN. 1896. q. free. Humphreys College, 6650 Inglewood Ave., Stockton, CA 95207. TEL 209-478-0800. FAX 209-478-8721. Ed. Pamela Knapp. circ. 20,000 (controlled). **Document type:** newsletter.
Description: Provides news and editorial regarding events, students, faculty, staff and alumni of Humphreys College.

378.1 US
HUNTER MAGAZINE. 1981. 2/yr. free. City University of New York, Hunter College, 695 Park Ave., New York, NY 10021. TEL 212-772-4070. Ed. Margo Viscusi. bibl.; charts; illus. circ. 73,000.
Supersedes: Newshunter (ISSN 0048-0274)

378.198 US
HURON UNIVERSITY ALPHOMEGA. 1883. m. membership. Huron University, Student Senate, Huron, SD 57350. TEL 605-352-8721. adv.; bk.rev. circ. 500. (tabloid format)
Formerly: Huron College Alphomega.

HUSKERS ILLUSTRATED. see SPORTS AND GAMES — Ball Games

378.2 370.196 SZ
▼**I B O PUBLICATIONS CATALOGUE.** (Text in English, French, Spanish) 1996. a. free. International Baccalaureate Organisation - Organisation du Baccalaureat International, Route des Morillons 15, CH-1218 Grand-Saconnex, Switzerland. TEL 41-22-7910274. FAX 41-22-7910277. E-mail: nancyw@ibo.org; URL: http://www.ibo.org. Ed. Nancy B. Weller. **Document type:** catalog.

378 UK
I C ENGINEER. s-a. membership. City Guilds College Association, Rm. 301, Shefield Bldg., Imperial College, London SW7 2AZ, England. TEL 44-171-594-6131. Ed. Joe Fernley. adv.; bk.rev. circ. 5,500. **Document type:** bulletin.
Formerly: Central.
Description: Covers news relating to Imperial College and City & Guilds Colleges as well as reports relating to association activities and features.

378 US
IDAHO ARGONAUT. 1899. 2/w. $18. University of Idaho, Student Publications, Student Union Bldg, University of Idaho, Moscow, ID 83843. TEL 208-885-7825. FAX 208-885-5896. adv.; bk.rev. circ. 8,000. (tabloid format) **Document type:** newspaper.

378 US ISSN 0744-5806
ILLINOIS BENEDICTINE MAGAZINE. 1971. q. free. Illinois Benedictine College, 5700 College Rd., Lisle, IL 60532. TEL 708-960-1500. FAX 708-960-1126. E-mail: candor@eagle.ibc.edu. Ed. Joseph Ursitti. adv. contact: Krissy Miller. circ. 15,000. **Document type:** academic/scholarly publication.

378.1 US ISSN 1047-4536
ILLINOIS QUARTERLY. 1907. 6/yr. $30 membership. University of Illinois at Urbana-Champaign, Alumni Association, University of Illinois, 1401 W. Green St., Urbana, IL 61801. TEL 217-337-1471. FAX 217-333-7803. E-mail: iq-uiuc@uiuc.edu. Ed. Vanessa Faurie; Pub. Louis D liay. R&P contact: Vanessa Faurie. adv. contact: Vanessa Faurie. bk.rev.; illus.; circ. 87,000 (controlled). **Document type:** academic/scholarly publication.
Formerly (until 1989): Illinois Alumni News (ISSN 0019-1841)

378.1 US
ILLINOIS STATE UNIVERSITY ALUMNI TODAY. 1966. q. free. Illinois State University, Alumni Office, Campus Box 3100, Normal, IL 61790-3100. TEL 309-438-2586. Ed. Barbara Tipsord Todd. circ. 85,000. (tabloid format)
Former titles: Illinois State University Today; Illinois State University Alumni Today; Illinois State University Alumni News; (1966-1974): Alumni Register (ISSN 0002-7235); American Alumni Newspaper.

378 CN
IMPACT (NORTH YORK). m. free. Seneca College, Student Federation Council, 1750 Finch Ave. E., North York, ON M2J 2X5, Canada. TEL 416-491-5050. FAX 416-756-2765. E-mail: impanews@learn.senecac.on.ca. Ed. Holly V. Pagnacco. adv. contact: Christopher York. bk.rev.; film rev.; circ. 5,000 (controlled). (tabloid format) **Document type:** newspaper.
Former titles: O B T; Oblique Times.
Description: Discusses student business and politics.
Refereed Serial

378 CN ISSN 0820-5116
IMPACT CAMPUS; le journal des etudiants et des etudiantes de l'Universite Laval. (Text in French) 1986. w. Can.$30. Impact Campus Inc., Bur. 1244, Pavillon Maurice-Pollack, Universite Laval, Quebec, PQ G1K 7P4, Canada. TEL 418-656-5079. FAX 418-656-2398. E-mail: impact-campus@public.ulaval.ca; URL: http://www.ulaval.ca/impact. Ed. Catherine Dube. adv. contact: Myriam Thiffault. circ. 15,000. (tabloid format; back issues avail.) **Document type:** newspaper.

378 CN
IMPRINT. 1978. w. University of Waterloo, CC140, Waterloo, ON N2L 3G1, Canada. TEL 519-885-1660. adv.; bk.rev.; film rev. (tabloid format)

783 US
IMPRINT (WALTHAM). 3/yr. Brandeis University, National Women's Committee, MS132, Box 9110, Waltham, MA 02254-9110. TEL 617-736-4160. Ed. Mary Pat Prado. **Document type:** newspaper.
Description: Contains news and articles about Brandeis University alumnae, along with information about activities to support the library.

378 US
IN MOTION (DAYTONA BEACH). 1991. m. $20. Daytona Beach Community College, 1200 International Spdy Blvd., Daytona Beach, FL 32114. TEL 904-255-8131. FAX 904-254-4458. Ed. Rosanne Garrity. adv. contact: Torrie Mathis. bk.rev.; film rev.; play rev.; circ. 5,000 (paid). (back issues avail.)
Description: Covers news, features, entertainment, sports of interest to DBCC community.

378.198 US
INDEPENDENT (DURANGO). 1931. w. $15. Fort Lewis College, College Heights, Box 7337, FLC, Durango, CO 81301. TEL 303-247-7405. Ed. Clara Woodmansee. adv. contact: Kitty Wild. bk.rev.; film rev.; illus.; play rev.; stat. circ. 3,000. **Document type:** newspaper.

378.1 US ISSN 0889-2423
THE INDEPENDENT FLORIDA ALLIGATOR. 1906. 5/w. $35. Campus Communications, Inc., Box 14257, Gainesville, FL 32604. TEL 904-376-4446. URL: http://www.alligator.org. Ed. C.E. Barber; Pub. C.E. Barber. R&P contact: C.E. Barber. adv. contact: Suzie Dean. bk.rev.; film rev.; play rev.; rec.rev. circ. 32,000. (tabloid format) **Document type:** newspaper.
Formerly: Florida Alligator (ISSN 0015-3877)

378.198 970.1 US ISSN 0364-8028
E97
INDIAN LEADER. 1897. fortn. $5. (Indian Leader Association) Haskell Indian Nation University, Box 258, Lawrence, KS 66046-4800. TEL 913-749-8477. FAX 913-749-8406. Ed. Darrel Deon James. adv. contact: Darrel Deon James. circ. 7,000. (also avail. in microfilm from BHP) **Document type:** newspaper.

378.1 US ISSN 0019-6517
INDIANA ALUMNI MAGAZINE. 1938. bi-m. Indiana University Alumni Association, 1000 E. 17th St., Bloomington, IN 47408. TEL 812-855-5785. FAX 812-855-4228. E-mail: iualumni@indiana.edu; URL: http://www.indiana.edu/-alumni/home.html. Ed. Judith Schroeder. R&P contact: Judith Schroeder. adv.; bk.rev.; illus. circ. 70,000.

378 US ISSN 0740-9664
INDIANA DAILY STUDENT. 1867. d. $50.90. Indiana University, Ernie Pyle Hall, Rm. 120, Bloomington, IN 47405. TEL 812-335-5507. circ. 10,500.

378.1 US ISSN 0019-6789
INDIANA STATESMAN. 1895. 3/w. $47. Indiana State University, Terre Haute, IN 47809. TEL 812-237-3025. FAX 812-237-7629. adv. contact: Paula Borman. bk.rev.; film rev.; play rev.; tr.lit. circ. 8,000. (tabloid format; also avail. in microform) **Document type:** newspaper.

378 CN
L'INDICE PENSABLE. (Text in French) m. Universite de Quebec Trois Rivieres, C.P. 500, Trois - Rivieres, Que. G9A 5H7, Canada. adv. circ. 2,500.

378 CN ISSN 0229-2068
L'INFOMANE. (Text in French) 1973. 10/yr. free. College de Bois-de-Boulogne, 10500 Av. Bois-de-Boulogne, Montreal, PQ H4N 1L3, Canada. TEL 514-332-3600 ext. 297. FAX 514-332-9579. Ed. Josiane Roulez. adv.: page Can.$200; adv. contact: Iloise LaRue. bk.rev.; film rev.; play rev. circ. 2,000. **Document type:** newspaper, academic/scholarly publication.
Description: Covers society, arts, student life and other topics.

378 CN
INFOMANE; le sixieme sens des etudiants de Bois-de-Boulogne. (Text in French) 1973. m. free. College de Bois-de-Boulogne, Infomane, 10555 ave. de Bois de Boulogne, Montreal, PQ H4N 1L3, Canada. TEL 514-332-3000 ext.297. FAX 514-332-9579. Ed. Josiane Roulez; Pub. Eloise LaRue. R&P contact: Josiane Roulez. adv.: page Can.$200; trim 11 x 15; adv. contact: Eloise LaRue. circ. 2,000. pp./issue: 20. Indexed: Lib.Lit. **Document type:** newspaper, academic/scholarly publication.
Description: Lists events, arts, movies, theatres, student life, etc.

378 AT
INFORMATION FOR OVERSEAS STUDENTS IN ARMIDALE. a. free. University of New England, International Programs Office, Armidale, N.S.W. 2351, Australia. TEL 61-67-733192. FAX 61-67-711238. E-mail: ipo@metz.une.edu.au.
Formerly: Information for Overseas Students and Their Families (ISSN 0816-3960)

378 US
INFORMATION X-III. 1990. bi-m. National Education Center, Tampa Technical Institute Campus, 2410 E. Busch Blvd., Tampa, FL 33612. TEL 813-935-5700. FAX 813-935-7415. Ed. Wiley E. Koon, Jr. circ. 2,000. **Document type:** newsletter.
Former titles: Information x-III-i; Information x-IV.
Description: News and information of interest to students, faculty and alumni of the institute.

378 UK
INKING. 1929. 3/yr. 50p. per no. Sheffield University, Students Union, Western Bank, Sheffield S10 2TG, England. TEL 0742-724076. FAX 0742-752506. adv.; bk.rev. circ. 1,500.
Formerly: Arrows.
Description: Arts and general interest for students

378 CN
INNIS HERALD. 1966. m. free. University of Toronto, Innis College Student Society, 2 Sussex Ave., Toronto, ON M5S 1A1, Canada. TEL 416-978-4748. FAX 416-978-5503. E-mail: innis.herld@utoronto.ca. Ed. Judy Josefowicz. adv.; film rev.; music rev.; circ. 1,500 (controlled). (tabloid format) **Document type:** newspaper.
Description: Aims to be an alternative to the news and politically oriented newspapers at the University of Toronto. Focuses on student lifestyles at the college, and also includes artistic, humourous and satirical content.

052 AT ISSN 0020-1618
INNOMINATE. 1946. irreg., approx. 7/yr. free. Sydney University Medical Society, Blackburn Bldg. D06, University of Sydney, Sydney, N.S.W. 2006, Australia. TEL 61-2-9351-2635. FAX 61-2-9351-6198. E-mail: innom@medsoc.usyd.edu.au; URL: http://www.blackburn.med.su.ua medsoc/innom/. Ed. Mitchell Lai. R&P contact: Mitchell Lai. adv. contact: Warwick Jonge. bk.rev.; circ. 800 (controlled). **Document type:** newspaper.
●Also available online.
Description: Includes medical news in local, national and international arenas.

COLLEGE AND ALUMNI

378 US ISSN 0046-9572
INNOVATOR (ANN ARBOR). 1969. irreg. free to alumni. University of Michigan, School of Education, E. & S. University Aves., Ann Arbor, MI 48109. TEL 313-763-4880. FAX 313-763-4062. Ed. Eric Warden. R&P contact: Eric Warden. circ. 49,000 (controlled). (tabloid format) **Document type:** newsletter.

378.198 US ISSN 0888-8469
INNOVATOR (UNIVERSITY PARK). 1969. fortn. free. Governors State University, University Pkwy., University Park, IL 60466. TEL 708-534-4517. FAX 708-534-8953. Ed. Sean Carr. R&P contact: Rita Nagy. adv. contact: Lisa Loschetter. bk.rev.; film rev.; play rev.; illus. circ. 3,000. (tabloid format) **Document type:** newspaper.

INSEAD ALUMNI ASSOCIATION ADDRESS BOOK. see BUSINESS AND ECONOMICS — Management

378.198 US
INSIDE BARUCH. s-a. free to qualified personnel. City University of New York, Baruch College, 17 Lexington Ave., New York, NY 10010. TEL 212-387-1182. circ. 5,000. **Document type:** newsletter.
 Description: College newspaper reporting on students, faculty and administration.

378 US ISSN 1070-6534
INSIDER (SKOKIE); careers, issues and entertainment for the next generation. 1984. bi-m. $24.99. Michiana Ventures, Inc., 4124 Oakton St., Skokie, IL 60076. TEL 847-673-3703. FAX 847-329-0358. E-mail: insideread@aol.com. Ed. Dave Glines; Pub. Mark Jansen. bk.rev.; circ. 1,018,350. **Document type:** consumer publication.
 Formerly: Collegiate Insider.

378 US
INSIGHT (FRESNO). 1969. w. California State University, Fresno, Department of Journalism, Business Bldg., Rm. 237, Fresno, CA 93740. TEL 209-294-2087. adv. (also avail. in microfilm from LIB)

378 UK
INTA-SITE; the magazine for students at De Montfort University. 1992. m. £4.50. Catch Student Publications, D.S.U., 4 Newarke Close, Leicester LE2 7BJ, England. TEL 0533-555576. FAX 0533-470926. Ed. Sue Lee. adv.; bk.rev.; film rev.; play rev.; illus. (back issues avail.)
 Formed by the merger of (1987-1992): Catch & Catch Monthly & Catchline.
 Description: Informs and entertains De Montfort University students and communicates the actions of the student union executive.

378.1 PR ISSN 8750-5428
INTERAMERICANA. (Text in English and Spanish) 1938. 7/yr. $3. (Inter American University of Puerto Rico, Public Relations Office) Media Sales Services, Galileo St., Jardines Metropolitanos, Rio Piedras, PR 00927. Ed. Ela Betancourt de Martinez. bk.rev.; illus. circ. 12,000.
 Supersedes (in 1979): Polygraph - I A U News; Which was formed by the 1971 merger of: Polygraph (ISSN 0032-3837); I A U News (ISSN 0018-8484)

658 334 CN ISSN 0703-9972
INTERET.* (Text in French) 1955. s-m. free. (Ecole des Hautes Etudes Commerciales) Publi-PEQ, 3575 bd. St. Laurent, Ste. 232, Montreal, PQ H2X 2T7, Canada. TEL 514-644-1000. Ed. Sophie Lemaire. adv.; bk.rev. circ. 5,000.
 Formerly: Lit-Pot-Hec.

378 UK ISSN 0952-6897
INTERFACE (GLASGOW). 1987. 2/yr. free. University of Stratclyde, External Affairs & Development, McCance Bldg., 16 Richmond St., Glasgow G1 1XQ, Scotland. TEL 0141-552-4400. FAX 0141-552-6558. Ed. Lorna B. Jaird. adv. circ. 42,000. (back issues avail.) **Document type:** bulletin.
 Description: College and alumni publication.

371.85 US
INTERFRATERNITY BULLETIN. 1950. m. (Sep.-May). $8. National Interfraternity Foundation, 3901 W. 86th St., Ste. 380, Indianapolis, IN 46268. TEL 719-846-0308. (Editorial addr.: 2405 W. Gregg Dr., Chandler, AZ 85224) Ed. Kris Brandt Riske. bk.rev. circ. 3,000. **Document type:** newsletter.
 Formerly: Interfraternity Research and Advisory Council. Bulletin.
 Description: Digest of articles on national Greek-letter fraternities and sororities, professional fraternities, campus and student trends; calendar of related events.

378.2 SZ
INTERNATIONAL BACCALAUREATE ORGANISATION. ANNUAL REPORT. (Text in English) 1968. a. 11 SFr.($9) International Baccalaureate Organisation - Organisation du Baccalaureat International, Route des Morillons 15, CH-1218 Grand-Saconnex, Switzerland. TEL 41-22-7910274. FAX 41-22-7910277. E-mail: nancyw@ibo.org; URL: http://www.ibo.org. (U.S. subscr. to: International Baccalaureate North America, 200 Madison Ave., New York, NY 10016) Ed. Nancy B. Weller. circ. 5,000 (approx.). **Document type:** corporate report.
 Former titles: International Baccalaureate Organisation. Annual Bulletin; International Baccalaureate Office. Annual Bulletin (ISSN 0074-1973); (until 1972): International Baccalaureate Office. Semi-Annual Bulletin.

INTERNATIONAL UNIVERSITY COLLEGIATE SPORTS REPORT. see SPORTS AND GAMES

378.1 US ISSN 0021-0358
IONIAN. 1946. bi-w. free. Iona College, 715 North Ave., New Rochelle, NY 10801. TEL 914-633-2370. FAX 914-633-2406. Ed. Angela Ciminello. adv.; bk.rev.; film rev.; play rev.; illus. circ. 4,000. (tabloid format) **Document type:** newspaper.

378 CN ISSN 0229-7493
IOTA. 1978. m. College d'Enseignement Generale et Professionnel, 1111 rue Lapierre, La Salle, Que. H8N 2J4, Canada.
 Formerly (until 1980): Meche (ISSN 0229-7485)

378 US
IOWA ALUMNI REVIEW. 1947. bi-m. membership. University of Iowa Alumni Association, Main Campus, Iowa City, IA 52242. FAX 3190335-3310. Ed. Carol Harker. adv. circ. 40,000.

378 US
IOWA STATE DAILY. 1871. d. $49.50. Iowa State Daily Publications Board, Inc., Hamilton Hall, Rm. 108, Ames, IA 50011. TEL 515-294-4120. FAX 515-294-4119. Ed. Jennifer Dukes. adv. contact: Kathy Davis. bk.rev. circ. 18,000. **Document type:** newspaper.

378 US ISSN 0746-2204
IOWA STATER. 1974. 3/yr. membership. Iowa State University, Ames, IA 50011. TEL 515-294-3129. FAX 515-294-9748. URL: htpp://www.iastate.edu/iastater. Ed. Linda A. Charles. R&P contact: Linda A. Charles. circ. 135,000 (controlled). **Document type:** newspaper.

378.198 UK
ISIS; the Oxford University magazine. 1892. 5/yr. £12. Isis Publications Ltd., 13 Bevington Rd., Oxford OX2 6NB, England. Eds. Briony Pope, Dov Waxman; Pub. Paddy Bullard. adv. contact: Ian Tester. bk.rev.; film rev.; play rev. circ. 7,500. (reprint service avail. from SCH) **Indexed:** Acad.Ind., Amer.Bibl.Slavic & E.Eur.Stud., Gen.Sci.Ind., Hum.Ind., Mid.East: Abstr.& Ind.

378.1 CU ISSN 0047-1542
ISLAS. 1958. 3/yr. $13 in N. and S. America; Europe $15. Universidad Central de las Villas, Faculty of Humanities, Santa Clara, 54830 Villa Clara, Cuba. Ed.Bd. bibl.; illus. circ. 2,500. **Indexed:** Amer.Hist.& Life (1970-1973), (1978-1990), (1994-), Hisp.Amer.Per.Ind. (1970-), Hist.Abstr. (1970-1973), (1978-1990), (1994-), IBR, Lang.& Lang.Behav.Abstr., Soc.Sci.Ind.

378.198 US
ITHACA COLLEGE QUARTERLY. 1983. q. free to alumni and parents. Ithaca College, Office of College Relations, Alumni Hall, Ithaca, NY 14850. TEL 607-274-3830. FAX 607-274-1490. URL: http://www.ithaca.edu. Ed. Marina B. Todd. R&P contact: Marina Todd. circ. 40,000. circ. 40,000 (controlled). **Document type:** academic/scholarly publication.
● **Also available online.**

378 US
IT'S ALLEN NEWSLETTER. q. Allen University, 1530 Harden St., Columbia, SC 29204. TEL 803-254-4165. FAX 803-376-5709. Eds. Rebecca Mbuh, Anne Coleman. (back issues avail.) **Document type:** newsletter.
 Description: For faculty-staff, alumni, students, parents and friends of the institution. Covers faculty and staff activities on and off campus.

371.85 US ISSN 0021-3276
IVY LEAF. 1921. q. $12. Alpha Kappa Alpha Sorority, Inc., 5656 S. Stony Island Ave., Chicago, IL 60637. Ed. Vanessa Lovelace. adv. contact: Connie L. Cochran. bk.rev.; circ. controlled.

378 US
J C S U NEWS. 1984. 4/yr. $6. Johnson C. Smith University, Communication Arts Department, 100 Beatties Ford Rd., Charlotte, NC 28216. TEL 704-378-1000. (Subscr. to: Johnson C. Smith University, Office of Alumni Affairs, Charlotte, NC 28216) circ. 1,800.

378 US
J U MAGAZINE. 1968. s-a. free. Jacksonville University, 2800 University Blvd. N., Jacksonville, FL 32211. TEL 904-745-7045. FAX 904-775-7047. Ed. Larry Marscheck. circ. 17,000 (controlled).
 Formerly (until 1997): Compass.
 Description: Informs alumni and parents of the activities and development of the administration, faculty, and alumni.

378 US
THE JAMBAR. 1930. fortn. $20. Youngstown State University, One University Plaza, Youngstown, OH 44555. TEL 330-742-3094. FAX 330-742-2322. Ed. Chalet Seidel. adv. contact: Amanda Manganaro. circ. 5,500. **Document type:** newspaper.

378 US
JAMESTOWN COLLEGE. ALUMNI & FRIENDS. q. free. (Jamestown College) 6093 College Lane, Jamestown, ND 58405. TEL 701-252-3467. FAX 701-253-4318. Ed. Kevin Thompson. R&P contact: Kevin C. Thompson. illus.; circ. 12,000 (controlled). (tabloid format) **Document type:** newsletter.
 Description: Covers college events, alumni and student news.

378 TS
JAMI'I. 1984. m. free. Emirates National Student Union, Emirates Branch - Al-Ittihad al-Watani li-Talabat al-Imarat, Far' al-Imarat, P.O. Box 15966, Al-Ain, United Arab Emirates. TEL 655508. Ed. Abd al-Aziz Harib al-Muhairi. circ. 5,000.
 Description: Covers student activities in the U.A.E.

051 US ISSN 0021-7255
LH1.J7
JOHNS HOPKINS MAGAZINE. 1950. bi-m. $18 (foreign $22); free to alumni. Johns Hopkins Magazine, 212 Whitehead Hall, 3400 N. Charles Streets, Baltimore, MD 21218-2692. TEL 410-516-7645. FAX 410-516-5251. Ed. Sue DiPasquale. adv.; bk.rev.; illus. circ. 93,000. (also avail. in microform from UMI; reprint service avail. from UMI) **Indexed:** P.A.I.S., Rehabil.Lit.
—UMI.
 Description: General interest magazine for faculty, alumni and friends of Johns Hopkins University.

378.1 US
JOHNSON C. SMITH NEWSLETTER. 1960? q. free. Johnson C. Smith University, Alumni Office, 100 Beatties Ford Rd., Charlotte, NC 28216. TEL 704-378-1000. Ed. Scott Scheer. circ. 7,500.

JORDAN UNIVERSITY NEWSLETTER/ANBA AL-JAMIAH. see EDUCATION — Higher Education

JOURNAL OF COLLEGE AND UNIVERSITY STUDENT HOUSING; A C U H O journal. see EDUCATION — Higher Education

COLLEGE AND ALUMNI

378.198 US
JUDSON CAMEO. 1974. s-a. free. Judson College, Bibb St., Marion, AL 36756. TEL 205-683-6161. Ed. Barbara Creswell. circ. 15,000.
Description: News on campus and features on alumnae of Judson College.

378 364 US
JUSTNOTES: NEWSLETTER OF THE DEPARTMENT OF CRIMINAL JUSTICE ADMINISTRATION. s-a. Sonoma State University, Department of Criminal Justice Administration, c/o Patrick Jackson, 1801 Cotati Ave., Rohnert Park, CA 94928-3609. TEL 707-664-2934. E-mail: jackson@sonoma.edu; URL: http://www.sonoma.edu/cja/.
Description: Contains news of the department and alumni as well as resources and opportunities related to criminal justice.

378 US
KA LEO O HAWAII/VOICE OF HAWAII. 1922. d. (Mon.-Fri.). $54 (effective 1997). University of Hawaii, Ka Leo Bldg., 1755 Pope Rd., 31-D, Honolulu, HI 96822. TEL 808-948-7235. FAX 808-956-9962. Ed. Genevieve Ancog. R&P contact: Jim Reis. adv. contact: Robert Lastimado. bk.rev. circ. 20,000. (tabloid format) **Document type:** newspaper.

378 US ISSN 8750-5746
KALAMAZOO COLLEGE QUARTERLY. 1934. q. free. Kalamazoo College, 1200 Academy St., Kalamazoo, MI 49006-3295. TEL 616-377-7304. FAX 616-337-7305. E-mail: aluminfo@kzoo.edu. Ed. Carol A.S. Derks. circ. 15,500 (controlled). **Document type:** academic/scholarly publication.
●Also available online.
Description: For alumni, parents, and friends of the college.
Refereed Serial

378 US
KALEIDOSCOPE (BIRMINGHAM). 1967. w. $25. University of Alabama at Birmingham, Box 76, University Center, Birmingham, AL 35294-1150. TEL 205-934-3354. Ed. Hunter Ford. adv.; circ. 8,000 (controlled). **Document type:** newspaper.

378 US ISSN 0745-3345
KANSAS ALUMNI MAGAZINE. 1902. 6/yr. $35. University of Kansas Alumni Association, 1266 Oread Ave., Lawrence, KS 66045-1600. Ed. Jennifer Jackson Sanner. bk.rev. circ. 40,000.

378 US
KANSAS STATE COLLEGIAN. 1893. d. (Mon.-Fri.). $70. (Kansas State University) Student Publications, Inc., Kedzie Hall, Kansas State University, Manhattan, KS 66506. TEL 913-532-6555. FAX 913-532-6236. Ed. Julie Long. adv. contact: Gloria Freeland. bk.rev. circ. 15,000. **Document type:** newspaper.

371.85 US ISSN 0022-894X
KAPPA DELTA EPSILON CURRENT. 1937. 3/yr. $5. Kappa Delta Epsilon, c/o Toni Gorrell, Ed., 201 Suelynn Dr., Normal, IL 61761. TEL 309-438-2164. FAX 309-438-8659. illus.; circ. 1,500 (controlled). **Document type:** newsletter.
Formerly (until 1947): Circle of Kappa Delta Epsilon.
Description: Newsletter of the activities of Kappa Delta Epsilon, a co-educational national honorary fraternity which emphasizes and promotes professional education.

371.8 XV ISSN 0022-9296
KATEDRA; akademiski casopis. (Text in Slovenian) 1961. m. 400 SLT($20) Akademska Zalozba - Katedra, Tyrseva 23, 62000 Maribor, Slovenia. FAX 38-62-22-742. Eds. Saso Dravinec, Petra Vidali. adv.; bk.rev. circ. 4,000.

378 IS
KAV P'NIM. (Text in Hebrew) 1968. m. Hebrew University of Jerusalem, Jerusalem 91905, Israel. Ed. Rivka Yuval. bk.rev.; charts; illus. circ. 10,000. (back issues avail.)
Formerly: Dushavon.

378.1 US
KENT ENGLISH NEWS. 1992. a. free. Kent State University, Department of English, Box 5190, Kent, OH 44242-0001. TEL 216-672-1212. Eds. Kyle Friedow, Timothy Adkins. **Document type:** newsletter.

378 US
KENTUCKY KERNEL. 1894. d. free. Kernel Press, Inc., 026 Journalism Bldg., University of Kentucky, Lexington, KY 40506. TEL 606-257-2871. FAX 606-323-1906. Ed. Tyrone Beason. bk.rev. circ. 18,000. **Document type:** newspaper.

378 US
KEUKA CONNECTION. 1929. q. free. Keuka College, Keuka Park, NY 14478. TEL 315-536-4411. FAX 315-536-5216. Ed. James P. Kuehl. **Document type:** newsletter.
Description: Information on the activities of the college.

371.85 US ISSN 0023-0804
LJ85.P2
KEY REPORTER. 1936. q. $3. Phi Beta Kappa Society, 1811 Q St. N.W., Washington, DC 20009. TEL 202-265-3808. FAX 202-986-1601. Ed. Priscilla S. Taylor. bk.rev.; cum.index: 1940-1950. circ. 435,000. (back issues avail) Indexed: Child.Lit.Abstr. **Document type:** academic/scholarly publication, newsletter.
Description: Contains news of the society's activities, feature articles, and scholarly book recommendations.

378.1 US ISSN 0023-1649
KINGSMAN. 1950. w. $20. City University of New York, Brooklyn College, c/o Michael Golub, Box 23-0200, Brooklyn, NY 11223. TEL 718-376-1429. adv.; bk.rev.; film rev.; play rev.; illus.; circ. 20,000 (controlled). (tabloid format) **Document type:** newspaper.

378.198 US
KNIGHT EXAMINER. 1966. s-w. $10. Jersey City State College, 2039 Kennedy Blvd., Jersey City, NJ 07305-1597. TEL 201-200-3575. FAX 201-200-3238. Ed. Larry D. Fowler. adv. contact: Larry D. Fowler. bk.rev.; film rev.; play rev.; illus. circ. 4,000. (tabloid format; back issues avail.) **Document type:** newspaper.
●Also available online.
Formerly: Gothic Times.

378 US
THE KNIGHT'S PAGE. 1897. m. (during school year). $6. Martin Luther College, 1884 College Heights, New Ulm, MN 56073. TEL 507-354-8221. FAX 507-354-8225. Ed. Dave Rau. adv.; bk.rev.; illus.; index. circ. 600. **Document type:** academic/scholarly publication.
Formerly (until vol.98, 1995): Black and Red.

378.1 US
KNOX ALUMNUS. 1917. 4/yr. free. Knox College, Office of Development and Alumni Affairs, Box 155, Knox College, Galesburg, IL 61401. TEL 309-341-7761. FAX 309-341-7770. Ed. David L. Amor. bk.rev.; illus. circ. 17,500. **Document type:** academic/scholarly publication.
Former titles: Knox Now and the Knox Alumnus; Knox Alumnus (ISSN 0047-3499)
Description: Focuses on Knox College, its alumni, faculty and students.

378 UK
KRED. w. University of Kent Students' Union, Mandela Bldg., University of Kent, Canterbury, Kent CT2 7NW, England. TEL 01227-765224. FAX 01227-464625. Ed. Alice Lythgoe-Goldstein. adv. contact: Andrew Green. bk.rev. circ. 3,000. (tabloid format; back issues avail.) **Document type:** newspaper.
Formerly: Kred Student.
Refereed Serial

378 500 JA ISSN 0911-8233
KWANSEI GAKUIN DAIGAKU RIGAKUBU TSUSHIN. 1970. 2/yr. free. Kwansei Gakuin University, School of Science - Kwansei Gakuin Daigaku Rigakubu Tsushin, 1-155 Uegahara-ichiban-cho, Nishinomiya-shi, Hyogo-ken 662, Japan. TEL 0798-53-6111. FAX 0798-51-0914. abstr.; circ. 1,200 (controlled). Indexed: MLA Intl.Bibl. **Document type:** newsletter.
Description: Contains news of the school.

378.1 UK ISSN 0023-639X
HB1
L S E MAGAZINE. 1951-1990; resumed. 2/yr. free. London School of Economics and Political Science, Houghton St., London WC2A 2AE, England. TEL 0171-405-7686. Ed. Doug Standring. adv.: B&W page £1000, color page £1500; trim 297 x 210. bk.rev.; illus. circ. 50,000. (reprint service avail. from KTO) Indexed: A.I.C.P. **Document type:** bulletin.

378.198 620 US ISSN 0023-6411
L S U ENGINEERING NEWS. 1966. 2/yr. free. (Louisiana State University, College of Engineering) Edward McLaughlin, Ed. & Pub., Baton Rouge, LA 70803. TEL 504-388-6003. FAX 504-388-5990. Ed. Amy Groves. circ. 14,200. **Document type:** newsletter.
Description: Contains news of engineering research carried out at the University, plus profiles of faculty, student activities, and alumni news.

378.1 US ISSN 8750-2526
L S U MAGAZINE. 1905. 4/yr. $35 (effective 1997). Louisiana State University, Alumni Association, 3838 W. Lakeshore Dr., Baton Rouge, LA 70808. TEL 504-388-3838. FAX 504-388-3816. E-mail: magazine@lsualumni.org. Ed. Andy Crawford. R&P contact: Andy Crawford. adv. contact: Kelly Lewis. bk.rev.; illus. circ. 22,000. **Document type:** trade publication.
Formerly (until 1984): L S U Alumni News (ISSN 0023-6403)
Description: Published for members and supporters of Louisiana State University to apprise them of current University events.

378 790.1 US ISSN 1055-3894
LA VERNE MAGAZINE. 1976. s-a. $7. University of La Verne, 1950 Third St., La Verne, CA 91750. TEL 909-392-2712. FAX 909-392-2706. Ed. Martha Fernandez; Pub. Dr. George Keeler. R&P contact: George Keeler. TEL 909-593-3511. circ. 1,600. (back issues avail.) **Document type:** consumer publication.
Description: Contains articles of interest to University of La Verne students and alumni and the La Verne community.

378.198 US ISSN 1046-1329
LAFAYETTE MAGAZINE. 1931. 3/yr. $2.50. Lafayette College, 17 Watson Hall, Easton, PA 18042. TEL 215-250-5126. FAX 215-250-5127. Ed. Allta Rusman. circ. 25,000.
Description: Covers higher education issues, news on alumni, and issues of interest to Lafayette College.

378.198 US
THE LAKELAND MIRROR. 1934. bi-w. free to students. Lakeland College, Box 359, Sheboygan, WI 53082-0359. TEL 414-565-1316. FAX 414-565-1206. Ed. Shannon Kring. adv.; bk.rev. circ. 1,300. (tabloid format) **Document type:** newspaper.
Formerly: Mirror (Sheboygan).

378 CN
LAMBDA. (Text in English and French) 1961. w. Laurentian University, Ramsey Lake Rd., Sudbury, ON P3E 2C6, Canada. TEL 705-673-6548. FAX 705-675-4849. Ed. Dominic Vidmar. adv.; bk.rev.; film rev. circ. 3,000. (tabloid format) **Document type:** newspaper.
Description: Bilingual student newspaper of the Laurentian University.

378.1 CN ISSN 0023-7493
LANCE. 1927. w. Can.$18($20) University of Windsor, Student Media Corp, Windsor, ON N9B 3P4, Canada. TEL 519-253-4232. FAX 519-971-3624 adv.: B&W page Can.$520, color page Can.$920. bk.rev.; film rev.; play rev.; circ. 10,000 (controlled

371.85 US ISSN 0023-8996
LAUREL OF PHI KAPPA TAU. 1919. q. $15. Phi Kappa Tau Foundation, 14 N. Campus Ave., Oxford, OH 45056-0030. TEL 513-523-1778. FAX 513-524-4812. E-mail: laurel_editor@phikappatau.org. Ed. Terri L. Nackid. R&P contact: Terri L. Nackid. adv.; circ. 50,000 (controlled).

378   CN   ISSN 0226-7934
LAURENTIAN UNIVERSITY. GAZETTE. (Text in English and French) 1970. bi-w. Laurentian University, Ramsey Lake Rd., Sudbury, ON P3E 2C6, Canada. TEL 705-673-6566. FAX 705-675-4840. Ed. Janet Sailian. circ. 1,600. (back issues avail.) **Document type:** newsletter.
   Description: Bilingual newsletter of Laurentian University.

378.1   CN   ISSN 0700-5105
LAURIER CAMPUS. 1962. 3/yr. free to college and alumni. Wilfrid Laurier University, University Advancement, 75 University Ave. W., Waterloo, ON N2L 3C5, Canada. TEL 519-884-1970. FAX 519-884-8848. E-mail: lhanna@machl.wlu.ca. Ed. Lynne Hanna. adv.; illus. circ. 40,000.
   Formerly: Waterloo Campus (ISSN 0043-146X)

378   US
LAW QUADRANGLE NOTES. 3/yr. free. University of Michigan, Law School, Hutchins Hall, Ann Arbor, MI 48109. TEL 313-647-3589. FAX 313-764-8309. E-mail: trogers@umich.edu; URL: http://www.law.umich.edu. Ed. Catherine Cureton. R&P contact: Tom Rogers. circ. 22,500 (controlled). (back issues avail.)
   Description: Covers news of the law school, faculty and alumni.

378   US
LAWRENCE TECHNOLOGICAL UNIVERSITY MAGAZINE. 1977. s-a. free. Lawrence Technological University, 21000 W. Ten Mile Rd., Southfield, MI 48075-1058. TEL 248-204-2200. Ed. Bruce Annett. circ. 28,000. **Document type:** academic/scholarly publication.
   Description: Information on the activities of the university, its students, alumni, and faculty.

378.198   US
LAWRENTIAN. 1906. q. Lawrenceville School, Box 6125, Lawrenceville, NJ 08648. Ed. Augustin Hedberg. **Document type:** academic/scholarly publication.
   Formerly: Lawrenceville Bulletin.
   Description: Provides news and information for alumni, parents, and friends of the school.

378   UK
LEEDS METROPOLITAN UNIVERSITY. ANNUAL REVIEW. a. Leeds Metropolitan University, Calverley St., Leeds LS1 3HE, England. TEL 44-113-283-2600. **Document type:** bulletin.
   Formerly: Leeds Metropolitan University. Review.

378.1   UK   ISSN 0041-6975
LEEDS STUDENT. 1970. w. Leeds University Union, P.O. Box 157, Leeds LS1 1UH, England. TEL 44-113-243-4727. FAX 44-113-246-7953. Ed. Ben East. adv.: B&Wpage £799, color page £949; adv. contact: Helen Whiteoak. bk.rev.; film rev.; play rev.; illus. circ. 40,000. (tabloid format) **Document type:** newspaper.
   Incorporates: Union News.
   Description: Student newspaper carrying news, current affairs, careers section and sports pages.

378   US
LEHIGH ALUMNI BULLETIN. 1912. q. Lehigh University, Alumni Association, 436 Broadhead Ave., Bethlehem, PA 18015. TEL 610-758-4838. FAX 610-758-4708. Ed. Robert W. Fisher. adv. contact: Suzanne Klein. circ. 50,000 (controlled).
   Description: Articles, essays, and photographs of general interest to educated readers, especially those with ties to the university. Covers Lehigh's intellectual, cultural and social life, and alumni news and announcements.

378.1   UK   ISSN 0024-0923
LEODIENSIAN. 1886. a. £3.20. Leeds Grammar School, Moorland Rd., Leeds LS6 1AN, England. Ed. Nigel Day. adv.; bk.rev.; illus.; stat. circ. 1,300. **Document type:** bulletin.

378.1   US   ISSN 0047-4452
LEX. vol.6, 1971. w. (during school term). John Jay College of Criminal Justice, Newspaper Society, City University of New York, 445 W. 59th St., New York, NY 10019. TEL 212-489-5183. adv.; illus. (tabloid format)

378.198   US
LEX REVIEW.* 1966. m. free. John Jay College, Lex Newspaper Society, 445 W. 59th St., New York, NY 10019. TEL 212-237-8308. Ed. Richard Durant. adv. **Document type:** newspaper.

378 335.5   SW   ISSN 1100-3693
LIBERTAS. 1988. bi-m. SEK 100 (effective 1995). Sveriges Socialdemokratiska Studentfoerbund, P.O. Box 11544, S-100 61 Stockholm, Sweden. TEL 46-8-714-48-40. FAX 46-8-714-95-08. Ed. Alexander Armiento. adv. contact: Max Elger. bk.rev. circ. 2,000. **Indexed:** Int.Polit.Sci.Abstr.
   Description: Serves as a forum for social-democratic debate.

378   GW
LIMA; liberales magazin. 1989. s-a. Bundesverband Liberaler Hochschulgruppen, Prinz-Albert-Str. 55, 53113 Bonn, Germany. TEL 0228-213744. FAX 0228-218491. adv.; stat. circ. 45,000. (back issues avail.)

378   US
LINFIELD REVIEW. 1895. w. (during school yr.). $16. Linfield College, 900 S. Baker St., Unit 395, McMinnville, OR 97128-6894. TEL 503-472-7715. FAX 503-472-3198. Ed. Jeff Cram. adv. contact: Amy Casterrline. bk.rev.; illus. circ. 1,700. (tabloid format) **Document type:** newspaper.
   Formerly (until 1967): Linews.

LINK (BURNABY). see EDUCATION

378   US   ISSN 1071-5487
LINK (NEW YORK, 1994); the college magazine. 1994. q. $15 (effective 1997-1998). Creative Media Generations, 110 Greene St., Ste. 407, New York, NY 10012-3838. TEL 212-966-1100; 800-943-LINK. FAX 212-966-1380. E-mail: editor@linkmag.com. Ed. Jeff Howe. R&P contact: Peter Kraft. adv.: Rob/Aronson. film rev.; rec.rev.; illus. circ. 1,000,000. **Document type:** consumer publication.

378.198   UK
LLAIS. 1974. m. free to students. South East Wales Students Association, Joint Students Union, Park Pl., Cardiff, Wales. adv.; bk.rev. circ. 8,000.
   Formerly: C A S A.

378   US
LOGOS (MASON CITY). 1968. m. North Iowa Area Community College, 500 College Dr., Mason City, IA 50401. TEL 515-421-4304. Ed. Melinda Bass. circ. 2,000. (reprint service avail from SCH)

378   US
LOGOS (SAN ANTONIO). 1932. bi-m. $5 free to students and community members. University of the Incarnate Word, 4301 Broadway, San Antonio, TX 78209. TEL 210-829-3964. E-mail: thelogos@universe.uiwtx.edu. Ed. Jennifer Walsh. adv.: B&W page $500; trim 10 X 14; adv. contact: Scarlett Flinn. bk.rev. circ. 3,000. (reprint service avail. from SCH) **Document type:** newspaper.

LONDON COLLEGE OF MUSIC MAGAZINE. see MUSIC

378   UK
LONDON STUDENT. 1952. fortn. free. University of London Union, Malet St., London WC1E 7HY, England. TEL 0171-580-7369. FAX 0171-436-4604. Ed. Liz Llewellyn. adv.; bk.rev.; film rev.; play rev. circ. 12,000. (tabloid format; back issues avail.) **Document type:** newsletter.

378.198   US   ISSN 1073-0249
LONGVIEW CURRENT. 1969. every 3 wks. free. Longview Community College, 500 Longview Rd., Lee's Summit, MO 64081. TEL 816-672-2303. FAX 816-672-2078. Ed. Kristin Hacker. adv. contact: Angie Richman. bk.rev.; film rev. circ. 2,000. (tabloid format) **Document type:** newspaper.
   Description: Prints news, features, and announcements pertaining to this Kansas City suburban community college.

378.198   US
THE LOOKOUT (LANSING). 1959. fortn. free. Lansing Community College, Student Personnel Bldg., Rm. 207, 430 N. Capitol Ave., Lansing, MI 48901. TEL 517-483-1290. FAX 517-483-1629. Ed. Erin Oakley; Pub. Bill Loewenstein. adv.: B&W page $468; adv. contact: Rick Cole. bk.rev.; film rev.; music rev.; play rev.; charts; illus. (tabloid format) **Document type:** newspaper.

LOS ANGELES COLLEGE OF CHIROPRACTIC. NEWS & ALUMNI REPORT. see MEDICAL SCIENCES — Chiropractic, Homeopathy, Osteopathy

378   US
LOS ANGELES LOYOLAN. 1923. w. $25 (free to students). Loyola Marymount University, 7101 W. 80th St., Los Angeles, CA 90045. TEL 213-338-2879. FAX 213-338-190. Ed. Beverly Butler. adv.; bk.rev.; film rev.; play rev. circ. 3,500. (back issues avail)

378.1   UK
LOUGHBOROUGH STUDENTS' UNION. NEWSPAPER. 1963. 34/yr. Loughborough Students' Union, Union Bldg., Ashby Rd., Loughborough, Leics. LE11 3TT, England. TEL 44-1509-217766. FAX 44-1509-235593. E-mail: lsu.news@lboro.ac.uk. Ed. Claire Tomlinson. R&P contact: Emily Dubberley. adv.: page £309; 283 x 206. bk.rev.; film rev.; play rev.; illus. circ. 3,000. **Document type:** newspaper.
   Former titles: Loughborough University. Newspaper; Fast Forward (ISSN 0950-5059); Loughborough Student; Venture (ISSN 0042-3548)
   Description: Reports news of interest to students.

378.1   UK
LOUGHBOROUGH UNIVERSITY GAZETTE. (Print edition ceased in 1994) 1966. a. free. Loughborough University, Loughborough, Leicestershire LE11 3TU, England. TEL 44-1509-222224. FAX 44-1509-223902. E-mail: j.allen2@lboro.ac.uk; URL: http://www.lboro.ac.uk/service/publicity/gazette.html. circ. 1,000. **Document type:** newsletter. ●Available only online.
   Formerly (until 1996): Loughborough University of Technology Gazette (ISSN 0024-6719)

378.198   US   ISSN 1054-7614
LOYOLA MAGAZINE. 1971. 3/yr. free. Loyola University Chicago, 820 N. Michigan Ave., Chicago, IL 60611. TEL 312-915-6407. FAX 312-915-7742. Ed. Bill Noblitt. bk.rev.; circ. 93,000 (controlled). (back issues avail.) **Document type:** consumer publication.
   Formerly: Loyola Today.
   Description: News and features of interest to Loyola University alumni and benefactors.

378   US
LUMBERJACK. 1929. w. $12 (effective 1996). Humboldt State University, Nelson Hall East 6, Arcata, CA 95521. TEL 707-826-3259. FAX 707-826-5921. Ed. Jackson Garland. R&P contact: Howard Seeman. adv. contact: Janet McIntosh. circ. 6,500. (also avail. in microfilm from LIB) **Document type:** newspaper.

378.1   AT   ISSN 1320-0747
LUMEN. 1952. 2/yr. free. University of Adelaide, Adelaide, S.A. 5005, Australia. TEL 61-8-83035174. FAX 61-8-82236437. E-mail: plyon@registry.adelaide.edu.au. Ed. Pamela Lyon. R&P contact: Pamela Lyon. adv.: B&W page Aus.$500, color page Aus.$900; adv. contact: Pamela Lyon. bk.rev.; stat. circ. 8,500. **Document type:** academic/scholarly publication.
   Former titles: University of Adelaide. Graduates Union. Monthly Newsletter and Gazette (ISSN 0001-8163); Adelaide University Graduates's Union. Gazette.

378.198   US
LUTHER ALUMNI MAGAZINE. 1964. 3/yr. free to qualified personnel. Luther College, Office of Publications, 700 College Dr., Decorah, IA 52101-1045. TEL 319-387-1350. FAX 319-387-1075. E-mail: http://www.luther.edu. Ed. Greg Vanney. circ. 30,500.
   Former titles (until 1997): Luther Alumni Quarterly; (until 1991): Luther; Luther Magazine.
   Description: For alumni and friends of the college. Contains college news, alumni news, and feature articles.

1960 COLLEGE AND ALUMNI

378.198 — US
M C C NEWS. 1930. q. free. Manhattan Christian College, c/o Laurin Hill, Dir. of Alumni and Public Relations, 1415 Anderson, Manhattan, KS 66502-4081. TEL 913-539-3571. FAX 913-539-0832. bk.rev.; circ. 15,000 (controlled). (tabloid format) **Document type:** newsletter.
  Description: Informational newsletter for constituents of the Manhattan Christian College.

378.198 — US
M C C POST. 1928. fortn. Mott Community College, 1401 E. Court St., Flint, MI 48502-2392. TEL 313-239-8224. adv. contact: Ben Kratz. bk.rev. circ. 4,000. (tabloid format; back issues avail.) **Document type:** newspaper.

378 610 — GW
M H H - INFO. 1972. m. Medizinische Hochschule Hannover, Carl-Neuberg-Str. 1, 30625 Hannover, Germany. TEL 49-511-532-3310. FAX 49-511-532-3852. TELEX 0922044-MEDHO-D. Eds. Christa Moeller, Christian Jung. bk.rev. circ. 2,600. **Document type:** newsletter.

378.198 — US
M S M C HAPPENINGS. 1972. q. free. Mount Saint Mary College, 330 Powell Ave., Newburgh, NY 12550. TEL 914-561-0800. FAX 914-562-6762. E-mail: coyne@msmc.edu; URL: http://www.msmc.edu. Ed. Brendan G. Coyne. bk.rev. circ. 10,000. **Document type:** newsletter.
  Formerly: Alumni Happenings.

378.1 — US — ISSN 0273-6977
M S U ALUMNI MAGAZINE. 1896. q. $30. Michigan State University, Alumni Association, Rm. 108, Student Union, E. Lansing, MI 48824-1029. TEL 517-355-8314. FAX 517-355-5265. Ed. Robert Bao. adv.; bk.rev.; circ. 44,000 (controlled).
  Formerly: Michigan State University Alumni Magazine (ISSN 0026-2463)

HA-MAAPIL. see POLITICAL SCIENCE

378 — US
MACALESTER TODAY. 1971. q. free. Macalester College, 1600 Grand Ave., St. Paul, MN 55105. TEL 612-696-6203. FAX 612-696-6192. Ed. Nancy A. Peterson. bk.rev. circ. 25,000.
  Formerly: Mac Today.

378 — CN — ISSN 0823-1672
MACEWAN JOURNALIST. 1973. bi-m. free. Grant MacEwan Community College, City Centre Campus, 10700-104 Ave., Edmonton, AB T5J 4S2, Canada. TEL 403-497-5644. Ed. Kathy Murrie; Pub. John Brittain. adv.: B&W page Can.$600; trim 10 3/8 x 15 1/2; adv. contact: Keith Burgess. circ. 1,800. **Document type:** newspaper.
  Formerly: MacEwan Journal (ISSN 0229-3439)

378 — CN — ISSN 1192-4608
MCGILL DAILY. French edition (ISSN 1192-4616) (Text in English) 1911. 3/w. English ed.; w. French ed. Daily Publications Society, 3480 McTavish, Montreal, PQ H3A 1X9, Canada. TEL 514-398-6784. FAX 514-398-8318. E-mail: daily@generation.net. Ed. Sonia Verma. R&P contact: Marian A. Schrier. adv.: B&W page Can.$950; adv. contact: Boris Shedov. bk.rev.; film rev. circ. 11,000. (tabloid format) **Document type:** newspaper.

378.1 — CN — ISSN 0024-9068
LH3.M2
MCGILL NEWS. 1919. q. Can.$25 for 2 years (effective 1996 & 1997). McGill Alumni Association, 3605 Mountain St., Montreal, PQ H3G 2M1, Canada. TEL 514-398-3552. FAX 514-398-7338. Ed. Janice Paskey. R&P contact: Janice Paskey. adv.: B&W page Can.$2000; trim 7 18 x 9 1/8; adv. contact: Donna Henchey. bk.rev.; charts; illus. circ. 70,000.

378 — CN — ISSN 0848-8436
MCGILL REPORTER. 1965. bi-w. $20. McGill University, University Relation Office, Rm. 110, Burnside Hall, 805 Sherbrooke St. W., Montreal, PQ H3A 2K6, Canada. TEL 514-398-6751. FAX 514-398-7364. URL: http://www.mcgill.ca/reporter. adv.; bk.rev. circ. 11,000. **Document type:** newspaper.
  Former titles (until 1989): Reporter (ISSN 0834-0773); (until 1984): McGill Reporter (ISSN 0580-8537); (until 1968): McGill University Reporter (ISSN 0541-6213)

378 — CN — ISSN 0843-0217
MCGILL UNIVERSITY GRADUATE SCHOOL OF LIBRARY AND INFORMATION STUDIES NEWSLETTER. 1981. a. free. McGill University, Graduate School of Library and Information Studies, 3459 McTavish St., Montreal, PQ H3A 1Y1, Canada. TEL 514-398-4204. FAX 514-398-7193. circ. 1,800. **Document type:** newsletter.
  Formerly (until 1985): McGill University Graduate School of Library Science Newsletter (ISSN 0715-481X)
  Description: Gives up-to-date information about the school and attempts to locate "lost" alumni.

378.198 — US
MACON JUNIOR COLLEGE COMMUTER. 1978. fortn. free to qualified personnel. Macon Junior College, Department of Developmental Studies, Macon, GA 31297. Ed. Whitney V. McMath. adv. circ. 3,500.

371.85 — US
THE MAGAZINE OF SIGMA CHI. 1881. q. $25 membership. Sigma Chi Fraternity, 1714 Hinman Ave., Box 469, Evanston, IL 60201. TEL 847-869-3655. E-mail: uncle_runkle@sigmachihq.org; URL: http://ww.sigmachihq.org/. Ed. Shelley L. Benson. adv. contact: Dan Shaver. bk.rev.; circ. 50,000 (paid).
  Description: Covers fraternity activities of its members and chapters.

378.198 — US
MAINESTREAM. 1975. w. University of Maine, 5 South St., Farmington, ME 04938. TEL 207-778-7330. Ed. Dan Ryder. R&P contact: Dan Ryder. adv. contact: Kerri Butler. bk.rev.; film rev.; play rev.; illus. circ. 2,000. (also avail. in diskette format; back issues avail.) **Document type:** newspaper.

378 — UK
MANCUNION. 1932. w. free. University of Manchester, Student Union, Oxford Rd., Manchester MI3 9PR, England. TEL 44-161-275-2943. FAX 44-161-275-2936. Ed. Juliet O'Brien. adv. contact: Jacqui Soo. bk.rev.; film rev.; play rev. circ. 20,000. (tabloid format; back issues avail.) **Document type:** newspaper.

378 — US
THE MANEATER. 1955. bi-w. $40 (free to students). University of Missouri at Columbia, A038 Brady Commons, Columbia, MO 65211. TEL 314-882-8500. FAX 314-882-5550. URL: http://www.cclabs.missouri.edu/~maneater/. Ed. Carmel Snyder. R&P contact: Barbara Burlison. TEL 573-882-4896. adv. contact: Rebecca Witte. circ. 14,000. (tabloid format) **Document type:** newspaper.
  Description: Contains news of the university campus.
  Refereed Serial

378 — US
MANHATTAN. 1974. q. free to qualified personnel. Manhattan College, Office of College Relations, Manhattan College Parkway, Riverdale, NY 10471. TEL 718-920-0235. FAX 718-548-4800. Ed. Darcy A. Lis. illus. circ. 40,000. (back issues avail.) **Document type:** newsletter.
  Description: Publishes institutional news and alumni features.

378.1 — CN — ISSN 0025-2298
MANITOBAN. 1913. w. Can.$40 (foreign Can.$50) (campus pickup free) (effective 1997). University of Manitoba, Students' Union, University Centre, Rm. 312, Winnipeg, MB R3T 2N2, Canada. TEL 204-474-6535. FAX 204-269-1299. E-mail: toban@cc.umanitoba.ca; URL: http://www.umanitoba.ca/manitoban. Ed. Ed. Janzen. adv. contact: Markian Saray. bk.rev.; film rev.; music rev.; play rev.; illus.; stat.; circ. 13,000 (controlled). (tabloid format) **Document type:** newspaper.
  Description: Includes news, sports, editorial opinions and letters.

378.1 — US
MANKATO STATE REPORTER. 1888. s-w. $25. Mankato State University, MSU Box 38, Mankato, MN 56002. TEL 507-389-1776. FAX 507-389-5812. Ed. Richard Price. adv. contact: Ken Stevermer. bk.rev.; film rev.; play rev.; illus.; stat. circ. 7,500. (tabloid format) **Document type:** newspaper.
  Former titles: Mankato State Independent; Mankato State Reporter; Mankato State Daily Reporter (ISSN 0025-231X)

378.1 — US — ISSN 0025-2867
MARCOLIAN. 1874. w. (during school yr.). $30. Marietta College, Box A-20, Marietta, OH 45750-4000. TEL 614-376-4937. FAX 614-376-4810. Ed. Melissa Kenreigh. adv.: B&W page $360; trim 13 x 21 1/2; adv. contact: Jeff Border. bk.rev. circ. 4,000. (tabloid format) **Document type:** newspaper.
  Refereed Serial

378 — US — ISSN 0889-2016
MAROON TIGER. 1898. every 3 wks. $10. Morehouse College, 830 Westview Dr., S.W., Atlanta, GA 30314. TEL 404-215-2681. Ed. Obinna Lewis. adv.: B&W page $338; adv. contact: Louis Clotman. bk.rev.; film rev.; play rev. circ. 2,500. (tabloid format; back issues avail.) **Document type:** newspaper.

378.1 — US — ISSN 0025-3995
MARQUETTE TRIBUNE. 1917. 2/w. $42. Marquette University, 1131 W. Wisconsin Ave., Milwaukee, WI 53233. TEL 414-288-7057. FAX 414-288-1979. Ed. Brent Killackey. adv.; circ. 7,500 (controlled). (tabloid format) **Document type:** newspaper.

378 — CN
MARTLET. 1946. w. (Sep.-Apr.). Can.$25($20) Martlet Publishing Society, P.O. Box 3035, Victoria, BC V8W 3P3, Canada. TEL 250-721-8360. FAX 250-472-4556. E-mail: martlet@uvic.ca; URL: http://kafka.uvic.ca/~martlet. Ed. Keith Woodley. R&P contact: Keith Powell. adv. contact: Todd Orchard. bk.rev.; film rev.; play rev.; circ. 10,000 (controlled). (tabloid format) **Document type:** newspaper.

MASSACHUSETTS COLLEGE OF PHARMACY. BULLETIN. see PHARMACY AND PHARMACOLOGY

378.1 — US — ISSN 0025-4797
MASSACHUSETTS DAILY COLLEGIAN. vol.96, 1968. d. (during school yr.). $75. Ware River News, 24 Water St., Palmer, MA 01069. TEL 413-545-3500. Ed. Meredith O'Brien. adv.; bk.rev.; illus. circ. 21,000. (also avail. in microfilm) **Document type:** newspaper.
  Formerly: Massachusetts Collegian.

378 — US
MASSACHUSETTS MAGAZINE. 1975. q. free. University of Massachusetts at Amherst, Massachusetts Magazine, 204 Munson Hall, Amherst, MA 01003. TEL 413-545-0155. FAX 413-545-3824. E-mail: massmag@dpc.umassp.edu. Ed. Patricia Wright. bk.rev. circ. 140,000. **Document type:** consumer publication.
  Formerly (until vol.14, no.4, 1989): Contact (Amherst).
  Description: Contains news and items of interest to alumni and friends of the University of Massachusetts at Amherst.

378 — IT — ISSN 0391-772X
IL MASSIMO. 1924. bi-m. free. Istituto Massimiliano Massimo, Via Massimiliano Massimo 7, 00144 Rome, Italy. TEL 06 592 5656. FAX 06-5914556.

378 — SA — ISSN 0025-5947
MATIELAND. 1957. 3/yr. free. University of Stellenbosch, Stellenbosch 7600, South Africa. adv. illus. circ. 29,000.

610 — US
MEDICINE ON THE MIDWAY. Variant title: University of Chicago. Pritzker School of Medicine. Alumni Association. Magazine. 1944. 3/yr. free. University of Chicago Hospitals, Office of Public Affairs, 5841 S. Maryland Ave., Mail Code 6063, Chicago, IL 60637. TEL 312-702-7322. FAX 312-702-3171. Ed. Carmen Marti. R&P contact: Carmen Marti. illus. circ. 14,000 (controlled). **Document type:** bulletin.
  Formerly: University of Chicago. Pritzker School of Medicine. Alumni Association. Bulletin (ISSN 0009-3734)
  Description: Covers news of graduates and their achievements, and updates alumni and alumnae on events of interest at the University of Chicago Hospital.
  Refereed Serial

COLLEGE AND ALUMNI

378.198 US
THE MEDIUM (NEW BRUNSWICK); the weekly entertainment paper. 1970? w. $5 for 14 nos. Rutgers University, Medium, LPO 16405-CN 5064, New Brunswick, NJ 08903. TEL 201-932-4721. Ed. Matt Valenti. adv.; bk.rev.; film rev.; play rev. circ. 10,000. (tabloid format) **Document type:** newspaper.
Description: Weekly news, features, announcements, and personals for Rutgers University and the campus of Livingston College.

378 CN ISSN 0841-2731
MEDIUM II.* 1974. w. free. (Erindale College) Campus Network, 315 Avenue Rd., Ste. 8, Toronto, ON M4V 2H2, Canada. TEL 416-924-2502. Ed. Norman B. Sanders. adv.; bk.rev.; film rev.; play rev. circ. 7,000. (tabloid format)

378.1 US ISSN 0025-8687
MEGAPHONE (CANTON). 1919. fortn. $15. Culver-Stockton College, Attn.: Steve Wiegenstein, Canton, MO 63435. TEL 217-231-6380. FAX 217-231-6611. E-mail: megaphone@culver.edu. Ed. Chris Lay. R&P contact: Steve Wiegenstein. adv. contact: Kelly Frey. bk.rev.; play rev.; illus.; circ. 1,000 (controlled). (tabloid format) **Document type:** newspaper.

378.1 US ISSN 0025-8709
MEGAPHONE (GEORGETOWN). 1906. w. Southwestern University, Student Publications, Box 6048, S.U. Sta., Georgetown, TX 78626. TEL 512-863-1345. FAX 512-863-5788. adv.; illus. circ. 1,300. (tabloid format) **Document type:** newspaper.

378 CN
MELIORIST. 1967. w. Can.$12. Meliorist Publishing Society, University of Lethbridge, Rm. SU-166, 4401 University Dr., Lethbridge, Alta. T1K 3M4, Canada. TEL 403-329-2334. FAX 403-329-2224. Ed. Rose Herbut; Pub. Times Taber. adv.; bk.rev.; film rev. circ. 3,000. (tabloid format)

378.18 CN ISSN 0228-8877
MEMORIAL UNIVERSITY OF NEWFOUNDLAND. GAZETTE. 1968. fortn. Memorial University of Newfoundland, Gazette, St. John's, NF A1C 5S7, Canada. TEL 709-737-8663. FAX 709-737-8669. E-mail: gazette@kean.ucs.mun.ca; URL: http://www.mun.ca/univrel/gazette. Ed. Pamela Frampton. R&P contact: Peter Morris. TEL 709-737-8665. adv. circ. 8,000. (tabloid format) **Document type:** newspaper.

378 GW
MENSA SPEZIAL - SOZIAL INFO. 1986. 11/yr. Studentenwerk Goettingen, Platz der Goettinger Sieben 4, 37073 Goettingen, Germany. TEL 49-551-390. FAX 49-551-395186. URL: http://www.stud.uni-goettingen.de. Ed. Christa Mirwald. adv. circ. 10,000. **Document type:** bulletin.
Formerly: Sozial Info.

378.1 US ISSN 0025-9853
MERCER CLUSTER; pacesetter of the seventies. 1920. w. $5. Students of Mercer University, Box 110, Macon, GA 31207. TEL 912-745-6811. adv.; bk.rev.; film rev.; play rev.; illus. circ. 2,000. (tabloid format)

378.002 UK
MERCHISTONIAN. 1866. s-a. Merchiston Castle School, Colinton, Edinburgh EH13 OPU, Scotland. Ed. M. Wilson. play rev. circ. 4,000. (back issues avail.)
Description: School magazine available to pupils, former pupils and others associated with the school.

378 US
MERCURY (GLENVILLE). 1929. w. $10. Glenville State College, 200 High St., Box 207, Glenville, WV 26351. TEL 304-462-7361. FAX 304-462-4407. Ed. Annie McCourt. adv. contact: Roger Carpenter. bk.rev. circ. 2,000. **Document type:** newspaper.

378 US
MESA LEGEND. 1964. bi-w. free to qualified personnel. Mesa Community College, 1833 W. Southern Ave., Mesa, AZ 85202. TEL 602-461-7330. FAX 602-461-7804. Ed. Lydia Kearney. adv. circ. 15,000. **Document type:** newspaper.
Description: Informs and entertains students and staff.

378.198 US
THE METER. 1950. bi-w. Tennessee State University, 304 Kean Hall, Nashville, TN 37209-1500. TEL 615-320-3861. FAX 615-320-3771. Ed. Moses Getahn. adv. circ. 4,000. (tabloid format; back issues avail.) **Document type:** newspaper.
Description: Covers campus news and events.

378.198 US
METHODIST COLLEGE TODAY. 1960. q. Methodist College, 5400 Ramsey St., Fayetteville, NC 28311. TEL 910-630-7043. FAX 910-630-2123. Ed. William Billings. circ. 15,000. (back issues avail.) **Document type:** bulletin.
Description: Contains news and features about the college and its alumni.

378.198 US
METROPOLITAN. 1979. w. Metropolitan State College, Student Publications, 1006 11th St., Box 4615-57, Denver, CO 80204. TEL 303-556-8361. FAX 303-556-2596. Dir. Kate Lutrey. adv.; bk.rev.; film rev. circ. 10,000. (tabloid format; back issues avail.)

378.1 US ISSN 1064-6442
MIAMI HURRICANE. 1926. s-w. $30. (University of Miami, Coral Gables Campus) Miami Hurricane, Box 248132, Miami, FL 33124. TEL 305-284-4401. FAX 305-284-4404. Ed.Bd. adv.; bk.rev.; illus. **Document type:** newspaper.

378 US
MIAMI STUDENT. 1826. 3/w. $25 (effective 1997). Miami University, 6 MacMillan Hall, Oxford, OH 45056. TEL 513-529-2210. FAX 513-529-1893. Ed. Emily Hebert. R&P contact: Brian Vass. adv. contact: Meredith Connor. circ. 10,000. **Document type:** newspaper.

378 US
MIAMIAN. 1982. 4/yr. free. Miami University, University Relations Division, Oxford, OH 45056. TEL 513-529-7592. FAX 513-529-1950. E-mail: miamian@muchio.edu. Ed. Donna J. Boen. circ. 100,000.
Refereed Serial

378.1 US ISSN 0745-967X
THE MICHIGAN DAILY. 1890. d. (Mon-Fri.). $165. University of Michigan, Board for Student Publications, 420 Maynard St., Ann Arbor, MI 48109. TEL 313-764-0552. FAX 313-764-4275. Ed.Bd. adv.; bk.rev. circ. 16,500. **Document type:** newspaper.

378 US
MICHIGAN REVIEW; the campus affairs journal of the University of Michigan. 1982. bi-w. $20 (effective Jan. 1992). Michigan Review, Inc., 911 N. University Ave., Ste. 1, Ann Arbor, MI 48109-1265. TEL 313-662-1909. FAX 313-936-2505. adv.; bk.rev.; music rev. circ. 10,000. (back issues avail.)
Description: Campus and local news coverage, editorials and opinion essays, sports coverage, interviews and informal opinion polls.

378 US
MICHIGAN TECH ALUMNUS. q. $25. Michigan Technological University, Alumni Association, 1400 Townsend Dr., Houghton, MI 49931. TEL 906-487-3327. FAX 906-487-3056. Ed. Dean Woodbeck. circ. 13,000. (back issues avail.)
Description: General interest publication for alumni, students, faculty and friends of the university, heavily oriented towards engineering and science.

378.198 US
MICHIGAN TIMES. 1971. bi-w. free to students. University of Michigan-Flint, 381 U C E N, Flint, MI 48503-2186. TEL 313-762-3475. FAX 313-762-3687. Ed. David Neil. adv. contact: Keith Bearup. film rev.; play rev.; charts; illus. circ. 3,500. (tabloid format; back issues avail.) **Document type:** newspaper.

378.1 US ISSN 0041-9850
MICHIGAN TODAY. 1968. q. free. University of Michigan, Office of University Relations, News and Information Services, 412 Maynard St., Ann Arbor, MI 48109. TEL 313-764-0105. FAX 313-764-7084. E-mail: johnwood@umich.edu; URL: http://www.umich.edu/~newsinfo/MT/mtfpg.html. Ed. John Woodford. adv. contact: Barbara Wilson. bk.rev.; illus. circ. 300,000. (tabloid format) **Document type:** academic/scholarly publication.
● Also available online.
Also available on CD-ROM.
Supersedes: Vital Margin.

378 US
MIDDLEBURY CAMPUS. w. $40 (foreign $60). Middlebury College, Drawer 30, Middlebury, VT 05753. Ed. Ryan D. Agosturo. circ. 3,200.

378.1 US ISSN 0745-2454
MIDDLEBURY COLLEGE MAGAZINE. 1926. q. free. Middlebury College, Wilson House, Middlebury, VT 05753. TEL 802-388-3711. FAX 802-388-6436. Ed. Tim Etchells. bk.rev.; illus. circ. 33,000.
Formerly: Middlebury College News Letter.

378 CN
THE MIKE. 1947. bi-w. Can.$25. Mike Publications Inc., 81 St. Mary Street, Toronto, ON M5S 1J4, Canada. TEL 416-926-7272. FAX 416-926-7276. Ed. Mark Slade. adv. contact: Grace McSorley. bk.rev.; film rev. circ. 5,000. (tabloid format) **Document type:** newspaper.

378.1 US
MILLS WEEKLY. 1917? w. $20. Mills College, Associated Students, P.O. Box 9974, 5000 MacArthur Blvd., Oakland, CA 94613. TEL 510-430-2246. FAX 510-430-3314. Ed. Colleen Almeida. adv.; bk.rev.; illus. circ. 1,200. (tabloid format)
Formerly: Mills Stream (ISSN 0026-430X)

378.1 US ISSN 0164-9450
MINNESOTA. 1901. bi-m. $30 membership. University of Minnesota Alumni Association, 501 Coffman Memorial Union, 300 Washington Ave. S.E., Minneapolis, MN 55455-0396. TEL 612-624-2323. FAX 612-626-8167. E-mail: umalumni@maroon.tc.umn.edu; URL: http://www.wmumaa.umn.edu. Ed. Tom Garrison. R&P contact: Teresa Scalzo. adv. contact: Sheila Farmer. bk.rev.; illus.; circ. 40,000 (paid). **Document type:** consumer publication.
Former titles (until 1978): Minnesota Alumni News (ISSN 0162-5209); (until 1977): University of Minnesota Alumni News (ISSN 0041-9869); Minnesota Alumni Weekly.

378.1 US
MINNESOTA DAILY. 1900. d. (Mon.-Fri.). $85. Minnesota Board of Directors, 2301 University Ave. S.E., Minneapolis, MN 55414. TEL 612-627-4080. FAX 612-627-4159. E-mail: rynerson@daily.umn.edu; URL: http://www.daily.umn.edu. Ed. R. Scott Rogers; Pub. Heather Burgess. R&P contact: Amy Rynerson. adv. contact: Chad Miyamoto. bk.rev.; illus. circ. 25,000. **Document type:** newspaper.

MINORITY TODAY. see *ETHNIC INTERESTS*

378.18 US
MIRROR (SOMERSET). 1966. s-m. membership. Somerset Community College, Communications Department, 808 Monticello Rd., Somerset, KY 42501. TEL 606-679-8501. Ed. Linda Stephens. film rev.; rec.rev. circ. 1,000.

378.1 US
MIRROR NEWS. 1967. bi-w. free. Henry Ford Community College, Student Center, Rm. C-4K, 5101 Evergreen, Dearborn, MI 48128. TEL 313-845-9639. FAX 313-845-9876. E-mail: layout@mail.henrford.cc.mi.us. Ed. Maria Reyes. R&P contact: Maria Reyes. adv. contact: Maria Reyes. bk.rev.; film rev.; play rev.; charts; illus. circ. 3,000. (tabloid format) **Document type:** newspaper.
Formerly: Ford Estate (ISSN 0015-6981)
Description: College news, local events, human interest, comics, puzzles, and college sports.
Refereed Serial

378.198 US
MISCELLANY MAGAZINE. 1983. s-a. Bowling Green State University, University Board of Student Publications, 214 W. Hall, Bowling Green, OH 43403. TEL 419-372-2601. FAX 419-372-0202. Ed. Andrea Wood. adv. contact: Todd Wise. circ. 5,000. (tabloid format)
  Formerly: Black Swamp Magazine.

378 US
MISSISSIPPI STATE UNIVERSITY ALUMNUS. 1926. q. $5. Mississippi State University, Alumni Association, Division of University Relations, Drawer AA, Mississippi State, MS 39762. Ed. Linsey Hardy Wright. circ. 56,000.

378 US
LH1.M63
MIZZOU MAGAZINE. 1912. q. $25. Publications & Alumni Communication, 407 D.W. Renolds Alumni & Visitor Center, Columbia, MO 65211. TEL 573-882-7357. FAX 573-882-7290. E-mail: mizzou@muccmail.missouri.edu. Ed. Karen Worley. adv.: B&W page $2400, color page $2950; trim 8 1/2 x 11; adv. contact: Tanya Stitt. circ. 125,000 (controlled). **Document type:** consumer publication.
  Formerly (until 1995): Missouri Alumnus (ISSN 0745-0583)
  Description: Covers happenings at the university. Includes articles on student life, teaching, research and educational issues.

378 US
MODERATOR. fortn. free. Mt. Marty College, 1105 W. 8th St., Yankton, SD 57078. TEL 605-668-1543. adv.; circ. 1,000 (controlled). **Document type:** newspaper.

371.805 US ISSN 1088-2839
MONITOR. 1985. m (10/yr.). free. Minnesota State University Student Association, Inc., 108 Como Ave., St. Paul, MN 55103. TEL 612-224-1518. FAX 612-224-9753. E-mail: msusa19@mail.idt.net.com. Ed. Ed Day. adv.: B&W page $796; adv. contact: Michael Howell. bk.rev.; charts; illus. circ. 22,000. cols./p.: 5; pp./issue: 12. (tabloid format; back issues avail.) **Document type:** newspaper.

371.8 362.1 US
THE MONTAGE. 1968. m. free. Essex Community College, Office of College Life, 7201 Rossville Blvd., Baltimore, MD 21237. TEL 410-780-6576. FAX 410-686-9503. Ed. Gwyneth B. Howard. adv.: B&W page $280; trim 11 x 13. circ. 3,500. cols./p.: 4; pp./issue: 28. (tabloid format)

378 US
MONTANA KAIMIN. 1898. d. (Tues.-Fri.). free to students. University of Montana, Journalism Bldg. 206, Missoula, MT 59812. TEL 406-243-6541. FAX 406-243-5475. bk.rev.; illus. circ. 6,000. (tabloid format) **Document type:** newspaper.

378.1 US
MONTANAN. 1969. 3/yr. free. University of Montana, Office of News and Publications, Missoula, MT 59812. TEL 406-243-2522. FAX 406-243-4520. URL: http://www.umt.edu. Ed. Caroline Patterson; Pub. Caroline/Patterson. R&P contact: Caroline Patterson. adv. contact: Caroline Patterson. bk.rev.; charts; illus. circ. 49,000. Indexed: Child.Auth.& Illus. **Document type:** academic/scholarly publication.
  Former titles: University; Profiles; U M Profiles (ISSN 0041-5200)
  Refereed Serial

378 CN ISSN 0838-9985
MONTREAL CAMPUS. (Text in French) 1980. s-m. Can.$24. Editions Montreal Camping Inc., C.P. 8888, Succ. Centre-Ville, Montreal, PQ H3C 3P8, Canada. TEL 514-987-7018. FAX 514-987-8210. E-mail: mtl.campus@uqam.ca. Ed. Isabelle Hachey. R&P contact: Remi Plourde. adv.: B&W page Can.$1070; 10 x 14; adv. contact: Remi Plourde. bk.rev. circ. 18,000. (tabloid format) **Document type:** newspaper.
  Refereed Serial

378 US ISSN 0886-8409
MORAVIAN (BETHLEHEM, 1912). Key Title: Moravian Alumni Quarterly. 1912. 3/yr. free to qualified personnel. Moravian College, Alumni Association, Bethlehem, PA 18018. TEL 215-861-1366. Ed. Susan Overath Woolley. charts; illus. circ. 17,500.
  Description: Moravian College Alumni Magazine

378.1 US ISSN 0027-1047
MOREHOUSE COLLEGE BULLETIN; the alumnus. 1926. q. free. Morehouse College, Public Relations and Alumni Affairs Office, 830 Westview Dr., S.W., Atlanta, GA 30314. TEL 404-688-3554. FAX 404-681-2800. Ed. Cason L. Hill. adv.; bk.rev.; charts; illus. circ. 6,500.
  Formerly: Alumnus.

378.198 US ISSN 0888-7780
MOSAIC (CLEVELAND). w. free. Cuyahoga Community College, 2900 Community College Ave., Cleveland, OH 44115. TEL 216-987-4231. Ed. Erick Sanders. adv.; bk.rev. circ. 3,500. (tabloid format; back issues avail.) Indexed: Curr.Adv.Ecol.Sci.

378 CN
LE MOTDIT.* (Text in French) 1975. s-m. free. Publi-Peq, 3575 bd. St. Laurent, Ste. 232, Montreal, PQ H2X 2T7, Canada. (Co-sponsor: College Edouard-Montpetit) circ. 3,000.

378 CN
MOTADIT. (Text in French) fortn. College d'Enseignement Generale et Professionnel (d'Ahuntsic), 9155 rue St. Hubert, Montreal, Que. H2M 1Y8, Canada. adv. circ. 3,000.

378.1 CN ISSN 0027-2485
MOUNT ALLISON RECORD. 1916. 3/yr. Can.$20 membership; newsstand price: Can.$7.50. Mount Allison University, Federated Alumni, Box 1140, Sackville, NB E0A 3C0, Canada. TEL 506-364-2345. FAX 506-364-2262. E-mail: cbourque@mta.ca. Ed. Carla Bourque. R&P contact: Gloria Jollymore. adv.: B&W page Can.$1000, color page Can.$1400; trim 8 1/2 x 11; adv. contact: Carla Bourque. bk.rev. circ. 18,000. **Document type:** consumer publication.

378.1 US ISSN 0027-2493
MOUNT HOLYOKE ALUMNAE QUARTERLY. 1917. q. free to members. Alumnae Association of Mount Holyoke College, 50 College St., South Hadley, MA 01075-1486. TEL 413-538-2251. FAX 413-538-2254. E-mail: scray@mhc.mt.holyoke.edu. Ed. Sabine Haberland Cray. R&P contact: Sabine H. Cray. bk.rev.; illus. circ. 29,000. **Document type:** bulletin.

378.198 US
MOUNT MAGAZINE. 1939. 3/yr. free. College of Mount St. Joseph, Office of Public Information, 5701 Delhi Pike, Cincinnati, OH 45233. TEL 513-244-4723. FAX 513-244-4654. E-mail: linda__liebau@mail.msj.edu. Ed. Linda B. Liebau. R&P contact: Linda B. Liebau. circ. 11,000. **Document type:** newsletter.
  Formerly (until 1985): Mountings.
  Description: College magazine for alumni, parents and friends of the institution.

378 CN ISSN 0826-2748
MOUTON NOIR.* (Text in French) 1978. m. free. Publi-Peq, 3575 bd. St. Laurent, Ste. 232, Montreal, PQ H2X 2T7, Canada. (Co-sponsor: College de Drummondville) circ. 1,400.

378 GW
MUENCHNER FREIHEIT; unabhaengige Studentenzeitung. 1986. q. DM.10. Akademischer Denk- und Presseverein zu Muenchen e.V., Hoerwarthstr. 4, 80804 Munich, Germany. Ed. Thomas Clement. adv.; bk.rev.; film rev.; play rev.; illus. circ. 10,000. (tabloid format; back issues avail.)

378 GW ISSN 0940-0141
MUENCHNER UNI MAGAZIN; Zeitschrift der Ludwig-Maximilians-Universitaet Muenchen. 1989. 8/yr. Universitaet Muenchen, Geschwister-Scholl-Platz 1, 80539 Munich, Germany. TEL 49-89-2180-3664. FAX 49-89-338297. Ed. Franziska Mueller-Haerlin. adv.: B&W page DM.1560, color page DM.3060; trim 260 x 245; adv. contact: Gisela Zeeb. circ. 11,000. **Document type:** academic/scholarly publication.

378 US
MUHLENBERG MAGAZINE. 1991. 4/yr. free. Muhlenberg College, Public Relations Office, 2400 Chew St., Allentown, PA 18104-5586. TEL 610-821-3230. FAX 610-821-3477. E-mail: bruckner@muhlberg.edu; berglaum@muhlberg.edu; URL: http://www.muhlberg.edu. Ed. Gary Kimball. R&P contact: Mike Bruckner. adv. contact: Mike Bruckner. illus. circ. 25,000. **Document type:** academic/scholarly publication.
  Formerly: Muhlenberg Door to Door.
  Description: Covers the history of the college and the people who shape it.

378 US
MULESKINNER. 1878. w. $20. Central Missouri State University, Warrensburg, MO 64093. TEL 816-543-4050. FAX 816-543-8663. (Subscr. to: Business Manager, CMSU Martin 30, Warrensburg, MO 64093. TEL 816-543-4051) adv. circ. 6,500. (tabloid format) **Document type:** newspaper.

378 CN ISSN 0820-5299
MUSE (ST. JOHN'S). 1950. w. Muse Board of Directors, Council of the Students' Union, Memorial University of Newfoundland, P.O. Box A-118, St. John's, NF A1C 5S7, Canada. TEL 709-737-8919. FAX 709-737-4743. E-mail: muse@morgan.ucs.mun.ca; URL: http:www.mun.ca/muse/muse.html. Ed. Kelly Batstone. R&P contact: Kelly Batstone. adv. contact: Sam Whiffen. bk.rev.; film rev. circ. 10,000. (tabloid format) **Document type:** newspaper.
  Description: Contains student related news, sports event, features and opinion.

378 US
MUSTANG DAILY. 1927. 5/w. $50. California Polytechnic State University, San Luis Obispo, CA 93407. TEL 805-756-1143. FAX 805-756-6784. Ed. Peter Hartlaub. adv. circ. 15,000. (tabloid format; also avail. in microfilm from LIB) **Document type:** newspaper.

378 US
N I C SENTINEL. bi-w. free. North Idaho College, 1000 W. Garden, Coeur D. Alene, ID 83814. TEL 208-769-3388. circ. 2,300 (controlled). **Document type:** newspaper.

378 US ISSN 0277-9749
N Y U PHYSICIAN. vol.24, 1969. s-a. free. New York University School of Medicine, 550 First Ave., New York, NY 10016. FAX 212-263-8425. Ed. Peter L. Ferrara. R&P contact: Gail Buckley. circ. 18,000 (controlled). **Document type:** academic/scholarly publication.
  Formerly (until 1980): New York University Medical Quarterly (ISSN 0028-7903)
  Description: Alumni magazine focusing on education, patient care and research at the NYU School of Medicine.
  Refereed Serial

378.1 US
N Y U TODAY. 1974. fortn. (Sep.-June). $12. New York University, Public Affairs Department, 25 W. Fourth St., New York, NY 10012. FAX 212-995-4021. Ed Craig Smith. circ. 15,000. (tabloid format)
  Former titles: New York University Report; Internal (ISSN 0020-5737)

378.198 US ISSN 1075-5004
NASSAU WEEKLY. 1978. w. $30. Nassau Inc., 317 Aaron Burr Hall, Princeton University, Princeton, NJ 08544. TEL 609-258-1899. Ed. Renee Kaplan; Pub. Steve Mercel. adv.: B&W page $200; trim 15 x 10. circ. 8,000. (tabloid format) **Document type:** newspaper.
  Description: Student-produced news, opinion, humor and cultural analysis.

378　　US　　ISSN 0162-1831
LJ85.P45
NATIONAL FORUM (AUBURN); the Phi Kappa Phi journal. 1913. q. $25. Honor Society of Phi Kappa Phi (Auburn), c/o Dr. James P. Kaetz, Ed., 129 Quad Center, Mell St., Auburn, AL 36849-5306. TEL 334-844-5200. FAX 334-844-5994. E-mail: kaetzjp@mallard.duc.auburn.edu; URL: http://www.auburn.edu/~kaetzjp/natforum.html. Ed. James Kaetz. R&P contact: Lourdes Barro. bk.rev.; circ. 120,000 (controlled). (also avail. in microform from UMI; back issues avail.; reprint service avail. from UMI) **Indexed:** Amer.Hist.& Life (1986-), Bk.Rev.Ind. (1979-), BPIA, C.I.J.E., Child.Bk.Rev.Ind. (1979-), Energy Info.Abstr., Environ.Abstr., Environ.Ind., High.Educ.Abstr., Hist.Abstr. (1986-), Lang.& Lang.Behav.Abstr., Mag.Ind., Manage.Cont., P.A.I.S., Phil.Ind., Sociol.Abstr., Tr.& Indus.Ind. **Document type:** academic/scholarly publication.
● Also available online. Vendor(s): Information Access Co., UMI.
— BLDSC (6023.642000); CIS; Genuine Article; UMI; UnCover. **Focus.**
Formerly: Phi Kappa Phi National Forum.
Description: Forum for analysis of issues of general social and scientific concerns such as education, public policy, medicine, and technology. A single theme treated in each issue.

378　　US　　ISSN 0300-6646
NATIONAL ON-CAMPUS REPORT. 1972. s-m. $119 (effective 1997). Magna Publications, Inc., 2718 Dryden Dr., Madison, WI 53704-3086. TEL 608-249-2455; 800-433-0499. FAX 609-249-0355. E-mail: editor@magnapubs.com; URL: http://www.magnapubs.com. Ed. Mary Lou Santovel; Pub. Richard Perkins. bk.rev. circ. 1,700. **Document type:** bulletin.
— CCC.
Description: Articles and news about college students for student service professionals.

378.1　　US
NEBRASKA. 1913. q. $30. University of Nebraska at Lincoln, Alumni Association, 1520 R St., Lincoln, NE 68588. TEL 402-472-2841. FAX 402-472-4635. E-mail: nebmag@unlinfo.unl.edu. Eds. Andrea W. Cranford, Robert Sheldon. illus.; circ. 23,000 (paid). (also avail. in microfilm)
Formerly (until Jan. 1994): Nebraska Alumnus (ISSN 0028-1794).

378.1　　NE　　ISSN 0028-2332
NEDERLANDSE VERENIGING VAN VROUWEN MET ACADEMISCHE OPLEIDING. MEDEDELINGEN. 1935. 7/yr. fl.40 membership. Nederlandse Vereniging van Vrouwen met Academische Opleiding - Netherlands Association of University Women, P.O. Box 13226, 3507 LE Utrecht, Netherlands. TEL 31-30-7215888. Ed. C.E.A.M. Raat. adv.; bk.rev.; charts; illus. circ. 5,500.
Description: Issues of concern to women with a background in higher education.

052　　UK
NERVE. 1991. m. free. Bournemouth University, Students Union, Talbot Campus, Fern Barrow, Poole, Dorset BH1 5BB, England. TEL 44-1202-5237555. FAX 44-1202-535990. Ed. Mike Gregory. adv.: page £290; adv. contact: Mike Gregory. bk.rev.; film rev.; play rev.; illus.; stat. circ. 3,000. (back issues avail.)
Description: Publishes news, features, student-related comedy, and music reviews of interest to students at Bournemouth University. Editorials are apolitical.

378.1　　AT　　ISSN 1036-4587
NEUCLEUS; U.N.E. student newspaper. (Supplement avail.: Kangaroo (ISSN 1036-3262)) 1936. 8/yr. free. University of New England, Armidale Students' Association, Armidale, N.S.W. 2351, Australia. TEL 61-67-732851. FAX 61-67-727633. Ed.Bd. R&P contact: Nigel Spence. adv. contact: Michael Epworth. bk.rev.; film rev.; play rev.; abstr.; index. circ. 2,500. (tabloid format) **Document type:** newspaper.

378　　CN
NEW EDITION. 1979. m. (during school year). Can.$20 (effective 1997). 2300 Yonge St., Box 67058, Toronto, ON M4P 1E0, Canada. TEL 416-598-1723. E-mail: the__new__edition@campuslife.utoronto.ca. Ed. Tom Conen; Pub. Will Steeves. R&P contact: Will Steevesk. adv.: page Can.$616; adv. contact: Tom Conen. bk.rev.; film rev.; music rev. circ. 10,000. **Document type:** newspaper.

378.1　　US　　ISSN 0028-6001
LH1
NEW JOURNAL. 1967. 5/yr. (Sep.-Apr.). $45. New Journal at Yale, Inc., Box 203432, New Haven, CT 06520. TEL 203-432-0519. FAX 203-432-0519. E-mail: tnj@yale.edu. adv.; bk.rev.; illus. circ. 10,000.

378.1　　US
NEW MEXICO DAILY LOBO. 1896. 5/w. during academic year. $35. University of New Mexico, Student Publications Board, Marron Hall, Rm. 131, Albuquerque, NM 87131-7061. TEL 505-277-5656. FAX 505-277-7530. adv.; bk.rev.; film rev. circ. 14,500. (tabloid format) **Document type:** newspaper.
Formerly: New Mexico Lobo (ISSN 0028-6230)
Description: Daily newspaper for the University of New Mexico.

378　　US　　ISSN 0883-6248
NEW SCHOOL OBSERVER. 1981. 9/yr. free. New School for Social Research, Public Relations Office, 55 W. 13th St., 7th Fl., New York, NY 10011-7958. TEL 212-229-5667. Ed. Ken Handel.
Description: Provides news and current information for the students, faculty, alumni and friends of the New School for Social Research, with campuses in New York and Paris.

378.1　　US
NEW TECH TIMES. m. free. New York City Technical College, 300 Jay St, Rm. A310, Brooklyn, NY 11201. TEL 718-260-5453. FAX 718-260-5455. Ed. Fred Sahakian. adv. contact: Pat Gay. bk.rev.; film rev.; circ. 8,000 (controlled). (tabloid format) **Document type:** newspaper.
Formerly (until 1975): Arts and Sciences (ISSN 0004-394X).

378.1　　CN　　ISSN 0028-6907
NEW TRAIL. 1942. 4/yr. Can.$15. University of Alberta Alumni Association, University of Alberta, 450 Athabasca Hall, Edmonton, AB T6G 2E8, Canada. TEL 403-492-3224. FAX 403-492-1568. Ed. Rick Pilger. R&P contact: Rick Pigler. adv. contact: Katherine Irwin. bk.rev.; charts; illus. circ. 97,500. **Document type:** bulletin.

378　　US
NEW UNIVERSITY. 1967. w. $15 per quarter. University of California, Irvine, 3100 Gateway Commons, Irvine, CA 92717. TEL 714-856-4285. FAX 714-856-4287. Ed. John Ronin. adv.; circ. 13,000 (controlled). (tabloid format; also avail. in microfilm from LIB) **Document type:** newspaper.

378.198　　US
NEW YORK LAW SCHOOL REPORTER. 1969. m. New York Law School, 57 Worth St., New York, NY 10013-2960. TEL 212-431-2118. adv. circ. 27,000. **Document type:** academic/scholarly publication.

378.198　　US
NEWS FROM HOPE COLLEGE. 1969. 6/yr. free. Hope College, 141 E. 12th St., Holland, MI 49423. TEL 616-395-7860. FAX 616-395-7991. E-mail: newsfromhope@hope.edu. Ed. Thomas L. Renner. R&P contact: Tom Renner. cum.index: 1969-1995; circ. 40,000 (controlled). (tabloid format; back issues avail.) **Document type:** newspaper.
Description: News of interest to alumni and friends of Hope College.

378　　US　　ISSN 0028-923X
NEWS, NOTES, AND QUOTES. 1956. q. membership only. Phi Delta Kappa, Inc., Box 789, Bloomington, IN 47402-0789. TEL 812-339-1156. FAX 812-339-0018. Ed. Donovan Walling. R&P contact: Terri Hampton. illus. circ. 130,000. (tabloid format) **Document type:** newsletter.

378　　US　　ISSN 0891-6063
NEWSBREAK (SAN FRANCISCO). 1986. fortn. (exc. Jun.-Aug., Dec., m.). free. University of California at San Francisco, Department of Public Affairs, 3333 California St., Ste. 103, San Francisco, CA 94143. TEL 415-476-3256. FAX 415-476-3541. Ed. Allen J. Balderson. bk.rev.; circ. 25,000 (paid). (tabloid format) **Document type:** newspaper.
Formerly: Today and Tomorrow.

378 620 790.1　　US　　ISSN 1093-0051
NEWSPEAK. 1909. w. $20. (Worcester Polytechnic Institute) W P I Newspeak Association, WPI Box 2700, 100 Institute Rd., Worcester, MA 01609. TEL 508-831-5464. FAX 508-831-5721. E-mail: newspeak@wpi.edu; URL: http://www.wpi.edu/~newspeak. Ed. Edward J. Cameron, Jr. adv.; bk.rev.; film rev.; play rev.; charts; illus.; stat. circ. 2,000. (tabloid format; back issues avail.) **Document type:** newspaper.

378　　CN
NEXUS (VICTORIA). (Text in English) 1990. 16/yr. Can.$18. Camosun College Student Society, Camosun College, 3100 Foul Bay Rd., Victoria, BC V8P 5J2, Canada. TEL 250-370-3591. FAX 250-370-3580. Ed. Barbara Risto. adv.; bk.rev.; film rev. circ. 4,000. **Document type:** newspaper.

378　　US
NICHOLS NEWS; newsletter for alumni, parents, and friends. 1932. 4/yr. free. Nichols College, Box 5000, Dudley, MA 01571. TEL 508-943-1560. Ed. Brian Rossetti. R&P contact: Brian Rossetti. circ. 10,000 (controlled). **Document type:** newsletter.
Formerly: Nichols Alumnus (ISSN 0300-6778)
Description: Includes general news of activities and events at the College including alumni events and class notes.

378　　CN　　ISSN 0845-8278
NOMAD. 1967. fortn. (Sep.-Apr.) free to current students. Student Association, St. Lawrence College, Kingston, ON K7L 5A6, Canada. TEL 613-544-5532. FAX 613-544-1763. Ed. Chris Price. adv.; bk.rev.; film rev.; music rev. circ. 1,000. pp./issue: 16. **Document type:** academic/scholarly publication.
Description: Contains campus news, events, sports, area news and events of interest to students, and Web surfing info.

378　　UK　　ISSN 0964-4652
NONESUCH. 1991. s-a. University of Bristol, Information Office, Senate House, Tyndall Ave., Bristol BS8 1TH, England. TEL 44-117-9287777. FAX 44-117-9292396. E-mail: info.office@bristol.ac.uk. Ed. Don Carleton. adv.: B&W page £1800, color page £2700; adv. contact: Laura Britton. bk.rev.; circ. 45,000. (back issues avail.) **Document type:** academic/scholarly publication, bulletin.

378　　GW　　ISSN 0944-8446
NORDRHEIN-WESTFAELISCHE AKADEMIE DER WISSENSCHAFTEN. JAHRBUCH. 1977. a. Westdeutscher Verlag GmbH (Leverkusen), Postfach 300944, 51338 Leverkusen, Germany. TEL 49-2171-44741. FAX 49-2171-48308. **Document type:** bulletin.
Formerly: Rheinisch-Westfaelische Akademie der Wissenschaften. Jahrbuch.

378　　UK
NORTH CIRCULAR. 1973. w. (during school yr.). free. Middlesex University, Bramley Rd., Oakwood, London N14 4YZ, England. FAX 44-181-362-6231. Ed. Michael Brown. adv. contact: Frank Jeffs. bk.rev. circ. 5,000. (back issues avail.) **Document type:** newspaper.

378.1　　US
NORTH TEXAS DAILY. 1852. d. (Tues.-Fri.). $20. University of North Texas, North Texas Daily, Box 5278, NT Sta., Denton, TX 76203. TEL 817-565-2353. E-mail: mercutio@nt__daily.unt.edu. adv.; bk.rev.; illus. circ. 11,000. **Document type:** newspaper.

378.1　　US
NORTH WIND. 1899. w. $21 (free on campus). Northern Michigan University, Marquette, MI 49855. TEL 906-227-2545. Ed. Ann Gonyer. adv.; bk.rev.; film rev.; play rev.; circ. controlled. (tabloid format) **Indexed:** M.L.A. **Document type:** newspaper.
Formerly (until 1971): Northern News (ISSN 0029-3202).

COLLEGE AND ALUMNI

378.1 US ISSN 0029-3032
NORTHEASTERN NEWS. 1921. w. $21. Northeastern University, 360 Huntington Ave., Boston, MA 02115. TEL 617-437-2648. FAX 609-437-2649. Ed.Bd. adv.; bk.rev.; illus. circ. 10,000. (tabloid format)

378 US ISSN 1069-3521
NORTHEASTERN UNIVERSITY MAGAZINE. 1975. bi-m. $20. Northeastern University, Office of University Relations, 360 Huntington Ave., 598 CP, Boston, MA 02115. TEL 617-373-5444. FAX 617-373-5430. URL: http://www.numag.neu.edu. Ed. Ken Gornstein. R&P contact: Edward Prewitt. adv. contact: Rickey Ezrin. bk.rev.; circ. 140,000 (controlled). **Document type:** consumer publication.
  Formerly: Northeastern Alumni Magazine.
  Description: News and features of interest to alumni.

378 US
NORTHERN IOWA TODAY. 1915. s-a. $12. University of Northern Iowa, Cedar Falls, IA 50614-0017. TEL 319-273-2311. Ed. Susan Chilcott. circ. 70,000.
  Formerly: Nonpareil.
  Description: Covers issues and trends in higher education.

378.1 US
NORTHERN IOWAN. 1874. s-w. $17.50. University of Northern Iowa, 112 Maucker Union, Cedar Falls, IA 50614. TEL 319-273-2157. adv. circ. 9,000. (tabloid format) **Document type:** newspaper.

378 US
NORTHERN NOW. 1900. q. free. Northern Illinois University, Office of Public Affairs, DeKalb, IL 60115. TEL 815-753-1681. FAX 815-753-3299. E-mail: nnow@niu.edu. Ed. Elizabeth Elving Bass. R&P contact: Elizabeth Elving Bass. charts; illus.; stat. circ. 150,000. (tabloid format; back issues avail.)
  Formerly: Alumni News.
  Description: Covers University news, faculty research, and higher education issues for alumni, parents, and friends.

378.1 US
NORTHERN STAR. 1899. d. $35. c/o Jim Killam, Adviser, Campus Life Bldg., Ste. 130, Northern Illinois University, De Kalb, IL 60115. TEL 815-753-0101. E-mail: star@wpo.cso.niu.edu; URL: http://star.niu.edu. adv.; bk.rev.; circ. 16,000. (tabloid format) **Document type:** newspaper.

378 US
NORTHWEST PHOENIX. 1959. fortn. Indiana University Northwest, 3400 Broadway, Moraine 110, Gary, IN 46408. TEL 219-980-6795. FAX 219-981-4233. E-mail: phoenix@iunlabl.iun.indiana.edu. Ed. Margaret Holland. R&P contact: Margaret Holland. adv. contact: Shelia Turner. bk.rev.; film rev.; software rev. circ. 3,500. (tabloid format; back issues avail.) **Document type:** newspaper.
  ●Also available online.
  Description: Deals with both campus and community issues.

378 US ISSN 0897-7488
NORTHWESTERN PERSPECTIVE. 1988. q. free to alumni and friends. Northwestern University, 555 Clark St., Evanston, IL 60208-1230. TEL 847-491-5000. FAX 847-491-2376. Ed. Alan . Cubbage. adv. contact: Nancy Isaacson. bk.rev.; circ. 95,624 (controlled). **Document type:** consumer publication.

378 US
NORWICH GUIDON. 1921. s-m. free. Norwich University, Communications Bldg., Northfield, VT 05663. TEL 802-485-2438. FAX 802-485-2580. adv.
  Formerly: Guidon.

378.1 US ISSN 0161-987X
NOTRE DAME MAGAZINE. vol.48, 1972. 4/yr. $20 to non-alumni. University of Notre Dame, Notre Dame Magazine, Main Bldg., Rm. 415, Notre Dame, IN 46556. TEL 219-631-6767. FAX 219-631-6767. E-mail: ndmag.iend-edu. Ed. Kerry Temple. R&P contact: Julie Ettl. illus.; circ. 135,000 (controlled). **Document type:** consumer publication.
  Formerly: Notre Dame Alumnus (ISSN 0029-4497)
  Description: In addition to campus news, each issue contains a dozen stories that reflect the university's Catholic intellectual tradition. Stories deal with current affairs, societal trends, and moral and ethical concerns.

378 US
NOTRE DAME REPORT. 1971. s-m. free to faculty and staff. University of Notre Dame, Office of the Provost, Notre Dame, IN 46556. TEL 219-631-5337. Ed. Linda M. Diltz. index; circ. 1,600. circ. 1,600 (controlled). **Document type:** newsletter.
  Incorporating: Office of the Provost at Notre Dame (ISSN 0034-5148)

378 CN ISSN 1185-717X
NOUVEAU QUARTIER LIBRE.* (Text in French) 1973. s-m. free. Publi-Peq, 3575 bd. St.Laurent, Montreal, PQ H2X 2T7, Canada. TEL 514-526-0235. (Co-sponsor: College de Rosemont) circ. 2,500.

378.1 US ISSN 0029-4985
NOVA (EL PASO). 1965. q. free. University of Texas at El Paso, El Paso, TX 79968-0522. TEL 915-747-5526. FAX 915-747-5969. Ed. Kathleen Rogers. bk.rev.; charts; illus. circ. 37,000. **Document type:** academic/scholarly publication.

NOVA NEWS NET. see JOURNALISM

378 US ISSN 1066-3347
NOW (LONGVIEW). 1936. q. free. LeTourneau University, Box 7001, Longview, TX 75607. TEL 903-233-3000. FAX 903-233-3618. E-mail: alumni@james.letu.edu. Ed. William Gibbs; Pub. Alvin O. Austin. (tabloid format; back issues avail.) **Document type:** newsletter.
  Description: For alumni and friends of LeTourneau University.

371.83 UK ISSN 0307-9244
LE NURB. 1973. 9/yr. free. Brunel University, Union of Brunel Students, Cleveland Rd., Uxbridge, Middlesex UB8 3PH, England. TEL 44-1895-462232. FAX 44-1895-810477. Ed. Jel McGill. adv. contact: Matt Osborne. bk.rev.; circ. 7,000. **Document type:** consumer publication.
  Former titles: Isam; Needle.

378.1 SA ISSN 0029-6716
NUX. 1948. m. free. University of Natal, Students Representative Council, P.O. Box 375, Pietermaritzburg, Natal, South Africa. adv.; bk.rev.; play rev.; illus.; circ. 2,500 (controlled). (tabloid format)

378.1 UK ISSN 0029-7380
OAKHAMIAN. 1883. 3/yr. £8. Oakham School, Chapel Close, Market Pl., Oakham, Leicestershire, England. Ed. D.N. Gilvary. adv. circ. 1,600. (tabloid format) **Document type:** newsletter.

378 US ISSN 1054-6480
OAKLAND UNIVERSITY MAGAZINE. 1982. q. $10 (free to qualified personnel). Oakland University, Publications Department, 109 N. Foundation Hall, Rochester, MI 48309-4401. TEL 248-370-3184. FAX 248-370-3182. E-mail: coutilis@oakland.edu. Ed. Theodore G. Coutilish. illus.; circ. 40,000 (controlled). (back issues avail.)
  Description: Covers campus activities, research projects, academic issues, and personalities of Oakland University.

378.1 US ISSN 0029-7518
OBERLIN ALUMNI MAGAZINE. 1904. q. $15 (alumni free). Oberlin College, 50 W. Lorain St., Bosworth 101, Oberlin, OH 44074-1089. TEL 216-775-8182. FAX 216-775-6907. E-mail: alummag@ocvaxc.cc.oberlin.edu; URL: http://www.oberlin.edu. Ed. Cynthia Nickoloff. R&P contact: Cynthia Nickoloff. bk.rev.; illus. circ. 30,500.
  Description: Covers news and issues affecting Oberlin College and its students and alumni.

378.1 US ISSN 0029-7526
OBERLIN REVIEW. 1874. w. $35 (free to Oberlin residents). Oberlin News Tribune, Wilder Box 90, Oberlin, OH 44074. TEL 216-775-8123. FAX 216-775-6733. E-mail: oreview@oberlin.edu; URL: http://www.oberlin.edu/~ocreview/. adv.; bk.rev.; film rev.; play rev.; illus. circ. 3,500. (tabloid format) **Document type:** newspaper.
  Description: Features college news, student life, local plays and music, and college sports.

378.1 US
OBSERVER (ELLENSBURG). 1927. w. $20. Central Washington University, Ellensburg, WA 98926-7435. TEL 509-963-1026. R&P contact: Christine Page. adv. contact: Christine Page. bk.rev.; film rev.; play rev. circ. 6,000. (tabloid format) **Document type:** newspaper.
  Formerly: Campus Crier (ISSN 0008-2503)

378 US
OBSERVER (FT. LAUDERDALE). 1986. bi-w. $15 (effective July 1994). Broward Community College Board of Trustees, 225 E. Las Olas Blvd., Ft. Lauderdale, FL 33301. TEL 305-973-2237. FAX 305-968-2448. (Subscr. to: 1000 Coconut Creek Blvd., Pompano Beach, FL 33066) Eds. Gary Band, Greta Penenori. adv. contact: Ann Chisholm. bk.rev.; circ. 10,000 (controlled). (tabloid format) **Document type:** newspaper.
  Description: Covers events, activities and other stories related to the BCC audience.

378 US
THE OBSERVER (NEW YORK). 1981. bi-w. Fordham College at Lincoln Center, 113 W. 60th St., Rm. 408, New York, NY 10023-7484. TEL 212-636-6015. FAX 212-636-7819. E-mail: zebulon@eworld.com. Ed. Adam C. Wolvek. adv. contact: Ben Billingsley. bk.rev.; dance rev.; film rev.; music rev.; play rev.; tele.rev.; charts; illus.; stat. circ. 10,000. (tabloid format; back issues avail.) **Document type:** newspaper.
  Description: Covers topics relevant to the college student, as a student and as a member of the NYC community.

378.198 US
OBSERVER (NEWARK). 1987. w. $10. Rutgers University, Newark College, 350 Dr. Martin Luther King Jr. Blvd., Newark, NJ 07102. TEL 201-648-5859. Ed. Steven Decillis. adv. (tabloid format)

378 US
OBSERVER (NOTRE DAME). (Supplement avail.: Irish Football) 1966. 5/w. $50 (free to students). University of Notre Dame - Saint Mary's College, 314 LaFortune Student Center, Box Q, Notre Dame, IN 46556. TEL 219-631-7471. FAX 219-631-6927. Ed. Liz Foran. R&P contact: Liz Foran. TEL 219-631-4542. adv. contact: Ellen Ryan. bk.rev. circ. 13,000. **Document type:** newspaper.
  Refereed Serial

378 US ISSN 1063-1631
OBSERVER (ROCK ISLAND). 1920. w. $12. Augustana College, Office of Communications, Rock Island, IL 61201. TEL 309-794-7485.
  Description: For students, contains campus news.

378.1 US ISSN 1072-3234
LD4249
OHIO STATE ALUMNI MAGAZINE. 1909. 9/yr. $35 membership. Ohio State University Alumni Association, Inc., 2400 Olentangy River Rd., Columbus, OH 43210-1061. TEL 614-292-3811. FAX 614-292-7697. Ed. Linda S. Crossley; Pub. Da L. Heinlen. adv.: B&W page $1240, color page $2365; adv. contact: Deborah S. Sawyer. circ. 113,000.
  Former titles: Ohio State (ISSN 0889-4116); O S U (ISSN 0744-8899); O S U Monthly (ISSN 0744-0758); (until 1980): Ohio State University Monthly (ISSN 0030-1167)

378.1 US ISSN 0030-1116
OHIO STATE LANTERN. 1881. d. $62. Ohio State University, School of Journalism, 242 W. 18th Ave., Columbus, OH 43210. TEL 614-292-2031. FAX 614-292-3722. URL: http://www.thelantern.com. R&P contact: Ray Catalino. TEL 614-292-6749. adv. contact: Chuck Kelley. bk.rev. film rev.; play rev.; charts; illus.; circ. 500 (paid); 30,000 (controlled). (also avail. in microfilm) **Document type:** newspaper.
  ●Also available online.

378.1 US ISSN 0030-1221
OHIO WESLEYAN MAGAZINE. 1923. q. free. Ohio Wesleyan University, Delaware, OH 43015. TEL 614-369-4431. Ed. Pamela Besel. bk.rev. circ. 26,000.

378.1 US ISSN 0030-171X
OKLAHOMA DAILY; a student newspaper serving the University of Oklahoma. 1916. d. $165 (effective 1997). University of Oklahoma, Student Publication Board, 860 Van Vleet, Norman, OK 73019. TEL 405-325-2521. FAX 405-325-7517. E-mail: Susan@ou.edu; URL: http://www.daily.ou.edu. Dir. Susan E. Sasso. R&P contact: Susan Sasso. adv. contact: Twila J. Smith. bk.rev.; circ. 13,500. (also avail. in microfilm) **Document type:** newspaper.

378.1 UK
OLD BRADFIELDIAN. 1994. s-a. Bradfield College, Old Bradfieldian Society, Bradfield, Berks. RG7 6AY, England. TEL 01734-744356. FAX 01734-744330. Ed. John Coldstream. **Document type:** consumer publication.
Description: Covers matters of interest to alumni of Bradfield College.

378 CN
OLD TIMES. 1940. s-a. free. Upper Canada College, 200 Lonsdale Rd., Toronto, ON M4V 1W6, Canada. TEL 416-484-8636. FAX 416-484-8611. Ed. M. Ridout. adv. circ. 8,500. **Document type:** academic/scholarly publication.

378.83 US
OLE MISS ALUMNI REVIEW. 1951. q. $25. University of Mississippi, Alumni Association, Rm. 172, Alumni House, University, MS 38677. TEL 601-232-7375. FAX 601-232-7756. Ed. Bill Dabney. adv.; B&W page 950; color page 1450; adv. contact: Bill Dabney. circ. 14,500 (60,000 Summer no.).
Description: For alumni and friends of the university. Covers campus events, alumni, activities, faculty research and activities and sports.

378 AT ISSN 0310-8864
ON CAMPUS. 1992. fortn. Flinders University of South Australia, Public Relations and Information Office, G.P.O. Box 2100, Adelaide, S.A. 5001, Australia. TEL 61-8-82012965. FAX 61-8-82013027. Ed. Charles Gent. circ. 1,600. **Document type:** newspaper.

378.1 AT ISSN 0030-2333
ON DIT. (Text in French) 1932. w. Aus.$8. University of Adelaide, Students Association, Adelaide, Australia. Ed.Bd. adv. contact: Luc Bondar. bk.rev.; film rev.; illus.; play rev.; stat.; tr.lit. circ. 6,000. (tabloid format) **Document type:** newspaper.

378.18 US
ON THE EDGE (MADISON). 1983. s-m. $5. Edgewood College, 855 Woodrow St., Madison, WI 53711. TEL 608-257-4861. adv.; bk.rev.; film rev.; play rev. circ. 650. (tabloid format) **Document type:** newspaper.
Formerly (until vol.7, 1989): Screed.

378 US
ON THE GREEN. 1952. q. free. Bloomfield College, Office of College Relations, Bloomfield, NJ 07003. TEL 201-748-9000. FAX 201-743-2040. URL: http://www.bloomfield.edu. Ed. Peggy F. Heller. adv. circ. 10,000. **Document type:** academic/scholarly publication, consumer publication.
Formerly: Bloomfield College. Bulletin.

378 US
ON WISCONSIN MAGAZINE. 1899. bi-m. $38 membership. Wisconsin Alumni Association, 650 N. Lake St., Madison, WI 53706. TEL 608-262-2551. FAX 608-262-3332. E-mail: pigorsch@facstaff.wisc.edu; URL: http://www.wisc.edu/waa/. Ed. Susan S. Pigorsch; Pub. Gayle M. Langer. R&P contact: Susan S. Pigorshc. adv.; B&W page $1250, color page $2650; adv. contact: Beth Vander Grinten. bk.rev.; illus.; circ. 42,500 (paid). (back issues avail.) **Document type:** consumer publication.
Former titles: Wisconsin Alumni Magazine; Wisconsin Alumnus.
Description: Directed to University of Wisconsin at Madison alumni, faculty and friends.

378 CN ISSN 0834-7603
ONTARION. 1951. w. Can.$20 (foreign Can.$65). Ontarion, Inc., University of Guelph, University Centre, Rm. 264, Guelph, ON N1G 2W1, Canada. TEL 519-824-4120. FAX 519-824-7838. E-mail: ontarion@uoguelph.ca; URL: http://tdg.res.uoguelph.ca/~ontarion/. Ed. Anicka Quin. R&P contact: Anicka Quin. adv. contact: Brigit Atkinson. bk.rev.; film rev.; play rev.; rec.rev.; circ. 12,000 (controlled). (tabloid format) **Document type:** newspaper.

378.1 US ISSN 0030-4069
OPTIMIST (ABILENE). 1912. s-w. $20. Abilene Christian University, Journalism & Mass Communication Department, Box 7618, ACU Sta., Abilene, TX 79699. TEL 915-674-2000. Ed. Gretchen Schultz. adv.; bk.rev. circ. 4,500. **Indexed:** Can.Wom.Per.Ind. **Document type:** newspaper.

378.1 US ISSN 0030-4662
OREGON DAILY EMERALD. 1907. d. (Mon.-Fri., Sep.-May). $70. Oregon Daily Emerald Publishing Co., Inc., University of Oregon, 300 Erb Memorial Union, Box 3159, Eugene, OR 97403. TEL 503-686-5511. FAX 503-346-5821. Ed.Bd. adv.; film rev.; play rev. circ. 11,500. (tabloid format; also avail. in microfilm) **Document type:** newspaper.

378 US
OREGON QUARTERLY; the Northwest perspective from the University of Oregon. 1919. q. $10 (foreign $25). University of Oregon, 5228 University of Oregon, Eugene, OR 97403-5228. TEL 503-346-5047. FAX 503-346-5571. E-mail: gmaynard@oregon.uoregon.edu; URL: http://www.uoregon.edu/~oq. Ed. Guy Maynard. adv. contact: Susan Thelen. circ. 100,000 (controlled). **Document type:** consumer publication.
Formerly (until Dec. 1993): Old Oregon.
Description: Covers the issues, problems, and accomplishments of higher education, with a special emphasis on the friends and alumni of the university.

378 US ISSN 0885-3258
S537
THE OREGON STATER. 1916. bi-m. $35. Oregon State University, Alumni Association, Administration Bldg. 416, Oregon State University, Corvallis, OR 97331. TEL 503-737-0780. FAX 503-737-2130. Ed. George P. Edmonston. bk.rev.; circ. 18,000 (paid). **Document type:** newspaper.

378 US
ORION (CHICO). 1975. w. $25. California State University, Chico, College of Communication, Department of Journalism, Chico, CA 95929-0600. TEL 916-898-5625. FAX 916-898-4839. URL: http://www.orion.csuchico.edu. Pub. Dave Waddell. adv.: page $750. bk.rev.; circ. 10,000 (controlled). **Indexed:** R.G.Abstr. **Document type:** newspaper.
●Also available online.

378.198 US
THE OSWEGONIAN. 1935. w. free. State University of New York, Oswego, 15B Hewitt Union, Oswego, NY 13126. TEL 315-341-3600. FAX 315-341-3542. E-mail: gonian@oswego.oswego.edu. Ed. Jennifer L. Fregoe. R&P contact: Jennifer L. Fegow. adv.: page $390; adv. contact: Faith Chaffee. circ. 6,000 (controlled). (tabloid format) **Document type:** newspaper.
Description: Directed to students and faculty of the college and the surrounding community.

378 CN
OTHER PRESS. 1976. m. free. Other Publications Society, Douglas College, Box 2503, 700 Royal Ave., New Westminster, B.C. V3L 5B2, Canada. TEL 604-525-3542. FAX 604-527-5095. adv.; bk.rev. circ. 5,000. **Document type:** newspaper.

378.18 US
OTTAWA CAMPUS. 1891. irreg. $7.50. Ottawa University, 1001 S. Cedar St., Ottawa, KS 66067. TEL 913-242-5200. adv. circ. 1,000. (tabloid format)

378 US
OUR BUSINESS. 1974. s-a. $25 membership. University of Oklahoma, College of Business Administration, 307 W. Brooks Hall, Rm. 208, Norman, OK 73019. TEL 405-253-5833. FAX 405-325-2096. E-mail: rgibson@uoknor.edu. Ed. Randy Gibson. circ. 22,000. **Document type:** newsletter.
Formerly (until Apr. 1990): Dialog (Norman).
Description: Discusses topics of interest to alumni both within the college and outside.

378 US
OUR LADY OF HOLY CROSS COLLEGE. JOURNAL. s-m. Our Lady of Holy Cross College, 4123 Woodland Dr., New Orleans, LA 70114. circ. 400.

378 UK ISSN 0268-1137
OXFORD MAGAZINE. 1986. 12/yr. £24($42) Oxford University Press, Oxford Journals, Walton St., Oxford OX2 6DP, England. TEL 44-1865-556767. FAX 44-1865-556646. TELEX 837330-OXPRES-G. E-mail: jnlorders@oup.co.uk. (U.S. subscr. to: Oxford University Press Inc., 2001 Evans Rd., Cary, NC 27513. TEL 919-677-0977. FAX 919-677-1714) Ed. T.J. Reed. adv.; bk.rev. **Document type:** academic/scholarly publication.
—BLDSC (6321.006110); UMI. **CCC.**
Description: Aims to show something of what goes on in one academic community, the kind of projects it pursues and the way it pursues them, providing a forum for debates, suggestions and criticisms.

378 UK ISSN 0954-1306
OXFORD TODAY. 1988. 3/yr. £15($30) (foreign £18) (effective 1997). (University of Oxford) Blackwell Publishers Ltd., 108 Cowley Rd., Oxford OX4 1JF, England. TEL 44-1865-791100. FAX 44-1865-791347. E-mail: jnlinfo@blackwellpublishers.co.uk; URL: http://www.blackwellpublishers.co.uk. adv. circ. 110,977. **Indexed:** Child.Lit.Abstr. **Document type:** bulletin. —CCC.
Description: Covers news and developments, alumni news, sports, finance, restaurants, museums and galleries.

P A S S; the first choice for Rart Qualified Accountants. (Professional Accountancy Student Service) see BUSINESS AND ECONOMICS — Accounting

378 US
P C C ALUMNI NEWS. 1961. q. free to alumni. Palmer College of Chiropractic, 1000 Brady St., Davenport, IA 52803. TEL 319-326-9662. FAX 319-322-8312. Ed. Christine Coleman. circ. 15,000.
Description: For college alumni and chiropractic professionals.

378.198 US
PACE PRESS. 1948. w. free. Pace University, Student Life Office, 41 Park Row, 8th Fl., New York, NY 10038. TEL 212-346-1553. FAX 212-346-1563. Ed. Ian B. Fernander.
Description: Covers students, faculty, and administrative activities at the university and the downtown NYC campus.

378 US
PACER. w. University of Tennessee at Martin, University Center, Rm. 263, Martin, TN 38238. TEL 901-587-7780.

378 US
PACER TIMES. w. University of South Carolina, 171 University Pkwy., Aiken, SC 29801.

378 US
PACIFIC LUTHERAN SCENE. 1970. q. Pacific Lutheran University, Tacoma, WA 98447-0003. TEL 206-535-7430. FAX 206-535-8331. E-mail: scene@plu.edu. Ed. Janet Prichard. illus. circ. 38,000. cols./p.: 4; pp./issue: 12. (tabloid format) **Document type:** consumer publication.
Formerly: Scene (Tacoma) (ISSN 0886-3369)
Description: Discusses academic issues and events of interest to alumni.

378 US ISSN 0030-8994
PACIFICAN. 1908. w. (Thu.). $30. Pacifican Publication Board, 3601 Pacific Ave., Stockton, CA 95211. TEL 209-946-2115. FAX 209-946-2195. E-mail: pacifican@uop.edu. Ed. Janell Bauer. R&P contact: James Simon. adv. contact: Melissa Batt. bk.rev. circ. 4,500. (tabloid format) **Document type:** newspaper.

COLLEGE AND ALUMNI

378 GW
PADERBORNER UNIVERSITAETS ZEITSCHRIFT. q. Universitaet-Gesamthochschule Paderborn, Warburger Str. 100, 33098 Paderborn, Germany. TEL 49-5251-602548. FAX 49-5251-603421. Ed. Tibor Werner Szolnoki. adv. contact: Martin Heynen. circ. 5,000. **Document type:** bulletin.

738 GW
PAEDAGOGISCHE HOCHSCHULE WEINGARTEN. PERSONEN- UND VORLESUNGSVERZEICHNIS. 1962. s-a. DM.3 per no. Paedagogische Hochschule Weingarten, Kirchplatz 2, 88250 Weingarten, Germany. TEL 49-751-501240. FAX 49-751-501200. E-mail: rektor@ph-nov1.ph.fh-weingarten.de. Ed. Dr. R. Meissner. adv. contact: Hubert Kaiserauer. circ. 2,500. **Document type:** directory.

378 US
PALADIN. w. (Sep.-May). $16.95. Furman University, Board of Student Communications, Box 28584, Greenville, SC 29613. TEL 864-294-2077. FAX 864-294-3001. Ed. David Coe. adv. circ. 3,000. **Document type:** newspaper.
Description: Student paper of campus events, issues and news.

PALATINATE. see *LITERATURE*

378 US
THE PAN - AMERICAN. 1927. s-w. University of Texas - Pan American, Student Publications, UC 322, Edinburg, TX 78539-2999. TEL 210-381-2541. FAX 210-316-7122. R&P contact: Robert Rollins. adv. contact: Juanita Sanchez. bk.rev. circ. 7,500. **Document type:** newspaper.

378.198 US ISSN 0031-062X
PS501
PANACHE (NEW YORK).* 1987. q. Win Records & Video, Inc., 1501 Broadway 8900, New York, NY 10036-5503. circ. 35,000.

378 617.6 US
PANKEY-GRAM. 1971. q. $10. L.D. Pankey Alumni Association, 785 Delaware Ave., Delmar, NY 12054. Ed. Robert C. King. circ. 8,000.

378 200.711 US ISSN 8755-0954
PANORAMA (PITTSBURGH). 1960. 5/yr. Pittsburgh Theological Seminary, 616 N. Highland Ave., Pittsburgh, PA 15206. TEL 412-362-5610. FAX 412-363-3260. Ed. Lisa Dormire Foster. **Document type:** newsletter.
Description: Provides news of the seminary, faculty and alumni activities, fundraising efforts and similar items of interest.

378 CN
THE PAPER CUT. 1981. fortn. Marianopolis College, Student Union, 3880 rue Cote des Neiges, Rm. G7, Montreal, PQ H3H 1W1, Canada. TEL 514-931-8792. FAX 514-931-6786. Eds. Danistan Saverimuthu, Marc Miresco. adv.: B&W page $180, color page $320; trim 10 x 15; adv. contact: Michael Tricot. bk.rev.; film rev. circ. 1,000. (tabloid format) **Document type:** newspaper.
Formerly (until 1995): Paper.
Description: Covers a wide range of topics, mostly related to college life, including sports, arts and entertainment, news and commentary sections.

600 378 PP ISSN 1019-5343
PAPUA NEW GUINEA UNIVERSITY OF TECHNOLOGY. REPORTER. no.34, 1979. w. Papua New Guinea University of Technology, P.O. Box 793, Lae, Papua New Guinea. FAX 675-424067. TELEX TLX 42428. Ed. Corney Lahies. adv.; charts; illus. circ. 1,500. (also avail. in microform) **Document type:** academic/scholarly publication.

378 US
THE PARTHENON. 1898. 4/w. $40. Marshall University, School of Journalism, 311 Smith Hall, Huntington, WV 25755. TEL 304-696-6696. FAX 304-696-2519. E-mail: parthenon@marshall.edu; URL: http://www.marshall.edu/parthenon/. Marilyn McClure, Adviser. adv. contact: Doug Jones. circ. 7,000. (also avail. in microfiche) **Document type:** newspaper.

378.1 US ISSN 0031-2657
PASQUINO. 1921. irreg. (10-11/yr.). $10. Potomac State College, Journalism Dept., Keyser, WV 26726. TEL 304-788-6966. Ed. Fred Jacoby. adv. circ. 2,000. (also avail. in microform from UMI)

378.18 CN ISSN 1194-8302
PASSPORT. 1940. q. free. Briercrest Family of Schools, 510 College Dr., Caronport, SK S0H 0S0, Canada. TEL 306-756-3200. FAX 306-756-3366. E-mail: briercrest@sasknet.sk.ca. Ed. Dwight Friesen; Pub. Ellery Pullman. R&P contact: Larry Hamm. bibl.; charts; illus.; stat.; circ. 27,000. (controlled). **Document type:** newsletter.
Former titles (until 1993): Briercrest Echo (ISSN 0821-5839); (until 1982): Echo (ISSN 0824-9288)
Description: Reports on news, events, alumni, academic, programs of Briercrest Family of Schools.

378 US
THE PATHFINDER (LEWISTON). bi-w. free. Lewis & Clark State College, Eighth Ave. & Sixth St., Lewiston, ID 83501. TEL 208-799-2470. Ed. Jeff Grygny. adv. **Document type:** newspaper.

378 US
PEABODY NEWS. 1981. 5/yr. free. Johns Hopkins University, Peabody Institute, 1 E. Mt. Vernon Place, Baltimore, MD 21202-2397. TEL 301-659-8163. FAX 301-783-8576. URL: http://www.peabody.jhv.edu. Ed. Anne Garside. R&P contact: Anne Garside. adv.; illus.; circ. 25,000. (controlled). **Document type:** newsletter.
Supersedes: Peabody Notes (ISSN 0031-3440)

378.1 US ISSN 0031-3459
LH1.G28
PEABODY REFLECTOR. 1927. s-a. free to qualified personnel. George Peabody College for Teachers, Alumni Association, Box 161, Nashville, TN 37203. TEL 615-322-2601. Ed. Jean Crawford. illus.; index; circ. 25,000. (controlled).

378.1 CN ISSN 0031-3629
PEAK. 1965. 39/yr. Can.$36. Peak Publications Society, Simon Fraser Univ., Burnaby, BC V5A 1S6, Canada. TEL 604-291-3598. FAX 604-291-3786. adv.; bk.rev. circ. 10,000. (tabloid format) **Document type:** newspaper.

378 US
PENDULUM. 1974. w. Elon College, Campus Box 2800, Elon College, NC 27244. TEL 910-584-2331. FAX 910-584-2467. E-mail: pendulum@vax1.elon.edu. adv.: B&W page $210. circ. 3,000. **Document type:** newspaper.
Description: Covers news of Elon College and the local community.

378 US
THE PENN. 1927. 3/yr (Fall, Spring, Summer). $50. Student Cooperative Association, 319 Pratt Dr., Indiana, PA 15701. TEL 412-349-6160. FAX 412-463-9597. Ed. Tom Charles. adv. contact: Mark Palmo. bk.rev. circ. 11,000. **Document type:** newspaper.

378.198 US
PENN STATER. 1910. bi-m. $30 membership. Penn State Alumni Association, 105 Old Main, University Park, PA 16802. TEL 814-865-2709. FAX 814-863-5690. E-mail: penn-stater@psu.edu; URL: http://www.alumni.alu.psu.edu. Ed. Tina Hay. R&P contact: Marjorie Sente. TEL 814-863-4546. adv. contact: Marjorie Sente. illus. circ. 125,000. **Document type:** consumer publication.
Description: Information about Penn State, the Penn State Alumni Association, and alumni.

378 US
PENNSYLVANIA GAZETTE. 1902. m. $28. University of Pennsylvania, Philadelphia, PA 19104. TEL 215-898-5555. Ed. Anthony A. Lyle. adv.; bk.rev. circ. 80,000. **Document type:** consumer publication.
Description: Contains articles for the alumni of the University of Pennsylvania.

378 AG ISSN 0327-9901
PENSAMIENTO UNIVERSITARIO. 1993. 3/yr. Arg.$10 per no.; foreign $75/yr. Casilla de Correo 333, Suc. 12-B, 1412 Buenos Aires, Argentina. TEL 54-1-8058429. FAX 54-1-8037001. Ed. Pedro Krotsch.

378 US
THE PERSPECTIVE (WAUKESHA). 1874. fortn. $18. Carroll College, 100 E. College Ave., Waukesha, WI 53186. TEL 414-524-7351. FAX 414-524-7139. Ed. Rene Schweitzer. adv.; bk.rev. circ. 1,200. **Document type:** newspaper.
Formerly: New Perspective.

378.18 US
PERSPECTIVES (INDIANAPOLIS). 1974. members only. Association of Fraternity Advisors, Inc., 3901 W. 86th St., Ste. 390, Indianapolis, IN 46268-1702. TEL 317-876-4691. FAX 317-872-1134. URL: http://sa.acusd.edu/afa/. Ed. Peter Smithhisler. R&P contact: Gayle Webb. circ. 950. **Document type:** newsletter.
Formerly: A F A Newsletter.
Description: Publishes articles pertaining to campus advisement of fraternities and sororities.

378 CN
LE PETIT MENSUEL. 1983. m. College d'Enseignement Generale et Professionnel, CEGEP St. Jean sur Richelieu, 1581 Dufresne, Montreal, Que. H2K 3J6, Canada. TEL 514-526-0235. adv. circ. 2,500.

378 CN ISSN 0712-2705
PETITE CAISSE.* (Text in French) 1980. s-m. free. Publi-Peq, 3575 bd. St. Laurent, Ste.232, Montreal, PQ H2X 2T7, Canada. TEL 514-845-8628. (Co-sponsor: Universite du Quebec a Chicoutimi) circ. 6,000.
Formerly: Alternatif.

371.85 US
PHI ETA SIGMA. FORUM. a. Auburn University at Montgomery, Montgomery, AL 36193. TEL 205-826-5856. circ. 20,000.

378 US
PHI GAMMA DELTA. 1879. q. $1 per no. Phi Gamma Delta Fraternity, Box 4599, Lexington, KY 40544-4599. TEL 606-255-1848. Ed. William Martin. circ. 79,000.
Description: Publishes college and fraternity news.

378 US ISSN 0093-5328
PHI KAPPA PHI NEWSLETTER. 1969. bi-m. membership Honor Society of Phi Kappa Phi (Baton Rouge), Box 16000, Louisiana State University, Baton Rouge, LA 70893. Ed. John E. Braithwaite, Jr. bk.rev. circ. 125,000. (back issues avail.) **Document type:** newsletter.
—CCC.
Description: Articles on outstanding Phi Kappa Phi members and national and regional organization activities.

371.85 US ISSN 0022-3581
R745
PHI RHO SIGMA. JOURNAL. Key Title: Journal of Phi Rho Sigma. 1900. q. membership only. Phi Rho Sigma Medical Society, Box 90264, Indianapolis, IN 46290-0264. TEL 317-255-4379. FAX 317-253-5067. Ed. Dr. James Jackson. bk.rev bibl.; illus.; circ. 16,000. (controlled).

378.1 US
PHILADELPHIA COLLEGE OF TEXTILES & SCIENCE. PORTFOLIO. 1988. s-a. free to alumni. Philadelphia College of Textiles & Science, Paul J. Gutman Library, 3243 School House Ln. & Henry Ave., Philadelphia, PA 19144-5497. TEL 215-951-285 FAX 215-951-2569. Ed. Christine Foy. circ. 15,000. **Document type:** newsletter.
Formerly: Alumni Update.
Description: Current news and events of the college, including features on faculty, alumni, students and staff.

378.1 PH ISSN 0031-7853
PHILIPPINE WOMEN'S UNIVERSITY ADMINISTRATIVE NEWS. q. Philippine Women's University, Taft Ave., Manila 2801, Philippines. Eds. Edgardo Ray Pedroche, Alegria A. Albano. illus. circ. 500.

378.1 PH ISSN 0031-8272
PHILWOMENIAN. (Text in English, Tagalog) m. free. Philippine Women's University, Taft Ave., Manila 2801, Philippines. Ed. Delia T. Arjona. illus.

378 CN ISSN 1189-9867
PHOENIX (ST. LAURENT). fortn. Vanier College, 821 Ste-Croix Blvd., St. Laurent, Que. H4L 3X9, Canad adv.; bk.rev.; film rev. circ. 4,000. (tabloid format) **Indexed:** SSCI.
Former titles: Issue (St. Laurent); End.

COLLEGE AND ALUMNI

371.805 US
THE PHOENIX (WESTMINSTER). 1981. bi-w. $15 (effective Sep. 1996). Western Maryland College, Attn: Phoenix, 2 College Hill, Westminster, MD 21157. TEL 410-751-8600. FAX 410-857-2729. Ed. Michelle Hamilton. adv.: page $47250; trim 15 x 10; adv. contact: Sara Gruber. dance rev.; film rev.; music rev.; play rev.; charts; illus. circ. 2,000. (tabloid format; back issues avail.) **Document type:** newspaper.
  Description: Student newspaper covering the school and student activities.

378 US
PHRENO - COSMIAN. 1906? 8/yr. $10. Dakota Wesleyan University, Mitchell, SD 57301. TEL 605-995-2814. Ed. Chad Larson. adv.; bk.rev. circ. 1,000. **Document type:** newspaper.

378 UK ISSN 0263-2128
PI; University College London students news. 1946. fortn. University College London Student Union, 25 Gordon Street, London WC1H 0AH, England. TEL 071-387-3611. FAX 071-383-3937. Ed. Luke Hoyland. adv.; bk.rev.; film rev.; play rev.; illus. circ. 3,500. (tabloid format)

378 US
PINE LOG. 1923. s-w. (Mon. & Thu.). $20 per academic yr. (free on campus). Stephen F. Austin State University, 13049 S.F.A. Sta., Nacogdoches, TX 75962. TEL 409-568-4703. FAX 409-568-1016. adv. circ. 7,000. (also avail. in microfiche) **Document type:** newspaper.

378.1 US
PIPE DREAM. 1970. s-w. $50 (effective 1995-1996). State University of New York at Binghamton, University Union, No.168, Binghamton, NY 13902. TEL 607-777-2515. FAX 607-777-2600. E-mail: pdream@binghamton.edu; URL: http://www.vive.com/connect/pipedream/. Ed. Carlos M. Granda. R&P contact: Kenneth S. Garson. adv.; bk.rev.; illus.; circ. 9,000 (controlled). (tabloid format; also avail. in microfiche) **Document type:** newspaper.

378 US
PITT MAGAZINE. 1986. q. $18. University of Pittsburgh, Department of University Relations, 400 Craig Hall, Pittsburgh, PA 15260. TEL 412-624-4147. FAX 412-624-1021. E-mail: pittmagt@pitt.edu; URL: http://www.pitt.edu/~pittmag/. Ed. Sally Ann Flecker. R&P contact: Sally Ann Flecker. adv. contact: Bill Young. bk.rev.; abstr.; charts; illus.; circ. 125,000 (controlled). (back issues avail.) **Indexed:** Environ.Abstr. **Document type:** academic/scholarly publication.
  Description: Covers the University, its alumni, and all subjects encompassed in the educational enterprise.

378.1 US
PITT NEWS. 1906. d. (Mon.-Thu.) (w. during Summer). $75. 434 William Pitt Union, University of Pittsburgh, Pittsburgh, PA 15260. TEL 412-648-7975. FAX 412-648-8491. R&P contact: Jim Tynen. adv.; bk.rev.; illus. (tabloid format) **Document type:** newspaper.

378 CN
THE PLANT (WESTMOUNT). 1971. w. Dawson College Student Union, 3040 Sherbrooke St. W., Westmount, PQ H3W 1A4, Canada. TEL 514-931-8731. FAX 514-931-1864. E-mail: paddie@dawsoncollege.qc.ca; URL: http://www.dawsoncollege/theplant/qc.ca. Ed.Bd. R&P contact: Paddie Chiara. adv.; bk.rev.; film rev. circ. 5,000. (tabloid format) **Indexed:** Can.B.P.I. **Document type:** newspaper.

081 US ISSN 0092-4318
AS36.K36 CODEN: PVREE7
PLATTE VALLEY REVIEW. 1973. s-a. $5. University of Nebraska at Kearney, Kearney, NE 68849. TEL 308-865-8295. E-mail: Plambeck@platte.UNK.edu. Ed. Vern Plambeck. illus. circ. 1,000. **Indexed:** M.L.A., MLA Intl.Bibl. **Document type:** academic/scholarly publication.
  —UnCover.

378 CN
PLUMBERS POT. 1904. 8/yr. Can.$4. McGill University, Engineering Undergraduate Society, McConnell Engineering Bldg., 3480 University, Montreal, Que. H3A 2A7, Canada. TEL 514-392-4311. Ed. Jeff Sprenger. adv. circ. 7,000. (tabloid format)

378 CN
LE POINGT.* (Text in French) s-m. free. Publi-Peq, 3575 bd. St. Laurent, Ste. 232, Montreal, PQ H2X 2T7, Canada. TEL 514-845-8628. (Co-sponsor: College de Shawinigan) circ. 800.

378.198 US
POINTER (WEST POINT). 1922. 6/yr. $20. United States Military Academy, Directorate of Cadet Activities, United States Corps of Cadet, West Point, NY 10996. TEL 914-938-2780. adv.; bk.rev. circ. 4,500. (back issues avail.)

378 CN
LE POLYSCOPE. (Text in French) 1967. w. (Sep.-Apr.). free. (Association des Etudiants de Polytechnique Inc.) Acces Media, 1124 Marie Anne Rd., East, Ste 31, Montreal, PQ H2J 2B7, Canada. TEL 514-340-4645. (Subscr. to: C.P. 6079 - Succ. A, Montreal, Que. H3C 3A7, Canada) adv. circ. 5,000. **Document type:** academic/scholarly publication.

378.198 US
POLYTECHNICABLE. 1970. q. Polytechnic University, 333 Jay St., Brooklyn, NY 11201. TEL 718-260-3400. circ. 35,000.
  Formerly (until Jul. 1987): Polytechnic Cable.

378.1 US
POMONA COLLEGE MAGAZINE. 1963. 3/yr. free. Pomona College, Alexander Hall 247, 550 N. College Ave., Claremont, CA 91711. TEL 909-621-8146. FAX 909-621-8203. Ed. Don Pattison. R&P contact: Donald Pattison. bk.rev.; illus. circ. 26,000.
  Former titles (until 1994): Pomona College Today (ISSN 1042-0827); (until 1988): Pomona Today (ISSN 0032-4183)

378 US
POOP SHEET SPORTS JOURNAL. 1977. fortn. $35. Sports Letter, Inc., Box 4323, Chapel Hill, NC 27515. TEL 919-967-7789. circ. 25,000. (tabloid format) **Document type:** newspaper.

378.1 US
POST (ATHENS). 1897. d. $35. (Ohio University) Derrick Cain, Ed. & Pub., 20 E. Union, Athens, OH 45701. TEL 614-593-4010. adv.; bk.rev.; film rev.; play rev.; charts; illus.; stat. circ. 12,000. (processed; also avail. in microform)
  Formerly: Ohio University Post (ISSN 0030-1205)

378 US
POST SCRIPT (COLUMBIA). 1947. fortn. $7.50. Columbia College, 312 Epworth, Columbia, SC 29203. TEL 803-786-3449. FAX 803-786-3674. Ed. Trish Willingham. adv. contact: Cindy Jamison. bk.rev. circ. 1,200. **Document type:** newspaper.

378 US
THE PRAIRIE. w. West Texas A&M University, Box 747, W.T. Sta., Canyon, TX 79016. TEL 806-656-2416. Ed. Jennifer Sicking. adv.: B&W page $236; adv. contact: Kevin D. Handley. **Document type:** newspaper.

378 CN ISSN 0383-7653
PRAIRIE HARVESTER. 1954. 4/yr. free. Prairie Bible Institute, Prairie Alumni Fellowship, Three Hills, AB T0M 2N0, Canada. TEL 403-443-5511. FAX 403-443-5540. Ed. Phil Callaway. bk.rev.; illus.; circ. 13,000 (controlled). **Document type:** newsletter.
  Description: News and information about Prairie Bible Institute for alumni and family.

378 US
PRATTFOLIO. 1983. 2/yr. free. Pratt Institute, Office of Alumni Resources, Brooklyn, NY 11205. R&P contact: Janet Fisher. circ. 27,000 (controlled). **Document type:** newsletter.

378 US ISSN 1071-4928
PRESBYTERIAN COLLEGE MAGAZINE. 1946. q. free. Presbyterian College, Office of Public Relations, Box 975, Clinton, SC 29325. TEL 864-833-2820. FAX 864-833-8481. E-mail: gvosburg@admin.presby.edu; URL: http://www.presby.edu. Ed. Grant Vosburgh. circ. 13,500 (controlled). **Document type:** academic/scholarly publication.
  Formerly (until 1993): Presbyterian College Report.
  Description: News of faculty, students, alumni, programs and achievements.

378.198 US
PRIDE (FAYETTEVILLE). s-m. Methodist College, 5400 Ramsey St., Fayetteville, NC 28311. TEL 910-630-7292. FAX 910-630-2123. Ed. Amanda Fellers. adv.; bk.rev. circ. 1,800. **Document type:** newspaper.
  Formerly: Small Talk.

378 US ISSN 0149-9270
LH1.P8
PRINCETON ALUMNI WEEKLY. 1900. 17/yr. $22 (foreign $26) (free to qualified personnel). Princeton Alumni Publications, 194 Nassau St., Princeton, NJ 08542. TEL 609-258-4885. FAX 609-258-2247. E-mail: paw@princeton.edu; URL: http://www.princeton.edu/~paw. Ed. J.I. Merritt. adv. contact: Beth Perrino. bk.rev.; illus.; circ. 59,000 (controlled). (back issues avail.) **Document type:** consumer publication.
  Supersedes: Alumni Princetonian.
  Description: Records news of the alumni and reviews without partiality the achievements and problems of the administration, the faculty, and the student body of Princeton University.

378 US
PRINCETON PARENTS. 1977. q. free to qualified personnel. Princeton University, Stanhoppe Hall, Princeton, NJ 08544. TEL 609-452-5734. Ed. Laurel Maston Cantor. circ. 13,000.

378.198 US
PRINCETON WEEKLY BULLETIN. 1975. 30/yr. $16 (free to qualified personnel). Princeton University, Stanhoppe Hall, Princeton, NJ 08544. TEL 609-452-3600. circ. 14,200.

378 SZ
PRISMA; Studentenzeitschrift der Universitaet St. Gallen. 1959. 7/yr. free. Universitaet St. Gallen, Hoehenweg 2, CH-9000 St. Gallen, Switzerland. TEL 41-71-2231727. FAX 41-71-2237470. E-mail: prisma@student.unisg.ch; URL: http://www.students.unisg.ch/~prisma/index.html. Ed. Patrick Mueller. R&P contact: Patrick Mueller. adv.: page 720 SFr.; adv. contact: Roger Bischof. (back issues avail.) **Document type:** bulletin.

378 US ISSN 0276-4830
AS30
PRO REGE. 1972. q. free. Dordt College, 498 Fourth Ave. N.E., Sioux Center, IA 51250. TEL 712-722-3771. FAX 712-722-1185. Ed. John Kok. circ. 3,000. **Indexed:** G.Soc.Sci.& Rel.Per.Lit. **Document type:** academic/scholarly publication.
  Description: Explores academic topics relevant to reformed Christian higher education.

378 CN ISSN 0032-9134
PRO TEM. (Text in English and French) 1961. w. (Sep.-Apr.). Can.$20. Glendon College, Student Union, 2275 Bayview Ave., Toronto, ON M4N 3M6, Canada. TEL 416-487-6736. adv.; bk.rev.; film rev.; play rev.; illus. circ. 4,000. (tabloid format) **Document type:** bulletin.

378 GW
PROFIL (BAD HARZBURG). 1964. q. DM.18. Werner-von-Siemens Gymnasium, Herzog-Wilhelm-Str. 25, 38667 Bad Harzburg, Germany. TEL 05322-4354. Ed. Eike Bruns. adv. (back issues avail.) **Document type:** bulletin.

378 US
THE PROFILE (CONWAY). 1913. bi-m. $25. Hendrix Student Association, Hendrix College, Conway, AR 72032. TEL 501-450-1269. Ed. Eric Dyer. adv. contact: Leslie Hager. bk.rev.; film rev.; music rev. circ. 1,200. (tabloid format; back issues avail.) **Document type:** newspaper.
  Description: Aims to cover campus news, issues and opinions. Serves as a medium for information, entertainment and debate.

378 US
PROMETHEAN (LOUDONVILLE). 1938. fortn. $4. Siena College, Loudonville, NY 12211. TEL 518-783-2560. circ. 2,400. **Document type:** newspaper.
  Formerly: Indian (Loudonville).

378 US
PROMETHEAN (SUPERIOR). 1920. w. $12 (effective Sep. 1996). University of Wisconsin at Superior, Holden Fine Arts Bldg., Superior, WI 54880. TEL 715-394-8387. FAX 715-394-8404. Ed.Bd. R&P contact: John Marder. adv. contact: Katie Gurgel. bk.rev. circ. 2,500. **Document type:** newspaper.

378.198 US
PROSPECTOR. 1914. s-w. $12. University of Texas at El Paso, Student Publications, 105 E. Union, UT, El Paso, TX 79968. TEL 915-747-5161. circ. 11,000. (tabloid format)

378 CN
PUBLI - P E Q.* 1981. irreg. free. Publi-PEQ, 3575 bd. St. Laurent, Ste. 232, Montreal, PQ H2X 2T7, Canada. TEL 514-845-8628. circ. 215,550. (tabloid format)

378.198 UK
THE PULSE. 1961. 6/yr. free. University of Sussex, Students Union, Falmer, Brighton, Sussex BN1 9QF, England. TEL 44-1273-678555. FAX 44-1273-678875. Ed. Jemima Kingsley. R&P contact: Jemima Kingsley. adv. contact: Nicola Stait. bk.rev.; film rev.; play rev.; illus. circ. 7,500. (tabloid format) **Document type:** consumer publication.
Former titles: Sussed; Unionews.

378 US ISSN 0883-6590
PULTENEY ST. SURVEY. 1973. q. free. Hobart & William Smith Colleges, 295 Pulteney St., Geneva, NY 14456. TEL 315-781-3540. FAX 315-781-3400. Ed. Dana Cooke. circ. 22,000.

378.1 US ISSN 0033-4502
LH1.P9
PURDUE ALUMNUS. 1912. 6/yr. membership. Purdue Alumni Association, Memorial Union Bldg. 160, W. Lafayette, IN 47906-6212. TEL 317-494-5175. FAX 317-494-9179. Ed. Tim Newton. adv. contact: Sharon Martin. circ. 65,000. **Indexed:** CAD CAM Abstr.

378 US
PURDUE EXPONENT. 1889. d. (during Fall & Spring). $45. Purdue University, 460 Northwestern Ave., Box 2506, W. Lafayette, IN 47906. TEL 317-743-1111. FAX 317-743-6087. circ. 22,000. **Document type:** newspaper.

378 CN ISSN 0706-8808
QUAD. 1953. a. Can.$12. Bishop's University, Students' Representative Council, c/o Box 2133, Lennoxville, PQ J1M 1Z7, Canada. TEL 819-569-9551. Ed. Eryn Whitehead. adv. circ. 1,050. **Document type:** newsletter.

378.1 US ISSN 0033-5045
QUAKER CAMPUS. 1914. w. $20 suggested donation. Whittier College, Quaker Campus, Box 8613, Whittier, CA 90608. TEL 310-907-4354. FAX 310-945-5301. adv.; bk.rev.; film rev.; play rev.; illus.; circ. 2,000 (controlled). (tabloid format)

378 CN ISSN 0843-8048
QUEEN'S ALUMNI REVIEW. 1927. bi-m. Can.$15 (effective 1997). Queen's University Alumni Association, Summerhill, 99 University Ave., Kingston, ON K7L 3N6, Canada. TEL 613-545-2060; 800-267-7837. FAX 613-545-6777. E-mail: cuthberk@post.queensu.ca. Ed. Ken Cuthbertson. adv.; bk.rev. circ. 80,000. (back issues avail.) **Document type:** consumer publication.
Description: Keeps Q.U. graduates up to date on new developments in all Faculties of the University, contains news of fellow graduates, and provides opinions and comments on news of current interest to grads.

378 CN
QUEEN'S JOURNAL. 1873. s-w. (Sep.-Apr.); w. (May-Aug.). Can.$12. Queen's University, Alma Mater Society Inc., Kingston, ON K7L 3N6, Canada. TEL 613-547-5511. Ed. Chris Armstrong. adv.; bk.rev.; film rev. circ. 9,500. (also avail. in microfiche)

378 CN
THE QUILL. 1910. w. Can.$20 (foreign Can.$30). Brandon University, 270 18th Ave., Brandon, MB R7A 6A9, Canada. TEL 204-727-9660. FAX 204-726-3498. Ed. Trevor Rinn. adv.; bk.rev.; film rev. circ. 2,000. (tabloid format) **Document type:** newspaper.

378.1 US
QUINCY UNIVERSITY BULLETIN. 1944. 4/yr. free. Quincy University, Office of Public Relations, Quincy, IL 62301. TEL 217-222-8020. FAX 217-228-5473. Ed. Pam Sherman. R&P contact: Pam Sherman. TEL 217-228-5275. illus. circ. 12,000. (processed) **Document type:** bulletin.
Formerly (until 1993): Quincy College Bulletin (ISSN 0033-6556)

R A U - RAPPORT. (Rand Afrikaans University) see EDUCATION — Higher Education

378 US
R U MAGAZINE. 1979. 3/yr. free. Radford University, Office of Public Information, Box 6916, Radford, VA 24142. TEL 703-831-5182. FAX 703-831-5036. Ed. Rob Tucker. adv.; bk.rev. circ. 48,000.
Formerly (until July 1993): Radford.

378.1 AT
RABELAIS. 1968. fortn. (during school term). Aus.$12. La Trobe University, Students Representative Council, Bundoora, Vic. 3083, Australia. Ed.Bd. adv.; bk.rev.; film rev.; play rev.; illus. circ. 15,000.

378.1 US ISSN 0033-930X
RACQUET (LA CROSSE). 1909. w. (during school yr.). free. University of Wisconsin at La Crosse, La Crosse, WI 54601. TEL 608-785-8378. adv. circ. 5,000. (tabloid format) **Indexed:** Sports Per.Ind., Sportsearch. **Document type:** newspaper.

378.1 US ISSN 0033-7447
RACQUETTE. 1926. w. free. State University of New York, College at Potsdam, 119 Borrington Student Union, Potsdam, NY 13676. TEL 315-267-8451. FAX 315-267-2170. Ed. Jude Kiah. adv.; bk.rev.; film rev.; play rev.; charts; illus.; circ. 3,500 (controlled). (tabloid format)

378.198 US ISSN 1042-3052
RADCLIFFE NEWS. 1980. q. free. Radcliffe College, Office of Communications, 10 Garden St., Cambridge, MA 02138. TEL 617-495-8608. FAX 617-496-4640. Ed. Liz Brown-Lavoie. illus.; circ. 50,000 (controlled). (tabloid format) **Document type:** newsletter.
Formerly: Second Century Radcliffe News.
Description: For alumnae and students. Covers events at the college.

378.1 US ISSN 0033-7528
LH1.R2
RADCLIFFE QUARTERLY. 1916. q. free. Radcliffe College, Alumnae Association, 10 Garden St., Cambridge, MA 02138. TEL 617-495-8608. FAX 617-496-0255. Ed. Diane Sherlock. bk.rev.; charts; illus.; circ. 35,000 (controlled). **Document type:** academic/scholarly publication.
Description: For students and alumnae. Covers issues of interest to educated women.

378 US
THE RAM PAGE. 1936. w. Angelo State University, Department of Communication, Drama and Journalism, 2601 W. Ave. N., San Angelo, TX 76909. TEL 915-942-2322. FAX 915-942-2078. E-mail: ram.page@mailserv.angelo.edu; URL: http://www.angelo.edu/aorg.rampage. Ed. Jerry Becker, Jr. adv. contact: Cindee Sharp. bk.rev.; circ. 4,500 (controlled). **Document type:** newspaper.

378.1 US
RANDOLPH-MACON COLLEGE. BULLETIN. 1930. 3/yr. free. Randolph-Macon College, Ashland, VA 23005. TEL 804-752-4721. FAX 804-752-3712. E-mail: levans@rmc.edu. Ed. Linda N. Evans. R&P contact: Linda N. Evans. circ. 12,100. **Document type:** bulletin.
Formerly: Randolph-Macon Alumni Bulletin (ISSN 0033-9180)

378 US
RANGER (AMARILLO). 1929. w. free. Amarillo College, Box 447, Amarillo, TX 79178. TEL 806-371-5290. FAX 806-371-5370. Ed. Elane Harvey. adv.; bk.rev. circ. 2,500. **Document type:** newspaper.

371.83 UK ISSN 0048-6809
RATCLIFFIAN. 1870. a. £6. Ratcliffe College, Syston, Leicestershire, England. TEL 44-1509-817000. FAX 44-1509-817004. Ed. Terence Stanford. ad. illus.; index. circ. 1,000. **Document type:** bulletin.

378 US
THE RATTLE. 1912. s-a. Theta Chi Funds for Leadership and Education, Inc., 3330 Founders R Indianapolis, IN 46268. TEL 317-824-1881. FAX 317-824-1908. E-mail: IHQ@thetachi.org; U http://www.a1.com/thetachi/. Ed. El Ahlwardt. R contact: El Ahlwardt. adv. contact: El Ahlwardt. bk.rev.; circ. 32,000 (controlled). **Document type:** trade publication.
Formerly: Rattle of Theta Chi.
Description: Provides leadership and education information in support of fundraising programs.

378.198 US
RAVEN REVIEW. 1987. 3/m. free. Coffeyville Community College, 400 W. 11th, Coffeyville, KS 67337. TEL 316-251-7700. FAX 316-251-779. E-mail: nancym@raven.ccc.cc.ks.us. Ed. Nancy March. circ. 8,000. (tabloid format; back issues avail.)
Description: Contains alumni news, faculty upda and campus information.

378.1 US
THE RECORD (BUFFALO). 1913. s-w. (Tue., Fri. durin school yr.). $20. State University of New York, College at Buffalo, United Students Government, I Cassety, Rm. 109, 1300 Elmwood Ave., Buffalo, 14222. TEL 716-878-4531. FAX 716-878-660C Ed. Margaret Coghlan. adv.: page $388; trim 5 x 16; adv. contact: Stephanie Brizard. bk.rev.; rev.; film rev.; illus. circ. 10,000. (tabloid format) **Document type:** newspaper.
Former titles: Buffalo State Record; State Univer: of New York. College at Buffalo. Record (ISSN 0039-0186)

378 US ISSN 0745-1679
THE RECORD OF SIGMA ALPHA EPSILON. 1880. q. free to qualified personnel. Sigma Alpha Epsilon Nation Fraternity, Box 1856, Evanston, IL 60204. TEL 708-475-1856. Ed. Pete C. Stevenson. circ. 81,000 (controlled).
—UnCover.
Description: Covers chapter news, alumni news, directory and major fraternity activities.

378 US
RED AND BLACK (ATHENS). (Supplements avail.: Between the Hedges, Apartment Life, Courtside Addition) 1893. d. (Mon.-Fri.). $30. 123 N. Jacks St., Athens, GA 30601. TEL 706-543-1791. FAX 706-548-7251. Ed. Harry Montevideo. adv. contact: Cathy Rauffman. circ. 16,000. **Document type:** newspaper.

378.198 US
RED AND BLACK (BALTIMORE). 1958. s-m. Catonsville Community College, 800 S. Rolling Rd., Baltimore, MD 21228. TEL 301-455-4485. Ed. Kitty William adv. circ. 4,000. (tabloid format)
Description: Covers campus news and sports, student organizations and clubs.

378.1 US ISSN 0034-1940
RED AND BLACK (WASHINGTON). 1909. s-m. free to students and faculty. Washington & Jefferson College, 60 S. Lincoln St., Washington, PA 15301. TEL 412-222-4400. adv.; film rev.; circ. 1,500 (controlled). (tabloid format)

378.1 US ISSN 0034-1959
RED AND GREEN. 1923. w. Minot State University, Publications Board, 500 University Ave. W., Minot, ND 58707. TEL 701-858-3354. FAX 701-858-3353. URL: http://www.misu.nodak.edu/redgreen/. adv. contact: Karen Holmen. bk.rev. play rev.; illus. circ. 3,000. **Document type:** newspaper.

378 UK
REDBRICK; the University of Birmingham student newspaper. 1950. bi-w. free. Birmingham University Guild of Students, Edgbaston Park Rd., Edgbaston, Birmingham B12 2TU, England. TEL 0121-472-1841. FAX 0121-472-2099. Ed. Roland Buerk. circ. 3,500. **Document type:** newspaper.

COLLEGE AND ALUMNI

378   CN
REFLECTOR. 1965. fortn. Can.$15. Reflector Publications Society, 4825 Richard Rd., S.W., Calgary, AB T3E 6K6, Canada. TEL 403-240-6268. FAX 403-240-6762. E-mail: reflecto@cadvision.com. Ed. Ivar Bergs. R&P contact: Ivar Bergs. adv. contact: Ivar Bergs. bk.rev.; film rev. circ. 10,000. (tabloid format) **Document type:** newspaper.

378   GW   ISSN 0557-6377
REGENSBURGER UNIVERSITAETSZEITUNG. 1976. 7/yr. DM.10 (effective 1997). Universitaet Regensburg, Pressestelle, 93040 Regensburg, Germany. TEL 49-941-943-2302. FAX 49-941-943-4929. E-mail: rudolf.dietze@verwaltung.uni-regensburg.de; URL: http://www.uni-regensburg.de. Ed. Rudolf Dietze. R&P contact: Rudolf Dietze. adv.: page DM.710. bk. rev. circ. 6,000. (back issues avail.) **Document type:** newspaper.
   Description: Review of research activities and academic affairs at the university.

387   US
REGIS TODAY. 1936. 3/yr. free to qualified personnel. Regis College, Publications Office, 235 Wellesley St., Weston, MA 02193. TEL 617-768-7000. URL: http://www.regiscollege.edu. Ed. Anne Souza. bk.rev. circ. 12,000.
   Description: Articles about and of interest to alumnae, students, parents, faculty and administration of the College.

378.1   US
RENSSELAER POLYTECHNIC. 1869. w. $40. Rensselaer Union, Box 35, Rensselaer Union, Troy, NY 12180-3590. TEL 518-276-8728. FAX 518-276-8728. Ed. Thanh Nguyen. adv.; bk.rev.; film rev.; play rev.; illus. circ. 10,000. (tabloid format) **Document type:** newspaper.
   Formerly: Polytechnic (ISSN 0032-4051)

378   CN
LA REPLIQUE.* (Text in French) m. free. Publi-Peq, 3575 bd. St. Laurent, Ste. 232, Montreal, PQ H2X 2T7, Canada. TEL 514-845-8628. (Co-sponsor: College de Victoriaville) circ. 500.

378   US
REPORT (OXFORD). w. Miami University, 213 Macmillan Hall, Oxford, OH 45056. Ed. Carolyn Riegel. (tabloid format) **Document type:** newspaper.
   Description: Covers events on the home campus and the university's campus in Luxembourg.

378   US
REPORTER (RIVER FOREST). 1923. bi-w. free. Rosary College, 7900 W. Division, River Forest, IL 60305. TEL 708-524-6035. FAX 708-366-5360. adv. (tabloid format; also avail. in microfilm) **Document type:** newspaper.

378   CN
REPUBLIQUE. (Text in French) m. College d'Enseignement Generale et Professionnel (Vieux-Montreal), P.O. Box 1444, Sta. N, Montreal, PQ H2X 3M8, Canada. TEL 514-982-3437. FAX 514-982-3448. Ed. Jean Pierre Couture. circ. 3,000. **Document type:** newspaper.
   Formerly: Mon Vieux Real (ISSN 0228-8745)

378   US
RESPONSE (SEATTLE). 1975. bi-m. free. Seattle Pacific University, Office of University Relations, Third Ave. W. & W. Nickerson, Seattle, WA 98119. Ed. Jennifer Johnson Gilnett. circ. 30,000.

378 600   CK   ISSN 0120-1557
REVISTA DE EGRESADOS. 1976. q. free. Universidad Tecnologica de Pereira, Asociacion de Egresados, Apdo. Aereo 97, Pereira Risaralda, Colombia. circ. 3,000.

378   BD
REVUE LE FLAMBEAU. (Text in French) q.? Association des Etudiants de Rumuri, B.P. 1550, Bujumbura, Burundi. **Indexed:** P.L.E.S.A.

378   CN
REVUE MATRICULE.* (Text in French) s-m. Publi-Peq, 3575 bd. St. Laurent, Ste. 232, Montreal, PQ H2X 2T7, Canada. TEL 514-526-0235. circ. 17,000.

378   US
RHODE ISLAND COLLEGE ALUMNI MAGAZINE. 1952. s-a. free to qualified personnel. Rhode Island College, Alumni Association, 600 Mt. Pleasant Ave., Providence, RI 02908. TEL 401-456-8086. FAX 401-456-8851. Ed. Ellie O'Neill. adv.; circ. 28,000 (paid). **Document type:** academic/scholarly publication, newsletter.
   Former titles: Perspectives (Providence); (until 1986): Rhode Island College Alumni Association. Alumni Review; Rhode Island College Alumni Association. Review (ISSN 0035-4589)

378.1   SA
RHODES NEWSLETTER. (Text in English) 1951. 2/yr. free. Rhodes University, P.O. Box 94, Grahamstown 6140, South Africa. TEL 27-461-318569. FAX 27-461-311902. E-mail: adlg@giraffe.ru.ac.za; URL: http://www.ru.ac.za. Ed. Lisl Griffioen Paterson. adv.; bk.rev. circ. 19,000. **Document type:** newsletter.
   Supersedes in part (in 1993): Rhodes Review; Which was formerly: Rhodes Newsletter (ISSN 0035-4678)

378.1   SA
RHODES TODAY. (Text in English) 1975. a. free. Rhodes University, P.O. Box 94, Grahamstown 6140, South Africa. TEL 27-461-318517. FAX 27-461-311902. E-mail: adbb@warthog.ru.ac.za. Ed. Mary Burnett. **Document type:** academic/scholarly publication.
   Supersedes in part (in 1996): Rhodes Review and Annual Report; Which supersedes in part (in 1993): Rhodes Review; Which was formerly: Rhodes Newsletter (ISSN 0035-4678)

378   SA
RHODES UNIVERSITY. ANNUAL REPORT. (Text in English) 1975. a. free. Rhodes University, Office of the Vice Chancellor, P.O. Box 94, Grahamstown 6140, South Africa. TEL 27-461-318517. FAX 27-461-311902. URL: http://www.ru.ac.za. circ. 24,000. **Document type:** corporate report.
   Supersedes in part (in 1996): Rhodes Review and Annual Report; Which supersedes in part (in 1993): Rhodes Review; Which was formerly: Rhodes Newsletter (ISSN 0035-4678)

378.198   US
RICE THRESHER. 1916. w. $40. Rice University, Student Publications, 6100 Main St., Houston, TX 77005. TEL 713-527-4801. FAX 713-285-5238. E-mail: thresher@rice.edu; URL: http://www.rice.edu/thresher. adv.; bk.rev.; film rev.; play rev. circ. 6,000. (tabloid format) **Document type:** newspaper.
● Also available online.

378.198   US   ISSN 1076-6677
RIDER UNIVERSITY MAGAZINE. 1991. q. free to alumni and friends. Rider University, 2083 Lawrenceville Rd., Lawrenceville, NJ 08648-3099. TEL 609-869-5165. FAX 609-895-5440. E-mail: kilmer@rider.edu; URL: http://www.rider.edu. Ed. Dana Kilmer. circ. 32,500 (controlled). **Document type:** academic/scholarly publication.
   Formerly (until 1994): Rider College Magazine (ISSN 1060-4316); Supersedes (1971-1991): Directions (Lawrenceville) (ISSN 0279-408X)

378   US
RIO (EDINBURG). a. University of Texas - Pan American, Student Publications, CAS 170, Edinburg, TX 78539-2999. TEL 210-381-2541. FAX 210-316-7122.
   Formerly: Rio (Edinburg).
   Description: Contains news and features about the University.

378   US   ISSN 1058-1855
RIPON MAGAZINE. 1968. 4/yr. free. Ripon College, Box 248, Ripon, WI 54971. TEL 414-748-8364. FAX 414-748-9262. Ed. Loren J. Boone. R&P contact: Loren J. Boone. bk.rev.; illus.; circ. 14,000 (controlled). **Document type:** bulletin.
   Formerly: Ripon College Magazine (ISSN 0300-7928)

378.1   US   ISSN 0035-7510
ROCKHURST HAWK. 1917. fortn. $4. Rockhurst College, 1100 Rockhurst Rd., Kansas City, MO 64110-2561. TEL 816-926-4051. E-mail: hawk@vax1.rockhurst.edu. Ed. Mark E. Costaldi. adv.; Robert J./Remack. bk.rev.; illus. circ. 1,500. (reprint service avail. from UMI,ISI) **Document type:** newspaper.

378.1   US   ISSN 0035-7936
ROLLINS SANDSPUR. 1894. w. $30. Rollins College Student Association, Rollins College, Box 2742, Winter Park, FL 32789. TEL 305-646-2000. Ed. Jonathan Chisdes. adv.; bk.rev.; illus. circ. 2,000. (also avail. in microfilm)

378   CN
ROTONDE. (Text in French) 1932. w. Can.$25. Federation Etudiante de l'Universite d'Ottawa, 85 University, Ottawa, ON K1N 6N5, Canada. TEL 613-562-5264. FAX 613-562-5265. E-mail: rotonde@aix2.uottawa.ca; URL: http://www.aix2.uottawa.ca/~rotonde/. Ed. Anik Lalonde. adv.; bk.rev.; film rev. circ. 8,000. (tabloid format) **Document type:** newspaper.

378   US   ISSN 1071-9369
ROTUNDA. 1921. w. $30. Longwood College, Box 1133, Farmville, VA 23901. TEL 804-395-2120. FAX 804-395-2237. adv.; bk.rev. circ. 3,000. **Indexed:** RILM.

378   US   ISSN 1053-5020
ROUND TABLE (BELOIT). 1853. w. (during school yr.) $15 (foreign $30). Beloit College, Box 109, Beloit, WI 53511. TEL 608-363-2475. adv. circ. 2,000. **Document type:** newspaper.

378   US   ISSN 0744-5555
ROUND UP. 1907. 2/w. $55. New Mexico State University, Box 30004, Dept. CC, University Park, NM 88003. TEL 505-646-6397. E-mail: roundup@nmsu.edu; URL: www.nmsu.edu/~roundup. Ed. Deanna Fisher. adv. contact: Mike Watson. **Document type:** newspaper.

378   US
ROYAL PURPLE. 1901. w. $15. University of Wisconsin at Whitewater, 268 E. University Center, Whitewater, WI 53190. TEL 414-472-5100. Ed. Aaron Hanson. adv. circ. 7,000.

378.1   AU   ISSN 0013-2489
RUNDBRIEF EHEMALIGER SCHUELER UND FREUNDE DER SCHULBRUEDER. 1948. s-a. S.90. Provinzialat der Brueder der Christlichen Schulen, Anton Boeckgasse 20, A-1215 Vienna, Austria. adv.; bk.rev.; abstr.; bibl.; charts; illus.; stat. circ. 3,000.

378.1   GW   ISSN 0035-998X
LH5.H4
RUPERTO-CAROLA. 1948. 4/yr. DM.60; newsstand price: DM.10. (Rektor der Universitaet Heidelberg) Universitaetsverlag C. Winter Heidelberg GmbH, Hans-Bunte-Str. 18, 69123 Heidelberg, Germany. TEL 49-6221-770260. FAX 49-6221-770269. E-mail: presse@urz.uni-heidelberg.de. Ed. Michael Schwarz. adv. contact: Edeltraud Conen. bk.rev.; abstr.; bibl.; charts; illus.; stat.; index, cum.index. circ. 2,200. **Indexed:** Amer.Hist.& Life (1955-1959), (1970-1978), Hist.Abstr. (1955-1959), (1970-1978), MLA Intl.Bibl. **Document type:** bulletin. —CCC.

378   GW   ISSN 0944-4181
RUPRECHT KARLS UNIVERSITAET HEIDELBERG. PERSONALVERZEICHNIS. a. DM.6. Universitaetsverlag C. Winter Heidelberg GmbH, Hans-Bunte-Str. 18, 69123 Heidelberg, Germany. TEL 49-6221-770260. FAX 49-6221-770269. adv. **Document type:** academic/scholarly publication.
   Formerly (until 1993): Ruprecht Karls Universitaet Heidelberg. Personal- und Informationsverzeichnis (ISSN 0178-5338)

367   US
RUTGERS MAGAZINE. 1914. 4/yr. $12. Rutgers University, Department of University Communications, Alexander Johnston Hall, New Brunswick, NJ 08903. TEL 908-932-7315. FAX 908-932-8412. E-mail: lcahmbe@communications.rutgers.edu. Ed. Lori Chambers. adv.; bk.rev.; illus.; circ. 110,000 (controlled). (back issues avail.)
   Former titles: Rutgers Alumni Magazine (ISSN 0036-0457); Rutgers Alumni Monthly; Rutger University. Alumni Quarterly; **Incorporates:** Matrix; Rutgers Today.

COLLEGE AND ALUMNI

378   CN
RYERSON MAGAZINE. 1962. 2/yr. free. Ryerson Polytechnic University, Office of University Advancement, 350 Victoria St., Toronto, ON M5B 2K3, Canada. TEL 416-979-5304.
FAX 416-979-5166. Ed. Ivana Benn. R&P contact: Ivana Benn. adv.: B&W page Can.$1680;
8 1/2 x 11; adv. contact: Ivana Benn. circ. 65,000 (controlled).
    Formerly: Ryerson Rambler (ISSN 0705-9191)
    Description: Focuses on university news and developments.

S A I S REVIEW; a journal of international affairs. (Paul H. Nitze School of Advanced International Studies) see POLITICAL SCIENCE — International Relations

378   US
S D S U ALUMNUS. 1910. 3/yr. free. South Dakota State University, Alumni Association, Tompkins Alumni Center, Box 515, Brookings, SD 57007. TEL 605-697-5198. FAX 605-697-5487. E-mail: Nan@foundation.SDstate.edu. Ed. Nan Steinley. adv. circ. 40,000. (tabloid format) **Document type:** newspaper.
    Description: Publishes campus news, university sports news, and alumni news.

378   US
S D S U MAGAZINE; for alumni and friends of San Diego State University. 1994. q. San Diego State University, University Communications, 5500 Campanile Dr., San Diego, CA 92182-0763. TEL 619-594-5204. FAX 619-594-5956. E-mail: sdsumag@mail.sdsu.edu. Ed. Rice Moore. adv.: page $3500; trim 8 1/2 x 10 3/4; adv. contact: Rick Moore. circ. 110,000 (controlled).
    Description: Contains features and news about the university.

378   CN
S R C BULLETIN. w. Bishop's University, Students' Representative Council, c/o Box 2133, Lennoxville, PQ J1M 1Z7, Canada. TEL 819-822-9697. **Document type:** newsletter.

378   GW
S V ZEITUNG. 1884. q. (Sondenhaeuser Verband) Georgi GmbH, Theaterstr. 77, 52062 Aachen, Germany. Ed. Johannes Zuehlsdorff. circ. 5,000.

378   US
SAGA OF SIGMA TAU GAMMA. 1927. q. $20 to libraries only. Sigma Tau Gamma Fraternity, Box 54, Warrensburg, MO 64093. TEL 816-747-2222. FAX 816-747-9599. E-mail: sigmatauagamma.org. Ed. Kyle Steinhouser; Pub. William P. Bernier. R&P contact: Kyle Steinhauser. adv. contact: Kyle Steinhauser. circ. 28,000 (controlled). **Document type:** newsletter.
    Description: Covers activities of the 86 chapters and 50,000 alumni members of the fraternity.

378   US
SAGAMORE. 1969. w. Indiana University, 425 Agnes St., Indianapolis, IN 46202. TEL 317-274-2976. circ. 12,000.

378   US
SAGEBRUSH. 1893. 2/w. $15. Associated Students of University of Nevada, Mail Stop 058, Reno, NV 89557. TEL 702-784-4033. FAX 702-784-4479. E-mail: gopher@unr.edu. Ed. James Welborn. adv.; bk.rev.; film rev. circ. 12,000. **Document type:** newspaper.

378.198   US   ISSN 0747-1025
ST. CLOUD STATE CHRONICLE. 1892. s-w. $20. St. Cloud State University, 13 Stewart Hall, St. Cloud, MN 56301. TEL 320-255-4086. Ed. Eric Hedlund. adv. contact: David Tjornhom. circ. 7,000. (tabloid format) **Document type:** newspaper.

378   UK
ST. EDWARDS SCHOOL CHRONICLE. 1863. s-a. St. Edwards School, Woodstock Rd., Oxford OX2 7NN, England. TEL 44-1865-319231.
FAX 44-1865-319202. Ed. N.R. Quartley. circ. 6,300. (back issues avail.) **Document type:** bulletin.

378.1   CN
ST. FRANCIS XAVIER UNIVERSITY ALUMNI NEWS. 1963. 3/yr. Can.$21. St. Francis Xavier University, P.O. Box 5000, Antigonish, NS B2G 2W5, Canada. TEL 902-867-2286. Eds. Kimberly Dickson, Verna MacDonald. adv.; bk.rev.; illus. circ. 21,500.
Document type: bulletin.
    Formerly: St. Francis Xavier University Contemporary and Alumni News (ISSN 0036-2824)

378   US
SAINT JOHN'S. 1961. q. free to alumni. Saint John's University, Collegeville, MN 56321.
TEL 612-363-2594. FAX 612-363-3446. Ed. Lee A. Hanley. bk.rev. circ. 22,000. **Document type:** newsletter.
    Description: Covers college activities and developments of interest to alumni.

ST. JOHN'S REPORTER. see EDUCATION — Higher Education

ST. JOHN'S REVIEW. see EDUCATION — Higher Education

378.1   CN   ISSN 0036-3138
SAINT MARY'S UNIVERSITY JOURNAL. 1935. w. Can.$35. Saint Mary's University, Journal Publishing Society, Ste. 517, SUB, Halifax, NS B3H 3C3, Canada. TEL 902-496-8200. FAX 902-496-8209. adv.; bk.rev.; film rev.; play rev. circ. 7,500. (tabloid format) **Document type:** newspaper.
    Description: Covers University news, arts, entertainment and sports; current affairs of Canadian universities.

378.198   US
SAINT PETER'S; the college magazine. vol.11, no.2, 1992. 3/yr. membership only. Saint Peter's College, Office of Communications, Dorothy Day House, 35 Glenwood Ave., Jersey City, NJ 07306.
TEL 201-915-9160. Ed. Rose Duger. **Document type:** consumer publication.
    Description: News of the college and its alumni.

378   US
SALEM STATE LOG. 1927. bi-w. free. Salem State College, Department of English, 352 Lafayette St., Salem, MA 01970-4589. TEL 508-741-7920. FAX 508-740-7204. Ed. Jon Zahlaway. R&P contact: Ellen Golub. circ. 4,000. **Document type:** newspaper.
    Description: College literary magazine.

378   IO
SALEMBA;* suratkabar kampus Universitas Indonesia. 1976. fortn. Rps.50 per no. University of Indonesia, Jalan Salemba Raya 4, Jakarta 10430, Indonesia.

378   US
SAMFORD CRIMSON. 1915. fortn. Samford University, Box 2269, Birmingham, AL 35229.
TEL 205-870-2474. Ed. Gina Dykeman.

371.85 378   US
SCALPEL. 1931. s-a. $3.50. Alpha Epsilon Delta, Jones Junior College, Ellisville, MS 39437.
TEL 601-426-6019. Ed. Hugh E. Bateman. adv.; bk.rev.; illus. circ. 8,500. **Indexed:** C.I.S. Abstr. **Document type:** academic/scholarly publication.

378.198   US
SCEPTER. 1968. m. free. City University of New York, Kingsborough Community College, 2001 Oriental Blvd., Brooklyn, NY 11235. TEL 718-934-5603. Ed. Thomas Vellios. adv.; bk.rev. circ. 10,000. (tabloid format; back issues avail.)

378   GW   ISSN 0448-1348
LH5.B7
SCHLESISCHE FRIEDRICH-WILHELMS-UNIVERSITAET. JAHRBUCH. 1955. a. DM.58. (Stiftung Kulturwerk Schlesien) Jan Thorbecke Verlag GmbH und Co., Postfach 546, 72482 Sigmaringen, Germany.
TEL 49-7571-728100. FAX 49-7571-728287. bk.rev. **Document type:** academic/scholarly publication.

378   US
SCHOLASTIC MAGAZINE. 1867. w. $30. University of Notre Dame, La Fortune Center, Notre Dame, 303 LaFortune Student Center, IN 46556-5635.
TEL 219-239-7569. FAX 219-63-9648. E-mail: scholastic.scholast.1@nd.edu. (Subscr. to: Business Manager, Scholastic, 303 La Fortune, Notre Dame, IN 46556) Ed. Steve Myers. R&P contact: Steve Myers. TEL 219-631-5029. adv. contact: Jenny Stachowiak. bk.rev.; film rev.; play rev. circ. 8,070. (back issues avail.)
    Description: Campus magazine highlighting the entertainment, student life, and sports concerning the University of Notre Dame.
    Refereed Serial

SCHOOL OF BUSINESS UPDATE. see BUSINESS AND ECONOMICS

378   US
SCOTS NEWSE. 1985. 3/yr. free. Monmouth College, Office of College Relations, Monmouth, IL 61462. TEL 309-452-2322. FAX 309-457-2330. E-mail: alumni@monm.edu; URL: http://www.monm.edu. Ed. Jeffrey D. Rankin. bk.rev. circ. 12,000. **Document type:** bulletin.

378.1   UK
SCRAPIE. 1967. bi-m. free. University of Bradford, Students' Union, Richmond Rd., Bradford, W. Yorks. BD7 1DP, England. TEL 44-1274-383254.
FAX 44-1274-308340. Ed. Helen Dalley. adv.: page £250; adv. contact: Elizabeth Tatlaw. bk.rev.; play rev.; illus. circ. 2,800. **Document type:** consumer publication.
    Former titles: Fleece; Javelin (ISSN 0047-1941)

378   US   ISSN 1083-6934
THE SCRIBE. 1937. bi-w. $25 (effective 1997-98). University of Bridgeport, Student Center, 244 University Ave., Bridgeport, CT 06601.
TEL 203-576-4382. FAX 203-576-4485. E-mail: scribe@cse.bridgeport.edu. Ed. Sharon Loh. R&P contact: Aurora Lee. adv.: page $252.80; adv. contact: Aurora Lee. bk.rev.; film rev.; play rev.; circ. 2,500. (controlled). (tabloid format) **Document type:** newspaper.
    ●Also available online.
    Description: Informs undergraduate and graduate students, faculty, and staff of news and events at the university and the community.
    Refereed Serial

378   US
SCROLL. 1888. w. (Wed.). $30. Ricks College, 160 Spori Bldg., Rexburg, ID 83460-0120.
TEL 208-356-2900. FAX 208-356-2911. E-mail: scroll@ricks.edu. R&P contact: Ron Bennett. adv.; bk.rev. circ. 5,000. (tabloid format) **Document type:** newspaper.
    Description: Covers a wide variety of topics of interest to students of the college.

371.85   US   ISSN 0036-9799
SCROLL OF PHI DELTA THETA. 1874. q. membership. Phi Delta Theta Fraternity, 2 So. Campus, Oxford, OH 45056. TEL 513-523-6345.
FAX 513-523-9200. URL: htttp://www.phidelt-ghq.com. Ed. Rob Pasquinucci. adv. contact: Bob Biggs. bk.rev.; circ. controlled. (processed)
    ●Also available online.

378   CR
SEMANARIO UNIVERSIDAD. (Supplements avail.: Forja, Libros, Crisol) 1970. w. $40 in Central America; N & S. America $50; elsewhere $60. Universidad de Costa Rica, Apdo. 21-2060, 2050 San Pedro de Montes de Oca, San Jose, Costa Rica.
TEL 506-207-5355. FAX 506-207-4774. TELEX 2544 UNICORI. URL: http://cariari.ucr.ac.cr/~semana/univ.html. Ed. Renato Cajas C.; Pub. Carlo Campos Vargas. adv.: B&W page Ch.$90000, color page Ch.$110000; adv. contact: Carlos Campos Vargas. bk.rev. circ. 15,000. **Document type:** newspaper.
    Description: Contains sections covering the nation culture, opinion, sports, foreign affairs, and letters to the editor.

COLLEGE AND ALUMNI

378.1   AT
SEMPER. 1932. 10/yr. Aus.$10. University of Queensland Union, Brisbane, Qld., Australia. FAX 07-371-4359. Ed.Bd. adv.; bk.rev.; film rev.; play rev.; illus. circ. 7,000. (tabloid format)
Formerly: Gamut; Incorporates: Semper Floreat (ISSN 0037-2013)
Description: A forum for student debate on local-campus and social, political issues, as well as containing student creative input in the form of humour, fiction, and photography.

378   US
THE SENATOR. 1921. a. Davis and Elkins College, Box 10, Elkins, WV 26241. TEL 304-636-1900. adv. circ. 1,000.

378   UK   ISSN 0267-033X
SESAME; the newspaper of the Open University. 1972. 6/yr. £5. Open University, Walton Hall, Milton Keynes, Bucks. MK7 6AA, England. TEL 44-1908-653761. FAX 44-1908-652247. Ed. Margaret Salter. adv.: page £1800; trim 375 x 270; adv. contact: Sheila Forman. bk.rev.; illus. circ. 140,000. (tabloid format) **Indexed:** High.Educ.Curr.Aware.Bull. **Document type:** newspaper.
—BLDSC (8253.096500).

378.1   US
SEWANEE. 1934. q. free. University of the South, 735 University Ave., Sewanee, TN 37383-1000. TEL 615-598-1286. Ed. Robert D. Bradford. R&P contact: Robert Bradford. illus. circ. 35,000. **Indexed:** Arts & Hum.Cit.Ind. **Document type:** consumer publication.
Formerly: Sewanee News (ISSN 0037-3044)
Description: Contains news and features of interest to alumni and friends.

378   US
THE SEWANEE PURPLE. bi-w. University of the South, 735 University Ave., Sewanee, TN 37383-1000. TEL 615-598-1204. Ed. Richard Nash. adv. contact: Ashley Saunders. **Document type:** newspaper.

079.62 059.927   UA
AP95.A6S395
AL-SHABAB AL-'ARABI; jaridat al-mab'uthin wal-mughtaribin wal-tullab al-'arab. (Text in Arabic) 1960. w. Majlis al-A'la lil-Shabab wal-Riyadiyyah, P.O. Box 1466, Cairo 61511, Egypt. TEL 20-2-3452426. illus. (tabloid format) **Document type:** newspaper.

SHANGHAI JIAOTONG DAXUE XUEBAO. see TECHNOLOGY: COMPREHENSIVE WORKS

378   CN
SHEAF. 1912. w. Can.$25 (effective 1997-98). Sheaf Publishing Society, University of Saskatchewan, 93 Campus Drive, Saskatoon, SK S7N 5B2, Canada. TEL 306-966-8688. FAX 306-966-8699. E-mail: ss__sheaf@duke.usask.ca; URL: http://www.usask.ca/~ss__sheaf. Eds. Gwen Howe, Jilaire Soucy. adv. contact: Don Charabin. bk.rev.; film rev.; music rev. circ. 10,000. (tabloid format) **Document type:** newspaper.
Refereed Serial

378.1   UK
SHEEPS CLOTHING. 1985. fortn. University of Wolverhampton, Students Union, Wulfruna St., Wolverhampton WV1 1LY, England. Ed. Yemi Adeleke. circ. 4,500. **Document type:** newspaper.
Formerly: Wolverhampton Polytechnic Students' Union Handbook.

378   US
THE SHEPHERD COLLEGE PICKET. 1896. m. free to students and college personnel. Shepherd College, Shepherdstown, WV 25443. TEL 304-876-2511. FAX 304-876-3262. Ed. Laura Gardner. adv.; bk.rev.; circ. 4,000 (controlled). (tabloid format; also avail. in microfilm) **Document type:** newspaper.

371.85   US   ISSN 8750-7536
SHIELD & DIAMOND. 1891. q. Pi Kappa Alpha Fraternity, 8347 W. Range Cove, Memphis, TN 38125. TEL 901-748-1868. Ed. Timothy J. McNary. adv. circ. 92,000.
Description: Provides news of general interest to members regarding chapter and alumni activities, fraternity's administration. Includes profiles and interviews of social alumni.

359   US   ISSN 0488-6720
VA49
SHIPMATE. 1938. 10/yr. $30. U S Naval Academy Alumni Association, Inc., Alumni House, Annapolis, MD 21402. TEL 301-263-4448. Ed. Nancy Gorum. R&P contact: Nancy Gorum. adv. contact: Bobbi Collins. bk.rev. circ. 30,000.

378.198 378   US   ISSN 0892-6603
THE SHORTHORN. 1919. 4/wk. $40. University of Texas at Arlington, Student Publications, c/o Dorothy Estes, 301 W. Second St., S.W. University Center, Box 19308, Arlington, TX 76019-0038. TEL 817-273-3188. FAX 817-794-5009. adv.; bk.rev. circ. 15,000. (back issues avail.) **Document type:** newspaper.

378   US
SIDELINES. 1912. 2/w. $17.50. Middle Tennessee State University, Box 42, Murfreesboro, TN 37132. TEL 615-898-2815. adv.; bk.rev. circ. 8,000.

378   GW   ISSN 0933-3983
DR279
SIEBENBUERGISCHE SEMESTERBLAETTER. 1987. s-a. DM.30($22) Arbeitskreis fuer Siebenbuergische Landeskunde e.V., Schloss Horneck, 74831 Gundelsheim, Germany. TEL 49-6269-42100. FAX 49-6269-421010. E-mail: haraldroth@aol.com. Eds. Harald Roth, Stefan Mazgareanu. adv.; bk.rev.; bibl.; index. circ. 250. (back issues avail.) **Document type:** academic/scholarly publication.

378.1   US   ISSN 0097-6563
LJ75.S82
SIGMA PHI EPSILON JOURNAL. 1902. 3/yr. membership. Sigma Phi Epsilon Fraternity, Inc., Box 1901, Richmond, VA 23215. TEL 804-353-1901. Ed. Dean Woodbeck. circ. 135,000. (also avail. in microfilm; back issues avail.)

378.1   US
SIGNATURES. 1918. 4/yr. free. Anderson University, 1100 E. 5th St., Anderson, IN 46012-3495. TEL 317-649-9071. Ed. Jack W. Williams. circ. 32,000. (tabloid format)
Formerly (until 1986): Anderson College News (ISSN 0003-293X)

SILHOUETTE. see LITERARY AND POLITICAL REVIEWS

378   US   ISSN 1054-3031
SILVER & BLUE MAGAZINE. 1983. bi-m. $15. University of Nevada at Reno, Office of Communications, Office No. 108, Reno, NV 89557-1447. TEL 702-784-1447. Ed. C.J. Hadley; Pub. Terry Maurer. adv. contact: Cynthia Kelley. bk.rev. circ. 30,000. (back issues avail.) **Document type:** academic/scholarly publication.

SIMMONS LIBRARIAN. see LIBRARY AND INFORMATION SCIENCES

378.1   US   ISSN 0049-0512
LH1.S45
SIMMONS REVIEW. 1921. 3/yr. free. Simmons College, 300 The Fenway, Boston, MA 02115. TEL 617-521-2363. FAX 617-521-3193. E-mail: pwalsh@simmons.edu. Ed. Patricia Walsh. bk.rev.; illus.; circ. 23,000 (controlled). **Document type:** academic/scholarly publication.

378.1   SI   ISSN 0049-0547
SINGAPORE UNDERGRAD. vol.6, 1972. 3/yr. S.$10. National University of Singapore, Students' Union, Kent Ridge Campus, Singapore 0511, Singapore. Ed. Jothi Rajah. adv.; illus.

378   US
THE SISKIYOU. 1938. w. $25. Southern Oregon State College, 1250 Siskiyou Blvd., Ashland, OR 97520. TEL 503-552-6307. FAX 503-552-6440. E-mail: siskiyou@tao.sosc.osshe.edu. Ed. Jessica Smith. adv.: page $511. bk.rev.; film rev.; play rev.; charts; illus. circ. 3,000. cols./p.: 5. (broadsheet format; back issues avail.) **Document type:** newspaper.

378   US
SLANT (MADISON). 1971. m. $10. Madison Area Technical College, 3550 Anderson St., Madison, WI 53704. TEL 608-246-6809. FAX 608-246-6880. adv. circ. 4,000.

378.198   US
SMITH ALUMNAE QUARTERLY. 1909. q. $35 membership. Smith College, Alumnae Association, Alumnae House, Northampton, MA 01063. FAX 413-585-2073. Ed. Judith Gingerich. bk.rev. circ. 20,000. **Document type:** consumer publication.

378   CN   ISSN 0838-4401
SOMMETS. (Text in French) 1988. q. free. Universite de Sherbrooke, Pavillon J.S. Bourque, 2500 bd. de l'Universite, Sherbrooke, PQ J1K 2R1, Canada. TEL 819-821-7388. FAX 819-821-7900. E-mail: bruno.levesque@courrier.usherb.ca; URL: http://www.usherb.ca/scsi/sommets/s-index.html. Ed. Bruno Levesque. adv.: B&W page Can.$1500, color page Can.$2100; adv. contact: France Champagne. bk.rev.; circ. 55,000 (controlled). **Document type:** academic/scholarly publication.
Description: Articles of interest to graduates and friends of the University.

378   US
SOUTH DAKOTAN. 1905. 3/yr. free. University of South Dakota Alumni Association, University of South Dakota, 414 E. Clark St., Vermillion, SD 57069. TEL 605-677-6714. FAX 605-677-6717. E-mail: http://www.usd.edu/foundation/alumni.html. Ed. Nancy H. McCahren. adv.; circ. 34,000; circ. 34,000 (controlled). **Document type:** newsletter.

051   US   ISSN 0038-3430
THE SOUTH END. 1969. d. (Mon.-Fri.). $75. Wayne State University, 6001 Cass Ave., Detroit, MI 48202. TEL 313-577-3494. FAX 313-577-6546. Ed. Terri Nichols. adv. contact: Robert Sharp. bk.rev.; charts; illus.; tr.lit. circ. 10,000. (tabloid format; also avail. in microfiche) **Document type:** newspaper.

378   US
SOUTH SURBURBAN COLLEGE COURIER. 1927. m. free. South Surburban College, 15800 S. State St., South Holland, IL 60473. TEL 708-596-2000. FAX 708-210-5758. adv.: page $400. bk.rev.; film rev.; play rev.; charts; illus. circ. 10,000. (tabloid format) **Document type:** newspaper.

SOUTHEASTERNER. see JOURNALISM

378.198   US
SOUTHERN DIGEST. 1928. w. $25. Southern University, Box 10188, Southern Branch P.O., Baton Rouge, LA 70813. TEL 504-771-2230. FAX 504-771-3253. Ed.Bd. adv. contact: Stephanie Cain. bk.rev. circ. 7,900. **Document type:** newspaper.

SOUTHERN GAMEPLAN. see SPORTS AND GAMES

378   US
SOUTHERN LIGHTS; the official alumni publication of Southern Nazarene University. 1977. q. free. Southern Nazarene University, 6729 N.W. 39th Expwy., Bethany, OK 73008. TEL 405-789-6400. FAX 405-491-6381. Ed. Marilyn Bergman. circ. 22,000. (back issues avail.) **Document type:** bulletin.
Description: Covers university life and developments, research, and alumni features.

378.1   US   ISSN 0038-4380
SOUTHERN NEWS AND VIEWS. 1961. q. University of Southern Mississippi, Alumni Association, Southern Station, Box 5013, Hattiesburg, MS 39406. TEL 601-266-5013. Ed. J. Claire Gerald. illus. circ. 48,500.
Description: Update on University of Southern Mississippi news, alumni meetings and alumni news.

378.198   US
SOUTHWEST BAPTIST UNIVERSITY OMNIBUS. w. $10. Southwest Baptist University, 623 Pike St., Bolivar, MO 65613. TEL 417-326-5281. FAX 417-326-1833. Ed. John Tucker. adv. contact: Ruth Ann Taylor. circ. 1,800 (controlled). **Document type:** newspaper.

378   US   ISSN 0038-4852
SOUTHWESTERN (GEORGETOWN). 1970. q. Southwestern University, Student Publications, Box 6048, S.U. Sta., Georgetown, TX 78626. TEL 512-863-1345. FAX 512-863-1347. illus. circ. 1,000. **Document type:** newspaper.

COLLEGE AND ALUMNI

378 — US
SPARTAN DAILY. (Weekly supplement avail.: Etc.) 1934. d. $25. San Jose State University, One Washington Sq., San Jose, CA 95192-0149. TEL 408-924-3275. FAX 408-924-3282. E-mail: greene@jmc.sjsu.edu. Ed. Genoa Barrow. R&P contact: C.E. Lawrence. adv. contact: Carissa Brayman. circ. 6,000. (also avail. in microfilm from LIB; back issues avail.)

378.1 — US
SPECTATOR (SEATTLE). 1933. w. $20. Seattle University, Broadway and Madison, Seattle, WA 98122. TEL 206-296-6470. FAX 206-296-2163. Ed. Teri Anderson. adv. contact: Meredith Burgin. bk.rev.; film rev.; play rev. circ. 3,200. (tabloid format)
Formerly: Seattle University Spectator (ISSN 0037-0479)

378.198 — US
SPECTRUM (FAIRFIELD). 1983. w. $20. Sacred Heart University, 5151 Park Ave., Fairfield, CT 06432. TEL 203-371-7963. adv.; bk.rev.; film rev.; play rev. circ. 2,500. (tabloid format) **Document type:** newspaper.
Formerly: Obelisk.

SPHINX; the student magazine for Liverpool. see *LITERARY AND POLITICAL REVIEWS*

378 — UK
SPIKE. 1968. every 3 wks. free. University of Bath, Students Union, Claverton Down, Bath BA2 7AY, England. TEL 0225-826151. FAX 0225-462508. Ed. Ellie Barker. adv.; bk.rev.; play rev. circ. 3,000. **Document type:** academic/scholarly publication.
Description: News and reviews of general interest.

SPORT SCOLAIRE. see *SPORTS AND GAMES*

378.1 — US
SPOTLIGHT (EMPORIA). 1920? 5/yr. (4 newspaper, 1 magazine format). membership. (Emporia State University, Alumni Association) Emporia State University Press, 1200 Commercial, Emporia, KS 66801-5087. TEL 316-341-5454. FAX 316-341-5589. Ed. Cora Shown. circ. 6,800. Indexed: Rehabil.Lit. **Document type:** newsletter.
Formerly: Kansas State Teachers College Alumni Association. Alumni News (ISSN 0022-8818)

378.1 — US
SPRING ARBOR COLLEGE JOURNAL. vol.50, 1970. q. free to alumni. Spring Arbor College, Spring Arbor, MI 49283. TEL 517-750-1200. FAX 517-750-6604. Ed. Shannon Scholten. illus. circ. 12,000.
Former titles: Spring Arbor College Update; Spring Arbor College Bulletin (ISSN 0038-8564)

378 — US
SPRINGHILLIAN. 1923. w. $25. Spring Hill College, 4000 Dauphin St., Mobile, AL 36608. TEL 334-380-3850. FAX 334-460-2185. E-mail: pmcgraw@shc.edu. Ed. Monique Curet. adv. contact: Pat McGraw. bk.rev.; circ. 2,100. (controlled). (tabloid format) **Document type:** newspaper.

378.198 — US — ISSN 0888-7411
STALL. 1969. 16/yr. (every 3 wks.). $5. Brookdale Community College, 765 Newman Springs Rd., Lincroft, NJ 07738. TEL 201-842-1900. Ed. Scott Poris. adv. contact: Meredith Monroe. bk.rev.; film rev.; play rev.; charts; illus. circ. 5,000. (also avail. in microfilm; back issues avail.)
Description: Contains reviews, sports items, entertainment, letters, comics, public opinions and classifieds.

378.198 — US — ISSN 1063-2778
STANFORD. 1973. bi-m. $24. Stanford Alumni Association, Bowman Alumni House, Stanford, CA 94305. TEL 415-723-2021. FAX 415-725-8676. URL: http://www.stanford.mag.org. Ed. Bob Cohn; Pub. Edie Barry. R&P contact: Leslie Endicott. adv. contact: Geoff WAII. bk.rev.; circ. 100,000. (controlled).
Formerly: Stanford Magazine (ISSN 0745-3981)

650 — US — ISSN 0883-265X
HF1134
STANFORD BUSINESS SCHOOL MAGAZINE. 1931. q. $10 (foreign $12). Stanford University, Graduate School of Business, Stanford, CA 94305-5015. FAX 415-725-6750. E-mail: gsb_newsline@gsb.stanford.edu; URL: http://gsb-www.stanford.edu/gsbhome.html. Ed. Cathy Castillo. bk.rev. circ. 20,000. **Document type:** bulletin.
—UnCover.
Former titles (until 1984): Stanford G S B (ISSN 0164-6605); (until 1979): Stanford Business School Alumni Bulletin (ISSN 0361-3615); Stanford University. Graduate School of Business. Bulletin (ISSN 0038-9803)
Description: Articles focus on the people, programs, events and ideas of the Business School.

378.1 — US — ISSN 0038-9757
STANFORD CHAPARRAL.* 1899. 4/yr. $11. Hammer and Coffin Society, Box 9916, Stanford, CA 94309-1696. TEL 415-723-1468. Ed. Aulde Boiy. adv.; bk.rev.; rec.rev.; film rev.; illus. circ. 14,000.
Description: Student humor magazine.

378 340 — US — ISSN 1061-3447
STANFORD LAW ALUM. 1992. a. Stanford University, Stanford Law School, Crown Quadrangle, Stanford, CA 94305-8610. Ed. Constance Hellyer. illus. circ. 9,000.
Description: Features news of Stanford Law School and its graduates.

378 — US
STATE NEWS. 1906. d. (Mon.-Fri.). $55. State News, Inc., 345 Student Services Bldg., East Lansing, MI 48824-1113. TEL 517-355-3447. FAX 517-353-2599. Ed. Kyle Melinn; Pub. Berl Schwartz. adv. contact: Laurel Tinker. bk.rev.; illus. circ. 36,000. **Document type:** newspaper.

378 — US
STATE PRESS. 1912. 5/w. (Mon.-Fri.). $39. Arizona State University, Matthews Center, Tempe, AZ 85287. TEL 602-965-2292. FAX 602-965-8484. adv. contact: Jackie Eldridge. bk.rev. circ. 21,000. (tabloid format) **Document type:** newspaper.

378 — US
STATE UNIVERSITY OF NEW YORK AT ALBANY. ALBANY. vol.2, 1988. s-a. free. State University of New York at Albany, Office of University Relations, AD233, Albany, NY 12222. TEL 518-442-3070. E-mail: jmb90@poppa.fab.albany.edu; URL: http://www.albany.edu. Eds. Mary Fiess, Christine McKnight; Pub. Joel M. Blumenthal. bk.rev.; circ. 70,000. (controlled). **Document type:** consumer publication.
Formerly (until 1991): Researcher (Albany).

378 — US
STATE UNIVERSITY OF NEW YORK AT ALBANY. UPDATE. 1977. bi-w. (Sep.-May). free. State University of New York at Albany, Department of University Relations, AD 233, State University of New York at Albany, Albany, NY 12222. TEL 518-442-3070. Ed. Vincent Reda. circ. 3,500. (tabloid format; back issues avail.) **Document type:** newsletter.
Description: Reports on university activities and achievements.

378.1 — US
STATEMENT (FREDONIA). 1971. 3/yr. free. State University of New York, College at Fredonia, Office of Public Information, Fredonia, NY 14063. TEL 716-673-3323. FAX 716-673-3156. URL: http://www.fredonia.edu. Ed. Christine Davis Mantai. illus. circ. 29,000. (tabloid format) **Document type:** newspaper.
Formerly: Fredonia Statement (ISSN 0046-4988)
Description: Covers alumni news.

378 — US
STATESMAN (WANTAGH). 1957. 2/w. $48. Box A.E., Stony Brook, NY 11790. TEL 516-632-6480. FAX 516-632-9128. (Street addr.: SUNY - Stony Brook, Student Union Bldg., Rm. 075, Wantagh, NY 11793) Ed. David Joachim. adv.; bk.rev. circ. 24,000. (tabloid format) **Document type:** newspaper.

378 — US
STEPHENS LIFE. 1929. w. $20. Stephens College, Box 2014, Columbia, MO 65215. TEL 314-876-7112. circ. 2,000. **Document type:** newspaper.
Description: College student newspaper.

STERN BUSINESS REPORT. see *BUSINESS AND ECONOMICS*

620 — US — ISSN 0039-1328
STEVENS INDICATOR. 1884. q. free to alumni, students, and other qualified personnel. Stevens Alumni Association, Castle Point, Hoboken, NJ 07030. TEL 201-216-5161. FAX 201-216-5374. E-mail: alumni-log@stevens-tech.edu. Ed. Ellen Usher Durkin. R&P contact: Ellen Usher Durkin. adv. contact: Harry W. Bodemann. bk.rev.; circ. 21,000. (controlled). **Document type:** consumer publication.
—Linda Hall.
Refereed Serial

378 — CN — ISSN 0710-4537
THE STRAND. 1958. fortn. Victoria University, 150 Charles St. West, Toronto, ON M5S 1K9, Canada. adv.; bk.rev.; film rev. (tabloid format)

378.1 — UK — ISSN 0039-2243
STRATHCLYDE TELEGRAPH. 1960. fortn. free. University of Strathclyde, Students' Association, 90 John St., Glasgow G1 1JH, Scotland. FAX 041-552-0775. adv.; bk.rev.; film rev.; play rev. circ. 6,000.

378.198 610 — US — ISSN 1054-7649
STRITCH M.D. 1986. s-a. free. Loyola University Chicago, Stritch School of Medicine, 2160 S. First Ave., Maywood, IL 60153. TEL 708-216-6700. FAX 708-216-8199. Ed. Tracy Binius. circ. 6,500. (controlled). (back issues avail.) **Document type:** bulletin.

053 — NE — ISSN 0165-6759
STUDENT; landelijk maandblad voor studenten. 1963. 10/yr. fl.18.25. De Studenten Uitgeverij, Smidstraat 12, 8746 NG Schraard, Netherlands. TEL 31-517-531583. FAX 31-517-532042. Ed. P.I. Bakker. adv.; bk.rev. circ. 65,000. **Document type:** academic/scholarly publication.

059.9277 — MM
THE STUDENT/L-ISTUDENT. 1977. 3/yr. University of Malta, University Students' Council, Msida, Malta.

378.198 — II
STUDENT ACTION. 1982. m. (All Indian Students Federation) Atul Kumar Anjan, 4-7 Asaf Ali Rd., New Dehli 110 002, India. Ed.Bd. film rev.

378 — US
▼**STUDENT AFFAIRS JOURNAL ONLINE.** 1996. irreg. 371-G North Barranca Ave., Azusa, CA 91702. E-mail: connect@digiserve.com; URL: http://www.digiserve.com/connect/sajo/. Ed. Steve Eubanks. ●Available only online.
Description: For professionals, practitioners and scholars in the field of college student affairs.

378 — US
STUDENT ECHO. w. University of Tennessee at Chattanooga, 641 Vine St., Chattanooga, TN 37402. TEL 615-755-4298.

378 — UK
STUDENT HACK. 1991. fortn. free. University of Bradford, Students' Union, Richmond Rd., Bradford, W. Yorks. BD7 1DP, England. TEL 44-1274-383254. FAX 44-1274-305340. Ed. Justin Coe. R&P contact: Justin Coe. circ. 2,500. **Document type:** newsletter.
Formerly: Lister.

368 — US — ISSN 1070-9657
STUDENT LEADER. 1993. 2/yr. $20. Oxendine Publishing, Inc., Box 14081, Gainesville, FL 32604-2081. TEL 352-373-6907. FAX 352-373-8120. Ed. W.H. Oxendine, Jr.; Pub. W.H. Oxendine. adv. contact: W.H. Oxendine, Jr. illus circ. 115,000. **Document type:** academic/scholarly publication, consumer publication.
Description: Covers issues of interest to student leaders and members of student governments throughout the U.S.

STUDENT LEADERSHIP JOURNAL. see *EDUCATION*

378.1 — US — ISSN 0039-2758
STUDENT LIFE (ST. LOUIS). 1878. s-w. $29. (Washington University) Student Life Publishers Board, Box 1039, St. Louis, MO 63130. TEL 314-889-5995. Ed. Laura Meckler. adv.; bk.rev.; film rev.; play rev.; illus. circ. 9,000. (also avail. in microform)

COLLEGE AND ALUMNI

378   US
STUDENT MAGAZINE (COSTA MESA). 1993. m. free. Box 1641, Costa Mesa, CA 92628-1641. TEL 714-548-9116. Ed. John Sinclair; Pub. Mike Dang. adv.: B&W page $595; trim 8 1/4 x 10 1/4; adv. contact: Cindy Hoff. circ. 20,000 (controlled). **Document type:** consumer publication.

378   US
STUDENT MAGAZINE (WASHINGTON, D.C.).* 1984. m. Collegiate Marketing Associates, 2629 Garfield St., N.W., Washington, DC 20008-4103. Ed. Carl Oesterle. adv. circ. 507,500.

378.198   US
STUDENT MOVEMENT. 1915. w. $18. Andrews University, Student Association, Berrien Springs, MI 49104. Ed. Patricia Nash. adv.; bk.rev. circ. 3,000. (tabloid format)

378   US
▼**STUDENT NET.** 1995. d. free. 254 College St., Ste. 400, New Haven, CT 06510. TEL 203-624-7650. FAX 203-624-8715. E-mail: advertising@student.net; URL: http://www.student.net. Ed. Stewart Ugelow. R&P contact: Stewart Ugelow. adv. contact: Eric Ng.
●Available only online.
  Description: Deals with campus issues, employment, humor, nostalgia and other topics of interest to college students.

378   US
STUDENT PRINTZ. 1910. bi-w. $15. University of Southern Mississippi, Box 5088, Southern Sta., Hattiesburg, MS 39406. TEL 601-266-4268. FAX 601-226-4263. Ed. Sean Murphy. adv. contact: Frank Louis. circ. 6,500. **Document type:** newspaper.
  Description: Informs students of events on campus.

371.8 796.3   SW
STUDENT PULSEN. 1983. q. membership. (Studentpulsen) S S I F - Stockholms Studenters I F, P.O. Box 50093, S-104 05 Stockholm, Sweden. TEL 46-8-15-10-75. FAX 46-8-15-76-28. Ed. Eva Wiklund. adv.: B&W page SEK 18000, color page SEK 21000; trim 250 x 375. circ. 52,500. cols./p.: 5; pp./issue: 24. (tabloid format)

378   UK
THE STUDENT TIMES; the Dundee students newspaper. 1967. 3/term. University of Dundee, Students Association, Airlie Pl., Dundee DD1 4HP, Scotland. adv. circ. 6,000. **Document type:** newspaper.
  Formerly (until 1995): Annasach.

378.1   PK   ISSN 0039-2790
STUDENT TIMES INTERNATIONAL. (Text in English) 1953. q.? Rs.4($1) Student Times Publications, 22D Block D, N. Nizamabad, Karachi, Pakistan. Ed. Qaseemuddim Pasha. circ. 16,000.

STUDENT TRAVELLER. see *TRAVEL AND TOURISM*

378.1   US   ISSN 0039-2804
STUDENT VOICE. 1916. w. $10. University of Wisconsin at River Falls, Stillwater Gazette, River Falls, WI 54022. TEL 715-425-3118. FAX 715-425-4486. Ed.Bd. bk.rev.; film rev.; illus. circ. 4,000. (also avail. in microform; broadsheet format) **Document type:** newspaper.

378   GW
STUDIEREN IN GOETTINGEN. 1965. a. free. Studentenwerk Goettingen, Platz der Goettinger Sieben 4, 37073 Goettingen, Germany. TEL 49-551-390. FAX 49-551-395186. URL: http://www.stud.uni-goettingen.de. Ed. Christa Mirwald. adv. circ. 9,000. **Document type:** bulletin.
  Description: Information for students of the University of Goettingen.

378   US
THE STUTE. 1904. w. $20. Stevens Institute of Technology, CastlePoint on the Hudson, Hoboken, NJ 07030. TEL 201-659-3404. E-mail: the___ stute@stevens-tech.edu. Ed. Michael Andreano. adv. contact: John Beek. circ. 2,500. (tabloid format) **Document type:** newspaper.
●Also available online.

378   GW
STUTTGARTER UNIKURIER. 1980. 5/yr. Universitaet Stuttgart, Referat fuer Presse- und Oeffentlichkeitsarbeit, Keplerstr. 7, 70174 Stuttgart, Germany. TEL 49-711-1212297. FAX 49-711-1212188. E-mail: presse@po.uni-stuttgart.de. Ed. Ursula Zitzler. adv. **Document type:** newsletter.

378.1   US   ISSN 0039-4289
STYLUS (BROCKPORT). 1931. w. $10 (per semester). (State University of New York at Brockport) Downtowner Publishing, 209 Student Union, Brockport, NY 14420. TEL 716-395-2230. FAX 716-395-2246. Ed. Andrew L. Simpson. adv.; bk.rev.; film rev.; play rev.; illus.; stat. circ. 5,000. (tabloid format)

378   GW   ISSN 0723-6816
SUEDDEUTSCHE STUDENTENZEITUNG. 1960. s-a. (1 double-no. per semester). DM.4. I. Wohlrabe Verlag, Eschenallee 31a, D-1000 Berlin 19, Germany. adv.

378   CN
SUITES; le magazine des diplomes de l'U Q A M. 1991. 3/yr. (Bureau des Diplomes de l'Universite du Quebec a Montreal) Editions Montreal Camping Inc., C.P. 8888, Succ. Centre-Ville, Montreal, PQ H3C 3P8, Canada. TEL 514-987-7018. FAX 514-987-8210. E-mail: magazine.suites@uqam.ca. Ed. Linda Mongeau. adv.: B&W page Can.$1570; trim 7 1/8 x 9 11/16; adv. contact: Rene Plourde. circ. 75,000.

378   US
SUMMIT. 1963. w. Grossmont College, 8800 Grossmont College Dr., El Cajon, CA 92020. TEL 619-465-1700. adv. circ. 3,600. **Document type:** newspaper.
  Formerly: G.

SUMMONS. see *LAW*

378   US
THE SUNDIAL. w. Randolph - Macon Women's College, 2500 Rivermont Ave., Box 396, Lynchburg, VA 24503. Ed. Lou Ann Graham. film rev.; play rev.; abstr. circ. 1,000. (looseleaf format; back issues avail.)

378   US
THE SUNFLOWER (WICHITA). 1896. 3/w. $21.50. Wichita State University, Box 134, Wichita, KS 67201. TEL 316-689-3640. FAX 316-689-3778. adv.; bk.rev. circ. 17,000. (tabloid format) **Document type:** newspaper.

378   US
SUSQUEHANNA TODAY. 1931. q. free to qualified personnel. Susquehanna University Alumni Association, Susquehanna University, Selinsgrove, PA 17870. TEL 717-372-4119. FAX 717-372-4048. E-mail: wells@susqu.edu. Ed. Gwenn E. Wells. circ. 16,000.
  Formerly: Susquehanna Alumnus.

378   US   ISSN 0888-2126
SWARTHMORE COLLEGE BULLETIN. 1938. q. free. Swarthmore College, Swarthmore, PA 19081-1397. TEL 610-328-8401. Ed. Jeffrey Lott. circ. 23,200. **Document type:** bulletin.

378   US
SWARTHMORE COLLEGE PHOENIX. 1881. w. $26. Swarthmore College, Swarthmore, PA 19081. TEL 610-328-8173. FAX 610-328-8674. circ. 2,700. (controlled). (tabloid format) **Document type:** newspaper.

378.1   US
SWEET BRIAR ALUMNAE MAGAZINE. 1931. q. free. Sweet Briar Alumnae Association, Sweet Briar College, Sweet Briar, VA 24595. TEL 804-381-6131. FAX 804-381-6132. E-mail: sbcmagazine@sbc.edu. Ed. Nancy Godwin Baldwin. R&P contact: Nancy G. Baldwin. TEL 804-381-6321. bk.rev.; illus. circ. 11,500. **Document type:** bulletin.
  Formerly: Sweet Briar College. Alumnae Magazine (ISSN 0039-7342)
  Description: Provides alumnae and friends of Sweet Briar College with news about the association, individual alumnae and the college.

051   US   ISSN 0740-2619
SYNAPSE (SAN FRANCISCO). 1955. w. $30 (foreign $40). University of California at San Francisco, Synapse Publication Board, Box 0376, San Francisco, CA 94143. TEL 415-476-2211. FAX 415-502-4537. E-mail: Synapse___ucsf@Quickmail.UCSF.edu. Ed. Fred Gardner. adv. contact: Adam Silve. bk.rev.; illus. circ. 5,000. (tabloid format) **Document type:** newspaper.

378   US
T C U MAGAZINE. 1956. q. Texas Christian University, Box 298940, Ft. Worth, TX 76129. TEL 817-921-7807. FAX 817-921-7110. (Subscr. to: Texas Christian University, Box 297044, Ft. Worth, TX 76129) Ed. John Ohendalski. circ. 51,000 (controlled). **Document type:** newsletter.
  Description: Provides information about TCU and topics of general interest to alumni.

378   GW
T U INTERN. 1985. m. Technische Universitaet Berlin, Presse- und Informationsreferat, Str. des 17. Juni 135, 10623 Berlin, Germany. TEL 49-30-31423922. FAX 49-30-314-23909. TELEX 184262-TUBLN-D. E-mail: pressestelle@tu-berlin.de; URL: http://www.tu-berlin.de/presse/. Ed. Kristina Zerges. adv. circ. 12,000. **Document type:** newsletter.

378   CN   ISSN 1187-8622
TABARET. (Text in English, French) 1949. q. Can.$6.50. University of Ottawa, Alumni and Development - Universite d'Ottawa, 190 Laurier, E., Ottawa, ON K1N 6N5, Canada. TEL 613-564-2316. FAX 613-564-9555. Ed. Pierre St-Cyr. adv.: B&W page Can.$960, color page Can.$1920; trim 7 x 9 1/2. bk.rev. circ. 57,000. **Document type:** academic/scholarly publication.
  Formerly: University of Ottawa. Alumni and Development. Alumni News. (ISSN 0832-7424)

378.198   US
TALLADEGA STUDENT STAR. 1921. m. $5. Talladega College, Communications Department, W. Battle St., Talladega, AL 35160. TEL 205-362-0206. adv.; bk.rev. circ. 1,000. (tabloid format)
  Formerly: Talladega Student.

378   US
TALLADEGAN. vol.93, 1975. q. free. Talladega College, 627 W. Battle St., Talladega, AL 35160. TEL 205-362-0206. FAX 205-362-2268. illus. circ. 5,000.

378   II
TAMIL CEITHI MALAR. (Text in Tamil) 1982. m. Rs.5($4) Tamil University, Thanjavur 613 001, Tamil Nadu, India.

378   II
TAMIL UNIVERSITY. NEWS BULLETIN. (Text in English) 1982. m. Rs.5($4) Tamil University, Thanjavur 613 001, Tamil Nadu, India. **Document type:** bulletin.

TE DEUM; alumni newsletter. see *RELIGIONS AND THEOLOGY — Protestant*

378.198   US   ISSN 0148-9607
T171
THE TECH. (Supplements avail.: Ideas; Year in Review) 1881. s-w. $20. Massachusetts Institute of Technology, Box 397029, Cambridge, MA 02139. TEL 617-253-1541. FAX 617-258-8226. Ed. Jeremy A. Hylton. adv.; bk.rev. circ. 9,000. (tabloid format; also avail. in microfiche) **Document type:** newspaper.

378   US
TECH COLLEGIAN. 1920. w. $17.50 free. West Virginia Institute of Technology, Student Service Center, Box 81 Old Main, Montgomery, WV 25136. TEL 304-442-3371. FAX 304-442-3464. E-mail: dibran@wit.wvnet.edu. Ed. Debra L. Brannon. adv.: B&W page $125, color page $180; 10 1/4 x 12 1/2. circ. 2,500.

378.1   US   ISSN 1062-077X
TECH TOPICS. 1971. 4/yr. free to qualified personnel. Georgia Tech Alumni Association, Alumni-Faculty House, Atlanta, GA 30332-0175. TEL 404-894-2391. FAX 404-894-5113. URL: http://www.gatech.edu/alumni/alumni.html. Ed. John Dunn. adv. contact: Robb Stanek. circ. 83,000. (tabloid format) **Document type:** newspaper.

COLLEGE AND ALUMNI

378   US   ISSN 1072-1916
TECHNICIAN; North Carolina State University's newspaper since 1920. 1920. 3/w. $50. North Carolina State University, Student Media Authority, Box 8608, Raleigh, NC 27695-8608. TEL 919-515-2411. FAX 919-515-5133. URL: http://www2.ncsu.edu/ncsu/stud_pubs/technician/. Ed. Chris Baysden. R&P contact: Chris Baysden. adv. contact: Robert Sadler. bk.rev.; film rev.; music rev.; play rev.; illus. circ. 18,500. (broadsheet format) **Document type:** newspaper.

378   US
TECHNIQUE (ATLANTA); the South's liveliest college newspaper. 1914. w. $15. Georgia Tech University, 225 North Ave., N.W., Box J, Atlanta, GA 30332. TEL 404-894-2830. Ed. James Cage. adv.; bk.rev.; film rev.; play rev.; illus. circ. 1,300. (tabloid format) **Indexed:** Phys.Ed.Ind., Sports Per.Ind.

378   US
TELLURIDE NEWSLETTER. 1912. 2/yr. membership. Telluride Association, 217 W. Ave., Ithaca, NY 14850. TEL 607-273-5011. Ed. Rachel J. Dickson. bk.rev. circ. 3,000. (looseleaf format) **Document type:** newsletter.

378   US
TEMPLE NEWS. 1920. d. (Tue.-Fri.). $25 per semester. Temple University, 405 Student Activity Center, 13th & Montgomery Ave., Philadelphia, PA 19122. TEL 215-204-7416. FAX 215-387-1663. adv. circ. 10,500. **Document type:** newspaper.

378.1   US   ISSN 0040-3156
TENNESSEE ALUMNUS. 1917. q. donation. University of Tennessee at Knoxville, National Alumni Association, 107 Communications Bldg., Knoxville, TN 37996. TEL 423-974-2225. FAX 423-974-6435. URL: http://loki.ur.utk.edu/alumnus/alumnus.html. Ed. Diane Ballard. adv. contact: Tom Looney. bk.rev. circ. 500,000.

378   GW   ISSN 0720-1303
TEX; die Zeitschrift der Fachhochschule fuer Technik und Wirtschaft. 1966. s-a. free. Fachhochschule fuer Technik und Wirtschaft, Alteburgstr. 150, 72762 Reutlingen, Germany. TEL 49-7121-271-0. FAX 49-7121-271224. (Co-sponsors: Betriebsverein des Technikums fuer Textilindustrie e.V., Vereinigung Reutlinger Ingenieure e.V.) adv.: B&W page DM.500; trim 270 x 185. circ. 2,500. (back issues avail.) **Document type:** academic/scholarly publication.

378   US   ISSN 0747-1661
TEXAS AGGIE. 1921. 8/yr. $50. Texas A & M University, Association of Former Students, Box 7368, College Sta., TX 77844. TEL 409-845-7514. FAX 409-845-9263. Ed. Jerry C. Cooper. adv. circ. 60,000.

378.1   US   ISSN 1061-561X
TEXAS ALCALDE. 1913. bi-m. $40 membership. Ex-Students' Association, Box 7278, University of Texas at Austin, Austin, TX 78713. TEL 512-471-3799. FAX 512-471-8088. Ed. Avrel Seale. adv.; bk.rev.; charts; illus. circ. 52,000. **Formerly:** Alcalde (ISSN 0002-497X) **Description:** Contains informational and feature articles about the programs, research, events, faculty, and students at the University of Texas at Austin.

378   US
T171
TEXAS TECHSAN MAGAZINE. 1948. bi-m. $25. Texas Tech University, Ex-Students Association, Box 45001, Lubbock, TX 79409. TEL 806-742-3641. FAX 806-742-3604. E-mail: mgustafson@ttu.edu. Ed. Marsha Gustafson; Pub. Bill Dean. R&P contact: Marsha Gustafson. adv.: B&W page $525, color page $850; trim 8 3/8 x 10 7/8; adv. contact: Curt Langford. bk.rev. circ. 18,000 (paid). **Formerly:** Texas Techsan (ISSN 0040-4721)

378 027.7   US
TEXAS WOMAN'S UNIVERSITY. SCHOOL OF LIBRARY AND INFORMATION STUDIES. ALUMNAE NEWSLETTER. 1978. a. Texas Woman's University, School of Library and Information Studies, Box 425438, Denton, TX 76204-5438. FAX 817-898-2611. E-mail: a_swigger@twu.edu. Ed. Keith Swigger. circ. 3,000. **Document type:** newsletter. **Formerly:** Texas Woman's University. School of Library Science. Alumnae Newsletter.

378   AT
THARUNKA. 1954. fortn. Aus.$3. University of New South Wales, Sydney, N.S.W. 2052, Australia. TEL 61-2-385-2840. FAX 61-2-662-2163. Ed.Bd. **Description:** Covers New South Wales Students Union events.

371.85   US
THEMIS. 1902. q. $2 to non-members. Zeta Tau Alpha, International Office, 3450 Founders Rd., Indianapolis, IN 46268. TEL 317-872-0540. FAX 371-876-3948. Ed. Lisa L. Elliott. bk.rev.; illus.; circ. 65,000(controlled). **Document type:** trade publication. **Description:** Presents news of college and alumnae chapters, their local and national philanthropic efforts, and general news of interest to women. *Refereed Serial*

378.198   CN   ISSN 0843-7092
THIRD DEGREE. vol.2, 1975. 2/yr. Can.$50 in U.S. and Canada; elsewhere Can.$75. University of Regina, Communications Office, Regina, SK S4S OA2, Canada. TEL 306-585-4403. FAX 306-585-4997. Ed. Therese Stecyk. R&P contact: Therese Stecyk. adv.; circ. 27,000 (controlled). (back issues avail.) **Document type:** academic/scholarly publication. **Formerly** (until 1989): Insight (Regina) (ISSN 0706-0262)

378.198   US
THE TICKER. fortn. City University of New York, Baruch College, 17 Lexington Ave., New York, NY 10010. TEL 212-387-1182. adv.; bk.rev.; film rev.; play rev. circ. 10,000. (tabloid format) **Document type:** newspaper. **Description:** Student newspaper of Baruch College.

378   US
THE TIGER. 1907. w. $30. Clemson University, Box 2097, Clemson, SC 29632. TEL 803-656-2150. FAX 803-656-4772. Ed. Greg Schmidt. adv. contact: Joel Moss. bk.rev. circ. 12,000. (also avail. in microfilm) **Document type:** newspaper.

378.1   US   ISSN 0040-7879
TIMES AND CHALLENGE. 1923. m. $12. Wesleyan College, Forsyth Rd., Macon, GA 31201. TEL 912-477-1110. Ed. Jaquis Dravis. adv.; bk.rev.; film rev.; play rev.; illus. circ. 800. (tabloid format) **Formerly:** Times and Chimes.

378.1   IS
▼**TOAR.** (Text in Hebrew) 1996. s-a. Hebrew University of Jerusalem, Department of Alumni Affairs and New Leadership, Jerusalem, Israel. E-mail: msbarach@pluto.mscc.huji.ac.il. adv.; circ. 60,000 (controlled). **Description:** Includes information on the university, its researchers, and graduates.

TODAY (KENT). see *CHILDREN AND YOUTH — For*

378   US
TORCH (SEGUIN). q. free. Texas Lutheran University, 1000 W. Court St., Seguin, TX 78155. TEL 830-372-8028. FAX 830-372-8096. Ed. Ralph Falkenberg. circ. 14,500.

378   US
THE TORCH (VALPARAISO). 1915. w. $40 (effective 1997 & 1998). Valparaiso University, 816 Union St., Valparaiso, IN 46383. TEL 219-464-5426. E-mail: torch@exodus.valpo.edu. Ed. Larry Mowry. R&P contact: Larry Mowry. adv.: B&W page $400; adv. contact: Kim Giles. bk.rev.; film rev.; play rev.; charts; illus.; stat. circ. 4,000. (tabloid format) **Document type:** newspaper. **Description:** Provides news, opinion pieces, sports stories, arts and entertainment features, and reviews to the students, faculty, and staff of Valparaiso University. *Refereed Serial*

378   CN   ISSN 1182-3836
TORCH (VICTORIA). 1986. 2/yr. free to alumni. University of Victoria, Public Relations & Information Services, Box 3060, 3775 Haro Rd., Victoria, BC V8W 3R4, Canada. TEL 250-721-7642. FAX 250-721-8955. E-mail: tmoore@uvic.ca; URL: http://www.kafka.uvic.ca/~prelatio/torch/index.html. Ed. Teresa Moore. adv.: B&W page Can.$1300; trim 8 x 10 1/2; adv. contact: Bev Grooms. circ. 41,000. **Document type:** academic/scholarly publication. **Formerly:** U Vic Torch. **Description:** News and information about the University of Victoria, the campus, faculty and researchers.

378   US
TORCH & TREFOIL. 1925. q. $2. Alpha Phi Omega, 14901 E. 42nd St., Independence, MO 64108. TEL 816-471-8667. Ed. Darrell Spoon. circ. 17,000 (controlled). **Description:** Contains information about college service fraternity activities.

378.198   US
TOWER. 1946. w. $25. Bethany College (Bethany), c/o Gael L. Cooper, Pub., Bethany, WV 26032. TEL 304-829-7951. Pub. Gael L. Cooper. R&P contact: Gael L. Cooper. adv.; stat.; tr.lit. circ. 1,200. (back issues avail.) **Document type:** newspaper.

378   IT
TRA NOI; alunni ed ex-alunni del Sociale. 1925. bi-m. free. Istituto Sociale, Corso Siracusa 10, 10136 Turin, Italy. TEL 011-357-835. FAX 011-327487. circ. 1,300.

378   US
▼**TRADITIONS.** 1995. q. free to alumni. University of Connecticut, 1266 Storrs Rd., Storrs, CT 06269-5144. TEL 860-486-3530. FAX 860-486-2063. E-mail: becher@univrel.pr.uconn.edu. Ed. Thomas Becher. circ. 120,000 (controlled). (tabloid format) **Document type:** newspaper. **Description:** Publishes features and news about the University of Connecticut for alumni, friends and supporters.

378   CN
TRAIT-D'UNION.* (Text in French) 1938. s-m. free. Publi-Peq, 3575 bd. St. Laurent, Ste. 232, Montreal, PQ H2X 2T7, Canada. TEL 514-845-8628. (Co-sponsor: College Maisonneuve) circ. 2,500.

371.85   US   ISSN 0041-1167
LJ121.C47
TRANSIT OF CHI EPSILON. 1928. s-a. $4. Chi Epsilon, c/o Neil J. Rowan, Ed., Civil Engineering Dept., Texas A & M University, College Sta., TX 77843. TEL 409-845-9883. illus. circ. 10,000.

378.198   US
TRANSITIONS (NEW YORK). 1989. q. Columbia University, School of General Studies, Box 405-S Lewisohn Hall, New York, NY 10027. Ed. Anthony Rainone.

378.198   US
TRIANGLE (DAYTON). 1978. bi-w. $12. Bryan College, Box 7000, Dayton, TN 37321. TEL 615-775-2041. FAX 615-775-7330. adv. contact: Tom Davis. bk.rev.; film rev.; play rev.; charts. circ. 500. (tabloid format) **Document type:** newspaper.

378   US
TRIANGLE (MARION). 1924. 5/yr. Judson College, Bibb St., Marion, AL 36756. TEL 205-683-6161. circ. 700.

378   UK
TRIBUTARY. 1974. fortn. £1.80. Tributary Publishing Co. Ltd., 13 Bevinton Rd., Oxford OX2 6NB, England. Ed. Sara Dracup. adv.; bk.rev. circ. 4,000.

378   US
TRIDENT OF DELTA DELTA DELTA. 1891. q. Box 5987, Arlington, TX 76005-5987. TEL 817-633-8001. FAX 817-652-0212. Ed. Karen Jenkins. circ. 125,000. **Document type:** consumer publication.

378   US
TRINITONIAN. 1942. w. $20. Trinity University, 715 Stadium Dr., Box 62, San Antonio, TX 78284. TEL 210-736-8556. FAX 210-736-0998. adv.; bk.rev. circ. 3,000. **Document type:** newspaper.

COLLEGE AND ALUMNI

378.1   IE   ISSN 0041-3062
TRINITY NEWS. 1953. w. (during school yr.). 10p. Trinity College, Dublin, Ireland. TEL 01-7022535. FAX 01-6778996. Ed. Barbara Collins. adv. contact: Barbara Collins. bk.rev.; charts; film rev.; illus.; play rev. circ. 8,000. (tabloid format) **Document type:** newspaper.

378.198   US
TRINITY REPORT (ELLENDALE). 1969. s-a. free. Trinity Bible College, Ellendale, ND 58436. TEL 701-349-3621. FAX 701-349-5443. Ed. Terry L. Terrell. bk.rev. (tabloid format) **Document type:** newsletter.
   Incorporates (1991-1995): Sermon of the Month; Formerly: Trinity Tidings.
   Description: Provides general college news to alumni and friends of the college, as well as prospective students.

378   US
TRINITY TRIPOD. 1863. w. $15. Trinity College, 300 Summit St., Box 1310, Hartford, CT 06106. adv.; bk.rev.; illus. circ. 3,000. (also avail. in microfilm; back issues avail.)

378   GW   ISSN 0930-3642
TUEBINGER BLAETTER. 1898. a. DM.12. Buerger- und Verkehrsverein Tuebingen e.V., An der Neckarbruecke, Postfach 2623, 72016 Tuebingen, Germany. TEL 07071-35011. FAX 07071-35070. Ed. Albrecht Locher. adv.: B&W page DM.1190, color page DM.1666; trim 185 x 270; adv. contact: Wolfgang Schuetz. bk.rev. circ. 4,500. **Document type:** consumer publication.

TULANE MEDICINE. see MEDICAL SCIENCES

378.1   US   ISSN 0041-4026
TULANIAN. 1927. q. free. Tulane University, University Relations, Hebert Hall, Rm. 300, New Orleans, LA 70118. TEL 504-865-5714. FAX 504-865-5621. E-mail: tulanian@mailhost.tcs.tulane.edu. Ed. Anne Yeoman. adv.: B&W page $2340; adv. contact: Suzanne Johnson. bk.rev.; circ. 75,000 (controlled).

378   US
TYLER JUNIOR COLLEGE NEWS. 1928. fortn. free. Tyler Junior College, Box 9020, Tyler, TX 75711. TEL 214-510-2335. FAX 903-510-2708. E-mail: izei@tjc.tyler.cc.tx.us. Ed. Jamie Melton; Linda K. Zeigler. R&P contact: Linda Zeigler. adv.; bk.rev.; circ. 3,500 (controlled). **Document type:** newspaper.
   Description: Covers junior college interests.

378   US
U A F ALUMNUS; information for University of Alaska Fairbanks graduates and former students. q. $35 membership. University of Alaska at Fairbanks, Alumni Association, Box 750126, Fairbanks, AK 99775-0126. TEL 907-474-7081. FAX 907-474-6712. URL: httpf://www.fyalum@ aurora.alaska.edu. Ed. Brenda Wilcox; Pub. Brenda Wilcox. R&P contact: Brenda Wilco. adv. contact: Brenda Wilcox. **Document type:** newsletter.
   Description: Contains information about the university and the alumni association; reports on new jobs, spouses, and residents of alumni.

378   GW   ISSN 0161-9810
HD6350.A8
U - A S T A - INFO. 1974. w. Allgemeiner Studentenausschuss der Albert-Ludwigs-Universitaet, Bertoldstr. 26, 79098 Freiburg, Germany. TEL 0761-203-3872. adv.; illus. circ. 2,000.

378   GW
J - A S T A - INFO FUER ERSTSEMESTER. s-a. Allgemeiner Studentenausschuss der Albert-Ludwigs-Universitaet, Bertoldstr. 26, 79098 Freiburg, Germany. TEL 0761-2033782. adv.; illus. circ. 3,500.

378   US
C DAVIS MAGAZINE. 1983. q. University of California at Davis, Davis, CA 95616. TEL 916-752-9839. (Subscr. to: Cal Aggie Alumni Association, Guilbert House, University of California at Davis, Davis, CA 95616) Ed. Maril Revette Stratton. circ. 115,000. **Document type:** newspaper.
   Formerly: Spectator (Davis).
   Description: Covers news and publishes feature stories about U.C.-Davis research, faculty, teaching programs, and alumni.

378   US   ISSN 1064-6205
U C S D GUARDIAN. 1967. s-w. $75. University of California at San Diego, Mail Code 0316 UCSD, La Jolla, CA 92093-0316. TEL 619-534-3466. FAX 619-534-7691. Ed. Douglas Alexander. adv. contact: Michael Foulks. circ. 12,000. **Document type:** newspaper.

378.1   US   ISSN 1067-4969
▼ **U I C ALUMNI MAGAZINE.** 1996. bi-m. University of Illinois at Chicago, Alumni Association, 322 S. Green St., Ste. 204, Chicago, IL 60607. TEL 312-413-2390; 800-556-2586. E-mail: uicaamag@uic.edu; URL: http://www.uic.edu:80/orgs/alumni/. Ed. Patricia Weismantel; Pub. Louis D. Liay. adv. contact: Debra Kozlowski.
   Description: Covers events related to the university and its alumni, including alumni working for the public good.

378   US
U OF L. 1982. q. University of Louisville, Alumni Association, Office of University Relations, 19 Development and University Relations Bldg., University of Louisville, Louisville, KY 40292. TEL 502-852-6171. FAX 502-852-7658. Ed. John Chamberlain. R&P contact: Oscar Bryant. adv. contact: Oscar Bryant. circ. 85,000 (controlled). **Document type:** academic/scholarly publication.

378.1   SA   ISSN 0041-5405
U P E N. (University of Port Elizabeth Newspaper) (Text in Afrikaans, English) 1968. fortn. free. University of Port Elizabeth, P.O. Box 1600, Port Elizabeth 6000, South Africa. TEL 27-41-5042173. FAX 27-41-5042574. Ed.Bd. adv.; bk.rev.; film rev.; play rev.; illus.; circ. 3,000 (controlled). (tabloid format) **Document type:** newspaper.

378   PH   ISSN 0117-245X
U P NEWSLETTER; the community newspaper of the University of the Philippines. (Text in English, Filipino) 1972. s-m. P.250($10) University of the Philippines, Information Office, 1st Fl. Mezzanine, Quezon Hall, U.P. Diliman, Quezon City, Philippines. FAX 96-15-72. E-mail: sio@nicole.upd.edu.ph. Ed. Helen E. Lopez. adv.; bk.rev. circ. 5,000. (tabloid format) **Document type:** newspaper, newsletter.
   ●Also available online.

378   CN
U Q A M JOURNAL. bi-m. (University of Quebec at Montreal) Access Media, 1124 Marie Anne Rd., East Ste 31, Montreal, PQ H2J 2B7, Canada. TEL 514-524-1182. FAX 514-524-7771. circ. 10,000.
   Formerly: U Q A M Hebdo.

378.1   US   ISSN 8750-7927
U S C TROJAN FAMILY. 1970. q. free. University of Southern California, U S C Magazines, University Park (KAP 249), Los Angeles, CA 90089-2537. TEL 213-740-2684. FAX 213-740-1746. Ed. Susan Heitman. illus. circ. 200,000. (avail. on records) **Document type:** academic/scholarly publication.
   Former titles: Trojan Family (ISSN 0042-0085); University of Southern California Alumni Review.

378   US
U S F ORACLE. 1965. d. University of South Florida, 4202 E. Fowler, CPR 472, Tampa, FL 33620. TEL 813-974-2617. FAX 813-974-4887. Ed. Michele Sager. R&P contact: Michele Sager. TEL 974-5190. adv. contact: Janet Gallagher. circ. 15,000. **Document type:** newspaper.

378   US
U S M ALUMNI NEWS. 1947. q. membership. University of Southern Mississippi, Alumni Association, Southern Station, Box 5013, Hattiesburg, MS 39406-5013. Ed. J. Claire Gerald. circ. 14,750.
   Description: Features and news for and about former students of the University of Southern Mississippi.

278   US
U S NAVAL ACADEMY ALUMNI ASSOCIATION. REGISTER OF ALUMNI. 1938. a. $35. U S Naval Academy Alumni Association, Inc., Alumni House, Annapolis, MD 21402. TEL 301-263-4448. Ed. Yvonne Parker. R&P contact: Yvonne Parker. adv. contact: Bobbie Collins. index. circ. 2,000. (processed) **Document type:** directory.

378.1   US   ISSN 0041-5561
U S U STAFF NEWS. vol.10, 1970. w. (not issued in summer). free to qualified personnel. Utah State University, Logan, UT 84322-0500. TEL 801-797-1352. FAX 801-797-1250. E-mail: chislop@relations.usu.edu; URL: http://www.usu.edu. Ed. Craig Hislop. circ. 3,500. **Document type:** newsletter.

378   US
U T DAILY BEACON. 1900. d. (Mon.-Fri.). $165. University of Tennessee at Knoxville, 5 Communications Bldg., Knoxville, TN 37996. TEL 615-974-3231. Ed. Irene McHugh. adv. contact: Lynne Nennstiel. bk.rev. circ. 16,000. **Document type:** newspaper.

378   US
U W M POST. (University of Wisconsin at Milwaukee) 1956. w. $50. U W M Post, Inc., Box 413, Union Box 88, Milwaukee, WI 53201. TEL 414-229-4578. FAX 414-229-4579. Ed. Paul Freitag. R&P contact: Gary Grass. adv. contact: Jacob Sutrick. bk.rev. circ. 10,000. **Document type:** newspaper.

378   CN   ISSN 1186-4745
UBYSSEY. 1918. s-w. Can.$40. University of British Columbia, Rm. 245 K, S.U.B., Vancouver, BC V6T 1Z1, Canada. TEL 604-822-6681. FAX 604-822-1658. Ed. Joe Clark. R&P contact: Fernie Pereira. adv. contact: Fernie Pereira. bk.rev.; film rev. circ. 12,000. (tabloid format) **Document type:** academic/scholarly publication, newspaper.
   Former titles (until 1949): Daily Ubyssey (ISSN 1186-4737); (until 1948): Ubyssey (ISSN 1186-4729)
   Refereed Serial

378   GW
UNI-FORUM. 1985. m. free. Justus-Liebig-Universitaet, Ludwigstr. 23, 35390 Giessen, Germany. TEL 49-641-9912040. FAX 49-641-9912049. E-mail: christel.lauterbach@admin.uni-giessen.de; URL: http://www.uni-giessen.de. Ed. Christel Lauterbach. adv. circ. 8,000. **Document type:** bulletin.

371.805   GW   ISSN 0943-4399
UNI-INFO. 1973. m. free. Carl von Ossietzky Universitaet Oldenburg, Ammerlaender Heerstr. 114, 26129 Oldenburg, Germany. TEL 49-441-7982417. FAX 49-441-7982435. E-mail: presse@admin.uni-oldenburg.de; URL: http://www.admin.uni-oldenburg.de/presse/uni-info. Ed. Gerhard Harms. adv.; circ. 4,500. **Document type:** academic/scholarly publication, newspaper.
   Description: University of Oldenburg politics, news, science and culture.

378   GW   ISSN 0176-036X
UNI ULM INTERN; Das Ulmer Universitaetsmagazin. 1971. m. (approx.). free. Universitaet Ulm, Pressestelle, Albert-Einstein-Allee 5, 89081 Ulm, Germany. TEL 49-731-5022020. FAX 49-731-5022016. E-mail: peter.pietschmann@rektoramt.uni-ulm.de. Ed. Peter Pietschmann. adv. contact: Sabine Kindermann. bk.rev. circ. 10,000. **Indexed:** Sci.Cit.Ind. **Document type:** newsletter.
   Description: Publication for university personnel, students, scientists, engineers, and freelance professionals. Features include education, current issues, research, student news, and calendar of events.

378   US
UNICORN (PHILADELPHIA). q. free to alumni. Peirce College, 1420 Pine St., Philadelphia, PA 19102-4699. TEL 215-545-6400. FAX 215-546-5996. Ed. Len McLean. **Document type:** newsletter.
   Formerly: Today (Philadelphia).

378   GW   ISSN 0939-4826
UNICUM. 1983. m. DM.30. Unicum Verlag GmbH, Willy-Brandt-Platz 5-7, 44787 Bochum, Germany. TEL 49-234-96151-0. FAX 49-234-60256. URL: http://www.unicum.de. Ed. Uwe Heinrich; Pub. Hermann-Josef Billstein. adv.: B&W page DM.16800; trim 210 x 295; adv. contact: Norbert Neuhaus. bk.rev.; illus.; circ. 333,000 (controlled). (back issues avail.) **Document type:** consumer publication.
   Description: Nationwide campus magazine for university students and alumni.

COLLEGE AND ALUMNI

378   **GW**
UNIJOURNAL. bi-m. Universitaet Trier, Pressestelle, 54286 Trier, Germany. TEL 49-651-2014239. FAX 49-651-2014247. E-mail: neyses@olewig.uni-trier.de; URL: http://www.uni-trier.de. Ed. Heidi Neyses. illus. **Document type:** bulletin.

378.1   **AT**   **ISSN 0041-7017**
UNION RECORDER. 1921. 13/yr. Aus.$30. University of Sydney Union, Sydney, N.S.W. 2006, Australia. TEL 61-2-5636111. FAX 61-2-5636109. E-mail: union@usyd.edu.au. Ed. Andrea Overall. R&P contact: Jason Harty. adv. contact: Kate Baird. bk.rev.; film rev.; play rev.; illus.; stat. circ. 9,000. **Document type:** academic/scholarly publication, newsletter.

378   **CN**   **ISSN 1181-8409**
UNISCOPE. 1981. 20/yr. University de Quebec a Hull, Service de l'Information et des Relations Publiques, C.P. 1250 succ. B, 170 rue Hotel de Ville, Hull, Que. J8X 3X7, Canada. TEL 819-595-3960. FAX 819-595-3924. Ed. Roger Labelle. circ. 600.
Formerly (until 1990): Nouvel Introspec (ISSN 0711-0162)

378   **GW**   **ISSN 0171-4880**
UNISPIEGEL. 1969. 6/yr. free. Rektor der Universitaet Heidelberg, Postfach 105760, 69047 Heidelberg, Germany. TEL 49-6221-542310. FAX 49-6221-542317. E-mail: presse@urz.uni-heidelberg.de; URL: http://www.uni-heidelberg.de. Ed. Michael Schwarz. adv. contact: Edeltraud Conen. bk.rev. circ. 25,000. **Document type:** newsletter.
Formerly: Unispiegel Aktuell.
Description: Higher education politics, college news, and general interest articles for students.

378   **CN**
L'UNITE.* (Text in French) 1975. s-m. (Universite du Quebec a Montreal) Publi-Peq, 3575 bd. St. Laurent, Ste. 232, Montreal, PQ H2K 3J6, Canada. adv.; bk.rev.; film rev.; play rev. circ. 10,000. (tabloid format; back issues avail.)

378.1   **CN**   **ISSN 0041-817X**
UNITER. (Text mainly in English, occasionally in French) 1947. bi-m. Can.$27.64. University of Winnipeg, Students Association, Rm. 230 Lockhart Hall, 515 Portage Ave., Winnipeg, MB R3B 2E9, Canada. TEL 204-786-9790. adv.; bk.rev.; film rev.; play rev.; illus. circ. 4,000. (tabloid format)

367 378   **UK**
UNIVERSAL POST.* 1992. fortn. Charlton Allison Publishing, Universal Post, 2 Ashwood Terrace, Sunderland, Tyne & Wear SR2 7NB, England. Ed. Colin Thorne. adv.: page £375; adv. contact: Maggie Edge. bk.rev.; film rev.; play rev.; illus.; circ. 5,000. (tabloid format; back issues avail.) **Document type:** newspaper.
Description: Aimed at the students and staff of the University of Sunderland.

378   **CR**
UNIVERSIDAD. 1970. w. Col.2000($40) Universidad de Costa Rica, Revista Universitaria, Apdo. 21, 2060 San Jose, Costa Rica. TEL 25-58-57. FAX 342382-340452. Ed. Carlos Morales. adv. contact: Carlos Campos. bk.rev. circ. 15,000. **Document type:** newspaper.

378   **CR**   **ISSN 1017-7507**
UNIVERSIDAD AUTONOMA DE CENTRO AMERICA. ACTA ACADEMICA.* 1987. biennial. Universidad Autonoma de Centro America, Apdo. 7637, San Jose 1000, Costa Rica.

378   **CK**
UNIVERSIDAD EXTERNADO DE COLOMBIA. INFORMATIVO. 3/yr. Universidad Externado de Colombia, Departamento de Publicaciones, Calle 12 No. 0-46 Este, Apdo. Aereo 034141, Bogota, Colombia. TEL 341-2610. FAX 2843769. **Document type:** newspaper.

500   **CK**
UNIVERSIDAD TECNOLOGICA DEL MAGDALENA.*
(Summaries in English and-or German) 1971. q. Universidad Tecnologica del Magdalena (UTEMAG), Apdo. Aereo No. 731, Santa Marta, Colombia. illus.

378   **GW**   **ISSN 0938-2569**
UNIVERSITAET AUGSBURG. PERSONEN- UND STUDIENVERZEICHNIS. 1970. s-a. DM.6.50. Presse Druck- und Verlagsgesellschaft mbH, Curt-Frenzel-Str. 2, 86167 Augsburg, Germany. TEL 49-821-777-0. FAX 49-821-7772383. Ed. Alois Zimmerman. adv. contact: Wolfgang Hoffmann. circ. 7,500. (back issues avail.) **Document type:** academic/scholarly publication.

378   **GW**   **ISSN 0931-0746**
UNIVERSITAET ERLANGEN - NUERNBERG. VORLESUNGSVERZEICHNIS. 1920. s-a. DM.4.80. Schlossplatz 4, 91054 Erlangen, Germany. TEL 09131-852131. TELEX 629830-UNIER-D.

378   **GW**   **ISSN 0947-1049**
UNIVERSITAET LEIPZIG. 8/yr. DM.25 (effective 1996); newsstand price: DM.3. (Universitaet Leipzig, Pressestelle) Leipziger Universitaetsverlag GmbH, Augustusplatz 10, 04109 Leipzig, Germany. TEL 49-341-2619964. FAX 49-341-9730099. Ed. Volker Schulte. adv.; circ. 9,000. **Document type:** academic/scholarly publication.

378   **GW**   **ISSN 0179-1109**
UNIVERSITAET PASSAU. VORLESUNGSVERZEICHNIS. s-a. Verlag Passavia, Vornholzstr. 40, 94036 Passau, Germany. TEL 0851-7002-0. FAX 0851-7002-77. **Document type:** directory.

378.1   **NE**   **ISSN 0920-7368**
UNIVERSITEITSKRANT GRONINGEN. Short title: U K. 1971. w. fl.42. Stichting Universiteitsblad, Postbus 80, 9700 AB Groningen, Netherlands. TEL 31-50-3636700. FAX 31-50-3636698. E-mail: uk@bureau.rug.nl; URL: http://docserver.ub.rug.nl/edoc/uk/inhoud.html. adv.; bk.rev.; illus. circ. 27,000. **Document type:** newspaper.
—KNAW.
Former titles: Rijksuniversiteit te Groningen. Universiteitskrant; Rijksuniversiteit te Groningen. Mededelingenblad (ISSN 0035-5348)

378.1   **PH**   **ISSN 0042-0360**
UNIVERSITY (PHILIPPINES). q. Philippine Women's University, Taft Ave., Manila 2801, Philippines. Ed. Edgardo Ray Pedroche. charts; illus. circ. 1,000.

UNIVERSITY AVIATION ASSOCIATION. NEWSLETTER. see TRANSPORTATION — Air Transport

378   **US**
UNIVERSITY DAILY. 1925. d. (Mon.-Fri.). $90. Texas Tech University, Student Publications, 103 Journalism Bldg., Texas Tech University, Lubbock, TX 79409. TEL 806-742-3388. FAX 806-742-2434. Ed. Megan Clark; Pub. Jan T. Childress. bk.rev. circ. 17,000. **Document type:** newspaper.

378   **US**   **ISSN 0746-4967**
UNIVERSITY DAILY KANSAN. 1889. d. (Mon.-Fri.). $120. University Daily Kansan, 119 Stauffer-Flint Hall, Lawrence, KS 66045-0001. TEL 913-864-4358. FAX 913-864-5261. URL: http://www.kansan.com. R&P contact: Tom Eblen. adv. contact: Dan Simon. circ. 13,000. **Document type:** newspaper.
●Also available online.
Description: Covers topics of interest to the university community.

378.198   **US**
THE UNIVERSITY NEWS. 1976. w. $32 (1997 & 1998). University of Dallas, University News, 1845 E. Northgate Dr., Box 732, Irving, TX 75062. TEL 972-721-5089. FAX 972-721-5048. URL: http://www.acad.udanas.edu. Ed. Aaron Deacon. R&P contact: Brian Bourque. adv.: page $400; adv. contact: Susannah West. bk.rev.; film rev. circ. 2,000. (tabloid format; reprint service avail.) **Document type:** newspaper.
Refereed Serial

378.1   **NZ**
UNIVERSITY OF AUCKLAND NEWS. 1971. m. (10/yr). NZ.$20 (foreign NZ.$30). University of Auckland, Private Bag, Auckland, New Zealand. TEL 64-9-3737599. FAX 64-9-3737047. Ed. A.H. Ashton. adv.; bk.rev. circ. 5,700.
Supersedes: University of Auckland Gazette (ISSN 0041-9397)

378   **UK**   **ISSN 0143-1951**
UNIVERSITY OF BRISTOL. NEWSLETTER. 1969. fortn. £17.50. University of Bristol, Information Office, Senate House, Tyndall Ave., Clifton, Bristol, Avon BS8 1TH, England. TEL 44-117-928-7777. FAX 44-117-929-2396. E-mail: info.office@bristol.ac.uk. Ed. Don Carleton. adv.: page £400; trim 256 x 205; adv. contact: Joanne Fryer. bk.rev.; film rev.; play rev.; illus.; stat. circ. 7,700. (back issues avail.) **Document type:** newsletter.
Description: Covers activities of the University of Bristol, and items of interest to members and friends of the university.

378   **CN**   **ISSN 0300-4333**
UNIVERSITY OF CALGARY GAZETTE. 1971. w. (Sep.-Apr.); fortn. (May-Aug.). Can.$30. University of Calgary, Public Affairs, 2500 University Dr., N.W., Calgary, Alta. T2N 1N4, Canada. TEL 403-220-3500. FAX 403-282-8413. E-mail: durquhar@acs.ucalgary.ca. Ed. Dennis Urquhart. adv.; bk.rev.; charts; illus.; stat. circ. 6,600. (tabloid format) **Document type:** newspaper.
●Also available online.

378.1   **US**   **ISSN 0041-9508**
LD908
UNIVERSITY OF CHICAGO MAGAZINE. 1907. bi-m. free to alumni. University of Chicago, 1313 E. 60th St., Chicago, IL 60637. TEL 773-702-2163. FAX 773-702-2166. E-mail: uchicago-magazine@uchicago.edu; URL: http://www2.uchicago.edu/alumni/alumni.mag//. Ed. Mary Ruth Yoe. adv.; bk.rev.; index. circ. 100,000.
—UnCover.
Description: Covers a variety of topics pertaining to the history of the university and its alumni.

UNIVERSITY OF CHICAGO RECORD. see EDUCATION — *Higher Education*

378   **US**
UNIVERSITY OF DELAWARE. STUDENT CENTER. REVIEW. 1882. 104/yr. 20. University of Delaware, Student Center, B-1 Student Ctr., Newark, DE 19716. TEL 302-451-2771. FAX 032-451-1396. adv.; bk.rev.; circ. 15,000 (controlled). **Document type:** newspaper.

378   **US**
UNIVERSITY OF DELAWARE MESSENGER. 1991. q. free to alumni. University of Delaware, Office of Public Relations, 150 S. College Ave., Newark, DE 19716. TEL 302-831-2791. FAX 302-831-1440. E-mail: themessenger@mvs.udel.edu; URL: http://www.udel.edu/pr. Ed. Cornelia Weil. adv. contact: Ed Stoner. circ. 85,000. (tabloid format) **Document type:** academic/scholarly publication.
Description: Reports on noteworthy alumni and college and university events.

378.1   **US**
UNIVERSITY OF DENVER JOURNAL. 1961. q. free to alumni. University of Denver, Office of Communications, Denver, CO 80208. TEL 303-871-2711. FAX 303-871-3827. E-mail: rbrant@du.edu. Ed. Rebecca Brant. bk.rev.; charts; illus.; circ. 70,000 (controlled). **Document type:** newspaper.
Former titles: University of Denver News (ISSN 0891-6020); University of Denver Alumni News (ISSN 0041-9532)

378   **UK**
UNIVERSITY OF EDINBURGH BULLETIN. m. University of Edinburgh, Old College, South Bridge, Edinburgh EH8 9YL, Scotland. TEL 44-131-650-2273. FAX 44-131-650-2253. URL: http://www.ed.ac.uk/edinfo/bull/bull_menu.html. Ed. Ray Footman. adv.; bk.rev. circ. 6,500. **Document type:** bulletin.

378   **UK**   **ISSN 0041-9567**
LH5.E4
UNIVERSITY OF EDINBURGH JOURNAL. 1925. s-a. £10 (effective 1997). University of Edinburgh, Graduates' Association, 5 Buccleuch Pl., Edinburgh EH8 9LW, Scotland. TEL 44-131-650-4292. Ed. Jean R. Guild. adv. contact: C. Tough. bk.rev.; index; circ. 3,000 (paid). **Document type:** academic/scholarly publication.

COLLEGE AND ALUMNI

378   US
UNIVERSITY OF HARTFORD OBSERVER. 1974. q. free to qualified personnel. University of Hartford, Office of University Affairs, 200 Bloomfield Ave., West Hartford, CT 06117-1599. TEL 860-768-5096. FAX 860-768-4378. E-mail: observer@uhavax.hartford.edu; URL: http://www.hartford.edu. Ed. Diana Simonds. R&P contact: Diana Simonds. circ. 70,000. **Document type:** newspaper.
    Description: Contains news, information, and feature articles pertaining to the university, its faculty, staff, alumni, and students.

378 617.6   US   ISSN 1088-9108
UNIVERSITY OF ILLINOIS AT CHICAGO. COLLEGE OF DENTISTRY. ALUMNI REPORT. 1985. s-a. $10 (free to alumni). University of Illinois at Chicago, College of Dentistry, 801 S. Paulina St., Chicago, IL 60612-7211. TEL 312-996-8495. FAX 312-996-1022. E-mail: billbike@uic.edu. Ed. William Bike; Pub. Irwin Robinson. R&P contact: William Bike. circ. 5,500. **Document type:** bulletin.

378.1   CN   ISSN 0706-9847
UNIVERSITY OF MANITOBA ALUMNI JOURNAL. 1936. q. Can.$35 to non-members. University of Manitoba, Alumni Association, 180 Dafoe Rd., Winnipeg, MB R3T 2N2, Canada. TEL 204-474-9946. FAX 204-261-6034. Ed. Chris Rutkowski. adv.; bk.rev.; illus. circ. 16,000. **Document type:** academic/scholarly publication.

378   US   ISSN 1048-9606
UNIVERSITY OF MARYLAND. MEDICAL ALUMNI ASSOCIATION. BULLETIN. vol.72, 1988. q. $15. University of Maryland, Medical Alumni Association, 522 W. Lombard St., Baltimore, MD 21201. TEL 410-706-7454. FAX 410-706-3658. Ed. Carole Miller. adv. circ. 8,000. (back issues avail.) **Document type:** bulletin.
    Formerly (until 1978): University of Maryland. School of Medicine. Bulletin (ISSN 1048-9614)

378   MF
UNIVERSITY OF MAURITIUS. JOURNAL. (Text in English and French; summaries in English) 1979. q. Rs.60. University of Mauritius, Reduit, Mauritius. circ. 250.

378.1   US   ISSN 0895-5409
UNIVERSITY OF NORTH DAKOTA. ALUMNI REVIEW. 1940. bi-m. free to alumni. University of North Dakota, Alumni Association and Foundation, Box 8157, Grand Forks, ND 58201. TEL 701-777-2611. FAX 701-777-4859. Ed. Jacqueline Flaten. adv.; bk.rev. circ. 76,000. (tabloid format) **Document type:** newsletter.

378.1   SA   ISSN 0259-1871
UNIVERSITY OF PRETORIA. ANNUAL REPORT/UNIVERSITEIT VAN PRETORIA. JAARVERSLAG. (Text in Afrikaans, English) 1954. a. free. University of Pretoria - Universiteit van Pretoria, Bureau for Public Relations, Pretoria 0002, South Africa. TEL 27-12-420-2252. FAX 27-12-432303. E-mail: manus@ccnet.up.ac.za. Ed. H.K. Myburgh. adv.; bibl. circ. 4,000. **Document type:** corporate report.
    Description: Reports on the activities, exchanges, students and faculties of the university.

UNIVERSITY OF QUEENSLAND. CALENDAR SERIES. DOCTOR OF PHILOSOPHY HANDBOOK. see EDUCATION — Higher Education

UNIVERSITY OF QUEENSLAND. CALENDAR SERIES. POSTGRADUATE STUDIES BOOK. see EDUCATION — Higher Education

UNIVERSITY OF QUEENSLAND. CALENDAR SERIES. STUDENT HANDBOOK - SURVIVAL GUIDE. see EDUCATION — Higher Education

378 266   US
UNIVERSITY OF ST. THOMAS MAGAZINE. 1985. q. free. University of St. Thomas, 2115 Summit Ave., St. Paul, MN 55105-1096. TEL 612-962-6741. FAX 612-962-6755. Ed.Bd. illus. circ. 39,000. (back issues avail.) **Document type:** consumer publication.
    Formerly (until 1990): College of St. Thomas. Magazine; Incorporates (1969-1990): Memorandum (St. Paul).
    Description: Keeps alumni informed about campus life.

378   US
UNIVERSITY OF SAN FRANCISCO MAGAZINE. 1975. q. free. University of San Francisco, Office of Public Affairs, 416 Corvell Hall, 2130 Fulton St., San Francisco, CA 94117. Ed. Mel Taylor. circ. 70,000.
    Formerly: University of San Francisco. Alumni Association. Alumnus; Which supersedes: U S F View; Which was formerly: View from the University of San Francisco.

378.1   UK
UNIVERSITY OF SHEFFIELD. DIARY OF EVENTS. 1961. 12/yr. membership. University of Sheffield, Sheffield S10 2TN, England. TEL 44-114-282-4015. FAX 44-114-279-8603. Ed. P.V. Broadhead. circ. 5,000. **Document type:** bulletin.
    Supersedes in part: University of Sheffield. Newsletter Diary (ISSN 0309-0191); University of Sheffield. Diary of Events (ISSN 0042-0034); University of Sheffield Reporter.

378.1   UK
UNIVERSITY OF SHEFFIELD. NEWSLETTER. 1976. 14/yr. University of Sheffield, Sheffield S10 2TN, England. TEL 44-114-282-4015. FAX 44-114-279-8603. Ed. Roger Allum. circ. 5,000. **Document type:** newsletter.
    Supersedes in part: University of Sheffield. Newsletter Diary (ISSN 0309-0191)

378.1   AT   ISSN 0042-0107
UNIVERSITY OF SYDNEY. GAZETTE. 1950. 2/yr. free. University of Sydney, Sydney, N.S.W. 2006, Australia. TEL 61-2-93513167. FAX 61-2-93513289. E-mail: m.theobald@publications.usyd.edu.au; URL: http://www.usyd.edu.au/su/exterel/gazette/. Ed. Marian Theobald. adv. contact: Jane O'Donnell. bk.rev. circ. 120,000. (tabloid format) **Document type:** newsletter.
    Description: Contains news of graduates, academic research, personality profiles etc.

UNIVERSITY OF TEXAS AT AUSTIN. GRADUATE SCHOOL OF LIBRARY AND INFORMATION SCIENCE. ALUMNI NEWS. see LIBRARY AND INFORMATION SCIENCES

378.1   CN
UNIVERSITY OF TORONTO BULLETIN. 21/yr. Can.$35. University of Toronto, Department of Public Affairs, 21 King's College Circle, Toronto, ON M5S 3J3, Canada. TEL 416-978-7016. FAX 416-978-7430. E-mail: janes@dur.utoronto.ca. Ed. Jane Stirling. adv. contact: Nancy Bush. bk.rev. circ. 16,500. (tabloid format) **Document type:** newspaper.
    ● Also available online.
    Description: News for faculty and staff about University events, announcements.

378.1   CN   ISSN 0840-562X
UNIVERSITY OF TORONTO MAGAZINE. 1967. q. Can.$20. University of Toronto, Department of Public Affairs, 21 King's College Circle, Toronto, ON M5S 3J3, Canada. TEL 416-946-3192. FAX 416-978-7430. E-mail: karen@dur.utoronto.ca. Eds. Karen Hanley, Karina Dahlin. adv. contact: Nancy Bush. bk.rev.; illus. circ. 200,000. (back issues avail.) **Document type:** consumer publication.
    Former titles: University of Toronto Alumni Magazine (ISSN 0833-4536); University of Toronto Graduate; University of Toronto News (ISSN 0042-0212)
    Description: Contains information about University activities for alumni.

378   US
UNIVERSITY OF VIRGINIA. DECLARATION. w. University of Virginia, Box 418 Newcomb Hall Sta., Charlottesville, VA 22901. TEL 804-924-7068.

378   US
UNIVERSITY OF WASHINGTON DAILY. 1909. d. (Mon.-Fri.). $90. University of Washington, Board of Student Publications, 144 Communications, Box 353720, Seattle, WA 98195. TEL 206-543-7666. FAX 206-543-2345. Ed. Kenneth Bogle; Pub. Oren Campbell. adv. contact: Carolynn Landwehr. circ. 18,000. (controlled). (tabloid format) **Document type:** newspaper.

378.198   CN   ISSN 0227-2199
UNIVERSITY OF WATERLOO COURIER. 1980. q. free. University of Waterloo, Waterloo, Ont. N2L 3G1, Canada. TEL 519-885-1211. circ. 50,000. (controlled).

378.198   CN   ISSN 0841-2715
UNIVERSITY OF WESTERN ONTARIO. GAZETTE. 1906. 4/w. Can.$60. University of Western Ontario, University Community Center, Rm. 263, London, ON N6A 3K7, Canada. TEL 519-661-3580. FAX 519-661-3825. E-mail: gazette@julian.uwo.ca. Ed. Jeremy Barker. adv.: page Can.$1800; adv. contact: Alex McKay. bk.rev.; film rev.; play rev. circ. 18,500. (tabloid format; also avail. in microfilm; back issues avail.) **Document type:** newspaper.

378   AT   ISSN 0313-6906
UNIVERSITY OF WOLLONGONG. ANNUAL REPORT. a. free. University of Wollongong, Northfields Ave., Wollongong, N.S.W. 2522, Australia. TEL 61-42-213555. FAX 61-42-213477. **Document type:** corporate report.
    Description: Reports on academic and research activities of the University.

378   AT   ISSN 1036-7985
UNIVERSITY OF WOLLONGONG. POSTGRADUATE CALENDAR. a. Aus.$8. University of Wollongong, Northfields Ave., Wollongong, N.S.W. 2522, Australia. TEL 61-42-213555. FAX 61-42-213477.
    Former titles: University of Wollongong. Postgraduate Handbook; University of Wollongong. Faculties Sector Postgraduate Handbook (ISSN 0726-1586); Which supersedes in part: University of Wollongong. Calendar (ISSN 0312-0007)
    Description: Provides description of postgraduate courses available at the university.

378   AT   ISSN 1032-0741
UNIVERSITY OF WOLLONGONG. RESEARCH REPORT. a. free. University of Wollongong, Northfields Ave., Wollongong, N.S.W. 2522, Australia. TEL 61-42-213386. FAX 61-42-214338.
    Description: Reports on research activities of the university.

378   AT   ISSN 1036-2371
UNIVERSITY OF WOLLONGONG. UNDERGRADUATE CALENDAR. a. Aus.$12. University of Wollongong, Northfields Ave., Wollongong, N.S.W. 2522, Australia. TEL 61-42-213555. FAX 61-42-213477.
    Former titles: University of Wollongong. Undergraduate Handbook (ISSN 0726-0717); University of Wollongong. Institute Sector Handbook (ISSN 0810-5294); Which supersedes in part: University of Wollongong. Calendar (ISSN 0312-0007)
    Description: Provides descriptions of undergraduate courses available at the university.

378   US
THE UNIVERSITY PACER. 1984. m. free. University of Rhode Island, Division of University Advancement, 22 Davis Hall, Kingston, RI 02881. TEL 401-874-2116. FAX 401-789-3435. E-mail: jredlich@dowis.uri.edu; URL: http://www.davis.uri.edu. Ed. Jhodi R. Redlich. R&P contact: Jhodi Redlich. circ. 24,000. **Document type:** newspaper.
    Description: Discusses events taking place at the University of Rhode Island.

378   US
UNIVERSITY SCOPE. 1933. q. Loma Linda University, Loma Linda, CA 92350. TEL 909-824-4526. URL: http://www.llu.edu/news/scope/. Eds. W. Augustus Cheatham, Richard W. Weismeyer. adv. circ. 35,000.

378   US
UNIVERSITY TIMES (CHARLOTTE). 1965. s-w. $30. University of North Carolina at Charlotte, Cone Center, 9201 Univ. City Blvd., Charlotte, NC 28223-0001. TEL 704-547-2663. Ed. Mike Twist. R&P contact: Wayne Maikranz. adv. contact: Dixie Tew. circ. 20,000. **Document type:** newspaper.
    Formerly: Forty-Niner Times.
    Description: Covers university news.

378.198   US
UNIVERSITY TIMES (LOS ANGELES). d. California State University, Los Angeles, 515 State University Dr., Los Angeles, CA 90032. TEL 213-343-4220. FAX 213-343-2670. adv.; bk.rev. circ. 10,000. (tabloid format; back issues avail.)

378   CN
L'UQUOI. (Text in French) m. Universite de Quebec a Hull, C.P. 1250 succ. B, 170 rue Hotel de Ville, Hull, Que. J8X 3X7, Canada. adv. circ. 2,000.

1978 COLLEGE AND ALUMNI

378.18 US ISSN 1082-1201
UTAH STATE UNIVERSITY MAGAZINE. 1969. q. $10 (free to alumni). Utah State University, Information Services, Logan, UT 84322-0500. TEL 801-797-1353. FAX 801-797-1250. E-mail: janek@relations.esu.edu. Ed. Jane Koerner. R&P contact: Jane Koerner. adv. contact: Scott Olsen. circ. 60,000 (controlled). **Document type:** consumer publication.
Formerly (until 1994): Outlook (Logan) (ISSN 1073-0281)

378 US
UTAH STATESMAN. 1902. 3/w. $45. Taggart Student Center, Rm. 317, Box 1249, Logan, UT 84322-0165. TEL 801-750-1743. FAX 801-750-2571. Pub. Jay Wamsley. adv. contact: Jay Wamsley. circ. 7,000. (tabloid format) **Document type:** newspaper.

378 US
V U U INFORMER. 1900. m. free. Virginia Union University, 1500 N. Lombardy St., Richmond, VA 23220-1790. TEL 804-257-5655. FAX 804-257-5818. Ed. A.H. Benson. adv. contact: A.H. Benson. bk.rev. circ. 2,000. (tabloid format; back issues avail.) **Document type:** newspaper.
Formerly: Campus Informer.
Description: Presents local, state, national, and international events as they relate to the university.

378.18 US
VALENCIA SOURCE; Valencia student press. 1978. fortn. $5. Valencia Community College, Box 3028, Orlando, FL 32802. TEL 407-299-5000. FAX 407-293-8839. Ed. Rich Grissom; Pub. Joe Gisondi. R&P contact: Joe Gisondi. adv.: page $300; adv. contact: Joe Gisondi. bk.rev.; film rev.; play rev. circ. 6,000. (tabloid format) **Document type:** newspaper.
Formerly: Paper.

378.198 US ISSN 0889-0935
THE VALLEY FORGE. 1965. bi-w. $15. Rock Valley Community College, 3301 N. Mulford, Rockford, IL 61114. TEL 815-654-4458. FAX 815-654-5245. Ed. Susan La Salla. adv.; bk.rev.; film rev.; music rev.; play rev.; illus. circ. 3,200. (looseleaf format) **Document type:** newspaper.

378.1 US ISSN 0042-2517
VANDERBILT HUSTLER. 1888. s-w. $80. Vanderbilt Student Communications, Inc., Box 1504-B, Nashville, TN 37235. TEL 615-322-2424. FAX 615-322-3762. Ed. Leah Stewart. adv.: page $375; adv. contact: Bryce Wells. bk.rev.; film rev.; play rev.; illus. circ. 10,000. (tabloid format) **Document type:** newspaper.
Description: Provides students with university news; includes a weekly arts and entertainment supplement.

378 US
VANDERBILT MAGAZINE. 1915. q. free to qualified personnel. Vanderbilt University, Box 91, Peabody Sta., Nashville, TN 37203. TEL 615-322-2601. FAX 615-343-8340. circ. 30,000.

378 US
VANGUARD (MOBILE). 1964. w. $30. University of South Alabama, University Board of Publications, c/o Student Media Manager Loran Lewis, Drawer U-25100, Mobile, AL 36688. TEL 334-460-6442. FAX 334-414-8293. E-mail: llewis@jaguar1.usouthal.edu; URL: http://www.usouthal.edu/. R&P contact: Loran Lewis. adv.: page $630; adv. contact: Amy Oliver. bk.rev. circ. 8,000. (also avail. in microfilm) **Document type:** newspaper.
●Also available online.

378 US
VANGUARD (PORTLAND). Variant title: Daily Vanguard. Seasonal edition: Summer Vanguard. vol.49, 1993. d. (Tues.-Fri.) during school yr.; w. during summer. $75. Portland State University, Publications Board, Box 347, Portland, OR 97207-0347. TEL 503-725-4531. FAX 503-725-5860. R&P contact: Judson Randall. TEL 503-725-5687. adv.: B&W page $622.40; trim 11 x 17. bk.rev.; illus. (tabloid format) **Document type:** newspaper.

378 US
EL VAQUERO. 1927. w. (during the academic year). $25. Glendale Community College, 1500 N. Verdugo Rd., Glendale, CA 91208-2894. TEL 818-240-1000. FAX 818-549-9436. adv.; circ. 3,500 (controlled).

378.1 CN ISSN 0042-2789
VARSITY. 1880. s-w. (during academic year). Can.$35. (University of Toronto) Varsity Publications Inc., 44 St. George St., Toronto, ON M5S 2E4, Canada. TEL 416-979-2831. adv.; bk.rev.; film rev.; play rev. circ. 25,000. (tabloid format; also avail. in microfilm; back issues avail.)

378.1 SA ISSN 0042-2797
VARSITY. (Text in English) 1940. fortn. R.10. (University of Cape Town, Students Representative Council) S R C Press, University of Cape Town, Rondebosch 7700, South Africa. TEL 021 698531. adv.; bk.rev.; film rev.; play rev.; illus.; circ. 7,500 (controlled). (tabloid format)

378 KE
VARSITY FOCUS. (Text in English) 1979. bi-m. free. (University of Nairobi, School of Journalism, Office of the Vice-Chancellor) Nairobi University Press, P.O. Box 30197, Nairobi, Kenya. TEL 254-2-230588. FAX 254-2-212604. TELEX VARSITY KE 22095. Ed. Josphat K. Kirimania. bk.rev. circ. 2,000. **Document type:** newsletter.

378 US
THE VARSITY NEWS. 1917. w. free. University of Detroit Mercy, 3800 Puritan, Detroit, MI 48238. TEL 313-993-3300. FAX 313-993-1120. E-mail: miomj@udmercy.edu. Ed. Kristie Dressler. R&P contact: Mathew J. Mio. adv.: page $369; adv. contact: Rachel Martin. film rev.; music rev.; play rev. circ. 10,000. cols./p.: 6. (broadsheet format) **Document type:** newspaper.
Description: Publishes entertainment stories on the people and events that affect the University of Detroit Mercy.

378 CN ISSN 0229-9119
VARSITY STUDENT HANDBOOK. 1980. a. free. (Varsity Newspaper) Varsity Publications Inc., 44 St. George St., Toronto, ON M5S 2E4, Canada. TEL 416-979-2831. Ed.Bd. adv.; film rev.; play rev.; illus. circ. 25,000. (back issues avail.)

378.1 US ISSN 0042-2851
LH1.V3
VASSAR QUARTERLY. 1916. q. $10. Vassar College, Alumnae and Alumni, Alumnae House, Poughkeepsie, NY 12603. TEL 914-437-5447. FAX 914-437-7425. Ed. Georgette Weir. bk.rev.; charts; illus. circ. 31,000. **Document type:** consumer publication.
Formerly: Vassar Alumnae Magazine.

378 US
VASSAR VIEWS. 1971. q. free. Vassar College, Office of College Relations, Poughkeepsie, NY 12604. TEL 914-437-7400. Ed. Susan DeKrey. illus. circ. 33,000. **Document type:** newsletter.

378 US ISSN 0892-3132
VERMONT CYNIC. 1883. w. $15. University of Vermont, Lower Billings, Burlington, VT 05405-0040. TEL 802-656-4413. FAX 802-656-7719. Ed. Alex Johnson. adv.; bk.rev.; film rev.; play rev.; illus. circ. 10,000. (tabloid format) **Document type:** newspaper.
Description: University of Vermont student newspaper.

378.1 UI ISSN 0042-5125
VICTORIAN. 1871. a. £10. Victoria College, School and Old Victorians' Association, Jersey, Channel Islands. TEL 44-1534-37591. FAX 44-1534-27448. URL: http://www.user.itl.net/~rcco/. Ed. T.A. Ozturk. adv. contact: Anthony Ozturk. bk.rev.; illus. circ. 2,000.
Description: Reports on activities of Victoria College, Jersey and its Old Boy Association. Includes sports reports, reviews of related art and theatre, and features.
Refereed Serial

378.198 US
THE VIKING PRESS. 1981. fortn. free. Barstow Community College District, 2700 Barstow Rd., Barstow, CA 92311. TEL 619-252-2411. FAX 619-252-1875. Ed. Vincent C. Lovato, Jr. adv.; play rev. circ. 8,000. (tabloid format; back issues avail.)
Formerly (until vol.9, no.5, 1990): Barstow College Collegiate.

378.198 US
LH1.V6
VIRGINIA (CHARLOTTESVILLE). 1912. q. $30 (effective 1997 & 1998). University of Virginia, Alumni Association, Box 3446, Charlottesville, VA 22903. TEL 804-971-9721. FAX 804-296-4577. E-mail: alumnews@virginia.edu. Ed. Kathleen D. Valenzi; Pub. John B. Syer. adv. contact: Bonnie Coggin. bk.rev.; illus. circ. 51,500. **Document type:** consumer publication.
Former titles: University of Virginia Alumni News; (until 1925): University of Virginia Alumni Bulletin (ISSN 0195-8798)

378 US
VIRGINIA TECH COLLEGIATE TIMES. 1903. s-w. $22. Virginia Polytechnic Institute and State University, 363 Squires Hall, Student Center, Blacksburg, VA 24061. TEL 703-231-9860. FAX 703-231-5057. Ed. Heather McElrath. adv.; bk.rev. circ. 14,000. (also avail. in microfiche) **Document type:** newspaper.

378.1 CN ISSN 0822-7896
VOICE. vol.7, 1970. w. (Sep.-Apr.). $15. Langara College, Journalism Department, Langara, 100 W. 49th Ave., Vancouver, BC V5Y 2Z6, Canada. TEL 604-323-5396. FAX 604-323-5398. R&P contact: Gene Keith. TEL 604-323-5415. adv.; bk.rev.; film rev.; play rev.; charts; illus. circ. 1,000. (tabloid format) **Document type:** newspaper.
Former titles: V C C Voice (ISSN 0821-5871) & Savant (ISSN 0036-5084)

378 US
VOICE (SIOUX CENTER). 1956. q. free. Dordt College, 498 Fourth Ave. N.E., Sioux Center, IA 51250. TEL 712-722-6020. FAX 712-722-1185. Ed. Sally Jongsma. circ. 35,000. **Document type:** newspaper.
Description: Covers news and events of interest to alumni and supporters.

378.18 US
VOICE - SOUTHEASTERN COMMUNITY COLLEGE - SOUTH. 1980. w. free. Southeastern Community College, South Campus, 335 Messenger Rd., Keokuk, IA 52632. TEL 319-524-3221. Ed. Thomas P. Gardner. circ. 300.

378.198 US
VOICES OF THE WILDCATS. m. Bethune-Cookman College, 640 Second Ave., Daytona Beach, FL 32014. TEL 904-255-1401.

378 US
VOLANTE. w. $14. Students Publications Board, Inc, University of South Dakota, 414 East Clark, Vermillion, SD 57069. TEL 605-677-5494. FAX 605-677-5105. E-mail: volant@sunbird.USD.Edu. Ed. Mary Jo Almquist. adv. contact: Katie Tobin circ. 6,500.

378.18 CN ISSN 0830-5315
VOX ME D A L. 1958. s-a. free to members. Dalhousie University, Dalhousie Medical Alumni Association, Dalhousie University, First Floor, Tupper Bldg., Halifax, NS B3H 4H7, Canada. TEL 902-494-8800. FAX 902-494-2033. E-mail: dilly.macfarlane@dal.ca; URL: http://www.medicine.dal.ca. Ed. D.E. MacFarlane. R&P contact: D.E. MacFarlane. adv. contact: D. MacFarlane. bk.rev.; circ. 6,700 (controlled). (back issues avail.) **Document type:** academic/scholarly publication, corporate report, newsletter.
●Also available online.
Formerly (until 1988): Me D A L (ISSN 0318-0735)

378.1 US
VOYAGER (PENSACOLA). 1966. w. $10. University of West Florida, Office of the Voyager, 11000 University Pkwy., Pensacola, FL 32514-5750. TEL 904-474-2191. Eds. Lloyd Goodman, Nancy Schwartz. adv.; bk.rev. circ. 4,000. (tabloid format)

378 US
LA VOZ (CUPERTINO). 1967. w. $7. De Anza College, 21250 Stevens Creek Blvd., Cupertino, CA 95014. TEL 408-996-4785. Ed. Ed Svoboda. adv. circ. 3,000.

378.1 US ISSN 0042-952X
W & L MAGAZINE. 1925. q. free to alumni. Washington and Lee University, 2 Lee Ave., Lexington, VA 24450. TEL 540-463-8957. FAX 540-463-8024. E-mail: randerson@wlu.edu. Ed. Dick Anderson. bk.rev. circ. 25,000.

COLLEGE AND ALUMNI

378   TS
AL-WA'I AL-TULLABI. 1978. s-m. free. United Arab Emirates University, Cultural Society, P.O. Box 15551, Al-Ain, United Arab Emirates. TEL 678333. Ed. Ahmad Muhammad Salih.
 Description: Covers topics of interest to students in the U.A.E., as well as regional development and cooperation issues.

378
WAR WHOOP. 1923. bi-m. $10. McMurry University, Box 248, McMurry Sta., Abilene, TX 79697. TEL 915-691-6375. FAX 915-691-6599. Ed. Steven Bristow. R&P contact: Bill Hartley. adv. contact: Stacey Nixon. circ. 1,000. **Document type:** newspaper.

378.198   US
WAREHOUSE JOURNAL. 1971. a. free to qualified personnel. Northern Virginia Community College, Alexandria Campus, 3001 N. Beauregard St., Alexandria, VA 22311. TEL 703-845-6239. circ. 2,000.

387   US
WASHINGTON SQUARE. q. San Jose State University, One Washington Sq., San Jose, CA 95192. TEL 408-924-1166. FAX 408-924-1168. Ed. Sylvia Hutchinson. circ. 115,000. **Document type:** newsletter.
 Formerly (until 1994): San Jose State University Digest.
 Description: Reports news of campus events, faculty research, athletics, fund-raising events, and alumni for alumni and friends of the university.

378.198   US
WASHINGTON SQUARE NEWS. 1979. d. (Mon.-Fri.) during school year. New York University, 566 LaGuardia Pl., Rm. 915, New York, NY 10012. TEL 212-998-4300. adv. circ. 18,500. **Document type:** newspaper.

378 071   US
WASHINGTON STATE UNIVERSITY. DAILY EVERGREEN. 1894. 5/wk. (Mon.-Fri.). $160. Washington State University, Student Publications Board, Box 2008 C.S., Pullman, WA 99165-2008. TEL 509-335-4573. FAX 509-335-7401. adv.; bk.rev. circ. 12,000. (tabloid format) **Document type:** newspaper.

378   US
LH1
WASHINGTON UNIVERSITY MAGAZINE AND ALUMNI NEWS. 1992. q. Washington University, Office of Publications, Campus Box 1086, One Brookings Dr., St. Louis, MO 63130-4899. TEL 314-935-5248. FAX 314-935-8533. E-mail: editor@@wuvmd.wustl.edu. Ed. Judy H. Watts. circ. 113,000 (controlled). Indexed: C.L.I., Leg.Per. **Document type:** academic/scholarly publication.
 Formed by the 1992 merger of: Washington University Alumni News; (1956-1992): Washington University Alumni Magazine (ISSN 0162-7570)
 Description: Describes university people and events for alumni, faculty, staff, parents, donors, university presidents, and the national media.

378   UK
WATT'S ON. 1986. bi-w. free. Heriot-Watt University Students' Association, The Union, Riccarton EH14 4AS, Scotland. TEL 0131-451-5333. Ed. Toby Jones. adv. contact: Keith Marshall. bk.rev. circ. 2,000. (back issues avail.) **Document type:** newspaper.

378.1   US
WAYNE STATE MAGAZINE. 1987. s-a. free to members. Wayne State University, Alumni Association, Office of Alumni Relations, Detroit, MI 48202. TEL 313-577-2300. FAX 313-577-2302. Ed. Duffy Ross. adv.; illus.; circ. 13,500 (controlled).

378.198   US   ISSN 0043-163X
WAYNE STATE UNIVERSITY ALUMNI NEWS. 1944. s-a. free to qualified personnel. Wayne State University, Alumni Association, Office of Alumni Relations, Detroit, MI 48202. TEL 313-577-2300. Ed. Duffy Ross. adv.; illus. circ. 120,000. (tabloid format)

378.1   CN
WEAL. 1926. w. Can.$15 free to students. (Southern Alberta Institute of Technology, Students' Association) S A I T S A Publications, 1301 16th Ave. N.W., Calgary, AB T2M 0L4, Canada. TEL 403-284-8458. FAX 403-284-8037. Ed. Allan Connery; Pub. Suzanne Trudel. adv. contact: Ron Burns. bk.rev.; film rev. circ. 2,600. (tabloid format; also avail. in microfiche) **Document type:** newspaper.
 Formerly: Emery Weal.

378.198
WEEKLY COLLEGIAN. 1979. w. $30. Collegian Inc., James Bldg., 123 S. Burrowes St., University Park, PA 16801-3882. TEL 814-865-2531. Ed. Rachel A. Hogan. circ. 5,369. (back issues avail.) **Document type:** newspaper.
 Description: College newspaper serving the branch campuses of Penn State, parents, alumni and sports fans.

378   CN
WELCOME BACK STUDENT MAGAZINE. 1983. a. Kingston Publications, P.O. Box 1352, Kingston, ON K7L 5C6, Canada. TEL 613-549-8442. Ed. Mary Laflamme. adv. contact: Ruth Kirkby. circ. 18,000 (controlled). **Document type:** directory.
 Formerly: Welcome Back Student Guide (ISSN 0839-1483)
 Description: Provides restaurant, night life & shopping info, and student related editorial to students & faculty at RMC, St. Lawrence College & Queens University.

378   US
WELLESLEY MAGAZINE. 1892. q. free to alumnae and friends. Wellesley College Alumnae Association, 106 Central St., Wellesley, MA 02181-8201. TEL 617-283-2341. FAX 617-283-3638. E-mail: lkatz@wellesley.edu. Ed. Alice Hummer. R&P contact: Laura Katz. TEL 617-283-2341. bk.rev. circ. 33,000. (back issues avail.) **Document type:** academic/scholarly publication.
 Description: Aims to connect the alumnae to the college and to each other.

378   GW
WER - WAS - WO. 2/yr. Studentenwerk Goettingen, Platz der Goettinger Sieben 4, 37073 Goettingen, Germany. TEL 49-551-390. FAX 49-551-395186. URL: http://www.stud.uni-oettingen.de. Ed. Christa Mirwald. circ. 12,500. **Document type:** academic/scholarly publication.

378   US
WESLEYAN UNIVERSITY ALUMNI MAGAZINE. 1916. q. free. Wesleyan University, Office of Public Information and Publications, Middletown, CT 06459. TEL 203-685-3699. FAX 203-685-3601. E-mail: wholder@weleyan.edu. Ed. William Holder. bk.rev. circ. 30,000. (back issues avail.) **Document type:** consumer publication.
 Formerly: Wesleyan University Alumnus.
 Description: Informs alumni of university and alumni developments.

378   US
WEST VIRGINIA FOURTH ESTATESMAN. 1941. q. free. West Virginia University, School of Journalism, 112 Martin Hall, Box 6010, Morgantown, WV 26506-6010. TEL 304-293-3505. FAX 304-293-3027. E-mail: wslater@wvnvm.wvu.edu; URL: http://www.wvu.edu/~journals. Ed. Ronda Weese; Pub. William T. Slater. circ. 3,500 (controlled). **Document type:** newsletter.
 Description: Covers alumni, student, and faculty news.

378.1   US
WEST VIRGINIA UNIVERSITY ALUMNI MAGAZINE. 1969. 3/yr. free. West Virginia University, 284 Prospect St., Morgantown, WV 26506. TEL 304-293-0111. FAX 304-293-6857. Ed.Bd. adv.; bk.rev.; charts; illus. circ. 105,000. **Document type:** bulletin.
 Former titles: West Virginia University Alumni Quarterly (ISSN 0163-366X); West Virginia University Magazine (ISSN 0043-3349)

378   US
WEST VIRGINIA UNIVERSITY ALUMNI NEWS. 1939. m. $30. West Virginia University Alumni Association, Erickson Center, Morgantown, WV 26506. TEL 304-293-4731. FAX 304-293-4733. Ed. Heather Cahill; Pub. Stephen L. Douglas. R&P contact: Heather Cahill. adv. contact: Will Armistead. circ. 28,000. **Document type:** newsletter.

378.1   CN   ISSN 1189-6272
WESTERN ALUMNI GAZETTE. 1939. 4/yr. free to alumni. University of Western Ontario, Department of Communications and Public Affairs, London, ON N6A 5B9, Canada. TEL 519-679-2111. FAX 519-661-3921. Ed. Alan Bass. adv.; bk.rev.; illus.; circ. 130,000 (controlled).
 Formerly: University of Western Ontario. Alumni Gazette (ISSN 0042-0344)
 Description: Aims to educate, inform, entertain and stimulate interest and positive attitudes among graduates toward the University and its goals.

378.198   US
WESTERN CAROLINIAN. 1893. w. $24. Western Carolina University, Box 66, Cullowhee, NC 28723. TEL 704-227-7267. FAX 704-227-7136. Ed. Blake Frizzell; Pub. Rudie Bax. adv. contact: Amy Moss. bk.rev.; film rev.; play rev. circ. 4,200. (tabloid format; also avail. in microfiche; back issues avail.) **Document type:** newspaper.

070   US
WESTERN CONCEPT. bi-w. Dickinson State University, Dickinson, ND 58601. TEL 701-227-2846. Ed. Diane Jandt. adv. contact: 700. (tabloid format) **Document type:** newspaper.

378   US
WESTERN HERALD. 1916. d. (Mon.-Thu.). $29 (out of state $30). Western Michigan University, 1523 Faunce Student Services Bldg., Kalamazoo, MI 49008. TEL 616-387-2092. FAX 616-387-2267. Ed. Dannielle Stap. circ. 12,500. **Document type:** newspaper.

378   US
WESTERN PRESS. 1962. w. Arizona Western College, Box 929, Yuma, AZ 85364. TEL 602-726-1000. circ. 1,000.

378.198   US
WESTERN STATE COLLEGE TOP O' THE WORLD. 1919. w. $8. Western State College, Student Government Association, Gunnison, CO 81231. TEL 303-943-3062. FAX 303-943-2702. Ed. Leah Neilson. adv. circ. 2,000. (tabloid format; also avail. in microfilm) **Document type:** newspaper.

378   US
WESTERN SUN. 1966. w. Golden West College, 15744 Golden West St., Huntington Beach, CA 92647. TEL 714-895-8786. FAX 714-895-8795. Ed. Vu Nguyen; Pub. Jim Tortolano. adv. contact: Mary Quinn. circ. 6,000.

378   US
WESTERN TEXAN. fortn. Western Texas College, Department of Journalism, Synder, TX 79549. TEL 915-573-8511.

378   US   ISSN 0279-3628
THE WESTERNER. 1980. a. Western Michigan University, 1201 Oliver St., Kalamazoo, MI 49001. TEL 616-387-4102. Ed. Jeanne M. Barron. circ. 100,000. (tabloid format; back issues avail.)
 Description: Presents a forum for the activities and events that relate to the alumni and friends of Western Michigan University.

378.198   US   ISSN 1062-6700
WESTMINSTER MAGAZINE. 1981. q. free. Westminster College, Office of Communication Services, New Wilmington, PA 16172. TEL 412-946-7226. FAX 412-946-7187. E-mail: wissinar@westminster.edu. Ed. Amy Rose Wissinger. circ. 20,225 (controlled). **Document type:** academic/scholarly publication.
 Supersedes (1932-1981): Blue and White.
 Description: Includes campus updates, features, and news items about student life and alumni.
 Refereed Serial

378   US
WESTMONT. 1977. q. free. Westmont College, 955 La Paz Rd., Santa Barbara, CA 93108-1089. TEL 805-565-6055. FAX 805-565-7049. E-mail: nphinney@westmont.edu; URL: http://www.westmont.edu. Ed. Nancy Lee Phinney. R&P contact: Nancy Phinney. circ. 21,000.
 Formerly (until 1996): Paz.
 Description: Provides college news and articles about and by alumni, students, faculty and friends of Westmont. Includes class notes for alumni.

COLLEGE AND ALUMNI — ABSTRACTING, BIBLIOGRAPHIES, STATISTICS

378 US
WHAT'S HAPPENING AT VASSAR. 1984. 3/yr. free. Vassar College, Office of College Relations, Poughkeepsie, NY 12604. TEL 914-437-7400. Ed. Susan DeKrey. illus. circ. 20,000. **Document type:** newsletter.

378 US
WHEATON ALUMNI. 1929. q. free to qualified personnel. Wheaton College, Wheaton, IL 60187-5593. TEL 708-752-5511. Ed. Georgia Douglass. bk.rev. circ. 27,000.

378 US
WHIRLWIND. 1978. m. free. State University of New York, A & T College at Cobleskill, Cobleskill, NY 12043. adv.; bk.rev.; film rev.; play rev. circ. 2,750. (tabloid format)

378 US
WHIT. 1938. w. free. Glassboro State College, Student Government, Student Center, Glassboro, NJ 08028. TEL 609-863-7105. Ed. Carol Katarsky. adv. contact: Ron Hayeck. circ. 4,000. (tabloid format) **Document type:** newspaper.
Formerly: Glassboro Whit.

378 US
WHITWORTH TODAY. 1973. s-a. free. Whitworth College, 300 W. Hawthorne Rd., Spokane, WA 99251-3102. FAX 509-466-3729. Ed. Pat Sturko. bk.rev. circ. 19,000. **Document type:** academic/scholarly publication.
Former titles: Today Whitworth College; Today (Spokane).

378.198 US
THE WHITWORTHIAN. 1910. w. $20 (free to qualified personnel). Associated Students of Whitworth College, Spokane, WA 99251. TEL 509-466-3248. FAX 509-466-3710. E-mail: whitworthian@whitworth.edu. Ed. Mark Jackson. R&P contact: Gordon Jackson. adv. contact: Carin Sepa. bk.rev. circ. 2,000. **Document type:** newspaper.

378 US
WICHITA STATE UNIVERSITY ALUMNI NEWS MAGAZINE. 1990. a. (plus irreg. newsletter, approx. 8/yr.). Wichita State University, Alumni Association, 1845 N. Fairmount, Campus Box 54, Wichita, KS 67260-0054. TEL 316-978-3290. FAX 316-978-3277. E-mail: white@twsuvm.uc.twsu.edu. Ed. Connie Kachel White. adv. circ. 53,000. **Document type:** newsletter.
Formerly (until 1992): Confluence (Wichita).
Description: Contains association news, university news and alumni profiles.

378 US
WICHITAN. 1922. w. $15 (effective 1997). Midwestern State University, Box 160, Wichita Falls, TX 76308-2099. TEL 817-689-4704. FAX 817-689-4511. Ed. Drew Myers. R&P contact: Jim Sernoe. adv.: page $463; adv. contact: Donna Payton. circ. 2,700. **Document type:** newspaper.

378.198 US
THE WICK. 3/yr. Hartwick College, Sponsor-Alumni Association, Clinton West St., Oneonta, NY 13820. TEL 607-431-4042. circ. 16,500.
Description: Directed to the alumni and friends of Hartwick College.

378.1 AU
WIENER BLAETTER; Forum fuer Kirche und Universitaet. 1946. 8/yr. S.120 students; S.400 all others. Katholische Hochschuljugend Oesterreichs, Ebendorferstr. 8, A-1010 Vienna, Austria. TEL 0222-4083587. Ed. Otto Friedrich. bk.rev.; illus. circ. 1,600.
Formerly: Katholische Hochschuljugend Oesterreichs - Blaetter (ISSN 0022-9393)

378.1 US
WILLIAMS ALUMNI REVIEW. 1909. q. free. Williams College, Society of Alumni, Mears House, 75 Park St., Box 38, Williamstown, MA 01267. TEL 413-597-4151. FAX 413-597-4158. E-mail: alumni.review@williams.edu; URL: http://www.williams.edu:803/AlumRev/review.html. Ed. Thomas W. Bleezarde. R&P contact: Thomas W. Bleezarde. TEL 413-597-4981. bk.rev.; circ. 29,000 (controlled). (back issues avail.) **Document type:** consumer publication.
Description: Provides news of the college and its alumni for distribution to all alumni, parents of undergraduates and friends.
Refereed Serial

378 US
THE WILLIAMS RECORD. 1886. w. $40. Williams College, Baxter Hall, Williamstown, MA 01267. TEL 413-597-2289. FAX 413-597-2450. Ed. Joshua Resnick. adv. contact: Barbara Shreve. circ. 3,950. **Document type:** newspaper.
Description: Reports issues concerning Williams College and its students and staff.

378 US
WINDOW (OMAHA). 1984. q. free to qualified personnel. Creighton University, Public Relations and Information, 2500 California Plaza, Omaha, NE 68178. FAX 402-280-2549. Ed. Steve Kline. circ. 55,000.

378 US
WINGSPAN (CHEYENNE). 1969. m. free. Laramie County Community College, 1400 E. College Dr., Cheyenne, WY 82007. TEL 307-778-1304. FAX 307-778-1399. E-mail: schliske@mail.lc.wheen.edu; URL: http://www/cc.wheen.edu/wing/wingsp.htm/. Eds. Linda Savell, Kelly Ruiz. adv.: B&W page $70. film rev.; play rev. circ. 2,000. (back issues avail.) **Document type:** newspaper.
Description: Covers student news at the college.

378 US
WISCONSIN SOUTH ASIAN AREA CENTER NEWS REPORT. 1975. 3/yr. Wisconsin South Asian Area Center, University of Wisconsin, 1242 Van Hise Hall, Madison, WI 53706. TEL 608-262-3384. circ. 2,000.
Description: Covers academic activities related to South Asia.

378 GW
WIWI-PRESS. 1972. bi-m. Johannes-Gutenberg-Universitaet Mainz, Allgemeine Studentausschuss, Saarstraase 21, 55122 Mainz, Germany. TEL 06131-39-4801. adv.; bk.rev.; play rev.; charts; illus.; stat. circ. 600.
Description: University news of interest to students of economics.

378 US
WOLF TALES. 1968. m. $10 (free to qualified personnel). Copiah-Lincoln Community College, Box 649, Wesson, MS 39191. TEL 601-643-8332. FAX 601-643-2366. adv. contact: Ann H. Hawkins. circ. 2,000. **Document type:** newspaper.
Description: College newspaper.

378.198 US ISSN 0894-8798
WOOSTER. 1886. 4/yr. free. College of Wooster, Wooster, OH 44691. TEL 330-263-2243. FAX 330-263-2594. E-mail: class-notes@acs.wooster.edu. Ed. Jeffery G. Hanna. bk.rev. circ. 26,000.
Formerly: Wooster Alumni Magazine.

THE WORD; the independent paper for all Oxford's students. see *GENERAL INTEREST PERIODICALS — Great Britain*

378.1 CN ISSN 0043-9886
XAVERIAN WEEKLY. 1895. 22/yr. $10. St. Francis Xavier University, Students' Union, P.O. Box 970, Antigonish, NS B2G 2W5, Canada. TEL 902-867-2412. adv.; bk.rev.; film rev.; play rev.; illus. circ. 3,500. (tabloid format) **Document type:** newspaper.

378 US ISSN 1075-1017
XAVIER. q. Xavier University, Office of Public Relations, 3800 Victory Pkwy., Cincinnati, OH 45227. TEL 513-745-3178. FAX 513-745-2083. Ed. Bill Noblitt.
Formerly (until 1993): Xavier Today.
Description: Covers news and activities of Xavier University for alumni, friends, and faculty.

378 US
Y C NEWS. m. free. Yavapai Community College, 1100 E. Sheldon St., Prescott, AZ 86301. TEL 602-776-2221. Ed. Debbie Ashcraft. adv.; bk.rev. circ. 6,500. (back issues avail.) **Document type:** newspaper.
Description: Student newspaper covering education, sports, and campus activities.

378.1 US ISSN 0044-0051
YALE ALUMNI MAGAZINE. 1891. 8/yr. $18.50 (foreign $26.50). Yale Alumni Publications, Inc., Box 1905, New Haven, CT 06509. TEL 203-432-0645. FAX 203-432-0651. E-mail: yam@yale.edu; URL: http://www.yale.edu/yam/. Ed. Carter Wiseman. R&P contact: Carolyn Butcher. adv. contact: Barbara Terry. bk.rev.; index; circ. 70,000 (paid). **Indexed:** Amer.Hist.& Life (1974-1976), Hist.Abstr. (1974-1976). **Document type:** academic/scholarly publication.

378.198 US ISSN 0890-2240
YALE DAILY NEWS. 1878. d. $65 (free to students on campus). Yale Daily News Publishing, Co., Inc., 202 York St., New Haven, CT 06511-4804. TEL 203-432-2424. FAX 203-432-7425. E-mail: ydn@minerva.cis.yale.edu; URL: http://www.cis.yale.edu/4dn. Ed. J. Sullivan; Pubs. J. Jewell, J. Kahr. adv.; bk.rev.; circ. 5,000 (paid). (also avail. in microfilm) **Document type:** newspaper.
Refereed Serial

378 US
YELLOW JACKET. w. Howard Payne University, Jennings Hall, Box 173, Brownville, TX 76801. TEL 915-646-2502.

378 CN ISSN 0827-522X
YORK GAZETTE. 1971. m. free. York University, Communication Department, Ste. A134, West Office Bldg., 4700 Keele St., North York, ON M3J 1P3, Canada. FAX 416-736-5681. bk.rev. circ. 5,100. (back issues avail.)

378 US
YOUNGTOWN EDITION. fortn. (during the spring and fall terms). County College of Morris, News Desk, Mail Sta. SCC 140, 214 Center Grove Rd., Randolph, NJ 07869-2086. TEL 201-328-5224. Ed.Bd. adv.; illus. cols./p.: 4; pp./issue: 12. **Document type:** newspaper.
Description: Covers campus news and events. Presents news and opinions on local, state, and national issues.

378 GW
Z V S - INFO. 1973. s-a. free. Zentralstelle fuer die Vergabe von Studienplaetzen, Sonnenstr. 171, 44128 Dortmund, Germany. TEL 49-231-10810. FAX 49-231-1081227. circ. 300,000 (paid). **Document type:** bulletin.
Description: Guide for application to German universities.

378 US
1766. s-a.? (Rutgers Alumni Association) Targum Publishing Company, 172 College Ave., New Brunswick, NJ 08903. TEL 201-932-7474.

COLLEGE AND ALUMNI — Abstracting Bibliographies, Statistics

COLLEGE MEDIA DIRECTORY. see *BIBLIOGRAPHIES*

COMMUNICABLE DISEASES

see *Medical Sciences–Communicable Diseases*

COMMUNICATIONS

see also *Communications–Computer Applications; Communications–Postal Affairs; Communications–Radio; Communications–Television and Cable Communications–Telephone and Telegraph; Communications–Video; Journalism*

A A F COMMUNICATOR. (American Advertising Federation) see *ADVERTISING AND PUBLIC RELATIONS*

384 378 US
▼A C U T A JOURNAL OF TELECOMMUNICATIONS IN HIGHER EDUCATION. 1997. q. $80 to non-members; members $60. Association of College and University Telecommunications Administrators, 152 W. Zandale Dr., Ste. 200, Lexington, KY 40503-2486. TEL 606-278-3338. FAX 606-278-3268. E-mail: pscott@acuta.org; URL: http://www.acuta.org. **Document type:** academic/scholarly publication.
Description: Focuses on telecommunications issues of significance to administrators, managers, and technical staff in higher education environments.

621.38 GW ISSN 0001-1096
TK7800 CODEN: AEUTAH
A E UE. (Archiv fuer Elektronik und Uebertragungstechnik); international journal of electronics and communication. (Text in English and German) 1947. bi-m. DM.780 (effective 1997). S. Hirzel Verlag, Postfach 101061, 70009 Stuttgart, Germany. TEL 49-711-2582-0. FAX 49-711-2582290. Ed. R. Pauli. adv.; bk.rev. circ. 1,020. (also avail. in microform from UMI) **Indexed:** ASCA, Curr.Cont., Eng.Ind., Excerp.Med., INIS Atomind., INSPEC (1971-), Sci.Cit.Ind. **Document type:** academic/scholarly publication.
—BLDSC (1605.500000); AskIEEE; CISTI; Ei; Genuine Article; KR SourceOne; Linda Hall; SWETS; UnCover. **CCC.**

621.38 SZ ISSN 0378-1291
CODEN: AENMAT
A G E N MITTEILUNGEN.* (Text in German, English and French) 1962. irreg., no. 19, 1975. free. (Arbeitsgemeinschaft fuer Elektrische Nachrichtentechnik) Gesellschaftsstelle der AGEN Institut fuer Technische Physik, Belpstr. 37, CH-3000 Bern 14, Switzerland. **Indexed:** Ind.Med., INSPEC. **Document type:** monographic series.

384 SP ISSN 0213-1226
A H C I E T REVISTA DE TELECOMUNICACIONES. 1984. q. 5300 ptas. Asociacion Hispanoamericana de Centros de Investigacion y Estudio de Telecomunicaciones, Guzman el Bueno 133, 28003 Madrid, Spain. **Indexed:** Ind.SST.

A I A A COMMUNICATIONS SATELLITE SYSTEMS CONFERENCE. TECHNICAL PAPERS. (American Institute of Aeronautics and Astronautics, Inc.) see AERONAUTICS AND SPACE FLIGHT

A M W A FREELANCE DIRECTORY. (American Medical Writers Association) see MEDICAL SCIENCES

A M W A JOURNAL. (American Medical Writers Association) see MEDICAL SCIENCES

A P C O BULLETIN. (Association of Public-Safety Communications Officials International, Inc.) see PUBLIC HEALTH AND SAFETY

384 621.3 JA ISSN 0915-2563
T R JOURNAL. (Text in Japanese) 1987. s-a. 700 Yen per no. Advanced Telecommunications Research Institute International - Kokusai Denki Tsushin Kiso Gijutsu Kenkyujo, Inuidani Sanpeidani, Seikacho, Soraku-gun, Kyoto 619-02, Japan.

621.38 BE ISSN 0778-0303
V INDUSTRIE. (Text in Dutch, French) 1989. bi-m. 1200 BEF. Making Magazines, Baudelostraat 29, 9000 Gent, Belgium. TEL 32-9-2338463. FAX 32-9-2338087. Ed. Patrick Verleye. adv.: B&W page 28000 BEF, color page 49000 BEF; trim 184 x 274. circ. 5,000. **Document type:** trade publication.
Description: For professionals in the audio-visual sector and related services.

380 UK ISSN 0956-9057
CAMEDIA RESEARCH MONOGRAPH. 1989. irreg., no.12, 1995. John Libbey Media, University of Luton, 75 Castle St., Luton, Bedfordshire LU1 3AJ, England. TEL 44-1582-743297. FAX 44-1582-743298. E-mail: john.libbey@luton.ac.uk. Ed.Bd. **Document type:** monographic series.
—BLDSC (0570.595700).
Description: Focuses on specific areas of media research.

TA WASAENSIA. see BUSINESS AND ECONOMICS — Economic Systems And Theories, Economic History

380 200 UK ISSN 0143-3253
ACTION NEWSLETTER. 1969. 10/yr. membership. World Association for Christian Communication, 357 Kennington Ln., London SE11 5QY, England. TEL 44-171-582-9139. FAX 44-171-735-0340. Ed. Kathy Lowe. bk.rev. circ. 2,200. **Document type:** newsletter.

621.38 US ISSN 1050-9496
TK5101.A1
ADVANCES IN TELEMATICS. 1991. irreg., vol.3, 1995. price varies. Ablex Publishing Corporation, Box 5297, Box 5297, CT 06831-0504. TEL 203-661-7602. FAX 203-661-0792. Eds. Jarice Hanson, Indu Singh. **Document type:** academic/scholarly publication.

ADVERTISING & MARKETING REVIEW. see ADVERTISING AND PUBLIC RELATIONS

AFRICA MEDIA MONOGRAPH SERIES. see JOURNALISM

301.16 KE ISSN 0258-4913
AFRICA MEDIA REVIEW. Abbreviated title: A M R. (Text, in English, summaries in French) 1987. 3/yr. $45 (outside Africa $60) (effective 1997). African Council for Communication Education - Conseil Africain pour l'Enseignement de la Communication, P.O. Box 47495, Nairobi, Kenya. TEL 254-2-227043. FAX 254-2-216135. TELEX 25148 ACCE KE. E-mail: acceb@arcc.permanet.org; acceb@form-net.com. Ed. Charles Okigbo. circ. 700. (back issues avail.) **Indexed:** Abstr.Anthropol., P.L.E.S.A. (1988-). **Document type:** academic/scholarly publication.
—BLDSC (0732.160950).
Description: Provides a forum for the study of communication theory, practice, and policy in African countries.
Refereed Serial

AFRICAN COUNCIL FOR COMMUNICATION EDUCATION. REPORTS ON WORKSHOPS - SEMINARS. see JOURNALISM

301.16 KE
AFRICOM. (Text in English, French) 3/yr. $30 (outside Africa $35) (effective 1997). African Council for Communication Education - Conseil Africain pour l'Enseignement de la Communication, P.O. Box 47495, Nairobi, Kenya. TEL 254-2-227043. FAX 254-2-216135. E-mail: acceb@arcc.permanet.org. Ed. Charles Okigbo. **Document type:** newsletter, academic/scholarly publication.
Description: Covers communications and media news in Africa.

AGENCY EXPERTISE. see ADVERTISING AND PUBLIC RELATIONS

384 II
ALPHA. vol.15, 1977. m. Rs.1.25 per no. Rajendra Prasad Institute of Communications, Bharatiya Vidya Bhavan, Bombay 400 007, India. Ed. G.S. Pohekar.

621.38 377 IN
ALPHA COMMUNICATIONS MONTHLY. (Text in English) 1964. m. Bharatiya Vidya Bhavan, Bhavan's College of Mass Communication, Kulapati K.M. Munshi Marg, Bombay 400007, India. Ed. M.K.B. Nairar.

ALTA FREQUENZA RIVISTA DI ELETTRONICA. see ELECTRONICS

808.53 US
AMERICAN FORENSIC ASSOCIATION NEWSLETTER. 1979. 3/yr. $22.50. American Forensic Association, Box 256, River Falls, WI 54022-0256. TEL 800-228-5424. FAX 715-425-9533. Ed. James Pratt. circ. 800. **Document type:** newsletter.

300 US ISSN 0740-5111
AMERICAN UNIVERSITY STUDIES. SERIES 15. COMMUNICATIONS. 1984. irreg. price varies. Peter Lang Publishing, Inc., 275 Seventh Ave., 28th Fl., New York, NY 10001. TEL 212-647-7700; 800-770-5264. FAX 212-647-7707. E-mail: customerservice@plang.com; URL: http://www.peterlang.com. Ed. Christopher Myers. **Document type:** academic/scholarly publication, monographic series.
Description: Delves into the study of various aspects of communications.

621.38 SZ ISSN 0003-4347
TK2 CODEN: ANTEAU
ANNALES DES TELECOMMUNICATIONS. (Text in English, French) 1946. bi-m. 170 SFr. (foreign 188 SFr.). Presses Polytechniques et Universitaires Romandes, EPFL - Ecublens, CH-1015 Lausanne, Switzerland. TEL 021-6934140. FAX 021-6934027. (Co-publisher: Centre National d'Etudes des Telecommunications (CNET)) bk.rev.; illus.; index. circ. 2,500. **Indexed:** Acoust.Abstr., ASCA, Chem.Abstr., Compumath, Comput.Cont., Curr.Cont., Eng.Ind., Ind.Sci.Rev., INIS Atomind., INSPEC (1968-), Math.R., PROMT, Sci.Cit.Ind., Zent.Math. **Document type:** academic/scholarly publication.
—BLDSC (1002.000000); AskIEEE; CASDDS; CISTI; Ei; Genuine Article; KR SourceOne; Linda Hall; SWETS.
Description: Disseminates research results and engineering developments in the field of telecommunications.
Refereed Serial

380 FR ISSN 1157-7002
ANNEES LASER; toute l'actualite audio video et laserdisc. 1991. 8/yr. 300 F.($65) 36 rue de Picpus, 75012 Paris, France. TEL 43-42-92-00. FAX 43-44-97-48. Ed. Patrick R. Marteau; Pub. Patrick Ribemont. adv.: page 22680 F.; adv. contact: Patrick Ribemont. circ. 40,000. (back issues avail.) **Document type:** consumer publication.

ANNUAIRE O.G.M.. (Office General de la Musique) see MUSIC

384 621.38 US
ANNUAL FORUM REPORTS. 1993. a. $475 (effective 1993). (International Engineering Consortium) Professional Education International, Inc., 549 W. Randolph St., Ste. 600, Chicago, IL 60661. TEL 312-559-4100. FAX 312-559-4111. Ed. Dan Coran. circ. 2,000. **Document type:** proceedings.
●Also available online.
Description: Publishes talks, speeches, lectures and invited papers on specific topics relevant to the information industry.

621.38 537 US ISSN 1073-0885
TK5
ANNUAL REVIEW OF COMMUNICATIONS. 1944. a. $195 (effective 1995). (International Engineering Consortium) Professional Education International, Inc., 549 W. Randolph St., Ste. 600, Chicago, IL 60661. TEL 312-559-4100. FAX 312-559-4111. R&P contact: Michael Janowiak. charts; index. circ. 4,000. (back issues avail.) **Document type:** proceedings.
●Also available online.
—BLDSC (1522.253000); CISTI; Linda Hall.
Former titles (until 1992): National Communications Forum. Proceedings (ISSN 0886-229X); National Electronics Conference National Communications Forum. Proceedings; (until 1979): National Electronics Conference. Proceedings (ISSN 0077-4413)
Description: Broad compilation of the latest technical and business thinking of experts in the telecommunications, computer and electronics fields.

ANRITSU TECHNICAL BULLETIN/ANRITSU TEKUNIKARU. see ENGINEERING — Electrical Engineering

621.38 SP
ANTENA DE PROFESIONALES, DE RADIO Y TELEVISION. 12/yr. Evaristo San Miguel 8, 1o, 28008 Madrid, Spain. TEL 248-98-38. Ed. E.G. Toledano.

621.38 384 SP
ANTENA DE TELECOMUNICACION. 1965. bi-m. free. Asociacion Espanola de Ingenieros de Telecomunicacion - Spanish Association of Telecommunications Engineers, General Arrando 38, 28010 Madrid, Spain. TEL 1-329-17-01. FAX 1-747-93-41. Ed. Carlos Dominquez. adv.; bk.rev.; charts; illus. circ. 3,000.

384 621.3 UK
ANTENNAS SERIES. irreg., vol.10, 1997. price varies. Research Studies Press Ltd., 24 Belvedere Rd., Taunton, Somerset TA1 1HD, England. TEL 44-1823-336197. FAX 44-1823-253252. E-mail: vaw@rspltd.demon.co.uk. (Dist. by John Wiley & Sons Ltd., Baffins Ln., Chichester, W. Sussex PO19 1UD, England. TEL 44-1243-779777. FAX 44-1243-775878) Ed. J.R. James. **Document type:** monographic series.

COMMUNICATIONS

301.16   FR   ISSN 0396-8995
ANTENNES. 12/yr. Telediffusion de France, 21-27 rue Barbes, B.P. 518, 92542 Montrouge Cedex, France. TEL 49-65-13-20. Ed. Philippe Baudelot.
    Description: Provides audio-visual information and new communication techniques.

301.16 700   BL   ISSN 0103-9652
ANUARIO DE INOVACOES EM COMUNICACOES E ARTES. 1989. a. Universidade de Sao Paulo, Escola de Comunicacoes e Artes, Av. Prof. Lucio Martins Rodrigues 443, Butanta 05508-900 Sao Paulo, Brazil. TEL 818-4112. FAX 814-1324. TELEX 80629 UVSI BR.

383 384   GW   ISSN 0943-2337
ARCHIV FUER POST UND TELEKOMMUNIKATION; Zeitschrift fuer Rechtsfragen des Postwesens, des Postbankbereichs und der Telekommunikation. 1948. q. DM.48. Deutsche Bundespost Telekom, Postfach 2000, 5300 Bonn 1, Germany. TEL 0228-1817320. FAX 0228-1817396. (Subscr. to: Verlagspostamt, 5000 Cologne 1, Germany) Ed. Joachim Schmidt. bk.rev. circ. 3,000. **Indexed:** INSPEC. **Document type:** academic/scholarly publication.
    —AskIEEE; KR SourceOne.
    Formerly (until 1992): Archiv fuer das Post- und Fernmeldewesen (ISSN 0170-8988)

420 808.53   US   ISSN 1051-1431
PN4171
ARGUMENTATION & ADVOCACY. 1964. q. $45. American Forensic Association, Box 256, River Falls, WI 54022-0256. TEL 800-228-5424. FAX 715-425-9533. Ed. Tom Goodnight. adv.; bk.rev.; bibl. circ. 1,500. (also avail. in microform from UMI; reprint service avail. from UMI) **Indexed:** C.I.J.E., IJCS (1964-). **Document type:** academic/scholarly publication.
    ●Also available online. Vendor(s): Information Access Co., UMI.
    —UMI; UnCover.
    Formerly (until vol.25, 1989): American Forensic Association. Journal (ISSN 0002-8353)

ARMY COMMUNICATOR; voice of the Signal Corps. see *MILITARY*

THE ART OF COMMUNICATION. see *PUBLIC ADMINISTRATION*

380 700   UK
ARTS AND MEDIA SERIES. 1988. irreg., no.6, 1994. John Libbey Media, University of Luton, 75 Castle St., Luton, Bedfordshire LU1 3AJ, England. TEL 44-1582-743297. FAX 44-1582-743298. E-mail: john.libbey@luton.ac.uk. **Document type:** monographic series.
    Description: Offers imaginative and provocative accounts of the relationships between art forms, popular cultural practices, technology and audiences.

384.5   US   ISSN 1080-370X
HE9721.A78
ASIA - PACIFIC SATELLITE DIRECTORY. 1994. a. $469 (effective 1996). Phillips Business Information, Inc., 1201 Seven Locks Rd., Potomac, MD 20854. TEL 301-424-3338. FAX 301-309-3847. E-mail: pbi@phillips.com. **Document type:** directory.

380   SI   ISSN 0129-2986
ASIAN JOURNAL OF COMMUNICATION. (Text in English) s-a. S.$24 (Asia S.$36; elsewhere $32) (effective 1996). Asian Media Information and Communication Centre, School of Communication Studies Bldg., Nanyang Technological University, Jurong Point Post Office, Box 360, Singapore 916412, Singapore. TEL 65-7927570. FAX 65-7927129. E-mail: amicline@singnet.com.sg. Ed. Vijay Menon. (back issues avail.)
    —BLDSC (1742.478000); UnCover.

301.16   SI   ISSN 0129-2056
ASIAN MASS COMMUNICATIONS BULLETIN; a newsletter. (Text in English) 1971. bi-m. S.$18 in Asia; elsewhere $22 (effective 1997). Asian Media Information and Communication Centre, School of Communication Studies Bldg., Nanyang Technological University, Jurong Point Post Office, Box 360, Singapore 916412, Singapore. TEL 65-7927570. FAX 65-7927129. TELEX AMICSI RS 55524. E-mail: amicline@singnet.com.sg. bk.rev.; bibl. circ. 1,500. **Document type:** newsletter.

301.16   US
PN4073
ASSOCIATION FOR COMMUNICATION ADMINISTRATION. JOURNAL. Abbreviated title: J A C A. 1972. 3/yr. $75 departmental membership; libraries $60 (effective 1997). Association for Communication Administration, 5105-F Backlick Rd., Annandale, VA 22003. TEL 703-750-0533. FAX 703-914-9471. Ed. Ronald Applbaum. R&P contact: Ellie Bruner. adv.; bk.rev. circ. 400. (also avail. in microfilm; reprint service avail. from UMI) **Indexed:** C.I.J.E., Educ.Tech.Abstr., High.Educ.Curr.Aware.Bull., IJCS (1972-). **Document type:** academic/scholarly publication.
    —UMI; UnCover.
    Former titles (until 1992): A C A Bulletin (ISSN 0360-0939); Association of Departments and Administrators in Speech Communication. Bulletin.
    Description: Incorporates information useful to academic administrators in all areas of the communication arts and sciences.

301.16   VE
ASUNTO. 1975. irreg. Universidad del Zulia, Escuela de Comunicacion Social, Maracaibo, Venezuela.

384.5   UK   ISSN 0956-2931
AUDIO VISUAL DIRECTORY. a. E M A P Vision Ltd., Box 109, Maclaren House, Scarbrook Rd., Croydon, Surrey CR9 1QH, England. TEL 081-760-9690. FAX 081-681-1672. TELEX 946665. **Document type:** directory.
    —BLDSC (1789.005700).

AUDIO VISUELLE MEDIA. see *ADVERTISING AND PUBLIC RELATIONS*

380   AT   ISSN 0726-3252
AUSTRALIAN COMMUNICATION REVIEW.* 1979. q. Aus.$70 to individuals; institutions Aus.$90. Australian Communication Association, c/o Univ. of Western Sydney, Information Officer, P.O. Box 10, Kingswood, N.S.W. 2750, Australia. TEL 062-573155. FAX 61-2-416-7174. (Subscr. to: c/o CRIA, G.P.O. Box 655, Canberra, A.C.T. 2601, Australia) Ed. Ray Archee. adv.; bk.rev. circ. 200.
    —UnCover.
    Description: Articles about communication issues of interest to communication scholars, specialists and practitioners.

380 070 659.1   AT   ISSN 0811-6202
P87   CODEN: AJCOEJ
AUSTRALIAN JOURNAL OF COMMUNICATION. 1982. 3/yr. Aus.$65. Queensland University of Technology, School of Communication, G.P.O. Box 2434, Brisbane, Qld. 4001, Australia. FAX 07-864-1810. Ed. Roslyn M. Petelin. adv.; bk.rev. circ. 400. **Indexed:** Aus.P.A.I.S. **Document type:** academic/scholarly publication.
    —BLDSC (1806.500000); UnCover.

380   GW
AUTO HIFI. 1990. bi-m. DM.45.90; newsstand price: DM.9. Vereinigte Motor-Verlage GmbH und Co. KG, Leuschnerstr. 1, 70174 Stuttgart, Germany. TEL 49-711-18201. FAX 49-711-1821669. (Subscr. to: Postfach 106036, 70049 Stuttgart, Germany) Ed. Karl Breh; Pub. Uwe Hagen. adv.: B&W page DM.6290, color page DM.11637; trim 185 x 248; adv. contact: Peter Michael Heyde. circ. 39,208. **Document type:** consumer publication.

380   AU
A3 BOOM. 8/yr. S.480 (foreign S.680). A3 Zeitschriftenverlags GmbH, Hagenauertalstr. 40, A-2372 Giesshuebl, Austria. TEL 43-2236-42528. FAX 43-2236-26311. circ. 18,000. **Document type:** bulletin.

A3 VOLT. see *ELECTRONICS*

380   UK   ISSN 0956-9065
HE8689.9.G7
B B C BROADCASTING RESEARCH. ANNUAL REPORT. (British Broadcasting Corporation) 1975. a. John Libbey Media, University of Luton, 75 Castle St., Luton, Bedfordshire LU1 3AJ, England. TEL 44-1582-743297. FAX 44-1582-743298. E-mail: john.libbey@luton.ac.uk. **Document type:** corporate report.
    Description: Provides empirical audience research information about broadcasting in Britain.

380   GW
B L M JAHRBUCH. 1992. a. DM.25. (Bayerische Landeszentrale fuer neue Medien) Verlag Reinhard Fischer, Weltistr. 34, 81477 Munich, Germany. TEL 49-89-7918892. FAX 49-89-7918310. E-mail: 106222.2504@compuserve.com. Ed. Johannes Kors. **Document type:** bulletin.

380   GW   ISSN 0939-8317
B L M SCHRIFTENREIHE. 1989. irreg. (Bayerische Landeszentrale fuer neue Medien) Verlag Reinhard Fischer, Weltistr. 34, 81477 Munich, Germany. TEL 49-89-7918892. FAX 49-89-7918310. E-mail: 106222.2504@compuserve.com. **Document type:** monographic series.

B M A MEMBERSHIP DIRECTORY AND RESOURCE GUIDE. (Business Marketing Association) see *BUSINESS AND ECONOMICS — Trade And Industrial Directories*

621.38   UK   ISSN 0265-0193
B T TECHNOLOGY JOURNAL. 1983. q. £70 (foreign $120) to individuals; institutions £165 (foreign $275); print & online eds. combined £200 (foreign $330) (effective 1998). (British Telecom) Thomson Science (Subsidiary of: International Thomson Publishing Group), 2-6 Boundary Row, London SE1 8HN, England. TEL 44-171-8650066. FAX 44-171-5229623. TELEX 290164 CHAPMA G. E-mail: journal@rapidcom.co.uk; URL: http://www.thomsonscience.com. (Dist. by: International Thomson Publishing Services Ltd., Cheriton House, North Way, Andover, Hants. SP10 5BE, England. TEL 44-1264-342713. FAX 44-1264-342807; Subscr. in US & Canada to: 10 Market St., Philadelphia, PA 19106. TEL 800-552-5866) Ed. Gerry White. (back issues avail.; reprint service avail.) **Indexed:** Abstr.Hum.Comp.Inter., Curr.Cont., INSPEC (1991-), Sci.Cit.Ind. **Document type:** academic/scholarly publication.
    ●Also available online.
    —AskIEEE; CISTI; Ei; Genuine Article; KR SourceOne; Linda Hall. CCC.
    Description: Contains research and review papers for development engineers, whether in companies, laboratories, or academic institutions involved in telecommunications and related technologies.
    Refereed Serial

621.38   CC   ISSN 1000-1506
BEIFANG JIAOTONG DAXUE XUEBAO/NORTH COMMUNICATIONS UNIVERSITY. JOURNAL. (Text in Chinese) q. Beifang Jiaotong Daxue, Xuebao Bianjibu, Xizhimenwai, Beijing 100044, People's Republic of China. TEL 8316622. Ed. Hu Shuliang. **Document type:** academic/scholarly publication.

621.38   CC   ISSN 1000-5145
BEIJING YOUDIAN XUEYUAN XUEBAO/BEIJING UNIVERSITY OF POSTS AND TELECOMMUNICATIONS. JOURNAL. (Text in Chinese) 1980. q. Y3 per no. Beijing University of Posts and Telecommunications, 42 Xueyuan Lu, Beijing 100088, People's Republic of China. TEL 861-2013388. FAX 061-2028643. Ed. Song Yamin. **Document type:** academic/scholarly publication.

301.16 070.43   GW   ISSN 0171-6786
BEITRAEGE ZUR KOMMUNIKATIONSWISSENSCHAFT UND MEDIENFORSCHUNG. 1995. irreg. Quintessenz Verlags GmbH, Ifenpfad 2-4, 12107 Berlin, Germany. TEL 49-30-76180646. FAX 49-30-76180692. E-mail: central@quinline.com; URL: http://www.quinline.com. **Document type:** monographic series.

589.2   SP   ISSN 1132-2179
BELARRA. 1987. a. free. Sociedad Micologica de Baracaldo, Apdo. 182, 48900 Baracaldo (Bilbao), Spain. **Indexed:** Ind.SST.

658.3   US   ISSN 1087-4798
▼**BETTER COMMUNICATION.** 1996. m. $36. Professional Training Associates, Inc., 210 Commerce Blvd., Round Rock, TX 78664-2189. TEL 512-255-6006. FAX 512-255-7532. Ed. Marilyn C. Johnson; Pub. Dennis E. Murphy. R&P contact: Dennis E. Murphy. **Document type:** newsletter.
    —CCC.

621.38   YU   ISSN 0406-3090
BILTEN TELEKOMUNIKACIJA. A. TEHNIKA TELEKOMUNIKACIJA. 1954. q. Zajednica Jugoslovenskih P T T, Palmoticeva 2, Belgrade, Yugoslavia. Ed. Radenko Kostic.

BLAETTERTEIG. see *JOURNALISM*

BOOKS IN THE MEDIA. see *PUBLISHING AND BOOK TRADE*

BORDER - LINES. see *ART*

BOVE & RHODES INSIDE REPORT ON DESKTOP PUBLISHING AND MULTIMEDIA. see *COMPUTERS — Microcomputers*

301.16   BL   ISSN 0103-9318
P92.B7
BRAZILIAN COMMUNICATION RESEARCH YEARBOOK. (Text in English) 1992. a. Universidade de Sao Paulo, School of Communications and Arts, Av. Prof. Lucio Martins Rodrigues 443, Butana, 05508 Sao Paulo SP, Brazil. TEL 813-3222. FAX 011-815-4272. TELEX 011-80629 UVSI BR. Ed. Jose Marques de Melo. **Document type:** academic/scholarly publication.

621.382   UK   ISSN 0262-401X
TK5101.A1   CODEN: BTEND4
BRITISH TELECOMMUNICATIONS ENGINEERING. 1908; N.S. 1982. q. £30 to individuals (overseas £35); institutions £50 (overseas £55) (effective 1997). Institution of British Telecommunications Engineers, 2-12 Gresham St., Rm. G012, London EC2V 7AG, England. TEL 44-171-356-7942. Ed. P.E. Nichols. adv.; bk.rev.; charts; index. circ. 20,000. **Indexed:** ASCA, Br.Tech.Ind., C.I.S. Abstr., CAD CAM Abstr., Comput.Cont., Curr.Cont., Eng.Ind., INSPEC (1968-), Int.Aerosp.Abstr., Met.Abstr., SSCI, Tel.Abstr. **Document type:** academic/scholarly publication.
—BLDSC (2345.527000); AskIEEE; CISTI; Ei; Genuine Article; KR SourceOne; Linda Hall; SWETS; UnCover. **CCC.**
   Formerly (until Jan. 1982): Post Office Electrical Engineers' Journal (ISSN 0032-5287)

621.38   CN   ISSN 0709-9797
                 CODEN: BRBEFI
BROADCAST TECHNOLOGY. 1975. 10/yr. $30 (foreign $45) (effective 1997). Diversified Publications Ltd., 6 Farmer's Lane, Box 420, Bolton, ON L7E 5T3, Canada. TEL 905-857-6076. Ed. Doug Loney; Pub. Doug Loney. adv. contact: Jacquie Loney. circ. 6,500 (controlled). **Indexed:** INSPEC (1979-1991). **Document type:** trade publication.
—BLDSC (2349.040000); CISTI; Ei.
   Formerly (until vol.4, no.6, 1979): Broadcast Equipment Today (ISSN 0383-9338)
   Description: Provides technical and general information for professional broadcasters.

301.16   CN
BROADCAST WEEK. w. Globe and Mail Publishing, 444 Front St. W., Toronto, ON M5V 2S9, Canada. TEL 416-585-5045. Ed. Trevor Cole. adv. contact: Irene Patterson. circ. 180,000. **Document type:** consumer publication.
●Also available online.

301.16   CE
BROADCASTER. (Text in English) 1978. m. Rs.17. Sri Lanka Broadcasting Corporation, Publications and Information, Box 574, Colombo, Sri Lanka.

384   UK
BROADCASTING AND TELECOMMUNICATIONS FOR CHINA. (Text in Chinese) a. £55. Sterling Publications Ltd., 86-88 Edgware Rd., London W2 2YW, England. TEL 44-171-915-9600. FAX 44-171-915-9619. circ. 10,000. **Document type:** trade publication.

301.16   UK   ISSN 0960-3999
BROADCASTING STANDARDS COUNCIL. ANNUAL REVIEW. a. John Libbey Media, University of Luton, 75 Castle St., Luton, Bedfordshire LU1 3AJ, England. TEL 44-1582-743297. FAX 44-1582-743298. E-mail: john.libbey@luton.ac.uk. Ed. Andrea Millwood Hargrave. **Document type:** corporate report.
—BLDSC (6967.820000).

380   UK   ISSN 0956-9073
BROADCASTING STANDARDS COUNCIL. MONOGRAPH. 1989. irreg., no.3, 1991. John Libbey Media, University of Luton, 75 Castle St., Luton, Bedfordshire LU1 3AJ, England. TEL 44-1582-743297. FAX 44-1582-743298. E-mail: john.libbey@luton.ac.uk. Ed. Andrea Hargrave. **Document type:** monographic series.
—BLDSC (2349.082500).

301.16   BX
BRUNEI DARUSSALAM NEWSLETTER. (Text in English) s-m. Information Department, Prime Minister's Office, Bandar Seri Begawan 2041, Brunei Darussalam. TEL 673-2-383400. FAX 673-2-382242. circ. 12,000. **Document type:** newsletter, government publication.

384   BU
BULGARIA. MINISTERSTVO NA INFORMATSIIATA I SUOBSHTENIIATA. SUOBSHTENIIA; nauchno i proizvodstveno-tekhnichesko spisanie. m. Komitet na Informatsiiata i Suobshteniiata, c/o Distributor: Foreign Trade Co. "Hemus", 1B Raiko Daskalov Sq., 1000 Sofia, Bulgaria. TEL 395-2-971686. FAX 359-2-9803319. illus.

BULGARSKI ZHURNALIST/BULGARIAN JOURNALIST. see *JOURNALISM*

BULLETIN S E V - V S E. (Schweizerischer Elektrotechnischer Verein) see *ENGINEERING — Electrical Engineering*

621.38   FR   ISSN 0007-5302
BULLETIN SIGNALETIQUE DES TELECOMMUNICATIONS. 1958. m. 885 F. (foreign 935 F.). Centre National d'Etudes des Telecommunications, Service de Documentation Interministerielle, Service des Abonnements, 38-40 rue du General Leclerc, 92131 Issy-les-Moulineaux Cedex, France. TEL 45-29-51-08. index. circ. 1,500.
●Also available online. Vendor(s): Telesystemes - Questel.
—Linda Hall.

380   US
BURRELLE'S MEDIA DIRECTORY. (In 3 vols.: vol 1: Newspapers and Related Media (Parts 1 & 2); vol. 2: Magazines and Newsletters; vol. 3: Radio, Television and Cable (Parts 1 & 2)) a. plus q. updates. $550 (CD-ROM $795). Burrelle's Media Directories, 75 E. Northfield Rd., Livingston, NJ 07039. TEL 202-992-6600; 800-USM-EDIA. Ed. James L. Hayes. adv. contact: James L. Hayes. (also avail. in diskette format) **Document type:** directory.
●Also available online.
Also available on CD-ROM. Producer(s): SilverPlatter Information, Inc.
   Description: Lists over 1,800 daily newspapers, 10,400 non-daily newspapers, and 12,500 magazines. Also includes 10,350 radio stations, 1,700 television stations, 1,000 cable systems, and all the related media.

BUSINESS COMMUNICATION QUARTERLY. see *BUSINESS AND ECONOMICS — Management*

384.3 004.6   GR
▼**THE BUSINESS INTERNET NEWSLETTER.** (Text in Greek) 1995. m. Dr.15000. Compupress S.A., 44 Syngrou, 117 42 Athens, Greece. TEL 30-1-9238-672. FAX 30-1-921-6847. Ed. M. Nikolaou; Pub. N.O. Manousos. adv. contact: V. Giakamozis. circ. 6,000 (paid). **Document type:** newsletter.
   Description: Covers topics on integrating business and the Internet and World Wide Web. Examines new opportunities or new ways of doing business with these online services. For entrepreneurs, marketers, and advertising professionals.

384   UK   ISSN 1364-0410
BUSINESS RATIO PLUS: TELECOMMUNICATIONS. 1980. a. I C C Business Publications Ltd., Field House, 72 Oldfield Rd., Hampton, Mddx. TW12 2HQ, England. TEL 44-181-783-0922. FAX 44-181-783-1940. charts; stat.
   Former titles (until 1995): Business Ratio Plus: Telecommunications Industry (ISSN 1355-8862); (until 1993): Business Ratio Report: Telecommunications Industry (ISSN 0261-9601)

THE BUSINESS - TO - BUSINESS MARKETER. see *ADVERTISING AND PUBLIC RELATIONS*

380 330   AT   ISSN 1035-9222
C B D. (Corporate Business Design) a. Aus.$60. Armadillo Publishers Pty. Ltd., 11 Dingley Dell Rd., Warrandyte North, Melbourne, Vic. 3113, Australia. TEL 61-3-98444558. FAX 61-3-98444638. illus.

C E P JOURNAL. (Communications, Energy and Paperworkers Union of Canada) see *PAPER AND PULP*

621.38   JA
C I A J ANNUAL REPORT. a. free. Communications Industry Association of Japan - Tsushin Kikai Kogyokai, Sankei, Bldg. Annex, 1-7-2 Ohte-machi, Chiyoda-ku, Tokyo 100, Japan. TEL 81-03-3231-3156. FAX 81-3231-3110. URL: http://www.ciaj.or.jp. Ed. Eizo Tamura.
   Formerly: Outline of Communications Industry.
   Description: Contains outline of recent CIAJ activities and major figures in Japan's telecommunications equipment industry.

621.38   US   ISSN 0095-9669
TK5104   CODEN: CSTRCQ
C O M S A T TECHNICAL REVIEW. (Communications Satellite) (Text in English; summaries in French, Spanish) 1971. a. $25. COMSAT Corporation, 22300 COMSAT Dr., Clarksburg, MD 20871-9471. TEL 301-428-4512. FAX 301-428-7747. TELEX 440696. E-mail: mike.onufry@comsat.com. URL: http:www.comsat.com. Ed. Michael Onufry. R&P contact: Michael Onufry. charts; illus. circ. 2,000. (also avail. in microfiche; reprint service avail. from ISI) **Indexed:** CAD CAM Abstr., Cadscan, Comput.Cont., Curr.Cont., Eng.Ind., INSPEC (1971-), Int.Aerosp.Abstr., Lead Abstr., Tel.Abstr., Zincscan. **Document type:** academic/scholarly publication.
●Also available online.
—BLDSC (3395.150000); AskIEEE; CISTI; Ei; KR SourceOne; Linda Hall; SWETS; UnCover.

301.16   US   ISSN 0271-4795
HE8689
C R I COMMUNICATIONS UPDATE SERVICE.* q. $15. Communications Research Institute, 515 Madison Ave., No. 3600, New York, NY 10022. Ed. Scott H. Robb.

384   IT   ISSN 0393-2648
TK5101.A1
C S E L T TECHNICAL REPORTS/C S E L T RAPPORTI TECNICI. (Text in English and Italian) 1973. bi-m. exchange basis. C S E L T - Centro Studi e Laboratori Telecomunicazioni S.p.A., Via Guglielmo Reiss Romoli 274, 10148 Turin, Italy. TEL 39-11-2285111. FAX 39-11-2285520. TELEX 220539. URL: http://www.cselt.stet.it. Ed.Bd. biennial index. circ. 1,300. (back issues avail.) **Indexed:** Eng.Ind., INSPEC, Int.Aerosp.Abstr. **Document type:** corporate report.
—BLDSC (3490.179100); AskIEEE; CISTI; Ei; KR SourceOne; Linda Hall.
   Formerly: C S E L T Rapporti Tecnici (ISSN 0390-1815)

621.382   CC   ISSN 1024-5847
▼**C T C NEWS.** (Text in English) 1995. 22/yr. $439. China Telecommunication Construction Publishers, 12-F, Sing Kui Commercial Bldg., 27 Des Voeux Rd. W., Hong Kong, People's Republic of China. TEL 852-2517-2095. FAX 852-2517-2101. (Alt. addr.: Ground Fl., 2A Qianhainanyan, Xicheng District, Beijing 100009, P.R. China. TEL 81-10-401-4103) Ed. S.Y. Cheung. **Indexed:** HongKongiana. **Document type:** newsletter.
   Description: Covers latest development of telecommunications in China.

004 384   UK   ISSN 1357-3128
K3
▼**C T L R.** (Computer and Telecommunications Law Review) 1995. bi-m. £195($325) Sweet & Maxwell, Mill St., Oxford OX2 0JU, England. TEL 44-1865-249248. FAX 44-1865-792301. E-mail: ctlr@smlawpub.co.uk. (Subscr. to: Sweet & Maxwell, Freepost, Andover, Hants SP10 5BR, England. TEL 44-1264-342899. FAX 44-1264-342761) Ed. Janet Phillips. **Document type:** academic/scholarly publication.
—BLDSC (3490.522450); UnCover.
   Refereed Serial

C W A NEWS. (Communications Workers of America) see *LABOR UNIONS*

CABLE & SATELLITE COMMUNICATIONS INTERNATIONAL. see *COMMUNICATIONS — Television And Cable*

COMMUNICATIONS

301.16   US   ISSN 1051-1938
CABLE OPTICS; covering worldwide developments in the application of fiber optics in cable television systems. 1989. m. $595 (foreign $645) (effective 1997). Information Gatekeepers, Inc., 214 Harvard Ave., Boston, MA 02134. TEL 617-232-3111; 800-323-1088. FAX 617-734-8562. E-mail: igiboston@aol.com; URL: http:///www.igigroup.com. Ed. Paul Polishuk. (back issues avail.) **Document type:** trade publication.
—CCC.
    Description: Covers fiber optics technology and applications to the CATV industry, new products, plans, regulations, standards, and business developments.

621.38   US   ISSN 1060-3050
TK5101.A1
CABLING BUSINESS MAGAZINE. 1991. m. free in US; Canada & Mexico $24; elsewhere $75. Cabling Publications Inc., 12035 Shiloh Rd., Ste. 350, Dallas, TX 75228. TEL 214-328-1717. FAX 214-319-6077. Ed. Stephen C. Paulov; Pub. Stephen S. Paulov. R&P contact: Stephen S. Paulov. adv.: B&W page $2765, color page $3855; trim 8 3/8 x 10 7/8; adv. contact: Russ Paulov. circ. 35,000. **Document type:** trade publication.
    Description: For users and providers of voice and data wiring and cabling.

301.16   FR
CAHIERS DE LA COMMUNICATION. 1981. 5/yr. 265 F. Centrale des Revues, Bordas-Dunod-Gauthier-Villars, 11 rue Gossin, 92543 Montrouge Cedex, France. Eds. Francis Balle, Jean-Marie Cotteret. adv.; bk.rev. circ. 1,000.

CANADIAN JOURNAL OF REMOTE SENSING. see *AERONAUTICS AND SPACE FLIGHT*

621.38   CN   ISSN 0836-0782
CANADIAN TELECOM. 1987. 6/yr. Can.$45($55) (effective 1997). A B Y Group, 36 Toronto St., Ste. 1160, Toronto, ON M5C 2C5, Canada. TEL 416-359-2911. FAX 416-359-9909. Ed. John Burry; Pub. John Burry. R&P contact: John Burry. adv. circ. 6,100. Indexed: Can.B.P.I. **Document type:** trade publication.
    Description: Addresses issues related to the application of communications technology to business. For managers of voice and data communications.

384   UN
CATALOGUE OF SOFTWARE FOR RADIO SPECTRUM MANAGEMENT. (Editions in English, French, Spanish) a. free. International Telecommunication Union, Place des Nations, CH-1211 Geneva 20, Switzerland. TEL 41-22-7306141. FAX 41-22-7305194. E-mail: sales@itu.ch; URL: http://www.itu.ch. **Document type:** catalog.

CATHOLIC MEDIA COUNCIL. INFORMATION BULLETIN. see *RELIGIONS AND THEOLOGY* — Roman Catholic

380   AG
CAUSAS Y AZARES; los lenguajes de la comunicacion y la cultura en (la) crisis. 1994. q. Arg.$7 per no. Ediciones El Cielo por Asalto, Lambare 873, 1185 Buenos Aires, Argentina. TEL 54-1-8657554. FAX 54-1-343-2999. Ed.Bd.

621.38   US
CELLULAR TELECOMMUNICATIONS. 1991. m. $595 (foreign $645) (effective 1997). Information Gatekeepers, Inc., 214 Harvard Ave., Boston, MA 02134. TEL 617-232-3111; 800-323-1088. FAX 617-734-8562. E-mail: igiboston@aol.com; URL: http://www.igigroup.com. Ed. Paul Polishuk. **Document type:** newsletter.
    Formerly: Wireless Cellular (ISSN 1058-6717)
    Description: Covers cellular mobile radio technology, markets, applications, services, standards, regulations, products, business developments.

621.38   CC   ISSN 1000-1794
CHANGCHUN YOUDIAN XUEYUAN XUEBAO/CHANGCHUN INSTITUTE OF POSTS AND TELECOMMUNICATIONS. JOURNAL. (Text in Chinese) q. Changchun Youdian Xueyuan, Xuebao Bianjibu, 20, Nanhu Dalu, Changchun, Jilin 130012, People's Republic of China. TEL 5551. Ed. Wang Zhihuai. **Document type:** academic/scholarly publication.

791.4   SI   ISSN 0129-3389
CHARACTERS - SINGAPORE AND MALAYSIA EDITIONS. (Text in Chinese) 1987. m. S.$30 for Singapore; West Malaysia M$36; East Malaysia M$43. Pioneers & Leaders (Publishers) Pte. Ltd., 42 MacTaggart Rd., 06-02 MacTaggart Bldg., Singapore 1336, Singapore. TEL 2866733. FAX 2895413. Ed. Sam Ng. adv.: B&W page S$550, color page S$1000. circ. 45,000.
    Description: Covers television, films, pop songs, fashion, cooking, furniture and tourism.

302.23   CC
CHINA MEDIA NEWSLETTER. (Text in English) 1993. 11/yr. $260. Art Text Pty. Ltd., Youyi Binguan, Ste. 40626, Beijing 100873, P.R. China. TEL 86-10-6849-8987. Ed. Bruce Doar. **Document type:** newsletter.
    Description: Provides up-to-date information on the Chinese media and publishing industries.

384   US   ISSN 1078-2214
CHINA TELECOM NEWSLETTER. 1994. m. $595 (foreign $645) (effective 1997). Information Gatekeepers, Inc., 214 Harvard Ave., Boston, MA 02134. TEL 617-232-3111; 800-323-1088. FAX 617-734-8562. E-mail: igiboston@aol.com; URL: http://www.igigroup.com. **Document type:** newsletter.

384   US   ISSN 1081-4094
CHINA TELECOM REPORT. 1994. m. $679 (effective 1997). International Technology Consultants, 4340 East-West Hwy., Ste. 220, Bethesda, MD 20814-4411. TEL 301-907-0060. FAX 301-907-6555. E-mail: 71011,2475@compuserve.com; itcuser@aol.com; URL: http://www.intl-tech.com. Ed. Kari Roe. adv. contact: William Thurmond. charts, stat. **Document type:** newsletter, trade publication.

CHURCHART PRO ON DISK. see *RELIGIONS AND THEOLOGY* — Protestant

CINE & MEDIA. see *MOTION PICTURES*

380   US
▼**CISCO WORLD.** 1995. m. $26 (foreign $76) (effective 1995). Publications & Communications, Inc., 12416 Hymeadow, Austin, TX 78750-1896. TEL 512-250-9023; 800-678-9724. FAX 512-331-3900. adv.: B&W page $3444, color page $4244; trim 10 3/4 x 14 1/2. (tabloid format) **Document type:** trade publication.

CLIENT DIRECTORY AND AGENCY LIST. see *ADVERTISING AND PUBLIC RELATIONS*

384   CN   ISSN 1024-0195
CLIPS. French edition (ISSN 1024-0187); Spanish edition (ISSN 1024-0179) 1992. 3/yr. $10. Videazimut, 3860 rue Jeanne Mance, Bur. 430, Montreal, PQ H2X 2K5, Canada. TEL 514-982-6660. FAX 514-982-6122. E-mail: videaz@web.net. Ed. Sylvia Roy. bk.rev. **Document type:** newsletter.
    Description: Promotes the democratic practice of communication. Aims to broaden the participation of communities and movements from the South and the North in sound and image production.

COGITO; das Online-Magazin fuer die Industrie. see *COMPUTERS*

COMMA; magazine voor communicatie in de publieke sector. see *PUBLIC ADMINISTRATION*

384   US
COMMTEXT SERIES. 1989. no.4. irreg., latest no.21. price varies. Sage Publications, Inc., 2455 Teller Rd., Thousand Oaks, CA 91320. TEL 805-499-0721. FAX 805-499-0871. E-mail: libraries@sagepub.com; URL: http://www.sagepub.com. (Overseas subscr. to: Sage Publications, 6 Bonhill St., London EC2A 4PU, England; Sage Publications India Pvt. Ltd., P.O. Box 4125, New Delhi 110 048, India) Ed. Everette E. Dennis. (back issues avail.) **Document type:** monographic series.
    Description: Discusses various aspects of mass communication.

380   SA   ISSN 0259-0069
COMMUNICARE; journal of communication sciences. (Text in Afrikaans, English; summaries in English) 1981. s-a. R.50 to individuals (foreign R.670); institutions R.150 (foreign R.160) (effective 1997). Southern African Communication Association, Department of Communication, Rand Afrikaans University, P.O. Box 524, Auckland Park 2006, South Africa. TEL 27-11-4892139. FAX 27-11-4892426. Ed. Sonja Verwey. R&P contact: Marianne Olivier. adv. contact: Marianne Olivier. bk.rev.; abstr.; charts; illus.; stat. circ. 400. (back issues avail.) Indexed: Ind.S.A.Per. **Document type:** academic/scholarly publication.
    Description: Academic journal of communication studies.
    Refereed Serial

070 384   BE   ISSN 0771-7342
COMMUNICATIE; tijdschrift voor communicatiewetenschap en mediacultuur. (Text in Dutch) 1970. q. 600 BEF (Netherlands fl.35.50; elsewhere 600 BEF). Katholieke Universiteit Leuven, Departement Communicatiewetenschap, E. Van Evenstraat 2A, 3000 Leuven, Belgium. TEL 32-16-323220. FAX 32-16-323312. E-mail: Roland.VanGompel@soc.kuleuven.ac.be. Ed.Bd. adv.; bk.rev.; bibl. circ. 500. (back issues avail.) **Document type:** academic/scholarly publication.
    Formerly (until 1975): Centrum voor Communicatiewetenschap. Informatie Bulletin (ISSN 0771-7334)
    Description: Publishes academic articles on communication science and culture.

301.16   SA   ISSN 0250-0167
COMMUNICATIO. (Text in Afrikaans, English) 1975. s-a. R.20 (overseas $6.31(£4.33)) (effective 1997). (University of South Africa, Department of Communication) Unisa Press, Periodicals, P.O. Box 392, Pretoria 0001, South Africa. TEL 27-12-4296565. FAX 27-12-4293346. TELEX 350068. E-mail: fouripj@risco.unisa.ac.za. Ed. Pieter J. Fourie. bk.rev.; circ. 1,800 (controlled). Indexed: Ind.S.A.Per., MLA Intl.Bibl. **Document type:** academic/scholarly publication.
    Description: Publishes articles reflecting communications research in Africa.
    Refereed Serial

301.161 070   CN   ISSN 1189-3788
P92.C3
COMMUNICATION; information - medias - theories - practiques. (Text in French; summaries in English, French, Spanish) 1975. s-a. Can.$30 to individuals (outside N. America Can.$35); institutions Can.$50 (outside N. America Can.$60); students Can.$25 (outside N. America Can.$30). (Universite Laval, Departement de Communication) Editions Saint-Martin, B-5420, Pavillon L.-J. Casault, Quebec, PQ G1K 7P4, Canada. TEL 418-656-7588. FAX 418-656-7807. E-mail: revue.communication@com.ulaval.ca. (Subscr. to: Les Editions Saint-Martin, 5000 Iverville, No. 203, Montreal, PQ H2H 2S6, Canada. TEL 514-529-0920. FAX 514-529-8384) Ed. Roger de la Garde. adv.; bk.rev.; bibl.; charts; illus.; cum.index. circ. 500. (back issues avail.) Indexed: Bull.Signal., Can.B.P.I., Can.Per.Ind., INSPEC (1993-), Lang.& Lang.Behav.Abstr., Pt.de Rep. (1982-), Sociol.Abstr. **Document type:** academic/scholarly publication.
    —BLDSC (3343.760000); AskIEEE; KR SourceOne
    Formerly (until 1991): Communication et Information (ISSN 0382-7798)
    Description: Covers Canadian media studies and journalism practices.

380   US   ISSN 0272-9830
P87
COMMUNICATION (BOCA RATON). (Subseries of: S I R Social Issues (ISSN 0740-3127)) 1976. a. price varies; a. supplement $19. Social Issues Resources Series, Box 2348, Boca Raton, FL 33427-2348. TEL 561-994-0079; 800-232-SIRS. FAX 561-994-4704. E-mail: custserve@sirs.com; URL: http://www.sirs.com. Ed. Trudy Collins; Pub. Eleanor Goldstein. R&P contact: Bonnie Milnes. (looseleaf format; back issues avail.) **Document type:** academic/scholarly publication.
    Description: Reprints articles that address all aspects of communication.

410 BE ISSN 0378-0880
P87
COMMUNICATION & COGNITION. (Text in English, French) 1968. q. 950 BEF to individuals; institutions 1050 BEF (effective 1996). (Rijksuniversiteit Gent) Communication and Cognition, Blandijnberg 2, 9000 Ghent, Belgium. TEL 32-9-2643952. FAX 32-9-2644197. Ed. Fernand Vandamme. adv.; bk.rev.; bibl. circ. 550. (reprint service avail. from ISI) **Indexed:** Bibl.Ling., Lang.& Lang.Behav.Abstr., Math.R., MLA Intl.Bibl., Phil.Ind, Psychol.Abstr. (1971-), Sage Fam.Stud.Abstr., Sociol.Abstr., SSCI. **Document type:** academic/scholarly publication.
—BLDSC (3359.260000); SWETS; UnCover. **CCC.**
Refereed Serial

380 658 US ISSN 0730-7799
CODEN: COBREC
COMMUNICATION BRIEFINGS;* a monthly idea source for decision-makers. 1981. m. $69 (Canada $79; elsewhere $99). 1101 King St., Ste. 110, Alexandria, VA 22314. TEL 703-548-3800. FAX 703-684-2136. Ed. Frank Grazian; Pub. Don Bagin. bk.rev.; index. circ. 45,000. (back issues avail.) **Document type:** newsletter.
—CASDDS; SWETS.
 Description: Articles, excerpts, news items, and departments on ideas and techniques to help improve writing, speaking, listening, organizing, problem-solving, and decision-making skills at the managerial and administrative levels.

380 US
HQ471.L56
COMMUNICATION CONCEPTS. irreg., no.5, 1993. Sage Publications, Inc., 2455 Teller Rd., Thousand Oaks, CA 91320. TEL 805-499-0721. FAX 805-499-0871. E-mail: libraries@sagepub.com; URL: http://www.sagepub.com. (Overseas subscr. to: Sage Publications Ltd., 6 Bonhill St., London EC2A 4PU, England; Sage Publications Pvt. Ltd., P.O. Box 4215, New Delhi 110 048, India) adv. contact: Margaret Travers. **Document type:** monographic series.

380 378 US
COMMUNICATION DISCIPLINES IN HIGHER EDUCATION: A DIRECTORY. 1987. irreg., 2nd ed., 1993. $15 to non-members; members $10. Association for Communication Administration, 5105-F Backlick Rd., Annandale, VA 22003. TEL 703-750-0533. FAX 703-914-9471. Ed. Garland C. Elmore. **Document type:** directory.
 Formerly: Communication Media in Higher Education: A Directory.
 Description: Lists communication programs, faculty, curriculum, majors, and organizational structures of over 1500 communications programs in the US and Canada.

COMMUNICATION EDUCATION. see *EDUCATION — Teaching Methods And Curriculum*

COMMUNICATION: JOURNALISM EDUCATION TODAY. see *EDUCATION*

COMMUNICATION LAW AND POLICY. see *LAW*

COMMUNICATION MONOGRAPHS. see *EDUCATION*

COMMUNICATION NEWS. see *BUSINESS AND ECONOMICS — Management*

COMMUNICATION QUARTERLY. see *EDUCATION*

COMMUNICATION REPORTS. see *LINGUISTICS*

301.16 US ISSN 0093-6502
P91 CODEN: CRESDG
COMMUNICATION RESEARCH. 1974. bi-m. $276 to institutions (effective Sep. 1996). Sage Publications, Inc., 2455 Teller Rd., Thousand Oaks, CA 91320. TEL 805-499-0721. FAX 805-499-0871. E-mail: libraries@sagepub.com; URL: http://www.sagepub.com. (Overseas subscr. to: Sage Publications Ltd., 6 Bonhill St., London EC2A 4PU, England; Sage Publications India Pvt. Ltd., P.O. Box 4215, New Delhi 110 048, India) Eds. Sandra J. Ball-Rokeach, Charles R. Berger. adv. contact: Margaret Travers. bk.rev.; illus.; bibl.; index. circ. 1,600. (back issues avail.; reprint service avail.) **Indexed:** Abstr.Anthropol., Abstr.Pop.Cult., Arts & Hum.Cit.Ind., ASCA, C.I.J.E., Commun.Abstr., Curr.Cont., Educ.Tech.Abstr., ERIC, Film Lit.Ind. (1989-), IJCS (1974-), Psychol.Abstr. (1974-), Sage Fam.Stud.Abstr., Sage Urb.Stud.Abstr., Soc.Sci.Ind., SSCI, Stud.Wom.Abstr., Tech.Educ.Abstr. **Document type:** academic/scholarly publication.
—BLDSC (3363.120000); Genuine Article; KR SourceOne; SWETS; UMI; UnCover. **CCC.**
 Description: Provides an interdisciplinary forum for scholars and professionals to present new research in communication.

301.16 US ISSN 0882-4096
COMMUNICATION RESEARCH REPORTS. (Packaged with: Communications Quarterly (ISSN 0146-3373)) 1984. q. $50 including Communication Quarterly (CQ). Eastern Communication Association, c/o Kathleen M. Long, Exec. Sec., Dept. of Communication & Marketing, West Virginia Wesleyan College, 59 College Ave., Buckhannon, WV 26201-2997. TEL 304-473-8234. FAX 304-473-8187. Ed. Jerry L. Allen. R&P contact: Kathleen Long. adv. contact: Sandra E. Presar. index. circ. 1,500. (also avail. in microfilm from UMI; back issues avail.) **Indexed:** Psychol.Abstr. (1984-). **Document type:** academic/scholarly publication.
—BLDSC (3363.133000); SWETS; UnCover.
 Description: Articles reporting research relating directly to human communication.

301.6 US ISSN 0144-4646
P91.3
COMMUNICATION RESEARCH TRENDS. 1980. q. $35 (effective 1997). Centre for the Study of Communication and Culture, Xavier Hall 325, St. Louis University, Box 59607, St. Louis, MO 63156-0907. TEL 314-977-7290. FAX 314-977-7296. E-mail: cscc@slu.edu. Ed. Fr. William E. Biernatzki; Pub. Fr. Paul J. Duffy. R&P contact: Fr. William E. Biernatzki. adv. contact: Marcia Deering. bk.rev.; bibl.; circ. 800 (paid); 600. **Indexed:** Film Lit.Ind. **Document type:** academic/scholarly publication, monographic series.
—BLDSC (3363.135000); SWETS.
 Formerly: Centre for the Study of Communication and Culture. Newsletter.
 Description: Each issue is a monographic review of the state-of-the-art in a sub-field of communications research.
Refereed Serial

301.16 NE ISSN 1071-4421
P87 CODEN: CURVEA
THE COMMUNICATION REVIEW. 1975. 4/yr. (in 1 vol.). $90 (effective 1998). Gordon and Breach - Harwood Academic, Amsteldisk 166, 1st Fl., 1079 LH Amsterdam, Netherlands. (Subscr. to: International Publishers Distributor, Box 32160, Newark, NJ 07102. TEL 800-545-8398. FAX 215-750-6343) Ed. Robert Horwitz. adv.; index. (also avail. in microfilm; back issues avail.) **Indexed:** Commun.Abstr., Psychol.Abstr. **Document type:** academic/scholarly publication.
—BLDSC (3363.141500); SWETS; UnCover. **CCC.**
 Formerly: Communication (Langhorne) (ISSN 0305-4233)
Refereed Serial

380 US
COMMUNICATION SERIES. irreg. Lawrence Erlbaum Associates, Inc., 10 Industrial Ave., Mahwah, NJ 07430-2262. TEL 201-236-9500; 800-926-6579. FAX 201-236-0072. E-mail: orders@erlbaum.com; URL: http://www.erlbaum.com. Eds. Jennings Bryant, Dolf Zillmann. **Document type:** monographic series.

301.16 370 US ISSN 1051-0974
PN4001 CODEN: CSTDEK
COMMUNICATION STUDIES. (Former name of issuing body: Central State Speech Association) 1949. q. $40 to libraries (foreign $50) (effective 1995). Boylor Universitg, Waco, TX 76798. TEL 405-332-8000. FAX 405-332-1623. E-mail: ADaniel@csca.ecok.edu. Ed. J. Kevin Barge. adv.; bk.rev.; bibl.; charts; stat.; tr.lit.; index. circ. 2,700. (also avail. in microform) **Indexed:** C.I.J.E., Commun.Abstr., Curr.Cont., IJCS (1949-), Lang.& Lang.Behav.Abstr., Mid.East: Abstr.& Ind., Psychol.Abstr., SSCI. **Document type:** academic/scholarly publication.
●Also available online. Vendor(s): UMI.
—UMI; UnCover.
 Formerly: Central States Speech Journal (ISSN 0008-9575)
Refereed Serial

301.16 GW ISSN 0341-2059
P87
COMMUNICATIONS; European Journal of Communication, Le Journal Europeen de la Communication, Die Europaeische Zeitschrift fuer Kommunikation. 1974. 4/yr. DM.186 (foreign DM.196; students DM.120) (effective 1996). (Deutsche Gesellschaft fuer Kommunikationsforschung) Quintessenz Verlags GmbH, Ifenpfad 2-4, 12107 Berlin, Germany. TEL 49-30-740646. FAX 49-30-7415080. (Co-sponsor: Internationale Vereinigung fuer Kommunikationswissenschaft) Eds. A. Silbermann, H. Neubert. adv.; bk.rev. (reprint service avail. from ISI) **Indexed:** Psychol.Abstr. **Document type:** academic/scholarly publication.
—BLDSC (3343.800000). **CCC.**
 Formerly (until 1976): International Journal of Communication Research (ISSN 0340-0158)

384 FR ISSN 0588-8018
P87
COMMUNICATIONS. 1961. s-a. 180 F. (foreign 205 F.). (Ecole Pratique des Hautes Etudes, Centre d'Etudes des Communications de Masse) Editions du Seuil, 27 rue Jacob, 75261 Paris Cedex 06, France. TEL 46-56-89-00. (Subscr. to: B.S.I., 49 rue de la Vanne, 92120 Montrouge, France) bk.rev.; bibl. **Indexed:** Int.Polit.Sci.Abstr., Intl.Ind.TV, Lang.& Lang.Behav.Abstr.
—BLDSC (3343.750000); SWETS. **CCC.**
 Description: Contains sociological and semiological studies of mass media.

621 UK ISSN 0962-3841
HE8461
COMMUNICATIONS AFRICA/COMMUNICATIONS AFRIQUE. (Text in English and French) 1987. bi-m. £43.50($75) Alain Charles Publishing Ltd., Alain Charles House, 27 Wilfred St., London SW1E 6PR, England. TEL 44-171-834-7676. FAX 44-171-973-0076. TELEX 297165 ACPLTD G. adv. circ. 3,781. **Indexed:** Ind.S.A.Per. **Document type:** trade publication.
 Description: Covers the telecommunications and broadcasting markets with practical information about ideas and the special requirements of managers throughout Africa.

301.16 340 US ISSN 0162-9093
K3 CODEN: COMLDE
COMMUNICATIONS AND THE LAW. 1979. q. $110 (foreign $120) (effective 1997). Fred B. Rothman & Co., 10368 W. Centennial Rd., Littleton, CO 80127. TEL 303-979-5657. FAX 303-978-1457. Ed. Theodore R. Kupferman. adv.; bk.rev. (also avail. in microfilm from PMC,WSH; microfiche from WSH; reprint service avail. from WSH) **Indexed:** ABI Inform., Abstr.Bk.Rev.Curr.Leg.Per., C.L.I., Film Lit.Ind. (1988-), INSPEC (1987-), L.R.I., Leg.Cont., Leg.Per.
●Also available online. Vendor(s): UMI.
—BLDSC (3359.314000); AskIEEE; KR SourceOne; SWETS; UMI; UnCover.

1986 COMMUNICATIONS

621.38 332.6   US
COMMUNICATIONS BUSINESS & FINANCE. bi-w. $547 (outside N. America $673). Telecommunications Reports (Subsidiary of: Business Research Publications, Inc.), 1333 H St., N.W., Ste. 100-E, Washington, DC 20005. TEL 800-822-6338. FAX 202-842-3023. E-mail: customerservice@tr.com; URL: http://www.tr.com. Ed. Victoria A. Mason. R&P contact: Jessica Bridges. **Document type:** newsletter.
●Also available online. Vendor(s): Information Access Co.
   Description: Deals exclusively with investment and finance activities in the converging telecom, cable television, wireless, and multimedia industries, tracking the performance of telecom mutual funds, deals in the making, and investment strategies.

384   UK   ISSN 1352-4399
COMMUNICATIONS COMPANIES ANALYSIS. MANUFACTURERS VOLUME. a. (plus m. updates). £695. M D I S Publications Ltd., MDIS House, City Fields Business Park, City Fields Way, Chichester, W. Sussex PO20 6FS, England. TEL 44-1243-533322. FAX 44-1243-533418. Ed. Neil Parker; Pub. Eric Wigart. R&P contact: Katie Sykes. **Document type:** directory.
●Also available on CD-ROM.

384   UK   ISSN 1352-4380
COMMUNICATIONS COMPANIES ANALYSIS. OPERATORS VOLUME. 1991. a. (plus m. upds.). £795 (effective 1997). M D I S Publications Ltd., MDIS House, City Fields Business Park, City Fields Way, Chichester, W. Sussex PO20 6FS, England. TEL 44-1243-533322. FAX 44-1243-533418. Ed. Neil Parker. R&P contact: Katie Sykes. circ. 3,000. (looseleaf format; also avail. in diskette format) **Document type:** directory.
●Also available online.
Also available on CD-ROM.

384   US   ISSN 1070-4426
COMMUNICATIONS INDUSTRIES REPORT.* (Former name of issuing body: National Audio-Visual Association) 1946. m. free. International Communications Industries Association, 11242 Waples Mill Rd., Ste. 200, Fairfax, VA 22030-6079. TEL 703-273-7200. FAX 703-278-8082. Ed. Dick Larsen. adv./bk.rev.; circ. 15,000 (controlled). (processed) **Document type:** trade publication.
—KR SourceOne.
   Formerly (until 1984): N A V A News (ISSN 0027-609X).
   Description: Provides information about the communications industry. Includes articles on video, multimedia, interactive technology and presentation, computer, audio-visual and teleconferencing.

621.38   UK   ISSN 0305-2109
TK5101.A1   CODEN: CINTDZ
COMMUNICATIONS INTERNATIONAL. 1974. m. £30 (overseas £45). E M A P Business & Computer Publications Ltd., 33-39 Bowling Green Ln., London EC1R 0DA, England. TEL 44-171-837-1212. FAX 44-171-278-4003. Ed. B. Whitehouse. adv. circ. 24,194. (also avail. in microform from UMI) **Indexed:** CAD CAM Abstr., INSPEC (1975-), PROMT, Tel.Abstr. **Document type:** trade publication.
●Also available online. Vendor(s): Information Access Co., Lexis-Nexis, UMI.
—BLDSC (3360.400000); AskIEEE; CISTI; Ei; KR SourceOne; Linda Hall; SWETS; UMI; UnCover. **CCC.**

621   US
COMMUNICATIONS: LATIN AMERICAN INDUSTRIAL REPORT. (Avail. for each of 22 Latin American countries) 1985. a. $435 per country report. Aquino Productions, Box 125, Rochester, VT 05767. Ed. Andres C. Aquino.

384 340   UK   ISSN 1361-9918
KD667.C65   CODEN: CLPRER
COMMUNICATIONS LAW. 1984. bi-m. £140 (foreign £149). Tolley Publishing Co. Ltd., Tolley House, 2 Addiscombe Rd., Croydon, Surrey CR9 5AF, England. TEL 44-181-686-9141. FAX 44-181-686-3155. E-mail: comms l@tolley.co.uk; URL: http://www.tolley.co.uk. Ed. David Goldberg. adv.; bk.rev. **Indexed:** C.L.I., Euro.LJI, INSPEC, LJI. **Document type:** trade publication.
—BLDSC (8863.685560); AskIEEE; KR SourceOne; SWETS.
   Former titles (until 1996): Tolley's Computer Law and Practice (ISSN 1359-5989); (until 1992): Computer Law and Practice (ISSN 0266-4801)
   Description: Covers all aspects of communications law and practice.

343.73 384   US   ISSN 0898-2457
COMMUNICATIONS LAW. a. $198 (effective 1996). Practising Law Institute, 810 Seventh Ave., New York, NY 10019. TEL 212-824-5700; 800-260-4754. FAX 800-321-0093. E-mail: info@pli.edu; URL: http://www.pli.edu.
   Former titles (until 1982): Annual Communications Law Institute (ISSN 0898-2449); (until 1981): Communications Law (ISSN 0160-2616)

COMMUNICATIONS LAW & POLICY IN AUSTRALIA. see LAW

COMMUNICATIONS LAWYER. see LAW

384 330.9   UK   ISSN 1356-3327
▼**COMMUNICATIONS MARKETS ANALYSIS.** 1995. a. (plus 2-4 upds. per m.). £695. M D I S Publications Ltd., MDIS House, City Fields Business Park, City Fields Way, Chichester, W. Sussex PO20 6FS, England. TEL 44-1243-533322. FAX 44-1243-533418. Ed. John Bennett. (looseleaf format; also avail. in diskette format) **Document type:** trade publication.
●Also available online.
Also available on CD-ROM.

380   UK   ISSN 0961-7590
COMMUNICATIONS MIDDLE EAST - AFRICA. m. £80($155) Angus House, 13 Tilehouse St., Hitchin, Herts. SG5 2DU, England. TEL 01462-420785. FAX 01462-420786. Ed. Mark Wiseman; Pub. Damon Thompson. adv. contact: Damon Thompson. bk.rev. circ. 14,073. (tabloid format; back issues avail.) **Document type:** newspaper, trade publication.
   Formerly (until 1991): Arabian Communications News.
   Description: Combines market news and technology features aimed at giving readers a total picture of telecommunications developments.

621.38   US   ISSN 0010-3632
TK5101.A1
COMMUNICATIONS NEWS. 1964. m. $50 (free to qualified personnel). Nelson Publishing Co., 2504 N. Tamiami Trail, Nokomis, FL 34275. TEL 813-966-9521. FAX 813-966-2590. E-mail: ripleyh@ix.netcom.com; URL: http://www.comnews.com. Ed. Curt Harler. adv.; bk.rev.; charts; illus.; stat. circ. 70,645. **Indexed:** B.P.I., Bus.Ind., Comput.Bus., Comput.Cont., Comput.Dtbs., Comput.Lit.Ind., INSPEC (1985-), PROMT, Tr.& Indus.Ind. **Document type:** trade publication.
●Also available online. Vendor(s): Information Access Co., Knight-Ridder Information, Inc.
—BLDSC (3361.300000); AskIEEE; Ei; Genuine Article; KR SourceOne; Linda Hall; SWETS; UMI; UnCover. **CCC.**
   Description: New developments in communications equipment, techniques and management for individuals involved in the design, engineering, construction, operation and maintenance of voice, video and data communications systems.

380   UK
COMMUNICATIONS NEWS. m. £40 (Europe £52; rest of world £75). Nexus Media Ltd., Nexus House, Azalea Dr., Swanley, Kent BR8 8HY, England. TEL 44-1322-660070. FAX 44-1322-667633. Ed. Steve Hamington. adv. contact: Chris Milton. circ. 31,600. **Indexed:** ASCA, B.P.I. **Document type:** trade publication.

380   IE   ISSN 1393-0745
COMMUNICATIONS TODAY. 1994. 10/yr. £29 (U.K. £37; Europe £42; rest of world £63($97)) (effective 1998). Blairford International Ltd., CPG House, Glenageary Office Park, Dun Laoghaire, Co. Dublin, Ireland. TEL 353-1-2847777. FAX 353-1-2847584. **Document type:** trade publication.

384   US   ISSN 1079-669X
▼**COMMUNICATIONS TODAY.** 1995. d. $1495 (effective 1996). Phillips Business Information, Inc., 1201 Seven Locks Rd., Potomac, MD 20854. TEL 301-424-3338. FAX 301-309-3847. E-mail: pbi@phillips.com. Ed. Ellen Mullally. **Document type:** newsletter.
—CCC.
   Incorporates (1993-1997): Washington Telecom News (ISSN 1069-7500); Which was formed by the merger of: Telecommunication Regulatory Monitor; (1991-1993): Spectrum Report (ISSN 1053-993X); (1980-1993): Telephone News (ISSN 0271-5430); Which incorporates (1983-1992): Long Distance Letter (ISSN 0740-6851) & (1984-1991): Tenant Communications (ISSN 0749-078X); (1984-1986): Digital Bypass Report (ISSN 0742-955X); (1971-1983): Inter-Connection (ISSN 0738-341X).

301.16 340   AT   ISSN 0815-1210
COMMUNICATIONS UPDATE; a monthly round-up of media and communications. 1985. m. Aus.$95 to individuals; institutions Aus.$160; students Aus.$60; foreign Aus.$180. Communications Law Centre, White House, University of New South Wales, Sydney, N.S.W. 2052, Australia. TEL 61-2-6630551. FAX 61-2-6626839. E-mail: comslaw@ozemail.com.au. (Co-sponsor: Media & Communications Council) Ed. Elisabeth Mealey. R&P contact: Amanda Butt. adv. contact: Amanda Butt. bibl.; stat. circ. 400. (back issues avail.) **Document type:** newsletter.
   Description: Covers policy developments and important initiatives in broadcasting and communications.

621.38   US   ISSN 0746-8121
HE7601
COMMUNICATIONSWEEK; the newspaper for the communications industry. 1984. w. $143. C M P Publications, Inc., 600 Community Dr., Manhasset, NY 11030. TEL 516-562-5000. FAX 516-562-5718. TELEX 647035 CMP PUB MAHA. Ed. Malcolm Laws. adv. circ. 150,000. **Indexed:** Tel.Abstr. **Document type:** trade publication, newspaper.
●Also available online. Vendor(s): Information Access Co., NewsNet (TE23).
—BLDSC (3363.468900); KR SourceOne; SWETS; UMI. **CCC.**

621.38   US   ISSN 1042-6086
HE7601   CODEN: CWEIEM
COMMUNICATIONSWEEK INTERNATIONAL. 1988. bi-w. $143. C M P Publications, Inc., 600 Community Dr Manhasset, NY 11030. TEL 516-562-5000. FAX 516-562-5474. TELEX 647035 CMP PUB MAHA. Ed. Malcolm Laws. circ. 20,000. (tabloid format) **Indexed:** Tel.Alert. **Document type:** trade publication.
●Also available online. Vendor(s): Data-Star, Information Access Co., Knight-Ridder Information, Inc., Lexis-Nexis, NewsNet (TE28).
—CCC.

621.38   UK   ISSN 0953-3699
     CODEN: CMMUES
COMMUNICATOR. 1965. 4/yr. £25 (foreign £35) (effective 1997). Institute of Scientific and Technical Communicators, King's Ct., 2/16 Goodge St., London W1P 1FF, England. TEL 44-171-435-4425. E-mail: istc@istc.org.uk; URL: http://www.istc.org.uk Ed. Dan Blackwell. R&P contact: Carol Battson. adv. contact: John Touze. bk.rev.; charts; illus. circ. 2,000. **Indexed:** INSPEC (1987-1992).
—BLDSC (3363.540600); Ei.
   Former titles: Communicator of Scientific and Technical Information (ISSN 0308-6925); Communicator of Technical Information (ISSN 0045-768X)

COMMUNICATOR (NEW DELHI). see COMMUNICATIONS — Radio

384 UK ISSN 0967-5841
COMMUNICATORS IN BUSINESS MAGAZINE. 1992. 3/yr. £35. British Association of Communicators in Business, 3 Locks Yard, High St., Sevenoaks, Kent TN13 1LT, England. TEL 44-1732-459331. FAX 44-1732-461757. Ed. Brendan Foley. adv. contact: Peter Barnes. circ. 3,000. **Document type:** trade publication.
  Description: Publishes features and news for policymakers in the communications industry.

621.38 US ISSN 0195-1009
COMMUNIQUE (DALLAS).* 1953. bi-m. membership. International Communications Association, 2755 Villa Creek Dr., Ste 200, Dallas, TX 75234. TEL 214-233-3889. FAX 214-233-2813. Ed. Naomi Sokol O'Sullivan. circ. 2,000. (back issues avail.)
  Description: Case studies and technical overviews of interest to large corporate users of voice, data and video communications.

380.5 SA
COMMUNITAS; joernaal vir gemeenskapskommunikasie - journal for community communication. (Text in Afrikaans, English) 1994. a. R.15. Universiteit van die Oranje-Vrystaat, Departement van Kommunikasiekunde, Einheid vir Gemeenskapskommunikasie - University of the Orange Free State, Department of Communications, Community Communications Unit, Posbus 339, Bloemfontein 9300, South Africa. **Indexed:** Ind.S.A.Per. **Document type:** academic/scholarly publication.

301.16 350 US ISSN 0736-7147
COMMUNITY RELATIONS REPORT. 1981. m. $160. Joe Williams Communications, Inc., Box 924, Bartlesville, OK 74005. TEL 918-336-2267. Ed. Joe Williams; Pub. Joe Williams. **Document type:** newsletter.
  Description: Reports on community relations ideas, programs, trends, and issues.

621.38 FR ISSN 0242-1283
TK5102.3.F8 CODEN: COTNDL
COMMUTATION ET TRANSMISSION. English edition: Switching and Transmission. 1947. q. 525 F. (effective 1996). S O T E L E C, 28 rue du Docteur Finlay, 75015 Paris, France. TEL 40-59-05-05. FAX 33-40-59-07-07. bibl.; charts; illus.; index. circ. 7,500. **Indexed:** ASCA, Curr.Cont., Eng.Ind., INSPEC (1979-). **Document type:** catalog.
  —AskIEEE; CISTI; Genuine Article; KR SourceOne; Linda Hall; UnCover.
  Formed by the 1979 merger of: Cables and Transmission (ISSN 0007-9308); Commutation et Electronique (ISSN 0010-3926)

COMPRESSION EXPRESS. see COMMUNICATIONS — Television And Cable

384 004 RH
COMPUTER AND TELECOM NEWS. m. Z.$81 (Africa Z.$106.80; elsewhere Z.$128.40) (effective 1997). Thomson Publications Zimbabwe (Pvt) Ltd., Thomson House, P.O. Box 1683, Harare, Zimbabwe. TEL 263-4-736835. FAX 263-4-752390. adv.

COMPUTER LAW MONITOR. see COMPUTERS

COMPUTER UND RECHT; Forum fuer die Praxis des Rechts der Datenverarbeitung, Kommunikation und Automation. see COMPUTERS

COMPUTERS AND COMMUNICATIONS IN AFRICA; the independent news magazine the African computer community. see COMPUTERS

COMPUTERS AND COMMUNICATIONS IN AFRICA YEARBOOK; yearbook of I.T. capability throughout the continent. see COMPUTERS

380 BL ISSN 0101-2657
COMUNICACAO E SOCIEDADE. (Text in Portuguese); abstracts in English and Portuguese) 1979. s-a. $12. Instituto Metodista de Ensino Superior, Curso de Pos-Graduacao em Comunicacao Social, Rua do Sacramento 230, Rudge Ramos, 09735-460 Sao Bernardo do Campo SP, Brazil. TEL 011-457-3733 ext. 78. FAX 455-3349. TELEX 11-47203 MTOD BR. Ed. Onesimo de Oliveira Cardoso. bibl. **Document type:** academic/scholarly publication.

301.16 VE ISSN 0251-3153
COMUNICACION. 1975. irreg. Centro de Comunicacion "Jesus M. Pellin.", Apdo. 4.838 Carmelitas, Caracas, Venezuela. Ed. Jose I. Rey. bk.rev. circ. 2,500.

621.38 SP
COMUNICACION DIRECTIVOS. 6/yr. Instituto Nacional de Industria, Pza. Marques de Salamanca 8, 28006 Madrid, Spain. TEL 1-401-40-04. Ed. Pablo Gonzalez.

380 621.3 US ISSN 0748-3104
HE7601
COMUNICACIONES; telecomunicaciones, comunicaciones de datos, computadoras y satelites. (Text in Spanish) 1979. q. $30 (free to qualified personnel). Intercom Corp., 9200 S. Dadeland Blvd., Ste. 309, Miami, FL 33156-2703. TEL 305-670-9444. FAX 305-670-9459. Ed. Thomas Will; Pub. Kenneth Bleakley. adv.: B&W page $4061, color page $4884; adv. contact: John Bull. circ. 12,250. (tabloid format; back issues avail.) **Document type:** trade publication.
  Description: Distributed throughout Latin America for the telecommunication and computer technologies.

384 SP ISSN 1130-4693
COMUNICACIONES DE TELEFONICA I & D. 1990. w. 1000 ptas. Telefonica I & D, Emilio Vargas 6, 28043 Madrid, Spain. **Indexed:** Ind.SST.

621.38 SP
COMUNICACIONES WORLD. 11/yr. I D G - C W Communications, Rafael Calvo 18, 4o, 28010 Madrid, Spain. TEL 3194014. FAX 3196104. Ed. Eduardo Barba.

380 IT
COMUNICAZIONE E MANAGEMENT. 1991. q. L.20000. Solofim s.r.l., Via G. Compagnoni 30, 20129 Milan, Italy. TEL 39-2-7383696. FAX 39-2-70100395. Ed. Umberto Frugiuele. adv.: B&W page L.3000000, color page L.4800000. circ. 13,900.

301 301.16 IT ISSN 0392-8667
P92.I8
COMUNICAZIONI SOCIALI. 1973. q. Lit.61000 (foreign Lit.88000($64)) (effective 1997); newsstand price: Lit.22000. (Universita Cattolica del Sacro Cuore) Vita e Pensiero, Largo Gemelli 1, 20123 Milan, Italy. TEL 39-2-72342370. FAX 39-2-72342974. TELEX 321033 UCATMI I. Ed. Gianfranco Bettettini. adv.; bk.rev. circ. 1,150. **Document type:** academic/scholarly publication.
  Description: Forum publishes scientific works elaborated from a secondary school setting. Focus is given to communication; cinema, television, radio, journalism, theater and advertising are analyzed through a theoretical and historical point of view.

CONFERENCING. see BUSINESS AND ECONOMICS — Office Equipment And Services

384 GW
CONNECT; Ratgeber zur Telekommunikation. 1992. m. DM.72 (effective 1997); newsstand price: DM.6. Vereinigte Motor-Verlage GmbH und Co. KG, Leuschnerstr. 1, 70174 Stuttgart, Germany. TEL 49-711-1821696. FAX 49-711-1821832. (Subscr. to: P M S GmbH, Postfach 290180, 47261 Duisburg, Germany. TEL 49-203-76908-0. FAX 49-203-7690830) Ed. Peter Waldleitner; Pub. Uwe Hagen. adv.: B&W page DM.7065, color page DM.12000; trim 185 x 248; adv. contact: Peter Michael Heyde. circ. 50,000. **Document type:** trade publication.

410 384 US
CONNECTIONS NEWSLETTER (MEMPHIS). 1980. 3/yr. $30 (free with subscr. to Southern Communication Journal). Southern States Communication Association, c/o Dr. Richard R. Ranta, Exec. Dir., College of Communication & Fine Arts, University of Memphis, Memphis, TN 38152. TEL 901-678-2350. FAX 901-678-5118. Ed. Richard R. Ranta. R&P contact: Richard R. Ranta. adv. contact: Jef Dolan. circ. 2,500. (back issues avail.) **Document type:** newsletter.
  ●Also available online.
  Description: Covers communications research.

301.16 384.55 GW
CORPORATE A V (YEAR). 1981. a. DM.13.50. Medienreport Verlags GmbH, Hegnacherstr. 30, 71336 Waiblingen, Germany. TEL 49-7151-23331. FAX 49-7151-23338. Ed. Rolf G. Lehmann. adv. circ. 4,200. **Document type:** newsletter.
  Formerly: A V - Branche (Year).

330 808.02 US
CORPORATE ANNUAL REPORT NEWSLETTER. 1986. m. $329. Ragan Communications, 212 W. Superior St., Ste. 200, Chicago, IL 60610-3533. TEL 800-878-5331. FAX 312-335-9583. Ed. Bob Ghelardi. circ. 500. **Document type:** newsletter.

658 UK ISSN 1356-3289
HD30.3
▼**CORPORATE COMMUNICATIONS**. 1996. q. £189($299) (foreign Aus.$369) (effective 1998). M C B University Press Ltd., 60-62 Toller Ln., Bradford, W. Yorks BD8 9BY, England. TEL 44-1274-777700. FAX 44-1274-785200. URL: http://www.mcb.co.uk. Ed. Sandra Oliver. **Document type:** academic/scholarly publication.
  —CCC.

CORPORATE I T UPDATE. see BUSINESS AND ECONOMICS

621.38 SP
CORREO C B. 12/yr. Los Yebenes 96, Apdo. 156193, 28047 Madrid, Spain. TEL 7183058.

380 US
COWLES - SIMBA MEDIA DAILY. d. Cowles - SIMBA Information (Subsidiary of: Cowles Business Media), 11 Riverbend Dr. S., Box 4949, Stamford, CT 06907-0949. TEL 203-358-9900; 800-307-2529. FAX 203-358-5811. E-mail: info@simbanet.com; URL: http://www.simbanet.com; http://www.mediacentral.com. (also avail. by fax and e-mail) **Document type:** trade publication.
  ●Also available online. Vendor(s): CompuServe, Inc., Information Access Co., NewsNet.
  Description: Reports news of the information industry, covering all media.

301.16 SA ISSN 0256-0046
P92.S58
CRITICAL ARTS; a journal for cultural studies. (Text in English) 1980. 2/yr. R.50 to individuals (foreign $45); institutions R.70 (foreign $80) (effective 1997 & 1998). (Critical Arts Projects) Centre for Cultural and Media Studies, University of Natal, King George V Ave., Durban 4001, South Africa. TEL 27-31-2602505. FAX 27-31-2601519. E-mail: roome@mtb.und.ac.za; govends@mtb.und.ac.za; URL: http://www.catalog.com/dsr/critical.htm. Ed. Keyan G. Tomaselli. R&P contact: Susan Govender. bk.rev. circ. 800. (back issues avail.) **Indexed:** Alt.Press Ind., Bibl.Engl.Lang.& Lit., Commun.Abstr., Film Lit.Ind. (1982-), HR Rep., Ind.S.A.Per., M.L.A., MLA Intl.Bibl. **Document type:** academic/scholarly publication.
  Description: Examines the relationship between texts and contexts of media in the Third World, cultural formations and popular forms of expression. Refereed Serial

384 US ISSN 0739-3180
P87
CRITICAL STUDIES IN MASS COMMUNICATION. 1984. q. $100 (foreign $110). Speech Communication Association, 5105 Backlick Rd., Bldg. E., Annandale, VA 22003. TEL 703-750-0533. FAX 703-914-9471. Ed.Bd. adv.; cum.index. circ. 2,800. **Indexed:** Amer.Hist.& Life (1985-), Arts & Hum.Cit.Ind., ASCA, C.I.J.E., Compumath, Curr.Cont., Fam.Ind., Hist.Abstr. (1985-), Hum.Ind., IJCS (1984-), SSCI. **Document type:** academic/scholarly publication.
  ●Also available online. Vendor(s): UMI.
  —BLDSC (3487.488000); Genuine Article; KR SourceOne; SWETS; UMI; UnCover.
  Refereed Serial

301.16 659.1 JA ISSN 0911-5625
CROSS AND TALK;* for communications between you and the world. (Text in Japanese) a. A L C Press Inc., Eifuku 2-chome, Suginami-ku, Tokyo 168, Japan. Ed.Bd.

CUADERNOS DE INFORMACION Y COMUNICACION. see JOURNALISM

CULTURAL INFORMATION SERVICE; the magazine for lifelong learners. see EDUCATION

301.16 621.38 US ISSN 0740-5405
CYRANO'S JOURNAL. 1982. q. $18 to individuals; libraries $24. New England Communications Task Force, Inc., Box 68, Westport, CT 06881. Ed. D.P. Greanville. adv.; bk.rev.; film rev.; abstr.; bibl.; charts; illus.; index. circ. 15,000. (back issues avail.) **Indexed:** Alt.Press Ind.

COMMUNICATIONS

621.38   DK   ISSN 0105-8541
DANMARKS TEKNISKE HOEJSKOLE. INSTITUTTET FOR TELETEKNIK. RAPPORT I T. irreg., vol.68, 1982. Danmarks Tekniske Hoejskole, Instituttet for Teleteknik - Technical University of Denmark. Institute of Circuit Theory and Telecommunication, Bygn 343, DK-2800 Lyngby, Denmark. FAX 45-45-93-03-55. illus.

DATA IN WORLD DATA CENTER C2 FOR IONOSPHERE. CATALOGUE. see EARTH SCIENCES — Geophysics

621.38   US
DATAPRO NETWORK MANAGEMENT. base vol. (plus bi-m. updates). $744 for new subscr.; renewals $674 (effective 1996). Datapro Information Services Group (Subsidiary of: McGraw-Hill, Inc.), 600 Delran Pkwy., Delran, NJ 08075. TEL 609-764-0100; 800-328-2776. FAX 609-764-8953.

621.38   US
DATAPRO NETWORK MANAGEMENT SYSTEMS. base vol. (plus bi-m. updates). $744 for new subscr.; renewals $674 (effectively 1996). Datapro Information Services Group (Subsidiary of: McGraw-Hill, Inc.), 600 Delran Pkwy., Delran, NJ 08075. TEL 609-764-0100; 800-328-2776. FAX 609-764-8953.

621.38   US
DATAPRO REPORTS ON INTERNATIONAL COMMUNICATIONS EQUIPMENT. 3 base vols. (plus m. updates). $1682 to new subscr.; renewals $1412 (effective 1996). Datapro Information Services Group (Subsidiary of: McGraw-Hill, Inc.), 600 Delran Pkwy., Delran, NJ 08075. TEL 609-764-0100; 800-328-2776. FAX 609-764-8953.

621.38   US
DATAPRO REPORTS ON INTERNATIONAL TELECOMMUNICATIONS. base vol. (plus m. updates). $779. Datapro Information Services Group (Subsidiary of: McGraw-Hill, Inc.), 600 Delran Pkwy., Delran, NJ 08075. TEL 609-764-0100; 800-328-2776. FAX 609-764-8953.

621.3 384   JA   ISSN 0911-7601
TK5101.A1
DENKI TSUSHIN/TELECOMMUNICATIONS. (Text in Japanese) 1938. m. 410 Yen per no. Denki Tsushin Kyokai - Telecommunications Association, 12-1, Yuraku-cho 1-chome, Chiyoda-ku, Tokyo 100, Japan.
—CCC.

621.38   JA   ISSN 0915-0935
AS552.C48784   CODEN: DTDKED
DENKI TSUSHIN DAIGAKU KIYO/UNIVERSITY OF ELECTRO-COMMUNICATIONS. BULLETIN. (Text in English, Japanese; summaries in English) 1950. s-a. Denki Tsushin Daigaku, 1-5-1 Chofugaoka, Chofu-shi, Tokyo 182, Japan. TEL 81-424-83-2161. FAX 81-424-84-3554. E-mail: ohashi@pc.uec.ac.jp. Ed. Mamoru Ohashi. circ. 481. **Indexed**: Chem.Abstr., INIS Atomind., INSPEC, Math.R. **Document type**: bulletin.
—BLDSC (2786.650000); AskIEEE; CASDDS; KR SourceOne.
Formerly (until 1988): Denki Tsushin Daigaku Gakuho (ISSN 0493-4253)

384   JA   ISSN 0918-7332
DENKI TSUSHIN FUKYU ZAIDAN KENKYU CHOSA HOKOKUSHO/TELECOMMUNICATIONS ADVANCEMENT FOUNDATION. RESEARCH REPORT. (Text in Japanese) 1986. a. Denki Tsushin Fukyu Zaidan - Telecommunications Advancement Foundation, 6-11, Nishishinbashi 1-chome, Minato-ku, Tokyo 105, Japan. Ed. Hiroshi Inaba. circ. 1,000. **Document type**: bulletin.

DENSHI JOHO TSUSHIN GAKKAI GIJUTSU KENKYU HOKOKU/INSTITUTE OF ELECTRONICS, INFORMATION AND COMMUNICATION ENGINEERS. TECHNICAL REPORT. see ENGINEERING — Electrical Engineering

DENSHI JOHO TSUSHIN GAKKAI TAIKAI KOEN RONBUNSHU/INSTITUTE OF ELECTRONICS, INFORMATION AND COMMUNICATION ENGINEERS. NATIONAL CONVENTION RECORD. see ELECTRONICS

621.38   CC   ISSN 1000-0801
DIANXIN KEXUE/TELECOMMUNICATIONS SCIENCE. (Text in Chinese) 1956. m. Y84; newsstand price: Y7. (China Institute of Communications) Renmin Youdian Chubanshe - People's Posts and Telecommunications Publishing House, 111 Nanzhugan Lane, Chaoyangmen-nei, Beijing 100700, People's Republic of China. TEL 86-10-5228738. FAX 86-10-5138139. (Dist. overseas by: China International Book Trading Corp., P.O. Box 399, Beijing, P.R. China) Ed. Gao Tandi. adv.: color page $2000; 210 x 285. index; circ. 30,000 (paid). **Document type**: academic/scholarly publication.

DIGITAL PUBLISHER. see PUBLISHING AND BOOK TRADE

380   SA
DIRECTORY OF CONTACTS. (Text in English) 1994. irreg. South African Communication Service, Directorate: Research, Private Bag X745, Pretoria 0001, South Africa. **Document type**: directory.

301.16   US   ISSN 0173-170X
DISORDERS OF HUMAN COMMUNICATION. 1980. irreg. price varies. Springer-Verlag, 175 Fifth Ave., New York, NY 10010. TEL 212-460-1500. FAX 212-473-6272. (Also: Berlin, Heidelberg, Tokyo and Vienna) Ed.Bd. (reprint service avail. from ISI) **Document type**: academic/scholarly publication.
—CCC.

301.16   BL   ISSN 0102-762X
RJ496.C67
DISTURBIOS DE COMUNICACAO. 1986. s-a. R.9. Editora da Pontificia Universidade Catolica de Sao Paulo, Rua Monte Alegre, 984, 05014 Sao Paulo, SP, Brazil. TEL 62-0280. Ed. Luiz Agusto de Paula Souza. **Document type**: academic/scholarly publication.

301.16   FR   ISSN 0767-4775
DOSSIERS DE L'AUDIOVISUEL. 6/yr. 355 F. (Europe 390 F., elsewhere 410 F.) (effective 1997). (Institut National de l'Audiovisuel) Documentation Francaise, 29-31 quai Voltaire, 75344 Paris Cedex 07, France. TEL 33-1-40157000. FAX 33-1-40157230. TELEX 215 666 DOCFRAN. (Subscr. to: 124 rue Henri Barbusse, 93308 Aubervilliers Cedex, France. TEL 33-1-48395600. FAX 33-1-48395601) (also avail. in microfiche from DFR) **Document type**: government publication.
—BLDSC (3619.754000).

DROIT DE L'INFORMATIQUE ET DES TELECOMS. see COMPUTERS

621.38 384.5   SZ   ISSN 1019-6587
E B U TECHNICAL REVIEW. French edition: U E R - Revue Technique (ISSN 1019-6595) (Text in English) 1958. q. 160 SFr. European Broadcasting Union, Case postale 67, CH-1218 Grand-Saconnex, Switzerland. TEL 41-22-7172111. FAX 41-22-7172200. E-mail: techreview@ebu.ch. Eds. Philip Laven, Mike Meyer. adv. contact: Richard McKillop. bk.rev.; index. circ. 3,700 (2,500 English ed.; 1,200 French ed.). (back issues avail.) **Indexed**: INSPEC, Int.Ind.Film Per. **Document type**: bulletin.
—BLDSC (3647.224500); CISTI; Ei; Linda Hall; SWETS; UnCover.
Formerly (until 1992): E B U Review, Technical (ISSN 1018-7391)
Description: Covers broadcast engineering, including radio, television and data broadcasting technologies, with reports of international standardization efforts and regulatory activities.
Refereed Serial

621.38 380.3   US   ISSN 8756-2537
CODEN: EMSYEO
E M M S. (Electronic Mail & Micro Systems) 1977. bi-w. $657 (foreign $816). Telecommunications Reports, 1333 H St., N.W., No.100-E., Washington, DC 20005. TEL 202-842-3022. FAX 202-842-1875. Ed. Rod Kuckro. (back issues avail.) **Indexed**: Comput.Cont., PROMT. **Document type**: newsletter.
●Also available online. Vendor(s): Information Access Co., NewsNet (EC32).
Formerly: Electronic Mail and Message Systems (ISSN 0163-9811); Incorporates (in 1992): Advanced Office Technologies Report (ISSN 1054-1462); And: Netline (ISSN 0892-9467); Which was formerly (1984-1987): P C Netline (ISSN 0749-8578); Incorporated: Telecom - Eye - Bee - Em (ISSN 0888-7292); Which was formerly: Telecom - I B M; Which incorporated: Download.
Description: Covers technology, users, product and legislative trends in graphic, record, and microcomputer communications.

E T R I JOURNAL. (Electronics and Telecommunications Research Institute) see ELECTRONICS

621.38 380.3   US
EAST EUROPEAN AND FORMER SOVIET TELECOM REPORT. 1990. m. $749 (effective 1997). International Technology Consultants, 4340 East-West Hwy., Ste. 220, Bethesda, MD 20814-4411. TEL 301-907-0060. FAX 301-907-6555. E-mail: 71011,2475@compuserve.com; itcuser@aol.com; URL: http://www.intl-tech.com. Ed. Davina Buivan. R&P contact: Ada Ghuman. adv. contact: William Thurmond. charts; stat. circ. 1,000. (back issues avail.) **Document type**: bulletin, newsletter, trade publication.
Former titles: Eastern European and Former Soviet Telecom Report & Eastern European and Soviet Telecom Report (ISSN 1054-6499)
Description: Contains information on regional telecommunications and information technology markets. Includes country surveys, market analyses, sectoral reports, business briefs and interviews.

621.38   FR   ISSN 0012-9283
TK5101.A1
ECHO DES RECHERCHES. 1950. 4/yr. 325 F. (foreign 375 F.) (effective 1995). Centre National d'Etudes des Telecommunications, 38-40 rue du General Leclerc, 92131 Issy-Les-Moulineaux Cedex, France. TEL 45-29-51-08. (Co-sponsor: Ecole Nationale Superieure des Telecommunications) Ed. J.P. Bloch. bibl.; charts; illus. **Indexed**: Cyb.Abstr., Excerp.Med., INSPEC.
—BLDSC (3647.500000); AskIEEE; CISTI; KR SourceOne; SWETS.

301.16   BL
ECO. 1992. s-a. (Universidade Federal de Rio de Janeiro, Escola de Comunicacao) Imago Editorial Ltda., Rua Santos Rodrigues, 201-A, 20250 Rio de Janeiro RJ, Brazil. TEL 293-1092. **Document type**: academic/scholarly publication.

380 621   JA   ISSN 0912-5094
EISEI TSUSHIN KENKYU/SATELLITE COMMUNICATIONS STUDY. (Text in Japanese) bi-m. 824 Yen per no. Kokusai Eisei Tsushin Kyokai - International Satellite Communications Society, 3-2, Nishishinjuku 2-chome, Shinjuku-ku, Tokyo 163-03, Japan. **Document type**: academic/scholarly publication.

380 621   JA
EISEI TSUSHIN NENPO/ANNUAL REPORT OF SATELLITE COMMUNICATION. (Text in Japanese) 1966. a. 5500 Yen. Kokusai Eisei Tsushin Kyokai - International Satellite Communications Society, 3-2 Nishishinjuku 2-chome, Shinjuku-ku, Tokyo 163-0, Japan.

384 621.3   UK   ISSN 1050-3420
ELECTROMAGNETIC APPLICATIONS SERIES. 1986. irreg., vol.3, 1988. £50. Research Studies Press Ltd., 24 Belvedere Rd., Taunton, Somerset TA1 1H, England. TEL 44-1823-336197. FAX 44-1823-253252. E-mail: vaw@rspltd.demo.co.uk. (Dist. by: John Wiley & Sons Ltd., Baffins Ln, Chichester, W. Sussex PO19 1UD, England. TEL 44-1243-779777. FAX 44-1243-775878) Ed. R Henderson. **Document type**: monographic series.

631.38 384.4   NE   ISSN 0013-5615
ELECTRONAUT. (Editions in Dutch and English) 1966. 3/yr. free. Radio Holland Group, Postbus 9094, 1069 CC Amsterdam, Netherlands. FAX 020-6678113. TELEX 13166. Ed. R. Westerhuis. adv.; charts; illus. circ. 15,000.
   Description: Surveys the Group's worldwide activities in maritime and land electronics.

380   US
ELECTRONIC ADVERTISING & MARKETPLACE REPORT. 1986. bi-w. $449 (outside N. America $499) (effective 1997). Cowles - SIMBA Information (Subsidiary of: Cowles Business Media), 11 Riverbend Dr. S., Box 4949, Stamford, CT 06907-0949. TEL 203-358-9900; 800-307-2529. FAX 203-358-5811. E-mail: simbainfo@simbanet.com; URL: http://www.simbanet.com. Ed. Karen Burka. **Document type:** newsletter.
   ●Also available online. Vendor(s): Information Access Co.
   —CCC.
   Former titles: Electronic Marketplace Report (ISSN 1071-247X); (until 1993): Electronic Directory and Classified Report.
   Description: Provides news, analysis, and opinion for the emerging business of electronic advertising, shopping and commerce.

384.554   CN
▼**ELECTRONIC TIMES REPORT.** 1996. 10/yr. Can.$38 (US $42; elsewhere $60) (effective 1998). Crailer Communications, 360 Dupont St., Toronto, ON M5R 1V9, Canada. TEL 416-966-9944. FAX 416-966-9946. E-mail: crailer@interlog.com; URL: http://www.nezmo/etr. Ed. Sheri Craig; Pub. Jack Ruttle. R&P contact: Jack Ruttle. adv.: B&W page Can.$2700; trim 8 x 10 3/4; adv. contact: John Bauslaugh. circ. 7,140. **Document type:** trade publication.
   Description: Reports on the broadcasting, cable and telecommunications industries.

ELECTRONICA Y COMUNICACIONES MAGAZINE. see ELECTRONICS

ELECTRONICS AND COMMUNICATIONS IN JAPAN. PART 1: COMMUNICATIONS. see ELECTRONICS

ELECTRONICS AND COMMUNICATIONS IN JAPAN. PART 2: ELECTRONICS. see ELECTRONICS

621.389   UK   ISSN 0261-2666
ELECTROSONIC WORLD. 1980. irreg., latest 1996. free. Electrosonic Limited, Hawley Mill, Hawley Rd., Dartford, Kent DA2 7SY, England. TEL 44-1322-222211. FAX 44-1322-282282. E-mail: Roberts@helvar.com; URL: http://www.helvar.com. Ed. R.S. Simpson. R&P contact: Yvonne Hegarty. illus.; circ. 80,000 (controlled). **Document type:** newspaper.
   Description: Directed to A/V professionals; lighting control, audio-visual, professional video, emphasizing business communications and leisure-time applications.

621.38 384.5   AU   ISSN 0374-3098
                       CODEN: EKITA9
AS ELEKTRON - INTERNATIONAL; Revue fuer Radio - Fernsehen - Elektronik und Elektroakustik. 1946. m. S.290. Elektron-Verlag, Postfach 156, A-4010 Linz, Austria. adv.; charts; illus. circ. 5,900. **Indexed:** INIS Atomind., INSPEC.
   —AskIEEE; KR SourceOne; Linda Hall.
   formerly (until 1969): Elektron (ISSN 0013-5607)

621.38   SW   ISSN 0281-1189
ELEKTRONIKVAERLDEN; hi-fi, video, datorer, praktisk elektronik. 1929. 10/yr. SEK 390 (effective 1997). Elektronikvaerlden Foerlag AB, P.O. Box 529, S-371 23 Karlskrona, Sweden. TEL 46-455-25800. FAX 46-455-14988. E-mail: ev@ev.se; URL: http://www.ev.se. (Subscr. to: Pressdata AB, Box 3263, S-103 65 Stockholm. TEL 46-8-29-37-30. FAX 46-8-28-59-74) Ed. Anders Albinsson. adv.; bk.rev. circ. 20,100. **Document type:** consumer publication.
   Former titles (until vol.4, 1983): Radio och Television; (until 1955): Populaer Radio och Television; (until 1954): Populaer Radio.

ELEKTRONTIDNINGEN. see ELECTRONICS

621.38   RU   ISSN 0013-5771
TK5101.A1   CODEN: EKVZAO
ELEKTROSVYAZ'. English translation: Telecommunications and Radio Engineering (US ISSN 0040-2508) 1938. m. $149 (effective 1998). (Nauchno-tekhnicheskoe Obshchestvo Radiotekhniki i Elektrosvyazi im. A.S. Popova) Izdatel'stvo Radio i Svyaz', Shchemilovskii 2-i per. 4-5, 103473 Moscow, Russia. TEL 7-095-9785351. adv.; bk.rev.; charts; illus.; index. circ. 4,000. **Indexed:** Chem.Abstr., Eng.Ind., INSPEC. **Document type:** academic/scholarly publication.
   —BLDSC (0399.030000); AskIEEE; CISTI; KR SourceOne.

ELETTRONICA E TELECOMUNICAZIONI. see ELECTRONICS

ELLIOT GOLD'S TELESPAN; a bulletin on teleconferencing. see COMPUTERS — Data Communications And Data Transmission Systems

301.16 371.42   US   ISSN 0882-3316
EMERGING PATTERNS OF WORK AND COMMUNICATIONS IN AN INFORMATION AGE. 1985. irreg. price varies. Greenwood Press, Inc. (Subsidiary of: Greenwood Publishing Group Inc.), 88 Post Rd. W., Box 5007, Westport, CT 06881-5007. TEL 203-226-3571. FAX 203-222-1502.

621.38   BL
EMPRESA BRASILEIRA DE TELECOMUNICACOES. RELATORIO ANUAL. 1972. a. (Empresa Brasileira de Telecomunicacoes S.A., Assessoria de Comunicacao Social) P L V Assessoria e Design, Rua das Marrecas, 36 Sala 401, Rio de Janeiro, RJ, Brazil. circ. 6,000.

621.38   PN   ISSN 1012-3547
HE7881
ESTADISTICA PANAMENA. SITUACION ECONOMICA. SECCION 334. COMUNICACIONES. 1985. a. Bl.0.50 (effective 1997). Direccion de Estadistica y Censo, Contraloria General, Apdo. 5213, Panama 5, Panama. FAX 507-269-7294. circ. 600. **Document type:** government publication, bulletin.
   Supersedes in part (in 1985): Estadistica Panamena. Situacion Economica. Seccion 333-334. Transporte y Comunicaciones (ISSN 0378-7389).
   Description: Contains statistics on the mail, telegraph, telephone, radio, and television systems in Panama.

ESTUDIOS DE TRANSPORTES Y COMUNICACIONES. see TRANSPORTATION

384.5   FR   ISSN 0999-582X
ETUDES TELECOM. 10/yr. Attis Communications, 14 rue des Reculettes, 75013 Paris, France. TEL 43-31-47-04. FAX 43-31-48-21. Ed. Leonid Tkatchenko. bk.rev. circ. 4,000.

384   UK   ISSN 0963-5734
EUROINFOTECH; the fortnightly newsletter on European Union policy in telecoms, IT and electronics. 1990. 23/yr. £500($750) (effective 1996). Wisedene Ltd., 27 Canfield Gardens, London NW6 3JP, England. TEL 44-171-624-8703. FAX 44-171-624-8703. E-mail: wisedene@neolith.demon.co.uk. Ed. Nigel Tutt; Pub. Richard Newstone. (looseleaf format; also avail. in diskette format) **Document type:** newsletter.
   Description: Covers European Union policies on telecommunications, computers, information technology and consumer electronics.

384   NE   ISSN 0926-9819
EUROPEAN COMMUNICATION POLICY RESEARCH SERIES. (Text in English) 1989. irreg., vol.6, 1996. price varies. I O S Press, Van Diemenstraat 94, 1013 CN Amsterdam, Netherlands. TEL 31-20-6382189. FAX 31-20-6203419. E-mail: market@iospress.nl; URL: http://www.iospress.nl/iospress. (In N. America: Box 10558, Burke, VA 22009-0558. TEL 703-323-5554. FAX 703-250-4705) (back issues avail.) **Document type:** monographic series, proceedings.
   Description: Covers changing telecommunications policies in Europe, as well as the impact of worldwide trends to deregulation.
   Refereed Serial

384 332   US
EUROPEAN INTERACTIVE MULLTIMEDIA. 1993. m. $695 (effective 1997). Kagan World Media, Ltd., 126 Clock Tower Pl., Carmel, CA 93923. TEL 408-624-1536. FAX 408-625-3225. E-mail: info@kagan.com. Ed. Robin Flynn. adv. contact: Lorraine Yglesias. **Document type:** trade publication.
   Description: Covers the convergence of computers, consumer electronics, communications, cable TV and content providers. Provides projections of growth of new products and platforms, analyses of strategic alliances, economic modelling of new corporate ventures, sources of capital and industry contacts.

301.06   UK   ISSN 0267-3231
P91.3   CODEN: EJCOET
EUROPEAN JOURNAL OF COMMUNICATION. (Text in English; summaries in English, French and German) 1986. q. £39($62) to individuals; institutions £135($216) (effective 1998). Sage Publications Ltd., 6 Bonhill St., London EC2A 4PU, England. TEL 44-171-374-0645. FAX 44-171-374-8741. E-mail: market@sagepub.co.uk; URL: http://www.sagepub.co.uk/. Ed.Bd. adv. contact: Bernie Folan. bk.rev.; charts. **Indexed:** Arts & Hum.Cit.Ind., ASCA, Commun.Abstr., Curr.Cont., IBZ, Int.Ind.Film Per., Int.Polit.Sci.Abstr., Intl.Bibl.S.S.Pol.Sci., Intl.Ind.TV., Lang.& Lang.Behav.Abstr., MLA Intl.Bibl., Sociol.Abstr., SSCI. **Document type:** academic/scholarly publication.
   —BLDSC (3829.728220); SWETS; UnCover.
   Description: Represents the best of communication theory and research in Europe in all its diversity. Promotes interchange among European scholars of different intellectual traditions and national backgrounds.
   Refereed Serial

THE EUROPEAN JOURNAL OF TELEWORKING. see BUSINESS AND ECONOMICS — Abstracting, Bibliographies, Statistics

EUROPEAN MEDIA BUSINESS & FINANCE. see BUSINESS AND ECONOMICS — Banking And Finance

384.5 338   US   ISSN 1050-0561
EUROPEAN RADIO. 1990. m. $695 (effective 1997). Kagan World Media, Ltd., 126 Clock Tower Pl., Carmel, CA 93923. TEL 408-624-1536. FAX 408-625-3225. E-mail: nfo@kagan.com. Ed. Bishop Cheen. adv. contact: Lorraine Yglesias. **Document type:** newsletter.
   Description: Covers and analyzes Europe's radio industry. Deals with regulatory changes, advertiser spending, station launches, demographics, ratings, market shares, ownership, and more

EUROPEAN SATELLITE DIRECTORY. see BUSINESS AND ECONOMICS — Trade And Industrial Directories

301.16   US   ISSN 1052-5068
EUROPEAN TELEVISION. 1989. m. $695 (effective 1997). Paul Kagan Associates, Inc., 126 Clock Tower Pl., Carmel, CA 93923. TEL 408-624-1536. FAX 408-625-3225. E-mail: info@kagan.com. Ed. Paul Kagan. adv. contact: Lorraine Yglesias.
   Formerly (until 1989): Euro TV Investor (ISSN 1043-9420)

621.38   IT   ISSN 1124-318X
TK5101.A1   CODEN: ETTTET
EUROPEAN TRANSACTIONS ON TELECOMMUNICATIONS. (Text in English) 6/yr. L.440000. Associazione Elettrotecnica ed Elettronica Italiana, Piazzale Morandi, 2, 20121 Milan, Italy. TEL 39-2-777901. FAX 39-2-798817. E-mail: rivisteaei@aei.it; URL: http://www.aei.it. Ed. Maurizio Decina. adv.; abstr.; bibl.; charts; illus.; index, cum.index. circ. 1,400. **Indexed:** Chem.Abstr., Curr.Cont., Eng.Ind., Excerp.Med., INIS Atomind., INSPEC.
   —BLDSC (3830.315000); AskIEEE; CASDDS; CISTI; Ei; Genuine Article; KR SourceOne; Linda Hall; SWETS; UMI; UnCover. CCC.
   Formerly (until 1995): European Transactions on Telecommunications and Related Technologies (ISSN 1120-3862); Formed by the merger of (1979-1997): N T Z Archiv (ISSN 0170-172X); (1932-1990): Alta Frequenza (ISSN 0002-6557)

380   EI   ISSN 1015-7328
EUROZOOM. 1988. bi-m. European Cinema and Television Year (ECTVY), Secretariat, Rue Guimard 10, B-1040 Brussels, Belgium. TEL 02-235-7021. FAX 02-236-1749. TELEX 20750 EYCTV B. Ed. Marina Znamensky.

COMMUNICATIONS

EVOLUTION OF COMMUNICATION; an international multidisciplinary journal. see *LINGUISTICS*

THE EXECUTIVE SPEECHWRITER NEWSLETTER; a newsletter of quotes, jokes, stories and ideas for the executive speechwriter. see *LITERATURE*

380 UK ISSN 1358-8915
EXPRESS; magazine for account holders of D H L International. q. (D H L International) Mediamark Publishing International Ltd., 35 Gresse St., Rathbone Pl., London W1P 1PN, England. TEL 44-171-580-3105. FAX 44-171-580-1695. E-mail: express@mediamark.co.uk; URL: http://www.mediamark.co.uk. Ed. Denise Curtis-Raleigh; Pub. Peter Moore. R&P contact: Susan Freegrove. adv. contact: Nicky Lane. circ. 50,000. **Document type:** consumer publication.

301.16 330 FR ISSN 0297-2301
EXPRESSION D'ENTREPRISE; le magazine de la communication. 1984. 10/yr. 850 F. Editions de l'Expression, 22 rue Plumet, 75015 Paris, France. TEL 47-34-02-70. FAX 47-34-00-46. Ed. Patrice Legendre. adv. contact: Francoise Casenave.
  Formerly (until 1985): Expression Audiovisuelle (ISSN 0762-9974)
  Description: For corporate spokespeople, marketing and communication directors.

384 US
F C C NEWS REPORT AND F C C HOTLINE REPORT. bi-m. $195 (outside N. America $250) (effective 1998). Seven Mountains Scientific, Inc., Box 650, Boalsburg, PA 16827. TEL 814-466-6559. FAX 814-466-2777.

380 350 US ISSN 1057-5766
KF2763.3.A2
F C C RECORD. 1986. fortn. $187 (foreign $233.75) (effective 1995). U.S. Federal Communications Commission, 1919 M St., Washington, DC 20554. (Subscr. to: Superintendent of Documents, U.S. Government Printing Office, Box 371954, Pittsburgh, PA 15250-7954. TEL 202-512-1800. FAX 202-512-2250) (back issues avail.) **Document type:** government publication.

340 US
F C C REPORT. (Federal Communications Commission); an exclusive report on domestic and international telecommunications policy and regulation. 1981. bi-w. (26/yr.) $649 (foreign $675) (effective 1998). Capitol Publications Inc., Telecom Publishing Group, 1101 King St., Ste. 444, Box 1455, Alexandria, VA 22313-2055. TEL 800-327-7205. FAX 703-739-6484. URL: http://www.telecommunications.com. Ed. Brenda Cardwell; Pub. Chris Vestal. R&P contact: Libby Lawbaugh. TEL 703-739-6542. adv. contact: Will Benton. (back issues avail.) **Document type:** newsletter.
  ●Also available online. Vendor(s): Information Access Co., Knight-Ridder Information, Inc., NewsNet (TE52).
  —CCC.
  Formerly: F C C Week (ISSN 0738-5714)

F I T C E FORUM. (Federation des Ingenieurs de Telecommunications de la Communaute Europeenne) see *ENGINEERING — Electrical Engineering*

380 BL
FACOM; revista de comunicacao. 1994. s-a. Fundacao Armando Alvares Penteado, Faculdade de Comunicacao, Rua Alagoas 903, Predio 5, 01242-001 Sao Paulo SP, Brazil. TEL 55-11-824-0233. FAX 55-11-8251636.

301.16 FR ISSN 1168-9951
FAXMEDIA. m. 1800 F. A Jour, 11 rue du Marche St. Honore, 75001 Paris, France. TEL 42-96-67-22. FAX 40-20-07-75. Ed. Marie-Agnes Giroud.

FEDERAL ACQUISITION REGULATION (WASHINGTON). see *PUBLIC ADMINISTRATION*

301.16 US ISSN 0098-3942
KF2763.35
FEDERAL COMMUNICATIONS COMMISSION REPORTS. Variant title: Cumulative Index Digest of Decisions and Reports of the Federal Communications Commission of the United States. 1934; N.S. 1965. irreg. price varies. U.S. Federal Communications Commission, 1919 M St., N.W., Washington, DC 20554. TEL 202-632-7000. (Orders to: Superintendent of Documents, U.S. Government Printing Office, Box 371954, Pittsburgh, PA15250-7954. TEL 202-512-1800. FAX 202-512-2250) (also avail. in microform from PMC) **Document type:** government publication.

621.38 GW ISSN 0015-010X
DER FERNMELDE-INGENIEUR; Zeitschrift fuer Ausbildung und Fortbildung. (Text in German; summaries in English, French, German) 1941. m. DM.115. Verlag fuer Wissenschaft und Leben Georg Heidecker, Rathenaustr. 20, 91052 Erlangen, Germany. TEL 09131-32162. FAX 09131-304144. Ed.Bd. abstr.; bibl.; charts; illus.; mkt.; index, cum.index. (tabloid format) **Indexed:** Eng.Ind., INSPEC.
  —BLDSC (3907.500000); AskIEEE; CISTI; KR SourceOne; Linda Hall.

301.16 US ISSN 1082-2119
FIBER IN THE LOOP, covering worldwide developments in bringing fiber to the home. 1989. s-m. $595 (foreign $645) (effective 1997). Information Gatekeepers, Inc., 214 Harvard Ave., Boston, MA 02134. TEL 617-232-3111; 800-323-1088. FAX 617-734-8562. E-mail: igiboston@aol.com; URL: http://www.igigroup.com. Ed. Paul Polishuk. (back issues avail.) **Document type:** newsletter.
  Formerly (until 1995): Fiber to the Home (ISSN 1051-192X)
  Description: Covers fiber to the home technology, products, trials, and services.

621.38 US ISSN 0275-0457
FIBER OPTICS AND COMMUNICATIONS. 1978. m. $595 (foreign $645) (effective 1997). Information Gatekeepers, Inc., 214 Harvard Ave., Boston, MA 02134. TEL 617-232-3111; 800-323-1088. FAX 617-734-8562. E-mail: igiboston@aol.com; URL: http://www.igigroup.com. Ed. Paul Polishuk. circ. 350. (back issues avail.) **Indexed:** Comput.Cont. **Document type:** newsletter.
  —BLDSC (3914.638500); SWETS; CCC.
  Description: Covers domestic and international news on fiber optics, communications and related fields.

621.3 US ISSN 8756-2049
FIBER OPTICS NEWS. 1981. w. $697 (foreign $730) (effective 1997). Phillips Business Information, Inc., 1201 Seven Locks Rd., Potomac, MD 20854. TEL 301-424-3338. FAX 301-424-4297. E-mail: pbi@phillips.com. Ed. Jennifer Whelen. (back issues avail.) **Indexed:** PROMT. **Document type:** newsletter.
  ●Also available online. Vendor(s): Information Access Co., Knight-Ridder Information, Inc., NewsNet (TE29).
  —CCC.
  Formerly: Fiber - Laser News (ISSN 0275-6099)

621.38 US ISSN 1051-189X
FIBER OPTICS WEEKLY UPDATE. Short title: F O W U. 1980. w. $595 (foreign $645) (effective 1997). Information Gatekeepers, Inc., 214 Harvard Ave., Boston, MA 02134. TEL 617-232-3111; 800-323-1088. FAX 617-734-8562. E-mail: igiboston@aol.com; URL: http://www.igigroup.com. Ed. Paul Polishuk. (back issues avail.) **Document type:** newsletter.
  —CCC.
  Formerly: Fiber Optics and Communications Weekly News Service (ISSN 0732-9407)
  Description: Covers news, information and market trends on fiber optics.

621.38 US ISSN 1075-5268
FIBER OPTICS YELLOW PAGES. 1978. a. $89.95 (foreign $104.95) (effective 1997). Information Gatekeepers, Inc., 214 Harvard Ave., Boston, MA 02134. TEL 617-232-3111; 800-323-1088. FAX 617-734-8562. Ed. Paul Polishuk. **Document type:** directory.
  —CISTI.
  Formerly (until 1993): Fiber Optics Handbook and Buyers Guide (ISSN 1075-525X)
  Description: Covers equipment and suppliers of fiber optics worldwide, reference materials, standards, sources of information, and review articles.

380 UK ISSN 0959-0188
FIBRE OPTICS COMMUNICATIONS AND USER SYSTEMS. 1990. bi-m. £30($52) (free to qualified personnel in the E.C.). F O C U S Publishing, Cotswold House, Kingston, Ringwood, Hants. BH24 3BQ, England. TEL 44-1425-473535. FAX 44-1425-480900. E-mail: 10046,3710@compuserve.com. Ed. Bob Yates; Pub. Bob Yates. R&P contact: Bob Yates. adv. contact: Alex Henner. **Indexed:** INSPEC (1990-). **Document type:** trade publication, directory.
  —BLDSC (3964.198600); AskIEEE; KR SourceOne.

380 GW ISSN 0931-7945
FLASCHENPOST; das authentische Massenmedium. 1987. irreg. DM.3. Lotharstr. 65, 47048 Duisburg, Germany. TEL 49-203-3792397. FAX 49-203-3793333. Ed. Ulrich Schmitz. adv. contact: Ulrich Schmitz. bk.rev.; film rev.; music rev.; circ. 1,000. (back issues avail.) **Document type:** academic/scholarly publication.
  Description: Examines all aspects of mass media.

301.16 808.5 US ISSN 1050-3366
PN4071
FLORIDA COMMUNICATION JOURNAL. 1973. s-a. $30 (effective 1997). Florida Communication Association, School of Communication, University of Central Florida, Orlando, FL 32816-1344. TEL 407-823-5958. FAX 407-823-6360. Ed. John B. O'Hara. adv.; bk.rev. circ. 400. (back issues avail.) **Document type:** academic/scholarly publication.
  Formerly (until 1987): Florida Speech Communication Journal (ISSN 0093-6138)
  Refereed Serial

384 IT
FONDAZIONE UGO BORDONI. ANNUAL REVIEW. a. Fondazione Ugo Bordoni, Via Baldassarre Castiglione 59, 00142 Rome, Italy. TEL 39-6-54801. FAX 39-6-54804400. **Document type:** corporate report.

808.53 US ISSN 0015-735X
PN4177
FORENSIC. 1915. q. $30 to non-members. Pi Kappa Delta, c/o Robert S. Littlefield, Box 5075, Univ. Sta., North Dakota State University, Fargo, ND 58105-5075. TEL 701-231-7783. FAX 701-231-7784. E-mail: rlittlef@badlands.nodak.edu. Ed. Steve Hunt. R&P contact: Robert S. Littlefield. adv.; bk.rev.; illus. circ. 1,700. (also avail. in microform from UMI) **Document type:** academic/scholarly publication.
  —UMI.

808.53 US ISSN 0196-304X
FORENSIC QUARTERLY. 1928. q. $24. National Federation of State High School Associations, 11724 N.W. Plaza Circle, Box 20626, Kansas City, MO 64195-6026. TEL 816-464-5400. FAX 816-464-5104. Ed. Richard G. Fawcett. R&P contact: Fritz McGinness. **Document type:** academic/scholarly publication.
  —UnCover.

621.38 FR
FRANCE TELECOM; revue francaise des telecommunications. (Text in French; summaries in English, Spanish) 1971. q. 100 F. (foreign 150 F.) France Telecom, Direction Generale des Telecommunications, 6, place d'Alleray, 75505 Par Cedex 15, France. TEL 1-44-44-22-22. FAX 1-48-42-51-26. Ed. Bruno Grassin Delyle. adv. bk.rev.; bibl.; stat.; index. circ. 35,000. **Indexed:** Key to Econ.Sci., PROMT.
  —CISTI.
  Formerly: Revue Francaise des Telecommunications (ISSN 0183-8636)
  Description: Covers the services, economics, world industry and history of telecommunications.

301.16 US
FREEDOM FORUM MEDIA STUDIES CENTER. OCCASIONAL PAPER. irreg., no.8, 1991. Colombia University, Freedom Forum Media Studies Center, 2950 Broadway, New York, NY 10027-7004. TEL 212-280-8392. FAX 212-678-6661. Ed. Martha FitzSimon.
  Formerly: Gannett Foundation. Occasional Paper.

FRIDAY MEMO. see *COMPUTERS*

384 004 GW ISSN 0016-2841
TK7800 CODEN: FUSHA2
FUNKSCHAU; Zeitschrift fuer Telekommunikationen und Unterhaltungselektronik. 1927. s-m. DM.157 (foreign DM.168) (effective 1997). Franzis Verlag GmbH, Dornacherstr. 3, 85622 Feldkirchen, Germany. TEL 49-89-99115-0. FAX 49-89-99115199. Ed. Michael Lang. adv.; bk.rev.; charts; illus.; mkt.; tr.lit.; index. circ. 31,000. **Indexed:** INSPEC. **Document type:** consumer publication.
—AskIEEE; CISTI; KR SourceOne; Linda Hall; SWETS; UMI. **CCC.**
    Description: Covers computers, television and telephones, with emphasis on electronic telecommunications. Includes readers' comments.

301.16 IT ISSN 0394-8234
G E C. (Giornale del Cartolaio) 1988. m. L.25000 (Europe L.50000; elsewhere L.70000) (effective 1997). Tecniche Nuove s.p.a., Via C. Menotti, 14, 20129 Milan, Italy. TEL 39-2-75701. FAX 39-2-7610351. E-mail: abbonamenti@tecnet.it; URL: http://www.tecnet.it. Ed. Enzo Guaglione. adv.: B&W page L.2760000; trim 267 x 375. circ. 5,000. (tabloid format) **Document type:** trade publication.
    Description: For wholesalers and retailers selling stationery products to the world of schools, offices, art and graphics.

621.38 001.644 US
G I G A B I T NEWS; covering worldwide developments in fiber distributed data interface. 1990. m. $595 (foreign $645) (effective 1997). Information Gatekeepers, Inc., 214 Harvard Ave., Boston, MA 02134. TEL 617-232-3111; 800-323-1088. FAX 617-734-8562. E-mail: igiboston@aol.com; URL: http://www.igigroup.com. Ed. Paul Polishuk. **Document type:** newsletter.
—**CCC.**
    Formerly: F D D I News (ISSN 1051-1903)
    Description: Covers FDDI and GIGABIT technology, markets, applications, products, standards, and business developments.

621.382
G P S DIRECTORY. (Global Positioning System) 1988. a. $167 (foreign $199) (effective 1997). Phillips Business Information, Inc., 1201 Seven Locks Rd., Potomac, MD 20854. TEL 301-424-3338. FAX 301-309-3847. **Document type:** directory.
    Description: Provides access to more than 700 product and service listings for 17 industries such as antennas, geodetic receivers, software, and supplemental GPS equipment.

G P S SOLUTIONS. (Global Positioning System) see GEOGRAPHY

621.38 CN ISSN 0845-1354
5 REPORT. bi-m. 187084 Ontario Inc., 26 Gailcrest Circle, Thorncille, ON L4J 5V1, Canada. TEL 416-764-1184. FAX 416-764-7339. adv. circ. 100,000.

778.5 770 384.5 US
ADNEY'S GUIDES TO INTERNATIONAL CONTESTS, FESTIVALS & GRANTS IN FILM & VIDEO, PHOTOGRAPHY, TV-RADIO BROADCASTING, WRITING & JOURNALISM. 1979. biennial. $15.95. Film-Video Publications, 7944 Capistrano Ave., West Hills, CA 91304-4603. TEL 818-340-6620. Ed. Alan Gadney; Pub. Alan Gadney. adv. circ. 15,000. **Document type:** directory.
    Former titles: Gadney's Guides to International Contests, Festivals and Grants in Film and Video, Photography, TV-Radio Broadcasting, Writing, Poetry, Playwriting and Journalism; Gadney's Guide to 1800 International Contests, Festivals and Grants in Film and Video, Photography, TV-Radio Broadcasting, Writing, Poetry, Playwriting and Journalism.

ZETTE; international journal for mass communication research. see JOURNALISM

BBIE PRESS ALL-IN-ONE DIRECTORY. see BUSINESS AND ECONOMICS — Trade And Industrial Directories

380 UK ISSN 0969-9880
HE8689.7.A8
GLOBAL AUDIENCES: RESEARCH FOR WORLDWIDE BROADCASTING. a. (B B C World Service, International Broadcasting Audience Research Department) John Libbey Media, University of Luton, 75 Castle St., Luton, Bedfordshire LU1 3AJ, England. TEL 44-1582-743297. FAX 44-1582-743298. E-mail: john.libbey@luton.ac.uk. Ed. Graham Mytton. **Document type:** corporate report.

384 UK ISSN 0969-7500
GLOBAL TELECOMS BUSINESS. 1993. bi-m. £120 (foreign $185) (effective 1996). Euromoney Publications plc., Nestor House, Playhouse Yard, London EC4V 5EX, England. TEL 44-171-779-8935. FAX 44-171-779-8541. (Dist. in US by: American Educational Systems, 173 W. 81st St., New York, NY 10024. TEL 800-717-2669. FAX 212-501-8926) **Document type:** trade publication.

621.38 US ISSN 1054-5921
TK5101.A1
GLOBECOM. I E E E GLOBAL TELECOMMUNICATIONS CONFERENCE. CONFERENCE RECORD. 1982. a. (I E E E, Communications Society) Institute of Electrical and Electronics Engineers, Inc., 345 E. 47th St., New York, NY 10017. TEL 212-705-7900. FAX 212-705-7682. (Subscr. to: Box 1331, 445 Hoes Lane, Piscataway, NJ 08855-1331. TEL 908-562-3948)
—BLDSC (4195.610000); UMI. **CCC.**
    Supersedes: National Telecommunications Conference. Record (ISSN 0895-1195); National Telemetering Conference. Record.
    Description: Discusses communication technology and its impact on the progress of scientific and industrial technical advances and development.

621.38 CC ISSN 1002-5561
GUANG TONGXIN JISHU/OPTICAL COMMUNICATIONS TECHNOLOGY. (Text in Chinese) 1977. q. Y15 (effective 1996). Guilin Institute of Optical Communications, P.O. Box 5, Guilin, Guangxi 541004, People's Republic of China. TEL 0773-5813838. FAX 0773-5812724. Ed. Zhou Shaohui. adv. circ. 5,000. **Document type:** academic/scholarly publication.
    Formerly (until 1984): Jiguang Tongxin - Laser Communications.
    Description: Covers optical communications in China.
    Refereed Serial

380 US
GUILFORD COMMUNICATION SERIES. irreg. (approx. 2/yr.). Guilford Publications, Inc., 72 Spring St., New York, NY 10012. TEL 212-431-9800; 800-365-7006. FAX 212-966-6708. E-mail: info@guilford.com. Eds. Theodore L. Glasser, Marshall Scott Poole. **Document type:** monographic series.
    Description: Studies, researches and analyzes communications in the arenas of work, society, relationships, media, law, politics, psychology, school and international relations.

621.38 CC ISSN 1002-4530
GUOJI GUANGBO DIANSHI JISHU/INTERNATIONAL BROADCASTING TECHNOLOGY; youxian yu weixing guangbo disnshi. (Text in Chinese; abstracts in Chinese and English) 1987. bi-m. $30 (effective 1997). Guangbo Yingshi Bu, Keji Xinxi Yanjiusuo - Ministry of Radio, Film and Television, Institute of Science and Technology Information, P.O. Box 2116, Beijing 100866, People's Republic of China. TEL 86-10-6092081. FAX 86-10-6092040. E-mail: crftmi@10.sti.ac.cn. Ed. Xiana Chen. adv.: color page $1400; trim 285 x 210. circ. 15,000. **Document type:** academic/scholarly publication.
    Description: Covers the development of new technologies and practical techniques in the field of radio and television.
    Refereed Serial

THE HARVARD INTERNATIONAL JOURNAL OF PRESS - POLITICS. see JOURNALISM

HERKENNING (THE HAGUE, 1948); journal for aircraft-, ship and A.F.V. recognition. see AERONAUTICS AND SPACE FLIGHT

621.3 HU ISSN 0018-2028
HIRADASTECHNIKA.* (Text in Hungarian; summaries in English, French, German) 1949. m. $43. Hiradastechnikai Tudomanyos Egyesulet, Kossuth Lajos ter 6-8, Pf. 451, 1055 Budapest, Hungary. TEL 1531027. (Subscr. to: Kultura, Box 149, H-1389 Budapest, Hungary) Ed. Gyula Boglar. adv.; bk.rev.; charts; illus. circ. 2,750. **Indexed:** Cyb.Abstr., INIS Atomind., INSPEC.
—AskIEEE; CISTI; KR SourceOne.
    Formerly (until 1961): Magyar Hiradastechnika (ISSN 0324-5403)

380 US
HISPANIC MEDIA UPDATE.* 1983. w. $99. Unimar, 190 S. La Salle St., Chicago, IL 60603-3410. TEL 312-988-9490. FAX 312-988-9854. Ed. Kevin D. Jenkins. adv. contact: Brad Saul. circ. 1,000. **Document type:** newsletter.

384 SP ISSN 1137-0734
HISTORIA Y COMUNICACION SOCIAL. a. 4000 ptas.($35) (effective 1997). Universidad Complutense, Facultad de Ciencias de la Informacion. Departamento de Historia de la Comunicacion Social, Servicio de Publicaciones, Calle Issac Peral s-n, Ciudad Universitaria, 28040 Madrid, Spain. TEL 34-1-3946934. FAX 34-1-3946954. (back issues avail.)
—CINDOC.
    Description: Covers communications from three different points of view; journalism, political science and history.

301.16 US ISSN 1064-6175
P87 CODEN: HJCOES
HOWARD JOURNAL OF COMMUNICATIONS. q. £79($130) to institutions (effective 1998). (Howard University) Taylor & Francis Inc., 1900 Frost Rd., Bristol, PA 19007-1598. TEL 215-785-5800; 800-821-8312. FAX 215-785-5515. E-mail: indo@tandf.co.uk; URL: http://www.tandf.co.uk/. (Subscr. in Europe to: Taylor & Francis Ltd., Rankine Rd., Basingstoke, Hants. RG24 8PR, England. TEL 44-1256-840366. FAX 44-1256-479438) Ed. William J. Starosta. **Indexed:** Mult.Ed.Abstr., Stud.Wom.Abstr. **Document type:** academic/scholarly publication.
—UnCover.
    Description: Emphasizes the link between communication and culture. Designed to foster exchange among scholars of all communications disciplines on theory, application, policy and pathology, especially from a cultural perspective.

410 US ISSN 0360-3989
P91.3
HUMAN COMMUNICATION RESEARCH. 1974. q. $197 to institutions (effective Sep. 1996). (International Communication Association) Sage Publications, Inc., 2455 Teller Rd., Thousand Oaks, CA 91320. TEL 805-499-0721. FAX 805-499-0871. E-mail: libraries@sagepub.com; URL: http://www.sagepub.com. (Overseas subscr. to: Sage Publications Ltd., 6 Bonhill St., London EC2A 4PU, England; Sage Publications India Pvt. Ltd., P.O. Box 4215, New Delhi 110 048, India) Ed. Cynthia Gallois. adv. contact: Margaret Travers. bk.rev.; abstr. circ. 3,700. (also avail. in microform from UMI; back issues avail.; reprint service avail. from UMI) **Indexed:** Abstr.Anthropol., Arts & Hum.Cit.Ind., ASCA, C.I.J.E. (1974-), IMFL, Lang.& Lang.Behav.Abstr., Mid.East: Abstr.& Ind., Mult.Ed.Abstr., Psychol.Abstr. (1975-), Sage Fam.Stud.Abstr., Sage Pub.Admin.Abstr., Soc.Sci.Ind. (1994-), SOMA, SSCI, SSCI. **Document type:** academic/scholarly publication.
—BLDSC (4336.043000); Genuine Article; KR SourceOne; SWETS; UMI. **CCC.**
    Description: Publishes important research and reports that contribute to the expanding body of knowledge about human communication.

384 NE ISSN 0925-7950
I A M C R NEWSLETTER. 1968. 2/yr. $25 to non-members. International Association for Mass Communications Research, c/o Prof. Cees Hamelink, P.O. Box 67006, 1060 JA Amsterdam, Netherlands. TEL 31-20-610-1581. FAX 31-20-610-1421. Eds. Robin Chessman, Janet Wasko. circ. 1,000. **Document type:** newsletter.
    Formerly: International Association for Mass Communications Research. Letter from the President (ISSN 0579-3742)

1992 COMMUNICATIONS

302.2309　　　　**NE**　　ISSN 1385-4038
I A M H I S T NEWSLETTER. 1991. q. $10 to individuals; institutions $20. (International Association for Media and History) Stichting Film Wetenskap - Film Research Foundation, Zeeburgerkade 8, 1019 HA Amsterdam, Netherlands. TEL 31-20-6652966. FAX 31-20-6659086. E-mail: pim.slot@sfw.nl. Ed. Pim Slot. adv.: B&W page $150. bk.rev.; circ. 400 (paid). **Document type:** newsletter.

384　　**EI**　　ISSN 1023-425X
TK5101.A1　　　　CODEN: XIMAEZ
I & T MAGAZINE. (Industrie et Telecoms) French edition (ISSN 1022-8713); German edition (ISSN 1023-4268); Italian edition (ISSN 1023-4276); Spanish edition (ISSN 1023-4284) (Supplement avail.: News Review (ISSN 1023-3008)) (Text in English) 1991. q. European Commission, Directorate-General for Telecommunications, Information Industries and Innovation (DG XIII), Rue de la Loi, 200, B-1049 Brussels, Belgium. E-mail: nke@dg13.cec.be. Ed. Michel Carpentier. adv.; bk.rev.; illus. **Indexed:** INSPEC (1993-).
●Also available online.
—BLDSC (4357.605000); AskIEEE; KNAW; KR SourceOne; SWETS.
Formerly (until 1993): X I I I Magazine (ISSN 1017-6950); Which was formed by the merger of: I & T T; (1985-1991): I E S News; (1985-1991): Information Market (ISSN 0256-5056); Which was formerly (1979-1985): Euronet Diane News (ISSN 0250-5789)
Description: Covers the activities and programs supported by DGXIII. Supplement provides information on current events, key decisions, new services, conferences, more.

384　　**EI**　　ISSN 1023-3008
I & T MAGAZINE NEWS REVIEW. (Supplement to: I & T Magazine (ISSN 1022-8713)) (Text in English) 1993. q. free. (European Commission, Directorate-General for Industry) Office for Official Publications of the European Commission, 2 rue Mercier, 2985 Luxembourg, Luxembourg. TEL 32-2-296-90-22. FAX 32-2-296-90-37. E-mail: kathleen.early@bxl.dg13.cec.be. Ed. Robert Verrue. bk.rev.
—BLDSC (4357.608000).

301.16　　**US**　　ISSN 0018-876X
P87
I C A NEWSLETTER. vol.22, 1973. q. $10. International Communication Association, 8140 Burnet Rd., Box 9589, Austin, TX 78766. TEL 512-454-8299. FAX 512-454-4221. Ed. Robert L. Cox. adv.; circ. controlled. **Document type:** newsletter.
Formerly: N S S C Newsletter.

I D A MEMBERSHIP AND SURVIVAL GUIDE. (International Documentary Association) see MOTION PICTURES

621.38　　**US**　　ISSN 0536-1486
TK5101.A1　　　　CODEN: CIDCD2
I E E E INTERNATIONAL CONFERENCE ON COMMUNICATIONS. CONFERENCE RECORD. 1965. a. price varies. (I E E E, Communications Society) Institute of Electrical and Electronics Engineers, Inc, 345 E. 47th St., New York, NY 10017-2394. TEL 212-705-7900. FAX 212-705-7682. (Subscr. to: Box 1331, 445 Hoes Lane, Piscataway, NJ 08855-1331. TEL 908-562-3948) bibl.; illus.
—BLDSC (4362.945000); Ei; UMI. **CCC**.
Formerly: International Conference on Communications. Conference Record.

621.3　　**US**　　ISSN 0733-8716
TK5101.A1　　　　CODEN: ISACEM
I E E E JOURNAL ON SELECTED AREAS IN COMMUNICATIONS. 1983. 9/yr. $320 to non-members (effective 1998). (I E E E, Communications Society) Institute of Electrical and Electronics Engineers, Inc., 345 E. 47th St., New York, NY 10017-2394. TEL 732-981-0060; 800-678-4333. FAX 908-981-9667. E-mail: customer.service@ieee.org; URL: http://www.ieee.org. (Subscr. to: Box 1331, 445 Hoes Lane, Piscataway, NJ 08855-1331) Ed. L.B. Milstein. (also avail. in microform) **Indexed:** Acoust.Abstr., ASCA, CAD CAM Abstr., Compumath, Curr.Cont., Ergon.Abstr., Ind.Sci.Rev., INSPEC, Int.Aerosp.Abstr., Robomat., SSCI, Tel.Abstr.
—BLDSC (4362.985000); AskIEEE; CISTI; Ei; Genuine Article; KR SourceOne; Linda Hall; SWETS; UMI; UnCover. **CCC**.
Description: Reports on the newest communications technologies. Covers fiber optics, digital satellite and computer communications, and local area networks.

I E E E MULTIMEDIA MAGAZINE. see COMPUTERS

I E E E NATIONAL RADAR CONFERENCE. PROCEEDINGS. see ENGINEERING — Electrical Engineering

380 004.16　　**US**　　ISSN 1070-9916
I E E E PERSONAL COMMUNICATIONS; the magazine of nomadic communications and computing. 1994. bi-m. $150 to non-members (effective 1998). Institute of Electrical and Electronics Engineers, Inc., 345 E. 47th St., New York, NY 10017-2394. TEL 732-981-0060; 800-678-4333. FAX 732-981-9667. E-mail: customer.service@ieee.org; URL: http://www.ieee.org. (Subscr. to: 445 Hoes Ln., Box 1331, Piscataway, NJ 08855-1331) Ed. Thomas F. LaPorta. adv. **Indexed:** ASCA, Curr.Cont., INSPEC (1994-).
—BLDSC (4363.012950); AskIEEE; CISTI; Ei; Genuine Article; KR SourceOne; Linda Hall; SWETS; UMI; UnCover. **CCC**.

I E E E PERSONAL COMPUTERS. see COMPUTERS — Personal Computers

I E E E POSITION LOCATION AND NAVIGATION SYMPOSIUM. RECORD. see ENGINEERING — Electrical Engineering

621.38　　**US**　　ISSN 0090-6778
TK5101.A1　　　　CODEN: IECMBT
I E E E TRANSACTIONS ON COMMUNICATIONS. 1953. a. $330 to non-members (effective 1998). (I E E E, Communications Society) Institute of Electrical and Electronics Engineers, Inc., 345 E. 47th St., New York, NY 10017-2394. TEL 732-981-0060; 800-678-4333. FAX 908-981-9667. E-mail: customer.service@ieee.org; URL: http://www.ieee.org. (Subscr. to: Box 1331, 445 Hoes Lane, Piscataway, NJ 08855-1331) Ed. D.P. Taylor. bk.rev.; abstr.; illus.; index. (also avail. in microform) **Indexed:** A.S.& T.Ind., Acoust.Abstr., Appl.Mech.Rev., ASCA, CAD CAM Abstr., Chem.Abstr., Compumath, Curr.Cont., Eng.Ind., Ind.Sci.Rev., INSPEC, Int.Aerosp.Abstr., Math.R., Nucl.Sci.Abstr., Sci.Cit.Ind., Tel.Abstr., Zent.Math.
—BLDSC (4363.170400); AskIEEE; CISTI; Ei; Genuine Article; KR SourceOne; Linda Hall; SWETS; UMI; UnCover. **CCC**.
Formerly: I E E E Transactions on Communication Technology (ISSN 0018-9332)
Description: State-of-the-art, archival and technical data covering the wide array of topics pertinent to the communications professional.

I E E REVIEW. (Institution of Electrical Engineers) see ENGINEERING — Electrical Engineering

384 621.38　　**UK**　　ISSN 0263-5852
　　　　　　　　　CODEN: ITESDS
I E E TELECOMMUNICATIONS SERIES. 1976. irreg., vol.34, 1996. INSPEC, I.E.E., Michael Faraday House, Six Hills Way, Stevenage, Herts. SG1 2AY, England. TEL 44-1438-313311. FAX 44-1438-313465. TELEX 825578 IEESTV G. E-mail: inspec@iee.org.uk; URL: http://www.iee.org.uk. (U.S. addr.: INSPEC Dept., IEEE Operations Center, 445 Hoes Ln., Box 1331, Piscataway, NJ 08855-1331. TEL 908-562-5553. FAX 908-562-8737) Ed.Bd. charts; stat. **Indexed:** INSPEC. **Document type:** monographic series, academic/scholarly publication.
—BLDSC (4362.769500).

621.38　　**UK**　　ISSN 0916-8516
　　　　　　　　　CODEN: ITRCEC
I E I C E TRANSACTIONS ON COMMUNICATIONS. (Text in English) 1976. m. £100 (foreign $170) (effective 1998). (Institute of Electronics, Information and Communication Engineers, JA - Denshi Joho Tsushin Gakkai) Oxford University Press, Academic Division, Great Clarendon St., Oxford OX2 6DP, England. TEL 44-1865-267907. FAX 44-1865-267485. E-mail: jnl.info@oup.co.uk; URL: http://www.oup.co.uk/journals. (Subscr. in N. America to: Oxford University Press Inc., 2001 Evans Rd., Cary, NC 27513. TEL 800-852-7323. FAX 919-677-1714) R&P contact: Joolz Longley. **Indexed:** ASCA, Compumath, Curr.Cont., Ind.Sci.Rev., INSPEC (1992-), Mat.Sci.Cit.Ind., SSCI. **Document type:** academic/scholarly publication.
—BLDSC (4363.240666); AskIEEE; CISTI; Ei; Genuine Article; KR SourceOne; Linda Hall; SWETS; UnCover. **CCC**.
Supersedes in part (in 1991): I E I C E Transactions on Communications Electronics Information and Systems (ISSN 0917-1673); Former titles (until 1991): Transactions of the Institute of Electronics, Information and Communication Engineers (ISSN 0913-574X); (until 1987): Transactions of the Institute of Electronics and Communication Engineers of Japan. Section E (ISSN 0387-236X); (until 1976): Transactions of the Institute of Electronics and Communication Engineers of Japan. Abstracts (ISSN 0418-6869); (until 1956): Journal of the Institute of Electrical Communication Engineers of Japan. Abstracts (ISSN 0914-5273).

621.38　　**II**
I E T E JOURNAL OF EDUCATION. 1959. q. Rs.75($25) Institution of Electronics and Telecommunication Engineers, 2, Institutional Area, Lodi Rd., New Delhi 110 003, India. TEL 91-11-463-1820. FAX 91-11-464-9429. TELEX 031-62747. E-mail: ietend@giasdl01.vsnl.net.in. Ed. T.V. Sreelatha. adv. bk.rev. circ. 16,000. **Indexed:** Chem.Abstr., Comput.Cont., Eng.Ind., INSPEC (1976-), Phys.Ber. **Document type:** academic/scholarly publication.
—BLDSC (8480.690000); AskIEEE; CISTI; Ei; KR SourceOne.
Formerly (until 1997): Institution of Electronics and Telecommunication Engineers. Students' Journal (ISSN 0970-1664)
Description: Contains tutorial type education articles for diploma and undergraduate level.

621.38　　**II**
TK5101　　　　CODEN: JIETAU
I E T E JOURNAL OF RESEARCH. 1955; N.S. 1984. bi-m. Rs.300($75) Institution of Electronics and Telecommunication Engineers, 2, Institutional Area, Lodi Rd., New Delhi 110 003, India. TEL 91-11-4631850. FAX 91-11-463-1810. TELEX 031-62747. E-mail: ietend@giasdl01.vsnl.net.in. circ. 7,000. **Indexed:** ASCA, CAD CAM Abstr. Chem.Abstr., Comput.Cont., Eng.Ind., INIS Atomind. INSPEC (1973-), Phys.Ber., Tel.Abstr. **Document type:** academic/scholarly publication.
—BLDSC (4792.600000); AskIEEE; CASDDS; CISTI; Ei; Genuine Article; KR SourceOne; Linda Hall; UnCover.
Formerly (until 1997): Institution of Electronics and Telecommunication Engineers. Journal (ISSN 0377-2063)
Refereed Serial

621.38　　**II**　　ISSN 0256-4602
I E T E TECHNICAL REVIEW. 1984. bi-m. Rs.300($75) Institution of Electronics and Telecommunication Engineers, 2, Institutional Area, Lodi Rd., New Delhi 110003, India. TEL 91-11-463-1850. FAX 91-11-464-9429. TELEX 031-62747. E-mail: ietend@giasdl01.vsnl.net.in. Ed. T.V. Sreelatha. adv. B&W page Rs.4000, color page Rs.5500; trim 232 x 180. bk.rev. circ. 7,000. **Indexed:** ASCA, Compumath, INIS Atomind., INSPEC (1984-), Tel.Abstr.
—BLDSC (4363.254000); AskIEEE; Ei; Genuine Article; KR SourceOne.
Description: Devoted to current research and developments in the field of electronics and telecommunications.

COMMUNICATIONS

808.5   US
I G A B NEWSLETTER. 1986. m. membership. International Group of Agencies and Bureaus, 6845 Parkdale Pl., Ste. A, Indianapolis, IN 46254. TEL 317-297-0872. FAX 317-387-3387. Ed. Jim D. Montoya. R&P contact: James D. Montoya. circ. 300. circ. 300 (controlled). **Document type:** newsletter.

301.16   II
I I M C BULLETIN. (Text in English) a. Rs.5. Indian Institute of Mass Communication, D-13, South Extension, Part II, New Delhi 110049, India. **Document type:** bulletin.

I M S A JOURNAL. (International Municipal Signal Association) see TRANSPORTATION — Roads And Traffic

621.38   US   ISSN 1075-5276
I S D N YELLOW PAGES. (Integrated Services Digital Network) Key Title: International ISDN Yellow Pages. 1986. a. $69.95 (foreign $98)(effective 1996). Information Gatekeepers, Inc., 214 Harvard Ave., Boston, MA 02134. TEL 617-232-3111; 800-323-1088. FAX 617-734-8562. Ed. Paul Polishuk. **Document type:** directory.
—CCC.
Formerly: I S D N Handbook and Buyers Guide.
Description: Worldwide directory of ISDN equipment and service suppliers, reference materials, applications, standards, publications, sources of information, and review articles.

621.38   CC
▼**T ASIA.** 12/yr. Newsources Investments Ltd., 1501 Shiu Lam Bldg., 23 Luard Rd., Wanchai, Hong Kong, People's Republic of China. TEL 852-2528-4808. FAX 852-2865-6832. Ed. Lim Kok Kiong; Pub. Lim Kok Kiong. adv. contact: Katherine Chan. **Document type:** trade publication.
Description: Covers the newly developing "Information Technology" field.

▼**T LAW TODAY.** (Information Technology) see COMPUTERS

384   UN   ISSN 1027-7420
▼**T U GLOBAL DIRECTORY.** (Text in English, French, Spanish) irreg., vol.12, 1997. 39 SFr. International Telecommunication Union, Place des Nations, CH-1211 Geneva 20, Switzerland. TEL 41-22-7306141. FAX 41-22-7305194. E-mail: sales@itu.ch; URL: http://www.itu.ch. **Document type:** directory.

384   UN   ISSN 1020-1173
HE7601   CODEN: TCJOA6
▼**T U NEWSLETTER.** 1934. 10/yr. International Telecommunication Union, Place des Nations, CH-1211 Geneva 20, Switzerland. TEL 41-22-7305239. FAX 41-22-7305321. E-mail: dominique.bourne@itu.int; URL: http://www.itu.ch. adv.; bk.rev.; bibl.; charts; illus. (also avail. in microfilm from PMC) **Indexed:** A.S.& T.Ind., ASCA, CAD CAM Abstr., Comput.Dtbs., Curr.Cont., INSPEC (1968-), SSCI, Tel.Abstr. **Document type:** newsletter. —AskIEEE; CISTI; Ei; KR SourceOne; Linda Hall; UnCover.
Former titles (until 1994): Telecommunication Journal (ISSN 0497-137X); U I T Journal.

384.6   UN
▼**T U STATISTICAL YEARBOOK/ANNUAIRE STATISTIQUE DES L'U I T.** (Each vol. cumulative over 10 yrs.) (Text in English, French and Spanish) a. 68 SFr. International Telecommunication Union, Place des Nations, CH-1211 Geneva 20, Switzerland. TEL 41-22-7306141. FAX 41-22-7305194. TELEX 421 000 UIT CH. E-mail: sales@itu.ch; URL: http://www.itu.ch. (also avail. in microfiche from CIS; diskette format) **Indexed:** IIS. **Document type:** corporate report.
Formerly (until 1995): Yearbook of Common Carrier Telecommunication Statistics (ISSN 0252-1563); Incorporates: Telecommunication Statistics.

384   UN
▼**U WEEKLY CIRCULAR AND SPECIAL SECTIONS.** (Text in English, French, Spanish) w. 4300 SFr. International Telecommunication Union, Place des Nations, CH-1211 Geneva 20, Switzerland. TEL 41-22-7306141. FAX 41-22-7305194. E-mail: sales@itu.ch; URL: http://www.itu.ch. **Document type:** bulletin.

380   UK
I V C A UPDATE. 1983. m. membership. International Visual Communications Association, Bolsover House, 5-6 Clipstone St., London W1P 7EB, England. TEL 0171-580-0962. FAX 0171-436-2606. Ed. Michael Smith. adv.; bk.rev. circ. 1,500. (back issues avail.) **Document type:** newsletter.
Supersedes: I V C A Magazine (ISSN 0952-7419); Which was formed by the 1987 merger of: B I S F A Magazine (ISSN 0263-502X); I T V A (UK).
Description: Reviews the state of the visual and business communication industry.

384 621.381   US
QA76.9.A25   CODEN: TDCREP
I-WAYS. Hungarian edition: T D R Hungary (ISSN 0866-4765) 1985. bi-m. $310. (Global Information Infrastructure Commission) Transnational Data Reporting Service, Inc., Box 10528, Burke, VA 22009-0528. TEL 703-323-9116. FAX 703-250-4705. E-mail: tgd@tdrs.com. Ed. Timothy G. Donovan; Pub. G. Russell Pipe. R&P contact: Timothy G. Donovan. bk.rev.; bibl.; charts; illus.; stat.; tr.lit.; index. **Indexed:** Commun.Abstr., Comput.Cont., Comput.Lit.Ind., ELLIS, INSPEC, Key to Econ.Sci., P.A.I.S. **Document type:** trade publication.
—AskIEEE; KR SourceOne; UnCover. **CCC.**
Formerly (until Mar. 1995): Transnational Data and Communications Report (ISSN 0892-399X); Which was formed by the merger of (1980-1984): Chronicle of International Communication (ISSN 0278-0011); (1978-1984): Transnational Data Report (ISSN 0167-6962)
Description: Focuses on the policies, politics, and technologies of all that moves across borders electronically.

380   IT
ICOM: ISTITUZIONI E COMUNICAZIONE. 1988. m. Presidenza del Consiglio dei Ministri, Dipartimento per l'Informazione e l'Editoria, Via Po, 14, 00198 Rome, Italy. TEL 39-6-85981. FAX 39-6-8553851.

384   IT
PN1795   CODEN: IRIFDT
IKON - RICERCHE SULLA COMUNICAZIONE. (Text in Italian; summaries in English and French) 1982. s-a. L.56000 (foreign L.70000) (effective 1993). (Istituto Agostino Gemelli) Franco Angeli Editore, Viale Monza 106, Casella Postale 17130, 20127 Milan, Italy. TEL 39-2-2827651. Ed. Giovanni Cesareo. bk.rev.; film rev.; charts; illus.; index. circ. 1,000. **Indexed:** Film Lit.Ind. (1973-).
Formed by the merger of (1948-1981): Ikon (ISSN 0019-1744) & Ricerche sulla Comunicazione.

301.16 407   US   ISSN 0145-5516
ILLINOIS SPEECH AND THEATRE ASSOCIATION. JOURNAL. a. $35 (effective 1998). Illinois Speech and Theatre Association, Bradley University, Dept. of Communication, IL 61625. TEL 309-677-2364. FAX 309-677-2330. E-mail: claussen@bradley.edu. Ed. Mary Pelias. R&P contact: Terry Perkins. adv. circ. 650. (back issues avail.) **Indexed:** ERIC. **Document type:** academic/scholarly publication. Refereed Serial

380.0981   BL   ISSN 0104-7140
IMAGENS. 1994. s-a. Editora da U N I C A M P, R. Caio Graco Prado 50, Caixa Postal 6070, 13083-970 Campinas SP, Brazil. TEL 55-019-788-2174. FAX 55-019-7882170. URL: http://www.editoras.com/unicamp/. Eds. Eduardo Guimaraes, Lucia Nagib; Pub. Fernao Ramos. R&P contact: Eduardo Guimaraes.
Description: Covers movies, television, newspapers and magazines in the Brazilian life.

301.16   FR
IMAGES JURIDIQUES. 10/yr. 135 bd. Pereire, 75017 Paris, France. TEL 46-22-52-52. FAX 42-67-48-81. TELEX 641 802. Ed. Jean-Pierre Fougea. circ. 8,000.

301.16   US
IMMEDIATE IMPACT. 1985. 4/yr. (Alternative Media Information Center) Media Network, 39 W. 14th St., Ste. 403, New York, NY 10011. TEL 212-929-2663. FAX 212-929-2732. Ed. Ilana Navaro. adv.; bk.rev. circ. 5,000. **Indexed:** Alt.Press Ind.
Former titles (until 1991): Mediactive (ISSN 0896-2375); Media Network Newsletter; What's in a Name.
Description: Explores the relationship between media and social change.

380   SA   ISSN 1021-4313
IN TOUCH. (Text in English) 1993. m. South African Communication Service, Private Bag X745, Pretoria 0001, South Africa.

384   US   ISSN 1083-4672
▼**INDIA TELECOM.** 1995. bi-w. $825 (foreign $870) (effective 1997). Information Gatekeepers, Inc., 214 Harvard Ave., Boston, MA 02134. TEL 617-232-3111; 800-323-1088. FAX 617-734-8562. E-mail: igiboston@aol.com; URL: http://www.igigroup.com. **Document type:** newsletter.

301.16   II
INDIAN INSTITUTE OF MASS COMMUNICATION. ANNUAL REPORT. (Text in English) a. Indian Institute of Mass Communication, D-13, South Extension, Part II, New Delhi 110049, India.

301.16   II
INDIAN JOURNAL OF COMMUNICATION ARTS. (Text in English) 1975. m. Rs.30($15) Hem Publishers Private Ltd., C-123 Greater Kailish I, New Delhi 110048, India. Ed. G.C. Awasthy. adv.; bk.rev.; illus. circ. 3,000.

301.16   US   ISSN 0740-5502
P87
INFORMATION AND BEHAVIOR. 1985. a. $54.95 (effective 1997). Transaction Publishers, Transaction Periodicals Consortium, Department 3092, Rutgers University, New Brunswick, NJ 08903. TEL 908-445-2280. FAX 908-445-3138. Ed. Brent D. Ruben. circ. 4,000. (back issues avail.) **Indexed:** Int.Polit.Sci.Abstr. **Document type:** academic/scholarly publication.
—BLDSC (4481.758500). **CCC.**
Description: Examines the forms, technologies, organization, and use of information, and their impact on human behavior. Coverage includes the impact of new technology on office and home life, regulation and control of information, and the economics of information.

380   JA
INFORMATION & COMMUNICATION IN JAPAN.* (Text in English) 1990. a. 4700 Yen. Infocom Research, Inc. - Joho Tsushin Sogo Kenkyujo, 12-31 Minami-Aoyama 1-chome, Minato-ku, Tokyo 107, Japan.

384 340   UK   ISSN 1360-0834
K12   CODEN: ICTLFX
INFORMATION AND COMMUNICATIONS TECHNOLOGY LAW. 1992. 3/yr. £48($88) to individuals; institutions £152 ($284) (effective 1997). Carfax Publishing Co., P.O. Box 25, Abingdon, Oxon OX14 3UE, England. TEL 44-1235-401000. FAX 44-1235-401550. E-mail: enquiries@carfax.co.uk. (Subscr. in N. America to: Carfax Publishing Co., 875-81 Massachusetts Ave., Cambridge, MA 02139(Ed. Indira Mahalingam. (back issues avail.) **Indexed:** Euro.LJI, Leg.Per., LJI. **Document type:** academic/scholarly publication.
—BLDSC (4481.763000); KR SourceOne; UnCover. **CCC.**
Formerly (until 1996, vol.5): Law, Computers and Artificial Intelligence (ISSN 0962-9580)

330   FR   ISSN 0924-3461
INFORMATION, COMPUTER AND COMMUNICATIONS POLICY. (Editions in English, French) 1971. irreg., no.32, 1993. price varies. Organization for Economic Cooperation and Development, Working Party on Information, Computers and Communications Policy, 2 rue Andre-Pascal, 75775 Paris Cedex 16, France. (U.S. subscr. to: O.E.C.D. Publications and Information Center, 2001 L St., N.W., Ste. 650, Washington, DC 20036-4922. TEL 202-785-6323) **Indexed:** IIS, INSPEC.
—BLDSC (4493.400000); CISTI.
Supersedes (in 1979): O E C D Informatics Studies Series.

1994 COMMUNICATIONS

384   NE   ISSN 0167-6245
INFORMATION ECONOMICS AND POLICY. (Text in English) 1984. q. fl.600($345) (effective 1998). North-Holland (Subsidiary of: Elsevier Science B.V.), P.O. Box 211, 1000 AE Amsterdam, Netherlands. TEL 31-20-4853911. FAX 31-20-4853598. TELEX 18582 ESPA NL. (Subscr. in the Americas to: Elsevier Science, Regional Sales Office, Box 945, New York, NY 10159-0945. TEL 212-633-3730. FAX 212-633-3680; Subscr. in Australasia and the Far East to: Elsevier Science (Singapore) Pte Ltd, No.1 Temasek Ave., No.17-01 Millenia Tower, Singapore 039192, Singapore. TEL 65-434-3727. FAX 65-337-2230; Subscr. in Japan to: Elsevier Science Japan, 9-15 Higashi-Azabu 1-chome, Minato-ku Tokyo 106, Japan. TEL 81-3-5561-5033. FAX 81-3-5561-5047) Ed. R.G. Noll. (also avail. in microform from UMI; back issues avail.; reprint service avail. from SWZ) **Indexed:** ABI Inform., C.R.E.J., Commun.Abstr., Comput.Cont., Geo.Abstr.H.G., INSPEC, Int.Polit.Sci.Abstr., J.of Econ.Lit., Polit.Sci.Abstr., Sage Pub.Admin.Abstr. **Document type:** academic/scholarly publication.
—BLDSC (4493.565300); AskIEEE; Ei; KR SourceOne; SWETS; UMI; UnCover. **CCC.**
Description: Provides an interdisciplinary and international forum for publications with telecommunications economics and policy as its core, including related issues on information economics and media policy.
Refereed Serial

621.38   UK
INFORMATION MANAGEMENT & TECHNOLOGY. 1967. bi-m. £80 (rest of Europe £85; elsewhere £102) (effective 1997). CIMTECH, University of Hertfordshire, 45 Grosvenor Rd., St. Albans, Herts. AL1 3AW, England. TEL 44-1727-813651. FAX 44-1727-813049. Ed. Anne Grimshaw. adv. contact: Cathy Godfrey. bk.rev.; abstr.; charts; illus.; index, cum.index. circ. 1,000. **Indexed:** C.I.S. Abstr., Consum.Ind., Educ.Tech.Abstr., Graph.Arts Lit.Abstr., Inform.Sci.Abstr., INSPEC, LISA, Photo.Abstr., Print.Abstr. **Document type:** trade publication.
—AskIEEE; CISTI; KR SourceOne; SWETS; UnCover. **CCC.**
Former titles: Information Media and Technology (ISSN 0266-6960); (until 1984): Reprographics Quarterly (ISSN 0306-2880); (until 1973): N R C D Bulletin (ISSN 0027-6928)
Description: Covers major developments in information management. Includes reviews of systems and equipment.

INFORMATION SOURCES (YEAR). see COMPUTERS

330   FR   ISSN 0985-8784
INFOS DE L'EXPRESSION D'ENTREPRISE. 1987. w. 2050 F. includes Expression of Entreprise. Editions de l'Expression, 22 rue Plumet, 75015 Paris, France. TEL 47-34-02-70. FAX 47-34-00-46. Ed. Patrice Legendre.
Description: Covers important meetings, key nominations, and current events in the world of corporate communications.

    SA
INFOSPEC; news for managers in the public service - nuus vir bestuurders in die staatsdiens. (Text in Afrikaans, English) 1992. bi-w. South African Communication Service - Suid-Afrikaanse Kommunikasiediens, Private Bag X745, Pretoria 0001, South Africa. **Document type:** government publication, newsletter.
Formerly (until 1994): Policy Guide - Beleidsgids.

621.38   GW
TK5981   CODEN: NTELAP
INGENIEUR DER KOMMUNIKATIONSTECHNIK; europaeische Zeitschrift fuer Informations- und Kommunikationstechnik. 1951. bi-m. DM.108 (foreign DM.138) (effective 1997). Verlag Technik GmbH, Am Friedrichshain 22, 10407 Berlin, Germany. TEL 49-30-42151-0. FAX 49-30-42151273. Ed. Frank Backasch. adv.: B&W page DM.5800; trim 178 x 256; adv. contact: Karin Patting. bk.rev.; charts; illus.; pat.; index. circ. 20,850. **Indexed:** Chem.Abstr., Cyb.Abstr., Eng.Ind., INSPEC, Lib.Sci.Abstr., PROMT. **Document type:** trade publication.
—AskIEEE; CASDDS; CISTI; Ei; KR SourceOne; Linda Hall. **CCC.**
Former titles: Nachrichtentechnik - Elektronik (ISSN 0323-4657); Nachrichtentechnik (ISSN 0027-7495)
Description: Covers all aspects of electronic communication engineering.

384   US   ISSN 1055-9000
HE7761
INSIDE THE INDEPENDENTS; status and trends. 1989. irreg., latest 1994. $995. Telecom Publishing Group, 1101 King St., Ste. 444, Alexandria, VA 22314. TEL 800-327-7205. FAX 800-645-4104.
Description: Reviews status and trends of the independent telephone industry, including competitive forces, acquisition and consolidation, network enhancements and business ventures.

621.38 364.4   SP   ISSN 0214-7181
INSTELEC. 1989. 8/yr. 7949 ptas. in Europe; elsewhere 18900 ptas. (effective 1997). Miller Freeman, S.A., Maria Auxiliadora 5, 28040 Madrid, Spain. TEL 1-4508837. FAX 4509429. Ed. Eloy Maestre. circ. 5,000. **Document type:** trade publication.

INSTITUTE OF ELECTRONICS, INFORMATION AND COMMUNICATION ENGINEERS. JOURNAL/DENSHI JOHO TSUSHIN GAKKAISHI. see ELECTRONICS

621.38   PL   ISSN 0020-451X
    CODEN: PILZAD
INSTYTUT LACZNOSCI. PRACE. (Text in Polish; summaries in English, French, German and Russian) 1954. 2/yr. 40 Zl.($12) per issue. Instytut Lacznosci, Ul. Szachowa 1, 04-894 Warsaw, Poland. TEL 48-22-128450. FAX 48-22-129969. Ed. Krystyna Plewko. R&P contact: Maria Lopuszniak. adv. contact: Maria Lopuszniak. circ. 350. (also avail. in microfilm) **Indexed:** INSPEC (1968-). **Document type:** proceedings.
—AskIEEE; KR SourceOne.
Refereed Serial

INTERACTIVE MULTIMEDIA INVESTOR. see BUSINESS AND ECONOMICS — *Investments*

380   US
INTERFACE (STORRS). 1974. q. free. University of Connecticut, Center for Instructional Media & Technology, UCIMT, U-1, 249 Glenbrook Rd., Storrs, CT 06269-2001. TEL 203-486-2530. FAX 203-486-1766. E-mail: pmiller@chronos.ucc.uconn.edu; URL: http://www.ucc.uconn.edu/~wwwucimt/ucimt.html. Ed. Patricia Miller. circ. 7,000 (controlled). (back issues avail.) **Document type:** newsletter.
Description: Newsletter for the University of Connecticut Media Center, for interested patrons of the film library. Includes details about the activities and productions (video and multimedia) at the center.

301.16   US   ISSN 0270-6075
HM258
INTERNATIONAL AND INTERCULTURAL COMMUNICATION ANNUAL. Short title: I I C Annual. 1974. a. (issued in Feb.). $24 (hardcover edition $52). Speech Communication Association, 5105 Backlick Rd., Bldg. E, Annandale, VA 22003. TEL 703-750-0533. FAX 703-914-9471. Ed.Bd. (back issues avail.) **Document type:** monographic series.

384   NE
INTERNATIONAL ASSOCIATION FOR MASS COMMUNICATIONS RESEARCH. MONOGRAPHS. irreg. International Association for Mass Communications Research, c/o Prof. Cees Hamelink, P.O. Box 67006, 1060 JA Amsterdam, Netherlands. TEL 31-20-610-1581. FAX 31-20-610-1421. **Document type:** monographic series.

INTERNATIONAL FEDERATION OF ADVERTISING AGENCIES. NEWSLETTER. see ADVERTISING AND PUBLIC RELATIONS

INTERNATIONAL GEOSCIENCE AND REMOTE SENSING SYMPOSIUM DIGEST. see GEOGRAPHY

301.16   II
INTERNATIONAL JOURNAL OF COMMUNICATION. (Text in English) 1991. s-a. Rs.250($6) Bahri Publications, 997-A St., No. 9, P.O. Box 4453, Gobindpuri, Kalkaji, New Delhi 110 019, India. TEL 91-11-6445710. FAX 91-11-6416116. Ed. Ujjal Singh Bahri. adv.; bk.rev. **Indexed:** MLA Intl.Bibl. **Document type:** academic/scholarly publication.
Description: Contains research articles on communications, cognition and language.

INTERNATIONAL JOURNAL OF INFORMATION MANAGEMENT. see COMPUTERS — *Information Science And Information Theory*

621.3 658   UK   ISSN 1055-7148
TK5105.5   CODEN: INMTEU
INTERNATIONAL JOURNAL OF NETWORK MANAGEMENT. 1991. bi-m. £445 (foreign £445) (effective 1998). John Wiley & Sons Ltd., Journals, Baffins Ln., Chichester, W. Sussex PO19 1UD, England. TEL 44-1243-779777. FAX 44-1243-775878. E-mail: info-assets@wiley.co.uk; URL: http://www.wiley.co.uk. (Subscr. in the Americas to: John Wiley & Sons, Inc., 605 Third Ave., New York, NY 10158. TEL 212-850-6645. FAX 212-850-6021) Ed. Gilbert Held. adv.: B&W page £595, color page £1495; trim 260 x 200; adv. contact: Bob Kern. circ. 237. (also avail. in microform from UMI; back issues avail.; reprint service avail. from SWZ) **Indexed:** INSPEC (1991-). **Document type:** academic/scholarly publication.
—BLDSC (4542.373300); AskIEEE; Ei; KR SourceOne; SWETS; UMI. **CCC.**
Description: Dedicated to the dissemination of practical information that enables readers to better manage, operate and maintain communications networks.
Refereed Serial

621.38   UK   ISSN 0737-2884
TK5104   CODEN: IJSCEF
INTERNATIONAL JOURNAL OF SATELLITE COMMUNICATIONS. 1983. bi-m. $995 (foreign $995) (effective 1998). John Wiley & Sons Ltd., Journals, Baffins Ln., Chichester, W. Sussex PO19 1UD, England. TEL 44-1243-779777. FAX 44-1243-775878. E-mail: info-assets@wiley.co.uk; URL: http://www.wiley.co.uk. (Subscr. in the Americas to: John Wiley & Sons, Inc., 605 Third Ave., New York, NY 10158. TEL 212-850-6645. FAX 212-850-6021) Ed. B.G. Evans. adv.: B&W page £595, color page £1495; trim 297 x 210; adv. contact: Bob Kern. bk.rev. circ. 800. (also avail. in microform from UMI; back issues avail.; reprint service avail. from SWZ) **Indexed:** ASCA, Curr.Cont., INSPEC, Int.Aerosp.Abstr., Tel.Abstr. **Document type:** trade publication.
—BLDSC (4542.542800); AskIEEE; CISTI; Ei; Genuine Article; KR SourceOne; Linda Hall; SWETS; UMI; UnCover. **CCC.**
Description: Provides rapid communication of new results and trends in the industry of satellite communications.

384   US   ISSN 1068-9605
TK5103.2   CODEN: IJWNEY
INTERNATIONAL JOURNAL OF WIRELESS INFORMATION NETWORKS. 1993. q. $225 (foreign $265) (effective 1998). Plenum Publishing Corp., 233 Spring St., New York, NY 10013-1578. TEL 212-620-8000. FAX 212-463-0742. TELEX 23-421139. URL: http://www.catchword.co.uk/. Ed. K. Pahlavan. **Document type:** academic/scholarly publication.
●Also available online.
—BLDSC (4542.701350); AskIEEE; CISTI; Ei; KR SourceOne; SWETS. **CCC.**
Formerly (until 1994): International Journal of Wireless Communication.
Description: Covers research advances affecting all aspects of wireless communication and information networks, including cellular phone networks.
Refereed Serial

384 300   US   ISSN 1092-6747
▼**INTERNATIONAL MASS MEDIA COMMUNICATIONS REVIEW.** 1997. q. $65. Inter-Com Publications, Box 1156, Anacortes, WA 98221. TEL 360-293-0732 FAX 360-293-8919. E-mail: intercom@cnw.com. Ed. Lester M. Goldsmith; Pub. B.P. Carter. R&P contact: Lester M. Goldsmith. **Document type:** academic/scholarly publication, monographic series.
Description: Publishes theory and research in the field of social sciences with a special emphasis on mass media.
Refereed Serial

INTERNATIONAL MEDIA LAW; bulletin on rights, clearances and legal practice. see LAW — *International Law*

621.38   US
INTERNATIONAL NETWORK MANAGEMENT. base vol. (plus m. updates). $2560 to new subscr.; renewal $2180. Datapro Information Services Group (Subsidiary of: McGraw-Hill, Inc.), 600 Delran Pkwy, Delran, NJ 08075. TEL 609-764-0100; 800-328-2776. FAX 609-764-8953.

| 621.38 | US |

INTERNATIONAL PROFESSIONAL COMMUNICATION CONFERENCE. CONFERENCE RECORD. Short title: I P C C. 1981. a. Institute of Electrical and Electronics Engineers, Inc., 345 E. 47th St., New York, NY 10017-2394. TEL 732-981-0060; 800-678-4333. FAX 732-981-9667. E-mail: customer.service@ieee.org; URL: http://www.ieee.org. (Subscr. to: Box 1331, 445 Hoes Lane, Piscataway, NJ 08855-1331)
  Formerly (until 1985): I E E E Professional Communication Society Conference. Record.
  Description: Discusses current issues and developments relevant to the creation, production, transmission and presentation of scientific and technical information.

| 621.38 629.1 | US |

INTERNATIONAL RADAR CONFERENCE. RECORD. Variant title: International Conference on Radar (Publication). (Alternately published by I E E E and I E E) 1973. a. price varies. (I E E E, Aerospace and Electronic Systems Society) Institute of Electrical and Electronics Engineers, Inc., 345 E. 47th St., New York, NY 10017-2394. TEL 732-981-0060; 800-678-4333. FAX 732-981-9667. E-mail: customer.service@ieee.org; URL: http://www.ieee.org. (Subscr. to: Box 1331, 445 Hoes Ln., Piscataway, NJ 08855-1331)

| 623.89 387.2 | UN |

INTERNATIONAL SAFETYNET MANUAL. (Text in English) irreg., 1994 edition. £8 (overseas £10). International Maritime Organization, 4 Albert Embankment, London SE1 7SR, England. TEL 0171-735-7611. FAX 0171-587-3210. TELEX 23588. illus.
  Description: Discusses the design and use of SafetyNET, an international automatic satellite-based navigation system to relay important navigation and meteorological information among ships.

INTERNATIONAL SATELLITE DIRECTORY; a complete guide to the satellite communications industry. see AERONAUTICS AND SPACE FLIGHT

| 383 051 | CN | ISSN 0823-1931 |

INTERNATIONAL SKYLINE. (Text in English and French) 1965. q. Can.$650. I.S.P. of Canada, 3738 - 39th Ave. W., Vancouver, BC V6N 3A7, Canada. Ed. J. Andrew de Lilio Rymsza. bk.rev.; bibl.; circ. 18,750 (controlled). (also avail. in microfiche)

| 301.16 | UN |

INTERNATIONAL TELECOMMUNICATION UNION. BOOKLETS. (Editions in English, French, Spanish) no.3, 1969. irreg., no.41, 1993. 12 SFr. International Telecommunication Union, Place des Nations, CH-1211 Geneva 20, Switzerland. TEL 41-22-7306141. FAX 41-22-7305194. TELEX 421 000 UIT CH. E-mail: sales@itu.int; URL: http://www.itu.int. Ed.Bd.

| 301.16 | UN |

INTERNATIONAL TELECOMMUNICATION UNION. SEMINARS. (Editions in English, French, Spanish) 1974. irreg., latest 1986. price varies. International Telecommunication Union, Place des Nations, CH-1211 Geneva 20, Switzerland. TEL 41-22-7306141. FAX 41-22-7305149. TELEX 421 000 UIT CH. E-mail: sales@itu.int; URL: http://www.itu.int. Ed.Bd.

| 384 | UK | ISSN 0268-9960 |

INTERNATIONAL TELECOMMUNICATIONS INTELLIGENCE. 1984. w. £595. M D I S Publications Ltd., MDIS House, City Fields Business Park, City Fields Way, Chichester, W. Sussex PO20 6FS, England. TEL 44-1243-533322. FAX 44-1243-533418. Ed. Neil Parker. adv.: page £250; trim 240 x 170; adv. contact: Helena Mancey. circ. 3,000. (looseleaf format; also avail. in diskette format; back issues avail.) **Document type:** trade publication, newsletter.
●Also available on CD-ROM.
—CCC.

| 384 | UK | ISSN 1361-603X |

INTERNATIONAL TELECOMS REVIEW. a. £75($135) (effective 1997). Euromoney Publications plc., Books, Nestor House, Playhouse Yard, London EC4V 5EX, England. TEL 44-171-779-8935. FAX 44-171-779-8541.
  Description: Covers developments in the international telecommunications market with contributions from financiers, lawyers, manufacturers and associations active in the market.

| 621.38 | US | ISSN 0884-5123 |
| TK399 | | CODEN: ITCOD6 |

INTERNATIONAL TELEMETERING CONFERENCE. (Includes: International Foundation for Telemetering Conference Proceedings (ITC-USA)) 1966. a. $170 to non-members; members $136. Instrument Society of America, 67 Alexander Dr., Box 12277, Research Triangle Park, NC 27709. TEL 919-549-8411. FAX 919-549-8288. TELEX 802540 ISA DURM. E-mail: info@isa.org; URL: http://www.isa.org. (reprint service avail. from ISI,UMI) **Indexed:** INSPEC. **Document type:** proceedings.
  —Ei. CCC.
  Supersedes: National Telemetering Conference Proceedings.
  Refereed Serial

| 621.38 | US |

INTERNATIONAL VOICE SYSTEMS REVIEW. 1989. q. $60. Media Dimensions, Inc., 1562 First Ave., No. 286, New York, NY 10028-4004. TEL 212-533-7481. FAX 212-475-1209. Ed. Jamese Glenn. **Indexed:** Abstr.Hum.Comp.Inter. **Document type:** newspaper.

INTERNET WEEK; news and analysis of internet business opportunities. see COMPUTERS — Computer Networks

| 621.382 | NE | ISSN 1385-9501 |

▼**INTEROPERABLE COMMUNICATION.** Announced for publication in 1998. s.a. 376 SFr. (effective 1998). Baltzer Science Publishers B.V., P.O. Box 221, 1400 AE Bussum, Netherlands. TEL 31-20-6370061. FAX 31-20-6323651. E-mail: subscribe@baltzer.nl; URL: http://www.baltzer.nl. **Document type:** academic/scholarly publication.

| 591 | US |

INTERSPECIES NEWSLETTER. 1978. q. $25. Interspecies Communication Inc., 273 Hidden Meadow, Friday Harbor, WA 98250. Ed. Jim Nollman. bk.rev. circ. 1,000. pp./issue: 8. (looseleaf format; back issues avail.) **Document type:** newsletter.
  Description: Relates field projects involving humans and other species seeking a common base for communication exchange. Networks writings on the perceptual bases of ecology.

| 301.16 371.91 | US |

IOWA JOURNAL OF COMMUNICATION. 1968. s-a. $15 (students $7). Iowa Communication Association, c/o Marvin D. Jensen, Dept. of Communication Studies, University of Northern Iowa, Cedar Falls, IA 50614. TEL 319-273-2593. FAX 319-273-2731. Ed. Fred Antczak. R&P contact: Marvin D. Jensen. adv. circ. 200. **Indexed:** Commun.Abstr. **Document type:** academic/scholarly publication.
  —UnCover. CCC.
  Formerly: Iowa Journal of Speech Communication (ISSN 0886-1943)
  Refereed Serial

| 301.16 | IT | ISSN 0374-3829 |

ISTITUTO SUPERIORE DELLE POSTE E DELLE TELECOMUNICAZIONI. NOTE RECENSIONI NOTIZIE. 1952. q. free. Istituto Superiore delle Poste e delle Telecomunicazioni, Viale Europa 190, 00144 Rome, Italy. TEL 39-6-59584370. FAX 39-6-5410904. TELEX 616250 ISTSUP I. Ed. Aldo Passaro. bk.rev. circ. 1,800. **Document type:** academic/scholarly publication.
  —AskIEEE; CISTI; Ei; KR SourceOne.
  Refereed Serial

| 621.38 | RU | ISSN 0130-6804 |
| TK5101.A1 | | |

ITOGI NAUKI I TEKHNIKI: ELEKTROSVYAZ'. irreg., vol.17, 1987. price varies. Vsesoyuznyi Institut Nauchno-Tekhnicheskoi Informatsii (VINITI), Ul. Baltiiskaya 14, Moscow A-219, Russia. (Subscr. to: Mezhdunarodnaya Kniga, Dimitrova ul. 39, 113095 Moscow, Russia)
  —Linda Hall.

| 384 | JA | ISSN 0913-8293 |

J A T E TSUSHIN/J A T E NEWS. (Text in Japanese) 1984. bi-m. 1200 Yen per no. (effective May 1996). Japan Approvals Institute for Telecommunications Equipment - Denki Tsushin Tanmatsu Kiki Shinsa Kyokai, 1-3, Toranomon 1-chome, Minato-ku, Tokyo 105, Japan. TEL 81-3-3591-4300. FAX 81-3-3591-4355. **Document type:** bulletin.

J U M - JUGEND UND MEDIEN; Lehrerzeitung des Buchklubs. see CHILDREN AND YOUTH — About

JANE'S RADAR AND ELECTRONIC WARFARE SYSTEMS. see MILITARY

| 384 | US | ISSN 1081-9983 |

▼**JAPAN TELECOM.** 1995. bi-w. $825 (foreign $870) (effective 1997). Information Gatekeepers, Inc., 214 Harvard Ave., Boston, MA 02134. TEL 617-232-3111; 800-323-1088. FAX 617-734-8562. E-mail: igiboston@aol.com; URL: http://www.igigroup.com. **Document type:** newsletter.

| 380 | JA | ISSN 0289-4513 |

JOHO TSUSHIN GAKKAISHI/JOURNAL OF INFORMATION & COMMUNICATION RESEARCH. (Text in English, Japanese) q. 1500 Yen per no. Joho Tsushin Gakkai - Society of Information and Communication Research, 8-3, Kiba 2-chome, Koto-ku, Tokyo 135, Japan.

| 384 | JA | ISSN 0914-6504 |

JOHO TSUSHIN JANARU/TELECOM JOURNAL. (Text in Japanese) 1984. m. 500 Yen per no. (Yuseisho, Tsushin Seisakukyoku - Ministry of Posts and Telecommunications, Communications Policy Bureau) Denki Tsushin Shinkokai - Association for the Promotion of Telecommunications, 3-10, Komagome 2-chome, Toshima-ku, Tokyo 170, Japan. TEL 81-3-3940-3951. FAX 81-3-3940-4055. circ. 6,500. **Document type:** government publication.
  Formerly (until 1988): Denki Tsushin Jiho (ISSN 0910-2590)

JOKESMITH. see LITERARY AND POLITICAL REVIEWS

| 301.16 | US | ISSN 0090-9882 |
| HM258 | | |

JOURNAL OF APPLIED COMMUNICATION RESEARCH. 1973. q. $100 (foreign $110). Speech Communication Association, 5105 Backlick Rd., Bldg. E, Annandale, VA 22003. TEL 703-750-0533. FAX 703-914-9471. Ed. David R. Seibold. adv.; abstr.; illus. circ. 2,000. (also avail. in microform from UMI; back issues avail.) **Indexed:** ASCA, C.I.J.E., Commun.Abstr., ERIC, Fam.Ind., IJCS (1973-), Lang.& Lang.Behav.Abstr., Sociol.Abstr. **Document type:** academic/scholarly publication.
  —BLDSC (4942.369000); Genuine Article; SWETS; UMI; UnCover.
  Refereed Serial

| 301.16 410 | US | ISSN 0957-6851 |
| P92.P16 | | CODEN: JACNEI |

JOURNAL OF ASIAN PACIFIC COMMUNICATION. 1990. q. £31($63) libraries £93($189). St. John's University, Institute of E S L Jamaica, NY 11439. TEL 718-990-1929. FAX 201-967-9829. Ed. Herbert D. Pierson. R&P contact: Marjukka Grover. adv. contact: Kathryn King. circ. 400. **Indexed:** C.I.J.E. **Document type:** academic/scholarly publication.
  —BLDSC (4947.247000). CCC.
  Description: Covers research into language issues and communication problems in the Asian Pacific region. Examines problems faced by Southeast Asian immigrants elsewhere in the world.
  Refereed Serial

JOURNAL OF BUSINESS AND TECHNICAL COMMUNICATION. see BUSINESS AND ECONOMICS

JOURNAL OF BUSINESS COMMUNICATION. see BUSINESS AND ECONOMICS — Management

| 621.38 | CC |

JOURNAL OF CHINA UNIVERSITIES OF POSTS AND TELECOMMUNICATIONS. (Text in English) 1994. s-a. Beijing University of Posts and Telecommunications, 42 Xueyuan Lu, Beijing 100088, People's Republic of China. TEL 861-203388. FAX 861-2028643. Ed. Shu Xianlin. **Document type:** academic/scholarly publication.

COMMUNICATIONS

384 US ISSN 0021-9916
P87
JOURNAL OF COMMUNICATION. 1951. q. $50 to individuals; institutions $115; students $30 (effective 1998). (International Communication Association) Oxford University Press, Journals, 2001 Evans Rd., Cary, NC 27513. TEL 919-677-0977; 800-852-7323. FAX 919-677-1714. E-mail: jnlorders@oup-usa.org; URL: http://www.oup-usa.org/. (Subscr. outside N. America to: Oxford University Press, Journals, Great Clarendon St., Oxford OX2 6DP, England. TEL 44-1865-267907. FAX 44-1865-267485) Ed. Alan Rubin. adv.; bk.rev.; charts; illus.; stat.; index. circ. 5,200. (also avail. in microform from UMI; reprint service avail. from UMI,KTO) **Indexed:** Acad.Ind., Amer.Bibl.Slavic & E.Eur.Stud., Amer.Hist.& Life (1974-), Arts & Hum.Cit.Ind., ASCA, Asian-Pac.Econ.Lit., Bk.Rev.Ind. (1980-), C.I.J.E., CAD CAM Abstr., Child.Bk.Rev.Ind. (1980-), Child.Lit.Abstr., Commun.Abstr., Curr.Cont., Educ.Ind., Excerp.Med., Film Lit.Ind. (1986-), Fut.Surv., Hist.Abstr. (1974-), Hum.Ind., IJCS (1951-), Ind.Med., Ind.Per.Art.Relat.Law, Inform.Sci.Abstr., Int.Ind.Film Per., Int.Polit.Sci.Abstr., Intl.Ind.TV, Lang.& Lang.Behav.Abstr., M.L.A., Mid.East: Abstr.& Ind., MLA Intl.Bibl., Mult.Ed.Abstr., Polit.Sci.Abstr., Psychol.Abstr. (1953-), Pub.Admin.Abstr., Rel.& Theol.Abstr., Sage Fam.Stud.Abstr., Sage Pub.Admin.Abstr., Soc.Sci.Ind., Sociol.Abstr., SSCI, Tel.Abstr. **Document type:** academic/scholarly publication.
●Also available online. Vendor(s): UMI.
—BLDSC (4961.500000); Genuine Article; KR SourceOne; SWETS; UMI; UnCover. **CCC.**
Description: Concerned with the study of communication research, theory, history and policy.
Refereed Serial

301.16 US ISSN 0196-8599
P87
JOURNAL OF COMMUNICATION INQUIRY. 1974. s-a. $18 to individuals; institutions $33; students $15 (effective 1997). Iowa Center for Communication Study, University of Iowa, School of Journalism and Mass Communication, Iowa City, IA 52242. TEL 319-335-5821. FAX 319-335-5210. Ed. Ralph Beliveau. adv.; bk.rev.; circ. 1,000 (paid). (back issues avail.) **Indexed:** Amer.Hist.& Life (1986-), Film Lit.Ind., Hist.Abstr. (1986-), MLA Intl.Bibl., Sociol.Abstr. **Document type:** academic/scholarly publication.
—BLDSC (4961.620000); SWETS; UnCover.
Description: Emphasizes interdisciplinary inquiry into communication and mass communication phenomena within cultural and historical perspectives.

JOURNAL OF COMMUNICATION MANAGEMENT. see
BUSINESS AND ECONOMICS — Management

621.38 RU ISSN 1064-2269
TK7800 CODEN: JTELEJ
JOURNAL OF COMMUNICATIONS TECHNOLOGY AND ELECTRONICS. English translation of: Radiotekhnika i Elektronika (RU ISSN 0033-8494) 1958. 16/yr. $1728 (Canada and Mexico $1888; elsewhere $1948 (effective 1996). (Russian Academy of Sciences, RU) Maika Nauka - Interperiodica, Mezhdunarodnyi Otdel, Ul. Profsoyuznaya, 90, 117864 Moscow, Russia. (Dist. by: Maik Nauka - Interperiodica, Subscription Office, Box 1831, Birmingham, AL 35201-1831. TEL 205-995-1567. FAX 205-995-1588) Ed. Rueben Glass. adv.; bk.rev.; bibl.; charts; illus.; pat.; index. circ. 500. (also avail. in microform from UMI) **Indexed:** Eng.Ind., INSPEC, INSPEC, Tel.Abstr. **Document type:** academic/scholarly publication.
—BLDSC (0414.227000); AskIEEE; CISTI; Ei; KR SourceOne; Linda Hall; SWETS; UMI; UnCover. **CCC.**
Former titles (until 1992): Soviet Journal of Communications Technology and Electronics (ISSN 8756-6648); (until 1984): Radio Engineering and Electronic Physics (ISSN 0033-7889); (until 1961): Radio Engineering and Electronics (ISSN 0097-2142)
Description: Deals with circuit theory, electrodynamics, wave propagation, magnetics, communications theory, antennas and waveguides, signal processing, solid-state theory and devices.

370 US
LB2847
JOURNAL OF EDUCATIONAL RELATIONS. 1975. q. $48 to individuals (foreign $52); institutions $60 (foreign $64). Educational Communication Center, Box 657, 1830 Walnut St., Camp Hill, PA 17011. TEL 717-761-6620. Ed. Albert E. Holliday. bk.rev.; illus.; index; circ. 1,000 (paid). (also avail. in microform from UMI; back issues avail.; reprint service avail. from UMI) **Indexed:** C.I.J.E., Cont.Pg.Educ., Educ.Admin.Abstr., ERIC. **Document type:** academic/scholarly publication.
—BLDSC (7352.072200); UMI; UnCover.
Former titles: Journal of Educational Public Relations (ISSN 0741-3653); (until 1984): Journal of Educational Communication (ISSN 0745-4058)
Description: Promotes student achievement through positive school-home-community relationships.
Refereed Serial

JOURNAL OF HEALTH COMMUNICATION. see *MEDICAL SCIENCES*

JOURNAL OF INFORMATION SCIENCE - PRINCIPLES AND PRACTICE. see *LIBRARY AND INFORMATION SCIENCES*

JOURNAL OF MARKETING COMMUNICATIONS. see *BUSINESS AND ECONOMICS — Marketing And Purchasing*

384 170 US ISSN 0890-0523
P94
JOURNAL OF MASS MEDIA ETHICS; exploring questions of media morality. 1985. q. $32 to individuals (foreign $62); institutions $180 (foreign $210) (effective 1997). Lawrence Erlbaum Associates, Inc., 10 Industrial Dr., Mahwah, NJ 07430-2262. TEL 201-236-9500; 800-926-6579. FAX 201-236-0072. E-mail: jamsel@erlbaum.com; URL: http://www.erlbaum.com. Eds. Ralph D. Barney, Jay Black. adv.: page $275; 5 x 8. bk.rev. (also avail. in microform from UMI) **Document type:** academic/scholarly publication.
—BLDSC (5012.179000); SWETS; UMI; UnCover. **CCC.**
Description: Stimulates mutually beneficial discussions about mass media ethics and morality among academic and professional groups in the various branches and subdisciplines of communication and ethics.
Refereed Serial

380 690 US ISSN 0899-7764
P96.E252
JOURNAL OF MEDIA ECONOMICS. q. $32 to individuals (foreign $62); institutions $135 (foreign $165) (effective 1997). (California State University, Fullerton, Department of Communications) Lawrence Erlbaum Associates, Inc., 10 Industrial Dr., Mahwah, NJ 07430-2262. TEL 201-236-9500; 800-926-6579. FAX 201-236-0072. E-mail: jamsel@erlbaum.com; URL: http://www.erlbaum.com. Ed. Robert G. Picard. adv.: page $300; 5 x 8. bk.rev. **Indexed:** ASCA, Curr.Cont. **Document type:** academic/scholarly publication.
—BLDSC (5017.044500); UnCover. **CCC.**
Description: Source for contemporary research and commentary about economic forces and policy affecting media.
Refereed Serial

621.38 GW ISSN 0173-4911
CODEN: JOCODG
JOURNAL OF OPTICAL COMMUNICATION. (Text in English) 1980. 6/yr. DM.660 (effective 1997). Fachverlag Schiele und Schoen GmbH, Markgrafenstr. 11, 10969 Berlin, Germany. TEL 49-30-253752-0. FAX 49-30-2517248. E-mail: 0302537520-0001@t-online.de. Ed. R.Th. Kersten. adv.; bk.rev. circ. 1,500. **Indexed:** Chem.Abstr., INSPEC. **Document type:** trade publication.
—BLDSC (5026.355000); AskIEEE; CASDDS; CISTI; Ei; KR SourceOne; Linda Hall; SWETS; UnCover. **CCC.**

JOURNAL OF PRAGMATICS; an interdisciplinary monthly of language studies. see *LINGUISTICS*

JOURNALISM AND MASS COMMUNICATION QUARTERLY; devoted to research and commentary in journalism and mass communication. see *JOURNALISM*

JOURNALISTEN JAHRBUCH. see *JOURNALISM*

JUMP CUT; a review of contemporary media. see *MOTION PICTURES*

K E S. (Kommunikations- und EDV Sicherheit) see *COMPUTERS — Computer Security*

384 JA
KAGAKU SHINBUN TSUSHIN JOHO/SCIENCE NEWS. TELECOMMUNICATION EDITION. (Text in Japanese) 1946. w. 600 Yen per mo. Kagaku Shinbunsha, 8-1, Hamamatsu-cho 1-chome, Minato-ku, Tokyo 105, Japan. **Document type:** newspaper.

KEP- ES HANGTECHNIKA. see *PHYSICS — Optics*

301.16 355 IS
KESHER ELEKTRONIKA MACHSHAVIM. q. Ministry of Defense Publishing House, 25 David Eleazer St., Hakirya, Tel Aviv, Israel. TEL 03-2045403. Ed. Avraham Granit. circ. 7,000.

KEY ABSTRACTS - BUSINESS AUTOMATION. see *COMPUTERS — Abstracting, Bibliographies, Statistics*

KEY ABSTRACTS - TELECOMMUNICATIONS. see *COMMUNICATIONS — Abstracting, Bibliographies, Statistics*

384 UK
KEY NOTE MARKET REPORT: TELECOMMUNICATIONS. Variant title: Telecommunications. irreg., no.10, 1995. £185. Key Note Ltd., Field House, 72 Oldfield Rd., Hampton, Middlesex TW12 2HQ, England. TEL 44-181-783-0755. FAX 44-181-783-1940. Ed. Donna Jones. **Document type:** trade publication.
●Also available online.
Also available on CD-ROM.
Formerly: Key Note Report: Telecommunications.

384 UK
KEY NOTE MARKET REVIEW: U K TELECOMMUNICATIONS. Variant title: U K Telecommunications. 1992. irreg. £410. Key Note Ltd., Field House, 72 Oldfield Rd., Hampton, Middlesex TW12 2HQ, England. TEL 44-181-783-0755. FAX 44-181-783-0049. **Document type:** trade publication.
●Also available online.
Also available on CD-ROM.

380 BO
KIPUS. 1993. m.? Bol.$5 per no. Universidad Mayor de San Andres, Facultad de Ciencias Sociales, Carrera de Comunicacion Social, Casilla 4787, La Paz, Bolivia. Dir. Mamani A. Constancio.

301.16 701 GW ISSN 0171-0834
P99
KODIKAS - CODE - ARS SEMEIOTICA; an international journal of semiotics. (Text in English, French, German) 1975; N.S. 1979. 4/yr. DM.84 to individuals; institutions DM.136. Gunter Narr Verlag Postfach 2567, 72015 Tuebingen, Germany. TEL 49-7071-9797-0. FAX 49-7071-75288. URL: http://www.narr.de. Ed.Bd. adv.; bk.rev.; illus. circ. 1,500. **Indexed:** Arts & Hum.Cit.Ind., Bibl.Ling., Can.Rev.Comp.Lit., Curr.Cont., IBR, MLA Intl.Bibl., Phil.Ind. **Document type:** academic/scholarly publication.
—Genuine Article; KR SourceOne; SWETS. **CCC.**
Formed by the 1982 merger of: Kodikas - Code; Ars Semeiotica.
Description: Focuses on the research and discussion of semiotical subjects related to the constitution of signs.

301.16 701 GW ISSN 0941-0139
KODIKAS - CODE SUPPLEMENT. (Supplement to: Kodikas (ISSN 0171-0834)) 1980. irreg., vol.23, 1997. price varies. Gunter Narr Verlag, Postfach 2567, 72015 Tuebingen, Germany. TEL 49-7071-97970. FAX 49-7071-75288. URL: http://www.narr.de. Ed.Bd. **Document type:** monographic series.

621.38 JA ISSN 0911-6850
KOKUSAI EISEI TSUSHIN JIDAI/INTERNATIONAL SATELLITE COMMUNICATIONS AGE. (Text in Japanese) q. 1030 Yen per no. Kokusai Eisei Tsushin Kyokai - International Satellite Communications Society, 3-2, Nishishinjuku 2-chome, Shinjuku-ku, Tokyo 163-03, Japan.

| 380 | SZ |

KOMMUNIKATION. 10/yr. B & L Verlags AG, Steinwiesenstr. 3, CH-8952 Schlieren, Switzerland. TEL 41-1-7333999. FAX 41-1-7333989. Ed. Peter Boll. circ. 18,000. **Document type:** trade publication.

KOMPASS PROFESSIONNEL. ELECTRICITE, ELECTRONIQUE, INFORMATIQUE. see *BUSINESS AND ECONOMICS* — *Trade And Industrial Directories*

KONTAKT. see *BUSINESS AND ECONOMICS* — *Labor And Industrial Relations*

KOREAN PRESS ANNUAL/HANGUK SINMUN PANGSONG YONGAM. see *JOURNALISM*

| 621.38 | US |

L E A TELECOMMUNICATIONS SERIES. 1994. irreg. Lawrence Erlbaum Associates, Inc., 10 Industrial Dr., Mahwah, NJ 07430-2262. TEL 212-236-9500. FAX 212-236-0072. E-mail: orders@erlbaum.com; URL: http://www.erlbaum.com. Ed. Christopher H. Sterling. **Document type:** academic/scholarly publication.
  Description: Book series dealing with all aspects of telecommunication, except engineering and mass communication. Subjects include management, policy, economics, finance, domestic and international facets, and historical considerations.

LANGUAGE & COMMUNICATION. see *LINGUISTICS*

| 384 | US | ISSN 1062-3884 |

LATIN AMERICA TELECOM REPORT. 1992. m. $679 (effective 1997). International Technology Consultants, 4340 East-West Hwy., Ste. 220, Bethesda, MD 20814-4411. TEL 301-907-0060. FAX 301-907-6555. E-mail: 71011,2475@compuserve.com; URL: http://www.intl-tech.com. Ed. J.J. Gullish. R&P contact: Ada Ghuman. adv. contact: William Thurmond. **Document type:** trade publication, bulletin, newsletter.
  Description: Contains information on Latin America and Caribbean telecommunications and information technology markets. Includes country surveys, market analyses, sectoral reports, business briefs and interviews.

LEADER IN ACTION. see *EDUCATION*

| 343.099 | FR | ISSN 1244-9288 |

LEGICOM; revue du droit de la communication d'enterprise. 1993. q. 1500 F. (effective 1997). Victoires - Editions, 38 rue Croix des Petits Champs, 75001 Paris, France. TEL 33-1-53458915. FAX 33-1-42962578.

| 343.0998 340 | FR | ISSN 0751-9478 |

LEGIPRESSE. m. (10/yr.). 1990 F. (effective 1997). Victoires - Editions, 38 rue Croix des Petits Champs, 75001 Paris, France. TEL 33-1-53458915. FAX 33-1-42962578.

| 621.38 | FR |

LETTRE DE L'AUDIOVISUEL. 1977. w. Societe des Gens de Lettres de France, 38 rue du Faubourg-Saint-Jacques, 75014 Paris, France. TEL 40-51-33-00. TELEX SCAMSGL 206963F. (Co-sponsor: Societe Civile des Auteurs Multimedia) Ed. Laurent Duvillier. **Document type:** newsletter.

LETTRE DU SPONSORING ET DU MECENAT; le 1er support francais sur le parrainage d'entreprise. see *BUSINESS AND ECONOMICS* — *Marketing And Purchasing*

LETTURE; mensile di informazione culturale, letteratura e spettacolo. see *BIBLIOGRAPHIES*

| 621.38 | LB |

LIBERIA. MINISTRY OF POSTS AND TELECOMMUNICATIONS. ANNUAL REPORT.* a. Ministry of Posts and Telecommunications, Monrovia, Liberia.

| 301.16 | PN |

LIBERTAD DE EXPRESION. 1988. m. Universidad de Panama, Facultad de Comunicacion Social, Estafeta Universitaria, Panama, Panama.

| 384.1 | US |
| Z713.5.U6 | | |

LIBRARY FAX ARIEL DIRECTORY. 1984. a. $42 (effective 1995). C B R Consulting Services, Inc., Box 22421, Kansas City, MO 64113. TEL 816-444-8246. FAX 816-444-8265. E-mail: leemapsi@aol.com. Ed. C. Lee Jones. **Document type:** directory.
  Former titles: Library Fax Directory; Directory of Telefacsimile Sites in North American Libraries (ISSN 1049-7218); (until 1988): Directory of Telefacsimile in Libraries in the United States and Canada (ISSN 1049-720X)

| 621.38 | US | ISSN 0741-5834 |
| TA1800 | | |

LIGHTWAVE; fiber optics technology and applications worldwide. 1984. m. $79 (foreign $105) (effective 1997). PennWell Publishing Co. (Nashua), 10 Tara Blvd., 5th Fl., Nashua, NH 03062-2801. TEL 603-891-0123. FAX 603-891-0587. (Subscr. to: Box 1260, Tulsa, OK 74101. TEL 918-835-3161. FAX 918-832-9295) Ed. George Miller; Pub. David Janoff. adv.: B&W page $4055, color page $5050; trim 11 x 14 1/4. bk.rev. circ. 31,000. Indexed: CAD CAM Abstr., Energy Info.Abstr., Tel.Abstr. **Document type:** trade publication.
  —CIS; CISTI; KR SourceOne; SWETS; UMI. **CCC.**
  Description: For producers and users of the technology enabling the transmission of information via light.

| 621.38 | US |

LIGHTWAVE BUYERS GUIDE. a. $68 (foreign $79) (effective 1997). PennWell Publishing Co. (Nashua), 10 Tara Blvd., 5th Fl., Nashua, NH 03062-2801. TEL 603-891-0123. FAX 603-891-0587. (Subscr. to: Box 1260, Tulsa, OK 74101. TEL 918-835-3161. FAX 918-832-9295) adv.; illus. **Document type:** directory.

| 384 | UN |

LIST OF COAST STATIONS. biennial, vol.15, 1996 (with 3/yr. updates). 79 SFr. International Telecommunication Union, Place des Nations, CH-1211 Geneva 20, Switzerland. TEL 41-22-7306141. FAX 41-22-7305194. E-mail: sales@itu.ch; URL: http://www.itu.ch. **Document type:** bulletin.

| 384 | UN |

LIST OF I T U - R RECOMMENDATIONS. a. free. International Telecommunication Union, Place des Nations, CH-1211 Geneva 20, Switzerland. TEL 41-22-7306141. FAX 41-22-7305194. E-mail: sales@itu.ch; URL: http://www.itu.ch. **Document type:** bulletin.
  ●Also available online.

| 384 | UN |

LIST OF SHIP STATIONS. (Text in English, French, Spanish) a. (with q. updates). 98 SFr. International Telecommunication Union, Place des Nations, CH-1211 Geneva 20, Switzerland. TEL 41-22-7306141. FAX 41-22-7305194. E-mail: sales@itu.ch; URL: http://www.itu.ch. **Document type:** bulletin.

| 301.16 | CU |

L M C. w. Ministerio de Comunicaciones, Centro de Informacion de Comunicaciones, Obispo no. 527, Apdo. 605, Havana, Cuba.

| 384.3 004.693 | US |

▼**M I N'S NEW MEDIA REPORT.** (Media Industry Newsletter) 1995. bi-w. $595 (foreign $630) (effective 1997). Phillips Business Information, Inc., 1201 Seven Locks Rd., Potomac, MD 20854. TEL 301-424-3338. FAX 301-309-3847. E-mail: pbi@phillips.com. Ed. Diane Schwartz. (back issues avail.) **Document type:** newsletter.
  Formerly: New Media Week (ISSN 1084-9637)

| 301.16 | CN |

McCARTHY TETRAULT REGULATORY REPORTER - BROADCASTING. 1989. s-m. Can.$295 (effective 1997). McCarthy Tetrault, 275 Sparks St., Ste. 1000, Ottawa, ON K1R 7X9, Canada. TEL 613-563-9386. FAX 613-563-7813. URL: kscantle@mccarthy.ca. Ed. Anthony H.A. Keenleyside. **Document type:** bulletin.
  Formerly: Clarkson, Tetrault Regulatory Reporter - Broadcasting.
  Description: Summary and analysis of all decisions orders and notices published by the Canadian Radio, Television and Telecommunications Commission in broadcasting.

| 621.38 | CN |

McCARTHY TETRAULT REGULATORY REPORTER - TELECOM. 1977. s-m. Can.$295 (effective 1997). McCarthy Tetrault, 275 Sparks St., Ste. 1000, Ottawa, ON K1R 7X9, Canada. FAX 613-563-7813. URL: kscantle@mccarthy.ca. Ed. Anthony H.A. Keenleyside. (back issues avail.)
  Former titles: Clarkson, Tetrault Regulatory Reporter - Telecom; Telecom Bulletin (ISSN 0831-0041)
  Description: Summary and analysis of all decisions, orders and notices with telecommunications applications published by the Canadian Radio, Television and Telecommunications Commission.

THE MAGAZINE HANDBOOK (YEAR). see *ADVERTISING AND PUBLIC RELATIONS*

MAGAZINE NEWS. see *ADVERTISING AND PUBLIC RELATIONS*

MANAGEMENT COMMUNICATION QUARTERLY. see *BUSINESS AND ECONOMICS* — *Personnel Management*

MANAGING THE HUMAN CLIMATE; guidelines on public relations and public affairs. see *ADVERTISING AND PUBLIC RELATIONS*

MARGARET GEE'S AUSTRALIAN MEDIA GUIDE. see *BUSINESS AND ECONOMICS* — *Trade And Industrial Directories*

MARKETING SIGNS; a newsletter at the crossroads of marketing, semiotics and consumer research. see *BUSINESS AND ECONOMICS* — *Marketing And Purchasing*

| 301.16 016.3354 | US | ISSN 0098-9509 |
| Z7164.S67 | | |

MARXISM AND THE MASS MEDIA; towards a basic bibliography. 1972. irreg. price varies. (International Mass Media Research Center, FR) International General, Box 350, New York, NY 10013. (And: 173 Ave. de la Dhuys, 93170 Bagnolet, France) Ed. Seth Siegelaub. circ. 2,000.

| 301.16 | US | ISSN 0193-7707 |
| P87 | | |

MASS COMM REVIEW. 1973. 3/yr. $20 (foreign $25). Association for Education in Journalism and Mass Communication, Le Conte College, Rm. 121, University of South Carolina, Columbia, SC 29208-0251. TEL 803-777-2005. Ed. Diana Tillinghast. adv.; bk.rev.; bibl.; charts; illus.; stat. (back issues avail.) Indexed: Commun.Abstr. **Document type:** academic/scholarly publication.
  —BLDSC (5387.900000); KR SourceOne; SWETS; UMI; UnCover.

MASSACHUSETTS INSTITUTE OF TECHNOLOGY. RESEARCH LABORATORY OF ELECTRONICS. R L E PROGRESS REPORT. see *ENGINEERING* — *Electrical Engineering*

MEDIA & MARKETING. see *ADVERTISING AND PUBLIC RELATIONS*

| 301.16 | US | ISSN 0890-7161 |

MEDIA AND SOCIETY SERIES. 1986. irreg. price varies. Praeger Publishers (Subsidiary of: Greenwood Publishing Group Inc.), 88 Post Rd. W., Box 5007, Westport, CT 06881-5007. TEL 203-226-3571. FAX 203-222-1502. **Document type:** monographic series.

1998   COMMUNICATIONS

301.16 200   US   ISSN 0149-6980
P94
MEDIA & VALUES.* 1977. q. $35 to individuals (Canada $47); institutions & libraries $25 (Canada $33) (effective Sep. 1993). Center for Media and Values, 4727 Wilshire Blvd., Ste. 403, Los Angeles, CA 90010-3873. TEL 310-559-2944. FAX 310-559-9396. (Subscr. in Canada to: c/o 85 St. Clair Ave. E., No. 500, Toronto, ON M4T 1M8, Canada) Ed. Rosalind Silver. bk.rev. circ. 10,000. Indexed: Alt.Press Ind. (1992-), R.G.Abstr.
— KR SourceOne; UnCover.
  Description: Analyzes the social impact of mass media and new technologies on family, youth and children.

011 070.5 070
301.16   SI   ISSN 0129-6612
P92.A7
MEDIA ASIA. (Text in English) 1974. q. $40 (effective 1997). Asian Media Information and Communication Centre, School of Communication Studies Bldg., Nanyang Technological University, Jurong Point Post Office, Box 360, Singapore 916412, Singapore. TEL 65-7927570. FAX 65-7927129. TELEX AMICSI-RS-55524. E-mail: amicline@singnet.com.sg. bk.rev.; index. circ. 1,500. (back issues avail.) Indexed: Commun.Abstr., IBR, Intl.Ind.TV, Rural Ext.Educ.& Tr.Abstr.
— BLDSC (5525.253000); SWETS; UnCover.

380.3   AT   ISSN 1038-6750
MEDIA AUSTRALIA. w. Aus.$385 (foreign Aus.$455). Information Australia, 45 Flinders Ln., Melbourne, Vic. 3000, Australia. TEL 61-3-96542800. stat. circ. 1,000. Document type: newsletter.
  Formed by merger of: Media Letter & Asian Media Survey.
  Description: Provides news of the latest developments in print and electronic media, public relations, promotions, advertising and communications.

MEDIA DATEN: REGIONALE MAERKTE UND MEDIEN. see *ADVERTISING AND PUBLIC RELATIONS*

380   UK   ISSN 0143-5558
BV4319
MEDIA DEVELOPMENT. 1970. q. $30 to individuals; institutions in Europe and N. America $60 (elsewhere £40). World Association for Christian Communication, 357 Kennington Ln., London SE11 5QY, England. TEL 44-171-582-9139. FAX 44-171-735-0340. Eds. Pradip Thomas, Philip Lee. bk.rev.; illus. circ. 2,000. Indexed: CERDIC, Chr.Per.Ind., Commun.Abstr. Document type: academic/scholarly publication.
— BLDSC (5525.257500); SWETS. **CCC**.
  Formerly: World Association for Christian Communication. Journal (ISSN 0092-7821)

380   BS
MEDIA DIRECTORY BOTSWANA (YEAR). (Text in English) 1992. biennial. Department of Information and Broadcasting, Private Bag 0060, Gaborone, Botswana. Ed. Tefo R. Mangope. circ. 20,000. Document type: directory, government publication.
  Description: Lists all public and private printers and broadcasters in Botswana.

MEDIA FACTS. see *ADVERTISING AND PUBLIC RELATIONS*

MEDIA INDUSTRY NEWSLETTER. see *ADVERTISING AND PUBLIC RELATIONS*

384   AT   ISSN 1324-5325
MEDIA INTERNATIONAL AUSTRALIA; quarterly journal of media research and resources. 1976. q. Aus.$80 to individuals; institutions Aus.$120; foreign Aus.$150. Australian Film, Television and Radio School, P.O. Box 126, North Ryde, N.S.W. 2113, Australia. TEL 61-2-98056611. FAX 61-2-98871030. E-mail: meredith.quinn@syd.aftrs.edu.au. Ed. Meredith Quinn. adv.; page Aus.$1250. bk.rev.; charts; stat.; index. circ. 1,000. (back issues avail.) Indexed: Aus.Educ.Ind., Aus.P.A.I.S., Commun.Abstr., Film Lit.Ind. (1989-), Int.Ind.Film Per., Intl.Ind.TV. Document type: academic/scholarly publication.
— BLDSC (5525.258185); UnCover.
  Former titles (until Sep. 1995): Media Information Australia (ISSN 0312-9616); (until 1976): Australian Media Notes (ISSN 0312-9241)
  Description: Publishes research, comment and information on media and telecommunications.

346   US   ISSN 0148-1045
KF2750
MEDIA LAW REPORTER. 1977. w. $1024. The Bureau of National Affairs, Inc., 1231 25th St., N.W., Washington, DC 20037. TEL 202-452-4200. FAX 202-822-8092. TELEX 285656 BNAI WSH. URL: http://www.bna.com/. (Subscr. to: 9435 Key West Ave., Rockville, MD 20850. TEL 800-372-1033) Ed. Cynthia J. Bolbach. index. (looseleaf format; back issues avail.) Indexed: L.R.I.
— CCC.
  Description: Reference service containing the full-text of federal and state court decisions and selected agency rulings affecting newspapers, magazines, radio, television, film and other media.

MEDIA MARKET RESEARCH. see *ADVERTISING AND PUBLIC RELATIONS*

659.1 070.5   US   ISSN 0895-4550
MEDIA MERGERS & ACQUISITIONS. m. $695 (effective 1997). Paul Kagan Associates, Inc., 126 Clock Tower Place, Carmel, CA 93923-8734. TEL 408-625-3225. FAX 408-624-1536. TELEX 408-625-3225.
  Description: Focuses on the status and value of major buyouts, swaps and sales in the entertainment, media, and publishing industries. Includes comprehensive historical databases and forecasts and valuations.

301.16   UK   ISSN 0958-6350
MEDIA MONITOR. w. £465($800) (overseas £500). Financial Times Telecoms & Media Publishing (Subsidiary of: Financial Times Group), Maple House, 149 Tottenham Court Rd., London W1P 9LL, England. TEL 0171-896-2234. FAX 0171-896-2256. Document type: newsletter, abstracting/indexing.
  • Also available online. Vendor(s): Data-Star.
  Description: Briefs readers on important news items and developments in the media and communications industry.

301.16 320   US
MEDIA MONITOR (WASHINGTON). 1987. 6/yr. $50. Center for Media and Public Affairs, 2100 L St., N.W., Ste. 300, Washington, DC 20037. TEL 202-223-2942. FAX 202-872-4014. URL: http://www.proxima.com/cmpa. Eds. S. Robert Lichter, Linda S. Lichter. R&P contact: Michelle Fernandez. Indexed: SRI. Document type: newsletter.
  Description: Analyzes how news and entertainment media treat social and political issues, relying on content analysis.

380   CH
MEDIA NEWS. (Text in Chinese) 1982. 2/w. (Tue. & Fri.) NT.$600($24) Ming Chuan University, No. 250 Chung Shan N. Rd., Sec. 5, Taipei, Taiwan, Republic of China. TEL 02-882-4564. FAX 02-881-8675. E-mail: lcmai@mcu.edu.tw. Ed. Charles Chih-Hung Yang; Pub. Lee Chuan. adv. contact: Li-Chuan Mai. bk.rev.; film rev.; illus.; circ. 3,000 (paid); 7,000 (controlled). (tabloid format) Document type: newspaper, trade publication.
  Description: Covers trends and important issues of the media industry in Taiwan for professionals and mass communications scholars and students.

301.16   US
MEDIA PEOPLE.* 1979. bi-m. $20. Media People Inc., 317 Madison Ave., Rm. 2300, New York, NY 10017-5301. TEL 212-719-5950. Ed. Charles Mandel. adv.; bk.rev. circ. 41,000.

MEDIA PLAN. see *ADVERTISING AND PUBLIC RELATIONS*

380   UK   ISSN 0967-0076
MEDIA POCKET BOOK. a. £24. N T C Publications Ltd., Farm Rd., Henley-on-Thames, Oxfordshire RG9 1EJ, England. TEL 01491-411000. FAX 01491-571188. Document type: trade publication.
  Description: Comprehensive statistical profile of British commercial media.

MEDIA REPORT TO WOMEN. see *WOMEN'S INTERESTS*

MEDIA REPORTER. see *JOURNALISM*

301.16
MEDIA STUDIES CENTER SPECIAL REPORT. 1986. irreg. free. Media Studies Center, 580 Madison Ave., New York, NY 10022. TEL 212-317-6500. FAX 212-317-6572.
  Formerly: Freedom Forum Media Studies Center. Special Report.

384   US   ISSN 1057-7416
P87
MEDIA STUDIES JOURNAL. (Former name of issuing body: Gannett Center for Media Studies) 1987. q. $32 (foreign $40); newsstand price: $8 (foreign $10). Media Studies Center, 580 Madison Ave., New York, NY 10022. TEL 212-317-6500. FAX 212-317-6572. E-mail: msj@ffnyc.mhs.compuserve.com; URL: http://www.mediastdies.org. Eds. Nancy Woodhull, Robert W. Snyder. R&P contact: Jennifer Sandberg. adv. contact: Sheila Owens. bk.rev. circ. 10,000. (back issues avail.) Indexed: ASCA, Curr.Cont., SSCI. Document type: academic/scholarly publication.
— BLDSC (5525.262500); Genuine Article; UnCover.
  Formerly (until 1991): Gannett Center Journal (ISSN 0893-8342)
  Description: For journalists, scholars and informed commentators. Discusses mass communications and technology issues of importance to the media and the public.

380   SZ
MEDIA TREND JOURNAL. 10/yr. Verlag Media-Daten AG, Kanzleistr. 80, CH-8026 Zurich, Switzerland. TEL 41-1-2417776. FAX 41-1-2417884. Ed. Raymond Ludi. circ. 1,500. Document type: trade publication.

384   US
▼**MEDIABOOK (YEAR).** 1997. a. $545. Cowles - Simba Information (Subsidiary of: Cowles Business Media), 11 Riverbend Dr., S., Box 4949, Stamford, CT 06907-0949. TEL 203-358-9900; 800-307-2529. FAX 203-358-5811. E-mail: info@simbanet.com; URL: http://www.simbanet.com.

MEDIACRITIC; the best and worst of America's journalism. see *BUSINESS AND ECONOMICS — Economic Situation And Conditions*

301.16   AU
MEDIACULT NEWS. (Text in English, French and German) 1972. 2/yr. free. Mediacult - Internationales Forschungsinstitut fuer Medien, Kommunikation und Kulturelle Entwicklung - International Research Institute for Media, Communication and Cultural Development, Schoenburgstr. 27-4, A-1040 Vienna, Austria. TEL 43-431-5041316. FAX 43-431-50413164. Ed. Robert Harauer. bk.rev. circ. 1,200. Indexed: Educ.Tech.Abstr. Document type: newsletter.
  Formerly: Mediacult Newsletter.

070 301   US   ISSN 0885-4610
MEDIAFILE. 1980. bi-m. $35 membership (effective 1997). Media Alliance, 814 Mission St., Ste. 205, San Francisco, CA 94103. TEL 415-546-6334. Ed Andrea Buffa. adv.; bk.rev.; film rev.; illus. circ. 4,200. (tabloid format) Indexed: Alt.Press Ind.
  Former titles (until 1980): Media Alliance News; (until 1979): Media Alliance Newsletter.

340 302.23   BE   ISSN 0777-7094
MEDIALEX; selectie van bronnen van de media- en infromatiewetgeving. (Editions in Dutch, French) 1990. biennial. latest 1994. 3440 BEF. Kluwer Rechtswetenschappen Belgie (Subsidiary of: Wolters Kluwer N.V.), Santvoortbeeklaan 21-25, 2100 Antwerp, Belgium. FAX 32-3-3600467. Document type: trade publication.
  Description: Covers national and international legal issues pertaining to the mass media.

380 340   SZ   ISSN 1420-3723
▼**MEDIALEX.** (Text in French, German) 1995. q. 115 SFr. (effective 1997). Staempfli AG, Hallerstr 7-9, CH-3012 Bern, Switzerland. TEL 41-31-3006666. FAX 41-31-3006699. Eds Denis Barrelet, Franz Riklin. circ. 600 (paid). Document type: bulletin.

301.16 370   GW   ISSN 0931-9808
MEDIENCONCRET; Magazin fuer die paedagogische Praxis. 1987. irreg. DM.35. Jugendfilmclub Koeln, Hansaring 82-86, 50670 Cologne, Germany. TEL 0221-120093. FAX 0221-132592. Ed. Sabine Sonnenschein. bk.rev. circ. 2,000. **Document type:** academic/scholarly publication.

380   GW   ISSN 0179-5724
MEDIENSPIEGEL. w. DM.542.40. (Institut der Deutschen Wirtschaft) Deutscher Instituts Verlag GmbH, Postfach 510670, 50942 Cologne, Germany. TEL 49-221-4981452. FAX 49-221-4981592. **Document type:** bulletin.

301.16   GW
MERCVRIVS; Informationsdienst der Motivgruppe Post- und Fernmeldewesen. 1960. q. DM.30. c/o Fritz Baeker, Ed. & Pub., Am Osterberg 19, 29386 Hankensbuettel, Germany. TEL 05832-2422. circ. 120. (back issues avail.) **Document type:** newsletter.

301.16   CU
MINISTERIO DE COMUNICACIONES DE CUBA. CENTRO DE INFORMACION DE COMUNICACIONES. COMUNICACIONES. s-a. $15 in N. and S. America; Europe $16. (Ministerio de Comunicaciones, Centro de Informacion de Comunicaciones) Ediciones Cubanas, Obispo No. 527, Apdo. 605, Havana, Cuba. TEL 32-5556-60.

808   US
MISSOURI SPEECH & THEATRE JOURNAL. 1970. biennial. $5. (Speech and Theatre Association of Missouri) Central Missouri State University, Warrensburg, MO 64093. TEL 816-429-4924. Ed. Marquita L. Byrd. adv.; bk.rev. circ. 175. **Document type:** academic/scholarly publication.
   Formerly: Missouri Speech Journal.

621.38   UK
MOBILE & SATELLITE SINGLE MARKET REVIEW. 1990. q. £20. Kline Publishing Ltd., 4-6 Station Parade, Balham High Rd., London SW12 9AD, England. TEL 081-673-7783. FAX 081-675-6466. TELEX 926319-KPL-G. Ed. Alexander Jardine. adv.; circ. 22,000 (controlled).
   Formerly (until 1991): Single Market Mobile and Satellite Review (ISSN 0958-9155)

621.38   UK   ISSN 0953-539X
MOBILE COMMUNICATIONS. Key Title: FinTech. 7, Mobile Communications. fortn. £670($1005) (effective 1995). Financial Times Telecoms & Media Publishing (Subsidiary of: Financial Times Group), Maple House, 149 Tottenham Court Rd., London W1P 9LL, England. TEL 44-171-896-2234. FAX 44-171-896-2256. Pub. Helen Nicol. (also avail. in microform from UMI) **Document type:** newsletter.
   •Also available online. Vendor(s): Information Access Co.
   —UMI.
   Description: Covers commercial aspects of the mobile communications industry, including cellular radio, private mobile radio, paging services, cordless telephones, airborne communications and satellite mobile services.

384   UK   ISSN 0958-157X
MOBILE COMMUNICATIONS INTERNATIONAL.* 1988. q. £40($120) (overseas £60). Cheerman Ltd., c/o Central Books, 99 Wallis Rd., London E9 5LN, England. **Document type:** trade publication.

301.16   US
MOBILE COMMUNICATIONS REPORT; news of aeronautical, maritime & land mobile satellite services. 1987. bi-w. $534 (foreign $557). Warren Publishing, Inc., 2115 Ward Court, N.W., Washington, DC 20037. TEL 202-872-9200. FAX 202-293-3435. Ed. Michael French. **Indexed:** Tel.Alert.
   •Also available online. Vendor(s): Data-Star, Information Access Co., Knight-Ridder Information, Inc., NewsNet (TE32).
   Former titles (until 1995): Mobile Satellite Reports (ISSN 1046-6061); (until 1988): Mobile Satellite News.
   Description: Provides information on regulatory, marketing and technological issues in this field.
   •Includes information on cellular services and PCS.

621.38   US
MOBILE ELECTRONICS RETAILER. 1983. m. (plus Factbook in Nov.) $28 (Canada $34; elsewhere $62). Bobit Publishing Company, 2512 Artesia Blvd., Redondo Beach, CA 90278-3210. TEL 213-376-8788. FAX 213-376-9043. E-mail: rprice@bobit.com. Ed. Michele Guido. circ. 23,000 (controlled). **Document type:** trade publication.
   Formerly: Installation News (ISSN 0887-2287)
   Description: Technical journal covering automotive aftermarket electronics.

621.38   UK   ISSN 1363-9927
▼**MOBILE MATTERS.** (Not avail. in print format) 1995. m. £100($170) (effective 1997). M2 Communications Ltd., P.O. Box 475, Coventry CV1 2ZW, England. TEL 44-1203-634700. FAX 44-1203-634144. E-mail: di@m2.com; URL: http://www.m2.com. Ed. Darren Ingram. **Document type:** trade publication.
   •Also available online.
   Description: Keeps track of developments affecting the high-growth mobile communications sector on a worldwide basis.

MOBILE NETWORKS & APPLICATIONS. see COMPUTERS — Computer Networks

384   AT
MOBILE'S IN CHINA NEWSLETTER. m. E-mail: moh1@tig.com.au; URL: http://homepages.tig.com.au/-moh1/index.html. Ed. Mike Haill. **Document type:** newsletter.
   •Available only online.
   Description: Reports developments in the mobile telecommunications market in China.

MODEM & TELECOMUNICAZIONI. see ELECTRONICS

MONITOR (OXFORD); an analytical review of current events in the online and electronic publishing industry. see COMPUTERS

MORALITY IN MEDIA NEWSLETTER. see LAW — Criminal Law

380   US
MOTIVATIONAL MANAGER. 1993. m. $119. Ragan Communications, 212 W. Superior St., Ste. 200, Chicago, IL 60610. TEL 800-878-5331. FAX 312-335-9583. E-mail: 10262.2730@compuserve.com. Ed. John Cowan. **Document type:** newsletter.
   Formerly: Speaker's Idea File.
   Description: Ideas and techniques for those who speak in public.

MULTILINGUA; journal of cross-cultural and interlanguage communication. see LINGUISTICS

621.38 001.6   JA   ISSN 0027-6421
N E C NEWS. (Text in English) 1963. q. free. Nippon Electric Company - Nippon Denki K.K., 7-1, Shiba 5-chome, Minato-ku, Tokyo 108-01, Japan. FAX 3-798-1510. TELEX NECTOK J22686. Ed. Masahiro Shinoda. charts; illus. circ. 23,500. (tabloid format) **Indexed:** CAD CAM Abstr.
   Description: Information on the new products and company's activities worldwide.

384   CN   ISSN 1198-6107
N F B ON T V. 1989. m. free. National Film Board of Canada - Office National du Film du Canada, P.O. Box 6100, Sta. Centre-Ville, Montreal, PQ H3C 3H5, Canada. TEL 514-496-4891. FAX 514-496-2573. Eds. Shawn Goldwater, Philip Lewis. circ. 4,700. pp./issue: 4. (back issues avail.) **Document type:** government publication, newsletter, trade publication.
   Description: Lists and describes films broadcast on Canadian television, including U.S. border stations.

621.38   JA   ISSN 0915-2334
TK5101.A1   CODEN: NTTREK
N T T REVIEW. (Text in English) 1959. bi-m. 10740 Yen. (Nippon Telegraph and Telephone Corporation - Nippon Denshin Denwa Kabushiki Kaisha) Telecommunications Association - Denki Tsushin Kyokai, Shin Yurakucho Bldg., 12-1, Yuraku-cho 1-chome, Chiyoda-ku, Tokyo 100, Japan. FAX 03-3201-6015. charts; index. circ. 5,000. **Indexed:** Alloys Ind., ASCA, CAD CAM Abstr., Comput.Cont., Curr.Cont., Eng.Ind., Eng.Mat.Abstr., Excerp.Med., Ind.Sci.Rev., INSPEC, Met.Abstr.Ind., Met.Abstr., Nonfer.Met.Alert, PCC Alert, Risk Abstr., Sci.Cit.Ind., Steels Alert, Tel.Abstr., World Alum.Abstr. **Document type:** trade publication.
   —BLDSC (6180.610100); AskIEEE; CASDDS; CISTI; Ei; Genuine Article; KR SourceOne; Linda Hall; SWETS; UnCover.
   Formerly (until vol.31, no.1, 1989): Japan Telecommunications Review (ISSN 0021-4744)

621.38   GW   ISSN 0948-728X
                          CODEN: NAZEAA
N T Z. (Nachrichtentechnische Zeitschrift); Telekommunikation und Informationstechnik. 1948. m. DM.340.20 (foreign DM.370.80) (effective 1998). V D E - Verlag GmbH, Bismarckstr. 33, 10625 Berlin, Germany. TEL 49-30-348001-0. FAX 49-30-3417093. E-mail: vertrieb@vde-verlag.de; URL: http://www.vde-verlag.de. Ed. Stephan Mayer. adv.: B&W page DM.4350, color page DM.6330; trim 270 x 189; adv. contact: Peter Schiro. bk.rev.; abstr.; charts; illus.; index. circ. 12,269. **Indexed:** Chem.Abstr., Cyb.Abstr., Eng.Ind., IBR, INSPEC, PROMT. **Document type:** trade publication.
   —BLDSC (6011.300000); AskIEEE; CISTI; KR SourceOne; Linda Hall; SWETS. **CCC.**
   Formerly (until 1995): N T Z - Nachrichtentechnische Zeitschrift (ISSN 0027-707X)

384   UK
NATIONAL COMMUNICATIONS UNION JOURNAL. 1916. 10/yr. £7.50. Greystoke House, 150 Brunswick Rd., London W5 1AW, England. TEL 44-181-998-2981. FAX 44-181-991-1410. Ed. Linda Quinn. adv.; bk.rev.; charts; illus.; stat.; tr.lit.; index. circ. 92,000. **Document type:** newsletter.
   Formerly: Post Office Engineering Union Journal (ISSN 0032-5295)
   Description: Provides news and views for the British post office, banks and telecommunications industry. Covers work, union and political issues.

808.53   US   ISSN 0749-1042
NATIONAL FORENSIC JOURNAL. 1983. s-a. $15 to non-members. National Forensic Association, Robinson Hall, Washington & Lee University, Lexington, VA 24450-0303. TEL 540-463-8812. Ed. Halford Ryan. adv.; bk.rev.; circ. 300 (paid). (back issues avail.) **Document type:** academic/scholarly publication.
   Description: Includes articles and reviews on individual events, speaking, and Lincoln-Douglas debating.
   Refereed Serial

384   ZA   ISSN 1010-8394
NATIONAL MIRROR. (Text in English) 1971. fortn. $19. Multimedia Zambia Registered Trustees, Box 320199, Lusaka, Zambia. TEL 253864. Ed. Fanwell Chembo. adv.; bk.rev. circ. 12,000.
   Formerly: With One Voice.

623.89 387.2   UN
NAVTEX MANUAL. (Editions in English, French, Spanish) 1988. irreg., 2nd edition, 1994. £8 (overseas £10). International Maritime Organization, 4 Albert Embankment, London SE1 7SR, England. TEL 44-171-735-7611. FAX 44-171-587-3210. TELEX 23588. illus.
   Description: Describes the design and use of NAVTEX, an automated information system to relay important navigational and meteorological warnings among ships.

2000 COMMUNICATIONS

621.38 NE ISSN 0374-3853
CODEN: NERTA9
NEDERLANDS ELEKTRONICA- EN RADIOGENOOTSCHAP. TIJDSCHRIFT. (Text in Dutch and English) 1920. bi-m. fl.75. Nederlands Elektronica- en Radiogenootschap, Box 39, Leidschendam, Netherlands. TEL 31-70-3325112. FAX 31-70-3326477. Ed. A.A. Spanjersberg. bk.rev.; bibl.; charts; illus.; index; circ. 900 (controlled). Indexed: INSPEC (1973-). **Document type:** academic/scholarly publication.
—BLDSC (8835.960000); AskIEEE; CISTI; KR SourceOne; Linda Hall; SWETS.
Formerly: Elektronica en Telecommunicatie (ISSN 0013-5623)

THE NET; the ultimate guide to the internet. see COMPUTERS — Computer Networks

NETCOM. see GEOGRAPHY

NETWORK CONTRACTS REPORT. see COMPUTERS — Computer Industry, Vocational Guidance

380 GW ISSN 0548-3093
NEUES VON ROHDE UND SCHWARZ. English edition: News from Rohde & Schwarz (ISSN 0028-9108); French edition: Actualites de Rohde et Schwarz (ISSN 0174-0660) 1961. 3/yr. free. Rohde und Schwarz, Muehldorfstr. 15, 81671 Munich, Germany. FAX 49-89-4129-3208. TELEX 523703-20. Eds. H. Wegener, G. Soennichsen. abstr.; charts; illus.; index. circ. 100,000. Indexed: INSPEC (1968-). **Document type:** bulletin.
—CCC.

621.38 JA ISSN 0912-0076
NEW ERA OF TELECOMMUNICATIONS IN JAPAN. (Text in English) s-m. $700. Telecommunications Association - Denki Tsushin Kyokai, Shin Yurakucho Bldg., 12-1, Yuraku-cho 1-chome, Chiyoda-ku, Tokyo 100, Japan. TEL 03-3215-5727. FAX 03-3201-6015. Ed. Kazuki Shibuta. circ. 500. **Document type:** newsletter.

NEW JERSEY MEDIA GUIDE. see BUSINESS AND ECONOMICS — Trade And Industrial Directories

380 JA ISSN 0289-1115
NEW MEDIA INFORMATION. (Text in Japanese) 1983. m. 1000 Yen per no. Kyoto Nyu Media Kondankai, Kyoto Shinbunsha, Ebisugawa Agaru, Karasuma Dori, Nakagyo-ku, Kyoto-shi, Kyoto 604, Japan.

NEW REVIEW OF HYPERMEDIA AND MULTIMEDIA. see COMPUTERS

384 US ISSN 1070-3683
HE7601 CODEN: NTQUFF
NEW TELECOM QUARTERLY. Variant title: N T Q. 1993. q. $120 (foreign $150). Technology Futures, Inc., 13740 Research Blvd., Ste. C-1, N. Highway 183, Austin, TX 78750-1859. TEL 800-835-3887. E-mail: editor@ntq.com; URL: http://www.ntq.com. Ed. Julia A. Marsh; Pub. Larry Vanston. R&P contact: Julia A. Marsh. charts; illus. (back issues avail.) **Document type:** trade publication.
—BLDSC (6180.606550); Ei. CCC.
Description: Focuses on national and international telecommunications issues, applications, markets, and technologies. Provides information on how technologies and markets can be expected to change over the next decade. Articles come from industry insiders as well as scholars.

NEW YORK GENERATOR. see LABOR UNIONS

581 JA ISSN 0915-4914
NEWSLETTER OF HIMALAYAN BOTANY. (Text in English) 1986. s-a. 3000 Yen. Society of Himalayan Botany - Himalaya Shokubutsu Kenkyukai, University Museum, University of Tokyo, 3-1, Hongo 7-chome, Bunkyo-ku, Tokyo 113, Japan. Ed. Shuichi Noshiro. R&P contact: Hideaki Ohba. adv. contact: Futoshi Miyamoto. bk.rev. **Document type:** newsletter.

301.16 US ISSN 1042-4326
NEWSPAPER INVESTOR. 1989. m. $695 (effective 1997). Paul Kagan Associates, Inc., 126 Clock Tower Pl., Carmel, CA 93923. TEL 408-624-1536. FAX 408-625-3225.

621.38 JA ISSN 0910-7215
NIKKEI COMMUNICATIONS. (Text in Japanese) 1985. s-m. 15100 Yen. Nikkei Business Publications, Inc. (Subsidiary of: Nihon Keizai Shimbun, Inc.), 2-7-6 Hirakawa-cho, Chiyoda-ku, Tokyo 102, Japan. TEL 81-3-5210-8073. FAX 81-3-5210-8229. URL: http://www.nikkeibp.co.jp/NCC. Ed. Koji Segawa; Pub. Norimichi Okai. adv.: B&W page 593000 Yen; color page 890000 Yen; trim 210 x 280; adv. contact: Kazuhiro Ono. circ. 36,685. **Document type:** trade publication.
Description: Contains technical and business-oriented reviews of the communications industry, including reports on equipment, framework, and regulatory environment.

621.38 384 385 JA ISSN 0288-5026
NIKKEI NEW MEDIA. 1983. w. 144000 Yen. Nikkei Business Publications, Inc. (Subsidiary of: Nihon Keizai Shimbun, Inc.), 2-7-6 Hirakawa-cho, Chiyoda-ku, Tokyo 102, Japan. TEL 81-3-5210-8502. FAX 81-3-5210-8119. URL: http://www.nikkeibp.co.jp/. (Subscr. to: Nikkei Business Pub. Inc., Reader Service Center, P.O. Box 20, Kasai Post Office, Tokyo 134-70, Japan) Ed. Takashi Takada; Pub. Tsunefumi Matsumoto. **Document type:** newsletter.
Description: Specializes in new electronic media.

380 JA ISSN 0387-0235
NIPPON SHINGO GIHO/NIPPON SIGNAL TECHNICAL JOURNAL. (Text in Japanese) 1977. q. 500 Yen per no. Nippon Shingo K.K., Gijutsu Kenkyu Senta - Nippon Signal Co., Ltd., Technical Research Center, 3-1, Marunouchi 3-chome, Chiyoda-ku, Tokyo 100, Japan.

301.6 SW ISSN 0349-5949
P91.5.S3
NORDICOM - INFORMATION; om masskommunikationsforskning i Norden. 1980. q. SEK 200 (effective 1997). Nordic Documentation Center for Mass Communications Research, University of Goeteborg, Spraengkullsgatan 21, S-411 23 Goeteborg, Sweden. TEL 46-31-773-12-19. FAX 46-31-773-46-55. E-mail: ulla.carlsson@jmg.gu.se. Ed. Ulla Carlsson. bk.rev. circ. 2,500. **Document type:** academic/scholarly publication.
Description: Articles on Nordic mass communication research; ongoing research projects; critical reviews; lists of new literature.

301.16 SW ISSN 0349-6244
NORDICOM REVIEW OF NORDIC MASS COMMUNICATION RESEARCH. (Text in English) 1981. s-a. free. Nordic Documentation Center for Mass Communication Research, University of Goeteborg, Spraengkullsgatan 21, S-411 23 Goeteborg, Sweden. TEL 46-31-773-12-19. FAX 46-31-773-46-55. E-mail: ulla.carlsson@jmg.gu.se. Ed. Ulla Carlsson. bk.rev. circ. 1,200. (back issues avail.) Indexed: Lang.& Lang.Behav.Abstr. **Document type:** academic/scholarly publication.
Description: Contains articles about Nordic mass communication research, reviews of the essential literature, surveys of literature, surveys of projects.

621.38 NE ISSN 0923-0068
NORTH-HOLLAND STUDIES IN TELECOMMUNICATION. (Text in English) 1982. irreg., vol.19, 1993. price varies. Elsevier Science B.V., Books Division, P.O. Box 211, 1000 AE Amsterdam, Netherlands. TEL 31-20-4853911. FAX 31-20-4853705. TELEX 18582 ESPA NL. E-mail: nlinfo-f@elsevier.nl; usinfo-f@elsevier.com; forinfo-kyf04035@niftyserve.or.jp; URL: http://www.elsevier.nl/. (Subscr. in the Americas to: Elsevier Science, Regional Sales Office, Box 945, New York, NY 10159-0945. TEL 212-633-3730. FAX 212-633-3680; Subscr. in Australasia and the Far East to: Elsevier Science (Singapore) Pte Ltd, No.1 Temasek Ave., No.17-01 Millenia Tower, Singapore 039192, Singapore. TEL 65-434-3727. FAX 65-337-2230; Subscr. in Japan to: Elsevier Science Japan, 9-15 Higashi-Azabu 1-chome, Minato-ku, Tokyo 106, Japan. TEL 81-3-5561-5033. FAX 81-3-5561-5047) **Document type:** monographic series.
—BLDSC (6150.024000).
Supersedes (in 1986): Studies in Telecommunications (ISSN 0923-005X)
Refereed Serial

301.16 SP ISSN 1130-8842
NOTICIAS DE LA COMUNICACION. 1991. 11/yr. 30000 ptas. (Europe 62000 ptas.; elsewhere 68000 ptas.). Noticias de la Comunicacion, S.A., Duque de Sesto 17, 28009 Madrid, Spain. TEL 34-1-4316624. FAX 34-1-5766724. Ed. Luis Muniz. adv. **Document type:** trade publication.
Description: Covers the communications industry, press, magazines, radio, TV and the media in general.

NOVINARSTVO. see JOURNALISM

380 JA
NYU MEDIA HAKUSHO/WHITE PAPER ON NEW MEDIUM. (Text in Japanese) 1984. a. 4800 Yen. (Nihon Joho Tsushin Shinko Kyokai - Japan Information & Communication Association) Nikkan Kogyo Shinbunsha, 8-10, Kudan Kita 1-chome, Chiyoda-ku, Tokyo 102, Japan.

659.2 301.16 CN ISSN 0381-8632
O C S NOUVELLES. (Text in French) 1970. q. Can.$25 (foreign Can.$35). Office des Communications Sociales, 1340 Est, bd. St-Joseph, Montreal, PQ H2J 1M3, Canada. TEL 514-524-8223. FAX 514-524-8522. E-mail: ocs@cam.org. Ed. Jacques Paquette. R&P contact: Jacques Paquette. adv. contact: Denis Dompierre. bk.rev.; film rev.; video rev.; bibl. circ. 900.
Description: Provides articles on current issues such as media literacy, ethics and media, information on Web sites, world media events and activities for its members.

OCEAN VOICE; maritime information technology and electronics. see TRANSPORTATION — Ships And Shipping

O'DWYER'S DIRECTORY OF CORPORATE COMMUNICATIONS. see BUSINESS AND ECONOMICS — Trade And Industrial Directories

420 US ISSN 0078-4052
PN4071
OHIO SPEECH JOURNAL. 1962. a. $20 in U.S. and Canada; elsewhere $25 (1996 & 1997). Speech Communication Association of Ohio, University of Akron, School of Communications, Akron, OH 44325. TEL 513-229-2340. Eds. Dudley Turner, David Ritchey. R&P contact: David Ritchey. adv. contact: Dudley Turner. bk.rev. circ. 200. Indexed: Lang.& Lang.Behav.Abstr. **Document type:** academic/scholarly publication.

380 JA
ON THE LINE. (Text in Japanese) 1953. 10/yr. free. K D D, Office of Public Relations, 3-2 Nishishinju-ku 2-chome, Shinjuku-ku, Tokyo 163-03, Japan. TEL 81-3-3504-6413. Ed. Yoshitada Ishida. circ. 25,000. **Document type:** corporate report.

384 US ISSN 1089-8980
OPERATOR; devoted to coverage of issues affecting the operator and enhanced services industry. 1991. m. $745 (foreign $820) (effective 1997). Whitaker Associates, 7700 Leesburg Pike, Ste. 109, Falls Church, VA 22043-2615. TEL 703-506-1220. E-mail: editor@whitaker.com; URL: http://www.whitaker.com. Ed. Stuart M. Whitaker; Stuart M. Whitaker. circ. 100 (paid). (looseleaf format; back issues avail.) **Document type:** newsletter.
Description: Focuses on news of technology, regulations, and competition in the telecommunications industry. Topics covered include directory assistance, the FCC, and the Telecommunications Act.

OPTOELECTRONICS CONFERENCE. TECHNICAL DIGEST. see ELECTRONICS

621.38 JA ISSN 0386-4987
Q4
OSAKA DENKI TSUSHIN DAIGAKU KENKYU RONSHU. SHIZEN KAGAKU HEN/OSAKA ELECTRO-COMMUNICATION UNIVERSITY. MEMOIRS. NATURAL SCIENCE. (Text in Japanese; summaries i English) 1965. a. Osaka Denki Tsushin Daigaku - Osaka Electro-Communication University, 18-8 Hatsu-cho, Neyagawa-shi, Osaka-fu 572, Japan. Indexed: Jap.Per.Ind.

LES OUVRAGES DE RADIOSIGNAUX. see TRANSPORTATION — Ships And Shipping

P A S C A L E 20: ELECTRONIQUE ET TELECOMMUNICATIONS. see ELECTRONICS

COMMUNICATIONS

621.38 US ISSN 1070-6607
P C S WEEK. (Personal Communications Systems) 1990. w. $697 (foreign $760) (effective 1997). Phillips Business Information, Inc., 1201 Seven Locks Rd., Potomac, MD 20854. TEL 301-424-3338. FAX 301-309-3847. E-mail: pbi@phillips.com. Ed. Mary McCormick. **Document type:** newsletter.
• Also available online. Vendor(s): Information Access Co., NewsNet (TE12).
—CCC.
Incorporates (1990-1995): Advanced Wireless Communications (ISSN 1058-7713); (in 1995): Personal Communications Report; Which was formerly: Microcell News; Formerly: P C S News (ISSN 1051-3833)
Description: Provides international information on cordless telephone, personal communications networks, microcellular technology and the wireless office.

380 SZ
P T T REVUE. (Text in French, German, Italian) m. Postes, Telephones et Telegraphes Suisses, Viktoriastr. 21, CH-3030 Bern, Switzerland. TEL 031-3383137. FAX 031-3386574. TELEX 911919-PTT-CH. circ. 85,000. **Document type:** newsletter.
Formerly: P T T Zeitschrift.

384 FR ISSN 0475-302X
P T T SYNDICALISTE. 10/yr. Force Ouvriere, 60 rue Vergniaud, 75640 Paris Cedex 13, France. TEL 40-78-30-57. FAX 40-78-30-58. TELEX 200 644 F. Ed. Bernard Vignaud. circ. 58,158.

380 SZ
P T T UND ZOLLBEAMTE. w. Postes, Telephones et Telegraphes Suisses, Monbijoustr. 130, CH-3007 Bern, Switzerland. TEL 031-452886. FAX 031-460592. Ed. Jean-Marc Eggenberger. circ. 12,242. **Document type:** bulletin.

380 SZ
P T T UNION. (Postes, Telephones et Telegraphes) w. Oberdorfstr. 32, CH-3072 Ostermundigen, Switzerland. TEL 031-9317272. FAX 031-9312782. Ed. Fred Feitknecht. circ. 20,000. **Document type:** bulletin.

384 FJ
PACIFIC ISLANDS COMMUNICATION JOURNAL. vol.14, 1986. irreg., vol.16, no.2, 1995. price varies. University of the South Pacific, Institute of Pacific Studies, P.O. Box 1168, Suva, Fiji. FAX 679-301594.

PARLIAMENTARY JOURNAL. see POLITICAL SCIENCE

380 BL ISSN 0553-8483
PESQUISAS: PUBLICACOES DE COMMUNICACOES. Key Title: Pesquisas. Communications. (Numbering continues those articles published in Pesquisas) 1957. irreg. (Universidade do Vale do Rio dos Sinos, Instituto Anchietano de Pesquisas) Unisinos, Av. Unisinos, 950, 93022-000 Sao Leopoldo RS, Brazil. TEL 55-51-5903333 ext. 1951. FAX 55-51-5921035. **Document type:** academic/scholarly publication.
—CISTI.
Supersedes in part (in 1960): Instituto Anchietano de Pesquisas. Pesquisas (ISSN 0480-1873)

PHILLIPS WORLD SATELLITE ALMANAC. see BUSINESS AND ECONOMICS — Trade And Industrial Directories

PHILOSOPHY AND RHETORIC. see PHILOSOPHY

621.38 658 US
PHONE SALES PRESENTATIONS FOR SERVICE-TYPE BUSINESSES, ETC. - A NEWSLETTER. 1991. irreg. $15.95 per no. Prosperity & Profits Unlimited Distribution Services, Box 416, Denver, CO 80201-0416. TEL 303-575-5676. Ed. A. Doyle. (looseleaf format) **Document type:** newsletter.
Description: Provides scripts for telemarketing presentations for various types of businesses.

384 CN ISSN 1206-0801
PHONE-TAP MAGAZINE. tapping into the power of telemarketing. 1996. m. Can.$5.95 per no. (foreign $6.95) (effective 1997). Canadian Telemarketing Corporation, 4 Dearbourne Ave., 1st Fl., Toronto, ON M4K 1M7, Canada. TEL 416-466-6943. Ed. Brian Wilson. adv. circ. 5,000.
Formerly: Phone-Taps.

THE PHONETICIAN. see LINGUISTICS

380 NQ
PIEDRA BOCONA; comunicacion para el desarrollo. 1991. m.? Apdo. 93, Granada, Nicaragua. TEL 2839. Ed. Ronald Puerto Lazo.

384 535 US ISSN 1064-1068
PLASTIC OPTICAL FIBER. Abbreviated title: P O F. 1993. bi-m. $250 (foreign $300) (effective 1996). Information Gatekeepers, Inc., 214 Harvard Ave., Boston, MA 02134. TEL 617-232-3111. FAX 617-734-8562. Ed. Paul Polishuk. (back issues avail.) **Document type:** newsletter.
Description: Covers industry news, trends and applications.

380 US
PODIUM. 2/yr. $45 membership. International Platform Association, Box 250, Winnetka, IL 60093. TEL 847-446-4321. circ. 10,000. **Document type:** newsletter.

POLICY MATTERS!. see COMPUTERS

384 US ISSN 0733-3315
TK9956
POPULAR COMMUNICATIONS. 1982. m. $22.95 (Canada & Mexico $32.95; elsewhere $34.95). (Scanner Association of North America) C Q Communications, Inc., 76 N. Broadway, Hicksville, NY 11801. TEL 516-681-2922. FAX 516-681-2926. Ed. Art Salsberg; Pub. Richard A. Ross. adv. contact: Margaret Milanese. bk.rev. circ. 92,238. **Indexed:** Ind.How To Do It (1989-). **Document type:** consumer publication.
—SWETS.
Incorporates: Scan Magazine.
Description: Devoted to users and enthusiasts of VHF scanners, short wave receivers, radar detectors, satellite TV and cellular telephones.

621.38 US ISSN 0891-5628
TR897.5
POST (PORT WASHINGTON); the magazine for animation, audio, film and video professionals. 1986. m. $40. Testa Communications, Inc., 25 Willowdale Ave., Port Washington, NY 11050. TEL 516-767-2500. FAX 516-767-9335. Ed. Ken McGorry. adv. circ. 25,000. **Document type:** trade publication.

POST- UND TELEKOMMUNIKATIONSGESCHICHTE. see COMMUNICATIONS — Postal Affairs

380.3 XR
POSTOVNI VESTNIK. (Text in Czech and Slovak) 1965. fortn. $54.20. Ministerstvo Hospodarstvi Ceske Republiky, Staromestske nam. 6, 110 15 Prague 1, Czech Republic. (Dist. by: Artia, Ve Smeckach 30, 111 27 Prague 1, Czech Republic) Ed. Ilona Stepanova.
Former titles (until 1993): Vestnik Spoju (ISSN 0862-4844); (until 1989): Federalni Ministerstvo Spoju. Vestnik (ISSN 0139-6927); (until 1970): Ustredni Sprava Spoju. Vestnik (ISSN 0042-4722)

PRAEGER SERIES IN POLITICAL COMMUNICATIONS. see POLITICAL SCIENCE

PRESSENS AARBOG. see HISTORY — History Of Europe

PREVISIONS GLISSANTES DETAILLEES EN PERSPECTIVES SECTORIELLES (VOL.14): TELECOMMUNICATIONS. see BUSINESS AND ECONOMICS — Economic Situation And Conditions

PREVISIONS GLISSANTES DETAILLEES EN PERSPECTIVES SECTORIELLES (VOL.32): INDUSTRIES DE LA COMMUNICATION. see BUSINESS AND ECONOMICS — Economic Situation And Conditions

384.5 IT ISSN 0390-3311
PRIMA COMUNICAZIONE. (Supplements avail.: Gli Uomini Comunicazione, Grande Libro della Stampa Italiana) 1973. m. (11/yr.) L.150000 (foreign L.300000). Editoriale Genesis, Via A. Saffi 12, 20123 Milan, Italy. TEL 39-2-48194401. FAX 39-2-4818658. Ed. Umberto Brunetti. adv.: B&W page L.7800000, color page L.10000000; adv. contact: Gianfranco Rizzini. bk.rev.; charts; illus. circ. 12,500. **Document type:** consumer publication.
Description: Covers news in media, newspapers, television, radio, advertising and communication. It's geared for publishers, editors, journalists, general managers, marketing managers and advertising agencies.

301.16 051 US ISSN 0886-6104
PRO MOTION; a quarterly newsletter for the Media Escort Network. 1985. q. $12. Beyond the Byte, c/o Emily Laisy, Ed., 2501 Laurel Brook Rd., Box 388, Fallston, MD 21047-0388. TEL 410-877-3524; 800-861-1235. FAX 410-877-7064. Ed. Emily Laisy; Pub. Emily Laisy. circ. 300 (controlled). (back issues avail.) **Document type:** trade publication, newsletter.
Description: News of the publishing and public relations media tours.

301.16 IT ISSN 0390-5195
PROBLEMI DELL'INFORMAZIONE. 1976. q. Lit.10000 (foreign L.180000) (effective 1997). Societa Editrice Il Mulino, Strada Maggiore, 37, 40125 Bologna, Italy. TEL 39-51-256511. FAX 39-51-256034. E-mail: riviste@mulino.it. Ed. Paolo Murialdi. adv.: B&W page Lit.2780000; adv. contact: M. Luisa Vezzali. index. circ. 1,500. (back issues avail.) **Indexed:** ELLIS, P.A.I.S.For.Lang.Ind.

621.38 US
PROCEEDINGS OF SPEECH TECH CONFERENCES.* a. $150. Media Dimensions, Inc., 1562 1st Ave., No. 286, New York, NY 10028-4004. TEL 212-533-7481. FAX 212-475-1209. **Document type:** proceedings.

PRODUCER'S MASTERGUIDE; the international production manual for motion pictures, television, commercials, cable and videotape industries in the United States, Canada, the United Kingdom, Bermuda, the Caribbean Islands, Mexico, South America, Europe, the Far East, Australia and New Zealand. see BUSINESS AND ECONOMICS — Trade And Industrial Directories

301.16 US ISSN 0891-1207
P94.5.W65
PROFESSIONAL COMMUNICATOR.* 1915. 4/yr. $18.50 (Canada & Mexico $22; overseas $26) (effective 1995). Women in Communications, Inc., 6900 Newman Rd., Clifton, VA 20124-1613. Ed.Bd. adv.; bk.rev.; illus.; circ. 11,200 (paid). **Document type:** trade publication.
—UnCover.
Former titles (until 1985): Pro - Comm; Matrix (ISSN 0025-598X)
Description: Gives members and subscribers an overview of issues, trends, and news in all areas of communications, including broadcast and print journalism; advertising, public relations, journalism curricula, and publishing. Also provides articles of interest to women communication professionals.

020 US ISSN 0163-5689
P87
PROGRESS IN COMMUNICATION SCIENCES. 1979. a., vol.12, 1993. price varies. Ablex Publishing Corporation, Box 5297, Greenwich, CT 06831-0504. TEL 203-661-7602. FAX 203-661-0792. Ed. George Barnett. (reprint service avail. from ISI) **Document type:** academic/scholarly publication.
—BLDSC (6867.810000).

380 UK ISSN 0810-9028
PROMETHEUS. 1983. 3/yr. £32($58) to individuals; institutions £88 ($148) (effective 1997). (Research School of Social Science, Urban Research Program, AT) Carfax Publishing Co., Abingdon, Oxon. OX14 3UE, England. TEL 44-1235-401000. FAX 44-1235-401550. E-mail: enquiries@carfax.co.uk. (N. American subscr. to: Carfax Publishing Co., 875-81 Massachusetts Ave., Cambridge, MA 02139. FAX 617-354-6875) Ed. Donald M. Lamberton. adv.; bk.rev.; circ. 500 (paid). **Indexed:** AESIS, Aus.P.A.I.S., INSPEC. **Document type:** academic/scholarly publication.
—BLDSC (6925.048000); AskIEEE; KR SourceOne; UnCover. CCC.
Description: Covers issues in technological change, innovation, information economics, communication and science policy.
Refereed Serial

PSYCHO-LINGUA; a biannual research journal devoted to communicative behavior. see LINGUISTICS

COMMUNICATIONS

380 070   GW   ISSN 0033-4006
PN4703
PUBLIZISTIK; Vierteljahreshefte fuer Kommunikationsforschung. 1956. q. DM.119 (students DM.91) (effective 1997). Westdeutscher Verlag GmbH, Postfach 1546, 65005 Wiesbaden, Germany. TEL 49-611-7878151. FAX 49-611-7878423. Ed.Bd. adv.; bk.rev.; bibl.; charts; illus.; index. circ. 1,900. (reprint service avail. from KTO) **Indexed:** E.I., IBR, Int.Polit.Sci.Abstr., Lang.& Lang.Behav.Abstr. **Document type:** academic/scholarly publication.
—SWETS. **CCC.**
    Description: Covers everything connected with communications and journalism from history to law.

THE QUARTERLY JOURNAL OF SPEECH. see *EDUCATION*

354   CN
QUEBEC (PROVINCE). MINISTERE DES COMMUNICATIONS. RAPPORT ANNUEL. 1972. a. price varies. Ministere des Communications, P.O. Box 1005, Quebec, PQ G1K 7B5, Canada. TEL 418-643-5150. illus.; stat.
    Formerly: Quebec (Province). Ministere des Communications. Rapport des Activites.

R S A REVIEW/R S A OORSIG. see *BUSINESS AND ECONOMICS — Economic Situation And Conditions*

RADIOCOMMUNICATIONS MARITIMES. see *TRANSPORTATION — Ships And Shipping*

RADIONAVIGATION. see *TRANSPORTATION — Ships And Shipping*

658 651   US   ISSN 0197-6060
RAGAN REPORT; a weekly survey of ideas and methods for communication executives. 1970. w. $287. Ragan Communications, 212 W. Superior St., Ste. 200, Chicago, IL 60610-3533. TEL 800-878-5331. FAX 312-335-9583. E-mail: 71154.2605@compuserve.com. Ed. David Murray. bk.rev. circ. 3,000. **Document type:** newsletter.

RAPID COMMUNICATIONS IN MASS SPECTROMETRY. see *PHYSICS — Optics*

384 346   GW   ISSN 0940-9122
RECHTSVORSCHRIFTEN DER TELEKOMMUNIKATION. bi-m. DM.248. Deutscher Wirtschaftsdienst, Marienburgerstr. 22, 50968 Cologne, Germany. TEL 49-221-93763-0. FAX 49-221-9376399. **Document type:** bulletin.

301.16   BO
RED DE RECURSOS DE COMUNICACION ALTERNATIVA. 1987. bi-m. $12 (effective 1993). Centro de Integracion de Medios de Comunicacion Alternativa, Apdo. 11365, La Paz, Bolivia. TEL 591-2-328318. bk.rev. film rev. circ. 400. **Document type:** bulletin.
    Description: Contains reviews from Latin America and the Caribbean and news of alternative media related events and competitions.

621.38 384.5   US   ISSN 1066-2731
TK6552
REFERENCE DATA FOR ENGINEERS;* radio, electronics, computer and communications. irreg., latest 7th ed., 1985. $99.95. Prentice Hall Computer Publishing, 201 W. 103rd St., Indianapolis, IN 46290-1094. TEL 317-298-5400. Ed. C. Jordan.
—CISTI.
    Formerly: Reference Data for Radio Engineers.

REPERTOIRE DES RADIOSIGNAUX. see *TRANSPORTATION — Ships And Shipping*

384 338.4   US   ISSN 1087-531X
▼**REPLICATION NEWS.** 1996. m. $30 in U.S. & Canada (foreign $42) (effective 1997). Miller Freeman P S N Inc (Subsidiary of: United News & Media Co.), 460 Park Ave. South, 9th Fl., New York, NY 10016-7415. TEL 212-378-0400. FAX 212-378-2160.
    Description: Covers the busines and technology issues encountered by the replicators and duplicators of the packageJ media.

001.5   UN   ISSN 0080-1356
REPORTS AND PAPERS ON MASS COMMUNICATIONS SERIES. French edition: Etudes et Documents d'Information (ISSN 0251-5105) (Consists of: An Unfinished Story: Gender Patterns in Media Employment; TV Transnationalization: Europe and Asia; Media and Democracy in Latin America and the Caribbean) 1953. irreg., no.110, 1995. price varies. UNESCO Publishing, 7 Place de Fontenoy, 75352 Paris 07 SP, France. TEL 33-1-45684300. FAX 33-1-45685741. URL: http://www.unesco.org/publications. (Dist. in U.S. by: Bernan Associates, 4611-F Assembly Dr., Lanham, MD 20706-4391. TEL 800-274-4888. FAX 800-865-3450) (also avail. in microfiche from CIS) **Indexed:** IIS.
—BLDSC (7638.092500).

384   UK   ISSN 0969-9864
P87   CODEN: RFJCE7
RESEAUX: FRENCH JOURNAL OF COMMUNICATION. 1993. irreg. £25 to individuals; institutions £45. John Libbey Media, University of Luton, 75 Castle St., Luton, Bedfordshire LU1 3AJ, England. TEL 44-1582-743297. FAX 44-1582-743298. E-mail: john.libbey@luton.ac.uk. Eds. Paul Beaud, Patrice Flichy. **Indexed:** Int.Polit.Sci.Abstr. **Document type:** academic/scholarly publication.
—BLDSC (7777.081500).
    Description: Covers all disciplines and fields of theoretical and empirical research on information and communication.

REVISTA CAILOR FERATE ROMNE. see *TRANSPORTATION*

301.16 700   BL   ISSN 0102-0897
P87
REVISTA COMUNICACOES E ARTES. Key Title: Comunicacoes e Artes. 1970. 3/yr. exchange basis. Universidade de Sao Paulo, Escola de Comunicacoes e Artes, Av. Prof. Lucio Martins Rodrigues 443, 05508-900 Sao Paulo SP, Brazil. TEL 818-4112. FAX 814-1324.
    Formerly: Universidade de Sao Paulo. Escola de Comunicacoes Culturais. Revista.

301.16 469   PO   ISSN 0870-7081
REVISTA DE COMUNICACAO E LINGUAGENS. 1985. irreg., no.13, 1990. Esc.700. Edicoes Cosmos, Rua da Emenda, 111, 1o, 1200 Lisbon, Portugal. TEL 3422050. FAX 3478255. Ed. Adriano Duarte Rodrigues.

380   MX   ISSN 0187-8190
REVISTA MEXICANA DE COMUNICACION. 1988. bi-m. Fundacion Manuel Buendia A.C., Apdo. Postal 1784, Admin. de Correos 1, 06700 Mexico DF, Mexico. TEL 208-4261. Ed. Miguel Angel Sanchez de Armas.

REVISTA TRANSPORTURILOR. AUTO, DRUMURI, NAVIGATIE. see *TRANSPORTATION*

384   TI   ISSN 0330-8480
P87
REVUE TUNISIENNE DE COMMUNICATION. (Text in Arabic, English, French) 1982. s-a. 10 din. Institut de Presse et des Sciences de l'Information (IPSI), 7 Impasse Mohamed Bachrouch Montleury, Tunis 1008, Tunisia. TEL 01-335216. FAX 01-348596. TELEX 15254 IPSI TN. Ed. Ridha Methnani. bibl. circ. 3,000. (back issues avail.) **Document type:** newsletter.
    Description: Covers issues affecting journalism and information sciences in the Arab world, Africa, the Third World, and other countries.

384   US   ISSN 1080-2169
HE8211
RUSSIAN TELECOM. 1994. m. $625 (foreign $695) (effective 1997). Information Gatekeepers, Inc., 214 Harvard Ave., Boston, MA 02134. TEL 617-232-3111; 800-323-1088. FAX 617-734-8562. E-mail: igiboston@aol.com; URL: http://igigroup.com. **Document type:** newsletter.

384 332.6   US
▼**RUSSIAN TELECOMMUNICATIONS INVESTOR'S GUIDE.** 1996. a. $1500 (effective 1996). Gist, Inc., 220 Wilson Blvd., Ste. 102-A, Arlington, VA 22201. TEL 703-527-7459. FAX 703-528-1477. Ed. David Bain. R&P contact: Michael Peil. adv. contact: Daniel Radack. (back issues avail.) **Document type:** directory.
    Description: Provides an overview of direct and portfolio investment opportunities in the Russian telecommunications sector, analysis of restructuring and privatization in the industry, surveys of leading public network operators.

384   US   ISSN 0099-1414
SAGE ANNUAL REVIEWS OF COMMUNICATION RESEARCH. 1972. a. $22.95 (hardcover edition $46) (effective 1996). Sage Publications, Inc., 2455 Teller Rd., Thousand Oaks, CA 91320. TEL 805-499-0721. FAX 805-499-0871. URL: http://www.sagepub.com. (Overseas subscr. to: Sage Publications Ltd., 6 Bonhill St., London EC2A 4PU, England; Sage Publications India Pvt. Ltd., P.O. Box 4215, New Delhi 110 048, India) Eds. James W. Carey, Peter V. Miller. adv. contact: Margaret Travers. (back issues avail.) **Document type:** monographic series.
—BLDSC (8069.216000).

301.16   US
SAGE SERIES IN INTERPERSONAL COMMUNICATION. 1983. irreg., vol.14, 1993. $22.95 (hardcover edition $46) (effective 1996). Sage Publications, Inc., 2455 Teller Rd., Thousand Oaks, CA 91320. TEL 805-499-0721. FAX 805-499-0871. E-mail: libraries@sagepub.com; URL: http://www.sagepub.com. (Overseas subscr. to: Sage Publications Ltd., 6 Bonhill St., London EC2A 4PU, England; Sage Publications India Pvt. Ltd., P.O. Box 4125, New Delhi 110 048, India) Ed. Mark L. Knapp. (back issues avail.) **Document type:** monographic series.

301.16 807   US   ISSN 1076-1810
P211
SAGE SERIES IN WRITTEN COMMUNICATION. 1986. irreg., vol.7, 1993. $22.95 (hardcover $48) (effective 1996). Sage Publications, Inc., 2455 Teller Rd., Thousand Oaks, CA 91320. TEL 805-499-0721. FAX 805-499-0871. E-mail: libraries@sagepub.com; URL: http://www.sagepub.com. Eds. Charles R. Cooper, Linda Brodkey. (back issues avail.) **Indexed:** Bibl.Engl.Lang.& Lit. **Document type:** monographic series.
—BLDSC (8069.271070).
    Formerly (until vol.7, 1993): Written Communication Annual (ISSN 0883-9298) *Refereed Serial*

301.16   CE
SANNIVEDANA. (Text in English or Sinhalese) a. Rs.3.50. University of Sri Lanka, Vidyalankara Campus, Department of Mass Communications, Kelaniya, Sri Lanka.

380 362.4   CC   ISSN 1003-109X
SANYUEFENG/SPRING BREEZES. (Text in Chinese) 1985. m. Y26.40. (Zhongguo Canjiren Lianhehui - China Disabled Persons' Federation) Disability in China, Inc., A-8 Huixin Li, Anwai, Chaoyang-qu, Beijing 100101, People's Republic of China. TEL 86-10-6496-8360. (Dist. in US by: China Books & Periodicals, Inc., 2929 24th St., San Francisco, CA 94110. TEL 415-282-2994) Ed. Li Zhiqi. circ. 50,000.
    Description: Coordinates interpersonal relations to create a harmonious social environment for the people.

621.38   US   ISSN 0147-7439
TK5104   CODEN: SACODH
SATELLITE COMMUNICATIONS. 1977. m. $42 (Canada and Mexico $62; elsewhere $102). Intertec Publishing Corp. (Atlanta), 6151 Powers Ferry Rd., N.W., Atlanta, GA 30339-2491. TEL 770-955-2500. FAX 770-955-0400. (Subscr. to: Box 41528, Nashville, TN 37204. TEL 615-377-3322) Ed. Lau Manuta. adv. circ. 17,991 (also avail. in microform from UMI; reprint service avail. from UMI) **Indexed:** ABI Inform., CAD CAM Abstr., Commun.Abstr., Comput.Cont., INSPEC, Int.Aerosp.Abstr., PROMT, Tel.Abstr. **Document type:** trade publication.
    ●Also available online. Vendor(s): Information Access Co., UMI.
—BLDSC (8076.560000); AskIEEE; CISTI; Ei; KR SourceOne; SWETS; UMI; UnCover. **CCC.**
    Description: Serves a broad spectrum of professionals involved with satellite transmission in the US and abroad.

SATELLITE INDUSTRY DIRECTORY. see *BUSINESS AND ECONOMICS — Trade And Industrial Directories*

621.38 658 US ISSN 0161-3448
SATELLITE NEWS. 1978. w. $897 (foreign $960) (effective 1997). Phillips Business Information, Inc., 1201 Seven Locks Rd., Potomac, MD 20854. TEL 301-424-3338. FAX 301-309-3847. E-mail: pbi@phillips.com. Ed. Dave Bross. (looseleaf format) **Indexed:** PROMT. **Document type:** newsletter.
●Also available online. Vendor(s): Information Access Co., NewsNet (TE03).
—CCC.
Incorporates: D B S News (ISSN 0733-9739)

384.51 US ISSN 1077-2278
▼**SATELLITE TIMES (BRASSTOWN).** 1995. bi-m. Grove Enterprises, Inc., Box 98, 7540 Hwy. 64 W., Brasstown, NC 28902-0098. TEL 704-837-9200. FAX 704-837-2216. E-mail: steditor@grove.net; URL: http://www.grove.net/hmpgst.html. Ed. Larry Van Horn; Pub. Bob Grove. adv. contact: Debbie Davis.
—BLDSC (8076.567360).

301.16 US ISSN 1075-5470
Q223 CODEN: SCICEQ
SCIENCE COMMUNICATION. 1979. q. $189 to institutions (effective Sep. 1996). Sage Publications, Inc., 2455 Teller Rd., Thousand Oaks, CA 91320. TEL 805-499-0721. FAX 805-499-0871. E-mail: libraries@sagepub.com; URL: http://www.sagepub.com. (Overseas subscr. to: Sage Publications Ltd., 6 Bonhill St., London EC2A 4PU, England; Sage Publications India Pvt. Ltd., P.O. Box 4125, New Delhi 110 048, India) Ed. Marcel LaFollette. adv. contact: Margaret Travers. bk.rev. circ. 800. (back issues avail.; reprint service avail.) **Indexed:** Arts & Hum.Cit.Ind., ASCA, C.I.J.E., Commun.Abstr., Compumath, Curr.Cont., Fut.Surv., Per.Islam. (1991-), Sage Pub.Admin.Abstr., SSCI. **Document type:** academic/scholarly publication.
—BLDSC (8141.807000); Genuine Article; KR SourceOne; SWETS; UMI; UnCover. CCC.
Formerly (until 1994): Knowledge (ISSN 0164-0259)
Description: Provides an interdisciplinary forum for critical and analytical articles addressing communication issues among scientists, scientific content in the mass media, and ethical issues related to the communication of science.
Refereed Serial

380 658 US ISSN 1069-210X
SE HABLA ESPANOL. 1993. q. $36. Hispanic Business, Inc., 360 Hope Ave., Ste. 300C, Santa Barbara, CA 93105. TEL 805-682-5843. FAX 805-563-1239. E-mail: info@hbinc.com. Ed. Hector Cantu; Jesus Chavarria. adv. contact: Robert Filiatreaux. **Document type:** newsletter.

301.16 US ISSN 1047-4692
Z6951
SENIOR MEDIA DIRECTORY. 1989. a. $99 (diskette $375). G E M Publishing Group, 250 E. Riverview Circle, Reno, NV 89509. TEL 702-786-7419. Ed. Gene Malott. (also avail. in diskette format) **Document type:** directory.

384 UK
SERVICE COMMUNICATIONS. 1993. bi-m. £249. M2 Communications Ltd., P.O. Box 475, Coventry CV1 2ZW, England. TEL 44-1203-634700. FAX 44-1203-634144. E-mail: info@m2.com; URL: http://www.m2.com. Pub. Darren Ingram. (also avail. in diskette format; magnetic tape; back issues avail) **Document type:** trade publication.
●Also available online.

808.5 US ISSN 0886-1501
SHARING IDEAS; the international newsmagazine for speakers, meeting planners, agents, bureaus, consultants, trainers, seminar leaders. 1978. bi-m. $95 for 2 yrs. (Canada & Mexico $124; elsewhere $175) (effective 1996). Royal Publishing Inc., 18825 Hicrest Ave., Box 1120, Glendora, CA 91740. TEL 818-335-8069. FAX 818-335-6127. Ed. Dorothy M. Walters; Pub. Dorothy M. Walters. adv. contact: Michael Walters. bk.rev. circ. 4,000. **Document type:** trade publication.
Description: Provides news, tips, and articles on speaking.

621.38 CC ISSN 1001-4802
SHIJIE DIANXIN/WORLD TELECOMMUNICATIONS. (Text in Chinese; abstracts in Chinese, English) 1988. bi-m. $60. Youdian-bu, Keji Qingbao Zhongxin - Ministry of Posts and Telecommunications, Science and Technology Information Center, 40 Xueyuan Rd., Haidian, Beijing 100083, People's Republic of China. TEL 86-10-6230-1569. FAX 86-10-6230-4077. Ed. Sen Zhang. adv.: B&W page $1000, color page $1500; adv. contact: Sen Zhang. circ. 20,000. **Document type:** academic/scholarly publication, trade publication.
Refereed Serial

380 US ISSN 1067-0440
PN2091.E4
SHOW TECHNOLOGY MAGAZINE. 1989. q. $15. High End Systems, 2217 W. Braker La., Austin, TX 78753. TEL 512-339-9535. FAX 512-837-5290. Ed. Bruce Jordahl. adv. contact: Lisa Davis. circ. 15,000. **Document type:** trade publication.
Description: An entertainment and technology magazine for the lighting, audio and production industry.

621.38 US ISSN 0037-4938
UG1 CODEN: SGNAAZ
SIGNAL (FAIRFAX). 1946. m. $44 to non-members; foreign $65. Armed Forces Communications and Electronics Association, 4400 Fair Lakes Court, Fairfax, VA 22033-3899. TEL 703-631-6100. FAX 703-631-6188. E-mail: signal@us.net; URL: http://www.us.net/signal. Ed. Clarence A. Robinson, Jr.; Pub. C. Norman Wood. R&P contact: Beverly Mowery. adv.: page $5005; trim 8 1/4 x 10 7/8; adv. contact: Louise Nelson. bk.rev.; illus.; tr.lit.; index, cum.index: 1989-1995; circ. 35,269 (paid). (also avail. in microform from UMI; reprint service avail.) **Indexed:** Air Un.Lib.Ind., INSPEC, Tel.Abstr. **Document type:** trade publication.
—BLDSC (8275.970000); CISTI; KR SourceOne; SWETS; UMI; UnCover. CCC.
Description: Covers communications-electronics with articles on research, innovative technologies and business trends, as well as their ramifications in defense, intelligence and geopolitics.

SINO-PLATONIC PAPERS. see HISTORY — History Of Asia

SISTEMI DI TELECOMUNICAZIONI. see ELECTRONICS

621.38 XR ISSN 0037-668X
CODEN: SLOZAE
SLABOPROUDY OBZOR/ELECTRONICS AND TELECOMMUNICATIONS REVIEW. (Text in Czech; summaries in English, French, German, Russian) 1933. m. $65.70. Akademie J.A. Komenskeho, Trziste 20, 118 43 Prague 1, Czech Republic. (Dist. by: Artia, Ve Smeckach 30, 111 27 Prague 1, Czech Republic) Ed. Petr Moos. adv.; bk.rev.; abstr.; bibl.; illus.; pat.; index. circ. 3,850. **Indexed:** C.I.S. Abstr., Chem.Abstr., INSPEC.
—BLDSC (8309.300000); AskIEEE; CASDDS; CISTI; KR SourceOne.

001.5 US
SOCIETY FOR TECHNICAL COMMUNICATION. ANNUAL CONFERENCE PROCEEDINGS. 1956. a. $60 for members; non-members $90. Society for Technical Communication, 901 N. Stuart St., Ste. 904, Arlington, VA 22203-1822. TEL 703-522-4114. bibl. circ. 2,500. (back issues avail.; reprint service avail. from PMC,UMI) **Indexed:** Eng.Ind. **Document type:** proceedings.
Formerly (until 1992): International Technical Communication Conference Proceedings.

384 UK
SOCIETY OF TELECOM EXECUTIVES. REVIEW. m. (10/yr.). £10($25) Society of Telecom Executives, 75-79 York Rd., London SE1 7AQ, England. TEL 44-171-928-9951. FAX 44-171-928-5440. E-mail: jane.mc@ge02.poptel.org.uk. (Subscr. addr.: 1 Park Rd., Teddington, Mddx. TW11 OAR, England. TEL 44-181-943-5181. FAX 44-181-943-2532) Ed. Jane McCarten. adv.: page £1250; adv. contact: T.G. Scott. circ. 24,000. (also avail. in audio cassette) **Document type:** newsletter.

301.16 IT ISSN 1121-1733
SOCIOLOGIA DELLA COMUNICAZIONE. 1982. s-a. L.50000 (foreign L.70000) (effective 1993). Franco Angeli Editore, Viale Monza 106, 20127 Milan, Italy. TEL 02-28-27-651. Ed. Enrico Mascilli Migliorini.

621.38 US
SONET NEWSLETTER. 1990. m. $595 (foreign $645) (effective 1997). Information Gatekeepers, Inc., 214 Harvard Ave., Boston, MA 02134. TEL 617-232-3111; 800-323-1088. FAX 617-734-8562. E-mail: igiboston@aol.com; URL: http://www.igigroup.com. Ed. Scott Clavenna. **Document type:** newsletter.
Formerly (until 1996): Metropolitan Area Networks (ISSN 1057-5383)
Description: Covers technology, products, applications, services, standards, regulations and business developments.

621.38 FR ISSN 0768-956X
SONOVISION. 1969. 11/yr. 480 F. (foreign 550 F.). Groupe Liaisons S.A., 1 av. Edouard Belin, 92856 Rueil Malmaison, France. TEL 33-1-47573166. FAX 33-1-47575055. Ed. Philippe Pelaprat. adv.; bk.rev.

SOUND & COMMUNICATIONS. see SOUND RECORDING AND REPRODUCTION

380 UK ISSN 1353-8799
THE SOUND & VISION YEARBOOK. 1994. a. £5 (foreign £10) (effective 1997). Sunrise Press, Spice House, 13 Belmont Rd., Exeter, Devon EX1 2HF, England. TEL 44-1392-411565. Ed. Andrew Emmerson. adv. contact: Jonathan Hill. circ. 3,000. **Document type:** directory.

SOURCES. see BUSINESS AND ECONOMICS — Trade And Industrial Directories

428.3 384 US ISSN 1041-794X
PN4071
SOUTHERN COMMUNICATION JOURNAL. 1935. q. $30. Southern States Communication Association, c/o Dr. Richard R. Ranta, Exec. Dir., College of Communication & Fine Arts, University of Memphis, Memphis, TN 38152. TEL 901-678-2350. FAX 901-378-5118. Ed. Craig Smith. R&P contact: Richard R. Ranta. adv. contact: Jef Dolan. bk.rev.; illus.; index. circ. 2,500. (also avail. in microform from KTO,UMI; reprint service avail. from KTO) **Indexed:** Abstr.Engl.Stud., Amer.Hist.& Life (1963-1991), C.I.J.E., Commun.Abstr., Hist.Abstr. (1963-1991), IJCS (1935-), Ind.Bk.Rev.Hum., Lang.& Lang.Behav.Abstr., Sociol.Abstr. **Document type:** academic/scholarly publication.
—UMI; UnCover.
(until 1988): Southern Speech Communication Journal (ISSN 0361-8269); (until 1971): Southern Speech Journal (ISSN 0038-4585)

SOUTHWESTERN MASS COMMUNICATION JOURNAL. see JOURNALISM

SPACE COMMUNICATIONS; an international journal. see AERONAUTICS AND SPACE FLIGHT

SPECTRA (ANNANDALE). see EDUCATION

SPEECHWRITER'S NEWSLETTER. see JOURNALISM

621.38 US
STATE & LOCAL COMMUNICATIONS REPORT. 1982. fortn. $599 (outside N. America $737). Telecommunications Reports (Subsidiary of: Business Research Publications, Inc.), 1333 H St., N.W., Ste. 100-E, Washington, DC 20005. TEL 800-822-6338. FAX 212-842-3023. E-mail: customerservice@tr.com; URL: http://www.tr.com. Ed. Lynn Stanton. R&P contact: Ellen Hartman. **Document type:** newsletter.
●Also available online. Vendor(s): NewsNet (TE59).
Formerly (until 1995): Telecommunications Week (ISSN 1040-418X)
Description: Covers communications franchising, licensing, construction, zoning, pre-emption issues at the state and local government level.

STATIONS RADIOMETEOROLOGIQUES. see TRANSPORTATION — Ships And Shipping

001.5 US ISSN 0081-5179
STATISTICS OF THE COMMUNICATIONS INDUSTRY IN THE UNITED STATES. 1939. a. price varies. U.S. Federal Communications Commission, 1919 M St., N.W., Washington, DC 20554. TEL 202-783-3238. (Subscr. to: Supt. of Documents, Washington, DC 20402)

COMMUNICATIONS

384 UK ISSN 1363-9064
STRATEGIC COMMUNICATION MANAGEMENT; a new information architecture. bi-m. Melcrum Publishing Ltd., Studio Bldg., 2nd Fl., 33 Parkgate Rd., London SW11 4NP, England. TEL 44-171-738-0555. FAX 44-171-738-2991. E-mail: 101745.3444@compuserve.com. (Subscr. in US to: 311 S. Wacker Dr., Ste. 4550, Chicago, IL 60606. TEL 312-697-4782. FAX 773-327-4817) Ed.Bd. **Document type:** trade publication.
—BLDSC (8474.031426).

384.3 371.425 US
▼**STRATEGIC NEWS SERVICE.** 1995. w. $195. Technology Alliance Partners, Box 1969, Friday Harbor, WA 98250. E-mail: markrander@aol.com. Ed. Mark R. Anderson.
●Available online only.
  Description: Contains predictions of trends of strategic events and issues for the computer and telecom industries.

301.16 US
STUDIES IN COMMUNICATION. 1984. irreg., vol.4, 1990. price varies. Ablex Publishing Corporation, Box 5297, Greenwich, CT 06831-0504. TEL 203-661-7602. FAX 203-661-0792. Ed. Sari Thomas. **Document type:** academic/scholarly publication.

380 SW ISSN 0280-5634
STUDIES IN COMMUNICATION. Abbreviated title: S I C. 1982. irreg. Linkoepings Universitet, Kommunikation, Kaarallen, S-581 83 Linkoeping, Sweden. **Document type:** monographic series.

301.16 US ISSN 0275-7982 P87
STUDIES IN COMMUNICATIONS; a research annual. 1980. irreg., vol.6, 1997. $73.25 to institutions. J A I Press Inc., 55 Old Post Rd., No. 2, Box 1678, Greenwich, CT 06830-1678. TEL 203-661-7602. FAX 203-661-0792. E-mail: jai@jaipress.com. (Subscr. in the UK and Europe to: JAI Press Ltd., 38 Tavistock St., Covent Garden, London WC2E 7PB, England. TEL 44-171-379-8834. FAX 44-171-379-8835) Ed. Thelma McCormack. **Indexed:** Lang.& Lang.Behav.Abstr., Sociol.Abstr. (1980-). **Document type:** academic/scholarly publication, monographic series.
—BLDSC (8490.171000). CCC.

STUDIES IN POPULAR CULTURE. see SOCIOLOGY

621.38 AT ISSN 1324-0471
SUPERHIGHWAYS AND TELECOMMUNICATIONS IN ASIA. a. Aus.$525 (US & Europe Aus.$555) (effective 1998). Paul Budde Communication Pty. Ltd., 2643 George Downes Dr., Bucketty, N.S.W. 2250, Australia. TEL 61-7-49988144. FAX 61-7-49988247. E-mail: pbc@budde.com.au; URL: http://www.budde.com.au.
  Description: Covers trends and developments in telecommunications, broadcasting and pay TV in 24 Asian countries.

621.38 SW
SWEDISH TELECOM. ANNUAL REPORT. * (Text in English) a. Televerket - Swedish Telecom Headquarters, Maarbackagatan 11, S-123 86 Farsta, Sweden. circ. 5,000. (back issues avail.) **Document type:** corporate report.
  Formerly: Sweden. Televerket. Annual Report (ISSN 0586-1926)

384 NE
▼**T I C.** (Trends In Communication) (Text in English) 1996. 2/yr. fl.35 per vol. to individuals (foreign fl.45); institutions fl.55 per vol. (foreign fl.65). Uitgeverij Boom, P.O. Box 400, 7940 AK Meppel, Netherlands. TEL 31-522-257012. FAX 31-522-253864.
  Description: Publishes thematic issues on subjects of interest in the fields of communication and information.

384 US
T R WIRELESS NEWS. (Telecommunications Reports) bi-w. $597 (outside N. America $735). Telecommunications Reports (Subsidiary of: Business Research Publications, Inc.), 1333 H St., N.W., Ste. 100-E, Washington, DC 20005. TEL 800-822-6338. FAX 202-842-3023. E-mail: customerservice@tr.com; URL: http://www.tr.com. Ed. Victoria Mason. R&P contact: Ellen Hartman. **Document type:** trade publication.
●Also available online. Vendor(s): Information Access Co., NewsNet (TE45).
  Description: Monitors regulatory, technological, and market developments in the wireless telecommunications industry.

TALKING MACHINE REVIEW INTERNATIONAL. see SOUND RECORDING AND REPRODUCTION

621.38 GW ISSN 0940-0311
TASCHENBUCH DER TELEKOM PRAXIS. 1963. a. DM.64 (effective 1997). Fachverlag Schiele und Schoen GmbH, Markgrafenstr. 11, 10969 Berlin, Germany. TEL 49-30-253752-0. FAX 49-30-2517248. E-mail: 0302537520-0001@t-online.de. Ed. B. Seiler. adv. circ. 4,000. **Document type:** trade publication.
—BLDSC (8606.568500).
  Formerly (until 1991): Taschenbuch der Fernmelde-Praxis (ISSN 0082-1764)

001.5 US ISSN 0049-3155
CODEN: TLCMBT
TECHNICAL COMMUNICATION. 1953. q. $60. Society for Technical Communication, 901 N. Stuart St., Ste. 904, Arlington, VA 22203-1822. TEL 703-522-4114. Ed. George Harhoe. adv.; bk.rev.; bibl.; illus.; index. circ. 17,000. (also avail. in microfiche from MIM,UMI,PMC; reprint service avail. from UMI) **Indexed:** Abstr.Anthropol., B.P.I., Bus.Ind., C.I.J.E., Comput.Abstr., Curr.Cont., Educ.Tech.Abstr., Int.Aerosp.Abstr., Mag.Ind.
●Also available online. Vendor(s): Information Access Co., UMI.
—BLDSC (8646.600000); CISTI; KR SourceOne; Linda Hall; SWETS; UMI; UnCover. CCC.

TECHNOLOGY, COMMUNICATION, DISABILITY/TEKNIK, KOMMUNIKATION, HANDIKAPP. see HANDICAPPED

384 004.693 US
▼**TECHNOLOGY FOR COMMUNICATORS.** 1995. m. $249. Ragan Communications, 212 W. Superior St., Ste. 200, Chicago, IL 60610. TEL 800-878-5331. FAX 312-335-9583. E-mail: 71154.2605@compuserve.com. Ed. Steve Crescenzo. **Document type:** newsletter.
  Description: Helps communicators get started and succeed using cyberspace technology.

TEL-COM - BRIEF; Telekommunikation, Datenverarbeitung und Organisation. see BUSINESS AND ECONOMICS — Office Equipment And Services

384 US
TELCO COMPETITION REPORT. bi-w. $596 (outside N. America $733). Telecommunications Reports (Subsidiary of: Business Research Publications, Inc.), 1333 H St., N.W., Ste. 100-E, Washington, DC 20005. TEL 800-822-6338. FAX 202-842-3023. E-mail: customerservice@tr.com; URL: http://www.tr.com. Ed. Brian Hammond. R&P contact: Ellen Hartman. **Document type:** newsletter.
●Also available online. Vendor(s): Information Access Co., NewsNet (TE62).
  Description: Provides news on regulatory decisions, legislative battles, interconnection, and business arrangements affecting local exchange industry.

621.38
TELE-COMMUNICATIONS ASSOCIATION. TECHNICAL BULLETIN. bi-m. Tele-Communications Association, 424 S. Pima Ave., West Covina, CA 91790. **Document type:** bulletin.

TELE TJENESTEN. see LABOR UNIONS

384 FR ISSN 0180-7234
TELE 7 JEUX. 1978. 12/yr. 200 F. Filipacchi Medias, 151 rue Anatole France, 92598 Levallois Perret Cedex, France. TEL 33-1-41347330. FAX 33-1-41347503. (Subscr. to: 5 rue Naracci, 59884 Lille Cedex 9, France. TEL 33-1-20121110. FAX 33-1-20121111) **Document type:** consumer publication.

621.38 SP
TELECAST & BROADCAST. 12/yr. Cardenal Herrera Oria 171, Ciudad de los Periodistas, Efc. Azorin, Torre 2, 28034 Madrid, Spain. TEL 1-730-71-77.

658 343.099 005.8 US ISSN 1081-5074
TELECOM & NETWORK SECURITY REVIEW. 1993. m. $290 (foreign $320). Pasha Publications Inc., 1616 N. Ft. Myer Dr., Ste. 1000, Arlington, VA 22209-3107. TEL 703-528-1244. FAX 703-528-1253. Ed. Beth McConnell. **Document type:** newsletter.
●Also available online.
  Description: Covers security of long-distance commercial telecommunications systems and computer networks that may be penetrated via telephone service.

621.38 US ISSN 1057-6002
TELECOM CALENDAR. 1980. q. $300 (foreign $350) (effective 1997). Information Gatekeepers, Inc., 214 Harvard Ave., Boston, MA 02134. TEL 617-232-3111; 800-323-1088. FAX 617-734-8562. Ed. Paul Polishuk. **Document type:** newsletter.
  Description: Presents worldwide 10-year calendar of telecommnunications, including computer, electronics, applications conferences and trade shows.

384 340 US
▼**TELECOM DEREGULATION & YELLOW PAGES (YEAR).** 1996. $1995 (effective 1997). Cowles - SIMBA Information (Subsidiary of: Cowles Business Media), 11 Riverbend Dr. S., Box 4949, Stamford, CT 06709-0949. TEL 203-358-9900; 800-307-2529. FAX 203-358-5811. E-mail: info@simbanet.com; URL: http://www.simbanet.com.
  Description: Assists publishers, consultants, lobbyists, and public policy staff at telecommunication companies understand what the changes in telephone industry regulations mean for their businesses.

384 CC ISSN 1021-1276
TELECOM SOURCES. (Text in Chinese, English) m. $65. Asian Sources Media Group, G.P.O. Box 12367, Hong Kong, People's Republic of China. TEL 852-2555-4777. E-mail: asmgroup@singnet.com.sg. (Subscr. to: Wordright Enterprises Inc., Box 3062, Evanston, IL 60204-3062. TEL 708-475-1900) Ed. Spenser Au. **Document type:** trade publication.
●Also available on CD-ROM.
  Description: Covers telecom, datacom and satellite products.

384 389.6 US ISSN 1064-1076
TELECOM STANDARDS NEWSLETTER. 1992. m. $595 (foreign $645) (effective 1997). Information Gatekeepers, Inc., 214 Harvard Ave., Boston, MA 02134. TEL 617-232-3111; 800-323-1088. FAX 617-734-8562. E-mail: igiboston@aol.com; URL: http://www.igigroup.com. **Document type:** newsletter.

384 UK ISSN 1361-1410
▼**TELECOMEUROPA'S DEVELOPING WORLD TELECOMMUNICATIONS;** the monthly bulletin on the development of the world's biggest machine. Variant title: Developing World Telecommunications. 1995. m. £495($740) Telecomeuropa News Bureau Publications, 3 Princes Bldgs., George St., Bath, Avon BA1 2ED, England. TEL 44-1225-445282. FAX 44-1225-445283. E-mail: 10014.3104@compuserve.com. (US subscr. to: Box 4948, Laguna Beach, CA 92652. TEL 714-499-1857) Ed. Annie Turner; Pub. Peter Purton. tr.lit. (back issues avail.) **Document type:** newsletter.
●Also available online.

384 332.6 UK ISSN 1361-1356
▼**TELECOMEUROPA'S INTERNATIONAL REGULATORY UPDATE;** your guide to telecoms liberalisation worldwide. Variant title: International Regulatory Update. 1995. m. £495($740) Telecomeuropa News Bureau Publications, 3 Princes Bldgs., George St., Bath, Avon BA1 2ED, England. TEL 44-1225-445282. FAX 44-1225-445283. E-mail: 10014.3104@compuserve.com. (US subscr. to: Box 4948, Laguna Beach, CA 92652. TEL 714-499-1857) Ed. Paul Chambers; Pub. Peter Purton. tr.lit. (back issues avail.) **Document type:** newsletter.
●Also available online.

621.382   UK   ISSN 1361-1402
▼**TELECOMEUROPA'S SATELLITE COMMUNICATIONS NEWSLETTER**; the monthly report for the global satellite communications industry. Variant title: Satellite Communications Newsletter. 1995. m. £495($740) (effective 1995). Telecomeuropa News Bureau Publications, 3 Princes Bldgs., George St., Bath, Avon BA1 2ED, England. TEL 44-1225-445282. FAX 44-1225-445283. E-mail: 100144.3104@compuserve.com. (US subscr. to: Box 4948, Laguna Beach, CA 92652. TEL 714-499-1857) Ed. John Williamson; Pub. Peter Purton. tr.lit. (back issues avail.) **Document type:** newsletter.
●Also available online.

384   UK   ISSN 1361-1348
TELECOMEUROPA'S TELECOMS STANDARDS MONITOR; the monthly update on telecoms and datacoms standards. Variant title: Telecoms Standards Monitor. 1994. m. £495($740) (effective 1995). Telecomeuropa News Bureau Publications, 3 Princes Bldgs., George St., Bath, Avon BA1 2ED, England. TEL 44-1225-445282. FAX 44-1225-445283. E-mail: 10014.3104@compuserve.com. (US subscr. to: Box 4948, Laguna Beach, CA 92652. TEL 714-499-1857) Ed. Annie Turner; Pub. Peter Purton. tr.lit. (back issues avail.) **Document type:** newsletter.
●Also available online.

384 332.6   UK   ISSN 1361-1380
▼**TELECOMEUROPA'S TELECOMS TARIFFS INNOVATION**; your guide to telecoms service pricing for profit. Variant title: Telecoms Tariffs Innovation. 1995. m. £495($740) (effective 1995). Telecomeuropa News Bureau Publications, 3 Princes Bldgs., George St., Bath, Avon BA1 2ED, England. TEL 44-1225-445282. FAX 44-1225-445283. E-mail: 10014.3104@compuserve.com. (US subscr. to: Box 4948, Laguna Beach, CA 92652. TEL 714-499-1857) Ed. Chris Thomas; Pub. Peter Purton. tr.lit. (back issues avail.) **Document type:** newsletter.
●Also available online.

621.38   AT   ISSN 0040-2486
TK5101.A1   CODEN: TCJAAW
TELECOMMUNICATION JOURNAL OF AUSTRALIA. 1935. 4/yr. Aus.$85 to non-members. Telecommunication Society of Australia Ltd., P.O. Box 4050, Melbourne, Vic. 3001, Australia. TEL 61-3-96390906. FAX 61-3-96391515. Ed. P. Gerrand. R&P contact: Tricia Collinson. adv. contact: Tricia Collinson. bk.rev.; charts; illus.; index, cum.index: 1935-1970, 1971-1980, 1981-1990. circ. 3,000. **Indexed:** CAD CAM Abstr., Comput.Cont., Eng.Ind., INSPEC, Int.Aerosp.Abstr., Tel.Abstr. **Document type:** academic/scholarly publication.
—BLDSC (8780.000000); AskIEEE; CISTI; Ei; KR SourceOne; Linda Hall; UnCover.
   Refereed Serial

380   FR   ISSN 0981-6895
TELECOMMUNICATIONS; la lettre des operateurs de services a valeur ajoutee. 1987. 22/yr. 2800 F. A Jour, 11 rue du Marche St. Honore, 75001 Paris, France. Ed. Jean-Claude Streicher. adv.; bk.rev.; index. circ. 1,500. (back issues avail.) **Indexed:** B.P.I.
   Formerly: Innovation et Produits Nouveaux (ISSN 0246-9715)

621.38 380.3   AT   ISSN 1034-7496
▼**TELECOMMUNICATIONS**; management and marketing newsletter. 1984. m. Aus.$398 (US Aus.$430; Europe Aus.$435) (effective 1998). Paul Budde Communication Pty. Ltd., 2643 George Downes Dr., Bucketty N.S.W. 2250, Australia. TEL 61-49-988-144. FAX 61-49-988-247. E-mail: pbc@budde.com.au; URL: http://www.budde.com.au. Ed. Paul Budde. index. circ. 250. (back issues avail.) **Indexed:** B.P.I. **Document type:** newsletter.
   Formerly: New Media Marketing Newsletter (ISSN 0816-6269)
   Description: Covers national and international management and marketing applications, trends and developments on optical fibres, HDTV, ISDN, optical media, EDI, videotex, pay TV, electronic publishing, mobile communications, teletext and satellite communications.

621.38   US   ISSN 0278-4831
TK5101.A1   CODEN: TLCOAY
TELECOMMUNICATIONS (NORTH AMERICAN EDITION). International edition (ISSN 0040-2494) 1967. m. $75 (foreign $135) (free to qualified personnel) (effective 1995). Horizon House Publications, Inc., 685 Canton St., Norwood, MA 02062. TEL 617-769-9750. FAX 617-762-9230. TELEX 951 659. Ed. James N. Budwey. adv.; charts; index. circ. 80,000. (also avail. in microform from UMI; reprint service avail.) **Indexed:** B.P.I, BMT, Bus.Ind., Comput.Bus., Comput.Cont., Comput.Lit.Ind., Eng.Ind., INSPEC, PROMT, Tel.Abstr., Tr.& Indus.Ind.
●Also available online. Vendor(s): Information Access Co., UMI.
—BLDSC (8781.012000); Ei; KR SourceOne; Linda Hall; SWETS; UMI; UnCover. **CCC**.
   Description: Covers telecommunications systems and research.

621.38   US   ISSN 0040-2508
    CODEN: TCREAG
TELECOMMUNICATIONS AND RADIO ENGINEERING. English translation of: Elektrosvyaz' (ISSN 0013-5771). 1962. m. $1488 (foreign $1674) (effective 1997). (Russian Society of Electronics and Communications Engineers, RU) Begell House Inc., 79 Madison Ave., Ste. 1205, New York, NY 10016-7892. TEL 212-725-1999. FAX 212-213-8368. E-mail: Begellhouse@worldnet.att.net. Ed. Reuben C. Glass. adv.; bk.rev.; bibl.; charts; illus. circ. 500. (also avail. in microform from UMI) **Indexed:** Eng.Ind., INSPEC (1968-), Sci.Cit.Ind., SSCI, Tel.Abstr. **Document type:** academic/scholarly publication.
—BLDSC (0426.010000); AskIEEE; CISTI; Ei; Genuine Article; KR SourceOne; Linda Hall; SWETS; UMI; UnCover. **CCC**.
   Formed by the 1963 merger of:
   Telecommunications and Radio Engineering. Part 1. Telecommunications (ISSN 0497-1396);
   Telecommunications and Radio Engineering. Part 2. Radio Engineering (ISSN 0497-140X)
   Description: Covers digital and analog wire, radio, video and optical communications, facsimile, micro- and millimeter-wave communications, switching and coding theory, signal processing, voice and pattern recognition, antennae and waveguides.

TELECOMMUNICATIONS DIRECTORY; an international descriptive guide to approximately 2,300 telecommunications organizations, systems, and services. see BUSINESS AND ECONOMICS — Trade And Industrial Directories

TELECOMMUNICATIONS IN EDUCATION NEWS. see EDUCATION — Computer Applications

384   UK   ISSN 0308-5961
HE7601   CODEN: TEPODJ
TELECOMMUNICATIONS POLICY. 1977. 10/yr. fl.1400($805) (effective 1998). Elsevier Science Ltd., Pergamon, P.O. Box 800, Kidlington, Oxford OX5 1DX, England. TEL 44-1865-843000. FAX 44-1865-843010. TELEX 83111 BHPOXF G. E-mail: nlinfo-f@elsevier.nl; usinfo-f@elsevier.com; forinfo-kyf04035@niftyserve.or.jp; URL: http://www.elsevier.nl/. (Subscr. to: Elsevier Science, Regional Sales Office, P.O. Box 211, 1000 AE Amsterdam, Netherlands. TEL 31-20-4853757. FAX 31-20-4853432; Subscr. in the Americas to: Elsevier Science, Regional Sales Office, Box 945, New York, NY 110159-0945. TEL 212-633-3730. FAX 212-633-3680; Subscr. in Australasia and the Far East to: Elsevier Science (Singapore) Pte Ltd, No.1 Temasek Ave., No.17-01 Millenia Tower, Singapore 039192, Singapore. TEL 65-434-3727. FAX 65-337-2230) Ed. Colin Blackman. adv.; bk.rev.; abstr. (also avail. in microform from UMI; back issues avail.) **Indexed:** ABI Inform., ASCA, CAD CAM Abstr., Comput.Cont., Curr.Cont., INSPEC (1977-), Int.Lab.Doc., Key to Econ.Sci., Mgmt.& Market.Abstr., P.A.I.S., Sci.Cit.Ind., SSCI, Tel.Abstr. **Document type:** academic/scholarly publication.
—BLDSC (8781.520000); AskIEEE; CISTI; Ei; Genuine Article; KR SourceOne; Linda Hall; SWETS; UMI; UnCover. **CCC**.
   Description: Takes an international interdisciplinary view of the social, economic, political and regulatory aspects of telecommunications and information systems.
   Refereed Serial

621.38   US
TELECOMMUNICATIONS PRODUCT REVIEW AND C P E STRATEGIES.* (Customer Premises Equipment) 1973. m. $199 (foreign $249). Aries Group - M P S G, 1823A Flower Hill Way, Gaithersburg, MD 20879-5334. TEL 301-840-0800. FAX 301-840-0809. Ed. Bryon W. Battles. index. circ. 700. (back issues avail.) **Indexed:** Comput.Cont., Tel.Abstr.
   Formerly: Telecommunications Product Review (ISSN 0736-4156); Incorporates: C P E Strategies.
   Description: Provides descriptions and analysis of telecommunications products and services. Covers industry trends and marketplace events.

621.38   US   ISSN 0163-9854
HE7775
TELECOMMUNICATIONS REPORTS. 1934. w. $1495 to institutions; educational and government organizations $895; outside N. America $1795. Telecommunications Reports (Subsidiary of: Business Research Publications, Inc.), 1333 H St., N.W., Ste. 100-E, Washington, DC 20005. TEL 800-822-6338. FAX 202-842-3023. E-mail: customerservice@tr.com; URL: http://www.tr.com. Ed. Victoria A. Mason. R&P contact: Ellen Hartman. bk.rev.; q. cum.index. (back issues avail.) **Indexed:** Comput.Cont., Tel.Alert. **Document type:** newsletter.
●Also available online. Vendor(s): Information Access Co., NewsNet (TE11).
   Description: Covers federal and state regulatory, legislative, technological, legal, and corporate news, as well as international telecommunications developments.

621.38   US   ISSN 1054-1942
HE7601
TELECOMMUNICATIONS REPORTS INTERNATIONAL. 1990. 25/yr. $1097 (foreign $1347). Telecommunications Reports (Subsidiary of: Business Research Publications, Inc.), 1333 H St., N.W., Ste.100-E, Washington, DC 20005. TEL 800-822-6338. FAX 202-842-3023. E-mail: customerservice@tr.com; URL: http://www.tr.com. Ed. John Alden. R&P contact: Ellen Hartman. **Document type:** newsletter.
●Also available online. Vendor(s): Information Access Co., NewsNet (TE14).
   Description: Provides a global perspective on telecommunications. Areas of coverage include trade battles, industry and government actions, liberalization and regulatory issues, satellites, new international telecom tariffs and services, financial development and more.

384.5   FR   ISSN 0982-8524
TELECOMS MAGAZINE.* 1987. 8/yr. Groupe Tests, 26 rue d'Oradour sur Glance, 75504 Paris Cedex 15, France. TEL 42-40-22-01. FAX 42-45-59-43. Ed. S. Heriard-Dubreuil. circ. 32,700.
   Incorporates (in 1989): Resources Informatiques (ISSN 0998-2361); Which was previously (until 1988): Resources, Temps Reel (ISSN 0766-6055); Which was formed by the merger of (1984-1985): Resources Informatiques (ISSN 0762-8110); (1980-1985): Temps Reel (ISSN 0247-4751).
   Description: Information on communication systems and services and research for business users.

621.38   FR   ISSN 1163-9180
TELECOMS RESEAUX INTERNATIONAL. 1986. m. (11/yr.). 748 F. (foreign 855 F.). I D G Communications France, 92051 Paris La Defense Cedex 65, France. TEL 49-04-79-00. FAX 49-04-78-00. TELEX 613234 F. Ed. Philippe Monnin. circ. 12,000.
—SWETS.
   Formerly (until 1991): Telecoms International (ISSN 0987-4119)

380.5   RM   ISSN 1220-8655
TELECOMUNICATII. (Text in Rumanian; summaries in English, French, German and Russian) m. Ministerul Transporturilor si Telecomunicatiilor, Calea Grivitei 193b, 78141 Bucharest, Rumania. (C.I.S. Abstr.; Dok.Str.) (Co-sponsor: Institutul de Cercetari si Proiectari Tehnologice in Transporturi) bibl.; charts; illus. **Document type:** government publication.
—Linda Hall.
   Supersedes in part (in 1989): Revista Transporturilor si Telecomunicatiilor (ISSN 0379-2390); Which was formed by the 1974 merger of: Posti si Telecomunicatii (ISSN 0048-492X); Transporturi Auto, Navale si Ariene (ISSN 0373-7136); Revista Cailor Ferate Romane (ISSN 0482-5020)

2006 COMMUNICATIONS

621.38 IT ISSN 0495-0186
TK5101.A1 CODEN: TLCZAX
TELECOMUNICAZIONI. 1962. q. free. Italtel Societa Italiana Telecomunicazioni, Piazzale Zavattari 12, Milan, Italy. Ed. Aldo Zana. bk.rev.; illus. circ. 5,000. **Indexed:** INSPEC.
—CISTI.

384.6 004.6 UK ISSN 1363-9900
TELECOMWORLDWIRE. 1994. d. £300 (effective 1997). M2 Communications Ltd., P.O. Box 475, Coventry CV1 2ZW, England. TEL 44-1203-634700. FAX 44-1203-634144. E-mail: info@m2.com; URL: http://www.m2.com. Ed. Darren Ingram. bk.rev. **Document type:** trade publication.
●Available only online.
Incorporates (1992-199?): Data Broadcasting News.
Description: International news service covering telecommunications and IT sectoral news and developments.

384 330 US ISSN 0739-7208
TELECONFERENCE MAGAZINE; the business communications magazine. Key Title: Tele Conference. 1981. m. $60 (effective 1997). Applied Business Communications, 2600 Kitty Hawk Rd., Ste. 110, Livermore, CA 94550. TEL 510-606-5150. FAX 510-606-9410. Ed. Corby Griffin; Pub. Patrick Portway. R&P contact: Corby Griffin. adv. contact: Larry Cookson. charts; illus.; stat.; tr.lit. circ. 10,000. (back issues avail.) **Document type:** trade publication, proceedings.
—BLDSC (8781.755000).
Description: Covers teleconferencing applications, trends and developments. Includes profiles of teleconferencing individuals.

621.38 NE
TELEKOMMUNIKATIE VISIE. q. free. Koning en Hartman Elektrotechniek B.V., P.O. Box 125, 2600 AC Delft, Netherlands. TEL 015-619194. circ. 3,200.

621.38 NO ISSN 0085-7130
TK6001 CODEN: TKTKAW
TELEKTRONIKK. (Text in English) 1904. q. NOK 600 (effective 1997). (Telenor Research) Telenor AS, P.O. Box 83, N-2007 Kjeller, Norway. TEL 47-63-84-84-00. FAX 47-63-81-00-76. E-mail: telektronikk@fou.telenor.no. Ed. Ola Espvik. index. circ. 5,000. **Indexed:** INSPEC.
—BLDSC (8782.900000); AskIEEE; CISTI; Ei; KR SourceOne.
Formerly (until 1959): Tekniske Meddelelser fra Telegrafstyret (ISSN 0802-6815)
Refereed Serial

621.38 US ISSN 0730-6156
HF5415.1265 CODEN: TELMES
TELEMARKETING; the magazine of integrated marketing. 1982. m. $49 (foreign $85). Technology Marketing Corporation, One Technology Plaza, Norwalk, CT 06854. TEL 203-852-6800. FAX 203-853-2845. E-mail: tmc@tmcnet.com; URL: http://www.tmcnet.com/telemark/telemktg.htm. Ed. Linda Driscoll; Pub. Nadji Tehrani. adv. contact: Ray Tomkins. **Indexed:** B.P.I., CAD CAM Abstr., Comput.Cont., PROMT. **Document type:** trade publication.
●Also available online. Vendor(s): Information Access Co.
—CASDDS; KR SourceOne; UMI; UnCover.

621.38 658 US ISSN 0736-167X
TELEMARKETING UPDATE. (Special editions avail.: Secretarial Script Presentations, Catering Service Script Presentations, Copier Service Business Script Presentations) 1985. a. $25. Update Publicare Co., c/o Prosperity & Profits Unlimited, Distribution Services, Box 416, Denver, CO 80201-0416. TEL 303-575-5676, Ed. E. A. Doyle. circ. 5,000. (looseleaf format) **Document type:** newsletter.
—CCC.
Description: Provides ideas on telemarketing, scripts and how to.

621.38 UK ISSN 0736-5853
TK5101.A1 CODEN: TEINEG
TELEMATICS AND INFORMATICS; an international journal. 1984. q. fl.1030($592) (effective 1998). Elsevier Science Ltd., Pergamon, P.O. Box 800, Kidlington, Oxford OX5 1DX, England. TEL 44-1865-843000. FAX 44-1865-843010. E-mail: nlinfo-f@elsevier.nl; usinfo-f@elsevier.com; forinfo-kyf04035@niftyserve.or.jp; URL: http://www.elsevier.nl/. (Subscr. to: Elsevier Science, Regional Sales Office, P.O. Box 211, 1000 AE Amsterdam, Netherlands. TEL 31-20-4853757. FAX 31-20-4853432; Subscr. in the Americas to: Elsevier Science, Regional Sales Office, Box 945, New York, NY 10159-0945. TEL 212-633-3730. FAX 212-633-3680; Subscr. in Australasia and the Far East to: Elsevier Science (Singapore) Pte Ltd, No.1 Temasek Ave., No.17-01 Millenia Tower, Singapore 039192, Singapore. TEL 65-434-3727. FAX 65-337-2230) Ed. Indu B. Singh. index. circ. 3,000. (also avail. in microfilm from UMI) **Indexed:** A.I.Abstr., Abstr.Hum.Comp.Inter., CAD CAM Abstr., Commun.Abstr., Comput.Abstr., Comput.Cont., Curr.Cont., Cyb.Abstr., IBR, INSPEC (1985-), Tel.Abstr. **Document type:** academic/scholarly publication.
—BLDSC (8782.955000); AskIEEE; CISTI; Ei; KR SourceOne; SWETS; UMI. **CCC.**
Description: Contains information on applied telecommunications and information technology, policy and legislation resource management. Examines the resulting socio-economic implications.
Refereed Serial

380 SZ
TELEMATIK. 2/yr. B & L Verlags AG, Steinwiesenstr. 3, CH-8952 Schlieren, Switzerland. TEL 41-1-7333999. FAX 41-1-7333989. Ed. Rainer Schulten. circ. 18,000. **Document type:** trade publication.

TELEMEDICINE & TELEHEALTH NETWORK. see *MEDICAL SCIENCES*

TELEMEDICINE BUSINESS NEWSLETTER. see *MEDICAL SCIENCES*

TELEMEDICINE TODAY. see *MEDICAL SCIENCES*

384 US
TELEPHONE I P NEWS. (Information Provider) m. $150 (outside N. America $165). Worldwide Videotex, Box 3273, Boynton Beach, FL 33424-3273. TEL 407-738-2276. Ed. Mark Wright; Pub. Mark Wright. bk.rev. **Document type:** newsletter.
●Also available online. Vendor(s): Information Access Co.
Description: Covers the telephone information provider industry, including new products and marketing strategies. Also reports on public service commission rulings.

TELEPROFESSIONAL INTERNATIONAL. see *BUSINESS AND ECONOMICS — Marketing And Purchasing*

TELEPROFESSIONAL MAGAZINE. see *BUSINESS AND ECONOMICS — Marketing And Purchasing*

621.38 DK ISSN 0040-2753
TK5101.A1
TELETEKNIK.. English edition (ISSN 0492-6110) (Text in Danish) 1950. 4/yr. Kr.30. (Post- og Telegrafvaesenet - Post and Telegraph Office) TELECOM, Telegade 2, DK-2630 Taastrup, Denmark. (Co-sponsor: Concessionary Telephone Companies in Denmark) Ed. Jens Kiil. charts; illus.; index annually for Eng. ed., biennially for Danish ed. circ. 5,300. **Indexed:** Eng.Ind., INSPEC, PROMT.
—BLDSC (8786.450000); AskIEEE; KR SourceOne.

384 GW ISSN 0942-5896
TELEVESTNIK; european magazine for telecommunications and information technology. (Text in Russian) 1992. q. DM.48($127) (foreign DM.60) (effective 1998). Verlag Technik GmbH, Am Friedrichshain 22, 10407 Berlin, Germany. TEL 49-30-42151-0. FAX 49-30-042151273. (Dist. by: Mezhdunarodnaya Kniga, B. Yakimanka 39, 117049 Moscow, Russia. TEL 7-095-2384967. FAX 7-095-2384634) Ed. Frank Backasch. adv.: B&W page DM.6400; trim 175 x 256; adv. contact: Frank Backasch. circ. 6,400. **Document type:** trade publication.

TELEVISION NEWS INDEX AND ABSTRACTS. see *COMMUNICATIONS — Abstracting, Bibliographies, Statistics*

TELEVIZIA A ROZHLAS; programovy tyzdennik. see *COMMUNICATIONS — Radio*

384 NE ISSN 0929-9459
TELEWERKEN. 1993. bi-m. fl.75; newsstand price: fl.11.50. Kommunicatie Service Nederland, P.O. Box 146, 5430 AC Cuijk, Netherlands. TEL 31-485-318008. FAX 31-485-313234. E-mail: ksn@nedernet.nl. Pub. J. Hijl. adv.: page fl.2500; adv. contact: Jan Heyda. bk.rev. circ. 23,000. (back issues avail.)
●Also available online.
—SWETS.
Description: Concerns management, labor organization, tele- and data-communications.

301.16 AT
TELSTRA CORPORATION LIMITED. ANNUAL REPORT. 1992. a. free. Telstra Corporation Limited, Corporate Headquarters, 242 Exhibition St., Melbourne, Vic. 3000, Australia. TEL 61-3-632-7711. FAX 61-3-634-4553. Eds. D. Hoare, F. Blount. circ. 40,000. **Document type:** corporate report.
Formerly: Australian and Overseas Telecommunications Corporation. Annual Report; Formed by the 1992 merger of: Overseas Telecommunications Commission. Report (ISSN 0404-1747); (1975-1992): Telecom Australia. Annual Report.

384 UY ISSN 0797-6488
TEMAS DE COMUNICACION. 1992. q.? Universidad de la Republica, Licenciatura de Ciencias de la Comunicacion, Aduardo Acevedo 928, 11200 Montevideo, Uruguay. TEL 5982-417995. FAX 5982-486796. Ed. Sergio Israel. **Document type:** academic/scholarly publication.

621.38 JA
TEREMATIKUSU SHINPOJUMU/TELEMATICS SYMPOSIUM. (Text in Japanese) 1988. irreg. Gazo Denshi Gakkai, Terematikusu Kenkyu Senmon linkai - Institute of Image Electronics Engineers of Japan, Telematics Committee, Waseda Daigaku Rikogakubu Denshi Tsushingakka Tominaga Kenkyushitsu, 4-1, Okubo 3-chome, Shinjuku-ku, Tokyo 169, Japan.

301.16 808.5 US ISSN 0363-8782
PN4071
TEXAS SPEECH COMMUNICATION JOURNAL. 1976. a. $10. Texas Speech Communication Association, c/o Dr. Martha Haun, Ed., 627 Arnold Hall, Univ. of Houston, Houston, TX 77204-3786. TEL 713-743-2886. FAX 713-743-2876. adv. circ. 650.

621.38 JA ISSN 0910-3732
THIS IS N E C (YEAR). 1989. a. Nippon Electric Company - Nippon Denki K.K., Kaigai Kikakubu, 7-1 Shiba 5-chome, Minato-ku, Tokyo 108-01, Japan. TEL 03-4541111. FAX 03-7986529. **Document type:** corporate report.
Description: Provides facts and figures on the communications equipment of this manufacturer. Major product areas are communications systems and equipment, computers and industrial electronic systems, electronic devices, and home electronics products.

384 GW
TIPS & TRENDS. 1982. 4/yr. membership. Deutsches Video Institut e.V., Budapester Str. 44, 10787 Berlin, Germany. TEL 49-30-230896-0. FAX 49-30-23089621. E-mail: 101566.1677@compuserve.com; URL: http://www.dvi.de. Ed. Imme Vogelsang. bk.rev. circ. 5,200. **Document type:** newsletter.
Formerly (until 1994): D V I - Infos.
Description: Trends and news for consumer electronics retailers on new products and their use.

808.5 659.2 US ISSN 0040-8263
PN4193.04
THE TOASTMASTER; for better listening, thinking, speaking. 1933. m. $36 membership. Toastmaster International, Box 9052, Mission Viejo, CA 92690. TEL 714-858-8255. FAX 714-858-1207. Ed. Suzanne Frey; Pub. Terrence McCann. R&P contact Suzanne Frey. adv. contact: Suzanne Frey. bk.rev.; illus.; index. circ. 175,000. **Indexed:** Intl.Mgmt.Info. **Document type:** trade publication.
Description: Covers public speaking, leadership, language usage, and communications in general.

TOHOKU DAIGAKU DENTSU DANWAKAI KIROKU/TOHOKU UNIVERSITY. RECORD OF ELECTRICAL AND COMMUNICATION ENGINEERING CONVERSAZIONE. see ENGINEERING — Electrical Engineering

537   JA
TOHOKU UNIVERSITY. RESEARCH INSTITUTE OF ELECTRICAL COMMUNICATION. TECHNICAL REPORT. (Text in English) 1964. irreg. exchange basis. Tohoku Daigaku, Denki Tsushin Kenkyujo - Tohoku University, Research Institute of Electrical Communication, 1-1 Katahira 2-chome, Sendai-shi, Miyagi-ken 980, Japan.

TOKYO DAIGAKU KOGAKUBU. DENKI KOGAKU DENSHI KOGAKU IHO/UNIVERSITY OF TOKYO. ELECTRICAL AND ELECTRONIC ENGINEERING DEPARTMENTS. BULLETIN. see ENGINEERING — Electrical Engineering

621.38   CC   ISSN 1000-436X
TONGXIN XUEBAO/CHINA INSTITUTE OF COMMUNICATIONS. JOURNAL. (Text in Chinese) 1980. bi-m. (Zhongguo Tongxin Xuehui) Renmin Youdian Chubanshe - People's Posts and Telecommunications Publishing House, 111 Nanzhuang Lane, Choyangmen-nei, Beijing 100700, People's Republic of China. TEL 86-10-5228738. FAX 86-10-5138139. (Dist. overseas by: China International Book Trading Corp., P.O. Box 399, Beijing, P.R. China) Ed. Zhou Jiongpan. **Document type:** academic/scholarly publication.
—BLDSC (4729.218500); AskIEEE; KR SourceOne.

380 659.1   UK
TOP 50 EUROPEAN MEDIA OWNERS. a. £430 (effective 1997). Zenith Media Ltd., 15 Chitty St., London W1P 1LJ, England. TEL 44-171-255-1221. FAX 44-171-637-0476. E-mail: publications@zenithmedia.co.uk; URL: http://www.zenithmedia.com. Ed. Adam Smith. **Document type:** trade publication.

384   UK   ISSN 0955-1670
TRANSAT; land mobile information technology. 1978. bi-m. free. Inmarsat, 99 City Rd., London EC1Y 1AX, England. TEL 44-171-728-1450. FAX 44-171-728-1344. E-mail: richard_scrase@inmarsat.org. (Dist. by: Virgin Mailing & Distribution, Aylesford, Kent ME20 7WZ, England) Ed. Richard Scrase; Pub. Lee Adamson. adv. contact: Peter Honeywell. circ. 18,000. (back issues avail.) **Document type:** trade publication.

621.38   CN
TRANSMITTER. 1978. 6/yr. free. Telecommunications Workers Union, 5261 Lane St., Burnaby, BC V5H 4A6, Canada. TEL 604-437-8601. FAX 604-435-7760. Ed. Myron Johnson. circ. 13,000. **Document type:** newsletter.

TRANSPORT AND COMMUNICATIONS. see TRANSPORTATION

TRANSPORT & COMMUNICATIONS BULLETIN FOR ASIA & THE PACIFIC. see TRANSPORTATION

380   UK   ISSN 0963-0317
TREND MONITOR REPORTS. COMMUNICATIONS. 1991. s-a. Trend Monitor International Ltd., 3 Tower St., Portsmouth, Hants PO1 2JR, England. TEL 01705-864714. FAX 01705-828009. E-mail: trendmon@cix.compulink.co.uk. Ed. Jan Wyllie. **Document type:** trade publication.

380   JA
TSUSHIN HAKUSHO/WHITE PAPER OF COMMUNICATIONS. (Text in Japanese) a. 2300 Yen. (Yuseisho - Ministry of Posts and Telecommunications) Okurasho Insatsukyoku - Ministry of Finance, Printing Bureau, 2-4, Toranomon 2-chome, Minato-ku, Tokyo 105, Japan. **Document type:** government publication.

380   JA
TSUSHIN NI KANSURU GENJO HOKOKU/CURRENT SURVEY ON COMMUNICATION. (Text in Japanese) a. Yuseisho - Ministry of Posts and Telecommunications, 3-2, Kasumigaseki 1-chome, Chiyoda-ku, Tokyo 100, Japan. **Document type:** government publication.

380   JA   ISSN 0916-5754
TSUSHIN SOGO KENKYUJO NENPO/JAPAN. MINISTRY OF POSTS AND TELECOMMUNICATIONS. COMMUNICATIONS RESEARCH LABORATORY. ANNUAL REPORT. (Text in Japanese) a. Yuseisho, Tsushin Sogo Kenkyujo - Ministry of Posts and Telecommunications, Communications Research Laboratory, 2-1 Nukui Kita-machi 4-chome, Koganei-shi, Tokyo 184, Japan. **Document type:** government publication.

301.16   GW
TUDUV-STUDIE. REIHE KOMMUNIKATIONSWISSENSCHAFTEN. 1986. irreg. price varies. Tuduv Verlagsgesellschaft mbH, Gabelsbergerstr. 15, 80333 Munich, Germany.

380 659.1   UK   ISSN 0968-2198
U K MEDIA YEARBOOK. 1988. a. £190 (effective 1997). Zenith Media Ltd., 15 Chitty St., London W1P 1LJ, England. TEL 44-171-255-1221. FAX 44-171-637-0476. E-mail: publications@zenithmedia.co.uk; URL: http://www.zenithmedia.com. Ed. Adam Smith. charts; circ. 500 (paid). (back issues avail.) **Document type:** trade publication.
Description: Facts and figures on the United Kingdom's advertising media.

301.16   NR
UNILAG COMMUNICATION REVIEW; a quarterly review of the communication media. 1977. q. £N10. University of Lagos, Department of Mass Communication, P.O. Box 12003, Lagos, Nigeria. adv.

301.16   SG   ISSN 0253-5858
UNIR CINE MEDIA; bulletin de la commission des moyens de communication sociale de la conference episcopale regionale de l'Afrique de l'ouest. 1982. s-a. 5000 Fr.CFA includes Unir Cinema. R.P. Jean Vast, Ed. & Pub., B.P. 160, 1 rue Neuville, Saint-Louis, Senegal. bk.rev.; film rev.; index.

U.S. ADMINISTRATIVE OFFICE OF THE UNITED STATES COURTS. REPORT ON APPLICATIONS FOR ORDERS AUTHORIZING OR APPROVING THE INTERCEPTION OF WIRE OR ORAL COMMUNICATIONS. see LAW — Judicial Systems

001.5   US   ISSN 0083-0607
U.S. FEDERAL COMMUNICATIONS COMMISSION. I N F BULLETINS. 1949. irreg., latest 1988. free. U.S. Federal Communications Commission, 1919 M St., N.W., Washington, DC 20554. TEL 202-632-7000. **Document type:** government publication, bulletin.

301.16   IT
UNIVERSITA DEGLI STUDI DI PARMA. CENTRO STUDI E ARCHIVIO DELLA COMUNICAZIONE. ARCHIVI DEL PROGRETTO - COLLANA. 1989. a. price varies. Universita degli Studi di Parma, Centro Studi e Archivi della Comunicazione, P.le della Pace 7A, 43100 Parma, Italy. TEL 0521-270847. FAX 0521-207125. **Document type:** academic/scholarly publication.

301.6   IT
UNIVERSITA DEGLI STUDI DI PARMA. CENTRO STUDI E ARCHIVIO DELLA COMUNICAZIONE. CATALOGHI. 1976. irreg., no.72, 1989. price varies. Universita degli Studi di Parma, Centro Studi e Archivio della Comunicazione, P.le della Pace 7A, 43100 Parma, Italy. TEL 0521-270847. FAX 0521-207125. **Document type:** catalog.

384   UK   ISSN 1363-7185
UNIVERSITY OF LEICESTER DISCUSSION PAPERS IN MASS COMMUNICATIONS. 1992. irreg. University of Leicester, Centre for Mass Communication Research, 104 Regent Rd., Leicester LE1 7LT, England. TEL 44-116-252-3863. FAX 44-116-252-3874. **Document type:** academic/scholarly publication, monographic series.
—BLDSC (5181.925700).

UNIVERSITY OF TECHNOLOGY, SYDNEY. RESEARCH REPORT. see TECHNOLOGY: COMPREHENSIVE WORKS

UNIVERSITY OF THE NORTH. DEPARTMENT OF BANTU LANGUAGES. COMMUNICATIONS. see LINGUISTICS

621.38   UY
URUGUAY. ADMINISTRACION NACIONAL DE TELECOMUNICACIONES. MEMORIA ANUAL. Short title: Memoria A N T E L Uruguay. a. Administracion Nacional de Telecomunicaciones, Fernandez Crespo 1534, Casilla de Correo 989, Montevideo, Uruguay. TELEX 23850 UY. **Document type:** government publication.

384 333.79   US   ISSN 1079-2937
UTILITIES TELECOMMUNICATIONS NEWS. 1994. m. $595 (foreign $635) (effective 1997). Information Gatekeepers, Inc., 214 Harvard Ave., Boston, MA 02134. TEL 617-232-3111; 800-323-1088. FAX 617-734-8562. E-mail: igiboston@aol.com; URL: http://www.igigroup.com. **Document type:** newsletter.

301.16   UK   ISSN 0177-7513
V H F COMMUNICATIONS. (Very High Frequency); a publication for the radio amateur, especially covering VHF, UHF and microwaves. 1969. q. £18 (effective 1997). K M Publications, 5 Ware Orchard, Barby, Nr. Rugby, Warks. CV23 8UF, England. TEL 44-1788-890365. FAX 44-1788-890365. URL: http://www.clearlight.com/~vhfcomm. (U.S. addr.: ATVQ Magazine, 3 N. Court St., Crown Point, IN 46182) Ed. Mike Wooding. R&P contact: Mike Wooding. adv. contact: Mike Wooding. index, cum.index: 1970-1989. circ. 4,500. (back issues avail.) Indexed: INSPEC (1994-). **Document type:** academic/scholarly publication.
—BLDSC (9231.590000); SWETS.
Description: Contains articles for radio amateurs, professionals and school personnel. Covers VHF, UHF and microwaves. Includes information about components.

VAASAN YLIOPISTO. JULKAISUJA. OPETUSMONISTEITA/UNIVERSITY OF VAASA. PROCEEDINGS. TEACHING AID SERIES. see BUSINESS AND ECONOMICS — Economic Systems And Theories, Economic History

VAASAN YLIOPISTO. JULKAISUJA. TUTKIMUKSIA/UNIVERSITY OF VAASA. PROCEEDINGS. RESEARCH PAPERS. see BUSINESS AND ECONOMICS — Economic Systems And Theories, Economic History

VAASAN YLIOPISTON JULKAISUJA. SELVITYKSIA JA RAPORTTEJA/PROCEEDINGS OF THE UNIVERSITY OF VAASA. REPORTS. see BUSINESS AND ECONOMICS — Economic Systems And Theories, Economic History

VARIETY'S ON PRODUCTION. see MOTION PICTURES

VERONIS, SUHLER & ASSOCIATES COMMUNICATIONS INDUSTRY FORECAST. see BUSINESS AND ECONOMICS

VERONIS, SUHLER & ASSOCIATES COMMUNICATIONS INDUSTRY REPORT. see BUSINESS AND ECONOMICS

VERONIS, SUHLER & ASSOCIATES COMMUNICATIONS INDUSTRY REPORT. see BUSINESS AND ECONOMICS

VERSO E REVERSO. see HUMANITIES: COMPREHENSIVE WORKS

621.38   RU   ISSN 0320-8141
    CODEN: VSVYAQ
VESTNIK SVYAZI. 1941. m. $116 (effective 1998). Izdatel'stvo Radion i Svyaz', Ul. Myasnitskaya 40, 101000 Moscow, Russia. TEL 258-5351. TELEX 411665. (Dist. by: Mezhdunarodnaya Kniga, B. Yakimanka 39, 117049 Moscow, Russia) Ed. M.N. Stoyanov. adv.; charts; illus.; tr.lit.; index. circ. 17,254.
—BLDSC (0033.750000); CASDDS; CISTI.

380   US
VIA FEDEX. q. free to Federal Express account holders; all others $7.50. (Federal Express) The Wells Group, 430 First Ave. N., Ste. 550, Minneapolis, MN 55401-1735. TEL 612-338-8300. FAX 612-338-6546. (Subscr. to: Box 727, Memphis, TN 38194-1862. TEL 901-395-3527) Eds. Joan McPeak, Marla Kinney. adv. contact: Lisa Svac. illus.; circ. 330,000 (controlled).

COMMUNICATIONS

621.38   US   ISSN 1041-0643
VIA SATELLITE. 1986. m. $49 in U.S. & Canada (elsewhere $69) (effective 1996). Phillips Business Information, Inc., 1201 Seven Locks Rd., Potomac, MD 20854. TEL 301-424-3338. FAX 301-340-0542. E-mail: pbi@phillips.com. Ed. Scott Chase. adv.; circ. controlled. (back issues avail.) **Document type:** trade publication.
—BLDSC (9231.756000); SWETS. **CCC.**
Description: Looks at commercial communication via satellite and competing technologies. Includes technical information, applications and case studies.

621.38   UK   ISSN 0267-3584
VIDEOTEX VIEWPOINT.* q. £15. Marathon Information Services, 243-253 Lower Mortlake Rd., Richmond, Surrey TW9 2LL, England. (back issues avail.) **Indexed:** Info.Media & Tech., INSPEC.
—AskIEEE; KR SourceOne.

VIDURA. see *GENERAL INTEREST PERIODICALS — India*

380   UK   ISSN 1350-6757
VINE (BATH); the european newsletter covering computer mediated communications. 1991. 10/yr. £425($635) Telecomeuropa Publications, 3 Princes Bldgs., George St., Bath, Avon BA1 2ED, England. TEL 44-1225-445282. FAX 44-1225-445283. E-mail: 100144.3104@compuserve.com. Ed. R.E. Walters; Pub. Peter Purton. **Document type:** newsletter.
Formerly (until 1993): Voice in Europe (ISSN 0966-9922).

428   US   ISSN 0022-2224
Z119   CODEN: VSLGAO
VISIBLE LANGUAGE; the quarterly concerned with all that is involved in our being literate. 1967. q. $30 to individuals (foreign $37); institutions $55 (foreign $62) (effective 1997). Illinois Institute of Technology, Institute of Design, 10 W. 35th St., Chicago, IL 60616. TEL 312-808-5317. FAX 312-808-5322. E-mail: poggenpohl@id.iit.edu. (Subscr. to: Rhode Island School of Design, Graphic Design Department, 2 College St., Providence, RI 02903. TEL 401-454-6171. FAX 401-454-6117) (Co-sponsor: Rhode Island School of Design, Graphic Design Department) Ed. Sharon H. Poggenpohl. adv.; bk.rev.; charts; illus.; stat.; index. circ. 1,600. (also avail. in microform from UMI) **Indexed:** Abstr.Engl.Stud., Art Ind., Artbibl., Artbibl.Mod., Arts & Hum.Cit.Ind., ASCA, Bibl.Ling., Bk.Rev.Dig., C.I.J.E., Curr.Cont., Ergon.Abstr., Graph.Arts Abstr., Graph.Arts Lit.Abstr., Inform.Sci.Abstr., INSPEC, Lang.& Lang.Behav.Abstr., M.L.A., MLA Intl.Bibl., Psychol.Abstr., SSCI. **Document type:** academic/scholarly publication.
—BLDSC (9240.895000); AskIEEE; Genuine Article; KR SourceOne; SWETS; UMI; UnCover. **CCC.**
Formerly (until 1970): Journal of Typographic Research.

384.5   SI
VISTAS. 1992. q. free. Telecommunication Authority of Singapore, 35 Robinson Rd., TAS Bldg., Singapore 0106, Singapore. TEL 65-323-3888. FAX 65-323-0941. Ed. Fum-Ko Joon Chin. circ. 8,000. **Document type:** newsletter.

VISUAL. see *ART*

380 020   IT   ISSN 1120-5512
P92.I8
VITA ITALIANA. ISTITUZIONI E COMUNICAZIONE. 1987. q. Presidenza del Consiglio dei Ministri, Dipartimento per l'Informazione e l'Editoria, Via Po, 14, 00198 Rome, Italy. TEL 39-6-85981. FAX 39-6-8553851.
Description: Covers problems in the information sciences and communications field.

384 004.6   II
VOICE & DATA. (Text in English) m. Cyber Media India Ltd., D-74 Panchsheel Enclave, New Delhi 110017, India. TEL 91-11-6433-9999. FAX 91-11-6469018. Ed. Ishan Ranjan. adv.: B&W page $473, color page $1008; trim 206 x 276; adv. contact: Shaji George.

384   UK
VOICE PLUS. 1994. 9/yr. free to qualified persons in Europe (non-qualified persons in Europe £76; others £107). Advanstar Communications, Advanstar House, Park West, Sealand Rd., Chester CH1 4RN, England. TEL 44-1244-378888. FAX 44-1244-370512. Ed. Stuart Sharrock; Pub. Fran Waldie. adv.: B&W page £2870, color page £3740; adv. contact: Jane Murphy. tr.lit. (reprint service avail.) **Document type:** trade publication.
Description: Focuses on the business benefits of voice automation and computer telephony.

384 006   US
VOICE TECHNOLOGY & SERVICES NEWS. 1989. bi-w. $497 (foreign $530) (effective 1997). Phillips Business Information, Inc., 1201 Seven Locks Rd., Potomac, MD 20854. TEL 301-424-3338. FAX 301-309-3847. E-mail: pbi@phillips.com. Ed. Mary Crowley. (back issues avail.) **Document type:** newsletter.
●Also available online. Vendor(s): Data-Star, Information Access Co., Knight-Ridder Information, Inc., NewsNet.
—CCC.
Formed by the 1995 merger of: Voice Technology News (ISSN 1045-1498) & Facsimile and Voice Services & Voice Processing Newsletter; Which was formerly: Voice Processing (ISSN 0884-6685)
Description: Publishes news of the voice processing industries, including messaging, response, synthesis and recognition.

301.16   US   ISSN 0734-3116
W U U A NEWSLETTER. 1982. q. World Union for a Universal Alphabet, Box 252, Cincinnati, OH 45201-0252. TEL 513-574-7638. Ed. Fred A. Sowder. adv.; bk.rev.; illus.; circ. 650 (controlled). (looseleaf format; back issues avail.) **Document type:** newsletter.
Description: Discusses the nature of the alphabet and the mode of its replacement, and alphabetic vs. post-alphabetic society. Includes news on telecommunications development.

380   US
WASHINGTON TELECOM WEEK. w. $695 (foreign $745) (effective 1997). Inside Washington Publishers, Box 7167, Ben Franklin Sta., Washington, DC 20044-7167. TEL 703-416-8500. FAX 703-416-8543. E-mail: service@iwpnews.com. **Document type:** newsletter.

WEB INFORMANT (PORT WASHINGTON). see *COMPUTERS — Computer Networks*

WEEKLY PLANET. see *COMPUTERS — Cybernetics*

380   AU
WERBUNG AKTUELL - PRINT & PRODUKTION. m. S.360 (foreign S.480). Media Emap Verlag GmbH, Loquaiplatz 12, A-1061 Vienna, Austria. TEL 01-59960-0. FAX 01-5996021. Ed. Birgit Salomon. adv. contact: Bernd Achter. circ. 13,000. **Document type:** trade publication.
Formed by the merger of: Werbung Aktuell & Print & Produktion.

WESTERN JOURNAL OF COMMUNICATION. see *LINGUISTICS*

380 330   UK   ISSN 0952-7001
WHAT'S NEW IN BUSINESS INFORMATION. 1987. 20/yr. £235($435) (effective 1997). Headland Business Information (Subsidiary of: Bowker-Saur), Customer Services Department, Maypole House, Maypole Rd., E. Grinstead, W. Sussex RH19 1HU, England. TEL 44-1342-330-100. FAX 44-1342-330-191. E-mail: custserv@bowker-saur.co.uk. (Subscr. to: World Wide Subscription Services Unit 4, Gibbs Reed Farm, Ticehurst, E. Sussex TN5 7HE, England) **Document type:** newsletter.
Description: Discusses new products, important reference works, online files, and information technology. Covers news affecting producers, distributors, and users of business information and alerts readers to important articles they may have missed.

621.38   AT
WHAT'S NEW IN COMMUNICATIONS. 1992. m. Aus.$60. Westwick-Farrow Pty. Ltd., Crn. Fox Valley Rd. and Kogle St., Wahroonga. N.S.W. 2076, Australia. TEL 61-2-94872700. FAX 61-2-94891265. Ed. Mike Smyth. adv. contact: Matthew Perkins. circ. 7,200 (controlled). (back issues avail.) **Document type:** trade publication.
Formed by the 1997 merger of: What's New in Telecommunications (ISSN 1038-1511) & What's New in Data Communications (ISSN 1038-152X)
Description: Provides new product information for communication engineers and communications management.

384.5   US   ISSN 1067-0793
WHAT'S ON SATELLITE. 1993. 3/yr. $125. Design Publishers, 800 Siesta Way, Sonoma, CA 95476-4413. TEL 707-939-9306. E-mail: design@satnews.com; URL: http://www.satnews.com. Ed. Silvano Payne; Pub. S. Payne. adv.; circ. 1,000 (paid). (back issues avail.) **Document type:** directory.
●Also available online.
Also available on CD-ROM.

380   US
WHO'S WHO IN THE MEDIA AND COMMUNICATIONS. 1997. biennial. $259.95. Marquis Who's Who, A Division of Reed Elsevier Inc., 121 Chanlon Rd., New Providence, NJ 07974. TEL 908-464-6800. FAX 908-665-6688. E-mail: info@reedref.com; URL http://www.reedref.com. (Subscr. to: Order Dept., Box 31, New Providence, NJ 07974-9903, TEL 800-521-8110) Ed. Lisa Weissbard.
Description: Contains biographies of people in the field of media and communications.

620   US   ISSN 0898-9850
TS270.A1   CODEN: WTINEI
WIRE TECHNOLOGY INTERNATIONAL. 1973. bi-m. $35 (foreign $70) (effective 1997). Initial Publications Inc., 3869 Darrow Rd., Ste. 109, Stow, OH 44224. TEL 216-686-9544. FAX 216-686-9563. E-mail: 104251.426@compuserve.com. Ed. Michael J. McNulty; Pub. John L. Jones. adv.; illus. circ. 10,000. **Indexed:** Alloys Ind., Eng.Mat.Abstr., INSPEC (1987-), Met.Abstr.Ind., Met.Abstr., Nonfer.Met.Alert, PCC Alert, Steels Alert, World Alum.Abstr. **Document type:** trade publication.
—BLDSC (9323.557000); AskIEEE; CISTI; KR SourceOne; Linda Hall. **CCC.**
Formerly: Wire Technology Newsletter (ISSN 0745-7510)

384   NE   ISSN 1383-4231
WIRELESS COMMUNICATION C D - R O M. irreg. 361 SFr. (effective 1998). Baltzer Science Publishers B.V., P.O. Box 221, 1400 AE Bussum, Netherlands. TEL 31-20-6370061. FAX 31-20-6323651. E-mail: subscribe@baltzer.nl URL: http://www.baltzer.nl. **Document type:** trade publication.
●Available only on CD-ROM.

WIRELESS DATA NEWS. see *COMPUTERS — Data Communications And Data Transmission Systems*

381   US   ISSN 1080-5249
TK6570.M6
WIRELESS: FOR THE CORPORATE USER. (Supplement avail.: Buyer's Guide) 1992. 10/yr. (plus update). $30 canada and Mexico $36; elsewhere $66 (free to qualified personnel). Wireless Publishing Co. (Subsidiary of: Probe Research, Inc.), 3 Wing Dr., Ste. 240, Cedar Knolls, NJ 07927. TEL 973-285-1500; 800-915-0999. FAX 973-285-1519. E-mail: dmkeller@aol.com. Pubs. Victor Schnee, Jack Killion. adv.: B&W page $4700, color page $5500; trim 8 3/8 x 10 7/8. charts; illus.; tr.lit.; circ. 9,000. circ. 34,000 (controlled). **Document type:** trade publication.
—KR SourceOne.
Description: Provides a comprehensive update on new and emerging wireless data and voice communications technologies and firms. Showcase new products and services.

384   US
WIRELESS INTEGRATION. m. $30 (Canada & Mexico $35; elsewhere $55) (effective 1997). PennWell Publishing Co., Box 1260, Tulsa, OK 74101. TEL 918-835-3161. FAX 918-832-9295. E-mail: subagent@pennwell.com.

COMMUNICATIONS

621.38 — US
WIRELESS LOCAL LOOP NEWSLETTER. 1991. m. $595 (foreign $645) (effective 1997). Information Gatekeepers, Inc., 214 Harvard Ave., Boston, MA 02134. TEL 617-232-3111; 800-323-1088. FAX 617-734-8562. E-mail: igiboston@aol.com; URL: http://www.igigroup.com. Ed. Paul Polishuk. **Document type:** newsletter.
Former titles: Spectrum Management Telecommunications & Wireless - Spectrum Management (ISSN 1058-6709)
Description: Covers radio spectrum management, regulatory developments, technology, applications, standards, worldwide developments, and spectrum auction and sale.

621.38 — US
WIRELESS MESSAGING REPORT. bi-w. $579 (outside N. America $715). Telecommunications Reports (Subsidiary of: Business Research Publications, Inc.), 1333 H St., N.W., Ste. 100-E, Washington, DC 20005. TEL 800-822-6338. FAX 202-842-3023. E-mail: customerservice@tr.com; URL: http://www.tr.com. R&P contact: Ellen Hartman. **Document type:** newsletter.

384 — NE — ISSN 1022-0038
TK5103.2 — CODEN: WINEF8
▼**WIRELESS NETWORKS**; the journal of mobile communication, computation and information. (Text in English) 1995. 6/yr. 395 SFr. (effective 1998). Baltzer Science Publishers B.V., P.O. Box 221, 1400 AE Bussum, Netherlands. TEL 31-20-6370061. FAX 31-20-6323651. E-mail: subscribe@baltzer.nl; URL: http://www.baltzer.nl. (Subscr. in N. America to: Baltzer Science Publishers, Box 8577, Red Bank, NJ 07701-8577) (Co-publisher: Association for Computing Machinery, US) Ed. Imrich Chlamtac. (back issues avail.) **Indexed:** INSPEC. **Document type:** academic/scholarly publication.
—BLDSC (9324.550000); AskIEEE; CISTI; KR SourceOne; SWETS. **CCC.**
Description: Publishes original articles addressing networks, systems, algorithms, and applications that support the symbiosis of portable computers, wireless networks, mobile communication and computation, and their integration into the global network of the future.

621.38 — US
WIRELESS SATELLITE AND BROADCASTING TELECOMMUNICATIONS. 1991. m. $595 (foreign $645) (effective 1997). Information Gatekeepers, Inc., 214 Harvard Ave., Boston, MA 02134. TEL 617-232-3111; 800-323-1088. FAX 617-734-8562. E-mail: igiboston@aol.com; URL: http://www.igigroup.com. Ed. Paul Polishuk. **Document type:** newsletter.
Former titles: Satellite and Broadcasting Telecommunications & Wireless - Satellite and Broadcasting (ISSN 1058-6695)
Description: Covers wireless applications for broadcasting, satellites, new technology, markets, regulations, products, standards, and business developments.

384 — CN — ISSN 1201-8538
WIRELESS TELECOM. 1968. q. Can.$40($50) to non-members. 275 Slater St., Ste. 2004, Ottawa, ON K1P 5H9, Canada. TEL 613-233-4888. FAX 613-233-2032. E-mail: chopwood@cwta.ca. Ed. Marc Choma. R&P contact: Marc Choma. adv. contact: Doug Seip. bk.rev. circ. 8,500. **Document type:** trade publication.
Former titles: Radiocomm Magazine (ISSN 1196-0809); Radiocomm in Canada (ISSN 0845-4531)
Description: Features articles on technology, market issues, industry news and events, new products, and the activities of government and regulatory agencies. Distributed to licensed radio common carriers in Canada, suppliers to the industry, governments, and regulatory agencies.
Refereed Serial

621.38 — US — ISSN 1057-5391
WIRELESS TELECOMMUNICATION. 1991. m. $595 (foreign $645) (effective 1997). Information Gatekeepers, Inc., 214 Harvard Ave., Boston, MA 02134. TEL 617-232-3111; 800-323-1088. FAX 617-734-8562. E-mail: igiboston@aol.com; URL: http://www.igigroup.com. Ed. Paul Polishuk. **Document type:** newsletter.
Description: Covers wireless applications such as LANs, building and point-of-sale technology, markets, standards, regulatory developments, and business developments.

384 — US — ISSN 1085-0473
▼**WIRELESS WEEK.** 1995. w. Chilton Publications, 825 Seventh Ave., 6th Fl., New York, NY 10019. TEL 212-887-8400.

WOMEN'S STUDIES IN COMMUNICATION. see *WOMEN'S STUDIES*

301.16 — II — ISSN 0043-7948
WORD. (Text in English) 1963. a. Rs.30. Bharatiya Vidya Bhavan, Kulapati K.M. Munshi Marg, Bombay 400007, India. Ed. G.S. Pohekar. adv.; bk.rev. circ. 1,000. **Indexed:** Curr.Cont.; Mid.East: Abstr.& Ind.

330 — US
WORKING COMMUNICATOR. 1981. m. $107. Ragan Communications, 212 W. Superior St., Ste. 200, Chicago, IL 60610-3533. TEL 800-878-5331. FAX 312-335-9583. E-mail: 102262.2730@compuserve.com. Ed. John Cowan. bk.rev. circ. 7,000. **Document type:** newsletter.
Former titles: Bottom Line Communicator; Business Writer.
Description: Provides advice on writing, speaking and editing better for those involved in organizational communications.

301.16 — US — ISSN 0882-4088
WORLD COMMUNICATION. 1984. s-a. World Communication Association, Ohio University, Athens, OH 45701. Ed. Don Stacks. circ. 1,500. (back issues avail.) **Document type:** newsletter.
—UnCover.
Formerly: Communication.
Description: Articles related to the study of human communication.

380 — UN — ISSN 1014-871X
P88.8
WORLD MEDIA HANDBOOK. 1990. a. United Nations Department of Public Information, Programme Evaluation and Communications Research Unit, Room 1072, New York, NY 10017. FAX 212-963-4361.
Description: Provides a summary of selected media and related data covering countries around the world.

384 004.16 — GR
▼**THE WORLD OF INTERNET.** (Text in Greek) 1995. m. Dr.15000 in Europe; Dr.17000U.S. (effective 1996). Compupress S.A., 44 Syngrou, 117 42 Athens, Greece. TEL 30-1-9238-672. FAX 30-1-9216-847. Ed. George Saklabanakis; Pub. N.O. Manousos. adv. contact: V. Giakamozis. circ. 12,000 (paid). **Document type:** consumer publication.
Description: Covers the Internet and the World Wide Web.

380 — UK
WORLD SATELLITE SERVICING (YEAR). a. U-View, 4 South Parade, Bawtry, Doncaster, S. Yorks DN10 6JH, England. TEL 01302-719997. FAX 01302-719995. Ed. Colin Barlow; Pub. Roger Yaxley. **Document type:** trade publication.
Formerly: Satellite Servicing.

621.38 — US
WORLDWIDE REPORT: TELECOMMUNICATIONS. irreg. (approx. 30/yr.) $7 per no. (foreign $14 per no.). U.S. Joint Publications Research Service, Box 12507, Arlington, VA 22209. TEL 703-487-4630. (Orders to: NTIS, Springfield, VA 22161)
Former titles: Worldwide Report: Telecommunications Policy. Research and Development; Telecommunications Policy. Research and Development.

301.16 807 — US — ISSN 0741-0883
P211
WRITTEN COMMUNICATION; a quarterly journal of research, theory, and application. 1984. q. $200 to institutions (effective Sep. 1996). Sage Publications, Inc., 2455 Teller Rd., Thousand Oaks, CA 91320. TEL 805-499-0721. FAX 805-499-0871. E-mail: libraries@sagepub.com; URL: http://www.sagepub.com. (Overseas subscr. to: Sage Publications Ltd., 6 Bonhill St., London EC2A 4PU, England; Sage Publications, India Pvt. Ltd., P.O. Box 4215, New Delhi 110 048 India) Eds. Deborah Brandt, Stephen P. Witte, Martin Nystrand. adv. contact: Margaret Travers. circ. 1,350. (back issues avail.; reprint service avail.) **Indexed:** Arts & Hum.Cit.Ind., ASCA, Bibl.Ling., C.I.J.E., Curr.Cont., Hum.Ind., Lang.& Lang.Behav.Abstr., Ling.Abstr., Sage Fam.Stud.Abstr., SSCI. **Document type:** academic/scholarly publication.
—BLDSC (9364.797000); Genuine Article; KR SourceOne; SWETS; UMI; UnCover. **CCC.**
Description: Provides a forum for ideas, theoretical viewpoints, and methodological approaches that better define and further develop thought and practice in the study of the written word.

621.38 — CC — ISSN 1001-2362
XINXI XITONG GONGCHENG/INFORMATION SYSTEM ENGINEERING. (Text in Chinese) 1988. q. $20. Guojia Xinxi Zhongxin - State Information Center, 39 Youyi Lu, Hexi Qu, Tianjin 300201, People's Republic of China. TEL 354273. FAX 344270. Ed. Zhou Hongren. adv.: B&W page $3,500.

302.2 808.5 — CC — ISSN 1006-4699
YANJIANG YU KOUCAI/SPEECH AND ELOQUENCE. (Text in Chinese) 1983. m. Y2.80 per no. Jilin Shifan Xueyuan, 3 Huangshan Lu, Jilin Dajie, Jilin, Jilin 132011, People's Republic of China. TEL 86-432-4661708. FAX 86-432-4666410. (Dist. overseas by: China International Book Trading Corp., P.O. Box 399, Beijing 100044, P.R. China) Ed. Shouyi Shao. R&P contact: Shouyi Shao. TEL 4666410. adv. contact: Shouyi Shao. circ. 1,050,000. pp./issue: 48.
Description: Aims to enhance people's speaking ability.

384 — UK
YEARBOOK OF EUROPEAN TELECOMMUNICATIONS. Variant title: Y E T: The Yearbook of European Telecommunications. a. £202 (outside Europe £211.50); with Communications Markets in Eastern Europe £365 (outside Europe £384). (Communications and Information Technology Ltd.) C I T Publications, 3 Colleton Cresc., Exeter, Devon EX2 4DG, England. TEL 01392-493444. FAX 01392-493626. E-mail: talk2us@cit.pubs.zynet.co.uk. Ed. Bettina Altemueller. charts. **Document type:** directory.
Description: Lists and profiles Western European telecommunicatons firms and the markets of the countries in which they operate.

301.16 — JA — ISSN 0289-551X
THE YOKE. (Text in English) 1983. bi-m. free. Yokohama Association for International Communications and Exchanges, Sangyo Boeki Center Bldg., 2 Yamashita-cho, Naka-ku, Yokohama 231, Japan. FAX 045-671-7187. TELEX 3822844-GREEN-J. Ed. Isao Tonooka. circ. 2,500. (back issues avail.) **Document type:** newsletter.
Description: Provides communication information about Japan and the city of Yokohama.

384 — JA — ISSN 0914-7721
YUSEISHO TSUSHIN SOGO KENKYUJO NYUSU/JAPAN. MINISTRY OF POSTS AND TELECOMMUNICATIONS. COMMUNICATIONS RESEARCH LABORATORY. NEWS. Key Title: C R L Nyusu. (Text in Japanese) 1976. m. Yuseisho, Tsushin Sogo Kenkyujo, 2-1, Nukui Kita-machi 4-chome, Koganei-shi, Tokyo 184, Japan. **Document type:** government publication.

ZEITSCHRIFT FUER SEMIOTIK. see *PHILOSOPHY*

COMMUNICATIONS — ABSTRACTING, BIBLIOGRAPHIES, STATISTICS

621.38 380.5 CC ISSN 1002-8617
ZHONGGUO JIAOTONG NIANJIAN/CHINA COMMUNICATIONS AND TRANSPORTATION YEARBOOK. (Text in Chinese) 1986. a. $120 (effective 1997). Zhongguo Jiaotong Yunshu Xiehui - China Communications and Transportation Association, 23 Shijin Huayuan Hutong, Dongsi, Beijing 100007, People's Republic of China. TEL 86-10-6401-4601. FAX 86-10-6405-3979. TELEX SPC CN 22552. Ed. J.T. Liu. adv.: page $1200. bk.rev. circ. 15,000. **Document type:** directory.
  Description: Covers the management and development of China's communication and transportation industries, including railroads, roads and traffic, air transportation, automobiles, ships and shipping, postal affairs, telecommunications, pipline transportation, and national defense transportation. Also contains related authoritative transportation statistics.

380 JA
ZUSETSU TSUSHIN HAKUSHO/ILLUSTRATED REPORT OF COMMUNICATIONS. (Text in Japanese) a. 850 Yen. (Yuseisho, Daijin Kanbo - Ministry of Posts and Telecommunications, Minister's Secretariat) Daiichi Hoki Shuppan - Dai-ichi Hoki Publishing Co., Ltd., 11-17, Minamiaoyama 2-chome, Minato-ku, Tokyo 107, Japan. **Document type:** government publication.

9-1-1 MAGAZINE. see *CRIMINOLOGY AND LAW ENFORCEMENT*

380 AG ISSN 0328-8323
P92.A6
60 X 60 - NOTICIAS DE MEDIOS Y COMUNICACION. 1990. m. $25 (America $40; elsewhere $50). Consigna - Comunicacion y Producciones Graficas, Cachimayo 11, 13o E, 1424 Buenos Aires C.F., Argentina. TEL 54-1-4326147. E-mail: consigna@fsoc.uba.ar. Dirs. Lorena Sanchez, Fernando Gigena. adv.: B&W page Arg.$1250; 250 x 370. circ. 20,000. **Document type:** newsletter.
  Supersedes (in 1996): Consignas - Medios y Comunicacion (ISSN 0327-5809); Formerly: Consignas de la Nueva Caledonia.
  Description: Contains national and international news about communication, media, advertising and culture.

2600; the quarterly journal of the American hacker. see *COMPUTERS — Computer Industry*

COMMUNICATIONS — Abstracting, Bibliographies, Statistics

016.3845 US ISSN 0891-8775
PN4888.T4
A B C NEWS INDEX. 1986. q. (with a. cumulation). $243.80. Primary Source Media, 12 Lunar Dr., Drawer AB, Woodbridge, CT 06525. TEL 203-397-2600; 800-444-0799. FAX 203-397-3893. (also avail. in microfiche from RPI; back issues avail.) **Document type:** abstracting/indexing.
  Description: Index to transcripts of ABC-TV news programs available in microfiche.

384.5 SA
A M P S RADIO DIARY. (All Media and Product Survey) (In 3 vols.) (Text in Afrikaans, English) 1976. a. R.1990 (effective 1996). S A Advertising Research Foundation, P.O. Box 98874, 2152 Sloane Park, South Africa. TEL 27-11-463-5340. FAX 27-11-463-5010. Ed. Mike Gorton. charts; stat. Indexed: Rel.& Theol.Abstr.
  ●Also available online.
  Supersedes: A M P S White - Colored - Asian Radio Diary & A M P S Black Radio and Television Diary; Which superseded in part: A M P S Broadcast Media; Formerly: Listening Index (ISSN 0047-4762)
  Description: Contains information on radio listening by South Africans.

A P T S PROJECT SUMMARIES. (Advanced Public Transportation Systems) see *TRANSPORTATION — Abstracting, Bibliographies, Statistics*

384.54 US
AMATEUR MASTER FILE. (Supplement avail.) s-a. $95 per issue in US, Canada, Mexico; elsewhere $190. (Federal Communications Commission) U.S. National Technical Information Service, 5825 Port Royal Rd., Springfield, VA 22161. TEL 703-487-4630. (microfiche)
  Description: Includes cross-reference by name, city and state as well as call sign sequences.

384.54 US
AMATEUR RADIO SERVICE MASTER FILE UPDATES. m. $290 per no. U.S., Canada, Mexico; elsewhere $580. (Federal Communications Commission) U.S. National Technical Information Service, 5825 Port Royal Rd., Springfield, VA 22161. TEL 703-487-4630. (magnetic tape)
  Description: Contains only additions and changes to the master file, not the master file itself. Limited to only those requiring a new license to be issued (approximately 95 per cent of the changes).

384.5 US ISSN 0738-8675
HE8698
AMERICAN RADIO. 1976. q. $350. Duncan's American Radio, Box 8446, Cincinnati, OH 45208-0446. TEL 513-731-1800. Ed. James H. Duncan, Jr. circ. 4,000. (also avail. in microfiche from CIS) **Document type:** directory.

384.54 US
ANTENNA SURVEY SYSTEM TOWER FILE REPORT. bi-m. $21.50 per no. in U.S., Canada, Mexico (elsewhere $43). (Federal Communications Commission) U.S. National Technical Information Service, 5825 Port Royal Rd., Springfield, VA 22161. TEL 703-487-4630. (microfiche) **Document type:** government publication.
  Description: Contains the following tower location data: latitude, longitude, height above ground and sea level, address, and FCC file and docket numbers, including painting and lighting specifications.

384.54 US
ANTENNA SURVEY TOWER FILE. q. $5900 per no. in U.S., Canada, Mexico (elsewhere $1180). (Federal Communications Commission) U.S. National Technical Information Service, 5825 Port Royal Rd., Springfield, VA 22161. TEL 703-487-4630. (magnetic tape) **Document type:** government publication.
  Description: Contains data on all towers requiring FCC or FAA clearance.

384.54 US
AVIATION MASTER FILE. q. $20 per no. in U.S., Canada, Mexico; elsewhere $40. (Federal Communications Commission) U.S. National Technical Information Service, 5825 Port Royal Rd., Springfield, VA 22161. TEL 703-487-4630.
  Description: Contains radio license data of aircraft records in FAA number sequence. Cross reference indexes are also included by fleet and name licensees.

BEIKOKU TOKKYO SHOROKU. DENSHI, TSUSHIN HEN/U.S. PATENT ABSTRACTS. ELECTRONICS, COMMUNICATIONS. see *PATENTS, TRADEMARKS AND COPYRIGHTS — Abstracting, Bibliographies, Statistics*

384.5 011 US ISSN 0742-4914
BIBLIOGRAPHY ON CABLE TELEVISION. Cover title: B C T V. 1975. a. $40 (effective 1996). Communications Institute, Communications Library, Lockbox 472139, Marina Station, San Francisco, CA 94147-2139. TEL 415-626-5050. Ed. T.S. Connelly. R&P contact: T.S. Connelly. index, cum.index: 1975-1992. (back issues avail.) **Document type:** bibliography, directory.
  Description: Open-ended, non-cumulative bibliography on access, advertising and marketing, audience and subscribers, programming, finance, law, technology and other issues of cable television.

332.6 384.55 US ISSN 0749-2936
BROADCAST STATS. 1984. m. $625 (effective 1997). Paul Kagan Associates, Inc., 126 Clock Tower Place, Carmel, CA 93923. TEL 408-625-3225. Ed. Paul Kagan.

621.3 IT ISSN 0391-5379
C S E L T INFOTEL; periodico d'informazione bibliografica nelle telecomunicazioni e scienze connesse. (Text in English, Italian) 1970. m. exchange basis. C S E L T - Centro Studi e Laboratori Telecomunicazioni S.p.A., Via Reiss Romoli, 274, 10148 Turin, Italy. TEL 39-11-2285111. FAX 39-11-2285095. TELEX 220539. URL: http://www.cselt.stet.it. Ed. Marco Melloni. **Document type:** abstracting/indexing.
  ●Also available online.

384.54 US
CABLE TV STATION AUTHORIZATION REPORT. q. $25 per no. in U.S., Canada, Mexico; elsewhere $50. (Federal Communications Commission) U.S. National Technical Information Service, 5825 Port Royal Rd., Springfield, VA 22161. TEL 703-487-4630. (microfiche)
  Description: Lists by call letters and locations the cable television stations authorized to broadcast programs.

384.554 US
CABLE TV STATION DISTRIBUTION FILE. s-a. $25 per no. in U.S., Canada, Mexico; elsewhere $40. (Federal Communications Commission) U.S. National Technical Information Service, 5825 Port Royal Rd., Springfield, VA 22161. TEL 703-487-4630. (microfiche)

384 US
CALLSIGN INDEX TO NON-GOVERNMENT MASTER FREQUENCY DATA BASE. (Supplement avail.) a. $25 per no. in U.S., Canada, Mexico; elsewhere $82. (U.S. Federal Communications Commission) U.S. National Technical Information Service, 5825 Port Royal Rd., Springfield, VA 22161. TEL 703-487-4630. (microfiche)

384 CN ISSN 0703-7244
HE8700.7.C6
CANADA. STATISTICS CANADA. CABLE TELEVISION/TELEDISTRIBUTION. (Text in English and French) 1967. a. Can.$42 (foreign $42) (effective 1998). Statistics Canada, Circulation Management, Jean Talon Bldg., 2-C12, Tunney's Pasture, Ottawa, ON K1A 0T6, Canada. TEL 613-951-7277; 800-267-6677. FAX 613-951-1584. URL: http://www.statcan.ca. (also avail. in microform from MML) **Document type:** government publication.
  Formerly: Canada. Statistics Canada. Community Antenna Television - Services de Television a Antenne Collective (ISSN 0575-8238)
  Description: Financial statistics on the Canadian cable television industry by area and revenue group.

384.097 CN ISSN 0380-0334
HE8861
CANADA. STATISTICS CANADA. COMMUNICATIONS. (Text in English and French) 1971. q. Can.$42 (foreign $42) (effective 1998). Statistics Canada, Operations and Integration Division, Circulation Management, Jean Talon Bldg., 2-C12, Tunney's Pasture, Ottawa, ON K1A 0T6, Canada. TEL 613-951-7277; 800-267-6677. FAX 613-951-1584. URL: http://www.statcan.ca. (also avail. in microform from MML) **Document type:** government publication.
  Description: Summary information on telecommunications, including the telephone industry and other carriers, radio and television broadcasting, cable TV. Includes methodology and data quality.

384.54 CN ISSN 0575-9560
HE8689.9.C3
CANADA. STATISTICS CANADA. RADIO AND TELEVISION BROADCASTING/RADIODIFFUSION ET TELEVISION. (Text in English and French) 1961. a. Can.$42 (foreign $42) (effective 1998). Statistics Canada, Operations and Integration Division, Circulation Management, Jean Talon Bldg., 2-C12, Tunney's Pasture, Ottawa, ON K1A 0T6, Canada. TEL 613-951-7277; 800-267-6677. FAX 613-951-1584. URL: http://www.statcan.ca. (also avail. in microform from MML) **Document type:** government publication.
  Formerly: Canada. Statistics Canada. Radio and Television Broadcasting Statistics (ISSN 0833-6784)
  Description: Presents detailed financial statistics on the Canadian radio and television industry by province and by revenue group, operational data on the privately owned radio and television industry and the C B C.

COMMUNICATIONS — ABSTRACTING, BIBLIOGRAPHIES, STATISTICS

384.6 CN ISSN 0707-9753
CANADA. STATISTICS CANADA. TELEPHONE STATISTICS/STATISTIQUE DU TELEPHONE. (Text in English and French) 1977. m. Can.$93 (foreign $93) (effective 1998). Statistics Canada, Operations and Integration Division, Circulation Management, Jean Talon Bldg., 2-C12, Tunney's Pasture, Ottawa, ON K1A 0T6, Canada. TEL 613-951-7277; 800-267-6677. FAX 613-951-1584. URL: http://www.statcan.ca. **Document type:** government publication.
Description: Presents monthly and year-to-date data aggregated from reports of 13 major telephone systems along with comparisons to data from the previous year.

384 UN
CATALOGUE OF I T U PUBLICATIONS. (Editions in English, French, Spanish) s-a. free. International Telecommunication Union, Place des Nations, CH-1211 Geneva 20, Switzerland. TEL 41-22-7306141. FAX 41-22-7305194. E-mail: sales@itu.ch; URL: http://www.itu.ch. **Document type:** catalog.
● Also available online.

CHILE. INSTITUTO NACIONAL DE ESTADISTICAS. ANUARIO DE TRANSPORTE Y COMUNICACIONES. see TRANSPORTATION — Abstracting, Bibliographies, Statistics

301.16 CL
CHILE. INSTITUTO NACIONAL DE ESTADISTICAS. CULTURA Y MEDIOS DE COMUNICACION. 1984. a. Ch.$1800 (US $12.50; elsewhere $14.90) (effective 1995). Instituto Nacional de Estadisticas, Av. Bulnes 418, Casilla 498, Correo 3 Santiago, Chile. TEL 56-2-6991441. FAX 56-2-6712169.

CHILE. INSTITUTO NACIONAL DE ESTADISTICAS. TRANSPORTE, COMUNICACIONES, TURISMO. see TRANSPORTATION — Abstracting, Bibliographies, Statistics

COLOMBIA. DEPARTAMENTO ADMINISTRATIVO NACIONAL DE ESTADISTICA. ANUARIO GENERAL DE ESTADISTICA - TRANSPORTES Y COMUNICACIONES. see TRANSPORTATION — Abstracting, Bibliographies, Statistics

384.54 US
COMMERCIAL MASTER FILE: RESTRICTED. s-a. $25 per no. in U.S., Canada, Mexico; elsewhere $137. (Federal Communications Commission) U.S. National Technical Information Service, 5825 Port Royal Rd., Springfield, VA 22161. TEL 703-487-4630. (microfiche)
Description: Documents listings of commercial and restricted operator licensees in operator name sequence. A cross-reference of commercial operators by serial number is also included. File only covers last seven years.

384.54 US
COMMERCIAL MASTER FILE SUPPLEMENT: RESTRICTED. m. $25 per no. in U.S., Canada, Mexico; elsewhere $40. (Federal Communications Commission) U.S. National Technical Information Service, 5825 Port Royal Rd., Springfield, VA 22161. TEL 703-487-4630. (microfiche)
Description: Documents additions and other changes made to records of commercial operators and restricted operator licensees since the release of the last Master File.

384.54 US
COMMON CARRIER INDIVIDUAL LAND MOBILE DATA BASE NAME SEQUENCE. m. $20 per issue in US, Canada, Mexico; elsewhere $40. (Federal Communications Commission, Board of Governors) U.S. National Technical Information Service, 5825 Port Royal Rd., Springfield, VA 22161. TEL 703-487-4630. (microfiche)
Description: Consists of various statistical and identifying data of common carrier individual land mobile subscriber records, in licensee name sequence.

384.54 US
COMMON CARRIER LAND MOBILE BASE STATION CUMULATIVE STAFF STUDY. m. price varies. (Federal Communications Commission, Common Carrier Bureau) U.S. National Technical Information Service, 5825 Port Royal Rd., Springfield, VA 22161. TEL 703-487-4630. (magnetic tape; diskette format)
Description: Covers weekly reports which discuss: frequency, longitude and latitude, state, applicant name, call sign, received and public notice date, file number and application type.

384.54 US
COMMON CARRIER LAND MOBILE BASE STATION CUMULATIVE STAFF STUDY LISTING. w. $20 per issue in US, Canada, Mexico; elsewhere $40. (Federal Communications Commission, Common Carrier Bureau) U.S. National Technical Information Service, 5825 Port Royal Rd., Springfield, VA 22161. TEL 703-487-4630. (microfiche)
Description: Lists base stations from the data base listed by frequency, longitude and latitude.

384.54 US
COMMON CARRIER LAND MOBILE BASE STATIONS DATA BASE (SUPPLIERS). m. $48 per issue in US, Canada, Mexico; elsewhere $96. (Federal Communications Commission, Common Carrier Bureau) U.S. National Technical Information Service, 5825 Port Royal Rd., Springfield, VA 22161. TEL 703-487-4630. (microfiche)
Description: Lists all telephone companies in the system that provide service to individual consumers. Includes various identifying information.

384.54 US
COMMON CARRIER MICROWAVE ANTENNA, LICENSEE, AND TRANSMITTER FILE. m. $350 per no. in U.S., Canada, Mexico; elsewhere $720. (Federal Communications Commission, Common Carrier Bureau) U.S. National Technical Information Service, 5825 Port Royal Rd., Springfield, VA 22161. TEL 703-487-4630. (magnetic tape)
Description: Contains identification and operating characteristics of acceptable transmitter types, and of antennae used at CCM stations. Includes names and addresses of licensees.

384.54 US
COMMON CARRIER MICROWAVE AUTHORIZATION FILE (LICENSEES). bi-m. $31.50 per no. in U.S., Canada, Mexico; elsewhere $63. (Federal Communications Commission, Common Carrier Bureau) U.S. National Technical Information Service, 5825 Port Royal Rd., Springfield, VA 22161. TEL 703-487-4630. (microfiche)
Description: Features authorization data such as licensee name, address, transmitter, receiver, path link and antenna information in state, country latitude and longitude sequence.

384.54 US
COMMON CARRIER MICROWAVE CONSTRUCTION PERMIT FILE. bi-m. $25 per no. in U.S., Canada, Mexico; elsewhere $40. (Federal Communications Commission, Common Carrier Bureau) U.S. National Technical Information Service, 5825 Port Royal Rd., Springfield, VA 22161. TEL 703-487-4630. index. (microfiche)
Description: Contains various common carrier microwave construction permit data.

384.54 US
COMMON CARRIER MICROWAVE DATA BASE. q. $820 per no. in U.S., Canada, Mexico; elsewhere $1640. (Federal Communications Commission, Common Carrier Bureau) U.S. National Technical Information Service, 5825 Port Royal Rd., Springfield, VA 22161. TEL 703-487-4630. (magnetic tape)
Description: Consists of station and antenna location and signal path information as well as technical operating characteristics of microwave radio stations licensed by the bureau.

384.54 US
COMMON CARRIER MICROWAVE PENDING APPLICATION DUMP. bi-m. $25 per no. in U.S., Canada, Mexico; elsewhere $40. (Federal Communications Commission, Common Carrier Bureau) U.S. National Technical Information Service, 5825 Port Royal Rd., Springfield, VA 22161. TEL 703-487-4630. (microfiche)
Description: Presents copies of pending application records not used in the production of the common carriers construction permit authorizations.

016 US ISSN 0162-2811
P87
COMMUNICATION ABSTRACTS. 1978. bi-m. $498 to institutions (effective Sep. 1996). Sage Publications, Inc., 2455 Teller Rd., Thousand Oaks, CA 91320. TEL 805-499-0721. FAX 805-499-0871. E-mail: libraries@sagepub.com; URL: http://www.sagepub.com. (Overseas subscr. to: Sage Publications Ltd., 6 Bonhill St., London EC2A 4PU, England; Sage Publications India Pvt. Ltd., P.O. Box 4215, New Delhi 110 048, India) Ed. Thomas F. Gordon. adv. contact: Margaret Travers. abstr.; bibl.; index. circ. 1,200. (back issues avail.; reprint service avail.) **Document type:** abstracting/indexing.
— BLDSC (3359.130000); UMI. **CCC**.
Description: Covers recent literature in all areas of communication studies, both mass and interpersonal. Includes expanded coverage of new communications technologies.

384.5 US ISSN 0748-657X
COMMUNICATION BOOKNOTES; recent titles in telecommunications, information & media. 1969. bi-m. $45 to individuals (foreign $50); institutions $95 (foreign $100). (Center for Advanced Study in Telecommunications) Christopher H. Sterling, Ed. & Pub., 5507 Airlie Way, Annandale, VA 22003. TEL 202-994-6211. FAX 703-255-5119. E-mail: cbooknotes@aol.com; URL: http://members.aol.com/cbooknotes/index.html. bk.rev.; abstr.; bibl.; index. circ. 700. (back issues avail.) **Document type:** bibliography.
Former titles: Mass Media Booknotes; Mass Media Publications Reporting Service; Which supersedes: Broadcasting Bibliophile's Booknotes (ISSN 0045-3188)

621.38 US ISSN 1041-7893
Z5632
COMMUNICATION SERIALS; an international guide to periodicals in communication, popular culture and the performing arts. 1992. biennial. $135. SovaComm, Inc., Box 64697, Virginia Beach, VA 23467-4697. TEL 804-420-0840. FAX 804-420-3564. Ed. Harry Sova. **Document type:** bibliography.
Description: Contains over 2,700 fully annotated publication titles in 40 areas of communication, popular culture, and the performing arts from 24 nations.

384.54 US
COMMUNITY UNIT CABLE: FULL RECORD. biennial. $51 per no. in U.S., Canada, Mexico; elsewhere $102. (Federal Communications Commission) U.S. National Technical Information Service, 5825 Port Royal Rd., Springfield, VA 22161. TEL 703-487-4630. (microfiche)
Description: Lists data on cable communities. Includes entrepreneurial, franchise, address statistics, and signal authorization information.

301.16 US ISSN 0732-4456
CONTRIBUTIONS TO THE STUDY OF MASS MEDIA AND COMMUNICATIONS. 1983. irreg. price varies. Greenwood Press, Inc. (Subsidiary of: Greenwood Publishing Group Inc.), 88 Post Rd. W., Box 5007, Westport, CT 06881-5007. TEL 203-226-3571. FAX 203-222-1502. bibl.; index.
— BLDSC (3461.454050).

384 383.4 PO
CORREIOS E TELECOMUNICACOES DE PORTUGAL. ANUARIO ESTATISTICO.* 1975. a. Correios e Telecomunicacoes de Portugal, Servico de Impressos e Publicacoes, Av. Casal Ribeiro, 28-1, 1000 Lisbon, Portugal. illus. circ. 1,000.

DENMARK. STATENS FILMCENTRAL. STATISTIK OVER UDLEJNING AF 16 MM FILM OG VIDEO OG OVERSIGT OVER 16 MM FILM OG VIDEOKASSETTER I DEPONERING. see MOTION PICTURES — Abstracting, Bibliographies, Statistics

384.54 US
DIRECTIONAL ANTENNA DATA BASE. m. $360 per no. in U.S., Canada, Mexico; elsewhere $720. (U.S. Federal Communications Commission) U.S. National Technical Information Service, 5825 Port Royal Rd., Springfield, VA 22161. TEL 703-487-4630. (magnetic tape)
Description: Includes indication of whether the TV station operates with a directional antenna pattern.

C

COMMUNICATIONS — ABSTRACTING, BIBLIOGRAPHIES, STATISTICS

621.38 016   RU   ISSN 0131-0208
EKSPRESS-INFORMATSIYA. KVANTOVAYA RADIOTEKHNIKA. 1971. 48/yr. 40.60 Rub. Vsesoyuznyi Institut Nauchno-Tekhnicheskoi Informatsii (VINITI), Baltiiskaya ul., 14, Moscow A-219, Russia. (Subscr. to: Mezhdunarodnaya Kniga, Dimitrova ul. 39, 113095 Moscow, Russia)
     Supersedes in part: Ekspress-Informatsiya. Radiotekhnika Sverkhvysokikh Chastot i Kvantovaya Radiotekhnika (ISSN 0013-371X)

384 016   RU   ISSN 0320-1058
EKSPRESS-INFORMATSIYA. PEREDACHA INFORMATSII. 1967. 48/yr. (effective 1996). Vsesoyuznyi Institut Nauchno-Tekhnicheskoi Informatsii (VINITI), Baltiiskaya ul., 14, Moscow A-219, Russia. (Subscr. to: Mezhdunarodnaya Kniga, Dimitrova ul. 39, 110395 Moscow, Russia)

621.38 016   RU   ISSN 0131-0437
EKSPRESS-INFORMATSIYA. RADIOTEKHNIKA SVERKHVYSOKIKH CHASTOT. 1962. 48/yr. 40.60 Rub. ($30) Vsesoyuznyi Institut Nauchno-Tekhnicheskoi Informatsii (VINITI), Baltiiskaya ul., 14, Moscow A-219, Russia. (Subscr. to: Mezhdunarodnaya Kniga, Dimitrova ul. 39, 113095 Moscow, Russia)
     Supersedes in part: Ekspress-Informatsiya. Radiotekhnika Sverkhvysokikh Chastot i Kvantovaya Radiotekhnika (ISSN 0013-371X)

621.38 016   US   ISSN 0361-3313
TK7800   CODEN: ECAJA
ELECTRONICS AND COMMUNICATIONS ABSTRACTS JOURNAL. (Includes annual index) 1967. m. $1045 (foreign $1095). Cambridge Scientific Abstracts, 7200 Wisconsin Ave., 6th Fl., Bethesda, MD 20814. TEL 301-961-6750. FAX 301-961-6720. E-mail: market@csa.com; URL: http://www.csa.com. (Co-publisher: Engineering Information, Inc.) Pub. Ted Caris. adv.; bk.rev.; abstr.; index. (also avail. in magnetic tape; back issues avail.) **Indexed:** Cal.Tiss.Abstr., Chemorec.Abstr., Oncol.Abstr. **Document type:** abstracting/indexing.
   ●Also available online. Vendor(s): STN International (ELCOM).
     —BLDSC (3703.160000); CISTI; Linda Hall.
     Formerly: Electronics Abstracts Journal (ISSN 0013-5097)
     Description: Covers theoretical and applied research in electronic systems, circuits, and devices; surveys all aspects of communications.

384.55 016   HU   ISSN 0231-066X
ELEKTRONIKAI ES HIRADASTECHNIKAI SZAKIRODALMI/ELECTRONICS & COMMUNICATIONS ABSTRACTS. 1974. m. 9900 Ft. Orszagos Muszaki Informacios Kozpont es Konyvtar (O.M.I.K.K.) - National Technical Information Centre and Library, Muzeum u. 17, P.O. Box 12, 1428 Budapest, Hungary. (Subscr. to: Kultura, Box 149, 1389 Budapest, Hungary) Ed. Ottmar Klavida. abstr.; index. circ. 320.
     Supersedes (in 1982): Muszaki Lapszemle. Hiradastechnika - Technical Abstracts. Telecommunication (ISSN 0303-2019)

384.54   US
F M ENGINEERING DATA BASE. m. $360 per no. in U.S., Canada, Mexico; elsewhere $720. (U.S. Federal Communications Commission) U.S. National Technical Information Service, 5825 Port Royal Rd., Springfield, VA 22161. TEL 703-487-4630. (magnetic tape; also avail. in diskette format)
     Description: Presents records for existing and proposed stations, allocations, rulemaking petitions and proposals, as well as translators and boosters.

384.54   US
F M ENGINEERING DATA BASE IN ORDER BY STATE. m. $20 per no. in U.S., Canada, Mexico; elsewhere $40. (Federal Communications Commission) U.S. National Technical Information Service, 5825 Port Royal Rd., Springfield, VA 22161. TEL 703-487-4630. (microfiche)
     Description: Includes vacant assignments, proposed rulemaking, and foreign facilities.

FACSIMILE FACTS AND FIGURES. see *BUSINESS AND ECONOMICS — Abstracting, Bibliographies, Statistics*

GREECE. NATIONAL STATISTICAL SERVICE. TRANSPORT AND COMMUNICATION STATISTICS. see *TRANSPORTATION — Abstracting, Bibliographies, Statistics*

I T S JOURNAL; R&D, operational testing and development of intelligent transportation systems. (Intelligent Transportation Society of America) see *TRANSPORTATION — Abstracting, Bibliographies, Statistics*

384.554   UK   ISSN 0143-5663
HE8700
INTERNATIONAL INDEX TO TELEVISION PERIODICALS. (Printed format ceased with 1990 edition) 1972. irreg. £220 for cumulative service (£40 with subscr. to International FilmArchive CD-ROM). International Federation of Film Archives (F I A F) - Federation Internationale des Archives du Film, 6 Nottingham St., London W1M 3RB, England. TEL 0171-224-1203. FAX 0171-224-0991. Ed. Michael Moulds. (microfiche; back issues avail.) **Document type:** abstracting/indexing.
   ●Also available on CD-ROM.

621.8 016   UN
INTERNATIONAL TELECOMMUNICATION UNION. CENTRAL LIBRARY. LIST OF PERIODICALS/UNION INTERNATIONALE DES TELECOMMUNICATIONS. BIBLIOTHEQUE CENTRALE. LISTE DES PERIODIQUES/UNION INTERNACIONAL DE TELCOMUNICACIONES. BIBLIOTECA CENTRAL. LISTA DE REVISTAS. (Text in English, French, Spanish) 1967. a. International Telecommunication Union, Central Library - Union Internationale des Telecommunications, Place des Nations, CH-1211 Geneva 20, Switzerland. TEL 41-22-7306141. FAX 41-22-7305194. TELEX 421 000 UIT CH. E-mail: sales@itu.ch; URL: http://www.itu.ch. Ed. A.G. el-Zanati. circ. 1,500. **Document type:** bibliography.

621.38 016   UN
INTERNATIONAL TELECOMMUNICATION UNION. CENTRAL LIBRARY. LIST OF RECENT ACQUISITIONS/UNION INTERNATIONALE DES TELECOMMUNICATIONS. BIBLIOTHEQUE CENTRALE. LISTE DES ACQUISITIONS RECENTES/UNION INTERNACIONAL DE TELECOMUNICACIONES. BIBLIOTECA CENTRAL. LISTA DE ADQUISICIONES RECIENTES. (Text in English, French and Spanish) 1972. q. International Telecommunication Union, Place des Nations, CH-1211 Geneva 20, Switzerland. TEL 41-22-7306141. FAX 41-22-7305194. TELEX 421 000 UIT CH. E-mail: sales@itu.ch; URL: http://www.itu.ch. Ed. A.G. el-Zanati. circ. 600. **Document type:** bibliography.

621.38 016   UN
INTERNATIONAL TELECOMMUNICATION UNION. LIST OF ANNUALS/UNION INTERNATIONALE DES TELECOMMUNICATIONS. LISTES DES PUBLICATIONS ANNUELLES/UNION INTERNACIONAL DE TELECOMUNICACIONES. LISTA DE PUBLICACIONES ANUALES. (Text in English, French and Spanish) 1972. a. International Telecommunication Union, Place des Nations, CH-1211 Geneva 20, Switzerland. TEL 41-22-7306141. FAX 41-22-7305194. TELEX 421 000 UIT CH. E-mail: sales@itu.ch; URL: http://www.itu.ch. Ed. A.G. el-Zanati. circ. 1,500. **Document type:** bibliography.

621.382 310   AT   ISSN 1326-6772
INTERNATIONAL TELECOMMUNICATIONS AND SUPERHIGHWAYS MARKETS. a. Aus.$495 (US Aus.$525; Europe Aus.$530) (effective 1998). Paul Budde Communication Pty. Ltd., 2643 George Downes Dr., Australia. TEL 61-7-49988144. FAX 61-7-49988247. E-mail: pbc@budde.com.au; URL: http://www.budde.com.au.
     Description: Provides statistical data on Asian, European and American telecommunications services and equipment markets.

380   IS   ISSN 0075-1308
ISRAEL. MINISTRY OF COMMUNICATIONS. STATISTICS/ISRAEL. MISRAD HA-TIKSHORET. STATISTIKAH. (Editions in English and Hebrew) 1955. a. Ministry of Communications, Jaffa Rd. 23, Jerusalem, Israel. circ. 300. **Document type:** government publication.

621   UK   ISSN 0950-4761
KEY ABSTRACTS - ANTENNAS & PROPAGATION. 1987. m. £120($200) (effective 1997). INSPEC, I.E.E., Michael Faraday House, Six Hills Way, Stevenage, Herts. SG1 2AY, England. TEL 44-1438-313311. FAX 44-1438-742840. TELEX 825578 IEESTV G. E-mail: inspec@iee.org.uk; URL: http://www.iee.org.uk. (Subscr. to: Publication Sales Dept., P.O. Box 96, Stevenage, Herts. SG1 2SD, England; U.S. addr.: INSPEC Dept., IEEE, Operations Center, 445 Hoes Ln., Box 1331, Piscataway, NJ 08855-1331. TEL 908-562-5549. FAX 908-562-8737) index. **Document type:** abstracting/indexing.
     Description: Covers radio links and equipment, radiowave propagation, antenna theory and antennas, radar, and radio navigation.

KEY ABSTRACTS - OPTOELECTRONICS. see *PHYSICS — Abstracting, Bibliographies, Statistics*

621.38 016   UK   ISSN 0950-4877
TK5101.A1
KEY ABSTRACTS - TELECOMMUNICATIONS. 1975. m. £120($200) (effective 1997). INSPEC, I.E.E., Michael Faraday House, Six Hills Way, Stevenage, Herts. SG1 2AY, England. TEL 44-1438-313311. FAX 44-1438-742840. TELEX 825578 IEESTV G. E-mail: inspec@iee.org.uk; URL: http://www.iee.org.uk. (U.S. addr.: INSPEC Dept., IEEE Operations Center, 445 Hoes Ln., Box 1331, Piscataway, NJ 08855-1331. TEL 908-562-5549. FAX 908-562-8737) index. **Document type:** abstracting/indexing.
     Formerly (until 1987): Key Abstracts - Communications Technology (ISSN 0306-5588)
     Description: Covers information theory, modulation, switching theory, applications of telecommunications, stations and equipment, switching centers, transmission line links, and optical communications.

KUWAIT. CENTRAL STATISTICAL OFFICE. ANNUAL STATISTICAL BULLETIN FOR TRANSPORT AND COMMUNICATION/KUWAIT. AL-IDARAH AL-MARKAZIYYAH LIL-IHSA'. AL-NASHRAH AL-IHSA'IYYAH AL-SANAWIYYAH LIL-NAQL WAL-MUWASALAT. see *TRANSPORTATION — Abstracting, Bibliographies, Statistics*

384.54   US
LICENSEE NAME INDEX TO NON-GOVERNMENT MASTER FREQUENCY DATA BASE. q. $25 per no. in U.S., Canada, Mexico; elsewhere $40. (Federal Communications Commission) U.S. National Technical Information Service, 5825 Port Royal Rd., Springfield, VA 22161. TEL 703-487-4630. (microfiche)
     Description: Includes frequency of service and call sign for use in finding detailed information about the station in Master Frequency Data Base.

384.54   US
M A P S DATA BASE. (Mid-Atlantic Preservation Service) 3/yr. $25 per no. in U.S., Canada, Mexico (elsewhere $40). (U.S. Federal Communications Commission, Private Radio Bureau) U.S. National Technical Information Service, 5825 Port Royal Rd., Springfield, VA 22161. TEL 703-487-4630. (microfiche)
     Description: Contains data in call sign sequence and includes name, address, transmitter information as well as data pertaining to the site and frequency path.

384.6   US
MARINE DATA BASE. q. $3000 for 1600 bpi in US, Canada, Mexico; elsewhere $6000. (Federal Communications Commission) U.S. National Technical Information Service, 5825 Port Royal Rd. Springfield, VA 22161. TEL 703-487-4630. (magnetic tape)
     Description: Contains data for applicants and licensees operating under the Marine (Telephone) Radio Service.

384.54   US
MARINE RADIO STATION MASTER FILE. q. $25 per no. in U.S., Canada, Mexico; elsewhere $40. (Federal Communications Commission) U.S. National Technical Information Service, 5825 Port Royal Rd. Springfield, VA 22161. TEL 703-487-4630. (microfiche)
     Description: Data sorted in vessel name sequence. Cross-reference indexes included by name of licensee, call sign, state and city, treasury number.

COMMUNICATIONS — ABSTRACTING, BIBLIOGRAPHIES, STATISTICS

380   SI   ISSN 0217-1287
Z5632
MASS COM PERIODICAL LITERATURE INDEX. s.a. Asian Media Information and Communication Centre, School of Communication Studies Bldg., Nanyang Technological University, Jurong Point Post Office, Box 360, Singapore 916412, Singapore. TEL 65-7927570. FAX 65-7927129. TELEX AMICSI RS 55524. E-mail: amicline@singnet.com.sg. **Document type:** abstracting/indexing.
Description: Provides up-to-date bibliographic information on articles relating to the field of mass communications.

384.54   US
MASTER FREQUENCY DATA BASE (FREQUENCY SEQUENCE). q. $25 per no. in U.S., Canada, Mexico; elsewhere $40. (Federal Communications Commission) U.S. National Technical Information Service, 5825 Port Royal Rd., Springfield, VA 22161. TEL 703-487-4630. (microfiche)
Description: Includes the following files: aviation, broadcast, auxiliary land transportation, public safety, experimental, miscellaneous. Also contains geographical information from the Tower File.

384.54   US
MASTER FREQUENCY DATA BASE (SERVICE GROUP CODE SEQUENCE). q. $25 per no. in U.S., Canada, Mexico; elsewhere $40. (Federal Communications Commission) U.S. National Technical Information Service, 5825 Port Royal Rd., Springfield, VA 22161. TEL 703-487-4630. (microfiche)
Description: Contains the non-government frequency assignments. Includes class, frequency, call sign, power, mobile units as well as other data. Does not include Tower File information.

621.38   GW   ISSN 0935-5936
MEDIA DATEN: RADIO - T V. 7/yr. DM.210. Media Daten Verlag GmbH, Klingenweg 4, 65396 Walluf, Germany. TEL 49-6123-700-0. FAX 49-6123-700122. **Document type:** directory.

384.5   NE
MEDIA NETWORK BOOKLIST; survey of publications international broadcasting. (Text in English) 1980. s-a. free. Stichting Radio Nederland Wereldomroep, English Section, P.O. Box 222, 1200 JG Hilversum, Netherlands. TEL 31-35-6724211. FAX 31-35-6724239. E-mail: letter@rnw.nl. Ed. Jonathan Marks. circ. 40,000. **Document type:** bibliography.
Description: Guide to books about international broadcasting.

MEXICO. CENTRO DE INFORMACION TECNICA Y DOCUMENTACION. INDICE DE REVISTAS. SECCION DE EDUCACION Y COMUNICACION. see *EDUCATION — Abstracting, Bibliographies, Statistics*

384.54   US
MICROWAVE APPLICATIONS. m. $25 per no. in U.S., Canada, Mexico; elsewhere $50. (Federal Communications Commission) U.S. National Technical Information Service, 5825 Port Royal Rd., Springfield, VA 22161. TEL 703-487-4630. (microfiche)
Description: Reports all outstanding (i.e. applied for, not yet granted) affecting stations. Includes call sign, purpose, last status, status date, licensee name, transmitter city and state.

384.54   US
MICROWAVE LICENSES ISSUED. (Supplement avail.: Microwave Licenses Issued Report) m. $25 per no. in U.S., Canada, Mexico; elsewhere $40. (Federal Communications Commission) U.S. National Technical Information Service, 5825 Port Royal Rd., Springfield, VA 22161. TEL 703-487-4630. (microfiche)

621.38 016   US
T I S ALERTS: COMMUNICATION. 1974. w. $135 (foreign $195). U.S. National Technical Information Service, 5285 Port Royal Rd., Springfield, VA 22161. TEL 703-487-4630. FAX 703-321-8527. TELEX 64617. bibl.; index. (also avail. in microform from NTI; back issues avail.) **Document type:** abstracting/indexing.
Former titles: Abstract Newsletter: Communication; Weekly Abstract Newsletter: Communication; Weekly Government Abstracts. Communication (ISSN 0364-4944)
Description: Contains summaries of the latest government-sponsored projects and their findings for professionals.

016.30116   DK   ISSN 0909-914X
Z5630
NORDICOM; bibliography of Nordic mass communication literature - bibliografi over nordisk massekommunikationslitteratur. 1976. a. DKK 150. Nordic Documentation Center for Mass Communication Research - Nordisk Dokumentationscentral for Massekommunikationsforskning, Statsbiblioteket, Universitetsparken, DK-8000 Aarhus C, Denmark. TEL 45-86-12-20-22. FAX 45-86-13-27-04. Ed. Claus Kragh Hansen. index. circ. 600. **Document type:** bibliography.
● Also available online.
Formed by the 1994 merger of: Nordicom Index (ISSN 0909-2773) & Nordicom Document List (ISSN 0105-1385)
Description: Covers publications in mass communications research.

NORWAY. STATISTISK SENTRALBYRAA. SAMFERDSELSSTATISTIKK/STATISTICS NORWAY. TRANSPORT AND COMMUNICATION STATISTICS. see *TRANSPORTATION — Abstracting, Bibliographies, Statistics*

PERFORMING ARTS BIOGRAPHY MASTER INDEX. see *THEATER — Abstracting, Bibliographies, Statistics*

PORTUGAL. INSTITUTO NACIONAL DE ESTATISTICA. ESTATISTICAS DOS TRANSPORTES E COMUNICACOES. see *TRANSPORTATION — Abstracting, Bibliographies, Statistics*

016.3845   US   ISSN 0897-9642
Z695.1.T24
PUBLIC TELEVISION TRANSCRIPTS INDEX. Variant title: P B S News Index. 1987. q. (with a. cumulation). $195. Primary Source Media, 12 Lunar Dr., Drawer AB, Woodbridge, CT 06525. TEL 203-397-2600. FAX 203-397-3893. (also avail. in microfiche from RPI; back issues avail.) **Document type:** abstracting/indexing.
Description: Index to transcripts of Public Television news programs available in microfiche.

621.38 016   RU   ISSN 0034-267X
REFERATIVNYI ZHURNAL. RADIOTEKHNIKA. 1955. m. 231 Rub. (294 Rub. including index). Vsesoyuznyi Institut Nauchno-Tekhnicheskoi Informatsii (VINITI), Baltiiskaya ul., 14, Moscow A-219, Russia. (Subscr. to: Mezhdunarodnaya Kniga, Dimitrova ul. 39, 113095 Moscow, Russia) **Document type:** abstracting/indexing.
—CISTI.

384.54   US
RESTRICTED - COMMERCIAL OPERATOR HISTORY FILE. a. $25 in U.S., Canada, Mexico; elsewhere $40. (Federal Communications Commission) U.S. National Technical Information Service, 5825 Port Royal Rd., Springfield, VA 22161. TEL 703-487-4630. (microfiche)
Description: Lists commercial operator and restricted operator licensees in operator name sequence. Includes a cross-reference of commercial operators by serial numbers. Contains licenses issued seven years ago or more.

380   CC
S R G CHINA MEDIA INDEX. (In 10 city editions: Beijing, Shanghai, Guangzhou, Shenyang, Tianjin, Shijiazhuang, Nanjing, Wuhan, Chengdu and Xiamen) (Text in English) 1986. a. $5500 for Guangzhou, Shanghai & Beijing eds; other city eds. $5000. S R G China Ltd., 2-F, Warwick House, 979 King's Rd., Quarry Bay, Hong Kong, People's Republic of China. TEL 852-2563-9688. FAX 852-2516-6856. Dir. Alic Lau. (back issues avail.) **Document type:** consumer publication.
Description: Multi-media survey provides a comprehensive picture of the media consumptions in key cities in China.

SAFETY ABSTRACTS. see *PUBLIC HEALTH AND SAFETY — Abstracting, Bibliographies, Statistics*

SIGNAL'NAYA INFORMATSIYA. RADIOFIZIKA I FIZICHESKIE OSNOVY ELEKTRONIKI. see *ELECTRONICS — Abstracting, Bibliographies, Statistics*

384.554   US   ISSN 1050-8015
HC101
SIMMONS STUDY OF MEDIA AND MARKETS. TECHNICAL GUIDE. 2/yr. Simmons Market Research Bureau, Inc., 309 W. 49th St., New York, NY 10019. TEL 212-373-8900. FAX 212-373-8918. **Document type:** trade publication.

384.554   US   ISSN 1050-799X
HC101
SIMMONS STUDY OF MEDIA & MARKETS (YEAR). 2/yr. Simmons Market Research Bureau, Inc., 309 W. 49th St., New York, NY 10019. TEL 212-373-8900. FAX 212-373-8918. **Document type:** trade publication.
● Also available online.

384.54   US
STATE INDEX TO NON-GOVERNMENT MASTER FREQUENCY DATA BASE. q. $25 per no. in U.S., Canada, Mexico; elsewhere $40. (Federal Communications Commission) U.S. National Technical Information Service, 5825 Port Royal Rd., Springfield, VA 22161. TEL 703-487-4630. charts. (microfiche)
Description: Contains transmitter location, frequency, service, call sign, licensee name and authorization for each station in the state. At the end of the fiche, a table showing the number of unique transmitter locations per state is printed.

SWEDEN. STATISTISKA CENTRALBYRAAN. STATISTISKA MEDDELANDEN. SERIE T, TRANSPORT OCH KOMMUNIKATIONER. see *TRANSPORTATION — Abstracting, Bibliographies, Statistics*

SYSDATA. see *COMPUTERS*

384.554   US
T V BROADCAST DATA BASE. m. $360 (foreign $620). (Federal Communications Commission) U.S. National Technical Information Service, 5825 Port Royal Rd., Springfield, VA 22161. TEL 703-487-4630. (magnetic tape; also avail. in diskette format)
Description: Contains records for existing and proposed stations, allocations, and rule-making petitions and proposals.

384.554   US
T V ENGINEERING DATA BASE IN ORDER BY STATE. m. $25 per no. in U.S., Canada, Mexico; elsewhere $40. (Federal Communications Commission) U.S. National Technical Information Service, 5825 Port Royal Rd., Springfield, VA 22161. TEL 703-487-4630. (microfiche)
Description: Includes vacant assignments, proposed rule-makings, and foreign facilities.

384.55   US   ISSN 1040-6123
T V PROGRAM STATS. 1988. m. $645 (effective 1997). Paul Kagan Associates, Inc., 126 Clock Tower Pl., Carmel, CA 93923. TEL 408-624-1536. FAX 408-625-3225. Ed. Larry Gerbrandt.
Description: Compiles statistics on the costs, ratings and revenues of TV programs. Analyzes network prime-time performance patterns and network licensing.

384.554   US
T V TRANSLATORS ENGINEERING DATA BASE IN ORDER BY STATE, CHANNEL, CALL. m. $25 per no. in U.S., Canada, Mexico; elsewhere $40. (Federal Communications Commission) U.S. National Technical Information Service, 5825 Port Royal Rd., Springfield, VA 22161. TEL 703-487-4630. (microfiche)

384.554   US
T V TRANSLATORS ENGINEERING DATA BASE IN ORDER BY STATE, CITY, CHANNEL. m. $25 per no. in U.S., Canada, Mexico; elsewhere $40. (Federal Communications Commission) U.S. National Technical Information Service, 5825 Port Royal Rd., Springfield, VA 22161. TEL 703-487-4630. (microfiche)

COMMUNICATIONS — COMPUTER APPLICATIONS

016.384 US ISSN 0085-7157
AI3
TELEVISION NEWS INDEX AND ABSTRACTS. 1968. m. $550 to individuals; institutions $330; microfilm $110. Vanderbilt University, Vanderbilt Television News Archive, 110 21st Ave. S., Ste. 704, Nashville, TN 37240-0007. TEL 615-322-2927. FAX 615-343-8250. E-mail: TVNews@TVNews.Vanderbilt.edu; URL: http://tvnews.vanderbilt.edu Ed. Andrew H. Pfeiffer. abstr.; index. circ. 250. (also avail. in microfilm) **Document type:** abstracting/indexing.
● Also available online.
Description: Guide to Vanderbilt's collection of network television evening news programs and other news broadcasts, including abstract and subject, person and place indexing.

U.S. DEPARTMENT OF TRANSPORTATION. INTELLIGENT VEHICLE HIGHWAY SYSTEMS PROJECTS. see TRANSPORTATION — Roads And Traffic

U.S. FEDERAL TRANSIT ADMINISTRATION. TECHNOLOGY SHARING PROGRAM. REPORT. see TRANSPORTATION — Abstracting, Bibliographies, Statistics

384 US ISSN 0896-0585
HE8801
UNITED STATES TELEPHONE ASSOCIATION. STATISTICS OF THE LOCAL EXCHANGE CARRIERS. 1954. a. $375 to non-members; members $275. United States Telephone Association, 1401 H St., N.W., Ste. 600, Washington, DC 20005. TEL 202-326-7300. FAX 202-326-7333. index. circ. 1,000. **Indexed:** SRI.
Formerly: United States Independent Telephone Association. Annual Statistical Volume (ISSN 0083-1298)

384.55 380.1 US
VIDEO INDUSTRY STATISTICAL REPORT. 1989. a. $385. Corbell Publishing, 4676 Admiralty Way, Ste. 300, Marina Del Rey, CA 90292. TEL 310-574-5337. FAX 310-574-5383. Ed. Deborah Rolfe; Pub. Maureen Healy. adv. contact: Joseph Daneshrad. charts. (looseleaf format) **Document type:** trade publication.
Description: Provides statistics on pre-recorded video, blank tape, video hardware, VCR's, laser discs, 8mm and penetration data.
Refereed Serial

384.55 US ISSN 0746-7680
VIDEOLOG. 1981. w. $252. Trade Service Corporation, 10996 Torreyana Rd., San Diego, CA 92121. TEL 619-457-5920. FAX 619-457-1320. Ed. Bonnie J. Dudley. adv. contact. circ. 5,250. (looseleaf format)
● Also available online.
Description: Bulletin of video industry news, containing reviews of video release listings.

COMMUNICATIONS — Computer Applications

A C U T A JOURNAL OF TELECOMMUNICATIONS IN HIGHER EDUCATION. (Association of College and University Telecommunications Administrators) see COMMUNICATIONS

380.3 378 US
A C U T A NEWS. 1982. m. $45. Association of College and University Telecommunications Administrators, 152 W. Zandale Dr., Ste. 200, Lexington, KY 40503-2486. TEL 606-278-3338. FAX 606-278-3268. E-mail: pscott@acuta.org; URL: http://www.acuta.org. Ed. Pat Scott. R&P contact: Pat Scott. bk.rev. circ. 1,900. **Document type:** newsletter.
● Also available online.
Description: Stories of new installations, applications, industry and regulatory updates, problems solved.

380.3 US ISSN 1042-0711
TK8315 CODEN: ADIMEZ
ADVANCED IMAGING. 1986. m. free to qualified personnel. P T N Publishing Corp., 445 Broad Hollow Rd., Ste. 21, Melville, NY 11747-4722. TEL 516-845-2700. FAX 516-845-2797. Ed. Barry Mazor; Pub. Charles Grecky. adv. circ. 60,050. **Indexed:** Info.Media & Tech., WPM. **Document type:** trade publication.
● Also available online. Vendor(s): Information Access Co.
—BLDSC (0696.854750); AskIEEE; CISTI; Ei; KR SourceOne; SWETS; UMI; UnCover.
Formerly (until 1988): Tech Photo Pro Imaging Systems (ISSN 1040-0141)
Description: Features real world video, photographic, and document electronic image acquisition, processing, display, storage, output transmission and communication for all application areas using imaging technologies.

AKADEMIA GORNICZO-HUTNICZA IM. STANISLAWA STASZICA. TELEKOMUNIKACJA CYFROWA - TECHNOLOGIA I USLUGI. see COMMUNICATIONS — Telephone And Telegraph

384.3 004 US ISSN 0893-0597
APPLICATIONS OF COMMUNICATIONS THEORY. 1980. irreg., latest 1995. price varies. Plenum Publishing Corp., 233 Spring St., New York, NY 10013-1578. TEL 212-620-8000. FAX 212-463-0742. TELEX 23-421139. E-mail: books@plenum.com. Ed. R.W. Lucky. (back issues avail.) **Document type:** monographic series.

AUDIOTEX DIRECTORY & BUYER'S GUIDE. see COMMUNICATIONS — Telephone And Telegraph

380.3 621.319
380.3 US ISSN 1045-5795
AUDIOTEX UPDATE. 1981. m. $150 (outside N. America $165) (effective 1995-1996). Worldwide Videotex, Box 3273, Boynton Beach, FL 33424-3273. TEL 407-738-2276. E-mail: markedit@juno.com. Ed. Mark Wright; Pub. Mark Wright. bk.rev. **Document type:** newsletter.
● Also available online. Vendor(s): Data-Star, Information Access Co., Knight-Ridder Information, Inc., NewsNet (TE16).
—CCC.
Description: Covers voice mail, voice recognition and response, automated telemarketing, dial-it-information, and talking yellow pages and gab lines.

AUSTRALIAN & NEW ZEALAND L A N MAGAZINE. see COMPUTERS — Personal Computers

B T TODAY. (British Telecommunications plc.) see COMMUNICATIONS — Telephone And Telegraph

004.678 US
▼**BITEY.** 1996. m. E-mail: bitey@bitey.com; URL: http://www.bitey.com.
● Available only online.
Description: Focuses on the internet community and issues that affect it.

380.3 US
BROADBAND NETWORKING. 1986. base vol. (plus m. updates). $621 to new subscr.; renewal $580 (effective 1996). Datapro Information Services Group (Subsidiary of: McGraw-Hill, Inc.), 600 Delran Pkwy., Delran, NJ 08075. TEL 609-764-0100; 800-328-2776. FAX 609-764-2814.
Formerly: Datapro Reports on Communications Alternatives.

380.3 US
▼**BROADBAND SYSTEMS & DESIGN.** 1995. 9/yr. $55 (outside N. America $70). Gordon Publications, Part of Cahners Publishing Company, Division of Reed Elsevier Inc., 301 Gibraltar Dr., Box 650, Morris Plains, NJ 07950-0650. TEL 973-292-5100 ext.334. FAX 973-605-1220. URL: http://www.broadbandmag.com. Ed. Aimee Kalnoskas; Pub. Jack Martin. circ. 24,600. **Document type:** trade publication.

BURTZ BIRTUAL ATELIER. see ART — Computer Applications

384.3 US
HD9999.I493
BUSINESS - PROFESSIONAL ONLINE SERVICES: REVIEW, TRENDS, FORECAST. 1990. a. $1295 (effective 1997). Cowles - SIMBA Information (Subsidiary of: Cowles Business Media), 11 Riverbend Dr. S., Box 4949, Stamford, CT 06907-0949. TEL 203-358-9900; 800-307-2529. FAX 203-358-5811. E-mail: info@simbanet.com; URL: http://www.simbanet.com. Ed. Karen Burka; Pub. Chris Elwell. charts; stat. (back issues avail.) **Document type:** trade publication.
—CCC.
Supersedes in part: Online Services: Review, Trends and Forecast (ISSN 1057-3666)
Description: Analyzes and forecasts online publishing various information industry segments including legal, brokerage, credit, marketing intelligence, financial news/research, agribusiness and healthcare and medical.

C C A I; the journal for the integrated study of artificial intelligence, cognitive science and applied epistemology. see COMPUTERS — Artificial Intelligence

C D - R O M PROFESSIONAL. see LIBRARY AND INFORMATION SCIENCES — Computer Applications

C M C NEWS. (Computers and the Media Center) see LIBRARY AND INFORMATION SCIENCES — Computer Applications

380.3 US
CARIBECOM NEWS. 1986. a. $5. Intercom Corp., 9200 S. Dadeland Blvd., Ste. 309, Miami, FL 33156-2703. TEL 305-670-9444. Ed. Thomas Will; Pub. Kenneth Bleakley. adv. contact: John Butt. circ. 4,000. **Document type:** newsletter.
Description: Dedicated to telecommunications and communication technology in the Caribbean.

COMMUNICATING TOGETHER. see EDUCATION — Computer Applications

371.5 US ISSN 0161-4126
COMMUNICATION OUTLOOK; focusing on communication aids and techniques. 1978. 4/yr. $18 (foreign $24) (effective 1996-97). Artificial Language Laboratory, 405 Computer Center, Michigan State University, E. Lansing, MI 48824-1042. TEL 517-353-0870. FAX 517-353-4766. E-mail: co@all.cps.msu.edu. Ed. John Eulenber. R&P contact: John Eulenber. adv contact: Carolyn Watt. bk.rev. circ. 1,000. (tabloid format; also avail. in microform from UMI; back issues avail.) **Indexed:** INSPEC (1984-), Rehabil.Lit. Yrbk.Assoc.Educ.& Rehab.Blind.
—BLDSC (3361.600000); AskIEEE; KR SourceOne.
Description: Covers technological developments for persons who experience communication handicaps due to neurological, sensory or neuromuscular conditions.

384.3 US
COMMUNICATION SYSTEMS DESIGN. 12/yr. $50 (Canada & Mexico $57; elsewhere $75). Miller Freeman, Inc. (Subsidiary of: United News & Media), 600 Harrison St., San Francisco, CA 94107. TEL 415-905-2200. FAX 415-905-2233. (Subscr. to: Box 420376, Palm Coast, FL 32142-0376. TE 800-829-9832. FAX 904-446-2774)

621.381 380.3 US ISSN 0743-0671
TK5103
COMMUNICATIONS PRODUCT REPORTS. 1984. m. $821. Management Information Corporation, 111 Marlkress Rd., Box 5062, Cherry Hill, NJ 08003-5602. TEL 609-424-1100. FAX 609-424-1999. Ed. Don Stuart. **Indexed:** Compumath.
Description: Provides evaluations of major voice and data communications products. Includes overviews and product evaluations relating to local area networks, data communication carriers and multiplexers.

384.3 CC
COMPUTER & COMMUNICATIONS; electronics international. w. China Computerworld Publishing & Servicing Co., 74 Lu Gu Rd., P.O. Box 750, Beijing 100036, People's Republic of China. TEL 86-10-885-2033. FAX 86-10-885-2055. Ed. Fulai Zhu. adv.: B&W page $3400; trim 275 x 39 circ. 80,000.

COMMUNICATIONS — COMPUTER APPLICATIONS

380.3   UK
COMPUTER AND COMMUNICATIONS TECHNOLOGY DOCUMENTS MICROFILE. (Text in English, French) 1982. s-a. Technical Indexes Ltd., Willoughby Rd., Bracknell, Berkshire RG12 8DW, England. TEL 44-1344-426311. FAX 44-1344-424971. E-mail: systems@techindex.co.uk; URL: http://www.techindex.co.uk. adv. contact: Gary Kearns. **Document type:** abstracting/indexing.
● Also available on CD-ROM.
Formerly: Computer and Communications Documents Microfile.

384.3   II
COMPUTERS & COMMUNICATIONS. (Text in English) 1987. m. newsstand price: Rs.15. Media Transasia (India) Pvt. Ltd., 103 Anand Lok, New Delhi 110049, India. TEL 011-6440110. FAX 011-6432950. TELEX 031-71313 MTIL IN, Ed. Murli Menon; Pub. Suresh Kumar Bhayana. adv.: B&W page Rs.10000, color page Rs.15000.

384.3   BU   ISSN 0861-3788
COMPUTERWORLD. (Quarterly supplement avail.: Networkworld) w. $30. I D G Technika Communications, Ltd., 1, Hristo Smirnenski Blvd., Fl. 11, 1421 Sofia, Bulgaria. TEL 359-2-9630886. FAX 359-2-9632841. Ed. Krassimir Bankov. R&P contact: Mila Pancheva. adv. contact: Mila Pancheva. **Document type:** consumer publication, newspaper.
Description: Provides executives, managers and professionals with national and international business oriented information.

004 650   BE
DATA NEWS; l'actualite informatique. (Editions in Dutch, French) 1979. w. 2000 BEF (foreign 4500 BEF). Diligentia Business Press N.V., 42 av. du Houx, 1170 Brussels, Belgium. TEL 32-2-6781611. FAX 32-2-6603600. Ed. Baudouin T. Elleboudt. adv.; bk.rev.; bibl.; circ. 23,400 (controlled). (tabloid format; back issues avail.)

004.6   CC
DATAPHILE; Internet in Asia. (Text in English) 1993. m. HK.$385($83); newsstand price: HK.$35. AsiaTech Publications Ltd., 23rd Fl., Citicorp Centre, 18 Whitfield Rd., North Point, Hong Kong, People's Republic of China. TEL 852-2837-8800. FAX 852-2520-5463. E-mail: editors@dataphile.com.hk; adverts@dataphile.com.hk; subs@dataphile.com.hk; URL: http://www.dataphile.com.hk. Ed. Eric Lai; Pub. Larry Campbell. R&P contact: Phil Ingram. adv.: color page $3950. circ. 44,500.
● Also available online.
Also available on CD-ROM.

384.3 794.8   US
▼**DIGITAL DINER.** 1996. bi-m. newsstand price: $2.95. Metropolis Publications, 643 Blair Island Rd., Ste. 301, Redwood City, CA 94063. TEL 415-568-7280. Ed. Andy Eddy. adv. **Document type:** consumer publication.
Description: Focuses on the influence of computers and digital technology within the entertainment industry.

384   US
▼**DIGITAL "VERSATILE" DISC (YEAR).** 1996. biennial. $1095 (effective 1997). Cowles - SIMBA Information (Subsidiary of: Cowles Business Media), 11 Riverbend Dr. S., Box 4949, Stamford, CT 06907-0949. TEL 203-358-9900; 800-307-2529. FAX 203-358-5811. E-mail: info@simbanet.com; URL: http://www.simbanet.com.

621.388   FR   ISSN 1164-0642
DIRECTORY OF FRENCH VIDEOTEX DATABASES FOR COMPANIES. (Text in English) 1991. irreg. 170 F. (effective 1997). Editions F L A Consultants, 27 rue de la Vistule, 75013 Paris, France. TEL 33-1-45827575. FAX 33-1-45824604. E-mail: flabases@iway.fr; URL: http://www.fla-consultants.fr. Ed. Beatrice Riou. **Document type:** directory.
Description: Identifies and presents in detail French videotex databases that can be useful to companies.

E M M S. (Electronic Mail & Micro Systems) see COMMUNICATIONS

380.3 621.3   US
EDITTECH INTERNATIONAL;* reporting worldwide on high technology. 1987. d. 1330 S. Bascom Ave., Ste. C, San Jose, CA 95128-4513. TEL 408-243-9788. FAX 408-985-5932. Ed. John Sterlicchi. (looseleaf format; back issues avail.)
Description: Information about computer technology, communication and electronics.

621.387   US   ISSN 1044-9892
ELECTRONIC MESSAGING NEWS. 1989. bi-w. $597 (foreign $630) (effective 1997). Phillips Business Information, Inc., 1201 Seven Locks Rd., Potomac, MD 20854. TEL 301-424-3338. FAX 301-309-3847. E-mail: pbi@phillips.com. Ed. Ruth Suarez. **Document type:** newsletter.
● Also available online. Vendor(s): NewsNet (TE05).
—CCC.
Description: Case studies and applications of recent developments in messaging technologies for corporate communications.

384.3 004.6   AT
ELECTRONIC TRADING MARKETS. 1984. a. Aus.$275 (US Aus.$295; Europe Aus.$300) (effective 1998). Paul Budde Communication Pty. Ltd., 2643 George Downes Dr., Bucketty, N.S.W. 2250, Australia. TEL 61-49-988144. FAX 61-49-988247. E-mail: pbc@budde.com.au; URL: http://www.budde.com.au. Ed. Paul Budde. stat. **Document type:** directory.
Formerly: Messaging and Transaction Services Market (Years) (ISSN 1326-6780); Supersedes in part: Directory of Electronic Services and Communications Networks in Australia and New Zealand (ISSN 1322-350X)
Description: Covers fax, e-mail, interactive voice response, voice mail, EDI, EFTPOS, computer reservation systems. Includes information on developments and trends.

ELEKTRISCHES NACHRICHTENWESEN; technisch-wissenschaftliche Zeitschrift. see ENGINEERING — Electrical Engineering

ELLIOT GOLD'S TELESPAN; a bulletin on teleconferencing. see COMPUTERS — Data Communications And Data Transmission Systems

380.3   US
FAX FACTS. 1982. q. Paper Manufacturers Company, 24 Triangle Park Dr., Cincinnati, OH 45256-3411. TEL 513-772-5057. FAX 513-772-5098. Ed. Tom Hoffman. circ. 10,000. **Document type:** newsletter.

380.3   US   ISSN 1051-1954
FIBER DATACOM. 1987. m. $595 (foreign $645) (effective 1997). Information Gatekeepers, Inc., 214 Harvard Ave., Boston, MA 02134. TEL 617-232-3111; 800-323-1088. FAX 617-734-8562. E-mail: igiboston@aol.com; URL: http://www.igigroup.com. circ. 350. (back issues avail.) **Document type:** newsletter.
—CCC.
Description: Publishes news and information on applications of fiber optics in data communications, building and campus wiring and high-speed LANs.

384.3   UK
▼**FIBRESYSTEMS.** 1996. bi-m. free to qualified readers. I O P Publishing Ltd., Dirac House, Temple Back, Bristol BS1 6BE, England. TEL 44-117-929-7481. FAX 44-117-929-4318. E-mail: custserv@ioppublishing.co.uk; URL: http://www.iop.org.
Description: Aimed at readers who are actively using and applying fibre-optic products or systems.

621.38   US   ISSN 0273-141X
TK1   CODEN: GAEJDG
G T E AUTOMATIC ELECTRIC WORLD-WIDE COMMUNICATIONS JOURNAL.* (General Telephone & Electronics) (Contents page in English, French, Italian and Spanish) 1948. 6/yr. G T E Communications Systems, 333 E. First St., Cenoa, IL 60135-1015. illus.; circ. 9,000 (controlled). (also avail. in microform from UMI; reprint service avail. from UMI) **Indexed:** Eng.Ind., INSPEC (1968-).
—AskIEEE; CISTI; KR SourceOne; Linda Hall; UMI.
Former titles (until 1979): G T E Automatic Electrical Journal (ISSN 0147-3328); (until 1977): G T E Automatic Electric Technical Journal (ISSN 0099-9490); (until 1971): Automatic Electric Technical Journal (ISSN 0005-1063)

384.3   GW
GATEWAY; Magazin fuer Daten- und Telekommunikation. 1989. 12/yr. DM.87 (foreign DM.105) (effective 1996). Verlag Heinz Heise GmbH und Co. KG, Helstorferstr. 7, 30625 Hannover, Germany. TEL 49-511-5352-0. FAX 49-511-5352129. Ed. Gerd Bausewein. adv. contact: Sonja Jansen. circ. 10,583 (paid). **Document type:** trade publication.

GUIDE INTERNATIONAL DES BANQUES DE DONNEES SUR LES BREVETS ET LES MARQUES. see PATENTS, TRADEMARKS AND COPYRIGHTS

380.3   US
HANDBOOK OF COMMUNICATIONS SYSTEMS MANAGEMENT. 1988. triennial (plus a. supplement). $144. Auerbach Publishers (Subsidiary of: Warren, Gorham & Lamont), One Penn Plaza, New York, NY 10119. TEL 212-971-5000. FAX 212-971-5024. (Subscr. to: 31 St. James Ave., Boston, MA 02116-4112. TEL 800-950-1218. FAX 617-423-1914) Ed. James Conard. **Document type:** trade publication.
Description: Covers all major aspects of communications issues and challenges - from strategic planning to network operations.

384 004.6   KO
HI-TECH INFORMATION. 1989. bi.w. Hi-Tech Information, Inc., 3-F, Woosung Bldg., 333 Cheong Jeon-dong, Mapo-ku, Seoul 135-270, S. Korea. TEL 2-3257300. FAX 2-3258475. Ed. Y.S. Gimm. adv.: B&W page $2000, color page $3000; trim 265 x 370; adv. contact: Junbin Kim. circ. 35,000.

HOBSONS I T CASEBOOK. see OCCUPATIONS AND CAREERS

I D C CHINA REPORT. see COMPUTERS — Computer Industry

380.3   US   ISSN 0743-166X
TK5105.5
I E E E INFOCOM. PROCEEDINGS. Variant title: Joint Conference of the I E E E Computer and Communications Societies. 1982. a. (Institute of Electrical and Electronics Engineers, Inc.) I E E E Computer Society Press, 10662 Los Vaqueros Circle, Los Alamitos, CA 90720-1264. TEL 714-821-8380. FAX 714-821-4641. (Co-sponsor: I E E E Communications Society) Ed. Cat Harris; Pub. Matt Loeb. adv. contact: Frieda Koester. **Document type:** proceedings.
—BLDSC (4362.934500); Ei; UMI. **CCC.**
Formerly (until 1982): I N F O C O M Proceedings.
Description: Presents recent advances in computer and communication disciplines.

380.3   US   ISSN 0893-4266
TK5101.A1
I E E E PACIFIC RIM CONFERENCE ON COMMUNICATIONS, COMPUTERS AND SIGNAL PROCESSING, CONFERENCE PROCEEDINGS. 1987. quadrennial. price varies. (I E E E, Victoria Section) Institute of Electrical and Electronics Engineers, Inc., 345 E. 47th St., New York, NY 10017-2394. TEL 732-981-0060; 800-678-4333. FAX 732-981-9667. E-mail: customer.service@ieee.org; URL: http://www.ieee.org. (Subscr. to: 445 Hoes Ln., Box 1331, Piscataway, NJ 08855-1331) **Indexed:** INSPEC. **Document type:** proceedings.
—UMI.
Description: Covers communications, computer technology, and signal processing as they relate to the Pacific Rim area.

380.3   US
I S A UPDATE. 1981. m. membership. Interactive Services Association, 8403 Colesville Rd., Ste. 865, Silver Spring, MD 20910-3368. TEL 301-495-4955. FAX 301-495-4959. bk.rev. circ. 230. (looseleaf format; back issues avail.)
Formerly: V I A Update.
Description: Examines online telecommunications and interactive services that are used anywhere for transmitting time-sensitive information, paying bills, gaining access to travel information, and much more.

COMMUNICATIONS — COMPUTER APPLICATIONS

380.3   US
I S ANALYZER. 1963. m. $325 (foreign $345). 400 Group, 175 Highland Ave., Needham, MA 02194. TEL 617-444-5755. FAX 617-444-8958. Ed. Joanne Cummings. index, cum.index. (also avail. in microform from UMI; Braille; reprint service avail. from UMI) Indexed: A.S.& T.Ind., ABI Inform., AESIS, B.P.I., Comput.Bus., Comput.Cont., Comput.Lit.Ind., INSPEC (1987-), Mgmt.& Market.Abstr., PROMT, Tr.& Indus.Ind. **Document type:** trade publication.
 —KR SourceOne. **CCC.**
 Formerly: E D P Analyzer (ISSN 0012-7523)
 Description: Offers management guidance for computer managers and MIS executives on strategic planning, systems architecture, distributed computing, new technologies, MIS productivity, and influencing corporate policies.

380.3   US   ISSN 0899-9554
I S D N NEWS. (Integrated Services Digital Network); strategies, marketing, applications. 1988. bi-w. $597 (foreign $630) (effective 1997). Phillips Business Information, Inc., 1201 Seven Locks Rd., Potomac, MD 20854. TEL 301-424-3338. FAX 301-309-3847. E-mail: pbi@phillips.com. Ed. Jennifer Whelen. charts; illus.; index. (back issues avail.) **Document type:** newsletter.
 ●Also available online. Vendor(s): Data-Star, Information Access Co., Knight-Ridder Information, Inc., NewsNet (TE90).
 —CCC.
 Description: Covers all aspects of ISDN, including applications, new products and RBOCS.

380.3 384   US   ISSN 1078-1005
I S D N USER NEWSLETTER. (Integrated Services Digital Network) 1987. bi-m. $90 (foreign $100) (effective 1996). Information Gatekeepers, Inc., 214 Harvard Ave., Boston, MA 02134. TEL 617-232-3111. FAX 617-734-8562. Ed. Paul Polishuk. adv. (back issues avail.) **Document type:** newsletter.
 —CCC.
 Formerly: I S D N User Magazine.
 Description: Covers technology trends, markets, products, standards, and applications of ISDN.

384.1   GW
INFO-SYS JOURNAL. 1994. bi-m. Dekotec GmbH, Gasstr. 18, Haus 1, 22761 Hamburg, Germany. TEL 040-891027. FAX 040-896069. Ed. Joern Fandrey. circ. 10,000. **Document type:** trade publication.

INFORMATION AND COMMUNICATIONS TECHNOLOGY LAW. see COMMUNICATIONS

INFORMATION INFRASTRUCTURE AND POLICY; an international journal on the development, adoption, use and effects of information technology. see COMPUTERS — Information Science And Information Theory

INFORMATION MANAGEMENT REPORT. see LIBRARY AND INFORMATION SCIENCES — Computer Applications

INFORMATION TECHNOLOGY MANAGEMENT; non-technical report on IT and its applications. see BUSINESS AND ECONOMICS — Office Equipment And Services

380.3   UK   ISSN 0950-9879
Z699.A1   CODEN: IWRED4
INFORMATION WORLD REVIEW; the information community newspaper. 1986. m. £28. Learned Information (Europe) Ltd., Woodside, Hinksey Hill, Oxford OX1 5BE, England. TEL 44-1865-388000. FAX 44-1865-736354. (Dist. in N. America by: Learned Information Inc., 143 Old Marlton Pike, Medford, NJ 08055) Eds. Peter Hyams, Simon Atkinson. adv.; bk.rev. (back issues avail.) Indexed: Abstr.Hum.Comp.Inter., Info.Media & Tech., Intl.Polym.Sci.& Tech., LISA, RAPRA, WPM. **Document type:** newspaper.
 —BLDSC (4496.412500); CASDDS; KR SourceOne; SWETS. UMI. **CCC.**
 Description: Reports on the information industry events and trends, software companies, electronic and optical publishing, new products, database, network, telecommunications developments and library automation.

INFORMATIZATION DEVELOPMENTS AND THE PUBLIC SECTOR. see PUBLIC ADMINISTRATION — Computer Applications

INTERACTIVE ADVERTISING SOURCE. see ADVERTISING AND PUBLIC RELATIONS

INTERACTIVE AGE; content, technology and communications for the information highway. see COMPUTERS — Computer Networks

INTERACTIVE HEALTHCARE INTERNET DIRECTORY. see MEDICAL SCIENCES — Computer Applications

(YEAR) INTERACTIVE TELEVISION INDUSTRY DIRECTORY. see BUSINESS AND ECONOMICS — Trade And Industrial Directories

384.55 621.38   NE
TK6679.I57
INTERNATIONAL WORKSHOP ON H D T V. PROCEEDINGS. (High Definition Television) Running title: Signal Processing of H D T V. (Text in English) irreg., 6th, Turin, Italy, 1994. price varies. Elsevier Science B.V., Books Division, P.O. Box 211, 1000 AE Amsterdam, Netherlands. TEL 31-20-4853911. FAX 31-20-4853705. TELEX 18582 ESPA NL. E-mail: nlinfo-f@elsevier.nl; usinfo-f@elsevier.com; forinfo-kyf04035@niftyserve.or.jp; URL: http://www.elsevier.nl/. (Subscr. in the Americas to: Elsevier Science, Regional Sales Office, Box 945, New York, NY 10159-0945. TEL 212-633-3730. FAX 212-633-3680; Subscr. in Australasia and the Far East to: Elsevier Science (Singapore) Pte Ltd, No.1 Temasek Ave., No.17-01 Millenia Tower, Singapore 039192, Singapore. TEL 65-434-3727. FAX 65-337-2230; Subscr. in Japan to: Elsevier Science Japan, 9-15 Higashi-Azabu 1-chome, Minato-ku, Tokyo 106, Japan. TEL 81-3-5561-5033. FAX 81-3-5561-5047) Eds. Y. Nimomiya, L. Chiariglione. **Document type:** proceedings.
 Refereed Serial

384.3 004.6   AT
INTERNET AND ONLINE SERVICES MARKET: AUSTRALIA AND NEW ZEALAND. 1984. a. Aus.$275 (US Aus.$295; Europe Aus.$300) (effective 1998). Paul Budde Communication Pty. Ltd., 2643 George Downes Dr., Bucketty, N.S.W. 2240, Australia. TEL 61-7-49988144. FAX 61-7-49988247. E-mail: pbc@budde.com.au; URL: http://www.budde.com.au. Ed. Paul Budde. stat. **Document type:** directory.
 Formerly: Electronic Information Sevices Market (ISSN 1326-6799); Supersedes in part: Directory of Electronic Services and Communications Networks in Australia and New Zealand (ISSN 1322-350X)
 Description: Covers online, Internet, bulletin boards and audiotex services. Includes information on developments and trends.

INTERNET BUSINESS ADVANTAGE; online solutions for business success. see COMPUTERS — Data Communications And Data Transmission Systems

INTERNET BUSINESS REPORT. see COMPUTERS — Data Communications And Data Transmission Systems

JAPAN ANNUAL REVIEWS IN ELECTRONICS, COMPUTERS & TELECOMMUNICATIONS. AMORPHOUS SEMICONDUCTOR TECHNOLOGIES & DEVICES. see ELECTRONICS

380.3   NE   ISSN 1058-7306
JAPANESE TECHNOLOGY REVIEWS: COMPUTERS AND COMMUNICATION (SECTION B). 1989. irreg. 60 ECU per vol. (effective 1993). Gordon and Breach - Harwood Academic, Amsteldisk 166, 1st Fl., 1079 LH Amsterdam, Netherlands. (Subscr. to: International Publishers Distributor, Box 32160, Newark, NJ 07102. TEL 800-545-8398. FAX 215-750-6343) Ed. Toshiaki Ikoma. (also avail. in microform) **Document type:** monographic series.
 —CISTI. **CCC.**
 Supersedes in part: Japanese Technology Review (ISSN 0898-5693)

380.31 370   US
PN4784.E5
JOURNAL OF MEDIATED COMMUNICATION.* 1984. q. $30 to individuals; libraries $100. (Duquesne University, Department of Communication) Edwards Company, Inc., 307 Sun Valley Dr., Cranberry Township, PA 16066-4947. adv.; bk.rev.; cum.index: 1984-1992. (back issues avail.) **Document type:** academic/scholarly publication.
 Formerly: News Computing Journal (ISSN 0888-1596)
 Description: Geared towards working journalists, journalism educators, and media researchers.

JOURNAL OF VISUAL COMMUNICATION AND IMAGE REPRESENTATION. see COMPUTERS — Computer Graphics

384.3   UK
KEY NOTE MARKET REPORT: C D - R O M. Variant title: C D - R O M. 1992. irreg. £185. Key Note Ltd., Field House, 72 Oldfield Rd., Hampton, Middlesex TW12 2HQ, England. TEL 44-181-783-0755. FAX 44-181-783-1940. **Document type:** trade publication.
 ●Also available online.
 Also available on CD-ROM.
 Formerly: Key Note Report: C D - R O M.

384.3   UK   ISSN 1357-1370
KEY NOTE MARKET REVIEW: MULTIMEDIA IN U K. Variant title: Multimedia in U K. 1994. irreg. £410. Key Note Ltd., Field House, 72 Oldfield Rd., Hampton, Middlesex TW12 2HQ, England. TEL 44-181-783-0755. FAX 44-181-783-0049. **Document type:** trade publication.
 ●Also available online.
 Also available on CD-ROM.

LOCAL AREA NETWORKING AND L A N INTERNETWORKING. see COMPUTERS — Personal Computers

LOGISTIK HEUTE. see BUSINESS AND ECONOMICS — Computer Applications

380.3   US
M I C - INFO. 1989. w. $2195. Management Information Corporation, 1111 Marlkress Rd., Box 5062, Cherry Hill, NJ 08003-5602. TEL 609-424-1111. FAX 609-424-1999. Ed. Jim Fidler. (diskette format)
 Description: Provides new product announcements for computers, and communications from over 3,000 companies. Includes organizational and financial information.

M I C - TECH-TELECOMMUNICATIONS. (Management Information Corporation) see COMMUNICATIONS — Telephone And Telegraph

MANAGING VOICE NETWORKS. see COMMUNICATIONS — Telephone And Telegraph

MICRO-GAZETTE. see COMPUTERS — Microcomputers

004   NE   ISSN 0923-8182
MULTI MEDIA COMPUTING MAGAZINE. 1972. m. fl.125. Nanton Press B.V., Leyenseweg 115C, 3721 BC Bilthoven, Netherlands. TEL 31-30-290644. FAX 31-30-286224. (Subscr. to: Postbus 93, 3720 AB Bilthoven, Netherlands) Ed. Anton Kriegsman. adv. contact: Anton Kriegsman. bk.rev. circ. 12,000. (back issues avail.)
 —SWETS.
 Incorporates (in 1991): Mini - Microcomputer (ISSN 0167-6547); Which was formed by the 1981 merger of: Microcomputer (ISSN 0167-3343) & Compu-techniek (ISSN 0165-9758); Incorporates: Informatronica (ISSN 0167-7225)

384.3   GW   ISSN 0940-5577
MULTIMEDIA; Informationsdienst fuer Medienintegration. 1991. s-m. DM.420 (foreign DM.504) (effective 1997). HighText Verlag, Ridlerstr. 55, 80339 Munich, Germany. TEL 49-89-500353-0. FAX 49-89-50035399. E-mail: info@hightext.de. Ed. Joachim Graf; Pub. Joachim Graf. R&P contact: Daniel Treplin. adv.: page DM.3150, color page DM.4650; trim 250 x 177; adv. contact: Erich Sommer. bk.rev.; index; circ. 1,500 (paid). (looseleaf format; back issues avail.) **Document type:** trade publication.
 ●Also available online.

384.3   UK   ISSN 1357-0080
MULTIMEDIA BUSINESS ANALYST. 1994. fortn. £495($738) Financial Times Telecoms & Media Publishing (Subsidiary of: Financial Times Group), Maple House, 149 Tottenham Court Rd., London W1P 9LL, England. TEL 0171-896-2234. FAX 0171-896-2256. Ed. Robin Arnfield. Indexed: WPM. **Document type:** newsletter.
 —SWETS.
 Description: Alerts readers to developments in the industry.

MULTIMEDIA ENTERTAINMENT & TECHNOLOGY REPORT. see COMPUTERS — Computer Industry

COMMUNICATIONS — COMPUTER APPLICATIONS

384.3   GW   ISSN 0946-4581
MULTIMEDIA MAGAZIN. (Supplement to: Multimedia (ISSN 0940-5577)) m. HighText Verlag, Ridlerstr. 55, 80339 Munich, Germany. TEL 49-89-500353-0. FAX 49-89-50035399. E-mail: info@hightext.de. Ed. Joachim Graf. R&P contact: Daniel Treplin. adv. contact: Erich Sommer. **Document type:** trade publication.
    Formerly (until 1993): M P C Multimedia Magazin (ISSN 0942-7449)

384.3   US
MULTIMEDIA PUBLISHER. m. $150 (outside N. America $165). Worldwide Videotex, Box 3273, Boynton Beach, FL 33424-3273. TEL 407-738-2276. Ed. Mark Wright; Pub. Mark Wright. bk.rev. **Document type:** newsletter.
● Also available online. Vendor(s): Information Access Co.
    Description: Covers all facets of multimedia publishing, exploring trends and marketing strategies.

380.3   US   ISSN 1087-4992
MULTIMEDIA TELECOMMUNICATION NEWS. 1991. m. $270 in US & Canada; elsewhere $300. Stoneridge Technical Services, Box 1891, Rockville, MD 20849. TEL 301-424-0114. FAX 301-424-8971. Ed. William W. Creitz; Pub. William W. Creitz. **Document type:** newsletter.
    Formerly: Integrated Messaging News (ISSN 1056-1412)
    Description: Covers mixed media messaging and communication involving combinations of text, image, video, voice and data. Provides information about technology, products, companies, and applications.

384.3   UK   ISSN 1358-6394
QA76.575
THE MULTIMEDIA YEARBOOK. 1992. a. £135($199) Macmillan Magazines Ltd., 4 Porters South, Crinan St., London N1 9XW. TEL 44-1256-29242. FAX 44-1256-842084. adv. contact: Mark Pearson. **Document type:** directory.
● Also available on CD-ROM.
—BLDSC (5983.149300).
    Formerly (until 1995): European Multimedia Yearbook (ISSN 0966-7709)
    Description: Evaluates the state of CD-ROM and multimedia in Europe.

N V R REPORTS. (National Video Resources) see COMMUNICATIONS — Video

384.3   US
NAUTILUS (DUBLIN). 1990. m. $136. Metatec, 7001 Discovery Blvd., Dublin, OH 43017. Ed. Mike Espindle. illus.
    Description: Covers computer applications in multimedia environments.

NETWORK WORLD. see COMPUTERS — Computer Networks

380.3   CN   ISSN 1187-2985
NETWORK WORLD CANADA. 1991. 24/yr. Can.$55($75) (foreign $95). Laurentian Technomedia Inc. (Subsidiary of: Laurentian Media Inc.), 501 Oakdale Rd., North York ON M3N 1W7, Canada. TEL 416-746-7360; 800-565-4007. FAX 416-746-1421. Ed. John Pickett. adv.: B&W page Can.$3950; trim 10 3/4 x 15; adv. contact: Gerald Chopik. circ. 12,000. (tabloid format) **Document type:** trade publication.
    Description: Provides strategic information on how to manage the enterprise network for competitive advantage.

380.3   US   ISSN 0888-8698
                                    CODEN: NALEEC
NEWSNET ACTION LETTER. 1983. m. free to qualified personnel. NewsNet, Inc., 945 Haverford Rd., Bryn Mawr, PA 19010. TEL 610-527-8030. FAX 610-527-0338. Ed. Raia King. **Document type:** newsletter.
● Also available online. Vendor(s): NewsNet (PB99).
—CASDDS.
    Description: Provides updates on NewsNet products available and service enhancements.

384.3   US   ISSN 1071-8990
QA75.5
O E M MAGAZINE. (Original Equipment Manufacturer) 1993. 8/yr. $59. C M P Publications, Inc., 600 Community Dr., Manhasset, NY 11030. TEL 516-562-5000. Ed. Rick Boyd-Merritt; Pub. Steve Weitzner. illus. circ. 35,000. **Document type:** trade publication.
—KR SourceOne. **CCC.**

OASIS (SURREY); the multimedia assets trade magazine. see PUBLISHING AND BOOK TRADE

384.3   US
▼**ON THE INTERNET: USER DEMOGRAPHICS & TRENDS.** 1995. irreg. $1001 (Canada and Mexico $1015; elsewhere $1031). Cowles - SIMBA Information (Subsidiary of: Cowles Business Media), 11 Riverbend Dr. S., Box 4949, Stamford, CT 06907-0949. TEL 203-358-9900; 800-307-2529. FAX 203-358-5811. E-mail: simba99@aol.com; URL: http://www.simbanet.com. **Document type:** trade publication.
    Description: Features detailed demographic studies of Internet users.

384.3   US
OPEN CHANNEL. 1981. m. University of Houston, Information Technology Information Services, Information Technology Division, Houston, TX 77204-1961. TEL 713-743-1500. E-mail: InfoServ@Jetson.UH.edu; URL: http://www.uhiedu/ toc. Ed. Rhonda Rubin; Pub. Jim Bradley. R&P contact: Rhonda Rubin. TEL 713-743-1505. **Document type:** newsletter.

384.3   JA
OPEN WORLD. bi-m. I D G Communications, Japan, 2-F, Shuwa Fujimicho Bldg., 1-2-27 Fujimu, Chiyoda-ku, Tokyo 102, Japan. TEL 81-3-3222-6411. FAX 81-3-3222-6566. Ed. Yoko Muramatsu. adv.: B&W page 320000 Yen, color page 520000; trim 210 x 282. circ. 36,000.

380.38   US
P C VIDEOLOG. 1988. m. updates on diskette. $240. Phonolog Publishing (Subsidiary of: Trade Service Corporation), 10996 Torreyana Rd., Box 85007, San Diego, CA 92138. TEL 619-457-5920.
    Formerly: Videoscan Database for IBM Compatible Computers.

PACIFIC TELECOMMUNICATIONS COUNCIL. CONFERENCE PROCEEDINGS. see COMMUNICATIONS — Telephone And Telegraph

PACIFIC TELECOMMUNICATIONS REVIEW. see COMMUNICATIONS — Telephone And Telegraph

380.3   US   ISSN 0896-582X
TK7885.A1
PHOENIX CONFERENCE ON COMPUTERS AND COMMUNICATIONS. CONFERENCE PROCEEDINGS. Variant title: International Phoenix Conference on Computers and Communications. Proceedings. 1982. a. price varies. Institute of Electrical and Electronics Engineers, Inc., 345 E. 47th St., New York, NY 10017-2394. TEL 732-981-0060; 800-678-4333. FAX 732-981-9667. E-mail: customer.service@ieee.org; URL: http://www.ieee. org. (Co-sponsor: I E E E Communications Society) (also avail. in microfiche) **Document type:** proceedings.
—CCC.
    Description: Covers a variety of topics in computers and communications.

384.3   GW   ISSN 0944-4033
POINT OF SALE. Short title: P O S. (Supplement to: Multimedia (ISSN 0940-5577)) m. HighText Verlag, Ridlerstr. 55, 80339 Munich, Germany. TEL 49-89-500353-0. FAX 49-89-50035399. E-mail: info@hightext.de. Ed. Joachim Graf. R&P contact: Daniel Treplin. adv. contact: Erich Sommer. **Document type:** trade publication.

070.5 384.3   US   ISSN 1090-7270
▼**PUBLISHING ENTREPRENEUR;** profit strategies for the information and publishing industries. 1995. bi-m. $29 in U.S.; Canada $38; Europe $45 (effective 1997); newsstand price: $3.50; Canada $4.50. Jenkins Group, Inc., 121 E. Front St., 4th Fl., Traverse City, MI 49684. TEL 616-933-0445; 800-706-4636. FAX 616-933-0448. E-mail: http:/ /www.smallpress.com. Ed. Mardi Link; Pub. Jerrold R. Jenkins. adv.: B&W page $1620; trim 8 1/4 x 10 7/8; adv. contact: Victoria Champagne Sutherland. illus. circ. 8,000. **Document type:** trade publication.
    Formerly (until 1996): Information Entrepreneur (ISSN 1086-1459)
    Description: Covers the profitable use of available and emerging information technologies.

380.3 330   FR   ISSN 0987-7401
REPERTOIRE DES BANQUES DE DONNEES TELETEL POUR L'ENTREPRISE. 1988. biennial. 295 F. (effective 1997). Editions F L A Consultants, 27 rue de la Vistule, 75013 Paris, France. TEL 33-1-45827575. FAX 33-1-45824604. E-mail: flabases@iway.fr; URL: http://www.fla-consultants.fr. Ed. Beatrice Riou. adv. contact: Beatrice Riou. **Document type:** directory.
● Also available online.
    Description: A tool to identify French Teletel databases which can be useful for companies.

380.3 621.381
384.6   US   ISSN 0741-8361
REPORT ON A T & T. (American Telephone and Telegraph); the independent bi-weekly reporting exclusively on the long-distance industry including AT&T and its competitors. 1983. bi-w (26/yr.). $759 (foreign $785) (effective 1998). Capitol Publications, Inc., Telecom Publishing Group, 1101 King St., Ste. 444, Box 1455, Alexandria, VA 22313-2055. TEL 800-327-7205. FAX 703-739-6490. URL: http://www. telecommunications.com. Ed. Mark Kellner. index, cum.index. **Document type:** newsletter.
● Also available online. Vendor(s): Information Access Co., NewsNet (TE50).
—CCC.
    Description: Independent "business intelligence" on all of AT&T's activities. Briefings on new products and services, computers and networking equipment, prices and marketing. Full coverage of long-distance activities, joint ventures, regulatory action, personnel decisions.

384 330   US   ISSN 1077-4653
RUSSIA ONLINE AND WIRELESS. 1994. m. $450 (effective 1996). Gist, Inc., 2200 Wilson Blvd., Ste. 102-G, Arlington, VA 22201. TEL 703-527-7459. FAX 703-528-1477. Ed. David K. Bain; Pub. David K. Bain. R&P contact: Michael Peil. adv. contact: Daniel Radack. index. (back issues avail.) **Document type:** newsletter.
    Description: Provides news of telecommunications and information markets in Russia and the New Independent States, analysis of investment opportunities and regulatory climate.

384.3   GW
SCREEN MULTIMEDIA. 1993. m. DM.99 (Europe DM.129) (effective 1996). MACup Verlag GmbH, Leverkusenstr. 54, 22761 Hamburg, Germany. TEL 49-40-85183350. FAX 49-40-85183399. Eds. Leo Jacobs, Henry Steinhau. adv.: B&W page DM.5900, color page DM.7900; adv. contact: Barbara Herpich. circ. 16,380 (paid). **Indexed:** WPM. **Document type:** trade publication.
    Description: Addresses the information and technical needs of the growing multimedia industry in Germany.

384.3   FR   ISSN 1167-2501
SOLUTIONS TELEMATIQUES; audiotex, bornes interactives, fax, micro, multimedia, RNIS, videotex. 1992. m. (11/yr.). 685 F. A Jour, 11 rue du Marche St. Honore, 75001 Paris, France. TEL 42-96-67-22. FAX 40-20-07-75.

COMMUNICATIONS — POSTAL AFFAIRS

384 005.13   NE   ISSN 0927-5444
STUDIES IN COMPUTER AND COMMUNICATIONS SYSTEMS. Running title: ADA Yearbook. 1992. irreg., vol.8, 1995. price varies. I O S Press, Van Diemenstraat 94, 1013 CN Amsterdam, Netherlands. TEL 31-20-6382189. FAX 31-20-6203419. E-mail: market@iospress.nl; URL: http://www.iospress.nl/iospress. (In N. America: Box 10558, Burke, VA 22009-0558. TEL 703-323-5554. FAX 703-250-4705) (back issues avail.) Indexed: Zent.Math. **Document type:** monographic series.
—BLDSC (8490.281500); CISTI.
    Description: Covers research in ADA programming language.
    Refereed Serial

384.3   US   ISSN 1070-096X
SUBMARINE FIBER OPTIC COMMUNICATIONS SYSTEMS. 1993. m. $595 (foreign $635) (effective 1997). Information Gatekeepers, Inc., 214 Harvard Ave., Boston, MA 02134. TEL 617-232-3111; 800-323-1088. FAX 617-734-8562. E-mail: igiboston@aol.com; URL: http://www.igigroup.com. **Document type:** newsletter.

380.31   US
SUPERCOMPUTING AND PARALLEL PROCESSING TODAY.* 1988. bi-m. $195 (foreign $235). Yellowstone Information Services, R.R. 2, Box 42A, Bloomingdale, OH 43910-9802. TEL 304-965-5548. FAX 304-965-7785. Ed. Roger C. Thibault. adv.; bk.rev.; index, cum.index. circ. 2,000. (back issues avail.)
    Description: Contains news and applications covering supercomputing and parallel processing.

380.3   CN
TECHNOLOGIES. (Text in French) 1983. m. Can.$39.95. Publications Transcontinental Inc., 1100 boul. Rene Levesque W., 24th Fl., Montreal, PQ H3B 4X9, Canada. TEL 514-392-9000. FAX 514-392-4726. Ed. Yan Barcelo. adv. circ. 86,550. (back issues avail.)

TECHSCAN NEWSLETTER; the manager's guide to technology. see *BUSINESS AND ECONOMICS — Computer Applications*

TELECOMBRIEF - TELEMATICS TRENDS. see *COMMUNICATIONS — Television And Cable*

004.692   UK   ISSN 1361-1364
▼**TELECOMEUROPA'S MESSAGING NEWSLETTER;** the monthly report on fixed and mobile messaging. Variant title: Messaging Newsletter. 1995. m. £495($740) (effective 1995). Telecomeuropa News Bureau Publications, 3 Princes Bldgs., George St., Bath, Avon BA1 2ED, England. TEL 44-1225-445282. FAX 44-1225-445283. E-mail: 10014.3104@compuserve.com. (US subscr. to: Box 4948, Laguna Beach, CA 92652. TEL 714-499-1857) Ed. Paul Rasmussen; Pub. Peter Purton. tr.lit. (back issues avail.) **Document type:** newsletter.
●Also available online.

TELECOMMUNICATIONS; management and marketing newsletter. see *COMMUNICATIONS*

384.3 004.6   AT   ISSN 1326-6810
TELECOMMUNICATIONS CARRIERS AND SERVICE PROVIDERS MARKET. 1984. a. Aus.$525 (US Aus.$555; Europe Aus.$560) (effective 1998). Paul Budde Communication Pty. Ltd., 2643 George Downes Dr., Bucketty, N.S.W. 2250, Australia. TEL 61-49-988144. FAX 61-49-988247. E-mail: pbc@budde.com.au; URL: http://www.budde.com.au. Ed. Paul Budde. **Document type:** directory.
    Supersedes in part: Directory of Electronic Services and Communications Networks in Australia and New Zealand (ISSN 1322-350X)
    Description: List over 100 telecommunications carriers and major service providers, Internet service providers, callback operators, MDS and pay TV licence holders in Australia.

621.38 384.3   AT   ISSN 1326-6802
TELECOMMUNICATIONS NETWORKS MARKET - AUSTRALIA AND NEW ZEALAND. 1984. a. Aus.$275 (US Aus.$295; Europe Aus.$300) (effective 1998). Paul Budde Communication Pty. Ltd., 2643 George Downes Dr., Bucketty, N.S.W. 2250, Australia. TEL 61-7-49988144. FAX 61-7-49988247. E-mail: pbc@budde.com.au; URL: http://www.budde.com.au. Ed. Paul Budde. stat. **Document type:** directory.
    Supersedes in part: Directory of Electronic Services and Communications Networks in Australia and New Zealand.
    Description: Covers voice, data, intelligent, broadband, satellite networks, resale, outsourcing, network management and facilities management services. Includes information on developments and trends.

TELECOMMUNICATIONS STRATEGIES REPORT; packaging of value added telecommunication & broadcasting services & networks. see *COMMUNICATIONS — Telephone And Telegraph*

TELEFACTS. see *COMMUNICATIONS — Telephone And Telegraph*

380.3   II   ISSN 0970-3934
TK5101.A1   CODEN: TELIEG
TELEMATICS INDIA. (Text in English) 1987. m. Rs.200($50) (effective 1995). Vimot Publishers Pvt. Ltd., 3Fl., Grandlay Complex, Community Centre, New Friends Colony, New Delhi 110 065, India. TEL 91-11-6924496. FAX 91-11-6836375. Ed. Rajendra Prabhu; Pub. B.K. Singhal. R&P contact: Rajendra Prabhu. adv. contact: Shashi Dharan. bk.rev.; charts; illus.; stat.; tr.lit.; index. circ. 21,000. (back issues avail.) **Document type:** trade publication.
—BLDSC (8782.956000); AskIEEE; CISTI; Ei; KR SourceOne.
    Description: Aims to fill information or technical gaps for professionals, laymen and college students.

384 004.6   NE
TELETRAFFIC SCIENCE AND ENGINEERING. (Text in English) 1994. irreg. price varies. (International Teletraffic Conference) Elsevier Science B.V., Books Division, P.O. Box 211, 1000 AE Amsterdam, Netherlands. TEL 31-20-4853911. FAX 31-20-4853705. TELEX 18582 ESPA NL. E-mail: nlinfo-f@elsevier.nl; usinfo-f@elsevier.com; forinfo-kyf04035@niftyserve.or.jp; URL: http://www.elsevier.nl/. (Subscr. in the Americas to: Elsevier Science, Regional Sales Office, Box 945, New York, NY 10159-0945. TEL 212-633-3730. FAX 212-633-3680; Subscr. in Australasia and the Far East to: Elsevier Science (Singapore) Pte Ltd, No.1 Temasek Ave., No.17-01 Millenia Tower, Singapore 039192, Singapore. TEL 65-434-3727. FAX 65-337-2230; Subscr. in Japan to: Elsevier Science Japan, 9-15 Higashi-Azabu 1-chome, Minato-ku, Tokyo 106, Japan. TEL 81-3-5561-5033. FAX 81-3-5561-5047) Ed. Paul J. Kuehn. **Document type:** monographic series, proceedings.
    Description: Publishes proceedings of world conferences, special conferences and selected monographs on topics relating to teletraffic theory and its applications to the design, planning and operation of telecommunications systems and networks.
    Refereed Serial

380.3   IS
TIKSHORET. s-a. Motorola Communication Israel Ltd., Customer Relations Manager, Rehov Karmanski 16, Tel Aviv 67 899, Israel. TEL 03-388257. Ed. Meir Eshkol.

004.6   UK
U K L U G NEWSLETTER. 1989? bi-m. £50 membership to institutions; non-member individuals £15. U K Online Users Group, Institute of Information Scientists, 44 Museum St., London WC1A 1LY, England. TEL 44-171-831-8003. E-mail: lby2@uk.ac.unn. (Subscr. to: Learned Information, Woodside, Hinksey Hill, Oxford OX1 5AU, England. TEL 44-1865-730275) (Co-sponsor: Institute for Information Scientists) Ed. Ian Winship. adv.: page £200; adv. contact: Ian Winship.
    Formerly (until 1994): U K Online User Group Newsletter (ISSN 0957-8544)

384.3   GW   ISSN 0946-5456
VIRTUAL REALITIES. 1993. m. HighText Verlag, Ridlerstr. 55, 80339 Munich, Germany. TEL 49-89-500353-0. FAX 49-89-50035399. E-mail: info@hightext.de. Ed. Joachim Graf. R&P contact: Daniel Treplin. **Document type:** trade publication.

384.3   FR   ISSN 1149-1566
VOCAL. 22/yr. 2800 F. A Jour, 11 rue du Marche St. Honore, 75001 Paris, France. TEL 42-96-67-22. FAX 40-20-07-75. Ed. Patricia Dreidemy.

380.3 621.319   US   ISSN 0886-2087
VOICENEWS. 1981. m. $297 in the U.S. and Canada; overseas $327. Stoneridge Technical Services, Box 1891, Rockville, MD 20849. TEL 301-424-0114. FAX 301-424-8971. Ed. William W. Creitz; Pub. William W. Creitz. **Document type:** newsletter.
    Description: Covers voice processing technology, products and companies. Offers information on voice mail, voice response, speech recognition and speech synthesis.

380.3   US
WIRELESS P C S TELECOMMUNICATIONS. (Personal Communications System) 1991. m. $595 (foreign $645) (effective 1997). Information Gatekeepers, Inc., 214 Harvard Ave., Boston, MA 02134. TEL 617-232-3111; 800-323-1088. FAX 617-734-8562. E-mail: igiboston@aol.com; URL: http://www.igigroup.com. Ed. Paul Polishuk. **Document type:** newsletter.
    Former titles: P C N Telecommunications & Wireless - Personal Communication Networks (ISSN 1058-6725)
    Description: Covers personal communications networks technology, regulatory developments, markets, products, standards, and business developments.

380.3   US
WORKSTATIONS & SERVERS. 2 base vols. (plus m. updates). $890 to new subscr.; renewals $797 (effective 1996). Datapro Information Services Group (Subsidiary of: McGraw-Hill, Inc.), 600 Delran Pkwy., Delran, NJ 08075. TEL 609-764-0100; 800-328-2776. FAX 609-764-2814.

621.381 001.6   US   ISSN 0731-7891
WORLDWIDE VIDEOTEX UPDATE. 1981. m. $150 (outside N. America $165). Worldwide Videotex, Box 3273, Boynton Beach, FL 33424-3273. TEL 407-738-2276. Ed. Mark Wright; Pub. Mark Wright. (back issues avail.) Indexed: Comput.Lit.Ind. **Document type:** newsletter.
●Also available online. Vendor(s): Data-Star, Information Access Co., Knight-Ridder Information, Inc., NewsNet (PB08).
—CCC.
    Description: Reports news and information on videotex, online services, electronic mail, satellite communications, and television-related technologies, such as teleconferencing and teletext.

COMMUNICATIONS — Postal Affairs

A G M. (Arbeitsgemeinschaft Malta im Bund Deutscher Philatelisten e.V.) see *PHILATELY*

383.12409489   DK   ISSN 0107-4350
ADRESSELOESE POSTFORSENDELSER. 1980. a. free. Post Danmark, Hovedkontoret, Tietgensgade 37, DK-1630 Copenhagen V, Denmark. TEL 45-33-75-44-75. FAX 45-33-75-44-50. illus. circ. 12,000.
    Supersedes in part: Postomdeling af Reklamer.

383 331.8   US   ISSN 0044-7811
HE6499
AMERICAN POSTAL WORKER. 1903. m. $3 to member (effective 1997-1998). American Postal Worker's Union, A F L - C I O, 1300 L St., N.W., Washington, DC 20005. TEL 202-842-4200. FAX 202-842-4297. Ed. Moe Biller. charts; illus.; tr.lit. circ. 300,000. (tabloid format) **Document type:** newspaper.
    Incorporated: Union Postal Clerk and Postal Transport Journal (ISSN 0041-6991)

383.12404989   DK
ANTAL MODTAGERE. 1985. q. free. Post Danmark, Hovedkontoret, Tietgensgade 37, DK-1566 Copenhagen V, Denmark. TEL 45-33-75-44-75. FAX 45-33-75-44-50. circ. 11,000.
    Formerly: Antal Modtagere, Adresseloese Postforsendelser (ISSN 0900-8829)

COMMUNICATIONS — POSTAL AFFAIRS

ARTISTAMP NEWS. see *ART*

383 US
ASSOCIATION OF PRIVATE POSTAL SYSTEMS. DIRECTORY.* 1975. a. Association of Private Postal Systems, 5580 Power Inn Rd., No. F, Sacramento, CA 95820-6748. TEL 916-929-3300. Dir. Donald F. Marford. **Document type:** directory.

383 US
ASSOCIATION OF PRIVATE POSTAL SYSTEMS. UPDATE.* 1975. m. Association of Private Postal Systems, 5580 Power Inn Rd., No. F, Sacramento, CA 95820-6748. TEL 916-929-3300.

383 BE
BELGIUM. POSTE. RAPPORT D'ACTIVITE. 1954. a. free. La Poste, Direction de la Communication, Centre Monnaie, 1000 Brussels, Belgium. Ed.Bd. illus. circ. 6,000. **Document type:** bulletin, corporate report.
  Supersedes: Belgium. Regie des Postes. Rapport d'Activite (ISSN 0377-337X)
  Description: Report on the activities of the Belgian Postal Service.

BERMUDA POST. see *PHILATELY*

383.12209489 DK ISSN 0908-7796
BREVE INDLAND. 1980-1983; resumed 1985. a. free. Post Danmark, Hovedkontoret, Tietgensgade 37, DK-1560 Copenhagen V, Denmark. TEL 45-33-75-44-75. FAX 45-33-75-44-50. illus. circ. 12,000.
  Former titles (until 1991): Adresserede Brevforsendelser (ISSN 0901-263X); (until 1985): Adresserede Forsendelser i Stoerre Antal (ISSN 0107-4369)

381 US ISSN 0068-4201
BULLINGER'S POSTAL AND SHIPPERS GUIDE FOR THE UNITED STATES AND CANADA. 1871. a. $360. Alber - Leland Publishing, 500 N. Skinner Blvd., St. Louis, MO 63130. Ed. D.L. Cundari. circ. 3,000. **Document type:** directory.
  Description: Lists approximately 200,000 place names throughout the United States and Canada.

383.4 US ISSN 0739-3873
CODEN: BMAREG
BUSINESS MAILERS REVIEW. 1980. bi-w. $279 (foreign $294) (effective 1997). Pasha Publications Inc., 1616 N. Ft. Myer Dr., Ste. 1000, Arlington, VA 22209-3107. TEL 703-816-8640. FAX 703-528-4926. E-mail: mailer@pasha.com. Ed. Kate Muth; Pub. Tod Sedgwick. R&P contact: Harry Baisden. TEL 703-816-8617. circ. 2,500 (paid). **Document type:** newsletter.
  ●Also available online. Vendor(s): Information Access Co.
  Description: Covers US Postal Service policy and activities as well as commercial postal vendors as they relate to the volume business mailer.

CALLIGRAPHER. see *HOBBIES*

383 CN
CANADA POSTAL GUIDE PART 1: POSTAL LAW AND REGULATIONS. irreg. Can.$31.75. Supply and Services Canada, Publishing Centre, Ottawa, ON K1A 0S9, Canada. TEL 613-997-2560. (looseleaf format)

383 CN
CANADA POSTAL GUIDE PART 2: INTERNATIONAL MAILS, RATES AND CONDITIONS. irreg. Can.$28. Supply and Services Canada, Publishing Centre, Ottawa, ON K1A 0S9, Canada. TEL 613-997-2560. (looseleaf format)

CANADIAN POSTMASTER/MAITRE DE POSTE CANADIEN. see *LABOR UNIONS*

383.4 US ISSN 1079-7661
▼**LA CATASTROPHE.** 1995. q. $15 (U.K. £10) (effective 1997). Wreck & Crash Mail Society, 132 Livingston Pl. W., Metairie, LA 70005. TEL 504-835-2856. E-mail: 74137.2275@compuserve.com. (Subscr. in UK to: 10 Lady Jane Park, Bradgate Rd., Newtown Linford, Leicester LE6 0HD, England) Ed. Henry J. Berthelot. R&P contact: Henry J. Berthelot. adv.; bk.rev.; illus.; maps; circ. 80. **Document type:** newsletter.
  Description: Contains articles on postal history including various aspects of damaged and delayed mail, especially mail service interruptions involving ships, trains, and airplanes.

CORREIOS E TELECOMUNICACOES DE PORTUGAL. ANUARIO ESTATISTICO. see *COMMUNICATIONS — Abstracting, Bibliographies, Statistics*

383 384.1 SP
CORREO POSTAL Y TELEGRAFICO. 12/yr. Palacio de Comunicaciones, Alcala 50, 28014 Madrid, Spain. TEL 1-531-50-39. FAX 1-396-21-32. Ed. Manuel Navalles-Castro.

383 UK ISSN 0011-0396
COURIER (LONDON); the post office newspaper. 1966. m. British Post Office, 130 Old St., 5th Fl., London EC1V 9PQ, England. TEL 44-171-320-7321. FAX 44-171-320-7322. Ed. John Schofield. adv.; bk.rev.; illus. circ. 320,000. (tabloid format) **Indexed:** So.Pac.Per.Ind. **Document type:** newspaper.

383 II ISSN 0011-5762
DAK TAR. (Editions in English and Hindi) 1956. m. Rs.12. Department of Posts & Telecommunications, Parliament St., New Delhi 110001, India. Ed. V. Naraynswamy. adv.; bk.rev.; illus. circ. 10,000.

DATA IN WORLD DATA CENTER C2 FOR IONOSPHERE. CATALOGUE. see *EARTH SCIENCES — Geophysics*

DEUTSCHE POST (FRANKFURT). see *LABOR UNIONS*

383.4 GW
DEUTSCHE POSTZEITUNG. m. (Deutsche Post AG) Vereinigte Verlagsanstalten GmbH, Hoeherweg 278, 40231 Duesseldorf, Germany. TEL 49-211-7357-0. FAX 49-211-7357223. circ. 45,000. **Document type:** newsletter.

383 350 US ISSN 1058-0867
CODEN: DMUSD4
DOMESTIC MAIL MANUAL. 1979. q. $37 (foreign $43.25) (effective 1995). U.S. Postal Service, 975 L'Enfant Plaza, S.W., DC 20260. TEL 202-783-3238. (Subscr. to: Superintendent of Documents, U.S. Government Printing Office, Box 371954, Pittsburgh, PA 15250. TEL 202-512-1800. FAX 202-512-2250) **Document type:** government publication.
  Description: Assists customers in obtaining maximum benefits from the U.S. Postal Service for domestic mailing. Includes regulation and rate information.

383 FR
ECOLE NATIONALE SUPERIEURE DES POSTES ET TELECOMMUNICATIONS. ASSOCIATION DES ELEVES ET ANCIENS ELEVES. CAHIERS D'ETUDES ET D'INFORMATION. (Not published during 1978) 1951. q. 20 F. Ecole Nationale Superieure des Postes et Telecomunications, Association des Eleves et Anciens Eleves, 46 rue Barrault, 75634 Paris Cedex 13, France. Ed. R. Fort. adv.; charts. circ. 30,525. **Document type:** academic/scholarly publication.
  Formerly (until 1978): Courrier: Cahiers d'Etudes et d'Informations (ISSN 0011-0469)

383.4 IT ISSN 1121-2624
GABBIANO. 1991. bi-m. L.50000. Emmeffe s.r.l., Via della Cavona 2, C.P. 3, 00040 Morena (RM), Italy. TEL 06-79840020. FAX 06-79840024. Ed. Enrico Veschi. adv.: color page L.28000000; adv. contact: Riccardo Marini. circ. 250,000.

383 GW ISSN 0940-4848
GERMANY. BUNDESMINISTERIUM FUER POST UND TELEKOMMUNIKATION. AMTSBLATT. 1846. s-w. DM.100. Bundesministerium fuer Post und Telekommunikation, Postfach 8001, 53105 Bonn, Germany. TEL 0228-145123. FAX 0228-146512. illus.; index. (looseleaf format) **Document type:** government publication.
  Former titles: Germany. Bundesminister fuer das Post- und Telekommunikation. Amtsblatt; Germany (Federal Republic, 1949-) Bundesministerium fuer das Post- und Fernmeldewesen. Amtsblatt (ISSN 0003-2263)

HOLY LAND POSTAL HISTORY. see *PHILATELY*

DER INGENIEUR DER DEUTSCHEN BUNDESPOST. see *ENGINEERING*

INTERNATIONAL ART POST. see *ART*

383 US ISSN 1058-0875
HE6445 CODEN: IMAMEA
INTERNATIONAL MAIL MANUAL. s-a. $20 (foreign $25) (effective 1995). U.S. Postal Service, 475 L'Enfant Plaza, S.W., Washington, DC 20260-1571. TEL 202-783-3238. (Subscr. to: Superintendent of Documents, U.S. Government Printing Office, Box 371954, Pittsburgh, PA 15250-7954. TEL 202-512-1800. FAX 202-512-2250) (looseleaf format; back issues avail.) **Document type:** government publication.
  Formerly: Directory of International Mail.

383.4 TS
ITTIHAD AL-BARIDI AL-ARABI/ARAB POSTAL UNION. REVIEW. (Text in Arabic) 1955. q. exchange basis. Arab Postal Union - Al-Ittihad al-Baridi al-Arabi, P.O. Box 7999, Dubai, United Arab Emirates. TEL 690508. TELEX 46284 BRDIM EM. Ed. Hussein Rashid al-Hamdani. circ. 3,000.
  Description: Covers news and activities of the Arab Postal Union, with a focus on modernization efforts.

JIAOTONG YUNSHU JINGJI, YOUDIAN JINGJI. see *TRANSPORTATION*

383.4 UK
KEY NOTE MARKET REPORT: COURIER & EXPRESS SERVICES. Variant title: Courier & Express Services. irreg., vol.6, 1995. £205. Key Note Ltd., Field House, 72 Oldfield Rd., Hampton, Middlesex TW12 2HQ, England. TEL 44-181-783-0755. FAX 44-181-783-0049. Ed. Kim Potts. **Document type:** trade publication.
  ●Also available online.
  Also available on CD-ROM.
  Formerly: Key Note Report: Courier and Express Services (ISSN 0957-7351)

383 701.68 US
LETTER BOMB.* (Text in various languages) 1979. q. $25. Transient Press Editions, Box 1049, Bridgehampton, NY 11932. Ed. Norman Conquest. bk.rev.; film rev.; charts; illus. circ. 500. (back issues avail.)
  Description: International magazine of mail art, experimental literature and pataphysics.

LETTER EXCHANGE; a magazine for letter writers. see *LITERATURE*

LONDON POSTAL HISTORY GROUP NOTEBOOK. see *PHILATELY*

383.4 769.56 US ISSN 1078-1692
LONG ISLAND POSTAL HISTORIAN. 1980. q. $15 (effective through 1998). Long Island Postal History Society, 144 Hamilton Ave., Clifton, NJ 07011. TEL 201-772-1413. Ed. Brad Arch. adv.; bk.rev. circ. 100.
  Refereed Serial

383 387.164 US ISSN 1051-824X
HF5761 CODEN: MSTTE8
M A S T. (Mailing and Systems Technology); for mailing professionals. Key Title: Mast. 1988. 6/yr. $27 (foreign $47) (free to qualified personnel). R B Publishing Company, 2701 E. Washington Ave., Madison, WI 57304-5002. TEL 604-241-8777. FAX 608-241-8666. Ed. Marll Thiede; Pub. Ron Brent. R&P contact: Linda Marx. adv.: B&W page $4280, color page $5530; trim 8 x 10 7/8; adv. contact: Ron Brent. illus.; tr.lit.; circ. 4,000 (paid); 36,000 (controlled). **Document type:** trade publication.

383 US ISSN 1053-0703
MAIL: THE JOURNAL OF COMMUNICATION DISTRIBUTION. 1989. 9/yr. $31 (foreign $72). Excelsior Publication, One Milstone Rd., Gold Key Box 2425, Milford, PA 18337-9607. TEL 717-686-2111. FAX 717-686-3495. Ed. Francis P. Ruggiero. **Document type:** trade publication.

383 MF
MAURITIUS. POSTS AND TELEGRAPHS DEPARTMENT. ANNUAL REPORT. (Text in English) a. Government Printing Office, Elizabeth II Ave., Port Louis, Mauritius. (Subscr. to: La Tour Koenig, Pointe aux Sables, Port Louis, Mauritius. TEL 2345294. FAX 2084011) **Document type:** government publication.

COMMUNICATIONS — POSTAL AFFAIRS

383 US
MEMO TO MAILERS. m. free. U.S. Postal Service, Corporate Relations, 475 L'Enfant Plaza, Rm. 10541, Washington, DC 20260-3100. (Subscr. to: U.S. Postal Service, National Address Information Center, 6060 Primacy Pkwy., Ste. 101, Memphis TN 38188-0001) charts; illus.; stat. circ. 100,000. **Document type:** trade publication.
  Description: Contains news articles and items on the latest issues and developments affecting U.S. Postal Service business and its customers.

MILITARY POSTAL HISTORY SOCIETY BULLETIN. see *PHILATELY*

383.4 769.56 US ISSN 1078-1625
HE6376.A1
N J P H. 1973. 5/yr. $15 (effective 1996 & 1997). New Jersey Postal History Society Inc., 144 Hamilton Ave., Clifton, NJ 07011. TEL 201-772-1413. Ed. Brad Arch. R&P contact: Brad Arch. adv. contact: Brad Arch. bk.rev. circ. 150.

333 CC ISSN 1000-1972
NANJING YOUDIAN XUEYUAN XUEBAO. (Text in Chinese) q. Nanjing Youdian Xueyuan, 38 Guangdong Lu, Nanjing, Jiangsu 210003, People's Republic of China. TEL 635561. Ed. Wang Hongsheng.

383 US ISSN 0731-9185
HE6361 CODEN: NFDDD3
NATIONAL FIVE DIGIT ZIP CODE AND POST OFFICE DIRECTORY. a. $15. U.S. Postal Service, Washington, DC 20260-6800. (Dist. by: Bernan, 4611-F Assembly Dr., Lanham, MD 20706. TEL 301-459-7666. FAX 301-459-0056) **Document type:** directory, government publication.
  —CASDDS; CISTI.
  Formerly: National Zip Code and Post Office Directory (ISSN 0191-6971); Formed by the 1979 merger of: National Zip Code Directory (ISSN 0160-6476); Directory of Post Offices.

383 US ISSN 0028-0089
HD6350.P77
THE NATIONAL RURAL LETTER CARRIER. 1903. bi-w. $15. National Rural Letter Carriers Association, 1630 Duke St., 4th Fl., Alexandria, VA 22314-3465. TEL 703-684-5545. Ed. Steven R. Smith. R&P contact: Steven R. Smith. adv.; illus.; stat. circ. 90,000. **Document type:** trade publication.

383 658 UK ISSN 0548-5924
NEW MANAGEMENT. 1968. m. £2.50. Communication Managers Association, Ltd., Hughes House, Twyford, Reading, Berkshire RG10 9JD, England. Ed. T.L. Deegan. adv.; bk.rev. circ. 20,000.

383 US ISSN 0049-5298
NEW YORK METRO AREA POSTAL UNION. UNION MAIL. Key Title: Union Mail. 1957. m. $1. New York Metro Area Postal Union, 460 W. 34th St., New York, NY 10001. TEL 212-563-7553. Ed. Robert Knolle. charts; illus. circ. 31,500. **Document type:** government publication, newspaper.
  Formerly: Manhattan - Bronx Postal Union. Union Mail.

383 US
NEWS AND IDEAS.* 1982. m. $160. Associated Mail & Parcel Centers, HC 75 Box 124, Chama, NM 87520-9708. TEL 505-294-6425. FAX 505-271-2050. Ed. James W. Baer. adv.; bk.rev. circ. 900. (back issues avail.) **Document type:** newsletter.
  Former titles: A C M R A News; (until 1987): Mail Center News.

NEWSPAPER AND MAIL DELIVERERS' UNION BULLETIN. see *LABOR UNIONS*

NONPROFIT MAILERS FEDERATION. NEWS UPDATE. see *CLUBS*

383 SW ISSN 0345-8539
NORDISK POSTTIDSSKRIFT; organ foer postfoervaltningarna i Norden: Danmark, Finland, Island, Norge, Sverige. Variant title: N P T. 1903. 8/yr. SEK 75 (effective 1991). Nordic Postal Union, S-105 00, Stockholm, Sweden. Ed. Lars Inge Svensson. bk.rev. circ. 3,600.
  Formerly (until 1919): Tidskrift foer Postvaesendet.

383 769.56 US
OFFICIALLY SEALED NOTES. 1978. q. $12 (foreign $15). Officially Sealed, c/o Fred Scheuer, Box 2356, Mesa, AZ 85204.

383.4 US
OPTIMUM DELIVERY; the newsletter for professionals competing with the postal service. 1990. bi-m. $89. Willow Bend Communications, Inc., Box 7977485, Dallas, TX 75379-7485. TEL 214-248-0451. FAX 214-733-0995. Ed. Alexander Thompson; Pub. Stephen Thompson. circ. 950. **Document type:** trade publication.
  Description: Discusses trends in private postal systems.

383 IT ISSN 0030-5634
ORIZZONTI PROFESSIONALI; rivista bimestrale di tecnica, cultura ed informazioni. 1960. bi-m. L.4000. Istituto Professionale di Stato per l'Industria e l'Artigianato "E. Ascione" Palermo, Via Leonardo da Vinci 364, 90143 Palermo, Italy. Dir. Giuseppe Maggio. illus.

P H S G NEWSLETTER. (Pearl Harbor Study Group) see *PHILATELY*

383 384 SZ
P T T I STUDIES. (Editions in English, French, Spanish, and German) 1973. irreg. free. Postal Telegraph and Telephone International, 38 av. du Lignon, Geneva, Switzerland. FAX 022-7963975. TELEX 418735-IPTT-CH. Ed. P. Bowyer. bibl. circ. 2,500.

P T T NOVICE; glasilo P T T delavcev Slovenije. see *COMMUNICATIONS — Telephone And Telegraph*

PARCEL SHIPPING & DISTRIBUTION; managing the package and document shipment process. see *TRANSPORTATION*

383.4 SA
POST OFFICE XPRESS. (Text in Afrikaans and English) 1971. m. free. S A Post Office, P.O. Box 9255, Pretoria 0001, South Africa. TEL 27-12-4217714. FAX 27-12-4217606. Ed. Martie Gilchrist. R&P contact: Martie Gilchrist. adv.; bk.rev.; illus.; circ. 33,000 (controlled). (tabloid format) **Document type:** newspaper.
  Formerly (until July 1991): Postel.
  Description: Covers postal matters for staff members.

383 SZ
POST, TELEFON UND TELEGRAFEN. AMTSBLATT. 1849. w. 25 SFr. (foreign 45 SFr.) (effective 1997). Swiss Posts, Telephones and Telegraphs (PTT), Postkonto 30-6450-2, CH-3030 Bern, Switzerland. TEL 41-31-626389. FAX 41-31-629059. circ. 24,000. **Document type:** government publication.

383.4 AU
POST UND TELEKOM. 1948. 10/yr. S.72. Post und Telekom Austria Aktiengesellschaft, Postgasse 8, A-1011 Vienna, Austria. TEL 43-1-515515040. FAX 43-1-5134052. Ed. Andreas Spannring; Pub. Karl Holleschek. adv.: page S.40000; trim 175 x 250; adv. contact: Werner Burmann. circ. 40,000. **Document type:** government publication.
  Formerly (until 1996): Postrundschau.

383 GW ISSN 0947-9945
HE6995
POST- UND TELEKOMMUNIKATIONSGESCHICHTE. 1953. s-a. DM.20 (effective 1997 & 1998). Deutsche Gesellschaft fuer Post- und Telekommunikationsgeschichte, Postfach 700262, 60552 Frankfurt a.M., Germany. TEL 49-69-611040. FAX 49-69-6060365. Ed. Gottfried North. R&P contact: Gottfried North. bk.rev.; index. circ. 45,000. (back issues avail.) Indexed: Amer.Hist.& Life (1989-1990), (1993-), Hist.Abstr. **Document type:** bulletin.
  Formerly (until 1995): Archiv fuer Deutsche Postgeschichte (ISSN 0003-8989)

769.56 383 US ISSN 0885-7385
HE6371
LA POSTA; a journal of American postal history. 1969. bi-m. $15. Posta Publications, Box 135, Lake Oswego, OR 97034. TEL 503-657-5685. Ed. Richard W. Helbock. circ. 1,000.

383 384 SA
POSTAL AND TELKOM HERALD/POS- EN TELKOMHERALD. (Text in Afrikaans, English) 1904. m. membership. Postal and Telkom Association of South Africa, Box 9186, Johannesburg 2000, South Africa. TEL 27-11-725-5422. FAX 27-11-725-6540. Ed. F.A. Gerber. adv. contact: F.A. Gerber. index. circ. 10,000. (tabloid format) **Document type:** newspaper, bulletin.
  Formerly: Postal and Telegraph Herald - Pos- en Telegraafherald (ISSN 0032-5317)

383 353.4 US ISSN 0364-863X
HE6311
POSTAL BULLETIN. 1880. fortn. $76 (foreign $95) (effective Jun. 1995). U.S. Postal Service, 475 L'Enfant Plaza, S.W., Washington, DC 20260-0010. TEL 202-268-2000. (Subscr. to: Superintendent of Documents, U.S Government Printing Office, Box 371954, Pittsburgh, PA 15250-7954. TEL 202-512-1800. FAX 202-512-2250) charts; illus. circ. 130,000. (back issues avail.) **Document type:** government publication, bulletin.
  —Genuine Article.
  Description: Contains current orders, instructions, and information relating to the U.S. Postal Service and on commemorative-stamp posters.

383 US ISSN 0032-5341
HE6001
POSTAL HISTORY JOURNAL. 1957. 3/yr. $30 (Canada & Mexico $35; elsewhere $40) (effective 1997). Postal History Society, Inc., c/o Kalman V. Illyefalvi, Sec.-Treas., 8207 Daren Ct., Pikesville, MD 21208. TEL 410-653-0665. Ed. Harlan F. Stone. R&P contact: Kalman V. Illyefalvi. adv. contact: Robert C. Danzer. bk.rev.; charts; illus.; cum.index: 1957-1993; circ. 600 (controlled). (also avail. in microform from UMI; reprint service avail. from UMI) Indexed: Stamp J.Ind. **Document type:** academic/scholarly publication.
  —UMI; UnCover.
  Description: Includes research articles on all aspects of postal history worldwide, society news, and commentary on writing and exhibiting.

383 353.4 350 US ISSN 0032-5368
HE6499
POSTAL LIFE; the magazine for postal employees. bi-m. $14. U.S. Postal Service, Communications Department, 475 L'Enfant Plaza West, S.W., Washington, DC 20260-0010. TEL 202-268-2000. (Subscr. to: Superintendent of Documents, U.S. Government Printing Office, Box 971354, Pittsburgh, PA 15250-7954. TEL 202-512-1800. FAX 202-512-2250) (also avail. in microform from MIM,UMI; reprint service avail. from UMI) Indexed: Ind.U.S.Gov.Per. **Document type:** government publication.
  —UMI.

POSTAL RECORD. see *LABOR UNIONS*

383 CH ISSN 0529-2786
HE6009.F6
POSTAL SERVICE TODAY/CHIN JIH YU CHENG. (Text in Chinese and English) 1958. m. NT.$400 in ROC; Hong Kong HK$.150; elsewhere $24 (effective 1992). 55 Chin Shan S. Rd. Sec.2, Taipei, Taiwan 106, Republic of China. FAX 02-34193400. Ed. W. Y. Fang. illus. circ. 20,000.

383 US ISSN 0554-8373
HE6187
POSTAL STATIONERY. 1948. bi-m. $10 to non-members. United Postal Stationery Society, Box 48, Redlands, CA 92373. Indexed: Stamp J.Ind.
  Formerly: Postal Stationery Journal (ISSN 0278-6362)

331.795 US ISSN 0032-5384
HE6001
THE POSTAL SUPERVISOR. 1911. m. $6. National Association of Postal Supervisors, 1727 King St., Ste. 400, Alexandria, VA 22314-2753. TEL 202-484-6070. Ed. Bob McLean. adv.: B&W page $800; 8 1/2 x 11. illus. circ. 35,000. Indexed: Work Rel.Abstr. **Document type:** trade publication.

383   US
POSTAL WORLD. 1974. bi-w. $349. United Communications Group, 11300 Rockville Pike, Ste. 1100, Rockville, MD 20852-3030. TEL 301-816-8950. Ed. Marcus J. Smith. illus. **Document type:** trade publication.
  Incorporates: E M World (Electronic Mail).
  Description: Provides information and advice to mail industry professionals; discusses how to trim postage costs, speed delivery, improve mailroom productivity, and plan for rate increases.

383 336   AU
POSTBUECHL. a. free. Steiger-Werbung Verlags- und Werbegesellschaft mbH, Hermanngasse 25, A-1070 Vienna, Austria. circ. 2,500,000.

383   SW   ISSN 0032-5503
POSTMAENNENS TIDNING. 1962. 7/yr. SEK 50 (effective 1994). Foereningen Kurskamraterna, P.O. Box 418, S-101 28 Stockholm, Sweden. Ed. Josef Lundell. adv.; charts; illus.; stat. circ. 5,000. **Document type:** trade publication.

383   US   ISSN 0032-5511
HE6001
POSTMASTERS ADVOCATE. 1894. m. $24 (foreign $34). National League of Postmasters, 1023 N. Royal St., Alexandria, VA 22314-1569. TEL 703-548-5922. FAX 703-836-8937. Ed. Allen T. Lanier. adv.: B&W page $700; 8 1/2 x 11. bk.rev.; illus.; circ. 23,000 (controlled). **Document type:** trade publication.

331.795   US   ISSN 0032-552X
HE6001
POSTMASTERS GAZETTE. 1903. m. (combined convention issue). $10. National Association of Postmasters of the United States, 8 Herbert St., Alexandria, VA 22305-2628. TEL 703-683-9027. FAX 703-683-6820. Ed. Harold McCraw; Pub. Ray Martin. R&P contact: Ray Martin. adv. contact: Ray Martin. illus. circ. 42,000. **Document type:** trade publication.

383.4   UK   ISSN 0269-1396
PRATIQUE. 1974. q. £12($32) (overseas £20). Disinfected Mail Study Circle, 25 Sinclair Grove, London NW11 9JH, England. TEL 44-181-455-9190. Ed. V. Denis Vandervelde; Pub. Malcolm Montgomery. R&P contact: V. Denis Vandervelde. adv.; bk.rev. circ. 160. (back issues avail.) **Document type:** academic/scholarly publication.

383   FR   ISSN 0983-1924
REFERENCES DE LA POSTE. 1983. q. 100 F. (foreign 120 F.). Direction Generale de la Poste, Direction du Reseau, 20 Av. de Segur, 75700 Paris, France. Ed. Bruno Faure. adv.; bk.rev. circ. 27,000. (back issues avail.)
  Formerly (until 1987): References (ISSN 0756-967X)

383   BE
REVUE DE LA POSTE/TIJDSCHRIFT VAN DE POST. 1937. bi-m. free. La Poste, Direction de la Communication, Centre Monnaie, 1000 Brussels, Belgium. TEL 32-2-2262226. FAX 32-2-2184962. Ed. Fred Lens; Pub. Monique Van Trappen. R&P contact: Monique Van Trappen. adv.; bk.rev. circ. 70,000. **Document type:** bulletin, corporate report.
  Formerly: Revue des Postes Belges - Tijdschrift der Belgische Posterijen (ISSN 0778-3817)

383.4 789.56   US
RHODE ISLAND POSTAL HISTORY JOURNAL. 1987. q. $10 includes membership (foreign $15). Rhode Island Postal History Society, c/o Thomas Greene, Ed., Box 113822, N. Providence, RI 02911. FAX 401-353-1161. **Document type:** academic/scholarly publication.

SCOTTISH POSTMARK GROUP. HANDBOOK. see *PHILATELY*

383   SP
SPAIN. DIRECCION GENERAL DE CORREOS Y TELECOMUNICACION. BOLETIN OFICIAL DE CORREOS Y TELECOMUNICACION. 1975. s-w. Direccion General de Correos y Telecomunicacion, Madrid, Spain.
  Formerly: Spain. Direccion General de Correos y Telecomunicacion. Boletin Oficial. Telecomunicacion.

383   US
STAR CARRIER. 1937. m. free to members. National Star Route Mail Contractors Association, 324 E. Capitol St., Washington, DC 20003. TEL 202-543-1661. FAX 202-543-8863. Ed. John V. Maraney. adv.; index; circ. 5,000 (controlled). (tabloid format) **Document type:** trade publication.
  Description: Provides news of association activities and relevant legislative changes.

383   UK   ISSN 0039-4335
SUB-POSTMASTER. 1897. m. £21; newsstand price: £1.75. National Federation of Sub-Postmasters, Evelyn House, 22 Windlesham Gardens, Shoreham-By-Sea, Sussex, England. TEL 44-1273-452324. FAX 44-1273-465403. Ed. R. Edmondson. adv.: B&W page £1437.65; trim 368 x 274; adv. contact: Lesley Hogan. charts; stat.; index; circ. 21,000 (controlled). **Document type:** newspaper.

383   GW
TELEFAXBUCH DER DEUTSCHEN TELEKOM AG. 1984. a. Deutsche Telekom Medien GmbH, Wiesenhuettenstr. 18, 60329 Frankfurt a.M., Germany. TEL 069-2682-0. FAX 069-26821101. Ed. Christine Pechel. adv. contact: Manfred Skudrzek. **Document type:** directory.
  ●Also available online.
  Also available on CD-ROM.
  Formerly: Amtliches Telefax- und Telebriefverzeichnis der Deutschen Bundespost Telecom.

383   UN   ISSN 0041-7009
UNION POSTALE. (Text and summaries in Arabic, Chinese, English, French, German, Russian and Spanish) 1875. 3/m. 21 SFr. Universal Postal Union - Union Postale Universelle, Weltpoststrasse 4, CH-3000 Berne 15, Switzerland. TEL 41-31-350-3111. FAX 41-31-350-3110. TELEX 912 761 UPU CH. E-mail: antoinebezencon@ib.upu.org. adv.; film rev.; bibl.; illus.; index. circ. 4,000.

383   UN   ISSN 0252-3973
UNION POSTALE UNIVERSELLE. ACTES. Spanish edition: Union Postal Universal. Actas (ISSN 1010-7428); English edition: Universal Postal Union. Acts (ISSN 0252-3981) 1874. quinquennial, 21st, Seoul 1994. 220 SFr. (effective 1996). Universal Postal Union - Union Postale Universelle, Weltpoststrasse 4, CH-3000 Berne 15, Switzerland. TEL 41-31-350-3111. FAX 41-31-350-3110. TELEX 912 761 UPU CH. E-mail: antoinebezencon@ib.upu.org.
  Formerly: Universal Postal Union. Documents du Congres (ISSN 0083-3878)

383   UN   ISSN 0252-3752
UNION POSTALE UNIVERSELLE. STATISTIQUE DES SERVICES POSTAUX. (Text in English, French) 1966. a. 75 SFr. Universal Postal Union - Union Postale Universelle, Weltpoststrasse 4, CH-3000 Berne 15, Switzerland. TEL 41-31-350-3111. FAX 41-31-350-3110. TELEX 912 761 UPU CH. E-mail: antoinebezencon@ib.upu.org. circ. 870. (also avail. in microfiche from CIS) **Indexed:** IIS.

383.2   US
U.S. POSTAL SERVICE. COST AND REVENUE ANALYSIS REPORT. 1970. a. U.S. Postal Service, Rates and Classification Department, 475 L'Enfant Plaza W., S.W., Washington, DC 20260-5327. TEL 202-245-4000. stat.
  Formerly: U.S. Postal Service. Support Group. Revenue and Cost Analysis (ISSN 0092-2765)

333   CC   ISSN 1000-6559
XIANDAI TONGXIN/COMMUNICATIONS TODAY. (Text in Chinese) 1981. m. Y12. Zhongguo Tongxin Xuehui - Chinese Society of Communications, No. 8, Lane 232, Bei Suzhou Lu, P.O. Box 085-253, Shanghai 200009, People's Republic of China. TEL 86-21-6324-0842. FAX 86-21-6324-8733. E-mail: sptjph@publicsta.net.ca. Ed. Xunjiong Zhong. adv. contact: Lihua Feng. circ. 100,000. **Document type:** government publication.

COMMUNICATIONS — RADIO

383   ZA
ZAMBIA. POSTS AND TELECOMMUNICATIONS CORPORATION. ANNUAL REPORT. 1963. a. k.50. Posts and Telecommunications Corporation, c/o Director-General, P.O. Box 71630, Ndola, Zambia. **Document type:** government publication.
  Formerly (until 1974): Zambia. General Post Office. Annual Report of the Postmaster-General (ISSN 0084-5019)

333   CC
ZHONGGUO YOUZHENG/CHINA POSTAL AFFAIRS. (Text in Chinese) bi-m. Renmin Youdian Chubanshe - People's Posts and Telecommunications Publishing House, 111 Nanzhugan Lane, Chaoyangmen-nei, Beijing 100700, People's Republic of China. TEL 5138139. Ed. Liu Guiping.

383 384.6
ZIP - AREA CODE DIRECTORY.* 1979. irreg., latest 1997. $7.95. Pilot Books, Box 2102, Greenport, NY 11944-0893. TEL 516-422-2225. FAX 516-422-2227. R&P contact: Anne Small. **Document type:** directory.
  Description: Numerically lists all zip codes in the U.S. along with the corresponding telephone area codes.

COMMUNICATIONS — Radio

A M P S RADIO DIARY. (All Media and Product Survey) see *COMMUNICATIONS — Abstracting, Bibliographies, Statistics*

384.54   US
A P R A NEWS. m. American Private Radio Association, Inc., Box 4221, Scottsdale, AZ 85261-4221. TEL 602-947-1100. FAX 602-947-3131. Ed. Mark W. Dobronski. circ. 9,000.

A R A LOG. (American Radio Association) see *LABOR UNIONS*

384   GW   ISSN 0066-5746
A R D - JAHRBUCH. 1969. a. DM.16.80. (Arbeitsgemeinschaft der Oeffentlich-Rechtlichen Rundfunkanstalten der Bundesrepublik Deutschland) Hans Bredow Institut, Heimhuderstr. 21, 20148 Hamburg, Germany. TEL 49-40-45021741. FAX 49-40-45021777. (Subscr. to: NOMOS Verlag, Postfach 610, 76484 Baden-Baden, Germany. TEL 49-7221-2104-0) Ed. Horst Halefeldt. circ. 13,000. **Document type:** trade publication.

621.38   US   ISSN 1048-1699
TK6565.A6
A R R L ANTENNA BOOK. 1939. irreg. American Radio Relay League, Inc., 225 Main St., Newington, CT 06111. TEL 860-594-0200. FAX 860-594-0303. E-mail: rdstraw@arrl.org; URL: http://www.arrl.org. Ed. R. Dean Straw. R&P contact: Mark Wilson. **Document type:** bulletin.

621.38   US   ISSN 1054-9293
TK9956
A R R L - D X X C COUNTRIES LIST. irreg. American Radio Relay League, Inc., 225 Main St., Newington, CT 06111. TEL 860-594-0200. FAX 860-594-0303. URL: http://www.arrl.org. (Co-sponsor: D X Century Club) R&P contact: Mark Wilson.

621.384   US
A R R L DIGITAL COMMUNICATIONS CONFERENCE. a. $12. American Radio Relay League, Inc., 225 Main St., Newington, CT 06111. TEL 860-594-0200. FAX 860-594-0303. URL: http://www.arrl.org. R&P contact: Mark Wilson. **Document type:** proceedings.
  Formerly (until 1993): A R R L Computer Networking Conference (ISSN 1080-5117)

621.384   US   ISSN 0890-3565
TK6550
A R R L HANDBOOK FOR RADIO AMATEURS. 1926. a. $38. American Radio Relay League, Inc., 225 Main St., Newington, CT 06111. TEL 860-594-0200. FAX 860-594-0303. E-mail: pdanzer@arrl.org; URL: http://www.arrl.org. Ed. Paul Danzer. R&P contact: Mark Wilson. illus.; index. circ. 30,000. **Document type:** bulletin.
  —CISTI; Linda Hall.
  Formerly (until 1985): Radio Amateur's Handbook (ISSN 0079-9440)

COMMUNICATIONS — RADIO

621.38 US
A R R L LICENSE MANUAL SERIES. a. American Radio Relay League, Inc., 225 Main St., Newington, CT 06111. TEL 860-594-0200. FAX 860-594-0303. E-mail: lwolfgang@arrl.org; URL: http://www.arrl.org. Ed. Larry Wolfgang. R&P contact: Mark Wilson. **Document type:** academic/scholarly publication.
Formerly: Radio Amateur's License Manual.

621.384 US
▼**(YEAR) A R R L PERIODICALS C D - R O M**; all (year) issues of three ARRL periodicals on one CD-ROM. 1996. a. $29.95 to non-members; members $19.95. American Radio Relay League, Inc., 225 Main St., Newington, CT 06111. TEL 860-594-0200. FAX 860-594-0303. URL: http://www.arrl.org. Ed. Mark Wilson. R&P contact: Mark Wilson. illus.; index. **Document type:** consumer publication.
●Available only on CD-ROM.

621.38 US ISSN 0190-3632
A R R L REPEATER DIRECTORY. a. $8. American Radio Relay League, Inc., 225 Main St., Newington, CT 06111. TEL 860-594-0200. FAX 860-594-0303. E-mail: jmabey@arrl.org; URL: http://www.arrl.org. Ed. Jay Mabey. R&P contact: Mark Wilson. circ. 55,000. **Document type:** directory.

384.5 II ISSN 0002-3620
AKASHI. (Text in Assamese) 1959. fortn. Rs.6. All India Radio, Akashvani Bhavan, Eden Gardens, Calcutta 700001, India. Ed. S.C. Basu. adv.; bk.rev.; charts; illus. circ. 175.

384.54
ALL OHIO SCANNER CLUB NEWSLETTER.* 1979. bi-m. $18.50 (Canada & Mexico $22, elsewhere $30). All Ohio Scanner Club, 20 Philip Dr., New Carlisle, OH 45544-9108. Ed. Dave Marshall; Pub. Dave Marshall. R&P contact: Dave Marshall. adv. contact: Dave Marshall. circ. 200. **Document type:** newsletter.
Description: Covers Ohio plus Illinois, Indiana, Kentucky, Michigan, Pennsylvania, West Virginia and Ontario. Nationwide coverage of federal government, military, land, sea and air transportation.

384.5 634 XR ISSN 0322-9572
AMATERSKE RADIO. 1952. m. $44 (effective 1996). Vydavatelstvi Magnet Press, Vladislavova 26, 113 66 Prague 1, Czech Republic. TEL 42-2-24239435. FAX 42-2-261226. Ed. Miroslav Wagner. circ. 80,000.

621.38 621.381 XR ISSN 0139-7087
AMATERSKE RADIO PRO KONSTRUKTERY. 1965. bi-m. $23 (effective 1996). Vydavatelstvi Magnet Press, Vladislavova 26, 113 66 Prague 1, Czech Republic. TEL 42-2-24239435. FAX 42-2-261226. Ed. Miroslav Wagner. circ. 50,000.
Formerly: (until 1976): Radiovy Konstrukter (ISSN 0033-8516).

621.384 AT ISSN 0002-6859
AMATEUR RADIO. 1933. m. Aus.$60. Wireless Institute of Australia, P.O. Box 2175, Caulfield Junction, Vic. 3161, Australia. TEL 61-3-95285962. FAX 61-3-95238191. Ed. W. Rice. adv.; bk.rev.; abstr.; illus.; cum.index every 5 yrs. circ. 5,000. Indexed: Pinpointer.
Description: A radio communication service for self training, intercommunication and technical investigation carried by amateurs.

621.384 UK ISSN 0264-2557
CODEN: AMRDEE
AMATEUR RADIO. 1982. m. £10.80. Goodhead Publications Ltd., 27 Murdock Rd., Bicester, Oxon, England. Ed. Richard Lamont. adv. circ. 30,000.

AMATEUR RADIO SERVICE MASTER FILE UPDATES. see COMMUNICATIONS — Abstracting, Bibliographies, Statistics

AMERICAN RADIO. see COMMUNICATIONS — Abstracting, Bibliographies, Statistics

384.54 US
AMERICAN SCANNERGRAM.* bi-m. $18.50 membership. All Ohio Scanner Club, 20 Philip Dr., New Carlisle, OH 45344-9108. Ed. Dave Marshall; Pub. Dave Marshall. R&P contact: Dave Marshall. adv. contact: Dave Marshall. circ. 867. **Document type:** newsletter.
Description: Helps the beginners in the scanning hobby, including topics about antennas and other improved reception techniques, and other subjects that are technical in nature.

384.54 US ISSN 8750-7471
ANTIQUE RADIO CLASSIFIED. 1984. m. $38.95 (Canada $49; elsewhere $55) (effective 1997). John V. Terrey, Ed. & Pub., Box 2, Carlisle, MA 01741. TEL 508-371-0512. FAX 508-371-7129. E-mail: arcmagazine@aol.com; URL: http://www.antiqueradio.com. R&P contact: John V. Terrey. adv. contact: Cindie Bryan. bk.rev. (back issues avail.)
Description: Covers old radios, TVs ham equipment, 40s and 50s radios, telegraph equipment, and books.

384.5 US
ASIA IMAGE. m. Cahners Publishing Company (Newton), Division of Reed Elsevier Inc., 275 Washington St., Newton, MA 02158-1630. TEL 617-964-3030. FAX 617-558-4506. (Asian addr.: 58A Smith St., Singapore 058962, Singapore. TEL 65-223-8823. FAX 65-220-5015) Ed. Nick Masters; Pub. Jonathan Hallett. circ. 5,220. **Document type:** trade publication.
Description: Business magazine for creative professionals in Asia's broadcast, production and post-production industries.

ASIA - PACIFIC BROADCASTING. see COMMUNICATIONS — Television And Cable

384.5 SW ISSN 0044-9989
AUDIENCE AND PROGRAMME RESEARCH. (Text in English) 1969. q. free. Sveriges Radio, Audience and Programme Research Department, S-105 10 Stockholm, Sweden. Eds. Charly Hulten, Claes Westrell. circ. 400.

AUDIOPHILE. see SOUND RECORDING AND REPRODUCTION

AUSTRALIAN FILM, TELEVISION AND RADIO SCHOOL ANNUAL REPORT. see EDUCATION — Higher Education

AUSTRALIAN FILM, TELEVISION AND RADIO SCHOOL HANDBOOK. see EDUCATION — Higher Education

384.54 AT ISSN 1035-106X
AUSTRALIAN RADIO TIMES. 1950. m. Aus.$10. Christian Broadcasting Association Ltd., 420 Lyons Rd., Five Dock, N.S.W. 2046, Australia. TEL 61-2-97121111. Ed. Rev. Vernon Turner OAm. circ. 10,000. **Document type:** newsletter.
Description: Covers matters of interest to radio listeners, particularly 2CBA-FM Sydney.

AVIATION MASTER FILE. see COMMUNICATIONS — Abstracting, Bibliographies, Statistics

384.54 305.8927 UK
▼**B B C AL-MUSHAHID.** (Text in Arabic) 1995. w. $150. (British Broadcasting Corporation, Arabic Service) Media World Services Ltd., Awdry House, 11 Kingsway, London WC2B 6YE, England. TEL 0171-240-4550. FAX 0171-240-4607. Ed. Nasr al-Majali; Pub. Ken Whittingham. adv. **Document type:** consumer publication.
Description: Contains current-affairs and general-interest articles and TV listings of interest to Arabic-speaking persons.

791.4 UK
PN1991
B B C ON AIR. 1939. m. £18($30) British Broadcasting Corporation, Bush House, Rm. 227 NW, Strand, London WC2B 4PH, England. TEL 44-171-257-2875. FAX 44-171-240-4899. E-mail: on.air.magazine@bbc.co.uk; URL: http://www.bbc.co.uk/worldservice/onair. Ed. Vicky Payne. adv. contact: Paul Cosgrove. bk.rev.; illus. circ. 130,000. **Document type:** consumer publication.
Supersedes (in June 1996): B B C Worldwide (ISSN 0967-5442); Which was formerly (until 1992): London Calling (ISSN 0024-600X)
Description: Contains full details of all forthcoming attractions on BBC World Service radio, BBC World, and BBC Prime international television channels. Includes frequency charts to help short wave listeners get the best reception, as well as news about the programmes presenters, correspondents and stars.

BACON'S RADIO & T V CABLE DIRECTORIES. see COMMUNICATIONS — Television And Cable

384.5 001.6
621.381 UK
BERNARDS AND BABANI PRESS RADIO & ELECTRONICS & COMPUTER BOOKS. 1942. 20/yr. price varies. Bernard Babani (Publishing) Ltd., The Grampians, Shepherds Bush Rd., London W6 7NF, England. TEL 0171-603-2581. FAX 0171-603-8203. **Document type:** monographic series.
Formerly: Bernards and Babani Press Radio and Electronics Books.

384.54 UK
BEST RADIO PLAYS OF (YEAR). a. £9.99. Methuen Drama, Michelin House, 81 Fulham Rd., London SW3 6RB, England. FAX 071-225-0933. (U.S. addr.: HEB, 361 Hanover St., Portsmouth, NH 03801)

384.5 II ISSN 0005-9773
BETAR JAGAT. (Text in Bengali) 1929. fortn. Rs.20. All India Radio, Akashvani Bhavan, Eden Gardens, Calcutta 700001, India. Ed. A.B. Ganguly. adv.; bk.rev.; charts, illus. circ. 33,000.

384.5 US ISSN 0006-0194
BETTER RADIO AND TELEVISION.* 1960. q. $6. National Association for Better Broadcasting, 1100 Graynold Ave., Glendale, CA 91202-2019. TEL 213-641-4903. Ed. Frank Orme. bk.rev.; illus. circ. 2,500.
—Linda Hall.

BOLLETTINO TECNICO GELOSO; pubblicazione trimestrale di radiofonia, televisione e scienze affini. see COMMUNICATIONS — Television And Cable

BRAILLE RADIO TIMES. see HANDICAPPED — Visually Impaired

621.38 NZ ISSN 0006-9523
BREAK-IN. 1928. m. NZ.$65. New Zealand Association of Radio Transmitters, Inc., P.O. Box 1733, Christchurch, New Zealand. Ed. J.R.L. Walker. R&P contact: J.R.L. Walker. adv. contact: Bob Allen. bk.rev.; charts; illus.; index. circ. 3,500. **Document type:** bulletin.
—CCC.
Description: Contains technical construction articles, news and general operating information.

384.5 NE
BREAKER; kontaktorgaan voor radiocommunicatie. 10/yr. J.V.D. Berg, Ed. & Pub., Brittenburg 2, 2804 ZX Gouda, Netherlands. bk.rev. circ. 250.

BRITAIN'S TELEVISION AND RADIO INDUSTRY. see BUSINESS AND ECONOMICS — Trade And Industrial Directories

BROADCAST BANKER - BROKER. see BUSINESS AND ECONOMICS — Banking And Finance

BROADCAST ENGINEERING; journal of broadcast technology. see COMMUNICATIONS — Television And Cable

BROADCAST ENGINEERING (SPANISH EDITION). see COMMUNICATIONS — Television And Cable

BROADCAST ENGINEERING EQUIPMENT REFERENCE MANUAL. see COMMUNICATIONS — Television And Cable

384.5　　　　UK　　ISSN 0269-493X
BROADCAST HARDWARE INTERNATIONAL. (Supplement avail.: Broadcast Hardware's U K Network) 1986. bi-m. £54. Hardware Industry Magazine Co. Ltd., 48 The Broadway, Maidenhead, Berks. SL6 1PW, England. TEL 44-1628-773935. FAX 44-1628-773537. Ed. David Sparks. R&P contact: Cathy Ward. adv. contact: Peter Gorland. circ. 15,500. (back issues avail.) **Document type:** trade publication.
　Description: Offers the international broadcast engineering industry information and news, as well as detailed equipment descriptions and updates.

384.5　　　　UK　　ISSN 0953-7627
BROADCAST HARDWARE'S U K NETWORK. (Supplement to: Broadcast Hardware International) 1988. bi-m. free to subscribers of Broadcast Hardware International. Hardware Industry Magazine Co. Ltd., 48 The Broadway, Maidenhead, Berks. SL6 1PW, England. TEL 44-1628-773935. FAX 44-1628-773537. Ed. David Sparks. R&P contact: Cathy Word. adv. contact: Peter Gorland. **Document type:** trade publication.
　Description: Offers news and information on U.K. product launches, recent equipment installations and major hardware sales to engineers, executives, and equipment users in broadcast, video productions, and video-audio postproduction fields in the U.K. and Ireland.

BROADCAST INVESTOR; newsletter on radio-TV station finance. see *BUSINESS AND ECONOMICS — Investments*

BROADCAST STATS. see *COMMUNICATIONS — Abstracting, Bibliographies, Statistics*

BROADCASTER. see *COMMUNICATIONS — Television And Cable*

BROADCASTING & CABLE. see *COMMUNICATIONS — Television And Cable*

BROADCASTING & CABLE INTERNATIONAL. see *COMMUNICATIONS — Television And Cable*

BROADCASTING & CABLE YEARBOOK. see *COMMUNICATIONS — Television And Cable*

384.5　　　　UK
BROADCASTING IN THE U K. irreg., no.2, 1995. £410. Key Note Ltd., Field House, 72 Oldfield Rd., Hampton, Middlesex TW12 2HQ, England. TEL 44-181-783-0755. FAX 44-181-783-0049. **Document type:** trade publication.
●Also available online.
Also available on CD-ROM.

384.54　　　US　　ISSN 0746-8911
TK6540
BUSINESS RADIO.* 1965. 10/yr. $65 (effective July 1992). Personal Communications Industry Association (P C I A), 500 Montgomery St., Ste. 700, Alexandria, VA 22314. TEL 703-739-0300. FAX 703-836-1608. Ed. A.E. Goetz. adv. contact: Robin E. Little. bk.rev.; illus. circ. 3,000. **Document type:** trade publication.
　Former titles: Business Radio - Action (ISSN 0093-0245); Action (ISSN 0567-8412).
　Description: Offers information of interest to two-way radio dealers, tower and site managers, operators of private carrier paging and specialized mobile radio systems, technicians, wireless systems integrators, system users, manufacturers and suppliers of mobile communications equipment and services.

384.4　　　　GW　　ISSN 0938-4022
C B FUNK. m. DM.69.60 (foreign DM.79.20) (effective 1997); newsstand price: DM.5.80. Verlag fuer Technik und Handwerk GmbH, Robert-Bosch-Str. 4, 76532 Baden-Baden, Germany. TEL 49-7221-5087-0. FAX 49-7221-508752. (Subscr. to: P M S GmbH, Postfach 290180, 47261 Duisburg, Germany. TEL 49-203-76908-0. FAX 49-203-7690830) Ed. Michael Buege. **Document type:** consumer publication.

621.38　　　　UK
C B NEWS. m. 60p. Crofts Publishers Ltd., 47 Derby Rd., Heanor, Derbyshire DE7 7QH, England. adv.

384.5　　　　US
C C I R PLENARY ASSEMBLY (PROCEEDINGS). quadrennial, 17th, 1990, Dusseldorf. $1659. (International Telecommunication Union, International Radio Consultative Service) U.S. National Technical Information Service, 5285 Port Royal Rd., Springfield, VA 22161. TEL 703-487-4630. FAX 703-321-8547. TELEX 64617. (Subscr. outside N. America to: International Telecommunications Union, Place des Nations, CH-1211 Geneva 12, Switzerland.)
　Formerly: C C I R Green Books.

621.38　　　CN　　ISSN 0045-3706
C I D X MESSENGER. 1962. m. membership. Canadian International DX Radio Club, 169 Grandview Ave., Winnipeg, Man. R2G 0L4, Canada. Ed. R. L. Jennings. adv.; bk.rev. circ. 1,100. (processed)

621.384　　　US　　ISSN 0007-893X
TK6540　　　　　　　　CODEN: CQCQAO
C Q; the radio amateurs' journal. 1945. m. $24.95 (Canada and Mexico $37.95; elsewhere $39.95). C Q Communications, Inc., 76 N. Broadway, Hicksville, NY 11801. TEL 516-681-2922. FAX 516-681-2926. Ed. Alan M. Dorhoffer; Pub. Richard A. Ross. adv. contact: Arnie Sposato. bk.rev.; charts; illus. circ. 113,309. **Indexed:** Ind.How To Do It (1979-), INSPEC. **Document type:** consumer publication.
　—BLDSC (3486.356000); AskIEEE; CISTI; Ei; KR SourceOne; Linda Hall; SWETS; UnCover.
　Description: For radio amateurs who are actively involved in operating, building and using amateur radio equipment and related devices.

621.384　　　GW　　ISSN 0178-269X
C Q - D L. 1928. m. DM.75 to non-members. Deutscher Amateur-Radio-Club, Postfach 1155, 34216 Baunatal, Germany. FAX 49-5603-933320. E-mail: 100737.3572@compuserve.com. adv.; bk.rev.; charts; illus.; tr.lit.; index, cum.index: 1951-1954, 1955-1959, 1960-1965, 1966-1970. circ. 60,000. **Document type:** bulletin.
　—SWETS.
　Formerly: D L - Q T C (ISSN 0011-4995)

621.384　　　JA　　ISSN 0007-8964
C Q HAM RADIO. (Text in Japanese) 1954. m. 13680 Yen. C Q Publishing Co., 14-2, Sugamo 1-chome, Toshima-ku, Tokyo 170, Japan. TEL 81-3-5395-2149. FAX 81-3-5395-2100. (Dist. outside Japan by: Nippon IPS Co., Ltd., 11-6, 3-chome, Iidabashi, Chiyoda-ku, Tokyo 102, Japan. TEL 81-3-3238-0700. FAX 81-3-3238-7944) Ed. Tadayuki Tominaga. adv.: B&W page $1750; color page $5775; trim 10 1/8 x 7 3/16. charts; illus. circ. 97,331.
　Description: Provides the latest technology, trends and equipments on ham radio.

621.38　　　CN　　ISSN 0318-0867
THE CANADIAN AMATEUR;* Canadian amateur radio from coast to coast. Short title: T C A. 1973. m. (Jul.& Aug. combined). Can.$28. (Canadian Amateur Radio Federation Inc.) C A R F Publications Ltd., 71 Main St., Box 730, Bloomfield, ON K0K 1G0, Canada. TEL 613-545-9100. Ed. George Sansom. adv.; bk.rev. circ. 5,000.
　Incorporates: V E News (ISSN 0049-576X)

CHART MAGAZINE; Canada's new music magazine. see *MUSIC*

CIRCUIT FERME; journal des employes de Radio-Canada. see *BUSINESS AND ECONOMICS — Personnel Management*

621.38　　　UK　　ISSN 0261-0361
CITIZENS' BAND. 1980. m. £21.60. Argus Specialist Publications Ltd. (Subsidiary of: Argus Press Group), Argus House, Boundary Way, Hemel Hempstead, Herts. HP2 7ST, England. TEL 01442-66551. FAX 01442-66998. (Subscr. to: Argus Subscription Services, Queensway House, 2 Queensway, Redhill, Surrey RH1 1QS, England. TEL 01737-768611) Ed. Tony Hethrington. adv.; bk.rev. (back issues avail.) **Document type:** consumer publication.
　Description: Covers all aspects of citizen's band radio.

COLLEGE BROADCASTER. see *COMMUNICATIONS — Television And Cable*

621.384　　　US　　ISSN 1053-9433
TK5101.A1
COMMUNICATIONS QUARTERLY; a journal of communications technology. 1990. q. $29.95 (foreign $39.95). C Q Communications, Inc., 76 N. Broadway, Hicksville, NY 11801. TEL 516-681-2926. FAX 516-681-2926. Ed. Terry Littlefield. circ. 8,100. **Document type:** consumer publication.
　Description: Technically-oriented amateur radio magazine that offers in-depth coverage of the science of communications.

621.38　　　US　　ISSN 1075-5721
COMMUNICATIONS STANDARDS SUMMARY. 1994. q. $250 (effective 1994). Communications Standards Review, 757 Greer Rd., Palo Alto, CA 94303-3024. TEL 415-856-9018. FAX 415-856-6591. E-mail: ebaskin@csrstds.com. Ed. Elaine Baskin; Pub. Elaine Baskin. circ. 150 (paid). (back issues avail.) **Document type:** directory.
　Description: Directory of all Telecommunications Industry Association active datacom and telecom standards projects.

384.54　　　II
COMMUNICATOR (NEW DELHI). (Text in English) 1965. q. Rs.20($10) (£8). Indian Institute of Mass Communication, Shaheed Jit Singh Marg, Sector XIII, J.N.U. Campus, New Delhi 110 067, India. Ed. Adarsh Kumar Varma. bk.rev.; bibl.; index.
　Description: Covers radio and other media in India.

COMMUNITY MEDIA REVIEW. see *COMMUNICATIONS — Television And Cable*

384.54　　　US
COMMUNITY RADIO NEWS. 1974. m. $75 to non-members. National Federation of Community Broadcasters, Ft. Mason Center No. D, San Francisco, CA 94123. TEL 415-771-1160. Ed. Lynn Chadwick. adv. circ. 500. **Document type:** newsletter.
　Former titles: N F C B News; N F C B Newsletter.
　Description: Covers public radio policy and issues. Includes information on programming, fundraising, management, volunteer coordination, and production.

384.5　　　　CR
CONTRAPUNTO. 1978. fortn. (Sistema Nacional de Radio y Television) Uruca, Apdo. 7-1980, San Jose, Costa Rica. TEL 31-3333. Dir. Fabio Munoz Campos. circ. 10,000.

CONVERGENCE; the journal of research into new media technologies. see *COMMUNICATIONS — Television And Cable*

621.38　　　UK　　ISSN 0959-843X
D-I-Y RADIO. 1992. bi-m. £9; newsstand price: £2. Radio Society of Great Britain, Lambda House, Cranborne Rd., Potters Bar, Herts EN6 3JE, England. TEL 44-1707-659015. FAX 44-1707-645105. Ed. M. Brimson. adv. contact: Malcolm Taylor. bk.rev.; circ. 10,000. (back issues avail.) **Document type:** bulletin.

DENPA GIJUTSU KYOKAIHO/RADIO ENGINEERING AND ELECTRONICS ASSOCIATION. JOURNAL. see *ELECTRONICS*

DENPA KOHO/ELECTRONIC NAVIGATION REVIEW. see *TRANSPORTATION — Ships And Shipping*

621.384　　　JA
DENPA TAIMUZU/DENPA TIMES. (Text in Japanese) 1950. 3/w. 3200 Yen per mo. 23-12, Nishishinbashi 3-chome, Minato-ku, Tokyo 105, Japan.

DIRECTORY OF RELIGIOUS MEDIA. see *BUSINESS AND ECONOMICS — Trade And Industrial Directories*

DIRITTO DELLE RADIODIFFUSIONI E DELLE TELECOMUNICAZIONI. see *LAW*

DUNCAN'S RADIO MARKET GUIDE. see *BUSINESS AND ECONOMICS — Trade And Industrial Directories*

COMMUNICATIONS — RADIO

621.38   GW   ISSN 0175-6877
DX MAGAZINE; monthly magazine for international radio-telecommunication. (Text mainly in English; occasionally in German) 1966. m. DM.30($18.50) Worldwide D X Club, Postfach 1214, 61282 Bad Homburg, Germany. TEL 49-6172-390918. FAX 49-6102-800999. E-mail: 100657.2376@compuserve.com; URL: http://ourworld.compuserve.com/homepages/wwdxc. Ed. Michael Bethge. R&P contact: Michael Bethge. adv. contact: Michael Bethge. bk.rev. circ. 500. (back issues avail.) **Indexed:** Ind.How To Do It (1990-). **Document type:** trade publication.
    Description: News about national and international radio stations, especially on longwave, mediumwave and shortwave.

384.5 790.13   US   ISSN 0899-9732
DX MONITOR.* 1964. 34/yr. $25. International Radio Club of America, Box 1831, Perris, CA 92572-1831. Ed. Ralph Sanserino. adv.; bk.rev.; charts; illus. circ. 275. (back issues avail.)
    Description: Covers the hobby of listening to distant stations on the AM broadcast band.

384.54   CN   ISSN 1183-0344
DX ONTARIO; monitoring the world via radio. 1975. m. Can.$35($28) Ontario DX Association, P.O. Box 161, Sta. A, Willowdale, ON M2N 5S8, Canada. TEL 416-293-8919. FAX 416-293-6603. Ed. Harold Sellers. R&P contact: Harold Sellers. adv.: page Can.$50; adv. contact: Harold Sellers. bk.rev.; index. circ. 1,300. (also avail. in magnetic tape) **Document type:** newsletter.
    Description: Provides transmission schedules, program information, equipment reviews and station profiles on international shortwave broadcasting and radio communications.

EKSPRESS-INFORMATSIYA. KVANTOVAYA RADIOTEKHNIKA. see COMMUNICATIONS — Abstracting, Bibliographies, Statistics

EKSPRESS-INFORMATSIYA. RADIOTEKHNIKA SVERKHVYSOKIKH CHASTOT. see COMMUNICATIONS — Abstracting, Bibliographies, Statistics

621.38 643   UK   ISSN 0013-4228
ELECTRICAL AND RADIO TRADING. 1890. w. £70. Reed Business Information (Subsidiary of: Reed Elsevier group), Quadrant House, The Quadrant, Sutton, Surrey SM2 5AS, England. TEL 44-181-652-8694. (Subscr. addr.: Oakfield House, Perrymount Rd., Haywards Heath, W. Sussex RH16 3DH, England) Ed. Frank Ogden; Pub. Jerry Gosney. R&P contact: Frank Ogden. adv. contact: Alan King. bk.rev.; illus.; tr.lit. circ. 8,083. **Document type:** trade publication.
    Description: Electrical retail magazine covering all aspects of the UK market.

621.384   NE   ISSN 0013-4767
ELECTRON; maandblad voor de Nederlandse radio-amateur. 1945. m. fl.70 membership. Vereniging voor Experimenteel Radio Onderzoek in Nederland, Postbus 1166, 6801 BD Arnhem, Netherlands. TEL 31-26-4426760. Ed. H.J. Duivenvoorden. adv.; bk.rev.; charts; illus.; tr.lit.; index. circ. 13,000. **Document type:** bulletin, newsletter.
    Description: For radio amateurs. Covers technology, amateur satellites, antennas, international news, reports of events and contest results. Includes a calendar of events and association library news.

ELECTRONIC MEDIA. see COMMUNICATIONS — Television And Cable

ELECTRONICS NOW; technology, audio, video, computers, projects. see ELECTRONICS

791.4   FR   ISSN 1144-5742
ELECTRONIQUE RADIO - PLANS. 1933. m. 364 F. (effective 1995). Publications Georges Ventillard, 2-12 rue de Bellevue, 75019 Paris, France. TEL 44-84-84-84. FAX 42-41-89-40. TELEX 220 409 F. adv.; charts; illus.; index. circ. 25,000.
    Formed by the 1989 merger of: Radio - Plans (ISSN 0033-7668); Electronique Applications (ISSN 0243-489X)

621.38   AU   ISSN 0373-8884
ELEKTRO RADIO HANDEL.* 1925. m. S.360. Erb Verlag GmbH, Eichenstr. 38, A-1120 Vienna, Austria. Ed. Gerhard Habliczek. adv.; bk.rev.; illus.; stat.; tr.lit.; circ. 9,000 (controlled).

ELEKTRONICA; markt en techniek. see ELECTRONICS

ELEKTRONIKK BRANSJEN. see ELECTRONICS

EUROFILE RADIO INDUSTRY DIRECTORY. see BUSINESS AND ECONOMICS — Trade And Industrial Directories

F F. see COMMUNICATIONS — Television And Cable

F M ENGINEERING DATA BASE. see COMMUNICATIONS — Abstracting, Bibliographies, Statistics

F M ENGINEERING DATA BASE IN ORDER BY STATE. see COMMUNICATIONS — Abstracting, Bibliographies, Statistics

791.4   US   ISSN 0014-5971
F M GUIDE.* (NY Edition) 1962. m. $10. Hampton International Communications, Inc., 4520 E. Grant Rd., Tucson, AZ 85712-2617. adv.; film rev.; play rev. circ. 72,000. (tabloid format)

384.5   FR
F M MAGAZINE. 4/yr. B.P. 28, 75362 Paris Cedex 08, France. TEL 42-93-39-45. Ed. Mlle. Chris Simon. circ. 8,000.

384.5   US   ISSN 0890-6718
FMEDIA!. 1987. m. $65. F M Atlas Publishing, Box 336, Esko, MN 55733-0336. TEL 218-879-7676. FAX 218-879-8333. Ed. Bruce F. Elving. R&P contact: Bruce F. Elving. circ. 300 (paid). **Document type:** newsletter.
    Description: Contains fact and opinion about FM radio and related technologies.

FACE TO FACE WITH TALENT. see COMMUNICATIONS — Television And Cable

FAMILY RADIO NEWS. see RELIGIONS AND THEOLOGY

384.54   US
FOLIO (BERKELEY). 1949. m. (except Sep.). $45. Pacifica Foundation, 1929 Martin Luther King, Jr. Way, Berkeley, CA 94704. TEL 510-848-6767. FAX 510-848-3812. Ed. Richard Wolinsky. adv.; bk.rev. circ. 23,000. (tabloid format; back issues avail.) **Indexed:** B.P.I., Tr.& Indus.Ind. **Document type:** consumer publication, newspaper.
    Description: Program guide for listener-sponsored KPFA-FM Pacifica community radio station.

384.5 780 640.73   US
FOLIO (NORTH HOLLYWOOD). (Text mainly in English; occasionally in Spanish) 1959? m. $50 membership. K P F K - F M (Pacifica Radio), 3729 Cahuenga Blvd., W., N. Hollywood, CA 91604. TEL 818-985-2711. Ed. Jill Smolin. adv. circ. 16,000. (also avail. in audio cassette; back issues avail.) **Indexed:** B.P.I.
    Formerly: Folio - K P F K (ISSN 0274-4856)

384.54   GW   ISSN 0342-1651
FUNK. 1977. m. DM.75.60 (foreign DM.81.60) (effective 1997); newsstand price: DM.6.30. Verlag fuer Technik und Handwerk GmbH, Robert-Bosch-Str. 4, 76532 Baden-Baden, Germany. TEL 49-7221-5087-0. FAX 49-7221-508752. (Subscr. to: P M S GmbH, Postfach 290180, 47261 Duisburg, Germany. TEL 49-203-76908-0. FAX 49-203-7690830) Ed. Michael Buege. **Document type:** consumer publication.

384.5   GW   ISSN 0016-2833
                     CODEN: FUAMBU
FUNK AMATEUR. m. Theuberger Verlag GmbH, Oberwasserstr. 12, 10117 Berlin, Germany. TEL 030-2082261. FAX 030-2071258. Ed. Hans Schwarz. adv. contact: Bettina Klink-von-Woyski. charts; illus.; circ. 29,000 (paid). **Document type:** consumer publication.
    —BLDSC (4058.110000).

384.5   GW
FUNK - SPOT; Radioservice des Instituts der deutschen Wirtschaft. w. DM.196.20. (Institut der Deutschen Wirtschaft) Deutscher Instituts Verlag GmbH, Postfach 510670, 50942 Cologne, Germany. TEL 49-221-4981452. FAX 49-221-4981592. **Document type:** bulletin.

621.384   JA
GEKKAN MUSEN SHUCHI/MONTHLY NEWS ON RADIO. (Text in Japanese) 1933. w. 800 Yen per no. (Senpaku Tsushinshi Rodo Kumiai - Marine Radio Officer's Union) Musen Tsushinsha - Radio News Agency, 14-8, Shibaura 1-chome, Minato-ku, Tokyo 105, Japan. TEL 81-3-3451-4729. FAX 81-3-3451-4727. Ed. Koumei Kikuta. **Document type:** bulletin.

621.38   JA   ISSN 0388-2306
HAM JOURNAL. (Text in Japanese) 1974. bi-m. 8520 Yen. C Q Publishing Co., 14-2 Sumago 1-chome, Toshima-ku, Tokyo 170, Japan. TEL 81-3-5395-2148. FAX 81-3-5395-2100. (Dist. outside Japan by: Nippon IPS Co., Ltd., 11-6, 3-chome, Iidabashi, Chiyoda-ku, Tokyo 102, Japan. TEL 81-3-3238-0700. FAX 81-3-3238-7944) Ed. Masao Hamada.
    Description: Discusses amateur radio operating.

621.38   UK   ISSN 0269-8269
HAM RADIO TODAY. 1983. m. £21.60. Argus Specialist Publications Ltd. (Subsidiary of: Argus Press Group), Argus House, Boundary Way, Hemel Hempstead, Herts. HP2 7ST, England. TEL 01442-66551. FAX 01442-66998. (Subscr. to: Argus Subscription Services, Queensway House, 2 Queensway, Redhill, Surrey RH1 1QS, England. TEL 01737-786111) Ed. Sheila Lorek. adv.; bk.rev. (back issues avail.) **Document type:** consumer publication.
    —BLDSC (4241.190000).
    Description: Features news, reviews, features and do-it-yourself projects for radio amateurs.

621.38   FR   ISSN 0337-1883
HAUT-PARLEUR. 1925. m. 415 F. (effective 1995). (Societe des Publications Radio-Electriques et Scientifiques) Publications Georges Ventillard, 2-12 rue Bellevue, 75940 Paris Cedex 19, France. TEL 444-84-84-84. FAX 42-41-89-40. TELEX PGV 220 409 F. adv. circ. 42,000.
    —BLDSC (4273.755000); SWETS.

HEARSAY. see HANDICAPPED — Visually Impaired

384.5   US
HEARTLAND. 1990. m. free. Susquehanna Radio Corp., 8120 Knue Rd., Indianapolis, IN 46250. TEL 317-842-9550. FAX 317-577-3361. adv.: B&W page $3500, color page $4150; trim 11 3/8 x 16 3/4; adv. contact: Kevin Isaacs. circ. 108,872 (controlled). **Document type:** consumer publication.

384.5   UN
HIGH FREQUENCY BROADCASTING SCHEDULE. (Text in English, French, Spanish) 1986. q. 231 SFr. International Telecommunication Union, Place des Nations, CH-1211 Geneva 20, Switzerland. TEL 41-22-7306141. FAX 41-22-7305194. TELEX 421 000 UIT CH. E-mail: sales@itu.ch; URL: http://www.itu.ch. Ed.Bd.

384   NE   ISSN 1382-2160
HILVERSUMMARY. (Text in English) 1987. q. free. Nederlandse Omroep Stichting, Postbus 26444, 1202 JJ Hilversum, Netherlands. TEL 31-35-6773197. FAX 31-35-6773586. E-mail: louis.heinsman@qsd.nos.nl; URL: http://www.omroep.nl/nos/rtv/voorlichting/hsumm. Ed. Louis Heinsman. (looseleaf format) **Document type:** newsletter.
● Also available online.
    Description: Provides information on developments in Dutch media, especially public service radio and TV of interest to foreign journalists and students of mass communications.

HISTORICAL JOURNAL OF FILM, RADIO AND TELEVISION. see HISTORY

HITMAKERS - WEEKLY TOP 40 RADIO & MUSIC INDUSTRY MAGAZINE. see MUSIC

384.5   GW   ISSN 0175-4564
HOERSPIELE IN DER A R D. a. (Deutsches Rundfunkarchiv) Max Niemeyer Verlag, Postfach 2140, 72011 Tuebingen, Germany. TEL 49-7071-989494. FAX 49-7071-989450. **Document type:** monographic series.
    Description: Transcripts of plays and other programs broadcast over the ARD radio network.

COMMUNICATIONS — RADIO

384.54 GW ISSN 0179-1869
HOERUEBERSICHT INTERNATIONAL; aktuelle Programmzeitschrift des Deutschsprachigen internationalen Rundfunks. 1978. q. $9. DX Listeners Service, P.O. Box 11 22, 34576 Homberg, Germany. TEL 05684-8215. adv.; bk.rev. circ. 3,000. (back issues avail.)

HORN SPEAKER; the newspaper for the hobbyist of vintage electronics and sound. see *ANTIQUES*

791.4 II ISSN 0019-4158
INDIA CALLING;* overseas programme journal. (Text in English) 1954. m. free. All India Radio, Akashvani Bhavan, Eden Gardens, Calcutta 700001, India. illus. circ. 10,000.

INFORMAZIONE RADIO TV; studi documenti e notizie. see *COMMUNICATIONS — Television And Cable*

384.5 US ISSN 0731-9312
INSIDE RADIO; the latest news, trends and management information. vol.12, 1987. d. $365. Inside Radio, Inc., 1930 E. Marlton Pike, Ste. S-93, Cherry Hill, NJ 08003. TEL 609-424-6800. FAX 609-424-2301. Ed. Tom Taylor; Pub. Jerry Del Colliano. adv. contact: Jerry Del Colliano. **Document type:** newsletter.

INSTYTUT TELE- I RADIOTECHNICZNY. PRACE. see *COMMUNICATIONS — Television And Cable*

621.384 US
INTERNATIONAL CALLBOOK. 1920. a. $29.95 includes update Service Editions, Radio Amateur Callbook, Inc., 1695 Oak St., Lakewood, NJ 08701-5925. adv.
Former titles: Foreign Callbook; Foreign Radio Amateur Callbook Magazine (ISSN 0015-7260)

384.54 GW ISSN 0178-9287
INTERNATIONAL LISTENING GUIDE; the basic directory of international short wave broadcasting. (Text in English) 1978. q. $15. DX Listeners Service, P.O. Box 11 22, 34576 Homberg, Germany. TEL 05684-8215. Ed. Bernd Friedewald. adv. circ. 4,500. (back issues avail.) **Document type:** directory.

384.5 UN
INTERNATIONAL RADIO CONSULTATIVE COMMITTEE. PLENARY ASSEMBLY. PROCEEDINGS. (Supplement avail.) (Text mainly in English, French, Spanish; occasionally in Chinese) 15th ed., 1982. quadrennial. price varies. International Telecommunication Union, International Radio Consultative Committee, Place des Nations, CH-1211 Geneva 20, Switzerland. TEL 41-22995111. FAX 41-22337256. TELEX 421000 UIT CH. Ed.Bd. **Document type:** proceedings.

621.38 BE ISSN 0074-9516
INTERNATIONAL UNION OF RADIO SCIENCE. PROCEEDINGS OF GENERAL ASSEMBLIES. (Text in English and French) 1928. triennial. 1500 BEF. International Union of Radio Science - URSI - Union Radio-Scientifique Internationale, c/o Ms. I. Heleu, University of Ghent (Intec), Sint-Pietersnieuwstraat 41, 9000 Ghent, Belgium. TEL 32-9-2643320. FAX 32-9-2644288. circ. 500. **Document type:** proceedings.
Formerly: International Scientific Radio Union. Proceedings of General Assemblies.

INTERNATIONALES HANDBUCH FUER HOERFUNK UND FERNSEHEN. see *COMMUNICATIONS — Television And Cable*

622 RU ISSN 0202-0769
TK6540
TOGI NAUKI I TEKHNIKI: RADIOTEKHNIKA. irreg., vols.39, 1989. price varies. Vsesoyuznyi Institut Nauchno-Tekhnicheskoi Informatsii (VINITI), Ul. Baltiiskaya 14, Moscow A-219, Russia. (Subscr. to: Mezhdunarodnaya Kniga, Dimitrova ul. 39, 113095 Moscow, Russia)
—CISTI.

AL-IZAA WAL-TELEVISION/RADIO AND TELEVISION. see *COMMUNICATIONS — Television And Cable*

621.384 537 KR ISSN 0021-3470
TK6540 CODEN: IVUZB5
IZVESTIYA VYSSHIKH UCHEBNYKH ZAVEDENII. SERIYA RADIOELEKTRONIKA. English translation: Radioelectronics and Communication Systems (US ISSN 0735-2727) 1958. bi-m. $199 (effective 1998). Politekhnichnyi Instytut, Prosp. Pobedy, 37, 252056 Kiev, Ukraine. TEL 38-44-4411263. charts; index. (tabloid format) **Indexed:** Chem.Abstr., Curr.Cont., Djerelo, INIS Atomind., INSPEC. —BLDSC (0077.780000); AskIEEE; CISTI; Genuine Article; KR SourceOne; Linda Hall. **CCC**.

384.5 GW ISSN 0948-3756
JAHRBUCH DER LANDESMEDIENANSTALTEN; privater Rundfunk in Deutschland. 1988. a. DM.49. (Arbeitsgemeinschaft der Landesmedienanstalten) Verlag Reinhard Fischer, Weltistr. 34, 81477 Munich, Germany. TEL 49-89-7918892. FAX 49-89-7918310. E-mail: 106222.2504@ compuserve.com. **Document type:** trade publication.
Formerly (until 1995): D L M Jahrbuch (ISSN 0940-287X)

384.5 659.1 US ISSN 1044-985X
JON SULLIVAN'S RADIO PROMOTION BULLETIN; ideas and inspiration for innovative broadcasters. 1989. m. $133 (foreign $168). The Sullivan Co., 5350 Pine Cliff Dr., Houston, TX 77084-3140. TEL 281-855-3475. FAX 281-855-2964. E-mail: radiobull@compassnet.com; URL: http://www.compassnet.com/radiobul. Ed. Jon Sullivan. R&P contact: Jon Sullivan. circ. 450 (paid). (looseleaf format) **Document type:** newsletter.
Description: Contains sales promotion ideas for commercial radio sales managers, marketing directors and promotion executives.

384 US ISSN 0010-1133
JOURNAL OF COLLEGE RADIO. 1941-1982; 1984-1987; resumed 1989. 4/yr. $12. Intercollegiate Broadcasting System, Inc., 367 Windsor Hwy., New Windsor, NY 12553-7900. TEL 914-565-0003. FAX 914-565-7446. Ed. Jeffrey N. Tellis; Pub. Fritz Kass. R&P contact: Fritz Kass. adv.; bk.rev.; abstr.; charts; illus.; tr.lit. circ. 2,500.
Formerly: College Radio.
Description: Contains articles for and about college radio stations.

384 GW ISSN 0343-9003
JUNGE RADIO-, FERNSEH- UND INDUSTRIE- ELEKTRONIKER. 1966. m. DM.70.80; newsstand price: DM.6.10. Frankfurter Fachverlag, Emil-Sulzbach-Str. 12, 60486 Frankfurt a.M., Germany. TEL 069-778410. FAX 069-702003. Ed. Lothar Starke; Pub. Erwin Kohl. circ. 18,000. **Document type:** trade publication.
—CCC.

K P B S ON AIR. see *COMMUNICATIONS — Television And Cable*

621.38 RU
K W ZHURNAL. (Supplement to: Radio (ISSN 0033-765X)) 1992. bi-m. 42000 Rub. (foreign $15) (effective 1997). Seliverstov per. 10, 103045 Moscow, Russia. TEL 7-095-2076889. FAX 7-095-2087713. E-mail: radio@sovam.com. Ed. Boris Stepanov. bk.rev.; charts; illus. circ. 5,000.

KATSO. see *COMMUNICATIONS — Television And Cable*

KEY ABSTRACTS - ANTENNAS & PROPAGATION. see *COMMUNICATIONS — Abstracting, Bibliographies, Statistics*

384.5 UK
KEY NOTE MARKET REPORT: COMMERCIAL RADIO. Variant title: Commercial Radio. irreg., no.4, 1995. £205. Key Note Ltd., Field House, 72 Oldfield Rd., Hampton, Middlesex TW12 2HQ, England. TEL 44-181-783-0755. FAX 44-181-783-0049. **Document type:** trade publication.
●Also available online.
Also available on CD-ROM.
Formerly: Key Note Report: Commercial Radio.

621.38 GW
KLINGENFUSS (YEAR) GUIDE TO UTILITY RADIO STATIONS. 1983. a. Joerg Klingenfuss Publications, Hagenlohrstr. 14, 72070 Tuebingen, Germany. **Document type:** directory.
Formerly (until 1994): Klingenfuss Guide to Utility Stations.

621.38 FI ISSN 0783-4632
KODINTEKNIIKKA. 1952. 10/yr. FIM 260. Radioliikkeiden Liitto r.y. - Radio Retailers Association, Vuorimiehenkatu 21, 00140 Helsinki 14, Finland. FAX 90-174233. Ed. Matti Ahtomies. adv.; bk.rev.; illus. circ. 1,800.
—BLDSC (5100.721500).
Formerly: Radiokauppias (ISSN 0355-6735)

384 PL ISSN 1230-9990
KROTKOFALOWIEC POLSKI. 1929. m. 300000 Zl. (foreign 500000 Zl.) (effective 1994). (Polski Zwiazek Krotkofalowcow - Polish Society of Radio Amateurs) Wydawnictwo C & J, P.O. Box 25, 04-520 Warszawa 106, Poland. TEL 48-22-120693. FAX 48-2-6132697. Ed. Wieslawa Janeczek; Pub. Zbigniew Jaworski. adv.; bk.rev.; illus. circ. 6,000. **Document type:** bulletin.
Formerly: Polski Zwiazek Krotkofalowcow. Biuletyn.

384.384 GW ISSN 0170-768X
KURIER (DUESSELDORF); Fachzeitschrift fuer Internationalen Rundfunkempfang. 1967. s-m. DM.69 (Europe DM.80; rest of world DM.100). A D D X e.V., Postfach 130124, 40551 Duesseldorf, Germany. TEL 0211-790636. FAX 0211-793272. Ed. Michael Schmitz. adv.; bk.rev. circ. 4,000. **Document type:** bulletin.

384.5 US
L C D. (Lowest Common Denominator) 1983. q. $10 contribution. W F M U, Box 1568, Montclair, NJ 07042. TEL 201-678-8264. E-mail: wfmu@wfmu.org. Ed. Kenneth Freedman. adv. contact: Douglas Schulkind. music rev.; illus.
Description: Program guide and articles of interest to listeners of independent, free-form radio station WFMU in the metro New York area.

384.54 US
THE LOWDOWN. m. Longwave Club of America, 45 Wildflower Rd., Levittown, PA 19057. Ed. Ken Stryker.

384.54 US ISSN 1052-7109
HE8698
THE M STREET JOURNAL. w. $139 (includes The M Street Radio Directory) (effective 1997). M Street Corporation, Box 479, Madison, TN 37116. TEL 615-865-1525; 800-248-4242. FAX 615-865-2598. Ed. Robert Unmacht. **Document type:** trade publication.
Description: Reports on AM and FM stations' format, technical, call letter and ownership changes; major decisions and actions taken by the FCC regarding radio broadcasting each week.

384.54 US ISSN 1052-7117
HE8698
THE M STREET RADIO DIRECTORY. a. $55.95. M Street Corporation, Box 479, Madison, TN 37116. TEL 615-865-1525; 800-248-4242. FAX 615-865-1525. Ed. Robert Unmacht. **Document type:** directory.
Description: Presents a guide to all radio stations in the U.S. and Canada.

384.5 US
▼**MANAGER'S BUSINESS REPORT.** 1997. m. $89. Box 782, Springfield, VA 22150. TEL 703-719-9500. FAX 703-719-7910.
Description: Covers management and operation issues pertaining to the radio.

MARINE DATA BASE. see *COMMUNICATIONS — Abstracting, Bibliographies, Statistics*

MARINE RADIO STATION MASTER FILE. see *COMMUNICATIONS — Abstracting, Bibliographies, Statistics*

MEDIA GUIDE (CLEVELAND). see *COMMUNICATIONS — Television And Cable*

384.5 643 NE
MEDIA NETWORK RECEIVER SHOPPING LIST; consumer survey of shortwave portable radios for international radio listening. (Text in English) 1980. s-a. free. Stichting Radio Nederland Wereldomroep, English Section, P.O. Box 222, 1200 JG Hilversum, Netherlands. TEL 31-35-6724211. FAX 31-35-6724239. E-mail: letters@rnw.nl. Ed. Jonathan Marks. circ. 45,000. **Document type:** catalog.

MEDIA PROFESSIONAL. see *JOURNALISM*

COMMUNICATIONS — RADIO

MERCATOR MEDIA FORUM. see *COMMUNICATIONS — Television And Cable*

384.5 US
MID-WEEK NEWS BRIEF. 1993. w. $89. Box 782, Springfield, VA 22150. TEL 703-719-9500. FAX 703-719-7910.
Description: Reports late-breaking news pertaining to the radio.

MILLECANALI; tv, radio, communicazione, spettacolo. see *COMMUNICATIONS — Television And Cable*

384.5 US ISSN 0745-7626
TK6570.M6 CODEN: MRTEFP
MOBILE RADIO TECHNOLOGY; technical information for paging, SMR and private wireless networks. 1983. m. $30 (free to qualified personnel in the US; all foreign $40). Intertec Publishing Corp., 9800 Metcalf, Overland Park, KS 66212-2215. TEL 913-341-1300. FAX 903-967-1898. Ed. Don Bishop. adv.; bk.rev.; tr.lit. circ. 24,458. (also avail. in microform from UMI) *Document type:* trade publication.
—BLDSC (5879.953840); AskIEEE; CISTI; KR SourceOne; UMI. **CCC.**
Description: Covers all aspects, technical as well as business, of wireless technology.

384.5 GW ISSN 0937-7042
MOBILFUNK NEWS. 1989. m. DM.300. Neue Mediengesellschaft Ulm mbH, Konrad-Celtis-Str. 77, 81369 Munich, Germany. TEL 49-89-74117190. FAX 49-89-74117195. Ed.Bd. circ. 5,000. *Document type:* trade publication.

621.384 JA
MOBIRU HAMU/RADIO AMATEUR'S MAGAZINE. (Text in Japanese) 1973. m. 520 Yen per no. Denpa Jikkensha, 15-4, Shimouma 6-chome, Setagaya-ku, Tokyo 154, Japan. TEL 81-3-3418-4111. FAX 81-3-3418-4702. Ed. Shinzaburo Kawai. adv. contact: Takashi Kimura. circ. 80,000.

MONITOR - RADIO T V. see *COMMUNICATIONS — Television And Cable*

384.5 UN
MONITORING INFORMATION SUMMARY. (Text in English, French, Spanish) q. 122 SFr. International Telecommunication Union, Place des Nations, CH-1211 Geneva 20, Switzerland. TEL 41-22-7306141. FAX 41-22-7305194. TELEX 421 000 UIT CH. E-mail: sales@itu.ch; URL: http://www.itu.ch. Ed.Bd. (microform)

621.384 US ISSN 0889-5341
TK6553
MONITORING TIMES. 1982. m. $23.95. Grove Enterprises, Inc., Box 98, Brasstown, NC 28902. TEL 704-837-9200. FAX 704-837-2216. Ed. Rachel Baughn. adv. contact: Beth Leinbach. bk.rev.; index. circ. 34,000. (back issues avail.) *Indexed:* Access (1991-).
Description: News on radio communications, scanner monitoring with loggings, international radio broadcast schedules, station, program, product, personality, technological profiles, and technical advice.

MUSIC & MEDIA; Europe's radio active newsweekly. see *MUSIC*

MUZIEK & WOORD. see *COMMUNICATIONS — Television And Cable*

621.38 NZ ISSN 0110-5337
N.Z.A.R.T. AMATEUR RADIO CALLBOOK. 1928. a. NZ.$65 includes monthly Break-In. New Zealand Association of Radio Transmitters, Inc., P.O. Box 1733, Christchurch, New Zealand. Ed. J.R.L. Walker. adv. contact: Bob Allen. bk.rev. circ. 3,800. *Document type:* bulletin.
Description: Lists amateur radio call-sign information in the South Pacific plus general radio and television information.

621.384 US ISSN 0899-0131
NATIONAL CONTEST JOURNAL. Short title: N C J. 1973. s-m. $12. American Radio Relay League, Inc., 25 Main St., Newington, CT 06111. TEL 860-594-0200. FAX 860-594-0303. E-mail: AA5Banana@aol.com; URL: http://www.arrl.org. Ed. Bruce Draper. R&P contact: Mark Wilson. *Document type:* bulletin.
●Also available on CD-ROM.

791.4 CN ISSN 0849-3952
NATIONAL RADIO GUIDE; guide to C B C radio and C B C stereo. 1981. m. Can.$32.10 (foreign Can.$55) (effective 1997). Core Group Publishers Inc., Box 48417, Bentall Centre, Vancouver, BC V7X 1A2, Canada. TEL 604-688-0382; 800-663-0354. FAX 604-688-3105. Eds. C. Robertson, Jane McIvor; Pub. Catherine Robertson. R&P contact: Jane McIvor. adv. contact: Jane McIvor. bk.rev. circ. 15,000. *Document type:* consumer publication.
Formerly: Radio Guide (ISSN 0711-642X)

384.5453 US ISSN 0889-2784
HE8664
NATIONAL RADIO PUBLICITY OUTLETS. 1972. a. $99. Morgan-Rand Inc., 1800 Byberry Rd., 800 Masons Mill Business Park, Huntingdon Valley, PA 19006. TEL 215-938-5500. FAX 215-938-5541. Ed. Nancy Sherker. adv.
Formerly (until 1986): National Radio Publicity Directory.

384.54 US
TK6540
NATIONAL SCANNING. 1990. 6/yr. $19.90 (effective 1997). L.J. Miller, Inc., Box 360, Wagontown, PA 19376. TEL 800-423-1331. E-mail: nscan@aol.com. Ed. Joe Nooney; Pub. L.J. Miller. adv. contact: Robin Miller. bk.rev. circ. 15,000.
Formerly (until 1996): National Scanning Report (ISSN 1066-5994)
Description: Non-technical magazine for those who enjoy monitoring police, fire, emergency medical and other communications on their scanners. Includes tips on hearing more, system profiles, frequency information, new products and a reader information exchange.

621.384 623.89 JA
NAVIGATIONAL RADIO AIDS. (Text in English) 1978. a. 9000 Yen per no. (Marine Radio Officer's Union - Senpaku Tsushinshi Rodo Kumiai) Radio News Agency - Musen Tsushinsha, 14-8, Shibaura 1-chome, Minato-ku, Tokyo 105, Japan. TEL 81-3-3451-4729. FAX 81-3-3451-4727. Ed. Koumei Kikuta.

384 NR ISSN 0331-4774
NIGERIAN RADIO - T V TIMES. 1958. m. Nigerian Broadcasting Corporation, P.O. Box 12504, Ikoyi, Lagos State, Nigeria. adv.; bk.rev. circ. 10,000.

621.384 JA ISSN 0287-1564
CODEN: NMGIDE
NIHON MUSEN GIHO/J R C REVIEW. (Text in Japanese; summaries in English) 1965. a. Nihon Musen K.K. - Japan Radio Co., Ltd., 17-22, Akasaka 2-chome, Minato-ku, Tokyo 107, Japan. TEL 03-3584-8836. FAX 03-3584-8878. TELEX 2425420 JRCTOK J. Ed. Kouhei Nishino; Pub. Hiroshi Yokomizo. *Indexed:* INSPEC (1985-). *Document type:* corporate report.
—BLDSC (5073.719000); AskIEEE; KR SourceOne.

621.384 JA
NIHON RAJIO SHINBUN/JAPAN RADIO NEWS. (Text in Japanese) 1946. 3/m. 10000 Yen. Nihon Rajio Shinbunsha, 14-15, Komagome 2-chome, Toshima-ku, Tokyo 170, Japan.

384.5 UN ISSN 0252-1814
NOMENCLATURE DES STATIONS DE RADIOCOMMUNICATIONS SPATIALES ET DES STATIONS DE RADIOASTRONOMIE/LIST OF SPACE RADIOCOMMUNICATION STATIONS AND RADIOASTRONOMY STATION/NOMENCLATOR DE LAS ESTACIONES DE RADIOCOMUNICACION ESPACIAL Y DE LAS ESTACIONES DE RADIOASTRONOMIA. (Text in English, French, Spanish) s-a. 736 Fr. International Telecommunication Union, Radiocommunication Bureau, Place des Nations, CH-1211 Geneva 20, Switzerland. TEL 41-22-730-5801. FAX 41-22-730-5785. TELEX 421 000 UIT CH. Ed.Bd. (microform)
Formerly: List of Radiocommunication Stations and Radioastronomy Stations.

621.38 US
NORTH AMERICAN CALLBOOK. 1920. a. $29.95. Radio Amateur Callbook, Inc., 1695 Oak St., Lakewood, NJ 08701-5925. adv.
Former titles: U S Callbook; Radio Amateur Callbook Magazine: U S Listings (ISSN 0033-7706)
Description: Now includes Canada, US, and Mexico.

384.54 780 640.73 US
OFF THE AIR. 1994. q. $6. Syracuse Community Radio, Box 6365, 205 Harvard Pl., Syracuse, NY 13210. TEL 315-474-9507. FAX 315-474-9507. E-mail: syrcomrad@aol.com. Ed. Frederic W. Noyes, IV. adv. contact: Frederic W. Noyes, IV. bk.rev.; dance rev.; film rev.; music rev.; play rev.; video rev.; stat. circ. 2,500. (back issues avail.) *Document type:* newsletter, trade publication.
Description: Covers trends in music, politics and broadcasting, including trends in independent and micro radio. Aims to support independent music labels and artists and increase awareness of community based listener responsive broadcasting.

621.38 US
OFFICIAL REGISTRY OF C B OPERATORS.* 1976. a. $5. M & O Communications, 120 E. 34th St., 7th Fl., New York, NY 10016. index.

384.54 NE
ON TARGET. (Text in English) s-a. Radio Netherlands, English Department, P.O. Box 222, 1200 JG Hilversum, Netherlands. TEL 31-35-6724222. FAX 31-35-6724239. E-mail: letters@rnw.nl; URL: http://www.rnw.nl. Ed. Jonathan Marks. illus. *Document type:* newsletter.
Description: News and programming schedules for Radio Netherlands external radio service.

384.54 030 US
ONE TO ONE (FRESNO); the journal of creative broadcasting. (Supplement avail.) 1976. w. $150 (effective Feb. 1991). CreeYadio Services, Box 9787, Fresno, CA 93794. TEL 209-448-0700. FAX 209-448-0761. E-mail: 71270.3707@compuserve.com. Ed. Jay Trachman. adv.; index. circ. 3,000. (back issues avail.) *Document type:* newsletter.
●Also available online. Vendor(s): CompuServe, Inc.
Formerly: Fruitbowl.
Description: Provides radio talent with guidance in delivery techniques; plus weekly humor, calendar and "Today in History," promotions, and artist biography.

384.54 030 US
ONE TO ONE II. (Supplement to: One to One) 1977. m. $65. CreeYadio Services, Box 9787, Fresno, CA 93794. TEL 209-226-0558. FAX 209-226-7481. Ed. Linda Richardson; Pub. Jay Trachman. circ. 300. (back issues avail.) *Document type:* newsletter.
Description: Contains humorous items for on-air and public speaking.

621.38 DK ISSN 0901-2567
OZ; tidsskrift for amatoer-radio. 1927. m. DKK 425. Landsforeningen Eksperimenterende Danske Radioamatoerer, Postbox 172, DK-5100 Odense C, Denmark. Ed. Flemming Hessel. adv.; bk.rev.; charts; illus.; index. circ. 6,000.
Formerly: Tidsskrift for Kortboelge Radio (ISSN 0040-7100)

P C I A BULLETIN; news and analysis for the personal communication industry. (Personal Communications Industry Association) see *COMMUNICATIONS — Telephone And Telegraph*

384.54 US ISSN 0897-0157
TK6555
PASSPORT TO WORLD BAND RADIO. 1984. a. $22.90. (International Broadcasting Services, Ltd.) I B S, Ltd., 825 Cherry Lane, Box 300, Penn's Park, PA 18943. TEL 215-794-3410. FAX 215-794-3396. Ed. Lawrence Magne. adv.; charts, illus, stat.; circ. 80,000 (paid). *Indexed:* Curr.Cont. *Document type:* consumer publication.
—BLDSC (6409.137000).
Formerly: Radio Database International.
Description: Refers to news, sports and entertainment shortwave broadcasts available from abroad.

PERFECT VISION. see *COMMUNICATIONS — Television And Cable*

PLAYBACK. see *COMMUNICATIONS — Television And Cable*

POPTRONIX EXPERIMENTERS HANDBOOK (YEAR). see *ELECTRONICS*

PROMAX INTERNATIONAL. see *COMMUNICATIONS — Television And Cable*

COMMUNICATIONS — RADIO

384.5 340   US
PUBLIC RADIO LEGAL HANDBOOK. irreg. $75 to non-members; members $50. National Federation of Community Broadcasters, Ft. Mason Center No. D, San Francisco, CA 94123. TEL 415-771-1160. index. (looseleaf format)
Formerly: N F C B Legal Handbook for Non-Commercial Stations.
Description: Reference checklist and explanation of FCC rules and regulations concerning regular station operation.

621.384   US
Q E X: A R R L EXPERIMENTERS' EXCHANGE. m. $15 to members. American Radio Relay League, Inc., 225 Main St., Newington, CT 06111. TEL 860-594-0200. FAX 860-594-0303. E-mail: jbloom@arrl.org; URL: http://www.arrl.org. Ed. John Bloom. R&P contact: Mark Wilson. circ. 4,000.
Document type: bulletin.
●Also available on CD-ROM.
—BLDSC (7163.603000); CISTI.
Formerly: Q E X: A R R L Experimenters' Exchange and A M S A T Satellite Journal (ISSN 0886-8093)

621.384   US   ISSN 0033-4812
TK1
QST; devoted entirely to amateur radio. 1915. m. $31. American Radio Relay League, Inc., 225 Main St., Newington, CT 06111. TEL 860-594-0200. FAX 860-584-0239. E-mail: mwilson@arrl.org; URL: http://www.arrl.org. Ed. Mark Wilson; Pub. David Summer. R&P contact: Mark Wilson. adv. contact: Brad Thomas. bk.rev.; charts; illus.; index. circ. 170,000. (also avail. in microform from UMI; reprint service avail. from UMI) **Indexed:** A.S.& T.Ind., Consum.Ind., INSPEC, MELSA. **Document type:** consumer publication.
●Also available on CD-ROM.
—BLDSC (7164.000000); CISTI; KR SourceOne; Linda Hall; SWETS; UMI; UnCover.

384.5   IT
QUI RAI. (Text in English) N.S. 1995. q. Rai International, Casella Postale 320, 00100 Rome, Italy. TEL 39-6-33171895. FAX 39-6-33171895. URL: http://www.planetitaly.com. Ed. Augusto Milana.
Description: News of Italian international radio and programs. Covers news from Italy for those abroad.

384.5   NE   ISSN 0927-9628
R A M. (Radio Amateur Magazine); magazine voor zend- en luisteramateurs. 27 MC en DX'ers. 1979. m. (CD-ROM a.). fl.59. Televak Uitgeverij N.V., Postbus 75985, 1070 AZ Amsterdam, Netherlands. TEL 31-20-6659220. FAX 31-20-6657316. Ed. J. Boers. adv. contact: Maarten Ponssen. index; circ. 25,000 (paid). **Document type:** consumer publication.
●Also available on CD-ROM.
—SWETS.
Former titles (until 1985): Radio Amateur Magazine (ISSN 0927-9644); (until 1982): Break Break (ISSN 0927-9636)

384.5   US
R C M A SCANNER JOURNAL. 1975. m. $27 (foreign $58). Radio Communications Monitoring Association, Box 542, Silverado, CA 92676. Ed. Carol Ruth. R&P contact: Carol Ruth. adv.; bk.rev.; index. circ. 2,100. **Document type:** newsletter.
Former titles: R C M A Journal; R C M A Newsletter.

384.54   US   ISSN 1060-0868
HE8811
C R CELLULAR HANDBOOK. (Radio Communications Report) 1977. a. $100. R C R Publications, Inc., 777 E. Speer Blvd., Denver, CO 80203-4214. TEL 303-733-2500. FAX 303-733-9941. Ed. Diane Hammer. adv.; index.
Supersedes in part (in 1991): Mobile Communications Handbook (ISSN 1048-0323); Which was formerly (until 1986): Mobile Radio Handbook.
Description: Provides information for the cellular communications industry, with listings of manufacturers, service providers, representatives, distributors, and cellular operators.

C R NEWSFAX. see COMMUNICATIONS — Telephone And Telegraph

C R - P C S HANDBOOK. (Radio Communications Report) see COMMUNICATIONS — Telephone And Telegraph

384.534   US   ISSN 1062-3779
TK6555
R C R PAGING HANDBOOK. (Radio Communications Report) 1977. a. $100. R C R Publications, Inc., 777 E. Speer Blvd., Denver, CO 80203-4214. TEL 303-733-2500. FAX 303-733-9941. adv.
Supersedes in part (in 1991): Mobile Communications Handbook (ISSN 1048-0323); Which was formerly (until 1986): Mobile Radio Handbook.

621.38   UK
R S G B AMATEUR RADIO CALL BOOK. 1951. a. £11.23. Radio Society of Great Britain, Lambda House, Cranborne Rd., Potters Bar, Herts. EN6 3JE, England. TEL 44-1707-659015. FAX 44-1707-645105. Ed. Brett Rider. adv. circ. 7,000. **Document type:** directory.
Description: Listing of names and addresses of UK radio amateurs and other useful information on UK amateur radio.

R T C A DIGEST. (Radio Technical Commission for Aeronautics) see AERONAUTICS AND SPACE FLIGHT

791.4   IE   ISSN 0033-7145
R T E GUIDE. (Text and summaries in English and Irish) 1961. w. Ir£40.80. Radio Telefis Eireann, Rm. 8, Annex 5, Donnybrook, Dublin 4, Ireland. TEL 353-1-2082919. FAX 353-1-2083085. Ed. Heather Parsons. adv.; film rev.; play rev.; illus. circ. 115,030. (tabloid format) **Document type:** consumer publication.

384   US   ISSN 0033-7153
PN4841
R T N D A COMMUNICATOR. 1946. m. $75. Radio - Television News Directors Association, 1717 K St., N.W., Washington, DC 20006. TEL 202-659-6510. FAX 202-223-4007. Ed. Bryan Moffett; Pub. Barbara S. Cochran. adv. contact: Ron T. Bardach. bk.rev.; abstr.; bibl.; illus. circ. 4,200.
Supersedes (in 1971): R T N D A Bulletin.

R T V; illustriertes Programm. see COMMUNICATIONS — Television And Cable

621.38   RU   ISSN 0033-765X
TK6540
RADIO. (Bi-monthly supplement avail.: K W Zhurnal) 1924. m. $84 (effective 1997). Seliverstov per. 10, 103045 Moscow, Russia. TEL 7-095-2076889. FAX 7-095-2087713. (Dist. by: Mezhdunarodnaya Kniga, B. Yakimanka 39, 117049 Moscow, Russia. TEL 7-095-2384967. FAX 7-095-2384634; Dist. in U.S. by: Victor Kamkin Inc., 4956 Boiling Brook Pkwy., Rockville, MD 20852. TEL 901-881-5973) Ed. A.V. Gorokhovsky. adv.; bk.rev.; charts; illus. circ. 60,000.
—Linda Hall.

384.54   UK   ISSN 0260-2423
RADIO ADVERTISERS' GUIDE. 1980. irreg. £25. Hamilton House Publishing, Staveley Way, Brixworth Industrial Park, Northampton NN6 9EU, England. illus.

RADIO ADVERTISING BUREAU. RADIO FACTS. see ADVERTISING AND PUBLIC RELATIONS — Abstracting, Bibliographies, Statistics

RADIO ADVERTISING BUREAU. RETAIL MARKETING KIT. see ADVERTISING AND PUBLIC RELATIONS

RADIO ADVERTISING SOURCE. see ADVERTISING AND PUBLIC RELATIONS — Abstracting, Bibliographies, Statistics

621.384 387   CN   ISSN 0033-7692
RADIO AIDS TO MARINE NAVIGATION. (Published in 2 editions; one dealing with the Atlantic and the Great Lakes, the other with the Pacific Area) (Atlantic area and Great Lakes edition avail. in French) vol.15, 1970. q. Can.$2.40 for each edition. Canadian Coast Guard, Telecommunications & Electronics Branch, Place de Ville, Ottawa, ON K1A 0N7, Canada. (Dist. by: Supply and Services Canada, Ottawa, ON K1A 0S9, Canada) Ed.Bd. charts; maps. circ. 10,000.

621.38   YU   ISSN 0033-8168
RADIO-AMATER. 1947. m. 3360 din.($30) (Savez Radio-Amatera Jugoslavije) Privredni Pregled, Marsala Birjuzova 3-5, 11000 Belgrade, Yugoslavia. Ed. Zarko Resanovic.

384 780   US   ISSN 0277-4860
PN1991.67.P67
RADIO & RECORDS. 1973. w. $299. Radio & Records, Inc., 10100 Santa Monica Blvd., 5th Fl., Los Angeles, CA 90067. TEL 213-553-4330. FAX 310-203-8727. E-mail: moreinfo@rronline.com; URL: http://www.rronline.com. Ed. Gail Mitchell. adv. contact: Michael Atkinson. circ. 9,000. **Document type:** trade publication, newspaper.

RADIO & T V. see COMMUNICATIONS — Television And Cable

RADIO AND TELEVISION CAREER DIRECTORY. see OCCUPATIONS AND CAREERS

384.5   US   ISSN 0741-8469
RADIO BUSINESS REPORT. 1983. w. $220 (foreign $280). Box 782, Springfield, VA 22150. TEL 703-719-9500. FAX 703-719-7910. Ed. Kathy Bachman; Pub. Jim Carnegie. R&P contact: Kathy Bachman. adv. contact: Ken Lee. circ. 5,200. **Document type:** trade publication.
Description: Covers radio and communications business and news for radio station and advertising personnel.

384.5   UK
RADIO BYGONES. bi-m. £18.50 (Europe £19.50; rest of world £23.75) (effective 1996). G.C. Arnold Partners, 9 Wetherby Close, Broadstone, Dorset BH18 8JB, England. TEL 44-1202-658474. FAX 44-1202-658474. (Subscr. in N. America to: Wise Owl Worldwide, 4314 W. 238th St., Torrance, CA 90505-4509, USA) **Document type:** bulletin.
Description: Contains articles on restoration and repair, history, circuit techniques, personalities, reminiscences and just plain nostalgia.

384.5   US   ISSN 1044-9647
PN1991.3.U6
RADIO - CHICAGO.* 1989. q. $12. Radio - Chicago, Inc., 233 E. Wacker Dr., Apt. 1112, Chicago, IL 60601-5107. TEL 312-939-5480. FAX 312-341-0222. Ed. Donna Walters. adv. circ. 15,000.
Description: Covers radio personalities and events in the Chicago metropolitan market.

621.38   US   ISSN 0033-779X
TK6540   CODEN: PRCAAO
RADIO CLUB OF AMERICA. PROCEEDINGS. 1920. s-a. $35 membership. Radio Club of America, Inc., c/o Gerri Hopkins, 3 Caro St., Red Bank, NJ 07701. TEL 732-842-5070. FAX 732-219-1938. E-mail: radioclubam@aol.com. Ed. Don Bishop. adv. contact: Mercy Contreras. bk.rev.; illus.; index; circ. 1,500 (controlled). **Indexed:** INSPEC. **Document type:** proceedings.
—AskIEEE; CISTI; KR SourceOne; Linda Hall. Refereed Serial

384.5 659.1   US
RADIO CO-OP SOURCES.* 1978. a. $15 membership. Radio Advertising Bureau, 261 Madison Ave., 23rd Fl., New York, NY 10016-2303. TEL 212-254-4800. FAX 212-254-8713. circ. 5,000. **Document type:** directory.
Description: Cooperative advertising fund directory for radio station sales people.

384.5   UK
TK6540   CODEN: RADCB7
RADIO COMMUNICATION. 1924. m. membership. Radio Society of Great Britain, Lambda House, Cranborne Rd., Potters Bar, Herts. EN6 3JE, England. TEL 44-1707-659015. FAX 44-1707-645105. Ed. Mike Dennison. adv.; bk.rev.; bibl.; charts; index. circ. 31,000. (also avail. in microform from UMI; reprint service avail. from UMI) **Indexed:** Br.Tech.Ind., INSPEC (1971-). **Document type:** bulletin.
—AskIEEE; CISTI; Ei; KR SourceOne; Linda Hall; SWETS; UMI; UnCover.
Former titles: RadCom; (until 1995): Radio Communication (ISSN 0033-7803)

384.54 380.1   US   ISSN 0146-6852
HE8698
RADIO CONTACTS (YEAR). 1970. a. (plus m. updates). $195. B P I Communications, Inc. (New York), 1515 Broadway, New York, NY 10036. TEL 212-536-5261; 800-BPI-4100. FAX 212-536-5294. Ed. Mitch Tebo. (looseleaf format) **Document type:** directory.
Description: Provides contact information for US and Canadian radio stations, national networks, syndicators and their programming.

COMMUNICATIONS — RADIO

384.5   HU   ISSN 0481-6048
RADIO ES TELEVIZIOUJSAG. 1924. w. 1668 Ft.($38.50) Brody S. u. 5-7, 1801 Budapest VIII, Hungary. TEL 36-1-138-8114. FAX 36-1-138-7349. (Subscr. to: HELIR, Lehel u. 1o-A, 1900 Budapest XIII, Hungary) Ed. Marta Boday. adv.: B&W page 420000 Ft., color page 520000 Ft.; adv. contact: Anna Samson. bk.rev.; film rev.; music rev.; play rev.; illus. circ. 650,000. **Document type:** consumer publication.
    Formerly (until 1957): Radio Ujsag (ISSN 0200-0415)
    Description: Provides detailed program information of Hungarian radio and television channels.

RADIO FERNSEHEN ELEKTRONIK; die Zeitschrift der Medienelektronik. see *ELECTRONICS*

RADIO FUN. see *HOBBIES*

621.384   US   ISSN 0079-9467
RADIO HANDBOOK.* 1935. irreg., 23rd ed., 1986. $39.95. Prentice Hall Computer Publishing, 201 W. 103rd St., Indianapolis, IN 46290-1094. TEL 317-298-5400. Ed. William I. Orr.

384.5   GW   ISSN 0944-0232
RADIO HOEREN; Hobby-Magazin fuer weltweiten Rundfunkempfang. m. DM.63 (foreign DM.75) (effective 1997); newsstand price: DM.5.25. Verlag fuer Technik und Handwerk GmbH, Robert-Bosch-Str. 4, 76532 Baden-Baden, Germany. TEL 49-7221-5087-0. FAX 49-7221-508752. (Subscr. to: P M S GmbH, Postfach 290180, 47261 Duisburg, Germany. TEL 49-203-76908-0. FAX 49-203-7690830) Ed. Rainer Pinkau. circ. 15,000. **Document type:** consumer publication.

384.54   ISSN 1064-587X
RADIO INK. 1986. fortn. $125 (foreign $199) (effective 1997). Streamline Publishing, Inc., 224 Datura St., Ste. 701, West Palm Beach, FL 33401. TEL 407-655-8778. FAX 407-655-6164. E-mail: radiolink@aol.com. Ed. B. Eric Rhoads; Pub. B. Eric Rhoads. R&P contact: John J. Montani. adv. contact: Tom Haymond. bk.rev. circ. 9,000. **Document type:** trade publication.
    Description: Provides news, interviews and features to help radio station owners, operators and managers.

384   JA   ISSN 0033-7927
RADIO JAPAN NEWS. (Editions in English, Japanese) 1956. m. free. Japan Broadcasting Corp. - Nippon Hoso Kyokai, 2-2-1 Jinnan, Shibuyu-ku, Tokyo 100, Japan. TEL 03-3465-1111. FAX 03-3481-1350. illus. circ. 14,000. (tabloid format)

RADIO - MEDIA. see *ADVERTISING AND PUBLIC RELATIONS*

791.4   NE
RADIO NETHERLANDS PROGRAMME SCHEDULE. (Editions in Dutch, English, Indonesian, and Spanish) 1949. s-a. free. Stichting Radio Nederland Wereldomroep, Public Relations Dept., P.O. Box 222, 1200 JG Hilversum, Netherlands. TEL 31-35-6724211. FAX 31-35-6724239. E-mail: letters@rnw.nl. circ. 200,000.
    Formerly: Radio Nederland (ISSN 0033-7951)

384.5   US
HE8698
RADIO ONLY MAGAZINE; the monthly management tool. 1978. m. $95 (foreign $150). Inside Radio, Inc., 1930 E. Marlton Pike, Ste. S-93, Cherry Hill, NJ 08003. TEL 609-424-6800. FAX 609-424-2301. Ed. Kyle Ruffin. tr.lit. (back issues avail.) **Document type:** trade publication.
    Former titles: Radio Magazine; Radio Only (ISSN 0731-8294)
    Description: Management information for radio executives and their sales representatives containing the latest trends and programming techniques.

384.55   CY
RADIO PROGRAMME. (Text in English, Greek) fortn. Cyprus Broadcasting Corporation (CyBC), Broadcasting House, P.O. Box 4824, Nicosia, Cyprus. TEL 357-2-422231. FAX 357-2-314050. TELEX 2333. circ. 21,000. **Document type:** consumer publication.
    Description: Greek-Cypriot radio and TV program news.

621.38 384   SA   ISSN 0033-7986
RADIO PROPAGATION PREDICTIONS FOR SOUTHERN AFRICA. (Text in Afrikaans, English) 1948. m. free. C S I R - Microelectronics & Telecommunications Technology, P.O. Box 395, Pretoria 0001, South Africa. TEL 27-12-841-2763. FAX 27-12-841-4720. TELEX 321312 SA. Ed. A. Delport. charts. circ. 300. (processed)

384.5   US   ISSN 1080-3025
RADIO RESOURCE INTERNATIONAL. 1987. 4/yr. free to qualified personnel. Pandata Corporation, 14 Inverness Dr. E., D-136, Englewood, CO 80112. TEL 303-792-2390. FAX 303-792-2391. Ed. Stacey Skillern; Pub. Paula Nelson-Shira. **Document type:** trade publication.
    Description: Covers the international mobile communications market.

384.5   US   ISSN 1080-3017
RADIO RESOURCE MAGAZINE. 1987. 8/yr. free to qualified personnel. Pandata Corporation, 14 Inverness Dr. E., D-136, Englewood, CO 80112. TEL 303-792-2390. FAX 303-792-2391. Ed. Stacey Skillern; Pub. Paulla Nelson-Shira. adv.; circ. 35,000 (controlled). **Document type:** trade publication.

621.384   IT   ISSN 0033-8036
RADIO RIVISTA. (Text mainly in Italian; occasionally in English) 1949. m. L.100000($60) (effective 1995). (Associazione Radioamatori Italiani) Ediradio, Via Scarlatti 31, 20124 Milan, Italy. TEL 2-6692894. FAX 2-66714809. Ed. Sergio Pesce. adv.; bk.rev.; bibl.; charts; illus.; pat.; index. circ. 25,000. **Document type:** academic/scholarly publication, proceedings.
    Refereed Serial

621.384   BE   ISSN 1024-4530
TK6540   CODEN: RABUEK
THE RADIO SCIENCE BULLETIN. (Text in English and French) 1994. q. 1500 BEF to libraries (free to qualified personnel) (effective 1994). International Union of Radio Science - URSI - Union Radio-Scientifique Internationale, c/o Ms. I. Heleu, University of Ghent (Intec), Sint-Pietersnieuwstraat 41, 9000 Ghent, Belgium. TEL 32-9-2643320. FAX 32-9-2644288. bk.rev. circ. 2,700. **Indexed:** INSPEC. **Document type:** bulletin.
    —BLDSC (7232.999600); AskIEEE; CISTI; KR SourceOne.
    Formerly: Radioscientist and Bulletin (ISSN 0779-9993); Formed by the merger of (1990-1994): Radioscientist (ISSN 1170-5833); (1938-1994): U R S I Information Bulletin (ISSN 0041-543X)

384.5   AA
RADIO SHQIP. fortn. 10 lek($3) Albanian Language Radio Union, Rruga Ismail Qemali 11 (pranie Radio Tiranes), Tirana, Albania. TEL 355-42-23239. FAX 355-42-23239. R&P contact: Buraj Skendaj. adv. contact: Bujar Skendaj. circ. 1,000. **Document type:** newspaper.
    Formerly (until 1996): Radio Perhapja.

384.5   BL
RADIO T V TECNICO. 1969. m. $300. Editora Signo Ltda., Caixa Postal 2483, 20001 Rio de Janeiro, Brazil. Ed. Apollon Fanzeres. bk.rev. circ. 80,000.
    Description: Instruction on radio technology for the radio technician.

RADIO TECHNICAL COMMISSION FOR AERONAUTICS. PROCEEDINGS OF THE ANNUAL TECHNICAL SYMPOSIUM. see *AERONAUTICS AND SPACE FLIGHT*

384   UK   ISSN 0033-8060
TK6540
RADIO TIMES. 1923. w. £52 (Europe & Ireland £90; rest of world £160) (effective 1997); newsstand price: £0.75. B B C Worldwide Publishing, Woodlands, 80 Wood Lane, London W12 0TT. TEL 44-181-576-3999. FAX 44-181-576-3160. URL: http://www.radiotimes.beeb.com. (Subscr. to: P.O. Box 425, Woking, Surrey GU21 1GP, England. TEL 44-1483-733720. FAX 44-1483-756792) Ed. Sue Robinson; Pub. Nicholas Brett. adv. contact: Ashley Munday. illus.; circ. 1,405,862 (paid). (also avail. in microform from CHL) **Indexed:** Child.Lit.Abstr., Int.Ind.Film Per., Intl.Ind.TV. **Document type:** consumer publication.
    ●Also available online.
    Description: Contains TV and radio listings plus related feature articles.

384.5 677.5   NR
RADIO - VISION TIMES. m. Western Nigeria Radio - Vision Service, Television House, P.O. Box 1460, Ibadan, Oyo State, Nigeria. Ed. Alton A. Adedeji. adv. circ. 20,000.

384.5   US   ISSN 1054-9048
RADIO WEEK. 1933. w. membership only. National Association of Broadcasters, 1771 N St., N.W., Washington, DC 20036. TEL 202-429-5350. FAX 202-429-5406. E-mail: tbutts@nab.org; URL: http://www.nab.org. Ed. Tom Butts. R&P contact: Ben Ivins. adv. contact: David Dziedzic. circ. controlled. (also avail. by fax) **Document type:** newsletter.
    ●Also available online.
    Incorporates (in 1988): Radioactive (ISSN 0747-4032); (in 1985): N A B Highlights; **Formerly:** N A B Today (Radio Edition).
    Description: Update on association news and broadcast industry news on Capitol Hill and at the FCC.

384.5   SZ
RADIO WELT. m. Postfach 758, CH-4127 Birsfelden, Switzerland. TEL 061-3121660. Ed. R. Birchel. circ. 15,000.

384.5   GW   ISSN 0176-800X
RADIO WELT. m. DM.69 (foreign DM.75). Beam Verlag, Bahnhofstr. 30, 35037 Marburg, Germany. TEL 06421-64026. FAX 06421-64647. Ed. Reinhard Birchel; Pub. Reinhard Birchel. adv. contact: Claudia Birchel. circ. 15,000. **Document type:** consumer publication.

621.38   US   ISSN 0274-8541
HE8698
RADIO WORLD. (International edition avail.) (Edition in English, Portuguese and Spanish) 1977. bi-w. $70 (foreign $90) (effective 1998). Industrial Marketing Advisory Services, Inc., 5827 Columbia Pike, Ste. 310, Falls Church, VA 22041. TEL 703-998-7600. FAX 703-998-2966. (Subscr. to: Box 1214, Falls Church, VA 22041) Ed. Lucra Cobo; Pub. Stevan B. Dana. adv. contact: Carmel King. bk.rev.; tr.lit. circ. 20,000. (tabloid format; back issues avail.) **Document type:** trade publication.
    Formerly: Broadcast Equipment Exchange (ISSN 0194-2190)

384.5   US   ISSN 0279-151X
RADIO WORLD INTERNATIONAL. 1990. m. free. Industrial Marketing Advisory Services, Inc.; 5827 Columbia Pike, Ste. 310, Falls Church, VA 22041. TEL 703-998-7600. FAX 703-998-2966. Ed. Alan Carter; Pub. Stevan B. Dana. adv. contact: Carmel King. circ. 20,000. (tabloid format; back issues avail.) **Document type:** trade publication.
    Description: Covers radio station technology, developments and applications. Geared toward radio station engineers, producers, technical staff and managers.

384.5 621.38   US
RADIO Y T V HISPANA. (Text in Spanish) 1987. m. $4 per no. Box 50656, Oxnard, CA 93031. TEL 805-986-2202. adv.: B&W page $1600; trim 9 3/5 x 13 2/5. circ. 4,800.
    Description: Covers the Hispanic radio and television industry and personalities. Includes music charts and play lists.

621.38   SA   ISSN 0033-815X
RADIO Z S. (Text in Afrikaans, English) 1947. m. R.15 membership. South African Radio League - Suid-Afrikaanse Radioliga, P.O. Box 807, Houghton 2041, South Africa. TEL 27-11-484-2830. FAX 27-11-484-2831. Ed. Reno Faber. adv.; bk.rev charts; index. circ. 3,000. **Document type:** newsletter.
    Description: Covers various aspects of amateur radio and electronics.

791.4   AU   ISSN 0033-8214
RADIOBOTE. 1947. s-a. free. F.O. Rothy, Ed. & Pub., A-4360 Grein, Austria. bk.rev.; tr.lit.; circ. 150,000 (controlled).

621.384   FR
RADIOCOMMUNICATIONS MAGAZINE. 6/yr. Societe d'Edition et de Publication Electronique, 87 rue Principale, 60360 Viefvillers, France. TEL 48-20-63-72. FAX 48-20-63-73. Ed. Yves Leclerc-Darras. circ. 8,000.

COMMUNICATIONS — RADIO

791.4   IT   ISSN 0033-8257
RADIOCORRIERE - T V. 1924. w. L.74500 (foreign L.250000). E R I Edizioni R A I, Via Arsenale 41, 10121 Turin, Italy. TEL 39-11-57101. FAX 39-11-534732. adv.: page L.24000000. circ. 150,446.

RADIOELECTRONICS AND COMMUNICATIONS SYSTEMS. see *ELECTRONICS*

621.384   PL   ISSN 0137-6802
RADIOELEKTRONIK; audio - hi-fi - video. 1924. m. 39 (foreign $36); newsstand price: 4.40 Zl. Radioelektronik Sp. z o.o., Ul. Switojerska 5-7, 00-236 Warsaw, Poland. TEL 48-22-314621. FAX 48-22-319337. E-mail: radelek@pol.pl. (Dist. by: Sigma - NOT Sp. z o.o., Zaklad Kolportazu, P.O. Box 1004, 00-950, Warsaw, Poland) Ed. Janusz Justat. R&P contact: Janusz Justat. adv.: B&W page 1930 Zl. ($1000); 205 x 286; adv. contact: Maria Tronina. bk.rev.; software rev.; charts; illus.; tr.lit.; index. circ. 68,000. (back issues avail.) **Document type:** consumer publication.
   Former titles (until 1979): Radioamator i Krotkofalowiec (ISSN 0483-8602); (until 1961): Radio Amator (ISSN 0481-5831)
   Description: Covers electronic components and applications, audio-video products and systems.

621.381   BW   ISSN 0236-4964
RADIOLYUBITEL'. (Text in Russian) 1991. m. $36 (effective 1995). Infotekh, P.O. Box 41, 220050 Minsk, Belarus. TEL 0172-786750. FAX 0172-783016. Ed. Valentin Benzar' adv. circ. 50,000.

384.5   UK
THE RADIOPHILE. bi-m. £18 (foreign £24) (effective 1996). Dept. NC, Larkhill, Newport Rd., Woodseaves, Stafford ST20 0NP, England. TEL 44-1785-284696. FAX 44-1785-284696. Ed. Chas. E. Miller. **Document type:** newsletter.
   Description: Covers all aspects of the vintage radio hobby.

621.38   RU   ISSN 0033-8486
TK5700   CODEN: RATEAO
RADIOTEKHNIKA.* English translation: Radio and Communications Technology (US ISSN 1087-7126) 1946. m. $653 (effective 1998). (Nauchno-tekhnicheskoe Obshchestvo Radiotekhniki i Elektrosvyazi im. A.S. Popova) Izdatel'stvo Radio i Svyaz', Shchemilovskii 2-i per. 4-5, 103473 Moscow, Russia. (Dist. by: Mezhdunarodnaya Kniga, B. Yakimanka 39, 117049 Moscow, Russia. TEL 7-095-2384967. FAX 7-095-2384634) Ed. A.L. Mikaelian. adv.; bk.rev.; charts; illus.; index. **Indexed:** Eng.Ind., INSPEC, Int.Aerosp.Abstr., Math.R. **Document type:** academic/scholarly publication.
   —AskIEEE; CISTI; KR SourceOne; Linda Hall.

621.38   RU   ISSN 0033-8494
TK7800   CODEN: RAELA4
RADIOTEKHNIKA I ELEKTRONIKA. English translation: Journal of Communications Technology and Electronics (US ISSN 1064-2269) (Contents page in English) 1956. m. $317 (effective 1998). (Rossiiskaya Akademiya Nauk) Izdatel'stvo Nauka, 90 Profsoyuznaya ul., 117864 Moscow, Russia. TEL 301-881-5973. FAX 301-881-1637. (Dist. in U.S. by: Victor Kamkin Inc., 4956 Boiling Brook Pkwy., Rockville, MD 20852. TEL 301-881-5973. FAX 301-881-1637) Ed. W.A. Kotelnikov. adv.; bk.rev.; charts; illus.; index. circ. 5,500. **Indexed:** ASCA, Chem.Abstr., Compumath, Curr.Cont., Eng.Ind., Ind.Sci.Rev., INSPEC, Int.Aerosp.Abstr., Math.R., Risk Abstr., Sci.Cit.Ind. **Document type:** academic/scholarly publication.
   —BLDSC (0139.000000); AskIEEE; CASDDS; CISTI; Genuine Article; KR SourceOne; Linda Hall. **CCC.**

384.5   SW
RATEKO & FOTO. 1955. m. SEK 350 (effective 1997). Elektronikfoerbundet Svenska, Box 6821, S-113 86 Stockholm, Sweden. TEL 46-8-441-51-80. FAX 46-8-441-51-91. E-mail: jan@elektronikforbundet.se; URL: http://www.elektronikforbundet.se. Ed. Jan Ljuhs. adv. circ. 5,300.
   Former titles (until vol. 10, 1994): Rateko (ISSN 0033-9962); (until vol. 3, 1983): Rateko med Radiohandlaren; (until vol. 5, 1967): Rateko.

...FERATIVNYI ZHURNAL. RADIOTEKHNIKA. see *COMMUNICATIONS — Abstracting, Bibliographies, Statistics*

RELIGIOUS BROADCASTING. see *COMMUNICATIONS — Television And Cable*

384   BL
REVISTA MONITOR DE RADIO E TELEVISAO. 1947. m. Instituto Radio Tecnico Monitor S.A., Rua Timbiras 263, Sao Paulo, SP, Brazil. Ed. Octavio A. De Toledo Assumpacao. adv. circ. 23,000.

384   SW   ISSN 0035-7839
ROESTER I RADIO T V; Sveriges radios programtidning, kabel-TV, Astra-parabol, Rymddoktorn. 1933. w. SEK 579 (effective 1991). Sveriges Radio, S-105 10 Stockholm, Sweden. Ed. Harry Straud. adv.; bk.rev.; film rev.; play rev.; abstr.; illus. circ. 120,000.
   Formerly (until 1957): Roester i Radio.
   Description: Program guide for radio and television in Sweden.

658.8   GW   ISSN 0035-9874
HE8690
RUNDFUNK UND FERNSEHEN. 1953. q. DM.100.20 (foreign DM.106.20) (effective 1996). (Hans Bredow Institut) Nomos Verlagsgesellschaft mbH und Co. KG, Waldseestr. 3-5, 76530 Baden-Baden, Germany. TEL 49-7221-2104-0. FAX 49-7221-210427. adv.; bk.rev.; bibl.; charts; stat.; note. circ. 1,100. **Indexed:** IBR, Int.Ind.Film Per. (until 1995), Intl.Ind.TV. **Document type:** trade publication.
   —BLDSC (8052.200000); SWETS. **CCC.**

384.5   GW   ISSN 0323-5998
RUNDFUNK- UND FERNSEHPROGRAMM. 1969. w. Deutscher Supplement Verlag GmbH, Breslauerstr. 300, 90471 Nuernberg, Germany. TEL 0911-89201-0. FAX 0911-8920135. adv. contact: Annelore Rupp. circ. 510,202. **Document type:** consumer publication.

S P E R ANNUAIRE. (Syndicat des Industries de Materiel Professionnel Electronique et Radioelectrique) see *ELECTRONICS*

384.5   GW
S R INFO. 1972. m. Saarlaendischer Rundfunk, Funkhaus Halberg, 66100 Saarbruecken, Germany. TEL 0681-6022040. FAX 0681-6022049. Ed. Rolf-Dieter Ganz. circ. 8,000. **Document type:** bulletin.

384.5 658.048   US   ISSN 0162-5934
S W L. (Shortwave Listener) 1959. m. $20 in US, Canada & Mexico; Europe & Russia $23; Pacific Rim $27. American Shortwave Listeners Club, 16182 Ballad Ln., Huntington Beach, CA 92649-2272. TEL 714-846-1685. E-mail: wdx6AA@aol.com. Ed. Stewart MacKenzie. adv.; bk.rev.; charts; illus.; stat. circ. 600. **Document type:** newsletter.
   Description: Contains logging of shortwave broadcast stations as reported by members. Includes feature articles on technology and equipment, club events and program schedules.

SAT - AUDIO - VIDEO; postepy w elektronice powszechnego uzytku. see *ELECTRONICS*

384   SZ
SCHWEIZERISCHE RADIO- UND FERNSEHGESELLSCHAFT. GESCHAEFTSBERICHT. (Editions in French, German) 1931. a. free. Schweizerische Radio- und Fernsehgesellschaft (S.R.G.) - Swiss Broadcasting Corporation (S.B.C.), P.O. Box, CH-3000 Bern 15, Switzerland. TEL 031-3509111. FAX 031-3509256. TELEX 911590-SSR-CH. circ. 11,500 (3,500 French ed.; 8,000 German ed.). (back issues avail.) **Document type:** corporate report.
   Formerly (until 1992): Schweizerische Radio- und Fernsehgesellschaft. Jahrbuch.

384.5   US
SHORTWAVE DIRECTORY; a frequency guide for the 10 kHz - 30 mHz spectrum. irreg., 8th ed. $19.95. Grove Enterprises, Inc., Box 98, Brasstown, NC 28902. TEL 704-837-9200. FAX 704-837-2216. **Document type:** directory.
   Description: Includes international broadcasting and VLF with emphasis on two-way communications (utilities).

384.5 790.13   US
SHORTWAVE RADIO TODAY; the DX radio magazine for active SWL'S. 1971. m. $23. Donald Thornton Ed. & Pub., 401 Amwell Rd., Bell Mead, NJ 08502. FAX 903-255-9220. (Subscr. to: Box 196, Du Bois, PA 15801-0196) bk.rev. circ. 500. **Document type:** bulletin.
   Formerly: Speedx (ISSN 0882-8091)
   Description: Provides up-to-date information on shortwave radio broadcasting, including schedules, rare catches of distant stations, and general radio news.

384.554 621.38   CN   ISSN 0831-0785
SON HI-FI VIDEO. 8/yr. Editions du Feu Vert, Inc., 5148 St. Laurent Blvd., Montreal, PQ H2T 1R8, Canada. TEL 514-273-9773. FAX 514-273-9268. Ed. Claude Corbeil. circ. 15,000. **Indexed:** Pt.de Rep. (1980-). **Document type:** consumer publication.
   Formerly: Son Hi-Fi Magazine.

384.54   FR
SON - MAGAZINE. 1969. m. N E M M, 63 av. des Champs-Elysees, 75008 Paris, France. adv.

384.5   US
THE SOURCE GUIDE. 1993. a. $129. Box 782, Springfield, VA 22150. TEL 703-719-9500. FAX 703-719-7910.

STEREO F M RADIO. see *MUSIC*

780   VC
STUDIO A - RADIOVATICANA MUSICA. 1986. bi-m. L.30000. Editore Radio Vaticana, 00120 Vatican City (Rome), State of the Vatican City. TEL 39-6-69883045. FAX 39-6-69884565. Ed. Pasquale Borgomeo. adv.: B&W page L.3000000, color page L.3000000; adv. contact: Lino D'Orazio. music rev. circ. 2,000. (back issues avail.) **Document type:** consumer publication, bulletin.
   Description: Lists musical programming from the Vatican Radio station.

384.5   GW
SUEDWESTDEUTSCHER EINZELHANDEL (FREIBURG). m. Landesgemeinschaft Radio-Elektro im Einzelhandel Baden-Wuerttemberg, Eisenbahnstr. 68-70, 79098 Freiburg, Germany.

384.5   GW
SUEDWESTFUNK JOURNAL. 1971. 10/yr. Suedwestfunk Journal Verlag, Hans-Bredow-Str., 76530 Baden-Baden, Germany. TEL 07221-92203. FAX 07221-922013. Ed. Arthur Landwehr. circ. 35,000. (back issues avail.) **Document type:** newsletter.
   Formerly: S W F Journal.

SUMMARY OF WORLD BROADCASTS. PART 1: FORMER U S S R (DAILY). see *BUSINESS AND ECONOMICS — Economic Situation And Conditions*

SUMMARY OF WORLD BROADCASTS. PART 1: FORMER U S S R (WEEKLY ECONOMIC REPORT). see *BUSINESS AND ECONOMICS — Economic Situation And Conditions*

SUMMARY OF WORLD BROADCASTS. PART 2: CENTRAL EUROPE, THE BALKANS (DAILY). see *BUSINESS AND ECONOMICS — Economic Situation And Conditions*

SUMMARY OF WORLD BROADCASTS. PART 2: CENTRAL EUROPE, THE BALKANS (WEEKLY ECONOMIC REPORT). see *BUSINESS AND ECONOMICS — Economic Situation And Conditions*

SUMMARY OF WORLD BROADCASTS. PART 3: ASIA - PACIFIC (DAILY). see *BUSINESS AND ECONOMICS — Economic Situation And Conditions*

SUMMARY OF WORLD BROADCASTS. PART 3: ASIA - PACIFIC (WEEKLY ECONOMIC REPORT). see *BUSINESS AND ECONOMICS — Economic Situation And Conditions*

SUMMARY OF WORLD BROADCASTS. PART 4: MIDDLE EAST (DAILY). see *BUSINESS AND ECONOMICS — Economic Situation And Conditions*

SUMMARY OF WORLD BROADCASTS. PART 4: MIDDLE EAST (WEEKLY ECONOMIC REPORT). see *BUSINESS AND ECONOMICS — Economic Situation And Conditions*

SUMMARY OF WORLD BROADCASTS. PART 5: AFRICA, LATIN AMERICA AND THE CARIBBEAN (DAILY). see BUSINESS AND ECONOMICS — Economic Situation And Conditions

SUMMARY OF WORLD BROADCASTS. PART 5: AFRICA, LATIN AMERICA AND THE CARIBBEAN (WEEKLY ECONOMIC REPORT). see BUSINESS AND ECONOMICS — Economic Situation And Conditions

621.38   SW   ISSN 0348-3177
SVENSK PRIVATRADIO. bi-m. Svenska Privatradiofoerbundet, c/o Elof Sjoestrand, Hornsgatan 35, S-502 41 Boras, Sweden. adv. circ. 15,626.

SYNDICAT DES INDUSTRIES DE MATERIEL PROFESSIONNEL ELECTRONIQUE ET RADIOELECTRIQUE. RAPPORT D'ACTIVITE. see ELECTRONICS

384.5   US
TALK SHOWS & HOSTS ON RADIO.* 1993. a. $37.95. Whitefoord Press, 23814 Michigan Ave., No. 314, Dearborn, MI 48124-1829. TEL 800-972-2584. FAX 313-274-9263. Ed. Annie M. Brewer; Pub. Annie M. Brewer. **Document type:** directory.
    Description: Lists radio talk shows and formats and contains biographical information on their hosts.

TELECOMMUNICATIONS AND RADIO ENGINEERING. see COMMUNICATIONS

TELEVIDENIE I RADIOVESHCHANIE. see COMMUNICATIONS — Television And Cable

384.5 791.45   XO   ISSN 0862-8122
TELEVIZIA A ROZHLAS; programovy tyzdennik. w. newsstand price: 8.50 Sk. Euroskop, Inc., Pribinova 25, 819 37 Bratislava, Slovakia. TEL 42-7-363677. FAX 42-7-2104192. Ed. Ladislav Balaj. adv.: B&W page 23000 Sk., color page 32000 Sk.; trim 212 x 270; adv. contact: Monika Tordova. film rev.; play rev.; illus. circ. 55,000. **Document type:** consumer publication.
    Description: Lists the week's television programs. Contains recipes and brief reviews.

TELEVIZIIA I RADIO. see COMMUNICATIONS — Television And Cable

621.384   CC   ISSN 1001-540X
TONGXIN JISHU YU FAZHAN/COMMUNICATION - TECHNOLOGY AND DEVELOPMENT. (Text in Chinese; abstracts in English) 1975. bi-m. Y54. Dianzi Gongye Bu, Wuxian Tongxin Zhuanye Qingbaowang - Ministry of Electronic Industry, Radio Communication Technology Information Exchange Organization, P.O. Box 174-215, Shijiazhuang, Hebei 050002, People's Republic of China. TEL 86-311-3033330. Ed. Zhao Hong. adv. contact: Cao Yutai. circ. 5,000.

384.5   NE   ISSN 0921-6677
TRANS WORD RADIO INFO BULLETIN. 1966. bi-m. Trans World Radio Nederland en Belgie, Noordersingel 90a, Postbus 91, 3780 BB Voorthuizen, Netherlands. TEL 31-342-478432. FAX 31-342-478343. **Document type:** bulletin.
    Former titles (until 1987): Toont de Wereld Haar Redder (ISSN 0921-6707); (until 1974): Trans World Radio (ISSN 0921-6715)

TRANS WORLD RADIO. see RELIGIONS AND THEOLOGY

621.38   DK   ISSN 0106-1968
TROPICAL BANDS SURVEY. 1973. a. DKK 50. Danish Shortwave Club International, Tavleager 31, DK-2670 Greve, Denmark. FAX 45-42-90-29-00. E-mail: dswci@centrum.dk; URL: http://www.sds.se/org/swl. Ed. Anker Petersen. circ. 800.

791.4   XR
TYDENIK ROZHLAS. 1923. w. 182 Kc. (effective 1992). Vydavatelstvi Radioservis, a.s., Na Florenci 3, 112 86 Prague 1, Czech Republic. TEL 232-32-37. FAX 235-64-67. (Subscr. to: PNS - Ustredni Expedice a Dovoz Tisku Praha, Zavod 01, Heliodora Piky 16, Prague, Czech Republic) Ed. Stanislav Pscheidt. circ. 170,000.
    Formerly: Rozhlas (ISSN 0231-6811)

384.5   UK
U K SCANNING DIRECTORY. irreg., vol.4, 1994. £21. Interproducts, 8 Abbot St., Perth PH2 0EB, Scotland. TEL 44-1738-441199. **Document type:** directory.

384.54   US   ISSN 1048-9908
U S SCANNER NEWS. 1988. m. $20. U S Scanner Publications, Box 14923, Portland, OR 97293-0923. TEL 503-203-8600; 800-890-6999. FAX 503-203-8631. Ed. Bob Gehri; Pub. Ken Gilbert. R&P contact: Ken Gilbert. adv.; bk.rev.; circ. 10,200 (paid). **Document type:** consumer publication.
    Description: Brings the scanner hobbyist the latest in related news and products reviews of equipment. For beginners through experts.

791.4   MY
UTUSAN RADIO DAN T V. fortn. 46M Jalan Lima, Off Jalan Chan Sow Lin, Kuala Lumpur, Malaysia. TEL 03-487055. Ed. Norshah Tamby. circ. 89,000.

621.38   CN   ISSN 0049-5778
V E 6. 1964. m. Can.$5. Amateur Radio League of Alberta, Box 447, Thorhild, AB T0A 3J0, Canada. Ed. Vic Prodanink. adv. circ. 500.
    Formerly (until 1971): Alberta Amateur (ISSN 0002-4716)

V R F INFO. (Verband des Radio-, Fernseh-, und Elektro-Fachhandels und Gewerbes Oesterreichs) see COMMUNICATIONS — Television And Cable

VERONICA; weekblad voor radio en TV. see COMMUNICATIONS — Television And Cable

384.5   US
W N Y C PROGRAM GUIDE. m. membership. W N Y C Membership, One Centre St., New York, NY 10007. TEL 212-669-7800. Ed. Lillie Balinova.
    Description: Contains schedules of public radio programs as well as commentary.

384.54   GW
W W F TRANSPARENT. 1988. bi-m. Westdeutsche Rundfunkwerbung GmbH, Ludwigstr. 11, 5000 Cologne 1, Germany. TEL 0221-2035208. FAX 0221-2035286. Ed. Thomas Straetling.

384.54   GW   ISSN 0170-1304
WELTWEIT HOEREN; internationale Fachzeitschrift fuer Rundfunk-Fernempfang. 1973. m. DM.48. Arbeitsgemeinschaft DX e.V., Postfach 1107, 91001 Erlangen, Germany. TEL 49-9131-992689. FAX 49-9131-49429. E-mail: 100665.2732@compuserve.com; URL: http://ourworld.compuserve.com/homepages/wwh/. Ed. Walter Eibl. R&P contact: Walter Eibl. adv. contact: Walter Eibl. bk.rev. circ. 2,300. (back issues avail.) **Document type:** trade publication.

621.384   AT   ISSN 1031-6353
WHAT'S NEW IN RADIO COMMUNICATIONS. 1982. bi-m. Aus.$36. Westwick-Farrow Pty. Ltd., Cnr. Fox Valley Rd. and Kiogle St., Wahroonga, N.S.W. 2076, Australia. TEL 61-2-94872700. FAX 61-2-94891265. E-mail: admin@westwick-farrow.com.au; URL: http://www.westwick-farrow.com.au. Ed. Mike Smyth. circ. 5,200 (controlled). (back issues avail.) **Document type:** trade publication.
    Description: New product information for radio communication engineers.

621.384   NE   ISSN 0929-6212
        CODEN: WPCOFW
WIRELESS PERSONAL COMMUNICATIONS; an international journal. (Text in English) 1994. 9/yr. fl.1260 to institutions; $646.50 to institutions in U.S. (effective 1998). Kluwer Academic Publishers, Postbus 17, 3300 AA Dordrecht, Netherlands. TEL 31-78-6392392. FAX 31-78-6392254. TELEX 29245 KAPG NL. E-mail: services@wkap.nl; URL: http://www.wkap.nl. (Dist. by: Kluwer Academic Publishers Group, P.O. Box 322, 3300 AH Dordrecht, Netherlands. TEL 31-78-6392392. FAX 31-78-6546474; N. America dist. addr.: Box 358, Accord Sta., Hingham, MA 02018-0358. TEL 617-871-6600. FAX 617-871-6528) Ed.Bd. **Document type:** academic/scholarly publication.
    —BLDSC (9324.700000); AskIEEE; CISTI; Ei; KR SourceOne; SWETS. CCC.
    Description: Publishes original archival-quality research studies considering theoretical, engineering and experimental aspects of wireless personal communications and radio communication of voice, data, images and multimedia combinations.
    Refereed Serial

384.5   UK   ISSN 1362-0983
WORLD MEDIA. BROADCASTING NEWS. Variant title: Broadcasting News. 1987. w. £410 (rest of Europe £440; elsewhere £456); online via Internet £425 (effective 1997). B B C Worldwide Monitoring, Caversham Park, Reading, Berks. RG4 8TZ, England. TEL 44-118-946-9289. FAX 44-118-946-3823. TELEX 848318. E-mail: marketing@mon.bbc.co.uk; URL: http://www.monitor.bbc.co.uk. Ed. MIke Elliott. R&P contact: Rosy Wolfe. adv. contact: Marian Martin. circ. 1,000. (back issues avail.) **Document type:** newspaper.
    ●Also available online. Vendor(s): Data-Star, Lexis-Nexis.
    Formerly (until 1996): Summary of World Broadcasts. Media. World Broadcasting Information (ISSN 1352-1438); Which superseded in part (in Sep. 1993): World Broadcasting Information: Broadcasting News and Transmission (ISSN 1350-8237)

384   US   ISSN 0144-7750
TK6540
WORLD RADIO T V HANDBOOK. 1947. a. $19.95. B P I Communications, Inc. (New York), 1515 Broadway, New York, NY 10036. TEL 212-764-7300; 800-344-7119. FAX 212-944-1719. Ed. A.G. Sennitt. circ. 55,000.
    —BLDSC (9358.700000); CISTI.
    Description: Complete guide to international broadcasting.

384.54   US   ISSN 1061-9240
WORLD SCANNER REPORT; a journal of VHF-UHF scanner technology & engineering. 1991. m. $35. Commtronics Engineering, Box 262478-C, San Diego, CA 92196-2478. E-mail: bcheek@cts.com; URL: http://ourworld.compuserve.com/homepages/bcheek. adv.; bk.rev. **Document type:** newsletter.
    Description: Features do-it-yourself mods, soup-ups, hints and kinks for serious scanner needs.

384.5   US
WORLDRADIO. 1971. m. $15 (foreign $25). Worldradio, Inc., 2120 28th St., Sacramento, CA 95818. TEL 916-457-3655. E-mail: kb6hp@NS.NET. Ed. LouAnn M. Keogh; Pub. Armond Noble. R&P contact: LouAnn M. Keogh. adv. contact: Rosalie Hernandez. bk.rev.; illus. circ. 33,000. **Document type:** consumer publication.
    Description: Contains articles for the amateur radio hobbyist.

621.384   CC   ISSN 0512-4174
WUXIANDIAN/RADIO. (Text in Chinese) m. Renmin Youdian Chubanshe - People's Posts and Telecommunications Publishing House, 111 Nanzhugan Lane, Chaoyangmen-nei, Beijing 100700, People's Republic of China. TEL 513839. Ed. Li Jun.

621.384   CC   ISSN 1003-3106
WUXIANDIAN GONGCHENG/RADIO ENGINEERING. (Text in Chinese) bi-m. Jixie Dianzi Gongye Bu, 54 Suo - Ministry of Engineering and Electronic Industry, Institute No. 54, 11 Zhongshan Xilu, P.O. Box 174-215, Shijiazhuang, Hebei 050002, People's Republic of China. TEL 33330. Ed. Cui Yuchang.

621.384   CC   ISSN 1003-3114
WUXIANDIAN TONGXIN JISHU/RADIO COMMUNICATION TECHNOLOGY. (Text in Chinese) bi-m. Jixie Dianzi Gongye Bu, 54 Suo - Ministry of Engineering and Electronic Industry, Institute No. 54, 11 Zhongshan Xilu, P.O. Box 174-215, Shijiazhuang, Hebei 050002, People's Republic of China. TEL 33330. Ed. Yang Bangzhen.

WUXIANDIAN YU DIANSHI/RADIO AND TELEVISION. see COMMUNICATIONS — Television And Cable

ZIMPEL. TEIL 3: FUNK UND FERNSEHEN. see COMMUNICATIONS — Television And Cable

384.5　　　　　AT　ISSN 1033-7539
24 HOURS. 1976. m. Aus.$49. Australian Broadcasting Corporation, G.P.O. Box 9994, Sydney, N.S.W. 2001, Australia. TEL 61-2-3332705. FAX 61-2-3332700. (Dist. by: Newsagents Direct Distribution Pty. Ltd., 150 Bourke Rd., Alexandria, N.S.W. 2015, Australia) Ed. John Nieuwenhuizen. adv.: B&W page Aus.$950, color page Aus.$1780. illus. circ. 30,000. (tabloid format; back issues avail.)
—UnCover.
　Former titles (until 1989): Australian Listener (ISSN 1032-108X); (until 1988): 24 Hours (ISSN 0313-1513)

621.384　　　　US　ISSN 1073-1024
50 MHZ DX BULLETIN. 1990. m. $20 (foreign $30) (effective 1997). Victor R. Frank, Ed. & Pub., 12450 Skyline Blvd., Woodside, CA 94062-4541. TEL 415-851-7031. E-mail: frank@sneezy.sri.com. R&P contact: Victor R. Frank. adv. contact: Victor R. Frank. circ. 300. (back issues avail.) **Document type:** bulletin, newsletter.
　Description: Dedicated to the understanding and utilization of long distance propagation in the 6-meter Amateur band.

621.384　　　　US　ISSN 1052-2522
TK9956　　　　　　CODEN: ARTAEG
73 AMATEUR RADIO TODAY.* 1960. m. $19.97. Wayne Greene Enterprises, 70 Route 202 N., Peterborough, NH 03458. (Subscr. to: Box 50330, Boulder, CO 80321-0330) Ed. David Cassidy. adv.: bk.rev.; illus.; index. circ. 65,000. (also avail. in microfilm from UMI; reprint service avail. from UMI) **Indexed:** INSPEC (1986-).
—BLDSC (9725.927600); AskIEEE; CISTI; KR SourceOne; UMI; UnCover. **CCC.**
　Former titles (until Oct. 1990): 73 Amateur Radio Magazine (ISSN 0889-5309); (until 1986): 73 for Radio Amateurs (ISSN 0883-234X); (until 1985): 73: Amateur Radio's Technical Journal (ISSN 0745-080X); (until 1982): 73 Magazine for Radio Amateurs (ISSN 0098-9010); (1974-1978): 73 Amateur Radio (ISSN 0037-3036)

1590 BROADCASTER. see COMMUNICATIONS — Television And Cable

COMMUNICATIONS — Telephone And Telegraph

A C U T A NEWS. (Association of College and University Telecommunications Administrators) see COMMUNICATIONS — Computer Applications

384.5 621.38　　UK　ISSN 1353-0356
A P T YEARBOOK. (Asia - Pacific Telecommunity) 1994. a. $195. Icom Publications Ltd., Chancery House, St. Nicholas Way, Sutton, Surrey SM1 1JB, England. TEL 44-181-642-1117. FAX 44-181-642-1941. E-mail: admin@icompub.demon.co.uk. Ed. A. Narayan. adv.: B&W page £4163, color page $5445; trim 210 x 148; adv. contact: Chris Ayres. **Document type:** directory.
　Description: Lists communications services in Asia.

384.6　　　　　US
A T & T NATIONAL TOLL-FREE DIRECTORY - BUSINESS BUYER'S GUIDE - BUSINESS EDITION. 1984. a. $24.99 (effective 1996). A T & T Yellow Page Directories, 4 Campus Dr., Parsippany, NJ 07054. TEL 800-562-2255. Pub. Patricia G. Selden. adv. **Document type:** directory.
　Former titles (until Sep. 1996): A T & T Toll-Free 800 National Directory - Business Edition & A T & T Toll-Free 800 Directory for Business.

384.6　　　　　US
A T & T NATIONAL TOLL-FREE DIRECTORY - SHOPPER'S GUIDE - CONSUMER EDITION. 1984. a. $14.99 (effective 1996). A T & T Yellow Page Directories, 4 Campus Dr., Parsippany, NJ 07054. TEL 800-562-2255. adv. **Document type:** directory.
　Former titles (until Sep. 1996): A T & T Toll-Free 800 National Directory - Consumer Edition; A T & T Toll-Free 800 Directory - Consumer Edition; A T & T Toll-Free 800 Directory for Consumers.

004.6 384.6　　　PL
▼**AKADEMIA GORNICZO-HUTNICZA IM. STANISLAWA STASZICA. TELEKOMUNIKACJA CYFROWA - TECHNOLOGIA I USLUGI.** 1997. q. 5 Zl. (effective 1997). Wydwnictwo A G H, Al. Mickiewicza 30, 30-059 Krakow, Poland. TEL 48-12-364038. FAX 48-12-364038. (Dist. by: Ars Polona, Krakowskie Przedmiescie 7, 00-068 Warsaw, Poland) Ed. A. Wichur. **Document type:** academic/scholarly publication.

384.6　　　　CN　ISSN 0002-4740
ALBERTA CALLS. 1920. w. free to qualified personnel. A G T Limited, Internal Communications Department, Fl. 26C Alberta Telephone Tower, 10020-100 St., Edmonton, AB T5J 0N5, Canada. TEL 403-493-4789. FAX 403-493-3006. Ed. J. Michael Warmington. bk.rev.; illus. circ. 10,000.

621.38　　　　FR　ISSN 1267-7167
TK5101.A1　　　　　CODEN: ANETE4
ALCATEL TELECOMMUNICATIONS REVIEW. German edition: Elektrisches Nachrichtenwesen (ISSN 1242-0557); Spanish edition: Comunicaciones Electricas (ISSN 1242-0573) (Text in English) 1922. q. $20. Alcatel, 54 rue de la Boetie, 75382 Paris Cedex 08, France. charts; illus.; index. circ. 31,000. (also avail. in microfilm from UMI; reprint service avail. from UMI) **Indexed:** A.S.& T.Ind., Acoust.Abstr., Br.Tech.Ind., CAD CAM Abstr., Cadscan, Chem.Abstr., Comput.Cont., Comput.Rev., Curr.Cont., Eng.Ind., INSPEC (1968-), Int.Aerosp.Abstr., Lead Abstr., SSCI, Tel.Abstr., Zincscan.
—BLDSC (0786.707500); AskIEEE; CISTI; Ei; Genuine Article; KR SourceOne; Linda Hall; UMI; UnCover.
　Former titles (until 1995): Electrical Communication (Paris) (ISSN 1242-0565); (until 1993): Electrical Communication (Romford) (ISSN 0013-4252)

AMERICAN TELEMARKETING ASSOCIATION. JOURNAL. see BUSINESS AND ECONOMICS — Marketing And Purchasing

384.6 621.385　US　ISSN 1075-5292
TK1　　　　　　CODEN: ANETE4
AMERICA'S NETWORK. 1909. s-m. $44 (effective 1996). Advanstar Communications, Inc., 7500 Old Oak Blvd., Cleveland, OH 44130. TEL 216-826-2839. FAX 216-891-2726. (Subscr. to: 1 E. First St., Duluth, MN 55802. TEL 800-346-0085) Ed. Paul McCloskey. adv.: page $3400. bk.rev.; illus.; tr.lit. rate. circ. 52,007. (also avail. in microfilm from UMI,PMC; back issues avail.) **Indexed:** ABI Inform., Bus.Ind., CAD CAM Abstr., INSPEC (1994-), PROMT, Tel.Abstr., Tr.& Indus.Ind. **Document type:** trade publication.
●Also available online. Vendor(s): Information Access Co., Knight-Ridder Information, Inc.
—BLDSC (0858.570000); AskIEEE; CISTI; KR SourceOne; Linda Hall; SWETS; UMI; UnCover. **CCC.**
　Formerly (until 1994): Telephone Engineer and Management (ISSN 0040-263X)
　Description: For the telephone operating industry: management, engineering, plant installation, commercial, marketing, traffic and accounting.

384 621.385　　US
AMERICA'S NETWORK DIRECTORY. 1935. a. $125 (effective 1996). Advanstar Communications, Inc., 7500 Old Oak Blvd., Cleveland, OH 44130. TEL 216-826-2839. FAX 216-891-2726. (Subscr. to: 131 W. First St., Duluth, MN 55082. TEL 800-346-0085) Ed. Paul McCloskey. adv. circ. 5,019. **Document type:** directory, trade publication.
●Also available online. Vendor(s): Knight-Ridder Information, Inc.
　Formerly (until 1994): Telephone Engineer and Management Directory (ISSN 0082-2655)

384.6　　　　　US
AMERICA'S PAY-PER-CALL DIRECTORY;* a billion dollar baby. 1991. a. $19.95. Infoman Publishing, c/o Barry Winton, Box 3707, Stateline, NV 89449-3707. **Document type:** directory.
　Description: Comprehensive listing of 900 and 976 phone numbers and the cost to make these phone calls.

384.6　　　　　US
ANSWER. 1958. q. $50 to non-members; members $30. Association of Telemessaging Services International, Inc., 1200 19th St., N.W., Washington, DC 20036-2412. TEL 202-429-5151. URL: http://206.69.91.109/icener/. Ed. Andy Briney; Pub. Herta Tucker. R&P contact: Andy Briney. TEL 202-857-1126. adv. contact: Stephanie Mattes. circ. 2,100. **Document type:** trade publication.
　Formerly: Super - Visor.

ARAB BANKING AND FINANCE DIRECTORY. see BUSINESS AND ECONOMICS — Banking And Finance

621.38　　　　UK
ASIA - PACIFIC MOBILE COMMUNICATIONS REPORT. bi-m. £990($1900) (effective 1997). E M C Publications, Holt Cottage, Kingston Hill, Kingston-upon-Thames, Surrey KT2 7JH, England. TEL 44-181-546-0841. FAX 44-181-549-8558. **Document type:** newsletter.
　Description: Analyzes the GSM, TACS, PDC, NMT, and PHS cellular markets in the Asia-Pacific region, reports on exhibitions and new products, provides subscriber statistics for the region, and contains updates on analogue, digital cellular, and PCN technologies.

384 621.38　　SI　ISSN 0217-510X
ASIA - PACIFIC TELECOMMUNICATIONS. 1990. m. $60 in Asia; elsewhere $70. Miller Freeman Pte. Ltd., 100 Beach Rd., 26-00 Shaw Towers, Singapore 0718, Singapore. TEL 294-3366. FAX 298-5534. Ed. Benidus Chong. circ. 10,738. (back issues avail.) **Document type:** trade publication.
　Description: Reports on the latest international and regional news and product and technical information on the world of telecommunications.

384.5　　　　　UK
ASIA - PACIFIC TELECOMMUNITY JOURNAL. Abbreviated title: A P T. 1989. q. £30($55) (Asia - Pacific Telecommunity) Icom Publications Ltd., Chancery House, St. Nicholas Way, Sutton, Surrey SM1 1JB, England. TEL 44-181-642-1117. FAX 44-181-642-1941. E-mail: admin@icompub.demon.co.uk. Ed. A. Narayan; Pub. Alec Barton. adv. contact: Christopher Ayres. circ. 1,172. **Document type:** trade publication.
　Description: Publishes research papers on telecommunications developments in Asia.

384.55 621.38　UK　ISSN 1355-0071
ASIA - PACIFIC TELECOMS ANALYST. 1994. fortn. £495($742) Financial Times Telecoms & Media Publishing, Maple House, 149 Tottenham Court Rd., London W1P 9LL, England. TEL 0171-896-2234. FAX 0171-896-2256. Ed. Jenny Walker. charts; stat. **Document type:** newsletter.
　Description: Covers business, legislative, and technical developments in the Asia-Pacific telecommunications market. Provides market analyses and forecasts.

384　　　　　UK　ISSN 0952-7516
ASIAN COMMUNICATIONS. (Text in English; summaries in Chinese and English) 1987. m. £60($110) (includes supplements). Icom Publications Ltd., Chancery House, St. Nicholas Way, Sutton, Surrey SM1 1JB, England. TEL 44-181-642-1117. FAX 44-181-642-1941. E-mail: ac@icompub.demon.co.uk. Ed. Diane Millis; Pub. Alec Barton. adv.: B&W page $4115, color page $5690; trim 297 x 210; adv. contact: Christopher Ayres. circ. 15,000. **Document type:** trade publication.
　Description: Contains news, product information and technical features.

384　　　　　US
AT THE L A T A LEVEL; news digest of telecommunications activities on a state-by-state basis. 50/yr. $365. United Communications Group, 11300 Rockville Pike, Ste. 1100, Rockville, MD 20852-3030. TEL 301-816-8950.

COMMUNICATIONS — TELEPHONE AND TELEGRAPH

380.3 621.3   US   ISSN 1042-6329
AUDIOTEX DIRECTORY & BUYER'S GUIDE. 1988. a. $55 (Canada $60; elsewhere $65). A D B G Publishing, Box 25929, Los Angeles, CA 90025. TEL 310-479-3533. FAX 310-479-0654. adv. circ. 10,000. **Document type:** directory.
   Description: Lists products and services in the audiotex, fax, and voice processing marketplace. Helps users locate hardware and software vendors, telephone companies, service bureaus, voiceover producers, consultants, and other support firms from over 1200 company listings.

384.5 658   US   ISSN 1063-1348
AUDIOTEX NEWS; the information & entertainment-by-phone newsletter. 1989. m. $249 (effective Jan. 1992). Audiotex News, 64 Division Ave., Ste. 7, Levittown, NY 11756. TEL 516-735-3398; 800-735-3398. FAX 516-735-3682. E-mail: carolg@spec.net. Ed. Carol Morse Ginsburg. R&P contact: Dory Kane. TEL 800-735-3398. bk.rev. circ. 1,000. (looseleaf format; also avail. in diskette format; back issues avail.; reprint service avail.) **Document type:** newsletter.
   Formerly: Ideal Dial.
   Description: Covers the domestic and international pay-per-call industry. Provides insights, analysis, information, news, trends and regulations, and related products.

780.8996073
305.896   US   ISSN 1063-1011
B R E. (Black Radio Exclusive) 1976. w. (47/yr.). $175 (Canada $250; elsewhere $350); newsstand price: $3. Sidney Miller's Black Radio Exclusive Corp., 15030 Ventura Blvd., Ste.864, Sherman Oaks, CA 91403. TEL 818-907-9959. FAX 818-907-9958. Ed. Heidi Butler; Pub. Sidney Miller. adv.: B&W page $2900, color page $3600; trim 8 3/4 x 11 3/4; adv. contact: Susan Miller. charts; dance rev.; film rev.; illus.; music rev.; play rev.; tele.rev.; video rev. (back issues avail.) **Document type:** consumer publication.
   Former titles (until 1988): Black Radio Exclusive (ISSN 0745-5992); Sidney Miller's Black Radio Exclusive (ISSN 0161-1526)
   Description: Covers the entire spectrum of the black music industry, with particular emphasis on the importance of black radio.

384 621   UK
B T TODAY. 1981. m. British Telecommunications plc., 81 Newgate St., Rm. A236, London EC14 7AJ, England. TEL 44-171-356-5307. TELEX 261127. Ed. Ken Runicles. adv.; bk.rev.; illus. circ. 270,000. (back issues avail.) **Document type:** newspaper.
   ●Also available online. Vendor(s): Data-Star, Knight-Ridder Information, Inc., NewsNet (TE40).
   Formerly (until Apr. 1991): Telecom Today.

621.38   US   ISSN 1089-7089
TK5101.A1   CODEN: BLTJFD
BELL LABS TECHNICAL JOURNAL. 1922. q. $69 to libraries and individuals (foreign $84) (effective 1998). Lucent Technologies, 600 Mountain Ave., Rm. 3C-412, Box 636, Murray Hill, NJ 07974-0636. TEL 908-582-4834. FAX 908-582-4430. URL: http://www.lucent.com/bltj. Ed. Frances A. Grimes. R&P contact: Sally Kempner. TEL 908-582-4823. bibl.; charts; illus.; index. circ. 35,000. (also avail. in microform from PMC,UMI) **Indexed:** A.I.Abstr., A.S.& T.Ind., Abstr.J.Earthq.Eng., Alloys Ind., Appl.Mech.Rev., ASCA, CAD CAM Abstr., Chem.Abstr., Comput.Abstr., Comput.Cont., Comput Dtbs., Curr.Cont.(1995-), Curr.Ind.Stat., Deep Sea Res.& Oceanogr.Abstr., Elec.& Electron Abstr., Electron.& Communic.Abstr.J., Eng.Ind., Eng.Mat.Abstr., Ergon.Abstr., GeoRef., Ind.Sci.Rev., INIS Atomind., INSPEC (1985-), Int.Aerosp.Abstr., J.Curr.Laser Abstr., Lang.& Lang.Behav.Abstr., Math.R., Met.Abstr.Ind., Met.Abstr., Nonfer.Met.Alert, PCC Alert, Psychol.Abstr., Sci.Cit.Ind., Sociol.Abstr., Solid St.Abstr., SSCI, Stat.Theor.Meth.Abstr. (1995-), Steels Alert, Tel.Abstr., World Alum.Abstr., Zent.Math. **Document type:** trade publication.
—BLDSC (1889.100000); AskIEEE; CASDDS; CISTI; Ei; Genuine Article; KR SourceOne; Linda Hall; SWETS; UMI. **CCC.**
   Former titles (until 1997): A T & T Technical Journal (ISSN 8756-2324); (until 1985): A T & T Bell Laboratories Technical Journal (ISSN 0748-612X); (until 1984): Bell System Technical Journal (ISSN 0005-8580)
   Description: Fosters technical excellence and innovation among the technical community of Lucent Technologies and promotes progress in communications fields worldwide.
   Refereed Serial

BETTER BUSINESS BY TELEPHONE. see BUSINESS AND ECONOMICS — Management

384   US   ISSN 0162-3885
HF5717   CODEN: BCORBD
BUSINESS COMMUNICATIONS REVIEW. 1971. m. $45. B C R Enterprises, Inc., 950 York Rd., Hinsdale, IL 60521-2939. TEL 312-986-1432. Ed. Fred S. Knight; Pub. Jerry Goldstone. adv. contact: Bob Horton. bk.rev.; index. circ. 13,759. (also avail. in microform from UMI; reprint service avail. from UMI; back issues avail.) **Indexed:** ABI Inform., B.P.I., CAD CAM Abstr., Comput.Cont., INSPEC (1984-), Tel.Abstr., Tel.Alert. **Document type:** trade publication.
●Also available online. Vendor(s): Information Access Co.
—BLDSC (2933.360000); AskIEEE; CASDDS; KR SourceOne; SWETS; UMI; UnCover. **CCC.**
   Description: Analysis of issues, trends, new products and services affecting telecommunications management.

621.382 621.385   US
C C I T T RED BOOKS. (International Telegraph and Telephone Consultative Committee) quadrennial. price varies. (International Telecommunication Union, International Telegraph and Telephone) U.S. National Technical Information Service, 3285 Port Royal Rd., Springfield, VA 22161. TEL 703-487-4630. (Subscr. outside North America to: International Telecommunication Union, Place des Nations, CH-1211 Geneva 12, Switzerland.)

384.5   US
C C M I GUIDE TO NETWORKING SERVICES. VOLUME 1: INTERLATA SWITCHED SERVICES. (Consists of 5 vols.) base vol. (plus m. updates). $629 (5-vol. set $2745). (Center for Communications Management Information) C C M I (Subsidiary of: United Communications Group), 11300 Rockville Pike, Ste. 1100, Rockville, MD 20852-3030. TEL 301-816-8950. FAX 301-816-8945. Ed. Belinda Jarvis; Pub. George David. R&P contact: Michael Peck. adv. contact: Betty Lehnus. (looseleaf format) **Document type:** directory.
   Former titles: Planning Guide 3. Value-Added Networks and Data Private Line. Telecommunications Rates Services; V A N and Resale Carrier Guide.
   Description: Provides the rates for AT&T, MCI, Sprint, Worldcom, Frontier, Vnet, VPN, SDN, Plat, Rate Plus, 800 services, Clarity, Premier, etc. Includes high-volume WATS and virtual networks. Includes interstate rates and intrastate, interLATA rates for each of the 48 continental states.

384.5   US
C C M I GUIDE TO NETWORKING SERVICES. VOLUME 2: INTRALATA SWITCHED SERVICES. (Consists of 5 vols.) base vol. (plus m. update). $629 (5-vol. set $2745). (Center for Communications Management Information) C C M I (Subsidiary of: United Communications Group), 11300 Rockville Pike, Ste. 1100, Rockville, MD 20852-3030. TEL 301-816-8950. FAX 301-816-8945. Ed. Belinda Jarvis; Pub. George David. R&P contact: Michael Peck. **Document type:** directory.
   Description: Gives rates for local calling plans for every Bell operated company for all states.

384.5   US
C C M I GUIDE TO NETWORKING SERVICES. VOLUME 3: INTERLATA PRIVATE LINE SERVICES. (Consists of 5 vols.) base vol. (plus m. updates). $629 (5-vol. set $2745). (Center for Communications Management Information) C C M I, 11300 Rockville Pike, Ste. 1100, Rockville, MD 20852-3030. TEL 301-816-8950. FAX 301-816-8945. Ed. Belinda Jarvis; Pub. George David. R&P contact: Michael Peck. (looseleaf format) **Document type:** directory.
   Description: Gives exact current rates for all the dedicated services offered by long-distance carrirs, Accunet, TDS, and Clearline digital services from fractional T-1 to T-45, plus DDS and voicegrade private line, exchange carrier special access and a special section on Frame relay from the IXCs and LECs.

384.5   US
C C M I GUIDE TO NETWORKING SERVICES. VOLUME 4: INTRALATA PRIVATE LINE SERVICES. (Consists of 5 vols.) base vol. (plus m. updates). $629 (5-vol. set $2679). (Center for Communications Management Information) C C M I, 11300 Rockville Pike, Ste. 1100, Rockville, MD 20851-3030. TEL 301-816-8950. FAX 301-816-8945. Ed. Belinda Jarvis; Pub. George David. R&P contact: Michael Peck. (looseleaf format) **Document type:** directory.
   Description: Describes high-capacity, DDS and voice grade services offered by local exchange carriers. Organized by Bell regional holding company.

384.5   US
C C M I GUIDE TO NETWORKING SERVICES. VOLUME 5: INTERNATIONAL SERVICES. (Consists of 5 vols.) base vol. (plus m. updates). $629 (5-vol. set $2745). (Center for Communications Management Information) C C M I, 11300 Rockville Pike, Ste. 1100, Rockville, MD 20852-3030. TEL 301-816-8950. FAX 301-816-8945. Ed. Belinda Jarvis; Pub. George David. R&P contact: Michael Peck. (looseleaf format) **Document type:** directory.
   Description: Gives rates for basic international toll and special services such as AT&T International Skynet. Other services covered include international Megacom, international SDN, international DDS, international Clarity from Sprint. A comprehensive Canadian section includes MTS, WATS and 800 services, plus private line services.

384.5   US
C C M I GUIDE TO NETWORKING SERVICES. VOLUME 6: REFERENCE FACTBOOK. (Consists of 5 vols.) base vol. (updates 4/yr.). $395. (Center for Communications Management Information) C C M I, 11300 Rockville Pike, Ste. 1100, Rockville, MD 20852-3030. TEL 301-816-8950. FAX 301-816-8945. Ed. Belinda Jarvis; Pub. George David. R&P contact: Michael Peck. (looseleaf format) **Document type:** directory.
   Description: Lists all the NPA-NXXs in the country; points of presence, with service available, for the Big Three; area codes organized numerically and alphabetically; a list of LATAs by state and states by LATAs; maps of all 50 states showing the territories of both Bell and independent operating companies.

621.38   UK
C E M A TELECOMMUNICATIONS. 1987. m. £2000. (Cores European Market Analysis) Portman Communications Ltd., 52 Foundling Ct., London WC1N 1AN, England. TEL 44-171-837-0815. FAX 44-171-278-9917. E-mail: 100141,676@compuserve. Ed. Philip Gallagher; Pub. Philip Gallagher. R&P contact: Philip Gallagher. bk.rev. circ. 500. **Document type:** newsletter.

COMMUNICATIONS — TELEPHONE AND TELEGRAPH

C S E L T INFOTEL; periodico d'informazione bibliografica nelle telecomunicazioni e scienze connesse. see COMMUNICATIONS — Abstracting, Bibliographies, Statistics

C S E L T TECHNICAL REPORTS/C S E L T RAPPORTI TECNICI. see COMMUNICATIONS

CANADA. STATISTICS CANADA. TELEPHONE STATISTICS/STATISTIQUE DU TELEPHONE. see COMMUNICATIONS — Abstracting, Bibliographies, Statistics

384   CN   ISSN 0825-3021
CANADIAN COMMUNICATIONS NETWORK LETTER. 1979. 40/yr. Can.$775. Evert Communications Ltd., 1296 Carling Ave., Ottawa, ON K1Z 7K8, Canada. TEL 613-728-4621. FAX 613-728-0385. E-mail: services@evert.com; URL: http://www.evert.com. Ed. Brant Scott. Indexed: CAD CAM Abstr., Comput.Dtbs., Tel.Abstr. **Document type:** newsletter.
   Formerly: Communications Week (ISSN 0227-0382)
   Description: Focuses on regulatory and policy issues in Canadian telecommunications.

CANADIAN NATIONAL ANNUAL REPORT. see TRANSPORTATION

384.6   US   ISSN 1054-7703
CELLULAR AND MOBILE INTERNATIONAL. 1991. 6/yr. free to qualified personnel. Intertec Publishing Corp., 9800 Metcalf, Overland Park, KS 66212-2215. TEL 913-341-1300. FAX 913-967-1898. Eds. Rhonda Wickham, Don Bishop. adv.: B&W page $2500, color page $3235; trim 8 x 10 7/8. circ. 10,400. (also avail. in microform from UMI) **Document type:** trade publication.
   —UMI. **CCC**.
   Description: Covers applications, technical aspects, and management for global cellular, mobile radio and paging industries.

384.6   US   ISSN 0741-6520
   HD9696.R363
CELLULAR BUSINESS; journal of cellular telecommunications. 1984. m. $24 (free to qualified personnel). Intertec Publishing Corp., 9800 Metcalf, Overland Park, KS 66212-2215. TEL 913-341-1300. FAX 913-967-1898. Ed. Rhonda Wickham. circ. 20,200. Indexed: ABI Inform., CAD CAM Abstr., Tel.Abstr. **Document type:** trade publication.
   ●Also available online. Vendor(s): UMI.
   —BLDSC (3097.926000); SWETS; UMI. **CCC**.

384.6 659.1   US   ISSN 0892-2683
CELLULAR SALES & MARKETING; cell the world! 1987. 10/yr. $347 (foreign $371) (effective 1995 & 1996). Creative Communications Inc. (Herndon), Box 1519-ULR, Herndon, VA 20172-1519. TEL 703-742-9696. Ed. Stuart F. Crump, Jr. (back issues avail.) **Document type:** newsletter.
   ●Also available online. Vendor(s): NewsNet (TE72).
   Description: News coverage of sales and marketing strategies in the industry.

384.5   US
THE CHANGING TIMES OF TELECOMMUNICATIONS. 1991. a. $395. Dun & Bradstreet Information Services (Murray Hill) (Subsidiary of: Dun & Bradstreet, Inc.), One Diamond Hill Rd., Murray Hill, NJ 07974. TEL 908-665-5224.
FAX 908-771-7599. Ed. Lynette Alvarez.
   Description: Examines the telecommunication industry from the deregulation of AT&T in the early 1980's to today's expansion of American telecommunication companies in foreign countries. Also covers cellular technology, satellite communications, microwave communication developments and innovations in fiber optics.

621.38   CC   ISSN 1017-5199
CHINA TELECOMMUNICATIONS CONSTRUCTION/ZHONGGUO DIANXIN JIANSHE. (Text in Chinese, English) 1988. 9/yr. $149 (effective 1998). (Beijing Dianxin Tongxin Xuehui) China Telecommunication Construction Publishers, 12-F, Sing Kui Commercial Bldg., 27 Des Voeux Rd. W., Hong Kong, People's Republic of China. TEL 852-2517-2093. FAX 852-2517-2101. Ed. Gao Xingzhong. adv.: B&W page $2300, color page $3200; trim 210 x 275. circ. 20,000. (back issues avail.) Indexed: HongKongiana. **Document type:** trade publication.
   Description: Covers the current and future development of telecommunication in China, co-operation project with Western countries, new products and technologies.

621.38   CC   ISSN 1025-7004
CHINA WIRELESS COMMUNICATIONS. (Text in Chinese, English) 6/yr. $79. (State Radio Regulatory Commission, CC) China Telecommunication Construction Publishers, 12-F, Sing Kui Commercial Bldg., 27 Des Voeux Rd. W., Hong Kong, People's Republic of China. FAX 852-2517-2101. E-mail: ctccwc@asiaonline.net. Ed. S.Y. Cheung. adv.: B&W page $2200, color page $2800. circ. 12,000.
   Description: Covers wireless communications including mobile, satellite and microwave in China, Hong Kong and Taiwan.

384.1   UN
CODES AND ABBREVIATIONS FOR THE USE OF THE INTERNATIONAL TELECOMMUNICATIONS SERVICES. (Editions in English, French, Spanish) irreg., 4th ed., 1982. 32 SFr. International Telecommunication Union, Place des Nations, CH-1211 Geneva 20, Switzerland. TEL 41-22-7306141.
FAX 41-22-7305194. TELEX 421 000 UIT CH. E-mail: sales@itu.ch; URL: http://www.itu.ch. Ed.Bd.

384.1 621.387   UK   ISSN 0966-4882
COMMUNICATIONS NETWORKS. 1984. m. £30; newsstand price: £3. E M A P Business & Computer Publications Ltd., 33-39 Bowling Green Ln., London EC1R 0DA, England. TEL 44-171-837-1212. FAX 44-171-278-4008. E-mail: 75300.243@compuserve.com. Ed. Maxwell Cooter. adv. circ. 20,000. Indexed: INSPEC (1991-). **Document type:** trade publication.
   —AskIEEE; KR SourceOne. **CCC**.
   Formerly (until 1991): Communications (ISSN 0266-8009)

621.38   US   ISSN 1081-4655
COMMUNICATIONS STANDARDS REVIEW - TELECOMMUNICATIONS. 1990. irreg. (8-9/yr.). $595 (effective 1995). Communications Standards Review, 757 Greer Rd., Palo Alto, CA 94303-3024. TEL 415-856-9018. FAX 415-856-6591. E-mail: ebaskin@csrstds.com. Ed. Ken Krechmer; Pub. Elaine Baskin. circ. 250 (paid). (also avail. in diskette format; back issues avail.) **Document type:** proceedings.
   Supersedes in part (in 1995): Communications Standards Review.
   Description: Reports on telecommunications standards works-in-progress in the Telecommunications Industry Association, International Telecommunications Union-Telecommunications, and European Telecommunications Standards Institute.

COMMUNICATIONS STANDARDS SUMMARY. see COMMUNICATIONS — Radio

383 621.382   SZ
   TK4
COMTEC. (Text in English, French, German, Italian; summaries in English) 1922. m. 80 SFr. Telecom P T T, Postfach 7216, CH-3001 Bern, Switzerland. TEL 41-31-3383137. FAX 41-31-3382779. TELEX 911010-PTT-CH. Ed. Hannes Gysling. adv.: bk.rev.; charts; illus.; index. circ. 4,000. Indexed: Eng.Ind., INSPEC. **Document type:** bulletin.
   —BLDSC (3395.158000); AskIEEE; CISTI; KR SourceOne.
   Former titles: ComTech (ISSN 1420-3715); (until 1995): Technische Mitteilungen P T T (ISSN 0040-1471)

384   PO
CORREIOS E TELECOMUNICACOES DE PORTUGAL. BOLETIM OFICIAL. 1948. m. Esc.240 or exchange basis. Correios e Telecomunicacoes de Portugal, Servico de Impressos e Publicacoes, Av. Casal Ribeiro, 28-1, 1000 Lisbon, Portugal. circ. 6,000. (also avail. in microform)
   Formerly: Portugal. Administracao Geral dos Correios e Telegrafos. Boletim Oficial dos C T T.

CORREO POSTAL Y TELEGRAFICO. see COMMUNICATIONS — Postal Affairs

COURIER (LONDON); the post office newspaper. see COMMUNICATIONS — Postal Affairs

384.6 537.5 001.6   IT
CRONACHE DAL GRUPPO STET. 1973. q. Societa Finanziaria Telefonica p.A., Via Aniene, 31, 00198 Rome, Italy. (Subscr. to: Via Corelli, 10, 00198 Rome, Italy) Dir. Giorgio Innamorati. bibl. circ. 125,000. (back issues avail.)
   Formerly: Cronache dal Gruppo (ISSN 0390-1777)

DAK TAR. see COMMUNICATIONS — Postal Affairs

621.38   JA
DENDEN KENSETSU NYUSU/TELEPHONE AND TELEGRAPH CONSTRUCTION NEWS. (Text in Japanese) 1967. s-m. 8400 Yen. Nihon Sogo Tsushinsha, 8-27, Kamata 1-chome, Ota-ku, Tokyo 144, Japan.

384.1 384.6   CC   ISSN 1000-1247
DIANXIN JISHU/TELECOMMUNICATION TECHNOLOGY. (Text in Chinese) m. $0.60 per no. Renmin Youdian Chubanshe - People's Posts and Telecommunications Publishing House, 111 Nanzhugan Lane, Chaoyangmen-nei, Beijing 100700, People's Republic of China. TEL 5130984. Ed. Zhang Xiufang.

384.6   US
DIRECT DIAL. 1990. m. (except Jan.). $20. United Advertising Publications, Inc., 15400 Knoll Trail, Ste. 500, Dallas, TX 75248. TEL 214-233-5131. FAX 214-788-5367. adv.: B&W page $1085; trim 7 5/8 x 10 3/4. circ. 25,000. **Document type:** trade publication.
   Description: Guide for buyers of business telecommunications products.

384   US
DOTS AND DASHES. 1950. q. $7. Morse Telegraph Club, Inc., 415 S. Rife St., Dillon, MT 59725. TEL 406-683-2798. FAX 406-683-2332. E-mail: dotndash@bmt.net. Ed. John M. IBarrows. bk.rev.; circ. 2,500 (controlled). (back issues avail.) **Document type:** newsletter.

621.38   UK
EDINBURGH P I C T RESEARCH REPORT SERIES. (Programme on Information & Communication Technologies) irreg., no.3. £20 (academics £5). University of Edinburgh, Research Centre for Social Sciences, Old Surgeons' Hall, High School Yards, Edinburgh EH1 1LZ, Scotland. **Document type:** monographic series.

621.38   UK   ISSN 0959-938X
EDINBURGH P I C T STUDENT PAPER SERIES. (Programme on Information & Communication Technologies) irreg., no.6, 1994. £5. University of Edinburgh, Research Centre for Social Sciences, Old Surgeons' Hall, High School Yards, Edinburgh EH1 1LZ, Scotland. **Document type:** monographic series.

EL & ENERGI. see ENGINEERING — Electrical Engineering

ELECTRONICS LETTERS. see ELECTRONICS

621.38   SW   ISSN 0014-0171
   CODEN: ERREAO
ERICSSON REVIEW. (Text in English) 1924. 4/yr. SEK 180($30) Telefonaktiebolaget L M Ericsson, 126 25 Stockholm, Sweden. TEL 46-8-7190000. FAX 46-8-6812710. Ed. P.O. Thyselius. charts; illus.; index. circ. 15,000. Indexed: Appl.Mech.Rev., CAD CAM Abstr., Comput.Cont., Curr.Cont., Eng.Ind., Ind.Sci.Rev., INSPEC, Met.Abstr., Sci.Cit.Ind., Tel.Abstr., World Alum.Abstr. **Document type:** trade publication.
   —BLDSC (3809.000000); AskIEEE; CISTI; Ei; KR SourceOne; Linda Hall; SWETS.
   Formerly (until 1933): L M Ericsson Review.

COMMUNICATIONS — TELEPHONE AND TELEGRAPH

384.5   UK   ISSN 0955-4041
EUROPEAN COMMUNICATIONS. a. £28. Harrington Kilbridge plc, The Publishing House, Highbury Station Rd., Islington, London N1 1SE, England. TEL 44-171-226-2222. FAX 44-171-226-1255. TELEX 263174 HKP G. Ed. Lynd Morley. circ. 15,048 (controlled). (back issues avail.) **Document type:** trade publication.
—BLDSC (3829.625000).
   Description: Serves officials of national governments and the European Commission, as well as senior management of major telecommunications firms.

621.38   UK
EUROPEAN MOBILE COMMUNICATIONS. 10/yr. £990($1900) (effective 1997). E M C Publications, Holt Cottage, Kingston Hill, Kingston-upon-Thames, Surrey KT2 7JH, England. TEL 44-181-546-0841. FAX 44-181-549-8558. TELEX 24667 IMPEMP G. Ed. Nigel Cawthorne. **Document type:** newsletter.

EUROPEAN TRANSACTIONS ON TELECOMMUNICATIONS. see COMMUNICATIONS

621.385   US
F C C TELEPHONE EQUIPMENT REGISTRATION LIST. q. $25 per no. in U.S., Canada, Mexico; elsewhere $40. (Federal Communications Commission) U.S. National Technical Information Service, 5825 Port Royal Rd., Springfield, VA 22161. TEL 703-487-4630. (microfiche)
   Description: Sequential file of all applications for approval to the telephone network. Listed in order of equipment type.

FACSIMILE FACTS AND FIGURES. see BUSINESS AND ECONOMICS — Abstracting, Bibliographies, Statistics

621.385   US
FAULKNER'S TELECOMMUNICATIONS WORLD. 1983. 3 base vols. (plus m. updates). $1260 (effective 1993). Faulkner Information Services, Inc., 114 Cooper Center, 7905 Browning Rd., Pennsauken, NJ 08109-4319. TEL 609-662-2070. FAX 609-662-3380. Ed. Tory Jenson. (looseleaf format)
●Also available on CD-ROM.
   Supersedes (in 1991): Telephone Cost and Call Management (ISSN 0736-8089); Telephone Equipment Selection Guide (ISSN 0737-4884)
   Description: Covers all aspects of telecommunications, networking, interconnection, and global communications. Includes product reports, management articles and coverage of new and evolving technologies.

FAXREPORTER. see BUSINESS AND ECONOMICS — Computer Applications

384.6   US   ISSN 1057-5375
FIBER OPTICS BUSINESS; bi-weekly newsletter covering fiber optics applications in military and government. 1986. bi-w. $595 (foreign $645) (effective 1997). Information Gatekeepers, Inc., 214 Harvard Ave., Boston, MA 02134. TEL 617-232-3111; 800-323-1088. FAX 617-734-8562. E-mail: igiboston@aol.com; URL: http://www.igigroup.com. Ed. Paul Polishuk. (back issues avail.) **Document type:** newsletter.
   Former titles: M F O C Newsletter; Military Fibercom.
   Description: Covers business developments in fiber optics, procurements, contract awards, price trends, markets, business developments, and conferences.

500 600   US   ISSN 0890-653X
TA1800
FIBEROPTIC PRODUCT NEWS. 1986. m. (13/yr.). $115 (Canada $123.05; Mexico $115; elsewhere $139) (effective 1996). Gordon Publications, Part of Cahners Publishing Company, Division of Reed Elsevier Inc., 301 Gibraltar Dr., Box 650, Morris Plains, NJ 07950-0650. TEL 973-292-5100 ext.317. FAX 973-292-0783. URL: http://www.fpnmag.com. Ed. Debra Norman; Pub. Terry McCoy. adv. circ. 35,000. (tabloid format; back issues avail.) **Document type:** newsletter, trade publication.
—KR SourceOne. **CCC.**
   Description: Reaches managers and supervisors of operations - manufacturing, engineering - technical, quality assurance, design, corporate and research and development in the fields of data and telecommunications equipment manufacturing, telecom services and end-users, test and measurement equipment, and suppliers of fiber, cable and fiberoptic components and system construction.

FILM UND FERNSEHEN; Zeitschrift fuer Theorie und Praxis des Film- und Fernsehschaffens. see MOTION PICTURES

FRANCE TELECOM; revue francaise des telecommunications. see COMMUNICATIONS

384.3   US   ISSN 1072-3080
VK562
GLOBAL POSITIONING & NAVIGATION NEWS. 1991. bi-w. $597 (foreign $630) (effective 1997). Phillips Business Information, Inc., 1201 Seven Locks Rd., Potomac, MD 20854. TEL 301-424-3338. FAX 301-309-3847. E-mail: pbi@phillips.com. Ed. Dave Brossehy. (looseleaf format) **Indexed:** Curr.Cont. **Document type:** newsletter.
●Also available online. Vendor(s): Information Access Co., NewsNet (DE24).
—CCC.
   Incorporates (in 1994): Marine Technology News (ISSN 1071-1333); **Formerly:** G P S Report (ISSN 1056-7127); Incorporates (in 1992): Geographic Information, Mapping, and Positioning Newsletter (ISSN 1045-6732)

384.6   US
GUIDE TO NETWORKING SERVICES. base vol. (plus m. supplement). $2195. United Communications Group, 1300 Rockville Pike, Ste. 1100, Rockville, MD 20852-3030. TEL 301-816-8950.
FAX 301-816-8945. Ed. David Rhodes.
   Description: Gives summaries of the most popular telecommunications services of the major telcos and carriers.

384.6   US
GUIDELINES. 1984. q. free to qualified personnel. Corning Inc., Opto-Electronics Group, M.P.-R.O.-02, Corning, NY 14831. TEL 607-974-7895.
FAX 607-974-7522. E-mail: fiber@corning.com. Ed. Paul Guggina. abstr.; bibl.; stat. circ. 20,000. **Document type:** trade publication.
   Description: Contains information on optical fiber for customers, end users, and others interested in the opto-electronics industry.

HEALTHCARE INFORMATION MANAGEMENT. see HOSPITALS

I D C CHINA REPORT. see COMPUTERS — Computer Industry

384   UK   ISSN 0964-6485
I P T C SPECTRUM. 1965. s-a. free to members and qualified personnel. International Press Telecommunications Council - Comite International des Telecommunications de Presse, 10 Sheet St., Windsor, Berks. SL4 1BG, England.
TEL 44-1753-833728. FAX 44-1753-833750.
E-mail: 100321.2156@compuserve.com; URL: www.iptc.org/iptc. Ed. H. Johnstone; Pub. David M. Allen. adv. contact: David M. Allen. circ. 250.
Indexed: Print.Abstr. **Document type:** newsletter.
   Former titles: I P T C News & I P T C Newsletter (ISSN 0579-6903)
   Description: Reviews I.P.T.C. activities.

I S A UPDATE. (Interactive Services Association) see COMMUNICATIONS — Computer Applications

384.6   GW   ISSN 0931-0827
I S D N REPORT. (Integrated Services Digital Network) 1987. m. DM.300. Neue Mediengesellschaft Ulm mbH, Konrad-Celtis-Str. 77, 81369 Munich, Germany. TEL 49-89-74117190.
FAX 49-89-74117195. Ed.Bd. circ. 3,050.
Document type: trade publication.
—SWETS.

I S D N USER NEWSLETTER. (Integrated Services Digital Network) see COMMUNICATIONS — Computer Applications

384   US
IMPACT (ROCKVILLE); analysis of communication common carrier rate changes and competitive offerings. At head of title: C C M I Reports. m. $325. United Communications Group, 11300 Rockville Pike, Ste. 1100, Rockville, MD 20852-3030. TEL 301-816-8950.

384.1   UN
INDICATORS FOR THE TELEGRAM RETRANSMISSION SYSTEM (TRS) - TELEX IDENTIFICATION CODES. (Supplements avail.) (Text in English, French and Spanish) 1966. triennial. 84 SFr. International Telecommunication Union, Place des Nations, CH-1211 Geneva 20, Switzerland.
TEL 41-22-7306141. FAX 41-22-7305194. TELEX 421 000 UIT CH. E-mail: sales@itu.ch; URL: http://www.itu.ch.
   Formerly: List of Destination Indicators and Telex Identification Codes (ISSN 0074-901X)

384.5   US
INDUSTRY BEAT. w. (50/yr.). $50 to non-members. Telecommunications Industry Association, 2500 Wilson Blvd., Ste. 300, Arlington, VA 22201-3836. TEL 703-907-7700. FAX 703-907-7727. (Co-sponsor: Electronic Industries Association) (only avail. by fax) **Document type:** bulletin.
   Description: Summarizes the week's industry and association news. Alerts telecommunications industry professionals to meetings and important notices.

621.38   US
INDUSTRY PULSE. 1979. 10/yr. $65 to non-members. Telecommunications Industry Association, 2500 Wilson Blvd., Ste. 300, Arlington, VA 22201-3836. TEL 703-907-7700. FAX 703-907-7727. E-mail: tia@tia.eia.org. (Co-sponsor: Electronic Industries Association) Ed. Sharon Grace. charts; illus.; stat.; tr.lit. circ. 4,500. (tabloid format) **Document type:** bulletin, newsletter.
   Description: Evaluates public policy, regulatory issues and trends affecting the telecommunications industry.

INFORMATION TECHNOLOGY & MANAGEMENT. see BUSINESS AND ECONOMICS — Office Equipment And Services

INFORMATION TECHNOLOGY MANAGEMENT; non-technical report on IT and its applications. see BUSINESS AND ECONOMICS — Office Equipment And Services

INSTITUTION OF ENGINEERS (INDIA). ELECTRONICS AN TELECOMMUNICATION ENGINEERING DIVISION. JOURNAL. see ELECTRONICS

INTERACTIVE HOME; consumer technology monthly. se TECHNOLOGY: COMPREHENSIVE WORKS

384.5 338.5   US   ISSN 1069-7136
INTERNATIONAL CELLULAR. 1991. m. $695 (effective 1997). Kagan World Media, Ltd., 126 Clock Tower Pl., Carmel, CA 93923. TEL 408-624-1536.
FAX 408-625-3225. E-mail: info@kagan.com. Ed. Sharon Armbrust. adv. contact: Lorraine Yglesias. stat. **Document type:** trade publication.
   Formerly: European Cellular (ISSN 1056-2281)
   Description: Compiles statistics on the economics technologies, marketing, companies, and countries involved in the cellular industry around the world.

COMMUNICATIONS — TELEPHONE AND TELEGRAPH

384.6 US ISSN 1047-8744
HE7621
INTERNATIONAL TELECOM DIRECTORY. a. $85 (foreign $90). Capitol Publications Inc., Telecom Publishing Group, 1101 King St., Ste. 444, Box 1455, VA 22313-2055. TEL 800-327-7205. FAX 703-739-6490. URL: http://www.telecommunications.com. Pub. Chris Vestal. adv. contact: Stuart Lilly. **Document type:** directory.
 Description: Lists titles of key officials, addresses, phone numbers, telex and telegraph numbers for telecom agencies in over 200 countries. Includes PTTs, satellite operating agencies, frequency allocation offices and standard organizations.

384.1 UN ISSN 0074-9044
INTERNATIONAL TELECOMMUNICATION UNION. LIST OF TELEGRAPH OFFICES OPEN FOR INTERNATIONAL SERVICE. (Preface in English, French and Spanish) 1869. quinquennial. 61 SFr. International Telecommunication Union, Place des Nations, CH-1211 Geneva 20, Switzerland. TEL 41-22-7306141. FAX 41-22-7305194. TELEX 421 000 UIT CH. E-mail: sales@itu.ch; URL: http://www.itu.ch.

384.1 UN ISSN 0047-1224
INTERNATIONAL TELECOMMUNICATION UNION. OPERATIONAL BULLETIN. (Editions in English, French, Spanish) 1966. fortn. 385 SFr. International Telecommunication Union, Place des Nations, CH-1211 Geneva 20, Switzerland. TEL 41-22-7306141. FAX 41-22-7305194. TELEX 421 000 UIT CH. E-mail: sales@itu.ch; URL: http://www.itu.ch. **Document type:** bulletin.
 ●Also available online.

384.1 UN ISSN 0085-2201
INTERNATIONAL TELECOMMUNICATION UNION. REPORT ON THE ACTIVITIES. Spanish edition: Union Internacional de Telecomunicaciones. Informe sobre las Actividades (ISSN 0252-1687); French edition: Union Internationale des Telecommunications. Rapport sur l'Activite. (ISSN 0252-1679) (Editions in English, French, Spanish) 1948. a. 5 SFr. International Telecommunication Union, Place des Nations, CH-1211 Geneva 20, Switzerland. TEL 41-22-7306141. FAX 41-22-7305464. E-mail: sales@itu.int. **Document type:** corporate report.

384.1 384.6 UN
INTERNATIONAL TELEGRAPH AND TELEPHONE CONSULTATIVE COMMITTEE. PLANS. (Text in English, French, Spanish) 1971. irreg., latest 1991. price varies. International Telecommunication Union, International Telegraph and Telephone Consultative Committee - Union Internationale des Telecommunications, Place des Nations, CH-1211 Geneva 20, Switzerland. TEL 41-22-730-5111. FAX 41-22-730-5149. TELEX 421 000 UIT CH. Ed.Bd.

384.1 384.6 UN
INTERNATIONAL TELEGRAPH AND TELEPHONE CONSULTATIVE COMMITTEE. PLENARY ASSEMBLY. PROCEEDINGS. (Supplement avail.) (Editions in Arabic, Chinese, English, French, Russian, Spanish) 1980. quadrennial. price varies. International Telecommunication Union, International Telegraph and Telephone Consultative Committee - Union Internationale des Telecommunications, Place des Nations, CH-1211 Geneva 20, Switzerland. TEL 41-22-730-5111. FAX 41-22-730-5149. TELEX 421 000 UIT CH. Ed.Bd. **Document type:** proceedings.

384 AT ISSN 0310-8031
INTERNATIONAL TELEX DIRECTORY. INTERNATIONAL SERVICE. 1972. a. Playfair Publishing Group, P.O. Box 52, Northbridge, N.S.W. 2063, Australia.

384.5 004.6 UK
INTERNET OPERATOR EUROPE. 1996. m. TechMedia, 52 Foundling Ct., London WC1N 1AN, England. TEL 44-171-837-0815. FAX 44-171-278-9917. E-mail: 100141.676@compuserve.com. Ed. Peggy Salz Trautman; Pub. Philip Gallagher. **Document type:** newsletter.
 ●Also available online.
 Formerly: Internet Business Europe (ISSN 1363-0180)
 Description: Covers European developments in Internet services and technologies.

384.55 GW
J & W BANKING INTERNATIONAL. INTERNATIONAL BANKING AND FINANCE COMMUNICATIONS DIRECTORY. 1993. a. $150. Telex - Verlag Jaeger & Waldmann GmbH, Birkenweg 8-10, 64295 Darmstadt, Germany. TEL 49-6151-3302-0. FAX 49-6151-3302-50. TELEX 419389-JWLX-D. E-mail: jwemail@aol.com. (Dist. by: Universal Media Div., Shamgar, Inc., 212 Broadway, Box 45, Bethpage, NY 11714) Ed. W. Lucius; Pub. W. Lich. **Document type:** directory.
 ●Also available on CD-ROM.

384.55 GW
▼**J & W BUSINESS INTERNATIONAL. INTERNATIONAL BUSINESS COMMUNICATIONS.** 1995. a. $210. Telex - Verlag Jaeger & Waldmann GmbH, Birkenweg 8-10, 64295 Darmstadt, Germany. TEL 49-6151-3302-0. FAX 49-6151-3302-50. TELEX 419389-JWLX-D. E-mail: jwemail@aol.com. (Dist. by: Universal Media Div., Shamgar Inc., 212 Broadway, Box 45, Bethpage, NY 11714) Ed. W. Lucius; Pub. W. Lich. **Document type:** directory.

384.55 GW
J & W TELEFAX INTERNATIONAL. INTERNATIONAL FAX DIRECTORY. 1985. a. $395. Telex - Verlag Jaeger & Waldmann GmbH, Birkenweg 8-10, 64295 Darmstadt, Germany. TEL 49-6151-3302-0. FAX 49-6151-3302-50. TELEX 419389-JWTLX-D. E-mail: jwemail@aol.com. (Dist. by: Universal Media Div., Shamgar Inc., 212 Broadway, Box 45, Bethpage, NY 11714) Ed. W. Lucius; Pub. W. Lich. **Document type:** directory.
 ●Also available on CD-ROM.
 Former titles: J & W Telefax International. International Facsimile Directory; Telefax International. International Telefax Directory; Jaeger and Waldmann International Telefax Directory (ISSN 0179-597X)

384.55 GW ISSN 0172-4134
J & W TELEX INTERNATIONAL. INTERNATIONAL TELEX AND TELETEX DIRECTORY. 1952. a. $275. Telex - Verlag Jaeger & Waldmann GmbH, Birkenweg 8-10, 64295 Darmstadt, Germany. TEL 49-6151-3302-0. FAX 49-6151-3302-50. TELEX 419389-JWTLX-D. E-mail: jwemail@aol.com. (Dist. by: Universal Media Div., Shamgar, Inc., 212 Broadway, Box 45, Bethpage, NY 11714) Ed. W. Lucius; Pub. W. Lich. **Document type:** directory.
 ●Also available on CD-ROM.
 Former titles: Telex and Teletex International. International Telex and Teletex Directory; Jaeger and Waldmann International Telex and Teletex Directory; Jaeger and Waldmann International Telex and Teletex Directory; Jaeger and Waldmann World Telex Directory (ISSN 0172-4142)

384.1 GW ISSN 0941-6889
J & W TRAVEL INTERNATIONAL; world guide of hotels, travel agents and tour operators. 1958. a. $135. Telex - Verlag Jaeger & Waldmann GmbH, Birkenweg 8-10, 64295 Darmstadt, Germany. TEL 49-6151-3302-0. FAX 49-6151-3302-50. TELEX 419389-JWTLX-D. E-mail: jwemail@aol.com. (Dist. by: Universal Media Div., Shamgar, Inc., 212 Broadway, Box 45, Bethpage, NY 11714) Ed. W. Lucius; Pub. W. Lich. **Document type:** directory.
 ●Also available on CD-ROM.
 Formerly (until 1989): Telex und Travel International (ISSN 0931-3192)

621.38 SZ
JOURNAL DES FONCTIONNAIRES DES P T T. w. Friedeggstr. 4, CH-3400 Burgdorf, Switzerland. TEL 034-225881. circ. 5,895.

621.38 JA ISSN 0917-2335
K D D TEKUNIKARU JANARU/K D D TECHNICAL JOURNAL. (Text in Japanese) 1990. q. 530 Yen per no. Kokusai Denshin Denwa K.K., Nettowaku Kaihatsu Honbu, 3-2, Nishishinjuku 2-chome, Shinjuku-ku, Tokyo 163-03, Japan. TEL 81-3-3347-7703. FAX 81-3-3347-6362. adv. circ. 5,500.
 —BLDSC (5088.301000); AskIEEE; KR SourceOne.

KEMPS FILM, T V AND VIDEO YEARBOOK. see MOTION PICTURES

384.6 UK
▼**KEY NOTE MARKET REPORT: MOBILE PHONES.** 1995. irreg. £205. Key Note Ltd., Field House, 72 Oldfield Rd., Hampton, Middlesex TW12 2HQ, England. TEL 44-181-783-0755. FAX 44-181-783-0049. Ed. Richard Caines. **Document type:** bulletin.

621.38 JA ISSN 0452-3431
KOKUSAI TSUSHIN NO KENKYU/K D D R & D. (Text in Japanese; summaries in English) 1953. s-a. 1240 Yen per no. Kokusai Denshin Denwa K.K., 3-2, Nishishinjuku 2-chome, Shinjuku-ku, Tokyo 163, Japan. TEL 03-3347-7111. FAX 03-3347-7000. Indexed: INSPEC (1992-).
 —BLDSC (5088.298000); AskIEEE; CISTI; KR SourceOne; Linda Hall.
 Description: Information on international telephone and telegraph communications as it relates to the company.

384 SW ISSN 0345-6471
KONTAKTEN. 1939. 20/yr. free. L.M. Ericsson AB, HF-LME-, 12625 Stockholm, Sweden. FAX 46-8-681-27-10. Ed. Lars-Goeran Hedin. adv. contact: Pia Rehnberg. illus. circ. 47,000. **Document type:** newsletter.
 Description: Internal magazine of the Ericsson Corporation.

621.38 US ISSN 1070-6593
LAND MOBILE RADIO NEWS. 1983. w. $597 (foreign $660) (effective 1997). Phillips Business Information, Inc., 1201 Seven Locks Rd., Potomac, MD 20854. TEL 301-424-3338. FAX 301-424-4297. E-mail: pbi@phillips.com. Ed. Mary McCormick. (back issues avail.) **Document type:** newsletter.
 ●Also available online. Vendor(s): Information Access Co., Knight-Ridder Information, Inc., NewsNet (TE13).
 —CCC.
 Formerly: Industrial Communications (ISSN 0737-0415)

384.1 UN ISSN 0074-9001
LIST OF CABLES FORMING THE WORLD SUBMARINE NETWORK. (Text in English, French and Spanish) 1877. irreg., 19th ed., 1977. 21 SFr. International Telecommunication Union, Place des Nations, CH-1211 Geneva 20, Switzerland. TEL 41-22-7306141. FAX 41-22-7305149. TELEX 421 000 UIT CH. E-mail: sales@itu.ch; URL: http://www.itu.ch.

384.1 UN ISSN 0074-9028
LIST OF INTERNATIONAL TELEPHONE ROUTES. (Text in English, French and Spanish) 1961. a. 44 SFr. International Telecommunication Union, Place des Nations, CH-1211 Geneva 20, Switzerland. TEL 41-22-7306141. FAX 41-22-7305194. TELEX 421 000 UIT CH. E-mail: sales@itu.ch; URL: http://www.itu.ch. **Document type:** bulletin.

384.6 US ISSN 1087-8998
LOCAL COMPETITION REPORT. 1992. bi-w. (26/yr.). $489 (foreign $515) (effective 1998). Capitol Publications Inc., Telecom Publishing Group, 1101 King St., Ste. 444, Box 1455, Alexandria, VA 22313-2055. TEL 800-327-7205. FAX 703-739-6484. URL: http://www.telecommunications.com. Ed. Kim Sunderland; Pub. Chris Vestal. R&P contact: Libby Lawbaugh. TEL 703-739-6542. adv. contact: Will Benton. **Document type:** newsletter.
 ●Also available online. Vendor(s): Information Access Co., NewsNet.
 Description: Reports regulation, technology, and competitive strategies in the local telephone exchange market. Features interviews with top decision makers. Covers CLACs, utilities competition, competitive telecom strategies, cable TV and wireless participation, and new technologies.

384.5 UK
M. 1991. m. £249. M2 Communications Ltd., P.O. Box 475, Coventry CV1 2ZW, England. TEL 44-1203-634700. FAX 44-1203-634144. E-mail: info@m2.com; URL: http://www.m2.com. Ed. Darren Ingram. bk.rev. (back issues avail.) **Document type:** trade publication.
 ●Also available online.
 Formed by the merger of: Satnews & Satnewswire

384.6 380.3 US
M I C - TECH-TELECOMMUNICATIONS. 1989. m. $920. Management Information Corporation, 1111 Marlkress Rd., Box 5062, Cherry Hill, NJ 08003-5602. TEL 609-424-1100. FAX 609-424-1999. Ed. Don Stuart. (diskette format)
 Description: Electronic telecommunication product reference. Provides specifications, features, strengths and weaknesses of PBX's, key sets, ACD's, call accounting and voice mail.

COMMUNICATIONS — TELEPHONE AND TELEGRAPH

384.6 CN ISSN 0849-6501
M T S ECHO. 1921. fortn. free. Manitoba Telephone System, 489 Empress St., Winnipeg, MB R3C 3V6, Canada. TEL 204-941-8256. FAX 204-775-0718. Ed. Mike Daly. circ. 6,000 (controlled). **Document type:** trade publication.
   Formerly (until 1990): Telephone Echo (ISSN 0381-4556)

384.6 380.3 US
MANAGING VOICE NETWORKS. 1985. m. $926 to new subscr.; renewals $843 (effective 1996). Datapro Information Services Group (Subsidiary of McGraw-Hill, Inc.), 600 Delran Pkwy., Delran, NJ 08075. TEL 609-764-0100; 800-328-2776. FAX 609-764-2814. circ. 2,000. (looseleaf format; back issues avail.) **Indexed:** Tel.Alert.
   Formerly: Datapro Management of Telecommunications.

MARCONI'S INTERNATIONAL REGISTER; linking buyers and sellers worldwide through fax and business listings. see *BUSINESS AND ECONOMICS — Trade And Industrial Directories*

384.6 CN
MARITIME TEL & TEL. BULLETIN. 1907. m. free to qualified personnel. Maritime Tel & Tel, P.O. Box 880, Station Central RPO, Halifax, NS B3J 2W3, Canada. TEL 902-421-4959. FAX 902-425-1274. Ed. Pearleen Mofford. circ. 5,200. **Document type:** newsletter.
   Formerly: Maritime Telegraph and Telephone. Bulletin.
   Description: News about the telephone industry in Nova Scotia.

384 MF
MAURITIUS. TELECOMMUNICATIONS DEPARTMENT. ANNUAL REPORT. (Text in English) a. Government Printing Office, Elizabeth II Ave., Port Louis, Mauritius.

MESSAGE (BRONX). see *LABOR UNIONS*

384 FR ISSN 1142-8538
HE6005
MESSAGES DES POSTES, DES TELECOMMUNICATIONS ET DE L'ESPACE. (Supplement avail.) (Text in French; summaries in English and Spanish) m. free. Ministere de l'Industrie, Postes, Telecommunications et Commerce Exterieur, Information et Communication, 20 av. de Segur, 75353 Paris Cedex 07, France. Ed. Annie Duperray. adv.; bk.rev.; charts; illus. circ. 380,000.
   Former titles (until 1988): Messages de la Poste, des Telecommunications et des Techniques de Communication (ISSN 1142-8511); (until 1976): Messages des Postes et Telecommunications (ISSN 0224-0807); (until 1976): Postes et Telecommunications (ISSN 0245-6028)

384 UK ISSN 0269-9567
MIDDLE EAST COMMUNICATIONS. (Text in English; summaries in Arabic) m. £60(£110) Icom Publications Ltd., Chancery House, St. Nicholas Way, Sutton, Surrey SM1 1JB, England. TEL 44-181-642-1117. FAX 44-181-642-1941. E-mail: mec@icompub.demon.co.uk. Ed. K. Anderson; Pub. Alec Barton. adv.: B&W page $3350, color page $4880; trim 210 x 297; adv. contact: A. Wand. circ. 10,200.
   Description: Covers voice and data communications, broadcasting, information technology and networking.

MINITEL NEWS INTERNATIONAL. see *COMPUTERS — Data Communications And Data Transmission Systems*

384.5 GW
MOBILCOM. m. DM.360 (effective 1997). Franzis Verlag GmbH, Dornacherstr. 3, 85622 Feldkirchen, Germany. TEL 49-89-99115-0. FAX 49-89-99115199. **Document type:** trade publication.

621.38 UK ISSN 1351-6515
MOBILE AND CELLULAR MAGAZINE. 1989. m. £38 (Europe £52; elsewhere £75). Nexus Business Comms, Warwick House, Swanley, Kent BR8 8HY, England. TEL 01322-660070. FAX 01322-667633. Ed. Paul O'Rourke; Pub. Christina Wood. adv. contact: Jon Rawling. bk.rev. circ. 8,809. **Indexed:** INSPEC (1991-). **Document type:** trade publication.

621.38 UK ISSN 1355-0039
MOBILE ASIA PACIFIC. 1993. 6/yr. £45. Nexus Media Ltd., Nexus House, Azalea Dr., Swanley, Kent BR8 8HY, England. TEL 44-1322-660070. FAX 44-1322-661257. E-mail: mobile.aap@nexusmedia.co.uk. Ed. Mike McLeod. adv. contact: Jon Rawling. **Document type:** trade publication.

621.38 UK ISSN 0957-4980
MOBILE BUSINESS. m. 134 Petherton Rd., Highbury, London N5 2RT, England. TEL 071-359-0493. FAX 071-354-2702. Ed. Ian White.

621.38 UK ISSN 1350-7362
MOBILE EUROPE. m. £60 in Europe; rest of world £75. Nexus Media Ltd., Warwick House, Azalea Dr., Swanley, Kent BR8 8HY, England. TEL 44-1322-660070. FAX 44-1322-661257. E-mail: mobile.europe@nexusmedia.co.uk. Ed. Peter Sayer. adv. contact: Jon Rawling. circ. 15,000. **Document type:** trade publication.
   Description: Provides information for those involved in the European mobile communications industry.

621.38 UK
▼**MOBILE MIDDLE EAST & AFRICA.** 1995. 4/yr. £45. Nexus Media Ltd., Nexus House, Azalea Dr., Swanley, Kent BR8 8HY, England. TEL 44-1322-660070. FAX 44-1322-661257. E-mail: mobile.mea@nexusmedia.co.uk. Ed. Mike McLeod. adv. contact: Jon Rawling. **Document type:** trade publication.

621.385 US ISSN 0737-5077
MOBILE PHONE NEWS. 1983. w. $697 (foreign $760) (effective 1997). Phillips Business Information, Inc., 1201 Seven Locks Rd., Potomac, MD 20854. TEL 301-424-3338. FAX 301-309-3847. E-mail: pbi@phillips.com. Ed. Mary McCormick. **Document type:** newsletter.
   ●Also available online. Vendor(s): Information Access Co., NewsNet (TE25).
   —CCC.
   Incorporates (1991-1997): Wireless Business and Finance (ISSN 1077-2235)

384.6 US ISSN 1073-1067
MOBILE PRODUCT ASIA. 1993. m. free to qualified personnel. Phillips Business Information, Inc., 1201 Seven Locks Rd., Potomac, MD 20854. TEL 301-340-1520. FAX 301-424-4297. E-mail: pbi@phillips.com. adv.; illus.; circ. controlled. **Document type:** trade publication.

384.6 US ISSN 1065-9188
MOBILE PRODUCT EUROPE. 1991. m. free to qualified personnel. Phillips Business Information, Inc., 1201 Seven Locks Rd., Potomac, MD 20854. TEL 301-340-1520. FAX 301-424-4297. E-mail: pbi@phillips.com. adv.; illus.; circ. controlled. **Document type:** trade publication.
   Formerly (until 1992): Mobile Products International (ISSN 1055-5285)

384 621.3 US ISSN 1046-5286
MOBILE SATELLITE NEWS (POTOMAC). 1989. bi-w. $597 (foreign $630) (effective 1997). Phillips Business Information, Inc., 1201 Seven Locks Rd., Potomac, MD 20854. TEL 301-424-3338. FAX 301-309-3847. E-mail: pbi@phillips.com. Ed. Dave Bross. **Document type:** newsletter.
   ●Also available online. Vendor(s): Information Access Co., NewsNet (TE27).
   —CCC.

621.385 AT ISSN 1036-014X
MOBILES. 1990. m. Aus.$425 (foreign Aus.$475). Teleresources Pty. Ltd., P.O. Box 693, Brookvale, N.S.W. 2100, Australia. TEL 61-2-99752230. FAX 61-2-99752240. E-mail: teleres@teleres.com.au. Ed. Maurie Dobbin. charts; stat. (back issues avail.) **Document type:** newsletter.
   Description: Analyses and reports on the Asia-Pacific mobile communication sector. Outlines details of new technologies, products and services and examines their impact on the region.

384 UK
MORSUM MAGNIFICAT. bi-m. £12 (Europe £12.75; rest of world £15.50) (effective 1996). G.C. Arnold Partners, 9 Wetherby Close, Broadstone, Dorset BH18 8JB, England. TEL 44-1202-658474. FAX 44-1202-658474. (Subscr. in N. America to: Wise Owl World, 4314 W. 238th St., Torrance, CA 90505-4509, USA) **Document type:** newsletter.
   Description: Devoted to Morse past, present and future.

MULTIMEDIA TELECOMMUNICATIONS SOURCEBOOK. see *BUSINESS AND ECONOMICS — Trade And Industrial Directories*

621.38 JA ISSN 0415-3200
TK5101.A1 CODEN: DTKKAA
MUSASHINO ELECTRICAL COMMUNICATION LABORATORIES TECHNICAL JOURNAL/KENKYU JITSUYOKA HOKOKU.* (Text in Japanese; summaries in English and Japanese) 1952. m. 12000 Yen. Musashino Kyodashi Kankokai, Musashino NTT, 3-9-11 Midor-cho, Musashino-shi, Tokyo, Japan. Ed. Iwao Shimizu. abstr.; bibl.; charts; illus.; pat.; index. circ. 4,500. **Indexed:** Chem.Abstr., INSPEC.
   —CASDDS; CISTI; Linda Hall.

621.38 JA ISSN 0029-067X
TK5101.A1 CODEN: RELTAN
MUSASHINO ELECTRICAL COMMUNICATION LABORATORY. REVIEW OF THE ELECTRICAL COMMUNICATION LABORATORY.* (Text in English) 1955. bi-m. 9000 Yen. Musashino Kyodashi Kankokai, Musashino NTT, 3-9-11 Midori-cho, Musashino-shi, Tokyo, Japan. (Subscr. to: Aoyama-Daiichi Publishing Co., Ltd., 3-12 Shirokane 3-chome, Minato-ku, Tokyo 108, Japan) Ed. Iwao Shimizu. abstr.; bibl.; charts; illus.; index. circ. 1,350. **Indexed:** Chem.Abstr., JCT, Met.Abstr.
   —CASDDS; CISTI; Linda Hall.

384.5 US
N T C A EXCHANGE. 1982. bi-m. $10 (effective 1992). National Telephone Cooperative Association, 2626 Pennsylvania Ave., N.W., Washington, DC 20037. TEL 202-298-2300. FAX 202-298-2320. Ed. Matthew W. Green, Jr. circ. 4,200. **Document type:** newsletter.

621.38 JA ISSN 0915-2318
TK5101.A1
N T T GIJUTSU JANARU/N T T TECHNICAL JOURNAL. (Text in Japanese) 1989. m. 720 Yen per no. (Nippon Denshin Denwa K.K., Kenkyu Kaihatsu Gijutsu Honbu, Gijutsu Joho Senta - Nippon Telegraph and Telephone Corp., Research and Development Headquarters, R & D Information, Patent and Licensing Center) Denki Tsushin Kyokai - Telecommunications Association, 12-1, Yuraku-cho 1-chome, Chiyoda-ku, Tokyo 100, Japan. **Document type:** trade publication.

621.38 JA
N T T KENKYUJO KONO ICHINEN/N T T TELECOMMUNICATIONS LABORATORIES. ANNUAL REPORT. (Text in Japanese) 1967. a. Nippon Denshin Denwa K.K., Kenkyu Kaihatsu Suishinbu - Nippon Telegraph and Telephone Corp., Research and Development Management Department, 19-2, 3-chome, Nishi-Shinjuku, Shinjuku-ku, Tokyo 163-19, Japan. TEL 81-3-5359-4200. FAX 81-3-5359-1185. E-mail: rd-annual@ecl-inet.ecl.ntt.co.jp; URL: http://www.nttinfo.ntt.co.jp/dlij/RD__J/. Ed. Toshimitsu Moroki. **Document type:** bulletin.

621.38 JA ISSN 0915-2326
TK5101.A1 CODEN: NTTDEC
N T T R & D. (Text in Japanese; summaries in English, Japanese) 1952. m. 1290 Yen per no. (Nippon Denshin Denwa K.K., Kenkyu Kaihatsu Gijutsu Honbu, Gijutsu Joho Senta - Nippon Telegraph and Telephone Corp., Research and Development Headquarters, R & D Information, Patent and Licensing Center) Denki Tsushin Kyokai - Telecommunications Association, 12-1, Yurakucho 1-chome, Chiyoda-ku, Tokyo 100, Japan. **Indexed:** INSPEC (1989-).
   —BLDSC (6180.610070); AskIEEE; CASDDS; CIS Ei; KR SourceOne.

COMMUNICATIONS — TELEPHONE AND TELEGRAPH

621.38   JA
N T T RESEARCH AND DEVELOPMENT. (Text in English) 1984. a. Nippon Telegraph and Telephone Corporation, Research and Development Management Department - Nippon Denshin Denwa K.K., Kenkyu Kaihatsu Suishinbu, 19-2, 3-chome, Nishi-shinjuku, Shinjuku-ku, Tokyo 163-19, Japan. TEL 81-3-5359-4200. FAX 81-3-5359-1185. E-mail: moroki@yamato.ntt.jp; URL: http://www.nttinfo.ntt.co.jp/RD/. Ed. Toshimitsu Moroki.

384.6   US   ISSN 0895-089X
N T T TOPICS.* q. free. (Nippon Telegraph & Telephone Company) Ruder, Finn & Rotman, N T T Information Desk, 301 E. 57th St., New York, NY 10022.
●Also available online. Vendor(s): Information Access Co.

384.5   US
NATIONAL EXCHANGE BULLETIN. m. price varies. (Center for Communications Management Information) C C M I, 11300 Rockville Pike, Ste. 1100, Rockville, MD 20852-3030. TEL 301-816-8950; 800-929-4824. FAX 301-816-8945. E-mail: listverv@usa.net. Ed. Juliana Cole; Pub. George David. R&P contact: Michael Peck. **Document type:** bulletin.

621.38   UK   ISSN 1360-1369
NETWORK BRIEFING. 1986. w. £495. A P T Data Group plc., 12 Sutton Row, 4th Fl., London W1V 5FH, England. TEL 44-171-208-4200. FAX 44-171-439-1105. (US subscr. to: APT Data Service Inc., 828 Broadway, Ste. 800, New York, NY 10010. TEL 212-677-0409. FAX 212-677-0463) Ed. Matthew Woollacott. circ. 2,000 (paid). **Document type:** newsletter.
●Also available online. Vendor(s): Information Access Co.
Former titles (until 1995): Network Week (ISSN 0965-3031); (until 1991): Telegram (ISSN 0953-5284)

621.38   US   ISSN 0195-7627
NEW JERSEY BELL.* 1927-19??; resumed 1978. q. New Jersey Telephone Co., 540 Broad St., Newark, NJ 07012-3178. illus. circ. 40,000.

384.6   NG
NIGER. OFFICE DES POSTES ET TELECOMMUNICATIONS. ANNUAIRE OFFICIEL DES TELEPHONES. a. Office des Postes et Telecommunications, Niamey, Niger.

384.1   UN   ISSN 0252-1792
NOMENCLATURE DES VOIES DE TELECOMMUNICATION UTILISEES POUR LA TRANSMISSION DES TELEGRAMMES/LIST OF TELECOMMUNICATION CHANNELS USED FOR THE TRANSMISSION OF TELEGRAMS/NOMENCLATOR DE LAS VIAS DE TELECOMUNICACION EMPLEADAS PARA LA TRANSMISION DE TELEGRAMAS. (Text in English, French, Spanish) irreg., latest 7th ed., 1988. 50 SFr. International Telecommunication Union - Unione Internationale des Communications, Place des Nations, CH-1211 Geneva 20, Switzerland. TEL 41-22-730-5111. FAX 41-22-730-5149. TELEX 421 000 UIT CH. Ed.Bd.

384.6   US
NORTH AMERICAN TELECOM NEWSWATCH. 1995. 24/yr. $293. (Center for Communications Management Information) C C M I, 11300 Rockville Pike, Ste. 1100, Rockville, MD 20852-3030. TEL 301-816-8950; 800-929-4824. FAX 301-816-8945. E-mail: cust_svc@evcg.com.
—CCC.
Incorporates: Telecommunications Alert (ISSN 0742-5384)
Description: Provides complete coverage of regulatory, wireless, business, local service, and long distance news for the US, Canadian and Mexican telecommunications industry.

384.6   US   ISSN 1066-1425
Z699.22
P A C DIRECTORY. 1991. a. $70 (effective 1997). Information Today, Inc., 143 Old Marlton Pike, Medford, NJ 08055-8750. TEL 609-654-6266. FAX 609-654-4309. **Document type:** directory.
—BLDSC (6265.740000); CISTI.
Formerly: Dial In (ISSN 1047-3424)

384.6 338   US   ISSN 1043-6073
HE8801
O P A S T C O ROUNDTABLE; the magazine of ideas for small telephone companies. 1988. bi-m. $27. Organization for the Promotion and Advancement of Small Telecommunications Companies, 21 Dupont Circle., N.W., Ste. 700, Washington, DC 20036. TEL 202-659-5990. FAX 202-659-4619. E-mail: roundtable@opastco.org. Ed. Linda M. Buckley. R&P contact: Linda M. Buckley. adv.: B&W page $1750, color page $2580; trim 8 1/4 x 11; adv. contact: Sue Partyke. bk.rev.; charts; illus.; tr.lit.; index. circ. 3,200. (back issues avail.)
Description: Covers business issues, new technology, regulations, and opportunities; for owners and managers of independent telephone companies.

384.6   US
ON THE LINE (LAKE HAVASU CITY). 1985. bi-m. $25 (foreign $30). California Payphone Association, 2610 Crow Canyon Rd., Ste. 150, San Ramon, CA 94583. Ed. Erica Robinson; Pub. Mary Lougheed. R&P contact: Mary Lougheed. adv.: B&W page $1000; adv. contact: Erica Robinson. bk.rev. circ. 5,300. (back issues avail.) **Document type:** trade publication.
Description: Covers regulatory and legislative issues, new products, and privately owned pay telephones.

621.385   US   ISSN 0747-8763
OUTSIDE PLANT MAGAZINE. 1983. m. $32 (Canada $50; elsewhere $80) (effective 1997). Practical Communications, Inc., Box 183, Cary, IL 60013-0183. TEL 847-639-2200. FAX 847-639-9542. Ed. John Saxtan. R&P contact: John Saxtan. adv. contact: Jim Queenan. circ. 20,000. **Document type:** trade publication.
Description: Focuses on the nation's 1300 local and interexchange telephone companies. Serves the construction, maintenance, outside plant planning and engineering people employed by these telephone companies and related contractors.

621.38   US   ISSN 0092-8828
TK6195
P B X SYSTEMS GUIDE.* (Vol. 1: PBX Systems; Vol. 2: Key Telephone & Hybrid Systems) 1972. 2 base vols. (plus updates 4-6/yr.). $695 for set (foreign $795); $399 per vol. (foreign $449). Aries Group - M P S G, 18223A Flover Hill Way, Gaithersburg, MD 20879-5334. TEL 301-840-0800. FAX 301-840-0890. (looseleaf format)

384.5 621.3   US   ISSN 1061-6438
P C I A BULLETIN;* news and analysis for the personal communication industry. w. $550. Personal Communications Industry Association, 500 Montgomery St., Ste. 700, Alexandria, VA 22314-1560. Ed. David Williams. adv.; illus. circ. 1,400. (looseleaf format) **Document type:** trade publication.
—CCC.
Formerly (until 1988): Filing and Grants Bulletin.
Description: Covers mobile and personal communication systems (e.g., pagers, cellular telephones, personal communication services, mobile data communications, and mobile satellite systems) as a business rather than a science or technology for executives and managers.

384.5   US   ISSN 1075-7821
TK6570.M6
P C I A JOURNAL.* 1977. m. $80. Personal Communications Industry Association, 500 Montgomery St., Ste. 700, Alexandria, VA 22314-1560. Ed. Lindsay Smith. adv.; charts; illus.; tr.lit.; circ. 3,500 (controlled). **Indexed:** HRIS. **Document type:** trade publication.
—UMI.
Formerly (until 1994): Telocator (ISSN 0193-1458); Which superseded (1958?-1977): National Association of Radiotelephone Systems. Communicator.

P T T I STUDIES. (Postal Telegraph and Telephone International) see COMMUNICATIONS — Postal Affairs

383 384   XV
P T T NOVICE; glasilo P T T delavcev Slovenije. (Text in Slovenian) 1970. fortn. Zdruzene P T T Organizacije Slovenije, Cigaletova 15, Ljubljana, Slovenia. Ed. Tatjana Pust.
Formerly: P T T - Zbornik (ISSN 0030-8390)

384   US
PACIFIC TELECOMMUNICATIONS COUNCIL. CONFERENCE PROCEEDINGS. Short title: P T C Proceedings. 1979. a., 18th, 1995, Honolulu. $225 to non-members ($125 in developing countries); members $125 ($50 to students or members in developing countries) (effective 1997). Pacific Telecommunications Council, 2454 S. Beretania St., Ste. 302, Honolulu, HI 96826-1596. TEL 808-941-3789. FAX 808-944-4874. E-mail: info@ptc.org. Eds. Dan Wedermeyer, Richard Nickelson. **Document type:** proceedings.
●Also available on CD-ROM.

384   US   ISSN 1066-3894
PACIFIC TELECOMMUNICATIONS REVIEW. 1980. q. $35 in North America; elsewhere $50. Pacific Telecommunications Council, 2454 S. Beretania, Ste. 302, Honolulu, HI 96826-1596. TEL 808-941-3789. FAX 808-944-4784. E-mail: info@ptc.org. Ed. Richard Nickelson. adv.; bk.rev. circ. 2,500. (back issues avail.) **Document type:** academic/scholarly publication.
—BLDSC (6946.595000).
Former titles: Pacific Telecommunications (ISSN 0899-434X); P T C Quarterly.
Description: Covers telecommunication developments and their impact on the Pacific region, specifically Asia, the Americas, and Oceania.

384.5   US
PHONE LOSERS OF AMERICA. 1994. bi-m. 1013 Kingswood Court, Celina, OH 45822. E-mail: bac@bright.net; URL: http://www.cocksoldier.com.
●Available only online.
Description: Covers telephone and computer insecurity issues.

394.6   US   ISSN 1046-2007
PHONE PLUS. 1987. m. $33. Taurus Publishing, Inc. (Subsidiary of: Virgo Publishing, Inc.), Box C-5400, Scottsdale, AZ 85261. TEL 602-483-0014. FAX 602-483-1247. Ed. Lee Stites. circ. 25,000. **Indexed:** Tel.Abstr.
Formerly: Telecommunications Equipment Retailer (ISSN 1045-0106)

384.6   US   ISSN 0897-0890
PHONEFACTS. a. $15 per no. to non-members; members $5. United States Telephone Association, 1401 H St., N.W., Ste. 600, Washington, DC 20005. TEL 202-326-7300. FAX 202-326-7333. Ed. Cheryl Sullivan. charts; illus.; stat. **Document type:** trade publication.
Formerly: Independent Phonefacts.

384   US
PLANNING GUIDE X-1. base vol. (plus m. updates). $345. United Communications Group, 11300 Rockville Pike, Ste. 1100, Rockville, MD 20852-3030. TEL 301-816-8950.
Formerly: Guide to Communication Services.

384   US
PLANNING GUIDE 1. INTER-L A T A TELECOMMUNICATIONS RATES AND SERVICES. base vol. (plus m. updates). $595. United Communications Group, 11300 Rockville Pike, Ste. 1100, Rockville, MD 20852-3030. TEL 301-816-8950.
Formerly: Executive Telecommunication Planning Guide.

384   US
PLANNING GUIDE 2. INTRA-L A T A TELECOMMUNICATIONS RATES AND SERVICES. base vol. (plus m. updates). $650. United Communications Group, 11300 Rockville Pike, Ste. 1100, Rockville, MD 20852-3030. TEL 301-816-8950.
Formerly: Guide to Intra L A T A Communications Services.

POLITECHNIKA GDANSKA. ZESZYTY NAUKOWE. ELEKTRONIKA. see COMPUTERS — Cybernetics

621.382 534   PL   ISSN 0324-9344
TK5101.A1   CODEN: PITKEC
POLITECHNIKA WROCLAWSKA. INSTYTUT TELEKOMUNIKACJI I AKUSTYKI. PRACE NAUKOWE. KONFERENCJE. (Text in Polish; summaries in English and Russian) 1973. irreg., no.23, 1993. price varies. Oficyna Wydawnicza Politechniki Wroclawskiej, Wybrzeze Wyspianskiego 27, 50-370 Wroclaw, Poland. TEL 48-71-222940. FAX 48-71-223664. TELEX 712559 PWRPL. (Dist. by: Ars Polona, Krakowskie Przedmiescie 7, Warsaw, Poland) Ed. Bronislaw Zoltogorski. R&P contact: Halina Dudek. adv. **Document type:** proceedings.
—BLDSC (6590.761000); Ei.

621.382 534   PL   ISSN 0324-9328
POLITECHNIKA WROCLAWSKA. INSTYTUT TELEKOMUNIKACJI I AKUSTYKI. PRACE NAUKOWE. MONOGRAFIE. (Text in Polish; summaries in English and Russian) 1969. irreg., no.42, 1996. price varies. Oficyna Wydawnicza Politechniki Wroclawskiej, Wybrzeze Wyspianskiego 27, 50-370 Wroclaw, Poland. TEL 48-71-222940. FAX 48-71-223664. TELEX 712559 PWRPL. (Dist. by: Ars Polona, Krakowskie Przedmiescie 7, Warsaw, Poland) R&P contact: Halina Dudek. adv. **Document type:** monographic series.
—CISTI.

621.382 534   PL   ISSN 0324-9336
POLITECHNIKA WROCLAWSKA. INSTYTUT TELEKOMUNIKACJI I AKUSTYKI. PRACE NAUKOWE. STUDIA I MATERIALY. (Text in Polish; summaries in English and Russian) 1971. irreg., no.12, 1980. price varies. Oficyna Wydawnicza Politechniki Wroclawskiej, Wybrzeze Wyspianskiego 27, 50-370 Wroclaw, Poland. TEL 48-71-222940. FAX 48-71-223664. TELEX 712559 PWRPL. (Dist. by: Ars Polona, Krakowskie Przedmiescie 7, Warsaw, Poland) R&P contact: Halina Dudek. adv. **Document type:** academic/scholarly publication.

POSTAL AND TELKOM HERALD/POS- EN TELKOMHERALD. see COMMUNICATIONS — Postal Affairs

621.38 383   IT   ISSN 0032-5406
POSTE E TELECOMUNICAZIONI. vol.45, 1977. q. L.35000 (effective 1995). Fondazione Ugo Bordoni, Via Baldassarre Castiglione 59, 00142 Rome, Italy. TEL 39-6-54801. FAX 39-6-54804400. TELEX 622539 FUB I. Dir. Elio Briganti. adv.; bk.rev.; charts; illus.; stat.; index. circ. 5,000. **Indexed:** Chem.Abstr.

384.6 621.388   US   ISSN 1077-3487
PRIVATE LINE (CARMICHAEL);* a journal of inquiry into the telephone system. 1994. bi-m. $27 (effective July 1995). Tom Farley, Ed. & Pub., Box 1059, Isleton, CA 95641. TEL 916-777-4420. E-mail: privateline@delphi.com; URL: etext.archive.umich.edu/pub/zines/PrivateLine. (Dist. by: 2605 Del Monte St., West Sacramento, CA 95691. FAX 916-373-3089) adv.: B&W page $100; adv. contact: Tom Farley. illus.; pat.; index; circ. 850 (paid). (back issues avail.) **Document type:** consumer publication.
●Also available online.
Description: An alternative magazine about the telephone system, concentrating on the technology of telecommunications.

384.6   US   ISSN 0896-7229
HE7601
PROCOMM ENTERPRISES MAGAZINE.* 1987. m. $39 (Canada $55; elsewhere $75) (effective 1993). Procomm Enterprises, 1655 Capitol St., N.E., Salem, OR 97303-6445. TEL 415-459-4669. FAX 415-459-4591. Ed. Jason Bray. adv.; bk.rev. circ. 28,200. **Document type:** trade publication.
Description: For the professional data and voice communications manager and consultant.

621.38   PL   ISSN 1230-3496
PRZEGLAD TELEKOMUNIKACYJNY I WIADOMOSCI TELEKOMUNIKACYJNE/TELECOMMUNICATION REVIEW & TELECOMMUNICATION NEWS; tele-radio-elektronika. (Text in Polish; summaries in English, Polish) 1992. m. $71.50. (Stowarzyszenie Elektrykow Polskich - Association of Polish Electrical Engineers) Wydawnictwo Czasopism i Ksiazek Technicznych SIGMA - NOT, Ul. Ratuszowa 11, P.O. Box 1004, 00-950 Warsaw, Poland. TEL 48-22-180918. FAX 48-22-192187. TELEX 814550 SIGMA PL. (Dist. by: SIGMA NOT Ltd., Ul. Bartycka 20, 00-716 Warsaw, Poland. TEL 48-22-403086) Ed. Krystyn Plewko. adv.: B&W page $1000. bk.rev.; circ. 2,000 (paid). **Indexed:** Ceram.Abstr., Chem.Abstr., INSPEC.
—BLDSC (6944.871000); AskIEEE; CISTI; KR SourceOne.
Formed by the merger of (1929-1992): Przeglad Telekomunikacyjny (ISSN 0033-2399); (1961-1992): Wiadomosci Telekomunikacyjne (ISSN 0043-5198); Which was formerly (1956-1959): Tele-Radio (ISSN 0492-5971); (1939-1956): Wiadomosci Telekomunikacyjne.

384.5   US   ISSN 1041-6943
HD9697.T453
PUBLIC COMMUNICATIONS MAGAZINE.* 1984. m. $39. Multimedia Publishing Corporation, 3721 Briarpark, Houston, TX 77042. TEL 713-783-8999. FAX 713-783-9567. Ed. Tracey Gahl. adv.: page $1965; adv. contact: Denise Fisher. bk.rev. circ. 5,000. **Document type:** trade publication.

621.38   UK   ISSN 0963-5084
PUBLIC NETWORK EUROPE. m. Axe and Bottle Ct., 70 Newcomen St., London SE1 1XT, England. TEL 071-403-5818. FAX 071-403-6104. Ed. Jim Chalmers. circ. 10,500.
—BLDSC (6967.783000); SWETS.

PUBLIC UTILITIES FORTNIGHTLY. see BUSINESS AND ECONOMICS — Management

384.6   FI   ISSN 0048-5977
PUHELIN/TELEPHONE.* (Text in Finnish, Swedish; summaries in English, Swedish) 1951. 8/yr. FIM 147. Puhelinlaitosten Liitto r.y. - Association of Telephone Companies in Finland, Sinebrychoffinkatu 11, Box 949, FIN-00101 Helsinki 10, Finland. FAX 358-0-228-11-244. adv. circ. 17,000. **Document type:** consumer publication.

384.6 380.1   US
QUICK GUIDE TO THE NEW TELECOM LINGO. irreg., latest 8th ed. $45. Capitol Publications Inc., Telecom Publishing Group, 1101 King St., Ste. 444, Box 1455, Alexandria, VA 22313-2055. TEL 800-327-7205. FAX 703-739-6490. URL: http://www.telecommunications.com. **Document type:** directory.
Description: Includes definitions and explanations of more than 800 telecom words and acronyms regarding voice and data communications.

384.5   US
R B O C UPDATE. (Regional Bell Operating Company) m. $150 (outside N. America $165). Worldwide Videotex, Box 3273, Boynton Beach, FL 33424-3273. TEL 407-738-2276. Ed. Mark Wright; Pub. Mark Wright. bk.rev. **Document type:** newsletter.
●Also available online. Vendor(s): Information Access Co.
Description: Covers all the activities of the regional Bell operating companies, including videotex trials, gateway operations, and their struggle in the courts to provide more services. Also covers marketing strategies.

384   US
R C R NEWSFAX. 1993. 200/yr. $125. R C R Publications, Inc., 777 E. Speer Blvd., Denver, CO 80203-4214. TEL 303-733-2500. FAX 303-733-9941. Ed. Tracy Anderson Ford. (only avail. by fax)

384   US
▼**R C R - P C S HANDBOOK.** (Radio Communications Report) 1997. a. $100. R C R Publications, Inc., 777 E. Speer Blvd., Denver, CO 80203-4214. TEL 303-733-2500. FAX 303-733-9941.

384   US   ISSN 0744-0618
RADIO COMMUNICATIONS REPORT. 1981. w. $49. R C R Publications, Inc., 777 E. Speer Blvd., Denver, CO 80203-4214. TEL 303-733-2500. FAX 303-733-9941. Ed. Tracy Anderson Ford; Pub. John Sudmeier. adv. **Indexed:** INSPEC. **Document type:** newspaper.
Supersedes: Two - Way Radio Dealer.

REPORT ON A T & T; the independent bi-weekly reporting exclusively on the long-distance industry including AT&T and its competitors. see COMMUNICATIONS — Computer Applications

621.382   AG   ISSN 0035-0516
                        CODEN: RTELB2
REVISTA TELEGRAFICA ELECTRONICA. 1912. m. $45. Arbo S.A.C.E.I., Avda. Martin Garcia 653, Buenos Aires, Argentina. Ed. Ariel Arbo. adv.; bk.rev.; abstr.; bibl.; charts; illus.; index. circ. 13,000. **Indexed:** INSPEC (1973-).
—AskIEEE; CISTI; KR SourceOne; Linda Hall.

RIVISTA TELETTRA REVIEW (ENGLISH EDITION); contributions to telecommunications development. see COMMUNICATIONS — Television And Cable

RIVISTA TELETTRA REVIEW (ITALIAN EDITION); contributi allo sviluppo delle telecomunicazioni. see COMMUNICATIONS — Television And Cable

621.38   IT   ISSN 0035-8185
RONZATORE.* 1953. q. free. Societa Generale di Telefonia ed Elettronica, Via Bernina 12, 20133 Milan, Italy. Ed. Gianluigi Rossi. bk.rev.; illus.; stat.; tr.lit.; index. circ. 4,000.

384.6   US   ISSN 0744-2548
HE8801
RURAL TELECOMMUNICATIONS. 1963. bi-m. $30 includes N T C A Exchange (effective 1992). National Telephone Cooperative Association, 2626 Pennsylvania Ave., N.W., Washington, DC 20037. TEL 202-298-2300. FAX 202-298-2320. Ed. Matt Green. adv.; bk.rev.; illus. circ. 4,700. **Indexed:** ABI Inform. **Document type:** trade publication.
●Also available online. Vendor(s): UMI.
—BLDSC (8052.640550); UMI.
Formerly (until 1982): Phone Call.

384   CN   ISSN 0080-6633
SASKATCHEWAN TELECOMMUNICATIONS. ANNUAL REPORT. 1947. a. free. Saskatchewan Telecommunications, 2121 Saskatchewan Dr., Regina, SK S4P 3Y2, Canada. TEL 306-777-2005. Ed. Evan Flude. circ. 10,000. **Document type:** corporate report.
—BLDSC (1432.008000).
Description: Provides an overview of the corporation's activities.

384   CN   ISSN 0036-4851
SASKTEL NEWS. 1960. m. free. Saskatchewan Telecommunications, 2121 Saskatchewan Dr., Regina, Sk S4P 3Y2, Canada. TEL 306-777-2006. Ed. Lee Cowie. charts; illus.; stat. circ. 5,100. **Document type:** newsletter.
Formerly: S.G.T.
Description: Highlights SaskTel's role in the telecommunications industry.

621.38   XR   ISSN 0036-9942
SDELOVACI TECHNIKA/TELECOMMUNICATIONS ENGINEERING. (Text in Czech or Slovak; summaries in English, French, German, Russian) 1953. m. $58.30. V Stihlach 1311-3, 142 00 Prague 4, Czech Republic. (Dist. by: Artia, Ve Smeckach 30, 111 27 Prague 1, Czech Republic) Ed. Petr Benes. bk.rev.; charts; illus.; mkt.; pat.; index in English and German. circ. 25,000. **Indexed:** C.I.S. Abstr., Cyb.Abstr., INSPEC.
—BLDSC (8213.500000); AskIEEE; CISTI; KR SourceOne.

384.1   IT
SELEZIONANDO S I P; giornale aziendale. 1950. bi-m. free. Societa Italiana per l'Esercizio delle Telecomunicazioni P.A., Via Flaminia 189, 00196 Rome, Italy. TEL 01139-636881. bk.rev. circ. 95,000.

384.6   BL   ISSN 0037-5764
SINO AZUL. 1928. 2/yr? free. Telecomunicacoes do R de Janeiro S.A., Av. Presidente Vargas, 2560-8 Andar, Rio de Janeiro, Brazil. Ed. Renato F. Goncalves. adv.; illus. circ. 10,000.

COMMUNICATIONS — TELEPHONE AND TELEGRAPH

621.38   JA
SODENSEN KENSETSU SHIRYO/TRANSMISSION LINE CONSTRUCTION ENGINEERING SOCIETY OF JAPAN. JOURNAL. (Text in Japanese) a. Sodensen Kensetsu Gijutsu Kenkyukai - Transmission Line Construction Engineering Society of Japan, 1-6, Kanda Surugadai, Chiyoda-ku, Tokyo 101, Japan.

384.6   US   ISSN 0038-3856
SOUTHERN BELL VIEWS. 1971. bi-m. free to qualified personnel. Southern Bell Telephone Co., 2850 Campbellton Rd., Atlanta, GA 30311. TEL 404-529-8611.

SPAIN. DIRECCION GENERAL DE CORREOS Y TELECOMUNICACION. BOLETIN OFICIAL DE CORREOS Y TELECOMUNICACION. see *COMMUNICATIONS — Postal Affairs*

384.1   US   ISSN 0741-8388
STATE TELEPHONE REGULATION REPORT. 1983. bi-w. (26/yr.). $589 (foreign $615) (effective 1998). Capitol Publications Inc., Telecom Publishing Group, 1101 King St., Ste. 444, Box 1455, Alexandria, VA 22313-2055. TEL 800-327-7205. FAX 703-739-6490. URL: http://www.telecommunications.com. Ed. Herb Kirchhoff. **Document type:** newsletter.
●Also available online. Vendor(s): Information Access Co., NewsNet (TE47).
—CCC.

T D I NATIONAL DIRECTORY OF T T Y NUMBERS (YEAR). (Telecommunications for the Deaf, Inc.) see *HANDICAPPED — Hearing Impaired*

384.1   UN   ISSN 0074-9052
TABLE OF INTERNATIONAL TELEX RELATIONS AND TRAFFIC. (Text in English, French and Spanish) 1964. a. price varies. International Telecommunication Union, Place des Nations, CH-1211 Geneva 20, Switzerland. TEL 41-22-7306141. FAX 41-22-7305149. TELEX 421 000 UIT CH. E-mail: sales@itu.ch; URL: http://www.itu.ch. (also avail. in microfiche from CIS) **Indexed:** IIS.

621.38   SZ
TEC - ASCOM TECHNICAL MAGAZINE. 1942. 2/yr. free. Ascom Holding Ltd., Belpstr. 37, CH-3000 Bern 14, Switzerland. TEL 41-31-9993244. FAX 41-31-9991835. E-mail: vongrote@tech.ascom.ch; karl-heinrich.vongrote@ascom.ch; URL: http://www.ascom.ch/hptecmag/tec.html. Ed. Karl Heinrich von Grote. circ. 6,500. **Indexed:** Chem.Abstr., Curr.Cont., Eng.Ind, INSPEC. **Document type:** bulletin.
—BLDSC (8614.633000); AskIEEE; CISTI; KR SourceOne. **CCC.**
Former titles (until 1991): Ascom Technische Mitteilungen (ISSN 1015-5473); (until 1989): Hasler Mitteilungen (ISSN 0017-8306)

384.6 658.8   US   ISSN 1073-8134
TELCO BUSINESS REPORT; executive briefings on the Bell operating companies - regional holding companies and independent telcos. 1985. bi-w. (26/yr.). $759 (foreign $785) (effective 1998). Capitol Publications Inc., Telecom Publishing Group, 1101 King St., Ste. 444, Box 1455, Alexandria, VA 22313-2055. TEL 800-327-7205. FAX 703-739-6490. URL: http://www.telecommunications.com. Ed. Jennifer Freer. (back issues avail.) **Document type:** newsletter.
●Also available online. Vendor(s): Information Access Co., Knight-Ridder Information, Inc., NewsNet (TE49).
—CCC.
Former titles (until 1993): Telephone Week (ISSN 1062-4724); (until 1992): B O C Week (ISSN 8755-3511); Incorporates (in 1992): Independent Telco News (ISSN 1051-3124); Formerly: Report on Telco Marketing.

384.6   US   ISSN 0882-1720
TELE;* the communications magazine for business. 1985. m. $24.97. Wayne Green Inc., 70 Rte. 202 N., Peterborough, NH 03458. TEL 603-924-0058. Ed. Dan Muse. adv. circ. 50,000. **Indexed:** CAD CAM Abstr., Tel.Abstr.

384.6   US
TELE-SERVICE NEWS. 1990. m. $150 (outside N. America $165). Worldwide Videotex, Box 3273, Boynton Beach, FL 33424-3273. TEL 407-738-2276. Ed. Mark Wright; Pub. Mark Wright. bk.rev. (back issues avail.) **Document type:** newsletter.
●Also available online. Vendor(s): Data-Star, Information Access Co., Knight-Ridder Information, Inc., NewsNet (TE21).
Description: Provides news and information on the telecommunications and telephone industry, with a focus on products, services, research and development, and business plans of regional Bell operating companies, long-distance carriers, and other industry vendors. Coverage includes cellular service, electronic data interchange, gateways, fiber optics, and effects of government regulations.

384.5   US
TELECOM ALTERNATIVES. 1992. q. $2215 (effective 1993). Faulkner Information Services, Inc., 114 Cooper Center, 7905 Browning Rd., Pennsauken, NJ 08109-4319. TEL 609-662-2070. FAX 609-662-3380. Ed. Tory Jenson. (looseleaf format)
Description: Profiles Competitive Access Providers (CAPs), regulatory issues, and major CAP applications.

621.38   UK
TELECOM ASIA. (Text in Chinese, English) q. 302 Whitchurch Ln., Edgware, Middlesex HA8 6QX, England. TEL 081-952-7991. Ed. Adrian Morant. circ. 12,000.

621.38   US
TELECOM GEAR. 1984. m. $31. United Advertising Publications, Inc., 15400 Knoll Trail., Ste. 500, Dallas, TX 75248. TEL 214-233-5131. FAX 214-233-5514. adv. circ. 40,000. **Document type:** trade publication.
Description: Information on the supply and demand of equipment in the telecommunications industry. Edited for a master list of end-users, interconnects, BOC's, OEM's and dealers.

TELECOM MARKETS. see *BUSINESS AND ECONOMICS — Production Of Goods And Services*

384.5   US
TELECOM NEWSFAX TODAY. d. (Mon.-Fri.). $249. (Center for Communications Management Information) C C M I, 11300 Rockville Pike, Ste. 1100, Rockville, MD 20852-3030. TEL 301-816-8950; 800-929-4824. FAX 301-816-8945. E-mail: cust_svc@vcg.com. Ed. Fritz McCormick; Pub. George David. adv. contact: Kristina Greggs.
Formerly: Daily Telecom News Bulletin.
Description: An exclusive daily executive briefing on the biggest telecom business news from the US and overseas.

384.6   US   ISSN 1078-523X
TELECOM PERSPECTIVES. Key Title: Northern Business Information's Telecom Perspectives. 1982. m. $995. Northern Business Information (Subsidiary of: McGraw-Hill, Inc.), 1221 Ave. of the Americas, No. 37, New York, NY 10020-1001. TEL 212-512-2898. FAX 212-512-2859. E-mail: poseyma@mcgraw-hill.com. Ed. Melanie A. Posey. R&P contact: Melanie A. Posey. charts; stat.; index. circ. 145. (back issues avail.) **Document type:** newsletter.
Formed by the 1994 merger of: Telecom Market Letter (ISSN 0712-3663) & Telecom Strategy Letter (ISSN 0739-683X)
Description: Designed to analyze competition and strategic developments in telecommunications.

384.6   IE   ISSN 0790-9268
TELECOM REPORT. (Supplement to: Irish Computer (ISSN 0332-0197)) 1977. q. $90. Computer Publications of Ireland Ltd., 66 Patrick St., Dun Laoghaire, Co. Dublin, Ireland. TEL 1-2800424. FAX 1-2808468. Ed. Donald McDonald. adv.; bk.rev.

384.6   US   ISSN 0898-9087
TELECOM RESOURCES. 1985. m. free to qualified personnel. Capitol Publications Inc., Telecom Publishing Group, 1101 King St., Ste. 444, Box 1455, Alexandria, VA 22313-2055. TEL 800-327-7205. FAX 703-739-6490. URL: http://www.telecommunications.com. Ed. Dick Stirba. **Document type:** bulletin, catalog.
Description: Covers current news stories and lists information products.

621.38   UK   ISSN 1355-3429
TELECOMEUROPA'S ADVANCED CORDLESS COMMUNICATIONS; digital cordless news for voice, data and image. Variant title: Advanced Cordless Communications. 1994. m. £595($940) Telecomeuropa Publications, 3 Princes Bldgs., George St., Bath, Avon BA1 2ED, England. TEL 44-1225-445282. FAX 44-1225-445283. E-mail: 100144.3104@compuserve.com. Ed. Ian Channing; Pub. Peter Purton. **Document type:** newsletter.
Description: Contains news and articles for developers, manufacturers, and users of cordless communications equipment.

621.38   UK   ISSN 0958-398X
TELECOMEUROPA'S COMMUNICATIONS NEWSLETTER; the newsletter for European telecommunications. s-m. £695($1090) Telecomeuropa Publications, 3 Princes Bldgs., George St., Bath, Avon BA1 2ED, England. TEL 44-1225-445282. FAX 44-1225-445283. E-mail: 100144.3104@compuserve.com. Ed. Carole Hewitt; Pub. Peter Purton. **Document type:** newsletter.
Former titles (until 1989): Communications Newsletter (ISSN 0956-7771); (until 1986): Telephony's Communications Newsletter (ISSN 0950-5717); Incorporates (in 1988): Telecommunications Week (ISSN 0269-9613); Which was (1985-1986): Telecommunications Newsweek (ISSN 0268-1404)
Description: For network operators; equipment manufacturers; regulators; persons from standards bodies; ministries; consultants; market researchers; corporate users; and banks and other funding agencies.

621.38   UK   ISSN 1357-3446
TELECOMEUROPA'S COMPUTER TELEPHONY WORLD REPORT; newsletter for computer and telephony integration. Variant title: Computer Telephony World Report. 1994. m. £595($940) Telecomeuropa Publications, 3 Princes Bldgs., George St., Bath, Avon BA1 2ED, England. TEL 44-1225-445282. FAX 44-1225-445283. E-mail: 100144.3104@compuserve.com. Ed. Bob Whitehouse; Pub. Peter Purton. **Document type:** newsletter.
Description: For vendors, manufacturers, and users of computer telephony equipment.

621.38   UK   ISSN 1354-1331
TELECOMEUROPA'S CUSTOMER CARE AND BILLING; monthly guide to successful telecoms service provision. Variant title: Customer Care and Billing. 1994. m. £595($940) Telecomeuropa Publications, 3 Princes Bldgs., George St., Bath, Avon BA1 2ED, England. TEL 44-1225-445282. FAX 44-1225-445283. E-mail: 10014.3104@compuserve.com. Ed. Chris Thomas; Pub. Peter Purton. **Document type:** newsletter.
Description: Covers customer care billing for mobile and fixed network operators and other telecom professionals.

621.38   UK   ISSN 0962-3825
TELECOMEUROPA'S EASTERN EUROPE NEWSLETTER; newsletter for Eastern European telecommunications. Variant title: Eastern Europe Newsletter. Abbreviated title: E E N. 1991. m. £595($940) Telecomeuropa Publications, 3 Princes Bldgs., George St., Bath, Avon BA1 2ED, England. TEL 44-1225-445282. FAX 44-1225-445283. E-mail: 100144.3104@compuserve.com. Ed. John Williamson; Pub. Peter Purton. **Document type:** newsletter.
Description: For telecoms operators, banks and other funding agencies, equipment manufacturers, regulators, consultants, ministries, and corporate users.

COMMUNICATIONS — TELEPHONE AND TELEGRAPH

621.38   UK   ISSN 1353-1336
TELECOMEUROPA'S G S M SERVICE MONITOR; newsletter for global digital mobile communications. Variant title: G S M Service Monitor. 1993. m. £595($940) Telecomeuropa Publications, 3 Princes Bldgs., George St., Bath, Avon BA1 2ED, England. TEL 44-1225-445282. FAX 44-1225-445283. E-mail: 100144.3104@compuserve.com. Ed. Paul Chambers; Pub. Peter Purton. **Document type:** newsletter.
   Description: For GSM network operators, PTTs, and non-PTT service providers; competing service providers; infrastructure manufacturers, terminal manufacturers, billing system suppliers, software suppliers, regulators, and consultants.

621.38   UK   ISSN 0958-8515
TELECOMEUROPA'S I S D N NEWSLETTER. Variant title: Telecomeuropa's Integrated Services Digital Networks Newsletter. 1990. m. £595($940) Telecomeuropa Publications, 3 Princes Bldgs., George St., Bath, Avon BA1 2ED, England. TEL 44-1225-445282. FAX 44-1225-445283. E-mail: 100144.3104@compuserve.com. Ed. Alan Spencer; Pub. Peter Purton. adv. contact: John Foley. **Document type:** newsletter.
   Description: Contains information for operators, corporate users, manufacturers of ISDN and terminal equipment, consultants, software developers, market researchers, regulators, and standards bodies.

621.38 659.1   UK   ISSN 1357-2865
TELECOMEUROPA'S MARKETING TELECOMS; newsletter for marketers of telecoms equipment and services. Variant title: Marketing Telecoms. 1994. m. £595($940) Telecomeuropa Publications, 3 Princes Bldgs., George St., Bath, Avon BA2 2ED, England. TEL 44-1225-445282. FAX 44-1225-445283. E-mail: 100144.3104@compuserve.com. Ed. Carole Hewitt; Pub. Peter Purton. **Document type:** newsletter.
   Description: For marketing, public relations, advertising, and publishing professionals.

384.5   UK   ISSN 1361-1372
▼**TELECOMEUROPA'S MOBILE PHONE MONITOR**; the monthly update on cellular handset developments worldwide. Variant title: Mobile Phone Monitor. 1995. m. £495($745) (effective 1995). Telecomeuropa News Bureau Publications, 3 Princes Bldgs., George St., Bath, Avon BA1 2ED, England. TEL 44-1225-445282. FAX 44-1225-445283. E-mail: 10014.3104@compuserve.com. (US subscr. to: Box 4948, Laguna Beach, CA 92652. TEL 714-499-1857) Ed. Kendrick Struthers-Watson; Pub. Peter Purton. tr.lit. (back issues avail.) **Document type:** newsletter.
● Also available online.

621.38   UK   ISSN 1350-9306
TELECOMEUROPA'S NEW NETWORK OPERATOR; newsletter for UK's deregulated telecoms industry. Variant title: New Network Operator. 1993. m. £595($940) Telecomeuropa Publications, 3 Princes Bldgs., George St., Bath, Avon BA1 2ED, England. TEL 44-1225-445282. FAX 44-1225-445283. E-mail: 100144.3104@compuserve.com. Ed. Alan Burlitt-Gray. **Document type:** newsletter.
   Description: For network operators, equipment makers, and regulators.

621.38   UK   ISSN 0958-8523
TELECOMEUROPA'S PERSONAL COMMUNICATIONS NEWSLETTER; newsletter for cordless communications. Variant title: Personal Communications Newsletter. 1990. s-m. £695($1091) Telecomeuropa Publications, 3 Princes Bldgs., George St., Bath, Avon BA1 2ED, England. TEL 44-1225-445282. FAX 44-1225-445283. E-mail: 100144.3104@compuserve.com. Ed. Peter Dykes; Pub. Peter Purton. **Document type:** newsletter.

TELECOMMAGAZINE; strategie en toepassingen van tele- en datacommunicatie. see *COMPUTERS — Data Communications And Data Transmission Systems*

621.38   SI
TELECOMMUNICATION AUTHORITY OF SINGAPORE. SINGAPORE TELECOM ANNUAL REPORT. 1974. a. price varies. Telecommunication Authority of Singapore, 35 Robinson Rd., TAS Bldg., Singapore 0106, Singapore. TEL 65-323-3888. FAX 65-323-0941. Ed. Fum-Ko Joon Chin. circ. 5,000. circ. controlled. **Document type:** government publication.
   Formerly (until 1992): Telecommunication Authority of Singapore. Telecoms Annual Report (ISSN 0217-3891); Formed by the 1974 merger of: Telecommunication Authority of Singapore. T A S Annual Report; Singapore Telephone Board Annual Report.

621.385   NE   ISSN 1018-4864
                 CODEN: TESYEV
TELECOMMUNICATION SYSTEMS. (Text in English) 1993. 8/yr. (in 2 vols.). 752 SFr. (effective 1998). Baltzer Science Publishers B.V., P.O. Box 221, 1400 AE Bussum, Netherlands. TEL 31-20-6370061. FAX 31-20-6323651. E-mail: subscribe@baltzer.nl; URL: http://www.baltzer.nl. (Subscr. in N. America to: Baltzer Science Publishers, Box 8577, Red Bank, NJ 07701-8577) Ed. Bezalel Gavish. Indexed: ASCA, Compumath, Curr.Cont., INSPEC (1993-). **Document type:** academic/scholarly publication.
   —BLDSC (8780.680000); AskIEEE; CISTI; Genuine Article; KR SourceOne; SWETS. **CCC.**
   Description: Publishes original research on the modelling, analysis, design and management of telecommunications systems.

384.1   II   ISSN 0497-1388
TELECOMMUNICATIONS. (Text in English) 1951. bi-m. Rs.15 per no. (foreign $7). Posts and Telegraphs Department, c/o Chief General Manager, Technical and Development Circle, Jabalpur, India. TEL 91-761-323440. FAX 91-761-322322. TELEX 81(765) 222. Ed. H.C. Soni. adv. circ. 9,300. Indexed: B.P.I., INSPEC.
   —BLDSC (8781.000000); AskIEEE; CISTI; KR SourceOne.
   Description: Publishes technical journals in the field of telecommunication.

621.38   UK
TELECOMMUNICATIONS AMERICAS. m. Portland House, Stag Pl., London SW1E 5XT, England. TEL 44-171-957-0030. FAX 44-171-957-0031. Ed. Steve McClelland. circ. 54,050. **Document type:** trade publication.
● Also available online. Vendor(s): UMI.
   Description: Provides coverage of communications applied technology and business topics.

384.5   UK   ISSN 1353-0097
TELECOMMUNICATIONS HERITAGE JOURNAL. irreg. Telecommunications Heritage Group, Unit 4, Travellers Close, Welham Green, Herts AL9 7LE, England. TEL 44-1707-287294. FAX 44-1707-287209. E-mail: thg@strowger.demon.co.uk. Ed. James Campbell. **Document type:** bulletin.
   Formerly (until 1993): Telecommunications Heritage Bulletin (ISSN 0969-238X)

621.38   UK
TELECOMMUNICATIONS INTERNATIONAL. m. $120. Portland House, Stag Pl., London SW1E 5XT, England. TEL 071-957-0030. FAX 071-957-0031. Ed. Steven McClelland. circ. 25,307. **Document type:** trade publication.
● Also available online. Vendor(s): UMI.
   Description: Provides coverage of communications applied technology and business topics worldwide.

621.38   UK   ISSN 0264-4568
TELECOMMUNICATIONS NEWS. 1983. 24/yr. 5 Riverside, Wooburn Moor, High Wycombe, Bucks. HP10 0NU, England. TEL 01628-523458. FAX 01628-523458. Ed. Alan Forberg. **Document type:** trade publication.

384 340   US   ISSN 1058-3181
KF2765.Z9
TELECOMMUNICATIONS POLICY AND REGULATION. 1990. a. Practising Law Institute, 810 Seventh Ave., New York, NY 10019.

384 340   AT
TELECOMMUNICATIONS REPORTER. 1990. 4/yr. (in 2 vols.). Aus.$695 plus updates. L B C Information Services, 50 Waterloo Rd., N. Ryde, N.S.W 2113, Australia. TEL 61-2-99366444. FAX 61-2-98889706. TELEX ASBOOK 27995. Ed.Bd. (looseleaf format)
   Description: For the telecommunications industry and lawyers practicing in this field.

651.2 621.38   AT   ISSN 1322-3518
TELECOMMUNICATIONS STRATEGIES REPORT; packaging of value added telecommunication & broadcasting services & networks. 1988. a. Aus.$595 (US Aus.$625; Europe Aus.$630) (effective 1998). Paul Budde Communication Pty. Ltd., 2643 George Downes Dr., Bucketty, N.S.W. 2250, Australia. TEL 61-49-988-144. FAX 61-49-988-247. E-mail: pbc@budde.com.au; URL: http://www.budde.com.au. Ed. Paul Budde. circ 500.
   Formerly: Strategic V A S - V A N S Report.
   Description: Covers Australian and New Zealand developments and strategies in telecommunication and broadcasting.

384.6   US
TELECOMMUNICATOR. 1950. bi-w. membership only. Association of Telemessaging Services International, Inc., 1200 19th St., N.W., Washington, DC 20036-2412. TEL 202-429-5151. URL: http://206.69.91.109/icenter/. Ed. Andy Briney; Pub. Herta Tucker. R&P contact: Andy Briney. TEL 202-857-1126. adv. contact: Stephanie Mattes. circ. 750. **Document type:** newsletter.
   Formerly: Telephone Secretary.

384.5   UK   ISSN 0969-5907
TELECOMS HERITAGE NEWS. 1991. q. Telecommunications Heritage Group, Unit 4, Travellers Close, Welham Green, Herts AL9 7LE, England. TEL 44-1707-287294. FAX 44-1707-287209. E-mail: thg@strowger.demon.co.uk. Ed. James Campbell. **Document type:** newsletter.

621.38   UK   ISSN 0968-0497
TELECOMS INDUSTRY. 1989. 6/yr. £28.80 (Europe £34.50; rest of world £45.90) (effective 1997). Stanworth Communications, P.O. Box 220, Walton-on-Thames, Surrey KT12 1YQ, England. TEL 44-1932-254400. FAX 44-1932-240294. Ed Paul Liptrot; Pub. Paul Liptrot. adv.: B&W page £1650, color page £2310; trim 297 x 210; adv. contact: Perry Sanger. bk.rev.; charts; illus.; stat.; tr.lit. circ. 12,500. (back issues avail.) **Document type:** trade publication.
   Description: Products, services, and marketing and business advice for the U.K. telecoms trade and industry.

384.6   CH   ISSN 0258-0284
TELECOMS TECHNICAL QUARTERLY.* Key Title: Dianxi Jishu Jikan. (Text in Chinese; summaries in English 1957. q. $25 in Hong Kong & Macao; elsewhere $30. Ministry of Transportation and Communications, Directorate General of Telecommunications, 31 Aikuo E. Rd., Taipei 10605, Taiwan, Republic of China. TEL 886-2-3443633. FAX 886-2-3519514. TEL 21733 GENTEL. bk.rev.; abstr.; illus. circ. 3,000.
   Formerly (until 1980): Taiwan Telecommunications Technical Quarterly.

384.1   US   ISSN 0740-9354
TK6001
TELECONNECT. 1983. m. $15. (Telcom Library Inc.) Gerald A. Friesen, Inc., 12 W. 21st St., New York, NY 10010. TEL 212-691-8215. adv.; tr.lit. circ. 35,000. Indexed: CAD CAM Abstr., Comput.Dtbs., Resour.Ctr.Ind., Tel.Abstr. **Document type:** trade publication.
● Also available online. Vendor(s): Information Acc Co.
   —BLDSC (8781.767000); KR SourceOne; SWETS UMI.

COMMUNICATIONS — TELEPHONE AND TELEGRAPH

621.38   UK
TELEFACTS. 1990. m. Datapro Research Group, McGraw-Hill House, Shoppenhangers Rd., Maidenhead, Berks. SL6 2QL, England. TEL 01628-773277. TELEX 01628-26865. E-mail: richarbj@mcgraw-hill.com. Ed. Angela Bailey. bk.rev. **Document type:** newsletter.
●Also available on CD-ROM.
    Formerly: Communications Equipment & Services.
    Description: Contains news of international activities and in-depth reviews of selected markets, technologies and companies, together with comprehensive country profiles.

621.385 643   IT
TELEFONO. 1991. bi-m. L.40000 (Europe L.80000; elsewhere L.120000). Studio Zeta s.r.l., Via S. Fruttuoso 10, 20052 Monza (MI), Italy. TEL 039-736451. FAX 49-30-2517248. Ed. Eugenio Zigliotto. adv.: B&W page L.3500000, color page L.6000000. circ. 25,000.

384   GW   ISSN 0948-3608
TELEKOMMUNIKATION JAHRBUCH FUER UNTERNEHMSMANAGEMENT IN EUROPE. 1970. a. DM.64. Fachverlag Schiele und Schoen GmbH, Markgrafenstr. 11, 10969 Berlin, Germany. TEL 49-30-253752-0. FAX 49-30-2517248. E-mail: 0302537520-0001@t-online.de. Ed. H. Bernd. adv. circ. 3,000. **Document type:** trade publication.
    Former titles: Verwaltungsjahrbuch fuer die Deutsche Bundespost (ISSN 0939-4400); Taschenbuch der Post- und Fernmelde-Verwaltung (ISSN 0082-190X); Taschenbuch fuer Fernmelde-Verwaltung.

384   XR   ISSN 0040-2591
TELEKOMUNIKACE; casopis pro pracovniky provozu, udrzby a vystavby telefonu, telegrafu, rozhlasu po drate a radiokomunikaci. 1962. m. 12 Kc.($27) (Federalni Ministerstvo Spoju) S P T Telecom, a.s., Plzenska 166, 150 00 Prague 5, Czech Republic. (Dist. by: Artia, Ve Smeckach 30, 111 27 Prague 1, Czech Republic) (Co-publisher: S T Bratislava, s.p., Slovakia) Ed. Vera Novotna. bk.rev.; abstr.; charts; illus.; stat.

384   YU   ISSN 0040-2605
TELEKOMUNIKACIJE. 1952. q. $5. Zajednica Jugoslovenskih Posta, Telegrafe i Telefona, Palmoticeva 2-2, Box 1110, 11001 Belgrade, Yugoslavia. FAX 22-636917. TELEX 11421. Ed. Bozidar Cavic. adv.; bk.rev.; charts; illus.; tr.lit. circ. 1,500. **Indexed:** INSPEC.
—AskIEEE; CISTI; KR SourceOne.

621.38   CN   ISSN 0840-5476
TELEMANAGEMENT; the Angus report on communications systems, services and strategies. 1983. 10/yr. Can.$297($260) Angus Telemanagement Group Inc., 8 Old Kingston Rd., Ajax, ON L1T 2Z7, Canada. TEL 905-686-5050. FAX 905-686-2655. E-mail: editors@angustel.ca; URL: http://angustel.ca. Eds. Ian Angus, Lis Angus. bk.rev.; index. (back issues avail.) **Document type:** newsletter.
—CISTI. CCC.
    Description: Provides practical guidance for managers of business telecommunications systems.

621.38   UK
TELEPHONE ENGINEER AND MANAGEMENT. 24/yr. 302 Whitchurch Ln., Edgware, Middlesex HA8 6QX, England. TEL 081-952-7991. FAX 081-9511490. Ed. Adrian Morant. circ. 40,000.

TELEPHONE INDUSTRY DIRECTORY. see *BUSINESS AND ECONOMICS — Trade And Industrial Directories*

384.6   TH
TELEPHONE ORGANIZATION OF THAILAND. ANNUAL REPORT. (Text in English and Thai) 1954. a. Telephone Organization of Thailand, Thanon Phloen Chit, Bangkok Metropolis 10500, Thailand. TEL 02-257-1000. Ed. Kamphonwut Sukhsong. **Document type:** corporate report.

TELEPHONE SELLING REPORT. see *BUSINESS AND ECONOMICS — Marketing And Purchasing*

384.6   IT
TELEPHONE TRADE. 1983. bi-m. L.50000($61) (foreign L.100000) (effective 1997). Stammer S.p.A., Via della Liberazione 1, 20068 Peschiera Borromeo (MI), Italy. TEL 39-2-55302606. FAX 39-2-55302700. E-mail: stammer@micronet.it; URL: http://stammer.convey.it. adv.: B&W page L.1780000, color page L.2430000; trim 210 x 297. circ. 5,000.
    Formerly: Giornale dell'Installatore Telefonico (ISSN 1120-219X)

384   US   ISSN 0040-2656
TK1   CODEN: TLPNAS
TELEPHONY; for today's competing network market. Variant title: Global Telephony. 1901. w. (51/yr.). $52 (foreign $92). Telephony Publishing (Subsidiary of: Intertec Publishing Corp.), One I B M Plaza, Chicago, IL 60611. TEL 312-595-1080. URL: http:/www.internettelephony.com. (Subscr. to: Intertec Publishing Corp., 9800 Metcalf, Overland Park, KS 66212-2215. TEL 800-441-0294. FAX 913-967-1903) Ed. Dir. Steve Titch. adv.; bk.rev.; illus.; stat.; s-a. index; circ. 48,307 (controlled). (also avail. in microform from UMI,PMC; reprint service avail. from UMI) **Indexed:** ABI Inform., B.P.I., Bus.Ind., CAD CAM Abstr., Comput.Bus., Comput.Cont., Comput.Dtbs., INSPEC, PROMT, SRI, Tel.Abstr., Tel.Alert, Tr.& Indus.Ind. **Document type:** trade publication.
●Also available online. Vendor(s): Information Access Co., UMI.
—BLDSC (8785.000000); AskIEEE; CASDDS; CISTI; Ei; KR SourceOne; Linda Hall; SWETS; UMI; UnCover. CCC.

621.38   UK
TELEPHONY. w. 71 Coval Ln., Chelmsford, Essex CM1 1TG, England. TEL 44-1245-283984. FAX 44-1245-257630. Ed. John Williamson. circ. 45,000. **Indexed:** B.P.I.

384   US
TELEPHONY'S BUYERS GUIDE. PUBLIC NETWORK TECHNOLOGY SOURCE.* 1895. a. $50. Intertec Publishing Corp. (Chicago), 1 E. IBM Plz., 23rd Fl., Chicago, IL 60611-3586. TEL 800-543-7771. adv. circ. 48,000. **Indexed:** SRI. **Document type:** directory.
    Former titles: Telephony's Directory and Buyers Guide for the Telecommunications Industry; Telephony's Directory and Buyer's Guide for the Telephone Industry; Telephony's Directory of the Telephone Industry (ISSN 0082-2671)

TELEPUBLISHING REPORT. see *PUBLISHING AND BOOK TRADE*

621.38   CN   ISSN 0040-2710
TK5101.A1   CODEN: TLSSAO
TELESIS (OTTAWA). 1967. 3/yr. free to qualified personnel. Bell-Northern Research Ltd., 3500 Carling Ave., Ottawa, ON K1Y 4H7, Canada. TEL 613-765-2520. FAX 613-763-2008. Ed. Jo-Anne Dyer. charts; illus.; circ. 35,000 (controlled). (reprint service avail. from UMI) **Indexed:** ABI Inform., CAD CAM Abstr., Chem.Abstr., Eng.Ind., INSPEC, Sci.Cit.Ind., Tel.Abstr.
●Also available online. Vendor(s): UMI.
—BLDSC (8785.700000); AskIEEE; CISTI; Ei; KR SourceOne; Linda Hall; UMI; UnCover.
    Description: Presents BNR's and Northern Telecom's technical progress to an international audience in telecommunications, office information management systems, industry and government.

384.6   US   ISSN 1074-5823
TK6401
TELETIMES. 1990. bi-m. $50 to non-members; members $10. United States Telephone Association, 1401 H St., N.W., Ste. 600, Washington, DC 20005. TEL 202-326-7300. FAX 202-326-7333. E-mail: csulliva@usta.org; URL: http://www.usta.org. Ed. Cheryl Sullivan.
    Description: Addresses the challenges and opportunities that face the rapidly changing telecommunications industry.

384.1   DK   ISSN 0109-8071
TELEX DANMARK/ANNUAIRE DES ABONNES TELEX DU DANEMARK. 1973. a. DKK 40. Danish Telecommunication Companies, c/o The Copenhagen Telephone Co., Publishing Dept., Ramsingsvej 7, DK-2500 Valby, Denmark.
    Formerly: Telexbog Danmark.

TOLL-FREE DIGEST. see *BUSINESS AND ECONOMICS — Trade And Industrial Directories*

384   FR   ISSN 0082-5980
TRANSTELEL: TRANSMISSIONS, TELECOMMUNICATIONS, ELECTRONIQUE EN FRANCE.* 1962. biennial. Bureau des Relations Exterieures et Sociales, 30 rue Bergere, 75009 Paris, France.

384.6 621.385   NE   ISSN 0920-2706
   CODEN: TRTLEK
TRENDS IN TELECOMMUNICATIONS.* 1985. 3/yr. free. A T & T and Network Systems International, Market Communications, P.O. Box 1168, 1200 BD Hilversum, Netherlands. FAX 31-35-875838. circ. 8,000.
—AskIEEE; KR SourceOne.

384   JA   ISSN 0041-381X
TSUSHIN KOGYO/C I A J JOURNAL. (Text in Japanese) 1953. m. 10800 Yen. Tsushin Kikai Kogyokai - Communications Industry Association of Japan, Sankei Bldg. Annex, 7-2, Ote-machi 1-chome, Chiyoda-ku, Tokyo 100, Japan. TEL 81-3-3231-3156. FAX 81-3-3231-3110. URL: http://www.ciaj.or.jp. Ed. Takayoshi Masuzawa. adv.; bk.rev.; stat.; circ. controlled. **Indexed:** JCT, JTA.
    Description: Contains articles on recent telecommunications developments, including CIAJ activities.

384.6   US   ISSN 0731-8251
HE8801
U.S. RURAL ELECTRIFICATION ADMINISTRATION. ANNUAL STATISTICAL REPORT. RURAL TELEPHONE BORROWERS. 1958. a. $12. U.S. Rural Electrification Administration, Department of Agriculture, Washington, DC 20250. TEL 202-382-8674. FAX 202-382-1915. (Subscr. to: Superintendent of Documents, U.S. Government Printing Office, Box 371954, Pittsburgh, PA 15250-7954. TEL 202-512-1800. FAX 202-512-2250) **Document type:** government publication.
    Formerly: U.S. Rural Electrification Administration. Annual Statistical Report. Rural Telephone Program (ISSN 0083-3185)

384.6   US
UNITED STATES TELEPHONE ASSOCIATION. HOLDING COMPANY REPORT. 1963. a. $75. United States Telephone Association, 1401 H St., N.W., Ste. 600, Washington, DC 20005. TEL 202-326-7300. FAX 202-326-7333. Ed. Amy Fabian. R&P contact: Emy Fabian. stat. circ. 3,000. **Indexed:** SRI. **Document type:** trade publication.
    Formerly: United States Independent Telephone Association. Holding Company Report.

UNITED STATES TELEPHONE ASSOCIATION. STATISTICS OF THE LOCAL EXCHANGE CARRIERS. see *COMMUNICATIONS — Abstracting, Bibliographies, Statistics*

384.6   UK   ISSN 1358-8923
UP TO DATE; one2one magazine for subscribers to mobile phone network. 1994. q. (One2one) Mediamark Publishing International Ltd., 35 Gresse St., Rathbone Pl., London W1P 1PN, England. TEL 44-171-580-3105. FAX 44-171-580-1695. E-mail: 121@mediamark.co.uk; URL: http://www.mediamark.co.uk. Ed. Denise Curtis-Raleigh; Pub. Peter Moore. R&P contact: Peter Moore. circ. 650,000. **Document type:** consumer publication.

384.6   US   ISSN 1058-9090
UTILITY AND TELEPHONE FLEETS. 1987. 8/yr. $22 (Canada $38; elsewhere $50) (effective 1997). Practical Communications, Inc., Box 183, Cary, IL 60013-0183. TEL 847-639-2200. FAX 847-639-9542. Ed. Alan Richter; Pub. Jim Queenan. R&P contact: Alan Richter. circ. 18,000. **Document type:** trade publication.
    Description: For fleet managers and maintenance supervisors employed by telephone companies, utilities, CATV operators, municipalities, public works, and related contractors.

2042 COMMUNICATIONS — TELEVISION AND CABLE

384.5 384.55   US   ISSN 0278-5013
PN1992
VIDEO AGE INTERNATIONAL; the business journal of film, TV broadcasting, cable, pay TV, PPV, home video, DBS, production. 1981. 10/yr. $30 in N. America; elsewhere $45 (includes Who's Who). T V Trade Media, Inc., 216 E. 75th St., Ste. PW, New York, NY 10021. TEL 212-288-3933. FAX 212-734-9033. TELEX 428669 VIDEO. (Alt. addr.: 1328 Westwood Blvd., Ste. 2, Los Angeles, CA 90024) Ed. Dom Serafini; Pub. Dom Serafini. R&P contact: Monica Gorghetto. adv. contact: Dianne Smolen. bk.rev. circ. 15,000. **Document type:** trade publication.
Description: International trade publication for the video industry, including profiles, information, and analysis.

384.6   US
VISIONS (OVERLAND PARK). 1968. bi-w. United Telephone - Midwest, (Subsidiary of: Sprint), 5454 W. 110th St., Overland Park, KS 66211. TEL 913-345-7801. Ed. Vicki Nelsen. circ. 3,900.
Formerly: Midwest Messenger.

VISTAS. see *COMMUNICATIONS*

384.6   MX
VOCES DE TELEFONOS DE MEXICO. 1953. m. free. Telefonos de Mexico, S.A., Via Parque 198, Mexico 5, D.F., Mexico. circ. 15,000.

621.38   UK   ISSN 0967-2052
HE8785
VOICE INTERNATIONAL. bi-m. £60 (outside Europe £68). 41-47 Kings Terrace, London NW1 OJR, England. TEL 44-171-911-6002. FAX 44-171-911-6020. E-mail: voice@emedia. demon.co.uk. Ed. Paul Newton. adv. contact: Jarvis Todd. circ. 15,000. **Document type:** trade publication.
Incorporates: World Telemedia (ISSN 0961-6284); Which was formerly: Audiotex Briefing.
Description: Provides information on voice-processing applications, including reports on product, technical and marketing developments worldwide.

VOICENEWS. see *COMMUNICATIONS — Computer Applications*

384.6 380.1   US   ISSN 8755-2876
HE7771
WASHINGTON TELECOM DIRECTORY. a. $35 (foreign $50). Capitol Publications Inc., Telecom Publishing Group, 1101 King St., Ste. 444, Box 1455, Alexandria, VA 22313-2055. TEL 800-327-7205. FAX 703-739-6490. URL: http://www. telecommunications.com. **Document type:** directory.
Description: Lists telecom contacts in Washington, D.C.: names, phone numbers and addresses for key people at the FCC, Departments of Commerce, Defense, Justice, International Trade Commission, other federal agencies, congressional committees, industry associations, international organizations and public interest groups.

621.385   UK   ISSN 0969-0859
WHAT CELLPHONE. Variant title: What Cellular Phone. 1993. m. £32 (Europe £50; rest of world £60) (effective 1997); newsstand price: £2.95. W V Publications and Exhibitions Ltd., 57-59 Rochester Pl., London NW1 9JU, England. TEL 44-171-485-0011. FAX 44-171-482-6269. (Orders to: ASM Ltd., Unit 6, Pipewell Rdoad Industrial Estate, Desborough, Northants NN14 2SW, England. TEL 44-1536-762860. FAX 44-1536-760306) **Document type:** consumer publication.

384.6   SA   ISSN 1023-179X
WHAT MOBILE AND CELLPHONE MAGAZINE; the magazine for mobile communications. 1994. m. R.53.70; newsstand price: R.8.95. Blah Publishing, P.O. Box 9573, Hennopsmeer 0046, South Africa. adv.; illus.; maps.

384.6   UK
WHAT MOBILE AND CELLPHONE MAGAZINE (UK EDITION). 1993. m. £29.95 (Europe £55; elsewhere £95) (effective 1997); newsstand price: £2.50. Blah Publishing Ltd., 20-26 Brunswick Pl., London N1 6DZ, England. TEL 44-171-251-6688. FAX 44-171-251-6699. E-mail: simon@blah.com. Ed. Simon Rockman; Pub. Simon Rockman. adv.: color page £2100; adv. contact: Chris Hanage. circ. 30,000 (paid). (back issues avail.) **Document type:** consumer publication.
Description: Offers persons looking to purchase mobile or cellular phone equipment and services practical advice. Includes phone and tariff tables.

384.6   US
WIRELESS BUSINESS & TECHNOLOGY. m. free to qualified personnel. Phillips Business Information, Inc., 1201 Seven Locks Rd., Potomac, MD 20854. TEL 301-424-3338. FAX 301-309-3847. E-mail: pbi@phillips.com. Ed. Cindy Stevens. adv.; circ. controlled. (tabloid format; back issues avail.) **Document type:** trade publication.
—CCC.
Incorporates (1989-1997): Wireless Product News (ISSN 1078-9782); Former titles (until 1994): Mobile Product News (ISSN 1044-1190); Mobile Communications Business (ISSN 0897-4802)
Description: Includes new products for the cellular, paging and two-way radio industries.

WIRELESS INDUSTRY DIRECTORY. see *BUSINESS AND ECONOMICS — Trade And Industrial Directories*

384.6 621.38   AT   ISSN 1326-6829
WIRELESS MARKETS - AUSTRALIA AND NEW ZEALAND. 1984. a. Aus.$275 (US Aus.$295; Europe Aus.$300) (effective 1998). Paul Budde Communication Pty. Ltd., 2643 George Downes Dr., Bucketty, N.S.W. 2250, Australia. TEL 61-49-988144. FAX 61-49-988247. E-mail: pbc@budde.com.au; URL: http://www.budde.com.au. Ed. Paul Budde. **Document type:** directory.
Supersedes in part: Directory of Electronic Services and Communications Networks in Australia and New Zealand (ISSN 1322-350X)
Description: Covers cellular, paging, satellite, mobile data, MDS and telemetry services and networks. Includes information on developments and trends.

WIRELESS PERSONAL COMMUNICATIONS; an international journal. see *COMMUNICATIONS — Radio*

384.6   US   ISSN 1075-413X
WIRELESS TELECOM INVESTOR. 1988. m. $795 (effective 1997). Paul Kagan Associates, Inc., 126 Clock Tower Place, Carmel, CA 93923. TEL 408-625-3225. FAX 408-625-3225.
Formerly: Cellular Investor (ISSN 0898-0403)
Description: Analyzes private and public values of cellular telephone companies, PCS, ESMR and paging companies.

621.38   UK
WORLD CELLULAR REPORTS. 5/yr. £7300($34700) (effective 1997). E M C Publications, Holt Cottage, Kingston Hill, Kingston-upon-Thames, Surrey KT2 7JH, England. TEL 44-181-546-0841. FAX 44-181-549-8558. **Document type:** trade publication.
Description: Analyzes and forecasts the following world markets: cellular networks, operators, and subscribers; cellular terminal manufacturers; GSM and DCS-1800 Markets and Forecasts; GSM terminals and distribution; TACS markets and products.

384.5   US
THE WORLD WIRELESS BEACON. 1989. q. $15 includes membership (effective Jan. 1994). Society of Wireless Pioneers, 6289 Olde Orchard Dr., Columbus, OH 43213-3416. TEL 614-866-6289. E-mail: w8tp@jun.com. (Subscr. to: Box 86, Geyserville CA 95441) Ed. Theodore Phelps; Pub. Theodore Phelps. R&P contact: Theodore Phelps. adv.; bk.rev. circ. 3,000. (also avail. in talking book; back issues avail.) **Document type:** newsletter.
Description: Includes experiences and anecdotes from members who are or were radio-telegraph operators in the U.S. Merchant Marine or military services. Also covers history of maritime and military communications.

384.6   US
WORLDWIDE TELECOM. 1989. m. $150 (outside N. America $165). Worldwide Videotex, Box 3273, Boynton Beach, FL 33424-3273. TEL 407-738-2276. Ed. Mark Wright; Pub. Mark Wright. bk.rev. (back issues avail.) **Document type:** newsletter.
●Also available online. **Vendor(s):** Data-Star, Information Access Co., Knight-Ridder Information, Inc., NewsNet (TE19).
Description: Provides the news and information on international telecommunications products, services, and contracts with emphasis on U.S. telecommunications companies doing business in foreign markets and on products with a potential market overseas.

ZIP - AREA CODE DIRECTORY. see *COMMUNICATIONS — Postal Affairs*

384   US
4 1 1 NEWSLETTER. 1979. bi-w. $379. (Center for Communications Management Information) C C M I, 11300 Rockville Pike, Ste. 1100, Rockville, MD 20852-3030. TEL 301-816-8950. FAX 301-816-8945. Ed. Steve Pastorkovich; Pub. George David. (back issues avail.) **Document type:** newsletter.
●Also available online. **Vendor(s):** Data-Star (PTBN), Knight-Ridder Information, Inc. (File no.636), NewsNet (TE95).
Formerly: Telephone Angles.
Description: Directed to telecom managers who oversee voice communications; it gives advice for trimming expenses, boosting productivity, buying equipment and the pros and cons of new systems.

384.6 621.387   UK   ISSN 0955-9760
1992 SINGLE MARKET COMMUNICATIONS REVIEW. 1989. q. £55($150) Kline Publishing Ltd., 4-6 Station Parade, Balham High Rd., London SW12 9AD, England. TEL 0181-673-7783. (Subscr. to: Tempest Public Relations, P.O. Box 601, London SW12 9BU, England) Ed. Hugh Chaloner. circ. 17,000. (back issues avail.)
—SWETS.

COMMUNICATIONS — Television And Cable

A B C NEWS INDEX. see *COMMUNICATIONS — Abstracting, Bibliographies, Statistics*

384.54   MY   ISSN 0126-6209
TK6630.A1
A B U TECHNICAL REVIEW. (Text in English) 1969. bi-m. M.$121.50($25) Asia - Pacific Broadcasting Union, P.O. Box 1164, 59700 Kuala Lumpur, Malaysia. TEL 60-3-2823108. FAX 60-3-2825292 TELEX MA-32227-ABU. Ed. O.P. Khushu. adv.; bk.rev.; index. circ. 1,000. (back issues avail.) **Indexed:** INSPEC (1992-). **Document type:** trade publication, newsletter.
—BLDSC (0570.300000); AskIEEE; CISTI; Ei; KR SourceOne.
Description: Contains news, technical developments and equipment trends in the field of engineering.

621.38 384   UK
A C E INTERNATIONAL. (Text in English, French, German, Italian) 1977. 10/yr. $50. A C E Publishing Ltd., Queensway House, 2 Queensway House, Redhill, Surrey RH1 1QS, England. Ed. Roge Packer. adv. circ. 25,000.

384.55   AT
A C T A C NEWSLETTER. 1974. 4/yr. Aus.$20. Australian Children's Television Action Committee, 569 Nicholson St., North Carlton, Vic. 3054, Australia. TEL 61-3-3870177. FAX 61-3-387865 Ed. Jo James. bk.rev. circ. 2,000. (back issues ava **Document type:** newsletter.

A F C NEWS. (Australian Film Commission) see *MOTIC PICTURES*

A F T R A. (American Federation of Television and Ra Artists) see *LABOR UNIONS*

A M I A NEWSLETTER. (Association of Moving Image Archivists) see *LIBRARY AND INFORMATION SCIENCES*

COMMUNICATIONS — TELEVISION AND CABLE

621.38　　　　US　　ISSN 1047-3076
TK9956
A M S A T JOURNAL. (Amateur Satellite) 1981. w. $30 (Canada $36; elsewhere $45). Radio Amateur Satellite Corporation, 850 Sligo Ave., No. 600, Silver Spring, MD 20910. TEL 301-589-6062. Ed. Russ Tillman. adv. circ. 7,000. (back issues avail.)
　Formerly: Amateur Satellite Report (ISSN 0889-6089)

621.389　　　　US
A-V ADVISOR. (Audio-Visual) m. 66 12th St., Atlanta, GA 30309. TEL 404-876-7841. FAX 404-875-5258. Ed. Bill Weber.

384.55　　　　NE　　ISSN 0928-8562
A V JOURNAAL; tweewekelijks nieuwsbulletin voor de audiovisuele branche. 1992. fortn. fl.85. Televak Uitgeverij N.V., Postbus 75985, 1070 AZ Amsterdam, Netherlands. TEL 31-20-6659220. FAX 31-20-6657316. Ed. J. Boers. adv. contact: Maarten Ponssen. illus.; tr.lit.; circ. 2,500 (paid). **Document type:** trade publication.

621.38　　　　GW
A V KANAL; Magazin fuer audiovisuelle Kommunikation. 1985. s-a. free. A V Studios GmbH, Reinsburgstr. 97, 70178 Stuttgart, Germany. Eds. Norbert W. Daldrop, Guenter Rein. bk.rev.; film rev. circ. 8,000. (back issues avail.) **Document type:** trade publication.

621.38　　　　NE　　ISSN 0923-7054
A V PROF. (Audio Visual); vakmagazine over professioneel beeld en geluid. 1987. 10/yr. fl.140 (effective 1997). Wegener Tijdschriften Groep B.V., Postbus 1860, 1110 CD Diemen, Netherlands. TEL 31-20-6603407. FAX 31-20-6606354. Ed. Tom Dalinghaus. circ. 3,043. **Document type:** trade publication.

791.4　　　　NE　　ISSN 0929-7758
A V R O BODE. Key Title: AVRO-Bode. (Text in Dutch) 1929. w. fl.72.45; newsstand price: fl.1.75. B.V. Programmabladen, Postbus 20002, 1202 AB Hilversum, Netherlands. TEL 31-35-6726715. FAX 31-35-6726712. Ed. P.A. Lichtenauer; Pub. F.N.W.M. Marechal. adv. page fl.19107, color page fl.33147; trim 212 x 262; adv. contact: A. Koopmans. film rev.; play rev.; illus.; circ. 799,121 (paid). **Document type:** consumer publication.
　Formerly: TeleVizier (ISSN 0049-3325)
　Description: Provides radio and television listings, as well as news and information on showbiz, movies, stars and related topics.

ACADEMY PLAYERS DIRECTORY. see MOTION PICTURES

ACTORS C D - R O M. see THEATER

ACTORS SPOTLIGHT CASTING DIRECTORY. see THEATER

ACTRESSES C D - R O M. see THEATER

ACTRESSES SPOTLIGHT CASTING DIRECTORY. see THEATER

AD - TIER NEWSLETTER. see ADVERTISING AND PUBLIC RELATIONS

384.55　　　　CN　　ISSN 0847-9097
ADBUSTERS QUARTERLY; journal of the mental environment. 1989. q. Can.$18 to individuals (foreign Can.$32); institutions Can.$36 (effective 1997). Adbusters Media Foundation, 1243 W. Seventh Ave., Vancouver, BC V6H 1B7, Canada. TEL 604-736-9401. FAX 604-737-6021. E-mail: adbusters@adbusters.org; URL: http://www.adbusters.org. Ed. Kalle Lasn; Pub. Kalle Lasn. R&P contact: Allan Macdonald. adv.: B&W page Can.$500, color page Can.$1000; 8 1/2 x 10 1/2; adv. contact: Allen Macdonald. bk.rev. circ. 30,000. Indexed: Alt.Press Ind., Can.B.P.I. **Document type:** consumer publication.
　—CCC.
　Description: For environmental, anti-commercial and media literacy groups, advertising executives and academics.

AGENCIES: WHAT THE ACTOR NEEDS TO KNOW. see BUSINESS AND ECONOMICS — Trade And Industrial Directories

AGENDA; magazine for media, education and culture. see EDUCATION — Adult Education

ALMANACCO DI FOTOGRAFARE. see PHOTOGRAPHY

384.54 621.389　　　IT
ALMANACCO DI STEREO. a. L.15000 per no. Editori Associati, Via Brenta 13, 00198 Rome, Italy. TEL 39-6-8417179. Ed. Egidio Mancianti. adv. contact: Paolo De Petris. **Document type:** consumer publication.

384　　　　IT
ALTRIMEDIA. 1976. m. L.35000. Media Edizioni srl., Via Gaffurio 4, 20124 Milan, Italy. Ed. Edoardo Fleischner. adv. circ. 42,000.

ANNUAIRE DU CINEMA, TELEVISION, VIDEO. see MOTION PICTURES

ANNUARIO DEGLI ATTORI/EUROPEAN PLAYERS' DIRECTORY. see MOTION PICTURES

384.55　　　　IT　　ISSN 1123-6523
ANNUARIO EUROSAT. 1993. a. L.120000 (effective 1997). Gruppo Editoriale J C E, Via Ferri 6, 20092 Cinisello Balsamo (MI), Italy. TEL 39-2-660251. FAX 39-2-6127620. E-mail: info@jce.it; URL: http://www.jce.it. Ed. Jacopo Castelfranchi. adv.: B&W page L.4800000, page color L.7500000; trim 210 X 276. circ. 80,000. **Document type:** consumer publication.
　Formerly (until 1995): Satellite Eurosat Annuario (ISSN 1123-1068)
　Description: Describes components of satellite reception equipments, interviews leaders of the field and provides with information on how to install a satellite reception equipment.

621.38　　　　IT　　ISSN 0003-5386
ANTENNA; rassegna mensile di tecnica elettronica. 1928. m. L.10000. Editrice Il Rostro, Via Monte Generoso 6-A, Milan, Italy. Ed. Alfonso Giovene. adv.; charts; illus.; index. circ. 25,000. Indexed: INSPEC. —CISTI.

384.5　　　　BL　　ISSN 0101-9112
ANTENNA - ELETRONICA POPULAR. 1926. m. R.27($30) for 6 nos. (effective 1996). Antenna Edicoes Tecnicas Ltda., Av. Marechal Floriano 143, 20080-005 Rio de Janeiro RJ, Brazil. TEL 55-21-223-2442. FAX 55-21-263-8840. adv. contact: Helio Santos. bk.rev.; s-a. index. circ. 19,550. **Document type:** consumer publication.
　—CCC.
　Formed by the merger of: Eletronica Popular (ISSN 0013-6085); Antenna (ISSN 0003-5378)

ARAB FILM AND TELEVISION CENTER NEWS. see MOTION PICTURES

384.5　　　　UK　　ISSN 0004-1335
ARIEL. vol.15, 1970. w. British Broadcasting Corp., 4 Cavendish Sq., Rm. 101A, London W1A 1AA, England. Ed. Robin Reynolds. adv.; bk.rev.; charts; illus. Indexed: Arts & Hum.Cit.Ind., Mid.East: Abstr.& Ind.

ASIA IMAGE. see COMMUNICATIONS — Radio

621.38　　　　SI
ASIA - PACIFIC BROADCASTING. m. $70 in Asia; elsewhere $80. Miller Freeman Pte. Ltd., 100 Beach Rd., 26-00 Shaw Towers, Singapore 0718, Singapore. TEL 294-3366. FAX 298-5534. Ed. Gary Hong. adv. contact: Ter Hui Peng. circ. 7,885. (back issues avail.) **Document type:** trade publication.
　Description: Reviews of hardware, software available to radio and TV studios, production houses, and recording studios.

384.55 621.388　　　UK
▼**ASIA - PACIFIC SATELLITE.** 1995. q. £30($55) Icom Publications Ltd., Chancery House, St. Nicholas Way, Sutton, Surrey SM1 1JB, England. TEL 44-181-642-1117. FAX 44-181-642-1941. E-mail: aps@icompub.demon.co.uk. Ed. D. Millis; Pub. Alec Barton. adv.: B&W page $3060, color page $4510; trim 297 x 210; adv. contact: C. Ayres. circ. 7,503 (controlled). **Document type:** trade publication.
　Description: Contains news, market reports, and technical and business features on the satellite market in the Asia-Pacific region.

621.388　　　　AT
AUSTRALASIAN SUPERHIGHWAYS NEWSLETTER. 1994. m. Aus.$398 (US Aus.$430; Europe Aus.$435) (effective 1998). Paul Budde Communication Pty. Ltd., 2643 George Downs Dr., Bucketty, N.S.W. 2250, Australia. TEL 61-49-988144. FAX 61-49-988247. E-mail: pbc@budde.com.au; URL: http://www.budde.com.au. R&P contact: Paul Budde. circ. 150. **Document type:** newsletter.
　Formerly: Australasian Cable and Pay T V Newsletter (ISSN 1322-3534)
　Description: Covers such topics as superhighways and superskyway; cable, satellite, pay TV and MDS; video-on-demand, video servers and set-top boxes; interactive TV, internet, online and hybrid ramps; multimedia; HDTV; teleconferencing; programming and content; homeshopping and consumer electronics regulatory issues; national and international developments.

AUSTRALIAN FILM, TELEVISION AND RADIO SCHOOL ANNUAL REPORT. see EDUCATION — Higher Education

AUSTRALIAN FILM, TELEVISION AND RADIO SCHOOL HANDBOOK. see EDUCATION — Higher Education

AVIATION WEEK VIDEO. see AERONAUTICS AND SPACE FLIGHT

B B C ON AIR. see COMMUNICATIONS — Radio

B F I FILM AND TELEVISION HANDBOOK (YEAR). (British Film Institute) see MOTION PICTURES

384.55　　　　US
B I B CHANNELS; what's new in domestic and international television programming and syndication. (Supplement to: B I B Television Programming Source Books; World Guide to Television) 1992. q. free to Television Programming Source Books subscribers. North American Publishing Co., 401 N. Broad St., Philadelphia, PA 19108. TEL 215-238-5300. FAX 215-238-5457.
　Description: Features updates on the latest program availabilities.

BACK STAGE; the performing arts weekly. see THEATER

BACK STAGE WEST; the performing arts weekly. see THEATER

621.38　　　　US
HE8689.8
BACON'S RADIO & T V CABLE DIRECTORIES. a. (in 2 vols.) $280. Bacon's Publishing Company, Inc., 332 S. Michigan Ave., Ste. 900, Chicago, IL 60604. TEL 312-922-2400. FAX 312-922-3127. Ed. Ruth McFarland. circ. 6,000. **Document type:** directory.
　Formerly: Bacon's Radio - T V Directory (ISSN 0891-0103)
　Description: Directory of all US broadcast media.

BETTER RADIO AND TELEVISION. see COMMUNICATIONS — Radio

621.388　　　　UK　　ISSN 1354-2605
BETTER SATELLITE. 1993. q. £9.20 (Europe £15; rest of world £19) (effective 1997); newsstand price: £2.50. W V Publications and Exhibitions Ltd., 57-59 Rochester Pl., London NW1 9JU, England. TEL 44-171-485-0011. FAX 44-171-482-6269. (Orders to: ASM Ltd., Unit 6, Pipewell Road Industrial Estate, Desborough, Northants NN14 2SW, England. TEL 44-1536-762860. FAX 44-1536-760306) **Document type:** consumer publication.

BIANCO E NERO. see MOTION PICTURES

BIBLIOGRAPHY ON CABLE TELEVISION. see COMMUNICATIONS — Abstracting, Bibliographies, Statistics

COMMUNICATIONS — TELEVISION AND CABLE

791.45 US
BIOGRAPHY (NEW YORK). m. $18; newsstand price: $2.99. Arts & Entertainment, 235 E. 45th St., New York, NY 10017. TEL 212-210-9759. E-mail: 0007536069@mcimail.com; URL: http://www.biography.com/read/read.html. (Subscr. to: Box 7418, Red Oak, IA 51591-0418. TEL 800-666-9264) Ed. Paulette McLeod; Pub. Paulette McLeod. adv. contact: Paulette McLeod. (back issues avail.) **Document type:** consumer publication.
Former titles (until 1997): A and E Monthly (ISSN 1083-1738); A and E Program Guide.
Description: Features current and historical stories and articles about the famous and the infamous. Includes program listings for the A&E Network and The History Channel.

BLUE BOOK OF BRITISH BROADCASTING. see *BUSINESS AND ECONOMICS — Trade And Industrial Directories*

384.5 US
BLUE LIGHTS. bi-m. Spotlight Starman, 16563 Ellen Springs Dr., Lower Lake, CA 95457. Ed. Vicki Werkley. **Document type:** newsletter.
Description: Covers TV and videotapes.

621.38 IT ISSN 0006-6877
BOLLETTINO TECNICO GELOSO;* pubblicazione trimestrale di radiofonia, televisione e scienze affini. 1932. q. L.500. Geloso S.p.A., Via Brenta 29, 20139 Milan, Italy. circ. 80,000.

621.384 SA
BOPHUTHATSWANA BROADCASTING CORPORATION. ANNUAL REPORT. a. Bophuthatswana Broadcasting Corporation, Private Bag X2150, 8681 Mmabatho, North West Province, South Africa. TEL 27-140-897111. FAX 27-140-897299. **Document type:** corporate report.

791.4 CN ISSN 1182-9893
BOW VALLEY THIS WEEK. 1987. w. Box 129, 223 Bear St., Banff, AB T0L 0C0, Canada. TEL 403-762-2453. FAX 403-762-5274. adv. circ. 10,450.
Description: Features television listings and entertainment news.

BRAILLE TELEVISION TIMES. see *HANDICAPPED — Visually Impaired*

BRITAIN'S TELEVISION AND RADIO INDUSTRY. see *BUSINESS AND ECONOMICS — Trade And Industrial Directories*

384 UK ISSN 0040-2788
BROADCAST. 1960. w. £85. E M A P Media (Subsidiary of: E M A P Business Communications), 33-39 Bowling Green Ln., London EC1R 0DA, England. TEL 44-171-505-8014. FAX 44-171-505-8050. E-mail: bcasted@media.emap.co.uk. (Subscr. to: RSS, Lansdowne Mews, 196 High St., Tonbridge, Kent TN9 1BR, England. TEL 44-1732-770523. FAX 44-1732-361708) Ed. Mike Jones; Pub. Jon Baver. adv.; bk.rev.; charts; illus.; stat.; tele.rev. circ. 11,042. **Indexed:** Int.Ind.Film Per. **Document type:** trade publication.
Formerly (until 1973): Television Mail; Incorporates (1983-1985): Television Weekly (ISSN 0264-2905).

BROADCAST BANKER - BROKER. see *BUSINESS AND ECONOMICS — Banking And Finance*

621.38 384 US ISSN 0007-1994
TK6540
BROADCAST ENGINEERING; journal of broadcast technology. Spanish edition (ISSN 1060-0787) 1959. m. $50 (free to qualified personnel). Intertec Publishing Corp., 9800 Metcalf, Overland Park, KS 66212-2215. TEL 913-341-1300. FAX 913-967-1898. Ed. Brad Dick. bk.rev.; charts; illus.; stat.; tr.lit.; index. circ. 35,500. (also avail. in microform from UMI; reprint service avail. from UMI) **Document type:** trade publication.
—BLDSC (2348.900000); CISTI; Linda Hall; SWETS; UMI; UnCover. **CCC.**

621.38 US ISSN 1060-0787
BROADCAST ENGINEERING (SPANISH EDITION). English edition (ISSN 0007-1994) (Editions in English, Spanish) 1988. s-a. Intertec Publishing Corp., 9800 Metcalf, Overland Park, KS 66212-2215. TEL 913-341-1300. FAX 913-967-1898. Ed. Carl Bentz. adv. circ. 7,500. **Document type:** trade publication.
—CCC.
Description: For management and technical personnel at radio and TV studios, recording studios, and government agencies throughout the Americas and in Spain and Portugal.

621.38 US
BROADCAST ENGINEERING EQUIPMENT REFERENCE MANUAL. (Special 13th issue of Broadcast Engineering) 1981. a. $20 (free to qualified personnel). Intertec Publishing Corp., 9800 Metcalf, Overland Park, KS 66212-2215. TEL 913-888-4664. FAX 913-541-6697. Ed. Carl Bentz. circ. 35,500. (back issues avail.) **Document type:** directory.
—UMI.
Formerly: Broadcast Engineering Spec Book.

621.38 AT ISSN 0155-3720
BROADCAST ENGINEERING NEWS. 1974. m. Aus.$66($104) (effective 1996). Reed Business Publishing Pty. Ltd. (Subsidiary of: Reed International PLC), P.O. Box 5487, W. Chatswood, N.S.W. 2057, Australia. TEL 61-2-372-5222. FAX 61-2-419-7399. Ed. Bill Dawes. circ. 3,648. (tabloid format)
Description: Reflects technological and legislative change in the areas of duplication, transmission and signal duplication, desktop video and multimedia, video production, professional audio and more.

BROADCAST INVESTOR; newsletter on radio-TV station finance. see *BUSINESS AND ECONOMICS — Investments*

621.38 332.6 US ISSN 0736-9069
BROADCAST INVESTOR CHARTS; monthly service showing price movements of broadcast stocks over two-year spans. 1983. m. $425. Paul Kagan Associates, Inc., 126 Clock Tower Place, Carmel, CA 93923. TEL 408-624-1536. FAX 408-625-3225. TELEX 408-625-3225. charts. (reprint service avail.)
Description: Chart service on stock price movements of 41 publicly held broadcast companies for the past two years.

338 UK ISSN 0967-2095
BROADCAST PRODUCTION GUIDE. 1982. a. £45. E M A P Media (Subsidiary of: E M A P Business Communications), 33-39 Bowling Green Ln., London EC1R 0DA, England. TEL 44-171-505-8328. FAX 44-171-505-8336. E-mail: bcasted@media.emap.co.uk. (Subscr. to: RSS, Lansdowne Mews, 196 High St., Tonbridge, Kent TN9 1BR, England. TEL 44-1732-770823. FAX 44-1732-361708) Pub. Martin Jackson. adv. **Document type:** directory.
Description: Lists names and addresses of independent production companies and facility houses for the broadcasting industry.

BROADCAST STATS. see *COMMUNICATIONS — Abstracting, Bibliographies, Statistics*

384 UK
BROADCAST YEARBOOK AND DIARY. 1961. a. £25. E M A P Media (Subsidiary of: E M A P Business Communications), 33-39 Bowling Green Ln., London EC1R 0DA, England. TEL 44-171-505-8014. FAX 44-171-505-8030. E-mail: bcasted@media.emap.co.ik. (Subscr. to: RSS, Lansdowne Mews, 196 High St., Tonbridge, Kent TN9 1BR, England. TEL 44-1732-770823. FAX 44-1732-361708) Pub. Jon Baver. adv. circ. 1,000. **Document type:** trade publication.

384.55 791.43 AT
BROADCASTAWAY. s-a. Techtonic Webzine, E-mail: jjc@merlin.com.au; URL: http://www.merlin.com.au/tech/index.html. Ed. Jeffrey Cook.
●Available only online.
Description: Publishes short articles on Australian and international film and television, culture and communications.

384.5 CN ISSN 0008-3038
BROADCASTER. 1942. m. (s-a. directory nos.). Can.$37($37) (foreign Can.$50) (effective 1997). Southam Magazine Group, 1450 Don Mills Rd., Don Mills, ON M3B 2X7, Canada. TEL 416-445-6641. FAX 416-442-2213. Ed. John Bugailiskis. adv.; bk.rev. circ. 7,844. (also avail. in microfilm from CML) **Indexed:** Can.B.P.I.
Formerly: Canadian Broadcaster.
Description: Covers radio and television communications industries in Canada.

384.5 US ISSN 1068-6827
TK6540
BROADCASTING & CABLE. 1931. w. $117 (foreign $320). Cahners Publishing Company (Washington), Entertainment Division, Division of Reed Elsevier Inc., 1705 DeSales St., N.W., Washington, DC 20036. TEL 202-659-2340. FAX 202-429-0651. E-mail: r.higgs@b&c.cahners.com; URL: http://www.broadcastingcable.com/. (Subscr. to: Box 6399, Torrence, CA 90504. TEL 800-554-5729) Ed. Donald West; Pub. Peggy Conlon. adv. contact: Gary Rubin. bk.rev.; charts; illus.; stat.; cum.index: 1972-1981; circ. 35,000 (paid). (also avail. in microfilm from UMI; microfiche from CIS; reprint service avail. from UMI) **Indexed:** ABI Inform. (1976-1977), Acad.Ind., B.P.I., Biog.Ind., Bus.Ind., CAD CAM Abstr., Chic.Per.Ind., Ind.Per.Art.Relat.Law, P.A.I.S., PROMT, SRI, Tel.Abstr., Tr.& Indus.Ind. (1981-). **Document type:** trade publication.
●Also available online. Vendor(s): Information Access Co., Knight-Ridder Information, Inc., Lexis-Nexis.
—BLDSC (2349.076300); KR SourceOne; SWETS; UMI; UnCover. **CCC.**
Former titles (until Mar. 1993): Broadcasting (Washington) (ISSN 0007-2028); (until Oct. 1957): Broadcasting Telecasting; (until 1948): Broadcasting - The News Magazine of the Fifth Estate; Incorporates (in 1961): Television; (in 1953): Telecast; (in 1933): Broadcast Reporter; Broadcast Advertising.
Description: Covers the broadcasting and cable industries in-depth, including news and reports on radio, television, cable and satellite. Features legislative updates, radio and television ownership changes, new stations, facilities changes, band allocations, classified, calendar of events and major meetings, and more.

384.5 US
BROADCASTING & CABLE INTERNATIONAL. 1983. bi-m. Cahners Publishing Company (New York), Division Reed Elsevier Inc., 245 W. 17th St., New York, NY 10011. TEL 212-337-6940. FAX 212-337-7028. URL: http://www.cahners.com/mainmag/bci.htm. Ed. Donald V. West; Pub. Peggy Conlon. adv.: page $1835; trim 7 7/8 x 10 1/2; adv. contact: Randi Schatz. film rev.; tele.rev.; charts; illus.; mkt.; tr.lit.; circ. 13,600. (back issues avail.) **Document type:** trade publication.
—CCC.
Formerly (until Sep. 1993): Broadcasting Abroad (ISSN 1064-6124)
Description: An international publication dedicated to providing global information on radio, television, cable and satellites.

791.4 US ISSN 0000-1511
HE8689
BROADCASTING & CABLE YEARBOOK. (Issued in 2 vols.) 1980. a. £160($179.95) R.R. Bowker, A Division of Reed Elsevier Inc., 121 Chanlon Rd., New Providence, NJ 07974. TEL 908-665-2823. FAX 908-771-7725. E-mail: info@bowker.com; URL: http://www.bowker.com. (Subscr. to: Order Dept., Box 31, New Providence, NJ 07974-9903. TEL 800-521-8110) adv. circ. 15,000. pp./issue: 2100. (also avail. in microfiche from CIS) **Indexed:** SRI. **Document type:** directory.
—BLDSC (2349.076600); CISTI. **CCC.**
Former titles (until 1993): Broadcasting and Cable Market Place (ISSN 0000-1384); (until 1992): Broadcasting Yearbook (ISSN 1051-1792); (until 1990): Broadcasting Cable Yearbook (ISSN 1045-9162); (until 1989): Broadcasting, Cablecasting Yearbook (ISSN 0732-7196); (until 1982): Broadcasting Cable Yearbook (ISSN 0277-3678); Which was formed by the merger of (1968-1980): Broadcasting Yearbook (ISSN 0068-2713); (19??-1980): Broadcasting, Cable Sourcebook (ISSN 0097-8132); Former titles: Broadcasting Yearbook - Marketbook Issue (ISSN 0731-6836); (until 1960): Broadcasting Yearbook Issue (ISSN 0731-6828); Which was formed by the 1958 merger of: Broadcasting Telecasting, Broadcasting Yearbook - Marketbook Issue (ISSN 0731-681X); Broadcasting Telecasting, Telecasting Yearbook - Marketbook Issue (ISSN 0731-6801); Which was formerly (until 1954): Broadcasting Telecasting, Telecasting Yearbook Issue (ISSN 0731-6569); (until 1953): Broadcasting Telecasting, Telecasting Yearbook (ISSN 0731-6542); Which superseded in part (1948-1951): Broadcasting Telecasting Yearbook (ISSN 0731-6534).
Description: Provides a comprehensive guide to the broadcasting and cable industries. Contains listings of U.S. and Canadian radio stations and television stations, top cable MSOs and their systems, satellite services, programming services, production services, manufacturing services, advertising and marketing services (including Arbitron and Nielsen market data), industry books, periodicals and videos, communications lawyers, industry trade shows and more. Includes yellow pages for radio, TV and cable stations and contacts.

384.55 UK ISSN 1071-9261
BROADCASTING & CABLE'S T V INTERNATIONAL NEWSLETTER. 1993. bi-m. $565. Baskerville Communications Corp. (Subsidiary of: Sage Publications Company), 2455 Teller Rd., Thousand Oaks, CA 91320. TEL 805-499-2622. FAX 805-499-9656. URL: http://www.baskerville.co.uk. (Alt. addr.: Baskerville Communications, Box 6589, Torrance, CA 90504-9960. TEL 310-978-6073. FAX 310-978-6072) Ed. Meredith Amdur; Pub. Tim Baskerville. R&P contact: Meredith Amdur. TEL 44-171-437-0493. adv. contact: Randi Schatz. circ. 1,500 (paid). **Document type:** newsletter.

384.5 US ISSN 0161-5823
KF2801.A3
BROADCASTING AND THE LAW. 1970. m. $150. Broadcasting and the Law, Inc., 1 S.E. Third Ave., Ste. 1450, Miami, FL 33131-1715. TEL 305-530-8322. FAX 305-530-9417. Ed. Edward S. Hammerman; Pub. Matthew Leibowitz. R&P contact: Edward S. Hammerman. index. circ. 7,000. (looseleaf format) **Document type:** newsletter.
Formerly (until 1985): Perry's Broadcasting and the Law.
Description: Provides current information about regulations and all aspects of station operations to help cut legal costs.

384.54 384.554 US
HE8689.8
BROADCASTING BOARD OF GOVERNORS. ANNUAL REPORT. a. free. Broadcasting Board of Governors, 330 Independence Ave. S.W., Ste. 3360, Washington, DC 20547. TEL 202-401-3736. **Document type:** government publication.
Formerly: Board for International Broadcasting. Annual Report (ISSN 0362-8272)

BROADCASTING IN THE U K. see *COMMUNICATIONS — Radio*

384.554 UK ISSN 0954-2620
BROADCASTING PRESS DIGEST. 1989. w. £850. Broadcasting Information Bureau, 3 Abbey Orchard St., Ste. 20, Westminster, London SW1P 2JJ, England. TEL 01-222-1330. Ed. Graham Lea.
Description: Aimed at broadcasting executives, independent producers, and others who need a summary of what is happening in the broadcasting world.

621.388 791.4 US
THE BULLET (NASHVILLE). 1982. 3/yr. $10. Andy Griffith Show Rerun Watchers Club, 9 Music Sq. S., Ste. 146, Nashville, TN 37203-3203. Ed. Jim Clark. bk.rev.; illus. circ. 15,000. (looseleaf format; back issues avail.) **Document type:** newsletter.
Description: Covers news and products of interest to fans of the Andy Griffith Show.

BURGUNDY BOOK OF EUROPEAN BROADCASTING. see *BUSINESS AND ECONOMICS — Trade And Industrial Directories*

384.55 US ISSN 1052-3138
HD30.34
THE BUSINESS TELEVISION DIRECTORY. 1988-199? a. Telehealth Associates, 11 Willow St., Needham, MA 02192. **Document type:** directory.

621.388 JA ISSN 0288-9323
C B C GIJUTSU HOKOKUKAI/C B C TECHNICAL INFORMATION. (Text in Japanese) 1953. a. Chubu - Nippon Broadcasting Co., 2-8, Shinsakae 1-chome, Naka-ku, Nagoya-shi, Aichi-ken 460, Japan.

384.55 UK ISSN 1352-2272
C C T V TODAY. 1994. bi-m. £34 (overseas £44) (effective 1998). Paramount Publishing Ltd., 17-21 Shenley Rd., Borehamwood, Herts. WD6 1RT, England. TEL 44-181-207-5599. FAX 44-181-207-2598. Ed. Ian Drury. R&P contact: Ian Drury. adv. contact: John McDowell. **Document type:** trade publication.

C D - R O M WORLD; the magazine and review for CD-ROM users. see *LIBRARY AND INFORMATION SCIENCES*

791 BE
C I L E C T NEWS. 1978. q. free. Centre International de Liaison des Ecoles de Cinema et de Television - International Liaison Centre for Cinema and Television Schools, CILECT Secretariat, Rue Theresienne, 8, 1000 Brussels, Belgium. TEL 32-2-5119839. FAX 32-2-5110035. E-mail: hver.cilect@skynet.be; URL: http://www.leland.stanford.edu/~hbreit/cilect/. Ed. Henry Verhasselt. R&P contact: Henry Verhasselt. bk.rev.; circ. 400 (controlled). **Document type:** newsletter.
Former titles: C I L E C T Newsletter (ISSN 1036-2215); C I L E C T News; Centre International de Liaison des Ecoles de Cinema et de Television. Bulletin d'Informations (ISSN 0528-4759)
Description: Contains information on film schools.

C I N C O M: COURSES IN COMMUNICATIONS. (Communications Institute) see *EDUCATION — Guides To Schools And Colleges*

C I R M. (Centro Internazionale Radio-Medico) see *MEDICAL SCIENCES*

C M J NEW MUSIC REPORT. (College Media Journal) see *MUSIC*

384.554 GW
C O M FUER EINSTEIGER. 1987. s-a. Neue Mediengesellschaft Ulm mbH, Konrad-Celtis-Str. 77, 81369 Munich, Germany. TEL 49-89-74117190. FAX 49-89-74117195. Ed. Guenter Goetz. circ. 40,000. **Document type:** trade publication.
Former titles: Btx fuer Einsteiger (ISSN 0948-521X); Bildschirmtext fuer Einsteiger (ISSN 0932-1977)

384 US
C P B TODAY. 1969. m. free. Corporation for Public Broadcasting, 901 E St., N.W., Washington, DC 20004-2037. TEL 202-879-9600. FAX 202-783-1039. Dir. Cristina DelSesto. bk.rev. circ. 15,000. **Document type:** newsletter.
Former titles (until Sep. 1993): C P B Report; (until Sep. 1974): Corporation for Public Broadcasting. Memo.

621.388 UK CODEN: CTEVB3
C T E. (Cable Telecommunication Engineering); the cable communications quarterly. q. £35 in Europe; elsewhere £45 (effective 1997). (Society of Cable Telecommunications Engineers) David Sheppard & Associates, 35 Picadilly, London W1V 1PB, England. TEL 44-171-734-6143. FAX 44-171-734-1737. Ed. Dan Smart. adv. contact: Nicola Heddle. bk.rev.; circ. 1,000 (paid); 1,400. **Indexed:** INSPEC (1968-1989). **Document type:** trade publication.
—AskIEEE; CISTI; KR SourceOne.
Former titles: Cable Television Engineering (ISSN 0308-4213); (until 1973): Relay Engineer (ISSN 0048-718X); (until 1971): Society of Relay Engineers. Proceedings (ISSN 0374-3985)
Description: Reports on developments in the industry.

C T V D: CINEMA - T V DIGEST; a quarterly review of the serious, foreign-language cinema-T V-press. see *MOTION PICTURES*

384.55 UK ISSN 0967-3245
CABLE & SATELLITE COMMUNICATIONS INTERNATIONAL. 1992. m. £75 (foreign £110). Route 104 Publishing, 104 City View, 463 Bethnal Green Rd., London E2 9QY, England. TEL 44-171-613-5553. FAX 44-171-729-7723. Ed. Joss Armitage; Pub. Marilyn Miller. adv.: B&W page £1300; trim 276 x 210; adv. contact: David Webster. bk.rev.; charts; illus.; stat. circ. 4,076. (back issues avail.) **Document type:** trade publication.
Description: Covers technical and business developments for professionals in the cable and satellite television industry.

384.55 UK ISSN 0956-6872
CABLE AND SATELLITE YEARBOOK. 1985. a. £115 (foreign £140). 21st Century Business Publications Ltd., 149 Tottenham Court Rd., London W1P 9LL, England. TEL 44-171-896-2700. FAX 44-171-896-2749. Ed. Chris Dziadul; Pub. Paul Nicholson. adv. contact: Tina Gamp. circ. 3,000 (paid). (back issues avail.) **Document type:** directory.
—BLDSC (2943.952000).
Description: Covers the cable and satellite broadcast, manufacturing and retailing industries.

791 US ISSN 1047-9902
HE8700.7.C6
CABLE AND STATION COVERAGE ATLAS. 1966. a. $440. Warren Publishing, Inc., 2115 Ward Ct., N.W., Washington, DC 20037. TEL 202-872-9200. FAX 202-293-3435. Ed. Albert Warren; Pub. Albert Warren. index. **Document type:** trade publication.
—CCC.
Former titles: Cable and Station Coverage Atlas and 35-Mile Zone Maps (ISSN 0193-3639); C A T V and Station Coverage Atlas and 35-Mile Zone Maps (ISSN 0068-4694)

384 US ISSN 1057-7378
CABLE AVAILS. 1991. m. Cowles Business Media, 11 River Bend Dr., S., Box 4949, Stamford, CT 06907-0949. TEL 203-358-9900. FAX 203-358-5811. **Document type:** trade publication.

621.38 384.5 CN ISSN 0318-0069
HE8700.7.C6
CABLE COMMUNICATIONS MAGAZINE. 1934. 6/yr. Can.$28 (foreign $35). Ter-Sat Media Publications Ltd., 57 Peachwood Court, Kitchener, ON N2B 1S7, Canada. TEL 519-744-4111. FAX 519-744-1261. Ed. Udo Salewsky. adv. contact: Udo Salewsky. bk.rev.; illus. circ. 6,900. **Indexed:** Can.B.P.I., Can.B.P.I. **Document type:** trade publication.
Former titles: Canadian Telephone and Cable Television Journal (ISSN 0008-5162); Canadian Telephone Journal.
Description: Coverage of cable television industry news, views, issues and developments in Canada, the United States and around the world.

384.6 790.1
CABLE CONNECTION MAGAZINE.* fortn. $35.40. P.O. Box 304, Fort Worth, TX 76101-0304. TEL 800-950-7999. **Document type:** consumer publication.
Description: Lists basic, premium, and pay-per-view programs available to subscribers to Sammons cable television. Contains Features on movies, stars, and shows.

COMMUNICATIONS — TELEVISION AND CABLE

384.55   US   ISSN 1053-9026
HE8700.72.U6
CABLE CONTACTS (YEAR). a. (plus m. updates). $150. B P I Communications, Inc. (New York), 1515 Broadway, New York, NY 10036. TEL 212-536-5261; 800-BPI-4100. FAX 518-536-5294. **Document type:** directory.

791.4 792   US   ISSN 0191-4871
CABLE GUIDE. 1982. m. $20. T V Syndicated Market, 309 Lakeside Dr., Horsham, PA 19044. TEL 215-443-9300; 800-540-5643. Ed. Jay Gissen; Pub. Michael Perlis. adv. circ. 4,200,000. (back issues avail.) **Document type:** consumer publication.
    Former titles: T V Entertainment (ISSN 1049-1163); T V Entertainment Monthly (ISSN 1044-0682); (until 1989): Cable Choice; (until 1986): Cabletime.
    Description: Lists programs on cable and pay TV. Includes feature articles and interviews.

CABLE IN THE CLASSROOM; teaching with television. see EDUCATION — Teaching Methods And Curriculum

CABLE INDUSTRY DIRECTORY. see BUSINESS AND ECONOMICS — Trade And Industrial Directories

CABLE MODEM REPORT: BUSINESS DIMENSIONS & MARKET OPPORTUNITIES. see COMPUTERS — Computer Networks

CABLE NETWORK INVESTOR. see BUSINESS AND ECONOMICS — Banking And Finance

791.4   US   ISSN 1089-5051
CABLE PLUS. 1980. bi-w. $29.92. T V Host, Inc., Box 1665, 3953 Jonestown Rd., Harrisburg, PA 17109. TEL 717-657-1700. FAX 717-657-2921. URL: http://www.tvhost.com. Ed. Mike Edkin; Pub. David W. Stefanic. adv. contact: Lou Pernik, Jr. circ. 25,000 (paid). **Document type:** consumer publication.
    Former titles (until 1984): CablePlus (ISSN 0884-8025); (until 1980): Caltec Cablevision (ISSN 8750-7102)

384.55   US   ISSN 0270-885X
HF6146.T42
CABLE T V ADVERTISING; newsletter on sale of commercial time by cable T V systems. 1980. m. $695 (effective 1997). Paul Kagan Associates, Inc., 126 Clock Tower Place, Carmel, CA 93923. TEL 408-624-1536. TELEX 408-625-3225. Ed. Larry Gerbrandt. charts; index. **Document type:** newsletter.
    Description: Examines the sale of commercial time by cable TV systems and networks. Includes local and national ad sales, case studies and projections.

CABLE T V AND NEW MEDIA; law & finance. see LAW

CABLE T V FACTS. see ADVERTISING AND PUBLIC RELATIONS

384.5 332   US   ISSN 1061-5652
HD8700.72.U6
CABLE T V FINANCE; newsletter on bank, insurance, commercial loans to cable operators. 1982. m. $745 (effective 1997). Paul Kagan Associates, Inc., 126 Clock Tower Place, Carmel, CA 93923. TEL 408-624-1536. FAX 408-625-3225. Ed. Paul Kagan. charts; index. **Document type:** newsletter.
    Former titles (until 1992): Cable T V Banker - Broker (ISSN 0893-2131); Cable T V Finance (ISSN 0734-6816)
    Description: Covers sources of funding for cable TV. Analysis of bank, insurance and bridge loans. Case studies of financing strategies.

384.554   US   ISSN 0736-8143
HE8700.7.C6
CABLE T V FINANCIAL DATABOOK; sourcebook for all key financial data on cable T V. 1980. a. $325 (effective 1997). Paul Kagan Associates, Inc., 126 Clock Tower Place, Carmel, CA 93923. TEL 408-624-1536. TELEX 408-625-3225. Ed. Mary Gagliardi. adv.; charts; stat. (back issues avail.)

537 332.6   US   ISSN 0731-0250
HE8700.72.U6
CABLE T V INVESTOR; newsletter on investments in cable T V systems and publicly held cable T V stocks. 1969. m. $895 (effective 1997). Paul Kagan Associates, Inc., 126 Clock Tower Place, Carmel, CA 93923. TEL 408-624-1536. FAX 408-624-1536. TELEX 408-625-3225. Eds. Paul Kagan, Sharon Armbrust. charts; index. **Document type:** newsletter.
    Formerly: Cablecast (ISSN 0146-0080)
    Description: Provides analysis of cash flow multiples and value per subscriber.

384.55 340   US   ISSN 0749-7652
KF2844.A59
CABLE T V LAW REPORTER. 1984. m. $695 (effective 1997). Paul Kagan Associates, Inc., 126 Clock Tower Pl., Carmel, CA 93923. TEL 408-624-1536. TELEX 408-625-3225.
    Description: Issues concerning cable TV. Includes anti-trust, first amendment, franchising, taxation, copyright, rate regulation, privacy and international law.

384.55   US   ISSN 0278-503X
PN1992.55
CABLE T V PROGRAMMING; newsletter on programs for pay cable T V and analysis of basic cable networks. 1981. m. $745. Paul Kagan Associates, Inc., 126 Clock Tower Place, Carmel, CA 93923. TEL 408-624-1536. FAX 408-625-3225. TELEX 408-625-3225. Ed. Paul Kagan. charts; index. (reprint service avail.) **Document type:** newsletter.
    Description: Covers the economics of basic and pay TV program networks. Gives case studies of cable system program valuations.

384.5   US   ISSN 1068-9826
KF2844.A15
CABLE T V REGULATION; newsletter on federal-state-city regulation of cable television. 1975. m. $675 (effective 1997). Paul Kagan Associates, Inc., 126 Clock Tower Place, Carmel, CA 93923. TEL 408-624-1536. TELEX 408-625-3225. Ed. John Mansell. charts; index. **Document type:** newsletter.
    Former titles (until 1993): Cable T V Franchising (ISSN 0731-0269); Cable T V Regulation (ISSN 0146-0102)
    Description: Reports on franchise awards and renewals and legal battles with cities and states. Includes listing of most cable TV rate increases.

384.55   US   ISSN 0276-5713
CABLE T V TECHNOLOGY; newsletter on technical advances, construction of new systems and rebuild of existing systems. 1981. m. $695 (effective 1997). Paul Kagan Associates, Inc., 126 Clock Tower Place, Carmel, CA 93923. TEL 408-624-1536. TELEX 408-625-3225. Ed. John Mansell. charts; index. **Document type:** newsletter.
    Description: Covers addressability updates and projections.

384.55   US   ISSN 1050-0553
CABLE - TELCO REPORT. 1990. bi-w. $599 (outside N. America $737). Telecommunications Reports (Subsidiary of: Business Research Publications, Inc.), 1333 H St., N.W., Ste. 100-E, Washington, DC 20005. TEL 800-822-6338. FAX 202-842-3023. E-mail: customerservice@tr.com; URL: http://www.tr.com. Ed. Michael Grebb. R&P contact: Ellen Hartman. **Document type:** trade publication.
    ●Also available online. Vendor(s): Information Access Co., NewsNet (TE106).
    Description: Covers the latest technologies, regulation, legislation and business deals affecting the delivery of video services.

384.55 658   US
CABLE THEFT NEWSLETTER.* m. $72. Skybridge Publishing Inc., c/o Schreff, 9 Frontier Rd., Cos Cob, CT 06807-1208.

CABLE TV STATION AUTHORIZATION REPORT. see COMMUNICATIONS — Abstracting, Bibliographies, Statistics

CABLE TV STATION DISTRIBUTION FILE. see COMMUNICATIONS — Abstracting, Bibliographies, Statistics

384.55   US   ISSN 0739-8166
HE8700.72.U6
CABLE VIDEO BRIEFS.* m. $72. Skybridge Publishing Inc., c/o Schreff, 9 Frontier Rd., Cos Cob, CT 06807-1208.

384   US   ISSN 1042-7228
HE8700.7
CABLE WORLD. 1989. w. $65. Cowles Business Media (Denver) (Subsidiary of: Cowles Media Company), 1905 Sherman St., Denver, CO 80203. TEL 303-837-0900. Ed. Bob Diddlebock. adv.; circ. 20,000 (controlled). **Document type:** trade publication.
    Description: Business news magazine for the cable television industry. Includes in-depth reports on trends and issues affecting the cable business.

384.55   CN   ISSN 0840-9153
CABLECASTER; Canada's cable magazine. 1989. 8/yr. Can.$29($29) (foreign Can.$39) (effective 1997). Southam Magazine Group, 1450 Don Mills Rd., Don Mills, ON M3B 2X7, Canada. TEL 416-445-6641. FAX 416-442-2213. Ed. Steve Pawlett; Pub. James Cook. adv.; bk.rev.; charts; illus.; stat.; tr.lit. circ. 6,075. (back issues avail.)
    Description: Covers the management, technology, regulation and programming of the Canadian cable television industry.

384.55   US   ISSN 1069-6644
CABLEFAX. (Distributed by facsimile.) 1990. d. (5/w.). $495 (effective 1997). Phillips Business Information, Inc., 1201 Seven Locks Rd., Potomac, MD 20854-1053. TEL 301-424-3338. FAX 301-309-3847. E-mail: pbi@phillips.com. Ed. Stephen Donohue. adv. **Document type:** newsletter.
    ●Also available online. Vendor(s): Information Access Co.
    Description: Covers industry news, legislation, finance, acquisitions, programming, hardware and personnel.

384.55   US   ISSN 0361-8374
HE8700.7.C6
CABLEVISION; the analysis and features bi-weekly of the cable television industry. 1975. bi-w. $55 (Canada $85; elsewhere $165). Capital Cities - A B C, Inc., Diversified Publishing Group, 825 Seventh Ave., New York, NY 10019. TEL 212-887-8400. FAX 212-887-8585. (Subscr. to: Cablevision Magazine, Box 7698, Riverton, NJ 08077-7698; And: 600 S. Cherry St., Ste. 400, Denver, CO 80222. TEL 303-393-7449) Ed. Craig Leddy; Pub. Larry Oliver. adv. contact: Richard Petralia. bk.rev. circ. 15,398. Indexed: Comput.Cont., SRI. **Document type:** trade publication.
    —BLDSC (2944.080000); UMI; UnCover.
    Description: Covers all fields related to cable television management: programming, pay per view, marketing and promotion, advertising sales, technology, operations, customer service, and policy and business.

621.88   US   ISSN 1073-3108
TK5103
CABLING INSTALLATION AND MAINTENANCE. 1993. $40 includes C I M Buyers Guide (foreign $47) (effective Jan. 1997). PennWell Publishing Co. (Nashua), 10 Tara Blvd., 5th Fl., Nashua, NH 03062-2801. TEL 603-891-0123. (Subscr. to: B 1260, Tulsa, OK 74101. TEL 918-835-3161. FAX 918-832-9295) **Document type:** trade publication.
—CCC.

384.55   UK
CABLING WORLD. m. £38 (Europe £60; rest of world £72). Nexus Media Ltd., Nexus House, Azalea Dr., Swanley, Kent BR8 8HY, England. TEL 44-1322-660070. FAX 44-1322-661257. E-mail: cabling@nexusmedia.co.uk. Ed. Rob Riggs; Pub. Christina Wood. R&P contact: Jeremy Cowan; adv. contact: Tony Barnes. circ. 14,000. **Document type:** trade publication.

CANADA. STATISTICS CANADA. CABLE TELEVISION/ TELEDISTRIBUTION. see COMMUNICATIONS — Abstracting, Bibliographies, Statistics

COMMUNICATIONS — TELEVISION AND CABLE

384.55   CN   ISSN 1194-3068
CANADA ON LOCATION. 1991. 2/yr. Brunico Communications Inc., 366 Adelaide St. W., Ste. 500, Toronto, ON M5V 1R9, Canada. TEL 416-408-2300. FAX 416-408-0870. E-mail: circ@brunico.com. Ed. Mary Maddever. adv.: B&W page Can.$2015, color page Can.$2640; trim 8 1/8 x 10 7/8. circ. 4,127. **Document type:** trade publication.
   Description: Covers production facilities, services and locations of the motion picture industry in Canada.

CANADIAN ACTORS' ANECDOTES. see *THEATER*

384.5   CN   ISSN 1193-5898
CANADIAN CABLE TELEVISION ASSOCIATION. COMMUNIQUE. (Editions in English, French) vol.5, 1975. every 6 wks. free. Canadian Cable Television Association, 360 Albert St., Ste.1010, Ottawa, ON K1R 7X7, Canada. TEL 613-232-2631. FAX 613-232-2137. Ed. Julia Ukrintz. adv.; illus. circ. 2,700. **Indexed:** Info.Media & Tech. **Document type:** newsletter, trade publication.
   Former titles: C C T A Cable Communique (ISSN 0710-2240); C C T A Communique; C C T A News.

384.55   CN   ISSN 0316-3083
CANADIAN COMMUNICATIONS REPORTS. 1973-1990; resumed 1993. 20/yr. Can.$475. Evert Communications Ltd., 1296 Carling Ave., Ottawa, ON K1Y 7K8, Canada. TEL 613-728-4621. FAX 613-728-0385. E-mail: evert@evert.com; URL: http://www.evert.com. Ed. Debbie Lawes. R&P contact: Gordon Hutchison. **Document type:** trade publication.
   Description: Details and analyzes developments in the provision of communications services in Canada.

384.54   CN   ISSN 0705-3657
P92.C3
CANADIAN JOURNAL OF COMMUNICATION. (Text in English; summaries in English, French) 1974. q. Can.$60 to individuals (foreign $60); institutions Can.$75 (foreign $75) (effective 1998). Wilfrid Laurier University Press, 75 University Ave. W., Waterloo, ON N2L 3C5, Canada. TEL 519-884-0710. FAX 519-725-1399. E-mail: press@mach1.wlu.ca. Ed. Jo-Anne Ray. adv.; bk.rev.; charts; stat.; index. circ. 460. (also avail. in microfiche) **Indexed:** Can.B.P.I., Can.Wom.Per.Ind., Commun.Abstr., Educ.Tech.Abstr., Film Lit.Ind. (1989-), INSPEC (1983-), Sage Fam.Stud.Abstr., Sage Pub.Admin.Abstr. **Document type:** academic/scholarly publication.
   —BLDSC (3031.045000); AskIEEE; KR SourceOne; SWETS; UnCover. **CCC.**
   Refereed Serial

384.5   371.912   US
APTION.* 1980. a. free. National Captioning Institute, Inc., 1900 Gallows Rd., Ste. 3000, Vienna, VA 22182-3865. FAX 703-998-2450. Ed. Morgan Bramlet. circ. 100,000 (controlled). (tabloid format)

384.55   US
APTION CENTER NEWS. 1989. s-a. free. Caption Center, 125 Western Ave., Boston, MA 02134. TEL 617-492-9225. FAX 617-562-0590. E-mail: caption@wgbh.org; URL: http://www.wgbh.org/caption. Ed. Mary Watkins. circ. 30,000. (looseleaf format; back issues avail.) **Document type:** newsletter.
● Also available online.
   Description: Information about captioning in television programming for corporate advertising, educators, and professionals.

AR STEREO REVIEW. see *ENGINEERING — Electrical Engineering*

384.55   621.88   330   UK
ARLTON COMMUNICATIONS PLC. ANNUAL REPORT AND ACCOUNTS. a. Carlton Communications Plc, 15 St. George St., Hanover Sq., London W1R 0LU, England. TEL 44-171-499-8050. FAX 44-171-895-9575. **Document type:** corporate report.
   Description: Discusses trends in broadcast television, home entertainment, video, and image processing, and the participation of the company in these fields. Includes information about the company's finances, personnel, and marketing.

384.55 792   UK   ISSN 0142-6079
CASTINGDEX. 1979. a. £18. P.O. Box 11, London N1 7JZ, England. TEL 44-171-566-8282. FAX 44-171-566-8284. (Subscr. to: P.O. Box 100, Broadstairs, Kent CT10 1UJ, England. TEL 44-1843-860885) Ed. Bobbi Dunn. **Document type:** directory.

384.55   US
▼ **CENTRAL PERKULATIONS.** 1996. bi-w. Y G H F, Box 17113, Memphis, TN 38187. E-mail: editor@yghf.com; URL: http://www.yghf.com/. Ed. Cat Wright.
● Available only online.
   Description: For the online fan of NBC TV's "Friends". Contains commentaries and articles, trivia contests, member participation sections, overseas updates, and the latest news on the cast members themselves.

791.45   US
CHILDREN'S ENTERTAINMENT BUSINESS. 1993. bi-m. $100 (effective 1993). American Academy of Children's Entertainment, Box 1257, Cooper Sta., New York, NY 10276. TEL 201-328-0204. FAX 201-328-0204. Ed. W.G. Weber; Pub. W.G. Weber. adv.: page $800; trim 8 1/2 x 11; adv. contact: W.G. Weber. bk.rev. circ. 1,500. (looseleaf format; back issues avail.) **Document type:** newsletter.
   Description: Business coverage for children's entertainment industry professionals.

THE CHRISTIANNET. see *MUSIC*

790.43 800   US
CHRONIC RIFT NEWSLETTER.* q. 135 W. 238th St., Apt. 4G, Bronx, NY 10463-4235. **Document type:** newsletter.
   Description: News, interviews and information relating to the science fiction discussion show.

CINE & TELE INFORME. see *MOTION PICTURES*

CINEGUIA; anuario espanol del espectaculo y audiovisuales. see *MOTION PICTURES*

CINEMA BLUE PRESENTS EROTIC STARS. see *MEN'S INTERESTS*

CINEMA BLUE PRESENTS RED-HOT COUPLES. see *MEN'S INTERESTS*

384.55   IT
CINEMA IN CASA. 1993. bi-m. L.54000 (foreign L.185000). Editore Progest s.r.l., Via Rovereto 6, 00198 Rome, Italy. TEL 39-6-8552084. FAX 39-6-8558885. Eds. Gianni Caserta, Giovanni B. Rodinis. adv.: B&W page L.7900000, color page L.12500000; 210 x 270. **Document type:** consumer publication.

CINEMA LOMBARDIA; periodico d'informazione a cura della sezione regionale dell'A.N.E.C. see *MOTION PICTURES*

CINEMA TECHNOLOGY. see *MOTION PICTURES*

791.43   FR
CINEMACTION T.V.. 1992. irreg. (approx. 4/yr.), no.13, 1995. 500 F. for 4 nos. Editions Corlet S.A., Z.I. Route de Vire, B.P. 86, 14110 Conde sur Noireau, France. TEL 31699127. FAX 31694129. Ed. Guy Hennebelle. (back issues avail.) **Document type:** monographic series.
   Description: In-depth coverage of topics relating to television.

CINESCAPE. see *MOTION PICTURES*

621   VE
CIRCUIT - FOTON. 1980. m. Bs.200($40) M.G. Ediciones Especializadas, S.A., Ave. Maturin, No. 15, Urb. Los Cedros, El Bosque, Caracas 1050, Venezuela. adv. circ. 3,500.
   Formerly: Circuit.

384.55   US   ISSN 1055-0461
COLLEGE BROADCASTER. 1989. 4/yr. $30 to individuals; institutions $75; students & faculty $20. National Association of College Broadcasters, 71 George St., Box 1824, Providence, RI 02912. TEL 401-863-2225. FAX 401-863-2221. E-mail: NACB@aol.com. Ed. Kelley Cunningham; Pub. Kelley Cunningham. R&P contact: Kelley Cunningham. adv.: B&W page $550; adv. contact: Mike Russo. bk.rev. circ. 3,500. (back issues avail.) **Document type:** trade publication, academic/scholarly publication.
   Description: Covers all aspects of college and school radio and television operations, broadcast and cable, the media industry, careers in media, and provides a forum for national communication among media students and faculty.

384.55   US
COLUMBO NEWSLETTER. 1992. q. $12 (foreign $16) (effective 1996). Box 1703, Pittsburgh, PA 15230-1703. Ed. Sheldon Catz. circ. 100. **Document type:** newsletter.
   Description: Covers the TV program Columbo, that stars Peter Falk as Lt. Columbo.

384.5   NE   ISSN 1380-9679
COMEDIA. 1989. m. (10/yr.). Commissariaat voor de Media, Postbus 1426, 1200 BK Hilversum, Netherlands. TEL 31-35-6721721. FAX 31-35-6721722. E-mail: cudm@cudm.nl; URL: http://www.cudm.nl/. circ. controlled. **Document type:** newsletter.
   Description: News on broadcasting and other media.

COMEDY WRITERS ASSOCIATION NEWSLETTER. see *LITERATURE*

COMEDY WRITERS BULLETIN. see *LITERATURE*

621.38   UK
HE8689
COMMONWEALTH BROADCASTER. 1966. q. $35 (effective 1998). Commonwealth Broadcasting Association, BBC Yalding House, Rm. 312, 152-156 Great Portland St., London W1N 6AJ. TEL 44-171-765-5144. FAX 44-171-765-5152. E-mail: cba@bbc.co.uk; URL: http://www.oneworld.org/cba/. Ed. Elizabeth Smith. adv. contact: Derek Inall. bk.rev. circ. 10,000. **Indexed:** Commun.Abstr., Int.Ind.Film Per., Intl.Ind.TV. **Document type:** newsletter.
   —BLDSC (3325.800000); UnCover.
   Formerly: Combroad (ISSN 0951-0826)

COMMUNICATION; information - medias - theories - practiques. see *COMMUNICATIONS*

COMMUNICATIONS BUSINESS & FINANCE. see *COMMUNICATIONS*

621.38   US   ISSN 0277-0679
COMMUNICATIONS DAILY; the authoritative news service of electronic communications. 1981. d. (5/w.). $2898 (foreign $3052). Warren Publishing, Inc., 2115 Ward Ct., N.W., Washington, DC 20037. TEL 202-872-9200. FAX 202-293-3435. Ed. Albert Warren. (looseleaf format) **Document type:** newsletter.
● Also available online. Vendor(s): Data-Star, Information Access Co., Knight-Ridder Information, Inc., Lexis-Nexis, NewsNet (TE01).
   —CCC.

621.388   US   ISSN 0191-5428
TK6675
COMMUNICATIONS ENGINEERING AND DESIGN. 1975. m. $54 (foreign $75). Chilton Communications (Denver), 600 S. Cherry St., Ste. 400, Denver, CO 80222. FAX 303-393-6654. URL: http://www.cedmagazine.com. Ed. Roger Brown; Pub. Robert Stuehrk. adv. contact: Scott Snyder. bk.rev.; illus. circ. 22,500. **Document type:** trade publication.
   —CISTI; Linda Hall.
   Formerly: Communications - Engineering Digest.
   Description: Written and edited for engineering and technical personnel involved in the evolving full service network of video, voice and data.

COMMUNICATIONS — TELEVISION AND CABLE

621.38 JA ISSN 0914-9260
QC973 CODEN: JCRLEX
COMMUNICATIONS RESEARCH LABORATORY. JOURNAL/TSUSHINSOGO KENKYUJO EIBUN RONBUNSHU. (Text in English) 1954. 3/yr. free or on exchange basis. Ministry of Posts and Telecommunications, Communications Research Laboratory, Technical Support Section - Yuseisho Tsushinsogo Kenkyujo, 2-1, Nukui Kita-machi 4-chome, Koganei-shi, Tokyo 184, Japan. TEL 81-423-21-1211. FAX 81-423-27-7603. TELEX 2832611-DEMPA-J. E-mail: pub@crl.go.jp. bibl.; charts; illus.; stat. circ. 1,000. **Indexed:** Curr.Cont., INIS Atomind., INSPEC (1988-), Int.Aerosp.Abstr., JCT, JTA. **Document type:** academic/scholarly publication.
—BLDSC (4731.704000); AskIEEE; CISTI; KR SourceOne; Linda Hall; UnCover.
Formerly: Radio Research Laboratory. Journal (ISSN 0033-8001).

384.55 US ISSN 0884-2272
TK6675
COMMUNICATIONS TECHNOLOGY. 1984. m. free to qualified personnel. (Society of Cable Television Engineers) Phillips Business Information, Inc., 1201 Seven Locks Rd., Potomac, MD 20854. TEL 301-424-3338. FAX 301-309-3847. E-mail: pbi@phillips.com. Ed. Laura Hamilton. adv.; charts; illus.; index. circ. 21,000. (back issues avail.) **Document type:** trade publication.
—CCC.
Description: Covers cable TV engineering and technology.

384.5 003 US ISSN 1074-9004
COMMUNITY MEDIA REVIEW. Short title: C M R. 1977. bi-m. $35 (Canada $45; elsewhere $55). Alliance for Community Media, 666 11th St., N.W., Ste. 806, Washington, DC 20001-4542. TEL 202-393-2650. FAX 202-393-2653. E-mail: AllianceCM@aol.com; URL: http://www.alliance.cm.org. Ed. T. James Goodwin. adv.; index. circ. 1,500. (back issues avail.) **Indexed:** Alt.Press Ind. **Document type:** academic/scholarly publication.
Formerly: Community Television Review.
Description: Devoted to media issues affecting community media workers and the empowerment of citizens through access to media.

384.55 UK ISSN 1358-1112
▼**COMPRESSION EXPRESS.** 1995. s-m. £310. Route 104 Publishing, 104 City View, 463 Bethnal Green Rd., London E2 9QY, England. TEL 44-171-613-5553. FAX 44-171-729-7723. Ed. Alan Burkitt-Gray; Pub. Marilyn Miller. **Document type:** newsletter.
Description: Delivers the latest news on digital broadcasting, consumer equipment, industry deals and standards.

384 CN ISSN 0708-0131
CONSEIL DE PRESSE DU QUEBEC. RAPPORT ANNUEL. (Text in French) 1977. a. free. Conseil de Presse du Quebec, 55 1-2, rue Saint Louis, Quebec, PQ G1R 3Z2, Canada. TEL 418-692-3008. FAX 418-692-5148. Ed. Sylvie Trottier. circ. 350. **Document type:** bulletin.

CONSORTIUM FOR DRAMA & MEDIA IN HIGHER EDUCATION. NEWSLETTER. see *THEATER*

384 US ISSN 1055-0666
CONSUMER MEDIA TECH. 1991. m. $645 (effective 1997). Paul Kagan Associates, Inc., 126 Clock Tower Place, Carmel, CA 93923. TEL 408-624-1536. FAX 408-625-3225. Ed. Paul Kagan.
Description: Analyzes trends in home entertainment and communication. Reports on the latest technologies, products and services.

CONTACTS; the media pipeline for public relations people. see *ADVERTISING AND PUBLIC RELATIONS*

CONTACTS. see *THEATER*

791.4 BL ISSN 0104-1444
CONTIGO. 1963. w. $155. Editora Azul, S.A., Av. Nacoes Unidas, 5777, 05479-900 Sao Paulo, SP, Brazil. TEL 55-11-8673000. FAX 55-11-8673311. TELEX 55-11-83178-EDAZ. E-mail: benjamin@emial.abril.com.br. (Subscr. to: Rua do Curtume 769, 05065-900 Sao Paulo SP, Brazil. TEL 011-823-9100) Ed. Airton Almeida. R&P contact: Benjamin Goncalvez. TEL 55-11-8673304. adv.: color page $12700; 227 x 299; adv. contact: Enio Vergeiro. film rev.; illus.; circ. 199,822 (paid).
Former titles (until July 1994): Contigo Superstar; (until May 1983): T V Contigo (ISSN 0010-7662)
Description: Guide to television broadcasts. Includes coverage of personalities.

384.55 US
CONTINENTAL CABLEVISION PROGRAM GUIDE. 1983. m. Pilot House, Lewis Wharf, Boston, MA 02110. TEL 617-574-9400. adv. contact: Henry James.

CONTRAPUNTO. see *COMMUNICATIONS — Radio*

384.55 UK ISSN 1354-8565
P96.T42
▼**CONVERGENCE;** the journal of research into new media technologies. 1995. s-a. £30 (N. America £40) to individuals; institutions £60 (N. America £60) (effective 1997). John Libbey Media, University of Luton, 75 Castle St., Luton, Bedfordshire LU1 3AJ, England. TEL 44-1582-743297. FAX 44-1582-743298. E-mail: john.libbey@luton.ac.uk; URL: http://www.luton.ac.uk/convergence. **Document type:** academic/scholarly publication.
—BLDSC (3463.544500).
Description: Provides a forum for the creative, social, political and pedagogical issues raised by the advent of new media technologies.

CORPORATE A V (YEAR). see *COMMUNICATIONS*

791.4 CC
COSMOS WEEKLY. (Text in Chinese) 1987. w. B2, 14-F, Fuk Keung Ind. Bldg., 66-68 Tong Mei Rd., Taikoktsui, Kowloon, Hong Kong, People's Republic of China. TEL 3905461. FAX 7893869. Ed. Vincent Leung. circ. 60,000.
Description: Covers entertainment.

CRONACHE; per il personale de Gruppo Philips. see *ENGINEERING — Electrical Engineering*

384.55 808.838 UK ISSN 1360-6530
▼**CULT TIMES.** 1995. m. £21 (U.S. & Canada $49; rest of world $26) (effective 1996). Visual Imagination Ltd., 9 Blades Ct., Deodar Rd., London SW15 2NU, England. TEL 44-181-875-1520. FAX 44-181-875-1588. (Subscr. to: P.O. Box 371, London SW14 8J, England; Subscr. in US & Canada to: Box 156, Manorville, NY 11949) Ed. John Ainsworth; Pub. Stephen Payne. R&P contact: Stephen Payne. adv.: B&W page £550, color page £825; trim 210 x 298. **Document type:** consumer publication.

384 US ISSN 0739-991X
LB1044.8
CURRENT (WASHINGTON, 1980). 1980. bi-w. $54 (Canada $115; Europe $145). (National Association of Educational Broadcasters) Current Publishing Committee, 1612 K St., N.W., Ste. 704, Washington, DC 20006. TEL 202-463-7055. FAX 202-463-7056. E-mail: currentron@aol.com; URL: http://www.current.org. Ed. Steve Behrens. adv. contact: Denese Scott. bk.rev.; illus.; circ. 6,000 (paid). (also avail. in microfilm) **Indexed:** G.Soc.Sci.& Rel.Per.Lit., PMR, R.G.Abstr., R.G. **Document type:** newspaper.
Former titles: N A E B Letter; National Association of Educational Broadcasters Newsletter (ISSN 0027-8610)
Description: News, features, and commentary about public television, public radio and noncommercial telecommunications.

CYRANO'S JOURNAL. see *COMMUNICATIONS*

D V S GUIDE. (Descriptive Video Services) see *HANDICAPPED — Visually Impaired*

384.554 791.43 US ISSN 0011-5509
PN1993
DAILY VARIETY; news of the entertainment industry. 1933. d. (Mon.-Fri.). $187 (foreign $289 surface; airmail $995). (Daily Variety Ltd.) Cahners Publishing Company (Los Angeles), Entertainment Division, Division of Reed Elsevier Inc., 5700 Wilshire Blvd., Ste. 120, Los Angeles, CA 90036. TEL 213-857-4403. FAX 213-857-0494. URL: http://www.cahners.com/mainmag/dvar.htm. (Subscr. to: Box 7550, Torrence, CA 90504-8950. TEL 800-552-3632) Ed. Peter Bart; Pub. Gerry Byrne. adv.: page $3225. bk.rev.; film rev.; music rev.; play rev.; tele.rev.; charts. circ. 24,700. (also avail. in microfilm from LIB) **Document type:** newspaper.
—UMI. **CCC.**
Description: Covers the entire scope of the entertainment business, including film, legitimate theatre, music, cable and home video.

DANGDAI XIJU/CONTEMPORARY DRAMA; xiju - dianshi shuangyuekan. see *THEATER*

384.554 US ISSN 1072-8104
DARK SHADOWS ANNOUNCEMENT. 1986. q. $20. (Dark Shadows Fan Club) Fan Club Publishing, Box 69A04, Dept. UL, W. Hollywood, CA 90069. TEL 213-650-5112. Ed. Louis Wendruck; Pub. Louis Wendruck. adv.; bk.rev. circ. 20,000. (back issues avail.) **Document type:** newsletter.
Description: Covers the Dark Shadows television show, a gothic soap opera from the 1960s, and Dark Shadows movies.

791.4 AT ISSN 0729-7920
DATA EXTRACT. 1980. 8/yr. Aus.$12; newsstand price: Aus.$2.50. Doctor Who Fan Club of Australia, G.P.O. Box 2870, Sydney, N.S.W. 2001, Australia. E-mail: neelix@eagles.bbs.net.au; URL: http://www.eagles.bbs.net.au/-draco/dwca. Ed. Neil Hogan. adv.; page Aus.$60. bk.rev.; video rev.; illus. circ. 700. (back issues avail.) **Document type:** newsletter.
Description: Alerts Australian afficianados of the British science fiction series Dr. Who to events of interest, including conventions, screenings of episodes, and appearances by the show's stars.

791.4 US
DAYTIME T V PRESENTS. 1969. bi-m. Sterling - Macfadden Partnership, 233 Park Ave. S., 6th Fl., New York, NY 10003. TEL 212-780-3500. (Suscr. to: 35 Wilbur St., Lynbrook, NY 11563. TEL 516-593-1220. FAX 516-593-0065) adv. **Document type:** consumer publication.
Description: For the entertainment of female readers. Concentrates on TV personalities.

384.5 US
DAYTIME T V'S GREATEST STORIES. bi-m. Sterling - Macfadden Partnership, 35 Wilbur St., Lynbrook, NY 11563. TEL 516-593-1220. FAX 516-593-0065. adv. **Document type:** consumer publication.
Description: Provides material of an entertaining and diversionary nature for women. Devoted to T.V. personalities.

384.55 US ISSN 0011-7129
DAYTIME TV.* 1970. bi-m. $14.95 (foreign $17.95). Sterling's Magazines, Inc., 233 Park Ave. S., New York, NY 10003. TEL 516-593-1220. Ed. Lucille Barilla; Pub. Allen Miller. adv. contact: Mel Goldman. **Document type:** consumer publication.
Description: Focuses on T.V. personalities. Aims to provide entertaining material for a primarily female audience.

384.5 CC ISSN 1003-4005
DAZHONG DIANSHI/POPULAR T V. (Text in Chinese) 1982. m. Y72. (Zhejiang Sheng Guangbo Dianshi-ting - Zhejiang Provincial Broadcasting and Television Bureau) Dazhong Dianshi Bianjibu, No. 31, Changsheng Lu, Hangzhou, Zhejiang 310006, People's Republic of China. TEL 86-571-706-5551. FAX 86-571-706-5558. (Dist. in US by: China Books & Periodicals, Inc., 2929 24th St., San Francisco, CA 94110. TEL 415-282-2994) Ed. Ruolin Ruan. adv. contact: Jinjun Xu. circ. 400,000 (paid). **Document type:** consumer publication.
Description: Covers movie, TV and pop song stars, new TV plays and series, and more.

COMMUNICATIONS — TELEVISION AND CABLE

384.554   US   ISSN 1065-1535
PN1992.3.U5
DESTINATION DISCOVERY. 1985. m. $19.95. (The Discovery Channel) Discovery Publishing, 7700 Wisconsin Ave., 7th Fl., Bethesda, MD 20814. TEL 301-986-0444. FAX 301-986-4628. circ. 200,000. **Document type:** consumer publication.
 Formerly (until Aug. 1992): Disney Channel Magazine (ISSN 0747-4644)

384   GW
DEUTSCHLANDFUNK. GESCHAEFTSBERICHT. 1962. biennial. Deutschlandfunk, Raderbergguertel 40, 50968 Cologne, Germany. TEL 0221-345-2110. **Document type:** corporate report.
 Formerly: Deutschlandfunk. Jahrbuch (ISSN 0084-9790)

DIANSHI DIANYING WENXUE/T V AND FILM LITERATURE. see MOTION PICTURES

384.5   CC
DIANSHI YUEKAN/TELEVISION MONTHLY. (Text in Chinese) 1982. m. $43.10. (Hubei Dianshi Tai) Dianshi Yuekan Zazhishe, Te-1, Zijincun, Liangdao Jie, Wuchang Qu, Wuhan, Hubei 430071, People's Republic of China. TEL 86-27-7816964. (Dist. overseas by: China International Book Trading Corp., P.O. Box 399, Beijing 100044, P.R. China; Dist. in US by: China Books & Periodicals, Inc., 2929 24th St., San Francisco, CA 94110. TEL 415-282-2994) Ed. Liu Chuncheng. adv. **Document type:** consumer publication.
 Description: General interest television entertainment magazine.

DIANYING, DIANSHI YISHU YANJIU. see MOTION PICTURES

384.55   UK   ISSN 1363-0199
▼**DIGITAL BROADCASTING EUROPE;** newsletter of DVB and DAB services & technologies. 1996. m. TechMedia, 52 Foundling Ct., London WC1N 1AN, England. TEL 44-171-837-0815. FAX 44-171-278-9917. E-mail: 100141.676@compuserve.com. Ed. George Cole; Pub. Philip Gallagher. **Document type:** newsletter.
 Description: Covers digital TV services and technologies.

778.59 621.388
006.6
TR899   US   ISSN 1075-251X
▼**DIGITAL VIDEO MAGAZINE.*** Partial Italian translation: Computer Gazette (IT ISSN 1123-4253) 1993. m. $29.97 (Canada $44.97; Mexico $42.97; overseas $84.97); newsstand price: $3.95; Can.$4.95. TechMedia Publishing, Inc. (Subsidiary of: I D G Company), 411 Borel Ave., San Mateo, CA 94402-3522. TEL 603-924-0100. FAX 603-924-4066. E-mail: lou@dv.com. (Subscr. to: Box 594, Mt. Morris, IL 61054-7902. TEL 815-734-1109) Ed. Louis R. Wallace; Pub. Peter Karnig. adv.: B&W page $4500, color page $5850; trim 8 x 10 3/4. software rev. circ. 40,000. (back issues avail.) **Document type:** consumer publication.
 —KR SourceOne. CCC.
 Formerly (until Jun. 1994): Desktop Video World (ISSN 1067-7720)
 Description: Covers the convergence of computers and video, providing information on digital video hardware and software for major platforms for videographers who are creating computer-enhanced videos. Includes graphics, animation, video capture and editing, image processing and multimedia.

DIRECTORY OF HISPANIC TALENT. see MOTION PICTURES

DIRECTORY OF RELIGIOUS MEDIA. see BUSINESS AND ECONOMICS — Trade And Industrial Directories

DIRITTO DELLE RADIODIFFUSIONI E DELLE TELECOMUNICAZIONI. see LAW

791.4   UK   ISSN 0957-9818
DOCTOR WHO MAGAZINE. 1979. 13/yr. £39(£69) Marvel Comics Ltd., Arundel House, 13-15 Arundel St., London WC2R 3DX, England. TEL 0171-497-2121. FAX 0171-497-2234. (Subscr. to: P.O. Box 503, Leicester LE94 0AD, England) Ed. Gary Russell. adv.; bk.rev.; circ. 33,000 (paid). (back issues avail.) **Document type:** consumer publication.
 Description: Covers the BBC Program "Doctor Who" as well as licensed off-shoots such as plays and film, actors involved, history of show, and related books.

DRAMA-LOGUE. see MOTION PICTURES

DREAM GUYS. see CHILDREN AND YOUTH — For

DUEL; mensile di cinema, immagini e televisione. see MOTION PICTURES

791.4   MP
DZAR BICHIG/PUBLICITY HERALD. (Text in Mongolian) 1991. w. National Information Centre, Ulan Bator, Mongolia.
 Description: Contains theater, cinema and TV programs and advertisements.

E B U TECHNICAL REVIEW. (European Broadcasting Union) see COMMUNICATIONS

E.P. MAGAZINE. see MUSIC

E T V; rivista di attualita-cultura-economia. (Educazione e Televisione) see EDUCATION

384.554   US
ED: ONE CLUB, ONE HORSE, ONE WORLD.* q. membership. Mr. Ed Fan Club, Box 720714, Dallas, TX 75372-0714. **Document type:** consumer publication.
 Description: Geared to fans of the television show Mr. Ed.

EDINBURGH P I C T RESEARCH REPORT SERIES. see COMMUNICATIONS — Telephone And Telegraph

EDINBURGH P I C T STUDENT PAPER SERIES. see COMMUNICATIONS — Telephone And Telegraph

EKRAN; revija za film in televizijo. see MOTION PICTURES

384.5   US   ISSN 0745-0311
PN1990
ELECTRONIC MEDIA. 1982. w. $99. Crain Communications, Inc. (Chicago), 740 N. Rush St., Chicago, IL 60611-2590. TEL 312-649-5200. FAX 312-649-5465. (Subscr. to: 965 E. Jefferson Ave., Detroit, MI 48207-3185. TEL 800-678-9595) Ed. P.J. Bednarski. adv. circ. 26,753. **Document type:** trade publication.
 ●Also available online. Vendor(s): Information Access Co., Lexis-Nexis.
 —UMI. CCC.
 Description: Written for the management of television and radio stations, broadcast networks, cable systems and the emerging electronic media, as well as advertising agency media executives and producers and syndicators of programming.

384.5   US
ELECTRONIC MEDIA DAILY FAX. 1991. 4/w. $99. Crain Communications, Inc. (Chicago), 740 Rush St., Chicago, IL 60611-2590. (Subscr. to: 965 E. Jefferson Ave., Detroit, MI 48207-3185) Ed. David Klein. adv. circ. 26,753. (fax)
 Description: Provides each day's breaking news, ratings results, and other timely information.

791.4   US
ELECTRONIC T V HOST; the television guide inside your computer. w. $49.95 (effective 1997-1998). T V Host, Inc., Box 1665, 3935 Jonestown Rd., Harrisburg, PA 17109. TEL 717-657-1700. FAX 717-657-2921. URL: http://www.tvhost.com; http://www.nytimes.com/maglife.html. adv. contact: Lou Pernik, Jr. illus. **Document type:** consumer publication.
 ●Available only online.
 Description: Informs readers on forthcoming programs on network and cable television. Contains articles of interest on shows and stars.

ELECTRONIC TIMES REPORT. see COMMUNICATIONS

ELECTRONICS & COMMUNICATION ENGINEERING JOURNAL. see ELECTRONICS

ELEKTRO JOURNAL. see ENGINEERING — Electrical Engineering

DAS ELEKTRON - INTERNATIONAL; Revue fuer Radio - Fernsehen - Elektronik and Elektroakustik. see COMMUNICATIONS

621.38   AU   ISSN 0254-4318
ELEKTRONIKSCHAU.* 1924. m. S.400. Erb Verlag GmbH, Eichenstr. 38, A-1120 Vienna, Austria. Ed.Bd. adv.; bk.rev.; bibl.; charts; illus.; pat.; circ. 16,000 (controlled). **Indexed:** Cyb.Abstr., INIS Atomind., INSPEC.
 —BLDSC (3717.833000); AskIEEE; CISTI; KR SourceOne.
 Former titles: Radioschau (ISSN 0033-846X); Radio Elektronik Schau.

791.45   US   ISSN 0896-2502
ELEVEN; WTTW Chicago member magazine. 1987. 10/yr. $40 membership. (Window To The World Communications, Inc.) General Learning Corporation, 900 Skokie Blvd., Ste. 200, Northbrook, IL 60062. TEL 847-205-3000. URL: http://www.wttw.com. Ed. Carol Spielman Lezak; Pb. Julian Berkin. adv. contact: Julian Berkin. bk.rev. circ. 162,000. **Document type:** consumer publication.
 ●Also available online.
 Description: Contains articles relating to programming on WTTW Channel 11 in Chicago (including a complete program listing) as well as articles on cuisine, family and at-home topics, travel, financial matters, education, fiction and communications.

384.554   US   ISSN 0164-3495
PN1992.3.U5
EMMY. 1979. bi-m. $28 (Canada $42; foreign $65). Academy of Television Arts & Sciences, 5220 Lankershim Blvd., N. Hollywood, CA 91601-3107. TEL 818-754-2800. FAX 818-761-2827. Ed. Hank Rieger; Pub. Hank Rieger. R&P contact: Gail Polevoi. adv. contact: John McCarthy. bk.rev.; illus. circ. 12,000. **Indexed:** Access (1979-), Int.Ind.Film Per., Intl.Ind.TV. **Document type:** trade publication.
 —UnCover.
 Description: Covers matters of interest to the television industry, including members of the academy.

ENCORE. see MOTION PICTURES

ENCORE DIRECTORY. see MOTION PICTURES

791.4   US   ISSN 8750-0280
THE ENTERTAINER. m. $24 (effective 1997-1998). T V Host, Inc., Box 1665, 3935 Jonestown Rd., Harrisburg, PA 17109. TEL 717-657-1700. FAX 717-657-2921. URL: http://www.tvhost.com. adv. contact: Lou Pernik, Jr. circ. 275,000 (paid). **Document type:** consumer publication.

ENTERTAINMENT INDUSTRY OUTLOOK. see BUSINESS AND ECONOMICS — Economic Situation And Conditions

ENTERTAINMENT LAW & FINANCE. see LAW

ENTERTAINMENT LAW REPORTER; movies, television, music, theater, publishing, multimedia, sports. see LAW

791.4 070.5   US   ISSN 0739-1897
KF4290.A152
ENTERTAINMENT, PUBLISHING AND THE ARTS HANDBOOK. a. $75. Clark - Boardman - Callaghan, 375 Hudson St., New York, NY 10014. TEL 212-929-7500; 800-422-2101. FAX 212-924-0460. Eds. Robert Thorne, John David Viera.
 Description: Covers copyright, right of publicity, privacy libel, music, motion pictures, television, contracts, entertainment and business.

791.45 384.55   US   ISSN 1058-109X
EPI-LOG;* the television magazine of science fiction, fantasy, comedy, drama and adventure. 1990. bi-m. $30 (Canada $35; elsewhere $40). Epi-log Communications, Inc., Box 456, Dunlap, TN 37327-0456. Ed. William E. Anchors, Jr.
 Description: Covers TV shows of science fiction, fantasy and adventure.

COMMUNICATIONS — TELEVISION AND CABLE

884.5 778.53   US
EL ESPECTACULAR.* (Text in Spanish) 1987. m. $20. Box 14029, Philadelphia, PA 19122-0029. TEL 215-455-8400. FAX 215-455-8402. Ed. Jonath Figueroa. adv. **Document type:** consumer publication.
   Description: Covers entertainment news and events.

621.384   SW   ISSN 0014-1658
ETER-AKTUELLT; tidningen foer DX-are och vaerldsradiolyssnare. 1958. m. SEK 135($20) Sveriges DX-Foerbund - Swedish DX Federation, P.O. Box 3108, S-103 62 Stockholm 3, Sweden. Ed. Paer Mattisson. adv.; bk.rev.; abstr.; charts; illus. circ. 1,500.

384.55 332   US   ISSN 1053-8313
EURO CABLE T V PROGRAMMING. 1990. m. $695 (effective 1997). Kagan World Media, Ltd., 126 Clock Tower Pl., Carmel, CA 93923. TEL 408-624-1536. FAX 408-625-3225. E-mail: info@kagan.com. Ed. Larry Gerbrandt. adv. contact: Lorraine Kagan. **Document type:** trade publication.
   Description: Analyzes programming economics, network values, carriage fees, viewer shares and the financial impact of changes in Europe's cable and DBS/DTH industries.

621.385   GW   ISSN 1021-5735
P92.E9
EUROPAEISCHES MEDIENINSTITUT. BULLETIN. French edition: Institut Europeen de la Communication. Bulletin (ISSN 1021-5727); English edition: European Institute for the Media. Bulletin (ISSN 1021-5719) 1984. q. DM.150. Europaeisches Medieninstitut e.V., Kaistr. 13, 40221 Duesseldorf, Germany. TEL 49-211-901040. FAX 49-211-9010456. E-mail: 100443.1703@compuserve.com. Ed. Bernd Peter Lange. R&P contact: Anne English. adv. contact: Anne English. bk.rev. circ. 2,000. **Document type:** bulletin.
   Formerly: Media Bulletin (ISSN 0267-5382)
   Description: News on the policies and economics of the media industry in Europe.

384.55   US   ISSN 1050-3579
EUROPEAN CABLE - PAY T V. 1988. m. $795 (effective 1997). Paul Kagan Associates, Inc., 126 Clock Tower Place, Carmel, CA 93923. TEL 408-624-1536. FAX 408-625-3225. E-mail: info@kagan.com. Ed. Paul Kagan. adv. contact: Lorraine Yglesias.
   Formerly (until 1990): Euromedia Investor (ISSN 1041-3014)
   Description: Economic analysis of European cable and pay TV, with valuations of public and private companies involved in international media.

384.55   US   ISSN 1055-2839
EUROPEAN HOME VIDEO. 1991. m. $695 (effective 1997). Kagan World Media, Ltd., 126 Clock Tower Pl., Carmel, CA 93923. TEL 408-624-1536. FAX 408-625-3225. E-mail: info@kagan.com. Ed. Paul Kagan. **Document type:** trade publication.
   Description: Analyzes the economics of the business, the revenues of the industry, the hardware growth and software distribution, retail updates, rentals, and sales. Offers insight into new competition from alternative home entertainment products.

621.385   GW   ISSN 1021-5700
EUROPEAN MEDIAFACTS. m. DM.150 (effective 1997). Europaeisches Medieninstitut e.V., Kaistr. 13, 40221 Duesseldorf, Germany. TEL 49-211-901040. FAX 49-211-9010456. E-mail: 100443.1703@compuserve.com. Ed. Bernd Peter Lange. R&P contact: Anne English. adv. contact: Anne English. **Document type:** bulletin.

384.55 338   US   ISSN 1050-298X
EUROPEAN T V SPORTS. 1990. m. $695 (effective 1997). Kagan World Media, Ltd., 126 Clock Tower Pl., Carmel, CA 93923. TEL 408-624-1536. FAX 408-625-3225. E-mail: info@kagan.com. Ed. Jay Stuart. adv. contact: Lorraine Yglesias. **Document type:** trade publication.
   Description: Current data on the business aspects of TV sports broadcasting. Includes rights fees, rights ownership, sponsorship, advertising spending, team revenues and profits, and regulatory changes.

384.55   UK   ISSN 0966-6257
EUROPEAN TELEVISION DIRECTORY. 1991. a. £68. N T C Publications Ltd., Farm Rd., Henley-on-Thames, Oxfordshire RG9 1EJ, England. TEL 01491-411000. FAX 01491-571188. **Document type:** directory.
   Description: Facts and figures on 115 channels in 27 countries.

384.55   XO
EUROTELEVIZIA. 1965. w. newsstand price: 12 Sk. Euroskop, Inc., Pribinova 25, 819 37 Bratislava, Slovakia. TEL 42-7-325405. FAX 42-7-21041522. Ed. Tana Lucka. adv.: B&W page 80000 Sk., color page 115000 Sk.; trim 212 x 270; adv. contact: Monika Tordova. film rev.; play rev.; illus. circ. 350,000. **Document type:** consumer publication.
   Formerly: Televizia (ISSN 0139-7451)
   Description: Provides the program information about more than twenty television channels, and interviews with film stars.

791.4   GW
F F. 1946. w. (Thu.). DM.70.20. Deutscher Supplement Verlag GmbH, Breslauerstr. 300, 90471 Nuernberg, Germany. TEL 0911-89201-0. FAX 0911-8920135. Ed. Alfred Wagner. adv. contact: Annelore Rupp. circ. 510,202. **Document type:** consumer publication.
   Former titles: F F Dabei (ISSN 0532-9140); (until 1969): Funk und Fernsehen (ISSN 0014-5823)

F K T; Fachzeitschrift fuer Fernsehen, Film und elektronische Medien. (Fernseh- und Kino-Technik) see *MOTION PICTURES*

384.5 700   CN   ISSN 0829-4747
FACE TO FACE WITH TALENT. 1970. biennial. Can.$50. Alliance of Canadian Cinema, Television and Radio Artists, Performers Guild, 2239 Yonge St., Toronto, ON M4S 2B5, Canada. TEL 416-489-1311. FAX 416-489-8076. E-mail: apg@actra.com. Ed. Ferne Downey. R&P contact: Ferne Downey. circ. 3,000. **Document type:** directory.
   Description: Features over 2,300 members of ACTRA and Canadian Actors' Equity Association, a significant proportion of the professional actors, performers and broadcasters in Canada. Includes photographs and contact information.

FAMA. see *MOTION PICTURES*

FATAL VISIONS. see *MOTION PICTURES*

791.4   CN   ISSN 1180-4785
FEATURE. 1990. m. Can.$15. Feature Publishing Ltd., Maison Astral, 2100 Rue Ste-Catherine Ouest, Bureau 900, Montreal, PQ H3H 2T3. TEL 514-939-5024. FAX 514-939-1515. Ed. David Sherman; Pub. Marvin Boisvert. R&P contact: Marvin Boisvert. adv.; circ. 460,000 (paid); 290,000 (controlled). **Document type:** consumer publication.
   Description: Stories about and descriptions of feature films on Eastern Canadian English Pay-TV.

384.554   US   ISSN 0147-4871
PN1990.83
FEEDBACK. vol.19, 1977. q. $20. Broadcast Education Association, 1771 N St., N.W., Washington, DC 20036-2891. TEL 202-429-5354. Ed. Jim Fletcher. bk.rev. circ. 1,000. **Document type:** trade publication.
   —BLDSC (3902.124800).
   Description: Provides a forum for the exchange of ideas among members on subjects relevant to educational programs and the industry.

791.4   GW   ISSN 0015-0134
FERNSEH-INFORMATIONEN. 1949. s-m. DM.288. Televisions-Verlag H. Schaefer, Rubenstr. 10, 81245 Munich, Germany. TEL 089-8503432. Ed. H. Schaefer. bk.rev. circ. 500.

384.55 792   XO   ISSN 0323-2921
FILM A DIVADLO. 1957. 26/yr. $78. (Theatre Institute in Bratislava) Obzor, Spitalska 35, 815 85 Bratislava, Slovakia.

FILM CANADA YEARBOOK. see *MOTION PICTURES*

FILM & TELEVISIE - VIDEO. see *MOTION PICTURES*

FILM LITERATURE INDEX. see *MOTION PICTURES — Abstracting, Bibliographies, Statistics*

FILMAARSBOKEN/FILM YEAR BOOK (YEAR). see *MOTION PICTURES*

FILMFAUST; internationale Filmzeitschrift. see *MOTION PICTURES*

791.45   SW   ISSN 1101-2943
FILMNET MAGAZINE. 1989. 11/yr. SEK 300 (effective 1991). Esselte Betal-TV, P.O. Box 9006, S-102 71 Stockholm, Sweden.

384.5 332   US
FINANCIAL MANAGER FOR THE MEDIA PROFESSIONAL. 1972. bi-m. $49. Broadcast Cable Financial Management Association, 701 Lee St., Ste. 640, Des Plaines, IL 60016. TEL 847-296-0200. FAX 847-296-7510. Ed. Marie Kuchel. R&P contact: Susan Solomon. adv. contact: Susan Solomon. illus.; stat.; index. circ. 1,800. **Document type:** trade publication.
   Formerly: Broadcast Cable Financial Journal.
   Description: For professional financial and business managers of broadcasting and cable properties.

791.4   US
FINE TUNING. 1983. m. $3. Channel 10-36 Friends, Inc., Box 122, Milwaukee, WI 53201. TEL 414-278-1468. FAX 414-225-1895. Ed. Steve Tighe. adv. circ. 56,000.

384.12   FI
FINNISH BROADCASTING COMPANY. PLANNING AND RESEARCH DEPARTMENT. RESEARCH REPORTS. (Text in English) irrege. free. Finnish Broadcasting Company, Kesakatu 2, 00260 Helsinki 26, Finland. Ed. Matti Oksanen. circ. 400.
   Formerly: Finnish Broadcasting Company. Section for Long-Range Planning. Research Reports (ISSN 0084-4225)

FOLLOW UP FILE. see *JOURNALISM*

FRICTION. see *MEN'S INTERESTS*

384.54   GH
G B C RADIO AND T V TIMES.* 1960. w. NC.10.40. Ghana Broadcasting Corporation, P.O. Box 1633, Accra, Ghana. TEL 233-21-221161. TELEX 2114. Ed. Ernest Asamoah. adv.; illus. circ. 5,000.
   Formerly: Ghana Radio and Television Times (ISSN 0435-9437)

791.4   US
G B H; the members' magazine. 1987. m. membership W G B H Educational Foundation, 125 Western Ave. Boston, MA 02134. TEL 617-492-2578. Ed. Diane Dion. adv. circ. 175,000. **Document type:** consumer publication.
   Description: Program guide and magazine for members of WGBH, Boston's PBS and NPR station. All editorial content is program-related and explores issues, events, personalities associated with station programming, which includes the arts, history, science, adventure, and public affairs.

GAMEPRO. see *COMPUTERS — Computer Games*

621.388   JA   ISSN 0385-3810
GEKKAN HOSO JANARU/MONTHLY BROADCASTING JOURNAL. (Text in Japanese) 1971. m. 1200 Yen per no. Hoso Janarusha, 3-13, Ginza 7-chome, Chuo-ku, Tokyo 104, Japan.

384.54 384.554   US
GENE PERRET'S ROUND TABLE; a gathering place for comedy writers and humorists. 1981. m. $54.95 (Canada $59.95; elsewhere $67) (effective 1997). 30941 Agoura Rd., Ste. 228, Westlake Village, CA 91361-4617. TEL 818-865-7833. FAX 818-865-0115. E-mail: rtcomedy@aol.com. Ed. Linda Perret; Pub. Linda Perret. bk.rev.; circ. 200 (paid). (back issues avail.) **Document type:** newsletter.

GET READY SHEET. see *PUBLISHING AND BOOK TRADE*

791.4   GW   ISSN 0017-1999
GONG; das aktuelle deutsche Fernseh-Magazin. (Supplement: Rundfunkhoerer und Fernseher) 194 w. (Fri.). DM.140.40 (effective 1997); newsstand price: DM.2.70. Gong Verlag GmbH, Innere Cramer-Klett-Str. 6, 90403 Nuernberg, Germany. TEL 49-911-5325-0. FAX 49-911-5325309. (Subscr. to: P M S GmbH, Postfach 290180, 47261 Duisburg, Germany. TEL 49-203-76908- FAX 49-203-7690830) Ed. Rainer Stiller. adv. contact: Werner Wittl. bk.rev.; film rev.; play rev.; bibl.; illus.; mkt. circ. 904,995. (tabloid format) **Document type:** consumer publication.

COMMUNICATIONS — TELEVISION AND CABLE

791.4   CC
GUANGDONG DIANSHI/GUANGDONG TELEVISION. (Text in Chinese) w. Guangdong Dianshi Tai - Guangdong Television Station, No. 686, Renmin Beilu, Guangzhou, Guangdong 510012, People's Republic of China. TEL 674356. Ed. Ma Yan.

GUARDIAN ENGEL. see *CLUBS*

791.4   IT   ISSN 1120-5121
GUIDA T V. 1976. w. newsstand price: Lit.1000. Arnoldo Mondadori Editore S.p.A, Corso Europa 7-7, 20121 Milan, Italy. TEL 39-2-7794426. FAX 39-2-7794474. E-mail: cavatort@amemail.mondadori.it. Ed. Aldo Gustavo Cimarelli. adv.: color page Lit.10800000. circ. 400,000.
    Formerly: Nuova Guida T V.

HASTINGS COMMUNICATIONS AND ENTERTAINMENT LAW JOURNAL (COMM - ENT). see *LAW*

HILVERSUMMARY. see *COMMUNICATIONS — Radio*

HISTORICAL JOURNAL OF FILM, RADIO AND TELEVISION. see *HISTORY*

HOLLYWOOD ACTING COACHES AND TEACHERS DIRECTORY. see *EDUCATION — Teaching Methods And Curriculum*

HOLLYWOOD REPORTER BLU-BOOK DIRECTORY. see *MOTION PICTURES*

384.55   IT
HOME CINEMA. 1993. s-a. Editore Progest s.r.l., Via Rovereto, 6, 00198 Rome, Italy. TEL 39-6-8551972. FAX 39-6-8558885. adv.: B&W page L.8500000, color page L.13400000; 210 x 270. **Document type:** directory.

384.55   IT
HOME THEATER. 1993. q. Editore Progest s.r.l., Via Rovereto, 6, 00198 Rome, Italy. TEL 39-6-8551972. FAX 39-6-8558885. adv.: B&W page L.790000, color page L.12500000; 210 x 270. **Document type:** trade publication.

HONG KONG. TELEVISION ADVISORY BOARD. ANNUAL REPORT. see *PUBLIC ADMINISTRATION*

791.4   BE   ISSN 0771-8179
HUMO; onafhankelijk weekblad voor radio en televisie. (Text in Dutch) 1936. w. 2750 BEF. Tijdschriften Vereniging Vlaanderen S.A., De Jonckerstr. 46, 1060 Brussels, Belgium. TEL 32-2-537-08-00. FAX 32-2-534-02-38. Ed. Guy Mortier; Pub. Louis Groonen. adv.: B&W page 160000 BEF, color page 394250 BEF; 180 x 243; adv. contact: Helene Piecha. film rev. circ. 231,931. (back issues avail.)

384.55   UK   ISSN 0951-3582
I B A TELEVISION RESEARCH MONOGRAPH. 1986. irreg. (Independent Broadcasting Authority) John Libbey Media, University of Luton, 75 Castle St., Luton, Bedfordshire LU1 3AJ, England. TEL 44-1582-743297. FAX 44-1582-743298. E-mail: john.libbey@luton.ac.uk. Ed. Josephine Langham. **Document type:** academic/scholarly publication.
    Description: Contains reviews of important broadcasting topics and reports of original research carried out by academic media researchers.

621.38   US   ISSN 0018-9316
TK6561   CODEN: IETBAC
I E E E TRANSACTIONS ON BROADCASTING. 1955. q. $50 to non-members (effective 1998). (I E E E, Broadcast Technology Society) Institute of Electrical and Electronics Engineers, Inc., 345 E. 47th St., New York, NY 10017-2394. TEL 732-981-0060; 800-678-4333. FAX 732-981-9667. E-mail: customer.service@ieee.org; URL: http://www.ieee.org. (Subscr. to: Box 1331, 445 Hoes Lane, Piscataway, NJ 08855-1331) Ed. Thomas L. Mann. bk.rev.; abstr.; illus.; index. (also avail. in microform from MIM,UMI,EEE) **Indexed:** A.S.& T.Ind., Acoust.Abstr., ASCA, Chem.Abstr., Curr.Cont., Eng.Ind., INSPEC, Int.Aerosp.Abstr., Math.R., Sci.Cit.Ind.
    —BLDSC (4363.161400); AskIEEE; CISTI; Ei; Genuine Article; KR SourceOne; Linda Hall; SWETS; UMI; UnCover. **CCC.**
    Description: Examines broadcast transmission systems engineering, including the design and utilization of equipment.

I E I C E TRANSACTIONS ON FUNDAMENTALS OF ELECTRONICS, COMMUNICATIONS AND COMPUTER SCIENCES. (Institute of Electronics, Information and Communication Engineers) see *ELECTRONICS*

384.54   UK
I T C ANNUAL REPORT & ACCOUNTS; licensing and regulating commercial television. 1954-1991; resumed 1993. a. free. Independent Television Commission, 33 Foley St., London W1P 7LB, England. TEL 0171-255-3000. FAX 0171-306-7800. **Document type:** corporate report.
    Formerly (until 1991): Independent Broadcasting Authority. Report and Accounts.

384.55   UK   ISSN 0962-7928
I T C TELEVISION RESEARCH MONOGRAPH. 1991. irreg., no.6, 1994. (Independent Television Commission) John Libbey Media, University of Luton, 75 Castle St., Luton, Bedfordshire LU1 3AJ, England. TEL 44-1582-743297. FAX 44-1582-743298. E-mail: john.libbey@luton.ac.uk. Ed.Bd. **Document type:** monographic series.

384.55   US
I T V A NEWS. 1970. bi-m. membership. International Television Association, 6311 N. O'Connor Rd., Ste. 230, Irving, TX 75039. TEL 972-869-1112. FAX 972-869-2980. E-mail: itvahq@worldnet.att.net; URL: http://www.itva.org. Ed. Rene Chapin; Pub. Fred Wehrli. R&P contact: Rene Chapin. adv.; bk.rev. circ. 8,500. **Document type:** newsletter.
    Former titles: International Television News; (until 1978): Industrial Television News (ISSN 0300-7685); N I T A News.
    Description: Carries information of interest to visual communications professionals in corporate and organizational settings and news of association events.

IMAGE TECHNOLOGY; technology of motion picture film, sound, television, audio, visual. see *MOTION PICTURES*

IN FOCUS (LOS ANGELES). see *MOTION PICTURES*

384.55   UK
IN THE VILLAGE. 1977; N.S. 1994. q. £27($45) (effective 1997). Six of One - Prisoner Appreciation Society, P.O. Box 66, Ipswich IP2 9TZ, England. (In U.S.: Prisoner Appreciation Society, c/o Bruce Clark, 871 Clover Dr., North Wales, PA 19454-2749. TEL 215-699-2527. FAX 215-699-2272) (Co-sponsor: Polygram TV International) Ed. David Healey. bk.rev.; tele.; rev.; video rev. circ. 3,000. (back issues avail.) **Document type:** consumer publication.
    Formerly (until 1994): Number Six.
    Description: Comprehensive interviews, production details and underlying symbolism concerning the 1967 British cult TV series "The Prisoner" starring Patrick McGoohan.

384.554   US   ISSN 1064-6833
INDEPENDENT TELEVISION. 1990. q. (Association of Independent Television Stations, Inc.) Crain Communications, Inc. (New York), 220 E. 42nd St., New York, NY 10017. TEL 212-210-0291. FAX 212-210-0400. William H. Dunlap. adv. —**CCC.**

INFORMATION TECHNOLOGY & MANAGEMENT. see *BUSINESS AND ECONOMICS — Office Equipment And Services*

INFORMATION TECHNOLOGY MANAGEMENT; non-technical report on IT and its applications. see *BUSINESS AND ECONOMICS — Office Equipment And Services*

384   IT   ISSN 0300-3973
INFORMAZIONE RADIO TV; studi documenti e notizie. 1970. s-a. free. R A I - Radiotelevisione Italiana, Documentazione e Studi, Viale Mazzini 14, 00195 Rome, Italy. FAX 06-3602460. Ed.Bd. bk.rev.; bibl.; illus.; stat.; index. circ. 1,000. (processed) **Indexed:** Intl.Ind.TV.

INSIDERS SPORTSLETTER. see *SPORTS AND GAMES*

INSTITUTE OF ELECTRONICS, INFORMATION AND COMMUNICATION ENGINEERS. TRANSACTIONS (SECTION A)/DENSHI JOHO TSUSHIN GAKKAI RONBUNSHI (A). see *ENGINEERING*

INSTITUTE OF ELECTRONICS, INFORMATION AND COMMUNICATION ENGINEERS. TRANSACTIONS (SECTION B-I)/DENSHI JOHO TSUSHIN GAKKAI RONBUNSHI (B-I). see *ELECTRONICS*

621.38   JA   ISSN 0915-1885
TK5101.A1   CODEN: DTBTEU
INSTITUTE OF ELECTRONICS, INFORMATION AND COMMUNICATION ENGINEERS. TRANSACTIONS (SECTION B-II)/DENSHI JOHO TSUSHIN GAKKAI RONBUNSHI (B-II). English translation (in part): Electronics and Communications in Japan - Part 3: Fundamental Electronic Science (US ISSN 1042-0967) (Text in Japanese) 1968. m. 2100 Yen. Institute of Electronics, Information and Communication Engineers - Denshi Joho Tsushin Gakkai, c/o Kikai Shinko Kaikan, 5-8 Shiba Koen, 3-chome, Minato-ku, Tokyo 105, Japan. Ed. Michiyuki Uenohara. **Indexed:** INSPEC (1989-), Int.Abstr.Oper.Res., JCT.
    —BLDSC (8939.441200); AskIEEE; CISTI; KR SourceOne. **CCC.**
    Supersedes in part (in 1989): Institute of Electronics, Information and Communication Engineers. Transactions. Section B (ISSN 0913-5715)

INSTITUTE OF ELECTRONICS, INFORMATION AND COMMUNICATION ENGINEERS. TRANSACTIONS (SECTION C-I)/DENSHI JOHO TSUSHIN GAKKAI RONBUNSHI (C-I). see *ELECTRONICS*

INSTITUTE OF ELECTRONICS, INFORMATION AND COMMUNICATION ENGINEERS. TRANSACTIONS (SECTION C-II)/DENSHI JOHO TSUSHIN GAKKAI RONBUNSHI (C-II). see *ELECTRONICS*

INSTITUTE OF ELECTRONICS, INFORMATION AND COMMUNICATION ENGINEERS. TRANSACTIONS (SECTION D-I)/DENSHI JOHO TSUSHIN GAKKAI RONBUNSHI (D-I). see *COMPUTERS — Computer Systems*

INSTITUTE OF ELECTRONICS, INFORMATION AND COMMUNICATION ENGINEERS. TRANSACTIONS (SECTION D-II)/DENSHI JOHO TSUSHIN GAKKAI RONBUNSHI (D-II). see *COMPUTERS — Information Science And Information Theory*

384.55   UK   ISSN 0969-9872
INSTITUTE OF LOCAL TELEVISION. RESEARCH MONOGRAPH. 1993. irreg. John Libbey Media, University of Luton, 75 Castle St., Luton, Bedfordshire LU1 3AJ, England. TEL 44-1582-743297. FAX 44-1582-743298. E-mail: john.libbey@luton.ac.uk. Ed. Dave Rushton. **Document type:** monographic series.

INSTITUTION OF ENGINEERS (INDIA). ELECTRONICS AND TELECOMMUNICATION ENGINEERING DIVISION. JOURNAL. see *ELECTRONICS*

621.38   PL   ISSN 0032-6259
    CODEN: PITRAT
INSTYTUT TELE- I RADIOTECHNICZNY. PRACE. (Contents pages in English and Russian) 1957. q. 40 Zl. Instytut Tele-i Radiotechniczny, Ratuszowa 11, 03-450 Warsaw, Poland. Ed. Stanislaw Kukacki. charts; illus.; index. circ. 370. **Indexed:** INSPEC.
    —AskIEEE; CISTI; KR SourceOne.

384.55 004.6   US   ISSN 1089-2540
▼**(YEAR) INTERACTIVE SOURCEBOOK.** 1995. a. $495 (effective 1998). North American Publishing Co., 401 N. Broad St., Philadelphia, PA 19108. TEL 215-238-5482; 800-777-8074. FAX 215-238-5412. Ed. Robin Whitmire. adv. **Document type:** directory.
    ●Also available on CD-ROM.
    Description: Lists suppliers of cable modems, interactive video systems, Internet and website software, merger and acquistion consultants, Internet home page designers, etc.

INTERLIT. see *RELIGIONS AND THEOLOGY*

COMMUNICATIONS — TELEVISION AND CABLE

384 UK ISSN 0309-118X
HE8689
INTERMEDIA. 1973. bi-m. £70. International Institute of Communications (IIC), Tavistock House., S., Tavistock Sq., London WC1H 9LF, England. TEL 44-171-388-0671. FAX 44-171-380-0623. TELEX 24578 IICLDN G. Eds.. Annelise Berendt, Rex Winsbury. adv.; B&W page £600; color page £1100. bk.rev.; bibl.; illus. circ. 1,500. (also avail. in microform from UMI; reprint service avail. from UMI) Indexed: CAD CAM Abstr., CLOSS, Commun.Abstr., Fut.Surv., Int.Ind.Film Per., Intl.Ind.TV, Tel.Abstr. **Document type:** academic/scholarly publication, trade publication.
—BLDSC (4534.480000); SWETS; UMI; UnCover.
Formerly: I B I Newsletter.
Description: Focuses on all aspects of international broadcasting, telecommunications, media developments, and communications in general.

INTERNATIONAL BLUEGRASS. see *MUSIC*

621.38 UK ISSN 0020-6229
INTERNATIONAL BROADCAST ENGINEER. 1958. 7/yr. £81($162) (overseas £84) (effective 1997). Argus Business Media Ltd. (Subsidiary of: D M G Exhibitions Group Ltd.), Queensway House, 2 Queensway, Redhill, Surrey RH1 1QS, England. TEL 44-1737-768611. FAX 44-1737-761989. Ed. David Kirk. adv.; bk.rev.; abstr.; charts; illus.; pat.; tr.lit.; tr.mk.; index. circ. 10,500. Indexed: Br.Tech.Ind., INSPEC. **Document type:** trade publication.
—BLDSC (4537.600000); AskIEEE; CISTI; KR SourceOne; SWETS.
Incorporates: International T V Technical Review.

621.38 UK ISSN 0957-4425
TK6540 CODEN: IBSODS
INTERNATIONAL BROADCASTING. 1978. m. £60. E M A P Media (Subsidiary of: E M A P Business Communications), 33 Bowling Green Ln., London EC1R 0DA, England. TEL 44-171-505-8073. FAX 44-171-833-4519. E-mail: 74431,1401@compuserve.com. (Subscr. to: Readerlink, Audit House, 260 Field End Rd., Eastcote, Ruislip, Mddx. HA4 9LT, England. TEL 44-181-868-4499. FAX 44-181-429-3117) Ed. Paul Marks. adv. contact: Julie Moore. circ. 10,000. Indexed: INSPEC. **Document type:** trade publication.
—BLDSC (4537.610000); AskIEEE; CISTI; KR SourceOne.
Former titles: International Broadcasting Systems and Operation (ISSN 0141-1748) & Broadcasting Systems and Operation.
Description: Comments on technological developments in the radio and television industry.

621.388 US ISSN 1069-5494
HE8700 CODEN: ICABE9
INTERNATIONAL CABLE. 1990. m. free to qualified personnel. (Society of Cable Television Engineers) Phillips Business Information, Inc., 1201 Seven Locks Rd., Potomac, MD 20854. TEL 301-424-3338. FAX 301-309-3847. E-mail: pbi@phillips.com. Ed. Shelley Ollig. adv.; bk.rev.; charts; illus.; circ. controlled. Indexed: Comput.Cont., INSPEC (1992-). **Document type:** trade publication.
—BLDSC (4538.386500); AskIEEE; KR SourceOne. CCC.

384.55 338.5 US ISSN 1053-8194
INTERNATIONAL CO-PRODUCTIONS. 1990. m. $695. Kagan World Media, Ltd., 126 Clock Tower Pl., Carmel, CA 93923. TEL 408-624-1536. FAX 408-625-3225. E-mail: info@kagan.com. Ed. Robin Flynn. adv. contact: Lorraine Yglesias. **Document type:** trade publication.
Description: Analyzes the deals, money, and people involved in worldwide program development. Covers deal structures, legal and tax issues, economics, U.S. networks and studios, and coproduction facilities - all with a focus on finance.

INTERNATIONAL DIRECTORY OF FILM AND T V DOCUMENTATION COLLECTIONS. see *MOTION PICTURES*

384.55 US
INTERNATIONAL EMMY ALMANAC. a. International Council - National Academy of Television, 142 W. 57th St., 16th Fl., New York, NY 10019-3300. adv.: B&W page $2500, color page $3800; trim 8 1/2 x 11; adv. contact: Gerry Brahney. stat.; tr.lit. **Document type:** trade publication.

384.5 UN ISSN 0252-7235
INTERNATIONAL FREQUENCY LIST/LISTE INTERNATIONALE DES FREQUENCES/LISTA INTERNACIONAL DE FRECUENCIAS. (Supplement avail.: Annex) (Text in English, French, Spanish) s-a. 400 SFr. International Telecommunication Union, Place des Nations, CH-1211 Geneva 20, Switzerland. TEL 41-22-7306141. FAX 41-22-7305464. E-mail: sales@itu.ch; URL: http://www.itu.ch. Ed.Bd. (microfiche) **Document type:** bulletin.
●Also available on CD-ROM.

384.5 UN ISSN 0252-1725
INTERNATIONAL FREQUENCY LIST. PREFACE. (Supplement avail.) (Editions in English, French, Spanish) 1970. irreg. 68 SFr. International Telecommunication Union, Place des Nations, CH-1211 Geneva 20, Switzerland. TEL 41-22-7306141. FAX 41-22-7305464. E-mail: sales@itu.ch; URL: http://www.itu.ch. **Document type:** bulletin.

INTERNATIONAL INDEX TO TELEVISION PERIODICALS. see *COMMUNICATIONS — Abstracting, Bibliographies, Statistics*

621.385 US ISSN 0275-0473
TK6271 CODEN: IITPDH
INTERNATIONAL TELECOMMUNICATIONS ENERGY CONFERENCE. PROCEEDINGS. Short title: I N T E L E C. (Published by other organizations when held outside of U.S.) 1978. a. price varies. (I E E E, Communications Society) Institute of Electrical and Electronics Engineers, Inc., 345 E. 47th St., New York, NY 10017-2394. TEL 732-981-0060; 800-678-4333. FAX 732-981-9667. E-mail: customer.service@ieee.org; URL: http://www.ieee.org. (Subscr. to: Box 1331, 445 Hoes Ln., Piscataway, NJ 08855-1331)
—BLDSC (4531.818700); Ei; UMI. **CCC.**
Formerly: International Telephone Energy Conference. Proceedings.
Description: Details state-of-the-art and future developments in the field of power supply for equipment and services.

384.55 US ISSN 0895-2213
HE8700
INTERNATIONAL TELEVISION & VIDEO ALMANAC; reference tool of the television and home video industries. 1956. a. $100. Quigley Publishing Co., 159 W. 53 St., New York, NY 10019. TEL 212-247-3100. FAX 212-489-0871. Ed. James Moser; Pub. Martin Quigley. adv. contact: James Moser. (also avail. in microfilm from BHP) **Document type:** trade publication.
Formerly: International Television Almanac (ISSN 0539-0761)

791 SZ ISSN 0082-0776
INTERNATIONAL TELEVISION SYMPOSIUM AND TECHNICAL EXHIBITION, MONTREUX. SYMPOSIUM RECORD. 1961. biennial. 200 Fr. International Television Symposium, Case Postale 97, CH-1820 Montreux, Switzerland. FAX 41-21-9638851. TELEX 453283. Ed.Bd. adv. circ. 4,000.

INTERNATIONAL WORKSHOP ON H D T V. PROCEEDINGS. see *COMMUNICATIONS — Computer Applications*

384.5 621.38 GW ISSN 0946-3348
HE8690
INTERNATIONALES HANDBUCH FUER HOERFUNK UND FERNSEHEN. 1957. biennial. DM.138. Hans Bredow Institut, Heimhuderstr. 21, 20148 Hamburg, Germany. TEL 49-40-45021741. FAX 49-40-45021777. (Subscr. to: NOMOS Verlag, Postfach 610, 76484 Baden-Baden, Germany. TEL 49-7221-2104-0) Ed. Christiane Matzen. adv. circ. 2,500. **Document type:** trade publication.
—CISTI.
Formerly: Internationales Handbuch fuer Rundfunk und Fernsehen (ISSN 0535-4358)

621.38 IE
IRISH ELECTRICAL REVIEW. 1962. m. I£22 (effective 1997). Sky Publishing Ltd., 5 Main St., Blackrock, Co. Dublin, Ireland. TEL 353-1-2836755. FAX 353-1-2836784. Ed. Patrick J. Codyre. adv. contact: Patrick J. Codyre. illus.; tr.lit. circ. 3,000. **Document type:** trade publication.
Formerly: Irish Electrical Industries Review (ISSN 0021-1141); Which incorporates: Irish Radio and Electrical Journal.

621.38 UA
AL-IZAA WAL-TELEVISION/RADIO AND TELEVISION. (Text in Arabic) 1935. w. 13 Sharia Muhammed Ezz El-Arab, Cairo, Egypt. Ed. Sakeena Fouad. adv. circ. 80,000.

JACK BENNY TIMES. see *CLUBS*

JAHRBUCH DER LANDESMEDIENANSTALTEN; privater Rundfunk in Deutschland. see *COMMUNICATIONS — Radio*

JEE: FILM & T V FORTNIGHTLY. see *MOTION PICTURES*

JOURNAL DES LETTRES ET DE L'AUDIOVISUEL. see *LITERATURE*

384 US ISSN 0883-8151
PN1991
JOURNAL OF BROADCASTING AND ELECTRONIC MEDIA. 1956. q. $75 (foreign $90). Broadcast Education Association, 1771 N St., N.W., Washington, DC 20036. TEL 202-429-5354. Ed. Dennis Davis. bk.rev.; charts; index, cum.index every 25 yrs. circ. 2,200. (also avail. in microform from UMI,PMC; microfilm from WSH; microfiche from WSH; reprint service avail. from UMI,WSH) Indexed: Acad.Ind., Arts & Hum.Cit.Ind., ASCA, C.I.J.E., C.L.I., Commun.Abstr., Crim.Just.Abstr., Curr.Cont., Educ.Tech.Abstr., Fam.Ind., Hum.Ind., IJCS (1956-), Int.Ind.Film Per., Intl.Ind.TV, L.R.I., Leg.Per., Mid.East: Abstr.& Ind., P.A.I.S., Per.Islam. (1990-), Psychol.Abstr. (1986-), Soc.Sci.Ind. (1994-), Sociol.Abstr., SSCI, Stud.Wom.Abstr. **Document type:** academic/scholarly publication, trade publication.
●Also available online. Vendor(s): UMI.
—BLDSC (4954.552000); Genuine Article; KR SourceOne; SWETS; UMI; UnCover.
Formerly (until 1985): Journal of Broadcasting (ISSN 0021-938X)
Description: Scholarly journal of communication and electronic media research, including media uses, effect, regulation, history, organization, advertising, technology, news, and entertainment.

384.55 371.33 UK ISSN 1358-1651
LB1044.7
JOURNAL OF EDUCATIONAL MEDIA. 1975. 3/yr. £68($148) to individuals; institutions I£158($438) (effective 1996). (Educational Television Association) Carfax Publishing Co., P.O. Box 25, Abingdon, Oxon. OX14 3UE, England. TEL 44-1235-401000. FAX 44-1235-401550. E-mail: enquiries@carfax.co.uk. (Subscr. in N. America to: Carfax Publishing Co., 875-81 Massachusetts Ave., Cambridge, MA 02139) Ed. M.M. Davies. bk.rev.; abstr.; illus.; index. (also avail. in microfiche; back issues avail.) Indexed: Arts & Hum.Cit.Ind., ASCA, Br.Educ.Ind., C.I.J.E., Child.Lit.Abstr., Cont.Pg.Educ., Curr.Cont, Educ.Tech.Abstr., Mult.Ed.Abstr., Res.High.Educ.Abstr., Sage Fam.Stud.Abstr., SOMA, SSCI, Stud.Wom.Abstr., Tech.Educ.Abstr. **Document type:** academic/scholarly publication.
—BLDSC (4973.157400); Genuine Article; SWETS; UMI; UnCover. **CCC.**
Formerly: Journal of Educational Television (ISSN 0260-7417)
Refereed Serial

621.388 JA
JOURNAL OF THREE DIMENSIONAL IMAGES/SURI D EIZO. (Text in English, Japanese) 1987. q. 1000 Yen per no. Forum for Advancement of Three Dimensional Image Technology and Arts - Sanjigen Eizo no Foramu, c/o Mr. Joji Hamasaki, Tokyo Daigaku Seisan Gijutsu Kenkyujo, 22-1, Roppongi 7-chome, Minato-ku, Tokyo 106.

JOURNALIST'S HANDBOOK. see *JOURNALISM*

JUNGE RADIO-, FERNSEH- UND INDUSTRIE-ELEKTRONIKER. see *COMMUNICATIONS — Radio*

384.55 US ISSN 1045-5744
K A E T MAGAZINE. 1975. m. $40 (effective 1997). (Arizona State University) K A E T, Box 1405, Tempe, AZ 85287-1405. TEL 602-965-3506. FAX 602-965-1000. URL: KAET2ASU.EDU. Ed. Sondra Mesnik. adv. circ. 50,000. (back issues avail.) **Document type:** consumer publication.

K & C. (Kunst en Cultuur) see *ART*

K C T S - NINE. see *GENERAL INTEREST PERIODICALS — United States*

COMMUNICATIONS — TELEVISION AND CABLE

384.5 791.4 US
K P B S ON AIR. 1969. m. $45 (effective 1997). K P B S - T V and F M Radio, San Diego State University, 5200 Campanile Dr., San Diego, CA 92182-5400. TEL 619-594-3766. Ed. Michael Good. adv. contact: Bruce Bauer. circ. 62,000 (paid). **Document type:** consumer publication, directory.
  Description: Publishes information about San Diego arts and entertainment and public television and radio programming for KPBS members.

384.5 GW ISSN 0177-9249
KABEL & SATELLIT. 1983. w. DM.728. Neue Mediengesellschaft Ulm mbH, Konrad-Celtis-Str. 77, 81369 Munich, Germany. TEL 49-89-74117190. FAX 49-89-74117195. Ed.Bd. adv.; bk.rev. circ. 1,500. **Document type:** trade publication.

384.55 NE ISSN 0165-439X
KABELVISIE; vakblad voor kabeltelevisie, omroep en telecommunicatie. 1973. m. fl.192.50 (foreign fl.200). Televak Uitgeverij N.V., Postbus 75985, 1070 AZ Amsterdam, Netherlands. TEL 31-20-6659220. FAX 31-20-6657316. Ed. J. Boers; Pub. M. de Rooij. adv. contact: Maarten Ponssen. illus.; index; circ. 2,000 (paid). **Document type:** trade publication.
  —SWETS.

791.4 LI
KALBA VILNIUS. 1956. w. Konarskio 49, Vilnius 232674, Lithuania. TEL (0122) 661-022. Ed. Algirdas Kratulis.

791.4 FI ISSN 0355-2969
KATSO. 1960. w. FIM 858; newsstand price: (effective 1997). A-Lehdet Oy, Hitsaajankatu 7, FIN-00081 A-Lehdet, Finland. FAX 358-0-781911. Ed. Dona Tuomi. circ. 62,295. **Document type:** consumer publication.
  Description: TV and radio guide for Finland.

384.55 658.8 UK
KEY NOTE MARKET REPORT: CABLE AND SATELLITE T V. Variant title: Cable and Satellite T V. 2nd ed., 1987. irreg., no.5, 1994. £205. Key Note Ltd., Field House, 72 Oldfield Rd., Hampton, Middlesex TW12 2HQ, England. TEL 44-181-783-0755. FAX 44-181-783-0049. **Document type:** trade publication.
  ●Also available online.
  Also available on CD-ROM.
  Former titles: Key Note Report: Cable and Satellite T V; Key Note Report: Cable T V - D B S Services.

384.55 UK
KEY NOTE MARKET REPORT: CABLING & WIRING. Variant title: Cabling & Wiring. 1996. irreg. £205. Key Note Ltd., Field House, 72 Oldfield Rd., Hampton, Middlesex TW12 2HQ, England. TEL 44-181-783-0755. FAX 44-181-783-0049. **Document type:** trade publication.

384.55 UK
KEY NOTE MARKET REPORT: COMMERCIAL T V. Variant title: Commercial T V. irreg., no.4, 1994. £205. Key Note Ltd., Field House, 72 Oldfield Rd., Hampton, Middlesex TW12 2HQ, England. TEL 44-181-783-0755. FAX 44-181-783-0049. **Document type:** trade publication.
  ●Also available online.
  Also available on CD-ROM.
  Formerly: Key Note Report: Commercial T V (ISSN 0954-5107).

384.55 778.53 UK
KEY NOTE MARKET REPORT: INDEPENDENT T V & FILM PRODUCTION. Variant title: Independent T V & Film Production. 1991. irreg. £185. Key Note Ltd., Field House, 72 Oldfield Rd., Hampton, Middlesex TW12 2HQ, England. TEL 44-181-783-0755. FAX 44-181-783-1940. **Document type:** trade publication.

KLIP. see *MOTION PICTURES*

384 UK ISSN 0966-3371
THE KNOWLEDGE. 1986. a. £73.50 (Europe £86; rest of world £94) (effective 1997). Miller Freeman Information Services (Subsidiary of: United News & Media), Riverbank House, Angel Ln., Tonbridge, Kent TN9 1SE, England. TEL 44-1732-362666. FAX 44-1732-767301. E-mail: info@mfplc.com; URL: http://www.mfplc.com. Ed. Gwen Young. adv.: B&W page £1625, color page £2025; 135 x 201; adv. contact: Elaine Soni. charts; maps. circ. 3,000. **Document type:** directory.
  ●Also available on CD-ROM.
  —BLDSC (5100.429800).
  Description: For companies and individuals working in the TV, film and video production industries in the UK. Includes over 10,000 crew and company contacts.

KURZWELLE AKTUELL. see *ADVERTISING AND PUBLIC RELATIONS*

384.55 332 US ISSN 1074-1135
LATIN AMERICAN CABLE & PAY T V. 1993. m. $795 (effective 1997). Kagan World Media, Ltd., 126 Clock Tower Pl., Carmel, CA 93923. TEL 408-624-1536. FAX 408-625-3225. E-mail: info@kagan.com. Ed. Robin Flynn. adv. contact: Lorraine Yglesias. **Document type:** trade publication.
  Description: Supplies economic analysis of the media industry in Latin American markets. Covers cable subscriber growth rates, basic cable and pay TV penetration; program network launches, satellite growth; mergers and acquisitions, regulatory developments, investment opportunities and contacts.

LEONARD MALTIN'S MOVIE AND VIDEO GUIDE. see *MOTION PICTURES*

384.5 US
LEWIS LETTER ON CABLE MARKETING.* 1977. m. $95. Lewis Associates, Inc., Box 567, Housatonic, MA 01236-0567. TEL 413-528-9445. Ed. Eiken Willner. (back issues avail.)
  Description: Marketing, public relations and advertising advice for cable companies.

LIFE VIDEO; przegląd sprzętu i kaset. see *ELECTRONICS*

LIGHTS!. see *THEATER*

791.4 RH ISSN 0024-6352
LOOK & LISTEN. 1966. fortn. Z.$64. Munn Publishing (Pvt.) Ltd., Box UA 589, Union Ave., Harare, Zimbabwe. TEL 263-4-752144. FAX 263-4-752062. TELEX 24748 ZW. E-mail: munn@masasa.samaro.co.zw. Ed. G. Peter. adv.; bk.rev.; illus. circ. 21,700. **Document type:** consumer publication.

384.55 UK
LOOK IN TELEVISION ANNUAL; for children. a. £3.95. I P C Magazines, Southbank Publishing Group (Subsidiary of: Reed Elsevier group), King's Reach Tower, Stamford St., London SE1 9LS, England. TEL 44-171-261-5000. FAX 44-1444-445599. Ed. Colin Shelbourn. **Document type:** consumer publication.

LOYOLA ENTERTAINMENT LAW JOURNAL. see *LAW*

LURZER'S INTERNATIONAL ARCHIVE; ads, TV and posters world-wide. see *ADVERTISING AND PUBLIC RELATIONS*

M. see *COMMUNICATIONS — Telephone And Telegraph*

383 US
M A I N. (Media Arts Information Network) 1991. m. membership only. National Alliance for Media Arts and Culture, 346 Ninth St., San Francisco, CA 94103-3809. TEL 415-431-1391. FAX 415-432-1392. Ed. Helen DeMichel. **Document type:** newsletter.

384 US
M H I S UPDATE. 1979. m. $300. Miller & Holbrooke Information Services, 1225 19th St., N.W., Ste. 400, Washington, DC 20036. TEL 202-785-8827. FAX 202-785-1234. Ed. Michael J. Goldrich. bk.rev.; bibl.; index. circ. 300. (back issues avail.) Indexed: PROMT.
  Former titles (until 1993): Cable Update; (until 1989): C T I C Reports; Cable Television Information Center. Urban Institute. Notes from the Center.
  Description: Contains reports, analysis and documents related to cable television and telecommunications of interest to state and local franchising authorities, municipal cable officers, libraries and other interested persons.

MASIFORM D. see *LITERATURE — Science Fiction, Fantasy, Horror*

621.38 II
MASS MEDIA IN INDIA. (Text in English) 1978. a. price varies. Ministry of Information & Broadcasting, Publications Division, Patiala House, Tilak Marg, New Delhi 110001, India. **Document type:** government publication.

384 301 UK ISSN 0163-4437
HM258
MEDIA CULTURE & SOCIETY. 1979. q. £40($64) to individuals; institutions £150($240) (effective 1998). Sage Publications Ltd., 6 Bonhill St., London EC2A 4PU, England. TEL 44-171-374-0645. FAX 44-171-374-8741. E-mail: market@sagepub.co.uk; URL: http://www.sagepub.co.uk/. Ed.Bd. adv. contact: Bernie Folan. bk.rev.; illus.; index. Indexed: Arts & Hum.Cit.Ind., ASCA, Commun.Abstr., Curr.Cont., DAAI, Film.Lit.Ind., IBR, IBZ, Int.Ind.Film Per., Int.Polit.Sci.Abstr., Intl.Bibl.S.S.Soc.Cult.Anthro., Intl.Ind.TV, Mult.Ed.Abstr., Soc.Sci.Ind., Sociol.Abstr., Sociol.Educ.Abstr., Sp.Ed.Needs Abstr., SSCI, SSCI. **Document type:** academic/scholarly publication.
  —BLDSC (5525.255500); KR SourceOne; SWETS; UnCover.
  Description: Provides a major international forum for the presentation of research and discussion concerning the media, including the newer information and communication technologies, within their political, economic, cultural and historical contexts.
  Refereed Serial

380 070 US ISSN 1072-3552
P92.U5
MEDIA CULTURE REVIEW. 4/yr. $16 to individuals; institutions $36. Institute for Alternative Journalism, 77 Federal St., San Francisco, CA 94107. TEL 415-284-1420. FAX 415-284-1414. Ed. Don Hazen. R&P contact: Don Hazen. **Document type:** newsletter.

384.5 070.5 US
MEDIA GUIDE (CLEVELAND). 1954. a. $25 (effective Jan. 1996). Federation for Community Planning, 614 W. Superior Ave., Ste. 300, Cleveland, OH 44113-1306. TEL 216-781-2944. FAX 216-781-2988. E-mail: jdawes@fcp.org. Ed. Jennie Dawes. R&P contact: Jennie Dawes. circ. 1,200. **Document type:** directory.
  Formerly: Publicity Guide.
  Description: Directory of local print and broadcast media along with advice on accessing media.

MEDIA IN EDUCATION & DEVELOPMENT. see *EDUCATION*

MEDIA INTERNATIONAL AUSTRALIA; quarterly journal of media research and resources. see *COMMUNICATIONS*

340 AT
MEDIA LAW AND PRACTICE. 1987. 5/yr. in 2 vols. Aus.$420. L B C Information Services, 50 Waterloo Rd., N. Ryde, N.S.W. 2113, Australia. TEL 61-2-99366444. FAX 61-2-98889706. TELEX ASBOOK 27995. Eds. J. McLachlan, P. Mallam. (looseleaf format)
  Formerly (until 1995): Broadcasting Law and Practice.
  Description: Examines laws relating to broadcasting, radio communications and other media related issues such as defamation, copyright, advertising and complaints. Includes commentary, legislation, standards, codes and guidelines.

MEDIA MAP DATAFILE. see *BUSINESS AND ECONOMICS — Marketing And Purchasing*

COMMUNICATIONS — TELEVISION AND CABLE

MEDIA MAP OF EASTERN EUROPE. see *BUSINESS AND ECONOMICS — Marketing And Purchasing*

MEDIA MAP OF WESTERN EUROPE. see *BUSINESS AND ECONOMICS — Marketing And Purchasing*

MEDIA MATTERS. see *ADVERTISING AND PUBLIC RELATIONS*

621.385 GW ISSN 0267-4467
MEDIA MONOGRAPH. French edition (ISSN 0267-4483) (Text in English) 1984. q. Europaeisches Medieninstitut e.V., Kaistr. 13, 40221 Duesseldorf, Germany. TEL 49-211-90104-0. FAX 49-211-9010456. Ed. Bernd Peter Lange. R&P contact: Anne English. adv. contact: Anne English. **Document type:** monographic series.
—BLDSC (5525.258300).

384.55 GW ISSN 0170-1754
P87
MEDIA PERSPEKTIVEN. 1970. m. Arbeitsgemeinschaft der ARD - Werbegesellschaften, Am Steinernen Stock 1, 60320 Frankfurt a.M., Germany. FAX 49-69-1552857. Ed. Klaus Berg. adv.; bk.rev.; index. circ. 7,000. (back issues avail.) **Indexed:** IBR, Int.Ind.Film Per. (until 1995). **Document type:** trade publication.
—BLDSC (5525.258550); SWETS.

MEDIA PROFESSIONAL. see *JOURNALISM*

MEDIA REPORTER. see *MOTION PICTURES*

384.5 US ISSN 0889-0951
MEDIA SPORTS BUSINESS. 1982. m. $645 (effective 1997). Paul Kagan Associates, Inc., 126 Clock Tower Place, Carmel, CA 93923. TEL 408-624-1536. TELEX 408-625-3225. Ed. John Mansell. charts; index.
Formerly: Pay T V Sports.
Description: Newsletter on the economic power struggle among sports teams and the electronic media. Analysis of the value of sports media rights.

MEDIAS POUVOIRS. see *JOURNALISM*

621.38 384.554
384.554 GW ISSN 0723-2128
MEDIEN BULLETIN; Fernsehen, Hoerfunk, Technik, Produktion. 1982. m. DM.183. Kellerer und Partner GmbH, Postfach 401080, 80710 Munich, Germany. TEL 49-89-38385416. FAX 49-89-38385428. Ed. Andreas Schuemchen. adv. contact: Heidelore Moeller. bk.rev. circ. 7,200. **Document type:** bulletin.

384 621.38 GW
MEDIEN DIALOG; Gespraech - Diskussion - Meinung - Information. 1987. m. DM.350. Wilfried Ahrens Verlag, Postfach 1360, 83046 Bruckmuehl, Germany. TEL 49-8062-6550. FAX 49-8062-6591. Ed. Wilfried Ahrens. adv.; bk.rev. circ. 3,500. **Document type:** trade publication.
Description: Covers media policy, TV and radio markets.

791.4 GW ISSN 0176-4918
P87
MEDIEN & ERZIEHUNG; Zweimonatsschrift fuer audiovisuelle Kommunikation. 1957. bi-m. DM.52 (students DM.41.60) (effective 1997). KoPaed Verlag, Pfaelzer-Wald-Str. 64, 81539 Munich, Germany. TEL 49-89-6891912. FAX 49-89-6891912. Ed. Erwin Schaar. adv.; bk.rev.; bibl.; film rev.; illus.; index. circ. 2,200. **Indexed:** Film Lit.Ind. (1973-), IBR. **Document type:** academic/scholarly publication.
—CCC.
Former titles (until 1984): M E R Z - Medien und Erziehung (ISSN 0723-399X); (until 1979): Medien und Erziehung (ISSN 0341-6860); Jugend Film Fernsehen (ISSN 0022-5886)
Description: Explores film, television, electronic games and computers as matters and instruments of learning.

MEDIEN UND RECHT INTERNATIONAL; Zeitschrift fuer das Recht der Medien und der Werbung. see *LAW*

MEDIENREPORT. see *BUSINESS AND ECONOMICS — Management*

384.5 028.1 GW ISSN 1431-5262
P87
MEDIENWISSENSCHAFT; Zeitschrift fuer Rezensionen ueber Veroeffentlichungen zu saemtlichen Medien. 1984. q. DM.98 (foreign DM.114) (effective 1998). Schueren Presseverlag GmbH, Deutschhausstr. 31, 35037 Marburg, Germany. TEL 49-6421-63084. FAX 49-6421-681190. E-mail: schueren.verlag@t-online.de. Ed.Bd. adv.; bk.rev.; index. circ. 800. (also avail. in diskette format) **Indexed:** IBR. **Document type:** academic/scholarly publication.
—CCC.
Formerly (until 1995): Medienwissenschaft: Rezensionen (ISSN 0176-4241)
Description: Reviews books in all fields of mass media communications, including radio, TV, motion pictures, and theater.

384.55 UK ISSN 1357-7220
P94.5.M552
▼**MERCATOR MEDIA FORUM.** 1996. a. £10. (University of Wales, Mercator Media) University of Wales Press, 6 Gwennyth St., Cathays, Cardiff CF2 4YD, Wales. TEL 44-1222-231919. FAX 44-1222-230908. E-mail: journals@press.wales.ac.uk; URL: http://www.swan.ac.uk/uwp/home.htm. Ed. George Jones. circ. 200 (paid). **Document type:** academic/scholarly publication.
Description: Promotes discussion and the flow of information between those in the European Union who work in the field of media.

METRO. see *EDUCATION — Teaching Methods And Curriculum*

METRO EDUCATION. see *EDUCATION — Teaching Methods And Curriculum*

384.554 CN ISSN 1191-7962
METRO WEEKLY TELECASTER. 1974. w. Fundy Group Publications, P.O. Box 128, 2 Second St., Yarmouth, NS B5A 4B1, Canada. TEL 902-742-7111. FAX 902-742-2311. Ed. Jeremy Akerman. circ. 16,000 (paid).
Former titles (until 1992): Metro Telecaster (ISSN 0708-2568); (until 1977): Metro Telecaster and Entertainment Guide (ISSN 0708-255X)

384.55 UK ISSN 0968-4344
MIDDLE EAST BROADCAST AND SATELLITE. (Text in English; summaries in Arabic) 1993. bi-m. £45($85) Icom Publications Ltd., Chancery House, St. Nicholas Way, Sutton, Surrey SM1 1JB, England. TEL 44-181-642-1117. FAX 44-181-642-1941. E-mail: mebs@icompub.demon.co.uk. Ed. K. Anderson; Pub. Alec Barton. adv.: B&W page $2720, color page $4250; trim 210 x 297; adv. contact: A. Wand. **Document type:** trade publication.
Description: Reports industry news and contains features and market data.

384.55 621.388 UK ISSN 1358-040X
▼**MIDDLE EAST SATELLITE TODAY.** 1995. bi-m. £45($85) Icom Publications Ltd., Chancery House, St. Nicholas Way, Sutton, Surrey SM1 1JB, England. TEL 44-181-642-1117. FAX 44-181-642-1941. E-mail: mest@icompub.demon.co.uk. Ed. K. Anderson; Pub. Alec Barton. adv.: B&W page $2525, color page $3630; trim 297 x 210; adv. contact: A. Wand. circ. 6,034 (controlled). **Document type:** trade publication.
Description: Supplies news, market reports, and technical and business features on the satellite distribution market in the Middle East.

384.5 IT ISSN 1122-9276
MILLECANALI; tv, radio, comunicazione, spettacolo. 1974. m. (11/yr.). L.120000 (effective 1997). Gruppo Editoriale J C E, Via Ferri 6, 20092 Cinisello Balsamo (MI), Italy. TEL 39-2-660251. FAX 39-2-6127620. TELEX 352376 JCE MIL I. E-mail: millecanali@jce.it; URL: http://www.jce.it. Ed. Mauro Roffi. adv.: B&W page 4000000, color page L.6500000; trim 210 x 280. circ. 15,000.
Description: Presents articles on radio, TV broadcasting, and audiovisual production.

MILLIMETER; the magazine of the motion picture and television production industries. see *MOTION PICTURES*

MINGAY'S ELECTRICAL RETAILER; covering sales and service in the home appliance radio and TV market. see *BUSINESS AND ECONOMICS — Marketing And Purchasing*

791.45 CN
MINI-DISH GUIDE. m. Can.$29.99 (effective 1997). T V Publishing Group, 201 - 4201 25A Ave., Vernon, BC V1T 7G8, Canada. TEL 250-542-0469; 800-663-4424. FAX 250-542-0942. Ed. Deeny Grazier; Pub. Tom Monahan. R&P contact: Deeny Grazier. adv. contact: Norm Metcalf.

780 IE
▼**MODEST PROPOSALS.** 1997. bi-w. Modest Proposals, Nua Ltd., Westland Court, S. Cumberland St., Dublin 2, Ireland. TEL 353-1-676-8996. FAX 353-1-661-3932. E-mail: modest@nua.ie; URL: http://www.nua.ie/modestproposals/. Ed. David Moore.
●Available only online.
Description: Encourages new and deeper thinking on the pressing cultural issues of the day: TV shows, advertisements, music, celebrities and other consumer products.

384.5 IT
MONITOR. 1978. m. free to qualified personnel. Media Edizioni srl., Via Gaffurio 4, 20124 Milan, Italy. Ed. Edoardo Fleischner. adv. circ. 12,500.

384.54 AT ISSN 1323-5435
MONITOR. 1937. bi-m. Institution of Radio and Electronics Engineers Society, Level 1, 118 Alfred St., Milsons Point, N.S.W. 2061, Australia. TEL 61-2-9290099. FAX 61-2-9290587. Ed. Cherie Morris. adv.: B&W page Aus.$675, color page Aus.$1080; 309 x 222.

384.5 IT ISSN 0394-0896
MONITOR - RADIO T V. 1978. m. L.75000 (effective 1997). Media Age s.r.l., Via S. Jacini 4, 20121 Milan, Italy. TEL 39-2-876038. FAX 39-2-86450149. E-mail: monitor_radiotv@compuserve.com; URL: http://ourworld.compuserve.com/homepages/monitor_radiotv. Ed. Enrico Callerio; Pub. Enrico Callerio. R&P contact: Maria Ronchetti. TEL 39-2-862534. adv.: B&W page L.3100000, color page L.4400000; adv. contact: Carlotta Pellizzari. bk.rev. circ. 15,000. **Document type:** trade publication.

MOTION PICTURE, T V & THEATRE DIRECTORY; for services & products. see *BUSINESS AND ECONOMICS — Trade And Industrial Directories*

MOVIE - T V MARKETING. see *MOTION PICTURES*

384 JA
MOVIE - T V MARKETING ANNUAL WORLDWIDE TELEVISION SURVEY. (Text in English) 1964. a. 10000 Yen. Movie - T V Marketing, Box 30, Central Post Office, Tokyo 100-91, Japan. TEL 03-3587-2855. FAX 03-3587-2820. Ed. Asia M. Ireton. adv. circ. 100,000. **Document type:** trade publication.
Formerly: Annual Worldwide T V Survey.

MOVIE - T V MARKETING GLOBAL MOTION PICTURE YEAR BOOK. see *MOTION PICTURES*

MOVING PICTURES TELEVISION. see *MOTION PICTURE*

384.55 US ISSN 0276-8593
HE8700.7.C6
MULTICHANNEL NEWS. 1980. w. $96 (foreign $195) Capital Cities - A B C, Inc., Diversified Publishing Group, 825 Seventh Ave., New York, NY 10019. TEL 212-887-8400. (Subscr. to: Box 10729, Riverton, NJ 08076-6129) Ed. Marianne Paskowski. Pub. Larry Oliver. adv. contact: Paul Audino. index. circ. 21,500. (also avail. in microfilm from FCM.) **Document type:** trade publication.
●Also available online. Vendor(s): Information Access Co.
—CCC.
Description: Covers all the related fields of cable television industry: programming, pay per view, marketing and promotion, advertising sales, technology, operations, customer service, policy and business.

MULTIMEDIA ENTERTAINMENT & TECHNOLOGY REPOR see *COMPUTERS — Computer Industry*

COMMUNICATIONS — TELEVISION AND CABLE

791 US ISSN 1072-8090
THE MUNSTERS & THE ADDAMS FAMILY REUNION.
1987. q. $20 (effective Jan. 1993). (Munsters and Addams Family Fan Club) Fan Club Publishing, Box 69A04, Dept. UL, W. Hollywood, CA 90069. TEL 213-650-5112. Ed. Louis Wendruck; Pub. Louis Wendruck. adv.; bk.rev. circ. 20,000. (back issues avail.) **Document type:** newsletter.
  Description: For fans of these two 1960's television comedy shows, and their more recent movies.

MUSIC VIDEO MAGAZINE. see *MUSIC*

384.5 791 BE
MUZIEK & WOORD. (Text in Dutch) 1974. m. 800 BEF. (Belgische Radio en Televisie) B R T N Persdienst, A. Reyerslaan 52, 1043 Brussels, Belgium. TEL 32-2-7415132. FAX 32-2-7415543. Ed. Leen Boereboom; Pub. Hugo Morrens. R&P contact: Leen Boereboom. adv. contact: Leen Boereboom. bk.rev.; film rev.; index. **Document type:** consumer publication.

N A B E T - C W A NEWS. (National Association of Broadcast Employees and Technicians - Communications Workers of America, A F L - C I O) see *LABOR UNIONS*

384.55 US
N A T P E PROGRAMMER.* 1965. 10/yr. $25. National Association of Television Program Executives, 2425 Olympic Blvd., Ste. 550E, Santa Monica, CA 90404-4030. Ed. Bill Strubbe. adv. circ. 2,400.
  Formerly: P.D. Cue.

621.38 UK
N B T V. 1976. q. £5. Narrow Bandwidth Television Association, 1 Burnwood Dr., Wollaton, Nottingham NG8 2DJ, England. TEL 44-115-9282896. Ed. D.B. Pitt. adv.; bk.rev. circ. 200. **Document type:** newspaper.

621.38 GW ISSN 0947-4765
TK7800 CODEN: NETTEN
N E T - ERFOLGREICHES KOMMUNIKATIONSMANAGEMENT. (Nachrichten - Elektronik - Telematik) 1946. 10/yr. DM.182 (foreign DM.194) (effective 1997). Huethig GmbH, Postfach 102869, 69018 Heidelberg, Germany. TEL 49-6221-489411. FAX 49-6221-489323. URL: http://www.huethig.de. Ed. Karel Charvat. adv.: B&W page DM.3700, color page DM.5650; trim 210 x 297; adv. contact: Isabell Pfisterer. bk.rev.; bibl.; illus.; pat.; tr.lit. circ. 5,201. **Indexed:** Chem.Abstr., Eng.Ind., INSPEC, PROMT. **Document type:** trade publication.
  —AskIEEE; CISTI; KR SourceOne; SWETS.
  Former titles (until 1993): N E T - Zeitschrift fuer Angewandte Telekommunikation (ISSN 0947-4757); (until 1989): N E T: Nachrichten - Elektronik und Telematik (ISSN 0177-5499); (until 1982): Nachrichten - Elektronik und Telematik (ISSN 0367-3383); (until 1976): Nachrichten - Elektronik (ISSN 0341-4035); (until 1963): Internationale Elektronische Rundschau (ISSN 0020-9236); (until 1955): Elektronische Rundschau (ISSN 0367-0686); (until 1947): Funk und Ton (ISSN 0367-3383).

621.388 JA
H K GIKEN DAYORI/N H K SCIENCE & TECHNICAL RESEARCH LABORATORIES. NEWS. (Text in Japanese) 1988. m. Nippon Hoso Kyokai, Hoso Gijutsu Kenkyujo - Japan Broadcasting Corp., Science & Technical Research Laboratories, 10-11, Kinuta 1-chome, Setagaya-ku, Tokyo 157, Japan. E-mail: okada@strl.nhk.or.jp; URL: http://www.strl.nhk.or.jp/.

621.38 JA ISSN 0914-7535
TK6630.A1 CODEN: NHKGDR
H K GIKEN R & D. (Text in Japanese) 1988. q. 1020 Yen per no. Nippon Hoso Kyokai, Hoso Gijutsu Kenkyujo - Japan Broadcasting Corp., Science and Technical Research Laboratories, 41-1 Udagawa-cho, Shibuya-ku, Tokyo 150, Japan. E-mail: okada@strl.nhk.or.jp; URL: http://www.strl.nhk.or.jp. **Indexed:** Chem.Abstr., INSPEC, JCT, JTA.
  —BLDSC (6109.475000); AskIEEE; CASDDS; CISTI; KR SourceOne; Linda Hall.
  Formed by the merger of (1949-1988): N H K Gijutsu Kenkyu - N H K Technical Journal (ISSN 0027-6553); (1958-1988): N H K Giken Geppo - N H K Technical Report (ISSN 0027-6561)

621.388 JA
N H K HOSO HAKUBUTSUKAN DAYORI/N H K BROADCAST MUSEUM NEWS. (Text in Japanese) 1964. a. Nippon Hoso Kyokai, Hoso Hakubutsukan - Japan Broadcasting Corp., Broadcast Museum, 1-1, Atago 2-chome, Minato-ku, Tokyo 105, Japan.

621.38 JA ISSN 0027-657X
N H K LABORATORIES NOTE. (Text in English) 1966. irreg. (10-12/yr.) exchange basis. Nippon Hoso Kyokai, Gijutsu Kenkyujo - Japan Broadcasting Corp., Science and Technical Research Laboratories, 10-11, Kinuta 1-chome, Setagaya-ku, Tokyo 157, Japan. FAX 81-3-5494-2418. Ed. Katsumi Nakabayashi. cum.index. circ. 1,000. (processed) **Indexed:** Excerp.Med., INSPEC, JCT, JTA, Sci.Cit.Ind. **Document type:** monographic series.
  —BLDSC (6109.495000); AskIEEE; CISTI; Ei; KR SourceOne; Linda Hall.

384.55 US
N J C T A. s-a.? New Jersey Cable Television Association, 132 W. State St., Trenton, NJ 08608. **Document type:** newsletter.
  Description: Discusses issues affecting cable television in New Jersey.

791.4 US
N J N GUIDE. 1971? m. $40. New Jersey Network, CN 777, Trenton, NJ 08625. TEL 609-777-5000. FAX 609-633-2927. Ed. Sandra Lanman.
  Description: Includes TV listings and articles for members of New Jersey Network, a public television network.

N T C A EXCHANGE. (National Telephone Cooperative Association) see *COMMUNICATIONS — Telephone And Telegraph*

N.Z.A.R.T. AMATEUR RADIO CALLBOOK. (New Zealand Association of Radio Transmitters, Inc.) see *COMMUNICATIONS — Radio*

NATIONAL FILM AND SOUND ARCHIVE NEWSLETTER. see *SOUND RECORDING AND REPRODUCTION*

384.554 659.1 US
NATIONAL NEWS. q. membership only. Association of Independent Commercial Producers, Kaufman Astoria Studios, 11 E. 22nd St., New York, NY 10010. TEL 212-475-2600. FAX 212-475-3910. URL: http://www.aicp.com. Ed. Renee Paley. **Document type:** newsletter.

621.388 JA ISSN 0918-4503
NETTOWAKU KONPYUTINGU. (Text in Japanese) 1990. m. Rikku Terekomu - R I C Telecom, 20-7, Yushima 3-chome, Bunkyo-ku, Tokyo 141, Japan.
  Formerly (until 1992): Komyunikeshon Tekunoroji - Communication Technology (ISSN 0916-4669)

791.4 US
NETWORK FUTURES & PROLOG.* w. $100. Television Index, Inc., 1515 Broadway 14th Fl., New York, NY 10036-8901. Ed. Timothy Hunter. **Document type:** trade publication.
  Formed by the merger of: Network Futures & T V Pro-Log (ISSN 0739-5574)

NEW ACTORS AND ACTRESSES. see *THEATER*

621.388 UK ISSN 0265-4717
NEW MEDIA MARKETS. s.m. £740($1110) (effective 1995). Financial Times Telecoms & Media Publishing (Subsidiary of: Financial Times Group), Maple House, 149 Tottenham Court Rd., London W1P 9LL, England. TEL 0171-896-2234. FAX 0171-896-2256. Pub. Helen Nicol. (also avail. in microform from UMI) **Document type:** newsletter.
  ●Also available online. Vendor(s): Information Access Co.
  Description: Provides global reporting on the commercial aspects of satellite television, terrestrial television, cable TV, programming and channel development.

NEW YORK CASTING - SURVIVAL GUIDE. see *THEATER*

791.4 CN ISSN 0824-3581
NEWFOUNDLAND HERALD. w. Sunday Herald Ltd., Box 2015, St. John's, Nfld. A1C 5R7, Canada. TEL 709-726-7060. FAX 709-726-5107. Ed. G.W. Stirling.
  Description: Family lifestyle magazine focusing on local and international entertainment scenes and provides full TV listings of all networks, cable and pay-TV channels throughout the province.

001.6 621.381 US ISSN 1060-7188
QA76.575
NEWMEDIA; technologies for the professional communicator. 1991. m. $29.95 (free to qualified persons). HyperMedia Communications, Inc., 901 Mariners Island, Ste. 365, San Mateo, CA 94404. TEL 415-573-5170. FAX 415-573-5131. URL: www.hyperstand.com. (Subscr. to: Box 1771, Riverton, NJ 08077-9771. TEL 800-253-6641) Ed. David Bunnell. adv.; circ. 40,000 (controlled). (back issues avail.; reprint service avail.)
  ●Also available online.
  —BLDSC (6084.477500); KR SourceOne.
  Formerly (until 1991): NewMedia Age (ISSN 1058-0492)
  Description: Discusses the social, economic, technical, legal, and philosophical issues concerning new digital media.

384.55 US
NEWS - BROADCAST NETWORK. q. 9431 Beloit Rd., Milwaukee, WI 53227-4365. TEL 414-321-6210. FAX 414-321-3608. Ed. Thomas Hill. circ. 2,000.

NEWSBANK REVIEW OF THE ARTS: FILM AND TELEVISION. see *MOTION PICTURES*

051 US ISSN 1073-7510
NICKELODEON MAGAZINE. 1993. bi-m. $9.97. Nickelodeon Magazine, Inc. (Subsidiary of: Viacom), 1515 Broadway, New York, NY 10036. TEL 212-258-7500; 800-832-6100. adv.; illus. **Document type:** consumer publication.

384.5 US
NIELSEN REPORT ON TELEVISION. 1955. a. Nielsen Media Research, 299 Park Ave., New York, NY 10171. TEL 212-708-7500. Ed. J. Loftus. circ. 30,000. **Indexed:** SRI. **Document type:** trade publication.
  Description: Summary of program audiences for broadcast network local and syndication, trends and related data on cable and VCR usage.

NIGERIAN RADIO - T V TIMES. see *COMMUNICATIONS — Radio*

621.388 JA
NIPPON HOSO KYOKAI HOSO GIJUTSU KENKYUJO KENKYU NENPO/N H K SCIENCE AND TECHNICAL RESEARCH LABORATORIES. ANNUAL REPORT. (Text in Japanese) 1946. a. Nippon Hoso Kyokai, Hoso Gijutsu Kenkyujo - Japan Broadcasting Corp., Science and Technical Research Laboratories, 10-11, Kinuta 1-chome, Setagaya-ku, Tokyo 157, Japan. E-mail: okada@strl.nhk.or.jp; URL: http://www.strl.nhk.or.jp/.

791.4 CN
NORTH ISLAND TELEVIEWER. 1981. w. North Island Gazette Ltd., Box 458, Port Hardy, BC V0N 2P0, Canada. TEL 609-949-6225. Rob/Giblak; Pub. Chuck Bennett. adv. circ. 3,683. **Document type:** newspaper.
  Description: Contains satellite TV listings.

NORTHWEST INDIANA CATHOLIC. see *RELIGIONS AND THEOLOGY — Roman Catholic*

NOTIZIE MESE. see *ETHNIC INTERESTS*

384.55 SP
NUEVO CLAN. 1987. w. Gran Via Carlos III, 124 5o, 08034 Barcelona, Spain. TEL 93-2800088. FAX 93-2805555. circ. 247,620.
  Formerly: Clan T V.

621.388 JA ISSN 0911-5943
O PLUS E. (Text in Japanese) 1979. m. 11000 Yen. New Technology Communications Co., Ltd. - Shin Gijutsu Komyunikeshonzu, 16-13, Hyakunin-cho 2-chome, Shinjuku-ku, Tokyo 169, Japan. E-mail: mich@magical.egg.or.jp. Ed. Motomu Matsushita; Pub. Motomu Matsushita. R&P contact: Motomu Matsushita. adv. contact: Sui Kim. circ. 13,500. **Document type:** academic/scholarly publication.
  Description: Covers optics, optoelectronics, imaging technology and more.

COMMUNICATIONS — TELEVISION AND CABLE

791.45   UK
OFFICIAL MAGAZINE OF CORONATION STREET. 1994. m. £21($59.90) (effective 1994). (Granada Television) Newsstand Publishing Services, Office Block One, Southlink Business Park, Southlink Rd., Oldham, Lancashire OL4 1DE, England. TEL 44-161-6240414. E-mail: truenews@passport.ca. (Dist. by: The Street in Canada Ltd., 72 Bellefair Ave., Toronto, ON M4L 3T8, Canada. TEL 416-694-8234; Subscr. to: P.O. Box 51545 RPO The Beaches, 2060 Queen St., E., Toronto, ON M4E 3V7, Canada. TEL 800-743-3552. FAX 416-684-7303; Sponsor addr.: Quay St., Manchester, Lancashire M6O 9EA, England. TEL 44-161-8327211) Ed. Brian Clark; Pub. Alan Young. circ. 60,000 (paid). **Document type:** consumer publication.
    Description: Coverage of Great Britain's television drama series "Coronation Street."

621.38   SZ   ISSN 0030-2007
OLD MAN. (Text in English, French, German and Italian) 1932. m. (11/yr.). 40 Fr. Union of Swiss Short Wave Amateurs, Postfach, 4511 Rumisberg, Switzerland. Eds. Werner Mueller, Peter Erni. adv.; bk.rev.; index. circ. 4,000.

384.55   US   ISSN 1076-0334
ON DEMAND. 1994. m. Cowles Business Media, 11 River Bend Dr., S., Box 4949, Stamford, CT 06907-0949. TEL 203-358-9900. FAX 203-358-5811. E-mail: ondemandms@aol.com. Ed. Matt Stump; Pub. Matt Stump. **Document type:** trade publication.

ON THE STREET. see *MUSIC*

791.4   IT   ISSN 0393-814X
ONDA TIVU. 1978. w. newsstand price: L.1200. Grafica Editoriale s.r.l., Via E. Mattei 106, 40138 Bologna, Italy. TEL 39-51-53651. Ed. Franco Di Bella. adv.: B&W page L.11000000, color page L.13000000. circ. 159,947.

621.38   FR   ISSN 0754-2623
ONDES COURTES INFORMATIONS. 1968. m. 235 Fr. Union des Radio-Clubs, 71 av. Orfila, 75020 Paris, France. adv.; bk.rev. circ. 3,000.

384.554   GW   ISSN 0948-2113
ONLINE AKTUELL. 1979. fortn. DM.449.40. Neue Mediengesellschaft Ulm mbH, Konrad-Celtis-Str. 77, 81369 Munich, Germany. TEL 49-89-74117190. FAX 49-89-74117195. Ed. Max Bold. circ. 1,500. **Document type:** trade publication.
    Incorporates (1991-1995): Audiotex News (ISSN 0941-6900); Former titles (until 1995): Btx Aktuell (ISSN 0935-6991); (until 1988): Bildschirmtext Aktuell (ISSN 0724-1828)

791.4   US
ONSAT - AMERICA'S WEEKLY SATELLITE GUIDE. 1984. w. $59.95 in N. America (effective 1997). Triple D Publishing, Inc., Box 2347, Shelby, NC 28151-2347. TEL 704-482-9673. FAX 704-484-8558. Ed. Jim H. Cothran. adv. circ. 370,000. **Document type:** consumer publication.
    Formerly: On Sat - America's Weekly Guide to Satellite T V (ISSN 0747-4059)
    Description: Includes listings and articles concerning satellite TV programming.

384   US
ORBITER. bi-m. membership. Society of Satellite Professionals International, 2200 Wilson Blvd., No. 102-258, Arlington, VA 22201. TEL 703-243-8948. FAX 703-528-4084. Ed. Carol McKibben. circ. 800. (looseleaf format; back issues avail.) **Document type:** newsletter.
    Description: Contains articles and news on the satellite industry.

P C I A BULLETIN; news and analysis for the personal communication industry. (Personal Communications Industry Association) see *COMMUNICATIONS — Telephone And Telegraph*

621.388 778.53   US
P W. (Production Weekly) w. URL: http://users.aol.com/prodwekly/pw/pw.htm.
    ●Available only online.
    Description: Breakdown of projects in pre-production, preparation and development for film, television, music videos, and commercials.

384.55   SW   ISSN 1100-3138
PAA T V. 1954. w. SEK 598; newsstand price: SEK 17.50. Medviks T V - Foerlag AB, P.O. Box 2155, Skeppsbron 32, S-103 14 Stockholm, Sweden. TEL 46-8-791-19-40. FAX 46-8-20-27-22. Ed. Bert Willborg. adv.: B&W page SEK 9000, color page SEK 12000; trim 140 x 210; adv. contact: Karin Brunnsjoe-Lind. circ. 63,000. pp./issue: 112.

384.554   US   ISSN 0146-0072
PAY T V NEWSLETTER; newsletter on developments in pay television. 1973. m. $745 (effective 1997). Paul Kagan Associates, Inc., 126 Clock Tower Place, Carmel, CA 93923. TEL 408-624-1536. TELEX 408-625-3225. Ed. Larry Gerbrandt. charts; index. **Document type:** newsletter.
    Description: Covers cable, over-the-air and direct satellite with analysis of the industry's subscribers, revenues and profits.

384.54 384.554   US   ISSN 0895-4143
PERFECT VISION. 1986. 4/yr. $22. Pearson Publishing Enterprises, Box 360, Sea Cliff, NY 11579. TEL 516-676-2830; 800-222-3201. FAX 516-676-5469. Ed. Harry Pearson. adv. circ. 20,000.
    —UnCover.

791.4 790.1   US   ISSN 0896-9973
PN2289
PERFORMANCE GUIDE. 1987. m. 1101 University Dr., Ste. 108, Ft. Worth, TX 76107-3000. TEL 817-338-9444. FAX 817-877-4273. Ed. Louis Marroquin. adv.

PHI PI EPSILON STAGE SCREEN & RADIO. see *LABOR UNIONS*

621.38 659.1   CN   ISSN 0836-2114
PLAYBACK; Canada's broadcast and production journal. 1986. 25/yr. Can.$59.50 (U.S. $93.50; elsewhere $186). Brunico Communications Inc., 366 Adelaide St. W., Ste. 500, Toronto, ON M5V 1R9, Canada. TEL 416-408-2300. FAX 416-408-0870. E-mail: circ@brunico.com. Ed. Mary Maddever. adv.: B&W page Can.$2840 ($3155), color page Can.$3680 ($3985); trim 8 1/8 x 10 7/8. illus.; stat.; circ. 9,800. (tabloid format; back issues avail.) **Indexed:** Can.B.P.I. **Document type:** trade publication.

384.5   IE   ISSN 0791-2161
PLAYBACK. 1989. 10/yr. Production Industry Publications Ltd., Prospect House, 1 Prospect Rd., Glasnevin, Ireland. TEL 303455. FAX 300888. adv.: B&W page $2529, color page $4427; trim 11 3/4 x 8 1/4; adv. contact: Stephen Roche. circ. 3,500.
    Description: Covers issues in broadcast TV and radio.

384.55   CN
PLAYBACK INTERNATIONAL. 1990. 2/yr. Brunico Communications Inc., 366 Adelaide St. W., Ste. 500, Toronto, ON M5V 1R9, Canada. TEL 416-408-2300. FAX 416-408-0870. E-mail: circ@brunico.com. Ed. Mary Maddever. adv.: B&W page Can.$2015, color page Can.$2640; trim 8 1/8 x 10 7/8. circ. 2,164. **Document type:** trade publication.
    Description: Covers broadcast programming products available for sale from Canadian producers.

PLUNKETT'S ENTERTAINMENT AND MEDIA INDUSTRY ALMANAC. see *BUSINESS AND ECONOMICS — Trade And Industrial Directories*

384   US   ISSN 1045-9545
P88.8
POWER MEDIA SELECTS. 1989. a. $166.50 (diskette $260). Broadcast Interview Source, 2233 Wisconsin Ave., N.W., Washington, DC 20007. TEL 202-333-4904. FAX 202-342-5411. E-mail: editor@yearbooknews.com; URL: http://www.yearbooknews.com. Ed. Mitchell P. Davis. (also avail. in diskette format) **Document type:** directory.
    Description: Directory of top contacts in the media, including newsletters, magazines, newspapers, radio and television.

384.4   UK   ISSN 0141-0857
PRACTICAL WIRELESS. 1932. m. £25 (Europe £28; elsewhere £30) (effective 1996). P W Publishing Ltd., Arrowsmith Ct., Sta. Approach, Broadstone, Dorset BH18 8PW, England. TEL 44-1202-659930. FAX 44-1202-659950. Ed. Rob Mannion. adv.: B&W page £745. circ. 20,000. **Indexed:** Br.Tech.Ind., INSPEC (1975-). **Document type:** consumer publication.
    —BLDSC (6596.995000); AskIEEE; KR SourceOne; SWETS. **CCC.**
    Formerly (until 1948): Practical Wireless and Practical Television.

PREMIERE VIDEO MAGAZINE. see *MOTION PICTURES*

791.4   US
PREVIEW (HARRISBURG). m. $24 (effective 1997-1998). T V Host, Inc., Box 1665, 3935 Jonestown Rd., Harrisburg, PA 17109. TEL 717-657-1700. FAX 717-657-2921. URL: http://www.tvhost.com. Ed. Mike Edkin. adv. contact. Lou Pernik, Jr. circ. 210,000. **Document type:** consumer publication.
    ●Also available online.

PREVIEW (RICHARDSON). see *MOTION PICTURES*

384.55   BL   ISSN 0032-812X
PREVISOES IONOSFERICAS M U F. 1955. m. Cr.$300($40) Ministerio da Marinha, Diretoria de Armamento e Comunicacoes, Rua 1 de Marco, 118. Rio de Janeiro, RJ, Brazil. FAX 021-216-5048. TELEX 021-215-217. charts; stat.; circ. 250 (controlled). (processed)

791.4   CN
PRIMETIME. 1983. m. Can.$19.26 (effective 1997). PrimeTime Publishing Inc., 5308 Calgary Tr., Riviera Plaza, Edmonton, AB T6H 4J8, Canada. TEL 403-434-7424. FAX 403-437-0123. Ed. Kare Paulgaard; Pub. Harold Roozen. adv. contact: Mario Da Ponte. circ. 290,000. **Document type:** consumer publication.
    Description: Pay-television program source carrying schedules and program descriptions for the Western Canadian movie channel and the major specialty networks.

384.55   CN
PRIMEURS MAGAZINE. 1984. m. Can.$18. Feature Publishing Ltd., Maison Astral, 2100 Rue Ste-Catherine Ouest, Bureau 900, Montreal, PQ H3 2T3, Canada. TEL 514-939-5024. FAX 514-939-1515. Ed. Mireille Duhamel; Pub. Marvin Boisvert. R&P contact: Marvin Boisvert. adv. circ. 300,000. **Document type:** consumer publication.
    Formerly: Super Ecran.
    Description: Pay-TV guide for French speaking Canadians in Eastern Canada.

384.55   US   ISSN 1080-9570
PRIVATE CABLE & WIRELESS CABLE. 1982. m. $24 (foreign $95). National Satellite Publishing Inc., 1909 Ave. G, Box 1489, Rosenberg, TX 77471-2535. TEL 713-342-9826. FAX 713-344-9227. Ed. Tanya J. Fluette; Pub. Lor T. Workin. R&P contact: Lori T. Workin. TEL 713-975-0030. adv. contact: Jennifer Hajovsky. circ. 12,200. **Document type:** trade publication.
    Formerly: Private Cable (ISSN 0745-8711); **Incorporates:** T V R O Technology (ISSN 0885-7598); **Incorporates:** Satellite T V (ISSN 0744-9739)

384.5   US   ISSN 1068-4514
PRIVATE CABLE INVESTOR. 1982. m. $645 (effective 1997). Paul Kagan Associates, Inc., 126 Clock Tower Place, Carmel, CA 93923. TEL 408-624-1536. TELEX 408-625-3225. Ed. John Mansell. charts; index. **Document type:** newsletter.
    Formerly: S M A T V News (ISSN 0734-5399)
    Description: Covers the economic, technical, marketing and legal issues that affect SMATV.

THE PRIZE. see *FOLKLORE*

PRODUCER. see *MOTION PICTURES*

PROFIFOTO; magazine for professional photography a electronic imaging. see *PHOTOGRAPHY*

COMMUNICATIONS — TELEVISION AND CABLE

791.45   PL   ISSN 1231-2142
PROGRAM T V. 1989. w. 20 Zl.; newsstand price: 0.55 Zl. Oficyna Wydawnicza Press - Media, UI. Trembeckiego 5, 35-234 Rzeszow, Poland. TEL 48-17-8520570. FAX 48-17-8525555. E-mail: pressmed@intertele.pl. Ed. Roman Oraczewski. adv.; film rev.; video rev.; circ. 450,000 (controlled).
  Description: TV Guide containing national, local, satellite and cable TV programs.

659.1 384.55   US
PROMAX INTERNATIONAL. 1985. q. membership. Promotion & Marketing Executives in the Electronic Media, 2029 Century Pk. E., Ste. 555, Los Angeles, CA 90067-2906. TEL 310-788-7600. FAX 310-788-7616. URL: http://www.promax.org. Ed. Dominick Morra; Pub. Jim Chabin. R&P contact: Dominick Morra. adv. contact: Suzanne Marie Gutierrez. bk.rev.; index; circ. 2,000 (controlled).
  Document type: trade publication.
  ●Also available online.
    Formerly: B P M E Image.
  Description: Directed to radio and TV stations and networks, cable systems, cable networks, radio, program distributors.
    Refereed Serial

384.55   US   ISSN 0193-3663
PN1990.9.P82
PUBLIC BROADCASTING REPORT. 1978. bi-w. $451 (foreign $474). Warren Publishing, Inc., 2115 Ward Ct., N.W., Washington, DC 20037. TEL 202-872-9200. FAX 202-293-3435. Ed. Patrick Ross; Pub. Charles Tepfer. index. **Document type**: newsletter.
  ●Also available online. Vendor(s): Information Access Co., NewsNet (PB04).
  —CCC.
  Incorporates (1967-1997): E T V Newsletter (Educational Television) (ISSN 0012-8023)

PUBLIC TELEVISION TRANSCRIPTS INDEX. see COMMUNICATIONS — Abstracting, Bibliographies, Statistics

621.38   US
Q C W A JOURNAL. 1954. q. membership. Quarter Century Wireless Association, Inc., 159 E. 16th Ave., Eugene, OR 97401-4017. TEL 503-683-0987. FAX 503-683-4181. Ed. J.C. Walsh. adv.; bk.rev. circ. 9,500.
    Formerly: Q C W A News.

621.384   SW   ISSN 0033-4820
Q T C. 1927. 12/yr. SEK 435 in Sweden; other Nordic and Baltic countries SEK 456; Europe SEK 4503 elsewhere SEK 586 (effective 1997). Foereningen Sveriges Saendareamatoerer SSA, Box 2021, SE-123 26 Farsta, Sweden. TEL 46-8-604-40-06. FAX 46-8-604-40-07. Ed. Robert Hulander. adv.; bk.rev.; illus. circ. 7,500. (also avail. in audio cassette)

U YI. see THEATER

790.1   GW
R & R SHOPPERS NEWS. (Rest & Relaxation) 1971. m. DM.100. R & R Communications GmbH, Kolpingstr. 1, 69181 Leimen, Germany. TEL 49-6224-706-0. FAX 49-6224-70616. Ed. Lenora Genovese. R&P contact: Lenora Genovese. adv.; B&W page DM.4300, color page DM.4700; trim 210 x 280; adv. contact: Ailsa Mattaj. film rev. circ. 66,000.
  Document type: consumer publication.
    Former titles: R and R Entertainment Digest; R and R Entertainment Digest - with Guide T V; Guide to T V and Easy Living.
  Description: Entertainment magazine for Americans and Canadians stationed in Germany.

384   CN
B WEEKENDER. w. Can.$35. Robinson-Blackmore Ltd., 18 O'Leary Ave., P.O. Box 8660, St. John's, Nfld. A1B 3T7, Canada. TEL 709-722-8500. FAX 709-722-2228. Ed. G. French. circ. 75,450.

658.8 621.38   GW   ISSN 0942-7295
F MAGAZIN FUER UNTERHALTUNGS- UND KOMMUNIKATIONSELEKTRONIK. 1957. m. Deutscher Radio- und Fernseh- Fachverband e.V., Sachsenring 89, 50677 Cologne, Germany. TEL 0221-3398115.
    Former titles (until 1991): R F Magazin fuer Unterhaltungs- und Informationselektronik (ISSN 0930-3898); (until 1980): Deutsche Rundfunk-Einzelhandel (ISSN 0012-0634)

R T E GUIDE. (Radio Telefis Eireann) see COMMUNICATIONS — Radio

R T N D A COMMUNICATOR. (Radio - Television News Directors Association) see COMMUNICATIONS — Radio

791.4   GW
R T V; illustriertes Programm. (Program supplement to 174 German newspapers) 1961. w. included in subscription to newspaper. Deutscher Supplement Verlag GmbH, Breslauerstr. 300, 90471 Nuernberg, Germany. TEL 0911-83301-0. FAX 0911-83301-60. TELEX 622061-DSV-D. Ed. Karlo Huck. adv.; illus. circ. 3,874,003.
    Formerly: Radio und Television (ISSN 0033-7757)

RAABTA. see MOTION PICTURES

385.5   SA
RADIO & T V. q. South African Broadcasting Corporation, Private Bag X1, Auckland Park 2006, South Africa. TEL 27-11-714-3741. FAX 27-11-714-6514. illus. **Document type**: consumer publication.
    Formerly: Interkom.

RADIO AND TELEVISION CAREER DIRECTORY. see OCCUPATIONS AND CAREERS

RADIO ES TELEVIZIOUJSAG. see COMMUNICATIONS — Radio

RADIO FERNSEHEN ELEKTRONIK; die Zeitschrift der Medienelektronik. see ELECTRONICS

RADIO PROGRAMME. see COMMUNICATIONS — Radio

621.384   FR   ISSN 0033-7994
RADIO R E F;* la revue des ondes courtes. 1925. 11/yr. 290 F. Reseau des Emetteurs Francais, B.P. 2129, 37021 Tours Cedex, France. TEL 47-41-88-73. adv.; bk.rev.; abstr.; charts; illus.; tr.lit.; index. circ. 10,000.

RADIO T V TECNICO. see COMMUNICATIONS — Radio

RADIO - VISION TIMES. see COMMUNICATIONS — Radio

RADIO Y T V HISPANA. see COMMUNICATIONS — Radio

RADIOCORRIERE - T V. see COMMUNICATIONS — Radio

RADIOLYUBITEL'. see COMMUNICATIONS — Radio

621.38 500   SP   ISSN 0211-3546
RADIORAMA; practica electronica - t.v. - radio - hi-fi - ciencia. 1967. 11/yr. $170 for 2 yrs. (Club de Radiorama) Ediciones Tecnicas Rede, S.A., Ecuador 91, 1o, 08029 Barcelona, Spain. TEL 3-410-3097. FAX -439-2813. TELEX 58642 SCTBE. Ed. Jose M. Prades. adv.; charts; illus.; tr.lit. circ. 7,000.

REGISTER OF STUNT PERFORMERS AND ARRANGERS. see THEATER

384 301   AU   ISSN 1025-2339
▼**RELATION**; Medien - Gesellschaft - Geschichte. 1995. s-a. S.340. Verlag der Oesterreichischen Akademie der Wissenschaften, Postfach 471, A-1011 Vienna, Austria. TEL 43-1-51581401. FAX 43-1-51581400. E-mail: verlag@oeaw.ac.at; URL: http://www.oeaw.ac.at/einheiten/verlag. Ed. Herbert Matis. **Document type**: academic/scholarly publication.
  Description: Provides a forum for all engaged in studying the relations between media, society and history.

384 200   US   ISSN 0034-4079
BV655
RELIGIOUS BROADCASTING. 1969. m. (10/yr.) $24 (foreign $48). National Religious Broadcasters, Inc., 7839 Ashton Ave., Manassas, VA 20109. TEL 703-330-7000. FAX 703-330-6996. Ed. Ron J. Kopczick; Pub. E. Brandt Gustavson. adv.; B&W page $1530; color page $1980; trim 8 3/8 x 10 7/8; adv. contact: Dick Reynolds. bk.rev.; charts; illus. circ. 9,320. (back issues avail.; reprint service avail. from UMI) **Indexed**: Chr.Per.Ind. **Document type**: trade publication.
  —UMI.
  Description: For Christian radio and television producers, station owners and operators, and others interested in religious broadcasting.

384.55   US
RESPONSE T V. 1992. m. $39 (effective 1996). Advanstar Communications, Inc., 7500 Old Oak Blvd., Cleveland, OH 44130. TEL 216-826-2839. FAX 216-891-2726. Ed. Jack Schember. adv.: B&W page $2290. circ. 16,000.
  ●Also available online. Vendor(s): Information Access Co.
  Description: Information on how to run your show and do two-minute commercials. Covers home-shopping networks and emerging interactive technologies.

384.55 781.64   US
▼**RETRO GENERATION**; dedicated to the connoisseurs of classic pop culture. 1996. bi-m. newsstand price: $4.99. Box 651, Gracie Sta., New York, NY 10028-0006. Ed. Michael O'Hara; Pub. Michael O'Hara. R&P contact: Michael O'Hara. adv. contact: Michael O'Hara. **Document type**: consumer publication.

384   US   ISSN 0149-9971
REVIEW OF INTERNATIONAL BROADCASTING.* (Text in English, Spanish) 1977. m. $18. Glenn Hauser, Ed. & Pub., Box 1684, Enid, OK 73702-1684. adv.; bk.rev.; charts; illus. circ. 2,000.

REVISTA MONITOR DE RADIO E TELEVISAO. see COMMUNICATIONS — Radio

384.55   BL   ISSN 0101-0093
REVISTA TELEBRAS. Spanish edition: Revista Telebras (ISSN 0102-6348) (Text in Portuguese) 1976. 3/yr. free. Telecomunicacoes Brasileiras S.A., S.A.S. Quadro 6, Bloco H, Lotes 5 a 8, Caixa Postal 11,1218, CEP 70, 313 Brasilia, DF, Brazil. Ed. Francisco Solano Borges Filho. circ. 12,000.

621.384   IT   ISSN 0392-8268
RIVISTA TELETTRA REVIEW (ENGLISH EDITION); contributions to telecommunications development. Italian edition (ISSN 0392-8276) 1953. s-m. free to qualified personnel. Telettra S.p.A., Via Fulvio Testi 136, 20092 Cinisello Balsamo (MI), Italy. TEL 02-320295. Ed. Mario Zanfi. circ. 5,000. (back issues avail.) **Indexed**: INSPEC.
    Formerly: Telettra Review.

621.384   IT   ISSN 0392-8276
RIVISTA TELETTRA REVIEW (ITALIAN EDITION); contributi allo sviluppo delle telecomunicazioni. English edition (ISSN 0392-8268) 1953. s-m. free to qualified personnel. Telettra S.p.A., Via Fulvio Testi 136, 20092 Cinisello Balsamo (MI), Italy. TEL 02-320295. FAX 02-26221777. TELEX 320295. Ed. Mario Zanfi. adv.; charts; illus.; stat. circ. 4,000. (back issues avail.) **Indexed**: INSPEC.
    Formerly: Rivista Telettra.
  Description: Technical forum featuring articles on technology and telecommunications, focusing on new technology and applications.

ROESTER I RADIO T V; Sveriges radios programtidning, kabel-TV, Astra-parabol, Rymddoktorn. see COMMUNICATIONS — Radio

791.4   US   ISSN 0035-8355
PN1992.3.U5
ROSS REPORTS TELEVISION; New York casting - national script contacts. 1949. m. $45; newsstand price: $6. B P I Communications, 1515 Broadway, New York, NY 10036. TEL 212-536-5199. Ed. Timothy Hunter; Pub. Steve Elish. R&P contact: Georgina Challis. adv. contact: Scott Berg. **Document type**: trade publication.

RUNDFUNK UND FERNSEHEN. see COMMUNICATIONS — Radio

RUNDFUNK- UND FERNSEHPROGRAMM. see COMMUNICATIONS — Radio

384.55 360   US
S E T FREE; the newsletter against television. 1982. q. $5 for 10 issues. Society for the Eradication of Television, Box 10491, Oakland, CA 94610-0491. TEL 510-763-8712. Ed. Steve Wagner. adv.; bk.rev. circ. 1,200. **Document type**: newsletter.
    Formerly: News and Notes From All Over.
  Description: Contains news and updates about television's harmful role in society with summaries of scholarly reports and empirical data.

COMMUNICATIONS — TELEVISION AND CABLE

384.55 322.44 US
S E T FREE!. 1994. q. Society for the Emancipation from Television, Southern California Chapter, Box 14472, Long Beach, CA 90803. TEL 310-987-1767. Ed. Bob Muller.
Description: Contains commentary on and against television and its place in society.

S M P T E JOURNAL. (Society of Motion Picture and Television Engineers) see MOTION PICTURES

384 US
S S P I UPDATE. m. membership. Society of Satellite Professionals International, 2200 Wilson Blvd., No. 102-258, Arlington, VA 22201. TEL 703-243-8948. FAX 703-528-4084. circ. 800. (looseleaf format; back issues avail.) **Document type:** newsletter.
Description: Provides updates covering the society's events.

SAT - AUDIO - VIDEO; postepy w elektronice powszechnego uzytku. see ELECTRONICS

384.554 IT
SATELLITE. 1988. 12/yr. L.72000 (Europe L.94000; elsewhere L.148000). Today S.r.l., Largo T. Antonelli 27 11, 00145 Rome, Italy. TEL 39-6-5417100. FAX 39-6-5940921. Ed. Daniel Caimi. adv.: B&W page L.5850000, color page L.7600000. circ. 45,000.

791.43 SA
SATELLITE. 1993. m. (Bop T V - Mmabatho T V) Bophuthatswana Broadcasting Corporation, Private Bag X2150, 8681 Mmabatho, Northwest Province, South Africa. TEL 27-140-897111. FAX 27-140-897299. Pub. Peter Godson. adv. contact: Thorsten Stamer. illus. **Document type:** consumer publication.

384.554 US ISSN 1075-1823
PN1992.3.U5
SATELLITE CHOICE. m. $52 (effective 1997). Fortuna Communications Corporation, 140 S. Fortuna Blvd., Fortuna, CA 95540-0308. TEL 707-725-6591. FAX 707-725-4311. Ed. James Scott; Pub. Patrick O'Dell. adv. contact: George Bryant. circ. 125,000.
Description: Contains listings and reviews for the 18-inch DSS Satellite System. Includes complete information on on DIRECTV and USSB Satellite programming.

621.385 US ISSN 0892-3329
SATELLITE DIRECT; the magazine of direct-broadcast satellite communications. 1983. m. $52. CommTek Publishing Co., Inc., 8330 Boone Blvd., Ste.600, Vienna, VA 22182. TEL 703-827-0511. FAX 703-356-6179. Ed. Tom Wiener; Pub. Phillip Swann. R&P contact: Angie Anderson. adv. contact: Christine Nolan. s-a. index. circ. 300,000. **Document type:** consumer publication.
Formerly (until 1987): Satellite Dealer (ISSN 0739-876X)

791.45 CN
SATELLITE DISH GUIDE. w. Can.$69.99 (effective 1997). T V Publishing Group, 201 - 4201 25A Ave., Vernon, BC V1T 7G8, Canada. TEL 250-542-0469; 800-663-4424. FAX 250-542-0942. Ed. Deeny Grazier; Pub. Tom Monahan. R&P contact: Deeny Grazier. adv. contact: Norm Metcalf.

384.55 IT ISSN 1122-9284
SATELLITE EUROSAT; tecnologia della televisione via satellite. 1985. m. L.98000 (effective 1997). Gruppo Editoriale J C E, Via Ferri 6, 20092 Cinisello Balsamo (MI), Italy. TEL 39-2-660251. FAX 39-2-6127620. E-mail: eurosat@jce.it; URL: http://www.jce.it. Ed. Amedeo Bozzoni. adv.: B&W page L.5500000, color page L.8500000; trim 210 X 276. circ. 115,000. **Document type:** consumer publication.
Description: Provides broad information on satellite TV, exhibitions, products and a programme guide.

791.4 US ISSN 0732-7668
PN1992
SATELLITE ORBIT; the magazine of c-band satellite. 1982. m. $57 (effective Sep. 1996). CommTek Publishing Co., Inc., 8330 Boone Blvd., Vienna, VA 22182. TEL 703-827-0511. FAX 703-356-6179. Ed. Linda Casey; Pub. Phillip Swann. R&P contact: Angie Anderson. adv. contact: Christine Nolan. circ. 300,000. (back issues avail.) **Document type:** consumer publication.
Supersedes (in 1985): Satguide.
Description: TV viewing guide for home satellite dish owners.

621.38 US ISSN 0890-1252
SATELLITE RETAILER. m. Triple D Publishing, Inc., 1300 S. DeKalb St., Box 2384, Shelby, NC 28151-2384. TEL 704-482-9673. FAX 704-484-8558. Ed. Theron Montgomeny. circ. 10,700. **Document type:** trade publication.
Description: Trade journal for satellite TV installation, service, and repair facilities.

384.55 UK ISSN 0268-8425
SATELLITE T V EUROPE. 1986. m. £28. Millenium Consumer Magazines, 531-533 Kings Rd., London SW10 0T2, England. TEL 44-171-351-3612. FAX 44-171-352-4883. (Subscr. to: RFS Ltd., 5 Riverpark Estate, Berkhamsted, Herts HP4 1HL, England. TEL 44-1442-879097) Ed. Louise Smith; Pub. Louise Smith. R&P contact: Louise Smith. adv. contact: Helen Read. circ. 140,000 (paid). (back issues avail.) **Document type:** consumer publication.

384.5 FR ISSN 0985-1542
SATELLITE T V EUROPE. 1987. m. Media Presse Informations, 17 quai Louis XVIII, 33000 Bordeaux, France. TEL 56-51-04-17. FAX 56-81-10-84. Ed. Veronique Le Vavasseur. circ. 10,000.

384.554 US ISSN 0744-7841
SATELLITE T V WEEK. 1981. w. $59.95 (effective 1997). Fortuna Communications Corporation, Box 308, Fortuna, CA 95540. TEL 707-725-6951. FAX 707-725-4311. Ed. James E. Scott; Pub. Patrick O'Dell. adv. contact: George Bryant. circ. 338,417 (paid). **Document type:** consumer publication.
Description: Reports television program listings for satellite channels. Includes editorial coverage of issues affecting the satellite industry, as well as entertainment features, sports coverage, consumer electronics and personality interviews.

384.55 US ISSN 0193-2861
SATELLITE WEEK. 1979. w. $937 (foreign $983). Warren Publishing, Inc., 2115 Ward Ct., N.W., Washington, DC 20037. TEL 202-872-9200. FAX 202-293-3435. Ed. Michael French. **Document type:** trade publication.
●Also available online. Vendor(s): Information Access Co., NewsNet (AE01).
—CCC.

384.554 US
SATVISION MAGAZINE. 1987. m. $35. Satellite Broadcasting and Communications Association, 225 Reinekers Ln., Ste. 600, Alexandria, VA 22314-2322. TEL 703-549-6990. FAX 703-549-7640. adv.; circ. 10,000 (controlled). (back issues avail.) **Document type:** trade publication.
Description: Provides information for satellite television dealers.

SCHULFERNSEHEN (MUNICH). see EDUCATION

SCHWEIZERISCHE RADIO- UND FERNSEHGESELLSCHAFT. GESCHAEFTSBERICHT. see COMMUNICATIONS — Radio

791.45 US ISSN 1075-8860
PN1995.9.S26
SCI-FI ENTERTAINMENT. 1994. bi-m. $14.95 (foreign $18.95) (effective 1994). (Sci-Fi Channel) Sovereign Media, 457 Carlisle Dr., Herndon, VA 22070. TEL 703-471-1556. FAX 703-471-1559. E-mail: flixman@dorsai.dorsai.org. (Dist. by: Warner Publisher Services, 1271 Ave. of the Americas, 39th Fl., New York, NY 10020. TEL 212-522-8900; Subscr. to: Box 709, Mt. Morris, IL, 61054-0709. TEL 800-933-6407) Ed. Edward Flixman; Pub. Mark Hintz. adv. contact: Mark Hintz. film rev, illus. circ. 75,000. (back issues avail.) **Document type:** consumer publication.
Description: Covers cable programming for the Sci-Fi Channel. Includes news, interviews and profiles of actors, filmmakers and writers, and articles about science fiction and horror films and TV series.

SCREEN. see EDUCATION — Teaching Methods And Curriculum

384.554 US ISSN 0276-153X
PN1995.9.P7
SCREEN. 1979. w. (plus a. directory). $70. 720 N. Wabash Ave., Chicago, IL 60611. TEL 312-664-5236. FAX 312-664-8425. URL: http://www.screenmag.com. Ed. Ruth Ratny; Pub. Maureen Canny. adv. contact: Maureen Canny. circ. 15,000. **Document type:** trade publication, directory.
Description: Covers film, video, and audiovisual production within the Chicagoland area: television commercials, industrial and corporate programs, audiovisuals, theatrical features.

384.554 770 UK
SCREEN DIGEST. 1971. m. £275 (foreign $495) (effective 1997). Screen Digest Ltd., 37 Gower St., London WC1E 6HH, England. TEL 44-171-580-2842. FAX 44-171-580-0060. Ed. David Fisher. R&P contact: Allan Hardy. bk.rev.; bibl.; charts; stat.; index. (back issues avail.) Indexed: WPM. **Document type:** newsletter.
●Also available online. Vendor(s): CompuServe, Inc., Data-Star, Information Access Co.
Description: Summaries of world news in film, television, video, satellite, multimedia and consumer electronics with statistical surveys and research data, along with lists of events and publications pertaining to screen media worldwide.

SCREEN INTERNATIONAL. see MOTION PICTURES

SCREEN INTERNATIONAL EUROGUIDE; the definitive guide to film, television and video in Europe. see MOTION PICTURES

SCRIPTWRITERS MARKET. see LITERATURE

SECOM ANNUAL REPORT (YEAR). see CRIMINOLOGY AND LAW ENFORCEMENT — Security

384.55 364.4 US
SECURE SIGNALS. (Supplements avail.) 1986. q. membership only. National Cable Television Association, Office of Cable Signal Theft, 1724 Massachusetts Ave., N.W., Washington, DC 20036. TEL 202-775-3684. FAX 202-775-3696. E-mail: ocst@iname.com. (Co-sponsor: Coalition Opposing Signal Theft) Ed. Staci M. Pittman. stat.; tr.lit. circ. 4,000. **Document type:** newsletter.
Description: Industry-oriented information covering legal and technical aspects of theft of cable television services and means of preventing losses.

384 IT
SETTIMANA T V. 1954. w. L.18000. Alberto Peruzzo Editore s.r.l., Via Marelli 165, 20099 Sesto San Giovanni, Italy. Ed. Ivano Davoli. adv. circ. 188,000.

384.55 UK ISSN 1363-0172
▼**SETTOP & SERVER BULLETIN.** 1996. m. TechMedia, 52 Foundling Ct., London WC1N 1AN, England. TEL 44-171-837-0815. FAX 44-171-278-9917. E-mail: 100141.676@compuserve.com. Ed. Paul Rasmussen; Pub. Philip Gallagher. **Document type:** newsletter.
●Also available online.
Description: Covers markets for technologies enabling interactive video and digital TV services.

384.55 CC
SHANGHAI DIANSHI/SHANGHAI TELEVISION. (Text in Chinese) m. $40.40. (Shanghai Dianshitai - Shanghai Television Station) Shanghai Dianshi Bianjibu, 651 Nanjing Xilu, Shanghai 200041, People's Republic of China. TEL 2562213. (Dist. in US by: China Books & Periodicals, Inc., 2929 24th St., San Francisco, CA 94110. TEL 415-282-2994)

SHICHOKAKU KYOIKU/AUDIO-VISUAL EDUCATION. see *EDUCATION*

SHOOT. see *ADVERTISING AND PUBLIC RELATIONS*

384.55 US
PN1998.A1
SHOOT DIRECTORY FOR COMMERCIAL PRODUCTION AND POSTPRODUCTION. 1965. a. $75. B P I Communications, Inc. (New York), 1515 Broadway, 12th Fl., New York, NY 10036. TEL 212-764-7300. FAX 212-536-5321. Ed. Theresa Pitti; Pub. Robert Griefer. adv. contact: Neal Greenberg. bk.rev. circ. 5,500. **Document type:** directory.
 Former titles: Shoot Commercial Production Directory & Back Stage Shoot Commercial Production Directory; Back Stage T V Film - Tape and Syndication Directory (ISSN 0098-5481)

681.384 UK ISSN 0037-4261
TK9956
SHORT WAVE MAGAZINE. 1937. m. £25 (Europe £28; elsewhere £30) (effective 1996). P W Publishing Ltd., Arrowsmith Ct., Sta. Approach, Broadstone, Dorset BH18 8PW, England. TEL 44-1202-659930. FAX 44-1202-659950. Ed. Dick Ganderton. adv.: B&W page £400. charts; illus. circ. 20,000. **Indexed:** Br.Tech.Ind., INSPEC (1983-). **Document type:** consumer publication.
 —BLDSC (8270.000000); AskIEEE; Ei; KR SourceOne; Linda Hall; SWETS.

SHOW BIZ NEWS AND MODEL NEWS. see *CLOTHING TRADE — Fashions*

SILVER SCREEN. see *BUSINESS AND ECONOMICS — Investments*

SINATRA INTERNATIONAL. see *BIOGRAPHY*

791.4 IC ISSN 1017-3617
SJONVARPSVISIR. 1987. m. free to qualified personnel. Islenska Utvarpsfelagid hf. - Stoed 2 - Icelandic Broadcasting Corp., Inc. - Channel 2, Lynghalsi 5, P.O. Box 10110, IS-130 Reykjavik, Iceland. TEL 354-515-6770. FAX 354-515-6870. E-mail: sjonvarpsvisir@ibc.is. Ed. Olafur Jon Jonsson; Pub. Jafet S. Olafsson. adv.: B&W page ISK 82960, color page ISK 117840; trim 11 1/2 x 8 1/4; adv. contact: Halldor Kristjansson. circ. 50,000 (controlled).
 Description: Guide for viewers of TV-Channel 2 in Iceland.

384 CI ISSN 0037-6523
SKOLSKA TELEVIZIJA. (Part 1: Predmetna Nastara; Part 2: Razredna Nastava) 1961. 4/yr. $1 per no. Radiotelevizija Zagreb, Cvjetna cesta 66, Zagreb, Croatia. Ed. Hrvoje Juracic. abstr.; charts; illus.; cum.index.

SKRIEN. see *MOTION PICTURES*

791.4 US ISSN 1074-4592
SKY-VIEW.* 1983. m. $27. O'Rourke Brothers, 1205 Fourth Ave., Moline, IL 61265. TEL 800-475-9484. adv. circ. 5,000. **Document type:** trade publication.
 Formerly: Satellite T V Pre Vue (ISSN 0896-3673)
 Description: Contains satellite television listings and articles.

SKYWAVES. see *RELIGIONS AND THEOLOGY*

790 US ISSN 0164-3584
SOAP OPERA DIGEST. 1975. bi-w. $49.90 (foreign $57.90). K-III Communications Corp., 745 Fifth Ave., New York, NY 10151. TEL 212-745-0100. (Subscr. to: Box 55125, Boulder, CO 80322. TEL 800-829-9095) Ed. Lynn Leahey. adv.; illus. circ. 1,300,000. (also avail. in microfiche from NBI; reprint service avail. from UMI) **Document type:** consumer publication.
 —UMI.
 Description: Covers TV soap operas, with synopses, interviews, and news items, with life-style features on beauty, fashion, food and parenting topics.

790 US
SOAP OPERA DIGEST SPECIAL ISSUE. 1988. q. newsstand price: $2.69 (Canada $2.95). K-III Magazines, 95 W. 25th St., New York, NY 10010. TEL 212-229-8400. Ed. Stephanie Sloane. circ. 500,000. (reprint service avail. from UMI) **Document type:** consumer publication.
 Formerly: Soap Opera Digest Presents (ISSN 0899-1979)
 Description: Each issue covers a particular soap opera theme.

051 US
SOAP OPERA ILLUSTRATED. 1992. bi-m. K-III Communications Corp., 745 Fifth Ave., New York, NY 10151. TEL 212-745-0100. **Document type:** consumer publication.

791.4 US ISSN 1057-9192
SOAP OPERA MAGAZINE. w. $39.84. S O M Publishing, Inc., 600 S. East Coast Ave., Lantana, FL 33462. TEL 407-586-1111. FAX 407-582-0126. Ed. Joseph J. Policy. adv.; illus. **Document type:** consumer publication.
 Description: Weekly record of daily television soap operas, featuring interviews with stars, previews, and behind the scenes gossip.

790 US ISSN 1092-3969
▼**SOAP OPERA NEWS.** 1997. w. $67.47 (Canada $79.47); newsstand price: $1.49. S O M Publishing, Inc., 660 White Plains Rd., Tarrytown, NY 10591. TEL 914-366-0620. FAX 914-366-0629. Ed. Richard Kaplan. adv. contact: Brian Carrigan. circ. 300,000 (paid). (back issues avail.) **Document type:** consumer publication.
 Description: Covers soap opera plotlines and personalities.

791.4 US ISSN 0199-3003
SOAP OPERA STARS. q. $9 (foreign $14). Sterling - Macfadden Partnership, 35 Wilbur St., Lynbrook, NY 11563. TEL 516-593-1220. FAX 516-593-0065. adv. **Document type:** consumer publication.
 Description: For the entertainment of female readers. Focuses on soap opera stars.

791.4 US ISSN 0898-1485
SOAP OPERA UPDATE. 1988. bi-w. $59. Bauer Publishing Company, L.P., 270 Sylvan Ave., Englewood Cliffs, NJ 07632-2513. TEL 201-569-6699. FAX 201-569-2510. Ed. Richard Spencer. adv. circ. 200,000. **Document type:** consumer publication.

790 US ISSN 1047-7128
PN1992.8.S4
SOAP OPERA WEEKLY. w. $56.68 in U.S.; Canada $88.47; elsewhere $84.24. K-III Communications Corp., 745 Fifth Ave., New York, NY 10151. TEL 212-745-0100. (Subscr. to: Box 54998, Boulder, CO 80322. TEL 800-829-9095) (also avail. in microfiche from NBI) **Document type:** consumer publication.
 Description: Devoted to the plots and personalities of TV soap operas, with interviews and a variety of feature columns.

384.5 384.55 AT ISSN 1032-3899
SOUND & IMAGE; Australia's magazine guide to home entertainment. 1988. bi-m. Horwitz Publications Pty. Ltd., 55 Chandos St., St. Leonards, N.S.W. 2065, Australia. Ed. Lesley Conran. adv.; bk.rev. **Document type:** consumer publication.

384.54 SA
SOUTH AFRICAN BROADCASTING CORPORATION. ANNUAL REPORT. (Text in Afrikaans, English) a. South African Broadcasting Corporation, Private Bag X1, Auckland Park 2006, South Africa. TEL 27-11-714-3741. FAX 27-11-714-6514. Ed. Des Celliers. charts; illus.; stat. **Document type:** corporate report.

SPECTATOR (LOS ANGELES); journal of film and television criticism. see *MOTION PICTURES*

384.5 UK
SPECTRUM (LONDON). 1991. q. Independent Television Commission, 33 Foley St., London W1P 7LB, England. TEL 071-255-3000. FAX 071-306-7800. **Document type:** bulletin.
 Formerly: Airwaves.
 Description: Discusses broadcasting policy and research.

SPOTLIGHT CHILDREN'S. see *THEATER*

SPOTLIGHT ON PRESENTERS. see *THEATER*

THE STAGE. see *THEATER*

STAGE SCREEN & RADIO. see *LABOR UNIONS*

791.43 US ISSN 1080-3793
STAR TREK COMMUNICATOR. 1980. bi-m. $19.95 (Canada $22.95; elsewhere $34.95) membership. Official Star Trek Fan Club, 3720 Revere St., Ste. B, Denver, CO 80239. TEL 303-574-0907. FAX 303-574-9442. Ed. Dan Madsen. adv.; bk.rev.; film rev.; illus. (back issues avail.) **Document type:** consumer publication.
 Formerly (until 1994): Star Trek 3 (ISSN 0883-3125)
 Description: Covers anything and everything pertaining to Star Trek: movies, TV and fandom.

791.43 US ISSN 1083-4486
STAR WARS INSIDER. bi-m. $19.95 membership. Official Star Wars Fan Club, 3720 Revere St., Ste. B, Denver, CO 80239. TEL 303-574-0907. FAX 303-574-9442. (Subscr. to: Box 111000, Aurora, CO 80017) Ed. Jon Bradley Synder; Pub. Dan Madsen. adv. contact: David Latimer. bk.rev.; film rev.; illus.; circ. 250,000 (paid). **Document type:** consumer publication.
 Formerly (until 1994): Lucasfilm Fan Club (ISSN 1041-5122)
 Description: Covers all matters connected to the science fiction trilogy, the new Star Wars Prequels and Star Wars Fandom.

384.554 778.5 US ISSN 0191-4626
STARLOG; magazine of the future. 1976. m. $39.97 (foreign $48.97). Starlog Group, Inc., 475 Park Ave. S., 8th Fl., New York, NY 10016. TEL 212-689-2830; 800-877-5549. FAX 212-889-7933. Ed. Michael Stewart. adv.; bk.rev.; film rev.; charts; illus. circ. 265,000. **Document type:** consumer publication.
 —UnCover.
 Description: Science fiction in TV and movies.

384.5 GW ISSN 0344-4252
STROM UND WELLE. m. Fachverband Elektrotechnische Handwerke Nordrhein-Westfalen, Hannoversche Str. 22, Postfach 110195, 44143 Dortmund, Germany. TEL 0231-593048.

301.16 JA ISSN 0585-7325
STUDIES OF BROADCASTING; an international annual of broadcasting science. (Text in English) 1963. a. exchange basis. Japan Broadcasting Corp., Broadcasting Culture Research Institute, Theoretical Research Center - Nippon Hoso Kyokai Hoso Bunka Kenkyujo, 1-1, Atago 2-chome, Minato-ku, Tokyo 105, Japan. TEL 81-3-5400-6800. FAX 81-3-3436-5880. bk.rev.; illus. circ. 1,000. **Indexed:** Int.Ind.Film Per., Intl.Ind.TV. **Document type:** academic/scholarly publication.
 —BLDSC (8489.720000).
 Description: Promotes the exchange of information on mass communications research.

STUDIO SOUND. see *SOUND RECORDING AND REPRODUCTION*

791.4 CN
SUNDAY SUN TELEVISION MAGAZINE (CALGARY). w. Can.$130. Calgary Sun, 2615-12 St. N.E., Calgary, Alta. T2E 7W9, Canada. TEL 403-250-4200. FAX 403-250-4180. Ed. Ray Djuff. adv. circ. 99,505. (tabloid format)

791.4 GW
SUPER - T V. w. newsstand price: DM 1.20. Burda Verlag GmbH, Postfach 1230, 77602 Offenburg, Germany. TEL 49-89-9250-0. FAX 49-89-92503519. (Subscr. to: Burda Medien Abo-Service, Postfach 1351, 88131 Lindau, Germany) adv. circ. 1,200,000. **Document type:** consumer publication.

COMMUNICATIONS — TELEVISION AND CABLE

621.388   AT   ISSN 1326-6764
SUPERHIGHWAYS STRATEGIES REPORT. a. Aus.$495 (US Aus.$525; Europe Aus.$530) (effective 1998). Paul Budde Communication Pty. Ltd., 2643 George Downes Dr., Bucketty, N.S.W. 2250, Australia. TEL 61-7-49988144. FAX 61-2-49988247. E-mail: pbc@budde.com.au; URL: http://www.budde.com.au. **Description:** Reports on Australian and New Zealand cable and pay TV markets: interactive TV, FSN's, ADSL and other interactive broadband developments.

791.4   SQ
SWAZI T V TIMES.* (Text in English) m. R.8. Swaziland Television Broadcasting Corporation, P.O. Box A146, Mbabane, Swaziland. Ed. Ann Thomas. adv.

SYSTEMS AND COMPUTERS IN JAPAN. see COMPUTERS — Computer Systems

384 659.2   US   ISSN 1054-4259
T V & CABLE PUBLICITY OUTLETS - NATIONWIDE. 1970. a. $99. Morgan-Rand Inc., 1800 Byberry Rd., 800 Masons Mill Business Park, Huntingdon Valley, PA 19006. TEL 215-938-5500. FAX 215-938-5549. Ed. Nancy Shenker. circ. 1,500.
Formerly: All T V Publicity Outlets - Nationwide; Formed by the merger of: T V Publicity Outlets - Nationwide (ISSN 0041-4514); (1982-1985): Cable T V Publicity Outlets - Nationwide.

T V & CABLE SOURCE. see ADVERTISING AND PUBLIC RELATIONS — Abstracting, Bibliographies, Statistics

384.55   UK
T V & SATELLITE WEEK. T V & Satellite Week. London - Anglia (ISSN 0968-851X); T V & Satellite Week. North West - Border (ISSN 0968-8528); T V & Satellite Week. South - South West (ISSN 0968-8536); T V & Satellite Week. Midlands - Wales and West (ISSN 0968-8544); T V & Satellite Week. Scotland - Ulster (ISSN 0968-8552) T V & Satellite Week. Yorkshire - Tyne - Tees (UK ISSN 0968-8560) 1993. w. I P C Magazines, Specialist Magazine Group (Subsidiary of: Reed Elsevier group), King's Reach Tower, Stamford St., London SE1 9LS, England. TEL 44-171-261-5000. FAX 44-1444-445599. TELEX 892084 REEDBP G. (Dist. by: Quadrant Subscription Services, Oakfield House, Perrymount Rd., Haywards Heath, W. Sussex RH16 3DH, England. TEL 44-1444-445555) Ed. Colin Tough. adv. contact: Rupert Miles. circ. 200,000. **Document type:** consumer publication. **Description:** Dedicated to full satellite program coverage, as well as terrestrial channels.

384.55   II
T V & VIDEO WORLD. (Text in English) 1983. m. Nariman Point Building Services & Trading Pvt. Ltd., 920 Tulsiani Chambers, Nariman Point, Bombay 400 021, India. Ed. Maneck Davar. adv.: B&W page Rs.10000, color page Rs.20000; trim 265 x 195.

791.4   GW
T V ANZEIGER; das regionale Fernsehmagazin. 1985. m. DM.36. Theodor-Hanloser-Str. 7, 78224 Singen, Germany. TEL 07731-41001. Ed. Roswitha Bosch. adv.; film rev. adv. circ. 80,000. **Description:** Television information and regional news.

384.554   AT
T V AUDIENCE PROFILES. 1989. 4/yr. Roy Morgan Research, P.O. Box 2282U, Melbourne, Vic. 3001, Australia. TEL 61-3-96296888. FAX 61-3-96291250.

384.55   GW
T V BUSINESS. 1991. 10/yr. Media Daten Verlag GmbH, Klingenweg 4, 6229 Walluf, Germany. TEL 06123-700-0. circ. 15,000. **Document type:** directory. **Description:** Directed to program planners, producers, production staff, advertisers and managers involved in the German-speaking Central European TV market.

384.554 790.13   US   ISSN 0887-5847
T V COLLECTOR. 1976. bi-m. $21 (Canada $23; elsewhere $30) (effective 1996). T V C Enterprises, Box 1088, 69 S. St., Easton, MA 02334. TEL 508-238-1179. E-mail: tvcollector@internetmci.com; URL: http://www.angelfire.com/ma/tvcollector. Ed. Diane L. Albert; Pub. Seven W. Albert. adv.: B&W page $65. bk.rev.; video rev.; circ. 2,000 (paid). (back issues avail.) **Document type:** consumer publication. **Description:** Provides in-depth articles, episode guides, interviews with stars of old TV series, actor profiles, tributes and interviews.

384.55   IT
T V COLOR.* 1978. a. L.3800($7) Gruppo Editoriale Suono s.r.l., Via Capo Peloro, 30, 00141 Rome, Italy. TEL 893608. adv.; illus. circ. 80,000.

384.55   US   ISSN 0884-1098
HE8700.8
T V DIMENSIONS. 1984. a. Media Dynamics, 322 E. 50th St., New York, NY 10022.

791.4   BE
T V EKSPRES. (Text in Dutch) 1970. w. 2860 BEF. Internationale Uitgevers Maatschappij, Jan Blockxstraat 7, 2018 Antwerp, Belgium. TEL 32-3-2474511. FAX 32-3-2474589. Ed. Lex Moolenaar. adv. circ. 183,224. **Document type:** consumer publication.

384.55   US   ISSN 0736-2986
HE8700.8
T V EXECUTIVE; a printed marketplace for programming and production. 1983. 2/yr. (subscr. includes Annual Directory Who's Who of Promo - Ad Executives). T V Trade Media, Inc., 216 E. 75th St., No. PW, New York, NY 10021. TEL 212-288-1549. FAX 212-734-9033. TELEX 428669 VIDEO. (Alt. addr.: 1328 Westwood Blvd., Ste. 2, Los Angeles, CA 90024. TEL 310-446-1532) Ed. Dom Serafini; Pub. Dom Serafini. R&P contact: Monica Gorghetto. adv. contact: Dianne Smolen. **Document type:** trade publication. **Description:** Contains news and information about the TV industry with profiles, analysis, and commentary.

791.4   CN
T V FACTS - LONDON. (Text in English) 1980. w. free. 533064 Ontario Ltd., 69 Wharncliffe Rd. S., London, Ont. N6J 2J8, Canada. TEL 519-637-2330. Ed. Mike Langley. adv. circ. 33,000. (back issues avail.)

791.4   PO   ISSN 0871-7362
T V GUIA. 1979. w. Esc.2652 (Europe Esc.5820; US Esc.7920) (effective 1997). T V Guia Editora, Av. Alm. Gago Coutinho, 113, 1700 Lisbon, Portugal. TEL 351-1-8474410. FAX 351-1-8474395. Ed. Rui Mendonca. adv.: B&W page Esc.750000. circ. 300,000. **Description:** Contains a program guide and entertainment features.

791.4   US   ISSN 0039-8543
T V GUIDE. 1953. w. $43.16 (effective 1997); newsstand price: $1.19. Murdoch Magazines (Radnor), Four Radnor Corporate Center, 100 Matsonford Rd., Box 500, Radnor, PA 19088. TEL 610-293-8500; 800-866-1400. FAX 610-688-3285. Ed. Jack Curry. adv. contact: Suzanne Grimes. bk.rev.; illus.; 38 yr. cum.index; circ. 15,800,000 (paid). (also avail. in microfilm) Indexed: Access (1975-1988), Mag.Ind., PMR, PROMT, R.G (1988-), R.G.Abstr. **Document type:** consumer publication.
—KR SourceOne; UMI; UnCover.
Description: Personality profiles and articles on television and entertainment of national interest. Published in regional editions with comprehensive listing of local network and cable TV programs.

791.4   US   ISSN 1191-5315
T V GUIDE (CANADIAN EDITION). (Published in 15 regional editions) 1953. w. Can. $54.24 (foreign Can.$65.98); newsstand price: Can.$0.99. News America Publications, Inc., 25 Shepard Ave., W., Ste. 100, North York, ON M2N 6S7, Canada. Ed. Debbie Morns; Pub. Suzanne M. Grimes. adv.; circ. 829,838 (paid). Indexed: R.G.Abstr. **Document type:** consumer publication.

791.4   CN   ISSN 0039-8551
T V HEBDO. 1960. w. Can.$52.63. Editions Telemedia, 2001 University, Ste. 900, Montreal, PQ H3A 2A6, Canada. TEL 514-499-0561. FAX 514-843-3529. Ed. Jean-Louis Podlesak. adv.; illus. circ. 220,757. (also avail. in microfilm from BNQ) **Document type:** consumer publication.

384.554   GW   ISSN 0940-0656
T V HOEREN UND SEHEN. 1962. w. (Fri.). newsstand price: DM.2.30. Heinrich Bauer Verlag, Burchardstr. 11, 20095 Hamburg, Germany. TEL 49-40-30193040. FAX 49-40-335923. (Dist. in UK by: Powers International, 517-523 Fulham Rd., London SW6 1HD, England. TEL 44-171-385-8855. FAX 44-171-381-5555) Ed. Marion Horn; Pub. Heinz Bauer. adv.: B&W page DM.44720, color page DM.71552; adv. contact: Karl Keller. circ. 2,157,793. **Document type:** consumer publication.

791.4   US
T V HOST MONTHLY. m. $24 (effective 1997-1998). T V Host, Inc., Box 1665, 3935 Jonestown Rd., Harrisburg, PA 17109. TEL 717-657-1700. FAX 717-657-2921. URL: http://www.tvhost.com; http://www.nytimes.cm/maglve.html. Ed. Mike Edkin. adv. contact: Lou Pernik, Jr. circ. 700,000 (paid). **Document type:** consumer publication.
●Also available online.
Supersedes in part: T V Host (ISSN 0744-7396)

791.4   US
T V HOST WEEKLY. w. $43 (effective 1997-1998). T V Host, Inc., Box 1665, 3935 Jonestown Rd., Harrisburg, PA 17109. TEL 717-657-1700. FAX 717-657-2921. URL: http://www.tvhost.com; http://www.nytimes.com/maglive.html. Ed. Suzanne Stefanic. adv. contact: Lou Pernik, Jr. circ. 130,000 (paid). **Document type:** consumer publication.
●Also available online.
Supersedes in part: T V Host (ISSN 0744-7396)

384.55   GW   ISSN 0947-1677
T V INTERAKTIV; Hintergrunddienst ueber interaktives Fernsehen. 1993. fortn. DM.1200. HighText Verlag, Ridlerstr. 55, 80339 Munich, Germany. TEL 49-89-500353-0. FAX 49-89-50035399. E-mail: info@hightext.de. Ed. Joachim Graf. R&P contact: Daniel Treplin. **Document type:** trade publication.

384.554   IT
T V KEY; mensile professionale di communicazione televisiva. 1982. m. (9/yr.). L.200000 (foreign L.280000; $175) includes Media Key Synthesis and Global. Media Key s.r.l., Via Filippino Lippi 33, 20131 Milan, Italy. TEL 39-2-236-66-25. FAX 39-2-236-26-62. Ed. Roberto Albano. adv. contact: Silvana Carazzina. index. circ. 10,500. **Document type:** trade publication.
Description: Covers commercial tv, new technology, production, marketing, programs and advertising.

384.55   GW   ISSN 0945-5981
T V KLAR. 1992. w. (Thu.). newsstand price: DM.1. Heinrich Bauer Verlag, Burchardstr. 11, 20095 Hamburg, Germany. TEL 49-40-30193040. FAX 49-40-335923. (Dist. in UK by: Powers International, 517-523 Fulham Rd., London SW6 1HD, England. TEL 44-171-385-8855. FAX 44-171-381-5555) Ed. Hartmut Klemann. adv.: color page DM.40354; adv. contact: Karl Keller. circ. 1,827,846. **Document type:** consumer publication.

791.4   NE   ISSN 0927-3204
T V KRANT. 1966. w. fl.40. Postbus 1313, 1000 BH Amsterdam, Netherlands. Ed. Wim Koesen. adv.; bk.rev.; charts; illus. circ. 750,000.
Formerly (until 1991): Tros-Kompas (ISSN 0041-3321)

791.4   JA
T V LIFE. (Text in Japanese) 1983. w. 6760 Yen. Gakken Co., Ltd., 40-5, 4 chome, Kamiikedai, Ohta-ku, Tokyo 145, Japan. Ed. Seiji Yokoyama.

791.4   CN   ISSN 0316-2397
T V MAGAZINE. 1967. w. Can.$50 (effective Nov. 1990). Spartan Printing, 101 Marsh Dr., Quesnel, B.C. V2J 3K3, Canada. TEL 604-992-2713. FAX 604-992-3902. Ed. J.P. Hartnett. adv.; illus. circ. 10,000.

COMMUNICATIONS — TELEVISION AND CABLE

791.4 028.5 JA
T V MAGAZINE. (Text in Japanese) 1971. m. Kodansha Ltd., 12-21 Otowa 2-chome, Bunkyo-ku, Tokyo 112, Japan. TEL 81-3-5395-3491. FAX 81-3-3492-7705. TELEX J34059 KODANSHA. Ed. Tohru Ogawa. circ. 360,000. **Document type**: consumer publication.
  Description: Children's TV magazine.

384.554 GW
T V MOVIE. 1991. fortn. newsstand price: DM.2.50. Heinrich Bauer Verlag, Burchardstr. 11, 20095 Hamburg, Germany. TEL 49-40-30193040. FAX 49-40-335923. (Dist. in UK by: Powers International, 517-523 Fulham Rd., London SW6 1HD, England. TEL 44-171-385-8855. FAX 44-171-381-5555) Ed. Michael Hopp. adv.: B&W page DM.64560, color page DM.80054; adv. contact: Karl Keller. circ. 3,301,715. **Document type**: consumer publication.

384.55 GW
T V NEU. 1992. w. (Thu.). newsstand price: DM.1. Axel Springer Verlag AG, Axel-Springer-Platz 1, 20355 Hamburg, Germany. TEL 49-40-3470-0. FAX 49-40-340224. Ed. Wili Schmitt. adv.: B&W page DM.10127, color page DM.16208; trim 212 x 280; adv. contact: Michael Bayer. circ. 810,215 (paid). **Document type**: consumer publication.

384.554 US
T V NEWS. (Geographic editions avail.) 1973. w. free. 80 Eighth Ave., Ste. 315, New York, NY 10011. TEL 212-243-6100. FAX 212-243-7457. Ed. Elizabeth Farkas; Pub. Allan Horwitz. R&P contact: Allan Horwitz. adv. contact: Allan Horwitz. bk.rev.; rec.rev.; circ. 331,000 (controlled). **Document type**: consumer publication.

791.4 384.554 US ISSN 1051-3590
PN4784.T4
T V NEWS CONTACTS (YEAR). 1970. a. (plus m. updates). $150. B P I Communications, Inc. (New York), 1515 Broadway, New York, NY 10036. TEL 212-536-5261; 800-BPI-4100. FAX 212-536-5294. Ed. Mitch Tebo. (looseleaf format) **Document type**: directory.

791.4
T V NEWS MAGAZINE;* Central Indiana, Eastern Illinois television listings. 1950. w. $23.70. Carter Publications, Inc., Box 1265, Indianapolis, IN 46206-1265. Ed. Jack Carter. adv. circ. 22,500.

791.4
T V OBSERVER. w. Bullivant - Wilde Publishing Ltd., Webb House, 20 Church Green E., Redditch, Worcs B98 8BP, England. TEL 0527-585588. (back issues avail.)
  Description: English television listings guide including editorial and features.

791.4 CN ISSN 0228-0116
T V PLUS. (Text in French) 1978. w. $42.90. Editions Telemedia, 2001 University, Ste. 900, Montreal, PQ H3A 2A6, Canada. TEL 514-499-0561. Ed. Therese Parisien. circ. 11,348. **Document type**: consumer publication.

384 791.4 US ISSN 0885-2340
T V PROGRAM INVESTOR. 1985. m. $695 (effective 1997). Paul Kagan Associates, Inc., 126 Clock Tower Pl., Carmel, CA 93923. TEL 408-624-1536. TELEX 408-625-3225. Ed. Larry Gerbrandt.
  Description: Covers trends in TV program syndication, values of TV networks and programs, public stocks and private companies in the TV program business, and analysis of mergers and acquisitions.

T V PROGRAM STATS. see *COMMUNICATIONS — Abstracting, Bibliographies, Statistics*

384.55 UK
T V QUICK. 1991. w. newsstand price: £0.60. H. Bauer Publishing Ltd., Shirley House, 6th Fl., 25-27 Camden Rd., London NW1 9LL, England. TEL 44-171-485-3774. FAX 44-171-284-0593. Ed. Lori Miles; Pub. H. Bauer. R&P contact: Lori Miles. adv.: page £10000; adv. contact: Louise Schofield. bk.rev.; tele.rev.; video rev.; circ. 800,000 (paid). **Document type**: consumer publication.
  Description: Provides T.V. listings and features.

384.554 US ISSN 1051-788X
T V R O DEALER. 1986. m. $18 (effective 1997). Fortuna Communications Corporation, 140 S. Fortuna Blvd., Fortuna, CA 95540. TEL 707-725-6591. FAX 707-725-4311. Ed. James Scott; Pub. Patrick O'Dell. adv.: B&W page $2200, color page $2800; trim 8 3/8 x 10 7/8; adv. contact: George Bryant. circ. 16,500. **Document type**: trade publication.
  Description: Serves the satellite television industry including satellite TV retailers, programmers, manufacturers, distributors, audio-video retailers, consumer electronic retailers and others.

791.4 CN
T V SCENE (VICTORIA). w. free with newspaper. Times-Colonist, 2621 Douglas St., Victoria, BC V8T 4M2, Canada. TEL 604-380-5211. FAX 604-380-5353. Ed. Ron Joiner; Pub. Paul Willcocks. adv. contact: Brian Hobbs. circ. 90,000. **Document type**: consumer publication.
  Description: Provides daily television listings, prime time charts for local cable and television programming in Victoria and Vancouver Island. Focuses on television and movie personalities, sports events and specials.

791.4 CN
T V 7 JOURS.* 1989. w. Trustar Ltd., 2020 rue Universite, 20th Fl., Montreal, PQ H3A 2A5, Canada. TEL 514-383-3400. FAX 514-383-1766. Ed. Claude Leclerc. adv.: B&W page Can.$2000, color page Can.$3450; trim 5 1/4 x 7 3/8. circ. 129,639 (paid); 255 (controlled). **Document type**: consumer publication.

384.554 PO
T V 7 DIAS. 1987. w. Esc.9360 (foreign 26780) (effective 1997). Impala Sociedade Editorial, Lda., Avda. Miguel Bombarda, 33-35, 2745 Queluz, Portugal. TEL 4364401. FAX 4365001. TELEX 16088 CENDIP P. (Distr. by: Electroliber, Rua Vasco da Gama, 4-A, 2685 Sacavem, Portugal. TEL 9425394) Ed. Antonio Mateus. adv. contact: consumer publication.

791.4 IT ISSN 0038-156X
T V SORRISI E CANZONI. Key Title: Sorrisi e Canzoni T V. 1952. w. L.33300; newsstand price: L.2000. Silvio Berlusconi Editore S.p.A., Corso Europa 5-7, 20122 Milan, Italy. TEL 39-2-77941. adv.: color page L.98000000; circ. 2,232,088.
  Formerly (until 1972): Sorrisi e Canzoni d'Italia (ISSN 1121-7502)

384.55 GW ISSN 0938-8729
T V SPIELFILM. fortn. DM.78 (effective 1997); newsstand price: DM.3. Verlagsgruppe Milchstrasse, Milchstr. 1, 20148 Hamburg, Germany. TEL 49-40-44198-0. FAX 49-40-458519. (Subscr. to: P M S GmbH, Postfach 290180, 47261 Duisburg, Germany. TEL 49-203-76908-0. FAX 49-203-7690830) Ed. Christian Hellmann; Pubs. Dirk Manthey, Joerg Altendorf. adv. contact: Rainer Gierke. circ. 1,785,161. **Document type**: consumer publication.

T V SPORTSFILE. see *SPORTS AND GAMES*

384.55 BE
T V STORY. (Text in Dutch) 1975. w. 2600 BEF. Tijdschriften Uitgevers Maatschappij N.V.I.U.M., Jan Blockxstraat 7, B-2018 Antwerp, Belgium. (U.S. addr.: Interactive Market Systems, 55 Fifth Ave., New York, NY 10003) Ed. L. van Raak. adv. circ. 180,416. **Document type**: consumer publication.
  Formerly: Story.

384.55 US
T V SUPERSTAR.* bi-m. $7.50. Sterling - Macfadden Partnership, 35 Wilbur St., New York, NY 10017. TEL 516-593-1220. **Document type**: consumer publication.

384.554 US ISSN 0887-1701
T V TECHNOLOGY. (International editions avail.) 1983. bi-w. $125 (foreign $150) (effective 1998). Industrial Marketing Advisory Services, Inc., 5827 Columbia Pike, Ste. 310, Falls Church, VA 22041. TEL 703-998-7600. FAX 703-998-2966. (Subscr. to: Box 1214, Falls Church, VA 22041) Ed. Richard Farrell; Pub. Stevan B. Dana. adv. contact: Carmel King. circ. 43,000. (reprint service avail.) **Document type**: trade publication.
  —KR SourceOne.

384.554 CN
T V TELESCOPE. 1979. w. Can.$49.99 (effective 1997). T V Publishing Group, 201 - 4201 25A Ave., Vernon, BC V1T 7G8, Canada. TEL 250-542-0469; 800-663-4424. FAX 250-542-0942. Ed. Deeny Grazier; Pub. Tom Monahan. R&P contact: Deeny Grazier. adv. contact: Norm Metcalf. circ. 36,000. (back issues avail.)
  Formerly: Tele-Scope Magazine.

791.5 UK ISSN 0039-8624
T V TIMES. 1955. w. £83.84 (Europe £99.71; elsewhere £151.73) (effective 1997). I P C Magazines, Weeklies Group (Subsidiary of: Reed Elsevier group), King's Reach Tower, Stamford St., London SE1 9LS, England. TEL 44-171-261-5000. FAX 44-171-261-7777. TELEX 892084 REEDBP G. (Dist. by: Quadrant Subscription Services, Oakfield House, Perrymount Rd., Haywards Heath, W. Sussex RH16 3DH, England. TEL 1444-445555) Ed. Liz Murphy. adv. contact: Kathryn Jacob. rec.rev.; illus. circ. 981,261. **Document type**: consumer publication.
  Description: Thirteen editions weekly listing all BBC, ITV, C4, and satellite broadcasts

791.4 US ISSN 1054-0008
T V TIMES (ST. PAUL). (In Regional Editions) 1967. w. $27. T V Times Publications, Inc., 1010 University Av., St. Paul, MN 55104. TEL 612-646-9629. Ed. Richard B. Beeson. adv.; illus. circ. 102,000.
  Formerly: T V Digest (ISSN 0041-4506)

384 US
T V TODAY. 1933. w. membership. National Association of Broadcasters, 1771 N St., N.W., Washington, DC 20036. TEL 202-429-5350. FAX 202-429-5406. E-mail: tbutts@nab.org; URL: http://www.nab.org. Ed. Tom Butts. R&P contact: Ben Ivins. adv. contact: David Dziedzic. circ. controlled. (only avail. by fax) **Document type**: newsletter.
  Incorporates (in 1985): N A B Highlights;
  Formerly: N A B Today (Television Edition).
  Description: Updates on association news and broadcast industry news at Capitol Hill and the FCC.

791.45 GW
T V TODAY. 1994. fortn. DM.58.50 (Europe DM.127.40; elsewhere DM.133.38). Magazin Verlag am Fleetrand GmbH, Stubbenhuk 5, 20459 Hamburg, Germany. TEL 49-40-37032324. FAX 49-40-37037844. E-mail: plathner@tvtoday.de; URL: http://www.co.guj.de/titel/tv_today. Ed. Andreas Schmidt. adv.: B&W page DM.22800, color page DM.28500; trim 224 x 295; adv. contact: Joerg Plathner. **Document type**: consumer publication.

791.4 FI ISSN 0788-6632
T V VECKAN OCH RADIO. 1934. w. FIM 386. Mannerheimv. 18, 00100 Helsinki 10, Finland. FAX 358-0-642930. Ed. Maj-Britt Paro. adv. contact: Bo Gerkman. circ. 9,200.
  Former titles (until 1990): Veckan med Radio och T V (ISSN 0356-0732); (until 1984): Radio - T V - Bladet.

791.4 AT ISSN 0810-249X
T V WEEK. 1957. w. Aus.$190.32 (foreign Aus.$213.20). Pacific Publications, 32 Walsh St., Melbourne, Vic. 3000, Australia. Ed. John Hall. circ. 743,000. (back issues avail) **Document type**: consumer publication.

791.4 CC
T V WEEK. (Text in Chinese) 1967. w. T V Week Ltd., 1 Leighton Rd., Hong Kong, People's Republic of China. TEL 8366188. FAX 8910421. circ. 62,000.

791.4 CN
T V WEEK MAGAZINE. 1976. w. Can.$37.95. Canada Wide Magazines & Communications Ltd., 4180 Lougheed Hwy., Ste. 401, Burnaby, BC V5C 6A7, Canada. TEL 604-299-7311. FAX 604-299-9188. Ed. Hardip Randhawa; Pub. Peter Legge. adv. contact: Harry van Hemmen. film rev.; play rev. circ. 86,600. **Document type**: consumer publication.
  Description: Television magazine with listings and television-related features.

COMMUNICATIONS — TELEVISION AND CABLE

384.55   UK   ISSN 0142-7466
HE8700
T V WORLD; international business magazine for television. 1977. 10/yr. £50 (rest of Europe £60; elsewhere £80). E M A P Media (Subsidiary of: E M A P Business Communications), 33-39 Bowling Green Ln., London EC1R ODA, England. TEL 44-171-505-8133. FAX 44-171-505-8139. E-mail: janem@media.emap.co.uk. (Subscr. to: Readerlink, Audit House, 260 Field End Rd., Eastcote, Ruislip, Mddx. HA4 9LT, England. TEL 44-181-956-3016. FAX 44-181-936-3020) Ed. Jane Millichip; Pub. Jon Baker. adv.: B&W page £3150; trim 272 x 204. (back issues avail.) Indexed: Int.Ind.Film Per. (until 1995), Intl.Ind.TV.
Document type: trade publication.
   Description: Reports on television programming developments worldwide.

791.45   CN
T V WORLD. w. Can.$48.99 (effective 1997). T V Publishing Group, 201 - 4201 25A Ave., Vernon, BC V1T 7G8, Canada. TEL 250-542-0469; 800-663-4424. FAX 250-542-0942. Ed. Deeny Grazier; Pub. Tom Monahan. R&P contact: Deeny Grazier. adv. contact: Norm Metcalf.

384.554   US
T V Y NOVELAS. (Editions avail. for Colombia, Mexico, Peru, Puerto Rico, US) (Text in Spanish) 1982. fortn. $27.95. Editorial Televisa, Vanidades Continental Bldg., 6355 N.W. 36th St., Virginia Gardens, FL 33166. TEL 305-871-6400. FAX 305-871-7146. E-mail: subscriptions@editorialtelevisa.com. Ed. Dora Luz Vargas. adv. circ. 1,237,000.
   Description: Covers the soap operas and their stars.

384.55 808.838   UK   ISSN 0957-3844
T V ZONE. 1989. m. £38 (U.S. and Canada $80; rest of world £44). Visual Imagination Ltd., 9 Blades Ct., Deodar Rd., London SW15 2NU, England. TEL 44-181-875-1520. FAX 44-181-875-1588. Ed. Jan Vincent-Rudzki. R&P contact: Stephen Payne. adv.: B&W page £550, color page £825; trim 210 x 298; adv. contact: James Ditchfield. illus.
Document type: consumer publication.
   Description: Covers cult television programs such as Star Trek, Quantum Leap, and Doctor Who.

384.55 808.838   UK   ISSN 0960-8230
T V ZONE SPECIAL. (Supplement to: T V Zone) 1990. q. Visual Imagination Ltd., 9 Blades Ct., Deodar Rd., London SW15 2NU, England. TEL 44-181-875-1520. FAX 44-181-875-1588. Ed. Jan Vincent-Rudzki. R&P contact: Stephen Payne. adv. contact: James Ditchfield. circ. 40,000 (paid).
Document type: consumer publication.

384.55   US   ISSN 1045-9553
PN1991.8.T35
TALK SHOW SELECTS. 1989. a. $185 (diskette $280). Broadcast Interview Source, 2233 Washington Ave., N.W., Washington, DC 20007-4104. TEL 202-333-4904. FAX 202-342-5411. E-mail: editor@yearbooknews.com; URL: http://www.yearbooknews.com. Ed. Mitchell P. Davis. R&P contact: Mitchell P. Davis. (also avail. in diskette format) **Document type:** directory.
   Description: Lists the top-rated radio and television news and talk programs in the United States.

384.55   US   ISSN 0896-3215
TECHLINE; a publication for the cable engineering community. 1979. bi-m. membership only. National Cable Television Association, 1724 Massachusetts Ave., N.W., Washington, DC 20036. TEL 202-775-3550. Ed. Katherine Rutkowski. bibl. circ. 2,500. **Document type:** newspaper.
   Description: Geared to the U.S. cable television engineering community.

TECHNOS; quarterly for education and technology. see
EDUCATION — Computer Applications

791.5   US   ISSN 1073-7669
TEENAGE GANG DEBS. 1989. a. $3 (effective 1995-1996). Erin & Don Smith, Eds. & Pubs., Box 1754, Bethesda, MD 20827-1754. bk.rev.; circ. 2,000 (paid). **Document type:** newsletter.
   Description: Carries articles, photos, interviews, satire, criticism, reviews, and letters.

621.38   RU   ISSN 0040-2249
CODEN: TKTEAE
TEKHNIKA KINO I TELEVIDENIYA/MOTION PICTURE AND TELEVISION TECHNOLOGY. (Text in Russian; summaries in English) 1957. m. $130 (effective 1998). (International Service Production Advertising S.A., SZ) Lerusha Ltd., 47, Leningradsky pr., 125167 Moscow, Russia. TEL 095-158-6225. FAX 096-157-3816. TELEX 411058 FILM. Ed. Valery V. Makartsev. R&P contact: Theodore Samoilov. adv. contact: Theodore Samoilov. bk.rev.; film rev.; rec.rev.; tele.rev.; video rev.; illus.; index. circ. 10,000. Indexed: Chem.Abstr., INSPEC, Photo.Abstr.
—BLDSC (0180.200000); AskIEEE; CASDDS; CISTI; KR SourceOne.

384.5   US
TELCOM HIGHLIGHTS INTERNATIONAL. 1978. w. $425. Box 527, Paramus, NJ 07653. TEL 201-265-7236. FAX 201-265-7236. Ed. George Chevalier; Pub. George Chevalier. bk.rev. circ. 425. **Document type:** newsletter.

791.4   MX
TELE GUIA; primera revista de la television mexicana. 1952. w. Mex.$4 per no. Editorial Television S.A. de C.V., Av. Vasco de Quiroga 200, Edif. E, 1o., Santa Fe, 01210 Mexico, D.F., Mexico. TEL 52-5-2612600. FAX 52-5-2612605. URL: http://www. Ed. Maria Eugenia Hernandez. circ. 375,000.

791.4   CN
TELE HORAIRE (MONTREAL). w. Journal de Montreal, 4545 Frontenac St., Montreal, Que. H2H 2R7, Canada. TEL 514-521-4545. FAX 514-525-5442. TELEX 05-827591. Ed. Gilles Crevier.
   Description: Provides daily coverage of daily television listings of all major Canadian and American networks.

791.4   CN
TELE HORAIRE (QUEBEC). 1982. w. Can.$1. Journal de Quebec, 450 Ave. Bechart, Ville Vanier, Que. G1M 2E9, Canada. TEL 418-683-1027. FAX 418-683-1573. FAX 418-683-1027. Ed. Serge Cote. adv. circ. 108,561. (also avail. in microfilm)
   Description: Guide for readers that includes TV listings and interviews with TV personalities, features on current TV shows, mini-series and films.

791.4   FR   ISSN 0297-8695
TELE LOISIRS. 1986. w. Prisma Presse, 6 rue Daru, 75008 Paris, France. TEL 33-1-44153000. FAX 33-1-47641042. Ed. Gilles de Prevaux. adv. circ. 1,415,000. **Document type:** consumer publication.
   Description: Provides TV listings and covers tourism, cars, fashion, beauty, health and fitness, cuisine, do-it-yourself activities, legal advice, horoscope, and games.

791.4   CN
TELE-MAGAZINE LE SOLEIL. w. Can.$504.35. Soleil, 925 chemin St-Louis, C.P. 1547 Terminus, Quebec, PQ G1K 7J6, Canada. TEL 418-686-3233. FAX 418-686-3260. Ed. Magella Soucy. adv.
Document type: consumer publication.
   Description: Carries articles of special interest to TV viewers. Included are: TV and movie listings, star profiles, films to see, behind the camera, choice of cable, pay-TV, TSN, inter-vision.

791.4   RE   ISSN 1246-4082
TELE MAGAZINE 7 REUNION. w. B.P. 405, 97469 Saint-Denis, Reunion. circ. 25,000. **Document type:** consumer publication.
   Former titles (until 1992): Tele 7 Jours Reunion (ISSN 0759-6669); (until 1983): Tele 7 Jours. Reunion, Maurice (ISSN 0182-0052); (until 1978): Tele 7 Jours - Reunion (ISSN 0398-4311)

791   BE   ISSN 0772-0963
TELE-MOUSTIQUE.* (Text in French) 1924. w. 3742 Fr.($62) Editions Jean Dupuis, S.A., Bd. Tirou 7, 6000 Charleroi, Belgium. Ed. Albert Desprechins. adv.; film rev.; abstr.; illus. circ. 190,000.
   Formerly: Moustique (ISSN 0027-2647)

791.4   FR
TELE - POCHE. 1966. w. 259 F. (effective 1997). E M A P France, 150 rue Gallieni, 92644 Boulogne Billancourt Cedex, France. TEL 33-1-41335000. FAX 33-1-41335749. TELEX 660 712. Ed. Jean-Charles Durand. adv. circ. 1,560,000.
Document type: consumer publication.

384.55   CN   ISSN 0049-3252
TELE PRESSE. 1969. w. free. Presse Ltee., 7 St. James St. W., Montreal, Que. H2Y 1K9, Canada. adv. circ. 238,755. (also avail. in microfilm)

621.385 384.554   GW   ISSN 0931-4733
TELE-SATELLIT; Europe's satellite magazine. 1981. m. DM.96. Tele-Audiovision, Postfach 801965, 81619 Munich, Germany. TEL 089-24013229. FAX 089-24013215. Ed. Alexander Wiese. adv. circ. 56,000. **Document type:** trade publication.
   Description: Technical periodical for satellite professionals and consumers.

791.4   FR   ISSN 0153-0747
TELE 7 JOURS. 1960. w. 480 F. Filipacchi Medias, 151 rue Anatole France, 92598 Levallois Peret Cedex, France. TEL 33-1-41347330. FAX 33-1-41347503. (Subscr. to: 5 rue Naracci, 59884 Lille Cedex 9, France. TEL 33-1-20121110. FAX 33-1-20121111) Ed. Alain Laville. circ. 3,335,000. **Document type:** consumer publication.

791.4   US
TELE VIEWING. 1975. s-w. $12. Paper Publishers, Inc., 200 E. Wilcox, Sierra Vista, AZ 85635. TEL 602-458-3340. FAX 602-458-9338. adv. circ. 37,200.

384   NE   ISSN 1382-9998
TELECOMBRIEF - TELEMATICS TRENDS. (Includes bi-m supplement: Combrief) 1980. 23/yr. fl.425. Broadcast Press Hilversum B.V., Postbus 576, 1200 AN Hilversum, Netherlands. TEL 31-35-6400015. FAX 31-35-6214559. E-mail: t_brief@euronet.nl. Ed. R.J. Landman; Pub. L. Derksen. R&P contact: Rob Bakker. adv. contact: A. van de Beek. bk.rev.; circ. 2,000 (paid). (back issues avail.) **Document type:** newsletter.
   Former titles (until 1993): Telecom-Brief (ISSN 0921-3651); (until 1987): Media-Info (ISSN 0921-366X)
   Description: Information on telecommunications, cable, satellite, and new media.

TELECOMMUNICATIONS STRATEGIES REPORT; packaging of value added telecommunication & broadcasting services & networks. see
COMMUNICATIONS — Telephone And Telegraph

384.554   LU
TELECRAN. (Text in German) 1978. w. 2200 Fr. (effective 1997). Editions Saint-Paul, S.A., 2 rue Christophe Plantin, L-2988 Luxembourg, Luxembourg. TEL 49-93-500. FAX 49-93-590. TELEX 3688-LIBO-LU. adv.; illus. circ. 43,000.

384.55   SP
TELEINDISCRETA. 1985. w. Publicaciones Ekdosis, S.A. Gran Via Carlos III, 124 5o, 08034 Barcelona, Spain. TEL 34-3-2800088. FAX 34-3-2800837. circ. 300,000.

384.5   US
TELEMEDIUM. 1953. 3/yr. membership. National Telemedia Council, Inc., 120 E. Wilson St., Madison, WI 53703. TEL 608-257-7712. Ed. Marieli Rowe. R&P contact: Marieli Rowe. bk.rev. circ. 600.
   Former titles (until 1984): Better Broadcasts New (ISSN 0006-0054); Better Broadcasts Newsletter.

384.554   BE
TELEMOUSTIQUE. (Text in French) 1924. w. 2750 BE Editions Francophones Belges S.A., Rue de Joncker 46, 1060 Brussels, Belgium. TEL 32-2-537-08-00 FAX 32-2-534-02-38. adv.: B&W page 102000 BEF, color page 165000 BEF; trim 180 x 243. circ. 189,116.

384.5   IT   ISSN 1121-1814
TELEPIU. 1987. w. L.38000 avail. in Italy only. Silvio Berlusconi Editore S.p.A., C.so Europa 5-7, 20122 Milan, Italy. TEL 39-2-77941. (Subscr. to: RCS Rizzoli Periodici S.p.a, Distribuzione e Abbonamenti Via Rizzoli 2, 20132 Milan, Italy) Ed. Paolo Cucco. adv.: color page L.18000000. circ. 434,682. **Document type:** consumer publication.

791.4   SP   ISSN 0040-2672
TELEPROGRAMA. 1966. w. 6000 ptas. (effective 1997). Hachette Filipacchi Revistas, Cardenal Herrera Oria 3, 28034 Madrid, Spain. TEL 34-1-5938462. FAX 34-1-5931028. E-mail: info@3.ibm.net; URL: http://www.hachette.es. Ed. Oscar Weinberg G. adv.; film rev.; play rev. circ. 1,150,000.

COMMUNICATIONS — TELEVISION AND CABLE

791.4   FR   ISSN 0040-2699
TELERAMA. 1950. w. 550 F. Publications de la Vie Catholique, 129 bd. Malesherbes, 75017 Paris, France. TEL 33-1-48884888.
FAX 33-1-40540645. Ed. Michel Houssin. adv.; bk.rev. circ. 526,000. **Indexed:** Int.Ind.Film Per. **Document type:** consumer publication.
—CCC.

384.554   CN   ISSN 0838-0953
TELEROMAN. q. Telemedia Publishing, 2001 University, Ste. 900, Montreal, PQ H3A 2A6, Canada. TEL 514-499-0561. FAX 514-499-1844. Ed. Therese Parisien. circ. 75,000.

TELESCOPE; l'hebdomadaire de television pour les enseignants, les parents et les educateurs. see EDUCATION — Teaching Methods And Curriculum

791.4   IT
TELESETTE. 1978. w. L.15500 (foreign L.140000). Casa Editrice Universo S.p.A., Via M. De Vizzi 35, 20092 Cinisello Balsamo (MI), Italy. Ed. Daniel Jarach. adv.: B&W page L.21400000, color page L.27600000. circ. 777,222. **Document type:** consumer publication.

384.55   IT
TELETUTTO. w. newsstand price: L.10000. Edizioni Internazionali Cioe s.r.l., Via Giovanni Fabbroni 24, 00191 Rome, Italy. TEL 39-6-3287250. FAX 39-6-3274576. Ed. Fabio Piscopo. adv.: page L.6500000. **Document type:** consumer publication.

384.5   RU
TELEVIDENIE I RADIOVESHCHANIE. 1952. m. Pyatnitskaya ul.25, 113326 Moscow, Russia. TEL (095) 292-82-68. Ed. N.S. Biryukov. circ. 50,000.

384.55   II
TELEVISION. (Text in Bengali) 1988. m. newsstand price: Rs.10. Aajkaal Publishers Ltd., 96, Raja Rammohan Sarani, Calcutta 700 009, India. TEL 3509803. Ed. Ashok Dasgupta. circ. 36,297.

384   UK   ISSN 0308-454X
TK6630.A1   CODEN: TELED3
TELEVISION (LONDON, 1927). 1927. 8/yr. £63 (foreign £75) (effective 1997). Royal Television Society, Holborn Hall, 100 Gray's Inn Rd., London WC1X 8AL, England. TEL 44-171-430-1000. FAX 44-171-430-0924. Ed. Peter Fiddick. R&P contact: Sue Griffith. adv.: B&W page £695, color page £990; trim 270 x 190; adv. contact: Sue Griffith. bk.rev.; abstr.; bibl.; charts; illus.; index. circ. 4,000. (also avail. in microfilm from CHL) **Indexed:** Br.Tech.Ind., Educ.Tech.Abstr., Eng.Ind., INSPEC, Int.Ind.Film Per., Intl.Ind.TV. **Document type:** trade publication.
—BLDSC (8788.052000); AskIEEE; CISTI; KR SourceOne; Linda Hall; SWETS.
Former titles: Royal Television Society. Journal (ISSN 0035-9270); Television Society. Journal.
Description: Provides news, views and features both technical and non-technical about the latest developments in the television industry.

384.5   UK   ISSN 0032-647X
CODEN: TELED3
TELEVISION (LONDON, 1934); servicing - projects - video - developments. 1934. m. £26 (overseas £30). Reed Business Information (Subsidiary of: Reed Elsevier plc), Quadrant House, The Quadrant, Sutton, Surrey SM2 5SA, England.
TEL 44-181-652-8120. FAX 44-181-652-8956. (Subscr. to: Quadrant Subscription Services, Oakfield House, Perrymount Rd., Haywards Heath, W. Sussex RH16 3DH, England. TEL 44-1444-445566) Ed. J.A. Reddihough; Pub. Susan Downey. adv. contact: Carol Nobbs. charts; illus.; circ. 25,000 (paid). **Indexed:** INSPEC, Int.Ind.Film Per., Pinpointer. **Document type:** trade publication.
—BLDSC (8786.950000); CASDDS. CCC.
Formerly (until 1969): Practical Television.

791   US   ISSN 1061-5741
TK6645
TELEVISION & CABLE ACTION UPDATE; the authoritative news service of actions affecting television stations and cable TV activities. Short title: T V & Cable Update. (Supplement to: Television & Cable Factbook) 1991. w. $462 (foreign $572). Warren Publishing, Inc., 2115 Ward Ct., N.W., Washington, DC 20037. TEL 202-872-9200.
FAX 202-293-3435. TELEX 650-217-2616-WUI. stat. (looseleaf format; back issues avail.) **Document type:** trade publication.
—CCC.
Formerly: Weekly Television and Cable Action Update.
Description: Highlights a weekly listing of new applications including permits, sales franchises, grants and regulatory changes.

791   US   ISSN 0732-8648
TK6540
TELEVISION AND CABLE FACTBOOK. 1945. a. $495. Warren Publishing, Inc., 2115 Ward Ct., N.W., Washington, DC 20037. TEL 202-872-9200. FAX 202-393-3435. Ed. Albert Warren. **Document type:** trade publication.
—CISTI. CCC.
Formerly: Television Factbook (ISSN 0082-268X)

384.55   US
TELEVISION ASIA. 10/yr. Cahners Publishing Company (Newton), Division of Reed Elsevier Inc., 275 Washington St., Newton, MA 02158-1630. TEL 617-964-3030. FAX 617-558-4506. URL: http://www.home1.pacific.net.sg/~tvasia. (Asian addr.: 58A Smith St., Singapore 058962, Singapore. TEL 65-223-8823. FAX 65-220-5015) Ed. Nick Masters; Pub. Jonathan Hallett. circ. 5,340.
Description: Offers in-depth coverage of Asian television broadcasting and programming.

384.55   UK   ISSN 1353-8586
THE TELEVISION BOOK (YEAR). 1993? a. £7.99. Edinburgh International Television Festival, 2nd Fl., 24 Neal St., London WC2H 9PS, England.
TEL 44-171-379-4519. FAX 44-171-836-0702. Ed. James Saynor; Pub. Wendy Hutton. **Document type:** academic/scholarly publication.
Description: Discusses various topics of television history, culture, and programming.

384.55   US   ISSN 0898-767X
TK6540
TELEVISION BROADCAST. 1978. m. $40 in U.S, and Canada (foreign $76) (effective 1997). Miller Freeman P S N Inc. (Subsidiary of: United News & Media Co.), 460 Park Ave. South, 9th Fl., New York, NY 10016-7315. TEL 212-378-0400.
FAX 212-378-2160. E-mail: tvbcast@psn.com. Ed. Michael Silbergleid; Pub. Paul Gallo. adv.; bk.rev.; circ. 30,800 (controlled). **Document type:** trade publication.
—KR SourceOne; UMI. **CCC.**
Former titles: Television - Broadcast Communications (ISSN 0746-5777); (until 1983): Broadcast Communications (ISSN 0164-999X)
Description: Covers news, products and applications in both the broadcast and narrowcast industries through a blend of hard news reporting, survey articles and news analysis columns.

384.55   UK   ISSN 0959-6917
TELEVISION BUYER; broadcast hardware for programme production. 1990. m. £30 (foreign £45); newsstand price: £3. E M A P Media (Subsidiary of: E M A P Business Communications), 33-39 Bowling Green Ln., London WC1R ODA, England.
FAX 44-171-833-4519. E-mail: 74431.1401@compuserve.com. (Subscr. to: Readerlink, Audit House, 240 Field End Rd, Eastcote, Ruislip, Mddx. HA4 9UY, England. TEL 44-181-868-4499. FAX 44-181-429-3117) Ed. Hilary Curtis; Pub. Steve Buckley. adv.: page £2135; 210 x 297; adv. contact: Julie Moore. tr.lit.; circ. 7,927 (controlled). (back issues avail.) **Document type:** trade publication.
—KR SourceOne.
Description: Covers all aspects of broadcast television production and reviews professional broadcasting and production equipment.

384.55   US
TELEVISION CONTACTS (YEAR). 1976. a. (plus m. updates). $195. B P I Communications, Inc. (New York), 1515 Broadway, New York, NY 10036.
TEL 212-536-5261; 800-BPI-4100.
FAX 212-536-5294. Ed. Mitch Tebo. circ. 5,000. **Document type:** directory.

384 643   US   ISSN 0497-1515
TELEVISION DIGEST WITH CONSUMER ELECTRONICS. 1945. w. $918 (foreign $983). Warren Publishing, Inc., 2115 Ward Ct., N.W., Washington, DC 20037. TEL 202-872-9200. FAX 202-293-3435. Ed. Albert Warren. **Indexed:** Bus.Ind., Tr.& Indus.Ind. **Document type:** trade publication.
•Also available online. Vendor(s): Information Access Co., NewsNet (PB01).
—CCC.
Formerly: Television Digest (ISSN 0497-1507)

TELEVISION DIRECTORS GUIDE. see BUSINESS AND ECONOMICS — Trade And Industrial Directories

384.55   UK
TELEVISION IN ASIA PACIFIC TO THE YEAR.... a. £220 (effective 1997). Zenith Media Ltd., 15 Chitty St., London W1P 1LJ, England. TEL 44-171-255-1221. FAX 44-171-637-0476. E-mail: publications@zenithmedia.co.uk; URL: http://www.zenithmedia.com. Ed. Adam Smith. **Document type:** trade publication.
Description: Forecasts the next five years of multichannel and pay television growth in the thirteen most important markets in the region.

384.55   UK   ISSN 0968-218X
TELEVISION IN EUROPE TO THE YEAR.... 1989. a. £250 (effective 1997). Zenith Media Ltd., 15 Chitty St., London W1P 1LJ, England. TEL 44-171-255-1221. FAX 44-171-637-0476. E-mail: publications@zenithmedia.co.uk; URL: http://www.zenithmedia.com. Ed. Adam Smith. **Document type:** trade publication.
Description: Facts and figures on today's audiences, channels and advertising in 25 markets, with long-range forecasts of satellite and cable growth for most western European countries.

384.5   ISSN 0739-5531
TELEVISION INDEX;* television network program and production reporting service. 1949. w. $250 (foreign $250) (effective 1997); newsstand price: $5. 1515 Broadway, New York, NY 10036-8901. Ed. Jonathan Miller. cum.index. **Document type:** trade publication.

384.55   US
TELEVISION INTERNATIONAL MAGAZINE. 1956. bi-m. $42. Television International Publications Ltd., Box 2430, Hollywood, CA 90028. TEL 213-462-1099. Ed. Josie Cory; Pub. Josie Cory. adv.; bk.rev.; bibl.; illus.; circ. 14,000 (controlled). **Indexed:** Intl.Ind.TV. **Document type:** consumer publication, trade publication.
Formerly: Telefilm International Magazine.

621.388   UK   ISSN 0961-589X
TELEVISION PRODUCER. 1984. m. £38. E M A P Vision Ltd., P.O. Box 109, Scarbrook Rd., Croydon, Surrey CR9 1QH, England. TEL 0181-760-9690. Ed. Fiona Matthias. adv.; bk.rev.; illus. circ. 8,000.
Formerly (until 1990): Television and Video Production (ISSN 0266-7460)
Description: Guide to television and radio production in England.

384.554   US   ISSN 1056-6104
PN1992.8.F5
(YEARS) TELEVISION PROGRAMMING SOURCE BOOKS. (Supplement avail.: B I B Channels) 1989. a. $895 for 4 vol. set; Film set $545 for 3 vol. set (CD-ROM version $1195) (effective 1997). North American Publishing Co., 401 N. Broad St., Philadelphia, PA 19108. TEL 215-238-5300. FAX 215-238-5457. Ed. D. Witzleben. adv. **Document type:** directory.
•Also available on CD-ROM.
Formed by the 1989 merger of: T V Feature Film Source Book (ISSN 0739-2400) & T V Series, Serials, and Packages (Domestic Edition) (ISSN 0895-2337); Which was formerly (until 1987): Series, Serials, and Packages (Domestic Edition) (ISSN 0162-9743) & T V Series, Serials, and Packages (Foreign Language Edition) (ISSN 0895-2345); Which was formerly (until 1987): Series, Serials, and Packages (Foreign Language Edition) (ISSN 0162-9751).
Description: Lists materials available for television programming, including films, series and miniseries.

COMMUNICATIONS — TELEVISION AND CABLE

384.55   US   ISSN 0040-2796
PN1992
TELEVISION QUARTERLY. 1962. q. $30 (foreign $35) (effective 1995). National Academy of Television Arts & Sciences, c/o Ed Eberung, 111 W. 57th St., Ste. 1020, New York, NY 10019. TEL 212-586-8424. FAX 212-246-8129. Ed. Richard Pack. adv.; bk.rev. circ. 11,500. (also avail. in microform from UMI; reprint service avail. from UMI) **Indexed:** ASCA, Bk.Rev.Ind. (1992-), Child.Bk.Rev.Ind. (1992-), Commun.Abstr., Curr.Cont., P.A.I.S., R.G.Abstr., R.G.
—KR SourceOne; SWETS; UMI; UnCover.
Description: Presents scholarly and professional views and interpretations of patterns and trends in the television industry, and provides a critique of industry performance.

TELEVISION SPONSORS DIRECTORY; product cross-reference directory. see BUSINESS AND ECONOMICS — Trade And Industrial Directories

TELEVISION WRITERS GUIDE. see BUSINESS AND ECONOMICS — Trade And Industrial Directories

384.55   BU   ISSN 0205-1281
TELEVIZIIA I RADIO. 1964. w. $78. Komitet za Televiziia i Radio - Bulgarian National Television, San Stefano St. 29, 1000 Sofia, Bulgaria. TEL 359-2-443294. (Dist. by: Foreign Trade Co. "Hemus", 1B Raiko Daskalov Sq., 1000 Sofia, Bulgaria. TEL 359-2-871686. FAX 359-2-9803319) Ed. St. Kolev. illus. circ. 70,300.

621.38   US
TENNESSEE BROADCASTER.* 1978. m. Tennessee Association of Broadcasters, Box 101015, Nashville, TN 37224-1015.

TEREBI GIJUTSU/TELEVISION TECHNICS & ELECTRONICS. see ELECTRONICS

621.388   JA   ISSN 0386-4227
TEREBIJON GAKKAI GIJUTSU HOKOKU/I T E J TECHNICAL REPORT. (Text in Japanese) 1977. irreg. Terebijon Gakkai - Institute of Television Engineers of Japan, 5-8, Shiba Koen 3-chome, Minato-ku, Tokyo 105, Japan.
—BLDSC (8792.302000).

621.388   JA   ISSN 0919-1879
TEREBIJON GAKKAI NENJI TAIKAI KOEN YOKOSHU/INSTITUTE OF TELEVISION ENGINEERS OF JAPAN. PROCEEDINGS OF ANNUAL CONVENTION. (Text in English, Japanese; summaries in English) a. 8000 Yen. Terebijon Gakkai - Institute of Television Engineers of Japan, 5-8, Shiba Koen 3-chome, Minato-ku, Tokyo 105, Japan. **Document type:** proceedings.
—BLDSC (6741.845000).
Formerly (until 1990): Terebijon Gakkai Zenkoku Taikai Koen Yokoshu.

621.388   JA   ISSN 0386-6831
TEREBIJON GAKKAISHI/INSTITUTE OF TELEVISION ENGINEERS OF JAPAN. JOURNAL. (Text in Japanese; summaries in English, Japanese) 1947. m. 1700 Yen per no. Terebijon Gakkai - Institute of Television Engineers of Japan, 5-8, Shiba Koen 3-chome, Minato-ku, Tokyo 105, Japan. **Indexed:** Eng.Ind, INSPEC.
—BLDSC (4787.600000); AskIEEE; CISTI; Ei; KR SourceOne; Linda Hall. **CCC.**

791.4   CN
THUNDER BAY GUIDE; Thunder Bay's television magazine. 1963. w. Can.$44.89. Amethyst Holdings Ltd., 1126 Roland St., Thunder Bay, ON P7B 5M4, Canada. TEL 807-623-5788. FAX 807-622-3140. Ed. Linda Tasa-Andrychuk; Pub. G.Dougall. R&P contact: A. Barrou. circ. 8,000 (paid). **Document type:** consumer publication.

384.55 790.1   US
THURSDAY MAGAZINE. 1982. w. Thursday Publications, Inc., 316 E St., Box 1061, N. Wilkesboro, NC 28659. TEL 910-667-0134. FAX 910-667-6694. Ed. Ken Welborn; Pub. Ken Welborn. R&P contact: Ken Welborn. adv. contact: Ken Welborn. circ. 22,500. (tabloid format) **Document type:** newspaper.
Description: Informs readers of events in Wilkes County, NC.

621.38   CC
TIANJIN BROADCASTING AND T V WEEKLY. 1955. w. 143 Weijing Lu, Tianjin, People's Republic of China. (Subscr. to: Tianjin Advertising Corp., 57 Hubei Lu, Tianjin, People's Republic of China) Ed. Zhang Jian-guo. circ. 1,340,000.

791.4   SU   ISSN 1319-1403
TILIVISYON AL-KHALIJ. Key Title: Magalat tilifizun al-halig. (Text in Arabic) q. Gulf Vision, P.O. Box 6802, Riyadh, Saudi Arabia. TEL 4032912.
Document type: consumer publication.
Formerly (until 1980): Gulfvision Nashrat al-Ma'lumat.

791   US   ISSN 1063-2883
TOTAL T V. 1990. w. price varies according to location. T V Syndicated Market, 309 Lakeside Dr., Horsham, PA 19044. TEL 215-443-9300; 800-540-5643. URL: http://www.total.com. Ed. Jay Gissen; Pub. Michael Perlis. **Document type:** consumer publication.
Formerly (until 1992): T V Times (Horsham) (ISSN 1054-8858); Incorporates (in 1993): Total.
Description: System-specific cable guide.

621.38   US
TRANSMITTER. 1982. q. $20 membership. Armed Forces Broadcasters Association, Box 447, Sun City, CA 92586-0447. TEL 909-679-5484. FAX 909-679-5484. Ed. Trent Christman. adv.; bk.rev. circ. 800. **Document type:** newsletter.
Description: Covers military broadcasting activities and projects. Provides a forum for ex-military broadcasters.

384.55   US   ISSN 1059-8286
HD9696.T443
TRANSPONDER. 1986. m. Terra Publishing, Inc., R.D. 1, Box 142, Center St. Ext., Salamanca, NY 14779. TEL 716-945-3488. FAX 716-945-5238. (Alt. addr.: Terra Publishing, Inc., Box 460, Salamanca, NY 14779) Ed. Sandra Jackson. R&P contact: Tim Jackson. adv. contact: Dodi McIntyre. circ. 14,500 (controlled). **Document type:** trade publication.
Description: Covers the satellite television industry.

621.38   JA   ISSN 0914-9279
QC676   CODEN: TSKKED
TSUSHIN SOGO KENKYUJO KIHO/COMMUNICATIONS RESEARCH LABORATORY. REVIEW. (Text in Japanese; summaries in English) 1954. q. exchange basis. Ministry of Posts and Telecommunications, Communications Research Laboratory - Yuseisho Tsushinsogo Kenkyujo, 2-1, Nukui Kita-machi 4-chome, Koganei-shi, Tokyo 184, Japan. TEL 81-423-21-1211. FAX 81-423-27-7603. TELEX 2832611-DEMPA-J. E-mail: pub@crl.go.jp. (Co-sponsor: Denki Tsushin Shinkokai - Association for the Promotion of Telecommunications) **Indexed:** INIS Atomind., INSPEC (1988-), Int.Aerosp.Abstr., JCT, JTA. **Document type:** academic/scholarly publication.
—BLDSC (7786.031000); AskIEEE; CISTI; KR SourceOne; Linda Hall.
Formerly (until 1988): Denpa Kenkyujo Kiho - Radio Research Laboratory. Review (ISSN 0033-801X)

070   US
THE TYNDALL REPORT. 1988. bi-m. $60. A D T Research, 135 Rivington St., New York, NY 10002. TEL 212-674-8913. FAX 212-979-7304. Ed. Bruno Pajaczkowski. circ. 500. (looseleaf format; back issues avail.)
Description: Analysis of television news: monitors the nightly newscasts of the three US broadcast networks with statistical data and commentary. Tracks trends in major news stories, social issues, domestic and foreign affairs, and politics.

384.55   UK
U K TELEVISION FORECASTS. 2/yr. £360 (effective 1997). Zenith Media Ltd., 15 Chitty St., London W1P 1LJ, England. TEL 44-171-255-1221. FAX 44-171-637-0476. E-mail: publications@zenithmedia.co.uk; URL: http://www.zenithmedia.com. Ed. Adam Smith. **Document type:** trade publication.
Description: Detailed forecasts along with backdata from the UK's largest buyers of TV airtime and audiences.

UTILITY AND TELEPHONE FLEETS. see COMMUNICATIONS — Telephone And Telegraph

UTUSAN RADIO DAN T V. see COMMUNICATIONS — Radio

384.54 621.38   AU
V R F INFO. q. Verband des Radio-, Fernseh-, und Elektro-Fachhandels und Gewerbes Oesterreichs, Goeschlgasse 12, A-1030 Vienna, Austria. TEL 786120.

384 780   NE
VERONICA; weekblad voor radio en TV. 1971. w. fl.72.75 (effective 1997). Veronica Blad B.V., P.O. Box 418, 1200 AK Hilversum, Netherlands. TEL 31-35-6723723. FAX 31-35-6214495. TELEX 7. E-mail: bladredactie@veronica.nl; URL: http://www.veronica.nl. Ed. Robert Briel; Pub. Maarten Tulen. R&P contact: Neidi Bast. adv. contact: Marlene Wickel. bk.rev.; film rev.; circ. 1,250,000 (paid). **Document type:** consumer publication.
Description: Contains features and radio and TV listings.

VIDEO & TELEVISION. see COMMUNICATIONS — Video

791.4   US   ISSN 1046-607X
HD9697.V543
VIDEO SOFTWARE MAGAZINE. 1985. m. free. Capital Cities - A B C, Inc., 825 Seventh Ave., 6th Fl., New York, NY 10019. TEL 212-887-8400. (And: 5519 Centinela Ave., Los Angeles, CA 90066) Ed. Jack Schember. adv.; film rev. circ. 42,000.
—CCC.
Formerly: Video Software Dealer (ISSN 0894-3001)
Description: Presents coverage of the home video industry to retailers and distributors. Includes information about market research, products and services, buyer's guides, release dates, and special feature articles.

384.5   DK   ISSN 0903-5117
VIDEO TRAILEREN. 1986. m. DKK 350($70) (effective 1997). Bladforlaget Nygaard ApS, Naestvedvej 12, P.O. Box 12, DK-Herlufmagle, Denmark. TEL 45-53-75-10-11. FAX 45-53-75-10-11. Ed. Jens Nygaard. adv.; B&W page DKK 4100, color page DKK 8300; trim 266 x 175. circ. 5,289. **Document type:** trade publication.

VISIE. see RELIGIONS AND THEOLOGY — Protestant

384.55   FI   ISSN 0780-4199
VISIO. 1971. 8/yr. FIM 580. Edita Ltd., P.O. Box 750, FIN-00043 Edita, Finland. TEL 358-0-56601. FAX 358-0-5660504. E-mail: timo.rinta@edita.fi; URL: http://www.edita.fi/visio. Ed. Timo M. Rinta. R&P contact: Timo M. Rinta. adv. contact: Arto Jarvenpaa. bk.rev. circ. 9,000. **Document type:** trade publication.
Formerly: Kuva ja Aani (ISSN 0357-2943)
Description: For A-V, video and new media professionals and users in Finland.

791.45 305.897   US   ISSN 1088-1824
▼**THE VISION MAKER.** 1995. q. Native American Public Telecommunications, 1800 N. 33rd St., Box 83111, Lincoln, NE 68501-3111. TEL 402-472-3522. FAX 402-472-8675. E-mail: jbauman@unlinfo.unl.edu; URL: http://www.indian.monterey.edu/napt. Ed. Jennifer Bauman.
Description: Informs, educates, and encourages awareness of tribal cultures, opportunities, histories, languages, and aspirations by employing educational and public telecommunications.

VOICE OF PROPHECY NEWS. see RELIGIONS AND THEOLOGY — Protestant

791.45   US   ISSN 1041-2700
PN1992.3.U5
W E T A MAGAZINE. m. W E T A, 3700 S. Four Mile Run Dr., Arlington, VA 22206. TEL 703-845-8084. FAX 703-379-5232. URL: http://www.wera.org. Ed. Pat Good. adv. contact: Ingrid Boud. circ. 125,000.
Formerly (until 1988): Dial W E T A (ISSN 0898-1779)

384.55   US   ISSN 1067-6252
WARREN'S CABLE REGULATION MONITOR; the authoritative weekly news service covering federal, state, and local cable activities and trends. 1993. w. $578 (foreign $624). Warren Publishing, Inc., 2115 Ward Ct., N.W., Washington, DC 20037. TEL 202-872-9200. FAX 202-293-3435. TELEX 6502173616. Ed. Michael Feazel. stat. **Document type:** newsletter.
●Also available online.
—CCC.
Description: Covers regulations at all levels of government affecting the cable industry.

791.43   US
WASHED - UPDATE. 1996. w. Box 2598, Seal Beach, CA 90740. E-mail: greg@bulmash.com; URL: http://us.imdb.com/washed-update.html; http://www.bulmash.com/washed. Ed. Greg Bulmash.
●Available only online.
   Description: Concentrates on the recent careers of popular celebrities of yesteryear.

WESTERNS & SERIALS. see MOTION PICTURES

621.388   UK
WHAT SATELLITE BOOK OF TESTS. a. £2.95 (effective 1997). W V Publications and Exhibitions Ltd., 57-59 Rochester Pl., London NW1 9JU, England. TEL 44-171-485-0011. FAX 44-171-482-6269. (Orders to: ASM Ltd., Unit 6, Pipewell Road Industrial Estate, Desborough, Northants NN14 2SW, England. TEL 44-1536-762860. FAX 44-1536-760306) Document type: consumer publication.

621.388   UK   ISSN 0956-2362
WHAT SATELLITE TV. 1986. m. £32 (Europe £50; rest of world £60) (effective 1997); newsstand price: £2.75. W V Publications and Exhibitions Ltd., 57-59 Rochester Pl., London NW1 9JU, England. TEL 44-171-485-0011. FAX 44-171-482-6269. (Subscr. to: ASM Ltd., Unit 6, Pipewell Road Industrial Estate, Desborough, Northants NN14 2SW, England. TEL 44-1536-762860. FAX 44-1536-760306) Ed. Geoff Bains. circ. 61,847. Document type: consumer publication.
—BLDSC (9309.758410).

791.5   UK
WHAT'S ON TV. 1991. w. £0.47 per week. I P C Magazines, Weeklies Group (Subsidiary of: Reed Elsevier group), King's Reach Tower, Stamford St., London SE1 9LS, England. TEL 44-171-261-5000. FAX 44-171-261-7739. TELEX 892084 REEDBP G. E-mail: wotv-postbag@ipc.co.uk. (Dist. by: Quadrant Subscription Services, Oakfield House, Perrymount Rd., Haywards Heath, W. Sussex RH16 3DH, England. TEL 44-1444-445555) Ed. Mike Hollingsworth. adv. contact: Rupert Miles. circ. 1,675,844. Document type: consumer publication.
   Description: TV listings service, plus features, puzzles and quizzes for the whole family.

384.5   791.4   US   ISSN 0887-4824
WHITMARK MAGAZINE.* (Annual Publication: Whitmark Directory) 1968. bi-m. $12. Whitmark Associates, 2908 McKinney Ave., Dallas, TX 75204-2431. TEL 214-871-8901. Ed. Eric Hirschhorn. illus. circ. 12,000.
   Former titles: Whitmark News and Views (ISSN 0192-9224); Talent News and Views (ISSN 0049-2876)
   Description: Reports from seven-state southwestern film-video industry on radio and television communications.

384.54   UK
WHO'S WHO IN COMMONWEALTH BROADCASTING.. 1976. a. $28 (effective 1998). Commonwealth Broadcasting Association, BBC Yalding House, Rm. 312, 152-156 Great Portland St., London W1N 6AJ. TEL 44-171-765-5144. FAX 44-171-765-5152. E-mail: cba@bbc.co.uk; URL: http://www.oneworld.org/cba/. Ed. Elizabeth Smith. adv. contact: Derek Hall. Document type: trade publication.
   Formerly (until 1995): Commonwealth Broadcasting Association. Handbook.

537   US   ISSN 1054-6960
WIRELESS CABLE INVESTOR. 1972. m. $645 (effective 1997). Paul Kagan Associates, Inc., 126 Clock Tower Place, Carmel, CA 93923. TEL 408-624-1536. TELEX 408-625-3225. Ed. George Eagle. charts; index. Document type: newsletter.
   Formerly: Multicast (ISSN 0146-0099)
   Description: Covers MDS, the FCC-regulated common carrier for pay TV and data services.

WIRELESS: FOR THE CORPORATE USER. see COMMUNICATIONS

WONDERFUL WORLD OF FLYING. see AERONAUTICS AND SPACE FLIGHT

384.5   US   ISSN 1050-012X
WORLD BROADCAST NEWS. m. (except July-Aug. combined). free to qualified personnel. Intertec Publishing Corp., 9800 Metcalf, Overland Park, KS 66212-2215. TEL 913-341-1300. FAX 913-967-1898. Ed. Gerald Walker. circ. 12,500 (controlled). (also avail. in microform from UMI) Document type: trade publication.
—KR SourceOne; UMI. CCC.
   Formerly: B M E's World Broadcast News.

384.55   US   ISSN 1084-9475
PN1992.1
(YEAR) WORLD GUIDE TO TELEVISION. (Supplement avail.: B I B Channels) 1990. a. $495 (effective 1997). North American Publishing Co., 401 N. Broad St., Philadelphia, PA 19108. TEL 215-238-5300. FAX 215-238-5474. Ed. Dana Witzleben. Document type: directory.
●Also available on CD-ROM.
   Former titles (until 1996): World Guide to Television and Film (ISSN 1072-6144); (until 1994): World Guide to Television and Programming (ISSN 1058-1944); (until 1992): T B I's World Guide (ISSN 1052-7192)
   Description: Guide to the international television marketplace including program buyers at every station around the world.

WORLD RADIO T V HANDBOOK. see COMMUNICATIONS — Radio

800   US
PN121
WRITTEN BY. 1963. 11/yr. $40. Writers Guild of America, West, 7000 W. Third St., W. Hollywood, Los Angeles, CA 90048. TEL 213-782-4522. E-mail: writtnby@wga.org. Ed. Lisa Chambers. R&P contact: Lisa Chambers. adv. contact: Dianna Hightower. illus. circ. 120,000. Document type: trade publication.
   Former titles (until 1996): Writers Guild of America, West. Journal (ISSN 1055-1948); (until Nov. 1988): Writers Guild of America, West. Newsletter (ISSN 0043-9533)
   Description: Looks at T.V. and screen writing for union members.

621.38   CC   ISSN 1000-1417
WUXIANDIAN YU DIANSHI/RADIO AND TELEVISION. (Text in Chinese) bi-m. Shanghai Scientific and Technical Publishers, Journal Department, 450 Ruijin 2 Lu, Shanghai 200020, People's Republic of China. TEL 4370160. Ed. Sun Heming.

384.554   US   ISSN 1051-4058
AS29.5
YEARBOOK OF EXPERTS, AUTHORITIES & SPOKESPERSONS; an encyclopedia of sources. 1984. a. $37.50. Broadcast Interview Source, 2233 Wisconsin Ave., N.W., Washington, DC 20007. TEL 202-333-4904. FAX 202-342-5411. E-mail: editor@yearbooknews.com; URL: http://www.yearbooknews.com. Ed. Mitchell P. Davis. R&P contact: Mitchell P. Davis. adv. circ. 10,000. Document type: directory.
●Also available online.
   Formerly (until 8th, 1990): Directory of Experts, Authorities and Spokespersons (ISSN 1045-9537)
   Description: Reviews 1,500 groups and individuals of interest to the media, and provides contact names and phone numbers.

384.55   II
YUGSHREE. (Text in Hindi) 1985. m. Ranchi Prakashan Pvt. Ltd., 55 Baralal St., Ranchi 834001, India. TEL 91-651-206320. FAX 91-651-203466. Ed. Vijay Maroo. adv.: B&W page Rs.8000, color page Rs.16000; trim 240 x 175; adv. contact: Rakesh Dosi. music rev.; tele.rev.; illus. circ. 30,000. cols./p.: 3; pp./issue: 72.
   Description: Guides people to TV programs, and commercial products.

384.554   GW   ISSN 0342-5886
Z D F JAHRBUCH. (Zweites Deutsches Fernsehen) 1964. a. DM.25. Z D F, Presse und Oeffentlichkeitsarbeit, Postfach 4040, 55100 Mainz, Germany. TEL 49-6131-702210. FAX 49-6131-705366. TELEX 4187930-ZDF-D. E-mail: info@zdf.de; URL: http://www.zdf.de. Eds. Peter Christian Hall, Jana Dietrich; Pub. Dieter Schwarzenau. Indexed: Int.Ind.Film Per. Document type: corporate report.
●Also available on CD-ROM.
   Formerly: Zweites Deutsches Fernsehen. Jahrbuch (ISSN 0514-8591)

COMMUNICATIONS — VIDEO

384.55   GW
▼ZAP! FERNSEHEN UND BUECHER. 1995. m. DM.2. Stiftung Lesen, Fischtorplatz 23, 55116 Mainz, Germany. TEL 06131-288900. FAX 06131-230333. circ. 10,000. Document type: consumer publication.

ZEITSCHRIFT FUER URHEBER- UND MEDIENRECHT. see LAW

621.388   UK   ISSN 0261-1686
ZERB. 1973. s-a. £3.75 per no. (foreign £6 per no.). Guild of Television Cameramen, 2 Burleigh Mead, Hatfield, Herts. AL9 5ED, England. TEL 01707-260216. FAX 01707-275091. E-mail: zerbadman@aol.com. (Subscr. to: 43 Mote Park, Saltash, Cornwall, England) Ed.Bd. adv.: B&W page £745, color page £1425; 270 x 185; adv. contact: John Constable. bk.rev.; illus. circ. 1,750. (back issues avail.) Document type: trade publication.
   Description: Official journal of the guild which aims to act as an authoritative source of advice and informtion on all matters of concern to television cameramen, and provide a forum for comments, ideas and criticism on the operational aspects of cameras, lenses, mountings and other equipment.

384.55   CC
ZHONGWAI DIANSHI/CHINESE & WORLD T V. (Text in Chinese) m. Y31.20 (foreign $58). (Zhongguo Dianshi Yishu Weiyuanhui - China Television Drama Committee) Zhongwai Dianshi Zazhishe, 2, Fuxingmenwai Dajie, Beijing 100866, People's Republic of China. TEL 867127. (Dist. in US by: China Books & Periodicals, Inc., 2929 24th St., San Francisco, CA 94110. TEL 415-282-2994) Ed. Ruan Ruolin.
   Description: Covers Chinese and foreign movie and TV scripts, stories, and profiles of movie stars and singers.

384.55   GW   ISSN 0177-0837
ZIMPEL. TEIL 3: FUNK UND FERNSEHEN. 1990. base vol. (plus bi-m. updates). DM.190 for base vol. (DM.275 with updates) (effective 1996). Verlag Dieter Zimpel, Angererstr. 36, 80796 Munich, Germany. TEL 49-89-3073445. FAX 49-89-302409. Ed. Ingrid Finsterwald. Document type: directory.

384.55   GW   ISSN 0946-6673
DIE ZWEI. w. (Thu.) DM.98.80 (foreign DM.163.80). Gong Verlag GmbH, Innere Cramer-Klett-Str. 6, 90403 Nuernberg, Germany. TEL 49-911-5325-0. FAX 49-911-5325309. Ed. Dieter Ulrich. adv. contact: Walter Krey. circ. 400,000. Document type: consumer publication.

384.5   AE
LES 2 ECRANS.* m. (10/yr.) 45 din. Radiodiffusion Television Algerienne (RTA), Immeuble RTA, 21, blvd. des Martyr, Algiers, Algeria. Ed. B. Abdou.

384.5   US
1590 BROADCASTER. 1964. w. $20 (effective 1992). 1590 Broadcasting Corp., 502 W. Hollis St., Box 548, Nashua, NH 03061. TEL 603-889-1590. FAX 603-883-4344. adv. contact: Maurice R. Parent. bk.rev.; circ. 63,500 (controlled). (tabloid format; back issues avail.) Document type: newspaper.

COMMUNICATIONS — Video

A F C NEWS. (Australian Film Commission) see MOTION PICTURES

A M I A NEWSLETTER. (Association of Moving Image Archivists) see LIBRARY AND INFORMATION SCIENCES

A V JOURNAAL; tweewekelijks nieuwsbulletin voor de audiovisuele branche. see COMMUNICATIONS — Television And Cable

COMMUNICATIONS — VIDEO

384.55 621.381
370 US ISSN 1090-7459
TK7881.4
A V VIDEO & MULTIMEDIA PRODUCER; production and presentation technology. 1996. m. $53. Knowledge Industry Publications, Inc., 701 Westchester Ave., White Plains, NY 10604. TEL 914-328-9157. Ed. Nick Dager; Pub. Patrick Dignan, R&P contact: Patrick Dignan. adv. contact: Jonathan Michaelis. circ. 101,420. (back issues avail.) **Document type:** trade publication.
● Also available online.
—KR SourceOne; SWETS; UMI; UnCover. **CCC.**
Formed by the merger of (1995-1996): Multimedia Producer (ISSN 1079-4689); (1984-1996): A V Video (ISSN 0747-1335); Which incorporated (in 1990): Video Management (ISSN 1047-7713); Which was formerly: Video Manager (ISSN 0747-3745); (until 1984): Video User (ISSN 0273-7817); (until 1980): V U Marketplace (ISSN 0149-6832); A V Video was formerly (until 1984): Audio Visual Directions (ISSN 0746-8989); (until 1980): Audio Visual Product News (ISSN 0164-6834).
Description: Covers all facets of the audio-video, multi-media interactive industry: video, presentation media, computer-graphics and audio services, with special emphasis on practical "how to" information.

AFTERIMAGE. see *PHOTOGRAPHY*

ALT OM FOTO & VIDEO. see *PHOTOGRAPHY*

ALTA FIDELIDAD EN AUDIO Y VIDEO. see *SOUND RECORDING AND REPRODUCTION*

384.55 US
ALTERNATIVE CINEMA. 1993. q. $18; newsstand price: $4.95. E.I. Film & Video Communications, Box 625, Lodi, NJ 07644. TEL 201-284-0240. FAX 201-338-5224. Ed. Jeffrey Faoro; Pub. Michael L. Raso. circ. 10,000. **Document type:** consumer publication.
Description: Covers home videos and independent films and film-makers.

AMERICAN FILM & VIDEO REVIEW. see *MOTION PICTURES*

THE AMIGA ONE. see *COMPUTERS — Computer Games*

ANNUAIRE DU CINEMA, TELEVISION, VIDEO. see *MOTION PICTURES*

ANNUARIO AUDIO & VIDEO. see *SOUND RECORDING AND REPRODUCTION*

ART ON SCREEN; the newsletter of film & video of the visual arts. see *MOTION PICTURES*

ATARIAN. see *COMPUTERS — Computer Games*

ATLANTA FILM AND VIDEO NEWS. see *MOTION PICTURES*

AUDIO VIDEO. see *SOUND RECORDING AND REPRODUCTION*

AUGEN-BLICK; Marburger Hefte zur Medienwissenschaft. see *MOTION PICTURES*

AUSTRALIAN CATALOGUE OF NEW FILMS AND VIDEOS. see *MOTION PICTURES*

384.55 AT
AUSTRALIAN VIDEOGRAPHY. 6/yr. Aus.$23 (foreign Aus.$70) (effective Aug. 1992). Gareth Powell Publishing, 21 Darley Rd., Randwick, N.S.W. 2031, Australia. TEL 02-398-5111. adv.: B&W page Aus.$1070, color page Aus.$1530; trim 273 x 210. **Document type:** consumer publication.
Description: Appeals to users and prospective purchasers of video camcorders, amateur video editing equipment, and high-band (super VHS and Hi 8) TV sets.

384.55 UK
BEST HOME CINEMA MAG ... EVER!. a. £3.50 (effective 1997). W V Publications and Exhibitions Ltd., 57-59 Rochester Pl., London NW1 9JU, England. TEL 44-171-485-0011. FAX 44-171-482-6269. (Orders to: ASM Ltd., Unit 6, Pipewell Road Industrial Estate, Desborough, Northants NN14 2SW, England. TEL 44-1536-762860. FAX 44-1536-760306) **Document type:** consumer publication.

BLUE LIGHTS. see *COMMUNICATIONS — Television And Cable*

778.53 US ISSN 1051-290X
PN1992.95
BOWKER'S COMPLETE VIDEO DIRECTORY; combining Variety's extensive listing of currently available entertainment titles with education and special interest videos for home, school, and business. (In 3 vols.; Vol.1: Entertainment; Vols. 2 and 3: Education - Special Interest) 1990. a. $249.95 for complete set; $124.95 for vol.1; $161.95 for vols.2 and 3. R.R. Bowker, A Division of Reed Elsevier Inc., 121 Chanlon Rd., New Providence, NJ 07974. TEL 908-464-6800. FAX 908-665-6688. TELEX 138 755. E-mail: info@bowker.com; URL: http://www.bowker.com. (Subscr. to: Order Dept., Box 31, New Providence, NJ 07974-9903. TEL 800-521-8110) **Document type:** directory.
● Also available on CD-ROM. Producer(s): Bowker Electronic Publishing.
Description: For libraries, schools, and video resource centers. Covers more than 140,000 videos, in all formats available, including VHS, Beta, 3/4", U-matic, 8mm, and laser disc.

384.55 658.8 UK ISSN 0954-1594
BUSINESS RATIO REPORT: COMMERCIAL AND VIDEO EQUIPMENT; an industry sector analysis. 1981. a. l C C Business Ratios Ltd., Freepost, Field House, Hampton, Mddx. TW12 1BR, England. TEL 081-783-0977. FAX 081-783-1940. charts; stat. **Document type:** trade publication.
Formerly (until 1988): Business Ratio Report: Audio-Visual Industry (ISSN 0261-7323)

384.55 US
C V C REPORT. 1983. s-m. $195 (foreign $245). Creative Video Consulting, Inc., 648 Broadway, New York, NY 10012-2314. TEL 212-533-9870. FAX 212-473-3772. Ed. Mitchell Rowen; Pub. Mitchell Rowen. adv. circ. 800. **Document type:** trade publication.

CABLE VIDEO BRIEFS. see *COMMUNICATIONS — Television And Cable*

621.388 US ISSN 1048-8804
TR882
CAMCORDER. 1985. m. $23. Miller Magazines, Inc., 4880 Market St., Ventura, CA 93003. TEL 805-644-3824. Ed. Bob Wolenik. adv. circ. 115,000. (back issues avail.)
Former titles (until 1989): Camcorder Report (ISSN 1047-8787); (until 1988): Super Television; (until 1987): Home Satellite TV.

CAMCORDER USER. see *ELECTRONICS*

CARLTON COMMUNICATIONS PLC. ANNUAL REPORT AND ACCOUNTS. see *COMMUNICATIONS — Television And Cable*

CATALOGUS FILMS EN VIDEO. see *MOTION PICTURES*

CHICAGO FILM & VIDEO NEWS. see *MOTION PICTURES*

CHILDREN'S ENTERTAINMENT BUSINESS. see *COMMUNICATIONS — Television And Cable*

028.5 384.55 US ISSN 0883-6922
CHILDREN'S VIDEO REPORT. 1985. 8/yr. $60. 370 Court St., No. 76, Brooklyn, NY 11231-4331. TEL 718-935-0600. FAX 718-243-0959. E-mail: CVReport@AOL.COM. Ed. Martha Dewing. circ. 1,200. **Document type:** newsletter.
Description: Reports on children and video from experts on child development and media.

791.45 US ISSN 0895-2094
CHILDREN'S VIDEO REVIEW NEWSLETTER. 1987. bi-m. $36 (Canada $40; elsewhere $46.80). Eveline P. Carsman, Ed. & Pub, 16765 Lena Ct., Grass Valley, CA 95949. TEL 916-273-7471. FAX 916-273-6542. E-mail: kidvid@nccn.net; kidvid@hotmail.com; URL: http://www.kid-video.com. R&P contact: Eveline P. Carsman. bibl.; cum.index; circ. 200 (paid). (looseleaf format; back issues avail.) **Document type:** newsletter.
Description: Reviews newly released children's videotapes for content and age-appropriateness (preschool through middle school).

CINEMA BLUE. see *MEN'S INTERESTS*

CINEMA IN CASA. see *COMMUNICATIONS — Television And Cable*

CINEMEDIA ACCESS COLLECTION. VIDEO CATALOG. see *MOTION PICTURES*

384.55 778.5 SP ISSN 0212-0143
CINEVIDEO 20. 1982. m. 6000 ptas. Comunicacion Audiovisual Iberoamericana, S.A., Apdo. 2016, 28080 Madrid, Spain. TEL 91-4150212. FAX 91-4155027. Dir. Fernando Campos. adv. contact: Victoria Vallejo. circ. 7,000.
Description: Reports on the latest in software and hardware, technology and business related to film, video, television and the multimedia.

COLLEGE BROADCASTER. see *COMMUNICATIONS — Television And Cable*

384.55 US
COMING ATTRACTIONS. 1984. m. Connell Communications, Inc. (Subsidiary of: International Data Group), 86 Elm St., Peterborough, NH 03548-1009. TEL 603-924-7271. FAX 603-924-7013. Ed. Melissa Stephenson; Pub. Jim Connell. adv.; bk.rev. circ. 450,000. **Document type:** consumer publication.
Description: Comprehensive guide to new releases on videocassette.

COMING SOON MAGAZINE. see *COMPUTERS — Computer Games*

COMMUNITY MEDIA REVIEW. see *COMMUNICATIONS — Television And Cable*

COMPUTER & VIDEO GAMES. see *COMPUTERS — Computer Games*

CONTEMPORARY VISUAL ARTS. see *ART*

621.388 UK ISSN 1363-0202
▼**D V D AND FUTURE C D.** 1996. m. TechMedia, 52 Foundling Ct., London WC1N 1AN, England. TEL 44-171-837-0815. FAX 44-171-278-9917. E-mail: 100141.676@compuserve.com. Ed. Tim Frost; Pub. Philip Gallagher. **Document type:** newsletter.
● Also available online.
Description: Covers developments in optical disc technologies.

DENMARK. STATENS FILMCENTRAL. S F C FILM KATALOGET. see *MOTION PICTURES*

DENMARK. STATENS FILMCENTRAL. STATISTIK OVER UDLEJNING AF 16 MM FILM OG VIDEO OG OVERSIGT OVER 16 MM FILM OG VIDEOKASSETTER I DEPONERING. see *MOTION PICTURES — Abstracting, Bibliographies, Statistics*

DENMARK. STATENS FILMCENTRAL. VIDEO (YEAR). see *MOTION PICTURES*

DETROIT FILM AND VIDEO NEWS. see *MOTION PICTURES*

DIGEST OF THE U F V A. see *MOTION PICTURES*

DIGITAL "VERSATILE" DISC (YEAR). see *COMMUNICATIONS — Computer Applications*

DIGITAL VIDEO MAGAZINE. see *COMMUNICATIONS — Television And Cable*

621.388 670 US
TS2301.A7
DIRECTORY OF VIDEO, COMPUTER AND AUDIO VISUAL PRODUCTS.* 1953. a. $65 to commercial non-members. International Communications Industries Association, 11242 Waples Mill Rd., Ste. 200, Fairfax, VA 22030-6079. TEL 703-273-7200. FAX 703-278-8082. Ed. Dian Smith. charts; illus.; stat.; index. circ. 12,000. (processed) **Document type:** directory.
—CISTI.
Former titles: Equipment Directory of Audio-Visual Computer and Video Products (ISSN 0884-2124); Audio-Visual Equipment Directory (ISSN 0571-8759)

DIRECTORY OF VIDEO RETAILERS. see *BUSINESS AND ECONOMICS — Trade And Industrial Directories*

EDUCATORS GUIDE TO FREE VIDEOTAPES. see *EDUCATION — Teaching Methods And Curriculum*

ENCORE. see *MOTION PICTURES*

COMMUNICATIONS — VIDEO

ENCORE DIRECTORY. see *MOTION PICTURES*

ETIN. see *LIBRARY AND INFORMATION SCIENCES*

621.388   FR   ISSN 1167-9468
F B I: FORTNIGHTLY BULLETIN ON INTERACTIVITY. Key Title: Fortnightly Bulletin on Interactivity. 22/yr. 2800 F. A Jour, 11 rue du Marche St. Honore, 75001 Paris, France. TEL 42-96-67-22. FAX 40-20-07-75. TELEX AJOUR 615887 F.
 Formerly: Vidotex International.

F V - FOTO VIDEO ACTUALIDAD. see *PHOTOGRAPHY*

FACETS FEATURES. see *MOTION PICTURES*

778.59   IT
FAREVIDEO; tecnica e cultura della videoregistrazione. m. L.60000 (Europe L.75000; elsewhere L.85000). Ediscreen s.r.l., Via Calderini, 68, 00196 Rome, Italy. TEL 06-3960328. FAX 06-390072. Ed. Enzo Perilli. adv.
 Formerly: Video Parade.

FATAL VISIONS. see *MOTION PICTURES*

FILM & VIDEO; the production magazine. see *MOTION PICTURES*

384.55 375   AU
FILM & VIDEO; Fachinformation ueber Informationsvideos und 16mm Filme. 1980. q. Oesterreichisches Filmservice KG, Schaumburgergasse 18, A-1040 Vienna, Austria. TEL 43-1-5055337-0. FAX 43-1-5055307. E-mail: ofs@magnet.at. Ed. Rudolf Kammel. adv.; B&W page S.15000; trim 210 x 296; adv. contact: Alexander Kammel. circ. 12,500 (paid). **Document type:** newsletter.
 Description: Contains information on educational, touristic and industrial films.

FILM AND VIDEO CAREER DIRECTORY. see *MOTION PICTURES*

FILM & VIDEO FINDER. see *EDUCATION — Abstracting, Bibliographies, Statistics*

FILM AND VIDEO MAKER. see *MOTION PICTURES*

FILM CLIPS; a publication for film & video professionals. see *MOTION PICTURES*

FILM & TELEVISIE - VIDEO. see *MOTION PICTURES*

FILM FAN SAT. see *MOTION PICTURES*

384.55 791.43   US
FILM THREAT VIDEO GUIDE. 1991. 4/yr. $24.95 (foreign $34.95) for 6 issues. Film Threat Video, 2805 W. Magnolia, Burbank, CA 91505. TEL 818-848-5522. FAX 818-848-5956. (Subscr. to: Box 3170, Los Angeles, CA 90078-3170) Ed. David E. Williams; Pub. Chris Gore. adv. contact: Merle Bertrand. illus. circ. 30,000. **Document type:** catalog, consumer publication.
 Description: Source for what's new and unusual on video.

FILM WORLD DIRECTORY OF ADULT FILM & VIDEO. see *BUSINESS AND ECONOMICS — Trade And Industrial Directories*

FILMS & FILMING. see *MOTION PICTURES*

FINANCIAL SURVEY. THE VIDEO AND AUDIO VISUAL INDUSTRY; company data for success. see *BUSINESS AND ECONOMICS — Trade And Industrial Directories*

FOTO. see *PHOTOGRAPHY*

FOTO VIDEO AUDIO NEWS (DUTCH EDITION). see *PHOTOGRAPHY*

FRAMELINE NEWS. see *MOTION PICTURES*

G P N EDUCATIONAL VIDEO CATALOG. ELEMENTARY - SECONDARY. (Great Plains National Instructional Television Library) see *EDUCATION — Teaching Methods And Curriculum*

GAME INFORMER MAGAZINE. see *COMPUTERS — Computer Games*

GEKKAN EBUI FURONTO/AUDIO VIDEO FRONT. see *SOUND RECORDING AND REPRODUCTION*

GIORNO POETRY SYSTEMS L P'S, C D'S, CASSETTES & GIORNO VIDEO PAK SERIES. see *LITERATURE — Poetry*

621.388 350   US   ISSN 1082-0493
GOVERNMENT INFORMATION AND IMAGING TECHNOLOGY.* 1992. bi-m. $25 (free to qualified personnel). 1224 Daleview Dr., McLean, VA 22102-1539. TEL 301-445-4405. FAX 301-445-5722. E-mail: wminami@aol.com. Ed. Wayde R. Minami; Pub. John McWilliams. adv. contact: John McWilliams. bk.rev.; circ. 34,000 (controlled). **Document type:** newspaper.
 Formerly: Government Imaging.
 Description: Provides up-to-date information on all aspects of the application of imaging technology within government organizations.

384.558   US   ISSN 1087-917X
GOVERNMENT VIDEO. 1989. m. $30 in U.S, and Canada (foreign $48) (effective 1997). Miller Freeman P S N Inc. (Subsidiary of: United News & Media Co.), 460 Park Ave. South, 9th Fl., New York, NY 10016-7315. TEL 212-378-0400. FAX 212-378-2160. E-mail: gmv@psn.com. Ed. Ron Merrell; Pub. Paul Gallo. adv.; B&W page $1990, color page $2440; trim 8 1/8 x 10 7/8; adv. contact: Joe Polombo. circ. 15,500. (back issues avail.) **Document type:** trade publication.
 Formerly: G M V - Government and Military Video (ISSN 1067-3407)
 Description: For video professionals in federal, state and city government and the military.

384.554   US   ISSN 1051-6050
GREAT AMERICAN VIDEO BUSINESS NEWSLETTER. 1990. s-a. $20. V. Parrish Publishing, 1900 S. Eads St., Arlington, VA 22202. TEL 703-892-1993. Ed. Vernon Parrish. adv. **Document type:** newsletter.
 Description: Provides issue analysis, feature stories, market evaluations, business and product news, and strategies for the video businessperson.

GUIDE TO POLITICAL VIDEOS. see *POLITICAL SCIENCE*

HI-FI AND VIDEO REVYEN. see *SOUND RECORDING AND REPRODUCTION*

HIFI & VIDEO MARKT; das Fachmagazin der Unterhaltungselektronik. see *ELECTRONICS*

HOME CINEMA. see *COMMUNICATIONS — Television And Cable*

621.388   UK   ISSN 1359-6276
HOME CINEMA CHOICE. 1995. m. £29 (Europe £45; rest of world £55) (effective 1997); newsstand price: £2.50. W V Publications and Exhibitions Ltd., 57-59 Rochester Pl., London NW1 9JU, England. TEL 44-171-485-0011. FAX 44-171-482-6269. (Orders to: ASM Ltd., Unit 6, Pipewell Road Industrial Estate, Desborough, Northants NN14 2SW, England. TEL 44-1536-762860. FAX 44-1536-760306) **Document type:** consumer publication.

HOME THEATER. see *COMMUNICATIONS — Television And Cable*

HUSTLER EROTIC VIDEO GUIDE. see *MEN'S INTERESTS*

I E E E TRANSACTIONS ON CIRCUITS AND SYSTEMS FOR VIDEO TECHNOLOGY. see *ELECTRONICS*

IN HER OWN IMAGE; films and videos empowering women for the future - a media network guide. see *WOMEN'S INTERESTS*

INDEPENDENT FILM AND VIDEO MONTHLY. see *MOTION PICTURES*

INDIEZINE. see *MOTION PICTURES*

384.55   US
INSTANT REPLAY; videocassette magazine. 1977. a. $1000 includes access to 30,000 hr. tape library. Instant Replay Publishing Inc., 6020 Lower Mountain Rd., New Hope, PA 18938-9617. TEL 215-794-3616. FAX 215-794-5279. Ed. Chuck Azar; Pub. Chuck Azar. R&P contact: Chuck Azar. bk.rev. (video cassette) **Document type:** consumer publication, trade publication.

INTERACTIVE VIDEO NEWS. see *BUSINESS AND ECONOMICS — Marketing And Purchasing*

INTERNATIONAL CONTACT - PHOTO, VIDEO, LAB TECHNOLOGY; independent journal for the international photographic market. see *PHOTOGRAPHY*

INTERNATIONAL TELEVISION & VIDEO ALMANAC; reference tool of the television and home video industries. see *COMMUNICATIONS — Television And Cable*

791.4   CN   ISSN 0847-3994
INTERNATIONAL VIDEOVUE MAGAZINE. 1989. m. Can.$18($24) (foreign $28). Thunder International Corporation, 238 Davenport Rd., Ste. 265, Toronto, Ont. M5R 1J6, Canada. TEL 416-474-5860. FAX 416-248-2381. adv. circ. 249,465.

JAHRBUCH FUER VIDEOFILMER. see *MOTION PICTURES*

JOURNAL OF FILM AND VIDEO. see *MOTION PICTURES*

KEMPS FILM, T V AND VIDEO YEARBOOK. see *MOTION PICTURES*

384.55   UK
KEY NOTE MARKET REPORT: VIDEO RETAIL & HIRE. Variant title: Video Retail & Hire. irreg., no.5, 1995. £205. Key Note Ltd., Field House, 72 Oldfield Rd., Hampton, Middlesex TW12 2HQ, England. TEL 44-181-783-0755. FAX 44-181-783-0049. **Document type:** trade publication.
 ●Also available online.
 Also available on CD-ROM.
 Formerly (until 1995): Key Note Report: Video Retail and Hire.

KINO - GLAZ. see *MOTION PICTURES*

LADYSLIPPER CATALOG AND RESOURCE GUIDE OF RECORDS, TAPES, COMPACT DISCS AND VIDEOS BY WOMEN. see *WOMEN'S INTERESTS*

384.55   US   ISSN 1077-5420
LASER VIEWS. 1988. 10/yr. $18 (foreign $42) (effective 1997). 831 State Route 10, Ste. 12, Whippany, NJ 07981-1154. TEL 800-899-4116. FAX 201-575-3505. E-mail: lvinfo@lascrviews.com. Ed. David Goodman; Pub. Joan Goodman. R&P contact: Joan Goodman. adv. contact: David Goodman. bk.rev.; circ. 30,000 (paid). **Document type:** consumer publication.

LEONARD MALTIN'S MOVIE AND VIDEO GUIDE. see *MOTION PICTURES*

384.55   FR   ISSN 1169-5293
LETTRE DU MULTIMEDIA. 18/yr. 2200 F. A Jour, 11 rue du Marche St. Honore, 75001 Paris, France. TEL 42-96-67-22. FAX 40-20-07-75. TELEX 615887F AJOUR. Ed. Marie-Jo Coutanceau.
 Formerly: Videodisque.

LIFE VIDEO; przeglad sprzetu i kaset. see *ELECTRONICS*

LOCATION UPDATE; the magazine of film and video production. see *MOTION PICTURES*

MARKEE. see *MOTION PICTURES*

MEAN MACHINES SEGA. see *COMPUTERS — Computer Games*

MEDIAMATIC. see *ART*

MEGATECH. see *COMPUTERS — Computer Games*

MESH; film - video - multimedia - art. see *MOTION PICTURES*

384.55 790.13   US   ISSN 0746-0325
MOVIE COLLECTORS WORLD. 1976. fortn. $45 (foreign $85) (effective 1997). Arena Publishing, Box 309, Fraser, MI 48026. TEL 313-774-4311. FAX 313-775-5450. Ed. Brian A. Bukantis; Pub. Brian A. Bukantis. R&P contact: Brian A. Bukantis. adv. contact: Dawn M. Bukantis. bk.rev. circ. 6,000. (tabloid format) **Document type:** newspaper.
 Incorporates: Video Shopper (Fraser); Which was formerly: Video Swapper; Film Collectors World.
 Description: Brings price results, events news, collector happenings, and the latest video releases.

MULTIMEDIA MONITOR. see *COMPUTERS — Computer Systems*

COMMUNICATIONS — VIDEO

384.55 US
N V R REPORTS. 1990. irreg. National Video Resources, 73 Spring St., Ste. 606, New York, NY 10012. TEL 212-274-8080. FAX 212-274-8081. E-mail: nvrinfo@nvr.org. Ed. Lisa Seagal. R&P contact: Delores A. Owens. circ. 5,700. **Document type:** newsletter.
  Description: Dedicated to increasing the public's access to quality independent works on videocassette and other formats.

384.55 US ISSN 0965-5506
O M N I. (Optical Media News and Information) 1991. m. B R P Publications, Inc., 65 Bleeker St., 5th Fl., New York, NY 10012. TEL 212-673-4700. FAX 212-475-1790. Ed. R.B. Selwyn. bk.rev.; abstr.; tr.lit. (back issues avail.) Indexed: Info.Media & Tech., Resour.Ctr.Ind. **Document type:** newsletter.
  Formed by the 1991 merger of: Optical Data Systems; Which was formerly (1981-1986): Videoinfo (ISSN 0261-393X); Document Image Processing (ISSN 0958-6156); Which was formerly (until 1989): Microinfo Microfilm News (ISSN 0951-4457); (1970-1987): Microinfo (ISSN 0047-7192).
  Description: Covers all aspects of image-management technology and markets including news of developments and events related to application of imaging techniques. Also includes coverage of all aspects of optical disk data storage and distribution techniques.

OBSCURE PUBLICATIONS AND VIDEO. see *PUBLISHING AND BOOK TRADE*

OFFICIAL VIDEO DIRECTORY & BUYER'S GUIDE. see *BUSINESS AND ECONOMICS — Trade And Industrial Directories*

384.55 CN ISSN 1194-3130
ON VIDEO. 1992. m. Can.$24. New Image Complete Print Services, 1314 Britannia Rd. E., Mississauga, Ont. L4W 1C8, Canada. TEL 416-564-1033. FAX 416-564-3398. Ed. Catherine Puddy. adv.: B&W page Can.$7000, color page Can.$7200; trim 8 1/8 x 10 3/4. circ. 160,000.

384.55 US ISSN 1094-3676
ONVIDEO. 1995. d. Box 17377, Beverly Hills, CA 90209. E-mail: onvideo@cyberpod.com; URL: http://www.cyberpod.com/cyberpod/onvideo. Ed. Harley W. Lond. adv.; video rev. **Document type:** consumer publication.
  ● Available only online.
  Description: Covers forthcoming home video releases; video industry news; complete resource guide to online and mail order home video sources.

P C GAMES. (Personal Computer) see *COMPUTERS — Computer Games*

384.55 GW ISSN 1430-5704
▼**P C VIDEO**; das Multimedia Magazin von Videofilmen. 1996. 2/yr. DM.21. Fachverlag Schiele und Schoen GmbH, Markgrafenstr. 11, 10969 Berlin, Germany. TEL 49-30-253752-0. FAX 49-30-2517248. E-mail: 0302537520-0001@t-online.de. Ed. E. Altenmueller. adv. circ. 24,000. **Document type:** consumer publication.

P C VIDEOLOG. see *COMMUNICATIONS — Computer Applications*

384.55 US ISSN 0898-302X
P R C NEWS. (Pre Recorded Cassette); a weekly news in brief for the video industry. 1988. w. $477. Corbell Publishing, 4676 Admiralty Way, Ste. 300, Marina Del Rey, CA 90292. TEL 310-574-5337. FAX 310-574-5383. Ed. Deborah Rolfe; Pub. Maureen Healy. adv. contact: Joseph Daneshrad. charts; illus. circ. 2,000. (looseleaf format; back issues avail.; reprint service avail.) **Document type:** newsletter.
  Description: Covers news, mergers and acquisitions, people on the move, calendar of events, statistics, new releases, and sell-through products.

791.43 US
PALMER VIDEO MAGAZINE. 1981. m. $15. Palmer Video Corp., 1767 Morris Ave., Union, NJ 07083. TEL 908-686-3030. FAX 908-686-2151. Eds. Susan Baar, Mary Schwartz. adv.; video rev.; circ. 203,915 (controlled).
  Formerly: Palmer Video News.

PERSISTENCE OF VISION. see *MOTION PICTURES*

791.43 US ISSN 1083-2920
THE PHANTOM OF THE MOVIES' VIDEOSCOPE; the ultimate genre video guide. 1993. q. $21.97 for 6 issues (Canada $28; elsewhere $38); newsstand price: $4.25. Phan Media, Inc., Box 216, Ocean Grove, NJ 07756. TEL 908-988-6264. FAX 908-988-9180. Ed. Joe Kane. R&P contact: Nancy Naglin. adv. contact: Nancy Naglin. bk.rev. circ. 10,000. **Document type:** consumer publication.
  Description: Reviews recent releases in genre video.

PHOTO & IMAGING RETAILER. see *PHOTOGRAPHY*

PHOTO VIDEO AUDIO NEWS (FRENCH EDITION). see *PHOTOGRAPHY*

PRE-RECORDED VIDEO SUPPLIERS DIRECTORY. see *BUSINESS AND ECONOMICS — Trade And Industrial Directories*

791.45 US ISSN 1070-4949
PN1995.9.H6
PSYCHOTRONIC VIDEO. no.11, 1991. bi-m. $22 (foreign $45). 3309 Rte. 97, Narrowsburg, NY 12764-6126. Ed. Michael Weldon. film rev.; video rev.
  Description: Covers unusual film and video releases.

PYRAMID FILM AND VIDEO CATALOG. see *MOTION PICTURES*

QUARTERLY REVIEW OF FILM AND VIDEO. see *MOTION PICTURES*

384 778 US
R T S VIDEO GAZETTE. 1985. m. $18. R T S, Box 93897, Las Vegas, NV 89193-3897. TEL 702-896-1300.
  Description: Industry insider's column of latest trends, new releases and information on pricing. Also covers obscure titles available for sale, including silents, serials, B movies in all genres, foreign and cult films.

REGENT ONLINE JOURNAL OF COMMUNICATION. see *MOTION PICTURES*

SAN JOSE FILM & VIDEO PRODUCTION BINDER. see *MOTION PICTURES*

SAT - AUDIO - VIDEO; postepy w elektronice powszechnego uzytku. see *ELECTRONICS*

384.5 SZ
SCHWEIZER VIDEO MAGAZIN. m. Schlagbaumstr. 6, CH-8201 Schaffhausen, Switzerland. TEL 053-248821. FAX 053-254977. Ed. Thomas Stemmle. circ. 12,000.

SEGA. see *COMPUTERS — Computer Games*

SET; cinema & video. see *MOTION PICTURES*

SHICHOKAKU JOHO KENKYUKAI KAIHO/AUDIO - VISUAL INFORMATION RESEARCH GROUP. NEWSLETTER. see *SOUND RECORDING AND REPRODUCTION*

384.55 AU
SKYTEC. 1989. 10/yr. S.350. Aram GmbH, Neustiftgasse 5, A-1070 Vienna, Austria. TEL 01-52342420. FAX 01-523424293. Ed. Gerry Weichselbaum. adv.; bk.rev.; circ. 6,000.

SMALFILM OG VIDEO. see *MOTION PICTURES*

SON HI-FI VIDEO. see *COMMUNICATIONS — Radio*

SOUND & VIDEO CONTRACTOR; the international management and engineering journal for sound and video contractors. see *SOUND RECORDING AND REPRODUCTION*

384.55 US ISSN 0883-2560
SPEC - COM JOURNAL.* 1967. bi-m. $20. Spec - Com Communications and Publishing Group, Ltd. (Subsidiary of: Donovan Group), Box 641, Fremont, NE 68025-0641. TEL 319-557-8791. FAX 319-583-6462. Ed. Gary Kaiser. adv. contact: Lynn Donovan. bk.rev. circ. 1,400. **Document type:** consumer publication.

384.55 621.389 US
STEREO REVIEW'S VIDEO BUYERS' GUIDE. 1984. a. newsstand price: $3.95. Hachette Filipacchi Magazines, Inc., 1633 Broadway, New York, NY 10009. TEL 212-767-6000. (Subscr. to: Box 55627, Boulder, CO 80322-5627) Ed. William Burton. adv. **Document type:** consumer publication.
  Description: Provides information on video equipment.

STEREOPHILE GUIDE TO HOME THEATER. see *MOTION PICTURES*

T V & VIDEO WORLD. see *COMMUNICATIONS — Television And Cable*

791.43 US
TAKE ONE; the video entertainment newspaper. 1981. m. Connell Communications, Inc. (Subsidiary of: International Data Group), 86 Elm St., Peterborough, NH 03458-1009. TEL 603-924-7271. FAX 603-924-7013. Ed. Melissa Stephenson; Pub. Jim Connell. adv.; illus. circ. 1,500,000. (tabloid format) **Document type:** newspaper, consumer publication.
  Description: Announces new movies released on videocassette each month.

TALKING PICTURES. see *MOTION PICTURES*

621.388 US
TECHFACTS; information about captioning for video professionals. 1989. irreg. (2-3/yr.). free. Caption Center, 125 Western Ave., Boston, MA 02134. TEL 617-492-9225. FAX 617-562-0590. E-mail: caption@wgbh.org; URL: http://www.wgbh.org/caption. Ed. Mary Watkins. (looseleaf format; back issues avail.) **Document type:** newsletter.

TECHNICIEN DU FILM ET DE LA VIDEO; magazine d'information des professionnels du cinema, de la television, et de l'audio-visuel. see *MOTION PICTURES*

621.388 UK ISSN 1361-1399
▼**TELECOMEUROPA'S INTERACTIVE VIDEO NEWSLETTER**; the monthly report on interactive multimedia communications. Variant title: Interactive Video Newsletter. 1995. m. £495($740) (effective 1995). Telecomeuropa News Bureau Publications, 3 Princes Bldgs., George St., Bath, Avon BA1 2ED, England. TEL 44-1225-445282. FAX 44-1225-445283. E-mail: 100144.3104@compuserve.com. (Subscr. in US to: Telecomeuropa, Box 4948, Laguna Beach, CA 92652. TEL 714-499-1857) Ed. Paul Rasmussen; Pub. Peter Purton. tr.lit. (back issues avail.) **Document type:** newsletter.
  ● Also available online.

THEY WON'T STAY DEAD. see *MOTION PICTURES*

384.554 IT
TOP VIDEO. 1987. m. L.49500 (foreign L.75000). Casa Editrice Universo S.p.A., Via M. De Vizzi 35, 20092 Cinisello Balsamo (MI), Italy. TEL 39-2-618331. Ed. Nicola De Feo. adv.: B&W page L.7000000, color page L.9500000. circ. 35,000.

384.55 IT
TOP VIDEO GUIDA. 1988. m. (11/yr.). Casa Editrice Universo S.p.A., Via M. de Vizzi 35, 20092 Cinisello Balsamo (MI), Italy. TEL 39-2-618331. FAX 39-2-6128931. Ed. Nicola De Feo. adv.: B&W page L.11200000, color page L.16000000. circ. 90,000. **Document type:** consumer publication.

TRIBUNE VIDEO DES ANGLICISTES. see *LINGUISTICS*

ULTRAHIGH SPEED AND HIGH SPEED PHOTOGRAPHY, PHOTONICS, AND VIDEOGRAPHY. see *PHOTOGRAPHY*

384.554 US ISSN 1041-1402
PN1992.93
V.* (Video); the guide to home videos. 1987. bi-m. $13.95. Fairfield Publishing Co., c/o Grenadier Association, 70 Seaview Ave., Stamford, CT 06902-6040. (Subscr. to: Box 270, Brewster, NY 10509) Ed. Peter Hauck. adv. circ. 400,000.

COMMUNICATIONS — VIDEO

384.55   GW
V K E; das Videoverzeichnis auf CD-ROM. 3/yr. DM.150 (effective 1997). Josef Keller Verlag, Postfach 1455, 82317 Starnberg, Germany. TEL 49-8151-771144. FAX 49-8151-771152. **Document type**: catalog.
● Available only on CD-ROM.

384.55   778.534   IT
V R. (Video Review); mensile di videoregistrazione creativa. 1985. m. L.60000($100) (effective Jan. 1990). Systems Comunicazioni, Via Olanda, 6, 20083 Gaggiano (MI), Italy. TEL 39-2-90841814. FAX 39-2-90841682. Ed. L. Fratti. adv.: B&W page L.6000000. circ. 34,000. (back issues avail.) **Document type**: consumer publication.
    Description: Covers home video and personal film making.

384.55   001.642   US   ISSN 1063-4193
V S D A VOICE.* 1983. bi-m. $19.95 (subscr. includes supplement 3/yr.). Video Software Dealers Association, 16530 Ventura Blvd., Encino, CA 91436-4551. TEL 609-231-7800. FAX 609-231-9791. circ. 5,000 (controlled). **Document type**: newsletter.
    Formerly (until 1992): V S D A Reports (ISSN 0896-4939)
    Description: Supplies information about association news, legislative and First Amendment issues, emerging technologies, and commentary.

VARIETY'S VIDEO DIRECTORY ON DISC. see *MOTION PICTURES*

384.55   FR   ISSN 0998-8483
VENTE PHOTO VIDEO LABO.* 10/yr. C.E.C., 70-76 Rie Brillat Savarin, 75013 Paris, France. TEL 33-5-45654600. FAX 33-5-45897285. TELEX 202 548 F. Ed. Jacques Hemon. circ. 9,500.

384.55   GW   ISSN 0172-4010
VIDEO; Sehen was Spass Macht. 1979. m. DM.78 (effective 1997); newsstand price: DM.6.50. Vereinigte Motor-Verlage GmbH und Co. KG, Leuschnerstr. 1, 70174 Stuttgart, Germany. TEL 49-711-18201. FAX 49-711-1821669. (Subscr. to: P M S GmbH, Postfach 290180, 47261 Duisburg, Germany. TEL 49-203-76908-0. FAX 49-203-7690830) Ed. Hans-Martin Burr; Pub. Uwe Hagen. adv.: B&W page DM.9410, color page DM.16468; trim size 185 x 248; adv. contact: Peter Michael Heyde. circ. 76,663. **Indexed**: R.G.Abstr.
Document type: consumer publication.

VIDEO AGE INTERNATIONAL; the business journal of film, TV broadcasting, cable, pay TV, PPV, home video, DBS, production. see *COMMUNICATIONS — Telephone And Telegraph*

778.59   GW   ISSN 0724-4398
VIDEO AKTIV. 1974-199?; resumed. m. newsstand price: DM.8. Vereinigte Motor-Verlage GmbH und Co. KG, Leuschnerstr. 1, 70174 Stuttgart, Germany. TEL 49-711-18201. FAX 49-711-1821759. (Subscr. to: Postfach 106036, 70049 Stuttgart, Germany) Ed. Tim Cole; Pub. Gernot Hempelmann. adv. contact: Peter Michael Heyde. circ. 37,000. (back issues avail.) **Document type**: consumer publication.
    Description: Test of camcorders, information on amateur video film-making.

VIDEO ALMANACCO. see *PHOTOGRAPHY*

VIDEO & MUSIC BUSINESS. see *BUSINESS AND ECONOMICS — Marketing And Purchasing*

384.5   SZ
VIDEO & SON. 8/yr. Atema Communications, Centre du Bief, CH-1110 Morges, Switzerland. TEL 021-8012665. Ed. Jean-Claude Marti. circ. 25,000.

621.388   US   ISSN 1046-3860
VIDEO & TELEVISION. Variant title: Orion Video & Television Blue Book. a. $144 (effective 1996). Orion Research Corp., 14555 N. Scottsdale Rd., Ste. 330, Scottsdale, AZ 85254. TEL 800-844-0759. FAX 800-375-1315. E-mail: orion@bluebook.com; URL: http://www.netzone.com/orion. (also avail. in diskette format) **Document type**: directory.
    Formerly: Video (ISSN 0883-5888)
    Description: Provides information on pricing used video and television equipment from 1968 to the present.

384.55   SZ
VIDEO - AUDIO - REVUE. m. Verband Schweizerischer Radio- und Televisions-Fachgeschaefte, Niklaus-Wengi-Str. 25, CH-2540 Grenchen, Switzerland. TEL 41-32-6542020. FAX 41-32-6542029. adv. **Document type**: trade publication.

384.55   FR   ISSN 0768-827X
VIDEO BROADCAST. 10/yr. Bernard Perrine, Ed. & Pub., 150 rue Gallieni, 92100 Boulogne, France. TEL 33-1-41861600. FAX 33-1-41861690. circ. 12,000.

384.55   338   US   ISSN 0279-571X
HD9697.V543
VIDEO BUSINESS. 1981. w. $70. Chilton Publications, 825 Seventh Ave., 6th Fl., New York, NY 10019. TEL 212-887-8400. Ed. Bruce Apar. adv.; charts; illus.; stat. circ. 40,369. (back issues avail.) **Document type**: trade publication.
—CCC.

VIDEO CAMERA. see *PHOTOGRAPHY*

384.5   US   ISSN 0896-2871
VIDEO CHOICE.* 1988. m. $24.95. Connell Communications, Inc. (Subsidiary of: International Data Group), 86 Elm St., Peterborough, NH 03458. TEL 603-924-7271. FAX 603-924-7013. Ed. Deborah Navas. adv. circ. 85,000.

VIDEO DISTRIBUTOR'S DIRECTORY (YEAR). see *BUSINESS AND ECONOMICS — Trade And Industrial Directories*

VIDEO DUPLICATION DIRECTORY. see *BUSINESS AND ECONOMICS — Trade And Industrial Directories*

384.55   FR   ISSN 1151-4760
VIDEO ECHOS. 21/yr. Editions du Gaillard, 29 rue de la Fontaine-au-Roi, 75011 Paris, France. TEL 43-38-99-77. FAX 43-38-50-13. Ed. Bruno Delamain. circ. 7,000.

778.59   US   ISSN 1045-2885
VIDEO EVENT. 1988. m. Connell Communications, Inc. (Subsidiary of: International Data Group), 86 Elm St., Peterborough, NH 03458. TEL 603-924-7271. FAX 603-924-7013. Ed. Melissa Stephenson; Pub. Jim Connell. adv. circ. 400,000. **Document type**: consumer publication.
    Description: Gives reviews of the box office hits being released on video.

VIDEO EYEBALL MAGAZINE. see *MOTION PICTURES*

790   US
VIDEO FILM MUSIC. Short title: V F M. 1992. bi-m. $5.95. Video Film Music Communications, Inc., 5231 E. Memorial Dr., Ste. 136, Stone Mountain, GA 30083. TEL 404-498-1729. Ed. David Deaton. adv. contact: David Deaton. circ. 20,000.

384.55   PO
VIDEO GUIA. 52/yr. Rua Palmira 33 2o Esq., 1100 Lisbon, Portugal. TEL 823978. Ed. Bernardo Britocunha.
    Description: Covers video and photographic equipment.

384.55   700   CN   ISSN 0228-6726
VIDEO GUIDE. 5/yr. Can.$16 (foreign Can.$20). Satellite Video Exchange Society, 1965 Main St., Vancouver, BC V5T 1C3, Canada. FAX 604-876-1185. adv.; bk.rev. circ. 2,000. (back issues avail.)

384.55   001.6   UK   ISSN 1351-3893
VIDEO HOME ENTERTAINMENT. 1981. w. £90 (Europe £150; Asia & U.S. $170). Video Business Publications Ltd., Strandgate, 18-20 York Bldgs., London WC2H 9JG, England. TEL 071-839-7774. FAX 071-839-4393. Ed. Sam Andrews. adv. contact: Chris Whitaker. circ. 7,500. (back issues avail.) **Document type**: trade publication.
    Formed by 1992 merger of: Video Business (ISSN 0950-2327) & Video Trade Weekly (ISSN 0262-4982)

VIDEO INDUSTRY STATISTICAL REPORT. see *COMMUNICATIONS — Abstracting, Bibliographies, Statistics*

384.5   US   ISSN 1042-7694
VIDEO INVESTOR. 1984. m. $695 (effective 1997). Paul Kagan Associates, Inc., 126 Clock Tower Pl., Carmel, CA 93923. TEL 408-624-1536. TELEX 408-625-3225.
    Formerly (until 1988): V C R Letter (ISSN 8755-9927)
    Description: Covers the economics of the home video industry and its impact on pay TV. Analyzes developments in hardware, software and retailing.

VIDEO LIBRARIAN; the video review guide for libraries. see *LIBRARY AND INFORMATION SCIENCES*

621.388   001.644   IT
VIDEO LINE. 6/yr. Esse 80 s.a.s., Via Gazzoletti 19, 38100 Trento, Italy. TEL 461-233936. FAX 461-236009. Ed. Marco Russolo. circ. 20,000.

384.55   US   ISSN 1044-7288
TK6630.A1
VIDEO MAGAZINE. 1978. m. (10/yr.). $17.94. Hachette Filipacchi Magazines, Inc., 1633 Broadway, 43rd. Fl., New York, NY 10019. TEL 212-767-6000. FAX 212-767-5619. (Subscr. to: Box 745, Mt. Morris, IL 61054. TEL 800-601-8345. FAX 815-734-1246) Ed. Bill Wolfe; Pub. Jay Rosenfeld. adv. contact: Jay Rosenfeld. bk.rev.; illus.; index. circ. 300,000. (reprint service avail. from UMI) **Indexed**: Mag.Ind. **Document type**: consumer publication.
● Also available online. Vendor(s): Information Access Co.
—CISTI; KR SourceOne; SWETS; UMI; UnCover.
    Formerly (until 1987): Video (New York) (ISSN 0147-8907)

384.55   US   ISSN 0738-7563
VIDEO NETWORKS. 1976. bi-m. $20. Bay Area Video Coalition, 1111 17th St., San Francisco, CA 94107. TEL 415-861-3282. FAX 415-861-4316. Ed. Karen Weiner. adv. circ. 10,000. (back issues avail.) **Document type**: newsletter.
    Description: Targets independent video producers and artists with valuable information and opportunities in production, exhibition, distribution, and fund raising.

700   384.55   370
320   CN
VIDEO OUT DISTRIBUTION CATALOGUE. 1983. a. $25. Satellite Video Exchange Society, 1965 Main St., Vancouver, BC V5T 1C3, Canada. Ed. Carla Wolf.

384.55   GW   ISSN 0935-803X
VIDEO PLUS. m. DM.60 (foreign DM.67.20); newsstand price: DM.5.50. Verlagsgruppe Milchstrasse, Milchstr. 1, 20148 Hamburg, Germany. TEL 040-44198-0. FAX 040-458519. Ed. Helmut Fiebig; Pubs. Dirk Manthey, Joerg Altendorf. adv. contact: Andre Hauke. circ. 12,193. **Document type**: consumer publication.

791.43   384.55   XR
VIDEO PLUS FILM; mesicnik pro audiovizualni tvorby a techniku. (Text in Czech; summaries in German and Russian) 1969. m. 48 Kc.($47.90) (Informaci a Poradenske Stredisko pro Mistni Kulturu) Vydavatelstvi a Nakladatelstvi Nezavisly Novinar III, Vodickova 34, 110 00 Prague 1, Czech Republic. TEL 42-2-276772. Ed. Vaclav Svoboda. adv.; bk.rev.; charts; illus.; index. circ. 4,500.
    Former titles: Amatersky Film a Video (ISSN 0862-187X); Amatersky Film (ISSN 0002-6794); **Supersedes**: Filmovym Objektivem.

788.59   SP   ISSN 1133-7079
VIDEO POPULAR. 1982. 5/yr. 3000 ptas.($40) (effective 1993-94). Mercacom S.L., Trav. Les Corts 322, 3-2, 08029 Barcelona, Spain. TEL 3-419-04-13. FAX 3-439-49-14. Ed. Arturo Paz Huguet. adv. contact: Monica Martin. bk.rev. circ. 9,000. **Indexed**: Ind.SST. **Document type**: consumer publication.

384.55   UK
VIDEO PRODUCTION TECHNIQUES. 3/yr. Pitman Publishing, 128 Long Acre, London WC2E 9AN, England. TEL 44-171-447-2000. FAX 44-171-240-5771. Ed. G. Elliott. cum.index. (looseleaf format) **Document type**: trade publication.

384.55   US
VIDEO RESERVED COLLECTION. 12/yr. T M Publishing, Inc., 2609 S. Highland, Box 18000-5, Las Vegas, NV 89109. TEL 702-796-9966. FAX 702-796-5655. Ed. M.S. Bram.

COMMUNICATIONS — VIDEO

384.55 US
VIDEO RETAILER SHOWCASE. 1986. m. Tel-Aire Publications, Inc., 3105 E. Carpenter Frwy., Irving, TX 75062. TEL 214-438-4111. FAX 214-579-7483. adv.; circ. 19,500 (paid); 19,500 (controlled).
Description: For retail video stores and chains across the continental US.

778.59 US ISSN 0277-3317
PN1992.95
VIDEO SOURCE BOOK. 1979. a (plus s-a supplement). $230. (National Video Clearinghouse, Inc.) Gale Research, 835 Penobscot Bldg., 645 Griswold St., Detroit, MI 48226-4094. TEL 313-961-2242; 800-877-4253. FAX 800-414-5043. E-mail: daniel_snyder@gale.com. Ed. Julia Furtan. adv.; index. circ. 6,000. (back issues avail.)
Description: Describes more than 125,000 currently available videotapes and discs, including feature movies, and instructional films.

384.554 US
VIDEO SPECIALIST - NEW TECHNOLOGY NEWSLETTER. 1981. m. $144 (foreign $156) (effective 1997). J. Lahm Consultants Inc., 2630 Coronado Dr., Fullerton, CA 92835. TEL 714-738-8422. FAX 714-738-4860. E-mail: vidspecnt@aol.com. Ed. James J. Lahm. adv.; bk.rev.; video rev. circ. 500. (looseleaf format; back issues avail.) **Document type:** newsletter, trade publication.
Formerly: Video Specialist Newsletter.
Description: Advisory news to retailers, manufacturers and executives in home video. Also covers industry trends, competitive developments, automatic merchandising systems, games, strategies, promotions, multimedia formats and new products and services.

384.55 US ISSN 0195-1750
HD9697.V543
VIDEO STORE; tomorrow's retailing today. 1979. w. (50/yr.) $62 (effective 1996). Advanstar Communications, Inc., 7500 Old Oak Blvd., Cleveland, OH 44130. TEL 216-243-8100; 800-854-3112. (Subscr. to: 131 W. First St., Duluth, MN 55802. TEL 800-346-8500) Ed. Thomas Arnald. circ. 44,287. (also avail. in microform from UMI; back issues avail.) **Indexed:** Account.Ind. (1986-). **Document type:** trade publication.
●Also available online. Vendor(s): Information Access Co., Knight-Ridder Information, Inc.
—UMI.
Description: For video retailers involved in home video sales. Includes proprietary market research, aggressive management, merchandising techniques, product buying information, industry people and news.

384.55 US ISSN 0361-0942
TK6680
VIDEO SYSTEMS; the magazine for video professionals. 1975. m. $45 (free to qualified personnel). Intertec Publishing Corp., 9800 Metcalf, Overland Park, KS 66212-2215. TEL 913-341-1300. FAX 913-967-1898. Ed. Ned Soseman. adv.; bk.rev.; illus. circ. 44,800. (also avail. in microfilm from UMI; reprint service avail. from UMI) **Indexed:** Educ.Tech.Abstr. **Document type:** trade publication.
—KR SourceOne; UMI. **CCC.**

621.3 384 US ISSN 1040-2772
VIDEO TECHNOLOGY NEWS. bi-w. $697 (foreign $732) (effective 1997). Phillips Business information, Inc., 1201 Seven Locks Rd., Potomac, MD 20854. TEL 301-424-3338. FAX 301-309-3847. E-mail: pbi@phillips.com. Ed. Craig Webb. **Document type:** newsletter.
●Also available online. Vendor(s): Data-Star, Information Access Co., Knight-Ridder Information, Inc., NewsNet (PB39).
—KR SourceOne. **CCC.**
Incorporates: H D T V Report (ISSN 1055-9280); Incorporates (1990-1992): Future Home Technology News (ISSN 1051-9971).
Description: Covers current developments in video technology, including broadcasting, cable, computers, satellites, consumer electronics, and telecommunications, and related business opportunities and trends.

384.55 GW
VIDEO TIP. 1982. m. Entertainment Media Verlag GmbH und Co. oHG, Stahlgruberring 11a, 81829 Munich, Germany. TEL 49-89-45114-0. FAX 49-89-45114444. Ed. Ulrich Hoecherl; Pub. Ulrich Scheele. adv. contact: Birgit Hagmann. film rev, play rev. circ. 21,883. (back issues avail.) **Document type:** consumer publication.

778.59 NE ISSN 0167-7039
VIDEO UIT & THUIS. 1981. m. fl.74 (foreign fl.140). Uitgeverij Scala bv, Postbus 28009, 3828 ZG Hoogland, Netherlands. TEL 31-33-4806896. FAX 31-33-4802281. Ed. F. Kraefft. adv.; film rev.; illus. circ. 21,000. **Document type:** consumer publication.
—SWETS.
Incorporates (1978-1986): Premiere (ISSN 0165-5361); Incorporates (in 1984): Videoaktief (ISSN 0920-8518); Which was formerly (until 1983): Film en Videotechniek (ISSN 0920-850X); (until 1982): Smalfilmen (ISSN 0165-5981); (1973-1979): Smalfilmen als Hobby (ISSN 0920-8496)
Description: Discusses video hardware and equipment.

384.554 US
VIDEO VIEWING.* 1984. m. free. View Publications, 4745 N. Seventh St., Ste. 110, Phoenix, AZ 85014. TEL 602-279-0841. FAX 602-277-8491. **Document type:** consumer publication.

621.3 US ISSN 0192-8899
VIDEO VOICE. 1980. m. $5. David Blumenthal Associates Inc., 30 E. 37th St., New York, NY 10016. TEL 212-686-8550. Ed. Paul Blumenthal. R&P contact: Phil Keaney. adv. contact: Renee Jarmin. **Document type:** trade publication.
Description: Provides up-to-date information on video-telecommunications industry.

791.43 US ISSN 1070-9991
VIDEO WATCHDOG; the perfectionist's guide to fantastic video. 1990. bi-m. $24 (foreign $33) (effective 1997 & 1998); newsstand price: $6.50. Box 5283, Cincinnati, OH 45205-0283. TEL 513-471-8989; 800-275-8395. FAX 513-471-8248. E-mail: videowd@aol.com; URL: http://www.cinemaweb.com/videowd. Ed. Tim Lucas; Pub. Donna Lucas. R&P contact: Tim Lucas. bk.rev.; bibl.; film rev.; illus.; music rev.; video rev. (back issues avail.) **Document type:** consumer publication.
Description: Helps consumers find the most complete version of their favorite films on videotape.

384.55 US ISSN 0196-5905
VIDEO WEEK. 1980. w. $882 (foreign $928). Warren Publishing, Inc., 2115 Ward Ct., N.W., Washington, DC 20037. TEL 202-872-9200. FAX 202-293-3435. Ed. Cindy Spielvogel. **Document type:** trade publication.
●Also available online. Vendor(s): Information Access Co., NewsNet (EL01).
—**CCC.**

384.55 AT ISSN 0729-1167
VIDEO WEEK. 1982. w. Aus.$200($150) General Magazine Company (Australia) Pty. Ltd., P.O. Box 1024, Richmond North, Vic. 3121, Australia. Ed. Geoffrey M. Gold. circ. 285.

384.55 658 US
VIDEOAGE. 1992. 10/yr. $149 (effective Mar. 1996). (Association of Professional Videographers) Triangle Media Group, Inc., 202 Lord Anson Dr., Raleigh, NC 27610. TEL 919-231-9245. FAX 919-231-8006. E-mail: aprovideo@aol.com. Ed. Sharon McMillan. adv.: page $300; trim 8 x 10 1/2; adv. contact: Stephen A. Short. bk.rev.; software rev.; video rev.; bibl.; charts; illus.; mkt.; stat.; tr.lit. circ. 800. (tabloid format; back issues avail.) **Document type:** trade publication, newsletter.
●Also available online.
Description: Serves as the official newsletter for the association. Includes event listings, business techniques, marketing tools, and equipment reviews.

621.388 GW
VIDEOAKTIV TESTJAHRBUCH. 1992. a. DM.14.80. Vereinigte Motor-Verlage GmbH und Co. KG, Leuschnerstr. 1, 70174 Stuttgart, Germany. TEL 49-711-1821226. FAX 49-711-1821349. Ed. Tim Cole; Pub. Gernot Hempelmann. adv. contact: Peter Michael Heyde. circ. 22,000. **Document type:** consumer publication.

VIDEOFASHION MONTHLY; news, men, specials. see *CLOTHING TRADE — Fashions*

384.55 GW ISSN 0176-3156
VIDEOFILMEN; das Magazin fuer aktive Videofilmer. 1984. bi-m. DM.34.80 (effective 1997). Fachverlag Schiele und Schoen GmbH, Markgrafenstr. 11, 10969 Berlin, Germany. TEL 49-30-253752-0. FAX 49-30-2517248. E-mail: 0302537520-0001@t-online.de. Ed. E. Altenmueller. adv. circ. 24,000. **Document type:** consumer publication.
—**CCC.**

VIDEOGAMES; the ultimate gaming magazine. see *COMPUTERS — Computer Games*

621.388 US ISSN 0363-1001
TK6630.A1
VIDEOGRAPHY. 1976. m. $30 in U.S. and Canada (foreign $48) (effective 1997). Miller Freeman P S N Inc. (Subsidiary of: United News & Media Co.), 460 Park Ave. South, 9th Fl., New York, NY 10016-7315. TEL 212-378-0400. FAX 212-378-2160. E-mail: videography@psn.com. Ed. Brian McKernan. adv. circ. 40,000. **Indexed:** Film Lit.Ind. (1977-), Ind.Per.Art.Relat.Law. **Document type:** trade publication.
—KR SourceOne; UMI; UnCover.
Description: For video professionals. Contains news, trends and analysis of the video industry, interviews with specialists, editorials, guest columns, a calendar of meetings and shows.

VIDEOHOUND'S GOLDEN MOVIE RETRIEVER. see *MOTION PICTURES*

VIDEOLOG. see *COMMUNICATIONS — Abstracting, Bibliographies, Statistics*

384.55 UK
VIDEOLOG. fortn. £220. Trade Service Information Ltd., Cherryholt Rd., Stamford, Lincs. PE9 2HT, England. TEL 44-1780-764331. FAX 44-1780-482067. E-mail: info@tsi-ltd.co.uk; URL: http://www.tsi-ltd.co.uk. Ed. Christine Morris. R&P contact: Russell Jackson. adv. contact: Tracey Armstrong. circ. 1,570 (paid). **Document type:** directory.
●Also available on CD-ROM.
Description: Directory of videos currently available for rent or retail in the U.K.

384.55 US
VIDEOLOG REPORTER. 1981. w. $252. Phonolog Publishing (Subsidiary of: Trade Service Corporation), 10996 Torreyana Rd., Box 85007, San Diego, CA 92138. TEL 619-457-5920. Ed. Bonnie J. Dudley.

384.55 US ISSN 0889-4973
TR845
VIDEOMAKER; the video camera user's magazine. 1986. m. $22.50 (Canada $32.50; elsewhere $42.50). Videomaker Inc., Box 4591, Chico, CA 95927. TEL 916-891-8410. FAX 916-891-8443. E-mail: editor@videomaker.com; URL: http://www.videomaker.com. (Subscr. to: Box 469026, Escondido, CA 92046) Ed. Stephen Muratore; Pub. Matthew York. R&P contact: Alice Greany. adv. contact: Rick Anderson. bk.rev.; illus. circ. 90,000. **Indexed:** Ind.How To Do It. **Document type:** consumer publication.
●Also available online. Vendor(s): CompuServe, Inc.
—KR SourceOne.
Description: Presents tools, tips and techniques for consumers and professionals involved with videomaking as a hobby, in business or in education. *Refereed Serial*

384.55 GW ISSN 0946-0993
VIDEOPLAY. 1983. m. DM.55 (foreign DM.60). Kinothek Zeitschriften Verlag GmbH, Karlstr. 26, 22085 Hamburg, Germany. TEL 040-227141-0. FAX 040-2203525. Ed. Klaus Krause; Pub. Wolfgang Schrader. adv. contact: Christine Rueter. circ. 11,689. **Document type:** consumer publication.

384.55 371.33 US ISSN 1043-9579
HF5001
VIDEOS FOR BUSINESS AND TRAINING; professional and vocational videos and how to get them. 1989. irreg. Gale Research, 835 Penobscot Bldg., 645 Griswold St., Detroit, MI 48226-4094. TEL 313-961-2242; 800-877-4253. FAX 800-414-5043. E-mail: daniel_snyder@gale.com. Ed. David Weiner.
●Also available online. Vendor(s): Human Resources Information Network (Video).

384.55 IT
VIDEOSAT; il mensile dell'home entertainment video e satellite. 1981. m. Lit.120000 (foreign Lit.160000) (effective 1997). Motta Periodici s.r.l., Via Branda Castiglioni, 2-A, 20156 Milan, Italy. TEL 39-2-38002901. FAX 39-2-38010437. adv.: color page L.9650000. **Indexed:** R.G.Abstr. **Document type:** consumer publication.
Formerly: Video.

384.55 IT ISSN 1121-7677
VIDEOSOFT. 2/yr. Ediscreen s.r.l., Via Calderini 68, 00196 Rome, Italy. TEL 6-39-60-409. FAX 6-39-00-72. Ed. Paola Gabrielli. circ. 20,000.

384.55 PO
VIDEOSOM. 12/yr. Av. da Republica, 47-1o Dto., 1100 Lisbon, Portugal. TEL 1-768911. FAX 1-732056. TELEX 65016 CEBRO P. Ed. Paulo Jorge Cruz. circ. 15,000.

384.55 IT
VIDEOTECNICA. 1989. m. L.85000 (foreign L.330000). Vidigest s.r.l., Via Brenta 13, 00198 Rome, Italy. TEL 39-6-8417179. FAX 39-6-8845585. Ed. Paolo de Petris. adv.: B&W page L.5886000, color page L.10584000. circ. 76,000. **Document type:** consumer publication.

621.388 FR ISSN 0247-4352
VIDEOTEX; news on videographic systems - bimensuel d'actualite des systemes videographiques. 1980. 30/yr. 3200 F. A Jour, 11 rue du Marche St. Honore, 75001 Paris, France. TEL 42-96-67-22. FAX 40-20-07-75. TELEX TELEXEL 615887F. Ed. Marie-Agnes Giroud. bk.rev.
—CCC.

384.55 GW ISSN 0941-0562
VIDEOWOCHE; das Nachrichtenmagazin fuer den Fachhandel. 1987. w. DM.396. Entertainment Media Verlag GmbH und Co. oHG, Stahlgruberring 11a, 81829 Munich, Germany. TEL 49-89-45114-0. FAX 49-89-45114444. Eds. Ulrich Scheele, Ulrich Hoecherl. film rev.; charts. circ. 5,000. **Document type:** trade publication.

384.55 GW
VIDI AKTUELL. (Video Digital) 1987. q. VIDI Video Digital Studio Technik GmbH, Roentgenstr. 104, 64291 Darmstadt, Germany. adv. contact: Bernd Poth. circ. 8,000. (tabloid format; back issues avail.) **Document type:** trade publication.

VISIO. see *COMMUNICATIONS — Television And Cable*

384.55 UK ISSN 0960-300X
VOX. 1990. m. £26.40 (foreign £40) (effective 1996). I P C Magazines, Specialist Magazine Group (Subsidiary of: Reed Elsevier group), King's Reach Tower, Stamford St., London SE1 9LS, England. TEL 44-171-261-5000. FAX 44-1444-445599. TELEX 892084 REEDBP G. (Subscr. to: Vox Subscriptions, Freepost CY1061, Haywards Heath, W. Sussex RH16 3ZA, England. TEL 44-1444-445555) Ed. Paul Colbert. adv. contact: Nick Watt. film rev. circ. 106,172. (back issues avail.) **Document type:** consumer publication.
Description: Covers all areas of popular music including rock, alternative, dance and world music, plus film, video, and comedy.

621.38833 UK ISSN 1365-8956
WHAT VIDEO AND TV. 1980. m. £30 (Europe £46; elsewhere £56) (effective 1997); newsstand price: £2.60. W V Publications and Exhibitions Ltd., 57-59 Rochester Pl., London NW1 9JU, England. TEL 44-171-485-0011. FAX 44-171-482-6269. (Subscr. to: ASM Ltd., Unit 6, Pipewell Road Industrial Estate, Desborough, Northants NN14 2SW, England. TEL 44-1536-762860. FAX 44-1536-760306) Ed. Kulwinder Singh Rai. adv. contact: Jason Grant. illus. circ. 43,000. **Document type:** consumer publication.
—BLDSC (9309.762000).
Former titles (until 1996): What Video and What Home Cinema (ISSN 1352-6162); (until 1993): What Video? (ISSN 0956-2354).

384.55 UK ISSN 0955-078X
WHAT VIDEO BOOK OF TESTS. 1986. a. £2.95 (effective 1997). W V Publications and Exhibitions Ltd., 57-59 Rochester Pl., London NW1 9JU, England. TEL 44-171-485-0011. FAX 44-171-482-6269. (Orders to: ASM Ltd., Unit 6, Pipewell Road Industrial Estate, Desborough, Northants NN14 2SW, England. TEL 44-1536-762860. FAX 44-1536-760306) **Document type:** consumer publication.

384.55 US
WIDESCREEN REVIEW. 1993. bi-m. $20. 26864 Mandelieu Dr., Murieta, CA 92562. Ed. Gary Reber. adv.; illus. **Document type:** consumer publication.

WORLDWIDE DIRECTORY OF FILM AND VIDEO FESTIVALS AND EVENTS. see *MOTION PICTURES*

WORLDWIDE VIDEOTEX UPDATE. see *COMMUNICATIONS — Computer Applications*

1000 VIDEOS. see *MOTION PICTURES*

COMPUTERS

see also Computers–Artificial Intelligence; Computers–Automation; Computers–Calculating Machines; Computers–Circuits; Computers–Computer Architecture; Computers–Computer Assisted Instruction; Computers–Computer Engineering; Computers–Computer Games; Computers–Computer Graphics; Computers–Computer Industry; Computers–Computer Industry Directories; Computers–Computer Industry, Vocational Guidance; Computers–Computer Music; Computers–Computer Networks; Computers–Computer Programming; Computers–Computer Sales; Computers–Computer Security; Computers–Computer Simulation; Computers–Computer Systems; Computers–Cybernetics; Computers–Data Base Management; Computers–Data Communications and Data Transmission Systems; Computers–Electronic Data Processing; Computers–Hardware; Computers–Information Science and Information Theory; Computers–Machine Theory; Computers–Microcomputers; Computers–Minicomputers; Computers–Personal Computers; Computers–Software; Computers–Theory of Computing; Computers–Word Processing

001.6 621.381 US ISSN 0736-721X
QA76.73.A35 CODEN: AALEE5
A C M ADA LETTERS. bi-m. membership. Association for Computing Machinery, 1515 Broadway, 17th Fl., New York, NY 10036. TEL 212-869-7440. FAX 212-869-0481. TELEX 421686. Ed. J. Kaye Grau. **Indexed:** INSPEC (1988-).
—AskIEEE; CISTI; Ei; KR SourceOne; SWETS; UnCover.

001.6425 621.381 US
A C M ADMINISTRATIVE DIRECTORY OF COLLEGE AND UNIVERSITY COMPUTER SCIENCE - DATA PROCESSING PROGRAMS AND COMPUTER FACILITIES. biennial. $17 (members $13). Association for Computing Machinery, 1515 Broadway, 17th Fl., New York, NY 10036. TEL 212-869-7440. FAX 212-869-0481. TELEX 421686. (Subscr. to: ACM Order Department, Box 64145, Baltimore, MD 21264)
Formerly: Administrative Directory of College and University Computer Science Departments and Computer Centers (ISSN 0190-6607)

004 US ISSN 0360-0300
QA76.5
A C M COMPUTING SURVEYS; the survey and tutorial journal of the ACM. 1969. q. $100 to non-members. Association for Computing Machinery, 1515 Broadway, 17th Fl., New York, NY 10036-5701. TEL 212-869-7440. FAX 212-944-1318. TELEX 421686. Ed. Salvatore T. March. index. circ. 33,000. (also avail. in microfiche from KTO; microfilm from WWS) **Indexed:** A.I.Abstr., A.S.& T.Ind., Abstr.Hum.Comp.Inter., ASCA, CAD CAM Abstr., Compumath, Compumath, Comput.Abstr., Comput.Cont., Comput Dtbs., Comput.Lit.Ind., Comput.Rev., Curr.Cont., Eng.Ind., Ergon.Abstr., Ind.Sci.Rev., INSPEC (1969-), Math.R., Oper.Res.Manage.Sci., Pr.& Indus.Ind., Qual.Contr.Appl.Stat., Sci.Cit.Ind.
—BLDSC (3395.130000); AskIEEE; CISTI; Ei; Genuine Article; KR SourceOne; Linda Hall; SWETS; UMI; UnCover. **CCC.**
Formerly: Computing Surveys (ISSN 0010-4892)
Description: Publishes new perspectives on hardware and software, computer systems organization, computer science theory, artificial intelligence, applications, and a spectrum of peripheral topics.

621.381 US ISSN 0572-4252
A C M MONOGRAPH SERIES. 1968. irreg., vol.21, 1981. (Association for Computing Machinery) Academic Press, Inc., 525 B St., Ste. 1900, San Diego, CA 92101-4495. TEL 619-231-0926. FAX 619-699-6715. (Subscr. to: Order Dept., 6277 Sea Harbor Dr., 4th Fl., Orlando, FL 32887. TEL 800-321-5068) Ed. Thomas A. Standish. (reprint service avail. from ISI) **Document type:** monographic series.
Refereed Serial

001.6 621.381 US ISSN 1049-3301
QA76.9.C65 CODEN: ATMCEZ
A C M TRANSACTIONS ON MODELING AND COMPUTER STIMULATION. q. $100 to non-members. Association for Computing Machinery, 1515 Broadway, 17th Fl., New York, NY 10036-5701. TEL 212-869-7440. FAX 212-944-1318. TELEX 421686. **Indexed:** INSPEC (1991-).
—BLDSC (0578.671000); AskIEEE; CISTI; Ei; KR SourceOne; Linda Hall; SWETS; UnCover. **CCC.**
Description: Covers research on aspects of computer simulation and modeling of complex systems. Includes applications, reviews and tutorials.

001.6 621.381 US ISSN 1061-7663
TS155.6
A-E-C SYSTEMS COMPUTER SOLUTIONS. (Architecture, Engineering, Construction); the computer applications and management journal for design and construction. 1991. q. free to qualified persons (outside the US $56) (effective 1996). A-E-C Systems, Inc., Box 310318, Newington, CT 06111. TEL 860-666-1326. FAX 860-666-4782. Ed. Charles R. Carroll, Jr.; Pubs. George S. Borkovich, Michael R. Hough. adv. contact: Gail Donahue. bk.rev. circ. 30,000. **Document type:** trade publication.
—BLDSC (0719.609000).
Description: Presents case studies, how-to and features to help management-level computer users in architecture, engineering, construction, facility management, and GIS mapping.

COMPUTERS

001.6 621.381 370 UK ISSN 1352-8971
QA75.5
A X I S. (Academic Computing and Information Systems) 1979. q. £50($95) to individuals; institutions £90($175) (effective 1998). (Universities and Colleges Information Systems Association) Whurr Publishers Ltd., 19b Compton Terrace, London N1 2UN, England. TEL 44-171-359-5979. FAX 44-171-226-5290. (Subscr. to: Turpin Distribution Services Ltd., Blackhorse Rd., Letchworth, Herts. SG6 1HN, England. TEL 44-1462-672555. FAX 44-1462-480947; Subscr. in N. America to: Whurr Publishers Ltd., Box 1897, Lawrence, KS 66044-8897. TEL 913-843-1221. FAX 913-843-1274) Ed. Mike Wells. adv.: page £175; adv. contact: Maggy Park. bk.rev.; illus.; index. circ. 350. (back issues avail.) **Indexed:** BMT, Compumath, Comput.Cont., Hort.Abstr., INSPEC (1984-). **Document type:** academic/scholarly publication.
—BLDSC (1840.979100); AskIEEE; CISTI; Genuine Article; KR SourceOne; UMI.
Former titles (until 1993): University Computing (ISSN 0265-4385); I U C C Bulletin (ISSN 0142-2464)
Description: Information about computing and IT related work carried out in higher education and research establishments and, where appropriate, the application of such work to business needs.
Refereed Serial

AALBORG UNIVERSITY. INSTITUTE FOR ELECTRONIC SYSTEMS. DEPARTMENT OF MATHEMATICS AND COMPUTER SCIENCE - REPORT. see *ENGINEERING — Electrical Engineering*

004 DK ISSN 0106-9969
AARHUS UNIVERSITET. INSTITUT FOR DE MATEMATISK FAG. DATALOGISK AFDELING. DAIMI IR. 1973. irreg. price varies. Aarhus Universitet, Institut for de Matematisk Fag, Datalogisk Afdeling, Bygn. 540, Ny Munkegade, DK-8000 Aarhus C, Denmark. **Document type:** academic/scholarly publication.

004 DK ISSN 0105-8525
AARHUS UNIVERSITET. INSTITUT FOR DE MATEMATISK FAG. DATALOGISK AFDELING. DAIMI MD. 1973. irreg. price varies. Aarhus Universitet, Institut for de Matematisk Fag, Datalogisk Afdeling, Ny Munkegade, DK-8000 Aarhus C, Denmark. **Document type:** academic/scholarly publication.

004 DK ISSN 0105-8517
AARHUS UNIVERSITET. INSTITUT FOR DE MATEMATISK FAG. DATALOGISK AFDELING. DAIMI PB. 1972. irreg. price varies. Aarhus Universitet, Institut for de Matematisk Fag, Datalogisk Afdeling, Ny Munkegade, DK-8000 Aarhus C, Denmark. **Document type:** academic/scholarly publication.

004 IE ISSN 0791-1254
ABAKUS. 1989. a. (University College Cork, Computer Science Department) Micromail, 7 Crawford Park, Bishop St., Cork. TEL 44-121-317686. FAX 44-121-310756. E-mail: willy@micromail.ie; URL: http://www.cis.ie/micromail. Eds. Colin McCormack, Brian Dowd. **Document type:** academic/scholarly publication.
—BLDSC (0537.724470).

001.6 621.381 US
ABLEX SERIES IN COMPUTATIONAL SCIENCES. 1990. irreg., latest 1996. price varies. Ablex Publishing Corporation, Box 5297, Greenwich, CT 06831-0504. TEL 203-661-7602. FAX 203-661-0792. Ed. Cheng-Ming Guo. **Document type:** academic/scholarly publication.

001.6 621.381 US
ACADEMY COMPUTING TIMES. 1986. 10/yr. free. Indiana University, Wrubel Computing Center, 10th St. & State Rd. 46 Bypass, Bloomington, IN 47405. TEL 812-855-9255. Ed. Janet Holloway-Smith.

ACCESS TO WANG; the magazine for Wang system users. see *COMPUTERS — Data Communications And Data Transmission Systems*

001.6 US ISSN 0163-6774
ACRONYMS. 1971. 7/yr. free. Michigan State University, Computer Laboratory, Computing Information Center, East Lansing, MI 48824. TEL 517-353-1800. FAX 517-353-9847. Ed. Linda Dunn. circ. 3,000. **Indexed:** Comput.Cont., Energy Ind., Energy Info.Abstr., Intl.Civil Eng.Abstr., Manage.Cont., Soft.Abstr.Eng.
Description: Addresses current mainframe, network and microcomputer topics of interest to MSU users; includes topics of more general appeal as well.

510 621.381 FI ISSN 1238-9803
QA3 CODEN: APSMFY
ACTA POLYTECHNICA SCANDINAVICA. MATHEMATICS, COMPUTING AND MANAGEMENT IN ENGINEERING SERIES. (Texts and summaries in English) irreg. (5-7/yr.). FIM 450 (effective 1997). Teknillisten Tieteiden Akatemia - Finnish Academy of Technology, Tekniikantie 12, FIN-02150 Espoo, Finland. Ed. Reijo Sulonen. index, cum.index: 1958-1994. circ. 500. (also avail. in microfilm from UMI; back issues avail.; reprint service avail. from UMI) **Indexed:** ASCA, CAD CAM Abstr., Compumath, Comput.Cont., Curr.Cont., I.M.M.Abstr., INIS Atomind., INSPEC (1981-), Math.R., Sci.Cit.Ind, Soft.Abstr.Eng., Zent.Math. **Document type:** monographic series.
—BLDSC (0661.263900); AskIEEE; CISTI; KR SourceOne; Linda Hall; UMI; UnCover.
Former titles: Acta Polytechnica Scandinavica. Mathematics and Computing in Engineering Series (ISSN 1237-2404); (until 1994): Acta Polytechnica Scandinavica. Mathematics and Computer Science Series (ISSN 0355-2713); (until 1975): Acta Polytechnica Scandinavica. Mathematics and Computing Machinery Series (ISSN 0001-6861)
Description: Presents research results in mathematical engineering and computer science.

001.64 621.381 US ISSN 0065-2458
QA76 CODEN: ADCOA7
ADVANCES IN COMPUTERS. 1960. irreg., vol.45, 1997. Academic Press, Inc., 525 B St., Ste. 1900, San Diego, CA 92101-4495. TEL 619-231-0926. FAX 619-699-6715. (Subscr. to: Order Dept., 6277 Sea Harbor Dr., 4th Fl., Orlando, FL 32887. TEL 800-321-5068) Ed. Marshall C. Yovits. index. (reprint service avail. from ISI) **Indexed:** ASCA, CAD CAM Abstr., Compumath, Deep Sea Res.& Oceanogr. Abstr., INSPEC, Zent.Math.
—BLDSC (0704.130000); CISTI; Linda Hall; SWETS; UnCover. CCC.
Refereed Serial

001.6 621.381 US ISSN 0741-9341
QA76.27
ADVANCES IN COMPUTING RESEARCH. 1983. a. $90.25 to institutions. J A I Press Inc., 55 Old Post Rd., No. 2, Box 1678, Greenwich, CT 06836-1678. TEL 203-661-7602. FAX 203-661-0792. (Addr. in the U.K. and Europe: J A I Press Ltd., The Courtyard, 28 High St., Hampton Hill, Mddx. TW12 1PD, England. TEL 44-81-943-9296. FAX 44-81-943-9317) Ed. Franco P. Preparata. **Indexed:** ASCA.
—BLDSC (0704.133000).

621.381 551 US ISSN 0882-6129
QC801
ADVANCES IN GEOPHYSICAL DATA PROCESSING; a research annual. 1984. a. $90.25 to institutions. J A I Press Inc., 36 Sherwood Pl., Greenwich, CT 06830. TEL 203-661-7602. Ed. Marwan Simaan. **Indexed:** INSPEC.
—CISTI.

001.6 621.381 US ISSN 1045-6821
QA276.A1
ADVANCES IN STATISTICAL ANALYSIS AND STATISTICAL COMPUTING. 1985. a. $73.25 to institutions. J A I Press Inc., 55 Old Post Rd., No. 2, Box 1678, Greenwich, CT 06836-1678. TEL 203-661-7602. FAX 203-661-0792. (Addr. in the U.K. and rest of Europe: J A I Press Ltd., The Courtyard, 28 High St., Hampton Hill, Mddx. TW12 1PD, England. TEL 44-81-943-9296. FAX 44-81-843-9317) Ed, Roberto S. Mariano.

001.6 629.8 US
AIXTRA. 1991. bi-m. $33. I B M Corporation (Roanoke), 5 W. Kirwood Blvd., MS 01-04-60, Roanoke, TX 76299. TEL 817-962-6551. FAX 817-962-7218. E-mail: bonziman@vnet.ibm.com; URL: http://pscc.dfw.ibm.com/aixtra. Ed. Alan E. Hodel; Pub. Melissa Cox. adv.: B&W page $3595, color page $4570; trim 8 3/8 x 10 7/8. circ. 40,000 (controlled). **Document type:** trade publication.
●Also available online.

001.6 621.381 US ISSN 0178-4617
QA75.5 CODEN: ALGOEJ
ALGORITHMICA; an international journal in computer science. m. $368 (effective 1998). Springer-Verlag, Science Journals, 175 Fifth Ave., New York, NY 10010. TEL 212-460-1500. FAX 212-473-6272. E-mail: orders@springer-ny.com; URL: http://www.springer-ny.com. (N. American subscr. to: Journal Fulfillment Services, Box 2485, Secaucus, NJ 07096-2485. TEL 800-777-4643. FAX 201-348-4505; Outside N. America to: Heidelberger Platz 3, 14197 Berlin, Germany. TEL 49-30-8207-0. FAX 49-30-8207448) Ed. C.K. Wong. R&P contact: Ian Gross. adv. contact: Robert Vrooman. (also avail. in microform from UMI; back issues avail.; reprint service avail. from SWZ) **Indexed:** ASCA, Compumath, Comput.Abstr., Curr.Cont., Cyb.Abstr., Eng.Ind., INSPEC (1986-), Math.R, Sci.Cit.Ind., Zent.Math. **Document type:** academic/scholarly publication.
—BLDSC (0787.337000); AskIEEE; CISTI; Ei; Genuine Article; KR SourceOne; Linda Hall; SWETS; UnCover. CCC.
Description: Publishes papers on algorithms, with a strong emphasis on practical application.
Refereed Serial

004 UK ISSN 0959-9630
AMIGA COMPUTING. 13/yr. £49.99($98) I D G Media, Media House, Adlington Park, Adlington, Macclesfield, Ches. SK10 4NR, England. TEL 44-1625-878888. FAX 44-1625-850652. E-mail: edit@acomp.demon.co.uk. Ed. Tim Hackett; Pub. Robin Wilkinson. adv. contact: Sue Horsefield. software rev.; circ. 22,000 (paid). (back issues avail.) **Document type:** consumer publication.
Description: Reviews Commodore Amiga computers, software and games.

004 FR ISSN 1164-1746
AMIGA NEWS & VIDEO NUMERIQUE. 1988. m. (11/yr.) 360 F. (foreign 365 F.) (effective 1997); newsstand price: 35 F. News Edition, 12 rue Barriere, 31200 Toulouse, France. TEL 61-47-25-67. FAX 61-47-25-69. E-mail: anews@club-internet.fr. Ed. Bruce Lepper; Pub. Bruce Lepper. adv. contact: Ms. Gimeno. software rev.; illus.; tr.lit.; index. (back issues avail.) **Document type:** consumer publication.
Description: Contains articles on the practical use of the range of Amiga computers, and alerts readers to new products.

004 NE ISSN 0254-5330
ANNALS OF OPERATIONS RESEARCH. (Text and summaries in English) 1984. 8/yr. 2216 SFr. (effective 1998). Baltzer Science Publishers B.V., P.O. Box 221, 1400 AE Bussum, Netherlands. TEL 31-20-6370061. FAX 31-20-6323651. E-mail: subscribe@baltzer.nl; URL: http://www.baltzer.nl. (Subscr. in N. America to: Baltzer Science Publishers, Box 8577, Red Bank, NJ 07701-8577) Ed. Peter L Hammer. **Indexed:** ASCA, Compumath, Cyb.Abstr., INSPEC (1984-), Oper.Res.Manage.Sci., Qual.Contr.Appl.Stat., Stat.Theor.Meth.Abstr. (1996), Zent.Math. **Document type:** academic/scholarly publication.
—BLDSC (1043.330000); AskIEEE; CISTI; Ei; Genuine Article; KR SourceOne; SWETS; UnCover. CCC.
Description: Presentation of trends in specific areas of operations research.

ANNUAL CONFERENCE ON STATISTICS, COMPUTER SCIENCE AND OPERATIONS RESEARCH. PROCEEDINGS. see *STATISTICS*

001.6 621.381 JA
ANNUAL SURVEY OF COMPUTER USERS. 1966. a. 10000 Yen. Japan Management Science Institute, 4-18-3-309 Minami-Aoyama, Minato-ku, Tokyo 107, Japan. Ed.Bd.

001.6 IT ISSN 1122-9268
APPLICANDO; la rivista per Macintosh. 1983. m. (11/yr.). L.96000 (effective 1997). Gruppo Editoriale J C E, Via Ferri, 6, 20092 Cinisello Balsamo (MI), Italy. TEL 39-2-660251. FAX 39-2-6127620. TELEX 352376 JCE MIL I. E-mail: applicando@jce.it; URL: http://www.jce.it. Ed. Fausto Gimondi. adv.: B&W page L.6400000, color page L.7950000; trim 210 x 276. circ. 40,000. (back issues avail.)
Description: Covers Mac pc world and MacOS products, and technology around the Apple market.

APPLIED CATEGORICAL STRUCTURES; a journal devoted to applications of categorical methods in algebra, analysis, order, topology and computer science. see MATHEMATICS — Computer Applications

004 UK ISSN 0961-8414
ARCHIMEDES WORLD. 1983. m. £35.40 (includes diskette). Argus Specialist Publications Ltd. (Subsidiary of: Argus Press Group), Argus House, Boundary Way, Hemel Hempstead, Herts. HP2 7SR, England. TEL 01442-66551. FAX 01442-66998. (Subscr. to: Argus Subscription Services, Queensway House, 2 Queensway, Redhill, Surrey RH1 1QS, England. TEL 01737-768611) Ed. Andrew Banner. adv. **Indexed:** INSPEC (1984-1989). **Document type:** consumer publication.
Formerly (until 1991): A and B Computing (ISSN 0264-4584)
Description: Covers all aspects of Acorn Risc OS computers and offers users technical information.

001.6 621.381 PL ISSN 0867-2121
ARCHIWUM INFORMATYKI TEORETYCZNEJ I STOSOWANEJ/ARCHIVES OF THEORETICAL AND APPLIED INFORMATICS. (Text in English; summaries in Polish) 1971. q. $52. (Polska Akademia Nauk, Instytut Informatyki Teoretycznej i Stosowanej) Wydawnictwo Naukowe P W N, Ul. Miodowa 10, 00-251 Warsaw, Poland. TEL 48-22-312738. FAX 48-22-6954288. TELEX 813763 PWN PL. Ed. Stefan Wegrzyn. circ. 420. **Indexed:** Alloys Ind., Eng.Mat.Abstr., INSPEC (1989-), Met.Abstr., Met.Mat.Ind., Nonfer.Met.Alert, PCC Alert, Steels Alert, World Alum.Abstr., Zent.Math.
—AskIEEE; CISTI; KR SourceOne; Linda Hall.
Formerly (until 1989): Podstawy Sterowania (ISSN 0374-4094)

001.6 621.381 SI ISSN 0129-5896
ASIA COMPUTER WEEKLY. 1979. w. $180 in Asia; elsewhere $199. Miller Freeman Pte. Ltd., 100 Beach Rd., 26-00 Shaw Towers, Singapore 0718, Singapore. TEL 294-3366. FAX 298-5534. TELEX RS-25280-ABPSIN. Ed. Raymond Tan. adv.: B&W page $7780, color page $8330; trim 280 x 406; adv. contact: Steve Milgrim. circ. 19,145. (tabloid format; back issues avail.) **Indexed:** J.of Ferroc.
Description: Reports on the latest news and happenings in the Asian computer industry.

003 658 SI ISSN 0217-5959
HD28 CODEN: APJRE3
ASIA - PACIFIC JOURNAL OF OPERATIONAL RESEARCH. 1973. s-a. $30 to individuals; institutions $60. National University of Singapore, Faculty of Business Administration, 10 Kent Ridge Crescent, Singapore 0511, Singapore. FAX 65-7771296. adv.; bk.rev. circ. 1,100. (also avail. in microform from UMI) **Indexed:** ASCA, Compumath, Curr.Cont., INSPEC (1986-), Int.Abstr.Oper.Res., J.Cont.Quant.Meth., Math.R., SSCI, Zent.Math. **Document type:** academic/scholarly publication.
—BLDSC (1742.260750); AskIEEE; Ei; Genuine Article; KR SourceOne; UMI.
Incorporates (in 1984): New Zealand Operational Research (ISSN 0110-6392)

SILOMAR CONFERENCE ON SIGNALS, SYSTEMS AND COMPUTERS. CONFERENCE RECORD. see COMPUTERS — Circuits

SSISTENZ. see BUSINESS AND ECONOMICS — Office Equipment And Services

SSISTIVE TECHNOLOGY RESEARCH SERIES. see HANDICAPPED — Computer Applications

621.3 004 US ISSN 0004-5411
QA76 CODEN: JACOAH
ASSOCIATION FOR COMPUTING MACHINERY. JOURNAL. 1954. q. $100 to non-members. Association for Computing Machinery, 1515 Broadway, 17th Fl, New York, NY 10036-5701. TEL 212-869-7440. FAX 212-944-1318. TELEX 421686. URL: http://www.acm.org/pubs/journals.html. Ed. D.J. Rosenkrantz. charts; illus.; index. circ. 16,000. (also avail. in microform from UMI,KTO,WWS; reprint service avail. from UMI) **Indexed:** A.S.& T.Ind., ASCA, B.P.I., CAD CAM Abstr., Compumath, Comput.Abstr., Comput.Cont., Comput.Rev., Curr.Cont., Eng.Ind., Ergon.Abstr., Ind.Sci.Rev., INIS Atomind., INSPEC (1968-), Int.Abstr.Oper.Res., Math.R., SSCI, Zent.Math.
—AskIEEE; CISTI; Ei; Genuine Article; KR SourceOne; Linda Hall; SWETS; UMI; UnCover. CCC.
Description: Papers covering research, development and applications of hardware, languages for information processing, scientific computation, automatic control and simulation of processes, artificial intelligence, operations research, computer systems and the recognition, storage and processing of data.

004 621.381 AT ISSN 1039-8767
AUSTRALIAN COMPUTER COMMENTARY; monthly review of significant developments in information technology. 1986. m. (10/yr.). Aus.$295. International Business Communications Pty Ltd., 14 Charles St., Redfern, N.S.W. 2016, Australia. TEL 02-319-3755. Ed. Reuven Blecher. bk.rev.; index. circ. 200. (back issues avail.)
Formerly (until 1992): Computer Commentary (ISSN 1036-8272)
Description: Provides concise summaries of information technology articles from the leading business, computer and management periodicals.

621.381 001.6 AT ISSN 0004-8917
QA76 CODEN: ACMJB2
AUSTRALIAN COMPUTER JOURNAL.* 1967. 4/yr. Aus.$65. (Australian Computer Society) Associated Business Publications Pty. Ltd., P.O. Box 440, Broadway, N.S.W. 2007, Australia. TEL 61-2-2122780. FAX 61-2-2814594. Ed. R. Cook. adv.; bk.rev.; charts; illus.; stat.; index. circ. 15,000. (also avail. in microform from UMI) **Indexed:** Appl.Mech.Rev., ASCA, Compumath, Comput.Abstr., Comput.Cont., Comput.Lit.Ind., Comput.Rev., Eng.Ind., INSPEC (1970-), Intl.Civil Eng.Abstr., Math.R., Soft.Abstr.Eng., Zent.Math. **Document type:** bulletin.
—BLDSC (1798.190000); AskIEEE; CISTI; Ei; Genuine Article; KR SourceOne; Linda Hall; SWETS; UMI; UnCover. CCC.

004 NE ISSN 0165-4683
AUTOMATISERING GIDS. 1967. w. (Fri.). fl.175 (foreign fl.325) (effective 1996). Ten Hagen & Stam b.v. (Subsidiary of: Wolters Kluwer N.V.), Postbus 34, 2501 AG The Hague, Netherlands. TEL 31-70-3045700. FAX 31-70-3045812. URL: http://www.worldaccess.nl/ths/. Ed. Jan Bakker. adv.: B&W page fl.32460, color page fl.37000; trim 420 x 300; adv. contact: Herman Voois. bk.rev.; circ. 34,750 (paid); 27,550 (controlled). **Indexed:** Key to Econ.Sci. **Document type:** trade publication.
—KNAW; SWETS.
Description: Reports on market developments and technological and management issues for computer industry professionals.

004 UK ISSN 0962-9475
CODEN: BACREA
B B C ACORN USER. 13/yr. £39.99; newsstand price: £3.75. I D G Media, Media House, Adlington Park, Macclesfield, Ches. SD10 4NP, England. TEL 44-1625-878888. FAX 44-1625-850652. E-mail: aueditos@idg.co.uk; URL: http://www.idg.co.uk/acornuser/. (Subscr. to: Database Direct, South Wirral L65 3EB, England. TEL 0151-357-1275) Ed. Steve Turnbull; Pub. Robin Wilkinson. R&P contact: Steve Turnbull. adv. contact: Carl Jackson. circ. 18,108 (paid). (back issues avail.) **Indexed:** INSPEC (1994-). **Document type:** consumer publication.
—AskIEEE; KR SourceOne.
Formerly (until 1994): Acorn User (ISSN 0263-7456)
Description: Contains articles from professional and dedicated users of RISCOS and ARM computer equipment for home and business use.

004 AT
B T W. m. Curtin University of Technology, Computing Centre, Kent St., Bentley, W.A. 6102, Australia. TEL 61-9-351-7915. FAX 61-9-3512495. E-mail: btw@info.curtin.edu.au; URL: http://www.curtin.edu.au/curtin/dept/cc/BTW/. Ed. Jo Winship.
●Available only online.

003 658 BE ISSN 0770-0512
BELGIAN JOURNAL OF OPERATIONS RESEARCH, STATISTICS AND COMPUTER SCIENCE. Running title: J O R B E L. (Text in English) 1961. 4/yr. Sogesci b.v.w.b., Av. de la Renaissance 30, 1040 Brussels, Belgium. **Indexed:** Curr.Cont.(1992-), Stat.Theor.Meth.Abstr. (1992-), Zent.Math. **Document type:** academic/scholarly publication.
—BLDSC (4673.287000); AskIEEE; KR SourceOne.
Former titles (until 1985): Revue Belge de Statistique, d'Information et de Recherche Operationnelle (ISSN 0373-9597); (until 1971): Revue Belge de Statistique et de Recherche Operationnelle (ISSN 0373-9589)

004 US ISSN 1066-0380
BENCHMARKS. 1980. bi-m. free. University of North Texas, Computing Center, Box 13495, Denton, TX 76203-6495. TEL 817-565-2324. FAX 817-565-4060. E-mail: lynch@unt.edu. Ed. Claudia Lynch. bk.rev.; index. circ. 1,000. (back issues avail.) **Document type:** newsletter.
●Also available online.
Description: Provides timely information about topics of interest to the academic computing community at the university.

BERNARDS AND BABANI PRESS RADIO & ELECTRONICS & COMPUTER BOOKS. see COMMUNICATIONS — Radio

004 US ISSN 1061-9216
HC79.I55
BEYOND COMPUTING; integrating business & information technology. 1992. 9/yr. $39.50 (Canada $49.50; elsewhere $59.50) (free to qualified personnel) (effective 1997); newsstand price: $4.95. International Business Machines (IBM) Corporation, 590 Madison Ave., New York, NY 10022. TEL 212-745-6326. FAX 212-745-6058. (Subscr. to: Box 3014, Northbrook, IL 60065-9984. TEL 708-564-1385) Ed. Eileen Feretic; Pub. Arthur Chassen. R&P contact: Jocelyn Glover. TEL 212-745-6347. adv.: color page $14675; trim 8 x 10 1/2; adv. contact: Clifford Benjamin. circ. 150,000. **Document type:** trade publication.
—BLDSC (1947.294240); KR SourceOne.
Description: Dedicated to the business issues surrounding the management of information technology and is targeted at I T executives and top corporate management.

003 SP ISSN 0214-3844
BINARY.* 1988. 12/yr. Haymarket, S.A., Travesera Gracia 17-21, 5o 2o, 08022 Barcelona, Spain. TEL 3-237-22-66. FAX 1-237-66-88. TELEX 51964 INK E. circ. 14,000.

004 621.381 DK ISSN 0006-3835
QA76 CODEN: NBITAB
BIT; nordisk tidskrift for informationsbehandling. (Text in English) 1961. q. $180 (effective 1997). Scandinavian Computer Societies, Postbox 113, DK-1004 Copenhagen K, Denmark. TEL 45-33-12-50-33. FAX 45-33-12-23-42. Ed. Carl-Erik Froeberg. bk.rev.; bibl.; charts; illus.; index, cum.index: 1961-1973, 1980-1989. circ. 1,000. (back issues avail.) reprint service avail. from ISI,SWZ) **Indexed:** Compumath, Comput.Abstr., Comput.Cont., Comput.Rev., INSPEC (1984-), Math.R.
—BLDSC (2095.400000); AskIEEE; CISTI; Genuine Article; KR SourceOne; SWETS; UnCover.
Description: Concentrates on the design and analysis of algorithms, programming languages, computer systems and numerical as well as non-numerical computation.

001.6 621.381 NZ ISSN 0111-9826
BITS AND BYTES. 1982. m. NZ.$55. Industrial Press Ltd., P.O. Box 9870, Newmarket, Auckland, New Zealand. TEL 64-9-3793880. FAX 64-9-3793884. Ed. Mark Lim. R&P contact: Phil Ryan. adv. contact: Brett MacLeod. bk.rev.; software rev. circ. 69,000. **Document type:** trade publication.

BOOKS & PERIODICALS ONLINE. see BIBLIOGRAPHIES

COMPUTERS

BOTTOMLINE (AUSTIN). see BUSINESS AND ECONOMICS — Accounting

004   DK   ISSN 0909-3206
▼**BRICS NOTES SERIES**. 1995. irreg. free. Aarhus University, Brics, Department of Computer Science, Ny Munkgade, Bygning 530, DK-8000 Aarhus C, Denmark. E-mail: brics@daaimi.aau.dk; URL: http://www.brics.aau.dk/brics/. Ed. Uffe Henrik Engberg. **Document type**: academic/scholarly publication.

004   DK   ISSN 0909-0878
▼**BRICS REPORT SERIES**. 1995. irreg. free. Aarhus University, Brics, Department of Computers Sciences, Ny Munkgade, Bygning 530, DK-8000 Aarhus C, Denmark. E-mail: brics@daimi.aau.dk; URL: http://www.brics.aau.dk/brics/. Ed. Uffe Henrik Engberg. **Document type**: academic/scholarly publication.

001.6 621.381   US
BURTON GROUP NEWS ANALYSIS. 1989. s-m. price varies. Burton Group, Box 3448, Salt Lake City, UT 84110-3448. TEL 801-943-1966. FAX 801-943-2425. E-mail: info@tbg.com. Ed. Jamie Lewis; Pub. Judith Burton. cum.index: 1992-1994; circ. 2,000 (paid). (looseleaf format) **Document type**: newsletter.
●Also available online.
Also available on CD-ROM.
    Formerly: Clarke Buton News Analysis.
    Description: Analyzes significant events and products in the PC network industry.

001.6 621.381   US
BURTON GROUP REPORT. m. price varies. Burton Group, Box 3448, Salt Lake City, UT 84110-3448. TEL 801-943-1966. FAX 801-943-2425. E-mail: info@tbg.com. Ed. Jamie Lewis; Pub. Judith Burton. cum.index: 1992-1994; circ. 1,500 (paid). (also avail. in diskette format) **Document type**: newsletter.
●Also available online.
Also available on CD-ROM.
    Formerly: Clarke Burton Report (ISSN 1048-4620)
    Description: Contains in-depth technology analysis of LAN architecture issues.

001.6 621.381
371.394   US
C A C REPORT.* bi-m. $20. Computer Aids Corporation, Box 1646, Branson, MO 65616-1646. (also avail. in audio cassette)
    Description: Articles and commentary on a wide range of topics in the computer field.

001.6 621.381   US
C M G CONFERENCE PROCEEDINGS. 1976. a. $125 membership. Computer Measurement Group, Inc., 414 Plaza Dr., Ste. 209, Westmont, IL 60559. TEL 800-436-7264. URL: http://www.cng.org. (Subscr. to: Department 77-6023, Chicago, IL 60678-6023) **Indexed**: Comput.Lit.Ind. **Document type**: proceedings.

001.6 621.381   US
C M G TRANSACTIONS. 1985. s-a. $125 membership. Computer Measurement Group, Inc., 414 Plaza Dr., Ste. 209, Westmont, IL 60559. TEL 800-436-7264. URL: http://www.cmg.org. (Subscr. to: Department 77-6023, Chicago, IL 60678-6023) **Indexed**: Comput.Abstr. **Document type**: proceedings.

004   US
▼**C O O L DOCTOR - COMPUTING ONLINE DOCTOR**. 1996. w. Kissware Works!, E-mail: cool@kww.com; URL: http://www.kww.com/cool/. Ed. Robert Zee.
●Available only online.
    Description: Covers topics related to computer use, hardware, software, programming, Internet and web.
    Refereed Serial

001.6 621.381   US
C O P I PRESS. (Communicator of the Electronic Printing Industry) 1989. bi-m. free. Computer Output Printing, Inc., 4828 Loop Central Dr., Ste. 150, Houston, TX 77081. TEL 713-666-0911. FAX 713-666-0957. Ed. William H. Young II. circ. 11,000.

001.6 621.381   II   ISSN 0970-647X
C S I COMMUNICATIONS.* (Text in English) 1965. m. Rs.20($10) Computer Society of India, 122 TV Industrial Estate, S.K. Ahire Marg, Whorli, Bombay 400 025, India. Ed. S. Venkatesh. adv.; bk.rev. circ. 3,000. **Indexed**: INSPEC (1993-).
—BLDSC (3490.183000); AskIEEE; KR SourceOne.
    Formerly (until 1978): C S I Newsletter.

001.6   GW   ISSN 0724-8679
C T; Magazin fuer Computer Technik. 1983. m. DM.97.20 (foreign DM.106.80). Verlag Heinz Heise GmbH und Co. KG, Helstorferstr. 7, 30625 Hannover, Germany. TEL 49-511-5352-0. FAX 49-511-5352-129. TELEX 923173-HEISE-D. Ed. Christian Perssn. adv. contact: Udo Elsner. circ. 277,344 (paid). **Document type**: consumer publication.
—SWETS.

C T L R. (Computer and Telecommunications Law Review) see COMMUNICATIONS

C W I TRACTS. (Centrum voor Wiskunde en Informatica) see MATHEMATICS

001.6 621.381   US
CALIFORNIA COMPUTER NEWS. 1983. m. California Computer News, Inc., 9719 Lincoln Village Dr., Ste. 500, Sacramento, CA 95827. TEL 916-363-5000. FAX 916-363-5197. adv.: B&W page $1500, color page $2100; adv. contact: Craig Miller. circ. 51,000. **Document type**: consumer publication.
    Description: Covers local and regional computer-related topics, new hardware and software products and industry news.

621.381 001.6   UK   ISSN 0266-3236
CAMBRIDGE COMPUTER SCIENCE TEXTS. 1972. irreg., no.21, 1985. price varies. Cambridge University Press, Edinburgh Bldg., Shaftesbury Rd., Cambridge CB2 2RU, England. TEL 44-1223-312393. FAX 44-1223-315052. TELEX 851817256. E-mail: information@cup.cam.ac.uk; URL: http://www.cup.cam.ac.uk. (N. American addr.: Cambridge University Press, Journals Dept., 40 W. 20th St., New York, NY 10011. TEL 212-924-3900. FAX 212-691-3239) Ed.Bd. R&P contact: Linda Nicol. **Indexed**: Zent.Math. **Document type**: monographic series.

001.6 621.381   IS
CHADASHOT TIKSHORET NITUNIM. q. Binat Co., 8 Hanichoshet St., Ramat Hachayal, Tel Aviv 69 710, Israel. TEL 03-498811.

004   IT
IL CHI E' DELL'I C T. 1992. Lit.25000 (foreign Lit.50000) (effective 1997). Editrice il Grogiolo S.r.l., Piazza Sant Agostino 22, 20123 Milan, Italy. TEL 39-2-48009805. FAX 39-2-48009749. E-mail: ilchie__ict@betacom.it; URL: http://www.betacom.it/ilchie__ict. Ed. Rodolfo Grigolato. adv.: page Lit.3500000; adv. contact: Roberto Zuin. circ. 3,150 (paid); 5,850 (controlled). **Document type**: directory.

004
QA75.5   US   ISSN 1073-0486
▼**CHICAGO JOURNAL OF THEORETICAL COMPUTER SCIENCE**. 1995. irreg. (1 vol./yr., 15-20 articles per vol.). $30 to individuals; institutions $125 (effective 1997). M I T Press, 5 Cambridge Center, Cambridge, MA 02142-1493. TEL 617-253-2889. FAX 617-577-1545. E-mail: journals-orders@mit.edu; URL: http://www-mitpress.mit.edu/jnls-catalog/chicago.html. Ed. Janus Simon. R&P contact: Paul Dzus. adv. **Indexed**: ASCA, Compumath, Curr.Cont. **Document type**: academic/scholarly publication.
●Available only online.
—Genuine Article.
    Description: Publishes original scholarship on theoretical computer science, including the mathematical foundations of computing, database theory, logics of programming, complexity theory, and related issues. Published on an article by article basis.
    Refereed Serial

CHINA COMPUTERWORLD. see COMPUTERS — Electronic Data Processing

004   PL   ISSN 1230-817X
CHIP; magazyn komputerowy. 1993. m. 45 Zl. (with CD-ROM 96 Zl.); newsstand price: 4.50 Zl. Vogel Publishing Sp. z o.o., Plac Czerwony 1-3-5, 53-661 Wroclaw, Poland. TEL 48-71-734475. FAX 48-71-557361. E-mail: chip@chip.voleg.pl; URL: http://www.chip.pl, http://www.vogel.pl. Ed. Marek Zimnak; Pub. Jerzy Karwelis. adv.: color page 4600 Zl.; 210 x 297; adv. contact: Marcin Hutnik. bk.rev.; software rev.; circ. 75,000 (controlled). (back issues avail.) **Document type**: trade publication.
●Also available on CD-ROM.
    Description: Aims to inform readers about products, applications and novelties on the Polish and international computer markets.

004   KR
▼**CHIP**. (Text in Russian) 1996. m. newsstand price: DM.1.50. Soft-Press, P.O. Box 596-2, 254205 Kiev, Ukraine. TEL 38-44-2940289. FAX 38-44-2940375. E-mail: 101472.2433@compuserve.com. Ed. Alexey Efetov; Pub. Ellina Shnourko-Tabakova. adv.: B&W page DM.1275, color page DM.1500; 185 x 266; adv. contact: Valeriy Brossel. circ. 10,000. **Document type**: trade publication.
    Description: Provides readers with the latest and most crucial information on all aspects of computer technology.

004   RM
CHIP; Computer Magazin. 1991. m. Vogel Publishing Srl., B-dul Victoriei 6, 2200 Brasov, Rumania. TEL 40-68-150886. FAX 40-68-153108. E-mail: 102404.3600@compuserve.com. Ed. Dan Badescu. adv.: B&W page DM.1380, color page DM.1550; 185 x 266; adv. contact: Zsolt Bodola. circ. 13,500. **Document type**: trade publication.
    Description: Offers the latest news in the fields of computers and software.

004   TU   ISSN 1300-9419
▼**CHIP**. 1996. m. Vogel Publishing Ltd. Sti, Peker Sokak, Akyildiz Apt. No.26, Levent, Istanbul, Turkey. TEL 90-212-2834244. FAX 90-212-2695021. E-mail: chipyaz@chip.com.tr. Ed. Sakir Batumlu. adv.: color page DM.2815; 180 x 270; adv. contact: Melih Sahin. circ. 20,000. **Document type**: trade publication.
    Description: Contains information on the Turkish software and hardware markets for beginners and professionals.

004   XR   ISSN 1210-0684
CHIP. 1991. m. 528 Kc. (effective 1997); newsstand price: 49 Kc. Vydavatelstvi Vogel Publishing, Vaclavske Nam. 56, Postbox 146, 111 21 Prague 1, Czech Republic. TEL 42-2-24032796. FAX 42-2-24231146. E-mail: inovotny@chip.anet.cz. Ed. Milan Loucky; Pub. Ivan Novotny. adv.: B&W page DM.2991, color page DM.3739; 183 x 265; adv. contact: Zuzana Paulinova. circ. 30,500 (paid). **Document type**: trade publication.

004   GR
CHIP. 1994. fortn. newsstand price: Dr.1500. Computer Verlag S.A., 8 Dimokratias Str., Athens 151 27, Greece. TEL 30-1-8033670. FAX 30-1-8034049. E-mail: chip@netor.gr. Pub. Petros Triantafillis. adv.: B&W page DM.2950, color page DM.3280; 200 x 266; adv. contact: Vassilis Arvanitopoulos. circ. 32,000 (paid). **Document type**: trade publication.
    Description: Covers trends and important details within the field of information technology.

004   HU   ISSN 0864-9421
CHIP; computer magazine. 1989. m. 5914 Ft.; newsstand price: 616 Ft. Vogel Publishing Kft, Hajo u.42-44 2nd Fl., 1139 Budapest, Hungary. TEL 36-1-2523731. FAX 36-1-2523731. E-mail: 75162.2344@compuserve.com. Ed. Peter Ivanov; Pub. Peter Ivanov. adv.: B&W page DM.2108, color page DM.2519; 185 x 266; adv. contact: Gabriella Olah. software rev, tele.rev, video rev, illus, mkt, sta circ. 23,000. (back issues avail.) **Document type**: newspaper.
●Also available online.
Also available on CD-ROM.
    Description: Contains information for users playin a role in making decisions concerning information technology investments.

004   XR   ISSN 1211-1307
▼CHIP WEEK. 1995. w. 380 Kc.; newsstand price: 12 Kc. Vydavatelstvi Vogel Publishing, Vaclavske Nam. 56, Postbox 146, 111 21 Prague 1, Czech Republic. TEL 42-2-24032796. FAX 42-2-24231146. E-mail: inovotny@chip.anet.cz. Ed. Jana Pelikanova; Pub. Ivan Novotny. adv.: B&W page DM.2450, color page DM.3060; 185 x 268; adv. contact: Zuzana Paulinova. circ. 15,000 (paid). Document type: trade publication.
 Description: Contains up-to-date information on products, entrepreneurs, trends, tests, and tips in the computer business.

621.39   UK   ISSN 1364-4009
CITY UNIVERSITY. COMPUTER SCIENCE TECHNICAL REPORTS. 1996. irreg. City University, Department of Computer Science, Northampton Square, London EC1V 0HB, England.
 —BLDSC (8715.107000).

004.36   UK   ISSN 1358-6505
▼CLIENT - SERVER MAGAZINE. 1995. m. Reed Business Information (Subsidiary of: Reed Elsevier group), Quadrant House, The Quadrant, Sutton, Surrey SM2 5AS, England. TEL 44-181-652-4800. FAX 44-181-652-4748.

001.6 621.381   GW   ISSN 0178-8325
COGITO; das Online-Magazin fuer die Industrie. bi-m. free. Verlag Hoppenstedt GmbH, Havelstr. 9, 64295 Darmstadt, Germany. TEL 49-6151-380-0. FAX 49-6151-380-360. Ed. Stefan Graf. Document type: trade publication.
 —SWETS.

COGNITION AND COMPUTING. see PSYCHOLOGY

COLIN'S MAGAZINE. see LITERATURE

004   AU   ISSN 1011-5641
COM.* 1984. m. S.420. Erb Verlag GmbH, Eichenstr. 38, A-1120 Vienna, Austria. Ed. Helmut Hackl. adv.; bk.rev.; bibl.; charts; illus. circ. 20,000.
 —CISTI.

004   GW
COM-POST; Zeitung fuer Computerkommunikation. 1990. bi-m. free. Ralph Wuttke Verlag, Postfach 1746, 53757 St. Augustin, Germany. TEL 02241-332034. FAX 02241-341047. Ed. Ralph Wuttke. circ. 200,000. Document type: trade publication.
 Formerly: Komm-Post.

621.39   US
COMMODORE HACKIN. 1991. q. Brain Innovations, Inc., 10710 Bruhn Ave., Bennington, NE 68007. E-mail: j.brain@ieee.org; URL: http://www.jbrain.com/chacking/. Ed. Jim Brain.
 ●Available only online.
 Description: Targets enthusiasts of the early 6502 based machines with hardware, software, and current events articles.

621.381 001.6   US   ISSN 1063-6390
CODEN: DCSIDU
COMPCON: I E E E COMPUTER SOCIETY INTERNATIONAL CONFERENCE. Title varies: Digest of Papers (spring). 1971. a. price varies. (Institute of Electrical and Electronics Engineers, Inc.) I E E E Computer Society Press, 10662 Los Vaqueros Circle, Los Alamitos, CA 90720-1264. FAX 714-821-4641. Ed. Cat Harris; Pub. Matt Loeb. adv. contact: Frieda Koester. Indexed: Comput.Cont., Comput.Lit.Ind., INSPEC. Document type: proceedings.
 —BLDSC (3363.922000). CCC.
 Former titles (until 1971): I E E E International Computer Society Conference. Conference Digest; (until 1970): I E E E International Computer Group Conference. Proceedings; (until 1969): Computer Group Conference. Digest; (until 1967): I E E E Computer Conference. Digest.
 Description: Disseminates recent advances in key computing fields.

001.6 621.381   US
COMPEURO. PROCEEDINGS. 1987. a. price varies. (Institute of Electrical and Electronics Engineers, Inc.) I E E E Computer Society Press, 10662 Los Vaqueros Circle, Los Alamitos, CA 90720-1264. TEL 714-821-8380. FAX 714-821-4641. Ed. Cat Harris; Pub. Matt Loeb. adv. contact: Frieda Koester. Indexed: INSPEC. Document type: proceedings.
 Description: Discusses the latest in computer technology, systems, and applications.

001.6 621.381   US   ISSN 0824-7935
Q334   CODEN: COMIE6
COMPUTATIONAL INTELLIGENCE/INTELLIGENCE INFORMATIQUE. (Text mainly in English, occasionally in French) 1985. 4/yr. $129.50 to individuals (foreign $143.50); institutions $280 (foreign $304.50) (effective 1997). (National Research Council of Canada, CN) Blackwell Publishers, 238 Main St., Cambridge, MA 02142. E-mail: subscript@blackwellpub.com; URL: http://www.cisti.nrc.ca/. Eds. Nick Cercone, Gordon McCalla. adv.; abstr.; bibl.; illus. circ. 650. (back issues avail.) Indexed: A.I.Abstr., Abstr.Hum.Comp.Inter., Art.Int.Abstr., CAD CAM Abstr., Comput.Abstr., INSPEC (1992-). Document type: academic/scholarly publication.
 —BLDSC (3390.595000); AskIEEE; CISTI; Ei; Genuine Article; KR SourceOne; SWETS; UMI. CCC.
 Description: Serves as a forum for experimental and theoretical research, surveys, and impact studies. Coverage ranges from the tools and languages of AI to its philosophical implications.

001.6 621.381   IT
COMPUTER. 1979. d. L.360000. Systems Comunicazioni, Via Olanda, 6, 20083 Gaggiano (MI), Italy. TEL 02-90841814. FAX 02-90841682. Ed. Michele di Pisa. adv.; bk.rev. circ. 12,000.
 Indexed: A.S.& T.Ind., Compumath.

621.3 004   US   ISSN 0018-9162
TK7885.A1   CODEN: CPTRB4
COMPUTER (LOS ALAMITOS). 1966. m. $455 to non-members (effective 1996). (Institute of Electrical and Electronics Engineers, Inc.) I E E E Computer Society Press, 10662 Los Vaqueros Circle, Box 3014, Los Alamitos, CA 90720-1264. TEL 714-821-8380; 800-678-4333. FAX 714-821-4641. E-mail: customer.service@ieee.org; webmaster@computer.org; URL: http://www.computer.org/pubs/computer/computer.htm. Ed. Ed Parrish. adv.: B&W page $4900, color page $6000. bk.rev.; abstr.; bibl.; charts; illus.; stat. circ. 96,859. (also avail. in microfilm from EEE) Indexed: A.I.Abstr., A.S.& T.Ind., Abstr.Hum.Comp.Inter., Compumath, Comput.Cont., Comput.Dtbs., Comput.Lit.Ind., Comput.Rev., Curr.Cont., Cyb.Abstr., Deep Sea Res.& Oceanogr.Abstr., Ergon.Abstr., Ind.Sci.Rev., INSPEC (1971-), Int.Aerosp.Abstr., J.of Ferroc., Mgmt.& Market.Abstr., Oper.Res.Manage.Sci., Qual.Contr.Appl.Stat., Risk Abstr., Sci.Cit.Ind., Soft.Abstr.Eng., SSCI, Tel.Abstr. Document type: trade publication.
 ●Also available online.
 —BLDSC (3390.650000); AskIEEE; CISTI; Ei; Genuine Article; KR SourceOne; Linda Hall; SWETS; UMI; UnCover. CCC.
 Former titles (until 1970): I E E E Computer; I E E E Computer Group News (ISSN 0537-9229)
 Description: Feature articles and papers cover the entire range of hardware and software design and applications. Circulates automatically to members of the IEEE Computer Society.

004   US   ISSN 0883-4881
COMPUTER (SCOTTSDALE). Variant title: Orion Computer Blue Book. q. $104 per issue. Orion Research Corp., 14555 N. Scottsdale Rd., Ste. 330, Scottsdale, AZ 85254-3457. TEL 800-844-0759. FAX 800-375-1315. E-mail: orion@bluebook.com; URL: http://www.netzone.com/orion. (also avail. in diskette format) Document type: directory.
 Description: Provides information on pricing used computer equipment.

004   GW   ISSN 0343-2564
COMPUTER ADDRESS.* 1973. s-a. DM.24. (Deutsches Computer Forum) Computer Magazin Verlag GmbH, Herdweg 15, 7000 Stuttgart 1, Germany. Ed. B. Neuner.

001.6 621.381   GR
COMPUTER AGE. (Text in Greek) 1980. m. $60. Infopublica S A, 4 Kartali Street, 11528 Athens, Greece. Ed. Kostas Kataras. adv. circ. 5,000.

004   LE
AL COMPUTER AND ELECTRONICS. (Text in Arabic) 1984. m. $125. Dar Assayad S.A.L., P.O. Box 1038, Hazmieh, Lebanon, Lebanon. FAX 961-1-456373. (UK addr.: c/o Contact PR & Mgt. (UK) Ltd., 3 Park Pl., 12 Lawn Ln., London SW8, England. TEL 071-582-2220) Ed. Antoine Butros. adv. contact: Salim Zreik. circ. 22,400.

COMPUTER AND TELECOM NEWS. see COMMUNICATIONS

004   US
COMPUTER BOOK BYTES. m. Baker & Taylor, Inc., Information and Entertainment Services, Box 734, Somerville, NJ 08876. TEL 908-218-0400; 800-775-1800. FAX 908-218-3980.
 Description: Provides up-to-date information on computer book titles.

028.1 001.6
621.381   US   ISSN 0737-0334
QA75.5
COMPUTER BOOK REVIEW. 1983. 6/yr. $30. Computer Book Review, Box 61067, Honolulu, HI 96839. E-mail: char@pixi.com; URL: http://www.bookwire.com/cbr. Ed. Carlene Char. adv.; bk.rev. (back issues avail.) Indexed: Bk.Rev.Ind. (1984-), Child.Bk.Rev.Ind. (1984-), Leg.Info.Manage.Ind. Document type: newsletter.
 ●Also available online. Vendor(s): Knight-Ridder Information, Inc.
 —BLDSC (3393.732000).
 Description: For computer professionals, users, librarians, managers and information specialists. Offers critical reviews of computer-related books.

001.6 621.381   UK   ISSN 0010-4531
QA76   CODEN: COBUAH
THE COMPUTER BULLETIN. 1957; N.S. 1974; N.S. 1985. bi-m. £65 (foreign $105) (effective 1998). (British Computer Society) Oxford University Press, Academic Division, Great Clarendon St., Oxford OX2 6DP, England. TEL 44-1865-267907. FAX 44-1865-267485. TELEX 837330-OXPRES-G. E-mail: jnl.info@oup.co.uk; URL: http://www.oup.co.uk/journals. (U.S. subscr. to: Oxford University Press Inc., 2001 Evans Rd., Cary, NC 27513. TEL 800-852-7323. FAX 919-677-1714) Ed. T.F. Goodwin; Pub. Martin Richardson. R&P contact: Joolz Longley. adv. contact: Ian Jones. bk.rev.; illus. circ. 36,000. (also avail. in microfilm from UMI; back issues avail.) Indexed: Abstr.Hum.Comp.Inter., BMT, Comput.Cont., Comput.Lit.Ind., Educ.Tech.Abstr., INSPEC (1974-), Mgmt.& Market.Abstr., Tech.Educ.Abstr. Document type: academic/scholarly publication.
 —BLDSC (3393.745000); AskIEEE; CISTI; Ei; KR SourceOne; Linda Hall; SWETS; UMI; UnCover. CCC.
 Incorporates: Computer Newsletter (Cambridge) (ISSN 0266-4631)
 Description: Technical, commercial and academic papers on advanced programming, computer science theory, hardware and logic design, and business applications.

COMPUTER CHESS REPORTS. see SPORTS AND GAMES

COMPUTER CONTRACTS PRINCIPLES AND PRECEDENTS. see LAW

004   US
COMPUTER CORNER. w. E-mail: news8@wfaa.com; URL: http://www.wfaa.com/ccindex.html. Document type: bulletin.
 ●Available only online.
 Description: Weekly look at news from the digital domain.

001.6 621.381   US   ISSN 1044-1794
KF320.A9A142
COMPUTER COUNSEL;* the journal of law office productivity and automation. 1988. m. $130. Computer Counsel, Inc., Box 819, Avon, CT 06001-0819. TEL 312-207-6900. FAX 312-207-1045. Ed. Tom O'Connor. adv. circ. 1,200. Document type: newsletter.
 ●Also available online. Vendor(s): West Group.
 —KR SourceOne.
 Description: Helps lawyers, managing partners of law firms, and MIS directors decide what software and hardware to buy to automate their offices, and how to improve productivity.

COMPUTER CRIME LAW REPORTER. see CRIMINOLOGY AND LAW ENFORCEMENT

001.6 621.381   US
COMPUTER DIGEST.* 1986. m. $5. Clark Publishing Company, 3930 Knowles Ave., Ste. 305, Kensington, MD 20895-2428. TEL 703-525-7900. FAX 703-525-9749. Ed. Bob Dietsch. adv.: B&W page $1485. bk.rev. circ. 50,000.
 Formerly: Capital Computer Digest.

COMPUTER EXPO (YEAR): EXHIBITION GUIDE. see MEETINGS AND CONGRESSES

COMPUTERS

004 NE ISSN 0924-3607
COMPUTER EXPRESS. 1988. bi-m. fl.40. Personeelsvereniging van Computergrbruikers van he Ministerie van Financien, Postbus 832, 7301 BB Apeldoorn, Netherlands. TEL 31-55-5788584. FAX 31-45-5712705. E-mail: josm@cuci.nl. Ed. John Smits. circ. 5,300 (paid). **Document type:** consumer publication, newsletter.

621.381 SZ
COMPUTER FORUM. 12/yr. 75 SFr. (foreign 95 SFr.). Diagonal Verlags AG, Industriestr. 21, CH-5507 Mellingen, Switzerland. circ. 18,000. **Document type:** trade publication.

004.16 CN ISSN 1192-585X
COMPUTER FREELANCER; Canada's information magazine for computing professionals. 1993. 8/yr. Can.$28($28); newsstand price: Can.$3.95. Box 55239, 1800 Sheppard Ave. E., North York, ON M2J 5B9, Canada. TEL 416-493-6752. FAX 416-493-7093. E-mail: info@freelancer.com; URL: http://www.freelancer.com. Ed. Jayanti Parmar; Pub. Alan Arthur. adv. **Document type:** trade publication.
   Description: Offers independent computer professionals practical advice on sources for landing a job, technical issues, contracts, the Internet and other areas.

004 GR ISSN 1105-5464
COMPUTER GIA OLOUS/COMPUTER FOR EVERYBODY. 1983. m. Dr.22000 in Europe; Dr.24000 in U.S. (effective 1996). Compupress S.A., 44 Syngrou, 117 42 Athens, Greece. TEL 30-1-9238-672. FAX 30-1-9216-847. Ed. George Christopoulos. adv.; bk.rev. circ. 25,000. (back issues avail.)
   Description: Business systems magazine covering developments and trends in the computer marketplace.

001.6 621.381 PH ISSN 0115-8686
COMPUTER ISSUES. (Text in English) 1983. s-a. P.60($4.40) (De La Salle University, College of Computer Studies) De La Salle University Press, 2401 Taft Ave., Manila, Philippines. TEL 2-59-48-32. bk.rev. circ. 300. **Document type:** academic/scholarly publication.
   Description: Presents scholarly articles reflecting significant quantitative or qualitative research. Includes speeches, research reports, and "state of the art" papers.

004 UK ISSN 0010-4620
QA76 CODEN: CMPJA6
THE COMPUTER JOURNAL. 1958. 8/yr. £350 (foreign $620) (effective 1998). (British Computer Society) Oxford University Press, Academic Division, Great Clarendon St., Oxford OX2 6DP, England. TEL 44-1865-267907. FAX 44-1865-267485. TELEX 837330-OXPRES-G. E-mail: jnl.info@oup.co.uk; URL: http://www.oup.co.uk/journals. (U.S. subscr. to: Oxford University Press Inc., 2001 Evans Rd., Cary, NC 27513. TEL 800-852-7323. FAX 919-677-1714) Ed. Keith Van Rijsbergen; Pub. Martin Richardson. R&P contact: Joolz Longley. adv. contact: Ian Jones. bk.rev.; illus.; index. circ. 10,000. (also avail. in microfiche from UMI,KTO; back issues avail.) **Indexed:** A.S.& T.Ind., Abstr.Hum.Comp.Inter., Account.& Data Proc.Abstr., Bk.Rev.Ind. (1984-1989), BMT, Br.Tech.Ind., Chem.Abstr., Compumath, Comput.Abstr., Comput.Cont., Comput.Lit.Ind., Comput.Rev., Cont.Pg.Manage., Curr.Cont., Cyb.Abstr., Educ.Tech.Abstr., Eng.Ind., Ergon.Abstr., Excerp.Med., INSPEC (1968-), Math.R., Mgmt.& Market.Abstr., Sci.Cit.Ind., SSCI, Zent.Math. **Document type:** academic/scholarly publication.
   ●Also available online.
   —BLDSC (3394.060000); AskIEEE; CISTI; Ei; Genuine Article; KR SourceOne; Linda Hall; SWETS; UMI; UnCover. **CCC.**

001.6 621.381 US ISSN 0748-9331
THE COMPUTER JOURNAL (LINCOLN). Short title: T C J. 1982. bi-m. $24 (Canada and Mexico $32; elsewhere $34). Box 3900, Citrus Heights, CA 95611-3900. TEL 916-645-1670; 800-424-8825. FAX 916-722-7480. E-mail: tcj@psyber.com; URL: http://www.psyber.com/~tcj/. Ed. Dave Baldwin; Pub. Bill Kibler. R&P contact: Dave Baldwin. adv. (back issues avail.) **Indexed:** A.S.& T.Ind.
   Description: Informs users of older Kaypro, ZCPR, S-100, PC-XT, and CoCo computers of ways to keep their machines running and improve their performance; alerts them of news and developments.

004.026 343.04 US ISSN 0361-7203
KF1890.C6
COMPUTER LAW & TAX REPORT; monthly newsletter covering computer-related law and tax issues. 1974. m. $297 (foreign $390). Roditti Reports Corp., Box 2066, New York, NY 10021. TEL 212-879-3325. FAX 212-879-4496. Ed. Esther Roditti; Pub. Esther Roditti. R&P contact: Ruth K. Darqis. bk.rev.; index. circ. 750. (looseleaf format; also avail. in microfiche from WSH) **Indexed:** Comput.Cont., Comput.Lit.Ind. **Document type:** newsletter.
   —CCC.
   Description: Features analyses of domestic and international computer law developments. Covers a wide range of legal and regulatory topics applicable to the computer industry, including software contracts, copyright, patent, trade secret protection, and federal and state taxes. Includes full citations.

004 340 US ISSN 0741-8809
KF390.5.C6
COMPUTER LAW MONITOR. 1982. q. $59.50 ($125 with reference casebook). Research Publications, Inc. (Asheville), 92 Fairway Dr., Asheville, NC 28805. TEL 704-298-8291. (Subscr to: Box 9267, Asheville, NC 28815) Ed. Julia P. Hardin. index; circ. 450 (paid). (looseleaf format; back issues avail.) **Indexed:** Comput.Lit.Ind. **Document type:** newsletter.
   Description: Reports and comments on selected court cases involving computers, electronic data or voice processing, telecommunications and information systems.

001.6 621.381 340 US ISSN 0739-7771
KF390.5.C6
COMPUTER LAW REPORTER; a monthly journal of computer law and practice, intellectual property, copyright and trademark law. 1983. m. $1550. Computer Law Reporter, Inc., 1601 Connecticut Ave., N.W., Ste. 602, Washington, DC 20009. TEL 202-462-5755. FAX 202-328-2430. Ed. John Noble. bk.rev.; index. circ. 200. (looseleaf format; back issues avail.) **Indexed:** Comput.Lit.Ind. **Document type:** newsletter.

004 340 NE ISSN 0927-0124
COMPUTER LAW SERIES. 1988. irreg., no.11, 1993. price varies. Kluwer Law International (Subsidiary of: Wolters Kluwer N.V.), Postbus 85889, 2508 CN The Hague, Netherlands. TEL 31-70-3081500. FAX 31-70-3081515. (Dist. by: Libresso Distribution Centre, P.O. Box 23, 7400 GA Deventer, Netherlands. TEL 31-570-633155. FAX 31-570-633834; In N. America: Kluwer Law International, 675 Massachusetts Ave., Cambridge, MA 02139. TEL 617-354-0140. FAX 617-354-8595) Eds. H.W.K. Kaspersen, A. Oskamp. **Document type:** monographic series.
   —BLDSC (3394.075830).
   Description: Deals with topical aspects of the interaction between information technology, telecommunications, technology and the law.

COMPUTER LAW STRATEGIST. see *LAW*

343.73 004 340 US ISSN 0742-1192
KF390.5.C6 CODEN: COLAEB
COMPUTER LAWYER. 1984. m. $374. Aspen Law & Business (Subsidiary of: Wolters Kluwer N.V.), 270 Sylvan Ave., Englewood Cliffs, NJ 07632-2513. TEL 800-223-0231. FAX 201-894-8666. Ed. Blanc Williams Johnston; Pub. Rick Kravitz. adv.; bk.rev. (also avail. in microfiche from WSH; back issues avail.) **Indexed:** Comput.Lit.Ind., L.R.I., Leg.Per. **Document type:** newsletter.
   ●Also available online. Vendor(s): Lexis-Nexis, West Group.
   —BLDSC (3394.075870); KR SourceOne; UnCover. **CCC.**
   Description: Aimed at lawyers working in the computer industry. Regularly discusses international developments in proprietary rights, finance, personnel issues, computer acquisitions, contracts and antitrust law.

001.6 621.381 TS
AL-COMPUTER LIL-MUBTADDI'IN/COMPUTER FOR BEGINNERS. (Text in Arabic) 1986. irreg. Dubai Educational Region - Mintaqat Dubai al-Ta'limiyyah, P.O. Box 3962, Dubai, United Arab Emirates. TEL 691405. Ed. Hamad Ahmed al-Shaibani. circ. 1,500.
   Description: Information to help new computer users, especially students.

001.6 621.381 GW ISSN 0937-9266
COMPUTER LIVE; aktuell - vielseitig - verstaendlich. 1983. m. DM.71.40 (foreign DM.85.80). Markt und Technik Verlag AG, Hans-Pinsel-Str. 2, 85540 Haar, Germany. TEL 089-4613-0. FAX 089-4613-775. **Document type:** consumer publication.
   Formerly (until 1990): Happy Computer (ISSN 0177-3658)

001.64 GW
COMPUTER MAGAZIN. 1972. m. DM.90. Basten Verlag, Ebertstr. 30, 52134 Herzogenrath, Germany. TEL 02407-5003. FAX 02407-8902. Ed. Kurt Emonts. adv.; bibl.; charts; illus. **Indexed:** PROMT.

001.6 CN ISSN 1187-5259
COMPUTER PAPER (ALBERTA EDITION); Canada's computer information source. 1988. m. Can.$24.95($60) Canada Computer Paper Inc., 3661 W. 4th Ave., Ste. 8, Vancouver, BC V6R 1P2, Canada. TEL 604-733-5596. FAX 604-732-4280. Ed. Douglas Alder. adv.: B&W page Can.$5691; color page Can.$8291; trim 10 1/4 x 12 5/8; adv contact: Hari Singh Khalsa.

004 CN ISSN 0840-3929
COMPUTER PAPER (B C EDITION); Canada's computer information source. 1988. m. Can.$24.95($60) (effective Jan. 1991). Canada Computer Paper Inc., 3661 W. 4th Ave., Ste. 8, Vancouver, BC V6R 1P2, Canada. TEL 604-733-5596. FAX 604-732-4280. Ed. Douglas Alder. adv.: B&W page Can.$5691; color page Can.$8291; trim 10 1/4 x 12 5/8; adv contact: Hari Singh Khalsa. circ. 235,000. **Document type:** newspaper.
   Description: For IBM, Macintosh, Atari, Amiga and Unix end users. Offers news, features and reviews.

001.6 CN ISSN 1196-0590
COMPUTER PAPER (MANITOBA EDITION); Canada's computer information source. 1988. m. Can.$24.95($60) Canada Computer Paper Inc., 3661 W. 4th Ave., Ste. 8, Vancouver, BC V6R 1P2 Canada. TEL 604-733-5596. FAX 604-732-4280 Ed. Douglas Alder. adv.: B&W page Can.$5691; color page Can.$8291; trim 10 1/4 x 12 5/8; adv contact: Hari Singh Khalsa.

001.6 CN ISSN 1195-3454
COMPUTER PAPER (ONTARIO EDITION). m. Can.$24.95($60) Canada Computer Paper Inc., 3661 W. 4th Ave., Ste. 8, Vancouver, BC V6R 1P2 Canada. TEL 604-733-5596. FAX 604-732-4280 Ed. Douglas Alder. adv.: B&W page Can.$5691; color page Can.$8291; trim 10 1/4 x 12 5/8; adv contact: Hari Singh Khalsa.

001.6　　　　　US　　ISSN 0899-126X
COMPUTER PROTOCOLS. 1988. m. $150 (outside N. America $165). Worldwide Videotex, Box 3273, Boynton Beach, FL 33424-3273. TEL 407-738-2276. Ed. Mark Wright; Pub. Mark Wright. bk.rev. **Document type:** newsletter.
●Also available online. Vendor(s): Data-Star, Information Access Co., Knight-Ridder Information, Inc., NewsNet (EC74).
　Description: Contains news and information about computer protocols and their related products, including LANs, gateways, and bridges.

001.64　　　　JA　　ISSN 0385-6658
COMPUTER REPORT/KONPYUTA REPOTO. (Text in Japanese) 1959. m. 8000 Yen. Japan Management Science Institute - Nihon Keiei Kagaku Kenkyujo, 4-18-3-3091 Minami-Aoyama, Minato-ku, Tokyo 107, Japan. Ed. Kotoshi Fujimi. **Indexed:** JCT, JTA.

621.3　　　　　US　　ISSN 1089-3350
▼**COMPUTER SCIENCE & ELECTRICAL ENGINEERING PROGRAMS.** 1997. a. $24.95. Peterson's, 202 Carnegie Center, Box 2123, Princeton, NJ 08543-2123. TEL 609-243-9111. FAX 609-243-9150. URL: http://www.petersons.com. Ed. Barbara Lawrence. **Document type:** directory.
　Description: Profiles of some 900 graduate computer science and electrical engineering programs in the U.S. and Canada.

001.6 510　　　　　US
COMPUTER SCIENCE AND SCIENTIFIC COMPUTING. 1971. irreg., latest 1997. Academic Press, Inc., 525 B St., Ste. 1900, San Diego, CA 92101-4495. TEL 619-231-0926. FAX 619-699-6715. (Subscr. to: Order Dept., 6277 Sea Harbor Dr., 4th Fl., Orlando, FL 32887. TEL 800-321-5068) Eds. Werner Reinboldt, Daniel Siewiorek. (reprint service avail. from ISI) **Indexed:** Math.R.
　Formerly: Computer Science and Applied Mathematics.

001.6 621.381　　US　　ISSN 0899-3408
COMPUTER SCIENCE EDUCATION. 1988. 2/yr. $37.50 to individuals; institutions $80 (effective 1997). Ablex Publishing Corporation, Box 5297, Greenwich, CT 06831-0504. TEL 203-661-7602. FAX 203-661-0792. Ed. Keith Barker. index. circ. 300. **Indexed:** Cont.Pg.Educ., Educ.Ind. **Document type:** academic/scholarly publication.
　—BLDSC (3394.270170); AskIEEE; KR SourceOne; SWETS. **CCC.**
　Description: Covers computer science education at college and university levels.

001.6 621.381　　US
COMPUTER SCIENCE TECHNICAL REPORT ANTHOLOGY. 1981. a. $7. University of Maryland, Department of Computer Science, College Park, MD 20742. TEL 301-405-2745. Ed. Betty Kellogg. bibl.; index, cum.index: 1963-1991. circ. 250. (also avail. in microfiche; back issues avail.)

004.05　　　　UK　　ISSN 1361-4339
COMPUTER SERVICES AND SOFTWARE ASSOCIATION. REFERENCE BOOK AND BUYERS' GUIDE. 1985. a. £65. Sterling Publications Ltd., 86-88 Edgware Rd., London W2 2YW, England. TEL 44-171-915-9600. FAX 44-171-915-9619. R&P contact: Sandy Tucker. circ. 6,000. **Document type:** trade publication.
　—BLDSC (6242.532000).
　Formerly (until 1995): Computing Services Association. Official Reference Book (ISSN 0266-7916)

COMPUTER SHOPPER; the computer magazine for direct buyers. see COMPUTERS — Computer Sales

621.381　　　　　SZ　　ISSN 1017-3803
COMPUTER SPECTRUM; the high tech magazine. (Text in German) bi-m. 98 SFr. c/o Oskar Baldinger, Ed. & Pub., Aarestr. 83, CH-5222 Umiken, Switzerland. TEL 41-56-4410043. FAX 41-56-4414854. adv.; bk.rev.; illus. circ. 11,000. **Document type:** trade publication.

003　　　　　NE　　ISSN 0920-5489
QA76.9.S8　　　　CODEN: CSTIEZ
COMPUTER STANDARDS AND INTERFACES; the international journal devoted to computer standards, their implementation and utilization. (Text in English) 1982. 7/yr. fl.1079($620) (effective 1998). Elsevier Science B.V., P.O. Box 211, 1000 AE Amsterdam, Netherlands. TEL 31-20-4853911. FAX 31-20-4853598. TELEX 18582 ESPA NL. E-mail: nlinfo-f@elsevier.nl; usinfo-f@elsevier.com; forinfo-kyf04035@niftyserve.or.jp; URL: http://www.elsevier.nl/. (Subscr. in the Americas to: Elsevier Science, Regional Sales Office, Box 945, New York, NY 10159-0945. TEL 212-633-3730. FAX 212-633-3680; Subscr. in Australasia and the Far East to: Elsevier Science (Singapore) Pte Ltd, No.1 Temasek Ave., No.17-01 Millenia Tower, Singapore 039192, Singapore. TEL 65-434-3727. FAX 65-337-2230; Subscr. in Japan to: Elsevier Science Japan, 9-15 Higashi-Azabu 1-chome, Minato-ku, Tokyo 106, Japan. TEL 81-3-5561-5033. FAX 81-3-5561-5047) Eds. John L. Berg, Harald Schumny. (also avail. in microform from UMI) **Indexed:** A.I.Abstr., ASCA, BMT, CAD CAM Abstr., Compumath, Comput.Abstr., Comput.Cont., Comput.Lit.Ind., INSPEC. **Document type:** academic/scholarly publication.
　—BLDSC (3394.276800); AskIEEE; CISTI; Ei; Genuine Article; KR SourceOne; Linda Hall; SWETS; UnCover. **CCC.**
　Formed by the 1986 merger of: Computers and Standards (ISSN 0167-8051); Interfaces in Computing (ISSN 0252-7308)
　Description: Provides information about the impact of international and national computer standards on technology, economics and trade.
　Refereed Serial

COMPUTER SUPPORTED COOPERATIVE WORK; an international journal. see SOCIAL SCIENCES: COMPREHENSIVE WORKS

004 621.39　　　　SW　　ISSN 0280-9982
COMPUTER SWEDEN. (Supplement avail.: Computer Sweden Extra) (Text in Swedish) 1980. 45/yr. SEK 545. C.W. Communications AB, S. Hamnv. 22, 115 41 Stockholm, Sweden. Ed. Bengt Marnfeldt. adv. circ. 17,000.
　—UMI.
　Formerly (until 1983): NovaGram.
　Description: Covers computer systems and related products, aimed at larger and middle size companies.

001.6 621.381　　　US　　ISSN 0278-9647
TK7885.A1
COMPUTER TECHNOLOGY REVIEW; the technologies for systems integrators - VAR's - OEM's. 1981. 16/yr. $150. West World Productions, Inc., 420 N. Camden Dr., Beverly Hills, CA 90210-4507. TEL 310-777-6670. Ed. George McNamara; Pub. Yuri Spiro. adv.; bk.rev.; tr.lit. circ. 70,000. (reprint service avail. from UMI) **Indexed:** ABI Inform, CAD CAM Abstr., Comput.Lit.Ind., Graph.Arts Lit.Abstr., Tel.Abstr. **Document type:** newsletter.
　●Also available online. Vendor(s): UMI.
　—BLDSC (3394.305000); CISTI; Ei; Linda Hall; UMI. **CCC.**
　Description: For systems, hardware and software systems integrators, OEMs, and engineering and corporate managers. Provides information on designing and utilizing computer-based systems.

001.6 621.38 340　　GW　　ISSN 0179-1990
KK164.C66　　　　CODEN: CRECE3
COMPUTER UND RECHT; Forum fuer die Praxis des Rechts der Datenverarbeitung, Kommunikation und Automation. 1986. m. DM.428 (effective 1997). (Graefe und Partner Verlagsgesellschaft mbH) Verlag Dr. Otto Schmidt KG, Unter den Ulmen 96-98, 50968 Cologne, Germany. TEL 49-221-9373801. FAX 49-221-93738943. E-mail: dr.otto.schmidt@t-online.de. index. circ. 1,900. **Indexed:** ELLIS, IBR. **Document type:** trade publication.
　—BLDSC (3394.335000); AskIEEE; KR SourceOne; SWETS. **CCC.**

004 375　　　　GW　　ISSN 0941-519X
COMPUTER UND UNTERRICHT. 1991. q. DM.92.60 (foreign DM.96.60). Erhard Friedrich Verlag GmbH, Im Brande 17, 30926 Seelze, Germany. TEL 49-511-40004-0. FAX 49-511-40004170. **Document type:** academic/scholarly publication.

001.6　　　　　IE
COMPUTER UPDATE. bi-m. 128 Lower Baggot St., Dublin 2, Ireland. TEL 619236. FAX 612417. Ed. John Low. circ. 6,000.

004　　　　　US　　ISSN 0742-5902
COMPUTER USER (MINNEAPOLIS). 1982. m. $24.95. M S P Communications, 220 S. 6th St., Ste. 500, Minneapolis, MN 55405. TEL 612-339-7571. FAX 612-339-5806. Ed. Steve Deyo. adv. contact: Michele Wachter. bk.rev. circ. 50,000. (tabloid format; back issues avail.) **Indexed:** Comput.Cont. —KR SourceOne.
　Formerly: Twin Cities Computer User.
　Description: Business-oriented microcomputer magazine for professionals in the Twin Cities and other metropolitan areas.

338.4 621.381　　　AT
COMPUTER WEEK. 1971. w. $85. Peter Isaacson Publications Pty. Ltd., 46-50 Porter St., Prahran, Vic. 3181, Australia. TEL 61-3-2457777. FAX 61-3-2457840. circ. 8,263. (reprint service avail. from UMI) **Indexed:** Comput.Cont.
　Former titles: Pacific Computer Weekly (ISSN 0817-6213) & Australian Computer Weekly (ISSN 0310-5865)

621.381 004　　UK　　ISSN 0010-4787
　　　　　　　　CODEN: COMWAA
COMPUTER WEEKLY. (Supplement avail.) 1966. w. £92.50 (overseas £129). Reed Business Information (Subsidiary of: Reed Elsevier group), Quadrant House, The Quadrant, Sutton, Surrey SM2 5AS, England. TEL 44-181-661-8642. FAX 44-181-661-8979. Ed. H. Sturridge. adv.; bk.rev. circ. 105,000. (also avail. in microform from UMI) **Indexed:** Account.& Data Proc.Abstr., Comput.Cont., Comput.Dtbs., Educ.Tech.Abstr., High.Educ.Curr.Aware.Bull., Info.Media & Tech., INSPEC (1972-1992), PROMT. **Document type:** trade publication.
　●Also available online. Vendor(s): Information Access Co.
　—BLDSC (3394.360000); CISTI; SWETS; UMI. **CCC.**
　Description: For information technology professionals, industry analysts, OEMs, value-added resellers, and end users of micro-, mini-, and mainframe computers. Covers industry developments, new product announcements, and company profiles.

621.39　　　　　PL　　ISSN 0867-2334
COMPUTER WORLD. 1990. w. $336 (effective 1998). I D G Poland S.A., P.O. Box 73, 04-228 Warsaw. TEL 48-22-152045. FAX 48-22-154495. (Dist. by: Mezhdunarodnaya Kniga, B. Yakimanka 39, 117049 Moscow, Russia. TEL 7-095-2384967. FAX 7-095-2384634) Ed. Janusz Kotarski. adv. circ. 20,000.

001.64 621.381　　GW　　ISSN 0341-5406
COMPUTER ZEITUNG. 1970. w. DM.223.60 (foreign DM.265.20) (effective 1997). Konradin Verlag Robert Kohlhammer GmbH, Ernst-Mey-Str. 8, 70771 Leinfelden-Echterdingen, Germany. TEL 49-711-7594-0. FAX 49-711-7594-390. Ed. Peter Welchering. adv.: B&W page DM.13700; trim 295 x 420; adv. contact: Dietmar Buettner. circ. 40,128. (back issues avail.) **Document type:** newspaper, trade publication.
　—SWETS. **CCC.**
　Description: Features systems, software, hardware, graphic systems, applications, marketing, techniques, and management information for professionals in the computer industry. Includes listing of positions.

001.64 621.381　　　US
COMPUTEREPORT. 1972. m. free. Virginia Commonwealth University, Academic Computing, 1015 Floyd Ave., Box 174, Richmond, VA 23284. TEL 804-786-4719. Ed. R.W. Duvall. circ. controlled.

COMPUTERS

001.6 621.381 UK ISSN 0268-716X
COMPUTERGRAM INTERNATIONAL; the daily newspaper for data processing, communications, and microelectronics professionals and investors. d. (Mon.-Fri.). $995. A P T Data Group plc., 12 Sutton Row, 4th Fl., London W1V 5FH, England. TEL 44-171-208-4200. FAX 44-171-439-1105. (US subscr. to: APT Data Services Inc., 828 Broadway, Ste. 800, New York, NY 10010. TEL 212-677-0409. FAX 212-677-0463) Ed. Tim Palmer. **Document type:** newspaper, trade publication.
●Also available online. Vendor(s): Information Access Co., NewsNet (EC72).
—BLDSC (3394.470000).

004 340 NE ISSN 0771-7784
COMPUTERRECHT; tijdschrift voor informatica en recht. French edition: Droit de l'Informatique et des Telecoms (ISSN 0991-2738) 1984. bi-m. fl.217.50 (effective 1996). Uitgeverij Kluwer B.V., Postbus 23, 7400 GA Deventer, Netherlands. TEL 31-570-647111. FAX 31-570-631419.
—SWETS.

004 384 UK
COMPUTERS AND COMMUNICATIONS IN AFRICA; the independent news magazine the African computer community. 1987. 10/yr. £30($45) (for 2 yrs.). A I T E C Exhibitions and Conferences, P.O. Box 18128, Nairobi, Kenya. (In South Africa: AITEC, P.O. Box 2802, Cresta 2118, Johannesburg, South Africa) Ed. Alan Dickinson. adv.: B&W page £1090, color page £1590; trim 297 x 210; adv. contact: Martin Williams. bk.rev.; stat. circ. 15,000. **Document type:** trade publication.
Formerly: Computers in Africa (ISSN 0953-3257)
Description: Covers all aspects of computing, including hardware, software, LAN development, Macintosh, computer fairs, international news and analysis of the developing computer infrastructure in specific African countries.

004 384 UK
COMPUTERS AND COMMUNICATIONS IN AFRICA YEARBOOK;* yearbook of I.T. capability throughout the continent. (Text in English; summaries in French) 1993. a. £10($15) A I T E C Exhibitions and Conferences, P.O. Box 18128, Nairobi, Kenya. Ed.Bd. adv. contact: Martin Williams. circ. 10,000. **Document type:** directory.
Description: Lists computer and communications vendors throughout Africa.

001.6 621.381
651.2 US
COMPUTERS & OFFICE EQUIPMENT: LATIN AMERICAN INDUSTRIAL REPORT. (Editions for each of 22 Latin American countries) 1985. a. $435 per country report. Aquino Productions, Box 125, Rochester, VT 05767.

003 658 UK ISSN 0305-0548
T57.6.A1 CODEN: CMORAP
COMPUTERS & OPERATIONS RESEARCH; and their application to problems of world concern. 1974. m. fl.2414($1387) (effective 1998). Elsevier Science Ltd., Pergamon, P.O. Box 800, Kidlington, Oxford OX5 1DX, England. TEL 44-1865-843000. FAX 44-1865-843010. E-mail: nlinfo-f@elsevier.nl; usinfo-f@elsevier.com; forinfo-kyf04035@niftyserve.or.jp; URL: http://www.elsevier.nl/. (Subscr. to: Elsevier Science, Regional Sales Office, P.O. Box 211, 1000 AE Amsterdam, Netherlands. TEL 31-20-4853757. FAX 31-20-4853432; Subscr. in the Americas to: Elsevier Science, Regional Sales Office, Box 945, New York, NY 10159-0945. TEL 212-633-3730. FAX 212-633-3680; Subscr. in Australasia and the Far East to: Elsevier Science (Singapore) Pte Ltd, No.1 Temasek Ave., No.17-01 Millenia Tower, Singapore 039192, Singapore. TEL 65-434-3727. FAX 65-337-2230) Ed. Samuel J. Raff. adv.; bk.rev.; charts; illus. circ. 1,000. (also avail. in microfilm from UMI) **Indexed:** ABI Inform., ASCA, Biol.Abstr., BPIA, Bus.Ind., Compumath, Comput.Cont., Comput.Dtbs., Curr.Cont., Cyb.Abstr., Excerp.Med., Fuel & Energy Abstr., INSPEC, Int.Abstr.Oper.Res., Intl.Civil Eng.Abstr., Manage.Cont., Math.R., Oper.Res.Manage.Sci., Qual.Contr.Appl.Stat., Sel.Water Res.Abstr., Soft.Abstr.Eng., SSCI, Tr.& Indus.Ind., Zent.Math. **Document type:** academic/scholarly publication.
—BLDSC (3394.770000); AskIEEE; CISTI; Ei; Genuine Article; KR SourceOne; Linda Hall; SWETS; UMI; UnCover. **CCC.**
Description: For researchers, teachers and practitioners. Provides international papers on the methodology used for determining solutions to problems using computers.
Refereed Serial

004 150 US
COMPUTERS AND PEOPLE SERIES. 1980. irreg., latest 1996. Academic Press, Inc., 525 B St., Ste. 1900, San Diego, CA 92101-4495. TEL 619-231-0926. FAX 619-699-6715. (Subscr. to: Order Dept., 6277 Sea Harbor Dr., 4th Fl., Orlando, FL 32887. TEL 800-321-5068) Ed. B. Gaines. (reprint service avail. from ISI) **Document type:** monographic series.

004 US
COMPUTERS, COGNITION AND WORK. irreg. Lawrence Erlbaum Associates, Inc., 10 Industrial Ave., Mahwah, NJ 07430-2262. TEL 201-236-9500; 800-926-6579. E-mail: orders@erlbaum.com; URL: http://www.erlbaum.com. Ed.Bd. **Document type:** monographic series.

001.6 621.381 II ISSN 0970-0129
COMPUTERS TODAY. (Text in English) 1985. m. Rs.144. Living Media India Pvt. Ltd., F-26 Connaught Place, New Delhi 110001, India. TEL 011-3315801. FAX 011-3316180. TELEX 31-61245 INTO IN. Ed. J.S. Raju. adv.: B&W page Rs.15000, color page Rs.24000; trim 197 x 273. circ. 18,000.

004 SA ISSN 0254-2188
COMPUTERWEEK. (Text in English) 1978. w. R.139.65. Systems Publishers (Pty) Ltd., P.O. Box 41345, Craighall 2024, South Africa. TEL 27-11-789-1808. FAX 27-11-789-4725. TELEX 4-24952. Ed. Frank Heydenrych. adv.; bk.rev.; illus. circ. 12,515. (tabloid format) **Indexed:** Comput.Cont. **Document type:** newspaper.
—CISTI.

004 GW ISSN 0170-5121
HD9696.C6
COMPUTERWOCHE. (Supplements avail.: Extra (ISSN 0935-1310); Focus (ISSN 0935-1329)) 1974. w. DM.406. Computerwoche Verlag GmbH, Brabanterstr. 4, 80805 Munich, Germany. TEL 49-89-36086-299. FAX 49-89-36086325. TELEX 5215250-COMW-D. Ed. Christoph Witte; Pub. Dieter Eckbauer. R&P contact: Karin Griffhorn. adv.: B&W page DM.28300, color page DM.33700; trim 280 x 381; adv. contact: Gabrielle Heilmann. circ. 48,956. **Indexed:** PROMT. **Document type:** newspaper.
—SWETS; UMI.
Description: Presents information about information processing, internetworking and client-server computing in the corporate environment. Aimed at IT managers, software specialists and communications professionals.

004 US ISSN 0010-4841
QA76 CODEN: CMPWAB
COMPUTERWORLD; newsweekly for information technology leaders. 1967. w. $48 (Canada $110; Mexico & S. America $150; elsewhere $295) (effective 1998). Computerworld, Inc. (Subsidiary of: I D G Communications, Inc.), 551 Old Connecticut Path, Box 9171, Framingham, MA 01701-9171. TEL 508-879-0700; 800-669-1002. FAX 508-875-8931. (Subscr. to: Box 2043, Marion, OH 43305-2043. TEL 614-382-3322) Ed. Paul Gillin; Pub. Kevin McPherson. adv. contact: Dave Peterson. bk.rev.; bibl.; charts; illus.; mkt.; pat.; stat.; circ. 147,000 (paid). (tabloid format; also avail. in microform from UMI; back issues avail.; reprint service avail. from UMI) **Indexed:** A.I.Abstr., ABI Inform, B.P.I., Bus.Comput.Ind., Bus.Ind., CAD CAM Abstr., Comput.Cont., Comput.Dtbs., Comput.Indus.Up., Comput.Lit.Ind., INSPEC, Microcomp.Ind., Microcomp.Indus.Up., PROMT, Resour.Ctr.Ind., Tel.Abstr., Tel.Alert. **Document type:** newspaper, trade publication.
●Also available online. Vendor(s): Knight-Ridder Information, Inc. (File no.674), Lexis-Nexis.
—BLDSC (3394.980000); CASDDS; CISTI; KR SourceOne; SWETS; UMI. **CCC.**
Description: Covers every aspect of the computer community and industry. Features in-depth reports, news, software, networking, systems, peripherals, and editorials.

001.6 621.381 DK ISSN 0107-5217
COMPUTERWORLD. 1981. 46/yr. DKK 785. I D G Danmark A-S, Carl Jacobsensvej 25, DK-2500 Valby, Denmark. TEL 45-36-19-91-00. FAX 45-36-44-20-33. TELEX 31566-CWDAD. Ed. Peter Hvidtfeldt. adv.; bk.rev.; circ. 26,000 (controlled). (reprint service avail.) **Indexed:** A.I.Abstr., Bus.Ind., Microcomp.Ind., PROMT, Tr.& Indus.Ind.

004 SI ISSN 0217-8362
COMPUTERWORLD.* 1984. fortn. $100. 04-07 Parkway Builders Centre, No.1, Marine Parade Central, Singapore 1544, Singapore. Ed. David Naidu. adv.; bk.rev. circ. 10,000.
—UMI.
Formerly (until 1985): Asian Computerworld (ISSN 0217-5665)

001.6 621.381 AG
COMPUTERWORLD ARGENTINA. (Text in Spanish) 1983. fortn. $70. C W Comunicaciones, Av. Belgrano 406, Piso 9, CP 1092 Buenos Aires, Argentina. FAX 1-331-7672. Ed. Ruben Argento. adv. circ. 7,000.

004 US ISSN 1077-5803
QA76.9.C55 CODEN: CLSJEI
COMPUTERWORLD CLIENT - SERVER JOURNAL. 1993. bi-m. $39.95. Computerworld, Inc. (Subsidiary of: I D G Communications, Inc.), 375 Cochituate Rd., Box 9171, Framingham, MA 01701-9171. TEL 508-879-0700. FAX 508-875-8931. E-mail: aalper@cw.com; 72303,1037@compuserve.com. Ed. Alan Alper; Pub. Kevin McPherson. adv.: B&W page $21700; adv. contact: James M. Hussey. circ. 133,000 (paid). **Document type:** trade publication.
—KR SourceOne.

004 CK ISSN 0122-2961
COMPUTERWORLD COLOMBIA. 1989. s-m. Col.$5000 (foreign $50) (effective 1997); newsstand price: Col.$2500. Iviarco Ltda., Carrera 90, No. 156-19, Piso 4, Santa Fe de Bogota, Colombia. TEL 57-1-6800399. FAX 57-1-6800399. Ed. Ciro Villate. adv.: page $1725; trim 350 x 250; adv. contact: Ciro Villate. bk.rev.; bibl. circ. 5,000. cols./p.: 4; pp./issue: 28. (tabloid format) **Document type:** consumer publication, newspaper.
Description: Covers computer systems applications, networking, the internet and computer related news.

001.6 US
COMPUTERWORLD DE MEXICO, S.A. DE C.V. fortn. $7. C W Communications, Inc., 375 Cochituate Rd., Box 9171, Framingham, MA 01701-9171. TEL 617-879-0700. adv. circ. 10,000.

COMPUTERWORLD - ESPANA. 1971. w. 18400 ptas. I D G - C W Communications, Rafael Calvo 18, p.4B, 28010 Madrid, Spain. TEL 91-3194014. FAX 91-3196104. Ed. Carlos de la Iglesia. adv. circ. 10,000.
   Former titles (until 1981): Informatica de la Pequena y Meidana Empresa (ISSN 0212-2472); (utnil 1977): Informatica (ISSN 0212-2464)

004   CH
COMPUTERWORLD - INFOWORLD TAIWAN. 1986. w. I D G Communications, Taiwan, 12-F, No. 4, Sect. 3, Min Sheng E. Rd., Taipei, Taiwan 10639, Republic of China. TEL 886-2-5019501. FAX 886-2-5056005. URL: http://www.idg.com.tw/cw/index.html. Ed. Margaret Tang; Pub. James Lai. adv.: B&W page NT.$96000; trim 265 x 375; adv. contact: Shirley Yeh. circ. 20,000. (tabloid format) **Document type:** newspaper.
   Description: For MIS people and channel managers. Contains up-to-date news and comprehensive coverage of all the latest developments in hardware, software, system integrator, networking and Internet-Intranet.

004   IT   ISSN 0392-8845
COMPUTERWORLD ITALIA; il settimanale per l'informatica italiana. 1982-1985 (Dec.); resumed. w. L.94000 (foreign L.371200). I D G Communications Italia s.r.l., Via G. Malipiero, 14, 20138 Milan, Italy. TEL 02-58011660. FAX 02-58011670. Ed. Brunello Bossi; Pub. Giulio Ferrari. adv.: B&W page L.9000000, color page L.13000000; trim 287 x 400; adv. contact: Sergio Rizzi. bk.rev. circ. 35,000. (tabloid format)
   Description: Covers news on PCs, workstations, mobile computing, software, LANs, and servers. Provides information on the computer industry: strategy, marketing and new products.

004   JA   ISSN 0286-4673
COMPUTERWORLD JAPAN. Key Title: Shukan Konpyutawarudo. (Text in Japanese) 1982. w. 15000 Yen($220) I D G Communications, Japan, 2-F, Shuwa Fujimiki Bldg., 1-2-27 Fujimi, Chiyoda-ku, Tokyo 102, Japan. TEL 81-3-3222-6411. FAX 81-3-3222-6566. Ed. Kimitaka Usui. adv. contact: Kazuhiro Hara. circ. 35,000.
   —UMI.

004   RM   ISSN 1222-4189
COMPUTERWORLD ROMANIA. 1993. bi-w. I D G Communications Publishing Group s.r.l., Calea Floreasca 167, et. 4 cam. 412, Sec. 2 Bucharest, Rumania. TEL 101-679-7140. FAX 01-312-76-12. adv.: B&W page $1100; 320 x 445. circ. 20,000. (tabloid format) **Document type:** newspaper.
   Description: Contains analyses of the Rumanian and worldwide computer markets, news and product comparisons.

001.6 621.381   US
COMPUTERWORLD VENEZUELA. bi-m. C W Communications, Inc., Computerworld Venezuela, Attn.: Diana La Muraglia, 375 Cochituate Rd., Box 9171, Framingham, MA 01701-9171. TEL 617-879-0700. circ. 5,000.

004   AU   ISSN 0010-485X
QA76   CODEN: CMPTA2
COMPUTING; archives for informatics and numerical computation/Archiv fuer Informatik und Numerik. (Supplements avail.) 1966. 8/yr. DM.1168 (effective 1998). Springer-Verlag, Sachsenplatz 4-6, P.O. Box 89, A-1201 Vienna, Austria. TEL 43-1-3302415. FAX 43-1-3302426. E-mail: springer@springer.co.at. (Subscr. in N. America to: Springer-Verlag New York, Inc., 175 Fifth Ave., New York, NY 10010. TEL 212-460-1500. FAX 212-473-6272) Ed. H.J. Stetter. adv.; bk.rev.; charts; illus.; index. (also avail. in microform from UMI; reprint service avail. from ISI,SWZ) **Indexed:** Abstr.Hum.Comp.Inter., Account.& Data Proc.Abstr., Appl.Mech.Rev., Compumath, Comput.Abstr., Comput.Rev., Curr.Cont., Cyb.Abstr., Ind.Sci.Rev., INIS Atomind., INSPEC (1968-), Int.Abstr.Oper.Res., Int.Aerosp.Abstr., Math.R., PROMT, Sci.Cit.Ind., Zent.Math. **Document type:** academic/scholarly publication.
   —BLDSC (3395.010000); AskIEEE; CISTI; Ei; Genuine Article; KR SourceOne; Linda Hall; SWETS; UMI; UnCover. **CCC.**
   Description: Publishes original papers from all fields of scientific computing.

001.6 621.381   UK
COMPUTING. 1973. w. £100 (foreign £120) (effective 1996). (British Computer Society) V N U Business Publications BV, VNU House, 32-34 Broadwick St., London W1A 2HG, England. TEL 44-171-439-4242. FAX 44-171-437-4841. Ed. Graham Cunningham. adv.; bk.rev.; charts; illus.; tr.lit. circ. 92,990. **Indexed:** BMT, Br.Tech.Ind., Comput.Rev., Curr.Cont., INSPEC, Key to Econ.Sci., PROMT. **Document type:** trade publication.
   —SWETS.
   Former titles: Computing Europe (ISSN 0307-8965); Computing.

004 621.39   SA   ISSN 0254-2196
COMPUTING S.A.. (Supplement avail.: Which Computer) 1979. w. R.125.36 (foreign R.437.36) (effective 1997). Thomson Publications (Subsidiary of: Times Media Ltd.), P.O. Box 56182, Pinegowrie 2123, South Africa. TEL 27-11-789-2144. FAX 27-11-789-3196. adv. circ. 17,723. **Indexed:** PROMT. **Document type:** trade publication.
   Formerly (until 1981): Computronics (ISSN 0250-0191)

001.6 621.381   US   ISSN 0344-8029
                             CODEN: COSPDM
COMPUTING SUPPLEMENTA. 1977. irreg. price varies. Springer-Verlag, 175 Fifth Ave., New York, NY 10010. TEL 212-460-1500. FAX 212-473-6272. (reprint service avail. from ISI) **Indexed:** INSPEC (1980-). **Document type:** academic/scholarly publication.
   —BLDSC (3395.129000); AskIEEE; CISTI; KR SourceOne; Linda Hall; SWETS; UMI.

621.381 001.6   JA   ISSN 0010-4906
COMPUTOPIA. (Text in Japanese) 1966. m. 28800 Yen. Computer Age Co., Ltd., Kasumigaseki Bldg., 30th Fl., 3-2-5 Kasumigaseki, Chiyoda-ku, Tokyo 100, Japan. Eds. Terutaka Kawabata, Teijiro Kubo. adv.; bk.rev. **Indexed:** JCT, JTA.

001.6   CN
COMPUVIEWS.* 1983. irreg. $8. J M G Software International, Inc., 892 Upper James, Hamilton, Ont. L9C 6C2, Canada. TEL 416-575-3200. Ed. George Geczy. illus.; stat. (looseleaf format)

COMUNICACIONES; telecomunicaciones, comunicaciones de datos, computadoras y satelites. see **COMMUNICATIONS**

CONTRACT PROFESSIONAL; the magazine for career contractors and consultants. see **BUSINESS AND ECONOMICS — Small Business**

621.381 001.6   US   ISSN 0734-757X
CONTRIBUTIONS TO THE STUDY OF COMPUTER SCIENCE. 1983. irreg. price varies. Greenwood Press, Inc. (Subsidiary of: Greenwood Publishing Group Inc.), 88 Post Rd. W., Box 5007, Westport, CT 06881-5007. TEL 203-226-3571. FAX 203-222-1502.
   —BLDSC (3461.453600); CISTI.

004   GW
COPERS - COMPUTERGESTUETZTE UND OPERATIVE PERSONALARBEIT. 1993. 8/yr. DM.128. Datakontext Fachverlag GmbH, Augustinusstr. 9d, 50226 Frechen-Koenigsdorf, Germany. TEL 49-2234-96610-0. FAX 49-2234-966109. Ed.Bd. adv.: B&W page DM.2400, color page DM.4350; trim 185 x 270; adv. contact: Gabriele Bender. circ. 4,000. **Document type:** trade publication.
   Formerly: CoPers - Computergestuetzte Personalarbeit (ISSN 0943-6669)

CRONACHE DAL GRUPPO STET. see **COMMUNICATIONS — Telephone And Telegraph**

001.6 621.381   GW   ISSN 0940-5062
D E C PROFESSIONELL. 1991. m. (Digital Equipment Corporation) Presse Professionelle Zeitschriften Gmblt & Co., St. Johanner Str. 58, Saarbruecken 6600, Germany. TEL 049068-14-23-24. FAX 049068-14-69-74. adv.: B&W page $3400, color page $4600; trim 8 1/4 x 10 3/4. circ. 6,500.
   Description: For buyers and users of DEC computers and related products and services.

001.6 621.381   FR   ISSN 1155-2549
D E C PROFESSIONNEL. 1991. 11/yr. (Digital Equipment Corporation) Presse Professionnelle SNC, 45 rue de Henri-de-Regnier, Versailles, France. TEL 39-53-95-26. FAX 39-02-39-71. Ed. Heinz Schiefer. adv.: B&W page $3700, color page $5000; trim 8 1/4 x 10 3/4. circ. 7,500 (controlled). **Document type:** trade publication.
   Description: For buyers and users of digital computers and related products and services.

001.6 621.381   UK   ISSN 0269-0489
                             CODEN: DETOEY
D E C TODAY. (Digital Equipment Corporation) 1986. m. £30 (foreign £50). C.W. Communication Ltd., 99 Grays Inn Rd., London WC1X 8UT, England. Ed. Charlie Brown. charts; illus.; pat.; stat.; tr.lit. circ. 12,501. (tabloid format; back issues avail.) **Indexed:** INSPEC (1986-).
   —AskIEEE; KR SourceOne.

001.6 621.381   IS   ISSN 0334-0996
D E C U S ISRAEL NEWS. (Text in English and Hebrew) q. Digital Equipment Computer Users Society, Digital House, Acadia Junction, Herzelia 46733, Israel. TEL 052-548222.

621.381 001.6   US
D E C U S MAGAZINE. 1962. q. membership. Digital Equipment Computer Users Society, Communications Organization, 334 South St., SHR3-1 - T25, Shrewsbury, MA 01545. TEL 508-841-3584. FAX 508-841-3357. E-mail: information@decus.org; URL: http://www.decus.org. Ed. Paula Morin. R&P contact: Paula Morin. adv.; bk.rev.; circ. 25,000 (controlled). **Document type:** newsletter.
   ●Also available online.
   —Linda Hall; UMI.
   Former titles: D E C U S '9X & DECUScope (ISSN 0011-7447)
   Description: Covers organization and committee news as well as symposia reports and technical articles of interest to the computing world.

621.381 001.6   UK   ISSN 0263-6530
D E C USER. (Digital Equipment Corp.); the independent guide to DEC computing. 1982. m. E M A P Business & Computer Publications Ltd., 33-39 Bowling Green Ln., London EC1R 0DA, England. TEL 44-171-837-1212. FAX 44-171-278-4008. TELEX 936566. adv.; bk.rev. circ. 13,000. (back issues avail.) **Indexed:** BMT, Comput.Dtbs., INSPEC (1983-). **Document type:** trade publication.
   —AskIEEE; CISTI; Ei; KR SourceOne. **CCC.**

003   GW   ISSN 0721-5924
T57.6.A1
D G O R. OPERATIONS RESEARCH PROCEEDINGS. 1972. a. (Deutsche Gesellschaft fuer Operations Research e.V.) Springer-Verlag, Heidelberger Platz 3, 14197 Berlin, Germany. TEL 49-30-82787-0. FAX 49-30-82787448. E-mail: subscriptions@springer.de. **Document type:** proceedings.
   —BLDSC (6269.365200).
   Formerly (until 1981): Proceedings in Operations Research (ISSN 0170-088X)

D G WORLD. (Data General Australia) see **COMPUTERS — Hardware**

001.6 621.381   US
D O S WORLD. 1991. bi-m. $23.70. Connell Communications, 86 Elm St., Peterborough, NH 03458. Ed. Jeff DeTray. adv.; illus. **Document type:** trade publication.
   Formerly: D O S Resource Guide (ISSN 1056-7364)

COMPUTERS

004 NE ISSN 0169-023X
QA76.9.D26 CODEN: DKENEW
DATA & KNOWLEDGE ENGINEERING. (Text and summaries in English) 1985. m. fl.1852($1064) (effective 1998). North-Holland (Subsidiary of: Elsevier Science B.V.), P.O. Box 211, 1000 AE Amsterdam, Netherlands. TEL 31-20-4853911. FAX 31-20-4853598. TELEX 18582 ESPA NL. (Subscr. in the Americas to: Elsevier Science, Regional Sales Office, Box 945, New York, NY 10159-0945. TEL 212-633-3730. FAX 212-633-3680; Subscr. in Australasia and the Far East to: Elsevier Science (Singapore) Pte Ltd, No.1 Temasek Ave., No.17-01 Millenia Tower, Singapore 039192, Singapore. TEL 65-434-3727. FAX 65-337-2230; Subscr. in Japan to: Elsevier Science Japan, 9-15 Higashi-Azabu 1-chome, Minato-ku Tokyo 106, Japan. TEL 81-3-5561-5033. FAX 81-3-5561-5047) Ed. Peter P. Chen. bk.rev. (reprint service avail. from SWZ) **Indexed:** A.I.Abstr., ASCA, Compumath, Comput.Abstr., Comput.Lit.Ind., Curr.Cont., Cyb.Abstr., Eng.Ind., INSPEC, Zent.Math. **Document type:** academic/scholarly publication.
—BLDSC (3534.250000); AskIEEE; CISTI; Ei; Genuine Article; KR SourceOne; Linda Hall; SWETS; UnCover. **CCC.**
 Description: Publishes original research results, technical advances and news items concerning data engineering, knowledge engineering, and the interface of these two fields.
 Refereed Serial

004 621.381 SW ISSN 0280-6622
DATA VAERLDEN. 1982. 12/yr. SEK 460; newsstand price: SEK 42. Affaersfoerlaget, P.O. Box 3188, A-103 63 Stockholm, Sweden.
TEL 46-8-736-56-00. FAX 46-8-14-12-43. Ed. Ulf Bergmark. adv.: B&W page SEK 36500, color page SEK 42800; trim 190 x 265. circ. 34,000. cols./p.: 4; pp./issue: 60.

DATALOGI O. see **EDUCATION — Computer Applications**

004 DK ISSN 0908-5491
DATALOGISKE NOTER. 1993. irreg. $10. Roskilde University, Department of Computer Science, P.O. Box 260, DK-4000 Roskilde, Denmark.
TEL 45-46-75-77-11. FAX 45-46-75-42-01. E-mail: troels@ruc.dk. Ed. Troels Andreasen. **Document type:** academic/scholarly publication.
 Description: Contains instructional material, lecture notes and textbooks.

004 DK ISSN 0109-9779
DATALOGISKE SKRIFTER. 1985. irreg. free. Roskilde University, Department of Computer Science, P. O. Box 260, DK-4000 Roskilde, Denmark.
TEL 45-46-75-77-11. FAX 45-46-75-42-01. E-mail: troels@ruc.dk. Ed. Troels Andreasen. circ. 200. **Document type:** academic/scholarly publication.
—BLDSC (3535.809800); AskIEEE; KR SourceOne.
 Description: Covers research activities in computer science at Roskilde University. Includes scientific papers and detailed reports.

001.64 621.381 II ISSN 0970-034X
DATAQUEST; the complete computer magazine. 1982. m. $50. Cyber Media India Ltd., D-74, Panchsheel Enclave, New Delhi 110 017, India. TEL 6433999. TELEX 031-71344 INDQ. Ed. Pravir Ganguly; Pub. H.C. Gupta. adv.: B&W page $1364, color page $1848; trim 196 x 266. bk.rev. circ. 40,000.

004 621.381 SW
DATATEKNIK. (Text in Swedish) 1980. fortn. SEK 589 (effective 1997). Ekonomi & Teknik Foerlag AB, S-106 12 Stockholm, Sweden.
TEL 46-8-796-66-80. FAX 46-8-613-30-38. Ed. Lennart Pettersson. adv.: B&W page SEK 33000, color page SEK 41900; adv. contact: Rolf Lindblom. bk.rev.; index. circ. 18,500. (back issues avail.) **Indexed:** INSPEC (1981-). **Document type:** trade publication.
—AskIEEE; KR SourceOne.
 Formerly (until 1991): I D - Industriell Datateknik (ISSN 0349-8476).
 Description: Covers the computer industry, technology, products and software.

001.6 621.381 NO ISSN 0332-8171
DATATID; norsk datatidende. 1979. m. NOK 560. Fasit Forlag AS, P.O. Box 2739 Stanshaugen, N-0131 Oslo, Norway. TEL 47-22-03-22-20.
FAX 47-22-03-22-21. URL: http://www.datatid.no. Ed. Svein-Erik Tosterud. adv. contact: Oystein Boe. bk.rev.; circ. 22,000 (controlled). (back issues avail.) **Indexed:** INSPEC, PROMT. **Document type:** trade publication.
—BLDSC (3535.828000); AskIEEE; CISTI; KR SourceOne. **CCC.**
 Formerly: Teknisk Ukeblad Data (ISSN 0800-532X)
 Description: Focuses on computer and information technology from the point of view of the professional user.

004.1 DK ISSN 0109-9213
DATATID. 1984. m.(11/yr.) DKK 425. Boersen Magasiner A-S, Moentergade 19, P.O. Box 2242, DK-1019 Copenhagen K, Denmark.
TEL 45-33-32-44-00. FAX 45-33-32-44-52. Ed. Leif Bomberg. adv.: B&W page DKK 13900, color page DKK 18000; trim 180 x 270; adv. contact: Christian Samsoe. circ. 15,000. (back issues avail.) **Document type:** trade publication.
 Incorporates (in 1991): Open Windows (ISSN 0907-1555)
 Description: Provides current information on EDP and computers in business and in the home.

DENSANKI RIYO NI KANSURU SHINPOJUMU KOENGAIYO/SYMPOSIUM OF COMPUTER RESEARCH. PROCEEDINGS. see **ENGINEERING — Civil Engineering**

001.6 US ISSN 1047-0735
QA76.8.A66 CODEN: DEVEFF
DEVELOP. 1990. q. Apple Computer, Inc., Box 531, Mt. Morris, IL 61054.

004 CC ISSN 1005-0043
DIANNAO AIHAOZHE/COMPUTER FANS.* (Text in Chinese) 1993. m. Zhongguo Kexueyuan, Jisuan Jishu Yanjiusuo - Chinese Academy of Sciences, Computing Tech Institute of Science, Zhongguancun Beirejei Rd., Beijing 100080, People's Republic of China. TEL 81-10-257-2123.
FAX 86-10-251-2124. adv.: color page $1500; trim 185-260. circ. 80,000.

004 621.381 CC ISSN 1006-5202
DIANNAO JISHU/COMPUTER TECHNOLOGY. (Text in Chinese) m. Shanghai Keji Jiaoyu Chubanshe - Shanghai Science and Technology Education Publishers, 393, Guanshengyuan Lu, Shanghai 200233, People's Republic of China.
TEL 86-21-4367970. FAX 86-21-4762835. Ed. Wu Zhiren. adv. contact: Wang Keping. **Document type:** academic/scholarly publication.

001.6 621.381 CC ISSN 1003-5850
DIANNAO KAIFA YU YINGYONG/COMPUTER DEVELOPMENT & APPLICATIONS. (Text in Chinese) 1985. q. $4 per no. Beifang Zidong Kongzhi Jishu Yanjiusuo, P.O. Box 8, Qi Xian (County), Shanxi 030900, People's Republic of China.
TEL 86-351-7043553. FAX 86-351-7042975. Ed. Tang Pengfei. adv. contact: Song Guolao. bk.rev.; circ. 9,500 (paid); 500 (controlled). **Document type:** academic/scholarly publication.

001.6 621.381 US ISSN 1084-9076
QA76.8.D43 CODEN: DECPDJ
DIGITAL AGE. 1982. m. $30 (free to qualified personnel in US) (Canada $36; foreign $96). Cardinal Business Media, Inc., 1300 Virginia Dr., Ste. 400, Ft. Washington, PA 19034-3225.
TEL 215-643-8000; 800-306-6332.
FAX 215-643-3901. URL: http://www.cardinal.com/digital_age; http://basix.com/decpro/. Ed. Charlie Simpson; Pub. Leslie Ringe. R&P contact: Charlie Simpson. adv. contact: Leslie Ringe. bk.rev.; tr.lit. circ. 50,000. **Indexed:** CAD CAM Abstr., Comput.Dtbs., Comput.Ind., Cyb.Abstr., INSPEC. **Document type:** trade publication.
●Also available online. Vendor(s): Information Access Co.
—AskIEEE; CASDDS; CISTI; KR SourceOne; SWETS; UMI; UnCover.
 Description: Features information on Open VMS, UNIX abd Windows NT for user of Digital Equipment Corporation) (ISSN 0744-9216)
 Description: Features information on Open VMS, UNIX abd Windows NT for user of Digital Equipment.

005 US ISSN 1086-9638
QA76.8.V37 CODEN: DSREFP
DIGITAL SYSTEMS REPORT; for Digital software professionals. 1979. bi-m. $95 (effective 1997). Computer Economics, Inc., 5841 Edison Pl., Carlsbad, CA 92008. TEL 760-438-8100.
FAX 760-431-1126. E-mail: dsr@compecon.com; URL: http://www.computereconomics.com. Ed. Mark McManus. adv. contact: Jeff Berman. bk.rev.; tr.lit.; index. circ. 7,370. (back issues avail.) **Indexed:** INSPEC (1992-). **Document type:** trade publication.
●Also available online. Vendor(s): Information Access Co.
—BLDSC (3588.397537); AskIEEE; CISTI; Ei; KR SourceOne; SWETS; UMI.
 Former titles (until vol.18, 1996): Digital Systems Journal (ISSN 1067-7224); (until 1992): V A X Professional (ISSN 8750-9628); V A X - R S T S Professional; R S T S Professional.
 Description: Provides insight and cost-effective performance tools for digital platforms.

001.603 658 UK
DIRECTORY OF TRAINING. 1982. a. £123. Directory of Training Ltd., 51 High St., Ruislip Middlesex HA4 7PL, England. Ed. Colin R. Steed. adv.; charts; illus.; index. circ. 3,000. (back issues avail.)
 Former titles: Directory of Computer Training & Directory of Management Training.

DIRITTO DELL'INFORMAZIONE E DELL'INFORMATICA. see **LIBRARY AND INFORMATION SCIENCES**

DISCRETE & COMPUTATIONAL GEOMETRY; an international journal of mathematics and computer science. see **MATHEMATICS**

006 621.39 GW ISSN 0178-2770
QA76.9.D5 CODEN: DICOEB
DISTRIBUTED COMPUTING. Online edition (GW ISSN 1432-0452) (Text in English) 1986. q. DM.336 (foreign DM.340.60) (effective 1998). Springer-Verlag, Heidelberger Platz 3, 14197 Berlin, Germany. TEL 49-30-82787-0.
FAX 49-30-82787448. E-mail: subscriptions@springer.de; URL: http://link.springer.de. (Subscr. in N. America to: Springer-Verlag New York, Inc., 333 Meadowlands Pkwy., Secaucus, NJ 07094. TEL 212-460-1500. FAX 212-473-6272) Ed. F.B. Schneider. **Indexed:** ASCA, Compumath, Comput.Abstr., Curr.Cont., Cyb.Abstr., Eng.Ind., INSPEC (1986-), Zent.Math. **Document type:** academic/scholarly publication.
●Also available online.
—BLDSC (3602.661200); AskIEEE; CISTI; Ei; Genuine Article; KR SourceOne; Linda Hall; SWETS; UMI; UnCover. **CCC.**
 Description: Topics covered include novel architectures of distributed systems and computer networks, communication protocols and hierarchies, distributed operating systems, and formal modeling, verification and synthesis of distributed systems.

004 UK
DISTRIBUTED COMPUTING DIRECTIONS. 1987. m. (10/yr.). £425 in Europe; rest of world £460 (effective 1997). Technology Appraisals Ltd., 82 Hampton Rd., Twickenham, Middlesex TW2 5QS, England. TEL 44-181-893-3986.
FAX 44-181-744-1149. E-mail: techapp@cix.compulink.co.uk. Ed. Peter Judge; Pub. Alan Paton. bk.rev. **Document type:** bulletin.
 Formerly: Open Systems Newsletter (ISSN 0952-1992)

001.6 FR ISSN 0757-309X
DISTRIBUTIQUE. 1983. m. (10/yr.). 500 F. (foreign 760 F.). I D G Communications France, 92051 Paris La Defense Cedex 65, France.
TEL 49-04-79-00. TELEX 613-234 F. Ed. Jacques Tillier. circ. 8,000.

340 FR ISSN 0991-2738
DROIT DE L'INFORMATIQUE ET DES TELECOMS. 4/yr. 680 F. Editions du Parques, 119 rue de Flandre, 75019 Paris, France. TEL 40-35-03-03.
FAX 40-38-96-43. circ. 3,340. **Indexed:** ELLIS.
 Formerly (until 1987): Droit de l'Informatique (ISSN 0772-4152)

001.6 621.381 500   UK   ISSN 0268-1110
QA871
DYNAMICS AND STABILITY OF SYSTEMS. 1986. q. £64($104) to individuals; institutions £212 ($384) (effective 1997). Carfax Publishing Co., P.O. Box 25, Abingdon, Oxon. OX14 3UE, England. TEL 44-1235-401000. FAX 44-1235-41550. E-mail: enequiries@carfax.co.uk. (N. American subscr. to: Carfax Publishing Co., 875-81 Massachusetts Ave., Cambridge, MA 02139) Eds. J. Stark, C. Sparrow. adv.; index. circ. 750. (also avail. in microfiche; back issues avail.) **Indexed:** ASCA, Comput.Abstr., Curr.Cont., Geo.Abstr.H.G., Math.R., Zent.Math. **Document type:** academic/scholarly publication.
—BLDSC (3637.143250); AskIEEE; CISTI; Ei; EMDOCS; Genuine Article; KR SourceOne; Linda Hall; SWETS; UMI; UnCover. **CCC.**
   Description: Disseminates original international research concerning the stability, instability, bifurcation and oscillatory behavior of natural and manmade systems.
   Refereed Serial

001.6 621.381   US
E A T C MONOGRAPHS IN THEORETICAL COMPUTER SCIENCE. 1984. irreg. price varies. Springer-Verlag, 175 Fifth Ave., New York, NY 10010. TEL 212-460-1500. FAX 212-473-6272. (Also: Berlin, Heidelberg, Tokyo and Vienna) (reprint service avail. from ISI) **Document type:** monographic series.

001.6 621.381 340   AU
E D V & RECHT; Zeitschrift fuer EDV-, Patentschutz- und Telekommunikationsrecht. 1986. irreg. (2-3/yr.) Medien und Recht Verlags GmbH, Danhausergasse 6-16, A-1041 Vienna, Austria. TEL 43-1-5052766. FAX 43-1-505276615. Ed. Heinz Wittmann. adv. contact: Ruth Rieder. bk.rev.; index. circ. 600. (back issues avail.) **Document type:** monographic series.

E D V UND KOMMUNIKATION FUER DAS HANDWERK. see *HOW-TO AND DO-IT-YOURSELF*

E E C S - E R L NEWS. (Electrical Engineering & Computer Sciences, Electronics Research Laboratory) see *ENGINEERING — Electrical Engineering*

004 621.39   UA   ISSN 0377-7154
QA76   CODEN: ECJODE
EGYPTIAN COMPUTER JOURNAL. 1973. 2/yr. £E5($15) Cairo University, Institute of Statistical Studies and Research, Tharwat St., Orman, Cairo, Egypt. FAX 20-2-3482533. TELEX 94372. Ed. Ibrahim Farag Eissa. bibl.; charts. (back issues avail.) **Indexed:** Comput.Cont., Comput.Rev., INSPEC. **Document type:** academic/scholarly publication.
—BLDSC (3664.234000); AskIEEE; KR SourceOne.

001.6   JA   ISSN 0366-9092
                          CODEN: DGSKAR
ELECTROTECHNICAL LABORATORY. BULLETIN/DENSHI GIJUTSU SOGO KENKYUJO IHO. (Text in English or Japanese; summaries in English) 1937. m. 21000 Yen. (Agency of Industrial Science and Technology, Electrotechnical Laboratory) Ohm-sha, 3-1, Kanda Nishiki-cho, Chiyoda-ku, Tokyo 101, Japan. circ. 1,150. **Indexed:** Alloys Ind., Chem.Abstr., Eng.Ind., Eng.Mat.Abstr., INIS Atomind., JCT, JTA, Met.Abstr.Ind., Met.Abstr., Nonfer.Met.Alert, PCC Alert, Steels Alert, World Alum.Abstr.
—BLDSC (2501.000000); AskIEEE; CASDDS; CISTI; Ei; KR SourceOne; Linda Hall.

621.39   XR   ISSN 0862-4607
ELEKTRONIKA. 1987. m. 228 Kc. I D G Czechoslovakia, A.S., Luzna 2, 160 00 Prague 6, Czech Republic. TEL 42-2-366251. FAX 42-2-3166246. E-mail: Martin__Kybal@idg.com; URL: http://infox.eunet.cz/idg. Ed. Martin Kybal. adv.: B&W page 55000 Kc.; trim 176 x 261; adv. contact: Eva Marikova. circ. 15,000.
   Description: Covers communications sytstems, new technology in the electronics industry.

001.6 621.381   IS   ISSN 0334-7680
TK4
ELEKTRONIKA UMACHSHAVIM/ELECTRICS & COMPUTERS. (Text in Hebrew) 1985. m. IS.120. Tzavta Publishing, P.O. Box 18287, Tel Aviv 61181, Israel. TEL 03-5622076. FAX 3-5618549. Ed. Y. Elyada. adv.; bk.rev.; circ. 8,500 (controlled).

621.39   UK
ENTERPRISE CLIENT - SERVER. 1993. m. £195 (U.S. $295). Xephon, 27-35 London Rd., Newbury,, Berks RG13 1JL, England. TEL 44-1635-38342. FAX 44-1635-38345. E-mail: 1000325.3711@compuserve.com; URL: http://www.hiway.co.uk/~xephon. (Subscr. in U.S. to: Xephon, 1301 W. Highway 407, Ste. 201-405, Lewisville, TX 75067. TEL 817-455-7050. FAX 817-455-2492) Ed. Trevor Eddolls. bk.rev. (back issues avail.) **Document type:** trade publication.
   Formerly: Mainframe Client - Server.

001.6 621.381   GW   ISSN 0949-9725
ERFOLGREICHE COMPUTER-PRAXIS. 1985. a. DM.78. Verlag Wirtschaft Recht und Steuern, Fraunhoferstr. 5, 82152 Planegg, Germany. TEL 49-89-89517-0. FAX 49-89-89517250. (Subscr. to: Postfach 1363, 82142 Planegg, Germany) **Document type:** trade publication.
   Formerly (until 1996): Computer-Praxis A B C (ISSN 0176-2508)

004 621.38   NE   ISSN 0926-9762
EURO COURSES. COMPUTER AND INFORMATION SCIENCE. (Text in English) 1990. irreg., vol.4, 1992. price varies. (Commission of the European Communities) Kluwer Academic Publishers, Postbus 17, 3300 AA Dordrecht, Netherlands. TEL 31-78-6392392. FAX 31-78-6392254. TELEX 29245 KAPG NL. E-mail: services@wkap.nl; URL: http://www.wkap.nl. (Dist. by: Kluwer Academic Publishers Group, P.O. Box 322, 3300 AH Dordrecht, Netherlands. TEL 31-78-6392392. FAX 31-78-6546474; N. America dist. addr.: Box 358, Accord Sta., Hingham, MA 02018-0358. TEL 617-871-6600. FAX 617-871-6528) **Document type:** proceedings.
   Refereed Serial

004   DK
▼**EUROCOMPUTER**; Nordens edb-avis. 1995. 6/yr. Media-Huset Solibraco a-s, Jyllingevej 55-57, P.O. Box 1670, DK-2720 Vanloese, Denmark. TEL 45-38-79-34-00. FAX 45-38-79-34-10. Ed. Ib Helge. adv.: B&W page DKK 21600, color page DKK 24000; trim 360 x 265; adv. contact: Kristian Larsen. circ. 40,803. **Document type:** newspaper.

001.6 621.381   US
EUROGRAPHIC SEMINARS. 1984. irreg. price varies. Springer-Verlag, 175 Fifth Ave., New York, NY 10010. TEL 212-460-1500. FAX 212-473-6272. (Also: Berlin, Heidelberg, Tokyo and Vienna) (reprint service avail. from ISI) **Document type:** monographic series.

EUROPEAN JOURNAL OF OPERATIONAL RESEARCH. see *BUSINESS AND ECONOMICS — Management*

001.6 621.381   NE
EUROTRADE COMPUTER. (Text in English) 1988. 10/yr. $40. Kluwer Technische Tijdschriften BV, Postbus 23, 7400 GA Deventer, Netherlands. TEL 5700-48750. FAX 5100-45547. adv.: B&W page $3780; trim 254 x 330. circ. 12,000.

FEDERAL COMPUTER WEEK; the newspaper for the government systems community. see *PUBLIC ADMINISTRATION — Computer Applications*

004   US
FOCUS: MANAGING AND USING DATA GENERAL SYSTEMS. 1985. m. $24. (North American Data General Users Group) Turnkey Publishing, Inc., Box 200549, Austin, TX 78720-0549. TEL 512-335-2286. FAX 512-335-3083. E-mail: nadgug@tkp.com; URL: http://www.dg.com/customers/nadgug. Ed. Germi M. Farman; Pub. Greg Farman. R&P contact: Geri M. Farman. adv.: B&W page $1265, color page $1765; adv. contact: Elizabeth Simmons. bk.rev.; charts; illus.; tr.lit. circ. 8,000. (back issues avail.) **Document type:** trade publication.
   Formerly: Focus (Austin, 1985).

FOCUS ON BRITISH ENGINEERING AND COMPUTER SCIENCES RESEARCH. see *BIBLIOGRAPHIES*

FORMAL ASPECTS OF COMPUTING; international journal of formal methods. see *COMPUTERS — Software*

004   UK
FREELANCE INFORMER. fortn. Reed Business Publishing Group (Subsidiary of: Reed Elsevier group), Quadrant House, The Quadrant, Sutton, Surrey SM2 5AS, England. TEL 44-181-652-4800. FAX 44-181-652-4748. **Document type:** trade publication.

001.6 301.16 070.5
340   US
FRIDAY MEMO. 1986. m. membership. Information Industry Association, 1625 Massachusetts Ave., N.W., Ste. 700, Washington, DC 20036-2212. TEL 202-986-0280. FAX 202-638-4403. Ed. Sheri Robey. circ. 4,500. (looseleaf format) **Document type:** bulletin.
   Former titles: Exchange; Videotex Voice; Database News; Information on Washington.
   Description: Provides news on industry happenings, government and policy issues as well as developments of the Information Industry Association.

004   NE
FUNDAMENTAL STUDIES IN COMPUTER SCIENCE. irreg., vol.3, 1984. price varies. Elsevier Science B.V., Books Division, P.O. Box 211, 1000 AE Amsterdam, Netherlands. TEL 31-20-4853911. FAX 31-20-4853705. TELEX 18582 ESPA NL. E-mail: nlinfo-f@elsevier.nl; usinfo-f@elsevier.com; forinfo-kyf04035@niftyserve.or.jp; URL: http://www.elsevier.nl/. (Subscr. in the Americas to: Elsevier Science, Regional Sales Office, Box 945, New York, NY 10159-0945. FAX 212-633-3680; Subscr. in Australasia and the Far East to: Elsevier Science (Singapore) Pte Ltd, No.1 Temasek Ave., No.17-01 Millenia Tower, Singapore 039192, Singapore. TEL 65-434-3727. FAX 65-337-2230; Subscr. in Japan to: Elsevier Science Japan, 9-15 Higashi-Azabu 1-chome, Minato-ku, Tokyo 106, Japan. TEL 81-3-5561-5033. FAX 81-3-5561-5047) **Indexed:** INSPEC. **Document type:** monographic series.
   Refereed Serial

FUNKSCHAU; Zeitschrift fuer Telekommunikationen und Unterhaltungselektronik. see *COMMUNICATIONS*

G M D NEWSLINE. see *COMPUTERS — Computer Systems*

001.6 621.381   GW   ISSN 0724-4339
G M D - SPIEGEL. (Text in English, German) 1971. q. free. (Gesellschaft fuer Mathematik und Datenverarbeitung) G M D - Forschungszentrum Informationstechnik GmbH, Schloss Birlinghoven, 53754 Sankt Augustin, Germany. TEL 49-2241-14-0. FAX 49-2241-14-2889. TELEX 889469-GMD-D. URL: http://www.gmd.de/muk/gmd-spiegel.inhalt.html. Ed. Siegfried Muench. adv.; bk.rev. circ. 6,000. (back issues avail.) **Document type:** academic/scholarly publication.
—CISTI.
   Description: Covers scientific research in computer science and mathematics. Includes association news, activities and projects, reports of events and exhibitions, and new publications.

001.6 621.381   BE   ISSN 0771-713X
GENEALOGIE AND COMPUTER. (Text in Dutch) 1984. bi-m. 300 Fr.($7) Vlaamse Vereniging voor Familiekunde, Centrum voor Familiegeschiedenis, Van Heybeeckstraat 3, Antwerp-Merksem, Belgium. Ed. Pieter A. Donche. adv.; bk.rev. circ. 300. (back issues avail.)
   Description: Information on the use of microcomputers for genealogical research for members of the Society.

GEOGRAPHICAL SOCIETY OF CHINA. BULLETIN. see *GEOGRAPHY*

001   FR   ISSN 1162-2784
GOLDEN. m. 320 F. (foreign 390 F.). I D G Communications France, 92051 Paris La Defense Cedex 65, France. TEL 49-04-79-00. FAX 49-04-78-00. TELEX 613 234 F.

COMPUTERS

001.6 621.381 CN
GOVERNMENT COMPUTING DIGEST; serving the government systems community in Canada. 1990. 6/yr. Can.$44. Synergistic Enterprises, 132 Adrian Cres., Markham, ON L3P 7B3, Canada. TEL 416-472-2801. FAX 416-472-3091. Ed. William Gadsby. adv.: B&W page Can.$1990, color page Can.$2590; trim 8 1/8 x 10 7/8; adv. contact: Bill Sherman. circ. 4,000. (back issues avail.) **Document type**: trade publication.
Description: For government computing professionals, featuring articles, columns and a news section.

004 GW
GRADUATE TEXTS IN COMPUTER SCIENCE. 1994. irreg. Springer-Verlag, Heidelberger Platz 3, 14197 Berlin, Germany. TEL 49-30-82787-0. FAX 49-30-82787448. E-mail: subscriptions@springer.de. (Subscr. in US to: Springer-Verlag New York, Inc., 333 Meadowlands Pkwy., Secaucus, NJ 07094. TEL 212-460-1500. FAX 212-473-6272) Eds. D. Gries, F. Schneider. **Document type**: monographic series.
Description: Provides information on topics covering all aspects of graduate-level computer science.

004 UK
GRADUATE TEXTS IN COMPUTER SCIENCE. irreg., vol.3, 1994. price varies. Oxford University Press, Walton St., Oxford OX2 6DP, England. TEL 44-1865-56767. FAX 44-1865-56646. (Subscr. in US to: Oxford University Press Inc. 2001 Evands Rd., Cary, NC27513. TEL 919-677-0977. FAX 919-677-1714) (back issues avail.) **Document type**: monographic series.

001.64 651.8 UK ISSN 0072-582X
GREAT BRITAIN. DEPARTMENT OF EDUCATION AND SCIENCE. COMPUTER BOARD FOR UNIVERSITIES AND RESEARCH COUNCILS. REPORT. 1968. irreg. H.M.S.O., 51 Nine Elms Ln., London SW8 5DR, England. (Co-sponsor: Department of Education and Science) **Document type**: government publication.
—CCC.

001.6 621.381 SP ISSN 0212-1549
GUIA DEL COMPRADOR DE INFORMATICA.* 1983. 52/yr. Haymarket, S.A., Travesera Gracia 17-21, 5o 2o, 08022 Barcelona, Spain. TEL 3-237-22-66. FAX 3-237-66-88.

001.6 621.381 475 US
GUIDE TO COMPUTER LAW. 1989. 2 base vols. (plus s-m. updates). $365. C C H Incorporated, 2700 Lake Cook Rd., Riverwoods, IL 60015. TEL 847-267-7000; 800-835-5224. FAX 800-224-8299. (looseleaf format)

001.6 621.381 US ISSN 0889-4108
GUIDE TO COMPUTER LIVING. m. Aquarian Communications, 3808 S.E. Licynrta Ct., Portland, OR 97222. TEL 206-654-5603.
Former titles (until 1986): Guide (Portland) (ISSN 0884-1446)

658.8 US ISSN 0748-6235
QA76.16
GUIDE TO FREE COMPUTER MATERIALS. 1983. a. $38.95. Educators Progress Service, Inc., 214 Center St., Randolph, WI 53956. TEL 414-326-3126. FAX 414-326-3127. Ed. Kathleen Suttles Nehmer.
Description: Covers free films, videotapes, pamphlets, charts and disks; plus a section on SHAREWARE.

004 UK
▼ **H C I LETTERS**. 1997. 6/yr. £140 (effective 1998). Springer-Verlag London Ltd., Sweetapple House, Cattashall Rd., Godalming, Surrey GU7 3DJ, England. TEL 44-1483-418822. FAX 44-1483-415151. E-mail: alex@svl.co.uk. (Subscr. in N. America to: Springer-Verlag New York, Inc., 333 Meadowlands Pkwy., Secaucus, NJ 07094. TEL 212-460-1500. FAX 212-473-6272) **Document type**: academic/scholarly publication.
● Also available online.
Description: Covers all aspects of human-computer interaction.
Refereed Serial

001.6 621.381 GW
H M D - ZEITSCHRIFT FUER WIRTSCHAFTSINFORMATIK. 1964. bi-m. DM.217.20 (foreign DM.228) (effective 1997). Huethig GmbH, Postfach 102869, 69018 Heidelberg, Germany. TEL 49-6221-489-417. FAX 49-6221-489481. URL: http://www.huethig.de. Ed. Reinhold Hammes. adv.: B&W page DM.1150; adv. contact: Isabell Pfisterer. circ. 2,000. **Document type**: trade publication.
—SWETS.
Former titles: H M D - Theorie und Praxis der Wirtschaftsinformatik (ISSN 0939-2602); Handbuch der Modernen Datenverarbeitung (ISSN 0723-5208)
Description: Applications of electronic data processing and its organization in business and industry.

621.39 US
HANDBOOK OF I B M TERMINOLOGY. s-a. $105 (effective Aug. 1996). Xephon, 1301 W. Hwy. 407, Ste. 201-450, Lewisville, TX 75067. TEL 817-455-7050. FAX 817-455-2492. **Document type**: trade publication.

003 658.4 NE ISSN 0927-0507
HANDBOOKS IN OPERATIONS RESEARCH AND MANAGEMENT SCIENCE. (Text in English) 1989. irreg., vol.9, 1995. price varies. Elsevier Science B.V., Books Division, P.O. Box 211, 1000 AE Amsterdam, Netherlands. TEL 31-20-4853911. FAX 31-20-4853705. E-mail: nlinfo-f@elsevier.nl; usinfo-f@elsevier.com; forinfo-kyf04035@niftyserve.or.jp; URL: http://www.elsevier.nl/. (Subscr. in the Americas to: Elsevier Science, Regional Sales Office, Box 945, New York, NY 10159-0945. TEL 212-633-3730. FAX 212-633-3680; Subscr. in Australasia and the Far East to: Elsevier Science (Singapore) Pte Ltd, No.1 Temasek Ave., No.17-01 Millenia Tower, Singapore 039192, Singapore. TEL 65-434-3727. FAX 65-337-2230; Subscr. in Japan to: Elsevier Science Japan, 9-15 Higashi-Azabu 1-chome, Minato-ku, Tokyo 106, Japan. TEL 81-3-5561-5033. FAX 81-3-5561-5047) **Indexed**: Zent.Math. **Document type**: monographic series.
—BLDSC (4250.956000).
Refereed Serial

004.7 681 US ISSN 1058-2444
TK7887.7
THE HARD COPY OBSERVER. 1991. m. $495 in N. America; elsewhere $535. Lyra Publishing, Box 9143, Newtonville, MA 02160. TEL 617-332-0708. FAX 617-332-0342. Ed. Charles LeCompte. **Document type**: newsletter.
—SWETS.

HASTINGS COMMUNICATIONS AND ENTERTAINMENT LAW JOURNAL (COMM - ENT). see *LAW*

HEALTHCARE INFORMATION MANAGEMENT. see *HOSPITALS*

HI-TECH COACHING & TRAINING. see *SPORTS AND GAMES*

001.6 621.381 US ISSN 1072-9755
HIGH-TECHNOLOGY SERVICES MANAGEMENT. m. Association for Services Management International, 1342 Colonial Blvd., Ste. 25, Ft. Myers, FL 33907. TEL 941-275-7887. FAX 941-275-0794. Ed. Leonard Mafrica; Pub. Leonard Mafrica. R&P contact: Leonard Mafrica. adv.: B&W page $2580, color page $3380; trim 8 x 10 7/8; adv. contact: Walter Donnelly. circ. 20,000. **Document type**: trade publication.
Description: Covers service management: planning, marketing, technical support, field operations.

004 GW ISSN 0941-9020
HIGHSCREEN HIGHLIGHTS. m. DM.73.50 (foreign DM.97.50; students DM.63) (effective 1997). Franzis Verlag GmbH, Dornacherstr. 3, 85622 Feldkirchen, Germany. TEL 49-89-99115-0. FAX 49-89-99115199. Ed. Alfons Schraeder; Pub. Michael Scharfenberger. adv. contact: Stefan Grajer. circ. 112,640. **Document type**: consumer publication.

001.6 UK ISSN 0957-0144
D16.12 CODEN: HICOFM
HISTORY AND COMPUTING (EDINBURGH). (Text in English; summaries in English, French, German) 1989. 3/yr. £21.50($40) to individuals (overseas £51.50); institutions £43 (overseas £47 ($80)) (effective 1996). (Association for History and Computing) Edinburgh University Press, 22 George Sq., Edinburgh EH8 9LF, Scotland. TEL 44-131-650-6207. FAX 44-131-662-0053. TELEX 727442 UNIVED G. Eds. Robert J. Morris, Stephen Baskerville; Pub. Vivian C. Bone. adv. contact: Kathryn MacLean. bk.rev.; software rev. circ. 500. (back issues avail.) **Indexed**: Amer.Hist.& Life (1989-), Educ.Tech.Abstr., Hist.Abstr. (1989-). **Document type**: academic/scholarly publication.
—BLDSC (4317.798020); AskIEEE; KR SourceOne; SWETS; UMI; UnCover. **CCC**.
Description: Aimed at historians using computers for research. Covers all aspects of computer applications in the field, from quantitative methods to free-text analysis and image processing.
Refereed Serial

004 CC
HONG KONG COMPUTER JOURNAL. (Text in English) 1985. m. Arting Publications Ltd., Ste. 709 Hong Man Industrial Bldg., 2 Hong Man St., Chawiwan, Wanchai, Hong Kong, People's Republic of China. TEL 852-2897-1127. FAX 852-2897-2980. Ed. Gordon Au. adv. contact: Paul Chan. circ. 16,200.

004 JA ISSN 0913-8420
HOSEI DAIGAKU KEISAN SENTA KENKYU HOKOKU/HOSEI UNIVERSITY. COMPUTER CENTER. BULLETIN. (Text in English, Japanese) 1987. a. Hosei Daigaku, Keisan Senta, 7-2, Kajinocho 3-chome, Koganei-shi, Tokyo 184, Japan. **Document type**: bulletin, academic/scholarly publication.
—BLDSC (2458.143400).

004 US
HOTWIRED. 1994. irreg. (updated d. or w.). free. Wired Ventures Ltd., 520 Third St., 4th Fl., San Francisco, CA 94107. TEL 415-222-6200. FAX 415-222-6369. E-mail: hotinfo@wired.com; URL: http://www.hotwired.com/. Eds. Chip Bayers, Louis Rossetto. illus. **Document type**: consumer publication.
● Available only online.
Description: Discusses and defines the future of the new medium of global interactive networks.

004 301.1 US ISSN 0737-0024
QA76.9.S88 CODEN: HCINE6
HUMAN - COMPUTER INTERACTION (MAHWAH); a journal of theoretical, empirical, and methodological issues of user psychology and of system design. 1985. q. $39 to individuals (foreign $69); institutions $230 (foreign $260) (effective 1997). Lawrence Erlbaum Associates, Inc., 10 Industrial Dr Mahwah, NJ 07430-2262. TEL 201-236-9500; 800-926-6579. FAX 201-236-0072. E-mail: jamsel@erlbaum.com; URL: http://www.erlbaum.com. Ed. Thomas P. Moran. adv.: page $400; 5 x 8 bk.rev. circ. 1,200. **Indexed**: Abstr.Hum.Comp.Inter. ASCA, C.I.J.E., Curr.Cont., INSPEC (1987-), Psychol.Abstr. (1985-). **Document type**: academic/scholarly publication.
—BLDSC (4336.043450); AskIEEE; CASDDS; CIST Ei; KR SourceOne; Linda Hall; SWETS; UnCover. **CC**
Refereed Serial

621.39 IS
I B E X BULLETIN. m. $430 (effective Aug. 1995). Xephon, 1301 W. Hwy. 407, Ste. 201-450, Lewisville, TX 75067. TEL 817-455-7050. FAX 817-455-2492. **Document type**: bulletin, trade publication.

001.6 621.381 UK
I B M COMPUTER TODAY. (International Business Machines Corp.) 1985. m. Reed Business Publishing Group, Quadrant House, The Quadrant, Sutton, Surrey SM2 5AS, England. TEL 44-181-652-866. FAX 44-181-652-8934. Ed. John Charlton. adv.; bk.rev. circ. 16,000. **Document type**: trade publication.
Description: For managers of IBM mainframes, minicomputers, and microcomputers. Includes corporate and industry news, new-product announcements, and programming and software tutorials.

621.381 001.6 US ISSN 0018-8646
TK7800 CODEN: IBMJAE
I B M JOURNAL OF RESEARCH AND DEVELOPMENT. 1957. bi-m. $80 (outside N. America $95) (effective 1996). International Business Machines Corp., Box 218, Yorktown Heights, NY 10598. TEL 914-945-3836. Ed. P.S. Hauge. abstr.; bibl.; index. circ. 25,000. (also avail. in microform from UMI; back issues avail.; reprint service avail. from UMI) **Indexed:** A.I.Abstr. (until 1992), A.S.& T.Ind., Abstr.Bull.Inst.Pap.Chem., Alloys Ind., Appl.Mech.Rev., ASCA, BMT, Bull.Signal., CAD CAM Abstr. (until 1992), Chem.Abstr., Chem.Cit.Ind., Compumath, Comput.Abstr., Comput.& Info.Sys., Comput.Cont., Comput.Dtbs., Comput.Lit.Ind., Comput.Rev., Curr.Cont., Cyb.Abstr., Data Process.Dig., Electron.& Communic.Abstr.J., Energy Info.Abstr., Eng.Ind., Eng.Mat.Abstr., Excerp.Med., Geo.Abstr., Graph.Arts Lit.Abstr., Ind.Sci.Rev., Inform.Sci.Abstr., INIS Atomind., INSPEC, Int.Aerosp.Abstr., Mat.Sci.Cit.Ind., Math.R., Met.Abstr., Met.Abstr.Ind., Nonfer.Met.Alert, Oper.Res.Manage.Sci., PCC Alert, Phys.Ber., PROMT, Qual.Contr.Appl.Stat., Ref.Zh., Robomat. (until 1992), Sci.Cit.Ind., Sci.Res.Abstr., Sh.& Vib.Dig., Solid St.Abstr., Steels Alert, Tel.Abstr., World Alum.Abstr., Zent.Math.
—BLDSC (4360.070000); AskIEEE; CASDDS; CISTI; Ei; Genuine Article; KR SourceOne; SWETS; UMI. **CCC.**
Refereed Serial

001.6 621.381 AT ISSN 0311-872X
I B M QUARTERLY. (International Business Machines) 1974. q. free. I B M Australia Ltd., Coonara Ave., West Pennant Hills, N.S.W. 2120, Australia. TEL 02-634-9111. FAX 02-899-1054. Ed. Henry Strasburger. adv.; bk.rev. circ. 20,000. (back issues avail.)
Description: For executive managers in industry, commerce, government and academia.

001.6 621.381 UK
I B M - READ ME. (International Business Machines) 1969. every 8 wks. free. I B M United Kingdom Ltd., P.O. Box 41, North Harbour, Portsmouth PO6 3AU, England. TEL 44-1705-563799. FAX 44-1705-385081. E-mail: gbib1s41@ibmmail.com. Ed. S. Austin. adv.; bk.rev.; circ. 29,000 (controlled). **Document type:** newsletter.
Formerly: I B M - U K News.

I B M SYSTEMS JOURNAL. (International Business Machines) see COMPUTERS — Computer Systems

004 UK ISSN 1364-310X
QA75.5 CODEN: ISJOF2
I C L SYSTEMS JOURNAL. 1978. s-a. £72 in Europe; elsewhere $120 (effective 1998). International Computers Ltd., Lovelace Rd., Bracknell, Berks. RG12 4SN, England, England. TEL 44-1344-472000. FAX 44-1344-472700. E-mail: v.a.j.maller@bra0114.wins.co.uk. (Alt. addr.: ICL House, 1 High St., Putney, London SW15 1SW) Ed. V.A.J. Maller. adv.; charts; illus.; circ. 1,250 (paid). (also avail. in microform from UMI; back issues avail.) **Indexed:** Abstr.Hum.Comp.Inter., Comput.Abstr., Comput.Cont., Ergon.Abstr., INSPEC (1978-), INSPEC. **Document type:** academic/scholarly publication.
—BLDSC (4362.047740); AskIEEE; CISTI; KR SourceOne; Linda Hall; UMI. **CCC.**
Former titles (until 1996): Ingenuity (ISSN 1354-9952); (until 1994): I C L Technical Journal (ISSN 0142-1557)
Description: Presents current practical applications and developments in the fields of computers and information science and technology.
Refereed Serial

I E COMPUTING SERIES. see ENGINEERING — Computer Applications

621.381 US ISSN 1058-6180
QA76.17 CODEN: IAHCEX
I E E E ANNALS OF THE HISTORY OF COMPUTING. 1979. q. $220 to non-members (effective 1998). Institute of Electrical and Electronics Engineers, Inc., 345 E. 47th St., New York, NY 10017-2394. TEL 732-981-0060; 800-678-4333. FAX 732-981-9667. E-mail: customer.service@ieee.org; URL: http://computer.org/pubs/annals/annals.htm. (Subscr. to: 445 Hoes Ln., Box 1331, Piscataway, NJ 08855-1331) Ed. Michel R. Williams. bk.rev.; charts; illus.; stat. circ. 1,400. (reprint service avail. from SWZ) **Indexed:** Amer.Hist.& Life (1979-), ASCA, Compumath, Comput.Cont., Comput.Lit.Ind., Curr.Cont., Hist.Abstr. (1979-), INSPEC, Math.R., SSCI.
●Also available online.
—BLDSC (4362.790000); AskIEEE; CISTI; Ei; Genuine Article; KR SourceOne; Linda Hall; SWETS; UMI; UnCover. **CCC.**
Formerly (until 1992): Annals of the History of Computing (ISSN 0164-1239)
Description: Chronicles vital contributions in computing and their impact on society.

004 US ISSN 1070-9924
TA329 CODEN: ISCEE4
I E E E COMPUTATIONAL SCIENCE & ENGINEERING. 1994. q. $350 to non-members (effective 1998). (I E E E, Computer Society) Institute of Electrical and Electronics Engineers, Inc., 345 E. 47th St., New York, NY 10017-2394. TEL 732-981-0060; 800-678-4333. FAX 732-981-9667. E-mail: customer.service@ieee.org; webmaster@computer.org; URL: http://www.ieee.org. (Subscr. to: 445 Hoes Ln., Box 1331, Piscataway, NJ 08855-1331) Ed. George Cybenko. adv.: B&W page $1200, color page $2300; adv. contact: Heidi Rex. (back issues avail.) **Indexed:** ASCA, Compumath, Curr.Cont., INSPEC (1994-). **Document type:** academic/scholarly publication.
●Also available online.
—BLDSC (4362.813500); AskIEEE; CASDDS; CISTI; Ei; Genuine Article; KR SourceOne; Linda Hall; SWETS; UMI; UnCover. **CCC.**
Description: Feature articles and papers covering developments in computation and algorithms, high-performance computer paradigms, performance evaluation and visualization techniques.

004 US ISSN 1070-986X
QA76.575 CODEN: IEMUE4
I E E E MULTIMEDIA MAGAZINE. 1994. q. $210 to non-members (effective 1996). (Institute of Electrical and Electronics Engineers, Inc.) I E E E Computer Society Press, 10662 Los Vaqueros Circle, Los Alamitos, CA 90720-1264. TEL 714-821-8380; 800-678-4333. FAX 714-821-4010. E-mail: customer.service@ieee.org; URL: http://www.ieee.org. (Subscr. to: IEEE, 445 Hoes Ln., Box 1331, Parsippany, NJ 08855-1331. TEL 908-981-0060. FAX 908-981-9667) Ed. Ramesh Jain. adv.: B&W page $1200, color page $2300; adv. contact: Heidi Rex. (also avail. in microfiche from EEE) **Indexed:** ASCA, Compumath, Curr.Cont.
—BLDSC (4363.006400); AskIEEE; CISTI; Ei; Genuine Article; KR SourceOne; Linda Hall; SWETS; UMI; UnCover. **CCC.**
Description: Feature articles and papers covering hardware and software for media compression, media storage and transport, workstation support for multimedia, data modeling, and abstractions to embed multimedia in application programs.

621.381 US ISSN 1051-9173
TK7895.M4
I E E E SYMPOSIUM ON MASS STORAGE SYSTEMS. DIGEST OF PAPERS. 4th, 1980. a. (Institute of Electrical and Electronics Engineers, Inc.) I E E E Computer Society Press, 10662 Los Vaqueros Circle, Los Alamitos, CA 90720-1264. TEL 714-821-8380. FAX 714-821-4641. Ed. Cat Harris; Pub. Matt Loeb. adv. contact: Frieda Koester. **Document type:** proceedings.
—Ei. **CCC.**
Description: Addresses the environments that are served by mass storage systems.

621.381 001.6 US ISSN 0018-9340
TK7885.A1 CODEN: ITCOB4
I E E E TRANSACTIONS ON COMPUTERS. 1952. m. $685 to non-members (effective 1998). (I E E E, Computer Society) Institute of Electrical and Electronics Engineers, Inc., 345 E. 47th St., New York, NY 10017-2394. TEL 732-981-0060; 800-678-4333. FAX 732-981-9667. E-mail: customer.service@ieee.org; URL: http://www.ieee.org. (Subscr. to: Box 1331, 445 Hoes Lane, Piscataway, NJ 08855-1331) Ed. Jane W.S. Liu. bk.rev.; abstr.; illus.; index. (also avail. in microform) **Indexed:** A.I.Abstr. (until 1992), A.S.& T.Ind., Appl.Mech.Rev., ASCA, CAD CAM Abstr. (until 1992), Chem.Abstr., Compumath, Comput.Abstr., Comput.Cont., Comput.Dtbs., Comput.Lit.Ind., Curr.Cont., Deep Sea Res.& Oceanogr.Abstr., Eng.Ind., Ergon.Abstr., Ind.Sci.Rev., INIS Atomind., INSPEC, Int.Aerosp.Abstr., Math.R., Neurosci.Cit.Ind., Oper.Res.Manage.Sci., Qual.Contr.Appl.Stat., Risk Abstr., Robomat. (until 1992), Sci.Cit.Ind., SSCI, Tel.Abstr., Zent.Math.
—BLDSC (4363.175000); AskIEEE; CASDDS; CISTI; Ei; Genuine Article; KR SourceOne; Linda Hall; SWETS; UMI; UnCover. **CCC.**
Former titles (until 1967): I E E E Transactions on Electronic Computers; (until 1962): I R E Transactions on Electronic Computers; (until 1954): I R E Professional Group on Electronic Computers. Transactions.
Description: Research and design papers in all areas of computation and information processing.

I E I C E TRANSACTIONS ON FUNDAMENTALS OF ELECTRONICS, COMMUNICATIONS AND COMPUTER SCIENCES. (Institute of Electronics, Information and Communication Engineers) see ELECTRONICS

I & I. (Informatie en Informatiebeleid) see BUSINESS AND ECONOMICS — Management

621.381 GW ISSN 0944-2774
QA76 CODEN: ITINEY
I T & T I; Computer, Systeme, Anwendungen. Variant title: Informationstechnik und Technische Informatik. 1958. bi-m. DM.306 (effective 1997). (Informationstechnische Gesellschaft im VDE (ITG)) R. Oldenbourg Verlag GmbH, Rosenheimerstr. 145, 81671 Munich, Germany. TEL 49-89-45051-0. FAX 49-89-45051207. (Subscr. to: Postfach 801360, 81613 Munich, Germany) Ed. R. Herschel. adv.; bk.rev.; charts; illus.; tr.lit.; index. circ. 2,400. (back issues avail.) **Indexed:** Appl.Mech.Rev., Comput.Abstr., Eng.Ind., INIS Atomind., INSPEC, Zent.Math. **Document type:** academic/scholarly publication.
—BLDSC (4496.634600); AskIEEE; CISTI; Ei; KR SourceOne; Linda Hall. **CCC.**
Former titles (until 1993): Informationstechnik - I T (ISSN 0179-9738); Elektronische Rechenanlagen mit Computer-Praxis (ISSN 0013-5720); Incorporates: Computer Praxis (ISSN 0010-4663)
Description: News on computer technology and application in all areas: mainframe, personal computers, hardware, software, data processing and more. Includes market news and calendar of events.

001.6 621.38 340 UK ISSN 0969-3297
KD667.C65
I T LAW TODAY. (Information Technology) 1984. 10/yr. £200 (foreign £225) (effective 1997). Monitor Press Ltd., Suffolk House, Church Field Rd., Sudbury, Suffolk CO10 6YA, England. TEL 44-1787-378607. FAX 44-1787-880201. Ed. Susan Singleton. bk.rev.; index. (back issues avail.) **Indexed:** Euro.LJI, LJI. **Document type:** newsletter.
—BLDSC (4587.613500).
Formerly (until 1993): Applied Computer and Communications Law (ISSN 0267-6621)
Description: Examines the laws governing information technology and the use of computers for suppliers and users of information processing equipment as well as legal practitioners.

004 389 DK ISSN 0905-3204
I T STANDARDNYT. (Supplement avil.: I T Standardnyt. Extra (ISSN 0908-9624)) 1989. 10/yr. DKK 3900. Dansk Standard - Danish Standards Association, Baunegaardsvej 73, DK-2900 Hellerup, Denmark. TEL 45-39-77-01-01. FAX 45-39-77-02-02. E-mail: ds@ds.dk. Ed. Hans Joern Reuss. bk.rev. circ. 300. **Document type:** newsletter.
Description: Publishes information about developments in information technology standards.

COMPUTERS

004   CN   ISSN 1198-8673
IN TOUCH (LONDON, ONTARIO). 1994. q. free. University of Western Ontario, Information Technology Services, Natural Sciences Centre, London, ON N6A 3K7, Canada. TEL 519-661-2151. FAX 519-661-3486. E-mail: in.touch@julian.uwo.ca; URL: http://www.uwo.ca/its/doc/newsletters/InTouch/. Ed. Merran Neville. index. circ. 2,000. (back issues avail.) Document type: newsletter.
   Formed by the merger of (1986-1994): I T S Focus (ISSN 0840-9595); And: C C S Focus (ISSN 0831-4926); Which was formerly (until 1986): Computing and Communications Services Newsletter (ISSN 0831-4225); (until 1985): Computing Centre Newsletter (ISSN 0706-5965); (1967-1979): University of Western Ontario Computing Centre Newsletter (ISSN 0833-8108)
   Description: Disseminates information to campus computer users regarding the activities of I.T.S. Covers areas of support for software and hardware on a wide variety of systems.
   Refereed Serial

621.381   UK   ISSN 0268-7860
   CODEN: INDCE2
INDUSTRIAL COMPUTING. 1986. m. E M A P Business & Computer Publications Ltd., 33-39 Bowling Green Ln., London EC1R 0DA, England. TEL 44-171-837-1212. FAX 44-171-278-4008. circ. 15,002 (controlled). (back issues avail.) **Indexed:** Comput.Dtbs. **Document type:** trade publication.
   —CISTI. **CCC.**

001.6 621.381   GW
INDUSTRIE MANAGEMENT; innovative Strategien fuer die Produktion. 1985. bi-m. DM.267 (effective 1997). (Technische Universitaet Berlin, Systemanalyse und EDV) G I T O Verlag, Kellenzeile 50A, 13437 Berlin, Germany. TEL 49-30-31425118. FAX 49-30-4148270. E-mail: ngronau@cs.tu-berlin.de; URL: http://www.iit.tu-cottbus.de/indman. Ed. Norbert Gronau. adv. contact: Andrea Gramoll. bk.rev. circ. 8,000. (back issues avail.) **Indexed:** Cyb.Abstr. **Document type:** academic/scholarly publication.
   —SWETS.
   Formerly (until 1995): C I M Management (ISSN 0179-2679)
   Description: Covers computer applications and organization in the production and manufacturing industries.
   Refereed Serial

INFO CANADA. see COMPUTERS — Electronic Data Processing

001.6 621.381   FR   ISSN 0981-6402
INFO P C. (Supplement avail.: Langages et Systemes) 1984. m. (11/yr.). 360 F. (foreign 600 F.). I D G Communications France, 92051 Paris La Defense Cedex 5, France. TEL 49-04-79-00. FAX 49-04-78-00. TELEX 613234F. Ed. Emmanuel Alexandre. circ. 70,000.
   —SWETS.
   Formerly: P C World France.

004   BL   ISSN 0103-3875
INFORMATICA. 1986. m. $80. Editora Abril, S.A., Av. Octaviano Alves de Lima 4400, 02909-900 Sao Paulo SP, Brazil. TEL 011-877-1322. FAX 011-877-1437. (Subscr. to: Rua do Curtume 769, 05065-900 Sao Paulo, Brazil. TEL 011-823-9100) Ed. Antonio Machado de Barros. adv.; charts; illus.; stat. circ. 170,000. **Document type:** consumer publication.
   Formerly (until 1993): Exame Informatica.
   Description: For computer users, professionals in administration, marketing, finance, human resources and industry.

004 003   NE   ISSN 0019-9907
INFORMATIE; maandblad voor informatievoorziening. 1958. 11/yr. (plus a. cumulation on CD-ROM). fl.207.50 includes CD-ROM (Belgium 4980 BEF) (effective 1996). Kluwer Bedrijfswetenschappen B.V. (Subsidiary of: Wolters Kluwer N.V.), Postbus 23, 7400 GA Deventer, Netherlands. TEL 31-570-648932. FAX 31-570-611504. E-mail: 74431.1162@compuserve.com. (Subscr. to: Intermedia bv, Postbus 4, 2400 MA Alphen aan den Rijn, Netherlands. TEL 31-172-466321. FAX 31-172-435527) (Co-sponsors: Nederlands Genootschap voor Informatica, Belgisch Studiecentrum voor Automatische Informatieverwerking, Nederlands Opleidingsinstituut voor Informatica) Ed. Joop Kuijs. adv.: B&W page fl.2980, color page fl.5130; trim 297 x 210; adv. contact: Ad Nuesink. bk.rev.; bibl.; charts; illus.; index. circ. 13,000. (also avail. in microform from UMI; reprint service avail. from UMI) **Indexed:** Account.& Data Proc.Abstr.; Cyb.Abstr.; INSPEC, Ref.Zh. **Document type:** trade publication.
   ●Also available on CD-ROM.
   —BLDSC (4481.300000); AskIEEE; CISTI; KR SourceOne; Linda Hall; SWETS; UMI.
   Description: Contains information and scientific articles on computer science, systems development, and EDP management.

004   GW
INFORMATIK (MANNHEIM). 1969. irreg., vol.98, 1994. DM.68. Spektrum Akademischer Verlag GmbH, Vangerowstr. 20, 69115 Heidelberg, Germany. TEL 49-6221-9126-0. FAX 49-6221-912638. E-mail: kaschura@spektrum-verlag.com; URL: http://www.spektrum-verlag.com. Ed.Bd. **Document type:** academic/scholarly publication.

001.6   US   ISSN 0343-3005
INFORMATIK-FACHBERICHTE. (Text in English or German) 1976. irreg. price varies. Springer-Verlag, 175 Fifth Ave., New York, NY 10010. TEL 212-460-1500. FAX 212-473-6272. (Also: Berlin, Heidelberg, Tokyo and Vienna) Ed. W. Brauer. (reprint service avail. from ISI) **Indexed:** INSPEC, Zent.Math. **Document type:** academic/scholarly publication.
   —CCC.

INFORMATION LAW ALERT. see PATENTS, TRADEMARKS AND COPYRIGHTS

INFORMATION LAW SERIES. see LAW

INFORMATION MANAGEMENT. see COMPUTERS — Data Base Management

INFORMATION PROCESSING LETTERS; devoted to the rapid publication of short contributions to information processing. see COMPUTERS — Electronic Data Processing

**001.6 301.16 070.5
340**   US   ISSN 0734-9637
HC102
INFORMATION SOURCES (YEAR). 1976. a. $125 (members $75) (effective 1997). Information Industry Association, 1625 Massachusetts Ave., N.W., Ste. 700, Washington, DC 20036-2212. TEL 202-986-0280. FAX 202-638-4403. Ed. Sheri Robey. adv. contact: Joe M. Carmack.
   Description: Annual directory of the members of the Information Industry Association; profiles of key executives, company descriptions, key products and services.

001.6 621.381   US
INFORMATION TECHNOLOGY DIGEST. 1971. 9/yr. free to University of Michigan community. University of Michigan, Information Technology Division, 535 W. William Argus Bldg., Ann Arbor, MI 48103. TEL 313-763-8980. FAX 313-763-8937. URL: http://www.itd.umich.edu/ITDigest/. Ed. Janet Eaton. circ. 5,500. (back issues avail.) **Document type:** newsletter.
   ●Also available online.
   Former titles (until 1991): University of Michigan. U - M Computing News; University of Michigan. Computing Center Newsletter.
   Description: Covers academic and administrative computing and telecommunications at the university. Intended for its faculty, staff, and students.

INFORMATION TECHNOLOGY FOR DEVELOPMENT. see BUSINESS AND ECONOMICS — International Development And Assistance

621.39   SA   ISSN 1022-2057
INFORMATION TECHNOLOGY REVIEW. Short title: I T Review. (Text in English) 1993. m. R.118. Primedia Publishing (Pty) Ltd., P.O. Box 784698, Sandton 2146, South Africa. TEL 27-11-8843857. FAX 27-11-8844677. E-mail: erich@is.co.za. Ed. Erich Viedge. adv. contact: Chris van Heusden. illus. **Document type:** trade publication.
   Refereed Serial

001.6 621.381   JA   ISSN 0918-3752
INFORMATIZATION WHITE PAPER. (Text in English) 1967. a. 5000 Yen. Japan Information Processing Development Center, 5-8, Shiba Koen 3-chome, Minato-ku, Tokyo 105, Japan. TEL 03-3432-9384. FAX 03-3432-9389. Ed. Eiji Kageyama. adv. contact: Yukie Hignchi. circ. 500. (back issues avail.) **Document type:** academic/scholarly publication.
   Formerly: Computer White Paper.
   Description: Reviews and updates the current status of Japan's information processing industry. Includes many graphs and tables to give a clear picture of the industry.

001.6 621.381   US   ISSN 1079-4573
INSIDE THE NEW COMPUTER INDUSTRY. 1988. m. (except July). $675 (foreign $725) (effective 1996). 25420 Via Cicindela, Carmel, CA 93923-8412. TEL 408-626-4361. FAX 408-626-4362. E-mail: aallison@mbay.net; URL: http://www.aallison.com. Ed. Andrew Allison; Pub. Andrew Allison. R&P contact: Andrew Allison. **Document type:** newsletter.
   ●Also available online.
   Formerly (until 1994): R I S C Management (ISSN 1051-1993)
   Description: Features strategic implications of impact of open systems technology on the computer industry, from PC's to mainframes.

001.6   FR   ISSN 0249-6399
INSTITUT NATIONAL DE RECHERCHE EN INFORMATIQUE ET EN AUTOMATIQUE. RAPPORTS DE RECHERCHE. (Text in English, French) 1974. irreg. free. Institut National de Recherche en Informatique et en Automatique, Sedis Diffusion, B.P. 105, 78153 Le Chesnay Cedex, France. TEL 33-1-39635511. FAX 33-1-39635228. TELEX 697 033 F. URL: http://www.inria.fr/RRRT/publications-fra.html; http://www.inria.fr/RRRT/publications-eng.html. bk.rev. circ. 4,000.
   ●Also available online.
   —BLDSC (7288.126860); CISTI; Ei.

331.1 621.381   US   ISSN 0098-2431
QA76
INSTITUTE FOR CERTIFICATION OF COMPUTING PROFESSIONALS. ANNUAL REPORT. Key Title: Annual Report - Institute for Certification of Computing Professionals. 1973. a. free. Institute for Certification of Computing Professionals, 2200 E. Devon Ave., Ste. 247, Des Plaines, IL 60018-4503. TEL 847-299-4227. FAX 847-299-4280. E-mail: 74040,3722@compuserve.com; URL: http://www.iccp.org. adv. contact: Cristi Herron. circ. 1,500. **Document type:** corporate report.

004   NE   ISSN 0953-5438
QA76.9.H85   CODEN: INTCEE
INTERACTING WITH COMPUTERS. (Text in English) 1989. q. fl.679($390) (effective 1998). (British Computer Society, H C I Specialist Group) Elsevier Science B.V., P.O. Box 211, 1000 AE Amsterdam, Netherlands. TEL 31-20-4853911. FAX 31-20-4853598. (Subscr. in the Americas to: Elsevier Science, Regional Sales Office, Box 945, New York, NY 10159-0945. TEL 212-633-3730. FAX 212-633-3680; Subscr. in Australasia and the Far East to: Elsevier Science (Singapore) Pte Ltd, No.1 Temasek Ave., No.17-01 Millenia Tower, Singapore 039192, Singapore. TEL 65-434-3727. FAX 65-337-2230; Subscr. in Japan to: Elsevier Science Japan, 9-15 Higashi-Azabu 1-chome, Minato-ku, Tokyo 106, Japan. TEL 81-3-5561-5033. FAX 81-3-5561-5047) Ed. Da Diaper. adv.; bk.rev.; abstr.; bibl.; charts; illus.; index (also avail. in microform from UMI; back issues avail.) **Indexed:** A.I.Abstr., Abstr.Hum.Comp.Inter., ASCA, Comput.Abstr., Curr.Cont., INSPEC (1989-), Psychol.Abstr. (1989-), SSCI. **Document type:** academic/scholarly publication.
   —BLDSC (4531.869750); AskIEEE; CISTI; Ei; Genuine Article; KR SourceOne; SWETS; UMI. **CCC.**
   Description: Emphasizes interdisciplinary topics applicable to industry, including research, techniques and tools.
   Refereed Serial

621.381 001.6   JA   ISSN 0387-9519
INTERFACE. (Text in Japanese) m. 13920 Yen. C Q Publishing Co., 1-14-2 Sugamo, Toshima-ku, Tokyo 170, Japan. TEL 81-3-5395-2122. FAX 81-3-5395-1255. (Dist. outside Japan by: Nippon IPS Co., Ltd., 11-6, 3-chome, Iidabashi, Chiyoda-ku, Tokyo 102, Japan. TEL 81-3-3238-0700. FAX 81-3-3238-7944) Ed. Kiyoshi Yamamoto. adv.: B&W page $1800, color page $3600; trim 10 1/8 x 7 3/16. circ. 27,664. **Indexed:** JCT, JTA, Pt.de Rep.
  Description: Provides readers with practical "how-to" articles on both hardware and software development and applications.

001.6 621.381 614   US   ISSN 0020-5419
INTERFACE (BETHESDA). 1968. 9/yr. free. U.S. National Institutes of Health, Division of Computer Research and Technology, Computer Center, Bldg. 12, Rm. 2244, Bethesda, MD 20892. TEL 301-496-5381. Ed. Joseph D. Naughton. bk.rev.; index. circ. 3,000. (looseleaf format)

001.6 621.381 364   US
INTERFACE (SACRAMENTO). 1975. s-a. free. Search Group, Inc., 7311 Greenhaven Dr., Ste. 145, Sacramento, CA 95831. TEL 916-392-2550. FAX 916-392-8440. URL: http://www.search.org. Ed. Twyla R. Cunningham. bk.rev.; bibl.; illus. circ. 3,500. **Document type:** newsletter.

INTERFACES (LINTHICUM). see BUSINESS AND ECONOMICS — Management

004   US
INTERNATIONAL CONFERENCE ON IMAGE MANAGEMENT AND COMMUNICATION IN PATIENT CARE. PROCEEDINGS. Short title: I M A C. 1989. biennial. price varies. (Institute of Electrical and Electronics Engineers, Inc.) I E E E Computer Society Press, 10662 Los Vaqueros Circle, Los Alamitos, CA 90720-1264. TEL 714-821-8380. FAX 714-821-4641. Ed. Cat Harris; Pub. Matt Loeb. adv. contact: Frieda Koester. **Document type:** proceedings.
  Description: Focuses on new technologies and their clinical effects on a number of different topics.

004   US
INTERNATIONAL JOURNAL OF COMPUTER RESEARCH. 1986. q. $245 (effective 1996). Nova Science Publishers, Inc., 6080 Jericho Tpke., Ste. 207, Commack, NY 11725-2808. TEL 516-499-3103. FAX 516-499-3146. E-mail: novasci1@aol.com. Pub. Frank Columbus. circ. 700. **Document type:** academic/scholarly publication.
  Former titles: Journal of Computer Abstracts and Research; (until vol.8): Computer Abstracts on Microfiche; (until vol.4): Computer Information Review (ISSN 0895-6588)

001.6   US
INTERNATIONAL LECTURE SERIES IN COMPUTER SCIENCE. 1981. irreg., vol.7. 1988. Academic Press, Inc., 525 B St., Ste. 1900, San Diego, CA 92101-4495. TEL 619-231-0926. FAX 619-699-6715. (Subscr. to: Order Dept., 6277 Sea Harbor Dr., 4th Fl., Orlando, FL 32887. TEL 800-321-5068) (reprint service avail. from ISI) **Indexed:** Math.R.
  Refereed Serial

621.3   US   ISSN 0731-3071
QA76.5   CODEN: DPFTDL
INTERNATIONAL SYMPOSIUM ON FAULT-TOLERANT COMPUTING. DIGEST OF PAPERS. Short title: F T C S. 1971. a. price varies. (Institute of Electrical and Electronics Engineers, Inc.) I E E E Computer Society Press, 10662 Los Vaqueros Circle, Box 3014, Los Alamitos, CA 90720-1264. TEL 714-821-8380. FAX 714-821-4641. Ed. Cat Harris; Pub. Matt Loeb. adv. contact: Frieda Koester. **Document type:** proceedings.
  —BLDSC (4047.398000); Ei; UMI. **CCC.**
  Former titles: International Symposium on Fault-Tolerant Computing. Proceedings (ISSN 0363-8928); International Symposium on Fault-Tolerant Computing. Digest (ISSN 0074-882X)
  Description: Addresses progress and potential of dependable computing research.

003 658   UK   ISSN 0969-6016
T57.6.A1   CODEN: ITORF9
INTERNATIONAL TRANSACTIONS IN OPERATIONAL RESEARCH. 1994. bi-m. fl.832($478) (effective 1998). (International Federation of Operational Research Societies) Elsevier Science Ltd., Pergamon, P.O. Box 800, Kidlington, Oxford OX5 1DX, England. TEL 44-1865-843000. FAX 44-1865-843010. E-mail: nlinfo-f@elsevier.nl; usinfo-f@elsevier.com; forinfo-kyf04035@niftyserve.or.jp; URL: http://www.elsevier.nl/. (Subscr. to: Elsevier Science, Regional Sales Office, P.O. Box 211, 1000 AE Amsterdam, Netherlands. TEL 31-20-4853757. FAX 31-20-4853432; Subscr. in the Americas to: Elsevier Science, Regional Sales Office, Box 945, New York, NY 10159-0945. TEL 212-633-3730. FAX 212-633-3680; Subscr. in Australasia and the Far East to: Elsevier Science (Singapore) Pte Ltd, No.1 Temasek Ave., No.17-01 Millenia Tower, Singapore 039192, Singapore. TEL 65-434-3727. FAX 65-337-2230) Ed. G.J. Bell. (also avail. in microform from UMI; back issues avail.) **Document type:** academic/scholarly publication.
  —BLDSC (4551.305950); AskIEEE; KR SourceOne; SWETS; UMI. **CCC.**
  Refereed Serial

001.6 621.381   US   ISSN 1051-9246
QA75.5
INTRODUCING COMPUTERS: CONCEPTS, SYSTEMS, AND APPLICATIONS. 1985. a. John Wiley & Sons, Inc., 605 Third Ave., New York, NY 10158. Ed. Robert H. Blissmer. index.
  —BLDSC (4557.486700); CISTI.
  Formerly (until 1989): Computer Annual (ISSN 0749-9221)

IRISH COMPUTER. see COMPUTERS — Microcomputers

001.6 621.381   GW   ISSN 0935-9680
IX; Multiuser - Multitasking - Magazin. 1988. m. DM.81 (foreign DM.88.80). Verlag Heinz Heise GmbH und Co. KG, Helstorferstr. 7, 30625 Hannover, Germany. TEL 49-511-5352-0. FAX 49-511-5352-129. Ed. Juergen Seeger. adv. contact: Michael Hanke. circ. 35,379 (paid). **Document type:** trade publication.
  —SWETS.

004   JA   ISSN 1340-3346
J I P D E C INFORMATIZATION QUARTERLY. 1970. q. 13000 Yen. Japan Information Processing Development Center, Kikai Shinko Kaikan Bldg., 5-8, Shiba Koen 3-chome, Minato-ku, Tokyo 105, Japan. TEL 03-3432-9384. FAX 03-3432-9389. (Co-sponsor: Japan Keirin Association) Ed. Yuji Yamadori. circ. 500. **Indexed:** Cyb.Abstr., INSPEC (1993-), JCT, JTA. **Document type:** academic/scholarly publication.
  —BLDSC (4669.153980); AskIEEE; CISTI; KR SourceOne.
  Former titles (until 1993): Japan Computer Quarterly (ISSN 0910-6707); (until 1984): J.I.P.D.E.C. Report (ISSN 0388-0494)

001.6 621.38   CC
JISUANJI SHIDAI/COMPUTER AGE. (Text in Chinese) q. Zhejiang Jisuan Jishu Yanjiusuo - Zhejiang Institute of Computing Technology, Xin 5, Huancheng Xilu, Hangzhou, Zhejiang 310006, People's Republic of China. TEL 754111. Ed. He Zhijun.

004   CC   ISSN 1002-1574
JISUANJI SHIJIE YUEKAN/P C WORLD CHINA. (Text in Chinese) 1985. m. China Computerworld, 3-F, Commercial Bldg., No. 2 Cuiwei Block, Wanshou Rd., P.O. Box 750, Beijing 100036, People's Republic of China. TEL 86-10-825-9412. FAX 86-10-825-9410. Ed. Yaying Lin. adv.: B&W page $3200, color page $4200; trim 185 x 260; adv. contact: Jinghua He. circ. 93,000.

001.6 621.381   CC   ISSN 1000-386X
JISUANJI YINGYONG YU RUANJIAN/COMPUTER APPLICATIONS AND SOFTWARE. (Text in Chinese) bi-m. Shanghai Jisuan Jishu Yanjiusuo - Shanghai Institute of Computing Technology, 546 Yuruan Lu, Shanghai 200040, People's Republic of China. TEL 520070.

001.6 621.381   US   ISSN 1041-1828
371.42
JOB EXPRESS. 1987. s-m. $49.50. C C N Publications, 105 N. Main St., Boonton, NJ 07005. TEL 201-299-1535; 800-836-0667. FAX 201-335-4866. Ed. Wendy Vandame. R&P contact: Wendy Vandame. adv. contact: Judy Green. (back issues avail.) **Document type:** newsletter.
  Description: Contains a survey of billing rates, a listing of available jobs and contracts and positions sought in computer consulting work.

004   GW
▼**JOURNAL FOR UNIVERSAL COMPUTER SCIENCE.** Short title: J U C S. Online edition (GW ISSN 0948-6968) (Text in English) 1995. m. online (plus a. print cumulation). Springer-Verlag, Heidelberger Platz 3, 14197 Berlin, Germany. TEL 49-30-82787-0. FAX 49-30-82787448. E-mail: subscriptions@springer.de; URL: http://link.springer.de. (Subscr. in N. America to: Springer-Verlag New York, Inc., 333 Meadowlands Pkwy., Secaucus, NJ 07094. TEL 212-460-1500. FAX 212-473-6272) abstr. (back issues avail.) **Document type:** academic/scholarly publication.
  ●Also available online.

JOURNAL OF BUSINESS LOGISTICS. see BUSINESS AND ECONOMICS — Marketing And Purchasing

003   US   ISSN 0022-0000
QA76.5   CODEN: JCSSBM
JOURNAL OF COMPUTER AND SYSTEM SCIENCES. 1967. bi-m. $800 (foreign $896) (effective 1997). Academic Press, Inc., Journal Division, 525 B St., Ste. 1900, San Diego, CA 92101-4495. TEL 619-230-1840. FAX 619-699-6800. E-mail: apsubs@acad.com; URL: http://www.apnet.com/www/journal/ss.htm; http://www.idealibrary.com/. (Subscr. to: Box 861213, Orlando, FL 32886-1213. TEL 407-347-4040. FAX 407-363-9661) Ed. Edward K. Blum. (back issues avail.) **Indexed:** ASCA, Biol.Abstr., Compumath, Comput.Cont., Curr.Cont., Curr.Cont., Cyb.Abstr., Eng.Ind., Excerp.Med., Ind.Sci.Rev., INSPEC, Int.Abstr.Oper.Res., Math.R., Sci.Cit.Ind., SSCI, Zent.Math. **Document type:** academic/scholarly publication.
  ●Also available online.
  —BLDSC (4963.600000); AskIEEE; CISTI; Ei; Genuine Article; KR SourceOne; Linda Hall; SWETS; UnCover. **CCC.**
  Description: Publishes original research papers on computer science and in system science, with emphasis on pertinent mathematical theory and its applications.
  Refereed Serial

685.22544   US
JOURNAL OF COMPUTER SCIENCE EDUCATION. 1987. q. $29 to non-members (foreign $39); members $20 (foreign $30). International Society for Technology in Education, Special Interest Groups for Computer Science, University of Oregon, 1787 Agate St., Eugene, OR 97403-1923. TEL 541-346-4414. FAX 541-346-5890. Ed. Charles Funkhouser. circ. 450. (back issues avail.) **Indexed:** C.I.J.E. **Document type:** newsletter.
  —**CCC.**
  Formerly: S I G C S Newsletter (ISSN 1040-7553)
  Description: Information for those teaching computer science at the pre-college level.

JOURNAL OF ELECTRONICS AND COMPUTER RESEARCH. see ELECTRONICS

JOURNAL OF INFORMATION & OPTIMIZATION SCIENCES. see MATHEMATICS

COMPUTERS

006 003 US ISSN 0743-7315
QA76.5 CODEN: JPDCER
JOURNAL OF PARALLEL AND DISTRIBUTED COMPUTING. 1984. 16/yr. $597 (foreign $669) (effective 1997). Academic Press, Inc., Journal Division, 525 B St., Ste. 1900, San Diego, CA 92101-4495. TEL 619-230-1840. FAX 619-699-6800. E-mail: apsubs@acad.com; URL: http://www.apnet.com/www/journal/pc.htm; http://www.idealibrary.com. (Subscr. to: Box 861213, Orlando, FL 32886-1213. TEL 407-347-4040. FAX 407-363-9661) Ed.Bd. (back issues avail.) Indexed: ASCA, Compumath, Curr.Cont., Ind.Sci.Rev., Sci.Cit.Ind., Zent.Math. **Document type:** academic/scholarly publication.
●Also available online.
—BLDSC (5028.620000); AskIEEE; CISTI; Ei; Genuine Article; KR SourceOne; Linda Hall; SWETS; UnCover. **CCC.**
Description: Directed to researchers, engineers, educators, managers, programmers, and users of computers who have particular interest in parallel process and, or distributed computing. Publishes original research papers and current review articles on theory, design, evaluation, and use of parallel and, or distributed computing systems.
Refereed Serial

006 621.39 US ISSN 0920-8542
QA76.88 CODEN: JOSUED
JOURNAL OF SUPERCOMPUTING; an international journal of supercomputing design, analysis and use. 1987. q. fl.680 to institutions; $349 to institutions in U.S. (effective 1998). (Supercomputing Research Center) Kluwer Academic Publishers Boston, Box 358, Accord Sta., Hingham, MA 02018-0358. TEL 617-871-6300. FAX 617-871-6528. TELEX 200190. E-mail: services@wkap.nl; URL: http://www.wkap.nl. (Dist. outside N. America by: Kluwer Academic Publishers Group, P.O. Box 322, 3300 AH Dordrecht, Netherlands. TEL 31-78-6392392. FAX 31-78-6546474) Eds. Harlow Freitag, John Riganati. adv.; illus. (also avail. in microform from UMI; back issues avail.; reprint service avail. from SWZ,UMI) Indexed: ASCA, Compumath, Comput.Abstr., Comput.Rev., Curr.Cont., Cyb.Abstr., Eng.Ind., Ind.Sci.Rev., Inform.Sci.Abstr., INSPEC (1987-), Ref.Zh., Sci.Cit.Ind., Zent.Math. **Document type:** academic/scholarly publication.
—BLDSC (5067.117000); AskIEEE; CISTI; Ei; Genuine Article; KR SourceOne; SWETS; UMI; UnCover. **CCC.**
Description: Archival technical journal publishing theoretical, practical, tutorial and survey papers on all aspects of supercomputing.
Refereed Serial

003 US ISSN 0899-1499
CODEN: OJCOE3
JOURNAL ON COMPUTING. Key Title: O R S A Journal on Computing. 1989. q. $69 to individuals (foreign $77); institutions $132 (foreign $140) (effective 1997). Institute for Operations Research and the Management Sciences, 901 Elkridge Landing Rd., Ste. 400, Linthicum, MD 21090-2909. TEL 410-850-0300; 800-343-0062. FAX 410-684-2963. (Subscr. to: Box 64794, Baltimore, MD 21264-4794) Ed. Bruce Golden. R&P contact: Fran Silverman. adv. contact: Kathye Long. charts; illus.; stat.; index. circ. 1,125. Indexed: INSPEC (1989-), Oper.Res.Manage.Sci., Qual.Contr.Appl.Stat., Zent.Math. **Document type:** academic/scholarly publication.
—AskIEEE; KR SourceOne; UnCover. **CCC.**
Description: Dedicated to the publication of research, surveys and applied articles on the interface between operations research and computer science.

JURIMETRICS JOURNAL; journal of law, science and technology. see *LAW*

001.6 350 310 FI ISSN 0357-9921
JYVASKYLA STUDIES IN COMPUTER SCIENCE, ECONOMICS AND STATISTICS. (Text in English) 1980. irreg. price varies. Jyvaskylan Yliopisto - University of Jyvaskyla, Publications Center, PL 35, 40100 Jyvaskyla 10, Finland. TEL 941-601-211. FAX 603-371. TELEX 28219 JYK SF. Ed.Bd. circ. 450. **Document type:** monographic series.

004 SU ISSN 1319-1578
KING SAUD UNIVERSITY. JOURNAL. COMPUTER AND INFORMATION SCIENCES/JAMI'AT AL-MALIK SA'UD. MAJALLAH. AL-'ULUM AL-HASIB WAL-MA'LUMAT. (Other sections avail.: Administrative Sciences, Agricultural Sciences, Architecture and Planning, Arts, Educational Sciences and Islamic Studies, Engineering Sciences, Science) (Text in Arabic, English) 1993. a. $5. King Saud University, University Libraries, P.O. Box 22480, Riyadh 11495, Saudi Arabia. TEL 966-1-4676148. FAX 966-1-4676162. TELEX 4010190 KSU SJ. Ed. Khalid A. Al-Dobaian. R&P contact: Saad A. Al-Dobaian. circ. 2,000. **Document type:** academic/scholarly publication.
Refereed Serial

621.3 NE ISSN 0893-3405
KLUWER INTERNATIONAL SERIES IN ENGINEERING AND COMPUTER SCIENCE. (Text in English) 1984. irreg., latest 1994. price varies. Kluwer Academic Publishers, Postbus 17, 3300 AA Dordrecht, Netherlands. TEL 31-78-6392254. FAX 31-78-6392392. TELEX 29245 KAPG NL. E-mail: services@wkap.nl; URL: http://www.wkap.nl. (Dist. by: Kluwer Academic Publishers Group, P.O. Box 322, 3300 AH Dordrecht, Netherlands. TEL 31-78-6392392. FAX 31-78-6546474; N. America dist. addr.: Box 358, Accord Sta., Hingham, MA 02018-0358. TEL 617-871-6600. FAX 617-871-6528) (back issues avail.) Indexed: INSPEC, Zent.Math. **Document type:** monographic series.
—BLDSC (5099.730000); CISTI. **CCC.**
Refereed Serial

004 DK ISSN 0107-8283
KOEBENHAVNS UNIVERSITET. DATALOGISK INSTITUT. RAPPORT. irregg. free. Koebenhavns Universitet, Datalogisk Institut, Universitetsparken 1, DK-2100 Copenhagen OE, Denmark. TEL 45-35-32-14-00. FAX 45-35-32-14-01. **Document type:** academic/scholarly publication.
—BLDSC (7264.280000).

004 IO
KOMPUTEK COMPUTERWORLD INDONESIA. (Text in Indonesian) w. P T Jawa Media Komputana, Jalan Kayun No. 24, Surabaya 60271, Indonesia. TEL 31-526041. FAX 31-519806. Ed. Edi Purwono. adv.: B&W page Rps.3800000, color page Rps.7600000; trim 285 x 415. circ. 15,000.

001.6 621.381 US ISSN 1045-3563
QA76.73.L23
L I S P POINTERS. 1987. q. Association for Computing Machinery, 1515 Broadway, 17th Fl., New York, NY 10036. TEL 212-869-7440. FAX 212-869-0481. TELEX 421686.
—SWETS; UnCover.

004 US
LAS VEGAS COMPUTER JOURNAL. 1994. m.; online version d. 4430-1 E Charleston, Ste. 101, Las Vegas, NV 89104. E-mail: compjour@vegas.infi.net; URL: http://www.computerjournal.com. Ed. Johanna Nezhoda.
●Also available online.
Description: Covers computer related topics.

LEARNING AND LEADING WITH TECHNOLOGY. see *COMPUTERS — Computer Assisted Instruction*

001.6 GW ISSN 0302-9743
CODEN: LNCSD9
LECTURE NOTES IN COMPUTER SCIENCE. Variant title: Lecture Notes in Artificial Intelligence. 1973. irreg. price varies. Springer-Verlag, Heidelberger Platz 3, 14197 Berlin, Germany. TEL 49-30-8207-0. FAX 49-30-8214091. E-mail: subscriptions@springer.de. (Orders in N. America to: Springer-Verlag New York, Inc., 44 Hartz Way, Secaucus, NJ 07096-2491. TEL 201-348-4033. FAX 201-348-4505) Eds. G. Goos, J. Hartmanis. (reprint service avail. from ISI; back issues avail.) Indexed: ASCA, Compumath, Comput.Cont., Cyb.Abstr., INSPEC, Neurosci.Cit.Ind., SSCI, Zent.Math. **Document type:** monographic series.
—BLDSC (5180.185000); CISTI; Ei; Genuine Article; SWETS. **CCC.**
Description: Reports on leading-edge research in artificial intelligence and other areas of computer science.

001.6 621.381 SI
LECTURE NOTES SERIES ON COMPUTING. (Text in English) irreg., vol. 5, 1994. price varies. World Scientific Publishing Co. Pte. Ltd., Farrer Rd., P.O. Box 128, Singapore 9128, Singapore. TEL 65-3825663. FAX 65-3825919. TELEX RS 28561 WSPC. E-mail: wspcsl@singnet.com.sg; sales@wspc2.demon.co.uk; wspc@wspc.com; URL: http://www.singnet.com.sg/~wspclib/. (UK addr.: 57 Shelton St., Covent Garden, London WC2H 9He, England. TEL 44-171-836-0888; US addr.: 1060 Main St., River Edge, NJ 07661. TEL 800-227-7562) Ed. D.T. Lee. Indexed: Zent.Math.

001.6 620 FR ISSN 1163-3867
LETTRE DE LA SURETE DE FONCTIONNEMENT. 1987. bi-m. 700 F. (foreign 750 F.) E C 2, 269, rue de la Garenne, 92024 Nanterre Cedex, France. TEL 47-80-70-00. FAX 1-47-80-66-29. Ed. Jean-Claude Rault. bk.rev. (back issues avail.) **Document type:** newsletter.

001.6 621.381 JA ISSN 0915-2296
LINKAGE; National Diet Library automation project news. (Text in Japanese) 1969. s-a. free. National Diet Library, Information Processing Division, 1-10-1 Nagata-cho, Chiyoda-ku, Tokyo 100, Japan. TEL 81-3-3581-2331. FAX 81-3-3581-3292. URL: http://www.ndl.go.jp. Ed. Masashi Murakami. circ. 1,000 (controlled). **Document type:** newsletter.
Formerly (until Mar. 1973): Gyomu Kikaika Junbishitsu Nyusu - Automation Project News.

001.6 808.87 US
M I S INFORMATION. 1988. 10/yr. $20 (effective 1997). Box 231, Rochester, MN 55903-0231. E-mail: misinfo@aol.com; URL: http://members.ad.com/misinfo/misinfo.html. Ed. Chris Miksanek; Pub. Chris Miksanek. adv.; bk.rev. circ. 1,000. **Document type:** newsletter.
Description: Newsletter devoted to computer humor. Specializes in satire, especially relating to trends in computing.

M I S QUARTERLY. (Management Information Systems) see *BUSINESS AND ECONOMICS — Management*

001.6 621.381 GW
M - U - M. (Menschen und Maus) 1984. bi-m. DM.100 Coconut e.V., Dornerhof 12, 47058 Duisburg, Germany. TEL 49-203-333575. FAX 49-203-333517. Ed. Klaus-Dieter Gogoll. bk.rev. circ. 2,500. **Document type:** bulletin.
Description: Information about software, hardware and programming.

MACHINE INTELLIGENCE AND PATTERN RECOGNITION. see *COMPUTERS — Artificial Intelligence*

006.3 621.39 US ISSN 0885-6125
Q325.5 CODEN: MALEEZ
MACHINE LEARNING; an international journal. Online edition (US ISSN 1383-7915) 1986. m. fl.1664 to institutions; $854 to institutions in U.S. (effective 1998). Kluwer Academic Publishers Boston, Box 358, Accord Sta., Hingham, MA 02018-0358. TEL 617-871-6300. FAX 617-871-6528. TELEX 200190. E-mail: kluwer@wkap.com; URL: http://mlis.wkap.nl. (Dist. outside N. America by: Kluwer Academic Publishers Group, P.O. Box 322, 3300 AH Dordrecht, Netherlands. TEL 31-78-6392392. FAX 31-78-6546474) Ed. Thomas G. Dietterich. adv.; bk.rev. (also avail. in microform from UMI; back issues avail.; reprint service avail. from SWZ,UMI) Indexed: A.I.Abstr. (un 1992), A.S.& T.Ind., ASCA, Compumath, Comput.& Info.Sys., Comput.Rev., Curr.Cont., Eng.Ind., INSPEC (1986-), Robomat. (until 1992), Sci.Cit.Ind., Sociol.Abstr., SSCI, Zent.Math. **Document type:** academic/scholarly publication.
●Also available online.
—BLDSC (5323.870000); AskIEEE; CISTI; Ei; Genuine Article; KR SourceOne; SWETS; UMI; UnCover. **CCC.**
Description: Disseminates international research computational approaches to learning, automated knowledge acquisition, and natural language processing.
Refereed Serial

006 US ISSN 1383-7915
MACHINE LEARNING ONLINE. "INS"/yr. $802 (effective 1998). Kluwer Academic Publishers Boston, Box 358, Accord Sta., Hingham, MA 02018-0358. TEL 617-871-6600. FAX 617-871-6528. E-mail: kluwer@wkap.com; URL: http://mlis.www.wkap.nl. (Dist. outside N. America by: Kluwer Academic Publishers Group, P.O. Box 322, 3300 AH Dordrecht, Netherlands. TEL 31-78-6392392. FAX 31-78-6546474) Document type: academic/scholarly publication.
●Available only online.
Refereed Serial

004 IS ISSN 0333-7413
MACHSHEVIM P C. (Text in Hebrew) 1980. m. $67. Merav Publishing Industries Ltd., 12 Yad Harutzim, Tel Aviv 67778, Israel. TEL 972-3-6382938. FAX 972-3-6382939. Ed. Nomi Epharati. adv. circ. 8,000.

001.6 629.8 IS
MAEDA VENITUNIM. 3/yr. I.B.M. Israel, I.B.M. House, 2 Weizmann St., Tel Aviv, Israel. TEL 03-618032. Ed. Yossi Shuval.

MAIL ADVERTISING SERVICE ASSOCIATION INTERNATIONAL. COMPUTER SURVEY. see ADVERTISING AND PUBLIC RELATIONS

001.6 621.381 GW ISSN 0939-7795
MANAGEMENT & SEMINAR. 1974. 11/yr. DM.56 (foreign DM.60). Verlag Neuer Merkur GmbH, Ingolstaedter Str. 63a, 80939 Munich, Germany. TEL 089-318905-0. FAX 089-31890553. Ed. Silke Bonarius. adv.; bk.rev. circ. 10,500. Document type: newsletter.
—BLDSC (5359.157500); SWETS.
Formerly (until 1991): Congress und Seminar.

MANUFACTURING AUTOMATION; the essential business resource on international manufacturing automation. see BUSINESS AND ECONOMICS — Marketing And Purchasing

MATHEMATICAL METHODS OF OPERATIONS RESEARCH. see MATHEMATICS — Computer Applications

658.4 003 US ISSN 0364-765X
T57.6.A1 CODEN: MOREDQ
MATHEMATICS OF OPERATIONS RESEARCH. 1976. q. $75 to individuals (foreign $84); institutions $132 (foreign $141) (effective 1997). Institute for Operations Research and the Management Sciences, 901 Elkridge Landing Rd., Ste. 400, Linthicum, MD 21090-2909. TEL 410-850-0300; 800-343-0062. Ed. Jan Karl Lenstra. R&P contact: Fran Silverman. adv. contact: Kathye Long. bibl.; charts; stat. Indexed: ABI Inform., ASCA, BPIA, Bus.Ind., Compumath, Comput.Cont., Cont.Pg.Manage., Curr.Cont., Cyb.Abstr., Ind.Sci.Rev., INSPEC, Int.Abstr.Oper.Res., J.Cont.Quant.Meth., Manage.Cont., Math.R., Oper.Res.Manage.Sci., Qual.Contr.Appl.Stat., Sci.Cit.Ind., SSCI, Tr.& Indus.Ind., Zent.Math. Document type: academic/scholarly publication.
—BLDSC (5406.150000); AskIEEE; CISTI; Ei; Genuine Article; KR SourceOne; Linda Hall; SWETS; UMI; UnCover. CCC.
Refereed Serial

378 621.381 US
MATRIX NEWSLETTER. 1983. s-a. free. Columbia University, Teachers College, Department of Communication, Computing and Technology in Education, 525 W. 120th St., Box 8, New York, NY 10027. TEL 212-678-3344. Ed. Marie M. Taylor. circ. 500. (back issues avail.)

004 IS ISSN 0333-7685
MAYDAON; Israeli journal for information on EDP. 1971. bi-m. IS.200 (effective 1997). Israeli Center for Information Systems, 30 Shderot Yehudit, Tel Aviv 67016, Israel. TEL 972-3-5618259. FAX 972-3-5616956. Ed. Benny H. Raab. bk.rev. circ. 3,000.

MERCHANT AND GOULD COMPUTER LAW NEWSLETTER. see PATENTS, TRADEMARKS AND COPYRIGHTS

004 PH ISSN 0116-1792
METROPOLITAN COMPUTER TIMES. (Text in English) 1985. w. Computer Connection Inc., 54 Don A Roces Snr. Ave., Quezon City, Metro Manila, Philippines. TEL 2-981509. Pub. Diana Roces Davila.

004 US ISSN 1087-481X
MICHIGAN COMPUTERUSER MAGAZINE. 1991. m. $12; newsstand price: free. Primetime Press, 500 Hickory, Box 597, Linden, MI 48451. TEL 810-735-9720. FAX 810-735-9720. E-mail: 70751,1271@compuserve.com; URL: http://www.michcu.com. Ed. Robert Gramer; Pub. Robert Gramer. adv.: page $1328.30; trim 10 x 14; adv. contact: Robert Gramer. bk.rev.; software rev.; charts; illus.; mkt.; pat.; stat. circ. 65,000. (tabloid format; back issues avail.) Document type: consumer publication, trade publication.
●Also available online.
Description: Business applications of computers and high technology.

001.6 621.381 JA ISSN 0285-6425
MICOMLIFE. (Text in Japanese) 1981. m. 6000 Yen. Gakken Co. Ltd., 40-5, 4-chome, Kamiikedai, Ohta-ku, Tokyo 145, Japan. Ed. Hajime Morita.

MICRO. see ELECTRONICS

004 FR
▼**MICRO PRATIQUE.** 1996. m. 279 F. (effective 1997). Editions Lariviere, 12 rue Mozart, 92587 Clichy Cedex, France. TEL 33-1-41403232. FAX 33-1-41403250. TELEX 211 678 F.
Description: Articles on domestic computers.

001.6 621.381 CL ISSN 0716-4777
MICROBYTE; todo computacion y telecomunicaciones. 1984. m. Esc.8500($55) Editora Microbyte Ltda., Passy - 056 - Providencia, Santiago, Chile. TEL 562-222-8556. FAX 562-222-2699. TELEX 243259 MICRO CL. Ed. Jose Kaffman. circ. 7,000. (back issues avail.)

621.39 US ISSN 1081-3497
▼**MICROSOFT CERTIFIED PROFESSIONAL MAGAZINE.** 1995. bi-m. $19.95 (effective 1996). Quick Start Technologies, Inc., 1500 Quail St., 6th Fl., Newport Beach, CA 92660-2738. TEL 714-476-1015; 888-462-7624. E-mail: mail@mcpmag.com. Ed. Linda Briggs. adv.; illus.; tr.lit. (back issues avail.)

621.39 355 UK
MILCOMP EUROPE (YEAR). CONFERENCE PROCEEDINGS; military computers, systems and software. a. Nexus Media, Nexus House, Azalea Dr., Swanley, Kent BR8 8HY, England. TEL 44-1322-660070. FAX 44-1322-667633. Document type: proceedings.

001.6 621.381 FR ISSN 0242-5769
MONDE INFORMATIQUE. (Annual supplement avail.: Guide du Monde Informatique) (Text in French) 1981. w. 850 F. (foreign 1550 F.). I D G Communications France, 2 place des Vosges Cedex 65, 92051 Paris La Defense Cedex 5, France. TEL 49-04-79-00. FAX 49-04-78-00. TELEX 613 234 F. Ed. Roland Schmitt. adv.; bk.rev. circ. 36,000.
—BLDSC (5907.025000). CCC.

001.6 AU ISSN 1021-271X
MONITOR; Zeitschrift fuer den erfolgreichen Computereinsatz. 1983. 13/yr. S.320. Monitor Verlag, Billrothstr. 58, A-1190 Vienna, Austria. TEL 0222-364450. FAX 0222-3644504. Ed. Michael Nobbe; Pub. Michael Nobbe. adv. contact: Christa Baumgartner. circ. 20,000. Document type: consumer publication.

001.6 621.38 UK ISSN 0260-6666
MONITOR (OXFORD); an analytical review of current events in the online and electronic publishing industry. 1981. m. £175. Learned Information (Europe) Ltd., Woodside, Hinksey Hill, Oxford OX1 5BE, England. TEL 44-1865-388000. FAX 44-1865-736354. (Dist. in N. America by: Learned Information Inc., 143 Old Marlton Pike, Medford, NJ 08055-8750. TEL 609-654-6266) Ed. Harry R. Collier. Indexed: INSPEC. Document type: newsletter.
—AskIEEE; KR SourceOne.
Description: Provides description and analysis of events in the sphere of information transfer via electronic media. Offers a comprehensive record of what is happening in the international information industry as well as interpretation of the month's news.

001.6 BL ISSN 0103-9741
MONOGRAFIAS EM CIENCIA DA COMPUTACAO. (Text in English and Portuguese) 1969. irreg. free. Pontificia Universidade Catolica do Rio de Janeiro, Departamento de Informatica, Rua Marques de Sao Vicente 225 - Gavea, 22453 Rio de Janeiro RJ, Brazil. FAX 55-21-511-5645. TELEX 021-31048. Ed. Carlos J.P. Lucena. circ. 200. Document type: academic/scholarly publication.
Formerly (until 1975): Monographs in Computer Science and Computer Applications.

MULTIMEDIA COMPUTING & PRESENTATIONS. see COMPUTERS — Software

MULTIMEDIA STRATEGIST. see COMPUTERS — Computer Networks

004 GW ISSN 0942-4962
CODEN: MUSYEW
MULTIMEDIA SYSTEMS. Online edition (GW ISSN 1432-1882) (Text in English) 1993. bi-m. DM.515.40 (foreign DM.520.80) (effective 1998). (Association for Computing Machinery) Springer-Verlag, Heidelberger Platz 3, 14197 Berlin, Germany. TEL 49-30-82787-0. FAX 49-30-82787448. E-mail: subscriptions@springer.de; URL: http://link.springer.de/link/service/journals/00530/index.htm. (Subscr. in N. America to: Springer-Verlag New York, Inc., 333 Meadowlands Pkwy., Secaucus, NJ 07094. TEL 212-460-1500. FAX 212-473-6272) Ed.Bd. (also avail. in microform from UMI) Indexed: ASCA, Curr.Cont. Document type: academic/scholarly publication.
●Also available online.
—BLDSC (5983.148500); AskIEEE; CISTI; Genuine Article; KR SourceOne; SWETS; UMI; UnCover. CCC.
Description: Serves as a forum for innovative research, emerging technologies, and state-of-the-art methods in all aspects of multimedia computing, communication, storage, and applications among researchers, engineers, and users.

N E C NEWS. (Nippon Electric Company) see COMMUNICATIONS

001.6 US
N I C E NEWS.* m? (National Information Conference) ConventionNews, 4341 Montgomery Ave., Bethesda, MD 20814-4401. Ed. Jawaid Awan. adv.

621.381 001.6 SZ ISSN 0028-3398
TJ212 CODEN: NETEA8
NEUE TECHNIK/NOUVELLES TECHNIQUES/NEW TECHNIQUES. (Text in German) 1959. m. 75 SFr. Diagonal Verlags AG, Industriestr. 21, CH-5507 Mellingen, Switzerland. Ed. Klaus Bucher. adv.; charts; illus.; index. circ. 12,000. Indexed: Chem.Abstr., Excerp.Med., Fuel & Energy Abstr., INSPEC. Document type: trade publication.
—CISTI; Linda Hall.

621.39 510 US ISSN 1061-5369
QA76.87 CODEN: NPACEM
NEURAL, PARALLEL & SCIENTIFIC COMPUTATIONS. 1993. 4/yr. $100 to individuals (foreign $140); institutions $250 (foreign $290). Dynamic Publishers, Inc., Box 48654, Atlanta, GA 30362. TEL 770-451-3616. Ed. M. Sambandham. Indexed: Zent.Math. Document type: academic/scholarly publication.
—BLDSC (6081.281010); AskIEEE; KR SourceOne; SWETS. CCC.
Description: Provides an international forum to computer science, engineering, mathematical, and other applied science communities to publish research papers.

001.6 621.381 UK ISSN 1361-4568
QA76.76.H92 CODEN: HYPEEW
NEW REVIEW OF HYPERMEDIA AND MULTIMEDIA. 1989. 3/yr. £70($130) Taylor Graham Publishing, 500 Chesham House, 150 Regent St., London W1R 5FA, England. Ed. Patricia Baird. adv.; bk.rev. Indexed: Abstr.Hum.Comp.Inter., Educ.Tech.Abstr., INSPEC (1989-), LISA, Tech.Educ.Abstr. Document type: academic/scholarly publication.
—BLDSC (6087.764200); AskIEEE; CISTI; KR SourceOne; SWETS.
Formerly (until 1995): Hypermedia (ISSN 0955-8543).
Description: Discusses the conceptual basis of hypertext systems: cognitive aspects, design strategies, knowledge representation, and link dynamics.

COMPUTERS

NEWMEDIA; technologies for the professional communicator. see COMMUNICATIONS — *Television And Cable*

001.6 621.381   JA   ISSN 0285-4619
HD9696.C63
NIKKEI COMPUTER. (Text in Japanese) 1981. 26/yr. 18400 Yen. Nikkei Business Publications, Inc. (Subsidiary of: Nihon Keizai Shimbun, Inc.), 2-7-6 Hirakawa-cho, Chiyoda-ku, Tokyo 102, Japan. TEL 81-3-5210-8502. FAX 81-3-5210-8119. URL: http://www.nikkeibp.co.jp/. (Subscr. to: Nikkei Business Pub. Inc., Reader Service Center, P.O. Box 20, Kasai Post Office, Tokyo 134-70, Japan) Ed. Yoshiyuki Furusawa; Pub. Shozo Watanabe. adv.: B&W page 778000 Yen, color page 1123000 Yen; trim 208 x280; adv. contact: Osamu Kujiraoka. circ. 69,045. **Indexed:** JCT, JTA. **Document type:** trade publication.
   Description: Provides technical and general information on computers, as seen from the viewpoint of systems, products, industry, and organizational management.

NIKKEI MICRODEVICES. see ELECTRONICS

---

004   FI   ISSN 1236-6064
NORDIC JOURNAL OF COMPUTING. (Text in English) 1994. q. FIM 350 to individuals; institutions FIM 650 (effective 1997). University of Helsinki, Department of Computer Science, P.O. Box 26, FIN-00014 University of Helsinki, Finland. TEL 358-9-70851. FAX 358-9-70844441. E-mail: njc@cs.helsinki.fi; URL: http://www.cs.helsinki.fi/njc/. Ed. Esko Ukkonen. R&P contact: Esko Ukkonen. circ. 150. **Document type:** academic/scholarly publication.
   —BLDSC (6117.926050); AskIEEE; CISTI; KR SourceOne.
   Description: Provides an international forum for original research within informatics.
   Refereed Serial

---

003 658.4   US
O R - M S TOMORROW. (Operations Research - Management Science) 1984. 2/yr. $5 (foreign $10). Institute for Operations Research and the Management Sciences, 901 Elkridge Landing Rd., Ste. 400, Linthicum, MD 21090-2909. TEL 410-850-0300. FAX 410-684-2963. (Subscr. to: Box 64794, Baltimore, MD 21264-4794) Ed. Peter Horner. R&P contact: Peter Horner. TEL 770-431-0867. **Document type:** trade publication.
   Formerly: O R S A Student Communications.

---

003   GW   ISSN 0171-6468
T57.6.A1   CODEN: ORSPD5
O R SPEKTRUM. (Operations Research) 1979. q. DM.469.60 (foreign DM.473.20) (effective 1998). (Deutsche Gesellschaft fuer Operations Research) Springer-Verlag, Heidelberger Platz 3, 14197 Berlin, Germany. TEL 49-30-82787-0. FAX 49-30-82787448. E-mail: subscriptions@springer.de. (Subscr. in N. America to: Springer-Verlag New York, Inc., 333 Meadowlands Pkwy., Secaucus, NJ 07094. TEL 212-460-1500. FAX 212-473-6272) Ed. G. Atrogge. **Indexed:** ASCA, INSPEC, Int.Abstr.Oper.Res., J.Cont.Quant.Meth., Math.R., Oper.Res.Manage.Sci., Qual.Contr.Appl.Stat., Zent.Math. **Document type:** academic/scholarly publication.
   —AskIEEE; CISTI; Genuine Article; KR SourceOne; SWETS; UMI. **CCC**.

621.39   US
O T J. Variant title: Oracle Technical Journal. 4/yr. $29.95 (Canada & Mexico $39.95; elsewhere $70) (effective 1996). Miller Freeman, Inc. (Subsidiary of: United News & Media), 600 Harrison St., San Francisco, CA 94107. TEL 415-905-2200. FAX 415-905-2233. (Subscr. to: Box 1181, Skokie, IL 60076-8181. TEL 800-250-2429. FAX 708-647-5972)

005.13   US   ISSN 1055-3614
CODEN: OBMAFO
OBJECT MAGAZINE; improving software quality through object technology. 1991. m. $45 to individuals (Canada & Mexico $70; elsewhere $88); institutions $119 (Canada & Mexico $144; elsewhere $159). Sigs Publications, Inc., 71 W. 23rd St., New York, NY 10010-4102. TEL 212-242-7447. FAX 212-242-7574. E-mail: subscriptions@sigs.com; info@sigs.com; URL: http://www.sigs.com. (Subscr. to: Box 5050, Brentwood, TN 37024-5050) Ed. Marie A. Lenzi; Pub. Hal Avery. adv.; bk.rev.; software rev. circ. 30,000. **Indexed:** INSPEC (1992-). **Document type:** trade publication.
●Also available online.
   —BLDSC (6197.007500); AskIEEE; KR SourceOne; SWETS. **CCC**.
   Description: Covers object technology, including analysis, design, methodology, databases, language comparisons, project management techniques and standardization efforts.

001.6   RU
OBRABOTKA SIMVOL'NOI INFORMATSII.* 1973. irreg. 0.47 Rub. Rossiiskaya Akademiya Nauk, Vychislitel'nyi Tsentr, Sepukhovskii raion, Pushchino, 142292 Moscow Oblast' TEL 234-05-84. illus.

OFFICE PRODUCTS ANALYST; a monthly report devoted to the analysis of office products. see BUSINESS AND ECONOMICS — *Office Equipment And Services*

---

004   US
OFFICE SYSTEMS RESEARCH ASSOCIATION. CONFERENCE PROCEEDINGS. 1983. a. $40. Office Systems Research Association, University of Nebraska, 529A Nebraska Hall, Lincoln, NE 68588-0515. TEL 402-472-3647. FAX 402-472-5907. URL: http://walden/mo.net/-osra. Ed. Donna Kizzier. circ. 250. **Indexed:** Bus.Educ.Ind. **Document type:** proceedings.

---

004   US   ISSN 0737-8998
HF5547.5.A1
OFFICE SYSTEMS RESEARCH JOURNAL. 1982. s-a. $35. Office Systems Research Association, University of Nebraska, 529A Nebraska Hall, Lincoln, NE 68588-0515. TEL 402-472-3647. FAX 402-472-5907. URL: http://walden.mo.net/-osra. Ed. B. McEwen. adv.; bk.rev.; abstr.; bibl.; illus. circ. 500. (also avail. in microform from UMI) **Indexed:** Abstr.Hum.Comp.Inter., Bus.Educ.Ind, C.I.J.E., INSPEC (1985-). **Document type:** academic/scholarly publication.
   —BLDSC (6237.685950); AskIEEE; KR SourceOne; UMI.
   Description: Articles on research of office systems technologies, problems, human factors, and office systems education.
   Refereed Serial

---

004   UK   ISSN 0160-5682
Q175   CODEN: OPRQAK
OPERATIONAL RESEARCH SOCIETY. JOURNAL. Key Title: Journal of the Operational Research Society. 1950. m. £451 (foreign £451($700)) to institutions (effective 1997). (Operational Research Society) Stockton Press (Subsidiary of: MacMillan Press Ltd.), Houndmills, Basingstoke, Hants. RG21 6XS, England. TEL 44-1256-351898. FAX 44-1256-328339. E-mail: jors@orsoc.org.uk. Ed. J.C. Ranyard; Pub. Harry Holt. adv. contact: Alison Reeves. bk.rev.; abstr.; bibl.; charts; index. (also avail. in microform from UMI) **Indexed:** ABI Inform., Account.& Data Proc.Abstr., Appl.Mech.Rev., ASCA, B.P.I., Biostat., BPIA, Br.Tech.Ind., Bus.Ind., Compumath, Comput.Cont., Cont.Pg.Manage., Curr.Cont. (1978-), Eng.Ind., Excerp.Med., HRIS, HRIS, Ind.Sci.Rev., INSPEC, Int.Abstr.Oper.Res., Intl.Civil Eng.Abstr., Intl.Mgmt.Info., ISMEC, J.Cont.Quant.Meth., Manage.Cont., Mark.Res.Abstr. (1978-), Oper.Res.Manage.Sci., Qual.Contr.Appl.Stat., Risk Abstr., Rural Recreat.Tour.Abstr., Sci.Cit.Ind., SCIMP, SSCI, Stat.Theor.Meth.Abstr. (1978-), Tr.& Indus.Ind., World Agri.Econ.& Rural Sociol.Abstr., World Bank.Abstr., Zent.Math. **Document type:** academic/scholarly publication.
   —BLDSC (4835.900000); AskIEEE; CISTI; Ei; Genuine Article; KR SourceOne; Linda Hall; SWETS; UMI; UnCover. **CCC**.
   Formerly (until vol.29, 1978): Operational Research Quarterly (ISSN 0030-3623)

---

003 658.4   US   ISSN 0030-364X
CODEN: OPREA1
OPERATIONS RESEARCH. 1952. bi-m. $109 to individuals (foreign $122); institutions $172 (foreign $185) (effective 1997). Institute for Operations Research and the Management Sciences, 901 Elkridge Landing Rd., Ste. 400, Linthicum, MD 21090-2909. TEL 410-850-0300; 800-343-0062. FAX 410-684-2963. (Subscr. to: Box 64794, Baltimore, MD 21264-4794) Ed. Patrick Harker. R&P contact: Fran Silverman. adv. contact: Kathye Long. bibl.; charts; stat.; index, cum.index. circ. 10,100. (also avail. in microform from KTO,WWS; back issues avail.; reprint service avail. from KTO) **Indexed:** A.S.& T.Ind., ABI Inform., Appl.Mech.Rev., ASCA, B.P.I., Biostat., Bk.Rev.Ind. (1965-1981), BMT, BPIA, Bus.Ind., Chem.Abstr., Comput.Cont., Cont.Pg.Manage., Curr.Cont., Energy Ind., Energy Info.Abstr., Eng.Ind., Ind.Sci.Rev., INSPEC, Int.Abstr.Oper.Res., Manage.Cont., Mark.Res.Abstr. (1963-1989), Math.R., Oper.Res.Manage.Sci., Psychol.Abstr., Pub.Admin.Abstr., Qual.Contr.Appl.Stat., Rural Recreat.Tour.Abstr., Sci.Cit.Ind., SCIMP (1978-), SSCI, Tr.& Indus.Ind., World Agri.Econ.& Rural Sociol.Abstr. **Document type:** academic/scholarly publication.
   —BLDSC (6269.360000); AskIEEE; CISTI; Ei; Genuine Article; KR SourceOne; Linda Hall; SWETS; UMI; UnCover. **CCC**.
   Formerly (until 1955): Operations Research Society of America. Journal (ISSN 0096-3984)
   Description: Information resource for practitioners and scholars in the disciplines of operations research and management science.
   Refereed Serial

---

003 658.4   NE
OPERATIONS RESEARCH COMPUTER SCIENCE INTERFACE. (Includes software diskette) (Text in English) 1993. irreg. price varies. Kluwer Academic Publishers, Postbus 17, 3300 AA Dordrecht, Netherlands. TEL 31-78-6392392. FAX 31-78-6392254. TELEX 29245 KAPG NL. E-mail: services@wkap.nl; URL: http://www.wkap.nl. (Dist. by: Kluwer Academic Publishers Group, P.O. Box 322, 3300 AH Dordrecht, Netherlands. TEL 31-78-6392392. FAX 31-78-6546474; N. America dist. addr.: Box 358, Accord Sta., Hingham, MA 02018-0358. TEL 617-871-6600. FAX 617-871-6528) Ed. Ramesh Sharda. (back issues avail.) **Indexed:** Zent.Math. **Document type:** monographic series.
   Refereed Serial

OPERESHONZU RISACHI/OPERATIONS RESEARCH SOCIETY OF JAPAN. COMMUNICATIONS. see BUSINESS AND ECONOMICS — *Management*

621.39   US   ISSN 1065-3171
ORACLE MAGAZINE. 1987. bi-m. free to qualified personnel. Oracle Corporation, 500 Oracle Pkwy., Box 659952, Redwood Shores, CA 94065. TEL 415-506-7000. FAX 415-506-7122. Ed. Juli B. Gibbs. R&P contact: Leslie Steere. adv.: B&W page $6260, color page $7160; trim 8 x 10 7/8 adv. contact: Kevin Canady. **Document type:** trade publication.
   —KR SourceOne.
   Description: Publishes practical, technical articles relating to applications of Oracle-based information management technology, as well as in-depth overviews and analysis of trends and issues affecting information managers.

---

004 621.381   FR   ISSN 0755-4249
ORDI 5. 6/yr. Editrace, 8 rue Saint-Marc, 75002 Paris, France. Ed. J.P. Nizard. circ. 25,000.

---

003 658.4   SA   ISSN 0259-191X
ORION. (Text and summaries in Afrikaans, English) 1985. s-a. $40 (effective 1996). Operations Research Society of South Africa, P.O. Box 850, Groenkloof 0027, South Africa. (Subscr. to: c/o W. Gevers, Business Ed., P.O. Box 610, Bellville 7535, South Africa. TEL 27-21-9184228. FAX 27-21-9184112) Ed. L.P. Fatti. R&P contact: W. Gevers. adv. contact: W. Gevers. circ. 450. **Indexed:** Ind.S.A.Per., Int.Abstr.Oper.Res., R.G.Abstr. **Document type:** academic/scholarly publication.
   —BLDSC (6291.279000).
   Description: Features success stories, case studies and methodological reviews in operations research.
   Refereed Serial

OXFORD APPLIED MATHEMATICS AND COMPUTING SERIES. see MATHEMATICS

001.6 621.381 GW ISSN 0930-5157
P I K: PRAXIS DER INFORMATIONSVERARBEITUNG UND KOMMUNIKATION; Fachzeitschrift fuer den Einsatz von DV-Systemen in Wirtschaft, Wissenschaft und Technik. 1978. q. DM.260. K.G. Saur Verlag KG, A member of the Reed Elsevier plc group, Ortlerstr. 8, 81373 Munich, Germany. TEL 49-89-76902-0. FAX 49-89-76902150. E-mail: 100730.1341@compuserve.com; URL: http://www.reed-elsevier.com. circ. 2,500. **Document type:** academic/scholarly publication.
—CCC.
Formerly: Rechenzentrum (ISSN 0343-317X)

001.6 621.38 SI ISSN 0129-6264
QA76.58 CODEN: PPLTEE
PARALLEL PROCESSING LETTERS. (Text in English) 1991. q. $99 to individuals and institutions of developing countries; institutions of developed countries $247. World Scientific Publishing Co. Pte. Ltd., Farrer Rd., P.O. Box 128, Singapore 9128, Singapore. TEL 65-382-5663. FAX 65-3825919. TELEX RS 28561 WPSC. E-mail: wspcsl@signet.com.sg; sales@wspc2.demon.co.uk; wspc@wspc.com; URL: http://www.singnet.com.sg/~wspclib. (UK addr.: 57 Shelton St., Covent Garden, London WC2H 9HE, England. TEL 44-171-836-0888. FAX 44-171-836-2020; US addr.: 1060 Main St., Ste. 1B, River Edge, NJ 07661. TEL 800-227-7562. FAX 201-487-9656) Ed. Michel Cosnard. **Indexed:** INSPEC (1991-). **Document type:** academic/scholarly publication.
—BLDSC (6404.833650); AskIEEE; CISTI; Ei; KR SourceOne; SWETS; UnCover. CCC.
Description: Aims to rapidly disseminate results in the field of parallel processing in the form of short letters. Covers the design and analysis of parallel and distributed algorithms, the theory of parallel computation, parallel programming languages, parallel programming environments and parallel architectures.

001.6 621.381 IS
PEOPLE & COMPUTERS WEEKLY. 1980. w. $175. Israel Peled Publishing, Pinsker 64, Tel Aviv 61 332, Israel. TEL 03-295145. FAX 03-295144. Ed. Israel Shalev. circ. 7,000.

004 NE ISSN 0166-5316
QA76.9.E95 CODEN: PEEVD9
PERFORMANCE EVALUATION. 1981. 16/yr. fl.2006($1153) (effective 1998). North-Holland (Subsidiary of: Elsevier Science B.V.), P.O. Box 211, 1000 AE Amsterdam, Netherlands. TEL 31-20-4853911. FAX 31-20-4853598. TELEX 18582 ESPA NL. (Subscr. in the Americas to: Elsevier Science, Regional Sales Office, Box 945, New York, NY 10159-0945. TEL 212-633-3730. FAX 212-633-3680; Subscr. in Australasia and the Far East to: Elsevier Science (Singapore) Pte Ltd, No.1 Temasek Ave., No.17-01 Millenia Tower, Singapore 039192, Singapore. TEL 65-434-3727. FAX 65-337-2230; Subscr. in Japan to: Elsevier Science Japan, 9-15 Higashi-Azabu 1-chome, Minato-ku Tokyo 106, Japan. TEL 81-3-5561-5033. FAX 81-3-5561-5047) Ed. Martin Reiser. (also avail. in microform from UMI; back issues avail.) **Indexed:** ASCA, Compumath, Comput.Abstr., Comput.Cont., Comput.Lit.Ind., Curr.Cont., Data Process.Dig., Inform.Sci.Abstr., INSPEC, Math.R., SSCI, Zent.Math. **Document type:** academic/scholarly publication.
—BLDSC (6423.760000); AskIEEE; CISTI; Ei; Genuine Article; KR SourceOne; Linda Hall; SWETS; UnCover. CCC.
Description: For system theorists, designers, implementers and analysts who are concerned with performing aspects of computer systems, computer communications, and distributed systems.
Refereed Serial

PERSONAL COMPUTER MARKETS. see BUSINESS AND ECONOMICS — Marketing And Purchasing

004 UK ISSN 0949-2054
PERSONAL TECHNOLOGIES. Online edition (UK ISSN 1433-3066). q. £140 (effective 1998). Springer-Verlag London Ltd., Sweetapple House, Catteshall Rd., Godalming, Surrey GU7 3DJ, England. TEL 44-1483-418822. FAX 44-1483-415151. E-mail: alex@svl.co.uk. (Subscr. in N. America to: Springer-Verlag New York, Inc., 333 Meadowlands Pkwy., Secaucus, NJ 07094. TEL 212-460-1500. FAX 212-473-6272) Ed.Bd. (back issues avail.) **Document type:** academic/scholarly publication.
●Also available online.
—BLDSC (6427.895500). CCC.
Description: Focuses on issues surrounding the innovation, design, use and evaluation of new generations of handheld and mobile computers, innovative information management devices, and range of information appliances.

001.6 621.381 US
PERSPECTIVES IN COMPUTING. irreg., vol.24, 1989. Academic Press, Inc., 525 B St., Ste. 1900, San Diego, CA 92101-4495. TEL 619-231-6616. FAX 619-699-6715. (Subscr. to: Order Dept., 6277 Sea Harbor Dr., 4th Fl., Orlando, FL 32887. TEL 800-321-5068) Ed. Werner Rheinboldt.
Formerly: Notes and Reports in Computer Science.
Refereed Serial

PERTH COMPUTING DIRECTORY. see BUSINESS AND ECONOMICS — Trade And Industrial Directories

621.381 001.642 UK ISSN 0958-3807
PICK RESOURCES GUIDE - INTERNATIONAL. 1985. a. £49.95. A L L M Systems and Marketing, 21 Beechcroft Rd., Bushey, Herts. WD2 2JU, England. TEL 44-1923-230150. FAX 44-1923-211148. E-mail: apritchard@cix.compulink.co.uk. Ed. Alan Pritchard; Pub. Alan Pritchard. bibl.; index. circ. 1,000. **Document type:** directory.
Formerly (until 1986): Pick Resources Guide.
Description: Lists hardware running the Pick Operating System, Pick-based software, and companies offering services to Pick community.

001.6 301.16 US
POLICY MATTERS!. 1993. q. membership. Information Industry Association, 1625 Massachusetts Ave., N.W., Ste. 700, Washington, DC 20036-2212. TEL 202-986-0280. circ. 400. **Document type:** bulletin.
Description: Reviews the IIA's public policy and government relations council activities.

001.6 621.381 PL ISSN 0138-0648
POLSKA AKADEMIA NAUK. INSTYTUT PODSTAW INFORMATYKI. PRACE/POLISH ACADEMY OF SCIENCES. INSTITUTE OF COMPUTER SCIENCE. REPORTS.* Key Title: Prace IPI PAN. (Text in English, Polish and Russian) 1969. irreg., no.650, 1988. free. Polska Akademia Nauk, Instytut Podstaw Informatyki, Ul. Ordona 21, 01-237 Warsaw, Poland. TEL 48-22-362841. FAX 48-22-376564. circ. 575. **Indexed:** Graph.Arts Lit.Abstr., Math.R., Ref.Zh.
Formerly (until 1977): Polska Akademia Nauk. Centrum Obliczeniowe. Prace (ISSN 0079-3175)

POLYSCOPE; computer - electronics - communication. see COMPUTERS — Automation

001.6 GW ISSN 0179-1133
PRAXIS COMPUTER. 1985. 7/yr. DM.54 (students DM.36) (effective 1997). Deutscher Aerzte-Verlag GmbH, Postfach 400265, 50532 Cologne, Germany. TEL 49-2234-7011-0. FAX 49-2234-7011255. Ed. Christa Kaul. adv.; bk.rev.; circ. 40,000 (controlled). **Document type:** academic/scholarly publication.
—SWETS.

PREVISIONS GLISSANTES DETAILLEES EN PERSPECTIVES SECTORIELLES (VOL.13): INFORMATIQUE. see BUSINESS AND ECONOMICS — Economic Situation And Conditions

PRINCETON SERIES IN COMPUTER SCIENCE. see COMPUTERS — Theory Of Computing

004 621.39 US
PRINCETON UNIVERSITY. DEPARTMENT OF COMPUTER SCIENCE. TECHNICAL REPORT SERIES. 1960. s-a. price varies. Princeton University, Department of Computer Science, 35 Olden St., Princeton, NJ 08544-2087. TEL 609-258-5030. FAX 609-258-1771.
—CISTI.
Former titles: Princeton University. Department of Computer Science. Technical Report Librarian; Princeton University. Computer Sciences Laboratory. Technical Report (ISSN 0079-5283)

PRIVACY EN REGISTRATIE. see LAW

PROCESS TECHNOLOGY PROCEEDINGS. see ENGINEERING — Industrial Engineering

001.6 621.381
331.8 US ISSN 0735-9381
PROCESSED WORLD. 1981. 2/yr. $15 for 4 nos. to individuals; libraries $18. 41 Sutter St., Ste. 1829, San Francisco, CA 94104. TEL 415-626-2999. FAX 415-626-2685. bk.rev. circ. 5,000. **Indexed:** Alt.Press Ind.
Description: Analysis, "tales of toil," fiction, poetry, graphics and humor exploring the impact of technology (including computers and biotechnology) on work and everyday life.

001.6 621.381 FR ISSN 1141-9636
PROCESSEURS. 1989. 42/yr. Porcedit, 182 rue du Fbg. Saint-Denis, 75010 Paris, France. TEL 40-35-09-49. FAX 40-35-08-62. Ed. Michel Ktitareff.

621.381 001.6 AT ISSN 0814-5822
PROFESSIONAL COMPUTING. 1977. 10/yr. $50. (Australian Computer Society) Associated Business Publications Pty. Ltd., 104-3 Smail St., Ultimo, N.S.W. 2007, Australia. TEL 61-2-2122780. circ. 13,665. (back issues avail) **Indexed:** Comput.Cont., Comput.Lit.Ind., INSPEC, Intl.Civil Eng.Abstr., Soft.Abstr.Eng.
—CISTI.
Formerly (until 1986): Australian Computer Bulletin (ISSN 0313-9050)
Description: Provides mid-range technical information as well as general comments on computer companies and their products.

004 US
PROMPT. 1980. m. $36 membership; newsstand price: $3. Pasadena I B M User Group, 2303 Glen Canyon Rd., Altadena, CA 91001-3539. TEL 818-791-1600. FAX 818-791-1600. E-mail: 71333.130@compuserve.com. Ed. Steve Bass. adv.: page $400; adv. contact: Steve Bass. circ. 6,000. (back issues avail.) **Document type:** newsletter.
●Also available online.
Description: Helps users of I.B.M.-compatible computers understand the potential of their systems.

PURE AND APPLIED MATHEMATIKA SCIENCES. see MATHEMATICS

R I C O LAW REPORTER. (Racketeer Influenced and Corrupt Organizations) see LAW — Corporate Law

RECHT DER DATENVERARBEITUNG; Zeitschrift fuer Praxis und Wissenschaft. see COMPUTERS — Computer Security

REFERENCE DATA FOR ENGINEERS; radio, electronics, computer and communications. see COMMUNICATIONS

RELIABLE COMPUTING. see COMPUTERS — Computer Engineering

001.6 621.381 US
RESEARCH REPORTS ESPRIT - PROJECT 322: CAD INTERFACES. 1986. irreg. price varies. Springer-Verlag, 175 Fifth Ave., New York, NY 10010. TEL 212-460-1500. FAX 212-473-6272. (Also: Berlin, Heidelberg, Tokyo and Vienna) (reprint service avail. from ISI) **Document type:** monographic series.

COMPUTERS

004 US ISSN 1071-2224
RETAIL SYSTEMS RESELLER; the news source for channel management. 1992. 10/yr. $36 (Canada $46; elsewhere $95). Edgell Enterprises, Inc., Ten W. Hanover Ave., Ste. 107, Randolph, NJ 07869. TEL 201-895-3300. FAX 201-895-7711. (Subscr. to: Circulation Services, Box 21644, St. Paul, MN 55121-9887) Ed. Michael Kachmar; Pub. Douglas C. Edgell. adv.: B&W page $3100, color page $3800; trim 8 1/8 x 10 7/8. illus.; software rev.; tr.lit. circ. 10,000. **Document type:** trade publication.
   Description: Teaches retailers how to present equipment and software packages. Also covers news, new products and new technologies.

REVISTA DE TECNOLOGIA EDUCATIVA. see COMPUTERS — Cybernetics

300 BE ISSN 0773-4379
P98
REVUE INFORMATIQUE ET STATISTIQUE DANS LES SCIENCES HUMAINES. (Text in English, French and Italian; summaries in French) 1966. q. 1000 BEF. Centre Informatique de Philosophie et Lettres, Laboratoire d'Analyse Statistique des Langues Anciennes, 32 Place du 20 Aout, 4000 Liege, Belgium. TEL 32-41-665211. FAX 32-41-665702. Ed. J. Denooz. **Indexed:** Mid.East: Abstr.& Ind. **Document type:** academic/scholarly publication.
   —SWETS.
   Formerly (until 1983): Organisation Internationale pour l'Etude des Langues Anciennes par Ordinateur. Revue (ISSN 0030-4972)

004 SA ISSN 1018-9564
S.A. COMPUTER BUYER. (South Africa) 1993. 11/yr. R.43.56. P.O. Box 16557, Vlaeberg 8018, South Africa. illus. **Indexed:** Ind.S.A.Per.
   Incorporates: Cape Computer Buyer.

001.6 621.381 US ISSN 1047-4544
QA76.73.F24 CODEN: SIFOEL
S I G FORTH. 1989. q. Association for Computing Machinery, Special Interest Group on Forth, 1515 Broadway, 17th Fl., New York, NY 10036. TEL 212-869-7440. FAX 212-869-0481. TELEX 421686. (Subscr. to: Box 12105, Church St. Sta., New York, NY 10249) **Indexed:** INSPEC (1989-).
   —UnCover.

001.6 US ISSN 1050-916X
QA76.6
S I G M I C R O NEWSLETTER. 1986. q. Association for Computing Machinery, 1515 Broadway, 17th Fl., New York, NY 10036. TEL 212-869-7440. FAX 212-869-0481. **Indexed:** INSPEC. **Document type:** newsletter.
   —BLDSC (8275.550000); CISTI; UnCover.
   Formerly (until 1987): S I G M I C R O, T C M I C R O Newsletter (ISSN 0892-3825)

001.6 621.381 US ISSN 0736-6892
QA75.5 CODEN: SSNRD3
S I G U C C S NEWSLETTER. q. $15. Association for Computing Machinery, Special Interest Group on University Computing Centers, 1515 Broadway, 17th Fl., New York, NY 10036. TEL 212-869-7440. FAX 212-302-5826. Ed. Alicia Towster. adv.; bk.rev. circ. 1,500. **Indexed:** INSPEC. **Document type:** newsletter.
   —BLDSC (8276.450000); AskIEEE; CISTI; KR SourceOne; SWETS; UnCover.
   Formerly: S I G U C C Newsletter (ISSN 0163-5832)

S PLUS - SICHERHEIT. see COMPUTERS — Computer Security

001.6 631.381 US
SCIENCE AND TECHNOLOGY SERIAL REPORTS: CENTRAL EURASIA. COMPUTERS. irreg. $206 in US, Canada & Mexico; elsewhere $432. (Joint Publications Research Service) U.S. National Technical Information Service, 5825 Port Royal Rd., Springfield, VA 22161. TEL 703-487-4630.
   Formerly: Science and Technology Serial Reports: U S S R: Computers.

621.39 UK ISSN 1356-7853
Q183.9 CODEN: SCWOEU
SCIENTIFIC COMPUTING WORLD. 1994. bi-m. free to qualified persons; other individuals and institutions £82 (effective 1997). (Institute of Physics) I O P Publishing Ltd., Dirac House, Temple Back, Bristol BS1 6BE, England. TEL 44-117-929-7481. FAX 44-117-927-4318. TELEX 449149 INSTP G. E-mail: scicomp@ioppublishing.co.uk; URL: http://www.iop.org. (US subscr. to: American Institute of Physics, Member and Subscriber Services, 500 Sunnyside Blvd., Woodbury, NY 11797-2900. TEL 516-349-7800) Ed. Vanessa Spedding; Pub. Mark Ware. adv. contact: S. Norrie. tr.lit./ circ. (controlled). **Document type:** academic/scholarly publication.
   ●Also available online.
   —BLDSC (8177.902600); AskIEEE; KR SourceOne.
   Formerly (until 1994): Scientific Computing (ISSN 1354-3520)
   Description: Covers computer languages, data analysis and storage, hardware, and software.

004 US
SELECTED BOOK REVIEWS. q. $10. Vector Graphiques, 206 Davison Ave., Lynbrook, NY 11563. Ed. John R. Cartmell, Jr. adv.: page $100. bk.rev.; circ. 1,000 (paid). (also avail. in diskette format) **Document type:** newsletter.
   Description: Reviews new books on software and other computer-related topics.

004 US ISSN 1068-2902
HD9696.C6
SERVICE & SUPPORT MANAGEMENT. Short title: S & S M. 1985. m. free in the U.S. (foreign $30). Publications & Communications, Inc., 12416 Hymeadow, Austin, TX 78750-1896. TEL 512-250-9023. FAX 512-331-3900. Ed. Dennis Smeltzer. adv.: B&W page $3965, color page $4900; trim 8 x 10 7/8. circ. 32,000. (back issues avail.) **Document type:** trade publication.
   —KR SourceOne; UMI.
   Former titles (until 1993): M S M - The Magazine of Computer Service Management (ISSN 0898-5499); (until 1988): M S M - The Magazine for Computer Service Managers (ISSN 0882-8105)

001.6 US ISSN 1048-3462
SERVICE INDUSTRY NEWSLETTER.* 1980. m. Ledgeway Publications, P.O. Box 5093, Westborough, MA 01581-5093. TEL 508-370-5555. FAX 508-370-6262. Ed. Jean Kane. circ. 800.
   Formerly (until 1989): Field Service Newsletter (ISSN 0889-3624)

621.381 658 US ISSN 1046-1965
HD9696.C63
SERVICE NEWS (YARMOUTH). 1981. m. $55 (foreign $125). United Publications, Inc., Box 995, Yarmouth, ME 04096. TEL 207-846-0600. FAX 207-846-0657. Ed. Karen Hamilton; Pub. Alison Harris. adv.; bk.rev. circ. 45,000. **Indexed:** Comput.Cont. **Document type:** trade publication.
   —KR SourceOne; UMI.
   Formerly: Computer-Electronic Service News (ISSN 0744-1584)

001.6 JA
SHUKAN COMPUTER.* m. Denpa Computerworld Co., 11-15 Higashi Gotanda, Shinagawa-ku, Tokyo 141, Japan. Ed. Mr. Takahashi. adv. circ. 35,000.

621.39 US
SMART ELECTRONICS. bi-m. newsstand price: $3.25. McMullen & Yee Publishing, 774 S. Placentia Ave., Placentia, CA 92670-6846. TEL 714-572-2255. FAX 714-572-1864.

004 SA ISSN 1015-7999
QA76 CODEN: SACJE3
SOUTH AFRICAN COMPUTER JOURNAL/SUID AFRIKAANSE REKENAARTYDSKRIF. (Text in Afrikaans, English) 1979. irreg. $15 per no. (effective 1994). Computer Society of South Africa, P.O. Box 1714, Halfway House 1685, South Africa. TEL 27-12-420-2504. FAX 27-12-436454. (Co-sponsor: South African Institute of Computer Scientists) Ed. D.G. Kourie. R&P contact: D.G. Kourie. adv.; bk.rev. circ. 500. (back issues avail.) **Indexed:** Ind.S.A.Per., INSPEC (1979-). **Document type:** academic/scholarly publication.
   —BLDSC (8334.191000); AskIEEE; Ei; KR SourceOne.
   Formerly (until 1989): Questiones Informaticae (ISSN 0254-2757)
   Description: Publishes original research papers in the fields of computer science and information systems.
   Refereed Serial

001.6 621.381 011 US ISSN 0177-7718
SPRINGER BOOKS ON PROFESSIONAL COMPUTING. 1984. irreg. price varies. Springer-Verlag, 175 Fifth Ave., New York, NY 10010. TEL 212-460-1500. FAX 212-473-6272. (reprint service avail. from ISI) **Document type:** monographic series.

003 658.4 GW
SPRINGER SERIES IN OPERATIONS RESEARCH. (Text in English) 1994. irreg. price varies. Springer-Verlag, Heidelberger Platz 3, 14197 Berlin, Germany. TEL 49-30-82787-0. FAX 49-30-82787448. E-mail: subscriptions@springer.de. (Subscr. in US to: Springer-Verlag New York, Inc., 333 Meadowlands Pkwy., Secaucus, NJ 07094. TEL 212-460-1500. FAX 212-473-6272) Ed. P. Glynn. **Document type:** monographic series.
   Description: Contains topics of interest to operations researchers and management scientists.

STATISTICS AND COMPUTING. see STATISTICS

003 NE ISSN 0141-1004
STUDIES IN OPERATIONS RESEARCH. 1972. irreg., latest vol.5. price varies. Gordon and Breach - Harwood Academic, Amsteldisk 166, 1st Fl., 1079 LH Amsterdam, Netherlands. (Subscr. to: International Publishers Distributor, Box 32160, Newark, NJ 07102. TEL 800-545-8398. FAX 215-750-6343) Ed. A. Ghosal. **Document type:** monographic series.
   Refereed Serial

004.16 US
QA76.5
SUNWORLD. (Print version ceased) 1988. m. free. Web Publishing Inc. (Subsidiary of: I D G Communications, Inc.), 501 Second St., Ste. 310, San Francisco, CA 94107. TEL 603-924-0100. FAX 603-924-8779. E-mail: carolyn.wong@sunworld.com; URL: http://www.sunworld.com. Ed. W.C. Wong. adv.: B&W page $6375; trim 8 x 10 3/4. bk.rev.
   ●Available only online.
   —CISTI; KR SourceOne.
   Former titles (until 1995): Advanced Systems (ISSN 1074-9306); (until 1994): SunWorld (ISSN 1054-5980); (until 1991): SunTech Journal (ISSN 1046-5456); SunTechnology (ISSN 0896-8950)
   Description: Provides news, features, and columns for Sun users, developers, and system administrators.

001.6 621.381 US ISSN 1043-2418
SUPER GROUP MAGAZINE (ENGLISH EDITION);* the magazine for the Hewlett-Packard 3000 user. 1981. bi-m. $60. Veritech Publications, Box 2141, Salt Lake City, UT 84121-0414. TEL 801-942-6655. FAX 801-942-8675. Ed. Kath Morrison. adv. circ. 3,500. (back issues avail.)
   Description: Covers software and productivity.

SURVEY OF LOGISTICS SOFTWARE. see BUSINESS AND ECONOMICS — Marketing And Purchasing

004 US ISSN 1072-2483
QA76.9.C55
SYBASE. 1993. q. Sybase, Inc., Kable Square, Mt. Morris, IL 61054.
   —KR SourceOne.

001.6 621.381   US
SYMPOSIUM ON APPLIED COMPUTING. Abbreviated title: S A C. 1990. a. price varies. (Institute of Electrical and Electronics Engineers, Inc.) I E E E Computer Society Press, 10662 Los Vaqueros Circle, Los Alamitos, CA 90720. TEL 714-821-8380. FAX 714-821-4010. adv. contact: Frieda Koester.
 Description: Addresses research and conclusions on a variety of advanced applied computer science areas.

SYMPOSIUM ON FOUNDATIONS OF COMPUTER SCIENCE. PROCEEDINGS. see COMPUTERS — Computer Engineering

651.8 001.6   SZ   ISSN 0254-2226
SYSDATA. 1901. 10/yr. 60 SFr. (foreign 116 SFr.) (effective 1996). Verlag Binkert AG, CH-5080 Laufenburg, Switzerland. TEL 41-62-8697272. FAX 41-62-8697333. Ed. Daniel Bohler. adv.: B&W page 3585 SFr., color page 4350 SFr.; trim 185 x 266; adv. contact: Ludwig Binkert. bk.rev.; abstr.; illus. circ. 12,000. **Indexed:** INSPEC. **Document type:** trade publication.
 —BLDSC (8589.079000); AskIEEE; KR SourceOne.
 Former titles: Sysdata und Buerotechnik; (until 1970): Buerotechnik (ISSN 0006-0003)
 Description: Trade publication for office technology and communication. Covers computer systems, automation, information processing, software, new products. Includes reports of events, positions available.

001.6 621.381   US   ISSN 1056-2699
TECH MARKET SOUTH. 1991. m. Jaye Publications, Inc., 550 Interstate North Pky., N.W., Ste. 150, Atlanta, GA 30339-5008. TEL 404-984-9444. FAX 404-933-9072. Ed. Mike Adkinson. adv.: B&W page $980, color $1700; trim 10 3/8 x 13 1/4. circ. 7,500.
 Description: Provides data, sales leads and prospect lists.

004   AT   ISSN 1038-5231
TECHNICAL COMPUTING. 1968. q. (A C A D S Association) National Publications Pty. Ltd., P.O. Box 297, Homebush W., N.S.W. 2140, Australia. TEL 02-764-111. FAX 02-763-1699. adv.; illus. **Document type:** trade publication.
 Former titles: (until 1991): A C A D S Quarterly (ISSN 0817-072X); (until 1984): Association for Computer Aided Design. Newsletter (ISSN 0818-2167)

TELECOMMUNICATIONS DIRECTORY; an international descriptive guide to approximately 2,300 telecommunications organizations, systems, and services. see BUSINESS AND ECONOMICS — Trade And Industrial Directories

TELECOMMUTING REVIEW. see BUSINESS AND ECONOMICS — Personnel Management

001.6 621.381   US   ISSN 0172-603X
TEXTS AND MONOGRAPHS IN COMPUTER SCIENCE. 1975. irreg. price varies. Springer-Verlag, 175 Fifth Ave., New York, NY 10010. TEL 212-460-1500. FAX 212-473-6272. (Also: Berlin, Heidelberg, Tokyo and Vienna) Eds. F.L. Bauer, D. Gries. **Indexed:** INSPEC, Math.R. **Document type:** monographic series.

004   US
THEORETICAL ISSUES IN COGNITIVE SCIENCE. 1986. irreg. price varies. Ablex Publishing Corporation, Box 5297, Greenwich, CT 06831-0504. TEL 203-661-7602. FAX 203-661-0792. Ed. Zenon W. Pylyshyn. **Document type:** academic/scholarly publication.

004.6 621.38028   FI   ISSN 0359-8543
TOIMIKKO. 1983. w. FIM 532 (effective 1997). Oy Talentum Ab, P.O. Box 920, FIN-00101 Helsinki, Finland. TEL 358-9-148-801. FAX 358-9-685-6605. Ed. Timo Tolsa. adv.: B&W page FIM 31200, color page FIM 46600; trim 315 x 420; adv. contact: Anssi Eskola. bk.rev.; circ. 27,304 (controlled). **Document type:** newspaper.
 Description: Provides essential product information for purchasing decision-makers and professionals who need to know about trends and developments in I.T., telecommunications and office automation.

TIPS & TRENDS. see COMMUNICATIONS

TOBA SHOSEN KOTO SENMON GAKKO KIYO/TOBA NATIONAL COLLEGE of MARITIME TECHNOLOGY. ANNUAL REPORTS. see TRANSPORTATION — Ships And Shipping

001.6 621.381   IC   ISSN 1021-724X
TOELVUMAL; timarit Skyrslutaeknifelags Islands. 1976. bi-m. membership. Skyrslutaeknifelag Islands - Icelandic Society for Information Processing, Baronsstig 5, IS-101 Reykjavik, Iceland. TEL 354-551-8820. FAX 354-562-7767. Ed. Gisli Ragnarsson. R&P contact: Svanhildur Johannesdottir. adv. contact: Svanhildur Johannesdottir. bk.rev.; index. circ. 1,100. **Document type:** trade publication.
 Description: Directed to data processing professionals, computer users and computer enthusiasts.

621.381   CN   ISSN 0833-3033
TORONTO COMPUTES.* 1984. m. Can.$17.07($24.50) ConText Publishing Inc., 99 Atlantic Ave., No. 408, Toronto, Ont. M4G 3J8, Canada. TEL 416-588-6818. Ed. Lawrence Bruner. adv.; bk.rev.; circ. 95,000 (controlled).
 ●Also available online.
 Description: Offers news, features, reviews and opinions for consumers of low-end desktop computer hardware and software.

621.39   IT
▼**TRADE NEWS;** news magazine per dealer, VAR, superstore e system integrator. 1995. m. (10/yr.). L.45000 (effective 1997). Gruppo Editoriale J C E, Via Ferri 6, 20092 Cinisello Balsamo (MI), Italy. TEL 39-2-660251. FAX 39-2-6127620. E-mail: tradenews@jce.it; URL: http://www.cje.it. Ed. Luisella Acquati. adv.: B&W page L.5000000, color page L.7500000; trim 285 X 420. circ. 14,800. (tabloid format) **Document type:** trade publication.
 Description: Presents information about dealers, var, distributors, software houses, system integrators, franchisess and superstors.

621.381 683.83   CH
TRADE WINNERS; the international trade weekly from Asia to the world. (Text in English) w. NT.$2400($80) P.O. Box 7-250, Taipei, Taiwan, Republic of China. TEL 02-7333988. FAX 02-7333968. TELEX 10596. (Subscr. in US to: P.O. Box 2868, Vancouver, WA 98668. TEL 503-735-0788) Ed. Kay K. Chen. adv.
 Description: Presents information and advertising for a wide range of Taiwan-made computers and peripherals, electronic components, and electrical appliances.

004   US   ISSN 1081-1109
TRI-CITY COMPUTING MAGAZINE; the Capital District's monthly computer connection. 1994. m. $21. A J A Consulting, 5208 W. Calavar Rd., Glendale, AZ 85306-4818. TEL 518-446-1944. E-mail: tricity@albany.net; URL: http://www.albany.net/~tricity/mast.html. Ed. Anthony J. Ardito; Pub. Josephine Soto. R&P contact: Anthony Ardito. adv. contact: Kevin Kiernan. bk.rev.; software rev. circ. 50,000. **Document type:** consumer publication.
 ●Also available online.
 Description: Informs computer users in the NY tri-state, NY region about industry news, local clubs and bulletin boards, and area events.

004 621.39   TU   ISSN 1300-0632
TK1   CODEN: ELEKF8
TURKISH JOURNAL OF ELECTRICAL ENGINEERING AND COMPUTER SCIENCES. 1993. 3/yr. $80 (effective 1997). Scientific and Technical Research Council of Turkey - TUBITAK - Turkiye Bilimsel ve Teknik Arastirma Kurumu, Ataturk Bulvari, No. 221, Kavaklidere, 06100 Ankara, Turkey. TEL 90-312-4685300. FAX 90-312-4276677. TELEX 46830 BTAK TR. E-mail: bdym@tubitak.gov.tr. (Co-sponsor: Chamber of Electrical Engineers) Ed. Kemal Leblebicioglu. abstr.; bibl.; charts; illus.; stat. circ. 1,000. **Indexed:** CHem.Abstr., Eng.Ind. **Document type:** academic/scholarly publication.
 —AskIEEE; CISTI; KR SourceOne.
 Formerly (until 1994): Elektrik - Doga Turkish Journal of Electrical Engineering and Computer Sciences.
 Refereed Serial

004 150   US
TUTORIAL MONOGRAPHS IN COGNITIVE SCIENCE. 1991. irreg. price varies. Ablex Publishing Corporation, Box 5297, Greenwich, CT 06831-0504. TEL 203-661-7602. FAX 203-661-0792. Ed. Nigel Shadbolt. **Document type:** academic/scholarly publication.

004 659.1   US   ISSN 1069-0417
QA76.76.063
UNIFORUM MONTHLY. 1981. m. $125 membership. UniForum, 2901 Tasman Dr., Ste. 205, Santa Clara, CA 95054-1100. TEL 408-986-8840. FAX 408-986-1645. E-mail: pubs@uniforum.org. Ed. Jeffrey Bartlett. adv. circ. 40,000.
 —KR SourceOne.
 Formerly: Communixations.

004   US   ISSN 1069-0395
UNINEWS. 1987. 24/yr. $125 membership. UniForum, 2901 Tasman Drive, Ste. 205, Santa Clara, CA 95054-1138. TEL 408-986-8840. FAX 408-986-1645. E-mail: pubs@uniforum.org or wwb: (url) http://www.uniforum.org. Ed. Don Dugdale. circ. 10,000.
 Formerly: U S R Digest.

001.6 621.381   BE   ISSN 0008-9737
T57.6   CODEN: CCROAT
UNIVERSITE LIBRE DE BRUXELLES. CENTRE D'ETUDES DE RECHERCHE OPERATIONNELLE. CAHIERS/OPERATIONS RESEARCH, STATISTICS AND APPLIED MATHEMATICS. (Text in English and French) 1958. q. 1300 Fr.($20) Universite Libre de Bruxelles, Centre d'Etudes de Recherche Operationnelle, c/o Institut de Statistique, Campus Plaine, C.P. 210, Bd. du Triomphe, B-1050 Brussels, Belgium. FAX 32-2-650-51-13. adv.; bk.rev.; charts; cum.index. **Indexed:** Comput.Rev., INSPEC, Zent.Math.
 —CISTI; Ei.

001.6 621.381   CN   ISSN 0829-5425
UNIVERSITY COMPUTING AND INFORMATION SERVICES NEWSLETTER. 1967. irreg. Dalhousie University, Computing Services, Halifax, NS B3H 3J5, Canada. TEL 902-424-3472. Ed. Ram Raju. adv.; bk.rev. circ. 900. (looseleaf format)
 Formerly: Dalhousie University. Computer Centre. Newsletter (ISSN 0384-8116)

001.6 621.381   CN   ISSN 0316-4683
UNIVERSITY OF ALBERTA. DEPARTMENT OF COMPUTING SCIENCE. TECHNICAL REPORTS. 1965. irreg. Can.$5 or on exchange. University of Alberta, Department of Computing Science, Edmonton, Alta. T6G 2H1, Canada. TEL 403-492-5198. FAX 403-492-1071. URL: ftp://ftp.cs.ualberta.ca/pub/techreports/. circ. 60.
 —CISTI.
 Formerly: University of Alberta. Department of Computing Science. Publication (ISSN 0065-6062)

004   SZ   ISSN 0940-9580
UNIVERSITY OF FRIBOURG. SERIES IN COMPUTER SCIENCE. (Text in English) 1992. irreg., vol.2, 1993. University of Fribourg, Institut pour l'Automation et la Recherche Operationnelle, Misericorde, CH-1700 Fribourg, Switzerland. FAX 41-37-219670. E-mail: hurlimann@cfruni51.bitnet. Ed.Bd. **Document type:** monographic series.
 —BLDSC (9110.075000); CISTI.

001.6 621.381   US
UNIVERSITY OF NEW MEXICO. C I R T NEWSLETTER. 1967. 5/yr. free. University of New Mexico, Computer & Information Resources & Technology, 2701 Campus Blvd., N.E., Albuquerque, NM 87131. TEL 505-277-8147. FAX 505-277-8101. Ed. Catherine Luther. bk.rev.; charts; illus.; stat.; index. circ. 3,000. (back issues avail.) **Document type:** newsletter.
 Former titles: University of New Mexico. C S I S Newsletter; University of New Mexico. Computing Center. Newsletter.
 Description: Provides general and higher education computer information to the computer operators of the University of Mexico.

COMPUTERS

621.381   UK
UNIVERSITY OF NEWCASTLE-UPON-TYNE. COMPUTING SCIENCE. TECHNICAL REPORT SERIES. 1969. irreg. £30 for 15 nos. University of Newcastle-upon-Tyne, Computing Science, Claremont Tower, Newcastle-Upon-Tyne NE1 7RU, England. TEL 091-222-8183. FAX 091-222-8232. Ed. I.A. Stewart. bibl. circ. 112. (also avail. in microfiche; reprint service avail. from NTIS) **Document type:** monographic series.
—BLDSC (8724.920000).
Formerly: University of Newcastle-upon-Tyne. Computing Laboratory. Technical Report Series (ISSN 0963-5068)

001.6 621.381   US
UNIX VIDEO QUARTERLY. q. $195 (foreign $310). Infopro Systems, Box 220, Rescue, CA 95672. TEL 916-677-5870. FAX 916-677-5873. bk.rev.
Description: Covers products, companies, people, and trade shows in the UNIX industry. Subscribers can watch hardware and software products in use, as well as see and hear interviews with vendor representatives.

UPDATE: THE EXECUTIVE'S PURCHASING ADVISOR. *see* BUSINESS AND ECONOMICS — Office Equipment And Services

UTILITAS MATHEMATICA; international journal of discrete and combinatorial mathematics and statistical design. *see* MATHEMATICS — Computer Applications

004   US   ISSN 0894-5802
HD9696.C63
V A R BUSINESS; technology & business decisions for solutions selling. 1987. 21/yr. $89; newsstand price: $5. C M P Publications, Inc., 600 Community Dr., Manhasset, NY 11030-3847. TEL 516-562-6700. FAX 516-562-8585. TELEX 647035 CMP PUB MAHA. Ed. Richard March; Pub. Michael S. Leeds. bibl. circ. 56,000. **Indexed:** Comput.Ind., Microcomp.Ind. **Document type:** trade publication.
● Also available online. Vendor(s): Information Access Co.
—BLDSC (9146.085000); KR SourceOne; UMI. **CCC.**

621.39   US
V M UPDATE. (Virtual Machine) 1986. m. $250 (effective Aug. 1996). Xephon, 1301 W. Hwy. 407, Ste. 201-450, Lewisville, TX 75067. TEL 817-455-7050. FAX 817-455-2492. bk.rev.; index. (back issues avail.) **Document type:** trade publication.

001.6 621.381   CN   ISSN 0822-8574
WHO'S WHO IN COMPUTING. (Avail. in 4 print editions) 1987. a. Can.$545. Whitsed Publishing, 268 Lakeshore Rd. E., Ste. 510, Mississauga, ON L5G 1H1, Canada. TEL 905-271-1601. FAX 905-271-4522. Ed. Roy Whitsed. (also avail. in diskette format) **Document type:** directory.

001.6 621.381   GW   ISSN 0941-9209
WIN; Alles ueber Windows. 1991. m. Vogel Verlag und Druck GmbH & Co. KG, Max-Planck-Str. 7-9, 97082 Wuerzburg, Germany. TEL 49-931-418-2335. FAX 49-931-418-2100. Ed. Reinhard Gloggengiesser. adv.: B&W page DM.8600, color page DM.10800; trim 185 x 266; adv. contact: Gabriele Groitzsch. circ. 135,208. **Document type:** consumer publication.
—SWETS.
Description: Offers tips on using Windows programs.

001.6 621.381   US   ISSN 1051-6425
WINDOWS JOURNAL. 1990. bi-m. $99 (Europe $145; Pacific $165). Wugnet Publications, Inc., Box 1967, Media, PA 19063. TEL 215-565-1861. FAX 215-565-7106. Ed. Howard Sobel. adv.; bk.rev. circ. 10,000.
● Also available online. Vendor(s): CompuServe, Inc.
Formerly: Wugnet Journal.

004   US   ISSN 1060-1066
QA76.76.W56   CODEN: WINMEV
WINDOWS MAGAZINE; hardware & software for graphical computing. 1990. 14/yr. $24.95 (foreign $42.94). C M P Publications, Inc. (Jericho), 1 Jericho Plaza, 3rd Fl., Jericho, NY 11753. TEL 516-733-6700. FAX 516-733-8390. TELEX 647035 CMP PUB MAHA. E-mail: melgan@cmp.com; URL: http://www.winmag.com. (Subscr. to: Reader Service Management Dept., Box 5006, Pittsfield, MA 01203-9951. TEL 800-829-9150) Ed. Michael R. Elgan. adv. circ. 80,000. **Indexed:** Comput.Ind.
● Also available online.
—CISTI; KR SourceOne; SWETS; UMI. **CCC.**
Formerly (until 1991): Windows and OS2 Magazine.
Description: Covers software, hardware and networking.

004   US   ISSN 1065-9641
QA76.76.W56
WINDOWS SOURCES; the magazine for windows experts. 1993. m. $16.97. Ziff-Davis Publishing Co., One Park Ave., New York, NY 10016. TEL 212-503-3500. FAX 212-503-4141. E-mail: wsonline@zd.com; URL: http://www.zdnet.com/wsources/. (Subscr. to: Box 59100, Boulder, CO 80322-9100. TEL 800-365-3414) Ed. Jim Louderback; Pub. Peter Weedfald. adv.: B&W page $6885, color page $8435; trim 7 7/8 x 10 1/2. circ. 400,000. **Document type:** consumer publication.
● Also available online. Vendor(s): Information Access Co.
—BLDSC (9319.332355); KR SourceOne; SWETS. **CCC.**

004   US   ISSN 1059-1028
TK5105.5   CODEN: WREDEM
WIRED. UK edition (ISSN 1357-0978) 1993. m. $39.95 to individuals (Canada and Mexico $64; elsewhere $79); institutions $80 (Canada and Mexico $103; elsewhere $110) (effective 1996). Wired Ventures Ltd., 520 Third St., 4th Fl., San Francisco, CA 94107. TEL 415-222-6200; 800-769-4733. FAX 415-222-6209. E-mail: editor@wired.com. (Subscr. to: Box 191826, San Francisco, CA 94119-9866) Ed. Russ Mitchell; Pub. Louis Rossetto. adv.: color page $22500; trim 9 x 10 3/4. illus.; circ. 325,000 (paid). **Indexed:** Access (1993-), WPM. **Document type:** consumer publication.
—BLDSC (9323.650000); KR SourceOne; SWETS; UnCover.
Description: Covers the people involved with the digital revolution and related changes in computer and communications technologies and life-styles.

004   US   ISSN 1073-2233
HF5548   CODEN: WPITE8
WORK PROCESS IMPROVEMENT TODAY; focusing on document, data capture, desktop and remittance processing. 1977. bi-m. $250 membership (effective 1995). Association for Work Process Improvement, 185 Devonshire St., Ste. 770, Boston, MA 02110. TEL 617-426-1167. FAX 617-521-8675. Ed. Franklin Cooper; Pub. Kerry C. Stackpole. R&P contact: Kerry C. Stackpole. adv.; bk.rev.; charts; illus.; tr.lit.; cum.index 1977-1996. circ. 10,000. (back issues avail.) **Indexed:** Comput.Cont., INSPEC. **Document type:** trade publication.
—BLDSC (9348.186500); AskIEEE; CASDDS; KR SourceOne.
Former titles: Remittance and Document Processing Today; Recognition Technologies Today (ISSN 0883-5594)
Description: Provides in-depth articles on topics such as applications of optical character recognition, magnetic ink character recognition, image and voice recognition and the other automated data technologies.

001.6 621.381   US   ISSN 0895-4372
THE WORKSHOP (MICROSOFT WORKS). 1988. m. $39 (foreign $59). Cobb Group, Inc., 9420 Bunsen Pkwy., Ste. 300, Louisville, KY 40220. TEL 502-493-3200. FAX 502-491-8050. (Subscr. to: Box 35160, Louisville, KY 40232-9720. TEL 800-223-8720) Ed. Jay Sedlaczek.

001.6 621.381   US   ISSN 1059-9959
WORKSTATION; independent news magazine for H P Apollo workstation and server users. 1985. m. $45 (foreign $75) (effective 1995). Publications & Communications, Inc., 12416 Hymeadow, Austin, TX 78750-1896. TEL 512-250-9023; 800-678-9724. FAX 512-331-3900. Ed. John Mitchell. adv.: B&W page $3401, color page $4201. bk.rev. circ. 10,000. (reprint service avail.) **Document type:** trade publication.
—KR SourceOne.
Former titles: H P Design and Automation (ISSN 0896-212X); H P Design and Manufacturing (ISSN 0892-2810); Chronicle Magazine.
Description: Contains in-depth articles and editorials about new and enhanced products from Hewlitt-Packard, Apollo, and third-party companies.

001.6 621.381   SI
WORLD SCIENTIFIC SERIES IN COMPUTER SCIENCE. (Text in English) 1985. irreg., vol.45, no.2, 1994. price varies. World Scientific Publishing Co. Pte. Ltd., Farrer Rd., P.O. Box 128, Singapore 9128, Singapore. TEL 65-3825663. FAX 65-3825919. TELEX RS 28561 WSPC. E-mail: wspcsl@singnet.com.sg; sales@wspc2.demon.co.uk; wspc@wspc.com; URL: http://www.singnet.com.sg/~wspclib/. (UK addr.: 57 Shelton St., Covent Garden, London WC2H 9HE, England. TEL 44-171-836-0888; US addr.: 1060 Main St., River Edge, NJ 07661. TEL 800-227-7562) **Indexed:** Zent.Math. **Document type:** monographic series.
Formerly (until vol.21): Series in Computer Science.

004   UK   ISSN 1363-9889
▼**WORLDWIDE COMPUTER PRODUCTS NEWS.** (Not avail in print format) 1995. m. £100($170) (effective 1997). M2 Communications Ltd., P.O. Box 475, Coventry CV1 2ZW, England. TEL 44-1203-634700. FAX 44-1203-634144. E-mail: di@m2.com; URL: http://www.m2.com. Ed. Darren Ingram. **Document type:** trade publication.
● Available only online.
Description: Monitors what new products are coming into the market within the competitive, fast-moving computer sector.

621.38 001.6   US   ISSN 0894-4326
YANKEE INGENUITY.* irreg. Yankee Group, 31 Saint James Ave., Boston, MA 02116-4101. TEL 617-367-1000.

004   US
▼**YEAR 2000 ANNOUNCEMENT LIST.** 1996. m. Tenagra Corporation, 1100 Hercules, Ste. 120, Houston, TX 77058. E-mail: cliff.kurtzman@year2000.com; URL: http://www.year2000.com/. Ed. Clifford Kurtzman. **Document type:** bulletin.
● Available only online.
Description: News about Year 2000 century date change computing issues.

003 658.4   YU   ISSN 0354-0243
YUGOSLAV JOURNAL OF OPERATIONS RESEARCH; an international journal dealing with theoretical and computational aspects of operations research, systems science, and management science. 1991. s-a. (2 nos. in 1 vol.). $60. University of Belgrade, Faculty of Organizational Sciences, Laboratory for Operations Research, Jove Ilica 154, 11000 Belgrade, Yugoslavia. TEL 38-11-465855. FAX 38-11-461221. (Subscr. to: Jugoslovenska Knjiga, Trg Republike 5-VIII, 11000 Belgrade, Yugoslavia. TEL 38-11-622696) Ed.Bd. bk.rev. **Indexed:** Zent.Math.
—BLDSC (9421.659370); Ei.
Description: Deals with all aspects of operations research, systems science, and management science.
Refereed Serial

621.39   US
▼**Z D NET ANCHORDESK.** 1996. 3/wk. Ziff - Davis Publications, Inc., 2300 130th Ave., N.E., Ste. 1-101, Bellevue, WA 98005. E-mail: info@anchordesk.com; URL: http://www.anchordesk.com Ed. Jesse Berst.
● Available only online.

001.6 621.381   IT   ISSN 0392-8497
ZEROUNO; mensile di informatica. 1982. m. (11/yr.). L.88000 (foreign L.111650). Mondadori Informatica S.p.A., Casella Postale 3686, 20090 Segrate (MI), Italy. TEL 39-2-21712270. FAX 39-2-21712275. E-mail: zerouno@mondadori.it. Ed. Francesco di Martile. adv. contact: Gianluca Ferranto. circ. 9,528. **Document type:** consumer publication.
Description: Covers client-server technology, databases and middleware.

004   US
▼**21ST, THE V X M NETWORK**. 1996. bi-m. V X M Technologies, Inc., Box 41, Boston, MA 02199. E-mail: 21st@vxm.com; URL: http://www.vxm.com. Ed. Franco Vitaliano.
●Available only online.
Description: Covers technology convergence, including computers, the Web, molecular computing, and more.

001.6 621.381   GW
64ER; das Magazin fuer Computer-Fans. 1984. m. DM.81 (foreign DM.105). Markt und Technik Verlag AG, Hans-Pinsel-Str. 2, 85540 Haar, Germany. TEL 089-4613-0. FAX 089-4613-774. circ. 208,677. **Document type:** consumer publication.
Description: For owners and users of Commodore 64, 128 and C16-Plus systems.

004 621.381   UK
4000 PLUS. 1987. m. £26.95. Future Publishing Ltd., 30 Monmouth St., Bath, Avon BA1 2BW, England. TEL 44-1224-442244. FAX 44-1224-462986. (Subscr. to: Future Publishing, Somerton, Somers. TA11 6BR, England. TEL 44-1225-822511) Pub. Simon Stansfield. adv.; charts; illus. circ. 30,583. (back issues avail.)
Description: Covers general-interest, programming, product reviews, business uses, and news.

COMPUTERS — Abstracting, Bibliographies, Statistics

001.64 016   US   ISSN 0149-1199
QA75.5
C M GUIDE TO COMPUTING LITERATURE; bibliographic listing, author index, keyword index, category index, proper noun subject index, reviewer index, source index. 1964. a. $190 to non-members. Association for Computing Machinery, 1515 Broadway, 17th Fl., New York, NY 10036-5701. TEL 212-869-7440. FAX 212-869-0481. TELEX 421686. (Subscr. to: Box 64145, Baltimore, MD 21264) Ed. Aaron Finerman. circ. 2,200. (back issues avail.)
●Also available online. Vendor(s): Knight-Ridder Information, Inc.
—BLDSC (0578.627000); Linda Hall; SWETS.
Formerly: Bibliography and Subject Index of Current Computing Literature (ISSN 0149-1202)
Description: Contains over 24,000 entries and listings for over 34,000 authors.

001.5 016   YU   ISSN 0351-3548
A P BIBLIOGRAFIJA/AUTOMATIC DATA PROCESSING. BIBLIOGRAPHY. (Automatska Obrada Podataka). 1974. bi-m. $190. Jugoslovenski Centar za Tehnicku i Naucnu Dokumentaciju - Yugoslav Center for Technical and Scientific Documentation (YCTSD), Sl. Penezica-Krcuna 29-31, Box 724, 11000 Belgrade, Yugoslavia. Ed. Ljiljana Kojic-Bogdanovic. circ. 200.
Formerly: O A P Automatika Obrada Podataka. Bibliografija (ISSN 0350-0403)

016.657 657   UK   ISSN 0961-2742
HF5635
ACCOUNTING & FINANCE ABSTRACTS. 1970. bi-m. £3199($4999) (foreign Aus.$6499) (effective 1998). M C B University Press Ltd., Anbar Electronic Intelligence, 60-62 Toller Ln., Bradford, W. Yorks BD8 9BY, England. TEL 44-1274-480916. FAX 44-1274-543576. TELEX 51317 MCBUNI G. URL: http://www.mcb.co.uk. Ed. Eric Sandelands. (looseleaf format) **Document type:** abstracting/indexing.
●Also available on CD-ROM.
—BLDSC (0900.065000).
Formerly: Accounting and Data Processing Abstracts (ISSN 0001-4796); Which superseded in part: Anbar Management Services Abstracts (ISSN 0003-2794)
Description: Contains abstracts of articles selected from more than 300 international management journals. Covers such topics as financial accounts, software, internal and external auditing, computer management, capital investment and data transmission.

AMERICAN STATISTICAL ASSOCIATION. STATISTICAL COMPUTING SECTION. PROCEEDINGS (OF THE ANNUAL MEETING). see STATISTICS

004 310   AT
AUSTRALIA. BUREAU OF STATISTICS. COMPUTING SERVICES INDUSTRY, AUSTRALIA. 1987. irreg., latest 1993. Aus.$20. Australian Bureau of Statistics, P.O. Box 10, Belconnen, A.C.T. 2616, Australia. **Document type:** government publication.

001.6 621.38   UK   ISSN 0957-3224
AUTOMATED OFFICE ABSTRACTS. 6/yr. £65. (National Computing Centre Ltd.) Techgnosis Ltd., Blade House, Battersea Rd., Stockport, Cheshire SK4 3AE, England. TEL 44-161-442-2639. FAX 44-161-443-1162. Ed. T. Drinkall. **Document type:** abstracting/indexing.
Formerly: Automated Office Profiles (ISSN 0265-167X)

004   US
BIBLIOGRAPHY OF COMPUTER AND AUTOMATED SYSTEMS TECHNICAL RESOURCES. a. free. Society of Manufacturing Engineers, One SME Dr., Box 930, Dearborn, MI 48121-0930. TEL 313-271-1500. FAX 313-271-2861. TELEX 297742 SME UR (VIA RCA). (Co-sponsor: Computer and Automated Systems Association) **Document type:** bibliography.

004   US
BIBLIOGRAPHY OF RAPID PROTOTYPING RESOURCES. a. free. Society of Manufacturing Engineers, One SME Dr., Box 930, Dearborn, MI 48121-0930. TEL 313-271-1500. FAX 313-271-2861. TELEX 297742 SME UR (VIA RCA). (Co-sponsor: Rapid Prototyping Association) **Document type:** bibliography.

629.892   US
BIBLIOGRAPHY OF ROBOTIC TECHNICAL RESOURCES. a. free. Society of Manufacturing Engineers, One SME Dr., Box 930, Dearborn, MI 48121-0930. TEL 313-271-1500. FAX 313-271-2861. TELEX 297742 SME UR (VIA RCA). (Co-sponsor: Robotics International) **Document type:** bibliography.

025.344025 016   US   ISSN 0891-8198
TK7882.C56
C D - R O M S IN PRINT. 1987. a. $145 (effective 1997). Gale Research, 835 Penobscot Bldg., 645 Griswold St., Detroit, MI 48226-4094. TEL 313-961-2242; 800-877-4253. FAX 800-414-5043. E-mail: daniel_snyder@gale.com. **Document type:** directory.
●Also available on CD-ROM.
—BLDSC (3096.306000); CISTI. **CCC**.

CINFOLINK ANNUAL REVIEW OF INFORMATION SERVICES IN CHINA. see BUSINESS AND ECONOMICS — Trade And Industrial Directories

COMPUMATH CITATION INDEX. see MATHEMATICS — Abstracting, Bibliographies, Statistics

004 016   UK   ISSN 0010-4469
Z6654.C17
COMPUTER ABSTRACTS. 1957. bi-m. £1999($2999) (foreign Aus.$3999) (effective 1998). M C B University Press Ltd., Anbar Electronic Intelligence, 60-62 Toller Ln., Bradford, W. Yorks BD8 9BY, England. TEL 44-1274-499821. FAX 44-1274-547143. E-mail: mwills@mcb.co.uk; URL: http://www.mcb.co.uk/compabs/home.htm. Ed. Chris Matthews. bk.rev.; pat.; tr.lit. circ. 1,200. (reprint service avail. from SWZ) **Indexed:** Comput.Rev. **Document type:** abstracting/indexing.
●Also available on CD-ROM.
—BLDSC (3390.680000).
Description: Presents abstracts from more than 200 English-language periodicals, as well as conference papers from around the world.

004 629.8   UK   ISSN 0036-8113
QA76   CODEN: CCABB8
COMPUTER & CONTROL ABSTRACTS. Alternative title: INSPEC. Section C. Represents: Science Abstracts. Section C. 1966. m. £1115 (effective 1997). INSPEC, I.E.E., Michael Faraday House, Six Hills Way, Stevenage, Herts. SG1 2AY, England. TEL 44-1438-313311. FAX 44-1438-742840. TELEX 825578 IEESTV G. E-mail: inspec@iee.org.uk; URL: http://www.iee.org.uk. (Subscr. to: Publication Sales Dept., P.O. Box 96, Stevenage, Herts. SG1 2SD, England; U.S. addr.: INSPEC Dept., IEEE Operations Center, 445 Hoes Ln., Box 1331, Piscataway, NJ 08855-1331. TEL 908-562-5553. FAX 908-562-8737) adv.; abstr.; bibl.; index, cum.index every 4 yrs. **Indexed:** Comput.Rev., Ergon.Abstr., Fluidex. **Document type:** abstracting/indexing.
●Also available online. Vendor(s): CEDOCAR, Data-Star, European Space Agency (File no.8/INSPEC), FIZ Technik, Knight-Ridder Information, Inc., Questel Orbit Inc., STN International.
Also available on CD-ROM. Producer(s): UMI.
—BLDSC (3393.550000); CASDDS; CISTI; Linda Hall. **CCC**.
Description: Provides abstracts, organized by subjects, of international technological information. Listings include publication details for acquisition purposes, author and number of references cited by the author.

651.8 016   US   ISSN 0191-9776
QA76
COMPUTER AND INFORMATION SYSTEMS ABSTRACTS JOURNAL; an abstract journal pertaining to the theory, design, fabrication and application of computer and information systems. 1962. m. $1045 (foreign $1350). Cambridge Scientific Abstracts, 7200 Wisconsin Ave., 6th Fl., Bethesda, MD 20814. TEL 301-961-6750. FAX 301-961-6720. E-mail: market@csa.com; URL: http://www.csa.com. (Co-publisher: Engineering Information, Inc.) Ed. Evelyn Beck; Pub. Ted Caris. adv.; bk.rev.; abstr.; index. (also avail. in magnetic tape; back issues avail.) **Indexed:** Cal.Tiss.Abstr., Chemorec.Abstr., Oncol.Abstr., Pollut.Abstr. **Document type:** abstracting/indexing.
●Also available online. Vendor(s): STN International.
—BLDSC (3393.580000); CISTI; Linda Hall; SWETS.
Former titles: Computer and Information Systems (ISSN 0010-4507); Information Processing Journal (ISSN 0362-8973)
Description: International reference publication devoted to complete and comprehensive coverage of the international literature.

COMPUTER BOOK REVIEW. see COMPUTERS

001.6 621.381
001.7   US
COMPUTER DATABASE. m. Information Access Company (Subsidiary of: Thomson Corporation), 362 Lakeside Dr., Foster City, CA 94404. TEL 415-378-5200; 800-227-8431. FAX 415-378-5369. (Or: Predicasts Europe, 8-10 Denman St., London W1V 7RF, England. TEL 44-171-494-3817) **Document type:** abstracting/indexing.
●Available only online. Vendor(s): Data-Star (CMPT), Knight-Ridder Information, Inc. (File no.275), Ovid Technologies, Inc. (CMPT).

COMPUTERS — ABSTRACTING, BIBLIOGRAPHIES, STATISTICS

004   XR   ISSN 1210-3721
COMPUTER INDEX; the latest computer news, articles, and tips from the U.S.A. (Text in English) 1992. q. 320 Kc. (effective 1995). Starman Bohemia Ltd., Ul. Konviktska 24, 110 00 Prague 1, Czech Republic. TEL 42-2-24231933. Ed. Frank Starman. adv.; bk.rev. circ. 1,500. **Document type:** abstracting/indexing.
   Description: Provides information and guidance on U.S. computer magazines and literature.

001.6 621.381   US   ISSN 0894-6213
HD9696.C6
COMPUTER INDUSTRY FORECASTS; the source for market information on computers, peripherals, internet, and software. 1984. q. $365 (foreign $405) (effective 1997 & 1998). Data Analysis Group, 5100 Cherry Creek Rd., Box 128, Cloverdale, CA 95425. TEL 707-539-3009. FAX 707-486-5618. URL: http://www.cif1.com. Ed. Reny Parker. abstr.; charts; stat.; cum.index. (also avail. in diskette format; back issues avail.) **Document type:** abstracting/indexing.
●Also available online. Vendor(s): Lexis-Nexis.
—CCC.
   Formerly: Computer Industry Abstracts (ISSN 0883-931X); Incorporates (as of 1985): Computer Industry Forecast (ISSN 0883-9301)

004 016   US   ISSN 0270-4846
QA76
COMPUTER LITERATURE INDEX. 1971. q. (plus a. cum.). $245. Applied Computer Research, Inc., Box 82266, Phoenix, AZ 85071-2266. TEL 800-234-2227. Ed. Phillip C. Howard. bk.rev. **Document type:** abstracting/indexing.
—CCC.
   Formerly (until 1979): Quarterly Bibliography of Computers and Data Processing (ISSN 0048-6132)
   Description: Bibliography of books, articles, and reports relating to computers and data processing.

001.6 621.381   UK   ISSN 0958-1413
COMPUTER SECURITY AND PRIVACY ABSTRACTS. 6/yr. £65. (National Computing Centre Ltd.) Techgnosis Ltd., Blade House, Battersea Rd., Stockport, Cheshire SK4 3AE, England. TEL 44-161-442-2639. FAX 44-161-443-1162. Ed. T. Drinkall. **Document type:** abstracting/indexing.
   Formerly: Computer Security and Privacy Profiles (ISSN 0265-1688)
   Description: Presents computer security and privacy issues, including legal aspects.

004   US   ISSN 1062-8509
QA75.5   CODEN: COSLEB
COMPUTER SELECT. 1988. m. $1250. Computer Library, One Park Ave., New York, NY 10016. TEL 212-503-4400; 800-827-7889. FAX 212-503-4414. bk.rev. **Document type:** abstracting/indexing, catalog.
●Available only on CD-ROM.
—CCC.
   Formerly (until 1991): Computer Library (ISSN 1062-8517)
   Description: Provides full text of more than 80 computer industry publications, with abstracts of articles from more than 40 other periodicals and four major newspapers. Also includes product specifications and company information for all sectors of the computer industry.

001.6 016   UK   ISSN 0309-8885
COMPUTING JOURNAL ABSTRACTS. 1969. m. £150. (National Computing Centre Ltd.) Techgnosis Ltd., Blade House, Battersea Rd., Stockport, Cheshire SK4 3AE, England. TEL 44-161-442-2639. FAX 44-161-443-1162. Ed. T. Drinkall. index. circ. 450. (also avail. in diskette format) **Indexed:** BMT, Mgmt.& Market.Abstr. **Document type:** abstracting/indexing.
   Description: Covers product reviews, surveys, case studies, new developments, company news, original research, professional awareness, events, and more.

621.381 001.6
011.7   US   ISSN 0010-4884
QA76   CODEN: CPGRA6
COMPUTING REVIEWS. 1960. m. $130 to non-members. Association for Computing Machinery, 1515 Broadway, 17th Fl., New York, NY 10036-5701. TEL 212-869-7440. FAX 212-944-1318. TELEX 421686. Ed. A. Finerman. adv.; bk.rev.; abstr.; index, cum.index. circ. 8,500. (also avail. in microfiche from KTO,WWS)
   Indexed: Abstr.Hum.Comp.Inter., Chem.Abstr., Ergon.Abstr.
●Also available online. Vendor(s): Knight-Ridder Information, Inc.
—BLDSC (3395.124000); CASDDS; UMI. **CCC.**
   Description: Reviews of current publications in all areas of computer science. Covers hardware, software, computer systems organization, theory of computation, information systems and computer applications.

651.8 629.8 016   UK   ISSN 0011-3794
QA75.5
CURRENT PAPERS ON COMPUTERS & CONTROL. Abbreviated title: C P C. 1969. m. £260 (effective 1997). INSPEC, I.E.E., Michael Faraday House, Six Hills Way, Stevenage, Herts. SG1 2AY, England. TEL 44-1438-313311. FAX 44-1438-742840. TELEX 825578 IEESTV G. E-mail: inspec@iee.org.uk; URL: http://www.iee.org.uk. (Subscr. to: Publication Sales Dept., P.O. Box 96, Stevenage, Herts. SG1 2SD, England; U.S. subscr. address: INSPEC Dept., IEEE Operations Center, 445 Hoes Ln., Box 1331, Piscataway, NJ 08855-1331. TEL 908-562-5549. FAX 908-562-8737) bk.rev.; index. **Indexed:** Agri.Eng.Abstr., Graph.Arts Lit.Abstr. **Document type:** abstracting/indexing.
   Description: Contains author, title, and bibliographic details of papers published in over 4,200 international journals and conference proceedings. Covers the latest research and development and applications in all areas of computing and control.

001.6 621.381   US   ISSN 1049-1244
C2C CURRENTS: JAPAN - COMPUTERS. 1990. m. $100. Scan C2C, 1001 Pennsylvania Ave., N.W., No. 1300, Washington, DC 20024-2025. TEL 800-525-3865. FAX 202-863-3855.
●Also available online. Vendor(s): Data-Star (JPTC), European Space Agency (File no.241), Knight-Ridder Information, Inc. (File no.582), Questel Orbit Inc. (JTEC).
Also available on CD-ROM. Producer(s): Knight-Ridder, Inc.
   Description: Provides a summary of the contents of leading scientific and business journals in Japan. Contains a table of contents for selected journals. Lists title, author, date of publication, number of pages, and source journal.

629.8 016   RU   ISSN 0131-0380
EKSPRESS-INFORMATSIYA. PRIBORY I ELEMENTY AVTOMATIKI I VYCHISLITEL'NOI TEKHNIKI. 1960. 24/yr. $168.20 (effective 1997). Vsesoyuznyi Institut Nauchno-Tekhnicheskoi Informatsii (VINITI), Baltiiskaya ul., 14, Moscow A-219, Russia. (Dist. by: Mezhdunarodnaya Kniga, B. Yakimanka 39, 117049 Moscow, Russia)

001.53 016   RU   ISSN 0131-0488
EKSPRESS-INFORMATSIYA. SISTEMY AVTOMATICHESKOGO UPRAVLENIYA. 1962. 48/yr. 40.60 Rub. Vsesoyuznyi Institut Nauchno-Tekhnicheskoi Informatsii (VINITI), Baltiiskaya ul., 14, Moscow A-219, Russia. (Subscr. to: Mezhdunarodnaya Kniga, Dimitrova ul. 39, 113095 Moscow, Russia)

001.53 016   RU   ISSN 0131-0577
EKSPRESS-INFORMATSIYA. TEKHNICHESKAYA KIBERNETIKA. 1965. 48/yr. 40.60 Rub. Vsesoyuznyi Institut Nauchno-Tekhnicheskoi Informatsii (VINITI), Baltiiskaya ul., 14, Moscow A-219, Russia. (Subscr. to: Mezhdunarodnaya Kniga, Dimitrova ul. 39, 113095 Moscow, Russia)

016.006   NE
EXCERPTA INFORMATICA; an abstract journal of recent literature on automation. (Abstracts in Dutch, English, French and German) 1960. m. fl.240. Tilburg University Press, Postbus 90153, 5000 LE Tilburg, Netherlands. bk.rev.; abstr.; bibl.; index, cum.index: 1961-1964; 1965-1968. circ. 1,500.
   Former titles (until 1985): New Literature on Automation (ISSN 0028-6095) (until 1967): Literature on Automation (ISSN 0377-1067)

001.6 621.381   GW   ISSN 0933-9507
FACHBUCHVERZEICHNIS INFORMATIK - DATENVERARBEITUNG (YEAR). 1900. a. DM.4. Rossipaul Kommunikation GmbH, Menzingerstr. 37, 80638 Munich, Germany. TEL 49-89-179106-0. FAX 49-89-17910622. Ed. Angela Sendlinger. circ. 30,000. **Document type:** trade publication.

001.6 314   HU   ISSN 0236-9842
HD9696.C63
HUNGARY. KOZPONTI STATISZTIKAI HIVATAL. SZAMITASTECHNIKAI STATISZTIKAI ZSEBKONYV. 1984. a. 156 Ft. Statisztikai Kiado Vallalat, Kaszasdulo u. 2, P.O. Box 99, 1300 Budapest 3, Hungary. TEL 36-1-180-3311. FAX 36-1-168-8635. TELEX 22-6699. (Subscr. to: Kultura, Box 149, H-1389 Budapest, Hungary) stat. circ. 1,200. **Document type:** government publication.
   Former titles: Hungary. Kozponti Statisztikai Hivatal. Szamitastechnikai Statisztikai Evkonyv (ISSN 0139-3286); Szamitastechnikai Evkonyv (ISSN 0133-9559)

004 410 410   CN   ISSN 1198-1083
INFOLINGUA. 1994. irreg. price varies. Infolingua Inc., P.O. Box 187, Snowdon, Montreal, PQ H3X 3T4, Canada. TEL 514-737-7745. FAX 514-737-7745. E-mail: 73651.2144@compuserve.com. Ed. Rolande Lamarche; Pub. Rolande Lamarche. R&P contact: Rolande Lamarche. **Document type:** bibliography.
   Description: Provides indexed bibliographies on computational linguistics, computational literature, computer mediated communication, computer assisted instruction, human-computer interaction, and information science.

INSPEC LIST OF JOURNALS AND OTHER SERIAL SOURCES. see ENGINEERING — Abstracting, Bibliographies, Statistics

003 016   UK   ISSN 0020-580X
Q500
INTERNATIONAL ABSTRACTS IN OPERATIONS RESEARCH. 1961. bi-m. £99($155) to individuals; institutions £250 (foreign £250($390)) (effective 1997). (International Federation of Operational Research Societies) Stockton Press (Subsidiary of: MacMillan Press Ltd.), Houndmills, Basingstoke, Hants. RG21 6XS, England. TEL 44-1256-351898. FAX 44-1256-328339. Ed. D. Smith; Pub. Harry Holt. adv. contact: Alison Reeves. index, cum.index. (also avail. in microform) **Document type:** abstracting/indexing.
—BLDSC (4535.580000); CISTI; Linda Hall. **CCC.**

001.6 621.381
001.7   UK   ISSN 0950-477X
Q334
KEY ABSTRACTS - ARTIFICIAL INTELLIGENCE. 1975. n. £120($200) (effective 1997). INSPEC, I.E.E., Michael Faraday House, Six Hills Way, Stevenage, Herts. SG1 2AY, England. TEL 44-1438-313311. FAX 44-1438-742840. TELEX 825578 IEESTV G. E-mail: inspec@iee.org.uk; URL: http://www.iee.org.uk. (Subscr. to: Publication Sales Dept., P.O. Box 9, Stevenage, Herts. SG1 2SD, England; U.S. addr.: INSPEC Dept., IEEE, Operations Center, 445 Hoes Ln., Box 1331, Piscataway, NJ 08855-1331. TEL 908-562-5549. FAX 908-562-8737) index. **Document type:** abstracting/indexing.
   Formerly (until 1987): Key Abstracts - Systems Theory (ISSN 0306-5553)
   Description: Presents abstracts on theory and applications of artificial intelligence, knowledge engineering, and expert systems.

COMPUTERS — ABSTRACTING, BIBLIOGRAPHIES, STATISTICS

001.6 621.381 UK ISSN 0954-9153
KEY ABSTRACTS - BUSINESS AUTOMATION. 1983. m. £120 (effective 1997). INSPEC, I.E.E., Michael Faraday House, Six Hill Way, Stevenage, Herts. SG1 2AY, England. TEL 44-1438-313311. FAX 44-1438-742840. TELEX 825578 IEESTV G. E-mail: inspec@iee.org.uk; URL: http://www.iee.org.uk. (U.S. addr.: INSPEC Dept., IEEE, Operations Center, 445 Hoes Ln., Box 1331, Piscataway, NJ 08855-1331. TEL 908-562-5549. FAX 908-562-8737) **Document type:** abstracting/indexing.
●Also available online. Vendor(s): CEDOCAR, Data-Star, European Space Agency, FIZ Technik, Knight-Ridder Information, Inc., Questel Orbit Inc., STN International.
Also available on CD-ROM. Producer(s): Knight-Ridder, Inc.
—BLDSC (5091.820490); Linda Hall.
Former titles: I T Focus (INSPEC, Section D); Information Technology Update for Managers; (until 1984): I T Focus (ISSN 0264-9152)

004 621.381 UK ISSN 0950-4788
KEY ABSTRACTS - COMPUTER COMMUNICATIONS AND STORAGE. 1987. m. £120($200) (effective 1997). INSPEC, I.E.E., Michael Faraday House, Six Hills Way, Stevenage, Herts. SG1 2AY, England. TEL 44-1438-313311. FAX 44-1438-742840. TELEX 825578 IEESTV G. E-mail: inspec@iee.org.uk; URL: http://www.iee.org.uk. (Subscr. to: Publication Sales Dept., P.O. Box 96, Stevenage, Herts.; SG1 2SD, England; U.S. addr.: INSPEC Dept., IEEE Operations Center, 445 Hoes Ln., Box 1331, Piscataway, NJ 08855-1331. TEL 908-562-5549. FAX 908-562-8737) index. **Document type:** abstracting/indexing.
Description: Covers multiprocessor systems, modern storage media, including optical disc, interfaces, networks, and network equipment.

004 621.381 UK ISSN 0950-4796
KEY ABSTRACTS - COMPUTING IN ELECTRONICS & POWER. 1987. m. £120($200) (effective 1997). INSPEC, I.E.E., Michael Faraday House, Six Hills Way, Stevenage, Herts. SG1 2AY, England. TEL 44-1438-313311. FAX 44-1438-742840. TELEX 825578 IEESTV G. E-mail: inspec@iee.org.uk; URL: http://www.iee.org.uk. (Subscr. to: Publication Sales Dept., P.O. Box 96, Stevenage, Herts. SG1 2SD, England; U.S. addr.: INSPEC Dept., IEEE Operations Center, 445 Hoes Ln., Box 1331, Piscataway, NJ 08855-1331. TEL 908-562-5549. FAX 908-562-8737) index. **Document type:** abstracting/indexing.
Description: Covers computer applications in communications, electrical engineering, electronics, and power engineering.

610 621.9 UK ISSN 0960-6572
KEY ABSTRACTS - FACTORY AUTOMATION. 1991. m. £120($200) (effective 1997). INSPEC, I.E.E., Michael Faraday House, Six Hills Way, Stevenage, Herts. SG1 2AY, England. TEL 44-1438-313311. FAX 44-1438-742840. TELEX 825578 IEESTV G. E-mail: inspec@iee.org.uk; URL: http://www.iee.org.uk. (Subscr. to: Publication Sales Dept. P.O. Box 96, Stevenage, Herts. SG1 2SD, England; U.S. addr.: INSPEC Dept., IEEE Operations Center, 445 Hoes Ln., Box 1331, Piscataway, NJ 08855-1331. TEL 908-562-5549. FAX 908-562-8737) Ed. John Deaves. **Document type:** abstracting/indexing.

001.6 621.381 UK ISSN 0964-0150
KEY ABSTRACTS - HUMAN-COMPUTER INTERACTION. 1992. m. £120($200) (effective 1997). INSPEC, I.E.E., Michael Faraday House, Six Hills Way, Stevenage, Herts. SG1 2AY, England. TEL 44-1438-313311. FAX 44-1438-742840. TELEX 825578 IEESTV G. E-mail: inspec@iee.org.uk; URL: http://www.iee.org.uk. (Subscr. to: Publication Sales Dept., P.O. Box 96, Stevenage, Herts. SG1 2SD, England; U.S. addr.: INSPEC Dept., IEEE Operations Center, 445 Hoes Ln., Box 1331, Piscataway, NJ 08855-1331. TEL 908-562-5549. FAX 908-562-8737) Ed. John Deaves. **Document type:** abstracting/indexing.

001.6 UK ISSN 0952-7052
KEY ABSTRACTS - MACHINE VISION. 1989. m. £120($200) (effective 1997). INSPEC, I.E.E., Michael Faraday House, Six Hills Way, Stevenage, Herts. SG1 2AY, England. TEL 44-1438-313311. FAX 44-1438-742840. TELEX 825578 IEESTV G. E-mail: inspec@iee.org.uk; URL: http://www.iee.org.uk. (Subscr. to: Publication Sales Dept., P.O. Box 96, Stevenage, Herts. SG1 2SD, England; U.S. addr.: INSPEC Dept., IEEE Operations Center, 445 Hoes Ln., Box 1331, Piscataway, NJ 08855-1331. TEL 908-562-5549. FAX 908-562-8737) Ed.Bd. (microfilm) **Document type:** abstracting/indexing.
Description: Summarizes recently published papers from more than 4,200 international journals and conference proceedings. Subjects covered include image processing, pattern recognition, information theory, computer vision, image-sensing devices, and applications.

006.3 UK ISSN 0964-0169
KEY ABSTRACTS - NEURAL NETWORKS. 1992. m. £120($200) (effective 1999). INSPEC, I.E.E., Michael Faraday House, Six Hills Way, Stevenage, Herts. SG1 2AY, England. TEL 44-1438-313311. FAX 44-1438-742840. TELEX 825578 IEESTV G. E-mail: inspec@iee.org.uk; URL: http://www.iee.org.uk. (Subscr. to: Publication Sales Dept., P.O. Box 96, Stevenage, Herts., SG1 2SD, England; U.S. addr.: INSPEC Dept., IEEE Operations Center, 445 Hoes Ln., Box 1331, Piscataway, NJ 08855-1331. TEL 908-562-5549. FAX 908-562-8737) Ed. Bob Beasley.

001.6 621.381
001.7 UK ISSN 0950-4842
Z5853.A8
KEY ABSTRACTS - ROBOTICS & CONTROL. 1975. m. £120($200) (effective 1997). INSPEC, I.E.E., Michael Faraday House, Six Hills Way, Stevenage, Herts. SG1 2AY, England. TEL 44-1438-313311. FAX 44-1438-742840. TELEX 825578 IEESTV G. E-mail: inspec@iee.org.uk; URL: http://www.iee.org.uk. (Subscr. to: Publication Sales Dept., P.O. Box 96, Stevenage, Herts. SG1 2SD, England; U.S. addr.: INSPEC Dept., IEEE Operations Center, 445 Hoes Ln., Box 1331, Piscataway, NJ 08855-1331. TEL 908-562-5549. FAX 908-562-8737) index.
Formerly (until 1987): Key Abstracts - Industrial Power and Control Systems (ISSN 0306-5596)
Description: Covers robots and their applications to materials handling, industrial production systems, and transportation systems.

001.6 621.381
001.7 UK ISSN 0950-4869
KEY ABSTRACTS - SOFTWARE ENGINEERING. 1987. m. £120($200) (effective 1997). INSPEC, I.E.E., Michael Faraday House, Six Hills Way, Stevenage, Herts. SG1 2AY, England. TEL 44-1438-313311. FAX 44-1438-742840. TELEX 825578 IEESTV G. E-mail: inspec@iee.org.uk; URL: http://www.iee.org.uk. (Subscr. to: Publication Sales Dept., P.O. Box 96, Stevenage, Herts. SG1 2SD, England; U.S. addr.: INSPEC Dept., IEEE Operations Center, 445 Hoes Ln., Box 1331, Piscataway, NJ 08855-1331. TEL 908-562-5549. FAX 908-562-8737) **Document type:** abstracting/indexing.
Description: Covers program support, high-level programming languages, operation systems, and database management systems.

MAGYAR KONYVTARI SZAKIRODALOM BIBLIOGRAFIAJA/BIBLIOGRAPHY ON HUNGARIAN LIBRARY LITERATURE. see LIBRARY AND INFORMATION SCIENCES — Abstracting, Bibliographies, Statistics

001.6 621.381 UK ISSN 0958-4668
MICRO ABSTRACTS. 1983. 6/yr. £65. (National Computing Centre Ltd.) Techgnosis Ltd., Blade House, Battersea Rd., Stockport, Cheshire SK4 3AE, England. TEL 44-161-442-2639. FAX 44-161-443-1162. Ed. T. Drinkall. **Document type:** abstracting/indexing.
Formerly: Microprofile (ISSN 0264-5629)
Description: Presents abstracts on the micro computer market, covering applications, developments and reviews.

004.16 016 US ISSN 1074-3995
QA75.5
MICROCOMPUTER ABSTRACTS. 1980. q. $199. Information Today, Inc., 143 Old Marlton Pike, Medford, NJ 08055. TEL 609-654-6266. FAX 609-654-4309. Eds. Judith W. Bouchard, John Eichornler. bk.rev.; index. (also avail. in magnetic tape; back issues avail.) **Document type:** abstracting/indexing.
●Also available online. Vendor(s): Knight-Ridder Information, Inc. (File no.233).
Also available on CD-ROM. Producer(s): SilverPlatter Information, Inc.
—CCC.
Formerly (until 1994): Microcomputer Index (ISSN 8756-7040)
Description: Contains abstracts of literature on the use of microcomputers in business, education, and the home. New products announcements, software and hardware reviews are included.

621.381 001.5 016 US
N T I S ALERTS: COMPUTERS, CONTROL & INFORMATION THEORY. w. $160 (foreign $225). U.S. National Technical Information Service, 5285 Port Royal Rd., Springfield, VA 22161. TEL 703-487-4630. FAX 703-321-8547. TELEX 64617. index. (also avail. in microform from NTI; back issues avail.)
Former titles: Abstract Newsletter: Computers, Control & Information Theory; Weekly Abstract Newsletter: Computers, Control and Information Theory; Weekly Government Abstracts. Computers, Control and Information Theory (ISSN 0364-796X)
Description: Contains abstracts on computer hardware, computer software, control systems and control theory, information processing standards, information theory, pattern recognition and image processing.

629.8 016 FR ISSN 0474-5868
O E C D LIBRARY SPECIAL ANNOTATED BIBLIOGRAPHY: AUTOMATION/O C D E BIBLIOTHEQUE BIBLIOGRAPHIE SPECIALE ANALYTIQUE: AUTOMATION. (Text in English, French) 1964. irreg. Organization for Economic Cooperation and Development, 2 rue Andre-Pascal, 75775 Paris Cedex 16, France. (U.S. orders to: O.E.C.D. Publications and Information Center, 2001 L St., N.W., Ste. 700, Washington, D.C. 20036-4910. TEL 202-785-6323) (also avail. in microfiche from OEC)

001.6 FR ISSN 1146-5417
Z5640
P A S C A L E 33. INFORMATIQUE. (Print edition ceased Jan. 1995) 1971. 10/yr. Centre National de la Recherche Scientifique, Institut de l'Information Scientifique et Technique, 2 allee du Parc de Brabois, 54514 Vandoeuvre-Les-Nancy Cedex, France. TEL 33-3-83504600. FAX 33-3-83504650. adv. contact: Veronique Guinvarc'h. (also avail. in microfiche) **Document type:** bibliography.
●Also available online. Vendor(s): European Space Agency, Knight-Ridder Information, Inc., Telesystemes - Questel.
Also available on CD-ROM.
Former titles (until 1989): P A S C A L Explore. E 33. Informatique (ISSN 0761-2052); P A S C A L Explore. Part 33: Informatique; Which supersedes in part (in 1984): Bulletin Signaletique. Part 110: Informatique - Automatique - Recherche Operationnelle - Gestion Economie (ISSN 0399-1563); Which was formerly (until 1978): Bulletin Signaletique. Part 110: Informatique - Automatique - Recherche Operationnelle - Gestion - Economie (ISSN 0301-3537); (until 1971): Bulletin Signaletique. Part 110: Mathematiques Appliques - Informatique - Automatique (ISSN 0007-5329).

COMPUTERS — ARTIFICIAL INTELLIGENCE

510 016 651.8 FR ISSN 1146-5425
Z5853
P A S C A L E 34. ROBOTIQUE, AUTOMATIQUE ET AUTOMATISATION DES PROCESSUS INDUSTRIELS. (Print edition ceased Jan. 1995) (Text in English, French) 1971. 10/yr. Centre National de la Recherche Scientifique, Institut de l'Information Scientifique et Technique, 2 allee du Parc de Brabois, 54514 Vandoeuvre-Les-Nancy Cedex, France. TEL 33-3-83504600.
FAX 33-3-83504650. adv. contact: Veronique Guinvarc'h. abstr. (also avail. in microform; reprint service avail. from KTO) **Document type:** bibliography.
●Also available online. Vendor(s): European Space Agency (File no.14), Knight-Ridder Information, Inc. (File no.144), Telesystemes - Questel.
Also available on CD-ROM.
Former titles: P A S C A L Explore. E 34: Robotique. Automatique et Automatisation des Processus Industriels (ISSN 0761-2060); P A S C A L Explore. Part 34: Robotique. Automatique et Automatisation des Processus Industriels; Which supersedes in part (in 1984): Bulletin Signaletique. Part 110: Informatique - Automatique - Recherche Operationnelle - Gestion Economie (ISSN 0399-1563); Which was formerly (until 1978): Bulletin Signaletique. Part 110: Informatique - Automatique - Recherche Operationnelle - Gestion - Economie (ISSN 0301-3537); (until 1971): Bulletin Signaletique. Part 110: Mathematiques Appliques - Informatique - Automatique (ISSN 0007-5329).

004 GW ISSN 0943-4887
DER P C INDEX. (Personal Computer) 1992. m. DM.298. Haimendorfstr. 8, 91126 Wolkersdorf, Germany. TEL 49-911-6320574.
FAX 49-911-6320574. E-mail: 100656.1023@compuserve.com. Ed. Bernhard Hefele; Pub. Bernhard Hefele. **Document type:** abstracting/indexing.

REFERATIVNYI ZHURNAL. AVTOMATIKA I VYCHISLITEL'NAYA TEKHNIKA. see ENGINEERING — Abstracting, Bibliographies, Statistics

001.53 016 RU
REFERATIVNYI ZHURNAL. TEKHNICHESKAYA KIBERNETIKA. English translation: Cybernetics Abstracts (UK ISSN 0011-4243) 1965. m. $74 (79.80 Rub. including index). Vsesoyuznyi Institut Nauchno-Tekhnicheskoi Informatsii (VINITI), Baltiiskaya ul., 14, Moscow A-129, Russia. (Subscr. to: Mezhdunarodnaya Kniga, Dimitrova ul. 39, 113095 Moscow, Russia) **Document type:** abstracting/indexing.
Formerly: Referativnyi Zhurnal. Kibernetika (ISSN 0486-2333)

001.539 510 JA
S S O R YOKOSHU/PROCEEDINGS OF S S O R. (Text in Japanese) a. Summer Symposium of Operation Research - S S O R Jimu-kyoku, c/o Mr. Yoshinobu Teraoka, Himeji Kogyo Daigaku Oyo Sugaku Kyoshitsu, 2167, Shosha, Himeji-shi, Hyogo-ken 671-22, Japan. abstr.

621.319 JA
SEIKEN N S T SHINPOJUMU KOEN KOGAISHU. (Numerical Simulation Turbulence) (Text in English and Japanese) 1986. a. Tokyo Daigaku, Seisan Gijutsu Kenkyujo, N S T Kenkyu Gurupu - University of Tokyo, Institute of Industrial Science, Numerical Simulation Turbulence Research Group, 22-1, Roppongi 7-chome, Minato-ku, Tokyo 106, Japan. abstr.
Description: Contains abstracts from the symposium of the group.

338 004 CN ISSN 1181-9847
HD9696.C63
SOFTWARE DEVELOPMENT AND COMPUTER SERVICE INDUSTRY/INDUSTRIE DE LA PRODUCTION DE LOGICIELS ET DES SERVICES INFORMATIQUES. (Text in English and French) 1972. a. Can.$33 (foreign $33) (effective 1998). Statistics Canada, Operations and Integration Division, Circulation Management, Jean Talon Bldg., 2-C12, Tunney's Pasture, Ottawa, ON K1A 0T6, Canada.
TEL 613-951-7277; 800-267-6677.
FAX 613-951-1584. URL: http://www.statcan.ca. charts. (also avail. in microform from MML) **Document type:** government publication.
Formerly (until 1991): Computer Service Industry (ISSN 0318-4064)
Description: Supplies the principal statistics for businesses providing computer services as a major activity.

001.6 UK ISSN 0958-465X
SOFTWARE SYSTEMS AND TECHNIQUES ABSTRACTS. 6/yr. £65. (National Computing Centre Ltd.) Techgnosis Ltd., Blade House, Battersea Rd., Stockport, Cheshire SK4 3AE, England.
TEL 44-161-442-2639. FAX 44-161-443-1162. Ed. T. Drinkall. **Document type:** abstracting/indexing.
Formerly: Software Systems and Techniques (ISSN 0265-1696)

001.6 621.381 UK ISSN 0957-4611
TELECOMMS ABSTRACTS. 1971. 6/yr. £65. (National Computing Centre Ltd.) Techgnosis Ltd., Blade House, Battersea Rd., Stockport, Cheshire SK4 3AE, England. TEL 44-161-442-2639.
FAX 44-161-443-1162. bk.rev.; illus.; stat; circ. controlled. (back issues avail.) **Indexed:** Anbar, Data Process.Dig. **Document type:** abstracting/indexing.
—CISTI.
Former titles: Telecomms Profile (ISSN 0265-170X); N C C-Interface (National Computing Centre) (ISSN 0027-6243); N C C Newsletter.

003 UK ISSN 0269-8862
TURING INSTITUTE ABSTRACTS IN ARTIFICIAL INTELLIGENCE. 1986. bi-m. £195. (Turing Institute) Springer-Verlag London Ltd., Sweetapple House, Catteshall Rd., Godalming, Surrey GU7 3DJ, England. TEL 44-1483-418800.
FAX 44-1483-415144. (U.S. subscr. to: Springer-Verlag New York, Inc., Box 2485, Secaucus, NJ 07096-2491. TEL 201-348-4033; Also Berlin, Heidelberg, Paris, Tokyo and Vienna) Ed. Jon Ritchie. **Document type:** abstracting/indexing.
●Also available online. Vendor(s): Data-Star.
—CCC.
Description: Abstracts material on artificial intelligence from journals, conference papers, research reports and monographs.

070.5 011 001.6 UK ISSN 0960-653X
Z286.E43 CODEN: WPMOED
WORLD PUBLISHING MONITOR. 1983. m. £570($913) includes Publishing and New Media Technology Newsletter (effective 1997). (International Electronic Publishing Research Centre) Pira International, Randalls Rd., Leatherhead, Surrey KT22 7RU, England. TEL 44-1372-802050.
FAX 44-1372-802239. E-mail: infocentre@pira.co.uk; URL: http://www.pira.co.uk/. Ed. Emma Foord; Pub. Marie Rushton. adv. (also avail. in microfilm from MIM,UMI) **Document type:** abstracting/indexing.
●Also available online. Vendor(s): Data-Star, FIZ Technik, Knight-Ridder Information, Inc., Questel Orbit Inc., STN International.
Also available on CD-ROM. Producer(s): Knight-Ridder, Inc.
—CASDDS; CISTI; UMI. **CCC.**
Formerly (until vol.9, 1991): Electronic Publishing Abstracts (ISSN 0739-2907)
Description: Provides summaries of the technical, scientific and business literature relating to international publishing.

COMPUTERS — Artificial Intelligence

see also Computers–Cybernetics

001.535 UK ISSN 0951-5666
CODEN: AISCEM
A I & SOCIETY. (Artificial Intelligence); the journal of human-centered systems and machine intelligence. 1987. q. £172 (effective 1998). Springer-Verlag London Ltd., Sweetapple House, Catteshall Rd., Godalming, Surrey GU7 3DJ, England.
TEL 44-1483-418800. FAX 44-1483-415144. Ed. Karamjit S. Gill. bk.rev. circ. 265. (also avail. in microform from UMI; back issues avail.; reprint service avail. from SWZ) **Indexed:**
Abstr.Hum.Comp.Inter., Comput.Abstr., INSPEC (1989-). **Document type:** academic/scholarly publication.
—BLDSC (0772.323500); AskIEEE; CISTI; Ei; KR SourceOne; SWETS; UMI; UnCover. **CCC.**
Description: Covers the issues, policy and management of artificial intelligence. Discusses social, economic, philosophical and political implications.

001.535 629.8 US ISSN 0738-4602
Q334
A I MAGAZINE. (Artificial Intelligence) 1979. q. $50. American Association for Artificial Intelligence, 445 Burgess Dr., Menlo Park, CA 94025.
TEL 415-328-3123. FAX 415-321-4457. E-mail: aimagazine@aaai.org; URL: http://www.aaai.org. Ed. Jude Shavlik; Pub. Carol Hamilton. R&P contact: Daphne Daily. adv.: B&W pag $1500, color page $2300; trim 8 3/8 x 10 7/8; adv. contact: David Hamilton. bk.rev.; bibl.; illus.; index. circ. 6,000. (also avail. in microform; back issues avail.) **Indexed:** A.I.Abstr. (until 1992), A.S.& T.Ind., Abstr.Hum.Comp.Inter., ASCA, Bus.Comput.Ind., Comput.Abstr., Comput.Lit.Ind., Curr.Cont., Eng.Ind., Ind.Sci.Rev., INSPEC (1985-), Oper.Res.Manage.Sci., Qual.Contr.Appl.Stat., Robomat. (until 1992), Sci.Cit.Ind. **Document type:** academic/scholarly publication.
●Also available online.
—BLDSC (0772.343000); AskIEEE; CISTI; Ei; Genuine Article; KR SourceOne; Linda Hall; SWETS; UMI; UnCover. **CCC.**
Description: Contains articles on all aspects of AI, focusing on state-of-the-art developments. Features include reports of research in progress, announcements of meetings and seminars, and information on job openings.

006.3 UK
A I PERSPECTIVES. (Artificial Intelligence) irreg., latest Mar. 1995. price varies. A I Intelligence, P.O. Box 95, Oxford OX2 7XL, England.
TEL 44-1865-791600. FAX 44-1865-791007. E-mail: aip@aiintelligence.com. Ed. Alex Goodall; Pub. Alex Goodall. R&P contact: Alex Goodall.
Document type: monographic series.
Description: Presents in-depth reports on important emerging issues in commercial artificial intelligence.

621.3 001.535 US ISSN 0893-6552
A I TODAY;* the magazine of applied artificial intelligence and expert systems. 1986. bi-m. $95 (foreign $135). Yellowstone Information Services, R.R. 2, Box 42A, Bloomingdale, OH 43910-9802.
TEL 304-965-5548. FAX 304-965-7785. Ed. Roge C. Thibault. adv.; bk.rev. circ. 5,000. (also avail. in magnetic tape; back issues avail.) **Indexed:** Comput.Lit.Ind.
Description: Covers natural language computer systems, applied expert systems, intelligent databases, robotics and artificial intelligence languages.

006.3 UK ISSN 1354-2001
A I WATCH. (Artificial Intelligence) 1992. m. £395 (academic institutions £270) (effective 1996). A I Intelligence, P.O. Box 95, Oxford OX2 7XL, England TEL 44-1865-791600. FAX 44-1865-791007.
E-mail: aip@aiintelligence.com. Ed. Alex Goodall; Pub. Alex Goodall. R&P contact: Alex Goodall. circ. 200 (paid). (back issues avail.) **Document type:** newsletter.
Incorporates (1984-1993): Machine Intelligence News (ISSN 0267-0429)
Description: Reports on commercial development in artificial intelligence, with emphasis on Europe.

001.535 US
ABLEX SERIES IN ARTIFICIAL INTELLIGENCE. 1985. irreg., latest 1996. price varies. Ablex Publishing Corporation, Box 5297, Greenwich, CT 06831-0504. TEL 203-661-7602.
FAX 203-661-0792. Ed. Yorick Wilks. **Indexed:** INSPEC. **Document type:** academic/scholarly publication.
Formerly: Advances in Artificial Intelligence.

COMPUTERS — Artificial Intelligence

591.51 006.3   US   ISSN 1059-7123
QL750   CODEN: ADBEEA
ADAPTIVE BEHAVIOR. 1992. q. $50 to individuals (foreign $66); institutions $148 (foreign $164); students and retired $35 (foreign $51) (effective 1997). M I T Press, 5 Cambridge Center, Cambridge, MA 02142. TEL 617-253-2889. FAX 617-577-1545. E-mail: journals-orders@mit.edu; URL: http://www-mitpress.mit.edu. Ed. Jean-Arcady Meyer. R&P contact: Paul Dzus. (also avail. in microfilm from UMI; back issues avail.) **Indexed:** Compumath, Curr.Cont., Ecol.Abstr., INSPEC (1992-), Psychol.Abstr. (1992-). **Document type:** academic/scholarly publication.
—BLDSC (0678.309000); AskIEEE; CISTI; Genuine Article; KNAW; KR SourceOne; UMI; UnCover. **CCC.**
    Description: International journal providing a forum for experimental and theoretical research on adaptive behavior in animals and autonomous artificial systems, with emphasis on mechanism, organizational principles, and architectures that can be expressed in computational, physical, or mathematical models.
Refereed Serial

001.535   SI
ADVANCED SERIES ON ARTIFICIAL INTELLIGENCE: ARCHITECTURES, LANGUAGES AND ALGORITHMS. (Text in English) irreg., latest vol. 2. World Scientific Publishing Co. Pte. Ltd., Farrer Rd., P.O. Box 128, Singapore 9128, Singapore. TEL 65-3825663. FAX 65-3825919. TELEX RS 28561 WSPC. (UK addr.: 73 Lynton Mead, Totteridge, London N20 8DH, England. TEL 44-181-446-2461; US addr.: 1060 Main St., River Edge, NJ 07661. TEL 800-227-7562) Ed. N.G. Bourbakis. **Document type:** monographic series.

006.3 330   US   ISSN 1078-7186
ADVANCES IN ARTIFICIAL INTELLIGENCE IN ECONOMICS, FINANCE, AND MANAGEMENT. 1994. irreg., vol.2, 1996. $73.25. J A I Press Inc., 55 Old Post Rd., No.2, Box 1678, Greenwich, CT 06830-1678. TEL 203-661-7602. FAX 203-661-0792. E-mail: jai@jaipress.com. (In Europe: JAI Press Ltd., 38 Tavistock St., Covent Garden, London WC2E 7PB, England. TEL 44-171-379-8834. FAX 44-171-379-8835) Eds. John Johnson, Andrew Whinston. **Document type:** monographic series.
—BLDSC (0699.267000).

006   US   ISSN 1057-6282
QA76.758
ADVANCES IN ARTIFICIAL INTELLIGENCE IN SOFTWARE ENGINEERING. 1990. a. $90.25. J A I Press Inc., 55 Old Post Rd., No. 2, Box 1678, Greenwich, CT 06830-1678. TEL 203-661-7602. FAX 203-661-0792. E-mail: jai@jaipress.com. **Document type:** monographic series.
—BLDSC (0699.270000); CISTI.

616.8 610   US   ISSN 1060-2410
QA76.87
ADVANCES IN CONNECTIONIST AND NEURAL COMPUTATION THEORY. 1991. irreg., vol.3, 1994. price varies. Ablex Publishing Corporation, Box 5297, Greenwich, CT 06831-0504. TEL 302-661-7602. FAX 203-661-0792. Ed. John Barnden. **Document type:** academic/scholarly publication.

001.535 616.8
ADVANCES IN CONTROL NETWORKS AND LARGE SCALE PARALLEL DISTRIBUTED PROCESSING MODELS. 1991. irreg. price varies. Ablex Publishing Corporation, Box 5297, Greenwich, CT 06831-0504. TEL 203-661-7602. FAX 203-661-0792. Ed. Martin Fraser. **Document type:** academic/scholarly publication, monographic series.

006.3 005.74   US
ADVANCES IN DATABASES AND ARTIFICIAL INTELLIGENCE. 1995. irreg. $90.25. J A I Press Inc., 55 Old Post Rd., No. 2, Box 1678, Greenwich, CT 06836-1678. TEL 203-661-7602. FAX 203-661-0792. Ed. Frederick Petry. **Document type:** academic/scholarly publication.

004.2 658   US   ISSN 1074-7532
QA76.76.E95
ADVANCES IN EXPERT SYSTEMS FOR MANAGEMENT. 1993. irreg., vol.2, 1996. $73.25. J A I Press Inc., 55 Old Post Rd., No. 2, Box 1678, Greenwich, CT 06830-1678. TEL 203-661-7602. FAX 203-943-9317. E-mail: jai@jaipress.com. (Addr. in Europe: J A I Press Ltd., 38 Tavistock St., Covent Garden, London WC2E 7PB, England. TEL 44-171-379-8834. FAX 44-171-379-8835) Ed. William A. Wallace. **Document type:** monographic series.

006.3   US
ADVANCES IN HUMAN AND MACHINE COGNITION. 1991. irreg. $90.25. J A I Press Inc., 55 Old Post Rd., No. 2, Box 1678, Greenwich, CT 06836-1678. TEL 203-661-7602. FAX 203-661-0792. Eds. Kenneth M. Ford, Patrick Hayes. **Document type:** academic/scholarly publication.

001.535 629.8   US
ADVANCES IN LOGIC PROGRAMMING AND AUTOMATED REASONING. 1992. a. price varies. Ablex Publishing Corporation, Box 5297, Greenwich, CT 06831-0504. TEL 203-661-7602. FAX 203-661-0792. Ed. Ralph Wilkerson. **Document type:** academic/scholarly publication.

001.535   US
ADVANCES IN SPATIAL REASONING. 1991. irreg. price varies. Ablex Publishing Corporation, Box 5297, Greenwich, CT 06831-0504. TEL 203-661-7602. FAX 203-661-0792. Ed. Su-Ching Chen. **Document type:** academic/scholarly publication.
Refereed Serial

006.3   IT
▼**ALMA;** scores of the unfinished thought. 1996. irreg. Via Tevere 68, 87036 Roges Rende (CS), Italy. E-mail: luigi@diemme.it;alma__mag@geocities.com; URL: http://www.diemme.it/~luigi/alma.html. Ed. Luigi Caputo.
●Available only online.
    Description: Covers artificial intelligence, neural networks and more.

001.535   NE   ISSN 1012-2443
                     CODEN: AMAIEC
ANNALS OF MATHEMATICS AND ARTIFICIAL INTELLIGENCE. (Text in English) 1990. 12/yr. (in 3 vols., 4 nos./vol.). 990 SFr. (effective 1998). Baltzer Science Publishers B.V., P.O. Box 221, 1400 AE Bussum, Netherlands. TEL 31-20-6370061. FAX 31-20-6323651. E-mail: subscribe@baltzer.nl; URL: http://www.baltzer.nl. (Subscr. in N. America to: Baltzer Science Publishers, Box 8577, Red Bank, NJ 07701-8577) Ed. M.C. Golumbic. (back issues avail.) **Indexed:** ASCA, Compumath, Curr.Cont., INSPEC (1991-), Zent.Math. **Document type:** academic/scholarly publication.
—BLDSC (1043.005000); AskIEEE; Ei; Genuine Article; KR SourceOne; SWETS; UnCover. **CCC.**
    Description: Presents research level coverage of artificial intelligence and mathematics.

001.535   US
ANNUAL CONFERENCE ON A I, SIMULATION AND PLANNING IN HIGH AUTONOMY SYSTEMS. 1990. a. price varies. (Institute of Electrical and Electronics Engineers, Inc.) I E E E Computer Society Press, 10662 Los Vaqueros Circle, Los Alamitos, CA 90720. TEL 714-821-8380. FAX 714-821-4641. Ed. Cat Harris; Pub. Matt Loeb. adv. contact: Frieda Koester. **Document type:** proceedings.
    Description: Examines integrated methods of simulation and planning that help automate basic decision-making processes in computer systems.

001.535   US   ISSN 0883-9514
Q334   CODEN: AAINEH
APPLIED ARTIFICIAL INTELLIGENCE. Online edition (US ISSN 1087-6545) 1987. 8/yr. £297($490) to institutions (£356($588) with online ed.) (effective 1998). Taylor & Francis Inc., 1900 Frost Rd., Ste. 101, Bristol, PA 19007-1598. TEL 215-785-5800; 800-821-8312. FAX 215-785-5515. E-mail: info@tandf.co.uk; URL: http://www.tandf.co.uk/. (Subscr. in Europe to: Taylor & Francis Ltd., Rankine Rd., Basingstoke, Hants. RG24 8PR, England. TEL 44-1256-840366. FAX 44-1256-479438) Ed. Robert Trappl. (also avail. in microform from UMI; back issues avail., reprint service avail. from UMI) **Indexed:** A.I.Abstr., Abstr.Hum.Comp.Inter., ASCA, CAD CAM Abstr., Compumath, Comput.Abstr., Curr.Cont., INSPEC (1987-), Robomat., SSCI. **Document type:** academic/scholarly publication.
●Also available online.
—BLDSC (1571.650000); AskIEEE; CISTI; Ei; Genuine Article; KR SourceOne; Linda Hall; SWETS; UnCover. **CCC.**
    Description: Evaluates current AI systems and tools; explores theoretical research relevant to potential applications; and covers the economic, social, and cultural impacts of AI.
Refereed Serial

006.3   US   ISSN 0924-669X
Q334   CODEN: APITE4
APPLIED INTELLIGENCE; the international journal of artificial intelligence, neural networks, and complex problem-solving technologies. 1991. bi-m. fl.820 to institutions; $421 to institutions in U.S. (effective 1998). Kluwer Academic Publishers Boston, Box 358, Accord Sta., Hingham, MA 02018-0358. TEL 617-871-6600. FAX 617-871-6528. TELEX 200190. E-mail: services@wkap.nl; URL: http://www.wkap.nl. (Dist. outside N. America by: Kluwer Academic Publishers Group, P.O. Box 322, 3300 AH Dordrecht, Netherlands. TEL 31-78-6392392. FAX 31-78-6546474) Ed. Moonis Ali. (also avail. in microform from UMI; back issues avail.; reprint service avail. from SWZ) **Indexed:** ASCA, Compumath, Compumath, Curr.Cont., Eng.Ind., INSPEC (1991-), Sci.Cit.Ind., Zent.Math. **Document type:** academic/scholarly publication.
—BLDSC (1573.210000); AskIEEE; CISTI; Ei; Genuine Article; KR SourceOne; SWETS; UMI; UnCover. **CCC.**
    Description: Provides a medium for exchanging scientific research and technological achievements accomplished by the international community. Focus is on research in artificial intelligence and neural networks.
Refereed Serial

COMPUTERS — ARTIFICIAL INTELLIGENCE

006.3　　　　　NE　ISSN 0004-3702
Q335　　　　　　　　CODEN: AINTBB
ARTIFICIAL INTELLIGENCE; an international journal. (Text in English) 1970. 18/yr. fl.3713($2134) (effective 1998). North-Holland (Subsidiary of: Elsevier Science B.V.), P.O. Box 211, 1000 AE Amsterdam, Netherlands. TEL 31-20-4853911. FAX 31-20-4853598. TELEX 18582 ESPA NL. URL: http://www.elsevier.nl:80/inca/publications/store/5/0/5/6/0/1/505601.pub.shtml. (Subscr. in the Americas to: Elsevier Science, Regional Sales Office, Box 945, New York, NY 10159-0945. TEL 212-633-3730. FAX 212-633-3680; Subscr. in Australasia and the Far East to: Elsevier Science (Singapore) Pte Ltd, No.1 Temasek Ave., No.17-01 Millenia Tower, Singapore 0391192, Singapore. TEL 65-434-3727. FAX 65-337-2230; Subscr. in Japan to: Elsevier Science Japan, 9-15 Higashi-Azabu 1-chome, Minato-ku, Tokyo 106, Japan. TEL 81-3-5561-5033. FAX 81-3-5561-5047) Ed. Daniel G. Bobrow. adv.: bk.rev. circ. 1,100. (also avail. in microform from UMI; back issues avail.; reprint service avail. from SWZ) **Indexed:** A.I.Abstr. (until 1992), A.S.& T.Ind., Abstr.Hum.Comp.Inter., ASCA, Bibl.Ling., Compumath., Comput.Abstr., Comput.Cont., Comput.Rev., Curr.Cont., Cyb.Abstr., Eng.Ind., Ergon.Abstr., Ind.Sci.Rev., INSPEC (1971-), Lang.& Lang.Behav.Abstr., Math.R., Psychol.Abstr. (1992-), Ref.Zh., Robomat. (until 1992), Sci.Cit.Ind., Sociol.Abstr., SSCI, Zent.Math. **Document type:** academic/scholarly publication.
—BLDSC (1735.035000); AskIEEE; CISTI; Ei; Genuine Article; KR SourceOne; SWETS; UnCover. **CCC.**
Formerly: Artificial Intelligence Journal.
Description: Presents technical papers for computer and research scientists and educators in AI. Includes robotics, software engineering, philosophy and logic, natural languages, cognitive psychology and vision.
Refereed Serial

006.3　　　　　US　ISSN 0272-1686
ARTIFICIAL INTELLIGENCE. irreg. Lawrence Erlbaum Associates, Inc., 10 Industrial Ave., Mahwah, NJ 07430-2262. TEL 201-236-9500; 800-926-6579. FAX 201-236-0072. E-mail: jamsel@erlbaum.com; URL: http://www.erlbaum.com. Ed. Roger Schank. **Document type:** monographic series.
—**CCC.**

ARTIFICIAL INTELLIGENCE AND LAW; an international journal. see *LAW*

006　　　　　　NE　ISSN 0921-7126
Q334　　　　　　　　CODEN: ACMMEE
ARTIFICIAL INTELLIGENCE COMMUNICATIONS. Short title: A I Communications. (Text in English) 1988. q. fl.340($194) (effective 1997). (European Coordinating Committee for Artificial Intelligence) I O S Press, Van Diemenstraat 94, 1013 CN Amsterdam, Netherlands. TEL 31-20-6382189. FAX 31-20-6203419. E-mail: market@iospress.nl; URL: http://www.iospress.nl.iospress. (In N. America: Box 10558, Burke, VA 22009-0558. TEL 703-323-5554. FAX 703-250-4705) Ed. R. Lopez de Mantaras. bk.rev.; abstr.; bibl.; charts; stat. circ. 10,000. **Indexed:** ASCA, Curr.Cont., INSPEC (1988-). **Document type:** academic/scholarly publication.
—BLDSC (0772.328000); AskIEEE; CISTI; Ei; Genuine Article; KR SourceOne; SWETS. **CCC.**
Description: Enhances contacts and information exchanges between artificial intelligence researchers and developers in Europe. Contains high level background material and topics of interest to those concerned with artificial intelligence and advanced information processing, at technical levels as well as those of opinions, policies, and news.
Refereed Serial

006　　　　　　UK　ISSN 0890-0604
TA174　　　　　　　CODEN: AIEMEG
ARTIFICIAL INTELLIGENCE FOR ENGINEERING DESIGN, ANALYSIS AND MANUFACTURING. Abbreviated title: A I E D A M. 5/yr. £145($249) (effective 1998). Cambridge University Press, The Edinburgh Bldg., Shaftesbury Rd., Cambridge CB2 2RU, England. TEL 44-1223-312393. FAX 44-1223-315052. TELEX 817256. E-mail: information@cup.cam.ac.uk; URL: http://www.cup.org/journals/CUPJNLS.html. (N. American addr.: Cambridge University Press, Journals Division, 40 W. 20th St., New York, NY 10011. TEL 212-924-3900. FAX 212-691-3239) Ed. Clive Dym. R&P contact: Linda Nicol. adv. contact: Rebecca Symons. bk.rev. (back issues avail.; reprint service avail. from UWZ) **Indexed:** ASCA, Compumath, Comput.Abstr., INSPEC (1989-), SSCI. **Document type:** academic/scholarly publication.
—BLDSC (1735.036200); AskIEEE; CISTI; Ei; Genuine Article; KR SourceOne; SWETS; UnCover. **CCC.**
Description: Covers the use of artificial intelligence in planning, design, finite-element analysis, simulation spatial reasoning and graphics, process planning, optimization and manufacturing.

006.3　　　　　NE
ARTIFICIAL INTELLIGENCE IN DESIGN (YEAR). a. Kluwer Academic Publishers, Postbus 17, 3300 AA Dordrecht, Netherlands. TEL 31-78-6392392. FAX 31-78-6392254. (Dist by: Kluwer Academic Publishers Group, P.O. Box 322, 3300 AA Dordrecht, Netherlands. TEL 31-78-6392392. FAX 31-78-6546474; N. America dist. addr.: Box 358, Accord Sta., Hingham, MA 02018-0358. TEL 617-871-6600. FAX 617-871-6528)
—BLDSC (1735.036050).

006.3　620　　　UK　ISSN 0954-1810
TA345　　　　　　　CODEN: AIENEJ
ARTIFICIAL INTELLIGENCE IN ENGINEERING. 1986. q. fl.880($506) to institutions; with Engineering Applications of Artificial Intelligence fl.1978 ($1137) (effective 1998). Elsevier Science Ltd., P.O. Box 800, Kidlington, Oxford OX5 1DX, England. TEL 44-1865-843000. FAX 44-1865-843010. E-mail: nlinfo-f@elsevier.nl; usinfo-f@elsevier.com; forinfo-kyf04035@niftyserve.or.jp; URL: http://www.elsevier.nl/. (Subscr. to: Elsevier Science, Regional Sales Office, P.O. Box 211, 1000 AE Amsterdam, Netherlands. TEL 31-20-4853757. FAX 31-20-4853432; Subscr. in the Americas to: Elsevier Science, Regional Sales Office, Box 945, New York, NY 10159-0945. TEL 212-633-3730. FAX 212-633-3680; Subscr. in Australasia and the Far East to: Elsevier Science (Singapore) Pte Ltd, No.1 Temasek Ave., No.17-01 Millenia Tower, Singapore 039192, Singapore. TEL 65-434-3727. FAX 65-337-2230) Eds. K.J. MacCallum, D. Sriram. adv. (also avail. in microform from UMI; back issues avail.) **Indexed:** A.I.Abstr., ASCA, CAD CAM Abstr., Compumath, Comput.Abstr., Comput.& Info.Sys., Curr.Cont., INSPEC (1989-). **Document type:** academic/scholarly publication.
—BLDSC (1735.036080); AskIEEE; CISTI; Ei; Genuine Article; KR SourceOne; Linda Hall; SWETS; UnCover. **CCC.**
Formerly (until 1991): International Journal for Artificial Intelligence in Engineering (ISSN 0267-9264)
Description: For engineers from all disciplines who are involved in research, development and implementation of computer systems for artificial intelligence.
Refereed Serial

ARTIFICIAL INTELLIGENCE IN MEDICINE. see *MEDICAL SCIENCES — Computer Applications*

006.3　　　　　NE　ISSN 0269-2821
Q334　　　　　　　　CODEN: AIRVE6
ARTIFICIAL INTELLIGENCE REVIEW; an international survey and tutorial journal. (Text in English) 1986. bi-m. fl.630 to institutions; $323.50 to institutions in U.S. (effective 1998). Kluwer Academic Publishers, Postbus 17, 3300 AA Dordrecht, Netherlands. TEL 31-78-6392392. FAX 31-78-6392254. TELEX 29245 KAPG NL. E-mail: services@wkap.nl; URL: http://www.wkap.nl. (Dist. by: Kluwer Academic Publishers Group, P.O. Box 322, 3300 AH Dordrecht, Netherlands. TEL 31-78-6392392. FAX 31-78-6546474; N. America dist. addr.: Box 358, Accord Sta., Hingham, MA 02018-0358. TEL 617-871-6600. FAX 617-871-6528) Eds. Masoud Yazdani, Tony Dodd. (also avail. in microform from UMI; reprint service avail. from SWZ) **Indexed:** A.I.Abstr., Abstr.Hum.Comp.Inter., Art.Int.Abstr., ASCA, Bull.Signal., Compumath, Comput.Abstr., Cont.Pg.Educ., Curr.Cont., Educ.Tech.Abstr., Eng.Ind., INSPEC (1987-1991), LISA, Psychol.Abstr., SSCI, Tech.Educ.Abstr., Zent.Math. **Document type:** academic/scholarly publication.
—BLDSC (1735.037300); AskIEEE; CISTI; Ei; Genuine Article; KR SourceOne; Linda Hall; SWETS; UMI; UnCover. **CCC.**
Description: Publishes commentary on issues and developments in artificial intelligence foundations and current research.
Refereed Serial

006.3　　　　　JA　ISSN 1433-5298
▼**ARTIFICIAL LIFE AND ROBOTICS.** (Text in English) 1997. q. DM.340 (effective 1998). Springer-Verlag Tokyo, 3-13, Hongo 3-chome, Bunkyo-ku, Tokyo 113, Japan. TEL 81-3-38120331. FAX 81-3-38120719. E-mail: svt-ebs@ppp.bekkoame.or.jp. (Subscr. to: Springer-Verlag, Heidelberger Platz 3, 14197 Berlin, Germany. TEL 49-30-82787-0. FAX 49-30-82787448) Ed. M. Sugisaka. **Document type:** academic/scholarly publication.
●Also available online.
Description: Publishes original technical papers and reviews on the development of new technologies concerning artificial life and robotics.

006.3　　　　　SI
AUSTRALIAN JOINT CONFERENCE ON ARTIFICIAL INTELLIGENCE. PROCEEDINGS. (Text in English) irreg. no.7, 1994. World Scientific Publishing Co. Pte. Ltd., Farrer Rd., P.O. Box 128, Singapore 912, Singapore. TEL 65-3825663. FAX 65-3825919. TELEX RS-28561-WSPC. (US addr.: 1060 Main St Ste. 1B, River Edge, NJ 07661. TEL 800-227-7562; UK addr.: 73 Lynton Mead, Totteridge, London N20 8DH, England. TEL 44-181-446-2461) **Document type:** proceedings.

006.3　　　　　NE　ISSN 0927-1023
AUTOMATED REASONING SERIES. (Text in English) 1991. irreg. price varies. Kluwer Academic Publishers, Postbus 17, 3300 AA Dordrecht, Netherlands. TEL 31-78-6392392. FAX 31-78-6392254. TELEX 29245 KAPG NL. E-mail: services@wkap.nl; URL: http://www.wkap.n (Dist. by: Kluwer Academic Publishers Group, P.O. Box 322, 3300 AH Dordrecht, Netherlands. TEL 31-78-6392392. FAX 31-78-6546474; N. America dist. addr.: Box 358, Accord Sta., Hingham, MA 02018-0358. TEL 617-871-6600. FAX 617-871-6528) Ed. William Pase. **Indexed:** Zent.Math. **Document type:** monographic series.
—BLDSC (1828.379600).
Refereed Serial

COMPUTERS — ARTIFICIAL INTELLIGENCE

006.3   NE   ISSN 0928-8910
QA76.758   CODEN: ASOEEA
AUTOMATED SOFTWARE ENGINEERING; the international journal of automated reasoning and artificial intelligence in software engineering. (Text in English) 1994. q. fl.690 to institutions; $354 to institutions in U.S. (effective 1998). Kluwer Academic Publishers, Postbus 17, 3300 AA Dordrecht, Netherlands. TEL 31-78-6392392. FAX 31-78-6392254. TELEX 29245 KAPG NL. E-mail: services@wkap.nl; URL: http://www.wkap.nl. (Dist. by: Kluwer Academic Publishers Group, P.O. Box 322, 3300 AH Dordrecht, Netherlands. TEL 31-78-6392392. FAX 31-78-6546474; N. America dist. addr.: Box 358, Accord Sta., Hingham, MA 02018-0358. TEL 617-871-6600. FAX 617-871-6528) Eds. W. Lewis Johnson, Anthony Finkelstein. (reprint service avail. from SWZ) **Document type:** academic/scholarly publication.
—BLDSC (1828.382000); AskIEEE; CISTI; Ei; KR SourceOne; SWETS. **CCC.**
   Description: Publishes reports of significant industrial experience in the application of automated reasoning, knowledge representation and artificial intelligence in software engineering.
Refereed Serial

AUTOMATIC DOCUMENTATION AND MATHEMATICAL LINGUISTICS. see LINGUISTICS — Computer Applications

AUTOMATIZACION. see COMPUTERS — Automation

AUTOMAZIONE OGGI; mensile di automazione, robotica, controllo di processo, controllo numerico. see COMPUTERS — Automation

621.38 440   BE   ISSN 0773-4182
C A I; the journal for the integrated study of artificial intelligence, cognitive science and applied epistemology. 1984. q. 1150 BEF to individuals; institutions 3050 BEF (effective 1996). (Rijksuniversiteit Gent) Communication and Cognition, Blandijnberg 2, 9000 Ghent, Belgium. TEL 32-9-2643952. FAX 32-9-2644197. Eds. Fernand Vandamme, Gertrudis Van de Vijver. adv.; bk.rev.; bibl. circ. 500. (also avail. in microform from ISI) **Indexed:** Lang.& Lang.Behav.Abstr., Math.R., Phil.Ind., Psychol.Abstr., Sage Fam.Stud.Abstr., Sociol.Abstr., SSCI. **Document type:** academic/scholarly publication.
—AskIEEE; CISTI; KR SourceOne.
   Description: Publishes articles relating to the evolving principles and techniques of artificial intelligence as enriched by research in such fields as mathematics, linguistics, logic, epistemology, the cognitive sciences and biology.

006.3   CN   ISSN 0823-9339
                                  CODEN: CARIEZ
CANADIAN ARTIFICIAL INTELLIGENCE. 1984. q. Can.$10 per no. Canadian Information Processing Society, 430 King St., W. Ste. 106, Toronto, ON M5V 1L5, Canada. TEL 416-593-4040. FAX 416-593-5184. R&P contact: Stan Matwins. **Indexed:** INSPEC (1989-). **Document type:** academic/scholarly publication.
—BLDSC (3017.270000); AskIEEE; CISTI; KR SourceOne.

001.535 629.892   US
CANADIAN INSTITUTE FOR ADVANCED RESEARCH IN ARTIFICIAL INTELLIGENCE AND ROBOTICS. 1988. irreg., latest 1990. price varies. Ablex Publishing Corporation, Box 5297, Greenwich, CT 06831-0504. TEL 203-661-7602. FAX 203-661-0792. Ed. Zenon W. Pylyshyn. **Document type:** academic/scholarly publication.

001.535   US   ISSN 0710-0825
Q334
CANADIAN SOCIETY FOR COMPUTATIONAL STUDIES OF INTELLIGENCE. PROCEEDINGS OF THE BIENNIAL CONFERENCE. 1986. biennial. price varies. Morgan Kaufmann Publishers, Inc., 340 Pine St., 6th Fl., San Francisco, CA 94104-3205. TEL 415-392-2665. FAX 415-982-2665. E-mail: orders@mkp.com; URL: http://www.mkp.com. Ed. Michael Morgan. R&P contact: Marilyn Alan. adv. contact: Lisa Schneider. **Document type:** proceedings.
—BLDSC (6842.530000).
Refereed Serial

006.3   NE
COMPUTATIONAL INTELLIGENCE. Represents: Proceedings of the International Symposium "Computational Intelligence". (Text in English) 1990. a., vol.3, 1991. Elsevier Science B.V., P.O. Box 211, 1000 AE Amsterdam, Netherlands. TEL 31-20-4853911. FAX 31-20-4853598. E-mail: nlinfo-f@elsevier.nl; usinfo-f@elsevier.com; forinfo-kyf04035@niftyserve.or.jp; URL: http://www.elsevier.nl/. (Subscr. in the Americas to: Elsevier Science, Regional Sales Office, Box 945, New York, NY 10159-0945. TEL 212-633-3730. FAX 212-633-3680; Subscr. in Australasia and the Far East to: Elsevier Science (Singapore) Pte Ltd, No.1 Temasek Ave., No.17-01 Millenia Tower, Singapore 039192, Singapore. TEL 65-434-3727. FAX 65-337-2230; Subscr. in Japan to: Elsevier Science Japan, 9-15 Higashi-Azabu 1-chome, Minato-ku, Tokyo 106, Japan. TEL 81-3-5561-5033. FAX 81-3-5561-5047) (back issues avail.) **Indexed:** ASCA, Compumath, Curr.Cont. **Document type:** proceedings.
Refereed Serial

COMPUTER-INTEGRATED MANUFACTURING SYSTEMS. see ENGINEERING — Computer Applications

006   XO   ISSN 0232-0274
COMPUTERS AND ARTIFICIAL INTELLIGENCE/POCITACE A UMELA INTELIGENCIA. (Text and summaries in English) 1982. bi-m. $68 (effective 1998). Slovenska Akademia Vied, Ustav Pocitacovych Systemov - Slovak Academy of Sciences, Institute of Comuter Systems, Dubravska cesta 9, 842 37 Bratislava, Slovakia. TEL 421-7-374703. FAX 421-7-371004. E-mail: upsycai@savba.sk. (Dist. by: Slovart GTG, Krupinska 4, P.O. Box 152, 052 99 Bratislava, Slovakia. TEL 421-7-839473; Dist. also by: Mezhdunarodnaya Kniga, B. Yakimanka 39, 117049 Moscow, Russia. TEL 7-095-2384967. FAX 7-095-2384634) Ed. Ivan Plander. R&P contact: Ivan Plander. bk.rev.; circ. 400 (paid). **Indexed:** Abstr.Hum.Comp.Inter., ASCA, Compumath, Comput.Abstr., INSPEC, Zent.Math. **Document type:** academic/scholarly publication.
—BLDSC (3394.647100); AskIEEE; Genuine Article; KR SourceOne.
   Description: Publishes new scientific papers related to the scope of computer science, artificial intelligence, and robotics. Topics covered include hardware, computer architecture, software, theory of computation, artificial intelligence, perception and pattern recognition, robotic systems and applications.
Refereed Serial

001.535 620 330   US   ISSN 1043-0989
Q334
CONFERENCE ON ARTIFICIAL INTELLIGENCE APPLICATIONS. PROCEEDINGS. 1984. a. price varies. (Institute of Electrical and Electronics Engineers, Inc.) I E E E Computer Society Press, 10662 Los Vaqueros Circle, Los Alamitos, CA 90720-1264. TEL 714-821-8380. FAX 714-821-4641. Ed. Cat Harris; Pub. Matt Loeb. adv. contact: Frieda Koester. **Document type:** proceedings.
—**CCC.**
   Description: Papers focus on the boundary between theory and practice; particularly on AI representations and problem solving techniques, and their demonstrated application to real problems. Addresses areas of engineering-manufacturing, business-decision support, and enabling technology.

006.33 121 511.3   US
Q334
CONFERENCE ON THE THEORETICAL ASPECTS OF REASONING ABOUT KNOWLEDGE. PROCEEDINGS. 1986. biennial. price varies. Morgan Kaufmann Publishers, Inc., 340 Pine St., 6th Fl., San Francisco, CA 94104-3205. TEL 415-392-2665. FAX 415-982-2665. E-mail: orders@mkp.com; URL: http://www.mkp.com. Ed. Michael B. Morgan. R&P contact: Marilyn Uffner Alan. **Document type:** proceedings.

006   UK   ISSN 0954-0091
QA76.87   CODEN: CNTSEU
CONNECTION SCIENCE; journal of neural computing, artificial intelligence, and cognitive research. Online edition (UK ISSN 1360-0494) 1989. q. £84($168) to individuals; institutions £272 ($488) (effective 1997). Carfax Publishing Co., P.O. Box 25, Abingdon, Oxon. OX14 3UE, England. TEL 44-1235-401000. FAX 44-1235-401550. E-mail: enquiries@carfax.co.uk. (Subscr. in N. America to: Carfax Publishing Co., 875-81 Massachusetts Ave., Cambridge, MA 02139) Ed. Noel Sharkey. adv.; bk.rev. (also avail. in microfiche) **Indexed:** Comput.Abstr., INSPEC (1989-), Psychol.Abstr. (1992-). **Document type:** academic/scholarly publication.
●Also available online.
—BLDSC (3417.662450); AskIEEE; CISTI; Ei; KR SourceOne; SWETS; UMI; UnCover. **CCC.**
   Description: Covers connectionist research in human and artificial intelligence, cognitive science, computational neuroscience and advanced computer science.
Refereed Serial

006 005.1   US   ISSN 1383-7133
▼**CONSTRAINTS.** 1996. q. fl.535 to institutions; $274.50 to institutions in U.S. (effective 1998). Kluwer Academic Publishers Boston, Box 358, Accord Sta., Hingham, MA 02018-0358. TEL 617-871-6600. FAX 617-871-6528. E-mail: kluwer@wkap.com; URL: http://www.wkap.nl. (Dist. outside N. America by: Kluwer Academic Publishers Group, P.O. Box 322, 3300 AH Dordrecht, Netherlands. TEL 31-78-6392392. FAX 31-78-6546474) **Document type:** academic/scholarly publication.
—BLDSC (3420.659700); AskIEEE; KR SourceOne.

CONTROL, CIBERNETICA Y AUTOMATIZACION. see COMPUTERS — Cybernetics

006   NE
DECENTRALIZED A I. Represents: European Workshop on Modelling Autonomous Agents in a Multi-Agent World. Proceedings. (Text in English) 1990. irreg., vol.3, 1992. price varies. Elsevier Science B.V., Books Division, P.O. Box 211, 1000 AE Amsterdam, Netherlands. TEL 31-20-4853911. FAX 31-20-4853705. E-mail: nlinfo-f@elsevier.nl; usinfo-f@elsevier.com; forinfo-kyf04035@niftyserve.or.jp; URL: http://www.elsevier.nl/. (Subscr. in the Americas to: Elsevier Science, Regional Sales Office, Box 945, New York, NY 10159-0945. TEL 212-633-3730. FAX 212-633-3680; Subscr. in Australasia and the Far East to: Elsevier Science (Singapore) Pte Ltd, No.1 Temasek Ave., No.17-01 Millenia Tower, Singapore 039192, Singapore. TEL 65-434-3727. FAX 65-337-2230; Subscr. in Japan to: Elsevier Science Japan, 9-15 Higashi-Azabu 1-chome, Minato-ku, Tokyo 106, Japan. TEL 81-3-5561-5033. FAX 81-3-5561-5047) Ed. Yves Demazeau. (back issues avail.) **Document type:** proceedings.

006.3 620   UK   ISSN 0952-1976
TA345   CODEN: EAAIE6
ENGINEERING APPLICATIONS OF ARTIFICIAL INTELLIGENCE. 1988. bi-m. fl.1318($757) (effective 1998). Elsevier Science Ltd., Pergamon, P.O. Box 800, Kidlington, Oxford OX5 1DX, England. TEL 44-1865-843000. FAX 44-1865-843010. E-mail: nlinfo-f@elsevier.nl; usinfo-f@elsevier.com; forinfo-kyf04035@niftyserve.or.jp; URL: http://www.elsevier.nl/. (Subscr. to: Elsevier Science, Regional Sales Office, P.O. Box 211, 1000 AE Amsterdam, Netherlands. TEL 31-20-4853757. FAX 31-20-4853432; Subscr. in the Americas to: Elsevier Science, Regional Sales Office, Box 945, New York, NY 10159-0945. TEL 212-633-3730. FAX 212-633-3680; Subscr. in Australasia and the Far East to: Elsevier Science (Singapore) Pte Ltd, No.1 Temasek Ave., No.17-01 Millenia Tower, Singapore 039192, Singapore. TEL 65-434-3727. FAX 65-337-2230) Ed. L. Motus. (also avail. in microfilm from UMI; back issues avail.) **Indexed:** A.I.Abstr., Abstr.Hum.Comp.Inter., ASCA, Compumath, Curr.Cont., INSPEC (1988-), SSCI. **Document type:** academic/scholarly publication.
—BLDSC (3755.704500); AskIEEE; CISTI; Ei; Genuine Article; KR SourceOne; SWETS; UMI. **CCC.**
   Description: Describes the practical application of AI methods in all branches of engineering.
Refereed Serial

2100 COMPUTERS — ARTIFICIAL INTELLIGENCE

620 UK ISSN 1363-2078
TK1 CODEN: IJEIEV
ENGINEERING INTELLIGENT SYSTEMS FOR ELECTRICAL ENGINEERING AND COMMUNICATIONS. 1993. q. £120 to institutions (outside E.C. nations £130). C R L Publishing Ltd., 108 Cowley Rd., P.O. Box 31, Market Harborough, Leics. LE16 9RQ, England. TEL 44-1858-525382. FAX 44-1858-525635. Ed. T.S. Dillon; Pub. T.S. Dillon. **Indexed:** ASCA, Curr.Cont. **Document type:** academic/scholarly publication.
—BLDSC (3763.150000); AskIEEE; CISTI; Ei; Genuine Article; KR SourceOne.
Formerly (until 1996): International Journal of Engineering Intelligent Systems for Electrical Engineering and Communications (ISSN 0969-1170)
Description: Addresses computer applications in electrical engineering, communication, and electrical power systems.

006 UK ISSN 0266-4720
QA76.76.E95 CODEN: EXSYEX
EXPERT SYSTEMS; the international journal of knowledge engineering and neural networks. 1984. q. £106($159) (effective 1997). Blackwell Publishers Ltd., 108 Cowley Rd., Oxford OX4 1JF, England. TEL 44-1865-791100. FAX 44-1865-791347. E-mail: jnlorders@blackwellpublishers.co.uk; URL: http://www.blackwellpublishers.co.uk. Ed.Bd. bk.rev. circ. 1,000. **Indexed:** A.I.Abstr. (until 1992), Abstr.Hum.Comp.Inter., Art.Int.Abstr., CAD CAM Abstr. (until 1992), Compumath, Comput.Abstr., Cont.Pg.Manage., Cyb.Abstr., INSPEC (1985-), Robomat. (until 1992). **Document type:** academic/scholarly publication.
—BLDSC (3842.004000); AskIEEE; CISTI; Genuine Article; KR SourceOne; Linda Hall; SWETS; UMI; UnCover. **CCC.**
Formerly: Expert Systems User; Which incorporates: Artificial Intelligence Business.
Description: Review of practical, technical information with papers, interviews, features, news and reviews.

001.535 UK ISSN 0268-2486
EXPERT SYSTEMS APPLICATIONS. 1985. m. £350 (foreign £500). I M L Group plc, Blair House, High St., Tonbridge, Kent TN9 1BQ, England. TEL 44-1732-359990. FAX 44-1732-770049. Ed. Andrew Bond; Pub. Peter Jago. R&P contact: M.T. Croucher. bk.rev.; circ. 90 (paid). **Indexed:** Curr.Cont. **Document type:** newsletter.
—AskIEEE; KR SourceOne.

006.3 NE ISSN 0922-6389
FRONTIERS IN ARTIFICIAL INTELLIGENCE AND APPLICATIONS. (Text in English) 1988. irreg., vol.33, 1996. price varies. I O S Press, Van Diemenstraat 94, 1013 CN Amsterdam, Netherlands. TEL 31-20-6382189. FAX 31-20-6203419. E-mail: market@iospress.nl; URL: http://www.iospress.nl/iospress. (In N. America: Box 10558, Burke, VA 22090-0558. TEL 703-323-5554. FAX 703-250-4705) (back issues avail.) **Indexed:** Zent.Math. **Document type:** monographic series, proceedings.
—Ei.
Description: Publishes studies and papers addressing issues at the forefront of artificial intelligence.

GENIE LOGICIEL ET SYSTEMES EXPERTS. see COMPUTERS — Computer Programming

001.535 616.8 CN
I A S T E D INTERNATIONAL CONFERENCE PROCEEDINGS. irreg. price varies. International Association of Science and Technology for Development, 4500 16th Ave., N.W., Ste. 80, Calgary, AB T3B 0M6, Canada. TEL 403-288-1195. FAX 403-247-6851. **Document type:** proceedings.

001.535 621.381 US
I C C V - INTERNATIONAL CONFERENCE ON COMPUTER VISION. 1982. biennial. price varies. (Institute of Electrical and Electronics Engineers, Inc.) I E E E Computer Society Press, 10662 Los Vaqueros Circle, Los Alamitos, CA 90720-1264. TEL 714-821-8380. FAX 714-821-4641. Ed. Cat Harris; Pub. Matt Loeb. adv. contact: Frieda Koester. **Document type:** proceedings.
Former titles: I E E E Computer Society Workshop on Computer Vision; (until 1985): Workshop on Computer Vision Representation and Control. Proceedings.
Description: Covers all areas of computer vision research including edge detection, neural networks, recognition, psychophysics and optical flow.

001.535 US ISSN 1094-7116
TK7874 CODEN: PCWIFE
I E E E INTERNATIONAL CONFERENCE ON INNOVATIVE SYSTEMS IN SILICON. 1989. a. price varies. Institute of Electrical and Electronics Engineers, Inc., 345 E. 47th St., New York, NY 10017-2394. TEL 732-981-0060; 800-678-4333. FAX 732-981-9667. E-mail: customer.service@ieee.org; URL: http://www.ieee.org. (Subscr. to: 445 Hoes Ln., Box 1331, Piscataway, NJ 08855-1331) (also avail. in microfiche) **Document type:** proceedings.
—Ei; UMI.
Formerly (until 1996): International Conference on Wafer Scale Integration. Proceedings (ISSN 1063-2204)
Description: Reports on the progress made in all aspects, including theory, technology, applications and products.

006.3 US ISSN 1063-6730
Q336
I E E E INTERNATIONAL CONFERENCE ON TOOLS WITH A I. Short title: T A I. 1989. a. price varies. (Institute of Electrical and Electronics Engineers, Inc.) I E E E Computer Society Press, 10662 Los Vaqueros Circle, Los Alamitos, CA 90720. TEL 714-821-8380. FAX 714-821-4641. Ed. Cat Harris; Pub. Matt Loeb. adv. contact: Frieda Koester. **Document type:** proceedings.
—Ei; UMI. **CCC.**
Formerly: I E E E International Conference on Tools for A I.
Description: Addresses both AI theory and application on designing, developing, and testing intelligent tools.

001.535 US ISSN 1063-6706
CODEN: IEFSEV
I E E E TRANSACTIONS ON FUZZY SYSTEMS. 1993. q. $250 to non-members (effective 1998). Institute of Electrical and Electronics Engineers, Inc., 345 E. 47th St., New York, NY 10017-2394. TEL 732-981-0060; 800-678-4333. FAX 732-981-9667. E-mail: customer.service@ieee.org; URL: http://www.ieee.org. (Subscr. to: Box 1331, 445 Hoes Lane, Piscataway, NJ 08855-1331) Ed. James C. Bezdek. adv. **Indexed:** ASCA, Curr.Cont., INSPEC (1993-).
—BLDSC (4363.187800); AskIEEE; CISTI; Ei; Genuine Article; KR SourceOne; Linda Hall; SWETS; UMI; UnCover. **CCC.**
Description: Covers theories and applications of fuzzy systems with emphasis on engineering systems and scientific applications.

001.535 US ISSN 1045-9227
QA76.87 CODEN: ITNNEP
I E E E TRANSACTIONS ON NEURAL NETWORKS. 1990. bi-m. $425 to non-members (effective 1998). Institute of Electrical and Electronics Engineers, Inc., 345 E. 47th St., New York, NY 10017-2394. TEL 732-981-0060; 800-678-4333. FAX 732-981-9667. E-mail: customer.service@ieee.org; URL: http://www.ieee.org. (Subscr. to: 445 Hoes Lane, Box 1331, Piscataway, NJ 08855-1331) Ed. Robert J. Marks. (also avail. in microform) **Indexed:** A.S.& T.Ind., ASCA, Compumath, Comput.Abstr., Curr.Cont., Ind.Sci.Rev., INSPEC (1990-), Neurosci.Cit.Ind., Oper.Res.Manage.Sci., Qual.Contr.Appl.Stat., Sci.Cit.Ind., SSCI.
—BLDSC (4363.207000); AskIEEE; CISTI; Ei; Genuine Article; KR SourceOne; Linda Hall; SWETS; UMI; UnCover. **CCC.**
Description: Covers self-organizing systems, neurobiological connections, network dynamics and architecture, speech recognition, electronic and photonic implementation, robotics and controls.

I E E PROCEEDINGS - CONTROL THEORY AND APPLICATIONS. see ENGINEERING — Electrical Engineering

006.3 US ISSN 1088-467X
INTELLIGENT DATA ANALYSIS. q. fl.694($399) (effective 1998). Elsevier Science Inc., Box 945, New York, NY 10159-0945. TEL 212-633-3730. FAX 212-633-3990. E-mail: editor@ida-il.com; URL: http://www-east.elsevier.com/ida/Menu.html. Ed. A. Famili.
●Available only online.
Description: Examines issues related to the research and applications of artificial intelligence techniques in data analysis across a variety of disciplines.
Refereed Serial

621.381 US ISSN 1052-7214
CODEN: INSSEN
INTELLIGENT SOFTWARE STRATEGIES; the monthly newsletter on Expert Systems, OOP, CASE, Neural Networks & Natural Language. 1985. m. $447 (foreign $507). Cutter Information Corp., 37 Broadway, Arlington, MA 02174. TEL 617-648-8700. FAX 617-648-1950. Ed. Curt Hall; Pub. Karen Fine Coburn. R&P contact: Carolyn Licata. charts, illus, software rev.; stat. (back issues avail.) **Indexed:** A.I.Abstr., Abstr.Hum.Comp.Inter., Robomat. **Document type:** newsletter.
●Also available online.
—BLDSC (4531.832100); CISTI; SWETS. **CCC.**
Formerly (until July 1990): Expert System Strategies (ISSN 0887-221X); Incorporates (in 1990): Spang Robinson Report (ISSN 0885-9957); Which was formed by the merger of (1983-1985): Artificial Intelligence Report (ISSN 0740-7556); (1983-1985): Target (Menlo Park).
Description: Discusses technology and market trends related to advanced "intelligent" software technologies, for example, artificial intelligence.

001.535 US ISSN 1054-8696
Q334
INTELLIGENT SYSTEMS REPORT. Abbreviated title: I S R 1990. m. $299 (foreign $349) (effective 1997). Lionheart Publishing, Inc., 2555 Cumberland Pkwy., Ste. 299, Atlanta, GA 30339. TEL 770-431-0967. FAX 770-432-6969. E-mail: lpi@lionhrtpub.com; URL: http://lionhrtpub.com/ISR/ISR-welcome.html. Ed. David Blanchard; Pub. John Llewellyn. R&P contact: David Blanchard. bk.rev. (back issues avail.) **Indexed:** A.I.Abstr. (until 1992), Abstr.Hum.Comp.Inter., CAD CAM Abstr. (until 1992), Compumath, Comput.Lit.Ind., Robomat. (until 1992). **Document type:** newsletter.
●Also available online.
—BLDSC (4531.832102); CISTI; Linda Hall. **CCC.**
Formed by the merger of (1989-1990): Neural Network News (ISSN 1051-5410); (1987-1990): I Week (ISSN 0897-3466); Which was formerly (1983-1987): Applied Artificial Intelligence Reporte (ISSN 0887-8986)
Description: Covers issues and events in the advanced computing field, such as expert systems, neural networks, fuzzy logic, virtual reality, speech recognition, and intelligent agents.

006.3 US
INTERNATIONAL CONFERENCE ON GENETIC ALGORITHMS. PROCEEDINGS. biennial. $49.95. (University of Illinois at Urbana - Champaign) Morgan Kaufmann Publishers, Inc., 340 Pine St., 6th Fl., San Francisco, CA 94104-3205. TEL 415-392-2665. FAX 415-982-2665. E-mail: orders@mkp.com; URL: http://www.mkp.com. Ed. Staphanie Forrest. (back issues avail.) **Document type:** proceedings.
Description: Presents research in this area of computer algorithms.

001.535 US
INTERNATIONAL JOINT CONFERENCE ON ARTIFICIAL INTELLIGENCE. ADVANCE PAPERS OF THE CONFERENCE. 1969. s-a. price varies. Morgan Kaufmann Publishers, Inc., 340 Pine St., 6th Fl., S Francisco, CA 94104-3205. TEL 415-392-2665. FAX 415-982-2665. E-mail: orders@mkp.com; URL: http://www.mkp.com. Ed. Michael B. Morgan. R&P contact: Marilyn Uffner Alan. adv. contact: Lisa Schneider. **Document type:** trade publication.

COMPUTERS — ARTIFICIAL INTELLIGENCE

001.535   US   ISSN 1045-0823
Q334
INTERNATIONAL JOINT CONFERENCE ON ARTIFICIAL INTELLIGENCE. PROCEEDINGS. 1969. biennial. price varies. Morgan Kaufmann Publishers, Inc., 340 Pine St., 6th Fl., San Francisco, CA 94104. TEL 415-392-2665. FAX 415-982-2665. E-mail: orders@mkp.com; URL: http://www.mkp.com. Ed. Michael B. Morgan. R&P contact: Marilyn Uffner Alan. adv. contact: Lisa Schneider.
—BLDSC (4541.440000); Ei. **CCC.**
Description: Provides a forum for the exchange of current research and groundbreaking results in the field.
Refereed Serial

006.3   US   ISSN 0888-613X
QA76.76.E95   CODEN: IJARE4
INTERNATIONAL JOURNAL OF APPROXIMATE REASONING. 1987. 8/yr. fl.1041($598) (effective 1998). (North American Fuzzy Information Processing Society) Elsevier Science Inc., Box 945, New York, NY 10159-0945. TEL 212-633-3730. FAX 212-633-3680. TELEX 420643 AEP UI. E-mail: usinfo-f@elsevier.com; URL: http://www.elsevier.nl/. (Subscr. outside the Americas to: Elsevier Science, Regional Sales Office, P.O. Box 211, 1000 AE Amsterdam, Netherlands. TEL 31-20-4853757. FAX 31-20-4853432; Subscr. in Australasia and the Far East to: Elsevier Science (Singapore) Pte Ltd, No.1 Temasek Ave., No.17-01 Millenia Tower, Singapore 039192, Singapore. TEL 65-434-3727. FAX 65-337-2230; Subscr. in Japan to: Elsevier Science Japan, 9-15 Higashi-Azabu 1-chome, Minato-ku, Tokyo 106, Japan. TEL 81-3-5561-5033. FAX 81-3-5561-5047) Ed. James C. Bezdek. bk.rev. (also avail. in microform from UMI; back issues avail.) **Indexed:** A.I.Abstr., ASCA, Compumath, Curr.Cont., INSPEC (1987-), Zent.Math. **Document type:** academic/scholarly publication.
—BLDSC (4542.102000); AskIEEE; CISTI; Ei; Genuine Article; KR SourceOne; Linda Hall; SWETS; UnCover. **CCC.**
Description: Represents all theoretical and applied approaches toward approximate reasoning in the design of (artificially) intelligent computer systems.
Refereed Serial

001.535   SI   ISSN 0218-2130
INTERNATIONAL JOURNAL OF ARTIFICIAL INTELLIGENCE TOOLS. Short title: I J A I T. (Text in English) 1992. q. $102 to individuals & institutions of developing countries; institutions of developed countries $254. World Scientific Publishing Co. Pte. Ltd., Farrer Rd., P.O. Box 128, Singapore 9128, Singapore. TEL 65-3825663. FAX 65-3825919. TELEX RS 28561 WSPC. E-mail: wspcsl@singnet.com.sg; sales@wspc2.demon.co.uk; wspc@wspc.com; URL: http://www.singnet.com.sg/~wspclib/. (UK addr.: 57 Shelton St., Covent Garden, London WC2H 9HE, England. TEL 44-171-836-0888. FAX 44-171-836-2020; US addr.: 1060 Main St., Ste. 1B, River Edge, NJ 07661. TEL 800-227-7562. FAX 201-487-9656) Ed. N.G. Bourbakis. **Document type:** academic/scholarly publication.
—BLDSC (4542.104900); AskIEEE; CISTI; KR SourceOne.
Description: Provides information on design, development tests, announcements, and improvement of tools for AI.

006.3   US   ISSN 1084-4589
QA76.76.E95
▼**INTERNATIONAL JOURNAL OF COMPUTATIONAL INTELLIGENCE AND ORGANIZATIONS.** 1996. q. $50 to individuals (foreign $80); institutions $150 (foreign $180) (effective 1997). Lawrence Erlbaum Associates, Inc., 10 Industrial Ave., Mahwah, NJ 07430-2262. TEL 201-236-9500; 800-926-6579. E-mail: jamsel@erlbaum.com; URL: http://www.ecst.csuchico.edu/~ijcio/aims.html. Ed. W. Raghupathi. adv.: page $275; trim 7 x 10. **Document type:** academic/scholarly publication.
●Also available online.
—**CCC.**
Description: Forum for exchanging research information relating to computational intelligence applied in business, government, and educational institutions worldwide.

001.6 621.381   US   ISSN 0894-9077
QA76.76.E95   CODEN: IJSYED
INTERNATIONAL JOURNAL OF EXPERT SYSTEMS; research and applications. q. $125 to individuals (foreign $145); institutions $265 (foreign $285) (effective 1998). J A I Press Inc., 55 Old Post Rd., No. 2, Box 1678, Greenwich, CT 06830-1678. TEL 203-661-7602. FAX 203-661-0792. E-mail: jai@jaipress.com. (Addr. in Europe: J A I Press Ltd., 38 Tavistock St., Covent Garden, London WC2E 7PB, England. TEL 44-171-379-8834. FAX 44-171-379-8835) Eds. Mehdi T. Harandi, Kenneth M. Ford. (also avail. in microform from UMI; back issues avail.) **Indexed:** Abstr.Hum.Comp.Inter., ASCA, Compumath, Comput.Abstr., Curr.Cont., INSPEC (1987-). **Document type:** academic/scholarly publication.
—BLDSC (4542.244850); AskIEEE; CISTI; Ei; Genuine Article; KR SourceOne; SWETS; UnCover. **CCC.**

006.3   SI   ISSN 0218-7965
▼**INTERNATIONAL JOURNAL OF INTELLIGENT CONTROL AND SYSTEMS.** Short title: I J I C S. 1996. 4/yr. $129 to individuals; institutions & libraries $322 (developing countries $193). World Scientific Publishing Co. Pte. Ltd., Farrer Rd., P.O. Box 128, Singapore 9128, Singapore. TEL 65-3825663. FAX 65-3825919. TELEX RS 28561 WSPC. E-mail: wspcsl@singnet.com.sg; sales@wspc2.demon.co.uk; wspc@wspc.com; URL: http://www.singnet.com.sg/~wspclib/. (UK addr.: 57 Shelton St., Covent Garden, London WC2H 9HE, England. TEL 44-171-836-0888. FAX 44-171-836-2020; US addr.: 1060 Main St., Ste. 1B, River Edge, NJ 07661. FAX 201-487-9656) Ed. Fei-Yue Wang. **Document type:** academic/scholarly publication.
—BLDSC (4542.310450).
Description: Publishes articles describing recent fundamental contributions and innovative applications in the field of intelligent control and systems.

006   US   ISSN 0884-8173
Q334   CODEN: IJISED
INTERNATIONAL JOURNAL OF INTELLIGENT SYSTEMS. 1986. m. $1140 (foreign $1350) (effective 1998). John Wiley & Sons, Inc., Journals, 605 Third Ave., New York, NY 10158. TEL 212-570-6645. FAX 212-850-6021. TELEX 12-7063. E-mail: SUBINFO@JWILEY.COM; URL: http://www.wiley.co.uk. (Subscr. outside the Americas to: John Wiley & Sons Ltd., Baffins Ln., Chichester, W. Sussex PO19 1UD, England. TEL 44-1243-779777. FAX 44-1243-776128) Ed. Ronald Yager. adv.: B&W page £640, color page £1515. bk.rev. circ. 525. (also avail. in microform from UMI; back issues avail.) **Indexed:** A.I.Abstr., Abstr.Hum.Comp.Inter., Arts & Hum.Cit.Ind., ASCA, Curr.Cont., INSPEC (1988-), SSCI, Zent.Math. **Document type:** academic/scholarly publication.
—BLDSC (4542.310500); AskIEEE; CISTI; Ei; Genuine Article; KR SourceOne; SWETS; UMI; UnCover. **CCC.**
Description: Promotes the development of the theory necessary for the construction of intelligence systems. Includes developmental, as well as theoretical issues.
Refereed Serial

003 006.3   SI   ISSN 0129-0657
QA76.87   CODEN: IJSZEG
INTERNATIONAL JOURNAL OF NEURAL SYSTEMS. (Text in English) 1989. 6/yr. $126 to individuals; institutions $316 (developing countries $190). World Scientific Publishing Co. Pte. Ltd., Farrer Rd., P.O. Box 128, Singapore 9128, Singapore. TEL 65-3825663. FAX 65-3825919. TELEX RS-28561-WSPC. E-mail: wspcsl@singnet.com.sg; sales@wspc2.demon.co.uk; wspc@wspc.com; URL: http://www.singnet.com.sg/~wspclib/. (US addr.: 1060 Main St., Ste. 1B, River Edge, NJ 07661. TEL 800-227-7562. FAX 201-487-9656; UK addr.: 57 Shelton St., Covent Garden, London WC2H 9HE, England. TEL 44-171-836-0888. FAX 44-171-836-2020) Eds. Benny Lautrup, S. Brunak. circ. 300. (back issues avail.) **Indexed:** ASCA, Ind.Med. (1993-), INSPEC (1989-), Neurosci.Cit.Ind., SSCI. **Document type:** academic/scholarly publication.
—BLDSC (4542.373700); AskIEEE; CISTI; Genuine Article; KR SourceOne; SWETS; UnCover. **CCC.**
Description: Contains original contributions on all aspects of information processing in natural and artificial neural systems.

006.3   SI   ISSN 0218-4885
Q375   CODEN: IJUSF6
INTERNATIONAL JOURNAL OF UNCERTAINTY, FUZZINESS AND KNOWLEDGE-BASED SYSTEMS. Short title: I J U F K S. 1993. q. $90 to individuals; institutions & libraries $180 (developing countries $108). World Scientific Publishing Co. Pte. Ltd., Farrer Rd., P.O. Box 128, Singapore 9128, Singapore. TEL 65-3825663. FAX 66-3825919. E-mail: wspcsl@singnet.com.sg; sales@wspc2.demon.co.uk; wspc@wspc.com; URL: http://www.singnet.com.sg/~wspclib/. (US addr.: 1060 Main St., River Edge, NJ 07661. TEL 800-227-7562. FAX 44-171-836-2020; UK addr.: 57 Shelton St., Covent Garden, London WC2H 9HE, England. TEL 44-171-836-0888. FAX 201-487-9656) Ed. B. Bouchon-Meunier. **Indexed:** ASCA. **Document type:** academic/scholarly publication.
—BLDSC (4542.526500); AskIEEE; Genuine Article; KR SourceOne. **CCC.**
Description: Researches the various methodologies for managing imprecise, vague, uncertain or incomplete information in neural networks and robotic systems.

006   NE   ISSN 1382-3434
▼**INTERNATIONAL SERIES IN INTELLIGENT TECHNOLOGIES.** Cover title: I S I T. (Text in English) 1995. irreg. price varies. Kluwer Academic Publishers, Postbus 17, 3300 AA Dordrecht, Netherlands. TEL 31-78-6392392. FAX 31-78-6392254. E-mail: services@wkap.nl; URL: http://www.wkap.nl. (Dist. by: Kluwer Academic Publishers Group, P.O. Box 322, 3300 AA Dordrecht, Netherlands. TEL 31-78-6392392. FAX 31-78-6546474; N. America dist. addr.: Box 358, Accord Sta., Hingham, MA 02018-0358. TEL 617-871-6600. FAX 617-871-6528) Ed. Hans-Juergen Zimmerman. **Document type:** monographic series.
—BLDSC (4549.237750).
Refereed Serial

006.3   FR   ISSN 1166-3081
JOURNAL OF APPLIED NON-CLASSICAL LOGICS. 1991. 4/yr. 1400 F. (foreign 1550 F.) (effective 1997). Editions Hermes, 14 rue Lantiez, 75017 Paris, France. TEL 33-1-42294466. FAX 33-1-42291556. Ed. Luis Farinas del Cerro. **Indexed:** Zent.Math.
—BLDSC (4943.400000); SWETS.

JOURNAL OF ARTIFICIAL INTELLIGENCE IN EDUCATION; an international journal of research and applications on using intelligent computer technologies in education. see EDUCATION — Computer Applications

006.3 621.399   US   ISSN 1076-9757
JOURNAL OF ARTIFICIAL INTELLIGENCE RESEARCH. Variant title: J A I R. 1993. s-a. $75 (effective 1997). Morgan Kaufmann Publishers, Inc., 340 Pine Street, 6th Fl., San Francisco, CA 94104. TEL 415-392-2665; 800-745-7323. FAX 415-982-2665. E-mail: orders@mkp.com; jair-ed@ptolemy.arc.nasa.gov; URL: http://www.jair.org/masthead.html; http://www.cs.washington.edu/research/jair/home.html. Ed. Steven Minton. **Document type:** academic/scholarly publication.
●Also available online.
—BLDSC (4947.211830); AskIEEE; KR SourceOne.
Description: Includes all areas of artificial intelligence, automated reasoning, cognitive modeling, knowledge representation, learning, natural language, neural networks, perception and robotics.

COMPUTERS — ARTIFICIAL INTELLIGENCE

006.3 NE ISSN 0168-7433
CODEN: JAREEW
JOURNAL OF AUTOMATED REASONING. (Text in English) 1985. bi-m. fl.870 to institutions; $447 to institutions in U.S. (effective 1998). Kluwer Academic Publishers, Postbus 17, 3300 AA Dordrecht, Netherlands. TEL 31-78-6392392. FAX 31-78-6392254. TELEX 29245 KAPG NL. E-mail: services@wkap.nl; URL: http://www.wkap.nl. (Dist. by: Kluwer Academic Publishers Group, P.O. Box 322, 3300 AH Hingham, MA 02018-0358. TEL 617-871-6600. FAX 617-871-6528) Ed. Deepak Kapur. adv.; bk.rev.; index. (also avail. in microform from UMI; reprint service avail. from SWZ) **Indexed:** A.I.Abstr., ASCA, Compumath, Comput.Abstr., Comput.& Info.Sys., Comput.Rev., Curr.Cont., Eng.Ind., IBR, INSPEC (1985-), Math.R., Robomat. (until 1992), Zent.Math. **Document type:** academic/scholarly publication.
—BLDSC (4949.558000); AskIEEE; CISTI; Ei; Genuine Article; KR SourceOne; Linda Hall; SWETS; UMI; UnCover. **CCC.**
Description: Focuses on different theories and applications in the field of automated reasoning, the objectives being the design and implementation of a computer program to assist in solving problems and answering questions that require reasoning.
Refereed Serial

JOURNAL OF COMPUTATIONAL INTELLIGENCE IN FINANCE; advanced technology in finance. see *BUSINESS AND ECONOMICS — Banking And Finance — Computer Applications*

JOURNAL OF COMPUTATIONAL NEUROSCIENCE. see *MEDICAL SCIENCES — Psychiatry And Neurology*

006.3 629.8 UK ISSN 0952-813X
Q334 CODEN: JEAIEL
JOURNAL OF EXPERIMENTAL & THEORETICAL ARTIFICIAL INTELLIGENCE. Short title: J E T A I. Online edition (UK ISSN 1362-3079) q. £218($360) to institutions (£262($432) with online ed.) (effective 1998). Taylor & Francis Ltd., 1 Gunpowder Sq., London EC4A 3DE, England. TEL 44-171-583-0490. FAX 44-171-583-0585. TELEX 858540. E-mail: info@tandf.co.uk; URL: http://turing.paccs.binghamton.edu/jetai/. (Subscr. in N. America to: Taylor & Francis Inc., 1900 Frost Rd., Ste. 101, Bristol, PA 19007-1598. TEL 800-821-8312. FAX 215-785-5515) Ed. Eric Dietrich. **Indexed:** A.I.Abstr., ASCA, INSPEC (1989-), Robomat., SSCI, Zent.Math. **Document type:** academic/scholarly publication.
● Also available online.
—BLDSC (4979.780000); AskIEEE; CISTI; Ei; Genuine Article; KR SourceOne; UnCover. **CCC.**
Description: Focuses on problem, perception, learning, representation, memory, and neural system modeling.
Refereed Serial

JOURNAL OF HEURISTICS. see *PHILOSOPHY*

006.3 629.8 NE ISSN 0921-0296
TJ210.2 CODEN: JIRSES
JOURNAL OF INTELLIGENT AND ROBOTIC SYSTEMS; theory and applications. (Text in English) 1988. m. fl.1440 to institutions; $739.50 to institutions in U.S. (effective 1998). Kluwer Academic Publishers, Postbus 17, 3300 AA Dordrecht, Netherlands. TEL 31-78-6392392. FAX 31-78-6392254. TELEX 29245 KAPG NL. E-mail: services@wkap.nl; URL: http://www.wkap.nl. (Dist. by: Kluwer Academic Publishers Group, P.O. Box 322, 3300 AH Dordrecht, Netherlands. TEL 31-78-6392392. FAX 31-78-6546474; N. America dist. addr.: Box 358, Accord Sta., Hingham, MA 02018-0358. TEL 617-871-6600. FAX 617-871-6528) Ed. Spyros G. Tzafestas. (also avail. in microform from UMI; back issues avail.; reprint service avail. from SWZ) **Indexed:** A.I.Abstr., Appl.Mech.Rev., ASCA, CAD CAM Abstr., Compumath, Comput.& Info.Sys., Curr.Cont., Eng.Ind., INSPEC (1988-), Psychol.Abstr. (1988-), Robomat., SSCI, Zent.Math. **Document type:** academic/scholarly publication.
—BLDSC (5007.538500); AskIEEE; CISTI; Ei; Genuine Article; KR SourceOne; Linda Hall; SWETS; UMI; UnCover. **CCC.**
Incorporates (in 1994): Mechatronics Systems Engineering (ISSN 0924-3992)
Description: Provides a source linking all fields where system intelligence plays a dominant role, and promotes interaction between workers carrying out theoretical and applied research in various areas.
Refereed Serial

006 US
JOURNAL OF INTELLIGENT CONTROL, NEUROCOMPUTING AND FUZZY LOGIC. 1993. q. $285 (effective 1996). Nova Science Publishers, Inc., 6080 Jericho Tpke., Ste. 207, Commack, NY 11725-2808. TEL 516-499-3103. FAX 516-499-3146. E-mail: novasci1@aol.com. **Document type:** academic/scholarly publication.

006 003 US ISSN 0925-9902
QA76.9.D3 CODEN: JIISEH
JOURNAL OF INTELLIGENT INFORMATION SYSTEMS; integrating artificial intelligence and database technologies. 1992. bi-m. fl.870 to institutions; $447 to institutions in U.S. (effective 1998). Kluwer Academic Publishers Boston, Box 358, Accord Sta., Hingham, MA 02018-0358. TEL 617-871-6600. FAX 617-871-6528. TELEX 200190. E-mail: services@wkap.nl; URL: http://www.wkap.nl. (Dist. outside N. America by: Kluwer Academic Publishers Group, P.O. Box 322, 3300 AH Dordrecht, Netherlands. TEL 31-78-6392392. FAX 31-78-6546474) Ed.Bd. (also avail. in microform from UMI; reprint service avail. from SWZ) **Indexed:** Comput.Rev., INSPEC, Zent.Math. **Document type:** academic/scholarly publication.
—BLDSC (5007.538510); AskIEEE; CISTI; Ei; KR SourceOne; SWETS; UMI. **CCC.**
Description: Focuses on the creation of intelligent information systems, including reasoning processes, and their application in database management processes.
Refereed Serial

JOURNAL OF INTELLIGENT MANUFACTURING. see *COMPUTERS — Automation*

001.535 UK ISSN 0955-792X
QA76.63 CODEN: JLCOEU
JOURNAL OF LOGIC AND COMPUTATION. 1990. bi-m. £240 (foreign $380) (effective 1998). Oxford University Press, Academic Division, Great Clarendon St., Oxford OX2 6DP, England. TEL 44-1865-267907. FAX 44-1865-267485. TELEX 837330-OXPRES-G. E-mail: jnl.info@oup.co.uk; URL: http://www.oup.co.uk/journals. (U.S. subscr. to: Oxford University Press Inc., 2001 Evans Rd., Cary, NC 27513. TEL 800-852-7323. FAX 919-677-1714) Ed. D.M. Gabbay; Pub. Steven Johnson. R&P contact: Joolz Longley. bk.rev. **Indexed:** Comput.Abstr., INSPEC (1990-), Zent.Math. **Document type:** academic/scholarly publication.
—BLDSC (5010.552200); AskIEEE; Ei; Genuine Article; KR SourceOne; SWETS; UMI; UnCover. **CCC.**

JOURNAL OF PRAGMATICS; an interdisciplinary monthly of language studies. see *LINGUISTICS*

JOURNAL OF ROBOTIC SYSTEMS. see *COMPUTERS — Robotics*

JOURNAL OF SEMANTICS. see *LINGUISTICS*

KNOWLEDGE-BASED SOFTWARE ENGINEERING CONFERENCE. PROCEEDINGS. see *COMPUTERS — Software*

003 NE ISSN 0950-7051
QA76.76.E95 CODEN: KNSYET
KNOWLEDGE-BASED SYSTEMS. (Text in English) 1987. 8/yr. fl.1115($641) (effective 1998). Elsevier Science B.V., P.O. Box 211, 1000 AE Amsterdam, Netherlands. TEL 31-20-4853911. FAX 31-20-4853598. (Subscr. in the Americas to: Elsevier Science, Regional Sales Office, Box 945, New York, NY 10159-0945. TEL 212-633-3730. FAX 212-633-3680; Subscr. in Australasia and the Far East to: Elsevier Science (Singapore) Pte Ltd, No.1 Temasek Ave., No.17-01 Millenia Tower, Singapore 039192, Singapore. TEL 65-434-3727. FAX 65-337-2230; Subscr. in Japan to: Elsevier Science Japan, 9-15 Higashi-Azabu 1-chome, Minato-ku, Tokyo 106, Japan. TEL 81-3-5561-5033. FAX 81-3-5561-5047) Ed. E.A. Edmonds. adv.; bk.rev. (also avail. in microform from UMI; back issues avail.) **Indexed:** A.I.Abstr., Abstr.Hum.Comp.Inter., ASCA, Compumath, Comput.Abstr., Comput.Lit.Ind., Curr.Cont., INSPEC (1987-), Sci.Cit.Ind., SSCI, Zent.Math. **Document type:** academic/scholarly publication.
—BLDSC (5100.442700); AskIEEE; CISTI; Ei; Genuine Article; KR SourceOne; SWETS; UMI; UnCover.
Description: Interdisciplinary and applications-oriented journal on fifth-generation computing, expert systems, knowledge-based methods in system design.
Refereed Serial

001.535 UK ISSN 0269-8889
QA76.76.E95 CODEN: KEREE3
KNOWLEDGE ENGINEERING REVIEW. vol.3, 1988. q. £112($194) (effective 1998). Cambridge University Press, Edinburgh House, Shaftesbury Rd., Cambridge CB2 2RU, England. TEL 44-1223-312393. FAX 44-1223-315052. TELEX 851817256. E-mail: information@cup.cam.ac.uk; URL: http://www.cup.cam.ac.uk. (N. America addr.: Cambridge University Press, Journals Dept., 40 W. 20th St., New York, NY 10011. TEL 212-924-3900. FAX 212-691-3239) Eds. John Fox, Adele E. Howe. R&P contact: Linda Nicol. adv. contact: Rebecca Symons. (reprint service avail. from SWZ) **Indexed:** ASCA, Compumath, Comput.Lit.Ind., INSPEC (1987-). **Document type:** academic/scholarly publication.
—BLDSC (5100.446000); AskIEEE; CISTI; Ei; Genuine Article; KR SourceOne; SWETS; UMI; UnCover. **CCC.**
Description: Monitors and promotes developments in the application of artificial intelligence techniques.

001.535 GW ISSN 0933-1875
KUENSTLICHE INTELLIGENZ; Forschung, Entwicklung, Erfahrungen. Short title: K I. 1987. 4/yr. DM.116. B O - Fachverlag fuer Buero- und Organisationstechnik GmbH, Hermannstr. 2, 7653 Baden-Baden, Germany. TEL 49-7221-271066. FAX 49-7221-33228. adv.; bk.rev.; index. circ. 6,000. (back issues avail.) **Document type:** bulletin.

LANGUAGES OF DESIGN; formalisms for word, images and sound. see *ART — Computer Applications*

001.6 621.381 FR ISSN 0767-4910
LETTRE DE L'INTELLIGENCE ARTIFICIELLE. 11/yr. 1450 F. (foreign 1500 F.). E C 2, 269, rue de la Garenne, 92000 Nanterre, France. TEL 33-1-47-80-70-00. FAX 33-1-47-80-55-29. Ed. Jean-Claude Rault. bk.rev. (back issues avail.) **Document type:** newsletter.

COMPUTERS — ARTIFICIAL INTELLIGENCE

003   NE   ISSN 0923-0459
MACHINE INTELLIGENCE AND PATTERN RECOGNITION. 1985. irreg., vol.13, 1992. price varies. Elsevier Science B.V., Books Division, P.O. Box 211, 1000 AE Amsterdam, Netherlands. TEL 31-20-4853911. FAX 31-20-4853705. TELEX 18582 ESPA NL. E-mail: nlinfo-f@elsevier.nl; usinfo-f@elsevier.com; forinfo-kyf04035@niftyserve.or.jp; URL: http://www.elsevier.nl/. (Subscr. in the Americas to: Elsevier Science, Regional Sales Office, Box 945, New York, NY 10159-0945. TEL 212-633-3730. FAX 212-633-3680; Subscr. in Australasia and the Far East to: Elsevier Science (Singapore) Pte Ltd, No.1 Temasek Ave., No.17-01 Millenia Tower, Singapore 039192, Singapore. TEL 65-434-3727. FAX 65-337-2230; Subscr. in Japan to: Elsevier Science Japan, 9-15 Higashi-Azabu 1-chome, Minato-ku, Tokyo 106, Japan. TEL 81-3-5561-5033. FAX 81-3-5561-5047) **Indexed:** Zent.Math. **Document type:** monographic series.
—BLDSC (5323.610000); CISTI.
Refereed Serial

MACHINE LEARNING; an international journal. see **COMPUTERS**

MACHINE LEARNING ONLINE. see **COMPUTERS**

006.3 004   NE   ISSN 0928-9119
MEDICAL ARTIFICIAL INTELLIGENCE. (Text in English) 1992. irreg., vol.2, 1995. price varies. Elsevier Science B.V., Books Division, P.O. Box 211, 1000 AE Amsterdam, Netherlands. TEL 31-20-4853911. FAX 31-20-4853705. E-mail: nlinfo-f@elsevier.nl; usinfo-f@elsevier.com; forinfo-kyf04035@niftyserve.or.jp; URL: http://www.elsevier.nl/. (Subscr. in the Americas to: Elsevier Science, Regional Sales Office, Box 945, New York, NY 10159-0945. TEL 212-633-3730. FAX 212-633-3680; Subscr. in Australasia and the Far East to: Elsevier Science (Singapore) Pte Ltd, No.1 Temasek Ave., No.17-01 Millenia Tower, Singapore 039192, Singapore. TEL 65-434-3727. FAX 65-337-2230; Subscr. in Japan to: Elsevier Science Japan, 9-15 Higashi-Azabu 1-chome, Minato-ku, Tokyo 106, Japan. TEL 81-3-5561-5033. FAX 81-3-5561-5047) Ed. K.S. Zadeh. **Document type:** monographic series.
—BLDSC (5526.245000).
Refereed Serial

006.3   NE   ISSN 0924-6495
Q334   CODEN: MMACEO
MINDS AND MACHINES; journal for artificial intelligence, philosophy and cognitive sciences. 1991. q. fl.650 to institutions; $333.50 to institutions in U.S. (effective 1998). (Society for Machines and Mentality, IT) Kluwer Academic Publishers, Postbus 17, 3300 AA Dordrecht, Netherlands. TEL 31-78-6392392. FAX 31-78-6392254. E-mail: services@wkap.nl; URL: http://www.wkap.nl. (Dist. by: Kluwer Academic Publishers Group, P.O. Box 322, 3300 AH Dordrecht, Netherlands. TEL 31-78-6392392. FAX 31-78-6546474; N. America dist. addr.: Box 358, Accord Sta., Hingham, MA 02018-0358. TEL 617-871-6600. FAX 617-871-6528) Eds. James H. Fetzer, William J. Rapaport. (also avail. in microform from UMI; back issues avail.; reprint service avail. from SWZ) **Indexed:** Arts & Hum.Cit.Ind., ASCA, Compumath, Curr.Cont., INSPEC (1991-), Neurosci.Cit.Ind., Phil.Ind., Psychol.Abstr. (1991-), Sci.Cit.Ind., SSCI. **Document type:** academic/scholarly publication.
—BLDSC (5775.593000); Ei; Genuine Article; KR SourceOne; SWETS; UMI; UnCover. **CCC.**
    Description: Discusses issues concerning machines and mentality, artificial intelligence, epistemology, simulation, and modeling.
Refereed Serial

006.3   US
NATIONAL CONFERENCE ON ARTIFICIAL INTELLIGENCE. PROCEEDINGS. 1980. a. $74.95. M I T Press, 5 Cambridge Center, Cambridge, MA 02142. URL: http://www-mitpress.mit.edu. abstr. circ. 3,000. (back issues avail.; reprint service avail. from UMI) **Document type:** proceedings.

006.3 616.8   US   ISSN 0899-7667
QA76.5   CODEN: NEUCEB
NEURAL COMPUTATION. 1989. 8/yr. $78 to individuals (foreign $106); institutions $250 (foreign $278); students $50 (foreign $78) (effective 1997). M I T Press, 5 Cambridge Center, Cambridge, MA 02142. TEL 617-253-2889. FAX 617-577-1545. E-mail: journals-orders@mit.edu; URL: http://www-mitpress.mit.edu. (Editorial addr.: Salk Institute, Box 85800, San Diego, CA 92186-5800) Ed. Terrence Sejnowski. R&P contact: Paul Dzus. circ. 1,800. (back issues avail.; reprint service avail. from UMI) **Indexed:** A.I.Abstr. (until 1992), ASCA, Comput.Abstr., Curr.Cont., Ind.Med. (1995-), Ind.Sci.Rev., INSPEC (1989-), Neurosci.Cit.Ind., Psychol.Abstr. (1989-), Sci.Cit.Ind., Zent.Math.
—BLDSC (6081.280200); AskIEEE; CISTI; Ei; Genuine Article; KR SourceOne; SWETS; UMI; UnCover. **CCC.**
    Description: Provides interdisciplinary forum for the dissemination of research results and for reviews of research in neural computation.
Refereed Serial

006.3   UK   ISSN 0941-0643
NEURAL COMPUTING AND APPLICATIONS. Online edition (UK ISSN 1433-3058) 1992. q. £196 (effective 1998). Springer-Verlag London Ltd., Sweetapple House, Catteshall Rd., Godalming, Surrey GU7 3DJ, England. TEL 44-1483-418800. FAX 44-1483-415144. (Subscr. in N. America to: Springer-Verlag New York, Inc., Box 2485, Secaucus, NJ 07096-2491. TEL 201-348-4033) Eds. D. Bounds, H. James. **Indexed:** ASCA, Compumath, Curr.Cont. **Document type:** trade publication.
● Also available online.
—BLDSC (6081.280250); CISTI; Genuine Article; SWETS. **CCC.**
    Description: Publishes innovations in theory and practice in the academic, commercial, and industrial fields; relates neural computing to its applications.

006   NE   ISSN 1210-0552
QA76.87   CODEN: NNWOFJ
NEURAL NETWORK WORLD. (Text in English) 1991. bi-m. DM.620 (effective 1997). V S P, P.O. Box 346, 3700 AH Zeist, Netherlands. TEL 31-30-6925790. FAX 31-30-6932081. E-mail: 100341.2372@compuserve.com. (Co-publisher: I D G, Prague) Ed. Mirko Novak. (back issues avail.) **Document type:** academic/scholarly publication.
—BLDSC (6081.280620); AskIEEE; Ei; KR SourceOne.
    Description: Covers the latest developments in the field of information technology, focusing on neurocomputing based on applications of artificial neural networks. Also covers related fields such as brain and neurophysiological research, artificial intelligence and massive parallel information processing.
Refereed Serial

006.3   UK   ISSN 0893-6080
QA76.5   CODEN: NNETEB
NEURAL NETWORKS. 1988. 9/yr. fl.1592($915) (effective 1998). (International Neural Networks Society) Elsevier Science Ltd., Pergamon, P.O. Box 800, Kidlington, Oxford OX5 1DX, England. TEL 44-1865-843000. FAX 44-1865-843010. E-mail: nlinfo-f@elsevier.nl; usinfo-f@elsevier.com; forinfo-kyf04035@niftyserve.or.jp; URL: http://www.elsevier.nl:80/inca/publications/store/8/4/1/841.pub.shtml. (Subscr. to: Elsevier Science, Regional Sales Office, P.O. Box 211, 1000 AE Amsterdam, Netherlands. TEL 31-20-4853757. FAX 31-20-4853432; Subscr. in the Americas to: Elsevier Science, Regional Sales Office, Box 945, New York, NY 10159-0945. TEL 212-633-3730. FAX 212-633-3680; Subscr. in Australasia and the Far East to: Elsevier Science (Singapore) Pte Ltd, No.1 Temasek Ave., No.17-01 Millenia Tower, Singapore 039192, Singapore. TEL 65-434-3727. FAX 65-337-2230) (Co-sponsors: European Neural Networks Society; Japanese Neural Networks Society) Ed.Bd. adv.: B&W page $600, color page $1400. circ. 3,000. (also avail. in microfilm from UMI; back issues avail.) **Indexed:** A.I.Abstr., A.S.& T.Ind., Abstr.Hum.Comp.Inter., ASCA, Biostat., Comput.Abstr., Curr.Cont., Excerp.Med. (1995-), Ind.Sci.Rev., INSPEC (1988-), Neurosci.Cit.Ind., Oper.Res.Manage.Sci., Psychol.Abstr. (1989-), Qual.Contr.Appl.Stat., Sci.Cit.Ind., SSCI, Telegen, Zent.Math. **Document type:** academic/scholarly publication.
—BLDSC (6081.280800); AskIEEE; CISTI; Ei; Genuine Article; KR SourceOne; Linda Hall; SWETS; UMI; UnCover. **CCC.**
    Description: Covers the modelling of brain and behavioral processes, and the application of these processes to computer and related technologies.
Refereed Serial

006   US   ISSN 1370-4621
NEURAL PROCESSING LETTERS. 1994. bi-m. fl.550 to institutions; $229 to institutions in U.S. (effective 1998). Kluwer Academic Publishers Boston, Box 358, Accord Sta., Hingham, MA 02018-0358. TEL 617-871-6600. FAX 617-871-6528. E-mail: services@kap.nl; URL: http://www.wkap.nl. (Dist. outside N. America by: Kluwer Academic Publishers Group, P.O. Box 322, 3300 AH Dordrecht, Netherlands. TEL 31-78-6392392. FAX 31-78-6546474) Eds. Francois Blayo, Michel Verleysen. **Indexed:** ASCA, Compumath. **Document type:** academic/scholarly publication.
—BLDSC (6081.281020); AskIEEE; Genuine Article; KR SourceOne.

006.3   NE   ISSN 0925-2312
QA76.87   CODEN: NRCGEO
NEUROCOMPUTING. 1989. 18/yr. fl.2004($1152) (effective 1998). North-Holland (Subsidiary of: Elsevier Science B.V.), P.O. Box 211, 1000 AE Amsterdam, Netherlands. TEL 31-20-4853911. FAX 31-20-4853598. TELEX 18582 ESPA NL. (Subscr. in the Americas to: Elsevier Science, Regional Sales Office, Box 945, New York, NY 10159-0945. TEL 212-633-3730. FAX 212-633-3680; Subscr. in Australasia and the Far East to: Elsevier Science (Singapore) Pte Ltd, No.1 Temasek Ave., No.17-01 Millenia Tower, Singapore 039192, Singapore. TEL 65-434-3727. FAX 65-337-2230; Subscr. in Japan to: Elsevier Science Japan, 9-15 Higashi-Azabu 1-chome, Minato-ku, Tokyo 106, Japan. TEL 81-3-5561-5033. FAX 81-3-5561-5047) Ed. V. David Sanchez. bk.rev. (also avail. in microform from UMI; back issues avail.; reprint service avail. from SWZ) **Indexed:** ASCA, Compumath, Curr.Cont., Excerp.Med. (1992-), INSPEC (1990-), Neurosci.Cit.Ind., Psychol.Abstr. (1993-), SSCI, Zent.Math. **Document type:** academic/scholarly publication.
—BLDSC (6081.365200); CISTI; Ei; EMDOCS; Genuine Article; KR SourceOne; SWETS; UnCover. **CCC.**
    Description: Publishes articles describing recent fundamental contributions in the field of neurocomputing.
Refereed Serial

COMPUTERS — ARTIFICIAL INTELLIGENCE

006.3 003   UK   ISSN 1361-0244
QA76.76.E95   CODEN: NRESF3
NEW REVIEW OF APPLIED EXPERT SYSTEMS. 1988. a. £65($125) Taylor Graham Publishing, 500 Chesham House, 150 Regent St., London W1R 5FA, England. E-mail: a.sangster@abdn.ac.uk; URL: http://www.agdn.ac.uk/~acc025/ijaes.html. Ed. Alan Sangster. abstr. **Indexed:** A.I.Abstr., Abstr.Hum.Comp.Inter., Comput.Abstr., Educ.Tech.Abstr., INSPEC (1988-), LISA. **Document type:** academic/scholarly publication.
—BLDSC (6087.763800); AskIEEE; KR SourceOne; SWETS.
    Former titles (until 1995): International Journal of Applied Expert Systems (ISSN 0969-9317); (until 1992): Expert Systems for Information Management (ISSN 0953-5551)
    Description: Discusses how expert system technologies relate to information processing and provision in the information sciences, business, the social sciences and the arts and humanities.

O E G A I JOURNAL. (Oesterreichische Gesellschaft fuer Artificial Intelligence) see *ENGINEERING — Computer Applications*

006   US   ISSN 0894-0711
            CODEN: PCAIE5
P C - A I MAGAZINE. (Personal Computer Artificial Intelligence); intelligent solutions for today's computers. 1987. bi-m. $32. Knowledge Technology, 3310 W. Bell Rd., Ste. 119, Phoenix, AZ 85023. TEL 602-971-1869. FAX 602-971-2321. E-mail: terry@pcai.com; URL: http://www.pcai.com/pcai/. Ed. Joseph Schmuller; Pub. Terry Hengl. R&P contact: Peggy Jackson. adv. contact: Robin Okun. bk.rev. circ. 20,000. (back issues avail.) **Indexed:** A.I.Abstr., CAD CAM Abstr. **Document type:** trade publication.
—BLDSC (6413.366100); CISTI; Ei; KR SourceOne; UnCover. **CCC.**
    Description: Topics covered include neural networks, expert systems, datamining, objected oriented development, fuzzy logic, languages and case-based reasoning.

001.535   US
PERSPECTIVES IN ARTIFICIAL INTELLIGENCE. 1989. irreg., vol.9, 1991. Academic Press, Inc., 525 B St., Ste. 1900, San Diego, CA 92101-4495. TEL 619-231-6616. FAX 619-699-6715. (Subscr. to: Order Dept., 6277 Sea Harbor Dr., 4th Fl., Orlando, FL 32887. TEL 800-321-5068) Ed. B. Chandrasekaran. (back issues avail.)
    Description: Focuses on artificial intelligence and attracts readers interested in cognitive science, psychology and computer science.
    Refereed Serial

001.535   GW   ISSN 0937-3225
PHILOSOPHY AND ARTIFICIAL INTELLIGENCE. 1990. 3/yr. DM.70($35) to individuals; institutions DM.140($70). Burgverlag, Postfach 1247, 49545 Tecklenburg, Germany. Ed. K.S. Zadeh.
    Description: Devoted to philosophical issues arising from the intersection of computer science and philosophy.

POLYTECHNISCH TIJDSCHRIFT - WERKTUIGBOUW; vakblad voor de ingenieur. see *ENGINEERING — Mechanical Engineering*

001.535   FR   ISSN 1240-3946
PRODUCTIQUE - AFFAIRES; actualite et strategie des entreprises de la productique. (Text in English, French) 1982. 18/yr. 2200 F. A Jour, 11 rue du Marche St. Honore, 75001 Paris, France. TEL 333-1-42-96-67-22. FAX 33-1-40-20-07-75. TELEX TELEXEL 615887F. Ed. Patrice Dacquin. adv.; bk.rev. circ. 2,500. (back issues avail.)
—CCC.
    Formerly: Robots (ISSN 0752-4978)

006.3 616.8   US   ISSN 1055-713X
QA76.87   CODEN: PNNEEX
PROGRESS IN NEURAL NETWORKS. 1991. irreg., vol.3, 1994. $75. Ablex Publishing Corporation, Box 5297, Greenwich, CT 06831-0504. TEL 203-661-7602. FAX 203-661-0792. Ed. Omid Omidvar. **Indexed:** INSPEC. **Document type:** academic/scholarly publication.

006.3   US
PROGRESS IN ROBOTICS AND INTELLIGENT SYSTEMS. 1991. a., vol.4, 1996. price varies. Ablex Publishing Corporation, Box 5297, Greenwich, CT 06831-0504. TEL 203-661-7602. FAX 203-661-0792. Eds. C.Y. Ho, George W. Zobrist. **Document type:** academic/scholarly publication.

001.535   US   ISSN 0268-7526
RESEARCH NOTES IN ARTIFICIAL INTELLIGENCE. 1985. irreg., latest 1989. price varies. Morgan Kaufmann Publishers, Inc., 340 Pine St., 6th Fl., San Francisco, CA 94104-3205. TEL 415-392-2665. FAX 415-982-2665. E-mail: orders@mkp.com; URL: http://www.mkp.com. (Co-publisher: Pitman Publishing) Ed. Michael B. Morgan. R&P contact: Marilyn Uffner Alan. adv. contact: Lisa Schneider. **Document type:** proceedings.
—CISTI.
    Description: Consists of primary research works in specific areas of AI.
    Refereed Serial

001.535   FR   ISSN 0992-499X
REVUE D'INTELLIGENCE ARTIFICIELLE. 1987. 4/yr. 1050 F. (foreign 1200 F.) (effective 1997). (Ministere de la Recherche et de l'Espace) Editions Hermes, 14 rue Lantiez, 75017 Paris, France. TEL 33-1-42294466. FAX 33-1-42291556. Ed. Marie-Odile Cordier.
—CISTI; Ei.

ROBOT EXPLORER. see *COMPUTERS — Robotics*

ROBOTICS AND COMPUTER-INTEGRATED MANUFACTURING; an international journal. see *COMPUTERS — Robotics*

001.535   CN
ROBOTRONICS AGE NEWSLETTER.* 1983. m. Twenty-First Century Media Communications, Inc., 548 Cardero St., Vancouver, B.C. V6N 2K3, Canada. TEL 604-261-5712. Ed. Ed Hawkes.
•Also available online. Vendor(s): NewsNet (EC16).

006.3   US   ISSN 1053-4830
Q334   CODEN: SIBUFK
S I G A R T BULLETIN. q. $40 to non-members; members $15 (students $8). Association for Computing Machinery, Special Interest Group on Artificial Intelligence, 1515 Broadway, 17th Fl., New York, NY 10036. TEL 212-869-7440. Ed. Lewis Johnson. bk.rev. circ. 9,600. **Indexed:** Abstr.Hum.Comp.Inter., CAD CAM Abstr., INSPEC.
—CISTI; SWETS; UnCover.
    Formerly (until 1990): S I G A R T Newsletter (ISSN 0163-5719)

006.3   NE   ISSN 0927-720X
SCANDINAVIAN CONFERENCE ON ARTIFICIAL INTELLIGENCE. (Subseries of: Frontiers in Artificial Intelligence (ISSN 0922-6389)) (Text in English) 1987. irreg., latest 1995. price varies. I O S Press, Van Diemenstraat 94, 1013 CN Amsterdam, Netherlands. TEL 31-20-6382189. FAX 31-20-6203419. E-mail: market@iospress.nl; URL: http://www.iospress.nl/iospress. (In N. America: Box 10558, Burke, VA 22009-0558. TEL 703-323-5554. FAX 703-250-4705) (back issues avail.) **Document type:** proceedings.
—BLDSC (8087.473300).
    Refereed Serial

SEMIOTIC AND COGNITIVE STUDIES. see *PHILOSOPHY*

SENSORS; the journal of applied sensing technology. see *INSTRUMENTS*

001.535   SI
SERIES ON MACHINE PERCEPTION AND ARTIFICIAL INTELLIGENCE. (Text in English) irreg., vol.25, 1996. price varies. World Scientific Publishing Co. Pte. Ltd., Farrer Rd., P.O. Box 128, Singapore 9128, Singapore. TEL 65-3825663. FAX 65-3825919. TELEX RS 28561 WSPC. E-mail: wspcsl@signet.com.sg; sales@wspc2.demon.co.uk; wspc@wspc.com; URL: http://www.singnet.com.sg/~wspclib/. (UK addr.: 57 Shelton St., Covent Garden, London WC2H 9HE, England. TEL 44-171-836-0888. FAX 44-171-836-2020; US addr.: 1060 Main St., River Edge, NJ 07661. TEL 800-227-7562. FAX 201-487-9656) Eds. H. Bunke, P.S.P. Wang. **Document type:** monographic series.

SISTEMI INTELLIGENTI; rivista quadrimestrale di scienze cognitive e intelligenza artificiale. see *PSYCHOLOGY*

001.535   US   ISSN 1075-606X
QA76.87
SIXTH GENERATION SYSTEMS; ultraparallel processing, neuroengineering news, sixth generation news. (Supplement avail.) 1987. m. $99 in the U.S. & Canada; elsewhere $129 (effective 1995). Box 155, Vicksburg, MI 49007. TEL 616-649-3772. FAX 616-649-3592. Ed. Derek F. Stubbs. bk.rev. circ. 500. (diskette format; back issues avail.) **Indexed:** A.I.Abstr. **Document type:** newsletter.
    Formerly (until 1990): Neurocomputers (ISSN 0893-1585)
    Description: Presents findings and news in the field of neural networks, whether natural, theoretical or artificial.

006.3   NE   ISSN 0924-3542
STUDIES IN COMPUTER SCIENCE AND ARTIFICIAL INTELLIGENCE. (Text in English) 1988. irreg., vol.10, 1994. price varies. Elsevier Science B.V., Books Division, P.O. Box 211, 1000 AE Amsterdam, Netherlands. TEL 31-20-4853911. FAX 31-20-4853705. TELEX 18582 ESPA NL. E-mail: nlinfo-f@elsevier.nl; usinfo-f@elsevier.com; forinfo-kyf04035@niftyserve.or.jp; URL: http://www.elsevier.nl/. (Subscr. in the Americas to: Elsevier Science, Regional Sales Office, Box 945, New York, NY 10159-0945. TEL 212-633-3730. FAX 212-633-3680; Subscr. in Australasia and the Far East to: Elsevier Science (Singapore) Pte Ltd, No.1 Temasek Ave., No.17-01 Millenia Tower, Singapore 039192, Singapore. TEL 65-434-3727. FAX 65-337-2230; Subscr. in Japan to: Elsevier Science Japan, 9-15 Higashi-Azabu 1-chome, Minato-ku, Tokyo 106, Japan. TEL 81-3-5561-5033. FAX 81-3-5561-5047) Ed.Bd. (back issues avail.) **Indexed:** INSPEC, Zent.Math. **Document type:** monographic series.
—BLDSC (8490.282000).
    Refereed Serial

006.3   GW
STUDIES IN FUZZINESS. (Text in English) irreg., vol.9, 1997. Physica-Verlag GmbH und Co., Postfach 105280, 69042 Heidelberg, Germany. TEL 49-6221-487492. FAX 49-6221-413982. E-mail: physica@springer.de. **Indexed:** Zent.Math. **Document type:** monographic series.
    Description: Covers various topics and research in the area of fuzzy logic.

006.3   US   ISSN 1074-3227
QA76.64   CODEN: TPOSF3
▼**THEORY & PRACTICE OF OBJECT BASED SYSTEMS.** 1995. q. $185 (foreign $225) (effective 1998). John Wiley & Sons, Inc., Journals, 605 Third Ave., New York, NY 10158. TEL 212-850-6645. FAX 212-850-6021. TELEX 12-7063. E-mail: SUBINFO@JWILEY.COM; URL: http://www.wiley.co.uk. (Subscr. outside the Americas to: John Wiley & Sons Ltd., Baffins Ln., Chichester, W. Sussex PO19 1UD, England. TEL 01243-779777. FAX 01243-776128) Eds. Karl Lieberherr, Roberto Zicari. adv.: B&W page £640, color page £1515; trim 279 x 216. circ. 850. (also avail. in microform from UMI; back issues avail.) **Document type:** academic/scholarly publication.
—BLDSC (8814.628470); AskIEEE; KR SourceOne
    Description: Covers programming languages and models; foundations, semantics and type theory; database management systems and database languages; concurrency; software development tool and environments; metrics and evaluation; analysis and design methods; novel applications and other areas of object based computing.
    Refereed Serial

TRENDS IN COGNITIVE SCIENCES. see *PSYCHOLOGY*

001.535   US
TUTORIAL MONOGRAPHS IN ARTIFICIAL INTELLIGENCE. 1992. irreg., latest 1995. price varies. Ablex Publishing Corporation, Box 5297, Greenwich, CT 06831-0504. TEL 203-661-7602. FAX 203-661-0792. Ed. Xingdong Wu. **Document type:** academic/scholarly publication.

006.3   UK
▼**UNCERTAINTY THEORY IN ARTIFICIAL INTELLIGENCE SERIES.** 1995. irreg. £49.50. Research Studies Press Ltd., 24 Belvedere Rd., Taunton, Somerset TA1 1HD, England. TEL 44-1823-336197. FAX 44-1823-253252. E-mail: vaw@rspltd.demon.co.uk. (Dist. by John Wiley & Sons Ltd., Baffins Ln. Chichester, W. Sussex PO19 1UD, England. TEL 44-1243-779777. FAX 44-1243-775878) Ed. J Baldwin. **Document type:** monographic series.

UNIVERSITY OF TEXAS. LINGUISTICS RESEARCH CENTER. QUARTERLY REPORT. see *LINGUISTICS*

UNMANNED SYSTEMS. see *MILITARY*

006.3   II   ISSN 0970-8618
VIVEK; a quarterly in artificial intelligence. (Text in English) 1988. q. Rs.100($20) National Centre for Software Technology, Gulmohar Cross Rd. No. 9, Juhu, Bombay 400 049, India. TEL 91-22-620-1606. FAX 91-22-621-0139. TELEX 81-011078260 NCST IN. E-mail: vivek@saathi.ncst.ernet.in; URL: http://konark.ncst.ernet.in. Ed. S. Ramani; Pub. Truptee C. Shah. R&P contact: Truptee Shah. adv.: page Rs.2000. bk.rev. circ. 400. **Document type:** academic/scholarly publication.
—BLDSC (9244.428000); AskIEEE; KR SourceOne.
    Description: Publishes articles on artificial intelligence and tutorials on areas of topical interest.
    Refereed Serial

VOICENEWS. see *COMMUNICATIONS — Computer Applications*

ZIDONGHUA XUEBAO/ACTA AUTOMATICA SINICA. see *COMPUTERS — Automation*

COMPUTERS — Automation

629.8   US
A D C NEWS. (Automatic Data Collection) m. Automatic Identification Manufacturers U.S.A., 634 Alpha Dr., Pittsburgh, PA 15238-2802. TEL 412-963-8588. FAX 412-963-8753. E-mail: andy.lambl@aimusa.org. Ed. Andrew F. Lambl. circ. 1,000. **Document type:** newsletter.
●Also available online.
    Formerly: A I M News.
    Description: Covers automatic data collection industry. Includes technical, membership and marketing events of the association.

A F R I LIAISON. (Association Francaise de Robotique Industrielle) see *COMPUTERS — Robotics*

A I MAGAZINE. (Artificial Intelligence) see *COMPUTERS — Artificial Intelligence*

629.8   US
A M - F M - G I S NETWORKS. 1984. $8 membership. A M - F M International, 14456 E. Evans Ave., Aurora, CO 80014. TEL 303-337-0513. FAX 303-337-1001. E-mail: amfmintl@aol.com. Ed. Liz Roberts; Pub. John Kayser. R&P contact: John Kayser. TEL 303-337-0513. circ. 2,000. (back issues avail.) **Document type:** newsletter.
    Description: Provides association members with technical news and association updates.

ADVANCED MANUFACTURING TECHNOLOGY. see *ENGINEERING — Electrical Engineering*

629.8   US
ADVANCES IN AUTOMATION AND ROBOTICS. 1985. irreg. $90.25. J A I Press Inc., 55 Old Post Rd., No. 2, Box 1678, Greenwich, CT 06830-1678. TEL 203-661-7602. FAX 203-661-0792. E-mail: jai@jaipress.com. Ed. George N. Saridis. **Document type:** monographic series.

004.01905   US   ISSN 0748-8602
QA76.9.I58
ADVANCES IN HUMAN - COMPUTER INTERACTION. 1985. irreg, vol.5, 1996. price varies. Ablex Publishing Corporation, Box 5297, Greenwich, CT 06831-0504. TEL 203-661-7602. FAX 203-661-0792. Ed. Jane Carey. **Document type:** academic/scholarly publication.
—BLDSC (0709.065000); CISTI.
    Refereed Serial

ADVANCES IN LIBRARY AUTOMATION AND NETWORKING. see *LIBRARY AND INFORMATION SCIENCES*

ADVANCES IN LOGIC PROGRAMMING AND AUTOMATED REASONING. see *COMPUTERS — Artificial Intelligence*

629.8   PL
AKADEMIA GORNICZO-HUTNICZA IM. STANISLAWA STASZICA. AUTOMATYKA. (Text and summaries in English, Polish) 1966-1994; resumed 1997. s-a. 5 Zl. per issue (effective 1997). Wydawnictwo A G H, Al. Mickiewicza 30, 30-059 Krakow, Poland. TEL 48-12-338100. FAX 48-12-331014. (Dist. by: Ars Polona, Krakowskie Przedmiescie 7, 00-068 Warsaw, Polnd) Ed. A. Wichur. illus. **Indexed:** Zent.Math. **Document type:** academic/scholarly publication.
—BLDSC (9512.150030).
    Formerly: Akademia Gorniczo-Hutnicza im. Stanislawa Staszica. Zeszyty Naukowe. Automatyka (ISSN 0454-4773).

629.8   US
ANNUAL AUTOMATION REPORT TO THE ARIZONA LEGISLATURE. a. State Department of Administration, Data Management Division, 1616 West Adams St., Phoenix, AZ 85007. TEL 602-542-5791.

629.892   PL   ISSN 1230-2384
TJ212
ARCHIVES OF CONTROL SCIENCES. (Text in English) 1956. q. $50. (Polska Akademia Nauk, Komitet Automatyki i Cybernetyki Technicznej) Wydawnictwo Naukowe P W Nowe, Miodowa 10, 00-251 Warsaw, Poland. Ed. Andrzej Wierzbicki. bibl.; charts; index. circ. 640. **Indexed:** Appl.Mech.Rev., Cyb.Abstr., Eng.Ind., INSPEC (1992-), Math.R., Zent.Math.
—BLDSC (1634.115200); AskIEEE; CISTI; KR SourceOne; Linda Hall.
    Former titles (until 1992): Archiwum Automatyki i Robotyki (ISSN 1230-0640); (until 1991): Archiwum Automatyki i Telemechaniki (ISSN 0004-072X)

001.6 629.8   UK   ISSN 0144-5154
TS178.4   CODEN: ASAUDL
ASSEMBLY AUTOMATION. 1980. q. £859($1339) (foreign Aus.$1689) (effective 1998). M C B University Press Ltd., 60-62 Toller Ln., Bradford, W. Yorks. BD8 9BY, England. TEL 44-1274-777700. FAX 44-1274-785200. TELEX 51317-MCBUNI-G. URL: http://www.mcb.co.uk. Ed. Clive Loughlin. adv. contact: Yvette Le Jeune. bk.rev.; charts; illus.; stat.; tr.lit.; index. (back issues avail.) **Indexed:** Alloys Ind., Anbar, ASCA, CAD CAM Abstr. (until 1992), Curr.Cont., Eng.Mat.Abstr., INSPEC (1981-), Met.Abstr., Met.Abstr.Ind., Nonfer.Met.Alert, PCC Alert, Robomat. (until 1992), Steels Alert, World Alum.Abstr. **Document type:** trade publication.
—BLDSC (1746.606200); AskIEEE; CISTI; Ei; Genuine Article; KR SourceOne; Linda Hall; SWETS; UMI; UnCover. **CCC.**
    Description: Charts international developments in dedicated and programmable assembly with emphasis on flexible manufacture.

001.6 629.8   SP
AUTOCAD MAGAZINE. 6/yr. 7500 ptas. Edimicros, S.L., C. Galileleo 281, Entlo. 2a, 08028 Barcelona, Spain. TEL 34-3-4908889. FAX 34-3-4901985. Ed. Angel Salada. adv.: B&W page 300000 ptas.; 210 x 297.

629.8 001.6   IT   ISSN 0005-1012
AUTOMAT; rivista italiana dell'automatico. 1962. m. L.150000 (foreign L.180000) (effective 1996-97). S A P A R, Sezioni Apparecchi per Pubbliche Attrazioni Ricreative, Via di Villa Patrizi 10, 00161 Rome, Italy. TEL 39-6-4403686. FAX 39-6-4402718. Ed. Maurizio Maneschi. adv.; bk.rev.; index. circ. 3,500. (back issues avail.) **Document type:** trade publication.
    Description: Covers industry trends, legal and fiscal problems, and association activities.

629.8 001.6   US   ISSN 0146-4116
TJ212   CODEN: ACCSCE
AUTOMATIC CONTROL AND COMPUTER SCIENCES. English translation of: Avtomatika i Vychislitel'naya Tekhnika (Riga) (LV ISSN 0132-4160) 1969. bi-m. $1170 (effective 1998). (Latvian Academy of Sciences, LV) Allerton Press, Inc., 150 Fifth Ave., New York, NY 10011. FAX 212-463-9684. Ed. I. Bilinskis. bk.rev.; bibl.; charts; illus.; index. **Indexed:** Appl.Mech.Rev., INSPEC (1976-), Math.R., Zent.Math. **Document type:** academic/scholarly publication.
—BLDSC (0404.840000); AskIEEE; CISTI; Ei; KR SourceOne; Linda Hall; SWETS; UnCover. **CCC.**
    Formerly: Automatic Control (ISSN 0005-1047)
    Description: For professionals in academia, scientific research, engineering and computer design. Provides technical papers on topics such as computer networks, control strategy, data communications and software.

001.6 629.8   US   ISSN 0890-9768
    CODEN: AIDNEE
AUTOMATIC I D NEWS; for automated data capture systems users. 1986. m. $41 (Canada $59; elsewhere $79) (effective 1996). Advanstar Communications, Inc., 7500 Old Oak Blvd., Cleveland, OH 44130. TEL 216-826-2839. FAX 216-891-2726. E-mail: AutoID@en.com; URL: http://Advanstar.com/AutoIDNews. (Subscr. to: 131 W. First St., Duluth, MN 55802. TEL 800-346-0085) Ed. Mark David; Pub. Diva Norwood. adv. circ. 56,024. (tabloid format; also avail. in microfilm; microform from UMI) **Document type:** trade publication.
●Also available online. Vendor(s): Information Access Co.
—BLDSC (1829.127000); AskIEEE; Ei; KR SourceOne; UMI. **CCC.**
    Description: For users and integrators to better understand all aspects of automated data capture. Includes applications, new products, technologies, industry news, and systems solutions.

001.6 629.8   UK
AUTOMATIC I D NEWS EUROPE; for automated data capture systems users. 1992. 9/yr. free to qualified persons in Europe (non-qualified persons in Europe £76; others £107). Advanstar Communications, Advanstar House, Park West, Sealand Rd., Chester CH1 4RN, England. TEL 44-1244-378888. FAX 44-1244-370512. Ed. Iestyn Armstrong-Smith; Pub. Fran Waldie. adv.: B&W page $6320; color page $7425; adv. contact: Sarah Blackhurst. tr.lit. circ. 22,000. (tabloid format; also avail. in microform from UMI; reprint service avail.) **Indexed:** Int.Packag.Abstr. **Document type:** trade publication.
    Incorporates: Auto I D Today.
    Description: Helps users and integrators in a multitude of industries worldwide better understand all aspects of automated data capture. Explores applications, new products and technologies, industry news, and system solutions by helping individuals in manufacturing, retail, government, health care, computers, service sectors and several vertical industries.

COMPUTERS — AUTOMATION

629.8 003   UK   ISSN 0005-1098
TJ212   CODEN: ATCAA9
AUTOMATICA. (Text in English, French, German, Russian) 1963. m. fl.2769($1591) to institutions; with Control Engineering Practice fl.4027 ($2314) (effective 1998). (International Federation for Automatic Control) Elsevier Science Ltd., Pergamon, P.O. Box 800, Kidlington, Oxford OX5 1DX, England. TEL 44-1865-843000. FAX 44-1865-843010. E-mail: nlinfo-f@elsevier.nl; usinfo-f@elsevier.com; forinfo-kyf04035@niftyserve.or.jp; URL: http://www.elsevier.nl:80/inca/publications/store/2/7/0/270.pub.shtml. (Subscr. to: Elsevier Science, Regional Sales Office, P.O. Box 211, 1000 AE Amsterdam, Netherlands. TEL 31-20-4853757. FAX 31-20-4853432; Subscr. in the Americas to: Elsevier Science, Regional Sales Office, Box 945, New York, NY 10159-0945. TEL 212-633-3730. FAX 212-633-3680; Subscr. in Australasia and the Far East to: Elsevier Science (Singapore) Pte Ltd, No.1 Temasek Ave., No.17-01 Millenia Tower, Singapore 039192, Singapore. TEL 65-434-3727. FAX 65-337-2230) Ed. G.S. Axelby. adv.; bk.rev.; charts; illus.; index. circ. 2,000. (also avail. in microfilm from UMI; back issues avail.) Indexed: Abstr.Bull.Inst.Pap.Chem., Abstr.Hum.Comp.Inter., Appl.Mech.Rev., ASCA, Compumath., Comput.Cont., Comput.Rev., Curr.Cont., Cyb.Abstr., Eng.Ind., Ergon.Abstr., Excerp.Med., Ind.Sci.Rev., INSPEC (1968-), Intl.Civil Eng.Abstr., Math.R., Oper.Res.Manage.Sci., Qual.Contr.Appl.Stat., Risk Abstr., Soft.Abstr.Eng., W.R.C.Inf., Zent.Math. **Document type:** academic/scholarly publication.
—BLDSC (1829.450000); AskIEEE; CISTI; Ei; Genuine Article; KR SourceOne; SWETS; UMI; UnCover. **CCC.**
   Description: Publishes papers on theoretical and experimental research and practical applications to all types of control systems.
   Refereed Serial

001.6 629.8   SP   ISSN 0213-3113
AUTOMATICA E INSTRUMENTACION; automatizacion, medida, control, instrumentacion, sistemas, tratamiento de informacion. (Supplements avail.: Anuario, TecnoMarket) 1968. 10/yr. plus 1 supplement. 19700 ptas. to non-members (Europe 17900; elsewhere 25700 ptas.) (effective 1997). (International Federation of Automatic Control, Comite Espanol) Cetisa - Boixareu S.A., Concepcion Arenal, 5, 08027 Barcelona, Spain. TEL 34-3-3527061. FAX 34-3-3492350. Ed. Laura Tremosa. R&P contact: Lluis Lleida. adv. contact: Xavier Cuatracasas. bk.rev.; abstr. circ. 5,000. Indexed: Ind.SST, INSPEC (1985-1992). **Document type:** consumer publication.
—BLDSC (1829.500000); AskIEEE; CISTI; KR SourceOne; SWETS.
   Formerly (until 1985): Tecnica de la Regulacion y Mando Automatico (ISSN 0040-1722)
   Description: Contains national and international new of the sector, technical and market trends, solutions, applications and new components and systems.

001.6 629.8   SP
AUTOMATICA & ROBOTICA. 12/yr. Promotora de Tecnologia Punta, C. Espartinas 3, 1o Dcha., 28001 Madrid, Spain. TEL 1-431-66-36. FAX 1-577-74-64. Ed. Pedro Hernanz Gomez.

629.8   NE   ISSN 0005-1128
CODEN: AUTOA7
AUTOMATIE; maandblad voor industriele en produktie automatisering, procestechniek en instrumentatie. 1957. m. fl.117.50. Uitgeverij Adex, Postbus 770, 3740 AT Baarn, Netherlands. TEL 31-35-5421212. FAX 31-35-5425545. Ed. H. van der Biezen. adv.; bk.rev.; abstr.; bibl.; charts; illus.; index. circ. 3,700. Indexed: Excerp.Med. (until 199?), INSPEC (1968-1992), Key to Econ.Sci., PROMT. **Document type:** trade publication.
—BLDSC (1829.700000); SWETS.

AUTOMATIK; industrial automation. *see ENGINEERING*

629.8 001.6   CI   ISSN 0005-1144
TJ212   CODEN: ATKAAF
AUTOMATIKA; journal of the Yugoslav Committee ETAN. (Text in English and Yugoslav languages) 1960. bi-m. $50. Jugoslovenski Savez za Elektroniku i Telekomunikacije, Automatizaciju i Nuklearnu Tehniku (ETAN), Unska 3, Zagreb, Croatia. FAX 041-611-369. TELEX 21234. Ed. Joze Cernelc. adv.; bk.rev.; charts; illus.; mkt.; tr.lit.; index. circ. 1,000. Indexed: Chem.Abstr., Comput.Abstr., Cyb.Abstr., INIS Atomind., INSPEC (1968-), Ref.Zh.
—BLDSC (1830.200000); AskIEEE; CISTI; KR SourceOne.

629.8 001.6   JA   ISSN 0473-5587
AUTOMATION. (Text in Japanese) 1956. m. 960 Yen per no. Industrial Daily News Ltd. - Nikkan Kogyo Shinbunsha, 1-8-10 Kudan Kita, Chiyoda-ku, Tokyo 102, Japan. Ed. Shigenori Yokota. adv. circ. 30,000. Indexed: JTA.
—Linda Hall.
   Description: Contains information on all aspects of robotics, automation and artificial intelligence applications.

629.881 004   SW   ISSN 0345-1011
AUTOMATION. 1973. 8/yr. SEK 220 (effective 1990). I T F - Instrumenttekniska Foereningen, P.O. Box 6076, 172 06 Sundbyberg, Sweden. Ed. Frits Niklasson. adv.; bk.rev. circ. 3,200.

001.6 629.8   NZ   ISSN 0110-6295
CODEN: AUCODR
AUTOMATION AND CONTROL. 1971. 11/yr. NZ.$44.55 plus postage. (Institute of Measurement and Control) Matrix Publishing Ltd., P.O. Box 99-731, Auckland, New Zealand. TEL 64-9-357-6006. FAX 64-9-358-0606. Ed. Ross MacKay. adv. contact: John Birch. bk.rev.; charts; illus.; tr.lit. circ. 6,000. Indexed: Comput.Cont., INSPEC (1976-). **Document type:** trade publication.
—BLDSC (1831.120000); Ei; Linda Hall; UnCover. **CCC.**
   Description: Contains practical information on control of industrial processes, electricity, instrumentation, computers, communications, pneumatics, and hydraulics.

629.8 003   US   ISSN 0005-1179
TJ212   CODEN: AURCAT
AUTOMATION AND REMOTE CONTROL. English translation of: Avtomatika i Telemekhanika (RU ISSN 0005-2310) 1957. 24/yr. $1795 (foreign $2100) (effective 1998). (Russian Academy of Sciences, RU) Plenum Publishing Corp., Consultants Bureau, 233 Spring St., New York, NY 10013-1578. TEL 212-620-8468. FAX 212-463-0742. TELEX 23-421139. URL: http://ns1.infor.com:6800/cgi/getrarec?ple.20000015. Ed. N.A. Kuznetsov. charts; illus.; index. (also avail. in microfilm from UMI; back issues avail.) Indexed: Appl.Mech.Rev., ASCA, CAD CAM Abstr., Chem.Abstr., Compumath., Comput.Abstr., Comput.& Info.Sys., Curr.Cont., Electron.& Communic.Abstr.J., Eng.Ind., Ind.Sci.Rev., INIS Atomind., INSPEC (1969-), Math.R., SSCI, Zent.Math. **Document type:** academic/scholarly publication.
—BLDSC (0405.000000); AskIEEE; CISTI; Ei; Genuine Article; KR SourceOne; Linda Hall; SWETS; UMI; UnCover. **CCC.**
   Description: Contains scholarly papers on such subjects as noise-tolerant data encoding, control of observable quantum systems, system constraints and algorithms.
   Refereed Serial

629.8 690   NE   ISSN 0926-5805
TH437   CODEN: AUCOES
AUTOMATION IN CONSTRUCTION; an international journal for the building industry. (Text in English) 1992. bi-m. fl.699($402) (effective 1998). Elsevier Science B.V., P.O. Box 211, 1000 AE Amsterdam, Netherlands. TEL 31-20-4853911. FAX 31-20-4853598. TELEX 18582 ESPA NL. E-mail: nlinfo-f@elsevier.nl; usinfo-f@elsevier.com; forinfo-kyf04035@niftyserve.or.jp; URL: http://www.elsevier.nl/. (Subscr. in the Americas to: Elsevier Science, Regional Sales Office, Box 945, New York, NY 10159-0945. TEL 212-633-3730. FAX 212-633-3680; Subscr. in Australasia and the Far East to: Elsevier Science (Singapore) Pte Ltd, No.1 Temasek Ave., No.17-01 Millenia Tower, Singapore 039192, Singapore. TEL 65-434-3727. FAX 65-337-2230; Subscr. in Japan to: Elsevier Science Japan, 9-15 Higashi-Azabu 1-chome, Minato-ku, Tokyo 106, Japan. TEL 81-3-5561-5033. FAX 81-3-5561-5047) (Co-sponsors: British Association for Automation and Robotics in Construction; International Association for Automation and Robotics in Construction; International Council for Building Research Studies and Documentation) Ed.Bd. (also avail. in microform from UMI; back issues avail.) Indexed: Alloys Ind., Eng.Mat.Abstr., Geo.Abstr.H.G., Geo.Abstr.P.G., INSPEC (1992-), Met.Abstr., Met.Abstr.Ind., Nonfer.Met.Alert, PCC Alert, Steels Alert, World Alum.Abstr. **Document type:** academic/scholarly publication.
—BLDSC (1831.228000); CISTI; Ei; EMDOCS; KR SourceOne; SWETS. **CCC.**
   Description: Covers computer applications in architecture and design, in the construction, maintenance and control of intelligent structures, and the construction industry.
   Refereed Serial

001.53 629.8   NO   ISSN 0333-3302
AUTOMATISERING. 1982. 9/yr. NOK 190. Teknisk Presse A.S, Box 6754, Roedelokke, N-0503 Oslo, Norway. TEL 47-2-52-10-40. FAX 47-2-50-66-48. Ed. Paul R. Bieker. adv.; bk.rev. circ. 17,842.
—**CCC.**
   Description: Focuses on the process industry and on specific fields of industrial automation.

629.8 001.6   XR   ISSN 0005-125X
CODEN: AUTMAZ
AUTOMATIZACE/AUTOMATION. (Text in Czech; summaries in English) 1958. m. 330 Kc. (foreign 105 DM). Automatizace s.r.o., Technicka 4, 160 00 Prague 6, Czech Republic. TEL 420-2-24352009. FAX 420-2-24355614. (Subscr. to: c/o M. Smejcky CONTRA, v Sareckem Udoli 64-196, 160 00 Prague 6, Czech Republic. TEL 420-2-24321321. FAX 420-2-24321321) Ed.Bd. R&P contact: Karel Suchy. adv.: B&W page 19000 Kc., color page 28000 Kc.; 210 x 290; adv. contact: Illona Grusova. bk.rev.; charts; illus.; mkt.; pat.; tr.mk.; index. circ. 2,000. Indexed: Appl.Mech.Rev., C.I.S.Abstr., Chem.Abstr., Cyb.Abstr., Excerp.Med., INIS Atomind., INSPEC (1968-), Met.Abstr., World Alum.Abstr.
—AskIEEE; CISTI; Ei; KR SourceOne; Linda Hall.
   Description: Covers industrial measurement and control systems design and operation in general.
   Refereed Serial

001.6 629.8   YU   ISSN 0005-1268
AUTOMATIZACIJA POSLOVANJA; unapredenje poslovne politike preduzeca. (Text in Serbo-Croatian) 1960. m. 500 din. Zavod za Ekonomske Ekspertize, Palmira Toljatija 3, Belgrade, Yugoslavia. Ed. Branislav Bakic. index. circ. 2,000.
—BLDSC (5093.410000).

006 629.8   SP
AUTOMATIZACION. 1985. 4/yr. $65 in Europe; America $83. Ediciones Tecnicas Izaro S.A., Mazustegui 21, 4o, 48006 Bilbao, Spain. TEL 34-4-4159022. FAX 34-4-4162743. Ed. Ramon Urizar. circ. 4,000.
   Formerly: Automatizacion de la Produccion (ISSN 0213-2672)
   Description: Covers robotics, numerical control and automation.

001.6 629.8   IT
AUTOMAZIONE COMPONENTI SICUREZZA. 6/yr. Via To 4, Varese, Italy. TEL 332-224-068. FAX 332-21-32-12. Ed. Franco Diari. circ. 6,300.

COMPUTERS — AUTOMATION

629.8 001.6 — IT — ISSN 0005-1284
TJ212 — CODEN: ATSZAS
AUTOMAZIONE E STRUMENTAZIONE. 1953. m. L.75000. (Associazione Nazionale Italiana per l'Automazione) Editrice B.I.A.S. s.a.s., Viale Premuda 2, 20129 Milan, Italy. Ed. Umberto Pellegrini. adv.; bk.rev.; bibl.; illus.; tr.lit.; index. **Indexed:** Appl.Mech.Rev., INIS Atomind., INSPEC (1968-).
—AskIEEE; CISTI; KR SourceOne; Linda Hall.

629.8 — IT — ISSN 0393-3911
AUTOMAZIONE INTEGRATA. 1968. 10/yr. L.75000 (Europe L.140000; elsewhere L.185000) (effective 1996). Tecniche Nuove s.p.a., Via Menotti 14, 20129 Milan, Italy. TEL 39-2-75701. FAX 39-2-7610351. E-mail: abbonamenti@tecnet.it; URL: http://www.tecnet.it. Ed. Enzo Guaglione. adv.: B&W page L.2380000, color page L.3808000; trim 210 x 297. bk.rev.; abstr.; charts; illus.; pat.; tr.lit. circ. 7,000. **Indexed:** Cyb.Abstr.
—CISTI.
Former titles: Controlli Numerici Macchine a C N Robot Industriali (ISSN 0392-6036); Controlli Numerici e Macchine (ISSN 0010-8081)
Description: Articles on advanced automation factories with employees, flexible working systems and robotics.

001.6 629.8 — IT — ISSN 0392-8829
AUTOMAZIONE OGGI; mensile di automazione, robotica, controllo di processo, controllo numerico. 1983. m. L.98000 (foreign L.196000). Gruppo Editoriale Jackson S.p.A., Via M. Gorki 69, 20092 Cinisello B. (MI), Italy. TEL 39-2-66034312. FAX 39-2-66034270. TELEX 316213 GEJIT 1. Ed. Pierantonio Palerma. adv.: B&W page L.2800000, color page L.3900000; 210 x 297. bk.rev.; cum.index: 1983-1984. circ. 11,186. (back issues avail.) **Indexed:** Alloys Ind., Cyb.Abstr., Eng.Mat.Abstr., Met.Abstr., Met.Abstr.Ind., Nonfer.Met.Alert, PCC Alert, Steels Alert, World Alum.Abstr. **Document type:** trade publication.
—CISTI.
Description: Covers all aspects of industrial automation from management and production systems to process control, numerical control, robots, CAD-CAM and flexible systems.

001.6 629.8 — RU — ISSN 0005-2310
TJ212 — CODEN: AVTEAI
AVTOMATIKA I TELEMEKHANIKA. (Text in Russian; table of contents and summaries in English) 1936. m. $357 (effective 1998). (Rossiiskaya Akademiya Nauk, Institut Avtomatiki i Telemekhaniki) Izdatel'stvo Nauka, 90 Profsoyuznaya ul., 117864 Moscow, Russia. (Dist. by: Mezhdunarodnaya Kniga, B. Yakimanka 39, 117049 Moscow, Russia; Dist. in U.S. by: Victor Kamkin Inc., 4956 Boiling Brook Pkwy., Rockville, MD 20852. TEL 301-881-5973. FAX 301-881-1637) Ed. V.A. Trapeznikov. adv.; bk.rev.; bibl. **Indexed:** Appl.Mech.Rev., Chem.Abstr., Cyb.Abstr., Eng.Ind., INIS Atomind., INSPEC (1968-), Math.R., Zent.Math.
—BLDSC (0001.060000); AskIEEE; CASDDS; CISTI; KR SourceOne; Linda Hall. **CCC.**

001.6 629.8 — LV — ISSN 0132-4160
TJ212 — CODEN: AVYTAK
AVTOMATIKA I VYCHISLITEL'NAYA TEKHNIKA. English translation: Automatic Control and Computer Sciences (US ISSN 0146-4116) (Text in Russian) 1967. bi-m. $90 (effective 1997). Latvian Academy of Sciences, Institute of Electronic and Computer Science, Dzerbenes iela, 14, Riga LV-1006, Latvia. TEL 371-2-554500. FAX 371-8828211. E-mail: avt@edzi.lza.lv; URL: http://www.edzi.lza.lv. Ed. Ivars Bilinskis. R&P contact: V. Pelipeiko. adv.: page $300; adv. contact: V. Pelipeiko. bk.rev.; charts; index; circ. 70,032 (paid). **Indexed:** Curr.Cont., Cyb.Abstr., INSPEC (1968-), Math.R., Zent.Math. **Document type:** academic/scholarly publication.
—BLDSC (0000.830000); AskIEEE; CASDDS; Genuine Article; KR SourceOne. **CCC.**
Refereed Serial

629.88 001.6 — BW — ISSN 0206-8214
AVTOMATIKA I VYCHISLITEL'NAYA TEKHNIKA. 1970. a. 3 Rub. (Minskii Radiotekhnicheskii Institut) Izdatel'stvo Vysheishaya Shkola, Pr. Masherava 11, 22600 Minsk, Belarus. TEL 0172-235415. **Indexed:** Math.R.
Formerly: Novye Elementy Sistem Avtomatiki, Telemekhaniki i Vychislitelnoi Tekhniki.

AVTOMATIKA, TELEMEKHANIKA I SVYAZ'. see TRANSPORTATION — Computer Applications

629.8 006.6 — RU — ISSN 1019-6455
T58.A2 — CODEN: MAVPAC
AVTOMATIZATSIYA I SOVREMENNYE TEKHNOLOGII. Abbreviated title: A S T. (Text in Russian; contents page in English) 1947. m. 30000 Rub.($147) (effective 1996). (Ministerstvo Nauki i Tehnicheskoi Politiki Rossiiskoi Federatsii) Izdatel'stvo Mashinostroenie, 4, Stromynsky per., 107076 Moscow, Russia. TEL 7-095-2697141. FAX 7-095-2694897. (Dist. by: Mezhdunarodnaya Kniga, B. Yakimanka 39, 1117049 Moscow, Russia. TEL 7-095-2384967. FAX 7-095-2384634) Ed. V.N. Kalchenko. adv.: back page $200. bk.rev.; abstr.; bibl.; charts; illus.; stat.; index. circ. 1,000. (microform) **Indexed:** Alloys Ind., Chem.Abstr., Eng.Mat.Abstr., INSPEC (1968-1991), Met.Abstr., Met.Abstr.Ind., Nonfer.Met.Alert, PCC Alert, Steels Alert, World Alum.Abstr. **Document type:** academic/scholarly publication.
—CASDDS; CISTI; Linda Hall.
Formerly (until 1992): Mekhanizatsiya i Avtomatizatsiya Proizvodstva (ISSN 0025-8873)
Description: Deals with the latest national and foreign developments in production automation and mechanization in diverse industries.

629.8 001.6 — RU — ISSN 0203-2406
AVTOMATIZIROVANNYE SISTEMY UPRAVLENIYA. 1974. irreg. 1.10 Rub. Sankt-Peterburgskii Universitet, Universitetskaya Nab. 7-9, St. Petersburg V-164, Russia. (Co-sponsor: Ministerstvo Vysshego i Srednego Spetsial'nogo Obrazovaniya) **Indexed:** Math.R.

BUILDING AUTOMATION. see BUILDING AND CONSTRUCTION

001.6 629.8 — US — ISSN 1066-8160
THE BULL BULLETIN; a semi-annual update on industrial automation. 1992. irreg. free. c/o Industrial Controls Consulting, Inc., 104 S. Main St., Ste. 320, Fond du Lac, WI 54935. TEL 414-929-6544. FAX 414-929-9344. Ed. Jonathan B. Bullock. R&P contact: Thomas B. Bullock. bk.rev.; circ. 4,000 (controlled). **Document type:** newsletter.
Description: Covers trends in factory automation, especially concerning controls and systems integration in discrete manufacturing.

001.6 629.8 — FR — ISSN 0303-1276
BULLETIN DE LIAISON DE LA RECHERCHE EN INFORMATIQUE ET EN AUTOMATIQUE. 1973. s-m. free. Institut National de Recherche en Informatique et en Automatique, U C I S, Domaine de Voluceau-Rocquencourt, B.P. 105, 78153 le Chesnay Cedex, France. TEL 33-1-39-63-55-11. FAX 33-1-39-63-52-28. TELEX 697 033 F. Ed. Nicole Ray. adv. contact: Alain Bensoussan. bk.rev. circ. 5,000. (also avail. in microfiche) **Indexed:** Cyb.Abstr., INSPEC (1987-). **Document type:** bulletin.
—AskIEEE; KR SourceOne.
Description: Provides articles on all aspects of automation. Topics may include algorithms, transport vehicles and the integration of automation.

629.8 — CH
C A D & AUTOMATION. (Computer Aided Design) (Text in Chinese) 1988. m. Acer T W P Corporation, 2-F, No. 19-1 Lane 231, Fu-Hsing N. Rd., Taipei, Taiwan 105, Republic of China. TEL 2-7136959. Ed. Wong Li Jul. adv.: B&W page $945, color page $1890; trim 210 x 298; adv. contact: David Tsai. circ. 10,800.

001.6 629.8 — UK — ISSN 0963-5750
C A D - C A M. 1982. m. E M A P Business & Computer Publications Ltd., 33-39 Bowling Green Ln., London EC1R 0DA, England. TEL 44-171-837-1212. FAX 44-171-278-4008. adv. circ. 12,000. (back issues avail.) **Indexed:** BMT, Br.Ceram.Abstr., Comput.Dtbs., INSPEC, Int.Packag.Abstr. **Document type:** trade publication.
—BLDSC (2946.265300); CISTI; SWETS. **CCC.**
Supersedes in part (in 1990): C A D - C A M International (ISSN 0261-6920)

001.6 629.8 — US
C A M - I CAMEOS.* bi-m. Computer Aided Manufacturing - International Inc., 3301 Airport Fwy., No. 324, Bedford, TX 76021-6032. Ed. Nancy Thomas. circ. 1,000.

006.6 — NE — ISSN 0925-7977
C A TECHNIEK; tijdschrift voor industriele automatisering. 1983. 10/yr. fl.150 (effective 1997). Array Publications B.V., Postbus 615, 2400 AP Alphen aan den Rijn, Netherlands. TEL 31-172-424177. FAX 31-172-424381. E-mail: cat@array.nl; URL: http://www.array.nl. Ed. H. Boland. adv.: B&W page fl.4600; adv. contact: H. van der Brugge. bk.rev.; charts; illus. circ. 2,500. (back issues avail.) **Document type:** trade publication.
—SWETS.
Former titles (until 1991): C A Techniek in Bedrijf (ISSN 0924-9605); (until 1990): C A D C A M in Bedrijf (ISSN 0924-9591)
Description: Covers practical information concerning industrial automation.

001.6 629.8 — UK
C D - R O M DIRECTORY. 1986. a. £135 (CD-ROM £175). Macmillan Reference Ltd., 25 Eccleston Pl., London SW1W 9NF, England. TEL 44-171-881-8000. FAX 44-171-881-8001. adv.; bk.rev. **Document type:** directory.
●Also available on CD-ROM.
Description: Lists CD-ROM and multimedia CD titles, companies, and related products and services worldwide.

001.6 629.8 — UK
C D - R O M FACTS AND FIGURES. 1991. a. £35. Macmillan Reference Ltd., 25 Eccleston Pl., London SW1W 9NF, England. TEL 44-171-881-8000. FAX 44-171-881-8001. **Document type:** trade publication.

629.8 — US — ISSN 1086-4806
C I M E. (Computer Integrated Manufacture and Engineering) q. $40 (Canada $45; Europe and Latin America $50; elsewhere $60) (effective 1997). Lionheart Publishing, Inc., 2555 Cumberland Pkwy., Ste. 299, Atlanta, GA 30339. TEL 770-431-0867. FAX 770-432-6969. E-mail: lpi@lionhrtpub.com; URL: http://lionhrtpub.com. Ed. Peter Horner; Pub. John Llewellyn. R&P contact: Peter Horner. adv. contact: Marvin Diamond. **Document type:** trade publication.
—CCC.

001.6 629.8 — FR — ISSN 0335-0479
C X P INFORMATIONS. 1973. m. 450 F. Centre d'Experimentation des Progiciels International, 19-21 rue du Rocher, 75008 Paris, France. TEL 33-1-43-87-90-28. FAX 33-1-44-70-91-10. Eds. Jean-Luc Alarcon, Alain Pauly; Pub. Armand Gambert. adv.: B&W page 11500 F., color page 19000 F.; adv. contact: Olivier de Colnet. circ. 8,000. **Document type:** consumer publication.
Description: Analyzes the software market and software products in France.

001.6 — UK — ISSN 1350-1291
CADDESK. 1991. m. £36. Electronic Design Automation Ltd., 31-33 High Holborn, London WC1V 6BD, England. TEL 44-171-404-0564. FAX 44-171-831-2057. Ed. Martyn Day. adv. contact: Nigel Jooper. bk.rev.; charts; illus.; stat. circ. 1,400. (back issues avail.)
Description: Helps managers and professional users get the most from Auto CAD and its associated family of applications software and utilites. Keeps readers abreast of product (both soft- and hardware) developments and draws attention to areas of key interest.

001.6 629.8 — US — ISSN 1044-064X
TJ212 — CODEN: CJAUEF
CHINESE JOURNAL OF AUTOMATION. Selective English translation of: Zidonghua Xuebao (CC ISSN 0254-4156) 1989. q. $545 (effective 1998). (Chinese Association of Automation) Allerton Press, Inc., 150 Fifth Ave., New York, NY 10011. TEL 212-924-3950. FAX 212-463-9684. Ed. Yang Jiachi. (back issues avail.) **Document type:** academic/scholarly publication.
—AskIEEE; CISTI; KR SourceOne; UnCover. **CCC.**
Description: Covers automation research in China, including control theory, system science, and information science.

001 629.8 — SP
COMPONENTES, EQUIPOS Y SISTEMAS DE AUTOMATICA Y ROBOTICA. 16/yr. Espartinas 3, 28001 Madrid, Spain. TEL 1-431-66-36. FAX 1-578-39-05. Ed. Francisco Venegas. circ. 10,000.

COMPUTERS — AUTOMATION

645 674 629.8   US
COMPUTERS IN FURNITURE AND CABINET MANUFACTURING. INTERNATIONAL SYMPOSIUM PROCEEDINGS. 1992. biennial. $65 (overseas $85). Wood Machining Institute, Box 476, Berkeley, CA 94701. TEL 510-943-5240. FAX 510-945-0947. Ed. Ryszard Szymani. R&P contact: R. Szymani. **Document type:** proceedings.
   Description: Disseminates the latest information on the use of computers in furniture and cabinet manufacturing worldwide.

CONDITION MONITOR. see *ENGINEERING*

629.8 001.6   CN   ISSN 0730-9538
TJ212   CODEN: CONCER
CONTROL AND COMPUTERS. 1972. 3/yr. $175 (effective 1996). International Association of Science and Technology for Development, 4500 16th Ave., N.W., Ste. 80, Calgary, AB T3B 0M6, Canada. TEL 403-288-1195. FAX 403-247-6851. (And: P.O. Box 354, CH-8053 Zurich, Switzerland; Box 2481, Anaheim, CA 92814-2481 USA) Ed. M.H. Hamza. adv. contact: M.H. Hamza. bk.rev.; charts; illus.; index. circ. 500. (back issues avail.) **Indexed:** ASCA, Compumath, Comput.Rev., Cyb.Abstr., Eng.Ind., INSPEC (1992-), Int.Aerosp.Abstr. **Document type:** academic/scholarly publication.
—BLDSC (3461.855000); AskIEEE; CISTI; Ei; KR SourceOne; SWETS.
   Formerly: Automatic Control: Theory and Applications (ISSN 0315-8934)
   Description: Covers control theory and its applications with emphasis on the areas of computers in control and control technology.
   Refereed Serial

629.8 001.6   UK   ISSN 0010-8022
TJ212   CODEN: CTLIAW
CONTROL AND INSTRUMENTATION. 1958. m. $190. Miller Freeman Technical Ltd. (Subsidiary of: Miller Freeman plc), Miller Freeman House, 30 Calderwood St., London SE18 6QH, England. TEL 44-181-855-7777. FAX 44-181-316-3422. Ed. Brian Tinham; Pub. Paul Grinsell. adv. contact: Jeremy Zielinski. bk.rev.; abstr.; charts; illus.; stat.; tr.lit.; index. circ. 19,501. (also avail. in microform from UMI) **Indexed:** AESIS, Agri.Eng.Abstr., Appl.Mech.Rev., ASCA, BMT, Br.Ceram.Abstr., Br.Tech.Ind., Chem.Abstr., Chem.Eng.Abstr., Curr.Cont., Cyb.Abstr., Ergon.Abstr., Excerp.Med., Fluidex, Fuel & Energy Abstr., INIS Atomind., INSPEC (1969-), Int.Build.Serv.Abstr., Photo.Abstr., PROMT, Robomat. (until 1992), T.C.E.A., World Surf.Coat., World Text.Abstr. **Document type:** trade publication.
●Also available online. Vendor(s): Information Access Co.
—BLDSC (3461.870000); AskIEEE; CISTI; Ei; Genuine Article; KR SourceOne; SWETS; UnCover. **CCC.**
   Formed by the merger of: Control and Measurement; Instrument Review.

629.8 001.6   US   ISSN 0010-8049
TJ212   CODEN: CENGAX
CONTROL ENGINEERING; covering control, instrumentation, and automation systems worldwide. 1954. m. $95.90 (Canada $134.90; Mexico $129.90; elsewhere $179.90). Cahners Publishing Company (Des Plaines), Division of Reed Elsevier Inc., 1350 E. Touhy Ave., Box 5080, Des Plaines, IL 60018-5080. TEL 847-390-2780. FAX 847-390-2618. URL: http://www.controleng.com. (Subscr. to: 8773 S. Ridgeline Blvd., Highlands Ranch, CO 80126. TEL 303-470-4000) Ed. Keith Larson; Pub. David A. Harvey. adv.: B&W page $8265; color page $10255. illus.; tr.lit. circ. 99,300. (also avail. in microform) **Indexed:** A.I.Abstr., A.S.& T.Ind., Agri.Eng.Abstr., API Abstr., API Catal., API Hlth.& Environ., API Oil., API Pet.Ref., API Pet.Subst., API Transport., ASCA, BMT, C.R.I.Abstr., C.R.I.Curr.Cont., CAD CAM Abstr., Chem.Abstr., Chem.Eng.Abstr., Comput.Cont., Comput.Lit.Ind., Curr.Cont., Cyb.Abstr., Energy Info.Abstr., Eng.Ind., Fluidex, Fuel & Energy Abstr., Gas Abstr., INSPEC, ISMEC, PROMT, Robomat., SSCI, T.C.E.A., Tr.& Indus.Ind. **Document type:** trade publication.
—BLDSC (3462.000000); AskIEEE; CISTI; Ei; EMDOCS; Genuine Article; KR SourceOne; Linda Hall; SWETS; UMI; UnCover. **CCC.**
   Description: Serves engineers who design and apply controls and instrumentation for the industrial marketplace. Provides facts and figures, and reports on most efficient controls and instrumentation.

629.8   US
CONTROL ENGINEERING (INTERNATIONAL EDITION). bi-m. Cahners Publishing Company (Des Plaines), Division of Reed Elsevier Inc., 1350 E. Touhy Ave., Box 5080, Des Plaines, IL 60018-5080. TEL 847-635-8800. FAX 847-390-2774. (Subscr. to: 8773 S. Ridgeline Blvd., Highlands Ranch, CO 80126. TEL 303-470-4000) Ed. Jane Gerold. circ. 31,000. (also avail. in microform from UMI) **Document type:** trade publication.

629.8   US
CONTROL ENGINEERING AUTOMATION REGISTER. a. Cahners Publishing Company (Des Plaines), Division of Reed Elsevier Inc., 1350 E. Touhy Ave., Box 5080, Des Plaines, IL 60018-5080. TEL 847-635-8800. FAX 847-390-2774. (Subscr. to: 8773 S. Ridgeline Blvd., Highlands Ranch, CO 80126. TEL 303-470-4000) **Document type:** directory.

629.8   US
CONTROL ENGINEERING CONFERENCE. PROCEEDINGS.* 1982. a. $50. Reed Exposition Companies (Subsidiary of: Reed International PLC), Division of Reed Publishing (USA) Inc., Box 6059, Norwalk, CT 06852-6059. TEL 203-964-8487. FAX 203-964-8287. Ed.Bd. **Document type:** proceedings.

CONTROL ENGINEERING PRACTICE. see *ENGINEERING — Computer Applications*

629.8 005.3029   US
CONTROL ENGINEERING SOFTWARE GUIDE. a. Cahners Publishing Company (Des Plaines), Division of Reed Elsevier Inc., 1350 E. Touhy Ave., Box 5080, Des Plaines, IL 60018-5080. TEL 847-635-8800. FAX 847-390-2774. (Subscr. to: 8773 S. Ridgeline Blvd., Highlands Ranch, CO 80126. TEL 303-470-4000) **Document type:** directory.

CONTROL SOFTWARE DIRECTORY FOR PROCESS CONTROL. see *BUSINESS AND ECONOMICS — Trade And Industrial Directories*

001.6 629.8   GW   ISSN 0935-0381
CONTROLLING; Zeitschrift fuer erfolgsorientierte Unternehmenssteuerung. 1989. bi-m. DM.184 (students DM.144) (effective 1997). Verlag C.H. Beck, 80791 Munich, Germany. TEL 49-89-38189-338. FAX 49-89-38189-398. Eds. Peter Horvath, Thomas Reichmann. adv.: B&W page DM.2400, color page DM.4200; trim 260 x 186. circ. 2,600. (back issues avail.) **Document type:** trade publication.
—SWETS.
   Description: Covers various aspects of control in computer engineering.

CYBERNETICS AND COMPUTING TECHNOLOGY. see *COMPUTERS — Cybernetics*

D L A BULLETIN. (Division of Library Automation) see *LIBRARY AND INFORMATION SCIENCES — Computer Applications*

DESIGN AUTOMATION FOR EMBEDDED SYSTEMS; an international journal. see *COMPUTERS — Computer Systems*

DIANLI XITONG ZIDONGHUA/AUTOMATION OF ELECTRIC POWER SYSTEMS. see *ENGINEERING — Electrical Engineering*

001.6 629.8   CC   ISSN 1000-3886
TK4   CODEN: DIZIE6
DIANQI ZIDONGHUA. (Text in Chinese) bi-m. Shanghai Dianqi Zidonghua Yanjiusuo, 414 Xietu Lu, Shanghai 200023, People's Republic of China. TEL 3779011. Ed. Li Xubao.

DIANZI YU ZIDONGHUA/ELECTRONICS AND AUTOMATION. see *ELECTRONICS*

001.6 629.8   US   ISSN 1063-6234
E C CADENCE.* 1992. 10/yr. £44. Ariel Communications, Inc., Box 203550, Austin, TX 78720-3550. TEL 512-250-1700. FAX 512-250-1016. Ed. Patrice Sarath. adv.: B&W page $8251, color page $9751; trim 8 1/4 x 10 7/8. tr.lit. circ. 105,000.

ELECTRONIC HOUSE; enhanced lifestyle through home automation. see *ELECTRONICS*

629.8 621.381   RM   ISSN 0254-2242
ELECTROTEHNICA, ELECTRONICA SI AUTOMATICA. AUTOMATICA SI ELECTRONICA. (Text in Rumanian; summaries in English, French, German and Russian) 1957. q. 30 lei($25) Institutul de Cercetare si Projectare pentru Electrotehnica, Splaiul Uniru 313, 74204 Bucharest, Rumania. FAX 40-1-3213769. TELEX 10486. (Subscr. to: ILEXIM, Str. 13 Decembrie Nr. 3, P.O. Box 136-37, Bucharest, Rumania) Ed. Florin Teodor Tanasescu. adv.; bk.rev.; abstr.; bibl.; charts; illus.; tr.lit.; index. circ. 300. **Indexed:** INSPEC.
—BLDSC (3709.740000); Linda Hall.
   Formerly: Automatica si Electronica (ISSN 0005-1101)
   Description: Covers innovations and product development, computing techniques, computer-aided analysis, CAD, quality assurance and automation

ENGINEERING AUTOMATION REPORT. see *ENGINEERING — Computer Applications*

001.6 629.8   US   ISSN 1066-1409
TK7874.6
EUROPEAN CONFERENCE ON DESIGN AUTOMATION. Abbreviated title: E D A C. 1990. a. price varies. (I E E E) Institute of Electrical and Electronics Engineers, Inc., 345 E. 47th St., New York, NY 10017-2394. TEL 732-981-0060; 800-678-4333. FAX 732-981-9667. E-mail: customer.service@ieee.org; URL: http://www.ieee.org. (Subscr. to: 445 Hoes Ln., Box 1331, Piscataway, NJ 08855-1331) **Document type:** proceedings.
—Ei. **CCC.**
   Formerly (until 1993): European Design Automation Conference Proceedings (ISSN 1066-1409)
   Description: Addresses all areas of the design process from concept to manufacture and includes information on CAD and DA tools.

620   GW   ISSN 0940-791X
FLEXIBLE AUTOMATION. 1982. 6/yr. DM.68 (foreign DM.108) (effective 1997). Henrich Publikationen GmbH, Schwanheimerstr. 110, 60528 Frankfurt a.M., Germany. TEL 49-69-96777234. FAX 49-69-96777111. E-mail: 106035.1254@compuserve.com. (Subscr. to: Vertriebsunion Meyner GmbH, Im Kappelhof 1, 65343 Eltrille, Germany. TEL 49-6123-9238-0. FAX 49-6123-923839) Ed. Michael Lind. R&P contact: Willy Schweitzer. adv. contact: Ralf Schoenfeld. **Document type:** trade publication.
   Former titles: Flexible Automation Flexible Fertigung; Flexible Automation.
   Description: Effects of technological innovations in industry. Features automation, flexible manufacturing systems, robots, and CIM. Includes reports of events.

670.42   US
FLEXIBLE AUTOMATION AND INTEGRATED MANUFACTURING (YEAR). a. Begell House, Inc., 79 Madison Ave., Ste. 120, New York, NY 10016-7892. TEL 212-725-1999. FAX 212-213-8368. E-mail: 74353.2052@compuserve.com. Eds. William G. Sullivan, M. Munir Ahmad; Pub. William Begell. **Document type:** proceedings.

001.6 629.8   IT
FUTURA. 1978. 6/yr. L.40000 (foreign L.80000). Go Creative Group, Via Tortona 14, 20144 Milan, Italy TEL 39-2-58106415. FAX 39-2-58106428. E-mail gri@mail.sko.it. Ed. Oreste Griotti. circ. 9,100. **Document type:** newsletter.
   Description: Covers high technology for managers Includes technology, research, science and environment.
   Refereed Serial

001.6 629.8   CC   ISSN 1001-182X
GONGYE KONGZHI JISUANJI/INDUSTRY CONTROL COMPUTER. (Text in Chinese) bi-m. Jiangsu Sheng Jisuan Jishu Yanjiusuo, Suojin Cun, Taipingmen Wa Nanjing, Jiangsu 210042, People's Republic of China. TEL 506450. Ed. Chan Weimin. **Document type:** academic/scholarly publication.

H A PRO. (Home Automation) see *ELECTRONICS*

HANDLING; Magazin fuer Automation, Handhabungstechnik und Logistik. see *ENGINEERING — Industrial Engineering*

COMPUTERS — AUTOMATION

629.8   NE   ISSN 0169-4693
I B M NIEUWS. (International Business Machines) 1964. 4/yr. free. I B M Nederland N.V., Johan Huizingalaan 765, P.O. Box 9999, 1000 AG Amsterdam, Netherlands. TEL 31-20-5133813. FAX 31-20-6177600. E-mail: MARC__BORN@NL.IBM.COM. Ed. Marc Born. bk.rev.; charts; illus.; cum.index; circ. 15,000 (controlled). **Indexed:** Key to Econ.Sci.
   Former titles (until 1982): I B M Monitor (ISSN 0166-0071); I B M Kwartaalschrift (ISSN 0018-8654)
   Description: For customers and prospects of IBM Nederland N.V., who use products, systems and/or services of IBM.

I D SYSTEMS; the magazine of automated data collection. see *BUSINESS AND ECONOMICS — Computer Applications*

I D SYSTEMS BUYERS GUIDE. see *BUSINESS AND ECONOMICS — Computer Applications*

I D SYSTEMS EUROPEAN EDITION. see *BUSINESS AND ECONOMICS — Computer Applications*

001.6 629.8   US   ISSN 1050-4729
TJ210.3
I E E E INTERNATIONAL CONFERENCE ON ROBOTICS AND AUTOMATION. PROCEEDINGS. 1984. a. price varies. (Institute of Electrical and Electronics Engineers, Inc.) I E E E Computer Society Press, 10662 Los Vaqueros Circle, Los Alamitos, CA 90720-1264. TEL 714-821-8380. FAX 714-821-4641. Ed. Cat Harris; Pub. Matt Loeb. adv. contact: Frieda Koester. **Document type:** proceedings.
  —BLDSC (4362.949900); Ei. **CCC.**
   Former titles (until 1985): I E E E International Conference on Robotics and Automation (ISSN 1049-3492); (until 1984): International Conference on Robotics. Proceedings (ISSN 1049-3484)
   Description: Covers all areas of robotics and flexible automation.

I E E E TRANSACTIONS ON AUTOMATIC CONTROL. see *ENGINEERING — Electrical Engineering*

I E E E TRANSACTIONS ON ROBOTICS AND AUTOMATION. see *COMPUTERS — Robotics*

I F A C WORKSHOP SERIES. (International Federation of Automatic Control) see *ENGINEERING — Mechanical Engineering*

I I E SOLUTIONS. (Institute of Industrial Engineers) see *ENGINEERING — Industrial Engineering*

001.6 629.8   US   ISSN 0748-0059
TA1632
IMAGE UNDERSTANDING. 1984. irreg., vol.3, 1990. price varies. Ablex Publishing Corporation, Box 5297, Greenwich, CT 06831-0504. TEL 203-661-7602. FAX 203-661-0792. Eds. Shimon Ullman, Whitman Richards. **Document type:** academic/scholarly publication.
  —CISTI.
   Description: Contains recent studies in computational vision or "image understanding". In addition to original articles, volumes include reprints of classical studies.

629.8 001.6   US   ISSN 0362-3858
                           CODEN: IMCNB
INCREMENTAL MOTION CONTROL SYSTEMS AND DEVICES NEWSLETTER. 1972. s-a. $10 (free to qualified personnel and institutions) (effective 1997). Incremental Motion Control Systems Society, Box 2772, Station A, Champaign, IL 61825. TEL 217-356-1523. FAX 217-356-2356. Ed. Benjamin C. Kuo. R&P contact: Benjamin C. Kuo. adv. contact: Benjamin C. Kuo. bk.rev. circ. 4,000. **Indexed:** INSPEC. **Document type:** newsletter.
  —AskIEEE; KR SourceOne.
   Description: Provides an up-to-date review of existing technology and hardware.

INDIAN SOCIETY OF STATISTICS AND OPERATIONS RESEARCH. JOURNAL. see *STATISTICS*

629.805   SI   ISSN 0218-3552
INDUSTRIAL AUTOMATION JOURNAL. (Text in English) 1992. q. $44. Singapore Industrial Automation Association, 151 Chin Swee Rd., No. 03-13 Manhattan House, Singapore 169876, Singapore. TEL 65-734-6911. FAX 65-235-5721. E-mail: sra__siaa@pacific.net.sg; URL: http://www.asia-mfg.com.sg/siaa. Ed. Stephen Teng; Pub. F.A. Vasenwala. R&P contact: Stephen Teng. adv. contact: Nicholas Neo. circ. 5,000. **Document type:** trade publication.
  —BLDSC (4445.428000).
   Description: Provides information on the availability and applications of automation systems and components.
   Refereed Serial

004 620   US   ISSN 1045-0203
TS176   CODEN: ICPCEJ
INDUSTRIAL COMPUTING. 1982. bi-m. $80 to non-members (foreign $100) (effective 1997). (Instrument Society of America) I S A Services, Inc., 67 Alexander Dr., Box 12277, Research Triangle Park, NC 27709. TEL 919-549-8411. FAX 919-832-0237. TELEX 802540 ISA DURM. Ed. Susan Colwell; Pub. Richard Simpson. R&P contact: Richard Simpson. adv. contact: Richard Simpson. bk.rev.; charts; illus.; pat.; tr.lit.; index; circ. 40,000 (controlled). (also avail. in microfilm from UMI; reprint service avail. from ISI,UMI) **Document type:** trade publication, directory.
  —Ei; KR SourceOne; UMI. **CCC.**
   Former titles: Programmable Controls (ISSN 0747-4458); P C User (St. Clair Shores) (ISSN 0744-5857)
   Description: Covers technology reports, and news on hardware and software products.

670.285   US   ISSN 1058-8655
TS155.6   CODEN: PINDET
INDUSTRIAL COMPUTING CONFERENCE. PROCEEDINGS. 1991. a. $95 to non-members; members $76. (Industrial Computing Society) I S A Services, Inc., 67 Alexander Dr., Box 12277, Research Triangle Park, NC 27709. TEL 919-549-8411. FAX 919-549-8288. TELEX 802540 ISA DURM. (Co-sponsor: Instrument Society of America) Ed. Edward Bassett; Pub. Richard Simpson. R&P contact: Richard Simpson. adv. contact: Richard Simpson. **Document type:** proceedings.
  —Ei. **CCC.**

001.6 629.8   US   ISSN 0745-8088
INDUSTRIAL NEWS (MONTROSE). m. $5. Industrial News Co., 2155 Verdugo, Montrose, CA 91020. TEL 818-957-4329. Ed. Tom Clement. adv. **Document type:** newspaper.
   Description: Covers robot design, CAD-CAM, worker safety, flexible assembly, machining and electronic manufacturing in the robotics industry.

INDUSTRIAL ROBOT; an international journal on industrial robot technology. see *COMPUTERS — Robotics*

001.6 629.8   SP   ISSN 0214-932X
                           CODEN: INAUE7
INFORMATICA Y AUTOMATICA. 1967. 4/yr. 6000 ptas. membership; institutions $40000 ptas. Asociacion Espanola de Informatica y Automatica - Spanish Association of Information Processing and Automation, Hortaleza, 104, 28004 Madrid, Spain. TEL 34-1-3192565. FAX 34-1-3083028. Ed. Juan Manuel Sanchez. adv. contact: Antonio Vaquero Sanchez. bk.rev. circ. 5,000. **Indexed:** Ind.SST, INSPEC (1990-). **Document type:** academic/scholarly publication.
  —BLDSC (4481.298570); AskIEEE; KR SourceOne.
   Formerly (until 1987): Revista de Informatica y Automatica (ISSN 0210-8712)
   Refereed Serial

003 629.8   US   ISSN 0890-5401
Q350   CODEN: INFCEC
INFORMATION AND COMPUTATION. 1957. 16/yr. $1300 (foreign $1456) (effective 1997). Academic Press, Inc., Journal Division, 525 B St., Ste. 1900, San Diego, CA 92101-4495. TEL 619-230-1840. FAX 619-699-6800. E-mail: apsubs@acad.com; URL: http://www.apnet.com/www/journal/ic.htm; http://www.idealibrary.com/. (Subscr. to: Box 620000, Orlando, FL 32891-8340. TEL 407-347-4040. FAX 407-363-9661) Ed. Albert R. Meyer. bk.rev.; bibl.; index. (back issues avail.) **Indexed:** ASCA, Chem.Abstr., Compumath., Comput.Cont., Comput.Rev., Curr.Cont., Eng.Ind., Excerp.Med., Ind.Sci.Rev., INIS Atomind., INSPEC, Math.R., Sci.Cit.Ind., SSCI, Zent.Math. **Document type:** academic/scholarly publication.
  ●Also available online.
  —BLDSC (4481.770000); AskIEEE; CASDDS; CISTI; Ei; Genuine Article; KR SourceOne; Linda Hall; SWETS; UnCover. **CCC.**
   Formerly: Information and Control (ISSN 0019-9958).
   Description: Provides technical papers on theoretical computer sciences, information and control theory.

001.6   FR
INFORMATIQUE - AUTOMATIQUE.* 1962-1980; resumed 19?? 2/yr. Europautomation, 83-85 av. d'Italie, 75013 Paris, France. TEL 45-87-29-22. Ed. R.J. Giffrain. circ. 3,000.

INSTITUTE OF ELECTRONICS, INFORMATION AND COMMUNICATION ENGINEERS. TRANSACTIONS (SECTION D-II)/DENSHI JOHO TSUSHIN GAKKAI RONBUNSHI (D-II). see *COMPUTERS — Information Science And Information Theory*

629.8 510.285   RM   ISSN 1223-5075
INSTITUTUL POLITEHNIC DIN IASI. BULETINUL. SECTIA 4. AUTOMATICA, CALCULATEARE. (Text in English, French, German, Italian, Russian, Spanish) 1946. s-a. exchange basis. Institutul Politehnic din Iasi, Bd. Copou 11, 6600 Jassy, Rumania. TEL 40-81-46577. FAX 40-81-47923. Eds. Alfred Braier, Hugo Rosman. bk.rev.

INTEGRATED MANUFACTURING SYSTEMS. see *MACHINERY — Computer Applications*

006 629.8   US   ISSN 1080-2797
INTEGRATED SYSTEM DESIGN. 1989. m. free to qualified personnel (foreign $130). The Verecom Group, 5150 El Camino Real, Ste. D-31, Los Altos, CA 94022-1527. TEL 415-903-0140. FAX 415-903-0151. E-mail: ASIC@asic.com. Ed. Jonah McLeod; Pub. James C. Uhl. adv.: B&W page $6710, color page $7705; trim 8 x 10 7/8; adv. contact: James DiFilippo. circ. 55,000 (controlled). **Document type:** trade publication.
  —BLDSC (4531.816203); KR SourceOne. **CCC.**
   Formerly: A S I C and E D A Technologies for System Design (ISSN 1067-9804); Incorporates (1989-1991): A S I C Technology and News (ISSN 1043-9617); (1990-1991): Design Automation (ISSN 1055-1530)
   Description: Provides hands-on articles and columns for users of ASIC, electronic design automation, and programmable logic products.

INTELLIGENT MANUFACTURING. see *BUSINESS AND ECONOMICS — Production Of Goods And Services*

001.6 629.8   AU   ISSN 0254-3109
INTERNATIONAL FEDERATION OF AUTOMATIC CONTROL. NEWSLETTER. 1976. bi-m. free. International Federation of Automatic Control, Schlossplatz 12, A-2361 Laxenburg 6, Austria. TEL 02236-71447. FAX 02236-72859. Ed. Gusztav Hencsey. bk.rev. circ. 8,000.
  —BLDSC (6107.448000).
   Description: Offers information on automation and automatic control in the workplace. Covers a broad range of pertinent topics.

COMPUTERS — AUTOMATION

001.6 629.8   US   ISSN 1055-8470
QA76.9.C65   CODEN: IJSIEX
INTERNATIONAL JOURNAL IN COMPUTER SIMULATION.
1991. q. $45 to individuals; institutions $140 (effective 1997). Ablex Publishing Corporation, Box 5297, Greenwich, CT 06831-0504. TEL 230-661-7602. FAX 203-661-0792. Ed. George W. Zobrist. adv.; abstr.; bibl. circ. 300. **Document type:** academic/scholarly publication.
—BLDSC (4542.175100); AskIEEE; KR SourceOne; SWETS.
     Description: Includes original work from industry, government, and academic contributors on state-of-the-art research and development, product development, and tutorials in computer simulation.

670.42 006   US   ISSN 1064-6345
TS155.6
INTERNATIONAL JOURNAL OF FLEXIBLE AUTOMATION AND INTEGRATED MANUFACTURING. 1992. q. $97.50 to individuals; institutions $395 (effective 1997). Begell House, Inc., 79 Madison Ave., Ste. 1205, New York, NY 10016-7892. TEL 212-725-1999. FAX 212-213-8368. E-mail: begellhouse@worldnet.att.net. Eds. M. Munir Ahmad, William G. Sullivan; Pub. William Begell. R&P contact: Jung Ra. adv. contact: Jung Ra. **Indexed:** Text.Tech.Dig. **Document type:** academic/scholarly publication.
—BLDSC (4542.251500); CISTI. CCC.

670.285   SI   ISSN 0218-3382
INTERNATIONAL JOURNAL OF MANUFACTURING SYSTEM DESIGN. (Text in English) 1994. q. $83 to individuals; institutions $207 (developing countries $124); World Scientific Publishing Co. Pte. Ltd., Farrer Rd., P.O. Box 128, Singapore 9128, Singapore. TEL 65-3825663. FAX 65-3825919. TELEX RS-28561-WSPC. E-mail: wspcsl@singnet.com.sg; sales@wspc2.demon.co.uk; wspc@wspc.com; URL: http://www.singnet.com.sg/~wspclib/. (US addr.: 1060 Main St., Ste. 1B, River Edge, NJ 07661. TEL 800-227-7562. FAX 201-487-9656; UK addr.: 57 Stelton St., Covent Garden, London WC2H 9HE, England. TEL 44-171-836-0888. FAX 44-171-836-2020) Ed. B. Wu. **Document type:** academic/scholarly publication.
     Description: Addresses the issues related to manufacturing system design, with the objective of providing a timely and encompassing source of references.
     Refereed Serial

001.6 629.8   CN   ISSN 0826-8185
TJ210.2   CODEN: IJAUED
INTERNATIONAL JOURNAL OF ROBOTICS AND AUTOMATION. 1986. q. $230 (effective 1996). International Association of Science and Technology for Development, 4500 16th Ave., N.W., Ste. 80, Calgary, AB T3B 0M6, Canada. TEL 403-288-1195. FAX 403-247-6851. (And: P.O. Box 354, CH-8053 Zurich, Switzerland; Box 2481, Anaheim, CA 92814-2481) Ed. R. Colbaugh. adv. contact: M.H. Hamza. bk.rev.; index. (back issues avail.) **Indexed:** A.I.Abstr., ASCA, Curr.Cont., INSPEC (1986-), Robomat. **Document type:** academic/scholarly publication.
—BLDSC (4542.538400); AskIEEE; CISTI; Ei; Genuine Article; KR SourceOne; Linda Hall; SWETS; UnCover.
     Description: Covers all aspects of robotics and automation including modelling, simulation, dynamics, design, and social implications and applications.

001.6 329.8   PO
JORNAL MICRO ELECTRONICA. 12/yr. Viv. Menela, Alto dos Campitos, Sao Joao do Estoril, 2765 Estoril, Portugal. Ed. Fernando D. Ferreria.

JOURNAL DE LA ROBOTIQUE ET INFORMATIQUE. see *COMPUTERS — Robotics*

629.8   JA
JOURNAL OF ADVANCED AUTOMATION TECHNOLOGY.
1989. bi-m. 72000 Yen. Fuji Technology Press Ltd., Daini Bunsei Bldg., 1-11-7, Toranomon, Minato-ku, Tokyo 105, Japan. TEL 81-3-3508-0051. FAX 81-3-3592-0648.

JOURNAL OF AUTOMATED REASONING. see *COMPUTERS — Artificial Intelligence*

629.8 003   US   ISSN 1064-2315
TJ212   CODEN: JAUIEP
JOURNAL OF AUTOMATION & INFORMATION SCIENCES.
English translation of: Problemy Upravleniya i Informatiki. vol.13, 1968. bi-m. $954 (foreign $1047) (effective 1997). (Ukrainian Academy of Sciences, Institut Kibernetiki, KR) Begell House Inc., 79 Madison Ave., Ste. 1205, New York, NY 10016-7892. TEL 212-725-1999. FAX 212-213-8368. E-mail: begellhouse@worldnet.att.net. Ed. Robert N. McDonough. adv.; bk.rev.; abstr.; bibl.; charts; illus.; pat.; index. circ. 275. (also avail. in microform from UMI) **Indexed:** A.I.Abstr., CAD CAM Abstr., Eng.Ind., INSPEC, Math.R., Tel.Abstr., Zent.Math. **Document type:** academic/scholarly publication.
—BLDSC (0414.220000); AskIEEE; CISTI; KR SourceOne; Linda Hall; SWETS; UMI; UnCover. CCC.
     Former titles (until 1992): Soviet Journal of Automation and Information Sciences (ISSN 0882-570X); (until 1985): Soviet Automatic Control (ISSN 0038-5328)
     Description: Contains translations of scholarly articles and research papers on systems analysis, digital modelling, control theory, dynamic systems, and image recognition. Papers include equations and graphs.

006 629.8   UK   ISSN 0956-5515
TS183   CODEN: JIMNEM
JOURNAL OF INTELLIGENT MANUFACTURING. 1990. bi-m. £365 (foreign $605) (effective 1998). Thomson Science (Subsidiary of: International Thomson Publishing Group), 2-6 Boundary Row, London SE1 8HN, England. TEL 44-171-8650066. FAX 44-171-5229624. TELEX 290164 CHAPMA G. E-mail: journal@rapidcom.co.uk; URL: http://www.thomsonscience.com. (Dist. by: International Thomson Publishing Services Ltd., Cheriton House, North Way, Andover, Hants. SP10 5BE, England. TEL 44-1264-342713. FAX 44-1264-342807; Subscr. in US & Canda to: 400 Market St., Philadelphia, PA 19106. TEL 800-552-5866) Ed. Andrew Kusiak. adv. contact: Helen Dixon. (back issues avail.; reprint service avail.) **Indexed:** ASCA, CAD CAM Abstr., Compumath, Curr.Cont., INSPEC (1990-), Robomat., SSCI. **Document type:** academic/scholarly publication.
● Also available online.
—BLDSC (5007.538530); AskIEEE; CISTI; Ei; Genuine Article; KR SourceOne; SWETS. CCC.
     Description: Informs readers about the effective design, development, and use of intelligent systems.
     Refereed Serial

001.6 629.8   US   ISSN 1052-6188
TJ1   CODEN: SOMSA4
JOURNAL OF MACHINERY MANUFACTURE AND RELIABILITY. English translation of: Problemy Mashinostroeniya i Nadezhnosti Mashin (RU ISSN 0235-7119) 1983. bi-m. $1115 (effective 1998). (Russian Academy of Sciences, Institute of Machine Science, RU) Allerton Press, Inc., 150 Fifth Ave., New York, NY 10011. TEL 212-924-3950. FAX 212-463-9684. Ed. K.V. Frolov. **Indexed:** Alloys Ind., Appl.Mech.Rev., Eng.Ind., Eng.Mat.Abstr., Fluidex, Met.Abstr., Met.Abstr.Ind., Nonfer.Met.Alert, PCC Alert, Steels Alert, World Alum.Abstr. **Document type:** academic/scholarly publication.
—BLDSC (0415.170000); CISTI; Linda Hall; SWETS. CCC.
     Formerly: Soviet Machine Science (ISSN 0739-8999)
     Description: Publishes the results of research conducted on all facets of machine science. Topics may include machine design, automation in design, computer-controlled machines, techniques of analysis and synthesis of mechanisms, as well as the theory of robots and manipulators.

JOURNAL OF ROBOTIC SYSTEMS. see *COMPUTERS — Robotics*

KEY ABSTRACTS - FACTORY AUTOMATION. see *COMPUTERS — Abstracting, Bibliographies, Statistics*

KIBERNETIKA I VYCHISLITEL'NAYA TEKHNIKA; respublikanskii mezhvedomstvennyi sbornik nauchnykh trudov. see *COMPUTERS — Cybernetics*

006 629.8   US   ISSN 0895-7533
           CODEN: LRAUEY
LABORATORY ROBOTICS AND AUTOMATION. 1989. bi-m. $399 (foreign $504) (effective 1998). John Wiley & Sons, Inc., Journals, 605 Third Ave., New York, NY 10158-0012. TEL 212-850-6645. FAX 212-850-6021. TELEX 12-7063. E-mail: subinfo@jwiley.com; URL: http://www.wiley.co.uk. (Subscr. outside the Americas to: John Wiley & Sons Ltd., Baffins Ln., Chichester, W. Sussex PO19 1UD, England. TEL 44-1243-779777. FAX 44-1243-776128) Ed. W. Jeffrey Hurst. adv.: B&W page £640, color page £1515; trim 279 x 210. circ. 855. **Indexed:** ASCA, Compumath, Curr.Cont., INSPEC (1989-). **Document type:** academic/scholarly publication.
—BLDSC (5141.595500); AskIEEE; CASDDS; CISTI; Ei; Genuine Article; KR SourceOne; SWETS; UnCover. CCC.
     Description: Serves as an international centralized source for advances and developments in automation and robotics for the laboratory.
     Refereed Serial

006.6 629.8   US
LINKAGE (PHOENIX). q. Honeywell, 6404 N. Black Canyon, Phoenix, AZ 85023. TEL 602-863-5104. Ed. Frances B. Emerson.

001.6 629.8   GW   ISSN 0935-7939
LOGISTIK SPEKTRUM; Management und Organisation. 1988. 6/yr. DM.216 (foreign DM.264). (Deutsche Gesellschaft fuer Logistik e.V.) Vereinigte Fachverlage GmbH, Lise-Meitner-Str. 2, 55129 Mainz, Germany. TEL 49-6131-992-0. FAX 49-6131-992100. Ed. Reiner Wesselowski. adv.: B&W page DM.9980, color page DM.12230; trim 265 x 185; adv. contact: Beatrice Thomas-Meyer. bk.rev. circ. 28,000. **Document type** consumer publication.

001.6 629.8   US   ISSN 0895-3805
HD30.2
MANAGING AUTOMATION. 1986. m. free to qualified personnel. Thomas Publishing Company, Five Penn Plaza, New York, NY 10001. TEL 212-629-0500. FAX 212-629-1551. Ed. William McIlvaine. circ. 104,000 (controlled). **Indexed:** A.I.Abstr., CAD CAM Abstr., Comput.Lit.Ind., INSPEC (1987-), Robomat Tel.Abstr. **Document type:** trade publication.
—BLDSC (5359.283000); AskIEEE; CISTI; Ei; KR SourceOne.
     Description: Assists in better management of automation equipment.

001.6 629.8   US
MANAGING AUTOMATION LITERATURE REVIEW. 1989. s-a. Thomas Publishing Company, 5 Penn Plaza, New York, NY 10001. TEL 212-629-1551. adv. circ. 92,250.
     Description: Covers the dissemination of catalogs and literature for the factory automation worker.

670 629.8   CN   ISSN 1192-5973
MANUFACTURING & PROCESS AUTOMATION. 1986. bi-m. $24 (effective 1997). Kerrwil Publications Ltd., 395 Matheson Blvd. E., Mississauga, ON L4Z 2H2, Canada. TEL 905-890-1846. FAX 905-890-5769. E-mail: mpa@kerrwil.com. Ed. Meg Mathur; Pub. Klaus Pirker. adv.: B&W page Can.$3220, color page Can.$3925; adv. contact: Klaus Pirker. circ. 21,000 (controlled). (tabloid format; also avail. in microfilm from MML; back issues avail.) **Indexed:** A.I.Abstr., Can.B.P.I., Robom. **Document type:** trade publication.
     Former titles (until 1993): Automation Systems (ISSN 1181-7003); (until 1990): Automation Products and Technology (ISSN 0847-5555); (un 1989): Industrial Automation Products and Technology (ISSN 0848-161X)
     Description: For plant manufacturing executives and engineers. Provides news, application and new product information relating to advanced manufacturing technology.

COMPUTERS — AUTOMATION

001.6 629.8 US ISSN 0195-2366
MATERIAL HANDLING PRODUCT NEWS. 1979. m. $25 (Canada $26.58; Mexico $25; elsewhere $48) (effective 1996). Gordon Publications, Part of Cahners Publishing Company, Division of Reed Elsevier Inc., 301 Gibraltar Dr., Box 650, Morris Plains, NJ 07950-0650. TEL 973-292-5100 ext.573. FAX 973-539-3476. URL: http://www.mhpn.com. Ed. Joseph Pagnotta; Pub. Barry Strobel. adv. circ. 100,500. (tabloid format) Indexed: Curr.Pack.Abstr. Document type: trade publication. —KR SourceOne. **CCC**.
  Description: Provides a listing of equipment and systems available for the material handling industry, storage areas and warehouses.

001.6 SZ
MESS UND REGELTECHNIK. 11/yr. Aida AG, Postfach 1710, CH-8640 Rapperswil, Switzerland. TEL 055-279627. FAX 055-271555. Ed. Peter Menzi. circ. 5,000.

629.8 001.6 FR ISSN 0755-219X
T2 CODEN: MRAUA7
MESURES. 1936. 10/yr. 670 F. (foreign 797 F.)(effective Jan. 1992). Group Tests, Immeuble Europais, 26 rue d'Oradour sur Glane, 75504 Paris Cedex 15, France. TEL 1-44-25-33-11. FAX 1-45-58-15-19. TELEX 270 589 F. Pub/ J. Weiss. adv. contact: M. Renaudineau. bk.rev. circ. 12,000. Indexed: Alloys Ind., C.I.S. Abstr., Eng.Mat.Abstr., Excerp.Med., INIS Atomind., INSPEC, Met.Abstr., Met.Abstr.Ind., Nonfer.Met.Alert, PCC Alert, Steels Alert, World Alum.Abstr.
—BLDSC (5682.890000); CASDDS; CISTI; Linda Hall; SWETS.
  Formerly (until 1983): Mesures Regulation Automatisme (ISSN 0026-0193)

N T I S ALERTS: MANUFACTURING TECHNOLOGY. (U.S. National Technical Information Service) see TECHNOLOGY: COMPREHENSIVE WORKS — Abstracting, Bibliographies, Statistics

OBSERVER (APTOS); office systems trends. see BUSINESS AND ECONOMICS — Office Equipment And Services

OFFICE AUTOMATION. see BUSINESS AND ECONOMICS — Office Equipment And Services

629.8 001.6 UK ISSN 0143-2087
QA402.3 CODEN: OCAMD5
OPTIMAL CONTROL APPLICATIONS AND METHODS. 1979. bi-m. $1365 (foreign $1365) (effective 1998). John Wiley & Sons Ltd., Journals, Baffins Ln., Chichester, W. Sussex PO19 1UD, England. TEL 44-1243-779777. FAX 44-1243-775878. E-mail: info-assets@wiley.co.uk; URL: http://www.wiley.co.uk. (Subscr. in the Americas to: John Wiley & Sons, Inc., 605 Third Ave., New York, NY 10148. TEL 212-850-6645. FAX 212-850-6021) Ed. Bion L. Pierson. adv.: B&W page £595, color page £1495; trim 254 x 178; adv. contact: Bob Kern. circ. 299. (also avail. in microform from UMI; back issues avail.; reprint service avail. from ISI,SWZ,UMI) Indexed: ASCA, Compumath., Comput.Abstr., Curr.Cont. (1992)-, INSPEC, Int.Abstr.Oper.Res., Int.Aerosp.Abstr., Math.R., SSCI, Stat.Theor.Meth.Abstr. (1992-), Zent.Math. Document type: academic/scholarly publication.
—BLDSC (6275.070000); AskIEEE; CISTI; Ei; EMDOCS; Genuine Article; KR SourceOne; Linda Hall; SWETS; UMI; UnCover. **CCC**.
  Description: Presents an interdisciplinary forum for the reporting of interesting optimal control applications emphasizing both the commonality of the underlying theory and the diversity of its applications.
  Refereed Serial

POLITECHNIKA GDANSKA. ZESZYTY NAUKOWE. ELEKTRONIKA. see COMPUTERS — Cybernetics

629.8 PL ISSN 0434-0760
TJ225 CODEN: ZNPIET
POLITECHNIKA SLASKA. ZESZYTY NAUKOWE. AUTOMATYKA. (Text in Polish; summaries in English, German, Russian) 1961. irreg. price varies. Politechnika Slaska, Katowicka 7, 44-100 Gliwice, Poland. FAX 371655. TELEX 036-304. (Dist. by: Ars Polona-Ruch, Krakowskie Przedmiescie 7, 00-068 Warsaw, Poland) Ed. Anna Skrzywan-Kosek. circ. 205. Indexed: Zent.Math.
—BLDSC (9512.325100); Linda Hall.
  Description: For engineers and scientists. Contains papers on various aspects of automation and artificial intelligence applications.

629.8 001.6 SZ
POLYSCOPE: computer - electronics - communication. 1969. 22/yr. 55 SFr. (foreign 120 SFr.) (effective 1996). Verlag Binkert AG, CH-5080 Laufenburg, Switzerland. TEL 41-62-8697272. FAX 41-62-8697333. Ed. Daniel Boehler. adv. contact: Ludwig Binkert. bk.rev.; abstr.; illus.; stat.; index. circ. 14,850. Indexed: INSPEC. Document type: trade publication.
  Formerly: Polyscope Automatik und Elektronik (ISSN 0032-4035)

629.8 PL ISSN 0032-4140
TJ1313 CODEN: PAUKAP
POMIARY - AUTOMATYKA - KONTROLA. 1955. m. $81. (Polski Komitet Pomiarow i Automatyki) Oficyna Wydawnicza SIMP Press, Ltd., Ul. Swietokrzyska 14A, 00-950 Warsaw, Poland. (Dist. by: Ars Polona-Ruch, Krakowskie Przedmiescie 7, Warsaw, Poland) (Co-sponsor: Sekcja Metrologii Automatyki i Mechaniki Precyzyjnej SIMP) Ed. Jan Bek. adv.: B&W page £1010. bk.rev.; bibl.; charts; illus.; index. circ. 2,000. Indexed: Appl.Mech.Rev., C.I.S. Abstr., Ceram.Abstr., Chem.Abstr., Cyb.Abstr., INSPEC, Sugar Ind.Abstr.
—AskIEEE; CASDDS; CISTI; KR SourceOne; Linda Hall.
  Description: Covers automatics in practice and theory, measurements, controls.

POPULAR HOME AUTOMATION; hands-on solutions for better living. see ELECTRONICS

001.6 621.381 AU
PRAEZISION IM SPIEGEL. q. Dynamis Werbe- und Verlagsgesellschaft mbH, Heinestr. 3, A-1020 Vienna, Austria. TEL 43-1-2143344. FAX 43-1-2167929. Ed. Friedrich Hubeni. circ. 13,200.

629.8 KR
TJ212 CODEN: AVTMA8
PROBLEMY UPRAVLENIYA I INFORMATIKI; nauchno-tekhnicheskii zhurnal. English translation: Journal of Automation & Information Sciences (US ISSN 1064-2315) (Text in Russian; summaries in English and Russian) 1956. bi-m. 6 Rub. Akademiya Nauk Ukrainy, Institut Kibernetiki im. V.M. Glushkova, Prosp. Akad. Glushkova, 40, 252207 Kiev, Ukraine. TEL 38-44-2652494. Ed. A.G. Ivakhnenko. Indexed: Cyb.Abstr., Djerelo, INIS Atomind., INSPEC, Math.R., Met.Abstr., World Alum.Abstr. Document type: academic/scholarly publication.
—CASDDS; CISTI; Genuine Article. **CCC**.
  Formerly: Avtomatika (ISSN 0572-2691)

001.6 629.8 FI ISSN 0357-4121
PROSESSORI. 1979. m. FIM 370. Helsinki Media Company Oy, Special Magazines, P.O. Box 2, FIN-00040 Helsinki Media, Finland. TEL 358-0-1205911. FAX 358-0-1205799. Ed. Jari Peltoniemi. adv. contact: Mia Kemppi. circ. 8,227. Document type: trade publication.
  Description: Directed to professionals in electronics and automation.

R A I R O: A P P I: JOURNAL EUROPEEN DES SYSTEMES AUTOMATISES. (Revue Francaise d'Automatique, d'Informatique et de Recherche Operationnelle) see COMPUTERS — Cybernetics

R I A QUARTERLY STATISTICS REPORT - ROBOTICS. (Robotic Industries Association) see COMPUTERS — Robotics

629.8 UK ISSN 0263-1377
RETAIL AUTOMATION. 1980. 6/yr. £95. R M D P Ltd., The Hideaway, Furze Hill, Hove, E. Sussex BN3 1PA, England. TEL 44-1273-722687. FAX 44-1273-821463. Ed. Elizabeth Mandeville. adv. contact: Peter Lumsden. bk.rev.; circ. 12,125. circ. 375 (paid). Document type: trade publication.
—AskIEEE; KR SourceOne.
  Description: Covers product reviews, market news, conference reports, diary and retail case studies.

006.6 629.8 FR
REVUE INTERNATIONALE DE C F A O ET D'INFORMATIQUE GRAPHIQUE. (Conception et Fabrication Assistees par Ordinateur) 1986. 6/yr. 1750 F. (foreign 1980 F.) (effective 1997). (Ministere de la Recherche et de l'Espace) Editions Hermes, 14 rue Lantiez, 75017 Paris, France. TEL 33-1-42294466. FAX 33-1-42291556. Ed. Yvon Gardan. circ. 3,000.
—CISTI.
  Formerly (until 1994): Revue Internationale de C F A O et d'Infographie (ISSN 0298-0924)
  Description: Covers mathematical aspects, problems of normalization, exchanges between systems, the development of databases.

006 629.8 GW
ROBOTER UND AUTOMATION; Zeitschrift fuer Automation. 1983. 4/yr. DM.124 (Europe DM.142; overseas DM.172). Verlag Moderne Industrie, Justus-von-Liebig-Str. 1, 86899 Landsberg, Germany. TEL 49-8191-125-0. FAX 49-8191-125-483. Ed. Helmut Augeli. adv.: B&W page DM.6360; trim 257 x 178; adv. contact: Klaus-Peter Egger. bk.rev. circ. 9,710. (back issues avail.) Document type: trade publication.
  Formerly: Roboter (ISSN 0724-1712)

ROBOTICS AND AUTONOMOUS SYSTEMS. see COMPUTERS — Robotics

ROBOTICS AND MANUFACTURING. see COMPUTERS — Robotics

629.8 001.6 US ISSN 0163-5700
QA267 CODEN: SIGNDM
S I G A C T NEWS. 1969. q. $35 to non-members; members $40 (students $7.50). Association for Computing Machinery, Special Interest Group on Automata and Computability Theory, 1515 Broadway, 17th Fl., New York, NY 10036. Ed. Ian Parberry. bk.rev.; charts; stat.; circ. 1,588 (controlled). (back issues avail.) Indexed: Abstr.Hum.Comp.Inter., INSPEC.
—AskIEEE; CISTI; KR SourceOne; SWETS; UnCover.

S T I N. see ENGINEERING — Mechanical Engineering

001.6 629.8 US ISSN 0273-3080
SCAN NEWSLETTER; the management newsletter for all industries involved with bar-code scanning and related technologies. (Former name of issuing body: Scanning, Coding & Automation Newsletter Ltd.) 1977. m. $195 (foreign $215) (effective 1995). Scan Newsletter Ltd., 11 Middle Neck Rd., Great Neck, NY 11021. TEL 516-487-6375. FAX 516-487-6393. Ed. George Goldberg; Pub. George Goldberg. bk.rev.; index. (back issues avail.) Document type: newsletter.
  Description: Contains information for all industries involved with bar-code scanning and other automatic identification technologies and applications.

SENSOR REPORT; Sensorik Messtechnik Automatisierung. see INSTRUMENTS

SENSOR REVIEW. see MACHINERY

SENSOR TECHNOLOGY; a monthly intelligence service. see COMPUTERS — Cybernetics

001.6 629.8 SI ISSN 0218-0197
SERIES IN AUTOMATION. (Text in English) 1988. irreg., vol.4, 1992. price varies. World Scientific Publishing Co. Pte. Ltd., Farrer Rd., P.O. Box 128, Singapore 9128, Singapore. TEL 65-3825663. FAX 65-3825919. TELEX RS 28561 WSPC. (UK addr.: 73 Lynton Mead, Totteridge, London N20 8DH, England. TEL 44-181-446-2461; US addr.: 1060 Main St., Ste. 1B, River Edge, NJ 07661. TEL 800-227-7562) Ed. S.S. Chen. Document type: monographic series.
—BLDSC (8250.151600); CISTI.

COMPUTERS — CALCULATING MACHINES

001.6 629.8   SI
SERIES IN ROBOTICS AND AUTOMATED SYSTEMS. (Text in English) 1991. irreg., vol.11, 1993. price varies. World Scientific Publishing Co. Pte. Ltd., Farrer Rd., P.O. Box 128, Singapore 9128, Singapore. TEL 65-3825663. FAX 65-3825919. TELEX RS 28561 WSPC. (UK addr.: 73 Lynton Mead, Totteridge, London N20 8DH, England. TEL 44-181-446-2461; US addr.: 1060 Main St., River Edge, NJ 07661. TEL 800-227-7562) Ed. T. Husband. **Document type:** monographic series.

SERVICE ROBOT; an international journal. see ENGINEERING — Industrial Engineering

629.8 003   JA   ISSN 0916-1600
SHISUTEMU SEIGYO JOHO/SYSTEMS, CONTROL AND INFORMATION. (Text in Japanese; summaries in English) 1957. m. 10800 Yen membership; newsstand price: 1400Yen. Shisutemu Seigyo Joho Gakkai - Institute of Systems, Control & Information Engineers, 14, Yoshida Kawaracho, Sakyo-ku, Kyoto 606, Japan. FAX 81-75-751-6037. E-mail: iscie@imel.kyoto-u.ac.jp. Eds. K. Akazawa, M. Araki. adv.; bk.rev.; abstr.; charts; illus.; index. circ. 2,500. (back issues avail.) **Indexed:** Fluidex, INIS Atomind., INSPEC, Math.R. **Document type:** academic/scholarly publication.
—BLDSC (8589.325500); AskIEEE; CISTI; KR SourceOne.
Former titles (until 1989): Shisutemu to Seigyo - Systems and Controls (ISSN 0374-4507); (until 1971): Seigyo Kogaku (ISSN 0021-4310)

SISTEMI E IMPRESA. see COMPUTERS — Computer Systems

SOFTAWARENESS; a CAD-CAM-CAE journal and buyer's guide. see COMPUTERS — Software

629.8 001.6   PL
STUDIA Z AUTOMATYKI I INFORMATYKI. (Text in Polish; summaries in English) 1969. irreg., vol.19, 1994. price varies. Poznanskie Towarzystwo Przyjaciol Nauk, Ul. Mielzynskiego 27-29, 61-725 Warsaw, Poland. (Dist. by: Ars Polona, Krakowskie Przedmiescie 7, 00-068 Warsaw, Poland) Ed. Andrzej Kasinski. bibl. circ. 300. **Indexed:** Math.R. **Document type:** bulletin.
—BLDSC (6582.930000); AskIEEE; KR SourceOne.
Former titles: Studia z Automatyki & Poznanskie Towarzystwo Przyjaciol Nauk. Komisja Automatyki i Informatyki. Prace (ISSN 0867-3977); Poznanskie Towarzystwo Przyjaciol Nauk. Komisja Automatyki. Prace (ISSN 0079-4589)

629.8 006.6   NE   ISSN 0167-4129
STUDIES IN AUTOMATION AND CONTROL. (Text in English) 1978. irreg., vol.10, 1993. price varies. Elsevier Science B.V., Books Division, P.O. Box 211, 1000 AE Amsterdam, Netherlands. TEL 31-20-4853911. FAX 31-20-4853705. TELEX 18582 ESPA NL. E-mail: nlinfo-f@elsevier.com; forinfo-kyf04035@niftyserve.or.jp; URL: http://www.elsevier.nl/. (Subscr. in the Americas to: Elsevier Science, Regional Sales Office, Box 945, New York, NY 10159-0945. TEL 212-633-3730. FAX 212-633-3680; Subscr. in Australasia and the Far East to: Elsevier Science (Singapore) Pte Ltd, No.1 Temasek Ave., No.17-01 Millenia Tower, Singapore 039192, Singapore. TEL 65-434-3727. FAX 65-337-2230; Subscr. in Japan to: Elsevier Science Japan, 9-15 Higashi-Azabu 1-chome, Minato-ku, Tokyo 106, Japan. TEL 81-3-5561-5033. FAX 81-3-5561-5047) **Indexed:** Cyb.Abstr., INSPEC, Zent.Math. **Document type:** monographic series.
—BLDSC (8489.575000).
Refereed Serial

SYMPOSIUM ON FOUNDATIONS OF COMPUTER SCIENCE. PROCEEDINGS. see COMPUTERS — Computer Engineering

SYSTEMS AND COMPUTERS IN JAPAN. see COMPUTERS — Computer Systems

SYSTEMS AND CONTROL LETTERS. see COMPUTERS — Computer Systems

SYSTEMS SCIENCE AND MATHEMATICAL SCIENCES. see MATHEMATICS

670.285 006.6   DK   ISSN 0909-1769
TECH WORLD. 1988. 11/yr. DKK 298 (effective 1997). I D G Danmark A-S, Carl Jacobsensvej 25, DK-2500 Valby, Denmark. TEL 45-36-19-91-00. FAX 45-36-44-20-33. Ed. Klavs Andersen. circ. 14,600. **Document type:** trade publication.
Formerly (until 1993): C A D - C A M World (ISSN 0903-8345)

TECNOLOGIE E TRASPORTI PER IL MARE. see TRANSPORTATION — Ships And Shipping

629.8   UK
U M I S T CONTROL SYSTEMS CENTRE SERIES. irreg., no.4, 1997. (University of Manchester Institute of Science and Technology) Research Studies Press Ltd., 24 Belvedere Rd., Taunton, Somerset TA1 1HD, England. TEL 44-1823-336197. FAX 44-1823-253252. E-mail: vaw@rspltd.demon.co.uk. (Dist. by: John Wiley & Sons Ltd., Baffins Ln., Chichester, W. Sussex PO19 1UD, England. TEL 44-1243-779777. FAX 44-1243-775878) Eds. M.B. Zarrop, P.E. Wellstead. **Document type:** monographic series.

629.8   RM   ISSN 1224-600X
UNIVERSITATEA POLITEHNICA DIN TIMISOARA. BULETINUL STIINTIFIC. SERIA CALCULATOARE SI AUTOMATICA. (Text in English, French, German, Rumanian) 1993. a. $20 (effective 1997). Universitatea Politehnica din Timisoara, Piata Victoriei 2, 1900 Timisoara, Rumania. TEL 40-56-200333. FAX 40-56-190321. bk.rev. circ. 500. **Document type:** bulletin.

629 629.8   RU   ISSN 0130-0415
TJ212   CODEN: VTSUD9
VOPROSY TEORII SISTEM AVTOMATICHESKOGO UPRAVLENIYA. 1974. irreg. 1 Rub. Sankt-Peterburgskii Universitet, Universitetskaya Nab. 7-9, St. Petersburg V-164, Russia. **Indexed:** Math.R., Zent.Math.
—CASDDS; Linda Hall.

003 658   NE   ISSN 1380-5304
▼**WORKFLOW MAGAZINE.** 1995. 8/yr. fl.130 (effective 1997). Array Publications B.V., Postbus 615, 2400 AP Alphen aan den Rijn, Netherlands. TEL 31-172-424177. FAX 31-172-424381. E-mail: wfm@array.nl; URL: http://www.array.nl. Ed. Arnoud van Gemeren. adv.: B&W page fl.3175; adv. contact: Robin Breij. circ. 3,000 (paid). **Document type:** trade publication.
—SWETS.
Description: Covers workflow automation and management.

XIANDAI TUSHU QINGBAO JISHU/NEW TECHNOLOGY OF LIBRARY AND INFORMATION SERVICE. see LIBRARY AND INFORMATION SCIENCES — Computer Applications

629.89   CC   ISSN 1002-0411
XINXI YU KONGZHI/INFORMATION AND CONTROL. (Text in Chinese) bi-m. Zhongguo Kexueyuan, Shenyang Zidonghua Yanjiusuo - Chinese Academy of Sciences, Shenyang Institute of Automation, 90, Sanhao Jie, Shenyang, Liaoning 110003, People's Republic of China. TEL 393591. Ed. Jiang Xinsong. **Indexed:** Acoust.Abstr.

001.6 629.8   CC   ISSN 0254-4156
TJ212   CODEN: ZIXUDZ
ZIDONGHUA XUEBAO/ACTA AUTOMATICA SINICA. English translation: Chinese Journal of Automation (US ISSN 1044-064X) (Text in Chinese; summaries in English) 1963. bi-m. $83.20. (Chinese Association of Automation) Science Press, Marketing and Sales Department, 16 Donghuangchenggen North St., Beijing 100717, People's Republic of China. TEL 4010642. FAX 4019810. adv. circ. 11,000. **Indexed:** INSPEC (1981-), Int.Aerosp.Abstr., Math.R., Zent.Math. **Document type:** academic/scholarly publication.
—BLDSC (0599.700000); AskIEEE; CISTI; KR SourceOne; Linda Hall.
Description: Covers automation research in mainland China, including control theory, systems science, information science, CAD-CAM, automatic detection instruments, and biocybernetics.
Refereed Serial

ZIDONGHUA YIBIAO/PROCESS AUTOMATION INSTRUMENTATION. see INSTRUMENTS

COMPUTERS — Calculating Machines

INSTITUTUL POLITEHNIC DIN IASI. BULETINUL. SECTIA 4. AUTOMATICA, CALCULATEARE. see COMPUTERS — Automation

INTERNATIONAL CALCULATOR COLLECTOR. see HOBBIES

COMPUTERS — Circuits

see also Computers–Computer Engineering

ANALOG DIALOGUE; a forum for the exchange of circuits, systems, and software for real-world signal processing. see COMPUTERS — Computer Engineering

621.381   US   ISSN 1058-6393
TK7801   CODEN: CCSCE2
ASILOMAR CONFERENCE ON SIGNALS, SYSTEMS AND COMPUTERS. CONFERENCE RECORD. 1967. a. price varies. (Institute of Electrical and Electronics Engineers, Inc.) I E E E Computer Society Press, 10662 Los Vaqueros Circle, Box 3014, Los Alamitos, CA 90720-1264. TEL 714-821-8380. FAX 714-821-4641. Ed. Cat Harris; Pub. Matt Loeb. adv. contact: Frieda Koester. **Indexed:** INSPEC. **Document type:** proceedings.
—BLDSC (1742.787170); Ei; UMI. **CCC.**
Former titles (until 1986): Asilomar Conference on Circuits, Systems and Computers. Conference Record; (until 1972): Asilomar Conference on Circuits and Systems. Conference Record (ISSN 0571-3218)
Description: Presents new ideas and preliminary research results in the general areas of signal, systems, and computers.

621.381   UK   ISSN 0263-6522
   CODEN: ICIIDZ
INTEGRATED CIRCUITS INTERNATIONAL; an international bulletin for suppliers and users of integrated circuits. 1976. m. £340($541) (effective 1996). Elsevier Science Ltd., P.O. Box 800, Kidlington, Oxford OX5 1DX, England. TEL 44-1865-843000. FAX 44-1865-843010. E-mail: nlinfo-f@elsevier.nl; usinfo-f@elsevier.nl; forinfo-kyf04035@niftyserve.or.jp; URL: http://www.elsevier.nl/. (Subscr. to: Elsevier Science, Regional Sales Office, P.O. Box 211, 1000 AE Amsterdam, Netherlands. TEL 31-20-4853757. FAX 31-20-4853432; Subscr. in the Americas to: Elsevier Science, Regional Sales Office, Box 945, New York, NY 10159-0945. TEL 212-633-3730. FAX 212-633-3680; Subscr. in Australasia and the Far East to: Elsevier Science (Singapore) Pte Ltd, No.1 Temasek Ave., No.17-01 Millenia Tower, Singapore 039192, Singapore. TEL 65-434-3727. FAX 65-337-2230) Ed. Patricia Harris. index. (back issues avail.) **Indexed:** Comput.Lit.Ind., INSPEC. **Document type:** trade publication, bulletin, newsletter.
●Also available online. Vendor(s): Data-Star, Information Access Co., Knight-Ridder Information, Inc.
—BLDSC (4531.809000); CISTI. **CCC.**
Incorporates: Microcomputer News International (ISSN 0260-8472); **Formerly:** Microcomputer Analysis (ISSN 0309-5444)
Description: Designed to keep all those involved with the design, manufacture and use of microtechnology, up-to-date with latest developments in the field.

621.39   UK
KEY NOTE MARKET REPORT: PRINTED CIRCUITS. Variant title: Printed Circuits. irreg., no.7, 1993. £205. Key Note Ltd., Field House, 72 Oldfield Rd., Hampton, Middlesex TW12 2HQ, England. TEL 44-181-783-0755. FAX 44-181-783-0049. **Document type:** trade publication.
●Also available online.
Also available on CD-ROM.
Formerly: Key Note Report: Printed Circuits.

COMPUTERS — COMPUTER ASSISTED INSTRUCTION

621.381 US
TK7895.S62
MOBILE COMPUTING TECHNOLOGY. 1991. bi-m. $36 (Canada and Mexico $56; elsewhere $96). Intertec Publishing Corp. (Atlanta), 6151 Powers Ferry Rd., N.W., Atlanta, GA 30339-2491. TEL 770-955-2500. FAX 770-955-0400. Ed. Tom Parrish. adv. circ. 20,171. **Document type:** trade publication.
—Ei; UMI. **CCC.**
  Former titles: I C Card Systems and Design (ISSN 1074-6269); (until 1993): Memory Card Systems and Designs (ISSN 1055-5188)
  Description: Covers integrated circuit memory card components and systems.

P C B INTERNATIONAL; electronics made in Europe. see *ELECTRONICS*

P C B MAGAZINE. see *ELECTRONICS*

COMPUTERS — Computer Architecture

see also Computers–Computer Engineering

621.381 621.815 US
COMPUTER DESIGN AND ARCHITECTURE SERIES. 1976. irreg. price varies. Elsevier Science Inc., Box 945, New York, NY 10159-0945. TEL 212-633-3730. FAX 212-633-3680. TELEX 420643 AEP UI. (Subscr. outside the Americas to: Elsevier Science, Regional Sales Office, P.O. Box 211, 1000 AE Amsterdam, Netherlands. TEL 31-20-4853757. FAX 31-20-4853432; Subscr. in Australasia and the Far East to: Elsevier Science (Singapore) Pte Ltd, No.1 Temasek Ave., No.17-01 Millenia Tower, Singapore 039192, Singapore. TEL 65-434-3727. FAX 65-337-2230; Subscr. in Japan to: Elsevier Science Japan, 9-15 Higashi-Azabu 1-chome, Minato-ku, Tokyo 106, Japan. TEL 81-3-5561-5033. FAX 81-3-5561-5047) Ed. Edward McCluskey. **Indexed:** INSPEC. **Document type:** monographic series.
  Refereed Serial

001.64 621.815 IT
INFORMATICA OGGI E UNIX; la rivista dei sistemi aperti. 1980-1996 (Oct.). m. (11/yr.). L.61600 (foreign L.123200). Gruppo Editoriale Jackson S.p.A., Via M. Gorki 69, 20092 Cinisello B. (MI), Italy. TEL 39-2-66034229. FAX 39-2-66034290. Ed. Claudio de Falco. adv.: B&W page L.4100000, color page L.6800000; trim 210 x 275. circ. 13,211. **Document type:** trade publication.
  Formerly: Informatica Oggi (ISSN 0392-8888)
  Description: Analyzes advanced technological and architectural solutions in modern data processing. Includes articles on hardware, software, UNIX and computer-aided tools.

INTERNATIONAL JOURNAL OF COMPUTER INTEGRATED MANUFACTURING. see *BUSINESS AND ECONOMICS — Computer Applications*

621.815 US ISSN 0884-7495
QA76.9.A73 CODEN: CPAAEV
INTERNATIONAL SYMPOSIUM ON COMPUTER ARCHITECTURE. CONFERENCE PROCEEDINGS. 1973. a. (Institute of Electrical and Electronics Engineers, Inc.) I E E E Computer Society Press, 10662 Los Vaqueros Circle, Los Alamitos, CA 90720-1264. TEL 714-821-8380. FAX 714-821-4641. (Co-publisher in alternate years: Association for Computing Machinery) Ed. Cat Harris; Pub. Matt Loeb. adv. contact: Frieda Koester. **Indexed:** INSPEC. **Document type:** proceedings.
  —BLDSC (1086.745000); Ei; UMI. **CCC.**
  Formerly (until 1982): Symposium on Computer Architecture. Conference Proceedings (ISSN 0149-7111)
  Description: Covers most aspects of computer architecture.

SUANJI XUEBAO. see *COMPUTERS — Theory Of Computing*

JOURNAL OF COMPUTER SCIENCE AND TECHNOLOGY. see *COMPUTERS — Theory Of Computing*

004.2 338 CH
LING YU YI KEJI ZASHI/0 & 1 TECHNOLOGY BYTE (CHINESE EDITION). (Text in Chinese) 1981. m. NT.$1400 (foreign NT.$4780). Third Wave Publishing Corp., 19-1, Lane 231, Fu-Hsing N. Rd., Taipei, Taiwan, Republic of China. TEL 886-2-7136959. FAX 886-2-7189467. Ed. Janet Wang. adv.: color page $1800. circ. 16,000. **Document type:** consumer publication.
  Description: Covers computer architecture, computer and electronics industries and technology in Taiwan.

621.381 US ISSN 0163-5964
QA76.9.A73 CODEN: CANED2
S I G A R C H COMPUTER ARCHITECTURE NEWS. Key Title: Computer Architecture News. q. $55. Association for Computing Machinery, Special Interest Group on Computer Architecture, c/o Texas Instruments, Inc., 429 Bellerive Dr., Dallas, TX 75287. TEL 214-917-6210. Ed. Doug de Groot. adv.; bk.rev. circ. 5,000. **Indexed:** Abstr.Hum.Comp.Inter., INSPEC (1981-). **Document type:** newsletter.
  —BLDSC (3393.700000); AskIEEE; CISTI; Ei; KR SourceOne; SWETS; UnCover.

621.815 US ISSN 0163-5743
CODEN: SIGDDQ
S I G D A NEWSLETTER. q. $5. Association for Computing Machinery, Special Interest Group on Design Automation, 1515 Broadway, 17th Fl., New York, NY 10036. TEL 212-869-7440. **Indexed:** Abstr.Hum.Comp.Inter., CAD CAM Abstr., INSPEC. **Document type:** newsletter.
  —AskIEEE; CISTI; KR SourceOne; SWETS; UnCover.

T G A - REPORT: die Kennziffer-Fachzeitschrift fuer technische Gebaeudeausruestung. see *ENGINEERING — Mechanical Engineering*

COMPUTERS — Computer Assisted Instruction

see also Education–Computer Applications

C A C REPORT. (Computer Aids Corporation) see *COMPUTERS*

371.394 US ISSN 1049-9059
CODEN: CLJOEM
C A E L L JOURNAL. (Computer Assisted English Language Learning) 4/yr. $35 to non-members (foreign $45); members $25 (foreign $35); student members $15. International Society for Technology in Education, 1787 Agate St., Eugene, OR 97403-1923. TEL 541-346-4414. FAX 541-346-5890. Ed. Gertrude Abramsor. R&P contact: Jodie Rogers. adv. contact: Judy Stickney. **Document type:** academic/scholarly publication.
  —BLDSC (2947.359000); AskIEEE; KR SourceOne; SWETS. **CCC.**
  Formerly: C A L L Digest.
  Description: Focuses on the most current issues facing computer-using English language teachers.

371.394 US
C A L I C O. MONOGRAPH SERIES. 1986. irreg. price varies. Computer Assisted Language & Instruction Consortium, 014 Language Bldg., Box 90267, Duke University, Durham, NC 27708-0267. TEL 919-660-3180. FAX 919-660-3183. Ed. Frank Borchardt. adv.; charts. (back issues avail.) **Document type:** monographic series.
  Description: Brochure on journals, monographs, software, programs, and symposia offered by the consortium.

C A L I REPORT. (Center for Computer-Assisted Legal Instruction) see *LAW — Computer Applications*

C U E NEWSLETTER; serving computer-using educators internationally. (Computer Using Educators, Inc.) see *EDUCATION — Computer Applications*

371.9 621.381 US ISSN 0897-3318
CATALYST (MENLO PARK). 1981. q. $12 to individuals; institutions $18 (Canada $22; elsewhere $24) (effective 1997). Western Center for Microcomputers in Special Education, Inc., 1259 El Camino Real, Ste. 275, Menlo Park, CA 94025. TEL 415-855-8064. Ed. Sue Swezey. bk.rev. **Indexed:** ERIC. **Document type:** newsletter.
  Description: Directed to educators and administrators interested in microcomputer applications to special education and rehabilitation.

370 US ISSN 1047-2452
COMPUTER-ASSISTED COMPOSITION JOURNAL. 1986. 3/yr. $15 (foreign $19). (Methodist College) Human Technology Interface, Ink Press, 163 Wood Wedge Way, Sanford, NC 27330. TEL 919-499-9216. Ed. Lynn Veach Sadler. software rev. circ. 500.
  Description: Publishes articles on the application of the computer to writing.

COMPUTER EDUCATION; a journal for teachers (especially of 11-18 age range) interested in computers & computing. see *EDUCATION — Computer Applications*

371.394 II
COMPUTER EDUCATION. (Text in English) 1991. bi-m. Rs.580($35) K.K. Roy (Private) Ltd., 55 Gariahat Road, P.O. Box 10210, Calcutta 700 019, India. Ed. K.K. Roy. adv.; abstr.; bibl.; index. circ. 1,490.
  Description: Discusses how schools and colleges are utilizing educational computer programs and systems. Describes new education software packages, including programs in sciences, social sciences, and humanities.

370 US ISSN 8755-4615
LB1576.7
COMPUTERS AND COMPOSITION; a journal for teachers of writing. 1983. 3/yr. $45 to individuals; institutions $79.50 (effective 1997). (Michigan Technological University, Department of Humanities) Ablex Publishing Corporation, Box 5297, Greenwich, CT 06831-0504. TEL 203-661-7602. FAX 203-661-0792. E-mail: hawisher@uruc.edu; cyselfe@mtu.edu. (Co-sponsor: University of Illinois, Urbana - Champaign) Eds. Gail Hawisher, Cynthia L. Selfe. bk.rev. circ. 450. (back issues avail.) **Indexed:** C.I.J.E., Educ.Ind., INSPEC (1987-). **Document type:** academic/scholarly publication.
  —BLDSC (3394.671000); AskIEEE; KR SourceOne; UnCover.
  Description: For teachers of writing. Includes information on subjects related to computer use in composition classrooms and programs.

COMPUTERS IN EDUCATION JOURNAL. see *EDUCATION — Computer Applications*

371.394 US
DIALOG FAST TRACK.* 1993. q. Dialog Information Services, Inc., 75 Wall St., 20th Fl., New York, NY 10005-2833. **Document type:** newsletter.
  Description: Covers news, regulatory issues, and intellectual property, and helps readers use Dialog more effectively and efficiently in the workplace.

371.394 621.381 US ISSN 1061-5008
LB1028.43
EDUCATION TECHNOLOGY NEWS. 1984. bi-w. $286 (effective Sep. 1992). Business Publishers, Inc., 951 Pershing Dr., Silver Spring, MD 20910-4464. TEL 301-587-6300. FAX 301-585-9075. Ed. David Ritchie. bk.rev. (looseleaf format) **Document type:** newsletter.
  ●Also available online. Vendor(s): Information Access Co., NewsNet.
  —**CCC.**
  Formerly: Education Computer News (ISSN 0742-0250)
  Description: For teachers and those interested in the educational uses of computers in the classroom. Feature articles on applications, educational software and pertinent programs.

ELECTRONIC LEARNING. see *EDUCATION — Computer Applications*

371.394 FR ISSN 1162-6496
GENIE EDUCATIF. 1991. 6/yr. 400 F. (foreign 450 F.). E C 2, 269, rue de la Garenne, 92024 Nanterre Cedex, France. TEL 33-1-47-80-70-00. FAX 33-1-47-80-66-29. Ed. Guy Gouarderes. (back issues avail.)

COMPUTERS — COMPUTER ENGINEERING

371.394 US
HUMAN - COMPUTER INTERACTION (NORWOOD). 1982. irreg. price varies. Ablex Publishing Corporation, Box 5297, Greenwich, CT 06831-0504. TEL 203-661-7602. FAX 203-661-0792. Ed. Ben Shneiderman. **Indexed:** A.I.Abstr., Compumath, Comput.Abstr. **Document type:** academic/scholarly publication.

371.941 US
HYPERNEXUS; journal of hypermedia and multimedia studies. q. $29 to non-members (foreign $39); members $20 (foreign $30); student members $12 (foreign $22). International Society for Technology in Education, HyperSIG, 1787 Agate St., Eugene, OR 97403-1923. TEL 541-346-4414. FAX 541-346-5890. Ed. David Moursund. R&P contact: Jodie Rogers. adv. contact: Lynda Ferguson. bk.rev.; software rev. **Document type:** academic/scholarly publication.
    Description: Features articles on projects, lesson plans and theoretical issues.

I S T E UPDATE; people, events and news in education technology. (International Society for Technology in Education) see EDUCATION

INNOVATIONS IN EDUCATION AND TRAINING INTERNATIONAL. see EDUCATION — Teaching Methods And Curriculum

371.394 UK ISSN 1362-7368
INTERNATIONAL JOURNAL OF COMPUTER ALGEBRA IN MATHEMATICS EDUCATION. 1994. 4/yr. £130($234) (effective 1997). Research Information Ltd., 222 Maylands Ave., Hemel Hempstead, Herts. HP2 7TD, England. TEL 44-1442-213222. FAX 44-1442-259395. E-mail: resinf@globalnet.co.uk. Ed. John Berry. adv. contact: J. Kumar Patel. circ. 300 (paid). **Document type:** academic/scholarly publication.
    —BLDSC (4542.173900); CISTI.
    Formerly (until 1997): International Derive Journal (ISSN 1351-0789)
    Description: Publishes articles on all aspects of the use of computer algebra systems in education and training.
    Refereed Serial

INTERNATIONAL JOURNAL OF COMPUTERS FOR MATHEMATICAL LEARNING. see MATHEMATICS — Computer Applications

INTERNATIONAL JOURNAL OF COMPUTERS IN ADULT EDUCATION AND TRAINING. see EDUCATION — Computer Applications

370 UK ISSN 0266-4909
LB1028.5 CODEN: JCALEG
JOURNAL OF COMPUTER ASSISTED LEARNING. 1985. q. £168.50($307) (foreign £185) (effective 1998). Blackwell Science Ltd., Osney Mead, Oxford OX2 0EL, England. TEL 44-1865-206206. FAX 44-1865-721205. E-mail: journals.cs@blacksci.co.uk; URL: http://www.black.co.uk. Ed. R. Lewis; Pub. Allen Stevens. R&P contact: Sarah Pollard. adv. contact: Martine Cariou-Keen. bk.rev.; illus.; charts; index. circ. 505. (also avail. in microform from UMI; back issues avail.) **Indexed:** ASCA, Br.Educ.Ind., C.I.J.E., Comput.Abstr., Cont.Pg.Educ., Curr.Cont., Educ.Tech.Abstr., INSPEC (1989-), Psychol.Abstr. (1985-), SOMA, Tech.Educ.Abstr. **Document type:** academic/scholarly publication.
    —BLDSC (4963.640000); AskIEEE; Genuine Article; KR SourceOne; SWETS; UMI; UnCover. **CCC.**
    Refereed Serial

JOURNAL OF COMPUTING IN TEACHER EDUCATION. see EDUCATION — Computer Applications

JOURNAL OF EDUCATIONAL TECHNOLOGY SYSTEMS. see EDUCATION — Computer Applications

JOURNAL OF SPECIAL EDUCATION TECHNOLOGY. see EDUCATION — Special Education And Rehabilitation

371.394 004 US ISSN 1082-5754
LB1028.5
LEARNING AND LEADING WITH TECHNOLOGY. 1979. 8/yr. $65 to non-members (foreign $75); members $38 (foreign $48); student members $23 (foreign $33). International Society for Technology in Education, University of Oregon, 1787 Agate St., Eugene, OR 97403-1923. TEL 541-346-4414. FAX 541-346-5890. Ed. Anita Best. R&P contact: Jodie Rogers. adv. contact: Judy Stickney. bk.rev.; charts; illus.; index. circ. 12,000. (also avail. in microform from UMI; back issues avail.) **Indexed:** C.I.J.E., Comput.Cont., Cont.Pg.Educ., Cyb.Abstr., Educ.Ind., Educ.Tech.Abstr., ERIC, INSPEC, Microcomp.Ind., PCR2, Tech.Educ.Abstr. **Document type:** academic/scholarly publication.
    —BLDSC (5179.325893); KR SourceOne; SWETS; UMI; UnCover. **CCC.**
    Formerly (until 1995): Computing Teacher (ISSN 0278-9175)
    Description: Provides feature articles and columns in language arts, Logo, science, mathematics, telecommunications, equity and international connections for the K-12 technology-using educator.

MEDIA & METHODS; educational products, technologies & programs for schools & universities. see EDUCATION — Teaching Methods And Curriculum

RECALL. see LINGUISTICS — Computer Applications

RECALL NEWSLETTER. see LINGUISTICS — Computer Applications

RECALL SOFTWARE GUIDE (YEAR). see LINGUISTICS — Computer Applications

370.285 CN ISSN 0831-7925
S A C E BULLETIN. 2/yr. Can.$20 (outside Saskatchewan Can.$30). (Saskatchewan Association for Computers in Education) Saskatchewan Teachers' Federation, 2317 Arlington Ave., Saskatoon, SK S7J 2H8, Canada. TEL 306-373-1660. adv. contact: **Document type:** bulletin.

S I G C U E OUTLOOK. (Special Interest Group on Computer Uses in Education) see EDUCATION — Computer Applications

SOCIETY FOR APPLIED LEARNING TECHNOLOGY. NEWSLETTER. see EDUCATION — Computer Applications

SOFTWARE AND NETWORKS FOR LEARNING. see EDUCATION — Computer Applications

T H E JOURNAL. (Technological Horizons in Education) see EDUCATION — Computer Applications

TECHNOLOGY AND LEARNING; the leading magazine of electronic education. see EDUCATION — Computer Applications

COMPUTERS — Computer Engineering

see also Computers–Computer Architecture

621.39 US ISSN 1073-0516
A C M TRANSACTIONS ON COMPUTER - HUMAN INTERACTION. (Part of A C M Series on Computing Methodologies) 1994. q. $100 to non-members & institutions (effective 1997). Association for Computing Machinery, 1515 Broadway, New York, NY 10036. TEL 212-869-7440. URL: http://www.acm.org. (Subscr. to: A C M, Box 12114, Church St. Sta., New York, NY 10257; Addr. in Europe: A C M European Services Center, Ave. Marcel Thiry 204, 1200 Brussels, Belgium. TEL 32-2-774-9602. FAX 32-2-774-9690) **Document type:** academic/scholarly publication.
    —BLDSC (0578.650000); CISTI; SWETS; UnCover. **CCC.**
    Description: Reports on research and theory on computer architecture, as it affects the end user.

621.381 US
ABLEX SERIES IN SOFTWARE ENGINEERING. 1987. irreg., latest 1989. price varies. Ablex Publishing Corporation, Box 5297, Greenwich, CT 06831-0504. TEL 203-661-7602. FAX 203-661-0792. Eds. Carolyn Rovee-Collier, Lewis P. Lipsitt. **Document type:** academic/scholarly publication.

ADVANCED SERIES IN ELECTRICAL AND COMPUTER ENGINEERING. see ENGINEERING — Electrical Engineering

621.3 US ISSN 0161-3626
  CODEN: ANDIDX
ANALOG DIALOGUE; a forum for the exchange of circuits, systems, and software for real-world signal processing. 1967. q. free to institutions, libraries, and qualified technical personnel. Analog Devices, Inc., 1 Technology Way, Box 9106, Norwood, MA 02062-9106. TEL 617-461-3392. FAX 617-326-8703. TELEX 924491. E-mail: dan.sheingold@analog.com; cammy.obrien@analog.com; URL: http://www.analog.com/publications/magazines/Dialogue/dialog.html. Ed. Daniel H. Sheingold; Pub. Daniel H. Sheingold. R&P contact: Daniel H. Sheingold. adv. contact: Daniel H. Sheingold. bk.rev.; bibl.; charts; illus.; tr.lit.; circ. 100,000 (controlled). (back issues avail.) **Indexed:** INSPEC (1975-).
    —BLDSC (0890.620000); AskIEEE; KR SourceOne. **CCC.**
    Description: Contains technical articles on semiconductor devices used in analog and digital processing of electrical signals in test, measurement, communications, computer electronics and audio-video.

621.39 UK ISSN 0941-0635
APPLIED SIGNAL PROCESSING; the international journal of analog and digital signal processing. 1994. q. £172 (effective 1998). Springer-Verlag London Ltd., Sweetapple House, Catteshall Rd., Godalming, Surrey GU7 3DJ, England. TEL 44-1483-418800. FAX 44-1483-415144. (Subscr. to: Heidelberger Platz 3, 14197 Berlin, Germany. TEL 49-30-8207-0. FAX 49-30-8214091; N. American subscr. to: Springer-Verlag New York, Inc., Box 2485, Secaucus, NJ 07096. TEL 800-777-4643. FAX 201-348-4505) Eds. M. Sandler, A.C. Davies. (also avail. in microform from UMI) **Document type:** academic/scholarly publication.
    —BLDSC (1578.110000); AskIEEE; CISTI; KR SourceOne. **CCC.**

ASPHALT INSTITUTE CATALOG OF PUBLICATIONS, AUDIO VISUALS, AND COMPUTER PROGRAMS. see ENGINEERING — Civil Engineering

621.39 620 UK ISSN 0958-1499
C A D - C A M ABSTRACTS. (Computer Aided Design - Computer Aided Manufacturing) 6/yr. £65. (National Computing Centre Ltd.) Techgnosis Ltd., Blade House, Battersea Rd., Stockport, Cheshire SK3 3AE, England. TEL 44-161-442-2639. FAX 44-161-443-1162. Ed. T. Drinkall. **Document type:** abstracting/indexing.
    Formerly: C A D - C A M Profiles (ISSN 0265-1718)

C A D YU ZIDONGHUA/C A D AND AUTOMATION. see COMPUTERS — Computer Graphics

CANADIAN JOURNAL OF ELECTRICAL AND COMPUTER ENGINEERING. see ENGINEERING — Electrical Engineering

621.381 US
COMPUTER AIDED ENGINEERING (NEW YORK). 1992. irreg., vol.5, 1994. price varies. Marcel Dekker, Inc 270 Madison Ave., New York, NY 10016. TEL 212-696-9000. FAX 212-685-4540. TELEX 421419. Ed. Russell Dekker; Pub. Graham Garratt R&P contact: Julia Mulligan. **Document type:** monographic series.

621.381 US
COMPUTER ENGINEERING AND COMPUTER SCIENCE. 1990. irreg., latest 1996. price varies. Ablex Publishing Corporation, Box 5297, Greenwich, CT 06831-0504. TEL 203-661-7602. FAX 203-661-0792. Ed. George W. Zobrist. **Document type:** academic/scholarly publication.

COMPUTERS — COMPUTER ENGINEERING 2115

621.39 003 US ISSN 1063-293X
TS176 CODEN: CRAPEM
CONCURRENT ENGINEERING: RESEARCH AND APPLICATIONS. 1993. q. $245 (foreign $293) (effective 1997); $265 (foreign $320) (effective 1998). (International Society for Productivity Enhancement, Concurrent Engineering Institute) Technomic Publishing Co., Inc., 851 New Holland Ave., Box 3535, Lancaster, PA 17604. TEL 717-291-5609; 800-233-9936. FAX 717-295-45638. TELEX 230 753565 (TECHNOMIC UD). E-mail: marketing@techpub.com; URL: http://www.techpub.com. Ed. Biren Prasad. circ. 310. Indexed: ASCA, Curr.Cont., INSPEC (1993-). **Document type:** academic/scholarly publication.
—BLDSC (3405.628000); AskIEEE; CISTI; Genuine Article; KR SourceOne; SWETS. CCC.
Description: Presents interdisciplinary research on all aspects of concurrency in enterprise modeling, information processing and computing.
Refereed Serial

621.381 NE ISSN 1383-7575
CODEN: TOESED
CONCURRENT SYSTEMS ENGINEERING SERIES. 1989. 2/yr. fl.324($195) (effective 1997). I O S Press, Van Diemenstraat 94, 1013 CN Amsterdam, Netherlands. TEL 31-20-6382189. FAX 31-20-6203419. E-mail: market@iospress.nl; URL: http://www.iospress.nl/iospress. (In N. America: Box 10558, Burke, VA 22009-0558. TEL 703-323-5554. FAX 703-250-4705) (back issues avail.) **Indexed:** Eng.Ind., Zent.Math. **Document type:** monographic series, academic/scholarly publication.
—CISTI; Ei.
Formerly (until vol.46, 1995): Transputer and Occam Engineering Series (ISSN 0925-4986)
Description: Monographic studies of advanced topics in high performance computing and communications.
Refereed Serial

621.39 US ISSN 0898-901X
QA76.8.D43
DIGITAL TECHNICAL JOURNAL. 1985. q. $40 (foreign $60). Digital Equipment Corporation, Ak02-3-B3, 50 Nagog Park, Acton, MA 01720-9843. TEL 508-264-7549. FAX 508-264-7493. E-mail: dtj@digital.com; URL: http://www.digital.com/info/dtj. Ed. Don Borst. charts; illus.; pat.; circ. 15,000 (controlled). (back issues avail.) **Indexed:** INSPEC (1988-). **Document type:** consumer publication, trade publication.
—BLDSC (3588.397540); AskIEEE; CISTI; Ei; KR SourceOne; Linda Hall; UnCover.
Description: Provides engineers and educators with practical insights into the application of scientific and engineering principles to the development of new computer technologies and products.
Refereed Serial

E-LETTER ON SYSTEMS, CONTROL, & SIGNAL PROCESSING. see COMPUTERS — Computer Systems

621.381 US ISSN 1040-3272
QA76.6 CODEN: EYPRE4
EMBEDDED SYSTEMS PROGRAMMING. 1988. m. $55 (Canada & Mexico $61; elsewhere $70). Miller Freeman, Inc. (Subsidiary of: United Newspapers), 600 Harrison St., San Francisco, CA 94107. TEL 415-905-2200. FAX 415-905-2232. (Subscr. to: Box 420046, Palm Court, FL 32142-0046. TEL 800-829-5537. FAX 904-446-2774) Ed. Tyler Sperry. circ. 30,000. **Indexed:** Comput.Ind., INSPEC (1992-). **Document type:** trade publication.
—BLDSC (3733.066000); AskIEEE; CISTI; KR SourceOne; SWETS; UMI; UnCover. CCC.
Description: Devoted to embedded applications - microprocessors wired into the electronics of a host of varied thingamajigs.

EMPIRICAL SOFTWARE ENGINEERING. see COMPUTERS — Software

621.39 NE ISSN 0924-5375
ENGINEERING APPLICATIONS OF SYSTEMS RELIABILITY AND RISK ANALYSIS. (Text in English) 1984. irreg. price varies. Kluwer Academic Publishers, Postbus 17, 3300 AA Dordrecht, Netherlands. TEL 31-78-6392392. FAX 31-78-6392254. TELEX 29245 KAPG NL. E-mail: services@wkap.nl; URL: http://www.wkap.nl. (Dist. by: Kluwer Academic Publishers Group, P.O. Box 322, 3300 AA Dordrecht, Netherlands. TEL 31-78-6392392. FAX 31-78-6546474; N. America dist. addr.: Box 358, Accord Sta., Hingham, MA 02018-0358. TEL 617-871-6600. FAX 617-871-6528) **Document type:** monographic series.
Refereed Serial

FINITE ELEMENTS IN ANALYSIS AND DESIGN; the international journal of applied finite elements and computer-aided engineering. see ENGINEERING — Computer Applications

628.281 US ISSN 1066-1395
TK7874.75 CODEN: PGVLEB
GREAT LAKES SYMPOSIUM ON V S L I. PROCEEDINGS. 1991. a. price varies. (Institute of Electrical and Electronics Engineers, Inc.) I E E E Computer Society Press, 10662 Los Vaqueros Circle, Los Alamitos, CA 90720-1264. TEL 714-821-8380. FAX 714-821-4641. **Document type:** proceedings.
—Ei. CCC.
Description: Showcases the research and development efforts in the Great Lakes region in the V L S I design field.

621.381 US ISSN 0740-7475
TK7885.A1
I E E E DESIGN & TEST OF COMPUTERS. 1984. q. $230 to non-members (effective 1996). (Institute of Electrical and Electronics Engineers, Inc.) I E E E Computer Society, 10662 Los Vaqueros Circle, Box 3014, Los Alamitos, CA 90720-1264. TEL 714-821-8380; 800-678-4333. E-mail: customer.service@ieee.org; webmaster@computer.org; URL: http://computer.org/pubs/d&t/d&t.htm. (And 345 E. 47th St., New York, NY 10017; Subscr. to: 445 Hoes Lane, Piscataway, NJ 08854) Ed. Ken Wagner. adv.: B&W page $1650, color page $2750; trim 8 1/8 x 10 7/8; adv. contact: Marian Tibayan. bk.rev.; bibl.; charts; illus.; tr.lit. circ. 6,046. (also avail. in microform; reprint service avail.) **Indexed:** Abstr.Hum.Comp.Inter., ASCA, Compumath, Comput.Cont., Comput.Dtbs., Curr.Cont., Cyb.Abstr., INSPEC, Int.Aerosp.Abstr., Oper.Res.Manage.Sci., Qual.Contr.Appl.Stat. **Document type:** trade publication.
●Also available online.
—BLDSC (4362.917500); AskIEEE; CISTI; Ei; Genuine Article; KR SourceOne; Linda Hall; SWETS; UMI; UnCover. CCC.
Description: Covers the methods, practical experience, research ideas and products that assist in the design and testing of assemblies and systems.
Refereed Serial

621.381 001.642 US ISSN 1094-7167
QA76.76.E95 CODEN: IEEXE7
I E E E INTELLIGENT SYSTEMS MAGAZINE. 1986. bi-m. $270 to non-members (effective 1996). (Institute of Electrical and Electronics Engineers, Inc.) I E E E Computer Society Press, 10662 Los Vaqueros Circle, Box 3014, Los Alamitos, CA 90720-1264. TEL 714-821-8380; 800-678-4333. FAX 714-821-4641. E-mail: customer.service@ieee.org;ah34; URL: http://computer.org/pubs/expert/expert.htm. Ed. Steve Cross. adv.: B&W page $2150, color page $3250; adv. contact: Frieda Koester. circ. 10,110. (also avail. in microform from EEE) **Indexed:** A.I.Abstr. (until 1992), Abstr.Hum.Comp.Inter., ASCA, CAD CAM Abstr. (until 1992), Compumath, Comput.Dtbs., Curr.Cont., INSPEC (1986-), Oper.Res.Manage.Sci., Qual.Contr.Appl.Stat., SSCI. **Document type:** proceedings.
●Also available online.
—BLDSC (4362.928000); AskIEEE; CASDDS; CISTI; Ei; Genuine Article; KR SourceOne; Linda Hall; SWETS; UMI; UnCover. CCC.
Formerly: I E E E Expert (ISSN 0885-9000)
Description: Covers knowledge engineering, database and data engineering, planning and problem solving, natural language processing, medical and industrial applications.

621.281 US ISSN 1063-6404
TK7888.4
I E E E INTERNATIONAL CONFERENCE ON COMPUTER DESIGN. V L S I IN COMPUTERS & PROCESSORS. PROCEEDINGS. Short title: I C C D. 1983. a. (Institute of Electrical and Electronics Engineers, Inc.) I E E E Computer Society Press, 10662 Los Vaqueros Circle, Los Alamitos, CA 90720-1264. TEL 714-821-8380. FAX 714-821-4641. Ed. Cat Harris; Pub. Matt Loeb. adv. contact: Frieda Koester. **Indexed:** CAD CAM Abstr. **Document type:** proceedings.
—CCC.
Formerly (until 1986): I E E E International Conference on Computer Design. V L S I in Computers. Proceedings; Which supersedes in part (1980-1982): I E E E International Conference on Circuits and Computers. I C C C Proceedings.
Description: Details all aspects of design and implementation of VLSI computer and processor systems.

621.381 II ISSN 0971-0469
TK7885.A1
INSTITUTION OF ENGINEERS (INDIA). COMPUTER ENGINEERING DIVISION. JOURNAL. (Text in English) 1984. s-a. Rs.60($20) Institution of Engineers (India), Computer Engineering Division, 8 Gokhale Rd., Calcutta 700 020, India. TEL 91-33-2238334. FAX 91-33-2238345. TELEX 0217885 IEIC-IN. Ed. S.P. Misra. adv.; charts; illus.; index. circ. 2,500. **Document type:** academic/scholarly publication.
—BLDSC (4794.017100); CISTI; Ei.
Refereed Serial

INSTYTUT AUTOMATYKI SYSTEMOW ENERGETYCZNYCH. PRACE. see ENGINEERING — Electrical Engineering

621.36 US ISSN 1069-2509
TA345 CODEN: ICAEEI
INTEGRATED COMPUTER-AIDED ENGINEERING. 1993. q. $220 (Canada & Mexico $260; elsewhere $286) (effective 1997). John Wiley & Sons, Inc., Journals, 605 Third Ave., New York, NY 10158. TEL 212-850-6645. FAX 212-850-6021. URL: http://www.wiley.co.uk. (Subscr. outside the Americas to: John Wiley & Sons Ltd., Baffins Ln., Chichester, W. Sussex PO19 1UD, England. TEL 44-1243-779777. FAX 44-1243-776128) Ed. Hojjat Adeli. adv.: B&W page £640, color page £1515; trim 279 x 210. circ. 400. (also avail. in microform from UMI; back issues avail.) **Indexed:** ASCA, Compumath, Curr.Cont. **Document type:** academic/scholarly publication.
—BLDSC (4531.810500); AskIEEE; CISTI; Genuine Article; KR SourceOne; SWETS. CCC.
Description: Seeks to integrate leading-edge and emerging computer technologies and innovative solutions of engineering problems in an interdisciplinary format. Covers such areas as biologically inspired computing, cognitive machine engineering, concurrent engineering, data engineering, distributed computing, fuzzy systems, genetic algorithms, intelligent and adaptive systems, knowledge engineering, machine learning, mechatronics, neurocomputing, object-oriented systems, parallel processing, symbolic processing, and virtual reality.
Refereed Serial

621.381 US ISSN 1063-6382
QA76.9.D3
INTERNATIONAL CONFERENCE ON DATA ENGINEERING (PROCEEDINGS). 1984. a. price varies. (Institute of Electrical and Electronics Engineers, Inc.) I E E E Computer Society Press, 10662 Los Vaqueros Circle, Los Alamitos, CA 90720-1264. TEL 714-821-8380. FAX 714-821-4641. Ed. Cat Harris; Pub. Matt Loeb. adv. contact: Frieda Koester. **Document type:** proceedings.
—Ei. CCC.
Description: Covers applications and issues in the field of data engineering.

INTERNATIONAL JOURNAL OF SPEECH TECHNOLOGY. see LINGUISTICS — Computer Applications

ULRICH'S INTERNATIONAL PERIODICALS DIRECTORY 1998

COMPUTERS — COMPUTER GAMES

621.3 US ISSN 0195-623X
QA9.45 CODEN: PSMLDF
INTERNATIONAL SYMPOSIUM ON MULTIPLE-VALUED LOGIC. PROCEEDINGS. 1971. a. (Institute of Electrical and Electronics Engineers, Inc.) I E E E Computer Society Press, 10662 Los Vaqueros Circle, Los Alamitos, CA 90720-1264. TEL 714-821-8380. FAX 714-821-4641. Ed. Cat Harris; Pub. Matt Loeb. adv. contact: Frieda Koester. **Indexed:** INSPEC. **Document type:** proceedings.
—BLDSC (6846.796000); Ei; UMI. **CCC.**
Formerly (until 1972): Symposium on the Theory and Applications of Multiple-Valued Logic Design. Conference Record.
Description: Information on multiple-valued logic, including algebra.

628.281 US
INTERNATIONAL SYMPOSIUM ON V L S I DESIGN. PROCEEDINGS. 1988. a. price varies. (Institute of Electrical and Electronics Engineers, Inc.) I E E E Computer Society Press, 10662 Los Vaqueros Circle, Los Alamitos, CA 90720-1264. TEL 714-821-8380. FAX 714-821-4641. Ed. Cat Harris; Pub. Matt Loeb. adv. contact: Frieda Koester. **Document type:** proceedings.
Description: Discusses the latest advances and recent technological opportunities in electronic design automation for V L S I designers, developers and users.

INVERSE PROBLEMS; inverse problems, inverse methods and computerized inversion of data. see *MATHEMATICS — Computer Applications*

621.381 CC ISSN 1000-3428
TK7885.A1 CODEN: JISGEV
JISUANJI GONGCHENG/COMPUTER ENGINEERING. (Text in Chinese) bi-m. $5. Shanghai Jisuanji Xuehui - Shanghai Computer Society, P.O. Box 800-209, Shanghai 201800, People's Republic of China. TEL 9528822. FAX 9529731. (Co-sponsor: Huadong Jisuanji Yanjiusuo - East China Research Institute of Computer Technology) Ed. Pufan Yu. adv. contact: Lieshen Diao. circ. 10,000. **Document type:** academic/scholarly publication.
Description: Covers AI theories, computer architecture, software development and applications, CAD technology, computer graphics and computer network.

621.381 CC ISSN 1000-1239
JISUANJI YANJIU YU FAZHAN/COMPUTER RESEARCH AND DEVELOPMENT. (Text in Chinese) 1978. m. $140.40. (Chinese Academy of Sciences, Institute of Computer Science) Science Press, Marketing and Sales Department, 16 Donghuangchenggen North St., Beijing 100717, People's Republic of China. TEL 86-1-4010642. FAX 86-1-4019810. adv. circ. 11,000. **Document type:** academic/scholarly publication.
Description: Covers computer science theory, study of hardware and software (including applied software), computer design and implementation, networking, data base systems, Chinese character processing, and image display. Emphasis is on applications.
Refereed Serial

THE KLUWER INTERNATIONAL SERIES IN SOFTWARE ENGINEERING. see *COMPUTERS — Software*

LABORATORY AUTOMATION AND INFORMATION MANAGEMENT. see *SCIENCES: COMPREHENSIVE WORKS — Computer Applications*

621.39 005.1 NE ISSN 1381-1142
LOOP TRANSFORMATIONS FOR RESTRUCTURING COMPILERS. (Text in English) 1993. irreg. price varies. Kluwer Academic Publishers, Postbus 17, 3300 AA Dordrecht, Netherlands. TEL 31-78-6392392. FAX 31-78-6392254. E-mail: services@wkap.nl; URL: http://www.wkap.nl. (Dist. by: Kluwer Academic Publishers Group, P.O. Box 322, 3300 AH Dordrecht, Netherlands. TEL 31-78-6392392. FAX 31-78-6546474; N. America dist. addr.: Box 358, Accord Sta., Hingham, MA 02018-0358. TEL 617-871-6600. FAX 617-871-6528) **Document type:** monographic series.
Refereed Serial

621.39 GW ISSN 0946-7076
CODEN: MCTCEF
▼**MICROSYSTEM TECHNOLOGIES;** sensors, actuators, systems integration. Online edition (GW ISSN 1432-1858) (Text in English, German) 1995. q. DM.475.60 (foreign DM.479.20) (effective 1998). Springer-Verlag, Heidelberger Platz 3, 14197 Berlin, Germany. TEL 49-30-82787-0.
FAX 49-30-82787448. E-mail: subscriptions@springer.de; URL: http://link.springer.de/link/service/journals/00542/index.htm. (Subscr. in N. America to: Journal Fulfillment Services, Meadowlands Pkwy., Secaucus, NJ 07094. TEL 212-460-1500. FAX 212-473-6272) Ed. A. Schubert. (also avail. in microform from UMI; reprint service avail.) **Document type:** academic/scholarly publication.
●Also available online.
—BLDSC (5760.840000); AskIEEE; KR SourceOne; SWETS. **CCC.**
Description: Deals with the development and production of miniaturized systems in information technology, telecommunications, medical, biotechnological, automotive, and environmental applications.
Refereed Serial

REAL-TIME ENGINEERING; computing with a deadline. see *COMPUTERS — Computer Networks*

621.39 004 NE ISSN 1385-3139
▼**RELIABLE COMPUTING.** (Text in English) 1996. q. fl.460 to institutions; $236 to institutions in U.S. (effective 1998). Kluwer Academic Publishers, Postbus 17, 3300 AA Dordrecht, Netherlands. TEL 31-78-6392392. FAX 31-78-6392254. E-mail: services@wkap.nl; URL: http://www.wkap.nl. (Dist. by: Kluwer Academic Publishers Group, P.O. Box 322, 3300 AH Dordrecht, Netherlands. TEL 31-78-6392392. FAX 31-78-6546474; N. America dist. addr.: Box 358, Accord Sta., Hingham, MA 02018-0358. TEL 617-871-6600. FAX 617-871-6528) (back issues avail.) **Document type:** academic/scholarly publication.
Refereed Serial

S I G A C T NEWS. (Special Interest Group on Automata and Computability Theory) see *COMPUTERS — Automation*

001.64 621.381 US ISSN 0163-5999
QA76.9.E94 CODEN: PEREDN
S I G M E T R I C S PERFORMANCE EVALUATION REVIEW. 1970. q. $25 to non-members; members $20. Association for Computing Machinery, Special Interest Group on Measurement and Evaluation, 1515 Broadway, 17th Fl., New York, NY 10036. TEL 212-869-7440. FAX 212-302-5826. Ed. Blaine D. Gaither. adv. circ. 2,400. **Indexed:** Comput.Cont., Comput.Lit.Ind., INSPEC (1980-).
—BLDSC (6423.780000); AskIEEE; CISTI; Ei; KR SourceOne; Linda Hall; SWETS; UnCover.

621.381 SI
STUDIES IN JOSEPHSON SUPERCOMPUTERS. (Text in English) 1991. irreg., vol.3, 1992. price varies. World Scientific Publishing Co. Pte. Ltd., Farrer Rd., P.O. Box 128, Singapore 9128, Singapore. TEL 65-3825663. FAX 65-3825929. TELEX RS 28561 WSPC. (UK addr.: 73 Lynton Mead, Totteridge, London N20 8DH, England. TEL 44-181-446-2461; US addr.: 1060 Main St., River Edge, NJ 07661. TEL 800-227-7562) **Document type:** monographic series.

SUPERCOMPUTER. see *COMPUTERS — Cybernetics*

SUPERCOMPUTER EUROPEAN WATCH. see *COMPUTERS — Cybernetics*

621.381 US ISSN 0272-5428
QA268.5 CODEN: ASFPDV
SYMPOSIUM ON FOUNDATIONS OF COMPUTER SCIENCE. PROCEEDINGS. 1960. a. price varies. (Institute of Electrical and Electronics Engineers, Inc.) I E E E Computer Society Press, 10662 Los Vaqueros Circle, Los Alamitos, CA 90720-1264. TEL 714-821-8380. FAX 714-821-4641. **Document type:** proceedings.
—BLDSC (1534.949000); Ei; UMI. **CCC.**
Former titles (until 1974): Annual Symposium on Switching and Automata Theory. Proceedings (ISSN 0272-4847); Symposium on Switching and Automata Theory; Switching and Automata Theory Conference. Record (ISSN 0082-0490); (until 1965): Symposium on Switching Circuit Theory and Logical Design.
Description: Contains papers presented at the symposium. Subjects include computational geometry, logistics, algorithms, circuits and graph problems. May occasionally contain information on automata theory.

TEST & MEASUREMENT EUROPE. see *ENGINEERING — Electrical Engineering*

TEST & MEASUREMENT WORLD. see *ENGINEERING — Electrical Engineering*

TEST & MEASUREMENT WORLD BUYER'S GUIDE. see *ENGINEERING — Electrical Engineering*

UNIVERSITY OF NEWCASTLE. DEPARTMENT OF ELECTRICAL AND COMPUTER ENGINEERING. TECHNICAL REPORT EE. see *ENGINEERING — Electrical Engineering*

628.281 NE ISSN 1065-514X
CODEN: VLDEEZ
V L S I DESIGN. (Very Large Scale Integration); an international journal of custom-chip design, simulation and testing. 1993. q. $118 (effective 1998). Gordon and Breach - Harwood Academic, Amsteldisk 166, 1st Fl., 1079 LH Amsterdam, Netherlands. URL: http://www.gbhap.com/VLSI_Design. (Subscr. to: International Publishers Distributor, Box 32160, Newark, NJ 07102. TEL 800-545-8398. FAX 215-750-6343) Ed. George W. Zobrist. (also avail. in microform) **Indexed:** ASCA, Curr.Cont. **Document type:** academic/scholarly publication.
●Also available online.
Also available on CD-ROM.
—BLDSC (9246.079800); AskIEEE; KR SourceOne.

XING DIANZI KEJI/MICRO ELECTRONICS. see *ELECTRONICS*

COMPUTERS — Computer Games

A P C T NEWS BULLETIN. (American Postal Chess Tournaments) see *SPORTS AND GAMES*

794.8 BL ISSN 0104-1630
ACAO GAMES. (Special issue avail.: Computer Player) 1991. m. Editora Azul, S.A., Av. Nacoes Unidas, 5777, 05479-900 Sao Paulo SP, Brazil. TEL 55-11-816-7866. FAX 55-11-8139115. E-mail: benjamin.gocalves@email.abril.br.com. Ed. Carlos C. Arruda. R&P contact: Benjamin Goncalvez. TEL 55-11-8673304. adv.: color page $7000; trim 227 x 299; adv. contact: Enio Vergeiro. charts; illus.; circ. 38,361 (paid). **Document type:** consumer publication.
Formerly: Acao.
Description: Covers the latest developments in the video games world, with news and articles on tips and strategies for all major systems, including PC and arcade games

794.8 GW ISSN 0946-6339
AMIGA GAMES. 1992. m. DM.79 (CD-ROM DM.139) (effective 1996). Computec Verlag, Isarstr. 32-34, 90451 Nuernberg, Germany. TEL 49-911-96832-0. FAX 49-911-6426333. Ed. Christian Geltenpoth. adv. contact: Thorsten Szameitat. circ. 43,501. **Document type:** consumer publication.
●Also available on CD-ROM.

794.8 GW
AMIGA JOKER. m. DM.63 (foreign DM.75). Joker Verlag, Bretonischer Ring 2, 85630 Grasbrunn, Germany. TEL 49-89-463700.
FAX 49-89-4604977. Ed. Michael Labiner; Pub. Michael Labiner. adv. contact: Brigitta Labiner. circ. 100,874. **Document type:** consumer publication.

COMPUTERS — COMPUTER GAMES

794   IT   ISSN 1121-1997
AMIGA MAGAZINE. 1988. 11/yr. L.107800 (foreign L.215600). Gruppo Editoriale Jackson S.p.A., Via M. Gorki 69, 20092 Cinisello B. (MI), Italy. TEL 39-2-660341. FAX 39-2-66034238. Ed. Pierantonio Palerma. adv.: B&W page L.3100000, color page L.4100000; 210 x 280. circ. 9,000. **Document type:** trade publication.
     Description: Covers computer games for Amiga users.

794   UK
THE AMIGA ONE. m. £47.40 (foreign £49) (effective 1996). E M A P - Images, Priory Ct., 30-32 Farringdon Ln., London EC1R 3AU, England. TEL 44-171-972-9700. FAX 44-171-972-6710. (Subscr. to: Tower Publishing Services Ltd., Tower House, Sovereign Park, Lathkill St., Market Harborough, Leics. LE16 9EF, England. TEL 44-1858-468811. FAX 44-1858-432164) circ. 52,476 (paid). **Document type:** consumer publication.
     Former titles: One for S T Games (ISSN 0962-2888); One (ISSN 0955-4084)

794.8   GW   ISSN 0942-8801
AMIGA PLUS. m. DM.101 (effective 1996). I C P - Innovativ Presse GmbH, Wendelstinstr. 3, 85591 Vaterstetten, Germany. TEL 49-8106-33954. FAX 49-8106-34238. Ed. Horst Brandl. adv. contact: Marie-Jeanne Jaminon-Brandl. circ. 45,000 (paid). **Document type:** consumer publication.

794.8   GW   ISSN 0949-6750
AMIGA PLUS C D - R O M. bi-m. DM.118.80 (effective 1996). I C P - Innovativ Presse GmbH, Wendelstinstr. 3, 85591 Vaterstetten, Germany. TEL 49-8106-33954. FAX 49-8106-34238. Ed. Horst Brandl. adv. contact: Marie-Jeanne Jaminon-Brandl. circ. 20,000 (paid). **Document type:** consumer publication.
     ●Available only on CD-ROM.

794   US   ISSN 1043-9064
ATARIAN.* 1989. bi-m. Atari Explorer Publications Corporation, 166 Baypointe Pkwy., San Jose, CA 95134-1621. Ed. David H. Ahl. circ. 100,000.
     Description: Provides information on Atari video games. Includes reviews of 8-10 new games with strategy tips for playing several games.

794   SW   ISSN 1102-2280
ATTACK; Mac, PC, Amiga, Atari, Konsoler. 1991. bi-m. SEK 232. C W - Communications AB, Soedra Hamnvaagen 22, S-115 41 Stockholm, Sweden. TEL 46-8-665-1037. FAX 46-8-665-3132. adv.: B&W page SEK 10500, color page SEK 13500; trim 185 x 265. circ. 25,000.

794.1   UK
CHESS COMPUTER WORLD. q. $20. Bryan Whitby, Ed. & Pub., 16 Manse Field Rd., Kingsley, Warrington, Ches. WA6 8BZ, England. adv.
     Description: Provides players with independent information about computerized chess. Contains articles, results, games and assessment of computer playing strength.

794.8   US
COMING SOON MAGAZINE. 1994. m. 130 Prim Rd., Ste. 211, Colchester, VT 05446. E-mail: t15@csoon.com; frederick@csoon.com; URL: http://www.csoon.com. Ed. Trevor Bennicke.
     ●Available only online.

794.8   US
COMPUTER & NET PLAYER. 1994. m. Air Age Publishing, 100 East Ridge, Ridgefield, CT 06877. TEL 203-431-9000. FAX 203-431-3000. **Document type:** consumer publication.
     Formerly: Computer Player (ISSN 1077-3967)

794   UK   ISSN 0261-3697
COMPUTER & VIDEO GAMES. Short title: C & V Games. 1981. m. £34 (foreign £48) (effective 1996). E M A P - Images, Priory Ct., 30-32 Farringdon Ln., London EC1R 3AU, England. TEL 44-171-972-6700. FAX 44-171-972-6710. (Subscr. to: Tower Publishing Services Ltd., Tower House, Sovereign Park, Lathkill St., Market Harborough, Leics. LE16 9EF, England. TEL 44-1858-468811. FAX 44-1858-432164) Ed. Paul Rand. adv.; illus.; circ. 104,000 (paid).
     —CCC.

794.1   UK
COMPUTER CHESS NEWS SHEET. 1985. bi-m. £18 (N. America £24). Eric Hallsworth, Ed. & Pub., The Red House, 46 High St., Wilburton, Cambs. CB7, England. E-mail: ERIC@elh <hess.demon.co.uk. adv. contact: Eric Hallsworth. circ. 600. **Document type:** consumer publication.
     Description: Provides a survey of the chess computer scene with emphasis on realistic assessments and comparisons of the different playing strengths of many machines; includes computer results, gradings and games.

794 338   US   ISSN 0890-2143
COMPUTER ENTERTAINER.* 1982. m. $35. Computer Entertainer and Video Game Update, 12115 Magnolia Blvd., Ste. 189, N. Hollywood, CA 91607-2609. TEL 818-761-1561. FAX 818-904-3682. Ed. Celeste Dolan. bk.rev. circ. 10,000.
     Formerly: Video Game Update and Computer Entertainer.
     Description: For computer and video game enthusiasts. Features articles on adventure, educational and quiz games, program descriptions.

794.8   US   ISSN 1069-4102
COMPUTER ENTERTAINMENT NEWS.* 1993. m. C E N Publishing, P.O. Box 20508, Oakland, CA 94620. TEL 510-601-9275. FAX 510-658-3757.

794   US   ISSN 1062-113X
COMPUTER GAME REVIEW. m. $36.95. Sendai Publishing Group, 1920 Highland Ave., Ste. 222, Lombard, IL 60148. TEL 708-916-7222. FAX 708-916-7227. adv. **Document type:** consumer publication.
     Incorporates: Super N E S Buyers Guide (ISSN 1063-8342); Which incorporated (in 1991): Super Gaming (ISSN 1060-4685)
     Description: Features the latest computer games. Includes previews, reviews, and tips for all game areas.

794.8   US   ISSN 0744-6667
GV1469.15
COMPUTER GAMING WORLD. 1981. 12/yr. $28. Ziff-Davis Publishing Co. (San Francisco), 135 Main St., San Francisco, CA 94105. TEL 415-357-4900. FAX 415-357-4977. E-mail: 76703,622@compuserve.com; URL: http://www.zdnet.com/~gaming. (Subscr. to: Box 57167, Boulder, CO 80322-7167) Ed. Johnny Wilson; Pub. Dale Strang. adv. contact: Lee Uniacke. circ. 175,000. **Document type:** consumer publication.
     ●Also available online. Vendor(s): Information Access Co.
     —CCC.
     Description: Articles on the latest developments in computer entertainment; reviews on computer hardware from a gamer's perspective.

794   GW   ISSN 0176-2400
COMPUTER-SCHACH UND -SPIELE. 1983. 6/yr. DM.66. Verlag Ernst Voegel GmbH, Postfach 1000, 93491 Stamsried, Germany. TEL 49-946694000. FAX 49-9466-1276. Eds. Frederic Friedel, Dieter Steinwender. adv.; bk.rev. circ. 7,000. **Document type:** consumer publication.
     Description: News about computer chess and other computer games.

794   GW   ISSN 0944-1743
COMPUTER-SPIELE PER POST; das Fachblatt fuer Computer- und Postspielfreunde. 1987. m. DM.4.20 (foreign DM.7.20). Verlag Computer-Spiele per Post, Alfred-Bucherer-Str. 63, 53115 Bonn, Germany. TEL 49-228-621392. FAX 49-228-621332. E-mail: h.topf@cspp.com. Ed. Harald Topf. adv. circ. 250. (back issues avail.) **Document type:** consumer publication.
     Description: Magazine for students and adults interested in playing games by mail and computer.

794.1   NE
COMPUTERSCHAAK. 1981. 6/yr. fl.44.50. Computer Chess Association, Postbus 22739, 1100 DE Amsterdam, Netherlands. TEL 31-20-6963953. FAX 31-20-6963953. (Subscr. to: C S V N, Lodewyek van Deyssellhoue 4, 3438 HS Nieuwegein, Netherlands) Ed. Minze bij de Weg. circ. 1,100.
     Description: Contains articles, chess games and problems.

CONNOTATIONS (PHOENIX); the quarterly science fiction, fantasy and convention magazine. see LITERATURE — Science Fiction, Fantasy, Horror

794.8   JA
DENGEKI COMIC GAO. (Text in Japanese) 1993. m. Shufunotomo Co., Ltd., 2-9 Kanda Surugadai, Chiyoda-ku, Tokyo 101, Japan. TEL 81-3-3294-1137. FAX 81-3-3291-5093. Ed. Fujio Mano. circ. 300,000. **Document type:** consumer publication.
     Description: A computer-game entertainment magazine for media conscious youngsters. Features comics popular with boys in their mid-teens.

794.8   JA
DENGEKI MEGA DRIVE. (Text in Japanese) 1993. bi-m. Shufunotomo Co., Ltd., 2-9 Kanda Surugadai, Chiyoda-ku, Tokyo 101, Japan. TEL 81-3-3294-1137. FAX 81-3-3291-5093. Ed. Fujio Mano. circ. 180,000. **Document type:** consumer publication.
     Description: A computer-game magazine published specifically for users of Mega Drive.

794.8   JA
DENGEKI-OH. (Text in Japanese) 1993. m. Shufunotomo Co., Ltd., 2-9 Kanda Surugadai, Chiyoda-ku, Tokyo 101, Japan. TEL 81-3-3294-1137. FAX 81-3-3291-5093. Ed. Fujio Mano. circ. 300,000. **Document type:** consumer publication.
     Description: A computer-game magazine aimed at teenagers. Introduces new game software, along with tips and "secret" techniques for enhancing the game.

794.8   JA
DENGEKI P C ENGINE. (Text in Japanese) 1993. m. Shufunotomo Co., Ltd., 2-9 Kanda Surugadai, Chiyoda-ku, Tokyo 101, Japan. TEL 81-3-3294-1137. FAX 81-3-3291-5093. Ed. Fujio Mano. circ. 220,000. **Document type:** consumer publication.
     Description: A computer-game magazine published specifically for users of P C Engine.

794.8   JA
DENGEKI SUPER FAMICOM. (Text in Japanese) 1993. bi-w. Shufunotomo Co., Ltd., 2-9 Kanda Surugadai, Chiyoda-ku, Tokyo 101, Japan. TEL 81-3-3294-1137. FAX 81-3-3291-5093. Ed. Fujio Mano. circ. 400,000. **Document type:** consumer publication.
     Description: A computer-game magazine aimed at teenagers. Published specifically for users of Super Famicom.

DIGITAL DINER. see COMMUNICATIONS — Computer Applications

794   US   ISSN 1074-1356
ELECTRONIC ENTERTAINMENT; the entertainment resource for the interactive age. 1988. m. $24.95. Infotainment World, Inc., 951 Mariner's Island Blvd., Ste. 700, San Mateo, CA 94404. Ed. Gina Smith. adv.: B&W page $3995, color page $5115; trim 8 x 10 3/4; adv. contact: John Seiling. **Document type:** consumer publication.
     —CCC.
     Former titles (until 1994): P C Games (ISSN 1042-2943); (until 1989): P C Resource's P C Games (ISSN 1042-1351)
     Description: Gives an inside look at hardware, multimedia titles and games in the market.

794   US   ISSN 1063-8326
GV1469.15
ELECTRONIC GAMES. 1992. bi-m. $24.95 (foreign $100). Decker Publications (Subsidiary of: Sendai Communications), 1920 Highland Ave., Ste. 222, Lombard, IL 60148. TEL 708-916-7222. Ed. Marc Camron. adv.; software rev.; circ. 250,000 (paid).

794   US   ISSN 1058-918X
ELECTRONIC GAMING MONTHLY. 1986. m. $23.95; newsstand price: $4.99. Sendai Publishing Group, 1920 Highland Ave., Ste. 222, Lombard, IL 60148. TEL 708-916-7222. FAX 708-916-7227. Ed. Ed Semrad. adv. **Document type:** consumer publication.
     —CCC.
     Description: Covers all games and game systems.

794.8 004.692
▼**EPLAY.** 1997. bi-m. newsstand price: $4.95. P C Press Inc., 249 E. Friendly Ave., Greensboro, NC 27401. TEL 910-272-0083. **Document type:** consumer publication.
     Description: Covers latest information on games and gaming services available through the Internet.

COMPUTERS — COMPUTER GAMES

EUROPE-ECHECS. see *SPORTS AND GAMES*

794.8   IS   ISSN 0792-9145
FRICK 2000. (Text in Hebrew) 1992. m. $35. Etzb'oni Publishing House, P.O. Box 28110, Tel Aviv 61280, Israel. FAX 972-3-5373906. Ed. Rami Shir. circ. 15,000.

794.8   US   ISSN 0183-5181
FULL THROTTLE. 1975. 7/yr. $29. Cobb Group, Inc., Box 35160, Louisville, KY 40232-9719. TEL 502-496-3200. FAX 502-491-8050. **Document type:** consumer publication.
Description: Offers users of Microsoft Flight Simulator tips on maximizing use of the software and advice on peripheral devices.

794.8   US   ISSN 1073-922X
GAME DEVELOPER. 1994. bi-m. $34.95 (Canada & Mexico $44.95; elsewhere $54.95) (effective 1996). Miller Freeman, Inc. (Subsidiary of: United News & Media), 600 Harrison St., San Francisco, CA 94107. TEL 415-905-2588. FAX 415-905-2165. URL: http://www.mfi.com/gdnag. (Subscr. to: Box 8024, Boulder, CO 80306-8024. TEL 800-334-8152. FAX 619-745-0685) Ed. Alex Dunne; Pub. Veronica Costanza. adv.: B&W page $2495; trim 8 x 10 7/8; adv. contact: Steve Nikkola. bk.rev.; software rev.; charts; illus.; tr.lit. circ. 20,000. (back issues avail.) **Document type:** trade publication.
●Also available online.
—KR SourceOne.
Description: Covers all areas of game development from music to graphics to team management. Aimed at game developers, designers and programmers.

794   US   ISSN 1067-6392
GAME INFORMER MAGAZINE. 1991. m. $19.98 (effective 1996); newsstand price: $3.95. Sunrise Publications, Inc., 10120 W. 76th St., Eden Prairie, MN 55344-3728. TEL 612-946-7274. FAX 612-946-8155. E-mail: gionline@winternet.com; URL: http://www.winternet.com/~gionline. Ed. Andrew McNamara; Pub. Richard A. Cihak. R&P contact: Terrie A. Maley. adv.: B&W page $4718, color page $5895; trim 8 x 10 3/4; adv. contact: Kimberly Thompson-Benike. bk.rev.; circ. 200,000 (paid). **Document type:** consumer publication.
Description: Provides news, reviews and information regarding forthcoming video game hardware and software. Also provides CD-ROM and multi-media coverage.

794.8   US   ISSN 1074-2425
GV1469.15
GAME PLAYERS SEGA NINTENDO. 1988. m. $26.50 (Canada $41.20). Imagine Publishing, Inc., 150 N. Hill Dr., Brisbane, CA 94005. TEL 415-468-4684. FAX 415-468-4686. Ed. Leslie Mizell. adv. circ. 400,000. **Document type:** consumer publication.
Formerly (until 1994): Game Players Nintendo Sega (ISSN 1068-1809); Formed by the merger of: Game Player's Guide to Nintendo (ISSN 1059-2172); Which incorporates (1990-1991): Game Player's Strategy Guide to Game Boy Games & Game Players Sega Guide (ISSN 1065-3376); Which was formerly (until 1992): Game Player's Sega Genesis Strategy Guide (ISSN 1052-763X)
Description: Provides hints and strategies for video games played on Super NES, Nintendo, Game Boy, Genesis, Sega CD and Game Gear systems. Includes game descriptions and screen shots to allow readers to preview games before purchasing.

794.8   IT
GAME POWER. 1991. m. newsstand price: L.5000. Studio V I T s.n.c., Via Aosta 2, 20155 Milan, Italy. TEL 39-2-33100413. FAX 39-2-33104726. Ed. Riccardo Albini. adv.: color page L.3300000; adv. contact: Marco Trabucchi. circ. 2,500,000.

794.8   US
▼**THE GAME REVIEW.** 1995. w. E-mail: ionizer@ns2.clever.net; URL: http://tgr.clever.net; http://ns2.clever.net/~ionizer. Ed. Ionizer.
●Available only online.
Description: Revises the games released to the internet scene.

794.8   US
GAME WORLD. q. free. T S R, Inc., Box 756, Lake Geneva, WI 53147. (Avail. in Europe from: T S R Ltd., 120 Church End, Cherry Hinton, Cambridge CB1 3LF, England) Ed. Thomas McLaughlin. software rev. (tabloid format) **Document type:** consumer publication.
Description: Previews and describes computer action and fantasy games from T S R.

794.8   US   ISSN 1042-8658
GAMEPRO. (Editions in English, Spanish) 1989. m. $24.95. Infotainment World, Inc., 951 Mariners Island Blvd., Ste. 700, San Mateo, CA 94404-1561. TEL 415-349-4300; 800-879-0499. FAX 415-349-7482. Ed. LeeAnne McDermott. adv. circ. 564,702. **Document type:** consumer publication.
Description: Information for young video game players on the newest games and the best tips for playing, with emphasis on Nintendo and Sega.

794.8   IT
GAMES MACHINE. 1988. m. L.50000. Xenia Edizioni s.r.l., Via Dell'Annunciata 31, 20121 Milan, Italy. TEL 39-2-66804505. FAX 39-2-66804478. Ed. Roberto Ferri. adv.: B&W page L.3000000, color page L.4700000. circ. 72,000. **Document type:** consumer publication.

794   US   ISSN 0742-6747
HI-RES. bi-m. $24 per no. Compupress Ltd., Box 162264, Altamonte Springs, FL 32716-2264. Ed. Anthony J. Nicholson.
Description: Current information on Atari, Commodore and IBM products. Includes futuristic fiction.

794.8   SP
HOBBY CONSOLAS. 1991. 12/yr. 5000 ptas. (Europe 13380 ptas.; elsewhere 11680 ptas.) (effective 1997). Hobby Press, S.A., C. de los Ciruelos, 4, 28700 San Sebastian de los Reyes (Madrid), Spain. TEL 34-1-6548199. FAX 34-1-6547272. Ed. Amalio Gomez. adv. contact: Maria Perera. circ. 68,067. **Document type:** consumer publication.
Description: Covers console video games: Sega, Nintendo, Playstation, and more.

794   NE   ISSN 0920-234X
I C C A JOURNAL. 1983. 4/yr. fl.60($40) (£25) to individuals; libraries $72); institutions $144 (effective 1996). International Computer Chess Association, c/o H.J. van den Herik, Ed., Universitiet Maastricht, Department of Computer Science, P.O. Box 616, 6200 MD Maastricht, Netherlands. TEL 31-43-883477. FAX 31-43-252392. E-mail: icca@cs.unimaas.nl. (U.S., U.K. and Canadian subscr. to: ICCA, c/o Don F. Beal, Dept. of Computer Science, Queen Mary and Westfield College, Mile End Rd., London E1 4NS, England) Ed. H.J. van den Herik. bk. rev. circ. 700. (reprint service avail. from ISI) Indexed: ASCA, Compumath, SSCI. **Document type:** newsletter.
—Genuine Article.
Description: For aficionados of computer chess.

794.8   US
▼**INTROSPECTION.** 1996. irreg. 32419 Seventh Ave. S.W., Federal Way, WA 98023. E-mail: akkbar@wa.net; URL: http://web.wa.net/~akkbar/. Ed. Dan Hardwicke. **Document type:** newsletter.
●Available only online.
Description: Dedicated to literary writing and opinion.

794.8   IT   ISSN 1122-1313
K.* 1988. m. L.50000 (foreign L.80000). R C S Libri, Via Mecenate 91, 20138 Milan, Italy. TEL 39-2-5095950. FAX 39-2-58012131. Ed. Riccardo Albini. adv.: color page L.5060000; adv. contact: Marco Trabucchi. circ. 61,000. **Document type:** consumer publication.

794.8 643   UK
KEY NOTE MARKET REPORT: ELECTRONIC GAMES.
Variant title: Electronic Games. 1994. irreg. £205. Key Note Ltd., Field House, 72 Oldfield Rd., Hampton, Middlesex TW12 2HQ, England. TEL 44-181-783-0755. FAX 44-181-783-0049. **Document type:** trade publication.
●Also available online.
Also available on CD-ROM.
Formerly: Key Note Report: Electronic Games (ISSN 1354-3350)

794   UK   ISSN 0967-9014
MEAN MACHINES SEGA. 1991. m £34 (foreign £40) (effective 1996). E M A P - Images, Priory Ct., 30-32 Farringdon Ln., London EC1R 3AU, England. TEL 44-171-972-6700. FAX 44-171-972-6710. (Subscr. to: Tower Publishing, Tower House, Sovereign Park, Lathkill St., Market Harborough, Leics. LE16 9EF, England. TEL 44-1858-468811. FAX 44-1858-432164) Ed. Richard Leadbetter. circ. 118,032 (paid). **Document type:** consumer publication.
Supersedes (in 1992): Mean Machines (ISSN 0960-4952)

794.8   GW   ISSN 0946-6282
MEGA FUN. m. DM.62 (effective 1996). Computec Verlag, Isarstr. 32-34, 90451 Nuernberg, Germany. TEL 49-911-96832-0. FAX 49-911-6426333. Ed. Christian Geltenpoth. adv. contact: Thorsten Szameitat. circ. 50,000. **Document type:** consumer publication.

794   UK   ISSN 0964-5764
MEGATECH.* 1991. m.? £27 (rest of Europe £38). E M A P Images (Subsidiary of: E M A P Consumer Publishing Group), Priory Ct., 30-32 Farringdon Ln., London EC1 R3AU, England. TEL 0171-972-6700. FAX 0171-972-6710. (Subscr. to: Tower Publishing, Tower House, Sovereign Pl., Lathkill St., Market Harborough, Leics. LE16 9EF, England) Ed. Steve Merrett. circ. 44,060 (paid). **Document type:** consumer publication.

MICHIGAN CHESS. see *SPORTS AND GAMES*

MINNESOTA CHESS JOURNAL. see *SPORTS AND GAMES*

MULTIMEDIA ENTERTAINMENT & TECHNOLOGY REPORT. see *COMPUTERS — Computer Industry*

794   GW   ISSN 0944-1735
DAS NAECHSTE SPIELEMAGAZIN. 1992. a. DM.7.50 (foreign DM.10.50). Verlag Computer-Spiele Per Post, Alfred-Bucherer-Str. 63, 53115 Bonn, Germany. TEL 49-228-621392. FAX 49-228-621332. E-mail: h.topf@cspp.com. Eds. Harald Topf, Heinz-Joachim Topf. circ. 1,250. (back issues avail.) **Document type:** consumer publication.
Description: For anyone interested in playing, producing or distributing computer games.

NEW ZEALAND CHESS. see *SPORTS AND GAMES*

794.8   US   ISSN 1078-9693
▼**NEXT GENERATION.** 1995. m. $34. Imagine Publishing, Inc., 150 N. Hill Dr., Brisbane, CA 94005. TEL 415-468-4684. FAX 415-468-4686. Ed. Neil West. adv.; illus. **Document type:** consumer publication.
—KR SourceOne.

NIKKEI ENTERTAINMENT!. see *MOTION PICTURES*

794.8   SP
NINTENDO ACCION. 1992. 12/yr. 4200 ptas. (effective 1997). Hobby Press, S.A., C. de los Ciruelos, 4, 28200 San Sebastian de los Reyes (Madrid), Spain. TEL 34-1-6548199. FAX 34-1-6547272. Ed. Juan Carlos Garcia. adv. contact: Maria Perera. circ. 40,000. **Document type:** consumer publication.
Description: Covers Nintendo Game Boy, N.E.S. and Super Nintendo video games.

794   UK   ISSN 0965-4240
NINTENDO MAGAZINE SYSTEM. 1992. m. £34 (elsewhere £40) (effective 1996). E M A P - Images, Priory Ct., 30-32 Farringdon Ln., London EC1R 3AU, England. TEL 44-171-972-6700. FAX 44-171-972-6710. (Subscr. to: Tower Publishing Services Ltd., Tower House, Sovereign Park, Lathkill St., Market Harborough, Leics. LE16 9EF, England. TEL 44-1858-468811. FAX 44-1858-432164) Ed. Tim Boone. circ. 110,384 (paid). **Document type:** consumer publication.

794   US   ISSN 1041-9551
NINTENDO POWER. 1988. 12/yr. $19.95. Nintendo of America Inc., Consumer Service Department, Box 97043, Redmond, WA 98073-9743. TEL 800-255-3700. (back issues avail.) **Document type:** consumer publication.

COMPUTERS — COMPUTER GRAPHICS 2119

794.8   GW   ISSN 0946-6290
P C ACTION. m. DM.79 (effective 1996). Computec Verlag, Isarstr. 32-34, 90451 Nuernberg, Germany. TEL 49-911-96832-0. FAX 49-911-6426333. Ed. Christian Geltenpoth. adv. contact: Thorsten Szameitat. circ. 108,835 (paid). **Document type:** consumer publication.
●Also available on CD-ROM.

794.8   IT
P C GAME PARADE. 1992. m. L.120000 (foreign L.300000). G R Edizioni s.r.l., Viale Espinasse 93, 20156 Milan, Italy. TEL 39-2-38010030. FAX 39-2-38010028. Ed. Gianluigi Zanfrognini. adv.: B&W page L.2800000, color page L.4200000. **Document type:** consumer publication.

794.8   GW   ISSN 0946-6304
P C GAMES. m. DM.108 (effective 1996). Computec Verlag, Isarstr. 32-34, 90451 Nuernberg, Germany. TEL 49-911-96832-0. FAX 49-911-6426333. E-mail: cngeltenpoth@pcgames.de; URL: http://www.pcgames.de. Ed. Christian Geltenpoth. adv. contact: Thorsten Szameitat. circ. 196,509. **Document type:** consumer publication.
●Also available online.
Also available on CD-ROM.

794   UK   ISSN 1351-0290
P C GAMES. (Personal Computer) 1994. m. £47.40 (foreign £55); CD-ROM edition £59.40 (foreign £67) (effective 1996). E M A P - Images, Priory Ct., 30-32 Farringdon Ln., London EC1R 3AU, England. TEL 44-171-972-6700. FAX 44-171-972-6710. (Subscr. to: Tower Publishing Services Ltd., Tower House, Sovereign Park, Lathkill St., Market Harborough, Leics. LE16 9EF, England. TEL 44-1858-468811. FAX 44-1858-432164) adv. (diskette format) **Document type:** consumer publication.
●Also available on CD-ROM.

794.8   GW
▼**P C GAMES PLUS.** 1996. m. DM.204 (effective 1996). Computec Verlag, Isarstr. 32-34, 90451 Nuernberg, Germany. TEL 49-911-96832-0. FAX 49-911-6426333. Ed. Christian Geltenpoth. adv. contact: Thorsten Szameitat. circ. 60,000 (paid). **Document type:** consumer publication.
●Also available on CD-ROM.

794.8   GW   ISSN 0943-6693
P C PLAYER. (Personal Computer) 1992. m. DM.72 (foreign DM.96; student DM.62) (effective 1997). Franzis Verlag GmbH, Dornacherstr. 3, 85622 Feldkirchen, Germany. TEL 49-89-99115-0. FAX 49-89-99115199. **Document type:** consumer publication.

794.8   GW
P C PLAYER PLUS. (Personal Computer) m. DM.129.60 (foreign DM.153.60; students DM.110.40) (effective 1997). Franzis Verlag GmbH, Dornacherstr. 3, 85622 Feldkirchen, Germany. TEL 49-89-99115-0. FAX 49-89-99115199. **Document type:** consumer publication.

794.8   GW
PLAY TIME. m. Computec Verlag GmbH, Isarstr. 32-34, 90451 Nuernberg, Germany. TEL 49-911-96832-0. FAX 49-911-6426333. Ed. Christian Geltenpoth. adv. contact: Thorsten Szameitat. circ. 56,002. **Document type:** consumer publication.

794.8   GW
PLAYSTATION. m. DM.138 (foreign DM.162; students DM.117.60) (effective 1997). Franzis Verlag GmbH, Dornacherstr. 3, 85622 Feldkirchen, Germany. TEL 49-89-99115-0. FAX 49-89-99115199. **Document type:** consumer publication.

794.1   SW
PLY: SVENSKA SCHACKDATORFOERINGEN. 1979. 4/yr. SEK 120. Swedish Computer Chess Association, c/o Thoralf Karlsson, Ed., Uttermarksgatan 31 C, S-633 51 Eskilstuna, Sweden. (Subscr. to: Mr. Goeran Grottling, Diabasv. 3, S-437 32 Lindome, Sweden) adv.; bk.rev. circ. 650.
Formerly: Ply - Svenska Schackdatorfoeringen.
Description: Contains annotated chess games, ratings, and news.

794   GW   ISSN 0937-9754
POWER PLAY. 1988. m. DM.70.80 (foreign DM.94.80). Markt und Technik Verlag AG, Hans-Pinsel-Str. 2, 85540 Haar, Germany. TEL 089-4613-0. FAX 089-4613-774. **Document type:** consumer publication.

794   GW   ISSN 0934-3237
S T - MAGAZIN; die Zeitschrift fuer den Atari ST. 1987. m. DM.77 (foreign DM.95). Markt und Technik Verlag AG, Hans-Pinsel-Str. 2, 85540 Haar, Germany. TEL 089-4613-0. FAX 089-4613-774. circ. 50,000. (back issues avail.) **Document type:** consumer publication.
Formerly: 6800er S T - Magazin.
Description: For owners and users of Atari systems.

794.8 004   US   ISSN 1070-1575
S.W.A.T.PRO; secret weapon and tactic guide. Variant title: SwatPro. 1991. bi-m. $20. Infotainment World, Inc., 951 Mariners Island Blvd., Ste. 700, San Mateo, CA 94404-1561. TEL 415-349-4300. **Document type:** consumer publication.

SAKKELET. see SPORTS AND GAMES

SCHWEIZERISCHE SCHACHZEITUNG; revue Suisse des echecs, revista scacchistica Svizzera. see SPORTS AND GAMES

794   UK   ISSN 1352-4267
SEGA. 1994. m. £34 (foreign £40) (effective 1996). E M A P - Images, Priory Ct., 30-32 Farringdon Ln., London EC1R 3AU, England. TEL 44-171-972-6700. FAX 44-171-972-6710. (Subscr. to: Tower Publishing Services Ltd., Tower House, Lathkill St., Market Harborough, Leics. LE16 9EF, England. TEL 44-1858-468811. FAX 44-1858-432164) adv. **Document type:** consumer publication.

794.8   GW   ISSN 0946-6274
SEGA MAGAZIN. m. DM.59 (effective 1996). Computec Verlag, Isarstr. 32-34, 90451 Nuernberg, Germany. TEL 49-911-96832-0. FAX 49-911-6426333. Ed. Christian Geltenpoth. adv. contact: Thorsten Szameitat. circ. 50,000. **Document type:** consumer publication.

794   US
SEGAVISIONS. 1990. bi-m. (Sega of America) Infotainment World, Inc., 951 Mariners Island Blvd., Ste. 700, San Mateo, CA 94404-1561. TEL 415-349-4300. Ed. Nic Lavaroff. software rev.; circ. 1,000,000 (controlled).

794   GW
SPIEL-EBENE; Spieleberatung und Information. 1986. q. DM.30($25) Im Alten Felde 13, 27607 Neuenwalde, Germany. TEL 04707-377. Eds. Hartmuth Seitz, Anna-Gesine Seitz. bk.rev. circ. 500. (also avail. in diskette format)
Description: Review of computer games to be used at schools.

794.8   US
STRATEGY PLUS. 1990. m. $36 (Canada $39). Strategy Plus, Inc., Box 21, Hancock, VT 05748. TEL 800-283-3542. Ed. Steve Bauman; Pubs. Yale Brozen, Marc Dultz. adv. contact: Russ Hoeffer. circ. 60,000. **Document type:** consumer publication.
Description: Reviews computer games for IBM, Macintosh, and Amiga and includes information on computer hardware.

794   GW
VIDEO GAMES. bi-m. DM.5.80 per no. Markt und Technik Verlag AG, Hans-Pinsel-Str. 2, 85540 Haar, Germany. TEL 089-4613-0. FAX 089-4613-774. **Document type:** consumer publication.

794.8   GW
VIDEO INTERAKTIV. 1993. a. DM.19.80. Vereinigte Motor-Verlage GmbH und Co. KG, Leuschnerstr. 1, 70174 Stuttgart, Germany. TEL 49-711-1821226. FAX 49-711-1821349. Ed. Tim Cole; Pub. Gernot Hempelmann. adv. contact: Peter Michael Heyde. circ. 30,000. **Document type:** consumer publication.

794.8   US   ISSN 1074-3774
GV1469.3
VIDEOGAMES; the ultimate gaming magazine. 1988. m. $19.95 (foreign $29.95); newsstand price: $4.95. Larry Flynt Publications, Inc., 9171 Wilshire Blvd., Ste. 300, Beverly Hills, CA 90210. TEL 310-858-7155. FAX 310-274-7985. Ed. Chris Gore; Pub. Larry Flynt. adv. **Document type:** consumer publication.
Formerly: Video Games and Computer Entertainment (ISSN 1059-2938)
Description: Presents articles and information on home video games.

X Y Z Z Y NEWS. see LITERATURE — Science Fiction, Fantasy, Horror

794.8   US
▼**2 X S**; an ezine by and for roll - role players. 1996. q. Box 392, Ector, TX 75439. E-mail: aramus@netexas.net; URL: http://www.netexas.net/rglaser/2xs/. Ed. Aramus Hudra.
●Available only online.

COMPUTERS — Computer Graphics

see also Printing–Computer Applications

001.644   US   ISSN 0730-0301
T385   CODEN: ATGRDF
A C M TRANSACTIONS ON GRAPHICS. 1982. q. $110 to non-members. Association for Computing Machinery, 1515 Broadway, 17th Fl., New York, NY 10036-5701. TEL 212-869-7440. FAX 212-944-1318. TELEX 421686. Ed. John C. Beatty. charts; illus.; index. circ. 9,000. Indexed: A.I.Abstr., A.S.& T.Ind., Abstr.Hum.Comp.Inter., ASCA, CAD CAM Abstr., Compumath, Comput.Abstr., Comput.Cont., Comput.Lit.Ind., Comput.Rev., Curr.Cont., Ergon.Abstr., INSPEC (1982-), Int.Aerosp.Abstr., Zent.Math.
—BLDSC (0578.665000); AskIEEE; CISTI; Ei; Genuine Article; KR SourceOne; Linda Hall; SWETS; UMI; UnCover. CCC.
Description: Provides coverage of various forms of graphics applications. Articles cover geometric modeling, design and analysis of algorithms, person-machine interaction techniques and computer graphics hardware.

006.6   NE   ISSN 0921-934X
CODEN: ACVLEM
ADVANCES IN C A D FOR V L S I. 1986. irreg., vol.8, 1994. price varies. Elsevier Science B.V., Books Division, P.O. Box 211, 1000 AE Amsterdam, Netherlands. TEL 31-20-4853911. FAX 31-20-4853705. TELEX 18582 ESPA NL. E-mail: nlinfo-f@elsevier.nl; usinfo-f@elsevier.com; forinfo-kyf04035@niftyserve.or.jp; URL: http://www.elsevier.nl/. (Subscr. in the Americas to: Elsevier Science, Regional Sales Office, Box 945, New York, NY 10159-0945. TEL 212-989-5800; Subscr. in Australasia and the Far East to: Elsevier Science (Singapore) Pte Ltd, No.1 Temasek Ave., No.17-01 Millenia Tower, Singapore 039192, Singapore; Subscr. in Japan to: Elsevier Science Japan, 9-15 Higashi-Azabu 1-chome, Minato-ku, Tokyo 106, Japan) (back issues avail.) Indexed: INSPEC. **Document type:** monographic series.
Refereed Serial

629.892 006   NE   ISSN 0926-9622
ADVANCES IN DESIGN AND MANUFACTURING. (Text in English) 1991. irreg., vol.6, 1995. price varies. I O S Press, Van Diemenstraat 94, 1013 CN Amsterdam, Netherlands. TEL 31-20-6382189. FAX 31-20-6203419. E-mail: market@iospress.nl; URL: http://www.iospress.nl/iospress. (In N. America: Box 10558, Burke, VA 22009-0558. TEL 703-323-5554. FAX 703-250-4705) (back issues avail.) **Document type:** monographic series.
—CISTI.
Description: Discusses the impact of computer and information technology on all sectors of the manufacturing industry.

COMPUTERS — COMPUTER GRAPHICS

006.6   NE   ISSN 0928-1479
ADVANCES IN IMAGE COMMUNICATION. (Text in English) 1993. irreg., vol.4, 1994. price varies. Elsevier Science B.V., Books Division, P.O. Box 211, 1000 AE Amsterdam, Netherlands. TEL 31-20-4853911. FAX 31-20-4853705. E-mail: nlinfo-f@elsevier.nl; usinfo-f@elsevier.com; forinfo-kyf04035@niftyserve.or.jp; URL: http://www.elsevier.nl/. (Subscr. in the Americas to: Elsevier Science, Regional Sales Office, Box 945, New York, NY 10159-0945. TEL 212-633-3730. FAX 212-633-3680; Subscr. in Australasia and the Far East to: Elsevier Science (Singapore) Pte Ltd, No.1 Temasek Ave., No.17-01 Millenia Tower, Singapore 039192, Singapore. TEL 65-434-3727. FAX 65-337-2230; Subscr. in Japan to: Elsevier Science Japan, 9-15 Higashi-Azabu 1-chome, Minato-ku, Tokyo 106, Japan. TEL 81-3-5561-5033. FAX 81-3-5561-5047) (back issues avail.) **Document type:** monographic series.
—BLDSC (0709.086000).

001.644 530   US
ADVANCES IN MAGNETIC RESONANCE IMAGING. 1989. irreg. price varies. Ablex Publishing Corporation, Box 5297, Greenwich, CT 06831-0504. TEL 203-661-7602. FAX 203-661-0792. Ed. Ephraim Feig. **Document type:** academic/scholarly publication.
Refereed Serial

006.6   US   ISSN 1049-0035
NC998.5.A1
BEFORE & AFTER; how to design cool stuff. 1990. 6/yr. $36 (Canada $40; elsewhere $54). PageLab, Inc., 1830 Sierra Gardens Dr., Ste. 30, Roseville, CA 95661-2942. TEL 916-784-3880. FAX 916-784-3995. Ed. Gaye McWade. **Document type:** trade publication.
Description: Practical graphic design advice, with particular emphasis on techniques and applications of Aldus PageMaker and FreeHand design software.

C A D - C A M. see *COMPUTERS — Automation*

006.6   GR   ISSN 1106-0077
C A D - C A M & COMPUTER GRAPHICS. (Text in Greek) 1991. q. Dr.15000 (effective 1996). Compupress S.A., 44 Syngrou, 117 42 Athens, Greece. TEL 30-1-9238-672. FAX 30-1-9216-847. Ed. Vassilis Sarmanadas; Pub. N.O. Manousos. adv. contact: Alexis Kanavos. software rev.; circ. 11,000 (paid). **Document type:** trade publication.
Description: Covers computer-aided design and illustration and reviews the necessary hardware and software.

006 005   BE
C A D - C A M & INDUSTRIAL SOFTWARE GUIDE. (Editions in Dutch, French) a. 650 BEF. Business & Management Editions Brussels s.p.r.l., Rue Stephanie, 17, 1020 Brussels, Belgium. TEL 32-2-4266115. FAX 32-2-4258226. circ. 25,000 (controlled). **Document type:** directory.

001.644   GW
C A D - C A M REPORT. (Computer Aided Design - Computer Aided Manufacturing); Nachrichtenmagazin fuer Computergraphik. 1982. m. DM.275. Dressler Verlag GmbH, Gaisbergstr. 55, 69115 Heidelberg, Germany. TEL 06221-91130. FAX 06221-911321. Ed. Gerhard Friederici. adv.; bk.rev.; circ. 19,700 (controlled). (back issues avail.) **Indexed:** Cyb.Abstr. **Document type:** consumer publication.

001.644   US
C A D - C A M UPDATE. (Computer-Aided Design - Computer-Aided Manufacturing) 1989. m. $120 (outside N. America $165). Worldwide Videotex, Box 3273, Boynton Beach, FL 33424-3273. TEL 407-738-2276. Ed. Mark Wright; Pub. Mark Wright. bk.rev. (back issues avail.) **Document type:** newsletter.
●Also available online. Vendor(s): Information Access Co., NewsNet (MG15).
Description: Provides timely news and information about the CAD-CAM industry, including CAD, CAM, CADD, CASE products, services, companies, marketing strategies, and research and development.

001.644   CN   ISSN 1183-9414
C A D SYSTEMS. (Text in English) 1982. bi-m. Can.$32.10($61) (effective 1997). Kerrwil Publications Ltd., 395 Matheson Blvd. E., Mississauga, ON L4Z 2H2, Canada. TEL 905-890-1846. FAX 905-890-5769. Ed. Karen Dalton; Pub. Karen Dalton. R&P contact: Karen Dalton. adv.: B&W page Can.$4715, color page Can.$5695; adv. contact: Phil Jarvis. circ. 18,000. (tabloid format) **Indexed:** Can.B.P.I. **Document type:** trade publication.
—CISTI; KR SourceOne.
Formed by the 1991 merger of: Architectural Engineering Construction Magazine (ISSN 1187-0524); Which was formerly: A E C Architectural Engineering Construction (ISSN 0847-4605) & C A D - C A M Systems (ISSN 0847-5547); Which was formerly: C A D - C A M and Robotics (ISSN 0822-0603)
Description: Provides news, application features, hardware and software reviews to CAD professionals in a range of disciplines, including mechanical design, AEC, facilities management and GIS.

001.6   IE
C A D UPDATE. 4/yr. 121 Lower Baggott St., Dublin 2, Ireland. TEL 810172. FAX 619192. Ed. Paul Condron. bk.rev.

006   UK   ISSN 0959-6259
C A D USER. (Computer-Aided Design) 1988. m. £39 (foreign £54). B.T.C., 24 High St., Beckenham, Kent BR3 1AY, England. TEL 44-181-663-3822. FAX 44-181-663-1394. E-mail: cod.user@btc.co.uk. Ed. John Richardson; Pub. John Richardson. R&P contact: John Richardson. TEL 44-181-663-3818. adv. contact: Ray Ibrahim. circ. 16,687.
—BLDSC (2946.220000); SWETS.
Description: Focuses on AutoCAD and its related hardware and software. Includes product reviews and launches, industry news and user profiles.

006.6   AT   ISSN 1037-8529
C A D USER AUSTRALIA NEW ZEALAND. 1990. 10/yr. Aus.$55; newsstand price: Aus.$5.95. Business & Communications, 283 Auburn Rd., Hawthorn, Vic. 3142, Australia. TEL 61-9-8132888. FAX 61-9-8132390. Ed. Steve Hunter. R&P contact: John Jaggurs. adv.: color page Aus.$2850; trim 297 x 210; adv. contact: Max Winter. software rev.; illus.; mkt.; tr.lit. circ. 10,000. (back issues avail.) **Document type:** trade publication.
Description: Provides information relating to professional use of AutoCAD and related hardware and software.

006.6   AT   ISSN 1323-0069
▼**C A D USER SOUTH EAST ASIA;** independent guide to Autodesk solutions. 1995. 6/yr. Aus.$40. Business & Technical Communications, 283 Auburn Rd., Howthorn, Vic. 3142, Australia. TEL 61-9-98132888. FAX 61-9-98132390. Ed. Steve Hunter. R&P contact: John Jageurs. adv.: color page Aus.$2850; trim 297 x 210; adv. contact: Edgar Yung. bk.rev.; software rev.; illus.; tr.lit. circ. 10,000. (back issues avail.) **Document type:** trade publication.

006.6 621.39   CH   ISSN 1022-291X
C A D YU ZIDONGHUA/C A D AND AUTOMATION. (Text in Chinese) 1988. m. NT.$1250 (foreign NT.$2950). Third Wave Publishing Corp., 19-1, Lane 231, Fu-Hsing N. Rd., Taipei, Taiwan, Republic of China. TEL 886-2-7136959. FAX 886-2-7189467. Ed. Teresa Fu. adv.: color page $1600. **Document type:** consumer publication.
Description: Serves Taiwan manufacturers, graphic artists and students.

001.644   US
C G PROFESSIONAL. (Computer Graphics) 1989. m. $89. Graphic Channels Inc., 1714 Stockton St., San Francisco, CA 94133. TEL 415-956-5350. Ed. Scott Lowe. circ. 25,000.
Description: Focuses on information relevant to the acquisition and utilization of computer graphics products and technologies.

001.644   US   ISSN 0820-5450
T385
CADALYST; professional management of AutoCAD and related industries. 1984. m. $39 (foreign $90) (effective 1996). Advanstar Communications, Inc., CADalyst, 859 Willamette St., Eugene, OR 97401. TEL 503-343-1200. FAX 503-686-5732. URL: http://www.cadonline.com. Ed. Gene Smarte; Pub. Dana Woodsmall. adv. contact: Lisa Anderson. bk.rev. circ. 67,805. (back issues avail.) **Document type:** trade publication.
●Also available online. Vendor(s): Information Access Co.
—CISTI; KR SourceOne; SWETS. **CCC.**
Description: Provides practical, hands-on information to users and managers of CAD systems using AutoCAD software, and the spectrum of application software built around these systems.

006.6   US
CADENCE (SAN FRANCISCO). 12/yr. $39.95 (Canada & Mexico $49.95; elsewhere $79.95) (effective 1996). Miller Freeman, Inc. (Subsidiary of: United News & Media), 600 Harrison St., San Francisco, CA 94107. TEL 415-905-2200. FAX 415-905-2233. (Subscr. to: Box 8024, Boulder, CO 80306-8024. TEL 800-289-0484. FAX 904-446-2774)

006.6 070.5   CN   ISSN 1190-8874
Z286.D47
CHRIS DICKMAN'S COREL DRAW JOURNAL. 1993. 10/yr. Can.$47. Kazak Communications, 16 Ottawa St., Toronto, ON M4T 2B6, Canada. TEL 416-924-0759. FAX 416-924-4875. Ed. Chris Dickman. bk.rev.; circ. 5,000 (paid). (also avail. in diskette format; back issues avail.) **Document type:** consumer publication.
Formerly (until 1994): Chris Dickman's Mastering Corel Draw (ISSN 1192-9006)
Description: Devoted solely to providing hands-on tips and techniques for those using the CorelDRAW graphics suite of applications.

006.6   NE   ISSN 1381-6446
COMPUTATIONAL IMAGING AND VISION. (Text in English) 1994. irreg., vol.3, 1995. price varies. Kluwer Academic Publishers, Postbus 17, 3300 AA Dordrecht, Netherlands. TEL 31-78-6392392. FAX 31-78-6392254. E-mail: services@wkap.nl; URL: http://www.wkap.nl. (Dist. by: Kluwer Academic Publishers Group, P.O. Box 322, 3300 AH Dordrecht, Netherlands. TEL 31-78-6392392. FAX 31-78-6546474; N. America dist. addr.: Box 358, Accord Sta., Hingham, MA 02018-0358. TEL 617-871-6600. FAX 617-871-6528) **Document type:** monographic series, proceedings.
—BLDSC (3390.594000).
Refereed Serial

006.6   UK   ISSN 0010-4485
TA174   CODEN: CAIDA5
COMPUTER-AIDED DESIGN. 1968. 14/yr. fl.1866($1072) (effective 1998). Elsevier Science Ltd., P.O. Box 800, Kidlington, Oxford OX5 1DX, England. TEL 44-1865-843000. FAX 44-1865-843010. TELEX 83111 BHPOXF G. E-mail: nlinfo-f@elsevier.nl; usinfo-f@elsevier.com; forinfo-kyf04035@niftyserve.or.jp; URL: http://www.elsevier.nl/. (Subscr. to: Elsevier Science, Regional Sales Office, P.O. Box 211, 1000 AE Amsterdam, Netherlands. TEL 31-20-4853757. FAX 31-20-4853432; Subscr. in the Americas to: Elsevier Science, Regional Sales Office, Box 945, New York, NY 10159-0945. TEL 212-633-3730. FAX 212-633-3680; Subscr. in Australasia and the Far East to: Elsevier Science (Singapore) Pte Ltd, No.1 Temasek Ave., No.17-01 Millenia Tower, Singapore 039192, Singapore. TEL 65-434-3727. FAX 65-337-2230) Ed. J. Hayes. adv.; bk.rev.; charts; illus.; stat.; index. (also avail. in microform from UMI; reprint service avail.) **Indexed:** A.I.Abstr., ASCA, BMT, Br.Tech.Ind., CAD CAM Abstr., Compumath., Comput.Abstr., Comput.Cont., Comput.Rev., Curr.Cont., Cyb.Abstr., Eng.Ind., Ergon.Abstr., Fluidex, INSPEC (1969-), Int.Aerosp.Abstr., Intl.Civil Eng.Abstr., ISMEC, Robomat., Soft.Abstr.Eng. **Document type:** academic/scholarly publication.
—BLDSC (3393.520000); AskIEEE; CISTI; Ei; Genuine Article; KR SourceOne; Linda Hall; SWETS; UMI; UnCover. **CCC.**
Description: Covers current developments and applications of computer-aided design in every field.
Refereed Serial

COMPUTERS — COMPUTER GRAPHICS

001.644 US ISSN 0276-749X
COMPUTER AIDED DESIGN REPORT. 1981. m. $189 (foreign $302). C A D - C A M Publishing, Inc., 1010 Turquoise St., Ste. 320, San Diego, CA 92109-1268. TEL 619-488-0533. FAX 619-488-6052. Ed. Jeannette Dewyze. bk.rev.; abstr.; bibl.; index. (back issues avail.) Indexed: CAD CAM Abstr. Document type: trade publication.
●Also available online. Vendor(s): Information Access Co.
—SWETS.
Description: Contains news and analysis of developments in the CAD-CAM field; includes information about firms using CAD to improve productivity; targeted toward engineers.

006.6 UK
COMPUTER AIDED DRAUGHTING & DESIGN. m. £27. Electronic Design Automation Ltd., 31-33 High Holborn, London WC1V 6BD, England. TEL 44-171-404-0564. FAX 44-171-831-2057. Ed. Geoff Walker. circ. 10,690. (back issues avail.; reprint service avail.) Document type: trade publication.
Formerly: Draughting and Design (ISSN 0951-5704)

COMPUTER-AIDED ENGINEERING (CLEVELAND). see ENGINEERING — Computer Applications

006.6 NE ISSN 0167-8396
CODEN: CAGDEX
COMPUTER-AIDED GEOMETRIC DESIGN. (Text in English) 1984. 9/yr. fl.885($509) (effective 1998). North-Holland (Subsidiary of Elsevier Science B.V.), P.O. Box 211, 1000 AE Amsterdam, Netherlands. TEL 31-20-4853911. FAX 31-20-4853598. TELEX 18582 ESPA NL. (Subscr. in the Americas to: Elsevier Science, Regional Sales Office, Box 945, New York, NY 10159-0945. TEL 212-633-3730. FAX 212-633-3680; Subscr. in Australasia and the Far East to: Elsevier Science (Singapore) Pte Ltd, No.1 Temasek Ave., No.17-01 Millenia Tower, Singapore 039192, Singapore. TEL 65-434-3727. FAX 65-337-2230; Subscr. in Japan to: Elsevier Science Japan, 9-15 Higashi-Azabu 1-chome, Minato-ku Tokyo 106, Japan. TEL 81-3-5561-5033. FAX 81-3-5561-5047) Eds. Robert E. Barnhill, Ing. Wolfgang Boehm. adv.; illus. (back issues avail.; reprint service avail. from SWZ) Indexed: Appl.Mech.Rev., CAD CAM Abstr., Compumath, Curr.Cont., Cyb.Abstr., Eng.Ind., Ind.Sci.Rev., INSPEC (1984-), Math.R., Zent.Math. Document type: academic/scholarly publication.
—BLDSC (3393.541500); AskIEEE; CISTI; Ei; Genuine Article; KR SourceOne; Linda Hall; SWETS; UnCover. **CCC.**
Description: Articles report on computer-aided geometric design applications in the design of automobiles, planes and ships, mathematical foundations, geometric aspects of CAD-CAM and robot cinematics.
Refereed Serial

COMPUTER ARTIST. see ART — Computer Applications

004 621.3 US ISSN 0010-4566
TK7888.3 CODEN: CMPDAM
COMPUTER DESIGN. 1962. m. $99 (foreign $195) (free to qualified personnel) (effective 1997). PennWell Publishing Co. (Nashua), Advanced Technology Group, 10 Tara Blvd., 5th Fl., Nashua, NH 03062-2801. TEL 603-891-9111. FAX 603-891-0514. (Subscr. to: Box 1260, Tulsa, OK 74101. TEL 918-835-3161. FAX 918-832-9295) Ed. John Miklosz. adv.: B&W page $10010, color page $11660; trim 7 x 10. bk.rev.; charts; illus.; tr.lit.; index; circ. 106,000 (controlled). (also avail. in microform from UMI; reprint service avail. from UMI) Indexed: A.I.Abstr., A.S.& T.Ind., ASCA, CAD CAM Abstr., Compumath., Comput.Bus., Comput.Cont., Comput.Dtbs., Comput.Lit.Ind., Comput.Rev., Curr.Cont., Eng.Ind., Ind.Sci.Rev., INSPEC (1993-), Robomat., Sci.Cit.Ind., Tel.Abstr. Document type: trade publication.
●Also available online. Vendor(s): Knight-Ridder Information, Inc.
—BLDSC (3393.870000); AskIEEE; CISTI; Ei; Genuine Article; KR SourceOne; Linda Hall; SWETS; UMI; UnCover. **CCC.**
Description: A magazine for engineers and engineering managers involved with developing computer-based electronics equipment and systems. Covers microcomputers in regular columns, as well as in occasional feature articles and special issues.

006.6 SA ISSN 1025-2738
COMPUTER GRAPHICS. (Text in English) 1990. 8/yr. free. Technews (Pty) Ltd., P.O. Box 626, Kloof 3640, South Africa. TEL 27-31-7640593. FAX 27-31-7640386. E-mail: technews@iafrica.com. Ed. Jenny Allebone. adv. contact: Rose Dunbar. illus.; circ. 4,685 (controlled). Indexed: Ind.S.A.Per. Document type: trade publication.
Description: Covers computer graphics technology and applications, including design, manufacture, mapping, construction and illustration.

006.6 US ISSN 0097-8930
T385 CODEN: CPGPBZ
COMPUTER GRAPHICS (NEW YORK). q. $95 (GRAPH members $59; students $50). Association for Computing Machinery, Special Interest Group on Graphics, 1515 Broadway, 17th Fl., New York, NY 10036. TEL 212-869-7440. FAX 212-869-0481. Ed. Sue Mair. Indexed: Abstr.Hum.Comp.Inter., Comput.Cont., Comput.Lit.Ind., Curr.Cont., GeoRef., INSPEC, PROMT. Document type: bulletin.
—BLDSC (3393.970000); AskIEEE; CISTI; Ei; KR SourceOne; Linda Hall; SWETS; UnCover.

001.644 US
COMPUTER GRAPHICS (SAN DIEGO). 1988. irreg., vol.3, 1991. Academic Press, Inc., 525 B St., Ste. 1900, San Diego, CA 92101-4495. TEL 619-231-6616. FAX 619-669-6715. (Subscr. to: Order Dept., 6277 Sea Harbor Dr., 4th Fl., Orlando, FL 32887. TEL 800-321-5068) Ed. Sol Sherr. (back issues avail.) Document type: monographic series.

001.644 UK ISSN 0167-7055
T385
COMPUTER GRAPHICS FORUM. 1982. 5/yr. £228($360) (foreign £228) (effective 1997). (Eurographics Association) Blackwell Publishers Ltd., 108 Cowley Rd., Oxford OX4 1JF, England. TEL 44-1865-791100. FAX 44-1865-791347. E-mail: jnlinfo@blackwellpublishers.co.uk; URL: http://www.blackwellpublishers.co.uk. Ed. Phillip Willis. bk.rev. (reprint service avail. from SWZ) Indexed: ASCA, CAD CAM Abstr., Compumath, Comput.Abstr., Comput.Lit.Ind., Cyb.Abstr., Data Process.Dig., Eng.Ind., INSPEC (1982-). Document type: academic/scholarly publication.
—BLDSC (3393.982000); AskIEEE; CISTI; Ei; Genuine Article; KR SourceOne; Linda Hall; SWETS; UMI; UnCover. **CCC.**
Description: Provides coverage of developments in the international computer graphics industry.
Refereed Serial

006.6 US ISSN 0271-4159
T385 CODEN: CGWODH
COMPUTER GRAPHICS WORLD. Partial Italian translation: Computer Gazette (IT ISSN 1123-4253) 1978. m. $50 (Canada $65; foreign $76; Pacific Rim $101) (effective 1997). PennWell Publishing Co. (Nashua), Advanced Technology Group, 10 Tara Blvd., 5th Fl., Nashua, NH 03062-2801. TEL 603-891-0123; 800-331-4463. FAX 603-891-0539. (Subscr. to: Box 1260, Tulsa, OK 74101. TEL 918-835-3161. FAX 918-832-9295) Ed. Steve Porter; Pub. Paul McPherson. adv.: B&W page $7610, color page $9320; trim 7 x 10. bk.rev. circ. 70,000. (also avail. in microform from UMI) Indexed: Abstr.Hum.Comp.Inter., ASCA, CAD CAM Abstr., Compumath, Comput.Cont., Comput.Dtbs., Comput.Lit.Ind., Graph.Arts Lit.Abstr., INSPEC, LAMP, Microcomp.Ind., PROMT. Document type: trade publication.
●Also available online. Vendor(s): Information Access Co., Knight-Ridder Information, Inc.
—BLDSC (3393.985000); AskIEEE; CISTI; Ei; Genuine Article; KR SourceOne; SWETS; UMI; UnCover. **CCC.**
Formerly: Computer Graphics (Eugene) (ISSN 0162-3273)
Description: For users and vendors of computer graphics software, hardware and services. Articles cover image processing, CAD-CAM, graphic arts, computerized modeling and software, multimedia, and animation.

006.6 US ISSN 0895-2760
T385
COMPUTER GRAPHICS WORLD BUYERS GUIDE. 1983. a. $100 (effective 1992). PennWell Publishing Co. (Nashua), 10 Tara Blvd., 5th Fl., Nashua, NH 03062-2801. TEL 613-891-9168. FAX 603-891-0539. Ed. Steve Porter. adv. circ. 2,000. (also avail. in microform from UMI) Document type: directory.
Formerly: Computer Graphics Directory (ISSN 0743-2836)

006.6 GW ISSN 0936-2770
COMPUTER GRAPHIK TOPICS; reports of the house of computer graphics. (Text in English, German) 1989. 6/yr. Wilhelminenstr. 7, 64283 Darmstadt, Germany. TEL 49-6151-155252. FAX 49-6151-155299. E-mail: lukacin@igd.fhg.de; URL: http://www.igd.fhg.de/www/pr/topics/topics_home.html. Ed. Bernad Lukacin; Pub. Jose Encarnacao. R&P contact: Bernad Lukacin. (also avail. in diskette format; back issues avail.) Document type: academic/scholarly publication.

006 US ISSN 1077-3142
TA1632 CODEN: CVIUF4
COMPUTER VISION AND IMAGE UNDERSTANDING. 1969. m. $525 (foreign $588) (effective 1997). Academic Press, Inc., Journal Division, 525 B St., Ste. 1900, San Diego, CA 92101-4495. TEL 619-230-1840. FAX 619-699-6800. E-mail: apsubs@acad.com; URL: http://www.apnet.com/www/journal/iv.htm; http://www.idealibrary.com/. (Subscr. to: Box 861213, Orlando, FL 32886-12123. TEL 407-347-4040. FAX 407-363-9661) Ed. Avinash C. Kak. Indexed: A.I.Abstr., A.S.& T.Ind., Abstr. Hum.Comp.Inter., ASCA, CAD CAM Abstr., Compumath, Curr.Cont., Geo.Abstr.P.G., Ind.Sci.Rev., INSPEC (1978-), Robomat., Sci.Cit.Ind., SSCI, Zent.Math. Document type: academic/scholarly publication.
●Also available online.
—BLDSC (3394.353500); AskIEEE; CISTI; Ei; Genuine Article; KR SourceOne; Linda Hall; SWETS; UnCover. **CCC.**
Formerly (until 1995): C V G I P: Image Understanding (ISSN 1049-9660); Which superseded in part (in 1991): Computer Vision, Graphics, and Image Processing (ISSN 0734-189X); Which was formerly (until 1983): Computer Graphics and Image Processing (ISSN 0146-664X)
Description: Focuses on the computer analysis of pictorial information.

COMPUTERS AND GEOTECHNICS. see ENGINEERING — Computer Applications

006.6 UK ISSN 0097-8493
T385 CODEN: COGRD2
COMPUTERS & GRAPHICS; international journal of systems applications in computer graphics. 1975. bi-m. fl.2051($1179) (effective 1998). Elsevier Science Ltd., Pergamon, P.O. Box 800, Kidlington, Oxford OX5 1DX, England. TEL 44-1865-843000. FAX 44-1865-843010. E-mail: nlinfo-f@elsevier.nl; usinfo-f@elsevier.com; forinfo-kyf04035@niftyserve.or.jp; URL: http://www.elsevier.nl/. (Subscr. to: Elsevier Science, Regional Sales Office, P.O. Box 211, 1000 AE Amsterdam, Netherlands. TEL 31-20-4853757. FAX 31-20-4853432; Subscr. in the Americas to: Elsevier Science, Regional Sales Office, Box 945, New York, NY 10159-0945. TEL 212-633-3730. FAX 212-633-3680; Subscr. in Australasia and the Far East to: Elsevier Science (Singapore) Pte Ltd, No.1 Temasek Ave., No.17-01 Millenia Tower, Singapore 039192, Singapore. TEL 65-434-3727. FAX 65-337-2230) Ed. Jose Encarnacao. bk.rev. circ. 1,050. (also avail. in microfilm from UMI) Indexed: Abstr.Hum.Comp.Inter., Appl.Mech.Rev., ASCA, BMT, Compumath, Comput.Abstr., Comput.Cont., Comput.Rev., Curr.Cont., Cyb.Abstr., Fluidex, INSPEC, LAMP, SSCI. Document type: academic/scholarly publication.
—BLDSC (3394.700000); AskIEEE; CISTI; Ei; Genuine Article; KR SourceOne; Linda Hall; SWETS; UMI; UnCover. **CCC.**
Description: Contains papers on the utilization of computer interactive graphics applications in industrial problem solving. Articles cover computer-aided design, person-machine communication techniques and information systems.
Refereed Serial

COMPUTERS — COMPUTER GRAPHICS

006.6 GW ISSN 0949-8958
▼**COREL DRAW.** 1995. bi-m. DM.98 (effective 1997). Verlag Wirtschaft Recht und Steuern, Fraunhoferstr. 5, 82152 Planegg, Germany. TEL 49-89-89517-0. FAX 49-89-89517250. (Subscr. to: Postfach 1363, 82142 Planegg, Germany) (looseleaf format) **Document type:** trade publication.

006.6 NE
COREL GRAPHICS MAGAZINE. 1994. m. fl.95. Uitgeverij Polanen B.V., P.O. Box 23, 2440 AA Woerden, Netherlands. TEL 31-348-453300. FAX 31-348-432133. adv.: color page fl.2000; adv. contact: H. Ketelaar. bk.rev.; index. (back issues avail.)
Description: Deals with all kinds of communications by computer. Also software like Corel, Adobe, Microsoft, MS Word, etc.

006.6 US ISSN 1063-7591
T385
COREL MAGAZINE. 1992. 10/yr. $39.95 (Canada & Mexico $49.95; elsewhere $99.95) (effective 1996 & 1997). Omray Inc., 9801 Anderson Mill Rd., Ste. 207, Austin, TX 78750. TEL 512-250-1700. FAX 512-219-3156. E-mail: scottc@jumpnet.com; URL: http://www.corelmag.com. Ed. D. Scott Campbell; Dave/Baceski. R&P contact: D. Scott Campbell. adv.: B&W page $3950, color page $4950; adv. contact: Mark Stacey. circ. 33,000 (paid); 7,000 (controlled). **Document type:** trade publication.
●Also available on CD-ROM.
Description: For users of CorelDraw, Photo-Paint and other graphics software from Corel Corp. Includes tutorials, technical and product solutions of interest to graphic design desktop publishing professionals.

006.6 760 UK ISSN 1355-4638
CREATIVE TECHNOLOGY. m. £27.50 (foreign £40) (effective 1997); newsstand price: £2.50. c/o Debbie Brown, Ed., 10 Barley Mow Passage, London W4 4PH, England. TEL 44-171-742-2885. FAX 44-171-995-3633. E-mail: creaT@cix.compulink.co.uk. (Subscr. to: Creative Technology Subscriptions, Fulham House, Goldworth Industrial Park, Goldsworth Rd., Woking, Surrey GU21 1LY, England. TEL 44-1483-733800) Pub. Kevin Marriot. R&P contact: Kevin Marriot. TEL 44-171-995-3632. adv. contact: Will Harries. illus.; software rev. **Indexed:** Int.Packag.Abstr., Print.Abstr., WPM.
—BLDSC (3487.247140).
Formerly (until Sept. 1994): X Y Z Direction (ISSN 0965-3848); Which was formed by the merger of (1991-1992): X Y Z (ISSN 1356-0441); Direction (Teddington) (ISSN 0952-7508); Which was formerly (1982-1986): Design and Art Direction.
Description: Covers the creation and application of graphic design and illustration on the computer. Reviews software and hardware.

006.6 AT ISSN 1320-3088
DESIGN GRAPHICS. 11/yr. $76.45. Design Graphics Pty. Ltd., 6 School Rd., Ferny Creek, Vic. 3786, Australia. TEL 61-3-97551149. FAX 61-3-97551155. E-mail: email@designgraphics.com.au; URL: http://www.designgraphics.com.au. (Dist. in US by: Mercury Air Freight Ltd., 2323 Randolph Ave., NJ 07001) Ed. Colin Wood; Pub. Colin Wood. circ. 32,000 (paid). **Indexed:** DAAI. **Document type:** trade publication.
Description: Devoted to all aspects of graphic design and digital imaging.

001.644 US
DESIGNER. q. $50 to individual members; institutions $500. University & College Designer's Association, 209 Commerce St., Alexandria, VA 22314-2909. TEL 703-548-1770. FAX 703-548-1934. E-mail: ucdadirect@aol.com. Ed. Jody Zamirowski. circ. 12,000 (paid). **Indexed:** DAAI. **Document type:** newsletter.

006.6 US
▼**DIGITAL CREATIVITY;** business solutions for imaging professionals. 1996. bi-m. $36. Cowles Business Media, 11 River Bend Dr., S., Box 4949, Stamford, CT 06097-0949. TEL 203-358-9900. FAX 203-358-5811. E-mail: michael_o'connor@cowlesbiz.com. Ed. Michael O'Connor. **Document type:** trade publication.

006.6 US ISSN 1084-5119
DIGITAL IMAGING; the magazine for users of graphics services. bi-m. $24.95 (free to qualified personnel). Micro Publishing, 2340 Plaza Del Amo, Ste. 100, Torrance, CA 90501-3452. TEL 310-371-5787. FAX 310-542-0849. Ed. James Carnoto. adv. contact: Ken Nicholas. **Document type:** trade publication.

621.3 004 NE ISSN 0141-9382
TK7882.I6 CODEN: DISPDP
DISPLAYS; technology and applications. (Text in English) 1979. q. fl.668($384) (effective 1998). Elsevier Science B.V., P.O. Box 211, 1000 AE Amsterdam, Netherlands. TEL 31-20-4853911. FAX 31-20-4853598. (Subscr. in the Americas to: Elsevier Science, Regional Sales Office, Box 945, New York, NY 10159-0945. TEL 212-633-3730. FAX 212-633-3680; Subscr. in Australasia and the Far East to: Elsevier Science (Singapore) Pte Ltd, No.1 Temasek Ave., No.17-01 Millenia Tower, Singapore 039192, Singapore. TEL 65-434-3727. FAX 65-337-2230; Subscr. in Japan to: Elsevier Science Japan, 9-15 Higashi-Azabu 1-chome, Minato-ku, Tokyo 106, Japan. TEL 81-3-5561-5033. FAX 81-3-5561-5047) Ed. Angela Jamieson. adv.; bk.rev.; abstr.; illus.; pat.; index. (also avail. in microform from UMI; back issues avail.) **Indexed:** Abstr.Hum.Comp.Inter., ASCA, CAD CAM Abstr., Chem.Abstr., Compumath., Curr.Cont., Cyb.Abstr., INSPEC, Int.Aerosp.Abstr., SSCI. **Document type:** academic/scholarly publication.
—BLDSC (3598.721500); AskIEEE; CASDDS; CISTI; Ei; Genuine Article; KR SourceOne; Linda Hall; SWETS; UMI; UnCover. **CCC.**
Description: Covers research and commercial development of display technology, including digital, alphanumeric, graphic and pictorial displays.
Refereed Serial

006.6 US ISSN 1068-7947
THE FUTURE IMAGE REPORT; the inside track in digital imaging. 1993. 10/yr. $275 (effective 1997). Future Image, Inc., 1020 Parrott Drive, Burlingame, CA 94010. TEL 415-579-0493; 800-749-3572. FAX 415-579-0566. E-mail: agfuture@aol.com. Ed. Alexis J. Gerard. circ. 400 (paid). **Document type:** trade publication.
Description: Covers photography, digital imaging information, and new products.

006 US ISSN 1077-3169
T385 CODEN: GMIPF4
GRAPHICAL MODELS AND IMAGE PROCESSING. 1969. bi-m. $342 (foreign $383) (effective 1997). Academic Press, Inc., Journal Division, 525 B St., Ste. 1900, San Diego, CA 92101-4495. TEL 619-230-1840. FAX 619-699-6800. E-mail: apsubs@acad.com; URL: http://www.apnet.com/www/journal/ip.htm; http://www.idealibrary.com/. (Subscr. to: Box 861213, Orlando, FL 32886-1213. TEL 407-347-4040. FAX 407-363-9661) Eds. Norman Badler, Rama Chellappa. (back issues avail.) **Indexed:** A.I.Abstr., A.S.& T.Ind., Abstr.Hum.Comp.Inter., ASCA, CAD CAM Abstr., Compumath, Comput.Cont., Comput.Dtbs., Comput.Rev., Curr.Cont., Cyb.Abstr., Ergon.Abstr., Geo.Abstr.P.G., Ind.Sci.Rev., INSPEC (1978-), Int.Aerosp.Abstr., Robomat., Sci.Cit.Ind., SSCI, Zent.Math. **Document type:** academic/scholarly publication.
●Also available online.
—BLDSC (4212.400000); AskIEEE; CISTI; Ei; EMDOCS; Genuine Article; KR SourceOne; Linda Hall; SWETS; UnCover. **CCC.**
Formerly (until 1995): C V G I P: Graphical Models and Image Processing (ISSN 1049-9652); Which supersedes in part (in 1991): Computer Vision, Graphics, and Image Processing (ISSN 0734-189X); Which was formerly (until 1983): Computer Graphics and Image Processing (ISSN 0146-664X)
Description: Focuses on the synthesis methods and computational models underlying computer-generated or -processed imagery.

001.644 US ISSN 0272-1716
T385 CODEN: ICGADZ
I E E E COMPUTER GRAPHICS AND APPLICATIONS. 1981. bi-m. $290 to non-members (effective 1996). (Institute of Electrical and Electronics Engineers, Inc.) I E E E Computer Society Press, 10662 Los Vaqueros Circle, Box 3014, Los Alamitos, CA 90720-1264. TEL 714-821-8380; 800-678-4333. FAX 714-821-4641. E-mail: customer.service@ieee.org; webmaster@computer.org; URL: http://www.ieee.org; http://www.computer.org/pubs/cg&a.htm. Ed. Bertram Herzog. adv.: B&W page $2150, color page $3250; adv. contact: Heidi Rex. bk.rev.; charts; illus.; stat. circ. 11,782. (also avail. in microfilm from EEE; back issues avail.) **Indexed:** A.I.Abstr., A.S.& T.Ind., Abstr.Hum.Comp.Inter., ASCA, CAD CAM Abstr., Compumath., Comput.Abstr., Comput.Cont., Comput.Dtbs., Comput.Lit.Ind., Curr.Cont., Cyb.Abstr., Deep Sea Res.& Oceanogr.Abstr., Ergon.Abstr., Ind.Sci.Rev., INSPEC, Int.Aerosp.Abstr., Intl.Civil Eng.Abstr., Soft.Abstr.Eng., SSCI. **Document type:** proceedings.
●Also available online.
—BLDSC (4362.814300); AskIEEE; CISTI; Ei; Genuine Article; KR SourceOne; Linda Hall; SWETS; UMI; UnCover. **CCC.**
Description: For professional users. Articles and columns present timely information on computer graphics research, technology and applications.

001.644 US ISSN 1063-6919
TA1650 CODEN: PIVRE9
I E E E COMPUTER SOCIETY CONFERENCE ON COMPUTER VISION AND PATTERN RECOGNITION. PROCEEDINGS. Short title: C V P R. 1983. a. price varies. (Institute of Electrical and Electronics Engineers, Inc.) I E E E Computer Society Press, 10662 Los Vaqueros Circle, Los Alamitos, CA 90720. TEL 714-821-8380. FAX 714-821-4641. Ed. Cat Harris; Pub. Matt Loeb. adv. contact: Frieda Koester. **Indexed:** A.I.Abstr., CAD CAM Abstr., Comput.Cont., Ind.Sci.Rev. **Document type:** proceedings.
—BLDSC (4362.816800); Ei. **CCC.**
Supersedes (1977-1982): I E E E Computer Society Conference on Pattern Recognition and Image Processing. P R I P. Proceedings; Which was formerly (until 1975): Conference on Computer Graphics, Pattern Recognition, and Data Structure. Proceedings.
Description: Papers submitted at the conference on all aspects of vision, pattern recognition and image processing.

001.644 US ISSN 1070-2385
T385
I E E E CONFERENCE ON VISUALIZATION. 1990. a. price varies. (Institute of Electrical and Electronics Engineers, Inc.) I E E E Computer Society Press, 10662 Los Vaqueros Circle, Los Alamitos, CA 90720. TEL 714-821-8380. FAX 714-821-4641. Ed. Cat Harris; Pub. Matt Loeb. adv. contact: Frieda Koester. **Document type:** proceedings.
—UMI. **CCC.**
Description: Explores the use of visualization strategies in a variety of applications to extract knowledge from data.

001.644 US ISSN 1063-6757
TK7874
I E E E INTERNATIONAL CONFERENCE ON COMPUTER-AIDED DESIGN. PROCEEDINGS. Short title: I C C A D. 1983. a. (Institute of Electrical and Electronics Engineers, Inc.) I E E E Computer Society Press, 10662 Los Vaqueros Circle, Los Alamitos, CA 90720-1264. TEL 714-821-8380. FAX 714-821-4641. Ed. Cat Harris; Pub. Matt Loeb. adv. contact: Frieda Koester. **Indexed:** CAD CAM Abstr. **Document type:** proceedings.
—**CCC.**
Supersedes in part (1980-1982): I E E E International Conference on Circuits and Computers. I C C C Proceedings.
Description: Covers computer-aided design for integrated circuit design.

COMPUTERS — COMPUTER GRAPHICS

006.6 US
I E E E JOURNAL OF TECHNOLOGY COMPUTER AIDED DESIGN. 1996. irreg. free. Institute of Electrical and Electronics Engineers, Inc., 345 E. 47th St., New York, NY 10017-2394. TEL 800-678-4333. E-mail: customer.service@ieee.org; URL: http://www.ieee.org/journal/tcal. (Subscr. to: 445 Hoes Ln., Box 1331, Piscataway, NJ 08855-1331. TEL 908-981-0060. FAX 908-981-9667) **Indexed:** INSPEC, INSPEC.
●Available only online.
Description: Covers modeling and simulation of basic semiconductor devices, materials and processes.
Refereed Serial

006.6 US ISSN 1057-7149
TA1632 CODEN: IIPRE4
I E E E TRANSACTIONS ON IMAGE PROCESSING. 1992. m. $475 to non-members (effective 1998). (I E E E, Signal Processing Society) Institute of Electrical and Electronics Engineers, Inc., 345 E. 47th St., New York, NY 10017-2394. TEL 732-981-0060; 800-678-4333. FAX 732-981-9667. E-mail: customer.service@ieee.org; URL: http://www.ieee.org. (Subscr. to: 445 Hoes Ln., Box 1331, Piscataway, NJ 08855-1331) Ed. A.C. Bovik. (also avail. in microform from IEE) **Indexed:** ASCA, Compumath, Curr.Cont. **Document type:** academic/scholarly publication.
—BLDSC (4363.190900); AskIEEE; CISTI; Ei; Genuine Article; KR SourceOne; Linda Hall; SWETS; UMI; UnCover. **CCC.**
Description: Covers the signal processing aspects of image processing, computed imaging, image scanning, display and printing.

001.644 US ISSN 0162-8828
Q327 CODEN: ITPIDJ
I E E E TRANSACTIONS ON PATTERN ANALYSIS AND MACHINE INTELLIGENCE. Short title: P A M I. 1979. m. $625 to non-members (effective 1998). (I E E E, Computer Society) Institute of Electrical and Electronics Engineers, Inc., 345 E. 47th St., New York, NY 10017-2394. TEL 732-981-0060; 800-678-4333. FAX 732-981-9667. E-mail: customer.service@ieee.org; URL: http://www.ieee.org. (Subscr. to: Box 1331, 445 Hoes Lane, Piscataway, NJ 08855-1331) Ed. Rangachar Kasturi. (also avail. in microform) **Indexed:** A.I.Abstr., A.S.& T.Ind., Abstr.Hum.Comp.Inter., ASCA, CAD CAM Abstr., Compumath, Comput.Abstr., Comput.Cont., Comput.Dtbs., Curr.Cont., Ergon.Abstr., Ind.Sci.Rev., INSPEC, Int.Aerosp.Abstr., Oper.Res.Manage.Sci., Qual.Contr.Appl.Stat., Risk Abstr., Robomat., Sci.Cit.Ind., SSCI, Zent.Math.
—BLDSC (4363.211400); AskIEEE; CISTI; Ei; Genuine Article; KR SourceOne; Linda Hall; SWETS; UMI; UnCover. **CCC.**

006.6 US ISSN 1077-2626
I E E E TRANSACTIONS ON VISUALIZATION AND COMPUTER GRAPHICS. 1995. q. $325 (effective 1998). Institute of Electrical and Electronics Engineers, Inc., 345 E. 47th St., New York, NY 10017-2394. TEL 732-981-0060; 800-678-4333. FAX 732-981-9667. E-mail: customer.service@ieee.org; URL: http://www.ieee.org. (Subscr. to: 445 Hoes Ln., Box 1331, Piscataway, NJ 08855-1331) Ed. Arie E. Kaufman. **Indexed:** ASCA, Compumath, Curr.Cont.
—AskIEEE; CISTI; Genuine Article; KR SourceOne; SWETS; UnCover.

001.644 US
I E E E WORKSHOP ON VISUAL MOTION. 1990. biennial. price varies. (Institute of Electrical and Electronics Engineers, Inc.) I E E E Computer Society Press, 10662 Los Vaqueros Circle, Los Alamitos, CA 90720. TEL 714-821-8380. FAX 714-821-4641. Ed. Cat Harris; Pub. Matt Loeb. adv. contact: Frieda Koester. **Document type:** proceedings.
Description: Examines key issues in the field, such as image-flow, optical flow, 3D motion, active vision and statistical estimation.

006.6 NE ISSN 0262-8856
TA1632
IMAGE AND VISION COMPUTING. (Text in English) 1982. m. fl.1649($948) (effective 1998). Elsevier Science B.V., P.O. Box 211, 1000 AE Amsterdam, Netherlands. TEL 31-20-4853911. FAX 31-20-4853598. (Subscr. in the Americas to: Elsevier Science, Regional Sales Office, Box 945, New York, NY 10159-0945. TEL 212-633-3730. FAX 212-633-3680; Subscr. in Australasia and the Far East to: Elsevier Science (Singapore) Pte Ltd, No.1 Temasek Ave., No.17-01 Millenia Tower, Singapore 039192, Singapore. TEL 65-434-3727. FAX 65-337-2230; Subscr. in Japan to: Elsevier Science Japan, 9-15 Higashi-Azabu 1-chome, Minato-ku, Tokyo 106, Japan. TEL 81-3-5561-5033. FAX 81-3-5561-5047) Ed. Keith Baker. adv.; bk.rev.; abstr.; illus.; index. (also avail. in microform from UMI; back issues avail.; reprint service avail.) **Indexed:** Abstr.Hum.Comp.Inter., ASCA, CAD CAM Abstr., Compumath, Comput.Abstr., Comput.Cont., Comput.Dtbs., Curr.Cont., Cyb.Abstr., Ind.Sci.Rev., INSPEC, LAMP, Robomat., SSCI. **Document type:** academic/scholarly publication.
—BLDSC (4368.991400); AskIEEE; CISTI; Ei; Genuine Article; KR SourceOne; Linda Hall; SWETS; UMI; UnCover. **CCC.**
Description: Focuses on the applications of electronically generated images on astronomy, biomedicine, robotics, remote sensing, broadcasting, metallurgy, seismology and radar.
Refereed Serial

006 US
▼**IMAGING BUSINESS**; the voice of the document imaging channel. 1995. m. free to qualified personnel. Phillips Business Information, Inc., 1201 Seven Locks Rd., Potomac, MD 20854. TEL 301-424-3338. FAX 301-309-3847. E-mail: pbi@phillips.com. adv.; illus.; circ. controlled. **Document type:** trade publication.
Formerly: Imaging Product News.

001.644 US ISSN 1063-4320
TK8315 CODEN: IMNYE9
IMAGING MAGAZINE; document solutions for business. 1992. m. $17.95 (Canada $25, Europe $50; elsewhere $60) (effective 1995); newsstand price: $2.95 (Can.$3.95). Telecom Library Inc., 12 W. 21st St., New York, NY 10010. TEL 212-691-8215; 800-542-7279. FAX 212-691-7279. (Subscr. to: Box 40706, Nashville, TN 37204) Ed. Harry Newton. adv.: B&W page $5800, color page $6650; trim 8 1/8 x 10 7/8. software rev. circ. 62,103. **Indexed:** INSPEC (1993-). **Document type:** trade publication.
—AskIEEE; CISTI; Ei; KR SourceOne; SWETS.
Description: For professionals who buy, implement and manage imaging products and services.

001.644 US
IMAGING UPDATE. 1989. m. $150 (outside N. America $165). Worldwide Videotex, Box 3273, Boynton Beach, FL 33424-3273. TEL 407-738-2276. Ed. Mark Wright; Pub. Mark Wright. bk.rev. (back issues avail.) **Document type:** newsletter.
●Also available online. Vendor(s): Data-Star, Information Access Co., Knight-Ridder Information, Inc., NewsNet (EC05).
Description: Provides news and information on the digitized image and computer graphics industry, covering new hardware and software products, as well as research and development. Special emphasis is on the marketing strategies of manufacturers and vendors, along with articles on publishing and information storage and retrieval.

001.644 US ISSN 1060-894X
IMAGING WORLD; electronic imaging, document management and workflow. m. $48 (free to qualified personnel) (foreign $96). Cardinal Business Media, Inc., 1300 Virginia Dr., Ste. 400, Fort Washington, PA 19034. TEL 215-643-8000. FAX 215-643-8099. URL: http://www.cardinal.com/iw. (Subscr. to: Box 3055, Northbrook, IL 60065-3055. TEL 847-291-5212. FAX 847-291-4816) Ed. Andy Moore; Pub. Bruce Taylor. circ. 85,000. (tabloid format)
●Also available online.
—KR SourceOne.
Description: Reports on new technologies, chronicles and evaluates them and delivers practical solutions.

INDUSTRIAL SYSTEMS. see ENGINEERING — *Industrial Engineering*

THE INTERACTIVE MULTIMEDIA SOURCEBOOK (YEAR). see BUSINESS AND ECONOMICS — *Trade And Industrial Directories*

006.6 US ISSN 1077-8047
QA76.76.I59
INTERACTIVITY; tools and techniques for interactive media developers. 1994. m. $59.95 (effective 1997); newsstand price: $4.95. Miller Freeman, Inc. (San Mateo) (Subsidiary of: United News & Media), 411 Borel Ave., Ste. 100, San Mateo, CA 94402. TEL 415-358-9500. FAX 415-655-4360. E-mail: interactivity@mfi.com; URL: http://www.eyemedia.com. (Subscr. to: Box 1174, Skokie, IL 60076. TEL 847-647-0818. FAX 847-647-5972) Ed. Dominic Milano; Pub. Thomas M. Edwards. adv.: B&W page $6825; trim 8 1/2 x 10 3/4; adv. contact: Alicia Langerards. software rev.; charts; illus.; circ. 55,000 (controlled). (back issues avail.) **Document type:** trade publication.
●Also available online.
—KR SourceOne.
Description: Written for professional digital media creators; digital entertainment, education, sales and marketing, and commerce applications.

001.5 651.8 US ISSN 1051-4651
Q327
INTERNATIONAL CONFERENCE ON PATTERN RECOGNITION. PROCEEDINGS. 1973. biennial. price varies. (Institute of Electrical and Electronics Engineers, Inc.) I E E E Computer Society Press, 10662 Los Vaqueros Circle, Los Alamitos, CA 90720-1264. TEL 714-821-8380. FAX 714-821-4641. Ed. Cat Harris; Pub. Matt Loeb. adv. contact: Frieda Koester. **Document type:** proceedings.
—BLDSC (4538.839560); Ei. **CCC.**
Formerly (1973-1978): International Joint Conference on Pattern Recognition. Proceedings.
Description: Fundamental research and industrial applications in the field of pattern recognition.

INTERNATIONAL IMAGING SOURCE BOOK (LARCHMONT). see BUSINESS AND ECONOMICS — *Production Of Goods And Services*

006 US
INTERNATIONAL IMAGING SOURCEBOOK (POTOMAC). 1985. a. $199 (foreign $223) (effective 1997). Phillips Business Information, Inc., 1001 Seven Locks Rd., Potomac, MD 20854. TEL 301-424-3338. FAX 301-309-3847. E-mail: pbi@phillips.com. **Document type:** directory.
Description: Provides over 400 pages of product and service information, competitive profiles, current market research, financial and operating facts, and access to executive personnel.

INTERNATIONAL JOURNAL OF COMPUTER INTEGRATED MANUFACTURING. see BUSINESS AND ECONOMICS — *Computer Applications*

INTERNATIONAL JOURNAL OF MICROWAVE AND MILLIMETER-WAVE COMPUTER AIDED ENGINEERING. see ENGINEERING — *Computer Applications*

001.5 651.8 SI ISSN 0218-0014
Q327 CODEN: IJPIEI
INTERNATIONAL JOURNAL OF PATTERN RECOGNITION AND ARTIFICIAL INTELLIGENCE. Abbreviated title: I J P R A I. (Text in English) 1987. 8/yr. $195 to individuals; institutions & libraries $490 (developing countries $294). World Scientific Publishing Co. Pte. Ltd., Farrer Rd., P.O. Box 128, Singapore 9128, Singapore. TEL 65-3825663. FAX 65-3825919. TELEX RS-28561-WSPC. E-mail: wspcsl@singnet.com.sg; sales@wspc2.demon.co.uk; wspc@wspc.com; URL: http://www.singnet.com.sg/~wspclib/. (UK addr.: 57 Shelton St., Covent Garden, London WC2H 9HE, England. TEL 44-171-836-0888. FAX 44-171-836-2020; US addr.: 1060 Main St., Ste. 1B, River Edge, NJ 07661. TEL 800-227-7562. FAX 201-487-9656) Eds. Patrick Shen-Pei Wang, Horst Bunke. bk.rev.; cum.index every 5 yrs. circ. 250. (back issues avail.) **Indexed:** ASCA, Comput.Abstr., INSPEC (1988-). **Document type:** academic/scholarly publication.
—BLDSC (4542.449700); AskIEEE; CISTI; Ei; Genuine Article; KR SourceOne; SWETS; UnCover. **CCC.**
Description: Disseminates pattern recognition and artificial intelligence, in particular when the two fields intersect. Emphasis on methodology and applications.
Refereed Serial

COMPUTERS — COMPUTER GRAPHICS

006.6   SI   ISSN 0218-6543
QA448.D38   CODEN: IJSMFC
INTERNATIONAL JOURNAL OF SHAPING MODELING. Short title: I J S M. (Text in English) 1994. 4/yr. $110 to individuals; institutions & libraries $220. World Scientific Publishing Co. Pte. Ltd., Farrer Rd., P.O. Box 128, Singapore 9128, Singapore. TEL 65-3825663. FAX 65-3825919. TELEX RS 28561 WSPC. E-mail: wspcsl@singnet.com.sg; sales@wspc2.demon.co.uk; wspc@wspc.com.sg; URL: http://www.singnet.com.sg/~wspclib/. (UK addr.: 57 Shelton St., London WC2H 9HE, England. TEL 44-171-836-0888. FAX 44-171-836-2020; US addr.: 1060 Main St., Ste. 1B, River Edge, NJ 07661. TEL 800-227-7562. FAX 201-487-9656) Ed. Bianca Galcidieno. **Document type:** academic/scholarly publication.
—BLDSC (4542.546000); AskIEEE; KR SourceOne. **CCC.**
   Description: Aims at creating a suitable environment for exchanging research results obtained in advanced theories and techniques devised for handling the shape of objects, pointing out the three main aspects of modeling: disciplines, roles and applications.

INTERNATIONAL JOURNAL OF VISUAL COMPUTING. see ART — Computer Applications

006.6   AT
▼**JOURNAL OF AUSTRALASIAN GRAPHICS IMAGERY.** 1997. irreg. Curtin University of Technology, School of Computing, Hayman Rd., Bentley, W.A. 6102, Australia. TEL 619-351-7680. E-mail: raytrace@cs.curtin.edu.au; URL: http://www.cs.curtin.edu.au/jagi/. Ed. Andrew Marriott. **Document type:** academic/scholarly publication.
●Available only online.
   Description: Contains scientific papers dealing with any area of computer graphics or computer vision research.
   Refereed Serial

JOURNAL OF COMPUTER - AIDED MATERIALS DESIGN. see CHEMISTRY — Computer Applications

JOURNAL OF COMPUTER - AIDED MOLECULAR DESIGN. see CHEMISTRY — Computer Applications

006.6   US   ISSN 1086-7651
T385
▼**JOURNAL OF GRAPHICS TOOLS.** 1996. q. $57.50 to individuals (outside N. America $70); institutions $127.50 (outside N. America $140); members $47.50 (foreign $60) (effective 1998). A K Peters, Ltd., 289 Linden St., Wellesley, MA 02181. TEL 617-235-2210. FAX 617-235-2404. E-mail: akpeters@tiac.net; URL: http://www.akpeters.com. Ed. Andrew Glassner. cum.index. (back issues avail.) **Document type:** academic/scholarly publication.
   Description: Reports techniques, research results and tricks of the trade of interest to computer graphics professionals.
   Refereed Serial

006.6 576   US   ISSN 0263-7855
QD461   CODEN: JMGRDV
JOURNAL OF MOLECULAR GRAPHICS. 1983. bi-m. fl.975($602) (effective 1997). (Molecular Graphics Society) Elsevier Science Inc., Box 945, New York, NY 10159-0945. TEL 212-633-3730. FAX 212-633-3680. E-mail: usinfo@elsevier.com; URL: http://www.elsevier.nl/. (Subscr. outside the Americas to: Elsevier Science, Regional Sales Office, P.O. Box 211, 1000 AE Amsterdam, Netherlands. TEL 31-20-4853757. FAX 31-20-4853432; Subscr. in Australasia and the Far East to: Elsevier Science (Singapore) Pte Ltd, No.1 Temasek Ave., No.17-01 Millenia Tower, Singapore 039192, Singapore. TEL 65-434-3727. FAX 65-337-2230; Subscr. in Japan to: Elsevier Science Japan, 9-15 Higashi-Azabu 1-chome, Minato-ku, Tokyo 106, Japan. TEL 81-3-5561-5033. FAX 81-3-5561-5047) Eds. Vivian Cody, W.G. Richards. adv.; bk.rev.; abstr.; illus.; index. (also avail. in microform from UMI; back issues avail.) **Indexed:** Chem.Abstr., Chem.Cit.Ind., Comput.Cont., Curr.Cont., Excerp.Med. (1992-), Ind.Sci.Rev., Sci.Cit.Ind. **Document type:** academic/scholarly publication.
—BLDSC (5020.713000); ADONIS; CASDDS; CISTI; Ei; EMDOCS; Genuine Article; Linda Hall; SWETS; UMI; UnCover. **CCC.**
   Description: Practical and theoretical research on the use of computer graphics for the investigation of molecular structure, function and interaction.
   Refereed Serial

006.6   US   ISSN 1047-3203
P93.5   CODEN: JVCRE7
JOURNAL OF VISUAL COMMUNICATION AND IMAGE REPRESENTATION. 1990. q. $240 (foreign $269) (effective 1997). Academic Press, Inc., Journal Division, 525 B St., Ste. 1900, San Diego, CA 92101-4495. TEL 619-230-1840. FAX 619-699-6800. URL: http://www.apnet.com/www/journal/vc.htm; http://www.idealibrary.com/. (Subscr. to: Box 861213, Orlando, FL 32886-1213. TEL 407-347-4040. FAX 407-363-9661) Eds. Yehoshua Y. Zeevi, T. Russell Hsing. (back issues avail.) **Indexed:** ASCA, Compumath, Curr.Cont., INSPEC (1990-). **Document type:** academic/scholarly publication.
—BLDSC (5072.493000); AskIEEE; CISTI; Ei; Genuine Article; KR SourceOne; SWETS; UnCover. **CCC.**
   Description: Publishes papers on the state-of-the-art of visual communication and image representation with emphasis on novel technologies and theoretical work in this multidisciplinary area of pure and applied research.
   Refereed Serial

001.644   UK   ISSN 1049-8907
TR897.5   CODEN: JVCAEO
THE JOURNAL OF VISUALIZATION AND COMPUTER ANIMATION. 1990. q. $595 (foreign $595) (effective 1998). John Wiley & Sons Ltd., Journals, Baffins Ln., Chichester, W. Sussex PO19 1UD, England. TEL 44-1243-779777. FAX 44-1243-775878. E-mail: info-assets@wiley.co.uk; URL: http://www.wiley.co.uk. (Subscr. in the Americas to: John Wiley & Sons, Inc., 605 Third Ave., New York, NY 10158. TEL 212-850-6645. FAX 212-850-6021) Eds. N.M. Thalmann, D. Thalmann. adv.: B&W page £1245, color page £2145; trim 297 x 210; adv. contact: Bob Kern. (also avail. in microform from UMI; back issues avail.; reprint service avail. from SWZ) **Indexed:** ASCA, Compumath, Geo.Abstr.H.G. **Document type:** academic/scholarly publication.
—BLDSC (5072.497000); AskIEEE; Ei; EMDOCS; Genuine Article; KR SourceOne; UMI. **CCC.**
   Description: Includes topics that range from scenario making to postproduction for those who apply animation techniques to science and art.
   Refereed Serial

006.6   US
JUST THE FAX. m. International Association of Presentation Professionals, 294 Arden Rd., Pittsburgh, PA 15210. TEL 403-266-5133. FAX 403-265-4012. E-mail: lesley@viacom.ca; URL: http://www.iapp.org. Ed. Lesley Hayes. (only avail. by fax) **Document type:** newsletter.

005.3   US   ISSN 0892-4635
QA76.73.L23   CODEN: LSCOEX
L I S P AND SYMBOLIC COMPUTATION; an international journal. 1988. q. fl.600 to institutions; $308 to institutions in U.S. (effective 1998). Kluwer Academic Publishers Boston, Box 358, Accord Sta., Hingham, MA 02018-0358. TEL 617-871-6600. FAX 617-871-6528. TELEX 200190. (Dist. outside N. America by: Kluwer Academic Publishers Group, P.O. Box 322, 3300 AH Dordrecht, Netherlands. TEL 31-78-6392392. FAX 31-78-6546474) Eds. Robert R. Kessler, Carolyn Talcott. (also avail. in microform from UMI; reprint service avail. from SWZ,UMI) **Indexed:** A.I.Abstr., ASCA, Chem.Abstr., Comput.Rev., Eng.Ind., INSPEC (1988-). **Document type:** academic/scholarly publication.
—BLDSC (5221.986300); AskIEEE; CISTI; Ei; KR SourceOne; SWETS; UMI; UnCover. **CCC.**
   Description: Presents a forum for current and evolving symbolic computing, focusing on LISP and object-oriented programming.
   Refereed Serial

006.6   GW   ISSN 0939-3846
LAYOUT; Corel User Magazin. 1989. bi-m. DM.55.80($160) Veda Verlag, Gartenstr. 5, 38729 Wallmoden, Germany. TEL 49-5383-8045. FAX 49-5383-8317. Ed. Alfred Goergens. adv. contact: Thomas Vieth. (also avail. in diskette format) **Document type:** consumer publication.

001.644
M C N: COMPUTER AUTOMATED SOLUTIONS FOR DESIGN ENGINEERING.* m. Ariel Communications, Inc., Box 203550, Austin, TX 78720-3550. TEL 512-250-1700. FAX 512-250-1016. Ed. Dave Baceski. adv.: page $4700. circ. 55,000.

001.644   IT
MONDO AUTOCAD. 1989. 5/yr. L.80000 (foreign L.160000) (effective 1997). Franco Ziviani Editore Srl, Via M. Gioia 168, 20125 Milan, Italy. TEL 39-2-6692329. FAX 39-2-66982879. E-mail: mc4467@mclink.it. Ed. Giovanni Gatti. adv. contact: Gian Pietro Grollo. circ. 9,000.

006.6   US   ISSN 1064-6639
   CODEN: MUWEEQ
MULTIMEDIA WEEK. 1992. w. (50/yr.) $697 (foreign $760) (effective 1997). Phillips Business Information, Inc., 1201 Seven Locks Rd., Potomac, MD 20854. TEL 301-424-3338. FAX 301-309-3847. E-mail: pbi@phillips.com. Ed. Seth Arenstein. bk.rev.; cum.index: 1979-1981. (back issues avail.) **Indexed:** CAD CAM Abstr., Comput.Lit.Ind., Graph.Arts Lit.Abstr. **Document type:** newsletter.
●Also available online. Vendor(s): Information Access Co.
—**CCC.**
   Incorporates (in 1994): Open Media Letter; Incorporates (in Nov. 1992): S. Klein Newsletter on Computer Graphics (ISSN 0731-9207); Which was formerly (1979-1982): Harvard Newsletter on Computer Graphics.
   Description: Covers computer graphics news, analysis, and commentary on everything from hardware and software to systems and services. Each issue covers the latest technology, product, market, application and finance data on CAD-CAM, multimedia, databases, business graphics and R&D.

MULTIMEDIA WORLD. see COMPUTERS — Personal Computers

001.644   JA   ISSN 0912-1609
NIKKEI COMPUTER GRAPHICS. Key Title: Nikkei C G. 1986. m. 13860 Yen. Nikkei Business Publications, Inc. (Subsidiary of: Nihon Keizai Shimbun, Inc.), 2-7-6 Hirakawa-cho, Chiyoda-ku, Tokyo 102, Japan. TEL 81-3-5210-8502. FAX 81-3-5210-8119. E-mail: http://www.nikkeibp.co.jp/. (Subscr. to: Nikkei Business Pub. Inc., Reader Service Center, P.O. Box 20, Kasai Post Office, Tokyo 134-70, Japan) Ed. Susumu Tajima; Pub. Shozo Watanabe. adv.: B&W page 355000 Yen, color page 498000 Yen; trim 208 x 280; adv. contact: Yoshio Mizuno. circ. 19,508. **Document type:** trade publication.
   Description: Contains comprehensive information on computer graphics and CG systems, and their applications in business.

001.644   US
P C GRAPHICS & VIDEO. 1991. 10/yr. $29.95 (effective 1996). Advanstar Communications, Inc., 7500 Old Oak Blvd., Cleveland, OH 44130. TEL 216-826-2839. FAX 216-891-2726. (Subscr. to: Box 7708, Riverton, NJ 08077-8708. FAX 503-683-8841) adv.: B&W page $6245, color page $7295; trim 8 1/8 x 10 7/8. bk.rev. circ. 75,000.
—KR SourceOne.
   Formerly (until 1993): High Color (ISSN 1060-5282)
   Description: Covers color applications of PC graphics systems for business presentations, multimedia, publishing, and creative arts.

001.644 621.381   US   ISSN 1056-6023
THE PAGE (LOUISVILLE). 1987. 10/yr. $59 (effective 1994). Cobb Group, Inc., 9420 Bunsen Pkwy., Ste. 300, Louisville, KY 40232-9720. TEL 502-493-3200. FAX 502-491-8050. (Subscr. to: Box 35160, Louisville, KY 40232-9720. TEL 800-223-8720) circ. 3,000. (looseleaf format)
   Description: Covers applications of computer graphics technologies and techniques for graphics arts designers and desktop publishers who use Macintosh systems.

001.644   UK   ISSN 1433-7541
▼**PATTERN ANALYSIS AND APPLICATIONS.** Announced for publication in 1998. q. £156 (effective 1998). Springer-Verlag London Ltd., Sweetapple House, Catteshall Rd., Godalming, Surrey GU7 3DJ, England. TEL 44-1483-418800. FAX 44-1483-415144. (Subscr. in N. America to: Springer-Verlag New York, Inc., Box 2485, Secaucus, NJ 07096-2485. TEL 800-777-4643. FAX 201-348-4505) **Document type:** academic/scholarly publication.
●Also available online.

COMPUTERS — COMPUTER GRAPHICS

006.4 UK ISSN 0031-3203
Q307
PATTERN RECOGNITION. 1968. m. fl.2798($1608) (effective 1998). (Pattern Recognition Society) Elsevier Science Ltd., Pergamon, P.O. Box 800, Kidlington, Oxford OX5 1DX, England. TEL 44-1865-843000. FAX 44-1865-843010. E-mail: nlinfo-f@elsevier.nl; usinfo-f@elsevier.com; forinfo-kyf04035@niftyserve.or.jp; URL: http://www.elsevier.nl/. (Subscr. to: Elsevier Science, Regional Sales Office, P.O. Box 211, 1000 AE Amsterdam, Netherlands. TEL 31-20-4853757. FAX 31-20-4853432; Subscr. in the Americas to: Elsevier Science, Regional Sales Office, Box 945, New York, NY 10159-0945. TEL 212-633-3730. FAX 212-633-3680; Subscr. in Australasia and the Far East to: Elsevier Science (Singapore) Pte Ltd, No.1 Temasek Ave., No.17-01 Millenia Tower, Singapore 039192, Singapore. TEL 65-434-3727. FAX 65-337-2230) Ed. Robert S. Ledley. adv.; bk.rev. circ. 1,500. (also avail. in microform from UMI; back issues avail.) **Indexed:** A.I.Abstr., Abstr.Hum.Comp.Inter., Appl.Mech.Rev., ASCA, Biol.Abstr., CAD CAM Abstr., Compumath, Comput.Abstr., Comput.Cont., Curr.Cont., Eng.Ind., Excerp.Med., Geo.Abstr.H.G., Ind.Sci.Rev., INSPEC, Neurosci.Cit.Ind., Robomat., Sci.Cit.Ind., SSCI, Zent.Math. **Document type:** academic/scholarly publication.
 —BLDSC (6412.981000); AskIEEE; CISTI; Ei; Genuine Article; KR SourceOne; Linda Hall; SWETS; UMI; UnCover. **CCC.**
 Refereed Serial

004 NE ISSN 0167-8655
TK7882.P3 CODEN: PRLEDG
PATTERN RECOGNITION LETTERS. (Text in English) 1983. 14/yr. fl.2142($1231) (effective 1998). (International Association for Pattern Recognition) North-Holland (Subsidiary of: Elsevier Science B.V.), P.O. Box 211, 1000 AE Amsterdam, Netherlands. TEL 31-20-4853911. FAX 31-20-4853598. TELEX 18582 ESPA NL. (Subscr. in the Americas to: Elsevier Science, Regional Sales Office, Box 945, New York, NY 10159-0945. TEL 212-633-3730. FAX 212-633-3680; Subscr. in Australasia and the Far East to: Elsevier Science (Singapore) Pte Ltd, No.1 Temasek Ave., No.17-01 Millenia Tower, Singapore 039192, Singapore. TEL 65-434-3727. FAX 65-337-2230; Subscr. in Japan to: Elsevier Science Japan, 9-15 Higashi-Azabu 1-chome, Minato-ku Tokyo 106, Japan. TEL 81-3-5561-5033. FAX 81-3-5561-5047) Eds. E. Backer, E.S. Gelsema. (also avail. in microform from UMI; back issues avail.) **Indexed:** A.I.Abstr., Abstr.Hum.Comp.Inter., Agri.Eng.Abstr., ASCA, CAD CAM Abstr., Compumath, Comput.Abstr., Curr.Cont., Cyb.Abstr., Geo.Abstr.H.G., INSPEC, Robomat., SSCI, Zent.Math. **Document type:** academic/scholarly publication.
 —BLDSC (6412.981840); AskIEEE; CISTI; Ei; EMDOCS; Genuine Article; KR SourceOne; Linda Hall; SWETS; UnCover. **CCC.**
 Description: Covers theoretical, methodological and empirical studies of image processing and pattern recognition.
 Refereed Serial

CABIA. see *ART*

001.644 FR ISSN 0992-1060
PIXEL. 1988. 11/yr. 360 F.($90) (foreign 450 F.) (effective 1997). Societe Pixel, 71 rue de Maubeuge, 75010 Paris, France. TEL 33-1-48786090. FAX 33-1-48781535. Ed. Pascal Guenee; Pub. Ben Kuhn. adv. contact: D. Choin. bk.rev.; circ. 15,000 (paid). **Document type:** trade publication.
 Description: Dedicated to computer graphics as it applies to television, cinema, and video-clips, as well as to scientific, medical, industrial and architectural publicity imagery.

006.6 CH ISSN 1024-8307
POWER MEDIA. (Text in Chinese) 1995. m. Acer T W P Corporation, 2-F, No. 19-1 Lane 231, Fu-Hsing N. Rd., Taipei, Taiwan 105, Republic of China. TEL 2-7136959. FAX 2-7189467. adv.: B&W page $860, color page $1720; trim 210 x 298; adv. contact: David Tsai. circ. 10,000.

001.644 760 US ISSN 0032-8510
Z119
PRINT; America's graphic design magazine. 1940. bi-m. $53. R C Publications, Inc., 104 Fifth Ave., 19th Fl., New York, NY 10011. TEL 212-463-0600. FAX 212-989-9891. (Subscr. to: 3200 Tower Oaks Blvd., Rockville, MD 20852. TEL 301-770-2900) Ed. Martin Fox; Pub. Howard Cadel. adv. contact: Ellen Saracino. bk.rev.; illus.; index. circ. 55,000. (also avail. in microform from UMI; back issues avail.; reprint service avail. from UMI) **Indexed:** Art Ind., Artbibl.Mod., DAAI, Film Lit.Ind. (1973-), Ind.Bk.Rev.Hum. **Document type:** trade publication.
 •Also available online. Vendor(s): Information Access Co.
 —BLDSC (6612.995000); CISTI; KR SourceOne; Linda Hall; SWETS; UMI; UnCover.
 Incorporates (in 1976): Packaging Design (ISSN 0030-9109)
 Description: Disseminates various aspects of graphic design programs with professional input on visual communication: film, animation, environmental and computer graphics.

001.644 US ISSN 1059-6399
RAPID PROTOTYPING REPORT; the newsletter of the desktop manufacturing industry. 1991. m. $295 (foreign $345). C A D - C A M Publishing, Inc., 1010 Turquoise St., Ste. 320, San Diego, CA 92109-1268. TEL 619-488-6052. FAX 619-488-6052. Ed. Geoff Smith-Moritz. **Document type:** newsletter.
 •Also available online. Vendor(s): Information Access Co.

006.6 UK ISSN 1077-2014
▼**REAL-TIME IMAGING.** 1995. bi-m. £56($83) to individuals; institutions £135 (effective 1998). Academic Press Ltd. (Subsidiary of: Harcourt Brace & Company Ltd.), 24-28 Oval Rd., London NW1 7DX, England. TEL 44-171-482-2893. FAX 44-171-267-0362. E-mail: apsubs@acad.com; laplante@njit.edu; alex@rtlab12.njit.edu; URL: http://www.hbuk.co.uk/ap/rti; http://europe.idealibrary.com/. (Subscr. to: Harcourt Brace & Company Ltd., Foots Cray High St., Sidcup, Kent DA14 5HP, England. TEL 44-181-300-3322. FAX 44-181-309-0807) Phillip A. Laplante, Alexander D. Stoyenko. R&P contact: Catherine John. adv. contact: Nik Screen. **Indexed:** Zent.Math. **Document type:** academic/scholarly publication.
 •Also available online.
 —BLDSC (7303.282648); AskIEEE; CISTI; Genuine Article; KR SourceOne; SWETS; UnCover. **CCC.**

SHOOTER'S RAG; the practical gazette for silver & digital photographers. see *PHOTOGRAPHY*

006.6 760 US ISSN 1057-7041
T385
SILICON GRAPHICS WORLD. 1991. bi-m. $45 (foreign $75) (effective 1995). Publications & Communications, Inc., 12416 Hymeadow, Austin, TX 78750-1896. TEL 512-250-9023; 800-678-9724. FAX 512-678-9724. adv.: B&W page $3202, color page $3952; trim 10 3/4 x 14 1/2. illus. (tabloid format) **Document type:** trade publication.
 —CISTI; KR SourceOne.

621.381 004 US ISSN 1071-0922
TK7882.I6 CODEN: JSIDE8
SOCIETY FOR INFORMATION DISPLAY. JOURNAL. 1963. q. $100 to non-members (foreign $110). Society for Information Display, 1526 Brookhollow Dr., Ste. 82, Santa Ana, CA 92705-5421. TEL 714-545-1526. FAX 714-545-1547. Ed. Alan Sobel. bk.rev.; abstr.; charts; illus.; index. circ. 4,500. (back issues avail.) **Indexed:** Comput.Cont., INSPEC. **Document type:** academic/scholarly publication, proceedings.
 —BLDSC (4889.100000); AskIEEE; CISTI; Ei; KR SourceOne; Linda Hall; SWETS; UnCover. **CCC.**
 Former titles (until 1991): Society for Information Display. Proceedings (ISSN 0734-1768); (until 1976): S I D Proceedings (ISSN 0036-1496)
 Description: Presents original work dealing with the theory and practice of information display.

SOFTAWARENESS; a CAD-CAM-CAE journal and buyer's guide. see *COMPUTERS — Software*

006.6 US
▼**TECHNICAL COMPUTING REPORT.** 1996. m. $129 (foreign $149). C A D - C A M Publishing, Inc., 1010 Turquoise St., San Diego, CA 92109-1268. TEL 619-488-0533. FAX 619-488-6052.
 Description: Focuses on computer hardware for CAD-CAM and CAE especially workstations.

686.2 US
TECHNOLOGY WATCH; for the graphic arts and information industries. 1980. m. $95. Technology Watch, Inc., Box 2206, Springfield, VA 22152. Ed. Henry B. Freedman; Pub. Henry B. Freedman. adv. contact: Henry B. Freedman. bk.rev. (avail. electronically on Electronet Information Systems) **Indexed:** Graph.Arts Lit.Abstr. **Document type:** newsletter.
 •Also available online.

VARIETY'S ON PRODUCTION. see *MOTION PICTURES*

VIDEO LINE. see *COMMUNICATIONS — Video*

006.37 621.399 US ISSN 1089-2788
▼**VIDERE;** a journal of computer vision research. 1997. q. $30 to individuals; institutions $125. M I T Press, 5 Cambridge Center, Cambridge, MA 02142. TEL 617-253-2889. FAX 617-577-1545. E-mail: journals-orders@mit.edu; URL: http://www-mit.edu.Ed.Bd.
 •Available only online.
 Description: Scope is all areas of computer vision.
 Refereed Serial

006.6 IT
VIRTUAL; il mensile dell'era digitale. 1993. m. L.95000 in Europe; elsewhere L.135000. Edizioni Wilson s.r.l., Via Carlo Ravizza 53-A, 20149 Milan, Italy. TEL 39-2-48010171. FAX 39-2-4982098. E-mail: info@virtual.it. Ed. Stefania Garassini. adv.: color page L.7000000. **Document type:** trade publication.

006.6 GW ISSN 0178-2789
T385 CODEN: VICOE5
THE VISUAL COMPUTER; international journal of computer graphics. Online edition (GW ISSN 1432-2315) (Text in English) 1985. 10/yr. DM.1149 (foreign DM.1158) (effective 1998). (International Computer Graphics Society) Springer-Verlag, Heidelberger Platz 3, 14197 Berlin, Germany. TEL 49-30-82787-0. FAX 49-30-82787448. E-mail: subscriptions@springer.de; URL: http://link.springer.de. (Subscr. in N. America to: Springer-Verlag New York, Inc., 333 Meadowlands Pkwy., Secaucus, NJ 07094. TEL 212-460-1500. FAX 212-473-6272) Ed. T.L. Kunii. (also avail. in microform from UMI; back issues avail.; reprint service avail. from ISI) **Indexed:** ASCA, Compumath, Comput.Abstr., Cyb.Abstr., INSPEC, Zent.Math. **Document type:** academic/scholarly publication.
 •Also available online.
 —BLDSC (9241.235000); AskIEEE; CISTI; Ei; Genuine Article; KR SourceOne; Linda Hall; SWETS; UMI. **CCC.**
 Description: Reports on the state-of-the-art technology in the fields of computer vision, graphics, and imaging, with a specific focus on applications.

001.644 UK ISSN 0953-2331
3 D. m. £36 (rest of Europe £59; elsewhere £68). E M A P - Business & Computer Publications Ltd., 33-39 Bowling Green Ln., London EC1R 0DA, England. TEL 44-171-837-1212. FAX 44-171-578-4008. **Document type:** trade publication.
 —BLDSC (9540.180000); CISTI; SWETS. **CCC.**
 Supersedes in part (in 1990): C A D - C A M International (ISSN 0261-6920)

006.6 US ISSN 1083-5288
3D DESIGN. 12/yr. $29.95 (Canada & Mexico $39.95; elsewhere $69.95) (effective 1996). Miller Freeman, Inc. (Subsidiary of: United News & Media), 600 Harrison St., San Francisco, CA 94107. TEL 415-905-2200. FAX 415-905-2233. (Subscr. to: Box 420432, Palm Coast, FL 32142-0432. TEL 800-829-2505. FAX 904-446-2774) **Document type:** trade publication.
 —KR SourceOne. **CCC.**

COMPUTERS — Computer Industry

338 621.381 US ISSN 1049-2135
HF5415.5
A F S M INTERNATIONAL; professional journal. 1975. m. $65 (foreign $89). Association for Services Management International, 1342 Colonial Blvd., Ste. 28, Fort Myers, FL 33907. TEL 813-275-7887. FAX 813-275-0794. Ed. Joseph Tiepik. adv.: B&W page $1090, color page $1800. bk.rev. circ. 5,800. (also avail. in microfiche; back issues avail.) —UMI.
Description: For executives, managers and professionals of the high-technology services industry.

004 338 US
TK5101.A1 CODEN: ASOCF5
ANDREW SEYBOLD'S OUTLOOK. 1981. m. $395 (Canada $410; elsewhere $425) (effective 1996 & 1997). Pinecrest Press, Inc., Box 917, Brookdale, CA 95007. TEL 408-338-7701. FAX 408-338-7806. URL: http://www.outlook.com. Ed. Andrew M. Seybold. R&P contact: Linda M. Seybold. bk.rev.; circ. 2,500 (paid). **Indexed:** Compumath, Comput.Bus., Comput.Cont., Comput.Dtbs., INSPEC (1987-). Document type: newsletter.
●Also available online.
—BLDSC (0900.407050); AskIEEE; KR SourceOne.
Formerly: Andrew Seybold's Outlook on Communications and Computing (ISSN 1080-4056); Formed by the 1995 merger of: Andrew Seybold's Outlook on Mobile Communications (ISSN 1066-8845) & Andrew Seybold's Outlook on Professional Computing (ISSN 0895-3821); Which was formerly (until 1987): Seybold Outlook on Professional Computing (ISSN 0887-5758); (until May 1986): Seybold Report on Professional Computing (ISSN 0736-5314)
Description: Newsletter for and about the mobile computer industry, with emphasis on data communications, including wireless technologies. Provides in-depth, hands-on evaluations, technology tutorials and analyses.

338 621.381 CC ISSN 0254-5586
HD9696.C63
ASIAN SOURCES COMPUTER PRODUCTS. 1983. m. $75. Asian Sources Media Group, G.P.O. Box 12367, Hong Kong, People's Republic of China. TEL 852-2555-4777. E-mail: asmgroup@signet.com.sg. (Subscr. to: Wordright Enterprises, Inc., Box 3062, Evanston, IL 60204-3062. TEL 708-475-1900) circ. 24,600. **Indexed:** HongKongiana. Document type: trade publication.
Description: Covers Asian made computer products, computers and peripherals, subassemblies and manufacturing.

338 621.381 US ISSN 1047-496X
BOCOEX INDEX.* 1986. w. $250. Boston Computer Exchange Index, 210 South St., 6th Fl., Boston, MA 02111. TEL 617-542-4414. FAX 617-542-8849. Ed. Alex Randall. (back issues avail.) Document type: bulletin.
●Also available online.
Description: News of industry; includes prices and product information.

338 UK
BUSINESS MONITOR: COMPUTER SERVICES. (Part of the Service and Distributive Monitors series) q. Office for National Statistics, C.S.O. Library, Government Bldgs., Cardiff Rd., Newport, Gwent NP9 1XG, Wales. TEL 44-1633-812973. FAX 44-1633-812599. TELEX 497121 ALBBSONPT G. E-mail: library@onls.gov.uk. (Subscr. to: Stationery Office Publications Centre, P.O. Box 276, London SW8 5DT, England. TEL 44-171-873-9090. FAX 44-171-873-8200) charts; stat. (back issues avail.) Document type: government publication.

338 658.8 UK ISSN 0267-8551
BUSINESS RATIO REPORT: COMPUTER EQUIPMENT DISTRIBUTORS; an industry sector analysis. 1978. a. I C C Business Ratios Ltd., Freepost, Field House, Hampton, Mddx. TW12 1BR, England. TEL 081-783-0977. FAX 081-783-1940. charts; stat. Document type: trade publication.
Incorporates in part (in 1985): Business Ratio Report: Computer Equipment Manufacturers (ISSN 0261-7706)

338 658.8 UK ISSN 0261-7676
BUSINESS RATIO REPORT: COMPUTER SERVICES; an industry sector analysis. 1979. a. I C C Business Ratios Ltd., Freepost, Field House, Hampton, Mddx. TW12 1BR, England. TEL 081-783-0977. FAX 081-783-1940. charts; stat. Document type: trade publication.

338 621.381 US ISSN 0893-4843
C D COMPUTING NEWS. (Compact Disc) 1987. m. $150 (outside N. America $165). Worldwide Videotex, Box 3273, Boynton Beach, FL 33424-3273. TEL 407-738-2276. Ed. Mark Wright; Pub. Mark Wright. (back issues avail.) Document type: newsletter.
●Also available online. Vendor(s): Information Access Co., Knight-Ridder Information, Inc., NewsNet (EC37).
—CCC.
Description: Covers CD-ROM technology, products, and news, with emphasis on marketing strategies.

005.74 658 338 CN ISSN 1195-6097
C I O CANADA. 1993. 10/yr. Laurentian Technomedia Inc. (Subsidiary of: Laurentian Media Inc.), 501 Oakdale Rd., North York ON M3N 1W7, Canada. TEL 416-746-7360. FAX 416-746-1421. Ed. John Pickett; Pub. Andrew White. R&P contact: John Pickett. adv.: B&W page Can.$4130, color page Can.$5025; trim 8 1/8 x 10 7/8; adv. contact: Gerald Chopik. circ. 7,600 (controlled). Document type: directory, trade publication.
Description: Directed to CIO, CEO, VP of MIS, all those looking for information technology solutions as applied in their business strategies.

621.39 UK
CE B I T NEWS. 1986. 3/yr. Portman Communications Ltd., 52 Foundling Ct., London WC1N 1AN, England. TEL 44-171-837-0815. FAX 44-171-278-9917. E-mail: 100141,676@compuserve.com. Ed. Philip Gallagher; Pub. Jim Charos. R&P contact: Philip Gallagher. adv.: B&W page $11125, color page $12370; trim 8 7/8 x 11 7/8; adv. contact: Jim Charos. bk.rev.; charts; stat.; software rev.; tr.lit.; circ. 50,000. circ. 50,000. cols./p.: 4; pp./issue: 140. Document type: trade publication.

621.39 UK
CERTIFICATION NEWS. 1975. q. $50. Institute for Certification of Computing Professionals, 2200 E. Devon Ave., Ste. 247, Des Plaines, IL 60018-4503. TEL 847-299-4227. FAX 847-299-4280. E-mail: 74040,3722@compuserve.com; URL: http://www.iccp.org. Cristi/Herron. adv. contact: Cristi Herron. circ. 25,000. Document type: consumer publication, newsletter.
Description: Offers updated information pertinent to the computer industry and international certification.

338 004.1 US ISSN 1045-2990
CHANNELMARKER LETTER. 1989. m. $499 in U.S. (foreign $599 (effective 1997). Merrin Information Services, Inc., 2275 E. Bayshore Rd., Ste. 101, Palo Alto, CA 94303. TEL 415-493-5050. FAX 415-493-5480. Ed. Terry Walton; Pub. Seymour Merrin. index, cum index: vols.1-7. (back issues avail.) Document type: newsletter.

COMPUTER & ONLINE INDUSTRY LITIGATION REPORTER; the national journal of record of computer industry litigation. see PATENTS, TRADEMARKS AND COPYRIGHTS

338 330 UK ISSN 1350-4665
COMPUTER BUSINESS REVIEW. 1993. m. £60 (rest of Europe £95; U.S. $105) (effective 1997). ComputerWire Plc., 12 Sutton Row, London W1V 5FH, England. TEL 44-171-208-4200. FAX 44-171-439-1105. E-mail: cbred@computerwire.com; URL: http://www.computerwire.com. Ed. Kenny MacIver; Pub. Tim Langford. adv. contact: Bill Hammond. bk.rev. Document type: trade publication.
●Also available online. Vendor(s): Information Access Co.
—BLDSC (3393.770200); AskIEEE; KR SourceOne.
Description: Examines the business side of the computer industry in depth. Analyzes corporate and market strategies, financial performances, M & A activities and other trends.

338 621.39 US
COMPUTER CURRENTS; computing in the real world. (Regional editions avail. for Bay Area (bi-w.), Southern California, Boston, New York, Chicago, Atlanta, Dallas-Ft. Worth, Houston and Austin) 1983. m. Computer Currents Publishing, Inc., 5720 Hollis St., Emeryville, CA 94608. TEL 510-547-6800; 800-365-7773. FAX 510-547-4613. E-mail: ccgenmail@currents.com; rluhn@aol.com; URL: http://www.currents.net. (East Coast Office: 125 Main St., Ste. J, Stoneham, MA 02180. TEL 800-372-0250. FAX 617-279-2353) Ed. Robert Luhn; Pub. Stan Politi. adv.: B&W page $22570; adv. contact: Amy Kavanagh Alynn. bk.rev. circ. 600,000.
●Also available online.

338 621.39 US ISSN 1090-7572
COMPUTER CURRENTS (BAY AREA EDITION); computing in the real world. bi-w. $19.95. Computer Currents Publishing, Inc., 5720 Hollis St., Emeryville, CA 94608. TEL 510-547-6800; 800-365-7773. FAX 510-547-4613. E-mail: editorial@compcurr.com; URL: http://www.currents.net. Ed. Robert Luhn; Pub. Stan Politi. adv. contact: Amy Kavanagh Flynn. (also avail. in microfiche from UMI)
●Also available online.
—KR SourceOne.
Formerly: Bay Area Computer Currents (ISSN 8756-0046)

338 621.39 US ISSN 1090-7602
COMPUTER CURRENTS (BOSTON EDITION). 1987. m. Computer Currents Publishing, Inc., 5720 Hollis St., Emeryville, CA 94608. TEL 510-547-6800. FAX 510-547-4613. E-mail: editorial@compcurr.com; URL: http://www.currents.net. Ed. Robert Luhn; Pub. Stan Politi. adv. contact: Amy Kavanagh Flynn.
●Also available online.
Formerly: Boston Computer Currents (ISSN 0897-9324)

338 US
COMPUTER CURRENTS (DALLAS - FT. WORTH EDITION). 1987. m. $16.95. Computer Currents Publishing, Inc., 5720 Hollis St., Emeryville, CA 94608. TEL 510-547-6800; 800-365-7773. FAX 510-547-4613. E-mail: editorial@compcurr.com; URL: http://www.currents.net. Ed. Cade Herzog; Pub. Roger Powers. adv.: B&W page $2185, color page $2935; trim 10 3/4 x 13 5/8; adv. contact: Connie Boyle. bk.rev.; film rev.; software rev.; charts. circ. 50,000. (also avail. in microfiche; back issues avail.) Document type: consumer publication.
●Also available online.
Formerly (until 1988): Texas Computing.
Description: Directed to business and professional personal computer users for the Dallas - Ft. Worth area.

338 621.39 US ISSN 1090-7580
▼**COMPUTER CURRENTS (NEW YORK METRO EDITION)**; computing in the real world. 1995. m. Computer Currents Publishing, Inc., 5720 Hollis St., Emeryville CA 94608. TEL 510-547-6800; 800-365-7773. FAX 510-547-4613. E-mail: editorial@compcurr.com; URL: http://www.currents.net. Ed. Robert Luhn; Pub. Stan Politi. adv. contact: Amy Kavanagh Flynn.
●Also available online.

338 621.39 US ISSN 1090-7599
COMPUTER CURRENTS (SOUTHERN CALIFORNIA EDITION). m. Computer Currents Publishing, Inc., 5710 Hollis St., Emeryville, CA 94608. TEL 510-547-6800; 800-365-7773. FAX 510-547-4613. E-mail: editorial@compcurr.com; URL: http://www.currents.net. Ed. Robert Luhr; Pub. Stan Politi. adv.
Formerly: Los Angeles Computer Currents (ISSN 0897-9308)

COMPUTER ENTERTAINER. see COMPUTERS — Computer Games

338 621.381 US
COMPUTER ENTREPRENEUR. 1983. m. $36. Computer Entrepreneur Publishing Company, Box 456, Grand Central Sta., New York, NY 10163. Ed. Richard Ho adv.; bk.rev. circ. 10,000.

COMPUTERS — COMPUTER INDUSTRY

338 US
COMPUTER INDUSTRY DAILY. (Not avail. in print format) 1994. d. $495 (effective 1997). Computer Economics, Inc., 5841 Edison Pl., Carlsbad, CA 92008. TEL 760-438-8100; 800-326-8100. FAX 760-431-1126. E-mail: editor@compecon.com; URL: http://www.computereconomics.com. (also avail. in diskette format)
●Also available online.
Description: Delivers daily news briefs on the latest technologies, vendor announcements, vendor strategies, and industry trends.

338 621.381 US
COMPUTER INDUSTRY WEEK.* w. Insight in Action, 15845 Cumberland Dr., Poway, CA 92064-2346. TEL 503-697-1136. FAX 503-638-7799. Ed. Tom Clarkson.

338 US
COMPUTER OPERATIONS MANAGEMENT COMMUNIQUE. 1987. bi-m. $155. (Association for Computer Operations Management) D C M S, Inc., 742 E. Chapman Ave., Orange, CA 92666. TEL 714-997-9743. FAX 714-997-9743. Ed. John J. Adams. circ. 2,600 (paid). **Document type:** newsletter.
Description: Provides data processing industry news, hardware and software product announcements, and AFCOM news.

338 US
COMPUTER OPERATIONS MANAGER. 1981. bi-m. $155. (Association for Computer Operations Management) D C M S, Inc., 742 E. Chapman Ave., Orange, CA 92666. TEL 714-997-7966. FAX 714-997-9743. Ed. Len Eckhaus. R&P contact: Leonard Eckhaw. adv. contact: Lucy Green. circ. 4,000. **Document type:** trade publication.
Description: Contains articles addressing technical and management issues for managers of integrated mainframe, midrange and client-server data center environments.

COMPUTERWORLD; newsweekly for information technology leaders. see COMPUTERS

COMPUTERWORLD. see COMMUNICATIONS — Computer Applications

338 CC ISSN 1023-4934
COMPUTERWORLD HONG KONG. (Text in English) 1984. w. HK.$200 (Asia $122; elsewhere $180). I D G Communications (HK) Ltd., Mount Parker House, Ste. 1011-15, 1111 King's Rd., Quarry Bay, Hong Kong, People's Republic of China. TEL 852-2861-3238. FAX 852-2861-0953. Ed. Don Tennant; Pub. Melvyn Bennett. R&P contact: Khrman Cheng. adv.: B&W page HK.$35600, color page HK.$43100; trim 292 x 407; adv. contact: Vera Chan. bk.rev.; circ. 11,500 (controlled). (tabloid format; back issues avail.; reprint service avail.) **Document type:** trade publication.
●Also available online.
Description: Provides information for technical professionals throughout Hong Kong and Asia.
Refereed Serial

338 621.381 SI
COMPUTERWORLD MALAYSIA. (Text in English) 1984. w. $250. I D G Communications (S) Pte. Ltd., 80 Masire Pasade Rd., 13-09 Parkway Parade, Singapore 1544, Singapore. TEL 65-345-8383. FAX 65-345-7097. Ed. Tim Wilson. adv.: B&W page M.$5000, color page M.$6200; trim 292 x 407; adv. contact: Chee Chaw Toh. **Document type:** trade publication.

338.4 004 SI
COMPUTERWORLD SINGAPORE. (Text in English) 1984. w. $250. I D G Communications (S) Pte. Ltd., 80 Masire Pasade Rd., 13-09 Parkway Parade, Singapore 1544, Singapore. TEL 65-345-8383. FAX 65-345-7097. Ed. Tim Wilson. adv.: B&W page S.$4600, color page S.$5700; trim 292 x 407; adv. contact: Jimmy Yu. circ. 24,793 (controlled). (tabloid format) **Document type:** trade publication.
Formerly: Computerworld Southeast Asia.

338 NE ISSN 0167-9759
DATA-INFO; nieuwsbrief voor de automatisering. CD-ROM edition: Mark.It. 1990. 20/yr. fl.295($200) Marketons B.V., Postbus 1310, 6501 BH Nijmegen, Netherlands. TEL 31-24-3224200. FAX 31-24-3603176. E-mail: redactie@marketons.nl; URL: http://www.marketons.nl. Ed. W.J. Veldkamp; Pub. W.J. Veldkamp. R&P contact: W.J. Veldkamp. circ. 1,500 (paid). (back issues avail.) **Document type:** newsletter.
●Also available on CD-ROM.
Description: News, analysis and commentary dealing with, and oriented toward, the IT industry.

DIGITAL INFORMATION GROUP'S INFORMATION INDUSTRY BULLETIN. see PUBLISHING AND BOOK TRADE — Computer Applications

DIRECTIONS ON MICROSOFT; the independent view of Microsoft technology & strategy. see COMPUTERS — Software

338 SZ
E C M A TECHNICAL REPORT. (Text in English) irreg., no.65, 1994. free. European Computer Manufacturers Association, 114 Rue du Rhone, CH-1204 Geneva, Switzerland. TEL 41-22-7353634. FAX 41-22-7865231. E-mail: helpdesk@ecma.ch. **Document type:** monographic series.

EUROPEAN SERVICES INDUSTRY. see BUSINESS AND ECONOMICS — Production Of Goods And Services

338 621.381 CC
I D C CHINA REPORT. 1982. 12/yr. $495. International Data Corporation China - Hong Kong Ltd., 30F, Universal Trade Center, Ste. 3004, 3 Arbuthnot Rd., Central, Hong Kong, People's Republic of China. TEL 852-2530-3831. FAX 852-2537-7347. (In U.S.: IDC Corporate HQ, 5 Speen St., Framingham, MA 01701. TEL 508-872-8200) Pub. Thompson Morrison. adv. circ. 300. (looseleaf format; back issues avail.) **Indexed:** Comput.Lit.Ind. **Document type:** newsletter.
Former titles: China Information; E D P China Report.

338 621.381 US
I D C JAPAN REPORT.* 1974. m. $495 (foreign $535). International Data Corporation, 5 Speen St., Framingham, MA 01701. TEL 508-875-5000. Ed. Yugi Ogino. adv. (looseleaf format; back issues avail.) **Indexed:** Comput.Lit.Ind.
●Also available online. Vendor(s): Information Access Co.
Formerly (until April 1989): E D P Japan Report.
Description: News and information on the fast-paced Japanese information technology market.

338 GW
I D G NEWSLINE; newsletter for the German computer market. (Text in English) q. I D G Communications Verlag AG, Rheinstr. 28, 80803 Munich, Germany. TEL 089-36086-0. FAX 089-36086325. **Document type:** newsletter.

INFOWORLD; the voice of personal computing in the enterprise. see COMPUTERS — Microcomputers

INSTITUTE FOR CERTIFICATION OF COMPUTING PROFESSIONALS. ANNUAL REPORT. see COMPUTERS

621.39 332.7
004.56 UK
▼**INTERNATIONAL SMART CARD INDUSTRY GUIDE**. 1995. irreg. £125. Smart Card News Ltd., 31 Ashdown Ave., Saltdean, Brighton BN2 8AH, England. TEL 44-1273-302503. FAX 44-1273-300991. Ed. Jack Smith; Pub. Patsy Everett. adv. contact: Albert Andoh. **Document type:** directory.

338 621.381 US ISSN 1073-1385
INTERVUE. 1984. q. free to qualified personnel. Intergraph Corporation, LR24C2, Huntsville, AL 35894. TEL 205-730-8172. FAX 205-730-9508. Ed. Thomas Gates. circ. 60,000 (controlled). **Document type:** consumer publication.
Description: Presents current trends in computer graphics hardware and software applications and information management technology.

IRISH COMPUTER. see COMPUTERS — Microcomputers

621.39 UK
KEY NOTE MARKET REPORT: COMPUTER SERVICES. Variant title: Computer Services. 1993. irreg., no.3, 1996. £205. Key Note Ltd., Field House, 72 Oldfield Rd., Hampton, Middlesex TW12 2HQ, England. TEL 44-181-783-0755. FAX 44-181-783-0049. **Document type:** trade publication.
●Also available online.
Also available on CD-ROM.
Formerly: Key Note Report: Computer Services (ISSN 1352-6553)

338 UK ISSN 1356-6229
KEY NOTE MARKET REVIEW: U K COMPUTER MARKET. Variant title: U K Computer Market. 1991. irreg., no.6, 1997. £410. Key Note Ltd., Field House, 72 Oldfield Rd., Hampton, Middlesex TW12 2HQ, England. TEL 44-181-783-0755. FAX 44-181-783-0049. **Document type:** trade publication.
●Also available online.
Also available on CD-ROM.

LING YU YI KEJI ZASHI/0 & 1 TECHNOLOGY BYTE (CHINESE EDITION). see COMPUTERS — Computer Architecture

338 US
MAINFRAME MARKET MONITOR. 1991. q. $1605 (effective Aug. 1996). Xephon, 1301 W. Hwy. 407, Ste. 201-450, Lewisville, TX 75067. TEL 817-455-7050. FAX 817-455-2492. Ed. Dave Bates. **Document type:** trade publication.

001.6 658.8 US ISSN 0895-5697
HD9696.C6
MARKETING COMPUTERS; communications, electronics and business systems. Variant title: Adweek's Marketing Computers. 1981. m. $42 (foreign $75) (effective 1997). B P I Communications, Inc. (New York), 1515 Broadway, New York, NY 10036. TEL 212-764-7300. Ed. Dave Dix. adv.; tr.lit. circ. 16,000. (reprint service avail.) **Indexed:** Comput.Indus.Up. **Document type:** trade publication.
●Also available online. Vendor(s): Information Access Co.
—BLDSC (5381.641300); KR SourceOne; UMI. CCC.
Former titles: Adweek's Computer and Electronics Marketing (ISSN 0884-5549); Computer and Electronics Marketing (ISSN 8750-1848); Incorporates: Computer Advertising News (ISSN 8750-9288)
Description: Features articles on advertising and marketing news in the high-tech industries.

621.39 US ISSN 1083-396X
▼**MICROSTATION WORLD**. 1995. q. $12.95 (effective June 1995); newsstand price: $4.95. Bentley Systems, Inc., 690 Pennsylvania Dr., Exton, PA 19341. TEL 610-458-2758. FAX 610-458-6284. E-mail: world@bentley.com; URL: http://www.bentley.com. Ed. Rachael Dalton. R&P contact: Rachael Dalton. adv. contact: Byron Mitchell. circ. 110,000. (also avail. in microfilm; back issues avail.) **Document type:** trade publication.
Description: Serves the information needs of managers, engineers, and users of the MicroStation line of computer-aided design products. Describes customer success in implementing technology and how to manage new technology.

COMPUTERS — COMPUTER INDUSTRY DIRECTORIES

338 384 794.8   US
▼**MULTIMEDIA ENTERTAINMENT & TECHNOLOGY REPORT.** 1997. w. (46/yr.) $549. Cowles - SIMBA Information (Subsidiary of: Cowles Business Media), 11 Riverbend Dr. S., Box 4949, Stamford, CT 06907-0949. TEL 203-358-9900; 800-307-2529. FAX 203-358-5811. E-mail: info@simbanet.com; URL: http://www.simbanet.com. Ed. Jennifer Doyle. **Indexed:** WPM. **Document type:** newsletter.
●Also available online. Vendor(s): Information Access Co.
—CCC.
  Formed by the merger of (1992-1997): Interactive Television Report (ISSN 1064-7457); (1992-1997): Multimedia Business Report (ISSN 1065-8300)
  Description: Covers the strategies companies use to profitably deliver games and interactive entertainment via the internet, DVD, CD-ROM and interactive TV. Monitors joint ventures, acquisitions, and licensing deals as well as marketing and sales trends. Evaluates how new technologies, tools, and interfaces affect content delivery, and what consumers are actually buying. Also covers intellectual property issues in multimedia.

338 621.381   US
MULTIMEDIA MARKETS: INTERNATIONAL FORECAST SUPPLEMENT. (Supplement to: Multimedia Opportunities) 1992. a. $990. Information Workstation Group, 501 Queen St., Alexandria, VA 22314. TEL 703-548-4320.
  Description: Provides a multimedia markets' forecast for Western Europe, Asia and other parts of the world.

338 621.381   US
MULTIMEDIA OPPORTUNITIES. a. $1890. Information Workstation Group, 501 Queen St., Alexandria, VA 22314. TEL 703-548-4320.
  Former titles: Multimedia Markets; (until 1991): Micro Multimedia.
  Description: Includes projections, market drivers and market barriers and in-depth implications of the forecast for vendors and end users.

338 621.381   US
MULTIMEDIA TECHNOLOGIES AND SYSTEMS. 1992. a. $490. Information Workstation Group, 501 Queen St., Alexandria, VA 22314. TEL 703-548-4320.
  Description: Introduces the multimedia technologies such as the CD, digital video-interactive, digital audio tape, and interactive television.

621.39   US
NATIONAL NEWSBYTES NEWSLETTER. 1986. m. membership. Association for Women in Computing, 41 Sutter St., Ste. 1006, San Francisco, CA 94104. TEL 415-905-4663. Ed. Margaret Hough. adv.; bk.rev.; circ. 1,500 (controlled).
  Formerly: National Newsbytes Magazine.

NEW EQUIPMENT REPORTER; new products industrial news. see COMPUTERS — Hardware

338   JA
▼**NIKKEI WATCHER COMPUTER MARKET.** (Text in Japanese) 1996. bi-w. 18000 Yen. Nikkei Business Publications, Inc. (Subsidiary of: Nihon Keizai Shimbun, Inc.), 2-7-6 Hirakawa-cho, Chiyoda-ku, Tokyo 102, Japan. TEL 81-3-5210-8025. FAX 81-3-5210-8119. URL: http://www.nikkeibp.co.jp/. Ed. Katsumi Tanaka; Pub. Shojo Watanabe. adv. contact: Kazuhisa Ogihara. **Document type:** trade publication.
  Description: Provides market news and trends vital to industry watchers.

338 621.381   US
OFFICE - DATA PROCESSING MACHINES: LATIN AMERICAN INDUSTRIAL REPORT. 1985. a. $235 per country report. Aquino Productions, Box 125, Rochester, VT 05767. Ed. Andres C. Aquino.

P C LETTER; the insider's guide to the personal computer industry. see COMPUTERS — Computer Sales

PROFESSIONAL COMPUTING. see COMPUTERS

PUBLISHING ENTREPRENEUR; profit strategies for the information and publishing industries. see COMMUNICATIONS — Computer Applications

REPORT ON I B M. see COMPUTERS — Hardware

338   US   ISSN 1072-9453
REPORT ON MICROSOFT; independent biweekly news and analysis of Microsoft Corporation. 1993. bi-w. $395 (outside N. America $443) (effective 1996). DataTrends Publications, Inc., Box 4460, Leesburg, VA 20175. TEL 703-779-0574; 800-766-8130. FAX 703-779-2267. Pub. Paul G. Ochs.
●Also available online. Vendor(s): Information Access Co.

621.381   US   ISSN 0160-2497
HD8039.D37   CODEN: CPPNB6
S I G C P R NEWSLETTER. q. $26 to non-members; members $20. Association for Computing Machinery, Special Interest Group on Computer Personnel Research, 1515 Broadway, 17th Fl., New York, NY 10036. TEL 212-869-7440. FAX 212-869-0481. TELEX 421686.
—BLDSC (3394.135000); AskIEEE; KR SourceOne; UnCover.

004.56 621.39   UK   ISSN 0967-196X
SMART CARD NEWS. 1992. m. £375 (foreign £395). Smart Card News Ltd., 40 Arundel Pl., Brighton BN2 1GO, England. TEL 44-1273-302503. FAX 44-1273-300991. Ed. Jack Smith; Pub. Patsy Everett. circ. 1,000. **Document type:** newsletter.

SOFTWARE FUTURES. see COMPUTERS — Software

SOUTH AFRICA. CENTRAL STATISTICAL SERVICE. CENSUS OF BUSINESS SERVICES - DATA PROCESSING SERVICES. see BUSINESS AND ECONOMICS — Abstracting, Bibliographies, Statistics

SOUTH AFRICA. CENTRAL STATISTICAL SERVICE. STATISTICAL RELEASE. CENSUS OF DATA PROCESSING SERVICES (YEAR). see BUSINESS AND ECONOMICS — Abstracting, Bibliographies, Statistics

338 621.39   TH
THAI COMPUTERWORLD. (Text in English) 1991. s-m. B.30. Media Transasia (Thailand) Ltd., 14th Fl., Orakarn Bldg., 26 Chidlorm Rd., Ploenchit, Bangkok 10330, Thailand. TEL 66-2-2519905. FAX 66-2-2535335. Ed. Pravir Ganguly. adv.: B&W page B.24000, color page B.35000; adv. contact: Pramodh Noronha. bk.rev. circ. 20,500. (tabloid format) **Document type:** consumer publication.
  Description: Provides up-to-date information on national and international happenings in the computer industry.

338 621.381   US   ISSN 0895-0334
UNISYS WORLD - EUROPE; an independent news monthly for Unisys users - Austria, Belgium, Denmark, Finland, France, West Germany, Greece, Ireland, Israel, Italy, Netherlands, Norway, Portugal, Spain, Sweden, Switzerland, United Kingdom. 1987. q. $72. Publications & Communications, Inc., 12416 Hymeadow Dr., Austin, TX 78750-1896. TEL 512-250-9023; 800-678-9724. FAX 512-331-3900. Ed. Larry Storer. adv.: B&W page $3312, color page $4062; tim 10 3/4 x 14 1/2. (tabloid format; reprint service avail.) **Document type:** trade publication.

338 621.381   US   ISSN 0896-2111
WANG IN THE NEWS; the independent newspaper of Wang computer users. 1987. m. $45 (foreign $75) (effective 1995). Publications & Communications, Inc., 12416 Hymeadow, Austin, TX 78750-1849. TEL 512-250-9023; 800-678-9724. FAX 512-331-3900. Ed. Larry Storer; Pub. Gary Putman. adv.: B&W page $2968, color page $3718; trim 10 3/4 x 14 1/2; adv. contact: Dan Martin. bk.rev. circ. 12,000. (tabloid format; reprint service avail.) **Document type:** newspaper, trade publication.
●Also available on CD-ROM.
—KR SourceOne.
  Formerly: Wang News (Marlin) (ISSN 0895-0318)

338 621.39   US   ISSN 0897-9316
WASHINGTON D.C. COMPUTER CURRENTS. 1988. m. Computer Currents Publishing, Inc., 5720 Hollis St., Emeryville, CA 94608. TEL 510-547-6800; 800-365-7773. FAX 510-547-4613. E-mail: editorial@compcurr.net; URL: http://www.currents.net. Ed. Robert Luhn. (also avail. in microfiche from UMI)
●Also available online.

338   US   ISSN 1054-0784
WINDOWS WATCHER. 1990. m. $495 (foreign $545) (effective 1997). Windows Watcher, 15127 N.E. 24th St., Ste. 344, Redmond, WA 98052-5547. TEL 206-881-7354. FAX 206-883-1452. E-mail: ddavis@sbexpos.com; URL: http://www.windowswatcher.com. (Subscr. to: Windows Watcher Customer Relations, Box 500, Media, PA 19063. TEL 800-575-5717. FAX 610-565-1858) Ed. Dwight Davis; Pub. Michela O'Connor Abrams. R&P contact: Robin Young. **Document type:** newsletter.
  Description: Reports and analyzes trends in the Windows software industry.

621.39   JA   ISSN 0915-051X
YUNISHISU NYUSU/UNISYS NEWS. (Text in Japanese) m. Nihon Yunishisu K.K. - Nihon Unisys Co., Ltd., 17-51, Akasaka 2-chome, Minato-ku, Tokyo 107, Japan.

621.39   CH   ISSN 1022-9698
0 YU 1 BYTE KEJI ZAZHI/0 & 1 TECHNOLOGY BYTE. Variant title: 0 & 1 Byte Magazine. (Text in Chinese) 1981. m. Acer T W P Corporation, 2-F, No. 19-1 Lane 231, Fu-Hsing N. Rd., Taipei, Taiwan 105, Republic of China. TEL 2-7136959. FAX 2-7189467. Ed. Angel Chen. adv.: B&W page $1042, color page $2175; trim 210 x 298; adv. contact: David Tsai. circ. 16,000.

338 621.38   US   ISSN 0749-3851
QA76.9.A25
2600; the quarterly journal of the American hacker. 1984. q. $21 to individuals; institutions $50. 2600 Enterprises, Inc., Box 752, Middle Island, NY 11953-0752. TEL 516-751-2600. FAX 516-474-2677. E-mail: info@2600.com. Ed. Emanuel Golstein; Pub. Emanuel Goldstein. adv.; bk.rev.; index. circ. 30,000. (back issues avail.) **Document type:** consumer publication.

COMPUTERS — Computer Industry Directories

338   FR
ANNUAIRE DES PROFESSIONNELS DU FAX. a. 600 F. A Jour, 11 rue du Marche St. Honore, 75001 Paris, France. TEL 42-96-67-22. FAX 40-20-07-75. **Document type:** directory.

338   FR   ISSN 1144-6552
ANNUAIRE DU C D - R O M. a. 220 F. A Jour, 11 rue du Marche St. Honore, 75001 Paris, France.

C D - R O M FUEHRER. see COMPUTERS — Software

338   US
CANADIAN DIRECTORY OF TOP COMPUTER EXECUTIVES. 1991. s-a. $285. Applied Computer Research, Inc., Box 82266, Phoenix, AZ 85071-2266. TEL 800-234-2227. **Document type:** directory.
  Description: Listing of top DP installations in Canada, including names and titles of MIS executives.

COMPULIFE'S MICROMARKET BLUE DISC. see COMPUTERS — Computer Sales

338   CN
COMPUTER DEALER NEWS SOURCE GUIDE. 1985. s-a. Plesman Publications Ltd., 2005 Sheppard Ave. E., 4th Fl., Willowdale, ON M2J 5B1, Canada. TEL 416-497-9562. FAX 416-497-9427. E-mail: cdnsales@plesman.com; URL: http://www.plesman.com. Ed. James Buchok; Pub. George Soltys. adv.: B&W page Can.$2615; adv. contact: Rob Groen. **Document type:** directory.
●Also available online.
  Description: Provides Canada's computer resellers with information on sources, trade names, products manufacturers and services.

001.6 338   US
COMPUTER DIRECTORY AND BUYER'S GUIDE.* (Supplement to: Computers and People) a. $35. Berkeley Enterprises, Inc., 368 Crescent St., 2, Waltham, MA 02154-3804. TEL 617-332-5453. Ed. Judith P. Callahan. adv.; illus. (reprint service avail. from UMI)
  Description: Alphabetical listing with names, addresses, phone numbers, size of offices (where available) and brief description of services and products of over 3,600 organizations in the computing and data processing field.

COMPUTERS — COMPUTER INDUSTRY DIRECTORIES

338 070.5   US   ISSN 0747-749X
COMPUTER MEDIA DIRECTORY. 1983. q. $395 (Canada $419; elsewhere $443). Morrissey Standard, 742 Gilman St., Berkeley, CA 94710-1327. TEL 510-525-4691. FAX 510-525-2501. Ed. Gary Berlind. circ. 1,200. (looseleaf format; also avail. in diskette format) **Document type:** directory.
 Description: Lists magazines, journals, tabloids and newsletters that deal with the high technology (computer and electronics) industry.

COMPUTER PRICE GUIDE; the blue book of used I B M computer prices. see COMPUTERS — Computer Sales

338   US
COMPUTER SOURCES. 1991. m. free to qualified personnel. Asian Sources Media Group, 1038 Leigh Ave., Ste. 100, San Jose, CA 95126-4155. TEL 408-295-5900. FAX 408-295-4595. Ed. Mary T. Lee. circ. 30,000 (controlled). **Indexed:** Comput.Ind. **Document type:** trade publication.
 Description: Informs resellers, original equipment manufacturers (OEMs) and value-added manufacturers about computer hardware and software supply issues, as well as buying decisions through targeted news, features and analysis.

651.8 621.381   UK   ISSN 0010-4760
**   CODEN: COSVA3**
COMPUTER SURVEY; list of digital computer installations world-wide. 1962. bi-m. £282 (effective 1996-1997). Inn Data Ltd., P.O. Box 372, Wimbledon, London SW19 6LH, England. TEL 44-181-780-2095. FAX 44-181-788-5243. Ed. Georgina A. Dodd; Pub. Barrie Lomas. R&P contact: Barrie Lomas. circ. 2,500. (also avail. in diskette format) **Indexed:** Bus.Ind., Comput.Cont., Comput.Lit.Ind., Curr.Cont., INSPEC. **Document type:** directory, trade publication.
 —BLDSC (3394.289000).

338   US   ISSN 1070-728X
QA76.25
COMPUTING AND SOFTWARE DESIGN CAREER DIRECTORY. 1993. biennial. Gale Research, 853 Penobscot Bldg., 645 Griswold St., Detroit, MI 48226-4094. TEL 313-961-2242; 800-877-4253. FAX 800-414-5043. E-mail: daniel_snyder@gale.com. Eds. Bradley J. Morgan, Joseph M. Palmisano.

ATA COMMUNICATIONS BUYERS' GUIDE. see COMPUTERS — Data Communications And Data Transmission Systems

001.6 621.381   US   ISSN 0744-1673
HD9696.C63   CODEN: DASODY
ATA SOURCES; the comprehensive guide to the data processing industry: hardware, data communications products, software, company profiles. 1981. 2/yr. $440. Ziff-Davis Publishing Co., One Park Ave., New York, NY 10016. TEL 212-503-5861. Ed. Kathy Thompson. **Indexed:** Comput.Lit.Ind.
 —CASDDS; CISTI. **CCC.**
 Description: Provides listings of over 43,000 hardware, software and data communications products as well as profiles on 10,000 companies.

338   US   ISSN 8755-7339
HD9696.C63
ATA SOURCES' GUIDE TO V A RS AND DISTRIBUTORS. (Value Added Resellers) 1985. 2/yr. $795. Ziff-Davis Publishing Co., One Park Ave., New York, NY 10016. TEL 212-503-5393. Ed. Kathy Thompson.
 —CCC.

ATANET. see COMPUTERS — Computer Networks

338 658.8 621.381   US
ATAPRO DIRECTORY OF MICROCOMPUTER HARDWARE. 1980. 2 base vols. (plus m. updates). $791. Datapro Information Services Group (Subsidiary of: McGraw-Hill, Inc.), 600 Delran Pkwy., Delran, NJ 08075. TEL 609-764-0100; 800-328-2776. **Document type:** directory.
 —CCC.
 Formerly: Datapro Directory of Small Computers (ISSN 0276-1866)
 Description: Offers comprehensive coverage of small computer systems for commercial, scientific and personal purposes.

338 005.36   US   ISSN 0730-8795
DATAPRO DIRECTORY OF MICROCOMPUTER SOFTWARE. 1981. 3 base vols. (plus m. updates). $1008 to new subscr.; renewals $973 (effective 1996). Datapro Information Services Group (Subsidiary of: McGraw-Hill, Inc.), 600 Delran Pkwy., Delran, NJ 08075. TEL 609-764-0100; 800-328-2776. FAX 609-764-2814. **Document type:** directory.
 ●Also available online. Vendor(s): Knight-Ridder Information, Inc.
 —CCC.
 Description: Designed for management and technical personnel on all levels. Offers comprehensive coverage on all varieties of proprietary microcomputer software.

338 004   US   ISSN 1067-1072
HD9696.C63
DIRECTORY OF COMPUTER RETAILERS, DEALERS & DISTRIBUTORS (YEAR). 1983. a. $290 (effective 1997). C S G Information Services (Subsidiary of: Lebhar-Friedman, Inc.), 3922 Coconut Palm Dr., Tampa, FL 33619. TEL 813-664-6800. FAX 813-664-6882. Eds. Michael Jarvis, Ashley Valdes. (also avail. in magnetic tape; diskette format) **Document type:** directory.
 ●Also available on CD-ROM.
 Formerly (until 1988): Directory of Computer and Software Retailers (ISSN 0738-839X)
 Description: Profiles on more than 2,200 computer retailers and dealers. Includes more than 400 computer and software distributors. Names and titles of over 8,000 key personnel and decision makers are listed. Listings identify sales volume, hardware brands carried, vertical market operations served, VAR activity, services provided, and more.

338.4702504   US   ISSN 1081-2024
KF242.A1
DIRECTORY OF ONLINE SERVICES. 1994. a. (plus q. updates). $9.95 (effective 1997). Lexis - Nexis Inc. (Subsidiary of: Reed Elsevier inc.), Box 933, Dayton, OH 45401. TEL 513-865-6800. FAX 513-865-6909. URL: http://www.lexis-nexis.com. Ed. Lorraine Gongala-Coppinger. circ. 225,000.
 Formerly (until 1995): Lexis-Nexis Library Contents, Alphabetical List, Quick Reference (ISSN 1078-3245)
 Description: Lists sources contained in Lexis-Nexis online services.

001.6 338   US   ISSN 0193-9920
HD9696.C63
DIRECTORY OF TOP COMPUTER EXECUTIVES. (Avail. in 2 editions, East and West) 1972. 2/yr. price varies. Applied Computer Research, Inc., Box 82266, Phoenix, AZ 85071-2266. TEL 800-234-2227. Ed. Alan Howard. (processed)
 Description: Listing of top MIS installations in the US, including names and titles of MIS executives.

DIRECTORY OF U.S. GOVERNMENT SOFTWARE FOR MAINFRAMES AND MICROCOMPUTERS. see BUSINESS AND ECONOMICS — Trade And Industrial Directories

DIRECTORY OF VIDEO, COMPUTER AND AUDIO VISUAL PRODUCTS. see COMMUNICATIONS — Video

FAIRPLAY MARINE COMPUTING GUIDE. see TRANSPORTATION — Ships And Shipping

338   US   ISSN 0897-4810
QA76.9.D32
FEDERAL DATA BASE FINDER. 1984. every 18 months. $125. Information U S A, Inc., Box E, Kensington, MD 20895-0418. TEL 301-924-0556. FAX 301-929-8907. Ed. Matthew Lesko. circ. 5,000.
 Description: A directory of free and fee-based data bases and files available from the federal government.

GALE DIRECTORY OF DATABASES. see COMPUTERS — Data Base Management

338   FR   ISSN 1169-6737
GUIDE DE LA TELEMATIQUE VOCALE. 1990. a. 180 F. A Jour, 11 rue du Marche St. Honore, 75001 Paris, France. TEL 42-96-67-22. FAX 40-20-07-75.

338   US
▼**HOOVER'S GUIDE TO COMPUTER COMPANIES.** 1995. a. $34.95. Reference Press, Inc., Box 140375, Austin, TX 78714-0375. TEL 512-454-7778. FAX 512-454-9401. E-mail: orders@hoovers.com; URL: http://www.hoovers.com. (also avail. in diskette format) **Document type:** directory.
 ●Also available online.
 Description: Profiles more than 1,100 top companies in the computer industry.

INFOPERSPECTIVES. see COMPUTERS — Computer Sales

338   US   ISSN 1051-6239
Z674.3   CODEN: IIDIEJ
INFORMATION INDUSTRY DIRECTORY. (Supplement avail.: Information Industry Directory Supplement) 1979. a. $475 (effective 1992). Gale Research, 835 Penobscot Bldg., 645 Griswold St., Detroit, MI 48226-4094. TEL 313-961-2242; 800-877-4253. FAX 800-414-5043. E-mail: daniel_snyder@gale.com. (Subscr. to: Box 33477, Detroit, MI 48232-5477. TEL 800-877-GALE) Ed. Bradley J. Morgan.
 —BLDSC (4493.607450); CISTI.
 Formerly (until 1990): Encyclopedia of Information Systems and Services (ISSN 0734-9068)
 Description: Guide to information systems and services in the US and internationally.

338   US
INFORMATION INDUSTRY DIRECTORY SUPPLEMENT. (Suppl. to: Information Industry Directory) 1979. s-a. $310. Gale Research, 835 Penobscot Bldg., 645 Griswold St., Detroit, MI 48226-4094. TEL 313-961-2242; 800-877-4253. FAX 800-414-5043. E-mail: daniel_snyder@gale.com. Ed. Bradley J. Morgan.
 Formerly (until 1990): New Information Systems and Services (ISSN 0190-8197)
 Description: Provides entries on newly formed and newly found information systems and services not listed in the main directory.

338   UK
KEY NOTE MARKET REPORT: ONLINE DATABASES. Variant title: Online Databases. irreg., no.5, 1990. £185. Key Note Ltd., Field House, 72 Oldfield Rd., Hampton, Middlesex TW12 2HQ, England. TEL 44-181-783-0755. FAX 44-181-783-1940. **Document type:** trade publication.

MACINTOSH C D - R O M GUIDE. see COMPUTERS — Data Base Management

001.642 621.831   US
MICROLEADS RESELLER DIRECTORY ON DISK. 1985. a. $595. Chromatic Communications Enterprises, Inc., Box 30127, Walnut Creek, CA 94598. TEL 800-782-3475. FAX 707-746-0542. Pub. Michael Shipp. (diskette format) **Document type:** directory.
 Formerly: Mircoleads Dealer Directory.

338 001.642
621.831   US   ISSN 1056-0386
HD9696.C63
MICROLEADS VENDOR DIRECTORY. 1983. a. $495. Chromatic Communications Enterprises, Inc., Box 30127, Walnut Creek, CA 94598. TEL 800-782-3475. FAX 707-746-0542. Ed. Michael Shipp. (diskette format) **Document type:** directory.
 Formerly: Personal Computer - An Industry Source Book (ISSN 0739-3687)
 Description: Directory for the microcomputer industry listing over 11,000 companies, 35,000 products, and 30,000 executives. Listings are arranged under eight cross-referenced sections: hardware, software, accessories, distributors, franchisors, support services, and publishers and periodicals.

NETZWERKFUEHRER. see COMPUTERS — Computer Networks

COMPUTERS — COMPUTER INDUSTRY, VOCATIONAL GUIDANCE

338.035 658.7 JA ISSN 1341-9919
▼**NIKKEI BEST P C.** (Text in Japanese) 1996. m. newsstand price: 480 Yen. Nikkei Business Publications, Inc. (Subsidiary of: Nihon Reizai Shimbun, Inc.), 2-7-6 Hirakawa-cho, Chiyoda-ku, Tokyo 102, Japan. TEL 81-3-5210-8560. FAX 81-3-5210-8119. URL: http://www.nikkeibp.co.jp/. Ed. Kazuo Kuniya; Pub. Koichi Shiraishi. adv.: B&W page 200000 Yen, color page 450000 Yen; adv. contact: Jun Mimura. **Document type**: consumer publication.
   Description: Assists consumers in their purchase of PCs, peripherals and software. Includes extensive coverage on retail prices and best buys.

338 US ISSN 1053-6809
NORTHWEST HIGH TECH (YEAR). 1988. a., 6th ed., 1996. $34.95. Resolution Business Press, Inc., 11101 N.E. Eighth St., Ste. 208, Bellevue, WA 98004. TEL 206-455-4611. FAX 206-455-9143. E-mail: info@respress.com; URL: http://www.respress.com. Ed. Karen Strudwick; Pub. Karen Strudwick. R&P contact: Karen Strudwick. adv. contact: Karen Strudwick. (also avail. in diskette format) **Document type**: directory.
   Description: Profiles more than 1800 software, hardware, sales and service companies in the Pacific Northwest and Western Canada.

338 US ISSN 0741-0077
QA76.55
ONLINE DATABASE SEARCH SERVICES DIRECTORY. irreg., 2nd ed., 1988. $155. Gale Research, 835 Penobscot Bldg., 645 Griswold St., Detroit, MI 48266-4094. TEL 313-961-2242; 800-877-4253. FAX 800-414-5043. E-mail: daniel_snyder@gale.com. Ed. Doris Morris Maxfield.
—CISTI.

338 621.381 621.3 US ISSN 1047-935X
HD9696.C63
RELEASE 1.0. Key Title: REIease 1.0. 1980. m. $595 (foreign $650). EDventure Holdings, 104 Fifth Ave., New York, NY 10011-6987. TEL 212-924-8800. FAX 212-924-0240. Ed. Esther Dyson; Pub. Daphne Kis. circ. 1,500. (back issues avail.) **Document type**: newsletter.
   ●Also available online. Vendor(s): Information Access Co.
—KR SourceOne.
   Formerly (until Mar. 1983): Rosen Electronics Letter (ISSN 0737-6677)
   Description: Covers software, wide-area networking, groupware, text management, connectivity, artificial intelligence, and intellectual property law.

SEKAI C D - R O M SORAN. see COMPUTERS — Computer Networks

SOFTWAREFUEHRER FUER PERSONAL-COMPUTER. see COMPUTERS — Software

SOFTWAREFUEHRER UNIX. see COMPUTERS — Software

338 SI ISSN 1394-1305
TIMES GUIDE TO COMPUTERS (MALAYSIA - THAILAND EDITION). (Text in English) a. $25. Times Trade Directories Pte. Ltd., Times Centre, One New Industrial Rd., Singapore 536196, Singapore. TEL 65-2848844. FAX 65-2850161. TELEX RS 25713 TIMES. Pub. Leslie Lim. R&P contact: Leslie Lim. adv. contact: Joseph Liang. **Document type**: directory.
   Description: Lists computer manufacturers, distributors, agents and dealers in Malaysia and Thailand. Also serves as a guide to buying computer hardware, software, networking systems, peripherals and other computer related products and services.

338 660 US
TODAY'S CHEMIST AT WORK. COMPUTERS IN CHEMISTRY BUYERS GUIDE. 1991. a. free. American Chemical Society, 1155 16th St., N.W., Washington, DC 20036. TEL 202-872-4600. Ed. Kathy Strum. adv.: page $4685; adv. contact: Bruce Poorman. circ. 102,000. **Document type**: directory.
   Formerly: Chempter Guide.
   Description: Lists the computers, peripherals, software, supplies and services used in the chemical processing industry for computer buyers and specifiers.

338 FR ISSN 1143-6360
VIDEOTEX GUIDE (YEAR). a. 120 F. A Jour, 11 rue du Marche St. Honore, 75001 Paris, France. TEL 42-96-67-22. FAX 40-20-07-75. **Document type**: directory.

001.6 621.381 338 UK ISSN 0262-2734
WHAT'S NEW IN COMPUTING. 1981. m. $130. Morgan-Grampian Technical Press Ltd. (Subsidiary of: Morgan-Grampian plc), Morgan-Grampian House, 30 Calderwood St., London SE18 6QH, England. TEL 44-181-855-7777. FAX 44-181-316-3102. Ed. Peter Bresser. adv. contact: Richard Hayes. illus. circ. 30,043. **Indexed**: INSPEC, Mgmt.& Market.Abstr. **Document type**: trade publication.
—AskIEEE; KR SourceOne. **CCC**.
   Incorporates (in Mar. 1985): What's New in Software; Whats New in Networking.
   Description: Provides new computer products information.

338 920 CN ISSN 1183-7837
WHO'S WHO IN SUPER SITES. 1992. a. Can.$595. Whitsed Publishing, 268 Lakeshore Rd. E., Ste. 510, Mississauga, ON L5G 1H1, Canada. TEL 905-271-1601. FAX 905-271-4522. Ed. Roy Whitsed. **Document type**: directory.

WINDOWSFUEHRER. see COMPUTERS — Software

COMPUTERS — Computer Industry, Vocational Guidance

see also Education; Occupations and Careers

371.425 UK
COMPUTER CONTRACTOR. 1989. fortn. £70 (foreign £80) (effective 1996). V N U Business Publications BV, VNU House, 32-34 Broadwick St., London W1A 2HG, England. TEL 44-171-439-4242. FAX 44-171-437-4841. **Document type**: trade publication.
   Description: Aimed at professionals who work on a freelance or temporary basis.

371.425 US
THE INDEPENDENT (ST. LOUIS). 1977. 6/yr. $30 to non-members. Independent Computer Consultants Association, 11131 S. Towne Sq., Ste. F, St. Louis, MO 63123-7817. TEL 314-892-1675. FAX 314-487-1345. Ed. Joyce Burkard. adv.; bk.rev. circ. 2,600. **Document type**: newsletter.

371.425 380 US
NETWORK CONTRACTS REPORT. bi-w. $385. Worldnet News Group, 27475 Ynez Rd., Ste. 290, Temecula, CA 92591-4632. TEL 909-672-3575; 800-539-NEWS. FAX 909-672-8058. E-mail: WORLDNET@DELPHI.COM. **Document type**: trade publication.
   Description: Aimed at computing and communications industry executives worldwide. Includes business news on major contract awards for network hardware, software, and services.

SPORTWISSENSCHAFT. see SPORTS AND GAMES

STRATEGIC NEWS SERVICE. see COMMUNICATIONS

COMPUTERS — Computer Music

see also Music–Computer Applications

786.7 NE ISSN 0929-8215
ML5 CODEN: JNEMEE
JOURNAL OF NEW MUSIC RESEARCH. (Text in English) 1972. q. fl.125($75) to individuals; institutions fl.504($306) (effective 1997). Swets & Zeitlinger bv, P.O. Box 825, 2160 SZ Lisse, Netherlands. TEL 31-252-435111. FAX 31-252-415888. TELEX 41325. E-mail: orders@swets.nl; URL: http://www.swets.nl/jnmr/jnmr.html. (Dist. in N. America by: Swets & Zeitlinger, Box 613, Royersford, PA 19468. TEL 610-644-4944) Eds. Marc Leman, Paul Berg. R&P contact: J.v.d. Valk. adv. contact: Patrick Kliean. bk.rev.; abstr.; bibl.; charts. circ. 1,000. (reprint service avail. from SWZ) **Indexed**: Arts & Hum.Cit.Ind., ASCA, Curr.Cont., INSPEC, Music Ind., RILM, RILM. **Document type**: academic/scholarly publication.
—BLDSC (5022.750000); AskIEEE; Genuine Article; KR SourceOne; SWETS; UnCover. **CCC**.
   Formerly (until 1993): Interface (ISSN 0303-3902); Which was formed by the merger of: Electronic Music Reports; Instituut voor Psychoakoestiek en Elektronische Muziek. Jaarboek.
   Description: Discusses developments in news music, including instrumental and electronic music, computer, interactive and multimedia systems, music-related DSP, psychoacoustics, and related topics such as music perception and music history.

PAGE. see ART — Computer Applications

ROLAND USERS GROUP MAGAZINE; the magazine for the electronic musician. see MUSIC — Computer Applications

SMALL COMPUTERS IN THE ARTS NEWS. see ART — Computer Applications

786.7 NE ISSN 1384-1203
▼**STUDIES IN NEW MUSIC RESEARCH**. (Text in English) 1996. irreg. price varies. Swets & Zeitlinger bv, P.O. Box 825, 2160 SZ Lisse, Netherlands. TEL 31-252-435111. FAX 31-252-415888. TELEX 41325 SZLIS NL. E-mail: orders@swets.nl; URL: http://www.swets.nl. (Dist. in N. America by: Swets & Zeitlinger, Box 613, Royersford, PA 19468. TEL 800-447-9387. FAX 610-524-5366) **Document type**: monographic series.
   Refereed Serial

COMPUTERS — Computer Networks

001.644 US ISSN 1057-2082
A B U I NETWORK NEWS. 1987. bi-m. $30 (Canada $42; elsewhere $52). (Association of Banyan Users International) Association of Banyan Users, Association Headquarters, 401 S. Michigan Ave., Chicago, IL 60611. TEL 312-644-6610. FAX 312-321-6869. Ed. Dave Meyer. adv.: B&W page $2090. circ. 16,000.
   Formerly: Network News (Sudbury).
   Description: Focuses on users and vendors of Vine's Networks and Banyan-compatible products.

004.6 US
A V E W D NEWSLETTER. 1994. m. free. E-mail: novsoft@cam.org; URL: http://www.cam.org/~novsoft/index.html. Ed. Alex Vasilesco.
   ●Available only online.
   Description: Includes Web events and trends, e-articles on theory about main Web issues.
   Refereed Serial

ACCESS TO WANG; the magazine for Wang system users. see COMPUTERS — Data Communications And Data Transmission Systems

004.6 SP
ACTUALIDAD INTERNET. w. E-mail: actualidad@infolanes; URL: http://www.infolanz.es/actualidad. **Document type**: newsletter.
   ●Available only online.
   Description: Focuses on news related to the Internet.

COMPUTERS — COMPUTER NETWORKS

004.678 808.87   US
▼**AD NAUSEAM.** 1995. m. 1176 Bird Ave., San Jose, CA 95125. E-mail: jnelson@crl.com; URL: http://www.crl.com/~jnelson/nauseam/. Ed. Jim Nelson.
●Available only online.
  Description: Contains humor and satire of the Internet and its phenomenal growth.

006.3   US   ISSN 1072-0030
ADVANCED INTELLIGENT NETWORK NEWS. 1991. bi-w. $597 (foreign $630) (effective 1997). Phillips Business Information, Inc., 1201 Seven Locks Rd., Potomac, MD 20854. TEL 301-424-3338. FAX 301-309-3847. E-mail: pbi@phillips.com. Ed. Jennifer Whelen. (looseleaf format) Document type: newsletter.
●Also available online. Vendor(s): Information Access Co., NewsNet (TE15).
—CCC.
  Formerly: A I N Report (ISSN 1056-7119)

006   NE   ISSN 0927-5452
QA76.58
ADVANCES IN PARALLEL COMPUTING. (Text in English) 1990. irreg., vol.8, 1993. price varies. Elsevier Science B.V., Books Division, P.O. Box 211, 1000 AE Amsterdam, Netherlands. TEL 31-20-4853911. FAX 31-20-4853705. TELEX 18582 ESPA NL. E-mail: nlinfo-f@elsevier.nl; usinfo-f@elsevier.nl; forinfo-kyf04035@niftyserve.or.jp; URL: http://www.elsevier.nl/. (Subscr. in the Americas to: Elsevier Science, Regional Sales Office, Box 945, New York, NY 10159-0945; Subscr. in Australasia and the Far East to: Elsevier Science (Singapore) Pte Ltd, No.1 Temasek Ave., No.17-01 Millenia Tower, Singapore 039192, Singapore; Subscr. in Japan to: Elsevier Science Japan, 9-15 Higashi-Azabu 1-chome, Minato-ku, Tokyo 106, Japan) Eds. G.R. Joubert, F.J. Peters. (back issues avail.) Indexed: Zent.Math.
Document type: monographic series.
—BLDSC (0709.578000).
  Refereed Serial

001.644   FR   ISSN 1145-4164
ANNUAIRE DU R N I S. 1989. a. 180 F. A Jour, 11 rue du Marche St. Honore, 75001 Paris, France. TEL 42-96-67-22. FAX 40-20-07-75. TELEX 615887F AJOUR.

004.6   IT
▼**ANOTHER WINDOWS 95 LINKS AND RESOURCES NEWSLETTER.** (Text in English) 1997. bi-m. TEL 39-81-5092318. E-mail: rhay@newage.it; URL: http://rhay.home.ml.org. Ed. Richard Hay. Document type: newsletter.
●Available only online.
  Description: Reviews a Windows 95 related web resource to allow readers a brief introduction.

001.644   US   ISSN 1060-1317
AUTO C A D WORLD. (Computer Aided Design) 1989. m. $38 (foreign $75) (effective 1995). Publications & Communications, Inc., 12416 Hymeadow, Austin, TX 78750-1896. TEL 512-250-9023; 800-678-9724. FAX 512-331-3900. Ed. Ken Chambers; Pub. Gary Pittman. adv.: B&W page $3042, color page $6842; trim 10 3/4 x 14 1/2; adv. contact: Gary Pittman, Jr. bk.rev.; software rev.; illus.; circ. 29,000 (controlled). (tabloid format; back issues avail.) Document type: newspaper, trade publication.
—KR SourceOne.
  Formerly (until 1992): Focus on A I X.
  Description: Provides news coverage of new products for the AutoCAD professional.

A U D. (Big Apple Users Digest) see COMPUTERS — Personal Computers

T A SOLUTIONS. (Business Technology Association) see BUSINESS AND ECONOMICS — Office Equipment And Services

EY. see COMMUNICATIONS — Computer Applications

SINESS - PROFESSIONAL ONLINE SERVICES: REVIEW, TRENDS & FORECAST. see BUSINESS & ECONOMICS — Computer Applications

004.678 330   US
SINESS TECH. m. $99. E-mail: btech@businesstech.om; URL: http://businesstech.com.
●Available only online.
  Description: Focuses on Internet business, emerging technology, and strategic planning.

001.644   US
C E R F NET NEWS. 1989. 6/yr. free. California Education and Research Federation Network, Box 85608, San Diego, CA 92186-9784. TEL 619-534-5087. circ. 1,000.
●Also available online.
  Description: Contains information pertinent to CERFnet users and INTERnet users, such as network technologies, a report on the latest activities of CERFnet, political and legislative related networking news, articles on different resources available on-line.

C O O L DOCTOR - COMPUTING ONLINE DOCTOR. see COMPUTERS

004.6   US
CABLE MODEM REPORT: BUSINESS DIMENSIONS & MARKET OPPORTUNITIES. a. $1095 (effective 1997). Cowles - SIMBA Information (Subsidiary of: Cowles Business Media), 11 Riverbend Dr. S., Box 4949, Stamford, CT 06907-0949. TEL 203-358-9900; 800-307-2529. FAX 203-358-5811. E-mail: info@simbanet.com; URL: http://www.simbanet.com. (Co-publisher: Cable World)

001.644 621.381   US   ISSN 0884-0830
CAPITAL P C MONITOR; users helping users. 1982. 12/yr. $35. Capital P C User Group, Inc., 51 Monroe St., Rockville, MD 20850. TEL 301-762-9372. Ed. Eldon Sarte. adv.; bk.rev. circ. 5,000. Document type: newsletter.
  Description: News, announcements, advertisements, and special features for users of IBM personal computers and compatibles.

004.65   US
CARD TECHNOLOGY; tracking the future of card systems and applications. bi-m. $79 uS & Canada; elsewhere $109. Faulkner & Gray, Inc (New York), 11 Penn Plaza, 17th Fl., New York, NY 10001-2006. TEL 212-631-1411; 800-535-8403. E-mail: faulknergray@mns.com; URL: http://www.faulknergray.com. Ed. John N. Frank; Pub. John Stewart.

004.6   CC
CHINA NETWORK WORLD. w. 74 Lu Gu Rd., P.O. Box 750, Beijing 100036, People's Republic of China. TEL 86-10-885-2033. FAX 86-10-885-2055. Ed. Fulai Zhu. adv.: B&W page $3400; trim 275 x 395. circ. 80,000.

004.678   US
CHIPNET ELECTRONIC MAGAZINE. 1994. every 6 wks. 650 Stadler Rd., Helena, MT 59602. E-mail: chipnet@aol.com; URL: http://www.tybee.com/chipnet. Ed. John Peck.
●Available only online.

004.6   UK   ISSN 0968-2082
HD66   CODEN: COLCEH
COLLABORATIVE COMPUTING. 1994. q. £55($99) to individuals; institutions in the E.U. £130 (N. America $225; elsewhere £145) (effective 1995). Chapman & Hall, Journals Department (Subsidiary of: International Thomson Publishing Group), 2-6 Boundary Row, London SE1 8HN, England. TEL 44-171-8650066. FAX 44-171-5229623. TELEX 290164 CHAPMA G. E-mail: jhelp@chall.co.uk; URL: http://www.chaphall.com/chaphall/journals.html. (Dist. by: International Thomson Publishing Services Ltd., Cheriton House, North Way, Andover, Hants. SP10 5BE, England. TEL 44-1264-342713. FAX 44-1264-342807; Subscr. in US & Canada to: 400 Market St., Philadelphia, PA 19106. TEL 800-552-5866) Ed.Bd. charts; illus. Document type: academic/scholarly publication.
●Also available online.
—AskIEEE; KR SourceOne. CCC.
  Description: Publishes innovative research in computer-supported cooperative work and computer-mediated communications, with emphasis on the development of computer and communication technologies to support group work.
  Refereed Serial

COMMERCE EXTRA. see BUSINESS AND ECONOMICS

004   AT
COMMS NETWORK. 1991. m. Aus.$57($104) (effective 1997). Reed Business Publishing Pty. Ltd. (Subsidiary of: Reed International PLC), P.O. Box 5487, W. Chatswood, N.S.W. 2057, Australia. TEL 61-2-372-5222. FAX 61-2-419-7399. adv. contact: Scott Forrest. circ. 5,979. (tabloid format; back issues avail.) Document type: trade publication.
  Formerly: Communications Engineer.
  Description: Contains technical information on hardware and software products for data communications, local area and wide area network systems applications.

001.644   US
COMMUNICATIONS NETWORKING SERVICES. base vol. (plus m. updates). $603 to new subscr.; renewal $563 (effective 1996). Datapro Information Services Group (Subsidiary of: McGraw-Hill, Inc.), 600 Delran Pkwy., Delran, NJ 08075. TEL 609-764-0100; 800-328-2776. FAX 609-764-2814.

004.693   US
▼**COMPUNOTES.** 1995. w. free. 1315 Woodgate Dr., St. Louis, MO 63122. E-mail: patrick.grote@supportu.com; URL: http://users.aol.com/compnote. Ed. Patrick Grote. Document type: newsletter.
●Available only online.
  Description: Features reviews, news, interviews, hot web sites, and cool FTP files.

004 005.3   GW
▼**COMPUTER & CO.** 1995. m. Hackenstr. 7, 80331 Muenchen, Germany. E-mail: computer-co@computer-co.m.eunet.de; URL: http://www.computer-co.de. Ed. Juergen Lewandowski.
●Available only online.
  Description: Covers news, interviews, hardware- and software-tests, games and CD-ROM.

COMPUTER CORNER. see COMPUTERS

004.6   NE   ISSN 0169-7552
TK5105.5   CODEN: CNISE9
COMPUTER NETWORKS AND I S D N SYSTEMS. (Integrated Service Digital Network); the international journal of computer and telecommunications networking. (Supplement avail.: Computer Networks for Research in Europe) (Text in English) 1976. bi-m. fl.2173($1249) (effective 1998). (International Council for Computer Communications) North-Holland (Subsidiary of: Elsevier Science B.V.), P.O. Box 211, 1000 AE Amsterdam, Netherlands. TEL 31-20-4853911. FAX 31-20-4853598. TELEX 18582 ESPA NL. (Subscr. in the Americas to: Elsevier Science, Regional Sales Office, Box 945, New York, NY 10159-0945. TEL 212-633-3730. FAX 212-633-3680; Subscr. in Australasia and the Far East to: Elsevier Science (Singapore) Pte Ltd, No.1 Temasek Ave., No.17-01 Millenia Tower, Singapore 039192, Singapore. TEL 65-434-3727. FAX 65-337-2230; Subscr. in Japan to: Elsevier Science Japan, 9-15 Higashi-Azabu 1-chome, Minato-ku, Tokyo 106, Japan. TEL 81-3-5561-5033. FAX 81-3-5561-5047) Ed. Philip H. Enslow, Jr. circ. 2,500. (also avail. in microform from UMI; back issues avail.; reprint service avail. from SWZ) Indexed: A.I.Abstr., ABI Inform., ASCA, CAD CAM Abstr., Commun.Abstr., Compumath, Comput.Abstr., Comput.Cont., Comput.Lit.Ind., Curr.Cont., Cyb.Abstr., Eng.Ind., Ergon.Abstr., INSPEC, Math.R., Sociol.Abstr., SSCI, SSCI, Tel.Abstr., Zent.Math. Document type: academic/scholarly publication.
—BLDSC (3394.117000); AskIEEE; CISTI; Ei; Genuine Article; KR SourceOne; Linda Hall; SWETS; UMI; UnCover. CCC.
  Formerly (until 1985): Computer Networks (ISSN 0376-5075)
  Description: Covers all aspects of the design, implementation, use and management of computer networks, communications subsystems and all other supporting activities.
  Refereed Serial

COMPUTERS — COMPUTER NETWORKS

004.6 NE
COMPUTER NETWORKS FOR RESEARCH IN EUROPE. (Supplement to: Computer Networks and I S D N Systems (ISSN 0169-7552)) (Text in English) 1994. 4/yr. fl.220($116) (effective 1995). North-Holland (Subsidiary of: Elsevier Science B.V.), P.O. Box 211, 1000 AE Amsterdam, Netherlands. TEL 31-20-4853911. FAX 31-20-4853598. TELEX 18582 ESPA NL. (Subscr. in the Americas to: Elsevier Science, Regional Sales Office, Box 945, New York, NY 10159-0945. TEL 212-633-3730. FAX 212-633-3680; Subscr. in Australasia and the Far East to: Elsevier Science (Singapore) Pte Ltd, No.1 Temasek Ave., No.17-01 Millenia Tower, Singapore 039192, Singapore. TEL 65-434-3727. FAX 65-337-2230; Subscr. in Japan to: Elsevier Science Japan, 9-15 Higashi-Azabu 1-chome, Minato-ku Tokyo 106, Japan. TEL 81-3-5561-5033. FAX 81-3-5561-5047) (also avail. in microform from UMI; back issues avail.) **Document type:** academic/scholarly publication.

COMPUTERWORLD COLOMBIA. see *COMPUTERS*

200 004.69 US
▼**COMPUTING TODAY.** 1997. bi-m. $9.95. Christianity Today, Inc., 465 Gundersen Dr., Carol Stream, IL 60188. TEL 630-260-6200. FAX 630-260-0114. E-mail: computing@aol.com; URL: http://www.christianity.met/compt. (Subscr. to: C D S, Box 37060, Boone, IA 50037-0060. TEL 800-523-7964) Ed. Richard Doebler. R&P contact: Cynthia Thomas. adv.: B&W page $2,500; adv. contact: Linda Schambach. **Document type:** consumer publication.
●Also available online.
Description: Aims to keep Christian computer users informed on Internet technology developments and resources for their ministries and personal lives.

001.644 US
CONFERENCE ON LOCAL COMPUTER NETWORKS (PROCEEDINGS). 1976. a. (Institute of Electrical and Electronics Engineers, Inc.) I E E E Computer Society Press, 10662 Los Vaqueros Circle, Los Alamitos, CA 90720-1264. TEL 714-821-8380. FAX 714-821-4641. (Co-sponsor: University of Minnesota. Computer Center) Ed. Cat Harris; Pub. Matt Loeb. adv. contact: Frieda Koester. **Document type:** proceedings.
Former titles (until 1979): Conference on Local Computer Networking; (until 1976): Conference on Experiments in New Approaches to Local Computer Networking.
Description: Topics include basic LAN issues: broadband, software, token rings, management and future directions.

004.6 US ISSN 0894-170X
CONNECTIONS (LOS GATOS); the newsletter for networking Macintoshes. 1987. 8/yr. $195 (outside N. America $250). Mactivity, Inc., 20 N. Santa Cruz Ave., Los Gatos, CA 95030. TEL 408-354-2500. FAX 408-354-2571. Ed. Paul Kent. index, cum.index; circ. 1,000 (paid). (back issues avail.)
●Also available online.
Description: Provides technical information to Macintosh network managers.

CONNEXION; the networking newspaper. see *COMPUTERS — Data Communications And Data Transmission Systems*

CYBERHOUND'S GUIDE TO ASSOCIATIONS AND NONPROFIT ORGANIZATIONS ON THE INTERNET. see *SOCIAL SERVICES AND WELFARE*

CYBERHOUND'S GUIDE TO COMPANIES ON THE INTERNET. see *BUSINESS AND ECONOMICS*

004.69 US
▼**CYBERHOUND'S GUIDE TO INTERNET DATABASES.** 1995. a. $99. Gale Research, 835 Penobscot Bldg., 645 Griswold St., Detroit, MI 48226-4094. TEL 313-961-2242; 800-877-4253. FAX 800-414-5043. E-mail: daniel_snyder@gale.com. Ed. Joanna Zakalik. **Document type:** directory.
—CISTI.
Formerly (until 1996): Gale Guide to Internet Databases (ISSN 1081-2385)
Description: Focuses on major government, academic, research and educational databases. Includes access paths, gopher, telnet, ftp, e-mail and URL addresses, as well as descriptive information on the databases.

004.6 US
▼**CYBERHOUND'S GUIDE TO INTERNET DISCUSSION GROUPS.** 1996. irreg. $79. Gale Research, 825 Penobscot Bldg., 645 Griswold St., Detroit, MI 48226-4094. TEL 313-961-2242; 800-877-4253. FAX 800-414-5043. E-mail: daniel_snyder@gale.com. **Document type:** directory.
Description: Provides information on nearly 4500 internet discussion groups.

004.6 US
CYBERHOUND'S GUIDE TO PEOPLE ON THE INTERNET. 1996. irreg. $95. Gale Research, 835 Penobscot Bldg., 645 Griswold St., Detroit, MI 48226-4094. TEL 313-961-2242; 800-877-4253. FAX 800-877-4253. E-mail: daniel_snyder@gale.com. **Document type:** directory.
Description: Provides information on online directories, databases and membership listings, personal websites, and listings of individuals accessible on the internet.

CYBERHOUND'S GUIDE TO PUBLICATIONS ON THE INTERNET. see *BIBLIOGRAPHIES*

004.692 US ISSN 1085-2417
CODEN: CYGUFF
▼**THE CYBERSKEPTIC'S GUIDE TO INTERNET RESEARCH.** 1995. 10/yr. $149 (non-profit organizations $99). BiblioData, Box 61, Needham Heights, MA 02194. TEL 617-444-1154. FAX 617-449-4584. E-mail: ina@bibliodata.com; URL: http://www.bibliodata.com. **Document type:** newsletter, directory.
Description: Aimed at business librarians, market researchers and those who use the Internet for serious purposes. Analyses various sites and compares using the Internet to using traditional online versions of those same sources.

004.6 700 US
▼**D T & G JOURNAL OF DESIGN, TYPOGRAPHY & GRAPHICS.** 1989. m. $39.99. Design & Publishing Center, 15 Southgate, Harrisonburg, VA 22801. E-mail: showker@graphic-design.com; URL: http://www.graphic-design.com/DTG/. Ed. Fred Showker.
●Available only online.
Description: For people who use computers for graphics, publishing, art, or communications.

DATA COMMUNICATIONS. see *COMPUTERS — Data Communications And Data Transmission Systems*

DATA COMMUNICATIONS BUYERS' GUIDE. see *COMPUTERS — Data Communications And Data Transmission Systems*

DATA SOURCES; the comprehensive guide to the data processing industry: hardware, data communications products, software, company profiles. see *COMPUTERS — Computer Industry Directories*

DATABASE AND NETWORK JOURNAL; an international journal of database and network practice. see *COMPUTERS — Data Base Management*

004.6 UK ISSN 0955-7415
DATACOM; the internetworking magazine. 1989. m. £48. E M A P Business Communications, E M A P Computing, Greater London House, Hampstead Rd., London NW1 7QZ, England. TEL 44-171-388-2430. FAX 44-171-388-2480. (Subscr. to: Ferrari House, Field End Rd., Eastcote, Ruislip, Mddx. HA4 9UX, England. TEL 44-181-868-4499) Ed. Jim Hayes; Pub. Danny Phillips. adv.: page £2756; trim 297 x 210; adv. contact: Peter Garner. circ. 21,000 (controlled). **Document type:** trade publication.
—AskIEEE; KR SourceOne.
Description: For specifiers and purchasers of networking hard- and software products and services. Supplies strategic management information on all areas of voice and data communications.

658.403 001.644 JA ISSN 0912-5833
DATANET. 1986. s-m. $550. PenLogue Publishing Corp., Futaba Building, 3-4-18, Mita, Minato-ku, Tokyo 108, Japan. TEL 81-3-3452-8080. FAX 81-3-3452-5728. E-mail: pdb01343@niftyserve.com. Ed. Minoru Nakamura. **Document type:** newsletter.

004.6 US
DATAPRO INTERNATIONAL NETWORK SERIES. (In 3 vols.: LANs and Internetworking; Network Services; Wide Area Communications) 3 base vols. (plus m. updates). $2443 to new subscr.; renewal $2279. Datapro Information Services Group (Subsidiary of: McGraw-Hill, Inc.), 600 Delran Pkwy., Delran, NJ 08075. TEL 609-764-0100; 800-328-2776. FAX 609-764-8953.

001.644 US
DATAPRO NETWORK MANAGEMENT INFORMATION SERVICE. 2 base vols. (plus m. updates). $1195 to new subscr.; renewal $1089 (effective 1996). Datapro Information Services Group (Subsidiary of: McGraw-Hill, Inc.), 600 Delran Pkwy., Delran, NJ 08075. TEL 609-764-0100; 800-328-2776. FAX 609-764-2814.

001.644 US
DATAPRO REPORTS ON INTERNATIONAL NETWORKS MANAGEMENT. 2 base vols. (plus m. updates & m. newsletter). $2465 to new subscr.; renewals $2100. Datapro Information Services Group (Subsidiary of: McGraw-Hill, Inc.), 600 Delran Pkwy., Delran, NJ 08075. TEL 609-764-0100; 800-328-2776. FAX 609-764-8953.

001.644 US
DATAPRO REPORTS ON INTERNATIONAL UNIX SYSTEMS. 2 base vols. (plus m. updates). $1050 to new subscr.; renewals $990. Datapro Information Services Group (Subsidiary of: McGraw-Hill, Inc.), 600 Delran Pkwy., Delran, NJ 08075. TEL 609-764-0100; 800-328-2776. FAX 609-764-8953.
Formerly: Datapro Reports on International UNIX & Open Systems.

004.678 US
▼**DIGITAL LIFE.** 1996. m. Marketsource Corporation, E-mail: access@phoenix.net; URL: http://www.taponline.com/tap/tech/net-tools/digital/digital.html. Ed. Steven E. Baker.
●Available only online.
Description: Covers the online world of Internet, technology and life.

025.04 DK ISSN 0107-7481
▼**DISPLAY;** database nyt fra INFOSCAN. 1982. 10/yr. DKK 350 (effective 1997). I N F O S C A N, Nordre Fasanvej 108-B, DK-2000 Frederiksberg, Denmark. TEL 45-38-16-06-06. FAX 45-38-16-06-07. E-mail infoscan@infoscan.dk; URL: http://www.infoscan.dk Ed. Karen Bonnis. adv. contact: Peter Raben. bk.rev illus. circ. 600. **Document type:** newsletter.
●Also available online.

004.69 EI
E C H O FACTS FOR USERS. q. free. European Commission Host Organization, P.O. Box 2373, L-1023 Luxembourg, Luxembourg. TEL 352-401162-200. FAX 352-401162-234. E-mail: echo@echo.lu; URL: http://www.echo.lu/. Ed. Jane Sanderson. **Document type:** newsletter.
●Also available online.
Formerly: E C H E News.

004.6 US ISSN 1081-3055
QA76.9.H85
THE ELECTRONIC JOURNAL ON VIRTUAL CULTURE. 1993. q. TEL 330-273-5932. E-mail: diane@kovacs.com; URL: http://rdz.stjohns.edu/ejvc/ejvc.html. Ed. Diane K. Kovacs. (back issues avail.) **Document type:** academic/scholarly publication.
●Available only online.
Formerly (until 1996): Arachnet Electronic Journ on Virtual Culture (ISSN 1068-5723)
Description: Covers the emerging social and cultural aspects of the internet and related compu applications.
Refereed Serial

COMPUTERS — COMPUTER NETWORKS

004.693 658   US
▼THE ELECTRONIC MARKETPLACE (YEAR): STRATEGIES FOR CONNECTING BUYERS & SELLERS. 1995. a. $1095 for print format; diskette $1295; both formats $1495 (effective 1997). Cowles - SIMBA Information (Subsidiary of: Cowles Business Media), 11 Riverbend Dr. S., Box 4949, Stamford, CT 06907-0949. TEL 203-358-9900; 800-307-2529. FAX 203-358-5811. E-mail: simbainfo@simbanet.com; URL: http://www.simbanet.com. (also avail. in diskette format) **Document type:** trade publication.
   Description: Offers an in-depth analysis of the emerging business of electronic commerce and shopping from a marketer's perspective.

ELECTRONIC RECRUITING NEWS. see BUSINESS AND ECONOMICS — Personnel Management

ELECTRONIC TRADING MARKETS. see COMMUNICATIONS — Computer Applications

004.6   US   ISSN 1085-2395
▼ENTERPRISE SOLUTIONS FOR MANAGERS OF WINDOWS NT. 1996. m. $34.95 (free to qualified personnel) (foreign $96). Cardinal Business Media, Inc., 1300 Virginia Dr., Ste. 400, Fort Washington, PA 19034. TEL 215-643-8000. FAX 215-643-8099. URL: http://www.cardinal.com/ent. (Subscr. to: Box 3008, Northbrook, IL 60065-3008. TEL 847-291-5212. FAX 847-291-4816) Ed. Al Gillen; Pub. Mark Durrick. circ. 80,000. **Document type:** trade publication.
●Also available online.
—KR SourceOne.
   Description: Identifies industry trends as they relate to the Windows NT environment.

EPLAY. see COMPUTERS — Computer Games

004.678   SZ
ETOY TANKSYSTEM. 1994. 4/yr. P.O. Box 3365, 8049 Zurich, Switzerland. E-mail: mailme@etoy.com; URL: http://www.etoy.com.
●Available only online.

004.6   US   ISSN 1088-2758
▼EVO. 1996. m. P Publishing, Box 566, Nebraska City, NE 68410-0566. E-mail: eVO@p-pub.com; URL: http://www.p-pub.com. Ed. Dave Prochnow.
●Available only online.
   Description: A professional designer's source book on the internet for how-to information, product reviews, and design world news.

004.678 659.1
658.8   US
▼EXPOSURE! (YAKIMA).* 1996. w. 129 Foothills Rd., Lake Oswego, OR 97034-3105. E-mail: exposure@usa.net; URL: http://www.exposure-usa.com/. Ed. Adam J. Boettiger. **Document type:** newsletter.
●Also available online.
   Description: Focuses on promotion of business on the internet through marketing and advertising mediums.

Y I FRANCE. see LIBRARY AND INFORMATION SCIENCES — Computer Applications

ASTLINK SOFTWARE UPDATE. see COMPUTERS — Software

001.644   US
▼IDO NEWS.* 1984. w. free. Fido Software, 55 Rodel Pl., San Francisco, CA 94103-3406. Ed. Tom Jennings. circ. 16,000. (back issues avail.)
●Available only online.
   Description: Contains news of the Fidonet computer network.

004.6   DK
▼FIRST MONDAY. (Not avail. in printed format) (Text in English) 1996. m. (CD-ROM a.). DKK 112 worldwide (effective 1997). Munksgaard International Publishers Ltd., Noerre Soegade 35, P.O. Box 2148, DK-1016 Copenhagen, Denmark. TEL 45-33-127030. E-mail: valauskas@firstmonday.dk; URL: http://www.firstmonday.dk. Ed. Edward Valauskas. illus. (back issues avail.) **Document type:** academic/scholarly publication.
●Also available online.
Also available on CD-ROM.
   Description: Publishes original articles about the Internet and the global information infrastructure, including political and regulatory issues, economic, technical and social factors, report on standards, and discuss the content of the internet.
   Refereed Serial

004.6   US   ISSN 1083-3501
FRONTIERS IN NETWORKING. q. $89.95. Academic Press, Inc, Journal Division, 525 B St., Ste. 1900, San Diego, CA 92101-4495. TEL 619-230-1840. URL: http://www.apnet.com. (Subscr. to: Box 861213, Orlando, FL 32886-1213. TEL 800-543-9534) **Document type:** academic/scholarly publication.
●Available only on CD-ROM.

G I G A B I T NEWS; covering worldwide developments in fiber distributed data interface. see COMMUNICATIONS

004.693   US   ISSN 1072-0413
G N N MAGAZINE.* 1993. q. Global Network Navigator (Subsidiary of: America OnLine), 22000 Aol Way, Dulles, VA 20166. TEL 510-883-7220. E-mail: info@ora.com; URL: http://gnn.com/.
●Available only online.

004.693   US   ISSN 1072-0421
G N N NEWS.* 1993. w. Global Network Navigator (Subsidiary of: America OnLine), 22000 Aol Way, Dulles, VA 20166. TEL 510-883-7220. E-mail: info@ora.com; URL: http://gnn.com/.
●Available only online.

GALE DIRECTORY OF DATABASES. see COMPUTERS — Data Base Management

004.6   US
▼GLEN COVE COMPUTING NEWS. 1995. m. Glen Cove Computing, 26 Castle Hill Ct., Vallejo, CA 94591. E-mail: editor@glencove.com; URL: http://www.glencove.com/gcctimes.htm. Ed. Todd L. Martini. **Document type:** newsletter.
●Available only online.
   Description: Features PC technical tips, Internet site reviews, and articles on the latest advances in Internet technologies.

004.6   UK
GOING ONLINE AND C D - R O M. 1980. irreg., 19th ed., 1994. Aslib, Association for Information Management, Publications Department, Information House, 20-24 Old St., London EC1V 9AP, England. TEL 44-171-253-4488. FAX 44-171-430-0514. Eds. Phil Bradley, Terry Hanson. **Document type:** trade publication.
   Formerly (until 1992): Going Online (ISSN 0953-3753)

001.644   CN   ISSN 0713-5424
QA76.9.I58
GRAPHICS INTERFACE. PROCEEDINGS - COMPTES RENDUS. Variant title: Graphic Interface Conference. Proceedings. (Text in English, French) 1969. a. Can.$45 to non-members; members $35. Canadian Information Processing Society, 430 King St., W., Ste. 106, Toronto, ON M5V 1L5, Canada. TEL 416-593-4040. FAX 416-593-5184. (Co-sponsors: Canadian Man-Computer Communications Society; National Computer Graphics Association of Canada) circ. 500. (back issues avail.) **Document type:** proceedings.
—BLDSC (4212.513000); Ei. **CCC.**
   Refereed Serial

HEALTH CARE ON THE INTERNET; a journal of methods and applications. see LIBRARY AND INFORMATION SCIENCES — Computer Applications

HI-TECH INFORMATION. see COMMUNICATIONS — Computer Applications

001.644   US   ISSN 1063-6692
TK5105.5   CODEN: IEANEP
I E E E - A C M TRANSACTIONS ON NETWORKING. 1993. 6/yr. $280 to non-members (effective 1998). (I E E E, Association for Computing Machinery, Special Interest Group on Data Communication) Institute of Electrical and Electronics Engineers, Inc., 345 E. 47th St., New York, NY 10017-2394. TEL 732-981-0060; 800-678-4333. FAX 732-981-9667. E-mail: customer.service@ieee.org; URL: http://www.ieee.org. (Subscr. to: 445 Hoes Ln., Box 1331, Piscataway, NJ 08855-1331) Ed. Simon S. Lam. adv. **Indexed:** ASCA, Compumath, Curr.Cont., INSPEC (1993-).
—BLDSC (4362.787550); AskIEEE; CISTI; Ei; Genuine Article; KR SourceOne; Linda Hall; SWETS; UMI; UnCover. **CCC.**
   Description: Contains high-quality papers on network architecture and design, communication protocols, network software, network technologies, services, operations and management.

001.644   US   ISSN 1092-3063
QA76.58   CODEN: IPDTEX
I E E E CONCURRENCY. 1993. q. $28 to members (effective 1997). (Institute of Electrical and Electronics Engineers, Inc.) I E E E Computer Society Press, 10662 Los Vaqueros Circle, Box 3014, Los Alamitos, CA 90720-1314. TEL 714-821-8380; 800-678-4333. FAX 714-821-4010. E-mail: customer.service@ieee.org; dprice@computer.org; URL: http://computer.org/pubs/p&dt/p&dt.htm. (Subscr. to: Box 1331, 445 Hoes Lane, Piscataway, NJ 08855-1331) Ed. Gul Agha; Pub. Matt Loeb. adv.: B&W page $1650, color page $2750; adv. contact: Patricia Garvey. (also avail. in microfiche; back issues avail.) **Indexed:** Curr.Cont., INSPEC (1993-).
●Also available online.
—AskIEEE; CISTI; Ei; Genuine Article; KR SourceOne; Linda Hall; UMI; UnCover. **CCC.**
   Formerly (until 1997): I E E E Parallel and Distributed Technology (ISSN 1063-6552)
   Description: Covers advances in parallel and distributed computing technology, and specifics on unique features and applications.

004.678   US
▼I E E E INTERNET COMPUTING. 1997. bi-m. (Institute of Electrical and Electronics Engineers, Inc.) I E E E Computer Society Press, 10662 Los Vaqueros Circle, Box 3014, Los Alamitos, CA 90720-1314. TEL 714-821-8380; 800-678-4333. FAX 714-821-4010. E-mail: petrie@cdr.stanford.edu; URL: http://www.computer.org/internet/. (Subscr. to: 445 Hoes Lane, Box 1331, Piscataway, NJ 08855-1331) Ed. Charles Petrie; Pub. Matt Loeb. adv. contact: Patricia Garvey. (also avail. in microfiche; back issues avail.)
●Also available online.
—BLDSC (4362.973900).
   Description: Covers internet technologies and their affect on engineers and engineering.

001.644   US   ISSN 0890-8044
TK5105.5   CODEN: IENEET
I E E E NETWORK; the magazine of global information exchange. 1987. bi-m. $130 to non-members (effective 1998). (I E E E, Communications Society) Institute of Electrical and Electronics Engineers, Inc., 345 E. 47th St., New York, NY 10017-2394. TEL 732-981-0060; 800-678-4333. FAX 732-981-9667. E-mail: customer.service@ieee.org; URL: http://www.ieee.org. (Subscr. to: Box 1331, 445 Hoes Lane, Piscataway, NJ 08855-1331) Ed. John N. Daigle. (also avail. in microform) **Indexed:** ASCA, Comput.Dtbs., Curr.Cont., Cyb.Abstr., INSPEC (1987-), Tel.Abstr.
—BLDSC (4363.007500); AskIEEE; CISTI; Ei; Genuine Article; KR SourceOne; Linda Hall; SWETS; UMI; UnCover. **CCC.**
   Description: Covers network protocols and architecture: protocol design and validation, communications software, network control, signaling and management, network implementation (LAN,MAN,WAN) and micro-to-host communications.

COMPUTERS — COMPUTER NETWORKS

001.644 　　　US 　　ISSN 1045-9219
QA76.58 　　　CODEN: ITDSEO
I E E E TRANSACTIONS ON PARALLEL AND DISTRIBUTED SYSTEMS. 1990. m. $625 to non-members (effective 1998). Institute of Electrical and Electronics Engineers, Inc., 345 E. 47th St., New York, NY 10017-2394. TEL 732-981-0060; 800-678-4333. FAX 732-981-9667. E-mail: customer.service@ieee.org; webmaster@computer; URL: http://www.ieee.org; http://www.computer.org/pubs/tpds.htm. (Subscr. to: 445 Hoes Lane, Box 1331, Piscataway, NJ 08855-1331) Ed. Duncan E. Lawrie. (also avail. in microform) Indexed: A.S.& T.Ind., ASCA, Compumath, Curr.Cont., Ind.Sci.Rev., INSPEC (1990-), SSCI.
●Also available online.
—BLDSC (4363.209000); AskIEEE; CISTI; Ei; Genuine Article; KR SourceOne; Linda Hall; SWETS; UMI; UnCover. **CCC.**
　Description: Design and implementation of multiprocessor systems, scheduling and task partitioning, performance measurement, reliability and fault tolerance, language and compilers.

004.6 070.5 　　US 　　ISSN 1090-8188
▼**I P NEWS (PRINT EDITION).** (Internet Publishing) Online edition: I P News (Internet Edition) (US ISSN 1090-8196) 1996. q. (plus m. updates for Internet Edition). $20. NetPubs International, LLC, 430 Canyon Ave., Ste. B, Ft. Collins, CO 80521-2625. TEL 970-416-7703. FAX 970-416-7754. E-mail: aterry@netpubsintl.com; URL: http://www.netpubsintl.com/ipnews.html. Ed. Barbara Meyers. adv. contact: Ana Arias Terry. **Document type:** newsletter.
●Also available online.
　Description: Provides independent coverage of electronic publishing and electronic commerce as they relate to the academic and professional publishing communities.

004.6 　　　AT
▼**I - WATCH NEWSLETTER.** 1996. w. Exton Enterprises, P.O. Box 394, Mt. Ommaney, Qld. 4074, Australia. E-mail: exton@gil.com.au; URL: http://www.gil.com.au/comm/eemall/iwatch/. Ed. Rohan Exton. **Document type:** newsletter.
●Available only online.
　Description: Provides internet users with a brief review of two useful internet sites each week.

004.678 　　　US
▼**IN SIGHT OF THE BIG EYE.** 1997. m. E-Mail Club, Inc., Box 2776, Sarasota, FL 34310. E-mail: emailclub@mailback.com; URL: http://www.bigeye.com. Ed. Charles Arnold.
●Available only online.
　Description: For E-Mail Club subscribers and friends and fans of the Big Eye.

004.6 　　　AT
INFO. q. University of Tasmania, Information Services Division, E-mail: tony.ryan@its.utas.edu.au; URL: http://info.utas.edu.au/docs/info/index.html. Ed. Tony Ryan. **Document type:** newsletter.
●Available only online.
　Description: Provides full-text articles and information about the internet and technology in general.

004.6 　　　US
▼**INFONATION MAGAZINE.** 1995. m. (plus w. updates). InfoNation Magazine, Inc., 2616 Harriet Ave., Ste. 119, Maples, MN 55408. TEL 612-871-4090. E-mail: canthony@info-nation.com; URL: http://www.info-nation.com. Eds. Charles Anthony, Charles Gimon. circ. 30,000.
●Also available online.
　Description: For people interested in the emerging computer culture.

004.6 　　　US
THE INFORMATION FREEWAY REPORT; free business and government information via modem. 1994. m. $160 (effective 1997). Washington Researchers, Ltd., Box 19005, 20th St. Sta., Washington, DC 20036-9005. TEL 202-333-3499. FAX 202-625-0656. E-mail: research@researchers.com; URL: http://www.researchers.com/pub/busintel/researchers.html. Ed. Walt Seager. R&P contact: Ellen O'Kane. s-a. index. **Document type:** newsletter.
●Also available online. Vendor(s): NewsNet.
　Description: Shows managers how to obtain free business information available online from electronic bulletin boards, databases and internet files.

006.3 　　　NE 　　ISSN 0922-6931
TK5105.5.I3422
INFORMATION NETWORK AND DATA COMMUNICATION. Represents: Proceedings of the International Conference on Information Network and Data Communication. 1987. irreg., vol.3, 1990. price varies. (International Federation for Information Processing, Technical Committee 6) Elsevier Science B.V., Books Division, P.O. Box 211, 1000 AE Amsterdam, Netherlands. TEL 31-20-4853911. FAX 31-20-4853705. TELEX 18582 ESPA NL. E-mail: nlinfo-f@elsevier.nl; usinfo-f@elsevier.com; forinfo-kyf04035@niftyserve.or.jp; URL: http://www.elsevier.nl/. (Subscr. in the Americas to: Elsevier Science, Regional Sales Office, Box 945, New York, NY 10159-0945. TEL 212-633-3730. FAX 212-633-3680; Subscr. in Australasia and the Far East to: Elsevier Science (Singapore) Pte Ltd, No.1 Temasek Ave., No.17-01 Millenia Tower, Singapore 039192, Singapore. TEL 65-434-3727. FAX 65-337-2230; Subscr. in Japan to: Elsevier Science Japan, 9-15 Higashi-Azabu 1-chome, Minato-ku, Tokyo 106, Japan. TEL 81-3-5561-5033. FAX 81-3-5561-5047) Ed. D. Khalkhar. **Document type:** proceedings.
　Refereed Serial

004.6 　　　US 　　ISSN 1078-6589
INFORMATION SUPERHIGHWAYS. 1994. m. $595 (foreign $645) (effective 1997). Information Gatekeepers, Inc., 214 Harvard Ave., Boston, MA 02134. TEL 617-232-3111; 800-323-1088. FAX 617-734-8562. E-mail: igiboston@aol.com; URL: http://www.igigroup.com. **Document type:** newsletter.

INFOSYS; the electronic newsletter for information systems. see COMPUTERS — *Information Science And Information Theory*

001.644 　　　FR 　　ISSN 1154-354X
INFOTECTURE EUROPE; fortnightly European newsletter on the on-line information industry. (Text in English) 1981. fortn. 2800 F. A Jour, 11 rue du Marche St. Honore, 75001 Paris, France. TEL 42-96-67-22. FAX 40-20-07-75. Ed. Sotires Eleftheriou. adv. Indexed: Comput.Cont. **Document type:** newsletter.
　Formerly (until 1987): Infotecture (European Edition) (ISSN 0294-7544)
　Description: Articles and newsbriefs on the online information industry in Europe. Contains database descriptions as well as information on database producers and host companies.

004.6 070.5 　　CN 　　ISSN 1205-6413
▼**INKLINGS;** newsletter for writers on the net. 1995. bi-w. free. Inkspot, Toronto, ON, Canada. E-mail: editor@inklings.com; URL: http://www.inkspot.com/-ohi/ink/inklings.html. Ed. Debbie Ridpath Ohi. **Document type:** newsletter.
●Available only online.

004.6 　　　US 　　ISSN 1087-9226
▼**INSIDE NETSCAPE NAVIGATOR.** 1996. m. $49 (foreign $69). Cobb Group, Inc., 9420 Bunsen Pkwy., Ste. 300, Louisville, KY 40220. TEL 502-493-3300; 800-223-8720. FAX 502-491-8050. E-mail: customer_relations@merlin.cobb.zd.com. Ed. Bruce Spencer; Pub. Mark Crane. **Document type:** newsletter.

004.6 　　　US 　　ISSN 1075-7902
TK5105.875.I57 　　CODEN: ININFR
INSIDE THE INTERNET. 1994. m. $49 (foreign $89). Cobb Group, Inc., 9420 Bunsen Pkwy., Ste. 300, Louisville, KY 40232-9720. TEL 502-493-3200. FAX 502-491-8050. URL: http://www.cobb.zd.com. (Subscr. to: Box 35160, Louisville, KY 40232-9720. TEL 800-223-8720) Ed. Bruce Spencer. **Document type:** consumer publication, trade publication.
—SWETS.
　Description: Each issue offers a feature story highlighting the newest and most exciting "stops" on the network; includes practical tips on how to retrieve information from the Internet, as well as coverage of the wide range of Internet tools available.

001.644 　　　US 　　ISSN 0735-1844
INTEGRATED SERVICE DIGITAL NETWORK; newsletter covering world trends in technology, markets and applications. Short title: I S D N. 1978-19??; resumed 1984. m. $595 (foreign $645) (effective 1997). Information Gatekeepers, Inc., 214 Harvard Ave., Boston, MA 02134. TEL 617-232-3111; 800-323-1088. FAX 617-734-8562. E-mail: igiboston@aol.com; URL: http://www.igigroup.com. Ed. Paul Polishuk. (looseleaf format; back issues avail.) **Document type:** newsletter.
—**CCC.**
　Formerly: International Data Networks News (ISSN 0270-2738); Incorporates: Transborder Data Flow News.
　Description: Offers the latest news on applications, products, the industry.

001.644 　　　UK
INTEGRATION. 1992. m. £50 (foreign £70). V N U Business Publications BV, VNU House, 32-34 Broadwick St., London W1A 2HG, England. TEL 0171-439-4242. FAX 0171-437-4841. Indexed: Compumath. **Document type:** trade publication.

INTENET. see COMPUTERS — *Data Communications And Data Transmission Systems*

004.6 　　　US
INTERACTIVE AGE; content, technology and communications for the information highway. 1994. m. $79 (free to qualified personnel). C M P Publications, Inc., 600 Community Dr., Manhasset, NY 11030. TEL 516-562-7743. FAX 516-562-7072. E-mail: interact@interact.cmp.com. (Subscr. to: Box 194, Skokie, IL 60076. TEL 708-647-6834) Ed. David Klein; Pub. Chuck Martin. adv.; illus. (tabloid format) **Document type:** trade publication.
　Description: Publishes news of technological and business developments relating to the integration of voice, video and data communication in the field of interactive computing.

004.6 　　　US
INTERACTIVE CONTENT. m. $555 (foreign $605) (effective 1997). Jupiter Communications, 627 Broadway, New York, NY 10012. TEL 212-780-6060; 800-488-4345. FAX 212-780-6075. URL: http://www.jup.com. Ed. Mark Mooradian; Pub. Gene DeRose. **Document type:** newsletter.
●Also available online. Vendor(s): Information Access Co.
　Description: Tracks business developments in consumer online services for the mass market.

INTERACTIVE PUBLICATIONS REVIEW (YEAR); an analysis of newspapers and magazines online. see *JOURNALISM*

(YEAR) INTERACTIVE SOURCEBOOK. see COMMUNICATIONS — *Television And Cable*

001.644 　　　US 　　ISSN 1059-1591
TK5103.7
INTERNATIONAL INTEGRATED SERVICES DIGITAL NETWORKS CONFERENCE & EXPOSITION. PROCEEDINGS. a. Information Gatekeepers, Inc., 214 Harvard Ave., Boston, MA 02134. TEL 617-232-3111. FAX 617-734-8562. **Document type:** proceedings.
　Formerly: International Integrated Services Digital Networks Exposition. Proceedings (ISSN 1059-1095)

001.644 　　　UK
INTERNATIONAL ONLINE INFORMATION MEETING (PROCEEDINGS). 1977. a. price varies. Learned Information (Europe) Ltd., Woodside, Hinksey Hill, Oxford OX1 5BE, England. TEL 44-1865-388000. FAX 44-1865-736354. TELEX 837704-INFORM-G (Dist. in N. America by: Learned Information Inc., 143 Old Marlton Pike, Medford, NJ 08055-8750. TEL 609-654-6266) (back issues avail.) **Document type:** proceedings.

COMPUTERS — COMPUTER NETWORKS

004.6 378   US
Z678.93.M53
INTERNET AND HIGHER EDUCATION; an quarterly review of innovations in post-secondary education. 1984. q. $50 (foreign $70) to individuals; institutions $175 (foreign $195) (effective 1998). J A I Press Inc., 55 Old Post Rd., No. 2, Box 1678, Greenwich, CT 06830-1678. TEL 203-661-7602. FAX 203-661-0792. E-mail: cchen@vmsvax. simmons.edu; jai@jaipress.com. Subscr. in the Uk and Europe to: JAI Press Ltd., 38 Tavistock St., Covent Garden, London WC2E 7PB, England. TEL 44-171-379-8834. FAX 44-171-379-8835) Ed. Ching-chih Chen. adv.; abstr.; bibl.; illus. circ. 500. (back issues avail.; reprint service avail.) **Indexed:** C.I.J.E., Comput.Abstr., Curr.Cont., ERIC, INSPEC, Lib.Lit., LISA, Microcmp.Ind.
—BLDSC (5758.520900); AskIEEE; KR SourceOne; Linda Hall; SWETS; UnCover. **CCC.**
Formerly: Microcomputers for Information Management (ISSN 0742-2342)
Description: For librarians and information specialists. Features articles on the applications of microcomputers in information processing, organization and dissemination, as well as information on microcomputer hardware and software.

INTERNET AND ONLINE SERVICES MARKET: AUSTRALIA AND NEW ZEALAND. see *COMMUNICATIONS — Computer Applications*

004.6   US
▼**INTERNET BANDWIDTH: TECHNOLOGY, FORECASTS AND THE IMPACT ON CONTENT, (YEAR)**. 1997. a. $1095 (effective 1997). Cowles - SIMBA Information (Subsidiary of: Cowles Business Media), 11 Riverbend Dr. S., Box 4949, Stamford, CT 06907-0949. TEL 203-358-9900; 800-307-2529. FAX 203-358-5811. E-mail: info@simbanet.com; URL: http://www.simbanet.com.

004.6   UK   ISSN 1363-9919
▼**INTERNET BUSINESS NEWS**. (Not avail. in print format) 1994. m. £100($170) (effective 1997). M2 Communications Ltd., P.O. Box 475, Coventry CV1 2ZW, England. TEL 44-1203-634700. FAX 44-1203-634144. E-mail: di@m2.com; URL: http://www.m2.com. Ed. Darren Ingram. **Document type:** trade publication.
●Available only online.
Description: Provides key insights into the commercial activities and benefits available through the Internet.

004.6   UK   ISSN 1363-2922
▼**INTERNET FOR BUSINESS**. 1996. bi-m. Financial Times Telecoms & Media Publishing (Subsidiary of: Financial Times Group), Maple House, 149 Tottenham Court Rd., London W1P 9LL, England. TEL 44-171-896-2234. FAX 44-171-896-2256. **Document type:** trade publication.

INTERNET HOMESTEADER. SERIES A: LIBRARY AND INFORMATION SCIENCE. see *LIBRARY AND INFORMATION SCIENCES*

004.6   US   ISSN 1088-0666
▼**INTERNET INFOSCAVENGER**; sites and insights for growing businesses. 1996. m. $99 (effective 1997). InfoScavenger Communications, Inc., 1153 Bergen Pkwy., Ste. 473, Evergreen, CO 80439. TEL 303-674-2794; 800-449-8533. FAX 303-674-4184. E-mail: info@infoscavenger.com; cathy@infoscavenger.com; URL: http://www.infoscavenger.com. Pub. Cathy D. Dupre. (back issues avail.) **Document type:** newsletter.
●Also available online.
Description: Offers tips, business leads, promotion strategies and business intelligence.

004.6   US
▼**INTERNET, JAVA AND ACTIVE X ADVISOR**. 1996. m. $49 (Canada $69; elsewhere $89). Advisor Publications Inc., 5675 Ruffin Rd., Ste. 200, San Diego, CA 92123. TEL 619-278-5600. FAX 619-278-0300. E-mail: subscribe@advisor.com; URL: http://www.advisor.com/ia.html. (Dist. by: International Periodical Distributors, 674 Via de la Valle, Ste. 204, Solana Beach, CA 92075) Ed. John L. Hawkins; Pub. William Ota. adv. contact: B.J. Ghiglione. circ. 37,000. **Document type:** trade publication.
●Also available online.
—KR SourceOne.
Former titles (until Apr. 1997): Internet and Java Advisor (ISSN 1090-6452); (until Apr. 1996): Internet Advisor (ISSN 1084-158X)
Description: For designing, building and deploying online applications. Provides application development guidance to users of the Internet, World Wide Web, Intranets and online development and deployment.

INTERNET LAWYER. see *LAW*

004.693   GW
INTERNET MAGAZIN. m. DM.52.80 (foreign DM.76.80; students DM.45.60) (effective 1997). Franzis Verlag GmbH, Dornacherstr. 3, 85622 Feldkirchen, Germany. TEL 49-89-99115-0. FAX 49-89-99115199. **Document type:** consumer publication.

658 004.6   US
▼**INTERNET MARKETING & TECHNOLOGY REPORT**. 1995. m. $387 (effective 1997). Computer Economics, Inc., 5841 Edison Pl., Carlsbad, CA 92008. TEL 760-438-8100; 800-326-8100. FAX 760-431-1126. URL: http://www.computereconomics.com. **Document type:** newsletter.
Description: Advises marketing, sales, and corporate executives with marketing success stories, demographic trends, sales tactics, and provides insider analyses from top business marketers and technical experts.

658 004.6   NE
INTERNET MARKETING DIGEST. fortn.
TEL 31-20-5128634. E-mail: info@informatiebank.nl; URL: http://www.informatiebank.nl/digest/indexgb.htm.
●Available only online.
Description: Contains articles on marketing and communications via the Internet.

INTERNET MEDICINE. see *MEDICAL SCIENCES*

004.6   IT
INTERNET NEWS. m. L.45000 (Europe L.80000; elsewhere L.100000) (effective 1997). Tecniche Nuove s.p.a., Via C. Menotti 14, 20129 Milan, Italy. TEL 39-2-75701. FAX 39-2-7610351. E-mail: abbonamenti@tecnet.it; URL: http://www.tecnet.it. adv.: B&W page L.3270000, color page L.5232000.

004.692 340   US   ISSN 1088-0615
▼**THE INTERNET NEWSLETTER: LEGAL & BUSINESS ASPECTS**. 1996. m. $129. New York Law Publishing Co., 345 Park Ave. S., New York, NY 10010. TEL 212-545-6170. FAX 212-696-1848. URL: http://www.ljx.com. Ed. Andy Hollander. (looseleaf format) **Document type:** newsletter.
Description: Covers legal, business and technological issues relating to the rapid development of the internet.

004.6   US   ISSN 1087-5301
Z674.75.I58   CODEN: IRSQFC
▼**INTERNET REFERENCE SERVICES QUARTERLY**; a journal of innovative information practice, technologies and resources. 1996. q. $36 to individuals (Canada $46.80; elsewhere $50.40); libraries and other institutions $48 (Canada $62.40; elsewhere $67.20) (effective 1997-1998). Haworth Press, Inc., 10 Alice St., Binghamton, NY 13904. TEL 607-722-5857; 800-342-9676. FAX 607-722-6362. E-mail: getinfo@haworth.com; URL: http://www.haworth.com. Ed. Lyn E. Martin; Pub. Bill Cohen. R&P contact: Ruthann Heath. adv.: B&W page $300; trim 4 3/8 x 7 1/8; adv. contact: Jackie Blakeslee. bk.rev. (also avail. in microform from HAW,UMI; reprint service avail. from HAW) **Document type:** academic/scholarly publication.
—BLDSC (4557.199819); AskIEEE; Haworth; KR SourceOne; UnCover.
Description: Highlights theoretical, research and practical application of internet-related information services, sources and resources.
Refereed Serial

004.693   GW
▼**INTERNET REPORT**; Branchendienst fuer Online-Profis. 1995. m. DM.240 (effective 1997). I W T Magazin Verlags GmbH, Bahnhofstr. 36, 85591 Vaterstetten, Germany. TEL 49-8106-350-0. FAX 49-8106-350126. URL: http://www.iwtnet.de. Ed. Tim Cole. circ. 7,000. **Document type:** trade publication.

004.6   UK   ISSN 1066-2243
TK5105.5   CODEN: IRESEF
INTERNET RESEARCH. 1991. 5/yr. £319($499) (foreign Aus.$619) (effective 1998). M C B University Press Ltd., 60-62 Toller Ln., Bradford, W. Yorks BD8 9BY, England. TEL 44-1274-777700. FAX 44-1274-785200. E-mail: peters@mcb.co.uk; URL: http://www.mcb.co.uk/liblink/intr/jourhome.htm. Ed. John Peters. **Indexed:** ASCA, C.I.J.E., Curr.Cont., INSPEC (1993-), Lib.Lit., SSCI, WPM. **Document type:** academic/scholarly publication.
●Also available online.
—BLDSC (4557.199820); AskIEEE; Genuine Article; KR SourceOne; SWETS; UnCover. **CCC.**
Formerly (until 1993): Electronic Networking (ISSN 1051-4805)
Description: Covers developments in information technology and communication, focusing on the use of telecommunications networks to provide information services and products. Publishes papers on policy and technical issues affecting electronic networks and potential applications.

INTERNET ROADSTOP: MAC ZINE AND INFORMATION. see *COMPUTERS — Personal Computers*

004.678   US
▼**INTERNET SCAMBUSTERS**. 1995. m. Netrageous Inc., 18113 Town Center Dr., Ste. 114, Olney, MD 20832. TEL 501-262-0463. E-mail: scambusters@scambusters.org; URL: http://www.scambusters.org/. Eds. Audri & Jim Lanford.

004.693 025   US
▼**INTERNET SHOPPER**. 1997. q. newsstand price: $4.95. Mecklermedia Corporation, 20 Ketchum St., Westport, CT 06880. TEL 203-226-6967. FAX 203-454-5840. Ed. Dan Rosenbaum. adv. **Document type:** consumer publication.
Description: Provides information and reviews on purchasing products or services online.

004.678   US
INTERNET SURVEYS. m. E-mail: web@nua.ie; URL: http://www.nua.ie/choice/surveys. **Document type:** newsletter.
●Available only online.
Description: A digest of the most interesting surveys containing data relating to the Internet.

004.678 658.8   US
▼**THE INTERNET TIMES**. 1996. s-m. Euro-Marketing Associates, 1850 Union St., Ste. 1229, San Francisco, CA 94123. TEL 415-680-2423. E-mail: ema@euromktg.com; URL: http://www.euromktg.com/eng/ed/it.html.
●Available only online.
Description: Covers the latest in Internet technology advances and their marketing applications, especially for the European market.

INTERNET TREND WATCH FOR LIBRARIES. see *LIBRARY AND INFORMATION SCIENCES*

COMPUTERS — COMPUTER NETWORKS

004.6 US
▼ **INTERNET UNDERGROUND.** 1995. m. $23.95; newsstand price: $4.99. Sendai Publishing Group, 1920 Highland Ave., Ste. 222, Lombard, IL 60148. TEL 708-916-7222. FAX 708-916-7227. **Document type:** consumer publication.
  Description: Highlights new locations and advances on the Internet.

004.693 384.3 US ISSN 1081-2474
▼ **INTERNET WEEK**; news and analysis of internet business opportunities. 1995. w. $697 (includes WWW access) (effective 1997). Phillips Business Information, Inc., 1201 Seven Locks Rd., Potomac, MD 20854. TEL 301-424-3338. FAX 301-309-3847. E-mail: pbi@phillips.com; URL: http://www.phillips.com/pbi/iw. Ed. Seth Arenstein. **Document type:** newsletter.
• Also available online.
  Incorporates (in Oct 1995): Internet Letter.

004.693 US ISSN 1064-3923
TK5105.5 CODEN: IERNE8
INTERNET WORLD. 1990. m. $29. Mecklermedia Corporation, 20 Ketchum St., Westport, CT 06880. TEL 203-226-6967. FAX 203-454-8540. URL: http://pubs.iworld.com/iw-online/. Ed. Michael Neubarth. (also avail. in microform from UMI) **Indexed:** ASCA, C.I.J.E., Curr.Cont., WPM. **Document type:** consumer publication.
—BLDSC (4557.199848); CISTI; Genuine Article; KNAW; KR SourceOne; Linda Hall; SWETS; UMI; UnCover. **CCC.**
  Formerly (until 1992): Research and Education Networking (ISSN 1051-4791)
  Description: Analyzes developments within the World-Wide Web, Internet, electronic networking, and publishing, as well as other emerging network issues of interest to the Internet end user.

001.644 US
INTERNETWORK. 1990. m. Cardinal Business Media, Inc., 1300 Virginia Dr., Ste. 400, Fort Washington, PA 19034. TEL 215-643-8000. FAX 215-643-3901. Ed. Evan Birkhead; Pub. Calvin Carr. adv. contact: Gloria Goodwin. circ. 80,000 (controlled). **Document type:** trade publication.
• Also available online. Vendor(s): Information Access Co.
—KR SourceOne.
  Formerly (until 1994): L A N Computing (ISSN 1055-1808)
  Description: Addresses the migration of enterprise networks to the Internet.

001.644 621.381 US
J U G NEWSLETTER.* m. membership. Jefferson State Computer Users Group, 1140 Sweet Rd., Medford, OR 97501-1849. (Subscr. to: Jefferson State Computer Users Group, Box 457, Gold Hill, OR 97525-0457.) Ed. John Newman. adv.
  Description: For Jefferson State Computer Users Group members. Features articles, news briefs and meeting notes.

JISUANJI XUEBAO. see COMPUTERS — Theory Of Computing

JOURNAL OF COMPUTER SCIENCE AND TECHNOLOGY. see COMPUTERS — Theory Of Computing

THE JOURNAL OF DATA MINING AND KNOWLEDGE DISCOVERY. see COMPUTERS — Information Science And Information Theory

004.6 NE ISSN 0926-6801
CODEN: JHSNEB
JOURNAL OF HIGH SPEED NETWORKS. 1992. q. fl.460($264) (effective 1997). I O S Press, Van Diemenstraat 94, 1013 CN Amsterdam, Netherlands. TEL 31-20-6382189. FAX 31-20-6203419. E-mail: market@iospress.nl; URL: http://www.iospress.nl/iospress. (In N. America: Box 10558, Burke, VA 22009-0558. TEL 703-323-5554. FAX 703-250-4705) Ed. Deepinder Sidhu. (back issues avail.) **Indexed:** INSPEC (1992-). **Document type:** academic/scholarly publication.
—BLDSC (4998.560000); AskIEEE; Ei; Genuine Article; KR SourceOne; SWETS. **CCC.**
  Description: Publishes work on theoretical and technical issues related to very-high-speed computer networks, optical networks and the control, management and operation of very-high-speed networks.
  Refereed Serial

JOURNAL OF INTERNET CATALOGING; the international quarterly of digital organization, classification, and access. see LIBRARY AND INFORMATION SCIENCES — Computer Applications

JOURNAL OF INTERNET PURCHASING. see BUSINESS AND ECONOMICS — Marketing And Purchasing

JOURNAL OF NETWORK AND SYSTEMS MANAGEMENT. see COMPUTERS — Computer Systems

001.644 US ISSN 1041-8334
TK5105.5 CODEN: JNMAEI
JOURNAL OF NETWORK MANAGEMENT.* 1989. q. $98. Frost & Sullivan, Inc., 90 West St., No. 1301, New York, NY 10005-1039. TEL 212-233-1080. **Indexed:** Comput.Abstr.
—KR SourceOne; Linda Hall.

JOURNAL OF TECHNOLOGY LAW AND POLICY. see PATENTS, TRADEMARKS AND COPYRIGHTS

KAIFANG XITONG YU WANGLU/OPEN SYSTEMS & NETWORK. see COMPUTERS — Computer Systems

KEY ABSTRACTS - NEURAL NETWORKS. see COMPUTERS — Abstracting, Bibliographies, Statistics

004.693 UK
KEY NOTE MARKET REPORT: INTERNET USAGE IN THE HOME. Variant title: Internet Usage in the Home. irreg. £205. Key Note Ltd., Field House, 72 Oldfield Rd., Hampton, Middlesex TW12 2HQ, England. TEL 44-181-783-0755. FAX 44-181-783-0049. **Document type:** trade publication.

004.6 UK
KEY NOTE MARKET REPORT: NETWORKS. Variant title: Networks. irreg. £205. Key Note Ltd., Field House, 72 Oldfield Rd., Hampton, Middlesex TW12 2HQ, England. TEL 44-181-783-0755. FAX 44-181-783-0049. **Document type:** trade publication.

004.678 US
▼ **THE KLEINMAN REPORT.** 1995. w. E-mail: geoff@kleinman.com; URL: http://www.kleinman.com. Ed. Geoffrey Kleinman.
• Available only online.
  Description: Covers Internet related topics.

004.6 UK ISSN 0968-6320
L A N MAGAZINE. (Local Area Network) 1993. m. E M A P Business Communications, E M A P Computing, Greater London House, Hampstead Rd., London NW1 7QZ, England. TEL 44-171-388-2430. FAX 44-171-383-5578. E-mail: letters.lan@computing.emap.co.uk. **Document type:** consumer publication.
—BLDSC (5145.316570); AskIEEE; KR SourceOne; SWETS. **CCC.**

004.6 NE ISSN 0926-308X
L A N MAGAZINE. (Local Area Network) 1989. 11/yr. fl.185. I D G Communications Nederland, Postbus 5446, 2000 GK Haarlem, Netherlands. TEL 31-23-5461111. FAX 31-23-5461155. Ed. D. Schievels; Pub. R. Gort. adv. circ. 7,800. **Document type:** trade publication.
—SWETS.

001.644 US
L A N PRODUCT NEWS. (Local Area Network) 1989. m. $150. Worldwide Videotex, Box 3273, Boynton Beach, FL 33424-3273. TEL 407-738-2276. Ed. Mark Wright; Pub. Mark Wright. bk.rev. (back issues avail.) **Document type:** newsletter.
• Also available online. Vendor(s): Data-Star; Information Access Co., Knight-Ridder Information, Inc., NewsNet (EC99).
  Description: Provides news and information on the computer local area network industry. Covers new hardware and software products, as well as research and development, with special emphasis on the marketing strategies of LAN manufacturers and vendors, user applications, and development of industry standards.

LAW AND ELECTRONIC COMMERCE. see LAW

004.6 658.8 US
LEARNING - FOUNTAIN REVIEWS. s-m. E-mail: soarsegl@ix.netcom.com; URL: http://www.tricky.com/lfm/newsletr.htm. Ed. Paul Siegel. **Document type:** newsletter.
• Available only online.
  Description: Helps readers do research on the Internet.

004.678 MX
LINK. m. $71 (effective 1997). Consorcio Sayrols, Mie y Pesado 126, Col. del Valle, 03100 Mexico, D.F., Mexico. TEL 52-5-6874699. FAX 52-5-5237045. E-mail: beatrizc@spin.com.mx; URL: http://www.sayrols.com.mx. Ed. Monica Mistretta. adv.: B&W page $1600, color page $2080; trim 205 x 270; adv. contact: Beatriz Coria. circ. 20,000. **Document type:** consumer publication.
  Description: Presents an internet guide that help users to find information in a faster and easier way.

LINK-UP; the newsmagazine for users of online service business, educational, personal. see COMPUTERS – Data Communications And Data Transmission Systems

004.678 US ISSN 1075-3583
LINUX JOURNAL. m. $22 (Canada & Mexico $27; elsewhere $32) (effective 1997). Specialized Systems Consultants, Box 85687, Seattle, WA 98145. TEL 206-782-7733. FAX 206-782-7191. E-mail: linux@ssc.com; URL: http://www.ssc.com. Ed. Jonathan Gross.
• Also available online.
  Incorporates (1996-1997): Websmith (ISSN 1086-1890)
  Description: Provides technical information on the Web, and articles and tutorials pertaining to Linux, the freely-available Unix operating system.

601.38 US ISSN 1051-1962
LOCAL AREA NETWORKS; newsletter covering worldwide technology trends, applications, and markets. Abbreviated title: L A N Newsletter. 1982. m. $59 (foreign $645) (effective 1997). Information Gatekeepers, Inc., 214 Harvard Ave., Boston, MA 02134. TEL 617-232-3111; 800-323-1088. FAX 617-734-8562. E-mail: igiboston@aol.com; URL: http://www.igigroup.com. Ed. Paul Polishuk. circ. 1,000 (paid). (looseleaf format; back issues avail.) **Indexed:** PROMT. **Document type:** newsletter.
—BLDSC (5289.600000). **CCC.**
  Description: Covers worldwide technology trends, applications, products, new developments, and markets for LANs.

004.69 US
LOCAL GOVERNMENT INTERNET CONNECTION. 1987. bi-m. $19. Innovation Groups, Inc., Box 16645, Tampa, FL 33687. TEL 813-622-8484. FAX 813-664-0051. Ed. Nicole Wooden. R&P contact: Nicole Wooden. adv. contact: Nicole Wooden. bk.rev.; video rev. circ. 700. pp./issue: 8 **Document type:** newsletter.
  Former titles: Local Government Newsnet; City County Communications; Video Letter (ISSN 1058-8515)
  Description: Features examples showing how city and county governments are using electronic communication services to improve the quality of service to and communication with citizens.

M I N'S NEW MEDIA REPORT. (Media Industry Newsletter) see COMMUNICATIONS

MAC NET JOURNAL. see COMPUTERS — Personal Computers

MACINTOSH C D - R O M GUIDE. see COMPUTERS — Data Base Management

006.3 US ISSN 1092-292X
▼ **MANAGED NETWORK SERVICES NEWS.** 1997. bi-w $597 (foreign $630) (effective 1997). Phillips Business Information, Inc., 1201 Seven Locks Rd. Potomac, MD 20854. TEL 301-424-3338. FAX 301-309-3847. E-mail: pbi@phillips.com. Ed John Spofford. (looseleaf format) **Document type:** newsletter.
• Also available online.

COMPUTERS — COMPUTER NETWORKS

004.69 658   US   ISSN 1082-9849
▼**MANAGING L A N COSTS**. 1995. m. $245 in U.S. & Canada; elsewhere $269. Institute of Management Administration, Inc., 29 W. 35th St., 5th fl., New York, NY 10001-2299. TEL 212-244-0360. FAX 212-564-0465.
   Description: Dedicated to helping LAN, MIS and DP managers and network administrators hold down costs and stay current on performance information. Covers hardware, software, wiring strategies, maintenance and service, and staff and training costs. Includes exclusive ratings on new technologies and surveys of salary information.

004.693 025   US
TK5105.875.I57
MECKLERMEDIA'S OFFICIAL INTERNET YELLOW PAGES. 1994. a. $45. Mecklermedia Corporation, 20 Ketchum St., Westport, CT 06880. TEL 203-226-6967. FAX 203-454-5840. URL: http://pubs.imworld.com. (In Europe: Mecklermedia Ltd., Artillery House, Artillery Row, London SW1P 1RT, England. TEL 44-171-976-0405. FAX 44-171-976-0506) **Document type:** directory.
   Formerly (until 1996): Internet World's on Internet (ISSN 1087-6111)
   Description: Guide to electronic journals, newsletters, texts, discussion lists and other resources on the Internet.

004.6   US
THE MESH. m. E-mail: themesh@aol.com; URL: http://www.albany.globalone.net/themesh/. **Document type:** newsletter.
●Available only online.
   Description: Features articles, reviews, columns, listings, and what's hot about the online world.

004.678   US
MESSAGES FROM THE FUTURE. 1994. w. E-mail: rhb@islandnet.com; URL: http://www.islandnet.com/~rhb/future__page.html.
●Available only online.
   Description: Features Internet investigative reporting.

001.644   US
MICHNET NEWS. 1986. q. free. Merit Network, Inc., c/o Mariella Wells, Ed., 4251 Plymouth Rd., Ann Arbor, MI 48105-2785. TEL 313-764-9430. FAX 313-647-3185. URL: http://www.merit.edu/michnet/michnet.news/. bk.rev. circ. 27,000. **Document type:** newsletter.
●Also available online.
   Formerly: Merit Network News.
   Description: Publishes information and documentation on MICHNET, feature articles on interesting network applications, the computing environments at the Merit member institutions, and information about recent developments in networking technology.

004.6   US
▼**MICROSOFT INTERACTIVE DEVELOPER**. 1996. m. $22.95 (effective 1997). 209 Hamilton Ave., Palo Alto, CA 94301-2500. TEL 800-848-5523. URL: http://www.windx.com. (Subscr. to: Box 56470, Boulder, CO 80321-6470) Pub. Lynne Matthes. **Document type:** trade publication.
   Description: Guide to Microsoft's internet technologies and more.

004.692 005   US
MICROSOFT INTERNET SERVER PROFESSIONAL. 1996. m. $199 includes companion diskette. Pinnacle Publishing, Inc., Box 888, Kent, WA 98035-0888. TEL 206-251-1900. FAX 206-251-5057. URL: http://www.pinpub.com. **Document type:** newsletter.

MICROSOFT SQL SERVER PROFESSIONAL. see COMPUTERS — Computer Programming

001.644   US
MIDRANGE SYSTEMS (INTERNATIONAL EDITION). 2 base vols. (plus m. updates). $1116 to new subscr.; renewals $1065 (effective 1996). Datapro Information Services Group (Subsidiary of: McGraw-Hill, Inc.), 600 Delran Pkwy., Delran, NJ 08075. TEL 609-764-0100; 800-328-2776. FAX 609-764-8953.

MINITEL NEWS INTERNATIONAL. see COMPUTERS — Data Communications And Data Transmission Systems

004.692 384.3   NE   ISSN 1383-469X
▼**MOBILE NETWORKS & APPLICATIONS**. (Text in English) 1996. 4/yr. 376 SFr. (effective 1998). Baltzer Science Publishers B.V., P.O. Box 221, 1400 AE Bussum, Netherlands. TEL 31-20-6370061. FAX 31-20-6323651. E-mail: subscribe@baltzer.nl; URL: http://www.baltzer.nl. (Co-publisher: Association for Computing Machinery, US) Ed. Imrich Chlamtac.
   —AskIEEE; KR SourceOne.
   Description: Publishes significant research in the area of mobile networking, nomadic computing and related topics.
   Refereed Serial

MODEM NOTES; on line to the business community. see COMPUTERS — Hardware

004.693   BE
MONTHLY REPORT ON INTERNET MATTERS IN BELGIUM AND EUROPE. (Text in Dutch, French) m. URL: http://www.best.be. **Document type:** bulletin.
●Available only online.
   Description: Guide to net and other telecom news in Europe.

MULTIMEDIA SCHOOLS; a practical journal of multimedia, CD-ROM, online and internet in K-12. see EDUCATION — Computer Applications

343 004.6   US   ISSN 1080-3904
KF390.5.C6
MULTIMEDIA STRATEGIST. 1994. m. $175. New York Law Publishing Co., 345 Park Ave. S., New York, NY 10010. TEL 212-545-6170. FAX 212-696-1848. URL: http://www.ljx.com. Eds. Julian S. Millstein, Jeffrey Neuburger. (looseleaf format) **Document type:** newsletter.
   Description: Covers legal, financial and business issues raised by multimedia technology.

MULTIMEDIA TOOLS AND APPLICATIONS; an international journal. see COMPUTERS — Software

006.3   US   ISSN 1076-2442
MULTIMEDIA WIRE. 1993. d. $495 (effective 1997). Phillips Business Information, Inc., 1201 Seven Locks Rd., Potomac, MD 20854. TEL 301-424-3338. FAX 301-309-3847. E-mail: pbi@phillips.com. Ed. Seth Arenstein. (only avail. by fax) **Document type:** newsletter.
   Incorporates (1995-1997): Interactive Daily (ISSN 1083-141X)

N O H U G NEWS. (New Orleans Heath Users Group) see COMPUTERS — Personal Computers

004.693 384.3   US   ISSN 1080-2681
▼**THE NET**; the ultimate guide to the internet. 1995. m. $24.95 (Canada $38.95; elsewhere $48.95); newsstand price: $4.95. Imagine Publishing, Inc., 150 North Hill Dr., Brisbane, CA 94005. TEL 415-468-4684. FAX 415-468-4686. adv. **Document type:** consumer publication.
   —KR SourceOne.

004.6   NE   ISSN 1381-5857
NET. 1994. 11/yr. fl.95. I D G Communications Nederland, Postbus 5446, 2000 GK Haarlem, Netherlands. TEL 31-23-5461111. FAX 31-23-5461155. Pub. Oscar Kneppers. adv. **Document type:** trade publication.
   —KNAW; SWETS.

004.678   MX
NET AT. fortn. $25 (effective 1997). Consorcio Sayrols, Mier y Pesado 126, Col. del Valle, 03100 Mexico, D.F., Mexico. TEL 52-5-6874699. FAX 52-5-5237045. E-mail: beatrizc@spin.com.mx; URL: http://www.sayrols.com.mx. Ed. Monica Mistretta. adv.: B&W page $2682, color page $3447; trim 320 x 260; adv. contact: Beatriz Coria. circ. 5,000. **Document type:** newspaper.
   Description: Includes news about internet, nets, and telecommunications and their impact in the business world.

NET BUSINESS DAILY. see BUSINESS AND ECONOMICS

004.6   US   ISSN 1093-2380
▼**NET CONNECT**. 1996. 5/yr. $49.95. Resource Communications Group, 3011 N. Lamar Blvd., Ste. 302, Austin, TX 78705. TEL 512-458-2021; 800-331-5076. FAX 512-458-2059. E-mail: rcg_NetConnect@austintx.net; URL: http://www.austintx.net/users/ResourceComm/NetConnectPage.htm. Ed. Jeanne Graves.
   Description: Contains interviews with librarians concerning various challenges posed in providing public access to the Internet. Includes reference sites, and success stories from librarians and Internet use.

004.678   US   ISSN 1078-7593
NETCETERA. 1994. w. 15400 S.E. 30th Pl., Ste. 202, Bellevue, WA 98007. E-mail: netcetera-feedback@nwnet.net; URL: http://www.nwnet.net/netcetera/. Ed. Sally Nordquist.
●Available only online.
   Description: Offers updates on new resources, services, and developments on the Internet, especially those that impact businesses.

NETCOM. see GEOGRAPHY

004.693   US   ISSN 1078-4632
NETGUIDE; the guide to the internet and online services. 1994. m. $22.97 (foreign $40.97) (effective 1996); newsstand price: $2.95. C M P Publications, Inc. (Jericho), 1 Jericho Plaza, 3rd. Fl., Jericho, NY 11753. TEL 516-733-6700. FAX 516-733-8390. TELEX 647035 CMP PUB MAHA. E-mail: netmail@netguide.cmp.com. (Subscr. to: Box 420355, Palm Coast, FL 32142-9371. TEL 800-829-0421) Ed. Patrice Adcroft; Pub. Donald F. Tydeman. adv.; software rev.; circ. 200,000 (paid). (back issues avail.) **Document type:** consumer publication.
   Description: Reviews Internet sites, online services and related hardware and software.

004.678   SP
▼**NETMANIA**. 1997. 12/yr. 6600 ptas. (Europe 10920 ptas.; elsewhere 13560 ptas.) (effective 1997). Hobby Press, S.A., C. de los Ciruelos, 4, 28700 San Sebastian de los Reyes (Madrid), Spain. TEL 34-1-6548199. FAX 34-1-6547272. Ed. Domingo Gomez. adv. contact: Mamen Perera. circ. 20,000. **Document type:** consumer publication.
   Description: Covers world wide web, the internet and more.

004.6   US
NETNEWS MAGAZINE. 1994. q. free. (International Business Machines Corporation) T D A Group, 289 S. San Antonio Rd., Ste. 204, Los Altos, CA 94022. TEL 415-948-3140. FAX 415-948-4280. E-mail: netnews@tdagroup.com. Ed. Lorrie Nelson; Pub. Bob Tabke. R&P contact: Pam Atkinson. adv. contact: Jeanine Bogart. charts; software rev.; circ. 250,000 (controlled). **Document type:** trade publication.
   Description: Helps network managers better evaluate and use networking technologies.

004.693   GW   ISSN 0948-4825
▼**NETRUNNER**. 1995. q. DM.26 (effective 1997). I W T Magazin Verlags GmbH, Bahnhofstr. 36, 85591 Vaterstetten, Germany. TEL 49-8106-350-0. FAX 49-8106-350126. URL: http://www.iwtnet.de. Ed. Roland Maeusl. circ. 50,500. **Document type:** trade publication.
   Description: For users of Novell products.

004.678   US
NETSURFER DIGEST. 1994. w. free. 333 Cobalt Way, Ste. 107, Sunnyvale, CA 94086. E-mail: editor@netsurf.com; URL: http://www.netsurf.com/nsd/. Eds. Arthur Bebak, Lawrence Nyveen.
●Available only online.
   Description: Guide to interesting news, places and resources online.

004.6   US   ISSN 1076-3422
                CODEN: NCONFZ
NETWARE CONNECTION. 1990? bi-m. free to qualified personnel. NetWare Users International, Inc., 1555 N. Technology Way, Orem, UT 84057. TEL 801-221-9634. Ed. Debbie Pearson; Pub. Michael Lans. R&P contact: Brian Smith. adv. contact: Brian Smith. illus.; circ. 140,000 (controlled). (back issues avail.)

COMPUTERS — COMPUTER NETWORKS

004.6 US ISSN 1058-2800
TK5105.7
NETWARE SOLUTIONS; the independent magazine for Novell system managers. 1991. m. $35.40 (foreign $50) (effective 1996). New Media Publications, 10711 Burnet Rd., No. 305, Austin, TX 78758-4459. TEL 512-873-7761. FAX 512-873-7782. Ed. Deni Connor; Pub. Floyd Sembler. R&P contact: Deni Connor. adv. contact: Beverly Thompson. circ. 40,000. **Document type:** trade publication.
—KR SourceOne.
  Description: Provides Novell, Novell-compatible, and Netware users with how-to articles on networking issues, new product and industry information.

004.6 US ISSN 1040-4503
QA76.76.063
NETWARE TECHNICAL JOURNAL. Short title: N T J. 1989-1990; resumed. bi-m. $44.95. McGraw-Hill Companies, 1221 Avenue of the Americas, New York, NY 10020. TEL 212-512-2000. Ed. Peter Clegg. **Document type:** trade publication.
—UMI.
  Description: Serves the NetWare segment of the network computing industry.

001.644 UK ISSN 0269-3089
CODEN: NWRKEA
NETWORK (LONDON, 1985). 1985. m. £60 (foreign £80). V N U Business Publications BV, VNU House, 32-34 Broadwick St., London W1A 2HG, England. TEL 44-171-439-4242. FAX 44-171-437-4841. adv.: B&W page $4570; trim 8.28 x 11.6. circ. 19,305. **Indexed:** INSPEC (1986-). **Document type:** trade publication.
—AskIEEE; KR SourceOne.
  Description: Services industry decision makers responsible for the management, development and purchasing of networking products and services.

NETWORK: COMPUTATION IN NEURAL SYSTEMS. see SCIENCES: COMPREHENSIVE WORKS — Computer Applications

001.644 US ISSN 1046-4468
TK5105.5
NETWORK COMPUTING (MANHASSET). 1990. 15/yr. $60. C M P Publications, Inc., 600 Community Dr., Manhasset, NY 11030. TEL 516-562-5000. FAX 516-365-4601. TELEX 647035 CMP PUB MAHA. (Subscr. to: Box 2040, Manhasset, NY 11030. TEL 708-647-6834) Ed. Patricia Schnaidt. circ. 175,425 (controlled). **Indexed:** Comput.Ind.
●Also available online. Vendor(s): Information Access Co.
—BLDSC (6077.203568); CISTI; KR SourceOne; UMI; UnCover. **CCC**.
  Description: For purchasers of computers, peripherals and software used in network environment. Focuses on the network as the basic business environment for computing. Articles cover connecting computers, networking opportunities and technical solutions for networking problems.

004.6 US
TK5105.7 CODEN: LANNER
NETWORK MAGAZINE. 1986. 13/yr. $29.95 (Canada & Mexico $43.95; elsewhere $47.95) (effective 1996). Miller Freeman, Inc. (Subsidiary of: United Newspapers), 600 Harrison St., San Francisco, CA 94107. TEL 415-905-2200. FAX 415-905-2233. URL: http://www.network-mag.com. (Subscr. to: Box 8024, Boulder, CO 80306-8024. TEL 800-234-9573) Ed. Alan Zeichicklen. adv.; bk.rev. circ. 82,718. **Indexed:** Comput.Ind., Microcomp.Ind., PCR2, Tel.Abstr. **Document type:** trade publication.
—CISTI; KR SourceOne; Linda Hall; SWETS; UMI; UnCover. **CCC.**
  Former titles (until May 1997): L A N Magazine (ISSN 1069-5621); (until 1993): Local Area Network Magazine (ISSN 0898-0012); Incorporates (in 1993): L A N Technology (ISSN 1042-4695); Which was formerly (1985-1989): Micro-Systems Journal (ISSN 8750-9482)
  Description: Devoted to products and solutions for the networking industry.

004.6 UK ISSN 1353-4858
TK5105.59
NETWORK SECURITY NEWSLETTER. (Includes s-m. E-mail update: Netsec News) 1994. m. fl.914($525) (effective 1998). Elsevier Science Ltd., Oxford Fulfillment Centre, P.O. Box 800, Kidlington, Oxford OX5 1DK, England. TEL 44-1865-843000. FAX 44-1865-843010. E-mail: nlinfo-f@elsevier.nl; usinfo-f@elsevier.com; forinfo-kyf04035@niftyserve.or.jp; URL: http://www.elsevier.nl/. (Subscr. to: Elsevier Science, Regional Sales Office, P.O. Box 211, 1000 AE Amsterdam, Netherlands. TEL 31-20-4853757. FAX 31-20-4853432; Subscr. in the Americas to: Elsevier Science, Regional Sales Office, Box 945, New York, NY 10159-0945. TEL 212-633-3730. FAX 212-633-3680; Subscr. in Australasia and the Far East to: Elsevier Science (Singapore) Pte Ltd, No.1 Temasek Ave., No.17-01 Millenia Tower, Singapore 039192, Singapore. TEL 65-434-3727. FAX 65-337-2230) Ed. John Meyer. (also avail. in microform from UMI; back issues avail.) **Document type:** newsletter.
—BLDSC (6077.203970); AskIEEE; KR SourceOne; SWETS.
  Description: Addresses technical and management issues relating to international network security problems.

004.6 US ISSN 1082-8818
TK5105.5
NETWORK V A R. 1993. m. $39 (Canada & Mexico $45; elsewhere $54) (effective 1996). Miller Freeman, Inc. (Subsidiary of: United Newspapers), 600 Harrison St., San Francisco, CA 94107. TEL 415-905-2200. FAX 415-905-2232. (Subscr. to: Box 1125, Skokie, IL 60076-8125. TEL 800-250-2429. FAX 708-647-5972) Ed. Dave Brambert. adv.: B&W page $3495, color page $4395; trim 8 x 10 3/4; adv. contact: Angela Young. circ. 30,000. **Document type:** trade publication.
●Also available online. Vendor(s): Information Access Co.
—KR SourceOne. **CCC.**
  Formerly (until 1996): Stacks (ISSN 1070-8596)

004.6 384.3 US ISSN 0887-7661
QA76
NETWORK WORLD. Online edition: Network World Fusion. 1983. w. (Mon.). $129 (Central & South America $150; Canada $160.50; Europe $205; elsewhere $300) (free to qualified personnel). Network World Inc., 161 Worcester Rd., 5th Fl., Framingham, MA 01701. TEL 508-875-6400. FAX 508-879-3167. URL: http://www.nwfusion.com. Ed. John Gallant; Pub. Evilee Thibeault. R&P contact: Donna Kirkey. adv.: B&W page $21950, color page $26050; trim 10 9/16 x 13 1/4; adv. contact: Carol Lasker. bk.rev.; circ. 150,210 (controlled). (tabloid format; also avail. in microform) **Indexed:** ABI Inform., Comput.Dtbs., Comput.Indus.Up., Comput.Lit.Ind., PSI, Tel.Abstr.; Tel.Alert. **Document type:** trade publication.
●Also available online. Vendor(s): Knight-Ridder Information, Inc. (File no.674), Lexis-Nexis, UMI. Also available on CD-ROM.
—BLDSC (6077.204380); KR SourceOne; UMI. **CCC.**
  Incorporates (in 1991): Connect; Former titles (until 1986): On Communications (ISSN 8750-7854); Computerworld on Communications.
  Description: Covers news, new technologies, products and services, trends, applications, electronic commerce, management strategies relating to network computing in the enterprise.

004.6 AT ISSN 1039-9607
NETWORK WORLD. irreg. Aus.$60 (foreign Aus.$150). I D G Communications Pty. Ltd., 88 Christie St., St. Leonards, N.S.W. 2065, Australia. TEL 02-439-5133. FAX 02-439-5512. Ed. David Beynon. **Document type:** trade publication.
—AskIEEE; KR SourceOne.
  Formerly: Windows World.

004.6 SA
NETWORK WORLD S.A.; enterprise network strategies. 1993. 11/yr. R.54.56 (foreign R.152.46) (effective 1997). Thomson Publications (Subsidiary of: Times Media Ltd.), P.O. Box 56182, Pinegowrie 2123, South Africa. TEL 27-11-789-2144. FAX 27-11-789-3196. adv.; illus. (tabloid format) **Document type:** trade publication.

004.6 IT ISSN 1121-5267
NETWORKING ITALIA; il mensile di reti e telecomunicazione. 1991. m. L.33000 (foreign L.128500) (effective 1996). I D G Communications Italia s.r.l., Via G. Malipiero, 14, 20138 Milan, Italy. TEL 39-2-58011660. FAX 39-2-58011670. Pub. Giulio Ferrari. adv. contact: Sergio Rizzi. circ. 17,400.
  Description: Devoted to the world of computer networks and telecommunications.

004.6 SA ISSN 1025-1790
NETWORKING S A. (Text in English) 1993. m. Technews (Pty) Ltd., P.O. Box 626, Kloof 3640, South Africa. TEL 27-31-7640593. FAX 27-31-7640386. E-mail: technews@iafrica.com. Ed. James Willimson. adv. contact: Viv Dorrington. illus. circ. 2,010. (tabloid format) **Document type:** trade publication.

004.6 JA
NETWORKS; personal computer communication magazine. 1986. m. 9360 Yen. Akio Fujii, A S C I I Publishing, 4-33-10 Yoyogi, Shibuya-ku, Tokyo 151-24, Japan. TEL 83-3-5351-8111.
  Formerly (until July 1993): NetWorker.

001.644 US
NETWORKS UPDATE. 1989. m. $150 (outside N. America $165). Worldwide Videotex, Box 3273, Boynton Beach, FL 33424-3273. TEL 407-738-2276. Ed. Mark Wright; Pub. Mark Wright. bk.rev. (back issues avail.) **Document type:** newsletter.
●Also available online. Vendor(s): Data-Star, Information Access Co., Knight-Ridder Information, Inc., NewsNet (EC95).
  Description: Includes national, international, public, private, and military network products, services, companies, marketing strategies, and research and development with specific applications items spanning a range of subjects such as ISDN, LANs, WANs, X.25, X.400, and OSI.

004.6 BU
NETWORKWORLD. (Supplement to: Computerworld (ISSN 0861-3788)) q. I D G Technika Communications, Ltd., 1, Hristo Smirnenski Blvd., Fl. 11, 1421 Sofia, Bulgaria. TEL 359-2-9630886. FAX 359-2-9632841. Ed. Krassmir Bankov. R&P contact: Mila Pancheva. adv. contact: Mila Pancheva (tabloid format; back issues avail.) **Document type:** consumer publication, newspaper.
  Description: Focuses on renovation of Bulgarian telecommunications, LAN implementations and services.

004.6 GW ISSN 0947-1383
NETZWERKFUEHRER. 1991. a. DM.79. Rossipaul Medien GmbH, Menzingerstr. 37, 80638 Munich, Germany. TEL 49-89-179106-0. FAX 49-89-179106-22. Ed. Hilla Hueber. adv. contact: Emmi Schmidbauer. circ. 15,000. **Document type:** directory.

NEWCASTLE MICROCOMPUTER CLUB. NEWSLETTER. see COMPUTERS — Personal Computers

NIKKEI ENTERTAINMENT!. see MOTION PICTURES

004.6 JA ISSN 1342-0100
▼**NIKKEI NETNAVIGATOR.** (Text in Japanese) 1996. m. newsstand price: 480 Yen. Nikkei Business Publications, Inc. (Subsidiary of: Nihon Keizai Shimbun, Inc.), 2-7-6 Hirakawa-cho, Chiyoda-ku, Tokyo 102, Japan. TEL 81-3-5210-8502. FAX 81-3-5210-8119. URL: http://www.nikkeibp.co.jp/. Ed. Toshiaki Sakurai; Pub. Zen'ichiro Tanaka. adv. contact: Haruo Isonuma. circ. 88,858. **Document type:** consumer publication.
  Description: Offers how-to and whereabouts information for internet surfers.

NORTH TEXAS P C NEWS. see COMPUTERS — Personal Computers

004.678 IE
▼**NUA INTERNET SURVEYS.** 1996. m. Westland Court, S. Cumberland St., Dublin 2, Ireland. TEL 353-1-676-8996. FAX 353-1-661-3932. E-mail: surveys@nua.ie; URL: http://www.nua.ie/surveys/. **Document type:** newsletter.
●Available only online.
  Description: Contains digests of the most important surveys and reports on the Internet.

COMPUTERS — COMPUTER NETWORKS

001.644 US ISSN 0731-8367
ON-LINE (DURHAM). 1975. q. $10 to non-members. University of New Hampshire, University Computing Department, Hamilton Smith Hall, Durham, NH 03824. TEL 603-862-3058. bk.rev.; index. circ. 1,500. (back issues avail.) Indexed: Mag.Ind., PROMT.
Description: Information on the local campus computing environment.

001.644 GW ISSN 0342-9393
HF5548.2
ONLINE; erfolgreiches Informationsmanagement. 1962. m. DM.175 (foreign DM.187) (effective 1997). Datacom Zeitschriften Verlag GmbH, Postfach 1502, 50105 Bergheim, Germany. TEL 49-2271-608-0. FAX 49-2271-608290. E-mail: info@datacom-verlag.de; URL: http://www.datacom-verlag.de. Ed. Joerg Hattwig; Pub. Klaus Lipinski. adv.; B&W page DM.6224; trim 180 x 272; adv. contact: Regina Longerich. bk.rev.; charts; illus. circ. 12,963. Indexed: Compumath., INSPEC, Microcomp.Ind., PROMT, SSCI, Tel.Abstr., Tr.& Indus.Ind. **Document type:** trade publication.
—CISTI; Linda Hall; SWETS.
Incorporates (1985-1992): Topix (ISSN 0179-8014); (1977-1985): O V D (ISSN 0342-9407); Which was formed by the merger of (1956-1977): A D L Nachrichten (ISSN 0514-9061); (1971-1977): Oeffentliche Verwaltung und Datenverarbeitung (ISSN 0340-3262); (1973-1977): Online (ISSN 0340-1545); Which was formerly: Zeitschrift fuer Datenverarbeitung (ISSN 0044-2453); (1963-1965): Datentraeger (ISSN 0340-1693).
Description: Reports on the strategic planning concepts of information management: outsourcing, downsizing and distributed systems.

004.6 US ISSN 0146-5422
Z699.A1 CODEN: ONLIDN
ONLINE (WILTON); the leading magazine for information professionals. 1977. bi-m. $110. Online, Inc., 462 Danbury Rd., Wilton, CT 06897. TEL 203-761-1466; 800-248-8466. FAX 203-761-1444. E-mail: info@onlineinc.com; URL: http://www.onlineinc.com/onlinemag. Ed. Susanne Bjorner. adv. contact: Andrew Pemberton. bk.rev.; index; circ. 5,500 (paid). (also avail. in microform from UMI; back issues avail; reprint service avail. from UMI) Indexed: AESIS, B.P.I., C.I.J.E., CINAHL, Compumath., Comput.Cont., Curr.Cont., Eng.Ind., ERIC, INSPEC, Int.Aerosp.Abstr., Intl.Polym.Sci.& Tech., Leg.Info.Manage.Ind., LHTN, Lib.Lit., LISA, Mag.Ind., PROMT, RAPRA, Soft.Abstr.Eng., SSCI, Tel.Abstr., WPM. **Document type:** trade publication.
•Also available online. Vendor(s): Information Access Co.
—BLDSC (6260.755000); AskIEEE; CASDDS; CISTI; Ei; Genuine Article; KNAW; KR SourceOne; Linda Hall; SWETS; UMI; UnCover. **CCC.**
Description: For online information systems users. Articles cover a variety of online applications for general and business use.

004.6 UK
ONLINE AND C D NOTES. 1978. 10/yr. £99($140) to non-members; members £80. Aslib, Association for Information Management, Publications Department, Information House, 20-24 Old St., London EC1V 9AP, England. TEL 44-171-253-4488. FAX 44-171-430-0514. E-mail: pubs@aslib.co.uk; URL: http://www.aslib.co.uk/. Ed. Monica Blake. R&P contact: Oliver Bond. adv. contact: Brian Thackray. bk.rev. circ. 400. Indexed: WPM.
—BLDSC (6260.760400). **CCC.**
Former titles: Online and C D - R O M Notes; (until 1994): Online Notes (ISSN 0144-025X)
Description: Contains news and reviews of online databases, with a diary of conferences and events.

004.6 UK ISSN 1353-2642
Z699.A1 CODEN: OLREDR
ONLINE & C D - R O M REVIEW; the international journal of online & optical information systems. 1977. bi-m. Learned Information (Europe) Ltd., Woodside, Hinksey Hill, Oxford OX1 5BE, England. TEL 44-1865-388000. FAX 44-1865-736354. E-mail: olr@learned.co.uk. (Dist. in US by: Learned Information, Inc., 143 Old Marlton Pike, Medford, NJ 08055-8750. TEL 609-654-6266. FAX 609-654-4309) Eds. Martha E. Williams, Forbes Gibb. adv.; bk.rev. (also avail. in microfiche; back issues avail.) Indexed: Arts & Hum.Cit.Ind., ASCA, C.I.J.E., CINAHL, Compumath., Comput.Cont., Comput.Lit.Ind., Curr.Cont., Excerp.Med., INSPEC, Key to Econ.Sci., Leg.Info.Manage.Ind., LHTN, Lib.Lit., LISA, SSCI, Tel.Abstr., W.R.C.Inf.
—BLDSC (6260.760500); AskIEEE; CASDDS; CISTI; Genuine Article; KR SourceOne; Linda Hall; SWETS; UMI; UnCover. **CCC.**
Formerly (until 1993): Online Review (ISSN 0309-314X)
Description: Covers the use and management of online & optical information retrieval systems; the training and education of online users; the development of search aids; the creation and marketing of databases; the policy affecting continued development of systems and networks; and the development of new standards for the profession.

001.644 US ISSN 1040-6646
Z699
ONLINE HOTLINE NEWS SERVICE. 1980. a. Information Intelligence, Inc., Box 31098, Phoenix, AZ 85046. TEL 602-996-2283. E-mail: order@infointelligence.com; URL: http://www.infointelligence.com/www/iii-info. Ed. Richard S. Huleatt. bk.rev.; index, cum.index. **Document type:** newsletter.
•Available only on CD-ROM.
—**CCC.**
Formerly: Information Intelligence Online Hotline (ISSN 0277-9501)
Description: Covers the online and CD-ROM fields.

004.693 GW ISSN 0947-7969
▼**ONLINE I S D N.** 1995. m. DM.49.80 (foreign DM.73.80; students DM.43.20) (effective 1997). Franzis Verlag GmbH, Dornacherstr. 3, 85622 Feldkirchen, Germany. TEL 49-89-99115-0. FAX 49-89-99115199. **Document type:** trade publication.

001.644 US CODEN: IIONDK
ONLINE NEWSLETTER. (CD-ROM ed. (ISSN 1040-6646)) 1980. 10/yr. $43.75 to individuals; institutions $62.50; students $25 (combined rates avail.). Information Intelligence, Inc., Box 31098, Phoenix, AZ 85046. TEL 602-996-2283. E-mail: order@infointelligence.com; URL: http://www.infointelligence.com/www/iii-info. Ed. Richard S. Huleatt. bk.rev.; index. (looseleaf format; back issues avail.) Indexed: INSPEC, LISA. **Document type:** newsletter.
•Also available online. Vendor(s): Data-Star, Dow Jones News Retrieval, European Space Agency, Information Access Co., Knight-Ridder Information, Inc., NewsNet (PB41).
Also available on CD-ROM.
—AskIEEE; CASDDS; KR SourceOne; UnCover. **CCC.**
Formerly: Information Intelligence Online Newsletter (ISSN 0194-0694)
Description: Covers all aspects of online use; features events, mergers, acquisitions, new products and relevant news.

004.678 NO
ONLINE WORLD MONITOR NEWSLETTER. 1994. bi-m. 4815 Saltrod, Norway. E-mail: presno@grida.no; URL: http://login.eunet.no/~presno/monitor.html. Ed. Odd de Presno.
•Available only online.
Description: For supporters of the online world shareware book.

004.6 NE ISSN 1383-648X
OPEN COMPUTING. 1992. 8/yr fl.106 (effective 1997). Array Publications B.V., Postbus 615, 2400 AP Alphen aan den Rijn, Netherlands. TEL 31-172-424177. FAX 31-172-424381. E-mail: oc@array.nl; URL: http://www.array.nl. Ed. Arnoud van Gemrren. adv.; B&W page fl.3400; adv. contact: Robin Breij. **Document type:** trade publication.
Formerly: P C Werkstation (ISSN 0927-7595)
Description: Covers open computing, networking and connectivity.

001.644 621.381 UK
P C L A N. m. £50 (foreign £70) (effective 1996). V N U Business Publications BV, VNU House, 32-34 Broadwick St., London W1A 2HG, England. TEL 44-171-439-4242. FAX 44-171-437-4841. adv.: B&W page $4190, color page $4580; trim 210 x 297. circ. 25,000. **Document type:** trade publication.
Description: Provides products, server and company reviews from the networker's point of view.

004.6 GW ISSN 0936-4315
P C NETZE. (Personal Computer) 1989. m. DM.98 (foreign DM.110) (effective 1997). Datacom Zeitschriften Verlag GmbH, Postfach 1502, 50105 Bergheim, Germany. TEL 49-2271-608-0. E-mail: info@datacom-verlag.de. Ed.Bd.; Pub. Ralf Ladner. adv.; B&W page DM.5600; trim 180 x 272; adv. contact: Gisela Bronckhorst. circ. 20,240. **Document type:** trade publication.
—SWETS.
Description: Covers important trends, developments and topics involving PC networks and professionals.

004.6 700 US
▼**PHOTOSHOP TIPS & TRICKS.** 1995. m. $39.95 includes DT&G Journal of Design, Topography & Graphics (effective 1997). Design & Publishing Center, 15 Southgate, Harrisonburg, VA 22801. E-mail: showker@graphic-desig.com; URL: http://www.graphic-design.com/Photoshop. Ed. Fred Showker.
•Available only online.
Description: Focuses on the process involved in using computers to create digital art for publishing.

004.678 US
▼**THE POCKET INTERNET.** 1996. m. 266 Main St., Medfield, MA 02052. E-mail: gadillon@tiac.net; URL: http://www.tiac.net/users/gadillon/pocket.htm. Ed. George Dillon.
•Available only online.

004.6 SA
PUB; the house of Internet zen. 1996. w. E-mail: g93m3425@thoth.ru.ac.za; URL: http://www.ru.ac.za/journprojects/pub/. Ed. Vincent Maher.
•Available only online.
Description: A weekly e-zine about life on the Web.

001.644 FR ISSN 0990-5243
R N I S. (Reseau Numerique a Integration de Services) 18/yr. 2200 F. A Jour, 11 rue du Marche St. Honore, 75001 Paris, France. TEL 42-96-67-22. FAX 40-20-07-75. TELEX 615887F AJOUR. Ed. Jean-Claude Streicher.

RAGAN'S INTERACTIVE PUBLIC RELATIONS. see ADVERTISING AND PUBLIC RELATIONS

004.6 621.39 US ISSN 1076-4429
REAL-TIME ENGINEERING; computing with a deadline. 1994. q. $24 (outside N. America $50) (free to qualified personnel) (effective 1997). Micrology P B T Inc., 2618 S. Shannon Dr., Tempe, AZ 85282. TEL 602-968-9265. E-mail: micrology@aol.com; URL: http://www.realtime-engineering.com. (Subscr. to: 25875 Jefferson, St. Clair Shores, MI 48081. TEL 810-774-8180. FAX 810-774-8182) Ed. John Black. R&P contact: John Black. adv. contact: Pat Hopper. illus.; tr.lit. **Document type:** trade publication.
Description: Covers developments, applications, software and hardware, and trends affecting the real-time computing industry.

REAL-TIME SAFETY CRITICAL SYSTEMS. see COMPUTERS — Computer Systems

004.678 US
▼**REALITY CHECK NETWORK.** 1995. bi-w. E-mail: staff@rcn.org; URL: http://www.rcn.org. Eds. Hitex & Rebel Chicken.
•Available only online.
Description: Covers the happenings in the Internet warez scene.

004.6 FR ISSN 0996-8210
RESEAUX (PARIS). m. 1800 F. A Jour, 11 rue du Marche St. Honore, 75001 Paris, France. TEL 42-96-67-22. FAX 40-20-07-75. Ed. Jean-Claude Streicher.

REVUSER; an independent journal for advanced Revelation and Revelation users. see COMPUTERS — Minicomputers

COMPUTERS — COMPUTER NETWORKS

004.6   IT
S M A U NEWS. 1994. 7/yr. Gruppo Editoriale J C E, Via Ferri 6, 20092 Cinisello Balsamo (MI), Italy. E-mail: info@jce.it; URL: http://www.jce.it. Ed. Annamaria Tasca; Pub. Jacopo Castelfranchi. circ. 290,000. (tabloid format)
    Description: Informs about new communications technology market.

004.6   US
S N A UPDATE. (Systems Network Architecture) q. $175 (effective Aug. 1996). Xephon, 1301 W. Hwy. 407, Ste. 201-450, Lewisville, TX 75067. TEL 817-455-7050. FAX 817-455-2492. **Document type**: trade publication.

SCHOOL NEWS. see EDUCATION

SEARCHER (MEDFORD); the magazine for database professionals. see COMPUTERS — Information Science And Information Theory

004.6   US
SEIDMAN'S ONLINE INSIDER. (Ed. Robert Seidman) 1994. w. C M P Media Inc., 1 Landmark Sq., Ste. 220, Port Chester, NY 10573. E-mail: robert@clark.net; URL: http://www.clark.net/pub/robert.
● Available only online.
    Description: Focuses on the current news in the online - internet world with analysis and commentary.

005.743 658.4   JA   ISSN 0915-9088
SEKAI C D - R O M SORAN. 1988. a. 23000 Yen. PenLogue Publishing Corp., Futaba Bldg., 3-4-18, Mita, Minato-ku, Tokyo 108, Japan. TEL 81-3-3452-8080. FAX 81-3-3452-5728. E-mail: pdb01343@nifty-serve.com.
    Description: Contains 3,500 Japanese CD-ROM titles and 2,400 foreign titles.

SOFTWARE AND NETWORKS FOR LEARNING. see EDUCATION — Computer Applications

004.6   US
▼**THE SUNSHINE POST**. 1995. bi-w. Box 5806, Jacksonville, AR 72078. E-mail: gandolf@lr.cleaf.com; jscott2957@aol.com; URL: http://home.sprynet.com/sprynet/mkuba/. Ed. Joshua Holt.
● Available only online.
    Description: Provides internet news.

SYSTEMS USER. see COMPUTERS — Computer Systems

004.6   US
TASTY BITS FROM THE TECHNOLOGY FRONT. w. E-mail: dawson@world.std.com; URL: http://www.tbtf.com/. **Document type**: newsletter.
● Available only online.
    Description: Presents bellwethers in computer and communications technology, with special attention to commerce on the Internet.

004.678 658.8   US   ISSN 1089-2176
TECHKNOW TIMES. w. E-mail: techknow-request@techknowtimes.com; URL: http://www.techknowtimes.com. **Document type**: newsletter.
● Available only online.
    Description: Covers news related to Internet and online marketing, WWW sites and design, and online technology and culture.

TECHNOLOGY FOR COMMUNICATORS. see COMMUNICATIONS

TELECOM & NETWORK SECURITY REVIEW. see COMMUNICATIONS

TELECOMMUNICATIONS CARRIERS AND SERVICE PROVIDERS MARKET. see COMMUNICATIONS — Computer Applications

TELECOMWORLDWIRE. see COMMUNICATIONS

TELETRAFFIC SCIENCE AND ENGINEERING. see COMMUNICATIONS — Computer Applications

TIDBITS. see COMPUTERS — Personal Computers

004.6   FI   ISSN 0788-6381
TIETOVERKKO. 1991. 11/yr. FIM 348 (effective 1997). Oy Talentum Ab, P.O. Box 920, FIN-00101 Helsinki, Finland. TEL 358-0-148-801. FAX 358-0-6856512. Ed. Kauko Niemi. adv.: B&W page FIM 12200, color page FIM 18300; trim 210 x 297; adv. contact: Anssi Eskola. circ. 12,819. **Document type**: trade publication.
    Description: Deals exclusively with organization performance and system integration from the point of view of telecommunications. Scope comprises the whole field from networking to transmission of data, text, speech and visual images and their integrated functions.

004.6   US
THE UNDERGROUND INFORMER. 1990. fortn. 4161 Tujunga Ave., No. 103, Studio City, CA 91604. E-mail: celeste@primenet.com; URL: http://www.primenet.com/~lonnie/ui/. Ed. Celeste Dolan Mookherjee. **Document type**: bulletin.
● Available only online.
    Description: Entertainment created by and for members of the online community.

UNDERGROUND ONLINE. see LITERARY AND POLITICAL REVIEWS

001.644 025.3   US   ISSN 0160-9742
    CODEN: NPPADM
U.S. LIBRARY OF CONGRESS. NETWORK PLANNING PAPERS. 1978. irreg. price varies. U.S. Library of Congress, Cataloging Distribution Service, Collection Services, Washington, DC 20540-4102. TEL 202-707-6100. FAX 202-707-1334. E-mail: cdsinfo@mail.loc.gov. (Dist. by: U.S. Library of Congress, Cataloging Distribution Service, Customer Services Section, Washington, DC 20541-5017. TEL 800-255-3666; And: Bernan, 4611-F Assembly Dr., Lanham, MD20706. TEL 800-274-4447. FAX 301-459-0026) Ed. Randall K. Barry. bibl.; charts; circ. 1,500 (paid). (also avail. in microfiche; back issues avail.) **Document type**: monographic series, proceedings, government publication.
—CASDDS.
    Description: Discusses various aspects of networking in library applications.

004.678   AT
▼**VICNET ZINE**. 1996. fortn. VicNet - Victoria's Network, 328 Swanston St., Melbourne, Vic. 3000, Australia. E-mail: richard@vicnet.net.au; URL: http://www.vicnet.net.au/vicnet/zine. Ed. Richard Hayward.
● Available only online.
    Description: Provides information about local events, as well as full-text editorials and news about internet development in the region.

004.6   US   ISSN 1087-4658
▼**VIRTUAL CITY**;* the city magazine of cyberspace. 1995. q. $11.80; newsstand price: $2.95. Virtual Communications, Inc., 888 Seventh Ave., New York, NY 10106-0001. E-mail: virtcity@aol.com; URL: http://www.virtcitnow.com. (Co-publisher: Newsweek, Inc.) Ed. Lewis D'Vorkin; Pub. Jonathan Sacks. adv.: B&W page $10000, color page $12500; adv. contact: Michael Hurley. illus. circ. 300,000. **Document type**: consumer publication.
    Description: User-friendly service-oriented lifestyle magazine and guide to the interactive world.

001.644   CN   ISSN 0843-803X
VISION INTERFACE CONFERENCE PROCEEDINGS - COMPTE RENDU. (Text in English, French) 1981. a. $45 to non-members; members $35. Canadian Information Processing Society, 430 King St., W., Ste. 106, Toronto, ON M5V 1L5, Canada. TEL 416-593-4040. FAX 416-593-5184. **Document type**: proceedings.

001.644   US
VOICE NETWORKING SYSTEMS. 2 base vols. (plus m. updates). $927 to new subscr.; renewals $867 (effective 1996). Datapro Information Services Group (Subsidiary of: McGraw-Hill, Inc.), 600 Delran Pkwy., Delran, NJ 08075. TEL 609-764-0100; 800-328-2776.

004.6 659   US
WEB ADVERTISING (YEAR): MARKET ANALYSIS & FORECAST. a. $1095 (effective 1997). Cowles - SIMBA Information (Subsidiary of: Cowles Business Media), 11 Riverbend Dr. S., Box 4949, Stamford, CT 06907-0949. TEL 203-358-9900; 800-307-2529. FAX 203-358-5811. E-mail: info@simbanet.com; URL: http://www.simbanet.com.

004.6   US
▼**WEB BOUND**. 1996. q. $29.95. N.A. International, 2001 Mentor Rd., Louisville, TN 37777. adv.; illus.

004.693   US   ISSN 1082-9415
TK5105.888
▼**WEB DEVELOPER**. 1996. q. Mecklermedia Corporation, 20 Ketchum St., Westport, CT 06880. TEL 203-226-6957. FAX 203-454-8540. **Document type**: consumer publication.
—KR SourceOne. CCC.

004.69   US
THE WEB DEVELOPER'S JOURNAL. (Print edition ceased 1994) 1992. d. Markland Communities, Inc., National Computer Tectonics, Rte. 1, Box 80, Burbank, SD 57010. E-mail: bmorris@usit.net; cmorris@webdevelopersjournal; URL: http://nctweb.com/webdev. Eds. Bruce Morris, Charlie Morris. **Document type**: bulletin.
● Available only online.
    Description: Reviews and news for people developing pages and products for the Internet.

004.6   US
▼**WEB GUIDE MAGAZINE**. 1997. bi-m. $19.95 (Canada $29.95). Box 500, Missouri City, TX 77459-9896. TEL 800-310-7047. **Document type**: consumer publication.

004.6   US
WEB INFORMANT (ELK GROVE); the complete monthly guide to web development. 1996. m. $39.95 (effective 1997). Informant Communications Group, Inc., 10519 E. Stockton Blvd., Ste. 100, Elk Grove, CA 95624-9703. TEL 916-686-6610. FAX 916-686-8497. E-mail: circulation@informant.com. Ed. Jerry Coffey. circ. 18,000 (paid). **Document type**: consumer publication.
    Description: Publishes programming for the World Wide Web with Java, Perl and other languages.

004.6   US
▼**WEB INFORMANT (PORT WASHINGTON)**. 1995. 3/m. 938 Port Washington Blvd., Port Washington, NY 11050. TEL 516-944-3407. E-mail: david@strom.com; URL: http://www.webinformant.com. Ed. David Strom.
● Available only online.
    Description: Analyzes recent trends with using the Internet and the web for public relations, advertising and marketing communications.

WEB - ONLINE SERVICES (YEAR): CONSUMER MARKET ANALYSIS & FORECAST. see BUSINESS AND ECONOMICS — Computer Applications

WEB PUBLISHING (YEAR): CONSUMER MARKET STRATEGIES & STATISTICS. see BUSINESS AND ECONOMICS — Computer Applications

004.6   US
WEB REVIEW; for people who make the Web work. w. E-mail: wr-info@webreview.com; URL: http://www.webreview.com. Ed. David Sims. (back issues avail.) **Document type**: trade publication.
● Available only online.
    Description: Provides information about the world wide web and the people who work for it, in it, and with it.

004.6   ISSN 1089-4861
▼**WEB SITE SOURCE BOOK (YEAR)**. 1996. a. $78. Omnigraphics, Inc., 2500 Penobscot Bldg., Detroit, MI 48226. TEL 313-961-1383; 800-234-1340. FAX 313-961-1340.
    Description: Lists 12,800 official web sites for businesses, organizations, agencies, institutions, and other information resources throughout the United States.

004.678   US
▼**WEB SOLUTIONS**. 1995. m. I S - O O P Group, 175 Osborn Ave., New Haven, CT 06511. E-mail: ssteinhardt@online-magazine.com; URL: http://www.online-magazine.com. Ed. Steve Steinhardt.
● Available only online.
    Description: Covers Internet related topics.

COMPUTERS — Computer Programming

004.6 US ISSN 1086-556X
▼WEB TECHNIQUES. 1996. 12/yr. $34.95 (Canada & Mexico $44.95; elsewhere $54.95) (effective 1996). Miller Freeman, Inc. (Subsidiary of: United News & Media), 600 Harrison St., San Francisco, CA 94107. TEL 415-905-2200. FAX 415-905-2233. E-mail: mfloyd@web-techniques.com; URL: http://www.webtechniques.com. (Subscr. to: Box 8024, Boulder, CO 80306-8024. TEL 800-365-1425) Ed. Michael Floyd. circ. 36,500 (paid). **Document type:** trade publication.
●Also available online.
—BLDSC (9283.982500); AskIEEE; KNAW; KR SourceOne.
Description: Offers technical advice for Web-site programmers and developers.

004.678 CN
▼WEB TIMES. (Avail. in 2 editions: Canada, International) 1995. d. 516 Centennial Pkwy., Delta, BC V4L 1L1, Canada. E-mail: djohnsto@unixg.ubc.ca; URL: http://www.webtimes.com. Ed. Devin Johnston.
●Also available online.
Description: Lists live Internet broadcasts and chats.

004.693 US
▼WEB WEEK. w. Mecklermedia Corporation, 20 Ketchum St., Westport, CT 06880. TEL 203-226-6957. FAX 203-454-8540. E-mail: tristan@iw.com; URL: http://pubs.iworld.com/ww-online/. **Document type:** trade publication.
●Also available online.

004.6 US
▼WEB - ZINE; the Internet & Web magazine. m. E-mail: chadz@nmsu.edu; URL: http://www.nmsu.edu/-czimmerm/Web-Zine/.
●Available only online.
Description: For internet users.

004.6 US
▼WEBDESIGN & REVIEW. 1997. m. $39.95 includes DT&G Journal of Design, Typography & Graphics (effective 1997). Design & Publishing Center, 15 Southgate, Harrisonburg, VA 22801. E-mail: showker@graphic-design.com; URL: http://www.graphic-design.com/WEB/. Ed. Fred Showker.
●Available only online.
Description: Focuses on design issues for producing web pages and web sites.

EBINK. see CHILDREN AND YOUTH — For

004.6 US
▼WEBMASTER. 1996. bi-m. $29.97. Box 9208, Framingham, MA 01701-9208. Ed. Lew McCreary. adv.; illus.; circ. controlled. **Document type:** trade publication.

004.6 US ISSN 1084-2063
▼WEBSIGHT. 1996. bi-m. $14.95. Navigate Media Inc., 9520 Jefferson Blvd., Culver City, CA 90232. URL: http://websight.com. **Document type:** consumer publication.
●Also available online.
Description: Provides information covering the exploration of the Web.

004.678 US
EEKEND WEB PICKS. w. (Fri.). E-mail: wwp@netogether.com; URL: http://www.netogether.com/picks.html.
●Available only online.

EEKLY PLANET. see COMPUTERS — Cybernetics

004.693 US ISSN 1072-043X
E WHOLE INTERNET CATALOGUE.* Variant title: G N N Whole Internet Catalogue. 1993. w. Global Network Navigator (Subsidiary of: America OnLine), 2200 Aol Way, Dulles, VA 20166. TEL 510-883-7220. E-mail: info@ora.com; URL: http://gnn.com/wic/index.html. Ed. Abbot Chambers. **Document type:** directory.
●Available only online.
Description: Descriptive guide to interesting and useful sites on the Internet.

004.693 US
THE WHOLE INTERNET USER'S GUIDE AND CATALOG. irreg., 2nd edition, 1994. $24.95. O'Reilly & Associates, 103 Morris St., Ste. A, Sebastopol, CA 95472. Ed. Ed Krol. **Document type:** consumer publication, catalog.
Description: Gives an overview of how to get connected with the Internet and what it offers.

WOMEN ONLINE. see WOMEN'S INTERESTS

001.644 US
WORKSTATIONS (INTERNATIONAL). base vol. (plus m. updates). $632 to new subscr.; renewals $581 (effective 1996). Datapro Information Services Group (Subsidiary of: McGraw-Hill, Inc.), 600 Delran Pkwy., Delran, NJ 08075. TEL 609-764-0100; 800-328-2776. FAX 609-764-8953.

004.6 US ISSN 1085-2301
CODEN: WWWFFI
▼WORLD WIDE WEB JOURNAL. 1996. q. $99.95 (Canada & Mexico $119.95; elsewhere $149.95) (effective 1997). (World Wide Web Consortium) O'Reilly & Associates, 103 Morris St., Ste. A, Sebastopol, CA 95472. TEL 707-829-0515; 800-998-9938. FAX 707-829-0104. E-mail: khare@w3.org; URL: http://www.w3.org/pub/www/journal. (Subscr. to: 101 Morris St., Sebastopol, CA 95472. TEL 800-998-9938 ext.261) Ed. Rohit Khare. (back issues avail.) **Document type:** academic/scholarly publication.
●Also available online.
—BLDSC (9360.225400).
Description: Publishes technical papers and articles on technological developments, intellectual property rights and censorship, and other issues relating to the World Wide Web.
Refereed Serial

004.6 US
▼WWWIZ. 1995. m. $48. 17971 Sky Park Circle, Bldg. 33B, Irvine, CA 92614. E-mail: wiz@wwwiz.com; URL: http://www.wiz.com. Ed. Don Hamilton. circ. 80,000 (paid). **Document type:** consumer publication.
●Also available online.
Description: Provides general interest stories on and about the World Wide Web.

004.6 US
▼YAHOO! INTERNET LIFE. 1995. q. $19.97. (Yahoo Corp.) Ziff-Davis Publishing Co., One Park Ave., New York, NY 10016. TEL 212-503-4804; 800-950-0484. FAX 212-503-5699. URL: http://www.zdnet.com/zdil. (Subscr. to: Box 53381, Boulder, CO 80323-3381) Ed. Barry Golson. adv.
●Also available online.
Also available on CD-ROM.
Formerly (until 1996): Z D Internet Life.
Description: Focuses on World Wide Web related issues. Provides information on Web sites.

004.6 II
ZANY ZINE. (Text in English) 1996. w. 2-421 Girja Bhavan, Bhaudaji Rd., Matunga, Maharashtra, Mumbai 400 019, India. E-mail: rashim@giasbm01.vsnl.net.in; URL: http://www.geocities.com/southbeach/4195. Ed. Nikunj Sanghvi. **Document type:** bulletin.
●Available only online.
Description: Source of online entertainment.

1ST STEPS: DAILY MARKETING AND DESIGN. see BUSINESS AND ECONOMICS — Marketing And Purchasing

1ST STEPS IN THE HUNT. see OCCUPATIONS AND CAREERS

COMPUTERS — Computer Programming

see also Computers–Software

001.642 US
QA76.7
A C M S I G P L A N NOTICES. 1965. m. $57 (plan members $30; students $10). Association for Computing Machinery, Special Interest Group on Programming Languages, 1515 Broadway, 17th Fl., New York, NY 10036. TEL 212-869-7440. FAX 212-302-5826. (Subscr. to: Box 12115, Church Street Sta., New York, NY 10249) Ed. Richard L. Wexelblat. bk.rev.; charts; illus.; stat.; circ. 11,600 (controlled). (back issues avail.) **Indexed:** Abstr.Hum.Comp.Inter., ASCA, Compumath, Comput.Abstr., INSPEC (1973-). **Document type:** bulletin.
—BLDSC (0578.640500); AskIEEE; CISTI; Genuine Article; KR SourceOne; SWETS; UnCover.
Formerly: S I G P L A N Notices (ISSN 0362-1340)

001.644 US ISSN 0164-0925
QA76.7 CODEN: ATPSDT
A C M TRANSACTIONS ON PROGRAMMING LANGUAGES AND SYSTEMS. 1979. q. $105 to non-members. Association for Computing Machinery, 1515 Broadway, 17th Fl., New York, NY 10036-5701. TEL 212-869-7440. FAX 212-944-1318. TELEX 421686. Ed. Susan L. Graham. charts; illus.; index. circ. 10,500. (also avail. in microform from WWS) **Indexed:** A.I.Abstr., A.S.& T.Ind., ASCA, BMT, CAD CAM Abstr., Compumath, Comput.Abstr., Comput.Cont., Comput.Dtbs., Comput.Lit.Ind., Curr.Cont., Educ.Tech.Abstr., Ergon.Abstr., Ind.Sci.Rev., INIS Atomind., INSPEC (1979-), Sci.Cit.Ind., Zent.Math.
—BLDSC (0578.675000); AskIEEE; CISTI; Ei; Genuine Article; KR SourceOne; Linda Hall; SWETS; UMI; UnCover. CCC.
Description: Provides a forum for the research in computer science areas. Publishes research and algorithms, programming languages and systems.

001.642 US ISSN 0067-2483
CODEN: ASDPDL
THE A P I C SERIES. 1961. irreg., vol.37, 1991. (Automatic Programming Information Centre) Academic Press, Inc., 525 B St., Ste. 1900, San Diego, CA 92101-4495. TEL 619-231-0926. FAX 619-699-6715. (Subscr. to: Order Dept., 6277 Sea Harbor Dr., 4th Fl., Orlando, FL 32887. TEL 800-321-5068) Eds. M. Shave, I. Wand. (reprint service avail. from ISI) **Indexed:** INSPEC.
—CISTI.
Former titles: A P I C Studies in Data Processing Series; Automatic Programming Information Center Studies in Data Processing Series.

001.642 US ISSN 0163-6006
QA76.73.A27 CODEN: APLQD9
A P L QUOTE QUAD. 1970. q. $35 to non-members; members $50. Association for Computing Machinery, Special Interest Group on Programming Languages, Technical Committee on A P L, 1515 Broadway, 17th Fl., New York, NY 10036. TEL 212-869-7440. FAX 212-302-5826. (Subscr. to: Box 12115, Church St. Sta., New York, NY 10249) Ed. Jon McGrew. bk.rev. circ. 1,600. **Indexed:** INSPEC.
—BLDSC (1568.579000); AskIEEE; CISTI; KR SourceOne; SWETS; UnCover.
Formerly: S I G P L A N - S T A P L Quote Quad.

005.13 UK ISSN 1381-6551
ADA USER JOURNAL. q. £110 (effective 1998). Ada Language UK Ltd., P.O. Box 322, York YO1 3GY, England. TEL 44-1904-412740. FAX 44-1904-426702. E-mail: admin@adauk.org.uk; URL: http://www.adauk.org.uk. Ed. J.S. Briggs. R&P contact: J.S. Briggs. bk.rev. **Indexed:** INSPEC (1993-). **Document type:** academic/scholarly publication.
—AskIEEE; CISTI; Ei; KR SourceOne; SWETS. CCC.
Formerly (until vol.15, no.1, 1994): Ada User (ISSN 0268-652X)
Description: Publishes material which promotes the effective development and use of the ADA language; includes news reports on significant ADA events and a calendar of activities.

COMPUTERS — COMPUTER PROGRAMMING

005.1 US
ADVANCES IN OBJECT TECHNOLOGY SERIES. irreg., latest no.8. Sigs Publications, Inc., 71 W. 23rd St., New York, NY 10010-4102. TEL 212-242-7447. FAX 212-242-2574. URL: http://www.sigs.com. Ed. Richard S. Wiener. (back issues avail.) **Document type:** monographic series.

005 US ISSN 1062-5895
ALPHA FORUM. 1992. m. $79 (effective 1996). Pinnacle Publishing, Inc., Box 888, Kent, WA 98035-0888. TEL 206-251-1900. FAX 206-251-5057. URL: http://www.pinpub.com. **Document type:** newsletter.
Description: For users of Alpha Four and Alpha Five software.

001.642 US ISSN 1048-5600
AMERICAN PROGRAMMER. 1988. m. $415 (foreign $515). Cutter Information Corp., 37 Broadway, Arlington, MA 02174. TEL 617-648-8700. FAX 617-648-1950. Ed. Edward Yourdon; Pub. Karen Fine Coburn. R&P contact: Carolyn Licata. (back issues avail.)
—BLDSC (0853.310000); AskIEEE; Ei; KR SourceOne. **CCC.**
Description: Covers high-level computer software; trends and forecasts; includes commentary.

005.13 UK ISSN 0066-4138
QA76 CODEN: ARVAAM
ANNUAL REVIEW IN AUTOMATIC PROGRAMMING. 1960. s-a. fl.406($250) (effective 1997). Elsevier Science Ltd., Pergamon, P.O. Box 800, Kidlington, Oxford OX5 1DX, England. TEL 44-1865-843000. FAX 44-1865-843010. E-mail: nlinfo-f@elsevier.nl; usinfo-f@elsevier.com; forinfo-kyf04035@niftyserve.or.jp; URL: http://www.elsevier.nl/. (Subscr. to: Elsevier Science, Regional Sales Office, P.O. Box 211, 1000 AE Amsterdam, Netherlands. TEL 31-20-4853757. FAX 31-20-4853432; Subscr. in the Americas to: Elsevier Science, Regional Sales Office, Box 945, New York, NY 10159-0945. TEL 212-633-3730. FAX 212-633-3680; Subscr. in Australasia and the Far East to: Elsevier Science (Singapore) Pte Ltd, No.1 Temasek Ave., No.17-01 Millenia Tower, Singapore 039192, Singapore. TEL 65-434-3727. FAX 65-337-2230) Ed. P. Brown. (also avail. in microform from UMI) **Indexed:** Comput.Cont., INSPEC. **Document type:** academic/scholarly publication.
—CISTI; Ei; Linda Hall; SWETS; UMI; UnCover. **CCC.**
Description: Provides substantive review articles on topics of interest to professionals in the field of computer software. Topics covered include distributed control systems, automation, software and real time systems, programming and applications.
Refereed Serial

001.64 001.642 JA ISSN 0385-6984
BIT. 1969. m. 9000 Yen. Kyoritsu Shuppan Co. Ltd., 4-6-19 Kohinata, Bunkyo-ku, Tokyo 112, Japan. Ed. Hiroyuki Iijima. adv. circ. 50,000. **Indexed:** Compumath, JCT, JTA.
—BLDSC (2095.500000); CISTI.

BITLUPE; Magazine fuer IBM-36 und AS-400 Anwender. see COMPUTERS — Software

001.642 US ISSN 1063-7273
QA76.7
BORLAND LANGUAGE EXPRESS.* 1990. q. Borland International, Inc., 100 Borland Way, Scotts Valley, CA 95066-3249. TEL 408-438-8400. FAX 408-439-9119. Ed. David Intersimone.
—CISTI.
Formerly (until vol.2, no.1, 1992): Turbo Technix (ISSN 0893-827X)

005.369 US
QA76.73.C15
C - C PLUS PLUS. 1981. m. $34.95 (Canada & Mexico $46; elsewhere $65) (effective 1996). Miller Freeman, Inc. (Lawrence), 1601 W. 23rd St., Ste. 200, Lawrence, KS 66046. TEL 913-841-1631. FAX 913-841-2624. E-mail: cujsub@mfi.com; URL: http://www.cuj.com. (Subscr. to: Box 8024, Boulder, CO 80306-8024. TEL 800-365-1364) Ed. Marc Briand; Pub. Martha Masinton. R&P contact: Marc Briand. adv.: B&W page $2500, color page $3045; adv. contact: Ed Day. bk.rev.; software rev.; circ. 40,000 (paid). (back issues avail.) **Document type:** trade publication.
●Also available online. Vendor(s): Information Access Co.
Also available on CD-ROM.
—CISTI; KR SourceOne; SWETS; UnCover. **CCC.**
Former titles: C - C Plus Plus Users Journal (ISSN 1075-2838); (until 1994): C Users Journal (ISSN 0898-9788); Which was formed by the Dec. 1987 merger of: C Journal (ISSN 8756-9736); C Users Group Newsletter.
Description: Discusses C and C Plus Plus programming at all levels, in addition to related software tools, books, public domain software and other products.

005.13 US
C I C S UPDATE. (Customer Information Control System) m. $240 (effective Aug. 1996). Xephon, 1301 W. Hwy. 407, Ste. 201-450, Lewisville, TX 75067. TEL 817-455-7050. FAX 817-455-2492. **Document type:** trade publication.

C PLUS PLUS JOURNAL. see COMPUTERS — Software

005.13 US
C PLUS PLUS PROGRAMMING LANGUAGE NEWSLETTER. every 3 wks. E-mail: majordomo@world.std.com; URL: http://www.rmii.com/~glenm. **Document type:** newsletter.
●Available only online.
Description: Contains information on C

005.13 US ISSN 1040-6042
QA76.73.C153 CODEN: CRPTE7
C PLUS PLUS REPORT; the international authority on C. 1988. 10/yr. $69 to individuals (Canada & Mexico $94; elsewhere $109); institutions $139 (Canada & Mexico $164; elsewhere $179). Sigs Publications, Inc., 71 W. 23rd St., New York, NY 10010-4102. TEL 212-242-7447. FAX 212-242-7574. E-mail: subscriptions@sigs.com; URL: http://www.sigs.com. (Subscr. to: Box 5050, Brentwood, TN 37024-5050) Ed. Doug Schmidt. adv.: B&W page $2770, color page $4270. software rev.; circ. 25,000 (paid). (back issues avail.) **Document type:** trade publication.
—BLDSC (2943.176500); AskIEEE; KR SourceOne; SWETS. **CCC.**
Description: Links C

005.13 400 UK ISSN 0096-0551
QA76.7 CODEN: COLADA
COMPUTER LANGUAGES. 1976. q. fl.1178($677) (effective 1998). Elsevier Science Ltd., Pergamon, P.O. Box 800, Kidlington, Oxford OX5 1DX, England. TEL 44-1865-843000. FAX 44-1865-843010. E-mail: nlinfo-f@elsevier.nl; usinfo-f@elsevier.com; forinfo-kyf04035@niftyserve.or.jp; URL: http://www.elsevier.nl/. (Subscr. to: Elsevier Science, Regional Sales Office, P.O. Box 211, 1000 AE Amsterdam, Netherlands. TEL 31-20-4853757. FAX 31-20-4853432; Subscr. in the Americas to: Elsevier Science, Regional Sales Office, Box 945, New York, NY 10159-0945. TEL 212-633-3730. FAX 212-633-3680; Subscr. in Australasia and the Far East to: Elsevier Science (Singapore) Pte Ltd, No.1 Temasek Ave., No.17-01 Millenia Tower, Singapore 039192, Singapore. TEL 65-434-3727. FAX 65-337-2230) Ed. Robert S. Ledley. adv.; bk.rev. circ. 1,025. (also avail. in microfilm from UMI) **Indexed:** Abstr.Hum.Comp.Inter., ASCA, Compumath, Comput.Abstr., Comput.Cont., Comput.Rev., Curr.Cont., Eng.Ind., Ergon.Abstr., INSPEC, Zent.Math. **Document type:** academic/scholarly publication.
—BLDSC (3394.070000); AskIEEE; CISTI; Ei; Genuine Article; KR SourceOne; Linda Hall; SWETS; UMI; UnCover. **CCC.**
Description: Original and review articles on programming systems and structures, programming languages and their theory. Contains abstract and full text of papers pertinent to the subject.
Refereed Serial

001.642 UK ISSN 0885-2308
TK7882.S65 CODEN: CSPLEO
COMPUTER SPEECH & LANGUAGE. 1986. q. £61($101) to individuals; institutions £160 (effective 1998). Academic Press Ltd. (Subsidiary of: Harcourt Brace & Company Ltd.), 24-28 Oval Rd., London NW1 7DX, England. TEL 44-171-267-4466. FAX 44-171-482-2293. TELEX 25775 ACPRES G. E-mail: apsubs@acad.com; URL: http://www.hbuk.co.uk/ap/csl; http://www.idealibrary.com/. (Subscr. to: Harcourt Brace & Company Ltd., Foots Cray High St., Sidcup, Kent DA14 5HP, England. TEL 44-181-300-3322. FAX 44-181-309-0807) Eds. S. Young, S. Levinson. R&P contact: Catherine John. adv. contact: Nik Screen. (reprint service avail. from SWZ) **Indexed:** Abstr.Hum.Comp.Inter., Art.Int.Abstr., ASCA, Compumath, INSPEC (1986-), Lang.& Lang.Behav.Abstr. (1987-), Ling.Abstr. **Document type:** academic/scholarly publication.
●Also available online.
—BLDSC (3394.276600); AskIEEE; CISTI; Ei; Genuine Article; KR SourceOne; SWETS; UnCover. **CCC.**
Description: Publishes papers of original research related to quantitative description of the recognition understanding, production, and coding of speech by humans or machines.

COMPUTERWORLD COLOMBIA. see COMPUTERS

003 US ISSN 0895-6340
QA76.73.063 CODEN: CMSYE2
COMPUTING SYSTEMS. 1988. q. $60 for non-members; institutions $75. (Usenix Association) M I T Press, 55 Hayward St., Cambridge, MA 02142-1399. TEL 617-253-2889. FAX 617-258-6779. E-mail: journals-orders@omit.edu; URL: http://www-mitpress.mit.edu/. Ed. David L. Presotto. adv.; charts; index; circ. 6,000 (paid). (back issues avail.; reprint service avail. from UMI) **Indexed:** ASCA, Compumath, Comput.Abstr., INSPEC (1988-). **Document type:** academic/scholarly publication.
—BLDSC (3395.131300); AskIEEE; CISTI; Ei; Genuine Article; KR SourceOne; Linda Hall; UnCover. **CCC.**
Description: Features research on advanced computing operating systems, architectures, network schemes, programming languages, tools and applications.
Refereed Serial

001.642 UK ISSN 1040-3108
QA76.58 CODEN: CPEXEI
CONCURRENCY: PRACTICE AND EXPERIENCE. 1989. 15/yr. $1295 (foreign $1295) (effective 1998). John Wiley & Sons Ltd., Journals, Baffins Ln., Chichester, W. Sussex PO19 1UD, England. TEL 44-1243-779777. FAX 44-1243-775878. E-mail: info-assets@wiley.co.uk; URL: http://www.wiley.co.uk. (Subscr. in the Americas to: John Wiley & Sons, Inc., 605 Third Ave., New York, NY 10158) TEL 212-850-6645. FAX 212-850-6021) Ed. Geoffrey C. Fox. adv.: B&W page £595, color page £1495; trim 260 x 200; adv. contact: Bob Kern. circ. 500. (also avail. in microform from UMI; back issues avail.; reprint service avail. from SWZ) **Indexed:** ASCA, Compumath, Comput.Abstr., INSPEC (1989-). **Document type:** academic/scholarly publication.
—BLDSC (3405.620000); AskIEEE; CISTI; Ei; Genuine Article; KR SourceOne; SWETS; UMI; UnCover. **CCC.**
Description: Relays practical experience of concurrent machines and focuses especially on concurrent solutions to specific probems, concurrent algorithms and computational methods, as well as programming environments and more.
Refereed Serial

001.642 US ISSN 0090-7383
CONFERENCE ON DATA SYSTEMS LANGUAGES. DATA BASE TASK GROUP. REPORT.* Key Title: Report - C.O.D.A.S.Y.L. Data Base Task Group. 1969. irreg latest 1971. $8. Association for Computing Machinery, Programming Language Committee, 1515 Broadway, 17th Fl., New York, NY 10036. TEL 212-869-7440. (And: British Computer Society, 29 Portland Pl., London W1N 4AP, England) illus.

CONSTRAINTS. see COMPUTERS — Artificial Intelligence

COMPUTERS — COMPUTER PROGRAMMING

001.642 621.381   US   ISSN 0895-4518
QA76.9.D3   CODEN: DPDEEZ
DATABASE PROGRAMMING & DESIGN. 1987. m. $47 (Canada & Mexico $57; elsewhere $62) (effective 1996). Miller Freeman, Inc. (Subsidiary of: United Newspapers), 600 Harrison St., San Francisco, CA 94107. TEL 415-905-2200. FAX 415-905-2233. (Subscr. to: Box 8024, Boulder, CO 80306-8024. TEL 800-289-0169. FAX 303-678-0439) Ed. David Stodder. adv. circ. 28,000. (also avail. in microfilm from UMI; reprint service avail. from UMI) Indexed: Comput.Lit.Ind., INSPEC (1990-). **Document type:** trade publication.
—BLDSC (3535.803560); AskIEEE; CASDDS; CISTI; Ei; KR SourceOne; SWETS; UMI. **CCC.**
   Description: Focuses on practical solutions for designing, using and maintaining database management systems.

DATABASED WEB ADVISOR. see *COMPUTERS — Software*

001.642   GW   ISSN 0930-1054
DIE DATENSCHLEUDER; das wissenschaftliche Fachblatt fuer Datenreisende. 1984. bi-m. DM.3.50 per no. Chaos Computer Club e.V., Schwenkestr. 85, 20355 Hamburg, Germany. TEL 49-40-4903757. FAX 49-40-4917689. Ed.Bd. charts; illus. circ. 1,500. (back issues avail.) **Document type:** bulletin.

005   US   ISSN 1082-4375
DELPHI DEVELOPER. 1995. m. $149 includes companion diskette. Pinnacle Publishing, Inc., Box 888, Kent, WA 98035-0888. TEL 206-251-1900. FAX 206-251-5057. URL: http://www.pinpub.com. **Document type:** newsletter.
   Description: For software developers using Delphi from Borland.

005.369   US   ISSN 1080-0662
DELPHI INFORMANT; the complete monthly guide of Delphi development. 1995. m. $49.95 (foreign $79.95) (effective 1995). Informant Communications Group, Inc., 10519 E. Stockton Blvd., Ste. 142, Elk Grove, CA 95624-9704. TEL 916-686-6610. FAX 916-686-8497. E-mail: 70461.7600@compuserve.com. Ed. Jerry Coffrey; Pub. Mitchell Koulouris. adv.: page $2175; trim size 8 x 10 3/4; adv. contact: Lynn Beaudoin. bk.rev. circ. 18,000. (also avail. in microform) **Document type:** trade publication.
●Also available on CD-ROM.
   Description: Contains articles with information on Delphi-related news, product reviews, Object Pascal programming tips and techniques, database application development, client-server application development, book reviews, and more.

005.1 004.16   CH   ISSN 1022-2901
SAN BO/THIRD WAVE MAGAZINE. (Text in Chinese) 1982. m. NT.$1350 (foreign NT.$2950). Third Wave Publishing Corp., 19-1, Lane 231, Fu-Hsing N. Rd., Taipei, Taiwan, Republic of China. TEL 886-2-7136959. FAX 886-2-7189467. Ed. Corena Lee. adv.: B&W page $1077, color page $2112; trim 190 x 260; adv. contact: Janet Wang. circ. 27,000 (paid). **Document type:** consumer publication.
   Description: Introduces PC software and hardware of all brands.

005.13   US   ISSN 1074-8911
DIGITAL UNIX NEWS. 1994. m. free in the U.S. (foreign $49). Publications & Communications, Inc., 12416 Hymeadow, Austin, TX 78750-1896. TEL 512-250-9023; 800-678-9724. FAX 512-331-3900. adv.: B&W page $3586, color page $4336; trim 10 3/4 x 14 1/2. (tabloid format) **Document type:** trade publication.
   Description: Deals with Digital Equipment Corp.'s Unix computer operating system and its advantages and disadvantages compared to other vendors' Unix systems and other operating systems.

005   US   ISSN 1077-6095
SY ACT! 1994. m. $79 (effective 1996). Pinnacle Publishing, Inc., Box 888, Kent, WA 98035-0888. TEL 206-251-1900. FAX 206-251-5057. URL: http://www.pinpub.com. **Document type:** newsletter.
   Description: Fors users of Symantec's ACT! software.

001.642   NE   ISSN 0921-2787
P98   CODEN: LANTEB
ELECTRIC WORD.* 1983. bi-m. $50 to individuals; institutions $80. Language Technology B.V., Emmalaan 21, 1075 AT Amsterdam, Netherlands. TEL 20-188225. FAX 20-838616. Ed. Louis Rossetto. adv.; bk.rev. circ. 1,000. Indexed: INSPEC (1989-), Lang.& Lang.Behav.Abstr.
—AskIEEE; KR SourceOne.
   Formerly: Language Technology; Incorporates (1983-1988): Language Monthly.
   Description: Informs professionals working with natural language about the current changes in their industry.

005.1   US   ISSN 1074-4916
EMBEDDED SYSTEMS PROGRAMMING PRODUCT NEWS. 1994. q. Miller Freeman, Inc., 600 Harrison St., San Francisco, CA 94107. TEL 415-905-2689. FAX 415-905-2232. Ed. Tyler Sperry. adv. contact: Eric Berg. **Document type:** trade publication.

EXPERT SYSTEMS; the international journal of knowledge engineering and neural networks. see *COMPUTERS — Artificial Intelligence*

001.642   US   ISSN 0740-4980
F T SYSTEMS. (Fault Tolerant) 1982. m. $695 worldwide (effective 1997). I T O M International Co., Box 1450, Los Altos, CA 94023. TEL 415-948-4516. FAX 415-948-9153. E-mail: omri@juno.com. Ed. Omri Serlin. index. (back issues avail.) **Document type:** trade publication.
   Description: Contains information about fault tolerant systems and on-line transaction processing.

001.6 001.642   US   ISSN 0884-0822
QA76.73.F24   CODEN: FODMD5
FORTH DIMENSIONS.* 1979. bi-m. $40 (Canada and Mexico $46; elsewhere $52). Forth Interest Group, 100 Dolores St. 183, Carmel, CA 93923-8665. TEL 510-893-6784. FAX 510-535-1295. Ed. Marlin Ouverson. adv. contact: Mike Elola. bk.rev.; index. circ. 2,000. (back issues avail.) Indexed: INSPEC. **Document type:** trade publication.
—BLDSC (4017.670000); AskIEEE; CISTI; Ei; KR SourceOne; UnCover.
   Description: For Forth programming language users and developers. Features articles on language implementation and optimization, applications incorporating Forth. Includes regular columns covering standards, new product announcements and reviews.

005.13   US   ISSN 1061-7264
QA76.73.F25
FORTRAN FORUM. 1982. q. $20. Association for Computing Machinery, Special Interest Group on Programming Languages, 1515 Broadway, 17th Fl., New York, NY 10036. TEL 212-869-7440. FAX 212-302-5826. (Subscr. to: Box 12115, Church Street Sta., New York, NY 10249)
—CISTI; SWETS.
   Formerly (until 1984): ForTec Forum (ISSN 0735-3761)

005 658.4031   US   ISSN 1042-6302
FOXTALK; a comprehensive monthly guide for users of Microsoft FoxPro. 1989. m. $149 includes companion diskette (Canada $159; elsewhere $169). Pinnacle Publishing, Inc., Box 888, Kent, WA 98035-0888. TEL 206-251-1900. FAX 206-251-5057. E-mail: foxtalk@pinpub.com; URL: http://www.pinpub.com. Ed. Whil Hentzen; Pub. Mickey Friedman. circ. 7,000 (paid). (looseleaf format; back issues avail.) **Document type:** newsletter.
●Also available on CD-ROM.
—CISTI.
   Description: Technical journal for Microsoft FoxPro software developers.

001.642 621.381   FR   ISSN 1166-4738
   CODEN: GLSEED
GENIE LOGICIEL ET SYSTEMES EXPERTS. 1985. q. 530 F. (foreign 580 F.). E C 2, 269 rue de la Garenne, 92000 Nanterre, France. TEL 47-80-70-00. FAX 47-80-66-29. Ed. Jean-Claude Rault. circ. 2,000. Indexed: INSPEC (1987-). **Document type:** trade publication.
—BLDSC (4116.070000); AskIEEE; CISTI; KR SourceOne.
   Formerly (until 1986): Genie Logiciel (ISSN 0295-6322)

001.642   US
ICON NEWSLETTER. 1978. 3/yr. free. University of Arizona, Department of Computer Science, Icon Project, Tucson, AZ 85721. TEL 602-621-8448. Eds. Ralph E. Griswold, Madge T. Griswold. circ. 1,500. (back issues avail.) **Document type:** newsletter.
   Description: Provides information about the implementation and application of the Icon programming language.

001.642 621.381   US   ISSN 0889-6836
INFOCUS (PHILADELPHIA); the technical journal for Prime Information, Universe and Unidata. bi-m. $48 in U.S.; Canada $58; elsewhere $75. Infocus, Inc., 37 S. Main St., Yardley, PA 19067. TEL 215-321-2200. FAX 215-321-2205. Ed. Lee J. Leitner.
   Incorporates (in 1992): S Select (ISSN 0895-7746)
   Description: Covers programming methodology, system administration, and discussions of programming tools.

INFORMATICA. see *MATHEMATICS — Computer Applications*

005.13   GW   ISSN 0942-8682
INFORMATIK UND SPRACHE. 1992. irreg., vol.4, 1994. price varies. Georg Olms Verlag, Hagentorwall 7, 31134 Hildesheim, Germany. TEL 49-5121-1501-0. FAX 49-5121-150150. (Subscr. in the U.S. to: 350 Fifth Ave., Ste. 3304, New York, NY 10118-0069. TEL 800-920-9334) Ed. Pius ten Hacken. **Document type:** monographic series.
   Description: Provides information on studies and research in the field of computer linguistics and data processing.

001.642   US   ISSN 1047-6067
INSIDE MICROSOFT BASIC. 1990. bi-m $49 (foreign $69). Cobb Group, Inc., 9420 Bunsen Pkwy., Ste. 300, Louisville, KY 40220. TEL 502-493-3200. FAX 502-491-8050. (Subscr. to: Box 35160, Louisville, KY 40232-9720. TEL 800-223-8720) Ed. Blake Ragsdell. **Document type:** consumer publication.
   Description: Contains tips and techniques exclusively for programmers using Microsoft BASIC and QuickBASIC.

001.642   US
INSIDE TURBO C PLUS PLUS. 1989. bi-m. $59 (foreign $79). Cobb Group, Inc., 9420 Bunsen Pkwy., Ste. 300, Louisville, KY 40220. TEL 502-493-3200. FAX 502-491-8050. (Subscr. to: Box 35160, Louisville, KY 40232-9720. TEL 800-223-8720) Ed. Bill Lamkin. **Document type:** consumer publication.
   Formerly (until 1991): Inside Turbo C (ISSN 1045-6791)
   Description: Contains tips and techniques aimed exclusively at programmers using Turbo C Plus Plus.

005   US   ISSN 1066-7555
INSIDE VISUAL BASIC FOR WINDOWS. 1991. m. $59 (foreign $79). Cobb Group, Inc., 9420 Bunsen Pkwy., Ste. 300, Louisville, KY 40220. TEL 502-493-3200. FAX 502-491-8050. (Subscr. to: Box 35160, Louisville, KY 40232-9720. TEL 800-223-8720) Ed. Blake Rasdell. **Document type:** consumer publication.
   Formerly (until 1993): Inside VisualBASIC (ISSN 1059-1788)
   Description: Contains tips and techniques exclusively aimed at programmers using VisualBASIC.

INTELLIGENT SOFTWARE STRATEGIES; the monthly newsletter on Expert Systems, OOP, CASE, Neural Networks & Natural Language. see *COMPUTERS — Artificial Intelligence*

005   US   ISSN 1072-5520
QA76.9.H85   CODEN: IERAE3
INTERACTIONS (NEW YORK). 1994. q. $70 to individual non-members; non-member institutions $135; members $45; student members $40. Association for Computing Machinery, 1515 Broadway, 17th Fl., New York, NY 10036-5701. TEL 212-369-7440. FAX 212-869-0481. E-mail: interactions@acm.org. Ed. John Rheinfrank; Pub. James Maurer. adv. contact: Walter Andrzejewski. Indexed: INSPEC (1994-).
—BLDSC (4531.871765); AskIEEE; CISTI; KR SourceOne; SWETS; UnCover. **CCC.**

COMPUTERS — COMPUTER PROGRAMMING

001.642 US ISSN 1074-8970
QA76.7 CODEN: PICLEW
INTERNATIONAL CONFERENCE ON COMPUTER LANGUAGES. PROCEEDINGS. 1986. biennial. price varies. (Institute of Electrical and Electronics Engineers, Inc.) I E E E Computer Society Press, 10662 Los Vaqueros Circle, Los Alamitos, CA 90720-1264. TEL 714-821-8380. FAX 714-821-4641. Ed. Cat Harris; Pub. Matt Loeb. adv. contact: Frieda Koester. **Indexed:** INSPEC. **Document type:** proceedings.
—Ei. **CCC.**
Formerly (until 1986): I E E E Computer Society International Conference on Computer Languages.
Description: Reports on new ideas, concepts, designs, implementations and experiments concerning languages used in various phases of the software life cycle.

001.642 SI ISSN 0129-0541
QA75.5 CODEN: IFCSEN
INTERNATIONAL JOURNAL OF FOUNDATIONS OF COMPUTER SCIENCE. Abbreviated title: I J F C S. (Text in English) 1990. q. $131 to individuals and institutions of developing countries; institutions of developed countries $329. World Scientific Publishing Co. Pte. Ltd., Farrer Rd., P.O. Box 128, Singapore 9128, Singapore. TEL 65-3825663. FAX 65-3825919. TELEX RS-28561-WSPC. E-mail: wspcs1@singnet.com.sg; sales@wspc2.demon.co.uk; wspc@wspc.com; URL: http://www.singnet.com.sg/~wspclib/. (UK addr.: 57 Shelton St., London WC2H 9HE, England. TEL 44-171-836-0888. FAX 44-171-836-2020; US addr.: 1060 Main St., Ste. 1B, River Edge, NJ 07661. TEL 800-227-7562. FAX 201-487-9656) Ed. D.T. Lee. cum.index every 5 yrs. circ. 150. (back issues avail.) **Indexed:** INSPEC (1990-), Zent.Math. **Document type:** academic/scholarly publication.
—BLDSC (4542.258000); AskIEEE; CISTI; KR SourceOne; SWETS. **CCC.**
Description: Publishes articles on all areas of the theoretical and mathematical foundations of computer science. Also publishes new results and proposals in these areas.

INTERNATIONAL JOURNAL OF HIGH SPEED COMPUTING. see COMPUTERS — Hardware

005.1 US ISSN 0885-7458
QA76.5 CODEN: IJPPE5
INTERNATIONAL JOURNAL OF PARALLEL PROGRAMMING. 1972. bi-m. $575 (foreign $670) (effective 1998). Plenum Publishing Corp., 233 Spring St., New York, NY 10013-1578. TEL 212-620-8000. FAX 212-463-0742. TELEX 23-421139. URL: http://ns1.infor.com:6800/cgi/getrarec/ple200000087. Ed.Bd. adv.; bibl.; charts; illus.; stat. (also avail. in microfilm from UMI; back issues avail.) **Indexed:** ABI Inform., ASCA, CAD CAM Abstr., Chem.Abstr., Compumath, Comput.Abstr., Comput.Cont., Comput.Rev., Curr.Cont., Cyb.Abstr., Ergon.Abstr., INSPEC, Lang.& Lang.Behav.Abstr., M.L.A., Math.R., Ref.Zh., Sci.Cit.Ind., Sociol.Abstr., Soft.Abstr.Eng., Zent.Math. **Document type:** academic/scholarly publication.
●Also available online.
—BLDSC (4542.441500); AskIEEE; CISTI; Ei; Genuine Article; KR SourceOne; Linda Hall; SWETS; UMI; UnCover. **CCC.**
Formerly (until 1987): International Journal of Computer and Information Sciences (ISSN 0091-7036)
Refereed Serial

INTERNATIONAL SYMPOSIUM ON MICROARCHITECTURE. PROCEEDINGS. see COMPUTERS — Microcomputers

005.13 US ISSN 1087-6944
▼**JAVA DEVELOPER'S JOURNAL.** Variant title: Internet Developer's Journal. 1996. m. $79. Sys-Con Publications, Inc., 39 E. Central Ave., Pearl River, NY 10965. TEL 914-735-1900. FAX 914-735-3922. E-mail: subscribe@sys-con.com; URL: http://www.sys-con.com/java/. adv.; bk.rev.; software rev.; illus.
●Also available online.
Description: Looks at techniques and tools for developing webpages with Java.

005.13 US ISSN 1086-4660
QA76.73.J38 CODEN: JREPFI
▼**JAVA REPORT.** 1996. 10/yr. $60 to individuals (Canada & Mexico $85; elsewhere $100); institutions $119 (Canada & Mexico $144; elsewhere $159). Sigs Publications, Inc., 71 W. 23rd St., 3rd Fl., New York, NY 10010-4102. TEL 212-274-0640. FAX 212-274-0646. E-mail: dfisco@sigs.com; URL: http://www.sigs.com/. Ed. David Fisco. adv.: B&W page $2800, color page $4100. illus.; tr.lit.; circ. 17,500 (paid). **Document type:** academic/scholarly publication, trade publication.
●Also available online.
—SWETS.
Description: Publishes studies and applications relating to Java development.
Refereed Serial

JOURNAL OF AUTOMATED REASONING. see COMPUTERS — Artificial Intelligence

005.1 US ISSN 1080-5230
▼**JOURNAL OF FUNCTIONAL AND LOGIC PROGRAMMING.** 1995. irreg. (1 vol./yr.). $30 to individuals; institutions $125 (effective 1996). M I T Press, 5 Cambridge Center, Cambridge, MA 02142. TEL 617-253-2889. FAX 617-577-1545. E-mail: journals-orders@mit.edu; URL: http://www-mitpress.mit.edu/jrnls-catalog/functional.html. Ed. Giorgio Levi. (reprint service avail.) **Document type:** academic/scholarly publication.
●Available only online.
Description: Publishes original research on functional and logic programming, including theoretical foundations. Articles are published on an article by article basis.
Refereed Serial

001.642 UK ISSN 0956-7968
QA76.62 CODEN: JFPRES
JOURNAL OF FUNCTIONAL PROGRAMMING. 1991. bi-m. £120($204) (effective 1998). Cambridge University Press, Edinburgh Bldg., Shaftesbury Rd., Cambridge CB2 2RU, England. TEL 44-1223-312393. FAX 44-1223-315052. TELEX 851817256. E-mail: information@cup.cam.ac.uk; URL: http://www.cup.cam.ac.uk. (N. American addr.: Cambridge University Press, Journals Dept., 40 W. 20th St., New York, NY 10011. TEL 212-924-3900. FAX 212-691-3239) Ed.Bd. R&P contact: Linda Nicol. adv. contact: Rebecca Symons. (also avail. in microform from UMI; back issues avail.) **Indexed:** INSPEC (1991-), Zent.Math. **Document type:** academic/scholarly publication.
—BLDSC (4986.820000); AskIEEE; CISTI; KR SourceOne; SWETS; UMI. **CCC.**
Description: Covers new languages and extensions, reasoning, proof and program transformation, program synthesis, implementation techniques, type theory, and parallelism.

005 US ISSN 0743-1066
CODEN: JLPRE2
JOURNAL OF LOGIC PROGRAMMING. 1984. m. fl.1629($936) (effective 1998). Elsevier Science Inc., Box 945, New York, NY 10159-0945. TEL 212-633-3730. FAX 212-633-3680. TELEX 420643 AEP UI. E-mail: usinfo-f@elsevier.com; URL: http://www.elsevier.nl/. (Subscr. outside the Americas to: Elsevier Science, Regional Sales Office, P.O. Box 211, 1000 AE Amsterdam, Netherlands. TEL 31-20-4853757. FAX 31-20-4853432; Subscr. in Australasia and the Far East to: Elsevier Science (Singapore) Pte Ltd, No.1 Temasek Ave., No.17-01 Millenia Tower, Singapore 039192, Singapore. TEL 65-434-3727. FAX 65-337-2230; Subscr. in Japan to: Elsevier Science Japan, 9-15 Higashi-Azabu 1-chome, Minato-ku, Tokyo 106, Japan. TEL 81-3-5561-5033. FAX 81-3-5561-5047) Eds. J.A. Robinson, J.L. Lassez. bibl.; charts; illus. circ. 1,000. (also avail. in microform from UMI; back issues avail.; reprint service avail. from SWZ) **Indexed:** A.I.Abstr., ASCA, CAD CAM Abstr., Compumath, Comput.Abstr., Comput.& Info.Sys., Comput.Rev., Curr.Cont., Eng.Ind., INSPEC, Math.R., SSCI, Zent.Math. **Document type:** academic/scholarly publication.
—BLDSC (5010.552300); AskIEEE; CISTI; Ei; Genuine Article; KR SourceOne; Linda Hall; SWETS; UnCover. **CCC.**
Description: Contains original research papers, survey and review articles, tutorial expositions and historical studies.
Refereed Serial

005.13 US ISSN 0896-8438
QA76.6 CODEN: JOOPEC
JOURNAL OF OBJECT - ORIENTED PROGRAMMING. 1988. 9/yr. $69 to individuals (Canada & Mexico $94; elsewhere $109); institutions $199 (Canada & Mexico $224; elsewhere $239). Sigs Publications, Inc., 71 W. 23rd St., New York, NY 10010-4102. TEL 212-242-7447. FAX 212-242-7574. E-mail: subscriptions@sigs.com; URL: http://www.sigs.com. (Subscr. to: Box 5050, Brentwood, TN 37024-5050) Ed. Richard S. Wiener. adv.: B&W page $2530, color page $3830. bk.rev. circ. 24,000. (back issues avail.) **Indexed:** ASCA, Compumath, Comput.Abstr., Curr.Cont., Data Process.Dig., INSPEC (1990-), SSCI. **Document type:** trade publication.
—BLDSC (5024.870000); AskIEEE; CASDDS; CISTI; Genuine Article; KR SourceOne; SWETS; UnCover. **CCC.**
Description: Evaluates research and developments in object-oriented programming methodologies.
Refereed Serial

005.1 UK ISSN 0963-9306
QA76.7 CODEN: JPLAER
JOURNAL OF PROGRAMMING LANGUAGES. 1992. q. £55($99) to individuals; institutions in the E.U. £130 (N. America $225; elsewhere £145) (effective 1995). Chapman & Hall, Journals Department (Subsidiary of: International Thomson Publishing Group), 2-6 Boundary Row, London SE1 8HN, England. TEL 44-171-8650066. FAX 44-171-5229623. TELEX 290164 CHAPMA G. E-mail: jhelp@chall.co.uk; URL: http://www.chaphall.com/chaphall/journals.html. (Dist. by: International Thompson Publishing Services Ltd., Cheriton House, North Way, Andover, Hants. SP10 5BE, England. TEL 44-1264-342713. FAX 44-1264-342807; Susbcr. in US & Canada to: 400 Market St., Philadelphia, PA 19106. TEL 800-552-5866) Eds. Des Watson, Jeanne Farrante adv.; bibl. (reprint service avail.) **Indexed:** ASCA, Compumath, Curr.Cont., INSPEC (1993-). **Document type:** academic/scholarly publication.
●Also available online.
—BLDSC (5042.735000); AskIEEE; CISTI; Genuine Article; KR SourceOne. **CCC.**
Formerly (until 1993): Journal of Programming Language Design and Implementation.
Description: Covers the design and implementation of programming languages.
Refereed Serial

JOURNAL OF SYSTEMS ARCHITECTURE. see COMPUTERS — Microcomputers

JOURNAL OF V L S I SIGNAL PROCESSING. see COMPUTERS — Data Communications And Data Transmission Systems

005 US ISSN 0899-9309
KERMIT NEWS. 1986. irreg., latest no.6, 1995. free. Columbia University Academic Information Systems Kermit Development and Distribution, 612 W. 115 St., New York, NY 10025. TEL 212-854-3703. FAX 212-663-8202. E-mail: cmg@columbia.edu; URL: http://www.columbia.edu/kermit/knews.html. Ed. Christine M. Gianone. R&P contact: Christine M Gianone. circ. 40,000. **Document type:** newsletter, bulletin.
●Also available online.
Description: Contains news about the university's Kermit communications software.

005.1 US ISSN 1057-4514
QA76.7 CODEN: ALPSE8
LETTERS ON PROGRAMMING LANGUAGES AND SYSTEMS. irreg. $105 to non-members. Association for Computing Machinery, 1515 Broadway, 17th F New York, NY 10036-5710. TEL 212-869-7440. FAX 212-944-1318. TELEX 421686. **Indexed:** INSPEC (1993-).
—AskIEEE; CISTI; Ei; KR SourceOne; UnCover. **CCC**
Description: Features rapid publication of significant short papers describing research and development efforts in programming languages and related systems.

001.642 FR ISSN 0981-0455
LETTRE ADA. 1987. 10/yr. 1150 F. E C 2, 269, rue de la Garenne, 92000 Nanterre, France. TEL 47-80-70-00. FAX 47-80-66-29. Ed. Jean-Claude Rault. bk.rev. circ. 300. (back issues avail.) **Document type:** newsletter.
Description: Dedicated to the Ada computer programming language.

COMPUTERS — COMPUTER PROGRAMMING 2145

LOGO EXCHANGE. see EDUCATION — Computer Applications

LOOP TRANSFORMATIONS FOR RESTRUCTURING COMPILERS. see COMPUTERS — Computer Engineering

004 621.381 610   US   ISSN 1072-3226
QA76.73.M15   CODEN: MCPUEF
M COMPUTING. 1978. 5/yr. M Technology Association, 1738 Elton Rd., Ste. 205, Silver Spring, MD 20903. TEL 301-431-4070. FAX 301-431-0017. Ed. Pam McIntyre. adv. contact: Marlo Brown. circ. 4,000. **Indexed:** INSPEC (1993-). **Document type:** academic/scholarly publication.
—BLDSC (5313.580000); AskIEEE; CISTI; KR SourceOne.
Former titles (until Feb. 1993): M U M P S Computing (Massachusetts General Hospital Utility Multi-Programming System) (ISSN 1060-7684) & M U G Quarterly (ISSN 0193-0885)
Description: Describes advances in M Technology, including systems, installations and programming techniques. Presents new product and industry information; announces meetings for M software users.
Refereed Serial

005.13   MM
▼**M WEB MAGAZINE.** 1996. q. 70 Triq il-Kosbor, Zonqor, Marsascala ZBR 09, Malta. FAX 356-639740. E-mail: mwm@mcenter.com; chrisb@4u.net; URL: http://www.geocities.com/siliconValley/7041/mwm.html. Ed. Chris Bonnici.
●Available only online.
Description: Contains programming tutorials, interviews, projects, FAQ, humor and more.

005.13   US   ISSN 1068-5669
MICROSOFT C - C PLUS PLUS DEVELOPER'S JOURNAL. 1990. m. $69 (foreign $89). Cobb Group, Inc., 9420 Bunsen Pkwy., Ste. 300, Louisville, KY 40220. TEL 502-493-3200. FAX 502-491-8050. (Subscr. to: Box 35160, Louisville, KY 40232-9720. TEL 800-223-8720) Ed. David Reid. **Document type:** consumer publication.
—CISTI.
Formerly (until 1993): Inside Microsoft C (ISSN 1047-6075)
Description: Contains tips and techniques aimed exclusively at programmers using Microsoft C.

MICROSOFT INTERNET SERVER PROFESSIONAL. see COMPUTERS — Computer Networks

005.369   US   ISSN 1085-1232
MICROSOFT MAGAZINE. 1994. q. $9.97 for registered Microsoft customers; non-registered $14.97. (Microsoft Corporation) T P D Publishing, 1300 Dexter Ave. N., Ste. 500, Seattle, WA 98109. TEL 206-284-1800. FAX 206-285-1900. E-mail: msmag@microsoft.com; URL: http://www.microsoft.com/magazine/. (Subscr. to: Microsoft Magazine, Box 1161, Skokie, IL 60076-8161. TEL 847-588-0302; Alt. addr.: Microsoft Corporation, One Microsoft Way, Redmond, WA 98052-6399) Ed. Jon Ganio; Pub. Karla Spormann. adv. contact: Celia Canfield.

005 004.692   US   ISSN 1081-9355
MICROSOFT SQL SERVER PROFESSIONAL. 1995. m. $199 includes companion diskette. Pinnacle Publishing, Inc., Box 888, Kent, WA 98035-0888. TEL 206-251-1900. FAX 206-251-5057. URL: http://www.pinpub.com. **Document type:** newsletter.

001.642   US   ISSN 0889-9932
QA76.5   CODEN: MSJOEB
MICROSOFT SYSTEMS JOURNAL. 1986. m. $50 (Canada & Mexico $65; elsewhere $75) (effective 1996). Miller Freeman, 411 Bord Ave., San Mateo, CA 94402. TEL 415-358-9500. FAX 415-358-9865. (Subscr. to: Box 8024, Boulder, CO 80306-8024. TEL 800-666-1084. FAX 303-678-0439) Ed. Eric Maffei. adv. circ. 45,000. (back issues avail.) **Indexed:** Comput.Ind. **Document type:** trade publication.
●Also available online. Vendor(s): Information Access Co.
—BLDSC (5760.602500); AskIEEE; CASDDS; CISTI; Ei; KR SourceOne; SWETS; UMI; UnCover. **CCC.**
Description: For advanced software developers.

001.642   JA
MICROSOFT SYSTEMS JOURNAL (JAPANESE EDITION). 1989. bi-m. 10800 Yen. Akio Fujii, A S C I I Publishing, 4-33-10 Yoyogi, Shibuya-ku, Tokyo 151-24, Japan. TEL 81-3-5351-8111.

003   US
N A S P A NEWS. q. National Systems Programmers Associations, 7044 S. 13th St., Oak Creek, WI 53154-1429. TEL 414-423-2420. Ed. Thom Ferris.

005.13   UK   ISSN 1351-3249
QA76.9.N38
▼**NATURAL LANGUAGE ENGINEERING.** 1995. q. £88($132) (effective 1998). Cambridge University Press, Edinburgh Bldg., Shaftesbury Rd., Cambridge CB22RU, England. TEL 44-1223-312393. FAX 44-1223-315052. TELEX 851817256. E-mail: information@cup.cam.ac.uk; URL: http://www.cup.cam.ac.uk. (N. American addr.: Cambridge University Press, Journals Dept., 40 W. 20th St., New York, NY 10011. TEL 212-924-3900. FAX 212-691-3239) Ed.Bd. R&P contact: Linda Nicol. adv. contact: Rebecca Symons. bk.rev. (reprint service avail. from ISI) **Document type:** academic/scholarly publication.
—BLDSC (6040.728100); AskIEEE; CISTI; KR SourceOne. **CCC.**
Description: Offers broad coverage of such topics as machine translation, information retrieval, speech recognition and generation, dialogue systems, knowledge bases for natural language processing, text analysis, and integrated systems.
Refereed Serial

NEW REVIEW OF APPLIED EXPERT SYSTEMS. see COMPUTERS — Artificial Intelligence

005.43   US
▼**O S - 2 COMPUTING! MAGAZINE.** 1996. m. free. E-mail: ronny@os2computing.com; URL: http://www.os2computing.com/magazine. Ed. Ronny Ko.
●Available only online.
Refereed Serial

005.13   US
▼**OBJECT CURRENTS;** the monthly on-line magazine. 1996. m. Sigs Publications, Inc., 71 W. 23rd St., New York, NY 10010. TEL 212-242-7447. FAX 212-242-7574. URL: http://www.sigs.com/. Ed. Bob Hathaway. adv. **Document type:** trade publication.
●Available only online.
Description: Comprehensive coverage of object technology and object oriented systems theory and applications.

005.1   UK   ISSN 0969-9767
QA76.64   CODEN: OOSYFD
OBJECT-ORIENTED SYSTEMS. 1994. q. £55($99) to individuals; institutions in the E.U. £130 (N. America $225; elsewhere £145) (effective 1995). Chapman & Hall, Journals Department (Subsidiary of: International Thomson Publishing Group), 2-6 Boundary Row, London SE1 8HN, England. TEL 44-171-8650066. FAX 44-171-5229623. TELEX 290164 CHAPMA G. E-mail: journal@chall.mhs.compuserve.com; URL: http://www.chaphall.com/chaphall/journals.html. (Dist. by: International Thomson Publishing Services, Ltd., N. Way, Andover, Hants. SP10 5BE, England. TEL 44-1264-342713. FAX 44-1264-342807; Subscr. in US & Canada to: 400 Market St., Philadelphia, PA 19106. TEL 800-552-5866) Ed. Russel Winder. adv. (reprint service avail.) **Indexed:** Geo.Abstr.H.G. **Document type:** academic/scholarly publication.
●Also available online.
—BLDSC (6197.009500); AskIEEE; CISTI; Genuine Article; KR SourceOne. **CCC.**
Description: Reports on all aspects of object orientation and fosters communication among researchers in object technology.
Refereed Serial

005   US   ISSN 1078-7518
ORACLE DEVELOPER. 1994. m. $199 includes companion diskette. Pinnacle Publishing, Inc., Box 888, Kent, WA 98035-0888. TEL 206-251-1900. FAX 206-251-5057. URL: http://www.pinpub.com. **Document type:** newsletter.

005.3   RU   ISSN 0361-7688
QA76.73   CODEN: PCSODA
PROGRAMMING AND COMPUTER SOFTWARE. English translation of: Programmirovanie (RU ISSN 0132-3474) 1975. bi-m. $825 in US; elsewhere $$965 (effective 1998). (Russian Academy of Sciences) Maik Nauka - Interperiodica, Mezhdunarodnyi Otdel, Ul. Profsoyuznaya, 90, 117864 Moscow, Russia. TEL 7-095-3360666. FAX 7-095-3360666. (Dist. by: Plenum Publishing Corp., 233 Spring St., New York, NY 10013-1578, U.S.A. TEL 212-620-8468. FAX 212-463-0742) Ed. V.P. Ivannikov. (also avail. in microfilm from UMI; back issues avail.) **Indexed:** ASCA, Compumath, Comput.Abstr., Comput.& Info.Sys., Comput.Cont., Curr.Cont., Eng.Ind., INSPEC (1975-), Intl.Civil Eng.Abstr., Math.R., Soft.Abstr.Eng., Zent.Math. **Document type:** academic/scholarly publication.
—BLDSC (0420.420000); AskIEEE; CISTI; Ei; Genuine Article; KR SourceOne; Linda Hall; SWETS; UMI; UnCover. **CCC.**
Refereed Serial

005.1   UK
PSYCHOLOGY OF PROGRAMMING INTEREST GROUP. PROCEEDINGS. irreg., no.9, 1997. Psychology of Programming Interest Group, Computing Research Centre, Sheffield Hallam University, 100 Napier St., Sheffield S11 8HD, England. E-mail: r.osborn@shu.ac.uk. Eds. Rick Osborn, Babak Khazaei. **Document type:** proceedings.

005.13   US
PURE JAVA DEVELOPER'S JOURNAL. m. $99. Cobb Group, Inc., 9420 Bunsen Pkwy., Ste. 300, Louisville, KY 40220. TEL 502-493-3200. FAX 502-491-8050. (Subscr. to: Box 35160, Lousville, KY 40232-9720. TEL 800-223-8720)
Description: Offers clear, concise, and practical articles that aim to help in developing applications and applets that are Java-compliant.

005.1   US   ISSN 1075-2528
QA76.64   CODEN: ROADFT
REPORT ON OBJECT ANALYSIS AND DESIGN. Variant title: R O A D. 1994. bi-m. $99 to individuals (Canada and Mexico $124; elsewhere $139); institutions $199 (Canada and Mexico $224; elsewhere $239). Sigs Publications, Inc., 71 W. 23rd St., New York, NY 10010-4102. TEL 212-242-7447. FAX 212-242-7574. E-mail: rsweiner@elbert.uccs.edu; URL: http://www.sigs.com. Ed. Richard S. Wiener; Pub. Hal Avery. adv.; bk.rev. circ. 6,000. **Document type:** trade publication, academic/scholarly publication.
—AskIEEE; KR SourceOne. **CCC.**
Description: Explores language-independent and object-oriented analysis and design.
Refereed Serial

005.1   NE   ISSN 0167-6423
QA76.6   CODEN: SCPGD4
SCIENCE OF COMPUTER PROGRAMMING. (Text in English) 1981. 9/yr. fl.1452($834) (effective 1998). North-Holland (Subsidiary of: Elsevier Science B.V.), P.O. Box 211, 1000 AE Amsterdam, Netherlands. TEL 31-20-4853911. FAX 31-20-4853598. TELEX 18582 ESPA NL. (Subscr. in the Americas to: Elsevier Science, Regional Sales Office, Box 945, New York, NY 10159-0945. TEL 212-633-3730. FAX 212-633-3680; Subscr. in Australasia and the Far East to: Elsevier Science (Singapore) Pte Ltd, No.1 Temasek Ave., No.17-01 Millenia Tower, Singapore 039192, Singapore. TEL 65-434-3727. FAX 65-337-2230; Subscr. in Japan to: Elsevier Science Japan, 9-15 Higashi-Azabu 1-chome, Minato-ku Tokyo 106, Japan. TEL 81-3-5561-5033. FAX 81-3-5561-5047) Ed. M. Sintzoff. bk.rev.; index. (also avail. in microform from UMI; back issues avail.; reprint service avail. from SWZ) **Indexed:** ASCA, Compumath, Comput.Abstr., Comput.Cont., Comput.Dtbs., Comput.Lit.Ind., Curr.Cont., Cyb.Abstr., INSPEC (1981-), Int.Abstr.Oper.Res., Zent.Math. **Document type:** academic/scholarly publication.
—BLDSC (8141.808000); AskIEEE; CISTI; Ei; Genuine Article; KR SourceOne; Linda Hall; SWETS; UnCover. **CCC.**
Description: Contains research papers, short notices, and occasional survey articles.
Refereed Serial

COMPUTERS — COMPUTER PROGRAMMING

001.642　　　　　US　ISSN 0894-2226
QA76.58
SERLIN REPORT ON PARALLEL PROCESSING. 1987. m. $695 worldwide (effective 1997). I T O M International Co., Box 1450, Los Altos, CA 94023. TEL 415-948-4516. FAX 415-948-9153. E-mail: omri@juno.com. Ed. Omri Serlin. index. (back issues avail.) **Document type:** trade publication.
　Description: Covers supercomputers and massively parallel systems.

005 621.39　　　NE　ISSN 0165-1684
TK5102.5　　　　　　CODEN: SPRODR
SIGNAL PROCESSING; an international journal devoted to the methods and applications of signal processing. (Text in English) 1979. 24/yr. fl.3352($1926) (effective 1998). (European Association for Signal Processing) Elsevier Science B.V., P.O. Box 211, 1000 AE Amsterdam, Netherlands. TEL 31-20-4853911. FAX 31-20-4853598. TELEX 18582 ESPA NL. E-mail: nlinfo-f@elsevier.nl; usinfo-f@elsevier.com; forinfo-kyf04035@niftyserve.or.jp; URL: http://www.elsevier.nl/. (Subscr. in the Americas to: Elsevier Science, Regional Sales Office, Box 945, New York, NY 10159-0945. TEL 212-633-3730. FAX 212-633-3680; Subscr. in Australasia and the Far East to: Elsevier Science (Singapore) Pte Ltd, No.1 Temasek Ave., No.17-01 Millenia Tower, Singapore 039192, Singapore. TEL 65-434-3727. FAX 65-337-2230; Subscr. in Japan to: Elsevier Science Japan, 9-15 Higashi-Azabu 1-chome, Minato-ku, Tokyo 106, Japan. TEL 81-3-5561-5033. FAX 81-3-5561-5047) Ed. Murat Kunt. adv.; bk.rev.; abstr.; bibl.; illus. circ. 1,500. (also avail. in microform from UMI) **Indexed:** Abstr.Hum.Comp.Inter., ASCA, Curr.Cont., Cyb.Abstr., INSPEC (1979-), Math.R., Tel.Abstr., Zent.Math. **Document type:** academic/scholarly publication.
　—BLDSC (8275.985300); AskIEEE; CISTI; Ei; Genuine Article; KR SourceOne; Linda Hall; SWETS; UnCover. **CCC.**
　Description: For researchers in signal processing, computer sciences, acoustics, automatic control, and electrical and electronics engineering.
　Refereed Serial

SIGNAL PROCESSING: IMAGE COMMUNICATION. see *COMPUTERS — Data Communications And Data Transmission Systems*

005.13　　　　　US　ISSN 1056-7976
QA76.73.S59
THE SMALLTALK REPORT; providing solutions to the smalltalk community. 1991. 9/yr. $89 to individuals (Canada & Mexico $114, elsewhere $129; institutions $199 (Canada & Mexico $224; elsewhere $239). Sigs Publications, Inc., 71 W. 23rd St., New York, NY 10010-4102. TEL 212-242-7447. FAX 212-242-7574. E-mail: subscriptions@sigs.com; URL: http://www.sigs.com. (Subscr. to: Box 5050, Brentwood, TN 37024-5050) Eds. John Pugh, Paul White. adv.; bk.rev. circ. 4,000. (back issues avail.) **Document type:** newsletter.
　—BLDSC (8310.187000); KR SourceOne. **CCC.**
　Description: Covers programming techniques, language issues, analysis and design, methodologies, project management, training and education, application case studies and experience reports.

005　　　　　　　US　ISSN 1066-7911
SMART ACCESS. 1993. m. $139 includes companion diskette. Pinnacle Publishing, Inc., Box 888, Kent, WA 98035-0888. TEL 206-251-1900. FAX 206-251-5057. URL: http://www.pinpub.com. (back issues avail.) **Document type:** newsletter.
　—SWETS.
　Description: For developers and power users working with Microsoft Access.

001.642　　　　　GW　ISSN 0945-8115
QA76.75　　　　　　CODEN: SCOTE5
SOFTWARE - CONCEPTS & TOOLS. 1982. q. DM.309.60 (foreign DM.313.20) (effective 1998). Springer-Verlag, Heidelberger Platz 3, 14197 Berlin, Germany. TEL 49-30-82787-0. FAX 49-30-82787448. E-mail: subscriptions@springer.de. (Subscr. in N. America to: Journal Fulfillment Services, 333 Meadowlands Pkwy., Secaucus, NJ 07094. TEL 212-460-1500. FAX 212-473-6272) Ed. Gustav Pomberger. adv.; bk.rev. circ. 1,500. (also avail. in microform from UMI) **Indexed:** Arts & Hum.Cit.Ind., ASCA, Compumath, Comput.Abstr., INSPEC (1994-), Zent.Math. **Document type:** academic/scholarly publication.
　—BLDSC (8321.450620); AskIEEE; Genuine Article; KR SourceOne; SWETS; UMI; UnCover. **CCC.**
　Supersedes: Structured Programming (ISSN 0935-1183); (until vol.11, no.6): Structured Language World (ISSN 0176-9375); Pascal Market News.
　Description: Aimed at Pascal and other structured language users. Offers information on programs, programming techniques, tutorials, operating system and new product news, as well as new products reviews.
　Refereed Serial

001.642 658.2　　　US　ISSN 0882-8415
SOFTWARE DEVELOPER'S MONTHLY.* 1985. m. $144. Sourceview Press (Subsidiary of: Sourceview Corporation), Box 4719, Walnut Creek, CA 94396-0713. Ed. M. Dean. adv.; bk.rev.; index. circ. 3,000.

SOFTWARE WORLD; an international journal of computer programs and packages. see *COMPUTERS — Software*

001.642　　　　　US　ISSN 1063-6870
QA267.7　　　　　　CODEN: PSTHE5
STRUCTURE IN COMPLEXITY THEORY CONFERENCE. PROCEEDINGS. 1986. a. price varies. (Institute of Electrical and Electronics Engineers, Inc.) I E E E Computer Society Press, 10662 Los Vaqueros Circle, Los Alamitos, CA 90720-1264. TEL 714-821-8380. FAX 714-821-4641. Ed. Cat Harris; Pub. Matt Loeb. adv. contact: Frieda Koester. (also avail. in microfiche) **Indexed:** INSPEC. **Document type:** proceedings.
　—Ei.
　Description: Focuses on structural properties of complexity classes and bonded reducibilities.

SURI KEIKAKU SHINPOJUMU RONBUNSHU/MATHEMATICAL PROGRAMMING SYMPOSIUM, JAPAN. PROCEEDINGS. see *MATHEMATICS*

005.43　　　　　US　ISSN 1061-2688
QA76.76.063　　　　CODEN: SYADE7
SYS ADMIN. Variant title: Sysadmin. 1992. m. $39 (Canada and Mexico $58; elsewhere $69) (effective 1997). Miller Freeman, Inc. (Lawrence), 1601 W. 23rd St., Ste. 200, Lawrence, KS 66046. TEL 913-841-1631. FAX 913-841-2624. E-mail: sasub@mfi.com; URL: http://www.samag.com. (Subscr. to: 8024, Boulder, CO 80306-8024. TEL 800-365-2210) Ed. Ralph Barker; Pub. Edwin Rothrock. R&P contact: Amber Ankerholz. TEL 913-838-7528. adv.: B&W page $1515; trim 8 x 10 7/8; adv. contact: Julie Thornton. circ. 22,000 (paid). (back issues avail.) **Document type:** trade publication.
　●Also available on CD-ROM.
　—CISTI; KR SourceOne; SWETS. **CCC.**
　Description: Provides technical information for UNIX administrators who seek to improve the performance or extend the capabilities of their UNIX systems; focuses on system-level processes.

001.642　　　　　US　ISSN 1079-3135
QA76.76.063
TECHNICAL SUPPORT MAGAZINE. Key Title: Na S P A Technical Support. 1987. m. $29.95 (Canada $44.95; elsewhere $54.95). Technical Enterprises, Inc., 7044 S. 13th St., Oak Creek, WI 53154-1429. TEL 414-423-2420. URL: http://www.naspa.net. Ed. Amy Birschbach; Pub. Jerry Seefeldt. R&P contact: Jerry Seefeldt. TEL 407-296-5050. adv. contact: Jerry Seefeldt. circ. 45,000. **Document type:** trade publication.
　Formed by the Oct. 1994 merger of: In-Depth Report. 370-390 Operating Systems (ISSN 1072-7647) & In-Depth Report. Computing Solutions (ISSN 1072-9100); Which incorporated (in Jun. 1993): Information Technologies (ISSN 1069-8140); Both of which superseded (in Apr. 1993): Technical Support (ISSN 1052-2581)
　Description: Serves and supports enterprise networks and operating ennvironments i.e. MVS, VM, VSE, LANs, etc.

005　　　　　　　US　ISSN 1076-5506
TICK, TICK, TICK...; the newsletter for millennial management. 1993. q. $100. 2000 Ad Inc., Box 020538, Brooklyn, NY 11202-0012. TEL 718-643-8425; 800-643-8425. URL: http://www.tickticktick.com. Ed. Bill Goodwin. adv.; bk.rev. circ. 350. (back issues avail.) **Document type:** newsletter.

005.3　　　　　　JA　ISSN 0913-0748
UNIX MAGAZINE. 1986. m. 8910 Yen. Akio Fujii, A S C I I Publishing, 4-33-10 Yoyogi, Shibuya-ku, Tokyo 151-24, Japan. TEL 81-3-5351-8111.

005.3　　　　　　US　ISSN 0742-3136
QA76.76.063　　　　CODEN: UNRED5
UNIX REVIEW. 1983. m. $55 (Canada and Mexico $60; elsewhere $75) (effective 1996). Miller Freeman, Inc. (Subsidiary of: United Newspapers), 600 Harrison St., San Francisco, CA 94107. TEL 415-905-2200; 800-829-5475. FAX 415-905-2232. (Subscr. to: Box 420029, Palm Coast, FL 32142-0029. TEL 800-829-5475. FAX 904-446-2774) Ed. Andrew Binstock. adv.; circ. 80,000 (controlled). **Indexed:** ABI Inform., Comput.Dtbs., INSPEC (1987-), Microcomp.Ind. **Document type:** consumer publication.
　●Also available online. Vendor(s): Information Access Co., UMI.
　—BLDSC (9120.493500); AskIEEE; CASDDS; CIST Ei; KR SourceOne; SWETS; UMI; UnCover. **CCC.**
　Description: For UNIX operating system users. Features articles on UNIX applications as well as compatible hardware and software coverage.

005.13　　　　　US
V S A M UPDATE. (Virtual Storage Access Method) q. $165 (effective Aug. 1996). Xephon, 1301 W. Hwy 407, Ste. 201-450, Lewisville, TX 75067. TEL 817-455-7050. FAX 817-455-2492. **Document type:** trade publication.

005.13　　　　　US
V S E UPDATE. (Virtual Storage Extended) q. $145 (effective Aug. 1996). Xephon, 1301 W. Hwy. 407 Ste. 201-450, Lewisville, TX 75067. TEL 817-455-7050. FAX 817-455-2492. **Document type:** trade publication.

005　　　　　　　US　ISSN 1077-6087
VISUAL BASIC DEVELOPER. 1994. m. $149 includes companion diskette. Pinnacle Publishing, Inc., Box 888, Kent, WA 98035-0888. TEL 206-251-1900 FAX 206-251-5057. URL: http://www.pinpub.com. **Document type:** newsletter.
　Description: For software developers using Visual Basic.

005.369　　　　　US　ISSN 1075-1955
VISUAL BASIC PROGRAMMER'S JOURNAL. 1991. m. $34.97 (Canada & Mexico $52.97; elsewhere $78.97). Fawcette Technical Publications, 209 Hamilton Ave., Palo Alto, CA 94301-2500. TEL 415-833-7100. FAX 415-853-0230. URL: http://www.windx.com.
　—BLDSC (9241.232000); CISTI; KR SourceOne; SWETS.
　Formerly (until 1993): Basic Pro (ISSN 1066-5978)

COMPUTERS — COMPUTER SALES 2147

005 US ISSN 1079-0608
VISUAL C PLUS PLUS DEVELOPER. 1994. m. $149 includes companion diskette. Pinnacle Publishing, Inc., Box 888, Kent, WA 98035-0888. TEL 206-251-1900. FAX 206-251-5057. URL: http://www.pinpub.com. **Document type:** newsletter.

005.1
▼**VISUAL DEVELOPER.*** 1996. bi-m. $21.95. 14455 N. Hayden Rd., Ste. 220, Scottsdale, AZ 85260-6949. TEL 602-483-0192. URL: http://www.coriolis.com/site/msie/comment.htm. Ed. Jeff Duntemann. **Document type:** trade publication.
●Also available online.
Description: Offers tips, techniques, expert advice and real source code for major visual development environments.

005.369 US ISSN 1083-9887
QA76.5
WINDOWS DEVELOPER'S JOURNAL. 1990. m. $34.99 (Canada & Mexico $45; elsewhere $64) (effective 1996). Miller Freeman, Inc. (Lawrence), 1601 W. 23rd St., Ste. 200, Lawrence, KS 66046. TEL 913-841-1631. FAX 913-841-2624. E-mail: wdsub@mfi.com; URL: http://www.wdj.com. (Subscr. to: Box 8024, Boulder, CO 80306-8024. TEL 800-365-1425) Ed. Ann Broecker; Pub. Martha Masinton. R&P contact: Ann Broecker. TEL 913-838-7550. adv.: B&W page $1750, color page $2215; adv. contact: Edward MacMillan. bk.rev.; circ. 22,000 (paid). (back issues avail.) **Document type:** trade publication.
●Also available online. Vendor(s): Information Access Co.
Also available on CD-ROM.
—KR SourceOne; SWETS. **CCC.**
Former titles: Windows - D O S Developers Journal (ISSN 1059-2407); (until Dec. 1991): Tech Specialist (ISSN 1049-913X)
Description: Provides practical, highly technical information for Windows developers.

005.13 US ISSN 1061-3501
QA76.76.W56
WINDOWS TECH JOURNAL. 1992. m. $29.95. Oakley Publishing Co., 150 N. Fourth St., Springfield, OR 97477. TEL 541-747-0800; 800-234-0386. FAX 541-746-0071. E-mail: 103716.3514@compuserve.com. Ed. J.D. Hildebrand; Pub. Bobbi Sinyard. adv. circ. 25,000. **Indexed:** Comput.Ind. **Document type:** trade publication.
—BLDSC (9319.332360); KR SourceOne.
Description: Technical resource for Windows application programmers and advanced users. Covers tools and techniques for programming.

005.13 US ISSN 1056-7003
QA76.76.W56 CODEN: XJOUEA
THE X JOURNAL; delivering open computing technology with the X window system. 1991. 7/yr. $39 to individuals (foreign $79); institutions $99 (foreign $139). Sigs Publications, Inc., 71 W. 23rd St., New York, NY 10010-4102. TEL 212-242-7447. FAX 212-242-7574. (Subscr. to: Box 5050, Brentwood, TN 37024-5050) Ed. Charles F. Bowman. adv.: B&W page $3630, color page $5400. circ. 35,000. **Document type:** trade publication.
—BLDSC (9365.575640); CISTI; KR SourceOne; SWETS. **CCC.**
Description: Covers X servers, window managers, X-based applications, X education, and software engineering in X.

COMPUTERS — Computer Sales

See also Business and Economics–Marketing and Purchasing

658.8 CN ISSN 0840-7312
CANADIAN COMPUTER RESELLER. 1987. 24/yr. Maclean-Hunter Ltd., Maclean-Hunter Bldg., 777 Bay St., Toronto, ON M5W 1A7, Canada. TEL 416-596-2643. FAX 416-593-3166. TELEX 06-219547. Ed. Kevin McKee. adv.: B&W page $1720. circ. 8,249. **Indexed:** Can.B.P.I.
—KR SourceOne.

658.8 338 621.381 US
COMPULIFE'S MICROMARKET BLUE DISC. 1982. q. $75. Compulife, 1050 140th Ave. N.E., Ste. H, Bellevue, WA 98005-2972. TEL 206-641-6101. Ed. Steve Sharp.
Description: Used microcomputer price guide for hardware and peripherals.

COMPUTER BUYER'S GUIDE AND HANDBOOK. see *COMPUTERS — Personal Computers*

658.8 US
COMPUTER CONNECTION.* 1993. m. $13. 11065 N.W. 21st. Pl., Coral Springs, FL 33071-5744. Ed. Sorensen. adv.: B&W page $210; trim 7 x 10.

658.8 IT ISSN 1122-3227
COMPUTER DEALER & V A R. m. L.82000 (foreign L.107000). A G E P E s.r.l. (Subsidiary of: Alfa Linea), Via Rosso di San Secondo 1-3, 20134 Milan, Italy. TEL 39-2-215621. FAX 39-2-70120032. Ed. Roberto Avanzo; Pub. Giorgio Artuffo. R&P contact: Roberto Avanzo. adv.: color page L.5450000; 225 x 310; adv. contact: Roberto Lenzi. circ. 11,780.

658.8 CN ISSN 1184-2369
COMPUTER DEALER NEWS. 1985. s-m. Can.$100($160) (foreign Can.$250). Plesman Publications Ltd., 2005 Sheppard Ave. E., 4th Fl., Willowdale, ON M2J 5B1, Canada. TEL 416-497-9562. FAX 416-497-9427. E-mail: cdnsales@plesman.com. Ed. James Buchok; Pub. George Soltys. adv.: page Can.$1695, color page Can.$2440; adv. contact: Robert Groen. circ. 8,100. **Indexed:** Can.B.P.I., Comput.Indus.Up.
●Also available online. Vendor(s): Information Access Co.
Formerly: Canadian Computer Dealer News (ISSN 0834-4612)

658.8 US
COMPUTER MANAGER. m. National Association of Purchasing Management Organization, E-mail: story@compumgr.com; URL: http://www.compumgr.com/index2.htm. circ. 25,000.
●Also available online.
Description: Computer equipment magazine for purchasing managers.

658.8 GW
▼**COMPUTER PARTNER.** 1995. 19/yr. Computerwoche Verlag GmbH, Brabanterstr. 4, 80805 Munich, Germany. TEL 49-89-36086299. FAX 49-89-36086325. TELEX 5215250-COMW-D. Ed. Damian Sicking. R&P contact: Thomas Perskowitz. adv.: B&W page DM.10200, color page DM.13200; trim 280 x 381; adv. contact: Gabrielle Heilmann. circ. 18,860. **Document type:** trade publication.
Formerly: Computer Business.
Description: Aimed at resellers who successfully sell high-tech products and services.

658.8 US ISSN 0045-7841
COMPUTER PRICE GUIDE; the blue book of used I B M computer prices. 1970. q. $125 (effective 1997). Computer Economics, Inc., 5841 Edison Place, Carlsbad, CA 92008. TEL 760-438-8100. FAX 760-431-1126. E-mail: custserv@compecon.com; URL: http://www.computereconomics.com. **Indexed:** Comput.Cont. **Document type:** catalog, newsletter.
Description: Provides price and market information for commonly traded IBM computers and peripherals.

001.6 658.8 US ISSN 0893-8377
HD9696.C6
COMPUTER RESELLER NEWS; the newspaper for microcomputer reselling. (Includes bi-m. supplement: Benchmarks Research Report (ISSN 1059-7573)) 1982. w. $189 (Europe $350; Asia $460). C M P Publications, Inc., 600 Community Dr., Manhasset, NY 11030. TEL 516-562-5000. FAX 516-733-6916. TELEX 647035 CMP PUB MAHA. URL: http://www.crn.com. (Subscr. to: Box 4037, Church Street Sta., New York, NY 10261-4037) Ed. Robert Faletra; Pub. John Russell. adv.: B&W page $9595, color page $11780; trim 10 3/4 x 14 3/8. circ. 104,000 (controlled). **Indexed:** Comput.Cont., Comput.Dtbs., Comput.Indus.Up., Microcomp.Ind., Microcomp.Indus.Up. **Document type:** trade publication.
●Also available online. Vendor(s): Information Access Co., NewsNet (EC07).
—BLDSC (3394.257200); KR SourceOne; UMI. **CCC.**
Incorporates (in 1992): Computer Reseller Sources (ISSN 1060-1376) & Macintosh News; Formerly (until 1986): Computer Retail News (ISSN 0744-673X)
Description: For dealers, VARS, distributors and vendors of microcomputer products. Provides news and comprehensive analysis on emerging market trends.

658.8 US ISSN 1066-7598
COMPUTER RETAIL WEEK. 1990. bi-m. $159. C M P Publications, Inc., 600 Community Dr., Manhasset, NY 11030. TEL 516-562-5000. FAX 516-562-5464. Ed. Keith Newman. adv.: B&W page $5395, color page $6290; trim 10 3/4 x 14 3/8. circ. 22,500. **Document type:** trade publication.
●Also available online. Vendor(s): Information Access Co.
—KR SourceOne; UMI. **CCC.**

004 US ISSN 0886-0556
QA76.5
COMPUTER SHOPPER; the computer magazine for direct buyers. 1979. m. $39.50. Coastal Associates Publishing, L.P., Computer Publications Division (Subsidiary of: Ziff-Davis Publishing Co.), One Park Ave., New York, NY 10016. TEL 800-999-7467. FAX 212-503-3999. (Subscr. to: Box 52568, Boulder, CO 80321) Ed. John Blackford. adv.; bk.rev.; charts; illus. circ. 502,618. (tabloid format) **Indexed:** Comput.Ind., PCR2.
●Also available online. Vendor(s): Information Access Co.
—BLDSC (3394.275280); KR SourceOne; SWETS. **CCC.**
Description: For individuals and companies interested in buying, reselling and using computer hardware, software and peripherals. Articles offer information on popular models of computers, software, new products, club news, network news and magazine reviews.

658.8 CN ISSN 0826-1547
COMPUTERWORLD CANADA. 1985. s-m. Laurentian Technomedia Inc. (Subsidiary of: Laurentian Media Inc.), 501 Oakdale Rd., North York ON M3N 1W7, Canada. TEL 416-746-7360. FAX 416-746-1421. Ed. John Pickett. R&P contact: John Pickett. adv. circ. 40,000. (tabloid format) **Document type:** trade publication.
Formerly: Direct Access (ISSN 0827-5033)
Description: Presents data processing news and career opportunities.

CULPEPPER LETTER. see *COMPUTERS — Software*

DATAPRO DIRECTORY OF MICROCOMPUTER HARDWARE. see *COMPUTERS — Computer Industry Directories*

DIRECTORY OF COMPUTER RETAILERS, DEALERS & DISTRIBUTORS (YEAR). see *COMPUTERS — Computer Industry Directories*

COMPUTERS — COMPUTER SECURITY

658.8   US
DISK - TREND REPORT. (Includes Disk Drive Array Report, Optical Disk Drive and Library Report, Rigid Disk Drive Report, and Removable Data Storage Report) 1977. a. $6432. Disk - Trend, Inc., 1925 Landings Dr., Mountain View, CA 94043. TEL 415-961-6209. FAX 415-969-2560. E-mail: dtinfo@disktrend.com; URL: http://www.disktrend.com. Pub. James N. Porter. (back issues avail.)
Description: Covers shipment, revenues and market trends for rigid disk drives, optical disk drives, flexible disk drives, and disk drive arrays.

658.8   US
EASY DATA COMPUTER COMPARISONS.* 1982. q. $120. (Easy Data Corporation) Dykstra Consultants, 545 Baywood Dr., Newport Beach, CA 92660-7141. stat.; charts; index. (back issues avail.)

658.8   US
FREQUENT BUYER. 1988. m. free to qualified personnel. Merisel, 200 Continental Blvd., El Segundo, CA 90245. TEL 213-615-3080. FAX 213-615-1263. Ed. W. Bryan Wadsworth. adv. circ. 13,000.
    Formerly: Softsell Reseller.
    Description: Designed to support the Merisel frequent buyer program.

658.5 335   US   ISSN 0733-9305
INFOPERSPECTIVES. 1980. m. $595 (foreign $630) (effective 1997). Technology News of America Co., Inc., 110 Greene St., New York, NY 10012. TEL 212-334-9750. Ed. Hesh Weiner. **Indexed:** Comput.Lit.Ind.
    Incorporates (1979-1997): Computer and Communications Buyer (ISSN 0272-4553)
    Description: Follows the use of mainframe and other large information processing devices at Fortune 1000 companies. Helps give MIS directors guidance in developing budgets and technical strategies for data processing.

IRISH COMPUTER. see *COMPUTERS — Microcomputers*

658.8 004   RU
KTO EST' KTO NA KOMP'YUTERNOM RYNKE; katalog. (In 2 vols.) (Text in Russian) 1994. s-a. 100000 Rub. Izdatel'stvo M G U, Bolshaya Nikitskaya ul., 5-7, 103009 Moscow, Russia. TEL 7-095-2030122. FAX 7-095-2030168. E-mail: pcmag@sovam.com. Ed. Alexander Zilbrman. adv.: page $5000; trim 150 x 210; adv. contact: Irina Adlerova. circ. 50,000. **Document type:** catalog, directory, trade publication.
    ● Also available on CD-ROM.
    Description: Lists Russian computer firms.

MICRO MONEY NEWSLETTER. see *COMPUTERS — Microcomputers*

MICRO SOFTWARE MARKETING. see *COMPUTERS — Software*

658.8 338 621.381   US   ISSN 8756-7822
P C LETTER; the insider's guide to the personal computer industry. 1985. 22/yr. $495 (foreign $575). 155 Bovet Rd., Ste. 800, San Mateo, CA 94402-3115. TEL 800-432-2478. FAX 415-312-0547. Ed. David Coursey; Pub. Stewart Alsop II. circ. 1,200. **Document type:** newsletter.
    ● Also available on CD-ROM.
    Description: Newsletter covering major shifts in the personal computer industry. Featuring news analysis of product design, business methods, financial trends and both industry and consumer perceptions.

001.6 658.8   US   ISSN 0736-0894
HD9696.C63
P C RETAILING.* (Personal Computer) 1983. m. free to qualified personnel. Bartex Publishing Group, 32 South St., Ste. 103, Waltham, MA 02154. TEL 617-890-5124. Ed. Neil Spann. adv.; bk.rev. circ. 45,000.
    Formerly (until 1984): Digital Retailing.
    Description: Aimed at IBM retailers.

001.6 658.8   US   ISSN 1042-7325
HD9696.C63
RESELLER MANAGEMENT; the magazine for profitable strategies for value added resellers. 1978. 14/yr. $69.90 (Canada $99.90). Cahners Publishing Company (Newton), Division of Reed Elsevier Inc., 275 Washington St., Newton, MA 02158. TEL 617-558-4497. FAX 617-558-4506. URL: http://www.resellermgmt.com. Ed. John Russell; Pub. Stephen Twombly. circ. 85,000. (back issues avail.) **Indexed:** Comput.Bus., Comput.Cont., LAMP. **Document type:** trade publication.
    —KR SourceOne. **CCC.**
    Formed by the merger of (1978-1989): Computer Dealer (ISSN 0160-8916); Computer Reseller Monthly (ISSN 0890-3980); Which was formerly (until 1986): Computer Merchandising Monthly (ISSN 0887-9974)
    Description: Feature articles on selling, marketing, the customer, technology, business, and vertical markets. Covers hardware, software, networking, and peripherals, as well as computer telephony and emerging technologies.

658.8   US
RESELLER QUARTERLY. 1991. q. free to qualified personnel. Merisel, 200 Continental Blvd., El Segundo, CA 90245. TEL 213-615-3080. FAX 213-615-1263. Ed. W. Bryan Wadsworth. adv. circ. 25,000.
    Description: Designed to support the Merisel customer base.

SOFT AD. (Software Advertiser) see *COMPUTERS — Software*

SOFT.LETTER; trends & strategies in software publishing. see *COMPUTERS — Software*

SOFTWARE DEVELOPER'S MONTHLY. see *COMPUTERS — Computer Programming*

SOFTWARE MAGAZINE. see *COMPUTERS — Software*

658.8   FR   ISSN 0762-5669
VENTE INFORMATIQUE.* 10/yr. L.N.E., 51 rue de l'Amiral Mouchez, 75013 Paris, France. TEL 33-5-45654400. TELEX 202 548 F. Ed. Yves Dupre. circ. 12,000.

COMPUTERS — Computer Security

658.478   US   ISSN 1063-9527
QA76.9.A25
ANNUAL CONFERENCE COMPUTER SECURITY APPLICATIONS. 1989. a. price varies. (Institute of Electrical and Electronics Engineers, Inc.) I E E E Computer Society Press, 10662 Los Vaqueros Circle, Los Alamitos, CA 90720. TEL 714-821-8380. FAX 714-821-4641. Ed. Cat Harris; Pub. Matt Loeb. adv. contact: Frieda Koester. **Document type:** proceedings.
    —BLDSC (1081.907000). **CCC.**
    Description: Covers various methods, issues, systems, designs and applications that contribute to the field of information security.

658.478   US   ISSN 0746-7281
AUERBACH DATA SECURITY MANAGEMENT. 1981. bi-m. $434. Auerbach Publishers (Subsidiary of: Warren, Gorham & Lamont), One Penn Plaza, New York, NY 10119. TEL 212-971-5000. FAX 212-971-5024. (Subscr. to: 31 St. James Ave., Boston, MA 02116-4112. TEL 800-950-1218. FAX 617-423-1914) Ed. Harold Tipton. (looseleaf format)
    —**CCC.**
    Formerly (until 1983): Data Security Management (ISSN 0736-363X)
    Description: Provides information on protecting data resources from human and computer error. Covers implementation of security measures, software packages, disaster-recovery planning, and security hardware.

005.8   GW   ISSN 0933-4033
BUNDESDATENSCHUTZGESETZ. 1977. irreg. DM.168. Erich Schmidt Verlag GmbH & Co. (Berlin), Genthiner Str. 30G, 10785 Berlin, Germany. TEL 49-30-250085-0. FAX 49-30-2500521. (looseleaf format) **Document type:** bulletin.

C I O CANADA. see *COMPUTERS — Computer Industry*

658.478   US   ISSN 0899-4595
C P R - J. (Contingency Planning & Recovery Journal) 1987. q. $65 (foreign $83) (effective 1997). (Contingency Planning & Recovery Institute) Management Advisory Publications, 57 Greylock Rd., Box 81151, Wellesley Hills, MA 02181. TEL 617-235-2895. Ed. J.F. Kuong. adv.; bk.rev. **Document type:** trade publication.
    Formerly: C P R - R (ISSN 0899-4994)
    Description: Devoted to issues of development, implementation, documentation and testing of computer contingency and recovery plans to protect business continuity and minimizing loss from computer and business disruptions. Includes tutorials and a thorough digest of literature sources published on the subject. Practical guidelines and practices are featured regularly.

658.478 341   CN   ISSN 0825-7361
JC596.2.C2
CANADA. PRIVACY COMMISSIONER. ANNUAL REPORT. (Text in English and French) 1983. a. free. Privacy Commissioner, 112 Kent St., 3rd Fl., Ottawa, ON K1A 1H3, Canada. TEL 613-995-2410; 800-267-0441. FAX 613-995-1501. Ed. Sally Jackson. adv. contact: Sally Jackson. stat. circ. 6,000. **Document type:** government publication.

658.478   US   ISSN 0738-4262
COM - S A C. (Computer Security, Auditing and Controls) 1974. q. $75 (Australasia $88; elsewhere $85) (effective 1997). Management Advisory Publications, 57 Greylock Rd., Box 81151, Wellesley Hills, MA 02181. TEL 617-235-2895. FAX 617-235-5446. Eds. J.F. Kuong, C. Winters. bk.rev.; circ. 1,000 (paid). **Indexed:** Account.Ind. (1979-), Data Process.Dig., INSPEC (1985-). **Document type:** trade publication.
    —BLDSC (3394.274910); AskIEEE; KR SourceOne.
    Description: Tutorials on computer security, audit and controls and comprehensive digest of all key articles and literature on the title subjects. Summary of new developments and product announcements in the field.

COMPASS: COMPUTER ASSURANCE (CONFERENCE). see *ENGINEERING — Electrical Engineering*

658.478 005.74   UK   ISSN 0960-2593
COMPUTER AUDIT UPDATE. 1988. m. fl.865($492) (effective 1998). Elsevier Science Ltd., P.O. Box 800, Kidlington, Oxford OX5 1DX, England. TEL 44-1865-843000. FAX 44-1865-843010. E-mail: nlinfo-f@elsevier.nl; usinfo-f@elsevier.com; forinfo-kyf04035@niftyserve.or.jp; URL: http://www.elsevier.nl/. (Subscr. to: Elsevier Science, Regional Sales Office, P.O. Box 211, 1000 AE Amsterdam, Netherlands. TEL 31-20-4853757. FAX 31-20-4853432; Subscr. in the Americas to: Elsevier Science, Regional Sales Office, Box 945, New York, NY 10159-0945. TEL 212-633-3730. FAX 212-633-3680; Subscr. in Australasia and the Far East to: Elsevier Science (Singapore) Pte Ltd, No.1 Temasek Ave., No.17-01 Millenia Tower, Singapore 039192, Singapore. TEL 65-434-3727. FAX 65-337-2230) Eds. Stephen Hinde, J. Meyer. adv. (also avail. in microform from UMI; back issues avail.) **Document type:** newsletter.
    ● Also available online. Vendor(s): Information Access Co.
    —BLDSC (3393.715500). **CCC.**
    Formerly (until 1991): Update On Computer Audit, Control and Security (ISSN 0953-5217)
    Description: Deals with topics such as: current and emerging threats to computer systems and how to guard against them, detailed technical methods, legal changes affecting IT installations. Also provides news, publication reviews and a listing of events.
    Refereed Serial

COMPUTERS — COMPUTER SECURITY

658.478 UK ISSN 1361-3723 CODEN: CFSBEK
COMPUTER FRAUD & SECURITY. 1978. m. fl.859($494) (effective 1998). Elsevier Science Ltd., P.O. Box 800, Kidlington, Oxford OX5 1DX, England. TEL 44-1865-843000. FAX 44-1865-843010. E-mail: nlinfo-f@elsevier.nl; usinfo-f@elsevier.com; forinfo-kyf04035@niftyserve.or.jp; URL: http://www.elsevier.nl/. (Subscr. to: Elsevier Science, Regional Sales Office, P.O. Box 211, 1000 AE Amsterdam, Netherlands. TEL 31-20-4853757. FAX 31-20-4853432; Subscr. in the Americas to: Elsevier Science, Regional Sales Office, Box 945, New York, NY 10159-0945. TEL 212-633-3730. FAX 212-633-3680; Subscr. in Australasia and the Far East to: Elsevier Science (Singapore) Pte Ltd, No.1 Temasek Ave., No.17-01 Millenia Tower, Singapore 039192, Singapore. TEL 65-434-3727. FAX 65-337-2230) Eds. Tina Monk, Harold J. Highland. bk.rev.; charts. (also avail. in microform from UMI; back issues avail.) Indexed: Comput.Lit.Ind., INSPEC. **Document type:** newsletter. ●Also available online. Vendor(s): Data-Star, Information Access Co., Knight-Ridder Information, Inc.
—BLDSC (3393.964600); AskIEEE; CISTI; KR SourceOne; SWETS. CCC.
Formerly (until Oct. 1995): Computer Fraud and Security Bulletin (ISSN 0142-0496)
Description: Provides information and advice on methods to combat computer crime and minimize risks.

658.478 UK ISSN 0267-3649
COMPUTER LAW & SECURITY REPORT. 1985. bi-m. fl.905($520) (effective 1998). Elsevier Science Ltd., P.O. Box 800, Kidlington, Oxford OX5 1DX, England. TEL 44-1865-843000. FAX 44-1865-843010. E-mail: nlinfo-f@elsevier.nl; usinfo-f@elsevier.com; forinfo-kyf04035@niftyserve.or.jp; URL: http://www.elsevier.nl/. (Subscr. to: Elsevier Science, Regional Sales Office, P.O. Box 211, 1000 AE Amsterdam, Netherlands. TEL 31-20-4853757. FAX 31-20-4853432; Subscr. in the Americas to: Elsevier Science, Regional Sales Office, Box 945, New York, NY 10159-0945. TEL 212-633-3730. FAX 212-633-3680; Subscr. in Australasia and the Far East to: Elsevier Science (Singapore) Pte Ltd, No.1 Temasek Ave., No.17-01 Millenia Tower, Singapore 039192, Singapore. TEL 65-434-3727. FAX 65-337-2230) Ed. Stephen Saxby, J. Matthews. adv.; index. circ. 500. (also avail. in microform from UMI; back issues avail.) Indexed: Euro.LJI, INSPEC (1985-), Leg.Per., LJI. **Document type:** academic/scholarly publication.
—BLDSC (3394.074900); AskIEEE; KR SourceOne; SWETS. CCC.
Description: Information technology law and computer security for general and financial managers.
Refereed Serial

COMPUTER LAW STRATEGIST. see *LAW*

005.8 658.478 US ISSN 0742-0633
QA76.9.A25
COMPUTER SECURITY ALERT. 1973. m. $197 membership (foreign $237 (effective 1997). (Computer Security Institute (San Francisco)) Miller Freeman, Inc., 600 Harrison St., San Francisco, CA 94107. TEL 415-905-2370. FAX 415-905-2234. (Subscr. to: Box 7703, San Francisco, CA 94120-7703. FAX 415-905-2562) Ed. Richard Power. R&P contact: Patrice Rapalus. adv. contact: Whitney Wilson. **Document type:** newsletter.
Formerly: Computer Security Newsletter.

005.8 US ISSN 1059-5317
QA76.9.A25
COMPUTER SECURITY BUYERS GUIDE. a. Computer Security Institute (San Francisco), 600 Harrison St., San Francisco, CA 94107. TEL 415-905-2370. FAX 415-905-2234. circ. 4,000. (looseleaf format) **Document type:** directory.
Description: Describes products and services designed for computer security practitioners.

658.478 US ISSN 0882-1453
QA76.9.A25
COMPUTER SECURITY DIGEST.* 1983. m. $125. Computer Protection Systems, Inc., 12275 Appletree Dr., Plymouth, MI 48170-3739. TEL 313-459-8787. FAX 313-459-2720. Ed. Jack Bologna; Pub. Jack Bologna. bk.rev.; index. (looseleaf format) **Document type:** newsletter.
Formerly: Corporate and Computer Fraud Digest.
Description: Provides digests of current incidents involving computer security breaches and computer-related crime.

005.8 US
COMPUTER SECURITY FOUNDATIONS WORKSHOP. PROCEEDINGS. 1988. a. price varies. (Institute of Electrical and Electronics Engineers, Inc.) I E E E Computer Society Press, 10662 Los Vaqueros Circle, Los Alamitos, CA 90720-1264. TEL 714-821-8380. FAX 714-821-4641. Ed. Cat Harris; Pub. Matt Loeb. adv. contact: Frieda Koester. **Document type:** proceedings.
Description: Explores fundamental issues in computer security.

658.478 005.8 US ISSN 0277-0865
QA76.9.A25 CODEN: CSJLDR
COMPUTER SECURITY JOURNAL. 1981. s-a. $85 (foreign $105) (effective 1997). (Computer Security Institute (San Francisco)) Miller Freeman, Inc., 600 Harrison St., San Francisco, CA 94107. TEL 415-905-2370. FAX 415-905-2234. (Subscr. to: Box 7703, San Francisco, CA 94120-7703. TEL 415-905-2751. FAX 415-905-2562) Ed. Richard Power. bk.rev. circ. 3,000. Indexed: Account.Ind. (1981-), Data Process.Dig., INSPEC. **Document type:** trade publication.
●Also available online. Vendor(s): UMI.
—BLDSC (3394.274920); AskIEEE; CASDDS; CISTI; Ei; KR SourceOne; SWETS; UMI.
Description: Presents ideas and information about current security practices and products.

658.478 UK ISSN 0167-4048
QA76.9.A25 CODEN: CPSEDU
COMPUTERS & SECURITY; the international journal devoted to the study of the technical and financial aspects of computer security. (Text in English) 1982. 8/yr. fl.914($525) (effective 1998). (International Federation for Information Processing, Technical Committee on Computer Security) Elsevier Science Ltd., P.O. Box 800, Kidlington, Oxford OX5 1DX, England. TEL 44-1865-843000. FAX 44-1865-843010. E-mail: nlinfo-f@elsevier.nl; usinfo-f@elsevier.com; forinfo-kyf04035@niftyserve.or.jp; URL: http://www.elsevier.nl/. (Subscr. to: Elsevier Science, Regional Sales Office, P.O. Box 211, 1000 AE Amsterdam, Netherlands. TEL 31-20-4853757. FAX 31-20-4853432; Subscr. in the Americas to: Elsevier Science, Regional Sales Office, Box 945, New York, NY 10159-0945. TEL 212-633-3730. FAX 212-633-3680; Subscr. in Australasia and the Far East to: Elsevier Science (Singapore) Pte Ltd, No.1 Temasek Ave., No.17-01 Millenia Tower, Singapore 039192, Singapore. TEL 65-434-3727. FAX 65-337-2230) Ed. Paul Evans. adv.; bk.rev.; abstr.; bibl.; index. (back issues avail.) Indexed: ABI Inform., Account.& Data Proc.Abstr., ASCA, Compumath, Comput.Abstr., Comput.Cont., Comput.Lit.Ind., Curr.Cont., Eng.Ind., INSPEC. **Document type:** academic/scholarly publication.
—BLDSC (3394.781000); AskIEEE; CASDDS; CISTI; Ei; Genuine Article; KR SourceOne; Linda Hall; SWETS; UMI; UnCover. CCC.
Description: Provides information about all phases of computer security.
Refereed Serial

658.478 US
HV8290
COMPUTING & COMMUNICATIONS: LAW & PROTECTION REPORT. 1975. m. $84 (Canada & Mexico $96; elsewhere $116) (effective 1996 & 1997). Assets Protection Publishing, Box 5323, Madison, WI 53705-0323. TEL 608-231-6730. Ed. Paul Shaw. R&P contact: Paul Shaw. bk.rev.; tr.lit. circ. 2,000. (also avail. in microfilm from UMI; microfiche from UMI; back issues avail.) Indexed: CJPI. **Document type:** newsletter.
—UMI.
Former titles: Computing and Communications Protection; Data Processing and Communications Security (ISSN 0749-1484)
Description: Devoted to the legal liability risks of inadequate or absent computer and telecommunications security, and civil and criminal laws affecting breaches of computer security.

CRYPTOLOGIA; a quarterly journal devoted to all aspects of cryptology. see *MATHEMATICS*

658.478 US ISSN 1065-9986
DATA SECURITY LETTER. 1988. 11/yr. $89 to individuals (foreign $114); institutions $345 (foreign $370). Trusted Information Systems, Inc., 3060 Rte. 97, Glenwood, MD 21738. TEL 301-854-6889. FAX 301-854-5363. E-mail: dsl@tis.com; URL: http://www.tis.com/. Ed. Sharon Osuna. bk.rev.; bibl.; index; circ. 350 (paid). (back issues avail.) **Document type:** newsletter, academic/scholarly publication.
Description: Focuses on information systems security, with emphasis on trends, research and development, and new technologies.
Refereed Serial

001.6 658.478 NE
DATA SECURITY MANUAL; guidelines and procedures for data protection. 1985. every 6 wks. fl.1213. Kluwer Academic Publishers, Postbus 17, 3300 AA Dordrecht, Netherlands. TEL 31-78-6392392. FAX 31-78-6392254. TELEX 29245 KAPG. E-mail: services@wkap.nl; URL: http://www.wkap.nl. (Dist. by: Kluwer Academic Publishers Group, P.O. Box 322, 3300 AH Dordrecht, Netherlands. TEL 31-78-6392392. FAX 31-78-6546474; N. America dist. addr.: Box 358, Accord Sta., Hingham, MA 02018-0358. TEL 617-871-6600)

658.478 US
DATAPRO REPORTS ON INFORMATION SECURITY INTERNATIONAL. 3 base vols. (plus m. updates). $1479 to new subscr.; renewals $1356 (effective 1996). Datapro Information Services Group (Subsidiary of: McGraw-Hill, Inc.), 600 Delran Pkwy., Delran, NJ 08075. TEL 609-328-2776; 800-328-2776. FAX 609-764-8953.

658.478 GW ISSN 0170-7256
DATENSCHUTZ-BERATER. 1978. m. DM.306. Handelsblatt GmbH, Kasernenstr. 67, 40213 Duesseldorf, Germany. TEL 49-2234-65240. FAX 49-2234-65531. (Subscr. to: Postfach 102717, 40018 Duesseldorf, Germany) Ed. Hans Gliss. circ. 3,500. **Document type:** trade publication.
—CCC.

005.8 GW ISSN 0173-7767
DATENSCHUTZ NACHRICHTEN. 1978. 6/yr. DM.50 (Europe DM.65; rest of world DM.95). Deutsche Vereinigung fuer Datenschutz, Reuterstr. 44, 53113 Bonn, Germany. TEL 49-228-222498. E-mail: dana@bg.bib.de. Ed. Heinz Alenfelder. adv.: page DM.1000. bk.rev.; index; circ. 500. (back issues avail.) **Document type:** bulletin.

658.478 GW
DATENSCHUTZ UND DATENSICHERUNG; Recht und Sicherheit der Informations und Kommunikationssysteme. Short title: D u D. 1978. m. DM.392 (effective 1997). Friedr. Vieweg und Sohn Verlagsgesellschaft mbH, Postfach 1546, 65005 Wiesbaden, Germany. TEL 49-611-7878151. FAX 49-611-7878423. Ed.Bd. Indexed: ELLIS, IBR. **Document type:** academic/scholarly publication.
—SWETS.
Former titles: Datenschutz und Datensicherung - Informationsrecht - Kommunikationssysteme; Datenschutz und Datensicherung Zugleich der Datenschutzbeauftragte (ISSN 0724-4371)

005.8 AU ISSN 1014-9333
DATENSCHUTZ UND INFORMATIONSRECHT. 1988. q. S.300. Oesterreichische Gesellschaft fuer Datenschutz, Sautergasse 20, A-1170 Vienna, Austria. TEL 43-1-4897893. FAX 43-1-4897891310. E-mail: info@adis.at; URL: http://www.adis.at/. Ed. Hans Zeger. bk.rev.; circ. 800. (back issues avail.) **Document type:** academic/scholarly publication.
●Also available online.

DIRECTORY OF CRIMINAL JUSTICE INFORMATION SOURCES. see *CRIMINOLOGY AND LAW ENFORCEMENT*

COMPUTERS — COMPUTER SECURITY

658.478 US ISSN 0736-6981
CODEN: EDPCDF
E D P A C S; the E D P audit, control and security newsletter. 1973. m. $166.25 (overseas $231.65) (effective 1995). (E D P Auditors Association) Auerbach Publishers (Subsidiary of: Warren, Gorham & Lamont), One Penn Plaza, New York, NY 10119. TEL 212-971-5000. FAX 212-971-5240. (Subscr. to: The Park Square Bldg., 31 St. James Ave., Boston, MA 02116-4112. TEL 800-950-1207) bk.rev.; index. circ. 5,000. (back issues avail.) **Indexed:** Comput.Cont., Comput.Lit.Ind., Data Process.Dig., INSPEC. **Document type:** newsletter.
—BLDSC (3661.115000); AskIEEE; KR SourceOne; UMI. **CCC.**
Description: Enables electronic data processing professionals to keep abreast of important topics and developments in computer audit, security, and control.

658.478 US ISSN 0278-7032
QA76.9.A25
I E E E SYMPOSIUM ON RESEARCH IN SECURITY AND PRIVACY. PROCEEDINGS. 1980. a. (Institute of Electrical and Electronics Engineers, Inc.) I E E E Computer Society Press, 10662 Los Vaqueros Circle, Los Alamitos, CA 90720-1264. TEL 714-821-8380. FAX 714-821-4641. Ed. Cat Harris; Pub. Matt Loeb. adv. contact: Frieda Koester. **Document type:** proceedings.
—UMI.
Former titles: I E E E Symposium on Security and Privacy. Proceedings.; (until 1985): Symposium on Security and Privacy. Proceedings.
Description: Covers advances in design, implementation, and application of secure computer systems.

I S AUDIT & CONTROL JOURNAL. (Information Systems) see COMPUTERS — Electronic Data Processing

658.478 US
I S S A JOURNAL.* q. membership. Information Systems Security Association, 1926 Waukegan Rd., Ste. 1, Glenview, IL 60025-1770. TEL 847-699-6441. FAX 847-699-6369. adv.; circ. controlled.
Formerly (until 1993): I S S A Access.

005.8 UK ISSN 1363-4127
QA76.9.A25
▼**INFORMATION SECURITY TECHNICAL REPORT.** 1996. q. fl.1308($752) (effective 1998). Elsevier Science Ltd., P.O. Box 800, Kidlington, Oxford OX5 1DX, England. TEL 44-1865-843000. FAX 44-1865-843000. E-mail: nlino-f@elsevier.nl; usinfo-f@elsevier.com; URL: http://www.elsevier.nl/. (Subscr. to: Elsevier Science, Regional Sales Office, P.O. Box 211, 1000 AE Amsterdam, Netherlands. TEL 31-20-4853757. FAX 31-20-4853432; Subscr. in the Americas to: Elsevier Science, Regional Sales Office, Box 945, New York, NY 10159-0945. TEL 212-633-3730. FAX 212-633-3680; Subscr. in Australasia and the Far East to: Elsevier Science (Singapore) Pte Ltd, No.1 Temasek Ave., No.17-01 Millenia Tower, Singapore 039192, Singapore. TEL 65-434-3727. FAX 65-337-2230) **Document type:** academic/scholarly publication, trade publication.
—BLDSC (4494.317500). **CCC.**

658.478 US ISSN 1065-898X
QA76.9.A25 CODEN: ISSEFH
INFORMATION SYSTEMS SECURITY. 1991. q. $155.50 (overseas $237.65) (effective 1995). Warren, Gorham & Lamont, One Penn Plaza, New York, NY 10119. TEL 212-971-5000. FAX 212-971-5113. (Subscr. to: The Park Sq. Bldg., 31 St. James Ave., Boston, MA 02116-4112. TEL 800-950-1207) **Document type:** trade publication.
—BLDSC (4496.368602); AskIEEE; KR SourceOne.
Formerly (until 1991): Journal of Information Systems Security.

658.478 NE ISSN 0926-227X
JOURNAL OF COMPUTER SECURITY. 1992. q. fl.400($229) (effective 1997). I O S Press, Van Diemenstraat 94, 1013 CN Amsterdam, Netherlands. TEL 31-20-6382189. FAX 31-20-6203419. E-mail: market@iospress.nl; URL: http://www.iospress.nl/iospress. (In N. America: Box 10558, Burke, VA 22009-0558. TEL 703-323-5554. FAX 703-250-4705) Eds. Sushil Jajodia, Jonathan Millen. **Document type:** academic/scholarly publication.
—BLDSC (4963.746000); AskIEEE; CISTI; KR SourceOne. **CCC.**
Description: Publishes advances in theory, architecture, design, implementation, analysis and application of secure computer and communication systems.

004.6 NE ISSN 0963-8687
HD30.213 CODEN: JSIYE3
JOURNAL OF STRATEGIC INFORMATION SYSTEMS. (Text in English) 1978. q. fl.524($301) (effective 1998). Elsevier Science B.V., P.O. Box 211, 1000 AE Amsterdam, Netherlands. TEL 31-20-4853911. FAX 31-20-4853598. (Subscr. in the Americas to: Elsevier Science, Regional Sales Office, Box 945, New York, NY 10159-0945. TEL 212-633-3730. FAX 212-633-3680; Subscr. in Australasia and the Far East to: Elsevier Science (Singapore) Pte Ltd, No. 1 Temasek Ave., No.17-01 Millenia Tower, Singapore 039192, Singapore. TEL 65-434-3727. FAX 65-337-2230; Subscr. in Japan to: Elsevier Science Japan, 9-15 Higashi-Azabu 1-chome, Minato-ku, Tokyo 106, Japan. TEL 81-3-5561-5033. FAX 81-3-5561-5047) Ed. Bob Galliers. adv.; bk.rev.; index. (also avail. in microform from UMI; back issues avail.) **Indexed:** ABI Inform., Abstr.Hum.Comp.Inter., Account.& Data Proc.Abstr., ASCA, BPIA, Commun.Abstr., Compumath, Comput.Abstr., Comput.Lit.Ind., Curr.Cont., INSPEC, Intl.Civil Eng.Abstr., Soft.Abstr.Eng., SSCI, Tel.Abstr. **Document type:** academic/scholarly publication.
—BLDSC (5066.872880); AskIEEE; CISTI; Ei; Genuine Article; KR SourceOne; SWETS; UMI. **CCC.**
Incorporates: International Information Systems; **Former titles** (until 1992): Journal of Strategic I T; (until 1990): Information Age (ISSN 0261-4103); (until Jan. 1982): Information Privacy (ISSN 0141-3406)
Description: Integrates academic findings and research with the practical needs of professionals attempting to create functional information systems.
Refereed Serial

621.38 384 GW ISSN 0177-4565
CODEN: KZKEED
K E S. (Kommunikations- und EDV Sicherheit) 1985. bi-m. DM.228 (foreign DM.260) (effective 1996). SecuMedia Verlags GmbH, Gaulsheimerstr. 17, 55218 Ingelheim-Sporkenheim, Germany. TEL 49-6725-9304-0. FAX 49-6725-5994. Ed. Peter Hohl. adv.; bk.rev.; bibl.; charts; illus.; stat.; index. circ. 4,200. (back issues avail.) **Document type:** trade publication.
—AskIEEE; CISTI; KR SourceOne; SWETS. **CCC.**
Description: Covers issues relating to communications and electronic data security.

005.8 340 GW ISSN 0947-9198
MARLY - RECHTSPRECHUNG ZUM COMPUTERRECHT. CD-ROM edition (GW ISSN 0947-9201) s-a. DM.468 (CD-ROM DM.698) (effective 1997). Verlag C.H. Beck, 80791 Munich, Germany. TEL 49-89-38189338. FAX 49-89-38189398. Ed. Jochen Marly. **Document type:** academic/scholarly publication.
●Available only on CD-ROM.

658.478 001.642 US ISSN 1068-3984
NATIONAL COMPUTER SECURITY ASSOCIATION. NEWSLETTER.* 6/yr. $25 to non-members. National Computer Security Association, 1200 Walnut Bottom Rd., No. 3, Carlisle, PA 17013-7635. TEL 717-258-1816. FAX 717-243-8642. **Document type:** newsletter.
Description: Covers computer security topics, including computer viruses.

PRIVACY JOURNAL; an independent monthly on privacy in a computer age. see POLITICAL SCIENCE — Civil Rights

658.478 340 GW ISSN 0178-8930
KK6071.5.A13
RECHT DER DATENVERARBEITUNG; Zeitschrift fuer Praxis und Wissenschaft. Short title: R D V. 1985. 5/yr. DM.198. (Gesellschaft fuer Datenschutz und Datensicherung e.V.) Datakontext Fachverlag GmbH, Augustinusstr. 9d, 50226 Frechen-Koenigsdorf, Germany. TEL 49-2234-96610-0. FAX 49-2234-966109. Ed. Georg Wronka. adv.: B&W page DM.1800, color page DM.3390; trim 255 x 186; adv. contact: Anja Loesener von Tempsky. index. circ. 4,000. **Document type:** trade publication.
—SWETS.

658.478 365.64 US
S I G S A C REVIEW. 1981. q. Association for Computing Machinery, Special Interest Group for Security Audit Control, 1515 Broadway, 17th Fl., New York, NY 10036. TEL 212-869-7440. FAX 212-869-0489. TELEX 421686. **Indexed:** INSPEC (1989-).

658.478 340 GW
▼**S PLUS - SICHERHEIT.** 1995. bi-m. DM.89 (effective 1996). Datakontext Fachverlag GmbH, Augustinusstr. 9d, 50226 Frechen-Koenigsdorf, Germany. TEL 49-2234-691961. FAX 49-2234-65531. Eds. Ralf Herweg, Thomas Muethlein. adv.: page DM.2500; trim 185 x 270; adv. contact: Anja Loesener von Tempsky. **Document type:** trade publication.
Formerly: R D V Praxis-Report.

SECOM ANNUAL REPORT (YEAR). see CRIMINOLOGY AND LAW ENFORCEMENT — Security

005.8 UK ISSN 1352-4097
SECURE COMPUTING; the international journal of computer security. 1994. m. £95 (foreign £225). West Coast Publishing Ltd., William Knox House, Britannic Way, Llandarcy, Swansea SA10 6EL, Wales. TEL 44-1792-324000. FAX 44-1792-324001. E-mail: 70007,5406@ compuserve.com. Ed. Paul Robinson. R&P contact: Paul Robinson. adv. contact: Kerry Hart. bk.rev.; circ 5,000. (paid). (back issues avail.) **Document type:** trade publication.
—BLDSC (8216.987500); AskIEEE; KR SourceOne.
Description: Deals with all aspects of computer security, including computer crime, hacking, fraud, viruses and software piracy.
Refereed Serial

SECURITE INFORMATIQUE. see BUSINESS AND ECONOMICS — Banking And Finance

SECURITY; the magazine for buyers of security products, systems and service. see CRIMINOLOGY AND LAW ENFORCEMENT — Security

658.4 GW
SICHERHEIT IN DER INFORMATIONS- UND KOMMUNIKATIONSTECHNIK. 1992. irreg., vol.4, 1994. DM.48. Spektrum Akademischer Verlag GmbH, Vangerowstr. 20, 69115 Heidelberg, Germany. TEL 49-6221-9126-0. FAX 49-6221-912638. E-mail: kaschura@ spektrum-verlag.com; URL: http://www.spektrum-verlag.com. Ed. Patrick Horster. **Indexed:** Zent.Math. **Document type:** monographic series.

SURVEILLANT; acquisitions and commentary for intelligence and security professionals. see POLITICAL SCIENCE — International Relations

TELECOM & NETWORK SECURITY REVIEW. see COMMUNICATIONS

COMPUTERS — COMPUTER SIMULATION

005.8   UK   ISSN 0956-9979
QA76.76.C68   CODEN: VBULE3
VIRUS BULLETIN; the international publication on computer virus prevention, recognition and removal. 1989. m. £195 (Europe £225; U.S. £185($295); elsewhere £245) (effective 1997). The Pentagon, Abingdon Science Park, Abingdon, Oxon OX14 3YP, England. TEL 44-1235-555139.
FAX 44-1235-531889. E-mail: alexandra@virusbtn.com; URL: http://www.virusbtn.com/. (Dist. in the U.S. by: Virus Bulletin, 590 Danbury Rd., Ridgefield, CT 06877. TEL 203-431-8720. FAX 203-431-8165) Ed. Ian Whalley. R&P contact: Alexandra Hothersall. adv. contact: Alexandra Hothersall. software rev. (back issues avail.) **Document type:** bulletin.
—BLDSC (9240.850300); AskIEEE; KR SourceOne; SWETS. **CCC.**
   Description: Dedicated to reporting and analyzing malicious computer programs.

005.8 005.3   AT
VIRUS WATCH. 1989. q. Aus.$14($10) (effective June 1995). Leprechaun Software Pty. Ltd., P.O. Box 826, Capalaba, Qld. 4157, Australia.
TEL 61-7-38231300. FAX 61-7-38231233. E-mail: intl@leprechaun.com.au; URL: http://www.leprechaun.com.au/ circ. 9,500. (also avail. in diskette format; back issues avail.) **Document type:** newsletter.
   Description: Provides product details, technical tips, and virus information.

COMPUTERS — Computer Simulation

003   US
A B S E L NEWS & VIEWS. s-a. Association for Business Simulation and Experiential Learning, University of Utah, Dept. of Management, Salt Lake City, UT 84112. Ed. Susan Chesteen. adv. contact: Susan A. Chesteen.
   Description: Published as a service to ABSEL members and others interested in simulation and experiential learning.

621.319   US
ADVANCES IN SIMULATION. vol.4, 1990. irreg. price varies. Springer-Verlag, 175 Fifth Ave., New York, NY 10010. TEL 212-460-1500.
FAX 212-473-6272. (N. American subscr. to: Journal Fulfillment Services, Box 2485, Secaucus, NJ 07096-2491. TEL 800-777-4643. FAX 201-348-4505; Subscr. outside N. America to: Heidelberger Platz 3, 1000 Berlin 33, Germany. TEL 030-8207-1. FAX 030-348-4505) Eds. P. Fishwick, R. Modjeski. (also avail. in microform from UMI) **Indexed:** Zent.Math. **Document type:** monographic series.

621.319   US
ANNUAL SIMULATION SYMPOSIUM. PROCEEDINGS. 1967. a. $80 to non-members; members $40. Society for Computer Simulation, Box 17900, San Diego, CA 92177. TEL 619-277-3888.
FAX 619-277-3930. Ed. Hildy Linn. (back issues avail.) **Document type:** proceedings.
   Description: Includes papers dealing with various techniques and applications of computer simulation.
Refereed Serial

AUDIOTEX UPDATE. see *COMMUNICATIONS — Computer Applications*

006 003   FR
CLONE. (Print edition ceased 1995) 1994. q. Alpha du Centaure, E-mail: clone@imaginet.fr.
●Available only online.
   Description: Covers virtual reality and cyberculture.

621.39   DK   ISSN 0106-357X
COMBINED SIMULATION. 1978. irreg. Koskilde Universitetscenter, Datalogi, 4000 Roskilde, Denmark.

COMMUNICATIONS IN STATISTICS. PART B: SIMULATION AND COMPUTATION. see *STATISTICS*

COMPLEXITY (NEW YORK). see *MATHEMATICS*

COMPUTATIONAL INTELLIGENCE/INTELLIGENCE INFORMATIQUE. see *COMPUTERS*

003   US   ISSN 1061-3099
CYBEREDGE JOURNAL. 1991. bi-m. $129 to individuals (foreign $149); institutions $249 (foreign $269) (effective 1997). CyberEdge Information Services, Inc., No. 1 Gate Six Rd., Ste. G, Sausalito, CA 94965-3100. TEL 415-331-3343.
FAX 415-331-3643. E-mail: info@cyberedge.com; URL: http://www.cyberedge.com. Ed. Ben Delaney. adv.; bk.rev.; index; circ. 1,000 (paid). (back issues avail.) **Document type:** newsletter.
—BLDSC (3506.343000); KR SourceOne; SWETS. **CCC.**
   Description: Covers virtual reality new product information, calendar of VR events and business updates.

003   US   ISSN 0278-2375
DEVELOPMENTS IN BUSINESS SIMULATION & EXPERIENTIAL EXERCISES. Represents: A B S E L Conference Proceedings. 1974. a. $15. (Association for Business Simulation and Experiential Learning) Oklahoma State University, Stillwater, College of Business Administration, Stillwater, OK 74078.
TEL 405-744-8647. FAX 405-744-5180. (Subscr. to: ABSEL, c/o Robert A. Wells, LB8152, Georgia Southern University, Statesboro, GA 30460-8152. TEL 916-681-5216) Eds. Precha Thavikulwat, John D. Overby. circ. 300 (paid). (back issues avail.) **Document type:** proceedings.
Refereed Serial

621.319   US
DIRECTORY OF SIMULATION SOFTWARE. 1993. a. $40 to non-members; members $20. Society for Computer Simulation, Box 17900, San Diego, CA 92177. TEL 619-277-3888. FAX 619-277-3930. Ed. Hildy Linn. R&P contact: William Gallagher. **Document type:** directory.
   Description: Provides a comprehensive listing of simulation-oriented software, with contact names, platforms, and prices.

621.381   US   ISSN 0924-6703
   CODEN: DEDAEE
DISCRETE EVENT DYNAMIC SYSTEMS: THEORY AND APPLICATIONS. 1991. q. fl.700 to institutions; $359 to institutions in U.S. (effective 1998). Kluwer Academic Publishers Boston, Box 358, Accord Sta., Hingham, MA 02018-0358. TEL 617-871-6600.
FAX 617-871-6528. TELEX 200190. E-mail: services@wkap.nl; URL: http://www.wkap.nl. (Dist. outside N. America by: Kluwer Academic Publishers Group, P.O. Box 322, 3300 AH Dordrecht, Netherlands. TEL 31-78-6392392. FAX 31-78-6546474) Ed. Yu-Chi Ho. (also avail. in microform from UMI; back issues avail.; reprint service avail. from SWZ) **Indexed:** ASCA, Curr.Cont., Eng.Ind., INSPEC (1991-), Zent.Math. **Document type:** academic/scholarly publication.
—BLDSC (3597.028000); AskIEEE; CISTI; Ei; Genuine Article; KR SourceOne; SWETS; UMI. **CCC.**
   Description: Publishes papers on the modeling and control of discrete event dynamic systems (DEDS), including engineering and mathematical models of manufacturing plants, communication and computer networks, management information databases, command-control-communication systems, and other man-made operational systems.
Refereed Serial

621.319   US
DISTRIBUTED SIMULATION. PROCEEDINGS. irreg., latest 1990. price varies. Society for Computer Simulation, Box 17900, San Diego, CA 92177.
TEL 619-277-3888. FAX 619-277-3930. Ed. Hildy Linn. (back issues avail.) **Document type:** proceedings.
   Description: Covers the latest developments in distributed simulation technologies.

621.3   KR   ISSN 0204-3572
QA75.5   CODEN: ELMODO
ELEKTRONNOE MODELIROVANIE: mezhdunarodni naucho-teoreticheskii zhurnal. English translation: Engineering Simulation (US ISSN 1063-1100) (Text in Russian; summaries in English, Russian, Ukrainian) 1979. bi-m. $240 (effective 1998). Akademiya Nauk Ukrainy, Institut Problem Modelyuvannya v Energetytsi, Ul. Generala Naumova, 15, 252680 Kiev, Ukraine.
TEL 38-44-4441466. FAX 38-44-4440586. E-mail: user@btk.kiev.ua. (Dist. by: Mezhdunarodnaya Kniga, B. Yakimanka 39, 117049 Moscow, Russia. TEL 7-95-2384600. FAX 7-95-2302117) Ed. G.E. Pukhov; Pub. V.F. Evdokimov. R&P contact: V.F. Evdokimov. adv. contact: V.V. Mokhor. bk.rev. circ. 300. **Indexed:** Cyb.Abstr., Djerelo, INSPEC. **Document type:** academic/scholarly publication.
—BLDSC (0398.975000); AskIEEE; CASDDS; CISTI; KR SourceOne; Linda Hall. **CCC.**
   Formerly: Matematicheskoe Modelirovanie i Teoriya Elektricheskikh Tsepei.
   Description: Informs about the newest achievements in theoretical and applied computer simulation.
Refereed Serial

621.319   NE   ISSN 0929-2268
EUROSIM - SIMULATION NEWS EUROPE; a European forum on simulation activities. Issued with: Simulation Practice and Theory (ISSN 0928-4869) 1990. 3/yr. membership. (Technical University of Vienna, Computer Center) Elsevier Science B.V., P.O. Box 211, 1000 AE Amsterdam, Netherlands. TEL 31-20-4853911. FAX 31-20-4853598. TELEX 18582 ESPA NL. E-mail: nlinfo-f@elsevier.nl; usinfo-f@elsevier.com; forinfo-kyf04035@niftyserve.or.jp; URL: http://www.elsevier.nl/. (Subscr. in the Americas to: Elsevier Science, Regional Sales Office, Box 945, New York, NY 10159-0945. TEL 212-633-3730. FAX 212-633-3680; Subscr. in Australasia and the Far East to: Elsevier Science (Singapore) Pte Ltd, No.1 Temasek Ave., No.17-01 Millenia Tower, Singapore 039192, Singapore. TEL 65-434-3727. FAX 65-337-2230; Subscr. in Japan to: Elsevier Science Japan, 9-15 Higashi-Azabu 1-chome, Minato-ku, Tokyo 106, Japan. TEL 81-3-5561-5033. FAX 81-3-5561-5047) Eds. F. Breitenecker, I. Husinsky. bk.rev.; software rev. circ. 2,500. **Document type:** newsletter.
—BLDSC (3830.428700).
   Description: Disseminates information on simulation to members of European simulation societies, interested research and development institutions, companies, and libraries.

001.6 621.381   US   ISSN 0177-6843
FACHBERICHTE SIMULATION. 1984. irreg. price varies. Springer-Verlag, 175 Fifth Ave., New York, NY 10010. TEL 212-460-1500. FAX 212-473-6272. (Also: Berlin, Heidelberg, Tokyo, Vienna) (reprint service avail. from ISI) **Indexed:** Zent.Math. **Document type:** academic/scholarly publication.

621.319   US
FAULKNER'S IMAGING SYSTEMS. 1992. base vol. (plus q. update). $615 (effective 1993). Faulkner Information Services, Inc., 114 Cooper Center, 7905 Browning Rd., Pennsauken, NJ 08109.
TEL 609-662-2070. FAX 609-662-3380. Ed. Janet Mann. (looseleaf format)
   Formerly: Image Systems.
   Description: Products and management guide for imaging systems technology. Includes advice for companies beginning to consider image technology, and coverage of all related hardware and software components and complete solutions.

003   UK   ISSN 0964-5640
FRACTAL REPORT. q. £20. Reeves Telecommunications Laboratories, West Towan House, Porthtowan, Truro, Cornwall TR4 8AX, England. E-mail: john@longevb.demon.co.uk; URL: http://ourworld.compuserve.com/homepages/johnder. Ed. John de Rivaz. **Document type:** academic/scholarly publication.
   Description: Provides a forum for the publication of computer programs for generating fractals and similar iterations in one or more dimensions.

COMPUTERS — COMPUTER SIMULATION

621.319   US
INTERNATIONAL EMERGENCY MANAGEMENT AND ENGINEERING CONFERENCE. PROCEEDINGS. 1983. irreg., vol. 10, 1993. $80 to non-members; members $40. Society for Computer Simulation, Box 17900, San Diego, CA 92177. TEL 619-277-3888. FAX 609-277-3930. Ed. James D. Sullivan. R&P contact: William Gallagher. adv. contact: Steven Branch. (back issues avail.) **Document type:** proceedings.
   Description: Covers papers on automation in emergency management and engineering.
   Refereed Serial

621.319 620
621.48   US
INTERNATIONAL SIMULATORS CONFERENCE. PROCEEDINGS. 1984. a. price varies. Society for Computer Simulation, Box 17900, San Diego, CA 92177. TEL 619-277-3888. FAX 619-277-3930. Ed. Ariel Sharon. R&P contact: William Gallagher. adv. contact: Steven Branch. (back issues avail.) **Document type:** proceedings.
   Description: Includes papers on simulation technology and methods in training, especially in the nuclear power industry.

621.319 500   JA   ISSN 0285-9947
JAPAN SOCIETY FOR SIMULATION TECHNOLOGY. JOURNAL. (Text in Japanese) 1982. 4/yr. 7400 Yen. (Japan Society for Simulation Technology) Japan Technical Information Service, Sogo Kojimachi No. 3 Bldg., 6th Fl., 1-6 Koji-machi, Chiyoda-ku, Tokyo 102, Japan. TEL 81-3-3239-4711. FAX 81-3-3239-4714. Ed. Shuich Iwata; Pub. Yoichi Yazaki. adv. contact: Michio Nakana. circ. 1,800. (back issues avail.) **Indexed:** INPSEC (1983-). **Document type:** academic/scholarly publication.
   ●Also available online. Vendor(s): JICST (JOIS).
   —BLDSC (4808.143000); AskIEEE; KR SourceOne; Linda Hall. **CCC.**
   Description: Research papers on the use of simulation methods in physical science and engineering.

621.319   US   ISSN 1040-7286
QH205.2   CODEN: JCMIEX
JOURNAL OF COMPUTER-ASSISTED MICROSCOPY. 1989. q. $325 (foreign $380) (effective 1998). Plenum Publishing Corp., 233 Spring St., New York, NY 10013-1578. TEL 212-620-8000. FAX 212-463-0742. TELEX 23-421139. Ed. Stanley M. Dunn. adv. (also avail. in microfilm from UMI) **Indexed:** Alloys Ind., Eng.Mat.Abstr., INSPEC (1989-), Met.Abstr., Met.Abstr.Ind., Nonfer.Met.Alert, PCC Alert, Steels Alert, World Alum.Abstr. **Document type:** academic/scholarly publication.
   —BLDSC (4963.645000); AskIEEE; CISTI; Ei; KNAW; KR SourceOne; Linda Hall; SWETS; UMI; UnCover. **CCC.**
   Description: Deals with various aspects of the application of computer methods to acquire, process, and measure images. Covers biology, microscopy, computer science, and geology.
   Refereed Serial

JOURNAL OF MATERIALS PROCESSING TECHNOLOGY. see *ENGINEERING — Mechanical Engineering*

519.5 028   NE   ISSN 0094-9655
QA276.A1   CODEN: JSCSAJ
JOURNAL OF STATISTICAL COMPUTATION AND SIMULATION. 1972. 16/yr. (in 4 vols., 4 nos./vol.). $381 (effective 1998). Gordon and Breach - Harwood Academic, Amsteldisk 166, 1st Fl., 1079 LH Amsterdam, Netherlands. URL: http://www.gbhap.com/Statistical__Computation__Simulation/. (Subscr. to: International Publishers Distributor, Box 32160, Newark, NJ 07102. TEL 800-545-8398. FAX 215-750-6343) Ed. Richard G. Krutchkoff. adv.; illus. (also avail. in microform) **Indexed:** ASCA, Compumath, Curr.Cont. (1973-), Curr.Ind.Stat., INSPEC, J.Cont.Quant.Meth., Math.R., Stat.Theor.Meth.Abstr. (1973-), Zent.Math.
   ●Also available online.
   Also available on CD-ROM.
   —BLDSC (5066.820000); CISTI; Ei; Linda Hall; SWETS; UnCover. **CCC.**
   Description: Contains papers on computer algorithms related to probability or statistics, studies in statistical inference and implementation of interactive statistical systems.
   Refereed Serial

003 621.39   NE   ISSN 0378-4754
QA76.4   CODEN: MCSIDR
MATHEMATICS AND COMPUTERS IN SIMULATION. (Text and summaries in English and French) 1959. 18/yr. fl.2404($1382) (effective 1998). (International Association for Mathematics and Computers in Simulation) North-Holland (Subsidiary of: Elsevier Science B.V.), P.O. Box 211, 1000 AE Amsterdam, Netherlands. TEL 31-20-4853911. FAX 31-20-4853598. TELEX 18582 ESPA NL. (Subscr. in the Americas to: Elsevier Science, Regional Sales Office, Box 945, New York, NY 10159-0945. TEL 212-633-3730. FAX 212-633-3680; Subscr. in Australasia and the Far East to: Elsevier Science (Singapore) Pte Ltd, No.1 Temasek Ave., No.17-01 Millenia Tower, Singapore 039192, Singapore. TEL 65-434-3727. FAX 65-337-2230; Subscr. in Japan to: Elsevier Science Japan, 9-15 Higashi-Azabu 1-chome, Minato-ku, Tokyo 106, Japan. TEL 81-3-5561-5033. FAX 81-3-5561-5047) Ed. R. Vichnevetsky. adv.; bk.rev.; charts; illus.; index every 2 yrs. circ. 1,000. (also avail. in microform from UMI; back issues avail.; reprint service avail. from SWZ) **Indexed:** Appl.Mech.Rev., ASCA, Biostat., Chem.Abstr., Compumath, Comput.Abstr., Comput.Cont., Curr.Cont. (1991)-, Cyb.Abstr., INSPEC (1968-), Int.Abstr.Oper.Res., Math.R., Oper.Res.Manage.Sci., Qual.Contr.Appl.Stat., SSCI, Stat.Theor.Meth.Abstr. (1991-), Zent.Math. **Document type:** academic/scholarly publication, proceedings.
   —BLDSC (5405.180000); AskIEEE; CISTI; Ei; Genuine Article; KR SourceOne; Linda Hall; SWETS; UnCover. **CCC.**
   Incorporates (in 1988): I M A C S News; Which was formerly: A I C A News; International Association for Mathematics and Computers in Simulation. Transactions (ISSN 0377-9114); (until 1975): International Association for Analog Computation. Proceedings (ISSN 0020-594X)
   Description: Provides an international forum for the dissemination of up-to-date information in the field of the computer simulation of systems.
   Refereed Serial

621.319   US   ISSN 0198-0092
TA343   CODEN: MSPCD4
MODELING AND SIMULATION. 1969. a. price varies. University of Pittsburgh, c/o Dr. Marlin Mickle, 348 Benedum Engineering Hall, Pittsburgh, PA 15261. (reprint service avail. from UMI, ISI and publisher)
   —CASDDS. **CCC.**

621.319   US   ISSN 0735-6773
QA76.9.C65
MODELING AND SIMULATION ON MICROCOMPUTERS. 1982. a. $150. Society for Computer Simulation, Box 17900, San Diego, CA 92177. TEL 619-277-3888. FAX 619-277-3930. Ed. Hildy Linn. circ. 500. (back issues avail.) **Document type:** proceedings.
   —CCC.

621.319   US
PARALLEL AND DISTRIBUTED SIMULATION WORKSHOP. PROCEEDINGS. 1987. a. price varies. Society for Computer Simulation, Box 17900, San Diego, CA 92177. TEL 619-277-3888. FAX 619-277-3930. Ed. Hildy Linn. (back issues avail.) **Document type:** proceedings.
   Description: Presents state-of-the-art papers on parallel simulation technologies used to improve execution of discreet-event simulation models.
   Refereed Serial

PATTERN RECOGNITION AND IMAGE PROCESSING SERIES. see *PHYSICS — Optics*

621.319   NE   ISSN 0928-2149
PROCESS SIMULATION & MODELING. (Text in English) 1992. irreg. price varies. Elsevier Science B.V., Books Division, P.O. Box 211, 1000 AE Amsterdam, Netherlands. TEL 31-20-4853911. FAX 31-20-4853705. TELEX 18582 ESPA NL. E-mail: nlinfo-f@elsevier.nl; usinfo-f@elsevier.com; forinfo-kyf04035@niftyserve.or.jp; URL: http://www.elsevier.nl/. (Subscr. in the Americas to: Elsevier Science, Regional Sales Office, Box 945, New York, NY 10159-0945. TEL 212-633-3730. FAX 212-633-3680; Subscr. in Australasia and the Far East to: Elsevier Science (Singapore) Pte Ltd, No.1 Temasek Ave., No.17-01 Millenia Tower, Singapore 039192, Singapore. TEL 65-434-3727. FAX 65-337-2230; Subscr. in U.S. and Canada to: Elsevier Science, Inc., Box 882, Madison Sq. Sta., New York, NY 10159. TEL 81-3-5561-5033. FAX 81-3-5561-5047) **Document type:** monographic series.
   —BLDSC (6849.990580).
   Refereed Serial

621.319   US
PROGRESS IN SIMULATION. 1992. a., vol.3, 1996. price varies. Ablex Publishing Corporation, Box 5297, Greenwich, CT 06831-0504. TEL 203-661-7602. FAX 203-661-0792. Eds. James V. Leonard, George W. Zorbist. **Indexed:** INSPEC. **Document type:** academic/scholarly publication.

SEIKEN N S T SHINPOJUMU KOEN KOGAISHU. see *COMPUTERS — Abstracting, Bibliographies, Statistics*

621.319   JA
SEIKEN N S T SHINPOJUMU KOEN RONBUNSHU. (Numerical Simulation Turbulence) (Text in Japanese) 1986. a. Tokyo Daigaku, Seisan Gijutsu Kenkyujo, N S T Kenkyu Gurupu - University of Tokyo, Institute of Industrial Science, Numerical Simulation Turbulence Research Group, 22-1, Roppongi 7-chome, Minato-ku, Tokyo 106, Japan.
   Description: Contains proceedings of the group's symposium.

621.39   US
SHORT CIRCUIT; the newsletter of empowered engineers. 1992. q. $25 (effective 1994). F E S Ltd., Box 158, Stuart, FL 34995. TEL 407-229-5654; 800-FES-LTD1. FAX 407-229-5636. E-mail: wilivingston@delphi.com. Ed. Carolyn Crosby; Pub. William Livingston. bk.rev.; illus.; circ. 300 (paid). (back issues avail.) **Document type:** newsletter.
   Description: Covers problem-solving science, technology and sociology.

621.319 006   US   ISSN 0037-5497
TA343   CODEN: SIMUA2
SIMULATION (SAN DIEGO). 1963. m. $149 (effective 1996). Society for Computer Simulation, Box 17900, San Diego, CA 92117-7900. TEL 619-277-3888. FAX 619-277-3930. Ed. Hild Linn. R&P contact: William Gallagher. adv. contact: Steve Branch. bk.rev.; index. cum.index. circ. 4,200. (also avail. in microfiche; reprint service avail. from UMI) **Indexed:** A.I.Abstr., A.S.& T.Ind., Abstr.Hum.Comp.Inter., Appl.Mech.Rev., Biostat., Bk.Rev.Ind. (1984-), BMT, CAD CAM Abstr., Chem.Abstr., Child.Bk.Rev.Ind. (1984-), Compumath, Comput.Cont., Comput.Rev., Curr.Cont., Data Process.Dig., Eng.Ind., Excerp.Med., High.Educ.Curr.Aware.Bull., INSPEC, Int.Abstr.Oper.Res., Int.Aerosp.Abstr., Lang.& Lang.Behav.Abstr., Nucl.Sci.Abstr., Oper.Res.Manage.Sci., Qual.Contr.Appl.Stat., Sci.Cit.Ind., Sociol.Abstr., Tech.Educ.Abstr., Zent.Math. **Document type:** trade publication.
   —BLDSC (8285.150000); AskIEEE; CASDDS; CIST; Ei; Genuine Article; KR SourceOne; Linda Hall; SWETS; UMI; UnCover. **CCC.**
   Formerly: S S S Newsletter (Simulation in the Service of Society) (ISSN 0036-1925)
   Description: Covers a wide variety of topics on the use of computer modeling and simulation.
   Refereed Serial

COMPUTERS — COMPUTER SYSTEMS

003   US   ISSN 1046-8781
H62   CODEN: SIGAEI
SIMULATION & GAMING; an international journal of theory, design and research. 1970. q. $59 to individuals; institutions $200 (effective 1996). (Association for Business Simulation and Experiential Learning) Sage Publications, Inc., 2455 Teller Rd., Thousand Oaks, CA 91320. TEL 805-499-0721. FAX 805-499-0871. E-mail: libraries@sagepub.com; URL: http://www.sagepub.com. (Overseas subscr. to: Sage Publications Ltd., 6 Bonhill St., London EC2A 4PU, England; Or: Sage Publications India Pvt. Ltd., P.O. Box 4215, New Delhi 110 048, India) (Co-sponsors: North American Simulation and Gaming Association; International Simulation and Gaming Association; Japan Asociation of Business and Gaming) Ed. David Crookall. adv. contact: Margaret Travers. bk.rev.; charts; index. circ. 1,600. (also avail. in microform from UMI; back issues avail.; reprint service avail. from UMI) **Indexed:** A.B.C.Pol.Sci., Abstr.Mil.Bibl., Adol.Ment.Hlth.Abstr., ASCA, Bk.Rev.Ind., C.I.J.E., Commun.Abstr., Comput.Cont., Comput.Rev., Curr.Cont., Educ.Admin.Abstr., Educ.Tech.Abstr., INSPEC (1970-), Int.Polit.Sci.Abstr., J.Cont.Quant.Meth., LAMP, Lang.& Lang.Behav.Abstr., M.M.R.I., Media Rev.Dig., Mid.East: Abstr.& Ind., P.A.I.S., PHRA, Psychol.Abstr. (1972-), Soc.Sci.Ind. (until 1994), Sociol.Abstr., SSCI, Tech.Educ.Abstr. **Document type:** academic/scholarly publication.
—BLDSC (8285.161000); AskIEEE; Genuine Article; KR SourceOne; SWETS; UMI; UnCover. **CCC.**
Formerly (until 1990): Simulation and Games (ISSN 0037-5500)
Description: Publishes theoretical and empirical papers related to man, man-machine, and machine simulations of social processes.

621.319   NE   ISSN 0928-4869
SIMULATION PRACTICE AND THEORY. (Text in English) 1993. 8/yr. fl.879($505) (effective 1998). (Federation of European Simulation Societies - EUROSIM) Elsevier Science B.V., P.O. Box 211, 1000 AE Amsterdam, Netherlands. TEL 31-20-4853911. FAX 31-20-4853598. TELEX 18582 ESPA NL. E-mail: nlinfo-f@elsevier.nl; usinfo-f@elsevier.com; forinfo-kyf04035@niftyserve.or.jp; URL: http://www.elsevier.nl/. (Subscr. in the Americas to: Elsevier Science, Regional Sales Office, Box 945, New York, NY 10159-0945. TEL 212-633-3730. FAX 212-633-3680; Subscr. in Australasia and the Far East to: Elsevier Science (Singapore) Pte Ltd, No.1 Temasek Ave., No.17-01 Millenia Tower, Singapore 039192, Singapore. TEL 65-434-3727. FAX 65-337-2230; Subscr. in Japan to: Elsevier Science Japan, 9-15 Higashi-Azabu 1-chome, Minato-ku, Tokyo 106, Japan. TEL 81-3-5561-5033. FAX 81-3-5561-5047) Ed. L. Dekker. software rev. (also avail. in microform from UMI; back issues avail.) **Indexed:** INSPEC (1993-), Zent.Math. **Document type:** academic/scholarly publication.
—BLDSC (8285.164600); AskIEEE; CISTI; Ei; KR SourceOne; SWETS. **CCC.**
Description: Publishes original research and tutorial papers in the field of simulation.
Refereed Serial

651.8 621.319   US   ISSN 0735-9276
                             CODEN: SMCPAX
SIMULATION SERIES. 1971. q. $192 (overseas $242). Society for Computer Simulation, Box 17900, San Diego, CA 92177. TEL 619-277-3888. FAX 619-277-3930. Ed. Hildy Linn. R&P contact: William Gallaghere. index. (reprint service avail. from UMI) **Indexed:** Appl.Mech.Rev., Comput.Cont., Comput.Rev., Curr.Cont., INSPEC, Int.Aerosp.Abstr., Nucl.Sci.Abstr. **Document type:** proceedings.
—BLDSC (8285.164800); CISTI; Ei; Linda Hall. **CCC.**
Formerly: Simulation Councils Proceedings (ISSN 0037-5519)
Description: Covers papers on special topic conferences.
Refereed Serial

001.6 621.319   US   ISSN 0272-4715
T57.62   CODEN: RASSDU
SIMULATION SYMPOSIUM. RECORD OF PROCEEDINGS. 1968. a. price varies. (Institute of Electrical and Electronics Engineers, Inc.) I E E E Computer Society Press, 10662 Los Vaqueros Circle, Los Alamitos, CA 90720-1264. TEL 714-821-8380. FAX 714-821-4641. (Co-sponsors: Annual Simulation Symposium, Inc.; Society for Computer Simulation) adv. contact: Frieda Koester. **Indexed:** INSPEC. **Document type:** proceedings.
—BLDSC (1530.850000); Ei; UMI. **CCC.**
Formerly: Annual Simulation Symposium. Proceedings.
Description: Provides information on the field of simulation with the primary focus on digital discrete simulation.

001.6 621.319   US   ISSN 0163-6103
QA76.9.C65   CODEN: SIMUD5
SIMULETTER. 1968. q. $25 to non-members; members $34. Association for Computing Machinery, Special Interest Group on Simulation, 1515 Broadway, 17th Fl., New York, NY 10036. TEL 212-869-7440. FAX 212-302-5826. Ed. Dana Wyatt. bk.rev. circ. 2,400. **Indexed:** INSPEC. **Document type:** newsletter.
—CISTI; UnCover.

621.319   US   ISSN 0740-6797
                            CODEN: TSCSEV
SOCIETY FOR COMPUTER SIMULATION. TRANSACTIONS. 1984. q. $145 (effective 1996). Society for Computer Simulation, Box 17900, San Diego, CA 92177. TEL 619-277-3888. FAX 619-277-3930. Ed. Paul Luker. R&P contact: William Gallagher. adv. contact: Steven Branch. circ. 1,000. **Indexed:** A.I.Abstr., ASCA, Biostat., CAD CAM Abstr., Compumath, Comput.Abstr., INSPEC (1984-). **Document type:** trade publication.
—BLDSC (9006.410000); AskIEEE; CISTI; Ei; Genuine Article; KR SourceOne; Linda Hall; SWETS; UnCover. **CCC.**
Refereed Serial

001.64 621.319   US   ISSN 0094-7474
QA76   CODEN: PSCCD6
SUMMER COMPUTER SIMULATION CONFERENCE. PROCEEDINGS. (Winter Simulation Conference. Proceedings also published annually; sponsoring body and publisher vary) 1967. a. $180. Society for Computer Simulation, Box 17900, San Diego, CA 92177. TEL 619-277-3888. FAX 619-277-3930. Ed. Hildy Linn. R&P contact: William Gallagher. adv. contact: Steven Branch. bk.rev.; illus.; index, cum.index. (back issues avail.) **Indexed:** Appl.Mech.Rev., Chem.Abstr., Comput.Cont., INSPEC. **Document type:** proceedings.
—BLDSC (8533.410000); CASDDS. **CCC.**

006 621.39   US
QA76.575
V R WORLD.* 1993. bi-m. $29 to individuals; institutions $59. Miller Freeman, Inc. (Subsidiary of: United News & Media), 600 Harrison St., San Francisco, CA 94107. TEL 415-905-2200. FAX 415-905-2562. (Subscr. to: Box 7703, San Francisco, CA 94120-7703) Ed. Sandra Kay Helsel. **Indexed:** INSPEC (1993-). **Document type:** consumer publication.
—AskIEEE; KR SourceOne. **CCC.**
Formerly: Virtual Reality World (ISSN 1060-9547)
Description: Devoted exclusively to virtual reality technology.

VIRTUAL; il mensile dell'era digitale. see COMPUTERS — Computer Graphics

006   UK   ISSN 1359-4338
▼**VIRTUAL REALITY;** research, development and applications. 1995. 2/yr. £65 (U.S. & Canada $110; elsewhere £70) to individuals; institutions £95 (U.S. & Canada $160; elsewhere £105). (Virtual Reality Society) Virtual Press Ltd., 147a High St., Waltham Cross, Hertfordshire EN8 7LN, England. FAX 44-1992-636557. Ed.Bd. adv. **Document type:** academic/scholarly publication.
—BLDSC (9240.727100).

004   US   ISSN 1065-271X
HD9696.C63
VIRTUAL REALITY MARKET PLACE. 1993. a. Mecklermedia Corporation, 20 Ketchum St., Westport, CT 06880-5808. TEL 203-226-6967. Ed. Sandra Kay Helsel. **Document type:** trade publication.

003 006   US
VIRTUAL REALITY NOW;* developments and applications. 1992. q. $65. Media Dimensions, Inc., 1562 First Ave., Ste. 286, New York, NY 10028-4004. TEL 212-533-7481. FAX 212-475-1209. Ed. Rory Stuart.
Description: Focuses on 3-dimensional reality through computers, headsets, suits and more.

003 006   UK   ISSN 1052-6242
QA76.9.C65
VIRTUAL REALITY REPORT.* 1990. 12/yr. Cydata Ltd., P.O. Box 2515, London N4 4JW, England. TEL 44-181-292-1498. (also avail. in microform from UMI) **Document type:** trade publication.
—UMI.
Description: Covers developments in the field of virtual reality and cyberspace.

VOICE TECHNOLOGY & SERVICES NEWS. see COMMUNICATIONS

621.319 001.53   US   ISSN 0891-7736
T57.62
WINTER SIMULATION CONFERENCE. PROCEEDINGS. (Earlier papers published in: IEEE Transactions on Systems Science and Cybernetics) 2nd, 1968. a. $150. Society for Computer Simulation, Box 17900, San Diego, CA 92117-7900. FAX 619-277-3930. Ed. Hildy Linn. R&P contact: William Gallagher. adv. contact: Steven Branch. circ. 1,050. **Document type:** proceedings.
—CCC.
Former titles (until 1970): Conference on the Applications of Simulation; (untl 1967): Conference on the Applications of GPSS.

COMPUTERS — Computer Systems

see also Computers–Computer Architecture

A C M TRANSACTIONS ON PROGRAMMING LANGUAGES AND SYSTEMS. (Association for Computing Machinery) see COMPUTERS — Computer Programming

621.381   AT   ISSN 0819-2898
A F M INFORMATION SYSTEMS SERIES (NO.). 1987. irreg. University of New England, Department of Accounting and Financial Management, Armidale, N.S.W. 2351, Australia. TEL 61-67-73221. FAX 61-67-733122. R&P contact: J.J. Staunton. TEL 61-67-733276. **Document type:** academic/scholarly publication.

621.381   US   ISSN 0749-6184
QA402   CODEN: ALSSEN
ADVANCES IN LARGE SCALE SYSTEMS. 1984. a. $90.25 to institutions. J A I Press Inc., 55 Old Post Rd., No. 2, Box 1678, Greenwich, CT 06836-1678. TEL 203-661-7602. Ed. Jose B. Cruz, Jr. **Indexed:** INSPEC.
—BLDSC (0709.255500); CISTI.

621.381   US   ISSN 1061-8929
QA75.5
ADVANCES IN THE IMPLEMENTATION AND IMPACT OF COMPUTER SYSTEMS; a research annual. 1991. a. $90.25. J A I Press Inc., 55 Old Post Rd., No.2, Box 1678, Greenwich, CT 06836-1678. TEL 203-661-7602. (U.K. addr.: J A I Press Ltd., 118 Pentonville Rd., London N1 9JN, England) Eds. Jonathan Morell, Mitchell Fleischer.

AIXPERT; IBM's technical magazine for AIX application developers. see COMPUTERS — Software

ANALOG DIALOGUE; a forum for the exchange of circuits, systems, and software for real-world signal processing. see COMPUTERS — Computer Engineering

621.381   SI   ISSN 0218-2599
ASIA - PACIFIC I.T. TIMES; today's technologies for the systems integration marketplace. 1991. s-m. $48. R M Technology Media Pte. Ltd., 1 North Bridge Rd., 24-06 High St. Ctr., Singapore 0617, Singapore. TEL 65-3340393. FAX 65-3343097. Ed. Lim Fung Meng. adv.: B&W page $4180, color page $4780; trim 275 x 375; adv. contact: Lynn Loke. circ. 21,468 (controlled). **Document type:** trade publication.
Description: Provides the latest, well-researched technology information and features that address aspects of today's systems integration marketplace.

COMPUTERS — COMPUTER SYSTEMS

ASILOMAR CONFERENCE ON SIGNALS, SYSTEMS AND COMPUTERS. CONFERENCE RECORD. see COMPUTERS — Circuits

004.16 US ISSN 0360-5280
QA76.5 CODEN: BYTEDJ
BYTE. 1975. m. $29.95 (Canada and Mexico $34.95; elsewhere $50) (effective 1997); newsstand price: $3.95. McGraw-Hill Companies, Byte Publications, One Phoenix Mill Ln., Peterborough, NH 03458. TEL 617-860-6336. FAX 617-860-6522. URL: http://www.byte.com. (Subscr. to: Box 550, Hightstown, NJ 08520-9886) Ed. Mark Schlack; Pub. David B. Egan. adv. contact: Lori Silverstein. bk.rev.; illus.; index. circ. 500,000. (also avail. in microform from UMI; reprint service avail. from UMI) **Indexed:** A.I.Abstr., A.S.& T.Ind., Abstr.Hum.Comp.Inter., Acad.Ind., Ap.Ind., ASCA, B.P.I., Bk.Rev.Ind. (1984-), BMT, Bus.Comput.Ind., Bus.Ind., CAD CAM Abstr., Can.B.P.I., Child.Bk.Rev.Ind. (1984-), Compumath, Compumath, Comput.Cont., Comput.Dtbs., Comput.Ind., Consum.Ind., Curr.Cont., Cyb.Abstr., Ergon.Abstr., Graph.Arts Lit.Abstr., IBM PC.Ind., Ind.How To Do It (1977-1984), Info.Media & Tech., INSPEC (1977-), LAMP, Mag.Ind., MELSA, Microcomp.Ind., Microcomp.Indus.Up., PC Abstr., PCR2, PMR, R.G.Abstr., Risk Abstr., Robomat., Sci.Cit.Ind., Soft.Abstr.Eng., SSCI, Tel.Abstr., TOM, Tr.& Indus.Ind., WPM. **Document type:** trade publication.
●Also available online. Vendor(s): Dow Jones News Retrieval, Knight-Ridder Information, Inc. (File no.624/McGRAW-HILL PUBLICATIONS ONLINE), Lexis-Nexis, NewsNet (EC34).
Also available on CD-ROM.
—BLDSC (2941.560000); AskIEEE; CASDDS; CISTI; Ei; Genuine Article; KNAW; KR SourceOne; Linda Hall; SWETS; UMI; UnCover. **CCC.**
Description: A broad-based microcomputer magazine for business and professional users emphasizing technical information, applications and products.

621.39 US
CLIENT SERVER NEWS; the new weekly newsletter for the windows NT marketplace worldwide. 1993. w. $595. G-2 Computer Intelligence Inc., Box 7, 3 Maple Place, Glen Head, NY 11545-0007. TEL 516-759-7025. FAX 516-759-7028. Ed. Stuart Zipper. **Document type:** newsletter.
Description: For industry executives, analysts and major end-users affiliated with the Windows NT operating system.

003 AT ISSN 1320-0682
QA267.7 CODEN: COINF2
COMPLEXITY INTERNATIONAL. irreg. free. c/o School of Information Techonology, Charles Sturt University, Panorama Ave., Bathurst, N.S.W. 2795, Australia. TEL 61-63-384272. FAX 61-63-384649. E-mail: ci-editor@csu.edu.au; URL: http://www.csu.edu.au/ci/ci.html. Ed. Terry Bossomaier. **Indexed:** Zent.Math. **Document type:** academic/scholarly publication.
●Available only online.
—CASDDS.
Description: Publishes papers dealing with complex systems research.
Refereed Serial

004 US
COMPUTER SYSTEMS SERIES. (In 4 vols.: Overviews, Systems, Peripherals, Software) 4 base vols. (plus m. updates). $1746 to new subscr.; renewals $1564 (effective 1996). Datapro Information Services Group (Subsidiary of: McGraw-Hill, Inc.), 600 Delran Pkwy., Delran, NJ 08075. TEL 609-764-0100; 800-328-2776. FAX 609-764-2814.

651.8 UK ISSN 0268-6821
THE COMPUTER USERS YEAR BOOK. 1969. a. £140. V N U Business Publications BV, VNU House, 32-34 Broadwick St., London W1A 2HG, England. Ed. Allan Wood. adv.; bk.rev. circ. 5,500. **Document type:** bulletin.
●Also available on CD-ROM.
—BLDSC (3394.350000).

621.39 UK ISSN 1352-9404
COMPUTING AND INFORMATION SYSTEMS. 1994. 3/yr. £50 (effective 1996). University of Paisley, Department of Computing and Information Systems, High St., Paisley PA1 2BE, Scotland. TEL 44-141-848-3301. FAX 44-141-848-3542. E-mail: mkc@paisley.ac.uk. Ed. M.K. Crowe. R&P contact: M.K. Crowe. circ. 120. **Document type:** academic/scholarly publication.
—BLDSC (3395.019800); AskIEEE; KR SourceOne.
Description: Contributions to research and occasional articles on development of academic subdisciplines.

COMPUTING SYSTEMS. see COMPUTERS — Computer Programming

CYBERNETICS AND SYSTEMS (BRISTOL); an international journal. see COMPUTERS — Cybernetics

CYBERNETICS AND SYSTEMS (NEW YORK). see COMPUTERS — Cybernetics

621.381 US ISSN 1055-0569
THE D O S AUTHORITY. 1991. m. $59. Cobb Group, Inc., 9420 Bunsen Pkwy., Ste. 300, Louisville, KY 40220. TEL 502-493-3200. FAX 502-491-8050. (Subscr. to: Box 35160, Louisville, KY 40232-9720. TEL 800-223-8720) **Document type:** consumer publication.
Description: Offers tips and techniques to advanced users of DOS.

DATABASE PROGRAMMING & DESIGN. see COMPUTERS — Computer Programming

621.381 001.642 US
DATAPRO REPORTS ON UNIX SYSTEMS & SOFTWARE. 2 base vols. (plus m. updates). $1077 to new subscr.; renewal $978. Datapro Information Services Group (Subsidiary of: McGraw-Hill, Inc.), 600 Delran Pkwy., Delran, NJ 08075. TEL 609-764-0100; 800-328-2776.

621.381 AU ISSN 0932-5581
DEPENDABLE COMPUTING AND FAULT-TOLERANT SYSTEMS. irreg. Springer-Verlag, Sachsenplatz 4-6, P.O. Box 89, A-1201 Vienna, Austria. TEL 43-1-3302415-0. FAX 43-1-3302426. E-mail: springer@springer.co.at. **Indexed:** Zent.Math. **Document type:** monographic series.
—BLDSC (3554.547000); CISTI.

621.39 NE ISSN 0929-5585
▼**DESIGN AUTOMATION FOR EMBEDDED SYSTEMS;** an international journal. (Text in English) 1996. q. fl.560 to institutions; $287.50 to institutions in U.S. (effective 1998). Kluwer Academic Publishers, Postbus 17, 3300 AA Dordrecht, Netherlands. TEL 31-78-6392390. FAX 31-78-6392254. E-mail: services@wkap.nl; URL: http://www.wkap.nl. (Dist. by: Kluwer Academic Publishers Group, P.O. Box 322, 3300 AH Dordrecht, Netherlands. TEL 31-78-6392392. FAX 31-78-6546474; N. America dist. addr.: Box 358, Accord Sta., Hingham, MA 02018-0358. TEL 617-871-6600. FAX 617-871-6528) Eds. Raul Camposano, Wayne Wolf. **Document type:** academic/scholarly publication.
—BLDSC (3559.922700); AskIEEE; CISTI; KR SourceOne; SWETS. **CCC.**
Description: Discusses the hardware, software and host aspects of embedded systems design.
Refereed Serial

DISTRIBUTED AND PARALLEL DATABASES; an international journal. see COMPUTERS — Data Base Management

004.6 US ISSN 1068-6266
TK5105.5
DISTRIBUTED COMPUTING MONITOR. 1986. m. $550 (foreign $585). Patricia Seybold Group, 85 Devonshire St. Fl. 5, Boston, MA 02109-3504. TEL 800-826-2424. TELEX 6503122583. E-mail: info@psgroup.comm. Ed. Anne Thomas; Pub. Patricia B. Seybold. (back issues avail.) **Indexed:** Comput.Lit.Ind. **Document type:** newsletter.
●Also available online.
Also available on CD-ROM.
—BLDSC (3602.661230); SWETS.
Former titles: Distributed Computing (ISSN 1058-4153); Patricia Seybold's Network Monitor (ISSN 0890-4685)
Description: Provides comprehensive analysis and objective evaluation of LAN products and vendor strategies. Takes a look ahead at advanced distributed computing technologies and implementation issues for objects, advanced client-server development tools, object request brokers, message-oriented middleware, and integrated distributed systems management.

621.319 US ISSN 0925-4668
CODEN: DYCOEL
DYNAMICS AND CONTROL; an international journal. 1991. q. fl.670 to institutions; $344 to institutions in U.S. (effective 1998). Kluwer Academic Publishers Boston, Box 358, Accord Sta., Hingham, MA 02018-0358. TEL 617-871-6600. FAX 617-871-6528. TELEX 200190. E-mail: services@wkap.nl; URL: http://www.wkap.nl. (Dist. outside N. America by: Kluwer Academic Publishers Group, P.O. Box 322, 3300 AH Dordrecht, Netherlands. TEL 31-78-6392392. FAX 31-78-6546474) Ed.Bd. (also avail. in microform from UMI; back issues avail.; reprint service avail. from SWZ) **Indexed:** ASCA, Compumath, Comput.Lit.Ind., Comput.Rev., Eng.Ind., Inform.Sci.Abstr., INSPEC (1991-), Math.R., Robomat. (until 1992), Zent.Math. **Document type:** academic/scholarly publication.
—BLDSC (3637.143085); AskIEEE; CISTI; Ei; Genuine Article; KR SourceOne; SWETS; UMI. **CCC.**
Description: Devoted to control of dynamical systems and to promoting the use of advanced dynamics in developing control methods. Papers cover both theory and applications.
Refereed Serial

003 621.3 NE
E-LETTER ON SYSTEMS, CONTROL, & SIGNAL PROCESSING. (Text in English) 1986. m. Eindhoven University of Technology, Department of Mathematics & Computing Science, P.O. Box 513, 5600 MB Eindhoven, Netherlands. TEL 31-10-472378. FAX 31-40-465995. E-mail: eletter-request@win.tue.nl. Ed. Anton A. Stoorvogel. (back issues avail.) **Document type:** newsletter.
●Available only online.

ELECTRONIC JOURNAL OF STRATEGIC INFORMATION SYSTEMS. see COMPUTERS — Information Science And Information Theory

EUROPEAN JOURNAL OF CONTROL. see ENGINEERING — Electrical Engineering

006.3 UK ISSN 0957-4174
QA76.76.E95 CODEN: ESAPEH
EXPERT SYSTEMS WITH APPLICATIONS; an international journal. 1990. 8/yr. fl.2460($1414) (effective 1998). Elsevier Science Ltd., Pergamon, P.O. Box 800, Kidlington, Oxford OX5 1DX, England. TEL 44-1865-843000. FAX 44-1865-843010. E-mail: nlinfo-f@elsevier.nl; usinfo-f@elsevier.com; forinfo-kyf04035@niftyserve.or.jp; URL: http://www.elsevier.nl/. (Subscr. to: Elsevier Science, Regional Sales Office, P.O. Box 211, 1000 AE Amsterdam, Netherlands. TEL 31-20-4853757. FAX 31-20-4853432; Subscr. in the Americas to: Elsevier Science, Regional Sales Office, Box 945, New York, NY 10159-0945. TEL 212-633-3730. FAX 212-633-3680; Subscr. in Australasia and the Far East to: Elsevier Science (Singapore) Pte Ltd, No.1 Temasek Ave., No.17-01 Millenia Tower, Singapore 039192, Singapore. TEL 65-434-3727. FAX 65-337-2230) Ed. J. Liebowitz. (also avail. in microfilm from UMI; back issues avail.) **Indexed:** A.I.Abstr., ASCA, Compumath, Comput.Abstr., INSPEC (1990-), Psychol.Abstr. (1990-), SSCI. **Document type:** academic/scholarly publication.
—BLDSC (3842.004220); AskIEEE; CISTI; Ei; Genuine Article; KR SourceOne; SWETS; UMI; UnCover. **CCC.**
 Description: For engineers, developers, researchers, scientists and consultants. Focuses on the exchange of information relating to expert systems worldwide.
 Refereed Serial

001.6 621.381 US ISSN 1042-721X
FEDERAL COMPUTER MARKET REPORT; intelligence and strategies for executives in government procurement. 1977. s-m. $495 (foreign $519). Computer Age & E D P News Services (Subsidiary of: Millin Publishing Group, Inc.), 714 Church St., Alexandria, VA 22314-4202. TEL 703-739-8500. FAX 703-739-8505. Ed. Michael E. Cotter; Pub. S.L. Millin. R&P contact: Michael E. Cotter. circ. 1,850. (back issues avail.) **Document type:** newsletter. ●Also available online. Vendor(s): Information Access Co.
—**CCC.**
 Formerly: Procurement Systems Digest (ISSN 0163-1489)
 Description: Analyzes government procurement regulations, technical evaluation criteria, minority subcontracting, RFP Instructions and other issues of interest to vendors and government buyers.

003 621.311 US ISSN 0925-9856
QA76.9.S88 CODEN: FMSDE6
FORMAL METHODS IN SYSTEM DESIGN; an international journal. 1992. bi-m. fl.910 to institutions; $467 to institutions in U.S. (effective 1998). Kluwer Academic Publishers Boston, Box 358, Accord Sta., Hingham, MA 02018-0358. TEL 617-871-6600. FAX 617-871-6528. TELEX 200190. E-mail: services@wkap.nl; URL: http://www.wkap.nl. (Dist. outside N. America by: Kluwer Academic Publishers Group, P.O. Box 322, 3300 AH Dordrecht, Netherlands. TEL 31-78-6392392. FAX 31-78-6546474) Ed.Bd. (also avail. in microform from UMI; back issues avail.; reprint service avail. from SWZ) **Indexed:** ASCA, Compumath, Comput.Rev., Eng.Ind., INSPEC (1992-), Zent.Math. **Document type:** academic/scholarly publication.
—BLDSC (4008.337500); AskIEEE; CISTI; Ei; Genuine Article; KR SourceOne; SWETS; UMI; UnCover. **CCC.**
 Description: International forum for research in the development and application of formal methods in VLSI hardware and software system design.
 Refereed Serial

621.381 NE ISSN 0167-739X
QA75.5
FUTURE GENERATION COMPUTER SYSTEMS. (Text in English) 1985. bi-m. fl.1027($590) (effective 1998). North-Holland (Subsidiary of: Elsevier Science B.V.), P.O. Box 211, 1000 AE Amsterdam, Netherlands. TEL 31-20-4853911. FAX 31-20-4853598. TELEX 18582 ESPA NL. (Subscr. in the Americas to: Elsevier Science, Regional Sales Office, Box 945, New York, NY 10159-0945. TEL 212-633-3730. FAX 212-633-3680; Subscr. in Australasia and the Far East to: Elsevier Science (Singapore) Pte Ltd, No.1 Temasek Ave., No.17-01 Millenia Tower, Singapore 039192, Singapore. TEL 65-434-3727. FAX 65-337-2230; Subscr. in Japan to: Elsevier Science Japan, 9-15 Higashi-Azabu 1-chome, Minato-ku Tokyo 106, Japan. TEL 81-3-5561-5033. FAX 81-3-5561-5047) Eds. L.O. Hertzberger, S. Ward. adv.; bk.rev.; illus. **Indexed:** A.I.Abstr., Art.Int.Abstr., ASCA, CAD CAM Abstr., Compumath, Comput.Abstr., Comput.Lit.Ind., Curr.Cont., Cyb.Abstr., INSPEC. **Document type:** academic/scholarly publication.
—BLDSC (4060.570000); AskIEEE; CISTI; Ei; Genuine Article; KR SourceOne; Linda Hall; SWETS; UnCover. **CCC.**
 Formerly: Fifth Generation Computer Systems.
 Description: Presents new developments in the field of computer systems. Includes models for new architectures and their analysis, as well as their hardware and software implementations.

621.381 001.6 US
G M D NEWSLINE. 1981. q. free to qualified personnel. G M D Systems International Inc., 3000 Atrium Way, Ste. 254, Mt. Laurel, NJ 08054-3926. Ed. Janet Creel. adv. circ. 22,000. **Document type:** newsletter.
 Former titles: G M D News and Information; G M D Newsletter.
 Description: Instructs IBM MAPICS system users.

621.381 US ISSN 0073-1129
TA168 CODEN: PHISD7
HAWAII INTERNATIONAL CONFERENCE ON SYSTEM SCIENCES. PROCEEDINGS. Short title: H I C S S. 1968. a. price varies. (Institute of Electrical and Electronics Engineers, Inc.) I E E E Computer Society Press, 10662 Los Vaqueros Circle, Los Alamitos, CA 90720-1264. TEL 714-821-8380. FAX 714-821-4641. Ed. Cat Harris; Pub. Matt Loeb. adv. contact: Frieda Koester. circ. 400. **Indexed:** INSPEC. **Document type:** proceedings.
—**CCC.**
 Description: Presents ideas, advances, and applications among academicians and practitioners in the information, computer and systems science fields.

001.535 621.381 US ISSN 1075-5888
TA167
HUMAN - TECHNOLOGY INTERACTION IN COMPLEX SYSTEMS. 1984-1989, resumed 1993. a. $90.25 to institutions. J A I Press Inc., 55 Old Post Rd., No. 2, Box 1678, Greenwich, CT 06836-1678. TEL 203-661-7602. FAX 203-661-0792. (In Europe: J A I Press Ltd., The Courtyard, 28 High St., Hampton Hill, Mddx. TW12 1PD, England. TEL 44-81-943-9296. FAX 44-81-943-9317) Ed. William B. Rouse. **Document type:** monographic series, academic/scholarly publication.
—BLDSC (4336.468300); CISTI. **CCC.**
 Formerly (until 1989): Advances in Man - Machine Systems Research (ISSN 0882-6137)

621.381 001.6 US ISSN 0018-8670
TA168 CODEN: IBMSA7
I B M SYSTEMS JOURNAL. 1962. q. $55 (foreign $70) (effective 1996). International Business Machines, Box 218, Yorktown Heights, NY 10598. TEL 914-945-3836. Ed. G. Hoffnagle. bk.rev.; abstr.; bibl.; charts; illus.; index, cum.index. circ. 60,000. (also avail. in microform from UMI; reprint service avail. from IBM, UMI) **Indexed:** A.I.Abstr., A.S.& T.Ind., ABI Inform., Acoust.Abstr., ASCA, BMT, CAD CAM Abstr., Chem.Abstr., Compumath, Comput.Abstr., Comput.& Info.Sys., Comput.Cont., Comput.Dtbs., Comput.Lit.Ind., Comput.Rev., Curr.Cont., Cyb.Abstr., Data Process.Dig., Eng.Ind., Ergon.Abstr., Excerp.Med., Inform.Sci.Abstr., INIS Atomind., INSPEC, Math.R., Oper.Res.Manage.Sci., PCR2, Qual.Contr.Appl.Stat., Ref.Zh., Sci.Cit.Ind., SSCI, Tel.Abstr., Zent.Math.
—BLDSC (4360.090000); AskIEEE; CASDDS; CISTI; Ei; Genuine Article; KR SourceOne; Linda Hall; SWETS; UMI; UnCover. **CCC.**
 Refereed Serial

COMPUTERS — COMPUTER SYSTEMS 2155

621.381 US ISSN 1063-8210
TK7874 CODEN: IEVSE9
I E E E TRANSACTIONS ON VERY LARGE SCALE INTEGRATION SYSTEMS. 1993. q. $290 to non-members (effective 1998). Institute of Electrical and Electronics Engineers, Inc., 345 E. 47th St., New York, NY 10017-2394. TEL 732-981-0060; 800-678-4333. FAX 732-981-9667. E-mail: customer.service@ieee.org; URL: http://www.ieee.org. (Subscr. to: Box 1331, 445 Hoes Ln., Piscataway, NJ 08855-1331) Ed. Bing Sheu. adv. **Indexed:** ASCA, Compumath, Curr.Cont., INSPEC (1993-).
—BLDSC (4363.231300); AskIEEE; CISTI; Ei; Genuine Article; KR SourceOne; Linda Hall; SWETS; UMI; UnCover. **CCC.**
 Description: Design and implementation of VLSI and microelectronic systems, system specifications, design and partitioning, high performance computing and communication systems.

INFOCUS (PHILADELPHIA); the technical journal for Prime Information, Universe and Unidata. see COMPUTERS — Computer Programming

001.6 621.381 FR ISSN 1247-0317
INGENIERIE DES SYSTEMES D'INFORMATION. 1993. 6/yr. 1250 F. (foreign 1450 F.) (effective 1997). (Association Francaise pour la Cybernetique Economique et Technique) Editions Hermes, 14 rue Lantiez, 75017 Paris, France. TEL 33-1-42294466. FAX 33-1-42291556. Eds. Arnold Rochfeld, Mokrane Bouzeghoub. adv. contact: Jean Philippe.
—BLDSC (4503.570000).

621.381 US ISSN 1049-5320
INSIDE D O S. (Disk Operating System) 1990. m. $49 (foreign $69). Cobb Group, Inc., 9420 Bunsen Pkwy., Ste. 300, Louisville, KY 40220. TEL 502-493-3200. FAX 502-491-8050. (Subscr. to: Box 35160, Louisville, KY 40232-9720. TEL 800-223-8720) Ed. Suzanne Thornberry. **Document type:** consumer publication.
 Description: Offers tips and techniques on using DOS 5.0.

621.381 US ISSN 1061-7647
INSIDE NETWARE. 1992. m. $89 (foreign $109). Cobb Group, Inc., 9420 Bunsen Pkwy., Ste. 300, Louisville, KY 40220. TEL 502-493-3200. FAX 502-491-8050. (Subscr. to: Box 35160, Louisville, KY 40232-9720. TEL 800-223-8720) **Document type:** consumer publication.

621.381 US ISSN 1063-3146
QA76.76.063
INSIDE O S - 2. 1992. m. $39 (foreign $59). Cobb Group, Inc., 9420 Bunsen Pkwy., Ste. 300, Louisville, KY 40220. TEL 502-493-3200. FAX 503-491-8050. (Subscr. to: Box 35160, Louisville, KY 40232-9720. TEL 800-223-8720) **Document type:** consumer publication.

004 US ISSN 1077-548X
INSIDE SCO UNIX SYSTEMS; tips & techniques for SCO open desktop, SCO open server, SCO UNIX, and SCO XENX systems. 1994. m. (10/yr.). $119 (foreign $139). Cobb Group, Inc., 9420 Bunsen Pkwy., Ste. 300, Louisville, KY 40220. TEL 502-493-3232; 800-223-8720. FAX 502-491-4200. E-mail: sco@merlin.cobb.ziff.com. Ed. August Mohr.

621.381 JA ISSN 0915-1915
TK5101.A1 CODEN: DJTJEK
INSTITUTE OF ELECTRONICS, INFORMATION AND COMMUNICATION ENGINEERS. TRANSACTIONS (SECTION D-I)/DENSHI JOHO TSUSHIN GAKKAI RONBUNSHI (D-I). English translation (in part): Systems and Computers in Japan (US ISSN 0882-1666) (Text in Japanese) 1968. m. 2100 Yen. Institute of Electronics, Information and Communication Engineers - Denshi Joho Tsushin Gakkai, c/o Kikai Shinko Kaikan, 5-8 Shiba Koen, 3-chome, Minato-ku, Tokyo 105, Japan. Ed. Michiyuki Uenohara. **Indexed:** Cyb.Abstr., INSPEC (1989-), Int.Abstr.Oper.Res., JCT, Tel.Abstr.
—BLDSC (8939.442100); AskIEEE; CISTI; KR SourceOne; Linda Hall.
 Supersedes in part (in 1989): Institute of Electronics, Information and Communication Engineers. Transactions (Section D) (ISSN 0913-5731)

COMPUTERS — COMPUTER SYSTEMS

621.381   US   ISSN 1063-6927
QA76.9.D5
INTERNATIONAL CONFERENCE ON DISTRIBUTED COMPUTING SYSTEMS. PROCEEDINGS. 1979. a. (Institute of Electrical and Electronics Engineers, Inc.) I E E E Computer Society Press, 10662 Los Vaqueros Circle, Los Alamitos, CA 90720-1264. TEL 714-821-8380. FAX 714-821-4641. Ed. Cat Harris; Pub. Matt Loeb. adv. contact: Frieda Koester. **Document type:** proceedings.
—BLDSC (4538.778900). **CCC.**
  Description: Addresses state-of-the-art and future technical developments in the field of distributed computing systems.

001.6   US
INTERNATIONAL CONFERENCE ON INFORMATION SYSTEMS. PROCEEDINGS. 1980. a. $25. (Society for Information Management) Association for Computing Machinery (Baltimore), 428 E. Preston St., Baltimore, MD 21202. TEL 301-528-4261. (Subscr. to: Box 64145, Baltimore, MD 21264. TEL 800-342-6626) Ed. Catherine A. Ross. circ. 700.

621.381   UK   ISSN 0267-6192
QA75.5   CODEN: CSSEEI
INTERNATIONAL JOURNAL OF COMPUTER SYSTEMS SCIENCE AND ENGINEERING. Short title: C S S E Journal. Computer Science and Engineering. 1985. bi-m. £199 to institutions (outside the EU £210). C R L Publishing Ltd., P.O. Box 31, Market Harborough, Leics. LE16 9RQ, England. TEL 44-8158-525382. FAX 44-1858-525635. Ed. T.S. Dillon; Pub. T.S. Dillon. adv.; bk.rev.; charts; illus.; index. (also avail. in microform from UMI; back issues avail.) **Indexed:** A.I.Abstr., CAD CAM Abstr., Comput.Abstr., Comput.Lit.Ind., Curr.Cont., INSPEC (1985-), Tel.Abstr., Zent.Math. **Document type:** academic/scholarly publication.
—BLDSC (3394.291700); AskIEEE; CISTI; Ei; Genuine Article; KR SourceOne; Linda Hall; SWETS; UMI.
  Description: Focuses on theory and applications in such areas as fault-tolerant systems, LAN engineering, parallel-processing, and multiple cooperating processor systems.
Refereed Serial

621.381   US   ISSN 0920-5691
TA1632   CODEN: IJCVEQ
INTERNATIONAL JOURNAL OF COMPUTER VISION. 1987. 15/yr. fl.2075 to institutions $1065 to institutions in U.S. (effective 1998). Kluwer Academic Publishers Boston, Box 358, Accord Sta., Hingham, MA 02018-0358. TEL 617-871-6600. FAX 617-871-6528. TELEX 200190. E-mail: services@kap.nl; URL: http://www.wkap.nl. (Dist. outside N. America by: Kluwer Academic Publishers Group, P.O. Box 322, 3300 AH Dordrecht, Netherlands. TEL 31-78-6392392. FAX 31-78-6546474) Eds. Takeo Kanade, Rodney Brooks. adv.; bk.rev. (also avail. in microform from UMI; back issues avail.; reprint service avail. from SWZ,UMI) **Indexed:** A.I.Abstr., A.S.& T.Ind., Abstr.Hum.Comp.Inter., ASCA, Compumath, Comput.Abstr., Comput.& Info.Sys., Comput.Rev., Curr.Cont., Eng.Ind., Ind.Sci.Rev., Ref.Zh., Sci.Cit.Ind. **Document type:** academic/scholarly publication.
—BLDSC (4542.175200); AskIEEE; CISTI; Ei; Genuine Article; KR SourceOne; SWETS; UMI; UnCover. **CCC.**
  Description: Provides a forum for the dissemination of new research results in the field of computer vision.

621.381   NE   ISSN 0308-1079
Q295   CODEN: IJGSAX
INTERNATIONAL JOURNAL OF GENERAL SYSTEMS; a comprehensive periodical devoted to general systems methodology, applications and education. 1974. 4/yr. (in 1 vol., 4 nos./vol.). $459 (effective 1998). Gordon and Breach - Harwood Academic, Amsteldisk 166, 1st Fl., 1079 LH Amsterdam, Netherlands. URL: http://www.gbhap.com/General_Systems/. (Subscr. to: International Publishers Distributors, Box 32160, Newark, NJ 07102. TEL 800-545-8398. FAX 215-750-6343) Ed. George J. Klir. adv.; bk.rev.; abstr.; bibl.; charts; illus.; index. (also avail. in microform from MIM,UMI; back issues avail.) **Indexed:** ASCA, Biol.Abstr., Compumath, Comput.Abstr., Comput.Rev., Curr.Cont., Geo.Abstr., Ind.Sci.Rev., INSPEC, Math.R., PHRA, Sci.Cit.Ind., SSCI, Zent.Math.
●Also available online.
Also available on CD-ROM.
—BLDSC (4542.266000); AskIEEE; CISTI; KR SourceOne; SWETS; UnCover. **CCC.**
Refereed Serial

621.39 005.3   GW   ISSN 1433-2779
▼**INTERNATIONAL JOURNAL ON SOFTWARE TOOLS FOR TECHNOLOGY TRANSFER.** 1997. q. DM.509.60 (foreign DM.513.20) (effective 1998). Springer-Verlag, Heidelberger Platz 3, 14197 Berlin, Germany. TEL 49-30-82787-0. FAX 49-30-82787448. E-mail: subscriptions@springer.de; URL: http://link.springer.de. (Subscr. in N. America to: Springer-Verlag New York, Inc., 333 Meadowlands Pkwy., Secaucus, NJ 07094. TEL 212-460-1500. FAX 212-473-6272) Eds. B. Steffen, W.R. Cleaveland. **Document type:** academic/scholarly publication.
●Also available online.
  Description: Forum for research and design professionals to discuss all aspects of tools that assist in the development of reliable and correct computer systems.

621.381   US
INTERNATIONAL SYMPOSIUM ON HIGH-PERFORMANCE DISTRIBUTED COMPUTING. PROCEEDINGS. Short title: H P D C. 1992. a. price varies. (Institute of Electrical and Electronics Engineers, Inc.) I E E E Computer Society Press, 10662 Los Vaqueros Circle, Los Alamitos, CA 90720-1264. TEL 714-821-8380. FAX 714-821-4641. Ed. Cat Harris; Pub. Matt Loeb. adv. contact: Frieda Koester. **Document type:** proceedings.
  Description: Addresses the latest research findings in all areas of high-performance distributed computing.

JOURNAL OF COMPUTER AND SYSTEM SCIENCES. see COMPUTERS

004 378   US   ISSN 0887-4417
QA76.27   CODEN: JCISE9
JOURNAL OF COMPUTER INFORMATION SYSTEMS. 1960. q. $50 to individuals; institutions $75. International Association for Computer Information Systems, 217 College of Business, Oklahoma State University, Stillwater, OK 74078. TEL 405-744-8632. FAX 405-744-5180. E-mail: jnord@okway.okstate.edu. Ed. Jeretta Horn Nord. adv.; bk.rev.; film rev.; index; circ. 1,000 (controlled). (also avail. in microform from UMI; reprint service avail. from UMI) **Indexed:** ASCA, Bus.Educ.Ind., Comput.Cont., INSPEC.
—BLDSC (4963.730000); AskIEEE; CISTI; Genuine Article; KR SourceOne; UMI; UnCover.
  Formerly (until 1985): Journal of Data Education (ISSN 0022-0310)
  Description: For collegiate information systems educators. Features articles on instruction, research, trends and information in information systems fields.
Refereed Serial

621.381 620   US   ISSN 1041-4673
JOURNAL OF MANUFACTURING;* issues, option and strategies. 1989. q. $98. Frost & Sullivan, Inc., 90 West St., No. 1301, New York, NY 10005-1039. TEL 212-233-1080. Ed. Hulas H. King.
  Description: Focuses on the dual role of technological innovation and managerial strategy in fostering business success in the automated manufacturing industry.

621.3 628.5   UK   ISSN 0278-6125
  CODEN: JMSYEB
JOURNAL OF MANUFACTURING SYSTEMS. 1982. bi-m. fl.838($481) (effective 1998). (Society of Manufacturing Engineers, Computer and Automated Systems Association, US) Elsevier Science Ltd., P.O. Box 800, Kidlington, Oxford OX5 1DX, England. TEL 44-1865-843000. FAX 44-1865-843010. E-mail: nlinfo-f@elsevier.nl; usinfo-f@elsevier.com; forinfo-kyf04035@niftyserve.or.jp; URL: http://www.elsevier.nl/; http://www.sme.org/. (Subscr. to: Elsevier Science, Regional Sales Office, P.O. Box 211, 1000 AE Amsterdam, Netherlands. TEL 31-20-4853757. FAX 31-20-4853432; Subscr. in the Americas to: Elsevier Science, Regional Sales Office, Box 945, New York, NY 10159-0945. TEL 212-633-3730. FAX 212-633-3680; Subscr. in Australasia and the Far East to: Elsevier Science (Singapore) Pte Ltd, No.1 Temasek Ave., No.17-01 Millenia Tower, Singapore 039192, Singapore. TEL 65-434-3727. FAX 65-337-2230) Ed. John G. Bollinger. adv.; bk.rev. circ. 1,000. **Indexed:** A.I.Abstr. (until 1992), A.S.& T.Ind., Alloys Ind., Appl.Mech.Rev., ASCA, CAD CAM Abstr. (until 1992), Curr.Cont., Eng.Ind., Eng.Mat.Abstr., INSPEC, Met.Abstr.Ind., Met.Abstr., Nonfer.Met.Alert, Oper.Res.Manage.Sci., PCC Alert, Qual.Contr.Appl.Stat., Robomat. (until 1992), Sci.Cit.Ind., Steels Alert, Text.Tech.Dig., World Alum.Abstr. **Document type:** academic/scholarly publication, trade publication.
●Also available online. Vendor(s): UMI.
—BLDSC (5011.650000); AskIEEE; CISTI; Genuine Article; KR SourceOne; Linda Hall; SWETS; UMI; UnCover. **CCC.**
  Description: For members of the Society and other practicing manufacturing engineers, researchers and educators. Covers such topics as integrating manufacturing processes into systems, hardware and component research and development, computer-aided manufacturing as well as sensors.
Refereed Serial

004.6   US   ISSN 1064-7570
TK5105.5   CODEN: JNSMEG
JOURNAL OF NETWORK AND SYSTEMS MANAGEMENT. 1993. q. $245 (foreign $285) (effective 1998). Plenum Publishing Corp., 233 Spring St., New York, NY 10013-1578. TEL 212-620-8000. FAX 212-463-0742. TELEX 23-421139. URL: http://www.catchword.co.uk/. Ed. Manu Malek. (also avail. in microfilm from UMI) **Indexed:** INSPEC (1993-). **Document type:** academic/scholarly publication.
●Also available online.
—BLDSC (5021.410700); AskIEEE; CISTI; Ei; KR SourceOne; SWETS. **CCC.**
  Description: Publishes original research, surveys and case studies discussing architecture, analysis, design, software, standards and migration issues related to the operation, management and control of distributed systems and communication networks for voice, data, image and networked computing.
Refereed Serial

JOURNAL OF SYSTEMS AND SOFTWARE. see COMPUTERS — Software

621.381   US   ISSN 0925-4676
  CODEN: JSINE4
JOURNAL OF SYSTEMS INTEGRATION; an international journal. 1991. q. fl.645 to institutions; $331 to institutions in U.S. (effective 1998). Kluwer Academic Publishers Boston, Box 358, Accord Sta., Hingham, MA 02018-0358. TEL 617-871-6600. FAX 617-871-6528. TELEX 200190. E-mail: services@kap.nl; URL: http://www.wkap.nl. (Dist. outside N. America by: Kluwer Academic Publishers Group, P.O. Box 322, 3300 AH Dordrecht, Netherlands. TEL 31-78-6392392. FAX 31-78-6546474) Ed.Bd. (also avail. in microform from UMI; back issues avail.; reprint service avail. from SWZ) **Indexed:** Eng.Ind., INSPEC (1991-). **Document type:** academic/scholarly publication.
—BLDSC (5068.075000); AskIEEE; CISTI; Ei; KR SourceOne; UMI. **CCC.**
  Description: Contains original, survey, application, and research papers on all topics related to system integration. Encompasses a collection of papers dispersed throughout a wide body of literature involving the interaction of disciplines, technologies, methods and machines necessary to integrate various constituent systems.
Refereed Serial

COMPUTERS — COMPUTER SYSTEMS

621.381   CC   ISSN 1004-3756
JOURNAL OF SYSTEMS SCIENCE AND SYSTEMS ENGINEERING. (Text in English) 1992. q. $140. (Systems Engineering Society of China) International Academic Publishers (IAP), 137 Chaonei Dajie, Beijing 100010, People's Republic of China. TEL 86-10-4035533. FAX 86-10-5063101. Ed. Liu Bao. **Document type:** academic/scholarly publication.
—BLDSC (5068.095500); AskIEEE; CISTI; KR SourceOne.
   Description: Carries papers on both theories and applications of SS and SE in management and planning of R&D, production, economy, education, demography, military activities involving various interdisciplinary theories, methodologies and techniques ranging from natural science to social science.

004 621.39   CH   ISSN 1022-968X
KAIFANG XITONG YU WANGLU/OPEN SYSTEMS & NETWORK. (Text in Chinese) 1991. m. NT.$1350 (foreign NT.$2950). Third Wave Publishing Corp., 19-1, Lane 231, Fu-Hsing N. Rd., Taipei, Taiwan, Republic of China. TEL 886-2-7136959. FAX 886-2-7189467. Ed. Samuel Huang. adv.: color page $2180. circ. 9,200. (back issues avail.) **Document type:** consumer publication.
   Description: Covers technical reports, market trends, product reviews, and new technologies.

TO EST' KTO NA KOMP'YUTERNOM RYNKE; katalog. see COMPUTERS — Computer Sales

KYBERNETES. see COMPUTERS — Cybernetics

LOGISTIK HEUTE. see BUSINESS AND ECONOMICS — Computer Applications

004   US   ISSN 0891-4710
                CODEN: MPCSEZ
M I T PRESS SERIES IN COMPUTER SYSTEMS. (Massachusetts Institute of Technology) Variant title: Computer Systems Series. 1984. irreg. price varies. M I T Press, 55 Hayward St., Cambridge, MA 02142. URL: http://www-mitpress.mit.edu/. R&P contact: Paul Dzus. **Document type:** monographic series.

MANAGING OPEN SYSTEMS. see COMPUTERS — Data Base Management

MANAGING SYSTEM DEVELOPMENT. see COMPUTERS — Electronic Data Processing

MEDIA COMPUTING; email report on emerging media markets. see COMPUTERS — Data Communications And Data Transmission Systems

621.381 001.642   US
MERRILL'S EDGAR ADVISOR; a publication for participants in the EDGAR and SEDAR systems for securities reporting. 1991. q. free. Merrill Corporation, One Merrill Circle, St. Paul, MN 55108. TEL 800-688-1933. FAX 612-644-1633. E-mail: edgar@merrillcorp.com; URL: http://www.merrillcorp.com. Ed. Richard Dargis. R&P contact: Richard Dargis. circ. 18,950. **Document type:** newsletter.
●Also available online.

MOBILE COMPUTING TECHNOLOGY. see COMPUTERS — Circuits

621.381   US   ISSN 0923-6082
TK5102.5   CODEN: MUSPE5
MULTIDIMENSIONAL SYSTEMS AND SIGNAL PROCESSING; an international journal. 1990. q. fl.640 to institutions; $328.50 to institutions in U.S. (effective 1998). Kluwer Academic Publishers Boston, Box 358, Accord Sta., Hingham, MA 02018-0358. TEL 617-871-6600. FAX 617-871-6528. TELEX 200190. E-mail: services@wkap.nl; URL: http://www.wkap.nl. (Dist. outside N. America by: Kluwer Academic Publishers Group, P.O. Box 322, 3300 AH Dordrecht, Netherlands. TEL 31-78-6392392. FAX 31-78-6546474) Ed. Nirmal K. Bose. (also avail. in microform from UMI; reprint service avail. from SWZ,UMI) **Indexed:** ASCA, Compumath, Comput.Lit.Ind., Comput.Rev., Eng.Ind., Inform.Sci.Abstr., INSPEC (1990-), Math.R., Sci.Cit.Ind., Zent.Math. **Document type:** academic/scholarly publication.
—BLDSC (5983.088000); AskIEEE; CISTI; Ei; Genuine Article; KR SourceOne; SWETS; UMI. CCC.
   Description: Publishes survey papers and original studies in fundamental and applied research in multidimensional systems, including mathematical modeling and the application of neural networks and artificial intelligence in signal and data processing.
Refereed Serial

621.38   US   ISSN 1071-0698
HD9696.V52   CODEN: DBALDA
MULTIMEDIA MONITOR. 1982. m. $395 (foreign $425) (effective 1997). Phillips Business Information, Inc., 1201 Seven Locks Rd., Potomac, MD 20854. TEL 301-424-3338. FAX 301-309-3847. E-mail: pbi@phillips.com. Ed. Richard Forgo. adv. contact: John Wilson. bk.rev.; circ. 3,000 (paid). (back issues avail.) **Indexed:** Educ.Tech.Abstr. **Document type:** newsletter.
●Also available online. Vendor(s): Information Access Co., Knight-Ridder Information, Inc., NewsNet (EC70).
Also available on CD-ROM.
—BLDSC (5983.147800); CASDDS; Linda Hall. CCC.
   Incorporates (1984-1997): Database Alert (ISSN 0737-951X); Former titles: Multimedia and Videodisc Monitor (ISSN 1054-7258); Videodisc Monitor (ISSN 0739-7089)
   Description: Provides worldwide coverage of interactive multimedia technologies and applications, business news, legal and regulatory issues, market statistics and industry analysis.

621.39   GW   ISSN 0258-1248
                   CODEN: NASFEG
N A T O ADVANCED SCIENCE INSTITUTES SERIES F: COMPUTER AND SYSTEMS SCIENCES. 1983. irreg., vol.147, 1995. price varies. (North Atlantic Treaty Organization, Scientific Affairs Division) Springer-Verlag, Heidelberger Platz 3, 14197 Berlin, Germany. TEL 49-30-8207-0. FAX 49-30-8214091. E-mail: subscriptions@springer.de. (Dist. by: Martinus Nijhoff International, P.O. Box 1853, 2700 CZ Zoetermeer, Netherlands. TEL 31-79-3684400. FAX 31-79-3615698) **Indexed:** INSPEC, Zent.Math. **Document type:** monographic series.
●Also available online. Vendor(s): European Space Agency (File no.128).
—BLDSC (6033.648800); CISTI. CCC.
   Formerly: N A T O Advanced Study Institute Series F: Computer and System Sciences.
   Description: Publishes cutting-edge research in various areas of computer systems science.
Refereed Serial

NETWORK COMPUTING (MANHASSET). see COMPUTERS — Computer Networks

621.381   JA   ISSN 0917-5342
NIKKEI JOHO SUTORATEJI/NIKKEI INFORMATION STRATEGY. (Text in Japanese) 1992. m. 12000 Yen. Nikkei Business Publications, Inc. (Subsidiary of: Nihon Keizai Shimbun, Inc.), 2-7-6 Hirakawa-cho, Chiyoda-ku, Tokyo 102, Japan. TEL 81-3-5210-8523. FAX 81-3-5210-8119. URL: http://www.nikkeibp.co.jp/. Ed. Takaki Kamimura; Pub. Takaki Kamimura. adv.: B&W page 399000 Yen, color page 570000 Yen; trim 210 x 280; adv. contact: Katsuyoshi Matsumura. circ. 23,050. **Document type:** trade publication.
   Description: Contains detailed information for successful construction and utilization of information systems.

621.381   NE
NORTH-HOLLAND SYSTEMS AND CONTROL SERIES. 1981. irreg., vol.10, 1987. price varies. Elsevier Science B.V., Books Division, P.O. Box 211, 1000 AE Amsterdam, Netherlands. TEL 31-20-4853911. FAX 31-20-4853705. TELEX 18582 ESPA NL. E-mail: nlinfo-f@elsevier.nl; usinfo-f@elsevier.com; forinfo-kyf04035@niftyserve.or.jp; URL: http://www.elsevier.nl/. (Subscr. in the Americas to: Elsevier Science, Regional Sales Office, Box 945, New York, NY 10159-0945. TEL 212-633-3730. FAX 212-633-3680; Subscr. in Australasia and the Far East to: Elsevier Science (Singapore) Pte Ltd, No.1 Temasek Ave., No.17-01 Millenia Tower, Singapore 039192, Singapore. TEL 65-434-3727. FAX 65-337-2230; Subscr. in Japan to: Elsevier Science Japan, 9-15 Higashi-Azabu 1-chome, Minato-ku, Tokyo 106, Japan. TEL 81-3-5561-5033. FAX 81-3-5561-5047) **Indexed:** Zent.Math. **Document type:** monographic series.
Refereed Serial

621.381   US   ISSN 1048-8928
TK7885.A1
O E M INTEGRATOR.* 1990. m. free to qualified personnel. TransAtlantic Publishers, 12 Main St., Leominster, MA 01453-5502. TEL 617-259-9207. Ed. W. Arnold. adv. contact: Barbara Arnold. **Document type:** trade publication.

004   US   ISSN 1073-1547
QA76.76.063
O S - 2 MAGAZINE. 1993. m. $39.95 (Canada & Mexico $49.95) (effective 1996). Miller Freeman, Inc. (Subsidiary of: United Newspapers), 600 Harrison St., San Francisco, CA 94107. TEL 415-905-2200. FAX 415-905-2499. (Subscr. to: Box 1079, Skokie, IL 60076-8079. TEL 708-647-5928. FAX 708-647-5972) Ed. Alan Zeichick. adv.: B&W page $4995. circ. 60,000 (paid). **Document type:** consumer publication.
—KR SourceOne; SWETS. CCC.
   Incorporates (1988-1996): I B M OS-2 Developer.

004.6   US   ISSN 1068-5553
                  CODEN: OINSET
OPEN INFORMATION SYSTEMS; a practical guide to implementing client-server computing. 1986. m. $550 (foreign $585). Patricia Seybold Group, 85 Devonshire St. 5th Fl., Boston, MA 02109-3504. TEL 800-826-2424. TELEX 6503122583. E-mail: info@psgroup.com. Ed. Susan E. Aldrich; Pub. Patricia B. Seybold. (back issues avail.) **Indexed:** Comput.Lit.Ind. **Document type:** newsletter.
●Also available online.
Also available on CD-ROM.
   Former titles: UNIX in the Office (ISSN 1058-4161); Patty Seybold's UNIX in the Office (ISSN 0887-3054)
   Description: Focuses on the realities of migrating from mainframe and proprietary systems to open-client and -server platforms. Takes a pragmatic business approach to the implementation of open platforms; standards; RDBMS; OLTP; systems and network management; and enterprise client-server, CASE, and 4GL development tools.

OPEN SYSTEMS & INFORMATION DYNAMICS. see COMPUTERS — Information Science And Information Theory

OPEN SYSTEMS AND INFORMATION DYNAMICS. see COMPUTERS — Information Science And Information Theory

001.6 621.381   US
OPEN SYSTEMS WORLD.* 1992. m. Open Systems Publishing, Box 9192, Framingham, MA 01701. TEL 617-482-8470.

621.381   NE   ISSN 1063-7192
                  CODEN: PAAPEC
PARALLEL ALGORITHMS AND APPLICATIONS. 1993. q. $126 (effective 1998). Gordon and Breach - Harwood Academic, Amsteldisk 166, 1st Fl., 1079 LH Amsterdam, Netherlands. URL: http://www.gbhap.com/Parallel__Algorithms__Applications/. (Subscr. to: International Publishers Distributor, Box 32160, Newark, NJ 07102. TEL 800-545-8398. FAX 215-750-6343) Ed. Graham M. Megson. (also avail. in microform)
●Also available online.
Also available on CD-ROM.
—BLDSC (6404.833020); CISTI; SWETS. CCC.
   Description: Publishes papers relating to parallel and multiprocessor computer systems covering the areas of parallel algorithms and parallel applications.

COMPUTERS — COMPUTER SYSTEMS

621.39   NE   ISSN 0167-8191
CODEN: PACOEJ
PARALLEL COMPUTING. (Text in English) 1984. 14/yr. fl.2235($1284) (effective 1998). North-Holland (Subsidiary of: Elsevier Science B.V.), P.O. Box 211, 1000 AE Amsterdam, Netherlands. TEL 31-20-4853911. FAX 31-20-4853598. TELEX 18582 ESPA NL. (Subscr. in the Americas to: Elsevier Science, Regional Sales Office, Box 945, New York, NY 10159-0945. TEL 212-633-3730. FAX 212-633-3680; Subscr. in Australasia and the Far East to: Elsevier Science (Singapore) Pte Ltd, No.1 Temasek Ave., No.17-01 Millenia Tower, Singapore 039192, Singapore. TEL 65-434-3727. FAX 65-337-2230; Subscr. in Japan to: Elsevier Science Japan, 9-15 Higashi-Azabu 1-chome, Minato-ku Tokyo 106, Japan. TEL 81-3-5561-5033. FAX 81-3-5561-5047) Ed. M. Feilmeier. adv. (back issues avail.; reprint service avail. from SWZ) **Indexed:** A.I.Abstr., ASCA, Compumath, Comput.Abstr., Curr.Cont., Cyb.Abstr., INSPEC (1984-), SSCI, Zent.Math. **Document type:** academic/scholarly publication.
—BLDSC (6404.833500); AskIEEE; CISTI; Ei; Genuine Article; KR SourceOne; Linda Hall; SWETS; UnCover. **CCC.**
Description: Presents theory and use of parallel computer systems, including vector, pipeline, array and fifth generation computers as well as high-speed computing.
Refereed Serial

PRAGMA'S PRODUCT PROFILES. see *COMPUTERS — Hardware*

621.381   RU   ISSN 0032-8154
CODEN: PRSUBT
PRIBORY I SISTEMY UPRAVLENIYA. (Text in Russian; contents page in English) 1956. m. $286 (effective 1998). (Mezhdunarodnoe N T O Proborostroitelei i Metrologov) Izdatel'stvo Mashinostroenie, 4, Stromynsky per., 107076 Moscow, Russia. TEL 7-095-2697141. FAX 7-095-2694897. Ed. M.S. Shkarbardnia. adv.: page DM.4500. bk.rev.; bibl.; charts; illus.; index. circ. 2,000. **Indexed:** Alloys Ind., Chem.Abstr., Eng.Mat.Abstr., INSPEC, Met.Abstr., Met.Abstr.Ind., Nonfer.Met.Alert, PCC Alert, Steels Alert, World Alum.Abstr. **Document type:** academic/scholarly publication.
—BLDSC (0131.670000); CASDDS; CISTI.
Description: Covers the state-of-the-art and trends in the development of instrument-making and the scientific-technical policy in this area.

621.381 355   US   ISSN 0199-7114
UC263
PROGRAM MANAGER. 1972. bi-m. $12 (foreign $15). Defense Systems Management College, Research and Information Division, c/o Superintendent of Documents, U.S. Government Printing Office, Box 371954, Pittsburgh, PA 15250-7954. TEL 202-512-1530. FAX 202-512-2250. E-mail: help@eids05.eids.gpo.gov; URL: http://www.access.gpo.gov. Ed. Catherine M. Clark. bk.rev.; charts; illus.; stat. circ. 11,599. (also avail. in microfiche; back issues avail.) **Indexed:** Air Un.Lib.Ind. **Document type:** government publication.
—BLDSC (6864.489000); UnCover.
Description: Serves as a vehicle for transmitting information on policies, trends, events, and current thinking affecting program management and defense systems acquisition.

004   BE   ISSN 1018-0303
REAL-TIME MAGAZINE. (Text in English) 1987. q. 8000 BEF. Real-Time Consult, Rue de la Justice 23, 1070 Brussels, Belgium. TEL 32-2-5205577. FAX 32-2-5208309. Eds. M. Timmerman. **Document type:** trade publication.
—BLDSC (7303.282649); AskIEEE; KR SourceOne; SWETS.
Formerly (until 1991): V M E Bus (ISSN 1013-364X)

004 621.39   NE
REAL-TIME SAFETY CRITICAL SYSTEMS. (Text in English) 1994. irreg., vol.2, 1994. price varies. Elsevier Science B.V., P.O. Box 211, 1000 AE Amsterdam, Netherlands. TEL 31-20-4853911. FAX 31-20-4853598. E-mail: nlinfo-f@elsevier.nl; usinfo-f@elsevier.com; forinfo-kyf04035@niftyserve.or.jp; URL: http://www.elsevier.nl/. (Subscr. in the Americas to: Elsevier Science, Regional Sales Office, Box 945, New York, NY 10159-0945. TEL 212-633-3730. FAX 212-633-3680; Subscr. in Australasia and the Far East to: Elsevier Science (Singapore) Pte Ltd, No.1 Temasek Ave., No.17-01 Millenia Tower, Singapore 039192, Singapore. TEL 65-434-3727. FAX 65-337-2230; Subscr. in Japan to: Elsevier Science Japan, 9-15 Higashi-Azabu 1-chome, Minato-ku, Tokyo 106, Japan. TEL 81-3-5561-5033. FAX 81-3-5561-5047) Ed. H. A. Hansson. (back issues avail.) **Document type:** monographic series.
Description: Serves as a forum for researchers and developers to report findings in the fields of computer systems development where failure of systems or software can involve loss of life or environmental damage.
Refereed Serial

621.39   US   ISSN 0922-6443
QA76.54   CODEN: RESYE9
REAL-TIME SYSTEMS; the international journal of time-critical computing systems. 1989. bi-m. fl.950 to institutions; $488 to institutions in U.S. (effective 1998). Kluwer Academic Publishers Boston, Box 358, Accord Sta., Hingham, MA 02018-0358. TEL 617-871-6600. FAX 617-871-6528. TELEX 200190. E-mail: services@wkap.nl; URL: http://www.wkap.nl. (Dist. outside N. America by: Kluwer Academic Publishers Group, P.O. Box 322, 3300 AH Dordrecht, Netherlands. TEL 31-78-6392392. FAX 31-78-6546474) Ed.Bd. (also avail. in microform from UMI; reprint service avail. from SWZ) **Indexed:** A.I.Abstr., ASCA, CAD CAM Abstr., Compumath, Comput.Lit.Ind., Comput.Rev., Curr.Cont., Eng.Ind., Inform.Sci.Abstr., INSPEC (1989-), Math.R., Psychol.Abstr., Zent.Math. **Document type:** academic/scholarly publication.
—BLDSC (7303.282660); AskIEEE; CISTI; Ei; Genuine Article; KR SourceOne; SWETS; UMI; UnCover. **CCC.**
Description: Consists of research papers, invited papers, reports on projects and case studies, standards and corresponding proposals for general discussion.
Refereed Serial

621.381   US   ISSN 1052-8725
QA76.54
REAL-TIME SYSTEMS SYMPOSIUM. PROCEEDINGS. Variant title: I E E E Real-Time Systems Symposium. Proceedings. 1981. a. (Institute of Electrical and Electronics Engineers, Inc.) I E E E Computer Society Press, 10662 Los Vaqueros Circle, Los Alamitos, CA 90720-1264. TEL 714-821-8380. FAX 714-821-4641. E-mail: cs.books@computer.org. (Orders to: I E E E Service Center, 445 Hoes Ln., Box 1331, Piscataway, NJ 08855-1331. TEL 908-981-1393. FAX 908-981-9667; Orders in Europe to: I E E E Computer Society, 13 ave. de l'Aquilon, B-1200 Brussels, Belgium. TEL 32-2-770-2198. FAX 32-2-770-8505) **Document type:** proceedings.
—CCC.
Description: Focuses on computer systems in charge of real-time applications.

003   FR   ISSN 1166-8636
REVUE DES SYSTEMES DE DECISION. 1992. 4/yr. 1150 F. (foreign 1300 F.) (effective 1997). Editions Hermes, 14 rue Lantiez, 75017 Paris, France. TEL 33-1-42294466. FAX 33-1-42291556. Ed. Jean-Charles Pomerol.
—BLDSC (7953.570000).

621.381   FR
REVUE INTERNATIONALE DE GEOMATIQUE. 1991. 4/yr. 1250 F. (foreign 1400 F.) (effective 1997). (Ministere de la Recherche et de l'Espace) Editions Hermes, 14 rue Lantiez, 75017 Paris, France. TEL 33-1-42294466. FAX 33-1-42291556. Ed. Chantal Menasce.
Former titles (until 1994): Revue de Geomatique (ISSN 1247-0589); (until 1992): Revue des Sciences de l'Information Geographique et de l'Analyse Spatiales (ISSN 1166-9624).

621.381   US   ISSN 1060-1074
QA76.75
S C O MAGAZINE.* (Santa Cruz Operation) (Supplement to: UNIX Today! (ISSN 1040-5038)) 1991. bi-m. C M P Publications, Inc., 600 Community Dr., Manhasset, NY 11030. TEL 516-562-5000. FAX 516-365-4601.
—KR SourceOne; UMI.

004   US   ISSN 1075-3265
S C O WORLD. (Santa Cruz Operation) 1994. m. $17.50 (Canada $24; elsewhere $49) (effective 1997); newsstand price: $2.95. Venture Publishing, Inc., 480 San Antonio Rd., Mountain View, CA 94040. TEL 415-941-1550. FAX 415-941-1504. E-mail: mikeb@scoworld.com. Ed. Michael Burgard; Pub. Bob Billhimer. R&P contact: Brenda Sloan. adv. B&W page $6995, color page $8050; trim 8 x 10 3/4. bk.rev.; circ. 50,000 (paid). **Document type:** trade publication.

621.381   CN   ISSN 0849-1801
S I BUSINESS. (Systems Integrator) 1989. 7/yr. Can.$75($110) (foreign $150). Plesman Publications Ltd., 2005 Sheppard Ave. E., 4th Fl., Willowdale, Ont. M2J 5B1, Canada. TEL 416-497-9562. FAX 416-497-9427. Ed. Charles P. Whaley. adv. contact: Leslie Davis. circ. 8,630. **Indexed:** Can.B.P.I.
Formerly (until 1990): Systems Integrator (ISSN 0846-5258)

001.6 621.381   US
S I G D O C NEWSLETTER. q. $24. Association for Computing Machinery, Special Interest Group on Systems Documentation, 1515 Broadway, 17th Fl., New York, NY 10036. TEL 212-869-7440. FAX 212-869-0481. TELEX 421686.

621.381   US
S I G LINK REVIEW. 1992. q. $40. Association for Computing Machinery, Special Interest Group for Hypertext - Hypermedia, 1515 Broadway, 17th Fl., New York, NY 10036. TEL 212-869-7440. FAX 212-869-0481. TELEX 421686. **Document type:** newsletter.

621.381   US   ISSN 0894-0819
HF5547.5.A1   CODEN: SIGBEL
S I G O I S BULLETIN. q. $30. Association for Computing Machinery, Special Interest Group for Office Information Systems, 1515 Broadway, New York, NY 10036. TEL 212-869-7440. FAX 212-869-0481. TELEX 421686. **Indexed:** INSPEC (1986-).
—BLDSC (8276.337000); AskIEEE; CISTI; KR SourceOne; SWETS; UnCover.
Former titles (until 1986): S I G O A Bulletin (ISSN 0893-2867); (until 1985): S I G O A Newsletter (ISSN 0737-819X)

621.381   US   ISSN 0270-7284
CODEN: SNAPEY
S N A PERSPECTIVE.* (Systems Network Architecture) 1980. m. $350 (foreign $385). Spc-Software Publishing Corp., Box 11044, San Jose, CA 95103-1044. Ed. Louise H. Wells. (back issues avail.)
—CASDDS.

621.381 001.64   US
SEMAPHORE SIGNAL. 1983. m. $10 (free to qualified personnel). Semaphore Corp., 207 Granada Dr., Aptos, CA 95003. TEL 408-688-9200. Ed. Mike Gabrielson. adv.; circ. 7,000 (controlled).
Formerly: Signal.
Description: For Apple Lisa and Apple Macintosh computer users. Provides news and information on current products.

SHISUTEMU SEIGYO JOHO/SYSTEMS, CONTROL AND INFORMATION. see *COMPUTERS — Automation*

621.381 629.8   IT   ISSN 0394-929X
SISTEMI E IMPRESA. 1955. m. (10/yr.) L.238000 (foreign L.360000). Edizioni Scientifiche Tecniche Europee s.r.l., Via Giorgio Vasari 15, 20135 Milan, Italy. TEL 39-2-55018039. FAX 39-2-5455644. E-mail: edizioni.este@iol.it. Ed. Franco Rebuffo. R& contact: Gianni Ceriani. adv. contact: Emma Samarati. bk.rev.; charts; illus.; index. circ. 9,500. **Indexed:** Cyb.Abstr., INSPEC.
—BLDSC (8286.420400); AskIEEE; KR SourceOn
Former titles (until 1988): Sistemi e Automazion (ISSN 0037-5896); (until 1967): Schede Perfora e Calcolo Elettronico.

621.381 US ISSN 0094-2898
QA402 CODEN: PASTDB
SOUTHEASTERN SYMPOSIUM ON SYSTEM THEORY. PROCEEDINGS. Key Title: Proceedings of the Annual Southeastern Symposium on System Theory. 1969. a. (Institute of Electrical and Electronics Engineers, Inc., Computer Society) I E E E Computer Society Press, 10662 Los Vaqueros Circle, Los Alamitos, CA 90720-1264. TEL 714-821-8380. FAX 714-821-4641. Ed. Cat Harris; Pub. Matt Loeb. adv. contact: Frieda Koester. **Indexed:** INSPEC. **Document type:** proceedings.
—BLDSC (8352.497000); UMI. **CCC.**
 Description: Covers system modeling, analysis, simulation and control.

003 NE ISSN 0923-0076
SPECIAL TOPICS IN SUPERCOMPUTING. (Text in English) 1987. irreg., vol.10, 1992. price varies. Elsevier Science B.V., Books Division, P.O. Box 211, 1000 AE Amsterdam, Netherlands. TEL 31-20-4853911. FAX 31-20-4853705. TELEX 18582 ESPA NL. E-mail: nlinfo@elsevier.nl; usinfo-f@elsevier.com; forinfo-kyf04035@niftyserve.or.jp; URL: http://www.elsevier.nl/. (Subscr. in the Americas to: Elsevier Science, Regional Sales Office, Box 945, New York, NY 10159-0945. TEL 212-633-3730. FAX 212-633-3680; Subscr. in Australasia and the Far East to: Elsevier Science (Singapore) Pte Ltd, No.1 Temasek Ave., No.17-01 Millenia Tower, Singapore 039192, Singapore. TEL 65-434-3727. FAX 65-337-2230; Subscr. in Japan to: Elsevier Science Japan, 9-15 Higashi-Azabu 1-chome, Minato-ku, Tokyo 106, Japan. TEL 81-3-5561-5033. FAX 81-3-5561-5047) Eds. G. Rodrigue, G. Michael. (back issues avail.) **Indexed:** Zent.Math. **Document type:** monographic series.
—BLDSC (8404.733000).
 Refereed Serial

004 IT
▼**START**; tutto Windows 95. 1995. m. (11/yr.). L.61000 (effective 1997). Gruppo Editoriale J C E, Via Ferri 6, 20092 Cinisello Balsamo (IT), Italy. TEL 39-2-660251. FAX 39-2-6127620. E-mail: start@jce.it; URL: http://www.jce.it. Ed. Fausto Gimondi. adv.: B&W page L.5000000, color page L.6500000; trim 210 X 276. circ. 43,000.
 Description: Covers new products, software upgrades, and everything supported by Windows 95.

STUDIES IN COMPUTER AND COMMUNICATIONS SYSTEMS. see *COMMUNICATIONS — Computer Applications*

004 JA ISSN 0918-5453
SUN WORLD/SANWARUDO. Variant title: Independent Journal of Sun and S P A R C Systems. (Text in Japanese) 1991. m. I D G Communications, Japan, 2-F, Shuwa Fujimicho Bldg., 1-2-27 Fujimi, Chiyoda-ku, Tokyo 102, Japan. TEL 81-3-3222-6411. FAX 81-3-3222-6566. Pub. Masashi Kobayashi. adv.: B&W page 450000 Yen, color page 580000 Yen; trim 210 x 280. circ. 28,000.

621.381 US ISSN 1063-9535
QA76.88
SUPERCOMPUTING PROCEEDINGS. 1988. a. price varies. (Institute of Electrical and Electronics Engineers, Inc.) I E E E Computer Society Press, 10662 Los Vaqueros Circle, Los Alamitos, CA 90720-1264. TEL 714-821-8380. FAX 714-821-4641. Ed. Cat Harris; Pub. Matt Loeb. adv. contact: Frieda Koester. **Indexed:** INSPEC. **Document type:** proceedings.
●Also available on CD-ROM.
—Ei. **CCC.**
 Description: Provides future directions and exchange information on supercomputing.

621.381 US ISSN 1043-6871
QA75.5
SYMPOSIUM ON LOGIC IN COMPUTER SCIENCE. PROCEEDINGS. 1986. a. price varies. (Institute of Electrical and Electronics Engineers, Inc.) I E E E Computer Society Press, 10662 Los Vaqueros Circle, Los Alamitos, CA 90720-1264. TEL 714-821-8380. FAX 714-821-4641. **Indexed:** INSPEC. **Document type:** proceedings.
—UMI.
 Description: Contains computer science issues broadly relating to logic, including algebraic and topological approaches.

621.381 001.6 US ISSN 0882-1666
QA75.5 CODEN: SCJAEP
SYSTEMS AND COMPUTERS IN JAPAN. (English translation of: Denshi Joho Tsushin Gakkai Ronbunshi (Section D-I) (ISSN 0915-1915), (Section D-II) (ISSN 0915-1923), and other Japanese material.) 1969. 14/yr. $2309 (foreign $2554) (effective 1998). (Institute of Electronics, Information and Communications Engineers of Japan, JA) John Wiley & Sons, Inc., Journals, 605 Third Ave., New York, NY 10158. TEL 212-850-6645. FAX 212-850-6021. E-mail: subinfo@jwiley.com; URL: http://www.wiley.co.uk. (Subscr. outside the Americas to: John Wiley & Sons Ltd., Baffins Ln., Chichester, W. Sussex PO19 1UD, England. TEL 44-1243-779777. FAX 44-1243-776128) Ed. C.H. Park. adv.; charts; illus.; index. circ. 300. (also avail. in microfilm from UMI; back issues avail.) **Indexed:** A.I.Abstr., ASCA, CAD CAM Abstr., Compumath, Comput.Abstr., Comput.Cont., Curr.Cont., Eng.Ind., INSPEC, Math.R., Robomat., Tel.Abstr. **Document type:** academic/scholarly publication.
—BLDSC (8589.292000); AskIEEE; CISTI; Ei; Genuine Article; KR SourceOne; Linda Hall; SWETS; UMI; UnCover. **CCC.**
 Formerly: Systems, Computers, Control (ISSN 0096-8765)
 Description: Covers computer architecture, large system design, advanced digital circuitry, data transmission, interface device, data processing, signal and speech processing.

004.6 NE ISSN 0167-6911
CODEN: SCLEDC
SYSTEMS AND CONTROL LETTERS. (Text in English) 1981. 15/yr. fl.1362($783) (effective 1998). North-Holland (Subsidiary of: Elsevier Science B.V.), P.O. Box 211, 1000 AE Amsterdam, Netherlands. TEL 31-20-4853911. FAX 31-20-4853598. TELEX 18582 ESPA NL. (Subscr. in the Americas to: Elsevier Science, Regional Sales Office, Box 945, New York, NY 10159-0945. TEL 212-633-3730. FAX 212-633-3680; Subscr. in Australasia and the Far East to: Elsevier Science (Singapore) Pte Ltd, No.1 Temasek Ave., No.17-01 Millenia Tower, Singapore 039192, Singapore. TEL 65-434-3727. FAX 65-337-2230; Subscr. in Japan to: Elsevier Science Japan, 9-15 Higashi-Azabu 1-chome, Minato-ku Tokyo 106, Japan. TEL 81-3-5561-5033. FAX 81-3-5561-5047) Ed. Jan C. Willems. adv.; index. (also avail. in microform from UMI; back issues avail.; reprint service avail. from SWZ) **Indexed:** Appl.Mech.Rev., CAD CAM Abstr., Compumath, Curr.Cont., Cyb.Abstr., INSPEC (1981-), Int.Aerosp.Abstr., Robomat., SSCI, Zent.Math. **Document type:** academic/scholarly publication.
—BLDSC (8589.294000); AskIEEE; CISTI; Ei; Genuine Article; KR SourceOne; Linda Hall; SWETS; UnCover. **CCC.**
 Description: Publishes theoretical, methodological and empirical studies and applications pertaining to systems.
 Refereed Serial

004 338.4 US ISSN 1087-4933
SYSTEMS & NETWORK MANAGEMENT REPORT. 1996. bi-w. $465 (foreign $513). DataTrends Publications, Inc., Box 4460, Leesburg, VA 20177. TEL 703-779-0574; 800-766-8130. FAX 703-779-2267. bk.rev. **Document type:** newsletter.
●Also available online. Vendor(s): Information Access Co.
—CCC.
 Formed by the merger of (1989-1996): Network Management Systems and Strategies (ISSN 1043-1217); (1988-1996): Distributed Systems Management Report; Which was formerly: O P E N (ISSN 1072-7760); (until 1992): O S I Product and Equipment News (ISSN 0898-0489)
 Description: Provides news on computer hardware and software products that work toward multivendor networking, and distributed networks and systems.

SYSTEMS CONTRACTOR NEWS; serving the electronic systems industry. see *ELECTRONICS*

621.381 US ISSN 0735-9985
SYSTEMS DEVELOPMENT MANAGEMENT. 1976. bi-m. $425. Auerbach Publishers (Subsidiary of: Warren, Gorham & Lamont), One Penn Paza, New York, NY 10119. TEL 212-971-5000. FAX 212-971-5024. (Subscr. to: 31 St. James Ave., Boston, MA 02116-4112. TEL 800-950-1218. FAX 617-423-1914) Ed. Paul Tinnirello. software rev. (looseleaf format) **Document type:** trade publication.
—CCC.
 Description: Articles present advice on how to develop, organize and implement the appropriate system for the user's needs. Contains information on cost-effective and efficient design techniques and tools, evaluating software, choosing hardware and training personnel.

003 658 UK ISSN 0731-7239
Q295 CODEN: SYREER
SYSTEMS RESEARCH. 1984. q. $265 (effective 1997). (International Federation for Systems Research) John Wiley & Sons Ltd., Journals, Baffins Ln., Chichester, W. Sussex PO19 1UD, England. TEL 44-1243-779777. FAX 44-1243-775878. E-mail: info-assets@wiley.co.uk; URL: http://www.wiley.co.uk. (Subscr. in the Americas to: John Wiley & Sons, Inc., 605 Third Ave., New York, NY 10158. TEL 212-850-6645. FAX 212-850-6021) Ed. Mike C. Jackson. adv.: B&W page £595, color page £1495; trim 260 x 200; adv. contact: Bob Kern. bk.rev.; charts; illus. (also avail. in microform from UMI) **Indexed:** ASCA, Compumath, Comput.Abstr., Comput.Cont., Curr.Cont., Excerp.Med., INSPEC (1984-), Int.Abstr.Oper.Res., SSCI, Zent.Math. **Document type:** academic/scholarly publication.
—AskIEEE; CISTI; Genuine Article; KR SourceOne; SWETS; UMI; UnCover. **CCC.**
 Formerly: International Journal of Systems Research.
 Description: Provides a forum for the exchange of new ideas and knowledge relating to the use of systems thinking in the development, management and assessment of activities, programs and organizations.
 Refereed Serial

001.6 621.381 US ISSN 0199-8951
QA75.5
SYSTEMS USER. 1980. m. $62 (foreign $98). Caulfield Publishing Ltd., 308 E. Van Buren St., Janesville, WI 53545-4047. Ed. Susan Lindsay. adv.; bk.rev. circ. 37,668. **Indexed:** Comput.Cont., Comput.Lit.Ind., INSPEC.
—CISTI; UMI.

621.381 US ISSN 0734-2071
QA76.9.S88 CODEN: ACSYEC
TRANSACTIONS ON COMPUTER SYSTEMS. Short title: T O C S. 1983. q. $110 to non-members. Association for Computing Machinery, 1515 Broadway, 17th Fl., New York, NY 10036-5701. TEL 212-869-7440. FAX 212-944-1318. TELEX 421686. Ed. Anita K. Jones. circ. 7,100. **Indexed:** A.I.Abstr., Abstr.Hum.Comp.Inter., CAD CAM Abstr., Compumath, Comput.Abstr., Comput.Lit.Ind., INSPEC (1983-), Tel.Abstr.
—BLDSC (0578.657000); AskIEEE; CISTI; Ei; Genuine Article; KR SourceOne; Linda Hall; SWETS; UMI; UnCover. **CCC.**
 Description: Publishes exploratory, theoretical, and conceptual papers on the design, architecture and organization of computer systems.

621.381 UK ISSN 1361-6153
UNIVERSITY OF MANCHESTER. DEPARTMENT OF COMPUTER SCIENCE. TECHNICAL REPORT SERIES. CD-ROM edition (UK ISSN 1363-8378) 1986. irreg. University of Manchester, Department of Computer Science, Oxford Rd., Manchester M13 9PL, England. TEL 44-161-275-6130. FAX 44-161-275-6236. E-mail: ulrich@cs.man.ac.uk; URL: http://www.cs.man.ac.uk/csonly/cstechrep/index.html. Ed. Ulrich Nehmzow. R&P contact: Jenny Fleet. circ. 100. **Document type:** abstracting/indexing, monographic series.
●Also available online.
Also available on CD-ROM.
 Description: Research reprints in computer science.
 Refereed Serial

621.381 GW ISSN 0934-8476
UNIX MAGAZIN; die unabhaengige Zeitschrift fuer Unix-Anwender. m. DM.84 (foreign DM.102). Markt und Technik Verlag AG, Hans-Pinsel-Str. 2, 85540 Haar, Germany. TEL 089-4613-0. FAX 089-4613-774. **Document type:** consumer publication.

COMPUTERS — CYBERNETICS

UNIX MAGAZINE. see *COMPUTERS — Computer Programming*

005.3   UK   ISSN 0956-2753
UNIX NEWS. 1989. m. 12 Sutton Row, 4th Fl., London W1V 5FH, England. TEL 44-171-867-9880. Ed. John Abbott; Pub. Beverly Harper. adv. contact: Oren Wolf. **Document type:** trade publication.
●Also available online. Vendor(s): Information Access Co.
—SWETS.

UNIX REVIEW. see *COMPUTERS — Computer Programming*

001.5 621.381   KR   ISSN 0130-5395
T58.6   CODEN: UPSMBC
UPRAVLYAYUSHCHIE SISTEMY I MASHINY. Short title: U S i M. (Text and summaries in English, Russian, Ukrainian) 1972. bi-m. $136 (effective 1999). Akademiya Nauk Ukrainy, Institut Kibernetiki im. V.M. Glushkova, Prosp. Akad. Glushkova, 6, 252207 Kiev, Ukraine. TEL 38-44-2660009. E-mail: scur@d410.icyb.kiev.ua. (Distr. in U.S. by: Victor Kamkin Inc., 4956 Boiling Brook Pkwy., Rockville, MD 20852. TEL 301-881-5973. FAX 301-881-1637) Ed. V.I. Skurikhin; Pub. V.I. Gritsenko. illus. circ. 859. **Indexed:** Appl.Mech.Rev., Chem.Abstr, Djerelo. **Document type:** academic/scholarly publication, proceedings.
—BLDSC (0385.032000); AskIEEE; CASDDS; CISTI; KR SourceOne; Linda Hall.
Description: Covers theories and methods of informatics, information technologies and real-time systems.

621.381   US   ISSN 0884-1357
TK7895.B87
V M E BUS SYSTEMS. 1985. bi-m. $24 in the U.S. and Canada; elsewhere $50 (free to qualified subscribers) (effective 1997). Micrology P B T Inc., 2618 S. Shannon Dr., Tempe, AZ 85282. TEL 602-967-5581. E-mail: micrology@aol.com; URL: http://www.primenet.com/~magpub. (Subscr. to; V M E Bus Systems, 25875 Jefferson, St. Clair Shores, MI 48081. TEL 810-774-8180. FAX 810-774-8182) Ed. John Black. R&P contact: John Black. adv. contact: Pat Hopper. bk.rev.; charts; illus.; tr.lit. circ. 18,000. (back issues avail.) **Document type:** trade publication.
—CISTI.

VOPROSY TEORII SISTEM AVTOMATICHESKOGO UPRAVLENIYA. see *COMPUTERS — Automation*

WINTER SIMULATION CONFERENCE. PROCEEDINGS. see *COMPUTERS — Computer Simulation*

621.381   CC   ISSN 1000-6788
XITONG GONGCHENG LILUN YU SHIJIAN/SYSTEM ENGINEERING THEORY AND PRACTICE. (Text in Chinese) 1981. bi-m. Y50.40. Zhongguo Xitong Gongcheng Xuehui - Systems Engineering Society of China, Xitong Yanjiusuo, Zhongguancun, Beijing 100080, People's Republic of China. TEL 2541828. FAX 2568364. Ed. Gu Jifa. **Document type:** academic/scholarly publication.
Description: Covers system engineering theory and its appliation.

621.381 510   CC   ISSN 1000-0577
Q295   CODEN: XKSHEW
XITONG KEXUE YU SHUXUE. English edition: Systems Science and Mathematical Sciences (ISSN 1000-9590) (Text in Chinese; summaries in English) 1981. q. $51.20. (Chinese Academy of Sciences, Institute of Systems Science) Science Press, Marketing and Sales Department, 16 Donghuachengmen North St., Beijing 100717, People's Republic of China. TEL 4010642. FAX 4019810. adv. circ. 6,000. **Document type:** academic/scholarly publication.
—Linda Hall.
Description: Presents original papers in mathematics from mainland China, including systems theory, system modeling, and system control.
Refereed Serial

001.6 621.381   US
YOURDON REPORT: journal of structured systems development. 1976. irreg. free. Yourdon Inc., c/o S R S Networks, 500 Fifth Ave., New York, NY 10110-0002. Ed. Wendy Eakin. circ. 10,000.

COMPUTERS — Cybernetics
Includes: Bionics.

see also Computers–Artificial Intelligence

001.53   US   ISSN 0066-0086
AMERICAN SOCIETY FOR CYBERNETICS. PROCEEDINGS OF THE ANNUAL SYMPOSIUM. 1967. irreg. price varies. American Society for Cybernetics, G. Washington University, Department of Management Science, Washington, DC 20052. TEL 202-994-7530. FAX 202-994-4030. E-mail: umpleby@gwis2.circ.gwu.edu. circ. 100.

001.53   HU   ISSN 0324-721X
Q300   CODEN: ACCYDX
ATTILA JOZSEF UNIVERSITY. ACTA CYBERNETICA. (Text in English, French, German and Russian) 1969. s-a. Attila Jozsef University, c/o E. Szabo, Exchange Librarian, Dugonics ter 13, P.O. Box 393, 6701 Szeged, Hungary. (Subscr. to: Kultura, Box 149, 1389 Budapest, Hungary) Ed. Ferenc Gecseg. bk.rev.; index. circ. 400. (back issues avail.) **Indexed:** Compumath, Comput.Rev., INSPEC (1987-), Math.R., Ref.Zh., Zent.Math.
—AskIEEE; Ei; KR SourceOne; Linda Hall.
Description: Presents scholarly papers on various aspects and applications of cybernetics. Covers such areas as rewriting systems, automata, attributed transformation, algebraic theories and mathematical systems theories.

AUTOMATISERING. see *COMPUTERS — Automation*

003 574   GW   ISSN 0340-1200
Q350   CODEN: BICYAF
BIOLOGICAL CYBERNETICS; communication and control in organisms and automata. Online edition (GW ISSN 1432-0770) (Text in English) 1961. m. DM.3384.80 (foreign DM.3395.60) (effective 1998). Springer-Verlag, Heidelberger Platz 3, 14197 Berlin, Germany. TEL 49-30-82787-0. FAX 49-30-82787448. E-mail: subscriptions@springer.de; URL: http://link.springer.de. (Subscr. in N. America to: Springer-Verlag New York, Inc., 333 Meadowlands Pkwy., Secaucus, NJ 07094. TEL 212-460-1500. FAX 212-473-6272) Ed. G. Hauske. adv.; bk.rev.; charts; illus.; index. (also avail. in microform from UMI; back issues avail.; reprint service avail. from ISI) **Indexed:** ASCA, Biol.Abstr., Compumath, Comput.Rev., Curr.Adv.Ecol.Sci., Curr.Cont., Dent.Ind., Excerp.Med., Ind.Med., Ind.Sci.Rev., INSPEC (1975-), Math.R., Neurosci.Cit.Ind., Rev.Appl.Entomol., SSCI, Zent.Math. **Document type:** academic/scholarly publication.
●Also available online.
—BLDSC (2075.170000); AskIEEE; CISTI; Ei; Genuine Article; KR SourceOne; Linda Hall; SWETS; UMI; Uncover. **CCC.**
Which supersedes: Kybernetik (ISSN 0023-5946)
Description: Provides experimental and theoretical information in the fields of quantitative analysis of behavior, quantitative physiological studies of information processing in receptors, neural systems and effectors, and computational studies of perceptual motor information processing tasks.

BULLETIN OF INFORMATICS AND CYBERNETICS. see *MATHEMATICS*

CLONE. see *COMPUTERS — Computer Simulation*

510 001.6   US
COMPUTATIONAL MATHEMATICS AND APPLICATIONS. 1977. irreg., latest 1994. Academic Press, Inc., 525 B St., Ste. 1900, San Diego, CA 92101-4495. TEL 619-231-0926. FAX 619-699-6715. (Subscr. to: Order Dept., 6277 Sea Harbor Dr., 4th Fl., Orlando, FL 32887. TEL 800-321-5068) Ed. J.R. Whiteman. (reprint service avail. from ISI) **Indexed:** Math.R.
Refereed Serial

COMPUTERS AND ARTIFICIAL INTELLIGENCE/POCITACE A UMELA INTELIGENCIA. see *COMPUTERS — Artificial Intelligence*

001.53   PL   ISSN 0324-8569
QA402.3   CODEN: CCYBAP
CONTROL AND CYBERNETICS. (Text in English) 1972. q. $125 (effective 1998). Polish Academy of Sciences, Systems Research Institute, Ul. Newelska 6, 01-447 Warsaw, Poland. TEL 48-22-364103. FAX 48-22-372772. TELEX 812397 IBS PL. E-mail: control@ibspan.waw.pl. (Dist. by: Ars Polona, Krakowskie Przedmiescie 7, 00-068 Warsaw, Poland; Dist. also by: Mezhdunarodnaya Kniga, B. Yakimanka 39, 117049 Moscow, Russia. TEL 7-095-2384967. FAX 7-095-2384634) Ed. Zbigniew Nahorski. R&P contact: Jan W. Owsinski. adv. contact: Jan W. Owsinski. bk.rev.; bibl. circ. 600. **Indexed:** Comput.Cont., Cyb.Abstr., INSPEC, Math.R., Zent.Math. **Document type:** academic/scholarly publication.
—BLDSC (3461.856000); AskIEEE; CISTI; KR SourceOne; UnCover.
Description: Publishes papers dealing with systems and control theory and systems control and management.
Refereed Serial

001.53   CU
CONTROL, CIBERNETICA Y AUTOMATIZACION. (Text in Spanish; summaries in English and French) 1967. s-a. $24 in S. America; N. America $26; elsewhere $30. (Ministerio de la Industria Basica, Instituto de Matematica, Cibernetica y Computacion) Ediciones Cubanas, Obispo No. 527, Apdo. 605, Havana, Cuba. Ed. Eduardo Canal Portuondo. adv.; charts; illus. circ. 2,000. **Indexed:** INSPEC.

CYBERARIAN'S GUIDE TO CYBER - MARKETING. see *BUSINESS AND ECONOMICS*

001.53   US   ISSN 0883-4202
CYBERNETIC. 1967. a. $25. American Society for Cybernetics, G. Washington University, Department of Management Science, Washington, DC 20052. TEL 202-994-7530. FAX 202-994-4030. E-mail: umpleby@gwis2.circ.gwu.edu. Ed. Paul Trachtman. bk.rev.; bibl.; illus. circ. 250.
Former titles: A S C Cybernetics Forum; (until vol.10, 1981): A S C Forum; (until vol.8, 1975): A C S Newsletter.

003   BE   ISSN 0011-4227
Q350   CODEN: CYBEA5
CYBERNETICA. (Text in English, French) 1958. q. 3000 BEF includes I A C Newsletter (effective 1994). International Association for Cybernetics - Association Internationale de Cybernetique, Palais des Expositions, Avenue Sergent Vrithoff 2, 5000 Namur, Belgium. TEL 32-81-735209. FAX 32-81-742045. bk.rev.; charts; illus.; index. **Indexed:** ASCA, Compumath, Comput.Cont., Curr.Cont., Eng.Ind., Excerp.Med., INSPEC, Math.R., SSCI, Zent.Math. **Document type:** academic/scholarly publication.
—BLDSC (3506.380000); AskIEEE; CISTI; KR SourceOne; Linda Hall; SWETS; UnCover.

001.53 001.6   US   ISSN 0739-8417
Q300
CYBERNETICS AND COMPUTING TECHNOLOGY. English translation of: Kibernetika i Vychislitel'naya Tekhnika (KR ISSN 0454-9910) 1982. q. $895 (effective 1997). (Ukrainian Academy of Sciences, KR) Allerton Press, Inc., 150 Fifth Ave., New York, NY 10011. TEL 212-924-3950. FAX 212-463-9684. Ed. V.S. Mikhalevich. **Indexed:** Appl.Mech.Rev., Eng.Ind., INSPEC (1984-), Math.R. **Document type:** academic/scholarly publication.
—BLDSC (0411.087500); AskIEEE; CISTI; KR SourceOne; Linda Hall. **CCC.**
Description: Provides papers on the application of control systems, computer science, CAD and AI to areas such as human factors engineering, transportation systems and medical diagnosis test procedures.

003　　　　　　　US　　ISSN 0196-9722
Q300　　　　　　　　　CODEN: CYSYDH
CYBERNETICS AND SYSTEMS (BRISTOL); an international journal. Online edition (US ISSN 1087-6553) 1971. 8/yr. £524($865) to institutions (£629($1038) with online ed.) (effective 1998). (Austrian Society for Cybernetic Studies, AU) Taylor & Francis Inc., 1900 Frost Rd., Ste. 101, Bristol, PA 19007-1598. TEL 215-785-5800; 800-821-8312. FAX 215-785-5515. E-mail: info@tandf.co.uk; URL: http://www.tandf.co.uk/jnls/cbs.htm. (Subscr. in Europe to: Taylor & Francis Ltd., Rankine Rd., Basingstoke, Hants. RG24 8PR, England. TEL 44-1256-840366. FAX 44-1256-479438) Ed. Robert Trappl. adv.; bk.rev.; abstr.; bibl.; charts; illus.; index. circ. 450. (also avail. in microform from UMI; back issues avail.; reprint service avail. from UMI) **Indexed:** Abstr.Hum.Comp.Inter., Appl.Mech.Rev., Biol.Abstr., Comput.Abstr., Curr.Cont., Cyb.Abstr., Eng.Ind., INSPEC, Math.R., Zent.Math. **Document type:** academic/scholarly publication.
●Also available online.
—BLDSC (3506.391000); AskIEEE; CISTI; Ei; Genuine Article; KR SourceOne; Linda Hall; SWETS; UnCover. **CCC.**
　Formerly (until June 1980): Journal of Cybernetics (ISSN 0022-0280)
　Description: Provides information on cybernetics applications for the scientific community. Topics covered include machine science, production systems, problem-solving in games, systems methodology and information systems.
　Refereed Serial

001.53　621.381　　NE
CYBERNETICS AND SYSTEMS (NEW YORK). (Subseries of: Abacus Press Series) 1979. irreg., vol.11, 1981. Gordon and Breach - Harwood Academic, Amsteldisk 166, 1st Fl., 1079 LH Amsterdam, Netherlands. (Subscr. to: International Publishers Distributor, Box 32160, Newark, NJ 07102. TEL 800-545-8398. FAX 215-750-6343) Ed. J. Rose. **Indexed:** A.I.Abstr., Curr.Cont. **Document type:** monographic series.
　Refereed Serial

003　　　　　　　US　　ISSN 1060-0396
Q300　　　　　　　　　CODEN: CYASEC
CYBERNETICS AND SYSTEMS ANALYSIS. English translation of: Kibernetika i Sistemnyi Analiz (KR ISSN 1019-5262) 1965. bi-m. $1455 (foreign $1700) (effective 1998). (Ukrainian Academy of Sciences, KR) Plenum Publishing Corp., Consultants Bureau, 233 Spring St., New York, NY 10013-1578. TEL 212-620-8468. FAX 212-463-0742. TELEX 23-421139. Ed. I.V. Sergienko. (also avail. in microform from UMI; back issues avail.) **Indexed:** Appl.Mech.Rev., ASCA, Compumath, Comput.& Info.Sys., Comput.Cont., Curr.Cont., Eng.Ind., INIS Atomind., INSPEC, Lang.& Lang.Behav.Abstr., Math.R., Sci.Cit.Ind., Zent.Math. **Document type:** academic/scholarly publication.
—BLDSC (0411.087800); AskIEEE; CISTI; Genuine Article; KR SourceOne; Linda Hall; SWETS; UMI; UnCover. **CCC.**
　Formerly: Cybernetics (ISSN 0011-4235)
　Description: Contains scholarly papers on all aspects of cybernetics. Topics include mathematical tools and models, computing algorithms, numeric software, specifications, computer applications and theorems.
　Refereed Serial

003　　　　　　　BE
CYBERNETICS: WORKS IN PROGRESS/CYBERNETIQUE: DOCUMENTS DE TRAVAIL. irreg., latest no.5. price varies. International Association for Cybernetics - Association Internationale de Cybernetique, Palais des Expositions, Avenue Sergent Vrithoff 2, 5000 Namur, Belgium. TEL 32-81-735209. FAX 32-81-742045. **Document type:** monographic series.

CLEXNEWS; learning and working in cybertime and cyberspace. see **EDUCATION — Computer Applications**

GEEKGIRL. see **WOMEN'S INTERESTS**

001.53　　　　　　KR　　ISSN 0207-0111
QA76.38　　　　　　　　CODEN: GVMKD2
GIBRIDNYE VYCHISLITEL'NYE MASHINY I KOMPLEKSY; respublikanskii mezhvedomstvennyi sbornik nauchnykh trudov. (Text in Russian) 1979. a. (Akademiya Nauk Ukrainy, Institut Problem Modelirovaniya v Energetike) Vidavnitstvo Naukova Dumka, Vul. Tereshchenkivska 3, 252601 Kiev, Ukraine. TEL 044-224-4068. FAX 044-224-7060. (Dist. by: Mezhdunarodnaya Kniga, B. Yakimanka 39, 117049 Moscow, Russia) Ed. G.E. Pukhov.
—CASDDS; Linda Hall. **CCC.**

001.53　　　　　　GW　　ISSN 0723-4899
GRUNDLAGENSTUDIEN AUS KYBERNETIK UND GEISTESWISSENSCHAFT; Humankybernetik. (Supplement avail.) 1960. 4/yr. DM.80. (Institut fuer Kybernetik) Akademia Libroservo - IfK Paderborn, Kleinenberger Weg 16, 33100 Paderborn, Germany. TEL 49-5251-64200. FAX 49-5251-1633533. E-mail: bfran2@pbhrz.uni-paderborn.de. Ed. Dr. Helmar Frank. R&P contact: Vera Barandovska. adv. contact: Baerbel Ehmke. bk.rev.; bibl.; charts. circ. 800. (back issues avail.) **Indexed:** IBR, Lang.& Lang.Behav.Abstr. **Document type:** academic/scholarly publication.
—CCC.
　Description: Covers the aesthetics of information, cybernetic educational theory, cybernetic linguistics, biocybernetics, as well as economic and juridical cybernetics.
　Refereed Serial

001.53　　　　　　US　　ISSN 1062-922X
Q300
I E E E INTERNATIONAL CONFERENCE ON SYSTEMS, MAN, AND CYBERNETICS. CONFERENCE PROCEEDINGS. 1971. a. (I E E E, Systems, Man, and Cybernetics Society) Institute of Electrical and Electronics Engineers, Inc., 345 E. 47th St., New York, NY 10017-2394. TEL 732-981-0060; 800-678-4333. FAX 732-981-9667. E-mail: customer.service@ieee.org; URL: http://www.ieee.org. (Subscr. to: 445 Hoes Ln., Box 1331, Piscataway, NJ 08855-1331) illus.
—BLDSC (4362.949950); Ei; UMI. **CCC.**
　Former titles (until 1989): I E E E International Conference on Systems, Man, and Cybernetics. Proceedings (ISSN 0884-3627); (until 1985): I E E E International Conference on Cybernetics and Society. Proceedings (ISSN 0884-3597); (until 1983): International Conference on Cybernetics and Society. Proceedings (ISSN 0360-8913); (until 1974): International Conference on Systems, Man, and Cybernetics. Proceedings; I E E E Systems, Man, and Cybernetics Group. Annual Conference Record; (in 1971): I E E E Systems, Man, and Cybernetics Group. Annual Symposium Record.
　Description: Examines human-machine interaction, behavioral decision making, robotics and manufacturing systems.

I E E E TRANSACTIONS ON SIGNAL PROCESSING. see **ENGINEERING — Electrical Engineering**

003　　　　　　　US　　ISSN 1083-4427
Q300　　　　　　　　　CODEN: ITSHFX
I E E E TRANSACTIONS ON SYSTEMS, MAN AND CYBERNETICS, PART A: SYSTEMS & HUMANS. 1971. bi-m. $225 to non-members (effective 1998). (I E E E, Systems, Man, and Cybernetics Society) Institute of Electrical and Electronics Engineers, Inc., 345 E. 47th St., New York, NY 10017-2394. TEL 732-981-0060; 800-678-4333. FAX 732-981-9667. E-mail: customer.service@ieee.org; URL: http://www.ieee.org. (Subscr. to: Box 1331, 445 Hoes Lane, Piscataway, NJ 08855-1331) Ed. Andrew P. Sage. bk.rev.; abstr.; illus.; index. (also avail. in microform) **Indexed:** A.I.Abstr. (until 1992), A.S.& T.Ind., Abstr.Hum.Comp.Inter., Biostat., CAD CAM Abstr. (until 1992), Chem.Abstr., Compumath, Comput.Abstr., Comput.Cont., Curr.Cont., Cyb.Abstr., Eng.Ind., Ergon.Abstr., Excerp.Med., Geo.Abstr., HRIS, Ind.Sci.Rev., INIS Atomind., INSPEC, ISMEC, Math.R., Neurosci.Cit.Ind., Oper.Res.Manage.Sci., Psychol.Abstr. (1971-), Psycscan, Qual.Contr.Appl.Stat., Robomat. (until 1992), Sci.Cit.Ind., SSCI, Tel.Abstr., Zent.Math.
—BLDSC (4363.225000); AskIEEE; CISTI; Ei; Genuine Article; KR SourceOne; Linda Hall; SWETS; UMI; UnCover. **CCC.**
　Supersedes in part (in 1996): I E E E Transactions on Systems, Man and Cybernetics (ISSN 0018-9472); Which was formed by the merger of (1968-1971): I E E E Transactions on Man-Machine Systems (ISSN 0536-1540); (1965-1971): I E E E Transactions on Systems Science and Cybernetics (ISSN 0536-1567)
　Description: Contains papers on the theoretical and practical considerations of natural and synthetic systems involving people and machines.

003　　　　　　　US　　ISSN 1083-4419
Q300　　　　　　　　　CODEN: ITSCFI
I E E E TRANSACTIONS ON SYSTEMS, MAN AND CYBERNETICS, PART B: CYBERNETICS. 1971. bi-m. $225 (effective 1998). (I E E E, Systems, Man and Cybernetics Society) Institute of Electrical and Electronics Engineers, Inc., 345 E. 47th St., New York, NY 10017-2394. TEL 732-981-0060; 800-678-4333. FAX 732-981-9667. E-mail: customer.service@ieee.org; URL: http://www.ieee.org. (Subscr. to: 445 Hoes Ln., Box 1331, Piscataway, NJ 08855-1331) Andrew P. Sage. **Indexed:** Zent.Math.
—BLDSC (4363.225050); AskIEEE; CISTI; Genuine Article; KR SourceOne; Linda Hall; SWETS; UnCover. **CCC.**
　Supersedes in part (in 1996): I E E E Transactions on Systems, Man and Cybernetics (ISSN 0018-9472); Which was formed by the merger of (1968-1971): I E E E Transactions on Man-Machine Systems (ISSN 0536-1540); (1965-1971): I E E E Transactions on Systems Science and Cybernetics (ISSN 0536-1567)

003　　　　　　　US　　ISSN 1094-6977
I E E E TRANSACTIONS ON SYSTEMS, MAN AND CYBERNETICS, PART C: APPLICATIONS AND REVIEWS. Announced for publication in 1998. q. $150. (I E E E, Systems, Man and Cybernetics Society) Institute of Electrical and Electronics Engineers, Inc., 345 E. 47th St., New York, NY 10017-2394. TEL 800-678-4333. E-mail: customer.service@ieee.org; URL: http://www.ieee.org. (Subscr. to: 445 Hoes Ln., Box 1331, Piscataway, NJ 08855-1331. TEL 732-981-0060. FAX 732-981-1209)
—AskIEEE; KR SourceOne; Linda Hall. **CCC.**
　Supersedes in part: I E E E Transactions on Systems, Man and Cybernetics (ISSN 0018-9472); Which was formed by the merger of (1968-1971): I E E E Transactions on Man-Machine Systems (ISSN 0536-1540); (1965-1971): I E E E Transactions on Systems Science and Cybernetics (ISSN 0536-1567)

003　　　　　　　BE
INTERNATIONAL ASSOCIATION FOR CYBERNETICS. NEWSLETTER/ASSOCIATION INTERNATIONALE DE CYBERNETIQUE. BULLETIN D'INFORMATION. (Text in English, French) q. 3000 BEF includes Cybernetica. International Association for Cybernetics - Association International de Cybernetique, Palais des Expositions, Avenur Sergent Vrithoff 2, 5000 Namur, Belgium. TEL 32-81-735209. FAX 32-81-742945. **Document type:** newsletter.

COMPUTERS — CYBERNETICS

003　　　　　　BE　　ISSN 0074-3380
INTERNATIONAL CONGRESS FOR CYBERNETICS. PROCEEDINGS/CONGRES INTERNATIONAL DE CYBERNETIQUE. ACTES. 1956. triennial, 14th, 1995. 9000 BEF. International Association for Cybernetics - Association Internationale de Cybernetique, Palais des Expositions, Avenue Sergent Vrithoff 2, 5000 Namur, Belgium. TEL 32-81-735209. FAX 32-81-742045. TELEX 59101 BEP NAMUR B. **Document type:** proceedings.

003
TA167　　　　UK　　ISSN 1071-5819
　　　　　　　　　　　　CODEN: IHSTEI
INTERNATIONAL JOURNAL OF HUMAN-COMPUTER STUDIES. 1969. m. £246($417) to individuals; institutions £773 (effective 1998). Academic Press Ltd. (Subsidiary of: Harcourt Brace & Company Ltd.), 24-28 Oval Rd., London NW1 7DX, England. TEL 44-171-2674466. FAX 44-171-4822293. TELEX 25775 ACPRES G. E-mail: apsubs@acad.com; URL: http://www.hbuk.co.uk/ap/iijhcs; http://www.europe.idealibrary.com/. (Subscr. to: Harcourt Brace & Company Ltd., Foots Cray High St., Sidcup, Kent DA14 5HP, England. TEL 44-181-300-3322. FAX 44-181-3090807) Ed. B.R. Gaines. R&P contact: Catherine John. adv. contact: Nik Screen. (reprint service avail. from SWZ) **Indexed:** A.I.Abstr. (until 1992), A.S.& T.Ind., Abstr.Hum.Comp.Inter., ASCA, Biol.Abstr., CAD CAM Abstr., Chem.Abstr., Commun.Abstr., Compumath, Comput.Abstr., Comput.Cont., Comput.Rev., Curr.Cont., Cyb.Abstr., Educ.Tech.Abstr., Eng.Ind., Ergon.Abstr., Excerp.Med., INSPEC, Psychol.Abstr. (1971-), Psycscan., Robomat (until 1992), SSCI, Tech.Educ.Abstr, Zent.Math. **Document type:** academic/scholarly publication.
●Also available online.
—BLDSC (4542.288100); AskIEEE; CISTI; Ei; Genuine Article; KR SourceOne; SWETS; UnCover. **CCC.**
Incorporates (1989-1995): Knowledge Acquisition (ISSN 1042-8143); **Formerly** (until 1994): International Journal of Man-Machine Studies (ISSN 0020-7373)
Description: Aimed at engineers, researchers, psychologists, and computer scientists. Contains articles on a broad range of pertinent topics, from person-machine interaction to management and medical information systems.

THE INTERNET LAW HANDBOOK NEWSLETTER. see LAW

001.53
TJ212　　　　RU　　ISSN 0130-6774
ITOGI NAUKI I TEKHNIKI: TEKHNICHESKAYA KIBERNETIKA. (Text in Russian) 1967. irreg., latest vols.26-28, 1989. price varies. Vsesoyuznyi Institut Nauchno-Tekhnicheskoi Informatsii (VINITI), Baltiiskaya ul. 14, Moscow A-219, Russia. (Subscr. to: Mezhdunarodnaya Kniga, Dimitrova ul. 39, 113095 Moscow, Russia) **Indexed:** Zent.Math.
—CISTI.

ITOGI NAUKI I TEKHNIKI: TEORIYA VEROYATNOSTEJ - MATEMATICHESKAYA STATISTIKA-TEORETICHESKAYA KIBERNETIKA. see MATHEMATICS

003
QA76　　　　GW　　CODEN: JICYE5
JOURNAL OF AUTOMATA, LANGUAGES AND COMBINATORICS. (Text in English, German) 1965. q. DM.110 to individuals; institutions DM.140 (effective 1996). Otto-von-Guericke-Universitaet Magdeburg, Fakultaet fuer Informatik, Postfach 4120, 39016 Magdeburg, Germany. TEL 49-391-6712851. FAX 49-391-6712810. E-mail: jalc@irb.cs.uni-magdeburg.de. Ed. Juergen Dassow. adv.; bk.rev.; charts; illus.; stat.; index. circ. 350. **Indexed:** Br.Ceram.Abstr., Comput.Rev., Cyb.Abstr., INSPEC (1968-), Math.R. **Document type:** academic/scholarly publication.
—AskIEEE; CISTI; Ei; KR SourceOne; Linda Hall; UnCover.
Former titles (until 1996): Journal of Information Processing and Cybernetics (ISSN 0863-0593); (until vol.23, 1987): Elektronische Informationsverarbeitung und Kybernetik (ISSN 0013-5712)

JOURNAL OF AUTOMATION & INFORMATION SCIENCES. see COMPUTERS — Automation

001.53 620
QA75.5　　　　RU　　ISSN 1064-2307
　　　　　　　　　　　　CODEN: JSSIE5
JOURNAL OF COMPUTER & SYSTEMS SCIENCES INTERNATIONAL. English translation of: Rossiiskaya Akademiya Nauk. Izvestiya. Tekhnicheskaya Kibernetika. 1963. bi-m. $1632 (foreign $1725) (effective 1997). (Russian Academy of Sciences, RU) Maik Nauka - Interperiodica, Mezhdunarodnyi Otdel, Ul. Profsoyuznaya, 90, 117864 Moscow, Russia. (Dist. by: Maik Nauka - Interperiodica, Subscription Office, Box 1831, Birmingham, AL 35201-1831. TEL 205-995-1567. FAX 205-995-1588) Eds. Robert N. McDonough, Reed K. Even. adv.; bk.rev.; abstr.; bibl.; charts; illus.; pat.; stat.; index. (also avail. in microform from UMI) **Indexed:** A.I.Abstr., Arts & Hum.Cit.Ind., ASCA, CAD CAM Abstr., Compumath, Curr.Cont., Eng.Ind., INIS Atomind, INSPEC, Math.R., Robomat., SSCI, Zent.Math. **Document type:** academic/scholarly publication.
—BLDSC (0414.230000); AskIEEE; CISTI; Ei; Genuine Article; KR SourceOne; Linda Hall; SWETS; UMI; UnCover. **CCC.**
Former titles (until 1992): Soviet Journal of Computer and Systems Sciences (ISSN 0882-4002); (until 1984): Engineering Cybernetics (ISSN 0013-788X)
Description: Contains papers on computer and systems science, control theory, and optimization studies. Specific topics include algorithms, design of computer and control systems, data processing, robotics, pattern recognition and applied mathematics.

006.3　　　　UK　　ISSN 0334-1860
　　　　　　　　　　　　CODEN: JISYEH
JOURNAL OF INTELLIGENT SYSTEMS. 1986. q. $270 (effective 1997). Freund Publishing House Ltd., Ste. 500, Chesham House, 150 Regent St., London W1R 5FA, England. E-mail: hs92jis@brunel.ac.uk; URL: http://http2.brunel.ac.uk:8080/-hs92jis/. (Alt. addr.: P.O. Box 35010, Tel Aviv, Israel. TEL 972-3-5628540. FAX 972-3-5628538) Ed. M. Wright. adv.; abstr. circ. 1,000. **Indexed:** Art.Int.Abstr., INSPEC (1987-), Psychol.Abstr. (1992-), Zent.Math. **Document type:** academic/scholarly publication.
—BLDSC (5007.538600); AskIEEE; CISTI; KR SourceOne; SWETS.

KEY ABSTRACTS - HUMAN-COMPUTER INTERACTION. see COMPUTERS — Abstracting, Bibliographies, Statistics

001.53
TJ212　　　　KR　　ISSN 1019-5262
　　　　　　　　　　　　CODEN: KBRNA5
KIBERNETIKA I SISTEMNYI ANALIZ, vsesoyuznyi nauchno-teoreticheskii zhurnal. (Text in Russian; summaries in English and Ukrainian) 1965. bi-m. $225 (effective 1998). Akademiya Nauk Ukrainy, Institut Kibernetiki im. V.M. Glushkova, Prosp. Akad. Glushkova, 40, 252650 Kiev, Ukraine. TEL 38-44-2666461. (Dist. by: Mezhdunarodnaya Kniga, B. Yakimanka 39, 117049 Moscow, Russia. TEL 7-095-2384967. FAX 7-095-2384634; Dist. in U.S. by: Victor Kamkin Inc., 4956 Boiling Brook Pkwy, Rockville, MD 20852. TEL 301-881-5973) Ed. V.S. Mikhalevich. index. **Indexed:** Biol.Abstr., Cyb.Abstr., Djerelo, INIS Atomind., INSPEC, Math.R., Zent.Math.
—BLDSC (0088.726500); CASDDS; CISTI; KNAW; Linda Hall.
Formerly (until 1991): Kibernetika (ISSN 0023-1274)

001.53
Q300　　　　KR　　ISSN 0454-9910
　　　　　　　　　　　　CODEN: KVYTAS
KIBERNETIKA I VYCHISLITEL'NAYA TEKHNIKA; respublikanskii mezhvedomstvennyi sbornik nauchnykh trudov. English translation: Cybernetics and Computing Technology (US ISSN 0739-8417) (Text in Russian) 1965. 4/yr. Akademiya Nauk Ukrainy, Institut Kibernetiki im. V.M. Glushkova, Prosp. Akad. Glushkova, 40, 252207 Kiev 207, Ukraine. TEL 38-44-2652494. Ed. V.S. Mikhalevich. **Indexed:** Cyb.Abstr., INSPEC, Math.R., Zent.Math.
—AskIEEE; CASDDS; CISTI; KR SourceOne; Linda Hall. **CCC.**

001.53
Q300　　　　UK　　ISSN 0368-492X
　　　　　　　　　　　　CODEN: KBNTA3
KYBERNETES. 1970. 9/yr. £2389($3549) (foreign Aus.$4659) (effective 1998). M C B University Press Ltd., 60-62 Toller Ln., Bradford, W. Yorks BD8 9BY, England. TEL 44-1274-777700. FAX 44-1274-785200. TELEX 51317-MCBUNI-G. URL: http://www.mcb.co.uk. Ed. Brian Ruddall. bk.rev.; index. circ. 750. (back issues avail.; reprint service avail. from SWZ) **Indexed:** Abstr.Hum.Comp.Inter., ASCA, Biol.Abstr., Chem.Abstr., Compumath, Curr.Cont., Cyb.Abstr., INSPEC, Math.R., SSCI, Zent.Math. **Document type:** academic/scholarly publication.
—BLDSC (5134.840000); AskIEEE; CISTI; Ei; Genuine Article; KR SourceOne; Linda Hall; UMI. **CCC**
Description: Concerned with the interdisciplinary study of cybernetics and systems. Topics covered include artificial intelligence, automation, cybernetic modelling, the philosophy of cybernetics and its interrelations with other sciences.

001.53
Q300　　　　XR　　ISSN 0023-5954
　　　　　　　　　　　　CODEN: KYBNAI
KYBERNETIKA/CYBERNETICS. (Text in Czech, English, French, German, Russian, Slovak) 1965. bi-m. DM.213. Ceska Akademie Ved, Ustav Teorie Informace a Automatizace, Pod Vodarenskou Vezi 4, 182 08 Prague 8, Czech Republic. (Dist. in Western countries by: Kubon & Sagner, P.O. Box 34 01 08, 8000 Munich 34, Germany) Ed. Stanislav Kubik. bk.rev.; bibl.; charts; illus.; index. circ. 1,250. **Indexed:** Appl.Mech.Rev., ASCA, Bibl.Ling., C.C.M.J., Compumath, Comput.Abstr., Curr.Cont. (1967-), Cyb.Abstr., Eng.Ind., Ind.Sci.Rev., INSPEC, Int.Aerosp.Abstr., Math.R., SSCI, Stat.Theor.Meth.Abstr. (1967-), Zent.Math.
—BLDSC (5134.852000); AskIEEE; CISTI; Genuine Article; KR SourceOne; Linda Hall; SWETS.
Description: Theoretical problems of cybernetics, information theory, systems and control theory, operations research, computer science (including automata and abstract languages), cybernetics in biology, medicine, and linguistics.

001.53 620
TA1632　　　　GW　　ISSN 0932-8092
　　　　　　　　　　　　CODEN: MVAPEO
MACHINE VISION & APPLICATIONS. Online edition (GW ISSN 1432-1769) (Text in English) 1988. bi-m. DM.515.40 (foreign DM.520.80) (effective 1998). (International Association for Pattern Recognition) Springer-Verlag, Heidelberger Platz 3, 14197 Berlin, Germany. TEL 49-30-82787-0. FAX 49-30-82787448. E-mail: subscriptions@springer.de; URL: http://link.springer.de. (Subscr. in N. America to: Springer-Verlag New York, Inc., 333 Meadowlands Pkwy., Secaucus, NJ 07094. TEL 212-460-1500. FAX 212-473-6272) Ed. M.M. Trivedi. adv. circ. 1,480. (also avail. in microform from UMI) **Indexed:** Abstr.Hum.Comp.Inter., ASCA, Compumath, Curr.Cont., INSPEC (1988-). **Document type:** academic/scholarly publication.
●Also available online.
—BLDSC (5326.570000); AskIEEE; CISTI; Ei; Genuine Article; KR SourceOne; Linda Hall; SWETS; UMI; UnCover. **CCC.**
Description: Covers applications and engineering aspects of image-related computing including original contributions dealing with scientific, commercial, industrial, military and biomedical applications.

MEDIA COMPUTING; email report on emerging media markets. see COMPUTERS — Data Communication And Data Transmission Systems

001.53
QA1　　　　US　　ISSN 0278-6419
　　　　　　　　　　　　CODEN: MUCTD4
MOSCOW UNIVERSITY COMPUTATIONAL MATHEMATICS AND CYBERNETICS. English translation of: Moskovskii Universitet. Vestnik. Seriya 15. Vychislitel'naya Matematika i Kibernetika. 1977. q. $1015 (effective 1998). (Moskovskii Universitet, RU) Allerton Press, Inc., 150 Fifth Ave., New York, NY 10011. TEL 212-924-3950. FAX 212-463-9684. Ed. D.P. Kostomarov. index. **Indexed:** INSPEC (1978-), Zent.Math. **Document type:** academic/scholarly publication.
—BLDSC (0416.238300); AskIEEE; KR SourceOne; Linda Hall; SWETS. **CCC.**
Description: Provides papers which report on the theoretical research of practical problems in computer technology, artificial intelligence, computation algorithms, system dynamics, etc.

COMPUTERS — CYBERNETICS

001.53   KR   ISSN 0374-3896
CODEN: NVIFB8
NAUKOVEDENIE I INFORMATIKA; respublikanskii mezhvedomstvennyi sbornik nauchnykh trudov. 1969. a. Akademiya Nauk Ukrainy, Institut Kibernetiki im. V.M. Glushkova, Prosp. Akad. Glushkova, 40, 252207 Kiev, Ukraine. TEL 38-44-2652494. (Dist. by: Mezhdunarodnaya Kniga, B. Yakimanka 39, 117049 Moscow, Russia) Ed. G.M. Dobrov. **Indexed:** INSPEC.
—AskIEEE; CASDDS; CISTI; KR SourceOne; Linda Hall.

001.53   UK   ISSN 0143-8115
NUMERICAL ENGINEERING. 1979. bi-m. £36. Numerical Engineering Society, 3 Priory Ct., Studley, Warwickshire B80 7BB, England. TEL 0527-854895. Ed. Keith Schofield. adv.; bk.rev.; circ. 700 (paid). **Indexed:** INSPEC. **Document type:** newsletter.
—CISTI.

001.53 001.6   KR   ISSN 0135-3071
CODEN: OTPIAE
OTBOR I OBRABOTKA INFORMATSII; respublikanskii mezhvedomstvennyi sbornik nauchnykh trudov. 1965. s-a. (Akademiya Nauk Ukrainy, Fiziko-mekhanicheskiy Institut) Vidavnitstvo Naukova Dumka, Vul. Tereshchenkivska 3, 252601 Kiev, Ukraine. TEL 044-224-4068. FAX 044-224-7060. (Dist. by: Mezhdunarodnaya Kniga, B. Yakimanka 39, 117049 Moscow, Russia) Ed. P.M. Soprunyuk. **Indexed:** INSPEC, Int.Aerosp.Abstr., Math.R.
—AskIEEE; CASDDS; KR SourceOne; Linda Hall. **CCC.**
Formerly (until 1987): Otbor i Peredacha Informatsii (ISSN 0474-8662)

001.53 629.8   PL   ISSN 0373-8698
POLITECHNIKA GDANSKA. ZESZYTY NAUKOWE. ELEKTRONIKA. (Text in English, Polish; summaries in Russian and one West-European language) 1967. irreg. price varies. Politechnika Gdanska, Ul. G. Narutowicza 11-12, 80-952 Gdansk 6, Poland. (Dist. by: Osrodek Rozpowszechniania Wydawnictw Naukowych PAN, Palac Kultury i Nauki, 00-901 Warsaw, Poland) bibl.; charts; illus.
—Linda Hall.
Description: Deals with cybernetics, automation, computer science, hydroacoustics, microwave technology, telecommunications and electronic equipment technology.

001.53 621.38   PL   ISSN 0324-9794
POLITECHNIKA WROCLAWSKA. INSTYTUT CYBERNETYKI TECHNICZNEJ. PRACE NAUKOWE. KONFERENCJE. (Text in Polish; summaries in English and Russian) 1973; N.S. 1996. irreg., no.1-2, 1996. price varies. Oficyna Wydawnicza Politechniki Wroclawskiej, Wybrzeze Wyspianskiego 27, 50-370 Wroclaw, Poland. TEL 48-71-222940. FAX 48-71-223664. TELEX 71-22-54 PWRPL. (Dist. by: Ars Polona, Krakowskie Przedmiescie 7, 00-068 Warsaw, Poland) Ed. Maria Lyko. R&P contact: Halina Dudek. adv. **Indexed:** Math.R. **Document type:** proceedings.
—AskIEEE; KR SourceOne.
Description: For automation engineers and scientists. Contains scholarly papers and-or abstracts on robotics, automation and artificial intelligence applications.

001.53   PL   ISSN 0324-9786
TJ212
POLITECHNIKA WROCLAWSKA. INSTYTUT CYBERNETYKI TECHNICZNEJ. PRACE NAUKOWE. MONOGRAFIE. (Text in Polish; summaries in English and Russian) 1974. irreg., no.25, 1997. price varies. Oficyana Wydawnicza Politechniki Wroclawskiej, Wybrzeze Wyspianskiego 27, 50-370 Wroclaw, Poland. TEL 48-22-222940. FAX 48-71-2223664. TELEX 712559 PWRPL. (Dist. by Ars Polona, Krakowskie Przedmiescie 7, 00-068 Warsaw, Poland) adv. circ. 675. **Indexed:** Math.R. **Document type:** monographic series.
—Linda Hall.
Description: Halina/Dudek

001.53 621.38   PL   ISSN 0324-9808
TJ212
POLITECHNIKA WROCLAWSKA. INSTYTUT CYBERNETYKI TECHNICZNEJ. PRACE NAUKOWE. STUDIA I MATERIALY. (Text in Polish; summaries in English and Russian) 1972. irreg., no.30, 1983. price varies. (Politechnika Wroclawska) Oficyna Wydawnicza Politechniki Wroclawskiej, Wybrzeze Wyspianskiego 27, 50-370 Wroclaw, Poland. TEL 48-71-222940. FAX 48-71-223664. TELEX 712559 PWRPL. (Dist. by: Ars Polona, Krakowskie Przedmiescie 7, 00-068 Warsaw, Poland) R&P contact: Halina Dudek. adv. **Indexed:** Math.R.
Document type: academic/scholarly publication.
—Linda Hall.
Description: For engineers and computer systems designers and planners. Contains scholarly papers on various aspects of automation, artificial intelligence and robotics.

003   BE
PRINCIPIA CYBERNETICA NEWSLETTER. 1990. irreg. free. Principia Cybernetica Project, c/o Free University of Brussels, Pleinlaan 2, 1050 Brussels, Belgium. TEL 32-2-6412525. FAX 32-2-6412489. E-mail: PCP@vnet3.vub.ac.be; URL: http://pespmc1.vub.ac.be/. Ed. Francis Heylighen. (back issues avail.) **Document type:** newsletter.
● Available only online.
Refereed Serial

001.53   BU   ISSN 0204-9848
TJ212   CODEN: PTKRDU
PROBLEMI NA TEKHNICHESKATA KIBERNETIKA I ROBOTIKA/PROBLEMS OF ENGINEERING CYBERNETICS AND ROBOTICS. (Text in various languages) 1975. irreg. 0.89 lv. per no. (Bulgarska Akademiia na Naukite) Publishing House of the Bulgarian Academy of Sciences, Acad. G. Bonchev St., Bldg. 6, 1113 Sofia, Bulgaria. circ. 470. (reprint service avail. from IRC) **Indexed:** Cyb.Abstr., Math.R., Zent.Math.
—BLDSC (0133.124500); AskIEEE; CISTI; KR SourceOne; Linda Hall.
Description: Provides scholarly papers on all aspects of robotics and cybernetics. Topics may include grippers, algorithms, automatic learning, and industrial and measuring robots.

003 629.8   FR
QA267.5.S4   CODEN: RAPIEK
R A I R O: A P P I: JOURNAL EUROPEEN DES SYSTEMES AUTOMATISES. (Revue Francaise d'Automatique, d'Informatique et de Recherche Operationnelle) (Text in French and English) 1966. 10/yr. 2700 F. (foreign 2950 F.) (effective 1997). (Association Francaise des Sciences et Technologies de l'Information et des Systemes) Gauthier - Villars, 5 rue Laromiguiere, 75005 Paris, France. TEL 33-1-40466200. FAX 33-1-40466201. Ed. P. Prevot. adv.; bibl.; charts. circ. 1,100. (also avail. in microfilm from UMI) **Indexed:** Compumath, Curr.Cont., Excerp.Med., INSPEC (1985-), Math.R., Zent.Math.
—AskIEEE; CISTI; Ei; Genuine Article; KR SourceOne; SWETS. **CCC.**
Formed by the merger of (1991-1996): Diagnostic et Surete de Fonctionnement (ISSN 1166-3049); (1988-1996): Revue d'Automatique et de Productique Appliquees (ISSN 0990-7009); (1985-1996): Automatique - Productique Informatique Industrielle (ISSN 0296-1598); Former titles: R A I R O Automatique (ISSN 0399-0524); (1972-1977): Revue Francaise d'Automatique, Informatique, Recherche Operationnelle. Automatique (ISSN 0397-9369).
Description: Covers the activities of the Association at the university and industry levels.

001.53   FR   ISSN 0988-3754
QA1   CODEN: RITAE4
R A I R O INFORMATIQUE THEORIQUE ET APPLIQUEE - THEORETICAL INFORMATICS AND APPLICATIONS. (Revue Francaise d'Automatique, d'Informatique et de Recherche Operationnelle) (Text in English and French) 1966. 6/yr. 1404 F. (foreign 1868 F.) (effective 1998). (Association Francaise des Sciences et Technologies de l'Information et des Systemes) Dunod, 5 rue Laromiguiere, 75005 Paris, France. TEL 33-1-40466200.
FAX 33-1-40466201. TELEX 634 916 F. E-mail: gauthier.villars.publisher@mail.sgip.fr; URL: http://www.gauthier-villars.fr. (Subscr. to: Societe de Periodiques Specialises, B.P. 22, 41354 Vineuil Cedex, France. TEL 33-2-54504612. FAX 33-2-54504611) Ed. C. Choffrut. bibl.; charts. circ. 1,025. (also avail. in microfilm from UMI) **Indexed:** ASCA, Compumath, Curr.Cont., Cyb.Abstr., INSPEC (1986-), Math.R., SSCI, Zent.Math.
—BLDSC (8814.559300); AskIEEE; CISTI; Ei; Genuine Article; KR SourceOne; Linda Hall; SWETS. **CCC.**
Formerly: R A I R O Informatique Theorique - Theoretical Informatics (ISSN 0399-0540) Supersedes in part (in 1972): Revue Francaise d'Informatique et de Recherche Operationnelle (ISSN 0035-3035)
Description: Contains research of high scientific level in theoretical computer science and its applications.

003   FR   ISSN 0399-0559
T57.6   CODEN: RSROD3
R A I R O RECHERCHE OPERATIONNELLE - OPERATIONS RESEARCH. (Text in English and French) 1966. 4/yr. 972 F. (institutions outside the Americas 1296 F.). (Association Francaise des Sciences et Technologies de l'Information et des Systemes) Gauthier - Villars, 5 rue Laromiguiere, 75005 Paris, France. TEL 33-1-40466200. FAX 33-1-40466201. TELEX 634 916 F. E-mail: gauthier.villars.publisher@mail.sgip.fr; URL: http://www.gauthier-villars.fr. (Subscr. to: Societe de Periodiques Specialises, B.P. 22, 41354 Vineuil Cedex, France. TEL 33-2-54504612. FAX 33-2-54504611) Ed. J. Abadie. adv.; bk.rev.; bibl.; charts. circ. 1,025. (also avail. in microfilm from UMI) **Indexed:** ASCA, Compumath, Curr.Cont., Cyb.Abstr., Ind.Sci.Rev., INSPEC, Int.Abstr.Oper.Res., Math.R., SSCI, Zent.Math.
—BLDSC (7253.215000); AskIEEE; CISTI; Ei; Genuine Article; KR SourceOne; Linda Hall; SWETS. **CCC.**
Formerly (1972-1977): Revue Francaise d'Automatique, Informatique et de Recherche Operationnelle; Supersedes in part (in 1972): Revue Francaise d'Informatique et de Recherche Operationnelle (ISSN 0035-3035)
Description: Covers all branches of operations research and scientific management. Includes all practical and theoretical aspects pertaining to mathematical theories as well as modelling, algorithms and computer science.
Refereed Serial

001.53   FR   ISSN 0752-4072
QA75.5   CODEN: TTSIDJ
R A I R O - TECHNIQUE ET SCIENCES INFORMATIQUES. (Text in English or French) 1967. 10/yr. 2150 F. (foreign 2350 F.) (effective 1997). (Association Francaise pour la Cybernetique Economique et Technique) Editions Hermes, 14 rue Lantiez, 75017 Paris, France. TEL 33-1-42294466.
FAX 33-1-42292556. Ed. Rene Jacquart. bibl.; charts. circ. 4,000. (also avail. in microfilm from UMI) **Indexed:** Curr.Cont., INSPEC (1982-), Math.R., Zent.Math.
—BLDSC (8740.008000); AskIEEE; CISTI; KR SourceOne; Linda Hall; SWETS. **CCC.**
Former titles: R A I R O Informatique - Computer Science (ISSN 0399-0532); (until 1977): Revue Francaise d'Automatique, Informatique et de Recherche Operationnelle. Informatique; Supersedes in part (in 1972): Revue Francaise d'Informatique et de Recherche Operationnelle (ISSN 0035-3035)
Description: Information on software engineering and programming; languages and compilers; operating, information and distributed systems; artificial intelligence as well as pattern recognition.

COMPUTERS — DATA BASE MANAGEMENT

001.53 371.3   PE   ISSN 0034-866X
REVISTA DE TECNOLOGIA EDUCATIVA. (Text in English, German and Spanish) 1967. s-a. exchange basis. Universidad Nacional de Trujillo, Seccion de Tecnologia Educacional, Apdo. 315, Trujillo, Peru. Ed. Atilio Leon Rubio. bk.rev.; charts; illus. circ. 600.
     Formerly (until vol.9, 1976): Revista de Pedagogia Cibernetica e Instruccion Programada.

003   RU
ROSSIISKAYA AKADEMIYA NAUK. IZVESTIIA. TEKHNICHESKAYA KIBERNETIKA. English translation: Journal of Computer & Systems Sciences International (US ISSN 1064-2307) 1963. bi-m. 39 Rub. (Otdelenie Mekhaniki i Protsessov Upravleniya) Izdatel'stvo Nauka, Mezhdunarodnyi Otdel, Profsoyuznaya 90, 117864 Moscow, Russia. (Dist. by: Mezhdunarodnaya Kniga, ul. B. Yakimanka 39, 117049 Moscow, Russia) Ed. Ve.A. Fedosov. **Indexed**: Chem.Abstr., Comput.Rev., Cyb.Abstr., INIS Atomind., Math.R., Zent.Math. **Document type**: academic/scholarly publication.
  —CISTI; KNAW; Linda Hall.
     Formerly (until 1992): Akademiya Nauk S.S.S.R. Izvestiya. Tekhnicheskaya Kibernetika (ISSN 0002-3388)

658.4 001.53   II   ISSN 0376-4087
S C I M A. (Text in English) 1972. s-a. $50. Society of Management Science and Applied Cybernetics, c/o CSIR Complex, New Delhi 110 012, India. Ed. A. Ghosal. adv.; bk.rev. circ. 500. **Indexed**: Zent.Math.

001.53   II
S C I M A SPECIAL SERIES. (Text in English) 1980. irreg. price varies. Society of Management Science and Applied Cybernetics, c/o CSIR Complex, New Delhi 110 012, India. Ed. A. Ghosal. circ. 1,000.

001.53 629.8   US   ISSN 8756-4017
SENSOR TECHNOLOGY; a monthly intelligence service. 1985. m. $610 (foreign $670). Technical Insights (Subsidiary of: John Wiley & Sons, Inc.), 32 N. Dean St., Englewood, NJ 07631-2807. TEL 201-568-4744. FAX 201-568-8247. URL: http://www.insights.com. Ed. Angelo DePalma; Pub. Peter Katz. bibl.; charts; pat.; stat.; tr.lit. (back issues avail.) **Document type**: newsletter.
  —BLDSC (8241.784000). **CCC**.
     Description: Follows rapidly evolving technological research and details complete advances.

SENSORS; the journal of applied sensing technology. see **INSTRUMENTS**

SENSOR'S BUYERS GUIDE. see **INSTRUMENTS**

001.53   NE   ISSN 0275-5807
STUDIES IN CYBERNETICS. 1982. irreg. latest vol.24. Gordon and Breach - Harwood Academic, Amsteldisk 166, 1st Fl., 1079 LH Amsterdam, Netherlands. (Subscr. to: International Publishers Distributor, Box 32160, Newark, NJ 07102. TEL 800-545-8398. FAX 215-750-6343) Ed. F.H. George. index. (also avail. in microform) **Indexed**: INSPEC, Zent.Math. **Document type**: monographic series.
  —BLDSC (8490.326000); CISTI.
     Refereed Serial

003 621.39   NE   ISSN 0168-7875
QA76.88   **CODEN: SPCOEL**
SUPERCOMPUTER. bi-m. fl.500 in Europe; elsewhere $310 (effective 1997). ASFRA B.V., Voorhaven 33, 1135 BL Edam, Netherlands. TEL 31-2993-72751. FAX 31-2993-72877. E-mail: asfra@pi.net. **Indexed**: ASCA, Compumath, Curr.Cont., INSPEC (1988-). **Document type**: academic/scholarly publication.
  —BLDSC (8547.068080); AskIEEE; Genuine Article; KR SourceOne; SWETS.
     Supersedes (in 1984): Supernieuwsbrief.
     Refereed Serial

003 621.39   NE   ISSN 0924-5553
SUPERCOMPUTER EUROPEAN WATCH. 1989. 11/yr. fl.525 in Europe; elsewhere $328 (effective 1998). ASFRA B.V., Voorhaven 33, 1135 BL Edam, Netherlands. TEL 31-299-372751. FAX 31-299-372877. E-mail: asfra@pi.net. **Document type**: academic/scholarly publication.

001.53   US   ISSN 1063-6889
QA76.9.C62
SYMPOSIUM ON COMPUTER ARITHMETIC. PROCEEDINGS. 3rd, 1975. biennial. price varies. (Institute of Electrical and Electronics Engineers, Inc.) I E E E Computer Society Press, 10662 Los Vaqueros Circle, Los Alamitos, CA 90720-1264. TEL 714-821-8380. FAX 714-821-4641. **Document type**: proceedings.
  —BLDSC (8585.163300). **CCC**.
     Description: Describes new and theoretical developments in computer arithmetic.
     Refereed Serial

003   PL   ISSN 0239-8044
TECHNIKI KOMPUTEROWE; biuletyn informacyjny. (Text in Polish; summaries in English, Polish) 1962-1989; resumed 1993. a. exchange basis. Instytut Maszyn Matematycznych, Ul. Krzywickiego 34, 02-078 Warsaw, Poland. TEL 48-2-6218441. FAX 48-22-6299270. TELEX 817880. E-mail: czajkowski@imm.org.pl. Ed. Roman Czajkowski. R&P contact: Roman Chajkowski. adv.; charts; illus. circ. 100. **Document type**: bulletin.
  —AskIEEE; KR SourceOne.

625.1 001.53   JA
TETSUDO NI OKERU SAIBANETIKKUSU RIYO KOKUNAI SHINPOJUMU RONBUNSHU/SYMPOSIUM ON THE USE OF CYBERNETICS ON THE RAILWAY. PAPERS. (Text in Japanese) 1964. a. Nihon Tetsudo Saibanetikkusu Kyogikai - Japan Railway Cybernetics Association, 28-6, Kameido 1-chome, Koto-ku, Tokyo 136, Japan.

003   NE   ISSN 0921-3406
THEORY AND DECISION LIBRARY. SERIES D: SYSTEM THEORY, KNOWLEDGE ENGINEERING AND PROBLEM SOLVING. (Text in English) 1973; N.S. 1987. irreg., vol.16, 1995. price varies. Kluwer Academic Publishers, Postbus 17, 3300 AA Dordrecht, Netherlands. TEL 31-78-6392392. FAX 31-78-6392254. TELEX 29245 KAPG NL. E-mail: services@wkap.nl; URL: http://www.wkap.nl. (Dist. by: Kluwer Academic Publishers Group, P.O. Box 322, 3300 AH Dordrecht. TEL 31-78-6392392. FAX 31-78-6546474; N. America dist. addr.: Box 358, Accord Sta., Hingham, MA 02018-0358. TEL 617-871-6600. FAX 617-871-6528) **Indexed**: Zent.Math. **Document type**: monographic series.
  —BLDSC (8814.628080).
     Supersedes in part (in 1987): Theory and Decision Library (ISSN 0921-3376)
     Refereed Serial

003   PL   ISSN 0208-4805
HB139
UNIWERSYTET GDANSKI. WYDZIAL EKONOMIKI PRODUKCJI. ZESZYTY NAUKOWE. CYBERNETYKA EKONOMICZNA I INFORMATYKA. (Text in Polish; summaries in English and Russian) 1972. irreg., latest no.7. price varies. Uniwersytet Gdanski, Wydzial Ekonomiki Produkcji, c/o Biblioteka Glowna, Ul. Armii Krajowej 110, 81-824 Sopot, Poland. TEL 51-0061. TELEX 051 2247 BMOR PL. (Dist. by: Ars Polona-Ruch, Krakowskie Przedmiescie 7, 00-680 Warsaw, Poland) Ed. Wieslawa Makac. **Document type**: academic/scholarly publication.
     Description: Covers statistical and econometrical investigations of economic processes, problems of cost analysis and computer science.

UPRAVLYAYUSHCHIE SISTEMY I MASHINY. see **COMPUTERS — Computer Systems**

V R WORLD. see **COMPUTERS — Computer Simulation**

VIRTUAL REALITY NOW; developments and applications. see **COMPUTERS — Computer Simulation**

VIRTUAL REALITY REPORT. see **COMPUTERS — Computer Simulation**

003 004.678 384   US
WEEKLY PLANET. (Text in English, Spanish) w. Arcadia Studios, E-mail: info@arcadiastudios.com; URL: http://www.arcadiastudios.com. **Document type**: newsletter.
  • Available only online.
     Description: Covers cybernetic, telecommunication, computer and internet news from Latin America and the Caribbean.

WINTER SIMULATION CONFERENCE. PROCEEDINGS. see **COMPUTERS — Computer Simulation**

COMPUTERS — Data Base Management

658.403   US   ISSN 0362-5915
QA76.9.D3   **CODEN: ATDSD3**
A C M TRANSACTIONS ON DATABASE SYSTEMS. 1976. q. $109 to non-members. Association for Computing Machinery, 1515 Broadway, 17th Fl., New York, NY 10036-5701. TEL 212-869-7440. FAX 212-944-1318. TELEX 421686. Ed. Gio Wiederhold. charts; illus.; index. circ. 9,600. (also avail. in microfiche from KTO; microfilm from WWS) **Indexed**: A.I.Abstr., A.S.& T.Ind., ASCA, CAD CAM Abstr., Compumath, Comput.Abstr., Comput.Cont., Comput.Dtbs., Comput.Lit.Ind., Comput.Rev., Curr.Cont., Ergon.Abstr., Ind.Sci.Rev., INSPEC (1976-Math.R., Sci.Cit.Ind., SSCI, Tel.Abstr., Zent.Math.
  —BLDSC (0578.660000); AskIEEE; CISTI; Ei; Genuine Article; KR SourceOne; Linda Hall; SWETS; UMI; UnCover. **CCC**.
     Description: Reports on work in database management and design. Covers the development and validation of abstractions and models to describe database applications, formalization and design methods which exploit the knowledge for effective processing of data.

005.74 331.2   US
A F C O M'S ANNUAL SURVEY OF DATA PROCESSING OPERATIONS SALARIES. 1981. a. $195. (Association for Computer Operations Management) D C M S, Inc., 742 E. Chapman Ave., Orange, CA 92666. TEL 714-997-7966. FAX 714-997-9743. Ed. Len Eckhaus. charts; stat. **Document type**: trade publication.
     Description: Provides statistics on current salaries and anticipated increases for data processing operation positions, as well as information on budgeting, current trends in automation, and outsourcing.

658.4   CN
A I X CASE NEWSLETTER. 1992. 3/yr. (I B M Software Solutions Division) I B M Canada Ltd., 844 Don Mills Rd., Sta. 23, North York, ON M3C 1V7, Canada. TEL 416-448-2170. FAX 416-448-2114. E-mail: patsmith@vnet.ibm.com. Ed. Patti Smith. **Document type**: newsletter.

658.403   US   ISSN 0197-1476
TK5105
ADVANCES IN DATA COMMUNICATIONS MANAGEMENT. irreg. Heyden & Sons, Inc., c/o John Wiley & Sons, 605 Third Ave., New York, NY 10016. TEL 215-382-6673.
  —CISTI.

ADVANCES IN DATA PROCESSING MANAGEMENT. see **COMPUTERS — Electronic Data Processing**

ADVANCES IN DATABASES AND ARTIFICIAL INTELLIGENCE. see **COMPUTERS — Artificial Intelligence**

658.403   US   ISSN 0197-1433
QA76.9.D5
ADVANCES IN DISTRIBUTED PROCESSING MANAGEMENT. irreg. Heyden & Sons, Inc., c/o John Wiley & Sons, 605 Third Ave., New York, NY 10016.
  —CISTI.

658.4031   US
QA76.758
APPLICATION DEVELOPMENT TRENDS.* Variant title: A D Trends. 1989. m. (plus a. supplement). $39 (Canada and Mexico $69; overseas $99). Software Productivity Group, Inc., 1 Apple Hill No. 301, Natick, MA 01760-2072. Ed. John Desmond; Pub. Eliot D. Weinman. adv.; bk.rev. circ. 34,000. (back issues avail.) **Indexed**: CAD CAM Abstr. **Document type**: trade publication.
  • Also available online.
  —KR SourceOne. **CCC**.
     Formerly (until Jan. 1994): C A S E Trends (ISSN 1046-5944)
     Description: Provides comprehensive coverage of developments in application development software technology.

COMPUTERS — DATA BASE MANAGEMENT

658.403 US
ASSOCIATION FOR COMPUTING MACHINERY. SPECIAL INTEREST GROUP FOR MANAGEMENT INFORMATION SYSTEMS. CONFERENCE PROCEEDINGS. 1969. irreg. (approx. a.). $38 to non-members. Association for Computing Machinery, Special Interest Group for Management Information Systems, 1515 Broadway, 17th Fl., New York, NY 10036. TEL 212-869-7440. FAX 212-869-0481. TELEX 421686. Eds. Ephraim McLean, Detmar Straub. adv.
 Formerly: Association for Computing Machinery. Special Interest Group for Business Processing and Management. Conference Proceedings.

658.4031 US ISSN 1054-2760
QA76.9.B84
BOARDWATCH MAGAZINE. 1987. 12/yr. $36 (foreign $99). 8500 W. Bowles Ave., Ste. 210, Littleton, CO 80123. TEL 303-973-6038. FAX 303-973-3731. E-mail: subscriptions@boardwatch.com; URL: http://www.boardwatch.com. Ed. Jack Rickard. adv.; bk.rev.; circ. 27,687 (paid).
 ●Also available online.
 —KR SourceOne.
 Formerly (until 1989): Denver P C Boardwatch (ISSN 0894-5209)
 Description: Covers online information services, the World Wide Web, and the Internet.

658.4031 US
BUSINESS RULES ALERT!. (Supplement to: Data Base Newsletter) bi-m. $99 (foreign $131). Database Research Group, Inc., 1 State St., Ste. 1150, Boston, MA 02109. TEL 617-227-2583. FAX 617-227-2396. Ed. Ronald G. Ross. (back issues avail.)
 Formerly: Data Management Update (ISSN 1057-9923)
 Description: Focuses on product-software news.

658.4031 621.381 US
C A F M SYSTEM & STRATEGIES (YEAR);* a manager's guide to facility management automation. 1983. a. $99. Graphic Systems Inc., 52 JFK St., Ste. 3, Cambridge, MA 02138-4953. TEL 617-492-1148. FAX 617-492-4044. Ed. Larry Yu. adv.; index. circ. 1,000.
 Formerly (until 1986): Design Compudata (Year).
 Description: Guide to the automation of facility management functions, written especially for the facility manager considering automation or maintaining an automated system.

C A U S E PROFESSIONAL PAPER SERIES. see
EDUCATION — Higher Education

C D - R O M INTERNATIONAL. see COMPUTERS — Electronic Data Processing

C I O CANADA. see COMPUTERS — Computer Industry

658.4031 UK ISSN 0951-6050
CAB INTERNATIONAL DATABASE NEWS. 1987. q. free. CAB International, Wallingford, Oxon. OX10 8DE, England. TEL 44-1491-832111. FAX 44-1491-826090. TELEX 847964 COMAGG G. E-mail: cabi@cabi.org; URL: http://www.cabi.org. (U.S. subscr. to: CAB International, North American Office, 198 Madison Ave., New York, NY 10016. TEL 212-726-6490. FAX 212-686-7993) Ed. Chris Ison. **Document type:** newsletter.
 Description: Focuses on the development, coverage and applications of the CAB Abstracts database. New products from the database and online search examples are discussed.

658.403 US
COMPUTER-BASED INFORMATION SYSTEMS IN ORGANIZATIONS. 1984. irreg., latest 1995. price varies. Ablex Publishing Corporation, Box 5297, Greenwich, CT 06831-0504. TEL 203-661-7602. FAX 203-661-0792. Ed. Michael J. Ginzberg. **Document type:** academic/scholarly publication.
 Formerly: Computer-Based Information Systems in Information Management.

658.463 620.11 US ISSN 1050-8112
TA404.25
COMPUTERIZATION AND NETWORKING OF MATERIALS DATABASES. 1989. biennial. American Society for Testing & Materials, 100 Barr Harbor Dr., W. Conshohocken, PA 19428-2959. TEL 610-832-9500. FAX 610-832-9555. E-mail: service@local.astm.org. **Indexed:** Mat.Sci.Cit.Ind.
 —CCC.

COWLES - SIMBA REPORT ON DATABASE MARKETING. see BUSINESS AND ECONOMICS — Marketing And Purchasing

003.5 DK ISSN 0907-0877
CYBERNETICS & HUMAN KNOWING; a journal of second order cybernetics & cyber-semiotics. (Text in English) 1992. q. DKK 270 to individuals in Nordic countries (Europe DKK 335; elsewhere DKK 380); institutions DKK 540 (Europe DKK 670; elsewhere DKK 760) (effective 1997). Soeren Brier, Ed. & Pub., Royal School of Librarianship, Langagervej 4, DK-9220 Aalborg Oest, Denmark. TEL 45-98-157922. FAX 45-98-151042. E-mail: sbr@db.dk; URL: http://www.db.dk/dbaa/sbr/cyber.htm. bk.rev.
 —BLDSC (3506.390300).

005.74 US
D B 2 UPDATE. m. $340 (effective Aug. 1996). Xephon, 1301 W. Hwy. 407, Ste. 201-450, Lewisville, TX 75067. TEL 817-455-7050. FAX 817-455-2492. **Document type:** trade publication.

005.74 US
QA76.9.D3
D M REVIEW. (Data Management) 1991. m. $35 (Canada $49; foreign $79) (free to qualified personnel). Powell Publishing, Inc., 617 S. 94th St., West Allis, WI 52314-1222. TEL 414-771-7687. FAX 414-771-8058. Ed. Jean Schaver; Pub. Ron Powell. R&P contact: Jean Schaver. adv. contact: Tracy Powell. circ. 59,308 (controlled). (back issues avail.) **Document type:** trade publication.
 —BLDSC (3534.666000); KR SourceOne.
 Former titles: Data Management Review (ISSN 1067-3717); (until 1993): Data Base Management (Milwaukee) (ISSN 1066-5498); 370 - 390 Data Base Management (ISSN 1056-974X)
 Description: Covers topics relating to data warehousing issues and solutions.
 Refereed Serial

658.403 US ISSN 0095-0033
QA76 CODEN: DTBSAN
DATA BASE. 1968. q. $25. Association for Computing Machinery, Special Interest Group on Business Information Technology, 1515 Broadway, New York, NY 10036. TEL 212-869-7440. FAX 212-869-0481. TELEX 421686. illus. **Indexed:** Compumath, Comput.Abstr., Comput.Cont., Comput.Lit.Ind., Curr.Cont., Data Process.Dig., INSPEC (1969-).
 —AskIEEE; CISTI; Ei; KR SourceOne; SWETS; UnCover.
 Supersedes: S I G B D P Newsletter.

001.6 658.43 US ISSN 0735-9977
DATA BASE MANAGEMENT (NEW YORK). 1976. bi-m. $434. Auerbach Publishers (Subsidiary of: Warren, Gorham & Lamont), One Penn Plaza, New York, NY 10119. TEL 212-971-5000. FAX 212-971-5024. (Subscr. to: 31 St. James St., Boston, MA 02116-4112. TEL 800-950-1218. FAX 617-423-1914) Ed. Susan McDermott. (looseleaf format) **Document type:** trade publication.
 —CCC.
 Description: Provides current guidance on how to select, install, implement, and maintain data base management systems and keep abreast of trends.

658.403 US ISSN 0735-3677
CODEN: DBNEDK
DATA BASE NEWSLETTER. (Supplement avail.: Business Rules Alert!) 1973. bi-m. $129 (foreign $156). Database Research Group, Inc., 1 State St., Ste. 1150, Boston, MA 02109. TEL 617-227-2583. FAX 617-227-2396. E-mail: 75401,174@compuserve.com. Ed. Ronald G. Ross. bk.rev.; charts; illus. circ. 1,750. (looseleaf format; back issues avail.) **Indexed:** Comput.Lit.Ind., INSPEC (1991-). **Document type:** newsletter.
 —AskIEEE; CASDDS; KR SourceOne.
 Description: Covers various current topics in data administration, current product and industry news.

621.381 NE ISSN 0922-3487
CODEN: DHSTEV
DATA HANDLING IN SCIENCE AND TECHNOLOGY. 1984. irreg., vol.16, 1995. price varies. Elsevier Science B.V., Books Division, P.O. Box 211, 1000 AE Amsterdam, Netherlands. TEL 31-20-4853911. FAX 31-20-4853705. TELEX 18582 ESPA NL. E-mail: nlinfo-f@elsevier.nl; usinfo-f@elsevier.com; forinfo-kyf04035@niftyserve.or.jp; URL: http://www.elsevier.nl/. (Subscr. in the Americas to: Elsevier Science, Regional Sales Office, Box 945, New York, NY 10159-0945. TEL 212-633-3730. FAX 212-633-3680; Subscr. in Australasia and the Far East to: Elsevier Science (Singapore) Pte Ltd, No.1 Temasek Ave., No.17-01 Millenia Tower, Singapore 039192, Singapore. TEL 65-434-3727. FAX 65-337-2230; Subscr. in Japan to: Elsevier Science Japan, 9-15 Higashi-Azabu 1-chome, Minato-ku, Tokyo 106, Japan. TEL 81-3-5561-5033. FAX 81-3-5561-5047) **Indexed:** INSPEC, Zent.Math. **Document type:** monographic series.
 —BLDSC (3534.588000); CASDDS.
 Refereed Serial

001.6 658.403 IT
DATA MANAGER; rivista di informatica professionale. 1975. 10/yr. L.80000 (foreign L.92000) (effective 1996). Fratelli Pini Editori s.r.l., Via L. Battista Alberti 10, 20149 Milan, Italy. TEL 39-2-33101836. FAX 39-2-3450749. Ed. Giordano Pini. adv. contact: Lilia Pini. bk.rev. circ. 20,000. (back issues avail.) **Document type:** trade publication.
 Description: Includes interviews with managers of leading companies. Offers developments in the art of Italian informatics, its applications, future trends and prospectives.

DATA SOURCES; the comprehensive guide to the data processing industry: hardware, data communications products, software, company profiles. see COMPUTERS — Computer Industry Directories

005.74 US ISSN 0162-4105
Z699.A1 CODEN: DTBSDQ
DATABASE (WILTON); the magazine of database reference and review. 1978. bi-m. $110. Online, Inc., 462 Danbury Rd., Wilton, CT 06897. TEL 203-761-1466. URL: http://www.onlineinc.com/database. Ed. Paula Hane. adv.; index; circ. 4,500 (paid). (back issues avail.) **Indexed:** A.S.& T.Ind., ABI Inform., B.P.I., C.I.J.E., CINAHL, Compumath, Comput.Cont., INSPEC, Key to Econ.Sci., Leg.Info.Manage.Ind., LHTN, Lib.Lit., LISA, Microcomp.Ind., SSCI, Tr.& Indus.Ind.
 ●Also available online. Vendor(s): Information Access Co., UMI.
 —BLDSC (3535.802200); AskIEEE; CASDDS; CISTI; Ei; Genuine Article; KR SourceOne; SWETS; UMI; UnCover. CCC.
 Description: Features articles on a variety of topics of interest to online database users. Includes database search aids.

004.6 658.403 UK ISSN 0265-4490
DATABASE AND NETWORK JOURNAL; an international journal of database and network practice. 1974. bi-m. £98($234) (overseas £117) (effective 1996). A.P. Publications Ltd., 377 St. John St., London EC1V 4LD, England. TEL 44-171-837-5921. FAX 44-171-837-1197. Ed. Ed Patterson. bk.rev.; bibl.; charts. circ. 1,400. **Indexed:** Agri.Eng.Abstr., BMT, CAD CAM Abstr., Comput.Cont., Comput.Lit.Ind., INSPEC (1975-), Tel.Abstr. **Document type:** academic/scholarly publication.
 —BLDSC (3535.802700); AskIEEE; CISTI; Ei; KR SourceOne; SWETS.
 Incorporates in part (in 1994): P C Business Software (ISSN 0954-2833); *Formerly* (until 1983): Database Journal (ISSN 0308-3314); P C Business Software was formerly titled: Mini Micro Software (ISSN 0265-6760); Small Systems Software.

658.403 US
DATABASE DISCUSSION. 1992. 2-3/yr. Institute for Scientific Information, 3501 Market St., Philadelphia, PA 19104-3389. TEL 800-336-4474. FAX 215-386-6362. (In U.K.: Brunel Science Park, Brunel University, Uxbridge UB8 3PH, England. TEL 895-270016) Ed. Michelle Brown. **Document type:** academic/scholarly publication, bibliography.
 Description: For subscribers to ISI databases.

COMPUTERS — DATA BASE MANAGEMENT

005.74   NE   ISSN 0925-6911
DATABASE MAGAZINE. 1990. 8/yr. fl.124 (effective 1997). Array Publications B.V., Postbus 615, 2400 AP Alphen aan den Rijn, Netherlands. TEL 31-172-424177. FAX 31-172-424381. E-mail: dbm@array.nl; URL: http://www.array.nl. Ed. Herbert Boland. adv.: B&W page fl.3400; adv. contact: J. Raaphorst. bk.rev.; index. circ. 6,000. (back issues avail.) **Document type:** trade publication.
—SWETS.
   Description: Covers applications, development and database management for systems developers, information managers and database administrators.

005.74   US
Z699.35
DATABASE SEARCHING SERIES. irreg. Libraries Unlimited, Inc., Box 6633, Englewood, CO 80155-6633. FAX 303-220-8843. Ed. Carol Tenopir. (back issues avail.) **Document type:** monographic series.
   Description: Covers theory and practice on the use of databases.

DATANET. see *COMPUTERS — Computer Networks*

DATAQUEST; the complete computer magazine. see *COMPUTERS*

005.74   US   ISSN 1078-0246
DBASE INFORMANT; the complete monthly guide to dbase for windows development. 1994. m. $44.95. Informant Communications Group, Inc., 10519 E. Stockton Blvd., Ste. 142, Elk Grove, CA 95624-9704. TEL 916-686-6610. FAX 916-686-8497. Ed. Jerry Coffey; Pub. Mitchell Koulouris. adv. contact: Lynn Beaudoin.

001.6 658.403   AU   ISSN 0419-9081
DIAGRAMM;* Fachzeitschrift fuer Datenverarbeitung und Organisation. 1969. 10/yr. S.450. Herbert O. Munk, Ed. & Pub., Rechte Wienzcile 85-6, A-1050 Vienna, Austria. adv. circ. 10,000. **Indexed:** Food Sci.& Tech.Abstr.

621.381 003   US   ISSN 0926-8782
QA76.9.D5   **CODEN: DAATES**
DISTRIBUTED AND PARALLEL DATABASES; an international journal. 1993. q. fl.595 to institutions; $305.50 to institutions in U.S. (effective 1998). Kluwer Academic Publishers Boston, Box 358, Accord Sta., Hingham, MA 02018-0358. TEL 617-871-6600. FAX 617-871-6528. TELEX 200190. E-mail: services@wkap.nl; URL: http://www.wkap.nl. (Dist. outside N. America by: Kluwer Academic Publishers Group, P.O. Box 322, 3300 AH Dordrecht, Netherlands. TEL 31-78-6392392. FAX 31-78-6546474) Ed. Ahmed K. Elmagarmid. (also avail. in microform from UMI; back issues avail.; reprint service avail. from SWZ) **Indexed:** ASCA, Compumath, Comput.Lit.Ind., Comput.Rev., Curr.Cont., Eng.Ind., Geo.Abstr., Inform.Sci.Abstr., INSPEC (1993-). **Document type:** academic/scholarly publication.
—BLDSC (3602.660800); AskIEEE; CISTI; Ei; Genuine Article; KR SourceOne; SWETS. **CCC.**
   Description: Presents new research results, systems developments and experiences in distributed and parallel database systems.
   Refereed Serial

005.74 658.4   UK   ISSN 1360-6786
DOCUMENT MANAGEMENT UPDATE. 1995. m. £345. Document Management Update, 1-1A, Brockley Cross Business Center, 96 Endwell Rd., London SE4 2PD, England. TEL 44-171-635-8886. FAX 44-171-277-6911. E-mail: dmu@pressfactory.co.uk. Ed. Stuart Draper. bk.rev. **Document type:** newsletter.
—BLDSC (3609.113021).

005.74   SZ
E T H INSTITUT FUER INFORMATIONSSYSTEME. DEPARTEMENT INFORMATIK. irreg. Eidgenoessische Technische Hochschule Zurich, Institut fuer Informationssysteme, ETH Zentrum, CH-8092 Zurich, Switzerland. TEL 01-6322756. FAX 01-2523404. E-mail: weikum, zabback@inf.ethz.ch. Ed. H.-J. Schek. **Document type:** bulletin.

004   US   ISSN 1076-0490
CODEN: EINREI
ELECTRONIC INFORMATION REPORT; empowering industry decision makers since 1979. 1979. w. (46/yr.). $499. Cowles - SIMBA Information (Subsidiary of: Cowles Business Media), 11 Riverbend Dr. S., Box 4949, Stamford, CT 06907-0949. TEL 203-358-9900; 800-307-2529. FAX 203-358-5811. E-mail: simbainfo@simbanet.com; URL: http://www.simbanet.com. Ed. Frances Katz. adv.; charts; stat. (looseleaf format; also avail. in diskette format; back issues avail.) **Indexed:** Comput.Dtbs., Comput.Lit.Ind., Key to Econ.Sci., PROMT, Tr.& Indus.Ind. **Document type:** newsletter.
   ●Also available online. Vendor(s): Information Access Co., Knight-Ridder Information, Inc., NewsNet (PB22).
—BLDSC (3702.568100). **CCC.**
   Former titles (until Mar. 1994): Electronic Information Week; (until Feb. 1994): I D P Report (ISSN 0197-0178)
   Description: Monitors, analyzes, and reports on information services, including storage and distribution media, databases, electronic publishing, value-added facsimile, online, multimedia, and voice services.

658.4031 620   US   ISSN 1061-9550
ENGINEERING DOCUMENT MANAGEMENT SYSTEM COMPARISON REPORT. 1988. q. $490. International Imaging, Inc., 1147 Manhattan Ave., Ste. 322, Manhattan Beach, CA 90266. TEL 310-937-7000. FAX 310-937-7001. (Subscr. to: 701 W. Foothill Blvd., Azusa, CA 91702. TEL 818-969-3078) Ed. Stephen J. Gilheany. bibl.; charts; tr.lit. (back issues avail.; reprint service avail.) **Document type:** newsletter.
   Formerly: Comparison Report on Engineering Scanning Systems (ISSN 1056-182X)
   Description: Reports on and compares all major electronic engineering document management, archive, and distribution systems currently available.

FOXTALK; a comprehensive monthly guide for users of Microsoft FoxPro. see *COMPUTERS — Computer Programming*

658.403 001.644   US   ISSN 1066-8934
QA76.9.D32   **CODEN: GDDAE6**
GALE DIRECTORY OF DATABASES. (In 2 vols.: Vol.1 Online Databases, Vol.2 CD-ROM, Diskette, Magnetic Tape, Batch Access and Handheld Database Products) a. (plus s-a. update) $280 for set (vol.1 $199, vol.2 $119) (effective Dec. 1992). Gale Research, 835 Penobscot Bldg., 645 Griswold St., Detroit, MI 48226-4094. TEL 313-961-2242; 800-877-4253. FAX 800-414-5043. E-mail: daniel__snyder@gale.com. Ed. Kathleen Young Marcaccio. charts; stat. (also avail. in magnetic tape; diskette format) **Indexed:** Comput.Lit.Ind. **Document type:** directory.
   ●Also available online. Vendor(s): Data-Star, Questel Orbit Inc., Telesystemes - Questel.
—BLDSC (4066.773000); CISTI; KNAW; Linda Hall. **CCC.**
   Formed by the merger of (1979-1992): Directory of Online Databases (ISSN 0193-6840); (1990-1992): Directory of Portable Databases (ISSN 1045-8352); (1978-1992): Computer Readable Databases (ISSN 0271-4477); Which was formerly: Computer Readable Bibliographic Data Bases.
   Description: Identifies 8,550 databases. Contains information on database selection and database descriptions, including producers and their addresses.

658.403   UK   ISSN 0950-303X
I B M SYSTEM USER. (International Business Machines) (Has m. supplement: Node (ISSN 0960-3786)) 1981. m. E M A P Business & Computer Publications Ltd., 33-39 Bowling Green Ln., London EC1R ODA, England. TEL 44-171-837-1212. FAX 44-171-278-4008. adv.; bk.rev. circ. 11,000. **Indexed:** Comput.Cont., Comput.Dtbs., Intl.Civil Eng.Abstr., Soft.Abstr.Eng. **Document type:** trade publication.
—BLDSC (4360.089800); AskIEEE; CISTI; KR SourceOne; SWETS. **CCC.**
   Formerly: I B M User (ISSN 0261-3654)

I C A S A NEWS. (International Consortium for Agricultural Systems Applications (ICASA)) see *AGRICULTURE — Crop Production And Soil*

658.4   UK   ISSN 0969-823X
I D P M JOURNAL. 1980. 6/yr. £19 (effective 1997). Institute of Data Processing Management, IDPM House, Edgington Way, Ruxley Corner, Sidcup, Kent DA14 5HR, England. TEL 44-181-308-0747. FAX 44-181-308-0604. E-mail: central@idpm.org.uk. Ed. David Campbell. R&P contact: V. J. Hymas. adv.: B&W page £800, color page £1200; trim 297 x 210. bk.rev. **Document type:** trade publication.
   Formerly (until 1992): Information Management Journal.

INDUSTRIAL MANAGEMENT & DATA SYSTEMS. see *BUSINESS AND ECONOMICS — Computer Applications*

005.74   US
▼**INFOBASE NEWS.** 1996. bi-m. Eureka, Box 57349, Sherman Oaks, CA 91413-2349. TEL 818-789-0269. FAX 818-789-2647. E-mail: editor@eurekapub.com; URL: http://www.eurekapub.com. Ed. Lance Hall. circ. 29,000 (paid). **Document type:** trade publication.
   Description: Covers all aspects of Folio Infobase technology.

658.403   US   ISSN 0891-6004
QA76.9.D3   **CODEN: IFDBEB**
INFODB;* the leading technical journal for database users. 1986. q. $475. DataBase Associates, P.O. Box 310, Morgan Hill, CA 95038-0310. TEL 408-779-0436. FAX 408-779-3274. Ed. Colin J. White. charts; stat.; tr.lit. circ. 500. (back issues avail.) **Indexed:** INSPEC (1988-). **Document type:** trade publication.
—BLDSC (4478.878780); AskIEEE; Ei; KR SourceOne.
   Incorporates (in Feb. 1994): DataBase Review (ISSN 1042-2595)
   Description: Covers key developments in the database marketplace, as well as information on technology directions and new products.

658.403 003   NE   ISSN 0378-7206
HD28   **CODEN: IMANDC**
INFORMATION AND MANAGEMENT; international journal of information systems applications. (Text in English) 1968. m. fl.1240($713) (effective 1998). (International Federation for Information Processing, Applied Information Processing Group) North-Holland (Subsidiary of: Elsevier Science B.V.), P.O. Box 211, 1000 AE Amsterdam, Netherlands. TEL 31-20-4853911. FAX 31-20-4853598. TELEX 18582 ESPA NL. (Subscr. in the Americas to: Elsevier Science, Regional Sales Office, Box 945, New York, NY 10159-0945. TEL 212-633-3730. FAX 212-633-3680; Subscr. in Australasia and the Far East to: Elsevier Science (Singapore) Pte Ltd, No.1 Temasek Ave., No.17-01 Millenia Tower, Singapore 039192, Singapore. TEL 65-434-3727. FAX 65-337-2230; Subscr. in Japan to: Elsevier Science Japan, 9-15 Higashi-Azabu 1-chome, Minato-ku, Tokyo 106, Japan. TEL 81-3-5561-5033. FAX 81-3-5561-5047) Ed. E.H. Sibley. adv.; bk.rev.; index. circ. 2,500. (also avail. in microform from UMI; back issues avail.; reprint service avail. from SWZ) **Indexed:** A.S.& T.Ind., Account.& Data Proc.Abstr., ASCA, Asian-Pac.Econ.Lit., Asian-Pac.Econ.Lit., BPIA, Compumath, Comput.Abstr., Comput.Cont., Comput.Lit.Ind., Cont.Pg.Manage., Curr.Cont., Cyb.Abstr., INSPEC, Int.Abstr.Oper.Res., Intl.Civil Eng.Abstr., Soft.Abstr.Eng., SSCI. **Document type:** academic/scholarly publication.
—BLDSC (4481.835000); AskIEEE; CISTI; Ei; Genuine Article; KR SourceOne; Linda Hall; SWETS; UMI; UnCover. **CCC.**
   Incorporates (1981-1985): Systems, Objectives, Solutions (ISSN 0165-7747); *Former titles* (until 1977): Management Datamatics (ISSN 0579-5486); (until 1975): Management Informatics; I A G Journal (ISSN 0018-8387)
   Description: For managers of information systems, researchers and systems designers. Provides information on new developments in applied information systems.
   Refereed Serial

INFORMATION AND SOFTWARE TECHNOLOGY; the international journal for computer managers. see *COMPUTERS — Electronic Data Processing*

COMPUTERS — DATA BASE MANAGEMENT

005.74 GW ISSN 0930-5181
INFORMATION MANAGEMENT. Variant title: I M - Information Management. 1986. q. I D G Communications Verlag AG, Rheinstr. 28, 80803 Munich, Germany. TEL 49-89-36086299. FAX 49-89-36086325. Ed. Dieter Eckbauer; Pub. Dieter Eckbauer. adv.: B&W page DM.24950, color page DM.29250; trim 260 x 356; adv. contact: Peter Townsend. circ. 44,000. **Document type:** trade publication.
—BLDSC (4493.686600); AskIEEE; KR SourceOne; SWETS.
Description: Covers information processing, internet networking, and client-server computing in the corporate environment.

INFORMATION SYSTEMS; data base: their creation, management and utilization. see LIBRARY AND INFORMATION SCIENCES — Computer Applications

003 US ISSN 8750-6874
QA75.5 CODEN: INFWE4
INFORMATION WEEK. 1979. w. $129 (effective 1996). C M P Publications, Inc., 600 Community Dr., Manhasset, NY 11030. TEL 516-562-5000. FAX 516-562-7013. TELEX 647035 CMP PUB MAHA. (Subscr. to: Box 1093, Skokie, IL 60076. TEL 800-292-3642) Ed. Joel Dreyfuss; Pub. Rebecca S. Barna. circ. 325,000. (tabloid format) **Indexed:** Comput.Bus., Comput.Cont., Comput.Dtbs., Comput.Indus.Up., Comput.Lit.Ind., Graph.Arts Lit.Abstr., INSPEC, Microcomp.Ind., PROMT, Resour.Ctr.Ind., Tel.Alert. **Document type:** trade publication.
•Also available online. Vendor(s): Information Access Co., NewsNet (TE34).
—BLDSC (4496.410100); AskIEEE; CASDDS; CISTI; KR SourceOne; SWETS; UMI; UnCover. **CCC.**
Incorporates (in 1994): Open Systems Today (ISSN 1061-0839); Which was formerly (1988-1992): UNIX Today (ISSN 1040-5038); (until 1984): Information Systems News (ISSN 0199-0691)

658.4 GW ISSN 0942-0207
INFORMATIONSVERARBEITUNG. 1992. bi-m. DM.98. Verlag Wirtschaft Recht und Steuern, Fraunhoferstr. 5, 82152 Planegg, Germany. TEL 49-89-89517-0. FAX 49-89-89517250. (Subscr. to: Postfach 1363, 82142 Planegg, Germany) (looseleaf format) **Document type:** trade publication.

651.8 658.403 US ISSN 0898-171X
HF5548.2
INSIDE D P M A; a monthly publication for DPMA and the information systems profession. 1951. m. $45 (foreign $75). Data Processing Management Association, 505 Busse Hwy., Park Ridge, IL 60068-3191. TEL 708-825-8124. FAX 708-825-1693. Ed. Susan Smith. R&P contact: Susan Smith. adv.: page $1700; 10 1/8 x 14; adv. contact: Susan Smith. bk.rev.; charts; illus.; stat.; index. circ. 22,000. (tabloid format; also avail. in microfilm from UMI; reprint service avail. from UMI) **Indexed:** B.P.I., Bus.Ind., Compumath, Comput.Bus., Comput.Cont., Comput.Lit.Ind., Curr.Cont., Data Process.Dig., INSPEC, LHTN, Resour.Ctr.Ind., Risk Abstr., Tel.Abstr. **Document type:** newspaper.
—CISTI; KR SourceOne; Linda Hall; UMI. **CCC.**
Former titles (until 1988): Data Management (ISSN 0148-5431); (until 1970): Journal of Data Management (ISSN 0449-2412)
Description: For mid and upper-level managers in information systems management. Articles focus on the manager's involvement in a computer environment.

005.7405 US ISSN 1047-7349
QA76.9.D3
INTERNATIONAL CONFERENCE ON VERY LARGE DATA BASES. PROCEEDINGS. 1982. a. price varies. Morgan Kaufmann Publishers, Inc., 340 Pine St., 6th Fl., San Francisco, CA 94104-3205. TEL 415-392-2665. FAX 415-982-2665. E-mail: orders@mkp.com; URL: http://www.mkp.com. Ed. Michael B. Morgan. R&P contact: Marilyn Uffner Alan. adv. contact: Lisa Schneider. **Document type:** trade publication.
—BLDSC (6845.076000); UMI. **CCC.**
Former titles (until 1987): Very Large Data Bases. Proceedings (ISSN 0730-9317); (until 1977): International Conference on Very Large Data Bases. Proceedings (ISSN 0278-2596)
Description: Forum for research in database system management design and programming.
Refereed Serial

INTERNATIONAL JOURNAL OF MICROGRAPHICS & OPTICAL TECHNOLOGY; including all aspects of electronic information transfer. see LIBRARY AND INFORMATION SCIENCES — Computer Applications

658.4 US ISSN 1050-9070
CODEN: ISPEEZ
INTERNATIONAL SPECTRUM; the business person's computer magazine. 1984. bi-m. $40 (foreign $50). International Database Management Association, 10675 Treena St., Ste. 103, San Diego, CA 92131. TEL 619-578-3152. FAX 619-271-1032. E-mail: multi-value@intl-spectrum.com; URL: http://www.intl-spectrum.com. Ed. Nichelle Johnson; Pub. Gus Giobbi. R&P contact: Monica Giobbi. adv. contact: Jill Dennis. bk.rev.; index. circ. 50,000. (back issues avail.) **Indexed:** Comput.Ind. **Document type:** trade publication.
—KR SourceOne.
Description: Covers software-hardware products for the business person using Pick-Unix - DOS.

658.403 US ISSN 0893-4274
INVESTEXT ADVISOR. 1987. 3/yr. free. Technical Data International, 11 Farnsworth St., Boston, MA 02210. TEL 617-330-7878. FAX 617-350-5011. TELEX 466199. Ed. Cynthia Costello. circ. 3,000.
Supersedes: InvesText News.

IX; Multiuser - Multitasking - Magazin. see COMPUTERS

658.403 US ISSN 1063-8016
QA76.9.D3 CODEN: JDAMEQ
JOURNAL OF DATABASE MANAGEMENT.* 1990. q. $65 to individuals; institutions $110. (Information Resources Management Association) Idea Group Publishing, 1331 E. Chocolate Ave., Hershey, PA 17033-1751. TEL 717-541-9150. FAX 717-541-9159. E-mail: 75364,3150@compuserve.com. Ed. Mehdi Khosrowpour. circ. 300 (controlled). (also avail. in microform from UMI) **Indexed:** Bus.Educ.Ind., INSPEC (1992-). **Document type:** academic/scholarly publication.
—BLDSC (4967.815000); AskIEEE; KR SourceOne; SWETS; UMI.
Formerly: Journal of Database Administration (ISSN 1047-9430)
Description: Provides those who design, develop, and administer DBMS-based information systems with state-of-the-art research.
Refereed Serial

JOURNAL OF INTELLIGENT INFORMATION SYSTEMS; integrating artificial intelligence and database technologies. see COMPUTERS — Artificial Intelligence

658.403 001.644 JA ISSN 0918-8002
MACINTOSH C D - R O M GUIDE. 1993. a. 3000 Yen. PenLogue Publishing Corp., Futaba Bldg., 3-4-18, Mita, Minato-ku, Tokyo 108, Japan. TEL 03-3452-8080. FAX 03-3452-5728.
Description: Contains 1,100 Japanese CD-ROM titles for Macintosh and 1,000 foreign titles.

658.403 IT ISSN 0391-6588
MANAGEMENT E INFORMATICA. 1961. m. L.135000 (foreign L.155000) (effective 1993). Franco Angeli Editore, Viale Monza 106, 20127 Milan, Italy. TEL 02-28-27-651. adv.; bk.rev.; charts; illus.; stat. circ. 3,000. **Indexed:** INSPEC.
—AskIEEE; KR SourceOne.
Formerly: Centri Meccanografici ed Elettronici (ISSN 0008-915X)

658.403 621.381 US
MANAGING OPEN SYSTEMS. 1992. 2 base vols. (plus m. updates). $875 (effective 1993). Faulkner Information Services, Inc., 114 Cooper Center, 7905 Browning Rd., Pennsauken, NJ 08109-4319. TEL 609-662-2070. FAX 609-662-3380. Ed. Janet Mann. (looseleaf format)
Description: Contains planning and how-to information for companies implementing open systems technology. Includes product and vendor analyses of those companies actively supporting open end architecture.

OEKONOMISTYRING OG INFORMATIK. see BUSINESS AND ECONOMICS — Management

621.387 US
ONLINE PRODUCT NEWS. 1981. m. $150 (outside N. America $165). Worldwide Videotex, Box 3273, Boynton Beach, FL 33424-3273. TEL 407-738-2276. Ed. Mark Wright; Pub. Mark Wright. bk.rev. (back issues avail.) **Document type:** newsletter.
•Also available online. Vendor(s): Information Access Co., NewsNet (TE27).
Description: Provides information and news on online services and on computer products, such as software and modems, used in accessing them. Focuses on industry trends and technology to help the online user.

658.4 AT
▼**ONLINE WORLD.** 1995. d. TEL 61-2-9281-6188. FAX 61-2-9281-6204. E-mail: info@widewest.com.au; URL: http://www.onlineworld.net.au. Ed. Geoggrey Ebbs.
•Available only online.
Description: Aimed primarily at professional users of IT, including news, reviews and discussion databases.

658.4031 GW ISSN 0930-3693
PASSWORD; Praxisberater fuer elektronische Informationsbeschaffung. 1986. m. DM.288. Verlagsgruppe Handelsblatt GmbH, Kasernenstr. 67, 40213 Duesseldorf, Germany. TEL 49-211-8870. FAX 49-211-374955. (Subscr. to: Postfach 102717, 40018 Duesseldorf, Germany) Ed. Willi Bredemeier. circ. 1,500. **Document type:** bulletin.

REPERTOIRE DES BANQUES DE DONNEES PROFESSIONNELLES/THE PROFESSIONAL DATABASES DIRECTORY. see BUSINESS AND ECONOMICS — Trade And Industrial Directories

005.74 658.403 US ISSN 0163-5808
CODEN: SRECD8
S I G M O D RECORD. q. $27 to non-members; members $20. Association for Computing Machinery, Special Interest Group on Management of Data, 1515 Broadway, 17th Fl., New York, NY 10036. TEL 212-869-7440. FAX 212-302-5826. E-mail: sigmod@bunny.cs.uiuc.edu; URL: http://bunny.cs.uiuc.edu/sigmod. bk.rev. **Indexed:** Comput.Abstr., INSPEC.
—BLDSC (8275.570000); AskIEEE; CISTI; Ei; KR SourceOne; SWETS; UnCover.
Formerly: S I G F I D E T Record.

SEKAI C D - R O M SORAN. see COMPUTERS — Computer Networks

658.403 US ISSN 1055-6338
QA76.9.D3
SIGACT - SIGMOD - SIGART SYMPOSIUM ON PRINCIPLES OF DATABASE SYSTEMS. PROCEEDINGS. 1987. a. Association for Computing Machinery, 11 W. 42nd St., New York, NY 10036. **Document type:** proceedings.
—BLDSC (6836.150780).

SYMPOSIUM ON RELIABLE DISTRIBUTED SYSTEMS. PROCEEDINGS. see COMPUTERS — Software

658.403 GW ISSN 1066-8888
CODEN: VLDBFR
THE V L D B JOURNAL. (Very Large Data Bases); the international journal on very large data bases. Online edition (GW ISSN 0949-877X) 1992. q. DM.275 (foreign DM.284.80) (effective 1998). (V L D B Endowment) Springer-Verlag, Heidelberger Platz 3, Berlin 14197, Germany. TEL 49-30-82787-0. FAX 49-30-82787448. E-mail: subscriptions@springer.de; URL: http://science.springer.de/vldb/vldb.html. Ed.Bd. (back issues avail.) **Document type:** academic/scholarly publication.
•Also available online.
—AskIEEE; KR SourceOne; SWETS. **CCC.**
Description: Dedicated to publishing scholarly contributions from around the world to the advancement of information system architectures, the effect of emerging technologies on information systems, and the development of novel applications.

658.403 US
WORLDWIDE DATABASES. 1990. m. $150 (outside N. America $165). Worldwide Videotex, Box 3273, Boynton Beach, FL 33424-3273. TEL 407-738-2276. Ed. Mark Wright; Pub. Mark Wright. bk.rev. (back issues avail.) **Document type:** newsletter.
●Also available online. Vendor(s): Data-Star, Information Access Co., Knight-Ridder Information, Inc., NewsNet (PB44).
Description: Reports on news and information dealing with online computer databases around the world. Includes articles on new database products and enhancements, developments, distribution agreements, and user applications.

COMPUTERS — Data Communications And Data Transmission Systems

A F M INFORMATION SYSTEMS SERIES (NO.). (Department of Accounting and Financial Management) see COMPUTERS — Computer Systems

001.6 621.381 JA ISSN 0386-5428
A S C I I. (American Standard Code for Information Interchange); home and office computer science magazine. 1977. m. 13200 Yen. Akio Fujii, A S C I I Publishing, 4-33-10 Yoyogi, Shibuya-ku, Tokyo 151-24, Japan. TEL 81-3-5351-8111. adv. circ. 280,000.
—BLDSC (1739.233000).

621.381 004 US ISSN 1052-6366
CODEN: AESSE8
ACCESS TO WANG; the magazine for Wang system users. 1983. m. $30 (foreign $40) (effective 1996). New Media Publications, 10711 Burnet Rd., No. 305, Austin, TX 78758-4459. TEL 512-873-7761. FAX 512-873-7782. Ed. Richard Zelade; Pub. Floyd Sembler. R&P contact: Floyd Sembler. adv. contact: Bonnie Gallaspy. charts; illus.; tr.lit. circ. 10,000. (back issues avail.) **Indexed:** INSPEC (1988-1989), Tel.Abstr. **Document type:** trade publication.
—KR SourceOne. **CCC.**
Former titles: Access (Year) (ISSN 0890-2321); Online Data Access (ISSN 0738-3843)
Description: For Wang computer users. Articles cover current product developments. Columns offer product announcements and reviews as well as interviews and a calendar of events.

621.39 US
ADVANCED TECHNOLOGY FOR DEVELOPERS; a monthly how-to newsletter for developers. m. $198. High-Tech Communications, 103 Buckskin Ct., Sewickley, PA 15143-9946. TEL 412-741-7699. FAX 412-741-6094. Ed. Jane Klimasauskas. **Document type:** newsletter.

621.381 US ISSN 0001-0782
QA76 CODEN: CACMA2
ASSOCIATION FOR COMPUTING MACHINERY. COMMUNICATIONS. 1958. m. $114 to non-members. Association for Computing Machinery, 1515 Broadway, 17th Fl., New York, NY 10036-5701. TEL 212-869-7440. FAX 212-944-1318. TELEX 421686. Ed. Peter J. Denning. adv.; charts; illus.; index. circ. 85,000. (also avail. in microfiche from KTO; back issues avail.) **Indexed:** A.I.Abstr., A.S.& T.Ind., Abstr.Hum.Comp.Inter., Appl.Mech.Rev., ASCA, B.P.I., BMT, CAD CAM Abstr., Compumath, Comput.Abstr., Comput.Cont., Comput.Lit.Ind., Comput.Rev., Curr.Cont., INIS Atomind., INSPEC (1968-), Int.Abstr.Oper.Res., Math.R., Oper.Res.Manage.Sci., Qual.Contr.Appl.Stat., Robomat.
●Also available online. Vendor(s): Information Access Co., UMI.
—BLDSC (3344.250000); AskIEEE; CASDDS; CISTI; Ei; Genuine Article; KR SourceOne; Linda Hall; SWETS; UMI; UnCover. **CCC.**
Description: Articles on all aspects of computing, including artificial intelligence, programming, human and social aspects of computing, operations research and management applications. Covers industry and ACM news.

621.39 US ISSN 1067-5221
ASYNCHRONOUS TRANSFER MODE NEWSLETTER. 1991. m. $595 (foreign $645) (effective 1997). Information Gatekeepers, Inc., 214 Harvard Ave., Boston, MA 02134. TEL 617-232-3111; 800-323-1088. FAX 617-734-8562. E-mail: igiboston@aol.com; URL: http://www.igigroup.com. Ed. Paul Polishuk. (back issues avail.) **Document type:** newsletter.
Description: Looks at products, trends, and industry news relating to ATM and its technology.

621.387 US ISSN 1059-0544
BROADBAND NETWORKING NEWS. 1991. bi-w. $597 (foreign $630) (effective 1997). Phillips Business Information, Inc., 1201 Seven Locks Rd., Potomac, MD 20854. TEL 301-424-3338. FAX 301-309-3847. E-mail: pbi@phillips.com. Ed. Jennifer Whalen. **Document type:** newsletter.
●Also available online. Vendor(s): Information Access Co., NewsNet (TE51).
—**CCC.**
Description: Covers developments, trends and applications of high-bandwidth data transmission and communications.

621.387 US ISSN 0744-2386
COMMLINE. 1972. q. $20 (free to qualified personnel). Numeridex, Inc, 241 Holbrook Dr., Box 11000, Wheeling, IL 60090. TEL 312-541-8840. Ed. June Loucks. adv. circ. 35,244. **Indexed:** Comput.Cont., INSPEC (1985-).
—AskIEEE; KR SourceOne.
Formerly: N-C Commline (ISSN 0191-6793)
Description: For engineers, managers and programmers in the numerical control and computerized manufacturing industry. Articles cover metalworking, cutting tools, computer control and CAD-CAM.

COMMUNICATIONS NETWORKS. see COMMUNICATIONS — Telephone And Telegraph

621.387 UK ISSN 1077-4696
COMMUNICATIONS STANDARDS NEWS; tcp/ip - lans - wans - multimedia - wireless - osi. 1982. bi-w. $497 (foreign $530) (effective 1996). Omnicom P B I, Rosemount House, Rosemount Ave., W. Byfleet, Surrey KT14 6NP, England. TEL 44-1932-355515. FAX 44-1932-355962. Ed. Mary Crowley. cum.index: 1982-1988. circ. 800. (looseleaf format; back issues avail.) **Document type:** newsletter.
●Also available online. Vendor(s): Information Access Co.
—**CCC.**
Incorporates (in July 1994): Open Systems Communications (ISSN 0741-2851); Incorporates (1990-1992): Open Systems Report (ISSN 1052-701X); Supersedes: Gateway (Ann Arbor) (ISSN 0890-2526); Formerly: O S I Communication (ISSN 0740-4433)

004 384.3 NE ISSN 0140-3664
TK5105.5 CODEN: COCOD7
COMPUTER COMMUNICATIONS; the international journal for the computer and telecommunications industry. (Text in English) 1978. 18/yr. fl.1976($1136) (effective 1998). Elsevier Science B.V., P.O. Box 211, 1000 AE Amsterdam, Netherlands. TEL 31-20-4853911. FAX 31-20-4853598. (Subscr. in the Americas to: Elsevier Science, Regional Sales Office, Box 945, New York, NY 10159-0945. TEL 212-633-3730. FAX 212-633-3680; Subscr. in Australasia and the Far East to: Elsevier Science (Singapore) Pte Ltd, No.1 Temasek Ave., No.17-01 Millenia Tower, Singapore 039192, Singapore. TEL 65-434-3727. FAX 65-337-2230; Subscr. in Japan to: Elsevier Science Japan, 9-15 Higashi-Azabu 1-chome, Minato-ku, Tokyo 106, Japan. TEL 81-3-5561-5033. FAX 81-3-5561-5047) Ed. Helen Hodge. adv.; bk.rev.; bibl.; illus.; index. (also avail. in microform from UMI; back issues avail.; reprint service avail.) **Indexed:** ASCA, CAD CAM Abstr., Compumath, Comput.Cont., Comput.Dtbs., Comput.Lit.Ind., Curr.Cont., Cyb.Abstr., Eng.Ind., INSPEC (1978-), Key to Econ.Sci., Mgmt.& Market.Abstr., Microcomp.Ind., PROMT, SSCI, Tel.Abstr. **Document type:** academic/scholarly publication.
—BLDSC (3393.831000); AskIEEE; Ei; Genuine Article; KR SourceOne; Linda Hall; SWETS; UMI; UnCover. **CCC.**
Description: Focuses on networking and distributed computing techniques, communications hardware and software, and standardization.
Refereed Serial

001.6 621.387 US ISSN 0146-4833
TK5105.5 CODEN: CCRED2
COMPUTER COMMUNICATIONS REVIEW. vol.8, 1978. q. $37. Association for Computing Machinery, Special Interest Group on Data Communication, 1515 Broadway, 17th Fl., New York, NY 10036. TEL 212-869-7440. FAX 212-869-0481. TELEX 421686. Ed. David Oran. **Indexed:** Comput.Cont., INSPEC (1981-), Tel.Abstr.
—BLDSC (3393.830000); AskIEEE; CISTI; KR SourceOne; SWETS; UnCover.

001.64 621.887 UK ISSN 0306-6886
COMPUTER REPORT. 1974. w. £49($110) European Communications Consultants Ltd., 2 Duncan Terrace, London N1 8BJ, England. Ed. Stacey Tanner. bk.rev. circ. 800. **Indexed:** Anbar.

621.387 AU
COMPUTERWELT. 1986. w. S.390 (foreign S.1250) (effective 1997). I D G Communications, Zieglergasse 6, A-1070 Vienna, Vienna. TEL 43-1-52316310. FAX 43-1-523050833. Ed. Gerhard Rainer. adv.: B&W page S.58900, color page S.79400; trim 199 x 270; adv. contact: Andreas Lenzenhofer. circ. 25,000. **Document type:** consumer publication.
Description: Information for data processing managers, engineers and students.

621.387 001.644 UK
CONNEXION; the networking newspaper. 1988. fortn. £60 (foreign £80). V N U Business Publications BV, VNU House, 32-34 Broadwick St., London W1A 2HG, England. TEL 44-171-316-9000. FAX 44-171-316-9003. Ed. John Caffrey; Pub. Tony Faure. adv.: B&W page £4920, color page £6310; trim 11 x 15 1/4; adv. contact: Richard Beagley. circ. 29,460. **Indexed:** INSPEC (1989-).

CONTEMPORARY TOPICS IN INFORMATION TRANSFER. see COMPUTERS — Information Science And Information Theory

CORPORATE I T UPDATE. see BUSINESS AND ECONOMICS

621.387 GW ISSN 0177-6894
D F N MITTEILUNGEN. (Text in English and German) 1985. q. free. Verein zur Foerderung eines Deutschen Forschungsnetzes, Pariserstr. 44, 10707 Berlin, Germany. TEL 49-30-88429924. FAX 49-30-884299-70. Ed. K.-E. Maass. bk.rev. circ. 7,000. **Document type:** newsletter.
Description: Examines data communication in science.

001.6 621.387 US ISSN 0736-3648
DATA CENTER OPERATIONS MANAGEMENT. 1977. bi-m. $434. Auerbach Publishers (Subsidiary of: Warren, Gorham & Lamont), One Penn Plaza, New York, NY 10119. TEL 212-971-5000. FAX 212-971-5024. (Subscr. to: 31 St. James Ave., Boston, MA 02116-4112. TEL 800-950-1218. FAX 617-423-1914) Ed. Layne Bradley. (looseleaf format) **Document type:** trade publication.
—**CCC.**
Description: Contains more than 85 articles on all areas of data center operations. Provides how-to information for data center operations, computer centers, and data processing operations managers.

COMPUTERS — DATA COMMUNICATIONS AND DATA TRANSMISSION SYSTEMS

001.6 621.387 330   US   ISSN 0363-6399
QA75.5   CODEN: DACODM
DATA COMMUNICATIONS. (International ed. avail.) 1972. m. $160 (effective 1996). McGraw-Hill Companies, 1221 Ave. of the Americas, New York, NY 10020. TEL 212-512-2000. (Subscr. to: Box 473, Hightstown, NJ 08520) Ed. Lee Keogh. adv.; index. circ. 65,000. (also avail. in microform from UMI; reprint service avail. from UMI) **Indexed:** ABI Inform., B.P.I., Bus.Ind., CAD CAM Abstr., Comput.Bus., Comput.Cont., Comput.Dtbs., Comput.Ind., Comput.Lit.Ind., Cyb.Abstr., INSPEC (1991-), LAMP, Mgmt.& Market.Abstr., Microcomp.Ind., PROMT, Tel.Abstr., Tel.Alert., Tr.& Indus.Ind. **Document type:** trade publication.
●Also available online. Vendor(s): Dow Jones News Retrieval, Knight-Ridder Information, Inc. (File no.624/McGRAW-HILL PUBLICATIONS ONLINE), Lexis-Nexis, NewsNet (TE37).
—BLDSC (3534.445000); AskIEEE; CASDDS; CISTI; Ei; Genuine Article; KR SourceOne; SWETS; UMI; UnCover. **CCC.**
Formerly: Data Communications Systems.
Description: Provides users and vendors with news and analysis of changing technology for the networking of computers.

001.6 338   US   ISSN 0194-195X
HD9696.T443
DATA COMMUNICATIONS BUYERS' GUIDE. 1978. s-a. $75. McGraw-Hill Companies, 1221 Ave. of the Americas, New York, NY 10020. TEL 212-512-2000. Ed. Brunny Ayala. adv. **Document type:** catalog, directory.
Description: Listing of vendors by types of products and services.

621.387   UK
DATA COMMUNICATIONS INTERNATIONAL. m. Wimbledon Bridge House, London SW19 3RU, England. TEL 081-545-6265. FAX 081-540-3833. TELEX 892191. Ed. Peter Heywood. circ. 80,000.

001.6 621.387   US   ISSN 0736-0002
DATA COMMUNICATIONS MANAGEMENT. 1975. bi-m. $434. Auerbach Publishers (Subsidiary of: Warren, Gorham & Lamont), One Penn Plaza, New York, NY 10119. TEL 212-971-5000. FAX 212-971-5024. (Subscr. to: 31 St. James Ave., Boston, MA 02116-4112. TEL 800-950-1218. FAX 617-423-1914) Ed. James Conard. (looseleaf format) **Document type:** trade publication.
—CCC.
Description: Contains more than 85 articles on all areas of data center operations. Provides how-to information.

004.6   US
DATA COMPRESSION CONFERENCE. PROCEEDINGS. 1991. a. price varies. (Institute of Electrical and Electronics Engineers, Inc.) I E E E Computer Society Press, 10662 Los Vaqueros Circle, Los Alamitos, CA 90720-1264. TEL 714-821-8380. FAX 714-821-4641. Ed. Cat Harris; Pub. Matt Loeb. adv. contact: Frieda Koester. **Document type:** proceedings.
Description: Presents current research, new techniques, and important studies on data compression and related areas.

001.6 621.387   US
DATA NETWORKING. 4 base vols. (plus m. updates). $1723 to new subscr.; renewals $1529 (effective 1996). Datapro Information Services Group (Subsidiary of: McGraw-Hill, Inc.), 600 Delran Pkwy., Delran, NJ 08075. TEL 609-764-0100; 800-328-3776. FAX 609-764-2814.
—CCC.
Formerly: Datapro Reports on Data Communications (ISSN 0730-8787)

621.387   GW   ISSN 0176-3288
DATACOM. 1984. m. DM.166 (foreign DM.182) (effective 1997). Datacom Zeitschriften Verlag GmbH, Postfach 1502, 50105 Bergheim, Germany. TEL 49-2271-608-0. FAX 49-2271-608290. E-mail: info@datacom-verlag.de; URL: http://www.datacom-verlag.de. Eds. Reinhold Hoelbling, Stefan Lueschow; Pub. Klaus Lipinski. adv.: B&W page DM.5600; trim 182 x 268; adv. contact: Andrea Schmidt-Dietrich. bk.rev. circ. 10,951. (back issues avail.) **Document type:** trade publication.
—SWETS.
Description: Special-interest magazine for data communication professionals covering topics such as in-house data transmission, the problems of LAN and WAN cabling, and long distance data transmission.

658.387   UK   ISSN 0959-6429
DATACOMMS BOOK (YEAR). 1986. a. £74. V N U Business Publications BV, 32-34 Broadway St., London W1A 2HG, England. TEL 44-171-439-4242. FAX 44-171-437-9638. Ed. Peter Chare. adv. (magnetic tape) **Document type:** trade publication.

621.387   US
DATAPRO MANAGEMENT OF INTERNATIONAL TELECOMMUNICATIONS. base vol. (plus bi-m. updates). $779. Datapro Information Services Group (Subsidiary of: McGraw-Hill, Inc.), 600 Delran Pkwy., Delran, NJ 08075. TEL 609-764-0100; 800-328-2776. FAX 609-764-8953.

621.387   US
DATAPRO REPORTS ON DOCUMENT IMAGING SYSTEMS. 2 base vols. (plus m. updates). $1008 to new subscr.; renewals $902 (effective 1996). Datapro Information Services Group (Subsidiary of: McGraw-Hill, Inc.), 600 Delran Pkwy., Delran, NJ 08075. TEL 609-764-0100; 800-328-2776. FAX 609-764-2814.

621.39   JA
▼**DIGITAL FACTORY.** (Text in Japanese) 1997. bi-m. free. Nikkei Business Publications, Inc. (Subsidiary of: Nihon Keizai Shimbun, Inc.), 2-7-6 Hirakawacho, Chiyoda-ku, Tokyo 102, Japan. TEL 81-3-5210-8031. FAX 81-3-5210-8119. URL: http://www.nikkeibp.co.jp. adv.: B&W page 478000 Yen, color page 694000 Yen. **Document type:** trade publication.
Description: Covers the designing and developing digital data for commercial use.

004.6   IT
DISTRIBUIRE OGGI; tecnologia dell'informazione. 1958. 5/yr. Gruppo Editoriale J C E, Via Ferri 6, 20092 Cinisello Balsamo (MI), Italy. TEL 39-2-660251. FAX 39-2-6127620. E-mail: info@jce.it; URL: http://www.jce.it. Ed. Vittorio Apuzzo; Pub. Marinella Zetti. adv.: B&W page L.2600000, color page L.5000000; trim 210 x 280. circ. 30,000.

004.6   US   ISSN 1071-1295
TK7882.C6   CODEN: DOIREO
DOCUMENT IMAGING REPORT. 1991. bi-w. $597 (foreign $630) (effective 1997). Phillips Business Information, Inc., 1201 Seven Locks Rd., Potomac, MD 20854. TEL 301-424-3338. FAX 301-309-3847. E-mail: pbi@phillips.com. Ed. Mary Crowley; Pub. Ellen Stuhlmann. **Document type:** newsletter.
●Also available online. Vendor(s): Information Access Co., NewsNet (EC02).
—BLDSC (3609.094500). **CCC.**
Incorporates (in 1993): Imaging Business Report (ISSN 1050-7019); **Formerly:** Electronic Imaging Report (ISSN 1057-0942)
Description: Discusses strategies and applications of imaging technology of interest to executives and corporate planners.

004.6   US   ISSN 1077-3452
DOT.COM; the gateway to on-line business. 1994. m. $375. Business Communications Co., Inc. (Norwalk), 25 Van Zant St., Ste. 13, Norwalk, CT 06855. TEL 203-853-4266. FAX 203-853-0348. E-mail: support@doctcom.vyne.com. Ed. Christiane Toenne. **Document type:** newsletter.
Description: Intended for business users seeking to identify investment opportunities. Provides information on the internet and other on-line resources.

004.6   GW
E D I CHANGE. (Electronic Data Interchange) q. DM.72. (Deutsches Institut fuer Normung e.V.) Beuth Verlag GmbH, Burggrafenstr. 6, 10787 Berlin, Germany. TEL 49-30-2601-0. FAX 49-30-26011260. Ed. Joerg Richter. adv. contact: Reinhardt Schultz. **Document type:** academic/scholarly publication.

004.6 300   US   ISSN 1048-3047
                       CODEN: EDFOE2
E D I FORUM; the journal of electronic data interchange. 1989. q. $250 (CD-ROM $150). E D I Group, Ltd., Box 710, Oak Park, IL 60302. TEL 708-848-0135. FAX 708-848-0270. E-mail: t.edigroup@resonet.com. Ed. Benjamin Wright. adv.; bk.rev. **Indexed:** INSPEC (1992-).
●Also available on CD-ROM.
—BLDSC (3660.576005); AskIEEE; Ei; KR SourceOne.
Description: Helps facilitate the conversion of business-to-business communication from paper- and mail-based processes to electronic processes, primarily Electronic Data Interchange, or EDI. Covers EDI and EFT (Electronic Funds Transfer), and focuses on the views of both EDI users and vendors.

004.6 340   NE   ISSN 0929-2233
K5   CODEN: EDLRE7
E D I LAW REVIEW. (Electronic Data Interchange); legal aspects of paperless communication. (Text in English) 1994. q. fl.386 to institutions; $198 to institutions in U.S. (effective 1998). Kluwer Law International (Subsidiary of: Wolters Kluwer N.V.), Postbus 85889, 2508 CN The Hague, Netherlands. TEL 31-70-3081500. FAX 31-70-3081515. E-mail: SERVICES@WKAP.NL. (Dist. by: Kluwer Academic Publishers Group, P.O. Box 322, 3300 AH Dordrecht, Netherlands. TEL 31-78-6392392. FAX 31-78-6546474; In N. America: Kluwer Law International, 675 Massachusetts Ave., Cambridge, MA 02139. TEL 617-354-0140. FAX 617-354-8595) Eds. Rob E. van Esch, Corien Prins. bk.rev.; abstr. (reprint service avail. from SWZ) **Document type:** academic/scholarly publication.
—BLDSC (3660.579000); AskIEEE; Ei; KR SourceOne; UnCover. **CCC.**
Description: Publishes studies and review articles addressing the legal ramifications of the increased use of EDI, including analysis of current and evolving legislation, and responses to unexpected legal consequences.
Refereed Serial

621.387   US   ISSN 0894-9212
E D I NEWS. (Electronic Data Interchange) 1987. bi-w. $597 (foreign $630) (effective 1997). Phillips Business Information, Inc., 1201 Seven Locks Rd., Potomac, MD 20854. TEL 301-424-3338. FAX 301-309-3847. E-mail: pbi@phillips.com. Ed. Ron Hudak. **Document type:** newsletter.
●Also available online. Vendor(s): Information Access Co., NewsNet (TE80).
—CCC.
Incorporates (1993-1996): Electronic Claims Processing Report (ISSN 1071-8524); (in 1992): E D I Executive; (1989-1992): Quick Response News; (1990-1991): Electronic Trade and Transport News (ISSN 1045-6643)
Description: Provides timely updates on EDI industry trends, events, new products and services, and advances in paperless trading technology.

ELECTRIC WORD. see COMPUTERS — Computer Programming

ELECTRONIC TRADING MARKETS. see COMMUNICATIONS — Computer Applications

301.16 380.3
621.381   US   ISSN 0749-9922
ELLIOT GOLD'S TELESPAN; a bulletin on teleconferencing. 1981. 40/yr. $357 to individuals (Canada and Mexico $367; elsewhere $397) (effective 1995). TeleSpan Publishing Corporation, 50 W. Palm St., Altadena, CA 91001-4337. TEL 818-797-5482. FAX 818-797-2035. E-mail: telespancp@aol.com. Ed. Shirley Singletary; Pub. Elliot Gold. bk.rev.; index. (also avail. in microform from UMI; back issues avail.) **Document type:** newsletter.

COMPUTERS — DATA COMMUNICATIONS AND DATA TRANSMISSION SYSTEMS

621.387   UK   ISSN 0960-5479
EUROPEAN COMMUNICATIONS NEWSFILE. 1989. fortn. £495 (effective 1997). (Communications and Information Technology Research Ltd.) C I T Publications, 3 Colleton Cres., Exeter, Devon EX2 4DG, England. TEL 44-1392-493444. FAX 44-1392-493626. E-mail: talk2us@citpubs.zynet.co.uk; URL: http://www.telecoms-data.com. Ed. Simon Sherrington. charts; stat.; index. **Document type:** newsletter.
   Incorporates: Value Added Networks Newsfile (ISSN 1352-8351)
   Description: Covers the European communications market. Includes news, company profiles, interviews with industry executives, and analysis.

621.387   US
FAULKNER'S ENTERPRISE NETWORKING. 1965. 3 base vols. (plus m. updates). $1275 (q. CD-ROM $1507). Faulkner Information Services, Inc., 114 Cooper Center, 7905 Browning Rd., Pennsauken, NJ 08109-4319. TEL 609-662-2070. FAX 609-662-3380. Ed. Larry Abbott. (looseleaf format)
   ●Also available on CD-ROM.
   Former titles: Data Communications Reports; Auerbach Data Communications Reports (ISSN 0004-7724)
   Description: Coverage of data communications hardware, software, services, and network facilities - strategies.

004.6   US
FEDERAL A D P AND TELECOMMUNICATIONS STANDARDS INDEX. s-a. $19.50. U.S. General Services Administration, G S A Bldg., 18th and F Sts., N.W., Washington, DC 20405. TEL 202-501-1231. (Subscr. to: Department of Commerce, National Technical Information Service, Springfield, VA 22161. TEL 703-487-4650) **Document type:** government publication, abstracting/indexing.
   Former titles (until 1995): A D P and Telecommunications Standards Index & Federal Information Resources Management Regulations.
   Description: Contains revised standards requirements.

004.6   FR   ISSN 1146-3031
G E D; la lettre de la gestion electronique de documents. 18/yr. 2200 F. A Jour, 11 rue du Marche St. Honore, 75001 Paris, France. TEL 42-96-67-22. FAX 40-20-07-75.

004.6   CC
I D N. (Text in English) 1994. bi-m. HK.$720($99) Systems Design Ltd., 5-9 Gresson St., Shop C, Wanchai, Hong Kong, People's Republic of China. TEL 852-2528-5744. FAX 852-2529-1296. URL: http://www.idnworld.com. Ed. Laurence Ng; Pub. Laurence Ng. adv. contact: Amy Cheung. circ. 16,000. **Document type:** consumer publication.
   Refereed Serial

004.6   SI   ISSN 1012-8328
I T ASIA. (Text in English) 1987. m. Newscom Pte. Ltd., 105 Boon Keng Rd., No. 04-17, Singapore 1233, Singapore. TEL 2919861. FAX 2931445. Ed. Austin Morais. adv.: B&W page $6545, color page $7415; trim 261 x 356; adv. contact: Desmond Wong. circ. 22,266.

621.387   UK
INFORMATION INTERCHANGE REPORT. 1993. m. £295 in Europe; rest of world £315 (effective 1997). Technology Appraisals Ltd., 82 Hampton Rd., Twickenham TW2 5QS, England. TEL 44-181-893-3986. FAX 44-181-744-1149. E-mail: techapp@cix.compulink.co.uk. **Indexed:** WPM. **Document type:** bulletin.
   Formerly: O I I Spectrum (ISSN 1351-0096)
   Description: Covers the technologies and markets for open information interchange and document interoperability.

INFORMATION NETWORK AND DATA COMMUNICATION. see COMPUTERS — Computer Networks

004.6   II
INFORMATION SYSTEMS COMPUTERWORLD. (Text in English) 1987. fortn. Media Transasia India Ltd., K-35 Green Park (Main), New Delhi - 110016, India. TEL 91-11-6868775. FAX 91-11-6867641. TELEX 031-73262. E-mail: pc.world@mtil.sprintrpg.ems.vsnl.net.in; pc.world@giaspl1.vsnl.net.in. (Subscr. to: 808, Dalamal Towers, 211 Nariman Point, Bombay, India. TEL 91-22-244947. FAX 91-22-2871302) Ed. Vinita Chawla. adv.: B&W page $750, color page $1000; trim 190 x 260; adv. contact: Pankaj Bhasin. circ. 18,000.
   Formerly: C and C.
   Description: Provides the Indian market with native IS management issues, technology solutions, availability and pricing information.

621.387   UK   ISSN 0959-4116
INFORMATION TECHNOLOGY REVIEW. Short title: I T Review. 1989. a. Price Waterhouse, 32 London Bridge St., London SE1 9SY, England. TEL 44-171-939-6283. FAX 44-171-403-5265. E-mail: brian_martin@europe.notes.pw.com. Ed. Brian Martin. circ. 25,000. **Document type:** bulletin.
   —BLDSC (6612.874600).
   Description: Annual review of IT budget and expenditure trends.

621.387 001.642   US
TK5101.A1
INTENET. 1990. m. Horizon - House Publications Inc., 685 Canton St., Norwood, MA 02062. TEL 617-769-9750. FAX 617-762-9071. adv. circ. 40,000. (tabloid format; also avail. in microfilm from UMI)
   —KR SourceOne.
   Former titles: Communications and Computer News (ISSN 1057-0071); Communications and Computer Product and Software News (ISSN 1059-5465)
   Description: Covers the local area network, wide area network and all aspects of internetworking.

004.33   UK   ISSN 0953-7856
INTERACTIVE MEDIA INTERNATIONAL. Key Title: I M I - Interactive Media International Newsletter. m. £125. Interactive Media Publications Ltd., 26 Rosebery Ave., London EC1R 4SX, England. TEL 44-171-837-3345. FAX 44-171-837-8901. E-mail: eps@epsitd.demon.co.uk. Ed. Hugh E. Look; Pub. David J. Powell. R&P contact: David J. Powell. **Indexed:** Info.Media & Tech.
   —BLDSC (4531.872300).
   Incorporates (in May 1997): E P Journal (ISSN 0954-3244)
   Description: Provides a source of news, project information and market analysis in the areas of interactive multimedia technology.

651.8   US
INTERNATIONAL CONFERENCE ON COMPUTER COMMUNICATIONS. (PROCEEDINGS). 1972. irreg. 5th, 1980, Atlanta. Elsevier Science Inc., Box 945, New York, NY 10159-0945. TEL 212-633-3730. FAX 212-633-3680. TELEX 420643 AEP UI. (Subscr. outside the Americas to: Elsevier Science, Regional Sales Office, P.O. Box 211, 1000 AE Amsterdam, Netherlands. TEL 31-20-4853757. FAX 31-20-4853432; Subscr. in Australasia to: Elsevier Science (Singapore) Pte Ltd, No.1 Temasek Ave., No.17-01 Millenia Tower, Singapore 039192, Singapore. TEL 65-434-3727. FAX 65-337-2230; Subscr. in Japan to: Elsevier Science Japan, 9-15 Higashi-Azabu 1-chome, Minato-ku, Tokyo 106, Japan. TEL 81-3-5561-5033. FAX 81-3-5561-5047) **Document type:** proceedings.
   Refereed Serial

INTERNATIONAL JOURNAL OF INFORMATION AND MANAGEMENT SCIENCES. see BUSINESS AND ECONOMICS — Management

004.678   IT
INTERNET. 1982. m. L.44000($44) (effective 1997); newsstand price: L.7000. Systems Comunicazioni, V. Olanda, 6, 20080 Gaggiana (MI), Italy. TEL 39-2-90841814. FAX 39-2-90841682. E-mail: redazione@systems.it. Ed. M. Di Pisa. adv.: page Lit.5000000; trim 21 x 28; adv. contact: Lilia Pini. (back issues avail.) **Document type:** consumer publication.
   ●Also available online.

INTERNET AND ONLINE SERVICES MARKET: AUSTRALIA AND NEW ZEALAND. see COMMUNICATIONS — Computer Applications

004.6   US   ISSN 1078-6422
INTERNET BUSINESS ADVANTAGE; online solutions for business success. 1994. m. $69 (foreign $89). Cobb Group, Inc., 9420 Bunsen Pkwy., Ste. 300, Louisville, KY 40220. TEL 502-493-3200; 800-223-8720. FAX 502-491-8050. Ed. Brian Schaffner. adv. contact: Tracee Bell Troutt. illus. **Document type:** newsletter.
   Description: Shows business professionals how to use the Internet to their company's advantage.

004.6 384.3   US
INTERNET BUSINESS REPORT.* bi-m. $395. C M P Publications, Inc., 600 Community Dr., Manhasset, NY 11030. TEL 516-562-5000.

004.678   US   ISSN 1080-8493
▼**INTERNET CONNECTION;** your guide to government resources. 1995. 10/yr. $69 (Canada and Mexico $79; elsewhere $89). Bernan Press, 4611-F Assembly Dr., Lanham, MD 20706-4391. TEL 800-274-4447. FAX 800-865-3450. E-mail: query@berman.com. Ed. E.I. Smith.

INTERNET OPERATOR EUROPE. see COMMUNICATIONS — Telephone And Telegraph

004.6   US   ISSN 1078-540X
INTERNET VOYAGER.* 1994? m. newsstand price: $4.95. Blue Dolphin Communications, Inc., 526 Boston Post Rd., Wayland, MA 01778-1833. TEL 508-443-6363. FAX 508-443-7286. E-mail: logan@BlueDolphin.com; URL: http://www.internetvoyager.com. Ed. Laura Logan. adv.: bk.rev.; software rev.; circ. 10,000 (paid). **Document type:** trade publication, consumer publication.
   ●Also available online.
   Description: Covers all aspects of using and searching on the Internet.

004.6 621.39   US   ISSN 0922-5773
TK5102.5   CODEN: JVSPED
JOURNAL OF V L S I SIGNAL PROCESSING. 1989. 9/yr. fl.1395 to institutions; $715.50 to institutions in U.S. (effective 1998). Kluwer Academic Publishers Boston, Box 358, Accord Sta., Hingham, MA 02018-0358. TEL 617-871-6600. FAX 617-871-6528. TELEX 200190. E-mail: services@wkap.nl; URL: http://www.wkap.nl. (Dist. outside N. America by: Kluwer Academic Publishers Group, P.O. Box 322, 3300 AH Dordrecht, Netherlands. TEL 31-78-6392392. FAX 31-78-6546474) Eds. Earl E. Swartzlander, S.Y. Kung. (also avail. in microform from UMI; reprint service avail. from SWZ,UMI) **Indexed:** ASCA, Compumath, Comput.Rev., Eng.Ind., INSPEC (1989 Zent.Math. **Document type:** academic/scholarly publication.
   —BLDSC (5072.504000); AskIEEE; CISTI; Ei; Genuine Article; KR SourceOne; SWETS; UMI; UnCover. **CCC.**
   Description: Publishes research and survey papers on the design and implementation of signal processing systems with VLSI circuits.
   Refereed Serial

621.387 001.644   US   ISSN 0739-988X
TK5105   CODEN: LIUPDL
LINK-UP; the newsmagazine for users of online service business, educational, personal. 1983. bi-m. $29.9 in U.S.; Canada and Mexico $36; elsewhere $54 (effective 1997). Information Today, Inc., 143 Old Marlton Pike, Medford, NJ 08055. TEL 609-654-6266. FAX 609-654-4309. E-mail: custserv@infotoday.com; 72105.1753@compuserve.com; URL: http://www.infotoday.com/lu/lunew.htm. Ed. Loraine Page. adv.: bk.rev. circ. 35,000. (tabloid format; also avail. in microform; reprint service avail. from UMI) **Indexed:** ABI Inform., Comput.Cont., Microcomp.Ind., PSI, Tel.Abstr.
   ●Also available online. Vendor(s): Lexis-Nexis, UMI.
   —BLDSC (5221.473570); CASDDS; Ei; UMI. **CCC.**
   Description: For individuals interested in small computer communications. Features articles on hardware, software, communications services and search methods. Regular columns cover local bulletin boards and clubs, information utility news.

621.387 US
M I C - TECH-DATA COMMUNICATIONS. 1990. m. $920. Management Information Corporation, 1111 Marlkress Rd., Box 5062, Cherry Hill, NJ 08003-5602. TEL 609-424-1100. FAX 609-424-1999. Ed. Michael Smith. circ. 5,000 (paid). (diskette format) **Document type:** directory.
Description: Provides product references, specifications, performance and prices on networks, multiplexers, and modems.

004 003 US ISSN 1090-4255
MEDIA COMPUTING; email report on emerging media markets. 1989. m. $495 (effective 1997). Dreamscape Net, 510 Woodhaven, Aptos, CA 95003. TEL 408-685-8818. E-mail: statsun@aol.com. Ed. Sherionn M. Tatsuno. charts; illus.; stat.; index. (avail. by e-mail only) **Document type:** newsletter.
●Available only online.
Former titles (until 1996): Pacific Rim Media (ISSN 1085-519X); (until 1994): NeoJapan.
Description: Offers an analysis of emerging technology and business trends in the multimedia and Internet markets.

621.388 FR ISSN 1162-843X
MINITEL NEWS INTERNATIONAL. (Text in English) 1990. m. France Telecom, Direction des Affaires Commerciales et Telematiques, 6 place d'Alleray, 75740 Paris Cedex 15, France.
Description: Highlights international news and front line reports from the industry's principal operators and key users.

621.39 UK
N P L REPORT C I S E. irreg. National Physical Laboratory, Centre for Information Systems Engineering, Teddington, Middlesex TW11 0LW, England. TEL 44-181-943-7002. FAX 44-181-977-7091. E-mail: cisegen@cise.npl.co.uk. **Document type:** monographic series.
—CISTI.
Former titles (until 1995): N P L Report D I T C (ISSN 0262-5369); (until 1982): N P L Report D N A C S (ISSN 0143-7348)

621.387 JA
NIKKEI DATAPRO: DATA COMMUNICATION STANDARDS. (Text in Japanese) data file with q. supplements plus m. newsletter. 143000 Yen to new subscr.; renewal 118000 Yen. Nikkei Business Publications, Inc. (Subsidiary of: Nihon Keizai Shimbun, Inc.), 2-7-6 Hirakawa-cho, Chiyoda-ku, Tokyo 102, Japan. TEL 03-5210-8502. FAX 03-5210-8119. URL: http://www.nikkeibp.co.jp/. Ed. Hisashi Okamura; Pub. Hisashi Okamura.

ONLINE I S D N. see COMPUTERS — Computer Networks

004.6 621.39 US ISSN 0032-9460
Q350 CODEN: PRITA9
PROBLEMS OF INFORMATION TRANSMISSION. English translation of: Problemy Peredachi Informatsii (RU ISSN 0555-2923) 1965. q. $1195 (foreign $1395) (effective 1998). (Russian Academy of Sciences, RU) Plenum Publishing Corp., Consultants Bureau, 233 Spring St., New York, NY 10013-1578. TEL 212-620-8468. FAX 212-463-0742. TELEX 23-421139. Ed. N.A. Kuznetsov. (also avail. in microfilm from UMI; back issues avail.) **Indexed:** Comput.& Info.Sys., Comput.Cont., Eng.Ind., INSPEC, Lang.& Lang.Behav.Abstr., Math.R., Zent.Math. **Document type:** academic/scholarly publication.
—BLDSC (0416.933000); AskIEEE; CISTI; KR SourceOne; Linda Hall; SWETS; UMI; UnCover. **CCC.**
Refereed Serial

SIGNAL PROCESSING; an international journal devoted to the methods and applications of signal processing. see COMPUTERS — Computer Programming

004.6 NE ISSN 0923-5965
TA1632 CODEN: SPICEF
SIGNAL PROCESSING: IMAGE COMMUNICATION. (Text in English; summaries in English, French, German) 1989. 8/yr. fl.1035($595) (effective 1998). (European Association for Signal Processing) Elsevier Science B.V., P.O. Box 211, 1000 AE Amsterdam, Netherlands. TEL 31-20-4853911. FAX 31-20-4853598. TELEX 18582 ESPA NL. E-mail: nlinfo-f@elsevier.nl; usinfo-f@elsevier.com; forinfo-kyf04035@niftyserve.or.jp; URL: http://www.elsevier.nl/. (Subscr. in the Americas to: Elsevier Science, Regional Sales Office, Box 945, New York, NY 10159-0945. TEL 212-633-3730. FAX 212-633-3680; Subscr. in Australasia and the Far East to: Elsevier Science (Singapore) Pte Ltd, No.1 Temasek Ave., No.17-01 Millenia Tower, Singapore 039192, Singapore. TEL 65-434-3727. FAX 65-337-2230; Subscr. in Japan to: Elsevier Science Japan, 9-15 Higashi-Azabu 1-chome, Minato-ku, Tokyo 106, Japan. TEL 81-3-5561-5033. FAX 81-3-5561-5047) Ed. Leonardo Chiariglione. illus.; cum.index. (also avail. in microfilm from UMI; back issues avail.) **Indexed:** ASCA, Compumath, Curr.Cont., Eng.Ind., INSPEC (1989-). **Document type:** academic/scholarly publication.
—BLDSC (8275.985600); AskIEEE; CISTI; Ei; Genuine Article; KR SourceOne; SWETS. **CCC.**
Description: Details all aspects of the design, implementation, and use of image transmission, storage, and display systems.
Refereed Serial

621.387 US ISSN 0896-4068
SILVERPLATTER EXCHANGE. 1988. irreg. SilverPlatter Information, Inc., 100 River Ridge Dr., Norwood, MA 02062-5026. TEL 617-769-2599; 800-343-0064. FAX 617-769-8763. (U.K. addr.: 10 Barley Mow Passage, Chiswick, London W4 4PH, England. TEL 44-181-995-8242) Ed. Elizabeth Morley. circ. 31,000. **Indexed:** LISA.
—BLDSC (8281.643000).
Description: Contains information for and about CD-ROM users.

SOLARIS. see LIBRARY AND INFORMATION SCIENCES — Computer Applications

005.3 JA ISSN 0917-7116
SUPER A S C I I; magazine for advanced computer users. 1990. m. 10560 Yen. Akio Fujii, A S C I I Publishing, 4-33-10 Yoyogi, Shibuya-ku, Tokyo 151-24, Japan. TEL 81-3-5351-8111.
—BLDSC (8547.054550).

621.39 CC
TELCOM ASIA. (Text in Chinese, English) 1989. m. C C I Asia-Pacific Ltd., Unit 101, 1-F, Pacific Plaza, 410 Des Vouex Rd., Hong Kong, People's Republic of China. TEL 852-2858-0789. FAX 852-2857-6309. Ed. Brian Washburn; Pub. Tom Gorman. adv.: B&W page $4800, color page $6150; trim 203 x 279. circ. 20,750.

TELECOM REPORT. see COMMUNICATIONS — Telephone And Telegraph

004 NE ISSN 0920-413X
TELECOMMAGAZINE; strategie en toepassingen van tele- en datacommunicatie. (Annual supplements avail.: Telecommagazine Service Guide, and ISDN Almanak) 1986. 10/yr. (foreign fl.200). V N U Business Publications B.V., Postbus 9194, 1006 CC Amsterdam, Netherlands. TEL 31-20-4875487. FAX 31-20-4875727. E-mail: telecommagazin@bpa.nl; URL: http://www.bpa.nl/telecommagazine. Ed. M. Kramer; Pub. A.H.W. van der Want. adv. contact: H. Citroen. bk.rev.; charts; illus.; circ. 17,000 (controlled). (back issues avail.) **Indexed:** Tel.Abstr. **Document type:** trade publication.
Incorporates: P C Netwerk (ISSN 0924-9737)
Description: Studies of data communications geared to the lay person.

TELECOMMUNICATIONS CARRIERS AND SERVICE PROVIDERS MARKET. see COMMUNICATIONS — Computer Applications

621.387 US
TOPICS IN INFORMATION SYSTEMS. 1984. irreg. price varies. Springer-Verlag, 175 Fifth Ave., New York, NY 10010. TEL 212-460-1500. FAX 212-473-6272. (Also: Berlin, Heidelberg, Tokyo and Vienna) (reprint service avail. from ISI) **Document type:** monographic series.

621.387 SP ISSN 1130-5401
VIDEOTEX COMUNICACION; revista del usuario. 1990. 12/yr. 2400 ptas. (effective 1993). Asociacion de Usuarios de Videotex de Espana, C. de Fernan Gonzalez, 22, 1o centro, 28009 Madrid, Spain. TEL 5043807. FAX 5773349. Ed. David Parra Valcarce. adv.: B&W page 300000 ptas.; 270 x 350. bk.rev. circ. 50,000. **Document type:** trade publication.

621.387 DK ISSN 0108-5220
VISUELT.* 1983. 4/yr. DKK 150. Blanketfolket, Forening for Visuel Data-Medie Kommunikation, c/o Bent Osholm, Ed., Lavager 15, DK-2620 Albertslund, Denmark. TEL 42-648927. FAX 42-64-89-27. illus. circ. 1,000. **Indexed:** DAAI.

VOICE & DATA. see COMMUNICATIONS

004.6 384 US ISSN 1069-3416
WIRELESS DATA NEWS. 1993. bi-w. $597 (foreign $630) (effective 1997). Phillips Business Information, Inc., 1201 Seven Locks Rd., Potomac, MD 20854. TEL 301-424-3338. FAX 301-309-3847. E-mail: pbi@phillips.com. Ed. Mary McCormick. (back issues avail.) **Document type:** newsletter.
●Also available online. Vendor(s): Information Access Co.
—CCC.
Incorporates (in 1995): Personal Devices Report; Which incorporates (1993-1994): Wireless Media and Messaging.

1992 SINGLE MARKET COMMUNICATIONS REVIEW. see COMMUNICATIONS — Telephone And Telegraph

COMPUTERS — Electronic Data Processing

see also Business and Economics–Banking and Finance–Computer Applications

A C M ADMINISTRATIVE DIRECTORY OF COLLEGE AND UNIVERSITY COMPUTER SCIENCE - DATA PROCESSING PROGRAMS AND COMPUTER FACILITIES. see COMPUTERS

A P D U NEWSLETTER. (Association of Public Data Users) see STATISTICS

004.7 US
ACTIVITIES. 1993. q. Association of Color Thermal Transfer Technology, Inc., 310 Commerce Dr., Amherst, NY 14228. TEL 716-691-5817. FAX 716-691-3395. **Document type:** newsletter.
Description: Provides information about developments in the color printer business with a special focus on thermal transfer technology.

001.64 658.403 US ISSN 0196-8696
HF5548.125
ADVANCES IN DATA PROCESSING MANAGEMENT. irreg. Heyden & Sons, Inc., c/o John Wiley & Sons, 605 Third Ave., New York, NY 10016. TEL 215-382-6673. **Indexed:** INSPEC.

004 DK ISSN 0109-2847
ALT OM DATA. 1983. 22/yr. DKK 668. Audio Media A-S, St. Kongensgade 72, DK-1264 Copenhagen K, Denmark. TEL 45-33-91-28-33. FAX 45-33-91-01-21. E-mail: redaktion@aod.dk; URL: http://www.aod.dk. Ed. Torben Okholm. adv. contact: Klaus Wiedemann. bk.rev.; circ. 40,000 (controlled). **Document type:** consumer publication.
Description: Covers all aspects of the Danish PC market, including reviews of hardware and software.

AMERICAN BANKERS ASSOCIATION. NATIONAL OPERATIONS & AUTOMATION CONFERENCE. PROCEEDINGS. see BUSINESS AND ECONOMICS — Banking And Finance — Computer Applications

AMERICAN BANKERS ASSOCIATION. OPERATIONS AND AUTOMATION DIVISION. CHECK PROCESSING. see BUSINESS AND ECONOMICS — Banking And Finance — Computer Applications

AMERICAN BANKERS ASSOCIATION. OPERATIONS AND AUTOMATION DIVISION. DATA PROCESSING - TELECOMMUNICATIONS. see BUSINESS AND ECONOMICS — Banking And Finance — Computer Applications

COMPUTERS — ELECTRONIC DATA PROCESSING

AMERICAN BANKERS ASSOCIATION. OPERATIONS AND AUTOMATION DIVISION. RETAIL OPERATIONS. see *BUSINESS AND ECONOMICS — Banking And Finance—computer Applications*

001.64   UK   ISSN 0953-4474
APPLE BUSINESS. m. E M A P Business & Computer Publications Ltd., 33-39 Bowling Green Ln., London EC1R 0DA, England. TEL 44-171-837-1212. FAX 44-171-278-4008. **Document type:** trade publication.

001.64   US   ISSN 0746-7265
AUERBACH E D P AUDITING. (Electronic Data Processing) 1978. bi-m. $434. Auerbach Publishers (Subsidiary of: Warren, Gorham & Lamont), One Penn Plaza, New York, NY 10119. TEL 212-971-5000. FAX 212-971-5024. (Subscr. to: 31 St. James Ave., Boston, MA 02116-4112. TEL 800-950-1218. FAX 617-423-1914) Ed. William E. Perry. charts. (looseleaf format) **Document type:** trade publication.
— CCC.
Formerly (until 1983): E D P Auditing (ISSN 0736-3656)
Description: Comprehensive and referenceable desktop aid for the working audit professional.

681   GW   ISSN 0178-2312
AUTOMATISIERUNGSTECHNIK; automatisierung Prozess. Short Title: A T. 1953. m. DM.478 (includes subscr. to Automatisierungstechnische Praxis) (effective 1997). R. Oldenbourg Verlag GmbH, Rosenheimerstr. 145, 81671 Munich, Germany. TEL 49-89-45051-0. FAX 49-89-45051207. (Subscr. to: Postfach 801360, 81613 Munich, Germany) Ed. F. Frueh. adv.; bk.rev.; abstr.; bibl.; charts; illus. circ. 3,000. **Indexed:** Appl.Mech.Rev., Chem.Abstr., Cyb.Abstr., Eng.Ind., Excerp.Med., INIS Atomind., INSPEC (1985-), Zent.Math. **Document type:** academic/scholarly publication.
—BLDSC (1831.584350); AskIEEE; CISTI; KR SourceOne; Linda Hall; SWETS. **CCC.**
Formerly (until 1985): Regelungstechnik (ISSN 0340-434X)
Description: Highly technical publication containing articles about the theory of automatic controls and automation and their industrial applications. Includes dissertations.

BANK OPERATIONS BULLETIN. see *BUSINESS AND ECONOMICS — Banking And Finance — Computer Applications*

BIT. see *COMPUTERS — Computer Programming*

001.64 910.03   US
BLACK DATA PROCESSING ASSOCIATES. DATA NEWS. q. Black Data Processing Associates, 1250 Connecticut Ave., N.W., Ste. 610, Washington, DC 20036-2603. TEL 202-775-4301.
Description: Includes information on word processing and data communications.

001.64 910.03   US
BLACK DATA PROCESSING ASSOCIATES. NATIONAL JOURNAL. q. Black Data Processing Associates, 1250 Connecticut Ave., N.W., Ste. 610, Washington, DC 20036-2603. TEL 202-775-4301.
Description: Includes word processing and data communications.

001.64   US
BOND INFORMATION DATABASE SERVICE. m. $1295. Moody's Investors Service (Subsidiary of: Dun & Bradstreet Corporation), 99 Church St., New York, NY 10007. TEL 212-553-0300. FAX 212-553-4700. (also avail. in magnetic tape)
● Also available on CD-ROM.
Description: Provides information on over 16,000 corporate, government, and agency convertible rated debt issues. Includes database management software.

658 001.6   SZ
BUEROSWISS; Fachzeitschrift fuer Buero und Automation. (Text in German) 1947. m. (11/yr.). 87 SFr. (Europe 103 SFr.; overseas 116 SFr.) (effective 1996). Fachpresse Goldach, Sulzstr. 12, CH-9403 Goldach, Switzerland. TEL 41-71-8449111. FAX 41-71-8449511. E-mail: 100442.1657@compuserve.com; URL: http://www.fachpresse.ch. Ed. Uwe Pawlowski. bk.rev.; illus. circ. 16,000. **Indexed:** Intl.Ind.TV. **Document type:** trade publication.
Former titles: Office Life; Information (ISSN 0379-248X)

004 658   UK
BUSINESS SOLUTIONS. q. 12-26 Lexington St., London W12 4HQ, England. TEL 0171-312-2720. FAX 0171-312-2724. Ed. Marc Beishon. circ. 15,000. **Indexed:** INSPEC. **Document type:** trade publication.
Description: For Unisys UK on strategic issues in information technology.

001.64   FR   ISSN 0986-847X
C D - R O M. 18/yr. 2200 F. A Jour, 11 rue du Marche St. Honore, 75001 Paris, France. Ed. Marie Jo Coutanceau.
Description: Covers manufacturers of discs and readers, new products, technologies and software and news on standardization.

001.64 658.4031   FR   ISSN 0987-8238
C D - R O M INTERNATIONAL. 18/yr. 2200 F. A Jour, 11 rue du Marche St. Honore, 75001 Paris, France. TEL 42-96-67-22. FAX 40-20-07-75. TELEX 615 887 AJOUR F. Ed. Sotires Eleftheriou. **Indexed:** Info.Media & Tech.
Description: Up-to-date international news on CD-ROM including new products, company profiles, technological developments, reports on major EC programs and market figures.

001.64   US   ISSN 1049-2194
QA76   CODEN: CAMRE3
CAPACITY MANAGEMENT REVIEW; a monthly report on managing computer performance. 1973. m. $295 (foreign $345) (effective 1997). Institute for Computer Capacity Management, 1020 8th Ave. S., Ste. 6, Naples, FL 34102. TEL 941-261-8945. FAX 941-261-5456. Ed. Tom Confrey; Pub. Mark Friedman. adv.; bk.rev.; charts; illus.; stat.; index. circ. 1,000. (also avail. in microfiche; back issues avail.) **Indexed:** ABI Inform., Comput.Lit.Ind., Comput.Rev., INSPEC (1990-). **Document type:** newsletter.
● Also available online. Vendor(s): UMI.
—BLDSC (3050.627750); AskIEEE; CISTI; Ei; KR SourceOne; UMI. **CCC.**
Formerly: E D P Performance Review (ISSN 0091-7206)

001.64   PO
CEREBRO. 12/yr. Av. Republica 47 - 1o Dto., 1000 Lisbon, Portugal. TEL 768911. FAX 732056. circ. 12,500.

621.381 030   CC
CHINA COMPUTERWORLD. (Text in Chinese) 1979. w. 3-F, Commercial Bldg., 2 Cuiwei Rd., Wanshou Rd., P.O. Box 750, Beijing 100036, People's Republic of China. TEL 86-10-825-9412. FAX 86-10-825-9410. Ed. Yaying Liu. adv.: B&W page $5300; trim 270 x 380; adv. contact: Jinghua He. circ. 130,000.

001.64   US
CIRCUIT NEWS DIGEST. 1984. bi-m. $50. Circuit News Inc., Rt. 1, Box 43C, Webb City, MO 64870. TEL 417-673-2860. FAX 417-673-4743. (Subscr. to: Drawer 48, Joplin, MO 64802-0048) Ed. Robert J. Blanset. adv. contact: Robert J. Blanset. bk.rev. circ. 10,009.
Former titles: Circuit News (ISSN 1058-9317); (until 1985): Printed Circuit News (ISSN 0891-7299)
Description: International coverage of electronic manufacturing, products, packaging, testing, and quality.

004   NE   ISSN 0169-3786
COMPUTABLE; automatiseringsvakblad voor de Benelux. 1968. w. (Fri.) fl.180 (foreign fl.290) (effective 1996). V N U Business Publications B.V., Postbus 9194, 1006 CC Amsterdam, Netherlands. TEL 31-20-4875487. FAX 31-20-4875700. TELEX 14407 PUBLI NL. Ed. M. Plekker; Pub. A.H.W. van der Want. adv. contact: Henk Vos. bk.rev.; illus.; index; circ. 806 (paid); 69,870 (controlled). (tabloid format) **Indexed:** Key to Econ.Sci. **Document type:** newspaper, trade publication.
—SWETS.
Former titles (until 1984): Weekblad Computable (ISSN 0165-5450); (until 1979): Computable (ISSN 0010-4450)

001.64   US
COMPUTER AND COMMUNICATIONS. 1969. m. $40 (free to qualified personnel). V N U Business Publications, Inc., 10 Mulholland Dr., Hasbrouck Heights, NJ 07604. TEL 201-393-6000. adv. circ. 100,000.
Description: Covers data processing.

001.64 657   II
COMPUTER DIGEST AND DATA PROCESSING. w. Rs.635($75) International Press Cutting Service, P.O. Box 121, Allahabad 211001, India. index. circ. 1,200. (processed) **Document type:** newsletter.
Formerly: Computer World - Data Processing - Accounting.

001.64   US   ISSN 0739-0874
    CODEN: CERTDR
COMPUTER ECONOMICS REPORT; the financial advisor of data processing users. (National and International eds. avail.) 1979. m. $595 (effective 1997). Computer Economics, Inc., 5841 Edison Pl., Carlsbad, CA 92008-6519. TEL 760-438-8100. FAX 760-431-1126. E-mail: cer@compecon.com; URL: http://www.computereconomics.com. charts; stat.; index. (back issues avail.) **Indexed:** Comput.Cont., Comput.Lit.Ind., INSPEC (1990-). **Document type:** newsletter.
—AskIEEE; CASDDS; KR SourceOne. **CCC.**
Incorporates (in 1996): Computer Economics Report International (ISSN 1054-5026)
Description: Provides financial advice for data processing users. Offers information on lease provisions, used and new equipment systems and management techniques.

651.8 001.64   US   ISSN 0889-082X
COMPUTER INDUSTRY REPORT. (Annual supplements avail.) 1964. 24/yr. $495. International Data Corporation, 5 Speen St., Framingham, MA 01701. TEL 508-935-4530. URL: http://www.idcresearch.com. Ed. Rick Miller. R&P contact: Rick Miller. charts index. (looseleaf format; back issues avail.) **Indexed:** Comput.Lit.Ind., Data Process.Dig., PROMT, Tr.& Indus.Ind. **Document type:** newsletter.
● Also available online. Vendor(s): Information Access Co.
Formerly: E D P Industry Report and Market Review (ISSN 0012-754X)
Description: Provides original research identifying and explaining important trends in the worldwide IT industry.

001.63   US   ISSN 0894-8941
Z5640
COMPUTERS AND COMPUTING INFORMATION RESOURCES DIRECTORY; a descriptive guide to live & print sources of information on general & specific applications of computers & data processing... 1986. biennial. $195 for main vol.; supplement $100. Gale Research, 835 Penobscot Bldg., 645 Griswold St., Detroit, MI 48226-4094. TEL 313-961-2242; 800-877-4253. FAX 800-414-5043. E-mail: daniel_snyder@gale.com. Eds. Martin Connors, Janice A. DeMaggio.
Description: Describes all sources of information about computer applications, including publications, associations, research organizations, consultants, trade shows, libraries, publishers, online services and teleprocessing networks.

005.3 664   US   ISSN 1051-6476
COMPUTERS, FOODSERVICE & YOU. 1990. bi-m. $119. 1201 S. Second St., Box 338, Raton, NM 87740. TEL 505-445-8252. Ed. Ann Rigdon; Pub. Mike J. Pappas. software rev.; index; circ. 400 (paid). **Document type:** newsletter.
Description: Provides computer information for the foodservice industry.

001.64   AT
COMPUTERWORLD. 1978. w. Aus.$95 (foreign Aus.$375). I D G Communications Pty. Ltd., 88 Christie St., St. Leonards, N.S.W. 2065, Australia. TEL 02-439-5133. FAX 02-439-5512. Ed. Steve Ireland. adv. circ. 9,146. **Document type:** trade publication.
—BLDSC (3394.979000); UMI.
Former titles: Computerworld Australia (ISSN 0813-295X); Australasian Computerworld.
Description: Newsweekly targeted to information systems professionals.

COMPUTERS — ELECTRONIC DATA PROCESSING

001.64 US ISSN 0887-2953
CONSULTANTS' AND CONTRACTORS' NEWSLETTER; a forum for data processing professionals. 1986. m. $79.95 (effective Jan. 1996). C C N Publications, 105 N. Main St., Boonton, NJ 07005. TEL 201-299-1535; 800-836-0667. FAX 201-335-4866. Ed. Wendy Vandame. R&P contact: Wendy Vandame. adv. contact: Wendy Vandame. bk.rev. (back issues avail.) **Document type:** newsletter.
Description: Covers tax, legal, and market information for data processing professionals.

004 UK
CORPORATE I T STRATEGY. (Information Technology); using information for business performance. m. £35 (Europe £60; rest of world £90). V N U Business Publications BV, VNU House, 32-34 Broadwick St., London W1A 2HG, England. TEL 44-171-316-9000. FAX 44-171-316-9380. Ed. Caroline Gabriel; Pub. Iain Blackhall. adv. contact: Brin Bucknor. **Document type:** trade publication.

001.64 PO ISSN 0870-8983
CORREIO INFORMATICO. 1986. 30/yr. Av. Republica, 47 - 1o Dto., 1000 Lisbon, Portugal. TEL 767339. FAX 7937519. Ed. Fernando Scares. circ. 10,000.

658 001.6 GW ISSN 0341-5449
D S W R. (Datenverarbeitung - Steuer - Wirtschaft - Recht); Zeitschrift fuer Praxisorganisation, Betriebswirtschaft und elektronische Datenverarbeitung. 1971. m. DM.89 (students DM.61) (effective 1997). Verlag C.H. Beck, 80791 Munich, Germany. TEL 49-89-38189-338. FAX 49-89-38189-398. Ed.Bd. adv.: B&W page DM.5600, color page DM.9800; trim 260 x 186. circ. 35,900. (back issues avail.) **Document type:** trade publication.
—SWETS.
Description: Covers organizational practice, management research, and the processing of electronic data.

004 US ISSN 1057-2554
HD9696.C63
DATA ENTRY - DATA CONVERSION SERVICES DIRECTORY. 1988. irreg. $33.95. Morgan-Rand Inc., 1800 Byberry Road, 800 Masons Mill Business Park, Huntingdon Valley, PA 19006. TEL 215-938-5500. FAX 215-938-5549. Ed. Shawn Phillips. adv. circ. 3,000.
Formerly: Data Entry Services Directory (ISSN 0899-4579)
Description: Lists over 600 companies worldwide that provide data entry and data conversion services. Indexed geographically, by services provided and areas of specialization.

001.64 330 US
DATA ENTRY MANAGEMENT ASSOCIATION. NEWSLETTER.* Short title: D E M A. 10/yr. $77 membership. Data Entry Management Association, 180 Devonshire St., Boston, MA 02110-1412. TEL 203-846-3777. FAX 203-846-6883. Ed. Beth Simone.
Description: Provides articles on data capture technology and management. Includes equipment survey, statistical compensation survey, and video terminal health survey.

DATA SOURCES; the comprehensive guide to the data processing industry: hardware, data communications products, software, company profiles. see COMPUTERS — Computer Industry Directories

001.64 UK
DATACOMS. m. E M A P Business & Computer Publications Ltd., 33-39 Bowling Green Ln., London EC1R ODA, England. TEL 44-171-837-1212. FAX 44-171-278-4008. **Document type:** trade publication.

001.64 US ISSN 0011-6963
T175 CODEN: DTMNAT
DATAMATION; the emerging technologies magazine for today's IS. International edition: Datamation International (ISSN 1062-8363) 1957. m. $75 (Canada, Mexico $110; Japan, Australia, New Zealand $195; elsewhere $165); free to qualified personnel. Cahners Publishing Company (Newton), Division of Reed Elsevier Inc., 275 Washington St., Newton, MA 02158-1630. TEL 617-558-4424. FAX 617-558-4506. URL: http://www.datamation.com. (Subscr. to: 8773 S. Ridgeline Blvd., Highlands Ranch, CO 80126. TEL 800-662-7776) Ed. Dennis Eskow; Pub. Carole M. Sacino. adv.; bk.rev.; charts; illus.; index. circ. 200,300. (also avail. in microform; microfiche from CIS; reprint service avail. from UMI) Indexed: A.I.Abstr., A.S.& T.Ind., AAR, ABI Inform., Acad.Ind., Account.& Data Proc.Abstr., Account.Ind. (1974-), AESIS, Appl.Mech.Rev., ASCA, ASEAN Manage.Abstr., B.P.I., BMT, Br.Ceram.Abstr., Bus.Comput.Ind., CAD CAM Abstr., Chem.Abstr., Compumath, Comput.Cont., Comput.Dtbs., Comput.Ind., Comput.Indus.Up., Comput.Lit.Ind., Curr.Cont., Cyb.Abstr., Data Process.Dig., Ergon.Abstr., Excerp.Med., Graph.Arts Lit.Abstr., Ind.Sci.Rev., INIS Atomind., INSPEC, Intl.Mgmt.Info., Law Ofc.Info.Svc., LHTN, Mag.Ind., Mgmt.& Market.Abstr., Microcomp.Ind., Oper.Res.Manage.Sci., PROMT, Qual.Contr.Appl.Stat., Robomat., Sci.Cit.Ind., SCIMP, SRI, SSCI, Tel.Abstr., Tr.& Indus.Ind. **Document type:** trade publication.
●Also available online. Vendor(s): Information Access Co., Knight-Ridder Information, Inc.
—AskIEEE; CASDDS; CISTI; Ei; Genuine Article; KR SourceOne; Linda Hall; SWETS; UMI; UnCover. **CCC**.
Description: Covers analysis, evaluation, implementation, and selection of technologies needed for companies to keep a competitive advantage with a focus on being the IT survival guide for today's IS management.

001.64 SP ISSN 0213-022X
DATAMATION (EDICION ESPANOLA).* 1985. 11/yr. Haymarket, S.A., Travesera Gracia 17-21, 5o 2o, 08022 Barcelona, Spain. TEL 3-237-22-66. FAX 1-237-66-88. Ed. J.M. Vila Solanes. circ. 10,000.

DATAPRO APPLICATION DEVELOPMENT SOFTWARE. see COMPUTERS — Software

001.64 US
DATAPRO INFORMATION MANAGEMENT AND WORKFLOW. 2 base vols. (plus m. updates). $2140 (effective 1996). Datapro Information Services Group (Subsidiary of: McGraw-Hill, Inc.), 600 Delran Pkwy., Delran, NJ 08075. TEL 609-764-0100. FAX 609-764-2814. Indexed: Resour.Ctr.Ind. **Document type:** trade publication.
—CCC.
Formed by the merger of: Datapro Management of Office Automation (ISSN 8750-6416); Which was formerly (until 1985): Datapro Automated Office Solutions (ISSN 0730-8833) & Datapro Reports on Office Automation; Which was formerly (until 1984): Datapro Reports on Office Systems (ISSN 0277-4984)

DATAPRO REPORTS ON BANKING AUTOMATION. see BUSINESS AND ECONOMICS — Banking And Finance — Computer Applications

001.64 US
DATAPRO REPORTS ON INFORMATION SECURITY. 1985. 3 base vols. (plus m. updates). $1264 to new subscr.; renewals $1141 (effective 1996). Datapro Information Services Group (Subsidiary of: McGraw-Hill, Inc.), 600 Delran Pkwy., Delran, NJ 08075. TEL 609-764-0100; 800-328-2776. FAX 609-764-2814.

DATAPRO REPORTS ON RETAIL AUTOMATION. see BUSINESS AND ECONOMICS — Computer Applications

001.64 US ISSN 0190-6585
QA76.5
DATAWORLD. 1978. 4 base vols. (plus m. updates). $1395 (q. CD-ROM $1507) (effective 1993). Faulkner Information Services, Inc., 114 Cooper Center, 7905 Browning Rd., Pennsauken, NJ 08109-4319. TEL 609-662-2070. FAX 609-662-3380. Ed. Betsy Yokum. (looseleaf format)
●Also available on CD-ROM.
Description: Covers information technology hardware, software, and communications equipment and service.

DATENSCHUTZ UND DATENSICHERUNG; Recht und Sicherheit der Informations und Kommunikationssysteme. see COMPUTERS — Computer Security

001.64 CN ISSN 0842-1951
DIRECTION INFORMATIQUE. 1988. m. Can.$60($90) Plesman Publications Ltd., 606 rue Cathcart, Ste. 533, Montreal, PQ H3B 1K9, Canada. TEL 514-875-4250. FAX 514-875-6751. Ed. Johanne DeLuca. adv.: B&W page $2842; adv. contact: Marc Meloche. circ. 17,000. Indexed: Pt.de Rep. (1988-).

001.64 US ISSN 1062-645X
E D I MONTHLY REPORT. (Electronic Data Interchange) 1988. m. $275 (foreign $335) (effective 1997). Congressional Information Bureau, Inc., 3030 Clarendon Blvd., Ste. 202, Arlington, VA 22201. TEL 703-516-4801. FAX 703-516-4804. E-mail: cibaech@erols.com; URL: http://www.cibpubs.com. Ed. R. Cazalas. circ. 500. (looseleaf format; back issues avail.)
—CCC.
Description: Devoted to education and developments of the uses of EDI.

651.8 001.64 US ISSN 0012-7558
E D P WEEKLY. (Electronic Data Processing); the leading weekly computer news summary. 1958. w. $495 (foreign $542). Computer Age & E D P News Services (Subsidiary of: Millin Publishing Group, Inc.), 714 Church St., Alexandria, VA 22314-4202. TEL 703-739-8500. FAX 703-739-8505. Ed. Michael E. Cotter; Pub. S.L. Millin. R&P contact: Michael E. Cotter. bk.rev. circ. 2,400. (also avail. in microform from UMI; back issues avail.; reprint service avail. from UMI) Indexed: Comput.Cont., Comput.Lit.Ind., Comput.Rev., PROMT. **Document type:** newsletter.
●Also available online. Vendor(s): Information Access Co.
—UMI. **CCC**.
Incorporates (1976-1989): Data - Comm Industry Report (ISSN 0149-9556); Which was formerly: Computer Age - Data Communications; (1975-1989): E F T S Industry Report; Which was formerly: E F T S Report (ISSN 0360-3784); (1976-1989): Mini-Micro Computer Report (ISSN 0363-7905); (1982-1989): Robotics Report (ISSN 0889-5759); (1970-1989): World Trade Report (Springfield); Which was formerly: Computer Age. World Trade (ISSN 0010-4477).
Description: Reports industry-wide corporate and governmental announcements, developments and strategies, with special features on mini and micro computers, electronic commerce, world trade, and market research.

001.64 US ISSN 1060-7870
E N N. (Electronic News Network) 1988. d. (Tue.-Fri.). $600 via fax. Circuit News Inc., Rt. 1, Box 43C, Webb City, MO 64870. TEL 417-673-2860. FAX 417-673-4743. Ed. Robert J. Blanset. adv. contact: Robert J. Blanset. **Document type:** newspaper.

384.3 005 UK ISSN 1361-2727
ELECTRONIC COMMERCE AND COMMUNICATIONS. 1990. 10/yr. $150. 10 Fourways, Canning Rd., Croydon CR0 6QB, England. TEL 44-181-655-4354. E-mail: johnkav@cix.compulink.co.uk. Ed. John Kavanagh; Pub. Terry Benson. bk.rev. circ. 10,000. **Document type:** consumer publication.
Formerly (until 1995): E D I Analysis (ISSN 0958-5052)
Description: For users and suppliers of products and services for electronic data interchange and electronic commerce.

COMPUTERS — ELECTRONIC DATA PROCESSING

004.93   US   ISSN 1086-2870
▼**ELECTRONIC COMMERCE TECHNOLOGY NEWS**. 1996. w. $697 (foreign $760) (effective 1997). Phillips Business Information, Inc., 1201 Seven Locks Rd., Potomac, MD 20854. TEL 301-424-3338. FAX 301-309-3847. E-mail: pbi@phillips.com. Ed. Mary Crowley. **Document type:** newsletter.
—BLDSC (3700.282000); SWETS. **CCC**.

ELECTRONIC CONTRACTING LAW; EDI and business transactions. see *PATENTS, TRADEMARKS AND COPYRIGHTS*

ELECTRONIC RETAILING. see *BUSINESS AND ECONOMICS — Marketing And Purchasing*

ELECTRONIC TECHNOLOGY. see *ELECTRONICS*

001.64   CU
ELECTRONICA Y PROCESOS DE DATOS EN CUBA. 3/yr. $26 in S. America; N. America $28; elsewhere $34. (C I D) Ediciones Cubanas, Obispo No. 527, Apdo. 605, Havana, Cuba.

001.642   US   ISSN 1053-6566
ENTERPRISE SYSTEMS JOURNAL; focusing on IBM host-based enterprise-wide computing. 1987. m. $60 (Canada & Mexico $72; elsewhere $125). Cardinal Business Media, Inc., 12225 Greenville Ave., Ste. 700, Dallas, TX 75243-9338. TEL 972-669-9000. FAX 972-669-9909. E-mail: 76130,221@compuserve.com. Ed. Debby English; Pub. George Dishman. R&P contact: Kathie Clark. adv. contact: Lynda Brown. bk.rev./ circ. 83,500 (controlled). **Indexed:** Comput.Lit.Ind. **Document type:** trade publication.
●Also available online. Vendor(s): Information Access Co.
—BLDSC (3776.631000); CISTI; KR SourceOne; SWETS.
Incorporates (1990-1991): Contingency Journal (ISSN 1050-2122); Which was formerly (until vol.5, no.9, 1990): Mainframe Journal (ISSN 0895-5751)
Description: Provides technical and information systems management information oriented to professionals associated directly with enterprisewide information systems.
Refereed Serial

004   US   ISSN 1068-3070
QA76.54
EUROMICRO - WORKSHOP ON REAL-TIME SYSTEMS. PROCEEDINGS. 1989. a. price varies. (Institute of Electrical and Electronics Engineers, Inc.) I E E E Computer Society Press, 10662 Los Vaqueros Circle, Los Alamitos, CA 90720-1264. TEL 714-821-8380. FAX 714-821-4641. Ed. Cat Harris; Pub. Matt Loeb. adv. contact: Frieda Koester. **Document type:** proceedings.
—BLDSC (3829.285930). **CCC**.
Description: Presents current research, new techniques and important studies on data compression and related areas.

001.64   CN   ISSN 1180-3711
CODEN: EIDRE2
EVANS REPORT. 1971. 12/yr. Can.$2495. Evans Research Corporation, 1 Eva Rd., Ste. 309, Etobicoke, ON M9C 4Z5, Canada. TEL 416-621-8814. FAX 416-621-8031. Ed. Bill Fournier. index, cum.index every 3 yrs. circ. 700. (looseleaf format; also avail. in microfiche) **Indexed:** Comput.Cont., Comput.Lit.Ind., INSPEC (1990-). **Document type:** trade publication.
—AskIEEE; KR SourceOne.
Formerly: E D P In-Depth Reports (ISSN 0315-3819)
Description: Focuses on key market statistics and trends in the information technology market.

001.64   CN
GOVERNMENT COMPUTER MAGAZINE. 1991. 11/yr. Can.$34.95 (US Can.$89.95, elsewhere Can.$120). 557 Cambridge St., S., Ste. 202, Ottawa, ON K1S 4J4, Canada. TEL 613-237-4862. FAX 613-237-4232. Ed. Tim Lougheed; Pub. Lee Hunter. adv.: B&W page Can.$1910, color page Can.$2790, trim 8 X 10 3/4; adv. contact: Lori Cunningham. bk.rev./ circ. 13,000 (controlled). **Document type:** trade publication.
Formerly: Hum Magazine (ISSN 1188-522X)

621.381   US   ISSN 0018-8689
CODEN: IBMTAA
I B M TECHNICAL DISCLOSURE BULLETIN. 1958. m. $1200 (effective 1997). International Business Machines Corp. (Thornwood), MD2-10, 500 Columbus Ave., Thornwood, NY 10594. TEL 914-742-6274. FAX 914-742-5826. E-mail: rossv@us.ibm.com; URL: http://www.ibm.com/ibm/licensing. Ed. V.W. Ross. charts; illus. **Indexed:** Eng.Ind., INIS Atomind., INSPEC (1968-1986). **Document type:** bulletin.
—CISTI; Linda Hall.

004   US   ISSN 1063-6374
QA76.58   CODEN: PSPDF8
I E E E SYMPOSIUM ON PARALLEL AND DISTRIBUTED PROCESSING. PROCEEDINGS. Short title: S P D P. 1989. a. price varies. (Institute of Electrical and Electronics Engineers, Inc.) I E E E Computer Society Press, 10662 Los Vaqueros Circle, Los Alamitos, CA 90720-1264. TEL 714-821-8380. FAX 714-821-4641. adv. contact: Frieda Koester. **Document type:** proceedings.
—Ei. **CCC**.
Description: Details important studies on subjects such as distributed programming, programming languages, modeling, scheduling, algorithms, fault tolerance and architectures.

004   CN   ISSN 0315-5986
T57.6.A1   CODEN: INFRCL
I N F O R JOURNAL/C O R S. (Text in English and French) 1963. q. Can.$75($80) to institutions (effective 1998). (Institute of Computer Science) University of Toronto Press, Journals Department, 5201 Dufferin St., Downsview, ON M3H 5T8, Canada. TEL 416-667-7710. FAX 416-667-7881. E-mail: journals@gpu.utcc.utoronto.ca. (U.S. addr.: 340 Nagel Dr., Cheektowaga, NY 14225) (Co-sponsors: Canadian Information Processing Society; Canadian Operational Research Society) Ed. D.J. Wright. adv.; bk.rev./ charts; illus.; index. circ. 2,742. **Indexed:** ABI Inform., Comput.Cont., Comput.Lit.Ind., Comput.Rev., Cont.Pg.Manage., Curr.Cont., Cyb.Abstr., Eng.Ind., INSPEC, Int.Abstr.Oper.Res., J.Cont.Quant.Meth., Oper.Res.Manage.Sci., Qual.Contr.Appl.Stat., Zent.Math. **Document type:** academic/scholarly publication.
●Also available online. Vendor(s): UMI.
—BLDSC (4478.880000); AskIEEE; CISTI; Ei; Genuine Article; KR SourceOne; Linda Hall; SWETS; UMI; UnCover. **CCC**.
Formed by the merger of: Canadian Information Processing Society. Quarterly Bulletin (ISSN 0008-3844); Canadian Journal of Operational Research and Information Processing (ISSN 0008-4638)

003 657   US   ISSN 1076-4100
CODEN: IACJET
I S AUDIT & CONTROL JOURNAL. (Information Systems) 1976. 6/yr. $75 (foreign $90) (effective 1997). (Information Systems Audit & Control Association) Information Systems Audit and Control Association, 3701 Algonquin Rd., Ste. 1010, Rolling Meadows, IL 60008. TEL 847-253-1545. FAX 847-253-1443. E-mail: publication@isaca.org; URL: http://www.isaca.org. Eds. P. Dahlberg, V. Greenland. adv.; bk.rev. circ. 17,000. **Indexed:** Account.Ind. (1974-), INSPEC (1994-).
—BLDSC (4582.115000); AskIEEE; KR SourceOne; SWETS; UnCover. **CCC**.
Former titles (until 1994): E D P Auditor Journal; E D P Auditor (ISSN 0885-0445)
Description: Addresses the information systems control community; includes IS audit, computer security and related fields.

001.64   US
I S CAPACITY MANAGEMENT HANDBOOK SERIES. (Information Systems) (Issued in six volumes: Vol. 1: Capacity Planning; Vol. 2: Performance Analysis & Tuning; Vol. 3: Cost Accounting & Chargeback; Vol. 4: Operations Management; Vol. 5: Data Network Performance - Capacity Management; Vol 6: Data Storage Performance - Capacity Management) 1978. q. $200 (foreign $250) for single volume (effective 1997). Institute for Computer Capacity Management, 1020 8th Ave. S., Ste. 6, Naples, FL 34102. TEL 941-261-8945. FAX 941-261-5456. Ed. Phillip C. Howard. (looseleaf format; back issues avail.) **Document type:** trade publication.
Formerly: E D P Performance Management Handbook (ISSN 0277-8920)
Description: For the mainframe performance and capacity management professional. Training aid for newcomers and a reference source for those needing to research methodologies, procedures, or tools.

004   US   ISSN 1071-6629
T58.5
I T A A MEMBERSHIP DIRECTORY. (Former name of issuing body: American Data Processing Service Organizations) 1963. a. $150 to non-members. Information Technology Association of America, Publications Dept., 1616 N. Ft. Myer Dr., Ste. 1300, Arlington, VA 22209-9998. TEL 410-543-0475. FAX 410-543-2921. circ. 10,000 (controlled). **Document type:** directory.
Former titles: A D A P S O Membership Directory; A D A P S O Membership; A D A P S O Directory; Directory of Data Processing Service Organizations (ISSN 0084-9901)
Description: Lists I.T.A.A. members involved in micro-, mini-, mainframe computer software, system integration, professional consulting services, data processing and network services. Cross-indexed by geographic regions served.

001.64 658   US
I T COST MANAGEMENT SOURCEBOOK. 1996. base vol. (plus m. updates). $2500. Computer Economics, Inc., 5841 Edison Pl., Carlsbad, CA 92008-6519. TEL 760-438-8100; 800-326-8100. FAX 760-431-1126. URL: http://www.computereconomics.com. Ed. Terrin Lovett. **Document type:** consumer publication.
Formed by the merger of (1987-1996): Computer Economics Sourcebook; (1990-1996): Residual Value Forecasts for D E C Systems and Peripherals; (1989-1996): Residual Value Forecasts for I B M Systems and Peripherals.
Description: Provides current financial guide to data processing equipment acquisition and control of data processing expenses.

004   US
I T COST MANAGEMENT STRATEGIES. (Information Technology); the planning assistant for IT directors. 1982. m. $495 (effective 1997). Computer Economics, Inc., 5841 Edison Pl., Carlsbad, CA 92008-6519. TEL 760-438-8100. FAX 760-431-1126. E-mail: editor@compecon.com URL: http://www.computereconomics.com. Ed. Edward Pesabew. charts; stat.; index. (back issues avail.) **Indexed:** Comput.Cont., Comput.Lit.Ind. **Document type:** newsletter.
—AskIEEE; KR SourceOne. **CCC**.
Incorporates (in 1996): Systems Reengineering Economics Letter (ISSN 1074-732X); **Former titles** (until Aug. 1996): I S Budget (Information Systems (ISSN 1076-2620); (until 1994): D P Budget (ISSN 0890-4316); (until 1986): Computer Executive Letter (ISSN 0739-2265)
Description: Provides financial advice and analyses to IT executives in charge of data processing budgets. Reports on and evaluates the financial management of IT operations, IT equipment acquisition methods and more.

004   AT
I T REVIEWS. (Information Technology); the enterprise technology journal. m. Aus.$20. A C P Computer Publications, Level 6, 54-58 Park St., Sydney, N.S.W. 2000, Australia. TEL 61-2-2889168. FAX 61-2-2674909. E-mail: itreview@acp.com.au. Ed. Chris Moriarty; Pub. Richard Walsh. adv.: B&W page Aus.$2900, color page Aus.$3800; trim 275 x 210; adv. contact: Matthew Chivers.
Description: Provides information on how to best implement technology from a management perspective.

COMPUTERS — ELECTRONIC DATA PROCESSING

001.64   US   ISSN 1055-8098
IMAGING SERVICE BUREAU NEWS; for users and suppliers of data conversion. 1988. bi-m. $190 (effective 1995 & 1996). Image Publishing, Inc., 105 Valley Rd., Box 3149, Westport, CT 06880-5133. TEL 203-222-9310. FAX 203-222-7871. E-mail: imagepub@futuris.net; URL: http://www.futuris.net/imagepub. Ed. David Miles; Pub. Charles Miles. adv.: page $960; adv. contact: David Miles. bk.rev. circ. 500. (back issues avail.) **Document type:** newsletter, trade publication.
Formerly: Data Conversion Newsletter (ISSN 0898-6509)
Description: Contains information on OCR scanning, image scanning, and media conversion.

004   CN   ISSN 1187-7081
QA75.5   CODEN: IFCAE3
INFO CANADA. (Supplement avail: Software Canada) 1969. m. Can.$50($90) Laurentian Technomedia Inc. (Subsidiary of: Laurentian Media Inc.), 501 Oakdale Rd., North York ON M3N 1W7, Canada. TEL 416-746-7360; 800-565-4007. FAX 416-746-1421. Ed. John Pickett. adv. contact: Gerald Chopik. bk.rev.; bibl.; charts; illus.; tr.lit.; index. circ. 30,000. (also avail. in microform from UMI) **Indexed:** ABI Inform., Can.B.P.I., Comput.Cont., Comput.Dtbs., Comput.Lit.Ind., INSPEC, PROMT. **Document type:** trade publication.
—AskIEEE; CISTI; KR SourceOne; UMI. **CCC.**
Incorporates (in Mar. 1994): I.T; Which was formerly titled: Canadian Datasystems (ISSN 0008-3364); Formerly (1976-1991): Computerdata.
Description: For information managers and professionals who use computers, office systems and data processing equipment. Provides information on hardware, software, office automation systems and data communication. Each issue is dedicated to a specific product review-comparison.

001.64   UK   ISSN 0260-7247
INFOMATICS. 1980. m. £33 (foreign £43) (effective 1996). V N U Business Publications BV, VNU House, 32-34 Broadwick St., London W1A 2HG, England. TEL 44-171-439-4242. FAX 44-171-734-5510. Ed. David Bannister. circ. 44,000. **Indexed:** Comput.Cont., INSPEC, Mgmt.& Market.Abstr., PROMT, World Text.Abstr. **Document type:** trade publication.
Description: Covers all aspects of the information industry. Includes articles on automation applications.

INFORMAA QUARTERLY. see BUSINESS AND ECONOMICS — Office Equipment And Services

621.38 001.64   HU   ISSN 0019-9753
INFORMACIO-ELEKTRONIKA. (Text in Hungarian; summaries in English and Russian) 1966. bi-m. 300 Ft. (Kozponti Statisztikai Hivatal) Statisztikai Kiado Vallalat, Kaszasdulo u. 2, P.O. Box 99, 1300 Budapest 3, Hungary. TEL 36-1-180-3311. FAX 36-168-8635. TELEX 22-6699. (Subscr. to: Kultura, Box 149, H-1389 Budapest, Hungary) adv.; bk.rev.; stat. circ. 1,820. **Indexed:** Comput.Rev., Data Process.Dig., INSPEC. **Document type:** government publication.
—AskIEEE; CISTI; KR SourceOne.

001.64   XO   ISSN 0323-1984
INFORMACNE SYSTEMY. (Text in Czech or Slovak; summaries in English and Russian) 1972. bi-m. $14. Institut Informatiky a Statistiky (INFOSTAT), Dubravska Cesta 3, 842 21 Bratislava, Slovakia. (Dist. by: Slovart, nam. Slobody 6, 817 64 Bratislava, Slovakia) illus.

001.64   IT
INFORMATICA.* 11/yr. Via Valdonega 117, 15046 San Salvatore, Monteferrato, Italy. TEL 2-58-11-12-83. Ed. Rodolfo Grigolato. circ. 21,894.

INFORMATICA OGGI E UNIX; la rivista dei sistemi aperti. see COMPUTERS — Computer Architecture

004   NE   ISSN 0925-8264
INFORMATIE MANAGEMENT; tijdschrift voor E D P management. 1984. 9/yr. fl.189 (foreign fl.360) (effective 1996). Ten Hagen & Stam b.v. (Subsidiary of: Wolters Kluwer N.V.), Postbus 34, 2501 AG The Hague, Netherlands. TEL 31-70-3045700. FAX 31-70-3045812. Ed. Jan Brogt. adv.: B&W page fl.3595, color page fl.6560; trim 280 x 210; adv. contact: Herman Voois. circ. 4,465 (paid). **Document type:** trade publication.
—SWETS.
Former titles (until 1990): Informatie Management Magazine (ISSN 0925-8256); (until 1989): A G Report (ISSN 0925-8248)
Description: For corporate and institutional EDP managers, data base managers, and computer science consultants.

INFORMATION AND MANAGEMENT; international journal of information systems applications. see COMPUTERS — Data Base Management

005.3   NE   ISSN 0950-5849
HF5548.2   CODEN: ISOTE7
INFORMATION AND SOFTWARE TECHNOLOGY; the international journal for computer managers. (Text in English) 1959. 15/yr. fl.1140($655) (effective 1998). Elsevier Science B.V., P.O. Box 211, 1000 AE Amsterdam, Netherlands. TEL 31-20-4853911. FAX 31-20-4853598. (Subscr. in the Americas to: Elsevier Science, Regional Sales Office, Box 945, New York, NY 10159-0945. TEL 212-633-3730. FAX 212-633-3680; Subscr. in Australasia to: Elsevier Science (Singapore) Pte Ltd, No.1 Temasek Ave., No.17-01 Millenia Tower, Singapore 039192, Singapore. TEL 65-434-3727. FAX 65-337-2230; Subscr. in Japan to: Elsevier Science Japan, 9-15 Higashi-Azabu 1-chome, Minato-ku, Tokyo 106, Japan. TEL 81-3-5561-5033. FAX 81-3-5561-5047) Ed. Jeremy Weightman. adv.; bk.rev.; abstr.; illus.; index. (also avail. in microform from UMI; back issues avail.; reprint service avail. from UMI) **Indexed:** A.I.Abstr., A.S.& T.Ind., ABI Inform., Abstr.Hum.Comp.Inter., Account.& Data Proc.Abstr., ASCA, BMT, Compumath, Comput.Abstr., Comput.Cont., Comput.Lit.Ind., Curr.Cont., Ergon.Abstr., INSPEC (1968-), Intl.Civil Eng.Abstr., Mgmt.& Market.Abstr., PROMT, Soft.Abstr.Eng., SSCI, Tel.Abstr. **Document type:** academic/scholarly publication.
—BLDSC (4481.865000); AskIEEE; CISTI; Ei; Genuine Article; KR SourceOne; Linda Hall; SWETS; UMI; UnCover. **CCC.**
Formerly: Data Processing (ISSN 0011-684X)
Description: Bridges the gap between software theory and application. Covers research, developments and implementation, and information systems management.
Refereed Serial

001.64   US
INFORMATION MANAGEMENT: STRATEGIES, SYSTEMS, AND TECHNOLOGIES. 1993. bi-m. (2 vols. per issue). $541. Auerbach Publishers (Subsidiary of: Warren, Gorham & Lamont), One Penn Plaza, New York, NY 10119. TEL 212-971-5000. FAX 212-971-5024. (Subscr. to: 31 St. Jemes Ave., Boston, MA 02116-4112. TEL 800-950-1218. FAX 617-423-1914) **Document type:** trade publication.
—CCC.
Formerly (until 1991): Data Processing Management (ISSN 0735-9993)
Description: Covers more than 150 topics pertaining to all aspects of data processing management. Provides latest information on current technology and management practices.

004   NE   ISSN 0020-0190
QA76   CODEN: IFPLAT
INFORMATION PROCESSING LETTERS; devoted to the rapid publication of short contributions to information processing. (Text in English) 1971. 24/yr. fl.2193($1230) (effective 1998). North-Holland (Subsidiary of: Elsevier Science B.V.), P.O. Box 211, 1000 AE Amsterdam, Netherlands. TEL 31-20-4853911. FAX 31-20-4853598. TELEX 18582 ESPA NL. (Subscr. in the Americas to: Elsevier Science, Regional Sales Office, Box 945, New York, NY 10159-0945. TEL 212-633-3730. FAX 212-633-3680; Subscr. in Australasia and the Far East to: Elsevier Science (Singapore) Pte Ltd, No.1 Temasek Ave., No.17-01 Millenia Tower, Singapore 039192, Singapore. TEL 65-434-3727. FAX 65-337-2230; Subscr. in Japan to: Elsevier Science Japan, 9-15 Higashi-Azabu 1-chome, Minato-ku, Tokyo 106, Japan. TEL 81-3-5561-5033. FAX 81-3-5561-5047) Ed.Bd. bk.rev.; bibl.; charts. (also avail. in microform from UMI; back issues avail.; reprint service avail. from SWZ) **Indexed:** ABI Inform., ASCA, Compumath, Comput.Abstr., Comput.Cont., Comput.Rev., Curr.Cont., Cyb.Abstr., Eng.Ind., Excerp.Med., INSPEC, Int.Abstr.Oper.Res., Math.R., SSCI, Zent.Math. **Document type:** academic/scholarly publication.
—BLDSC (4493.898000); AskIEEE; Ei; Genuine Article; KR SourceOne; Linda Hall; SWETS; UMI; UnCover. **CCC.**
Description: Concise reports of interesting results in the field of information processing.
Refereed Serial

001.64   JA   ISSN 0387-5806
QA75.5
INFORMATION PROCESSING SOCIETY OF JAPAN. TRANSACTIONS. (Text in Japanese, English) m. 17010 Yen to non-members; members 6930 Yen (effective Apr. 1997). Information Processing Society of Japan - Joho Shori Gakkai, 7th Fl., Shibaura-Maekawa Bldg., 3-16-20, Shibaura, Minato-ku, Tokyo 108, Japan. TEL 81-3-5484-3535. FAX 81-3-5484-3534. E-mail: editt@ipsj.or.jp; URL: http://www.ipsj.or.jp. Ed. Norio Shiratori; Pub. Hiroshi Iizuka. R&P contact: Yoshio Iwase. circ. 6,000. **Indexed:** Comput.Abstr., INSPEC (1979-), Zent.Math. **Document type:** academic/scholarly publication.
—AskIEEE; CISTI; KR SourceOne. **CCC.**
Description: Contains original research papers and review articles in the field of computer, information science and technology.
Refereed Serial

INFORMATION STRATEGY: THE EXECUTIVE'S JOURNAL. see BUSINESS AND ECONOMICS — Management

001.64   US
INFORMATION SYSTEMS AUDIT & CONTROL ASSOCIATION. CONTROL OBJECTIVES; for information and related technology. (Former name of issuing body: E D P Auditors Association) irreg. $255 (foreign $395) (effective 1997). Information Systems Audit & Control Association, 3701 Algonquin Rd., Ste. 1010, Rolling Meadows, IL 60008. TEL 847-253-1545. FAX 847-253-1443. E-mail: research@isaca.org; URL: http://www.isaca.org.
Formerly (until 1992): E D P Auditors Association. Control Objectives.

001.64 658   US
INFORMATION SYSTEMS SPENDING; an analysis of trends and strategies. 1990. a. $1595 for vols.1,2,3; vols.1,2 $1295; vol.3 $595 (effective 1997). Computer Economics, Inc., 5841 Edison Pl., Carlsbad, CA 92008-6519. TEL 760-438-8100; 800-326-8100. FAX 760-431-1126. URL: http://www.computereconomics.com.
Description: Provides an inside look at the complexities and successful strategies of information systems budget management.

001.64   UK   ISSN 0961-740X
INFORMATION TECHNOLOGY SOLUTIONS EUROPE. 1989. a. £55. Sterling Publications Ltd., 86-88 Edgware Rd., London W2 2YW, England. TEL 44-171-915-9600. FAX 44-171-915-9619. R&P contact: Sandy Tucker. circ. 15,000. **Document type:** trade publication.
Formerly (until 1991): Information Technology Applications Europe (ISSN 0953-6094)

COMPUTERS — ELECTRONIC DATA PROCESSING

001.64   FR   ISSN 0756-7677
INRIATHEQUE; revue de signalement du Centre de Documentation de l'INRIA. 44/yr. 964.80 F. (outside EU 1100 F.) (effective 1997). Institut National de Recherche en Informatique et en Automatique, S E D I S Diffusion, Domaine de Voluceau-Rocquencourt, B.P. 105, 78153 Le Chesnay Cedex, France. TEL 33-1-39635627. FAX 33-1-39635228. TELEX 697 033 F. E-mail: dif.ges-dif@inria.fr; URL: http://www.inria.fr. (also avail. in microfiche)
Description: Provides a listing of mathematical and computer oriented periodicals along with a copy of the contents page. Serves as a reference guide for those users wanting further information on the listings.

001.64   FR   ISSN 0299-0733
INSTITUT NATIONAL DE RECHERCHE EN INFORMATIQUE ET EN AUTOMATIQUE. COLLECTION DIDACTIQUE. irreg. price varies. Institut National de Recherche en Informatique et en Automatique, Sedis Diffusion, B.P. 105, 78153 Le Chesnay Cedex, France. TEL 33-1-39635627. FAX 33-1-39635330.
Indexed: Zent.Math.
—CISTI.

001.64   US   ISSN 0279-2664
INTERACT; the magazine for users of HP3000 computers. 1981. m. $49.50. (H P 3000 International Users Group) Interex, Publications Department, 1192 Borregas Ave., Sunnyvale, CA 94089. TEL 408-747-0227. FAX 408-747-0947. TELEX 4971527. Ed. Connie Wright. adv.; tr.lit. circ. 14,000. **Indexed:** Abstr.Hum.Comp.Inter. **Document type:** consumer publication.

001.64   US   ISSN 1049-8982
INTEREXPRESS; the news publication for HP users worldwide. 1980. m. $30.50. Interex, Publications Department, 1192 Borregas Ave., Sunnyvale, CA 94089. TEL 408-747-0227. FAX 408-747-0947. TELEX 4971527. Ed. Connie Wright. circ. 8,000.
Document type: consumer publication.
Formerly: Interrupt.
Description: Examines the HP role in industry.

621.381   US   ISSN 0190-3918
QA76.6   CODEN: PCPADL
INTERNATIONAL CONFERENCE ON PARALLEL PROCESSING. PROCEEDINGS. 1972. a. price varies. (Institute of Electrical and Electronics Engineers, Inc.) C R C Press, Inc., 2000 Corporate Blvd., N.W., Boca Raton, FL 33431. TEL 561-994-0555; 800-272-7737. FAX 561-998-9784. **Indexed:** INSPEC. **Document type:** proceedings.
—BLDSC (6844.900000); Ei; UMI. **CCC.**
Formerly (until 1975): Sagamore Computer Conference on Parallel Processing. Proceedings.

INTERNATIONAL GEOSCIENCE AND REMOTE SENSING SYMPOSIUM DIGEST. see *GEOGRAPHY*

004   SI   ISSN 0218-7957
▼**INTERNATIONAL JOURNAL OF INFORMATION TECHNOLOGY.** Short title: I J I T. (Text in English) 1995. 2/yr. $55 to individuals; institutions & libraries $92 (developing countries $55). World Scientific Publishing Co. Pte. Ltd., Farrer Rd., P.O. Box 128, Singapore 9128, Singapore. TEL 65-3825663. FAX 65-3825919. TELEX RS 28561 WSPC. E-mail: wspcsl@singnet.com.sg; sales@wspc2.demon.co.uk; wspc@wspc.com; URL: http://www.wspc.com.sg/~wspclib/. (UK addr.: 57 Shelton St., Covent Garden, London WC2H 9HE, England. TEL 44-171-836-0888. FAX 44-171-836-2020; US addr.: 1060 Main St., Ste. 1B, River Edge, NJ 07661. TEL 800-227-7562. FAX 201-487-9656) Ed. Robert K. L. Gay.
Document type: academic/scholarly publication.
—BLDSC (4542.304970); AskIEEE; KR SourceOne.
Description: Publishes original research articles on application and development of information technology.

004   US   ISSN 1063-7133
QA76.58
INTERNATIONAL PARALLEL PROCESSING SYMPOSIUM. PROCEEDINGS. Short title: I P P S. 1987. a. price varies. (Institute of Electrical and Electronics Engineers, Inc.) I E E E Computer Society Press, 10662 Los Vaqueros Circle, Los Alamitos, CA 90720-1264. TEL 714-821-8380. FAX 714-821-4641. Ed. Cat Harris; Pub. Matt Loeb. adv. contact: Frieda Koester. **Document type:** proceedings.
—UMI. **CCC.**
Formerly (until 1991): International Parallel Processing Workshop.
Description: Covers new developments in parallel processing technology, including architectures, algorithms, modeling, neural networks and V L S I systems.

004   US   ISSN 1048-5120
ITEM PROCESSING REPORT. 1990. bi-w. $595 (foreign $630) (effective 1997). Phillips Business Information, Inc., 1201 Seven Locks Rd., Potomac, MD 20854. TEL 301-424-3338. FAX 301-309-3847. E-mail: pbi@phillips.com. Ed. Mary Crowley. **Document type:** newsletter.
●Also available online. Vendor(s): Data-Star, Information Access Co., Knight-Ridder Information, Inc., NewsNet (EC19).
—**CCC.**
Incorporates (in 1992): Powell Report.

001.64   JA   ISSN 0447-8053
QA75.5
JOHO SHORI/INFORMATION PROCESSING SOCIETY OF JAPAN. JOURNAL. (Text in Japanese) 1960. m. 19600 Yen to non-members; exchange basis for academic & government institutions. Information Processing Society of Japan - Joho Shori Gakkai, 7th Fl., Shibaura-Maekawa Bldg., 3-16-20, Shibaura, Minato-ku, Tokyo 108, Japan.
TEL 81-3-5484-3535. FAX 81-3-5484-3534. E-mail: editj@ipsj.or.jp; URL: http://www.ipsj.or.jp. Ed. Motoi Suwa; Pub. Hiroshi Iizuka. R&P contact: Keiko Ushiro. circ. 30,000. **Indexed:** INIS Atomind., INSPEC, JCT, JTA. **Document type:** academic/scholarly publication.
—AskIEEE; CISTI; KR SourceOne. **CCC.**
Description: Presents papers and results of research on the theoretical fundamentals and applications of computers, with emphasis on information processing. Aims to promote the international exchange of information processing.
Refereed Serial

JOURNAL OF AUTOMATA, LANGUAGES AND COMBINATORICS. see *COMPUTERS — Cybernetics*

004   **657**   US
JOURNAL OF I S FINANCIAL MANAGEMENT. 1990. 3/yr. membership only. I S Financial Management Association, Box 27543, San Francisco, CA 94127-0543. TEL 415-731-3706. Eds. Susan J. Quinlan, Terence A. Quinlan. R&P contact: Terence A. Quinlan. bibl.; circ. 650 (paid). (back issues avail.) **Document type:** academic/scholarly publication, trade publication.
Formerly: Journal of Financial Management for Data Processing (ISSN 1078-5736).
Description: Provides specialized financial literature for this unique profession. Informs on association activities.

006.3   UK   ISSN 0959-1524
TS156.8   CODEN: JPCOEO
JOURNAL OF PROCESS CONTROL. 1990. bi-m. fl.1062($610) (effective 1998). Elsevier Science Ltd., P.O. Box 800, Kidlington, Oxford OX5 1DX, England. TEL 44-1865-843000.
FAX 44-1865-843010. TELEX 83111 BHPOXF G. E-mail: nlinfo-f@elsevier.nl; usinfo-f@elsevier.com; forinfo-kyf04035@niftyserve.or.jp; URL: http://www.elsevier.nl/. (Subscr. to: Elsevier Science, Regional Sales Office, P.O. Box 211, 1000 AE Amsterdam, Netherlands. TEL 31-20-4853757. FAX 31-20-4853432; Subscr. in the Americas to: Elsevier Science, Regional Sales Office, Box 945, New York, NY 10159-0945. TEL 212-633-3730. FAX 212-633-3680; Subscr. in Australasia and the Far East to: Elsevier Science (Singapore) Pte Ltd, No.1 Temasek Ave., No.17-01 Millenia Tower, Singapore 039192, Singapore. TEL 65-434-3727. FAX 65-337-2230) Ed. J.D. Perkins. (also avail. in microform from UMI; back issues avail.) **Indexed:** ASCA, Compumath, Curr.Cont. **Document type:** academic/scholarly publication.
—BLDSC (5042.645000); AskIEEE; CASDDS; Ei; Genuine Article; KR SourceOne; SWETS; UMI. **CCC.**
Description: Covers the application of control theory, operations research, computer science and engineering principles to the solution of process-control problems.
Refereed Serial

004   UK
KEY NOTE MARKET REPORT: I T TRAINING. Variant title: I T Training. irreg. £205. Key Note Ltd., Field House, 72 Oldfield Rd., Hampton, Middlesex TW12 2HQ, England. TEL 44-181-783-0755.
FAX 44-181-783-0049. **Document type:** trade publication.

001.64 621.381   AT
KOMPASS INFORMATION TECHNOLOGY. 1977. a. $85. Peter Isaacson Publications Pty. Ltd., 46-50 Porter St., Prahran, Vic. 3181, Australia.
TEL 61-3-2457777. FAX 61-3-2457840. adv. circ. 6,000.
Former titles: Information Technology Index (ISSN 1036-0352) & D P Index and Software Register (ISSN 0813-4758); (until 1983): D P Index (ISSN 0314-1578)

001.64 651.8   JA
KYOTO UNIVERSITY. DATA PROCESSING CENTER. REPORT/KYOTO DAIGAKU OGATA KEISANKI SENTA EIBUN REPOTO. (Text in English) irreg. exchange basis. Kyoto University, Data Processing Center - Kyoto Daigaku Ogata Keisanki Senta, Yoshida Hon-cho, Sakyo-ku, Kyoto-shi 606, Japan.

621.381 001.64   IT   ISSN 0392-9027
LINEA E D P; settimanale di informatica. 1978. w. L.85000 (foreign L.132000). A G E P E s.r.l. (Subsidiary of: Alfa Linea), Via Rosso di San Secondo 1-3, 20134 Milan, Italy. TEL 39-2-215621. FAX 39-2-70120032. Ed. Roberto Avanzo; Pub. Giorgio Artuffo. R&P contact: Roberto Avanzo. adv.: color page L.15450000; trim 274 x 350; adv. contact: Roberto Lenzi. circ. 40,670.

001.64   US
M I C - TECH-COMPUTERS. 1989. m. $1570. Management Information Corporation, 1111 Marlkress Rd., Box 5062, Cherry Hill, NJ 08003. TEL 609-424-1100. FAX 609-424-1999. Ed. Jim Fidler. (diskette format)
Description: Electronic computer product reference. Provides specifications, performance and pricing on personal computers, laptops, portables, workstations, minicomputers, mainframes, and super computers.

004   IS
MA'ASEH CHOSHEV. (Text in English and Hebrew) vol.4. 1976. bi-m. $10. Information Processing Association of Israel, Kfar Hamacabia, Ramat Gan 52109, Israel. Ed. Batsheva Shezaf. adv.

001.64   US
MANAGING DATA NETWORKS. 1979. 2 base vols. (plus m. updates). $1031 to new subscr.; renewals $97. (effective 1996). Datapro Information Services Group (Subsidiary of: McGraw-Hill, Inc.), 600 Delran Pkwy., Delran, NJ 08075. TEL 609-764-0100; 800-328-2776. FAX 609-764-2814.
Former titles (until 1991): Datapro Management of Data Communications; (until 1985): Datapro Communications Solutions.

001.64 US
MANAGING INFORMATION TECHNOLOGY. 2 base vols. (plus m. updates). $937 to new subscr.; renewals $885 (effective 1996). Datapro Information Services Group (Subsidiary of: McGraw-Hill, Inc.), 600 Delran Pkwy., Delran, NJ 08075. TEL 609-764-0100; 800-328-2776. FAX 609-764-2814.
 Former titles (until 1991): Datapro Management of E D P Systems; (until 1985): Datapro E D P Solutions.

MANAGING OFFICE TECHNOLOGY; integrating technology & human resources for total office quality. see BUSINESS AND ECONOMICS — Office Equipment And Services

001.64 621.381 US
QA76.9.S88
MANAGING SYSTEM DEVELOPMENT. 1981. m. $245 (foreign $220). Applied Computer Research, Inc., Box 82266, Phoenix, AZ 85071-2266. TEL 800-234-2227. Ed. Phillip C. Howard. bk.rev. circ. 1,000. (tabloid format; back issues avail.) **Indexed:** Comput.Lit.Ind., INSPEC. **Document type:** newsletter.
 —AskIEEE; CISTI; Ei; KR SourceOne; UMI. **CCC.**
 Formerly (until 1993): System Development (ISSN 0275-6617)
 Description: Covers issues and trends in software programming management in industry and government.

001.64 IT ISSN 0393-0599
MEDIA DUEMILA. 1983. 11/yr. Corso Massimo d'Azeglio 60, 10126 Turin, Italy. TEL 11-560-44-30. Ed. Oscar Gonzalbo. circ. 24,000. **Indexed:** WPM.

MICROSYSTEMS. see COMPUTERS — Microcomputers

001.64 US ISSN 1059-4108
OBJECT-ORIENTED STRATEGIES; the monthly newsletter for managers and developers of object-oriented systems. 1991. m. $497 (foreign $567). Cutter Information Corp., 37 Broadway, Arlington, MA 02174. TEL 617-648-8700. FAX 617-648-1950. URL: http://www.cutter.com. Ed. Paul Harmon; Pub. Karen Fine Coburn. R&P contact: Carolyn Licata. (back issues avail.) **Document type:** newsletter.
 ●Also available online.
 —**CCC.**
 Description: Covers new technologies, new products, market developments and industry trends in the capabilities and uses of object-oriented software technologies. Includes discussion of techniques and methodologies.

001.64 UK ISSN 0968-3038
ONLINE MANUAL. 1992. a. £145. Blackwell Publishers Ltd., 108 Cowley Rd., Oxford OX4 1JF, England. TEL 44-1865-791100. FAX 44-1865-791347. E-mail: jnlinfo@blackwellpublishers.co.uk; URL: http://www.blackwellpublishers.co.uk. **Document type:** trade publication.

M S TODAY. (Policy Management Systems Corp.) see BUSINESS AND ECONOMICS — Computer Applications

388 004.16 US ISSN 1063-9470
PC-TRANS. 1991. q. free. Kansas University Transportation Center, 2011 Learned Hall, Lawrence, KS 66049. TEL 913-864-5655. FAX 913-864-3199. E-mail: pctrans@kuhub.cc.ukans.edu; URL: http://kuhub.cc.ukans.edu. Ed. Lisa Harris. adv.: B&W page $600; trim 7 x 9 3/16; adv. contact: Mehrdad Givechi. software rev.; mkt. circ. 13,500. (back issues avail.) **Document type:** trade publication.

PHARMACY CLAIM STANDARD. see PHARMACY AND PHARMACOLOGY

004 659.1 US
PROCESSOR. 1979. w. $59. Peed Corporation, Box 85518, Lincoln, NE 68501. TEL 402-479-2141; 800-247-4880. adv. rev. circ. 180,000. (tabloid format) **Document type:** trade publication.

004 US
▼**PRODUCT DATA MANAGEMENT REPORT.** 1997. m. $345 (foreign $550). C A D - C A M Publishing, Inc., 1010 Turquoise St., San Diego, CA 92109-1268. TEL 619-488-0533. FAX 619-488-6052.
 Description: Designed to keep readers current on PDM technology, track suppliers for the industry, reports on what other companies are doing with PDM, and tips on streamlining.

004 US ISSN 0898-8439
RETAIL SYSTEMS ALERT; a monthly update on automation news and trends for retailers. 1987. m. $295 (effective 1995 & 1996). Ardea Research Corp., 77 Oak St., Ste. 201, Box 332, Newton Upper Falls, MA 02164. TEL 617-527-8102. FAX 617-527-8102. Ed. Eric L. Olson; Pub. Thomas H. Friedman. bk.rev.; charts; stat.; index. circ. 700. (back issues avail.) **Document type:** newsletter.
 Description: Focuses on how retailers are using information technology systems to streamline their operations.
 Refereed Serial

001.64 PO
RS232 INFORMATICA. 11/yr. Calcada de Palma de Baixo, 15 c-c Dnta., 1600 Lisbon, Portugal. TEL 726-46-52. TELEX 13011 VASSIS P. Ed. Carlos M.S. Aguda. circ. 15,000.

S I BUSINESS. (Systems Integrator) see COMPUTERS — Computer Systems

001.64 US
THE SCANNING SOURCEBOOK.* (In two vols.) 1986. a. $925. Disc Company, 21 Red Maple Rd., Hilton Head Island, SC 29928. TEL 703-237-0682. FAX 703-532-5447.
 Description: Provides all product and service specifications and company information to assist those comparing products or making buying decisions related to data conversion systems and services.

001.64 PO ISSN 0871-6218
SEMANA INFORMATICA. 1989. 44/yr. Ferreira e Bento Lda., Rua D. Estefania 32-1o, 1000 Lisbon, Portugal. TEL 544-307. FAX 522643. TELEX 64198. Ed. Antonio Panciarelli. circ. 308,000.

SEMAPHORE SIGNAL. see COMPUTERS — Computer Systems

001.64 GW ISSN 0343-5202
P98 CODEN: SPDADH
SPRACHE UND DATENVERARBEITUNG. (Text in English and German) 1977. 2/yr. DM.85. Institut fuer angewandte Kommunikations- und Sprachforschung e.V., Poppelsdorfer Allee 47, 53115 Bonn, Germany. TEL 49-228-735645. FAX 49-228-735639. E-mail: iks@uni-bonn.de; URL: http://www.ikp.uni-bonn.de/iks. Eds. Ulrich Schmitz, C. Gerhardt. adv.; bk.rev. **Indexed:** Bibl.Ling., INSPEC, Lang.& Lang.Behav.Abstr., MLA Intl.Bibl. **Document type:** academic/scholarly publication.
 —BLDSC (8419.868500); AskIEEE; KR SourceOne.

001.64 US
STORAGE MANAGEMENT. m. $495 (foreign $545) (effective 1997). Institute for Computer Capacity Management, 1020 8th Ave. S., Ste. 6, Naples, FL 34102. TEL 941-261-8945. FAX 941-261-5456. **Document type:** newsletter.

TAIWAN COMPUTER; providing the latest Taiwan trade information. see COMPUTERS — Hardware

001.64 PO
UNIX COMPUTER WORLD. 12/yr. Oceanus - Publicacoes e Edicoes Ltda., Rua Quinta das Palmeiras 76-4, 2780 Oeiras, Portugal. TEL 2466072. FAX 246-61-22. TELEX 63840 OCEANU P. Ed. Maria Diniz. circ. 15,000.

001.64 PO
VIDA INFORMATICA. w. Travessa de Santo Ildefonso, no. 1, 1200 Lisbon, Portugal. TEL 676315. FAX 66-74-20. TELEX 66036. Ed. J.E. Aparicio. circ. 10,000.
 Description: Contains news on all aspects of computers.

651.8 001.6 GW ISSN 0937-6429
QA76.5 CODEN: WIINE9
WIRTSCHAFTSINFORMATIK. (Text in German; summaries in English) 1959. bi-m. DM.366 (students DM.183) (effective 1997). Friedr. Vieweg und Sohn Verlagsgesellschaft mbH, Postfach 1546, 65005 Wiesbaden, Germany. TEL 49-611-7878151. FAX 49-611-7878423. Ed.Bd. adv.; bk.rev.; index. circ. 5,000. **Indexed:** ASCA, Compumath, Comput.Abstr., Comput.Rev., Curr.Cont., Cyb.Abstr., Eng.Ind., Excerp.Med., INSPEC, Int.Abstr.Oper.Res., SSCI. **Document type:** academic/scholarly publication.
 —BLDSC (9325.524500); AskIEEE; CISTI; Ei; Genuine Article; KR SourceOne; Linda Hall; SWETS. **CCC.**
 Former titles: Angewandte Informatik (ISSN 0013-5704); Elektronische Datenverarbeitung.

651.8 004 US ISSN 1068-9699
HF5548.125 CODEN: WOCREX
WORKGROUP COMPUTING REPORT; applying technology to business processes. 1978. m. $440 (foreign $475). Patricia Seybold Group, 85 Devonshire St., 5th Fl., Boston, MA 02109-3504. TEL 800-826-2424. TELEX 6503122583. E-mail: info@psgroup.comm. Ed. Ronni T. Marshak; Pub. Patricia B. Seybold. software rev.; charts; illus. (looseleaf format; back issues avail.) **Indexed:** Comput.Bus., Comput.Cont., Comput.Dtbs., INSPEC. **Document type:** newsletter.
 ●Also available online. Vendor(s): Information Access Co., NewsNet.
 Also available on CD-ROM.
 —BLDSC (9348.527790); AskIEEE; KR SourceOne; SWETS.
 Former titles: Office Computing Report (ISSN 1057-8889); Patricia Seybold's Office Computing Report (ISSN 0894-9921); Patricia Seybold's Office Systems Report (ISSN 1040-2594); (until 1986): Patty Seybold's Office Computing Report (ISSN 0887-3062); (until 1985): Seybold Report Office Systems (ISSN 0736-7279); (until 1982): Seybold Report on Word Processing (ISSN 0160-4572).
 Description: Provides in-depth coverage of office and word processing systems; occasionally contains articles on automation applications.

004 GW ISSN 0945-9448
X-CHANGE; Magazin fuer elektronischen Geschaeftsverkehr. 1994. q. DM.78. (Deutsche E D I Gesellschaft e.V.) Beuth Verlag GmbH, Burggrafenstr. 6, 10787 Berlin, Germany. TEL 030-24399786. FAX 030-24399926. (Co-sponsor: Deutsches Institut fuer Normung e.V.) Ed. Christian-Hinrich Dorner. adv. contact: Birgit Heller. **Document type:** trade publication.

COMPUTERS — Hardware
Includes: Analog Computers, Digital Computers, Disk Drives, Input-Output Systems, Memory Structures, Modems, Monitors, Peripherals, Printers, Tape Decks, Terminals.

004 005 US
A S - 400 HOT SHEET.* bi-m. $139 (foreign $169). D G C Inc., 25 Lawrence Ave., Lawrence, NY 11559-1446. TEL 516-295-0296. FAX 516-295-0348. Ed. David Greenblatt. **Document type:** newsletter.

COMPUTERS — HARDWARE

621.381 US ISSN 0925-1030
TK7874 CODEN: AICPEF
ANALOG INTEGRATED CIRCUITS AND SIGNAL PROCESSING; an international journal. 1991. 9/yr. fl.1350 to institutions/ $693. to institutions in U.S. (effective 1998). Kluwer Academic Publishers Boston, Box 358, Accord Sta., Hingham, MA 02018-0358. TEL 617-871-6600. FAX 617-871-6528. E-mail: services@wkap.nl; URL: http://www.wkap.nl. (Dist. by: Kluwer Academic Publishers Group, P.O. Box 322, 3300 AH Dordrecht, Netherlands; Dist. outside N. America by: Kluwer Academic Publishers Group, P.O. Box 322, 3300 AH Dordrecht, Netherlands. TEL 31-78-6392392. FAX 31-78-6546474) Eds. Mohammed Ismail, David Haigh. (also avail. in microform from UMI; reprint service avail. from SWZ) Indexed: ASCA, Compumath, Curr.Cont., INSPEC (1991-), SSCI. **Document type:** academic/scholarly publication.
—BLDSC (0890.630000); AskIEEE; CISTI; Ei; Genuine Article; KR SourceOne; SWETS; UMI. **CCC**.
  Description: Research and tutorial papers on the design and applications of analog integrated circuits and signal processing circuits and systems.
  Refereed Serial

621.9 US
ASSOCIATION FOR COMPUTING MACHINERY. COMPUTER SERVICE. q. Association for Computing Machinery, 1515 Broadway, 17th Fl., New York, NY 10036. TEL 212-869-7440.

621.9 US
ASSOCIATION FOR COMPUTING MACHINERY. CONFERENCE PROCEEDINGS. a. Association for Computing Machinery, 1515 Broadway, 17th Fl., New York, NY 10036. TEL 212-869-7440.

BINARY: COMPUTING IN MICROBIOLOGY. see *BIOLOGY — Microbiology*

621.381 UK
BRITAIN'S D I Y INDUSTRY. 1986. irreg., latest 1991. £50. Jordan & Sons Ltd., 21 St. Thomas St., Bristol BS1 6JS, England. TEL 44-117-923-0600. FAX 44-117-923-0063. **Document type:** directory.

621.381 US
BUZZBYTES. 1989. s-w. Charles Mann & Associates, 113 Wattenbarger Rd., Sweetwater, TN 37874-6135. Ed. C.W. Mann. circ. 417,421. **Document type:** newspaper.

C D - R O M DIRECTORY. see *COMPUTERS — Automation*

C D - R O M FACTS AND FIGURES. see *COMPUTERS — Automation*

004 BE
C P N - EUROPE. (Text in English) 1977. 9/yr. 3000 BEF($95) (free to qualified personnel). Pan European Publishing Co. (Subsidiary of: Reed Elsevier plc), Rue Verte 216, 1030 Brussels, Belgium. TEL 32-2-2402611. FAX 32-2-2427111. Ed. J. Lobell. adv.; bk.rev. circ. 50,003 (controlled). **Document type:** trade publication.
  Formerly (until vol.19, 1995): Computer Product News.
  Description: Reports exclusively on new computer hardware, software and data communication products from manufacturers throughout the world.

CLIENT - SERVER COMPUTING. see *BUSINESS AND ECONOMICS — Office Equipment And Services*

004 US
COMPAQ COMPASS. q. free. Compaq Computer Corporation, Box 4400, Kearneysville, WV 25430.
  Description: Discusses applications of all types of Compaq computers and announces new models.

COMPULIFE'S MICROMARKET BLUE DISC. see *COMPUTERS — Computer Sales*

COMPUTER & CO. see *COMPUTERS — Computer Networks*

621.381 FR ISSN 0988-3452
COMPUTER DATA STORAGE NEWSLETTER; the monthly news report on the worldwide magnetic and optical disk and tape industry. (Text in English) 1988. 12/yr. 1650 F.($325) (effective 1996). Micro-Journal S.a.r.l., 11, rue de Provence, 75009 Paris, France. TEL 1-42-46-30-56. FAX 1-48-24-22-76. E-mail: 100565.3667@compuserve.com; URL: www.mosarca.com/storagenews. Ed. Jean-Jacques Maleval. R&P contact: Jean-Jacques Maleval. bk.rev. circ. 500. (back issues avail.) **Document type:** newsletter.
  Description: News report on the international computer data storage industry; includes new products, new technologies, marketing and distribution trends, market studies, reports of major industry events, and worldwide developments.

621.381 US
THE COMPUTER HARDWARE INDUSTRY. 1990. a. $395. Dun & Bradstreet Information Services (Murray Hill) (Subsidiary of: Dun & Bradstreet, Inc.), One Diamond Hill Rd., Murray Hill, NJ 07974. TEL 908-665-5224. FAX 908-771-7599. Ed. Matthew Gowen.
  Description: Covers super computers, mainframes, mid-ranges, workstations and personal computers. Analyzes the future and new technological advances.

621.381 UK
COMPUTER PERIPHERALS. 2/yr. Peripheral Suppliers Association, Owles Hall, Buntingford, Herts. SG9 9PL, England. Ed. H.M.W Gibbons. adv.

621.381 ISSN 0093-416X
TK7885.A1 CODEN: CMRVCK
COMPUTER REVIEW. 1961. a. $385 to new subscr. (foreign $415); renewal $355 (foreign $395) (effective 1998). Computer Review, 19 Pleasant St., Box 260, Gloucester, MA 01930. TEL 508-283-2100. FAX 508-281-3125. E-mail: info@computerreview.com; URL: http://www.computerreview.com. Ed. Alexander Luhowy. charts; index. circ. 1,000. (also avail. in diskette format) Indexed: Comput.Rev., INSPEC. **Document type:** directory.
  —Linda Hall; SWETS.
  Incorporates (1983-1991): Microcomputer Review (ISSN 8755-7525); (1973-1991): Computer Terminals Review (ISSN 0147-9415); Which was formerly (until 1976): Terminals Review (ISSN 0093-2337); (1974-1991): Computer Peripherals Review (ISSN 0149-5054); Which was formerly: Peripherals Review; Also incorporates (1988-1991): Computer-Specs; Former titles (until 1973): Computer Characteristics Review (0010-454X); (until 1969): Computer Characteristics Quarterly.
  Description: Profiles computer, telecommunications, and new media companies and reviews their products and services.

COMPUTER SURVEY; list of digital computer installations world-wide. see *COMPUTERS — Computer Industry Directories*

621.39 US ISSN 0899-9783
COMPUTER WORKSTATIONS. 1988. m. $150 (outside N. America $165). Worldwide Videotex, Box 3273, Boynton Beach, FL 33424-3273. TEL 407-738-2276. Ed. Mark Wright; Pub. Mark Wright. bk.rev. **Document type:** newsletter.
  ●Also available online. Vendor(s): Information Access Co.
  Description: Provides information on computer workstations used in network applications, computer-aided design, computer-aided engineering, and other business and industrial applications to improve productivity.

004.7 US ISSN 1070-0994
CONNECT (ANN ARBOR); the modem user's resources. 1993. 9/yr. $18 (effective 1994). Pegasus Press, Inc., 3487 Braeburn Circle, Ann Arbor, MI 48108. TEL 313-973-8825. FAX 313-973-0411. Ed. William Rail. adv. contact: Mary Caro. bk.rev. circ. 65,000. (back issues avail.) **Document type:** consumer publication.
  ●Also available online.
  Description: Covers commercial on-line services, the Internet, and bulletin board systems and networks from a user's perspective.

621.381 001.6 AT
D G WORLD. 1978. 4/yr. free. Data General Australia, 100 Dorcas St., South Melbourne, Vic. 3205, Australia. Ed. Susan Collins. adv. circ. 8,000.
  Formerly (until 1988): Data General News.

D V D AND FUTURE C D. see *COMMUNICATIONS — Video*

DATA NEWS; l'actualite informatique. see *COMMUNICATIONS — Computer Applications*

621.39 US ISSN 1078-0920
TK7895.M4
DATA STORAGE. 1994. 9/yr. $118 includes Buyers Guide (Canada & Mexico $158; elsewhere $204) (effective 1997). PennWell Publishing Co. (Nashua), Advanced Technology Group, 10 Tara Blvd., 5th Fl., Nashua, NH 03062. TEL 603-891-0123. FAX 603-891-0539. (Subscr. to: Box 1260, Tulsa, OK 74101. TEL 918-835-31616. FAX 918-832-9295) adv.: B&W page $2700. circ. 12,000. **Document type:** trade publication.

621.381 US ISSN 0267-5447
DATA STORAGE REPORT. 1985. m. $385 (foreign $424) (effective 1996 & 1997). Jonas Press Publishing Company, 53 Park Belmont Pl., San Jose, CA 95136-2506. TEL 408-629-8249. FAX 408-629-8249. E-mail: jonah@asic.com. Ed. Jonah McLeod. bk.rev.; charts; stat. (back issues avail.) **Document type:** newsletter.
  ●Also available online. Vendor(s): Information Access Co., Knight-Ridder Information, Inc.
  Description: Covers all aspects of the mass storage industry; technology, legislation, finance and marketing.

621.381 GW ISSN 0933-8640
DECKBLATT; die unabhaengige Zeitschrift fuer Anwender von D E C Systemen. 1986. m. DM.98 (foreign DM.116). Markt und Technik Verlag AG, Hans-Pinsel-Str. 2, 85540 Haar, Germany. TEL 089-4613-0. FAX 089-4613-775. **Document type:** consumer publication.

621.381 US ISSN 1055-9329
TK7874
DEFECT AND FAULT TOLERANCE IN V L S I SYSTEMS. 1989. irreg., vol.2, 1990. prcie varies. Plenum Publishing Corp., 233 Spring St., New York, NY 10013-1578. TEL 212-620-8000. FAX 212-463-0742. E-mail: books@plenum.com. **Document type:** monographic series.

621.381 001.642 GW ISSN 0933-8667
DESIGN UND ELEKTRONIK; Spezialisten Zeitschrift fuer Hard- und Softwareentwickler. 1985. fortn. DM.163.80 (foreign DM.215.80). Markt und Technik Verlag AG, Hans-Pinsel-Str. 2, 85540 Haar, Germany. TEL 089-4613-0. FAX 089-4613-774. Ed. Johann Wiesboeck. circ. 18,000. (back issues avail.) **Document type:** trade publication.

DISPLAYS; technology and applications. see *COMPUTERS — Computer Graphics*

DOCUMENT IMAGING REPORT. see *COMPUTERS — Data Communications And Data Transmission Systems*

004 US ISSN 0892-4856
GREGORY'S A-SERIES TECHNICAL JOURNAL. 1986. 9/yr. $225 (foreign $255). Gregory Publishing Company, 333 Cobalt Way no.107, Sunnyvale, CA 94086. (back issues avail.)
  Description: Provides technical information for Unisys A-Series computer users.

621.381 001.642 US ISSN 1065-6189
THE H P PALMTOP PAPER. (Hewlett-Packard) 1986. bi-m. $39 (Canada and Mexico $45; elsewhere $57); diskette format $100 (overseas $118) (subscr. includes one Subscribers Disk and 2 bonus issues). Thaddeus Computing, Inc., c/o Wayne Kneeskern, Controller, Box 869, Fairfield, IA 52556-0869. TEL 515-472-6330. FAX 515-472-1879. E-mail: letters@thaddeus.com; URL: http://www.thaddeus.com. Ed. Hal Goldstein. cum.index: 1986-1996. circ. 15,000. (also avail. diskette format; back issues avail.) **Document type:** newsletter.
  Description: Covers computer hardware and software for Hewlett Packard 95 LX, 100 LX, and 200 LX palmtop computers.

COMPUTERS — HARDWARE

004 **US**
H P - U X - USR. bi-m. $49.50 (foreign $99.50). (International Association of Hewlett-Packard Computer Users) Interex, Publications Department, 1192 Borregas Ave., Sunnyvale, CA 94089. TEL 408-747-0227. FAX 408-747-0947. TELEX 4971527. Ed. Michael Ehrhardt. adv. contact: Brian Hallin.

004 005.3 **US** **ISSN 1093-2585**
HANDHELD P C MAGAZINE. 1997. bi-m. $35 (Canada & Mexico $41; elsewhere $53) (effective 1997). Thaddeus Computing, Inc., c/o Wayne Kneeskern, Controller, Box 869, Fairfield, IA 52556-0869. TEL 525-472-6330. FAX 515-472-1879. E-mail: letters@thaddeus.com; URL: http://www.thaddeus.com.
Description: Covers computer hardware and software with the Windows C E operating system.

621.381 005.3 **UK** **ISSN 1350-2387**
TK1 **CODEN: ICDTEA**
E E PROCEEDINGS - COMPUTERS AND DIGITAL TECHNIQUES. (Institution of Electrical Engineers) Online edition (UK ISSN 1359-7027) (Subseries of: I E E Proceedings) 1980. bi-m. £395 (effective 1997). I.E.E., Michael Faraday House, Six Hills Way, Stevenage, Herts. SG1 2AY, England. TEL 44-1438-313311. FAX 44-1438-742840. TELEX 825578 IEESTV G. E-mail: inspec@iee.org.uk; URL: http://www.iee.org.uk. (Subscr. to: Publication Sales Dept., P.O. Box 96, Stevenage, Herts. SG1 25D, England; U.S. addr.: INSPEC Dept., IEEE Operations Center, 445 Hoes Ln., Box 1331, Piscataway, NJ 08855-1331. TEL 908-562-5553. FAX 908-562-8737) Eds. E.L. Dagless, D.A. Nicole. adv.; bk.rev.; index. circ. 4,000. Indexed: A.S.& T.Ind., ASCA, BMT, Br.Tech.Ind., Compumath, Comput.Cont., Curr.Cont., Excerp.Med., INSPEC, Int.Aerosp.Abstr., Math.R., Sci.Cit.Ind. **Document type:** proceedings.
●Also available online.
—BLDSC (4362.751860); AskIEEE; CISTI; Ei; Genuine Article; KR SourceOne; Linda Hall; SWETS; UMI; UnCover. **CCC**.
Formerly: I E E Proceedings E (Computers and Digital Techniques) (ISSN 0143-7062)
Description: Covers hardware and software for digital systems, theory design and application of computers, minicomputers, microprocessors, computer languages, computer architecture, VLSI and CAD of VLSI, logic circuits, and digital subsystems.

004.7 686.2 **US**
IMAGING NEWS (VENTURA). 1993. m. $55 (foreign $85). Diamond Research Corporation, 4864 Market St., Ste. C, Ventura, CA 93003. TEL 805-650-9081. FAX 805-650-1607. E-mail: drc@west.net; URL: http://www.imagingnews.com/drc. Ed. Arthur S. Diamond. R&P contact: Arthur S. Diamond. adv. contact: Dorothy Bacchilega. bk.rev. **Document type:** trade publication.
Formerly: R and R News (Remanufacturing and Recycling) (ISSN 1086-0355)
Description: Covers developments in laser and ink jet cartridge recycling and remanufacturing industry, and trends in paper and film products for the imaging industry.

004.7 **UK** **ISSN 0960-6645**
IHAND. 1985. bi-m. £98 (N. America £108) (effective June 1994). 31 Randolph Dr., Southwood, Farnborough, Hants. GU14 0QQ, England. TEL 01252-518960. FAX 01252-518960. Ed. Keith Goodyear. adv.: page £770; 268 x 190; adv. contact: Keith Goodyear. circ. 10,000. (back issues avail.) **Document type:** trade publication.
●Also available online.
Description: Covers hand-held computer devices used for bar-code scanning.

621.381 **US** **ISSN 1074-0511**
INDUSTRIAL CONTROLS INTELLIGENCE AND THE P L C INSIDER'S NEWSLETTER. (Programmable Logic Controller); informing the industrial controls industry since 1981. 1981. m. $195. Carefree Communications, Inc., Box 5268, Carefree, AZ 85377. TEL 602-488-1462. FAX 602-488-5376. E-mail: jgrenard@aol.com; URL: http://www.control.com/carefree. Ed. Jack Grenard. R&P contact: Jack Grenard. bk.rev. (looseleaf format; also avail. in diskette format) **Document type:** newsletter.
Former titles (until 1994): Controls Digest (ISSN 1067-3121); (until 1993): P L C Insider's Newsletter (ISSN 1040-9718); P C Insider's Newsletter.
Description: For marketing and other executives who make and sell industrial controls, peripherals, and industrial computers.

621.381 **NE** **ISSN 0167-9260**
INTEGRATION; the VLSI journal. (Text in English) 1983. q. fl.894($514) (effective 1998). Elsevier Science B.V., P.O. Box 211, 1000 AE Amsterdam, Netherlands. TEL 31-20-4853911. FAX 31-20-4853598. TELEX 18582 ESPA NL. E-mail: nlinfo-f@elsevier.nl; usinfo-f@elsevier.com; forinfo-kyf04035@niftyserve.or.jp; URL: http://www.elsevier.nl/. (Subscr. in the Americas to: Elsevier Science, Regional Sales Office, Box 945, New York, NY 10159-0945. TEL 212-633-3730. FAX 212-633-3680; Subscr. in Australasia and the Far East to: Elsevier Science (Singapore) Pte Ltd, No.1 Temasek Ave., No.17-01 Millenia Tower, Singapore 039192, Singapore. TEL 65-434-3727. FAX 65-337-2230; Subscr. in Japan to: Elsevier Science Japan, 9-15 Higashi-Azabu 1-chome, Minato-ku, Tokyo 106, Japan. TEL 81-3-5561-5033. FAX 81-3-5561-5047) Ed. R.H.J.M Otten. adv.; illus.; index. (also avail. in microform from UMI; back issues avail.; reprint service avail. from SWZ) Indexed: Compumath, Comput.Abstr., Curr.Cont., Eng.Ind., INPSEC (1983-), Sci.Cit.Ind., Zent.Math. **Document type:** academic/scholarly publication.
—BLDSC (4542.816270); AskIEEE; CISTI; Ei; Genuine Article; KR SourceOne; Linda Hall; SWETS; UnCover. **CCC**.
Description: Covers every aspect of the VLSI design and testing field.
Refereed Serial

006 **SI** **ISSN 0129-0533**
QA76.5 **CODEN: IHSCEZ**
INTERNATIONAL JOURNAL OF HIGH SPEED COMPUTING. Abbreviated title: I J H S C. (Text in English) 1989. q. $147 to individuals; institutions & libraries $367 (developing countries $220). World Scientific Publishing Co. Pte. Ltd., Farrer Rd., P.O. Box 128, Singapore 9128, Singapore. TEL 65-3825663. FAX 65-3825919. TELEX RS-28561-WSPC. E-mail: wspcsl@signet.com.sg; sales@wspc2.demon.co.uk; wspc@wspc.com; URL: http://www.singnet.com.sg/-wspclib/. (UK addr.: 57 Shelton St., Covent Garden, London WC2H 9HE, England. TEL 44-171-836-0888. FAX 44-171-836-2020; US addr.: 1060 Main St., Ste. 1B, River Edge, NJ 07661. TEL 800-227-7562. FAX 201-487-9656) Ed.Bd. circ. 200. (back issues avail.) **Indexed:** ASCA, Comput.Abstr., Curr.Cont., INSPEC (1989-), Zent.Math. **Document type:** academic/scholarly publication.
—BLDSC (4542.280500); AskIEEE; CISTI; Genuine Article; KR SourceOne; SWETS. **CCC**.
Description: Covers parallel computation, algorithms, program restructuring, and compiler technology, performance evaluation, scheduling and resource allocation. Provides insight into the fields of supercomputing and other high speed parallel computing for computer scientists, electrical engineers, and physicists.

JISUANJI YANJIU YU FAZHAN/COMPUTER RESEARCH AND DEVELOPMENT. see *COMPUTERS — Computer Engineering*

JOURNAL OF CIRCUITS, SYSTEMS AND COMPUTERS. see *ENGINEERING*

KEY ABSTRACTS - COMPUTER COMMUNICATIONS AND STORAGE. see *COMPUTERS — Abstracting, Bibliographies, Statistics*

KEY ABSTRACTS - MACHINE VISION. see *COMPUTERS — Abstracting, Bibliographies, Statistics*

004 **UK**
KEY NOTE MARKET REPORT: COMPUTER HARDWARE. Variant title: Computer Hardware. irreg. £205. Key Note Ltd., Field House, 72 Oldfield Rd., Hampton, Middlesex TW12 2HQ, England. TEL 44-181-783-0755. FAX 44-181-783-0049. **Document type:** trade publication.

004.7 **US**
M V S UPDATE. (Multiple Virtual Storage) m. $450 (effective Aug. 1996). Xephon, 1301 W. Hwy. 407, Ste. 201-450, Lewisville, TX 75067. TEL 817-455-7050. FAX 817-455-2492. **Document type:** trade publication.

621.381 **US**
MAINFRAME COMPUTING. 1988. m. $150 (outside N. America $165). Worldwide Videotex, Box 3273, Boynton Beach, FL 33424-3273. TEL 407-738-2276. Ed. Mark Wright; Pub. Mark Wright. **Document type:** newsletter.
●Also available online. Vendor(s): Data-Star, Information Access Co., Knight-Ridder Information, Inc., NewsNet (EC87).
Description: Reports on computer mainframes, including supercomputers. Covers new hardware peripherals, as well as applications software, operating systems, and network systems. Emphasis is on the marketing strategies of mainframe and peripheral vendors.

003 **UK** **ISSN 1355-1507**
MEDIA INDUSTRIES TRENDS. 6/yr. (in 2 vols., 3 nos./vol.) £105 per no. Aslib, Association for Information Management, Publications Department, Information House, 20-24 Old St., London EC1V 9AP, England. TEL 44-171-253-4488. FAX 44-171-430-0574. E-mail: pubs@aslib.co.uk; URL: http://www.aslib.co.uk/aslib/. Ed. Jan Wyllie.
Former titles (until 1993): Trend Monitor Reports (ISSN 0963-0325) & Trend Monitor (ISSN 0954-7479)

MICRO CONTROL JOURNAL. see *MATHEMATICS — Computer Applications*

004 005.3 **US**
TK7800
MICROCOMPUTER JOURNAL; the magazine for computer enthusiasts. 1984. bi-m. $29.70 (Canada & Mexico $36; elsewhere $38) for 8 nos. C Q Communications, Inc., 76 N. Broadway, Hicksville, NY 11801. TEL 516-681-2922. FAX 516-681-2926. Ed. Arthur Salsberg; Pub. Richard A. Ross. adv. contact: Donald Allen. circ. 50,000. Indexed: Ind.How To Do It (1984-). **Document type:** consumer publication.
—CISTI; SWETS.
Former titles (until Dec. 1993): Computercraft (ISSN 1055-5072); (until 1992): Modern Electronics (ISSN 0149-2357)
Description: For readers actively involved in upgrading and expanding personal computer, microcontrollers and related equipment for both home and work.

621.381 001.644 **US** **ISSN 0741-580X**
QA76.55
MODEM NOTES; on line to the business community. 1983. m. $36. Cache Data Products, Inc., 403 Oxford Rd., E. Lansing, MI 48823-2628. Ed. Katherine Ackerman. adv.; bk.rev.
Description: For personal computer users. Features articles on modems and their applications. Offers information and reviews of databases that can be accessed online.

621.381 **US**
MODEM USER NEWS. 1989. m. $150 (outside N. America $165). Worldwide Videotex, Box 3273, Boynton Beach, FL 33424-3273. TEL 407-738-2276. Ed. Mark Wright; Pub. Mark Wright. bk.rev. (back issues avail.) **Document type:** newsletter.
●Also available online. Vendor(s): Data-Star, Information Access Co., Knight-Ridder Information, Inc., NewsNet (EC97).
Description: Provides the latest news and information on software, hardware, supplies, and services for individuals and companies who communicate via modems in computer or facsimile applications.

COMPUTERS — INFORMATION SCIENCE AND INFORMATION THEORY

621.381 US ISSN 1040-0966
CODEN: MODIE3
MONOSSON REPORT ON D E C AND I B M. (Digital Equipment Corporation and International Business Machines) 1981. 12/yr. $495 (foreign $545). Monosson Technology Enterprise, 20 Overland St., Box 71, Kenmore Sta., Boston, MA 02215. TEL 617-267-2900. FAX 617-2672370. Ed. Sheila Osmundsen. index. circ. 400.
 Formerly (until June 1988): Monosson on D E C (ISSN 0884-4097)

621.381 338 669 US
NEW EQUIPMENT REPORTER;* new products industrial news. 1943. m. De Roche Publications, 12 Del Italia, Irvine, CA 92714-5355. Ed. David De Roche. circ. 18,034.

621.381 IT ISSN 1121-8649
NEWS 3X-400; mensile per utenti di sistemi IBM 34-36-38 e AS-400. Key Title: New 3X-400. 1988. m. Duke Italia s.r.l., Viale Lunigiana 42, 20125 Milan, Italy. TEL 02-66711222. FAX 02-66801323. adv.; B&W page L.3590000, color page L.5180000; trim 177 x 253. circ. 21,415.

621.381 US ISSN 1084-7626
NEWS - 400. 1982. 16/yr. $129. Duke Communications International, 221 E. 29th St., Ste. 242, Loveland, CO 80538. TEL 970-663-4700. FAX 970-663-3285. E-mail: editors@news400.com; URL: http://www.news400.com. Ed. Kathy Nelson; Pub. Wayne Madden. R&P contact: Kathy Nelson. adv. contact: David Blansfield. bk.rev.; index. circ. 30,500. (also avail. in microfiche; reprint service avail.) Indexed: Comput.Lit.Ind. Document type: trade publication.
 ●Also available online.
 Also available on CD-ROM.
 —CISTI; KR SourceOne; SWETS.
 Former titles: News 3X-400 (ISSN 1040-6093); News 34-38 (ISSN 8750-1678)
 Description: Publishes technical articles explaining and interpreting AS-400, with coverage of new releases.
 Refereed Serial

621.381 US ISSN 0163-5980
QA76.6 CODEN: OSRED8
OPERATING SYSTEMS REVIEW. vol.4, 1970. 5/yr. $39 to non-members; members $18. Association for Computing Machinery, Special Interest Group on Operating Systems, 1515 Broadway, 17th Fl., New York, NY 10036. TEL 212-869-7440. FAX 212-302-5826. E-mail: acmbelp@acm.org; URL: http://www.acm.org/catalog/. Ed. William Waite. adv.; bk.rev.; bibl.; charts. circ. 8,000. Indexed: Abstr.Hum.Comp.Inter., Comput.Cont., INSPEC.
 —BLDSC (6267.895000); AskIEEE; CISTI; KR SourceOne; Linda Hall; SWETS; UnCover. **CCC**.

004.7 US ISSN 0741-5869
CODEN: OMNEEF
OPTICAL MEMORY NEWS. 1982. bi-w. $597 (foreign $630) (effective 1997). Phillips Business Information, Inc., 1201 Seven Locks Rd., Potomac, MD 20854. TEL 301-424-3338. FAX 301-309-3847. E-mail: pbi@phillips.com. Ed. Mary Crowley. circ. 1,000. (back issues avail.) Indexed: Info.Media & Tech. Document type: newsletter.
 ●Also available online. Vendor(s): Information Access Co., NewsNet (EC50).
 —BLDSC (6273.330000); CASDDS; KR SourceOne. **CCC**.
 Incorporates (1990-1991): Optical and Magnetic Report (ISSN 1047-5117); Formerly: Optical Memory Newsletter.
 Description: Covers the optical storage marketplace from the vendor perspective, including industry trends, new products, and corporate alliances and partnerships.

621.381 US ISSN 1042-3575
QA76.9.E94
P C DIGEST RATINGS REPORT. 1987. m. $450 (foreign $470). National Software Testing Laboratories, Inc., Plymouth Corporate Center, Box 1000, Plymouth Meeting, PA 19462. TEL 215-941-9600. FAX 215-941-9752. Pub. Linda DiBasio. index.
 —CCC.
 Formerly (until 1989): P C Digest (ISSN 0891-575X)
 Description: Reports test ratings of microcomputer systems and peripherals.

P C MAGAZINE. see COMPUTERS — Personal Computers

621.381 US
PERIPHERALS (INTERNATIONAL). base vol. (plus m. updates). $632 to new subscr.; renewals $581 (effective 1996). Dataproject Information Services Group (Subsidiary of: McGraw-Hill, Inc.), 600 Delran Pkwy., Delran, NJ 08075. TEL 609-764-0100; 800-328-2776. FAX 609-764-8953.

PICK RESOURCES GUIDE - INTERNATIONAL. see COMPUTERS

621.381 US
PRAGMA'S PRODUCT PROFILES. 1984. m. free to qualified personnel. Semaphore Corp., 207 Granada Dr., Aptos, CA 95003. TEL 408-688-9200. Ed. Mike Gabrielson. adv.; circ. 4,000 (controlled).
 Description: For Pick Operating Systems users. Provides news and information on current systems. Also covers hardware and user groups.

621.381 US ISSN 0742-5341
REPORT ON I B M. 1984. w. $775 (foreign $825) (effective 1996). DataTrends Publications, Inc., Box 4460, Leesburg, VA 20175. TEL 703-779-0574. FAX 703-779-2267. Indexed: Comput.Lit.Ind. Document type: newsletter.
 ●Also available online. Vendor(s): Information Access Co.
 —CCC.
 Incorporates (in 1992): A D - Solutions Report; Mainframe Communications Report.
 Description: Independent newsletter reporting and providing analysis on the activities and plans of the IBM Corporation.

THE SOLUTION. see PRINTING

SOLUTION INTERNATIONALE. see PRINTING

SVENSKA MACPRESSEN. see COMPUTERS — Microcomputers

SYSTEMS & NETWORK MANAGEMENT REPORT. see COMPUTERS — Computer Systems

621.381 001.64 CH
TAIWAN COMPUTER; providing the latest Taiwan trade information. Cover title: T C. m. NT.$2200($60) in Asia, Oceania, Middle East; elsewhere $75. United Pacific International Inc., P.O. Box 81-417, Taipei, Taiwan, Republic of China. TEL 02-715-0751. FAX 866-2-7125591. TELEX 28784-UNIPAINC. (Dist. in US by: Perfect Seller Mr. John Huang, 5422 Commercial Drive, Huntington Beach, CA 92649) adv.
 Formerly (until Mar. 1990): Target Electronics Industry Computer.
 Description: Contains information and advertising on Taiwan-made computers and Taiwan's computer industry. Mainly concerned with IBM-compatible PC's. Includes a trade-show calendar.

921.381 DK ISSN 0900-3762
TECHNICAL PRODUCT UPDATE. m. free. Digital Equipment Corporation A-S, Aadalsvej 99, DK-2970 Hoersholm, Denmark.

621.381 US
TORONTO SYSTEMS LETTER.* 1960. bi-m. membership. Association for Systems Management, Toronto Chapter, 1433 W. Bagley Rd., Berca, OH 44017. TEL 416-364-4018. FAX 416-862-0315. Ed. Jon Witteker. adv.; bk.rev. circ. 400. (tabloid format)
 Description: Delves into technical and management issues of information systems management.

TRADE WINNERS; the international trade weekly from Asia to the world. see COMPUTERS

UNISYS WORLD; an independent news monthly for Unisys system users. see COMPUTERS — Microcomputers

621.39 US
VIDEOGAMES.* m. newsstand price: $3.95. Larry Flynt Publications, Inc., 8484 Wilshire Blvd., Ste. 900, Beverly Hills, CA 90211-3227. TEL 310-858-7100. FAX 310-275-3857. adv. Document type: consumer publication.

004 US
▼**THE VIEW (FEDERAL WAY).** 1996. d. 1089 S.W. 330 Ct., Federal Way, WA 98023. E-mail: danielf@the-view.com; URL: http://www.the-view.com. Ed. Daniel W. Finley.
 ●Available only online.
 Description: Covers computer hardwares for those interested in buying hardware.

VOICENEWS. see COMMUNICATIONS — Computer Applications

621.381 CN ISSN 0828-5624
WATCOM NEWS. (Waterloo Computing) 1982. q. Can.$10($10) W A T C O M Products Inc., 415 Phillip St., Waterloo, ON N2L 3X2, Canada. TEL 519-886-3700. Ed. Janet Cater. circ. 6,000.
 Formerly: Infowat.
 Description: Newsletter featuring information on Watcom software.

WHAT'S NEW IN COMPUTING. see COMPUTERS — Computer Industry Directories

WORKSTATION; independent news magazine for H P Apollo workstation and server users. see COMPUTERS

WORLD BUSINESS SOLUTION. see PRINTING

621.381 US ISSN 1051-9637
TK5105.5
3 TECH. 1990. q. 3 Com Corp., 540 Bayfront Plaza, Box 58145, Santa Clara, CA 95052-8145.

COMPUTERS — Information Science And Information Theory

see also Computers

003 FR ISSN 1166-7664
A F C E T INTERFLASH. (Former name of issuing body: Association Francaise pour la Cybernetique Economique et Technique) irreg. Association Francaise des Sciences et Technologies de l'Information et des Systemes, 156 bd. Pereire, 75017 Paris, France. TEL 47-66-24-19. FAX 42-67-93-12.
 —AskIEEE; KR SourceOne.
 Former titles (until 1992): A.F.C.E.T. Interfaces (ISSN 0751-0268); A.F.C.E.T. (ISSN 0154-0386)

A I & SOCIETY; the journal of human-centered systems and machine intelligence. (Artificial Intelligence) see COMPUTERS — Artificial Intelligence

A S O R BULLETIN. (Australian Society for Operations Research Inc.) see BUSINESS AND ECONOMICS — Management

003 GW ISSN 0001-5903
QA76 CODEN: AINFA2
ACTA INFORMATICA. Online edition (GW ISSN 1432-0525) (Text in English) 1971. m. DM.1514.80 (foreign DM.1525.60) (effective 1998). Springer-Verlag, Heidelberger Platz 3, 14197 Berlin, Germany. TEL 49-30-82787-0. FAX 49-30-82787448. E-mail: subscriptions@springer.de; URL: http://link.springer.de. (Subscr. in N. America to: Springer-Verlag New York, Inc., 333 Meadowlands Pkwy., Secaucus, NJ 07094. TEL 212-460-1500. FAX 212-473-6272) Ed. M. Broy. adv. (also avail. in microform from UMI; back issues avail.; reprint service avail. from ISI) Indexed: ASCA, Compumath, Comput.Abstr., Comput.Cont., Comput.Rev., Curr.Cont., Eng.Ind., Ind.Sci.Rev., INSPEC (1971-), Int.Abstr.Oper.Res., Math.R., Sci.Cit.Ind. Document type: academic/scholarly publication.
 ●Also available online.
 —BLDSC (0627.850000); AskIEEE; CASDDS; Ei; Genuine Article; KR SourceOne; Linda Hall; SWETS; UMI; UnCover. **CCC**.

ADVANCES IN ACCOUNTING INFORMATION SYSTEMS. see BUSINESS AND ECONOMICS — Accounting

COMPUTERS — INFORMATION SCIENCE AND INFORMATION THEORY

001.539   GW   ISSN 0938-5495
ADVANCES IN KNOWLEDGE ORGANIZATION. 1990. irreg., vol.5, 1996. DM.88. (International Society for Knowledge Organization) Ergon Verlag, Grombuehlstr. 7, 97080 Wuerzburg, Germany. TEL 49-931-280084. FAX 49-931-282872. E-mail: ergon-verlag@t-online.de. **Document type:** monographic series.
—BLDSC (0709.254500).

001.539   US   ISSN 1080-7772
HD30.3
ADVANCES IN MANAGERIAL COGNITION AND ORGANIZATIONAL INFORMATION PROCESSING. 1984. irreg. $73.25 to institutions. J A I Press Inc., 55 Old Post Rd., No. 2, Box 1678, Greenwich, CT 06836-1678. TEL 203-661-7602. FAX 203-661-0792. (In Europe : J A I Press Ltd., The Courtyard, 28 High St., Hampton Hill, Mddx. TW12 1PD, England. TEL 44-181-943-9296. FAX 44-181-943-9317) Ed.Bd. (back issues avail.) **Document type:** academic/scholarly publication.
—CCC.
Formerly (until 1994): Advances in Information Processing in Organizations (ISSN 0747-9778)

003   PL
▼**AKADEMIA GORNICZO-HUTNICZA IM. STANISLAWA STASZICA. INFORMATYKA.** (Text and summaries in English and Polish) 1997. a. 5 Zl. (effective 1997). Wydawnicto A G H, Al. Mickiewicza 30, 30-059 Krakow, Poland. TEL 48-12-364038. FAX 48-12-364038. (Dist. by: Ars Polona, Krakowskie Przedmiescie 7, 00-068 Warsaw, Poland) Ed. A. Wichur. **Document type:** academic/scholarly publication.

AMERICAN SOCIETY FOR INFORMATION SCIENCE. JOURNAL. see *LIBRARY AND INFORMATION SCIENCES*

003   GW
ANGEWANDTE INFORMATIK. 1988. irreg., vol.14, 1994. DM.78. Spektrum Akademischer Verlag GmbH, Vangerowstr. 20, 69115 Heidelberg, Germany. TEL 49-6221-9126-0. FAX 49-6221-912638. E-mail: kaschura@spektrum-verlag.com. Ed. Helmut Balzert. **Indexed:** Zent.Math. **Document type:** monographic series.

ANNALS OF LIBRARY SCIENCE AND DOCUMENTATION. see *LIBRARY AND INFORMATION SCIENCES*

003   GW
ASPEKTE KOMPLEXER SYSTEME. 1994. irreg., vol.2, 1994. DM.58. Spektrum Akademischer Verlag GmbH, Vangerowstr. 20, 69115 Heidelberg, Germany. TEL 49-6221-9126-0. FAX 49-6221-912638. E-mail: kaschura@spektrum-verlag.com. Ed. Thomas Beth. **Indexed:** Zent.Math. **Document type:** monographic series.

001.539   US   ISSN 1045-7879
HD30.2
AUERBACH INFORMATION MANAGEMENT SERIES. 1972. 8 base vols. (plus bi-m. updates for each vol.). $3103. Auerbach Publishers (Subsidiary of: Warren, Gorham & Lamont), One Penn Plaza, New York, NY 10119. TEL 212-971-5000. FAX 212-971-5024. (Subscr. to: 31 St. James Ave., Boston, MA 02116-4112. TEL 800-950-1218. FAX 617-423-1914) Ed. Deb Rhoades. (looseleaf format) **Document type:** trade publication.
—CCC.
Incorporated (in 1989): Managing the Information System Resource; End-User Computing Management; Which was formerly: Managing the Information Center Resource.
Description: Addresses all critical management and technical issues involved in starting up and running a successful information center.

N A'S ELECTRONIC INFORMATION POLICY & LAW REPORT. see *LAW — Civil Law*

003 370   GW   ISSN 0935-8757
▼**BIBLIOGRAPHIE INFORMATIK FUER SCHULE, HOCHSCHULE UND WEITERBILDUNG.** (Text in English, German) 1987. bi-m. DM.64. Fachinformationszentrum Karlsruhe, Gesellschaft fuer Wissenschaftlich-Technische Information mbH, 76344 Eggenstein-Leopoldshafen, Germany. TEL 07247-808333. FAX 07247-808135. TELEX 724710-FIZKA. **Document type:** abstracting/indexing.

BRITISH JOURNAL OF HEALTHCARE COMPUTING & INFORMATION MANAGEMENT. see *MEDICAL SCIENCES — Computer Applications*

003   NE   ISSN 0922-5366
C W I QUARTERLY. 1988. q. fl.100 (effective 1994). Centrum voor Wiskunde en Informatica - Centre for Mathematics and Computer Science, P.O. Box 94079, 1090 GB Amsterdam, Netherlands. FAX 31-20-5924199. TELEX 12571 MATCTR NL. Ed. Nico Tenne. R&P contact: Miente Bakker. adv. contact: Miente Bakker. bk.rev. circ. 600. **Indexed:** Curr.Cont.(1988-), Stat.Theor.Meth.Abstr. (1988-), Zent.Math. **Document type:** academic/scholarly publication.
—Linda Hall.
Formerly: Centrum voor Wiskunde en Informatica Newsletter.

CAHIER V G I. see *HISTORY — Computer Applications*

CHICAGO JOURNAL OF THEORETICAL COMPUTER SCIENCE. see *COMPUTERS*

001.539   US   ISSN 0899-0182
HD30.2   CODEN: CIOJEB
CHIEF INFORMATION OFFICER JOURNAL. 1988. q. $99 (foreign $124) (effective 1993). Faulkner & Gray, Inc. (New York), 11 Penn Plaza, 17th Fl., New York, NY 10001. TEL 212-967-7000. FAX 212-967-7155. Ed. Robert Scott. adv.: B&W page $1700, color page $2550; trim 8 1/8 x 10 7/8. bk.rev.; circ. 3,905 (paid); 8,095 (controlled).
—UMI; UnCover.
Description: Provides strategies and tactics, insights and guidance from information system professionals.

COMMUNITY MEDIA REVIEW. see *COMMUNICATIONS — Television And Cable*

COMPUTER ISSUES. see *COMPUTERS*

003 621.39   PH   ISSN 0117-3308
COMPUTERWORLD PHILIPPINES; journal of information systems management. (Text in English) 1991. fortn. P.1290 (other Asian countries $175; US $300; elsewhere $350). W S Computer Publishing Corp., Rm. 704, Sedcco Bldg., Rada Corner Legazpi Sts., Legazpi Village, Makati, 1229 Metro Manila, Philippines. TEL 632-812-8401. FAX 632-817-6430. E-mail: dcg@vasia.com; URL: http://www.powerhouse.net/comwor. Ed. Chin Wah Wong. adv.: B&W page $3029, color page $4846; trim 290 x 430; adv. contact: Delia C. Gutierree. circ. 12,000. (tabloid format; back issues avail.) **Document type:** trade publication, newspaper.
Description: Covers local and international news and analysis of interest to Philippine information technology professionals and observers.

CONCURRENT ENGINEERING: RESEARCH AND APPLICATIONS. see *COMPUTERS — Computer Engineering*

004.6   NE   ISSN 0167-7438
CONTEMPORARY TOPICS IN INFORMATION TRANSFER. 1982. irreg., vol.5, 1987. price varies. Elsevier Science B.V., Books Division, P.O. Box 211, 1000 AE Amsterdam, Netherlands. TEL 31-20-4853911. FAX 31-20-4853705. TELEX 18582 ESPA NL. E-mail: nlinfo-f@elsevier.nl; usinfo-f@elsevier.com; forinfo-kyf04035@niftyserve.or.jp; URL: http://www.elsevier.nl/. (Subscr. in the Americas to: Elsevier Science, Regional Sales Office, Box 945, New York, NY 10159-0945. TEL 212-633-3730. FAX 212-633-3680; Subscr. in Australasia and the Far East to: Elsevier Science (Singapore) Pte Ltd, No.1 Temasek Ave., No.17-01 Millenia Tower, Singapore 039192, Singapore. TEL 65-434-3727. FAX 65-337-2230; Subscr. in Japan to: Elsevier Science Japan, 9-15 Higashi-Azabu 1-chome, Minato-ku, Tokyo 106, Japan. TEL 81-3-5561-5033. FAX 81-3-5561-5047) **Indexed:** INSPEC. **Document type:** monographic series.
Refereed Serial

003   SP   ISSN 0210-4210
DOCUMENTACION DE LAS CIENCIAS DE LA INFORMACION. 1976. a. 1500 ptas.($17) (effective 1997). Universidad Complutense, Facultad de Ciencias de la Informacion. Departamento de Biblioteconomia y Documentacion, Servicio de Publicaciones, Calle Isaac Peral s-n, Ciudad Universitaria, 28040 Madrid, Spain. TEL 34-1-3946934. FAX 34-1-3946954. (back issues avail.)
—CINDOC.
Description: Publishes theoretical work on documentation and information sciences. Includes also journalism, mass media and up-to-date technology as a tool.

003   UK   ISSN 0969-7977
ELECTRONIC JOURNAL OF STRATEGIC INFORMATION SYSTEMS. Variant title: S I S E-Journal. 1994. irreg. (1 vol./yr.). free. University of Sheffield, Information Studies Department, 211 Portobello St., Regents Court, Rm. 315, Sheffield S10 2UH, England. TEL 44-742-768555. FAX 44-742-780300. E-mail: L.Zeredo@sheffield.ac.uk. (Co-sponsor: Newcastle University) Ed. Luis Zeredo. (back issues avail.) **Document type:** academic/scholarly publication.
●Available only online.
Refereed Serial

004 658   UK   ISSN 0960-085X
T58.5   CODEN: EISYEU
EUROPEAN JOURNAL OF INFORMATION SYSTEMS. 1991. q. £85($130) to individuals; institutions £140 (foreign £160($250)) (effective 1997). (Operational Research Society) Stockton Press (Subsidiary of: MacMillan Press Ltd.), Houndmills, Basingstoke, Hants. RG21 6XS, England. TEL 44-1256-351898. FAX 44-1256-328339. Eds. J. Liebenau, S. Smithson; Pub. Harry Holt. adv. contact: Alison Reeves. bk.rev.; abstr.; illus.; index. (also avail. in microfilm; back issues avail.) **Indexed:** ASCA, Compumath, Cont.Pg.Manage., Curr.Cont.(1991-), Educ.Tech.Abstr., INSPEC (1991-), Stat.Theor.Meth.Abstr. (1991-), Tech.Educ.Abstr. **Document type:** academic/scholarly publication.
—BLDSC (3829.730400); AskIEEE; CISTI; Genuine Article; KR SourceOne; Linda Hall; SWETS; UMI; UnCover. **CCC.**
Incorporates: Journal of Applied Systems Analysis (ISSN 0308-9541)
Description: Provides information on theory and practice of information systems for professionals in academia, industry, commerce and government.

001.539   US
EXECUTIVE BRIEF. vol.3, 1987. q. membership. Society for Information Management, 401 N. Michigan Ave., Chicago, IL 60611-4267. TEL 312-644-6610. FAX 312-245-1083. URL: http://www.simnet.org. Ed. Lisa Suarez. circ. 2,700.
●Also available online.
Formerly (until 1990): S I M Spectrum.

003   GW   ISSN 0172-2204
F I Z - K A BERICHTE. 1979. irreg., no.17, 1992. DM.15. Fachinformationszentrum Karlsruhe, Gesellschaft fuer Wissenschaftlich-Technische Information mbH, 76344 Eggenstein-Leopoldshafen, Germany. TEL 07247-808333. FAX 07247-808135. TELEX 724710-FIZKA. **Document type:** monographic series.

003 658   US   ISSN 1088-128X
   CODEN: FLLMFQ
▼**FAILURE & LESSONS LEARNED IN INFORMATION TECHNOLOGY MANAGEMENT.** 1997. q. $145 (foreign $175) (effective 1998). Cognizant Communication Corporation, 3 Hartsdale Rd., Elmsford, NY 10523. TEL 914-592-7720. FAX 914-592-8981. Ed. Jay Liebowitz. **Document type:** academic/scholarly publication.
—CCC.
Description: Reports on failures in information technology projects and discusses relevant management, technology, organizational and social issues.
Refereed Serial

FUNDAMENTA INFORMATICAE. see *MATHEMATICS — Computer Applications*

H I C. (Health Informatics Conference) see *MEDICAL SCIENCES — Computer Applications*

HEALTH INFORMATICS EUROPE. see *MEDICAL SCIENCES — Computer Applications*

COMPUTERS — INFORMATION SCIENCE AND INFORMATION THEORY

003 153   NE   ISSN 0923-8433
HUMAN FACTORS IN INFORMATION TECHNOLOGY. (Text in English) 1989. irreg., vol.12, 1996. price varies. Elsevier Science B.V., Books Division, P.O. Box 211, 1000 AE Amsterdam, Netherlands. TEL 31-20-4853911. FAX 31-20-4853705. TELEX 18582 ESPA NL. E-mail: nlinfo-f@elsevier.nl; usinfo-f@elsevier.com; forinfo-kyf04035@niftyserve.or.jp; URL: http://www.elsevier.nl/. (Subscr. in the Americas to: Elsevier Science, Regional Sales Office, Box 945, New York, NY 10159-0945. TEL 212-633-3730. FAX 212-633-3680; Subscr. in Australasia and the Far East to: Elsevier Science (Singapore) Pte Ltd, No.1 Temasek Ave., No.17-01 Millenia Tower, Singapore 039192, Singapore. TEL 65-434-3727. FAX 65-337-2230; Subscr. in Japan to: Elsevier Science Japan, 9-15 Higashi-Azabu 1-chome, Minato-ku, Tokyo 106, Japan. TEL 81-3-5561-5033. FAX 81-3-5561-5047) Eds. Hans-Jorg Bullinger, Peter G. Polson. (back issues avail.) **Indexed:** Zent.Math. **Document type:** monographic series.
—BLDSC (4336.081300).
     Refereed Serial

I D P M JOURNAL. (Institute of Data Processing Management) see *COMPUTERS — Data Base Management*

016.003   US   ISSN 0271-4655
Q350
I E E E INTERNATIONAL SYMPOSIUM ON INFORMATION THEORY. ABSTRACTS OF PAPERS. 1967. a. (I E E E, Information Theory Group) Institute of Electrical and Electronics Engineers, Inc., 345 E. 47th St., New York, NY 10017-2394. TEL 732-981-0060; 800-678-4333. FAX 732-981-9667. E-mail: customer.service@ieee.org; URL: http://www.ieee.org. (Subscr. to: 445 Hoes Ln., Box 1331, Piscataway, NJ 08855-1331)
—BLDSC (4362.972000); UMI. **CCC**.
     Description: Recent advances in areas such as coding, Shannon theory, modulation and stochastic processes.

001.539   US   ISSN 0018-9448
Q350   CODEN: IETTAW
I E E E TRANSACTIONS ON INFORMATION THEORY. 1953. 7/yr. $445 to non-members (effective 1998). (I E E E, Information Theory Group) Institute of Electrical and Electronics Engineers, Inc., 345 E. 47th St., New York, NY 10017-2394. TEL 732-981-0060; 800-678-4333. FAX 732-981-9667. E-mail: customer.service@ieee.org; URL: http://www.ieee.org. (Subscr. to: Box 1331, 445 Hoes Lane, Piscataway, NJ 08855-1331) Ed. A.R. Calderbank. bk.rev.; abstr.; illus.; index. (also avail. in microform) **Indexed:** A.S.& T.Ind., Appl.Mech.Rev., ASCA, BMT, CAD CAM Abstr., Chem.Abstr., Compumath, Comput.Abstr., Comput.Cont., Curr.Cont., Cyb.Abstr., Eng.Ind., Ergon.Abstr., Excerp.Med., Ind.Sci.Rev., INSPEC, Int.Aerosp.Abstr., Math.R., Oper.Res.Manage.Sci., Qual.Contr.Appl.Stat., Sci.Cit.Ind., Tel.Abstr., Zent.Math.
—BLDSC (4363.197500); AskIEEE; CISTI; Ei; Genuine Article; KR SourceOne; Linda Hall; SWETS; UMI; UnCover. **CCC**.
     Former titles (until 1962): I R E Transactions on Information Theory; (until 1955): I R E Professional Group on Information Theory Transactions.
     Description: Theoretical and experimental aspects of transmission, processing and utilization.

621.38   UK   ISSN 0916-8532
                                   CODEN: ITISEF
I E I C E TRANSACTIONS ON INFORMATION AND SYSTEMS. 1976. m. £100 (foreign $170) (effective 1998). (Institute of Electronics, Information and Communication Engineers, JA - Denshi Joho Tsushin Gakkai) Oxford University Press, Academic Division, Great Clarendon St., Oxford OX2 6DP, England. TEL 44-1865-267907. FAX 44-1865-267485. E-mail: jnl.info@oup.co.uk; URL: http://www.oup.co.uk/journals. (Subscr. in N. America to: Oxford University Press Inc., 2001 Evans Rd., Cary, NC 27513. TEL 800-852-7323. FAX 919-677-1714) Ed. Michiyuki Uenohara. **Indexed:** ASCA, Curr.Cont., Cyb.Abstr., INSPEC, Int.Abstr.Oper.Res., JCT, Tel.Abstr.
—BLDSC (4363.240675); AskIEEE; CISTI; Ei; Genuine Article; KR SourceOne; Linda Hall; UnCover. **CCC**.
     Supersedes in part (in 1991): I E I C E Transactions on Communications Electronics Information and Systems (ISSN 0917-1673); Former titles (until 1991): Transactions of the Institute of Electronics, Information and Communication Engineers (ISSN 0913-574X); (until 1987): Transactions of the Institute of Electronics and Communication Engineers of Japan. Section E (ISSN 0387-236X); (until 1976): Transactions of the Institute of Electronics and Communication Engineers of Japan. Abstracts (ISSN 0418-6869); (until 1956): Journal of the Institute of Electrical Communication Engineers of Japan. Abstracts (ISSN 0914-5273).

003   AU   ISSN 0304-7121
T57.6.A1
I I A S A ANNUAL REPORT. (Text in English) 1973. a. free. International Institute for Applied Systems Analysis, A-2361 Laxenburg, Austria. TEL 43-2236-807-0. FAX 43-2236-73149. URL: http://www.iiasa.ac.at. Eds. Christoph Schneider, Mary Ann Williams. illus. circ. 7,000. **Indexed:** Energy Ind., Energy Info.Abstr., Geo.Abstr., INSPEC, Sport Fish.Abstr., Wild.Rev., Zent.Math. **Document type:** corporate report.
—CISTI.

003   NE
I T LOGISTIEK. q. Misset (Subsidiary of: Reed Elsevier plc), Postbus 4, 7000 BA Doetinchem, Netherlands. TEL 31-314-349371. FAX 31-314-363638. adv.: B&W page 3280, color page fl.4240; trim 215 x 285; adv. contact: Cor van Nek. circ. 8,500.

003   US   ISSN 1070-0013
INFOMANAGE; the international management newsletter for the information services professional. (Supplement avail.) 1993. m. $137.50 (Canada $152.50; elsewhere $167.50) (effective 1997). S M R Publishing (Subsidiary of: S M R International), Murray Hill Station (948), New York, NY 10156. TEL 212-683-6285. FAX 212-683-2987. E-mail: 73042.67@compuserve.com; URL: http://www.mindspring.com/~smrintl/smr.html. Ed. Guy St. Clair; Pub. Guy St. Clair. bk.rev.; software rev.; index. **Document type:** newsletter.
—BLDSC (4478.878999). **CCC**.

001.539   SA
INFORM. (Text in English) 1964. m. free. I S M, P.O. Box 1419, Johannesburg 2000, South Africa. Ed. Mark Ingle. adv. circ. 13,000. (back issues avail.) **Indexed:** Lib.Lit. **Document type:** trade publication.

001.539 658   US   ISSN 0892-3876
TR835   CODEN: INFREN
INFORM (SILVER SPRING); the magazine of information and image management. (Former name of issuing body: National Micrographics Association) 1967. m. $85 (foreign $105). Association for Information and Image Management, 1100 Wayne Ave., Ste. 1100, Silver Spring, MD 20910. TEL 301-587-8202. Ed. John Harney. adv.; bk.rev.; bibl.; charts; illus. circ. 9,000. (also avail. in microform from UMI; reprint service avail.) **Indexed:** Chem.Abstr., Comput.Cont., Comput.Lit.Ind., Curr.Cont., Eng.Ind., INSPEC, Leg.Info.Manage.Ind., LHTN, Lib.Lit., Resour.Ctr.Ind. **Document type:** trade publication.
—BLDSC (4478.886500); AskIEEE; CASDDS; CISTI; Ei; KR SourceOne; Linda Hall; SWETS; UMI; UnCover. **CCC**.
     Former titles (until 1986): Journal of Information and Image Management (Short title: J I I M) (ISSN 0745-9963); (until 1983): Journal of Micrographics (ISSN 0022-2712); N M A Journal; Incorporates (as of vol.15): Micrographics Today (ISSN 0149-9300); Which was formerly: Micro News Bulletin (ISSN 0026-2544); And which incorporated: N M A Annual Report.
     Description: Covers document and image processing and information management applications. Examines micrographic, optical digital computer technology and systems.

INFORMAA QUARTERLY. see *BUSINESS AND ECONOMICS — Office Equipment And Services*

003   PL   ISSN 1230-2090
Z699.4.C17
INFORMACJA NAUKOWA/INFORMATION SCIENCE. (Text in Polish; summaries in English, French, Russian) 1991. irreg. Instytut Informacji Naukowej, Technicznej i Ekonomicznej, Ul. Zurawia 4a, 00-503 Warsaw, Poland. TEL 48-22-6295624. FAX 48-22-6297989. E-mail: iinte@cc.cup.gov.pl. **Document type:** monographic series.
     Description: Covers computer science, information science, computer information systems, and information-retrieval languages.

INFORMATICA; revista de computacion y sistemas. see *LIBRARY AND INFORMATION SCIENCES — Computer Applications*

INFORMATICS IN HEATHCARE AUSTRALIA. see *MEDICAL SCIENCES — Computer Applications*

INFORMATIE; maandblad voor informatievoorziening. see *COMPUTERS*

003   GW   ISSN 0863-503X
INFORMATIK (BERLIN, 1992). 1992. irreg., vol.7, 1993. Akademie Verlag GmbH, Muehlenstr. 33-34, 13187 Berlin, Germany. TEL 49-30-47883948. FAX 49-30-47889357. E-mail: info@akademie-verlag.de. **Indexed:** Zent.Math. **Document type:** monographic series.
—CISTI.
     Supersedes (in 1992): Research in Informatics (ISSN 0863-4300)

003   GW   ISSN 0178-3564
                                   CODEN: IFENEI
INFORMATIK - FORSCHUNG UND ENTWICKLUNG. Key Title: Informatik (Berlin, 1986). Online edition (GW ISSN 0949-2925) 1986. q. DM.469.60 (foreign DM.473.20) (effective 1998). (Gesellschaft fuer Informatik) Springer-Verlag, Heidelberger Platz 3, 14197 Berlin, Germany. TEL 49-30-82787-0. FAX 49-30-82787448. E-mail: subscriptions@springer.de; URL: http://science.springer.de/ife/ife-main.htm. (Subscr. in N. America to: Springer-Verla New York, Inc., 333 Meadowlands Pkwy., Secaucus NJ 07094. TEL 212-460-1500. FAX 212-473-6272) Ed. A. Endres. adv. **Indexed:** BMT, INSPEC (1986-), Zent.Math. **Document type:** academic/scholarly publication.
●Also available online.
—BLDSC (4481.366000); AskIEEE; Ei; KR SourceOne; SWETS; UMI. **CCC**.

INFORMATION AND SYSTEMS ENGINEERING. see *ENGINEERING — Electrical Engineering*

COMPUTERS — INFORMATION SCIENCE AND INFORMATION THEORY

003 384   NE   ISSN 1383-7605
HC79.I55   CODEN: IIPOFU
INFORMATION INFRASTRUCTURE AND POLICY; an international journal on the development, adoption, use and effects of information technology. (Text in English) 1991. 4/yr. fl.400($229) (effective 1997). I O S Press, Van Diemenstraat 94, 1013 CN Amsterdam, Netherlands. TEL 31-20-6382189. FAX 31-20-6203419. E-mail: market@iospress.nl; URL: http://www.iospress.nl/iospress. (In N. America: Box 10558, Burke, VA 22009-0558. TEL 703-323-5554. FAX 703-250-4705) Ed.Bd. bk.rev. (also avail. in microfiche; back issues avail.) **Indexed:** INSPEC (1991-). **Document type:** academic/scholarly publication.
—BLDSC (4493.607650); AskIEEE; KR SourceOne; SWETS. **CCC.**
  Formerly (until vol.4, 1995): Informatization and the Public Sector (ISSN 0925-5052)
  Description: Publishes articles on political, economic, legal, organizational and policy issues related to developments in information infrastructure, including information resources management, data and privacy protection and security, and relevant applications of technology to large databases and communications infrastructures, and analyses of automation issues in public administration.
Refereed Serial

651.8   IS   ISSN 0073-7879
INFORMATION PROCESSING ASSOCIATION OF ISRAEL. NATIONAL CONFERENCE ON DATA PROCESSING. PROCEEDINGS. (Text in Hebrew and English) 1964. a. £15. Information Processing Association of Israel, Kfar Hamacabia, Ramat Gan 52109, Israel. **Document type:** proceedings.

003 029.7   US   ISSN 0020-0255
Z699.A1   CODEN: ISIJBC
INFORMATION SCIENCES; an international journal. (In 3 sections, A: Informatics and Computer Science, B: Intelligent Systems, C: Applications) 1969. 32/yr. fl.4218($4242) (effective 1998). Elsevier Science Inc., Box 945, New York, NY 10159-0945. TEL 212-633-3730. FAX 212-633-3680. TELEX 420643 AEP UI. E-mail: usinfo-f@elsevier.com; URL: http://www.elsevier.nl/. (Subscr. outside the Americas to: Elsevier Science, Regional Sales Office, P.O. Box 211, 1000 AE Amsterdam, Netherlands. TEL 31-20-4853757. FAX 31-20-4853432; Subscr. in Australasia and the Far East to: Elsevier Science (Singapore) Pte Ltd, No.1 Temasek Ave., No.17-01 Millenia Tower, Singapore 039192, Singapore. TEL 65-434-3727. FAX 65-337-2230; Subscr. in Japan to: Elsevier Science Japan, 9-15 Higashi-Azabu 1-chome, Minato-ku, Tokyo 106, Japan. TEL 81-3-5561-5033. FAX 81-3-5561-5047) Ed. Paul Wang. adv.; bk.rev.; abstr.; charts; illus. (also avail. in microform from UMI; reprint service avail. from SWZ) **Indexed:** ASCA, Chem.Abstr., Compumath, Comput.Abstr., Comput.Cont., Comput.Rev., Curr.Cont., Cyb.Abstr., Eng.Ind., Geo.Abstr.P.G., Ind.Sci.Rev., INSPEC (1968-), Intl.Civil Eng.Abstr., Lang.& Lang.Behav.Abstr., M.L.A., Math.R., Sci.Cit.Ind., Sociol.Abstr., Soft.Abstr.Eng., SSCI, Zent.Math. **Document type:** academic/scholarly publication.
—BLDSC (4494.250000); AskIEEE; CISTI; Ei; Genuine Article; KR SourceOne; Linda Hall; SWETS; UnCover. **CCC.**
  Incorporates (1994-1995): Information Sciences - Applications (ISSN 1069-0115)
  Description: Explores data structures, database management, distributed and image processing.

003 020   NE   ISSN 0167-5265
Z699.A1   CODEN: ISUDX8
INFORMATION SERVICES & USE. (Text in English) 1981. 4/yr. fl.440($254) (effective 1997). I O S Press, Van Diemenstraat 94, 1013 CN Amsterdam, Netherlands. TEL 31-20-6382189. FAX 31-20-6203419. E-mail: market@iospress.nl; URL: http://www.iospress.nl/iospress. (In N. America: Box 10558, Burke, VA 22009-0558. TEL 703-323-5554. FAX 703-250-4705) Ed. A.W. Elias, T. Cawkell. adv.; bk.rev. (also avail. in microform from UMI) **Indexed:** AESIS, BPIA, Bus.Ind., C.I.J.E., Comput.Abstr., Comput.Cont., Comput.Lit.Ind., Fluidex, INSPEC (1981-), Key to Econ.Sci., Leg.Info.Manage.Ind., LHTN, LISA, Manage.Cont., Mgmt.& Market.Abstr., Tr.& Indus.Ind. **Document type:** academic/scholarly publication.
—BLDSC (4495.950000); AskIEEE; CASDDS; CISTI; Ei; KR SourceOne; Linda Hall; SWETS. **CCC.**
  Incorporates (1987-1993): Infomediary (ISSN 0169-2763)
  Description: Contains data on international developments in information management and its applications. Articles cover on-line systems, library automation, word processing, micrographics, videotex and telecommunications.
Refereed Serial

003 020   US   ISSN 0197-2243
Z668   CODEN: INSCD8
THE INFORMATION SOCIETY; an international journal. Online edition (US ISSN 1087-6537) 1981. q. £85($140) to institutions (£102($168) with online ed.) (effective 1998). Taylor & Francis Inc., 1900 Frost Rd., Ste. 101, Bristol, PA 19007-1598. TEL 215-785-5800; 800-821-8312. FAX 215-785-5515. E-mail: info@tandf.co.uk; URL: http://www.ics.uci.edi/~kling/tis.html. (Subscr. in Europe to: Taylor & Francis Ltd., Rankine Rd., Basingstoke, Hants. RG24 8PR, England. TEL 44-1256-840366. FAX 44-1256-479438) Ed. Robert Kling. adv.; bk.rev.; abstr. **Indexed:** ABI Inform., Abstr.Hum.Comp.Inter., CAD CAM Abstr., Commun.Abstr., Comput.Cont., Inform.Sci.Abstr., INSPEC, LISA, Mgmt.& Market.Abstr., P.A.I.S., Ref.Zh., Tel.Abstr. **Document type:** academic/scholarly publication.
●Also available online.
—BLDSC (4496.310000); AskIEEE; Genuine Article; KR SourceOne; Linda Hall; SWETS; UMI; UnCover. **CCC.**
  Description: Provides a forum for such topics on information as transborder flow and regulatory issues.
Refereed Serial

003   UK   ISSN 1350-1917
INFORMATION SYSTEMS JOURNAL; an international journal promoting the study and practice of information systems. 1991. q. £159($290) (foreign $175) (effective 1998). Blackwell Science Ltd., Osney Mead, Oxford OX2 OEL, England. TEL 44-1865-206206. FAX 44-1865-721205. E-mail: journals.cs@blacksci.co.uk; URL: http://www.black.co.uk. Eds. D. Avison, G. Fitzgerald; Pub. Allen Stevens. R&P contact: Sarah Pollard. adv. contact: Martine Cariou-Keen. bk.rev.; bibl.; illus.; index. circ. 345. (also avail. in microform from UMI) **Indexed:** ASCA, Comput.Abstr., Curr.Cont., Geo.Abstr.P.G., INSPEC (1994-), Tech.Educ.Abstr. **Document type:** academic/scholarly publication.
—BLDSC (4496.368300); AskIEEE; Genuine Article; KR SourceOne; SWETS; UMI; UnCover. **CCC.**
  Formerly (until 1993): Journal of Information Systems (ISSN 0959-2954)
  Description: Aims to promote the study of, and interest in, information systems and to publish articles that reflect the wide and interdisciplinary nature of the subject.
Refereed Serial

001.539   US   ISSN 1047-7047
QA76.27   CODEN: ISYREH
INFORMATION SYSTEMS RESEARCH. 1990. q. $75 to individuals (foreign $82); institutions $116 (foreign $123) (effective 1997). Institute for Operations Research and the Management Sciences, 901 Elkridge Landing Rd., Ste. 400, Linthicum, MD 21090-2909. TEL 410-850-0300; 800-343-0062. Ed. John L. King. R&P contact: Fran Silverman. adv. contact: Kathye Long. circ. 1,490. **Indexed:** ASCA, Compumath, Curr.Cont. **Document type:** academic/scholarly publication.
—BLDSC (4496.368601); AskIEEE; KR SourceOne; SWETS; UnCover. **CCC.**

INFORMATION TECHNOLOGY AND LIBRARIES. see
LIBRARY AND INFORMATION SCIENCES

INFORMATION TECHNOLOGY CATALOGUE. see
TRANSPORTATION — Air Transport

001.539 370   AT   ISSN 1037-616X
INFORMATION TECHNOLOGY, EDUCATION AND SOCIETY. 1994. s-a. $60 to individuals; institutions $120. James Nicholas Publishers, P.O. Box 244, Alberst Park, Vic. 3206, Australia. TEL 61-3-6995545. FAX 61-3-6992040. E-mail: razajda@jamesnicholaspublishers.com.au; URL: http://www.jamesnicholaspublishers.com.au. Ed. Rea Zajda; Pub. Rea Zajda. R&P contact: Mary Berchmann. adv. contact: Dorothy Murphy. bk.rev.; index. **Document type:** academic/scholarly publication.
  Description: Concerned with major and current issues in information technology and its relation to education and society, by critically examining the nexus between both formal and informal educational processes and outcomes and information technology.
Refereed Serial

INFORMATION TECHNOLOGY OUTLOOK/PERSPECTIVES DES TECHNOLOGIES DE L'INFORMATION. see
LIBRARY AND INFORMATION SCIENCES — Computer Applications

INFORMATION TECHNOLOGY REVIEW. see
COMPUTERS — Data Communications And Data Transmission Systems

001.539   US
INFORMATION TECHNOLOGY SERIES. 1976. irreg., latest vol.6. price varies. (American Federation of Information Processing Societies) Springer-Verlag, 175 Fifth Ave., New York, NY 10010. TEL 212-460-1500. FAX 212-473-6272. (Also: Berlin, Heidelberg, Tokyo and Vienna) **Document type:** monographic series.

003   PL   ISSN 0542-9951
INFORMATYKA. 1965. m. $144 (effective 1998). (Polski Komitet Automatycznego Przetwarzania Informacji NOT) Wydawnictwo Czasopism i Ksiazek Technicznych SIGMA - NOT, Ul. Ratuszowa 11, P.O. Box 1004, 00-950 Warsaw, Poland. (Dist. by: SIGMA NOT Ltd., Ul. Bartycka 20, 00-716 Warsaw, Poland; Dist. also by: Mezhdunarodnaya Kniga, B. Yakimanka 39, 117049 Moscow, Russia. TEL 7-095-2384967. FAX 7-095-2384634) (Co-sponsor: Krajowe Biuro Informatyki) Ed. Wladyslaw Klepacz. adv.: B&W page $1260. circ. 5,250. **Indexed:** Cyb.Abstr., INIS Atomind., INSPEC.
—BLDSC (4496.915000); AskIEEE; KR SourceOne.

003 004.6   NZ   ISSN 1173-3764
INFOSYS; the electronic newsletter for information systems. 1994. w. free. Massey University, Information Systems Department, Albany, New Zealand. TEL 64-9-4418150. FAX 64-9-4418181. E-mail: d.viehland@massey.ac.nz. Ed. Dennis Viehland. circ. 5,200. **Document type:** newsletter.
●Available only online.
  Description: For faculty, students, and practitioners in the field of information systems. Publishes news items, announcements, requests for assistance, calls for papers, notices of professional meetings and conferences, position announcements, and other items of interest to the global information systems community.

003   US
INSIGHT I S. (Information Technology) m. $370 (effective Aug. 1996). Xephon, 1301 W. Hwy. 407, Ste. 201-450, Lewisville, TX 75067. TEL 817-455-7050. FAX 817-455-2492. **Document type:** trade publication.
  Formerly: Insight I B M.

COMPUTERS — INFORMATION SCIENCE AND INFORMATION THEORY

621.3   JA   ISSN 0915-1923
TK5101.A1   CODEN: DTGDE7
INSTITUTE OF ELECTRONICS, INFORMATION AND COMMUNICATION ENGINEERS. TRANSACTIONS (SECTION D-II)/DENSHI JOHO TSUSHIN GAKKAI RONBUNSHI (D-II). English translation (in part): Systems and Computers in Japan (US ISSN 0882-1666) (Text in Japanese) 1968. m. 2100 Yen. Institute of Electronics, Information and Communication Engineers - Denshi Joho Tsushin Gakkai, c/o Kikai-Shinko-Kaikan Bldg., 5-8 Shiba Koen, 3-chome, Minato-ku, Tokyo 105, Japan. TEL 81-3-3433-6691. FAX 81-3-3433-6659. Ed. Michiyuki Uenohara. adv.; bk.rev. circ. 8,700. **Indexed:** INSPEC (1989-), Int.Abstr.Oper.Res., JCT. —BLDSC (8939.442200); AskIEEE; CISTI; KR SourceOne.
    Supersedes in part (in 1989): Institute of Electronics, Information and Communication Engineers. Transactions (Section D) (ISSN 0913-5731)

INTERNATIONAL JOURNAL OF COMPUTER APPLICATIONS IN TECHNOLOGY. see *COMPUTERS — Software*

001.539   SI
QA76.9.D3
INTERNATIONAL JOURNAL OF COOPERATIVE INFORMATION SYSTMES. Abbreviated title: I J C I S. (Text in English) 1992. q. $115 to individuals & institutions of developing countries; institutions of developed countries $288. World Scientific Publishing Co. Pte. Ltd., Farrer Rd., P.O. Box 128, Singapore 9128, Singapore. TEL 65-3825663. FAX 65-3825919. TELEX RS 28561 WSPC. E-mail: wspcsl@singnet.com.sg; sales@wspc2.demon.co.uk; wspc@wspcc.com; URL: http://www.singnet.com.sg/~wspclib/. (UK addr.: 57 Shelton Rd., Covent Garden, London WC2H 9HE, England. TEL 44-171-836-0888. FAX 44-171-836-2020; US addr.: 1060 Main St., Ste. 1B, River Edge, NJ 07661. TEL 800-227-7562. FAX 201-487-9656) Eds. M.P. Papazoglou, G. Schlageter. **Indexed:** ASCA, INSPEC (1992-). **Document type:** academic/scholarly publication. —AskIEEE; CISTI; Genuine Article; KR SourceOne. **CCC.**
    Formerly (until vol.4, no.1, 1995): International Journal of Intelligent and Cooperative Information Systems (ISSN 0218-2157)
    Description: Provides a forum where both the AI and DBS research communities can come to understand the intricacies of intelligent cooperative work.

003 658   UK   ISSN 0268-4012
H61.9
INTERNATIONAL JOURNAL OF INFORMATION MANAGEMENT. 1980. bi-m. fl.826($475) (effective 1998). Elsevier Science Ltd., Pergamon, P.O. Box 800, Kidlington, Oxford OX5 1DX, England. TEL 44-1865-843000. FAX 44-1865-843010. TELEX 83111 BHPOXF G. E-mail: nlinfo-f@elsevier.nl; usinfo-f@elsevier.com; forinfo-kyf04035@niftyserve.or.jp; URL: http://www.elsevier.nl/. (Subscr. to: Elsevier Science, Regional Sales Office, P.O. Box 211, 1000 AE Amsterdam, Netherlands. TEL 31-20-4853757. FAX 31-20-4853432; Subscr. in the Americas to: Elsevier Science, Regional Sales Office, Box 945, New York, NY 10159-0945. TEL 212-633-3730. FAX 212-633-3680; Subscr. in Australasia and the Far East to: Elsevier Science (Singapore) Pte Ltd, No.1 Temasek Ave., No.17-01 Millenia Tower, Singapore 039192, Singapore. TEL 65-434-3727. FAX 65-337-2230) Eds. P. Hills, R.E. Wiggins. index. (also avail. in microform from UMI; back issues avail.) **Indexed:** ASCA, ASSIA, Cont.Pg.Manage., Geo.Abstr., INSPEC, Int.Lab.Doc., Int.Polit.Sci.Abstr., LISA, P.A.I.S., Sociol.Abstr., SSCI, Tech.Educ.Abstr. **Document type:** academic/scholarly publication. —BLDSC (4542.304900); AskIEEE; Ei; Genuine Article; KR SourceOne; SWETS; UMI; UnCover. **CCC.**
    Formerly (until 1985): Social Science Information Studies (ISSN 0143-6236)
    Description: Promotes corporate efficiency and individual productivity by addressing questions of information, systems, organization and management, planning and decision-making, and interpersonal communications.
    Refereed Serial

IRYO JOHO SHISUTEMU KENKYU KAIHATSU HOKOKUSHO/REPORT OF RESEARCH AND DEVELOPMENT OF MEDICAL INFORMATION SYSTEM. see *MEDICAL SCIENCES*

001.539   JA
JOHO RIRON TO SONO OYO SHINPOJUMU YOKOSHU/SYMPOSIUM ON INFORMATION THEORY AND ITS APPLICATIONS. PROCEEDINGS. (Text in English, Japanese) a. Joho Riron to Sono Oyo Gakkai - Society of Information Theory and Its Applications, c/o Suguru Arimoto, Tokyo Daigaku, 7-3-1, Hongo, Bunkyo-ku, Tokyo 113, Japan. **Document type:** proceedings.

001.539   US   ISSN 0163-5956
QA76.9.D6
JOURNAL OF COMPUTER DOCUMENTATION. q. $24 to non-members; members $44. Association for Computing Machinery, Special Interest Group for Documentation (SIGDOC), 1515 Broadway, New York, NY 10036. TEL 212-869-7440. FAX 212-869-0481. TELEX 421686. Ed. Russell Borland.
—SWETS.

JOURNAL OF CRYPTOLOGY. see *MATHEMATICS*

003 004.6   US   ISSN 1384-5810
▼**THE JOURNAL OF DATA MINING AND KNOWLEDGE DISCOVERY**. Announced for publication in 1997. q. fl.690 to institutions; $354 to institutions in U.S. (effective 1998). Kluwer Academic Publishers Boston, Box 358, Accord Sta., Hingham, MA 02018-0358. TEL 617-871-6600. FAX 617-871-6528. E-mail: services@wkap.nl; URL: http://www.wkap.nl. (Dist. outside N. America by: Kluwer Academic Publishers Group, P.O. Box 322, 3300 AH Dordrecht, Netherlands. TEL 31-78-6392392. FAX 31-78-6546474) **Document type:** academic/scholarly publication. —BLDSC (3534.726000).
    Description: Publishes articles on all aspects of knowledge discovery in databases and data mining methods for extracting high-level representations from data.
    Refereed Serial

JOURNAL OF INFORMATION & OPTIMIZATION SCIENCES. see *MATHEMATICS*

004   JA   ISSN 0021-7298
    CODEN: JOKAAB
JOURNAL OF INFORMATION PROCESSING AND MANAGEMENT/JOHO KANRI. (Text in Japanese, summaries in English) 1958. m. $175. Japan Science and Technology Corporation, Information Center for Science and Technology - Kagaku Gijutsu Shinko Gigyodan, 5-3, Yonbancho, Chiyoda-ku, Tokyo 102, Japan. TEL 81-3-5214-8413. FAX 81-3-5214-8410. adv.; bk.rev.; abstr.; charts; illus.; index. circ. 5,000. **Indexed:** Chem.Abstr., INIS Atomind., INSPEC, JTA, Math.R. —BLDSC (5006.772200); AskIEEE; CASDDS; KR SourceOne; UnCover.
    Formerly: Information and Documentation.

003   US   ISSN 0888-7985
    CODEN: JINFE3
THE JOURNAL OF INFORMATION SYSTEMS. 1986. s-a. $35. American Accounting Association, 5717 Bessie Dr., Sarasota, FL 34233-2399. TEL 941-921-7747. FAX 941-923-4093. R&P contact: Mary Cole. **Indexed:** INSPEC (1989-). —BLDSC (5006.777000); AskIEEE; KR SourceOne; SWETS; UnCover.

001.539   US   ISSN 1042-1319
T58.64
JOURNAL OF INFORMATION TECHNOLOGY MANAGEMENT.* 1990. q. $125. Maximilian Press, Box 64841, Virginia Beach, VA 23467-4841. Ed. Karin E. Klenke. adv. contact: Willem A. Hamel. circ. 1,500. **Document type:** academic/scholarly publication.
—BLDSC (5006.795000).

JOURNAL OF INTERNATIONAL INFORMATION MANAGEMENT. see *BUSINESS AND ECONOMICS — Management*

JOURNAL OF LAW AND INFORMATION SCIENCE. see *LAW*

003 658   US   ISSN 0742-1222
    CODEN: JMISEB
JOURNAL OF MANAGEMENT INFORMATION SYSTEMS. Abbreviated title: J M I S. 1984. q. $63 to individuals (foreign $84); institutions $280 (foreign $320) (effective 1997). M.E. Sharpe, Inc., 80 Business Park Dr., Armonk, NY 10504. TEL 914-273-1800; 800-541-6563. FAX 914-273-2106. URL: http://www.stern.nyu.edu/jmis. Ed. Vladimir Zwass. adv.: page $300; 6 x 9. charts; illus.; index. (back issues avail.) **Indexed:** Account.& Data Proc.Abstr., Comput.Lit.Ind., IBR, INSPEC (1984-), Oper.Res.Manage.Sci., Qual.Contr.Appl.Stat., SCIMP (1991-). **Document type:** academic/scholarly publication.
●Also available online. Vendor(s): UMI.
—BLDSC (5011.350000); AskIEEE; KR SourceOne; SWETS; UMI; UnCover. **CCC.**
    Description: Presents research that advances the practice and understanding of organizational information systems. Aims to serve those investigting new models of information delivery and the changing landscape of information policy making, as well as practitioners and executives managing information resources.
    Refereed Serial

003   JA
KYUSHU UNIVERSITY. RESEARCH INSTITUTE OF FUNDAMENTAL INFORMATION SCIENCE. RESEARCH REPORT. (Text in English) 1968. biennial. Kyushu University, Faculty of Science, Research Institute of Fundamental Information Science - Kyushu Daigaku Rigakubu Fuzoku Kiso Johogaku Kenkyu Shisetsu, 10-1, Hakozaki 6-chome, Fukuoka-shi, Fukuoka-ken 812, Japan.

L I T A LINE. (Library and Information Technology Association) see *LIBRARY AND INFORMATION SCIENCES — Computer Applications*

L I T A NEWSLETTER. (Library and Information Technology Association) see *LIBRARY AND INFORMATION SCIENCES*

001.539   UK   ISSN 1361-4576
TK5105.5   CODEN: JIFNEL
THE NEW REVIEW OF INFORMATION NETWORKING. 1993; N.S. 1995. 3/yr. £65($125) Taylor Graham Publishing, 500 Chesham House, 150 Regent St., London W1R 5FA, England. Ed. Michael Breaks. (back issues avail.) **Indexed:** Educ.Tech.Abstr., INSPEC (1993-). **Document type:** academic/scholarly publication.
—BLDSC (6087.764555); AskIEEE; KR SourceOne.
    Formerly (until 1994): Journal of Information Networking (ISSN 0966-9248)

001.539   UK   ISSN 0263-2187
ON LINE (SUNBURY-ON-THAMES). 1978. 3/yr. B O C Computer Services, 99 Staines Rd. W., Sunbury-on-Thames, Middlesex, England. charts; illus.

003 004   NE
OPEN SYSTEMS & INFORMATION DYNAMICS. 1992. q. fl.420 to institutions; $250 to institutions in U.S. (effective 1997). (Society for Open Systems & Information Dynamics) Kluwer Academic Publishers Postbus 17, 3300 AA Dordrecht, Netherlands. TEL 31-78-6392392. FAX 31-78-6392254. E-ma services@wkap.nl; URL: http://www.wkap.nl. (Dist. by: Kluwer Academic Publishers Group, P.O. Box 322, 3300 AH Dordrecht, Netherlands. TEL 31-78-6392392. FAX 31-78-6546474; N. America dist. addr.: Box 358, Accord Sta., Hingham MA 02018-0358. TEL 617-871-6600. FAX 617-871-6528) **Document type:** academic/scholarl publication.
    Refereed Serial

003 004   PL   ISSN 1230-1612
OPEN SYSTEMS AND INFORMATION DYNAMICS. (Text i English) 1993. q. fl.460 to institutions; $236 to institutions in U.S. (effective 1998). Uniwesytet Mikolaja Kopernika, Wydawnictwo, Ul. Gagarina 11 87-100 Torun, Poland. TEL 48-56-14295. FAX 21224. (Dist. by: Osrodek Rozpowszechniania Wydawnictw Naukowych PAN, Palac Kultury i Nauk 00-901 Warsaw, Poland)

COMPUTERS — INFORMATION SCIENCE AND INFORMATION THEORY

003 AU ISSN 0252-9572
OPTIONS. 1978. q. free. International Institute for Applied Systems Analysis, A-2361 Laxenburg, Austria. TEL 43-2236-807-0. FAX 43-2236-73149. E-mail: options@iiasa.ac.at; URL: http://www.iiasa.ac.at. Eds. Christoph Schneider, Mary Ann Williams. circ. 8,000. (back issues avail.) **Document type:** newsletter.
●Also available online.
—BLDSC (6275.270000); CISTI.

DER ORGANISATOR. see *BUSINESS AND ECONOMICS — Management*

003 SZ ISSN 0379-2501
OUTPUT; Fachjournal fuer die professionelle Informationsverarbeitung. (Text in German) 1972. m. 133 SFr. (Europe 143 SFr.; overseas 157 SFr.) (effective 1997). Fachpresse Goldach, Sulzstr. 12, CH-9403 Goldach, Switzerland. TEL 41-71-8449111. FAX 41-71-8449511. E-mail: 100442.1657@compuserve.com; URL: http://www.fachpresse.ch. Ed. Karlheinz Pichler. adv. circ. 12,000. **Indexed:** INSPEC. **Document type:** trade publication.
—BLDSC (6314.594000); AskIEEE; KR SourceOne.

003 PH
PHILIPPINE I.T. JOURNAL. (Information Technology) m.? P.320 (foreign $80). Science and Technology Information Institute, Department of Science and Technology, P.O. Box 3596, Manila, Philippines. TEL 822-0954. (Subscr. to: Dept. of Science and Technology, Bicutan, Taguig, P.O. Box 2131, Manila, Philippines) **Document type:** trade publication.
Description: A technical journal for Philippine information technology professionals.

003 PL ISSN 0860-0082
POLITECHNIKA LODZKA. ZESZYTY NAUKOWE. INFORMATYKA. (Text in English; summaries in English and Russian) 1991. irreg. price varies. Wydawnictwo Politechniki Lodzkiej, Ul. Wolczanska 223, 93-005 Lodz, Poland. (Dist. by: Ars Polona-Ruch, Krakowskie Przedmiescie 7, 93-085 Lodz, Poland) Ed. Edward Kacki. circ. 296. **Document type:** academic/scholarly publication.

003 PL ISSN 0208-7286
Z699.A1 CODEN: ZNPIET
POLITECHNIKA SLASKA. ZESZYTY NAUKOWE. INFORMATYKA. (Text in Polish; summaries in English, German, Russian) 1980. irreg. price varies. Politechnika Slaska, Katowicka 2, 44-100 Gliwice, Poland. FAX 0371655. TELEX 036304. (Distributed by: Ars Polona-Ruch, Krakowskie Przedmiescie 7, 00-068 Warsaw, Poland) Ed. Marcin Skowronek. circ. 300.
—BLDSC (9512.327500); Linda Hall.

003 519 NE ISSN 0231-9969
QA273
PRAGUE CONFERENCE ON INFORMATION THEORY, STATISTICAL DECISION FUNCTIONS, RANDOM PROCESSES. TRANSACTIONS. Running title: Information Theory, Statistical Decision Functions, Random Processes. (Text in English) 1956. irreg., vol.11, 1992. price varies. Kluwer Academic Publishers, Postbus 17, 3300 AA Dordrecht, Netherlands. TEL 31-78-6392392. FAX 31-78-6392254. TELEX 29245 KAPG NL. E-mail: services@wkap.nl; URL: http://www.wkap.nl. (Dist. by: Kluwer Academic Publishers Group, P.O. Box 322, 3300 AH Dordrecht, Netherlands. TEL 31-78-6392392. FAX 31-78-6546474; N. America dist. addr.: Box 358, Accord Sta., Hingham, MA 02018-0358. TEL 617-871-6600. FAX 617-871-6528) **Document type:** proceedings.
—Linda Hall.
Formerly: Conference on Information Theory, Statistical Decision Functions, Random Processes (ISSN 0573-3634)
Refereed Serial

006 US ISSN 1054-7460
TA167 CODEN: PSENEG
PRESENCE: TELEOPERATORS AND VIRTUAL ENVIRONMENTS. 1992. s-m. $75 to individuals (foreign $97); institutions $210 (foreign $232); students $48 (foreign $70) (effective 1997). M I T Press, 5 Cambridge Center, Cambridge, MA 02142-1399. TEL 617-253-2889. FAX 617-577-1545. E-mail: journals-orders@mit.edu; URL: http://www-mitpress.mit.edu. Ed.Bd. R&P contact: Paul Dzus. **Indexed:** Curr.Cont. **Document type:** academic/scholarly publication.
—BLDSC (6609.709700); CISTI; Genuine Article; SWETS; UMI. **CCC.**
Description: Contains research and designs applicable to advanced eletromechanical and computer systems, incorporating perspectives from physics to philosophy.

PROBABILITY IN THE ENGINEERING AND INFORMATIONAL SCIENCES. see *ENGINEERING — Abstracting, Bibliographies, Statistics*

003 US ISSN 1048-6542
CODEN: PACRES
THE PUBLIC - ACCESS COMPUTER SYSTEMS REVIEW. 1990. irreg, vol.8, no.2, 1997. free. University Libraries, University of Houston, Houston, TX 77204-2091. TEL 713-743-9762. FAX 713-743-9673. E-mail: plensor@uh.edu; twilson@uh.edu; URL: http://info.lib.uh.edu/pacsrev.html. Eds. Pat Ensor, Thomas C. Wilson. circ. 10,912.
●Also available online.
—KR SourceOne.

001.539 CC ISSN 1000-8489
Z671 CODEN: QKJIEF
QINGBAO KEXUE/INFORMATION SCIENCE.* (Text in Chinese; summaries and table of contents in English) 1980. bi-m. Y2.60. 30, Yinhang Jie, Nangang Qu, Harbin, Heilongjiang 150001, People's Republic of China. (Dist. outside China by: China International Book Trading Corp., P.O. Box 399, Beijing, P.R.C.) adv.; bk.rev.; bibl.; charts. circ. 5,000.
—CASDDS.
Description: Reports on the theory method and technology of information collecting, processing, searching, analyzing, and transmitting, as well as the construction of information systems and networks, and the management of information work and policy.

001.6 IT
QUADERNI D'INFORMATICA. 3/yr. Honeywell Information Systems Italia, 20010 Pregnana Milanese, Italy. Ed. Franco Filippazzi.

REFERENCE INFORMATION REVIEW SOUTHERN AFRICA; a sourceguide fo informationists and managers. see *LIBRARY AND INFORMATION SCIENCES — Computer Applications*

RESEARCH REPORTS ON INFORMATION SCIENCE AND ELECTRICAL ENGINEERING/KYUSHU DAIGAKU DAIGAKUIN SHISUTEMU JOHO KAGAKU KENKYUKA HOKOKU. see *ENGINEERING — Electrical Engineering*

001.539 510 JA ISSN 0912-2370
RESEARCH REPORTS ON INFORMATION SCIENCES. SERIES A, MATHEMATICAL SCIENCE. (Text and summaries in English) irreg Tokyo Kogyo Daigaku, Rigakubu, Joho Kagakka - Tokyo Institute of Technology, Faculty of Science, Department of Information Sciences, 12-1, Ookayama 2-chome, Meguro-ku, Tokyo 152, Japan. **Indexed:** INSPEC.
—AskIEEE; KR SourceOne.

003 JA ISSN 0912-2389
RESEARCH REPORTS ON INFORMATION SCIENCES. SERIES B, OPERATIONS RESEARCH. (Text and summaries in English) irreg Tokyo Kogyo Daigaku, Rigakubu, Joho Kagakka - Tokyo Institute of Technology, Faculty of Science, Department of Information Sciences, 12-1, Ookayama 2-chome, Meguro-ku, Tokyo 152, Japan. **Indexed:** INSPEC.
—AskIEEE; KR SourceOne.

001.539 JA ISSN 0912-2397
RESEARCH REPORTS ON INFORMATION SCIENCES. SERIES C, COMPUTER SCIENCES. (Text and summaries in English) irreg. Tokyo Kogyo Daigaku, Rigakubu, Joho Kagakka - Tokyo Institute of Technology, Faculty of Science, Department of Information Sciences, 12-1, Ookayama 2-chome, Meguro-ku, Tokyo 152, Japan. **Indexed:** INSPEC.
—BLDSC (7769.541630); AskIEEE; KR SourceOne.

003 SP ISSN 0213-070X
REVISTA DE CIENCIAS DE LA INFORMACION. (Supplement avail.: Revista de Ciencias de la Informacion. Numero Extraordinario (ISSN 1133-1577) 1984. 4/yr. 6000 ptas.($66) (effective 1997). Universidad Complutense, Facultad de Ciencias de la Informacion, Servicio de Publicaciones, Calle Issac Peral s-n, Ciudad Universitaria, 28040 Madrid, Spain. TEL 34-1-3946934. FAX 34-1-3946954. (back issues avail.)
Description: Publishes original articles on information, library and computer sciences, mainly written by the faculty members.

003 SP ISSN 1133-1577
REVISTA DE CIENCIAS DE LA INFORMACION. NUMERO EXTRAORDINARIO. (Supplement to: Revista de Ciencias de la Informacion (ISSN 0213-070X)) 1988. a. Universidad Complutense, Facultad de Ciencias de la Informacion, Servicio de Publicaciones, Calle Isaac Peral s-n, Ciudad Universitaria, 28040 Madrid, Spain. TEL 34-1-3946934. FAX 34-1-3946954. (back issues avail.)

001.6 IT ISSN 0390-668X
RIVISTA DI INFORMATICA. (Text in Italian; summaries in English) 1970. q. L.123000($117) to individuals; institutions $177 (effective 1997). (Associazione Italiana per l'Informatica e il Calcolo Automatico) Masson S.p.A., Divisione Periodici, Via Flli. Bressan 2, 20126 Milan, Italy. TEL 39-2-270741. FAX 39-2-27074210. Eds. L. Dadda, F.A. Schreiber. adv.: B&W page L.1430000; trim 170 x 240. bk.rev. circ. 2,700. **Indexed:** INSPEC, Phys.Ber. **Document type:** academic/scholarly publication.
—BLDSC (7986.830000); AskIEEE; Ei; KR SourceOne.

001.539 US ISSN 0163-5840
Z699.5.E6 CODEN: FASRDV
S I G I R FORUM. q. $32 to non-members; members $65. Association for Computing Machinery, Special Interest Group on Information Retrieval, 1515 Broadway, 17th Fl., New York, NY 10036. TEL 212-869-7440. FAX 212-869-0481. TELEX 421686. **Indexed:** INSPEC.
—BLDSC (8275.330000); AskIEEE; Ei; KR SourceOne; SWETS; UnCover.

001.539 US
S I M NETWORK. bi-m. membership. Society for Information Management, 401 N. Michigan Ave., Chicago, IL 60611-4267. TEL 312-644-6610. FAX 312-245-1083. URL: http://www.simnet.org. Ed. Mary Rose Mazza. circ. 2,700.
●Also available online.

003 GW ISSN 0931-4326
S T NEWS. 1985. bi-m. Fachinformationszentrum Karlsruhe, Gesellschaft fuer Wissenschaftlich-Technische Information mbH, 76344 Eggenstein-Leopoldshafen, Germany. TEL 07247-808333. FAX 07247-808135. TELEX 724710-FIZKA. **Document type:** bulletin.

003 US ISSN 1070-4795
Z699.A1 CODEN: SMDPE8
SEARCHER (MEDFORD); the magazine for database professionals. 1993. 10/yr. $59.95 (Canada and Mexico $71; elsewhere $82) (effective 1997). Information Today, Inc., 143 Old Marlton Pike, Medford, NJ 08055. TEL 609-654-6266. FAX 609-654-4309. URL: http://www.infotoday.com. (Outside N. America subscr. to: Woodside, Hinksey Hill, Oxford OX 15AU, England) Ed. Barbara Quint; Pub. Thomas H. Hogan. adv. contact: Michael Zarrello. **Document type:** consumer publication.
—BLDSC (8214.625500); CISTI; Ei; Genuine Article; KR SourceOne; SWETS; UnCover. **CCC.**
Description: Explores and deliberates on a comprehensive range of issues important to the professional database searcher. Includes all electronic media--online, CD-ROM, diskette, tape leasing.

2186 COMPUTERS — MACHINE THEORY

THE SOFTWARE QUALITY ADVISOR; the "how-to" newsletter of software quality assurance. see COMPUTERS — Software

STUDIES IN VISUAL INFORMATION PROCESSING. see MEDICAL SCIENCES — Psychiatry And Neurology

001.539   GW
TERMINOLOGY AND KNOWLEDGE ENGINEERING. (Text in English) irreg., no.96, 1996. DM.82.40. (International Society for Knowledge Organization) Ergon Verlag, Grombuehlstr. 7, 97080 Wuerzburg, Germany. TEL 49-931-280084. FAX 49-931-282872. E-mail: ergon-verlag@t-online.de. **Document type:** monographic series.

THEORY AND DECISION LIBRARY. SERIES D: SYSTEM THEORY, KNOWLEDGE ENGINEERING AND PROBLEM SOLVING. see COMPUTERS — Cybernetics

004   US   ISSN 0749-9531
HT390
U R I S A NEWS. 1982. bi-m. Urban and Regional Information Systems Association, URISA Secretariat, 900 Second St., N.E., Ste. 304, Washington, DC 20002. TEL 202-289-1689. FAX 202-842-1850. E-mail: member@urisa.org. Ed. Bob Lima. adv. contact: Tegan Parodi. **Document type:** newsletter. **Description:** Covers association news and events.

003   UK
▼**UNIVERSITY OF CENTRAL ENGLAND IN BIRMINGHAM. FACULTY OF COMPUTING & INFORMATION STUDIES. RESEARCH PAPERS.** 1996. irreg. £10 for paper version; paper and floppy £15. University of Central England in Birmingham, Faculty of Computing & Information Studies, Perry Barr, Birmingham B42 2SU, England. TEL 44-121-331-5300. FAX 44-121-356-2875. TELEX 334684 UCEBIR. (also avail. in diskette format)

003   SA   ISSN 1021-1500
UNIVERSITY OF TRANSKEI. DEPARTMENT OF INFORMATION SCIENCE. OCCASIONAL PAPERS. (Text in English) 1993. irreg. University of Transkei, Department of Information Science, Private Bag X1, Umtata 5100, South Africa. **Document type:** academic/scholarly publication.

UNIWERSYTET GDANSKI. WYDZIAL EKONOMIKI PRODUKCJI. ZESZYTY NAUKOWE. CYBERNETYKA EKONOMICZNA I INFORMATYKA. see COMPUTERS — Cybernetics

001.539   US
URBAN & REGIONAL INFORMATION SYSTEMS ASSOCIATION. ANNUAL CONFERENCE PROCEEDINGS. 1980. a. (in several vols.). $50 to non-members; members $25. Urban & Regional Information Systems Association, URISA Secretariat, 900 Second St., N.E., Ste. 304, Washington, DC 20002. TEL 202-289-1685. FAX 202-289-1850. adv. contact: Tegan Parodi. abstr. **Document type:** proceedings. **Description:** Includes papers on the use of information systems technology in all facets of land-use planning.

COMPUTERS — Machine Theory

001.534   US   ISSN 1041-4517
QA75.5
A C M ANNUAL COMPUTER SCIENCE CONFERENCE. PROCEEDINGS. 1984. a. Association for Computing Machinery, 1515 Broadway, 17th Fl., New York, NY 10036. TEL 212-869-7440. FAX 212-869-0481. TELEX 421686.
—BLDSC (0578.623000).

THEORETICAL COMPUTER SCIENCE. see COMPUTERS — Theory Of Computing

COMPUTERS — Microcomputers

see also Computers–Personal Computers

A P L QUOTE QUAD. see COMPUTERS — Computer Programming

001.6   621.381   US   ISSN 1086-881X
QA75.5
A S - 400 SYSTEMS MANAGEMENT. 1973. m. $42 (Canada $54; Europe $102; elsewhere $198) (free to qualified personnel) (effective 1997). Hunter Publishing Limited Partnership, 2101 S. Arlington Heights Rd., Ste 150, Arlington Heights, IL 60005. TEL 847-427-9512. FAX 847-427-2097. E-mail: 71333.730@compuserve.com. Ed. Renee Robbins. adv.; bk.rev. circ. 55,279. **Indexed:** ABI Inform., Comput.Cont., Comput.Lit.Ind., Graph.Arts Lit.Abstr., INSPEC, Resour.Ctr.Ind. **Document type:** trade publication.
—BLDSC (1738.547000); CISTI; KR SourceOne; UMI; UnCover. **CCC.**
    Formerly (until Dec. 1995): 3 X - 400 Systems Management (ISSN 1070-6097); Systems 3X - 400 (ISSN 1055-7768); Systems 3X and A S World (ISSN 1044-1239); Small System World (ISSN 0272-5444); System - 3 World.
    Description: For managers of IBM minicomputers, RS-6000 workstations and related products.

A T M USER. (Asynchronous Transfer Mode) see COMPUTERS — Personal Computers

A V VIDEO & MULTIMEDIA PRODUCER; production and presentation technology. see COMMUNICATIONS — Video

621.381   001.642   US   ISSN 0741-997X
ABSOLUTE REFERENCE; the journal for 1-2-3 and Symphony users. 1983. m. $60. Que Publishing Corporation, Box 90, Carmel, IN 46032-0090. TEL 800-428-8331. Ed. David Maguiness. adv. (back issues avail.) **Indexed:** Comput.Lit.Ind.
—CCC.
    Description: For 1-2-3 and Symphony users. Features instructional articles as well as columns on spreadsheets and product reviews.

621.381   US
ACCESS (NEW YORK, 1983); the consulting services newsletter. 1983. m. $24. Charles River Computers, 575 Lexington Ave., Ste. 4, New York, NY 10022-6102. TEL 212-371-3500. Ed. Mark Dobson. adv.; bk.rev. circ. 9,706. (back issues avail.) **Description:** Primarily for Charles River Computers clients. Offers evaluations and comparisons of different software, hardware and peripheral packages for personal computer.

ACCESS (RESEARCH TRIANGLE PARK). see SCIENCES: COMPREHENSIVE WORKS — Computer Applications

621.381   US
ACCESS (ROCKVILLE). m. United Communications Group, 11300 Rockville Pike, Ste. 1100, Rockville, MD 20852. TEL 301-816-8950. Ed. Doug O'Boyle. adv.: page $1130.

ACCESS TO WANG; the magazine for Wang system users. see COMPUTERS — Data Communications And Data Transmission Systems

621.381   001.642   US   ISSN 1043-0768
ACKNOWLEDGE THE WINDOW LETTER. 1989. m. $245 (Canada $275; elsewhere $330). Mendham Technology Group, 144 Talmadge Rd., Box 11, Mendham, NJ 07945. TEL 201-543-2273. FAX 201-543-6033. Ed. Carole Patton. bk.rev. circ. 2,500. (looseleaf format)
●Also available online. Vendor(s): Information Access Co.
Also available on CD-ROM.
    Description: Covers news, product reviews, and presents information on new software applications for users of Microsoft Windows and Presentation Manager.

ANDREW SEYBOLD'S OUTLOOK. see COMPUTERS — Computer Industry

APPLE EDUCATION NEWS; an information service for educators and trainers. see COMPUTERS — Personal Computers

AUSTRALIAN & NEW ZEALAND P C USER. see COMPUTERS — Personal Computers

AUSTRALIAN MACWORLD. see COMPUTERS — Personal Computers

AUSTRALIAN PERSONAL COMPUTER. see COMPUTERS — Personal Computers

A2 - CENTRAL. see COMPUTERS — Personal Computers

B A U D. (Big Apple Users Digest) see COMPUTERS — Personal Computers

621.381   001.642   SP   ISSN 0210-3923
B I T. (Boletin Informativo de Telecomunicacion) (Editions in Italian, Japanese, Spanish) 1976. bi-m. 5300 ptas. Asociacion Espanola de Ingenieros de Telecomunicacion, C. General Arrando, 38, 28010 Madrid, Spain. TEL 91-4197418. FAX 1-410-11-55. Ed. Carmen Fernandez Ruiz. circ. 6,000. **Indexed:** Ind.SST.

B U G NEWSLETTER. (Brevard Users Group) see COMPUTERS — Personal Computers

BALTIMORE SANYO USER'S NEWSLETTER. see COMPUTERS — Personal Computers

621.381   BE
BELGIUM MICRO.* (Text in English, Flemish and French) 10/yr. Informatic Assistance, Rue J. Cuylits 39, 1180 Brussels, Belgium. circ. 110,000.

BOCOEX INDEX. see COMPUTERS — Computer Industry

070.5 384 621.381   US   ISSN 1043-6065
BOVE & RHODES INSIDE REPORT ON DESKTOP PUBLISHING AND MULTIMEDIA. 1986. m. $395. Bove & Rhoades, Box 1289, Gualala, CA 95445-1289. TEL 707-884-4413; 800-222-4863. FAX 707-884-4421. Eds. Tony Bove, Cheryl Rhodes. **Document type:** newsletter.
    Formerly (until 1988): Bove and Rhodes Inside Report.

BUG REPORT. see COMPUTERS — Personal Computers

BUILDERS' COMPUTER NEWSLETTER. see BUILDING AND CONSTRUCTION

621.381   US   ISSN 1053-1343
BUSINESSMAC. 1990. m. John G. Catalano, Ed. & Pub., 148 Bon Air Center, Greenbrae, CA 94904. TEL 415-461-2227. FAX 415-461-2249. bk.rev. circ. 1,500. **Document type:** newsletter.

BYTE. see COMPUTERS — Computer Systems

C A L I C O JOURNAL. (Computer Assisted Language & Instruction Consortium) see EDUCATION — Computer Applications

C U AMIGA. see COMPUTERS — Personal Computers

621.381   US   ISSN 0887-9141
T385   CODEN: CADEEL
CADENCE (AUSTIN).* 1986. m. $39.95 (Canada and Mexico $49.95; elsewhere $105). Ariel Communications, Inc., Box 203550, Austin, TX 78720-3550. TEL 512-250-1700. FAX 512-250-1016. Ed. Kathleen Maher. adv.: B&W page $3500, color page $4500. circ. 60,000. **Indexed:** Microcomp.Ind.
—BLDSC (2946.380000); CISTI; KR SourceOne; SWETS; UMI; UnCover. **CCC.**

CAMPUS-WIDE INFORMATION SYSTEMS. see LIBRARY AND INFORMATION SCIENCES — Computer Applications

CAPITAL P C MONITOR; users helping users. see COMPUTERS — Computer Networks

CATALYST (MENLO PARK). see COMPUTERS — Computer Assisted Instruction

621.381   US   ISSN 1071-7749
CHICAGO COMPUTER GUIDE.* m. Micro Computer Learning Center, Inc., 954 W. Washington Blvd., St 510, Chicago, IL 60607-2224. TEL 312-332-0419. Ed. Armond Mussey. adv.: pa $1400. circ. 50,000.
—KR SourceOne.

001.6 621.381   GW   ISSN 0170-6632
CODEN: CHIPDP
CHIP; das Mikrocomputer-Magazin. 1978. m. DM.120. Vogel Verlag und Druck GmbH & Co. KG, Max-Planck-Str. 7-9, 97082 Wuerzburg, Germany. TEL 49-931-4182335. FAX 49-931-4182905. (Subscr. to: Vogel Verlag, 97064 Wuerzburg, Germany; Dist. in US by: Vogel Europublishing, Inc., 632 Sunflower Ct., San Ramos, CA 94583. TEL 510-648-1170. FAX 510-648-1171) Ed. Rainer Grabowski. adv.: B&W page DM.15890, color page DM.22130; trim 266 x 185; adv. contact: Gabriele Groitzsch. bk.rev.; circ. 227,888 (controlled). (back issues avail.) **Indexed:** INSPEC (1979-1992).
Document type: trade publication.
—BLDSC (3181.123600); AskIEEE; CISTI; KR SourceOne; SWETS. **CCC.**

621.381   US   ISSN 0896-8985
QA76.76.A65
CIRCUIT CELLAR INK; the computer applications journal. 1988. m. $21.95 (Canada & Mexico $31.95; elsewhere $49.95) (effective 1998); newsstand price: $3.95. Circuit Cellar, Inc., 4 Park St., Ste. 20, Vernon, CT 06066. TEL 860-875-2199. FAX 860-871-0411. E-mail: edit@circellar.com; URL: http://www.circellar.com/. Ed. Ken Davidson; Pub. Daniel Rodrigues. adv.: B&W page $2100, color page $2350; trim 7 x 10; adv. contact: Sue Hodge. illus.; index; circ. 35,000 (paid). (back issues avail.) **Indexed:** Comput.Ind. **Document type:** trade publication.
—BLDSC (3198.835587); KR SourceOne; SWETS.
Description: Dedicated to high-tech hardware design and software applications.

CLOSING THE GAP. see EDUCATION — Computer Applications

621.381 200   US   ISSN 1053-752X
COMMUNAL COMPUTING NEWS. 1987. q. Communal Computing, Inc., 3222 Brooklawn Court, Chevy Chase, MD 20815. TEL 301-656-9524. FAX 301-656-9564. Ed. Glenn S. Easton. adv.: page $695. circ. 3,500. **Document type:** newsletter.

COMPULIFE'S MICROMARKET BLUE DISC. see COMPUTERS — Computer Sales

COMPUTER (LOS ALAMITOS). see COMPUTERS

621.381   US   ISSN 1067-389X
COMPUTER JOURNAL (TULSA). 1989. m. $24 (foreign $36). Adventure Publishing (Tulsa), Box 700686, Tulsa, OK 74170-0686. TEL 918-621-2131; 800-726-7667. FAX 918-621-2134. E-mail: tcj@tcpi.com. Ed. Cheryl Cooper. R&P contact: Cheryl Cooper. adv. contact: Cheryl Cooper. circ. 70,000. (tabloid format) **Indexed:** A.S.& T.Ind. **Document type:** trade publication.
Description: Shows business people how computing technology can address their business needs. Presents the latest technology and trends in a non-technical way.

621.381   US
COMPUTER LETTER; business issues in technology. 1985. 40/yr. $595 (foreign $695). Technologic Partners, Inc., 120 Wooster St., 6th Fl., New York, NY 10012. TEL 212-343-1900. FAX 212-343-1915. E-mail: klein@technologicp.com. Ed. Richard A. Shaffer; Pub. Richard A. Shaffer. R&P contact: Matthew Klein. (looseleaf format; back issues avail.) **Document type:** newsletter.
Description: Guide to business issues in computing and examines strategic planning.

COMPUTER RETAILERS' GUIDE. see COMPUTERS — Personal Computers

COMPUTER SHOPPER; the computer magazine for direct buyers. see COMPUTERS — Computer Sales

COMPUTER USER (MINNEAPOLIS). see COMPUTERS

COMPUTERS AND THE HUMANITIES. see HUMANITIES; COMPREHENSIVE WORKS — Computer Applications

COMPUTERS IN ACCOUNTING. see BUSINESS AND ECONOMICS — Computer Applications

004 020   US   ISSN 1041-7915
Z678.9.A1   CODEN: CPLIE8
COMPUTERS IN LIBRARIES. Variant title: C I L. 1981. 10/yr. $89.95 in U.S.; Canada and Mexico $99.95; elsewhere $107.95 (effective 1997). Information Today, Inc., 143 Old Marlton Pike, Medford, NJ 08055-8750. TEL 609-654-6266. FAX 609-654-4309. Ed. David Hoffman. adv.; bk.rev.; software rev.; bibl. astr. circ. 5,100. (back issues avail.) **Indexed:** C.I.J.E., C.L.I., Comput.Cont., Comput.Lit.Ind., INSPEC, Leg.Info.Manage.Ind., Leg.Per., LHTN, Lib.Lit., LISA, Microcomp.Ind., PCR2, Tr.& Indus.Ind.
●Also available online. Vendor(s): Information Access Co., NewsNet, UMI.
—BLDSC (3394.924000); AskIEEE; CISTI; KR SourceOne; Linda Hall; SWETS; UMI; UnCover. **CCC.**
Formerly (until 1989): Small Computers in Libraries (ISSN 0275-6722); Which incorporated (1986-1988): Systems Librarian and Automation Review (ISSN 0890-8354); (1985-1987): Bulletin Board Systems (ISSN 0882-990X); And (1986-1987): Public Computing (ISSN 0884-9498).
Description: Covers the use of microcomputers in libraries, with applications, practical information and procedures.

COMPUTERS IN THE SCHOOLS; the interdisciplinary journal of practice, theory, and applied research. see EDUCATION — Computer Applications

COMPUTERTALK DIRECTORY OF MEDICAL COMPUTER SYSTEMS. see MEDICAL SCIENCES — Computer Applications

COMPUTERTALK FOR THE PHARMACIST. see PHARMACY AND PHARMACOLOGY — Computer Applications

COMPUTERTALK PHARMACY SYSTEMS BUYERS GUIDE. see PHARMACY AND PHARMACOLOGY — Computer Applications

COMPUTERWORLD; newsweekly for information technology leaders. see COMPUTERS

COMPUTERWORLD CLIENT - SERVER JOURNAL. see COMPUTERS

621.381   US
COMPUTING TIMES. m. $10.50 (effective Jul. 1995). Triad Publications, Box 14018, Tulsa, OK 74159-1018. TEL 918-585-8564. Ed. Brent Morrison; Pub. Brent Morrison. adv. contact: Paul Karady. bk.rev. circ. 40,000. **Document type:** trade publication.
●Also available online.

621.381   US
COMPUTOREDGE. 1982. w. $85. Byte Buyer, Inc., Box 83086, San Diego, CA 92138-1833. TEL 619-573-0315. FAX 619-573-0205. E-mail: editor@computoredge.com. Ed. John San Filippo; Pub. John Dunning. R&P contact: Leah Steward. adv.: page $1157; adv. contact: Elvira Phipps. circ. 80,000. **Document type:** consumer publication.
Description: Contains non-technical, entertaining articles on all aspects of computers: hardware, software, technology, productivity, advice, and personal experience.

CYBERLOG; library of applied medical software. see MEDICAL SCIENCES — Computer Applications

D E C U S MAGAZINE. (Digital Equipment Computer Users Society) see COMPUTERS

D E C USER; the independent guide to DEC computing. (Digital Equipment Corp.) see COMPUTERS

621.381   US
D XERS MAGAZINE.* m. $15. D Xers Magazine, RR 1 Box 121-A, Elloree, SC 29047-9801. Ed. Gus Browning.

DATAPRO DIRECTORY OF MICROCOMPUTER HARDWARE. see COMPUTERS — Computer Industry Directories

DATAPRO DIRECTORY OF MICROCOMPUTER SOFTWARE. see COMPUTERS — Computer Industry Directories

621.381   US
DATAPRO HARDWARE VENDOR DIRECTORY. 3 base vols. (plus m. updates). $1008. Datapro Information Services Group (Subsidiary of: McGraw-Hill, Inc.), 600 Delran Pkwy., Delran, NJ 08075. TEL 609-764-0100; 800-328-2776. **Document type:** directory.
Formerly: Datapro Reports on Microcomputers.

DEAL; il mensile di informatica e telecomunicazioni. see BUSINESS AND ECONOMICS — Office Equipment And Services

621.381   FR   ISSN 1148-4675
DECISION MICRO.* 1982. w. Groupe Tests, 26 rue d'Oradour sur Glance, 75504 Paris Cedex 15, France. TEL 42-40-22-01. FAX 42-45-59-43. TELEX 215 205 GRTESTS F. Ed. Jean-Francois Ruiz. circ. 25,474.
—SWETS. **CCC.**
Formerly (until 1990): Decision Informatique (ISSN 0293-3896)

DENTAL COMPUTER NEWSLETTER. see MEDICAL SCIENCES — Computer Applications

621.381   US   ISSN 1061-1118
TA174   CODEN: DESNEQ
DESIGN NET.* 1987. m. $34.95 (Canada $44.95; elsewhere $105). Ariel Communications, Inc., Box 203550, Austin, TX 78720-3550. TEL 512-250-1700. FAX 512-250-1016. Ed. Aubrey McAuley. adv. circ. 50,000. **Indexed:** Microcomp.Ind.
—AskIEEE; CISTI; KR SourceOne.
Formerly (until 1991): Microcad News (ISSN 0895-4151)

621.381 070.5   US   ISSN 1042-3923
DESKTOP COMMUNICATIONS.* 1989. bi-m. $24. International Desktop Communications, Ltd., 342 Madison Ave., Ste. 622, New York, NY 10173-0002. TEL 212-768-7666. FAX 272-768-0288. Ed. Pauline Ores. adv.: B&W page $3900, color page $5000. bk.rev. circ. 73,000. **Indexed:** Abstr.Bull.Inst.Pap.Chem.
—KR SourceOne.
Formerly: I T C Desktop.
Description: Helps small business, corporate and individual computer users design and implement innovative and effective newsletters, reports, presentations and other business communications, including graphics.

621.381   GW   ISSN 0936-8833
DESKTOP DIALOG. 1987. m. DM.115 (foreign DM.142) (effective 1996). Druckspiegel Verlagsgesellschaft mbH und Co., Borsigstr. 1-3, 63150 Heusenstamm, Germany. TEL 49-6104-606303. FAX 49-6104-606399. E-mail: 100547.3200@compuserve.com. Ed. Manfred Diehl. adv.: B&W page DM.5400, color page DM.6900; trim 188 x 270. circ. 10,900. (back issues avail.) **Indexed:** WPM. **Document type:** trade publication.
Description: Provides information for digital publishing and multimedia users.

621.381   US
DESKTOP SOFTWARE & SOLUTIONS (INTERNATIONAL). 2 base vols. (plus m. updates). $1121 to new subscr.; renewals $958 (effective 1996). Datapro Information Services Group (Subsidiary of: McGraw-Hill, Inc.), 600 Delran Pkwy., Delran, NJ 08075. TEL 609-764-0100; 800-328-3776. FAX 609-764-8953.

004   US
DIGITAL CHICAGO;* the resource for Chicagoland's creative community. 1989. bi-m. $15. Peregrine Marketing Associates, 5225 Old Orchard Rd., Ste. 39, Skokie, IL 60077-1027. TEL 847-439-6575. E-mail: jdees@digitalchi.com. Ed. Jennifer Dees. R&P contact: Jennifer Dees. adv.: page $1265; adv. contact: Phyllis Wier. bk.rev. circ. 20,000. **Document type:** trade publication.
Formerly (until 1996): Mac - Chicago (ISSN 1045-5825)
Description: Provides local and regional information, including news and reviews of software and hardware, profiles of local users, and a resource directory.

COMPUTERS — MICROCOMPUTERS

070.5 004.16 686.2 SA   ISSN 1024-8552
DIGITAL IMAGING & PUBLISHING. (Text in English) 1988. 9/yr. R.104 (southern Africa R.170; elsewhere R.540) (effective 1997). Graphix Publications (Pty) Ltd., P.O. Box 751119, Gardenview 2047, South Africa. TEL 27-11-6224800. FAX 27-11-6222480. E-mail: graphix@aztec.co.za. Ed. Colleen Bate; Pub. Brian Strickland. adv. contact: Dyelan Copeland. **Indexed:** WPM. **Document type:** trade publication.
    Formerly: D T P Today (ISSN 1016-1287)
    Description: Covers electronic publishing and pre-press.

621.381   US   ISSN 1056-7038
    CODEN: DMEDEG
DIGITAL MEDIA: A SEYBOLD REPORT. m. $395 (Canada $401; elsewhere $413). Seybold Publications, 528 E. Baltimore Ave., Box 644, Media, PA 19063. TEL 610-565-2480; 800-325-3830. FAX 610-565-1858. Ed. Mitch Radcliffe; Pub. Jonathan Seybold. **Indexed:** INSPEC (1991-). **Document type:** trade publication.
    ●Also available online. Vendor(s): Information Access Co.
    —AskIEEE; KR SourceOne; SWETS.

004.16   US
DIMENSIONS. 1984. q. free (foreign $30). Pick Systems Inc., 1691 Browning, Irvine, CA 92606. TEL 714-261-7425. FAX 714-250-8187. E-mail: dmagazine@picksys.com. Ed. M. Dennis Hill. R&P contact: M. Dennis Hill. adv. contact: Sharm Cressy. circ. 25,000. **Document type:** trade publication.
    —KR SourceOne.
    Formerly: Pickworld (ISSN 1066-2154)

621.381   US
DISKETTE GAZETTE.* 1986. m. free. International Datawares Inc., 804 Hamann Dr., San Jose, CA 95117-2025. TEL 408-262-6660. FAX 408-262-8906. Ed. Delfina Daves. bk.rev. circ. 75,000.

658.478   US   ISSN 1044-789X
QA76.5   CODEN: DDJOEB
DR. DOBB'S JOURNAL; software tools for the professional programmer. 1977. m. $34.95 (Canada & Mexico $45; elsewhere $70) (effective 1996). (Markt and Technik Verlag Akiengeselltschaft, GW) Miller Freeman, Inc., 600 Harrison St., San Francisco, CA 94107. TEL 415-905-2200; 800-956-1215. FAX 415-905-2232. (Subscr. to: Box 8024, Boulder, CO 80306-8024. TEL 800-456-1215. FAX 303-661-1885) Ed. Jonathan Ericson. adv.; bk.rev.; charts; illus.; stat. circ. 184,050. (also avail. in microform from UMI; back issues avail.; reprint service avail.) **Indexed:** ASCA, Compumath, Comput.Cont., Comput.Dtbs., Comput.Ind., INSPEC, Microcomp.Ind., PMR. **Document type:** trade publication.
    ●Also available online. Vendor(s): Information Access Co.
    —BLDSC (3606.590000); AskIEEE; CISTI; Ei; Genuine Article; KR SourceOne; Linda Hall; SWETS; UMI; UnCover. CCC.
    Former titles: (until 1989): Dr. Dobb's Journal of Software Tools (ISSN 0888-3076); (until 1986): Dr. Dobb's Journal: Software Tools for Advanced Programmers; (in 1984): Dr. Dobb's Journal for the Experienced in Microcomputing (ISSN 0278-6508); (until 1984): Dr. Dobb's Journal for Users of Small Computer Systems; (until 1981): Dr. Dobb's Journal of Computer Calisthenics and Orthodontia (ISSN 0190-1435)
    Description: Delivers the latest programming languages, algorithms, program listings, operating systems, and more.

EARLY CHILDHOOD TEACHER; instructor's magazine for preschool and primary professionals. see *EDUCATION*

EDUCATION TECHNOLOGY NEWS. see *COMPUTERS — Computer Assisted Instruction*

621.381 621.381   UK
EMBEDDED SYSTEMS ENGINEERING. 1985. m. £15. Electronic Design Automation Ltd., 31-33 High Holborn, London WC1V 6BD, England. TEL 44-171-404-0564. FAX 44-171-831-2057. Ed. J. Kenyon. circ. 12,757. (back issues avail.) **Document type:** trade publication.
    Incorporates (in 1993): Microsystem Design (ISSN 0269-1477)

004.16   GW
ENGINEERING TODAY. bi-m. DM.56 (effective 1997). I W T Magazin Verlags GmbH, Bahnhofstr. 36, 85591 Vaterstetten, Germany. TEL 49-8106-350-0. FAX 49-8106-350126. URL: http://www.iwtnet.de. Ed. Karl Mayer. **Document type:** trade publication.
    Formerly: MicroStation Journal.
    Description: For all MicroStation users, decision makers, dealers and education companies.

621.381   US
FAULKNER'S LOCAL AREA NETWORKING. 1985. base vol. (plus m. updates). $715 (effective 1993). Faulkner Information Services, Inc., 114 Cooper Center, 7905 Browning Rd., Pennsauken, NJ 08109-4319. TEL 609-662-2070. FAX 609-662-3380. Ed. Larry Abbott. (looseleaf format)
    ●Also available on CD-ROM.
    Formerly: Microcomputer Communications.
    Description: Product and management reports describing microcomputer communications technology and services; includes LAN hardware and software, micro-host links, gateways, bridges, routers, and asynchronous communications software packages.

621.381   US
FAULKNER'S MICROCOMPUTERS AND SOFTWARE. 1983. 2 base vols. (plus m. updates). $925 (bi-m. CD-ROM $1013) (effective 1993). Faulkner Information Services, Inc., 114 Cooper Center, 7905 Browning Rd., Pennsauken, NJ 08109-4319. TEL 609-662-2070. FAX 609-662-3380. Ed. Betsy Yokum. (looseleaf format) **Indexed:** Comput.Lit.Ind.
    ●Also available on CD-ROM.
    Former titles: Faulkner Report on Microcomputers and Software; (until 1987): MicroWorld (ISSN 0738-0453)
    Description: Analysis and interpretation of the leading PC systems, PC-based software packages and peripherals.

621.381   US
FAULKNER'S MINICOMPUTERS REPORTS. 1970. 2 base vols. (plus m. updates). $1065 (effective 1993). Faulkner Information Services, Inc., 114 Cooper Center, 7905 Browning Rd., Pennsauken, NJ 08109-4319. TEL 609-662-2070. FAX 609-662-3380. Ed. Janet Mann. (looseleaf format)
    Formerly: Auerbach Minicomputers Report.
    Description: Management and product reports covering mid-level computers, workstations, and related peripherals.

621.381   US
FLEXLINES. 1984. 6/yr. $30 (foreign $60). Data Access Corporation, 14000 S.W. 119th Ave., Miami, FL 33186. TEL 305-238-0012. FAX 305-238-0017. TELEX 469021 DATA ACCESS CI. Ed. Beverly Horning-Gore; Pub. C.L. Casanave. adv.; bk.rev. circ. 5,000. **Document type:** trade publication.

FORTH DIMENSIONS. see *COMPUTERS — Computer Programming*

621.381   US
FROBBER.* q. $195. (Tri-Comp Polytechnical Inc.) FROBCO, c/o Embarcadero Venture, Box 2600, Menlo Park, CA 94026-2600. Ed. Candace L. Brown. adv.; circ. 200 (controlled).
    Description: Instructs Atari computer users.

G R M U G NEWSLETTER. (Great River Microcomputer Users Group) see *COMPUTERS — Personal Computers*

621.381   IT   ISSN 1122-9195
GUIDA ALLE APPLICAZIONI MACINTOSH. Variant title: Pagine Mac. 1990. s-a. Gruppo Editoriale J C E, Via Ferri 6, 20092 Cinisello Balsmao (MI), Italy. TEL 39-2-660251. FAX 39-2-6127620. TELEX 352376 JCE MIL I. E-mail: info@jce.it; URL: http://www.jce.it. Ed. Fausto Gimondi. adv.: B&W page L.5500000, color page L.7000000; trim 210 X 280. circ. 28,000 (paid).
    ●Also available on CD-ROM.

H A L - P C USER JOURNAL. (Houston Area League of P C Users, Inc.) see *COMPUTERS — Personal Computers*

621.381   US   ISSN 0892-2829
QA76.8.H48
THE H P CHRONICLE. (Hewlett-Packard); the independent newspaper for Hewlett-Packard computers users. 1983. m. $45 (foreign $75) (effective 1995 & 1996). Publications & Communications, Inc., 12416 Hymeadow Dr., Austin, TX 78750-1896. TEL 512-250-9023; 800-678-9724. FAX 512-331-3900. adv.: B&W page $3586, color page $4336; trim 10 3/4 x 14 1/2. circ. 17,000. (tabloid format; back issues avail.) **Document type:** trade publication.
    —KR SourceOne; SWETS.
    Formerly: Chronicle (Austin) (ISSN 0741-0522)

621.381   US   ISSN 0896-145X
QA76.8.H48
H P PROFESSIONAL; the independent magazine for Hewlett-Packard computing professionals. vol.6, 1992. m. free to qualified personnel; foreign $60. Cardinal Business Media, Inc., 1300 Virginia Dr., Ste. 400, Fort Washington, PA 19034-3225. TEL 215-643-8000. FAX 215-643-4827. Ed. Charlie Simpson; Pub. Leslie Ringe. R&P contact: Charlie Simpson. adv. contact: Leslie Ringe. circ. 30,000. **Indexed:** Microcomp.Ind. **Document type:** trade publication.
    ●Also available online. Vendor(s): Information Access Co.
    —BLDSC (4335.262230); KR SourceOne; SWETS; UMI.

004   US
H - SCOOP. 1980. m. $28 (Canada $32; elsewhere $42). Quikdata, Inc., 2618 Penn Circle, Sheboygan, WI 53081. TEL 414-452-4172. FAX 414-452-4344. Ed. Henry Fale. bk.rev. circ. 2,900. **Document type:** newsletter.
    Description: For Heath-Zenith computer users. Articles cover hardware, software and applications.

621.381   US   ISSN 0018-1153
QA76.8.H16   CODEN: HPJOAX
HEWLETT-PACKARD JOURNAL. 1949. bi-m. free to qualified personnel. Hewlett Packard Co. (Palo Alto), 3000 Hanover St., Palo Alto, CA 94304. TEL 415-857-2387. FAX 415-857-2157. E-mail: Steve_Beitler@hp.com; URL: http://www.hp.com/hpj/journal.html. Ed. Steve Beitler. R&P contact: Susan Wright. charts; illus.; stat.; index; circ. 130,000 (controlled). (also avail. in microform from UMI; reprint service avail. from ISI,UMI) **Indexed:** AESIS, ASCA, CAD CAM Abstr., Comput.Cont., Comput.Dtbs., Curr.Cont., INSPEC, Intl.Civil Eng.Abstr., Sh.& Vib.Dig., Soft.Abstr.Eng., Tel.Abstr. **Document type:** academic/scholarly publication, corporate report.
    ●Also available online. Vendor(s): Information Access Co., Knight-Ridder Information, Inc. Also available on CD-ROM.
    —BLDSC (4302.000000); AskIEEE; CISTI; Ei; Genuine Article; KR SourceOne; Linda Hall; UMI; UnCover.
    Description: Technical contributions by HP personnel.

001.6 621.381   US   ISSN 0747-055X
HOME COMPUTER MAGAZINE.* 1981. 10/yr. $25. Emerald Valley Publishing Co., Box 21705, Eugene, OR 97402-0411. TEL 503-485-8796. Ed. Gary Kaplan. bk.rev. circ. 250,000. (back issues avail.)
    Former titles: 99'er Home Computer Magazine; 99'er Magazine.

HOME OFFICE COMPUTING; building better businesses with technology. see *COMPUTERS — Personal Computers*

COMPUTERS — MICROCOMPUTERS

621.381 US ISSN 0272-1732
QA76.5 CODEN: IEMIDZ
I E E E MICRO. 1981. bi-m. $270. (Institute of Electrical and Electronic Engineers, Inc.) I E E E Computer Society Press, 10662 Los Vaqueros Circle, Box 3014, Los Alamitos, CA 90720-1264. TEL 714-821-8380; 800-678-4333. FAX 714-821-4641. E-mail: customer.service@ieee.org; webmaster@computer.org; URL: http://computer.org/pubs/micro/micro.htm. Ed. Stephen Diamond. adv.: B&W page $2290, color page $3390; adv. contact: Heidi Rex. bk.rev.; bibl.; charts; illus.; tr.lit.; index. circ. 16,342. (also avail. in microfilm from EEE; back issues avail.) Indexed: A.I.Abstr., A.S.& T.Ind., ASCA, Compumath., Comput.Bus., Comput.Cont., Comput.Dtbs., Curr.Cont., Cyb.Abstr., Ind.Sci.Rev., INSPEC, PCR2, Robomat., Sci.Cit.Ind., SSCI. **Document type:** proceedings.
● Also available online.
—BLDSC (4362.999500); AskIEEE; CISTI; Ei; Genuine Article; KR SourceOne; Linda Hall; SWETS; UMI; UnCover. **CCC.**
Description: For advanced microcomputer users. Articles on chips, systems, applications, software, hardware design, new technical developments and microcomputer law and standards.

I E E PROCEEDINGS - SOFTWARE ENGINEERING. (Institution of Electrical Engineers) see COMPUTERS — Software

I E SOLUTIONS. (Institute of Industrial Engineers) see ENGINEERING — Industrial Engineering

INDIVIDUAL INVESTOR'S GUIDE TO COMPUTERIZED INVESTING. see BUSINESS AND ECONOMICS — Investments

621.381 GW ISSN 0941-6048
INFODOC; Technologien fuer Information und Dokumentation. 6/yr. DM.162 (foreign DM.174) (effective 1996). F B O - Fachverlag fuer Buero- und Organisationstechnik GmbH, Taunusstr. 54, 65183 Wiesbaden, Germany. TEL 49-611-534-0. FAX 49-611-534430. Ed. Heinz Scharfenberg. adv. contact: Cornelia Maschke. bk.rev. (back issues avail.) **Document type:** academic/scholarly publication.
—AskIEEE; KR SourceOne; SWETS.
Formerly (until 1992): Mikrodok (ISSN 0344-8010)

621.381 US ISSN 0895-8726
INFONETICS.* 1987. irreg. Infonetics Research Institute, 255 W. Julian St., Ste. 402, San Jose, CA 95110-2406. TEL 408-298-7999. FAX 408-298-2073. Ed. Michael Howard.

621.381 352 US
INFOTECH REPORT. m. $130 (effective 1997). International City - County Management Association, 777 N. Capitol St., N.E., Ste. 500, Washington, DC 20002-4201. TEL 202-962-3595; 800-745-8780. FAX 202-962-3500. Ed. Christine Ulrich. R&P contact: Christine Ulrich. index. (back issues avail.) **Document type:** newsletter.
Formerly: Microsoftware News.
Description: Devoted to computer and telecommunications applications for local governments and public agencies.

INFOTECTURE EUROPE; fortnightly European newsletter on the on-line information industry. see COMPUTERS — Computer Networks

621.381 338 US ISSN 0199-6649
QA75.5 CODEN: INWODU
INFOWORLD; the voice of personal computing in the enterprise. 1979. w. $145. InfoWorld Publishing (Subsidiary of: I D G Communications), 155 Bovet Rd., Ste. 800, San Mateo, CA 94402. TEL 415-572-7341; 800-227-8365. FAX 415-358-1269. URL: http://192.216.48.63/. Ed. Ed Foster; Pub. Sandy Reed. adv.; bk.rev.; illus.; stat.; index. circ. 205,000. (also avail. in microfilm from UMI; back issues avail.; reprint service avail. from UMI) Indexed: ABI Inform., Bus.Comput.Ind., CAD CAM Abstr., Can.B.P.I., Comput.Bus., Comput.Cont., Comput.Dtbs., Comput.Indus.Up., INSPEC, LAMP, Microcomp.Ind., Pers.Lit., PROMT, PSI, Resour.Ctr.Ind., Robomat., Tel.Abstr. **Document type:** newspaper, trade publication.
● Also available online. Vendor(s): Information Access Co., Lexis-Nexis, UMI.
—BLDSC (4499.360000); AskIEEE; CASDDS; CISTI; Genuine Article; KR SourceOne; UMI. **CCC.**
Formerly (until vol.2): Intelligent Machines Journal.
Description: News and reviews on PC hardware, software, peripherals and networking.

INTERNATIONAL JOURNAL OF MINI AND MICROCOMPUTERS. see COMPUTERS — Minicomputers

005 US ISSN 1072-4451
QA76.6 CODEN: PSMIE7
INTERNATIONAL SYMPOSIUM ON MICROARCHITECTURE. PROCEEDINGS. 4th, 1971. a. price varies. (Institute of Electrical and Electronics Engineers, Inc.) I E E E Computer Society Press, 10662 Los Vaqueros Circle, Los Alamitos, CA 90720-1264. TEL 714-821-8380. FAX 714-821-4641. (Co-publisher in alternate years: Association for Computing Machinery, Special Interest Group on Microcomputers) Ed. Cat Harris; Pub. Matt Loeb. adv. contact: Frieda Koester. bibl.; charts. Indexed: Comput.Cont. **Document type:** monographic series.
—BLDSC (5756.773000); Ei; UMI. **CCC.**
Former titles: Microprogramming and Microarchitecture Workshop. Proceedings; Microprogramming Workshop. Proceedings; (until 1983): Annual Microprogramming Workshop. Proceedings (ISSN 0194-1895); (1978-1982): Workshop on Microprogramming. Proceedings; (1974-1976?): Micro Proceedings (ISSN 0361-2163); (until 1973): Annual Workshop on Microprogramming. Preprints; (until 1972): Annual Workshop on Microprogramming. Conference Record; (until 1969): Joint A C M - SIGMICRO - I E E E Workshop on Microprogramming (Proceedings); (until 1968): A C M Workshop on Microprogramming (Proceedings).

INTERNATIONAL SYMPOSIUM ON MINI AND MICROCOMPUTERS. PROCEEDINGS. see COMPUTERS — Minicomputers

621.381 658.8 IE ISSN 0332-0197
CODEN: IRCODQ
IRISH COMPUTER. (Supplement avail.: Telecom Report (ISSN 0790-9268)) 1977. 12/yr. I£37 (U.K. £47; Europe £54; rest of world £79($119)) (effective 1998). Blairford International Ltd., CPG House, Glenageary Office Park, Dun Laoghaire, Co. Dublin, Ireland. TEL 353-1-2847777. FAX 353-1-2847584. Ed. Declan McColgan. adv.; bk.rev. circ. 6,000. Indexed: INSPEC (1981-). **Document type:** consumer publication.
—BLDSC (4571.250000); AskIEEE; KR SourceOne.
Incorporates: Micro News (ISSN 0790-6323); Which was formerly: Micro News and Market (ISSN 0790-0864)

J U G NEWSLETTER. (Jefferson State Computer Users Group) see COMPUTERS — Computer Networks

004.16 330 US ISSN 1063-2239
QA76.9.M3 CODEN: JEUCEZ
JOURNAL OF END USER COMPUTING;* the international journal of information user management. 1989. q. $65 to individuals; institutions $110. (Information Resources Management Association) Idea Group Publishing, 1331 E. Chocolate Ave., Hershey, PA 17033-1117. TEL 717-541-9150. FAX 717-541-9159. E-mail: 75364,3150@compuserve.com. Ed. Mo Adam Mahmood. adv.; bk.rev. circ. 250. (also avail. in microform from UMI) Indexed: B.P.I., Bus.Educ.Ind., INSPEC (1992-), Oper.Res.Manage.Sci., Qual.Contr.Appl.Stat. **Document type:** academic/scholarly publication.
—BLDSC (4977.870000); AskIEEE; Ei; KR SourceOne; SWETS; UMI; UnCover.
Formerly (until 1992): Journal of Microcomputer Systems Management (ISSN 1043-6464)
Description: Focuses on providing coverage of research findings and expert advice on the development, utilization and management of end-user computing in organizations.
Refereed Serial

004.693 UK ISSN 1084-8045
QA76.5 CODEN: JNCAF3
JOURNAL OF NETWORK AND COMPUTER APPLICATIONS. 1977. q. £76($128) to individuals; institutions £220 (effective 1998). Academic Press Ltd. (Subsidiary of: Harcourt Brace & Company Ltd.), 24-28 Oval Rd., London NW1 7DX, England. TEL 44-171-267-4466. FAX 44-171-482-2293. TELEX 25775 ACPRES G. URL: http://www.hbuk.co.uk/ap/jnca; http://www.europe.idealibrary.com/. (Subscr. to: Harcourt Brace & Company Ltd., Foots Cray High St., Sidcup, Kent DA14 5HP, England. TEL 44-181-300-3322. FAX 44-181-309-0807) Ed. H. Maurer. R&P contact: Catherine John. adv. contact: Nik Screen. (reprint service avail. from SWZ) Indexed: Abstr.Hum.Comp.Inter., ASCA, BMT, Br.Ceram.Abstr., Compumath, Comput.Abstr., Comput.Cont., Curr.Cont., Cyb.Abstr., INSPEC, SSCI. **Document type:** academic/scholarly publication.
—BLDSC (5021.410600); AskIEEE; CISTI; Ei; Genuine Article; KR SourceOne; Linda Hall; SWETS; UnCover. **CCC.**
Formerly (until vol.19, 1996): Journal of Microcomputer Applications (ISSN 0745-7138)
Description: Provides an interdisciplinary forum for the presentation of full-length papers and shorter communications on software engineering and on hardware design.

005.1 NE ISSN 1383-7621
QA76.5 CODEN: MMICDT
JOURNAL OF SYSTEMS ARCHITECTURE. 1975. m. fl.1334($767) (effective 1998). (European Association for Micro-Processing and Micro-Programming) North-Holland (Subsidiary of: Elsevier Science B.V.), P.O. Box 211, 1000 AE Amsterdam, Netherlands. TEL 31-20-4853911. FAX 31-20-4853598. TELEX 18582 ESPA NL. (Subscr. in the Americas to: Elsevier Science, Regional Sales Office, Box 945, New York, NY 10159-0945. TEL 212-633-3730. FAX 212-633-3680; Subscr. in Australasia and the Far East to: Elsevier Science (Singapore) Pte Ltd, No.1 Temasek Ave., No.17-01 Millenia Tower, Singapore 039192, Singapore. TEL 65-434-3727. FAX 65-337-2230; Subscr. in Japan to: Elsevier Science Japan, 9-15 Higashi-Azabu 1-chome, Minato-ku, Tokyo 106, Japan. TEL 81-3-5561-5033. FAX 81-3-5561-5047) Eds. G. Sami, L. Richter. adv.; bk.rev.; index. circ. 1,250. (also avail. in microform from UMI; back issues avail.; reprint service avail. from SWZ) Indexed: A.I.Abstr., ABI Inform., Abstr.Hum.Comp.Inter., ASCA, CAD CAM Abstr., Compumath, Comput.Abstr., Comput.Lit.Ind., Curr.Cont., Eng.Ind., INSPEC, Intl.Civil Eng.Abstr., Soft.Abstr.Eng. **Document type:** academic/scholarly publication.
—BLDSC (5068.066000); AskIEEE; CISTI; Ei; Genuine Article; KR SourceOne; Linda Hall; SWETS; UMI; UnCover. **CCC.**
Former titles (until 1996): Microprocessing and Microprogramming (ISSN 0165-6074); Euromicro Journal (ISSN 0167-3858); Euromicro Newsletter (ISSN 0303-1268)
Description: Publishes papers presenting the results of original research and technological progress.
Refereed Serial

COMPUTERS — MICROCOMPUTERS

621.381 US
K C COMPUTER USER. 1990. m. $12.95. Computer Reporter, Box 7810, Shawnee Mission, KS 66207-0810. TEL 913-451-1337. FAX 913-451-1698. Ed. Ron Goertzen. circ. 40,000. **Document type:** newspaper.

LIBRARY SOFTWARE REVIEW. see COMPUTERS — Software

LIBRARY TECHNOLOGY. see LIBRARY AND INFORMATION SCIENCES — Computer Applications

LINK-UP; the newsmagazine for users of online service - business, educational, personal. see COMPUTERS — Data Communications And Data Transmission Systems

004.16 US ISSN 0886-4144
LOADSTAR; the monthly software collection for people who love their Commodores. 1984. m. $89.95. Softdisk, Inc., Box 30008, Shreveport, LA 71130-0008. TEL 318-221-8718. Ed. Fender Tucker. circ. 20,000. (diskette format)

LOCAL AREA NETWORKS; newsletter covering worldwide technology trends, applications, and markets. see COMPUTERS — Computer Networks

004.16 SZ
M & K COMPUTERMARKT; Schweizer Fachzeitschrift fuer Computer und Kommunikation. (Text in German) 1979. m. 75 SFr. (foreign 85 SFr.). M & K Computer Verlag AG, Seeburgstr. 12, CH-6000 Luzern 15, Switzerland. TEL 041-311846. FAX 041-317268. Ed. Daniel Schwarzentruber. adv.: B&W page 3570 SFr., color page 4470 SFr.; trim 185 x 285. circ. 15,000. **Indexed:** INSPEC. **Document type:** trade publication.
—AskIEEE; CISTI; KR SourceOne; UMI.
Formed by the merger of: Mikro- und Klein-Computer (ISSN 0251-0006) & Computermarkt (ISSN 0254-5012); Mikro-Klein Computer.

621.381 IT
M C - MICROCOMPUTER. 1981. m. (11/yr.) L.72000 (Europe L.170000; America L.235000) (effective 1996). Technimedia s.r.l., Via Carlo Perrier, 9, 00157 Rome, Italy. TEL 396-418921. FAX 396-41732169. Eds. Paolo Nuti, Marco Marinacci. adv. circ. 85,000. (back issues avail.)

M COMPUTING. see COMPUTERS — Computer Programming

M.D. COMPUTING (NEW YORK). see MEDICAL SCIENCES — Computer Applications

004.165 070.5 US
MAC PUBLISHING AND PRESENTATIONS.* 1992. bi-m. $18. International Desktop Communications, Ltd., 342 Madison Ave., Ste. 622, New York, NY 10173-0002. TEL 212-768-7666. FAX 212-768-0288. Ed. Pauline Ores. circ. 50,000.
Description: For Macintosh desktop publishers; provides histories, product recommendations and reviews; publishes solutions and profiles on how to select and use Mac-based desktop technology.

MACROCOSM. see COMPUTERS — Personal Computers

621.381 US ISSN 1065-3929
MACROMEDIA USER JOURNAL; for multimedia developers and users of macromedia programs. m. Bove & Rhoades, Box 1289, Gualala, CA 95445-1289. TEL 707-884-4413; 800-222-4863. FAX 707-884-4421. Eds. Tony Bove, Cheryl Rhodes.
Formerly (until 1992): Macromind.

MACUSER; the Macintosh resource. see COMPUTERS — Personal Computers

MACWORLD. see COMPUTERS — Personal Computers

MACWORLD DANMARK. see COMPUTERS — Personal Computers

MACWORLD SWEDEN. see COMPUTERS — Personal Computers

621.381 US
MANAGING L A NS. 2 base vols. (plus m. updates). $838 to new subscr.; renewals $832 (effective 1996). Datapro Information Services Group (Subsidiary of: McGraw-Hill, Inc.), 600 Delran Pkwy., Delran, NJ 08075. TEL 609-764-0100; 800-328-2776. FAX 609-764-2814.
Former titles (until 1992): Datapro Management of Microcomputer Systems; (until 1985): Datapro Management of Small Computer Systems.

MAPLE ORCHARD; Canadian publication on Apple and Macintosh /computing. see COMPUTERS — Personal Computers

004.16 UK ISSN 0956-3881
MICRO COMPUTER MART. 1985. w. £57 (Europe £100; rest of world £180) (effective 1997); newsstand price: £0.80. Micromart (UK) Ltd., 24 Richmond Rd., Olton, Solihull, W. Midlands B92 7RP. TEL 44-121-706-1433. FAX 44-121-765-4057. E-mail: mcmeditor@micromart.co.uk; URL: http://micromart.co.uk/. Ed. Andrew Shorter; Pub. Fiona Nicol. adv.: B&W page £417.35; trim 297 x 210; adv. contact: Aron Nassim. bk.rev.; software rev (back issues avail.) **Document type:** consumer publication.
Description: Contains news, reports and information on available new and used computers.

001.6 621.381 IT
MICRO E PERSONAL COMPUTER. m. (11/yr.). L.67000. Gruppo Editoriale Suono s.r.l., Via Capo Peloro, 30, 00141 Rome, Italy. TEL 06-86-899-705. FAX 06-86-899-711. TELEX 621348 EDSUON I. Ed. Ugo Stella. adv. **Document type:** consumer publication.

621.381 GW ISSN 0172-0899
MICRO EXTRA; Zeitschrift fuer Mikrocomputertechnik. (Text in English and German) 1976. bi-m. DM.32. Feltron Elektronik - Zeissler und Co. GmbH, Auf dem Schellerod 22, 53842 Troisdorf, Germany. TEL 02241-4867-0. FAX 02241-404241. Ed. U. Zeissler. adv.; bk.rev. circ. 10,000. (back issues avail.) **Document type:** trade publication.

621.381 380.3 CN ISSN 0836-3587
MICRO-GAZETTE. (Text in French) 1986. 10/yr. Can.$29.96 (foreign Can.$75). Micro Gazette Inc., 785 Plymouth Ave., Ste. 117, Town of Mount Royal PQ H4P 1B3, Canada. TEL 514-735-2992. FAX 514-735-1269. E-mail: ggauthier@micro-gazette.com; URL: http://www.micro-gazette.com. Ed. Gerald Gauthier; Pub. Gerald Gauthier. R&P contact: Agnes Anger. adv. contact: Gerald Gauthier. bk.rev.; circ. 11,000 (paid). (back issues avail.) **Indexed:** Pt.de Rep.
—CISTI.
Description: Publication of interest to heads of enterprises and professionals. Contains information on the benefits of micro-computing and telecommunications in the office and the home office.

MICRO MEDICAL NEWSLETTER. see MEDICAL SCIENCES — Computer Applications

621.381 US ISSN 0742-9398
MICRO MONEY NEWSLETTER.* 1983. 10/yr. $55. H O W Publishing Company Inc., 232 Briargate Rd., Washington, IL 61571-3118. Ed. Harry Wahl. (looseleaf format; back issues avail.)
Description: Explains how to make money with microcomputers and their related products.

621.381 FR ISSN 0765-2887
MICRO P C. m. Editions Verona, 69 rue de Rome, 75008 Paris, France. TEL 45-22-55-33. Ed. Eric von Ascheberg. circ. 40,000.

MICRO SOFTWARE MARKETING. see COMPUTERS — Software

621.381 001.642 FR ISSN 0183-5084
MICRO SYSTEMES. 11/yr. 2-12 rue de Bellevue, 75019 Paris, France. TEL 42-00-33-05. FAX 42-41-89-40. Ed. Pascal Rosier. circ. 96,000.
—CISTI.

MICROAGE QUARTERLY. see COMPUTERS — Minicomputers

MICROBANKER; the research letter on financial end-user computing. see BUSINESS AND ECONOMICS — Banking And Finance — Computer Applications

621.381 US
MICROBRARY. q. 19 N. Broadway, Box 306, Red Hook, NY 12571. TEL 914-758-5567.

MICROCOMPUTER ABSTRACTS. see COMPUTERS — Abstracting, Bibliographies, Statistics

001.6 621.381 CN ISSN 0820-0750
QA76.5
MICROCOMPUTER APPLICATIONS. 1982. 3/yr. $160 (effective 1996). International Society for Mini and Microcomputers (ISMM), 4500 16th Ave., N.W., Ste. 80, Calgary, AB T3B 0M6, Canada. TEL 403-288-1195. FAX 403-247-6851. (And: P.O. Box 354, CH-8053 Zurich, Switzerland; Box 2481, Anaheim, CA 92814-2481, USA) Ed. L. Miller. adv. contact: M Hamza. bk.rev.; index. (back issues avail.) **Indexed:** CAD CAM Abstr., Comput.Abstr., Comput.Cont., INSPEC, Intl.Civil Eng.Abstr., LAMP, Soft.Abstr.Eng. **Document type:** academic/scholarly publication.
—BLDSC (5758.495000); AskIEEE; CISTI; Ei; KR SourceOne; Linda Hall; SWETS; UnCover.
Description: Covers all aspects of microcomputer applications including engineering, science, business, management, robotics, manufacturing and personal computers.

004.16 338.025 US ISSN 1066-1824
QA76.215
MICROCOMPUTER MARKET PLACE (YEAR); the complete guide to PC software and hardware vendors, service providers, and information sources. 1993. a. $29.95. Random House, Electronic Publishing, 201 E. 50th St., New York, NY 10022. (Dist. by: Reference Press, Inc., 6448 Hwy. 290 E., Ste. E-104, Austin, TX 78723. TEL 512-454-7778. FAX 512-454-9401) **Document type:** directory.
Description: Lists major companies and providers of software, hardware, and microcomputer service.

004.16 US ISSN 1055-3258
THE MICROCOMPUTER TRAINER. 1991. m. (11/yr.). $195. Systems Literacy Inc., 696 Ninth St., Box 2487, Secaucus, NJ 07096-2487. TEL 201-330-8963. FAX 201-330-0163. Ed. Loretta Weiss-Morris; Pub. Loretta Weiss-Morris. R& contact: Barbara Schinke. bk.rev. (back issues avail.) **Document type:** newsletter.
Description: Offers practical solutions and strategies for professional trainers and technical support staff responsible for building end-user skills.

MICROELECTRONICS AND SIGNAL PROCESSING. see ELECTRONICS

MICROPENDIUM; covering the T199/4A, the Myarc 9640 and compatibles. see COMPUTERS — Personal Computers

MICROPROCESSOR - BASED AND INTELLIGENT SYSTEM ENGINEERING. see ENGINEERING

621.381 US ISSN 1049-2445
MICROPROCESSOR I C'S D.A.T.A. DIGEST. (Integrated Circuits) 1981. s-a. $205. D.A.T.A. Business Publishing (Subsidiary of: Information Handling Services), 15 Inverness Way E., Box 6510, Englewood, CO 80155-6510. TEL 800-447-466 FAX 303-799-4082. TELEX 4322083 IHS UI. Ed Paul Magin. adv. contact: Kevin Asbjornson.
●Also available on CD-ROM.
—CISTI.
Formerly: Microprocessor I C's D.A.T.A. Book (IS 0276-511X)
Description: Reference guide covering up to 20 technical parameters on over 20,300 devices from more than 185 manufacturers.

621.381	US	ISSN 0899-9341
MICROPROCESSOR REPORT; the insiders' guide to microprocessor hardware. 1987. 17/yr. $595 (Europe £450; elsewhere £695) (CD-ROM $395) (effective 1997). 874 Gravenstein Hwy. So., Ste.14, Sebastopol, CA 95472. TEL 707-824-4004. FAX 707-823-0504. E-mail: cs@mdr.zd.com; URL: http://www.MDRonline.com. Ed. Linley Gwennap; Pub. Michael Slater. R&P contact: Kathy Acuff. TEL 408-328-3910. adv. contact: Joseph McIntyre. circ. 2,500 (paid). (back issues avail.) **Document type:** newsletter.
●Also available online. Vendor(s): Information Access Co.
Also available on CD-ROM.
—BLDSC (5759.755000); SWETS.
   Description: Reports on emerging microprocessor technology.
   Refereed Serial

004.6 621.3	NE	ISSN 0141-9331
QA76.5		CODEN: MIMID5
MICROPROCESSORS & MICROSYSTEMS. 1976. 10/yr. fl.882($507) (effective 1998). Elsevier Science B.V., P.O. Box 211, 1000 AE Amsterdam, Netherlands. TEL 31-20-4853911. FAX 31-20-4853598. (Subscr. in the Americas to: Elsevier Science, Regional Sales Office, Box 945, New York, NY 10159-0945. TEL 212-633-3730. FAX 212-633-3680; Subscr. in Australasia and the Far East to: Elsevier Science (Singapore) Pte Ltd, No.1 Temasek Ave., No.17-01 Millenia Tower, Singapore 039192, Singapore. TEL 65-434-3727. FAX 65-337-2230; Subscr. in Japan to: Elsevier Science Japan, 9-15 Higashi-Azabu 1-chome, Minato-ku, Tokyo 106, Japan. TEL 81-3-5561-5033. FAX 81-3-5561-5047) Ed. Steve Hitchcock. bk.rev.; abstr.; illus. (also avail. in microform from UMI; back issues avail.) **Indexed:** A.I.Abstr., ASCA, BMT, Br.Ceram.Abstr., Br.Tech.Ind., CAD CAM Abstr., Compumath, Comput.Abstr., Comput.Cont., Curr.Cont., INSPEC, Intl.Civil Eng.Abstr., LAMP, Robomat., Soft.Abstr.Eng.
—BLDSC (5759.771000); AskIEEE; CISTI; Ei; Genuine Article; KR SourceOne; Linda Hall; SWETS; UMI; UnCover. **CCC.**
   Formerly: Microprocessors (ISSN 0308-5953)
   Description: Serves the professional computing and engineering community with practical papers on the design and implementation of microprocessor-based computer and control systems.
   Refereed Serial

MICROPUBLISHING NEWS; the newsmonthly for electronic designers and publishers. see *PUBLISHING AND BOOK TRADE — Computer Applications*

621.381	UK	ISSN 0269-5766
MICROSCOPE. 1982. w. £75. Dennis Publishing Ltd., 19 Bolsover St., London W1E 4UZ, England. TEL 44-171-631-1433. FAX 44-171-636-5668. adv. circ. 10,000. **Indexed:** World Surf.Coat.

621.381 001.64	FR
MICROSYSTEMS. (Text in French) 11/yr. S.P.E., 2 - 12 rue Bellevue, 75940 Paris Cedex 19, France. Ed. J.P. Ventillard. adv. circ. 317,978. **Indexed:** Intl.Civil Eng.Abstr., PROMT, Soft.Abstr.Eng.

621.381	US	ISSN 1065-0148
MICROTIMES; California's computer magazine. 1984. 14/yr. $65. Bam Publications, Inc., 3470 Buskirk Ave., Pleasant Hill, CA 94523. TEL 510-934-3700. FAX 510-934-2974. Ed. Mary Eisenhart; Pub. Chloe Vezo. adv. contact: Sara Tassione. circ. 235,000. **Document type:** consumer publication.
   Description: Includes interviews, company profiles, hands-on reviews, and new product announcements.

621.381 330	CN	ISSN 0836-5482
MICROVIEW; journal for micro users in business. 10/yr. Can.$195 (foreign Can.$205). Canadian Institute of Chartered Accountants, 277 Wellington St. W., Toronto, Ont. M5V 3H2, Canada. TEL 416-977-3222. FAX 416-977-8585. Eds. Hugh Hardie, Blair Whelan. **Document type:** newsletter.
   Description: Informative publication on microcomputers. Covers applications, reviews and evaluations of new products.

001.6 621.381	SW	ISSN 0348-4009
MIKRODATORN; foer dig som anvaender datorer i jobbet. m. SEK 455 (effective 1991). C W - Communications AB, Soedra Hamnvaagen 22, S-115 41 Stockholm, Sweden. Ed. Bengt Marnfeldt. adv. circ. 16,665. (also avail. in audio cassette) —UMI.
   Description: Presents information for microcomputer users.

MODELING AND SIMULATION ON MICROCOMPUTERS. see *COMPUTERS — Computer Simulation*

N O H U G NEWS. (New Orleans Heath Users Group) see *COMPUTERS — Personal Computers*

NEW ENGLAND WORLD OF SANYO. see *COMPUTERS — Personal Computers*

006	JA	ISSN 0288-3635
QA76.5
NEW GENERATION COMPUTING; an international journal. 1983. q. DM.534.20 (Germany DM.526) (effective 1998). Ohmsha, Ltd., 3-1 Kanda Nishiki-cho, Chiyoda-ku, Tokyo 101, Japan. TEL 81-3-3233-0641. (Dist. by: Springer-Verlag, Tokyo, 3-13, Hongo 3-chome, Bunkyo-ku, Tokyo 113, Japan. TEL 81-3-3812-0331. FAX 81-3-3812-0719; Dist. in N. America by: Springer-Verlag New York, Inc., 333 Meadowlands Pkwy., Secaucus, NJ 07094-1897. TEL 201-348-4033. FAX 201-348-4505; Dist. elsewhere by: Springer-Verlag, Heidelberger Platz 3, D-14197 Berlin, Germany. TEL 49-30-82787-273. FAX 49-30-82787-448) Ed. H. Tanaka. (also avail. in microfiche from UMI; reprint service avail. from ISI) **Indexed:** A.I.Abstr., Abstr.Hum.Comp.Inter., ASCA, CAD CAM Abstr., Compumath, Comput.Abstr., Curr.Cont., Cyb.Abstr., INSPEC (1983-), SSCI, Zent.Math. **Document type:** academic/scholarly publication.
—BLDSC (6084.211200); AskIEEE; CISTI; Ei; Genuine Article; KR SourceOne; Linda Hall; SWETS; UMI; UnCover. **CCC.**
   Description: Covers the fields of software engineering, artificial intelligence, computer architecture, data base systems, parallel processing, VLSI, and natural language processing.

NEWCASTLE MICROCOMPUTER CLUB. NEWSLETTER. see *COMPUTERS — Personal Computers*

621.381	US
NEWS & REVIEW. 1987. m. $35 (foreign $75). Thurman Marketing Services Inc., 145 Columbia, Ste.100, Aliso Viejo, CA 92656-1490. TEL 714-362-3993. FAX 714-362-4151. E-mail: compnews@newsrev.com; URL: http://www.hewsrev.com. Ed. Stanley Goodrich; Pub. Phyllis Thurman. R&P contact: Phyllis Thurman. adv.: B&W page $1650, color page $2680; adv. contact: Scott Thurman. bk.rev. circ. 25,000. (tabloid format) **Document type:** newspaper.
   Description: Aimed at mainstream computer users worldwide. Focuses on DBMS news with other departments on client-server computing, networking and the internet.

621.381	US
NEWS I S. w. $480 (effective Aug. 1996). Xephon, 1301 W. Hwy. 407, Ste. 201-450, Lewisville, TX 75067. TEL 817-455-7050. FAX 817-455-2492. E-mail: 100325.3711@compuserve.com; URL: http://www.xephon.co.uk. Ed. Trevor Eddolls. bk.rev.; circ. 1,500 (paid). **Document type:** trade publication.
●Available only online.
   Formerly: News I B M.

NEWSLINK (WESTERVILLE). see *COMPUTERS — Personal Computers*

004.16	JA	ISSN 0918-581X
NIKKEI OPEN SYSTEMS. (Text in Japanese) 1993. m. 10700 Yen. Nikkei Business Publications, Inc. (Subsidiary of: Nihon Keizai Shimbun, Inc.), 2-7-6, Hirakawa-cho, Chiyoda-ku, Tokyo 102, Japan. TEL 81-3-5210-8528. FAX 81-3-5210-8119. URL: http://www.nikkeibp.co.jp/. Ed. Norio Inaba; Pub. Shozo Watanabe. adv.: B&W page 260000 Yen, color page 480000 Yen; trim 210 x 280; adv. contact: Toru Kato. circ. 33,165. **Document type:** trade publication.
   Description: Offers practical information for construction and utilization of open systems consisting of workstations, PCs, and LANs.

NORTH TEXAS P C NEWS. see *COMPUTERS — Personal Computers*

NORTH TEXAS SANYO USERS GROUP. NEWSLETTER. see *COMPUTERS — Personal Computers*

621.381	UK	ISSN 1065-075X
Z678.93.M53		CODEN: OSSEEE
O C L C SYSTEMS AND SERVICES. (Online Computer Library Center, Inc.) 1985. q. £169($259) (foreign Aus.$329) (effective 1998). M C B University Press Ltd., 60-62 Toller Ln., Bradford, W. Yorks BD8 9BY, England. TEL 44-1274-777700. FAX 44-1274-785200. URL: http://www.mcb.co.uk. Ed. John Peters. adv.; bk.rev.; index. circ. 2,250. **Indexed:** INSPEC (1993-), Lib.Lit., LISA, Microcomp.Ind. **Document type:** trade publication.
—BLDSC (6235.137500); AskIEEE; KR SourceOne; Linda Hall; UMI; UnCover. **CCC.**
   Formerly: O C L C Micro (ISSN 8756-5196)
   Description: For librarians using OCLC Workstations, IBM PC's and compatibles, and microcomputers other than MS-DOS computers. Provides "how to" tips, short cuts, programs and solutions. Contains information on product compatibility and availability. Publishes articles on systems and services produced by Online Computer Library Center, Inc. in Dublin, Ohio.

621.381	AU
OESTERREICHISCHE MIKRO COMPUTER MAGAZIN. q. Johann L. Bondi und Sohn, Industriestr. 2, A-2380 Perchtoldsdorf, Austria. TEL 01-864921. FAX 01-86492144. TELEX 131136. circ. 40,500.

ON-LINE (DURHAM). see *COMPUTERS — Computer Networks*

ONLINE & C D - R O M REVIEW; the international journal of online & optical information systems. see *COMPUTERS — Computer Networks*

ONLINE HOTLINE NEWS SERVICE. see *COMPUTERS — Computer Networks*

ONLINE NEWSLETTER. see *COMPUTERS — Computer Networks*

OPEN SYSTEMS WORLD. see *COMPUTERS — Computer Systems*

004.16	SA
P C & OFFICE TECHNOLOGY.* (Text in English) 1982. m. R.25. Systems Publishers (Pty) Ltd., P.O. Box 41345, Craighall 2024, South Africa. Ed. David Briston. adv.; bk.rev. circ. 7,500. **Indexed:** Comput.Cont.
   Incorporates: Microcomputer Owner.

P C CHRONICLES. see *COMPUTERS — Personal Computers*

P C LETTER; the insider's guide to the personal computer industry. see *COMPUTERS — Computer Sales*

P C M; premier personal computer magazine for Tandy computer users. see *COMPUTERS — Personal Computers*

P C MAGAZINE. see *COMPUTERS — Personal Computers*

P C MAGAZINE AUSTRALIA. see *COMPUTERS — Personal Computers*

P C MAGAZINE: THE INDEPENDENT GUIDE TO I B M - STANDARD PERSONAL COMPUTING. see *COMPUTERS — Personal Computers*

P C PUBLISHING AND PRESENTATIONS; desktop publishing. see *PUBLISHING AND BOOK TRADE — Computer Applications*

P C RETAILING. (Personal Computer) see *COMPUTERS — Computer Sales*

P.C. REVIEW; evaluations of new personal computer products. see *COMPUTERS — Software*

COMPUTERS — MICROCOMPUTERS

004.16 UK ISSN 0964-4547
P C REVIEW. m. £47.40 (foreign £55); CD-ROM edition £59.40 (foreign £67) (effective 1996). E M A P - Images, Priory Ct., 30-32 Ferringdon Ln., London EC1R 3AU, England. TEL 44-171-837-1212. FAX 44-171-972-6710. (Subscr. to: Tower Publishing Services Ltd., Tower House, Sovereign Park, Lathkill St., Market Harborough, Leics. LE16 9EF, England. TEL 44-1858-468811. FAX 44-1858-432164) Ed. Christina Erskine. circ. 45,000 (paid). (diskette format) **Document type:** consumer publication.
●Also available on CD-ROM.

621.381 UK ISSN 0263-5720
P C USER; all you need to know about IBM personal computing. (Has m. supplement: P C Marketplace (ISSN 0969-1839)) 1983. fortn. E M A P Business & Computer Publications Ltd., 33-39 Bowling Green Ln., London EC1R ODA, England. TEL 44-171-278-4008. TELEX 936566. adv.; bk.rev. circ. 45,000. (back issues avail.) **Indexed:** Comput.Cont., Comput.Dtbs., INSPEC (1983-), Intl.Civil Eng.Abstr., PCR2, Soft.Abstr.Eng. **Document type:** trade publication.
●Also available online. Vendor(s): Information Access Co.
—AskIEEE; CISTI; KR SourceOne; SWETS. **CCC**.

P C WEEK; Australia's newspaper of corporate computing. see COMPUTERS — Personal Computers

P C WELT. see COMPUTERS — Personal Computers

P C WORLD. see COMPUTERS — Personal Computers

621.381 UK
P C YEAR BOOK. HARDWARE VOLUME. 1985. a. £50. V N U Business Publications BV, 32-34 Broadwick St., London W1A 2HG, England. TEL 071-439-4242. FAX 071-734-5510. Ed. Peter Chave. circ. 3,500. **Document type:** trade publication.
Supersedes: P C Year Book; Microcomputer User's Year Book.

621.381 UK
P C YEAR BOOK. SOFTWARE VOLUME. 1985. a. £50. V N U Business Publications BV, 32-34 Broadwick St., London W1A 2HG, England. TEL 071-439-4242. FAX 071-734-5510. Ed. Peter Chave. circ. 3,500. **Document type:** trade publication.
Supersedes: P C Year Book.

PERSONAL COMPUTER MAGAZINE; het computerblad voor Nederland en Belgie. see COMPUTERS — Personal Computers

PLUNKETT'S INFOTECH INDUSTRY ALMANAC. see BUSINESS AND ECONOMICS — Trade And Industrial Directories

621.381 001.642 GW ISSN 0934-8654
POCKET & LAPTOP COMPUTER; Zeitschrift fuer mobile Datensysteme. 1985. bi-m. DM.72 (foreign DM.84). A D C C Fischel GmbH, Kaiser-Friedrich-Str. 54a, 10627 Berlin, Germany. TEL 030-3236029. FAX 030-3240928. circ. 20,000. (back issues avail.) **Document type:** consumer publication.

001.6 621.381 US ISSN 0732-7501
PORTABLE COMPANION;* for Osborne computer users. 1982-1983; N.S. 1984. bi-m. $25. Osborne Computer Corp., c/o Ed Walsh, 1255 Post St., No. 948, San Francisco, CA 94109-6712. (Co-sponsor: T U G Inc.) Ed. Tony Bove. adv.; bk.rev. circ. 18,000. **Indexed:** Comput.Cont.
 Description: For Osborne computer users. Features articles on hardware, peripherals, programs and applications. Includes a column by Adam Osborne as well as new product announcements.

THE PORTABLE COMPUTING LETTER. see COMPUTERS — Personal Computers

PRE-K TODAY. see EDUCATION

004.16 DK ISSN 0909-1777
PRIVAT COMPUTER. 1985. m. DKK 425. Audio Media A-S, St. Kongensgade 72, DK-1264 Copenhagen K, Denmark. TEL 45-33-91-28-33. Ed. Kenneth Bernhols. circ. 40,000. (back issues avail.) **Document type:** consumer publication.
Former titles: Nye Computer (ISSN 0905-6009); Computer Commodore Magazine (ISSN 0900-8284)

070.5 686.2 004.16 US ISSN 0897-6007
Z286.D47 CODEN: PBLIEJ
PUBLISH; the how-to magazine of desktop publishing. 1986. m. $39.90. Integrated Media, Inc., Publish! (Subsidiary of: I D G Communications Group), 501 Second St., Ste. 310, San Francisco, CA 94107. TEL 415-243-0600; 800-656-7495. (Subscr. to: Box 5039, Brentwood, TN 37024. TEL 800-685-3435) Ed. Jake Widman. R&P contact: Candace Krom. adv.: B&W page $11445, color page $12820. circ. 98,819. (back issues avail.) **Indexed:** Abstr.Bull.Inst.Pap.Chem., B.P.I., Bus.Educ.Ind., Comput.Dtbs., Microcomp.Ind., PCR2. **Document type:** consumer publication.
—BLDSC (7156.040500); CISTI; KR SourceOne; SWETS; UMI; UnCover.
Formerly (until 1986): Desktop Publishing (ISSN 0884-0873)

235.621 381 UK ISSN 0966-1913
R I S C USER. (Reduced Instruction Set Computer) 1987. 10/yr. £24 (rest of Europe £35; Middle East £41; Americas & Africa £44; elsewhere £46). Beebug Ltd., 117 Hatfield Rd., St. Albans, Herts AL1 4JS, England. TEL 44-1727-840303. FAX 44-1727-860263. E-mail: ruser@beebug.co.uk. Ed. Richard Hallas. adv. contact: Helen O'Sullivan. bk.rev.; index. circ. 7,000. **Document type:** consumer publication.

621.381 US ISSN 1061-0030
HF5548.4.I25
R S - MAGAZINE; power PC magazine for IBM workstation users. 1992. m. $60. Computer Publishing Group, 320 Washington St., Brookline, MA 02146-3202. TEL 617-739-7001. FAX 617-739-7003. Ed. Cris Casatelli; Pub. S. Henry Sacks. R&P contact: Doug Pryor. adv.: B&W page $4720; adv. contact: Linda Liebich. circ. 40,000 (controlled). **Indexed:** Comput.Ind. **Document type:** trade publication.
—CISTI; KR SourceOne.
Description: Targets IBM RS/6000 users, OEMs, and workstation buyers. Focuses on peripherals, new products, languages and networks.

REAL ESTATE COMPUTER REVIEW. see REAL ESTATE

RELEASE 1.0. see COMPUTERS — Computer Industry Directories

REPORT ON A T & T; the independent bi-weekly reporting exclusively on the long-distance industry including AT&T and its competitors. see COMMUNICATIONS — Computer Applications

ROOT DIRECTORY. see COMPUTERS — Personal Computers

S V M MAC. (Science et Vie Micro) see COMPUTERS — Personal Computers

621.381 FR ISSN 0760-6516
S V M SCIENCE ET VIE MICRO. 1983. 11/yr. 224 F.($62) (foreign 320 F.). Excelsior Publications, 1 rue du Colonel Pierre Avia, 75503 Paris Cedex 15, France. TEL 46-48-48-48. FAX 46-48-48-09. TELEX 631 994 F. Eds. Seymour Dinnematin, Yann Garret. adv. contact: Gilles de Keranflach. bk.rev. circ. 102,010. **Indexed:** Pt.de Rep. (1983-). **Document type:** trade publication.
—CISTI; SWETS.
Description: For the professional end-user.

SAN FRANCISCO BAY AREA SANYO GROUP NEWSLETTER. see COMPUTERS — Personal Computers

SANYO P C HACKERS NEWSLETTER. see COMPUTERS — Personal Computers

SANYO SOURCE. see COMPUTERS — Personal Computers

621.381 US
SAWTOOTH NEWS. 1985. 3/yr. free. Sawtooth Technologies, 1007 Church St., Ste. 402, Evanston, IL 60201-3624. TEL 847-866-0870. FAX 847-866-0876. E-mail: info@sawtooth.com; URL: http://www.sawtooth.com. Ed. Suzanne Weiss. R&P contact: Suzanne Weiss. TEL 847-866-0870. circ. 8,000. **Document type:** newsletter.
Description: Covers topics of interest to persons in P.C. interviewing and analysis, such as computer interviewing, conjoint analysis, and data clustering.

621.381 US
SCARLETT.* 1982. m. $12. Big Red Apple Club, 1401 Charolais Dr., Norfolk, NE 68701-2348. TEL 402-379-4680. Ed. John Wrenholt. adv.; bk.rev. circ. 9,000.
Formerly: Scarlett Letter.
Description: For club members as well as owners of Apple, Franklin and Basis computers. Covers current news and trends.

686.2 070.5 US ISSN 0889-9762
Z286.D47 CODEN: SRDFED
SEYBOLD REPORT ON DESKTOP PUBLISHING. 1986. m. $245 (Canada $251; elsewhere $263). Seybold Publications, 428 E. Baltimore Ave., Box 644, Media, PA 19063. TEL 610-565-2480; 800-325-3830. FAX 610-565-1858. Ed. Peter E. Dyson; Pub. Jonathan Seybold. cum.index: vols. 1-7. **Indexed:** Abstr.Bull.Inst.Pap.Chem., INSPEC (1986-). **Document type:** trade publication.
●Also available online. Vendor(s): Information Access Co.
—AskIEEE; CASDDS; KR SourceOne. **CCC**.
Description: Reports and analyzes developments in standard, mass-market hardware and software products used to create, revise, and print documents.

001.6 621.381 US ISSN 0736-6957
CODEN: SBCNDL
SMALL BUSINESS COMPUTER NEWS. 1975. m. $721. Management Information Corporation, 1111 Marlkress Rd., Box 5062, Cherry Hill, NJ 08003. TEL 609-424-1100. FAX 609-424-1999. Ed. Al Powell. circ. 2,000 (paid). (looseleaf format; also avail. in magnetic tape; diskette format; back issues avail.) **Indexed:** Compumath, Comput.Bus., Comput.Lit.Ind., INSPEC. **Document type:** directory.
—AskIEEE; KR SourceOne.
Description: For business and professional users. Offers evaluations of business mini and microcomputers, describing hardware and system software, pricing and analysis of systems advantages, disadvantages and capabilities.

004.16 US ISSN 0893-9462
SMART CARD MONTHLY. (Annual special issues avail.) 1987. m. $595 (foreign $655). Smart Card Concepts, Box 548, Lopez, WA 98261-0548. TEL 206-468-3570. FAX 206-468-3571. Ed. Stephan Seidman; Pub. Stephan Seidman. bk.rev.; circ. 300 (paid). (back issues avail.) **Document type:** newsletter.
Description: Covers the technology, applications and markets of smart cards, memory cards and optical cards.

SOFT & MICRO. see COMPUTERS — Personal Computers

SOFT.LETTER; trends & strategies in software publishing. see COMPUTERS — Software

621.381 US
SOFTWARE CATALOG: MICROCOMPUTERS. 1983. irreg latest 1990. fl.510. Elsevier Science Inc., Box 945, New York, NY 10159-0945. TEL 212-633-3730. FAX 212-633-3680. TELEX 420643 AEP UI. E-mail: usinfo-f@elsevier.com; URL: http://www.elsevier.nl/. (Subscr. outside the Americas to: Elsevier Science, Regional Sales Office, P.O. Box 211, 1000 AE Amsterdam, Netherlands. TEL 31-20-4853757. FAX 31-20-4853432; Subscr. in Australasia and the Far East to: Elsevier Science (Singapore) Pte Ltd, No.1 Temasek Ave., No.17-01 Millenia Tower, Singapore 039192, Singapore. TEL 65-434-3727. FAX 65-337-2230; Subscr. in Japan to: Elsevier Science Japan, 9-15 Higashi-Azabu 1-chome, Minato-ku, Tokyo 106, Japan. TEL 81-3-5561-5033. FAX 81-3-5561-5047) Ed. Joe Claypool. adv. **Indexed:** Comput.Lit.Ind. **Document type:** catalog.
●Also available online. Vendor(s): CompuServe, Inc Knight-Ridder Information, Inc.
Description: Provides up-to-date information on the availability, applications, prices and compatibility of over 25,000 program units.

SOFTWARE DIGEST; the independent, comparative ratings report for PC and LAN software. see COMPUTERS — Software

SOURCEVIEW JOURNAL OF SOFTWARE EVALUATIONS, REVIEWS & RATINGS. see COMPUTERS — Software

COMPUTERS — MINICOMPUTERS

621.381 001.64   US   ISSN 0734-0125
SPREADSHEET.* m. $52. International Electronic Spreadsheet Users Group (InterCalc), 25 Roxbury Rd., Scarsdale, NY 10583. TEL 914-472-0038. Ed. Roger Clark. circ. 2,500.

STACK. see COMPUTERS — *Personal Computers*

STUDIO CITY FOR THE II GS. see COMPUTERS — *Personal Computers*

621.381   US   ISSN 1058-5400
THE SUN OBSERVER. 1988. m. $45 (foreign $75) (effective 1995). Publications & Communications, Inc., 12416 Hymeadow, Austin, TX 78750-1896. TEL 512-250-9023. FAX 512-331-6779. Ed. Jonathan Roe. adv.: B&W page $3684, color page $4484; trim 10 3/4 14 1/2. circ. 30,000. (tabloid format) **Document type:** trade publication.
—KR SourceOne.
Description: Covers news and technical issues relating to the use of Sun Microsystems and SPARC-compatible computer systems.

621.381   US   ISSN 1053-9239
SUNEXPERT; serving the client/server UNIX workstation network. 1989. m. $60. Computer Publishing Group, 320 Washington St., Brookline, MA 02146-3202. TEL 617-739-7001. FAX 617-739-7003. Ed. Douglas Pryor; Pub. S. Henry Sacks. R&P contact: Doug Pryor. adv.: B&W Page $6875; adv. contact: S. Henry Sacks. circ. 69,000 (controlled). (back issues avail.) **Document type:** trade publication.
—CISTI; KR SourceOne.
Description: Independent forum for open systems serving the client/server UNIX workstation network with particular emphasis on Sun's workstations. Covers technical trends, emerging applications and business issues.

004.1 005.3   SW   ISSN 1101-1416
VENSKA MACPRESSEN. 1990. m. SEK 349 (effective 1997); newsstand price: SEK 34.50. Fakta - Press AB, P.O. Box 2048, S-550 02 Jonkoeping, Sweden. TEL 46-36-16-50-08. FAX 46-36-71-93-33. E-mail: macpressen@faktapress.se; URL: http://www. macpressen.se. Ed. Valter Bengtsson. adv.: B&W page SEK 22000, color page SEK 26000; trim 240 x 360; adv. contact: Aasa Antonsson. bk.rev. circ. 18,700. cols./p.: 5; pp./issue: 96. **Document type:** newspaper, consumer publication.
●Also available online.

621.381   US
SOP NEWS... AND CYBER WORLD REPORT. m. $20 (Canada $35; elsewhere $45); newsstand price: $2.95. B B S Press Service Inc., 8125 S.W. 21st St., Topeka, KS 66615-1515. TEL 913-478-3157. Ed. Alan R. Bechtold. circ. 35,000. (tabloid format) **Document type:** trade publication.
Formerly: Info-mat Magazine.
Description: For professional and amateur operators of online information services including Internet, World Wide Web and BBSes.

621.381   US
RGET AN AIM 65 NEWSLETTER. bi-m. $7. Target Publications, 1176 Bay Circle, Lima, OH 45801. adv. circ. 500.

RONTO SYSTEMS LETTER. see COMPUTERS — *Hardware*

621.381   US
JLY PORTABLE. bi-m. Rachel Holmen, Ed. & Pub., 6540 Dana Street, P.O. Box 2916, Oakland, CA 94609-1108. TEL 415-658-1889. bk.rev. circ. 1,000.

621.381   HU   ISSN 1217-7598
ALAPLAP; computing. (Includes a floppy disk with each issue.) 1983. m. $58 (effective 1993). Uj Alaplap Kiado Kft., P.O. Box 571, 1539 Budapest, Hungary. TEL 36-1-3224417. E-mail: alaplap@mail. datanet.hu; URL: http://www.alaplap.hu. Ed. Pal aklen. adv.: B&W page $1000; trim 203 x 295. bk.rev. circ. 11,000. **Document type:** trade publication.
Former titles (until 1993): Alaplap (ISSN 865-9788); (until 1990): Mikroszamitogep lagazin (ISSN 0236-6088)
Description: Covers mainly software information and general computing topics for programmers and advanced computer users.

004 330   US   ISSN 0892-2845
UNISYS WORLD; an independent news monthly for Unisys system users. 1980. m. $92 (foreign $140) (effective 1995). Publications & Communications, Inc., 12416 Hymeadow, Austin, TX 78750-1896. TEL 512-250-9023; 800-678-9724. FAX 512-331-3900. Ed. Larry Storer. adv.: B&W page $3312, color page $4062; trim 10 3/4 x 14 1/2. circ. 13,500. (tabloid format; reprint service avail.) **Indexed:** Comput.Cont., Intl.Civil Eng.Abstr., Soft.Abstr.Eng. **Document type:** trade publication.
—KR SourceOne.
Formerly: Burroughs World (ISSN 0743-9474); Incorporates (1982-1989): Unisys World Software Directory (ISSN 0892-2799); Which was formerly: Burroughs Software Directory.
Description: Features product news, corporate news, technical articles and software, hardware reviews for users of Unisys systems. Provides coverage of the entire range of Unisys and third-party vendor products.

USER MAGAZIN. see COMPUTERS — *Personal Computers*

VIC-NIC NEWS. see COMPUTERS — *Personal Computers*

VIDEOGRAPHY. see COMMUNICATIONS — *Video*

WATCOM NEWS. (Waterloo Computing) see COMPUTERS — *Hardware*

621.381   CC
WEI JISUANJI XINXI/INFORMATION ON MICROCOMPUTERS. (Text in Chinese) q. China INTEL Computer Users Association, P.O. Box 20, Changzhi, Taiyuan 046000, People's Republic of China. Ed. Zhuang Zixin.

004.16   CC   ISSN 1003-1944
WEIJISUANJI YINGYONG/MICROCOMPUTER APPLICATIONS. (Text in Chinese) 1980. bi-m. P.O. Box 2712, Beijing 100080, People's Republic of China. TEL 86-10-284573. FAX 86-10-256-1457. TELEX 222525 IOAAS CN. adv. contact: Xiaoxia Wang. circ. 50,000.

621.381   UK
WHAT P C? AND SOFTWARE. 1982. m. £18.90 (Europe £36) (effective 1995). V N U Business Publications BV, VNU House, 32-34 Broadwick St., London W1A 2HG, England. TEL 44-171-316-9000. E-mail: 70007,5417@compuserve.com. (Subscr. in US to: Global Media Representatives, Inc., 611 Veterans Blvd., Ste.205, Redwood City, CA 94063. TEL 415-306-0880. FAX 415-306-0890) Ed. Mick Andon; Pub. Jon Ross. adv. contact: Paula Devine. bk.rev. circ. 48,512. (back issues avail.) **Indexed:** INSPEC (1992-). **Document type:** trade publication.
—AskIEEE; KR SourceOne.
Former titles (until 1995): What P C; (until 1992): What Micro? (ISSN 0264-441X)
Description: Buyers' guide to business microcomputers and software; includes tables on products available in the UK.

621.381   US
THE YELLOWSTONE WINDOWS LETTER.* 1991. bi-m. $49.95 (foreign $89.95). Yellowstone Information Services, R.R. 2, Box 42A, Bloomingdale, OH 43910-9802. TEL 304-965-5548. FAX 304-965-7785. Ed. Roger Thibault.

COMPUTERS — Minicomputers

AMY D. WOHL'S TRENDS LETTER. see COMPUTERS — *Personal Computers*

621.381   UK   ISSN 0950-5482
D E C COMPUTING. (Digital Equipment Corporation); midrange newspaper. 1985. w. £60 (foreign £80) (effective 1996). V N U Business Publications BV, VNU House, 32-34 Broadwick St., London W1A 2HG, England. TEL 44-171-439-4242. FAX 44-171-437-4841. Ed. C. Gabriel. adv.: B&W page $4590, color page $5790; trim 11 x 15 1/4; adv. contact: David Weekes. bk.rev. circ. 15,717. **Indexed:** INSPEC (1986-). **Document type:** trade publication.
—AskIEEE; KR SourceOne.
Description: Contains news coverage and analysis, features on industry developments, a buyer's guide and product reviews.

001.6 621.381   CN   ISSN 0702-0481
QA76.5   CODEN: IJMMDE
INTERNATIONAL JOURNAL OF MINI AND MICROCOMPUTERS. 1979. 3/yr. $185 (effective 1996). International Society for Mini and Microcomputers (ISMM), 4500 16th Ave., N.W., Ste. 80, Calgary, AB T3B 0M6, Canada. TEL 403-288-1195. FAX 403-247-6851. (And: P.O. Box 354, CH-8053 Zurich, Switzerland; Box 2481, Anaheim, CA 92814, USA) Ed. B. Furht. adv. contact: M. Hamza. bk.rev.; index. (back issues avail.) **Indexed:** Chem.Abstr., Comput.Abstr., Comput.Cont., Comput.Rev., Cyb.Abstr., Eng.Ind., INSPEC, Int.Aerosp.Abstr. **Document type:** academic/scholarly publication.
—BLDSC (4542.363000); AskIEEE; CISTI; Ei; KR SourceOne; SWETS; UnCover.
Description: Covers all aspects of mini and microcomputers including technology, hardware, software, systems, education, networks, distributed processing and applications.

621.381   CN
INTERNATIONAL SYMPOSIUM ON MINI AND MICROCOMPUTERS. PROCEEDINGS. 1975. a. price varies. International Society of Mini and Microcomputers, 80-4500 16th Ave., N.W., Calgary, AB T3B 0M6, Canada. TEL 403-288-1195. FAX 403-247-6851. (And: P.O. Box 354, CH-8053 Zurich, Switzerland; Box 2481, Anaheim, CA 92814-2481, USA) Ed. M.H. Hamza. **Document type:** proceedings.

M I C - TECH-COMPUTERS. (Management Information Corporation) see COMPUTERS — *Electronic Data Processing*

001.6 621.381   US
MICROAGE QUARTERLY.* 1985. q. MicroAge Computer Centers, Inc., 2400 S. Microage Way, Tempe, AZ 85282. TEL 602-968-3168. FAX 602-966-7339. Ed. Jay O'Callaghan. adv. circ. 300,000.

621.381   US   ISSN 1052-3561
MIDRANGE COMPUTING. 1983. m. $99 (Canada and Mexico $129; elsewhere $149) (effective 1993). Fleming Enterprises, 5650 El Camino Real, Ste. 225, Carlsbad, CA 92008. TEL 619-931-8615. FAX 619-931-9935. adv. circ. 30,000. (back issues avail.) **Document type:** trade publication.
—KR SourceOne.
Description: Provides technical information in IBM AS-400 to MIS professionals.

621.381   US
MIDRANGE COMPUTING'S SHOWCASE. 1992. 9/yr. free to M.C. subscribers. Fleming Enterprises, 5650 El Camino Real, Ste. 225, Carlsbad, CA 92008. TEL 619-932-8615. FAX 619-931-9935. adv.: B&W page $3600; trim 10 3/4 x 13 1/2. circ. 80,000. **Document type:** trade publication.
Description: Contains news of goods and services offered to the midrange industry.

621.381   US   ISSN 1041-8237
CODEN: MISYEG
MIDRANGE SYSTEMS; the independent newspaper for IBM AS-400 and RS-6000 server computing. 1988. 18/yr. free to qualified personnel. Cardinal Business Media, Inc., 1300 Virginia Dr., Ste. 400, Fort Washington, PA 19034-3225. TEL 215-643-8000. FAX 215-643-3901. Ed. Al Gillen; Pub. Doug Johnson. adv. contact: Mike Boucher. circ. 50,000 (controlled). **Document type:** trade publication, newspaper.
●Also available online. Vendor(s): Information Access Co.
—BLDSC (5761.435722); KR SourceOne; UMI.
Description: For users and buyers of IBM AS-400 and RS-6000 computers and related products and services.

001.6 621.381   SP
MINI DATA REPORT; boletin informativo de proceso de datos. no.7, 1973. q. Siemens, S.A., Calle Orense No. 2, Madrid 20, Spain. circ. controlled. (looseleaf format)

OPEN SYSTEMS WORLD. see COMPUTERS — *Computer Systems*

COMPUTERS — PERSONAL COMPUTERS

621.381 001.644   US   ISSN 1051-8118
REVUSER; an independent journal for advanced Revelation and Revelation users. bi-m. $35. Infocus, Inc., 37 S. Main St., Yardley, PA 19067. TEL 215-321-2200. FAX 215-321-2205. Ed. Lee J. Leitner.
Description: For users of Revelation and Advanced Revelation. Publishes technical information about personal computers, workstations, networking and applications.

621.381   US
SOFTWARE CATALOG: MINICOMPUTERS. irreg., latest 1987. price varies. Elsevier Science Inc., Box 945, New York, NY 10159-0945. TEL 212-633-3730. FAX 212-633-3680. TELEX 420643 AEP UI. E-mail: usinfo-f@elsevier.com; URL: http://www.elsevier.nl/. (Subscr. outside the Americas to: Elsevier Science, Regional Sales Office, P.O. Box 211, 1000 AE Amsterdam, Netherlands. TEL 31-20-4853757. FAX 31-20-4853432; Subscr. in Australasia and the Far East to: Elsevier Science (Singapore) Pte Ltd, No.1 Temasek Ave., No.17-01 Millenia Tower, Singapore 039192, Singapore. TEL 65-434-3727. FAX 65-337-2230; Subscr. in Japan to: Elsevier Science Japan, 9-15 Higashi-Azabu 1-chome, Minato-ku, Tokyo 106, Japan. TEL 81-3-5561-5033. FAX 81-3-5561-5047) **Indexed:** Comput.Lit.Ind. **Document type:** catalog.
Description: Contains in-depth descriptions including the availability, applications, price and compatibility of over 7,800 programs for minicomputers.

621.381   US   ISSN 0279-1579
QA76.8.U55
UNISPHERE; the magazine for Unisys users. 1981. m. free to qualified personnel in U.S. & Canada; elsewhere $80. Cardinal Business Media Inc., 12225 Greenville Ave., Ste. 700, Dallas, TX 75243. TEL 972-669-9000. FAX 972-669-9909. Eds. Dean Lampman, Debby English. R&P contact: Debby English. adv. contact: Mary Thomas. bk.rev. circ. 12,000. (back issues avail.) **Document type:** trade publication.
—BLDSC (9090.784700); AskIEEE; CISTI; Ei; KR SourceOne; UMI.
Description: Contains new product news, technical articles and features relating to Unisys computer systems.

621.381   CC   ISSN 1000-1220
XIAOXING WEIXING JISUANJI XITONG/MICROCOMPUTER SYSTEMS. (Text in Chinese) m. Zhongguo Kexueyuan, Shenyang Jisuan Jishu Yanjiusuo - Chinese Academy of Sciences, Shenyang Institute of Computing Technology, 18 Sanhao Jie, Hepingqu, Shenyang, Liaoning 110003, People's Republic of China. TEL 86-24-392758. Ed. Luan Guixing. adv.: B&W page $1000. circ. 23,000. **Document type:** academic/scholarly publication.
—BLDSC (5797.755000); AskIEEE; KR SourceOne.

COMPUTERS — Personal Computers

see also Computers–Microcomputers

A C E INTERNATIONAL. see COMMUNICATIONS — Television And Cable

621.381   US   ISSN 0273-8708
A M U S LOG.* 1978. m. $75. Alpha Micro User Society, 210 N. Iris Ave., Rialto, CA 92376-5727. TEL 303-678-7066. FAX 303-678-9420. E-mail: slg@indra.com. Ed. Claudia Previn. adv. contact: Jim Randazzo. circ. 1,400 (paid). (back issues avail.) **Document type:** trade publication.
Description: For Alpha Micro computer users - beginners through advanced.

A P L QUOTE QUAD. see COMPUTERS — Computer Programming

004.6   US   ISSN 1068-5189
A T M USER. (Asynchronous Transfer Mode) 1982. m. $395 in U.S. and Canada; elsewhere $440 (effective 1997). Jeffries Research, 2263 Callender Rd., Arroyo Grande, CA 93420. TEL 805-343-5444. FAX 805-343-2118. E-mail: info@atm-user.com; URL: http://www.ATM-user.com. Ed. Ron Jeffries. bk.rev. circ. 1,000. **Document type:** newsletter.
Formerly (until 1993): Jeffries Report (ISSN 0734-4589)
Description: Features reports and reviews on asynchronous transfer mode (ATM) for LANs and internetworks.

ABSOLUTE REFERENCE; the journal for 1-2-3 and Symphony users. see COMPUTERS — Microcomputers

ACCESS (RESEARCH TRIANGLE PARK). see SCIENCES: COMPREHENSIVE WORKS — Computer Applications

621.381   UK   ISSN 0957-4867
AMIGA FORMAT. 1988. m. £48.75 (rest of Europe £71.27; elsewhere £86.27). Future Publishing Ltd., 30 Monmouth St., Bath, Avon BA1 2BW, England. TEL 44-1224-442244. FAX 44-1224-462986. (Subscr. to: Future Publishing, Somerton, Somers. TA11 6BR, England. TEL 44-1225-822511) Pub. Simon Stansfield. circ. 115,158. **Indexed:** WPM.
Supersedes in part (in 1989): S T Amiga Format (ISSN 0954-805X)
Description: Covers aspects of the Amiga computer range. Reviews games and technical products.

621.381   GW
AMIGA MAGAZIN. m. DM.83.40 (foreign DM.109.20). Markt und Technik Verlag AG, Hans-Pinsel-Str. 2, 85540 Haar, Germany. TEL 089-4613-0. FAX 089-4613-774. Ed. Albert Absmeier. Pubs. Carl-Franz von Quadt, Otmar Weber. adv. contact: Peter Kusterer. circ. 104,798. **Document type:** consumer publication.

004.16   US
AMIGA REPORT MAGAZINE. 1993. bi-w. 1203 Alexander Ave., Streamwood, IL 60107. FAX 847-741-0689. E-mail: jcompton@xnet.com; URL: http://www.cucug.org/ar/. Ed. Jason Compton. **Document type:** trade publication.
•Available only online.
Description: Contains information, news, reviews, and views directed at users of the Amiga computer.

621.381   SP   ISSN 1130-1074
AMIGA WORLD. 11/yr. C. Rafael Calvo, 18 4oB, 28010 Madrid, Spain. TEL 1-319-40-14. FAX 1-319-61-04. Ed. Juan Miguel Urraca. circ. 18,000.

621.381   US
AMY D. WOHL'S TRENDS LETTER. m. $495 (foreign $530) (effective 1997). Wohl Associates, 915 Montgomery Ave., Ste. 309, Narbeth, PA 19072. TEL 610-667-4842. FAX 610-667-3081. Ed. Amy D. Wohl. bk.rev. **Document type:** newsletter.
Formerly (until 1991): Wohl Report on End User Computing.

621.381   US
APPLE DIRECT; an information resource from Apple developers services. m. Apple Computer, Inc., 10381 Bandley Dr., Cupertino, CA 95014. TEL 408-974-2552. Ed. Lisa Raleigh.
Description: For Apple users. Feature articles on pertinent software, hardware, new product developments, marketing and news clips as well as listings of upcoming events pertinent to developers.

621.381 370   US
APPLE EDUCATION NEWS; an information service for educators and trainers. q. free. Apple Computer, Inc., 10381 Bandley Dr., Cupertino, CA 95014. TEL 408-974-2552. Ed. Lori Deuchar. bk.rev. circ. 100,000.
Description: For educators and trainers using Apple computers. Features articles on projects and innovative applications created by schools using Apple computers.

APPLE IIGS. see COMPUTERS — Software

621.381   FR
APPLE - LE MAGAZINE. 11/yr. 31 rue du Petit Music, 75004 Paris, France. TEL 40-27-99-99. FAX 40-27-96-99. Ed. Pascal Boucher. circ. 100,000.

APPLE LIBRARY USERS GROUP NEWSLETTER. see LIBRARY AND INFORMATION SCIENCES — Computer Applications

621.381   AU
APPLE TIME; business and communication. (Text in German) 1987. bi-m. S.210. Page Verlag Inc., Hermann-Gasse 18, A-1070 Vienna, Austria. TEL 01-52626500. FAX 01-5262536. Ed. Peter Pisecker; Pub. Renato Zappella. adv.: B&W page S.2430, color page S.3880; trim 185 x 265; adv. contact: Renate Hartlieb. circ. 35,000. **Document type:** trade publication.
Description: For business and Apple computer users.

004.16   NE   ISSN 0926-8588
APPLE WORLD MAGAZINE. Cover title: A W M - Apple World Magazine. 1984. m. fl.75 (900 BEF) (effective 1993). Nanton Press B.V., Leyenseweg 115C, 3721 BC Bilthoven, Netherlands. TEL 31-30-29064. FAX 31-30-286224. (Subscr. to: Postbus 93, 3720 AB Bilthoven, Netherlands) Ed. Anton Kriegsman. adv. contact: Anton Kriegsman. bk.rev. circ. 16,000.
—SWETS.
Former titles (until 1991): Apple Macintoshblad (ISSN 0926-857X); (until 1990): Apple Blad 2 - Macintosh Blad (ISSN 0168-8308)

004.16   AT   ISSN 1328-3049
APPLESAUCE. Online edition (AT ISSN 1328-3057) 1980. m. (except Jan.). Aus.$30 membership. South Australian Apple Users Club, P.O. Box 322, Prospect, S.A. 5082, Australia. TEL 61-8-84434298. E-mail: pcarter@acslink.net.au; URL: http://www.webmedia.com.au/applesauce/ (Editorial addr.: c/o Pelagos Productions, P.O. Box 133, Brooklyn Park, S.A. 5032, Australia) Ed. P.J. Carter. R&P contact: P.J. Carter. **Document type:** newsletter.
•Also available online.
Description: Contains club news, product reviews, hints and tips for club members.

621.381   JA   ISSN 0916-0302
ASAHI PASOKON/ASAHI PERSONAL COMPUTERS. (Text in Japanese) 1988. s-m. $150.50. Asahi Shimbun Publishing Co., 3-2 Tsukiji 5-chome, Chuo-ku, Tokyo 104-11, Japan. (Order to: Japan Publications Trading Co., Ltd., Box 5030, Tokyo International, Tokyo, Japan) Ed. Keijiro Mori.

621.381 380.3   AT   ISSN 1038-359X
AUSTRALIAN & NEW ZEALAND L A N MAGAZINE. Variant title: L A N magazine. m Aus.$45. A C P Computer Publications, Level 6, 54-58 Park St., Sydney, N.S.W. 2000, Australia. TEL 61-2-2889168. FAX 61-2-2674909. E-mail: lanmag@acp.com.au. Ed. Chris Moriarty; Pub. Richard Walsh. adv.: B&W page Aus.$2700, color page Aus.$3600; trim 275 x 210; adv. contact: M. Chivers. circ. 15,250 —UnCover.
Description: Covers local networking industry - networking news, product updates, relevant business news and coverage of industry events.

621.381 001.642   AT   ISSN 1039-2149
AUSTRALIAN & NEW ZEALAND P C USER. Variant title: C User. m. Aus.$65. A C P Computer Publications, Level 6, 54-58 Park St., Sydney, N.S.W. 2000, Australia. TEL 61-2-2889137. FAX 61-2-2674909. E-mail: pcuser@acp.com.au. Ed. Glenn Rees; Pub. Richard Walsh. adv.: B&W page Aus.$2595, color page Aus.$3440; trim 275 x 210; adv. contact: Tom Di Terlizzi. circ. 35,218.
Formerly: Australian P C User (ISSN 1034-4703)
Description: For the business user and other end users of personal computers. Ideal companion for the small office, home office computer user.

621.381   AT   ISSN 1034-3806
AUSTRALIAN COMMODORE AND AMIGA REVIEW. 198_ m. Aus.$34. Gareth Powell Pty Ltd., 21 Darley Rd, Randwick, N.S.W. 2031, Australia. TEL 02-398-5_ Ed. Andrew Farrell. adv.; bk.rev. circ. 11,500. (back issues avail.)
Formerly: Australian Commodore Review.

COMPUTERS — PERSONAL COMPUTERS

621.381 AT ISSN 0814-9356
AUSTRALIAN MACWORLD. 1985. m. Aus.$54 (foreign Aus.$150). I D G Communications Pty. Ltd., 88 Christie St., St. Leonards, N.S.W. 2065, Australia. TEL 02-439-5133. FAX 02-439-5512. Pub. Robert Wells. circ. 12,000. **Document type:** trade publication.
—CCC.
Description: Aimed at users and potential users of the Apple Macintosh; primarily for people in business and professions.

621.381 AT ISSN 0813-1384
AUSTRALIAN P C WORLD. 1984. fortn. Aus.$59.40 (foreign Aus.$150). I D G Communications Pty. Ltd., 88 Christie St., St. Leonards, N.S.W. 2065, Australia. TEL 02-439-5133. FAX 02-439-5512. Ed. Robert Thirlwell. circ. 17,230. **Document type:** trade publication.

621.381 AT ISSN 0725-4415
AUSTRALIAN PERSONAL COMPUTER. 1980. m. Aus.$55. A C P Computer Publications, Level 6, 54-58 Park St., Sydney, N.S.W. 2000, Australia. TEL 61-2-2889123. FAX 61-2-2674909. E-mail: apc@acp.com.au; URL: http://www.com.au/apc/. Ed. Jeremy White; Pub. Richard Walsh. adv.; B&W page Aus.$3200, color page Aus.$4280; trim 275 x 210; adv. contact: David O'Sullivan. bk.rev. circ. 39,608. (back issues avail.)
—UnCover.

004.16 US ISSN 1066-730X
A2 - CENTRAL.* 1985. m. $59.95. Resource Central, Inc., 7118 Main St., Kansas City, MO 64114-1406. TEL 913-649-6502. FAX 913-469-6507. Pub. Tom Weishaar. bk.rev.; charts; illus. circ. 10,000. (diskette format)
—CCC.
Formerly: Open-Apple (ISSN 0885-4017)
Description: For Apple II users. Features software reviews, programming information as well as letters, questions and tips from readers. Includes management of the Apple II areas on Genie.

621.381 001.644 US
A U D.* (Big Apple Users Digest) 1979. m. membership. Big Apple Users Group (BAUG), 345 W. 58th St., Apt. 5L, New York, NY 10019-1132. FAX 212-924-2690. Ed. Michael Callery. adv. circ. 300.
Description: Provides news, information and commentary for users of Apple computers: Apple II and Macintosh.

621.381 US
B S MAGAZINE. (Bulletin Board Systems) 1990. m. $26 to individuals (foreign $10); institutions $31 (foreign $41). Callers Digest, Inc., 701 Stokes Rd., Medford, NJ 08055. TEL 609-953-9110. FAX 609-953-7961. E-mail: http://www.bbsmag.com. (Subscr. to: The National Interest, Box 622, Shrub Oak, NY 10588) Ed. Rick Robinson; Pub. Richard Paguette. adv. contact: John Carcione. bk.rev. circ. 46,000. (back issues avail.) **Document type:** consumer publication.
Formerly: B B S Callers Digest (ISSN 1055-2812)
Description: Used by modem owners to call local bulletin board systems.

004.16 BE
I. (Bureau Informatique); information management systems magazine. Dutch edition: B I Buro Informatika (ISSN 0777-9216) (Text in French) vol.34, 1994. 10/yr. 2150 BEF (foreign 2900 BEF); newsstand price: 200 BEF. Business & Management Editions Brussels s.p.r.l., Rue Stephanie, 17, 1020 Brussels, Belgium. TEL 32-2-4266115. FAX 32-2-4258226. Ed. Jean-Luc Manise; Pub. Philippe Fabry. adv.; software rev.; illus. circ. 24,000. **Document type:** trade publication.
Former titles: B M B Bureau Informatique (ISSN 0777-9208); (until 1990): B M B Bureau Magazine (ISSN 0777-9186); B M B (ISSN 0771-0682)
Description: Covers new software and hardware products, data communication, network applications, legal issues and other news affecting business computer users.

621.381 US ISSN 1076-089X
J G NEWSLETTER. 1983. m. $20 includes membership. Brevard Users Group, Box 37211, Satellite Beach, FL 32937. TEL 407-727-1591. E-mail: jbeck@tng.net. Ed. John Beck. R&P contact: John Beck. adv. contact: Richard DeSaulnier. bk.rev. circ. 350. **Document type:** newsletter.

621.381 US
BALTIMORE SANYO USER'S NEWSLETTER.* m. membership. Baltimore Sanyo User's Group, c/o Mark Kurzmack, Ed., 5037 W. County Rd. 54G, Laporte, CO 80535-9552.

004.16 US
▼**BIG SKY MAC E - ZINE.** 1995. m. B - Smug, Big - Sky Mac User Group, Box 80553, Billings, MT 59108. E-mail: bgskymac@imt.net; URL: http://www.imt.net/~bgskymac/BigSky_MacEzine.html. Ed. Bud Henley.
● Available only online.
Description: Covers Macintosh computer related topics.
Refereed Serial

621.381 US
BUG REPORT. 1983. m. $12.50. Greater South Bay P C Users Group, Box 6950, Torrance, CA 90504-6950. TEL 310-329-2804. Ed. Lindsey Barlow. adv.; bk.rev. circ. 400.
Formerly: G S B U G.
Description: For IBM and clone computer users.

004.16 US
BUGNET. 1994. m. Box 393, Sumas, WA 98295. E-mail: bugnet@bugnet.com; cb@bugnet.com; URL: http://www.bugnet.com/free1.html. Ed. Bruce Brown. **Document type:** newsletter.
● Available only online.
Description: Global resource for PC bugs, glitches, incompatibilities, and their fixes.

621.381 GW
BUS; Computernutzung an Schulen. 1979. s-a. DM.19.80. (Zentralstelle fuer Computer im Unterricht) Bayerischer Schulbuch-Verlag, Hubertusstr. 4, 80639 Munich, Germany. Eds. Udo Karl, Werner Liessel. circ. 3,500. **Indexed:** Pt.de Rep. **Document type:** academic/scholarly publication.

THE BUSINESS INTERNET NEWSLETTER. see *COMMUNICATIONS*

BYTE. see *COMPUTERS — Computer Systems*

C A D - C A M & COMPUTER GRAPHICS. see *COMPUTERS — Computer Graphics*

C A L I C O JOURNAL. (Computer Assisted Language & Instruction Consortium) see *EDUCATION — Computer Applications*

004.16 UK
C E M A PERSONAL COMPUTERS AND PERIPHERALS. 1986. m. £2000($3500) (Cores European Market Analysis) Portman Communications Ltd., 52 Foundling Ct., London WC1N 1AN, England. TEL 44-171-837-0815. FAX 44-171-278-9917. E-mail: 100141,676@compuserve. Ed. Keith Waller; Pub. Philip Gallagher. R&P contact: Philip Gallagher. bk.rev.; charts; stat.; software rev.; circ. 400 (paid). **Document type:** newsletter.

C E P SOFTWARE DIRECTORY. (American Institute of Chemical Engineers) see *CHEMISTRY — Computer Applications*

621.381 UK ISSN 0963-0090
C U AMIGA. 1981. m. £47.40 (foreign £55) (effective 1996). E M A P - Images, Priory Ct., 30-32 Farringdon Ln., London EC1R 3AU, England. TEL 44-171-972-6700. FAX 44-171-972-6710. (Subscr. to: Tower Publishing Services Ltd., Tower House, Sovereign Park, Lathkill St., Market Harborough, Leics. LE16 9EF, England. TEL 44-1858-468811. FAX 44-1858-432164) adv. circ. 111,400. **Indexed:** INSPEC. **Document type:** consumer publication.
Former titles (until 1991): C U Amiga-64 (ISSN 0957-5103); (until 1989): Commodore User (ISSN 0265-721X)

CAFE MAGAZINE. see *GENERAL INTEREST PERIODICALS — Great Britain*

CAMPUS-WIDE INFORMATION SYSTEMS. see *LIBRARY AND INFORMATION SCIENCES — Computer Applications*

CAPITAL P C MONITOR; users helping users. see *COMPUTERS — Computer Networks*

CATALYST (MENLO PARK). see *COMPUTERS — Computer Assisted Instruction*

CHANNELMARKER LETTER. see *COMPUTERS — Computer Industry*

621.381 IT ISSN 1122-9241
CHIP; mensile di microinformatica. 1974-1989; resumed 1990. m. (11/yr.). L.76000 (effective 1997). Gruppo Editoriale J C E, Via Ferri 6, 20092 Cinisello Balsamo (MI), Italy. TEL 39-2-660251. FAX 39-2-6127620. TELEX 352376 JCEMIL I. E-mail: chip@jce.it; URL: http://www.jce.it. Ed. Gerald Dick. adv.: B&W page L.5500000, color page L.7500000; trim 210 x 246. circ. 50,000.
Description: Presents tips and product tests about internet and multimedia.

004.16 IT ISSN 1123-8518
▼**CLIC!.** 1995. m. L.66000 (foreign L.89700). Mondadori Informatica S.p.A., Casella Postale 3686, 20090 Segrate (MI), Italy. TEL 39-2-21712240. FAX 39-2-21712245. E-mail: clic@mondadori.it. Ed. Francesco Di Martile. adv. contact: Gianluca Ferrauto. circ. 121,847. **Document type:** consumer publication.
Description: For home computer users who want to have fun with their computers.

COMMUNICATIONS PRODUCT REPORTS. see *COMMUNICATIONS — Computer Applications*

621.381 FR ISSN 0985-7443
COMPATIBLES P C MAGAZINE. 1987. 11/yr. Sepcom, 5-7 rue de l'Amiral-Courbet, 94160 Saint-Mande, France. TEL 43-98-22-22. FAX 43-28-72-12. Ed. Jean Kaminsky. circ. 125,000.

621.381 US
COMPUTACION PERSONAL. (Text in Spanish) m. C W Communications, Inc., Computacion Personal, Attn.: Diana La Muraglia, 375 Cochituate Rd., Box 9171, Framingham, MA 01701-9171. TEL 617-879-0700. circ. 5,000.

004.16 US ISSN 0738-9213
QA76.5 CODEN: CBGHEI
COMPUTER BUYER'S GUIDE AND HANDBOOK. 1982. m. $36. Bedford Communications, Inc., 150 Fifth Ave., New York, NY 10011. TEL 212-807-8220. FAX 212-807-1098. Ed. David Finck; Pub. Ed Brown. R&P contact: David Finck. adv. contact: Carol Berman. circ. 45,000. **Document type:** consumer publication.
—CASDDS; KR SourceOne.

COMPUTER GAMING WORLD. see *COMPUTERS — Computer Games*

621.381 IT ISSN 1123-4253
COMPUTER GAZETTE. Italian translation in part of: Computer Graphics World (US ISSN 0271-4159) and: Digital Video Magazine (US ISSN 1075-251X) 1986. 11/yr. L.180000 in Europe; elsewhere L.240000. I H T Gruppo Editoriale, Via Monte Napoleone 9, 20121 Milan, Italy. TEL 39-2-794181. FAX 39-2-784021. E-mail: cg@iht.it; URL: http://www.iht.it. Pub. Massimiliano Lisa. adv.: B&W page $2018, color page $3045; adv. contact: Massimiliano Lisa. bk.rev. circ. 36,000. **Document type:** consumer publication.
Formerly: Commodore Gazette (ISSN 0394-6991)
Description: Covers computer graphics, CAD-CAM, multimedia, digital audio-video for all platforms.

621.381 GW ISSN 0722-0987
COMPUTER PERSOENLICH. fortn. DM.67.20 (foreign DM.91.20). Markt und Technik Verlag AG, Hans-Pinsel-Str. 2, 85540 Haar, Germany. TEL 089-4613-0. FAX 089-4613-774. Ed. Michael Pauly. adv. contact: Philipp Schiede. **Indexed:** Cyb.Abstr. **Document type:** consumer publication.
Incorporates (in 1991): P C Plus Technik (ISSN 0940-9238); Which was formerly (until 1990): P C Magazin Plus (ISSN 0934-8468)
Description: Reports about personal computers in offices, research, planning, construction and the sciences.

004.16 US ISSN 0748-8610
QA76.5
COMPUTER RETAILERS' GUIDE.* 1984. q. C M P Publications, Inc., 600 Community Dr., Manhasset, NY 11030. TEL 516-562-5000. FAX 516-365-4601. TELEX 647035 CMP PUB MAHA.
Formerly (until 1985): Computer Retail News. Retailers Guide (ISSN 0884-7444)

COMPUTERS — PERSONAL COMPUTERS

COMPUTER SHOPPER; the computer magazine for direct buyers. see COMPUTERS — Computer Sales

004.16   NE   ISSN 0927-2739
COMPUTER! TOTAAL. 1992. 11/yr. (Hobby Computer Club) I D G Communications Nederland, Postbus 5446, 2000 GK Haarlem, Netherlands. TEL 31-23-5461111. FAX 31-23-5461155. Pub. R. Gort. circ. 107,000. **Document type:** consumer publication.
—SWETS.
    Formed by the merger of (1984-1991): P C World Benelux (ISSN 0169-3417); (1977-1992): H C C Nieuwsbrief (ISSN 0928-2688); (1990-1991): P C Thuis (ISSN 0926-3101)

COMPUTER USER (MINNEAPOLIS). see COMPUTERS

004   US   ISSN 1053-3834
COMPUTER USER'S SURVIVAL MAGAZINE. 1980. m. $60. Enterprises Publishing, 400 E. 59th St., Ste. 9F, New York, NY 10022. TEL 212-755-4363. FAX 212-755-4365. Ed. Tom Weston. circ. 300,000. **Document type:** consumer publication.
●Also available online.

001.642 070   US   ISSN 8756-7911
COMPUTERITER; microcomputer news and views for the writer-editor. 1984. m. $40. Creative Business Communications, Box 476, Columbia, MD 21045. TEL 301-596-5591. FAX 301-997-7946. Ed. Linda J. Elengold. bk.rev. circ. 7,000. (looseleaf format; back issues avail.)

COMPUTERLAND MAGAZINE. see BUSINESS AND ECONOMICS — Computer Applications

004.16   US   ISSN 1076-9862
COMPUTERLIFE. 1994. m. Ziff-Davis Publishing Co., One Park Ave., New York, NY 10016. TEL 212-503-5100. circ. 300,000 (paid). **Document type:** consumer publication.
—KR SourceOne. **CCC**.

COMPUTERS IN ACCOUNTING. see BUSINESS AND ECONOMICS — Computer Applications

621.381 025   US
COMPUTERS IN LIBRARIES: BUYERS GUIDE & CONSULTANT DIRECTORY. 1986. a. Information Today, Inc., 143 Old Marlton Pike, Medford, NJ 08055-8750. TEL 609-654-6266. FAX 609-654-4309. circ. 30,000. (reprint service avail. from WSH) **Document type:** directory.
    Formerly (until 1988): Small Computers in Libraries: Buyers Guide and Consultant Directory (ISSN 0896-9485)
    Description: Lists products and services available to libraries and information centers, broken down by computers, peripherals, software, consultants, online database systems and services; covers furniture and other products as well.

COMPUTERS IN THE SCHOOLS; the interdisciplinary journal of practice, theory, and applied research. see EDUCATION — Computer Applications

COMPUTERWORLD; newsweekly for information technology leaders. see COMPUTERS

COMPUTERWORLD CLIENT - SERVER JOURNAL. see COMPUTERS

CONNECTIONS (LOS GATOS); the newsletter for networking Macintoshes. see COMPUTERS — Computer Networks

004.16   UK   ISSN 0953-1378
CONNECTIVITY. 1983. m. £40 to individuals; institutions £150. Taylor Associates, P.O. Box 13281, London N3 3TD, England. TEL 44-70-500-40035. FAX 44-70-500-28485. E-mail: andrew@taylor.co.uk. Ed. Andrew Taylor. R&P contact: Andrew Taylor. adv. contact: Paul Savill. bk.rev. circ. 10,000. (back issues avail.) **Document type:** consumer publication.
    Description: Articles with a technical bias on personal computers, peripherals, software and networks for professionals and enthusiasts.

621.381   US   ISSN 0899-8159
QA76.9.A25
CRYPTOSYSTEMS JOURNAL. 1988. irreg. $45 (foreign $65). 485 Middle Holland Rd., Holland, PA 18966. TEL 215-579-9888. E-mail: crypto@compuserve.com; URL: http://ourworld.compuserve.com/homepages/crypto. Ed. Tony Patti; Pub. Tony Patti. bk.rev. (also avail. in diskette format; back issues avail.) **Document type:** academic/scholarly publication.
●Also available on CD-ROM.
    Description: Covers the implementation of cryptographic systems (encryption, decryption, key generation) on IBM-PCs. Includes one or more diskettes with complete source code.

CYBERLOG; library of applied medical software. see MEDICAL SCIENCES — Computer Applications

D XERS MAGAZINE. see COMPUTERS — Microcomputers

DATAPRO DIRECTORY OF MICROCOMPUTER HARDWARE. see COMPUTERS — Computer Industry Directories

004.16   SW   ISSN 1104-3784
DATORMAGAZIN; tidningen foer dig som har Amiga eller PC. 1986. m. SEK 369; newsstand price: SEK 34. Broedrena Lindstroems Foerlags AB, Industrig. 2A, S-112 85 Stockholm, Sweden. TEL 46-8-692-01-40. FAX 46-8-650-97-05. E-mail: pk@dmz.medstroms.se. (Subscr. to: Titel Data AB, Industrig. 2A, 112 86 Stockholm, Sweden. TEL 46-8-652-43-00) Ed. Peter Kerschbaumer. adv.: B&W page SEK 16000; adv. contact: Bjoren Wenstroem. (back issues avail.) **Document type:** consumer publication.
    Formerly (until 1992): Datormagazin C64-128-Amiga (ISSN 0283-3379)

DI SAN BO/THIRD WAVE MAGAZINE. see COMPUTERS — Computer Programming

004.16   CH   ISSN 1024-3879
DIANNAO SHIJIE ZAZHI/P C WORLD - WINDOWS WORLD TAIWAN. (Text in Chinese) 1988. m. I D G Communications, Taiwan, 12-F, No.2, Sec.3, Min Sheng E. Rd., Taipei, Taiwan 10639, Republic of China. TEL 886-2-5019501. FAX 886-2-5056005. URL: http://www.idg.com.tw/pcw/index.html. Ed. Charles Chan. adv.: B&W page NT.$33600, color page NT.$64800; trim 210 x 280. circ. 30,000.
    Description: Provides analysis and reports on software, hardware, market development, and operations for audience in sectors such as IT, service, manufacturing, military, public service, academics, and students.

DR. DOBB'S JOURNAL; software tools for the professional programmer. see COMPUTERS — Microcomputers

DUN'S DATALINE. see BUSINESS AND ECONOMICS — Computer Applications

004.16 330   US
DVORAK DIRECTORY. a. $4. Dvorak International, Box 44, Poultney, VT 05764-0044. TEL 802-287-2343. E-mail: DvorakInt@aol.com. **Document type:** directory.
    Former titles: Dvorak Products List & Dvorak International. Typing Manual for Computer and Typewriter.
    Description: Comprehensive listing of sources for Dvorak related products.

EDUCATION TECHNOLOGY NEWS. see COMPUTERS — Computer Assisted Instruction

621.381   US   ISSN 0886-9812
CODEN: EELLEU
EXCELLENCE (MICROSOFT EXCEL). 1985. m. $49 (foreign $79). Cobb Group, Inc., 9420 Bunsen Pkwy., Ste. 300, Louisville, KY 40220. TEL 502-493-3200. FAX 502-491-8050. (Subscr. to: Box 35160, Louisville, KY 40232-9720. TEL 800-223-8720) Ed. Steven Cobb. **Document type:** consumer publication.
    Description: Offers tips and techniques for users of Microsoft Excel for the Macintosh.

EXECUTIVE COMPUTING; ideas you can use about small computers. see BUSINESS AND ECONOMICS — Computer Applications

004.16   US   ISSN 1076-7754
QA76.5
FAMILY P C. Key Title: FamilyPC. 1994. 10/yr. $14.95 (Europe $24.95) (effective 1997); newsstand price: $2.95. FamilyPC (Subsidiary of: Disney Computer Magazine, Inc.), 1 Park Ave., New York, NY 10016. TEL 212-503-3500. E-mail: familypc@aol.com; URL: http://www.zdnet.com/-familypc. (Subscr. to: Box 400454, Des Moines, IA 50340-0454. TEL 800-825-6450) (Co-publisher: Ziff-Davis Publishing Co.) Ed. Robin Raskin. adv.: B&W page $11860, color page $15810; trim 7 7/8 x 10 1/2. software rev.; illus.; tr.lit.; circ. 300,000 (paid). **Document type:** consumer publication.
—KR SourceOne; UnCover. **CCC**.
    Description: Provides information on new hardware and software products for families using personal computers, with emphasis on multimedia applications, educational and entertainment software.

004.16   US
FAMILY P C'S ULTIMATE FAMILY SOFTWARE GUIDE. a. newsstand price: $3.95. Walt Disney Magazine Publishing Group, 500 S. Buena Vista, Burbank, CA 91521-6012. TEL 818-973-4320. (Co-publisher: Ziff-Davis Publishing Co.) adv.
    Description: Provides guidance to the year's most notable software products.

FORTH DIMENSIONS. see COMPUTERS — Computer Programming

621.381   US
G R M U G NEWSLETTER. irreg. Great River Microcomputer Users Group, 47 Lake Dr. S., Rte. 9, Quincy, IL 62301. Ed. David N. Wexler.

GLEN COVE COMPUTING NEWS. see COMPUTERS — Computer Networks

004.16   US
GW2K: THE GATEWAY MAGAZINE. q. Gateway 2000, Inc., 610 Gateway Dr., North Sioux City, SD 57049. TEL 800-846-2000. FAX 605-232-2023. E-mail: editor@gw2k.com. Ed. Ann VanderWiel. adv. contact: Nick Hofer. **Document type:** newsletter.

621.381   US   ISSN 1069-3467
H A L - P C USER JOURNAL.* 1983. m. $40 membership. Houston Area League of P C Users, Inc., 2200 Post Oak Blvd., Ste. 512, Houston, TX 77056-4706. TEL 713-963-4155. FAX 713-623-4251. E-mail: cevans@hal-pc.org; URL: http://www.hal-pc.org. Ed. Charles W. Evans. R&P contact: Charles Evans. adv. contact: Kevin Upp. bk.rev.; circ. 20,000 (paid). **Document type:** trade publication.
    Formerly: H A L - P C Newsletter.
    Refereed Serial

621.381   US   ISSN 0895-0342
H P CHRONICLE - EUROPE; the independent newspaper for Hewlett-Packard computer users in the U K and Western Europe. 1987. m. $45 (foreign $75) (effective 1995 & 1996). Publications & Communications, Inc., 12416 Hymeadow, Austin, TX 78750-1896. TEL 512-250-9023. FAX 512-331-3900. Ed. Brian Simpson. adv. (tabloid format; reprint service avail.) **Document type:** trade publication.

H - SCOOP. see COMPUTERS — Microcomputers

HOME AUTOMATION NEWS. see ELECTRONICS

COMPUTERS — PERSONAL COMPUTERS

004 US ISSN 0899-7373
QA76.5
HOME OFFICE COMPUTING; building better businesses with technology. 1983. m. $19.97 (foreign $27.97); newsstand price: $2.95. Scholastic Inc., 555 Broadway, New York, NY 10012-3999. TEL 212-505-3000. URL: http://www.samlloffice.com/. (Subscr. to: Box 51344, Boulder, CO 80321-1344. TEL 800-288-7812) Ed. Dennis Eskow. adv.; bk.rev. circ. 500,000. (also avail. in microform from UMI; reprint service avail. from UMI) Indexed: Mag.Ind., Microcomp.Ind., PCR2, R.G.Abstr. **Document type:** trade publication.
●Also available online. Vendor(s): Information Access Co., UMI.
—BLDSC (4326.104900); KR SourceOne; SWETS; UMI; UnCover.
Former titles (until 1988): Family and Home Office Computing (ISSN 0896-6028); (until 1987): Family Computing (ISSN 0738-6079)
Description: Aimed at professionals who use computers and do business at home. Features articles on a variety of topics, from applications and maintenance to profiles of families and their experiences with computers.

004.16 US ISSN 1073-1784
HOME P C. 1994. m. C M P Publications, Inc. (Jericho), 1 Jericho Plaza, 3rd. Fl., Jericho, NY 11753. TEL 516-733-6700. FAX 516-733-8390. TELEX 647035 CMP PUB MAHA. URL: www.winmag.com. (Subscr. to: Reader Service Management Dept., Box 5006, Pittsfield, MA 01203-9951. TEL 800-829-9150) software rev. **Document type:** consumer publication.
—KR SourceOne. **CCC**.

004.16 US ISSN 1056-8573
HD9696.C6
HOW TO BUY AND PRICE A USED COMPUTER. 1992. irreg. $39. Orion Research Corp., 14555 N. Scottsdale Rd., Ste. 330, Scottsdale, AZ 85254. TEL 800-844-0759. FAX 800-375-1315. E-mail: orion@bluebook.com.

E E E MICRO. see COMPUTERS — Microcomputers

E E E PERSONAL COMMUNICATIONS; the magazine of nomadic communications and computing. see COMMUNICATIONS

004.16 380 US
E E E PERSONAL COMPUTERS. 1994. q. $75 to non-members. Institute of Electrical and Electronics Engineers, Inc., 345 E. 47th St., New York, NY 10017. TEL 908-981-0060. FAX 908-981-9667. (Subscr. to: Box 1331, 445 Hoes La., Piscataway, NJ 08855-1331) Ed. Hamid Ahmadi. adv.
Description: Personalized, location-independent communications in all media. Portable telephones, communicating palm-top computers, protocols, messaging, communications and personalized traffic filtering, spectrum allocation, industry structure and technology evolution.

621.381 AU
S S B AMIGA MAGAZINE. bi-m. Kirchengasse 27, A-1070 Vienna, Austria. TEL 02732-853273. FAX 02732-85327. Ed. Marcello Isidori. circ. 30,000.

621.381 FR
ONES; des souries et des hommes. 6/yr. Dynamots, 13 ave Delory, 59100 Roubaix, France. TEL 20-70-54-90. FAX 20-70-43-96. Ed. J.P. Grevet. circ. 25,000.
Description: For Macintosh Apple users.

FOTECTURE EUROPE; fortnightly European newsletter on the on-line information industry. see COMPUTERS — Computer Networks

621.381 001.642 US ISSN 1052-9470
QA76.8.M3
SIDE HYPERCARD. 1991. m. $59 (foreign $79). Cobb Group, Inc., 9420 Bunsen Pkwy., Ste. 300, Louisville, KY 40220. TEL 502-493-3200. FAX 502-491-8050. (Subscr. to: Box 35160, Louisville, KY 40232-9720. TEL 800-223-8720) Ed. Jim Pile. **Document type:** consumer publication.
Description: Offers tips and techniques on using Claris HyperCard.

SIDE MARKET DATA; the newsletter of real-time market data. see BUSINESS AND ECONOMICS — Banking And Finance — Computer Applications

INSIDE MICROSOFT WINDOWS. see COMPUTERS — Software

INSIDE MICROSOFT WINDOWS; tips and tricks for Microsoft Windows. see COMPUTERS — Software

621.381 US ISSN 1046-9648
INSIDE MICROSOFT WORKS (MACINTOSH EDITION). 1989. m. $39 (foreign $59). Cobb Group, Inc., 9420 Bunsen Pkwy., Ste. 300, Louisville, KY 40220. TEL 502-493-3200. FAX 502-491-8050. (Subscr. to: Box 35160, Louisville, KY 40232-9720. TEL 800-223-8720) Ed. Mike Stephens. **Document type:** consumer publication.
Description: Contains tips and techniques aimed exclusively to users of Microsoft Works for the Macintosh.

621.381 US ISSN 1061-5873
INSIDE MICROSOFT WORKS FOR WINDOWS. 1992. m. $39 (foreign $59). Cobb Group, Inc., 9420 Bunsen Pkwy., Ste. 300, Louisville, KY 40220. TEL 502-493-3200. FAX 502-491-8050. (Subscr. to: Box 35160, Louisville, KY 40232-9720. TEL 800-223-8720) **Document type:** consumer publication.

621.381 US ISSN 1053-1467
INSIDE QUATTRO PRO. 1988. m. $59 (foreign $79). Cobb Group, Inc., 9420 Bunsen Pkwy., Ste. 300, Louisville, KY 40220. TEL 502-493-3200. FAX 502-491-8050. (Subscr. to: Box 35160, Louisville, KY 40232-9720. TEL 800-223-8720) Ed. Steven Cobb. **Document type:** consumer publication.
Formerly (until 1990): Quattro (ISSN 0895-5603)
Description: Contains tips and techniques aimed exclusively to users of Borland's Quattro Pro.

INSIDE VISUAL BASIC FOR WINDOWS. see COMPUTERS — Computer Programming

621.381 US ISSN 0893-9349
INSIDE WORD (MACINTOSH EDITION). 1987. m. $49 (foreign $89). Cobb Group, Inc., 9420 Bunsen Pkwy., Ste. 300, Louisville, KY 40220. TEL 502-493-3200. FAX 502-491-8050. (Subscr. to: Box 35160, Louisville, KY 40232-9720. TEL 800-223-8720) Ed. Jody Gilbert. **Document type:** consumer publication.
Description: Contains tips and techniques aimed exclusively at users of Microsoft Word for the Macintosh.

004.16 US
THE INSIDE WORD (MICROSOFT WORD 5.5 & 6.0). 1988. m. $69 (foreign $89). Cobb Group, Inc., 9420 Bunsen Pkwy., Ste. 300, Louisville, KY 40220. TEL 502-493-3200. FAX 502-491-8050. (Subscr. to: Box 35160, Louisville, KY 40232-9720. TEL 800-223-8720) Ed. Mike Stephens. **Document type:** consumer publication.
Formerly (until 1993): Word for Word (Microsoft Word 5.0) (ISSN 0896-7717)
Description: Offers tips and techniques on using Microsoft Works.

004.16 US ISSN 1052-7605
THE INSIDE WORD (P C EDITION - MICROSOFT WORD 5.5 & 6.0). 1991. m. $69 (foreign $89). Cobb Group, Inc., 9420 Bunsen Pkwy., Ste. 300, Louisville, KY 40220. TEL 502-493-3200. FAX 502-491-8050. (Subscr. to: Box 35160, Louisville, KY 40232-9720. TEL 800-223-8720) **Document type:** consumer publication.

621.381 001.642 US ISSN 1049-0795
CODEN: IWWIE8
INSIDE WORD FOR WINDOWS. 1990. m. $59 (foreign $79). Cobb Group, Inc., 9420 Bunsen Pkwy., Ste. 300, Louisville, KY 40220. TEL 502-493-3200. FAX 502-491-8050. (Subscr. to: Box 35160, Louisville, KY 40232-9720. TEL 800-223-8720) Ed. Jody Gilbert. Indexed: INSPEC (1994-).
Document type: consumer publication.
Description: Contains tips and techniques aimed exclusively to users of Microsoft Word for Windows.

621.381 US ISSN 1046-9656
CODEN: INWOEV
INSIDE WORDPERFECT. 1990. m. $69 (foreign $89). Cobb Group, Inc., 9420 Bunsen Pkwy., Ste. 300, Louisville, KY 40220. TEL 502-493-3200. FAX 502-491-8050. (Subscr. to: Box 35160, Louisville, KY 40232-9720. TEL 800-223-8720) Ed. Greg Geis. **Document type:** consumer publication.
Description: Offers tips and techniques for using WordPerfect.

621.381 US ISSN 1063-2727
INSIDE WORDPERFECT FOR WINDOWS. 1992. m. $59 (foreign $79). Cobb Group, Inc., 9420 Bunsen Pkwy., Ste. 300, Louisville, KY 40220. TEL 502-493-3200. FAX 502-491-8050. (Subscr. to: Box 35160, Louisville, KY 40232-9720. TEL 800-223-8720) **Document type:** consumer publication.

621.381 001.642 US ISSN 1052-2662
INSIDE 1-2-3 RELEASE 3 (3.1 & 3.4). 1990. m. $49 (foreign $69). Cobb Group, Inc., 9420 Bunsen Pkwy., Ste. 300, Louisville, KY 40220. TEL 502-493-3200. FAX 502-491-8050. (Subscr. to: Box 35160, Louisville, KY 40232-9720. TEL 800-223-8720) Ed. Stuart Vessels. **Document type:** consumer publication.
Description: Offers tips and techniques for using Lotus 1-2-3 version 3.

004.16 004.678 US
INTERNET ROADSTOP: MAC ZINE AND INFORMATION. m. E-mail: roadstop@digiserve.com; URL: http://digiserve.com/roadstop. Ed. Ben Wilson.
●Available only online.
Description: Provides articles, reviews, columns focusing on the upgrading of the Macintosh, pros and cons of different operating systems, and internet tools.

J U G NEWSLETTER. (Jefferson State Computer Users Group) see COMPUTERS — Computer Networks

004.16 UK
KEY NOTE MARKET REPORT: PERSONAL COMPUTERS & WORKSTATIONS. Variant title: Personal Computers & Workstations. irreg., no.8, 1990. £185. Key Note Ltd., Field House, 72 Oldfield Rd., Hampton, Middlesex TW12 2HQ, England.
TEL 44-181-783-0755.
FAX 44-181-783-1940604.

621.381 001.642
658.8
KEY NOTE REPORT: HOME COMPUTERS - SOFTWARE. Variant title: Home Computers - Software. 3rd ed., 1987. every 18 mos. £155 per no. Key Note Publications Ltd., Field House, 72 Oldfield Rd., Hampton, Middlesex TW12 2HQ, England. TEL 0181-783-0755. Fax 0181-783-1940. **Document type:** trade publication.
Description: Industry information on home computers and software. Covers marketing, major manufacturers, distribution and promotion, market size and trends, and recent developments.

621.381 US ISSN 1040-5917
L A N TIMES. (Local Area Network); information source for network users. 1984. bi-w. $65 in Canada; elsewhere $150; free in U.S. McGraw-Hill Companies, 1221 Ave. of the Americas, New York, NY 10020. TEL 212-512-2000; 800-525-5003. (Subscr. to: 1900 O'Farrell St., San Mateo, CA 94403. TEL 415-513-6800) Ed. Susan Breidenbach. adv.; bk.rev. circ. 153,845. Indexed: Comput.Ind., Tel.Abstr. **Document type:** trade publication.
●Also available online. Vendor(s): Dow Jones News Retrieval (LNTM), Knight-Ridder Information, Inc. (LAN), Lexis-Nexis (LANTME), NewsNet (EC42).
—BLDSC (5145.317000); KR SourceOne; SWETS; UMI. **CCC**.
Description: Contains industry news and information on new-product development.

621.381 JA
LAPTOP; notebook personal computer magazine. 1990. m. 9360 Yen. Akio Fujii, A S C I I Publishing, 4-33-10 Yoyogi, Shibuya-ku, Tokyo 151-24, Japan. TEL 81-3-5351-8111.

COMPUTERS — PERSONAL COMPUTERS

621.381 US
LAPTOP BUYER'S GUIDE. m. $36. Bedford Communications, Inc., 150 Fifth Ave., New York, NY 10011. TEL 212-807-8220. FAX 212-807-1098. Ed. David Finck; Pub. Ed Brown. R&P contact: David Finck. adv. contact: Carol Berman. **Document type:** consumer publication.

621.381 SZ
LAPTOP MAGAZIN. 2/yr. B & L Verlags AG, Steinwiesenstr. 3, CH-8952 Schlieren, Switzerland. TEL 41-1-7333999. FAX 41-1-7333989. Ed. Rainer Schulten. circ. 18,000. **Document type:** trade publication.

LINK-UP; the newsmagazine for users of online service - business, educational, personal. see COMPUTERS — Data Communications And Data Transmission Systems

621.381 IT
LIST SOLUZIONI PER INFORMATICA. 11/yr. Editore Edicomp s.r.l., Via Sannio 79, 00183 Rome, Italy. TEL 2-66-92-041. FAX 2-66-98-14-78. Ed. Renzo Rubeo. circ. 34,580.

LOADSTAR; the monthly software collection for people who love their Commodores. see COMPUTERS — Microcomputers

LOADSTAR QUARTERLY. see COMPUTERS — Software

621.381 380.3 US
LOCAL AREA NETWORKING AND L A N INTERNETWORKING. 1986. 3 base vols. (plus m. issues). $1224 to new subscr.; renewal $1113 (effective 1996). Datapro Information Services Group (Subsidiary of: McGraw-Hill, Inc.), 600 Delran Pkwy., Delran, NJ 08075. TEL 609-764-0100; 800-328-2776. FAX 609-764-2814.
   Former titles: Datapro Reports on P C and L A N Communications; Datapro Reports on P C Communications.

LOCAL AREA NETWORKS; newsletter covering worldwide technology trends, applications, and markets. see COMPUTERS — Computer Networks

621.381 SZ
LOGIC TIMES. 3/yr. Buckhauserstr. 24, CH-8048 Zurich, Switzerland. TEL 01-4927616. FAX 01-4930660. circ. 40,000.

M.D. COMPUTING (NEW YORK). see MEDICAL SCIENCES — Computer Applications

004.16 US ISSN 1088-548X
▼**MAC ADDICT.** 1996. m. $29.95 includes m. diskette (effective 1997). Imagine Publishing, Inc., 150 North Hill Dr., Brisbane, CA 94005. TEL 415-468-4684. FAX 415-468-4686. E-mail: subscribe@imagine-inc.com; URL: http://www.macaddict.com. Ed. Cheryl England; Pub. Patricia Neuray. adv. contact: Patricia Neuray. bk.rev.; software rev.; charts; illus. (back issues avail.). **Document type:** consumer publication.

004.16 US
MAC DISKWORLD. m. $89.95. Softdisk, Inc., Box 30008, Shreveport, LA 71130-0008. TEL 318-221-8718.

004.16 US ISSN 1074-0392
MAC HOME JOURNAL. 1993. m. $23.95; newsstand price: $3.95. 612 Howard St., 6th Fl., San Francisco, CA 94105-3905. TEL 415-957-1911. FAX 415-882-9502. adv.; bk.rev. circ. 55,000. **Document type:** consumer publication.
   Description: For the home Mac user.

004.1 004.678 US
▼**MAC NET JOURNAL.** 1995. m. (Bottom Line Online) White Rabbit Publishing, 3711 N. Mullen St., Tacoma, WA 98407. TEL 206-752-6402. E-mail: mchuff@wolfenet.com; URL: http://www.blol.com/web__mnj/. Ed. Rob McNair-Huff.
   ●Available only online.
   Description: Contains informative articles on how to get more out of Macintosh computers for home and business use.

621.381 JA
MAC POWER. 1990. m. 12000 Yen. Akio Fujii, A S C I I Publishing, 4-33-10 Yoyogi, Shibuya-ku, Tokyo 151-24, Japan. TEL 81-3-5351-8111.

621.381 US ISSN 1062-452X
THE MACAUTHORITY. 1992. m. $49 (foreign $69). Cobb Group, Inc., 9420 Bunsen Pkwy., Ste. 300, Louisville, KY 40220. TEL 502-493-3200. FAX 502-491-8050. (Subscr. to: Box 35160, Louisville, KY 40232-9720. TEL 800-223-8720) **Document type:** consumer publication.

004.16 CN
▼**MACCENTRAL.** 1995. d. 6526 Roslyn Rd., Halifax, NS B3L 2M9, Canada. TEL 902-455-9169. E-mail: email@maccentral.com; URL: http://www.maccentral.com. Ed. Stan Flack. **Document type:** bulletin.
   ●Available only online.
   Description: Provides a platform from which to promote, discuss, inform, and generally wonder at the world which is Macintosh.

004.16 US
▼**MACCOM.** 1996. m. E-mail: maccom@maccom.net; URL: http://www.maccom.net. Ed. Aaron Gibbons.
   ●Available only online.
   Description: Macintosh e-mail magazine with reviews, articles, ads, tips, contests and more.
   Refereed Serial

621.381 GW
▼**MACEASY.** 1995. m. DM.99 (Europe DM.129) (effective 1996). MACup Verlag GmbH, Leverkusenstr. 54, 22761 Hamburg, Germany. TEL 49-40-85183250. FAX 49-40-85183299. Eds. Frank Lohstoeter, Claus Heitmann. adv.: B&W page DM.4300, color page DM.5000; adv. contact: Tanja Fellgiebel. circ. 47,055 (paid). **Document type:** consumer publication.

621.381 US ISSN 0899-725X
MACINTOSH BUSINESS REVIEW. 1988. m. $38. V N U Business Publications, Inc., Ten Holland Dr., Hasbrouck Heights, NJ 07604. TEL 201-393-6000. (Subscr. to: Box 1716, Riverton, NJ 08077-7316) Ed. Sandra R. Reed. adv.; charts; illus.; stat.; tr.lit. (also avail. in microfilm) Indexed: Microcomp.Ind.
   —CCC.
   Description: Directed to business users of Apple Macintosh personal computers.

004.16 US ISSN 1070-7425
MACINTOSH TIPS & TRICKS. (Print edition ceased.) 1992. irreg. free online. Giles Road Press, 520 Palm Dr., Apt. 3, Wickenburg, AZ 85390-2432. TEL 520-684-1011. FAX 520-684-3965. E-mail: gilesrdprs@aol.com; URL: http://www.intac.com/~gilesrd/. Ed. Maria Langer; Pub. Maria Langer. R&P contact: Maria Langer. bk.rev. circ. 12,500. **Document type:** newsletter.
   ●Also available online.
   Also available on CD-ROM.
   Description: News and productivity for the Apple Macintosh computer.

621.381 SZ
MACINTOUCH. 1987. bi-m. 42 SFr. (foreign 48 SFr.). Macintouch Verlag, Birkenweg 2, CH-8304 Wallisellen, Switzerland. TEL 01-8305600. FAX 01-8305458. E-mail: ricford@macintouch.com; URL: http://www.macintouch.com. Ed. Roger Klein. adv.; bk.rev. circ. 11,000. **Document type:** consumer publication.
   ●Also available online.
   Description: Provides information for users of Apple Macintosh systems.

621.381 FI ISSN 0786-3683
MACMAAILMA. 1989. 10/yr. FIM 310. Helsinki Media Company Oy, Special Magazines, P.O. Box 2, FIN-00040 Helsinki Media, Finland. TEL 358-0-1205911. FAX 358-0-1205799. Ed. Eskoensio Pipatti. adv. contact: Mia Kemppi. circ. 4,829. **Document type:** consumer publication.
   Description: For Macintosh users.

004.16 US ISSN 1072-5466
MACROCOSM. 1993. m. $59.95. Resource Central, Inc., 7118 Main St., Kansas City, MO 64114-1406. TEL 913-469-6502. FAX 913-469-6507. Pub. Tom Weishaar. software rev. (diskette format) **Document type:** newsletter.
   Description: News, tips, tricks, letters, freeware and shareware for the Macintosh community.

621.381 GW ISSN 0935-6282
MACUP. 1985. m. DM.96 (foreign DM.126) (effective 1996). MACup Verlag GmbH, Leverkusenstr. 54, 22761 Hamburg, Germany. TEL 49-40-85183200. FAX 49-40-85183249. Ed. Frank Lohstoeter; Pub. Thomas Rehder. adv.: B&W page DM.7800, color page DM.10600; adv. contact: Christine Homann. circ. 77,920. (back issues avail.) **Document type:** consumer publication.
   —SWETS.

621.381 GW
MACUP BUYER'S GUIDE. 1988. 2/yr. DM.18 (effective 1996). MACup Verlag GmbH, Leverkusenstr. 54, 22761 Hamburg, Germany. TEL 49-40-85183-0. FAX 49-40-85183199. adv. contact: Christine Homann. (back issues avail.) **Document type:** consumer publication.

621.381 GW ISSN 0935-6290
MACUP EXTRA. q. DM.18 per no. MACup Verlag GmbH, Grosse Elbstr. 277, 22767 Hamburg, Germany. TEL 040-3910901. FAX 040-39109150. adv.: B&W page DM.5460; trim 185 x 265. **Document type:** consumer publication.
   Description: Highlights one area of special interest to Macintosh users.

004 US ISSN 0884-0997
QA76.8.M3 CODEN: MCUSEY
MACUSER; the Macintosh resource. 1985. m. $19.97. Ziff-Davis Publishing (San Francisco), 50 Beale St., 14th Fl., San Francisco, CA 94105-1813. TEL 415-378-5600; 800-627-2247. (Subscr. to: Box 56986, Boulder, CO 80322. TEL 800-627-2247) Ed. Jim Bradbury. adv.; bk.rev.; illus.; software rev.; circ. 311,253 (controlled). Indexed: Acad.Ind., Comput.Dtbs., Comput.Ind., Microcomp.Ind., PCR2, WPM. **Document type:** consumer publication, trade publication.
   ●Also available online. Vendor(s): Information Access Co.
   —CASDDS; CISTI; KR SourceOne; SWETS; UnCover. CCC.
   Formerly: MacLetter.
   Description: For Apple Macintosh computer users. Features articles on a variety of applications.

621.381 SP ISSN 0214-9966
MACUSER (EDICION ESPANOLA). 1989. 11/yr. 13975 ptas. Editorial America Iberica, Miguel Yuste 26, 28037 Madrid, Spain. TEL 34-1-3045542. FAX 34-1-3272402. Ed. Daniel Alonso. R&P contact: Carlos Gonzalez. adv. contact: Blanca Samperiz. circ. 15,000. **Document type:** consumer publication.

004.16 US ISSN 0892-8118
QA76.8.M3 CODEN: MWEEEI
MACWEEK; the newsweekly for Macintosh network managers. 1987. w. $125 (Canada and Mexico $225; elsewhere $350) (effective 1995). Coastal Associates Publishing, L.P. (Subsidiary of: Ziff-Davis Publishing Co.), One Park Ave., New York, NY 10016. TEL 212-503-3500. (Subscr. to: Box 10634, Riverton, NJ 08076-0634. TEL 609-786-8230) Ed. Mark Hall. adv. circ. 50,000. Indexed: Comput.Dtbs., Microcomp.Ind. **Document type:** trade publication.
   ●Also available online. Vendor(s): Information Access Co., Lexis-Nexis.
   —BLDSC (5330.796250); KR SourceOne; SWETS. CCC.

004.6 GW ISSN 0937-4906
MACWELT. 1990. m. DM.90. I D G Communications Verlag AG, Rheinstr. 28, 80803 Munich, Germany. TEL 089-36086234. FAX 089-36086304. Ed. Stefan Scherzer; Pub. Stefan Scherzer. adv.: B&W page DM.7200, color page DM.9450; trim 266 x 185; adv. contact: Siggi Poeschel. circ. 47,526. **Document type:** consumer publication, trade publication.
   —SWETS.
   Description: Provides information to Macintosh users at home, in business, research, design publishing and media.

004.16　　　　　US　　ISSN 0741-8647
QA76.8.M3　　　　　　CODEN: MACWEA
MACWORLD. 1984. m. $30. Macworld Communications, 501 Second St., Ste. 500, San Francisco, CA 94107. TEL 415-243-0505. URL: http://www.macworld.com. (Subscr. to: Box 54529, Boulder, CO 80322-4529) Ed. Adrian Mello. adv.; illus.; software rev.; tr.lit. circ. 575,000. (also avail. in microfiche from NBI) Indexed: Ap.Ind., B.P.I., Comput.Dtbs., Comput.Ind., Mag.Ind., Microcomp.Ind., PCR2, R.G.Abstr., TOM, WPM. **Document type:** consumer publication, trade publication.
● Also available online. Vendor(s): Information Access Co., UMI.
— BLDSC (5330.796300); CASDDS; CISTI; Ei; KR SourceOne; SWETS; UMI; UnCover. **CCC**.
Description: For Macintosh personal computer users. Features articles on applications and hardware. Regular columns include new products, questions and answers, hardware and software reviews.

004.16　　　　　DK　　ISSN 0905-0515
MACWORLD DANMARK. 1989. 11/yr. DKK 448 (effective 1997). I D G Danmark A-S, Carl Jacobsensvej 25, DK-2500 Valby, Denmark. TEL 45-36-19-91-00. FAX 45-36-44-27-97. Ed. Marianne Fejstrup. circ. 9,000. **Document type:** consumer publication.
Description: For the professional and general user alike.

004.16　　　　　IT　　ISSN 1121-5259
MACWORLD ITALIA; mensile per l'utente Macintosh. 1991. m. L.88000 (foreign L.198000) (effective 1996). I D G Communications Italia s.r.l., Via G. Malipiero 14, 20138 Milan, Italy. TEL 39-2-58011660. FAX 39-2-58011670. adv.: B&W page L.5200000, color page L.6900000; adv. contact: Costantino Cialfi. circ. 10,500.
Description: Provides the latest news from Italy and the world. Contains reviews of single products, advice, tips, tricks and explanations.

004.16　　　　　JA
MACWORLD JAPAN. m. I D G Communications, Japan, 2-F, Shuwa Fujimicho Bldg., 1-2-27 Fujimi, Chiyoda-ku, Tokyo 102, Japan. TEL 81-3-3222-6411. FAX 81-3-3222-6566. Ed. Osamu Homma. adv.: B&W page 260000 Yen, color page 530000 Yen; trim 208 x 280; adv. contact: Bonnie Shishido. circ. 120,000.

004.16　　　　　KO
MACWORLD KOREA. m. Hi-Tech Information, Inc., 3-F, Woosung Bldg., 333 Cheong Jeon-dong, Mapo-ku, Seoul 135-270, S. Korea. TEL 2-3257300. FAX 2-3258475. Pub. Y.S. Gimm. adv.: B&W page $1800, color page $2100; trim 213 x 277; adv. contact: Junbin Kim. circ. 30,000.

004.16　　　　　NE　　ISSN 0927-1066
MACWORLD MAGAZINE. 1991. 11/yr. fl.89.50. I D G Communications Nederland, Postbus 5446, 2000 GK Haarlem, Netherlands. TEL 31-23-5461111. FAX 31-23-5461155. Pub. Oscar Kneppers. adv. circ. 13,500. **Document type:** trade publication.
Incorporates: Macintosh Magazine (ISSN 0926-3098)

621.381　　　　　SW
MACWORLD SWEDEN. 1986. m. SEK 004.16. International Data Group AB, Sturegatan 11, S-106 71 Stockholm, Sweden. TEL 46-8-453-60-00. FAX 46-8-453-60-05. Ed. Nicklas Mattsson. adv. contact: Magnus Wallen. circ. 15,000. **Document type:** consumer publication, trade publication.
Description: Focuses on tests of products and services. Reports on news and provides articles on how-to in the Mac-World.

MAKINTOSH. see PUBLISHING AND BOOK TRADE — Computer Applications

MANAGING OFFICE TECHNOLOGY; integrating technology & human resources for total office quality. see BUSINESS AND ECONOMICS — Office Equipment And Services

621.381　　　　　CN　　ISSN 0827-1755
MAPLE ORCHARD; Canadian publication on Apple and Macintosh computing. 1982. m. Can.$15 to non-members. Loyal Ontario Group Interested in Computers Inc. (LOGIC), P.O. Box 958, Thornhill, ON L3T 4A5, Canada. TEL 416-323-0828. Ed. Ken Nelson. adv.; bk.rev. circ. 350. **Document type:** newsletter.
● Also available online.

MICRO E PERSONAL COMPUTER. see COMPUTERS — Microcomputers

621.381　　　　　US　　ISSN 1081-518X
MICRO MATERIALS UPDATE. 1985. s-a. free. American Printing House for the Blind, Inc., 1839 Frankfort Ave., Box 6085, Louisville, KY 40206-0085. TEL 502-895-2405. FAX 502-899-2274. E-mail: info@aph.org. Ed. Venus Elder. circ. 3,700. (also avail. in audio cassette; diskette format; large print edition in 14 pt.) **Document type:** newsletter.
Description: Contains articles about computer products designed for visually impaired users.

MICRO MEDICAL NEWSLETTER. see MEDICAL SCIENCES — Computer Applications

MICROBANKER; the research letter on financial end-user computing. see BUSINESS AND ECONOMICS — Banking And Finance_computer Applications

MICROLEADS RESELLER DIRECTORY ON DISK. see COMPUTERS — Computer Industry Directories

MICROLEADS VENDOR DIRECTORY. see COMPUTERS — Computer Industry Directories

621.381　　　　　SP
MICROMANIA. 1982. 12/yr. 7140 ptas. (Europe 14484 ptas.; elsewhere 18972 ptas. (effective 1997). Hobby Press, S.A., C. de los Ciruelos, 4, 28700 San Sebastian de los Reyes (Madrid), Spain. TEL 34-1-6548199. FAX 34-1-6547272. Ed. Domingo Gomez. adv. contact: Maria Perera. circ. 35,100. **Document type:** consumer publication.
Description: Covers computer games, music, software and personal computers.

621.381　　　　　US　　ISSN 1043-2299
MICROPENDIUM; covering the T199/4A, the Myarc 9640 and compatibles. 1984. bi-m. $35 (Canada$42.50; Mexico $40.25; elsewhere $40; air mail $52). Burns-Koloen Communications, Inc., Box 1343, Round Rock, TX 78680. TEL 512-255-1512. E-mail: jkoloen@io.com. Ed. Laura Burns; Pub. John Koloen. R&P contact: Laura Burns. adv. contact: Laura Burns. bk.rev.; charts; illus.; circ. 2,000 (paid). (back issues avail.) **Document type:** consumer publication.
Formerly: Home Computer Compendium.

004.16　　　　　FI　　ISSN 0785-9988
MIKRO P C. Key Title: Mikro PC. 1983. m. FIM 376 (effective 1997). Oy Talentum Ab, P.O. Box 920, FIN-00101 Helsinki, Finland. TEL 358-9-148-801. FAX 358-9-685-6605. URL: http://www.talentum.fi. Ed. Kari Tyllila. adv.: B&W page FIM 19400, color page FIM 28600; trim 210 x 297; adv. contact: Anssi Eskola. bk.rev.; index; circ. 59,090 (controlled). **Document type:** trade publication, consumer publication.
Formerly (until 1988): Mikro (ISSN 0780-6663)
Description: Reports on extensive product tests in concrete user situations and carries out broad product comparisons on PCs, peripherals and software.

621.381　　　　　FI　　ISSN 0781-2078
MIKROBITTI. 1984. 12/yr. FIM 295. Helsinki Media Company Oy, Special Magazines, P.O. Box 2, FIN-00040 Helsinki Media, Finland. TEL 358-0-1205911. FAX 358-0-1205799. Ed. Markku Alanen. adv. contact: Mia Kemppi. circ. 47,712. **Document type:** consumer publication.
Description: For home computer users.

MIKRODATORN; foer dig som anvaender datorer i jobbet. see COMPUTERS — Microcomputers

621.381　　　　　US
MINI' APP'LES. m. $25. Minnesota Apple Computer User's Group, Inc., Box 796, Hopkins, MN 55343. TEL 612-229-6952. adv. contact: Eric Knopp. circ. 500. **Document type:** newsletter.

MODEM NOTES; on line to the business community. see COMPUTERS — Hardware

MULTIMEDIA & C D - R O M. see COMPUTERS — Software

004.16 006　　　　　US　　ISSN 1073-4759
QA76.575
MULTIMEDIA WORLD. CD-ROM edition: Multimedia World Live! 1991. m. $9.97. I D G Communications Inc. (San Francisco), 501 Second St., San Francisco, CA 94107. TEL 415-281-8650. FAX 415-281-3915. Ed. Russel Giltman. adv.: color page $13715. circ. 180,000 (paid). **Document type:** consumer publication, trade publication.
● Also available on CD-ROM.
— KR SourceOne; UnCover. **CCC**.
Former titles (until 1993): M P C World (ISSN 1060-2194); (until 1992): M P C
Description: Features informative articles, how-to clinics, new product reviews and special departments on multimedia personal computing.

006
▼ **MULTIMEDIA WORLD LIVE!**. 1995. m. $79.95. I D G Communications Inc. (San Francisco), 501 Second St., San Francisco, CA 94107. TEL 415-281-8650. FAX 415-281-3915. Ed. Russell Giltman. adv.; circ. 100,000 (paid). **Document type:** consumer publication.
● Available only on CD-ROM.

621.381　　　　　SP　　ISSN 1134-2749
MUY ESPECIAL. 1990. 4/yr. 1200 ptas. (Europe 2450 ptas.; elsewhere 3350 ptas.) (effective 1997). G y J Espana Ediciones, S.L., Marques de Villamagna 4, 28001 Madrid, Spain. TEL 34-1-4369898. FAX 34-1-5752617. Ed. Miguel Ruiz. adv. contact: Elena Sanchez Fabres. circ. 150,000. **Document type:** consumer publication.

621.381 001.644　　　　　US
N O H U G NEWS.* m. New Orleans Heath Users Group, Heathkit Electronics Center, 1 Packard Bell Way, Sacramento, CA 95828-0903.

621.381　　　　　US
NEW ENGLAND WORLD OF SANYO. 1984. m. $15. Sanyo New England Users Club, 46 Asbury St., Lexington, MA 02173. Ed. R.E. Zapolin. adv.; bk.rev. circ. 250.

004　　　　　US　　ISSN 1064-0444
NEW JERSEY COMPUTERUSER. 1992. m. $12. Burr - Cooke Associated Publishers, Inc., 1655-245 Oaktree Rd., No. 119, Edison, NJ 08820. TEL 908-287-6565. FAX 908-287-6566. Ed. Steve Deyo; Pub. Eric Burris. adv. contact: Lance Burris. bk.rev.; software rev. circ. 52,000. cols./p.: 4; pp./issue: 28. (tabloid format) **Document type:** newspaper, trade publication.
Description: Contains practical and humorous articles of interest to computer enthusiasts in New Jersey. Informs readers of forthcoming conferences and events.

621.381 001.644　　　　　AT
NEWCASTLE MICROCOMPUTER CLUB. NEWSLETTER. m. membership. Newcastle Microcomputer Club, P.O. Box 293, Hamilton, N.S.W. 2303, Australia.

621.381　　　　　US
NEWSLINK (WESTERVILLE).* 1984. m. $20. Sanyo Users of Central Ohio, 6128 Headington Pl., Gahanna, OH 43230-6329. Ed. Tom Peet. adv.; bk.rev. circ. 100.
Formerly: Link (Westerville).

004.16　　　　　US
NEWTNEWS. 1994. w. 5375 Hewlett Dr., San Diego, CA 92115. E-mail: newtnews@pobox.com; URL: http://www.ridgecrest.ca.us/NewtNews/. Ed. Steve Holden. **Document type:** newsletter.
● Available only online.
Description: A weekly freeware newsletter that focuses on the Apple Newton and related technologies.

COMPUTERS — PERSONAL COMPUTERS

621.381 JA ISSN 0289-6508
NIKKEI BYTE. (Text in Japanese) 1984. m. 11600 Yen. Nikkei Business Publications, Inc. (Subsidiary of: Nihon Keizai Shimbun, Inc.), 2-7-6 Hirakawa-cho, Chiyoda-ku, Tokyo 102, Japan. TEL 81-3-5210-8038. FAX 81-3-5210-8119. URL: http://www.nikkeibp.co.jp/. (Subscr. to: Nikkei Business Pub. Inc., Reader Service Center, P.O. Box 20, Kasai Post Office, Tokyo 134-70, Japan) Ed. Shigeru Ishii; Pub. Koichi Shiraishi. adv.: B&W page 570000 Yen, color page 861000 Yen; trim 208 x 280; adv. contact: Akira Okamoto. circ. 82,041. **Document type:** trade publication.
  Description: Contains updates and reviews of advanced technologies in personal computing for both professionals and laymen.

004.16 005.3 JA ISSN 1340-8372
NIKKEI CLICK. (Text in Japanese) 1994. m. 480 Yen per no. Nikkei Business Publications, Inc. (Subsidiary of: Nihon Keizai Shimbun, Inc.), 2-7-6 Hirakawacho, Chiyoda-ku, Tokyo 102, Japan. TEL 81-3-5210-8560. FAX 81-3-5210-8119. URL: http://www.nikkeibp.co.jp/. Ed. Tohru Saino; Pub. Koichi Shiraishi. adv.: B&W page 410000 Yen, color page 700000 Yen; adv. contact: Naoto Kawajiri. circ. 165,429. **Document type:** consumer publication.
  Description: Offers an easy guide to enjoying PCs as a multimedia tool, introducing electronic communication and CD-ROM.

004.16 JA ISSN 0918-8894
NIKKEI MAC. (Text in Japanese) 1993. m. 12900 Yen. Nikkei Business Publications, Inc. (Subsidiary of: Nihon Keizai Shimbun, Inc.), 2-7-6, Hirakawa-cho, Chiyoda-ku, Tokyo 102, Japan. TEL 81-3-5210-8536. FAX 81-3-5210-8119. URL: http://www.mac.nikkeibp.co.jp. Ed. Nobuo Hayashi; Pub. Koichi Shiraishi. adv.: B&W page 210000 Yen, color page 480000 Yen; trim 208 x 280; adv. contact: Haruo Isonuma. circ. 63,161. **Document type:** trade publication.
  Description: Focuses on the efficient use of Apple Computer's Macintosh in business fields.

NIKKEI OPEN SYSTEMS. see *COMPUTERS — Microcomputers*

004.16 JA ISSN 1341-9900
▼NIKKEI P C 21. (Text in Japanese) 1996. m. newsstand price: 480 Yen. Nikkei Business Publications, Inc. (Subsidiary of: Nihon Keizai Shimbun, Inc.), 2-7-6 Hirakawa-cho, Chiyoda-ku, Tokyo 102, Japan. TEL 81-3-5210-8502. FAX 81-3-5210-8119. URL: http://www.nikkeibp.co.jp/. Ed. Shun'ich Fujita; Pub. Koichi Shiraishi. adv. contact: Haruo Isonuma. circ. 115,182. **Document type:** consumer publication.
  Description: Targets businesspeople working at the front lines of the information society with reports on the inner workings of PCs and how to make the most of this key business tool.

621.381 JA ISSN 0287-9506
NIKKEI PERSONAL COMPUTING. 1983. 24/yr. 11400 Yen. Nikkei Business Publications, Inc. (Subsidiary of: Nihon Keizai Shimbun Inc.), 2-7-6 Hirakawa-cho, Chiyoda-ku, Tokyo 102, Japan. TEL 81-3-5210-8027. FAX 81-3-5210-8119. URL: http://www.nikkeibp.co.jp/npc. (Subscr. to: Nikkei Business Pub. Inc., Reader Service Center, P.O. Box 20, Kasai Post Office, Tokyo 134-70, Japan) Ed. Tamio Ohta; Pub. Tamio Ohta. adv.: B&W page 915000 yen, color page 1327000 Yen; trim 208 x 280; adv. contact: Yasuo Harada. circ. 233,611. **Document type:** trade publication.
  Description: Provides practical guidelines on the use of personal computers, as well as related business opportunities and applications.

004.16 JA ISSN 1341-1497
▼NIKKEI WINPC. (Text in Japanese) 1995. m. 680 Yen. Nikkei Business Publications, Inc. (Subsidiary of: Nihon Keizai Shimbun Inc.), 2-7-6 Hirakawacho, Chiyoda-ku, Tokyo 102, Japan. TEL 81-3-5210-8560. FAX 81-3-5210-8119. URL: http://www.nikkeibp.co.jp/. Ed. Makoto Kawakami; Pub. Koichi Shiraishi. adv. contact: Shun'ich Ono. circ. 89,037. **Document type:** consumer publication.
  Description: Provides Window users "how-to" information on Windows and detailed and practical tips for immediate application.

621.381 001.644 US
NORTH TEXAS P C NEWS. 1982. m. $24. North Texas P C Users Group Inc., 2025 Rockcreek Dr., Arlington, TX 76010. TEL 817-275-4109. Ed. J.P. Pribyl. adv.; bk.rev. circ. 1,500.
  Description: Each issue includes feature articles, special interest groups' reports, software reviews and a directory of key group officials.

621.381 US
NORTH TEXAS SANYO USERS GROUP. NEWSLETTER. m. membership. North Texas Sanyo Users Group, 4323 Middleton Rd., Dallas, TX 75229. Ed. Craig W. Stahre.

ON DISK MONTHLY. see *COMPUTERS — Software*

ONLINE & C D - R O M REVIEW; the international journal of online & optical information systems. see *COMPUTERS — Computer Networks*

ONLINE HOTLINE NEWS SERVICE. see *COMPUTERS — Computer Networks*

ONLINE NEWSLETTER. see *COMPUTERS — Computer Networks*

621.381 SP ISSN 0211-9579
ORDENADOR PERSONAL. 1982. m. 3000 ptas. P C Disc, S.A., Ferraz, 11, 28008 Madrid, Spain. TEL 541 34 00. FAX 248-11-23. Ed. Francisco Javier San Roman y Perez. adv.; bk.rev. circ. 20,000.

004.16 FR ISSN 0183-570X
ORDINATEUR INDIVIDUEL.* m. Groupe Tests, 26-40 rue d'Oradour sur Glane, 75504 Paris Cedex 15, France. TEL 33-4-42402201. FAX 33-4-42455943. TELEX 215 105 F GR TEST. Ed. Jacques Eltabet. circ. 100,000.
  —CISTI; SWETS.

004.16 GW ISSN 0944-7075
P C AKTIV. m. DM.68.40 (foreign DM.82.70). Tronic Verlagsgesellschaft mbH, Hessenring 32, 37269 Eschwege, Germany. TEL 05651-929-0. FAX 05651-929140. Ed. Ottfried Schmidt; Pub. Christian Widuch. adv. contact: Anja Seiler. circ. 85,000. **Document type:** consumer publication.

621.381 US
P C CHRONICLES.* 1982. m. membership. Greater Cleveland P C Users Group, c/o Roy McCartney, 6542 Carter Blvd., Mentor, OH 44060. TEL 216-944-5173. Ed. Ward Larkin. adv.; bk.rev. circ. 350.
  Description: Instructs IBM PC users.

004 US ISSN 0899-1847
QA76.5 CODEN: PCMPEI
P C - COMPUTING.* 1988. m. $24.97. Ziff-Davis Publishing (San Francisco), Computer Publications Division, 50 Beale St., 14th Fl., San Francisco, CA 94105-1813. TEL 415-578-7000. FAX 415-578-7059. (Subscr. to: Box 5300, Boulder, CO 80322. TEL 800-365-2770) Ed. Jack Lyon. adv. contact: David NcCaman. bk.rev. **Indexed:** CAD CAM Abstr., Comput.Dtbs., Comput.Ind., Microcomp.Ind., R.G.Abstr., Tel.Abstr. **Document type:** trade publication.
  ●Also available online. Vendor(s): Information Access Co.
  —BLDSC (6413.366445); CISTI; KR SourceOne; SWETS; UnCover. **CCC.**
  Description: Aimed at personal computer business users; covers various computer applications.

621.381 UK ISSN 0950-5474
P C DEALER. 1986. w. £100 (foreign £120) (effective 1996). V N U Business Publications BV, VNU House, 32-34 Broadwick St., London W1A 2HG, England. TEL 44-171-439-4242. FAX 44-171-437-4841. adv.: B&W page $4164, color page $5564; trim 10 x 14.04. circ. 6,195. **Indexed:** WPM. **Document type:** trade publication.
  Description: Provides news and information to senior business computer resellers and distributors.

004.16 PH ISSN 0117-0996
P C DIGEST; P C world Philippines. (Text in English) 1989. m. P.1020. W S Computer Publishing Corp., Rm. 704, Sedcco Bldg., Rada Corner Legazpi Sts., Legazpi Village, Makati, Metro Manila, Philippines. TEL 632-812-8401. FAX 632-817-6430. Ed. P.W. Wong. adv.: B&W page $1928, color page $2897; trim 215 x 280; adv. contact: Delia C. Gutierree. index. circ. 10,000. (back issues avail.) **Document type:** consumer publication.
  Description: Contains practical and informative materials of interest to corporate and individual users of DOS-based personal computers.

621.381 UK ISSN 0964-1661
P C DIRECT. 1991. m. Ziff-Davis UK Ltd., Cottons Centre, Hay's Ln., London SE1 2QT, England. TEL 4471-378-6800. FAX 4471-403-0668. Ed. Tony Westbrooke. adv.: B&W page $2690, color page $3120; trim 8 1/4 x 11 5/8. circ. 62,290.
  —BLDSC (6413.367700); SWETS.

621.381 FR ISSN 1164-6977
P C DIRECT. 1992. m. Ziff-Davis France S.A.R.L., 10 Rue Thierry le Luron, 92593 Levallois-Perret Cedex, France. TEL 46-39-55-00. FAX 46-39-00-33. Ed. Thierry Crouzet. adv.: B&W page $3535, color page $4420; trim 8 1/4 x 11 1/4. circ. 50,000.

621.381 GW ISSN 0943-4038
P C DIREKT; the up-to-date buyer's magazine. 1991. m. Ziff-Davis Verlag GmbH, Riesstr. 25, 80992 Munich Germany. TEL 49-89-14312-655. FAX 49-89-14312-659. Ed. Elke Huff; Pub. Martha Kleinwort. adv. contact: Gerhard Layer. circ. 120,008. **Document type:** trade publication.
  Description: For active buyers of PC hardware and software.

621.381 SP
P C DISC; publicacion con programas para P C compatibles. 1987. m. (10/yr.). 7420 ptas. P C Disc, S.A., Ferraz, 11, 28008 Madrid, Spain. TEL 541 34 00. FAX 248-11-23. Dir. Gilberto Sanchez. adv.; bk.rev. circ. 13,000.

621.381 IT
P C DISK MAGAZINE. 10/yr. Via Ferri 6, 20092 Cinisello Balsamo (Milan), Italy. TEL 2-660-251. FAX 2-660-103-53. TELEX 352-376 JCE MIL I. Ed. Silvia Vigano. circ. 17,000.

621.381 CK
P C DISTRIBUTOR. (Text in English, Portuguese, Spanish) 1990. bi-m. free. Empresar Editores Ltda Carrera 11, No. 94-02, L-123, Bogota, Colombia. TEL 2182730. FAX 610-1958. Ed. Hernando Bahamon. circ. 5,000 (controlled).
  Description: For distributors of personal computers in Latin America.

621.381 SP
P C DOS DISK MAGAZINE.* 12/yr. Infodisc Informatica S.L., Ferraz 11, 1o, 28088 Madrid, Spain. TEL 3-347-92-79. FAX 3-433-05-92. Ed. Alberto Rodriguez.
  Description: For users of IBM, Amstrad and compatibles.

621.381 FR ISSN 1164-6969
P C EXPERT. 1992. 11/yr. Ziff-Davis France S.A.R.L., 10 rue Thierry Le Luron, 92593 Levallois-Perret Cedex, France. TEL 46-39-55-00. FAX 46-39-00-33. Ed. Emmanuel Alexandre. adv.: B&W page $4950, color page $6190; trim 8 1/4 x 11 1/4. circ. 60,000.
  —SWETS.

621.381 SP
P C FLOPPY. 12/yr. Grupo Editorial Jackson, Conde d Penalver 52 3o, 28006 Madrid, Spain. TEL 1-401-73-65. FAX 1-401-27-87. Ed. Carmen de la Ossa.

621.381 IT
P C FLOPPY. 11/yr. L.115500 (foreign L.231000). Gruppo Editoriale Jackson S.p.A., Via M. Gorki 69 20092 Cinisello B. (MI), Italy. TEL 39-2-660229. FAX 39-2-66034448. Ed. Pierantonio Palerma. **Document type:** trade publication.

621.381 SP ISSN 0214-1434
P C FORUM.* 1987. 11/yr. Editorial Planeta, S.A., Corcega 273-277, 08008 Barcelona, Spain. TEL 3-433-12-28. FAX 3-433-00-86. circ. 20,00

COMPUTERS — PERSONAL COMPUTERS 2201

621.381 US
GV1469.2
P C GAMER. 1988. m. newsstand price: $7.95. Imagine Publishing, Inc., 150 North Hill Dr., Brisbane, CA 94005. TEL 415-468-4684. FAX 415-468-4686. Ed. Selby Bateman. adv. circ. 170,000. **Document type:** consumer publication.
—KR SourceOne.
Former titles (until May 1994): Game Player's P C Entertainment (ISSN 1059-2180); (until 1991): Game Player's P C Strategy Guide.
Description: Covers computer games and educational products for IBM PC and compatible computers. Includes hints and tips to improve readers' scores, coverage of popular PC games, and previews of forthcoming games.

621.381 GW ISSN 0949-2461
▼**P C INTERN.** (Personal Computer) 1995. m. DM.84 (foreign DM.108) (effective 1997). Data Becker GmbH, Merowingerstr. 30, 40223 Duesseldorf, Germany. TEL 49-211-933470. FAX 49-211-9334710. E-mail: pcintern@pcintern.de; URL: http://www.pcintern.de. Ed. Oliver Kuerten; Pub. Achim Becker. adv. contact: Michale Manke. circ. 20,533 (paid). **Document type:** consumer publication.
●Also available online.
Description: Provides regular information on the latest developments in the high-end computer market and the specialist areas of networking, programming and multimedia.

004.16 NE ISSN 0928-7051
▼**C KOOP;** uw koop adviseur voor computer hard- en software. 1991. 11/yr. fl.54.50 (Europe fl.165). V N U Business Publications B.V., Postbus 9194, 1006 CC Amsterdam, Netherlands. TEL 31-20-4875487. FAX 31-20-4875700. E-mail: pckoop@marketing.vnu.com. Ed. M. Heffers; Pub. A.H.W. van der Want. adv.: B&W page fl.3837, color page fl.5892; trim 210 x 285; adv. contact: C. van den Berg. circ. 60,000 (paid). **Document type:** trade publication.

004.16 PL ISSN 0867-0153
C KURIER. 1989. bi-w. 2.11 Zl. per issue. Wydawnictwo Lupus sp. z o.o., Ul. Stepinska 22-30, 00-739 Warsaw, Poland. TEL 48-22-415121. FAX 48-22-410374. TELEX 813527. E-mail: pckurier@lupus.waw.pl. Ed. Zbigniew Blewonski; Pub. Tomasz Zielinski. adv.: B&W page 2750 DM.; trim 170 x 250; adv. contact: Piotr Roszczyk. software rev. circ. 50,000. (back issues avail.) **Document type:** newspaper.
Description: Provides technical information for PC users. Focuses on Polish computer market.

C L A N. see COMPUTERS — Computer Networks

621.381 US ISSN 1043-1314
C LAPTOP COMPUTERS.* m. $24.95 (foreign $34.95). Larry Flynt Publications, Inc., 8484 Wilshire Blvd., Ste. 900, Beverly Hills, CA 90211-3227. TEL 310-858-7100. FAX 310-274-7985. Ed. Michael Goldstein. adv. **Document type:** consumer publication.
—KR SourceOne. **CCC.**
Description: Covers all aspects of portable computers.

C LETTER; the insider's guide to the personal computer industry. see COMPUTERS — Computer Sales

621.381 US
C LIFEBOAT. 1983. irreg. (6-10/yr.). $26. National P C Users Group, Box 1076, Lemont, PA 16851. TEL 814-237-5511. (Subscr. to: Box 376, Lemont, PA 16851) Ed. Richard Shoemaker. adv.; bk.rev. circ. 5,000. (also avail. in diskette format; back issues avail.)
Formerly: Epson LifeBoat; **Incorporates:** Amigahelp.
Description: Provides a communication network for Epson and MS-DOS clone owners interested in new hardware and software products, and programming tips.

004 US ISSN 0747-0460
QA76.5
P C M; premier personal computer magazine for Tandy computer users. m. $34 (effective Oct. 1991). Falsoft, Inc., The Falsoft Bldg., Box 385, Prospect, KY 40059. TEL 502-228-4492. FAX 502-228-5121. Ed. Lawrence C. Falk. software rev.; index. circ. 87;046. (back issues avail.)
Indexed: Microcomp.Ind., PCR2. **Document type:** consumer publication.
—KR SourceOne.
Description: For Tandy MS-DOS and portable computer users. Covers languages, business, communications, education, games, graphics, and desktop publishing.

004.16 GW ISSN 0177-0977
P C MAGAZIN. m. DM.88.50 (foreign DM.120; students DM.75) (effective 1997). Franzis Verlag GmbH, Dornacherstr. 3, 85622 Feldkirchen, Germany. TEL 49-89-99115-0. FAX 49-89-99115199. **Document type:** consumer publication.
●Also available online. Vendor(s): Knight-Ridder Information, Inc.
—SWETS.
Description: For professional PC-users.

621.381 001.642 IT
P C MAGAZINE. m. (11/yr.). L.53900 (foreign L.107800). Gruppo Editoriale Jackson S.p.A., Via M. Gorki 69, 20092 Cinisello B. (MI), Italy. TEL 39-2-66034229. FAX 39-2-66034448. Ed. Pierantonio Palerma. adv.: B&W page L.5000000, color page L.8300000; trim 210 x 280. circ. 52,387 (controlled). **Document type:** trade publication.
Formerly: P C World Magazine.
Description: Analyzes news concerning both hardware and software of computer products, specifically dedicated to standard IBM computers, MS-DOS-OS2 and Olivetti N24, as well as other compatibles.

621.381 UK
P C MAGAZINE (U.K.). 1992. m. $1.50 per no. Ziff-Davis UK Ltd., Cottons Centre, Hay's Ln., London SE1 2QT, England. TEL 44-171-378-6800. FAX 44-171-403-0668. Ed. Stephen Malone. adv. circ. 80,000.
●Also available online. Vendor(s): Information Access Co.

004.16 AT
P C MAGAZINE AUSTRALIA. m. Aus.$55. A C P Computer Publications, Level 6, 54-58 Park St., Sydney, N.S.W. 2000, Australia. TEL 61-2-2889161. FAX 61-2-2674909. E-mail: pcmag@acp.com.au. Ed. Bill Bennett; Pub. Richard Walsh. adv.: B&W page Aus.$2820, color page Aus.$3750; adv. contact: Anthony McLennan. circ. 25,022.
Description: Provides comprehensive product information.

004.165 US ISSN 0888-8507
QA76.8.I1015 CODEN: PCMGEP
P C MAGAZINE: THE INDEPENDENT GUIDE TO I B M - STANDARD PERSONAL COMPUTING. Key Title: P C Magazine. Spanish edition: P C Magazine en Espanol (ISSN 1069-9953) (Network edition also avail.) 1982. bi-w. $29.97. Ziff-Davis Publishing Co., One Park Ave., New York, NY 10016. TEL 212-503-5100. (Subscr. to: Box 54093, Boulder, CO 80322. TEL 800-289-0429) Ed. Michael Miller. adv.; bk.rev.; illus. circ. 750,000. **Indexed:** Acad.Ind., CAD CAM Abstr., Comput.Bus., Comput.Cont., Comput.Dtbs., Info.Media & Tech., INSPEC, Mag.Ind., Microcomp.Ind., PCR2, TOM, Tr.& Indus.Ind.
—BLDSC (6413.367600); CASDDS; CISTI; Ei; KNAW; Linda Hall; SWETS; UnCover. **CCC.**
Formerly (until 1986): P C: The Independent Guide to I B M Personal Computers (ISSN 0745-2500)
Description: For IBM Personal Computer users. Feature articles are comparative reviews of computer hardware and general business software programs such as word processing, spreadsheets, graphics, CAD and communications.

621.381 330 UK ISSN 0269-0640
P C MANAGEMENT; corporate strategy, connectivity and analysis. 1984. m. E M A P Business & Computer Publications Ltd., 33-39 Bowling Green Ln., London EC1R 0DA, England. TEL 44-171-837-1212. FAX 44-171-278-4008. circ. 15,000. (back issues avail.) **Document type:** trade publication.
—CCC.

621.381 SP
P C MANIA. (Includes 2 CD-ROM discs and 1 diskette.) 1992. 12/yr. 11940 ptas. (Europe 22092 ptas.; elsewhere 28296 ptas. (effective 1997). Hobby Press, S.A., C. de los Ciruelos, 4, 28700 San Sebastian de los Reyes (Madrid), Spain. TEL 34-1-6548199. FAX 34-1-6547272. Ed. Domingo Gomez. adv.: page 550000 ptas.; 190 x 245; adv. contact: Jeronimo Mediavilla. circ. 60,293. **Document type:** consumer publication.
Description: Covers games, music, and software for personal computers.

621.381 AU
P C MARKT. m. Sommerhaidenweg 124, A-1190 Vienna, Austria. TEL 01-4432950. FAX 01-442825. circ. 42,000.

621.381 GR ISSN 1105-5472
P C MASTER. (Text in Greek) 1989. m. Dr.21000 in Europe; Dr.22000 in U.S. (effective 1996) (includes diskette). Compupress S.A., 44 Syngrou, 117 42 Athens, Greece. TEL 30-1-9238-672. FAX 30-1-9216-847. Ed. G. Patrikos; Pub. N.O. Manousos. adv. contact: Alexis Kanavos. circ. 20,000. **Document type:** consumer publication.
Description: Covers topics and applications relevant to the low-end PC market.

004.16 BE ISSN 0771-4254
P C MICRO MAGAZINE.* Dutch edition (ISSN 0771-4408) (Text in French) 1982. m. 760 BEF. Ecopress S.A., Rue Gabrielle 114, 1180 Brussels, Belgium. FAX 32-2-3442451. (Subscr. to: A M P Abonnements, 1 rue de la Petite Ile, 1170 Brussels, Belgium) Ed. Renee Baguette. adv.; circ. 15,000 (controlled). (back issues avail.)

004.16 GW ISSN 0949-8427
P C MOBIL UND KOMMUNIKATION. (Personal Computer) 1994. 8/yr. DM.68 (effective 1997). I W T Magazin Verlags GmbH, Bahnhofstr. 36, 85591 Vaterstetten, Germany. TEL 49-8106-350-0. FAX 49-8106-350126. URL: http://www.iwtnet.de. Ed. Ulrich Smyrek. circ. 31,000. **Document type:** trade publication.
Formerly (until 1995): P C Mobil (ISSN 0945-2621)

621.381 IS
P C MONTHLY; Israeli monthly for PC computers. (Text in Hebrew) m. IS.56.60. Technosdar Inc., P.O.B. 31684, Tel Aviv, Israel. TEL 03-622418. Ed. Dan Halevy.
Description: For owners of personal computers.

P C NETZE. (Personal Computer) see COMPUTERS — Computer Networks

004 US ISSN 1052-1186
QA76.5.P364
P C NOVICE; personal computers in plain English. 1990. m. $29 (foreign $49). Peed Corporation, 120 W. Harvest Dr., Lincoln, NE 68521. TEL 800-848-1478. (Subscr. to: Box 85380, Lincoln, NE 68501-5380. TEL 800-424-7900. FAX 402-479-2104) Ed. Ronald D. Kobler. **Indexed:** R.G.Abstr.
—KR SourceOne. **CCC.**

004.16 IT ISSN 1123-7600
▼**P C OPEN.** 1995. m. L.77000 (foreign L.108000) (effective 1996). A G E P E s.r.l., Via Rosso di San Secondo 1-3, 20134 Milan, Italy. Ed. Pasquale Laurelli; Pub. Giorgio Artuffo. adv.: color page L.6500000; 224 x 297; adv. contact: Roberto Lenzi.

621.381 US
P C OPPORTUNITIES. 1984. m. $25. Opportunities Publishing, Inc., 305 W. Jackson Ave., Oxford, MS 38655. TEL 601-236-5510. adv. circ. 19,102.

COMPUTERS — PERSONAL COMPUTERS

621.381 IS
P C PLUS/ANASHIM VEMACHSHEVIM; people and computers magazine weekly. (Text in Hebrew) 1981. m. $135. Israel Peled Publishing, P.O.B. 33325, Tel Aviv 61 332, Israel. TEL 03-295145. FAX 03-295144. Ed. Israel Peied. circ. 9,500.
Formerly: People and Computers Magazine.

621.381 GW ISSN 0940-6743
P C PRAXIS. (Personal Computer) 1984. m. DM.75 (foreign DM.96) (effective 1997). Data Becker GmbH, Merowingerstr. 30, 40223 Duesseldorf, Germany. TEL 49-211-933470. FAX 49-211-9334710. E-mail: pcpraxis@pcpraxis.de; URL: http://www.pcpraxis.de. Ed. Juergen Grollius; Pub. Achim Becker. adv. contact: Markus Yaguee-Bosch. bk.rev. circ. 208,201. **Document type:** consumer publication.
●Also available online.
Former titles (until 1989): Data Welt (ISSN 0930-4975); (until 1985): Neue Datewelt (ISSN 0176-4187)
Description: Aims to provide professional PC users, decision makers and dealers with articles concerning the practical side of computing.

004.16 US
P C PRESENTATIONS PRODUCTIONS. 1993. m. free. Pisces Publishing Group, Inc., 417 Bridgeport Ave., Devon, CT 06460-4105. TEL 203-877-1927. FAX 203-877-1927. E-mail: piscespub@msn.com; URL: http://www.cadvision.com/nolimits/pcpp.html. Ed. Don S. Johnson. adv.; bk.rev. **Document type:** consumer publication.
●Available only online.
Description: Includes how-to graphics design and desktop video.

004.16 UK ISSN 1355-4603
P C PRO. 1994. m. £15.99 (effective 1995); newsstand price: £2.50. Dennis Publishing Ltd., 19 Bolsover St., London W1P 7HJ, England. TEL 44-171-631-1433. FAX 44-171-636-5668. E-mail: writeon@pcpro.co.uk; URL: http://www.pcpro.co.uk. (Dist. by: S M Magazine Distribution, 6 Leigham Court Rd., Streatham, London SW16 2PG, England. TEL 44-181-677-8111; Subscr. to: Subscriptions Department, Bradley Pavilions, Pear Tree Rd., Bradley Stoke North, Bristol, Avon BS12 OBQ, England. TEL 44-1454-620070. FAX 44-1454-622080) Ed. Derek Cohen; Pub. Guy Phillips. adv.: page £2650; adv. contact: Adrian Jenkins. software rev.; cum. index; circ. 80,000 (paid). (back issues avail.) **Document type:** consumer publication.
—AskIEEE; KR SourceOne.
Description: Covers all aspects of computing for PC users, including product reviews.

004.16 IT ISSN 1121-3337
P C PROFESSIONALE. 1991. m. L.88000 (foreign L.128150). Mondadori Informatica S.p.A., Casella Postale 3686, 20090 Segrate (MI), Italy. TEL 39-2-21712230. FAX 39-2-21712235. E-mail: pcpno@mondadori.it. Ed. Roberto Mazzoni. adv. contact: Gianluca Ferrauto. circ. 71,864. **Document type:** trade publication.

621.381 GW ISSN 0939-5822
P C PROFESSIONELL; the independent magazine for PC specialists. 1991. m. Ziff-Davis Verlag GmbH, Riesstr. 25, 80992 Munich, Germany. TEL 49-89-14312-655. FAX 49-89-14312659. Ed. Alfons Schraeder; Pub. Marg Ann Phillips. adv. contact: Petra Seeger. circ. 165,730. **Document type:** consumer publication.
—SWETS.
Description: For professional computer buyers.

P C PUBLISHING AND PRESENTATIONS; desktop publishing. see *PUBLISHING AND BOOK TRADE — Computer Applications*

004.16 II ISSN 0971-216X
P C QUEST. (Text in English) 1987. m. Rs.240($60) (effective 1997). Cyber Media India Ltd., D-74 Panchsheel Enclave, New Delhi 110017, India. TEL 91-11-6433999. FAX 91-11-6475765. E-mail: pcq@pobox.com; URL: http://www.pcquest.com. Ed. Shyam Malhotra; Pub. Pradeep Gupta. adv.: B&W page $1100, color page $1535; trim 296 x 266; adv. contact: Swati Shrivstava. circ. 38,076. **Document type:** consumer publication.
●Also available online.

621.381 CK
P C REGIONAL. (Text in English, Portuguese, Spanish) 1990. bi-m. Col.$9600 (foreign Col.$14000) (effective 1992). Empresar Editores Ltda., Carrera 11, No. 94-02, L-123, Bogota, Colombia. TEL 2182730. FAX 6101958. Ed. Hernando Bahamon. adv. circ. 10,000. (back issues avail.) **Description:** For users of personal computers.

004.16 SA
P C REPORT; South Africa's independent information source for PC professionals. (Text in English) 1993. m. R.96. Systems Publishers (Pty) Ltd., P.O. Box 41345, Craighall 2024, South Africa. TEL 27-11-7891808. FAX 27-11-7894725. adv.; illus. **Document type:** trade publication.

P C RETAILING. (Personal Computer) see *COMPUTERS — Computer Sales*

P.C. REVIEW; evaluations of new personal computer products. see *COMPUTERS — Software*

621.381 US
P C S ADVISOR. (Progressive Computer Software) 3/yr. P C S Technologies, 4250 Wissahickon Ave., Philadelphia, PA 19129-1215. TEL 215-226-2222. FAX 215-225-2339. Ed. Robert J. Evans.

004.16 MX
P C SEMANAL. w. $100 (effective 1997). Consorcio Sayrols, Mier y Pesado 126, Col. del Valle, 03100 Mexico D.F., Mexico. TEL 52-5-6874699. FAX 52-5-5237045. E-mail: beatrizc@spin.com.mx; URL: http://www.sayrols.com.mx. Ed. Monica Mistretta. R&P contact: Roberto Davo. TEL 52-5-5236714. adv.: B&W page $2235, color page $2873; 320 x 260; adv. contact: Beatriz Coria. circ. 15,000. (tabloid format) **Document type:** newspaper.
Description: Includes news, new products, information regarding the Mexican computer market.

621.381 CC
P C SPECIAL MONTHLY. m. HK.$360($71) in South East Asia; elsewhere $87. Interface Electronic Publisher, Flat 8, 13th Fl., Yeung Yiu Chung no.8, Ind. Bldg., 20 Wang Hoi Rd., Kowloon Bay, Kowloon, Hong Kong. People's Republic of China. TEL 3-7955582. FAX 3-7952962. Ed. K.C. Wong. adv.; circ. controlled.
Description: Features recent technical innovations and breakthroughs in personal computer products, including leading enterprises in the trade.

004.16 US
P C SUPPORT EXPERT. 1993. bi-m. $89 (Canada and Mexico $109; elsewhere $129). Fleming Enterprises, 5650 El Camino Real, Ste. 225, Carlsbad, CA 92008. TEL 619-931-8615. FAX 619-931-9935. Ed. Craig Pelkie. **Document type:** newsletter.
Description: Contains information on IBM's PC Support-400 and Client Access-400 products.

621.381 US
P C TECH JOURNAL DIRECTORY. (Personal Computer) a. Ziff-Davis Publishing Co., One Park Ave., New York, NY 10016. TEL 212-503-5346.

621.381 MX
P C - TIPS; ideas y recomendaciones para optimizar el uso de su computadora personal. vol.4, 1991. m. Mex.$600000. Editora y Comercializadora de Bienes de Informatica, S.A., Goldsmith No. 38, 3r piso, Col. Polanco, 11560 Mexico, D.F., Mexico. TEL 259-14-48. FAX 2026970. TELEX 1763259 ADIRME. (Subscr. to: Admin. de Correos 105, 11581 Mexico D.F., Mexico) Ed. Areli Gaona Castillo. adv.; tr.lit. circ. 11,000.

004.16 US ISSN 1040-6484
QA76.5
P C TODAY; computing for small business. 1987. m. $24. Peed Corporation, 120 W. Harvest Dr., Box 85380, Lincoln, NE 68501-5380. TEL 800-424-7900. FAX 402-477-9252. URL: http://www.peed.com/pctoday.html. adv. circ. 44,183. **Document type:** trade publication.
—KR SourceOne. **CCC.**
Formerly: P C Catalog.
Description: Shows how to increase productivity and decrease costs, maximize return on investment, utilize software more effectively; presents new technology.

621.381 UK ISSN 0960-0124
P C TODAY. 1987. 13/yr. £45.50 (foreign £84.50). Europress Publications Ltd., Europa House, Adlington Park, Adlington, Macclesfield, Ches. SK10 4NP, England. TEL 0625-878888. FAX 0625-879966. (Subscr. to: Europress Direct, P.O. Box 2, Ellesmere Port, South Wirral L65 3EA, England) Ed. Alex France. adv. contact: John Singh. illus.; tr.lit. circ. 35,779. (back issues avail.) **Document type:** consumer publication.
Formerly: Personal Computing with the I B M - P C and Compatibles.
Description: Covers all business aspects of computing with a personal computer.

004.16 IT
▼**P C TRADE**. 1996. m. Mondadori Informatica S.p.A., Casella Postale 3686, 20090 Segrate (MI), Italy. TEL 39-2-21712280. FAX 39-2-21712285. E-mail: pctrade@mondadori.it. Ed. Emilio Mango. adv. contact: Gianluca Ferrauto. circ. 12,000. **Document type:** trade publication.
Description: For dealers and resellers. Provides a market overview, opportunities, and business news.

004.16 US ISSN 1067-0998
TK7887.5
P C UPGRADE; the guide to building and expanding computer systems. 6/yr. $17.95. Bedford Communications, Inc., 150 Fifth Ave., New York, NY 10011. TEL 212-807-8220. FAX 212-807-1098. Ed. David Finck; Pub. Ed Brown. R&P contact: David Finck. adv. contact: Carol Berman. **Document type:** consumer publication.
—KR SourceOne.
Formerly: Desktop Publishing - Office Automation Buyer's Guide and Handbook.

621.381 US ISSN 0740-1604
QA75.5
P C WEEK; the national newspaper of corporate computing. 1984. w. $195 (Canada & Mexico $250; elsewhere $395) (free to qualified personnel); newsstand price: $6. Ziff-Davis Publishing Co., One Park Ave., New York, NY 10016-5146. TEL 212-503-5100; 800-451-1032. E-mail: elundquist@zd.com; URL: http://www.pcweek.com/. (Subscr. to: Box 1770, Riverton, NJ 08077. TEL 609-829-0667. FAX 609-786-2081) Ed. Dan Farber; Pub. Donald J. Byrnes. adv.; circ. 128,277 (controlled). (tabloid format; also avail. in microform from UMI) **Indexed:** Bus.Ind., Comput.Dtbs., Comput.Indus.Up., Mag.Ind Microcomp.Ind., PCR2, Tel.Alert, Tr.& Indus.Ind. **Document type:** trade publication.
●Also available online. Vendor(s): CompuServe, Inc. Information Access Co.
Also available on CD-ROM.
—BLDSC (6413.374700); CISTI; KR SourceOne; SWETS. **CCC.**
Description: Covers all aspects of computers for corporate users. Covers a wide variety of topics, including software, hardware, industry news, business strategies and hardware, software reviews.

621.381 UK ISSN 0269-3011
CODEN: PCWKEJ
P C WEEK. 1985. w. £100. V N U Business Publications BV, VNU House, 32-34 Broadwick St., London W1A 2HG, England. TEL 44-171-439-4242. FAX 44-171-437-7906. adv.; B&W page £3245; trim 10 x 14.16. circ. 50,675. **Document type:** trade publication.
Description: For corporate DP-MIS purchasers an PC buyers. Includes reviews and up-to-date product-based news.

621.381 001.642 AT ISSN 1030-6137
P C WEEK; Australia's newspaper of corporate computing. 1988. m. Aus.$99. A C P Computer Publications, Level 6, 54-58 Park St., Sydney, N.S.W. 2000, Australia. TEL 61-2-2889119. FAX 61-2-2674909. E-mail: pcweek@acp.com.au. Ed. Chris Bowes; Pub. Richard Walsh. adv.: B&W page Aus.$3625, color page Aus.$4875; trim 355 x 275; adv. contact: Jon Fox. circ. 8,696. **Document type:** trade publication.
Description: For people in charge of purchasing large quantities of personal computer and related products for corporate, government and small business organizations.

COMPUTERS — PERSONAL COMPUTERS

001.64   SP   ISSN 1133-8113
P C WEEK (EDICION ESPANOLA). 1988. w. 27950 ptas. (effective 1997). Editorial America Iberica, Miguel Yuste 26, 28037 Madrid, Spain. TEL 34-1-3045542. FAX 34-1-3272462. Ed. Carmen Cristobal. adv. circ. 12,000. **Document type:** newspaper.

621.381   CC   ISSN 1012-8336
P C WEEK ASIA. (Text in English) 1987. s-m. $100 (foreign $123). Newsources Investments Ltd., 1501 Shiu Lam Bldg., 23 Luard Rd., Wanchai, Hong Kong, People's Republic of China. TEL 852-2528-4808. FAX 852-2865-6832. TELEX 66784 NEWS MX. (Subscr. to: 105 Boon Keng Rd., No. 04-17, Singapore 339776. TEL 291-9861) Ed. Tan Lay Leng; Pub. Katherine Chan. adv. contact: Bernie Lim. bk.rev.; circ. 21,429 (controlled). (tabloid format; back issues avail.) **Document type:** trade publication.
Description: Covers corporate computing for decision-making MIS managers, and DP professionals in end-user organizations.

004.16   IT
P C WEEK ITALIA. 1987. w. L.107500 (foreign L.161500). Mondadori Informatica S.p.A., Casella Postale 3686, 20090 Segrate (Milan), Italy. TEL 39-2-21712250. FAX 39-2-21712255. E-mail: pcweek@mondadori.it. Ed. Stefano Maruzzi. adv. contact: Gianluca Ferrauto. circ. 34,492. **Document type:** trade publication.
Description: Contains worldwide news, product tests, market and company analyses.

004.16   GW   ISSN 0175-0496
P C WELT. 1983. m. DM.72 (foreign DM.90) (effective 1997); newsstand price: DM.6.60. I D G Communications Verlag AG, Brabanterstr. 4, 80805 Munich, Germany. TEL 49-89-36086-222. FAX 49-89-36086372. Ed. Michael Klein. adv.: B&W page DM.14800, color page DM.19800; trim 264 x 180; adv. contact: Christoph Burkhart. circ. 311,000 (paid). **Document type:** consumer publication, trade publication.
—BLDSC (6413.374780); SWETS.
Description: Aimed specifically at PC experts. Reports feature systems operating under MS-DOS, Windows and OS-2.

C WINDOWS. see COMPUTERS — Software

005   US   ISSN 0737-8939
QA76.8.I2594   CODEN: PCWDDV
C WORLD; the no. 1 source for definitive how-to-buy, how-to-use advice on Personal Computing systems and software. 1982. m. $29.90 (Canada and Mexico $49.90; elsewhere $75.90); newsstand price: $3.95. D J Communications, Inc., One Exeter Plaza, Boston, MA 02116. TEL 617-534-1200. URL: http://www.pcworld.com/. (Subscr. to: Box 55029, Boulder, CO 80322-5029. TEL 800-234-3498) Ed. Philip Lemmons. adv. contact: Jeff Edman. software rev.; circ. 915,639 (paid). (also avail. in microform from UMI; back issues avail.) **Indexed:** Abstr.Bull.Inst.Pap.Chem., B.P.I., Comput.Bus., Comput.Cont., Comput.Dtbs., Comput.Ind., Comput.Indus.Up., IBM PC.Ind., INSPEC, LHTN, Microcomp.Ind., Microcomp.Indus.Up., PC Abstr., PCR2, R.G.Abstr., WPM. **Document type:** consumer publication.
●Also available online. Vendor(s): CompuServe, Inc. (GO PWOFORUM), Information Access Co.
—BLDSC (6413.375000); AskIEEE; CASDDS; CISTI; Ei; KR SourceOne; Linda Hall; SWETS; UMI; UnCover. CCC.
Incorporates (1985-1992): Lotus (ISSN 8756-7334); (in 1991): Windows (San Francisco); (1987-1990): P C Resource (ISSN 0892-0575)
Description: For IBM personal Computer users. Features articles on applications. Regular columns contain news, systems information, questions-and-answers, product announcements and hardware updates, with a regular section on Lotus software news and applications.

621.381   DK   ISSN 0904-4191
C WORLD. (Text in Danish) 1985. 20/yr. DKK 698. I D G Danmark A-S, Carl Jacobsensvej 25, DK-2500 Valby, Denmark. TEL 45-36-19-91-00. FAX 45-36-44-27-97. TELEX 31566-CWDAN. Ed. Mads Christensen. adv. circ. 20,000. (reprint service avail.) **Indexed:** B.P.I., Comput.Indus.Up., Microcomp.Ind., R.G.Abstr.

621.381   PO
P C WORLD. 12/yr. Rua D. Estefania 32, 1o, 1000 Lisbon, Portugal. TEL 544307. FAX 522643. TELEX 64198. Ed. Antonio Panciarelli. **Indexed:** B.P.I., R.G.Abstr.

004.16   BU
P C WORLD. m. $30. I D G Technika Communications, Ltd., 1, Hristo Smirnenski Blvd., Fl. 11, 1421 Sofia, Bulgaria. TEL 359-2-96308866. FAX 359-2-9632841. Ed. Nelly Vacheva. R&P contact: Yanka Petrovska. adv. contact: Yanka Petrovska. (back issues avail.) **Document type:** consumer publication.
Description: Provides professionals with products reviews and purchasing guides.

621.381   NR   ISSN 0795-4077
P C WORLD AFRICA; Africa's business magazine of information technology, products and applications. 1991. m. £N300($30) (foreign £35) (effective Mar. 1991). I D G Communications (West Africa), P.O. Box 71729, Victoria Island, Lagos State, Nigeria. TEL 234-1-883585. FAX 234-1-883014. Ed. S.A. Ochapa. adv.; bk.rev. circ. 15,000. (back issues avail.) **Document type:** trade publication.
Description: Examines computer products and applications, communications systems, and telecommunications; computers as they relate to African businesses and the role of computers in education.

621.381   SP   ISSN 0213-1307
P C WORLD ESPANA; magazine for the IBM PC compatible user in Spain. 1983. m. $73. I D G - C W Communications, Rafael Calvo 18, p.4B, 28010 Madrid, Spain. TEL 91-3194014. FAX 91-3196104. (In U.S.: C W Communications Inc, c/o Diana La Muraglia, 375 Cochituate Rd., Box 9171, Framingham, MA 01701-9171. TEL 617-879-0700) Ed. Juan M. Saez. circ. 84,000.
Formerly (until 1988): MicroSistemas.

621.381   CC   ISSN 1023-4942
P C WORLD HONG KONG. (Text in English) 1992. m. HK.$350 (Asia $85; elsewhere $95). I D G Communications (HK) Ltd., Mount Parker House, Ste. 1011-15, 1111 King's Rd., Quarry Bay, Hong Kong, People's Republic of China. TEL 852-2861-3238. FAX 852-2861-0953. Ed. Peter Gloster; Pub. Melvyn Bennett. R&P contact: Karman Cheng. adv.: B&W page HK.$17900, color page HK.$23100; trim 205 x 277; adv. contact: Vera Chan. circ. 12,000. **Document type:** consumer publication.
Description: Provides products and PC productivity hints for PC users in Hong Kong.

621.381   IT   ISSN 1120-8066
P C WORLD ITALIA; il mensile per l'utente di PC e workstation. 11/yr. L.88000 (foreign L.203500). I D G Communications Italia s.r.l., Via G. Malipiero, 14, 20138 Milan, Italy. TEL 39-2-58011660. FAX 39-2-58011670. Pub. Mario Toffoletti. adv. contact: Costantino Cialfi. circ. 34,225. (back issues avail.)
Description: Helps PC users buy and use microcomputer and workstation hardware and software. Contains previews, trials and comparisons of products from Italian and international companies.

004.16   KO
P C WORLD KOREA. 1990. m. Hi-Tech Information, Inc., 3-F, Woosung Bldg., 333 Cheong Jeon-dong, Mapo-ku, Seoul 135-270, S. Korea. TEL 2-3257300. FAX 2-3258475. adv.: B&W page $1500, color page $2500; trim 190 x 258. circ. 40,000.

621.381   SI
P C WORLD MALAYSIA. (Text in English) 1992. m. M.86. Communication Resources Pte. Ltd., Blk. 1008, Toa Payoh North, No. 07-01, Singapore 318996, Singapore. TEL 65-256-6201. FAX 65-251-0348. E-mail: pcworld@po.jaring.my; URL: http://www.jaring.my/pcworld. (Malaysia addr.: 21A Jalan 17-45, 46400 Petaling Jaya, Selangor Darn'l Ehsan, Malaysia) Ed. James Miller; Pub. Tan Tee Seng. R&P contact: James Miller. adv.: B&W page M.$3000, color page M.$4000; trim 215 x 279; adv. contact: Mahendran Sivanesan. circ. 15,000. **Document type:** consumer publication.
●Also available online.
Description: Provides latest product information and PC productivity hints for PC users in Malaysia.

004.16   PK
P C WORLD PAKISTAN. (Text in English) m. Micro Publications, 33-C Main Gulberg, Lahore, Pakistan. TEL 42-5711147. FAX 42-5760277. adv.: B&W page $950, color page $1350; trim 205 x 275. circ. 5,000.

004.16   RM
P C WORLD ROMANIA. (Personal Computer) 1990. bi-m. I D G Communications Publishing Group s.r.l., Calea Floreasca 167, et. 4, cam. 412, Sec. 2 Bucharest, Rumania. TEL 01-679-7140. FAX 01-312-76-12. Ed. Ion Diamandi. adv.: B&W page $896, color page $1125; trim 8 1/4 x 11 5/8. circ. 15,000.
Formerly (until 1993): Infoclub (ISSN 1220-8639)

621.381   SI
P C WORLD SINGAPORE. (Text in English) 1992. m. S.$68. Communication Resources Pte. Ltd., Blk. 1008, Toa Payoh North, No. 07-01, Singapore 318996, Singapore. TEL 65-2566201. FAX 65-251-0348. E-mail: marketing@comres.com.sg; URL: http://www.comres.com.sg/pcworld. Ed. James Miller; Pub. James Miller. adv.: B&W page S.$2450, color page S.$3200; trim 215 x 279; adv. contact: Lynn Teo. circ. 15,000. **Document type:** consumer publication.
●Also available online.
Description: Provides latest product information and PC productivity hints for PC users in Singapore.

004.16   VN
P C WORLD VIETNAM. (Text in Vietnamese) m. H C M City Information and Telecommunications, 79 Truong Dinh District, 1 Ho Chi Minh City, Socialist Republic of Vietnam. TEL 8297629. FAX 8291957. (Co-sponsor: H C M City Committee for Sciences & Technology) Ed. Nguyen Trong. adv.: B&W page $600, color page $1400; trim 200 x 280. circ. 15,000.

621.381   GW   ISSN 0935-6274
PAGE; Publizieren und Praesentieren mit dem Personal Computer. 1986. m. DM.132. MACup Verlag GmbH, Leverkusenstr. 54, 22761 Hamburg, Germany. TEL 49-40-85183400. FAX 49-40-85183449. Ed. Albert Dommer. adv.: B&W page DM.6200, color page DM.8300; adv. contact: Christine Homann. circ. 23,660. (back issues avail.) **Document type:** consumer publication.
Description: Information on creative multiplatform publishing on PC.

THE PAGE (LOUISVILLE). see COMPUTERS — Computer Graphics

004.16   US   ISSN 1074-7257
PAGE P C. 1994. m. $69 (foreign $89). Cobb Group, Inc., 9420 Bunsen Pky., Louisville, KY 40220. TEL 502-493-3200; 800-223-8720. FAX 502-491-8050. Ed. Mike O'Mara. pp./issue: 16. **Document type:** trade publication.
Description: Contains newsletter design ideas, techniques and shortcuts for using any of the featured software. Covers illustration tech, pre-press issues, reviews, new versions of major software.

621.381   US   ISSN 1051-9696
PARADOX DEVELOPER'S JOURNAL. 1990. 12/yr. $119 (foreign $139). Cobb Group, Inc., 9420 Bunsen Parkway, Ste. 300, Louisville, KY 40220. TEL 502-493-3200. FAX 502-491-8050. (Subscr. to: Box 35160, Louisville, KY 40232. TEL 800-223-8720) Ed. David Brown. **Document type:** consumer publication.
Description: Addresses the specific needs of experienced Paradox developers and sophisticated PAL programmers.

621.381   US   ISSN 0889-2911
PARADOX USER'S JOURNAL. 1986. m. $69 (foreign $89). Cobb Group, Inc., 9420 Bunsen Pkwy., Ste. 300, Louisville, KY 40220. TEL 502-493-3200. FAX 502-491-8050. (Subscr. to: Box 35160, Louisville, KY 40232-9720. TEL 800-223-8720) Ed. David Brown. **Document type:** consumer publication.
Description: Provides tips and timesaving ideas, new applications and techniques, for users of Paradox.

COMPUTERS — PERSONAL COMPUTERS

621.381 FI ISSN 1235-1199
PELIT. 1992. 10/yr. FIM 258. Helsinki Media Company Oy, Special Magazines, P.O. Box 2, FIN-00040 Helsinki Media, Finland. TEL 358-0-1205911. FAX 358-0-1205795. Ed. Tuija Linden. adv. contact: Mia Kemppi. circ. 27,156. **Document type:** consumer publication.

621.381 IT
PERSONAL COMPUTER; mensile d'informatica. 1986. m. L.60000($80) Systems Comunicazioni, Via Olanda, 6, 20083 Gaggiano (MI), Italy. TEL 02-90841814. FAX 02-90841682. Ed. Michele di Pisa. adv. circ. 24,000. (reprint service avail.)

004.16 IT
PERSONAL COMPUTER - ANNUARIO. s-a. L.15000. Systems Comunicazioni, Via Olanda 6, 20083 Vigano di Gaggiano (MI), Italy. TEL 39-2-90841814. FAX 39-2-90841682. Ed. Agostina Ronchetti. adv.: B&W page L.3600000, color page L.5400000.

004.16 NE ISSN 0772-8077
PERSONAL COMPUTER MAGAZINE; het computerblad voor Nederland en Belgie. 1983. 11/yr. fl.84.50 (outside Europe fl.180). V N U Business Publications B.V., Postbus 9194, 1006 CC Amsterdam, Netherlands. TEL 31-20-4875487. FAX 31-20-4875700. E-mail: pcmmarketing@pcm.vnu.com. Ed. M. Heffels; Pub. A.H.W. van der Want. adv. contact: C. van den Berg. circ. 125,000 (paid). **Document type:** trade publication.
—KNAW; SWETS.
Description: Independent and professional special interest magazine on personal computers and software.

621.381 UK ISSN 0957-2279
PERSONAL COMPUTER MAGAZINE. 1982. m. £24 (foreign £50). V N U Business Publications BV, VNU House, 32-34 Broadwick St., London W1A 2HG, England. TEL 0171-439-4242. FAX 0171-437-7906. adv.: B&W page £3035, color page £3735; trim 297 x 210. circ. 100,552. **Indexed:** INSPEC (1988-). **Document type:** trade publication.
—CCC.
Description: Covers Unix and OS-2, and mini and mainframe connectivity.

621.381 UK ISSN 0142-0232
CODEN: PCWODU
PERSONAL COMPUTER WORLD. 1978. m. £24.95 (effective 1996). V N U Business Publications BV, VNU House, 32-34 Broadwick St., London W1A 2HG, England. TEL 44-171-439-4242. FAX 44-171-437-7906. Ed. Jane Bird. adv.: B&W page £2255, color page £2955; trim 297 x 210. bk.rev. circ. 112,306. **Indexed:** Br.Tech.Ind., Build.Manage.Abstr., Info.Media & Tech., INSPEC, LAMP, Microcomp.Ind., WPM. **Document type:** trade publication.
—BLDSC (6427.860000); AskIEEE; Ei; KR SourceOne; SWETS.

004.16 MX
PERSONAL COMPUTING MEXICO; la revista de los sistemas personales. m. $71 (effective 1997). Consorcio Sayrols, Mier y Pesado 126, Col. del Valle, 03100 Mexico D.F., Mexico. TEL 52-5-6874699. FAX 52-5-5237045. E-mail: beatrizc@spin.com.mx; URL: http://www.sayrols.com.mx. Ed. Monica Mistretta. R&P contact: Roberto Davo. TEL 52-5-5236714. adv. contact: B&W page $3465, color page $4500; trim 205 x 270. circ. 25,000. **Document type:** consumer publication.
Description: Includes a buyer's guide of products available in Mexico. Contains news on new products, LAN, and Macintosh.

621.381 US ISSN 0748-0016
TA345 CODEN: PEGNEU
PERSONAL ENGINEERING & INSTRUMENTATION NEWS. 1984. m. $50 in U.S.; Canada and Mexico $75; elsewhere $125. P E C Inc., Box 430, Rye, NH 03870-0430. TEL 603-427-1377. FAX 603-427-1388. E-mail: pgpserseng@aol.com. Ed. Paul Schreier; Pub. Al Shackil. adv.: bk.rev.; circ. 50,000 (controlled). **Document type:** trade publication.
—BLDSC (6427.862850); Ei; KR SourceOne. **CCC.**
Description: Covers PC-based hardware and software used by scientists and engineers for technical applications. Focuses on data acquisition and control, design automation and instrumentation.

PINKERTON EYE ON TRAVEL. see TRAVEL AND TOURISM

PORTABLE COMPANION; for Osborne computer users. see COMPUTERS — Microcomputers

621.381 US
THE PORTABLE COMPUTING LETTER.* 1991. bi-m. $49.95 (foreign $89.95). Yellowstone Information Services, R.R. 2, Box 42A, Bloomingdale, OH 43910-9802. TEL 304-965-5548. FAX 304-965-7785. Ed. Roger Thibault.

PRIVAT COMPUTER. see COMPUTERS — Microcomputers

PROMPT; P C Zeitschrift. see HANDICAPPED — Visually Impaired

004 US ISSN 0886-8174
QA75.5
PUGET SOUND COMPUTERUSER; business technology, office automation, computers. Key Title: Puget Sound Computer User. 1986. m. $12 (Canada $36); free to qualified personnel. K F H Publications, Inc., 3530 Bagley Ave. N., Seattle, WA 98103. TEL 206-547-4950. FAX 206-545-6591. Ed. John Shaw; Pub. Stan Kehl. adv.: B&W page $2595, color page $3245; trim 11 x 15; adv. contact: Lora Cheney. index. circ. 95,000. (tabloid format; back issues avail.) **Document type:** consumer publication.
Description: Covers new developments in computer hardware and software, industry trends, personnel and management issues, consumer electronics, and more.

R I S C USER. (Reduced Instruction Set Computer) see COMPUTERS — Microcomputers

004.16 US
READ ME FIRST. irreg. E-mail: jgamble@midusa.net; dbudin@spiritone.com; URL: http://www.spiritone.com/~dbudin/. Eds. John Gamble, Dave Budin.
●Available only online.
Description: Provides reviews of various Mac software products.

621.381 US ISSN 0899-014X
RECREATIONAL & EDUCATIONAL COMPUTING; a mathemagical panoply of computer recreations for thinking readers. Short title: R E C. (Supplements avail. on diskette) 1986. 6/yr. $27 (Canada $29; elsewhere in Americas $33; elsewhere $36). Dr. Michael W. Ecker, Ed. & Pub., 909 Violet Terr., Clarks Summit, PA 18411. TEL 717-586-2784. E-mail: MWE1@psu.edu. R&P contact: Michael W. Ecker. adv.: bk.rev.; software rev. (back issues avail.) **Document type:** newsletter.
Formerly: R E C Newsletter.
Description: Presents applications of mathematics and computers in a recreational format, reviews of games and correspondence.

REPORT ON A T & T; the independent bi-weekly reporting exclusively on the long-distance industry including AT&T and its competitors. see COMMUNICATIONS — Computer Applications

004 FR ISSN 1164-6950
REVUE DE L'UTILISATEUR P C. 10/yr. Softin Communications, 2 rue d'Amsterdam, 75009 Paris, France. TEL 42-81-54-27. Ed. Roger Christophe. circ. 50,000.
Formerly (until 1991): Revue de l'Utilisateur de l'IBM - P C (ISSN 0760-775X)

621.381 US
ROOT DIRECTORY. 1985. m. $20. (Manatee P C User's Group, Inc.) Daniel L. Crumpler, Ed. & Pub., 411 67th St., N.W., Bradenton, FL 34209-1652. TEL 813-795-0063. adv.: bk.rev. circ. 1,000.
Formerly (until 1989): Letter (Bradenton).

004.16 US ISSN 0893-2875
QA76.5
S I G SMALL - P C NOTES. 1984. q. $14 to non-members. Association for Computing Machinery, Special Interest Group on Small and Personal Computing Systems and Applications, 1515 Broadway, 17th Fl., New York, NY 10036. TEL 212-869-7440. (Subscr. to: Box 12115, Church St. Sta., New York, NY 10249) **Indexed:** INSPEC. **Document type:** newsletter.
—AskIEEE; CISTI; KR SourceOne; UnCover.
Formed by the merger of (1978-1984): S I G P C Notes (ISSN 0163-5816); (1978-1984): S I G Small Newsletter (ISSN 0272-720X); Which was formerly (1975-1978): S I G Mini Newsletter (ISSN 0163-576X)
Description: A newsletter for those interested in the technical considerations of personal computing. Articles cover design, technology and applications of computer systems for personal uses.

621.381 UK ISSN 0957-4859
S T FORMAT. 1988. m. £33 (rest of Europe £45; elsewhere £54.95). Future Publishing Ltd., 30 Monmouth St., Bath, Avon BA1 2BW, England. TEL 44-1224-442244. FAX 44-1224-462986. (Subscr. to: Future Publishing Ltd., Somerton, Somers. TA11 6BR, England. TEL 44-1225-822511) Ed. Karen Levell; Pub. Simon Stansfield. adv.; circ. 38,671 (paid). (back issues avail.) **Document type:** consumer publication.
Supersedes in part (in 1989): S T Amiga Format (ISSN 0954-805X)
Description: Covers Amiga ST computing, programming and games.

621.381 FR
S V M MAC. (Science et Vie Micro) 1988. 11/yr. 282 F. (foreign 376 F.)(effective 1992). Excelsior Publications, 1 rue du Colonel Pierre Avia, 75503 Paris Cedex 15, France. TEL 46-48-48-48. FAX 46-48-48-09. TELEX 631 994 F. Ed. Andreas Pfeiffer. adv. contact: Gilles de Keranflech. circ. 44,087. **Indexed:** Pt.de Rep.
Formerly: S V M Macintosh (ISSN 0992-5120)

S V M SCIENCE ET VIE MICRO. see COMPUTERS — Microcomputers

S.W.A.T.PRO; secret weapon and tactic guide. see COMPUTERS — Computer Games

621.381 US
ST. LOUIS COMPUTING. 1983. m. $12. Wikman Publishing, Inc., 8045 Big Bend Blvd., Ste. 110, St. Louis, MO 63119-2714. TEL 314-968-0706. FAX 314-968-5316. Ed. Carol Ellerman; Pub. Thomas M. Jozwik. adv. circ. 49,000.

004 BE ISSN 0776-1503
SAMSOM PERSONAL COMPUTER (EDITION FRANCAISE). Flemish edition (ISSN 0774-9929) s-m. 4770 BEF. C E D Samsom (Subsidiary of: Wolters Samsom Belgie n.v.), Kouterveld 14, B-1831 Diegem, Belgium. TEL 32-2-7231111. index.

004 BE ISSN 0774-9929
SAMSOM PERSONAL COMPUTER (VLAAMSE EDITIE). French edition (ISSN 0776-1503) 1986. 10/yr. 4134 BEF. C E D Samsom (Subsidiary of: Wolters Samsom Belgie n.v.), Kouterveld 14, B-1831 Diegem, Belgium. TEL 32-2-7231111.

621.381 US
SAN FRANCISCO BAY AREA SANYO GROUP NEWSLETTER. m. San Francisco Bay Area Sanyo Group, 1260 Westwood St., Redwood City, CA 94061. Ed. Barbara Valley.

621.381 US ISSN 1054-4232
SANYO P C HACKERS NEWSLETTER. 1984. m. $20 (Canada $25; elsewhere $30) (effective 1997). Victor R. Frank, Ed. & Pub., 12450 Skyline Blvd., Woodside, CA 94062-4541. TEL 415-851-7031. E-mail: frank@sneezy.sri.com. (Alt. addr. for items requiring trip to post office: Sanyo PC Hackers Newsletter, Box 762, Menlo Park, CA 94026) R&P contact: Victor R. Frank. adv. contact: Victor R. Frank. bk.rev. circ. 70. (back issues avail.) **Document type:** newsletter.
Description: Devoted to information exchange about Sanyo computers and software, primarily the MBC-550 series.

621.381 US
SANYO SOURCE. s-m. $32. Computer User Services, 230 Anderson St., Hackensack, NJ 07601.

COMPUTERS — ROBOTICS 2205

SCARLETT. see COMPUTERS — Microcomputers

SCRIPT - CENTRAL. see COMPUTERS — Software

621.381 US
SELLING NETWORKS. (Supplement to: L A N Times) 1994. bi-m. McGraw-Hill Companies, 1221 Ave. of the Americas, New York, NY 10020. TEL 212-512-2000. (Subscr. to: 1900 O'Farrell St., San Mateo, CA 94403. TEL 415-513-6800) **Document type:** trade publication.

621.381 US ISSN 1042-0681
QA76.753
SHAREWARE MAGAZINE;* best buys in software for the IBM and compatible. 1982. bi-m. $14.95. P C - S I G, Inc., 955 W. Chandler Blvd., Ste. 9, Chandler, AZ 85224-5345. TEL 408-730-9291. FAX 408-730-2107. TELEX 5106013509PCSIG. Ed. Michael Callahan. adv. contact: Jerry Pearson. bk.rev.; software rev. circ. 90,000. **Document type:** consumer publication.
—UnCover.
  Former titles: P C - S I G Magazine; P C - S I G Newsletter.
  Description: For beginners to sophisticated users of Shareware marketed software. Covers educational uses, Macintosh applications, comparisons of commercial and shareware packages.

621.381 640.73 US ISSN 0882-5939
SLOANE REPORT; an off-line access to computing. 1985. 10/yr. (plus 8 supplements). $279 (effective July 1990). Sloane Report, 8306 Mills Dr., Ste. 518, Miami, FL 33183. TEL 305-251-2199. FAX 305-238-6039. Ed. E. Sloane. adv.; bk.rev.; cum.index: 1985-1990. circ. 10,000. (back issues avail.)
  Description: Reports on and analyzes events in the computer industry, specifically Apple, Commodore, IBM and Tandy.

621.381 FR ISSN 0755-3579
SOFT & MICRO. 1984. 11/yr. 326 F. (foreign 483 F.)(effective 1992). Excelsior Publications, 1 rue du Colonel Pierre Avia, 75503 Paris Cedex 15, France. TEL 46-48-48-48. FAX 46-48-48-09. TELEX 631 994 F. Eds. Seymour Dinnematin, Yann Garret. adv. contact: Gilles de Keranflech. circ. 41,063.
  Description: Covers how to choose PC hardware and software for professional applications.

SOFT.LETTER; trends & strategies in software publishing. see COMPUTERS — Software

SOFTDISK; the monthly software collection for people who love their Apple II's. see COMPUTERS — Software

SOFTWARE DIGEST; the independent, comparative ratings report for PC and LAN software. see COMPUTERS — Software

SOURCEVIEW JOURNAL OF SOFTWARE EVALUATIONS, REVIEWS & RATINGS. see COMPUTERS — Software

SPREADSHEET. see COMPUTERS — Microcomputers

004.16 NE ISSN 0923-2214
ST; onafhankelijk tijdschrift van en voor gebruikers van Atari ST computers. 1986. bi-m. fl.40 ($40 in U.S.). Stichting ST, Postbus 11129, 2301 EC Leiden, Netherlands. TEL 31-71-5130045. Ed. Han Driesen. circ. 3,000 (paid). **Document type:** consumer publication.
  Description: For serious Atari ST users and programmers.

621.381 US
STACK. 1975. m. $25 includes membership. Long Island Computer Association, Inc., Box 71, Hicksville, NY 11802. TEL 516-293-9368. Ed. Al Levy. adv.; bk.rev. circ. 5,000. (also avail. in diskette format) **Document type:** bulletin.

004.16 US
STRIKING HOME. q. $12. Dvorak International, Box 44, Poultney, VT 05764-0044. TEL 802-287-2343. E-mail: DvorakInt@aol.com.
  Formerly: Dvorak International. Quarterly.
  Description: Contains studies comparing the Dvorak keyboard layout to Qwerty, product reviews, first person accounts from Dvorak typists.

004.16 US ISSN 1066-7334
STUDIO CITY FOR THE II GS.* Macintosh version: Studio City for the Mac (ISSN 1072-5458) 6/yr. $49.95. Resource Central, Inc., 7118 Main St., Kansas City, MO 64114-1406. FAX 913-469-6507. Pub. Tom Weishaar. (diskette format)
  Formerly: Stack - Central.
  Description: Current news for creators of HyperStudio stacks; includes tutorials, examples, clip art and sounds.

621.381 620 US
SURVEY (LA JOLLA).* 1984. bi-m. K V A Associates, c/o Amatneek, 2356 Torrey Pines Rd. No. 17, La Jolla, CA 92037-3412. **Indexed:** CERDIC.

004.12 SW ISSN 0281-9015
SVENSKA P C WORLD; allt om P C familjens Haard- och Mjukvara. 1984. 10/yr. SEK 435 (effective 1990). C W - Communications AB, Soedra Hamnvaagen 22, S-115 41 Stockholm, Sweden. Ed. Bo Nordin. circ. 10,550.
—UMI.

004.16 004.678 US
TIDBITS. (Text in Chinese, Dutch, English, French, German, Japanese, Spanish) w. E-mail: webmaster@tidbits.com; URL: http://www.tidbits.com/. Eds. Adam Engst, Tonya Engst.
  ●Available only online.
  Description: Focuses on Internet-related topics. Provides information about software and hardware bugs along with tips for Mac users.

004 621.381 FI ISSN 0359-4947
TIETOKONE. 1982. 12/yr. FIM 379. Helsinki Media Company Oy, Special Magazines, P.O. Box 2, FIN-00040 Helsinki Media, Finland. TEL 358-0-1205911. FAX 358-0-1205799. Ed. Eskoensio Pipatti. adv. contact: Mia Kemppi. circ. 32,149. **Document type:** consumer publication.
  Description: For professional PC users.

004.16 US ISSN 1066-7326
TIMEOUT - CENTRAL.* 6/yr. $49.95. Resource Central, Inc., 7118 Main St., Kansas City, MO 64114-1406. TEL 913-469-6502. FAX 913-469-6507. Ed. Randy Brandt; Pub. Tom Weishaar. (diskette format)
  Description: Provides the latest AppleWorks and TimeOut tips, macros, and ware.

621.381 PO
UPDATE. 12/yr. Rua D. Estefania 32, 1o, 1000 Lisbon, Portugal. TEL 572763. FAX 522643. Ed. Antonio Panciarelli. circ. 15,000.

004.16 JA
UPLINK; personal computer magazine with a 3.5" companion disk. 1993. m. 9360 Yen. Akio Fujii, A S C I I Publishing, 4-33-10 Yoyogi, Shibuya-ku, Tokyo 151-24, Japan. TEL 81-3-5351-8111.

621.381 GW
USER MAGAZIN.* 1979. 8/yr. DM.120. J.P. Kern, Schwannstr. 28, 41460 Neuss, Germany. Ed. Rolf Hermann. adv.; bk.rev. circ. 1,200. **Document type:** newsletter.
  Description: For Apple, Macintosh, and AT computer users.

621.381 US
VIC-NIC NEWS.* 1982. 12/yr. $10. Dennis E. McCormack, Ed. & Pub., 30 Dorset, Dorchester, MA 02125-0009. circ. 2,000.
  Description: Aimed at Commodore Vic-20 users.

VIDEOGAMES; the ultimate gaming magazine. see COMPUTERS — Computer Games

621.381 US ISSN 1088-0992
QA76.76.D47
VISUAL DEVELOPER MAGAZINE. 1990. bi-m. $21.95 (Canada $29.95; elsewhere $39.95). Coriolis Group, 14455 N. Hayden Rd., Ste. 220, Scottsdale, AZ 85260-6949. TEL 602-483-0192. FAX 602-483-0193. Ed. Jeff Duntemann. adv.: B&W page $2595, color page $3195; adv. contact: Kelly Mero. bk.rev.; illus. circ. 35,000. (back issues avail.) **Indexed:** Comput.Ind. **Document type:** trade publication.
—KR SourceOne.
  Formerly (until 1996): P C Techniques (ISSN 1053-6205)
  Description: Serves the needs of software and database developers on DOS, Windows and OS/2 platforms. Articles answer the questions "how does it work and how do I do it," in plain, informal English with abundant code examples and drawn technical figures.

WANG IN THE NEWS; the independent newspaper of Wang computer users. see COMPUTERS — Computer Industry

WATCOM NEWS. (Waterloo Computing) see COMPUTERS — Hardware

621.381 UK ISSN 0956-5248
WHAT PERSONAL COMPUTER?. (Has m. supplement: P C Marketplace (ISSN 0969-1839)) m. £24 (foreign £35). E M A P Business & Computer Publications Ltd., 33-39 Bowling Green Ln., London EC1R 0DA, England. TEL 44-171-837-1212. FAX 44-171-278-4008. **Document type:** trade publication.
—BLDSC (9309.757450); AskIEEE; KR SourceOne. CCC.

WINDOWS DEVELOPER'S JOURNAL. see COMPUTERS — Computer Programming

WINDOWS MAGAZINE; MS - windows magazine. see COMPUTERS — Software

004.16 JA ISSN 1340-4857
WINDOWS WORLD JAPAN/GEKKAN WINDOZU WARUDO. (Text in Japanese) 1993. m. I D G Communications, Japan, 2-F, Shuwa Fujimicho Bldg., 1-2-27 Fujimi, Chiyoda-ku, Tokyo 102, Japan. TEL 81-3-3222-6411. FAX 81-3-3222-6566. Ed. Yoko Muramatsu; Pub. Masashi Kobayashi. adv.: B&W page 280000 Yen, color page 518000; trim 210 x 277. circ. 80,000.

621.381 GW
WORKOUT; unabhaengige Personal Workstation Magazin. q. DM.48. MACup Verlag GmbH, Grosse Elbstr. 277, 22767 Hamburg, Germany. TEL 040-3910901. FAX 040-39109150. adv.: B&W page DM.7200; trim 185 x 265. circ. 40,000. **Document type:** consumer publication.

THE WORLD OF INTERNET. see COMMUNICATIONS

THE YELLOWSTONE WINDOWS LETTER. see COMPUTERS — Microcomputers

001.6 621.381 AT ISSN 0725-3931
YOUR COMPUTER. 1981. m. Aus.$59.40. Federal Publishing Company, 180 Bourke Rd., Alexandria, N.S.W. 2015, Australia. TEL 61-2-93536666. FAX 61-2-93174615. Ed. Jake Kennedy; Pub. Michael Hannan. R&P contact: Mark Marshall. adv. contact: Gary Lupos. bk.rev. circ. 17,423. (back issues avail.)
—UMI.

COMPUTERS — Robotics

629.8 FR
A F R I LIAISON. 1982. q. membership. Association Francaise de Robotique Industrielle, 4 place Jussieu, Tour 66, 75252 Paris Cedex 05, France. TEL 43-54-71-70. FAX 43-54-71-70. Ed. Gerard Bourgeois. bk.rev. circ. 2,000.
  Description: Contains international coverage of the industrial robotics industry. Articles cover product developments, automation, systems design and market news. Features include a calendar of events, employment opportunities and a listing of available literature.

COMPUTERS — ROBOTICS

629.8 US ISSN 0885-5684
ADVANCED MANUFACTURING TECHNOLOGY; monthly report. 1979. m. $630 (foreign $690). Technical Insights (Subsidiary of: John Wiley & Sons, Inc.), 32 N. Dean St., Englewood, NJ 07631-2807. TEL 201-568-4744. FAX 201-568-8247. E-mail: amtinfo@insights.com; URL: http://www.insights.com. Ed. Pamela Frost; Pub. Peter Katz. pat.; stat. (back issues avail.) **Document type:** newsletter.
—BLDSC (0696.896500). **CCC.**
   Formerly: Industrial Robots International (ISSN 0197-9280)
   Description: Focuses on technological advances that can ensure manufacturing competitiveness, e.g., desktop manufacturing, computer graphics, flexible automation, computer-integrated manufacturing, and other techniques for cutting costs, improving the quality of manufactured products, and increasing productivity.

629.892 NE ISSN 0169-1864
CODEN: ADROEI
ADVANCED ROBOTICS. (Text in English) 1986. 8/yr. DM.780 (effective 1997). (Robotics Society of Japan) V S P, P.O. Box 346, 3700 AH Zeist, Netherlands. TEL 31-30-6925790. FAX 31-30-6932081. E-mail: 100341.2372@compuserve.com. Ed. T. Fukuda. adv. (back issues avail.) **Indexed:** A.I.Abstr. (until 1992), Abstr.Hum.Comp.Inter., ASCA, CAD CAM Abstr. (until 1992), Compumath, Curr.Cont., INSPEC (1987-), Robomat. (until 1992). **Document type:** academic/scholarly publication.
—BLDSC (0696.926500); AskIEEE; CISTI; Ei; Genuine Article; KR SourceOne; Linda Hall; SWETS; UnCover.
   Description: Interdisciplinary coverage of research on robotics science and engineering.
   Refereed Serial

ADVANCES IN AUTOMATION AND ROBOTICS. see COMPUTERS — Automation

ADVANCES IN DESIGN AND MANUFACTURING. see COMPUTERS — Computer Graphics

AKADEMIA GORNICZO-HUTNICZA IM. STANISLAWA STASZICA. AUTOMATYKA. see COMPUTERS — Automation

ARCHIVES OF CONTROL SCIENCES. see COMPUTERS — Automation

629.8 AT ISSN 0726-3716
AUSTRALIAN ROBOT ASSOCIATION. NEWSLETTER. 1982. q. Aus.$50. Australian Robot Association Inc., G.P.O. Box 1527, Sydney, N.S.W. 2001, Australia. TEL 61-2-99593239. FAX 61-2-99594632. E-mail: MichaelK@zip.com.au; URL: http://www.cs.uow.edu.au/isase/ara. Ed. Michael Kassler. adv.; page Aus.$275; adv. contact: Michael Kassler. bk.rev.; stat. circ. 500. (back issues avail.) **Document type:** newsletter.
   Description: Covers robotics in Australia and New Zealand.

AUTOMATICA & ROBOTICA. see COMPUTERS — Automation

003 629.892 NE ISSN 0929-5593
AUTONOMOUS ROBOTS. (Text in English) 1994. q. fl.625 to institutions; $321 to institutions in U.S. (effective 1998). Kluwer Academic Publishers, Postbus 17, 3300 AA Dordrecht, Netherlands. TEL 31-78-6392392. FAX 31-78-6392254. E-mail: services@wkap.nl; URL: http://www.wkap.nl. (Dist. by: Kluwer Academic Publishers Group, P.O. Box 322, 3300 AH Dordrecht, Netherlands. TEL 31-78-6392392. FAX 31-78-6546474; N. America dist. addr.: Box 358, Accord Sta., Hingham, MA 02018-0358. TEL 617-871-6600. FAX 617-871-6528) Ed. George A. Bekey. (back issues avail.) **Indexed:** Eng.Ind., INSPEC (1994-). **Document type:** academic/scholarly publication.
—BLDSC (1835.061600); AskIEEE; CISTI; Ei; Genuine Article; KR SourceOne. **CCC.**
   Description: Publishes papers on the theory and application of robotic systems incorporating self-sufficiency.
   Refereed Serial

BIBLIOGRAPHY OF ROBOTIC TECHNICAL RESOURCES. see COMPUTERS — Abstracting, Bibliographies, Statistics

629.892 658.8 UK ISSN 0269-9133
BUSINESS RATIO REPORT: INDUSTRIAL ROBOTS; an industry sector analysis. 1986. a. I C C Business Ratios Ltd., Freepost, Field House, Hampton, Mddx. TW12 1BR, England. TEL 081-783-0977. FAX 081-783-1940. charts; stat. **Document type:** trade publication.

CANADIAN INSTITUTE FOR ADVANCED RESEARCH IN ARTIFICIAL INTELLIGENCE AND ROBOTICS. see COMPUTERS — Artificial Intelligence

629.892 621 JA
CHINO IDO ROBOTTO SHINPOJUMU SHIRYO/INTELLIGENT ROBOT SYMPOSIUM. PROCEEDINGS. (Text in Japanese) 1982. biennial. 2500 Yen per no. Nihon Kikai Gakkai - Japan Society of Mechanical Engineers, 4-9, Yoyogi 2-chome, Shibuya-ku, Tokyo 151, Japan. **Document type:** proceedings.

COMPONENTES, EQUIPOS Y SISTEMAS DE AUTOMATICA Y ROBOTICA. see COMPUTERS — Automation

621.48 US ISSN 0069-8644
TK9151.6 CODEN: CRSTBJ
CONFERENCE ON REMOTE SYSTEMS TECHNOLOGY. PROCEEDINGS. 1951. a. $110. American Nuclear Society, 555 N. Kensington Ave., La Grange Park, IL 60525. TEL 708-352-6611. FAX 708-352-0499. R&P contact: Mary Beth Gardner. circ. 500. (back issues avail.; reprint service avail.) **Indexed:** Biol.Abstr., Chem.Abstr., INSPEC. **Document type:** proceedings.
—CASDDS; Ei. **CCC.**
   Description: Presents full scientific papers on robotics and other remote technologies used in the context of nuclear engineering.
   Refereed Serial

629.892 US ISSN 1077-2642
TS171.A1 CODEN: EDAUFU
▼**ENGINEERING DESIGN & AUTOMATION.** 1995. q. $350 (foreign $420) (effective 1998). John Wiley & Sons, Inc., Journals, 605 Third Ave., New York, NY 10158. TEL 212-850-6645. FAX 212-850-6021. TELEX 12-7063. E-mail: SUBINFO@JWILEY.COM; URL: http://www.wiley.co.uk. (Subscr. outside the Americas to: John Wiley & Sons Ltd., Baffins Ln., Chichester, W. Sussex PO19 1UD, England. TEL 44-1243-779777. FAX 44-1243-776128) Ed. Hamid R. Parsaei. adv.: B&W page £640, color page £1515; trim 279 x 210. circ. 855. (also avail. in microform from UMI; back issues avail.) **Document type:** academic/scholarly publication.
—BLDSC (3758.952000); AskIEEE; KR SourceOne.
   Refereed Serial

I E E E INTERNATIONAL CONFERENCE ON ROBOTICS AND AUTOMATION. PROCEEDINGS. see COMPUTERS — Automation

629.892 US ISSN 1070-9932
TJ210.2 CODEN: IRAMEB
I E E E ROBOTICS AND AUTOMATION MAGAZINE. 1994. q. $95 to non-members (effective 1998). Institute of Electrical and Electronics Engineers, Inc., 345 E. 47th St., New York, NY 10017-2394. TEL 732-981-0060; 800-678-4333. FAX 732-981-9667. E-mail: customer.service@ieee.org; URL: http://www.ieee.org. (Subscr. to: Box 1331, 445 Hoes Ln., Piscataway, NJ 08855-1331) Ed. Kimon P. Valavanis. adv. (microform) **Indexed:** ASCA, Curr.Cont.
—BLDSC (4363.062300); AskIEEE; CISTI; Ei; Genuine Article; KR SourceOne; SWETS; UMI; UnCover.
   Description: Prototyping, demonstration and evaluation, and commercialization of robotic and automation technology and systems, application of theory to real-world systems, with emphasis on implementation.

629.8 US ISSN 1042-296X
TJ210.2 CODEN: IRAUEZ
I E E E TRANSACTIONS ON ROBOTICS AND AUTOMATION. 1985. bi-m. $275 to non-members (effective 1998). (I E E E, Robotics and Automation Council) Institute of Electrical and Electronics Engineers, Inc., 345 E. 47th St., New York, NY 10017-2394. TEL 732-981-0060; 800-678-4333. FAX 732-981-9667. E-mail: customer.service@ieee.org; URL: http://www.ieee.org. (Subscr. to: Box 1331, 445 Hoes Lane, Piscataway, NJ 08855-1331) Ed. Richard A. Volz. bk.rev. (also avail. in microform) **Indexed:** A.I.Abstr., A.S.& T.Ind., ASCA, CAD CAM Abstr., Compumath, Comput.Dtbs., Curr.Cont., Cyb.Abstr., INSPEC (1989-), Robomat., SSCI.
—BLDSC (4363.219600); AskIEEE; CISTI; Ei; Genuine Article; KR SourceOne; Linda Hall; SWETS; UMI; UnCover. **CCC.**
   Formerly (until 1988): I E E E Journal of Robotics and Automation (ISSN 0882-4967)
   Description: Features theory and applications in robotic dynamics and control.

629.892 SW
HD9696.R62
I F R ROBOTICS NEWSLETTER. (Text in English) 1989. 4/yr. $60. International Federation of Robotics, Secretariat, c/o Sveriges Verkstadsindustrier, P.O. Box 5510, S-114 85 Stockholm, Sweden. TEL 46-8-782-08-00. FAX 46-8-660-33-78. adv.: B&W page $1000. circ. 2,000. **Indexed:** Robomat. (until 1992). **Document type:** newsletter.
   Formerly (until 1991): Yearbook on Industrial Robot Statistics.

629.8 003 UK ISSN 0143-991X
CODEN: IDRBAT
INDUSTRIAL ROBOT; an international journal on industrial robot technology. 1973. bi-m. £1099($1699) (foreign Aus.$2149) (effective 1998). M C B University Press Ltd., 60-62 Toller Ln., Bradford, W. Yorks BD8 9BY, England. TEL 44-1274-777700. FAX 44-1274-785200. TELEX 51317-MCBUNI-G. URL: http://www.mcb.co.uk. Ed. Clive Loughlin. adv.; bk.rev.; abstr.; bibl.; charts; illus.; pat.; index. circ. 1,000. **Indexed:** A.I.Abstr., A.S.& T.Ind., Appl.Mech.Rev., ASCA, Br.Tech.Ind., CAD CAM Abstr., Comput.Cont., Curr.Cont., Eng.Ind., Fluidex, Ind.Sci.Rev., INSPEC, Int.Packag.Abstr., Paper & Bd.Abstr., Print.Abstr., Sci.Cit.Ind. **Document type:** trade publication.
—BLDSC (4462.200000); AskIEEE; CISTI; Ei; Genuine Article; KR SourceOne; Linda Hall; SWETS; UMI; UnCover. **CCC.**
   Description: Offers comprehensive international coverage of the robot industry. Regularly contains industry news, a spotlight article on a specific company, international updates, technological developments.

INTEGRATED MANUFACTURING SYSTEMS. see MACHINERY — Computer Applications

629.8 JA
INTERNATIONAL CONFERENCE ON ADVANCED ROBOTICS. PROCEEDINGS. irreg. 10500 Yen. Japan Robot Association - Nihon Robotto Kogyokai, Kikaishinko Bldg., 3-5-8 Shibakoen, Minato-ku, Tokyo 105, Japan. TEL 81-3-3434-2919. FAX 81-3-3578-1404. **Document type:** proceedings.

INTERNATIONAL JOURNAL OF ROBOTICS AND AUTOMATION. see COMPUTERS — Automation

COMPUTERS — ROBOTICS

629.892 003   US   ISSN 0278-3649
TJ211
INTERNATIONAL JOURNAL OF ROBOTICS RESEARCH. 1982. bi-m. $82 to individuals (foreign $104); institutions $230 (foreign $252); students and retired $50 (foreign $72) (effective 1997). M I T Press, 5 Cambridge Center, Cambridge, MA 02142. TEL 617-253-2889. FAX 617-577-1545. E-mail: journals-orders@mit.edu; URL: http://www-mitpress.mit.edu/. (Editorial addr.: Robotics Research, Department of Engineering Science, Oxford University, 19 Parks Rd., Oxford, OX1 3PJ, England) Ed. J. Michael Brady. circ. 1,340. (also avail. in microform from UMI; back issues avail.; reprint service avail. from UMI) **Indexed:** A.I.Abstr. (until 1992), A.S.& T.Ind., Appl.Mech.Rev., ASCA, CAD CAM Abstr. (until 1992), Compumath, Comput.Rev., Curr.Cont., Eng.Ind., Ind.Sci.Rev., INSPEC, Int.Aerosp.Abstr., Robomat. (until 1992), Sci.Cit.Ind. **Document type:** academic/scholarly publication. —BLDSC (4542.538500); AskIEEE; CISTI; Ei; Genuine Article; KR SourceOne; Linda Hall; SWETS; UMI; UnCover. **CCC.**
    Description: Interdisciplinary approach to the study of robotics for researchers, scientists and students.
Refereed Serial

001.535 629.8   JA
INTERNATIONAL SYMPOSIUM ON AUTOMATION AND ROBOTICS IN CONSTRUCTION. PROCEEDINGS. irreg. 20600 Yen. Japan Robot Association - Nihon Robotto Kogyokai, Kikaishinko Bldg., 3-5-8 Shibakoen, Minato-ku, Tokyo 105, Japan. TEL 81-3-3434-2919. FAX 81-3-3578-1404. **Document type:** proceedings.

629.8   JA
INTERNATIONAL SYMPOSIUM ON INDUSTRIAL ROBOTS. PROCEEDINGS. irreg. price varies. Japan Robot Association - Nihon Robotto Kogyokai, Kikaishinko Bldg., 3-5-8 Shibakoen, Minato-ku, Tokyo 105, Japan. TEL 81-3-3434-2919. FAX 81-3-3578-1404. **Document type:** proceedings.

629.8   JA
J A R A ROBOT NEWS; robots and application systems. (Text in English) 1984. bi-m. 2100 Yen. Japan Robot Association - Nihon Robotto Kogyokai, Kikaishinko Bldg., 3-5-8, Shibakoen, Minato-ku, Tokyo 105, Japan. TEL 81-3-3434-2919. FAX 81-3-3578-1404. **Indexed:** Robomat. (until 1992). **Document type:** newsletter.
    Formerly: J I R A Robot News.

629.892   CC   ISSN 1002-0446
JIQIREN/ROBOT. (Text in Chinese) bi-m. Zhongguo Kexueyuan, Shenyang Zidonghua Yanjiusuo - Chinese Academy of Sciences, Shenyang Institute of Automation, 90, Sanhao Jie, Shenyang, Liaoning 110003, People's Republic of China. TEL 393591. Ed. Jiang Xinsong.

629.8 004   FR
JOURNAL DE LA ROBOTIQUE ET INFORMATIQUE. 11/yr. Saincy Communication, 15 rue d'Hauteville, 75010 Paris, France. TEL 48-24-02-40. FAX 45-23-57-42. Ed. Maurice Duron. circ. 10,000.
    Description: Provides news and applications of the robotics and computer industries.

JOURNAL OF INTELLIGENT AND ROBOTIC SYSTEMS; theory and applications. see COMPUTERS — Artificial Intelligence

003 629.8   US   ISSN 0741-2223
TJ210.3
JOURNAL OF ROBOTIC SYSTEMS. (Text in English and Japanese; summaries in English and Japanese) 1984. m. $1200 (foreign $1410) (effective 1998). John Wiley & Sons, Inc., Journals, 605 Third Ave., New York, NY 10158. TEL 212-692-6645. FAX 212-850-6021. TELEX 12-7063. E-mail: SUBINFO@JWILEY.COM; URL: http://www.wiley.co.uk. (Subscr. outside the Americas to: John Wiley & Sons Ltd., Baffins Ln. Chichester, W. Sussex PO19 1UD, England. TEL 44-1243-779777. FAX 44-1243-776128) Eds. Gerardo Beni, Susan Hackwood. adv.: B&W page £640, color page £1515; trim 254 x 165. bk.rev. circ. 750. (also avail. in microform from UMI; back issues avail.) **Indexed:** A.I.Abstr. (until 1992), A.S.& T.Ind., ASCA, CAD CAM Abstr. (until 1992), Compumath, Curr.Cont., Ind.Sci.Rev., INSPEC, Int.Aerosp.Abstr., Robomat. (until 1992), Sci.Cit.Ind., Zent.Math. **Document type:** academic/scholarly publication. —BLDSC (5052.110000); AskIEEE; CISTI; Ei; Genuine Article; KR SourceOne; SWETS; UMI; UnCover. **CCC.**
    Description: For computer scientists, electrical, mechanical, manufacturing and industrial engineers. Presents research results on all aspects of design, realization and use of robots, robot components and systems.
Refereed Serial

629.892   JA   ISSN 0915-3942
JOURNAL OF ROBOTICS AND MECHATRONICS. (Text in English) 1989. bi-m. 72000 Yen. Fuji Technology Press Ltd., 11-7, Toranomon 1-chome, Minato-ku, Tokyo 105, Japan. TEL 81-3-3508-0051. FAX 81-3-3592-0648.
—BLDSC (5052.112000); CISTI.

629.8 690   JA
KENSETSU ROBOTTO SHINPOJUMU RONBUNSHU/SYMPOSIUM ON CONSTRUCTION ROBOTICS IN JAPAN. PROCEEDINGS. (Text in Japanese; summaries in English) 1990. a. 10300 Yen. Japan Robot Association - Nihon Robotto Kogyokai, Kikaishinko Bldg., 3-5-8 Shibakoen, Minato-ku, Tokyo 105, Japan. TEL 81-3-3434-2919. FAX 81-3-3578-1404. **Document type:** proceedings.

KOMPASS PROFESSIONNEL. MACHINES - OUTILS, ROBOTIQUE, MECANIQUE GENERALE. see BUSINESS AND ECONOMICS — Trade And Industrial Directories

LABORATORY ROBOTICS AND AUTOMATION. see COMPUTERS — Automation

629.8 355   US   ISSN 0896-0348
MILITARY ROBOTICS NEWSLETTER; covering government and defense applications of robotics. 1987. s-m. $350 in U.S. and Canada; elsewhere $375. L & B Limited, 19 Rock Creek Church Rd., N.W., Washington, DC 20011-6005. TEL 202-723-1600. FAX 202-726-2979. Ed. Joseph A. Lovece. circ. 250. (reprint service avail.) **Document type:** newsletter.
    ●Also available online. Vendor(s): Information Access Co., Knight-Ridder Information, Inc. (NL0650); NewsNet (DE14).
    Description: Covers military and government use of robotics.

MOBILE ROBOTS. see PHYSICS — Optics

P A S C A L. E 34. ROBOTIQUE, AUTOMATIQUE ET AUTOMATISATION DES PROCESSUS INDUSTRIELS. see COMPUTERS — Abstracting, Bibliographies, Statistics

PROBLEMI NA TEKHNICHESKATA KIBERNETIKA I ROBOTIKA/PROBLEMS OF ENGINEERING CYBERNETICS AND ROBOTICS. see COMPUTERS — Cybernetics

PROGRESS IN ROBOTICS AND INTELLIGENT SYSTEMS. see COMPUTERS — Artificial Intelligence

629.892   US
R I A QUARTERLY STATISTICS REPORT - ROBOTICS. q. $50. Robotic Industries Association, 900 Victors Way, Box 3724, Ann Arbor, MI 48106. TEL 313-994-6088. FAX 313-994-3338. E-mail: ria@robotics.org; URL: http://www.robotics.org.

003 006.3   US   ISSN 1060-4375
ROBOT EXPLORER. 1992. 8/yr. $14.95 in US, Canada, Mexico; elsewhere $29.95. Appropriate Solutions, Inc., 145 Grove St., Box 458, Peterborough, NH 03458. TEL 603-924-6079. FAX 603-525-4923. E-mail: apsol@apsol.com. Ed. Ray Cote; Pub. Andrew Taylor. R&P contact: Raymond Cote. adv. contact: Elizabeth S. Alpaugh-Cote. bk.rev.; circ. 500 (paid). **Document type:** newsletter.
    Description: Targets the non-industrial usages of robotics. Topics include commercial, research, and educational projects.

629.892   US
ROBOT TIMES. q. membership. Robotic Industries Association, 900 Victors Way, Box 3724, Ann Arbor, MI 48106. TEL 313-994-6088. FAX 313-994-3338. E-mail: ria@robotics.org; URL: http://www.robotics.org. **Indexed:** CAD CAM Abstr.
    Description: Contains information for members about workshops, conferences, symposia, industry standards, publications and trade shows.

629.892   AT
ROBOTIC AGE. 1983. q. P.O. Box 1024, Richmond North, Vic. 3121, Australia. TEL 03-429-5599. FAX 03-427-0332. Ed. Geoffrey M. Gold. circ. 8,000.

629.8   UK   ISSN 0263-5747
TJ210.2
ROBOTICA. 1983. bi-m. £204($350) (effective 1998). Cambridge University Press, Edinburgh Bldg., Shaftesbury Rd., Cambridge CB2 2RU, England. TEL 44-1223-312393. FAX 44-1223-315052. TELEX 851817256. E-mail: information@cup.cam.ac.uk; URL: http://www.cup.cam.ac.uk. (N. American addr.: Cambridge University Press, Journals Dept., 40 W. 20th St., New York, NY 10011. TEL 212-924-3900. FAX 212-691-3239) Ed. J. Rose. R&P contact: Linda Nicol. adv. contact: Rebecca Symons. bk.rev. (back issues avail.; reprint service avail. from SWZ) **Indexed:** A.I.Abstr., Abstr.Hum.Comp.Inter., ASCA, Br.Tech.Ind., CAD CAM Abstr., Comput.Cont., Curr.Cont., Int.Aerosp.Abstr., Robomat. **Document type:** academic/scholarly publication. —BLDSC (8000.452300); AskIEEE; CISTI; Ei; Genuine Article; KR SourceOne; Linda Hall; SWETS; UMI; UnCover. **CCC.**
    Description: Contains robotics, automation industrial research and educational programs results for students and professionals.

629.8   NE   ISSN 0921-8890
TJ210.2   CODEN: RASOEJ
ROBOTICS AND AUTONOMOUS SYSTEMS. (Text in English) 1985. 16/yr. fl.1984($1140) (effective 1998). North-Holland (Subsidiary of: Elsevier Science B.V.), P.O. Box 211, 1000 AE Amsterdam, Netherlands. TEL 31-20-4853911. FAX 31-20-4853598. TELEX 18582 ESPA NL. URL: http://www.elsevier.nl:80/inca/publications/store/5/0/5/6/2/2/505622.pub.shtml. (Subscr. in the Americas to: Elsevier Science, Regional Sales Office, Box 945, New York, NY 10159-0945. TEL 212-633-3730. FAX 212-633-3680; Subscr. in Australasia and the Far East to: Elsevier Science (Singapore) Pte Ltd, No.1 Temasek Ave., No.17-01 Millenia Tower, Singapore 039192, Singapore. TEL 65-434-3727. FAX 65-337-2230; Subscr. in Japan to: Elsevier Science Japan, 9-15 Higashi-Azabu 1-chome, Minato-ku Tokyo 106, Japan. TEL 81-3-5561-5033. FAX 81-3-5561-5047) Ed. T.M. Knasel. adv.; bk.rev. circ. 1,200. (back issues avail.; reprint service avail. from SWZ) **Indexed:** A.I.Abstr. (until 1992), Abstr.Hum.Comp.Inter., ASCA, CAD CAM Abstr. (until 1992), Compumath, INSPEC (1985-), Int.Packag.Abstr., Robomat. (until 1992). **Document type:** academic/scholarly publication. —BLDSC (8000.453180); AskIEEE; CISTI; Ei; Genuine Article; KR SourceOne; Linda Hall; SWETS; UnCover. **CCC.**
    Formerly (until 1988): Robotics (ISSN 0167-8493)
    Description: Provides information on the international robotics industry. Focuses on applications in business and technology.
Refereed Serial

COMPUTERS — SOFTWARE

629.8   UK   ISSN 0736-5845
TS191.8
ROBOTICS AND COMPUTER-INTEGRATED MANUFACTURING; an international journal. 1984. 6/yr. fl.1272($731) (effective 1998). Elsevier Science Ltd., Pergamon, P.O. Box 800, Kidlington, Oxford OX5 1DX, England. TEL 44-1865-843000. FAX 44-1865-843010. E-mail: nlinfo-f@elsevier.nl; usinfo-f@elsevier.com; forinfo-kyf04035@niftyserve.or.jp; URL: http://www.elsevier.nl/. (Subscr. to: Elsevier Science, Regional Sales Office, P.O. Box 211, 1000 AE Amsterdam, Netherlands. TEL 31-20-4853757. FAX 31-20-4853432; Subscr. in the Americas to: Elsevier Science, Regional Sales Office, Box 945, New York, NY 10159-0945. TEL 212-633-3730. FAX 212-633-3680; Subscr. in Australasia and the Far East to: Elsevier Science (Singapore) Pte Ltd, No.1 Temasek Ave., No.17-01 Millenia Tower, Singapore 039192, Singapore. TEL 65-434-3727. FAX 65-337-2230) Ed.Bd. adv.; bk.rev.; bibl.; pat. circ. 2,500. (also avail. in microfilm from UMI) **Indexed**: A.I.Abstr. (until 1992), A.S.& T.Ind., ASCA, CAD CAM Abstr. (until 1992), Comput.Cont., Curr.Cont., INSPEC (1985-), Manage.Cont., Robomat. (until 1992). **Document type**: academic/scholarly publication.
—BLDSC (8000.453200); AskIEEE; CISTI; Ei; Genuine Article; KR SourceOne; Linda Hall; SWETS; UMI; UnCover. **CCC**.
   Description: Features original international papers on theoretical, experimental and applied robotics and on computer-integrated manufacturing, with an emphasis on flexible manufacturing systems.
Refereed Serial

629.8   US   ISSN 1052-4150
TJ210.3
ROBOTICS AND MANUFACTURING. 1988. biennial. A S M E Press, 22 Law Dr., Box 2300, Fairfield, NJ 07007-2300. **Document type**: catalog.

629.892   UK
ROBOTICS AND MECHATRONICS SERIES. 1993. irreg. £50. Research Studies Press Ltd., 24 Belvedere Rd., Taunton, Somerset TA1 1HD, England. TEL 44-1823-336197. FAX 44-1823-253252. E-mail: vaw@rspltd.demon.co.uk. (Dist. by: John Wiley & Sons Ltd., Baffins Ln., Chichester, W. Sussex PO19 19 1UD, England. TEL 44-1243-779777. FAX 44-1243-775878) Ed. J. Billingsley. **Document type**: monographic series.

629.892   US   ISSN 0193-6913
TS191   CODEN: ROTODJ
ROBOTICS TODAY. 1979. q. $60 to non-members. Society of Manufacturing Engineers, One SME Dr., Box 930, Dearborn, MI 48121-0930. TEL 313-271-1500. FAX 313-271-2861. TELEX 297742 SME UR (VIA RCA). Ed. Robert N. Stauffer. adv.; bk.rev.; charts; illus.; stat.; tr.lit. circ. 15,000. (also avail. in microfiche; microform from UMI) **Indexed**: A.I.Abstr., ABI Inform., Appl.Mech.Rev., CAD CAM Abstr., Comput.Cont., Comput.Dtbs., Cyb.Abstr., Eng.Ind., INSPEC (1982-), Met.Abstr., PROMT, Robomat., World Alum.Abstr. **Document type**: trade publication.
—AskIEEE; KR SourceOne; UMI. **CCC**.
   Description: Offers comprehensive information on the application of robotics in automated manufacturing.

629.892 621   JA
ROBOTIKUSU MEKATORONIKUSU KOENKAI KOEN RONBUNSHU/ANNUAL CONFERENCE ON ROBOTICS AND MECHATRONICS. PROCEEDINGS. (Text in English) 1989. a. 14000 Yen. Nihon Kikai Gakkai - Japan Society of Mechanical Engineers, 4-9, Yoyogi 2-chome, Shibuya-ku, Tokyo 151, Japan.

629.892   JA   ISSN 0387-1940
                                CODEN: ROBBDQ
ROBOTTO/ROBOT. (Text in Japanese; summaries in English, Japanese) 1971. bi-m. 1200 Yen per no. Japan Robot Association - Nihon Robotto Kogyokai, Kikaishinko Bldg., 5-8, Shiba Koen 3-chome, Minato-ku, Tokyo 105, Japan. TEL 81-3-3434-2919. FAX 81-3-3578-1404. **Indexed**: INSPEC (1984-).
—BLDSC (8000.450000); AskIEEE; Ei; KR SourceOne; Linda Hall.

629.892   JA
ROBOTTO SENSA SHINPOJUMU YOKOSHU/ROBOT SENSOR SYMPOSIUM. PREPRINTS. (Text in Japanese; summaries in English) 1988. biennial. Keisoku Jido Seigyo Gakkai - Society of Instrument and Control Engineers, 35-28-303, Hongo 1-chome, Bunkyo-ku, Tokyo 113, Japan.

629.892   JA
SANGYOYO ROBOTTO RIYO GIJUTSU KOSHUKAI TEKISUTO/TEXT OF LECTURES ON UTILIZATION TECHNIQUES OF INDUSTRIAL ROBOTS. (Text in Japanese) 3/yr. 2100 Yen. Nihon Sangyoyo Robotto Kogyokai - Japan Industrial Robot Association, Kikaishinko Bldg., 5-8, Shiba Koen 3-chome, Minato-ku, Tokyo 105, Japan. TEL 81-3-3434-2919. FAX 81-3-3578-1404.

SERIES IN ROBOTICS AND AUTOMATED SYSTEMS. see *COMPUTERS — Automation*

629.8   JA
SPECIFICATIONS & APPLICATIONS OF INDUSTRIAL ROBOTS IN JAPAN: MANUFACTURING FIELDS (YEAR). (Text in English) 1973. biennial. 20,600 Yen. Japan Robot Association - Nihon Robotto Kogyokai, Kikaishinko Bldg., 3-5-8, Shibakoen, Minato-ku, Tokyo 105, Japan. TEL 81-3-3434-2919. FAX 81-3-3578-1404.
   Supersedes in part: Specifications and Applications of Industrial Robots in Japan.
   Description: Contains 501 specs and 229 applications of industrial robots manufactured by members of the association. Provides current information concerning industrial robots in Japan.

629.8   JA
SPECIFICATIONS & APPLICATIONS OF INDUSTRIAL ROBOTS IN JAPAN: NON-MANUFACTURING FIELDS (YEAR). (Text in English) 1973. biennial. 10300 Yen. Japan Robot Association - Nihon Robotto Kogyokai, Kikaishinko Bldg., 3-5-8, Shibakoen, Minato-ku, Tokyo 105, Japan. TEL 81-3-3434-2919. FAX 81-3-3578-1404.
   Supersedes in part: Specifications and Applications of Industrial Robots in Japan.
   Description: Contains 185 specs and 183 applications of industrial robots in the fields of mining, construction, electricity, gas services and more.

TECH WORLD. see *COMPUTERS — Automation*

629.892   SZ
WORLD INDUSTRIAL ROBOTS. (Text in English) 1989. a. $120. International Federation of Robotics, c/o United Nations Economic Commission for Europe, Palais des Nations, CH-1211 Geneva 10, Switzerland. TEL 41-22-917-3285. FAX 41-22-917-0040. E-mail: publications@un.org. Ed. Jan Karlsson. R&P contact: Anne Cunningham. TEL 212-963-0869. **Document type**: bulletin.
   Former titles: World Robot Statistics; I F R World Industrial Robot Statistics (ISSN 1020-1076)
   Description: Contains a collection of data from more than 20 national robotics associations. Provides statistics from 1984 to 1995 and forecast to 1999.

COMPUTERS — Software

see also Computers–Computer Programming

A B A - UNIX - GROUP NEWSLETTER. see *LAW — Computer Applications*

005.3 510   US   ISSN 0098-3500
QA76.6   CODEN: ACMSCU
A C M TRANSACTIONS ON MATHEMATICAL SOFTWARE. 1975. q. $109 to non-members. Association for Computing Machinery, 1515 Broadway, 17th Fl., New York, NY 10036-5701. TEL 212-869-7440. FAX 212-944-1318. TELEX 421686. E-mail: boisvert@nist.gov; URL: http://gams.nist.gov/toms/Overview.html. Ed. John Rice. charts; illus. circ. 5,500. (also avail. in microfiche from KTO; microfilm from WWS) **Indexed**: A.S.& T.Ind., ASCA, Compumath, Comput.Abstr., Comput.Cont., Comput Dtbs., Comput.Rev., Curr.Cont., Cyb.Abstr., Ind.Sci.Rev., INSPEC (1975-), Int.Abstr.Oper.Res., Int.Aerosp.Abstr., Math.R., Sci.Cit.Ind., Zent.Math. **Document type**: academic/scholarly publication.
●Also available online.
—BLDSC (0578.670000); AskIEEE; CISTI; Ei; Genuine Article; KR SourceOne; Linda Hall; SWETS; UMI; UnCover. **CCC**.
   Description: Disseminates the original work of computer scientists that forms the theoretical foundations of subsequent applications.

005.3   US   ISSN 1049-331X
QA76.758   CODEN: ATSMER
A C M TRANSACTIONS ON SOFTWARE ENGINEERING AND METHODOLOGY. 1992. q. $90 to non-members. Association for Computing Machinery, 1515 Broadway, 17th Fl., New York, NY 10036-5701. TEL 212-869-7440. FAX 212-944-1318. TELEX 421686. **Indexed**: INSPEC (1992-).
—BLDSC (0578.675100); AskIEEE; CISTI; Ei; KR SourceOne; SWETS; UnCover. **CCC**.
   Description: Publishes research on the mechanisms, tools and processes involved in supporting complex systems of scale and longevity that require substantial investments in definition, design, development, maintenance, and related support activities.

005.302   GW   ISSN 0933-1867
A S M. (Aktueller Software Markt) m. DM.79.20 (foreign DM.95.50). Tronic Verlagsgesellschaft mbH, Hessenring 32, 37269 Eschwege, Germany. TEL 05651-929-0. FAX 05651-929140. Ed. Peter Schmitz; Pub. Christian Widuch. adv. contact: Gerlinde Rachow. circ. 97,819. **Document type**: consumer publication.

A S - 400 HOT SHEET. see *COMPUTERS — Hardware*

ABSOLUTE REFERENCE; the journal for 1-2-3 and Symphony users. see *COMPUTERS — Microcomputers*

005.3   US
QA76.9.D3
ACCESS - OFFICE - V B ADVISOR. (Visual Basic) 1994. m. $39 (Canada $59; elsewhere $79). Advisor Publications Inc., 5675 Ruffin Rd., Ste.200, San Diego, CA 92123. TEL 619-278-5600. FAX 619-278-0300. E-mail: subscribe@advisor.com; URL: http://www.advisor.com. (Dist. by: International Periodical Distributors, 674 Via de la Valle, Ste. 204, Solana Beach, CA 92075) Ed. John L. Hawkins; Pub. William Ota. adv. contact: B.J. Ghiglione. **Document type**: trade publication.
—KR SourceOne; SWETS.
   Former titles: Access - Visual Basic Advisor (ISSN 1078-2990); (until 1995): Access Advisor (ISSN 1066-7253)
   Description: Explains how to build business solutions with Microsoft application development tools. For users of Microsoft Access, Visual Basic, Office, Internet, Windows 95 - NT and SQL Server.

ACKNOWLEDGE THE WINDOW LETTER. see *COMPUTERS — Microcomputers*

005.3   US   ISSN 1081-4477
Z286.D47
ADOBE MAGAZINE. 1989. bi-m. $35. Adobe Systems, 411 First Ave., S., Seattle, WA 98104. TEL 206-622-5500. FAX 206-343-3273. Ed. Nicholas Allism; Pub. Carla Noble. R&P contact: Retsu Takahashi. adv.: B&W page $12695, color page $15200; adv. contact: Allan Routh. bk.rev.; circ. 23,361 (controlled). **Indexed**: WPM. **Document type**: trade publication.
—KR SourceOne.
   Formerly: Aldus Magazine (ISSN 1046-0616)
   Description: Covers desktop design techniques, product specific question and answer, customer profile, and new product information.
Refereed Serial

COMPUTERS — SOFTWARE

005.3   UK
ADVANCED SOFTWARE DEVELOPMENT SERIES. 1989. irreg., vol.5, 1996. price varies. Research Studies Press Ltd., 24 Belvedere Rd., Taunton, Somerset TA1 1HD, England. TEL 44-1823-336197. FAX 44-1823-253252. E-mail: vaw@rspltd.demon.co.uk. (Dist. by: John Wiley & Sons Ltd., Baffins Ln., Chichester, W. Sussex PO19 1UD, England. TEL 44-1243-779777. FAX 44-1243-775878) Ed. J. Kramer. **Document type:** monographic series.

ADVANCED TECHNOLOGY IN WASHINGTON STATE. see BUSINESS AND ECONOMICS — Trade And Industrial Directories

ADVANCES IN ARTIFICIAL INTELLIGENCE IN SOFTWARE ENGINEERING. see COMPUTERS — Artificial Intelligence

ADVANCES IN ENGINEERING SOFTWARE. see ENGINEERING — Computer Applications

005.3   US
ADVANCES IN SOFTWARE ENGINEERING. 1985. a. $90.25 to institutions. J A I Press Inc., 55 Old Post Rd., No. 2, Box 1678, Greenwich, CT 06836-1678. TEL 203-661-7602. Ed. Stephen S. Yau. **Document type:** academic/scholarly publication.
    Refereed Serial

005.3   US   ISSN 1044-7997
QA76.75
ADVANCES IN SOFTWARE SCIENCE AND TECHNOLOGY. 1989. irreg., vol.5, 1994. (Japanese Society for Software Science and Technology, JA) Academic Press, Inc., 525 B St., Ste. 1900, San Diego, CA 92101-4495. TEL 619-231-6616. FAX 619-699-6715. (Subscr. to: Order Dept., 6277 Sea Harbor Dr., 4th Fl., Orlando, FL 32887. TEL 800-321-5068) (back issues avail.) **Document type:** monographic series.
    —BLDSC (0711.407000); CISTI.
    Refereed Serial

AIR QUALITY DATA MANAGEMENT SOFTWARE REPORT. see ENVIRONMENTAL STUDIES — Pollution

005.3 004   US   ISSN 1081-6283
AIXPERT; IBM's technical magazine for AIX application developers. (Not avail. in print format) 1991. q. $29.95 (foreign $34.95). I B M Corporation (Austin), Izip 1034, 11400 Burnet Rd., Austin, TX 78758. TEL 512-823-6840. FAX 512-823-6520. E-mail: geo@austin.ibm.com; URL: http://www.developer.ibm.com/library/aixpert/. Ed. George Noren. R&P contact: George Noren. adv.: B&W & color, B&W page $2795; trim 8 1/2 x 11. circ. 10,000. **Document type:** trade publication.
    ●Also available online.
    Also available on CD-ROM.

ANDREW SEYBOLD'S OUTLOOK. see COMPUTERS — Computer Industry

005.3   NE   ISSN 1022-7091
▼**ANNALS OF SOFTWARE ENGINEERING.** (Text in English) 1995. 2/yr. 592 (effective 1998). Baltzer Science Publishers B.V., P.O. Box 221, 1400 AE Bussum, Netherlands. TEL 31-20-6370061. FAX 31-20-6323651. E-mail: subscribe@baltzer.nl; URL: http://www.baltzer.nl. (Subscr. in N. America to: Baltzer Science Publishers, Box 8577, Red Bank, NJ 07701-8577) Ed. Osman Balci. (back issues avail.) **Indexed:** INSPEC (1995-). **Document type:** academic/scholarly publication.
    —BLDSC (1044.240000); AskIEEE; CISTI; KR SourceOne; SWETS. **CCC.**
    Description: Publishes state-of-the-art survey and tutorial papers, industrial and academic research and application papers, covering all aspects of software engineering.
    Refereed Serial

005.3 004.16   US
APPLE IIGS. q. $39.95. Softdisk, Inc., Box 30008, Shreveport, LA 71130-0008. TEL 318-221-8718. (diskette format)
    Description: Programs and software for owners of Apple IIgs computers.

005.1   US
APPLICATIONS SOFTWARE REPORTS. 1971. base vol. (plus m. updates). $670. Faulkner Information Services, Inc., 114 Cooper Center, 7905 Browning Rd., Pennsauken, NJ 08109-4319. TEL 609-662-2070. FAX 609-662-3380. Ed. Betsy Yokum. (looseleaf format)
    Formerly: Auerbach Applications Software Reports; Supersedes in part: Auerbach Software Reports (ISSN 0004-7775)
    Description: Accounting, human resource management, project management, word processing, decision support - EIS, and manufacturing software for mainframe, mini, and micro computers.

005.3   IT
▼**APPLIWARE.** 1996. m. (6/yr.) L.89000 (effective 1997). Gruppo Editoriale J C E, Via Ferri 6, 20092 Cinisello Balsamo (MI), Italy. TEL 39-2-660251. FAX 39-2-6127620. E-mail: appliware@jce.it; URL: http://www.jce.it. Ed. Fausto Gimondi. adv.: color page L.6100000; trim 210 X 276. circ. 20,000. **Document type:** trade publication.
    ●Also available on CD-ROM.
    Description: Provides complement software with practical examples and shareware programs.

ARTIFICIAL INTELLIGENCE IN ENGINEERING. see COMPUTERS — Artificial Intelligence

ASIAN CLASSICS INPUT PROGRAM. see RELIGIONS AND THEOLOGY — Buddhist

ASTROTALK BULLETIN. see ASTROLOGY

001.642   US
AUTHORWARE.* 1988. q. $20 (foreign $30). Authorware, Inc., 600 Townsend St., San Francisco, CA 94103-4945. TEL 415-595-3101. FAX 415-595-3077. Ed. Kathy Nordgaard. adv.: bk.rev. circ. 5,000.
    Formerly: Co Action Magazine.
    Description: Focuses on interactive multi-media authoring software, computer-aided instruction (CAI), and computer-based training (CBT).

001.642   GW   ISSN 0934-1749
AUTOCAD MAGAZIN; das unabhaengige Magazin der C A - Techniken. 1988. bi-m. DM.78 (effective 1996). I W T Magazin Verlags GmbH, Bahnhofstr. 36, 85591 Vaterstetten, Germany. TEL 49-8106-350-0. FAX 49-8106-350126. URL: http://www.iwtnet.de. Ed. Alexander Psdera. circ. 22,000. (back issues avail.) **Document type:** trade publication.
    —SWETS.
    Description: For those interested in CAD systems.

005.3   CN   ISSN 1198-0869
AUTOCAD USER. 1993. 4/yr. Can.$18($20) (US $20, elsewhere $25) (effective 1997). Swan Erickson Publishing Inc., 1011 Upper Middle Rd. E., Ste. 1235, Oakville, ON L6H 5Z9, Canada. TEL 905-475-4231. FAX 905-475-3512. Ed. Robert Erickson; Pub. Robert Erickson. adv.: B&W page Can.$2600, color page Can.$3400; trim 8 1/8 x 10 7/8; adv. contact: Mike Swan. **Document type:** trade publication.

005.3   SP
AUTODESK NOTICIAS. (Supplement avail.: Guia de Soluciones) q. Edimicros, S.L., C. Galileo, 281, Entlo. 2a, 08028 Barcelona, Spain. TEL 34-3-4908889. FAX 34-3-4901985. adv.: page 450000 ptas.; 271 x 394. circ. 12,000 (paid).

B I T. (Boletin Informativo de Telecomunicacion) see COMPUTERS — Microcomputers

005.3   BE
BELGOSOFT. (Editions in Dutch, French) a. 950 BEF (diskette 2000 BEF) (effective 1995). Business & Management Editions Brussels s.p.r.l., Rue Stephanie, 17, 1020 Brussels, Belgium. TEL 32-2-4266115. FAX 32-2-4258226. adv. circ. 25,000. (also avail. in diskette format) **Document type:** directory.
    Description: Lists more than 4000 software programs, with complete information on Belgian software distributors.

BINARY: COMPUTING IN MICROBIOLOGY. see BIOLOGY — Microbiology

BIOTECHNOLOGY SOFTWARE & INTERNET JOURNAL; the computer software journal for scientists. see BIOLOGY — Biotechnology

001.642   GW
BITLUPE; Magazine fuer IBM-36 und AS-400 Anwender. 1986. q. free. Gruenblicher Software-Systeme GmbH, Westendstr. 34, 86916 Kaufering, Germany. TEL 08191-66991. FAX 08191-65250. Ed. Josef Gruenblicher. circ. 10,000. (video cassette)
    Formerly: Guenbichler's Bitlupe.

005.3   US   ISSN 1088-5439
QA75.5
BOOT. 1993. m. $29.95. Imagine Publishing, Inc., 150 N. Hill Dr., Brisbane, CA 94005. TEL 415-468-4684. FAX 415-468-4686. E-mail: editor@bootnet.com; URL: http://www.bootnet.com. Ed. David Vincent. adv.: B&W page $7140, color page $8920; trim 8 3/8 x 10 7/8; adv. contact: Patricia Neuray. illus.; circ. 123,000 (paid). **Document type:** consumer publication.
    ●Also available online.
    —KR SourceOne; UnCover.
    Formerly (until 1996): C D - R O M Today (ISSN 1069-4099)
    Description: Features, reviews and news to inform end users of CD-ROM software and hardware.

001.624   UK   ISSN 0264-1283
BRITISH MICRO SOFTWARE NEWS. 1984. fortn. £135($250) (avail. in the U.K. only). Ferndown Publications, 302 Bramhall Ln. S., Bramhall, Stockport SK7 3DL, England. TEL 0161-439-4926. Ed. P. Smith. **Document type:** newsletter.
    Description: Lists new software products for the business microcomputer.

BUS; Computernutzung an Schulen. see COMPUTERS — Personal Computers

005.3 658.8   UK   ISSN 0950-6543
BUSINESS RATIO REPORT: COMPUTER SOFTWARE HOUSES; an industry sector analysis. 1986. a. I C C Business Ratios Ltd., Freepost, Field House, Hampton, Mddx. TW12 1BR, England. TEL 081-783-0977. FAX 081-783-1940. charts; stat. **Document type:** trade publication.

C A D - C A M & INDUSTRIAL SOFTWARE GUIDE. see COMPUTERS — Computer Graphics

005.3   UK
C A D DES. (Computer - Aided Design) 1990. m. £30. Electronic Design Automation Ltd., 31-33 High Holborn, London WC1V 6BD, England. TEL 44-171-404-0564. FAX 44-171-831-2057. Ed. Geoff Walker. (back issues avail.) **Document type:** trade publication.
    Description: Covers Auto CAD for managers and other design professionals.

C A F M SYSTEM & STRATEGIES (YEAR); a manager's guide to facility management automation. see COMPUTERS — Data Base Management

005.3 236   US   ISSN 8755-5727
HD9697.P56   CODEN: CDDRED
C D DATA REPORT;* a monthly newsletter covering the compact disc (CD-ROM) industry and related optical storage technologies. 1984. 12/yr. $395 in N. America; foreign $495. Disc Company, 21 Red Maple Rd., Hilton Head Island, SC 29928. TEL 703-237-0682. FAX 703-532-5447. Ed. Linda W. Helgerson. bk.rev. circ. 1,500. **Document type:** newsletter.
    Description: For the CD-ROM industry. Reports services, products, projects and applications, and provides information on what others are doing in CD-ROM.

005.3 338   GW
C D - R O M FUEHRER. 1993. irreg. DM.78. Rossipaul Medien GmbH, Menzingerstr. 37, 80638 Munich, Germany. TEL 49-89-179106-0. FAX 49-89-17910622. Ed. Hilla Hueber. adv. contact: Ursula Rossipaul. circ. 15,000. **Document type:** directory.

COMPUTERS — SOFTWARE

001.642   UK
C D - R O M NEWSLETTER. 1989. bi-m. £85 (foreign £95). Microinfo Ltd., P.O. Box 3, Omega Park, Alton, Hants GU34 2PG, England. TEL 44-1420-86848. FAX 44-1420-89889. Ed. R.B. Selwyn. (back issues avail.) **Document type:** newsletter.
Description: Reviews worldwide CD-ROM technology and markets covering news of developments and events related to application of CD techniques.

C D - R O M PROFESSIONAL. see *LIBRARY AND INFORMATION SCIENCES — Computer Applications*

C D - R O M WORLD; the magazine and review for CD-ROM users. see *LIBRARY AND INFORMATION SCIENCES*

C E P SOFTWARE DIRECTORY. (American Institute of Chemical Engineers) see *CHEMISTRY — Computer Applications*

001.642   US   ISSN 0730-3157
QA76.6
C O M P S A C/I E E E COMPUTER SOCIETY'S INTERNATIONAL COMPUTER SOFTWARE & APPLICATIONS CONFERENCE. PROCEEDINGS. 1977. a. price varies. (Institute of Electrical and Electronics Engineers, Inc.) I E E E Computer Society Press, 10662 Los Vaqueros Circle, Los Alamitos, CA 90720-1264. TEL 714-821-8380. FAX 714-821-4641. Ed. Cat Harris; Pub. Matt Loeb. adv. contact: Frieda Koester. **Indexed:** Comput.Lit.Ind. **Document type:** proceedings.
—BLDSC (3368.300000); UMI. CCC.
Description: Provides papers primarily dealing with software engineering and developmental themes, along with major applications areas.

001.642   US   ISSN 1050-3048
QA76.73.C153   CODEN: CJOUEH
C PLUS PLUS JOURNAL.* 1990. q. $32 (foreign $52). c/o Image Soft Inc., 6-57 158th St., Flushing, NY 11357-1349. TEL 516-767-7107. FAX 516-944-3050. Ed. Livleen Singh. adv.; bk.rev.
—KR SourceOne; SWETS.

CATALOGUE OF SOFTWARE FOR RADIO SPECTRUM MANAGEMENT. see *COMMUNICATIONS*

005.302 371.3   US   ISSN 1069-9430
QA76.76.C54
CHILDREN'S SOFTWARE REVUE. 1993. 6/yr. $24 (foreign $33). Active Learning Associates, 44 Main St., Flemington, NJ 08822. TEL 908-284-0404. FAX 908-284-0405. URL: http://www.microweb.com/pepsite. Ed. Warren Buckleitner. circ. 4,400 (paid). **Document type:** consumer publication.
Description: Covers software and hardware for parents and teachers of children 3 to 14 years old.

005.3   US   ISSN 1074-7443
QA76.75   CODEN: CJSRES
CHINESE JOURNAL OF ADVANCED SOFTWARE RESEARCH. (Text in English) 1994. q. $310 (effective 1998). (Chinese Computer Society) Allerton Press, Inc., 150 Fifth Ave., New York, NY 10011. TEL 212-924-3950. FAX 212-463-9684. Ed. Xu Kongshi. **Document type:** academic/scholarly publication.
—BLDSC (3180.290300); AskIEEE; CISTI; KR SourceOne. CCC.
Description: Covers both theoretical and applied aspects of computer science and software techniques.

005.3   PL   ISSN 1427-7301
▼**CHIP SPECIAL.** 1995. irreg. Vogel Publishing Sp. z o.o., Plac Czerwony 1-3-5, 53-661 Wroclaw, Poland. TEL 48-71-734475. FAX 48-71-557361. E-mail: special@vogel.pl. Ed. Jaromir Lanski. adv.: color page 3500 Zl.; 210 x 297; adv. contact: Marcin Hutnik. software rev. (back issues avail.)
●Also available on CD-ROM.
Description: Every issue is dedicated to one topic and includes CD-ROM with software concerning the overall subject.

CHURCH BUSINESS. PRODUCTS & TECHNOLOGY. see *RELIGIONS AND THEOLOGY*

005.3   US
COMING TO ORDER. 1989. bi-m. $55. EyeOn Associates, Inc., 660 Fairmont Ave., Westfield, NJ 07090. TEL 908-232-4674. Ed. Lauren Flast. circ. 1,000. (back issues avail.)

COMPUTER & CO. see *COMPUTERS — Computer Networks*

COMPUTER-ASSISTED COMPOSITION JOURNAL. see *COMPUTERS — Computer Assisted Instruction*

COMPUTER PERIPHERIE SOFTWARE; Produktinformation ueber Computer, Peripherie, Software OEM-Produkte und Kommunikations-Technik. see *BUSINESS AND ECONOMICS — Office Equipment And Services*

001.642   JA   ISSN 0289-6540
COMPUTER SOFTWARE. (Text in Japanese) 1984. q. 5500 Yen. (Nihon Sofutowea Kagakukai - Japan Society for Software Science and Technology) Iwanami Shoten Publishers, 2-5-5 Hitotsubashi, Chiyoda-ku, Tokyo 101-02, Japan. FAX 03-3239-9618. (Dist. overseas by: Japan Publications Trading Co., Ltd., Box 5030, Tokyo International, Tokyo 100-31, Japan; Or: 1255 Howard St., San Francisco, CA 94103) adv.; bk.rev.; charts.

COMPUTERS, FOODSERVICE & YOU. see *COMPUTERS — Electronic Data Processing*

004   CN   ISSN 0319-0161
COMPUTING CANADA; software report. 1975. bi-w. Can.$60($90) (foreign Can.$130). Plesman Publications Ltd., 2005 Sheppard Ave. E., 4th Fl., Willowdale, ON M2J 5B1, Canada. TEL 416-497-9562. FAX 416-497-9427. Ed. Charles P. Whaley. adv. contact: Carmen Girard. bk.rev. circ. 33,000. **Indexed:** ABI Inform., Can.B.P.I., Can.Per.Ind., Comput.Cont., PROMT, PSI.
●Also available online. Vendor(s): Information Access Co.
—BLDSC (3395.031000); CISTI; KR SourceOne; UMI.

001.642   US   ISSN 1063-6773
QA76.76.S64
CONFERENCE ON SOFTWARE MAINTENANCE. PROCEEDINGS. 1983. a. price varies. (Institute of Electrical and Electronics Engineers, Inc., Computer Society) I E E E Computer Society Press, 10662 Los Vaqueros Circle, Los Alamitos, CA 90720-1264. TEL 714-821-8380. FAX 714-821-4641. Ed. Cat Harris; Pub. Matt Loeb. adv. contact: Frieda Koester. **Document type:** proceedings.
—CCC.
Formerly (until 1983): Software Maintenance Workshop. Record.
Description: Presents current experiences, and highlights promising approaches in software maintenance.

CONTROL ENGINEERING SOFTWARE GUIDE. see *COMPUTERS — Automation*

005.3   UK   ISSN 1367-0263
COREL USER. 1992. m. (10/yr.). £58.75 to individuals (rest of Europe £60; elsewhere £70); institutions £235 (effective 1997). (Corel Ventura Users (C V U)) V P U Ltd., 49 Olney Rd., Emberton, Olney, Bucks. MK46 5BU, England. TEL 44-1234-241234. FAX 44-1234-713757. E-mail: 100012.1554@compuserve.com; URL: http://www.enterprise.net/cvu. Ed. Alex Gray. R&P contact: Anne Gray. adv. contact: Leigh Foster. bk.rev.; illus.; software rev.; circ. 1,000 (paid). **Document type:** consumer publication.
Formerly (until 1996): Tagline! (ISSN 0968-0349)
Description: Reviews Corel desktop publishing software products. Offers users tips, informs of new packages in the works, and announces C.V.U. meetings and events.

001.642 658.8   US   ISSN 8750-3697
CULPEPPER LETTER.* no.21, 1984. m. $295 (effective 1995 & 1996). Culpepper & Associates, Inc., 1000 Mansell Exchange W., No. 210, Alpharetta, GA 30202. E-mail: ginger@culpepper.com. Ed. Ginger Kernachan; Pub. Warren Culpepper. bk.rev.; index. circ. 3,000. **Indexed:** Comput.Lit.Ind. **Document type:** newsletter.
—CCC.
Formerly (until 1984): Salt 'n' Pepper.
Description: For computer software and services executives. Articles, survey-based reports, and columns offer views, statistics, and ideas on how to improve growth and profits in the software industry.

CYBERLOG; library of applied medical software. see *MEDICAL SCIENCES — Computer Applications*

001.642   US   ISSN 1041-5173
QA76.9.D3   CODEN: DBMSEO
D B M S. (Database Management Systems); client-server computing. (Includes Database Buyers Guide) 1986. 13/yr. $24.95 (Canada and Mexico $35; elsewhere $60) (effective 1996). Miller Freeman Inc. (San Mateo) (Subsidiary of: United Newspapers Group), 411 Borel Ave. Ste. 100, San Mateo, CA 74402. TEL 415-358-9500. FAX 415-358-9855. (Subscr. to: Box 1182, Skokie, IL 60076-8182. TEL 708-647-5928. FAX 708-647-5872) Ed. David R. Kalman. adv.: B&W page $6775, color page $7925. circ. 56,360 (controlled). (back issues avail.; reprint service avail. from UMI) **Indexed:** Comput.Dtbs., Comput.Ind., INSPEC (1988-), Microcomp.Ind. **Document type:** trade publication.
●Also available online. Vendor(s): Information Access Co.
—BLDSC (3535.871200); AskIEEE; CISTI; Ei; KR SourceOne; SWETS; UMI; UnCover. CCC.
Formerly (until 1988): Business Software.
Description: Targets the needs of database developers, serious end users, and DP-MIS managers and staff. Contains innovative programming tips, insights, and product reviews.

001.642   GW
D E R: DISC-EDV-REPORT; Softwarezeitschrift auf Diskette fuer IBM-PC, XT-AT & Kompatible. 1987. m. DM.140. Verlag Erwin Simon, Daimlerstr. 24, 89079 Ulm, Germany. TEL 0731-40180-60. FAX 0731-40180-65. Ed. Andreas Hirtz. (back issues avail.)

001.642   US   ISSN 1065-0776
D O S SOFTWARE CONNECTION. (Disk Operating System) 1992. m. $59 (foreign $79). Cobb Group, Inc., 9420 Bunsen Pkwy., Ste. 300, Louisville, KY 40220. TEL 502-493-3200. FAX 502-491-8050. (Subscr. to: Box 35160, Louisville, KY 40232-9720. TEL 800-223-8720) (diskette format) **Document type:** consumer publication.

DATA NEWS; l'actualite informatique. see *COMMUNICATIONS — Computer Applications*

001.642   US   ISSN 1090-6436
QA76.9.D3
DATABASED WEB ADVISOR. 1983. m. $39 (Canada $59; elsewhere $79). Advisor Publications Inc., 5675 Ruffin Rd., Ste. 200, San Diego, CA 92123. TEL 619-278-5600. FAX 619-278-0300. E-mail: subscribe@advisor.com; URL: http://www.advisor.com/. (Dist. by: International Periodical Distributors, 674 Via de la Valle, Ste. 204, Solana Beach, CA 92075) Ed. John L. Hawkins; Pub. William T. Ota. adv.: B&W page $3450, color page $5185; adv. contact: B.J. Ghiglione. bk.rev.; circ. 35,556 (paid). **Indexed:** INSPEC. **Document type:** trade publication.
●Also available online.
—CISTI; Ei; KR SourceOne.
Formerly: Data Based Advisor (ISSN 0740-5200)
Description: Provides guidance for designing, deploying and maintaining on-line applications. Including articles on such vital topics as database security; distributed data; data warehouse and mart; client-server and other web database related topics.

005.3 658   US
DATAPRO APPLICATION DEVELOPMENT SOFTWARE. base vol. (plus m. updates). $738 to new subscr.; renewal $603. Datapro Information Services Group (Subsidiary of: McGraw-Hill, Inc.), 600 Delran Pkwy, Delran, NJ 08075. TEL 609-764-0100; 800-328-2776. FAX 609-764-8953.

DATAPRO DIRECTORY OF MICROCOMPUTER SOFTWARE see *COMPUTERS — Computer Industry Directories*

005.3   US   ISSN 0730-8779
    CODEN: DDSODL
DATAPRO DIRECTORY OF SOFTWARE. 1975. 3 base vols. (plus m. updates). $949 (effective 1996). Datapro Information Services Group (Subsidiary of: McGraw-Hill, Inc.), 600 Delran Pkwy., Delran, NJ 08075. TEL 609-764-0100; 800-328-2776. FAX 609-764-2814. **Document type:** directory.
●Also available online. Vendor(s): Knight-Ridder Information, Inc.
—CCC.

COMPUTERS — SOFTWARE

005.3   US   ISSN 8756-6516
DATAPRO MANAGEMENT OF APPLICATIONS SOFTWARE. 1979. 2 base vols. (plus m. updates). $937 to new subscr.; renewal $897 (effective 1996). Datapro Information Services Group (Subsidiary of: McGraw-Hill, Inc.), 600 Delran Pkwy., Delran, NJ 08075. TEL 609-764-0100; 800-328-2776. FAX 609-764-2814.
—CCC.
Formerly (until 1984): Datapro Applications Software Solutions (ISSN 0730-8760)

DATAPRO REPORTS ON UNIX SYSTEMS & SOFTWARE. see COMPUTERS — Computer Systems

001.642   US   ISSN 1052-195X
QA76.75
DATAPRO SOFTWARE FINDER. 1991. q. Datapro Information Services Group (Subsidiary of: McGraw-Hill, Inc.), 600 Delran Pkwy., Delran, NJ 08075. TEL 800-328-2776.
●Available only on CD-RQM.

DESIGN UND ELEKTRONIK; Spezialisten Zeitschrift fuer Hard- und Softwareentwickler. see COMPUTERS — Hardware

DIGITAL TECHNICAL JOURNAL. see COMPUTERS — Computer Engineering

005.3 338   US   ISSN 1077-4394
DIRECTIONS ON MICROSOFT; the independent view of Microsoft technology & strategy. 1992. m. $595 (outside N. America $643) (effective 1996). Redmond Communications Inc., 15127 N.E. 24th, Ste. 293, Redmond, WA 98052. TEL 206-882-3396. FAX 206-885-0848. E-mail: redcom@msn.com. Ed. Robert Horwitz; Pub. Jeff Parker. R&P contact: Jeff Parker. abstr.; index; circ. 2,000 (paid). (back issues avail.) **Document type:** newsletter.
Formerly: Microsoft Directions.
Description: Provides news and analysis of business and technology issues relating to the Microsoft Corporation.

DIRECTORY OF COMPUTER RETAILERS, DEALERS & DISTRIBUTORS (YEAR). see COMPUTERS — Computer Industry Directories

DIRECTORY OF COMPUTER SOFTWARE. see BUSINESS AND ECONOMICS — Trade And Industrial Directories

005.302   US   ISSN 1078-795X
DO IT WITH LOTUS SMARTSUITE. 1994. m. $69 (Canada $89; overseas $109) (effective 1996). I D G Newsletter Corporation, 77 Franklin St., Boston, MA 02110. TEL 617-482-8785; 800-807-0771. FAX 617-338-0164. E-mail: idgcust@pcworld.com; URL: http://idgnews.com. Ed. Valerie Murray; Pub. Craig Pierce. adv. contact: Scott Tharler. (looseleaf format) **Document type:** consumer publication.
Description: Tips and techniques for users of Lotus SmartSuite.

005.13   US   ISSN 1085-3200
DO IT WITH LOTUS 1-2-3. 1991. m. $69 (Canada $89; elsewhere $99) (effective 1996). I D G Newsletter Corporation, 77 Franklin St., Boston, MA 02110. TEL 617-482-8785; 800-807-0771. FAX 617-338-0164. E-mail: idgcust@pcworld.com; URL: http://idgnews.com. Ed. Richard Cranford; Pub. Craig Pierce. adv. contact: Scott Tharler. circ. 10,000. (looseleaf format) **Document type:** newsletter.
Formerly (until 1995): 1-2-3 for Windows Report (ISSN 1057-2333)
Description: Tips and techniques for users of Lotus 1-2-3 software.

005.302   US   ISSN 1081-7905
DO IT WITH MACINTOSH SYSTEM 7.5. 1995. m. $69 (Canada $89; overseas $109) (effective 1996). I D G Newsletter Corporation, 77 Franklin St., Boston, MA 02110. TEL 617-482-8785; 800-807-0771. FAX 617-338-0164. E-mail: idgcust@pcworld.com; URL: http://idgnews.com. Ed. Scott Fields; Pub. Craig Pierce. adv. contact: Scott Tharler. (looseleaf format) **Document type:** consumer publication.
Description: Tips, advice and hands-on guidance on Macintosh System 7.5.

005.302   US   ISSN 1080-398X
▼**DO IT WITH MICROSOFT OFFICE.** 1995. m. $69 (Canada $89; overseas $109) (effective 1996). I D G Newsletter Corporation, 77 Franklin St., Boston, MA 02110. TEL 617-482-8785; 800-807-0771. FAX 617-338-0164. E-mail: idgcust@pcworld.com; URL: http://idgnews.com. Ed. Jim Pile; Pub. Craig Pierce. adv. contact: Scott Tharler. (looseleaf format) **Document type:** consumer publication.
Description: Tips and techniques for Microsoft Office users.

005.302   US   ISSN 1078-7968
DO IT WITH MICROSOFT PUBLISHER. 1994. m. $69 (Canada $89; overseas $109) (effective 1996). I D G Newsletter Corporation, 77 Franklin St., Boston, MA 02210. TEL 617-482-8785; 800-807-0771. FAX 617-338-0164. E-mail: idgcust@pcworld.com; URL: http://idgnews.com. Ed. Scott Fields; Pub. Craig Pierce. adv. contact: Scott Tharler. (looseleaf format) **Document type:** consumer publication.
Description: Tips and techniques for Microsoft Publisher users.

005.302   US
▼**DO IT WITH WINDOWS 95.** 1995. m. $69 (Canada $89; overseas $109) (effective 1996). I D G Newsletter Corporation, 77 Franklin St., Boston, MA 02110. TEL 617-482-8785; 800-707-8065. FAX 617-338-0164. E-mail: idgcust@pcworld.com; URL: http://idgnews.com. Ed. Valerie Murray; Pub. Craig Pierce. adv. contact: Scott Tharler. (looseleaf format) **Document type:** consumer publication.

EARLY CHILDHOOD TEACHER; instructor's magazine for preschool and primary professionals. see EDUCATION

EDUCATIONAL SOFTWARE REVIEW. see EDUCATION — Computer Applications

ELECTRICAL UTILITY INDUSTRY SOFTWARE DIRECTORY. see ENERGY — Computer Applications

005.3   US
THE ELECTRONIC EDGE. q. free to qualified personnel. R.R. Bowker Electronic Publishing, A Division of Reed Elsevier Inc., 121 Chanlon Rd., New Providence, NJ 07974. TEL 908-665-2810; 800-323-3288. FAX 908-665-3575. E-mail: adagostino@reedref.com; URL: http://www.reedref.com. Ed. Angela D'Agostino. circ. 12,000 (controlled). **Document type:** newsletter.
Formerly: PLUS Extensions.
Description: Annnounces new CD-ROM and online publications, and reports on news, technical tips and other information of interest to information specialists.

005.3 621.3   US   ISSN 1382-3256
▼**EMPIRICAL SOFTWARE ENGINEERING.** 1996. q. fl.535 to institutions; $274.50 to institutions in U.S. (effective 1998). Kluwer Academic Publishers Boston, Box 358, Accord Sta., Hingham, MA 02018-0358. TEL 617-871-6600. FAX 617-871-6528. E-mail: services@wkap.nl; URL: http://www.wkap.nl. (Subscr. outside N. America to: Kluwer Academic Publishers Group, P.O. Box 322, 3300 AH Dordrecht, Netherlands. TEL 31-78-6392392. FAX 31-78-6546474) **Document type:** academic/scholarly publication.
—BLDSC (3737.024150); AskIEEE; KR SourceOne. CCC.
Refereed Serial

ENGINEERING & INDUSTRIAL SOFTWARE DIRECTORY. see BUSINESS AND ECONOMICS — Trade And Industrial Directories

ENTERPRISE SYSTEMS JOURNAL; focusing on IBM host-based enterprise-wide computing. see COMPUTERS — Electronic Data Processing

ENVIRONMENTAL COMPLIANCE AUDITING SOFTWARE REPORT. see LAW

ENVIRONMENTAL COST ESTIMATING SOFTWARE REPORT. see ENVIRONMENTAL STUDIES

ENVIRONMENTAL MODELLING & SOFTWARE. see ENVIRONMENTAL STUDIES — Computer Applications

ENVIRONMENTAL SOFTWARE GUIDE. see ENVIRONMENTAL STUDIES — Computer Applications

ENVIRONMENTAL SOFTWARE REPORT. see ENVIRONMENTAL STUDIES — Computer Applications

005.302   GW   ISSN 0946-6800
EXCEL. 1994. bi-m. DM.98. Verlag Wirtschaft Recht und Steuern, Fraunhoferstr. 5, 82152 Planegg, Germany. TEL 49-89-89517-0. FAX 49-89-89517250. (Subscr. to: Postfach 1363, 82142 Planegg, Germany) (looseleaf format) **Document type:** trade publication.

EXE; software developers magazine. see BUSINESS AND ECONOMICS — Computer Applications

005.3   US
THE EXPERT RESOURCE DISK. m. $49 (foreign $69). Cobb Group, Inc., 9420 Bunsen Pkwy., Ste. 300, Louisville, KY 40220. TEL 502-493-3200. FAX 502-491-8050. (Subscr. to: Box 35160, Louisville, KY 40232-9720. TEL 800-223-8720) (diskette format) **Document type:** consumer publication.

005.3   US   ISSN 1070-8383
EXPLORING WINDOWS N T; tips & techniques for users of Microsoft Windows N T. 1993. m. $119 (foreign $139). Cobb Group, Inc., 9420 Bunsen Pkwy., Ste. 300, Louisville, KY 40220. TEL 502-493-3200. FAX 502-491-8050. (Subscr. to: Box 35160, Louisville, KY 40232-9720. TEL 800-223-8720) Ed. Blake Ragsdell. (back issues avail.) **Document type:** consumer publication.

FARM COMPUTING. see AGRICULTURE — Computer Applications

005.3 004.678   US
FASTLINK SOFTWARE UPDATE. w. free. E-mail: customer@symgroup.com; URL: http://www.symgroup.com/ng/html/newsletter.html. **Document type:** newsletter.
●Available only online.
Description: Provides links to the download sites to get softwares, and links to companies of interest to the readers.

005.1 003 004.2   US
FAULKNER'S SYSTEMS SOFTWARE REPORTS. 1971. base vol. (plus m. updates). $670 (effective 1993). Faulkner Information Services, Inc., 114 Cooper Center, 7905 Browning Rd., Pennsauken, NJ 08109-4319. TEL 609-662-2070. FAX 609-662-3380. Ed. Betsy Yokum. (looseleaf format)
Formerly: Auerbach Systems Software Reports; Supersedes in part: Auerbach Software Reports (ISSN 0004-7775)
Description: Describes and evaluates systems software products for mainframe, mini and micro computer environments; includes DBMS, performance management, systems development, communications and CASE.

005.302 332.1   UK
FINANCIAL SOFTWARE AND SYSTEMS GUIDE. 1986. biennial. £85. V N U Business Publications BV, 32-34 Broadwick St., London W1A 2HG, England. TEL 44-171-439-4242. FAX 44-171-734-5510. Ed. Ann Maher.
Formerly: Software Guide for Accountants.

005.3   US
▼**FINESSE MARKETPLACE JOURNAL.** 1995. bi-m. free. E-mail: webmaster@fingraphics.com; URL: http://www.fingraphics.com. Ed. Leon Fainbuch. software rev.
●Available only online.
Description: Includes Mac and Windows tips and tricks.

COMPUTERS — SOFTWARE

001.642 UK ISSN 0934-5043
QA75.5 CODEN: FACME5
FORMAL ASPECTS OF COMPUTING; international journal of formal methods. 1989. bi-m. £216 (effective 1998). (British Computer Society) Springer-Verlag London Ltd., Sweetapple House, Catteshall Rd., Godalming, Surrey GU7 3DJ, England. TEL 44-1483-418800. FAX 44-1483-415144. Ed. Cliff Jones. adv.; bk.rev. circ. 207. (also avail. in microform from UMI; back issues avail.; reprint service avail. from SWZ) **Indexed:** Comput.Abstr., INSPEC (1990-), Zent.Math. **Document type:** trade publication.
—BLDSC (4008.335800); AskIEEE; Ei; KR SourceOne; SWETS; UnCover. **CCC.**
Description: Promotes growth of computer science through the application of formalisms.

005.3 GW
FORSCHUNG IN DER SOFTWARETECHNIK. 1993. irreg., vol.2, 1994. DM.68. Spektrum Akademischer Verlag GmbH, Vangerowstr. 20, 69115 Heidelberg, Germany. TEL 49-6221-9126-0. FAX 49-6221-912638. E-mail: kaschura@spektrum-verlag.com; URL: http://www.spektrum-verlag.com. **Document type:** monographic series.

005.3 US ISSN 1066-7261
QA76.9.D3
FOXPRO ADVISOR; the magazine for using microsoft FoxPro. 1993. m. $49 (Canada $69; elsewhere $89). Advisor Publications Inc., 5675 Ruffin Rd., Ste. 200, San Diego, CA 92131. TEL 619-278-5600. FAX 619-278-0300. E-mail: subscribe@advisor.com; URL: http://www.advisor.com. (Dist. by: International Periodical Distributors, 674 Via de la Valle, Ste. 204, Solana Beach, CA 92075) Ed. John L. Hawkins; Pub. William T. Ota. adv. contact: B.J. Ghiglione.
—KR SourceOne; SWETS.
Description: Explains how build database solutions with Microsoft FoxPro. For users of Microsoft FoxPro, ranging from new users to advanced developers.

005.3 US ISSN 1070-0315
FOXPRO DEVELOPER'S JOURNAL; tips & techniques for FoxPro. MS-DOS and Windows. 1993. m. $89 (foreign $109). Cobb Group, Inc., 9420 Bunsen Pkwy., Ste. 300, Louisville, KY 40220. TEL 502-493-3200. FAX 502-491-8050. (Subscr. to: Box 35160, Louisville, KY 40232-9720. TEL 800-223-8720) Ed. Darren McGee. (back issues avail.) **Document type:** consumer publication.

005.3 US
FOXPRO DEVELOPER'S RESOURCE DISK. m. $49 (foreign $69). Cobb Group, Inc., 9420 Bunsen Pkwy., Ste. 300, Louisville, KY 40220. TEL 502-493-3200. FAX 502-491-8050. (Subscr. to: Box 35160, Louisville, KY 40232-9720. TEL 800-223-8720) (diskette format) **Document type:** consumer publication.

001.642 IT
FREE SOFTWARE COMPUTER MAGAZINE. 6/yr. Via Ferri 6, 20092 Cinisello Balsamo (Milan), Italy. TEL 2-66-02-51. FAX 2-612-76-20. TELEX 352376 JCE MIL I. Ed. Marinella Zetti.

005.3 US
G U I PROGRAM NEWS. (Graphic User Interface) m. $150 (outside N. America $165). Worldwide Videotex, Box 3273, Boynton Beach, FL 33424-3273. TEL 407-738-2276. Ed. Mark Wright; Pub. Mark Wright. bk.rev. **Document type:** newsletter.
●Also available online. Vendor(s): Information Access Co.
Description: Reports on the popular graphic user interfaces and the growing number of associated applications for microcomputers and workstations.

005.3 IT
▼**GUIDA ALLE APPLICAZIONI OS-2 WARP**. 1996. s-a. Gruppo Editoriale J C E, Via Ferri 6, 20092 Cinisello Balsamo (MI), Italy. TEL 39-2-660251. FAX 39-2-6127620. E-mail: guidawarp@jce.it; URL: http://www.jce.it. Ed. Fausto Gimondi. adv.: B&W page L.5500000, color page L.7000000; trim 210 X 280. circ. 35,000. **Document type:** trade publication.
Description: Provides an overview of OS/2 Warp platform products, IBM operative system with special focus on workgroup, network management and the Internet.

005.302 IT ISSN 1122-9187
GUIDA ALLE APPLICAZIONI WINDOWS. 1993. s-a. L.15000 per no. Gruppo Editoriale J C E s.r.l., Via Ferri 6, 20092 Cinisello Balsamo (MI), Italy. TEL 39-2-660251. FAX 39-2-6127620. E-mail: guidawin@jce.it; URL: http://www.jce.it. Ed. Fausto Gimondi. adv.: B&W page L.5500000, color page L.7000000. circ. 30,000. **Document type:** consumer publication.
Description: Provides an overview of Windows products, from 3.1 to 95, including accounting, desktop publishing, science, industry, multimedia, and entertainment.

GUIDE TO REAL ESTATE & MORTGAGE BANKING SOFTWARE. see *BUSINESS AND ECONOMICS — Banking And Finance__computer Applications*

THE H P PALMTOP PAPER. see *COMPUTERS — Hardware*

H - SCOOP. see *COMPUTERS — Microcomputers*

HANDHELD P C MAGAZINE. see *COMPUTERS — Hardware*

001.642 370 US ISSN 1060-9504
LB1028.7
HIGH - SCOPE BUYER'S GUIDE TO CHILDREN'S SOFTWARE; survey of computer programs for children ages 3 to 7. 1984. a. $19.95 (effective 1997). (High - Scope Educational Research Foundation) High - Scope Press, 600 N. River St., Ypsilanti, MI 48198-2898. TEL 800-407-7377. FAX 800-442-4329. URL: http://www.info@highscope.org. Ed. Lynn Taylor. R&P contact: Emily Koepp. TEL 313-485-2000.
Description: Designed to help readers save time and money when making decisions about purchasing developmentally appropriate software for young children. Over 500 titles reviewed.

HONG KONG COMPUTER DIRECTORY (YEAR). see *BUSINESS AND ECONOMICS — Trade And Industrial Directories*

005.3 SP
▼**HOT SHAREWARE**. 1995. 12/yr. 7140 ptas. (Europe 10380 ptas.; elsewhere 12360 ptas.) (effective 1997). Hobby Press, S.A., C. de los Ciruelos, 4, 28700 San Sebastian de los Reyes (Madrid), Spain. TEL 34-1-6548199. FAX 34-1-6547272. Ed. Domingo Gomez. adv.: page 300000 ptas.; 210 x 275; adv. contact: Maria Perera. circ. 18,000. **Document type:** consumer publication.

005.3 639.2 PH ISSN 0116-6964
I C L A R M SOFTWARE. (Text in English) 1987. irreg. International Center for Living Aquatic Resources Management, M.C.P.O. Box 2631, 0718 Makati City, Philippines. TEL 63-2-812-86-41. FAX 63-2-816-31-83. URL: http://www.cgiar.org/iclarm/.

005 US
I D U G SOLUTIONS JOURNAL; for users of DB2 technology. 1994. q. newsstand price: $3.95. (International DB2 Users Group) Design Liberte, 5048 W. Coyle Ave., Skokie, IL 60077. TEL 847-677-9326. Eds. Doug Stacey, Michael Cotignola; Pub. Linda Pearlstein. adv. contact: Shawn Rogers. illus. circ. 30,000. **Document type:** trade publication.
Refereed Serial

I E E E INTELLIGENT SYSTEMS MAGAZINE. (Institute of Electrical and Electronics Engineers, Inc.) see *COMPUTERS — Computer Engineering*

001.642 US ISSN 0740-7459
QA76.75 CODEN: IESOEG
I E E E SOFTWARE. 1984. bi-m. $305 to non-members (effective 1996). (Institute of Electrical and Electronics Engineers, Inc.) I E E E Computer Society Press, 10662 Los Vaqueros Circle, Box 3014, Los Alamitos, CA 90720-1264. TEL 714-821-8380; 800-678-4333. FAX 714-821-4641. E-mail: customer.service@ieee.org; webmaster@computer.org; URL: http://computer.org/pubs/software/software.htm. Ed. Alan Davis. adv.: B&W page $2290, color page $3390; adv. contact: Heidi Rex. bk.rev.; illus.; tr.lit. circ. 25,719. (also avail. in microfiche; microfilm from EEE) **Indexed:** A.S.& T.Ind., Abstr.Hum.Comp.Inter., ASCA, BMT, Comput.Cont., Comput.Lit.Ind., Curr.Cont., Cyb.Abstr., INSPEC, Oper.Res.Manage.Sci., Qual.Contr.Appl.Stat., SSCI. **Document type:** proceedings.
●Also available online.
—BLDSC (4363.066560); AskIEEE; CISTI; Ei; Genuine Article; KR SourceOne; Linda Hall; SWETS; UMI; UnCover. **CCC.**
Description: Covers programming, methodology, software project management, programming environment, hardware and software monitoring, and programming tools.

005.1 US ISSN 0098-5589
QA76.6 CODEN: IESEDJ
I E E E TRANSACTIONS ON SOFTWARE ENGINEERING. 1975. m. $615 to non-members (effective 1998). (I E E E Computer Society) Institute of Electrical and Electronics Engineers, Inc., 345 E. 47th St., New York, NY 10017-2394. TEL 732-981-0060; 800-678-4333. FAX 732-981-9667. E-mail: customer.service@ieee.org; URL: http://www.ieee.org. (Subscr. to: Box 1331, 445 Hoes Lane, Piscataway, NJ 08855-1331) Ed. Richard A. Kemmerer. (also avail. in microform) **Indexed:** A.I.Abstr., A.S.& T.Ind., ABI Inform., ASCA, BMT, CAD CAM Abstr., Compumath, Comput.Abstr., Comput.Cont., Comput.Dtbs., Comput.Lit.Ind., Curr.Cont., Cyb.Abstr., Ind.Sci.Rev., INSPEC, Int.Aerosp.Abstr., Math.R., Oper.Res.Manage.Sci., Qual.Contr.Appl.Stat., Risk Abstr., Tel.Abstr., Zent.Math.
—BLDSC (4363.220500); AskIEEE; CISTI; Ei; Genuine Article; KR SourceOne; Linda Hall; SWETS; UMI; UnCover. **CCC.**
Description: Details specification, development, management, test, maintenance and documentation of computer programs.

I E E PROCEEDINGS - COMPUTERS AND DIGITAL TECHNIQUES. (Institution of Electrical Engineers) see *COMPUTERS — Hardware*

005.1 UK ISSN 1364-5080
QA76.758 CODEN: SEJOED
I E E PROCEEDINGS - SOFTWARE ENGINEERING. (Institution of Electrical Engineers) 1981. bi-m. £395 (effective 1997). I.E.E., Michael Faraday House, Six Hills Way, Stevenage, Herts. SG1 2AY, England. TEL 44-1438-313311. FAX 44-1438-742840. TELEX 825578 IEESTV G. E-mail: inspec@iee.org.uk; URL: http://www.iee.co.uk/publish/profjrnl/ieeproc.html. (Subscr. to: Publication Sales Dept., P.O. Box 96, Stevenage, Herts. SG1 2SD, England; U.S. addr.: INSPEC Dept. IEEE Operations Center, 445 Hoes Ln., Box 1331, Piscataway, NJ 08855-1331. TEL 908-562-5553. FAX 908-562-8737) (Co-sponsor: British Computer Society) Ed. J.A. McDermid. **Indexed:** Abstr.Hum.Comp.Inter., ASCA, CAD CAM Abstr., Compumath, Comput.Abstr., Comput.Cont., Curr.Cont., INSPEC, Pub.Admin.Abstr. **Document type:** trade publication.
—AskIEEE; CISTI; Ei; Genuine Article; KR SourceOne; Linda Hall; SWETS; UnCover. **CCC.**
Formerly (until 1997): Software Engineering Journal (ISSN 0268-6961); Which incorporates: Software and Microsystems (ISSN 0261-3182)
Description: Covers all aspects of the software cycle, including design, development, implementation and maintenance.

I T A A MEMBERSHIP DIRECTORY. (Information Technology Association of America) see *COMPUTERS — Electronic Data Processing*

001.642 US
I T A A NEW PRODUCTS AND SERVICES GUIDE. 3/yr. Information Technology Association of America, 1616 N. Fort Myer Dr., Ste. 1300, Arlington, VA 22209-9998. TEL 410-543-0475. FAX 410-543-2921.
Description: Highlights new and established software products, computer services and business support services for high technology companies.

001.642 US
I T A A SOFTWARE INDUSTRY REPORTS. irreg. price varies. Information Technology Association of America, 1616 N. Fort Myer Dr., Ste. 1300, Arlington, VA 22209-9998. TEL 410-543-0475. FAX 410-543-2921.

I T REVIEWS; the enterprise technology journal. (Information Technology) see COMPUTERS — Electronic Data Processing

005.3 US
THE ICON ANALYST. 1990. bi-m. $25 (foreign $35). Icon Project, Department of Computer Science, University of Arizona, Tucson, AZ 85721. TEL 602-621-6609. FAX 602-621-4426. Eds. Ralph & Madget Griswold. index; circ. 160 (paid). (back issues avail.) **Document type:** academic/scholarly publication.
Description: Covers the Icon programming language, along with techniques and implementation. Aimed at high-level computer programmers.

ICON NEWSLETTER. see COMPUTERS — Computer Programming

IMAGING BUSINESS; the voice of the document imaging channel. see COMPUTERS — Computer Graphics

INDUSTRIAL CONTROLS INTELLIGENCE AND THE P L C INSIDER'S NEWSLETTER; informing the industrial controls industry since 1981. see COMPUTERS — Hardware

005.3 NE ISSN 1386-3681
INFORMATION SYSTEMS. (Text in English) 1973. irreg. Stichting Mathematisch Centrum, Centrum voor Wiskunde en Informatica, Department of Computer Science, P.O. Box 94079, 1090 GB Amsterdam, Netherlands. TEL 31-20-5924128. FAX 31-20-5924199. URL: http://www.cwi.nl. abstr. **Document type:** academic/scholarly publication.
Supersedes in part: Centrum voor Wiskunde in Informatica. Department of Computer Science. Report (ISSN 0169-118X); Which was formerly (until 1984): Stichting Mathematisch Centrum. Afdeling Informatica. Rapport (ISSN 0376-4028)

005.3 US ISSN 1071-0728
INSIDE AUTO C A D; tips & techniques for users of AutoCAD. 1993. m. $99. Cobb Group, Inc., 9420 Bunsen Pkwy., Ste. 300, Louisville, KY 40220. TEL 502-493-3200. FAX 502-491-8050. (Subscr. to: Box 35160, Louisville, KY 40232-9720. TEL 800-223-8720) Ed. David Reid. adv. contact: Tracee Bell. (back issues avail.) **Document type:** consumer publication.

001.642 US ISSN 1061-3293
QA76.9.D3
INSIDE DBASE. 1992. m. $69 (foreign $89). Cobb Group, Inc., 9420 Bunsen Pkwy., Ste. 300, Louisville, KY 40220. TEL 502-493-3200. FAX 502-491-8050. (Subscr. to: Box 35160, Louisville, KY 40232-9720. TEL 800-223-8720) **Document type:** consumer publication.

005.3 US ISSN 1068-6908
INSIDE FILEMAKER PRO; tips & techniques for users of Claris FileMaker Pro for the Macintosh. 1993. m. $59 (foreign $79). Cobb Group, Inc., 9420 Bunsen Pkwy., Ste. 300, Louisville, KY 40220. TEL 502-493-3200. FAX 502-491-8050. (Subscr. to: Box 35160, Louisville, KY 40232-9720. TEL 800-223-8720) Ed. Ron Wilder. (back issues avail.) **Document type:** consumer publication.

INSIDE HYPERCARD. see COMPUTERS — Personal Computers

005.3 US ISSN 1067-8204
INSIDE MICROSOFT ACCESS; tips & techniques for Microsoft Access & Windows. 1993. m. $59 (foreign $79). Cobb Group, Inc., 9420 Bunsen Pkwy., Ste. 300, Louisville, KY 40220. TEL 502-493-3200. FAX 502-491-8050. (Subscr. to: Box 35160, Louisville, KY 40232-9720. TEL 800-223-8720) Ed. David Brown. adv. (back issues avail.) **Document type:** consumer publication.

005.3 US
INSIDE MICROSOFT ACCESS RESOURCE DISK. m. $49 (foreign $69). Cobb Group, Inc., 9420 Bunsen Pkwy., Ste. 300, Louisville, KY 40220. TEL 502-493-3200. FAX 502-491-8050. (Subscr. to: Box 35160, Louisville, KY 40232-9720. TEL 800-223-8720) (diskette format) **Document type:** consumer publication.

INSIDE MICROSOFT BASIC. see COMPUTERS — Computer Programming

001.642 621.381 US ISSN 1051-9734
INSIDE MICROSOFT WINDOWS. 1990. m. $49 (foreign $69). Cobb Group, Inc., 9420 Bunsen Pkwy., Ste. 300, Louisville, KY 40220. TEL 502-493-3200. FAX 502-491-8050. (Subscr. to: Box 35160, Louisville, KY 40232-9720. TEL 800-223-8720) Ed. Curt Havlin. **Document type:** consumer publication.
Description: Contains tips and techniques aimed exclusively to users of Windows.

621.381 UK ISSN 0966-968X
INSIDE MICROSOFT WINDOWS; tips and tricks for Microsoft Windows. 1992. m. £39 (other E.C. nations £42; elsewhere £45). Cobb Group U K, Cottons Centre, Hay's Ln., London SE1 2QT, England. TEL 0171-378-6800. FAX 0171-378-8779. (Subscr. to: Tower House, Sovereign Park, Market Harborough, Leics. LE16 9EF, England. TEL 0158-468888. FAX 0158-434958) Ed. Elisa Williams. illus. **Document type:** newsletter.
—BLDSC (4518.152410).
Description: Informs users how to best employ and operate Microsoft Windows; offers time-saving tips.

005.3 US ISSN 1068-4697
INSIDE NORTON DESKTOP FOR WINDOWS. 1993. m. $39. Cobb Group, Inc., 9420 Bunsen Pkwy., Ste. 300, Louisville, KY 40220. TEL 502-493-3200. FAX 502-491-8050. (Subscr. to: Box 35160, Louisville, KY 40232-9720. TEL 800-223-8720) **Document type:** consumer publication.

001.642 US ISSN 1061-5865
INSIDE P C TOOLS. 1992. m. $39 (foreign $59). Cobb Group, Inc., 9420 Bunsen Pkwy., Ste. 300, Louisville, KY 40220. TEL 502-493-3200. FAX 502-491-8050. (Subscr. to: Box 35160, Louisville, KY 40232-9720. TEL 800-223-8720) **Document type:** consumer publication.

005.3 US ISSN 1070-8375
INSIDE P C TOOLS FOR WINDOWS; tips and techniques for users of PC Tools for Windows. 1993. m. $39. Cobb Group, Inc., 9420 Bunsen Pkwy., Ste. 300, Louisville, KY 40220. TEL 502-493-3200. FAX 502-491-8050. (Subscr. to: Box 35160, Louisville, KY 40232-9720. TEL 800-223-8720) Ed. Greg Shultz. adv. contact: Tracee Bell-Troutt. (back issues avail.) **Document type:** consumer publication.

005.3 US
INSIDE PARADOX FOR WINDOWS. 1993. m. $79. Cobb Group, Inc., 9420 Bunsen Pkwy., Ste. 300, Louisville, KY 40220. TEL 502-493-3200. FAX 502-491-8050. (Subscr. to: Box 35160, Louisville, KY 40232-9720. TEL 800-223-8720) **Document type:** consumer publication.

005.3 US ISSN 1066-5218
INSIDE QUATTRO PRO FOR WINDOWS. 1993. m. $59. Cobb Group, Inc., 9420 Bunsen Pkwy., Ste. 300, Louisville, KY 40220. TEL 502-493-3200. FAX 502-491-8050. (Subscr. to: Box 35160, Louisville, KY 40232-9720. TEL 800-223-8720) **Document type:** consumer publication.

INSIDE TURBO C PLUS PLUS. see COMPUTERS — Computer Programming

INSIDE VISUAL BASIC FOR WINDOWS. see COMPUTERS — Computer Programming

THE INSIDE WORD (MICROSOFT WORD 5.5 & 6.0). see COMPUTERS — Personal Computers

THE INSIDE WORD (P C EDITION - MICROSOFT WORD 5.5 & 6.0). see COMPUTERS — Personal Computers

INSIDE WORD FOR WINDOWS. see COMPUTERS — Personal Computers

005.3 US
INSIDE WORD FOR WINDOWS SOFTWARE CONNECTION. m. $59 (foreign $79). Cobb Group, Inc., 9420 Bunsen Pkwy., Ste. 300, Louisville, KY 40220. TEL 502-493-3200. FAX 502-491-8050. (Subscr. to: Box 35160, Louisville, KY 40232-9720. TEL 800-223-8720) (diskette format) **Document type:** consumer publication.

INSIDE WORDPERFECT. see COMPUTERS — Personal Computers

INSIDE 1-2-3 RELEASE 3 (3.1 & 3.4). see COMPUTERS — Personal Computers

005.3 US
INTERACTION (SAN FRANCISCO). 1994. q. free. (Sierra On-Line) I D G Communications Inc. (San Francisco), 501 Second St., San Francsico, CA 94107. TEL 415-281-8650. FAX 415-281-3915. **Document type:** trade publication.

INTERACTIVE AGE; content, technology and communications for the information highway. see COMPUTERS — Computer Networks

INTERNATIONAL CONFERENCE ON COMPUTER LANGUAGES. PROCEEDINGS. see COMPUTERS — Computer Programming

001.642 US ISSN 0270-5257
QA76.6 CODEN: PCSEDE
INTERNATIONAL CONFERENCE ON SOFTWARE ENGINEERING. PROCEEDINGS. 1975. a. (Institute of Electrical and Electronics Engineers, Inc.) I E E E Computer Society Press, 10662 Los Vaqueros Circle, Los Alamitos, CA 90720-1264. TEL 714-821-8380. FAX 714-821-4641. Ed. Cat Harris; Pub. Matt Loeb. adv. contact: Frieda Koester. **Document type:** proceedings.
—BLDSC (4538.883800); Ei; UMI; UnCover. **CCC**.
Formerly: National Conference on Software Engineering. Proceedings.
Description: Covers advances in the software and hardware of methodological and linguistic tools.

005.3 CN ISSN 1198-5577
INTERNATIONAL JOURNAL OF APPLIED SOFTWARE TECHNOLOGY. 1995. q. $100 to individuals (foreign $120); institutions $250 (effective 1996). International Academic Publishing Company, Inc., 1025 McNicoll Ave., Ste. 201, Scarborough, ON M1W 3W6, Canada. (Subscr. to: International Academic Publishing Company, Inc., 10 Musgrave St., St. John's, NF, Canada) Ed. Si-Wei Lu.
—BLDSC (4542.100900); AskIEEE; KR SourceOne.

001.642 001.539 SZ ISSN 0952-8091
CODEN: IJCTEK
INTERNATIONAL JOURNAL OF COMPUTER APPLICATIONS IN TECHNOLOGY. (Text in English) 1988. bi-m. $290 in N. America; elsewhere DM.500. (International Network of Centres for Computer Applications) Inderscience Enterprises Ltd., World Trade Centre Bldg., 110 Ave. Louis Casai, Case Postale 306, CH-1215 Geneva-Aeroport, Switzerland. FAX 41-22-7910885. (Co-sponsor: Unesco) Ed. M.A. Dorgham. R&P contact: Jeannette Brooks. adv. contact: M.A. Dorgham. bk.rev.; abstr.; charts; illus. circ. 10,000. (back issues avail.) Indexed: A.I.Abstr. (until 1992), Abstr.Hum.Comp.Inter., Alloys Ind., ASCA, CAD CAM Abstr. (until 1992), Compumath, Curr.Cont., Eng.Mat.Abstr., INSPEC (1988-), Met.Abstr.Ind., Met.Abstr., Nonfer.Met.Alert, PCC Alert, Robomat. (until 1992), Steels Alert, World Alum.Abstr. **Document type:** academic/scholarly publication.
—BLDSC (4542.174400); AskIEEE; CISTI; Ei; Genuine Article; KR SourceOne; Linda Hall; SWETS.
Description: Information on computer applications: advanced manufacturing systems and technology, information technology and systems, software engineering and management, communications, as well as computer-aided learning.
Refereed Serial

INTERNATIONAL JOURNAL OF FOUNDATIONS OF COMPUTER SCIENCE. see COMPUTERS — Computer Programming

INTERNATIONAL JOURNAL OF HIGH SPEED COMPUTING. see COMPUTERS — Hardware

001.642   SI   ISSN 0218-1940
QA76.758   CODEN: ISEKEW
INTERNATIONAL JOURNAL OF SOFTWARE ENGINEERING AND KNOWLEDGE ENGINEERING. Short title: S E K E. 1991. q. $100 to individuals; institutions & libraries $251 (developing countries $151). World Scientific Publishing Co. Pte. Ltd., Farrer Rd., P.O. Box 128, Singapore 9128, Singapore. TEL 65-3825663. FAX 65-3825919. TELEX RS-28561-WSPC. E-mail: wspcsl@singnet.com.sg; sales@wspc2.demon.co.uk; wspc@wspc.com; URL: http://www.singnet.com.sg/~wspclib/. (UK addr.: 57 Shelton St., Covent Garden, London WC2H 9HE, England. TEL 44-171-836-0888. FAX 44-171-836-2020; US addr.: 1060 Main St., Ste. 1B, River Edge, NJ 07661. TEL 800-227-7562. FAX 201-487-9656) Ed. S.K. Chang. index. **Indexed:** ASCA, INSPEC (1991-), SSCI. **Document type:** academic/scholarly publication.
—BLDSC (4542.585000); AskIEEE; CISTI; Genuine Article; KR SourceOne; SWETS. **CCC.**
    Description: Serves as a forum for researchers, practitioners, and developers to exchange ideas and results for the advancement of software engineering and knowledge engineering.

004.1   US   ISSN 1078-3482
QA76.5   CODEN: IJSCFG
INTERNATIONAL JOURNAL OF SUPERCOMPUTER APPLICATIONS AND HIGH-PERFORMANCE COMPUTING. Variant title: S A H P C. 1987. q. $222 to institutions. Sage Publications, Inc., Sage Science Press, 2455 Teller Rd., Thousand Oaks, CA 91320. TEL 805-499-0721. FAX 805-499-0871. E-mail: order@sagepub.com; URL: http://www.sagepub.com. (Overseas subscr. to: Sage Publications Inc., 6 Bonhill St., London EC2A 4PU, England; Sage Publications India Pvt. Ltd., P.O. Box 4215 New Delhi, 110 048, India) Eds. Jack Dongarra, Joanne L. Martin. R&P contact: Cris Anderson. adv. contact: Susan Hanscom. bk.rev. circ. 650. (also avail. in microform from UMI; back issues avail.; reprint service avail. from UMI) **Indexed:** A.I.Abstr., Appl.Mech.Rev., ASCA, CAD CAM Abstr., Curr.Cont., Cyb.Abstr., Inform.Sci.Abstr., INIS Atomind., INSPEC (1988-), Sci.Cit.Ind., SSCI. **Document type:** academic/scholarly publication.
●Also available online. Vendor(s): Knight-Ridder Information, Inc.
—BLDSC (4542.684250); AskIEEE; CISTI; Ei; Genuine Article; KR SourceOne; Linda Hall; SWETS; UMI; UnCover.
    Formerly (until 1994): International Journal of Supercomputer Applications (ISSN 0890-2720)
    Description: Interdisciplinary forum for the exchange of experiences in supercomputing, with emphasis on software techniques.
    Refereed Serial

INTERNATIONAL JOURNAL ON SOFTWARE TOOLS FOR TECHNOLOGY TRANSFER. see COMPUTERS — Computer Systems

INTERNATIONAL SMART CARD INDUSTRY GUIDE. see COMPUTERS — Computer Industry

005.3   US   ISSN 1074-6005
    CODEN: PWRPED
INTERNATIONAL WORKSHOP IN RAPID SYSTEM PROTOTYPING. PROCEEDINGS. Short title: R S P. 1990. a. price varies. (Institute of Electrical and Electronics Engineers, Inc.) I E E E Computer Society Press, 10662 Los Vaqueros Circle, Los Alamitos, CA 90720-1264. TEL 714-821-8380. FAX 714-821-4641. adv. contact: Frieda Koester. **Document type:** proceedings.
—Ei. **CCC.**
    Description: Documents current research trends and reports on system specifications, system modeling, system design and design validation.

005.3   US   ISSN 1066-1387
QA76.758   CODEN: PIWEE9
INTERNATIONAL WORKSHOP ON COMPUTER-AIDED SOFTWARE ENGINEERING. PROCEEDINGS. Short title: CASE. 1989. biennial. price varies. (Institute of Electrical and Electronics Engineers, Inc.) I E E E Computer Society Press, 10662 Los Vaqueros Circle, Los Alamitos, CA 90720-1264. TEL 714-821-8380. FAX 714-821-4641. Ed. Cat Harris; Pub. Matt Loeb. adv. contact: Frieda Koester. **Document type:** proceedings.
—**CCC.**
    Description: Covers the overriding issues of software engineering and CASE.

JISUANJI YANJIU YU FAZHAN/COMPUTER RESEARCH AND DEVELOPMENT. see COMPUTERS — Computer Engineering

JISUANJI YINGYONG YU RUANJIAN/COMPUTER APPLICATIONS AND SOFTWARE. see COMPUTERS

JOURNAL OF CHEMICAL EDUCATION: SOFTWARE. SERIES B; for MS-DOS - IBM PC compatible computers. see EDUCATION — Computer Applications

JOURNAL OF CHEMICAL EDUCATION: SOFTWARE. SERIES C; for Apple Macintosh computers. see EDUCATION — Computer Applications

JOURNAL OF CHEMICAL EDUCATION: SOFTWARE. SERIES D; for Windows. see EDUCATION — Computer Applications

JOURNAL OF CHEMICAL EDUCATION: SOFTWARE. SPECIAL ISSUE SERIES. see EDUCATION — Computer Applications

001.642   UK   ISSN 1040-550X
QA76.76.S64   CODEN: JSMPEU
JOURNAL OF SOFTWARE MAINTENANCE: RESEARCH AND PRACTICE. 1989. bi-m. $885 (foreign $885) (effective 1998). John Wiley & Sons Ltd., Journals, Baffins Ln., Chichester, W. Sussex PO19 1UD, England. TEL 44-1243-779777. FAX 44-1243-775878. E-mail: info-assets@wiley.co.uk; URL: http://www.wiley.co.uk. (Subscr. outside the Americas to: John Wiley & Sons, Inc., 605 Third Ave, New York, NY 10158. TEL 212-850-6645. FAX 212-850-6021) Ed. K.H. Bennett, N. Chapin; Pub. Rosie Altoft. adv.: B&W page £595, color £1495; trim 260 x 200; adv. contact: Bob Kern. circ. 400. (also avail. in microform from UMI; back issues avail.; reprint service avail. from SWZ) **Indexed:** ASCA, Compumath, Comput.Abstr., INSPEC (1989-). **Document type:** academic/scholarly publication.
—BLDSC (5064.938000); AskIEEE; CISTI; Ei; Genuine Article; KR SourceOne; SWETS; UMI. **CCC.**
    Description: Devoted to sustaining the viability of software and conveys the results of academic research and practical experience into the computing community.
    Refereed Serial

005   UK   ISSN 0960-0833
    CODEN: JTREET
JOURNAL OF SOFTWARE TESTING, VERIFICATION AND RELIABILITY. 1991. q. $345 (foreign $345) (effective 1998). John Wiley & Sons Ltd., Journals, Baffins Ln., Chichester, W. Sussex PO19 1UD, England. TEL 44-1243-779777. FAX 44-1243-843232. E-mail: cs-journals@wiley.co.uk; URL: http://www.wiley.co.uk. (Subscr. in the Americas to: John Wiley & Sons, Inc., 605 Third Ave., New York, NY 10158. TEL 212-850-6645. FAX 212-850-6021) Ed. M. Woodward; Pub. Rosie Altoft. adv.: B&W page £590, color page £1495; 230 x 170; adv. contact: Bob Kern. bk.rev. circ. 420. (also avail. in microform from UMI; back issues avail.) **Indexed:** INSPEC (1992-). **Document type:** academic/scholarly publication.
—BLDSC (8321.457500); AskIEEE; CISTI; Ei; KR SourceOne; SWETS; UMI. **CCC.**
    Description: Provides information on research and experience for those who wish to measure the progress in the important fields of software testing and reliability.
    Refereed Serial

005.4   US   ISSN 0164-1212
QA76.5   CODEN: JSSODM
JOURNAL OF SYSTEMS AND SOFTWARE. 1979. m. fl.1650($948) (effective 1998). Elsevier Science Inc., Box 945, New York, NY 10159-0945. TEL 212-633-3730. FAX 212-633-3680. TELEX 420643 AEP UI. E-mail: usinfo-f@elsevier.com; URL: http://www.elsevier.nl/. (Subscr. outside the Americas to: Elsevier Science, Regional Sales Office, P.O. Box 211, 1000 AE Amsterdam, Netherlands. TEL 31-20-4853757. FAX 31-20-4853432; Subscr. in Australasia and the Far East to: Elsevier Science (Singapore) Pte Ltd, No.1 Temasek Ave., No.17-01 Millenia Tower, Singapore 039192, Singapore. TEL 65-434-3727. FAX 65-337-2230; Subscr. in Japan to: Elsevier Science Japan, 9-15 Higashi-Azabu 1-chome, Minato-ku, Tokyo 106, Japan. TEL 81-3-5561-5033. FAX 81-3-5561-5047) Ed. Robert Glass. (also avail. in microform from UMI; reprint service avail. from SWZ) **Indexed:** ABI Inform., ASCA, Compumath, Comput.Abstr., Comput.Cont., Comput.Dtbs., Comput.Lit.Ind., Comput.Rev., Curr.Cont., Cyb.Abstr., Eng.Ind., INSPEC, Intl.Civil Eng.Abstr., Math.R., Soft.Abstr.Eng. **Document type:** academic/scholarly publication.
—BLDSC (5068.065000); AskIEEE; CISTI; Ei; Genuine Article; KR SourceOne; Linda Hall; SWETS; UMI; UnCover. **CCC.**
    Description: Covers all aspects of programming methodology, software engineering and related hardware topics.
    Refereed Serial

KEY ABSTRACTS - SOFTWARE ENGINEERING. see COMPUTERS — Abstracting, Bibliographies, Statistics

005.302   UK
KEY NOTE MARKET REPORT: COMPUTER SOFTWARE. 1993. irreg. £185. Key Note Ltd., Field House, 72 Oldfield Rd., Hampton, Middlesex TW12 2HQ, England. TEL 44-181-783-0755. FAX 44-181-783-1940. Ed. Samantha Miller. **Document type:** trade publication.
●Also available online.
Also available on CD-ROM.
    Formerly: Key Note Report: Computer Software (ISSN 1352-6936)

KEY NOTE REPORT: HOME COMPUTERS - SOFTWARE. see COMPUTERS — Personal Computers

005.3   US   ISSN 0197-7342
HA32
KEYWORDS (CHICAGO); for users of S P S S software products. 1974. q. free. S P S S Inc., 444 N. Michigan Ave., Chicago, IL 60611. TEL 312-329-2400. FAX 312-329-3668. Ed. Davi Pittman. circ. 25,000.
    Description: For SPSS software users. Articles mainly cover specific applications. Regular columns contain questions-and-answers and new product announcements.

005.3 621.39   NE
▼**THE KLUWER INTERNATIONAL SERIES IN SOFTWARE ENGINEERING.** (Text in English) 1996. irreg. price varies. Kluwer Academic Publishers, Postbus 17, 3300 AA Dordrecht, Netherlands. TEL 31-78-6392392. FAX 31-78-6392254. E-ma services@wkap.nl; URL: http://www.wkap.nl. (Dist. by: Kluwer Academic Publishers Group, P.O. Box 322, 3300 AH Dordrecht, Netherlands. TEL 31-78-6392392. FAX 31-78-6546474; N. America dist. addr.: Box 358, Accord Sta., Hingham MA 02018-0358. TEL 617-871-6600. FAX 617-871-6528) Ed. Victor R. Basili. **Document type** monographic series.
    Description: Publishes important research and applications in the field of software engineering.
    Refereed Serial

COMPUTERS — SOFTWARE

005.3 US ISSN 1068-3062
QA76.758 CODEN: PKECFU
KNOWLEDGE-BASED SOFTWARE ENGINEERING CONFERENCE. PROCEEDINGS. Short title: K B S E. 1986. a. price varies. (Institute of Electrical and Electronics Engineers, Inc.) I E E E Computer Society Press, 10662 Los Vaqueros Circle, Los Alamitos, CA 90720-1264. TEL 714-821-8380. FAX 714-821-4641. Ed. Cat Harris; Pub. Matt Loeb. adv. contact: Frieda Koester. **Document type:** proceedings.
—Ei. CCC.
 Description: Examines the role of AI and new techniques for improving the productivity of software processes.

KOMPASS INFORMATION TECHNOLOGY. see COMPUTERS — Electronic Data Processing

001.642 FR ISSN 1154-4724
LETTRE D'EXCEL. (Each issue includes diskette) 1990. bi-m. 990 F. (effective 1997). Editions M E V, 12 rue d'Anjou, 78000 Versailles, France. TEL 33-1-39512443. FAX 33-1-39495465. Ed. Herve Thiriez. illus. (looseleaf format)

001.642 FR ISSN 1167-654X
LETTRE DE WINDOWS. (Each issue includes diskette) 1992. bi-m. 1485 F. (effective 1997). Editions M E V, 12 rue d'Anjou, 78000 Versailles, France. TEL 33-1-39512443. FAX 33-1-39495465. Ed. Alain Pinaud. illus. (looseleaf format)

001.642 FR ISSN 1156-6477
LETTRE DE WORD. (Each issue includes diskette) 1991. bi-m. 990 F. (effective 1997). Editions M E V, 12 rue d'Anjou, 78000 Versailles, France. TEL 33-1-39512443. FAX 33-1-39495465. Ed. Pierre Brandeis. illus. (looseleaf format)

001.642 US
QA76.6
LIBRARY OF PROGRAMMERS AND DEVELOPERS TOOLS. 1983. a. $275. Applied Computer Research, Inc., Box 82266, Phoenix, AZ 85071-2266. TEL 800-234-2227.
—CCC.
 Formerly: Guide to Software Productivity Aids (ISSN 0740-8374)
 Description: Lists commercial software packages that improve productivity of systems development.

005.3 025.04 370 US ISSN 0742-5759
QA76.6 CODEN: LSREEA
LIBRARY SOFTWARE REVIEW. 1981. q. $170 to institutions (effective Sep. 1996). Sage Publications, Inc., 2455 Teller Rd., Thousand Oaks, CA 91320. TEL 805-499-0721. FAX 805-499-0871. E-mail: libraries@sagepub.com; URL: http://www.sagepub.com. (Overseas subscr. to: Sage Publications Ltd., 6 Bonhill St., London EC2A 4PU, England; Sage Publications India Pvt. Ltd., P.O. Box 4315, New Delhi 110 048, India) Ed. Marshall Breeding. adv. contact: Margaret Travers. bk.rev. circ. 1,850. (back issues avail.; reprint service avail.) **Indexed:** ASCA, C.I.J.E., Compumath, Comput.Cont., Comput.Lit.Ind., INSPEC, Leg.Info.Manage.Ind., Lib.Lit., LISA, Mgmt.& Market.Abstr., Microcomp.Ind., Soft.Abstr.Eng., SSCI, Tr.& Indus.Ind.
●Also available online. Vendor(s): Information Access Co.
—BLDSC (5205.488800); AskIEEE; CISTI; Ei; Genuine Article; KR SourceOne; Linda Hall; SWETS; UMI; UnCover. CCC.
 Formerly (until 1984): Software Review (Westport) (ISSN 0278-2634)
 Description: For libraries and educators. Covers the topics of software evaluation, procurement, applications and installation decisions.

LITIGATION APPLICATIONS. see LAW — Computer Applications

005.3 004.16 US
LOADSTAR QUARTERLY. q. $39.95. Softdisk, Inc., Box 30008, Shreveport, LA 71130-0008. TEL 318-221-8718. (diskette format)
 Description: For owners of Commodore Loadstar 128 computers.

005.3 US
▼**LOCKERGNOME'S FREE WINDOWS 95 - N T E-ZINE.** 1996. w. free. Box 63, Hudson, IA 50643. E-mail: chris@lockergnome.com; URL: http://www.lockergnome.com/. Ed. Christopher Pirillo. **Document type:** newsletter.
●Available only online.
 Description: For Windows 95/NT users, with information about software, web sites, themes, fonts, updates and patches, tips and tricks, news and more.

005.3 CN ISSN 0836-6853
LOGIBASE; repertoire des logiciels quebecois. (Text in French) 1985. a. Can.$25. Services Documentaires Multimedia Inc., 75 Port-Royal E., bureau 300, Montreal, PQ H3L 3T1, Canada. TEL 514-382-0895. FAX 514-384-9139. E-mail: info@sdm.qc.ca; URL: http://www.sdm.qc.ca. adv. circ. 700. (back issues avail.) **Document type:** directory.
●Also available online.
 Description: Directory of software developed in Quebec or available in French, for all computer systems and-or applications: 3600 detailed descriptions from 750 software firms, with complete Canadian addresses.

001.642 FR ISSN 0996-8490
LOGICIELS & BUSINESS. 6/yr. Publinews, 3 av. Gallieni, 92000 Nanterre, France. TEL 47-29-88-11. FAX 47-29-88-18. Ed. Ange Galula. circ. 20,000.

005.3 US
 CODEN: LNADFO
▼**LOTUS NOTES & DOMINO ADVISOR.** 1995. bi-m. $39 (Canada $49; elsewhere $59). Advisor Publications Inc., 5675 Ruffin Rd., Ste. 200, San Diego, CA 92123. TEL 619-278-5400. FAX 619-278-0300. E-mail: subscribe@advisor.com; URL: http://www.advisor.com/. (Dist. by: International Periodical Distributors, 674 Via de la Valle, Ste. 204, Solana Beach, CA 92075) Ed. John L. Hawkins; Pub. William T. Ota. adv. contact: B.J. Ghiglione. **Document type:** trade publication.
—KR SourceOne.
 Formerly: Lotus Notes Advisor (ISSN 1079-235X)
 Description: Technical publication that explains how to take advantage of the power of Lotus Notes and Domino. For developers and power users who are customizing Lotus Notes to serve their organizations.

005.302 IT
M C - MICROCOMPUTER SOFTWARE. 1990. m. (11/yr.). L.35000 per no. (effective 1996). Technimedia s.r.l., Via Carlo Perriuer 9, 00157 Rome, Italy. TEL 396-418921. FAX 396-41732169. Ed. Marco Marinacci. adv. circ. 15,000. (back issues avail.)

001.642 US
M I C - TECH-UNIX. 1989. m. $877. Management Information Corporation, 1111 Marlkress Rd., Box 5062, Cherry Hill, NJ 08003-5602. TEL 609-424-1100. FAX 609-424-1999. Ed. Mark Kostre. (diskette format)
 Description: Electronic UNIX product reference. Provides specifications and pricing of UNIX system software.

005.3 628 US ISSN 1074-1984
▼**M S D S SOFTWARE REPORT.** (Materials Safety Data Sheets) 1997. s-a. $239. Donley Technology, Box 152, Colonial Beach, VA 22443. TEL 804-224-9427; 800-201-1595. FAX 804-224-7958. E-mail: donleytech@donleytech.com. Eds. Elizabeth Donley, John Donley.
 Description: Describes and compares 64 software systems for managing and creating material safety data sheets. Includes 18 tables comparing systems' features.

MAC DISKWORLD. see COMPUTERS — Personal Computers

MAC POWER. see COMPUTERS — Personal Computers

001.642 US ISSN 1063-2700
MACAUTHORITY SOFTWARE CONNECTION. 1992. m. $59 (foreign $79). Cobb Group, Inc., 9420 Bunsen Pkwy., Ste. 300, Louisville, KY 40220. TEL 502-493-3200. FAX 502-491-8050. (Subscr. to: Box 35160, Louisville, KY 40232-9720. TEL 800-223-8720) (diskette format) **Document type:** consumer publication.

005.3 US
THE MAGIC CARPET BAG. 1994. bi-m. $24.95; newsstand price: $6. Cobb Group, Inc., 9420 Bunsen Pkwy., Ste. 300, Louisville, KY 40220. TEL 502-493-3200. FAX 502-491-8050. Ed. Clyde Zeller; Pubs. Mark Crane, Jon Pyles. **Document type:** consumer publication.
 Description: Provides information on Microsoft's Creative Writer and Fine Artist software packages for children ages 8 to 14.

005.13 US ISSN 0891-7973
MAPICS THE MAGAZINE. 1986. 9/yr. $95 ($160 to Canada & Central America; Europe $175; elsewhere $208) (effective 1995). Phoenix Publishing, Inc., 1855 McFarland-400 Dr., Alpharetta, GA 30201. TEL 770-442-1211. FAX 770-442-5046. Ed. Anna Jones. R&P contact: Anna Jones. adv. contact: Janet Creel. software rev. circ. 5,300. **Document type:** trade publication.
 Description: Targets manufacturing industry personnel who use and manage Marcam's MAPICS software.

005.3 US
QA155.7.E4
MAPLE TECH. 1987. a. (3 nos./vol) $71 (foreign SFr.89). (Waterloo Maple Software) Birkhaeuser, 675 Massachusetts Ave., Cambridge, MA 02139-3309. TEL 800-777-4643. FAX 210-348-4505. Ed. Tony Scott. **Document type:** academic/scholarly publication.
—Genuine Article; UMI.
 Former titles: Maple Tech: The Maple Technical Newsletter (ISSN 1061-5733); (until 1991) Maple Newsletter (ISSN 1074-3790)

MATHEMATICA IN EDUCATION AND RESEARCH. see MATHEMATICS

MERRILL'S EDGAR ADVISOR; a publication for participants in the EDGAR and SEDAR systems for securities reporting. see COMPUTERS — Computer Systems

005.13 658.8 US ISSN 0738-6354
MICRO SOFTWARE MARKETING. 1982. m. $147 (foreign $157) (effective 1997). Box 380, Congers, NY 10920. TEL 914-268-5925. Ed. Scott Witt; Pub. Scott Witt. bk.rev. **Indexed:** Comput.Indus.Up. **Document type:** newsletter.
 Description: For marketing directors involved with the marketing of software for microcomputers. Features articles on telemarketing, promotions, marketing services and related news briefs.

MICRO SYSTEMES. see COMPUTERS — Microcomputers

MICROCOMPUTER JOURNAL; the magazine for computer enthusiasts. see COMPUTERS — Hardware

MICROCOMPUTERS IN CIVIL ENGINEERING. see ENGINEERING — Computer Applications

MICROLEADS RESELLER DIRECTORY ON DISK. see COMPUTERS — Computer Industry Directories

MICROLEADS VENDOR DIRECTORY. see COMPUTERS — Computer Industry Directories

MICROSOFT C - C PLUS PLUS DEVELOPER'S JOURNAL. see COMPUTERS — Computer Programming

MICROSOFT SYSTEMS JOURNAL. see COMPUTERS — Computer Programming

MICROSOFT SYSTEMS JOURNAL (JAPANESE EDITION). see COMPUTERS — Computer Programming

MOODY'S COMPANY DATA. see BUSINESS AND ECONOMICS — Computer Applications

001.642 CN
MUGSHOTS; the Medianet Users Group newsletter. q. Dymaxion Research Ltd., 5515 Cogswell St., Halifax, NS B3J 1R2, Canada. TEL 902-429-1973. FAX 902-421-1267. E-mail: medianet@dymaxion.com; URL: http://www.dymaxion.com/medianet. R&P contact: Peter Mason. (looseleaf format) **Document type:** newsletter.

COMPUTERS — SOFTWARE

005.3 004.16   GR
▼ **MULTIMEDIA & C D - R O M**. (Includes CD-ROM) (Text in Greek) 1995. m. Dr.26000 in Europe; Dr.2800 in U.S. (effective 1996) (includes CD). Compupress S.A., 44 Syngrou, 117 42 Athens, Greece. TEL 30-1-9238-672. FAX 30-1-9216-847. Ed. John Patrikos; Pub. N.O. Manousos. adv. contact: V. Giakamozis. software rev.; circ. 16,000 (paid). **Document type:** consumer publication.
Description: Covers multimedia technology.

004.16 005.36   US   ISSN 1051-953X
MULTIMEDIA COMPUTING & PRESENTATIONS.* 1988. bi-m. $449 (foreign $499). Multimedia Computing Corporation, P.O. Box 60369, Sunnyvale, CA 94088-0369. TEL 408-737-7575. FAX 408-739-8019. Ed. Nick Arnett. bk.rev.
●Also available online.
Also available on CD-ROM.
—CCC.
Description: For high level executives who make decisions about emerging multimedia technologies. Covers the opportunities and challenges these new technologies present in communications, entertainment, publishing, advertising, education, and other areas.

005.3   US   ISSN 1085-1453
THE MULTIMEDIA DIRECTORY;* software producers, publishers & tele-media firms. 1994. s-a. Carronade Group, 7840 E. Ring St., Long Beach, CA 90808-3137. TEL 213-935-7600. FAX 213-939-6705. Eds. Jon Samsel, Clancy Fort. **Document type:** directory.

005.3 004.6   NE   ISSN 1380-7501
▼ **MULTIMEDIA TOOLS AND APPLICATIONS;** an international journal. (Text in English) 1995. bi-m. fl.980 to institutions; $503 to institutions in U.S. (effective 1998). Kluwer Academic Publishers, Postbus 17, 3300 AA Dordrecht, Netherlands. TEL 31-78-6392392. FAX 31-78-6392254. E-mail: services@wkap.nl; URL: http://www.wkap.nl. (Dist. by: Kluwer Academic Publishers Group, P.O. Box 322, 3300 AH Dordrecht, Netherlands. TEL 31-78-6392392. FAX 31-78-6546474; N. America dist. addr.: Box 358, Accord Sta., Hingham, MA 02018-0358. TEL 617-871-6600. FAX 617-871-6528) Ed. Borko Furht. **Document type:** academic/scholarly publication.
—BLDSC (5983.148820); AskIEEE; CISTI; Genuine Article; KR SourceOne; SWETS. **CCC.**
Description: Publishes original research articles on multimedia development and performance measurement tools, user interfaces, and case studies of multimedia applications.
Refereed Serial

NATIONAL COMPUTER SECURITY ASSOCIATION. NEWSLETTER. see *COMPUTERS — Computer Security*

NEW GENERATION COMPUTING; an international journal. see *COMPUTERS — Microcomputers*

001.642   CN   ISSN 1201-1916
NEW MEDIA CANADA; CD-ROM and multimedia for schools, libraries and information centres. 1985. bi-m. Can.$45($45) (overseas $60). (University of Western Ontario, School of Library and Information Science) Pelican Island, Box 24004, London, ON N6H 2J3. TEL 519-679-9107. FAX 519-697-9107. E-mail: 71722,2122@ compuserve.com. Ed. Paul Nicholls; Pub. Paul Nicholls. adv.: B&W page Can.$400. bk.rev.; circ. 500 (paid). **Document type:** newsletter.
Supersedes (in 1995): Canadian C D - R O M News (ISSN 0848-8649); Which was formerly (until 1989): Canadian C D - R O M Newsletter (ISSN 0832-5979); (until 1987): Canadian Libraries C D - R O M Interest Group Newsletter (ISSN 0832-5987)
Description: Provides articles and up-to-date information on CD-ROM titles and software, the CD-ROM industry and other news concerning CD-ROMs.

NIKKEI CLICK. see *COMPUTERS — Personal Computers*

005.3   JA
▼ **NIKKEI WINDOWS N T**. (Text in Japanese) 1997. m. 12000 Yen; newsstand price: 1100 Yen. Nikkei Business Publications, Inc. (Subsidiary of: Nihon Keizai Shimbun, Inc.), 2-7-6, Hirakawacho, Chiyoda-ku, Tokyo 102, Japan. TEL 81-3-5210-8560. FAX 81-3-5210-8119. URL: http://www.nikkeibp.co.jp. Ed. Makoto Kawakami; Pub. Koichi Shiraishi. adv.: B&W page 320000 Yen, color page 550000 Yen; adv. contact: Shun'ichi Ono. **Document type:** trade publication.
Description: Covers the latest Windows NT products; explains the usage of Windows NT.

005.3   GW   ISSN 1431-1798
▼ **NOTES MAGAZIN**. 1996. bi-m. DM.62 (effective 1997). I W T Magazin Verlags GmbH, Bahnhofstr. 36, 85591 Vaterstetten, Germany. TEL 49-8106-350-0. FAX 49-8106-350126. URL: http://www.iwtnet.de. Ed. Peter von Bechen. circ. 31,000 (paid). **Document type:** trade publication.
Description: For existing and potential Lotus Notes users.

005.3   CN   ISSN 1203-5696
▼ **O S - 2 E - ZINE!**. 1995. m. Haligonian Media, 26 Victoria Rd., Dartmouth, NS B2Y 2V9, Canada. E-mail: editor@haligonian.com; URL: http://www.haligonian.com/os2/. Ed. Trevor Smith.
●Available only online.
Description: Contains news, reviews, tips and interviews for novice and experienced OS-2 users.

005.3   US
▼ **O S - 2 SOFTWARE CONNECTION**. m. $59 (foreign $79). Cobb Group, Inc., 9420 Bunsen Pkwy., Ste. 300, Louisville, KY 40220. TEL 502-493-3200. FAX 502-491-8050. (Subscr. to: Box 35160, Louisville, KY 40232-9720. TEL 800-223-8720) (diskette format) **Document type:** consumer publication.

005.3   GW   ISSN 0949-3328
▼ **O S - 2 SOFTWAREFUEHRER**. 1995. irreg. DM.49.80. Rossipaul Medien GmbH, Menzingerstr. 37, 80638 Munich, Germany. TEL 49-89-179106-0. FAX 49-89-17910622. Ed. Rainer Rossipaul. adv. contact: Ulrike Mauksch. circ. 20,000. **Document type:** directory.

005.3   GW   ISSN 0941-1968
OFFENE SYSTEME; Zeitschrift deutschsprachiger UNIX-Benutzer-Vereinigungen. 1992. q. DM.353.60 (foreign DM.357.20) (effective 1998). Springer-Verlag, Heidelberger Platz 3, 14197 Berlin, Germany. TEL 49-30-82787-0. FAX 49-30-82787448. E-mail: subscriptions@springer.de. (Subscr. in N. America to: Journal Fulfillment Services, Meadowlands Pkwy., Secaucus, NJ 07094. TEL 212-460-1500. FAX 212-473-6272) Pub. B. Stork. (also avail. in microform from UMI; reprint service avail.) **Document type:** academic/scholarly publication.
—UMI. **CCC.**
Description: Covers both the technical and applications-oriented aspects of the development of UNIX-based open systems.
Refereed Serial

005.3 004.16   US
ON DISK MONTHLY. 1986. m. $89.95. Softdisk, Inc., Box 30008, Shreveport, LA 71130-0008. TEL 318-221-8718. Ed. Daniel Tobias. circ. 20,000. (diskette format)
Formerly (until 1994): Big Blue Disk (ISSN 0893-2212)
Description: Software resources for owners of IBM PC and compatibles.

005.3 371.3   US   ISSN 1053-4326
ONLY THE BEST; the annual guide to the highest-rated educational software and multimedia. 1985. a. Association for Supervision and Curriculum Development, 1250 N. Pitt St., Alexandria, VA 22314-1453. TEL 703-549-9110; 800-933-2723. FAX 703-299-8631. E-mail: member@acsd.org; URL: http://www.ascd.org. (back issues avail.) **Document type:** academic/scholarly publication, consumer publication.
●Also available online.
Also available on CD-ROM.
Description: Identifies and rates educational software and multimedia programs.

005.3   US   ISSN 1080-0654
▼ **ORACLE INFORMANT**; the independent monthly guide to Oracle development. 1996. m. $49.95. Informant Communications Group, Inc., 10519 E. Stockton Blvd., Ste. 100, Elk Grove, CA 95624-9703. TEL 916-686-6610. FAX 916-686-8497. E-mail: circulation@informant.com. Ed. Jerry Coffey. adv.: page $2000; trim 8 x 10 3/4; adv. contact: Lynn Beaudoin. bk.rev.; software rev.; circ. 15,000 (paid). (back issues avail.) **Document type:** trade publication.
●Also available on CD-ROM.
Description: Covers technical issues facing the Oracle developer.

P C MAGAZINE. see *COMPUTERS — Personal Computers*

001.642 621.381   US   ISSN 1052-357X
P.C. REVIEW;* evaluations of new personal computer products. m. $195. Amanda C. Hixson, Ed. & Pub., 18870 Pendergast Ave., Cupertino, CA 95014. (Subscr. addr.: 50 West Palm St., Altadena, CA 91001. TEL 818-797-8452)

001.642   FR
P C T E NEWSLETTER. 1989. q. E C 2, 269, rue de la Garenne, 92024 Nanterre Cedex, France. TEL 33-1-47-80-70-00. FAX 33-1-47-80-66-29. Ed. Ian Campbell. (back issues avail.) **Document type:** newsletter.

005.3   GW
P C WINDOWS. m. DM.67.20 (foreign DM.91.20). Markt und Technik Verlag AG, Hans-Pinsel-Str. 2, 85540 Haar, Germany. TEL 089-4613-0. FAX 089-4613100. Ed. Albert Absmeier. adv. contact: Philipp Schiede. circ. 150,000. **Document type:** consumer publication.

005.3 004.16   IT
P C WINDOWS. 1991. m. L.120000. G R Edizioni s.r.l., Viale Espinasse 93, 20156 Milan, Italy. TEL 39-2-38010030. FAX 39-2-38010028. Ed. Gianluigi Zanfrognini. adv.: B&W page L.3400000, color page L.5200000. **Document type:** consumer publication.

005.3   SA
P C WORLD. (Personal Computer) (Text in English) 1994. m. R.72 (foreign R.160.24) (effective 1997. T M L Trade Publishing (Subsidiary of: Times Media Ltd.), P.O. Box 182, Pinegowrie 2123, South Africa TEL 27-11-789-2144. FAX 27-11-789-3196. adv. illus. **Document type:** trade publication.
Formerly: Software World (ISSN 1023-0661)

P M S TODAY. (Policy Management Systems Corp.) see *BUSINESS AND ECONOMICS — Computer Applications*

005.302   US   ISSN 1058-7071
PARADOX INFORMANT;* the complete monthly guide to Paradox for DOS and Windows. 1990. m. $49.95 (Canada $54.95; Mexico $74.95; elsewhere $119.95) (effective Feb. 1991). Informant Communications Group, 10519 E. Stockton Blvd., Ste. 100, Elk Grove, CA 95624-9703. TEL 916-686-6610. FAX 916-686-8497. E-mail: 70304,3633@compuserve.com. Ed. Jerry Coffey; Pub. Mitchell Koulouris. adv.: B&W page $2165, color page $2565; trim 8 3/8 x 10 7/8; adv. contact: Lynn Beaudoin. bk.rev. circ. 18,000. **Document type:** trade publication.
—KR SourceOne.
Description: Contains articles with information on Paradox-related news, product, reviews, ObjectPal and Pal Programming tips, techniques and insights into interactive Paradox, programming multi-user applications, Client-Server application development.

PENNSYLVANIA BUSINESS AND TECHNOLOGY. see *TECHNOLOGY: COMPREHENSIVE WORKS*

PERSONAL COMPUTER MAGAZINE; het computerblad voor Nederland en Belgie. see *COMPUTERS — Personal Computers*

001.642   US   ISSN 0743-6750
TN860
PETROLEUM SOFTWARE DIRECTORY. 1984. a. $165. PennWell Publishing Co., Box 1260, Tulsa, OK 74101. TEL 918-835-3161. Ed. Jonelle Moore. adv. circ. 1,000.
—BLDSC (6435.717000). **CCC.**

PICK RESOURCES GUIDE - INTERNATIONAL. see *COMPUTERS*

COMPUTERS — SOFTWARE   2217

POCKET & LAPTOP COMPUTER; Zeitschrift fuer mobile Datensysteme. see *COMPUTERS — Microcomputers*

005.3   US   ISSN 1078-1889
POWERBUILDER DEVELOPER'S JOURNAL. m. $119 (Canada and Mexico $139; elsewhere $167); newsstand price: $12. Sys-Con Publications, Inc., 39 E. Central Ave., Pearl River, NY 10965. TEL 914-735-1900. FAX 914-735-3922. E-mail: subscribe@sys-con.com; URL: http://www.sys-con.com. Ed. Michael Griffith; Pub. Fuat A. Kircaali. R&P contact: Mary Ann MacBride. adv. contact: Diane Baird. software rev.; illus. (back issues avail.) **Document type:** trade publication.

PRE-K TODAY. see *EDUCATION*

005.302 658   UK   ISSN 1354-2109
THE PRICE WATERHOUSE SALES AND MARKETING SOFTWARE HANDBOOK (YEAR). 1991. a. Pitman Publishing, 128 Long Acre, London WC2E 9AN, England. TEL 44-171-447-2000. FAX 44-171-240-5771. Eds. Debbie Gorski, Jonathan Ingram. **Document type:** directory.

001.642   US
PRODUCTIVITY SOFTWARE. 1988. m. $150 (outside N. America $165). Worldwide Videotex, Box 3273, Boynton Beach, FL 33424-3273. TEL 407-738-2276. Ed. Mark Wright; Pub. Mark Wright. bk.rev. (back issues avail.) **Document type:** newsletter.
●Also available online. Vendor(s): Data-Star, Information Access Co., Knight-Ridder Information, Inc., NewsNet (EC80).
  Description: Provides information and news on the latest business software products for microcomputers, minicomputers, and mainframes to increase productivity and cost-effectiveness. Covers the vendors who develop and market the programs and the end user.

PROGRAMMING AND COMPUTER SOFTWARE. see *COMPUTERS — Computer Programming*

001.642   JA   ISSN 0910-7223
PROMPT. (Text in Japanese) 1985. m. Nikkan Kogyo Shinbunsha, 8-10, Kudan Kita, 1-chome, Chiyoda-ku, Tokyo 102, Japan. TEL 03-263-2311. FAX 03-262-4603. TELEX NIKKANKO J29687. Ed. Norio Shishido. circ. 50,000.
  Description: For personal computers users.

QUANTUM P C REPORT FOR C P AS. see *BUSINESS AND ECONOMICS — Accounting*

RECALL SOFTWARE GUIDE (YEAR). see *LINGUISTICS — Computer Applications*

REQUIREMENTS ENGINEERING. see *ENGINEERING — Computer Applications*

REVISTA CANARIA DE ESTUDIOS INGLESES. see *LINGUISTICS*

005.3   BL   ISSN 0104-8732
▼**REVISTA DO C D - R O M;** informatica pratica e descomplicada. 1995. m. $110 includes a CD-ROM (effective 1997). Editora Europa Ltda., Rua M.M.D.C., 12115, 05510-021 Sao Paulo SP, Brazil. TEL 55-11-8166767. FAX 55-11-8678583. E-mail: revista.cd-rom@sti.com.br. Ed. Aydano Roriz. adv.: B&W page $7398, color page $10200; trim 205 x 275; adv. contact: Givaldo Fernandez. circ. 98,000 (paid).
  Description: For people who do not want to read complicated computer book guides. Covers games, computing tips, new computing programs, service features for PC users, and the latest software and hardware.

001.642   CC   ISSN 1003-6970
RUANJIAN/SOFTWARE. (Text in Chinese) m. Tianjin Dianzi Xuehui - Tianjin Electronics Society, 151 Jiefang Beilu, Tianjin 300040, People's Republic of China. TEL 86-22-3112605. FAX 86-22-3112605. E-mail: swjour@public.tpt.tj.cn; URL: http://www.softmag.com. Ed. Zhang Shangren.

005.3   CC   ISSN 1005-2348
RUANJIAN SHIJIE/SOFTWARE WORLD. (Text in Chinese) 1993. m. Software World Magazine Agency, P.O. Box 162, Beijing, People's Republic of China. TEL 86-10-821-2233. FAX 86-10-821-1386. circ. 50,000.

001.642   CC
RUANJIAN XUEBAO/JOURNAL OF SOFTWARE. (Text in Chinese; summaries in English) 1990. q. Y9 (effective 1998). Ruanjian Xuebao Bianjibu, P.O. Box 8718, Beijing 100080, People's Republic of China. TEL 86-10-6256-2563. FAX 86-10-6256-3916. E-mail: xuebao@ns.ict.ac.cn. (Dist. overseas by: P.O. Box 399, Beijing 100044, P.R. China) Ed. Yulan Ju. adv. circ. 3,000.
  Description: Covers research in both theoretical and applied aspects of computer science and software techniques.
  Refereed Serial

005.3   US
THE S T LABS REPORT. bi-m. S T Labs, Inc., Sterling Plaza, 3rd Fl., 3535 128th Ave., S.E., Bellevue, WA 98006. E-mail: pruec@stlabs.com. **Document type:** trade publication.

001.642   CN
SASKATCHEWAN SOFTWARE DIRECTORY. 1988. a. free. Saskatchewan Economic Development, 206-15 Innovation Blvd., Saskatoon, SK S7N 2X8, Canada. TEL 306-933-7200. FAX 306-933-8244. (back issues avail.)
  Description: Provides an inventory of products, services and capabilities of the Software Developers of Saskatchewan.

005.1 620   US   ISSN 1058-9244
QA76.6   CODEN: SCIPEV
SCIENTIFIC PROGRAMMING: TOOLS & TECHNIQUES. 1992. q. $196 (Canada & Mexico $236; elsewhere $262) (effective 1997). John Wiley & Sons, Inc., Journals, 605 Third Ave., New York, NY 10158. TEL 212-850-6645. FAX 212-850-6021. TELEX 12-7063. URL: http://www.wiley.co.uk. (Subscr. outside the Americas to: John Wiley & Sons Ltd., Baffins Ln., Chichester, W. Sussex PO19 1UD, England. TEL 44-1243-779777. FAX 44-1243-776128) Eds. Robert Babb, Ron Perrot. adv.: B&W page £640, color page £1515; trim 279 x 210. circ. 550. (also avail. in microform from UMI; back issues avail.) **Document type:** academic/scholarly publication.
—BLDSC (8190.220000); AskIEEE; CISTI; Ei; KR SourceOne; UnCover. **CCC.**
  Description: Provides a meeting ground for research in, and practical experience with, software engineering environments, tools, languages, and models of computation aimed specifically at supporting scientific and engineering computing.
  Refereed Serial

005.13   US   ISSN 1066-7318
SCRIPT - CENTRAL.* 6/yr. $49.95. Resource Central, Inc., 7118 Main St., Kansas City, MO 64114-1406. Pub. Tom Weishaar. (diskette format)
  Description: Covers Apple's HyperCard IIgs and HyperTalk, its scripting language.

005.302   US
SEARCH SOFTWARE. 1991. biennial. $35. Information Sources Inc., 1173 Colusa Ave., Box 8120, Berkeley, CA 94707. TEL 510-525-6220. FAX 510-525-1568. Ed. Ruth K. Koolish; Pub. Ruth K. Koolish. R&P contact: Ruth K. Koolish. (looseleaf format) **Document type:** directory.

001.642 620   SI
SERIES ON SOFTWARE ENGINEERING & KNOWLEDGE ENGINEERING. (Text in English) irreg., vol.6, no.3, 1996. price varies. World Scientific Publishing Co. Pte. Ltd., Farrer Rd., P.O. Box 128, Singapore 9128, Singapore. TEL 65-3825663. FAX 65-3825919. TELEX RS 28561 WSPC. E-mail: wspcsl@singnet.com.sg; sales@wspc2.demon.co.uk; wspc@wspc.com; URL: http://www.singnet.com.sg/~wspclib/. (UK addr.: 57 Shelton St., Covent Garden, London WC2H 9HE, England. TEL 44-171-836-0888. FAX 44-171-836-2020; US addr.: 1060 Main St., River Edge, NJ 07661. TEL 800-227-7562. FAX 201-487-9656) Ed. S.K. Chang. **Document type:** monographic series.

005.3029   US
▼**SHAREPAPER.** 1996. d. E-mail: webmaster@sharepaper.com; URL: http://www.sharepaper.com. Ed. Lars Mathiassen. software rev.
●Available only online.
  Description: Contains reviews of low cost, high quality software, tips and related links.
  Refereed Serial

SMART CARD NEWS. see *COMPUTERS — Computer Industry*

001.642 658.8   US
SOFT AD.* (Software Advertiser) bi-m. $6.95. 1644 Massachusetts Ave., Lexington, MA 02173-5353.

004 621.381 070.5   US   ISSN 0882-3499
SOFT.LETTER; trends & strategies in software publishing. 1983. s-m. $345 (foreign $380) (effective 1997). Mercury Group, Inc., 17 Main St., Watertown, MA 02172-4491. TEL 617-924-3944. FAX 617-924-7288. Ed. Jeffrey Tarter. bk.rev.; index. circ. 1,500. (looseleaf format; back issues avail.) Indexed: Comput.Lit.Ind. **Document type:** newsletter.
●Also available online. Vendor(s): Information Access Co.
  Description: For managers of software companies. Covers news, trends and strategies in the software publishing field.

005.3 629.8   US   ISSN 1065-7290
SOFTAWARENESS; a CAD-CAM-CAE journal and buyer's guide. 1992. m. Ariel Communications, Inc., 12710 Research Blvd., Ste. 250, Austin, TX 78759. TEL 512-250-1700. FAX 512-250-1016. adv.: B&W page $1250, color page $2000; trim 5 1/4 x 6 7/8. circ. 20,000. **Document type:** trade publication.

005.3 004.16   US   ISSN 0886-4152
SOFTDISK; the monthly software collection for people who love their Apple II's. 1981. m. $89.95. Softdisk, Inc., Box 30008, Shreveport, LA 71130-0008. TEL 318-221-8718. Ed. James Weiler. circ. 20,000. (diskette format)

621.381 001.642   US
QA76.75
SOFTWARE & C D - R O M REVIEWS ON FILE. 1985. m. $249. Facts on File, Inc., 11 Penn Plaza, 15th Fl., New York, NY 10001. TEL 212-967-8800. cum.index. circ. 1,300. (looseleaf format) Indexed: Comput.Lit.Ind.
  Formerly: Software Reviews on File (ISSN 8755-7169)
  Description: For library, business, school or home use. Contains condensations of software reviews that appeared in any of over 150 publications. Features software for all major microcomputer systems and programming languages.

SOFTWARE AND NETWORKS FOR LEARNING. see *EDUCATION — Computer Applications*

SOFTWARE DEVELOPER'S MONTHLY. see *COMPUTERS — Computer Programming*

005.3   US   ISSN 1070-8588
QA76.76.D47
SOFTWARE DEVELOPMENT. 1993. m. $39 (Canada & Mexico $45; elsewhere $54) (effective 1996). Miller Freeman, Inc., 600 Harrison St., San Francisco, CA 94107. TEL 415-905-2200. FAX 415-905-2232. E-mail: 73611.633@compuserve.com; URL: http://www.sdmagazine.com/. (Subscr. to: Box 1126, Skokie, IL 60076-8126. TEL 800-250-2429. FAX 708-647-5972) Ed. Larry O'Brien. adv.: B&W page $5400. circ. 72,000. **Document type:** trade publication.
●Also available online.
—BLDSC (8321.450660); CISTI; KR SourceOne; SWETS; UMI. **CCC.**
  Description: Focuses on products to streamline the development process and increase productivity and practices for the corporate developer.

COMPUTERS — SOFTWARE

005.3   UK   ISSN 0964-6841
SOFTWARE DEVELOPMENT MONITOR. 1992. 12/yr. £495($738) (effective 1995). Elsevier Science Ltd., P.O. Box 800, Kidlington, Oxford OX5 1DX, England. TEL 44-1865-843000. FAX 44-1865-843010. E-mail: nlinfo-f@elsevier.nl; usinfo-f@elsevier.com; forinfo-kyf04035@niftyserve.or.jp; URL: http://www.elsevier.nl/. (Subscr. to: Elsevier Science, Regional Sales Office, P.O. Box 211, 1000 AE Amsterdam, Netherlands. TEL 31-20-4853757. FAX 31-20-4853432; Subscr. in the Americas to: Elsevier Science, Regional Sales Office, Box 945, New York, NY 10159-0945. TEL 212-633-3730. FAX 212-633-3680; Subscr. in Australasia and the Far East to: Elsevier Science (Singapore) Pte Ltd, No.1 Temasek Ave., No.17-01 Millenia Tower, Singapore 039192, Singapore. TEL 65-434-3727. FAX 65-337-2230) Ed. T. Monk. bk.rev.; software rev. (also avail. in microform from UMI; back issues avail.) Document type: academic/scholarly publication.
—CCC.
    Description: In-depth analysis of emerging technologies and market trends relevant to commercial software development.
    Refereed Serial

005   US
QA76.76.E93
SOFTWARE DIGEST; the independent, comparative ratings report for PC and LAN software. 1983. 12/yr. $450. National Software Testing Laboratories, Inc. (Subsidiary of: McGraw-Hill, Inc.), Plymouth Corporate Center, Box 1000, Plymouth Meeting, PA 19462. TEL 215-941-9600; 800-257-9402. FAX 215-941-9950. Pub. Linda DiBasio. cum.index.
—CCC.
    Former titles (until Mar. 1995): Software Digest Ratings Report (ISSN 0893-6455); Software Digest Ratings Newsletter (ISSN 0742-0676); Which supersedes in part: Software Digest.

001.642   US   ISSN 1052-3227
HD9696.C63
SOFTWARE DIRECTORY. INDUSTRY SPECIFIC APPLICATIONS.* 1990. 3/yr. International Computer Programs, Inc., 9 Shore Center, Carmel, IN 46033-3640. TEL 317-251-7727. FAX 317-251-7813. Document type: directory.
    Formerly: I C P Software Directory. Mainframe and Minicomputer Series. Industry Specific Applications (ISSN 1045-7518).

001.642   US   ISSN 1065-6146
       CODEN: SECLE3
SOFTWARE ECONOMICS LETTER; maximizing your return on corporate software. 1992. m. $395 (effective 1997). Computer Economics, Inc., 5841 Edison Pl., Carlsbad, CA 92008-6519. TEL 760-438-8100. FAX 760-431-1126. E-mail: swn@compecon.com; 72360.3303@compuserve.com; URL: http://www.computereconomics.com. Ed. Mark Mcmanus; Pub. Bruno Bassi. (back issues avail.) Indexed: INSPEC (1992-). Document type: newsletter.
—BLDSC (8321.451187); AskIEEE; KR SourceOne. CCC.
    Incorporates (in 1996): Client - Server Economics Letter (ISSN 1074-3138)
    Description: Provides the corporate and IS communities with a concise analysis of software issues and enables them to stay informed of the latest trends in software and software licensing.

005.36   US   ISSN 0000-006X
QA76.753
SOFTWARE ENCYCLOPEDIA; a guide for personal, professional, and business users. (Issued in 2 vols.) 1985. a. $255 for 1997-98 ed. R.R. Bowker, A Division of Reed Elsevier Inc., 121 Chanlon Rd., New Providence, NJ 07974. TEL 908-464-6800. FAX 908-665-3502. TELEX 138 755. E-mail: info@bowker.com; URL: http://www.reedref.com. (Subscr. to: Order Dept., Box 31, New Providence, NJ 07974-9903. TEL 800-521-8110) (also avail. in magnetic tape) Document type: bibliography, directory.
●Also available online. Vendor(s): Knight-Ridder Information, Inc. (File no.278).
—BLDSC (8321.451190); CISTI. CCC.
    Description: Provides annotated listings for microcomputer software, along with contact information. Indexed by title, compatible systems, and applications.

005.3   NE   ISSN 1386-369X
SOFTWARE ENGINEERING. (Text in English) 1973. irreg. Stichting Mathematisch Centrum, Centrum voor Wiskunde en Informatica, Department of Computer Science, P.O. Box 94079, 1090 GB Amsterdam, Netherlands. TEL 31-20-5924128. FAX 31-20-5924199. URL: http://www.cwi.nl. abstr. Document type: academic/scholarly publication.
—CISTI.
    Supersedes in part: Centrum voor Wiskunde en Informatica. Department of Computer Science. Report (ISSN 0169-118X); Which was formerly (until 1984): Stichting Mathematisch Centrum. Afdeling Informatica. Rapport (ISSN 0376-4028)

005.1   US   ISSN 0163-5948
QA76.758   CODEN: SFENDP
SOFTWARE ENGINEERING NOTES. q. $30. Association for Computing Machinery, Special Interest Group on Software Engineering (SIGSOFT), 1515 Broadway, 17th Fl., New York, NY 10036. TEL 212-869-7440. FAX 212-869-0481. TELEX 421686. Indexed: Abstr.Hum.Comp.Inter., Comput.Lit.Ind., INSPEC.
—BLDSC (8321.451500); AskIEEE; CISTI; Ei; KR SourceOne; SWETS; UnCover.

005.3 621.39   UK   ISSN 0965-6545
SOFTWARE FUTURES. 1991. m. £395 (N. America £495). A P T Data Group plc., 12 Sutton Row, 4th Fl., London W1V 5FH, England. TEL 44-171-528-7083. FAX 44-171-439-1105. E-mail: sfutures@power.globalnews.com. (US subscr. to: APT D Services Inc., 828 Broadway, Ste. 800, New York, NY 10010. TEL 212-677-0409. FAX 212-677-0463) Ed. Clare Haney; Pub. Dominic Sharp. circ. 2,000. (also avail. in diskette format; back issues avail.) Document type: newsletter.
●Also available online. Vendor(s): Information Access Co.
    Description: Enables software developers to keep abreast of all developments, from CASE to 4GLs to object orientation and software quality. Aimed at professional package authors and user-based development teams on diverse platforms.
    Refereed Serial

001.642   US   ISSN 0883-5772
       CODEN: SOIBE5
SOFTWARE INDUSTRY BULLETIN.* 1985. w. $395. Digital Information Group, Box 110235, Stamford, CT 06911-0235. TEL 203-348-2751. Ed. Jeff Silverstein. Document type: bulletin.
—CASDDS.
    Description: For managers and executives in the computer software industry field. Provides current information on the computer software industry. Features software news and analysis, proprietary statistics, financial statements, and information on new product releases.

001.642   US
SOFTWARE INDUSTRY BUSINESS PRACTICE SURVEY. a. $400. Information Technology Association of America, 1616 N. Fort Myer Dr., Ste. 1300, Arlington, VA 22209-9998. TEL 410-543-0475. FAX 410-543-2921.
    Description: Includes information about products, pricing, development and testing, types of support, methods of maintenance, marketing, strategic alliances, management, growth and finance.

001.642   US
SOFTWARE INDUSTRY FACTBOOK.* a. $395. Digital Information Group, Box 110235, Stamford, CT 06911-0235. TEL 203-348-2751. Pub. Jeff Silverstein.

005.3 338.4   US   ISSN 1042-7252
SOFTWARE INDUSTRY REPORT; a comprehensive information management analysis of the computer software industry. 1968. s-m. $495 (foreign $519). Computer Age & E D P News Services (Subsidiary of: Millin Publishing Group, Inc.), 714 Church St., Alexandria, VA 22314-4202. TEL 703-739-8500. FAX 703-739-8505. Ed. Michael E. Cotter; Pub. S.L. Millin. R&P contact: Michael E. Cotter. bk.rev. (back issues avail.) Indexed: Comput.Cont. Document type: newsletter.
●Also available online. Vendor(s): Information Access Co.
—CCC.
    Former titles: Computer Age - Software Digest; Software Digest (Annandale) (ISSN 0038-0636)
    Description: Tracks worldwide industry and government software activities and opportunities, with an emphasis on innovative strategies for MIS executives, market research and new developments in systems technology.

005.3   US   ISSN 0897-8085
QA76.75   CODEN: SMWMEQ
SOFTWARE MAGAZINE. 1981. m. $65 in U.S.; Canada $75; elsewhere $125 (free to qualified personnel). Sentry Publishing Company, Inc., 1 Research Dr., Ste. 400B, Westborough, MA 01581-3907. TEL 508-366-2031. FAX 508-836-4732. Ed. Mike Bucken; Pub. Donald Fagan. R&P contact: Barbara Gagne. adv. contact: Bill Orth. bk.rev.; circ. 91,000 (controlled). (also avail. in microform from UMI; reprint service avail. from UMI) Indexed: ABI Inform., Comput.Cont., Comput.Dtbs., Comput.Ind., Comput.Indus.Up., Comput.Lit.Ind., Microcomp.Ind., PCR2, PROMT. Document type: trade publication.
●Also available online. Vendor(s): Information Access Co., UMI.
—BLDSC (8321.451700); CISTI; Ei; KR SourceOne; SWETS; UMI; UnCover. CCC.
    Formerly (until 1987): Software News (Hudson) (ISSN 0279-9782)
    Description: For business and professional users. Feature articles offer information on software applications and industry developments. Also contains news briefs and new software package announcements for mainframe, mini and microcomputers.

005.1   UK   ISSN 0038-0644
QA76.5   CODEN: SPEXBL
SOFTWARE: PRACTICE & EXPERIENCE. 1971. 15/yr. $1545 (foreign $1545) (effective 1998). John Wiley & Sons Ltd., Journals, Baffins Ln., Chichester, W. Sussex PO19 1UD, England. TEL 44-1243-779777. FAX 44-1243-775878. E-mail: info-assets@wiley.co.uk; URL: http://www.wiley.co.uk. (Subscr. in the Americas to: John Wiley & Sons, Inc., 605 Third Ave., New York, NY 10158. TEL 212-850-6645. FAX 212-850-6021) Eds. A. Wellings, Douglas E. Comer; Pub. Rosie Altoft. adv.: B&W page £595, color page £1495; trim 260 x 200; adv. contact: Bob Kern. bk.rev.; illus.; index. circ. 1,784. (also avail. in microform from UMI; back issues avail.; reprint service avail. from ISI,SWZ,UMI) Indexed: A.S.& T.Ind., Abstr.Hum.Comp.Inter., ASCA, BMT, Compumath, Comput.Abstr., Comput.Cont., Comput.Lit.Ind., Curr.Cont., Cyb.Abstr., Educ.Tech.Abstr., Eng.Ind., INSPEC (1971-), Intl.Civil Eng.Abstr., J.of Ferroc., Soft.Abstr.Eng., Zent.Math. Document type: academic/scholarly publication.
—BLDSC (8321.453000); AskIEEE; CISTI; Ei; Genuine Article; KR SourceOne; SWETS; UMI. CCC.
    Description: Concerned with the details and experience of the tools or methods used to achieve the results for all those who design, implement, or maintain software.
    Refereed Serial

COMPUTERS — SOFTWARE

005.3　　　　　UK　　ISSN 1077-4866
QA76.75　　　　　　CODEN: SPIPFL
▼**SOFTWARE PROCESS IMPROVEMENT AND PRACTICE.** 1995. q. £225 (foreign £225) (effective 1998). John Wiley & Sons Ltd., Journals, Baffins Ln., Chichester, W. Sussex PO19 1UD, England. TEL 44-1243-779777. FAX 44-1243-775878. E-mail: info-assets@wiley.co.uk; URL: http://www.wiley.co.uk. (Subscr. in the Americas to: John Wiley & Sons., Inc., 605 Third Ave., New York, NY 10158. TEL 212-850-6645. FAX 212-850-6021) Eds. D.E. Perry, W. Schafer. adv.: B&W page £595, color page £1495; trim 297 x 210; adv. contact: Bob Kern. (also avail. in microform from UMI; back issues avail.) **Document type:** academic/scholarly publication.
—BLDSC (8321.453300); SWETS. **CCC.**
　Description: Aims to foster improvement in the quality, productivity, performance and assessment of the software development process.
　Refereed Serial

005.3 003　　　US　　ISSN 1068-400X
THE SOFTWARE QUALITY ADVISOR; the "how-to" newsletter of software quality assurance. 1991. q. $36 (effective 1996). Rice Consulting Services, Inc., Box 891284, Oklahoma City, OK 73189. TEL 504-692-7331. FAX 405-692-7570. E-mail: rcs@telepath.com; URL: http://www.telepath.com/rcs. Ed. Randall W. Rice; Pub. Randall W. Rice. R&P contact: Randall W. Rice. bk.rev.; software rev. circ. 500. (back issues avail.) **Document type:** newsletter.
　Description: Focuses on software testing and quality assurance. Aims to provide practical and proven methods for ensuring quality for software testers, QA analysts, developers, and end-users.

005.14　　　UK　　ISSN 0963-9314
QA76.76.Q35　　　　　CODEN: SQJOET
SOFTWARE QUALITY JOURNAL. 1992. q. £215 (E.U. £260; rest of world $435) for print and online eds. combined (effective 1998). Thomson Science (Subsidiary of: International Thomson Publishing Group), 2-6 Boundary Row, London SE1 8HN, England. TEL 44-171-8650066. FAX 44-171-5229623. TELEX 290164 CHAPMA G. E-mail: journal@rapidcom.co.uk; URL: http://www.thomsonscience.com. (Dist. by: International Thomson Publishing Services Ltd., Cheriton House, North Way, Andover, Hants. SP10 5BE, England. TEL 44-1264-342713. FAX 44-1264-342807; Subscr. in US & Canada to: 400 Market St., Philadelphia, PA 19106. TEL 800-552-5866) Eds. K. Croucher, W. Harrison. adv. contact: Gemma Heiser. bk.rev.; software rev. (back issues avail.; reprint service avail.) **Indexed:** ASCA, Compumath, Comput.Lit.Ind., Curr.Ind.Stat., INSPEC (1992-). **Document type:** academic/scholarly publication.
●Also available online.
—BLDSC (8321.453050); AskIEEE; CISTI; Genuine Article; KR SourceOne; UnCover. **CCC.**
　Description: Contains practical and researched-based material on software-quality and related issues.
　Refereed Serial

005　　　　　NE　　ISSN 1385-1659
▼**SOFTWARE RELEASE.** 1996. 8/yr. fl.110 (effective 1997). Array Publications B.V., Postbus 615, 2400 AP Alphen aan den Rijn, Netherlands. TEL 31-172-424177. FAX 31-172-424381. E-mail: srm@array.nl; URL: http://www.array.nl. Ed. Rene Moscou. adv.: B&W page fl.3400; adv. contact: J. Raaphorst. circ. 5,000. **Document type:** trade publication.
　Description: Covers issues and techniques in corporate software development.

005.3　　　　　US　　ISSN 1087-2493
▼**SOFTWARE STRATEGIES.** Key Title: Software Strategies for Running Industry on Windows. 1996. q. Putman Publishing Co., 301 E. Erie St., Chicago, IL 60611. TEL 312-644-2020. FAX 312-644-1131. Ed. Keith Larson; Pub. Peggy Smedley.
—KR SourceOne.

001.642　　　　　US　　ISSN 1068-8544
　　　　　　　　　CODEN: SOSUEA
SOFTWARE SUCCESS; increasing profits for software entrepreneurs. 1988. m. $197. United Communications Group, 11300 Rockville Pike, Ste. 1100, Rockville, MD 20852. TEL 617-444-5755. FAX 617-444-8958. Ed. Robert D. Shapiro. index. circ. 2,500. (back issues avail.) **Document type:** newsletter.
—**CCC.**
　Former titles (until 1992): David H. Bowen's Software Success (ISSN 0896-4386); (until 1987): David H. Bowen's Software Strategies (ISSN 0896-4378)
　Description: Offers advice on software sales and marketing, covering management and finance tactics software entrepreneurs can use to increase profits.

621.381　　　　　US
SOFTWARE TIMES. 1978. 4/yr. free. Sterling Software, Systems Software Marketing Division, 11050 White Rock Rd., Ste. 100, Rancho Cordova, CA 95670-6095. TEL 916-635-5535. FAX 916-635-5604. Ed. James G. Hanchett. circ. 20,000.

001.642　　　UK　　ISSN 0268-6708
THE SOFTWARE USERS YEAR BOOK. 1985. a. £150. V N U Business Publications BV, 32-34 Broadwick St., London W1A 2HG, England. TEL 071-439-4242. FAX 071-437-7906. Ed. Anne Maher. circ. 3,500. **Document type:** directory.
●Also available on CD-ROM.
—BLDSC (8321.459000); SWETS.
　Formerly: Microcomputer Software Directory - International Directory of Software.

005.3　　　　　UK　　ISSN 0038-0652
QA76　　　　　　CODEN: SOFWBG
SOFTWARE WORLD; an international journal of computer programs and packages. 1969. bi-m. £98($234) (overseas £117) (effective 1996). A.P. Publications Ltd., 377 St. John St., London EC1V 4LD, England. TEL 44-171-837-5921. FAX 44-171-837-1197. Ed. Ed Patterson. adv.; bk.rev.; software rev.; illus. circ. 1,033. (also avail. in microform from UMI; reprint service avail. from UMI) **Indexed:** Agri.Eng.Abstr., BMT, Comput.Cont., Comput.Lit.Ind., INSPEC. **Document type:** academic/scholarly publication.
—BLDSC (8321.460000); AskIEEE; CISTI; Ei; KR SourceOne; Linda Hall; SWETS; UMI.
　Incorporates in part (in 1994): P C Business Software (ISSN 0954-2833); Which was formerly: Mini Micro Software (ISSN 0265-6760); Small Systems Software (ISSN 0308-3314).
　Description: Discusses software programs and packages for use in many installations. Includes business news.

005.3 338　　　GW　　ISSN 0178-1766
SOFTWAREFUEHRER FUER PERSONAL-COMPUTER. 1985. a. DM.49.80. Rossipaul Medien GmbH, Menzingerstr. 37, 80638 Munich, Germany. TEL 49-89-179106-0. FAX 49-89-179106-22. Ed. Hilla Hueber. adv. contact: Emmi Schmidbauer. circ. 40,000. **Document type:** directory.

005.3　　　　　GW　　ISSN 0944-2367
SOFTWAREFUEHRER UNIX. 1989. a. DM.98. Rossipaul Medien GmbH, Menzingerstr. 37, 80638 Munich, Germany. TEL 49-89-179106-0. FAX 49-89-179106-22. Ed. Hilla Hueber. adv. contact: Emmi Schmidbauer. circ. 30,000. **Document type:** directory.
　Formerly (until 1990): UNIX Softwarefuehrer (ISSN 0939-0367)

005.3　　　　　US　　ISSN 1064-8860
SOFTWATCH; keeping managers abreast of state-of-the-art software development. 1992. q. $95. Applied Computer Research, Inc., 11242 N. 19th Ave., Phoenix, AZ 85029. TEL 602-216-9100. FAX 602-216-9200. (Subscr. to: Box 82266, Phoenix, AZ 85071-2266) Ed. Alan Howard. (back issues avail.) **Document type:** trade publication.
—**CCC.**
　Description: Reports on over 200 periodicals in the computer industry. Abstracts and summaries of the significant and unique articles in the application development field are covered.

001.642 621.381　　　US
SOURCEVIEW JOURNAL OF SOFTWARE EVALUATIONS, REVIEWS & RATINGS.* 1985. m. $36. SourceView Software International (Subsidiary of: SourceView Corporation), Box 4713, Walnut Creek, CA 94596-0713. TEL 800-929-8117. Ed. Paul Elmore. adv.; bk.rev.; software rev. circ. 50,000.
　Former titles: Sourceview (ISSN 0742-3772); Sourceview Magazine.
　Description: For professional software developers and users. Features articles on industry trends, copyright laws and manufacturing.

SPREADSHEET. see *COMPUTERS — Microcomputers*

001.642　　　　　US
STANDARD FOR TESTING APPLICATION SOFTWARE. 1985. a. $158. Auerbach Publishers (Subsidiary of: Warren, Gorham & Lamont), One Penn Plaza, New York, NY 10119. TEL 212-791-5000. FAX 212-971-5024. (Subscr. to: 31 St. James Ave., Boston, MA 02116-4112. TEL 800-950-1218. FAX 617-423-1914) Ed. William E. Perry. **Document type:** trade publication.
　Description: Provides experienced programmers with a structured testing program.

005.3　　　　　IT
▼**STARTWARE.** 1996. m. (6/yr.) L.66000 (effective 1997). Gruppo Editoriale J C E, Via Ferri 6, 20092 Cinisello Balsamo (MI), Italy. TEL 39-2-660251. FAX 39-2-6127620. E-mail: startware@jce.it; URL: http://www.jce.it. Ed. Fausto Gimondi. adv.: color page L.6100000; trim 210 X 276. circ. 23,000. **Document type:** trade publication.
　Description: Includes shareware written in Italian and a multimedia catalogue.

STUDIO CITY FOR THE II GS. see *COMPUTERS — Personal Computers*

SUPER A S C I I; magazine for advanced computer users. see *COMPUTERS — Data Communications And Data Transmission Systems*

SUPERMARKET SOFTWARE DIRECTORY. see *FOOD AND FOOD INDUSTRIES — Grocery Trade*

SVENSKA MACPRESSEN. see *COMPUTERS — Microcomputers*

621.381　　　　　US
SWIFT'S DIRECTORY OF EDUCATIONAL SOFTWARE FOR THE I B M - P C.* a. (plus s-a. updates). $19.95. D.C. Heath & Company, 222 Berkeley St., Boston, MA 02116-3748. TEL 617-862-6650.

001.642　　　　　US　　ISSN 1054-3902
SYMANTEC. 1990. q. $16. Symantec Corporation, 10201 Torre Ave., Cupertino, CA 95014-2132. TEL 408-253-9600. FAX 408-253-3968. Ed. Hugh R. Bethell. adv.; circ. 650,000 (controlled).
　Description: Directed to owners of Symantec and Peter Norton personal computer software.

001.642 658.381　　　US　　ISSN 1060-9857
QA76.9.D5　　　　　CODEN: PRDSFK
SYMPOSIUM ON RELIABLE DISTRIBUTED SYSTEMS. PROCEEDINGS. 1981. a. price varies. (Institute of Electrical and Electronics Engineers, Inc.) I E E E Computer Society Press, 10662 Los Vaqueros Circle, Los Alamitos, CA 90720-1264. TEL 714-821-8380. FAX 714-821-4641. (Co-sponsors: Association for Computing Machinery; University of Pittsburgh) **Document type:** proceedings.
—BLDSC (6849.629000); Ei. **CCC.**
　Formerly (until 1987): Symposium on Reliability in Distributed Software and Database Systems. Proceedings (ISSN 1073-4899)

001.642 370　　　　　US
LB1028.7
T E S S. (The Educational Software Selector) (Print version ceased) 1984. a. $82.50 for 1996 ed.; upgrade $32.50. Educational Products Information Exchange (EPIE) Institute, 103-3 W. Montauk Hwy., Hampton Bays, NY 11946-4006. TEL 516-728-9100. FAX 516-728-9228. index. (back issues avail.) **Document type:** directory.
●Available only on CD-ROM.
　Former titles: Latest and Best of T E S S & Educational Software Selector (ISSN 8755-5107)
　Description: Contains descriptions of software for all grade levels, preschool through postgraduate.

T W I C E. (This Week in Consumer Electronics) see *ELECTRONICS*

COMPUTERS — SOFTWARE

005.3   GW   ISSN 1432-9638
▼**TELEWORX**; das Magazin fuer Telearbeit. 1997. q. DM.31. I W T Magazin Verlags GmbH, Bahnhofstr. 36, 85591 Vaterstetten, Germany. TEL 49-8106-350-0. FAX 49-8106-350126. URL: http://www.iwtnet.de. Ed. Ulrich Pesch. circ. 50,000 (paid). **Document type:** trade publication.

005.3   US
▼**THE TESTERS' NETWORK**. 1996. m. S T Labs, Inc., Sterling Plaza, 3rd Fl., 3535 128th Ave., S.E., Bellevue, WA 98006. E-mail: pruec@stlabs.com; URL: http://www.stlabs.com/testnet.htm. Ed. Prue Cuper. **Document type:** trade publication.
●Available only online.
  Description: Contains articles, links, product reviews, and other information for software quality assurance professionals.

TICK, TICK, TICK...; the newsletter for millennial management. see COMPUTERS — Computer Programming

TIMEOUT - CENTRAL. see COMPUTERS — Personal Computers

005.3   UK
TRENDS IN SOFTWARE. irreg., no.3, 1995. price varies. John Wiley & Sons Ltd., Journals, Baffins Ln., Chichester, W. Sussex PO19 1UD, England. TEL 44-1243-779777. FAX 44-1243-843232. E-mail: cs-journals@wiley.co.uk; URL: http://www.wiley.co.uk. Ed. Balachander Krishnamurthy. **Document type:** monographic series.

005.3   US   ISSN 1090-6444
▼**UNICENTER T N G ADVISOR**. 1996. bi-m. $39 (Canada $49; elsewhere $59). Advisor Publications, Inc., 5675 Ruffin Rd., Ste. 200, San Diego, CA 92123. TEL 619-278-5600; 800-336-6060. FAX 619-278-0300. E-mail: subscribe@advisor.com; URL: http://www.advisor.com/. Pub. William Ota. adv. contact: B.J. Ghiglione. **Document type:** consumer publication.
  Formerly: C A - Unicenter Advisor.

001.642 330   US   ISSN 0952-3359
UNIGRAM.X; the weekly information newsletter for the UNIX community worldwide. 1984. w. $495. G-2 Computer Intelligence Inc., 3 Maple Place, P.O. Box 7, Glen Head, NY 11545-0007. TEL 516-759-7025. FAX 516-759-7028. Ed. William Fellows. cum.index. circ. 100,000.
●Also available online.
  Description: Directed at UNIX hardware and software marketers.

UNISYS WORLD; an independent news monthly for Unisys system users. see COMPUTERS — Microcomputers

001.642   GW   ISSN 0176-8654
UNIX - MAIL; die Zeitschrift fuer offene Systeme. 1983. bi-m. DM.183. Carl Hanser Verlag, Kolbergerstr. 22, 81679 Munich, Germany. TEL 49-89-998300. FAX 49-89-984809. (Subscr. to: Postfach 860420, 81631 Munich, Germany) Ed. Axel-Tobias Schreiner. adv.; bk.rev.; charts. circ. 2,000. **Document type:** trade publication.
—Ei. **CCC**.

001.642   US
UNIX SOFTWARE JOURNAL.* 1988. q. $15. FourGen Software Inc., 115 N.E. 100th St., Seattle, WA 98125-8013. TEL 206-774-9209. FAX 206-672-4950. Ed. Gary Gagliardi. adv. circ. 15,000.
  Formerly (until 1990): Unix Journal.
  Description: Covers the latest software technology, applications, and issues of interest to users in the Unix marketplace.

005.3   US
UNIX UPDATE. m. $150 (outside N. America $165). Worldwide Videotex, Box 3273, Boynton Beach, FL 33424-3273. TEL 407-738-2276. Ed. Mark Wright; Pub. Mark Wright. **Document type:** newsletter.
●Also available online. Vendor(s): Information Access Co.
  Description: Provides news and information on UNIX-based computer systems and products around the world. Covers research and development, as well as new hardware and software products and enhancements.

005.3   US
UPDATE WEEKLY MAC. (In 2 editions: Free Edition; Supported Edition) w. E-mail: update@level6.com; URL: http://www.webcom.com/level6/. Ed. Kevin Garrett. adv. **Document type:** newsletter.
●Available only online.
  Description: Covers updates to Mac platform software, utilities, applications and firmware for Macintosh network managers, consultants, and VARs.

005   US
▼**V B TECH JOURNAL**; your Visual Basic resource. 1995. m. $24.95 (Canada & Mexico $34.95; elsewhere $64.95). Oakley Publishing Co., Box 70167, Eugene, OR 97401-0111. TEL 503-747-0800; 800-234-0386. FAX 503-746-0071. (Subscr. to: Box 70087, Eugene, OR 97401-0143) Ed. J.D. Hildenbrand; Pub. Bobbi Sinyard. adv. **Document type:** trade publication.

V S D A VOICE. (Video Software Dealers Association) see COMMUNICATIONS — Video

VIRUS WATCH. see COMPUTERS — Computer Security

005.3   NE   ISSN 0921-0490
W G S NEWSLETTER. 1985. s-a. Working Group on Software, c/o Mr. Ruth Kool, Secy., Eindhoven University of Technology, Dept. of Mathematics and Computing Science, P.O. Box 513, 5600 MB Eindhoven, Netherlands. FAX 31-40-2465995. E-mail: rkool@win.tue.nl. **Document type:** newsletter.
●Also available online.
—BLDSC (9309.553500).

W S S RESEARCH SERIES. (Water Software Systems) see ENGINEERING — Electrical Engineering

WASTE MANIFEST SOFTWARE REPORT. see ENVIRONMENTAL STUDIES — Waste Management

WATER SOFTWARE SYSTEMS RESEARCH REPORTS. see ENGINEERING — Electrical Engineering

WHAT P C? AND SOFTWARE. see COMPUTERS — Microcomputers

WHAT'S NEW IN COMPUTING. see COMPUTERS — Computer Industry Directories

621.381   JA
WINDOWS MAGAZINE; MS - windows magazine. 1991. m. 12000 Yen. Akio Fujii, A S C I I Publishing, 4-33-10 Yoyogi, Shibuya-ku, Tokyo 51-24, Japan. TEL 81-3-5351-8111.

001.642   US   ISSN 1065-0784
WINDOWS SOFTWARE CONNECTION. 1992. m. $59 (foreign $79). Cobb Group, Inc., 9420 Bunsen Pkwy., Ste. 300, Louisville, KY 40220. TEL 502-493-3200. FAX 502-491-8050. (Subscr. to: Box 35160, Louisville, KY 40232-9720. TEL 800-223-8720) (diskette format) **Document type:** consumer publication.

005.3 338   GW   ISSN 0947-1391
WINDOWSFUEHRER. 1992. a. DM.49.80. Rossipaul Medien GmbH, Menzingerstr. 37, 80638 Munich, Germany. TEL 49-89-179106-0. FAX 49-89-17910622. Ed. Hilla Hueber. adv. contact: Emmi Schmidbauer. circ. 30,000. **Document type:** directory.

005.4   SW   ISSN 1102-7991
WINDOWSTIDNINGEN. 1991. 10/yr. SEK 299 (effective 1994); newsstand price: SEK 39. Media Marketing - Skalin Eklund AB, P.O. Box 6001, S-191 06 Sollentuna, Sweden. TEL 46-8-626-91-21. FAX 46-8-754-69-30. Ed. Viktor Pylypenko. adv.: B&W page SEK 32000, color page SEK 36000; trim 254 x 385; adv. contact: Joachim Blomberg. circ. 14,000. cols./p.: 5. **Document type:** consumer publication.

005.302   US
▼**WINSURFER**. 1995. m. $49. I D G Newsletter Corporation, 77 Franklin St., Boston, MA 02110. TEL 617-482-8785; 800-807-0771. FAX 617-338-0164. E-mail: idgcust@pcworld.com; URL: http://idgnews.com. Ed. Jim Pile; Pub. Craig Pierce. adv. contact: Scott Tharler. **Document type:** consumer publication.
  Description: Systems-level tips, bug reports, networking advice about Windows 95 and Windows NT.

005.302   GW   ISSN 0945-4322
WORD FUER WINDOWS. 1993. bi-m. DM.78. Verlag Wirtschaft Recht und Steuern, Fraunhoferstr. 5, 82152 Planegg, Germany. TEL 49-89-89517-0. FAX 49-89-89517250. (Subscr. to: Postfach 1363, 82142 Planegg, Germany) (looseleaf format) **Document type:** trade publication.

WORD PROGRESS. see LAW — Computer Applications

WORDPERFECT FOR THE LAW OFFICE. see LAW — Computer Applications

005.3   US   ISSN 1058-9783
Z52.5.W65
WORDPERFECT FOR WINDOWS MAGAZINE. 1992. m. $27.97 (Canada and Mexico $35.97; elsewhere $51.97) (effective 1997). Ivy International Communications, Inc., 270 W. Center St., Orem, UT 84057. TEL 801-228-9626. FAX 801-227-3478. E-mail: wpwinmag@wpmag.com; URL: http://www.wpmag.com. Ed. Oleah Clegg; Pub. Edie Rockwood. R&P contact: Julie Valdes. adv. contact: Rachel Duncan Catledge. circ. 200,000 (paid). **Document type:** consumer publication.
●Also available online. Vendor(s): CompuServe, Inc. Also available on CD-ROM.
—CISTI; SWETS.
  Description: Offers solutions to word processing problems for WordPerfect users. Includes information on software and hardware.

005.3   US   ISSN 1042-5152
Z52.5.W65   CODEN: WORPEY
WORDPERFECT MAGAZINE. 1989. m. $27.97 (Canada $35.97; elsewhere $51.97) (effective 1997). Ivy International Communications, Inc., 270 W. Center St., Orem, UT 84057. TEL 801-228-9626. FAX 801-227-3478. E-mail: wpmag@wpmag.com; URL: http://www.wpmag.com. Ed. Lisa Bearnson; Pub. Edie Rockwood. adv. contact: Rachel Duncan Catledge. index. circ. 160,000. Indexed: Bus.Educ.Ind. **Document type:** consumer publication.
●Also available online.
Also available on CD-ROM.
—CISTI; KR SourceOne; Linda Hall; SWETS; UnCover
  Description: For executives, mid-level managers and word processing personnel. Provides step-by-step solutions for business software problems, addressing specific WordPerfect applications.

001.642   US   ISSN 1063-2719
WORDPERFECT SOFTWARE CONNECTION. 1992. m. $59 (foreign $79). Cobb Group, Inc., 9420 Bunsen Pkwy., Ste. 300, Louisville, KY 40220. TEL 502-493-3200. FAX 501-491-8050. (Subscr. to: Box 35160, Louisville, KY 40232-9720. TEL 800-223-8720) (diskette format) **Document type:** consumer publication.

001.642   US   ISSN 1061-1053
THE WORDPERFECTIONIST. 1986. m. $59 (foreign $79). Cobb Group, Inc., 9420 Bunsen Pkwy., Ste. 300, Louisville, KY 40220. TEL 502-493-3200. FAX 502-491-8050. (Subscr. to: Box 35160, Louisville, KY 40232-9720. TEL 800-223-8720) **Document type:** consumer publication.
—SWETS.

WRITER'S N W; news and reviews for the community of the printed word. see PUBLISHING AND BOOK TRADE

005.302   GW
▼**ZIMPEL. SOFTWARE: Z DATA**. 1996. m. Verlag Dieter Zimpel, Angererstr. 36, 80796 Munich, Germany. TEL 49-89-3073445. FAX 49-89-302409. Eds. Ingrid Finsterwald, Petra Baumgartner. **Document type:** directory.
●Also available on CD-ROM.

001.642   US
1-2-3 SOFTWARE CONNECTION. 1992. m. $59 (foreign $79). Cobb Group, Inc., 9420 Bunsen Pkwy., Ste. 300, Louisville, KY 40220. TEL 502-493-3200. FAX 502-491-8050. (Subscr. to: Box 35160, Louisville, KY 40232-9720. TEL 800-223-8720) (diskette format) **Document type:** consumer publication.

001.642 US ISSN 0891-5121
1-2-3 USER'S JOURNAL; up to release 2.4. 1986. m. $59 (foreign $79). Cobb Group, Inc., 9420 Bunsen Pkwy., Ste. 300, Louisville, KY 40220. TEL 502-493-3200. FAX 502-491-8050. (Subscr. to: Box 35160, Louisville, KY 40232-9720. TEL 800-223-8720) Ed. Stuart Vessels. **Document type**: consumer publication.
Description: Offers tips and techniques on using Lotus 1-2-3.

005.3 GW ISSN 1432-1734
▼**3D LIVE**; das Computer-Magazin fuer 3d-Anwender. 1996. bi-m. DM.36 (effective 1997). I W T Magazin Verlags GmbH, Bahnhofstr. 36, 85591 Vaterstetten, Germany. TEL 49-8106-350-0. FAX 49-8106-350126. URL: http://www.iwtnet.de. Ed. Alexander Pschera. circ. 25,000 (paid). **Document type**: trade publication.
Description: For professional multimedia users.

COMPUTERS — Theory Of Computing

003 US ISSN 0737-8017
QA267 CODEN: CATCDQ
ANNUAL A C M SYMPOSIUM ON THE THEORY OF COMPUTING. PROCEEDINGS. 1969. a. price varies. Association for Computing Machinery, Special Interest Group on Automata and Computability Theory, 1515 Broadway, 17th Fl., New York, NY 10036. TEL 212-869-7440. bibl.; charts. **Document type**: proceedings.
—BLDSC (1073.870000); Ei. **CCC**.
Former titles (until 1982): Annual A C M Symposium on Theory of Computing. Conference Proceedings (ISSN 0734-9025); (until 1980): Annual A C M Symposium on Theory of Computing. Conference Record (ISSN 0277-0261)

COMPUTATIONAL INTELLIGENCE/INTELLIGENCE INFORMATIQUE. see *COMPUTERS*

003 CC ISSN 0254-4164
QA75.5 CODEN: JIXUDT
JISUANJI XUEBAO. (Text in Chinese; summaries in Chinese, English) 1978. bi-m. $168.60. (Chinese Academy of Sciences, Chinese Computer Federation) Science Press, Marketing and Sales Department - Science Press, 16 Donghuangchenggen North St., Beijing 100717, People's Republic of China. TEL 86-10-4010630. FAX 86-10-4012180. TELEX 210247-SPBJ-CN. Ed. Paysu Shaw. adv.: B&W page $500, color page $900; 187 x 260; adv. contact: Yuanyaun Liu. circ. 15,000. (back issues avail.) **Indexed**: INSPEC, Math.R. **Document type**: academic/scholarly publication.
—BLDSC (3180.310000); AskIEEE; KR SourceOne; Linda Hall.
Description: Covers theoretical foundations and applications, hardware architecture, software, networking, CAD, and other applications.
Refereed Serial

JOURNAL OF COMBINATORIAL MATHEMATICS AND COMBINATORIAL COMPUTING. see *MATHEMATICS*

003 CC ISSN 1000-9000
QA75.5 CODEN: JCTEEM
JOURNAL OF COMPUTER SCIENCE AND TECHNOLOGY. (Text in English) 1986. q. $340 (foreign $410) (effective 1996). (Academia Sinica, Chinese Computer Federation) Science Press, Marketing and Sales Department, 16 Donghuangchenggen North St., Beijing 100717, People's Republic of China. TEL 4010642. FAX 4019810. (US office: Science Press New York, Ltd., 84-04 58th Ave., Elmhurst, NY 11373. TEL 718-476-0238; Exclusively dist. outside P.R. China by: Allerton Press, 150 Fifth Ave., New York, NY 10011, USA. TEL 212-924-3950. FAX 212-463-9684) (Co-publisher: Allerton Press, Inc.) Ed. Xia Peisu. adv. circ. 6,000. (back issues avail.) **Indexed**: INSPEC (1988-), Zent.Math. **Document type**: academic/scholarly publication.
—BLDSC (4963.744000); AskIEEE; Ei; KR SourceOne; UnCover. **CCC**.
Description: Covers all aspects of computer science and technology, including theoretical foundations of information processing computer hardware and architecture, computer software and various computer applications.
Refereed Serial

004 US
PRINCETON SERIES IN COMPUTER SCIENCE. irreg. price varies. Princeton University Press, 41 William St., Princeton, NJ 08540. TEL 609-258-4900. FAX 609-258-6305. URL: http://pup.princeton.edu. Eds. David Hanson, Robert Tarjan. **Document type**: monographic series.

003 NE ISSN 0304-3975
QA267 CODEN: TCSCDI
THEORETICAL COMPUTER SCIENCE. 1975. 38/yr. fl.7063($4059) (effective 1998). North-Holland (Subsidiary of: Elsevier Science B.V.), P.O. Box 211, 1000 AE Amsterdam, Netherlands. TEL 31-20-4853911. FAX 31-20-4853598. TELEX 18582 ESPA NL. (Subscr. in the Americas to: Elsevier Science, Regional Sales Office, Box 945, New York, NY 10159-0945. TEL 212-633-3730. FAX 212-633-3680; Subscr. in Australasia and the Far East to: Elsevier Science (Singapore) Pte Ltd, No.1 Temasek Ave., No.17-01 Millenia Tower, Singapore 039192, Singapore. TEL 65-434-3727. FAX 65-337-2230; Subscr. in Japan to: Elsevier Science Japan, 9-15 Higashi-Azabu 1-chome, Minato-ku, Tokyo 106, Japan. TEL 81-3-5561-5033. FAX 81-3-5561-5047) Ed. M. Nivat. (also avail. in microform from UMI; back issues avail.; reprint service avail. from SWZ) **Indexed**: Compumath, Comput.Abstr., Comput.Cont., Comput.Dtbs., Curr.Cont., Cyb.Abstr., Ind.Sci.Rev., INSPEC (1975-), Math.R., Sci.Cit.Ind., SSCI, Zent.Math. **Document type**: academic/scholarly publication.
—BLDSC (8814.556000); AskIEEE; CISTI; Ei; Genuine Article; KR SourceOne; Linda Hall; SWETS; UnCover. **CCC**.
Description: Presents research papers on theoretical and mathematical aspects of computer science. Focuses on the problems of practical computation. Subjects covered include automata, formal languages, semantics of programming languages and algorithms.
Refereed Serial

003 510 US
QA1
THEORY OF COMPUTING SYSTEMS; an international journal. Online edition (US ISSN 1433-0490) 1966. bi-m. $301 (effective 1998). Springer-Verlag, Science Journals, 175 Fifth Ave., New York, NY 10010. TEL 212-460-1500. FAX 212-473-6272. E-mail: orders@springer-ny.com; URL: http://www.springer-ny.com. (N. American subscr. to: Journal Fulfillment Services, Box 2485, Secaucus, NJ 07096-2485. TEL 800-777-4643. FAX 201-348-4505; Elsewhere: Heidelberger Platz 3, 14197 Berlin, Germany. TEL 49-30-82787358. FAX 49-30-82787448) Ed. Arnold L. Rosenberg. R&P contact: Ian Gross. adv. contact: Robert Vrooman. (also avail. in microform from UMI; reprint service avail. from ISI,SWZ) **Indexed**: ASCA, Compumath, Curr.Cont., Ind.Sci.Rev., INSPEC, Math.R., Sci.Cit.Ind., Zent.Math. **Document type**: academic/scholarly publication.
●Also available online.
—AskIEEE; CISTI; Genuine Article; KR SourceOne; Linda Hall; UMI; UnCover. **CCC**.
Formerly (until 1997): Mathematical Systems Theory (ISSN 0025-5661)
Description: Features original research from all areas of theoretical computer science.
Refereed Serial

COMPUTERS — Word Processing

ARCHIV FUER STENOGRAFIE, TEXTVERARBEITUNG, BUEROTECHNIK. see *EDUCATION — Teaching Methods And Curriculum*

WORDPERFECT FOR WINDOWS MAGAZINE. see *COMPUTERS — Software*

WORDPERFECT MAGAZINE. see *COMPUTERS — Software*

651.8 US ISSN 0890-524X
WORDSTAR SCROLL. 1985. bi-m. $30 (effective 1996). WordStar Processing Users' Group, Inc., 7958 S.W. 105th Pl., Miami, FL 33173. TEL 305-274-0099. FAX 305-271-8904. E-mail: cbabbage@gix.netcom.com. (Subscr. to: Box 16-1443, Miami, FL 33116-1443) Ed. Emerson Boardman; Pub. David Rafky. R&P contact: David Rafky. adv. contact: David Rafky. bk.rev. circ. 4,000. (looseleaf format; back issues avail.) **Document type**: newsletter.
Description: Serves as the official publication for the WordStar Processing Users' Group.

WORKGROUP COMPUTING REPORT; applying technology to business processes. see *COMPUTERS — Electronic Data Processing*

CONSERVATION

see also Environmental Studies; Forests and Forestry; Water Resources

A C A REVIEW. (Anglers' Conservation Association) see *FISH AND FISHERIES*

333.7 US
A N J E C REPORT. 1969. q. $15. Association of New Jersey Environmental Commissions, Box 157, Mendham, NJ 07945. TEL 201-539-7547. FAX 201-539-7713. Ed. Sandy Batty. adv.: bk.rev. circ. 2,200. **Document type**: academic/scholarly publication, newsletter.
Former titles (until 1977): Association of New Jersey Environmental Commissions Newsletter; Association of New Jersey Conservation Commissions Newsletter (ISSN 0044-9636)
Description: Contains information on a variety of environmental subjects with a special focus on New Jersey.

A S P I TECHNICAL SERIES. (Appalachia - Science in the Public Interest) see *ENVIRONMENTAL STUDIES*

333.7 PL ISSN 0208-6131
ACTA UNIVERSITATIS LODZIENSIS: FOLIA SOZOLOGICA. 1955-1974; N.S. 1983. irreg. Wydawnictwo Uniwersytetu Lodzkiego, Ul. Jaracza 34, Lodz, Poland. TEL 331671. (Dist. by: Ars Polona-Ruch, Krakowskie Przedmiescie 7, Warsaw, Poland) Ed.Bd. **Document type**: academic/scholarly publication.
—BLDSC (0585.208770); CISTI; Linda Hall.
Supersedes in part: Uniwersytet Lodzki. Zeszyty Naukowe. Seria 2: Nauki Matematyczno-Przyrodnicze (ISSN 0076-0366)
Description: Devoted to problems of theory and practice of biological conservation in Poland.

333.7 PL ISSN 0208-533X
ACTA UNIVERSITATIS NICOLAI COPERNICI. NAUKI HUMANISTYCZNO-SPOLECZNE. ZABYTKOZNAWSTWO I KONSERWATORSTWO. 1966. irreg. price varies. Uniwersytet Mikolaja Kopernika, Wydawnictwo, Ul. Gagarina 11, 87-100 Torun, Poland. TEL 48-56-14295. TELEX 21224. (Dist. by: Osrodek Rozpowszechniania Wydawnictw Naukowych PAN, Palac Kultury i Nauki, 00-901 Warsaw, Poland) **Document type**: academic/scholarly publication.
Formerly (until 1973): Uniwersytet Mikolaja Kopernika. Nauki Humanistyczno-Spoleczne. Zeszyty Naukowe. Zabytkoznawstwo i Konserwatorstwo (ISSN 0563-9506)

ACTION ALERT (SAN FRANCISCO). see *ENVIRONMENTAL STUDIES*

ACT'IONLINE. see *ANIMAL WELFARE*

ADELAIDE BOTANIC GARDEN BOARD. ANNUAL REPORT. see *BIOLOGY — Botany*

ADIRONDAC. see *SPORTS AND GAMES — Outdoor Life*

CONSERVATION

333.7 591   UK   ISSN 0141-6707
QL337.E25   CODEN: AJOEDE
AFRICAN JOURNAL OF ECOLOGY. 1962. q. £236.50($431.50) (foreign £260) (effective 1998). (East African Wildlife Society) Blackwell Science Ltd., Osney Mead, Oxford OX2 0EL, England. TEL 44-1865-206206. FAX 44-1865-721205. E-mail: journals.cs@blacksci.co.uk; URL: http://www.blacksci.co.uk/products/journals/afje.html. Ed. F.I.B. Kayanja; Pub. Allen Stevens. R&P contact: Sarah Pollard. adv. contact: Martine Cariou-Keen. bk.rev.; cum.index. circ. 395. (also avail. in microform from UMI; back issues avail; reprint service avail. from ISI) **Indexed:** Abstr.Anthropol., Anim.Breed.Abstr., ASCA, Biol.Abstr., Curr.Adv.Ecol.Sci., Curr.Cont., Curr.Ref.Fish Res., Dairy Sci.Abstr., Ecol.Abstr., Environ.Per.Bibl. (1989-), Field Crop.Abstr., Forest.Abstr., Forest Prod.Abstr., Geo.Abstr., Geol.Abstr., Helminthol.Abstr., Herb.Abstr., IDA, Ind.Sci.Rev., Ind.Vet., Nutr.Abstr., Rev.Appl.Entomol., Sci.Cit.Ind., Sel.Water Res.Abstr., Soils & Fert., Sport Fish.Abstr., Vet.Bull., Wild Life Rev., Wild.Rev., Zoo.Rec. **Document type:** academic/scholarly publication.
—BLDSC (0732.519000); EMDOCS; Genuine Article; Linda Hall; SWETS; UMI; UnCover. **CCC.**
    Formerly: East African Wildlife Journal (ISSN 0070-8038)
    Refereed Serial

333.7 591.1   SA   ISSN 0002-0273
                     CODEN: AFWLAA
AFRICAN WILDLIFE. (Text in English) 1946. bi-m. R.110 individual membership; institutions R.200. Wildlife and Environment Society of South Africa, P.O. Box 394, Howick 3290, South Africa. TEL 27-332-303911. FAX 27-332-304576. E-mail: wildmag@em.co.za; URL: http://www.wildlifesociety.org.za. Ed. Ms Sandie Anderson. adv.; bk.rev.; charts; illus.; index. circ. 15,000. (also avail. in microform from UMI; back issues avail.) **Indexed:** Biol.Abstr., Curr.Adv.Ecol.Sci., Environ.Abstr., Environ.Per.Bibl. (1991-), Ind.S.A.Per., Key Word Ind.Wildl.Res., Sport Fish.Abstr., Wild.Rev., Zoo.Rec.
—BLDSC (0735.000000); Linda Hall; UMI; UnCover.
    Refereed Serial

333.7   US
KF5640.A15
AFRICAN WILDLIFE NEWS. 1963. 5/yr. $25 donation. African Wildlife Foundation, 1717 Massachusetts Ave., N.W., Washington, DC 20036. TEL 202-265-8394. FAX 202-265-2361. TELEX 1504TEMBO. URL: http://www.awf.com. Ed. Rebecca Villarreal. R&P contact: Rebecca Villarreal. bk.rev. circ. 40,000. **Document type:** newsletter.
    Former titles: Wildlife News (ISSN 0270-0360); African Wildlife News (ISSN 0065-4086)

333.7   ET
AGAZEN. (Text in Amharic, English) s-a. $1 per issue (free to Ethiopian students). Ethiopian Wildlife and Natural History Society, P.O. Box 60074, Addis Ababa, Ethiopia. Ed. Zewditu Tessema. adv.; bk.rev.; charts; illus.
    Description: Publishes short articles on conservation and environmental issues for a secondary school and undergraduate audience.

639.9 796   US   ISSN 0894-8356
ALABAMA WILDLIFE. 1985. q. $25. Box 1109, Montgomery, AL 36102. FAX 334-832-9454. Ed. Dan Dumont. R&P contact: Dan Dumont. adv. contact: Barbara Harrington.
    Description: Covers outdoors, wildlife and related topics.

333.7   US
ALASKA. DEPARTMENT OF FISH AND GAME. WILDLIFE NOTEBOOK SERIES. irreg. Department of Fish and Game, Division of Wildlife Conservation, Box 25526, Juneau, AK 99802-5526. TEL 907-465-4190.
    Formerly: Alaska. Department of Fish and Game. Wildlife Booklet Series (ISSN 0084-0130)

333.95   US   ISSN 0362-6962
SK367
ALASKA. DIVISION OF WILDLIFE CONSERVATION. ANNUAL REPORT OF SURVEY - INVENTORY ACTIVITIES. Key Title: Annual Report of Survey - Inventory Activities. 1970. a. free. Department of Fish and Game, Division of Wildlife Conservation, Box 22526, Juneau, AK 99802-2526. TEL 907-465-4190. Ed. Mary Hicks. illus. circ. 300. **Document type:** government publication.
    Formerly (until 1991): Alaska. Division of Game. Annual Report of Survey - Inventory Activities.

333.7   US
ALASKA CENTER FOR THE ENVIRONMENT. CENTER NEWS. 1972. 5/yr. $30 (effective Jan. 1990). Alaska Center for the Environment, 519 W. 8th Ave., Ste. 201, Anchorage, AK 99501-3549. TEL 907-274-3621. FAX 907-274-8733. Ed. Cliff Eames. adv.; bk.rev. circ. 1,000. **Document type:** newsletter.

ALASKA FISHERIES ENHANCEMENT PROGRAM ANNUAL REPORT. see *FISH AND FISHERIES*

333.7   CN   ISSN 0318-5540
                     CODEN: ALNAEC
ALBERTA NATURALIST. 1970. q. Can.$20 membership. Federation of Alberta Naturalists, P.O. Box 1472, Edmonton, AB T5J 2N5, Canada. TEL 403-453-8629. FAX 403-453-8553. E-mail: fan@freenetEdmonton.ab.ca. Ed. R. Edrea Daniel. adv.: page Can.$75; adv. contact: Glen Semenchuk. bk.rev.; cum.index: 1970-1980, 1981-1985, 1986-1990, 1991-1995; circ. 500 (paid). (back issues avail.) **Indexed:** Key Word Ind.Wildl.Res., Sport Fish.Abstr., Wild.Rev., Zoo.Rec. **Document type:** newsletter, proceedings.
—CISTI. **CCC.**
    Description: Covers conservation, nature, rare plants, animals, birds, insects and environmental issues.

ALBURY & DISTRICT HISTORICAL SOCIETY. BULLETIN. see *HISTORY — History Of Australasia And Other Areas*

333.91   US
ALONG THE TOWPATH. 1969. q. membership. Chesapeake & Ohio Canal Association, Inc., Box 366, Glen Echo, MD 20812-0366. Ed. Donald Besom. bk.rev.; charts; illus.; stat. circ. 800. (looseleaf format)

333.7 613.1   GW
DAS ALTERNATIVE BRANCHENBUCH. 1985. a. DM.19.80. A L T O P Verlags mbH, Gotzinger str. 48, 81371 Munich, Germany. TEL 089-746611-0. FAX 089-7256246. Ed.Bd. adv. **Document type:** directory.

333.7 350.086   FR   ISSN 0044-7463
AMENAGEMENT ET NATURE. 1966. q. 200 F. (foreign 240 F.). Association pour les Espaces Naturels, 21 rue du Conseiller Collignon, 75116 Paris, France. TEL 33-01-45201500. FAX 33-01-45204536. Ed. Roland Bechmann. R&P contact: Bernard Cesari. adv.; bk.rev.; bibl.; illus.; cum.index: nos.1-120. circ. 2,300. **Indexed:** Acid Pre.Dig., Pt.de Rep. (1978-).
—CISTI.

AMERICAN CURRENTS. see *BIOLOGY — Zoology*

AMERICAN HAWKWATCHER. see *BIOLOGY — Ornithology*

639.9   US   ISSN 0065-9150
AMERICAN LITTORAL SOCIETY. SPECIAL PUBLICATIONS. 1962. irreg. (approx. 4/yr.). $25 to individuals; institutions and libraries $30 (effective 1996 & 1997). American Littoral Society, Sandy Hook, Highlands, NJ 07732. TEL 908-291-0055. Ed. D.W. Bennett. adv.; bk.rev. circ. 7,500. (reprint service avail. from UMI) **Indexed:** Biol.Abstr.
—Linda Hall.

AMERICAN SOCIETY FOR CONSERVATION ARCHAEOLOGY REPORT. see *ARCHAEOLOGY*

AMERICAN UNIVERSITY STUDIES. SERIES 21. REGIONAL STUDIES. see *ETHNIC INTERESTS*

AMERICAN WHITE WATER. see *SPORTS AND GAMES — Boats And Boating*

AMOEBA. see *BIOLOGY*

ANBLICK; Zeitschrift fuer Jagd, Fischerei, Jagdhundwesen und Naturschutz. see *SPORTS AND GAMES — Outdoor Life*

333.95   UK   ISSN 1367-9430
ANIMAL CONSERVATION. q. £78($124) (effective 1998). Cambridge University Press, Edinburgh Bldg., Shaftesbury Rd., Cambridge CB2 2RU, England. TEL 44-1223-312393. FAX 44-1223-312052. E-mail: information@cup.cam.ac.uk; URL: http://www.cup.org/journals/CUPJNLS.html. (N. America addr.: 40 W. 20th St., New York, NY 10011-4211. TEL 212-924-3900. FAX 212-691-3239)

ANIMAL KEEPERS' FORUM. see *BIOLOGY — Zoology*

333.7 614.7   US
ANTARCTICA PROJECT. 1992. q. $30 membership. (Antarctic & Southern Ocean Coalition) Antarctica Project, Box 76920, Washington, DC 20013. TEL 202-544-0236. FAX 202-544-8483. E-mail: antarctica@igc.org. Dir. Beth Marks. R&P contact: Berh Marks. illus. circ. 1,000. (looseleaf format) **Document type:** newsletter.
    Description: Covers current events of Antarctica and the international campaign for its protection.

APPALACHIAN ALTERNATIVES. see *ENVIRONMENTAL STUDIES*

333.91 578.76   UK   ISSN 1052-7613
QH541.5.W3   CODEN: AQCOEY
AQUATIC CONSERVATION: MARINE AND FRESHWATER ECOSYSTEMS. 1991. bi-m. £425 (foreign $425) (effective 1998). John Wiley & Sons Ltd., Journals, Baffins Ln., Chichester, W. Sussex PO19 1UD, England. TEL 44-1243-779777. FAX 44-1243-775878. E-mail: cs-journals@wiley.co.uk; URL: http://www.wiley.co.uk. (Subscr. in the Americas to: John Wiley & Sons, Inc., 605 Third Ave., New York, NY 10158. TEL 212-850-6645. FAX 212-850-6021) Eds. Philip Boon, Roger Mitchell; Pub. Helen Bailey. adv.: B&W page £595, color page £1495; trim 260 x 200; adv. contact: Bob Kern. circ. 500. (also avail. in microform from UMI; back issues avail.; reprint service avail. from SWZ) **Indexed:** ASCA, Ecol.Abstr., Environ.Per.Bibl. (1993-), Geo.Abstr.H.G., Geo.Abstr.P.G., IDA, Sport Fish.Abstr., W.R.C.Inf., Wild.Rev., Zoo.Rec. **Document type:** academic/scholarly publication.
—BLDSC (1582.371000); EMDOCS; Genuine Article; SWETS; UMI; UnCover. **CCC.**
    Description: Dedicated to publishing original paper that relate specifically to freshwater, brackish or marine habitats and encouraging work that spans these ecosystems.
    Refereed Serial

AQUATIC ENVIRONMENT PROTECTION; analytical methods. see *ENVIRONMENTAL STUDIES*

635   US
AQUILEGIA. 1976. 6/yr. membership only. Colorado Native Plant Society, Box 200, Ft. Collins, CO 80522. Ed. Tamara Naumann. **Document type:** newsletter.
    Formerly: Colorado Native Plant Society. Newsletter.

333.7   US
ARBOR DAY. bi-m. membership. National Arbor Day Foundation, 100 Arbor Ave., Nebraska City, NE 68410. TEL 402-474-5655. FAX 402-474-0820. **Document type:** newsletter.
    Formerly: Arbor Day News.
    Description: Serves as a communication link for members, promoting tree-planting projects throughout the United States.

ARID SOIL RESEARCH AND REHABILITATION. see *AGRICULTURE — Crop Production And Soil*

333.7 639.2 614.7   US   ISSN 0882-5572
SK51
ARIZONA WILDLIFE VIEWS. 1953. m. $8.50 (foreign $15). Game and Fish Department, 2221 W. Greenway Rd., Phoenix, AZ 85023. TEL 602-942-3000. Ed. Roberta Dobolek. R&P contact: Roberta Dobolek. charts; illus.; stat.; circ. 20,000 (paid). **Document type:** government publication.
    Description: Articles on Arizona wildlife, hunting, fishing and boating.
    Refereed Serial

CONSERVATION

333.95   UK   ISSN 0306-8870
THE ARK. 1974. q. £15 (foreign £25). Rare Breeds Survival Trust, National Agricultural Centre, Kenilworth, Warwickshire CV8 2LG, England. TEL 44-1203-696551. FAX 44-1203-696706. Ed. Richard Lutwyche. R&P contact: Richard Lutwyche. adv. contact: Paul Dunning. bk.rev.; index; circ. 10,000. **Document type:** bulletin.
—BLDSC (1668.750000); UnCover.
Description: Promotes conservation of endangered breeds of British farm animals.

333.7 799   US   ISSN 0884-9145
ARKANSAS OUTDOORS. 1946. w. free to qualified personnel. Game and Fish Commission, No. 2 Natural Resource Dr., Little Rock, AR 72205. TEL 501-223-6342. FAX 501-223-6447. Ed. Joe Mosby. circ. 1,200. **Document type:** newsletter.

333.7 799   US   ISSN 1063-0953
SK371
ARKANSAS WILDLIFE. 1968. q. $8. Game and Fish Commission, No. 2 Natural Resource Dr., Little Rock, AR 72205. TEL 501-223-6406. FAX 301-223-6447. Ed. Keith Sutton. charts; illus.; stat. circ. 35,000. **Indexed:** Sport Fish.Abstr., Wild.Rev. **Document type:** consumer publication.
—UnCover.
Formerly (until 1992): Arkansas Game & Fish Magazine (ISSN 0004-1807)

333.7   US
THE ARROW (CEDAR KNOLLS). 1989. q. Morris 2000, 2 Ridgedale Ave., Cedar Knolls, NJ 07927. TEL 201-984-2000. Dir. Carol J. Rufener. **Document type:** newsletter.
Description: Presents information on public policy issues in Morris County on which Morris 2000 is currently working.

ASIAN-PACIFIC ENVIRONMENT; newsletter of the Asia Pacific people's environment network. see *ENVIRONMENTAL STUDIES*

639.9 179.3   SZ
ASIAN PRIMATES. 4/yr. International Union for Conservation of Nature and Natural Resources, Species Survival Commission - Primate Specialist Group, Rue Mauverney 28, CH-1196 Gland, Switzerland. TEL 41-22-9990001. FAX 41-22-9990002. TELEX 419624-IUCN-CH. (Subscr. to: Ardith Eudey, 164 Dayton St., Upland, CA 91786, USA) **Document type:** academic/scholarly publication.

333.78   US
ASSOCIATION OF MIDWEST FISH AND WILDLIFE AGENCIES. PROCEEDINGS. (Notes: Publisher varies according to host state.) 1934. a. price varies. Association of Midwest Fish and Wildlife Agencies, Box 30028, Lansing, MI 48909. circ. 25.
Former titles: Association of Midwest Fish and Wildlife Commissioners. Proceedings; Association of Midwest Fish and Game Commissioners. Proceedings (ISSN 0066-9601)

596.0973   US   ISSN 0097-7136
QL671   CODEN: AUDUAD
AUDUBON. 1899. bi-m. $20 includes membership. National Audubon Society, 700 Broadway, New York, NY 10003. TEL 212-979-3126. FAX 212-477-9069. (Subscr. to: Box 52529, Boulder, CO 80322. TEL 800-274-4201) Ed. Michael W. Robbins. adv.: B&W page $14610; adv. contact: James Fishman. bk.rev.; charts; illus.; index. circ. 4,545,790. (also avail. in microform from UMI,PMC) **Indexed:** Acad.Ind., Biol.Abstr., Bk.Rev.Ind. (1965-), Child.Bk.Rev.Ind. (1965-), Curr.Adv.Ecol.Sci., Deep Sea Res.& Oceanogr.Abstr., Energy Info.Abstr., Energy Rev., Environ.Abstr., Environ.Per.Bibl. (1973-), Gard.Lit. (1992-), Gen.Sci.Ind., Key Word Ind.Wildl.Res., Mag.Ind., PMR, R.G.Abstr., R.G, TOM. **Document type:** consumer publication.
●Also available online. Vendor(s): Information Access Co., UMI.
Also available on CD-ROM. Producer(s): UMI.
—BLDSC (1789.850000); KR SourceOne; Linda Hall; UMI; UnCover.
Formerly (until 1961): Audubon Magazine (ISSN 0004-7694)
Description: Covers environment, wildlife and preservation of wildlife habitat.

333.7   US   ISSN 0274-502X
AUDUBON SOCIETY OF RHODE ISLAND. REPORT. 1966. 6/yr. $10 to non-members. Audubon Society of Rhode Island, 12 Sanderson Rd., Smithfield, RI 02917-2606. TEL 401-949-5454. FAX 401-949-5788. Ed. Ken Weber. bk.rev. circ. 5,000.
Formerly: Rhode Island Audubon Report (ISSN 0556-8587)
Description: Articles focus on natural history and environmental issues in Rhode Island.

333.7   US
AULLWOOD NOTES. 1962. bi-m. membership. (Friends of Aullwood, Inc.) Aullwood Audubon Center and Farm, 1000 Aullwood Rd., Dayton, OH 45414. TEL 513-890-7360. Ed. John C. Ritzenthaler. bk.rev. circ. 1,500. (processed) **Document type:** newsletter.

333.7   AT   ISSN 0587-5846
AUSTRALIAN CONSERVATION FOUNDATION. ANNUAL REPORT. 1968. a. Australian Conservation Foundation, 340 Gore St., Fitzroy, Vic. 3065, Australia. TEL 61-3-94161166. FAX 61-3-94160767. R&P contact: Louise Ray. illus. **Document type:** corporate report.
Description: Annual report of the Australian Conservation Foundation.

333.7   AT
AUSTRALIAN MARINE CONSERVATION SOCIETY. BULLETIN. 1978. 6/yr. Aus.$25. Australian Marine Conservation Society Inc., P.O. Box 3139, Yeronga, Qld. 4104, Australia. TEL 61-7-38485235. FAX 61-7-38925814. Eds. E. Hegerl, D. Tarte. bk.rev. circ. 750. **Document type:** bulletin.
Formerly: Australian Littoral Society. Bulletin (ISSN 0157-308X)
Description: Contains commentary on Australian marine and coastal conservation issues, particularly the management of the Great Barrier Reef Marine Park and Australian Mangroves.

333.7   AT   ISSN 0313-7414
AUSTRALIAN NATIONAL UNIVERSITY. CENTRE FOR RESOURCE AND ENVIRONMENTAL STUDIES. WORKING PAPERS. 1974. irreg. free. Australian National University, Centre for Resource and Environmental Studies (C.R.E.S.), Canberra, A.C.T. 0200, Australia. TEL 61-6-2494277. FAX 61-6-2490757. E-mail: publications@cres.anu.edu.au. Ed. Gordon Sheldon. circ. 500.

639.9   AT   ISSN 1320-9736
AUSTRALIAN NATURE CONSERVATION AGENCY. ANNUAL REPORT. 1976. a. Australian Government Publishing Service, G.P.O. Box 84, Canberra, A.C.T. 2601, Australia. TEL 61-6-295-4411. FAX 61-6-295-4455. TELEX AA62013. illus. **Document type:** government publication.
—CCC.
Formerly: Australian National Parks and Wildlife Service. Report (ISSN 0314-1322)

333.78   AT   ISSN 0311-8223
AUSTRALIAN PARKS & RECREATION. 1964. q. Aus.$40 (foreign Aus.$48) to non-members. Royal Australian Institute of Parks & Recreation, Bldg. E, National Exhibition Centre, Flemington Rd., Lyneham, A.C.T. 2602, Australia. TEL 61-06-241-4371. FAX 61-06-241-5817. (Subscr. to: P.O. Box 603, Dickson, A.C.T. 2602, Australia) Ed.Bd.; Pub. Eva Smith. R&P contact: Eva Smith. adv. contact: Eva Smith. bk.rev.; illus.; index; circ. 1,800 (controlled). (back issues avail.) **Indexed:** Forest.Abstr., Forest Prod.Abstr., Geo.Abstr.H.G., Rural Recreat.Tour.Abstr., Sportsearch (1979-), World Agri.Econ.& Rural Sociol.Abstr. **Document type:** trade publication.
—BLDSC (1817.651000); UnCover.
Formerly: Australian Parks (ISSN 0004-9956)
Refereed Serial

AUSTRALIAN PRIMATOLOGY. see *BIOLOGY — Zoology*

579 333.7   AT   ISSN 0155-266X
AUSTRALIAN WILDLIFE NEWSLETTER. 1966. q. Aus.$20 membership. Wildlife Preservation Society of Australia, G.P.O. Box 3428, Sydney, N.S.W. 2001, Australia. TEL 61-43-434708. Ed. Pat Medway. bk.rev.; circ. 1,000 (paid). **Document type:** newsletter.

B B C WILDLIFE. see *BIOLOGY — Zoology*

333.7 340   US   ISSN 1049-3972
BACK FORTY. 1990. bi-m. $110. c/o Hastings College of Law, 200 McAllister St., San Francisco, CA 94102. TEL 415-565-4857. FAX 415-565-4818. Ed. William T. Hutton. R&P contact: Dana M. Landrum. adv. contact: Dana M. Landrum. index. circ. 500. (looseleaf format; back issues avail.) **Document type:** newsletter.

333.7 614.7   US   ISSN 0885-615X
BEAR NEWS. 1983. q. $25. Great Bear Foundation, Box 1289, Bozeman, MT 59771. TEL 406-586-5533. FAX 406-586-6103. E-mail: great bears@aol.com. Ed. Matthew Reid. adv. contact: Tom Shands. bk.rev.; circ. 2,000. circ. 5,000 (paid). (tabloid format; back issues avail.) **Indexed:** Environ.Abstr. **Document type:** newsletter.
Description: Conservation of 8 species of wild bears and bear habitat around the world.

THE BEAVER DEFENDERS; they shall never be trapped anymore. see *ANIMAL WELFARE*

333.7   BE   ISSN 0771-355X
BEENBREEK; Natuur 2000. (Text in Dutch, summaries in English) 1969. bi-m. 950 BEF($25) Natuur 2000, Bervoetstraat 33, 2000 Antwerp, Belgium. TEL 32-3-2312604. FAX 32-3-2336499. Ed. Julius-Anton Smeyers. adv.: B&W page 9000 BEF; adv. contact: Mart Pauwels. bk.rev.; illus.; index. circ. 2,500. (back issues avail.) **Document type:** bulletin.
Description: Includes articles on the study and conservation of nature in Belgium and the world, coming events agenda, new products information, etc.

BEFRIENDING CREATION. see *RELIGIONS AND THEOLOGY*

333.7   GW   ISSN 0525-4736
BEITRAEGE ZUR LANDESENTWICKLUNG. 1966. irreg., no.51, 1996. price varies. (Landschaftsverband Rheinland, Umweltamt) Rheinland Verlag GmbH, Abtei Brauweiler, Postfach 2140, 50250 Pulheim, Germany. TEL 49-2234-9854265. FAX 49-2234-82503. (Dist. by: Dr. Rudolf Habelt GmbH, Am Buchenhang 1, 53115 Bonn, Germany. TEL 49-228-232016. FAX 49-228-9238322) **Document type:** monographic series.

333.7   GW   ISSN 0405-6779
BEWAEHRUNGSHILFE; Fachzeitschrift fuer Bewaehrungs-, Gerichts- und Straffaelligenhilfe. 1953. q. DM.87.50 (effective 1997). (Deutsche Bewaehrungshilfe e.V.) Forum Verlag Godesberg GmbH, Parkstr. 55, 41061 Moenchengladbach, Germany. TEL 49-2161-206669. FAX 49-2161-209183. **Indexed:** Abstr.Crim.& Pen., IBR. **Document type:** newspaper.

BILTEN DOKUMENTACIJE. ZASTITA COVEKOVE OKOLINE I ISKORISCENJE OTPADAKA/BULLETIN OF DOCUMENTATION. ENVIRONMENTAL PROTECTION AND WASTE UTILIZATION. see *CONSERVATION — Abstracting, Bibliographies, Statistics*

577   CR   ISSN 0250-6963
BIOCENOSIS. 1979. 2/yr. Col.1700 (Central America $13; N. and S. America $15; Europe $20; Africa and Asia $21) (effective 1997). Universidad Estatal a Distancia, Oficina de Extencion Comunitaria y Conservacion del Medio Ambiente, Apdo. 474-2050, 2050 San Pedro de Montes de Oca, San Jose, Costa Rica. TEL 506-2532121. FAX 506-2346547. E-mail: biocenos@arenal.uned.ac.cr. Ed. Martha Camacho. R&P contact: Oscar Raul Hernandez. adv. contact: Oscar Raul Hernandez. **Document type:** academic/scholarly publication.

CONSERVATION

333.7 UK ISSN 0960-3115
CODEN: BONSEU
BIODIVERSITY AND CONSERVATION. 1991. 9/yr. £60($99) to individuals; institutions in the E.U. £215 (N. America $365; elsewhere £235) (effective 1995). Chapman & Hall, Journals Department (Subsidiary of: International Thomson Publishing Group), 2-6 Boundary Row, London SE1 8HN, England. TEL 44-171-8650066. FAX 44-171-5229623. TELEX 290164 CHAPMA G. E-mail: jhelp@chall.co.uk; URL: http://www.chaphall.com/chaphall/journals.html. (Dist. by: International Thomson Publishing Services, Ltd., Cheriton House, North Way, Andover, Hants. SP10 5BE, England. TEL 44-1264-342713. FAX 44-1264-342807; Subscr. in US & Canada to: 400 Market St., Philadelphia, PA 19106. TEL 800-552-5866) Eds. Alan T. Bull, Ian R. Swingland. adv. (reprint service avail.). **Indexed:** ASCA, Bibl.Agri., Curr.Cont., Ecol.Abstr., Environ.Abstr., Environ.Per.Bibl. (1993-), Geo.Abstr.H.G., IDA, SSCI. **Document type:** academic/scholarly publication.
●Also available online.
—BLDSC (2071.700000); ADONIS; CISTI; EMDOCS; Genuine Article; SWETS; UnCover. CCC.
Description: Devoted to papers on biological diversity in all its aspects, its description, analysis and conservation, and its controlled and rational use by man.
Refereed Serial

639.9 UK ISSN 0006-3207
S900 CODEN: BICOBK
BIOLOGICAL CONSERVATION. 1969. m. fl.2343($1347) (effective 1998). Elsevier Science Ltd., P.O. Box 800, Kidlington, Oxford OX5 1DX, England. TEL 44-1865-843000. FAX 44-1865-843010. E-mail: nlinfo-f@elsevier.nl; usinfo@elsevier.com; forinfo-kyf04035@niftyserve.or.jp; URL: http://www.elsevier.nl/. (Subscr. to: Elsevier Science, Regional Sales Office, P.O. Box 211, 1000 AE Amsterdam, Netherlands. TEL 31-20-4853757. FAX 31-20-4853432; Subscr. in the Americas to: Elsevier Science, Regional Sales Office, Box 945, New York, NY 10159-0945. TEL 212-633-3730. FAX 212-633-3680; Subscr. in Australasia and the Far East to: Elsevier Science (Singapore) Pte Ltd, No.1 Temasek Ave., No.17-01 Millenia Tower, Singapore 039192, Singapore. TEL 65-434-3727. FAX 65-337-2230) Ed. Dr. Eric Duffey. adv.; bk.rev.; charts; illus. (also avail. in microform from UMI; back issues avail.). **Indexed:** Acid Pre.Dig., ASCA, Bio-Contr.News & Info., Biol.Abstr., Biol.& Agr.Ind., Curr.Adv.Ecol.Sci., Curr.Cont., Deep Sea Res.& Oceanogr.Abstr., Ecol.Abstr., Energy Ind., Energy Info.Abstr., Energy Rev., Environ.Per.Bibl. (1975-), Excerp.Med., Field Crop Abstr., Forest.Abstr., Forest Prod.Abstr., Geo.Abstr.H.G., Geo.Abstr.P.G., GeoRef., Herb.Abstr., IDA, Ind.Sci.Rev., Ind.Vet., Key Word Ind.Wildl.Res., Plant Breed.Abstr., Sci.Cit.Ind., Sel.Water Res.Abstr., Soils & Fert., Sport Fish.Abstr., SSCI, Vet.Bull., W.R.C.Inf., Weed Abstr., Wild.Rev., Zoo.Rec. **Document type:** academic/scholarly publication.
—BLDSC (2075.100000); CISTI; EMDOCS; Genuine Article; KR SourceOne; Linda Hall; SWETS; UnCover. CCC.
Description: Publishes original papers dealing with the preservation of wildlife and the conservation or wise use of biological and allied natural resources.
Refereed Serial

HABIOSPHERA. see *ENVIRONMENTAL STUDIES*

639.9 CN ISSN 0824-1600
QH75.A1
BIOSPHERE. (Text in French) 1985. 5/yr. $26.75 (effective 1996). (Canadian Wildlife Federation - Federation Canadienne de la Faune) Malcolm Publishing Inc., 11 450 Albert-Hudon Blvd., Montreal N., PQ H1G 3J9, Canada. TEL 514-327-4464. FAX 514-327-7592. Ed. Sylvie Berube. adv.; bk.rev. circ. 20,000. **Indexed:** Pt.de Rep. (1987-). Incorporates: Biosphere en Bref.
Description: Full-colour magazine dealing with the environment, wildlife, and the conservation of natural resources.

BIRD WATCHING. see *BIOLOGY — Ornithology*

BIRDLIFE INTERNATIONAL. STUDY REPORT. see *BIOLOGY — Ornithology*

BIRDWATCHER'S YEARBOOK AND DIARY. see *BIOLOGY — Ornithology*

BLUE BILL. see *BIOLOGY — Ornithology*

639.9 US ISSN 0196-3430
BLUE GOOSE FLYER. 1975. q. $25. National Wildlife Refuge Association, 1000 Thomas Jefferson St., N.W., Ste. 311, Washington, DC 20007-7835. TEL 202-298-8095. FAX 202-298-8155. E-mail: nwra@dittusgroup.com; URL: http://www.RefugeNET.com. R&P contact: Anne Criss. bk.rev. circ. 2,000. **Document type:** newsletter.
Description: Provides informational and educational material on issues concerning the National Wildlife Refuge System, individual refuge units, refuge personnel changes, and association news.

333.7 GW ISSN 0935-2171
BODENSCHUTZ. 1988. irreg. DM.196. Erich Schmidt Verlag GmbH & Co. (Berlin), Genthiner Str. 30G, 10785 Berlin, Germany. TEL 49-30-250085-0. FAX 49-30-25008521. (looseleaf format) **Document type:** bulletin.

333.7 614.7 AT ISSN 0159-6586
BOGONG. 1980. q. Aus.$15 to individuals; school libraries Aus.$18; institutions Aus.$20 (effective 1997). Canberra and South East Region Environment Centre, G.P.O. Box 1875, Canberra, A.C.T. 2601, Australia. TEL 61-6-2480885. FAX 61-6-2480885. Ed. Tamsin Salehian, Sharon Ford. R&P contact: Tamsin Salehian. adv.; bk.rev. circ. 500. (back issues avail.) **Indexed:** Alt.Press Ind. **Document type:** academic/scholarly publication, consumer publication.
Description: Covers primarily local and regional with some national and international environmental and related social issues.

BOMENNIEUWS. see *GARDENING AND HORTICULTURE*

333.7 NE
BOS- EN NATUURBEHEER IN NEDERLAND. N.S. 1994. irreg., vol.6, 1997. price varies. Backhuys Publishers, P.O. Box 321, 2300 AH Leiden, Netherlands. TEL 31-71-5170208. FAX 31-71-5171856. E-mail: backhuys@euronet.nl; URL: http://www.euronet.nl/users/backhuys/. **Document type:** monographic series.
Supersedes: Reeks Natuurbeheer in Nederland.

333.7 US ISSN 0899-2681
BOUNDARY WATERS JOURNAL; the magazine of America's favorite wilderness area. 1987. q. $13 (effective 1993). Boundary Waters Journal Publishing Co., 9396 Rocky Ledge Rd., Ely, MN 55731. TEL 218-365-6184. Ed. Stuart Ostroff. circ. 18,500. (back issues avail.)
Description: Covers canoeing, camping, fishing, and natural resource management for both the expert, as well as the novice.

333.7 628 CN ISSN 0824-5126
BRANTA; Canada's forum for environmental awareness. 1983? s-a. Can.$40 individual membership; families Can.$60; newsstand price: Can.$2.50. Fort Whyte Foundation Inc., 1961 McCreary Rd., Winnipeg, MB R3P 2K9, Canada. TEL 204-989-8355. FAX 202-895-4700. Ed. Kimberly Palmer. R&P contact: Kimberly Palmer. adv. contact: Kimberly Palmer. illus. circ. 5,000. **Document type:** newsletter.
Description: Covers environmental wildlife themes.

333.7 CN ISSN 1195-4825
GE190.C2
BRITISH COLUMBIA. MINISTRY OF ENVIRONMENT, LANDS AND PARKS. ANNUAL REPORT. 1964. a. free. Ministry of Environment, Lands and Parks, Public Affairs and Communications Branch, 810 Blansfard St., 1st Fl., Victoria, BC V8V 1X4, Canada. TEL 604-387-9422. FAX 604-356-6464. circ. 3,000. **Document type:** government publication.
—BLDSC (1352.878000).
Former titles (until 1992): British Columbia. Ministry of Environment. Annual Report (ISSN 1181-8336); (until 1989): British Columbia. Ministry of Environment and Parks. Annual Report (ISSN 0838-1933); British Columbia. Ministry of Environment. Annual Report (ISSN 0227-7506); British Columbia. Department of Lands, Forests and Water Resources. Water Resources Service. Report (ISSN 0068-1873)

333.7 US
BROADSIDES. 4/yr. $25 includes membership. Great Old Broads for Wilderness, 1942 Broadway St. 206, Boulder, CT 80302-5213. TEL 406-543-4205. E-mail: gobsmt@aol.com. Ed. Michael J. Hoffer. R&P contact: Paula Hoffer Raines. **Document type:** newsletter.

BROOKER'S RESOURCE MANAGEMENT GAZETTE. see *LAW*

799.2 US ISSN 0889-6445
BUGLE (MISSOULA); journal of elk and the hunt. 1984. q. $35. Rocky Mountain Elk Foundation, Box 8249, Missoula, MT 59807-8249. TEL 406-523-4568. FAX 406-523-4550. URL: http://www.rmef.org. Ed. Dan Crockett. adv. contact: Tara Sheridan. circ. 150,000 (paid). **Document type:** consumer publication.
—UnCover.
Description: Focuses on conserving elk, other wildlife and their habitat, from the viewpoints of hunters, naturalists and all those who care about elk.

BUILDINGS ENERGY TECHNOLOGY; a current awareness bulletin. see *BUILDING AND CONSTRUCTION*

639.9 FR ISSN 0767-2861
CODEN: BFPPE2
BULLETIN FRANCAIS DE LA PECHE ET DE LA PISCICULTURE. (Text in French; summaries in English, French) 1928. q. 220 F. (foreign 280 F.) (effective 1997). Conseil Superieur de la Peche, Centre du Paraclet, B.P. 5, 80440 Boves, France. TEL 33-3-22353480. FAX 33-3-22353484. (Subscr. to: Conseil Superieur de la Peche, Attn: Mlle. Gentil, 134 avenue de Malakoff, 75116 Paris, France. TEL 33-1-45022020. FAX 33-1-45012723) Ed. Erick Vigneux. R&P contact: Erick Vigneux. bk.rev.; bibl.; illus.; index. circ. 1,000. (back issues avail.) **Indexed:** Anim.Breed.Abstr., Aqua.Sci. & Fish.Abstr., ASCA, Biol.Abstr., Bull.Signal., Curr.Adv.Ecol.Sci., Curr.Cont., Curr.Ref.Fish Res., Excerp.Med., Ind.Vet., Nutr.Abstr., Sport Fish.Abstr., Vet.Bull., W.R.C.Inf., Wild.Rev., Zoo.Rec. **Document type:** bulletin.
—CASDDS; Genuine Article.
Formerly (until 1985): Bulletin Francais de Pisciculture (ISSN 0373-0514)

BULLETIN G C I D. (Greek National Committee) see *WATER RESOURCES*

333.7 700 AU
BURGENBOTE; Oesterreichs Bindenschild. vol.5, 1973. 4/yr. membership. Burgen- und Schloessererhaltungsverein, Stadtamt, A-2070 Retz, Austria. Ed. Fred Borth. adv.; illus. circ. 1,000. **Document type:** bulletin.

333.7 US
BUSINESS ASSOCIATE; partners in land conservation. 1984. s-a. membership. Western Pennsylvania Conservancy, 209 Fourth Ave., Pittsburgh, PA 15222-1707. TEL 412-288-2777. FAX 412-281-1792. Ed. Bill Randour. circ. 1,000. (back issues avail.) **Document type:** newsletter.
Description: Reports on various environmental activities of member companies for the corporate members of the Western Pennsylvania Conservancy.

639.9 179.3 SZ ISSN 0254-0878
CODEN: BUSTEW
BUSTARD STUDIES. 1983. a. £10. Birdlife International Wellbrook Ct., Girton Rd., Cambridge CB3 0NA, England. **Document type:** academic/scholarly publication.

333.7 SW ISSN 0345-7982
BYGD OCH NATUR; tidskrift foer hembygdsvaard. 1920. 5/yr. SEK 150 (effective 1997). Sveriges Hembygdsfoerbund, S H F - National Association for the Preservation of Swedish Culture and Nature, P.C Box 6167, S-102 33 Stockholm, Sweden. TEL 46-8-34-55-11. FAX 46-8-34-74-74. Eds. Henrik Axioe, Gunilla Lindberg, Peter Johansson. adv.; bk.rev. circ. 12,000.
Formerly (until 1939): Tidskrift foer Hembygdsvaard (ISSN 0007-7453)

CONSERVATION

577 AT ISSN 1320-145X
C A L M SCIENCE. (Conservation and Land Management) Variant title: CALMScience. 1994. irreg. Aus.$30 per issue. Department of Conservation and Land Management, Locked Bag 104, Bentley Delivery Centre, W.A. 6893, Australia. TEL 61-9-334-0333. FAX 61-9-334-8296. Ed. Marianne Lewis. circ. 500. (back issues avail.) **Indexed:** Aus.Sci.Ind., Biol.Abstr., Forest.Abstr., Forest Prod.Abstr., Sport Fish.Abstr., Wild.Rev., Zoo.Rec. —BLDSC (3015.446000).
Formed by the merger of (1985-1994): Western Australia. Department of Conservation and Land Management. Technical Report (ISSN 0816-6757); Which was formerly: Western Australia. Department of Conservation and Land Management. Occasional Paper (ISSN 0816-9675); (1986-1994): Western Australia. Department of Conservation and Land Management. Research Bulletin (ISSN 1032-8106); Which was formerly (until 1986): Western Australia. Department of Conservation and Land Management. Bulletin (ISSN 0816-9675); Western Australia. Forest Department. Bulletin (ISSN 0085-8129).
Description: For those interested in nature conservation, sustainable utilization and land management.
Refereed Serial

639.9 US
C B E ENVIRONMENTAL REVIEW. 1972. 3/yr. $30 to individuals; students and seniors $20. Citizens for a Better Environment, 3255 Hennepin Ave., S., Ste. 150, Minneapolis, MN 55408. TEL 612-824-8637. FAX 612-824-0506. Ed. Sarah Johanneson. bk.rev. circ. 48,000. **Indexed:** Alt.Press Ind. **Document type:** newsletter.

639.9 179.3 SZ
C B S G NEWS. (Captive Breeding Specialist Group) (Text in English) 4/yr. $25. International Union for Conservation of Nature and Natural Resources, Species Survival Commission, Rue Mauverney 28, CH-1196 Gland, Switzerland. TEL 41-22-9990001. FAX 41-22-9990002. TELEX 419624-IUCN-CH. (Subscr. to: 12101 Johnny Cake Ridge Rd., Apple Valley, MN 55124, USA) **Document type:** newsletter.

C C I NEWSLETTER/BULLETIN DE L'I C C. see *MUSEUMS AND ART GALLERIES*

C C I NOTES/NOTES DE L'I C C. see *MUSEUMS AND ART GALLERIES*

C C I TECHNICAL BULLETINS/I C C BULLETINS TECHNIQUES. (Canadian Conservation Institute) see *MUSEUMS AND ART GALLERIES*

333.7 US
C E A S E NEWS. 1980. 3/yr. $10. Concerned Educators Allied for a Safe Environment, c/o Peggy Schirmer, Ed., 17 Gerry St., Cambridge, MA 02138. TEL 617-864-0999. bk.rev. circ. 900. **Document type:** newsletter.
Description: Provides a forum for the exchange of ideas on how to help children become peaceful and constructive citizens, with a sense of responsibility towards their environment.

C E L S S JOURNAL/C E L S S GAKKAISHI. (Japan Society for Controlled Ecological and Life Support Systems) see *BIOLOGY*

C E L S S NEWS. (Japan Society for Controlled Ecological and Life Support Systems) see *BIOLOGY*

C N P S INVENTORY OF RARE AND ENDANGERED VASCULAR PLANTS OF CALIFORNIA. (California Native Plant Society) see *BIOLOGY — Botany*

179 333.7 US
C - PAPER. (Inserted in the Civil Abolitionist) 1983. q. Coalition to Protect Animals in Parks & Refuges, Box 26, Swain, NY 14884-0026. TEL 607-545-6213. Ed. Bina Robinson. bk.rev. circ. 2,300. **Document type:** bulletin.
Formerly: Coalition to Protect Animales in Parks and Refuges.
Description: Current information on wildlife and environmental issues.

333.78 US ISSN 0887-9176
S P R A NEWSLETTER. 1968. bi-m. $36. California State Park Rangers Association, Box 292010, Sacramento, CA 95829-2010. TEL 916-558-3734. FAX 916-387-1179. Ed. Doug Bryce. bk.rev. circ. 700. (tabloid format; back issues avail.) **Document type:** newsletter.

333.9 630 US
C T F A STRAIGHT TALK. 1994. bi-m. $50 membership. Committee for Truth in Farmland Assessment, Box 238, Cream Ridge, NJ 08514-0238. Ed. Sandra Borah. **Document type:** newsletter.
Description: Works to promote and improve New Jersey's 1964 Farmland Assessment Act, encouraging maintenance of open space at little or no cost to all taxpayers in the state.

333.91 US ISSN 1052-5823
CALIFORNIA COAST & OCEAN. 1985. q. $18 (foreign $33) (effective 1997). California State Coastal Conservancy, 1330 Broadway, Ste. 1100, Oakland, CA 94612-2530. TEL 510-286-0934. FAX 510-286-0470. E-mail: calcoast@igc.apc.com; URL: http://www.coastalcauseway.ca.gov. Ed. Rasa Gustaitis. R&P contact: Rasa Gustaitis. bk.rev.; illus.; index. circ. 9,300. **Indexed:** Environ.Per.Bibl.
Formerly (until 1990): California WaterfrontAge (ISSN 8756-0852)
Description: Covers California coastal environmental issues.

639.9 591 US ISSN 0008-1078
SK373 CODEN: CAFGAX
CALIFORNIA FISH AND GAME. 1914. q. $15. Department of Fish and Game, 1416 Ninth St., Sacramento, CA 95814. TEL 916-653-7664. bk.rev.; bibl.; illus.; index. circ. 1,000. (also avail. in microform from UMI; reprint service avail. from UMI) **Indexed:** ASCA, Biol.Abstr., Cal.Per.Ind. (1978-), Chem.Abstr., Curr.Adv.Ecol.Sci., Curr.Cont., Curr.Ref.Fish Res., Deep Sea Res.& Oceanogr.Abstr., Environ.Abstr., Environ.Per.Bibl. (1972-), Forest.Abstr., Forest Prod.Abstr., Helminthol.Abstr., Ind.Vet., Key Word Ind.Wildl.Res., Nutr.Abstr., Sci.Cit.Ind., Sel.Water Res.Abstr., Sport Fish.Abstr., Vet.Bull., W.R.C.Inf., Wild.Rev., Zoo.Rec. —BLDSC (3013.000000); Genuine Article; Linda Hall; UMI; UnCover.

333.7 US
CALIFORNIA FISH AND GAME CODE. SUPPLEMENT. a. $19.95 (effective Jan. 1996). (Department of Fish and Game) Gould Publications, 1333 N. U.S. Hwy. 17-92, Longwood, FL 32750-3724. TEL 407-695-9500. FAX 407-695-2906. index. (looseleaf format)

CALIFORNIA PARKS & RECREATION. see *LEISURE AND RECREATION*

CALIFORNIA TODAY. see *ENVIRONMENTAL STUDIES*

333.95 628 CN ISSN 1194-2258
CALL OF THE LOON. 1991. m. Ontario Federation of Anglers & Hunters, 4601 Guthrie Dr., P.O. Box 2800, Peterborough, ON K9J 8L5, Canada. TEL 705-748-6324. FAX 705-748-9577. E-mail: ofah@oncomdis.on.ca. Ed. Mark Holmes. R&P contact: Mark Holmes. adv.: page Can.$500; adv. contact: Mark Holmes. charts, illus, maps, stat, tr.lit.; circ. 1,300 (controlled). cols./p.: 5; pp./issue: 8. (tabloid format; back issues avail.) **Document type:** newsletter.
Description: Disseminates club project news, issues and event information.

639.9 US ISSN 1074-9209
THE CALLER. 1990. q. $25 membership. National Wild Turkey Foundation, Inc., Box 530, 770 Augusta Rd., Edgefield, SC 29824-0530. TEL 803-637-3106. FAX 803-637-0034. E-mail: nwtf@gab.net. Ed. Shannon Geiger. adv. contact: Danny Young. stat.; circ. 137,000 (paid). (tabloid format; back issues avail.)
Description: Includes articles submitted by volunteer members and state conservation agencies.

CALYPSO LOG. see *ENVIRONMENTAL STUDIES*

639.9 796.5 BL ISSN 0104-1541
OS CAMINHOS DA TERRA. Short title: Terra. 1992. m. $60. Editora Azul, S.A., Av. Nacoes Unidas, 5777, 05479-900 Sao Paulo SP, Brazil. TEL 55-11-867300. FAX 55-11-8673311. TELEX 55-11-83178-EDAZ. E-mail: benjamin.goncalvez@email.abril.br.com. (Subscr. to: Rua do Curtume 769, 05065-900 Sao Paulo SP, Brazil. TEL 011-823-9100) Ed. Jorge de Souza. R&P contact: Benjamin Goncalvez. TEL 55-11-8673304. adv.: color page $11500; 202 x 266; adv. contact: Enio Vergeiro. illus.; circ. 112,482 (paid). **Document type:** consumer publication.
Description: Covers nature, ecology, adventure travel, and exotic places.

639.9 CN ISSN 0703-6027
CANADA. CANADIAN WILDLIFE FEDERATION. PUBLICATION LIST. 1974. a. Can.$26.75 (foreign Can.$34.75). Malcolm Publishing Inc., 11 450 Albert-Hudon Blvd., Montreal, PQ H1G 3J9, Canada. TEL 514-327-4464. FAX 514-327-7592. Ed. Martin Silverstone. adv. contact: Gaby Gagnon. circ. 45,000 (paid). **Document type:** consumer publication.
Formerly: Canada. Federal-Provincial Wildlife Conference. Wildlife Management Papers.
Refereed Serial

333.91 CN ISSN 0227-4787
TC426
CANADA WATER ACT. ANNUAL REPORT. (Text in English and French) 1973. a. Environment Canada, 351 St. Joseph Blvd., 18th Fl., Place Vincent Massey, Hull, PQ K1A 0H3, Canada. TEL 819-953-1610. FAX 819-953-7253. E-mail: jim.moyes@ec.gc.ca. (Subscr. to: Environmental Protection Publications, Technology Transfer Office, Environmental Technology Advancement Directorate, Environment Canada, Ottawa, ON K1A 0H3, Canada. TEL 819-953-5750) **Document type:** government publication.
—CISTI; Linda Hall.
Formerly (until 1974): Canada. Department of the Environment. Report of Operations Under the Canada Water Act (ISSN 0714-1114)

333.7 CN
CANADIAN HUNTING AND FISHING TRADE NEWS. 1995. q. Ontario Federation of Anglers & Hunters, 4601 Guthrie Dr., P.O. Box 2800, Peterborough, ON K9J 8L5, Canada. TEL 705-748-6324. FAX 705-748-9577. E-mail: ofah@oncomdis.on.ca. Ed. Mark Holmes. R&P contact: Mark Holmes. circ. 3,000. (tabloid format)
Description: Explores the topic of conservation and natural resources and their impact on outdoor retailers and manufacturers.

639.9 CN ISSN 0318-5133
CANADIAN SOCIETY OF ENVIRONMENTAL BIOLOGISTS NEWSLETTER. 1958. q. Can.$35 (foreign Can.$45). Canadian Society of Environmental Biologists, P.O. Box 962, Stn. F, Toronto, ON M4Y 2N9, Canada. TEL 403-481-1253. Ed. Katrina Hodgson. R&P contact: Gerry Leering. TEL 705-743-9834. adv. contact: Gary Ash. bk.rev. circ. 500. **Document type:** newsletter.
Formerly: Canadian Wildlife and Fisheries Newsletter Bulletin (ISSN 0045-5571)
Description: Deals with national issues and practice of environmental management from an ecological perspective.

639.9 CN ISSN 1201-673X
CANADIAN WILDLIFE. 1965. 5/yr. Can.$26.75 membership (effective 1996). (Canadian Wildlife Federation) Malcolm Publishing Inc., 11 450 Albert-Hudon Blvd., Montreal, PQ H1G 3J9, Canada. TEL 514-327-4464. FAX 514-327-7592. Ed. Martin Silverstone. bk.rev. circ. 77,000.
—CISTI.
Formerly: International Wildlife (Canadian Edition); Incorporates: Wildlife Update; Formerly: Canadian Chronicle; Supersedes: Wildlife News (ISSN 0043-5503)
Description: Contains wide range of subjects including articles on wildlife, wild areas, nature-related research, endangered species, wildlife management, land use issues, character profiles and the science and politics of conservation.

639.9 CN ISSN 0576-6370
CODEN: CWOPAL
CANADIAN WILDLIFE SERVICE. OCCASIONAL PAPERS. (Editions in English, French) 1966. irreg., no.76, 1992. free. Canadian Wildlife Service, Environment Canada, Ottawa, ON K1A 0H3, Canada. TEL 819-997-1095. FAX 819-953-6283. Ed. Pat Logan. circ. 2,000. **Indexed:** Biol.Abstr., Curr.Adv.Ecol.Sci., Ecol.Abstr., Key Word Ind.Wildl.Res., Nutr.Abstr., Rural Recreat.Tour.Abstr., Sport Fish.Abstr., Wild.Rev., World Agri.Econ.& Rural Sociol.Abstr., Zoo.Rec. **Document type:** government publication.
—BLDSC (6215.500000); CISTI; Linda Hall.
Description: Contains research results of major CWS wildlife studies.

CONSERVATION

639.9   CN   ISSN 0069-0023
CODEN: CWPNBL
CANADIAN WILDLIFE SERVICE. PROGRESS NOTES/SERVICE CANADIEN DE LA FAUNE. CAHIERS DE BIOLOGIE. (Editions in English, French) 1967. irreg., no.203, 1993. free. Canadian Wildlife Service, Environment Canada, Ottawa, ON K1A 0H3, Canada. TEL 819-997-1095. FAX 819-953-6283. Ed. Pat Logan. circ. 2,000. **Indexed:** Biol.Abstr., Curr.Adv.Ecol.Sci., IBR, Key Word Ind.Wildl.Res., Sport Fish.Abstr., Wild.Rev., Zoo.Rec. **Document type:** government publication, monographic series.
—Linda Hall.
  Description: Contains data and conclusions from C.W.S. wildlife studies.

639.9   CN   ISSN 0384-1480
CANADIAN WOLF DEFENDERS. NEWSLETTER.* 1963. q. membership. Canadian Wolf Defenders, 3819 112 A St., Edmonton, Alta. T6J 1K4, Canada. Ed. Dick Dekker. bk.rev.; bibl.; illus.; stat.; tr.lit. circ. 900. (tabloid format)

CAPITALISM, NATURE, SOCIALISM; a journal of socialist ecology. see *POLITICAL SCIENCE*

639.9 179.3   SZ
CAPRINAE NEWS. a. $10. International Union for Conservation of Nature and Natural Resources, Species Survival Commission - Caprinae Specialist Group, Rue Mauverney 28, CH-1196 Gland, Switzerland. TEL 41-22-9990001. FAX 41-22-9990002. TELEX 419624-IUCN-CH. (Subscr. to: Sandro Lovari, Dept. of Evol. Biology, University of Siena, Via P.A. Mattioli 4, 53100 Siena, Italy) **Document type:** newsletter.

333.7   BB
CARIBBEAN CONSERVATION ASSOCIATION. ANNUAL REPORT. 1991. a. Caribbean Conservation Association, Savannah Lodge, The Garrison, St. Michael, Barbados, W.I. TEL 246-426-9633. FAX 246-429-8483. E-mail: cca@caribsurf.com; URL: http://www.tidco.cao.tt/local/seduweb/cca/cca.html. **Document type:** corporate report.
  Description: Provides information on programs and activities for the year. Includes audited financial statements.

CARIBBEAN RESEARCH INSTITUTE. REPORT. see *HISTORY — History Of North And South America*

333.7 363.73   US
CARRYING CAPACITY NETWORK. NETWORK BULLETIN. 1991. bi-m. $25 to individuals; institutions $85; students $20. Carrying Capacity Network, Inc., 2000 P St., N.W., Ste. 240, Washington, DC 20036. TEL 202-296-4548. FAX 202-296-4609. E-mail: ccn@igc.apc.org. Ed. David F. Durham; Pub. Ed Lytvak. R&P contact: Ed Lytvak. adv. contact: Leon Kolankiewicz. illus.; charts. circ. 5,000. **Document type:** newsletter.
  Formerly: Carrying Capacity Network Clearinghouse Bulletin (ISSN 1066-5404)
  Description: Provides current information on developments in fields such as national revitalization, population stabilization, immigration restriction, resource conservation and economic sustainability.

639.9 179.3   SZ
CARTA NOTICIAS. (Text in Spanish) 2/yr. International Union for Conservation of Nature and Natural Resources, Species Survival Commission - South American Camelid Specialist Group, Rue Mauverney 28, CH-1196 Gland, Switzerland. TEL 41-22-9990001. FAX 41-22-9990002. (Subscr. to: Dra. Silvia Puig, CRICYT, Casilla de Correo 507, 5500 Mendoza, Argentina) **Document type:** academic/scholarly publication.

639.9 179.3   SZ
CAT NEWS. (Text in English) 2/yr. 54 SFr.($40) International Union for Conservation of Nature and Natural Resources, Species Survival Commission - Cat Specialist Group, Rue Mauverney 28, CH-1196 Gland, Switzerland. TEL 41-22-9990001. FAX 41-22-9990002. TELEX 419624-IUCN-CH. E-mail: peterjackson@gn.apc.org. (Subscr. to: Peter Jackson, CH-1172 Bougy Villars, Switzerland). **Indexed:** Key Word Ind.Wildl.Res. **Document type:** newsletter.

333.7   US   ISSN 1087-8491
CENTRAL ATLANTIC ENVIRONMENTAL DIRECTORY. 1996. biennial. $18.50. Harbinger Communications, Box 8175, Missoula, MT 59807. TEL 406-721-0440. FAX 406-721-0440. E-mail: ned@ism.net. index. (also avail. in diskette format) **Document type:** directory.
  ●Also available online.
  Description: Annotated listings of citizen groups, government agencies in New Jersey, New York and Pennsylvania.

333.78   US
CENTRAL PARK CONSERVANCY. a. Central Park Conservancy, The Arsenal, Central Park, New York, NY 10021. **Document type:** corporate report.

639.9 179.3   SZ   ISSN 1071-8443
QL666.C5   CODEN: CCOBED
CHELONIAN CONSERVATION BIOLOGY. s-a. International Union for Conservation of Nature and Natural Resources, Species Survival Commission - Tortoise and Freshwater Turtle Specialist Group, Rue Mauverney 28, CH-1196 Gland, Switzerland. TEL 41-22-9990001. FAX 41-22-9990002. TELEX 419624-IUCN-CH. (Subscr. to: Dr. John Behler, New York Zoological Society, Bronx, NY 10460, USA) **Document type:** academic/scholarly publication.
—BLDSC (3133.451900); UnCover.
  Description: Covers all aspects of turtle and tortoise research, particularly concerning their conservation, systemic relationships, diversity, geographic distribution, natural history, reproduction, and morphology.
  Refereed Serial

CHILDREN'S WHALEWATCH. see *CHILDREN AND YOUTH — For*

CHILEANS. see *GARDENING AND HORTICULTURE*

333.7 634.9   JA
CHISAN KENKYU HAPPYOKAI RONBUNSHU/FORESTRY CONSERVATION CONFERENCE, AICHI PREFECTURE. PROCEEDINGS. (Text in Japanese) a. Aichiken Nochi Rinmubu - Aichi Prefectural Government, Agricultural Land and Forestry Administration Division, 1-2, Sannomaru 3-chome, Naka-ku, Nagoya-shi, Aichi-ken 460, Japan. **Document type:** proceedings.

CHRIS AND TILDE STUART'S GUIDE TO SOUTHERN AFRICAN GAME & NATURE RESERVES. see *TRAVEL AND TOURISM*

333.7   PL   ISSN 0009-6172
CODEN: CPZOAO
CHRONMY PRZYRODE OJCZYSTA. (Text in Polish; summaries in English) 1945. bi-m. $20. Polska Akademia Nauk, Instytut Ochrony Przyrody, Ul. Lubicz 46, 31-512 Krakow, Poland. TEL 48-12-210348. FAX 48-12-210348. TELEX 322630 PANZO. (Co-sponsor: Panstwowa Rada Ochrony Przyrody) Ed. Z. Dennisiuk. R&P contact: Elzbieta Skorek. bk.rev.; bibl.; charts; illus.; index. circ. 6,270. **Indexed:** AgroLibrex, Biol.Abstr., Sport Fish.Abstr., Wild.Rev., Zoo.Rec. **Document type:** academic/scholarly publication.

333.78   US   ISSN 1083-3889
CITIZENS FOR CONTROLLED DEVELOPMENT. BULLETIN; saving land in Morris County from overdevelopment. 1990. 3/yr. $20 individual membership. Citizens for Controlled Development, Inc., Box 1101, Morristown, NJ 07962-1101. TEL 973-560-9520. Ed. Peter S. Lemmo. R&P contact: Peter S. Lemmo. circ. 3,000. **Document type:** newsletter.
  Description: Addresses development problems and preservation and land-conservation efforts in Morris County, NJ.

333.78   US
CLEARING HOUSE NEWSLETTER. 1975. m. $100 membership only (effective 1997). National Institute on Park & Grounds Management, Box 1936, Appleton, WI 54913. TEL 414-733-2301. Ed. Barbara Walters. R&P contact: Barbara Walters. adv. circ. 1,100. **Document type:** newsletter.
  Description: Provides information on large outdoor grounds management.

CLEARWATER NAVIGATOR. see *ENVIRONMENTAL STUDIES*

COASTAL SOCIETY BULLETIN. see *ENVIRONMENTAL STUDIES — Pollution*

333.91   US   ISSN 0045-723X
COASTAL ZONE MANAGEMENT; newsletter of coastal resource development, conservation & enhancement. 1969. 3/m. (every 10 days) $355 (foreign $379) (effective 1998). Nautilus Press, Inc., 1201 National Press Bldg., Washington, DC 20045. TEL 202-347-6643. Ed. John R. Botzum. bk.rev.; pat. (processed) **Indexed:** Deep Sea Res.& Oceanogr.Abstr., Environ.Per.Bibl., GeoRef., Ind.Per.Art.Relat.Law, P.A.I.S. **Document type:** newsletter.
  Incorporates: Environmental Monitor.
  Description: Specializes in reporting on federal-state relationships in the U.S. Coastal Zone and Exclusive Economic Zone, including information on oil, gas, and mineral activities on the outer continental shelf; also covers technical side of coastal management community development, and certain aspects of tourism.

COASTLINES (STONY BROOK). see *EARTH SCIENCES — Oceanography*

333.7   US   ISSN 0084-8875
SK375   CODEN: CWSPA7
COLORADO. DIVISION OF WILDLIFE. SPECIAL REPORT. 1962. irreg., no.67, 1991. $2. Division of Wildlife, 317 W. Prospect, Ft. Collins, CO 80526. TEL 303-484-2836. Ed. Nancy W. McEwen. bibl.; charts; illus.; stat. circ. 1,200. (back issues avail.) **Indexed:** Biol.Abstr., Key Word Ind.Wildl.Res., Sport Fish.Abstr., Wild Life Rev., Wild.Rev., Zoo.Rec.
—Linda Hall.

333.7 639.9   US   ISSN 0084-8883
COLORADO. DIVISION OF WILDLIFE. TECHNICAL PUBLICATION. 1955. irreg., no.39, 1991. $2 per issue. Division of Wildlife, 317 W. Prospect, Ft. Collins, CO 80526. TEL 303-484-2836. Ed. Nancy W. McEwen. bibl.; charts; illus.; stat. circ. 1,200. **Indexed:** Biol.Abstr., Sport Fish.Abstr., Wild Life Rev., Wild.Rev., Zoo.Rec.
—BLDSC (8706.180000); Linda Hall.

COLORADO. DIVISION OF WILDLIFE. TERRESTRIAL AND AQUATIC WILDLIFE RESEARCH. RESEARCH REVIEW. see *FISH AND FISHERIES*

COLORADO OUTDOORS. see *SPORTS AND GAMES — Outdoor Life*

340   US   ISSN 0164-3193
COLORADO WILDLIFE. 1981. bi-m. $25 membership (foreign $30). Colorado Wildlife Federation, 445 Union Blvd., Ste. 302, Lakewood, CO 80228-1243. TEL 303-987-0400. FAX 303-987-0200. E-mail: cwfed@aol.com. Ed. Diane Gansauer. R&P contact: Diane Gansauer. adv. contact: Carolyn Greene. bk.rev. circ. 5,500. **Document type:** newspaper.
  Description: Updates on wildlife-related and natural resource conservation issues in Colorado, particularly issues of interest to Colorado Wildlife Federation members.

333.7 301.35   US   ISSN 0893-276X
COLUMBIANA; bioregional journal for the Intermountain Northwest. 1987. bi-m. $15 (Canada $17). Columbia Bioregional Education Project, Chesaw Rte., Box 83F, Oroville, WA 98844. TEL 509-485-3844. Ed. Geraldine Payton. adv. contact: Stuart R. Gillespie. bk.rev. circ. 6,000.
  Supersedes (1978-1986): Okanogan Natural News.
  Description: Lifestyle and ecology of the intermountain Northwest region.

333.7 614.7   US   ISSN 0198-9103
COMPENDIUM NEWSLETTER; your guide to the world's environmental crisis. 1972. bi-m. $20. Educational Communications, Inc. (Los Angeles), Box 351419, Los Angeles, CA 90035-9119. TEL 310-559-9160. FAX 310-559-9160. E-mail: ecnp@aol.com. Ed. Nancy Pearlman. bk.rev. circ. 800. **Document type:** newsletter.
  Description: Contains ecological news and information.

333.7   US
CONDOR CALL. 10/yr. $5. Sierra Club, 645 C Costal del Mar, Santa Barbara, CA 93103. Ed. Art Benkeim.

CONSCIENCE CANADA NEWSLETTER. see *POLITICAL SCIENCE — Civil Rights*

CONSERVATION 2227

333.7   SA   ISSN 0258-3313
S934.S6
CONSERVA. (Text in Afrikaans and English) 1974. q. free. Department of Environmental Affairs and Tourism, Private Bag X447, Pretoria 0001, South Africa. TEL 27-12-3103415. FAX 27-12-3222476. bk.rev. circ. 30,000. (back issues avail.) **Document type:** government publication.
   Formerly (until 1986): Environment R S A.
   Description: Educational and informational coverage of current environmental issues and problems, as well as research regarding environmental matters.

333.7 570   US   ISSN 0888-8892
QH75.A1   CODEN: CBIOEF
CONSERVATION BIOLOGY. (Text in English; abstracts in Spanish) 1986. q. $250 (foreign $280) (effective 1996). Blackwell Science Inc., 350 Main St., Malden, MA 02148. TEL 617-876-7000. FAX 617-388-8255. Ed. Reed Noss. index. circ. 5,000. (back issues avail.; reprint service avail.) **Indexed:** Anim.Breed.Abstr., ASCA, Bibl.Agri., Biol.& Agr.Ind., Curr.Cont., Ecol.Abstr., Environ.Abstr., Environ.Ind., Environ.Per.Bibl. (1989-), Geo.Abstr.H.G., Geo.Abstr.P.G., IDA, Ind.Sci.Rev., Key Word Ind.Wildl.Res., Sel.Water Res.Abstr., Sport Fish.Abstr., SSCI, Wild.Rev., Wildlife & Conserv.Biol.Abstr. (1986-), Zoo.Rec. **Document type:** academic/scholarly publication.
   —BLDSC (3417.999000); CISTI; EMDOCS; Genuine Article; KR SourceOne; SWETS; UMI; UnCover. **CCC.**

333.7   US   ISSN 0027-6537
CONSERVATION COMMISSION NEWS. 1967. q. $5. New Hampshire Association of Conservation Commissions, 54 Portsmouth St., Concord, NH 03301. TEL 603-224-7867. FAX 603-228-0423. Ed. Marjory M. Swope. adv.; bk.rev.; charts; illus. circ. 1,650. (tabloid format) **Document type:** newsletter.
   Description: Deals with matters of interest to municipal conservation commissioners.

333.7   CN
CONSERVATION COUNCIL OF ONTARIO. CONFERENCE PROCEEDINGS. irreg. price varies. Conservation Council of Ontario, 489 College St., Ste. 506, Toronto, Ont. M6G 1A5, Canada. TEL 416-969-9637. FAX 416-960-8053. **Document type:** proceedings.

333.7   CN
CONSERVATION COUNCIL OF ONTARIO. REPORTS. irreg. price varies. Conservation Council of Ontario, 489 College St., Ste. 506, Toronto, Ont. M6G 1A5, Canada. TEL 416-969-9637. FAX 416-960-8053.

333.7   US   ISSN 0069-911X
S920
CONSERVATION DIRECTORY; a listing of organizations, agencies and officials concerned with natural resource use and management. 1955. a. $55. National Wildlife Federation, 8925 Leesburg Pike, Vienna, VA 22184-0001. TEL 703-790-4000; 800-477-5560. FAX 703-442-7332. E-mail: gordonr@nwf.org; URL: http://www.nwf.org. Ed. Rue Gordon. circ. 13,000. **Document type:** directory.
   —CISTI.

333.7   US   ISSN 1195-5449
CONSERVATION ECOLOGY. q. free. E-mail: info@consecol.org; URL: http://journal.biology.carleton.ca/journal/overview.html. Ed. C.S. Holling.
   ●Available only online.
   Description: Covers the conservation of ecosystems, landscapes, species, populations and genetic diversity; restoration of ecosystems and habitats; and the management of resources.
   Refereed Serial

333.7   UK   ISSN 0262-2203
CONSERVATION EDUCATION; a bulletin for teachers and youth leaders. 1981. 2/yr. £1 (free to schools). Young People's Trust for the Environment and Nature Conservation, 8 Leapale Rd., Guildford, Surrey GU1 4JX, England. TEL 44-1483-39600. FAX 44-1483-301992. Ed. Cyril Littlewood. bk.rev.; illus. circ. 40,000. **Document type:** bulletin.
   Description: A bulletin for teachers, youth leaders and young people.

333.7   UK   ISSN 0309-2224
AM141
CONSERVATION NEWS. 1976. 3/yr. £52. United Kingdom Institute for Conservation, 6 Whitehorse Mews, Westminster Bridge Rd., London SE1 7QD, England. TEL 071-620-3371. Ed. Victoria Todd. adv.; bk.rev. circ. 1,300. **Document type:** newsletter.
   —BLDSC (3418.071000).

CONSERVATION NEWS DIGEST; news briefs for non-industrial private woodland owners across the nation. see FORESTS AND FORESTRY

333.7 614.7   AT   ISSN 0816-875X
CONSERVATION NORTH QUEENSLAND. 1975. m. Aus.$15. North Queensland Conservation Council Inc., P.O. Box 364, Townsville, Qld. 4810, Australia. TEL 61-77-716226. FAX 61-77-7121713. Ed.Bd. bk.rev. circ. 250. (back issues avail.) **Document type:** newsletter.
   Description: Focuses on North Queensland environmental issues and concerns.

CONSERVATION VOTER. see ENVIRONMENTAL STUDIES

333.7   UK   ISSN 0140-0096
N8554
THE CONSERVATOR. 1977. a. £49 to individuals; institutions £60; students £20. United Kingdom Institute for Conservation, 6 Whitehorse Mews, Westminster Bridge Rd., London SE1 7QD, England. TEL 071-620-3371. Ed. Victoria Todd. bk.rev. circ. 950. **Indexed:** Art & Archaeol.Tech.Abstr., Avery Ind.Archit.Per., Br.Archaeol.Abstr., Key to Econ.Sci. **Document type:** academic/scholarly publication.

333.78   US
CONSERVE;* water, land, life. 1971. s-a. membership. Western Pennsylvania Conservancy, 209 Fourth Ave., Pittsburgh, PA 15222-1707. Ed. Bill Randour. circ. 20,000. (tabloid format) **Document type:** newsletter.

333.7   US   ISSN 1093-1007
CONSERVE WILDLIFE. 1978. q. free. Department of Environmental Protection, Division of Fish, Game and Wildlife, CN 400, Trenton, NJ 08625-0400. TEL 609-292-9400. FAX 908-735-5689. Ed. Michael Valent. circ. 41,500. **Document type:** government publication, newsletter.
   Formerly: Nongame News (ISSN 1061-0928)
   Description: Contains articles pertaining to the research, protection and management of native endangered, threatened and nongame wildlife in N.J., with occasional coverage of relevant national and international topics.

333.7   UK   ISSN 0143-4144
CONSERVER; the magazine for people working for a better environment. 1972. q. membership. British Trust for Conservation Volunteers, 36 St. Mary's St., Wallingford, Oxon. OX10 0EU, England. TEL 44-1491-839766. FAX 44-1491-839646. Ed. Melanie Rowe. R&P contact: Melanie Rowe. adv.; bk.rev.; circ. 20,000. (controlled). **Document type:** consumer publication.
   Description: Aims to keep the members and everyone interested in practical conservation up-to-date with news and issues.
   Refereed Serial

CONTEXT (LETCHWORTH). see ARCHITECTURE

333.7 550   II
CORSONAT. (Text in English) 1979. q. Rs.10($2) Corbett Society of Naturalists, 342 Shivaji Rd., Meerut 250 001, India. Ed. Y.M. Rai. adv.; bk.rev. circ. 300.
   Description: Discusses conservation and all aspects of animal and plant life in India.

333.7   US
COUNTRY ROAD GAZETTE. 1993. m. Meadow Ridge Graphics, R.R. 1, Box 345, Milford, PA 18337. TEL 717-828-7782. FAX 717-828-7959. Pub. Elaine Torretta. adv.: B&W page $390; trim 11 1/2 x 15. circ. 9,000 (paid). **Document type:** consumer publication.

333.78   UK
COUNTRYSIDE. 1983. q. free. Countryside Commission, John Dower House, Crescent Pl., Cheltenham, Glos. GL50 3RA, England. TEL 44-1242-521381. FAX 44-1242-584270. Ed. Calvin Pugsley. adv.; bk.rev. circ. 13,000. (back issues avail.) **Document type:** newsletter.
   —CCC.
   Formerly: Countryside Commission News (ISSN 0264-8822)
   Description: Focuses on the work and policies of the Commission and presents debates on issues affecting the countryside.

333.7   UK   ISSN 0268-5795
COUNTRYSIDE CAMPAIGNER. 1962. 3/yr. membership. Council for the Protection of Rural England, Warwick House, 25 Buckingham Palace Rd., London SW1W OPP, England. TEL 071-976-6433. FAX 071-976-6373. Ed. Nicola S. Frank. adv.; bk.rev.; illus. circ. 24,000. **Indexed:** RICS. **Document type:** newsletter.
   —BLDSC (3482.040000).
   Former titles: Council for the Protection of Rural England. Quarterly Bulletin (ISSN 0010-9916); Council for the Preservation of Rural England. Monthly Bulletin.
   Description: Covers issues and activities for people who want to protect rural England.

COVERED BRIDGE TOPICS. see HISTORY — History Of North And South America

CULTURAL HERITAGE MANAGEMENT BULLETIN. see PUBLIC ADMINISTRATION

333.7   US
CURRENTS & EDDIES. 1952. q. membership. Connecticut River Watershed Council, Inc., 1 Ferry St., Easthampton, MA 01027-1244. TEL 413-529-9500. FAX 413-529-9501. E-mail: crwc@k12.ucs.umass.edu. Ed. Whitty Sanford. bk.rev.; circ. 2,000 (controlled). **Document type:** newsletter.
   Formerly: Valley Newsletter.

CURTIS'S BOTANICAL MAGAZINE. see GARDENING AND HORTICULTURE

333.7   SA   ISSN 1022-5315
CUSTOS (ENGLISH EDITION). Custos (Afrikaans Edition) (ISSN 1022-5307) 1971. bi-m. R.106. National Parks Board - Nasionale Parkeraad, P.O. Box 787, Pretoria 0001, South Africa. TEL 27-12-343-9770. FAX 27-12-343-9958. TELEX 321931 SA. E-mail: janines@parks-sa.co.za. Ed. Janine Smit. adv.; bk.rev.; illus. circ. 10,000. **Indexed:** Curr.Adv.Ecol.Sci., Ind.S.A.Per. **Document type:** consumer publication.
   Supersedes (in 1993): Custos (ISSN 0379-9921)

CYCLE (NEW YORK, 1970). see ENVIRONMENTAL STUDIES — Waste Management

CYPRUS. DEPARTMENT OF FISHERIES. ANNUAL REPORT ON THE DEPARTMENT OF FISHERIES AND THE CYPRUS FISHERIES. see FISH AND FISHERIES

DAL COMUNE-NOTIZIE. see ENVIRONMENTAL STUDIES

339.49   UK   ISSN 0070-3001
DAWN SONG AND ALL DAY.* 1949. irreg. World Bird Research Station, Glanton, Northumberland, England.
   Formerly: Dawn Song.

639.9   US   ISSN 0162-6337
S960   CODEN: DEFEDZ
DEFENDERS. 1930. q. $20 membership. Defenders of Wildlife, 1101 14th St., N.W., Ste. 1400, Washington, DC 20005-5601. TEL 202-682-9400. FAX 202-682-1331. E-mail: info@defenders.org; URL: http://www.defenders.org. Ed. James G. Deane. R&P contact: James G. Deane. bk.rev.; illus. circ. 130,000. (back issues avail.) **Indexed:** Biol.Abstr., Biol.Dig., Environ.Abstr., Environ.Per.Bibl. (1972-), Sport Fish.Abstr., Wild.Rev., Zoo.Rec.
   —BLDSC (3546.210500); CIS; UMI; UnCover.
   Former titles: Defenders of Wildlife Magazine (ISSN 0162-6329); Defenders of Wildlife News (ISSN 0011-7528)
   Description: Features in-depth report on wildlife conservation issues, primarily in the U.S.

DELAWARE SEA GRANT REPORTER. see FISH AND FISHERIES

CONSERVATION

639.9 US ISSN 0418-7598
SK305.M6
DESERT BIGHORN COUNCIL. TRANSACTIONS. 1957. a. $26. Desert Bighorn Council, c/o Bighorn Institute, 51000 Highway 74, Palm Desert, CA 92260. TEL 702-646-3401. Ed. Ray Boyd. bk.rev.; cum.index; circ. 300 (paid). (back issues avail.) **Indexed:** Sport Fish.Abstr., Wild.Rev. **Document type:** academic/scholarly publication.
Refereed Serial

DESIGN EXCHANGE. see *ENVIRONMENTAL STUDIES*

333.7 GW ISSN 0939-3501
DEUTSCHER JUGENDBUND FUER NATURBEOBACHTUNG. NATURKUNDLICHE BEITRAEGE. 1978. s-a. DM.30. Deutscher Jugendbund fuer Naturbeobachtung, Justus-Strandes-Weg 14, 22337 Hamburg, Germany. TEL 040-506764. bk.rev. (back issues avail.) **Document type:** bulletin.

DEUTSCHER RAT FUER LANDESPFLEGE. SCHRIFTENREIHE. see *ENVIRONMENTAL STUDIES*

333.7 US ISSN 1075-1653
GE180 CODEN: FOWAEV
DIFFERENT DRUMMER MAGAZINE. 1980. q. $27.50 (foreign $37.50). Thoreau Institute, 14417 S.E. Laurie, Oak Grove, OR 97267. TEL 503-652-7049. E-mail: rot@ti.rog; URL: http://www.teleport.com/~rot. Ed. Randal O'Toole. bk.rev.; cum.index. circ. 1,500. (back issues avail.) **Document type:** monographic series.
—UnCover.
Former titles (until 1994): Forest Watch (ISSN 1057-2724); Forest Planning (ISSN 0738-0585)
Description: Analysis and proposed reforms of natural resource agencies and policies.

614.7 333.7 US ISSN 0270-1111
GE1
DIRECTORY OF ENVIRONMENTAL ORGANIZATIONS. 1975. bi-m. $30 (zip or subject code index $10; on diskette $300; on labels $200). Educational Communications, Inc. (Los Angeles), Box 351419, Los Angeles, CA 90035-9119. TEL 310-559-9160. FAX 310-559-9160. Ed. Nancy Pearlman, Lynn Cason. adv. circ. 500. **Document type:** directory.
Description: Contains a comprehensive, alphabetical zip or subject list of more than 6,000 names, addresses, and telephone numbers of international, national, state, regional, and local organizations concerned with environmental issues.

THE DIRECTORY OF NATIONAL ENVIRONMENTAL ORGANIZATIONS. see *ENVIRONMENTAL STUDIES*

DISCOVERY. see *SCIENCES: COMPREHENSIVE WORKS*

639.9 SW ISSN 0281-1545
DJURENS VAERLD. 1958-1974; resumed 1981. q. SEK 30 membership. Svenska Djurskyddsfoereningen, P.O. Box 10081, S-100 55 Stockholm, Sweden. Ed. Lars Smit; Pub. Goesta Bengtsson. bk.rev.; illus. circ. 8,000. **Document type:** newsletter.
Incorporates (in 1983): Djurexpressen (ISSN 0012-432X)

333.7 UI ISSN 0265-5640
QL76.5.C55 CODEN: DODODN
DODO. 1977. a. £12 (effective 1997). Jersey Wildlife Preservation Trust, Les Augres Manor, Trinity, Jersey JE3 5BP, Channel Islands. TEL 44-1534-864666. FAX 44-1534-864161. Eds. Jeremy J.C. Mallinson, Anna T.C. Feistner. R&P contact: Jeremy Mallinson. charts; illus. (reprint service avail.) **Indexed:** Sport Fish.Abstr., Wild.Rev., Zoo.Rec.
—BLDSC (3614.290000); Genuine Article.
Description: Topics covered include: breeding and husbandry of endangered species, field studies, capture expeditions and reintroduction programs, behavioral studies, reproductive biology, and population management.

DOLPHIN LOG. see *CHILDREN AND YOUTH — For*

DOWN TO EARTH NORTH EAST AUSTRALIA NEWSLETTER. see *NEW AGE PUBLICATIONS*

DROUGHT NETWORK NEWS. see *WATER RESOURCES*

333.7 700 913 YU
DRUSTVO KONZERVATORA SRBIJE. GLASNIK. (Text in Serbo-Croatian) 1978. a. $10. Drustvo Konzervatora Srbije, Bozidara Adzije 11, 11000 Belgrade, Yugoslavia. TEL 011-451-642. abstr.; bibl.; illus. circ. 600. (back issues avail.)

639.9 US ISSN 0012-6950
DUCKS UNLIMITED. 1938. bi-m. $25 membership. Ducks Unlimited, Inc., 1 Waterfowl Way, Memphis, TN 38120-2351. TEL 901-758-3825. FAX 901-758-3909. URL: http://www.ducks.org/. Ed. Lee Salber. adv.; bk.rev.; illus.; stat. circ. 500,000.
—UnCover.
Description: Highlights waterfowl conservation.

333.79 NE ISSN 0168-7948
DUIN. 1978. q. fl.35. Stichting Duinbehoud, Postbus 11059, 2301 EB Leiden, Netherlands. TEL 31-71-5131800. FAX 31-71-5131707. Ed. H. Wijkhuisen. bk.rev.; index.
—BLDSC (3630.943900); SWETS.
Description: Covers dune and coastal conservation.

E A N H S BULLETIN. (East Africa Natural History Society) see *BIOLOGY*

E P A POLICY ALERT. (Environmental Protection Agency) see *ENVIRONMENTAL STUDIES*

EAGLE (GALENA). see *ENVIRONMENTAL STUDIES*

333.7 US ISSN 1054-0067
TD169
THE EARTH CARE ANNUAL. 1990. a. National Wildlife Federation, 8925 Leesburg Pike, Vienna, VA 22184. TEL 703-790-4000; 800-432-6564. FAX 703-442-7332. E-mail: gordonr@nwf.org; URL: http://www.nwf.org.

333.7 614.7 US ISSN 1055-8411
HC110.E5
EARTH FIRST!; the radical environmental journal. 1980. 8/yr. $25 to individuals (foreign $35); institutions $45. Box 1415, Eugene, OR 97440-1415. TEL 541-741-9191. FAX 541-741-9192. E-mail: earthfirst@igc.apc.org; URL: http://www.envirolink.org/orgs/ef. Ed.Bd. adv. contact: Jim Flynn. bk.rev. circ. 15,000. (tabloid format; back issues avail.) **Indexed:** Alt.Press Ind., Environ.Abstr., Per.Islam. (1991-). **Document type:** newspaper.
Former titles (until 1990): Earth First! Journal (ISSN 1055-8845); (until 1989): Earth First! (ISSN 1047-7195)
Description: Covers the cutting edge of radical environmental action and thought.
Refereed Serial

628 333.7 UK
EARTH HERITAGE. 1968. s-a. free. English Nature, Northminster House, Peterborough, Cambs. PE1 1UA, England. TEL 44-1733-340345. FAX 44-1733-68834. TELEX 931 2130132 NC G. **Indexed:** Geo.Abstr. **Document type:** academic/scholarly publication.
Formerly (until Jan. 1994): Earth Science Conservation (ISSN 0142-2324)

EARTH ISLAND JOURNAL; an international environmental news magazine. see *ENVIRONMENTAL STUDIES*

EARTH NEWS. see *ENVIRONMENTAL STUDIES*

EARTHLIGHT; exploring the relationship of spirituality and ecology. see *RELIGIONS AND THEOLOGY — Other Denominations And Sects*

333.7 628 AT
ECO ECHO; the green voice of the Sunshine Coast. 1984. q. Aus.$12. Sunshine Coast Environmental Council, P.O. Box 269, Nambour, Qld. 4560, Australia. TEL 61-7-54415747. FAX 61-7-54417478. E-mail: jillyr@squirrel.com.au. Ed. Jillian Rossiter. R&P contact: Jillian Rossiter. adv.: page Aus.$140; adv. contact: Jillian Rossiter. bk.rev. circ. 600. (back issues avail.) **Document type:** bulletin.
Description: Contains issues, articles and news pertaining to the Sunshine Coast and South East Queensland.

333.7 US
ECO-HUMANE LETTER. 1976. irreg. $15. International Ecology Society, 1471 Barclay St., St. Paul, MN 55106-1405. Ed. R.J.F. Kramer. adv.; bk.rev. circ. 17,000. **Document type:** newsletter.
Formerly: Eco-Letter.

ECOLOGIA. see *BIOLOGY*

ECOLOGICAL ECONOMICS. see *ENVIRONMENTAL STUDIES*

ECOLOGICAL PSYCHOLOGY. see *PSYCHOLOGY*

THE ECOLOGISTS. see *BIOLOGY*

333.78 614.7 UK ISSN 0144-6258
ECOLOGY & CONSERVATION STUDIES. 1980. q. membership. Ecology and Conservation Studies Society, c/o J. Gadsby, Gen. Sec., 36 The Windings, Sanderstead, Surrey CR2 0HU, England. Ed. Shirley Goodwin. bk.rev. circ. 250.
—BLDSC (3650.040500).

333.7 UK ISSN 0143-9073
ECOS; a review of conservation. 1980. q. £15 membership. British Association of Nature Conservationists, Nature Conservation Bureau, 36 Kingfisher Court, Hambridge Rd., Newbury, Berks. RG14 5SJ, England. Ed. Rick Minter. adv.; bk.rev. circ. 900. (back issues avail.) **Indexed:** Deep Sea Res.& Oceanogr.Abstr., Ecol.Abstr., Environ.Abstr., Environ.Per.Bibl. (1982-), Forest.Abstr., Geo.Abstr.H.G., IDA, Irr.& Drain.Abstr., Maize Abstr., Rural Ext.Educ.& Tr.Abstr., Rural Recreat.Tour.Abstr. Soils & Fert., Triticale Abstr., World Agri.Econ.& Rural Sociol.Abstr.
—BLDSC (3659.531300); CISTI.

333.7 614 AT ISSN 1323-7594
ECOSPHERE. 1973. q. Aus.$45. Queensland Conservation Council, P.O. Box 12046, Elizabeth St Brisbane, Qld. 4002, Australia. TEL 61-7-32210188. FAX 61-7-32297992. Ed. Imogen Zethoven. R&P contact: Rose Kvlak. adv. contact: Rose Kvlak. bk.rev. circ. 2,000. **Document type:** newsletter.
Former titles: Queensland Conservation Council Newsletter; Eco Info (ISSN 0310-0294)
Description: Covers all conservation issues relevant to Queensland, with reports on conservation groups activities, environmental law battles and relevant work on government and industry committees.

ECOTHEOLOGY. see *RELIGIONS AND THEOLOGY*

ECOVILLAGE NEWSLETTER. see *HOUSING AND URBAN PLANNING*

333.7 SZ ISSN 1016-3166
EIDGENOESSISCHE FORSCHUNGSANSTALT FUER WALD SCHNEE UND LANDSCHAFT. BERICHTE. (Text in German; summaries in English, French and Italian) 1968. irreg. price varies. Eidgenoessische Forschungsanstalt fuer Wald, Schnee und Landschaft, Zuercherstr. 111, CH-8903 Birmensdorf, Switzerland. TEL 01-7392111. Ed. Rodolphe Schlaepfer. cum.index. (back issues avail.) **Indexed:** Biol.Abstr., Curr.Adv.Ecol.Sci., Ecol.Abstr., Forest.Abstr., Geo.Abstr.P.G., Key Word Ind.Wildl.Re **Document type:** monographic series.
—BLDSC (1919.030000).
Formerly (until 1990): Eidgenoessische Anstalt fuer das Forstliche Versuchswesen. Berichte (ISSN 0259-3092)

333.7 SZ ISSN 1016-3174
EIDGENOESSISCHE FORSCHUNGSANSTALT FUER WALD SCHNEE UND LANDSCHAFT. JAHRESBERICHT. (Text in German) 1946. a. free. Eidgenoessische Forschungsanstalt fuer Wald, Schnee und Landschaft, Zuercherstr. 111, CH-8903 Birmensdorf, Switzerland. TEL 01-7392111. FAX 01-7392215. Ed. Rodolphe Schlaepfer. bk.rev. circ. 700. **Indexed:** Forest Prod.Abstr. **Document type:** monographic series.
Formerly (until 1989): Eidgenoessische Anstalt fuer das Forstliche Versuchswesen. Jahresbericht (ISSN 1011-9124)

333.7   SZ   ISSN 1016-3158
SD1   CODEN: MEFLEK
EIDGENOESSISCHE FORSCHUNGSANSTALT FUER WALD, SCHNEE UND LANDSCHAFT. MITTEILUNGEN. (Text in German; summaries in English, French, German and Italian) 1891. irreg. 50 SFr. Eidgenoessische Forschungsanstalt fuer Wald, Schnee und Landschaft, Zuercherstr. 111, CH-8903 Birmensdorf, Switzerland. TEL 01-7392111. FAX 01-7392215. Ed. Rodolphe Schlaepfer. bk.rev.; charts; illus.; stat.; index, cum.index. circ. 750. (back issues avail.) **Indexed:** Geo.Abstr.H.G., GeoRef. **Document type:** monographic series.
  Former titles (until 1990): Switzerland. Eidgenoessische Anstalt fuer das Forstliche Versuchswesen. Mitteilungen (ISSN 0251-4133); Switzerland. Schweizerische Anstalt fuer das Forstliche Versuchswesen. Mitteilungen (ISSN 0080-7257)

333.7   ES
EL SALVADOR. MINISTERIO DE AGRICULTURA Y GANADERIA. DIRECCION GENERAL DE RECURSOS NATURALES RENOVABLES. PLAN ANUAL OPERATIVO.* a. Ministerio de Agricultura y Ganaderia, Direccion General de Recursos Naturales Renovables, c/o OSPA 31, Avda. del Sur, 627, San Salvador, El Salvador.

ELECTRICITY CONSERVATION QUARTERLY. see ENGINEERING — Electrical Engineering

333.7   UK   ISSN 0969-1340
ENACT; managing land for wildlife. 1993. q. £12 (overseas £15). English Nature, Northminster House, Peterborough, Cambs. PE1 1UA, England. TEL 44-1733-340345. FAX 44-1733-68834. TELEX 931-2130132 NC G. (Subscr. to: Administration Office, Communication House, Works Rd., Letchworth, Herts. SG6 1LB, England) Ed.Bd. adv. (back issues avail.) **Document type:** consumer publication.
  —BLDSC (3738.230000).
  Description: Covers wildlife conservation and other land-management issues.

333.7 639.9   US
ENDANGERED SPECIES BULLETIN. 1976. 6/yr. free to qualified State & Federal government agencies. U.S. Fish and Wildlife Service, Division of Endangered Species, 452 Arlington Sq., Washington, DC 20240. TEL 703-358-2390. URL: http://www.fws.gov. Ed. Mike Bender. **Document type:** government publication, bulletin.
  Formerly (until 1994): Endangered Species Technical Bulletin (ISSN 0145-9236).

333.7 639.9   US   ISSN 1081-3705
QL81.5   CODEN: ESUPEF
ENDANGERED SPECIES UPDATE. 1983. 6/yr. $23 to individuals (foreign $28); students and senior citizens $18 (foreign $23) (effective 1996 & 1997). University of Michigan, School of Natural Resources & Environment, 430 E. University, Dana Bldg., Ann Arbor, MI 48109-1115. TEL 313-763-3243. FAX 313-936-2195. E-mail: mmcphee@umich.edu; URL: http://www.umich.edu/ ~esupdate. Ed. M.E. McPhee. bk.rev. circ. 1,200. (looseleaf format; back issues avail.) **Indexed:** Environ.Abstr., Environ.Per.Bibl. (1989-), Gard.Lit. (1992-). **Document type:** newsletter.
  Formerly (until Jul. 1987): Endangered Species Technical Bulletin Reprint.
  Description: Reprints the Endangered Species Bulletin with additional material on endangered species. Provides a forum for the exchange of information and ideas on endangered species issues, management and conservation.

333.7   SA   ISSN 1016-1902
ENDANGERED WILDLIFE. 1983. 3/yr. R.120($50) Endangered Wildlife Trust, Private Bag X11, Parkview 2122, South Africa. TEL 27-11-486-1102. FAX 27-11-486-1506. Ed. David Holt Biddle. adv. contact: Lynn Ras. bk.rev. circ. 6,000. (back issues avail.) **Indexed:** Ind.S.A.Per., Sport Fish.Abstr., Wild.Rev. **Document type:** academic/scholarly publication.
  —UnCover.
  Formerly (until 1990): Quagga.
  Description: Studies conservation of wildlife in Africa, with a focus on endangered species.

333.7   SZ
ENERGIE EXTRA. (Text in French, German) 1977. bi-m. free. Office Federal de l'Energie, CH-3003 Bern, Switzerland. TEL 41-31-3225664. FAX 41-31-3824307. charts; stat. circ. 35,000. **Document type:** government publication.
  Formerly (until 1996): Courrier de l'Antigaspillage.
  Description: Government publication covers political and technical aspects of energy with special emphasis on savings.

ENERGY AND HOUSING REPORT; the national newsletter on residential energy conservation and consumption trends. see ENERGY

333.7   US
ENERGY CONSERVATION AND UTILIZATION TECHNOLOGIES. 6/yr. $90 in U.S., Canada, Mexico; elsewhere $180. (Department of Energy, Energy Conservation and Utlization Technologies Program) U.S. National Technical Information Service, 5825 Port Royal Rd., Springfield, VA 22161. TEL 703-487-4630.
  Description: Examines combustion, thermal sciences, materials, biocatalysis, and tribology. Includes digests and citations to technical reports in all five areas.

ENERUGI SHIGEN/ENERGY AND RESOURCES. see ENERGY

333.7   UK
ENGLISH NATURE SCIENCE. irreg., no.18, 1993. English Nature, Northminster House, Peterborough PE1 1UA, England. TEL 44-1733-340345. FAX 44-1733-68834. **Document type:** monographic series.

333.7   US
S930
ENVIROACTION. 1980. m. $10 basic membership (foreign $13). National Wildlife Federation, 8925 Leesburg Pike, Vienna, VA 22184-0001. TEL 703-790-4000; 800-432-6564. FAX 703-772-7332. E-mail: gordonr@nwf.org; URL: http://www.nwf.org. Ed. Tim McLean. index. circ. 37,000. (also avail. in microform from UMI) **Document type:** newsletter.
  Supersedes: National Wildlife's Conservation (ISSN 0736-9522); Which was formerly (1938-1983): Conservation Report (ISSN 0010-6488)

ENVIRONMENT & POLICY. see ENVIRONMENTAL STUDIES

ENVIRONMENT NEW JERSEY; news of New Jersey's natural and historic resources. see ENVIRONMENTAL STUDIES

ENVIRONMENT NEWSLETTER. see ENVIRONMENTAL STUDIES

ENVIRONMENT SOUTH AUSTRALIA. see ENVIRONMENTAL STUDIES

ENVIRONMENTAL AND RESOURCE ECONOMICS. see ENVIRONMENTAL STUDIES

ENVIRONMENTAL AND RESOURCE ECONOMICS. see ENVIRONMENTAL STUDIES

ENVIRONMENTAL AWARENESS. see ENVIRONMENTAL STUDIES

333.7   US
ENVIRONMENTAL BULLETIN. 1971. m. $35. New Jersey Conservation Foundation, 170 Longview Rd., Far Hills, NJ 07931. E-mail: njcf@aol.com. Ed. Pat Baxter. circ. 700. **Indexed:** World Surf.Coat. **Document type:** bulletin.
  Description: Provides information on hearings, legislative action on environmental bills, and legislation introduced. Includes a calendar of public hearings and meetings.

ENVIRONMENTAL CONSERVATION; international journal devoted to maintaining global vitality through exposing and countering environmental deterioration resulting from human population pressure and unwise technology. see ENVIRONMENTAL STUDIES

ENVIRONMENTAL HISTORY. see HISTORY

ENVIRONMENTAL LANDSCAPE NEWS. see GARDENING AND HORTICULTURE

ENVIRONMENTAL NEWS DIGEST. see ENVIRONMENTAL STUDIES

ENVIRONMENTAL OPPORTUNITIES. see ENVIRONMENTAL STUDIES

ENVIRONMENTAL PROGRESS (SPRINGFIELD). see ENVIRONMENTAL STUDIES

500.9   IS   ISSN 0334-9578
ERETZ MAGAZINE. (Editions in English, Hebrew) 1985. bi-m. $45. Eretz Ha-Tzvi Inc., P.O. Box 565, 26 Taiber St., Givatayim 53104, Israel. TEL 972-3-5712681. FAX 972-3-5714184. (Subscr. in the U.S. to: SFC, 100 Cooper Center, 7905 Browning Rd., Pennsauken, NJ 08109-4319. TEL 609-488-1881) Ed. Yadin Roman. R&P contact: Yadin Roman. adv. contact: Dita Kohl. circ. 40,000 (25,000 English ed.; 15,000 Hebrew ed.). **Indexed:** Zoo.Rec. **Document type:** consumer publication.
  Incorporates (1976-1991): Israel - Land and Nature (ISSN 0333-6867)
  Description: Covers the culture, geography, history, nature, archaeology and people of Israel.

639.9 622   US   ISSN 1073-7227
TA760
EROSION CONTROL; the journal for erosion & sediment control professionals. 1973. bi-m. $60 (foreign $75) (effective 1997). (International Erosion Control Association) Forester Communications, Inc., 5638 Hollister Ave., Ste. 301, Goleta, CA 93117-3474. TEL 805-681-1300; 800-546-4679. FAX 805-681-1312. E-mail: erosion@1x.netcom.com. (Subscr. to: Box 3100, Santa Barbara, CA 93130-3100) Ed. John Trotti; Pub. Daniel Waldman. R&P contact: Daniel Waldman. adv. contact: Daniel Waldman. bk.rev.; bibl.; illus.; circ. 20,000 (controlled). (tabloid format) **Indexed:** Environ.Per.Bibl. **Document type:** trade publication. —CISTI.
  Formerly (until 1993): I E C A Report (ISSN 0733-8910)
  Description: Features articles on erosion-control techniques and technologies, problems and solutions, national programs around the world, and member profiles, as well as association news, and information on new products.

639.9   UK   ISSN 0961-6004
ESSEX WILDLIFE MAGAZINE. 1982. w. (48/yr.). membership. Essex Wildlife Trust Ltd., Fingringhoe Wick Nature Reserve, S. Green Rd., Fingringhoe, Colchester, Essex CO5 7DN, England. TEL 01206-729678. Ed. Sue Newton. adv. contact: Kevin Davis. bk.rev.; illus. circ. 12,000. (reprint service avail. from UMI) **Document type:** consumer publication.
  Formerly (until 1991): Watch Over Essex (ISSN 0264-2700); **Supersedes:** Essex Naturalists' Trust Bulletin.

333.7   ET
ETHIOPIAN WILDLIFE AND NATURAL HISTORY SOCIETY. NEWSLETTER. m. membership. Ethiopian Wildlife and Natural History Society, P.O. Box 60074, Addis Ababa, Ethiopia. Ed. Zewditu Tessema. **Indexed:** Sport Fish.Abstr., Wild.Rev. **Document type:** newsletter.
  Description: Presents news of society meetings and outdoor activities and conservation news affecting Ethiopia.

EURO-UNION GICEF; la revue qui est dan le vent pour une meilleure qualite de vie. see SPORTS AND GAMES — Outdoor Life

333.78 614.7   US
EVERGLADES REPORTER.* 1969. a. $1 membership (effective May 1995). Friends of the Everglades, Inc., 244 Westward Dr., Ste. A, Miami Springs, FL 33166-5260. TEL 305-888-1230. Ed. Joe Podgor. bk.rev.; circ. 5,000 (paid). (back issues avail.) **Document type:** newsletter.
  Description: Dedicated to the restoration and protection of the Everglades and associated natural systems.

EXPLORER (CLEVELAND). see SCIENCES: COMPREHENSIVE WORKS

FAELTBIOLOGEN. see ENVIRONMENTAL STUDIES

CONSERVATION

799.2 US ISSN 1077-3274
FAIR CHASE. 1986. q. $25. Boone and Crockett Club, 250 Station Dr., Missoula, MT 59801-2753. TEL 406-542-1888. FAX 406-542-0784. E-mail: bcclub@montana.com; URL: http://www.boone-crockett.org. Ed. George Bettas. R&P contact: Julie L. Tripp. adv. contact: Julie L. Tripp. bk.rev.; illus. **Document type:** newsletter.
Former titles (until 1994): Boone and Crockett Club News Journal (ISSN 1067-2958); (until 1993): Boone and Crockett Club Associates Newsletter.
Description: Features hunting stories, conservation topics, and recently accepted trophies.

333.95 598.91 UK
THE FALCONERS AND RAPTOR CONSERVATION MAGAZINE. 1989. q. £14 (Europe £18; elsewhere £26); newsstand price: £2.95. Falcon Publishing, 20 Bridle Rd., Burton Latimer, Kettering, Northants. NN15 5QP, England. TEL 01536-722794. Eds. David Wilson, Lyn Wilson. adv.: B&W page £450, color page £490; trim 210 x 297; adv. contact: Lyn Wilson. bk.rev.; video rev.; tr.lit. circ. 5,000. (back issues avail.) **Document type:** consumer publication.
Description: Publishes informational and nostalgic articles on raptor conservation.

333.7 SZ ISSN 0014-715X
FAMILIENBLATT; Monatszeitschrift des Blauen Kreuzes. 1885. m. 30 SFr. Blaukreuz Verlag, Lindenrain 5A, CH-3001 Bern, Switzerland. TEL 41-31-3005866. FAX 41-31-3005869. Ed. Else Schoenthal. illus. circ. 4,000. **Document type:** newsletter.

333.7 634.9 US ISSN 0740-3690
SB482.A4F43
FEDERAL PARKS & RECREATION. 1983. fortn. $187. Resources Publishing Co., 1010 Vermont Ave., N.W., Ste. 708, Washington, DC 20005. TEL 202-638-7529. FAX 202-393-2075. E-mail: coffinj@clark.net; URL: http://www.plnfpr.com. Ed. James B. Coffin; Pub. James B. Coffin. R&P contact: James B. Coffin. (looseleaf format; back issues avail.) **Document type:** newsletter.

333.7 SZ ISSN 0014-9756
SK219
FELD WALD WASSER; schweizerische Jagdzeitung. 1949. m. 75 SFr. (foreign 84 SFr.) (effective 1997). Steigstr. 59, CH-8200 Schaffhausen, Switzerland. Ed. Dr. Jakob Reiff; Pub. Dr. Jakob Reiff. adv.; bk.rev.; illus.; stat. circ. 7,400. **Indexed:** Key Word Ind.Wildl.Res. **Document type:** consumer publication.

FIELD NOTES (BETHESDA). see ENVIRONMENTAL STUDIES

372.357 SP ISSN 1136-5552
▼**THE FIRST WORD BULLETIN.** (Text in English) 1995. q. 1000 ptas.($12) (effective 1997); newsstand price: $3.50. First Word Bulletin Associates, Calle Domingo Fernandez, 5, Box 500, 28036 Madrid, Spain. TEL 34-1-3596418. FAX 34-1-3208961. (Alt. addr.: PDS, Mary H. Swain, 2046 Lothbury Dr., Fayetteville, NC 28304-5666) Ed. G.W. Amick; Pub. G.W. Amick. adv.: page $200; trim 120 x 170; adv. contact: G.W. Amick. circ. 3,000. (also avail. in diskette format; back issues. avail.) **Document type:** consumer publication, bulletin.
Description: Covers environmental studies, problems with aging, youth education, and human relationships with animals.

639.9 179.3 SZ
FISH. irreg. (1-2/yr.). International Union for Conservation of Nature and Natural Resources, Species Survival Commission - Freshwater Fish Specialist Group, Rue Mauverney 28, CH-1196 Gland, Switzerland. TEL 41-22-9990001. FAX 41-22-9990002. TELEX 419624-IUCN-CH. (Subscr. to: Dr. C. Andrews, Freshwater Fish Specialist Group, National Aquarium Baltimore, 501 E. Pratt St., Baltimore, MD 21202 USA) **Document type:** newsletter.

333.7 179 FR
FLAMINGO RESEARCH. a. c/o Dr. Alan Johnson, Station Biologique de la Tour du Valat, Le Sambuc, 13200 Aries, France. **Document type:** newsletter.

333.7 340 US
FLORIDA FISH AND WILDLIFE NEWS. vol.7, 1979. m. $15. Florida Wildlife Federation, Box 6870, Tallahassee, FL 32314-6870. TEL 904-656-7113. Ed. Richard Farren. circ. 9,500. (reprint service avail.)
Former titles: Wildlife Notes; Florida Out of Doors.

FLORIDA LAND USE RESTRICTIONS. see LAW

333.7 591 US ISSN 0015-4172
QH105.F6 CODEN: FLNAAT
FLORIDA NATURALIST. 1927. q. $25 includes membership; libraries $18 (effective 1997). Florida Audubon Society, 1331 Palmetto Ave., Ste. 110, Winter Park, FL 32789-4963. TEL 407-539-5700. FAX 407-539-5701. Ed. Sandy Bogan. adv.; bk.rev.; illus.; stat.; index. circ. 30,000. (also avail. in microform from UMI; reprint service avail. from UMI) **Indexed:** Biol.Abstr., Curr.Adv.Ecol.Sci. **Document type:** newsletter, trade publication.
—UMI.

639.9 US ISSN 0015-4369
SK1
FLORIDA WILDLIFE. 1947. bi-m. $12 (effective 1997). Game and Fresh Water Fish Commission, 620 S. Meridian St., Tallahassee, FL 32399-1600. TEL 904-488-5563. FAX 904-488-1961. E-mail: subletd@mail.state.Fl.us. Ed. Dick Sublette. bk.rev.; illus.; circ. 25,000 (paid). **Indexed:** Sport Fish.Abstr., Wild.Rev. **Document type:** government publication.
—UnCover.
Description: Presents informational articles on state wildlife conservation and its interaction with fishing and hunting. Includes news on legislative and regulatory developments and provides legal guidance in the practice of these sports; natural history and status of threatened and endangered species.

FOCUS (INDIANAPOLIS). see SPORTS AND GAMES — Outdoor Life

333.7 US ISSN 0273-009X
FOCUS (MOSCOW); on renewable natural resources. 1975. a. free. University of Idaho, Forest, Wildlife and Range Experiment Station, Moscow, ID 83844-1130. TEL 208-885-6673. FAX 208-885-6226. TELEX 218228 COLFOR UR. E-mail: ortiz@uidaho.edu. Ed. Denise Ortiz. R&P contact: Denise Ortiz. illus, charts, maps, stat, bibl. circ. 2,500. (back issues avail.) **Document type:** academic/scholarly publication.
—Linda Hall.
Description: Lists publications, research, scientists, and continuing education activities. Contains information on ways to improve land management for all of Idaho's renewable resource interests, their industries, and related economic enterprises.

333.7 US ISSN 0744-3315
QL81.5
FOCUS (WASHINGTON, 1977). 1977. bi-m. $15 membership only. World Wildlife Fund, 1250 24th St., N.W., Washington, DC 20037. TEL 202-293-4800. FAX 202-293-9211. Ed. David Slater. bk.rev. circ. 1,000,000. **Indexed:** Mid.East: Abstr.& Ind. **Document type:** newsletter.
Description: Discusses W.W.F. conservation activities worldwide.

333.7 363.73 US ISSN 1062-7472
HC79.E5
FOCUS: CARRYING CAPACITY SELECTIONS. 1991. q. $20. Carrying Capacity Network, Inc., 2000 P St., N.W., Ste. 240, Washington, DC 20036. TEL 202-296-4548. FAX 202-296-4609. E-mail: ccn@igc.apc.org. Ed. David F. Durham; Pub. Ed Lytvak. R&P contact: Ed Lytvak. adv. contact: Leon Kolankiewicz. circ. 1,000. **Indexed:** C.I.J.E., Environ.Abstr. **Document type:** academic/scholarly publication.
Description: Features current and classic writings on a range of carrying capacity issues (environmental protection, population stabilization, and resource conservation), furnishes challenging point-counterpoint discussions, including reports as well as interviews with thought-provoking personalities.

333.7 US
FOOTPRINTS (FAR HILLS). 1973. bi-m. $25 membership. New Jersey Conservation Foundation, 170 Longview Rd., Far Hills, NJ 07931. E-mail: njcf@aol.com. Ed. Patricia J. Baxter. circ. 6,000. **Document type:** newsletter.
Description: Discusses legislative developments encouraging or impeding the preservation of ecologically diverse land in New Jersey, and covers the foundation's activities.

333.7 598.2 NZ ISSN 0015-7384
CODEN: FRBDAK
FOREST AND BIRD. 1923. q. NZ.$47 (effective 1997). Royal Forest and Bird Protection Society of New Zealand Inc., P.O. Box 631, Wellington, New Zealand. TEL 64-4-385-7374. FAX 64-4-385-7373. E-mail: office@wn.forest-bird.org.nz. Ed. Ian Close. R&P contact: Ian Close. adv. contact: Jill Wood. bk.rev.; index; circ. 23,000 (paid). **Indexed:** Curr.Adv.Ecol.Sci., Environ.Per.Bibl., Geo.Abstr., Sport Fish.Abstr., Wild.Rev., Zoo.Rec. **Document type:** consumer publication.
—BLDSC (3989.115000); UnCover. **CCC.**

FOREST HISTORY TODAY. see FORESTS AND FORESTRY

FOREST NOTES; New Hampshire's conservation magazine. see FORESTS AND FORESTRY

333.7 634.9 US
FOREST STEWARD. bi-m. $10. National Arbor Day Foundation, 100 Arbor Ave., Nebraska City, NE 68410. TEL 402-474-5655. FAX 402-474-0820. **Document type:** newsletter.
Description: Dedicated to sustainable natural resource management on privately owned, non-industrial forest lands.

FORTH NATURALIST AND HISTORIAN SERIES. see SCIENCES: COMPREHENSIVE WORKS

333.7 SZ ISSN 1021-2256
FORUM FUER WISSEN. 1991. a. free. Eidgenoessische Forschungsanstalt fuer Wald, Schnee und Landschaft, Zuercherstr. 111, CH-8903 Birmensdorf, Switzerland. TEL 01-7392111. FAX 01-7392215. Ed. Rodolphe Schlaepfer. **Document type:** proceedings.

333.7 614.7 CN ISSN 0822-7284
FRANC - VERT. (Text in French) 1984. bi-m. Can.$23.93. Union Quebecoise Pour la Conservatio de la Nature, 690 Grande Allee Est, Quebec City, PQ G1K 2K5, Canada. TEL 418-648-2104. FAX 418-648-0991. Ed. Louise Desautels. adv. contact: Helene Savard. bk.rev. circ. 6,000. **Indexed** Can.B.P.I., Pt.de Rep. (1991-). **Document type:** consumer publication.
Formerly (until 1990): Franc - Nord.
Description: Discusses the conservation of wilderness areas, parklands, waterways, and other natural resources in Quebec.

FRENCH INSTITUTE, PONDICHERRY. PONDY PAPERS IN ECOLOGY. see BIOLOGY

639.9 US ISSN 0016-1284
FRIEND O'WILDLIFE. 1959. bi-m. $5. North Carolina Wildlife Federation, Inc., Box 10626, Raleigh, NC 27605. TEL 919-833-1923. FAX 919-829-1192. Ed. Eddie Nickens. adv.; bk.rev.; illus. circ. 40,000.

333.7 790 US
FRIENDS OF PARKS & RECREATION. 1990. q. $15. National Recreation and Park Association, 2775 S. Quincy St., No. 300, Arlington, VA 22206. TEL 703-820-4940. FAX 703-671-6772. (Co-sponsor: National Recreation Foundation) Ed. Sylvia Somerville.
Description: Covers topics of interest to volunteer and participants in parks, recreation and leisure services.

333.7 179 SZ
FROGLOG. q. International Union for Conservation of Nature and Natural Resources, Species Survival Commission - Task Force on Declining Amphibians Populations, Rue Mauverney 28, CH-1196 Gland, Switzerland. TEL 41-22-9990001. FAX 41-22-9990002. TELEX 419624-IUCN-CH. (Subscr. to: Tim Halliday, Dept. of Biology, The Open University, Walton Hall, Milton Keynes MK7 6AA, England) **Document type:** newsletter.

CONSERVATION

333.7 574   UK   ISSN 0269-8463
QH540   CODEN: FECOE5
FUNCTIONAL ECOLOGY. 1987. bi-m. £255($465) (foreign £280) (effective 1998). (British Ecological Society) Blackwell Science Ltd., Osney Mead, Oxford OX2 0EL, England. TEL 44-1865-206206. FAX 44-1865-721205. E-mail: journals.cs@blacksci.co.uk; URL: http://www.black.co.uk. Eds. P. Calow, J. Grace; Pub. Allen Stevens. R&P contact: Sarah Pollard. adv. contact: Martine Cariou-Keen. circ. 1,315. (also avail. in microform from UMI; back issues avail.) **Indexed:** Apic.Abstr., ASCA, Curr.Cont., Ecol.Abstr., Environ.Per.Bibl. (1989-), Geo.Abstr.P.G., Hort.Abstr., Ind.Sci.Rev., Irr.& Drain.Abstr., Key Word Ind.Wildl.Res., Sel.Water Res.Abstr., Sport Fish.Abstr., Wild.Rev., Zoo.Rec. **Document type:** academic/scholarly publication.
—BLDSC (4055.616000); CISTI; EMDOCS; Genuine Article; SWETS; UMI; UnCover. **CCC**.
   Description: Contains articles on ecological sciences for research workers and advanced students.
   Refereed Serial

340 636   US
FUND FOR ANIMALS QUARTERLY. 1969. s-a. $20 to adults; students $10. Fund for Animals Inc., 200 W. 57th St., New York, NY 10019. TEL 212-246-2096. illus. circ. 180,000.

FUNDACION MIGUEL LILLO. SERIE CONSERVACION DE LA NATURALEZA. see *BIOLOGY — Botany*

FUR INFORMATION COUNCIL OF AMERICA. NEWSLETTER. see *LEATHER AND FUR INDUSTRIES*

639.9 179.3   SZ
GAJAH. (Text in English) 2/yr. International Union for Conservation of Nature and Natural Resources, Species Survival Commission - Asian Elephant Specialist Group, Rue Mauverney 28, CH-1196 Gland, Switzerland. TEL 41-22-9990001. FAX 41-22-9990002. TELEX 419624-IUCN-CH. (Subscr. to: Dr. Charles Santiapillai, AESG, 110 Wattarentenne Rd., Kandy, Sri Lanka) **Document type:** newsletter.
   Formerly: International Union for Conservation of Nature and Natural Resources. Species Survival Commission - Asian Elephant Specialist Group. Newsletter.

333.7   US   ISSN 1087-1276
GAME BIRD AND CONSERVATIONISTS GAZETTE. 1952. m. $20. Allen Publishing Co., Box 171227, Salt Lake City, UT 84117. TEL 801-575-1111. R&P contact: George Allen. adv. contact: Jim Wilson. bk.rev.; charts; illus.; tr.lit.; index. circ. 18,000. (back issues avail.) **Indexed:** Sport Fish.Abstr., Wild.Rev. **Document type:** trade publication.
   Former titles: Game Birds Breeders and Conservationists Gazette (ISSN 1074-2077) & Game Bird Breeders, Aviculturists, Zoologists, and Conservationists Gazette (ISSN 0164-3711)

639.2 598.2   UK
GAME CONSERVANCY MAGAZINE. s-a. £35 membership (includes Game Conservancy Review). Game Conservancy Trust, Burgate Manor, Fordingbridge, Hants. SP6 1EF, England. TEL 44-425-652381. FAX 44-25-655848. Ed. Sophia Miles. R&P contact: Sophia Miles. adv. contact: Sophia Miles. circ. 24,000. **Document type:** consumer publication.
   Formerly: Game Conservancy Newsletter.
   Description: Promotes the conservation of game bird habitat.

639.9 598.2   UK
CODEN: GCANAJ
GAME CONSERVANCY REVIEW. 1968. a. £35 membership (includes Game Conservancy Magazine). Game Conservancy Trust, Burgate Manor, Fordingbridge, Hants. SP6 1EF, England. TEL 44-425-652381. FAX 44-425-655848. URL: http://www.game-conservancy.org.UK/. Ed. Sophia Miles. adv.; illus.; stat.; index. circ. 24,000. (back issues avail.) **Indexed:** Biol.Abstr., Sport Fish.Abstr., Wild.Rev., Zoo.Rec. **Document type:** corporate report.
   Description: Discusses the organization's efforts to promote the conservation of game bird habitats.

GAN NO SHINPOJUMU/SYMPOSIUM ON WILD GEESE. (Text in Japanese) irregg. Gan o Hogosurukai - Japanese Association for Wild Geese Protection, c/o Mr. Kurechi, 16 Kawaminami Minamimachi, Wakayanagimachi, Kurihara-gun, Miyagi-ken 989-55, Japan. TEL 81-228-32-2004. FAX 81-228-32-3294. E-mail: hgh02256@niftyserve.or.jp.
   Description: Reprints of articles on geese from other periodicals.

333.95 179   JA

333.95 591   JA
GAN NO TAYORI/GOOSE LETTER. (Text in Japanese) 1971. 2/yr. 1000 Yen (effective 1997 & 1998). Gan o Hogosurukai - Japanese Association for Wild Geese Protection, c/o Mr. Kurechi, 16 Kawaminami Minamimachi, Wakayanagimachi, Kurihara-gun, Miyagi-ken 989-55, Japan. TEL 81-228-32-2004. FAX 81-228-32-3294. E-mail: hgh02256@niftyserve.or.jp. Ed. Yoshihiko Miyabayashi. bk.rev. circ. 600. **Document type:** newsletter.
   Description: Newsletter on the goose species in Japan and east Asia, their habitat, as well as conservation issues and activities of the Association.

333.95 591   JA
GANKAMOKA NO CHORUI NO CHOSA HOKOKUSHO/ANNUAL CENSUS ON WILD GEESE, DUCKS AND SWANS IN JAPAN ADVOCATED BY THE ENVIRONMENTAL AGENCY. (Text in Japanese) a. Kankyocho, Shizen Hogokyoku - Environmental Agency, Nature Conservation Bureau, 2-2 Kasumigaseki 1-chome, Chiyoda-ku, Tokyo 100, Japan.

333.7   IT
GEOS. 1993. m. L.78000 (with video L.126000). Edizioni Ecos s.r.l., Via Garigliano 74-A, 00198 Rome, Italy. TEL 39-6-8841766. FAX 39-6-8557394. Ed. Vito Bruschini. adv.: B&W page L.8500000, color page L.12000000; adv. contact: Antonio Carriero. circ. 65,000. **Document type:** consumer publication.

GESELLSCHAFT FUER VERANTWORTUNG IN DER WISSENSCHAFT. SCHRIFTEN. see *ENVIRONMENTAL STUDIES*

GETTY CONSERVATION INSTITUTE NEWSLETTER. see *ART*

GIBIER FAUNE SAUVAGE/GAME AND WILDLIFE. see *BIOLOGY — Zoology*

GLOBAL BIODIVERSITY MAGAZINE. see *BIOLOGY*

GLOBUS - BEGLEITHEFTE. see *ENVIRONMENTAL STUDIES*

639.9 179.3   SZ   ISSN 1017-2718
GNUSLETTER. Variant title: Antelope Specialist Group Gnusletter. (Text in English) 1981. 3/yr. $10. International Union for Conservation of Nature and Natural Resources, Species Survival Commission - Antelope Specialist Group, Rue Mauverney 28, CH-1196 Gland, Switzerland. TEL 41-22-9990001. FAX 41-22-9990002. TELEX 419624-IUCN-CH. (Subscr. to: Dr. Richard D. Estes, 5 Granite St., Peterborough, NH 03458 USA) **Document type:** newsletter.

333.95 591   JA
GOOSE STUDY. (Text in Japanese) 1990. 2/yr. 2000 Yen (effective 1997 & 1998). Gan o Hogosurukai - Japanese Association for Wild Geese Protection, c/o Mr. Kurechi, 16 Kawaminami Minamimachi, Wakayanagimachi, Kurihara-gun, Miyagi-ken 989-55, Japan. TEL 81-228-32-2004. FAX 81-228-32-3294. E-mail: hgh02256@niftyserve.or.jp. Ed. Yoshihiko Miyabayashi. bibl. circ. 300. **Document type:** bulletin.
   Description: Contains reports of research work by the Association members as well as reviews of scientific studies on goose species published in other languages.

508   US
GRASSROOTS (ST. LOUIS).* q. Grassroots Institute, Box 1866, E. St. Louis, IL 62208-0066. TEL 618-235-7775. Ed. Don Pierce.

333.7   US   ISSN 1080-5664
GREAT LAKES ENVIRONMENTAL DIRECTORY. 1995. biennial. $25 (effective 1997). Harbinger Communications, Box 8175, Missoula, MT 59807. TEL 406-721-0440. FAX 406-721-0440. E-mail: ned@ism.net. index. (also avail. in diskette format) **Document type:** directory.
   •Also available online.
   Description: Annotated listings of citizen groups and government agencies in Illinois, Indiana, Michigan, Minnesota, Ohio, Wisconsin and Ontario.

333.7   US   ISSN 1091-5605
GREAT LAKES UNITED; an international coalition to conserve and protect the Great Lakes - St. Lawrence River ecosystem. 1986. q. $25 in US & Canada; libraries $35 (effective 1997). Great Lakes United, Buffalo State College, Cassety Hall, 1300 Elmwood Ave., Buffalo, NY 14222. TEL 716-886-0142. FAX 716-886-0303. E-mail: glu@igc.org; URL: http://www.great-lakes.net/glu. Ed. Reg Gilbert. adv.: page $400. bk.rev. circ. 3,000. **Document type:** newsletter.
   •Also available online.
   Description: Includes news and in-depth articles about the Great Lakes Basin.

GREEN ANARCHIST; global anarcho-primitivist 'zine. see *POLITICAL SCIENCE*

GREEN BOOK: THE DIRECTORY OF NATURAL HISTORY AND GENERAL STOCK PHOTOGRAPHY. see *PHOTOGRAPHY*

333.7   UK   ISSN 0263-0095
GREEN DRUM; the green paper for people who care. 1974. q. £3.50. Greenspur Enterprise, 18 Cofton Lake Rd., Birmingham, England. circ. 2,000.
   Formerly: Good Earth.

333.7   AT   ISSN 0727-0119
GREEN PAGES: DIRECTORY OF NON-GOVERNMENT ENVIRONMENTAL GROUPS IN AUSTRALIA. 1970. irreg., latest 1996. Aus.$20. Australian Conservation Foundation, 340 Gore St., Fitzroy, Vic. 3065, Australia. TEL 61-3-94161166. FAX 61-3-94160767. Ed. Chris Smyth. R&P contact: Louise Ray. **Document type:** directory.
   Formerly: Australian Conservation Foundation. Conservation Directory.
   Description: Addresses and telephone numbers of Australian conservation and environmental groups.

GREEN POLITICS. see *POLITICAL SCIENCE*

333   US   ISSN 0899-0190
QH75.A1
GREENPEACE QUARTERLY. 1981. 4/yr. $30. Greenpeace, National Office, 1436 U St., N.W., Washington, DC 20009. TEL 202-462-1177. FAX 202-462-4507. URL: http://www.greenpeace.org/-usa. Ed. Jay Townsend. adv. circ. 900,000. **Indexed:** Alt.Press Ind., Energy Rev., Environ.Abstr., Environ.Per.Bibl. **Document type:** newsletter.
   Formerly: Greenpeace Examiner (ISSN 0828-7988)
   Description: International environmental group protesting the destruction and abuse of the environment. Provides current news and articles on activities the world over.
   Refereed Serial

333.78   US   ISSN 0031-2150
SB482.A4
GRIST. q. $30. National Recreation & Park Association, Park Practice Program, 2775 S. Quincy St., No. 300, Arlington, VA 22206. TEL 703-820-4940. FAX 703-671-6772. Ed. Kathleen Pleasant. **Indexed:** Sportsearch (1983-).

GROUND WATER MONITOR; legislation, regulation, litigation, technology. see *WATER RESOURCES*

333.7   AT   ISSN 1320-7849
THE GROWING IDEA. 1992. q. free to members. Greening Australia - Queensland Inc., 431 Montague Rd., West End, Qld. 4101, Australia. TEL 61-7-8440211. FAX 61-7-8440727. E-mail: goqldinc@eis.net.au; URL: http://www2.eis.net.au/~goqldinc/. Ed. Rebecca Ho. **Document type:** newsletter.
   Description: Covers activities of Greening Australia and issues in vegetation management.

CONSERVATION

333.7 — **GW** — ISSN 0943-2949
GRUENER WEG 31A. 1987. q. DM.40. Institut und Studienarchiv Arbeiterkultur und Oekologie, Gruener Weg 31A, 34225 Baunatal, Germany. TEL 49-5601-87510. FAX 49-5601-87726. Ed. Klaus-Peter Lorenz. bk.rev.; bibl.; illus.; index; circ. 900 (paid). (back issues avail.) **Document type:** academic/scholarly publication.
  Formerly (until 1992): Arbeiterkultur und Oekologie (ISSN 0937-6798)
  Description: Reports on social movements and the protection of natural resources.

639.9 333.77 — **GW** — ISSN 0178-1421
GRUENSTIFT (BERLIN); das Umweltmagazin fuer Berlin und Brandenburg. 1983. m. DM.50($50) Stiftung Naturschutz Berlin, Potsdamerstr. 68, 10785 Berlin, Germany. TEL 49-30-2626001. FAX 49-30-2615277. Ed. Klaus-Dieter Heise. R&P contact: Joerg Goetting-Frosinski. adv. contact: Sabine Braun. bk.rev. circ. 10,000. (back issues avail.) **Document type:** consumer publication.
  Description: Promotes natural conservation and environmental protection in Berlin and the state of Brandenburg.

333.7 — **UK** — ISSN 0269-0934
DA873
GUIDE TO OVER 100 PROPERTIES. 1931. a. membership. National Trust for Scotland, 5 Charlotte Sq., Edinburgh EH2 4DU, Scotland. TEL 44-131-226-5922. FAX 44-131-243-9501. URL: http://www.scotland.net/sntrust. Ed. Hilary Horrocks. circ. 250,000. **Document type:** directory.
  Formerly: National Trust for Scotland Yearbook (ISSN 0077-5916)
  Description: Details facilities and attractions available at properties owned by the National Trust for Scotland.

GUILFOYLE REPORT. see PHOTOGRAPHY

333.7 — **AT** — ISSN 0310-2939
QH77.A8 — CODEN: HAAUE7
HABITAT AUSTRALIA. 1973. bi-m. Aus.$49. Australian Conservation Foundation, 340 Gore St., Fitzroy, Vic. 3065, Australia. TEL 61-3-94161166. FAX 61-3-94160767. Ed. Chris Smyth. R&P contact: Louise Ray. adv. contact: Peggy Nichols. illus. circ. 16,000. **Indexed:** Aus.P.A.I.S., Aus.Rd.Ind., Gdlns., Geo.Abstr. Sport Fish.Abstr., Wild.Rev., Zoo.Rec. **Document type:** consumer publication.
  —BLDSC (4237.370000); UnCover.
  Formerly: Habitat.
  Description: Concerned with environment, conservation, ecologically sustainable alternatives to current industry and consumer practices.

333.7 — **JA** — ISSN 0388-4732
HAKUSAN/HAKUSAN NATURE CONSERVATION CENTER. NEWS. (Text in Japanese) 1973. q. Ishikawa-ken Hakusan Shizen Hogo Senta - Hakusan Nature Conservation Center, Ishikawa Prefecture, Kinamiri, Yoshinodanimura, Ishikawa-gun, Ishikawa-ken 920-23, Japan. TEL 81-7619-5-5321. FAX 81-7619-5-5323. **Document type:** newsletter.

HANA NO WA/HIROSHIMA CITY PARK ASSOCIATION. NEWS. see BIOLOGY — Botany

HARAMATA - BULLETIN OF THE DRYLANDS. see ENVIRONMENTAL STUDIES

333.7 508 — **UK** — ISSN 0141-3503
CODEN: HESNAW
THE HASTINGS & EAST SUSSEX NATURALIST. 1906. a. £4 membership. Hastings and East Sussex Natural History Society, c/o John A.B. Gale, Argosy, 11 Rockmead Rd., Fairlight, Hastings, E. Sussex TN35 4DJ, England. circ. 150. **Indexed:** Sport Fish.Abstr., Wild.Rev., Zoo.Rec. **Document type:** academic/scholarly publication.

HAWK MIGRATION STUDIES. see BIOLOGY — Ornithology

HAWK MOUNTAIN NEWS. see BIOLOGY — Ornithology

333.7 — **SZ** — ISSN 0017-9817
HEIMATSCHUTZ/SAUVEGARDE. (Text in French and German) 1906. q. 20 SFr. Schweizer Heimatschutz - Ligue Suisse du Patrimoine National, Merkurstr. 45, CH-8032 Zurich, Switzerland. Ed. Marco Badilatti. bk.rev.; charts; illus. circ. 20,000. **Document type:** bulletin.

HERITAGE CANADA. see ARCHITECTURE

333.7 796 — **AT** — ISSN 1321-2354
HERITAGE HIGHLIGHTS. 1992. free. New South Wales National Parks and Wildlife Service, 43 Bridge St., Hurstville, N.S.W. 2220, Australia. TEL 61-2-5856444. FAX 61-2-5856447. Ed. Anita Ray. circ. 800. **Document type:** government publication.
  Description: Presents a summary of N S W National Parks and Wildlife Service achievements.

HERITAGE NEWS. see ARCHITECTURE

333.7 — **US**
HI SIERRAN. 1950. m. $12. Sierra Club, San Diego Chapter, 3820 Ray St., San Diego, CA 92104-3623. TEL 619-233-7143. FAX 619-299-1742. Ed. Jackie Main; Pub. Jackie Main. adv. contact: Bill Schaul. bk.rev. circ. 15,000. **Document type:** newsletter.

333.7 — **US** — ISSN 0161-9896
HIGHLANDS VOICE. 1968. m. $15. West Virginia Highlands Conservancy, Inc., Box 306, Charleston, WV 25321-0306. TEL 304-824-3571. Ed. Bill Ragette. adv.; bk.rev.; index. circ. 1,000. **Document type:** newsletter.

333.7 — **JA** — ISSN 0286-0627
HOKKAIDO NO SHIZEN/NATURE IN HOKKAIDO. a. Hokkaido Shizen Hogo Kyokai - Nature Conservation Society of Hokkaido, 064 Kamori Bldg., Nishi (West) II, Kita (North) 3, Chuoh-ku (Central Ward), Sapporo, Japan.

333.7 — **US** — ISSN 1092-6623
HOLISTIC MANAGEMENT QUARTERLY. 1983. q. $25 (foreign $30) (effective 1997 & 1998). Center for Holistic Management, Box 7128, Albuquerque, NM 87194. TEL 505-842-5252. FAX 505-843-7900. E-mail: jodybs@igc.agc.org. Ed. Jody Butterfield. R&P contact: Sandra Halpin. adv.: page $660; trim 7 1/4 x 10; adv. contact: Jeff Coriell. bk.rev.; charts; illus.; circ. 2,000 (paid). (tabloid format; back issues avail.) **Document type:** newsletter.
  Former titles (until 1996): Holistic Resource Management Quarterly (ISSN 1069-2789); (until 1993): Holistic Resource Management Newsletter (ISSN 1048-8472); (until 1989): Savory Letter.
  Description: Examines issues related to agriculture, economics and the environment using the HRM model, and updates HRM practitioners on new developments.

333.7 634.9 — **US** — ISSN 0073-3369
S900
HORACE M. ALBRIGHT CONSERVATION LECTURESHIP. 1961. a. free. University of California at Berkeley, Department of Forestry and Resource Management, 145 Mulford Hall, Berkeley, CA 94720. TEL 415-642-0376. **Indexed:** Forest.Abstr. **Document type:** academic/scholarly publication.

333.7 — **JA** — ISSN 0287-0606
CODEN: HKAGDY
HOZON KAGAKU/SCIENCE FOR CONSERVATION. (Text in Japanese; summaries in English and Japanese) 1964. a. Agency for Cultural Affairs, Tokyo National Research Institute of Cultural Properties - Bunka-cho Tokyo Kokuritsu Bunkazai Kenkyujo Hozon Kagakubu, 13-27 Ueno Park, Taito-ku, Tokyo 110, Japan. TEL 81-3-3823-2241. FAX 81-3-3828-2434. E-mail: miura@tobunken.go.jp. Dir. Sadatoshi Miura. **Indexed:** Chem.Abstr. **Document type:** bulletin.
  —CASDDS.

THE HUMAN ECOLOGIST. see ENVIRONMENTAL STUDIES

333.7 — **AT** — ISSN 0085-1663
HUNTER VALLEY RESEARCH FOUNDATION. MONOGRAPHS. 1959. irreg. price varies. Hunter Valley Research Foundation, P.O. Box 302, Hamilton DC, N.S.W. 2303, Australia. TEL 61-49-694566. FAX 61-49-694566. E-mail: oukhvrf@cc.newcastle.edu.au. **Indexed:** Aus.Sci.Ind. **Document type:** monographic series.

333.7 — **AT** — ISSN 0310-0111
HUNTER'S HILL TRUST JOURNAL. 1971. 3/yr. Aus.$15 to individuals. Hunter's Hill Trust, P.O. Box 85, Hunter Hill, N.S.W. 2110, Australia. TEL 61-2-98162796. FAX 61-2-98162796. Ed. Megan Martin. R&P contact: Megan Martin. adv.; bk.rev.; circ. 500 (paid). (back issues avail.) **Document type:** newsletter.
  Description: Covers environmental and architectural matters, especially regarding Hunters Hill, N.S.W., Australia.

I C A S A L S NEWSLETTER. (International Center for Arid and Semiarid Land Studies) see AGRICULTURE

639.9 — **US**
I P P L NEWS. 1973. q. $20. International Primate Protection League, Box 766, Summerville, SC 29484. TEL 803-871-2280. FAX 803-871-7988. E-mail: ippl@sc.net; URL: http://www.sims.net/organizations/ippl/ippl.html. Ed. Shirley McCreal. R&P contact: Shirley McCreal. bk.rev. circ. 13,000. (back issues avail.)
  Formerly: International Primate Protection League Newsletter (ISSN 1040-3027)
  Description: Conservation and protection of primates.

639 — **US** — ISSN 0073-4527
IDAHO. DEPARTMENT OF FISH AND GAME. FEDERAL AID INVESTIGATION PROJECTS. PROGRESS REPORTS AND PUBLICATIONS. 1948. irreg., approx. a. free. Department of Fish and Game, Box 25, Boise, ID 83707. TEL 208-334-3746. FAX 208-334-2148. E-mail: dronayne@idfg.state.id.us; URL: http://www.state.id.us/fishgame/fishgame.html. circ. controlled. (also avail. in microfiche) **Document type:** government publication.

333.7 — **US**
IDAHO BUREAU OF LAND MANAGEMENT TECHNICAL BULLETIN. 1985. irreg., latest 1996. free. U.S. Bureau of Land Management, Idaho State Office, 1387 S. Vinnell Way, Boise, ID 83709. TEL 208-373-3827. FAX 208-373-3805. E-mail: a1thom@id.blm,gov. Ed. Allan Thomas. circ. 200. **Document type:** monographic series.
  Description: Contains information about natural resources.
  Refereed Serial

639.9 — **US** — ISSN 8755-2469
SK387
IDAHO WILDLIFE. 1978. bi-m. $12.95. Department of Fish and Game, Box 25, Boise, ID 83707. TEL 208-334-3748. FAX 208-334-2148. E-mail: dronayne@idfg.state.id.us; URL: http://www.state.id.us/fishgame/fishgame.html. Ed. Diane Ronayne. R&P contact: Diane Ronayne. charts; illus.; index. circ. 25,000. **Indexed:** Sport Fish.Abstr., Wild.Rev. **Document type:** consumer publication.
  —Linda Hall; UnCover.
  Supersedes: Idaho Wildlife Review (ISSN 0019-1248)

333.7 977 — **US**
ILLINOIS. NATURAL HISTORY SURVEY. REPORTS. 1962 6/yr. free. Department of Natural Resources, Natur History Survey, Natural Resources Bldg., 607 E. Peabody Dr., Champaign, IL 61820. TEL 217-244-2115. FAX 217-333-4949. Ed. Charles Warwick. circ. 2,200. **Indexed:** Sport Fish.Abstr., Wild.Rev. **Document type:** newsletter, trade publication.
  Description: Reports current research undertaken at the Illinois Natural History Survey, for a non-specialist audience.

639.9 — **US** — ISSN 1061-9801
ILLINOIS AUDUBON. 1897. q. $20. Illinois Audubon Society, Box 2418, Danville, IL 61834-2418. TEL 217-446-5085. FAX 217-446-6375. Ed. Debbie Scott Newman. R&P contact: Debbie Scott Newman. adv. contact: Debbie Scott Newman. bk.rev.; stat. circ. 3,000. (back issues avail.) **Indexed:** Sport Fish.Abstr., Wild.Rev. **Document type:** bulletin.
  —UnCover.
  Formerly: Illinois Audubon Bulletin.

ILLINOIS PARKS & RECREATION. see SPORTS AND GAMES — Outdoor Life

CONSERVATION

333.7 US ISSN 1058-9309
S932.I3
ILLINOIS STEWARD. 1992. q. $10 (foreign $18) (effective 1997). Illinois Stewardship Committee, W503 Turner Hall, 1102 S. Goodwin Ave., Urbana, IL 61801. TEL 217-333-2778.
FAX 217-244-3219. Ed. Mike Bolin. R&P contact: Mike Bolin. adv. contact: Michael Bolin. illus.; index. circ. 4,000. **Document type:** consumer publication.
Description: Articles pertaining to the understanding and care of Illinois' natural resources and heritage.
Refereed Serial

639.9 US ISSN 0019-2317
ILLINOIS WILDLIFE. 1945. m. $10. Illinois Wildlife Federation, 123 S. Chicago, Rossville, IL 60963. TEL 217-748-6365. FAX 217-748-6304. E-mail: wildlife@cu-online.com; URL: http://www.cu-online.com/~wildlife/iwf.htm. Ed. Tom Mills; Pub. Tom Mills. R&P contact: Tom Mills. adv. contact: Tom Mills. bk.rev.; illus.; circ. 12,500 (controlled). (tabloid format) **Indexed:** Biol.Dig. **Document type:** newspaper.

333.7 BL
IMAGENS DA AMAZONIA. bi-m. Editora Ecopress, Rua Jose Bonifacio 209, Sala 1009, 01003-902 Sao Paulo SP, Brazil. TEL 55-11-352221.
FAX 55-11-342059. Ed. Tania Nomura.

333.78 UK ISSN 0966-2200
IN PRACTICE (NEWBURY). Variant title: Ecology and Environmental Management in Practice. 1991. q. £70 to non-members (effective 1996 & 1997). Institute of Ecology and Environmental Management, 36 Kingfisher Ct., Newbury, Berks. RG14 5SJ, England. TEL 44-1635-37715.
FAX 44-1635-550230. E-mail: ieem@naturebureau.co.uk. Ed. Sue Everett. adv.: page £320; trim 260 x 184; adv. contact: Martin Harvey. bk.rev.; bibl.; illus. circ. 750. (back issues avail.) **Document type:** bulletin.
Description: Contains news and articles of interest to professional ecologists. Offers vocational advice and covers professional standards.

333.9 RE ISSN 0750-4586
INFO-NATURE. 1974. irreg. 40 Fr. Societe Reunionnaise pour l'Etude et la Protection de l'Environnement, B.P. 1109, 97482 Saint Denis Cedex, Reunion. illus.

INSTITUTO ECUATORIANO DE CIENCIAS NATURALES. CONTRIBUCIONES. see *SCIENCES: COMPREHENSIVE WORKS*

333.7 SP ISSN 0210-0134
INTEGRAL. 1978. m. 4900 ptas. (foreign 21000 ptas.); newsstand price: 500 ptas. R B A Revistas, S.A., Perez Galdos 36, 08012 Madrid, Spain. TEL 34-3-4147374. FAX 34-3-2177378. Ed. Josan Ruiz. R&P contact: Ila Matthiasdottir. adv.: page 485000 ptas.; trim 220 X 300; adv. contact: Adriana Hernandez. bk.rev. circ. 375,180.
Description: Covers ecology, personal development and alternative cultures.

333.7 639.9 US ISSN 0161-3332
SK352
INTERNATIONAL ASSOCIATION OF FISH AND WILDLIFE AGENCIES. PROCEEDINGS OF THE CONVENTION. 1946. a. $20. International Association of Fish and Wildlife Agencies, 444 N. Capitol St., N.W., Ste. 544, Washington, DC 20001. TEL 202-624-7890.
FAX 202-624-7891. Eds. Mark J. Reeff, Harold Nesbitt. circ. 600. (back issues avail.) **Document type:** proceedings.
—BLDSC (6843.479000).
Formerly: Convention of the International Association of Fish and Wildlife Agencies (ISSN 0163-8653)

333.7 370.196 AT ISSN 1040-5208
INTERNATIONAL ASSOCIATION OF ZOO EDUCATORS. JOURNAL. 1974. s-a. membership only. International Association of Zoo Educators, c/o Melbourne Zoo Education Service, P.O. Box 74, Parkville, Vic. 3052, Australia. TEL 61-3-92859355.
FAX 61-3-92859340. E-mail: mzes@zoo.org.au. Ed. Greg Hunt. bk.rev. circ. 220. **Indexed:** Sport Fish.Abstr., Wild.Rev. **Document type:** academic/scholarly publication.
Formerly: International Association of Zoo Educators. Newsletter.
Description: Aimed at zoo and aquarium educators and other professionals.
Refereed Serial

INTERNATIONAL BEAR NEWS. see *BIOLOGY — Zoology*

639.97978 SZ
INTERNATIONAL BEAR NEWS. (Text in English) 1990. 2/yr. International Union for Conservation of Nature and Natural Resources, Species Survival Commission - Bear Specialist Group, Rue Mauverney 28, CH-1196 Gland, Switzerland. TEL 41-22-9990001. FAX 41-22-9990002. TELEX 419624-IUCN-CH. (Subscr. to: Sterling Miller, 333 Raspberry Rd., Anchorage, AK 99518-1599, USA) **Document type:** newsletter.
Formerly: International Union for Conservation of Nature and Natural Resources. Species Survival Commission - Bear Specialist Group Newsletter.

INTERNATIONAL CENTRE OF INSECT PHYSIOLOGY AND ECOLOGY. ANNUAL REPORT. see *BIOLOGY — Entomology*

INTERNATIONAL COMMISSION FOR THE CONSERVATION OF ATLANTIC TUNAS. REPORT. see *BIOLOGY — Zoology*

639.9 622 US ISSN 1050-2106
INTERNATIONAL EROSION CONTROL ASSOCIATION. CONFERENCE PROCEEDINGS. 1974. a. $45 to non-members; members $35 (effective 1997). International Erosion Control Association, Box 4904, Steamboat Springs, CO 80477-4904.
TEL 970-879-3010; 800-455-4322.
FAX 970-879-8563. E-mail: ecinfo@ieca.org; URL: http://www.ieca.org. Ed. David Williams. circ. 1,500. (back issues avail.) **Document type:** proceedings.

INTERNATIONAL EROSION CONTROL ASSOCIATION. PRODUCTS & SERVICES DIRECTORY. see *BUSINESS AND ECONOMICS — Trade And Industrial Directories*

INTERNATIONAL INSTITUTE FOR ENVIRONMENT AND DEVELOPMENT. DRYLANDS PAPER. see *ENVIRONMENTAL STUDIES*

INTERNATIONAL INSTITUTE FOR ENVIRONMENT AND DEVELOPMENT. PASTORAL LAND TENURE SERIES. see *ENVIRONMENTAL STUDIES*

INTERNATIONAL JOURNAL OF ENVIRONMENT AND POLLUTION. see *ENVIRONMENTAL STUDIES — Pollution*

INTERNATIONAL JOURNAL OF GLOBAL ENERGY ISSUES. see *ENERGY*

INTERNATIONAL JOURNAL OF RURAL STUDIES. see *SOCIOLOGY*

INTERNATIONAL JOURNAL OF SUSTAINABLE DEVELOPMENT AND WORLD ECOLOGY. see *ENVIRONMENTAL STUDIES*

333.9 628 US ISSN 1086-5519
INTERNATIONAL JOURNAL OF WILDERNESS. 1995. q. Can.$30 to individuals; institutions and libraries Can.$50 (effective 1997). International Wilderness Leadership Foundation, 2162 Baldwin Rd., Ojai, CA 93023. FAX 805-649-1757. E-mail: wild@fishnet.net. (Editorial addr.: University of Idaho, Wilderness Research Center, Moscow, ID 83844-1144. TEL 208-885-2267. FAX 208-885-2268) Ed. John C. Hendee. (back issues avail.)
—BLDSC (4542.701230).
Description: Offers a forum for reporting and discussing wilderness ideas and events; planning, management and allocation strategies; education; and research and policy aspects of wilderness stewardship.

333.7 628 US ISSN 1046-8366
THE INTERNATIONAL PERMACULTURE SOLUTIONS JOURNAL. Variant title: T I P S Journal. irreg. $25. Yankee Permaculture, Hemenway - Permaculture, Box 2052, Ocala, FL 34478-2052. Ed. Dan Hemenway. R&P contact: Dan Hemenway. **Document type:** academic/scholarly publication.
Supersedes in part (in 1990): T I P S Y: International Permaculture Species Yearbook (ISSN 0896-5781)
Description: Provides information, ideas, and tools for solutions to the environmental crisis.

333.7 SZ ISSN 0074-929X
INTERNATIONAL UNION FOR CONSERVATION OF NATURE AND NATURAL RESOURCES. PROCEEDINGS OF THE GENERAL ASSEMBLY. 1948. triennial; 19th, Buenos Aires, Argentina, 1994. International Union for Conservation of Nature and Natural Resources, Rue Mauverney 28, CH-1196 Gland, Switzerland. TEL 41-22-9990001. FAX 41-22-9990002. TELEX 419624-IUCN-CH. **Document type:** proceedings.

639.9 179.3 SZ
INTERNATIONAL UNION FOR CONSERVATION OF NATURE AND NATURAL RESOURCES. SPECIES SURVIVAL COMMISSION - CACTI AND SUCCULENT SPECIALIST GROUP NEWSLETTER. 2/yr. International Union for Conservation of Nature and Natural Resources, Species Survival Commission - Cacti and Succulent Specialist Group, Rue Mauverney 28, CH-1196 Gland, Switzerland. TEL 41-22-9990001. FAX 41-22-9990002. TELEX 419624-IUCN-CH. (Subscr. to: Dr. Edward Anderson, Desert Botanical Garden, 1201 N. Galvin Pkwy., Phoenix, AZ 85008, USA) **Document type:** newsletter.

639.9 179.3 SZ
INTERNATIONAL UNION FOR CONSERVATION OF NATURE AND NATURAL RESOURCES. SPECIES SURVIVAL COMMISSION - CROCODILE SPECIALIST GROUP NEWSLETTER. 4/yr. International Union for Conservation of Nature and Natural Resources, Species Survival Commission - Crocodile Specialist Group, Rue Mauverney 28, CH-1196 Gland, Switzerland. TEL 41-22-9990001.
FAX 41-22-9990002. TELEX 419624-IUCN-CH. (Subscr. to: Dr. J.P. Ross, Florida Museum of Natural History, Gainesville, FL 32611 USA. FAX 904-392-9367) **Document type:** newsletter.

333.7 179 SZ
INTERNATIONAL UNION FOR CONSERVATION OF NATURE AND NATURAL RESOURCES. SPECIES SURVIVAL COMMISSION - CANID SPECIALIST GROUP. NEWSLETTER. Variant title: Canid News. 3/yr. £12. Species Survival Commission - Canid Specialist Group, Rue Mauverney 28, CH-1196 Gland, Switzerland. TEL 41-22-9990001.
FAX 41-22-9990002. TELEX 419624-IUCN-CH. (Subscr. to: Dr. David Macdonald, Wildlife Conservation Research Unit, Dept. of Zoology, Oxford University, South Parks Rd., Oxford OX1 3PS, England) **Document type:** newsletter.

639.9 179.3 SZ
INTERNATIONAL UNION FOR CONSERVATION OF NATURE AND NATURAL RESOURCES. SPECIES SURVIVAL COMMISSION - DEER SPECIALIST GROUP. NEWSLETTER. 1975. a. International Union for Conservation of Nature and Natural Resources, Species Survival Commission - Deer Specialist Group, Rue Mauverney 28, CH-1196 Gland, Switzerland. TEL 41-22-9990001.
FAX 41-22-9990002. TELEX 419624-IUCN-CH. (Subscr. to: Dr. C.M. Wemmer, National Zoological Park, Front Royal, VA 22630, USA) **Document type:** newsletter.

639.9 179.3 SZ
INTERNATIONAL UNION FOR CONSERVATION OF NATURE AND NATURAL RESOURCES. SPECIES SURVIVAL COMMISSION - HYAENA SPECIALIST GROUP BULLETIN. (Text in English) irreg. International Union for Conservation of Nature and Natural Resources, Species Survival Commission - Hyaena Specialist Group, Rue Mauverney 28, CH-1196 Gland, Switzerland. TEL 41-22-9990001. FAX 41-22-9990002. TELEX 419624-IUCN-CH. (Subscr. to: Dr. M.G.L. Mills, Kruger National Park, P. Bag X402, Skukuza, 1350, South Africa) **Document type:** bulletin.

639.9 179.3 SZ
INTERNATIONAL UNION FOR CONSERVATION OF NATURE AND NATURAL RESOURCES. SPECIES SURVIVAL COMMISSION - OTTER SPECIALIST GROUP BULLETIN. (Text in English) 1984. a. International Union for Conservation of Nature and Natural Resources, Species Survival Group - Otter Specialist Group, Rue Mauverney 28, CH-1196 Gland, Switzerland. TEL 41-22-9990001.
FAX 41-22-9990002. TELEX 419624-IUCN-CH. (Subscr. to: Arno Gutleb, Institute for Medical Chemistry, University of Veterinary Medicine, Linke Bahngasse 11, A-1030 Vienna, Austria) **Document type:** bulletin.

CONSERVATION

693.9 179.3 US
INTERNATIONAL UNION FOR CONSERVATION OF NATURE AND NATURAL RESOURCES. SPECIES SURVIVAL COMMISSION - SPECIALIST GROUP ON STORKS, IBISES, AND SPOONBILLS NEWSLETTER. (Text in English) 1988. 2/yr. International Union for Conservation of Nature and Natural Resources, Species Survival Commission - Specialist Group on Storks, Ibises, and Spoonbills, c/o Malcom Coulter, SREL, Drawer E, Aiken, SC 29802. **Document type:** newsletter.

333.7 179 SZ
INTERNATIONAL UNION FOR CONSERVATION OF NATURE AND NATURAL RESOURCES. SPECIES SURVIVAL COMMISSION - VETERINARY SPECIALIST GROUP. NEWSLETTER. a. $5. Rue Mauverney 28, CH-1196 Gland, Switzerland. TEL 41-22-9990001. FAX 41-22-9990002. TELEX 419624-IUCN-CH. (Subscr. to: Dr. M. Woodford, Care of the Wild, 500 23rd St., N.W., Washington, DC 20037 USA) **Document type:** newsletter.

INTERNATIONAL WHALING COMMISSION. ANNUAL REPORT. see *FISH AND FISHERIES*

333.7 639.9 US ISSN 0020-9112
QL81.5   CODEN: INWLAI
INTERNATIONAL WILDLIFE; dedicated to the conservation of the world's natural resources. 1971. bi-m. $22. National Wildlife Federation, 8925 Leesburg Pike, Vienna, VA 22184-0001. TEL 703-790-4000; 800-588-4000. FAX 703-790-4075. E-mail: pubs@nwf.org; URL: http://www.nwf.org. Ed. Bob Strohm; Pub. Bob Strohm. R&P contact: Kelly Hartley. TEL 703-790-4510. adv. contact: Thuy Senser. charts; illus.; pat.; index. circ. 380,000. (also avail. in microform from UMI; microfiche from NBI; reprint service avail from UMI) **Indexed:** Acad.Ind., Acid Pre.Dig., Biol.Abstr., Biol.Dig., Can.B.P.I., Deep Sea Res.& Oceanogr.Abstr., Environ.Abstr., Environ.Per.Bibl. (1972-), Gen.Sci.Ind., Ind.Child.Mag., Ind.Sci.Rev., Jun.High.Mag.Abstr., Mag.Ind., Mid.East: Abstr.& Ind., PMR, R.G., R.G.Abstr., Zoo.Rec. **Document type:** consumer publication.
● Also available online. Vendor(s): Information Access Co.
—BLDSC (4552.120000); KR SourceOne; Linda Hall; SWETS; UnCover.

333.7 599.74442 US
INTERNATIONAL WOLF. 1990. q. $12 (foreign $19) (effective until further notice). International Wolf Center, 5930 Brooklyn Blvd., Minneapolis, MN 55429. TEL 612-560-7374; 800-ELY-WOLF. FAX 612-569-7368. E-mail: wolfinfo@wolf.org; URL: http://www.wolf.org. Ed. Mary Ortiz. adv. contact: Sheri LeVasseur.
Description: Submissions including international reintroduction plans and updates, human/wolf contact interest stories, wolf research updates, future wolf conferences and events, literature reviews and ongoing international Wolf Center and other wolf organizational activities.
Refereed Serial

IOWA SIERRAN. see *CLUBS*

639.9 UK ISSN 0260-986X
IRISH HARE. 1978. 3/yr. membership. Ulster Wildlife Trust, 3 New Line, Crossgar BT30 9EP, N. Ireland. Ed. William McNamara. adv.; bk.rev.; illus. circ. 1,200. **Document type:** newsletter.

IRRIGATION NEWS. see *WATER RESOURCES*

333.7 JA ISSN 0286-8660
ISHIKAWA-KEN HAKUSAN SHIZEN HOGO SENTA KENKYU HOKOKU/HAKUSAN NATURE CONSERVATION CENTER, ISHIKAWA PREFECTURE. ANNUAL REPORT. (Text in Japanese; summaries in English and Japanese) 1974. a. Ishikawa-ken Hakusan Shizen Hogo Senta - Hakusan Nature Conservation Center, Ishikawa Prefecture, Kinameri, Yoshinodanimura, Ishikawa-gun, Ishikawa-ken 920-23, Japan. TEL 81-7619-5-5321. FAX 81-7619-5-5323. **Document type:** academic/scholarly publication.

639.9 799.2 BE ISSN 0770-6693
JACHT EN NATUURBEHEER. 1909. m. Koninklijke Sint-Hubertusclub van Belgie, Jan Jacobsplein 1, 1000 Brussels, Belgium.
Formerly (until 1970): Koninklijke Sint-Hubertusclub van Belgie (ISSN 0770-8440)

577 JM ISSN 1018-1261
JAMAICA NATURALIST. 1991. s-a. J.$120($15) Natural History Society of Jamaica, c/o Peter Vogel, Ed., Department of Zoology, University of the West Indies, Kingston 7, Jamaica, W.I. TEL 809-927-1202. FAX 809-927-1640. adv. contact: Adam Hyde. bk.rev. circ. 2,000. (back issues avail.; reprint service avail.)
Description: Covers fauna and flora of Jamaica, natural heritage, conservation of tropical biodiversity, and sustainable use of natural resources.

333.7 US
JERSEY SIERRAN. bi-m. $7.50 to non-members. Sierra Club, New Jersey Chapter, 57 Mountain Ave., Princeton, NJ 08540. TEL 609-924-3141. Ed. Mary Penney. adv.; bk.rev. circ. 15,000.
Description: Covers conservation issues on a statewide and national basis, including information on the state legislative agenda. Also lists club hikes, meetings, and events statewide.

333.7 II ISSN 0970-5945
    CODEN: JNCOEA
JOURNAL OF NATURE CONSERVATION; an international journal devoted to nature, natural resource conservation and environment. (Text in English) 1989. s-a. Rs.100 to individuals (foreign $50); institutions Rs.200 (foreign $100). Journal of Nature Conservation, c/o G.R. Shukla, Mng. Ed., 1351 South Civil Lines, Circular Rd., Charan Singh Colony, Muzaffarnagar 251 001, India. TEL 0131-401414. Ed. S.R. Verma. adv.: page Rs.500 ($175). bk.rev. circ. 300. **Indexed:** Ecol.Abstr. **Document type:** academic/scholarly publication.
—BLDSC (5021.302000).

JOURNAL OF PARK AND RECREATION ADMINISTRATION. see *SPORTS AND GAMES — Outdoor Life*

JOURNAL OF RANGE MANAGEMENT; covering the study, management, and use of rangeland ecosystems and range resources. see *BIOLOGY*

JOURNAL OF RURAL STUDIES. see *SOCIOLOGY*

333.7 II ISSN 0022-457X
S954.I5   CODEN: JSWIAL
JOURNAL OF SOIL AND WATER CONSERVATION IN INDIA. (Text in English) 1952. q. Rs.100 to individuals (foreign $70); institutions Rs.500 (foreign $500). Soil Conservation Society of India, B-19 Paryat Apts., Pilampura, 4 Outer Ring Rd., New Delhi 110034, India. TEL 91-11-5743811. Ed. T.K. Sarkar. adv.; charts; illus circ. 1,500. (back issues avail.) **Indexed:** Biol.Abstr., Chem.Abstr., GeoRef., SSCI. **Document type:** academic/scholarly publication.
—CASDDS; CISTI; Linda Hall.
Refereed Serial

333.7 US ISSN 1044-0046
S494.5.S86   CODEN: JSAGEB
JOURNAL OF SUSTAINABLE AGRICULTURE. 1990. q. (in 2 vols.) $40 to individuals (Canada $52; elsewhere $56); institutions $60 (Canada $78; elsewhere $84); libraries $145 (Canada $188.50; elsewhere $203) (effective 1997). Haworth Press, Inc., 10 Alice St., Binghamton, NY 13904. TEL 607-722-5857; 800-342-9676. FAX 607-722-6362. E-mail: getinfo@haworth.com; URL: http://www.haworth.com. Ed. Raymond P. Poincelot; Pub. Bill Cohen. R&P contact: Ruthann Heath. adv.: B&W page $300; trim 4 3/8 x 7 1/8; adv. contact: Jackie Blakeslee. bk.rev. circ. 448. (also avail. in microfiche from UMI; microform from HAW; reprint service avail. from HAW) **Indexed:** ASCA, Ecol.Abstr., Energy Info.Abstr., Environ.Abstr., Environ.Per.Bibl. (1990-), Food Sci.& Tech.Abstr., Geo.Abstr.H.G., Geo.Abstr.P.G., IDA, Ref.Zh., SOPODA, SSCI. **Document type:** academic/scholarly publication.
—BLDSC (5067.730000); Genuine Article; Haworth; SWETS; UnCover.
Description: Devoted to the study and application of sustainable agriculture for solutions to the problems of resource depletion and environmental misuse.
Refereed Serial

JOURNAL OF WILDLIFE DISEASES. see *VETERINARY SCIENCE*

639.9 US ISSN 0022-541X
SK351   CODEN: JWMAA9
JOURNAL OF WILDLIFE MANAGEMENT. 1937. q. $120 (foreign $130) (effective 1997) (includes Wildlife Monographs). Wildlife Society, 5410 Grosvenor Ln., Bethesda, MD 20814. TEL 301-897-9770. FAX 301-530-2471. Ed. Mark S. Boyce. bk.rev.; bibl.; charts; illus.; stat.; index. circ. 7,000. (also avail. in microform from UMI; back issues avail.; reprint service avail. from UMI) **Indexed:** Agroforest.Abstr., Anim.Breed.Abstr., ASCA, Biol.Abstr., Biol.& Agr.Ind., Cadscan, Chem.Abstr., Curr.Adv.Ecol.Sci., Curr.Cont., Curr.Ref.Fish Res., Dairy Sci.Abstr., Deep Sea Res.& Oceanogr.Abstr., Ecol.Abstr., Energy Rev., Environ.Per.Bibl. (1983-), Excerp.Med., Field Crop Abstr., Forest.Abstr., Forest Prod.Abstr., Gen.Sci.Ind., Geo.Abstr.H.G., Helminthol.Abstr., Herb.Abstr., IBR, Ind.Sci.Rev., Ind.Vet., INIS Atomind., Int.Aerosp.Abstr., Key Word Ind.Wildl.Res., Lead Abstr., Maize Abstr., Mid.East: Abstr.& Ind., Nutr.Abstr., Pig News & Info., Poult.Abstr., Rev.Appl.Entomol., Sci.Cit.Ind., Sel.Water Res.Abstr., Soils & Fert., Sport Fish.Abstr., Triticale Abstr., Vet.Bull., Weed Abstr., Wild.Rev., Wildlife & Conserv.Biol.Abstr. (1937-), Zincscan, Zoo.Rec. **Document type:** academic/scholarly publication.
—BLDSC (5072.630000); CASDDS; CISTI; EMDOCS; KR SourceOne; Linda Hall; SWETS; UMI; UnCover.
Refereed Serial

JUNGLE; a journal for promotion of tourism and nature study. see *TRAVEL AND TOURISM*

639.9 AT
JUNIOR NATURALIST. m. Australian Wildlife Club, 2 Coolgardie Place, Sutherland, N.S.W. 2232, Australia.

639.9 KE
K W S NEWSLETTER. (Text in English) 1979. q. donation. Kenya Wildlife Service, Nairobi Education Centre, P.O. Box 40241, Nairobi, Kenya. TEL 254-2-501081. FAX 254-2-505866. TELEX 22804 KE. circ. 2,000 (controlled).
Formerly (until 1989): Kenya. Ministry of Tourism and Wildlife. Department of Wildlife Conservation and Management. Newsletter.

333.7 JA ISSN 0914-8744
KANAGAWA-KENRITSU SHIZEN HOGO SENTA HOKOKU/KANAGAWA PREFECTURAL NATURE CONSERVATION CENTER. BULLETIN. (Text in Japanese) 1984. a. Kanagawa-kenritsu Shizen Hogo Senta, 657 Nanasawa, Atsugi-shi, Kanagawa-ken 243-01, Japan. TEL 81-462-48-0323. FAX 81-462-48-2560.
Description: Presents research reports of the center.

333.7 JA
KANAGAWA SHIZEN HOZEN KENKYUKAI HOKOKUSHO/KANAGAWA NATURAL PRESERVATION SOCIETY. JOURNAL. (Text in Japanese; summaries in English, Japanese) 1981. a. Kanagawa Shizen Hozen Kenkyukai - Kanagawa Natural Preservation Society, c/o Mr. Hidemaro Toshima, 27-5 Kamiyabe 5-chome, Sagamihara-shi, Kanagawa-ken 229, Japan.

KANSAS SCHOOL NATURALIST. see *EDUCATION*

639.9 US ISSN 0898-6975
SK397   CODEN: KWPAE5
KANSAS WILDLIFE & PARKS. 1938. bi-m. $10 (effective 1997). Department of Wildlife & Parks, Information - Education, 512 S.E. 25th Ave., Pratt, KS 67124-8174. TEL 316-672-5911. FAX 316-672-6020. Ed. Mike Miller. bk.rev.; illus. circ. 46,000. **Indexed:** Sport Fish.Abstr., Wild.Rev., Zoo.Rec.
—BLDSC (5085.651600); UnCover.
Former titles: Kansas Wildlife (ISSN 0279-9030); Kansas Fish and Game (ISSN 0022-8591)
Description: Main objective is to increase individual awareness of responsibility towards the land by examining the issue of conservation and the use of natural resources.

KENTUCKY AFIELD; the magazine. see *SPORTS AND GAMES — Outdoor Life*

CONSERVATION

346.036 US
KENTUCKY FISH AND WILDLIFE STATUTES. a. $22. Michie, A Division of Reed Elsevier Inc., Box 7587, Charlottesville, VA 22906-7587. TEL 804-972-7566; 800-562-1197. FAX 800-643-1280. E-mail: custserv@michie.com; URL: http://www.michie.com. Ed. George Harley.
Description: Contains statutes covering fish and wildlife resources, boats and boating, and more.

639.9 ZA ISSN 1015-5546
KOBUS. 1987. bi-m. $20. Wildlife Conservation Society of Zambia, P.O. Box 30255, Lusaka, Zambia. TEL 01-254226. FAX 01-222906. E-mail: 5:761/1.91@FIDONET. Ed. Mwape Sichilongo. **Document type:** newsletter.

508 SA ISSN 0075-6458
QL337.S65 CODEN: KOEDB2
KOEDOE; navorsingstydskrif vir nasionale parke in die Republiek van Suid-Afrika - research journal for national parks in the Republic of South Africa. (Supplement avail.) (Text in English) 1958. 2/yr. R.50 (foreign R.70) (effective 1997). National Parks Board - Nasionale Parkeraad, P.O. Box 787, Pretoria 0001, South Africa. TEL 27-12-343-9770. FAX 27-12-343-2832. TELEX 321931 SA. E-mail: kobier@parks-sa.ca.za. Ed. J.C. Rautenbach. abstr.; bibl.; charts; cum.index: vols.1-25 in vol.25, 1982; vols.26-35 in vol.35, 1992. circ. 1,200. **Indexed:** Bio-Contr.News & Info., Biol.Abstr., Curr.Adv.Ecol.Sci., Ecol.Abstr., Field Crop Abstr., Forest.Abstr., Forest Prod.Abstr., Geo.Abstr.H.G., Helminthol.Abstr., Herb.Abstr., IBR, IDA, Ind.S.A.Per., Ind.Vet., Irr.& Drain.Abstr., Key Word Ind.Wildl.Res., Rev.Appl.Entomol., Soils & Fert., Sport Fish.Abstr., Vet.Bull., W.R.C.Inf., Weed Abstr., Wild.Rev., Zoo.Rec. **Document type:** academic/scholarly publication.
—CIS; UnCover.
Description: Presents original papers concerned with the perpetuation of wildlife and the conservation of biological and associated natural resources. *Refereed Serial*

500.9 SA ISSN 0075-6466
CODEN: KOEDAZ
KOEDOE. MONOGRAPHS. 1966. irreg. R.25. National Parks Board - Nasionale Parkeraad, P.O. Box 787, Pretoria 0001, South Africa. TEL 27-12-343-9770. FAX 27-12-343-9958. TELEX 321931 SA. Ed. J.C. Rautenbach. circ. 2,000. **Indexed:** Biol.Abstr., Sport Fish.Abstr., Wild.Rev., Zoo.Rec. **Document type:** monographic series.

333.7 IS
KOL ATAR; bulletin of the National Park Authority. 1973. s-a. free. National Park Authority, P.O. Box 7028, Tel Aviv 61 070, Israel. TEL 03-252281. Ed. S. Raviv. circ. 5,000.

639.9 KE
KOMBA. (Text in English) 1969. 3/yr. $1. Wildlife Clubs of Kenya Association, P.O. Box 20184, Nairobi, Kenya. TEL 254-2-891904. Ed. Ibrahim M. Ali. adv.; bk.rev. circ. 6,000. **Document type:** academic/scholarly publication.
Formerly (until 1978): Wildlife Clubs of Kenya Association. Newsletter.

333.7 KN ISSN 0023-4036
KOREAN NATURE.* 1967. q. Korean Association for Conservation of Nature, Pyongyang, N. Korea. charts; illus.

639.9 SA
QH195.A323
KWAZULU - NATAL WILDLIFE. 1960. bi-m. R.100 membership. Wildlife and Environment Society of Southern Africa, Natal Branch - Natuurlewevereniging van Suidelike Afrika, 100 Brand Rd., Durban 4001, South Africa. TEL 27-31-213126. FAX 27-31-219525. Ed. Els Van Asseltty. adv.; bk.rev.; circ. 5,000 (paid).
Formerly: Natal Wildlife (ISSN 0027-8343).
Description: Includes news from all of the society's branches and from other organizations concerned with the environment.

333.7 VE ISSN 0047-3898
LAGO. 1967. bi-m. free. Instituto para la Conservacion del Lago de Valencia, Apartado 761, Valencia, Venezuela. Ed. Octavio Jelambi. adv.; bk.rev.; charts; illus. circ. 1,500.

639.9 179.3 SZ
LAGOMORPH NEWSLETTER. (Text in English) 1980. 2/yr. $5. International Union for Conservation of Nature and Natural Resources, Species Survival Commission - Lagomorph Specialist Group, Rue Mauverney 28, CH-1196 Gland, Switzerland. TEL 41-22-9990001. FAX 41-22-9990002. TELEX 419624-IUCN-CH. (Subscr. to: Dr. Andrew Smith, Dept. of Zoology, Arizona State University, Tempe, AZ 85287-1501, USA) **Document type:** newsletter.

333.91 US ISSN 0743-7978
GB1601
LAKE LINE. 1981. q. $35 membership. North American Lake Management Society, Box 5443, Madison, WI 53705-5443. Ed. Jeffrey Thornton. adv.; bk.rev. circ. 2,300. (back issues avail.)
—BLDSC (5143.946320).
Description: Environmental issues and developments in lake management for a general audience.

333.7 SA ISSN 0075-7780
QH195.N3 CODEN: LMGYA3
LAMMERGEYER. (Text in English) 1960. irreg., no.42, 1993. R.12 (foreign $20). Natal Parks Board - Natalse Parkeraad, P.O. Box 662, Pietermaritzburg 3200, South Africa. TEL 27-331-471961. FAX 27-331-471037. Ed. D.N. Johnson. R&P contact: D.N. Johnson. circ. 453. **Indexed:** Biol.Abstr., Curr.Adv.Ecol.Sci., Curr.Cont., Ind.S.A.Per., Ind.Vet., Key Word Ind.Wildl.Res., Rev.Appl.Entomol., Sel.Water Res.Abstr., Soils & Fert., Sport Fish.Abstr., Vet.Bull., Wild Life Rev., Wild.Rev., Zoo.Rec. **Document type:** academic/scholarly publication.
—BLDSC (5144.300000); CISTI; UnCover.
Description: Nature conservation research in Natal. *Refereed Serial*

333.7 US ISSN 0192-9453
CODEN: LAWAEX
LAND & WATER. 1959. 6/yr. $20 (foreign $32) (effective 1997). Land and Water, Inc., Box 1197, Ft. Dodge, IA 50501. TEL 515-576-3191. FAX 515-576-2606. E-mail: landandwater@dodgenet.com; URL: http://www.landandwater.com. Ed. Teresa Doyle; Pub. Amy Dencklau. adv. contact: Gail Henry. bk.rev.; illus.; stat. circ. 20,000. **Indexed:** Excerp.Med., HRIS. **Document type:** trade publication.
—BLDSC (5146.765000); Linda Hall.
Former titles: Land and Water Development (ISSN 0023-7590); Land and Water Contracting.
Description: Edited for contractors, engineers, architects, government officials and those working in the field of natural resource management and restoration from idea stage through project completion and maintenance. *Refereed Serial*

333.7 US
LAND AND WATER CONSERVATION FUND GRANTS MANUAL. 1965. irreg. $45. U.S. National Park Service, U.S. Department of the Interior, Washington, DC 20240. TEL 202-343-1100. (looseleaf format) **Document type:** government publication.
Formerly: U.S. Bureau of Outdoor Recreation. Recreation Grants-in-Aid Manual.

333.7 333.91 II
▼**LAND HUSBANDRY;** international journal of soil and water conservation. (Text in English) 1996. s-a. $69. Oxford & I.B.H. Publishing Co. Pvt. Ltd., 66 Janpath, New Delhi 110 001, India. TEL 91-11-3315310. FAX 91-11-3713275. E-mail: oxford.publ@axcess.net.in; oxford.editor@axcess.net.in. Ed. K.J. Tejwani. R&P contact: Raju Primlani.
Description: Devoted to the advancement of the science and practice of land husbandry, soil and water conservation, wasteland reclamation and rehabilitation, and environment management with respect to land, water, forests and crops.

333.7 US ISSN 0890-7625
LAND LETTER; the newsletter for natural resource professionals. 1982. 34/yr. (12 monthly eds., 10 special reports, 11 status reports). $165. Conservation Fund, 1800 N. Kent St., Ste. 1120, Arlington, VA 22209. TEL 703-522-8008. FAX 703-525-4610. Ed. Jason Rylander. adv. contact: Jason Rylander. index. **Document type:** newsletter, trade publication.

DE LANDEIGENAAR; maandblad voor beheer van het buitengebied. see *REAL ESTATE*

333.7 NE ISSN 0169-2046
HT166 CODEN: LUPLEZ
LANDSCAPE AND URBAN PLANNING; an international journal on landscape design, conservation and reclamation, planning and urban ecology. (Text in English) 1974. 16/yr. fl.1740($1074) (effective 1997). Elsevier Science B.V., P.O. Box 211, 1000 AE Amsterdam, Netherlands. TEL 31-20-4853911. FAX 31-20-4853598. TELEX 18582 ESPA NL. E-mail: nlinfo-f@elsevier.nl; usinfo-f@elsevier.com; forinfo-kyf04035@niftyserve.or.jp; URL: http://www.elsevier.nl/. (Subscr. in the Americas to: Elsevier Science, Regional Sales Office, Box 945, New York, NY 10159-0945. TEL 212-633-3730. FAX 212-633-3680; Subscr. in Australasia and the Far East to: Elsevier Science (Singapore) Pte Ltd, No.1 Temasek Ave., No.17-01 Millenia Tower, Singapore 039192, Singapore. TEL 65-434-3727. FAX 65-337-2230; Subscr. in Japan to: Elsevier Science Japan, 9-15 Higashi-Azabu 1-chome, Minato-ku, Tokyo 106, Japan. TEL 81-3-5561-5033. FAX 81-3-5561-5047) Eds. M.M. McCarthy, J.R. Rodiek. adv.; bk.rev.; bibl.; charts; illus.; index. (reprint service avail. from SWZ) **Indexed:** Acid Pre.Dig., Agri.Eng.Abstr., Agroforest.Abstr., ASCA, Avery Ind.Archit.Per., Biol.Abstr., Br.Tech.Ind., Curr.Adv.Ecol.Sci., Curr.Cont., Ecol.Abstr., Energy Ind., Energy Info.Abstr., Energy Rev., Environ.Abstr., Environ.Per.Bibl. (1975-), Excerpt.Med., Field Crop Abstr., Forest.Abstr., Geo.Abstr.H.G., Geo.Abstr.P.G., GeoRef., Herb.Abstr., IDA, Ind.Sci.Rev., Irr.& Drain.Abstr., Ornam.Hort., Rural Recreat.Tour.Abstr., Soils & Fert., Soyabean Abstr., Sport Fish.Abstr., SSCI, Weed Abstr., Wild.Rev., World Agri.Econ.& Rural Sociol.Abstr., Zoo.Rec. **Document type:** academic/scholarly publication.
—BLDSC (5153.134000); CASDDS; CISTI; Ei; EMDOCS; Genuine Article; Linda Hall; SWETS; UnCover. **CCC.**
Incorporates (in 1988): Reclamation and Revegetation Research (ISSN 0167-644X); (in 1986): Urban Ecology (ISSN 0304-4009); **Formerly:** Landscape and Planning (ISSN 0304-3924)
Description: Concerned with conceptual, scientific and design approaches to land use.

LANDSCAPE ARCHITECTURAL REVIEW/REVUE D'ARCHITECTURE DE PAYSAGE. see *ARCHITECTURE*

LANDSCHAP; tijdschrift voor landschapsecologie en milieukunde. see *ENVIRONMENTAL STUDIES*

333.7 US
LEAGUE LEADER. 5/yr. Izaak Walton League of America, 707 Conservation Ln., Gaithersburg, MD 20878-2983. TEL 301-548-0150. FAX 301-548-0146. Ed. Paul Hansen. adv. contact: Denny Johnson. circ. 2,000. (back issues avail.)

333.7 GW ISSN 0303-4283
LEBEN UND UMWELT; unabhaengige Zeitschrift fuer Biologie, Umwelt und Lebensschutz. 1964. q. DM.24. Biologie-Verlag, Schlossallee 10a, 65388 Schlangenbad, Germany. Ed. Herbert Bruns. adv.; bk.rev.; illus.; index. **Indexed:** Biol.Abstr. **Document type:** academic/scholarly publication.
—Linda Hall.
Formerly: Leben (ISSN 0023-9887)

333.7 GW
LEBENSBAUM; literarische Zeitschrift fuer Natur-Bewusstsein. 1987. 2/yr. DM.5. Markgrafenstr. 21, 91438 Bad Windsheim, Germany. TEL 09841-2974. Ed. Erwin Bauereiss; Pub. Erwin Bauereiss. circ. 300. **Document type:** academic/scholarly publication.

LEISURE MANAGER. see *LEISURE AND RECREATION*

333.7 DK ISSN 0108-7991
LEVENDE NATUR; tidsskrift for international naturbevarelse. 1983. q. DKK 175. Verdensnaturfonden - World Wide Fund for Nature, Denmark, Ryesgade 3F, DK-2200 Copenhagen N, Denmark. TEL 45-35-36-36-35. FAX 31-39-20-62. Ed. Nanet Poulsen. adv.; illus. circ. 24,000. **Document type:** consumer publication.
Formerly: Panda-Nyt (ISSN 0105-7936)

CONSERVATION

333.7 NE ISSN 0024-1520
LEVENDE NATUUR; tijdschrift voor natuurbehoud en natuurbeheer. (Text in Dutch; summaries in English) 1896. 6/yr. fl.50 in the Netherlands and Belgium; elsewhere fl.57.50. Vereniging tot Behoud van Natuurmonumenten, Noordereinde 60, 1243 JJ 's-Graveland, Netherlands. TEL 31-58-2673946. FAX 31-58-2666856. Ed. H.L. Schimmel. adv.; bk.rev.; charts; illus. circ. 1,850. **Indexed:** Biol.Abstr.
—BLDSC (5185.500000); SWETS.
Description: Journal of nature conservation and management.

333.7 020 UK ISSN 0265-041X
LIBRARY CONSERVATION NEWS. 1983. q. £20 (foreign £24) (effective 1997). British Library, National Preservation Office, Great Russell St., London WC1B 3DG, England. TEL 44-171-412-7612. FAX 44-171-412-7796. E-mail: npo@bl.uk. (Subscr. to: Turpin Distribution Services Ltd., Blackhorse Rd., Letchworth, Herts. SG6 1HN, England. TEL 44-1462-672555. FAX 44-1462-480947) Ed. Hazel Podmore. R&P contact: Hazel Podmore. bk.rev.; bibl. circ. 1,000. (back issues avail.) **Indexed:** LISA. **Document type:** newsletter.
—BLDSC (5198.550000).
Description: Promotes current preservation awareness among librarians with news, features, abstracts, announcements of forthcoming events, and periodical contents listings.

333.95 UK
LIFEWATCH. 1989. 4/yr. £22. London Zoo, Regent's Park, London NW1 4RY, England. TEL 44-171-586-4443. FAX 44-171-586-6177. Ed. Gina Guarnieri. adv. contact: Gina Guarnieri. circ. 28,000 (paid). (back issues avail.) **Document type:** newsletter.

LIVING WITH THE SHORE. see *ENVIRONMENTAL STUDIES*

639.9 CE ISSN 0024-6514
SK1 CODEN: LRISAU
LORIS; a journal on Ceylon wildlife. (Text in English) 1936. s-a. $10 (annual membership). Wildlife & Nature Protection Society of Sri Lanka, Chaitiya Rd., Fort, Colombo 1, Sri Lanka. TEL 25248. FAX 941-580721. TELEX 22933-METALIX-CE. Ed. Mrs. Sirancee Gunawardena. adv.; bk.rev.; illus. circ. 2,000. **Indexed:** Biol.Abstr., Sport Fish.Abstr., Sri Lanka Sci.Ind., Wild.Rev., Zoo.Rec.
Refereed Serial

333.7 US ISSN 0024-6778
LOUISIANA CONSERVATIONIST. 1923. bi-m. $10. Department of Wildlife and Fisheries, Box 98000, Baton Rouge, LA 70898-9000. TEL 504-765-2918. FAX 504-763-3568. Ed. Bob Dennie. charts; illus.; stat.; circ. 45,000 (paid). **Indexed:** Biol.Dig., Chem.Abstr. **Document type:** government publication.
—Linda Hall; UnCover.
Description: Articles on hunting, fishing, and outdoor recreation in the state. Covers the laws and regulations that govern the management of the state's natural resources.

LOV I RIBOLOV. see *SPORTS AND GAMES* — *Outdoor Life*

LUDWIG BOLTZMANN-INSTITUT FUER UMWELTWISSENSCHAFTEN UND NATURSCHUTZ. MITTEILUNGEN. see *ENVIRONMENTAL STUDIES*

333.7 US ISSN 0744-5288
MACKINAC. 1966. q. $10 to non-members; members $1. Sierra Club, Mackinac Chapter, 300 N. Washington Sq., Ste. 411, Lansing, MI 48933-1223. TEL 517-484-2372. FAX 517-484-3108. E-mail: mackinac.chapter@ sfsierra.sierraclub.org. Ed. Cathy Semer. adv. contact: Gary Semer. bk.rev. circ. 12,000. (tabloid format; back issues avail.) **Indexed:** Mich.Mag.Ind. **Document type:** newsletter.
Description: Covers environmental issues of the chapter's educational and outdoor activities.

MADAGASCAR PRIMATES. see *BIOLOGY* — *Zoology*

570 SX ISSN 1011-5498
 CODEN: MADOAL
MADOQUA; journal of arid zone biology and nature conservation research. (Text in English) 1969. 2/yr. R.25 (effective 1993). Ministry of Environment and Tourism, Directorate of Resource Management and Research, Private Bag 13306, Windhoek, Namibia. TEL 061-63131. FAX 061-63195. TELEX 50-908-3180. Ed. C.J. Brown. bk.rev. circ. 750. (back issues avail.) **Indexed:** Biol.Abstr., Curr.Cont., Curr.Tit.Ocean, Field Crop Abstr., Herb.Abstr., Ind.S.A.Per., Ind.Vet., Key Word Ind.Wildl.Res., Soils & Fert., Sport Fish.Abstr., Vet.Bull., Wild.Rev., Zoo.Rec. **Document type:** academic/scholarly publication.
—BLDSC (5330.969000).
Supersedes: Madoqua. Series 2 (ISSN 1010-2302); (as of vol.9, 1975): Madoqua. Series 1; Namib Desert Research Station. Scientific Papers.
Description: Publishes papers on original and applied research concerning nature conservation in Namibia and adjacent countries, and on arid zone biology with a focus on the Namib desert.

333.7 US ISSN 0898-7742
MAINE ENVIRONMENT; news bulletin of Maine's leading conservation organization. 1960. 6/yr. $28. Natural Resources Council of Maine, 271 State St., Augusta, ME 04330. TEL 207-622-3101. Ed. Leslie Hahn. bk.rev.; bibl.; illus. circ. 8,000. **Document type:** newsletter.

639.9 US ISSN 0360-005X
SH11 CODEN: MFWIDY
MAINE FISH AND WILDLIFE. 1959. q. $9. Department of Inland Fisheries and Wildlife, Station 41, 284 State St., Augusta, ME 04333. TEL 207-289-2871. Ed. V. Paul Reynolds. illus.; index, cum.index. circ. 12,000. **Indexed:** Sport Fish.Abstr., Wild.Rev., Zoo.Rec. **Document type:** government publication.
—UnCover.
Formerly: Maine Fish and Game Magazine (ISSN 0025-0643)
Description: Natural history, research and management programs.

MALAWI. DEPARTMENT OF FORESTRY AND GAME. REPORT. see *FORESTS AND FORESTRY*

581 598 333.7 CN ISSN 0823-2911
MANITOBA NATURALISTS SOCIETY BULLETIN. 1975. m. (11/yr.) Can.$35 membership. Manitoba Naturalists Society, 401 63 Albert St., Winnipeg, MB R3B 1G4, Canada. TEL 204-943-9029. FAX 204-949-9052. Ed. Kevin Hill. adv.: page Can.$200; trim 9 1/2 x 7 1/4; adv. contact: Coleen Pilawski. bk.rev. circ. 1,500. (back issues avail.)
Description: Covers natural history topics, outdoor recreation activities, natural history lectures and workshops and environmental protection issues.

MARIN PABIRION/MARINE PAVILION. see *EARTH SCIENCES* — *Oceanography*

333 639 US
MARINE BULLETIN. 1973. bi-m. membership. National Coalition for Marine Conservation, 3 W. Market St., Leesburg, VA 22075-2901. TEL 703-777-0037. Ed. Ken Hinman. circ. 1,200.
Formerly (until 1985): Right Rigger.

MARINE CONSERVATION. see *BIOLOGY*

333.7 US
MARINE CONSERVATION NEWS; "for all at last returns to the sea - the beginning and the end." Rachel Carson. 1976. 4/yr. membership. Center for Marine Conservation, 1725 DeSales St., N.W., Washington, DC 20036. TEL 202-429-5609. FAX 202-872-0619. Ed. Rose Bierce. circ. 100,000.
Former titles: C E E Report; Whale Report.
Description: News and articles on legislation, policy, and regulations pertaining to the conservation of marine species and their habitats.

MARINE FISHERIES REVIEW. see *FISH AND FISHERIES*

340 639.9 US ISSN 0196-4690
QL713.2
MARINE MAMMAL PROTECTION ACT OF 1972 ANNUAL REPORT. a. U.S. National Marine Fisheries Service, National Oceanic and Atmospheric Administration, Office of Protected Resources, 1335 East-West Hwy., Silver Spring, MD 20910. TEL 301-713-2332. **Document type:** government publication.
Formerly: Administration of the Marine Mammal Protection Act of 1972 (ISSN 0148-186X)

333.9 387.2 UN
MARPOL 73 - 78 AMENDMENTS. (Editions in: Arabic, Chinese, English, French, Russian, Spanish) 1991. irreg. £8 (overseas £10). International Maritime Organization, 4 Albert Embankment, London SE1 7SR, England. illus.
Description: Covers amendments enacted by the I.M.O. Marine Environment Protection Committee.

353.9 US
MARYLAND. DEPARTMENT OF NATURAL RESOURCES. ANNUAL ACTIVITIES REPORT. 1971. a. free. Department of Natural Resources, Tawes State Office Bldg., D-4, 580 Taylor Ave., Annapolis, MD 21401. TEL 301-974-3990. FAX 301-974-5206. Ed. R.L. Gould. illus. circ. 1,500.

333.7 340 US
MARYLAND DEPARTMENT OF NATURAL RESOURCES LAWS. a., latest 1995 ed. $18. Michie, A Division of Reed Elsevier Inc., Box 7587, Charlottesville, VA 22906-7587. TEL 804-977-7566; 800-562-1197. FAX 800-643-1280. E-mail: custserv@michie.com; URL: http://www.michie.com. Ed. George Harley. index.
Description: Contains selected titles from the Natural Resources Articles.

333.78 US
MASSACHUSETTS. DIVISION OF FISHERIES AND WILDLIFE. ANNUAL REPORT. 1866. a. $6. Division of Fisheries and Wildlife, One Rabbit Hill Rd., Westborough, MA 01581. TEL 508-792-7270. FAX 508-792-7275. Ed. Peter G. Mirick. circ. 18,700.
Formerly: Massachusetts. Division of Fisheries and Game. Annual Report (ISSN 0076-4957)

333.7 US ISSN 1071-9229
MASSACHUSETTS SIERRAN. 1970. 10/yr. $10 to non-members. Sierra Club, Boston Chapter, 3 Joy St., Boston, MA 02108. TEL 617-227-5339. adv. **Document type:** newsletter.
Formerly: New England Sierran (ISSN 0164-4491)

799 574.92 US ISSN 0025-4924
SK407
MASSACHUSETTS WILDLIFE. 1949. q. $6 (foreign $50 (effective 1997). Division of Fisheries and Wildlife, Field Headquarters, One Rabbit Hill Rd., Westborough, MA 01581. TEL 508-792-7270. FAX 508-792-7275. E-mail: pmirick@state.ma.us. Ed. Peter G. Mirick. bk.rev.; charts; illus. circ. 20,000. (back issues avail.) **Document type:** government publication.

639.9 700 IT ISSN 1121-2373
MATERIALI E STRUTTURE; problemi di conservazione. 1991. 3/yr. L.100000 (effective 1997). L'Erma di Bretschneider, Via Cassiodoro 19, Rome, Italy. TEL 39-6-6874127. FAX 39-6-6874129. Ed.Bd.

333.7 636.7 AT ISSN 0725-8739
MERIGAL; a voice for the dingo. 1977. q. Aus.$15. Australian Native Dog Conservation Society Ltd., Dingo Sanctuary, 590 Arina Rd., Bargo, N.S.W. 2574, Australia. TEL 046-841156. Ed. David Steward. R&P contact: David Stewart. circ. 300. (back issues avail.) **Document type:** bulletin.
Description: Promotes conservation of the Australian dingo.

639.9 FI ISSN 0047-6986
METSASTAJA. Swedish edition: Jaegaren (ISSN 0355-2683) (Text in Finnish and Swedish) 1951. bi-m. FIM 80 membership (effective 1997). Metsastajain Keskusjarjesto - Jaegarnas Centralorganisation - Hunters' Central Organisation 01100 Oestersundom, Helsinki, Finland. FAX 358-9-877-7617. Eds. Esa Niemela, Klaus Ekman. adv.; bk.rev. circ. 290,000.

333.7   US   ISSN 0275-8180
SK351   CODEN: MGNRB
MICHIGAN NATURAL RESOURCES MAGAZINE. 1931. bi-m. $11.50. (Department of Natural Resources) Kolka & Robb, Inc., 30600 Telegraph Rd., Ste. 1255, Bingham Farms, MI 48025-4531. TEL 810-642-9580. FAX 810-642-5290. Ed. Richard Morscheck; Pub. Vicki Robb. adv. contact: Thomas Strong. bk.rev.; charts; illus.; index every 2 yrs. circ. 90,000. Indexed: Mich.Mag.Ind. **Document type:** consumer publication.
   Former titles (until 1977): Michigan Natural Resources (ISSN 0026-2358); Michigan Conservation.
   Description: Focuses on the natural resources of Michigan and outdoor recreation.

333.7   US   ISSN 0026-2382
MICHIGAN OUT-OF-DOORS. 1947. m. $25 (effective 1997). Michigan United Conservation Clubs Inc, Box 30235, Lansing, MI 48909. TEL 517-371-1041. FAX 517-371-1505. Ed. Dennis C. Knickerbocker. adv. contact: J. William Donahue. bk.rev.; illus. circ. 132,000. (also avail. in microfiche) Indexed: Mich.Mag.Ind., PMR. **Document type:** consumer publication.
   Description: Features, news, and departments on hunting, fishing and conservation activities in the state.

MICROBIAL UTILIZATION OF RENEWABLE RESOURCES. see *BIOLOGY — Biotechnology*

MIDDLE EAST SCIENCE POLICY SERIES. see *PUBLIC ADMINISTRATION*

333.7   NE   ISSN 0165-9545
MILIEUDEFENSIE. 1972. m. fl.56. Vereniging Milieudefensie, Postbus 19199, 1000 GD Amsterdam, Netherlands. TEL 31-20-6221366. FAX 31-20-6275287. E-mail: redactie@foenl.antenna.nl. Ed. Koen Vink. R&P contact: Jelle van der Meer. adv.; bk.rev.; illus. circ. 20,000. (tabloid format) Indexed: Excerp.Med., Key to Econ.Sci. **Document type:** consumer publication.
   —SWETS.

MINING RECORD. see *MINES AND MINING INDUSTRY*

333.7   US
MINNESOTA OUT-OF-DOORS. 1954. bi-m. $20 (effective 1997). Minnesota Conservation Federation, 551 S. Snelling Ave., St. Paul, MN 55116-1887. TEL 612-690-3077. Ed. Dan Hinton. adv. contact: Dan Hinton. circ. 2,500. **Document type:** newsletter.
   Description: Provides the latest information on conservation issues in Minnesota and outdoor recreation opportunities.

333.7   US   ISSN 0196-593X
S916.M6
THE MINNESOTA VOLUNTEER. 1940. 6/yr. free to Minnesota residents; out of state $15. Department of Natural Resources, 500 Lafayette Rd., St. Paul, MN 55155-4046. TEL 612-296-3336. FAX 612-296-0902. Ed. Kathleen Weflen. bk.rev.; illus.; index. circ. 155,000. **Document type:** government publication.
   —Linda Hall; UnCover.
   Formerly: Conservation Volunteer (ISSN 0010-6496)

MISSISSIPPI. DEPARTMENT OF WILDLIFE CONSERVATION. ANNUAL REPORT. see *FISH AND FISHERIES*

MISSISSIPPI NATIVE PLANTS. see *GARDENING AND HORTICULTURE*

639.9   US   ISSN 1041-9306
SH11.M7
MISSISSIPPI OUTDOORS. 1935. bi-m. $6. Department of Wildlife, Fisheries and Parks, Box 451, Jackson, MS 39205. TEL 601-364-2123. Ed. David L. Watts. bk.rev.; charts; illus. circ. 40,000. Indexed: Sport Fish.Abstr., Wild.Rev.
   —Linda Hall; UnCover.
   Former titles (until 1987): MS Outdoors (ISSN 0732-6602); Mississippi Outdoors (ISSN 0199-3240); (until 1981): Mississippi Game and Fish (ISSN 0026-6256)

333.7   US   ISSN 0085-3496
QH76.5.M8
MISSOURI. DEPARTMENT OF CONSERVATION. ANNUAL REPORT. 1937. a. $1. Department of Conservation, Outreach and Education, Box 180, Jefferson City, MO 65102. TEL 573-751-4115. FAX 573-751-2260. Ed. Kathy Love. circ. 800. (processed) Indexed: GeoRef. **Document type:** government publication.
   —Linda Hall.

333.7   US   ISSN 0026-6515
SK351   CODEN: MOCOAC
MISSOURI CONSERVATIONIST. 1938. m. $5 outside Missouri. Department of Conservation, Outreach and Education, Box 180, Jefferson City, MO 65102. TEL 573-751-4115. FAX 573-751-2260. Ed. Kathy Love. charts; illus.; index. circ. 400,000. Indexed: Biol.Abstr., Sport Fish.Abstr., Wild.Rev., Zoo.Rec. **Document type:** government publication.
   —Linda Hall; UnCover.

333.7   US
MISSOURI WILDLIFE. 1939. bi-m. $10. Conservation Federation of Missouri, 728 W. Main, Jefferson City, MO 65101. TEL 573-634-2322. FAX 573-634-8205. Ed. Charles F. Davidson. R&P contact: Charles F. Davidson. adv.; adv. page $475; adv. contact: Irene Schneiders. bk.rev. circ. 40,000. (tabloid format) **Document type:** newspaper.
   Description: Editorials, news commentary, and informational articles on environment and conservation in the state and on the preservation of land for hunting, fishing, and other outdoor recreational activities.

333.7   NE   ISSN 0169-6459
MOLENS. 1954. q. fl.3.50. Vereniging tot Behoud van Molens in Nederland - Association for the Preservation of Windmills in the Netherlands, Sarphatistraat 634, 1018 AV Amsterdam, Netherlands. TEL 31-20-6238703. Ed. L.M. Endedijk. adv.; bk.rev. circ. 13,000.
   Formerly (until 1986): Molennieuws - Windmill News (ISSN 0026-8992)

MONOGRAPHS ON SOIL AND RESOURCES SURVEY. see *AGRICULTURE — Crop Production And Soil*

333.7 639.9   AT   ISSN 0311-032X
MOONBI. 1971. q. Aus.$10. Fraser Island Defender's Organization, Ltd., P.O. Box 301, West End, Qld. 4101, Australia. TEL 7-870-2820. Ed. J. Sinclair. circ. 500.
   Description: Issues concerning the conservation of Fraser Island, Cooloola and the Great Sandy Region.

MOOREANA; journal of the Palmetum. see *BIOLOGY — Botany*

MOTHER EARTH. see *ENVIRONMENTAL STUDIES*

MOUNTAINEER (SEATTLE); to explore, study, preserve and enjoy the natural beauty of the Northwest and beyond. see *SPORTS AND GAMES — Outdoor Life*

333.78 628.168   US
MUSCONETCONG RIVER NEWS. 1992. q. membership. Musconetcong Watershed Association, Box 87, Washington, NJ 07882. TEL 908-689-3260. Ed. Victoria Reiners. charts; illus. **Document type:** newsletter.
   Description: Reports on efforts to preserve the quality of the Musconetcong River, one of the most important waterways in the highlands of northern New Jersey.

333.7 799.2   XR   ISSN 0323-214X
MYSLIVOST. 1953. m. $16.70. Cesky Myslivecky Svaz, Husova 7, 110 00 Prague 1, Czech Republic. TEL 26 59 51. (Subscr. to: Artia, Ve Smeckach 30, 111 27 Prague 1, Czech Republic) Ed. Ladislav Janostik. charts; illus. circ. 100,000.
   Description: Focuses on hunting.

N B I A NEWSLETTER. (New Brunswick Institute of Agrologists) see *AGRICULTURE*

373.78 634.9   US
N F R A NEWSLETTER. 1949. q. membership. National Forest Recreation Association, Box 409, Mammoth Lakes, CA 93546. TEL 619-934-2887. Ed. Robert C. Tanner. circ. 2,000. (looseleaf format; back issues avail.) **Document type:** newsletter.

N J AUDUBON. see *BIOLOGY — Ornithology*

333.7   CN   ISSN 0702-732X
N.S. CONSERVATION. 1977. q. free. Nova Scotia Natural Resources, P.O. Box 68, Truro, NS B2N 5B8, Canada. TEL 902-893-5660. FAX 902-893-6102. bk.rev. circ. 19,000. **Document type:** bulletin.
   Description: Dedicated to the wise use and understanding of Nova Scotia's wildlife and forests.

631.4   US   ISSN 0047-8733
NATIONAL ASSOCIATION OF CONSERVATION DISTRICTS. TUESDAY LETTER. 1952. w. $35. National Association of Conservation Districts, Box 855, League City, TX 77574-0855. TEL 713-332-3402. FAX 713-332-5259. Ed. Laurie Adcox. R&P contact: Laurie Adcox. adv.; bk.rev.; illus. circ. 25,000. **Document type:** newsletter.
   Formerly: National Association of Soil and Water Conservation Districts. Tuesday Letter (ISSN 0027-8661)
   Description: Monitors issues, programs and activities of interest to the nation's 3000 soil and water conservation districts.
   Refereed Serial

333.78   US
NATIONAL ASSOCIATION OF STATE PARK DIRECTORS. ANNUAL INFORMATION EXCHANGE. 1978. a. membership only. National Association of State Park Directors, c/o Ney C. Landrum, Exec. Dir., 126 Mill Branch Rd, Tallahassee, FL 32312. circ. 400 (controlled). Indexed: SRI.
   Description: Provides information on state park systems throughout the United States.

NATIONAL GEOGRAPHIC WORLD. see *GEOGRAPHY*

NATIONAL PARKS. see *LEISURE AND RECREATION*

333.7 796   AT   ISSN 1323-2118
NATIONAL PARKS & WILDLIFE NEWS. Short titles: N P W News. 1994. 2/yr. free. New South Wales National Parks and Wildlife Service, 43 Bridge St., Hurstville, N.S.W. 2220, Australia. TEL 61-2-5856444. FAX 61-2-5856447. Ed. Anita Ray. bk.rev. **Document type:** newspaper.
   Description: Focuses on issues, activities, events in national parks. Provides general information to community.

333.78   AT   ISSN 0047-9012
NATIONAL PARKS JOURNAL. 1959. 6/yr. membership. National Parks Association of N.S.W., P.O. Box A96, Sydney South, N.S.W. 2000, Australia. TEL 61-2-2334660. FAX 61-2-2334880. E-mail: npansw@msn.com. Ed. K. Fook. R&P contact: Kathy Fook. adv.; bk.rev. circ. 7,000. Indexed: C.I.J.E., Curr.Adv.Ecol.Sci., Environ.Per.Bibl. (1982-1995). **Document type:** newsletter.
   —UnCover.
   Description: Dedicated to preserving the natural heritage.

333.7   UK   ISSN 0954-3597
NATIONAL PRESERVATION OFFICE SEMINAR PAPERS. 1987. a. £9.95. British Library, National Preservation Office, Great Russell St., London WC1B 3DG, England. TEL 44-171-412-7612. FAX 44-171-412-7796. E-mail: npo@bl.uk. (Orders to: Turpin Distribution Services Ltd., Blackhorse Rd., Letchworth, Herts. SG6 1HN, England) R&P contact: Geraldine Kenny. **Document type:** proceedings.
   Description: Publishes papers on various topics in conservation presented at annual seminars organized by the National Preservation Office.

NATIONAL RESEARCH INSTITUTE OF FAR SEAS FISHERIES. BULLETIN. see *FISH AND FISHERIES*

NATIONAL RESEARCH INSTITUTE OF FAR SEAS FISHERIES. S SERIES. see *FISH AND FISHERIES*

333.7   US
NATIONAL RIVERS HALL OF FAME NEWSLETTER. 1985. q. $25. National Rivers Hall of Fame, c/o Dubuque County Historical Society, Box 266, Dubuque, IA 52004-0266. TEL 319-583-1241. Ed. Jerome A. Enzler. bk.rev. circ. 900. **Document type:** newsletter.
   Formerly: River Yarns.
   Description: For those interested in the people of the inland waters of America: inventors, artists, conservationists.

NATIONAL SOCIETY FOR THE PRESERVATION OF COVERED BRIDGES NEWSLETTER. see *HISTORY — History Of North And South America*

2238 CONSERVATION

333.7 — UK — ISSN 0266-8068
NATIONAL TRUST. 1968. 3/yr. £7 to non-members (includes National Trust Handbook). National Trust for Places of Historic Interest or National Beauty, 36 Queen Anne's Gate, London SW1H 9AS, England. TEL 44-171-222-9251. FAX 44-171-222-5097. URL: http://www.ukindex.co.uk/nationaltrust. Ed. Gina Guarnieri. adv.; bk.rev. circ. 1,400,000. **Indexed:** Archit.Per.Ind., Avery Ind.Archit.Per. **Document type:** newsletter.
  Formerly (until 1972): National Trust News.
  Description: Promotes the conservation of nature and history, with an emphasis on the countryside (gardens, uplands and country houses).

NATIONAL TRUST NEWS. see HISTORY — History Of Australasia And Other Areas

333.7 — AT — ISSN 1036-9880
NATIONAL TRUST OF AUSTRALIA (NEW SOUTH WALES) NATIONAL TRUST QUARTERLY. no.58, 1973. q. Aus.$41 (effective 1991). National Trust of Australia (New South Wales), G.P.O. Box 518, Sydney, N.S.W. 2001, Australia. FAX 2511110. Ed. Julain Faigan. adv.; bk.rev.; bibl.; illus. circ. 25,000.
  —BLDSC (6033.191000).
  Former titles: National Trust of Australia (New South Wales) National Trust Magazine (ISSN 0811-0964) & National Trust of Australia (New South Wales) National Trust Bulletin (ISSN 0047-9128)

639.9 333.7 — US — ISSN 0028-0402
S964.U6
NATIONAL WILDLIFE; dedicated to the conservation of our nation's natural resources. 1962. bi-mo. $16 (foreign $22). National Wildlife Federation, 8925 Leesburg Pike, Vienna, VA 22184-0111. TEL 703-790-4000; 800-588-1650. FAX 703-790-4075. E-mail: pubs@nwf.org; URL: http://www.nwf.org. Ed. Bob Strohm; Pub. Bob Strohm. R&P contact: Kelly Hartley. TEL 703-790-4510. adv. contact: Thuy Senser. charts; illus.; pat.; tr.mk.; index. circ. 675,000. (also avail. in microfiche from NBI,UMI; reprint service avail. from UMI) **Indexed:** Acad.Ind., Acid Pre.Dig., Acid Rain Abstr., Acid Rain Ind., Biol.Abstr., Biol.Dig., C.I.J.E., Deep Sea Res.& Oceanogr.Abstr., Environ.Abstr., Environ.Ind., Environ.Per.Bibl. (1972-), Gen.Sci.Ind., Ind.Child.Mag., Ind.Sci.Rev., Jun.High.Mag.Abstr., Mag.Ind., Mid.East: Abstr.& Ind., R.G.Abstr., R.G., Soc.Sci.Ind., TOM. **Document type:** consumer publication.
  ●Also available online. Vendor(s): Information Access Co.
  —BLDSC (6033.350000); KR SourceOne; SWETS.

NATUR OG MILJOE. see ENVIRONMENTAL STUDIES

333.7 — GW
NATUR-SPIEGEL. q. DM.8. (Naturschutzbund Deutschland e.V.) Stuenings Verlag GmbH, Luisenstr. 100-104, 47799 Krefeld, Germany. TEL 49-2151-853-0. FAX 49-2151-853103. (Co-sponsor: Bezirksverband Krefeld-Viersen e.V.) **Document type:** newsletter.

333.7 — GW — ISSN 0028-0615
QH77.G3
NATUR UND LANDSCHAFT; Zeitschrift fuer Naturschutz, Landschaftspflege und Umweltschutz. 1925. m. DM.118 (students DM.79) (effective 1997). (Bundesanstalt fuer Naturschutz und Landschaftsoekologie) W. Kohlhammer GmbH, Hessbruehlstr. 69, 70565 Stuttgart, Germany. TEL 49-711-7863-1. FAX 49-711-7863263. Eds. Dr. W. Mrass, Marlies Petzoldt. bk.rev.; charts; index. **Indexed:** Biol.Abstr., Curr.Adv.Ecol.Sci., Dok.Str., Excerp.Med., Forest.Abstr., Geo.Abstr., Key Word Ind.Wildl.Res., Ocean.Abstr., Pollut.Abstr., Rural Recreat.Tour.Abstr., World Agri.Econ.& Rural Sociol.Abstr. **Document type:** bulletin.
  —SWETS. CCC.

NATURAL AREAS JOURNAL. see ENVIRONMENTAL STUDIES

333.7 — ZA
NATURAL HERITAGE. 1993. irreg. latest no.2. $2. National Heritage Conservation Commission, P.O. Box 60124, Livingstone, Zambia. TEL 260-320354. FAX 260-324509. Ed. Lawrence Sumpa. R&P contact: Maxwell Zulu. adv. contact: Maxwell Zulu.

333.7 — CN — ISSN 0701-8002
NATURAL LIFE. 1976. 6/yr. Can.$21 (foreign $21 effective 1997). R.R. 1, St. George, ON NOE 1N0, Canada. TEL 519-448-4001. E-mail: altpress@netroute.net; URL: http://www.netroute.net/natlife. Ed. Wendy Priesnitz; Pub. Wendy Priesnitz. adv.; bk.rev. circ. 25,000. **Indexed:** Can.B.P.I. **Document type:** consumer publication.
  Incorporates (in 1995): Earthkeeper (ISSN 1181-7828)

338 — NE
NATURAL RESOURCE MANAGEMENT AND POLICY. (Text in English) 1993. irreg., vol.4, 1994. price varies. Kluwer Academic Publishers, Postbus 17, 3300 AA Dordrecht, Netherlands. TEL 31-78-6392392. FAX 31-78-6392254. TELEX 29245 KAPG NL. E-mail: services@wkap.nl; URL: http://www.wkap.nl. (Dist. by: Kluwer Academic Publishers Group, P.O. Box 322, 3300 AH Dordrecht, Netherlands. TEL 31-78-6392392. FAX 31-78-6546474; N. America dist. addr.: Box 358, Accord Sta., Hingham, MA 02018-0358. TEL 617-871-6600. FAX 617-871-6528) Eds. Ariel Dinar, David Zilberman. (back issues avail.) **Document type:** monographic series.
  Refereed Serial

340 — US — ISSN 0882-3812
K14
NATURAL RESOURCES & ENVIRONMENT. 1968. q. $30 (foreign $35) (effective 1997). American Bar Association, Natural Resources, Energy, and Environmental Law Section, 750 N. Lake Shore Dr., Chicago, IL 60611. TEL 312-988-5000. URL: http://www.abanet.org. Ed. Lori T. King. R&P contact: Richard Vitterson. circ. 15,500. (also avail. in microfiche from WSH,PMC; microfilm from WSH,PMC; reprint service avail. from WSH) **Indexed:** Acid Rain Abstr., Acid Rain Ind., C.L.I., Curr.Cont., Deep Sea Res.& Oceanogr.Abstr., Energy Info.Abstr., Environ.Abstr., Environ.Ind., GeoRef., L.R.I., Leg.Cont., Leg.Per., Mar.Aff.Bibl., Sel.Water Res.Abstr., Sport Fish.Abstr., SSCI, Wild.Rev. **Document type:** academic/scholarly publication.
  ●Also available online. Vendor(s): West Group.
  —BLDSC (6040.746400); KR SourceOne; SWETS.
  Supersedes (in 1985): Natural Resources Lawyer (ISSN 0028-0747)
  Description: Covers the latest developments in the fields of natural resources, energy, and environmental law.

NATURAL RESOURCES FORUM. see GEOGRAPHY

333.7 — US — ISSN 0028-0739
K14 — CODEN: NRJOAB
THE NATURAL RESOURCES JOURNAL. 1961. q. $32 (foreign $35). University of New Mexico, School of Law, 1117 Stanford N.E., Albuquerque, NM 87131. TEL 505-277-4820. FAX 505-277-0068. Ed. Albert E. Utton. adv. contact: Barbara A. Jacques. bk.rev.; charts; index, cum.index every 10 yrs. circ. 2,000. (also avail. in microfiche from WSH,PMC; microfilm from WSH,PMC; reprint service avail. from WSH) **Indexed:** A.B.C.Pol.Sci., Acid Pre.Dig., AESIS, ASCA, Bk.Rev.Ind. (1965-), C.L.I., Child.Bk.Rev.Ind. (1965-), Cont.Pg.Manage., Curr.Adv.Ecol.Sci., Curr.Cont., Deep Sea Res.& Oceanogr.Abstr., Ecol.Abstr., Econ.Abstr., Energy Info.Abstr., Energy Rev., Environ.Abstr., Environ.Ind., Environ.Per.Bibl. (1989-), Excerp.Med., Geo.Abstr.H.G., Geo.Abstr.P.G., GeoRef., IBR, IDA, J.of Econ.Lit., L.R.I., Leg.Cont., Leg.Per., Mar.Aff.Bibl., P.A.I.S., Petrol.Abstr., Risk Abstr., Sel.Water Res.Abstr., Sport Fish.Abstr., SSCI, W.R.C.Inf., Wild.Rev. **Document type:** academic/scholarly publication.
  —BLDSC (6040.750000); CIS; CISTI; Genuine Article; KR SourceOne; SWETS; UnCover.

340 333 — US — ISSN 0077-6084
NATURAL RESOURCES LAW NEWSLETTER. 1967. 6/yr. membership only. American Bar Association, Natural Resources, Energy, and Environmental Law Section, 750 N. Lake Shore Dr., Chicago, IL 60611. TEL 312-988-5000. circ. 15,500. **Indexed:** Acid Pre.Dig., C.L.I., Deep Sea Res.& Oceanogr.Abstr., L.R.I. **Document type:** newsletter.
  Description: Provides news and a calendar of events for members of the law section.

NATURAL RESOURCES MANAGEMENT AND POLICY. see ENVIRONMENTAL STUDIES

NATURAL RESOURCES RESEARCH. see EARTH SCIENCES

333.78 — UK — ISSN 0261-7358
CODEN: NAWOET
NATURAL WORLD. 1969. 3/yr. £16 membership. R S N C - The Wildlife Trusts Partnership, 20 Upper Ground, London SE1 9PF, England. TEL 44-171-805-5555. FAX 44-171-805-5565. Ed. Linda Bennett. R&P contact: Linda Bennett. adv. contact: Jane Washbourn. bk.rev.; circ. 154,200 (controlled). **Indexed:** Sport Fish.Abstr., Wild.Rev., Zoo.Rec. **Document type:** bulletin.
  Former titles: Royal Society for Nature Conservation. Technical Publications; Society for the Promotion of Nature Conservation. Technical Publications; Society for the Promotion of Nature Reserves. Technical Publications (ISSN 0081-1513)

639.9 — SA — ISSN 1013-6444
CODEN: NTULB4
NATURALIST. (Text in English) 1955. 3/yr. R.15($20) Wildlife Society of Southern Africa, Eastern Province Branch, 2B Lawrence St., Port Elizabeth 6001, South Africa. TEL 27-41-559606. FAX 27-41-5633228. Ed. Irene De Moor. adv.; bk.rev.; charts; illus.; index. circ. 2,000. (back issues avail) **Indexed:** Environ.Per.Bibl (1991-), Ind.S.A.Per., Sport Fish.Abstr., Wild.Rev., Zoo.Rec. **Document type:** academic/scholarly publication.
  —BLDSC (6042.400000); UnCover.
  Formerly (until 1959): Eastern Cape Naturalist (ISSN 0012-8724)

339.49 — EI — ISSN 0252-0575
NATURE AND ENVIRONMENT SERIES. (Editions in English, French) 1967. irreg. price varies. (Council of Europe) Council of Europe Publishing, F-67075 Strasbourg Cedex, France. TEL 33-3-88412263. FAX 33-3-88412780. TELEX 870 943F. (Dist. in U.S. by: Manhattan Publishing Co., 468 Albany Post Rd., Croton-on-Hudson, NY 10520. FAX 914-271-5856) **Indexed:** Key Word Ind.Wildl.Res., Rural Ext.Educ.& Tr.Abstr.
  Formerly: Conservation of Nature and Natural Resources (ISSN 0069-9144)

333.7 — UK — ISSN 0547-9665
CODEN: NAREB5
NATURE AND RESOURCES (ENGLISH EDITION); international news about research on environment, resources, and conservation of nature. 1958. q. £45($78) to individuals; institutions £85($145) (effective 1998). (UNESCO) Parthenon Publishing Group, Casterton Hall, Carnforth, Lancs. LA6 2LA, England. TEL 44-152-427-2084. FAX 44-152-427-1587. URL: http://www.parthpub.com/natres/home.html. (In US: Box 1564, Pearl River, NY 10544. TEL 914-735-9363. FAX 914-735-1385) adv. contact: Margaret Clarke. bk.rev. **Indexed:** Abstr.Rural Dev.Trop, AESIS, Agri.Eng.Abstr., ASCA, Biol.Abstr., Curr.Adv.Ecol.Sci., Environ.Per.Bibl. (1972-), Excerp.Med., Field Crop Abstr., Forest.Abstr., Forest Prod.Abstr., Geo.Abstr.H.G., Geo.Abstr.P.G., Herb.Abstr., IBR, IDA, Int.Abstr.Biol.Sci., Irr.& Drain.Abstr., Per.Islam. (1994-), Plant Breed.Abstr., Rural Recreat.Tour.Abstr., Sel.Water Res.Abstr., So.Pac.Per.Ind., Soils & Fert., Sport Fish.Abstr., SSCI, W.R.C.Inf., Wild.Rev., World Agri.Econ.& Rural Sociol.Abstr., Zoo.Rec. **Document type:** bulletin.
  —BLDSC (6046.095000); CISTI; Genuine Article; SWETS; UnCover.
  Formerly: Nature and Resources and Man and Biosphere Programme. Bulletin (ISSN 0028-0844)

333.7 — CN — ISSN 0374-9894
CODEN: NTCNBM
NATURE CANADA. 1972. 4/yr. Can.$33 (foreign Can.$43) (effective 1997). Canadian Nature Federation, 1 Nicholas St., Ste. 520, Ottawa, ON K1N 7B7, Canada. TEL 613-562-3447. FAX 613-562-3371. E-mail: cnf@web.net; URL: http://www.web.net/~cnf. Ed. Tracy Trottier-Whit. R&P contact: Barbara Stevenson. adv. contact: Christie Chute. bk.rev.; bibl.; charts; illus.; stat.; circ. 18,500 (paid). (also avail. in microform from UMI; reprint service avail. from UMI) **Indexed:** Acid Pre.Dig., Biol.Abstr., Biol.Dig., Can.B.P.I., Can.Per.Ind., CMI, Environ.Per.Bibl. (1972-), Ind.Child.Mag., Key Word Ind.Wildl.Res., Mag.Ind., Ref.Zh. **Document type:** consumer publication.
  —CISTI; Linda Hall; UMI; UnCover.
  Formerly: Canadian Audubon.

CONSERVATION

333.7   US
NATURE CONSERVANCY MAGAZINE. 1951. bi-m. $25 membership (effective 1993). Nature Conservancy, 1815 N. Lynn St., Arlington, VA 22209. TEL 703-841-5300. Ed. Ron Geatz. illus. circ. 800,000. **Indexed:** Biol.Dig., Environ.Abstr., Environ.Per.Bibl. (1988), Gard.Lit. (1992-). **Document type:** consumer publication.
●Also available online.
—UnCover.
Formerly (until 1987): Nature Conservancy News (ISSN 0028-0852)
Description: Membership magazine covering biological diversity and related conservation issues.

333.7 614.7   AT
NATURE CONSERVATION NEWS. 1972. 3/mo. Aus.$15. Nature Conservation Council of New South Wales, 39 George St., Sydney, N.S.W. 2000, Australia. TEL 61-2-92474206. FAX 61-2-92475945. bk.rev. circ. 450.
Former titles: Nature Conservation Council of N.S.W. Newsletter & Nature Conservation Council of N.S.W. Bulletin (ISSN 0311-0745)
Description: Gives an update on environmental and conservation issues in NSW. It also serves as a notice of events, and as an agenda for council activities.

333.7   UN
NATURE ET FAUNE; international journal on nature conservation in Africa. (Text in English, French) 1984. q. free. Food and Agriculture Organization of the United Nations, Regional Office for Africa, P.O. Box 1628, Accra, Ghana. (Co-sponsor: United Nations Environment Programme) Ed. J.D. Keita. circ. 1,500.
Description: Covers wildlife conservation and management in Africa.

639.9   US   ISSN 0890-3735
NATURE SOCIETY NEWS; North America's backyard journal. 1966. m. $12. Nature Society, Griggsville, IL 62340. TEL 217-833-2323. FAX 217-833-2123. Ed. Harry Wright. bk.rev.; illus. (tabloid format) **Document type:** newspaper.
Former titles: Purple Martin News; Purple Martin Capital News.

NATURE STUDY. see ENVIRONMENTAL STUDIES

333.7   US
NATURE'S BEST. q. National Wildlife Federation, 1400 16th St., N.W., Washington, DC 20036. TEL 202-797-6800. URL: http://www.nwf.org/nwf. (Subscr. to: Box 774, Mt. Morris, IL 61054-0774. TEL 800-588-1650; Dist. in Canada by: Canadian Wildlife Federation, 2740 Queensview Dr., Ottawa, ON K2B 1A2, Canada) Ed. Stephen Freleigh. illus. **Document type:** academic/scholarly publication.

NATUREZA; revista dos amantes da natureza. see GARDENING AND HORTICULTURE

NATURFREUNDE. see SPORTS AND GAMES — Outdoor Life

333.7   EI   ISSN 0250-7102
NATUROPA. German edition (ISSN 0250-7099) English edition (ISSN 0250-7072); Italian edition (ISSN 0250-7080); French edition (ISSN 0250-7102) 1968. 3/yr. free. (Council of Europe, Centre Naturopa) Council of Europe Publishing, F-67075 Strasbourg Cedex, France. TEL 33-3-88412263. FAX 33-3-88412780. TELEX 870 943 F. Ed. Jean Pierre Ribaut. illus. circ. 25,000. **Indexed:** Biol.Dig., Curr.Adv.Ecol.Sci., Deep Sea Res.& Oceanogr.Abstr., Environ.Abstr., Environ.Per.Bibl. (1981-), Excerp.Med., Geo.Abstr., Key Word Ind.Wildl.Res., Ocean.Abstr., Pollut.Abstr., Rural Recreat.Tour.Abstr., Sport Fish.Abstr., Wild.Rev., World Agri.Econ.& Rural Sociol.Abstr., Zoo.Rec. (until 19??). **Document type:** monographic series.
Formerly: Nature in Focus (ISSN 0250-7064)

333.7   GW   ISSN 0934-8883
NATURSCHUTZ HEUTE. 1969. q. DM.72 (effective 1996). Naturschutzbund Deutschland e.V., Postfach 301054, 53190 Bonn, Germany. TEL 49-228-9756141. FAX 49-228-9756194. Ed. J. Michael Schroeren. adv. contact: Anne Schoenhofer. bk.rev.; circ. 180,000. **Indexed:** Key Word Ind.Wildl.Res. **Document type:** bulletin.

333.7   SW   ISSN 0347-5301
NATURVAARDSVERKETS FOERFATTNINGSSAMLING. irreg. price varies. Swedish Environmental Protection Agency, Blekholmsterrassen 36, S-106 48 Stockholm, Sweden. FAX 46-8-6981400. Pub. Ingvar Bingman. **Document type:** government publication.

333.7   NE   ISSN 0166-2570
NATUUR EN MILIEU. 1977. 10/yr. fl.50. Stichting Natuur en Milieu - Association for Nature and Environment, Donkerstraat 17, 3511 KB Utrecht, Netherlands. TEL 31-30-2331328. FAX 31-30-2331311. E-mail: snm@gn.apc.org. Ed. M. Jehae. adv. contact: Buro Case Hoorn. bk.rev.; charts; illus.; index. circ. 10,500. **Indexed:** Biol.Abstr., Excerp.Med., Key to Econ.Sci.
—SWETS.
Formed by the merger of: Natuur en Landschap (ISSN 0028-1077); Natuur en Milieuzorg (ISSN 0304-4890)

333.7   US   ISSN 0047-9217
NEBRASKA RESOURCES. q. Natural Resources Commission, 301 Centennial Mall South, Box 94876, Lincoln, NE 68509. TEL 402-471-2081. illus. **Document type:** government publication.

799   US   ISSN 0028-1964
NEBRASKALAND. 1926. 10/yr. $14. Game and Parks Commission, Box 30370, Lincoln, NE 68503. TEL 402-471-0641. FAX 402-471-5528. Ed. Donald Cunningham. adv.; bk.rev.; charts; illus.; tr.lit. circ. 51,000. **Document type:** consumer publication, government publication.
Formerly: Outdoor Nebraskaland.
Description: Covers outdoor recreation in the state. Includes history, wildlife and conservation.

DE NEDERLANDSE JAGER; tijdschrift over natuur, wildbeheer en jachthonden. see SPORTS AND GAMES — Outdoor Life

NEOTROPICAL PRIMATES. see BIOLOGY — Zoology

NEW CITY MAGAZINE. see HOUSING AND URBAN PLANNING

333.7   US   ISSN 1078-4616
NEW ENGLAND ENVIRONMENTAL DIRECTORY. 1995. biennial. $18.50. Harbinger Communications, Box 8175, Missoula, MT 59807. TEL 406-721-0440. FAX 406-721-0440. E-mail: ned@ism.net. index. (also avail. in diskette format) **Document type:** directory.
●Also available online.
Description: Annotated listings of citizen groups, government agencies in Connecticut, Massachusetts, Maine, Rhode Island, New Hampshire and Vermont.

333.7   US   ISSN 0077-8362
NEW HAMPSHIRE. FISH AND GAME DEPARTMENT. BIENNIAL REPORT. 1865. biennial. Fish and Game Department, 2 Hazen Dr., Concord, NH 03301. TEL 603-271-3211; 800-735-2964. FAX 603-271-1438. E-mail: info@wildlife.state.nh.us; URL: http://www.wildlife.state.n.h.us. Dir. Wayne R. Vetter. R&P contact: Judy Stokes. circ. 4,000.

639.9 598.2   US   ISSN 0162-5284
NEW HAMPSHIRE AUDUBON. 1966. bi-m. $30 to individuals; families $45. Audubon Society of New Hampshire, 3 Silk Farm Rd., Concord, NH 03301-8200. TEL 603-224-9909. FAX 603-226-0902. E-mail: nhaudubon@igc.apc.org. Ed. Miranda Levin. bk.rev.; charts; illus. circ. 7,000. **Indexed:** Sport Fish.Abstr., Wild.Rev. **Document type:** newsletter.
Formerly: New Hampshire Audubon News (ISSN 0028-520X)

333.7   US
NEW JERSEY CONSERVATION FOUNDATION (YEAR) ANNUAL REPORT. a. New Jersey Conservation Foundation, 170 Longview Rd., Far Hills, NJ 07931. E-mail: njcf@aol.com. Ed. Patricia J. Baxter. **Document type:** corporate report.

333.7   US
NEW JERSEY LAND FORUM; focusing on protection of agriculture and natural lands. 1984. q. free. New Jersey Conservation Foundation, 170 Longview Rd., Far Hills, NJ 07931. E-mail: njcf@aol.com. Ed. Patricia J. Baxter. charts; stat. circ. 2,000. **Document type:** newsletter.
Former titles: Land Forum & Farmland Forum.
Description: Addresses issues facing the conservation of farms and tracts of natural lands.

639.9   US   ISSN 0028-6338
SK427   CODEN: NMWIAN
NEW MEXICO WILDLIFE. 1961. bi-m. $10. Department of Game and Fish, Box 25112, Sante Fe, NM 87504. TEL 505-827-7911. FAX 505-827-7915. bk.rev.; charts; illus.; index. circ. 10,000. (also avail. in microform from UMI; reprint service avail. from UMI) **Indexed:** Biol.Abstr., Sport Fish.Abstr., Wild.Rev., Zoo.Rec. **Document type:** government publication.
—Linda Hall; UMI; UnCover.

333.7 628   AT   ISSN 0158-0965
NEW SOUTH WALES NATIONAL PARKS AND WILDLIFE SERVICE. ANNUAL REPORT. 1967. a. Aus.$15 (effective Dec. 1995). New South Wales National Parks and Wildlife Service, 43 Bridge St., Hurstville, N.S.W. 2220, Australia. TEL 61-2-5856444. FAX 61-2-5856447. Ed. Anita Ray. circ. 1,000. **Document type:** corporate report, government publication.
Description: Reports on achievements, projects and financial situation.

NEW YORK ENVIRONMENTAL CONSERVATION LAW. see LAW

333.7   US
QH76.5.N7
NEW YORK STATE CONSERVATIONIST. 1946. bi-m. $10 (effective 1997 & 1998). Department of Environmental Conservation, 50 Wolf Rd., Albany, NY 12233. TEL 518-457-5547. FAX 518-457-0858. (Subscr. to: Box 1500, Latham, NY 12110. TEL 800-678-6399) Ed. R.W. Groneman. R&P contact: Maria Lamb. bk.rev.; charts; illus. circ. 140,000. (also avail. in microform from UMI) **Indexed:** Acid Pre.Dig., Biol.Abstr., Biol.Dig., C.I.J.E., Curr.Adv.Ecol.Sci., Energy Rev., Environ.Abstr., Environ.Per.Bibl. (1973-1995), Gen.Sci.Ind., GeoRef., Ind.Sci.Rev., Mag.Ind., PMR, R.G., R.G.Abstr., Sport Fish.Abstr., Wild.Rev., Zoo.Rec. **Document type:** government publication, consumer publication.
●Also available online. Vendor(s): UMI.
—KR SourceOne; Linda Hall; UMI; UnCover.
Formerly (until vol.50, no.1, 1995): Conservationist (ISSN 0010-650X)
Refereed Serial

639.9   US
NEWS TO USE; a newsletter for members of the International Erosions Control Association. q. International Erosion Control Association, Box 4904, Steamboat Springs, CO 80477-4904. TEL 970-879-3010; 800-455-4322. FAX 970-879-8563. E-mail: ecinfo@ieca.org; URL: http://www.ieca.org.

712.5   CN   ISSN 0078-0502
NIAGARA PARKS COMMISSION. ANNUAL REPORT. 1886. a. free. Niagara Parks Commission, P.O. Box 150, Niagara Falls, Ont. L2E 6T2, Canada. TEL 416-356-2241. FAX 416-354-6041. Ed. George Bailey. circ. 500.

NIHON SEITAI GAKKAI KANTO CHIKUKAI KAIHO/ECOLOGICAL SOCIETY OF JAPAN. KANTO BRANCH. NEWS. see BIOLOGY

NIHON SEITAI GAKKAI KYUSHU CHIKUKAI KAIHO/ECOLOGICAL SOCIETY OF JAPAN. KYUSHU BRANCH. BULLETIN. see BIOLOGY

NIHON SEITAI GAKKAI TOHOKU CHIKUKAI KAIHO/ECOLOGICAL SOCIETY OF JAPAN. TOHOKU BRANCH. NEWS. see BIOLOGY

333.7   UK
NORFOLK WILDLIFE TRUST. ANNUAL REVIEW. a. £16 membership. Norfolk Naturalists Trust, 72 Cathedral Close, Norwich NR1 4DF, England. TEL 441603-625540. FAX 441603-614430. Ed. Anne Bloomfield. adv. circ. 10,000. **Document type:** corporate report.
Formerly: Norfolk Naturalists Trust. Annual Review.

CONSERVATION

NORTH AMERICAN SWANS. see *BIOLOGY — Ornithology*

333.7 US ISSN 0078-1355
SK351 CODEN: NAWTA6
NORTH AMERICAN WILDLIFE AND NATURAL RESOURCES CONFERENCE. TRANSACTIONS. 1915. a. $35. Wildlife Management Institute, 1101 14 St., N.W., Ste. 801, Washington, DC 20005. TEL 202-371-1808. FAX 202-408-5059. Ed. Kelly G. Wadsworth. cum.index. circ. 1,000. (reprint service avail. from ISI) **Indexed:** Biol.Abstr., Curr.Adv.Ecol.Sci., Forest.Abstr., Forest Prod.Abstr., Protozool.Abstr., Sel.Water Res.Abstr., Sport Fish.Abstr., Wild.Rev., Wildlife & Conserv.Biol.Abstr. (1936-), Zoo.Rec. **Document type:** proceedings.
—BLDSC (9020.551000); Linda Hall; UnCover.
Former titles (until 1936): Transactions of the American Game Conference; North American Wildlife Conference. Transactions (ISSN 0097-6830); North American Wildlife Conference. Proceedings.

333.7 US
NORTH CAL-NEVA RESOURCE CONSERVATION AND DEVELOPMENT AREA. ANNUAL WORK PLAN. Variant titles--Plan of Action; Program of Action. 1968. a. free. North Cal-Neva Resource Conservation and Development Area, 1030 N. Main, Ste. 101, Alturas, CA 96101. FAX 916-233-2709. Ed. Jan Dybdahl. illus. circ. 500.
Formerly: North Cal-Neva Resource Conservation and Development Project. Annual Work Plan (ISSN 0097-7268)

333.7 US ISSN 0029-2761
SK351 CODEN: NDODA7
NORTH DAKOTA OUTDOORS. 1933. 10/yr. $7. Game and Fish Department, 100 N. Bismarck Expressway, Bismarck, ND 58501. TEL 701-328-6300. FAX 701-328-6352. Ed. Harold Umber. bk.rev.; charts; illus.; index. circ. 19,000. **Indexed:** Sport Fish.Abstr., Wild.Rev., Zoo.Rec.
—BLDSC (6149.393000); Linda Hall; UnCover.

333.7 639.9 US ISSN 0029-2958
NORTH WOODS CALL. 1953. fortn. $25. North Woods Call, Inc., Rt. 1, 00509 Turkey Run, Charlevoix, MI 49720. TEL 616-547-9797. FAX 616-547-0367. Ed. Glen Sheppard. adv.; bk.rev.; circ. 10,000 (paid). (tabloid format) **Indexed:** Mich.Mag.Ind. **Document type:** newspaper.
Description: Advocates an environmentally sensitive response to all issues involving natural resources.

NORTHEAST MEMO. see *SPORTS AND GAMES — Outdoor Life*

639.9 AT
NORTHERN TERRITORY. PARKS AND WILDLIFE COMMISSION. ANNUAL REPORT. 1978. a. free. Parks and Wildlife Commission, P.O. Box 496, Palmerston, N.T. 0830, Australia. TEL 61-08-89994508. FAX 61-08-89994510. E-mail: krisainne.abbott@nt.gov.au; URL: http://www.nt.gov.au/paw/. Ed. Kathy Williams. circ. 575. **Document type:** government publication.
Former titles: Northern Territory. Conservation Commission. Annual Report (ISSN 0159-8821); Northern Territory. Territory Parks and Wildlife Commission. Annual Report.

NOTICIAS DE GALAPAGOS. see *SCIENCES: COMPREHENSIVE WORKS*

NOVA SCOTIA TRAPPERS NEWSLETTER. see *LEATHER AND FUR INDUSTRIES*

NOW AND THEN. see *LITERATURE*

639.9 MW ISSN 0251-1924
QH195.M47 CODEN: NYALEA
NYALA. (Text in English) 1975. s-a. K.30($12) Wildlife Society of Malawi, c/o Museums of Malawi, P.O. Box 30360, Blantyre 3, Malawi. Ed. Cornell Dudley. adv.; bk.rev. circ. 625. **Indexed:** Sport Fish.Abstr., Wild.Rev., Zoo.Rec. **Document type:** academic/scholarly publication.

O D I NATURAL RESOURCE PERSPECTIVES. (Overseas Development Institute) see *BUSINESS AND ECONOMICS — International Development And Assistance*

333.7 US
O F W I M NEWSLETTER. irreg. $25 individual membership. Organization of Fish and Wildlife Information Managers, 26 Snow St., Penacook, NH 03303. E-mail: jeffs@gis.dep.state.nj.us. Ed. Jeff Smith. **Document type:** newsletter.
Description: Promotes the management and conservation of natural resources by facilitating technology and information exchange among managers of fish and wildlife information.

578.0913 US
O T S LIANA. 1967. 3/yr. $30. Organization for Tropical Studies, Box 90632, Durham, NC 27708-0632. TEL 919-684-5774. FAX 919-684-5661. Eds. Jonathan Giles, Carol Mozell. bk.rev. circ. 3,500. (back issues avail.) **Document type:** newsletter.

333 614.7 770 IT
OASIS; mensile di natura, ecologia, fotografia e viaggi. 1985. m. (10/yr.). L.59000 (foreign L.100000). Industrie Grafiche Editoriali Musumeci S.p.A., Loc. Amerique 99, 11020 Quart (AO), Italy. TEL 0165-765-853. FAX 0165-765-106. Dir. Pietro Giglio. adv.: color page L.15700000. circ. 65,000.

OCEAN AND COASTAL LAW MEMO. see *LAW — Maritime Law*

333.91 US ISSN 0738-9833
OCEAN REALM; international magazine of the sea. q. $39.95 (foreign $49.95) (effective 1997); newsstand price: $7. Friends of the Sea, Inc., 4067 Broadway, San Antonio, TX 78209. TEL 210-824-8099; 800-680-3522. FAX 210-820-3522. E-mail: oceanica@eden.com. (Subscr. to: Box 99275 Collingswood, NJ 08108-9803. TEL 800-681-7727. FAX 609-488-6188) Eds. Charlene deJori, Cheryl Schorp. adv.: color page $2875 trim 8 7/8 X 10 7/8; adv. contact: Cheryl Schorp. illus.; circ. 30,000. circ. 27,457 (paid); 2,543 (controlled). (back issues avail.) **Document type:** consumer publication.
—UnCover.
Description: Focuses on conservation and the protection of marine ecosystems by increasing awareness on issues of concern in the marine environment.

339.49 PL ISSN 0078-3250
CODEN: OCPZAE
OCHRONA PRZYRODY. (Text in English or Polish; summaries in English) 1920. a. $15. Polska Akademia Nauk, Instytut Ochrony Przyrody, Ul. Lubicz 46, 31-512 Krakow, Poland. TEL 48-12-210348. FAX 48-12-210348. TELEX 322630 PANZO. Ed. Z. Alexandrowicz. R&P contact: Elzbieta Skorek. bibl.; charts; illus. **Indexed:** AgroLibrex, Biol.Abstr., Sport Fish.Abstr., Wild.Rev., Zoo.Rec. **Document type:** academic/scholarly publication.
—BLDSC (6235.110000).

333.7 322.4 GW
OEKOLOGIEPOLITIK. 1984. bi-m. DM.20 (effective 1996). Oekologisch - Demokratische Partei, Bundesgeschaeftsstelle, Marienstr. 41, 40210 Duesseldorf, Germany. TEL 49-211-134375. FAX 49-211-134376. Ed. Peter Amsler. bk.rev. circ. 7,500. **Document type:** newsletter.
Formerly: Oekologie und Politik.
Description: Political ecology and party-related information for party members and others interested in environmental politics.
Refereed Serial

333.7 GW ISSN 0935-7602
OEKOWERKMAGAZIN;* Naturschutz in Berlin und Brandenburg. 1987. m. DM.36. Natur und Text Verlags GmbH, Im Dol 50, 14195 Berlin, Germany. adv.; bk.rev. circ. 10,000. (back issues avail.)

639 AU
OESTERREICHISCHE TIERSCHUTZZEITUNG; vereinsunabhaengige illustrierte Monatsschrift fuer den Tierfreund. m. S.92. Franz Abele, Ed. & Pub., Neuer Markt 9, A-1010 Vienna, Austria.

OF THE WORLD SERIES. see *BIOLOGY — Zoology*

OHIO ENVIRONMENTAL REPORT. see *ENVIRONMENTAL STUDIES*

333.7 591 US ISSN 0085-4468
CODEN: OFWRBD
OHIO FISH AND WILDLIFE REPORT. 1971. irreg., no.12, 1995. free. Department of Natural Resources, Division of Wildlife, 1840 Belcher Dr., Columbus, OH 43224-1329. TEL 614-265-6300. circ. 1,000. **Indexed:** Biol.Abstr., Sport Fish.Abstr., Wild Life Rev., Wild.Rev., Zoo.Rec. **Document type:** monographic series, government publication.
—BLDSC (6246.320000).
Formed by the merger of: Ohio Fish Monographs (ISSN 0078-4028); Ohio Game Monographs (ISSN 0078-4036); **Supersedes:** Game Research in Ohio (ISSN 0473-9442)

363.7 333.95 US
OHIO NATURALIST. 1994. bi-m. $15. Box 429142, Cincinnati, OH 45242. Ed. Jane Van Coney; Pub. Jane Van Coney. circ. 150. **Document type:** newsletter.

333.7 JA ISSN 0912-4071
OKAYAMA NO SHIZEN/NATURE IN OKAYAMA. (Text in Japanese) bi-m. 300 Yen. Okayama no Shizen o Mamoru Kai - Study Group of Nature Protection in Okayama, 1-21 Tsushima Minami 1-chome, Okayama-shi, Okayama-ken 700, Japan.

333.9 US ISSN 0095-442X
S916.05
OKLAHOMA. CONSERVATION COMMISSION. BIENNIAL REPORT. 1941. biennial. free. Conservation Commission, 2800 Lincoln, Ste. 160, Oklahoma City, OK 73105. TEL 405-521-2384. Ed. Mason Mungle. stat.; circ. 175 (controlled). **Document type:** government publication.

333.7 US
ON THE EDGE (PHILADELPHIA). 1976. 3/yr. $25 membership (effective 1997). Wildlife Preservation Trust International, 3400 W. Girard Ave., Philadelphia, PA 19104. TEL 215-222-3636; 800-978-4275. FAX 215-222-2191. E-mail: WPTI@aol.com; URL: http://www.columbia.edu/cu/cerc/wpti.html. Ed. Mary C. Pearl. circ. 3,000. **Document type:** newsletter.

ON THE WILD SIDE. see *ENVIRONMENTAL STUDIES*

333.7 CN ISSN 0383-6479
ONTARIO CONSERVATION NEWS. 1975. 6/yr. Can.$25 to individuals; institutions Can.$100. Conservation Council of Ontario, 489 College St., Ste. 506, Toronto, Ont. M6G 1A5, Canada. TEL 416-969-9637. FAX 416-960-8053. Ed. Chris Winter. bk.rev.; illus. circ. 1,000.
Formerly: Conservation News (ISSN 0317-5839)

333.7 CN
ONTARIO OUT OF DOORS HOTLINE. 1989. m. free to members. Ontario Federation of Anglers and Hunters, P.O. Box 2800, Station Main, Peterborough, ON K9J 8L5, Canada. TEL 705-748-6324. FAX 705-748-9577. E-mail: ofah@oncomdis.on.ca. Ed. Mark Holmes. R&P contact: Mark Holmes. circ. 74,000 (paid). (back issues avail.) **Document type:** newsletter.

333.78 UK ISSN 0265-8445
OPEN SPACE. 1927. 3/yr. £7.50 in UK; rest of Europe £10; elsewhere £15 (effective 1997). Open Spaces Society, 25A Bell St., Henley-on-Thames, Oxon. RG9 2BA, England. TEL 44-1491-573535. Ed. Kate Ashbrook. adv. contact: Karen Baum. bk.rev. circ. 3,000. **Indexed:** Rural Recreat.Tour.Abstr., World Agri.Econ.& Rural Sociol.Abstr. **Document type:** corporate report.
—UMI.
Formerly (until 1982): Commons, Open Spaces and Footpaths Preservation Society. Journal (ISSN 0010-3322); **Incorporates:** Commons, Open Spaces and Footpaths Preservation Society. Annual Report.
Description: Journal of general interest to environmentalists concerned with land and public recreational access, especially commons, village greens and rights of way.

ORION (GREAT BARRINGTON); people and nature. see *ENVIRONMENTAL STUDIES*

333.7 US
▼**ORION SOCIETY NOTEBOOK.** 1995. s-a. Orion Society, 195 Main St., Great Barrington, MA 01230. TEL 413-528-4422. FAX 413-528-0676. E-mail: orion@bcn.net. Ed. Jennifer Sahn. R&P contact: Jennifer Sahn. **Document type:** newsletter.

ORNITHOLOGISCHER VEREIN ZU HILDESHEIM. MITTEILUNGEN. see *BIOLOGY — Ornithology*

639.9 UK ISSN 0030-6053
QL81.5 CODEN: ORYXAM
ORYX. 1903-1913; N.S. 1921; N.S. 1950. q. £110($201) (foreign £121) (effective 1998). (Flora and Fauna International) Blackwell Science Ltd., Osney Mead, Oxford OX2 0EL, England. TEL 44-1865-206206. FAX 44-1865-721205. E-mail: journals.cs@blacksci.co.uk; URL: http://www.black.co.uk. Ed. J. Morris; Pub. Allen Stevens. R&P contact: Sarah Pollard. adv. contact: Martine Cariou-Keen. bk.rev.; bibl.; charts; illus.; index. circ. 2,920. **Indexed:** Anim.Breed.Abstr., Biol.Abstr., Biol.Dig., Curr.Adv.Ecol.Sci., Ecol.Abstr., Environ.Abstr., Environ.Per.Bibl. (1972-), Forest.Abstr., Forest Prod.Abstr., Geo.Abstr.H.G., Geo.Abstr.P.G., IDA, Ind.Vet., Key Word Ind.Wildl.Res., Sport Fish.Abstr., Vet.Bull., Wild.Rev., Zoo.Rec. **Document type:** academic/scholarly publication.
—BLDSC (6296.700000); CIS; EMDOCS; Genuine Article; Linda Hall; UMI; UnCover. **CCC.**
Formerly (until 1950): Society for the Restoration of the Fauna of the Empire. Journal.
Refereed Serial

333.95 179 US
OTTER RAFT. 1969. s-a. $15 to members. Friends of the Sea Otter, 2150 Garden Rd., B-4, Monterey, CA 93940. TEL 408-373-2747. FAX 408-373-2749. E-mail: fndseaottr@aol.com. Ed. Susan Brown. bk.rev.; charts; illus.; circ. 4,500 (paid). **Document type:** newsletter.
Description: Presents science and educational material on the sea otter and marine habitats. Focuses on protecting the species.

OUR PLANET. see *ENVIRONMENTAL STUDIES*

333.7 US ISSN 0002-4171
SH11.A6 CODEN: ALCNAQ
OUTDOOR ALABAMA. 1929. q. $8. Conservation Department, 64 N. Union St., Montgomery, AL 36130. TEL 334-242-3151; 800-262-3151. FAX 334-242-0999. (Subscr. to: 64 N. Union St., Montgomery, AL 36130) Ed. Cindy Thompson. charts; illus.; index, cum.index. circ. 11,000. **Indexed:** Biol.Abstr., Sport Fish.Abstr., Wild.Rev. **Document type:** consumer publication.
—UnCover.
Formerly: Alabama Conservation.

333.7 639.9 US ISSN 0021-3314
SK1
OUTDOOR AMERICA. 1922. q. $25. Izaak Walton League of America, 707 Conservation Ln., Gaithersburg, MD 20878-2983. TEL 301-548-0150. FAX 301-548-0146. Ed. Paul Hansen. adv. contact: Denny Johnson. illus. circ. 58,000. **Indexed:** Acid Pre.Dig., Acid Rain Abstr., Acid Rain Ind., Environ.Abstr., Sportsearch.
—BLDSC (6314.410000); UnCover.
Formerly: Izaak Walton Magazine.
Description: Devoted to national environmental issues, recreation and conservation; covers current issues and membership news.

333.95 US ISSN 0030-7025
SH11
OUTDOOR CALIFORNIA. 1953. bi-m. $12. Department of Fish and Game, 1416 Ninth St., Sacramento, CA 95814. TEL 916-653-6420. (Subscr. to: Box 944209, Sacramento, CA 94244-2090) Ed. Alexia E. Retallack. R&P contact: Alexia E. Retallack. illus.; index. circ. 28,000. **Indexed:** Cal.Per.Ind. (1978-), Sport Fish.Abstr., Wild.Rev.
—Linda Hall; UnCover.

OUTDOOR CANADA. see *SPORTS AND GAMES — Outdoor Life*

333.7 US ISSN 1068-3240
OUTDOOR DELAWARE. 1956. q. $6. Department of Natural Resources and Environmental Control, 89 Kings Hwy., Box 1401, Dover, DE 19903. TEL 302-739-4506. FAX 302-739-6242. Ed. Kathleen M. Jamison. R&P contact: Kathleen M. Jamison. circ. 6,000 (paid). (tabloid format) **Indexed:** Environ.Abstr., Sport Fish.Abstr., Wild.Rev. **Document type:** consumer publication.
—UnCover.
Formerly (until 1991): Delaware Conservationist (ISSN 0045-9852)

333.7 639.9 US ISSN 1072-7175
OUTDOOR ILLINOIS. 1972. m. $10 (effective Jan. 1994). Department of Natural Resources, 524 S. Second St., Rm. 510, Springfield, IL 62701-1787. TEL 217-782-7454. FAX 217-785-9236. (Subscr. to: Illinois Department of Natural Resources, Box 19225, Dept. NL, Springfield, IL 62794-9225) Ed. Gary Thomas. bk.rev. circ. 35,000. **Document type:** government publication.
Formerly (until vol.21, no.9, 1993): Illinois. Department of Conservation. Outdoor Highlights (ISSN 0279-8700)
Description: Provides information on hunting, fishing, camping, birding, hiking and other outdoor activities in Illinois. Includes profiles on conservation personalities, permit applications, and editorials.

333.7 US ISSN 0030-7068
HC107.I6
OUTDOOR INDIANA. 1934. 6/yr. $10 (foreign $18) (effective 1996-1997). Department of Natural Resources, 402 W. Washington St., W 255B, Indianapolis, IN 46204-2748. TEL 317-232-4004. FAX 317-232-8036. Ed. Steve Sellers. bk.rev.; charts; illus.; cum.index: 1966-1981. circ. 29,000. **Document type:** government publication.
Description: Covers the natural resources and cultural history of the state. Reviews an Indiana trail each month.

333.7 796 US ISSN 0279-9065
OUTDOOR NEWS. 1951. m. $25. Oklahoma Wildlife Federation, 3900 N. Santa Fe, Oklahoma City, OK 73118. TEL 405-524-7009. FAX 405-521-9270. Ed. Margaret Ruff. R&P contact: Margaet Ruff. adv.; bk.rev.; circ. 10,000 (paid). (tabloid format) **Document type:** newspaper.
Description: Provides timely information on national, state and local conservation and environmental issues.

333.7 796 US ISSN 0030-7092
OUTDOOR NEWS BULLETIN. 1947. m. free to members and qualified media representatives. Wildlife Management Institute, 1101 14 St., N.W., Ste. 801, Washington, DC 20005. TEL 202-371-1808. FAX 202-408-5059. Ed. Lonnie L. Williamson. bk.rev. circ. 4,000. (processed; reprint service avail. from ISI) **Document type:** bulletin.

333.7 US ISSN 0030-7106
OUTDOOR OKLAHOMA. 1945. bi-m. $8 (foreign $12). Department of Wildlife Conservation, 1801 N. Lincoln, Oklahoma City, OK 73105. TEL 405-521-3855. FAX 405-521-6535. (Co-sponsor: Oklahoma Wildlife Conservation Commission) Ed. Steve Wagner. bk.rev.; illus.; circ. 21,500 (controlled). (also avail. in microform from UMI; reprint service avail. from UMI) **Indexed:** Biol.Abstr., Environ.Abstr., Sport Fish.Abstr., Wild.Rev. **Document type:** government publication.
—UMI; UnCover.
Formerly: Oklahoma Wildlife.
Description: Covers hunting, fishing, the environment, and conservation.

OUTDOOR REPORT. see *LEISURE AND RECREATION*

333.7 US ISSN 0030-7181
OUTDOORS UNLIMITED. 1940. m. membership. Outdoor Writers Association of America, Inc., 2017 Cato Ave., Ste. 101, State College, PA 16801. TEL 814-234-1011. Ed. Carol J. Kersavage. bk.rev.; film rev.; bibl.; illus. circ. 2,600. (back issues avail.) **Indexed:** Acid Rain Abstr., Acid Rain Ind., Sportsearch. **Document type:** newsletter.

333.7 US
OUTDOORS WEST. 1977. s-a. $10. Federation of Western Outdoor Clubs, 512 Boylston E., No. 106, Seattle, WA 98102. TEL 206-332-3041. Ed. Hazel A. Wolf. bk.rev. circ. 800. (tabloid format) **Document type:** newsletter.

P I N. see *SPORTS AND GAMES*

591 179.3 SZ ISSN 1026-2881
PACHYDERM. (Text in English) 2/yr. International Union for Conservation of Nature and Natural Resources, Species Survival Commission - African Elephant and Rhino Specialist Group, Rue Mauverney 28, CH-1196 Gland, Switzerland. TEL 41-22-9990001. FAX 41-22-9990002. TELEX 419624-IUCN-CH. (Subscr. to: WWF Regional Office, Box 62440, Nairobi, Kenya) **Indexed:** P.L.E.S.A. (1989-). **Document type:** newsletter.
—BLDSC (6328.292000).

333.95 AT ISSN 1038-2097
QH77.P3 CODEN: PCOBEK
PACIFIC CONSERVATION BIOLOGY. 1993. q. Aus.$175 (foreign $218). Surrey Beatty & Sons, 43 Rickard Rd., Chipping Norton, N.S.W. 2170, Australia. TEL 61-2-96023888. FAX 61-2-982112553. Ed. Craig Moritz; Pub. Ivor Beatty. R&P contact: Ivor Beatty. adv.: page Aus.$250; trim 897 x 210; adv. contact: Ivor Beatty. bibl.; charts; illus.; index. circ. 500. (back issues avail.) **Indexed:** Zoo.Rec. **Document type:** academic/scholarly publication.
—BLDSC (6329.075000).
Description: Publishes news and views, forum essays, research papers on conservation and land management in the Pacific region.
Refereed Serial

333.7 US ISSN 1091-0301
PACIFIC NORTHWEST ENVIRONMENTAL DIRECTORY. 1996. biennial. $18.50. Harbinger Communications, Box 8175, Missoula, MT 59807. TEL 406-721-0440. FAX 406-721-0440. E-mail: ned@ism.net. index. (also avail. in diskette format) **Document type:** directory.
●Also available online.
Description: Annotated listings of citizen groups, government agencies in Oregon, Washington and British Columbia

333.7 EI
PAN-EUROPEAN BIOLOGICAL AND DIVERSITY STRATEGY BULLETIN. (Editions in English, French, Italian, German and Russian) 1997. 6/yr. free. (Council of Europe, Centre Naturopa) Council of Europe Publishing, F-67075 Strasbourg Cedex, France. TEL 33-3-88412000. FAX 33-3-88412715. TELEX 870 943 F. Ed. Jean-Pierre Ribaut. circ. 20,000. **Document type:** newsletter.

333.7 IT
PANDA. 1966. bi-m. L.40000. Fondo Mondiale per la Natura - World Wildlife Fund, Via Salaria 290, 00199 Rome, Italy. TEL 06-852492. Ed. Fulco Pratesi. adv.: B&W page L.9000000, color page L.11000000.

333.7 IT
PANDA JUNIOR. 1966. bi-m. L.30000. Fondo Mondiale per la Natura - World Wildlife Fund, Via Salaria 290, 00199 Rome, Italy. TEL 39-6-852492. Ed. Fulco Pratesi. adv.: B&W page L.9000000, color page L.11000000.

PARK AND RECREATION OPPORTUNITIES JOB BULLETIN. see *OCCUPATIONS AND CAREERS*

333.78 US ISSN 0363-0617
SB481.A1
PARKS; an international journal for managers of national parks, historic sites and other protected areas. French edition: Parcs. Spanish edition: Parques. 1976. q. U.S. National Park Service, Interior Bldg., Washington, DC 20240. TEL 202-343-1100. (Co-sponsors: Organization of American States; Eastern National Park and Monument Association) (also avail. in microfilm from UMI; reprint service avail. from UMI) **Indexed:** Biol.Abstr., Curr.Adv.Ecol.Sci., Environ.Abstr., Forest.Abstr., Forest Prod.Abstr., Geo.Abstr., IDA, Rural Recreat.Tour.Abstr., World Agri.Econ.& Rural Sociol.Abstr.
—Linda Hall; UMI.

333.78 UK ISSN 0960-233X
SB481.A1 CODEN: PARKEE
PARKS; the international magazine dedicated to the protected areas of the world. (Text in English; summaries in English, French, Spanish) 1990. 3/yr. £18 (effective 1997 & 1998). (I U C N - World Conservation Union, World Commission on Protected Areas) Nature Conservation Bureau Ltd., 36 Kingfisher Ct., Hambridge Rd., Newbury, Berks. RG14 5SJ, England. TEL 44-1635-550380. FAX 44-1635-550230. E-mail: parks@naturebureau.co.uk. Ed. Paul Goriup. adv.: B&W page £240; 208 x 138; adv. contact: Martin Harvey. bk.rev. circ. 1,700. (back issues avail.) **Document type:** bulletin.
—BLDSC (6406.794000).
Description: Publishes papers and news items relating to national parks and other protected areas. Aimed at parks managers, policy-makers, administrators, and campaigners.

PARKS AND GROUNDS; technical magazine for landscape design, construction and maintenance. see *GARDENING AND HORTICULTURE*

CONSERVATION

333.7   AT   ISSN 1324-4361
PARKWATCH.* 1952. q. Aus.$18($20) Victorian National Parks Association Inc., 10 Tasma Terr., Parliament Pl., E. Melbourne, Vic. 3002, Australia. TEL 61-3-6508296. FAX 61-3-6546843. (Subscr. addr.: G.P.O. Box 785F, Melbourne, Vic. 3001, Australia) Ed. James Calde. adv.; bk.rev. circ. 3,400.

PASHOSH. see CHILDREN AND YOUTH — For

333.91   US
PASSAIC RIVER REVIEW. 1981. s-a. free. Passaic River Coalition, 246 Madisonville Rd., Basking Ridge, NJ 07920. TEL 908-766-7550. FAX 908-766-7550. Ed. Ella Filippone. bk.rev. circ. 1,500. (looseleaf format) **Document type:** newsletter.
   Formerly: Passaic River Restoration Newsletter.
   Description: Publishes news and information on organization activities.

333.7   US   ISSN 1077-5110
PATHWAYS TO OUTDOOR COMMUNICATION. Key Title: New York State Outdoor Education Association's Pathways to Outdoor Communication. 1991. s-a. membership. New York State Outdoor Education Association, 418 Meery Rd., Amsterdam, NY 12010. TEL 518-842-0501. Ed. Susan Amtower. Indexed: C.I.J.E.
   —BLDSC (6412.860200).
   Formerly (until 1994): Pathways to Outdoor Communication (ISSN 1077-5102); Supersedes: Outdoor Communicator.

333.7   US
PEAK AND PRAIRIE. 1970? bi-m. $5 to non-members. Sierra Club, Rocky Mountain Chapter, 777 Grant St., Ste. 606, Denver, CO 80203. TEL 303-861-8819. FAX 303-861-2436. E-mail: mary.romano@rmc.sierraclub.org; barry.satlow@rmc.sierraclub.org; fran.baxter@rmc.sierr@cluborg; URL: http://www.sierraclub.org/chapters/co/. Eds. Barry Satlow, Fran Baxter; Pub. Diane Benjamin. adv. contact: Mary Romano. bk.rev.; film rev. circ. 14,000. **Document type:** newsletter.
   Description: Covers environmental issues, legislative news, chapter activities, and events.

333.7   IE   ISSN 0791-2757
PEATLAND NEWS. 1986. s-a. I£16 (effective 1997). Irish Peatland Conservation Council, 119 Chapel St., Dublin 1, Ireland. TEL 353-1-8722397. FAX 353-1-8722397. E-mail: ipcc@indigo.ie; URL: http://indigo.ie/~ipcc. Ed. Catherine O'Connell. R&P contact: Peter Foss. adv. contact: Catherine O'Connell. bk.rev.; circ. 1,300 (paid). **Document type:** newsletter.

PEDAL UPDATE. see SPORTS AND GAMES — Bicycles And Motorcycles

333.7   US   ISSN 1041-701X
PENNSYLVANIA STATE UNIVERSITY. ENVIRONMENTAL RESOURCES RESEARCH INSTITUTE. NEWSLETTER. 1970. q. free. Pennsylvania State University, Environmental Resources Research Institute, 125 Land and Water Research Bldg., University Park, PA 16802-4900. TEL 814-863-0291. FAX 814-865-3378. E-mail: jrr131@ceres.erri.psu.edu; URL: http://www.erri.psu.edu. Ed. Joy R. Drohan. R&P contact: Joy R. Drohan. circ. 2,500. **Document type:** newsletter.
   ●Also available online.
   Formerly: Pennsylvania State University. Institute for Research on Land and Water Resources. Newsletter (ISSN 0020-2614)

333.7 598.2   US
PEREGRINE FUND NEWSLETTER. 1970. s-a. $25. Peregrine Fund, Inc., 5666 W. Flying Hawk Ln., Boise, ID 83709. TEL 208-363-3716. FAX 208-362-2376. E-mail: tpf@peregrinefund.org; URL: http://www.peregrinefund.org. Ed. William Burnham. R&P contact: William Burnham. **Document type:** newsletter.
   Description: Discusses programs of the organization for conservation of natural resources and wildlife.

333.7 628   US
PERMACULTURE REVIEW, OVERVIEW AND DIGEST. Short title: P R O D. 4/yr. $15. Yankee Permaculture, Hemenway - Permaculture, Box 2052, Ocala, FL 34478-2052.
   Description: Includes digests of articles and other information sources.

PHILIPPINES. BUREAU OF MINES. ANNUAL REPORT. see MINES AND MINING INDUSTRY

PHILIPPINES. MINISTRY OF NATURAL RESOURCES. ANNUAL REPORT. see ENVIRONMENTAL STUDIES

333.7 614.7   PH
PHILIPPINES. MINISTRY OF NATURAL RESOURCES. PLANS AND PROGRAMS. 1976. a. Department of Natural Resources, Diliman, Quezon City, Philippines. charts; stat.

340   UN   ISSN 1015-5082
PILOT (NAIROBI); newsletter of the marine mammal action plan. 1987. q. United Nations Environment Programme, P.O. Box 30552, Nairobi, Kenya. circ. 5,000.
   —BLDSC (6500.971000).

333.7   US
▼**THE PINES POST.** 1996. 2/yr. membership. Pinelands Preservation Alliance, 114 Hanover St., Pemberton, NJ 08068. TEL 609-894-8000. Ed. Lisa Thibault. **Document type:** newsletter.
   Description: Covers news, activities, events funding, and legislative issues relating to efforts to preserve the New Jersey Pinelands.

631   IT   ISSN 0048-4334
SD123.3
PLANT GENETIC RESOURCES NEWSLETTER. (Text in English or French or Spanish) 1957. q. free. International Plant Genetic Resources Institute, Via delle Sette Chiese 142, 00145 Rome, Italy. TEL 39-6-51892233. FAX 39-6-575009. TELEX 4900005332 IBR UI. E-mail: p.stapleton@cgnet.com; URL: http://www.cgiar.org/ipgri. Ed. Paul Stapleton. bk.rev.; abstr.; bibl.; charts; illus.; circ. 5,000 (controlled). (processed) Indexed: Biol.Dig., Cott.& Trop.Fibr.Abstr., Environ.Abstr., Field Crop Abstr., Herb.Abstr., Hort.Abstr., Maize Abstr., Plant Breed.Abstr., Rice Abstr., Seed Abstr., Sorghum & Millets Abstr., Telegen, Triticale Abstr., Trop.Oil Seeds Abstr. **Document type:** academic/scholarly publication.
   —BLDSC (6517.800000); UnCover.
   Formerly: Plant Introduction Newsletter.
   Description: Publishes research articles, short articles, and reports on all aspects of plant genetic resources work, including news and conference reports.

PLANT TALK; news and views on plant conservation worldwide. see BIOLOGY — Botany

POTOMAC APPALACHIAN. see SPORTS AND GAMES — Outdoor Life

POWDER RIVER BREAKS. see ENVIRONMENTAL STUDIES

POWER LINE. see ENERGY

PRACTICAL QUEENSLAND LANDSCAPE DESIGN CONSTRUCTION AND MAINTENANCE; the newsmagazine for Queensland's landscaping industry. see GARDENING AND HORTICULTURE

333.7   GW   ISSN 0032-6542
AM1   CODEN: PPTRAA
DER PRAEPARATOR. (Text in English and German) 1955. q. DM.40 (foreign DM.48) (effective 1996). Verband Deutscher Praeparatoren e.V., Middeweg 36, 46240 Bottrop, Germany. TEL 49-2041-96651. FAX 49-2041-29716. Ed. Siegfried Eckardt. adv.; bk.rev.; charts; illus.; index every 2 yrs. circ. 2,000. (tabloid format) Indexed: Art & Archaeol.Tech.Abstr., Chem.Abstr., GeoRef. **Document type:** bulletin.
   —BLDSC (6601.650000).

796.5   US   ISSN 0032-6607
PRAIRIE CLUB BULLETIN; organized for the promotion of outdoor recreation in the form of walks, outings, camping and canoeing. no.45, 1915. bi-m. $15. Prairie Club of Chicago, 203 N. Wabash St., Ste. 1620, Chicago, IL 60601-2416. TEL 312-899-1539. FAX 312-899-1541. bk.rev.; illus. circ. 1,000. **Document type:** bulletin, newsletter.

333.7 340   US
PRESERVING LANDS: LEGAL ISSUES. 1990. q. $35. Preserving Family Lands, Box 2242, Boston, MA 02107. TEL 617-244-7553. FAX 617-728-9797. Ed. Stephen J. Small.
   Description: News and legal developments concerning tax issues in land ownership, including estate planning, environmental and conservation easements, and wildlife preservation strategies.

639.9 179.3   SZ   ISSN 0898-6207
QL737.P9
PRIMATE CONSERVATION. (Text in English) 1985. a. $15. International Union for Conservation of Nature and Natural Resources, Species Survival Commission - Primate Specialist Group, Rue Mauverney 28, CH-1196 Gland, Switzerland. TEL 41-22-9990001. FAX 41-22-9990002. TELEX 419624-IUCN-CH. (Subscr. to: Dr. Russell A. Mittermeier, Conservation International, 1015 18th St., N.W., Ste. 1000, Washington, DC 20036, USA) **Document type:** newsletter.
   —BLDSC (6612.916000); UnCover.

333.7   BW
PROBLEMY BIOSPHERY. (Text in Russian) 1972. biennial. 3200 Rub. (Akademiya Navuk Belarusi - Byelorussian Academy of Sciences) Vydavetstvo Navuka i Tekhnika, Zhodzinskaya, 18, 220067 Minsk 67, Belarus. TEL 39-55-17. FAX 252494. TELEX 252277 NAUKA. Dir. F.I. Savitsky. bibl.; charts; illus.; index. circ. 150. **Document type:** academic/scholarly publication.
   Formerly (until 1992): Problemy Poles'ya (ISSN 0131-3010)
   Description: Presents papers on scientific problems of environmental protection, rational use of natural resources of Byelarus.

PRZEGLAD PRZYRODNICZY. see BIOLOGY

333.7 634.9   US   ISSN 0270-8094
PUBLIC LANDS NEWS. 1976. fortn. $217. Resources Publishing Co., 1010 Vermont Ave., N.W., Ste. 708, Washington, DC 20005. TEL 202-638-7529. FAX 202-393-2075. E-mail: coffinj@clark.net; URL: http://www.plnfpr.com. Ed. James B. Coffin; Pub. James B. Coffin. R&P contact: James B. Coffin. (looseleaf format; back issues avail.) **Document type:** newsletter.
   Formerly: Public Lands Use.

719.32   US   ISSN 0270-1308
E51
PUBLICATIONS IN ARCHAEOLOGY. 1951. irreg. U.S. National Park Service, Interior Bldg., Washington, DC 20240. TEL 202-343-1100. (Orders to: Supt. Doc Washington, DC 20402) **Indexed:** GeoRef.
   Formerly: U.S. National Park Service. Archaeological Research Series (ISSN 0083-2308)

PUDDLER. see CHILDREN AND YOUTH — For

PULPWOOD HIGHLIGHTS. see PAPER AND PULP

QUEBEC (PROVINCE). MINISTERE DES FORETS. DIRECTION DE LA RECHERCHE. MEMOIRE DE RECHERCHE FORESTIERE. see FORESTS AND FORESTRY

QUEBEC (PROVINCE). MINISTERE DES RESSOURCES NATURELLES. DIRECTION DE LA RECHERCHE FORESTIERE. GUIDE. see FORESTS AND FORESTRY

333.7 570   US   ISSN 0079-9211
QUETICO-SUPERIOR WILDERNESS RESEARCH CENTER, ELY, MINNESOTA. ANNUAL REPORT. 1949. irreg. free. Wilderness Research Foundation, c/o F.B. Hubachek, Jr., 111 W. Monroe St., Chicago, IL 60603. Ed. Clifford E. Ahlgren. **Indexed:** Biol.Abstr. **Document type:** corporate report.

333.7   US   ISSN 0079-922X
QUETICO-SUPERIOR WILDERNESS RESEARCH CENTER, ELY, MINNESOTA. TECHNICAL NOTES. 1952. irreg. no.5, 1968. Wilderness Research Foundation, c/o F.B. Hubachek, Jr., 111 W. Monroe St., Chicago, IL 60603. Ed. Clifford E. Ahlgren. **Indexed:** Biol.Abstr

CONSERVATION

**639.2 634.9 970.1   US   ISSN 1083-012X
QUINAULT NATURAL RESOURCES.** 1978. 3/yr. donation. (Quinault Indian Nation, Department of National Resources) Quinault Indian Nation Publishing Co., Box 189, Taholah, WA 98587-0189. TEL 360-276-8211. FAX 360-276-4682. Ed. Larry J. Workman. R&P contact: Larry J. Workman. bk.rev. circ. 1,500. **Document type:** government publication.
   Description: Educational information on environment-related issues, including ecology, forestry, fisheries and development of the natural resources of the Quinault Indian Nation.

**333.7   US
QUINNEHTUKQUT.** 1970. bi-m. $35 membership. Sierra Club, Connecticut Chapter, 118 Oak St., Hartford, CT 06106. TEL 203-527-9788. FAX 203-549-3094. Ed. Faith Vis. adv.; bk.rev. circ. 8,400. (also avail. in diskette format) **Document type:** newsletter.
   Description: Contains environmental, political, and local group news. Includes information on Sierra Club outings, and other events of interest to the Connecticut Sierra Club members.

R C O UPDATE. (Recycling Council of Ontario) see ENVIRONMENTAL STUDIES — Waste Management

**333.7   UK   ISSN 0965-5727
RAMBLING TODAY.** 1949. 4/yr. membership. Ramblers' Association, 1-5 Wandsworth Rd., London SW8 2XX, England. TEL 44-171-582-6878. FAX 44-171-820-1004. Ed. Annabelle Birchall. adv. contact: Peter Raven. bk.rev.; illus. circ. 90,000. **Document type:** newsletter.
   Former titles: Rambler; Rucksack (ISSN 0006-7334)
   Description: Covers walks in the countryside, long distance trails and access to wild country. Focuses on the conservation of the countryside.

RANGER RICK. see CHILDREN AND YOUTH — For

THE RAPTOR REPORT. see BIOLOGY — Ornithology

**639.9 179.3   SZ
RE-INTRODUCTION NEWS.** (Text in English) 1990. 2/yr. International Union for Conservation of Nature and Natural Resources, Species Survival Commission - Re-introduction Specialist Group, Rue Mauverney 28, CH-1196 Gland, Switzerland. TEL 41-22-9990001. FAX 41-22-9990002. TELEX 419624-IUCN-CH. (Subscr. to: African Wildlife Foundation, P.O. Box 48177, Nairobi, Kenya. FAX 0254-2-332294) Ed. Minoo Rahbar. **Document type:** newsletter.

**333.7   CN   ISSN 1180-5722
RECOVER;** the environmental magazine. 1990. q. Can.$10. Recover Enterprises, 114 Dollery Court, North York, Ont. M2R 3P1, Canada. Eds. Nancy Phillips, Heather Sangster. **Indexed:** Environ.Abstr.

RECREATION AND PARKS LAW REPORTER. see LAW

RECYCLING RELATED NEWSLETTERS, PUBLICATIONS, PERIODICALS; an updating reference. see ENVIRONMENTAL STUDIES

REGENWALD REPORT. see FORESTS AND FORESTRY

REMEDIATION REVIEW; a newsletter of hazardous waste remediation. see ENVIRONMENTAL STUDIES — Waste Management

**333.7   BE   ISSN 0772-9472
         CODEN: RENAEE
RESERVES NATURELLES/NATURRESERVATEN.** 1974. bi-m. 600 BEF membership. Reserves Naturelles et Ornithologiques de Belgique, 105 rue Royale Ste-Marie, 1030 Brussels, Belgium. Ed. Jean Rommes; Pub. Jean Rommes. **Indexed:** Zoo.Rec. **Document type:** consumer publication.
   Formerly (until 1979): Feuille de Contact des Reserves Naturelles et Ornithologiques de Belgique (ISSN 0773-0225)
   Description: Covers wildlife and landscape preservation in Belgium, organization activities and news, including international conservation initiatives.

**333.7   NE   ISSN 0142-2391
HC10   CODEN: RMOPDH
RESOURCE MANAGEMENT AND OPTIMIZATION;** an international journal. 4/yr. (in 1 vol.; 4 nos./vol.). $239 (effective 1998). Gordon and Breach - Harwood Academic, Amsteldisk 166, 1st Fl., 1079 LH Amsterdam, Netherlands. (Subscr. to: International Publishers Distributor, Box 32160, Newark, NJ 07102. TEL 800-545-8398. FAX 215-750-6343) Ed.Bd. stat. (also avail. in microfilm; microfiche). **Indexed:** AESIS, Agri.Eng.Abstr., Curr.Adv.Ecol.Sci., Curr.Cont., Energy Ind., Energy Info.Abstr., Environ.Abstr., Environ.Per.Bibl. (1991-1993), Excerp.Med., Forest.Abstr., Forest Prod.Abstr., Geo.Abstr., Int.Lab.Doc., Irr.& Drain.Abstr., Rural Recreat.Tour.Abstr., Soils & Ferts., Sport Fish.Abstr., Wild.Rev., World Agri.Econ.& Rural Sociol.Abstr., Zoo.Rec. **Document type:** academic/scholarly publication.
   —BLDSC (7777.602700); Linda Hall. **CCC**.
   Refereed Serial

RESOURCE RECOVERY REPORT. see ENVIRONMENTAL STUDIES — Waste Management

RESOURCE RECYCLING; North America's recycling and composting journal. see ENVIRONMENTAL STUDIES — Waste Management

**333.7 614.7   US   ISSN 0048-7376
RESOURCES (WASHINGTON).** 1959. q. free. Resources for the Future, Inc., 1616 P St., N.W., Washington, DC 20036. TEL 202-328-5025. FAX 202-939-3460. E-mail: info@rff.org; URL: http://www.rff.org. Ed. Richard Getrich. charts; illus.; cum.index. circ. 26,000. (also avail. in microform from UMI; reprint service avail. from UMI) **Indexed:** Abstr.Bull.Inst.Pap.Chem., Energy Info.Abstr., Energy Rev., Environ.Per.Bibl. (1989-), P.A.I.S. **Document type:** newsletter.
   —BLDSC (7777.606500); CIS; KNAW; Linda Hall; UMI; UnCover. **CCC**.
   Description: Includes feature articles and briefer pieces on matters of the environment, natural resources, conservation, energy, etc. Reports on the activities and research performed at Resources for the Future.

RESOURCES, CONSERVATION AND RECYCLING. see ENVIRONMENTAL STUDIES — Waste Management

**333.7 570   US   ISSN 0733-0707
QH76   CODEN: RMNOEA
RESTORATION AND MANAGEMENT NOTES.** 1981. s-a. $24 to individuals; institutions $66. (University of Wisconsin at Madison, Arboretum) University of Wisconsin Press, Journal Division, 114 N. Murray St., Madison, WI 53715. TEL 608-262-4952. FAX 608-262-7560. Ed. William R. Jordan, III. adv.; bk.rev.; index. circ. 2,400. (also avail. in microform from UMI; back issues avail.; reprint service avail. from UMI) **Indexed:** Curr.Tit.Ocean, Ecol.Abstr., Energy Rev., Environ.Abstr., Environ.Per.Bibl. (1985-), Gard.Lit. (1992-), Geo.Abstr.H.G., Geo.Abstr.P.G., Sport Fish.Abstr., Wild.Rev., Zoo.Rec. **Document type:** academic/scholarly publication.
   —BLDSC (7777.820000); CIS; Linda Hall; UMI; UnCover. **CCC**.
   Refereed Serial

RESTORATION ECOLOGY. see ENVIRONMENTAL STUDIES

**333.7 796.6   US   ISSN 0748-9846
RIDE ON!.*** 1972. m. $20 (effective 1990). Washington Bicycling Association, 818 Connecticut Ave., N.W., Washington, DC 20006. TEL 202-872-9830. FAX 202-862-9762. Eds. B. Nevel, T. Wallace. adv. circ. 1,100. (tabloid format; back issues avail.) **Document type:** consumer publication.
   ●Also available online.
   Description: Advocates bicycling as an alternate means of transportation in the interest of environmental conservation.

**352   AT
RIVERLANDER NOTES.** 1946. q. Aus.$30. Murray Darling Association for Conservation and Sustainable Development, P.O. Box 359, Albury, N.S.W. 2640, Australia. TEL 060-213655. FAX 060-212025. Ed. Adrian Wells. adv. contact: Adrian Wells. bk.rev.; illus.; index. circ. 3,500. **Document type:** newsletter.
   Formerly: Riverlander (ISSN 0035-5682)

**333.7   US   ISSN 1067-4322
ROCKY MOUNTAIN ENVIRONMENTAL DIRECTORY.** 1992. biennial. $22.50 (effective 1997). Harbinger Communications, Box 8175, Missoula, MT 59807. TEL 406-721-0440. FAX 406-721-0440. E-mail: ned@ism.net. index. (also avail. in diskette format) **Document type:** directory.
   ●Also available online.
   Description: Annotated listings of citizen groups, governement agencies in Colorado, Idaho, Montana, Utah and Wyoming.

**052 622   SX   ISSN 0257-2001
ROSSING MAGAZINE.** (Text in English) 1979. 2/yr. free. Rossing Uranium Ltd., Corporate Affairs, P.O. Box 22391, Windhoek 9000, Namibia. TEL 264-61-236760. FAX 264-61-228147. Eds. Dorian Haarhoff, Anne Haarhoff. R&P contact: Gida Sekandi. illus.; circ. 4,000 (controlled). **Document type:** consumer publication.
   Description: Aims to contribute to a broader knowledge of Namibia, its people, and the environment. Each issue illustrates various aspects of the country.

**333.7   GW
DIE ROTE MAPPE;** Kritischer Jahresbericht zur Situation der Heimatpflege in unserem Land. 1960. a. free. Niedersaechsischer Heimatbund e.V., Goseriede 15, 30159 Hannover, Germany. TEL 49-511-131565. FAX 49-511-17475. Ed. Roswitha Sommer. R&P contact: Roswitha Sommer. circ. 7,000. (looseleaf format; back issues avail.) **Document type:** bulletin.

**333.7   UK   ISSN 0267-4807
RURAL FORUM.** q. £12.50. Rural Forum Ltd., Highland House, St. Catherines Rd., Perth PH1 5RY, Scotland. Ed. Amanda Anderson. adv. circ. 1,800. **Document type:** bulletin.

**333.7 614.7   UK
RURAL WALES - CYMRU WLEDIG.** (Text in English and Welsh) 3/yr. £15 membership (overseas £20). Campaign for the Protection of Rural Wales, 31 High St., Welshpool, Powys, Wales SY21 7YD. TEL 44-1938-552525. FAX 44-1938-552741. E-mail: cprw@mcrl.poptel.org.uk. Ed. Merfyn Williams. adv. contact: Jenny Smith. bk.rev. circ. 4,000. **Document type:** newsletter.
   Former titles: Rural Wales (ISSN 0142-0100); C P R W News; Council for the Protection of Rural Wales. Newsletter.
   Description: Discusses actions that need to be taken to protect the Welsh countryside. For planners and decision-makers.

RUSSELL REVIEW. see HISTORY — History Of Australasia And Other Areas

**333.7   SA
S.A. WILD/S.A. GAME.** (Text in Afrikaans, English) 1994. q. R.5.70 per issue. J L O Uitgewers, P.O. Box 4722, Pretoria 0001, South Africa. illus. **Indexed:** Ind.S.A.Per.

**333.7 613.1   UK   ISSN 0955-226X
S C E N E S - SCOTTISH ENVIRONMENT NEWS.** 1988. m. £22 to individuals; institutions £38 (effective 1997). Strome House, North Strome, Lochcarron, Ross-shire IV54 8YJ, Scotland. TEL 44-1520-722588. FAX 44-1520-722660. Eds. Michael Scott, Sue Scott. bk.rev.; circ. 610 (paid). (back issues avail.) **Document type:** abstracting/indexing, newsletter.
   Description: Reports topical information on the Scottish environment.

S P R E P ENVIRONMENTAL CASE STUDIES. (South Pacific Regional Environment Programme) see ENVIRONMENTAL STUDIES

S P R E P FACT SHEET. (South Pacific Regional Environment Programme) see ENVIRONMENTAL STUDIES

S P R E P MEETING REPORTS. (South Pacific Regional Environmental Programme) see ENVIRONMENTAL STUDIES

S P R E P OCCASIONAL PAPERS. see ENVIRONMENTAL STUDIES

S P R E P TOPIC REVIEW. see ENVIRONMENTAL STUDIES

S P R E P TRAINING REPORTS. see ENVIRONMENTAL STUDIES

CONSERVATION

SALAR. see *FISH AND FISHERIES*

333.7 US ISSN 0085-5898
SAN FRANCISCO BAY CONSERVATION AND DEVELOPMENT COMMISSION. ANNUAL REPORT. 1971. a. free. San Francisco Bay Conservation and Development Commission, 30 Van Ness Ave., San Francisco, CA 94102. TEL 415-557-3606. Ed. R.A. Abramson. illus. circ. 10,000.

639.9 US ISSN 0272-8966
QH76.5.N45 CODEN: SNCTEM
SANCTUARY. 1961. 6/yr. membership. Massachusetts Audubon Society, South Great Rd., Lincoln, MA 01773. TEL 617-259-9500. Ed. John Hanson Mitchell. R&P contact: John H. Mitchell. adv.; bk.rev. circ. 55,000. **Indexed:** Sport Fish.Abstr., Wild.Rev., Zoo.Rec.
—Linda Hall; UnCover.
Formerly (until 1980): Massachusetts Audubon Newsletter (ISSN 0076-4892)

SAUMONS. see *BIOLOGY — Zoology*

SAVON LUONTO. see *BIOLOGY*

SAVONIA. see *BIOLOGY*

639.9 UK ISSN 0143-1234
CODEN: SCWIEC
SCOTTISH WILDLIFE. 1964. 3/yr. membership. Scottish Wildlife Trust, Cramond House, Kirk Cramond, Cramond Glebe Rd., Edinburgh EH4 6NS, Scotland. TEL 44-131-312-7765. FAX 44-131-312-8705. Ed. Andy Reynolds; Pub. Andy Reynolds. adv.: B&W page £425, color page £650; adv. contact: Kirstin Norrie. bk.rev. circ. 12,000. **Indexed:** Sport Fish.Abstr., Wild.Rev., Zoo.Rec. **Document type:** consumer publication.
—UnCover.
Formerly: Scottish Wildlife Trust. Newsletter.
Description: Focuses on the flora and fauna of Scotland.
Refereed Serial

333.7 669 US
SCRAP. 1944. bi-m. $32.95 to non-members; Canada and Mexico $38.95; elsewhere $104.95 (effective 1997); newsstand price: $7.50. Institute of Scrap Recycling Industries, 1325 G St., N.W., Ste. 1000, Washington, DC 20005. TEL 202-737-1770. FAX 202-626-0900. Ed. Kent Kiser; Pub. Tim Fowler. adv. contact: Tim Fowler. illus. circ. 6,200. (back issues avail.) **Indexed:** Abstr.Bull.Inst.Pap.Chem., Alloys Ind., CAD CAM Abstr., Eng.Mat.Abstr., Environ.Abstr., Met.Abstr., Met.Abstr.Ind., Nonfer.Met.Alert, PCC Alert, Steels Alert, World Alum.Abstr. **Document type:** trade publication.
—UnCover.
Former titles (until 1996): Scrap Processing and Recycling (ISSN 0898-0756); (until 1988): Scrap Age (ISSN 0036-9527)
Description: Covers the scrap industry (paper, metals, plastics) and market trends. Profiles notable persons and companies, large and small.

639.9 CN
SEASONS; the nature & outdoors magazine. 1963. 4/yr. Can.$34 (foreign Can.$40) (effective 1997). Federation of Ontario Naturalists, 355 Lesmill Rd., Don Mills, ON M3B 2W8, Canada. TEL 416-444-8419. FAX 416-444-9866. URL: http://www.web.net/fon. Ed. Margaret Webbs. R&P contact: Margaret Webb. adv. contact: Carolyn Ford. bk.rev.; bibl.; illus. circ. 12,000. (also avail. in microform from UMI; reprint service avail. from UMI) **Indexed:** Biol.Dig., Can.B.P.I., Can.Per.Ind., CMI. **Document type:** consumer publication.
—CISTI; UMI.
Formerly: Ontario Naturalist (ISSN 0030-3046); Incorporates (1965-1975): Federation of Ontario Naturalists. Newsletter (ISSN 0046-3574)

333.7 634.9 US
SEEDLING NEWS. 1974. q. $25 membership. TreePeople, 12601 Mulholland Dr., Beverly Hills, CA 90210. TEL 818-753-4600. FAX 818-753-4625. Ed. Rena Kilmor. R&P contact: Kate Hahn. circ. 21,000. (tabloid format; back issues avail.) **Document type:** newsletter.
Former titles: TreePeople News; Seedling News.

SEINE. see *BIOLOGY — Zoology*

SHENGTAI HUANJING YU BAOHU/ECOLOGICAL ENVIRONMENT AND ITS PROTECTION. see *ENVIRONMENTAL STUDIES*

639.9 JA ISSN 0916-8265
SHINRIN YASEI DOBUTSU KENKYUKAISHI/JAPANESE WILDLIFE RESEARCH SOCIETY. JOURNAL. (Text in English, Japanese) 1972. a. 3500 Yen. Shinrin Yasei Dobutsu Kenkyukai - Japanese Wildlife Research Society, Historical Museum of Hokkaido, Atsubetsuku, Sapporo 004, Japan. TEL 81-11-898-0456. FAX 81-11-898-2657. Ed. Masaaki Kadosaki. **Document type:** academic/scholarly publication.

333.7 JA
SHIZEN AIGO/NATURE OF KAGOSHIMA. (Text in Japanese) 1975. a. Kogoshimaken Shizen Aigo Kyokai - Society for the Preservation of Nature of Kagoshima, Kagoshima Daigaku Nogakubu, Kachiku Kaibogaku Kyoshitsu, 50-20 Shimoaratacho 4-chome, Kagoshima-shi, Kagoshima-ken 890, Japan.

SHOKUCHU SHOKUBUTSU KENKYUKAI KAISHI/INSECTIVOROUS PLANT SOCIETY. JOURNAL. see *BIOLOGY — Botany*

SHUITU BAOCHI TONGBAO/BULLETIN OF SOIL AND WATER CONSERVATION. see *AGRICULTURE — Crop Production And Soil*

SHUITU BAOCHI YANJIU/RESEARCH OF SOIL AND WATER CONSERVATION. see *AGRICULTURE — Crop Production And Soil*

SHUTTERBUG'S OUTDOOR & NATURE PHOTOGRAPHY. see *PHOTOGRAPHY*

333.7 GW
SIEBENSTERN; Vereinszeitschrift fuer Heimatpflege, Heimatkunde, Wandern und Naturschutz. 1927. bi-m. Fichtelgebirgsverein e.V., Auguststrasse 6, 95028 Hof, Germany. TEL 09281-2531. adv.; bk.rev.; index. circ. 13,000. (back issues avail.)

333.7 US ISSN 0161-7362
F868.S5
SIERRA. 1893. bi-m. $15 to non-members (foreign $20). Sierra Club, 85 Second St., San Francisco, CA 94105-3441. TEL 415-977-5500. FAX 415-977-5794. E-mail: information@sierraclub.org; URL: http://www.sierraclub.org. Ed. Joan Hamilton. R&P contact: Bob Schildgen. TEL 415-977-5691. adv. contact: Frank Noto. bk.rev.; illus.; tr.lit.; cum.index (vols. 35-61, 1978). circ. 550,000. (also avail. in microform from UMI; reprint service avail. from UMI) **Indexed:** Acad.Ind., Acid Rain Abstr., Acid Rain Ind., ASCA, Biog.Ind., Biol.Abstr., Biol.Dig., Bk.Rev.Ind. (1978-), C.I.J.E., Cal.Per.Ind. (1987-), Child.Bk.Rev.Ind. (1978-), Energy Rev., Environ.Abstr., Environ.Per.Bibl. (1980-), Gen.Sci.Ind., Geo.Abstr., Mag.Ind., PMR, R.G.Abstr., R.G., TOM. **Document type:** consumer publication.
●Also available online. Vendor(s): Information Access Co., UMI.
—BLDSC (8274.050000); CIS; KR SourceOne; SWETS; UMI; UnCover.
Formerly: Sierra Club Bulletin (ISSN 0037-4725)
Description: Provides commentary on environmental issues and articles on nature and the wilderness. Includes legislative developments, stories of outdoor adventures, and profiles of environmental activists.

333.7 US ISSN 0164-825X
SIERRA ATLANTIC. 1974. q. $5 membership. Sierra Club, Atlantic Chapter, 353 Hamilton St., Albany, NY 12210. TEL 518-426-9144. (Subscr. to: Sierra Club, 730 Polk St.. San Francisco, CA 94109) Ed. Ann Botshon. adv.; bk.rev.; film rev. circ. 40,000. **Document type:** newsletter.
Formerly: Subway Sierran.
Description: Chapter newsletter on environmental issues of interest to club members in New York State.

333.7 CN ISSN 1194-6148
SIERRA REPORT. 1973? q. Can.$15. Sierra Club, Western Canada Chapter, 1525 Amelia St., Victoria, BC V8W 2K1, Canada. TEL 604-386-5255. FAX 604-386-4453. Ed. Geraldine Irby. adv.; bk.rev. circ. 5,000. **Document type:** consumer publication.
Formerly (until 1982): Sierra Club. Western Canada Chapter. Quarterly Newsletter.
Description: Covers environmental issues in the prairie provinces, Yukon, and British Columbia. Liaison with Alaska chapter on transboundary issues.

639.9 179.3 SZ ISSN 1017-3439
SIRENEWS. (Text in English) 1983. 2/yr. International Union for Conservation of Nature and Natural Resources, Species Survival Commission - Sirenia Specialist Group, Rue Mauverney 28, CH-1196 Gland, Switzerland. TEL 41-22-9990001. FAX 41-22-9990002. TELEX 419624-IUCN-CH. (Subscr. to: Dr. Daryl P. Domning, Dept. of Anatomy, Howard University, Washington, DC 20059, USA) **Document type:** newsletter.

333.7 599.5 US
SKYHOPPER. 1980. q. $35 membership. American Cetacean Society, Box 1391, San Pedro, CA 90733-1391. TEL 310-548-6279. FAX 310-548-6950. E-mail: acs@pobox.com. Ed. Sue Hayter. circ. 2,000. **Document type:** newsletter.
Formerly: Whale News (ISSN 1061-5970)
Description: Current information on whale and dolphin research, education, and conservation.

639.9 179.3 SZ ISSN 1019-5041
SMALL CARNIVORE CONSERVATION. (Text in English) s-a. $15. International Union for Conservation of Nature and Natural Resources, Species Survival Commission - Mustelid, Viverrid, and Procyonid Specialist Group, Rue Mauverney 28, CH-1196 Gland, Switzerland. TEL 41-22-9990001. FAX 41-22-9990002. TELEX 419624-IUCN-CH. (Subscr. to: Harry von Rompaey, Jan Verbertlei, 15, 2650 Edegem, Belgium) **Document type:** newsletter.
Formerly: Mustelid and Viverrid Conservation.

SOCIETY AND NATURAL RESOURCES. see *ENVIRONMENTAL STUDIES*

SOIL - PLANT ANALYST. see *AGRICULTURE — Crop Production And Soil*

SOIL SURVEY HORIZONS. see *AGRICULTURE — Crop Production And Soil*

SOLAR PROGRESS; renewable energy for Australasia. see *ENERGY — Solar Energy*

333.7 SA
SOUTH AFRICA. NATIONAL PARKS BOARD. ANNUAL REPORT. a. free to qualified personnel. National Parks Board - Nasionale Parkeraad, P.O. Box 787, Pretoria 0001, South Africa. TEL 27-12-343-9770 FAX 27-12-343-9958. TELEX 321931 SA. illus.; stat.; circ. controlled. **Document type:** government publication.

333.7 SA ISSN 0379-4369
SK575.S5 CODEN: SAJRDR
SOUTH AFRICAN JOURNAL OF WILDLIFE RESEARCH/SUID-AFRIKAANSE TYDSKRIF VIR NATUURNAVORSING. (Text and summaries in English) 1971. q. R.118 to individuals; institutions R.138 (foreign $45) (effective 1997). (Southern African Wildlife Management Association) Foundation for Education, Science & Technology, P.O. Box 1758, Pretoria 0001, South Africa. TEL 27-12-3226404. FAX 27-12-3207803. E-mail buro@shuttle.up.ac.za. Ed. N. Fairall. adv. contact: Fairall. charts; illus. circ. 800. **Indexed:** Abstr.Anthropol., Anim.Breed.Abstr., ASCA, Biol.Abstr., Curr.Cont., Ecol.Abstr., Energy Ind., Energy Info.Abstr., Forest.Abstr., Forest Prod.Abstr Geo.Abstr., Helminthol.Abstr., Herb.Abstr., IBR, IDA Ind.S.A.Per., Ind.Vet., Key Word Ind.Wildl.Res., Poult.Abstr., Protozool.Abstr., Sci.Cit.Ind., Seed Abstr., Sport Fish.Abstr., Vet.Bull., Wild Life Rev., Wild.Rev., Zoo.Rec. **Document type:** academic/scholarly publication.
—BLDSC (8340.330000); Genuine Article; Linda Hall; UnCover. CCC.
Former titles: South African Journal of Wildlife Management; (until vol.6, 1976): Southern Africa Wildlife Management Association. Journal.

CONSERVATION

333.7 614.7   US   ISSN 0887-9249
SOUTH CAROLINA OUT-OF-DOORS. 1974. m. $15 membership. South Carolina Wildlife Federation, 715 Woodrow St., Columbia, SC 29205-1733. TEL 803-771-4417. FAX 803-771-6120. Ed. Patricia Jerman. adv. contact: Mike Willis. bk.rev.; circ. 7,000 (paid). (tabloid format) **Document type:** newsletter.

639.9   US   ISSN 0038-3198
SK1
SOUTH CAROLINA WILDLIFE. 1954. bi-m. $10. Department of Natural Resources, Box 167, Columbia, SC 29202. TEL 803-734-3972. Ed. John Davis. circ. 60,000 (paid). **Indexed:** Sport Fish.Abstr., Wild.Rev. **Document type:** government publication.
—UnCover.

333.7   US   ISSN 0038-3279
SOUTH DAKOTA CONSERVATION DIGEST. 1934. bi-m. $5. Game, Fish and Parks Department, 523 E Capitol, Pierre, SD 57501-3182. TEL 605-773-3485. Ed. Bruce Coonrod. R&P contact: Bruce Coonrod. bk.rev.; illus. circ. 20,000. **Indexed:** Biol.Abstr. **Document type:** government publication.
—UnCover.

333.7   US   ISSN 1082-7196
SOUTHEAST ENVIRONMENTAL DIRECTORY. 1995. biennial. $18.50. Harbinger Communications, Box 8175, Missoula, MT 59807. TEL 406-721-0440. FAX 406-721-0440. E-mail: ned@ism.net. index. (also avail. in diskette format) **Document type:** directory.
●Also available online.
Description: Annotated listings of citizen groups, government agencies in Alabama, Arkansas, Florida, Georgia, Kentucky, Louisiana, Mississippi, North Carolina, South Carolina and Tennessee.

SOUTHEASTERN ASSOCIATION OF FISH AND WILDLIFE AGENCIES. PROCEEDINGS. see FISH AND FISHERIES

SOUTHERN BIRDS. see BIOLOGY — Ornithology

333.7   US   ISSN 1073-6875
SOUTHERN SIERRAN.* 1945. m. (11/yr.). $5. Sierra Club, Los Angeles Chapter, 3345 Wilshire Blvd., No. 508, Los Angeles, CA 90010-1816. FAX 213-387-5383. Ed. Gregg Solkovits. adv.; bk.rev. circ. 59,000. (tabloid format)

SPEAK. see SOCIOLOGY

333.8   US
SPECIAL PLACES. q. membership. Trustees of Reservations, 290 Argilla Rd., Box 563, Ipswich, MA 01938-4351. TEL 508-921-1944. FAX 508-921-1948. Ed. Marah Ren. circ. 20,000. **Document type:** newsletter.
Formerly: Trustees of Reservations. Newsletter.
Description: Directed to members and contributors to the Massachusetts land conservation organization. Covers specific management practices, new land acquisitions, and events on the organization's 78 properties.

333.7   SZ   ISSN 1016-927X
SPECIES. 1983. s-a. 25 SFr.($18) International Union for Conservation of Nature and Natural Resources, Rue Mauverney 28, CH-1196 Gland, Switzerland. TEL 41-22-9990001. FAX 41-22-9990002. TELEX 419624-IUCN-CH. (Subscr. to: Species Survival Commission, c/o Chicago Zoological Society, 3300 S. Golf Rd., Brookfield, IL 60513, USA) Eds. Diane Cavalieri, Timothy Sullivan. circ. 3,000. **Indexed:** Key Word Ind.Wildl.Res., Sport Fish.Abstr., Wild.Rev. **Document type:** newsletter.

SPILL TECHNOLOGY NEWSLETTER/BULLETIN DE LA LUTTE CONTRE LES DEVERSEMENTS. see SCIENCES: COMPREHENSIVE WORKS

333.720   CN   ISSN 1185-5762
GE160.C2
STATE OF THE ENVIRONMENT REPORT FOR MANITOBA.* 1991. a. Manitoba Environment, 139 Tuxedo Ave., Winnipeg, MB R3N 0H6, Canada. Ed.Bd.
Description: Contains a description of Manitoba's environmental quality and activities related to present environmental issues as well as future environmental issues, projected trends and environmental management activities.

720   AU   ISSN 0039-1026
STEINE SPRECHEN. (Supplement avail.: Steinschlag) 1962. q. S.240 (effective 1996 & 1997). Oesterreichische Gesellschaft fuer Denkmal und Ortsbildpflege, Karlsplatz 5, A-1010 Vienna, Austria. TEL 43-1-587-96630. FAX 43-1-5232374. Ed. Mario Schwarz. adv. contact: Mario Schwarz. bk.rev. circ. 1,200. **Document type:** bulletin.
Description: Covers the history, the care and upkeep of historical monuments, buildings, and gardens.
Refereed Serial

639.9 333.95   PL
CODEN: SNPPD6
STUDIA NATURAE. WYDAWNICTWA NAUKOWE. (Text in English and Polish; summaries in English) 1952. irreg., no.40, 1993. $10. Polska Akademia Nauk, Instytut Ochrony Przyrody, Ul. Lubicz 46, 31-512 Krakow, Poland. TEL 48-12-210348. FAX 48-12-210348. TELEX 322630 PANZO. Ed. R. Kazmierczakowa. bibl.; charts. circ. 320. **Document type:** academic/scholarly publication.
Formerly: Studia Naturae. Seria A. Wydawnictwa Naukowe; Supersedes in part: Studia Naturae (ISSN 0081-6760)

333.7 338.91   MY   ISSN 0127-6409
SUARA SAM; Malaysia's leading environmental newspaper. (Text in English, Malay) 1979. q. M.$16($30) Sahabat Alam Malaysia - Friends of the Earth Malaysia, 19 Kelawai Rd., 10250 Pulau Pinang, Malaysia. TEL 6-04-376930. FAX 6-04-375705. adv.; bk.rev.; charts; illus. circ. 2,500. (back issues avail.)

SUIRI KAGAKU/WATER SCIENCE. see WATER RESOURCES

SUPERFUND WEEK. see ENVIRONMENTAL STUDIES

333.7   SW   ISSN 0039-6974
QH169   CODEN: SVNAA4
SVERIGES NATUR. 1910. 6/yr. SEK 240 to non-members; members SEK 230; with yearbook, non-members SEK 315; members SEK 325. Svenska Naturskyddsfoereningen - Swedish Society for Nature Conservation, P.O. Box 4625, S-116 91 Stockholm, Sweden. TEL 08-7026500. FAX 08-702-2702. E-mail: Sveriges.Natur@snf.se. adv.: B&W page SEK 24300, color page SEK 29900; trim 185 x 256; adv. contact: Kjell Dahlin. bk.rev.; index, cum.index: 1910-1959; circ. 150,200 (controlled). (also avail. in audio cassette) **Indexed:** Biol.Abstr., Sport Fish.Abstr., Wild.Rev., Zoo.Rec.
—BLDSC (8571.800000).

333.7   KE   ISSN 1018-6174
SWARA. (Text in English) 1978. bi-m. KShs.1000 thoughout East Africa (rest of Africa ($48); Europe £35; Canada Can.$85; elsewhere $50) (effective 1996-1997). East African Wild Life Society, P.O. Box 20110, Nairobi, Kenya. TEL 254-2-748170. FAX 254-2-746868. E-mail: eawls@arso.gn.apc.org; eawls@elci.gn.apc.org. Ed. Louisa Lockwood. R&P contact: Louisa Lockwood. adv.: B&W page Ksh.35000, color page Ksh.45000; 270 x 189. bk.rev. circ. 40,000. **Document type:** academic/scholarly publication.
Description: Publishes popular articles on wildlife and conservation in East Africa.

333   SW   ISSN 0282-7298
SWEDEN. SWEDISH ENVIRONMENTAL PROTECTION AGENCY. REPORT. (Text in Swedish; occasionally in English) irreg. price varies. Swedish Environmental Protection Agency, Blekholmsterrassen 36, S-106 48 Stockholm, Sweden. FAX 46-8-6981400. Pub. Ingvar Bingman. **Document type:** government publication.
—CISTI.
Formerly: Sweden. National Environmental Protection Board. Report.

SYDNEY'S KOALA CLUB NEWS. see BIOLOGY — Zoology

333.7   US
SYLVANIAN. 1983. bi-m. $10 to non-members. Sierra Club, Pennsylvania Chapter, 305 Jefferson St., Export, PA 15632. TEL 717-232-0101. Ed. Chris De Cristopher. adv. circ. 19,000. **Document type:** newsletter.
Description: Discusses the activities of the Sierra Club Pennsylvania Chapter and state environmental highlights.

TALL TIMBERS RESEARCH STATION. MISCELLANEOUS PUBLICATION. see FORESTS AND FORESTRY

639.9 179.3   SZ
TAPIR CONSERVATION. (Text in English) 1990. a. $15. International Union for Conservation of Nature and Natural Resources, Species Survival Commission - Tapir Specialist Group, Rue Mauverney 28, CH-1196 Gland, Switzerland. TEL 41-22-9990001. FAX 41-22-9990002. TELEX 419624-IUCN-CH. (Subscr. to: Rod Mast, Conservation International, 1015 18th St., N.W., Washington, DC 20036, USA) **Document type:** newsletter.
Formerly: International Union for Conservation of Nature and Natural Resources. Species Survival Commission - Tapir Specialist Group. Newsletter.

333.7 614.7   AT   ISSN 0725-0355
TASMANIAN CONSERVATIONIST. 1969. 6/yr. Aus.$25 to individuals; institutions Aus.$50. Tasmania Conservation Trust Inc., 102 Bathurst Street, Hobart, Tas. 7000, Australia. TEL 61-02-343552. FAX 61-02-312491. Ed.Bd. adv. contact: Suzy Manigian. bk.rev. circ. 500. (back issues avail.) **Document type:** newsletter.
Formerly (until 1981): Tasmania Conservation Trust Inc. Newsletter (ISSN 0726-2442)
Description: Covers a broad range of local, national and global environmental issues affecting Tasmania.

333.7 338.4   AG
TEMA VERDE. 1994. q.? free. Fundacion para el Desarrollo Turistico y el Medio Ambiente, Calle 15, No. 568, La Plata, Argentina. TEL 54-21-40714. Dir. Angel Merlo.

333.7   US   ISSN 0040-3202
THE TENNESSEE CONSERVATIONIST; nature, environmental issues. 1937. bi-m. $10; newsstand price: $2.25. Department of Environment & Conservation, Nashville, TN 37243-0440. TEL 615-532-0060. FAX 615-532-0046. Ed. Louise Zepp. R&P contact: Valary Marks. bk.rev.; circ. 14,500 (paid). **Indexed:** Environ.Abstr. **Document type:** government publication.
—Linda Hall.
Description: Provides news items and nature, historical, environmental conservation and preservation articles and photo layouts.

333.7   US
TENNESSEE NATIVE PLANT SOCIETY. NEWSLETTER. 1978. bi-m. $15 to individuals; institutions $20; students and senior citizens $10. Tennessee Native Plant Society, University of Tennessee at Knoxville, Department of Botany, Knoxville, TN 37996-1100. TEL 615-598-5532. Ed. Candy Swan. adv.; bk.rev. circ. 250. **Document type:** newsletter.
Description: Botanical news on the native flora of Tennessee.

333.7   US   ISSN 0363-101X
TK1425.M8
TENNESSEE VALLEY AUTHORITY. ANNUAL REPORT. 1934. a. free. Tennessee Valley Authority, 400 W. Summit Hill Dr., Knoxville, TN 37902. TEL 615-632-8039. FAX 615-632-6783. Ed. Dennis McCarthy. circ. 75,000. **Indexed:** Soils & Fert. **Document type:** corporate report.
Description: Includes chapters on the agency's work in energy, the environment, and economic development.

639.9 179.3   SZ   ISSN 0958-5079
TENTACLE. (Text in English) 1989. 2/yr. International Union for Conservation of Nature and Natural Resources, Species Survival Commission - Mollusc Specialist Group, Rue Mauverney 28, CH-1196 Gland, Switzerland. TEL 41-22-9990001. FAX 41-22-9990002. TELEX 419624-IUCN-CH. (Subscr. to: Dr. Robert Cowie, Dept. of Natural Sciences, Bishop Museum, 1525 Bernice St., P.O. Box 19000A, Honolulu, Hawaii) **Document type:** newsletter.

333.7 910.91   FR   ISSN 0981-4140
TERRE SAUVAGE. 1986. m. Bayard Presse, 3 rue Bayard, 75393 Paris Cedex 08, France. TEL 33-1-44356060. FAX 33-1-44356091. TELEX 648 094 F. (Subscr. to: Bayard Presse International, B.P. 12, 99505 Paris Entreprises, France. TEL 33-1-44216000. FAX 33-3-20274192) Ed. Elena Adam. circ. 112,500.
Description: Reports on far away places and offers itineraries to help travelers enjoy the earth's natural beauties.

CONSERVATION

TEXAS. NATURAL RESOURCES INFORMATION SYSTEM. NEWSLETTER. see *ENVIRONMENTAL STUDIES*

333.7 639.9   US   ISSN 0040-4586
SK1
TEXAS PARKS AND WILDLIFE MAGAZINE. 1942. m. $12.95. Parks and Wildlife Department, 4200 Smith School Rd., Austin, TX 78744. TEL 512-389-4800. FAX 512-707-1913. Ed. David Baxter. adv.; bk.rev.; charts; illus.; index. circ. 175,000. **Indexed:** Sport Fish.Abstr.; Wild.Rev. **Document type:** government publication, consumer publication.
—UnCover.

THREATENED BIRDS OF AFRICA AND RELATED ISLANDS; the ICBP-IUCN Red Data Book. see *BIOLOGY — Ornithology*

THREATENED BIRDS OF THE AMERICAS; the ICBP-IUCN Red Data Book. see *BIOLOGY — Ornithology*

333.78 628.168   US
THE TIDAL EXCHANGE. 1991. s-a. free. (New York - New Jersey Harbor Estuary Program) Hudson River Foundation, 40 W. 20th St., 9th Fl., New York, NY 10011. TEL 212-924-8290. FAX 212-924-8325. (Co-sponsors: U.S. Environmental Protection Agency, NY Bight Restoration Plan) Ed. Clay Hiles. R&P contact: Nancy Steinberg. charts; illus.; maps. **Document type:** newsletter.
Description: Reports on local- and state-level efforts to preserve the quality of New York's and New Jersey's waterways and the flora and fauna that inhabit them.

614.7 799.1   US
TIDE. 1977. bi-m. membership. Coastal Conservation Association, 4801 Woodway, Ste. 220 W, Houston, TX 77056. TEL 713-626-4222. FAX 713-961-3801. Ed. Doug Pike. adv. contact: Ben Kocian. circ. 40,000.
Description: Focuses on current conservation issues and activities from Texas to Florida and Maine. Includes information on programs in education, legislation, support for law enforcement and restocking.

TIDINGS (BOSTON). see *ENVIRONMENTAL STUDIES*

TIERRA AMIGA. see *ENVIRONMENTAL STUDIES*

333.79   UN   ISSN 1014-2789
QL84.5.A1   CODEN: TIGEE7
TIGER PAPER. 1974. q. $12 (effective 1997). Food and Agriculture Organization of the United Nations, Regional Office for Asia and the Pacific, Maliwan Mansion, 39 Phra Atit Rd., Bangkok 10200, Thailand. TEL 662-281-7844. FAX 662-280-0445. TELEX 82815 FOODAG TH. E-mail: fao-rap@field.fao.org. Ed. Mrs. J. Naewboonnien. R&P contact: Mrs. J. Naewboonnien. bk.rev. circ. 2,000. **Indexed:** Key Word Ind.Wildl.Res., Sport Fish.Abstr., Wild.Rev., Zoo.Rec. **Document type:** bulletin.
—BLDSC (8835.040000).
Description: Dedicated to the exchange of information relating to wildlife and national parks management for the Asia-Pacific Region.

028.5 333.7   SA   ISSN 0256-0437
TOKTOKKIE. (Text in English) 1979. bi-m. R.50 membership. Wildlife & Environment Society of South Africa, P.O. Box 44189, Linden 2104, South Africa. TEL 27-11-4863294. FAX 27-11-4863369. Ed. Roberta Griffiths. R&P contact: Roberts Griffiths. TEL 27-21-7011397. adv. contact: Robert Griffiths. bk.rev. circ. 5,000. (back issues avail.) **Document type:** consumer publication.
Description: Environmental magazine for junior school members and environmental clubs.

333.7   JA
TOKUSHIMA-KEN SHIZEN HOGO KYOKAI CHOSA HOKOKU. (Text in Japanese) 1974. 3/yr. Tokushima-ken Shizen Hogo Kyokai, Tokushima Daigaku Kyoikugakubu, 1-1 Minami Josanjima-cho, Tokushima-shi, Tokushima-ken 770, Japan.
Description: Contains reports of the society.

TORONTO FIELD NATURALIST. see *BIOLOGY*

TORTOISE; the conservation magazine. see *ENVIRONMENTAL STUDIES*

TOSHI KAIHATSU CHIIKI KAIHATSU KANKYO KOGAI KANKEI INDEKKUSU/CITY DEVELOPMENT, REGIONAL DEVELOPMENT AND ENVIRONMENTAL POLLUTION INDEX. see *ENVIRONMENTAL STUDIES*

333.7   US   ISSN 0040-9723
TOTEM.* 1958. q. free. Department of Natural Resources, c/o Virginia Forestry Association, 8810 Patterson Ave., Ste. B, Richmond, VA 23229-6322. illus.; stat. circ. 36,000. **Document type:** government publication.

TOURISM AND WILDLIFE. see *TRAVEL AND TOURISM*

TRACES (JACKSON). see *CLUBS*

TRAESKYDD; aktuellt fraan Traeskyddsinstituttet. see *FORESTS AND FORESTRY*

333.7   CN   ISSN 0041-0748
TRAIL AND LANDSCAPE. 1967. 4/yr. Can.$23 effective 1997. Ottawa Field-Naturalists' Club, Box 35069, Westgate P.O., Ottawa, ON K1Z 1A2, Canada. TEL 613-722-3050. Ed. F. Brodo. charts; illus.; index. circ. 950. (back issues avail.) **Indexed:** Sport Fish.Abstr., Wild.Rev.

TRAIL AND TIMBERLINE. see *SPORTS AND GAMES — Outdoor Life*

TRAIL WALKER; news of hiking and conservation. see *SPORTS AND GAMES — Outdoor Life*

333.7   US
TREE CITY U S A BULLETIN. bi-m. membership. National Arbor Day Foundation, 100 Arbor Ave., Nebraska City, NE 68410. TEL 402-474-5655. FAX 402-474-0820. **Document type:** bulletin.
Description: Encourages communities to actively participate in the urban forestry movement by providing advice on pruning and other means of maintaining the health of their town's trees.

333.7   UK   ISSN 0041-221X
TREES; the magazine for tree-lovers. (Former name of issuing body: Men of the Trees) 1937. a. £12.50 individual membership; institutions £20. International Tree Foundation, Sandy Ln., Crawley Down, W. Sussex RH10 4HS, England. TEL 01342-712536. FAX 01342-718282. Ed. A. Godschalk. adv.; bk.rev.; bibl.; illus. circ. 5,000. **Document type:** newsletter.

333.7   AT   ISSN 0814-4680
S934.A8
TREES AND NATURAL RESOURCES. 1959. q. Aus.$22.50 (foreign Aus.$25). Natural Resources Conservation League of Victoria, 593-615 Springvale Rd., Springvale South, Vic. 3172, Australia. TEL 03-547-8791. Ed. Felicity Anderson. adv.; bk.rev.; charts; illus. circ. 6,500. (also avail. in microfiche; back issues avail.) **Indexed:** Aus.P.A.I.S., Aus.Rd.Ind., Biol.Abstr., Forest.Abstr., Geo.Abstr., GeoRef., Irr.& Drain.Abstr., Rural Ext.Educ.& Tr.Abstr., World Agri.Econ.& Rural Sociol.Abstr.
—UnCover.
Former titles: Trees and Victoria's Resources (ISSN 0725-0045); Victoria's Resources (ISSN 0042-5230)

TRENDS (ARLINGTON). see *LEISURE AND RECREATION*

333.7   NE   ISSN 0166-8358
TRIAS. 1973. q. fl.25. Jeugdbond voor Natuur- en Milieustudie - Youth Federation for Nature and Environmental Study, Oude Gracht 42, 3511 AR Utrecht, Netherlands. TEL 030-368925. FAX 030-343986. bk.rev.; illus. circ. 2,500.

TROFEO; caza - naturaleza. see *SPORTS AND GAMES — Outdoor Life*

639.9   US   ISSN 0041-3364
TROUT. 1959. q. $30 (Canada $35; elsewhere $50). Trout Unlimited, 1500 Wilson Blvd., Arlington, VA 22209. TEL 703-522-0200. FAX 703-284-9400. E-mail: trout@tu.org; URL: http://www.tu.org/trout/. Ed. Peter A. Rafle, Jr. R&P contact: Peter A. Rafle, Jr. adv. contact: Tony Hill. bk.rev.; illus. circ. 95,000. **Indexed:** Sport Fish.Abstr., Wild.Rev. **Document type:** consumer publication.
—UnCover.
Description: Includes articles on trout, salmon, and steelhead angling, fish behavior and natural history, and environmental issues affecting fish and fishing.

TURANG QINSHI YU SHUITU BAOCHI XUEBAO/JOURNAL OF SOIL EROSION AND SOIL AND WATER CONSERVATION. see *AGRICULTURE — Crop Production And Soil*

TURKEY CALL. see *BIOLOGY — Ornithology*

333.95   CN
TURKEY TALK. 1997. q. Ontario Federation of Anglers & Hunters, 4601 Guthrie Dr., P.O. Box 2800, Peterborough, ON K9J 8L5, Canada. TEL 705-748-6324. FAX 705-748-9577. E-mail: ofah@oncomdis.on.ca. Ed. Mark Holmes. R&P contact: Mark Holmes. circ. 1,000. (tabloid format) **Document type:** newsletter.
Description: Provides educational material and club-related activities on wild turkey reintroduction.

333.7 300   UK
TURNING POINT 2000. 1976. 2/yr. £5 (foreign £6). The Old Bakehouse, Cholsey, Oxon OX10 9NU, England. TEL 44-1491-652346. FAX 44-1491-651804. Eds. James Robertson, Alison Pritchard. bk.rev. circ. 1,200. (back issues avail.) **Document type:** newsletter.

U.K. IRRIGATION ASSOCIATION QUARTERLY. see *WATER RESOURCES*

333.7   UK   ISSN 0963-8083
U K NATURE CONSERVATION. 1992. irreg., no.9, 1994. Joint Nature Conservation Committee, Monkstone House, City Rd., Peterborough PE1 1JY, England. E-mail: nhbs@nhbs.co.uk; URL: http://www.nhbs.co.uk. (Dist. by: Natural History Book Service Ltd., 2-3 Wills Rd., Totnes, Devon TQ9 5XN, England. TEL 44-1803-865913. FAX 44-1803-865280) Ed. John Bratton. R&P contact: John Bratton. **Document type:** academic/scholarly publication.
—BLDSC (9082.665175).
Refereed Serial

333.9   US   ISSN 1045-8077
HT390   CODEN: URJOEO
U R I S A JOURNAL. 1989. s-a. $30 to individuals (foreign $38); institutions $77. (Urban and Regional Information Systems Association) University of Wisconsin Press, Journal Division, c/o Institute for Environmental Studies, WARF Bldg., Rm. 1048, 610 Walnut St., Madison, WI 53705. TEL 608-263-6843. (Subscr. to: 900 Second St., N.E., Ste. 304, Washington, DC 20002. TEL 202-289-1685. FAX 202-842-1850) (Co-sponsor: Portland State University) Ed. Kenneth J. Dueker. bk.rev.; maps. circ. 3,800. **Indexed:** Geo.Abstr.H.G., Geo.Abstr.P.G., INSPEC (1991-). **Document type:** academic/scholarly publication.
—BLDSC (9124.328000); AskIEEE; KR SourceOne.
Description: Covers electronic information systems for managers, users, developers, and educators. Discusses improved systems that can be developed and used effectively and equitably at all levels of government.
Refereed Serial

U S A C O R FORUM. (U S Association for the Club of Rome) see *POLITICAL SCIENCE — International Relations*

U T A INTERNATIONAL. (Umwelt Technologie Aktuell) see *ENVIRONMENTAL STUDIES*

UMWELT TECHNOLOGIE AKTUELL. see *ENVIRONMENTAL STUDIES*

333.7   GW
UMWELTBRIEF; Fakten, Hintergruende und Entscheidungshilfen fuer Wirtschaft und Verwaltung. m. DM.330. (Industrie-Initiative fuer Umweltschutz) Deutscher Wirtschaftsdienst, Marienburgerstr. 22, 50968 Cologne, Germany. TEL 49-221-93763-0. FAX 49-221-9376399. bk.rev. circ. 5,000. (back issues avail.) **Document type:** bulletin.
Formerly: I W L - Umweltbrief (ISSN 0179-3462)

333.7   CN
UNIT SCHEME AND CONSERVATION ORDER OUTLINES. a. Can.$4.50. Ministry of Employment and Investment, Energy and Minerals Division, 7th Fl., 1810 Blanshard St., Victoria, BC V8W 9N3, Canada. (Subscr. to: Crown Publications, 546 Yates St., Victoria, BC V8W 1K8, Canada. TEL 604-386-4636) (looseleaf format) **Document type:** government publication.
Description: Includes schemes such as approved water disposal, gas conservation orders, good engineering practice and unitization.

CONSERVATION 2247

333.7　　　　　UN　　ISSN 0255-9250
TED NATIONS. ECONOMIC AND SOCIAL COMMISSION FOR ASIA AND THE PACIFIC. DEVELOPMENT PAPERS. 1981. irreg., no.16. price varies. United Nations Economic and Social Commission for Asia and the Pacific (ESCAP), United Nations Bldg., Rajadamnern Ave., Bangkok 2, Thailand. (Dist. by: United National Publications, Rm. DC2-0853, New York, NY 10017; or Distribution and Sales Section, Palais des Nations, CH-1211 Geneva 10, Switzerland; or Conference Services Unit, E.S.C.A.P., Bangkok) index. (back issues avail.) **Document type:** monographic series.

333.7　　　　　US
BUREAU OF RECLAMATION. ANNUAL REPORT. 1949. a. U.S. Bureau of Reclamation (Denver), Reclamation Service Center, Box 25007, Denver Federal Center, Bldg. 67, Denver, CO 80225-0007. TEL 303-236-7000. (Subscr. to: National Technical Information Service, 5285 Port Royal Rd., Springfield, VA 22161. TEL 703-487-4650. FAX 703-321-8547) **Document type:** government publication, corporate report.
　Former titles: U.S. Water and Power Resources Service. Annual Report; Federal Reclamation Projects: Water and Land Resource Accomplishments.

333.7　　　　　US
DEPARTMENT OF AGRICULTURE. WETLANDS RESERVE PROGRAM. REPORT TO CONGRESS. a. U.S. Department of Agriculture, Agricultural Stabilization and Conservation Service, Box 2415, Washington, DC 20013. TEL 202-720-7093. (Subscr. to: Superintendent of Documents, U.S. Government Printing Office, Box 317954, Pittsburgh, PA 15250-7954. TEL 202-783-3238. FAX 202-512-2233) **Document type:** government publication.

333.7　　　　　US　　ISSN 0092-9433
D223
ENVIRONMENTAL PROTECTION AGENCY. CLEAN WATER: REPORT TO CONGRESS. a. U.S. Environmental Protection Agency, Water Planning Division, 401 M St., S.W., Washington, DC 20460. TEL 202-655-4000. (Orders to: National Technical Information Service, 5285 Port Royal Rd., Springfield, VA 22161. TEL 703-487-4650. FAX 703-321-8547) circ. 15,000. **Indexed:** GeoRef. **Document type:** government publication.

FISH AND WILDLIFE SERVICE. SELECTED LIST OF FEDERAL LAWS AND TREATIES RELATING TO SPORT FISH AND WILDLIFE. see *LAW*

333.7　　　　　US　　ISSN 1078-6295
HC110.E5
NATIONAL COMMITTEE FOR MAN AND THE BIOSPHERE PROGRAM. BULLETIN. Short title: U.S. M A B Bulletin. 1976. irreg. (3-4/yr.). free. U.S. National Committee for the Man and the Biosphere Program, Man and the Biosphere Secretariat, U.S. Department of State, SA-44C, 1st Fl., Washington, DC 20522-4401. TEL 202-776-8318. FAX 202-776-8367. Ed. Antoinette J. Condo. abstr. circ. 10,500. (tabloid format) **Document type:** government publication, bulletin.
　Also available online.
　Description: Reports on program directorates of the U.S. Man and the Biosphere Program, which include biosphere reserves, high-latitude research, human-dominated ecological systems research, marine and coastal research, temperate and tropical areas research, and other items of interest, including publications.

333.7　　　　　US　　ISSN 0361-9737
SB482
NATIONAL PARK SERVICE. PUBLIC USE OF THE NATIONAL PARK SYSTEM: CALENDAR YEAR REPORT. 1972. a. free. National Park Service, Interior Bldg., Washington, DC 20240. TEL 202-343-1000. circ. 2,000.

333.7　　　　　US　　ISSN 0093-3074
SB482
NATIONAL PARK SERVICE. PUBLIC USE OF THE NATIONAL PARK SYSTEM: FISCAL YEAR REPORT. Key Title: Public Use of the National Park System (Washington). 1972. a. National Park Service, Interior Bldg., Washington, DC 20240. TEL 202-343-1100. illus.; stat. circ. 2,000.

333.7　　　　　US
U.S. NATIONAL PARK SERVICE. RESEARCH REPORTS BY SERVICE PERSONNEL. 5-10/yr. U.S. National Park Service, Interior Bldg., Washington, DC 20240. TEL 202-343-1100. (Orders to: NTIS, Springfield, VA 22161)

333.7　　　　　UK　　ISSN 0142-3649
UNIVERSITY COLLEGE LONDON. DISCUSSION PAPERS IN CONSERVATION. 1972. irreg. University College London, Gower St., London WC1E 6BT, England. TEL 44-171-380-7707. FAX 44-171-413-8392. **Document type:** monographic series.

333.7　　　　　US　　ISSN 0073-4586
SD12
UNIVERSITY OF IDAHO. FOREST, WILDLIFE AND RANGE EXPERIMENT STATION, MOSCOW. STATION BULLETIN. 1965. irreg., no.57, 1996. price varies. University of Idaho, Forest, Wildlife and Range Experiment Station, Moscow, ID 83841-1130. TEL 208-885-6673. Ed. Denise Ortiz. R&P contact: Denise Ortiz. circ. 1,000. **Indexed:** Biol.Abstr., Forest.Abstr. **Document type:** academic/scholarly publication, bulletin.
　—Linda Hall.
　Description: Research results on forestry, forest products, fisheries, wildlife, and resource and tourism recreation management.

333.7　　　　　US　　ISSN 0073-4594
UNIVERSITY OF IDAHO. FOREST, WILDLIFE AND RANGE EXPERIMENT STATION, MOSCOW. STATION NOTE. 1965. irreg., no.40, 1990. free. University of Idaho, Forest, Wildlife and Range Experiment Station, Moscow, ID 83844-1130. TEL 208-885-6673. Ed. Denise Ortiz. R&P contact: Denise Ortiz. circ. 1,000. **Indexed:** Biol.Abstr., Forest.Abstr. **Document type:** academic/scholarly publication.
　—Linda Hall.
　Description: Research results on forestry, forest products, fisheries and wildlife.

UNIVERSITY OF MINNESOTA. CENTER FOR NATURAL RESOURCE POLICY AND MANAGEMENT. WORKING PAPERS. see *WATER RESOURCES*

337.7　　　　　AT　　ISSN 0811-580X
UNIVERSITY OF TASMANIA. CENTRE FOR ENVIRONMENTAL STUDIES. PROJECT REPORT. Key Title: Environmental Studies Project Report. 1975. irreg., latest 1992. price varies. University of Tasmania, Centre for Environmental Studies, G.P.O. Box 252C, Hobart, Tas. 7001, Australia. FAX 61-02-202989. Ed. John Todd. circ. 50. (back issues avail.) **Document type:** academic/scholarly publication.
　Description: Records the results of short research projects.
　Refereed Serial

333.7 614.7　　　AT　　ISSN 0313-5780
UNIVERSITY OF TASMANIA. CENTRE FOR ENVIRONMENTAL STUDIES. WORKING PAPERS. 1976. irreg., no.24, 1993. price varies. University of Tasmania, Centre for Environmental Studies, G.P.O. Box 252C, Hobart, Tas. 7001, Australia. TEL 61-02-202834. FAX 61-02-202989. Ed. John Todd. circ. 100. (back issues avail.) **Indexed:** Forest Prod.Abstr. **Document type:** academic/scholarly publication.
　—BLDSC (3791.691000); CISTI.
　Description: Results of long-term research projects.

UNIVERSITY OF WALES. WELSH INSTITUTE OF RURAL STUDIES. WORKING PAPER. see *SOCIOLOGY*

UNIVERSITY OF WATERLOO. DEPARTMENT OF GEOGRAPHY. PUBLICATION SERIES. see *GEOGRAPHY*

333.7　　　　　AU　　ISSN 0042-0484
UNSER NEUSTADT. 1957. q. $8. Wiener Neustaedter Denkmalschutzverein, Schneeberggasse 2, A-2700 Wiener Neustadt, Austria. Ed. Gerta Haring. bk.rev. circ. 600. (tabloid format) **Document type:** bulletin.

UPWELLINGS. see *WATER RESOURCES*

URBAN ECOLOGIST; the journal of urban ecology. see *HOUSING AND URBAN PLANNING*

URBAN FOCUS. see *ENVIRONMENTAL STUDIES*

333.7　　　　　UK　　ISSN 0268-2664
URBAN WILDLIFE NEWS. 1984. q. free. English Nature, Northminster House, Peterborough, Cambs. PE1 1UA, England. TEL 44-1733-4340345. FAX 44-1733-68845. Ed. G.M.A Barker. bk.rev. circ. 5,000. **Document type:** newsletter.
　Description: Contains news items and informational articles on ecological conservation and management in architectural and landscape planning in and around urban areas with announcements of relevant seminars, publications, and events.

URBAN WILDLIFE NEWS. see *BIOLOGY — Zoology*

333.77　　　　　UK
URBAN WILDLIFE REVIEW; the journal of urban nature conservation, habitat and land restoration. 1987. q. £15 to individuals; libraries and institutions £45. Packard Publishing Ltd., Forum House, Stirling Rd., Chichester, W. Sussex PO19 2EN, England. TEL 01243-537977. Ed. Michael Packard. adv.; bk.rev. circ. 350. **Document type:** newsletter.
　—BLDSC (9123.754400); CISTI.
　Formerly (until 1995): Urban Wildlife (ISSN 0951-6425)

333.7　　　　　DK　　ISSN 0908-7761
VAND OG JORD/WATER & SOIL. 1994. bi-m. DKK 315 to individuals worldwide; institutions DKK 600 (effective 1997). (Selskabet for Vand & Jord) Munksgaard International Publishers Ltd., 35 Noerre Soegade, P.O. Box 2148, DK-1016 Copenhagen K, Denmark. TEL 45-33-127030. FAX 45-33-129387. E-mail: fsub@mail.munksgaard.dk. (In N. America: Commerce Place, 350 Main St., Malden, MA 02148-5018. TEL 617-388-8273. FAX 617-388-8274) adv.; bk.rev.; illus.

333.7　　　　　XV　　ISSN 0506-4252
VARSTVO NARAVE/NATURE CONSERVATION. (Text in Slovenian; summaries in English) 1962. a. DM.10. Zavod Slovenije za Varstvo Naravne in Kulturne Dediscine, Plecnikov trg 2, Box 176, 61001 Ljubljana, Slovenia. FAX 38-61-213-120. Ed. Jelka Habjan. adv.; bk.rev.; bibl.; illus. circ. 800.

VATTEN/WATER; tidskrift foer vattenvaard/journal of water management and research. see *WATER RESOURCES*

333.7 628　　　　GW　　ISSN 0300-8665
　　　　　　　　　　　CODEN: SVWLAE
VEREIN FUER WASSER-, BODEN- UND LUFTHYGIENE. SCHRIFTENREIHE. irreg. price varies. Gustav Fischer Verlag, Wollgrasweg 49, 70599 Stuttgart, Germany. TEL 49-711-458030. FAX 49-711-4580334. (Subscr. to: Postfach 720143, 70577 Stuttgart, Germany; U.S. addr.: Lubrecht & Cramer Ltd., 38 Rte. 48, Forestburgh, NY 12777-6400) Ed. F. Meinck. **Indexed:** Food Sci.& Tech.Abstr., Ind.Med. **Document type:** monographic series.
　—BLDSC (8104.000000); CASDDS; CISTI; Linda Hall; SWETS; UMI. **CCC.**

339.49　　　　　GW
VEREIN ZUM SCHUTZ DER BERGWELT. JAHRBUCH. 1900. a. DM.50. Verein zum Schutz der Bergwelt e.V., Praterinsel 5, 80538 Munich, Germany. TEL 49-89-479053. FAX 49-89-479053. Ed. Hans Smettan. circ. controlled. **Indexed:** Biol.Abstr., IBR, Key Word Ind.Wildl.Res. **Document type:** bulletin.
　—CISTI.
　Formerly: Verein zum Schutze der Alpenpflanzen und Tiere. Jahrbuch (ISSN 0083-5625)

VERGEL; revista de ciencias naturales visualizada. see *AGRICULTURE*

VERMONT FISH & WILDLIFE LAWS AND REGULATIONS. see *SPORTS AND GAMES — Outdoor Life*

333.7　　　　　GW　　ISSN 0342-684X
QH77.G3
VEROEFFENTLICHUNGEN FUER NATURSCHUTZ UND LANDSCHAFTSPFLEGE IN BADEN-WUERTTEMBERG. 1925. a. price varies. Landesanstalt fuer Umweltschutz, Postfach 210752, 76157 Karlsruhe, Germany. TEL 49-721-983-0. FAX 49-721-9831456. Pub. Dr. Winfried Krahl. bk.rev. circ. 2,000. **Document type:** academic/scholarly publication, government publication.
　—BLDSC (9194.405000).

VIRGINIA ENVIRONMENTAL LAW JOURNAL. see *LAW*

CONSERVATION

333.7 340   US
VIRGINIA GAME, INLAND FISH AND BOAT LAWS AND REGULATIONS. a. $32.50. Michie, A Division of Reed Elsevier Inc., Box 7587, Charlottesville, VA 22906-7587. TEL 804-972-7566; 800-562-1197. FAX 800-643-1280. E-mail: custserv@michie.com; URL: http://www.michie.com. Ed. George Harley.

VIRGINIA NATIVE PLANT SOCIETY. BULLETIN. see *BIOLOGY — Botany*

333.7   US
VIRGINIA OUTDOORS PLAN (YEAR). 1965. quinquennial. $20. Department of Conservation & Recreation, Division of Planning and Recreation Resources, 203 Governor St., Ste. 326, Richmond, VA 23219. TEL 804-786-2556. FAX 804-371-7899. R&P contact: John Davy. illus.; tr.lit. **Document type:** government publication.
Formerly: Virginia's Common Wealth.
Description: Attempts to project future needs and to identify emerging trends and issues that may have an effect upon open space, natural resources and outdoor recreational resources, planning and management.

639.9   US   ISSN 0042-6792
SK137
VIRGINIA WILDLIFE. 1947. m. $10. Department of Game and Inland Fisheries, Box 11104, Richmond, VA 23230-1104. TEL 804-367-1000. FAX 804-367-0488. E-mail: rjefferson@dgif/index.htm. Ed. Riche Jefferson. R&P contact: Rich Jefferson. bk.rev.; illus., index. circ. 40,000. **Indexed:** Biol.Abstr., Biol.Dig., Sport Fish.Abstr., Wild.Rev. **Document type:** government publication.
—Linda Hall; UnCover.
Description: Covers resource management, hunting and fishing.

333.7 614.7 790.1   US
VIRGINIA WILDLIFE FEDERATION. FEDERATION RECORD. 1938. m. $5. Virginia Wildlife Federation, Inc., 1001 E. Broad St., No. LL5, Richmond, VA 23219-1928. TEL 804-648-3136. Nancy J. Loveless. circ. 15,000. (tabloid format) **Document type:** newspaper.

VISION (STAMFORD). see *ENVIRONMENTAL STUDIES*

333.79   SA   ISSN 1022-1115
VISION OF WILDLIFE, ECOTOURISM AND THE ENVIRONMENT IN SOUTHERN AFRICA. 1994. a. R.99($22) Endangered Wildlife Trust, Private X11, Parkview 2122, South Africa. TEL 27-11-4861102. FAX 27-11-4861506. Ed. David Holt Biddle. adv. contact: Lynn Ras. illus.; maps.

VITAL SIGNS (YEAR); the environmental trends that are shaping our future. see *ENVIRONMENTAL STUDIES*

VOGEL UND UMWELT; Zeitschrift fuer Vogelkunde und Naturschutz in Hessen. see *BIOLOGY — Ornithology*

VOGELS. see *BIOLOGY — Ornithology*

333.78   US   ISSN 0898-6193
THE VOICE OF WALDEN. 1981. q. membership. Walden Forever Wild, Inc., Box 275, Concord, MA 01742. TEL 508-429-2839. FAX 860-487-1629. Ed. Mary P. Sherwood. bk.rev.; bibl.; illus.; circ. controlled. (back issues avail.) **Document type:** newsletter.
Description: Provides support for changing the status of Walden from a recreational park to a nature-preserve sanctuary.

VULTURE NEWS. see *BIOLOGY — Ornithology*

W A N D BULLETIN. (Women's Action for Nuclear Disarmament) see *WOMEN'S INTERESTS*

639.9   US   ISSN 1062-0435
W E A LEGEND; developing outdoor leaders and educating wilderness users. 1988. q. $30 membership for individuals; institutions $100; students $15. Wilderness Education Association, Colorado State University, Department of Natural Resource Recreation and Tourism, Colorado State University, Ft. Collins, CO 80523. TEL 970-223-6252. FAX 970-223-6252. E-mail: wea@lamar.colostate.edu. Ed. Kent Clement. adv. contact: Kent Clement. bk.rev.; circ. 2,000 (paid). **Document type:** newsletter.
Description: Promotes wilderness education and preservation through leadership training in the outdoor classroom.
Refereed Serial

639.9   JA   ISSN 0916-7846
W W F. (World Wide Fund) (Text in Japanese) 1971. m. 300 Yen per no. Sekai Shizen Hogo Kinkin Nihon linkai - World Wide Fund for Nature Japan, 1-14 Shiba 3-chome, Minato-ku, Tokyo 105, Japan.

W W F INDIA QUARTERLY. (World Wide Fund for Nature - India) see *ENVIRONMENTAL STUDIES*

639.9 614.7   UK
W W F NEWS. 1962. q. £19 membership. World Wide Fund For Nature, Weyside Park, Godalming, Surrey GU7 1XR, England. TEL 01483-426444. FAX 01483-426409. Ed. Philip Smith. bk.rev. circ. 180,000. (back issues avail.) **Indexed:** Environ.Abstr. **Document type:** newspaper.
Formerly: World Wildlife News (ISSN 0952-3170)

333.7 613.1   GW   ISSN 0922-7989
WADDEN SEA NEWSLETTER. (Text in English) 1989. q. Common Wadden Sea Secretariat, Virchowstr. 1, 26382 Wilhelmshaven, Germany. TEL 49-4421-9108-0. FAX 49-4421-910830. URL: http://www.de/cwss/. Ed. Bettina Reineking. bk.rev. circ. 1,200. **Document type:** newsletter.
—BLDSC (9261.181000).

333.7 949.23   NE   ISSN 0166-4824
WADDENBULLETIN. 1965. 4/yr. fl.37.50. Waddenvereniging, Postbus 90, 8860 AB Harlingen, Netherlands. TEL 31-45178-15541. FAX 31-45178-17977. Ed. Jan Abrahamse. adv.; bk.rev. circ. 60,000. **Document type:** bulletin.
—SWETS.
Description: Covers conservation and cultural history issues relating to the Waddensee and the North coast of Holland.

WAKOU; pour les petits curieux de nature. see *CHILDREN AND YOUTH — For*

WALIA. see *ENVIRONMENTAL STUDIES*

WAPITI; un oeil fute sur la nature. see *CHILDREN AND YOUTH — For*

WASHINGTON (STATE). DEPARTMENT OF FISH AND WILDLIFE. ANNUAL REPORT. see *FISH AND FISHERIES*

WASHINGTON LAND USE AND ENVIRONMENTAL PRACTICE. see *LAW*

333.78   US
WASHINGTON RECREATION AND PARK ASSOCIATION. SYLLABUS. 1969. 10/yr. membership. Washington Recreation and Park Association, Inc., 350 S. 333rd St., Ste. 103, Federal Way, WA 98003. TEL 206-874-1283. FAX 206-661-3929. Ed. Jim Webster. R&P contact: Jim Webster. adv. contact: Jim Webster. bk.rev.; charts; illus. circ. 1,050. **Document type:** newsletter.
Former titles: Washington Recreation and Park Association. Bulletin; Washington Recreation and Park Society. News (ISSN 0042-9805)

WASTELINE. see *ENVIRONMENTAL STUDIES — Waste Management*

WATER NEWSLETTER; water supply, waste disposal, conservation, pollution. see *WATER RESOURCES*

WATER RESOURCES JOURNAL. see *WATER RESOURCES*

WATER, WOODS & WILDLIFE. see *BIOLOGY — Botany*

WATERFOWL. see *BIOLOGY — Ornithology*

333.7   US
WATERSHED. 1994. q. $15 membership. Friends of the Santa Clara River, 660 Randy Dr., Newbury Park, CA 91320-3036. TEL 805-498-4323. Ed. Barbara Wampole. **Document type:** newsletter.

WATERSHED FOCUS. see *ENVIRONMENTAL STUDIES — Pollution*

333.7   CN   ISSN 1188-360X
WATERSHED SENTINEL. 1990. 6/yr. Can.$12($16); newsstand price: Can.$3.50. P.O. Box 39, Whaletown, BC V0P 1Z0, Canada. TEL 604-935-6992; 604-935-6992. E-mail: wss@rfu.org. Ed. Delores Broten; Pub. Delores Broten. adv.; B&W page Can.$170; trim 8 1/2 x 10. bk.rev.; charts, illus. circ. 3,000. (back issues avail.)
Description: Focus on forestry, toxics, pulp and paper and ozone.

333.7   GW   ISSN 0256-7059
WATTENMEER INTERNATIONAL. 1983. q. free. Umweltstiftung W W F Deutschland, Norderstr. 3, 25813 Husum, Germany. TEL 49-4841-62073. FAX 49-4841-4736. E-mail: husum@wwf.de. Ed. Hans-Ulrich Roesner. R&P contact: Sybille Mielke. **Document type:** newsletter.

WEIDWERK. see *SPORTS AND GAMES*

333.7   US   ISSN 0198-6600
SK351   CODEN: WPAAED
WESTERN ASSOCIATION OF FISH AND WILDLIFE AGENCIES. PROCEEDINGS. 1940. a. $10. Western Association of Fish and Wildlife Agencies, c/o Sandra J. Wolfe, Dept. of Fish & Game, 1416 Ninth St., Sacramento, CA 95814. TEL 916-653-9388. cum.index: 1940-1969. circ. 400. (processed) **Indexed:** Forest.Abstr., Forest Prod.Abstr., Sport Fish.Abstr., Wild.Rev., Zoo.Rec. **Document type:** proceedings.
—BLDSC (6833.800000).
Formerly: Western Association of State Game and Fish Commissioners. Proceedings (ISSN 0085-8102)

333.7   AT   ISSN 0815-4465
S934.A8
WESTERN AUSTRALIA. DEPARTMENT OF CONSERVATION AND LAND MANAGEMENT. LANDSCOPE. 1970. 4/yr. Aus.$24 (foreign Aus.$44) (effective 1997). Department of Conservation and Land Management Locked Bag 104, Dertley Delivery Centre, W.A. 6893, Australia. TEL 61-9-334-0333. FAX 61-9-334-0498. circ. 15,000. **Indexed:** Forest.Abstr., Rural Recreat.Tour.Abstr., Sport Fish.Abstr., Wild.Rev., World Agri.Econ. & Rural Sociol.Abstr.
—UnCover.
Formerly (until 1985): Western Australia. Forest Department. Forest Focus (ISSN 0049-7320)
Description: General information on conservation, forests and national parks.

333.7 614.7   AT
WESTERN AUSTRALIA. DEPARTMENT OF ENVIRONMENTAL PROTECTION. ANNUAL REPORT. 1994. a. free. Department of Environmental Protection, 8th Fl., Westralia Sq., 141 St. George's Terr., Australia. FAX 61-9-2227000. Ed. Rodney Hughes. **Document type:** government publication.

333.7 614.7   AT
WESTERN AUSTRALIA. ENVIRONMENTAL PROTECTION AUTHORITY. ANNUAL REPORT. 1972. a. free. Environmental Protection Authority, Westralia Sq., 141 St. George's Terr., Perth, W.A. 6000, Australia. FAX 61-9-322-1598. circ. 1,000. **Indexed:** AESIS. **Document type:** government publication.
Formerly: Western Australia. Department of Conservation and Environment. Annual Report; Which incorporated: Western Australia. Conservation and Environment Council. Annual Report; Formerly: Western Australia. Environmental Protection Council. Annual Report.

WESTERN AUSTRALIA. FISHERIES DEPARTMENT. REPORT. see *FISH AND FISHERIES*

333.7   US   ISSN 0083-8934
WESTERN LANDS AND WATERS SERIES. 1959. irreg. price varies. Arthur H. Clark Co., Box 14707, Spokane, WA 99214. Ed. Robert A. Clark. R&P contact: Robert A. Clark. index. **Document type:** monographic series.

WHALEWATCH. see *ANIMAL WELFARE*

340   US   ISSN 0273-4419
QL737.C4
WHALEWATCHER. 1967. q. $35 membership. American Cetacean Society, Box 1391, San Pedro CA 90733-1391. TEL 310-548-6279. FAX 310-548-6950. E-mail: acs@pobox.com. Ed. Maura Leos. adv.; bk.rev.; charts; illus.; index. circ. 2,000. **Document type:** academic/scholarly publication.
—BLDSC (9309.554500).

WHITESHELL ECHO. see *SPORTS AND GAMES — Outdoor Life*

CONSERVATION

36.8   UK   ISSN 0260-7492
. CAT. 1977. s-a. £5 (foreign £7). Cat Survival
rust, The Centre, Codicote Rd., Welwyn, Herts AL6
TU, England. TEL 44-143-871-6873.
AX 44-143-871-7535. Ed. T. Moore. adv. contact:
. Watkiss. bk.rev.; circ. 1,800 (paid). **Document
ype:** academic/scholarly publication.
Refereed Serial

14.7   US   ISSN 1055-1166
H75.A1   CODEN: WIEAEI
D EARTH. 1991. q. $25 to individuals (Canada
30; elsewhere $45). Cenozoic Society, Inc., Box
55, Richmond, VT 05477. TEL 802-434-4077.
d. John Davis; Pub. Dave Foreman. R&P contact:
om Butler. adv. contact: Tom Butler. bk.rev. circ.
,000. (also avail. in microform from UMI) **Indexed:**
lt.Press Ind., Environ.Abstr., Environ.Per.Bibl.
1993-), Zoo.Rec. **Document type:**
cademic/scholarly publication.
—BLDSC (9317.208000). **CCC.**
  Description: Serves academic and grassroots
lements within the conservation movement:
dvocates the restoration and protection of natural
iodiversity and wilderness.

D FLOWER NOTES. see *BIOLOGY — Botany*

D HORSE AND BURRO DIARY. see *ANIMAL WELFARE*

333.7   CN   ISSN 1192-6287
D LANDS ADVOCATE. 1968. q. Can.$25 individual
nembership; institutional Can.$100. Alberta
Vilderness Association, Box 6398, Sta. D, Calgary,
AB T2P 2E1, Canada. TEL 403-283-2025.
AX 403-270-2743. E-mail: awa@web.net. Ed.
Vendy Adams. adv.; bk.rev.; illus.; stat. circ. 4,000.
tabloid format; back issues avail.) **Indexed:**
iportsearch. **Document type:** newsletter.
  Former titles: Wilderness Alberta (ISSN
0830-8284); Alberta Wilderness Association.
Newsletter (ISSN 0380-562X)
  Description: Covers conservation issues of concern
o Albertans, with the aim to protect wilderness
areas.

D OUTDOOR WORLD (W.O.W.). see *CHILDREN AND
YOUTH — For*

333.7   US
D RANCH REVIEW. 1991. q. $15. Tim Haugh, Ed. &
Pub., Box 91, Gulnare, CO 81042. **Document type:**
newsletter.
  Description: Offers in-depth profiles of grass-roots
environmental groups.

DBIOLOGIE. see *BIOLOGY — Zoology*

639.9   US   ISSN 0194-3030
DERNESS RECORD. 1976. m. $30. California
Vilderness Coalition, 2655 Portage Bay E., Ste. 5,
Davis, CA 95616. TEL 916-758-0380.
AX 916-758-0382. E-mail: cwc@wheel.dcn.davis.
ca.us; URL: http://www.dcn.davis.ca.us/~cwc. Ed.
Herb Walker. R&P contact: Herb Walker. adv.
contact: Jim Eaton. bk.rev.; illus.; circ. 3,000 (paid).
Document type: newsletter.
●Also available online.
  Description: Covers California's existing and
potential wilderness areas.
Refereed Serial

333.7   PK
LDFIELDS.* (Text in English) m. Rs.2 per no. 15
Dayaram Gidumac Road, Karachi 3, Pakistan. Ed.
Mansoorul Hasan. adv.

333.7   US   ISSN 1074-942X
LDFIRE MAGAZINE (TITUSVILLE);* a "plus" network
magazine. 1961. q. $16 (effective 1996). Wild Fire
Publishing, Inc., Box 759, Titusville, FL
32781-0759. URL: http://www.onetinc.com/col/
iteweb/wildfire.html. Ed. Elizabeth Robinson; Pub.
Rick McBride. adv.; bk.rev. circ. 10,000. (also avail.
in microfilm from UMI; back issues avail.) **Indexed:**
Key Word Ind.Wildl.Res. **Document type:** consumer
publication.
  Former titles (until Dec. 1995): Wildfire (Spokane)
(ISSN 0889-7867); (until 1984): Many Smokes
(ISSN 0025-2670)
  Description: Covers earth issues as it relates to
human beings.

333.78   CN   ISSN 0316-3350
WILDLAND NEWS. 1968. q. Can.$35. Wildlands
League, 380-401 Richmond St. W., Toronto, ON
M5V 3A8, Canada. TEL 416-971-9453.
FAX 416-979-3155. E-mail: wildland@web.apc.org;
URL: http://web.idirect.can/~wildland. Ed. Sarah Ives.
R&P contact: Tim Gray. adv.; bk.rev.; illus.; circ.
4,000 (paid). **Document type:** newsletter.
  Description: News and views on current wilderness,
forest management, forest policy and park issues in
Ontario.

333.7   US
WILDLANDS NEWS. 1973. q. free. Plymouth County
Wildlands Trust, Box 2282, Duxbury, MA 02331.
TEL 617-934-9018. Ed. Lois Woods. circ. 1,300
(controlled). **Document type:** newsletter.

333.7 796.95   US
WILDLIFE AND BOATING SAFETY LAWS OF TENNESSEE.
a. $18. Michie, A Division of Reed Elsevier Inc., Box
7587, Charlottesville, VA 22906-7587.
TEL 804-972-7566; 800-562-1197.
FAX 800-643-1280. E-mail: custserv@michie.com;
URL: http://www.michie.com. Ed. George Harley.

639.9 591   AT   ISSN 0043-5481
QL338
WILDLIFE AUSTRALIA. 1963. q. Aus.$25 (foreign
Aus.$35). Wildlife Preservation Society of
Queensland, 2nd Fl., 133 George St., Brisbane, Qld.
4000, Australia. TEL 61-7-221-0194.
FAX 61-7-221-0701. Ed. Michelle Ryan. R&P
contact: Michelle Ryan. TEL 61-7-38407602. adv.
contact: Michelle Ryan. bk.rev.; illus. circ. 6,500.
Indexed: Biol.Abstr., Gdlns, Key Word Ind.Wildl.Res.
Document type: consumer publication.
—UnCover.

WILDLIFE BIOLOGY. see *BIOLOGY — Zoology*

639.9 333.95   US   ISSN 1048-4949
QL1   CODEN: WICOEG
WILDLIFE CONSERVATION. 1897. bi-m. $17.98
(effective 1995). Wildlife Conservation Society,
Wildlife Conservation Park, Bronx, NY 10460.
TEL 718-220-5121. FAX 718-584-2625. (Subscr.
to: Box 14267, Dayton, OH 45413) (Affiliate:
Wildlife Conservation Society) Ed. Joan Downs; Pub.
Joan Downs. adv. contact: Charles Merber. bk.rev.;
illus.; index; circ. 150,000 (paid). (also avail. in
microfiche from UMI; back issues avail.) **Indexed:**
Biol.Abstr., Biol.Dig., Environ.Per.Bibl. (1991-),
Gen.Sci.Ind., Key Word Ind.Wildl.Res., Sport
Fish.Abstr., Wild.Rev., Zoo.Rec. **Document type:**
consumer publication.
—BLDSC (9317.330000); KR SourceOne; Linda
Hall; SWETS; UnCover.
  Formerly (until 1989): Animal Kingdom (ISSN
0003-3537); Which was formed by the 1942
merger of: New York Zoological Society. Journal &
New York Zoological Society. Bulletin.
  Description: Popular articles about wildlife
conservation worldwide, for the general public.
Refereed Serial

WILDLIFE CRUSADER. see *SPORTS AND GAMES —
Outdoor Life*

639.9   US   ISSN 0043-549X
SK351
WILDLIFE IN NORTH CAROLINA. 1938. m. $7.50. North
Carolina Wildlife Resources Commission, Archdale
Bldg., 512 N. Salisbury St., Raleigh, NC
27604-1188. TEL 919-733-7380. Ed. Jim Dean.
bk.rev.; charts; illus.; index. circ. 80,000. **Indexed:**
Sport Fish.Abstr., Wild.Rev.
—UnCover.
  Description: Articles on wildlife, the outdoors,
hunting, fishing and conservation.

333.7 799   US   ISSN 0084-0173
QL1   CODEN: WLMOAF
WILDLIFE MONOGRAPHS. 1958. irreg., no.128, 1995.
$120 (foreign $130) (effective 1997) (includes
Journal of Wildlife Management). Wildlife Society,
5410 Grosvenor Ln., Bethesda, MD 20814-2197.
TEL 301-897-9770. FAX 301-530-2471. Ed. Roy
L. Kirkpatrick. circ. 7,000. (back issues avail.)
Indexed: Biol.Abstr., Curr.Adv.Ecol.Sci., Curr.Cont.,
Ecol.Abstr., Energy Ind., Energy Info.Abstr.,
Environ.Per.Bibl. (1983-), Geo.Abstr., Ind.Sci.Rev.,
Ind.Vet., Key Word Ind.Wildl.Res., Nutr.Abstr.,
Sci.Cit.Ind., Sport Fish.Abstr., Vet.Bull., Wild.Rev.,
Wildlife & Conserv.Biol.Abstr. (1958-), Zoo.Rec.
Document type: monographic series.
—BLDSC (9317.450000); CASDDS; Linda Hall;
SWETS; UnCover.
Refereed Serial

333.7   AT
**WILDLIFE PRESERVATION SOCIETY OF QUEENSLAND.
NEWSLETTER.** 1968. q. Aus.$25. Wildlife
Preservation Society of Queensland, 2nd Fl., 133
George St., Brisbane, Qld. 4000, Australia.
TEL 61-7-2210194. FAX 61-7-2210701. R&P
contact: David Andrew. adv. contact: David Andrew.
Document type: newsletter.

WILDLIFE REHABILITATION TODAY. see *VETERINARY
SCIENCE*

639.9   CN   ISSN 1188-5106
WILDLIFE RESCUE. 1979. q. Can.$20 individual
membership. Wildlife Rescue Association of British
Columbia, 5216 Glencarin Dr., Burnaby, BC V5B
3C1, Canada. TEL 604-526-7275.
FAX 604-524-2890. E-mail: wra@vcn.bc.ca; URL:
http://www.vcn.bc.ca/wra. Ed. David Wells. R&P
contact: Jim Heaton. adv.; bk.rev.; circ. 2,000
(controlled). (looseleaf format) **Document type:**
newsletter.
  Description: Reviews the organization's activities in
wildlife rehabilitation and education.
Refereed Serial

639.9   AT   ISSN 1035-3712
QL338   CODEN: WRESEX
WILDLIFE RESEARCH. 1974. bi-m. Aus.$320($320)
(effective 1998). (C.S.I.R.O. Australia) C.S.I.R.O.
Publishing, 150 Oxford St., Collingwood, Vic. 3066,
Australia. TEL 61-3-96627622.
FAX 61-3-96627611. E-mail: dwm@publish.csiro.
au; URL: http://www.publish.csiro.au/journals/wr.
Eds. D.W. Morton, S.L. Farrer. adv.; charts; illus.;
index. circ. 1,350. (also avail. in microform from
UMI; back issues avail.) **Indexed:** ASCA, Biol.Abstr.,
Curr.Adv.Ecol.Sci., Curr.Cont., Ecol.Abstr., Energy
Ind., Energy Info.Abstr., Environ.Abstr., Forest.Abstr.,
Forest Prod.Abstr., Geo.Abstr., Helminthol.Abstr.,
Ind.Sci.Rev., Ind.Vet., Key Word Ind.Wildl.Res., Maize
Abstr., Nutr.Abstr., Sci.Cit.Ind., Sci.Cit.Ind, Seed
Abstr., Sport Fish.Abstr., Triticale Abstr., Vet.Bull.,
Wild.Rev., Zoo.Rec. **Document type:**
academic/scholarly publication.
●Also available online.
—BLDSC (9317.466500); CASDDS; CIS; CISTI;
EMDOCS; Genuine Article; Linda Hall; SWETS; UMI;
UnCover. **CCC.**
  Former titles: Australian Wildlife Research (ISSN
0310-7833); C S I R O Wildlife Research (ISSN
0007-9103)
  Description: Covers biology and management of
wild vertebrates, primarily in Australia.

590 333.954   US
WILDLIFE RESEARCH REPORT. irreg., latest no.90-1.
Wildlife Resource Agency, Box 40747, Nashville, TN
37204. TEL 615-781-6502. FAX 615-741-4606.

CONSERVATION

639.9 591 US ISSN 0091-7648
SK351 CODEN: WLSBA6
WILDLIFE SOCIETY BULLETIN. 1973. q. $90 (foreign $100) (effective 1997). Wildlife Society, 5410 Grosvenor Ln., Bethesda, MD 20814-2197. TEL 301-897-9770. FAX 301-530-2471. Ed. Edwin J. JOnes. bibl.; index. circ. 6,000. (back issues avail.; reprint service avail. from UMI) **Indexed:** ASCA, Bibl.Agri., Biol.Abstr., Curr.Adv.Ecol.Sci., Curr.Cont., Ecol.Abstr., Energy Ind., Energy Info.Abstr., Environ.Per.Bibl. (1983-), Excerp.Med., Geo.Abstr.H.G., Geo.Abstr.P.G., Ind.Sci.Rev., Ind.Vet., InterActions Bibl. (1989-), Key Word Ind.Wildl.Res., Risk Abstr., Rural Recreat.Tour.Abstr., Sci.Cit.Ind., Sel.Water Res.Abstr., Sport Fish.Abstr., SSCI, W.R.C.Inf., Wild.Rev., Wildlife & Conserv.Biol.Abstr. (1973-), World Agri.Econ. & Rural Sociol.Abstr., Zoo.Rec. **Document type:** academic/scholarly publication.
—BLDSC (9317.488000); CISTI; EMDOCS; Linda Hall; SWETS; UnCover.
Refereed Serial

333.7 US
WILDLIFE WATCH. q. $15 membership. International Wildlife Coalition, 70 E. Falmouth Hwy., East Falmouth, MA 02536. TEL 508-548-8328. Ed. Stephen Best. (back issues avail.)
Description: Describes IWC's wildlife rescue, rehabilitation and protection programs, and provides updates on critical issues facing wildlife around the world for IWC members.

639.9 US ISSN 0163-6359
WILDLIFER. 1939. bi-m. $40 membership (effective 1997). Wildlife Society, 5410 Grosvenor Ln., Bethesda, MD 20814-2197. TEL 301-897-9770. FAX 301-530-2471. Ed. Harry E. Hodgdon. **Document type:** newsletter.
—Linda Hall.
Formerly: Wildlife Society News (ISSN 0043-552X)

333.7 NE
WINDMOLEN. 1975. 4/yr. fl.20 membership. Vereniging tot Behoud van Molens in Zeeland, Ten Ankerweg 43, 4691 GV Tholen, Netherlands. Ed. F.D.M. Weemaes. bk.rev. circ. 40.

333.7 US
WINGS (PORTLAND); essays on invertebrate conservation. 1987. 2/yr. $25 membership. Xerces Society, 4828 S.E. Hawthorne Blvd., Portland, OR 97215-3252. TEL 503-232-6639. FAX 503-233-6794. E-mail: xerces@teleport.com. Ed. Mary Troychak. R&P contact: Mary Troychak. bk.rev.; circ. 5,000 (paid).
Description: Dedicated to protecting invertebrates as the major component of biological diversity.

333.7 628 US ISSN 0084-0564
SK463 CODEN: WDNTAD
WISCONSIN. DEPARTMENT OF NATURAL RESOURCES. TECHNICAL BULLETIN. Key Title: Technical Bulletin - Department of Natural Resources (Madison). 1950. irreg. free. Department of Natural Resources, Box 7921, Madison, WI 53707. TEL 608-266-3369. FAX 608-264-6293. E-mail: sperld@dnr.state.wi.us; URL: http://www.dnr.state.wi.us/wnr. Ed. David L. Sperling. R&P contact: David L. Sperling. circ. 1,500. **Indexed:** Biol.Abstr., Ocean.Abstr., Pollut.Abstr., Sport Fish.Abstr., Wild.Rev., Zoo.Rec. **Document type:** government publication.
—CISTI; Linda Hall; UnCover.

WISCONSIN ENVIRONMENTAL DECADE. see *ENVIRONMENTAL STUDIES*

333.7 628 US ISSN 0736-2277
HC107.W6
WISCONSIN NATURAL RESOURCES. 1936. bi-m. $8.97. Department of Natural Resources, Box 7921, Madison, WI 53707. TEL 608-266-1510. Ed. David L. Sperling. bk.rev.; illus.; index. circ. 82,000. **Indexed:** Biol.Abstr., Sport Fish.Abstr., Wild.Rev. **Document type:** government publication.
—Linda Hall; UnCover.
Formerly (until 1977): Wisconsin Conservation Bulletin (ISSN 0043-6410)

639.9 US
THE WOLF SANCTUARY REVIEW. 1972. q. $25 (foreign $15) (effective 1997). Washington University Tyson Research Center, Wild Canid Survival Research Center, Box 760, Eureka, MO 63025. TEL 314-938-5900. FAX 314-938-6490. URL: http://www.wolfsanctuary.org. Ed. Sarah Newman; Pub. Barbara Miller. R&P contact: Susan Lindsey. bk.rev.; circ. 3,000 (paid). **Document type:** newsletter.
Former titles: Wolf Sanctuary Newsletter; (until 1985): Wolf Sanctuary's Bulletin; W C S R C News; W C S R C Bulletin.
Description: Offical publication of the WCSRC. Summarizes captive breeding and reintroductions of federally sanctioned recovery programs (and WCSRC animals) as well as general (i.e. educational) activities of the organization.

WOMEN IN NATURAL RESOURCES; a journal of professional women in forestry, wildlife, fisheries, range, soils and the social sciences as they pertain to natural resources. see *WOMEN'S INTERESTS*

333.7 US ISSN 0030-7157
SK461
WONDERFUL WEST VIRGINIA. 1936. m. $15. Department of Natural Resources, State Capitol, Charleston, WV 25305. TEL 304-558-9152. Ed. Nancy Clark. illus. circ. 60,000. (also avail. in microfiche from UMI)
Formerly: Outdoor West Virginia.

WORLD BIRDWATCH. see *BIOLOGY — Ornithology*

333.7 SZ ISSN 1027-0965
QH75.A1
WORLD CONSERVATION. (Editions in English, French, Spanish) 1952. q. 66 SFr.($60) International Union for Conservation of Nature and Natural Resources, Rue Mauverney 28, CH-1196 Gland, Switzerland. TEL 41-22-9990001. FAX 41-22-9990002. TELEX 419624-IUCN-CH. Ed. Nikki Meith. bk.rev.; index. circ. 6,000. **Indexed:** Biol.Abstr., Environ.Abstr., Key Word Ind.Wildl.Res. **Document type:** bulletin.
—CIS; CISTI; UnCover.
Formerly (until 1996): I U C N Bulletin (ISSN 0020-9058)

333.7 US ISSN 0092-0908
S920
WORLD DIRECTORY OF ENVIRONMENTAL ORGANIZATIONS; a handbook of national and international organizations and programs, governmental and non-governmental, concerned with protecting the earth's resources. 1973. irreg., 5th ed., 1996. $60 (foreign $65; £50). California Institute of Public Affairs, Box 189040, Sacramento, CA 95818. TEL 916-442-CIPA. FAX 916-442-2478. (Published in the U.K. by: Earthscan Publications Ltd., 120 Pentonville Rd., London N1 9JN, England. TEL 44-171-278-0433. FAX 44-171-278-1142) (Co-sponsors: Sierra Club; International Union for Conservation of Nature and Natural Resources; IUCN - The World Conservation Union) (Affiliate: The Claremont Graduate School) Ed. Thaddeus C. Trzyna. circ. 3,000. **Document type:** directory.
Description: Provides a comprehensive global guide to organizations concerned with the environment and natural resources, covering more than 2,100 governmental and nongovernmental organizations in over 200 countries.

WORLD GUIDE TO COVERED BRIDGES. see *HISTORY — History Of North And South America*

WORLD MAGAZINE; the magazine of mankind. see *TRAVEL AND TOURISM*

639.9 SA
WORLD OF BIRDS WILDLIFE SANCTUARY C.C., SOUTH AFRICA. NEWSLETTER. 1978. m. R.150. World of Birds Wildlife Sanctuary C.C., Valley Rd., Hout Bay 7800, South Africa. TEL 27-21-7902730. FAX 27-21-7904839. Ed. Walter Mangold. circ. 1,000. **Document type:** newsletter.

WORLD RAINFOREST REPORT. see *ENVIRONMENTAL STUDIES*

WORLD RESOURCE REVIEW. see *ENVIRONMENTAL STUDIES*

333.7 UK ISSN 0887-0403
HC10 CODEN: WORSE9
WORLD RESOURCES (YEAR). 1986. biennial, latest 1994. $21.95 paperbound. (World Resources Institute) Oxford University Press, Walton St., Oxford OX2 6DP, England. TEL 44-1865-56767. FAX 44-1865-56646. (Subscr. in US to: Oxford University Press Inc., 2001 Evans Rd., Cary, NC 27513. TEL 919-677-0977. FAX 919-677-1714) **Indexed:** SRI. **Document type:** academic/scholarly publication.
—CISTI.

333.78 US
WORLD RIVERS REVIEW. bi-m. $35 to individuals; institutions $100; non-profit organizations $50. International Rivers Network, 1857 Berkeley Way, Berkeley, CA 94703. TEL 510-848-1155. FAX 510-848-1008. E-mail: irn@irn.org; URL: http://www.irn.org. Ed. Lori Pottinger. bk.rev. (back issues avail.) **Document type:** newsletter.
Formerly: International Rivers Network (ISSN 0890-6211)

WORLD WATCH; working for a sustainable future. see *ENVIRONMENTAL STUDIES*

WORLDWATCH PAPERS. see *ENVIRONMENTAL STUDIES*

639.9 591 US ISSN 0043-9819
CODEN: WYWLA
WYOMING WILDLIFE. 1936. m. $10. Game and Fish Department, 5400 Bishop Blvd., Cheyenne, WY 82006. TEL 307-777-4544. Ed. Chris Madson. bk.rev.; charts; illus.; index. circ. 40,000. (also avail. in magnetic tape; back issues avail.) **Indexed:** Biol.Abstr., Sport Fish.Abstr., Wlld.Rev., Zoo.Rec. **Document type:** bulletin, government publication.
—BLDSC (9365.550000); UnCover.
Formerly: Wyoming Game and Fish Commission. Bulletin.

YEDIOT KEREN KAYEMIT LEYISRAEL. see *FORESTS AND FORESTRY*

333.95 NZ ISSN 1171-4131
YELLOW-EYED PENGUIN NEWS. 1989. s-a. NZ.$15 to individuals; students $8. Yellow-Eyed Penguin Trust, P.O. Box 5409, Dundin, New Zealand. TEL 64-3-4790011. FAX 64-3-2790019. Ed. Cla Freser. charts; illus.; maps. circ. 2,000. **Document type:** newsletter.
Description: Covers conservation of the yellow-eye penguin in New Zealand.

333.7 IS ISSN 0334-0554
YIDION; rashut shmuret hateva. 1975. 3/yr. free. Nature Reserves Authority, Rehov Yermeyahn 78, Jerusalem 94 467, Israel. TEL 972-2-5005444. FAX 972-2-5374887. Ed. Ms Dina Winstaine. bk.rev. circ. 500.
Description: Information on the Israeli nature reserves and the activities of the Authority.

333.79 SA ISSN 1022-5293
YOUNG CUSTOS. Afrikaans edition: Jong Custos (ISSN 1022-5285) 1993. bi-m. R.47. National Parks Board - Nasionale Parkeraad, P.O. Box 787, Pretoria 0001, South Africa. TEL 27-12-343-9770. FAX 27-12-343-9958. E-mail: janines@parks-sa.c za. illus.; maps. **Document type:** academic/scholarly publication.

354.689 ZA ISSN 0084-4586
ZAMBIA. COMMISSION FOR THE PRESERVATION OF NATURAL AND HISTORICAL MONUMENTS AND RELICS. ANNUAL REPORT. 1948. a. K.3.00. Commission for the Preservation of Natural and Historical Monuments and Relics, P.O. Box 60124, Livingstone, Zambia. **Document type:** government publication.

333.7 ZA
ZAMBIA. NATIONAL HERITAGE CONSERVATION COMMISSION. ANNUAL REPORT. 1948. a. National Heritage Conservation Commission, P.O. Box 60124, Livingstone, Zambia. TEL 260-320354. FAX 260-324509. Ed. Maxwell Zulu. R&P contact: Maxwell Zulu. adv. contact: Maxwell Zulu. **Document type:** government publication.

333.7 ZA
ZAMBIA. NATURAL RESOURCES DEPARTMENT. ANNUAL REPORT. 1964-1973; resumed 1976. a. K.200. Zambia Government Printing Department, P.O. Box 30136, Lusaka, Zambia. **Document type:** government publication.
  Former titles: Zambia. Natural Resources Advisory Board. Annual Report (ISSN 0377-1709); Zambia. Office of the Conservateur of Natural Resources. Annual Report (ISSN 0377-3906); Zambia. Natural Resources Board. Annual Report (ISSN 0084-4993)

333.7 ZA
ZAMBIA HERITAGE. 1991. 2/yr. $4. National Heritage Conservation Commission, P.O. Box 60124, Livingstone, Zambia. TEL 260-320354. FAX 260-324509. Ed. Maxwell Zulu. R&P contact: Maxwell Zulu. adv. contact: Maxwell Zulu. circ. 2,000 (paid).

ZEITSCHRIFT FUER OEKOLOGIE UND NATURSCHUTZ. see ENVIRONMENTAL STUDIES

333.7 NE ISSN 1383-3340
ZELFZWICHTER. 1976. q. fl.25 membership. Vereniging van Vrienden van de Groninger Molens, Mezenlaan 43, 9663 CM Nieuwe Pekela, Netherlands. (Co-sponsor: Stichting Groninger Molenvrienden) Ed. H.A. Hachmer. bk.rev. circ. 800. **Document type:** bulletin.
  Description: Publishes news and information on the history and restoration of mills in the Groningen area.

333.7 RH
ZIMBABWE. MINISTRY OF LANDS AND NATURAL RESOURCES. REPORT OF THE SECRETARY FOR LANDS AND NATURAL RESOURCES. 1968. a. Z.$1.05. Government Printer, P.O. Box CY 341, Causeway, Harare, Zimbabwe. stat. circ. 400. **Document type:** government publication.
  Supersedes in part: Rhodesia. Ministry of Mines and Lands. Report of the Secretary for Mines and Lands.

333.7 RH
ZIMBABWE WILDLIFE. (Text in English) 1973. 4/yr. Z.$250 (overseas $50). Wildlife Society of Zimbabwe, P.O. Box HG996 Highlands, Harare, Zimbabwe. TEL 263-4-747500. FAX 263-4-747500. Ed. Clive Wilson. adv.; bk.rev. circ. 5,500. **Indexed:** Zoo.Rec.
  Formerly: Wild Rhodesia.

333.7 CC ISSN 1000-0038
ZIRAN ZIYUAN/NATURAL RESOURCES. (Text in Chinese) 1977. bi-m. $68.40. (Zhongguo Kexueyuan, Zonghe Kaocha Weiyuanhui) Science Press, Marketing and Sales Department, 16 Donghuangchenggen North St., Beijing 100717, People's Republic of China. TEL 4010642. FAX 4019810. adv.; bk.rev. circ. 11,000. **Document type:** academic/scholarly publication.
  Description: Publishes articles on China's earth, water, biological, and atmospheric resources; results of research into their development, utilization, and protection; methods of investigations; and application of new technology in such investigations.

333.7 CC ISSN 1005-8141
ZIYUAN KAIFA YU SHICHANG/RESOURCE DEVELOPMENT AND MARKET. (Text in Chinese) 1985. bi-m. $30. (Sichuansheng Ziran Ziyuan Yanjiusuo - Sichuan Institute of Natural Resource) Resource Development and Market Press, 24, Yihuan Lu Nan Erduan, Chengdu, Sichuan 610015, People's Republic of China. TEL 86-28-555-3285. FAX 86-28-558-9983. TELEX 60219 STEC CN. Ed. Lu Yongji. adv. contact: Lin Shangqun. bk.rev.
  Formerly: Ziyuan Kaifa yu Baohu (ISSN 1001-3822)
  Description: Covers development, protection and utilization of natural resources including water, soil, air, energy, living organisms, as well as tourism and land management planning.

ZO ANVERS. see BIOLOGY — Zoology

ZO VIEW. see ANIMAL WELFARE

333.95 591 US ISSN 0044-5282
QL1 CODEN: ZONOA
ZOONOOZ. 1926. m. $15 (foreign $18). Zoological Society of San Diego, Box 551, San Diego, CA 92112. TEL 619-231-1515. Ed. Thomas L. Scharf. R&P contact: Thomas L. Scharf. bk.rev.; charts; illus.; index. circ. 250,000. **Document type:** academic/scholarly publication.
  —BLDSC (9531.000000); Linda Hall; UnCover.

333.72 639.9 XR ISSN 1210-5538
ZPRAVY PAMATKOVE PECE.* (Text in Czech; summaries in English, French, German, Russian) 1976. bi-m. $26. Statni Ustav Pamatkove Pece, Valdstejnske Nam. 4, 110 00 Prague 1, Czech Republic. TEL 42-2-513-1111. illus. **Indexed:** Art & Archaeol.Tech.Abstr., Br.Tech.Ind.
  Formerly (until 1992): Pamatky a Priroda (ISSN 0139-9853); Formed by the merger of (1962-1976): Pamatkova Pece (ISSN 0231-7966); (1946-1976): Ochrana Prirody (ISSN 0029-8204)

CONSERVATION — Abstracting, Bibliographies, Statistics

AQUATIC SCIENCES & FISHERIES ABSTRACTS. PART 1: BIOLOGICAL SCIENCES AND LIVING RESOURCES. see WATER RESOURCES — Abstracting, Bibliographies, Statistics

333.7 YU ISSN 0352-1036
BILTEN DOKUMENTACIJE. ZASTITA COVEKOVE OKOLINE I ISKORISCENJE OTPADAKA/BULLETIN OF DOCUMENTATION. ENVIRONMENTAL PROTECTION AND WASTE UTILIZATION. 1971. bi-m. $264. Jugoslovenski Centar za Tehnicku i Naucnu Dokumentaciju - Yugoslav Center for Technical and Scientific Documentation (YCTSD), Sl. Penezica-Krcuna 29-31, Box 724, 11000 Belgrade, Yugoslavia. Ed. Ljiljana Kojic-Bogdanovic.
  Formerly: Bilten Dokumentacije. Iskoriscenje Otpadaka (ISSN 0350-0209)

CURRENT ADVANCES IN ECOLOGICAL AND ENVIRONMENTAL SCIENCES. see ENVIRONMENTAL STUDIES — Abstracting, Bibliographies, Statistics

333.7 016 GW ISSN 0936-0948
DOKUMENTATION NATUR UND LANDSCHAFT. 1950. q. DM.84 (students DM.56) (effective 1997). (Bundesanstalt fuer Naturschutz) W. Kohlhammer GmbH, Hessbruehlstr. 69, 70565 Stuttgart, Germany. TEL 49-711-7863-0. FAX 49-711-7863263. Ed. Rainer Flueeck. bk.rev.; abstr.; index. circ. 800. **Indexed:** Forest.Abstr., Forest Prod.Abstr. **Document type:** abstracting/indexing, government publication.
  —CISTI. **CCC.**
  Former titles (until 1988): Dokumentation fuer Umweltschutz und Landespflege (ISSN 0026-6957); (until 1970): Mitteilungen zur Landschaftspflege.
  Description: Contains reviews of current publications concerned with ecological subjects, including nature conservation and landscape management.

ESSENTIAL WILDLIFE & CONSERVATION BIOLOGY ABSTRACTS. see BIOLOGY — Abstracting, Bibliographies, Statistics

333.7 550 US
N T I S ALERTS: NATURAL RESOURCES & EARTH SCIENCES. w. $140 (foreign $195). U.S. National Technical Information Service, 5285 Port Royal Rd., Springfield, VA 22161. TEL 703-487-4630. FAX 703-321-8547. TELEX 64617. abstr.; index. (back issues avail.)
  Former titles: Abstract Newsletter: Natural Resources and Earth Sciences (ISSN 0163-1438); Weekly Abstract Newsletter: Natural Resources and Earth Sciences; Weekly Government Abstracts. Natural Resources and Earth Sciences; Weekly Government Abstracts. Natural Resources (ISSN 0364-4979)

333.7 310 CN
NEW BRUNSWICK. TOURISM RECREATION & HERITAGE. TECHNICAL SERVICES BRANCH. PROVINCIAL PARK STATISTICS. 1971. a. free. Tourism Recreation & Heritage, Technical Services Branch, P.O. Box 12345, Fredericton, N.B. E3B 5C3, Canada. TEL 506-453-2730. FAX 506-453-2416. Ed. Phillip Ossinger. illus. circ. 200.
  Formerly: New Brunswick. Field Services Branch. Provincial Park Statistics.

REFERATIVNYI ZHURNAL. OKHRANA PRIRODY I VOSPROIZVODSTVO PRIRODNYKH RESURSOV. see ENVIRONMENTAL STUDIES — Abstracting, Bibliographies, Statistics

333.7 639.9 US
RESOURCE CONSERVATION RECOVERY ACT NOTIFICATION DATA FILE. Short title: R C R A. m. $2000 for 1600 bpi in US, Canada, Mexico; elsewhere $4000. (U.S. Environmental Protection Agency) U.S. National Technical Information Service, 5825 Port Royal Rd., Springfield, VA 22161. TEL 703-487-4630. (only avail. on tape)
  Description: Includes names and addresses of the facility owner and operator as well as the contact name and number. Indicates the status of each facility: generator, treatment-storer-disposer, and or transporter of hazardous wastes.

333.7 639.9 US ISSN 0043-5511
SK351
WILDLIFE REVIEW (FORT COLLINS); an indexing service for wildlife management. 1935. bi-m. $32 (foreign $40) (effective 1995). U.S. National Biological Service, Information Transfer Center, 1201 Oak Ridge Dr., No. 200, Ft. Collins, CO 80525-5562. TEL 970-226-9401. FAX 970-226-9455. E-mail: wildlifereview@nbs.gov. (Subscr. to: Superintendent of Documents, U.S. Government Printing Office, Box 371954, Pittsburgh, PA 15250-7954. TEL 202-512-1800. FAX 202-512-2250) Ed. Terry N. Sexson. bk.rev.; cum.index: 1935-1951, 1952-1955, 1956-1960, 1961-1970, 1971-1975, 1976-1980. circ. 4,600. (also avail. in microform from UMI; back issues avail.) **Indexed:** Biol.Dig., Key Word Ind.Wildl.Res. **Document type:** abstracting/indexing, government publication, academic/scholarly publication.
  ●Also available on CD-ROM. Producer(s): NISC (Wildlife Worldwide).
  —CISTI; Linda Hall; UMI.
  Description: Indexes articles from more than 1,300 journals and magazines and more than 500 books and symposia proceedings dealing with natural resources topics.

WILDLIFE WORLDWIDE. see BIOLOGY — Abstracting, Bibliographies, Statistics

CONSTITUTIONAL LAW

see Law–Constitutional Law

CONSUMER EDUCATION AND PROTECTION

A B A CONSUMER BANKING DIGEST. (American Bankers Association) see BUSINESS AND ECONOMICS — Banking And Finance

640.73 US
AD SACK. w. 3040 S. Padre Island Dr., Corpus Christi, TX 78415. TEL 512-854-0137.

ADVANCES IN CONSUMER RESEARCH. see BUSINESS AND ECONOMICS — Marketing And Purchasing

640.73 US ISSN 1044-7385
HC110.C63
ADVANCING THE CONSUMER INTEREST. 1989. s-a. $70 to individuals; institutions $170 (includes Journal of Consumer Affairs, Consumer News and Reviews, Consumer Interests Annual) (effective 1997 & 1998). American Council on Consumer Interests, c/o Anita Metzen, Exec.Dir., 240 Stanley Hall, University of Missouri, Columbia, MO 65211. TEL 573-882-3817. FAX 573-884-6571. E-mail: acci@showme.missouri.edu; URL: http://acci.ps.missouri.edu. (Editorial addr.: c/o Dept. of Consumer Science, University of Wisconsin, 1300 Linden Dr., Madison, WI 53706. TEL 608-265-6515. FAX 608-262-5335) Ed. Rima Apple. **Indexed:** C.I.J.E. **Document type:** academic/scholarly publication.
  —BLDSC (0712.209500); SWETS; UnCover.
  Description: Focuses on the application of knowledge and analysis of current consumer issues.

2252 CONSUMER EDUCATION AND PROTECTION

640.73 US ISSN 1047-031X
ALABAMA LIVING. 1948. m. $6 to non-members; members $3 (effective 1997-1998). Alabama Rural Electric Association of Cooperatives, Box 244014, Montgomery, AL 36124. TEL 334-215-2732. FAX 334-215-2737. Ed. Darryl Gates; Pub. Fred Clark. R&P contact: Darryl Gates. adv. contact: Lee Berry. bk.rev. circ. 315,000. (back issues avail.)
Formerly (until 1989): A R E A Magazine (ISSN 0883-7392)
Description: Dedicated to members of rural electric cooperatives in Alabama.

AMERICAN DEMOGRAPHICS; consumer trends for business leaders. see POPULATION STUDIES

AQUA INDUSTRY GUIDE. see PHYSICAL FITNESS AND HYGIENE

640.73 CC
ASIAN SOURCES.* 1970. m. $25. Asian Sources Trade Journals, ASIMAG Ltd., P.O. Box 12367, Hong Kong, People's Republic of China. TEL 852-555-4777. FAX 852-873-0488. Ed. R.S. Day. adv.; illus. circ. 23,500.

640.73 US
AUSTIN GREENSHEET. w. free. Gordon Publications (Austin), Box 140721, Austin, TX 78714-0721. TEL 512-454-1003. FAX 512-454-2442. Pub. Kathleen Douglass. circ. controlled. **Document type:** consumer publication.

640.73 AT
AUSTRALIAN CAPITAL TERRITORY ATTORNEY-GENERAL'S DEPARTMENT ANNUAL REPORT. a. Australian Capital Territory Attorney-General's Department, Consumer Affairs Bureau, G.P.O. Box 158, Canberra, A.C.T. 2601, Australia. TEL 61-6-2070400. circ. 300. **Document type:** government publication.
Formerly: Consumer Affairs Council of the Australian Capital Territory. Annual Report.
Description: Provides information to the public on the operations and performance of the department, for the prior year ending 30 June.

THE AVIATION CONSUMER. see AERONAUTICS AND SPACE FLIGHT

BANKCARD BAROMETER. see BUSINESS AND ECONOMICS — Banking And Finance

BANKCARD UPDATE. see BUSINESS AND ECONOMICS — Banking And Finance

BARGAIN HUNTERS & BUDGETEERS OPPORTUNITY NEWSLETTER. see HOME ECONOMICS

640.73 381 AT ISSN 0159-6861
BARGAIN SHOPPER'S GUIDE TO MELBOURNE. biennial. Aus.$6.95. Universal Magazines Pty. Ltd., 64 Talavera Rd., Macquarie Park, N.S.W. 2113, Australia. TEL 02-805-0399. FAX 02-035-0714. —CCC.

640.73 381 AT ISSN 0158-7358
BARGAIN SHOPPERS GUIDE TO SYDNEY. 1985. biennial. Aus.$6.95. Universal Magazines Pty. Ltd., 64 Talavera Rd., Macquarie Park, N.S.W. 2113, Australia. TEL 02-805-0399. FAX 02-805-0714.

640.73 US ISSN 0730-9376
BAY AREA CONSUMERS' CHECKBOOK. 1984. s-a. $30 for 2 yrs.; newsstand price: $6.95. Center for the Study of Services, 733 15th St N.W., Ste. 820, Washington, DC 20005-2112. TEL 202-347-9612. Ed. Kevin Brasler; Pub. Robert Krughoff. R&P contact: Dorothy Miller. TEL 510-763-7979. charts; illus.; mkt.; stat.; cum.index. circ. 38,000. (back issues avail.) **Document type:** consumer publication.

640.73 YU
BEOGRAD (BELGRADE, 1966); informativni list. 1966. m. Robna Kuca "Beograd", Marsala Tolbuhina 51-61, Belgrade, Yugoslavia. Ed. Mira Cemerikic.

640.73 US
THE BEST FOR LESS; a newsletter for creative bargain hunters. 1982. m. $33; newsstand price: $5. 14 Washington Pl., New York, NY 10003. TEL 212-673-6297. Ed. Lydia Cherniakova; Pub. Lydia Cherniakova. R&P contact: Lydia Cherniakova. bk.rev. (looseleaf format; back issues avail.) **Document type:** consumer publication, newsletter.

917.1 380 CN ISSN 1182-1124
BINGO NEWS & GAMING HI-LITES. 1984. m. Can.$25 (outside Alberta, Can.$30). Bingo Hi-Lites Ltd., 101, 10171 Saskatchewan Dr., Box 106, Edmonton, AB T6E 4R5, Canada. TEL 403-986-5088. FAX 403-986-5089. Ed. Lorraine B. Kramer-Kalmbach. adv.: B&W page Can.$1245; trim 8 x 10 1/2; adv. contact: Lorraine B. Kramer-Kalmbach. circ. 25,000. (controlled). (also avail. in microfiche) **Document type:** consumer publication.
Former titles (until 1991): Alberta Bingo Gaming News and Hi-Lites (ISSN 1182-1132); (until 1989): Alberta Bingo Hi-Lites Gaming News (ISSN 1182-1140)
Description: Provides up-to-date news on bingo and gaming issues.

640.73 US ISSN 1069-8191
BOYCOTT QUARTERLY. 1993. q. $20 (Canada $27; foreign $40) (effective 1997). Center for Economic Democracy, Box 30727, Seattle, WA 98103-0727. E-mail: boycottguy@aol.com; URL: http://www.speakeasy.com/boycottq. Ed. Zachary Lyons. R&P contact: Zachary Lyons. bk.rev. circ. 3,000. **Indexed:** Alt.Press Ind. **Document type:** consumer publication.
Description: Researches and reports on boycotts and economic democracy topics. Provides listings of ongoing boycotts.

640.73 BE ISSN 0772-9383
BUDGET ET DROITS. Dutch edition: Budget en Recht (ISSN 0772-9391) (Text in French) bi-m. 2424 BEF in Belgium and Luxembourg (elsewhere 2676 BEF). Association des Consommateurs - Verbruikersunie, Rue de Hollande 13, 1060 Brussels, Belgium. TEL 32-2-5423211. FAX 32-2-5423250. TELEX 26771. **Document type:** consumer publication.
Formerly (until 1985): Test Achats Budget (ISSN 0772-9766)

640.73 BE ISSN 0773-0748
BUDGET HEBDO. Dutch edition: Budget Week. (Text in French) w. 6588 BEF in Belgium and Luxembourg (elsewhere 7190 BEF). Association des Consommateurs - Verbruikersunie, Rue de Hollande 13, 1060 Brussels, Belgium. TEL 32-2-5423211. FAX 32-2-5423250. TELEX 26771. **Document type:** consumer publication.

BUSINESS & EMPLOYMENT LAW NEWS. see LAW — Corporate Law

640.73 JA
BUYER'S GUIDE OF TOKYO (YEAR). a. Tokyo Foreign Trade Association, Tokyo Trade Center, 1-7-8 Kaigan, Minato-ku, Tokyo 105, Japan. TEL 03-3438-2026. FAX 03-3433-7164.

640.73 AT
BUYING FOR BABY. 1987. a. $5.95. Magazine House Pty. Ltd., P.O. Box 1067, Crows Nest, N.S.W. 2065, Australia. TEL 61-2-94382399. FAX 61-2-94363014. Ed. Carol Fallows. adv.: B&W page Aus.$3600, color page Aus.$4900; adv. contact: Lee Vecchiet. (back issues avail.) **Document type:** consumer publication.
Formerly (until 1992): Parents Shopping Guide (ISSN 1030-1968)

640.73 US
C E P REPORTS AND C E P BOOKS. 1969. m. $100 to libraries (includes Research Reports). Council on Economic Priorities, 30 Irving Pl., New York, NY 10003. TEL 212-420-1133. FAX 212-420-0988. Ed. Alice Tepper Marlin. R&P contact: Thomas W. Knowlton. **Indexed:** P.A.I.S. **Document type:** newsletter.
Former titles: C E P Reports and C E P Studies; Economic Priorities Report.
Description: In-depth, unbiased analysis of such vital issues as corporate social responsibility, military spending and the environment.

640.73 US ISSN 0898-4328
C E P RESEARCH REPORT. 1974. m. price varies. Council on Economic Priorities, 30 Irving Pl., New York, NY 10003. TEL 212-420-1133. FAX 212-420-0988. Ed. Alice Tepper Marlin. R&P contact: Thomas W. Knowlton. illus. (back issues avail.)
Former titles (until 1987): Council on Economic Priorities Newsletter (ISSN 8755-3538); C E P Newsletter (ISSN 0193-4066)
Description: Concise, objective research on such vital issues as corporate social responsibility, military spending and the environment.

640.73 US ISSN 0732-8281
C F A NEWS (WASHINGTON). 1970? 8/yr. $25. Consumer Federation of America, 1424 16th St., N.W., Washington, DC 20036. TEL 202-387-6121. Ed. Barbara Roper. bk.rev. circ. 1,500.
Description: News articles on legislative, regulatory and policy issues pertaining to consumer issues.

640.73 070.48 JA
CADET. (Text in Japanese) 1985. m. Kodansha Ltd., 12-21, Otowa 2-chome, Bunkyo-ku, Tokyo 112, Japan. TEL 03-5395-3475. FAX 03-3944-5489. TELEX J34509 KODANSHA. Ed. Michio Yoshioka. circ. 150,000. **Document type:** consumer publication.
Formerly (until 1990): Accele.
Description: Provides consumer goods information for men.

MA CAISSE; revue d'information des caisses populaires et des caisses d'economie Desjardins. see BUSINESS AND ECONOMICS — Banking And Finance

640.73 658.7 US
CALIFORNIA. DEPARTMENT OF CONSUMER AFFAIRS. ANNUAL REPORT. 1975. a. free. Department of Consumer Affairs, 400 R St., Ste. 3060, Sacramento, CA 95814-6213. TEL 916-324-1691 FAX 916-445-8796. Ed. Nancy Hardaker. R&P contact: Nancy Hardaker. circ. 1,000. **Document type:** government publication.

CALIFORNIA PRODUCTS LIABILITY ACTIONS. see LAW

CANADIAN BUSINESS LIFE. see BUSINESS AND ECONOMICS

CANADIAN MONEYSAVER; your personal finance guide. see BUSINESS AND ECONOMICS — Investments

640.73 AT ISSN 0008-5413
CANBERRA CONSUMER. 1963. q. Aus.$6. Canberra Consumers, Inc., G.P.O. Box 591, Canberra, A.C.T. 2601, Australia. TEL 61-6-281-5604. bk.rev.; bibl. charts; illus.; circ. 900 (paid). **Indexed:** Aus.P.A.I.S. **Document type:** consumer publication.

640.73 388.3 US ISSN 0893-1208 TL162
CAR BOOK (YEAR); an indispensable guide to the safes most economical new cars. 1980. a. $16.95. Center for Auto Safety, 2001 S St., N.W., Ste. 410 Washington, DC 20009. TEL 202-328-7700.
Description: Covers leasing versus buying, price comparisons, showroom strategies, insurance guide and warranties.

CARDSEARCH. see BUSINESS AND ECONOMICS — Banking And Finance

CARDTRAK. see BUSINESS AND ECONOMICS — Banking And Finance

640.73 US
CASHSAVER.* 1994. bi-m. $9.95. Larry Flynt Publications, Inc., 8484 Wilshire Blvd., Ste. 900, Beverly Hills, CA 90211-3227. TEL 310-858-032 FAX 310-274-7985. Ed. Michael Goldstein. adv.: B&W page $2500, color page $2950. circ. 170,000 (paid). **Document type:** consumer publication.

640.73 US ISSN 0743-989X
CAVEAT EMPTOR CONSUMERS BULLETIN; the environmental and consumer protection monthly. 1970. m. $10. Consumer Education Research Center, 439 Clark St., South Orange, NJ 07079. E Robert Berko. bk.rev. circ. 20,000. **Indexed:** Bk.Rev.Ind. (1981-1982).
—UMI.
Formerly: Caveat Emptor (ISSN 0045-6004)

640.73 US ISSN 1083-897X
CHEAPSKATE MONTHLY. 1992. m. $18 (Canada $24 elsewhere $30) (effective 1997). Hunt Publishing Co., Box 2135, Paramount, CA 90703-8135. TEL 562-630-8845. FAX 562-630-3433. E-mail: cheapsk8@ix.netcom.com; URL: http://www.cheapsk8.com. Ed. Mary Hunt. R&P contact: Cathy Hollenbeck. bk.rev.; index. (looseleaf format) **Document type:** newsletter.
Description: Helps those who are struggling to li within their means find practical and realistic methods and solutions to their financial problems.

CONSUMER EDUCATION AND PROTECTION

640.73 368.382 US ISSN 0740-3925
CHECKBOOK'S GUIDE TO HEALTH INSURANCE PLANS FOR FEDERAL EMPLOYEES. 1979. a. $8.95. Center for the Study of Services, 733 15th St., N.W., Ste. 820, Washington, DC 20005-2112. TEL 202-347-9612. Ed. Walton Francis; Pub. Robert Krughoff. R&P contact: Dorothy Miller. charts; illus.; stat. (back issues avail.) **Document type:** consumer publication.
  Description: Compares health plans offered through the Federal Employee Health Benefits Program.

917.1 028.5 CN
CHILD AND FAMILY MAGAZINE. 1984. q. Can.$30. Literati Publishing Corp., 50 Charles St. E., Ste. 966, Toronto, ON M4Y 2N9, Canada. TEL 416-963-5988. (Co-publisher: Ontario Child and Parent Publications Ltd.) Ed. Joseph Holmes. adv. **Document type:** consumer publication.
  Description: For parents of children age 5 - 15.

CHILD SAFETY REVIEW. see *CHILDREN AND YOUTH — About*

640.73 AT ISSN 0009-496X
CHOICE. 1960. m. Aus.$48 to individuals; institutions Aus.$66. Australian Consumers' Association, 57 Carrington Rd., Marrickville, N.S.W. 2204, Australia. TEL 61-2-558-0099. FAX 61-2-558-9341. Ed. Jane Mackenzie. cum.index. circ. 160,000. **Indexed:** Aus.P.A.I.S., Aus.Rd.Ind., Gdlns, Lib.Lit., Pinpointer. —UnCover.

640.73 CC
CHOICE. m. $110. Consumer Council, 19th Fl., Tower 6, China Hong Kong City, 33 Canton Rd., Tsimshatsui, Kowloon, Hong Kong, People's Republic of China. TEL 7363322. FAX 7367700. TELEX 72036. circ. 45,000. (also avail. in microfiche) **Indexed:** Bk.Rev.Dig., Lib.Lit.

640.73 US ISSN 1079-2953
R726.C66
CHOICES (NEW YORK). (Former names of issuing body: Concern for Dying; Concern for Dying - Society for the Right to Die) 1975. 4/yr. $25. Choice in Dying, Inc., 200 Varick St., New York, NY 10014. TEL 212-366-5540; 800-989-WILL. FAX 212-366-5337. E-mail: cid@choices.org; URL: http://www.choices.org. Ed. Mary Meyer. R&P contact: Mary Meyer. bk.rev.; illus. circ. 80,000. **Indexed:** R.G.Abstr. **Document type:** newsletter.
  ●Also available online.
  —UMI.
  Former titles (until 1994): Choice in Dying News; Concern for Dying - Society for the Right to Die Newsletter; (until 1985): Concern for Dying Newsletter (ISSN 0192-1096); (until 1978): Euthanasia News (ISSN 0164-1581)

640.73 PH
CITIZEN VOLUNTEER. (Text in English) 1990. m. free. Department of Trade and Industry, Trade & Industry Information Center, 4th Fl., Industry & Investment Bldg., 385 Sen. Gil J. Puyat Ave., Makati, Metro Manila 3117, Philippines. TEL 863611. FAX 856487. Ed. Minerva R. Fajardo. R&P contact: Alfonso M. Valenzueia. adv. contact: Alfonso M. Valenzuela. circ. 5,000. **Document type:** government publication, newsletter.
  Description: Covers consumer laws, activities of consumer groups, government's action on consumer grievances, and other consumer-related news around the country.

640 SP ISSN 0212-4114
CIUDADANO; revista consumo y calidad de vida. 1973. m. 4290 ptas. (Europe 4890 ptas.; elsewhere 5355 ptas.) (effective Oct. 1994). Fundacion Ciudadano, C. Atocha 26, 28012 Madrid, Spain. TEL 34-1-3691285. FAX 34-1-3690827. Ed. Carmen Martin Carrobles. adv. contact: Ana Quilez H. charts; illus.; stat.; index; circ. 70,000 (controlled). (some back issues avail.)

051 US ISSN 1053-6507
CLOTHING FOR LESS NEWSLETTER. 1990. biennial. $5. Continuus, c/o Prosperity & Profits Unlimited Distribution Services, Box 416, Denver, CO 80201-0416. TEL 303-575-5676. Ed. A.C. Doyle. circ. 3,999. (looseleaf format) **Document type:** newsletter.
  Description: Contains ideas on buying clothing for less.

COMMITTEE TO RESTORE THE CONSTITUTION. BULLETIN. see *POLITICAL SCIENCE*

COMMUNITY RIGHT-TO-KNOW NEWS. see *SOCIAL SERVICES AND WELFARE*

640.73 US
CONFIDENT CONSUMER MAGAZINE.* m. 113 Blue Bird Dr., Dothan, AL 36303-1389. TEL 205-671-4944. Ed. Jimmy Davis.

640.73 US
CONN P I R G CHANNEL.* irreg. free. Connecticut Public Interest Research Group, Box 6000, 300 Summit St., Hartford, CT 06106. TEL 203-247-2735. Ed. Greg Stan. (tabloid format)

640.73 US ISSN 1059-6623
CONSCIOUS CONSUMER; products and services that help the earth and society. (Print edition ceased in 1995) 1990. q. free. New Consumer Institute, Inc., Box 51, Wauconda, IL 60084. TEL 847-526-0522. FAX 847-487-0010. URL: http://www.envirolink. com/sbn. Ed. John F. Wasik; Pub. John F. Wasik. R&P contact: John F. Wasik. stat. **Document type:** newsletter.
  ●Available only online.
  Description: Serves as a clearing house for socially responsible and environmentally sound product information. Covers national trends, business and product news, media and legislative issues.

640.73 FR
CONSEIL NATIONAL DE LA CONSOMMATION. ANNUAL REPORT. 1989. a. free. Conseil National de la Consommation, DGCCRF, Carre Diderot, 5, Bd. Diderot, 75572 Paris Cedex 12, France. FAX 1-44-87-33-66. circ. 6,000.
  Description: Includes studies, opinions and structure of the council.

640.73 IT
CONSUMATORI. 1983. m. L.20000. Editrice Consumatori, Via A. Moro, 16, 40127 Bologna, Italy. TEL 39-51-511026. FAX 39-51-6570109. Ed. Diego Passini. adv.: B&W or color page L.27000000. circ. 1,150,000.

CONSUMENTEN REISGIDS. see *TRAVEL AND TOURISM*

640.73 NE ISSN 0165-6775
CONSUMENTENGIDS. 1953. m. fl.63 to members. Consumentenbond, Postbus 1000, 2500 BA The Hague, Netherlands. TEL 31-70-4454545. FAX 31-70-3841282. URL: http://www. consumatenbond.nl. circ. 650,000. (also avail. in audio cassette) **Document type:** consumer publication. —SWETS.

640.73 NZ ISSN 0110-5949
CONSUMER. m. (except Jan.) NZ.$51.50 (effective 1997). Consumers' Institute, Private Bag 6996, Wellington 6035, New Zealand. TEL 64-4-384-7963. FAX 64-4-385-8752. E-mail: editor@consumer.org.nz. Ed. Simon Wilson. circ. 87,000 (paid). **Document type:** consumer publication.
  Description: Covers consumer testing and research: products, legislation, finance, food, health, safety, environment, welfare.

640.73 NZ
CONSUMER ACTION. 1989. irreg. Ministry of Consumer Affairs, P.O. Box 1473, Wellington, New Zealand. TEL 64-4-4742750. FAX 64-4-4739400. circ. 1,500. **Document type:** consumer publication.

640.73 AT
CONSUMER AFFAIRS COUNCIL. ANNUAL REPORT. 1971. a. free. Consumer Affairs Council, 99 Bathurst St., Hobart, Tas. 7000, Australia. TEL 002-33-4567. FAX 002-33-4509. stat. circ. 1,000. (back issues avail.)

640.73 US ISSN 0270-0999
CONSUMER AFFAIRS LETTER; monthly report to management on issues, activities, strategies, etc. of consumer groups. 1980. m. $125 to non-profit institutions; corporations $247. Box 65313, Washington, DC 20035. TEL 202-362-4279. Ed. George Idelson. bk.rev. (back issues avail.) **Document type:** newsletter.

640.73 IE ISSN 0790-486X
CONSUMER CHOICE. 1970. m. I£45. Consumers Association of Ireland Ltd., 45 Upper Mount St., Dublin 2, Ireland. TEL 353-1-6612090. FAX 353-1-6612464. Ed. Kieran Doherty. R&P contact: Kieran Doherty. circ. 11,000 (controlled). (processed) **Indexed:** Lib.Lit. **Document type:** consumer publication.
  Formerly: Inform.
  Description: Independent resource for information on products, services and issues of interest to Irish consumers.

640.73 AT ISSN 0045-8236
CONSUMER COMMENT. 1970. q. Aus.$12 (foreign Aus.$14) (effective 1997 & 1998). Consumers' Association of Victoria Inc., P.O. Box 2339, Mt. Waverley, Vic. 3149, Australia. TEL 61-3-96226990. E-mail: yyharris@werple.net.au. Ed.Bd. bk.rev.; cum.index. circ. 300. **Document type:** consumer publication, newsletter.

CONSUMER CREDIT DELINQUENCY BULLETIN. see *BUSINESS AND ECONOMICS — Banking And Finance*

CONSUMER CREDIT GUIDE REPORTS. see *LAW*

641 MY ISSN 0128-1143
CONSUMER CURRENTS. 1980. 10/yr. $50 (non-profit groups in the Third World $10; in industrial countries $20). Consumers International, Regional Office for Asia and Pacific, P.O. Box 1045, 10830 Penang, Malaysia. TEL 60-4-229-1296. FAX 60-4-228-6506. E-mail: ciroap@pc.jaring.my. (Subscr. to: Regional Office for Asia & Pacific, P.O. Box 1045, Penang, Malaysia) Ed. Loh Cheng Kooi. R&P contact: Loh Cheng Hooi. bk.rev. circ. 450. **Indexed:** HR Rep. **Document type:** newsletter.
  Description: Contains news of relevance to groups and individuals who serve the consumer interest particularly in the Third World.
  Refereed Serial

CONSUMER FINANCE BULLETIN. see *BUSINESS AND ECONOMICS — Banking And Finance*

CONSUMER INFORMATION CATALOG. see *BIBLIOGRAPHIES*

640.73 US
HC110.C63
CONSUMER INTERESTS ANNUAL. 1957. a. $30 (effective 1997 & 1998). American Council on Consumer Interests, c/o Anita Metzen, Exec. Dir., 240 Stanley Hall, University of Missouri, Columbia, MO 65211. TEL 573-882-3817. FAX 573-884-6571. E-mail: acci@showme.missouri.edu; URL: http://acci.ps.missouri.edu. Ed. Irene Leech. circ. 1,200. (also avail. in microfilm) **Indexed:** BPIA.
  —BLDSC (1082.050000).
  Former titles: American Council on Consumer Interests. Proceedings of the Annual Conference (ISSN 0275-1356); Council on Consumer Information. Proceedings of Annual Conference.
  Refereed Serial

CONSUMER LAW TODAY - THE FAIR TRADING MONITOR. see *LAW*

640.73 US ISSN 1086-9107
HC110.C6
CONSUMER NEWS AND REVIEWS. 1953. bi-m. $70 to individuals; institutions $140 (includes Journal of Consumer Affairs, Consumer Interests Annual, Advancing the Consumer Interest) (effective 1997 & 1998). American Council on Consumer Interests, c/o Anita Metzen, Exec.Dir., 240 Stanley Hall, University of Missouri, Columbia, MO 65211. TEL 573-882-3817. FAX 573-884-6571. E-mail: acci@showme.missouri.edu; URL: http://acci.ps.missouri.edu. Ed. Les Dlabay. bk.rev. circ. 1,600. (processed; also avail. in microfilm; back issues avail.) **Document type:** newsletter.
  —UMI.
  Former titles (until 1989): A C C I Newsletter (ISSN 0010-9975); (until 1969): Council on Consumer Information. Newsletter.
  Description: Offers information on the latest developments in the consumer field, and news of ACCI and other consumer organizations. Federal and state consumer activities, annotated listings of consumer resource materials, and special focus sections are included in each issue.

CONSUMER EDUCATION AND PROTECTION

640.73 UK ISSN 0961-1134
CONSUMER POLICY REVIEW. 1991. bi-m. £35($52) to individuals; institutions £85 ($145). (Consumers' Association) Which? Ltd., 2 Marylebone Rd., London NW1 4DF, England. TEL 44-171-830-6000. FAX 44-171-830-6220. (Subscr. to: Consumers' Association, Castlemead, Gascoyne Way, Herts. SG14 1LH, England. TEL 44-171-830-8500) Ed.Bd. R&P contact: Gill Rowley. **Indexed:** Cont.Pg.Manage., LJI, Stud.Wom.Abstr.
• Also available online. Vendor(s): UMI.
—BLDSC (3424.318680).

640.73 US ISSN 0162-119X
CONSUMER PRODUCT SAFETY GUIDE. 1972. w. $972. C C H Incorporated, 2700 Lake Cook Rd., Riverwoods, IL 60015. TEL 847-267-7000; 800-835-5224. FAX 800-224-8299. (looseleaf format)

363.19 640.73 US
▼**CONSUMER PRODUCT SAFETY REVIEW.** 1996. q. $9 (foreign $11.25). (U.S. Consumer Product Safety Commission) National Injury Information Clearinghouse, 4330 East-West Hwy., Bethesda, MD 20814. TEL 301-504-0990; 800-638-2772. E-mail: info@cpsc.gov; URL: http://www.cpsc.gov. **Document type:** government publication.
• Also available online.
Description: Informs consumers, public health and medical professionals, and industry about injuries and deaths associated with consumer products.

343.0721 346.07
640.73 US
CONSUMER PROTECTION, ANTITRUST & UNFAIR BUSINESS PRACTICES NEWSLETTER.* 1974. q. $10. Washington State Bar Association, 2101 Fourth Ave., Ste. 400, Seattle, WA 98121-2330. TEL 206-727-8239. FAX 206-727-8320. circ. 330. (looseleaf format; back issues avail.) **Document type:** newsletter.
Formerly: Antitrust Law Section Newsletter.

640.73 US ISSN 0362-157X
KFW2630.A59
CONSUMER PROTECTION REPORT. 1980. 10/yr. $145 (effective June 1997). National Association of Attorneys General, 444 N. Capitol St., Ste. 339, Washington, DC 20001. TEL 202-434-8000. FAX 202-434-8008. Ed. Emmit Carlton. (looseleaf format; back issues avail.) **Document type:** newsletter.

640.73 US ISSN 0010-7174
TX335.A1 CODEN: CONRAY
CONSUMER REPORTS. (Annual Buying Guide avail.) 1936. m. (except s-m. Dec.) $30 includes Annual Buying Guide. Consumers Union of the United States, Inc., 101 Truman Ave., Yonkers, NY 10703-1057. TEL 914-378-2000. FAX 914-378-2900. (Subscr. to: Box 53029, Boulder, CO 80322-3016) Ed. Joel Gurin. R&P contact: Wendy Wintman. charts; illus.; index, cum.index. circ. 5,000,000. (also avail. in microfiche from NBI; reprint service avail.) **Indexed:** Abr.R.G., Acad.Ind., Bank.Lit.Ind., Can.B.P.I., CHNI, CINAHL, Consum.Ind., Curr.Pack.Abstr., Environ.Abstr., Film Lit.Ind. (1973-), Hlth.Ind., I.P.A., Ind.Per.Art.Relat.Law, Jun.High.Mag.Abstr., Key to Econ.Sci., Mag.Ind., P.A.I.S., PROMT, R.G., R.G.Abstr., TOM.
• Also available online. Vendor(s): Information Access Co., Knight-Ridder Information, Inc. (File no.646), Lexis-Nexis.
Also available on CD-ROM.
—BLDSC (3424.500000); CASDDS; CISTI; KR SourceOne; Linda Hall; SWETS; UnCover.
Description: Features objective comparative evaluations of consumer items, ranging from small household appliances to automobiles.

640.73 US
CONSUMER REPORTS BUYING GUIDE. a. included with subscr. to Consumer Reports; newsstand price: 8.95. Consumers Union of the United States, Inc., 101 Truman Ave., Yonkers, NY 10703-1057. TEL 914-378-2000. FAX 914-378-2906.
Description: Rates and reviews various consumer goods, offering informed consumers practical, objective advice on such matters as value and reliability.

CONSUMER REPORTS NEW CAR YEARBOOK. see TRANSPORTATION — Automobiles

CONSUMER REPORTS ON HEALTH. see PHYSICAL FITNESS AND HYGIENE

CONSUMER REPORTS TRAVEL LETTER. see TRAVEL AND TOURISM

640.73 US
CONSUMER REPORTS YARD & GARDEN EQUIPMENT BUYING GUIDE. a. $8.99. Consumers Union of the United States, Inc., 101 Truman Ave., Yonkers, NY 10703-1057. TEL 914-378-2000. FAX 914-378-2906.

640.73 US ISSN 0738-0518
HC110.C63
CONSUMER SOURCEBOOK. 1974. irreg., 7th ed., 1991. $195. Gale Research, 835 Penobscot Bldg., 645 Griswold St., Detroit, MI 48226-4094. TEL 313-961-2242; 800-877-4253. FAX 800-414-5043. E-mail: daniel_snyder@gale.com. Ed. Shawn Brennan.
Description: Entries identify and describe more than 7300 programs and services available at little or no cost.

640.73 US ISSN 0010-7182
TX335.A1
CONSUMERS DIGEST; best buys, best prices, best reports, for people who demand value. 1959. bi-m. $15.97 (foreign $25.97). Consumers Digest, Inc., 8001 N. Lincoln Ave., 6th Fl., Skokie, IL 60077-3657. TEL 847-763-9200. (Subscr. to: Box 3074, Harlan, IA 51593-4138) Ed. John Manos; Pub. Randy Weber. adv. contact: Howard Plissner. bk.rev.; illus.; cum.index; circ. 1,250,000 (paid). (also avail. in microform from UMI; back issues avail.) **Indexed:** Consum.Ind., Hlth.Ind., Mag.Ind., PMR, R.G.Abstr. **Document type:** consumer publication.
• Also available online. Vendor(s): Information Access Co.
—KR SourceOne; UMI; UnCover.

640.73 KE
CONSUMER'S DIGEST. m. Nangina House, P.O. Box 50795, Nairobi, Kenya. TEL 21431. Ed. Eunice Mathu. circ. 17,000.

640.73 PH
CONSUMERS FEDERATED GROUPS OF THE PHILIPPINES. NEWSLETTER. q. Consumers Federated Groups of the Philippines, 962 Josefa Llanes Escoda St., Ermita, Manila 2801, Philippines.

640.73 368 US
CONSUMERS FOR HEALTH CARE REFORM NEWSLETTER.* 1991. m. $24. Personal Best Press, 1301 First St. N., Fargo, ND 58102-2720. TEL 701-280-3818. Ed. D.K. Haugen.
Description: Covers fiscal, policy and administrative issues affecting the cost of consumer health care.

640.73 362.11 US ISSN 1070-2644
CONSUMERS' GUIDE TO HOSPITALS. 1988. irreg., approx. biennial. $12. Center for the Study of Services, 733 15th St., N.W., Ste. 820, Washington, DC 20005-2112. TEL 202-347-9612. Ed. Robert Krughoff; Pub. Robert Krughoff. R&P contact: Dorothy Miller. charts; illus.; stat. (back issues avail.) **Document type:** consumer publication.
Description: Gives death rates at 5500 US hospitals as well as information on how to choose a hospital, how to get the best care wherever you go, and how to keep costs down.

640.73 US ISSN 0095-2222
TX335.A1 CODEN: CRMZA6
CONSUMER'S RESEARCH MAGAZINE; analyzing consumer issues. 1927. m. $24 (foreign $32). Consumers' Research, Inc., 800 Maryland Ave., N.E., Washington, DC 20002. TEL 202-546-1713. FAX 202-546-1638. (Subscr. to: Box 5025, Brentwood, TN 37024) Ed. Peter Spencer. adv.; bk.rev.; charts; illus.; index, cum.index. circ. 14,000. (also avail. in microfilm from UMI; microfiche from NBI; Braille; back issues avail.) **Indexed:** Acad.Ind., Consum.Ind., Film Lit.Ind. (1973-), Hlth.Ind., Key to Econ.Sci., Mag.Ind., PMR, R.G.Abstr., R.G., Text.Tech.Dig., TOM. **Document type:** consumer publication.
• Also available online. Vendor(s): Information Access Co., UMI.
Also available on CD-ROM. Producer(s): UMI.
—KR SourceOne; Linda Hall; SWETS; UMI; UnCover.
Formerly (1957-1973): Consumer Bulletin (ISSN 0010-7123)
Description: Includes articles on health, safety, finance, home, auto, and products.

640.73 AT ISSN 0728-3008
CONSUMING INTEREST. 1981. q. Aus.$27. Australian Consumers' Association, 57 Carrington Rd., Marrickville, N.S.W. 2204, Australia. TEL 61-2-5580099. FAX 61-2-558-9341. Ed. L. Rist. circ. 3,000. (back issues avail.)
—UnCover.

640.73 US
CO-OP NEWS (HANOVER). 1937. 7/yr. $5. Hanover Consumer Cooperative Society, 45 S. Park St., Box 633, Hanover, NH 03755-0633. TEL 603-643-2667. Ed. Harrison Drinkwater. bk.rev. circ. 4,700. (tabloid format; back issues avail.)

381 US
HC110.C63
COUNCIL OF BETTER BUSINESS BUREAUS. BUSINESS ADVISORY SERIES; tips on consumer information series. 1972. m. $2 per no. Council of Better Business Bureaus, Publications Department, 4200 Wilson Blvd., Arlington, VA 22203-1804. TEL 703-276-0100. **Document type:** consumer publication.
Formerly: Council of Better Business Bureaus. Annual Report (ISSN 0094-8853)
Description: Over 80 titles on subjects of interest to consumers and businesses.

640.73 658.8 US ISSN 1053-6523
COUPON TREASURE HUNT NEWSLETTER. 1990. biennial. $3. Continnuus, c/o Prosperity & Profits Unlimited Distribution Services, Box 416, Denver, CO 80201-0416. TEL 303-575-5676. Ed. A.C. Doyle. R&P contact: A. Doyle. circ. 1,500. (looseleaf format) **Document type:** newsletter.
Description: Information on finding and redeeming coupons.

640.73 340 II
CURRENT CONSUMER CASES. (Text in English) 1994. m. $120 (effective 1998). International Law Book Co., Nijhawan Bldg., 1562 Church Rd., Kashmere Gate, New Delhi 110 006, India. TEL 91-11-2967810. E-mail: lakshmin@giasdla.vsnl.net.in.
Description: Contains judgments, whether reportable or nonreportable of the National Consumer Disputes Redressal Commission, Supreme Court of India, and more.

CUSTOMER SERVICE MANAGER'S LETTER. see BUSINESS AND ECONOMICS — Management

640.73 US
DALLAS GREENSHEET.* w. free. Gordon Publications (Dallas), 7929 Brookriver Dr., Ste. 700, Dallas, TX 75247-4900. TEL 214-905-8200. (Or: Box 560727, Dallas, TX 75356)

DEALERNEWS BUYERS GUIDE. see SPORTS AND GAMES — Bicycles And Motorcycles

DENKEN EN DOEN. see WOMEN'S INTERESTS

640.73 DK ISSN 0905-2860
DENMARK. FORBRUGERSTYRELSEN. JURIDISK AARBOG. 1975. a. DKK 150. Forbrugerstyrelsen, 56 Amagerfaelledvej, DK-2300 Copenhagen S, Denmark. TEL 45-31-570100. FAX 45-32-96023 circ. 3,500. **Document type:** academic/scholarly publication.
Incorporates (in 1989): Forbrugerklagenaevnet. Juridisk Aarbog.

640.73 DK ISSN 0904-8529
DENMARK. FORBRUGERSTYRELSEN. PJECER. 1936. 4/yr. DKK 30. Forbrugerstyrelsen, 56 Amagerfaelledvej, DK-2300 Copenhagen S, Denmark. TEL 45-31-57-01-00. FAX 45-32-96-02-32. illus. circ. 65,000. **Document type:** consumer publication.
Formerly (until 1989): Denmark. Statens Husholdningsraad. Pjecer (ISSN 0106-1887)

CONSUMER EDUCATION AND PROTECTION

640.73   DK   ISSN 0904-986X
DENMARK. FORBRUGERSTYRELSEN. TEKNISKE MEDDELELSER. (Supplement to: Raad og Resultater (ISSN 0033-748X)) (Text in Danish; summaries in English) 10/yr. DKK 88 (includes Raad og Resultater). Forbrugerstyrelsen, 56 Amagerfaelledvej, DK-2300 Copenhagen S, Denmark. TEL 45-31-570100. FAX 45-32-960232. Ed. L. Krayboerre. **Document type:** consumer publication.
    Formerly: Denmark. Statens Husholdningsraad. Tekniske Meddelelser (ISSN 0106-1895)

640.73   DK   ISSN 0033-748X
DENMARK. STATENS HUSHOLDNINGSRAAD. RAAD OG RESULTATER. (Supplement avail.: Tekniske Meddelelser - Forbrugerstyrelsen (ISSN 0904-986X)) 1961. 10/yr. DKK 60 (effective 1997). (Statens Husholdningsraad) Forbrugerstyrelsen, 56 Amagerfaelledvej, DK-2300 Copenhagen S, Denmark. TEL 45-31-570100. FAX 45-32-960232. URL: http://www.forbrugerstyrelsen.dk. Ed. Lissi Krayborre. R&P contact: Lissi Krayborre. adv. contact: J. Larsen. cum.index. circ. 74,000. **Document type:** consumer publication, government publication.

DIAMOND INSIGHT; penetrating the multi-faceted world of diamonds. see *JEWELRY, CLOCKS AND WATCHES*

DIRECTORY OF INFORMATION AND REFERRAL AGENCIES IN THE UNITED STATES AND CANADA. see *SOCIAL SERVICES AND WELFARE*

640.73   US   ISSN 0196-8203
DISCLOSURE (CHICAGO); the national newspaper of neighborhoods. 1974. bi-m. $15 to individuals; institutions $30. National Training and Information Center, 810 N. Milwaukee, Chicago, IL 60622. TEL 312-243-3035. FAX 312-243-7044. Ed. Gordon Mayer. R&P contact: Gordon Mayer. bk.rev.; charts; stat. circ. 6,000. (tabloid format; also avail. in microform from UMI; back issues avail.) **Indexed:** Alt.Press Ind. **Document type:** newsletter.
  ●Also available online. Vendor(s): UMI.

ENERGIEDEPESCHE. see *ENERGY*

ENERGY USER NEWS. see *ENERGY*

640.73 170.73   UK   ISSN 0955-8608
THE ETHICAL CONSUMER. 1989. bi-m. £17 (rest of Europe £22; elsewhere £26); with supplements £29 (rest of Europe £34; elsewhere £38) (effective 1998). E C R A Publishing Ltd., 41 Old Birley St., Unit 21, Manchester M15 5RF, England. TEL 44-161-226-2929. FAX 44-161-226-6277. E-mail: ethicon@mcr1.poptel.org.uk. Ed. Rob Harrison; Pub. Bruce Bingham. R&P contact: Rob Harrison. adv. contact: Simon Birch. bk.rev.; abstr.; charts; stat. circ. 3,750. (back issues avail.) **Document type:** consumer publication.
    Description: Researches and disseminates information for consumers and how they can act to promote corporate ethics and responsibility for animal and human rights, the environment, and social well-being.

640.73   US
EXCHANGE (FAYETTEVILLE). w. $15. Exchange, Inc., Box 490, 408 S. Main St., Fayetteville, TN 37334. TEL 615-433-9737.

353.84   US   ISSN 0362-1332
HD9000.9.U5   CODEN: FDACBH
F D A CONSUMER. 1967. m. (Jul.-Aug. and Jan.-Feb. issues combined). $15 (foreign $18.75). U.S. Food and Drug Administration, Office of Public Affairs, 5600 Fishers Ln., Rockville, MD 20857. TEL 301-443-3220. (Subscr. to: Superintendent of Documents, U.S. Government Printing Office, Box 371954, Pittsburgh, PA 15250. TEL 202-512-1800. FAX 202-512-2250) Ed. Judith Levine Willis. illus.; cum.index: vols. 1-22; circ. 28,000 (paid). (also avail. in microform from UMI; back issues avail.; reprint service avail. from UMI) **Indexed:** Acad.Ind., Bibl.Agri., BPIA, CHNI, Curr.Lit.Fam.Plan., Curr.Pack.Abstr., Excerp.Med., Food Sci.& Tech.Abstr., Gen.Sci.Ind., Hlth.Ind., I.P.A., Ind.U.S.Gov.Per., Mag.Ind., MEDOC, NRN, P.A.I.S., PMR, R.G.Abstr., R.G., Telegen. **Document type:** government publication.
  ●Also available online. Vendor(s): Information Access Co., Knight-Ridder Information, Inc., UMI.
  —BLDSC (3901.292000); CISTI; Genuine Article; KR SourceOne; Linda Hall; SWETS; UMI; UnCover.
    Formerly: F D A Papers (ISSN 0014-5750)
    Description: Designed to inform the public of the Food and Drug Administration activities on behalf of consumers.

640.73   US
F D A WEEK. (Food and Drug Administration) w. $495 (foreign $545) (effective 1997). Inside Washington Publishers, Box 7167, Ben Franklin Sta., Washington, DC 20044-7167. TEL 703-416-8500. FAX 703-416-8543. E-mail: service@iwpnews.com. **Document type:** newsletter.

F E B BULLETIN. (Federation des Entreprises de Belgique) see *BUSINESS AND ECONOMICS — Production Of Goods And Services*

F M O NEWS. (Federation of Mobile Home Owners of Florida) see *REAL ESTATE*

640.73   US
FACTORY OUTLET SHOPPING GUIDE FOR NEW ENGLAND.* 1973. a. $3.95. Factory Outlet Shopping Guide Publications, 11 Tory Ln., Newtown, CT 06470. Ed. Jean D. Bird. adv.; bk.rev. circ. 25,000.

FAMILY ECONOMICS AND NUTRITION REVIEW. see *HOME ECONOMICS*

FEDERATION DES ENTREPRISES DE BELGIQUE. RAPPORT ANNUEL. see *BUSINESS AND ECONOMICS — Production Of Goods And Services*

FINANCIAL AND ESTATE PLANNING FOR THE MATURE CLIENT IN ONTARIO. see *LAW — Estate Planning*

640   GW   ISSN 0939-1614
FINANZTEST. 1991. bi-m. DM.72 (foreign DM.84) (effective 1997). Stiftung Warentest, Luetzowplatz 11-13, 10785 Berlin, Germany. TEL 49-30-26312408. FAX 49-30-26312428. circ. 225,000. **Document type:** consumer publication.
    Description: Comparative analyses and other reports on financial services, private savings and investment, insurance, taxes and legal matters.

FLORIDA CONSUMER LAW MANUAL. see *LAW*

FONDS ET SICAV. see *BUSINESS AND ECONOMICS — Banking And Finance*

640.73 664 659   US
FOOD & WATER JOURNAL. 1992. q. $25 (foreign $40) (effective Apr. 1992). Food and Water, Inc., R.R. 1, Box 68D, Walden, VT 05873. TEL 802-426-3700. FAX 802-426-3711. Ed. Michael Colby. bk.rev.; charts; illus. circ. 15,000. (looseleaf format; back issues avail.) **Document type:** newsletter.
    Formerly: Safe Food News.
    Description: Covers food irradiation, pesticides, bovine growth hormone, and the activities of the company.

FOOD FREE OR CHEAP NEWSLETTER. see *HOME ECONOMICS*

640.73 658.8   US
FOODWATCH UPDATE.* 1992. q. $18 to non-members. Agriculture Council of America, 11020 King St., Ste. 205, Overland Park, KS 66210-1201. TEL 202-682-9200. FAX 202-289-6648. Ed. Mark Bennett. R&P contact: Mark Bennett. circ. 10,000 (controlled). (back issues avail.) **Document type:** newsletter.
    Description: For those who are interested in food safety.

640.73   DK   ISSN 0105-9122
FORBRUGERINDEKS. (Supplements avail.) 1978. a. DKK 776 includes supplements (effective 1996). Dansk BiblioteksCenter as, Tempovej 7-11, DK-2750 Ballerup, Denmark. TEL 45-44-867777. FAX 45-44-867892. E-mail: dbc@dan.bib.dk.

640.73   NO   ISSN 0046-449X
FORBRUKER-RAPPORTEN. (Text in Norwegian; summaries in English) 1958. 10/yr. NOK 55. Forbrukerraadet - Consumer Council, Boks 8104, Oslo 1, Norway. illus. circ. 185,000.
  —CCC.

640.73   US   ISSN 0148-2092
FREEBIES; the magazine with something for nothing. 1977. 5/yr. $8.95 (effective Jan. 1992). Freebies Publishing Co., 1135 Eugenia Place, Box 5025, Carpinteria, CA 93014-5025. TEL 805-566-1225. FAX 805-566-0305. Ed. Abel Magana; Pub. Harry Short. R&P contact: Harry Short. adv. contact: Harry Short. bk.rev. circ. 350,000. **Document type:** consumer publication.

640.73 658.8   US   ISSN 1058-0271
FRONT LINES (PORTLAND). 1977. bi-m. free. Food Front Cooperative Grocery, 2375 N.W. Thurman, Portland, OR 97210-2572. TEL 503-222-5658. FAX 503-227-5140. Ed. Joel Dippold. adv. contact: Judy Rose. bk.rev. circ. 3,000. (looseleaf format; back issues avail.) **Document type:** newsletter.
    Formerly: Food Front.
    Description: Consumer education regarding the natural foods industry, including product information, coverage of key issues and related environmental concerns.

FRUGAL CONSUMERS DOLLAR-STRETCHING POSSIBILITY NEWSLETTER. see *HOME ECONOMICS*

640.73 332   NE
GELD (YEAR). 1985. 2/yr. fl.13.90. Service Pers B.V., Postbus 9044, 1800 GA Alkmaar, Netherlands. TEL 31-72-5158084. FAX 31-72-5157540. Ed. P. Hagtingius. adv.; bk.rev. circ. 90,000. **Document type:** consumer publication.

GOODE'S CONSUMER CREDIT LEGISLATION. see *LAW*

640.73   BE
GUIDE DU CONTRIBUABLE. a. Association des Consommateurs - Verbruikersunie, Rue de Hollande 13, 1060 Brussels, Belgium. TEL 32-2-5423211. FAX 32-2-5423250. TELEX 26771.

640.73   US
GUIDE TO BAY AREA RESTAURANTS. 1989. irreg., approx. triennial. $7.95. Center for the Study of Services, 733 15th St., N.W., Ste. 820, Washington, DC 20005-2112. TEL 510-763-7979. Ed. Sue Remick; Pub. Robert M. Krughoff. R&P contact: Dorothy Miller. charts; illus.; stat. (back issues avail.) **Document type:** consumer publication.
    Description: Reports restaurant ratings from a local survey. Restaurants are rated for food, service, ambience, and value, and write-ups include remarks from professional restaurant critics.

640.73   US
GUIDE TO WASHINGTON AREA RESTAURANTS. 1988. irreg., approx. triennial. $7.95. Center for the Study of Services, 733 15th St., N.W., Ste. 820, Washington, DC 20005-2112. TEL 202-347-9612. Ed. Geneva Collins; Pub. Robert M. Krughoff. R&P contact: Dorothy Miller. charts; illus.; stat. (back issues avail.) **Document type:** consumer publication.
    Description: Reports restaurant ratings from a local survey. Restaurants are rated for food, service, ambience, and value, and write-ups include remarks from professional restaurant critics.

640.73   BE
GUIDES PRATIQUES. q. Association des Consommateurs, Rue de Hollande 13, 1060 Brussels, Belgium. TEL 32-2-5423211. FAX 32-2-5423250. TELEX 26771.

CONSUMER EDUCATION AND PROTECTION

640.73 JA
HANAKO. (Text in Japanese) 1988. w. newsstand price: 350Yen. Magazine House, 3-13-10, Ginza, Chuo-ku, Tokyo 104, Japan. TEL 81-3-3545-7070. FAX 81-3-3545-7498. Ed. Koji Tomono. circ. 301,000. **Document type:** consumer publication.

640.73 JA
HANAKO - WEST. (Text in Japanese) 1991. m. newsstand price: 380Yen. Magazine House, 3-13-10 Ginza, Chuo-ku, Tokyo 104-03, Japan. TEL 81-3-3545-7061. FAX 81-6-371-8759. (Alt. addr.: Magazine House Osaka Office, 2F Yodogawa 5 Bankan, 3-2-1, Toyosaki, Kitaku, Osaka 531, Japan. TEL 81-6-371-8750) Ed. Kyotaro Takechi. circ. 178,000. **Document type:** consumer publication.

HARVEST TIMES. see FOOD AND FOOD INDUSTRIES — Grocery Trade

HEALTH LETTER (WASHINGTON). see MEDICAL SCIENCES

HEALTH LITERATURE REPORTS. see MEDICAL SCIENCES

HOT TOPICS; burning legal issues in plain language. see LAW

051 US
HOUSING CHEAP OR ON A BUDGET NEWSLETTER. 1990. biennial. $6. Center for Self-Sufficiency, Publishing Division, c/o Prosperity & Profits Unlimited, Distribution Services, Box 416, Denver, CO 80201-0416. TEL 303-575-5676. Ed. A.C. Doyle. R&P contact: A. Doyle. circ. 4,500. (looseleaf format) **Document type:** newsletter.
Description: Ideas on cheap housing.

HUIS (YEAR). see REAL ESTATE

THE HUMAN ECOLOGIST. see ENVIRONMENTAL STUDIES

640.73 FR ISSN 1145-0673
I N C HEBDO CONSOMMATEURS ACTUALITES. w. 620 F. (foreign 760 F.) (effective 1997). Institut National de la Consommation, 80 rue Lecourbe, 75732 Paris Cedex 15, France. TEL 33-1-45662020. FAX 33-1-45662120. E-mail: inc3@club-internet.fr. Ed. Marie-Jeanne Husset; Pub. Marc Deby. **Document type:** consumer publication, newsletter.
Formerly: Consommateurs Actualites (ISSN 0339-154X)

917.1 CN ISSN 0704-7428
IMAGE DE LA MAURICIE. m. Can.$15. Publicite G.M. Inc., 564 Blvd. des Prairies, Cap-de-la-Madeleine, Que. G8T 1K9, Canada. TEL 819-378-2176. Ed. Gilles Mercier. adv.; circ. 10,000 (controlled).
Formerly (until 1977): Mauricie Touristique (ISSN 0700-3188)

IMPACT (WASHINGTON). see TRANSPORTATION — Automobiles

640.73 US ISSN 0162-1300
IMPACT JOURNAL. 1972. irreg. $15. Impact Journal, 301 Lynn Manor Dr., Rockville, MD 20850-4430. TEL 301-309-6790. Ed. A. Louis Ripskis. bk.rev.
Description: Includes exposes on waste and mismanagement, fraud and rip-offs, and occasional travel articles.

640.73 EI ISSN 1018-5755
HC240.9.C63
INFO - C (ENGLISH EDITION). French edition (ISSN 1018-5747); German edition (ISSN 1021-2248) 1991. bi-m. free. European Commission, DG XXIV Consumer Policy, Unit 3, Rue de la Loi 200, 1049 Brussels, Belgium. TEL 32-2-2957080. FAX 32-2-2991857. E-mail: sheila.reynolds@dg24.cec.be. Ed. Nicolas Geneva y. bk.rev. circ. 10,000. **Document type:** bulletin.
—BLDSC (4478.876555).
Description: Covers issues of consumer policy within the EU, including consumer protection. Reviews case laws.

640.73 IT ISSN 0020-1871
INSIEME (ROME). 1959. m. L.100000($62) Editoriale Italiana, Via Viglieno 10, 00192 Rome, Italy. TEL 39-6-3230177. FAX 39-6-3211359. Ed. Giordano Treveri Gennari. charts; illus.; index. circ. 20,000. **Document type:** consumer publication.
Formerly: Rassegna dell'Economo Cattolico (ISSN 0392-8381)

640.73 387.7 CN
INTER - CANADIAN. (Text in English, French) 1989. 6/yr. R.E.P. Communications Inc., 1623 De Maricourt St., Montreal, Que. H4E 1V6, Canada. TEL 514-762-1667. FAX 514-769-9490. Ed. Andre Vigneau. adv.: B&W page Can.$2625, color page Can.$3500; trim 8 x 10 7/8. circ. 25,000.
Formerly: Intair.
Description: Covers consumer protection, education and general interest topics.

343.071 NE
INTERNATIONAL CONSUMER PROTECTION. (Text in English) 2 base vols. (plus irreg. supplements). (Center for International Legal Studies) Kluwer Law International (Subsidiary of: Wolters Kluwer N.V.), Postbus 85889, 2508 CN The Hague, Netherlands. TEL 31-70-3081500. FAX 31-70-3081515. E-mail: services@wkap.nl; URL: http://www.wkap.nl. (Dist. by: Libresso Distribution Centre, P.O. Box 23, 7400 GA Deventer, Netherlands. TEL 31-570-633155. FAX 31-570-633834; In N. America: Kluwer Law International, 675 Massachusetts Ave., Cambridge, MA 02139. TEL 617-354-0140. FAX 617-354-8595) Ed. Dennis Campbell. (looseleaf format)
Description: Examines the area of consumer protection law in an international context.

640.73 614 NE ISSN 0929-8347
HC79.C63
INTERNATIONAL JOURNAL FOR CONSUMER SAFETY. (Text in English) 1994. 4/yr. fl.480($291) (effective 1997). (European Consumer Safety Association) Aeolus Press (Subsidiary of: Swets & Zeitlinger bv), Postbus 740, 4116 ZJ Buren, Netherlands. TEL 31-344-572055. FAX 31-344-572562. E-mail: orders@swets.nl; URL: http://www.swets.nl. (Subscr. to: Swets & Zeitlinger bv, P.O. Box 825, 2160 SZ Lisse, Netherlands. TEL 31-252-435111. FAX 31-252-415888; Dist. in N. America by: Swets & Zeitlinger, Box 613, Royersford, PA 19468. TEL 800-447-9387. FAX 610-524-5366) Ed. Wim Rogmans; Pub. J.K.W. van Leeuwen. R&P contact: C.E. van Leeuwen-Meyren. adv. contact: Patrick Kleian. bk.rev. (back issues avail.) **Document type:** academic/scholarly publication.
—BLDSC (4542.175920). **CCC.**
Supersedes: E C O S A Newsletter.
Description: Publishes original papers, review articles, short communications and news items relating to research in the etiology of accidents in everyday life, policy development and implementation of prevention strategies.
Refereed Serial

917.1 028.5 CN ISSN 0838-5505
ISLAND PARENT MAGAZINE. 1988. m. Can.$26.75 (in US Can.$35) (effective 1997). Island Parent Group Enterprises Ltd., 941 Kings Rd., Victoria, BC V8T 1W7, Canada. TEL 604-388-6905. FAX 604-388-4391. Ed. Selinde Krayenhoff. R&P contact: Mada Johnson. adv. contact: Paul Abra. bk.rev. circ. 25,000. **Document type:** consumer publication.
Description: Written for and by parents on Vancouver Island. Covers education, recreation, discipline, relationships, work, birth, grandparenting and family finance.
Refereed Serial

640.73 SZ
J'ACHETE MIEUX. 1959. 10/yr. 60 SFr. (effective 1996). Federation Romande des Consommateurs, Route de Geneve 7, Case postale 2820, CH-1002 Lausanne, Switzerland. TEL 41-21-3128006. FAX 41-21-3128004. circ. 43,000. **Document type:** consumer publication.

JOURNAL D'ECONOMIE MEDICALE. see MEDICAL SCIENCES

640.73 US ISSN 0022-0078
HC110.C6
JOURNAL OF CONSUMER AFFAIRS. 1967. s-a. $70 to individuals; institutions $170 (includes Consumer News and Reviews, Advancing the Consumer Interest, Consumer Interests Annual) (effective 1997 & 1998). American Council on Consumer Interests, 240 Stanley Hall, University of Missouri, Columbia, MO 65211. TEL 573-882-3817. FAX 573-884-6571. E-mail: acci@showme.missouri.edu; URL: http://acci.ps.missouri.edu. (Editorial addr.: 102 Erikson Hall, Univ. of Kentucky, Lexington, KY 40506-0050) Ed. Claudia Peck-Heath. adv.; bk.rev.; abstr.; bibl.; charts; stat. circ. 1,600. (also avail. in microform from MIM,UMI; reprint service avail. from UMI,KTO) **Indexed:** ABI Inform., Arts & Hum.Cit.Ind., ASCA, B.P.I., Bk.Rev.Ind. (1980-1990), BPIA, Bus.Educ.Ind., Bus.Ind., C.I.J.E., Child.Bk.Rev.Ind. (1980-1990), Commun.Abstr., Consum.Ind., Curr.Cont., Curr.Pack.Abstr., J.of Econ.Lit., Manage.Cont., Mkt.Inform.Guide., P.A.I.S., Ref.Pt.Food Indus.Abstr., Risk Abstr., SSCI, Tr.& Indus.Ind. **Document type:** academic/scholarly publication.
—BLDSC (4965.210000); Genuine Article; KR SourceOne; SWETS; UMI; UnCover.
Description: Interdisciplinary academic journal that fosters and disseminates professional thought and scholarly research having implications for government, household, or business policy.
Refereed Serial

640.73 NE ISSN 0168-7034
HF5415.3 CODEN: JCPODV
JOURNAL OF CONSUMER POLICY; consumer issues in law, economics and behavioral sciences. (Text in English) 1977. q. fl.415($247) to institutions (effective 1997). Kluwer Academic Publishers, Postbus 17, 3300 AA Dordrecht, Netherlands. TEL 31-78-6392392. FAX 31-78-6392254. TELEX 29245 KAPG NL. E-mail: services@wkap.nl; URL: http://www.wkap.nl. (Dist. by: Kluwer Academic Publishers Group, P.O. Box 322, 3300 AH Dordrecht, Netherlands. TEL 31-78-6392392. FAX 31-78-6546474; N. America dist. addr.: Box 358, Accord Station, Hingham, MA 02018-0358. TEL 617-871-6600. FAX 617-871-6528) Ed.Bd. adv.; bk.rev.; index. (also avail. in microform from UMI; reprint service avail. from SWZ) **Indexed:** ABI Inform., ASCA, Bibl.Agri., BPIA, Curr.Cont., ELLIS, Euro.LJI, Fam.Ind., IBR, IBZ, P.A.I.S., SSCI, Tr.& Indus.Ind. **Document type:** academic/scholarly publication.
●Also available online. Vendor(s): Information Access Co.
—BLDSC (4965.212000); Genuine Article; SWETS; UMI; UnCover. **CCC.**
Formerly (until 1983): Zeitschrift fuer Verbraucherpolitik (ISSN 0342-5843)
Description: Publishes research in a broad range of issues relating to consumer affairs, including discussion of social and economic structures influencing the consumer interest, and the impact of policies and actions of consumers, industry, organizations, government and educational institutions. Includes extensive systematic coverage of issues in consumer law and legislation in transnational communities such as the EC.
Refereed Serial

640 UK ISSN 0309-3891
JOURNAL OF CONSUMER STUDIES & HOME ECONOMICS. 1977. q. £173($315) (foreign £190) (effective 1998). Blackwell Science Ltd., Osney Mead, Oxford OX2 OEL, England. TEL 01865-206206. FAX 01865-721205. E-mail: journals.cs@blacksci.co.uk; URL: http://www.black.co.uk. Ed. Ann Maree Rees; Pub. Allen Stevens. R&P contact: Sarah Pollard. adv. contact: Martine Cariou-Keen. abstr.; bibl.; index. circ. 365. (also avail. in microform from UMI; back issues avail.; reprint service avail. from ISI) **Indexed:** Educ.Tech.Abstr., Excerp.Med., Fam.Ind Food Sci.& Tech.Abstr., P.A.I.S., Stud.Wom.Abstr., Tech.Educ.Abstr., World Text.Abstr. **Document type:** academic/scholarly publication.
—BLDSC (4965.217000); SWETS; UMI; UnCover. **CCC.**
Refereed Serial

JOURNAL OF INTERNATIONAL CONSUMER MARKETING. see BUSINESS AND ECONOMICS — Marketing And Purchasing

640.73 II
KARNATAKA CONSUMER VOICE. m. Karnataka Consumer Service Society, 877 Hal. 3rd Stage, Bangalore 560 075, India. TEL 576224.

CONSUMER EDUCATION AND PROTECTION

HRUS; the magazine for the kosher consumer. see *OOD AND FOOD INDUSTRIES*

40.73　　　　　CY　ISSN 0255-8408
ANALOTIS/CONSUMER. (Text in Greek) 1977. bi-m. O. Box 4874, 28 Gladstone St., Nicosia 162, yprus. TEL 0245-1092. FAX 0246-7080. circ. 000.

40.73　　　　　II
MAT; consumer's voice. (Text in English) 1972. m. embership. Consumer Guidance Society, Hutment Mahapalika Marg, Mumbai 400 001, India. EL 91-22-262-1612. FAX 91-22-265-9715. Ed. ynthia Rodrigues. bk.rev. circ. 2,000. **Document** pe: consumer publication.

40.73　　　　　AU
SUMENT. 1961. m. S.486 (effective 1997). Verein er Konsumenten-Information, Mariahilfer Str. 81, -1060 Vienna, Austria. TEL 43-1-588770. Ed. erhard Frueholz. bk.rev. circ. 115,000. **Document** pe: consumer publication.

40.73　　　　　LU
KONSUMENT. (Text in French, German, uxembourgish) 1963. 18/yr. 1000 Fr. Union uxembourgeoise des Consommateurs, 55 rue des ruyeres, 1274 Howald, Luxembourg. EL 49-60-22. FAX 49-49-57. TELEX 2966. circ. 5,000. (looseleaf format)

40.73　　　　　NE　ISSN 0929-0001
ISCH CONSUMEREN. 1982. 8/yr. fl.44. lternatieve Konsumenten Bond, Postbus 61236, 005 HE Amsterdam, Netherlands. EL 31-20-6863338. FAX 31-20-6867361. E-mail: kb@xs4all.nl. Ed. Peter Beekman. R&P contact: eter Beekman. bk.rev.; circ. 2,500 (paid). (back ssues avail.) **Document type:** consumer publication.
Former titles (until 1992): Voeding en Milieu (ISSN 926-0447); (until 1990): Alternatieve onsumentengids (ISSN 0168-0676)
Description: Provides information on issues relating o responsible consumerism, including the nvironment, Third World, animal welfare, and the orking environment.

A C NEWSLETTER. (Legal Information Access Centre) ee *LAW*

DER'S PRODUCT LIABILITY LAW AND STRATEGY. see *BUSINESS AND ECONOMICS — Production Of oods And Services*

AL PLAN LETTER. see *LAW*

ON AID MAGAZINE. see *TRANSPORTATION — utomobiles*

ON TIMES. see *TRANSPORTATION — Automobiles*

NG ABROAD; the Daily Telegraph guide. see *TRAVEL ND TOURISM*

640.73　　　　　US
ING CHEAP NEWS. 1992. 10/yr. $12 in U.S.; Canada $15; elsewhere $19 (effective 1997). iving Cheap Press, 7232 Belleview Ave., Kansas City, MO 64114-1218. TEL 816-523-3161. AX 816-523-0224. E-mail: livcheap@aol.com. Ed. arry Roth. bk.rev.; circ. 1,800 (paid). **Document** ype: consumer publication, newsletter.
Description: Eclectic frugality newsletter containing money-saving tips with emphasis on "doing without," smarter, cheaper ways to buy, travel, live.

OKOUT - FOODS. see *FOOD AND FOOD INDUSTRIES*

D R WATCH; an independent guide to medical device reporting. (Medical Device Reporting) see *MEDICAL SCIENCES*

640.73　　　　　IS
KADAI. 4/yr. IS.10. Israel Consumer Board, 28 Albert Mendeler St., Hakirya, Tel Aviv, Israel. TEL 03-266138. circ. 10,000.

917.1　　　　　CN　ISSN 0832-557X
AGAZINE LE CLAP. 1986. bi-m. Cinema Le Clap, 2360 chemin Ste-Foy, Ste. Foy, PQ G1V 4H2, Canada. TEL 418-653-2470. FAX 418-653-6018. adv. circ. 59,400.

E MARKET GUIDE. see *BUSINESS AND ECONOMICS — Investments*

MASS CYCLIST. see *SPORTS AND GAMES — Bicycles And Motorcycles*

MASSCITIZEN. see *ENVIRONMENTAL STUDIES*

MEIO AMBIENTE. see *ENVIRONMENTAL STUDIES*

640.73　　　　　US
MERCHANDISER. w. Box 1289, Center, TX 75935. TEL 409-598-3377. Ed. Leon Aldridge.

640.73　　　　　SW　ISSN 1102-2930
MERSMAK. 1953. 6/yr. Konsumentfoereningen Stockholm, Magnus Ladulaasg. 67, S-102 61 Stockholm, Sweden. TEL 46-8-743-50-00. Ed. Rune Struck. adv.: B&W page SEK 34900, color page SEK 43500; trim 185 x 240; adv. contact: Anne-Marie Sandstroem. circ. 384,400. cols./p.: 3; pp./issue: 48.
Formerly (until 1990): Storstaden (ISSN 0491-113X)

MILLER'S PRODUCT LIABILITY & SAFETY ENCYCLOPAEDIA. see *LAW*

640.73　　　　　CN　ISSN 0705-6109
KE1610.A13
MISLEADING ADVERTISING BULLETIN. (Text in English and French) 1974. q. free. Department of Industry Canada, Bureau of Competition Policy, Marketing Practices Branch, 50 Victoria St., Hull, PQ K1A 0C9, Canada. TEL 819-953-8549. FAX 819-953-2557. Ed. Danielle Dubois. adv. contact: Claire Payette. circ. 5,000. **Indexed:** CS Ind. **Document type:** government publication.
Description: Covers current policies, practices, convictions and alternative case resolutions related to the misleading advertising and deceptive marketing practices provisions of the Competition Act of Canada.

MONEY (NEW YORK). see *BUSINESS AND ECONOMICS — Banking And Finance*

640.73 381　　　　　US
MONEY SAVER. w. Box 152, Bolivar, TN 38008.

640.73　　　　　US　ISSN 0026-9646
TX335
MONEYSWORTH. 1970. q. $10. Avant-Garde Media, Inc., 80 Central Park W., Ste. 16B, New York, NY 10023. Ed. Ralph Ginzburg. adv.; bk.rev. circ. 900,000. (tabloid format; also avail. in microfilm from UMI) **Indexed:** Hlth.Ind., Mag.Ind.
—UMI. **CCC.**

640.73　　　　　US　ISSN 0739-392X
N A C A A NEWS. 1978. 10/yr. $75 to individuals; businesses $95. National Association of Consumer Agency Administrators, 1010 Vermont Ave., N.E., Ste. 514, Washington, DC 20005. TEL 202-347-7395. Dir. Anna Flores. index. circ. 300. (tabloid format; back issues avail.) **Document type:** newsletter.
Description: What's happening in state, local and federal consumer protection agencies.

N A P O NEWS/ECHO DE L'O N A P. (National Anti-Poverty Organization) see *SOCIAL SERVICES AND WELFARE*

640.73 332　　　　　US　ISSN 1090-2740
N C F E MOTIVATOR. 1982. q. $10. National Center for Financial Education, Box 34070, San Diego, CA 92163-4070. TEL 619-232-8811. URL: http://www.ncfe.org. Ed. Paul Richard; Pub. Loren Dunton. bk.rev/; circ. 7,600 (paid). **Document type:** newsletter.
Description: Dedicated to helping people improve their spending behavior, decrease reliance on credit and increase their savings.

N C L C ENERGY & UTILITY UPDATE. (National Consumer Law Center) see *LAW*

N C L C REPORTS: BANKRUPTCY & FORECLOSURES. (National Consumer Law Center) see *LAW*

N C L C REPORTS: CONSUMER CREDIT & USURY. (National Consumer Law Center) see *LAW*

N C L C REPORTS: DEBT COLLECTION & REPOSESSIONS. (National Consumer Law Center) see *LAW*

N C L C REPORTS: DECEPTIVE ACTS & WARRANTIES. (National Consumer Law Center) see *LAW*

640.73　　　　　US　ISSN 1044-3134
N Y P I R G AGENDA. 1978. q. $25 membership. New York Public Interest Research Group, Inc., 9 Murray St., 3rd Fl., New York, NY 10007-2272. TEL 212-349-6460. FAX 212-349-1366. Ed. Tracy Peel. bk.rev. circ. 75,000. **Indexed:** Alt.Press Ind. **Document type:** newsletter.
Formerly: Agenda for Citizen Involvement (ISSN 0745-368X)
Description: Provides updates on group's programs, including consumer protection, environmental preservation, energy conservation, food safety, government accountability, fairness in standardized testing, and citizen participation.

640.73　　　　　US　ISSN 1055-923X
NATIONAL CONSUMERS LEAGUE BULLETIN. 1937. bi-m. $20 to individuals; corporations $100. National Consumers League, Inc., 1701 K St., N.W., Ste. 1200, Washington, DC 20006. TEL 202-835-3323. FAX 202-835-0747. E-mail: nclncl@aol.com; URL: http://www.nationalconsumersleague.org. Eds. Cleo Manuel, Kim Michalski. R&P contact: Cleo Manuel. bk.rev. circ. 5,000. **Document type:** bulletin.
Description: Investigates, educates and advocates consumer and worker rights on marketplace and workplace issues.

NATIONAL LIQUOR NEWS. see *BEVERAGES*

NEW SOUTH WALES & AUSTRALIAN CAPITAL TERRITORY RETAIL DIRECTORY. see *BUSINESS AND ECONOMICS — Trade And Industrial Directories*

640.73　　　　　US　ISSN 0095-5590
HC107.N73
NEW YORK (STATE). CONSUMER PROTECTION BOARD. ANNUAL REPORT. Key Title: Annual Report - State Consumer Protection Board. 1976. a. free to NY state residents. Consumer Protection Board, Albany, NY 12210. illus. circ. 500. **Document type:** government publication.

640.73　　　　　IC　ISSN 1021-7223
NEYTENDABLADID. 1953. bi-m. ISK 1900 membership. Neytendasamtoekin, Skulagata 26, IS-101 Reykjavik, Iceland. TEL 354-562-5000. FAX 354-562-4666. Ed. Johannes Gunnarsson. circ. 24,500. (back issues avail.) **Document type:** consumer publication.

640.73　　　　　FR　ISSN 0184-9832
NOUS. (Supplement avail.: Femmes Chefs de Famille (ISSN 0184-9824)) 1969. bi-m. 65 F. (Confederation Syndicale des Familles) Editions Garibaldi, 53 rue Riquet, 75019 Paris, France. TEL 40-35-33-99.

640.73 691　　　　　GW
▼**OEKO-HAUS;** bauen, wohnen, renovieren. 1997. q. DM.35; newsstand price: DM.9.50. Oeko-Test Verlag GmbH und Co. KG, Kasselerstr. 1a, 60486 Frankfurt a.M., Germany. TEL 49-69-97777-0. FAX 49-69-97777139. E-mail: oet.verlag@oekotest.de; URL: http://www.oekotest.de. Ed. Thomas Schmitz-Guenther. adv. contact: Renate Zoerb. circ. 90,000 (paid). **Document type:** consumer publication.

640.73　　　　　GW　ISSN 0178-7608
OEKO-TEST MAGAZIN; oekologische Verbraucherzeitschrift. 1985. m. DM.72 (foreign DM.87; CD-ROM DM.50) (effective 1997); newsstand price: DM.6.50. Oeko-Test Verlag GmbH und Co. KG, Kasselerstr. 1a, 60486 Frankfurt a.M., Germany. TEL 49-69-97777-0. FAX 49-69-97777139. E-mail: oet.verlag@oekotest.de; URL: http://www.oekotest.de. Ed. Juergen Stellpflug. adv. contact: Renate Zoerb. bk.rev.; index; circ. 140,000 (paid). (back issues avail.) **Document type:** consumer publication.
●Also available on CD-ROM.
—SWETS.
Description: Tests products for consumer health and environmental safety.

OFF THE AIR. see *COMMUNICATIONS — Radio*

640.73　　　　　US
OKLAHOMA. COMMISSION ON CONSUMER CREDIT. ANNUAL REPORT. a. Commission on Consumer Credit, 4545 N. Lincoln, No. 104, Oklahoma City, OK 73105. TEL 405-521-3653; 800-448-4904.
Formerly: Oklahoma. Commission on Consumer Affairs. Annual Report.

CONSUMER EDUCATION AND PROTECTION

641.1   US
P C C SOUND CONSUMER. 1974. m. $12 to non-members. Puget Consumers Co-op, 4201 Roosevelt Way, N.E., Seattle, WA 98105-6008. TEL 206-547-1222. FAX 206-545-7131. Ed. Kim Runciman. adv. contact: Nancy Gaynat. bk.rev.; illus. circ. 43,000. (tabloid format; back issues avail.) **Document type:** newspaper.
     Formerly: Puget Consumers Co-op Newsletter.

640.73   IT
PANIERE; mensile di informazione del consumatore. 1976. m. L.3300. Rodi S.p.A., Via G.B. Soresina 9, 20144 Milan, Italy. TEL 39-2-48195639. FAX 39-2-48195657. Ed. Armando Bonacina. adv.: B&W page L.3000000, color page L.10000000. circ. 310,000. **Document type:** consumer publication.

640.73 381   US
PEDDLER. Box 701, Cookville, TN 38503-0701. TEL 615-526-5910.

PENSIONERS VOICE. see SOCIAL SERVICES AND WELFARE

614 640.73 360   US   ISSN 0736-4873
PEOPLE'S MEDICAL SOCIETY NEWSLETTER. 1983. bi-m. $20 (effective 1996 & 1997). People's Medical Society, 462 Walnut St., Allentown, PA 18102-5488. TEL 610-770-1670. FAX 610-770-0607. Ed. Jennifer Hay. R&P contact: Jennifer Hay. charts; stat.; index. circ. 65,000. (looseleaf format; back issues avail.) **Indexed:** CHNI, Hlth.Ind. **Document type:** newsletter.
     ●Also available online. Vendor(s): Information Access Co.
     Description: Provides medical consumers with previously unavailable medical information so that they can make informed decisions about their own health care.

640.73   US
POCKET CHANGE INVESTOR. 1990. q. $12.95. Good Advice Press, Box 78, Elizaville, NY 12523. TEL 914-758-1400. Ed. Marc Eisenson; Pub. Nancy Castleman. bk.rev.; charts; stat. (looseleaf format; back issues avail.) **Document type:** newsletter, consumer publication.
     Formerly: Banker's Secret Bulletin (ISSN 1054-8920)
     Description: Teaches consumers how to save money on mortgages, credit cards, and other debts. Focuses on painless ways to save on other expenses, such as taxes, cars and insurance.

POWER LINE. see ENERGY

658   US   ISSN 0748-4755   CODEN: PRADER
PRICING ADVISOR. 1984. m. $195 in U.S. and Canada; elsewhere $295 (effective 1994). 3277 Roswell Rd., Ste. 620, Atlanta, GA 30305-1840. TEL 404-509-9933. FAX 404-509-1862. (Subscr. to: Box 1831, Birmingham, AL 35201-1831. TEL 800-633-4931) Ed. Eric G. Mitchell. R&P contact: Eric Mitchell. bk.rev. **Document type:** newsletter.

640.73 332   US   ISSN 0195-5934
PRIME TIMES MAGAZINE. 1978. q. $15. (National Association for Retired Credit Union People) Grote Publishing, 634 W. Main St., Ste. 207, Madison, WI 53703-2634. TEL 608-257-4640. FAX 608-257-4670. Ed. Barbara Walsh. R&P contact: Barbara Walsh. adv. contact: Frances Healy. circ. 80,000 (controlled). **Document type:** consumer publication.
     Description: Covers consumer education, health, travel, lifestyle, and money management for credit union members 50 and over.

640.73   SW   ISSN 0348-3312
PRIVATA AFFAERER. 1978. m. SEK 390 (effective 1995). Affaersfoerlaget, P.O. Box 3188, S-103 63 Stockholm, Sweden. (Subscr. to: Pressdata AB, P.O. Box 3217, S-103 64 Stockholm, Sweden) Ed. Anders Andersson. adv. circ. 50,000.

PRODUCT ALERT. see FOOD AND FOOD INDUSTRIES

PRODUCT LIABILITY AUSTRALIA. see LAW

PRODUCTS LIABILITY LAW JOURNAL. see LAW

640.73   CN   ISSN 0701-8517
PROTEGEZ-VOUS. (Text in French) 1973. m. Can.$19.95. Office de la Protection du Consommateur, 5199 Sherbrooke St. E., Ste. 2580, Montreal, PQ H1T 3X1, Canada. TEL 514-873-7771. FAX 514-873-3429. Ed. Jacques Elliot. circ. 150,000. **Indexed:** Can.B.P.I., Can.Per.Ind., CMI, Pt.de Rep. (1979-), Sportsearch (1984-).
     Description: Provides information on consumer rights and issues, comparative product tests, and product and service buying guides.

640.73   SZ
PRUEF MIT. 1969. 10/yr. 42 SFr. (foreign 52 SFr.); newsstand price: 5.70 SFr. Konsumentinnenforum Schweiz KF, Postfach, CH-8024 Zurich, Switzerland. TEL 01-2523914. FAX 01-2611279. Eds. Doris Huber, Christine Ruf Erne. circ. 44,000. **Document type:** consumer publication.

320   US   ISSN 0738-5927   HC79.C63
PUBLIC CITIZEN. 1976. bi-m. $25 (foreign $35). Public Citizen, Inc., 1600 20th St., N.W., Washington, DC 20009. TEL 202-833-3000. FAX 202-296-1727. URL: http://www.essential.org/ public_citizen/; gopher://gopher.essential.org/hh/ ftp/pub/public_citizen. Ed. Melissa W. Kaye. R&P contact: Melissa W. Kaye. bk.rev.; illus. circ. 100,000. (tabloid format) **Indexed:** Alt.Press Ind., Med. Care Rev. **Document type:** consumer publication.
     Incorporates (1979-1987): Congress Watcher (ISSN 0278-1093)
     Description: Articles for the politically active consumer; public investigation articles on consumer rights, safety and protection.

640.73 345.01   US
PUBLIC EYE (MADISON).* 1975. q. $20. Center for Public Representation, Box 260049, Madison, WI 53726-0049. TEL 608-251-4009. FAX 608-251-1263. Ed. Nicole Graper; Pub. Michael Pritchard. circ. 1,200 (paid). **Document type:** newsletter.
     Description: Reports on broad range of consumer and legal issues of interest to residents of Wisconsin.

THE QUAD REPORT; covering efficiency, demand-side management, and energy policy. see ENERGY

640.73   US   ISSN 0736-1688
REFUNDING UPDATE. 1983. s-a. $4. Update Publicare Co., c/o Prosperity & Profits Unlimited, Distribution Services, Box 416, Denver, CO 80201-0416. TEL 303-575-5676. Ed. A. Doyle. adv.; bibl. circ. 3,000. (looseleaf format; also avail. in microfiche; back issues avail.) **Document type:** newsletter.

640.73   US   ISSN 0194-0139
REFUNDLE BUNDLE. 1973. bi-m. $10. Box 140, Centuck Sta., Yonkers, NY 10710. TEL 914-472-2227. Eds. Susan J. Samtur, Stephen M. Samtur; Pub. Susan J. Samtur. R&P contact: Susan J. Samtur. adv. contact: Susan J. Samtur. circ. 70,000. (tabloid format; back issues avail.)
     Description: Provides coupon and refund information on all current offers.

RENTAL DEALER NEWS. see BUSINESS AND ECONOMICS — Marketing And Purchasing

650 640   US
REPORT TO BUSINESS. 1975. q. free. Better Business Bureau of Metropolitan New York Inc., 257 Park Ave. S., New York, NY 10010. TEL 212-533-7500. Ed. Carrie Getty. stat.; circ. controlled.
     Formerly: Report to Business and Consumer Information; Formed by the merger of: Better Business Bureau of Metropolitan New York. Report to Business (ISSN 0045-1819); Consumer Information for Employees.

640.73   US
RESOURCES (NASHVILLE); a consumer information source for customers of financial institutions. 1983. q. free. F I S I - Madison Financial (Subsidiary of: C U C International), Box 40726, Nashville, TN 37204. TEL 615-371-2658. (Or: 200 Powell Place, Brentwood, TN 37027) Ed. Melany Klinck. circ. 1,200,000 (controlled). (looseleaf format) **Document type:** newsletter.
     Description: Consumer and lifestyle information for bank customers over 50. Provides practical solutions to the challenges of saving, spending and earning. **Refereed Serial**

REVUE EUROPEENNE DE DROIT DE LA CONSOMMATION. see LAW

RIGHT-TO-KNOW PLANNING GUIDE (SERIES). see SOCIAL SERVICES AND WELFARE

640.73   RU
S P R O S. (Sovety Potrebitelyam, Reitingi, Obzory, Situatsii); spravochno-informatsionnoe izdanie dlya potrebitelei. (Text in Russian) 1992. m? Ul. Varvarka, 14, 103690 Moscow, Russia. TEL 7-95-2984957. Ed. Larisa Leonova. circ. 200,000.

640.73   DK   ISSN 0036-3944
SAMVIRKE. 1928. 12/yr. free to members. F D B - Faellesforeningen for Danmarks Brugsforeninger - Danish Consumers Cooperative Movement, c/o Poul Dines, Ed., Roskildevej 65, DK-2620 Albertslund, Denmark. TEL 45-43-86-43-86. FAX 45-43-86-44-89. TELEX 33311FDBHK DK. E-mail: fdb@fdb.dk. Ed. Poul Dines. adv.; index. circ. 800,000. **Document type:** newsletter.

640.73   IT
SCELTE DEL CONSUMATORE (DAILY). 1976. d. L.300000 includes monthly review. Unione Nazionale Consumatori, Via Andrea Doria 48, 00192 Rome, Italy. TEL 39-6-39737021. FAX 39-6-39733329. Ed. Vincenzo Dona. bk.rev. circ. 5,100. **Document type:** consumer publication.
     Formerly: U N C Notizie.

SCHRIFTTUMS FUER DEN BEREICH HAUSHALT UND VERBAUCH. BIBLIOGRAPHIE. see HOME ECONOMICS

SENIOR SUN. see ENERGY

640.73   NE   ISSN 0922-1646
SERVICESERIE. (Consists of: Auto; Geld; Huis; Lekker) 1978. 7/yr. Service Pers B.V., Postbus 9044, 1800 GA Alkmaar, Netherlands. TEL 31-72-158084. FAX 31-72-157540. Ed. Peter Hooft. adv. **Document type:** consumer publication.
     Description: Publishes information for consumers on automobiles, housing, money and restaurants.

SHEDDING LIGHT ON LEGISLATION. see PUBLIC HEALTH AND SAFETY

640.73   US   ISSN 1056-8832   TX356
SHOPPING FOR A BETTER WORLD; a quick and easy guide to socially responsible supermarket shopping. a. $14. Council on Economic Priorities, 30 Irving Pl, New York, NY 10003. TEL 800-729-4237. FAX 212-420-0988. Ed. Alice Tepper Marlin. R&P contact: Thomas W. Knowlton.

SLOANE REPORT; an off-line access to computing. see COMPUTERS — Personal Computers

SURVIVE & WIN. see BUSINESS AND ECONOMICS — Computer Applications

T UE V AUTOREPORT; Sicherheitsanalyse, 78 Modelle des In- und Auslandes. (Vereinigung der Technische Ueberwachungs-Vereine e.V.) see TRANSPORTATION — Automobiles

TAX HOTLINE; the inside report for people who need to be on top of every tax break the law allows. see BUSINESS AND ECONOMICS — Public Finance, Taxation

640.73   FI   ISSN 0355-4287
TEKNIIKAN MAAILMA. 21/yr. FIM 516. Yhtyneet Kuvalehdet Oy, Maistraatinportti 1, FIN-00240 Helsinki, Finland. TEL 358-0-156-6524. FAX 358-0-156-6505. TELEX 121364. Ed. Mauri Salo. adv.: B&W page FIM 24600, color page FIM 36200. circ. 115,179. **Document type:** consumer publication.
     Description: Covers automobiles, home electronic, videos and cameras for the prospective buyer.

640.73   US
TENNESSEE CONSUMER PROTECTION ACT AND RELATED LAWS. a. $8. Michie, A Division of Reed Elsevier Inc., Box 7587, Charlottesville, VA 22906-7587. TEL 804-972-7566; 800-562-1197. FAX 800-643-1280. E-mail: custserv@michie.com; URL: http://www.michie.com. Ed. George Harley.

CONSUMER EDUCATION AND PROTECTION — ABSTRACTING, BIBLIOGRAPHIES, STATISTICS

640   GW   ISSN 0040-3946
TEST; die Zeitschrift fuer den Verbraucher. 1966. m. DM.68.40 (foreign DM.80.40) (effective 1997). Stiftung Warentest, Luetzowplatz 11-13, 10785 Berlin, Germany. TEL 49-30-26312408. FAX 49-30-26312428. (Co-Sponsor: Bundesministerium fuer Wirtschaft) adv.; bk.rev.; charts; illus.; stat. circ. 1,100,000. **Indexed:** Chem.Abstr., Curr.Ind.Stat., Key to Econ.Sci. **Document type:** consumer publication.
—BLDSC (8796.327000); SWETS.

640.73   BE   ISSN 0772-9413
TEST AANKOOP MAGAZINE. French edition: Test Achats Magazine (ISSN 0772-9405) 1958. m. 2256 BEF in Belgium and Luxemburg (elsewhere 2608 BEF). Verbruikersunie - Association des Consommateurs, Rue de Hollande 13, 1060 Brussels, Belgium. TEL 32-2-5423211. FAX 32-2-5423250. TELEX 26771.
Formerly (until 1984): Test Aankoop (ISSN 0772-9758)

640.73   BE   ISSN 0772-9405
TEST ACHATS MAGAZINE. Dutch edition: Test Aankoop Magazine (ISSN 0772-9413) 1958. m. 2256 BEF in Belgium and Luxemburg (elsewhere 2608 BEF). Association des Consommateurs - Verbruikersunie, Rue de Hollande 13, 1060 Brussels, Belgium. TEL 32-2-5423211. FAX 32-2-5423250. TELEX 26771. **Document type:** consumer publication.
Formerly (until 1984): Test Achats (ISSN 0772-974X)

640   GW
TEST JAHRBUCH (YEAR). a. DM.14. Stiftung Warentest, Luetzowplatz 11-13, 10785 Berlin, Germany. TEL 49-30-26312408. FAX 49-30-26312428. circ. 420,000. **Document type:** consumer publication.

TEST SANTE. see PUBLIC HEALTH AND SAFETY

640.73 663   AT   ISSN 0313-0568
THOMSON'S LIQUOR GUIDE. 1976. m. Aus.$110. Thomson Business Publishing, 47 Chippen St., Chippendale, N.S.W. 2008, Australia. TEL 02-699-2411. FAX 02-698-3920. Ed. Glynis Macri. adv.; stat. circ. 994. (back issues avail.)

TIGHTWAD LIVING. see HOME ECONOMICS

343.071   NE   ISSN 0169-1570
TIJDSCHRIFT VOOR CONSUMENTENRECHT. 1985. 5/yr. fl.0.71 per page (effective 1996). Uitgeverij Kluwer B.V., Postbus 23, 7400 GA Deventer, Netherlands. TEL 31-570-633155. FAX 31-570-633834. adv.; circ. 550 (paid). (back issues avail.) **Indexed:** ELLIS. **Document type:** academic/scholarly publication.
—SWETS.

TOPICS IN SAFETY, RISK, RELIABILITY AND QUALITY. see OCCUPATIONAL HEALTH AND SAFETY

TOUREN-FAHRER; Reportagen - Test - Technik. see SPORTS AND GAMES — Bicycles And Motorcycles

UNABHAENGIGE BAUERNSTIMME; eine Zeitung von Baeuerinnen und Bauern. see AGRICULTURE

640.73   JM
VALUE. q. National Consumers' League, 6 Hope Rd., Kingston 10, Jamaica, W.I. TEL 809-92-66388.

VEGETARIAN JOURNAL. see NUTRITION AND DIETETICS

640.73   GW
VERBRAUCHER AKTUELL. 1981. m. DM.15 (effective 1996). Verbraucher - Zentrale Nordrhein-Westfalen Landesarbeitsgemeinschaft der Verbraucherverbaende, Mintropstr. 27, 40215 Duesseldorf, Germany. TEL 49-211-38090. FAX 49-211-3809172. Ed. Bernd Huppertz. R&P contact: Bernd Huppertz. adv.; charts. **Document type:** consumer publication.

640   GW   ISSN 0042-3653
VERBRAUCHER POLITISCHE KORRESPONDENZ. 1953. fortn. DM.198.50. Arbeitsgemeinschaft der Verbraucherverbaende e.V., Heilsbachstr. 20, 53123 Bonn, Germany. TEL 49-228-6489-0. FAX 49-228-644258. Ed. Helga Kuhn. adv.; stat.; index. circ. 2,400. **Document type:** consumer publication, newsletter.

640   GW   ISSN 0042-3661
VERBRAUCHER RUNDSCHAU. 1957. m. DM.29. Arbeitsgemeinschaft der Verbraucherverbaende e.V. (AgV), Heilsbachstr. 20, 53123 Bonn, Germany. TEL 49-228-6489-0. FAX 49-228-644258. Ed. Ileana von Puttkauer-Wigger. bk.rev.; abstr.; charts; illus.; mkt.; pat.; stat.; tr.mk.; index. circ. 10,000. **Indexed:** Excerp.Med. **Document type:** consumer publication.
—BLDSC (9155.770000).

640.73   GW   ISSN 0943-2116
VERBRAUCHER TELEGRAMM. 1987. m. membership. (Verbraucher Initiative e.V.) V I Verlags und Handels GmbH, Breitestr. 51, 53111 Bonn, Germany. TEL 49-228-7263393. FAX 49-228-7263399. E-mail: 100575.242@compuserve.com. adv.; bk.rev. **Document type:** consumer publication.

VICTORIAN TASMANIAN RETAIL DIRECTORY. see BUSINESS AND ECONOMICS — Trade And Industrial Directories

917.1   CN   ISSN 0849-5920
VOIR (MONTREAL). 1986. w. Communications Voir Inc., 4130 St. Denis, Montreal, PQ H2W 2M5, Canada. TEL 514-848-0805. FAX 514-848-9004. Ed. Richard Martineau; Pub. Pierre Paquet. adv.; B&W page Can.$2400; adv. contact: Claudia Pharand. circ. 100,000. (also avail. in microfilm from BNQ) **Document type:** consumer publication.

917.1   CN   ISSN 1188-5017
VOIR (QUEBEC CITY). (Text in French) 1992. w. Can.$70 (U.S. Can.$150; foreign Can.$250). Communications Voir Inc., 4130 St. Denis, Montreal, PQ H2W 2M5, Canada. TEL 514-848-0805. FAX 514-848-9004. Ed. Jean-Simon Gagne; Pub. Pierre Paquet. adv.; B&W page Can.$1475; adv. contact: Claudia Pharand. circ. 50,000. **Document type:** consumer publication.

640.73   IO   ISSN 0126-3455
WARTA KONSUMEN. 1974. m. Rs.1500. Yayasan Lembaga Konsumen Indonesia - Indonesian Consumer Organization, Jalan Pembangunan I No. 1, Duren Tiga, Jakarta 12760, Indonesia. TEL 62-021-7971378. FAX 62-021-7981038. bk.rev. circ. 300.

640.73   US
WASH P I R G REPORTS.* 1981. q. $15. Washington Public Interest Research Group, 5200 University Way N.E., Ste. 201, Seattle, WA 98105-3547. TEL 206-322-9064. Ed. K. Krushas. circ. 30,000. (tabloid format)
Description: Works to identify, research, analyze, and pursue solutions to consumer protection problems, environmental protection and preservation concerns, and corporate and governmental accountability.

640.73   US   ISSN 0272-0469
WASHINGTON CONSUMER'S CHECKBOOK. s-a. $30 for 2 yrs.; newsstand price: $6.95. Center for the Study of Services, 733 15th St., N.W., Ste. 820, Washington, DC 20005-2112. TEL 202-347-7283. Ed. Kevin Brasler; Pub. Robert Krughoff. R&P contact: Dorothy Miller. charts; illus.; mkt.; stat.; cum.index. circ. 55,000. (back issues avail.) **Document type:** consumer publication.

640.73   UK   ISSN 0043-4841
TX335.A1
WHICH?. 1957. m. £59. (Consumers' Association) Which? Ltd., 2 Marylebone Rd., London NW1 4DF, England. TEL 44-171-830-6000. FAX 44-171-830-6220. (Subscr. to: Consumers' Association, Castlemead, Gascoyne Way, Herts. SG14 1LH, England. TEL 44-171-830-8500) Ed. Helen Parker. charts; illus.; index. circ. 686,000. (also avail. in microfiche) **Indexed:** Archit.Per.Ind., Art.Hosp.& Tour., Br.Ceram.Abstr., Consum.Ind., Key to Econ.Sci., RICS, World Surf.Coat., World Text.Abstr. **Document type:** consumer publication.
—BLDSC (9310.800000); CISTI; SWETS.
Description: Deals with consumer education and protection based on testing of goods and services.

640.73   SZ
WIRTSCHAFT UND ENERGIE. irreg. Schweizerischer Energie- Konsumentenverband von Industrie und Wirtschaft, Baumleingasse 22, 4001 Basel, Switzerland. TEL 233060.

WORLD SKI DIRECTORY. see SPORTS AND GAMES — Outdoor Life

640.73   CC
XIANDAI SHENGHUO YONGPIN/MODERN DAILY NECESSITIES. (Text in Chinese) 1981. bi-m. Y8.28($6) (Liaoning Science & Technology Information Institute) Xiandai Shenghuo Yongpin Zazhishe, 9, Heping Dajie 3 Duan, Heping-qu, Shenyang, Liaoning 110003, People's Republic of China. TEL 22818. Ed. Lu Yuanli. illus. circ. 100,000. (reprint service avail.)
Description: Contains articles on interior furniture, home appliances, clothing, toys, food, arts and crafts, daily-use chemicals, and various other products. Introduces new products and new design.

640.73   CC   ISSN 1002-7882
XIAOFEI ZHINAN/CONSUMPTION GUIDE.* (Text in Chinese) m. Xiaofei Zhinan Zazhishe, A-3, Huangsi Dajie, Andingmenwai, Beijing, People's Republic of China. TEL 4218114. (Dist. outside China by: China International Book Trading Corp., P.O. Box 399, Beijing, P.R.C.. TEL 8413063)

640.73 332.67   US   ISSN 1057-123X
HG179
YOUR MONEY. 1979. bi-m. $15.97 (foreign $25.97). Consumers Digest, Inc., 8001 N. Lincoln Ave., 6th Fl., Skokie, IL 60077-3657. TEL 847-763-9200. (Subscr. to: Box 3084, Harlan, IA 51537-3084. TEL 800-777-0025) Ed. Dennis Fertig; Pub. Randy Weber. adv.; B&W page $9885, color page $14820. bk.rev.; charts; illus.; cum.index; circ. 500,000 (paid). (also avail. in microfiche; back issues avail.) **Document type:** consumer publication.
—UMI.
Formerly (until 1991): Money Maker (ISSN 0730-692X)
Description: Personal finance magazine, providing advice on savings and investment opportunities, including mutual funds and stock recommendations.

640.73   US
ZHONGGUO XIAOFEIZHE BAO. (Text in Chinese) 3/w. $101. China Books & Periodicals, Inc., 2929 24th St., San Francisco, CA 94110. TEL 415-282-2994. FAX 415-282-0994. **Document type:** newspaper.

ZILLIONS. see CHILDREN AND YOUTH — For

640.73   FR   ISSN 1267-8066
60 MILLIONS DE CONSOMMATEURS. Variant title: Soixante Millions de Consommateurs. 11/yr. 224 F. (foreign 289 F.) (effective 1997). Institut National de la Consommation, 80 rue Lecourbe, 75732 Paris Cedex 15, France. TEL 33-1-45662020. FAX 33-1-45662120. E-mail: inc1@club-internet.fr. Ed. Marie-Jeanne Husset; Pub. Marc Deby. **Indexed:** Key to Econ.Sci. **Document type:** consumer publication, newsletter.
Formerly: 50 Millions de Consommateurs (ISSN 0339-1531)

CONSUMER EDUCATION AND PROTECTION — Abstracting, Bibliographies, Statistics

640.73 310   JA   ISSN 0289-1336
ANNUAL REPORT ON THE CONSUMER PRICE INDEX (YEAR). 1989. a. 4587 Yen. Nihon Tokei Kyokai - Japan Statistical Association, Crest 21, 6-21, Yocho-machi, Shinjuku-ku, Tokyo 162, Japan. TEL 81-3-5269-3051. FAX 81-3-5269-3058. (Co-sponsor: Somu-cho Tokei-kyoku - Statistics Bureau, Management and Coordination Agency) Ed. Hideshi Honda. R&P contact: Hideshi Honda. adv. contact: Hideshi Honda. **Document type:** government publication.

640.73   EI   ISSN 1013-3402
CONSUMER PRICE INDEX; statistics in focus: economics and finance. French edition: Indice des Prix a la Consommation (ISSN 1010-2787) English quarterly edition (EI ISSN 1011-7725) (Supplement avail. (ISSN 0258-0861)) (Text in English, French) m. $105. Office for Official Publications of the European Communities, L-2985 Luxembourg, Luxembourg. (Dist. in US by: Unipub, 4611-F Assembly Dr., Lanham, MD 20706-4391. TEL 800-274-4888. FAX 301-459-0056) (also avail. in microfiche from CIS) **Indexed:** IIS.
—BLDSC (3424.319000).

COOPERATIVES

640.73   **CN**   ISSN 0703-9352
CONSUMER PRICE INDEX (OTTAWA). 1935. m. Can.$93($112) (foreign $130). Statistics Canada, Operations and Integration Division, Circulation Management, Jean Talon Bldg., 2-C12, Tunney's Pasture, Ottawa, ON K1A 0T6, Canada. TEL 613-951-7277; 800-267-6677. FAX 613-951-1584. URL: http://www.statcan.ca.
Description: Provides a descriptive capsule summary of retail price movements and the factors underlying them.

640.73   **CN**
CONSUMER PRICE INDEX (VICTORIA). 12/yr. Can.$60 (effective 1997). Ministry of Finance and Corporate Relations, B C Stats, P.O. Box 9410, Stn. Prov. Govt., Victoria, BC V8W 9V1, Canada. TEL 250-387-0359. FAX 250-387-0380. E-mail: bcstats@fincc04.fin.gov.bc.ca; URL: http://www.bcstats.gov.bc.ca. **Document type:** government publication.
Description: Price trends in British Columbia, Vancouver and Victoria for various categories of consumer spending. Includes historical summaries and comparisons with major Canadian cities.

640.73 016   **US**   ISSN 0094-0534
TX335
CONSUMERS INDEX; to product evaluations and information sources. 1973. q. (plus a cumulation). $129 ($231 with cumulation). Pierian Press, Box 1808, Ann Arbor, MI 48106. TEL 313-434-5530. FAX 313-434-6409. Ed. Mary Hashman. (also avail. in magnetic tape) **Document type:** abstracting/indexing.
● Also available online. Vendor(s): OCLC.
Also available on CD-ROM. Producer(s): NISC (Consumers Reference Disc).
Description: Evaluations, descriptions and tests of a variety of products.

640.73 016   **US**   ISSN 1053-1424
CONSUMERS REFERENCE DISC. s-a. $695. National Information Services Corporation (NISC), 3100 St. Paul St., Ste. 806, Baltimore, MD 21218. TEL 410-243-0797. FAX 410-243-0982. **Document type:** abstracting/indexing.
● Available only on CD-ROM. Producer(s): NISC.
Description: Provides access to records from Consumers Index and Consumer Health & Nutrition Index from 1985 to the present.

640.73   **JA**
NIKKEI ANTHROPOS. (Text in Japanese) m. Nikkei Home Publishing, Inc. (Subsidiary of: Nihon Keizai Shimbun, Inc.), 2-2-7 Kanda Tsukasa-cho, Chiyoda-ku, Tokyo 101, Japan. TEL 03-3258-7818. **Document type:** consumer publication.
Description: Helps readers enhance business sense, predict life-style trends, and extend their people network.

640.73   **JA**   ISSN 0288-920X
HB235.J3
SHOHISHA BUKKA SHISU GEPPO/JAPAN. STATISTICS BUREAU. MONTHLY REPORT ON THE CONSUMER PRICE INDEX. (Text in Japanese) m. Somucho, Tokeikyoku - Management and Coordination Agency, Statistics Bureau, 19-1, Wakamatsu-cho, Shinjuku-ku, Tokyo 162, Japan. TEL 81-3-3203-1111. FAX 81-3-5273-1180.
Formerly (until 1983): Shohisha Bukka Shisu (ISSN 0448-7222)

640.73 011   **GW**   ISSN 0171-4163
TEST-INDEX. 1980. bi-m. DM.65. Deutsches Bibliotheksinstitut, Abt. 1 - Publikationen, Alt-Moabit 101A, 10559 Berlin, Germany. TEL 49-30-39077-0. FAX 49-30-39077100. circ. 300. **Document type:** bulletin.

640.73   **NN**
VANUATU. STATISTICS OFFICE. REPORTS ON CONSUMER PRICES INDEXES. (Text in English and French) 1976. a. 500 vatu($5) (effective 1996). Statistics Office, Private Mail Bag 19, Port Vila, Vanuatu. TEL 678-22110. FAX 678-24583. Ed. Jacob Isaiah. adv. contact: Tali Saurei. stat. circ. 300. **Document type:** government publication.
Former titles: Vanuatu. National Planning and Statistics Office. Consumer Prices Indexes; Vanuatu. Condominium Bureau of Statistics. Consumer Price Indexes.
Description: Provides information on movements in retail prices of goods and services commonly purchased by the wage and salary earner households living in the urban areas.

COOPERATIVES

see Business and Economics—Cooperatives

CORPORATE LAW

see Law—Corporate Law

CRIMINAL LAW

see Law—Criminal Law

CRIMINOLOGY AND LAW ENFORCEMENT

see also Criminology and Law Enforcement—Security; Education—Special Education and Rehabilitation; Medical Sciences—Forensic Sciences

364 370   **US**
A C J S TODAY. q. membership. Academy of Criminal Justice Sciences, c/o Patricia DeLancey, Exec. Dir., 402 Nunn Hall, Northern Kentucky University, Highland Heights, KY 41099-5998. TEL 606-572-5634; 800-757-ACJS. Ed. Jeff Walker. adv. **Document type:** newsletter.
Formerly: Placement News.
Description: Provides articles, news releases and information on events and job opportunities.

364   **US**   ISSN 0270-2991
A M S STUDIES IN CRIMINAL JUSTICE. 1975. irreg., vol.3, 1980. price varies. A M S Press, Inc., 56 E. 13th St., New York, NY 10003. TEL 212-777-4700. FAX 212-995-5413. (back issues avail.) **Document type:** monographic series.
Description: Series of monographs, reference works and bibliographies designed for the study of forensic science and law enforcement.

364 340.6 614.19   **JA**   ISSN 0302-0029
CODEN: HAZAAY
ACTA CRIMINOLOGIAE ET MEDICAE LEGALIS JAPONICA/HANZAIGAKU ZASSHI. (Text in English, Japanese) 1928. bi-m. $55 (effective 1992). Japanese Association of Criminology - Nihon Hanzai Gakkai, c/o Department of Criminal Psychiatry, Tokyo Medical and Dental University, 2-3-10 Kanda-Surugadai, Chiyoda-ku, Tokyo 101, Japan. FAX 03-3291-5799. Ed. A. Yamagami. adv.; bk.rev. circ. 800. **Indexed:** Abstr.Crim.& Pen., Biol.Abstr., Chem.Abstr., Excerp.Med. (1996-), Jap.Per.Ind. **Document type:** academic/scholarly publication.
—CASDDS; EMDOCS.

364 345   **SA**   ISSN 1012-8093
ACTA CRIMINOLOGICA. 1988. s-a. R.30 (overseas $8.70(£6)) (effective 1997). (Criminological Society of Southern Africa) Unisa Press, Periodicals, P.O. Box 392, Pretoria 0001, South Africa. TEL 27-12-4293111. FAX 27-12-4293221. E-mail: unisa-press@unisa.ac.za. (Co-sponsor: University of South Africa, Department of Criminology) Ed. H.J. Prinsloo. circ. 1,300. (back issues avail.) **Indexed:** Ind.S.A.Per. **Document type:** academic/scholarly publication.
Refereed Serial

364.4   **US**
ACTION LINE (SACRAMENTO); a crime and violence prevention newsjournal. 1981. 2/yr. free. Attorney General's Office, Crime Prevention Center, Box 944255, Sacramento, CA 94244-2550. TEL 916-324-7863. FAX 916-327-2384. Ed. Daphne Hom. illus. circ. 10,000.
Former titles (until Fall, 1993): Senior's Action Alert; Sentinel (Sacramento).

363.2   **FR**   ISSN 0339-7858
ACTUALITE POLICIERE. 1948. bi-m. Caserne de la Cite, 11 rue de Ursins, 75004 Paris, France. Ed. Serge Maciet. adv. circ. 20,000.
Formerly (until 1975): Actualite Policiere. Police de Paris (ISSN 0339-784X)
Description: Discusses police administration.

364   **US**   ISSN 0894-2366
HV6001
ADVANCES IN CRIMINOLOGICAL THEORY. a. $44.95 (effective 1997). Transaction Publishers, Transaction Periodicals Consortium, Department 3092, Rutgers University, New Brunswick, NJ 08903. TEL 908-445-2280. FAX 908-445-3138. Eds. Freda Adler, William S. Laufer. **Document type:** academic/scholarly publication.
—CCC.
Description: Provides a forum for the dissemination of original work on criminological theory.

ALARM/ALLARME/ALARME; modern fire protection and security systems bulletin. see *FIRE PREVENTION*

353.9   **US**   ISSN 0095-3415
HV8691.U5
ALASKA. VIOLENT CRIMES COMPENSATION BOARD. ANNUAL REPORT. Key Title: Annual Report - State of Alaska. Violent Crimes Compensation Board. 1973. a. Violent Crimes Compensation Board, Box 111200, Juneau, AK 99811. TEL 907-465-3040. illus.

364   **NE**   ISSN 0002-5283
ALGEMEEN POLITIEBLAD VAN HET KONINKRIJK DER NEDERLANDEN. 1852. bi-w. free to qualified personnel. Ministerie van Justitie, Postbus 20301, 2500 EH The Hague, Netherlands. Ed. J. van Schie. circ. 40,000. **Indexed:** Abstr.Crim.& Pen., Key to Econ.Sci. **Document type:** government publication.

ALIBI. see *LAW — Criminal Law*

365 616.8   **US**
AMERICAN ASSOCIATION OF MENTAL HEALTH PROFESSIONALS IN CORRECTIONS. MONOGRAPH SERIES. 1940. q. $60. Martin Psychiatric Research Foundation, Box 3365, Fairfield, CA 94533. TEL 707-864-0910. FAX 707-964-0910. Ed. Dr. Clyde Verne Martin. circ. 4,000. **Document type:** academic/scholarly publication, monographic series.
Description: For professionals working in correctional settings.

364   **US**
HV8987
AMERICAN CORRECTIONAL ASSOCIATION. THE STATE OF CORRECTIONS. PROCEEDINGS A C A ANNUAL CONFERENCES. 1870. a. $25 to non-members; members $20. American Correctional Association, 4380 Forbes Blvd., Lanham, MD 20706-4322. TEL 301-918-1800. R&P contact: Gabriella Daley. circ. 2,000. (also avail. in microfilm from BHP; reprint service avail. from KTO) **Document type:** proceedings.
Former titles: American Correctional Association. Winter Conference and Annual Congress of Correction. Proceedings; American Correctional Association. Annual Congress of Correction. Proceedings (ISSN 0065-7948)
Description: Covers speeches and papers presented at annual Summer congress and Winter conference.

343   **US**   ISSN 0164-0364
K1
AMERICAN CRIMINAL LAW REVIEW. 1962. q. $30 (foreign $38) (effective 1998). Georgetown University Law Center, 600 New Jersey Ave., N.W., Washington, DC 20009. TEL 202-662-9468. Ed. Ariadne Makris. adv.; bk.rev. circ. 2,153. (also avail in microfilm from RRI,UMI; microfiche from WSH; reprint service avail. from RRI,UMI,WSH; back issues avail.) **Indexed:** Abstr.Crim.& Pen., C.L.I., Crim.Just.Abstr., Curr.Cont., L.R.I., Leg.Cont., Leg.Per., SSCI. **Document type:** academic/scholarly publication.
● Also available online. Vendor(s): Information Access Co., West Group (ACRIMLREV).
—BLDSC (0812.680000); Genuine Article; KR SourceOne; SWETS; UMI; UnCover.
Formerly: American Criminal Law Quarterly (ISSN 0002-8118)

CRITICOLOGY AND LAW ENFORCEMENT

365   US   ISSN 1056-0319
HV8745
AMERICAN JAILS. 1987. bi-m. $30 (Canada $36; elsewhere $42). American Jail Association, 2053 Day Rd., Ste. 100, Hagerstown, MD 21740-9795. TEL 301-790-3930. FAX 301-790-2941. Ed. Ken Kerle. R&P contact: Ken Kerle. adv.; bk.rev. circ. 10,000. Indexed: Crim.Just.Abstr. Document type: trade publication.
   Description: Covers jail programs, crowding, training, direct supervision, management, jail research, and standards.

364   US   ISSN 0092-2315
K1
AMERICAN JOURNAL OF CRIMINAL LAW. 1972. 3/yr. $25 (foreign $28). University of Texas at Austin, School of Law Publications, Box 149084, Austin, TX 78714-9084. TEL 512-471-1106. FAX 512-471-6988. adv.; bk.rev.; cum.index. circ. 900. (also avail. in microform from MIM,UMI,WSH,PMC; microfiche from WSH; back issues avail.; reprint service avail. from WSH) Indexed: Abstr.Crim.& Pen., C.L.I., CJPI, Crim.Just.Abstr., Curr.Cont., L.R.I., Leg.Cont., Leg.Per., SSCI. Document type: academic/scholarly publication.
   —BLDSC (0824.200000); KR SourceOne; UMI; UnCover.

364.128   US
AMERICAN POLYGRAPH ASSOCIATION NEWSLETTER. 1966. bi-m. $45 (foreign $55). American Polygraph Association, Box 8037, Chattanooga, TN 37414-0037. TEL 410-647-4581. Ed. Norman Ansley. R&P contact: Norman Ansley. adv.; bk.rev. circ. 3,500. (also avail. in microform from UMI; back issues avail.; reprint service avail. from UMI) Document type: newsletter.
   Description: Covers current cases, legal changes, news of technical interest, worldwide activities, and training.

AMERICAN SERIES OF FOREIGN PENAL CODES. see LAW — Criminal Law

365.976317   US   ISSN 0402-4249
HV9475.L22
ANGOLITE; the prison newsmagazine. 1952. bi-m. $20 in the U.S.; Canada $30; elsewhere $40 (effective 1997). (Department of Corrections) Louisiana State Penitentiary, Angola, LA 70712. TEL 504-655-4411. Ed. Wilbert Rideau. bk.rev. circ. 2,000. Indexed: Ind.Per.Art.Relat.Law.
   Description: Louisiana State Penitentiary's uncensored official prisoner publication.
   Refereed Serial

ANNALES DES FALSIFICATIONS DE L'EXPERTISE CHIMIQUE ET TOXICOLOGIQUE. see MEDICAL SCIENCES — Forensic Sciences

364   FR   ISSN 0003-4452
ANNALES INTERNATIONALES DE CRIMINOLOGIE/INTERNATIONAL ANNALS OF CRIMINOLOGY/ANALES INTERNACIONALES DE CRIMINOLOGIA. (Text in English, French and Spanish) 1962. s-a. 600 F. (effective 1998). International Society of Criminology - Societe Internationale de Criminologie, c/o Rachida Touahria, 4-14 rue Ferrus, 75014 Paris, France. TEL 33-1-45880023. FAX 33-1-45894076. bk.rev.; bibl. Indexed: Crim.Just.Abstr., P.A.I.S.For.Lang.Ind. Document type: newsletter.
   —BLDSC (4535.795000); SWETS.

364   US   ISSN 0272-3816
HV8138
ANNUAL EDITIONS: CRIMINAL JUSTICE. 1976. a. $12.95. Dushkin Publishing Group, Sluice Dock, Guilford, CT 06437-9989. TEL 203-453-4351. FAX 203-453-6000. Eds. John J. Sullivan, Joseph L. Victor; Pub. Ian Nielsen. illus. Document type: academic/scholarly publication.
   Formerly: Annual Editions: Readings in Criminal Justice.
   Refereed Serial

364   US
ANNUAL EDITIONS: VIOLENCE AND TERRORISM. 1990. a. $12.95. Dushkin Publishing Group, Sluice Dock, Guilford, CT 06437-9989. TEL 203-453-4351. FAX 203-453-6000. Eds. Bernard Schechterman, Martin Slann; Pub. Ian Nielsen. illus. Document type: academic/scholarly publication.
   Refereed Serial

365   KE
ANNUAL REPORT ON THE ADMINISTRATION OF PRISONS IN KENYA. (Text in English) a. (Ministry of Home Affairs) Government Printing and Stationery Department, P.O. Box 30128, Nairobi, Kenya. Document type: government publication.

364.4   IT   ISSN 0391-6227
ANTIFURTO; rivista mensile di studio dei problemi antifurto e antirapina. 1974. m. L.195000. Edizioni di Protezione Civile s.r.l., Via dell'Acqua Traversa 187-189, 00135 Rome, Italy. TEL 39-6-3313000. FAX 39-6-3313212. TELEX 626462 EPCINF. Ed. Laura Lavarello; Pub. Pier Roberto Pais. adv. contact: Roberto Barberini. bk.rev. circ. 8,000. Document type: trade publication.

365 364.4   SW
APROPAA.* 1975. 6/yr. free. Brottsfoerebyggande Raadet, P.O. Box 6494, S-113 82 Stockholm, Sweden.
   Former titles: Brottsfoerebyggande Raadets Tidskrift Apropaa (ISSN 0283-3352); (until 1986): B R Aa - Apropaa (ISSN 0346-9360)

364   II   ISSN 0003-7540
ARAKSHA.* (Text in Bengali & English) 1969. bi-m. Rs.10($12) Criminalistics Research Institute, c/o Indian Law Institute, Opp. Supreme Court, Bhagwandas Rd., New Delhi 110 001, India. Ed. S.K. Chatterjee. circ. 2,000.

364   GW   ISSN 0003-9225
HV6003   CODEN: ARKRAI
ARCHIV FUER KRIMINOLOGIE; unter besonderer Beruecksichtigung der gerichtlichen Physik, Chemie und Medizin. 1897. 6/yr. DM.441 (foreign DM.445) (effective 1996). Schmidt-Roemhild Verlag, Mengstr. 16, 23552 Luebeck, Germany. TEL 49-451-703101. FAX 49-451-7031253. Ed. Friedrich Geerds. adv.; bk.rev.; bibl.; charts; illus.; index. circ. 1,000. (also avail. in microfiche from BHP; reprint service avail. from KTO,SCH) Indexed: Abstr.Crim.& Pen., Biol.Abstr., Chem.Abstr., Crim.Just.Abstr., Excerp.Med., IBR, Ind.Med. Document type: academic/scholarly publication.
   —BLDSC (1615.650000); CASDDS; EMDOCS; SWETS.

ARCHIVOS DE CRIMINOLOGIA, NEURO-PSIQUIATRIA Y DISCIPLINAS CONEXAS. see MEDICAL SCIENCES — Psychiatry And Neurology

364   PL   ISSN 0066-6890
ARCHIWUM KRYMINOLOGII. (Text in Polish; summaries in English) 1960. irreg., vol.18, 1992. price varies. Polska Akademia Nauk, Instytut Nauk Prawnych - Polish Academy of Sciences, Institute of Law Studies, Ul. Nowy Swiat 72, 00-330 Warsaw, Poland. TEL 48-22-268484. FAX 48-22-267853. Ed. J. Jasinski. bk.rev. circ. 500. Indexed: Abstr.Crim.& Pen., IBR. Document type: academic/scholarly publication.
   Description: Research into problems of criminology in various spheres of life in Poland and in the world.

ARCHIWUM MEDYCYNY SADOWEJ I KRIMINOLOGII. see MEDICAL SCIENCES — Forensic Sciences

364   US   ISSN 8755-8300
KF9625.A59
ARREST LAW BULLETIN. 1976. m. $60. Quinlan Publishing Co., Inc., 23 Drydock Ave, 2nd Fl., Boston, MA 02210-2387. TEL 617-542-0048; 800-229-2084. FAX 617-345-9646. index. (looseleaf format; also avail. in microform from UMI; back issues avail.) Indexed: CJPI. Document type: newsletter.
   —UMI. CCC.
   Description: Summaries of current cases discussing arrest procedures. Written for non-lawyer law enforcement personnel.

364   US
ARRESTS OF YOUTH (YEAR). a. U.S. Department of Justice, Office of Juvenile Justice and Delinquency Prevention, 633 Indiana Ave., N.W., Washington, DC 20531. TEL 202-307-5929. (Subscr. to: Superintendent of Documents, U.S. Government Printing Office, Box 371954, Pittsburgh, PA 15250-7954. TEL 202-512-1800. FAX 202-512-2250). stat. Document type: government publication.

ARSON REPORTER; arson cases and legislation. see LAW

364.36   UK   ISSN 0143-8387
ATTENDANCE CENTRE NEWS. 1979. irreg. Home Office, 50 Queen Anne's Gate, London SW1H 9AT, England. TEL 071-273-3877. Ed. John Race. circ. 4,000. Document type: government publication.

364   AT   ISSN 0004-8658
HV6001
AUSTRALIAN AND NEW ZEALAND JOURNAL OF CRIMINOLOGY. 1968. 3/yr. Aus.$155 (foreign Aus.$165) (effective 1997). Butterworths, Division of Reed International Books Australia Pty. Ltd. (Subsidiary of: Reed Elsevier Australia Pty. Ltd.), 271-273 Lane Cove Rd., North Ryde, N.S.W. 2113, Australia. TEL 61-2-93354444. FAX 61-2-93354655. E-mail: tom.smith@ butterworths.com.au. (Dist. in N. America by: Wm. W. Gaunt & Sons, Inc., Law Book Dealers & Subscription Agents, Gaunt Bldg., 3011 Gulf Dr., Homes Beach, FL 34217-2199) Ed. Peter Sallmann. adv. contact: Rebecca Browning. bk.rev.; abstr.; charts; illus.; stat.; index. (reprint service avail. from WSH) Indexed: Abstr.Bk.Rev.Curr.Leg.Per., Abstr.Crim.& Pen., ASCA, Aus.P.A.I.S., C.L.I., Crim.Just.Abstr., Curr.Cont., Curr.Cont., Fam.Ind., HRIS, L.R.I., Leg.Per., SSCI. Document type: academic/scholarly publication.
   —BLDSC (1796.885000); Genuine Article; UnCover. CCC.

364   AT
AUSTRALIAN CRIMINAL LAW - FEDERAL OFFENCES. 1985. 7/yr. Aus.$775. L B C Information Services, 50 Waterloo Rd., N. Ryde, N.S.W. 2113, Australia. TEL 61-2-99366555. FAX 61-2-98889706. TELEX ASBOOK 27995. Eds. R.S. Watson, P. Coghlan.
   Description: Definitive treatment of all offenses created by commonwealth laws, both Acts of Parliament and by Regulations.

340   AT   ISSN 0159-6667
AUSTRALIAN CRIMINAL REPORTS. 1980. 7/yr. Aus.$250 per vol. L B C Information Services, 50 Waterloo Rd., N. Ryde, N.S.W. 2113, Australia. TEL 61-2-99366444. FAX 61-2-98889706. TELEX ASBOOK 27995. Ed. Fiori Rinaldi. cum.index: vols.1-50, vols.51-75. (back issues avail.)
   Description: Provides a comprehensive series of reports on the criminal decisions made by the High Court, Federal Court and the supreme courts of all Australian states and territories.

364   AT   ISSN 0311-449X
HV7171
AUSTRALIAN INSTITUTE OF CRIMINOLOGY. ANNUAL REPORT. a. Aus.$20. Australian Institute of Criminology, G.P.O. Box 2944, Canberra, A.C.T. 2601, Australia. TEL 61-6-2609256. FAX 61-6-2609260. E-mail: aicpress@aic.gov.au. (Dist. in US by: Criminal Justice Press, Box 249, Monsey, NY 10952) Document type: corporate report.
   Incorporates (1972-1996): Criminology Research Council. Annual Report (ISSN 0311-4481)

364   AT   ISSN 1034-5086
AUSTRALIAN INSTITUTE OF CRIMINOLOGY. CONFERENCE PROCEEDINGS (NO.). Variant title: A I C Conference Proceedings (No.). 1990. irreg. Aus.$50. Australian Institute of Criminology, G.P.O. Box 2944, Canberra, A.C.T. 2601, Australia. TEL 61-6-2609256. FAX 61-6-2609260. E-mail: aicpress@aic.gov.au. (Dist. in US by: Criminal Justice Press, Box 249, Monsey, NY 10952) Ed.Bd. Document type: proceedings.
   —BLDSC (0773.068800).
   Formed by the merger of (1984-1990): A I C Seminar. Report (ISSN 0813-7013); Which was formerly (1974-1984): A I C Report on Training Project (ISSN 0311-4597); (1983-1990): A I C Seminar. Proceedings (ISSN 0813-7005); Which was formerly (197?-1983): A I C Proceedings, Training Project (ISSN 0725-475X)

364   AT
HV9873
AUSTRALIAN INSTITUTE OF CRIMINOLOGY. RESEARCH AND PUBLIC POLICY. 1996. irreg. Aus.$20. Australian Institute of Criminology, G.P.O. Box 2944, Canberra, A.C.T. 2601, Australia. TEL 61-6-274-0260. FAX 61-6-274-0260. E-mail: aicpress@aic.gov.au. Ed. David McDonald. Document type: academic/scholarly publication.
   Formed by the merger of (1992-1996): Deaths in Custody Australia (ISSN 1038-667X); And part of (1990-1992): Homicides in Australia (ISSN 1038-6912)

CRIMINOLOGY AND LAW ENFORCEMENT

363.2　　　　　　AT　ISSN 0005-0024
HV7551
AUSTRALIAN POLICE JOURNAL. 1946. q. Aus.$14 (foreign Aus.$22) (effective 1998). New South Wales Police Service, G.P.O. Box 45, Sydney, N.S.W. 2001, Australia. TEL 61-2-3390277. FAX 61-2-3395564. Ed. Phil T. Peters. adv. contact: P.T. Peters. bk.rev.; illus. circ. 23,000. **Indexed:** Abstr.Crim.& Pen., Excerp.Med.
—BLDSC (1818.070000).
　　Description: Covers all aspects of law enforcement: child abuse, narcotics control, homicide and firearms.

364　　　　　　　AT
AUSTRALIAN POLICE WORLD. 1965. q. Aus.$0.10 per no. (International Police Association, Australian Section) Percival Publishing Co. Pty. Ltd., 862-870 Elizabeth St., Waterloo, N.S.W. 2017, Australia.

365　　　　　　　AT　ISSN 0813-2364
HV9872
AUSTRALIAN PRISONERS. a. price varies. Australian Bureau of Statistics, P.O. Box 10, Belconnen, A.C.T. 2616, Australia.
　　Description: For all working in the fields of criminology, corrections, probation and parole.

364　　　　　　　AT
AUSTRALIAN STUDIES IN LAW, CRIME AND JUSTICE. irreg. (1-2/yr.). price varies. Australian Institute of Criminology, G.P.O. Box 2944, Canberra, A.C.T. 2601, Australia. TEL 61-6-2609256. FAX 61-6-2609260. E-mail: aicpress@aic.gov.au. (Dist. in US by: Criminal Justice Press, P.O. Box 249, Monsey, NY 10952) **Document type:** monographic series.

345.73　　　　　　US　ISSN 0098-8049
KF9219.3
B A R - B R I BAR REVIEW. CRIMINAL LAW. a. $395. B A R - B R I Bar Review, 3280 Motor Ave., Los Angeles, CA 90034-3710. TEL 213-477-2542. **Indexed:** Curr.Cont.

346　　　　　　　US　ISSN 0098-7611
KF1250.Z9
B A R - B R I BAR REVIEW. TORTS. a. $395. B A R - B R I Bar Review, 3280 Motor Ave., Los Angeles, CA 90034-3710. TEL 213-477-2542.

364　　　　　　　US　ISSN 0742-7271
B J S BULLETIN. 1981? m. U.S. Department of Justice, Bureau of Justice Statistics, 633 Indiana Ave., N.W., 11th Fl., Washington, DC 20531. (Orders to: Bureau of Justice Statistics Clearinghouse, Box 179, Department BJS C-1, Annapolis Junction, MD 20701-0179. FAX 410-792-4358) stat. (back issues avail.) **Indexed:** Crim.Just.Abstr. **Document type:** bulletin, government publication.

364　　　　　　　US
B J S CRIME DATA BRIEF. irreg.? U.S. Department of Justice, Bureau of Justice Statistics, 633 Indiana Ave., N.W., Washington, DC 20531. (Orders to: Bureau of Justice Statistics Clearinghouse, Box 179, Department BJS C-1, Annapolis Junction, MD 20701-0179. FAX 410-792-4358) stat. (back issues avail.) **Document type:** government publication, monographic series.

364　　　　　　　US
B J S DISCUSSION PAPER. irreg. U.S. Department of Justice, Bureau of Justice Statistics, 633 Indiana Ave., N.W., 11th Fl., Washington, DC 20531. (Orders to: Bureau of Justice Statistics Clearinghouse, Box 179, Department BJS C-1, Annapolis Junction, MD 20701-0179) stat. (back issues avail.) **Document type:** government publication, monographic series.

364　　　　　　　US
B J S EXECUTIVE SUMMARY. irreg. U.S. Department of Justice, Bureau of Justice Statistics, 633 Indiana Ave., N.W., 11th Fl., Washington, DC 20531. (Orders to: Bureau of Justice Statistics Clearinghouse, Box 179, Department BJS C-1, Annapolis Junction, MD 20701-0179. FAX 410-792-4358) stat. (back issues avail.) **Document type:** government publication.

364　　　　　　　US
B J S SELECTED FINDINGS. irreg. U.S. Department of Justice, Bureau of Justice Statistics, 633 Indiana Ave., N.W., 11th Fl., Washington, DC 20531. (Orders to: Bureau of Justice Clearinghouse, Box 179, Department BJS C-1, Annapolis Junction, MD 20701-0179. FAX 410-792-4358) stat. (back issues avail.) **Document type:** government publication.

364　　　　　　　US
B J S SPECIAL REPORT. irreg. stat. U.S. Department of Justice, Bureau of Justice Statistics, 633 Indiana Ave., N.W., 11th Fl., Washington, DC 20531. (Orders to: Bureau of Justice Statistics Clearinghouse, Box 179, Department BJS C-1, Annapolis Junction, MD 20701-0179. FAX 410-792-4358) stat. circ. 17,000. (also avail. in microfiche; back issues avail.) **Document type:** government publication.

364.4　　　　　　NE　ISSN 0005-4259
BALANS; personeelsblad van de Directie Delinquentenzorg en Jeugdinrichtingen. 1970. m. fl.5. Ministerie van Justitie, Redactie Balans, Terminal Noord Kamer N 452, Postbus 20301, 2500 EH The Hague, Netherlands. TEL 31-70-3702613. Ed.Bd. adv.; bk.rev.; charts; illus. circ. 5,400.

363.2　　　　　　US
BARS AND STRIPES. 1965. m. $10. Detroit Police Lieutenants & Sergeants Association, 28 W. Adams St., No. 1308, Detroit, MI 48226. Ed. Joseph E. Wolff. adv.; circ. 2,900 (controlled).

364　　　　　　　GW
BAYERNS POLIZEI. 1990. 5/yr. Bayerisches Staatsministerium des Innern, Odeonsplatz 3, 80524 Munich, Germany. TEL 49-89-21922644. FAX 49-89-21922870. E-mail: stmi.vi5@polizei.bayern.de. Ed. Wolfgang Schlee. bk.rev. **Document type:** bulletin.

364　　　　　　　US
BEST SCENE. 1954. bi-m. $5. Best Scene, Box 400, Rawlins, WY 82301-0400. TEL 308-324-1441. Ed. J.E. Boyette. circ. 1,200.

BEZBEDNOST. see *LAW — Criminal Law*

364　　　　　　　US
BLACKS IN LAW ENFORCEMENT; a living tribute to Black history. 1986. a. $5.50. Blacks in Law Enforcement, Inc., 256 E. McLemore Ave., Memphis, TN 38106-2833. TEL 800-533-4649. FAX 901-774-1139. Ed. Clyde R. Venson. adv. circ. 25,000. (back issues avail.)
　　Formerly: Top Blacks in Law Enforcement.
　　Description: To document, acknowledge and publish the contributions made to law enforcement by Black officers.

363.2　　　　　　CN　ISSN 0847-8538
BLUE LINE MAGAZINE. 1988. m. Can.$25 foreign Can.$35) (effective 1997). Blue Line Magazine, 4981 Hwy. 7 E., Unit 12A, No. 254, Markham, ON L3R 1N1, Canada. TEL 905-640-3048. FAX 905-640-7547. Ed. Morley S. Lymburner; Pb. Morley S. Lymburner. adv. contact: Mary Lymburner. bk.rev. circ. 10,000. **Document type:** trade publication.
　　Description: Covers law enforcement throughout Canada, featuring case law, news, feature articles, and product information.

363.2　　　　　　UK
BLUEPRINT (WINFRITH). 1974. 4/yr. free. Dorset Police, Force Headquarters, Winfrith, Nr. Dorchester DT2 8DZ, England. FAX 44-1929-463755. Ed. Mike Maber. R&P contact: Mike Maber. bk.rev.; circ. 4,000 (controlled). **Indexed:** Br.Tech.Ind. **Document type:** government publication.

BOLLETTINO PER LE FARMACODIPENDENZE E L'ALCOOLISMO. see *DRUG ABUSE AND ALCOHOLISM*

351.74　　　　　　BS　ISSN 0068-046X
BOTSWANA. COMMISSIONER OF THE POLICE. ANNUAL REPORT. 1885. a. P.10. Commissioner of the Police, c/o Assistant Commissioner, Police Headquarters, Gaborone, Botswana. circ. 250. **Document type:** corporate report, government publication.

364　　　　　　　UK　ISSN 0007-0955
HV6001　　　　　　　　CODEN: BJCDAR
THE BRITISH JOURNAL OF CRIMINOLOGY; delinquency and deviant social behaviour. 1950. q. foreign $145) (effective 1998). (Institute for the Study and Treatment of Delinquency) Oxford University Press, Academic Division, Great Clarendon St., Oxford OX2 6DP, England. TEL 44-1865-267907. FAX 44-1865-267485. TELEX 837330-OXPRES-G. E-mail: jnl.info@oup.co.uk; URL: http://www.oup.co.uk/journals. (U.S. subscr. to: Oxford University Press Inc., 2001 Evans Rd., Cary, NC 27513. TEL 800-852-7323. FAX 919-677-1714) Ed. Joanna Shapland; Pub. Martin Green. R&P contact: Joolz Longley. adv. contact: Jane Parker. bk.rev.; abstr.; bibl.; index. circ. 1,850. (also avail. in microform; back issues avail.; reprint service avail. from SWZ,WSH) **Indexed:** Abstr.Crim.& Pen., Adol.Ment.Hlth.Abstr., ASCA, ASSIA, Br.Educ.Ind., Br.Hum.Ind., CJPI, Crim.Just.Abstr., Curr.Adv.Ecol.Sci., Curr.Cont., Euro.LJI, IBR, IMFL, L.R.I., Leg.Per., LJI, Mid.East: Abstr.& Ind., Mult.Ed.Abstr., P.A.I.S., Psychol.Abstr. (1960-), Soc.Sci.Ind., SSCI, Stud.Wom.Abstr. **Document type:** academic/scholarly publication.
　　●Also available online. Vendor(s): Information Access Co.
—BLDSC (2307.300000); Genuine Article; KR SourceOne; SWETS; UMI; UnCover. **CCC**.
　　Supersedes (in 1960): British Journal of Delinquency.
　　Description: Focuses on British and international criminology, including social deviance.

363.2 345 320　　　GW　ISSN 0932-5409
BUERGERRECHTE & POLIZEI. (Text in German; summaries in English) 1978. 3/yr. DM.36 to individuals; institutions DM.63. Verlag C I L I P, c/o FU Berlin, Malteserstr. 74-100, 12249 Berlin, Germany. TEL 49-30-7792462. FAX 49-30-7751073. Ed. Otto Diederichs. adv.; bk.rev.; index. circ. 1,200. (also avail. in microfiche; back issues avail.) **Indexed:** Abstr.Crim.& Pen. **Document type:** academic/scholarly publication.
　　Description: Review of the structure, function and daily work of Germany's police and intelligence agencies.

364　　　　　　　GW
BUNDESPOLIZEI. 1979. m. DM.10. Bundesgrenzschutz Verband e.V., Kreuzbergweg 17, 53115 Bonn, Germany.

BUSINESS ESPIONAGE REPORT; controls and countermeasures training for managers. see *BUSINESS AND ECONOMICS — International Commerce*

363　　　　　　　US　ISSN 1059-2423
HV9960.E85
C J EUROPE. 1991. 6/yr. $24 (foreign $42). (University of Illinois at Chicago) Office of International Criminal Justice, 1333 S. Wabash, Box 53, Chicago, IL 60605. TEL 312-996-8420. FAX 312-413-0458. Ed. Dennis Rowe. R&P contact Jeffrey Builta. adv. contact: Beth Pachowski. **Indexed** Abstr.Crim.& Pen., Euro.LJI. **Document type:** newsletter.
—BLDSC (3274.271200); UMI.
　　Description: Focuses on criminal justice issues in Europe.

364　　　　　　　US　ISSN 1079-1574
C J MANAGEMENT & TRAINING AIDS DIGEST. (Criminal Justice) s-m. $295 (Canada $301) (includes q. Calendar of Events) (effective 1998). Washington Crime News Services, 3918 Prosperity Ave., Ste. 318, Fairfax, VA 22031-3334. TEL 703-573-1600; 800-422-9267. FAX 703-573-1604. Ed. Betty B. Bosarge; Pub. Richard J. O'Connell. (also avail. in microform from UMI; reprint service avail. from UMI) **Indexed:** CJPI. **Document type:** newsletter.
—UMI.
　　Formed by the merger of (1976-1995): Training Aids Digest (ISSN 0889-5732); (1985-1995): Criminal Justice Digest (ISSN 0889-5724); Which was (1982-1985): Criminal Justice Journal.
　　Description: Discusses various aspects of criminal justice training and management, including professional tactics, legal issues and narcotics investigations. Includes job listings.

CRIMINOLOGY AND LAW ENFORCEMENT

364 US ISSN 0896-9922
C J THE AMERICAS. 1988. 6/yr. $24 (foreign $42). (University of Illinois at Chicago) Office of International Criminal Justice, 1333 S. Wabash, Box 53, Chicago, IL 60605. TEL 312-996-8420. FAX 312-413-0458. Ed. Jess Machan. R&P contact: Jeffrey Builta. **Document type:** newsletter.
—UMI.
Description: Focuses on criminal justice issues in Central, North and South America.

364 US ISSN 0194-1682
CALIFORNIA CORRECTIONAL NEWS. 1946. 10/yr. $18 to non-members; libraries $15. California Probation, Parole and Correctional Association, 211 Lathrop Way, Ste. M, Sacramento, CA 95815-4242. TEL 916-927-4888. FAX 916-927-8123. Ed. Romel White. R&P contact: Romel White. adv. contact: Renee Bitton. bk.rev. circ. 2,900. **Indexed:** Cal.Per.Ind. (1990-). **Document type:** newsletter.

CALIFORNIA CRIMINAL DEFENSE PRACTICE. see *LAW — Criminal Law*

CALIFORNIA CRIMINAL DEFENSE PRACTICE REPORTER. see *LAW — Criminal Law*

364 US
CALIFORNIA DISTRICT ATTORNEYS ASSOCIATION. CASE DIGEST. s-m. $135. California District Attorneys Association, 731 K St., Ste. 300, Sacramento, CA 95814-3402. TEL 916-443-2017. FAX 916-443-0540. R&P contact: Cat Karnezis. index. circ. 2,500. (back issues avail.)
Description: Summarizes California case decisions.

363.2 US ISSN 0008-1140
CALIFORNIA HIGHWAY PATROLMAN. 1937. m. $18 (foreign $26). (California Association of Highway Patrolmen) Jon Hamm, Pub., Box 161209, Sacramento, CA 95816. TEL 916-452-6751. Ed. Carol Perri. R&P contact: Diane Wolff. adv.: B&W page $1150, color page $1850; trim 8 1/2 x 11; adv. contact: Diane Wolff. illus. circ. 20,000. **Indexed:** HRIS.
Description: Covers articles about the California Highway Patrol, its programs, policies and personnel.

THE CALIFORNIA PRISONER. see *LAW — Constitutional Law*

364.4 US ISSN 0739-0394
HV8290
CAMPUS LAW ENFORCEMENT JOURNAL; professional publication for campus law enforcement administrators. (Former name of issuing body: International Association of College and University Security Directors) 1970. bi-m. $30 (foreign $35) (effective 1997). International Association of Campus Law Enforcement Administrators, 638 Prospect Ave., Hartford, CT 06105. TEL 860-586-7517. FAX 860-586-7550. E-mail: ljohnson@iaclea.org; URL: http://www.iaclea.org. Ed. Peter J. Berry. R&P contact: Lisa Johnson. adv. contact: Lisa Johnson. bk.rev. circ. 1,500. (also avail. in microform from UMI; reprint service avail. from UMI) **Indexed:** CJPI. **Document type:** trade publication.

354.71 CN ISSN 0383-4379
HV7315
CANADA. CORRECTIONAL INVESTIGATOR. ANNUAL REPORT. (Text in English, French) 1974. a. (Correctional Investigator) Supply and Services Canada, Ottawa, ON K1A 0S9, Canada. TEL 613-993-6425. illus. circ. 2,500.

364 CN ISSN 0843-8439
CANADIAN CRIMINAL JUSTICE ASSOCIATION. BULLETIN/ASSOCIATION CANADIENNE DE JUSTICE PENALE. BULLETIN. (Text in English, French) 1989. bi-m. membership. Canadian Criminal Justice Association, 383 Parkdale Ave., Ste. 304, Ottawa, ON K1Y 4R4, Canada. TEL 613-725-3715. FAX 613-725-3720. circ. 1,100. **Document type:** bulletin.
Description: Contains brief news and information items on criminal justice for some categories of association members.

364 365 CN ISSN 0704-9722
HV6001
CANADIAN JOURNAL OF CRIMINOLOGY/REVUE CANADIENNE DE CRIMINOLOGIE. (Text in English, French) 1958. q. Can.$50 to individuals; institutions $100 (effective 1996). Canadian Criminal Justice Association - Association Canadienne de Justice Penale, 383 Parkdale Ave., Ste. 304, Ottawa, ON K1Y 4R4, Canada. TEL 613-725-3715. FAX 613-725-3720. adv.; bk.rev.; charts; illus.; index, cum.index. circ. 1,300. (also avail. in microform from UMI; reprint service avail. from UMI) **Indexed:** Abstr.Crim.& Pen., Abstr.Soc.Work, Amer.Hist.& Life (1986-1989), ASCA, ASSIA, C.L.I., Can.B.P.I., Can.Per.Ind., CJPI, CMI, Crim.Just.Abstr., Curr.Cont., Hist.Abstr. 1986-1989), Human Resour.Abstr., Ind.Can.L.P.L., L.R.I., Periodex, Psychol.Abstr. (1972-), Risk Abstr., Sage Pub.Admin.Abstr., Sage Urb.Stud.Abstr., Soc.Sci.Ind. (until 1994), Soc.Work Res.& Abstr., SSCI. **Document type:** academic/scholarly publication.
● Also available online. Vendor(s): Information Access Co., UMI.
—BLDSC (3031.125000); Genuine Article; KR SourceOne; SWETS; UMI; UnCover. **CCC**.
Former titles (until vol.19): Canadian Journal of Criminology and Corrections; (until vol.13): Canadian Journal of Corrections (ISSN 0008-4069)

364 CN ISSN 0713-4517
CANADIAN POLICE CHIEF NEWSLETTER. (Text in English; occasionally in French) 1930. q. Can.$53.50 (in US Can.$60, elsewhere Can.$70) (effective 1997). Canadian Association of Chiefs of Police, 130 Albert St., Ste 1710, Ottawa ON K1P 5G4, Canada. TEL 613-233-1106. FAX 613-233-6960. Ed. Bryan McConnell. R&P contact: Fred Schultz. adv.: B&W page Can.$500; trim 8 1/2 x 11. bk.rev. circ. 1,300. (back issues avail.) **Indexed:** Crim.Just.Abstr. **Document type:** newsletter.
Formerly (until 1982): Canadian Police Chief (ISSN 0315-2464)

CANADIAN SOCIETY OF FORENSIC SCIENCE JOURNAL/SOCIETE CANADIENNE DES SCIENCES JUDICIAIRES JOURNAL. see *LAW*

CANINE COURIER. see *PETS*

365 US ISSN 0198-9693
K3 CODEN: CULRDZ
CAPITAL UNIVERSITY LAW REVIEW. 1972. q. $24. Capital University, Law School, 665 S. High St., Columbus, OH 43215. TEL 614-445-8836. FAX 614-445-7125. Ed. Eric Keller. R&P contact: Matthew T. Schaeffer. adv. contact: Bill Nicolozakes. bk.rev. circ. 1,200. (also avail. in microfiche from WSH; reprint service avail. from WSH) **Indexed:** C.L.I., Crim.Just.Abstr., L.R.I., Leg.Cont., Leg.Per., Mar.Aff.Bibl. **Document type:** academic/scholarly publication.
● Also available online. Vendor(s): National Data Corp., West Group.
—BLDSC (3050.669500); KR SourceOne; UnCover.
Description: A scholarly compilation of legal articles written by jurists, distinguished scholars and prominent members of the law profession.

364 343 VE ISSN 0798-9598
CAPITULO CRIMINOLOGICO. 1973. a. Bs.200($10) Universidad del Zulia, Instituto de Criminologia, Apdo. 526, Maracaibo, Venezuela. TEL 423913. circ. 1,000.
Description: Covers sociology, psychology and history of criminology and political science and penal law.

365 US
CATALYST (WASHINGTON); for community crime and drug prevention. 1980. 10/yr. free. National Crime Prevention Council, 1700 K St., N.W., 2nd Fl., Washington, DC 20006-3817. TEL 202-466-6272. FAX 202-296-1356. E-mail: marvin@ncpc.org; URL: http://www.weprevent.org. Ed. Mary Jo Marvin. R&P contact: Jean O'Neil. circ. 15,000 (controlled). **Document type:** newsletter.
● Also available online.
Description: News and resources for community anti-crime initiatives.

364 VE ISSN 0798-9202
CENTRO DE INVESTIGACIONES PENALES Y CRIMINOLOGICAS. REVISTA. Variant title: Revista C E N I P E C. 1976. a. $9. Universidad de los Andes, Centro de Investigaciones Penales y Criminologicas, Apdo. 730, Merida 5101, Venezuela. FAX 58-74-402055. E-mail: gabaldon@faces.ula.ve. (Subscr. to: Av. Andres Bello, Consejo de Publicaciones, Via la Parroqquia, Merida, Venezuela) Ed. Luis Gerardo Gabaldon. bk.rev. circ. 1,000. **Document type:** academic/scholarly publication.
Refereed Serial

CHAMPION. see *LAW — Criminal Law*

CHARTERED INSTITUTE OF PUBLIC FINANCE AND ACCOUNTANCY. ADMINISTRATION OF JUSTICE. ESTIMATES & ACTUALS. see *CRIMINOLOGY AND LAW ENFORCEMENT — Abstracting, Bibliographies, Statistics*

364.4 RU
CHASTNYI SYSK, OKHRANA, BEZOPASNOST'. (Text in Russian; summaries in English) 1992. m. 18000 Rub. Izdatel'stvo Chastnyi Sviet, Skatertnyi per., 15, 121069 Moscow, Russia. TEL 7-095-2031865. FAX 7-095-2031625. Ed. Sergei Guryanov; Pub. Nikolai Krayushenko. adv.: page $2400; adv. contact: Alexander Vlasov. bibl.; illus.; index. circ. 27,000. (back issues avail.)
Description: Provides information about security: industry, equipment, technics, law, and detective agencies.

363.2 US ISSN 0889-9207
CHIEF OF POLICE. 1986. bi-m. National Association of Chiefs of Police, 3801 Biscayne Blvd., Miami, FL 33137. TEL 305-573-0070. FAX 305-573-9819. Ed. Jim Gordon. circ. 22,500. **Document type:** trade publication.
Formerly: Police Command.

CHILDREN'S COURT OF NEW SOUTH WALES INFORMATION BULLETIN. see *LAW — Criminal Law*

364.6 CR
CIENCIAS PENALES. 1989. m.? Asociacion de Ciencias Penales de Costa Rica, c/o Corte Suprema de Justicia, 4-1003 San Jose, Costa Rica.

363.2 US ISSN 0091-8806
HV7586
CINCINNATI. DIVISION OF POLICE. ANNUAL REPORT. Key Title: Annual Report of the Division of Police (Cincinnati). 1929. a. free. Division of Police, Department of Safety, Records Section, 310 Ezzard Charles Dr., Cincinnati, OH 45214. TEL 513-352-3519. FAX 513-352-1422. stat. circ. 2,000.
Description: Reports of the division's organizational structure, budget, crime statistics and brief historical information.

CIVIL R I C O LITIGATION REPORTER; the national journal of record of litigation brought under the Federal Racketeer Influenced Corrupt Organizations Act. see *LAW — Civil Law*

CIVIL REMEDIES IN DRUG ENFORCEMENT REPORT. see *LAW — Civil Law*

CLEARWAY; traffic magazine of the metropolitan police. see *TRANSPORTATION — Roads And Traffic*

364 345 US
COALITION FOR PRISONERS' RIGHTS NEWSLETTER. 1976. m. $12 to individuals; institutions $25; free to prisoners. Coalition for Prisoners' Rights, Box 1911, Santa Fe, NM 87504-1911. TEL 505-982-9520. circ. 3,000. (back issues avail.) **Document type:** newsletter.
Description: Discusses politics and prison conditions, including prison and death penalty abolition issues, resources for prisoners, and commentary and analysis from prisoners.

CRIMINOLOGY AND LAW ENFORCEMENT

364.4   UK   ISSN 1012-2710
HV6652
COMMERCIAL CRIME INTERNATIONAL. 1983. m. £95($160) International Maritime Bureau (IMB), Maritime House, One Linton Rd., Barking, Essex IG11 8HG, England. TEL 0181-591-3000. FAX 0181-594-2833. TELEX 8956492 IMBLDN G. Ed. Andy Holder. bk.rev. circ. 700. (back issues avail.) Document type: trade publication.
—CCC.
Former titles: International Cargo Crime Prevention (ISSN 0266-3988); Business and Crime: Cargoes.
Description: Directed to senior executives, risk managers, insurance managers, security directors and all who are concerned with crime prevention.

364.4   US   ISSN 1079-1612
COMMUNITY POLICING DIGEST; a semi-monthly summary of significant news of community anti-crime programs. 1973. s-m. $295 (Canada $301) (effective 1998). Washington Crime News Services, 3918 Prosperity Ave., Ste. 318, Fairfax, VA 22031-3334. TEL 703-573-1600; 800-422-9267. FAX 703-573-1604. Ed. Susan Kernus. Document type: newsletter.
Formerly (until 1995): Community Crime Prevention Digest (ISSN 0889-5767)
Description: Focuses on federal and state budgets, and programs for the community crime-policing and -prevention professional.

364   US   ISSN 1059-6569
COMPILER. 1979. q. free. Illinois Criminal Justice Information Authority, 120 S. Riverside Plaza, Rm. 1016, Chicago, IL 60606-3997. TEL 312-793-8550. FAX 312-793-8422. E-mail: ddighton@icjia.state.il.us; URL: http://www.cjia.state.il.us. Ed. Daniel Dighton. R&P contact: Daniel Dighton. bk.rev.; stat.; circ. 9,000 (controlled). (back issues avail.) Document type: newsletter.
Description: Newsletter of criminal justice research and information issues.

346 004   US
COMPUTER CRIME LAW REPORTER. 1985. a. $140. National Center for Computer Crime Data, 1222 17th Ave., Ste. B, Santa Cruz, CA 95062. TEL 408-475-4557. FAX 408-475-5336. Ed. J.J. Bloombecker. circ. 200 (paid). (looseleaf format; back issues avail.) Document type: trade publication.

364 364 387   US   ISSN 1065-9455
CONFIDENTIAL A-I-R LETTER. 1993. irreg. (approx 7/yr.) $108 (effective 1996). Air Incident Research, Box 4745, East Lansing, MI 48826. TEL 517-336-9375. FAX 517-336-9375. Ed. Michael Morris; Pub. Maureen MacLaaughlin. bk.rev.; circ. 120 (paid). Document type: academic/scholarly publication, newsletter.
Description: Presents specialist research analysis and comment on terrorism and untoward events in aviation.
Refereed Serial

364   US   ISSN 0090-2756
HV7256
CONNECTICUT. DEPARTMENT OF CORRECTION. PUBLICATIONS. 1970. irreg. Department of Corrections, Research Section, 340 Capitol Ave., Hartford, CT 06115. TEL 203-566-5710. Ed. James Harris. stat. circ. 200 (controlled). (processed)

364   UK
CONSTABULARY. 1980. m. National Press Publishers, Peel House, 5 Balfour Rd., Weybridge, Surrey KT13 8HE, England. TEL 44-1932-859155. FAX 44-1932-859661. Ed. Chris Locke. adv.; bk.rev.; play rev. circ. 55,000. Document type: trade publication.

363.2   UK   ISSN 0010-6607
HV7551
CONSTABULARY GAZETTE; Ulster police magazine. 1933. m. £6. Howard Publications, 39 Boucher Rd., Belfast BT12 6UT, Northern Ireland. Ed. W.M. Williams. adv.; bk.rev.; film rev.; illus. circ. controlled. Document type: consumer publication.

364   US   ISSN 0732-4464
CONTRIBUTIONS IN CRIMINOLOGY AND PENOLOGY. 1983. irreg., no.28, 1992. price varies. Greenwood Press, Inc. (Subsidiary of: Greenwood Publishing Group Inc.), 88 Post Rd. W., Box 5007, Westport, CT 06881-5007. TEL 203-226-3571. FAX 203-222-1502.
—BLDSC (3458.295500).

CONTROLLED SUBSTANCES HANDBOOK. see *DRUG ABUSE AND ALCOHOLISM*

364   US
CONVICTIONS;* by and for prisoners and their people. 1989. s-a. $12 to individuals; institutions $17; prisoners $10. 67 Wall St., Ste. 2411, New York, NY 10005-3101. Ed. James M. Trappe. adv.; bk.rev.; illus. circ. 2,500.
Description: Showcase for prisoner talent; includes fiction, issues, humor, art, tattoo flash.

CORHEALTH. see *MEDICAL SCIENCES*

CORRECTIONAL FOODSERVICE MAGAZINE. see *FOOD AND FOOD INDUSTRIES*

364   US
CORRECTIONAL POPULATIONS IN THE U S (YEAR). (Subseries of: National Crime Victimiztion Survey Report) 1985. a. free. U.S. Department of Justice, Bureau of Justice Statistics, 633 Indiana Ave., N.W., 11th Fl., Washington, DC 20531. (Subscr. to: Superintendent of Documents, U.S. Government Printing Office, Box 371954, Pittsburgh, PA 15250-7954. TEL 202-512-1800. FAX 202-512-2250) stat. circ. 17,000. (also avail. in microfiche) Document type: government publication.

364   US   ISSN 0272-9822
HV9471
CORRECTIONS. (Subseries of: S I R S Social Issues (ISSN 0740-3127)) 1974. a. price varies; a. supplement $19. Social Issues Resources Series, Box 2348, Boca Raton, FL 33427-2348. TEL 561-994-0079; 800-232-SIRS. FAX 561-994-4704. E-mail: custserve@sirs.com; URL: http://www.sirs.com. Ed. Trudy Collins; Pub. Eleanor Goldstein. R&P contact: Bonnie Milnes. (looseleaf format; back issues avail.) Document type: academic/scholarly publication.
Description: Reprints important articles on problems and developments in criminal justice.

364   US   ISSN 0738-8144
CORRECTIONS COMPENDIUM; the national journal for corrections. 1976. m. $60. C E G A Publishing, 3900 Industrial Ave., N., 2nd Fl., Box 81826, Lincoln, NE 68501-1826. TEL 402-464-0602. FAX 402-464-5931. Ed. Greg Wees; Pub. Gary Hill. R&P contact: Greg Wees. adv. contact: Greg Wees. charts; illus.; stat.; tr.lit.; circ. 2,000 (paid) (back issues avail.) Indexed: Crim.Just.Abstr. Document type: newsletter.

365   US   ISSN 0010-9045
CORRECTIONS DIGEST; the only independent news service for the corrections professional. 1970. w. (51/yr.). $345 (Canada $355) (includes q. Calendar of Events) (effective 1998). Washington Crime News Services, 3918 Prosperity Ave., Ste. 318, Fairfax, VA 22031-3334. TEL 703-573-1600; 800-422-9267. FAX 703-573-1604. Ed. Betty B. Bosarge; Pub. Richard J. O'Connell. bk.rev. (looseleaf format; also avail. in microform from UMI; reprint service avail. from UMI) Indexed: CJPI. Document type: newsletter.
—UMI.
Description: Discusses U.S. and foreign legal and corrections topics. Includes job listings.

365   US   ISSN 1072-9275
CORRECTIONS FORUM. 1992. bi-m. $60. Corrections Forum, 320 Broadway, Bethpage, NY 11714. TEL 516-942-3601. FAX 516-942-5968. Ed. Tom Kapinos; Pub. Tom Kapinos. R&P contact: Tom Kapinos. adv.: B&W page $1550, color page $2440; trim 8 1/8 x 10 7/8; adv. contact: Sue Shelly. bk.rev.; circ. 12,000 (controlled). Indexed: Abstr.Crim.& Pen. Document type: trade publication.
Description: Presents and promotes the latest developments in corrections.

364   US
▼**CORRECTIONS JOURNAL**. 1996. s-m. $249. Pace Publications, 443 Park Ave. S., New York, NY 10016. TEL 212-685-5450. FAX 212-679-4701. Ed. Vincent Taylor. Document type: newsletter.

365   US   ISSN 0190-2563
HV7231
CORRECTIONS TODAY. 1939. bi-m. $25 or membership. American Correctional Association, 4380 Forbes Blvd., Lanham, MD 20706-4322. TEL 301-918-1800. Ed. Gabrielle deGoot. R&P contact: Gabriella Daley. adv. contact: Marge Restivo. bk.rev.; illus.; index. circ. 20,000. (also avail. in microform from MIM,KTO; reprint service avail. from KTO) Indexed: Abstr.Bk.Rev.Curr.Leg.Per., CJPI, Crim.Just.Abstr., Ind.Per.Art.Relat.Law, P.A.I.S., Soc.Sci.Ind. Document type: trade publication.
●Also available online. Vendor(s): Information Access Co., UMI.
—BLDSC (3472.166000); KR SourceOne; UMI; UnCover.
Former titles (until 1979): American Journal of Correction (ISSN 0002-9203); (until 1954): Prison World; (until 1941): Jail Association Journal.
Description: Covers adult, juvenile and community corrections and criminal justice.

364   US   ISSN 0272-9849
HV6201
CRIME. (Subseries of: S I R S Social Issues (ISSN 0740-3127)) 1975. a. price varies; a. supplement $19. Social Issues Resources Series, Box 2348, Boca Raton, FL 33427-2348. TEL 561-994-0079; 800-232-SIRS. FAX 561-994-4704. E-mail: custserve@sirs.com; URL: http://www.sirs.com. Ed. Trudy Collins; Pub. Eleanor Goldstein. R&P contact: Bonnie Milnes. (looseleaf format; back issues avail.) Document type: academic/scholarly publication.
Description: Reprints articles that explore how crime affects society.

364   US   ISSN 0011-1287
HV6001   CODEN: CRDLAL
CRIME & DELINQUENCY. 1955. q. $211 to institutions (effective Sep. 1996). (National Council on Crime and Delinquency) Sage Publications, Inc., 2455 Teller Rd., Thousand Oaks, CA 91320. TEL 805-499-0721. FAX 805-499-0871. E-mail: libraries@sagepub.com; URL: http://www.sagepub.com. (Overseas subscr. to: Sage Publications Ltd., 6 Bonhill St., London EC2A 4PU, England; Sage Publication India Pvt. Ltd., P.O. Box 4215, New Delhi 110 048, India) Ed. Don C. Gibbons. adv. contact: Margaret Travers. bk.rev.; charts; index. circ. 2,900 (also avail. in microfilm from PMC,WSH; microfiche from WSH; back issues avail.; reprint service avail. from KTO,WSH) Indexed: Abstr.Crim.& Pen., ASCA, ASSIA, C.I.J.E., C.L.I., CJPI, Crim.Just.Abstr., Curr.Cont., Excerp.Med., Fam.Ind., IMFL, L.R.I., Lang.& Lang.Behav.Abstr., Leg.Per., P.A.I.S., Psychol.Abstr. (1966-), Sage Fam.Stud.Abstr., Sage Urb.Stud.Abstr., Soc.Sci.Ind., SSCI, Viol.& Abuse Abstr. Document type: academic/scholarly publication.
●Also available online. Vendor(s): UMI.
—BLDSC (3487.337000); Genuine Article; KR SourceOne; SWETS; UMI; UnCover. CCC.
Formerly (until 1960): National Probation and Parole Association Journal.
Description: Addresses specific policy or program implications or issues (social, political, and economic) of great topical interest to professionals in the criminal justice system.

364   US   ISSN 0192-3234
HV6001
CRIME AND JUSTICE; a review of research. 1979. irreg. (1-3/yr.), vol.22, 1997. price varies. University of Chicago Press, Journals Division, 5720 S. Woodlawn Ave., Chicago, IL 60637. TEL 773-702-7600. FAX 773-702-0172. E-mail: subscriptions@journal.uchicago.edu. (Subscr. to: Box 37005, Chicago, IL 60637. TEL 773-753-3347. FAX 773-753-0811) Ed. Michael Tonry. adv.; bk.rev. (back issues avail.; reprint service avail. from UMI,ISI,WSH) Indexed: ASCA, C.L.I. Document type: academic/scholarly publication.
—BLDSC (3487.340300); UMI; UnCover.
Formerly: Studies in Crime and Justice.
Description: Treats important developments in the criminal justice system. Covers legal, psychological, biological, sociological, historical and ethical considerations.
Refereed Serial

CRIMINOLOGY AND LAW ENFORCEMENT

364 US
CRIME & JUSTICE INTERNATIONAL. 1985. m. $59 (foreign $89) (effective 1998). (University of Illinois at Chicago) Office of International Criminal Justice, 1333 S. Wabash, Box 53, Chicago, IL 60605. TEL 312-996-8420. FAX 312-413-0458. Ed. Sean Malinowski. R&P contact: Jeffrey Builta. index. **Indexed:** Abstr.Crim.& Pen., Crim.Just.Abstr. **Document type:** newsletter.
—UMI.
C J International (ISSN 0882-0244)
Description: Focuses on criminal justice issues in Asia, Africa and other countries outside of Europe.

364 US
CRIME AND THE NATION'S HOUSEHOLDS (YEAR). (Subseries of: National Crime Victimization Survey Report) 1973. a. free. U.S. Department of Justice, Bureau of Justice Statistics, 633 Indiana Ave., N.W., 11th Fl., Washington, DC 20531. (Orders to: Superintendent of Documents, U.S. Government Printing Office, Box 371954, Pittsburgh, PA 15250-7954. TEL 202-512-1800. FAX 202-512-2250) stat. circ. 17,000. (also avail. in microfiche) **Document type:** government publication.

364 US ISSN 0011-1295
KF9223.C92
CRIME CONTROL DIGEST; a comprehensive and independent news summary for the law enforcement professional. 1967. w. (51/yr.). $345 (Canada $355) (includes q. Calendar of Events) (effective 1998). Washington Crime News Services, 3918 Prosperity Ave., Ste. 318, Fairfax, VA 22031-3334. TEL 703-573-1600; 800-422-9267. FAX 703-573-1604. Ed. Richard J. O'Connell; Pub. Richard J. O'Connell. bk.rev.; tr.lit. (looseleaf format; also avail. in microform from UMI; reprint service avail. from UMI) **Indexed:** CJPI. **Document type:** newsletter.
—UMI.
Description: Reviews current criminal laws and criminal-justice issues.

364 US ISSN 0146-5759
HV7296
CRIME IN VIRGINIA.* a. Department of State Police, Uniform Crime Reporting Section, Box 27472, Richmond, VA 23261-7472. TEL 804-323-2031. (also avail. in microfiche from CIS) **Indexed:** SRI.

CRIME LABORATORY DIGEST. see MEDICAL SCIENCES — Forensic Sciences

364 343 360 NE ISSN 0925-4994
HV6001 CODEN: CSCJEL
CRIME, LAW AND SOCIAL CHANGE; an international journal. (Text in English) 1977. 8/yr. fl.930 to institutions; $477 to institutions in U.S. (effective 1998). Kluwer Academic Publishers, Postbus 17, 3300 AA Dordrecht, Netherlands. TEL 31-78-6392392. FAX 31-78-6392254. TELEX 29245 KAPG NL. E-mail: services@wkap.nl; URL: http://www.wkap.nl. (Dist. by: Kluwer Academic Publishers Group, P.O. Box 322, 3300 AH Dordrecht, Netherlands. TEL 31-78-6392392. FAX 31-78-6546474; N. America dist. addr.: Box 358, Accord Sta., Hingham, MA 02018-0358. TEL 617-871-6600. FAX 617-871-6528) Ed. Alan Block. bk.rev.; index. (also avail. in microform from UMI; reprint service avail. from SWZ) **Indexed:** A.B.C.Pol.Sci., Abstr.Crim.& Pen., Amer.Hist.& Life (1988-1993), Arts & Hum.Cit.Ind., ASCA, Crim.Just.Abstr., Curr.Cont., Hist.Abstr. (1988-1993), IBR, Int.Polit.Sci.Abstr., Lang.& Lang.Behav.Abstr., Left Ind. (1982-), P.A.I.S., Sociol.Abstr., SSCI. **Document type:** academic/scholarly publication.
—BLDSC (3487.342795); Genuine Article; SWETS; UMI; UnCover. **CCC.**
Formerly: Contemporary Crises (ISSN 0378-1100); Incorporates (1986-1992): Corruption and Reform (ISSN 0169-7528)
Refereed Serial

364.4 UK
CRIME PREVENTION NEWS. 1969. q. Home Office, 50 Queen Anne's Gate, London SW1H 9AT, England. TEL 071-273-2946. circ. 65,000. **Document type:** government publication.

364 AT ISSN 1031-5330
CRIME PREVENTION SERIES. irreg. price varies. Australian Institute of Criminology, G.P.O. Box 2944, Canberra, A.C.T. 2601, Australia. TEL 61-6-2609256. FAX 61-6-2609260. E-mail: aicpress@aic.gov.au. (Dist. in US by: Criminal Justice Press, Box 249, Monsey, NY 10952) **Document type:** monographic series.

364 US ISSN 1065-7029
CRIME PREVENTION STUDIES. 1993. s-a. $47.50 per vol. Criminal Justice Press, Box 249, Monsey, NY 10952. TEL 914-354-9139. FAX 914-362-8376. Ed. Ronald V. Clarke; Pub. Richard Allinson. **Document type:** academic/scholarly publication.
—BLDSC (3487.343650).
Description: Covers international research and practice on situational crime prevention and other measures to limit opportunities for crime. Papers include prevention-oriented analyses of specific crime problems, evaluations of crime prevention programs, and theoretical discussions of the philosophy and methods of situational crime prevention.

364 FR ISSN 1244-5770
LES CRIMES DE L'ANNEE. 1992. a. 68 F. (Bibliotheque des Literatures Policieres) Agence Culturelle de Paris, 6 rue Francois Miron, 75004 Paris, France. TEL 33-1-44788050. FAX 33-1-44788055. (Sponsor addr.: 48-50 rue du Cardinal Lemoine, 75005 Paris, France. TEL 33-1-42349300. FAX 33-1-40518123) bibl.

364 UK ISSN 0070-1521
KD7865.A2
CRIMINAL APPEAL REPORTS. 1908. 6/yr. (in 2 vols., 3 nos./vol.). £190. Sweet & Maxwell, South Quay Plaza, 7th Fl., 183 Marsh Wall, London E14 9FT, England. TEL 071-538-8686. FAX 071-538-9508. Ed. Rebecca Hough. adv. contact: Jackie Wood. index. **Document type:** bulletin.
•Also available online. Vendor(s): Lexis-Nexis.
—BLDSC (3487.346000). **CCC.**

CRIMINAL BEHAVIOUR AND MENTAL HEALTH. see MEDICAL SCIENCES — Psychiatry And Neurology

365 UK ISSN 0264-987X
CRIMINAL JUSTICE. 1970. 4/yr. £10 membership. Howard League, 708 Holloway Rd., London N19 3NL, England. TEL 44-171-281-7722. E-mail: howard.league@ukonline.co.uk; URL: http://web.ukonline.co.uk/howard.league. Ed. Frances Crook. adv.; bk.rev.; illus. circ. 2,000. (also avail. in microform from UMI) **Indexed:** C.L.I., CJPI, Hum.Ind.
—BLDSC (3487.346800); UMI.
Formerly (until 1983): Howard League for Penal Reform Newsletter.
Description: Reports on prison facilities and administration.

345 US
KFI1762.A15I55
CRIMINAL JUSTICE (SPRINGFIELD). 1957. bi-m. $18 to members; members $68. Illinois State Bar Association, Section on Criminal Justice, Illinois Bar Center, Springfield, IL 62701. TEL 217-525-1760. FAX 217-525-0712. Ed.Bd. circ. 2,350. (looseleaf format; back issues avail.)

364 150 US ISSN 0093-8548
HV9261 CODEN: CJBHAB
CRIMINAL JUSTICE & BEHAVIOR; an international journal. 1974. q. $195 to institutions (effective Sep. 1996). (American Association of Correctional Psychologists) Sage Publications, Inc., 2455 Teller Rd., Thousand Oaks, CA 91320. TEL 805-499-0721. FAX 805-499-0871. E-mail: libraries@sagepub.com; URL: http://www.sagepub.com. (Overseas subscr. to: Sage Publications Ltd., 6 Bonhill St., London EC2A 4PU, England; Sage Publications India Pvt. Ltd., P.O. Box 4215, New Delhi 110 048, India) (Affiliate: American Correctional Association) Ed. David S. Glenwick. adv. contact: Margaret Travers. bk.rev.; index. circ. 1,600. (also avail. in microfiche from WSH; microfilm from UMI,WSH,PMC; back issues avail.; reprint service avail. from KTO,UMI) **Indexed:** Abstr.Bk.Rev.Curr.Leg.Per., Abstr.Crim.& Pen., ASCA, ASSIA, C.I.J.E., C.L.I., CJPI, Crim.Just.Abstr., Curr.Cont., Excerp.Med., Fam.Ind., Ind.Per.Art.Relat.Law, L.R.I., Leg.Cont., Mid.East: Abstr.& Ind., Mult.Ed.Abstr., P.A.I.S., PHRA, Psychol.Abstr. (1974-), Psychol.R.G., Sage Fam.Stud.Abstr., Sage Urb.Stud.Abstr., Soc.Sci.Ind., Sociol.Abstr., Sp.Ed.Needs Abstr., SSCI, Viol.& Abuse Abstr. **Document type:** academic/scholarly publication.
—BLDSC (3487.348000); Genuine Article; KR SourceOne; SWETS; UMI; UnCover. **CCC.**
Supersedes: Correctional Psychologist (ISSN 0589-8218)
Description: Covers criminal justice relating to mental health, personality assessment, and changes.

CRIMINAL JUSTICE ETHICS. see PHILOSOPHY

364.9 US ISSN 0194-0953
HV7921
CRIMINAL JUSTICE HISTORY; an international annual. 1980. a. $59.50. Greenwood Press, Inc. (Subsidiary of: Greenwood Publishing Group Inc.), 88 Post Rd., W., Box 5007, Westport, CT 06881-9990. TEL 203-226-3571. FAX 203-222-1502. Ed.Bd. **Indexed:** Amer.Hist.& Life (1980-), Hist.Abstr. (1980-).
—BLDSC (3487.350200); UnCover.

364 UK ISSN 0962-7251
CRIMINAL JUSTICE MATTERS. Abbreviated title: C J M. 1988. q. £15 to non-members (rest of Europe £21; elsewhere £27) (effective 1997); newsstand price: £4. Institute for the Study and Treatment of Delinquency, King's College London, Strand, London WC2R 2LS, England. TEL 44-171-873-2822. FAX 44-171-873-2823. Ed. Julia Braggins. R&P contact: Julia Braggins. adv. contact: Julia Braggins. circ. 1,400. (back issues avail.) **Document type:** academic/scholarly publication.
—BLDSC (3274.273400).
Incorporates: I S T D Bulletin.
Description: Provides information and informed opinion on all aspects of criminal justice, including the policy, the magistracy, crime prevention, forensic psychiatry, prisons, victims, and women and crime, both in the UK and abroad.

364 US ISSN 0045-9038
K3
CRIMINAL JUSTICE NEWSLETTER. 1970. s-m. $198. Pace Publications, 443 Park Ave. S., New York, NY 10016. TEL 212-685-5450. FAX 212-679-4701. Ed. Craig Fischer. bk.rev.; index. **Indexed:** C.L.I., CJPI, L.R.I. **Document type:** newsletter.
Description: Systemwide perspective on the criminal justice system, covering law enforcement, courts, and corrections.

CRIMINAL LAW FORUM; an international journal. see LAW — Criminal Law

364 US ISSN 0192-3323
K3
CRIMINAL LAW REVIEW. 1979. a. $160. Clark - Boardman - Callaghan, 375 Hudson St., New York, NY 10014. TEL 212-929-7500; 800-422-2101. FAX 212-924-0460. Ed. James G. Carr. (reprint service avail. from WSH) **Indexed:** ASSIA, Crim.Just.Abstr., SSCI.
—CCC.
Description: Contains the most significant articles on criminal law published within the past year.

CRIMINOLOGY AND LAW ENFORCEMENT

364   US   ISSN 1073-8290
CRIMINAL ORGANIZATIONS. 1985. q. $25 membership. International Association of the Study of Organized Crime (IASOC), University of Illinois at Chicago, OICJ (M-C 777), 1033 W. Van Buren St., Chicago, IL 60607-2919. TEL 516-299-2594. FAX 516-299-2587. Ed. Paul Clare. adv. contact: Jeff Builta. bk.rev. circ. 600. (back issues avail.) **Indexed:** Crim.Just.Abstr. **Document type:** newsletter.
    Formerly: International Association for the Study of Organized Crime. Update.
    Description: Includes articles, book reviews, news and notes, member network and summaries on organized crime issues.

364   CN   ISSN 0316-0041
HV6002
CRIMINOLOGIE. (Text in French; abstracts in English) 1968. 2/yr. Can.$32 to individuals; institutions Can.$53. Presses de l'Universite de Montreal, C.P. 6128, Succ. Centre-Ville, Montreal, PQ H3C 3J7, Canada. TEL 514-343-6933. FAX 514-343-2232. E-mail: pumedit@ere.umontreal.ca; URL: http://www.pum.umontreal.ca/pum/. Ed. Serae Brochu. R&P contact: Lise Bergevin. adv. contact: Lise Bergevin. circ. 1,000. (reprint service avail. from UMI) **Indexed:** Abstr.Crim.& Pen., Crim.Just.Abstr., Ind.Can.L.P.L., P.A.I.S.For.Lang.Ind., Pt.de Rep. (1983-). **Document type:** academic/scholarly publication.
—BLDSC (3487.369000); SWETS; UMI.
    Formerly: Acta Criminologica (ISSN 0065-1168)

364   UK   ISSN 0011-1376
THE CRIMINOLOGIST. 1966-1975; N.S. 1987. q. £36.75 (effective 1997). Barry Rose Law Periodicals, Little London, Chichester, W. Sussex PO19 1PG, England. TEL 44-1243-783637. FAX 44-1243-779278. E-mail: jp@barry-rose-law.co.uk. Ed. R. Stone. R&P contact: Jean Harbut. adv. contact: Dora Curtis. bk.rev.; bibl.; charts; illus.; stat.; index. (back issues avail.) **Indexed:** Abstr.Crim.& Pen., Crim.Just.Abstr., Euro.LJI, Excerp.Med., LJI, SSCI. **Document type:** academic/scholarly publication.
—BLDSC (3487.372000).
    Former titles: Crime; Detection.
    Description: Covers whole spectrum of criminal behavior in a practical and philosophical manner.

364   US   ISSN 0164-0240
CRIMINOLOGIST. 1976. bi-m. $7.50 (foreign $10). American Society of Criminology, 1314 Kinnear Rd., Ste. 212, Columbus, OH 43212. TEL 614-292-9207. FAX 614-292-6767. Ed. Miriam A. DeLone. adv. circ. 2,800. (back issues avail.) **Document type:** newsletter.

364   US   ISSN 0011-1384
HV6001   CODEN: CRINYA
CRIMINOLOGY; an interdisciplinary journal. 1963. q. $50 to individuals; institutions $90. American Society of Criminology, 1314 Kinnear Rd., Columbus, OH 43212. TEL 614-292-9207. Ed. Charles R. Tittle. R&P contact: Sarah Hall. index. circ. 4,000. (also avail. in microfilm from UMI; back issues avail.; reprint service avail. from RRI,UMI,WSH) **Indexed:** Abstr.Bk.Rev.Curr.Leg.Per., Abstr.Crim.& Pen., Abstr.Soc.Work, ASCA, ASSIA, C.L.I., Chic.Per.Ind., CJPI, Crim.Just.Abstr., Crim.Just.Abstr., Crime Delinq.Abstr., Curr.Cont., Excerp.Med., L.R.I., Leg.Per., Mid.East: Abstr.& Ind., P.A.I.S., Psychol.Abstr., Risk Abstr., Soc.Sci.Ind., Sociol.Abstr., SSCI. **Document type:** academic/scholarly publication.
●Also available online. Vendor(s): UMI.
—BLDSC (3487.374000); KR SourceOne; SWETS; UMI; UnCover.
    Formerly: Criminologica.

364   US
CRIMINOLOGY AND CRIME CONTROL POLICY. 1992. irreg. price varies. Praeger Publishers (Subsidiary of: Greenwood Publishing Group Inc.), 88 Post Rd. W., Box 5007, Westport, CT 06881-5007. TEL 203-226-3571. FAX 203-222-1502. **Document type:** monograph series.

364   UK
CROPWOOD ROUND-TABLE CONFERENCE PAPERS. 1968. irreg., no. 21, 1993. £11.50. University of Cambridge, Institute of Criminology, 7 West Rd., Cambridge CB3 9DT, England. TEL 44-1223-335375. FAX 44-1223-335356. (back issues avail.) **Document type:** academic/scholarly publication, monograph series.

364   AT   ISSN 1034-5329
HV7231
CURRENT ISSUES IN CRIMINAL JUSTICE. 1967. 3/yr. Aus.$70($840) (foreign Aus.$85) (effective 1997). University of Sydney, Institute of Criminology, Faculty of Law, 173-175 Phillip St., Sydney, N.S.W. 2000, Australia. TEL 61-2-93510239. FAX 61-2-93510200. E-mail: dawnk@law.usyd.edu.au; URL: http://www.law.usyd.edu.u/~criminology/. (Dist. in US by: Wm. Gaunt & Sons, Inc., Gaunt Building, 3011 Gulf Dr., Holmes Beach, FL 34217-2199) adv.; bk.rev.; cum.index. circ. 2,000. (back issues avail.; reprint service avail. from WSH) **Indexed:** Aus.P.A.I.S., Crim.Just.Abstr., L.R.I. **Document type:** academic/scholarly publication.
—BLDSC (3499.061000); UnCover. **CCC.**
    Supersedes (in 1989): University of Sydney. Institute of Criminology. Proceedings (ISSN 0085-7033)
    Description: Presents papers in the criminal justice fields, focusing on timely and critical concerns in a range of areas, from juvenile justice to Aboriginal issues, domestic violence, corporate crime and others.
    Refereed Serial

364.6 323.4   US
KF9725.D432
DEATH ROW U.S.A. REPORTER. 1975. irreg. (3-5/yr.). $50 (effective 1995). (N A A C P Legal Defense Educational Fund) William S. Hein & Co., Inc., 1285 Main St., Buffalo, NY 14209. TEL 716-883-2600; 800-882-7571. FAX 716-883-8100. TELEX 91-209 WM S HEIN BUF. (looseleaf format; back issues avail.; reprint service avail. from WSH) **Document type:** newsletter.

364   GW
DEI DELITTI E DELLE PENE. (Annual English edition avail.) 1982-1987; N.S. 1991. 3/yr. L.70000 (foreign L.110000) (effective 1995). Universitaet des Saarlandes, 66041 Saarbruecken, Germany. TEL 0681-3023153. FAX 0681-3024510. Ed. Alessandro Baratta.

DELIKT EN DELINKWENT; tijdschrift voor strafrecht. see *LAW — Criminal Law*

364   MX   ISSN 0045-9992
DERECHO PENAL CONTEMPORANEO.* bi-m. Mex.$60($6.) Universidad Nacional Autonoma de Mexico, Facultad de Derecho, Ciudad Universitaria, 04510 Mexico DF, Mexico. bk.rev.

364   BG
DETECTIVE. (Editions in Bengali and English) 1960. w. East Pakistan Police Co-Operative Society, Polwell Bhaban, Naya Paltan, Dhaka 2, Bangladesh. TEL 2-402757. Ed. Syed Amjad Hossain. adv.; charts; illus. circ. 3,000. **Indexed:** CJPI.

364 340   US   ISSN 0742-552X
KF9730.A15
DETENTION REPORTER; a monthly resource for detention & corrections. 1983. m. $48. C R S, Inc., Box 1180, Washington Grove, MD 20880-1180. TEL 301-977-9090. FAX 301-527-1962. Ed. Rod Miller. bk.rev. circ. 700. (back issues avail.) **Document type:** newsletter.
    Description: Summaries of news, special issues and court decisions for detention and corrections.

363.2   GW   ISSN 0012-057X
DEUTSCHE POLIZEI. 1951. m. DM.57.60. (Gewerkschaft der Polizei) Verlag Deutsche Polizeiliteratur GmbH, Forststr. 3a, 40721 Hilden, Germany. bk.rev.; bibl.; charts; illus. circ. 174,000.
—**CCC.**

363.2   GW   ISSN 0175-4815
DEUTSCHES POLIZEIBLATT; Fachzeitschrift fuer die Aus- und Fortbildung des Polizeibeamten. Short title: D Pol Bl. 1983. bi-m. DM.54. Richard Boorberg Verlag (Stuttgart), Scharrstr. 2, 70563 Stuttgart, Germany. TEL 0711-7385-0. Ed. Gert Taures. (back issues avail.) **Document type:** trade publication.
—**CCC.**

DEVIANT BEHAVIOR; an interdisciplinary journal. see *SOCIOLOGY*

364   US
DICTIONARY OF CRIMINAL JUSTICE. irreg., 3rd ed., 1991. $14.95. Dushkin Publishing Group, Sluice Dock, Guilford, CT 06437-9989. TEL 203-453-4351. FAX 203-453-6000. Ed. George E. Rush; Pub. Rick Connelly. illus. **Document type:** academic/scholarly publication.

364   US   ISSN 1071-3530
HV9463
DIRECTORY - JUVENILE AND ADULT CORRECTIONAL DEPARTMENTS, INSTITUTIONS, AGENCIES, AND PAROLING AUTHORITIES. 1939. a. $80 to non-members; members $64. American Correctional Association, 4380 Forbes Blvd., Lanham, MD 20706-4322. TEL 301-918-1800. Ed. Gabriella Daley. R&P contact: Gabriella Daley. adv. contact: Marge Restivo. circ. 5,000. (also avail. in microfiche from CIS) **Indexed:** SRI. **Document type:** directory.
    Former titles (until 1992): Directory - Juvenile and Adult Correctional Departments, Institutions, Agencies, and Paroling Authorities of the United States and Canada (ISSN 0190-2555); Directory - Juvenile and Adult Correctional Departments, Institutions, Agencies, and Paroling Authorities of the United States and Canada (ISSN 0362-9287); (until 1973): Directory - Juvenile Adult Correctional Institutions and Agencies of the United States of America, Canada, and Great Britain (ISSN 0090-4872); (until 1972): Directory of Correctional Institutions and Agencies of the United States of America, Canada, and Great Britain (ISSN 0070-5373); American Correctional Association Directory: State and Federal Correctional Institutions (ISSN 0065-7956)

364 658.478   US   ISSN 0191-4553
HV9950
DIRECTORY OF CRIMINAL JUSTICE INFORMATION SOURCES. 1972. biennial. U.S. Department of Justice, National Institute of Justice, National Criminal Justice Reference Service, Box 6000, Rockville, MD 20849-6000. TEL 800-851-3420. (also avail. in microfiche)

344 343   US
DIRECTORY OF CRIMINAL JUSTICE ISSUES IN THE STATES. 1984. a. $25. Justice Research Statistics Association, Inc., 444 N. Capitol St., N.W., Ste. 445, Washington, DC 20001. TEL 202-624-8560. FAX 202-624-5269. Ed. Karen F. Maline. circ. 1,000. **Document type:** directory.

DIRECTORY OF SERVICES FOR VICTIMS OF CRIME/REPERTOIRE DES SERVICES AUX VICTIMES D'ACTES CRIMINELS. see *SOCIAL SERVICES AND WELFARE*

364   NQ
DOCUMENTOS PENALES Y CRIMINOLOGICOS. 1993. 3/yr. Apdo. Postal A-113, Managua, Nicaragua. Dirs. Diego-Manuel Luzon Pena, Sergio J. Cuarezma Teran.
    Description: Promotes scientific discussion of penal and criminological sciences.

DRUG AND CRIME PREVENTION FUNDING NEWS. see *DRUG ABUSE AND ALCOHOLISM*

DRUG DETECTION REPORT. see *BUSINESS AND ECONOMICS — Personnel Management*

DRUG ENFORCEMENT ADMINISTRATION REGISTRATION FILE - ACTIVE. see *MEDICAL SCIENCES*

365   US   ISSN 0894-1300
HV5825
DRUG ENFORCEMENT REPORT. 1984. s-m. $197. Pace Publications, 443 Park Ave. S., New York, NY 10016. TEL 212-685-5450. FAX 212-679-4701. Ed. Dean Boyd. (back issues avail.) **Indexed:** Hlth.Ind. **Document type:** newsletter.
    Description: Reports on federal developments in drug enforcement policy.

364   US   ISSN 1070-2377
EAGLE INVESTIGATORS' NEWS; an international journal of private investigation, security and counter-espionage. 1988. q. $15 (foreign $25). International Security & Detective Alliance - I S D A, Box 6303, Corpus Christi, TX 78466-6303. TEL 512-888-6164. Ed. H. Roehm. adv.; bk.rev. circ. 2,000. **Document type:** newsletter.
    Formerly (until 1990): Eagle (Corpus Christi).
    Description: Covers news relevant to security and private investigation and security professionals, counter-espionage specialists, police science.

CRIMINOLOGY AND LAW ENFORCEMENT

365 US ISSN 0046-1059
ECHO (HUNTSVILLE). 1929. m. $2.50. Department of Corrections, Box 40-MC, Huntsville, TX 77340. TEL 713-295-6371. Ed. J.T. Sullivan. bk.rev.; film rev. circ. 38,000.

364 US
EIGHTEEN-ELEVEN. 1978. m. membership. Federal Law Enforcement Officers Association, 106 Cedarhurst Ave., Selden, NY 11784. TEL 516-698-0179. Ed. Alan B. Bernstein. circ. 5,000.
Description: Covers subjects of interest to federal law enforcement officers and criminal investigators.

ELSEVIER SERIES IN FORENSIC AND POLICE SCIENCE. see MEDICAL SCIENCES — Forensic Sciences

ELSEVIER SERIES IN PRACTICAL ASPECTS OF CRIMINAL & FORENSIC INVESTIGATION. see MEDICAL SCIENCES — Forensic Sciences

EMPLOYEE TESTING & THE LAW; reporting legal, technical, and business developments in employee testing. see BUSINESS AND ECONOMICS — Personnel Management

364 BL
ESCOLA DO SERVICO PENITENCIARIO DO RIO GRANDE DO SUL. REVISTA. 1990. q. Escola do Servico Penitenciario do Rio Grande do Sul, Av. Borges de Medeiros, 1501, 9o andar, Ala N, 90068 Porto Alegre RS, Brazil. TEL 0512-26-7563.

363.2 FR ISSN 0338-1595
ESSOR DE LA GENDARMERIE NATIONALE. 4/yr. 132 rue du Faubourg St. Denis, 75481 Paris Cedex 10, France. TEL 40-36-44-64. FAX 40-36-90-20. Ed. Jacques Revise. circ. 40,000.
Formerly (until 1971): Essor de la Gendarmerie et de la Garde (ISSN 0338-1587)

364 PL ISSN 0860-3723
EUROCRIMINOLOGY. (Text in English) 1987. a. Instytut Problematyki Przestepczosci - Institute of Crime Problems, Ul. Kozia 9-17, 00-070 Warsaw, Poland. TEL 48-22-279701. (Dist. in U.S. by: Criminal Justice Press, 124 Willow Tree Rd., Monsey, NY 10952. TEL 914-354-9139. FAX 914-362-8376) Ed. Brunon Holyst. Indexed: Abstr.Crim.& Pen., Crim.Just.Abstr. Document type: academic/scholarly publication.

EUROPEAN JOURNAL OF CRIME, CRIMINAL LAW AND CRIMINAL JUSTICE. see LAW — Criminal Law

364 345 NE ISSN 0928-1371
EUROPEAN JOURNAL ON CRIMINAL POLICY AND RESEARCH. (Text in English) 1993. 4/yr. $112.50 (effective 1996). (Ministry of Justice, Research and Documentation Centre) Kugler Publications B.V., P.O. Box 11188, 1001 GD Amsterdam, Netherlands. TEL 31-20-6278070. FAX 31-20-6380524. Ed.Bd. (back issues avail.) Indexed: Crim.Just.Abstr. Document type: academic/scholarly publication.
—BLDSC (3829.728240).
Description: Provides a platform for discussion and information exchange on the crime problem in Europe.

364 US ISSN 0014-5688
HV6201
F B I LAW ENFORCEMENT BULLETIN. 1935. m. $19 (foreign $23.75). U.S. Federal Bureau of Investigation, F B I Academy, Madison Bldg., Rm. 209, Quantico, VA 22135. TEL 703-640-8666. FAX 703-640-1474. E-mail: leb@fbi.gov. (Subscr. to: Superintendent of Documents, U.S. Government Printing Office, Box 371954, Pittsburgh, PA 15250. TEL 202-512-1800. FAX 202-512-2250) Ed. Kathryn E. Sulewski. R&P contact: Brian Parmell. bk.rev. circ. 60,000. (also avail. in microform from MIM,UMI; back issues avail.; reprint service avail. from UMI) Indexed: Abstr.Crim.& Pen., CJPI, Crim.Just.Abstr., Excerp.Med., Ind.U.S.Gov.Per., P.A.I.S., Soc.Sci.Ind. Document type: government publication, bulletin.
●Also available online. Vendor(s): Information Access Co., UMI.
—BLDSC (3901.007000); KR SourceOne; UMI; UnCover.
Description: Discusses current issues in law enforcement.

F C L ACTION ALERTS. (Friends Committee on Legislation of California) see POLITICAL SCIENCE

364 US ISSN 1057-9397
F D A ENFORCEMENT REPORT. w. $92 (foreign $115) (effective 1995). U.S. Food and Drug Administration, Office of Public Affairs, Rm. 15A-11, Parklawn Bldg., 5600 Fishers Ln., Rockville, MD 20857. TEL 301-443-3285. (Subscr. to: Superintendent of Documents, U.S. Government Printing Office, Box 371954, Pittsburgh, PA 15250-7954. TEL 202-512-1800. FAX 202-512-2250) Document type: government publication.
●Also available online. Vendor(s): Information Access Co., Ovid Technologies, Inc. (DIOG).
Description: Lists actions taken in connection with agency regulatory activities.

FAMILY VIOLENCE & SEXUAL ASSAULT BULLETIN. see SOCIAL SERVICES AND WELFARE

364.4 CC
FAZHI LIAOWANG/LEGAL OUTLOOK. (Text in Chinese) bi-m. Y6. Fazhi Liaowang Zazhishe, Xihu Jingbianting, Fuzhou, Fujian 350003, People's Republic of China. (Dist. overseas by: Jiangsu Publications Import & Export Corp., 56 Gao Yun Ling, Nanjing, Jiangsu, P.R.C.)
Formerly: Fujian Cifa.
Description: Publishes results of criminological research and discussions of legal issues in special economic zones and focuses on special laws covering Taiwan and Hong Kong.

365 US ISSN 0014-9128
HV9261 CODEN: FDEPA
FEDERAL PROBATION; a journal of correctional philosophy and practice. 1937. q. $8 (foreign $10) (effective 1997). U.S. Administrative Office of the United States Courts, Federal Corrections and Supervision Division, Washington, DC 20402-9371. TEL 202-273-1627. FAX 202-273-1603. (Subscr. to: Superintendent of Documents, U.S. Government Printing Office, Box 371954, Pittsburgh, PA 15250-7954. TEL 202-512-1800. FAX 202-512-2250) Ed. Karen S. Henkel. R&P contact: Karen S. Henkel. bk.rev.; abstr.; bibl.; index; cum.index every 5 yrs. circ. 6,500. (also avail. in microform from MIM,UMI; back issues avail.; reprint service avail. from KTO,UMI,WSH) Indexed: Abstr.Crim.& Pen., Adol.Ment.Hlth.Abstr., ASCA, C.L.I., CJPI, Crim.Just.Abstr., Curr.Cont., Energy Ind., Energy Info.Abstr., Excerp.Med., Fam.Ind., IBR, Ind.U.S.Gov.Per., L.R.I., Leg.Per., Mid.East: Abstr.& Ind., P.A.I.S., Psychol.Abstr. (1983-), Soc.Sci.Ind., SSCI. Document type: government publication, academic/scholarly publication.
●Also available online. Vendor(s): Information Access Co.
—BLDSC (3901.932000); Genuine Article; KR SourceOne; SWETS; UMI; UnCover.
Formerly: U.S. Probation System. News Letter.
Description: Focuses on criminal justice and corrections issues including community corrections, alternatives to incarceration, and sentencing.

340 US ISSN 1053-9867
KF9685.A59
FEDERAL SENTENCING REPORTER. 1988. bi-m. $146 (foreign $152) (effective July 1997). (Vera Institute of Justice) University of California Press, Journals Division, 2120 Berkeley Way, No. 5812, Berkeley, CA 94720-5812. TEL 510-643-7154. FAX 510-642-9917. E-mail: journal@ucop.edu; URL: http://library.berkeley.edu:8080/ucalpress/journals. Ed. Daniel J. Freed. circ. 2,450 (paid) (also avail. in microform from UMI; back issues avail.; reprint service avail. from UMI,WSH) Document type: academic/scholarly publication.
●Also available online. Vendor(s): Lexis-Nexis, West Group.
—UMI. CCC.
Description: Provides up-to-date information on and thorough analysis of contemporary federal sentencing issues.
Refereed Serial

363.2 IT
FIAMME D'ARGENTO. m. Associazione Nazionale Carabinieri, Via Legnano 1-a, 00192 Rome, Italy. Ed. Efisio Anedda.

363.24 614.19 UK ISSN 0951-1288
FINGERPRINT WORLD. 1975. q. £17 to non-member individuals in E.C. nations (elsewhere $40); non-member institutions in E.C. nations £20 (elsewhere $60) (effective 1996). Fingerprint Society, Merseyside Police, Fingerprint Bureau, Canning Pl., Liverpool L1 8JX, England. (Subscr. to: Vivienne Galloway, The Fingerprint Society, 5 Slate Close, Glenfield, Leics. LE3 8QQ, England) Ed. Graham Hughes. R&P contact: Graham Hughes. adv. contact: Steve Mewett. bk.rev. circ. 1,200. Document type: academic/scholarly publication.

364 343 US ISSN 1059-7298
HV8079.A7
FIRE AND ARSON INVESTIGATOR.* 1949. q. $55 membership for first yr.; $40 per yr. thereafter. (International Association of Arson Investigators, Inc.) V.G. Reed and Sons Inc., 300 S. Broadway, Ste. 100, St. Louis, MO 63102-2808. Ed. Linda Koch. adv.; bk.rev. circ. 7,500. (back issues avail.) Indexed: Abstr.Crim.& Pen., Crim.Just.Abstr.
Description: Covers all fields related to arson investigation.

FIRE AND POLICE PERSONNEL REPORTER. see BUSINESS AND ECONOMICS — Personnel Management

363.2 US
THE FLORIDA POLICE CHIEF. 1961. m. $20 (effective Oct. 1997). Florida Police Chiefs Association, c/o Assoc. Ed. Karen Price, 2300 Centerville Rd., Tallahassee, FL 32308. TEL 904-385-9046. FAX 904-386-3272. (Subscr. to: Box 14038, Tallahassee, FL 32317-4038) adv.: B&W page $600, color page $1200; trim 8 1/4 x 11. circ. 1,000. (back issues avail.) Document type: trade publication.
Description: Informs and educates on law enforcement trends in the state.

363.2 CN ISSN 0703-4725
FLUTE. (Text in French) 1945. m. free. Montreal Urban Community Policemen's Brotherhood Inc. - Fraternite des Policiers de la Communaute Urbaine de Montreal, 480 Gilford St., Montreal, PQ H2J 1N3, Canada. TEL 514-527-4161. FAX 514-527-7830. Ed. Gerald Deslandes. illus. circ. 9,000.
Formerly: Revue des Agents de Police (ISSN 0035-1903)

FORENSIC ACCOUNTING REVIEW. see BUSINESS AND ECONOMICS

365 US ISSN 0015-8275
FORTUNE NEWS. 1967. q. $40 to non-members (free to inmates). Fortune Society, 39 W. 19th St., New York, NY 10011. TEL 212-206-7070. Ed. Ken Bloomfield. adv.; bk.rev. circ. 40,000. (tabloid format) Document type: newspaper.
Description: Reports on prison facilities, criminal justice issues, and root causes of crime.

365 CN ISSN 0847-0464
HV7231
FORUM ON CORRECTIONS RESEARCH. French edition: Forum, Recherche sur l'Actualite Correctionnelle (ISSN 0847-0472) 1989. 3/yr. free. Correctional Service of Canada - Service Correctionnel Canada, Research Division, Correctional Research and Development, 2B-340 Laurier Ave. W., Ottawa, ON K1A 0P9, Canada. TEL 613-995-3975. FAX 613-941-8477. URL: http://www.csc-scc.gc.ca. Ed. Larry Motiuk. R&P contact: Larry Motiuk. TEL 613-995-4694. circ. 6,000. Indexed: Crim.Just.Abstr. Document type: academic/scholarly publication, government publication.
—BLDSC (4024.085160).

363.2 FR ISSN 0240-4729
J341
FRANCE. MINISTERE DE L'INTERIEUR. REPERTOIRE MENSUEL. 1979. m. (11/yr.). 450 F. (effective 1997). (Ministere de l'Interieur, Service d'Information et de Relations Publiques) Publications Paul Dupont, 38 rue Croix des Petits Champs, 75001 Paris, France. TEL 33-1-42962578. FAX 33-1-42601041.
Formerly: France. Ministere de l'Interieur. Repertoire.

CRIMINOLOGY AND LAW ENFORCEMENT

364.4 658   US
FRESNO DAILY LEGAL REPORT.* 1886. d. $130. G.M. Webster Jr., P.O. Box 126, Fresno, CA 93707. TEL 209-237-0114. Ed. G.M. Webster, Jr. adv. circ. 1,125.
Description: Covers court and commercial interests.

363.2   CC
FUJIAN GONG'AN/FUJIAN PUBLIC SECURITY. (Text in Chinese) 1949. m. Y15.60. (Fujian Sheng Gong'an Ting - Fujian Provincial Bureau of Public Security) Fujian Gong'an Publishing House, 12 Hualin Rd., Fuzhou, Fujian 350003, People's Republic of China. TEL 8093063. (Dist. overseas by: Jiangsu Publications Import & Export Corp., 56 Gao Yun Ling, Nanjing, Jiangsu, P.R.C.) Ed. Li Jiaju. circ. 65,000. **Document type:** consumer publication.

364   US   ISSN 0883-3087
G D G REPORT.* 1985. q. $40. G.D. Gawkowski, Ed. & Pub., Box 277, Beacon Falls, CT 06403-0277. TEL 203-371-0136. bk.rev. circ. 1,000. (back issues avail.)

362.2   IE   ISSN 0332-463X
GARDA NEWS. 10/yr. Association of Garda Sergeants & Inspectors, Phibsboro Tower, 6th Fl., Dublin 7, Ireland. TEL 303752. FAX 303465. Ed. Austin Kenny. circ. 5,000.
Formerly (until 1982): Horizon (ISSN 0332-4621)

363.2   IE
GARDA REVIEW. 1924. m. £7.50. Garda Review Ltd., Philsboro Tower, 5th Fl., Philsboro, Dublin 7, Ireland. TEL 01-303533. Ed. Catherine Fox. adv.; bk.rev.; charts; illus.; tr.lit. circ. 12,000. **Document type:** trade publication.
Formerly: Iris an Gharda (ISSN 0021-101X)
Description: Monthly publication of the Irish police force, or Garda.

365   UK
GATELODGE. 1939. bi-m. £6 (Scotland £8; foreign £16) to non-members; retirees £6 (effective 1996). Prison Officers' Association, Cronin House, 245 Church St., Edmonton, London N9 9HW, England. TEL 0181-803-0255. FAX 0181-803-1761, Ed. David Evans. adv.; bk.rev. circ. 17,500. **Indexed:** Abstr.Crim.& Pen. **Document type:** trade publication.
Formerly (until 1986): Prison Officers Magazine (ISSN 0032-8863)

365   US
GATEWAY ALLIANCE NEWSLETTER. 1966-1979?; resumed 1984. q. free. Correctional Association of New York, 135 E. 15th St., New York, NY 10003. TEL 212-254-5700. FAX 212-473-2807. (Co-sponsor: Osborne Association) Ed. Anthony J. Scanlon. bk.rev.; bibl.; illus. circ. 5,500. **Document type:** newsletter.
Former titles (until Mar. 1993): Correctional Association of New York. News Bulletin; Correctional Association of New York. Newsletter.

GEND'INFO. see MILITARY

GLOBAL JOURNAL ON CRIME AND CRIMINAL LAW. see LAW — Criminal Law

364   GW   ISSN 0017-1956
K7
GOLTDAMMER'S ARCHIV FUER STRAFRECHT. 1853. m. DM.390.60 (foreign DM.403.80) (effective 1996). R. v. Decker's Verlag Huetig GmbH, Im Weiher 10, 69121 Heidelberg, Germany. TEL 49-6221-489281. FAX 49-6221-489279. Ed. P.G. Poetz. adv.; bk.rev.; bibl.; charts; illus.; stat.; index. circ. 800. **Indexed:** IBR. **Document type:** academic/scholarly publication.
—SWETS.

364 970   US   ISSN 0146-762X
GRASSY KNOLL GAZETTE. 1981. bi-m. $10 (foreign $12). Cutler Designs, Box 1465, Manchester, MA 01944. TEL 508-526-1521. Ed. R.B. Cutler. circ. 150 (paid); 250 (controlled).
Description: Publishes continuing research into US assassinations.

364.1   UK   ISSN 0959-597X
GREAT BRITAIN. HOME OFFICE. POLICE RESEARCH GROUP. CRIME PREVENTION UNIT. PAPERS. no.32, 1992. irreg. price varies. Home Office, Police Research Group, Crime Prevention Unit, 50 Queen Anne's Gate, London SW1H 9AT, England. **Document type:** government publication, monographic series.

365   UK   ISSN 0265-573X
HV9649.E5
GREAT BRITAIN. HOME OFFICE. PROBATION STATISTICS ENGLAND & WALES (YEAR). Key Title: Probation Statistics England & Wales (Year). a. Home Office, Publications Office, 50 Queen Anne's Gate, London SW1 9AT, England. (Subscr. to: Home Office, Research and Statistics Department, Lunar House, Croydon, Surrey CR0 9YD, England. TEL 081-760-2850) **Document type:** government publication.
—BLDSC (6617.256500).

GREAT BRITAIN. HOME OFFICE. RESEARCH AND PLANNING UNIT. PROGRAMME (YEAR). see PUBLIC ADMINISTRATION

GREAT BRITAIN. HOME OFFICE. RESEARCH AND PLANNING UNIT. RESEARCH FINDINGS. see PUBLIC ADMINISTRATION

GREAT BRITAIN. HOME OFFICE. RESEARCH AND STATISTICS DEPARTMENT. RESEARCH BULLETIN. see PUBLIC ADMINISTRATION

364   UK   ISSN 0072-6435
GREAT BRITAIN. HOME OFFICE. RESEARCH STUDIES. 1969. irreg. Home Office, Research and Statistics Department, Research and Planning Unit, 50 Queen Anne's Gate, London SW1 9AT, England. (Orders to: H.M.S.O., P.O. Box 276, London SW8 5DT, England. TEL 44-171-873-0011. FAX 44-171-873-8200) (reprint service avail. from UMI) **Document type:** government publication, monographic series.
—BLDSC (4326.110000). CCC.
Description: Publishes results of studies on social and operational research on the criminal justice system and community relations.

GUIDE TO FEDERAL FUNDING FOR ANTI-DRUG PROGRAMS. see DRUG ABUSE AND ALCOHOLISM

364   UK
H M INSPECTORATE OF PROBATION. QUALITY & EFFECTIVENESS INSPECTION REPORTS. irreg. (H M Inspectorate of Probation) Home Office Publications Unit, 50 Queen Anne's Gate, Rm. 1024, London SW1H 9AT, England. TEL 44-171-273-2302.

353.9   US   ISSN 0098-5708
HV8688
HAWAII. CRIMINAL INJURIES COMPENSATION COMMISSION. ANNUAL REPORT.* Key Title: Annual Report - Criminal Injuries Compensation Commission. 1967. a. Criminal Injuries Compensation Commission, 333 Queen St., Rm. 404, Honolulu, HI 96813. TEL 808-587-1143. FAX 808-548-8102.

HOME OFFICE. RESEARCH AND STATISTICS DIRECTORATE. STATISTICAL BULLETIN. see PUBLIC ADMINISTRATION — Abstracting, Bibliographies, Statistics

364.021   US   ISSN 0098-8537
HV6533.C2
HOMICIDE IN CALIFORNIA. 1963. irreg. free. Department of Justice, Bureau of Criminal Statistics and Special Services, 3301 C St, Box 13427, Sacramento, CA 95813. TEL 916-227-3509. illus.; stat.

364.1   US   ISSN 1088-7679
▼**HOMICIDE STUDIES.** Announced for publication in 1997. q. $160 to institutions (effective 1997). Sage Publications, Inc., 2455 Teller Rd., Thousand Oaks, CA 91320. TEL 805-499-0721. FAX 805-499-0871. E-mail: order@sagepub.com; URL: http://www.sagepub.com. (Overseas subscr. to: Sage Publications Ltd., 6 Bonhill St., London EC2A 4PU, England; Sage Publications Ltd., P.O. Box 4215, New Delhi 110 048, India) Ed. M. Dwayne Smith. **Document type:** academic/scholarly publication.
—BLDSC (4326.177900).

364 340   US   ISSN 0895-3171
HOTLINE (STONY BROOK); news service on the missing children field. 1980. q. free. Children's Rights of New York, Inc., 15 Arbutus Lane, Stony Brook, NY 11790-1408. TEL 516-751-7840. Ed. John E. Gill. bk.rev. circ. 1,700. (looseleaf format; back issues avail.)

364   US
HOW TO FIND ANYONE ANYWHERE; secret sources & techniques for locating missing persons. 1981. a. $20. (National Association of Investigative Specialists) Thomas Publishing (Austin), Box 33244 Austin, TX 78764. TEL 512-832-0355. Ed. Ralph Thomas. circ. 2,500.
Description: Contains how-to tips for investigators.

365   UK   ISSN 0265-5527
HV8995.A1
THE HOWARD JOURNAL OF CRIMINAL JUSTICE. 1941. q. £119($229) (foreign £145) (effective 1997). (Howard League for Penal Reform) Blackwell Publishers Ltd., 108 Cowley Rd., Oxford OX4 1JF, England. TEL 44-1865-791100. FAX 44-1865-791347. E-mail: jnlinfo@ blackwellpublishers.co.uk; URL: http://www. blackwellpublishers.co.uk. Eds. Nigel Fielding, Leslie Wilkins. adv.; bk.rev.; cum.index 1941-1975. circ. 1,700. (also avail. in microform from UMI; reprint service avail. from KTO,UMI) **Indexed:** Abstr.Crim.& Pen., ASSIA, C.L.I., CJPI, Crim.Just.Abstr., Euro.LJI, Fam.Ind., L.R.I., LJI, P.A.I.S. **Document type:** academic/scholarly publication.
—BLDSC (4335.244300); SWETS; UMI; UnCover. CCC.
Formerly (until Feb. 1984): Howard Journal of Penology and Crime Prevention (ISSN 0073-3741)
Description: Offers commentary and reviews on both the theory and the practice of criminal justice and the study of criminals. Reports academic research and makes complex material accessible to criminal-justice professionals.

HUMAN KINDNESS FOUNDATION NEWSLETTER; a little news. see RELIGIONS AND THEOLOGY

363.2   US
I A C P - B J A POLICY ISSUES.* bi-m. $15 to non-members; members $12. International Association of Chiefs of Police, Inc., 515 N. Washington St., Ste. 400, Alexandria, VA 22314-2340. TEL 703-243-6500. circ. controlled.

363.2   US
I A C P TRAINING KEY.* m. $5. International Association of Chiefs of Police, Inc., 515 N. Washington St., Ste. 400, Alexandria, VA 22314-2340. TEL 703-243-6500. circ. controlled. **Indexed:** CJPI.

364   US
I D CHECKING GUIDE (INTERNATIONAL). 1993. s-a. $32.95 (foreign $34.95). Drivers License Guide Company, 1492 Oddstad Dr., Redwood City, CA 94063. TEL 415-369-4849.
Description: Features full-color coverage of driver's licenses for countries outside of the U.S. and Canada.

343 364.4   US   ISSN 1041-5793
HV8074
I D CHECKING GUIDE (YEAR); U.S. & Canadian edition. 1971. a. $21.95 (foreign $25). Drivers License Guide Company, 1492 Oddstad Dr., Redwood City, CA 94063. TEL 415-369-4849. Ed. Keith Doerge. circ. 50,000.
Formerly: Drivers License Guide (ISSN 0276-1696)
Description: Full color coverage of all driver's licenses valid-in-use in U.S. and Canada.

I F A R REPORTS; and the art loss register. (International Foundation for Art Research, Inc.) see ART

363.2   GW
I P A AKTUELL. 1955. 6/yr. DM.48.80. A. Bernecker Verlag, Unter dem Schoeneberg 1, 34212 Melsungen, Germany. TEL 49-5661-731-0. FAX 49-5661-73189. Ed. Gerd Thielmann. adv.; bk.rev.; circ. 54,500 (controlled). **Document type:** bulletin.

364.4 346.01　　　SW　　ISSN 0284-9887
I P A - JOURNAL. 1964. bi-m. SEK 75 membership (effective 1990). International Police Association, Svenska Sektionen, P.O. Box 5254, S-200 72 Malmoe, Sweden.
 Formerly (until vol.3, 1988): International Police Association.

364.12　　　　　US　　ISSN 0019-1450
IDENTIFICATION NEWS.* 1960. m. membership (official police libraries). International Association for Identification, Box 6054, Kinston, NC 28501-0054. Ed. Walter M. Thomas. bk.rev.; charts; illus.; stat.; tr.lit. circ. 2,500.
 —UMI.

363.2　　　　　US　　ISSN 0019-2171
HV7551
ILLINOIS POLICE ASSOCIATION. OFFICIAL JOURNAL.* 1945. bi-m. $10. Illinois Police Association, 220 Yosemite Cir. N., Minneapolis, MN 55422-5032. Ed. E.B. Hoffman. adv.; bk.rev.; circ. 17,000 (controlled).

363.2　　　　　AU
ILLUSTRIERTE RUNDSCHAU DER OESTERREICHISCHEN GENDARMERIE. 1948. m. S.550. Hahngasse 6, A-1090 Vienna, Austria. TEL 31 85 20. Eds. Dr. Kavar, E. Lutschinger. adv.; bk.rev.; illus.; index. circ. 5,000. **Indexed:** Abstr.Crim.& Pen.
 Formerly: Illustrierte Rundschau der Gendarmerie (ISSN 0019-2511)

364　　　　　　II　　ISSN 0376-9844
HV6201　　　　　　　　CODEN: IJOCDS
INDIAN JOURNAL OF CRIMINOLOGY. (Text in English) 1973. s-a. $20. Indian Society of Criminology, c/o Department of Psychology, University of Madras, Madras 600 005, India. TEL 044-566-988. E-mail: Unimad!ArulKali@iitem.ernet.in. Ed. K.V. Kaliappan. bk.rev.; bibl. circ. 700. **Indexed:** ASSIA, Crim.Just.Abstr., IBR.
 —BLDSC (4410.900000).

363.2　　　　　II　　ISSN 0537-2429
HV7551
INDIAN POLICE JOURNAL. (Text in English) 1954. q. Rs.7. Ministry of Home Affairs, Intelligence Bureau, 25 Akbar Rd., New Delhi 110 011, India. bk.rev.; illus. **Indexed:** Pub.Admin.Abstr. **Document type:** government publication.

365　　　　　　IT　　ISSN 0019-7084
K9
INDICE PENALE. 1967. 3/yr. L.150000 (foreign L.200000) (effective 1997). Casa Editrice Dott. Antonio Milani, Via Jappelli 5-6, 35121 Padua, Italy. TEL 39-49-656677. FAX 39-49-8752900. Ed. Mario Pisani. circ. 700.
 Description: Review of law, criminal procedure and criminology.

364　　　　　　GW
INFO INTERN. 1951. 10/yr. DM.80. Bundesverband Deutscher Detektive e.V., Koehlstr. 16, 53125 Bonn, Germany. TEL 49-228-298085. FAX 49-228-298091. Ed. Josef Riehl. adv.: page DM.450; adv. contact: Josef Riehl. circ. 250 (paid). **Document type:** bulletin.

INNER VOICES; a new journal of prison literature. see LITERATURE

INSIDER (HARRISBURG). see FOOD AND FOOD INDUSTRIES

364.4 301　　　YU　　ISSN 0350-2694
INSTITUT ZA KRIMINOLOSKA I SOCIOLOSKA ISTRAZIVANJA. ZBORNIK. (Text in Serbo-Croatian; summaries in English, French and Russian) 1972. a. $4. Institut za Kriminoloska i Socioloska Istrazivanja, Gracanicka 18, 11000 Belgrade, Yugoslavia. TEL 626-543. Ed. Aleksandar Mihajlovski. bk.rev.

365　　　　　　PL
INSTYTUT BADANIA PRAWA SADOWEGO. ZESZYTY NAUKOWE. (Text in Polish; summaries in English and Russian) 1974. s-a. 300 Zl.($20) Wydawnictwo Prawnicze, Ul. Wisniowa 50, 02-520 Warsaw, Poland. TEL 48-22-494705. FAX 48-22-499410. (Dist. by: Ars Polona-Ruch, Krakowskie Przedmiescie 7, Warsaw, Poland) circ. 1,200.

INTELLIGENCE NEWSLETTER. see MILITARY

364　　　　　　NG　　ISSN 0534-4816
INTER-AFRICAN CONFERENCE ON THE TREATMENT OF OFFENDERS. MEETINGS. REUNION.* Title varies slightly; some issues called reports. 1953. irreg. (Commission for Technical Co-Operation in Africa South of the Sahara) Maison de l'Afrique, B.P. 878, Niamey, Niger.

364　　　　　　GW　　ISSN 0937-0773
INTERDISZIPLINAERE BEITRAEGE ZUR KRIMINOLOGISCHEN FORSCHUNG. 1989. irreg., no.2, 1989. price varies. (Kriminologisches Forschungsinstitut Niedersachsen) Nomos Verlagsgesellschaft mbH und Co. KG, Waldseestr. 3-5, 76530 Baden-Baden, Germany. TEL 49-7221-2104-0. FAX 49-7221-210427. (reprint service avail. from IRC) **Document type:** monographic series.

INTERFACE (SACRAMENTO). see COMPUTERS

364　　　　　　US
INTERNATIONAL COMMUNITY CORRECTIONS ASSOCIATION. JOURNAL. 1967. 4/yr. $50 (effective 1997 & 1998). International Community Corrections Association, c/o Peter Kinziger, Ed., Box 1987, La Crosse, WI 54602. TEL 608-785-0200. FAX 608-784-5335. adv.; bk.rev.; bibl.; stat. circ. 3,000. (tabloid format) **Document type:** trade publication.
 Former titles: International Association of Residential and Community Alternatives. Journal; International Halfway House Association. Newsletter.

364　　　　　　US　　ISSN 0538-7191
INTERNATIONAL DIRECTORY OF PRISONERS AID AGENCIES.* irreg. International Prisoners Aid Association, U. of Louisville, Dept. of Sociology, Louisville, KY 40292.

364.4　　　　　US　　ISSN 0148-4648
HV5800
INTERNATIONAL DRUG REPORT. (Text in English, French and Spanish) 1960. q. $35 (foreign $50) (effective 1997). International Narcotic Enforcement Officers Association, 112 State St., Ste. 1200, Albany, NY 12207. TEL 518-463-6232. Ed. Celeste Morga. R&P contact: Celeste Morga. bk.rev.; film rev.; charts; stat.; index. circ. 10,000. (tabloid format) **Document type:** newsletter.
 Supersedes: International Narcotic Conference. Report: Proceedings of Annual Conference (ISSN 0074-7114); Former titles: International Narcotic Report (ISSN 0020-806X); International Drug Reporter.

364　　　　　　US　　ISSN 0192-4036
HV6001
INTERNATIONAL JOURNAL OF COMPARATIVE AND APPLIED CRIMINAL JUSTICE. 1977. s-a. $25 to individuals (foreign $30); institutions $40 (foreign $45); students $20 (foreign $25) (effective 1997). Wichita State University, Department of Administration of Justice, Box 135, Wichita, KS 67260-0135. TEL 316-978-6517. Ed. Dae H. Chang; Pub. Dae H. Chang. R&P contact: Dae H. Chang. adv. contact: Dae H. Chang. bk.rev.; bibl.; charts; stat. circ. 500. (also avail. in microform from UMI; back issues avail.; reprint service avail. from UMI) **Indexed:** Abstr.Crim.& Pen., C.L.I., CJPI, Crim.Just.Abstr., Crime Delinq.Abstr., L.R.I. **Document type:** academic/scholarly publication, abstracting/indexing.
 —BLDSC (4542.172700); UnCover.

364　　　　　　CN　　ISSN 1201-9607
INTERNATIONAL JOURNAL OF COMPARATIVE CRIMINOLOGY. s-a? De Sitter Publications, 374 Woodsworth Rd., Willowdale, ON M2L 2T6, Canada.

363.2　　　　　CN　　ISSN 1198-8975
　　　　　　　　　　　　CODEN: IJFEFP
▼**INTERNATIONAL JOURNAL OF FORENSIC DOCUMENT EXAMINERS.** 1995. q. $30 to individuals (outside N. America $35); to libraries worldwide $40 (effective 1997). Shunderson Communications, P.O. Box 42057, Ottawa, ON K1K 4L8, Canada. TEL 613-830-4750. FAX 613-830-9654. Ed. Joel S. Harris. (back issues avail.) **Indexed:** Chem.Abstr., Curr.Cont. **Document type:** academic/scholarly publication.
 ●Also available online. Vendor(s): West Group.
 —BLDSC (4542.257100); CASDDS.
 Description: Publishes research articles, technical reports, and case studies on various subjects of forensic-document examination.
 Refereed Serial

616.8 364.3　　　US　　ISSN 0306-624X
HV9261　　　　　　　　CODEN: IOTCAH
INTERNATIONAL JOURNAL OF OFFENDER THERAPY AND COMPARATIVE CRIMINOLOGY. 1957. q. $130 to institutions (effective Sept. 1996). Sage Publications, Inc., 2455 Teller Rd., Thousand Oaks, CA 91320. TEL 805-499-0721. FAX 805-499-0871. (Overseas subscr. to: Sage Publications Ltd., 6 Bonhill St., London EC2A 4PU, England; Sage Publications India Pvt. Ltd., P.O. Box 4215, New Delhi 110 048, India) Ed. Dr. Edward M. Scott; Pub. Robert Matloff. adv. contact: Marian Robinson. bk.rev.; bibl.; stat.; index, cum.index: 1957-1975. circ. 1,000. (also avail. in microform from UMI; back issues avail.; reprint service avail. from RRI,UMI,WSH) **Indexed:** Abstr.Bk.Rev.Curr.Leg.Per., Abstr.Crim.& Pen., ASCA, ASSIA, C.L.I., CJPI, Crim.Just.Abstr., Curr.Cont., IMFL, Ind.Per.Art.Relat.Law, L.R.I., Lang.& Lang.Behav.Abstr., Leg.Per., Mid.East: Abstr.& Ind., Psychol.Abstr. (1967-), Soc.Sci.Ind. (1994-), SSCI, Viol.& Abuse Abstr.
 —BLDSC (4542.424000); Genuine Article; KR SourceOne; SWETS; UMI; UnCover. CCC.
 Former titles (until 1972): International Journal of Offender Therapy (ISSN 0020-7497); (until 1966): Journal of Offender Therapy; (until 1961): Association for Psychiatric Treatment of Offenders. Journal.
 Description: International forum for research, discussion, and treatment of variables associated with crime and delinquency, with an emphasis on the theoretical and clinical treatment of the offender.
 Refereed Serial

363.2　　　　　US
RC480.6
INTERNATIONAL JOURNAL OF POLICE NEGOTIATIONS AND CRISIS MANAGEMENT. 1984. s-a. $45 to non-member individuals; institutions $65 (effective 1997). Society of Police and Criminal Psychology, c/o Dr. Wayman Mullins, Managing Editor, Southwest Texas State University, Hines Academy Center, Rm. 120, TX 75367-0292. TEL 512-245-2174. FAX 512-245-8063. (Alt. addr.: c/o Dr. James L. Greenstone, Ed., Box 670292, Dallas, TX 75367-0292. TEL 214-361-0209. FAX 214-361-0209) R&P contact: James L. Greenstone. adv. contact: James L. Greenstone. bk.rev.; index. circ. 400. (also avail. in microform from UMI; back issues avail.) **Indexed:** Psychol.Abstr. **Document type:** academic/scholarly publication.
 —UMI.
 Formerly (until Fall 1995): Journal of Crisis Negotiations (ISSN 1083-5067); Which supersedes (in 1995): Emotional First Aid (ISSN 0739-828X)
 Refereed Serial

364.4　　　　　US
INTERNATIONAL NARCOTIC ENFORCEMENT OFFICERS ASSOCIATION DIRECTORY. a. membership only. International Narcotic Enforcement Officers Association, 112 State St., Ste. 1200, Albany, NY 12207. TEL 518-463-6232. Ed. Celeste Morga. circ. 10,000. **Document type:** directory.

340　　　　　　US
INTERNATIONAL NARCOTICS CONTROL STRATEGY REPORT. a. U.S. Department of State, Bureau for International Narcotics and Law Enforcement Affairs, 2201 C St., N.W., Washington, DC 20520. TEL 202-647-6575. E-mail: usdosweb@uic.edu; URL: http://www.state.gov. **Document type:** government publication.
 ●Also available online.

363.2　　　　　UK
▼**INTERNATIONAL POLICE REVIEW.** 1997. bi-m. £110 (E.U. £120; rest of world £130) (effective 1997). Police Review Publishing Co., Celcon House, 5th Fl., 289-293 High Holborn, London WC1V 7HU, England. TEL 44-171-440-4700. FAX 44-171-405-7163. E-mail: fabiana.angelini@policereview.co.uk. Ed. Stephen Ulph; Pub. Fabiana Angelini. R&P contact: Sergio De Oliveira. adv. contact: Alice Codrington. circ. 3,000 (paid). **Document type:** trade publication.
 Description: Promotes communications between law and order professionals and provides a forum for the dissemination of expertise.

INTERNATIONAL PRISONERS AID ASSOCIATION. NEWSLETTER. see SOCIAL SERVICES AND WELFARE

CRIMINOLOGY AND LAW ENFORCEMENT

364   UN   ISSN 0074-7688
JX1977
INTERNATIONAL REVIEW OF CRIMINAL POLICY. French edition: Revue Internationale de Politique Criminelle (ISSN 0482-8208); Russian edition: Mezhdunarodnyi Obzor Ugolovnoi Politiki (ISSN 0251-7639); Spanish edition: Revista Internacional de Politica Criminal (ISSN 0251-7620) (Text in English) 1946. a. $25 (effective 1997). (United Nations, Department of Economic and Social Affairs) United Nations Publications, Sales and Marketing Section, Room DC2-0853, New York, NY 10017. TEL 212-963-8302; 800-253-9646. FAX 212-963-3489. E-mail: publications@un.org; URL: http://www.un.org/publications. (Or: Palais des Nations, CH-1211 Geneva 10, Switzerland) (also avail. in microform from UMI; reprint service avail. from KTO,UMI) **Indexed:** Abstr.Crim.& Pen., C.L.I., Crim.Just.Abstr., Excerp.Med., Leg.Per., Mid.East: Abstr.& Ind.
—BLDSC (4547.020000); SWETS; UMI.

364   360   UK   ISSN 0269-7580
HV6250   CODEN: IRVIE2
INTERNATIONAL REVIEW OF VICTIMOLOGY. 1990. q. £89($179) A B Academic Publishers, P.O. Box 42, Bicester, Oxon. OX6 7NW, England. TEL 44-1869-320949. Ed.Bd. **Indexed:** Abstr.Crim.& Pen., Crim.Just.Abstr., Fam.Ind., L.R.I., Mult.Ed.Abstr., Per.Islam. (1992-), Stud.Wom.Abstr., Viol.& Abuse Abstr. **Document type:** academic/scholarly publication.
—BLDSC (4547.980000).
Description: Covers all aspects of victimological research, victimization surveys, broader theoretical issues and philosophy of victimology, criminal justice, compensation, and more.

364   FR   ISSN 0539-032X
INTERNATIONAL SOCIETY OF CRIMINOLOGY. BULLETIN. irreg. International Society of Criminology, c/o Rachida Touahria, 4-14 rue Ferrus, 75014 Paris, France. TEL 33-1-45880023. FAX 33-1-45894076.

364   FR
INTERNATIONAL SOCIETY OF CRIMINOLOGY. RAPPORTS ANNUELS. (Text in English and French) a. International Society of Criminology, c/o Rachida Touahria, 4-14 rue Ferrus, 75014 Paris, France. TEL 33-1-45880023. FAX 33-1-45894076.
Formerly: International Society of Criminology. Rapport Quinquennaux.

INTERNATIONAL SYMPOSIUM ON WOUND BALLISTICS. PROCEEDINGS. see *MEDICAL SCIENCES — Forensic Sciences*

INTERPOL - MOSKVA. see *LITERATURE — Mystery And Detective*

364   US   ISSN 0882-1356
INVESTIGATOR (SUISUN). 1960. m. $25. Luna Ventures, P.O. Box 398, Suisun, CA 94585-0398. TEL 707-425-6657. **Document type:** newsletter.

364   US
INVESTIGATOR'S INTERNATIONAL ALL-IN-ONE DIRECTORY OF THE INVESTIGATIVE INDUSTRY. 1981. a. $30. (National Association of Investigative Specialists) Thomas Publishing (Austin), Box 33244, Austin, TX 78764. TEL 512-832-0355. Ed. Ralph D. Thomas. circ. 2,000.

363.2   US   ISSN 0021-0633
IOWA POLICE JOURNAL. 1969. q. $4. Iowa State Policeman's Association, Box 1768, Fort Dodge, IA 50501. Ed. Michael R. Hoffman. adv.; bk.rev.; stat. circ. 5,000.

ISSUES IN CHILD ABUSE ACCUSATIONS. see *CHILDREN AND YOUTH — About*

364   US
J R S A FORUM. (Former name of issuing body: Criminal Justice Statistics Association, Inc.) q. free. Justice Research Statistics Association, Inc., 444 N. Capitol St., N.W., Ste. 445, Washington, DC 20001. TEL 202-624-8560. FAX 202-393-7616. Ed. Karen F. Maline. circ. 750. **Document type:** newsletter.
Formerly: C J S A Forum.
Description: Addresses the concerns and interests of state level criminal justice researchers and analysts, and UCR managers.

345   340   US   ISSN 0739-0998
KF9730.A15
JAIL AND PRISONER LAW BULLETIN. 1976. m. $188 (effective Sep. 1997). Americans for Effective Law Enforcement, Inc., 5519 N. Cumberland Ave., Ste. 1008, Chicago, IL 60656-1471. TEL 773-763-2800. FAX 773-763-3225. E-mail: aele@aol.com. Ed. Bernard Farber. index. circ. 1,100. (looseleaf format; back issues avail.) **Document type:** bulletin.
Description: Reviews cases which have an effective impact upon jail and prison personnel and their attorneys.

364   US
JAIL INMATES (YEAR). (Subseries of: National Crime Victimization Survey Report) 1973. a. free. U.S. Department of Justice, Bureau of Justice Statistics, 633 Indiana Ave., N.W., 11th Fl., Washington, DC 20531. (Orders to: Superintendent of Documents, U.S. Government Printing Office, Box 371954, Pittsburgh, PA 15250-7954. TEL 202-512-1800. FAX 202-512-2250) stat. circ. 15,000. (also avail. in microfiche) **Document type:** government publication.

365.068   370   US
JAIL OPERATIONS BULLETIN. 1988. a. $63 to non-members; members $39. American Jail Association, 2053 Day Rd., Ste. 100, Hagerstown, MD 21740-9795. TEL 301-790-3930. FAX 301-790-2941. Ed. Debra Goldentyer. **Document type:** bulletin.
Description: Used for in-service training, formal classroom study, and individual study by jail officers.

JOURNAL OF ADDICTIONS & OFFENDER COUNSELING. see *PSYCHOLOGY*

363.2   US   ISSN 0449-5063
JOURNAL OF CALIFORNIA LAW ENFORCEMENT. 1966. q. $35 (foreign $50) (effective 1996). California Peace Officers Association, 1455 Response Rd., Ste. 190, Sacramento, CA 95815. TEL 916-923-1825. FAX 916-263-6090. Ed. Leslie McGill. R&P contact: Leslie McGill. circ. 1,100 (paid). **Indexed:** Abstr.Crim.& Pen., Crim.Just.Abstr. **Document type:** trade publication.
—UMI.
Refereed Serial

JOURNAL OF CLINICAL FORENSIC MEDICINE. see *MEDICAL SCIENCES — Forensic Sciences*

JOURNAL OF CONTEMPORARY CRIMINAL JUSTICE. see *LAW — Criminal Law*

JOURNAL OF CORRECTIONAL EDUCATION. see *EDUCATION*

JOURNAL OF CORRECTIONAL HEALTH CARE. see *MEDICAL SCIENCES*

364   US   ISSN 1064-508X
HV9470
JOURNAL OF CORRECTIONAL TRAINING. * 1986. q. American Association of Correctional Training Personnel, Eastern Kentucky University, 217 Perkins Bldg., 521 Lancaster Ave., Richmond, KY 40475-3101.

364   US   ISSN 0735-648X
HV6201
JOURNAL OF CRIME & JUSTICE. 1981. s-a. $35 to individuals; libraries $65. (Midwestern Criminal Justice Association) Anderson Publishing Co., 2035 Reading Rd., Cincinnati, OH 45202. TEL 513-421-4142. FAX 513-562-8116. Ed. Dean Champion. adv. **Indexed:** Abstr.Crim.& Pen., CJPI, Crim.Just.Abstr., Curr.Cont., Fam.Ind. **Document type:** academic/scholarly publication.
—BLDSC (4965.526000); UnCover.

JOURNAL OF CRIMINAL JUSTICE; an international journal. see *LAW — Criminal Law*

364   US   ISSN 1051-1253
HV7419.5
JOURNAL OF CRIMINAL JUSTICE EDUCATION. 1990. s-a. $45. Academy of Criminal Justice Sciences, c/o Patricia DeLancey, Exec. Dir., 402 Nunn Hall, Northern Kentucky University, Highland Heights, KY 41099-5998. TEL 606-572-5634; 800-757-ACJS. FAX 606-572-6665. Ed. Dorothy Bracey. adv. circ. 2,800. **Indexed:** Crim.Just.Abstr. **Document type:** academic/scholarly publication.
—BLDSC (4965.535000); UnCover.
Description: Features scholarly articles on criminal justice education.

JOURNAL OF CRIMINAL LAW/KEIHO ZASSHI. see *LAW — Criminal Law*

343   US   ISSN 0091-4169
K10   CODEN: JCRLA
JOURNAL OF CRIMINAL LAW & CRIMINOLOGY. Short title: J C L C. 1910. q. $35 (foreign $38) (effective 1994). Northwestern University, School of Law - Office of Legal Publications, 357 E. Chicago Ave., Chicago, IL 60611. TEL 312-503-8463. R&P contact: Edward Kerros. TEL 312-503-0186. bk.rev.; abstr.; bibl.; illus.; index, cum.index: vols.1-24 (1910-1934). circ. 2,700. (also avail. in microform from UMI; microfilm from RRI,WSH; reprint service avail. from RRI,WSH) **Indexed:** A.B.C.Pol.Sci., Abstr.Crim.& Pen., ASCA, ASSIA, C.L.I. CJPI, Crim.Just.Abstr., Curr.Cont., Excerp.Med., IBR, L.R.I., Leg.Cont., Leg.Per., Mult.Ed.Abstr., P.A.I.S., Psychol.Abstr., Soc.Sci.Ind., SSCI. **Document type:** academic/scholarly publication.
●Also available online. Vendor(s): Information Access Co., UMI, West Group.
—BLDSC (4965.590000); KR SourceOne; SWETS; UMI; UnCover.
Formerly (until 1972): Journal of Criminal Law, Criminology and Police Science (ISSN 0022-0205)

301.4   US   ISSN 0885-7482
HQ809   CODEN: JFVIEV
JOURNAL OF FAMILY VIOLENCE. q. $255 (foreign $300) (effective 1998). Plenum Publishing Corp., 233 Spring St., New York, NY 10013-1578. TEL 212-620-8000. FAX 212-463-0742. TELEX 23-421139. (Editorial addr.: c/o Center for Psychological Studies, Nova Southeastern Univ., 3301 College Ave., Ft. Lauderdale, FL 33314) Eds. Vincent B. Van Hasselt, Michel Hersen. adv.; bk.rev. (also avail. in microfilm from UMI; back issues avail. **Indexed:** ASCA, Crim.Just.Abstr., Curr.Cont., Fam.Ind IMFL, Ind.Per.Art.Relat.Law, Psychol.Abstr. (1986-), Soc.Sci.Ind. (1994-), SSCI, Viol.& Abuse Abstr. **Document type:** academic/scholarly publication.
—BLDSC (4983.746000); Genuine Article; SWETS; UMI; UnCover. **CCC.**
Refereed Serial

364   250   301   US   ISSN 0886-2605
HV6618
JOURNAL OF INTERPERSONAL VIOLENCE; concerned with the study and treatment of victims and perpetrators of physical and sexual violence. 1986. bi-m. $189 to institutions (effective Sep. 1997). Sage Publications, Inc., 2455 Teller Rd., Thousand Oaks, CA 91320. TEL 805-499-0721. FAX 805-499-0871. E-mail: libraries@sagepub.com URL: http://www.sagepub.com. (Overseas subscr. to Sage Publications Ltd., 6 Bonhill St., London EC2A 4PU, England; Sage Publications India Pvt. Ltd., P.O. Box 4215, New Delhi 110 048, India) Ed. Jon R. Conte. adv. contact: Margaret Travers. circ. 5,300. (back issues avail.; reprint service avail.) **Indexed:** Abstr.Crim.& Pen., ASCA, C.I.J.E., Crim.Just.Abstr., Curr.Cont., Fam.Ind., IMFL, Int.Nurs.Ind., Mult.Ed.Abstr., Psychol.Abstr. (1986-), Soc.Sci.Ind. (1994-), Soc.Work Res.& Abstr., Sociol.Abstr., Sp.Ed.Needs Abstr., SSCI, Stud.Wom.Abstr., Viol.& Abuse Abstr. **Document type:** academic/scholarly publication.
—BLDSC (5007.693500); Genuine Article; KR SourceOne; SWETS; UMI; UnCover. **CCC.**
Description: Provides a forum for the discussion of the concerns and activities of professionals and researchers working in domestic violence, child sexual abuse, rape and sexual assault, physical child abuse, and other violent crimes.

364   US   ISSN 1043-500X
HV9304
JOURNAL OF OFFENDER MONITORING. 1988. q. Box 1013, Warrensburg, MO 64093. Ed. Joseph B. Vaughn. **Indexed:** Crim.Just.Abstr.

CRIMINOLOGY AND LAW ENFORCEMENT

364   362.8   US   ISSN 1050-9674
HV9261   CODEN: JOFHEB
JOURNAL OF OFFENDER REHABILITATION; a multidisciplinary journal of innovation in research, services, and programs in corrections and criminal justice. 1976. q. $45 to individuals (Canada $58.50; elsewhere $63); institutions $125 (Canada $162.50; elsewhere $175); libraries $225 (Canada $292.50; elsewhere $315) (effective 1996-1997). Haworth Press, Inc., 10 Alice St., Binghamton, NY 13904. TEL 607-722-5857; 800-342-9676. FAX 607-722-6362. E-mail: getinfo@haworth.com; URL: http://www.haworth.com. Ed. Nathaniel J. Pallone; Pub. Bill Cohen. R&P contact: Ruthann Heath. adv.: B&W page $300; trim 4 3/8 x 7 1/8; adv. contact: Jackie Blakeslee. bk.rev.; index. circ. 450. (also avail. in microfiche from UMI; microform from HAW; reprint service avail. from HAW) **Indexed:** Abstr.Crim.& Pen., Abstr.Crim.& Pen., Abstr.Soc.Work, Adol.Ment.Hlth.Abstr., Alt.Press Ind., Behav.Abstr., Bull.Signal., C.I.J.E., CERDIC, Chic.Per.Ind., Chicago Psychoanal.Lit.Ind., CJPI, Crim.Just.Abstr., Curr.Cont., Human Resour.Abstr., IMFL, Lang.& Lang.Behav.Abstr., Past.Care & Couns.Abstr., Psychol.Abstr. (1976-), Ref.Zh., Sage Fam.Stud.Abstr., Sage Pub.Admin.Abstr., Soc.Work Res.& Abstr., Sociol.Abstr.
—BLDSC (5026.218000); Haworth; SWETS; UnCover.
Former titles (until 1990): Journal of Offender Counseling, Services and Rehabilitation (ISSN 0195-6116); (until 1980): Offender Rehabilitation (ISSN 0364-3093)
Description: Publishes research and concepts on the rehabilitation of criminal offenders, both in custodial and community settings.
Refereed Serial

364   US   ISSN 0882-0783
HV6001
JOURNAL OF POLICE AND CRIMINAL PSYCHOLOGY. 1985. s-a. $50. Society of Police and Criminal Psychology, c/o Wayman C. Mullins, Managing Ed., Southwest Texas State University, Hines Academy Center, Rm. 120, San Marcos, TX 78666. TEL 512-245-2174. FAX 512-245-8063. R&P contact: Wayman C. Mullins. adv. contact: Wayman C. Mullins. circ. 200. (also avail. in microfilm from UMI) **Indexed:** Crim.Just.Abstr. **Document type:** academic/scholarly publication.
—UMI; UnCover.
Refereed Serial

365   US   ISSN 0838-164X
JOURNAL OF PRISONERS ON PRISONS. 1988. s-a. $10 to individuals; institutions $20. University of Manitoba, University Centre, Box 54, Winnipeg, MB R3T 2N2, Canada. E-mail: arrakis@synapse.net; URL: http://www.synapse.net/~arrakis/jpp/jpp.html. (back issues avail.) **Indexed:** Alt.Press Ind.
●Also available online.

364   US   ISSN 0748-4518
CODEN: JQCRE6
JOURNAL OF QUANTITATIVE CRIMINOLOGY. 1984. q. $315 (foreign $370) (effective 1998). Plenum Publishing Corp., 233 Spring St., New York, NY 10013-1578. TEL 212-620-8000. FAX 212-463-0742. TELEX 23-421139. Eds. James Alan Fox, John H. Laub. adv. (also avail. in microfilm from UMI; back issues avail.; reprint service avail. from WSH) **Indexed:** Abstr.Crim.& Pen., ASCA, Crim.Just.Abstr., Curr.Cont., Fam.Ind., Ind.Per.Art.Relat.Law, Psychol.Abstr. (1985-), Sociol.Abstr. **Document type:** academic/scholarly publication.
—BLDSC (5043.696000); Genuine Article; SWETS; UMI; UnCover. **CCC.**
Refereed Serial

364   US   ISSN 1061-3455
HV8074
JOURNAL OF QUESTIONED DOCUMENT EXAMINATION. 1988. s-a. $40. Independent Association of Questioned Document Examiners, Inc., 10809 S. Sandusky, Tulsa, OK 74137-6834. TEL 918-299-9663. Ed. Glenda C. Portman. R&P contact: Glenda C. Portman. bk.rev. circ. 75. **Document type:** academic/scholarly publication.
Formerly (until 1992): Independent Association of Questioned Document Examiners. Journal (ISSN 1056-8972)
Description: Contains papers and information on document examination and handwriting identification.
Refereed Serial

364   US   ISSN 0022-4278
HV6001
JOURNAL OF RESEARCH IN CRIME AND DELINQUENCY. 1964. q. $198 to institutions (effective Sep. 1996). (National Council on Crime and Delinquency) Sage Publications, Inc., 2455 Teller Rd., Thousand Oaks, CA 91320. TEL 805-499-0721. FAX 805-499-0871. E-mail: libraries@sagepub.com; URL: http://www.sagepub.com. (Overseas subscr. to: Sage Publications Ltd., 6 Bonhill St., London, EC2A 4PU, England; Sage Publications India Pvt. Ltd., P.O. Box 4215, New Delhi 011 048, India) Ed. Jeffrey Fagan. charts; illus.; stat. circ. 1,700. (also avail. in microform from PMC; microfilm from WSH; microfiche from WSH; back issues avail.; reprint service avail. from KTO,WSH) **Indexed:** Abstr.Crim.& Pen., Adol.Ment.Hlth.Abstr., ASCA, ASSIA, C.I.J.E., C.L.I., CJPI, Crim.Just.Abstr., Curr.Cont., Excerp.Med., Fam.Ind., IMFL, Lang.& Lang.Behav.Abstr., Leg.Per., Mid.East: Abstr.& Ind., Psychol.Abstr. (1978-), Sage Urb.Stud.Abstr., Soc.Sci.Ind., Soc.Work Res.& Abstr., SSCI, Viol.& Abuse Abstr. **Document type:** academic/scholarly publication.
—BLDSC (5052.005000); Genuine Article; KR SourceOne; SWETS; UMI; UnCover. **CCC.**
Description: Reports on original research in crime and deliquency, new theory, and the critical analyses of theories and concepts pertinent to research development in the field.

JOURNAL OF SEXUAL AGGRESSION. see *PSYCHOLOGY*

JUBILEE; the monthly newsletter of Prison Fellowship. see *RELIGIONS AND THEOLOGY — Protestant*

JUDICIAL INTERIM RELEASE: BAIL MANUAL. see *LAW — Criminal Law*

364   YU   ISSN 0022-6076
JUGOSLOVENSKA REVIJA ZA KRIMINOLOGIJU I KRIVICNO PRAVO. (Text in Serbo-Croatian; summaries in English) 1963. q. $70. (Savez Udruzenja za Krivicno Pravo i Kriminologiju Jugoslavije) Slavija - Press, Trg Toze Markovicz br. 5, Novi Sad, Vojvodina, Yugoslavia. (Co-sponsor: Institut za Kriminoloska i Socioloska Istrazivanja) Ed. Vesna Nikolic-Ristanovic. adv.; bk.rev.; index. circ. 1,000.
—BLDSC (5073.852000).
Description: Covers original papers and studies in criminal law.

364   AT   ISSN 0814-0278
JUSTICE AND THE J.P. 1983. bi-m. Aus.$50. State Council of the Queensland Justices' and Community Legal Officers' Association Inc. (QJA), Level 2, 349 Queen St., Brisbane, Qld. 4000, Australia. TEL 61-7-32297061. FAX 61-7-32297048. (Subscr. to: G.P.O. Box 653, Brisbane, Qld. 4001, Australia) Ed. Peter H. MacDonald. adv. contact: Carlo Marchese. bk.rev. circ. 10,000. **Document type:** newsletter.

JUSTICE - DIRECTORY OF SERVICES/JUSTICE - REPERTOIRE DES SERVICES. see *SOCIAL SERVICES AND WELFARE*

JUSTICE IN AMERICA SERIES. see *LAW*

364   340   US   ISSN 0741-8825
HV7231
JUSTICE QUARTERLY. 1984. q. $100. Academy of Criminal Justice Sciences, c/o Patricia DeLancey, Exec.Dir., 402 Nunn Hall, Northern Kentucky University, Highland Heights, KY 41099-5998. TEL 606-572-5634; 800-757-ACJS. Ed. Vic Kappeler. adv.; bk.rev. circ. 3,000. (also avail. in microform; back issues avail.) **Indexed:** Abstr.Crim.& Pen., Crim.Just.Abstr. **Document type:** academic/scholarly publication.
—BLDSC (5075.673700); UMI; UnCover.
Description: Features scholarly articles on issues of criminal justice, criminology and justice studies.

365   CN   ISSN 0823-9436
HV9960.C2
JUSTICE REPORT/ACTUALITES JUSTICE. (Text in English, French) 1971. q. Can.$35 to libraries; others membership only. Canadian Criminal Justice Association - Association Canadienne de Justice Penale, 383 Parkdale Ave., Ste. 304, Ottawa, ON K1Y 4R4, Canada. TEL 613-725-3715. FAX 613-725-3720. Ed.Bd. bk.rev.; bibl. circ. 1,000. **Indexed:** Ind.Can.L.P.L. **Document type:** bulletin.
—BLDSC (5075.674400).
Former titles (until 1991): Canadian Association for the Prevention of Crime. Bulletin - Societe Canadienne pour la Prevention du Crime. Bulletin (ISSN 0705-9094); Canadian Criminology and Corrections Association. Bulletin (ISSN 0045-463X); Correctional Process (ISSN 0045-8635); Readaption (ISSN 0034-0367)
Description: Contains information and opinions for members of the association written by professional journalists.

JUSTNOTES: NEWSLETTER OF THE DEPARTMENT OF CRIMINAL JUSTICE ADMINISTRATION. see *COLLEGE AND ALUMNI*

JUVENILE AND FAMILY COURT JOURNAL. see *LAW — Family And Matrimonial Law*

JUVENILE AND FAMILY JUSTICE TODAY. see *LAW — Family And Matrimonial Law*

364.36   US   ISSN 0094-2413
JUVENILE JUSTICE DIGEST; an independent summary of significant events in the field of juvenile delinquency prevention. 1973. s-m. $195 (Canada $201) (includes q. Calendar of Events) (effective 1998). Washington Crime News Services, 3918 Prosperity Ave., Ste. 318, Fairfax, VA 22031-3334. TEL 703-573-1600; 800-422-9267. FAX 703-573-1604. Ed. Susan M. Kernus; Pub. Richard J. O'Connell. bk.rev. (looseleaf format; also avail. in microform from UMI; reprint service avail. from UMI) **Indexed:** Adol.Ment.Hlth.Abstr., CJPI, Crim.Just.Abstr. **Document type:** newsletter.
—UMI.
Description: Focuses on deliquency issues. Includes job listings.

364.4   JA   ISSN 0451-1999
HV6005
KAGAKU KEISATSU KENKYUJO HOKOKU BOHAN SHONEN HEN/NATIONAL RESEARCH INSTITUTE OF POLICE SCIENCE. REPORT. RESEARCH ON PREVENTION OF CRIME AND DELINQUENCY. (Text in Japanese; summaries in English) 1960. s-a. Kagaku Keisatsu Kenkyujo - National Research Institute of Police Science, 6 Sanban-cho, Chiyoda-ku, Tokyo 102, Japan. TEL 81-3-3261-9986. FAX 81-3-3221-1245. Ed. Taizo Nagano. circ. 900. **Indexed:** Psychol.Abstr. (1980-). **Document type:** academic/scholarly publication.
—BLDSC (7570.222800).

364   JA   ISSN 0453-0667
KAGAKU KEISATSU KENKYUJO NENPO/NATIONAL RESEARCH INSTITUTE OF POLICE SCIENCE. ANNUAL REPORT. (Text in Japanese) 1948. a. Kagaku Keisatsu Kenkyujo - National Research Institute of Police Science, 6 Sanban-cho, Chiyoda-ku, Tokyo 102, Japan. TEL 81-3-3261-9986. FAX 81-3-3221-1245. circ. 1,000. **Document type:** bulletin.

363.2   KE   ISSN 0023-0448
KENYA POLICE REVIEW. 1956. q. 180s.($4) (effective 1995). Kenya Police Force, Force Headquarters, P.O. Box 30083 NBI, Nairobi, Kenya. TEL 254-2-335124. FAX 254-2-330495. TELEX 22720 COMPOL KE. Ed. M.N. Kabetu. adv.; bk.rev.; circ. 30,000 (paid). **Document type:** newsletter.
Description: Seeks to advocate for the officers of the Kenya Police Force.

345   DK   ISSN 0904-1990
HV8437
KRIMINALFORSORGENS AARSBERETNING. 1910. a. free. Direktoratet for Kriminalforsorgen, Justitsministeriet, Klareboderne 1, DK-1115 Copenhagen K, Denmark. TEL 33-11-55-00. FAX 45-33-14-03-45. bk.rev.; illus. circ. 3,300. **Document type:** government publication, corporate report.
Formerly: Denmark. Direktoratet for Kriminalforsorgen. Kriminalforsorgen (ISSN 0107-511X)

CRIMINOLOGY AND LAW ENFORCEMENT

364   GW   ISSN 0722-3501
DER KRIMINALIST. 1969. m. DM.50. (Bund Deutscher Kriminalbeamter) Schmidt-Roemhild Verlag, Mengstr. 16, 23552 Luebeck, Germany. TEL 49-451-703101. FAX 49-451-7031253. Ed. G. Rudnick. adv.; bk.rev.; illus. circ. 18,000. (reprint service avail. from SCH) **Indexed:** Abstr.Crim.& Pen. **Document type:** trade publication.

364   GW   ISSN 0023-4699
KRIMINALISTIK; Zeitschrift fuer die gesamte kriminalistische Wissenschaft und Praxis. 1946. 11/yr. DM.187 (foreign DM.199.10) (effective 1997). Kriminalistik Verlag Huethig GmbH, Im Weiher 10, 69121 Heidelberg, Germany. TEL 49-6221-489416. FAX 49-6221-489624. Ed. Waldemar Burghard. adv.; bk.rev.; bibl.; charts; illus.; index. circ. 4,523. (reprint service avail. from SCH) **Indexed:** Abstr.Crim.& Pen., ASCA, Crim.Just.Abstr., Excerp.Med., IBR, INIS Atomind., SSCI. **Document type:** academic/scholarly publication.
—BLDSC (5118.235000); Genuine Article; SWETS. **CCC.**

364.4 346   SW   ISSN 0347-2612
KRIMINALVAARDSVERKETS FOERFATTNINGSSAMLING. 1976. irreg. free. Kriminalvaardsstyrelsen, S-601 80 Norrkoeping, Sweden. TEL 46-8-738-53-72. FAX 46-11-19-36-63.

364   GW   ISSN 0454-5265
KRIMINALWISSENSCHAFTLICHE ABHANDLUNGEN. 1967. irreg., vol.28, 1993. DM.98. Schmidt-Roemhild Verlag, Mengstr. 16, 23552 Luebeck, Germany. TEL 49-451-703101. FAX 49-451-7031253. Ed. Friedrich Geerds. **Document type:** monographic series.

364   GW
KRIMINALWISSENSCHAFTLICHE STUDIEN. irreg., no.14, 1992. DM.37. N.G. Elwert Verlag, Reitgasse 7-9, 35037 Marburg, Germany. TEL 49-6421-17090. FAX 49-6421-15487. E-mail: elwert@ibm.net. **Document type:** monographic series.

364   GW   ISSN 0341-1966
KRIMINOLOGISCHES JOURNAL. 1969. q. DM.87 (foreign DM.99) (effective 1998). (Arbeitskreis Junger Kriminologen) Juventa Verlag GmbH, Ehretstr. 3, 69469 Weinheim, Germany. TEL 49-6201-61035. FAX 49-6201-13135. E-mail: juventa@t-online.de; URL: http://www.juventa@t-online.de. adv.; bk.rev.; index. circ. 1,000. (reprint service avail. from SCH) **Indexed:** Abstr.Crim.& Pen., Crim.Just.Abstr., IBR. **Document type:** bulletin.
—SWETS. **CCC.**

KRONIEK VAN HET STRAFRECHT. see *LAW — Criminal Law*

363.2   UK
LANCASHIRE CONSTABULARY JOURNAL. 1936. 4/yr. free. Lancashire Constabulary, County Police Headquarters, P.O. Box 77, Hutton, Preston PR4 5SB, England. TEL 44-1772-618444. FAX 44-1772-618356. Ed. Roger Blaxall. R&P contact: Roger Blaxall. adv.; bk.rev.; circ. 4,000 (controlled). **Document type:** newsletter.
Description: News, views and features from Lancashire Constabulary.

352 363.2   US   ISSN 0023-9194
HV7551
LAW AND ORDER; for those involved in law enforcement. 1953. m. $20. Hendon, Inc., 1000 Skokie Blvd., Wilmette, IL 60091. TEL 708-256-8555. FAX 708-256-8574. Ed. Bruce Cameron; Pub. H.S. Kingwill. adv. contact: Pete Kingwill. bk.rev.; illus.; index. circ. 29,214. (also avail. in microform from UMI; reprint service avail. from UMI) **Indexed:** Abstr.Crim.& Pen., Crim.Just.Abstr. **Document type:** trade publication.
●Also available online. Vendor(s): CompuServe, Inc.
—BLDSC (5161.360000); UMI; UnCover.
Description: Police procedures and administration.

345 346   US   ISSN 1070-9967
KF9614
LAW ENFORCEMENT LEGAL REVIEW. (Former issuing body: International Association of Chiefs of Police) 1970. bi-m. $98 (effective 1998). Law Enforcement Legal Publications, 421 Ridgewood Ave., Ste. 100, Glen Ellyn, IL 60137-4900. TEL 630-858-6392. FAX 630-858-6392. E-mail: lelp@xnet.com; URL: http://www.xnet.com/~lelp. Ed. James P. Manak; Pub. James P. Manak. adv. contact: James P. Manak. bibl.; index. circ. 500. **Indexed:** CJPI. **Document type:** trade publication.
—UnCover.
Formerly (until 1990): I A C P Law Enforcement Legal Review.
Description: Covers criminal law and civil liability.

LAW ENFORCEMENT LIABILITY REPORTER. see *LAW — Civil Law*

363.2   US   ISSN 0364-1724
HV8138
LAW ENFORCEMENT NEWS. 1975. 22/yr. $18. John Jay College of Criminal Justice, 899 Tenth Ave., New York, NY 10019. TEL 212-237-8442. Ed. Peter Dodenhoff. adv.; bk.rev.; charts; illus. circ. 7,000. (also avail. in microform from UMI; reprint service avail. from UMI) **Indexed:** CJPI.
—UMI.
Formerly: John Jay College of Criminal Justice. Criminal Justice Center. Monographs.

364.6   US   ISSN 1060-5126
LAW ENFORCEMENT PRODUCT NEWS. 1990. bi-m. free to qualified personnel. General Communications, Inc., 100 Garfield St., Denver, CO 80206-5550. TEL 303-322-6400. FAX 303-322-0627. Ed. Toni Stephenson. R&P contact: Toni Stephenson. adv. contact: Michael George. bk.rev.; circ. 40,000 (controlled). **Document type:** trade publication.
Incorporates (1990-1991): Inside Product News.
Description: Covers new products, equipment and services for the law enforcement and corrections markets.

363.2   US
LAW ENFORCEMENT PRODUCT NEWS. 1990. bi-m. free in N. America; elsewhere $40 (effective 1997). General Communications, Inc., 100 Garfield St., 3rd. Fl., Denver, CO 80206. E-mail: mlg@qreal.com. Ed. Grey Monroe. adv.: B&W page $3276, color page $3436; trim 10 7/8 x 15 3/4; adv. contact: Michael George. software rev, video rev, abstr, bibl, charts, illus, maps, mkt, pat, stat, tr.mk. (tabloid format; back issues avail.) **Document type:** trade publication.
●Also available online.
Description: Presents new products, equipment and services for the law enforcement, corrections and private security market.

364   US   ISSN 0747-3680
LAW ENFORCEMENT TECHNOLOGY. 1974. bi-m. $60. P T N Publishing Corp., 445 Broad Hollow Rd., Ste. 21, Melville, NY 11747-4722. TEL 516-845-2700. FAX 516-845-7109. Ed. Trica Walsh; Pub. Pat Bernardo. adv.; bk.rev. circ. 25,050. **Document type:** trade publication.
—UMI.
Formerly (until 1984): Law Enforcement Communications (ISSN 0193-0540)
Description: Management, operations and technical information for senior law enforcement personnel.

364   US
LAW ENFORCEMENT VOLUNTEERS. q. American Association of Retired Persons, Criminal Justice Services, 601 E St., N.W., Washington, DC 20049. TEL 202-662-4842.
Description: For, about, and by volunteers who work with law enforcement agencies and officials.

363.2   US   ISSN 0145-6571
KF9202
LAW OFFICER'S BULLETIN. 1976. bi-w. $147. The Bureau of National Affairs, Inc., 1231 25th St., N.W., Washington, DC 20037. TEL 202-452-4200. FAX 202-822-8092. TELEX 285656 BNAI WSH. URL: http://www.bna.com/. (Subscr. to: 9435 Key West Ave., Rockville, MD 20850. TEL 800-372-1033) Ed. Robert L. Goebes. (looseleaf format; back issues avail.) **Indexed:** CJPI. **Document type:** newsletter.
—CCC.
Description: Provides an update of court decisions, Justice Department proposals and congressional actions involving law enforcement officers, describing the legal reasoning and explaining the impact on the law enforcement community.

364   MF
LAZOL; the prison magazine. irreg. c/o T. Printers Co. Ltd., Residence de 5 Palmiers, 198 Route Royale, Beau-Bassin, Mauritius. **Indexed:** P.L.E.S.A.

LEGAL AND CRIMINOLOGICAL PSYCHOLOGY. see *PSYCHOLOGY*

LEX. see *COLLEGE AND ALUMNI*

LEX REVIEW. see *COLLEGE AND ALUMNI*

363.2   FR   ISSN 0024-1717
LIAISONS; revue d'information et de relations publiques. 1963. m. 51.50 F. Prefecture de Police, 9 bd. du Palais, 75195 Paris, France. FAX 43-54-63-78. Dir. M. Vinzerich. charts; illus.; stat. circ. 17,500.
Description: Information concerning public relations, edited by French chiefs of police.

LOKALES; Stadtzeitung fuer Babenhausen. see *POLITICAL SCIENCE*

LOW INTENSITY CONFLICT & LAW ENFORCEMENT. see *POLITICAL SCIENCE — International Relations*

364.4 345   US   ISSN 1074-8083
THE MCGRUFFLETTER (NATIONAL EDITION); the nation's crime prevention newsletter. 1987. q. $12. (U.S. National Crime Prevention Council) Jam Communications, 75 Varick St., 11th Fl., New York, NY 10013. TEL 212-941-6080. (Or: National Crime Prevention Council, 1700 K St., N.W., 2nd Fl. Washington, DC 20006-3817. TEL 202-496-6272 Ed. Joseph A. Mangini. adv. circ. 12,000. **Document type:** newsletter.
Supersedes: McGruffletter (ISSN 1063-2999)
Description: Provides crime-prevention information for people who do not want to become victims.

363.2   GW   ISSN 0944-8764
MAGAZIN FUER DIE POLIZEI; internationales unabhaengiges Fachmagazin. 1970. m. DM.30. Almanach Verlagsgesellschaft, Postfach 35, 63701 Aschaffenburg, Germany. TEL 49-6021-3807-0. FAX 49-6021-380720. Ed. Robert Hamischmacher. adv.; bk.rev.; charts; illus. circ. 3,000. **Document type:** trade publication.
Formerly: Polizeimagazin (ISSN 0032-3543)

365   MK
MAJALLAT AL-SHURTAH. 1976. q. free. Royal Oman Police, Directorate of Public Relations, P.O. Box 2, 113 Muscat, Sultanate of Oman. TEL 968-569216. FAX 968-563352. TELEX 5377 COMPOL MB. Ed. Maj. Abdullah Amor al-Kasbi. circ. 9,000 (controlled). **Document type:** government publication.
Formerly: Al-Shurtah.

364   MW   ISSN 0076-308X
MALAWI. POLICE FORCE. ANNUAL REPORT. a. (Police Force) Malawi. Government Printer, P.O. Box 37, Zomba, Malawi. **Document type:** government publication.

364   GW   ISSN 0172-8563
MANNHEIMER HEFTE FUER SCHRIFTVERGLEICHUNG. 1975. q. DM.106 (foreign DM.109) (effective 1996). Schmidt-Roemhild Verlag, Mengstr. 16, 23552 Luebeck, Germany. TEL 49-451-703101. FAX 49-451-7031253. Ed. Lothar Michel. **Indexed:** IBr. **Document type:** bulletin.
—BLDSC (5361.048500).

364   IS
MAROTE HAMISHTARAH. (Text in Hebrew) q. free. Israel National Police, c/o Chief Education Officer, Central Police Headquarters, Jerusalem, Israel. Ed. Oded Neev. adv.; bk.rev. circ. 22,000.

CRIMINOLOGY AND LAW ENFORCEMENT

...TIN'S RELATED CRIMINAL STATUTES. see *LAW — Criminal Law*

53.9 US ISSN 0362-9198
V7270
...RYLAND. DIVISION OF CORRECTION. REPORT.* Key title: Report - Maryland Division of Correction. a. ...ivision of Correction, 6776 Reisterstown Rd., Ste. ...09, Baltimore, MD 21215-2306.

...SSACHUSETTS CRIMINAL DEFENSE. see *LAW — Criminal Law*

63.2 MF
...URITIUS POLICE FORCE. ANNUAL REPORT. (Text in ...nglish) a. Police Force, Police Headquarters, Line ...arracks, Port Louis, Mauritius.

63.2 MF
...URITIUS POLICE MAGAZINE. (Text in English and ...rench) 1953. a. Rs.35. Police Force, Police ...eadquarters, Line Barracks, Port Louis, Mauritius. ...dv. circ. 6,000.

63.2 CN ISSN 1201-5318
...TROPOLITAN TORONTO POLICE ASSOCIATION. NEWS **& VIEWS**. 1962. m. Can.$44.94 (U.S. Can.$53.50; ...verseas Can.$64.20) (effective 1995). ...etropolitan Toronto Police Association, 180 ...orkland Blvd., North York, ON M2J 1R5, Canada. ...EL 416-491-4301. FAX 416-494-4948. Ed. ...lizabeth Alexander. R&P contact: Elizabeth ...lexander. adv.: B&W page Can.$850, color page ...an.$1500; trim 8 1/8 x 10 7/8; adv. contact: ...rian Shugar. bk.rev. circ. 9,400. **Document type:** newsletter.
Refereed Serial

353.9 US
...CHIGAN. DEPARTMENT OF STATE POLICE. ANNUAL **REPORT**. 1919. a. Department of State Police, 714 ...S. Harrison Rd., East Lansing, MI 48823. ...EL 517-332-2521. illus.; circ. controlled.
Formerly: Michigan. State Police. Annual Report.

...CHIGAN JOURNAL OF INTERNATIONAL LAW. see *LAW — International Law*

364 US
...CHIGAN POLICE CHIEFS NEWSLETTER. 1979. m. $30 (effective 1997). Michigan Association of Chiefs of Police, 2133 University Dr., No. 200, Okemos, MI 48864. TEL 517-349-9420. Ed. Thomas A. Hendrickson. adv. circ. 1,600. **Document type:** newsletter.
Formerly: Michigan Police Journal (ISSN 0085-3380)

363.2 US
...NNESOTA POLICE CHIEF. 1981. q. $20 (avail. only to qualified personnel and libraries). (Minnesota Chiefs of Police Association) Callan Publishing, Inc., 6465 Wayzata Blvd., Ste. 220, Minneapolis, MN 55426. TEL 612-920-4848. FAX 612-541-0435. Dir. Toni Johnson. adv.; bk.rev. circ. 2,500.

363.2 US ISSN 0026-5624
...NNESOTA POLICE JOURNAL. 1928. bi-m. $13 (subscr. avail. only to qualified personnel and libraries). Minnesota Police & Peace Officers Association, 375 Selby Ave., St. Paul, MN 55102. TEL 612-291-1119. FAX 612-291-0227. Ed. Dennis J. Flaherty. adv. contact: Stan Burzynski. bk.rev. circ. 6,500.
Description: Law enforcement and police administration.

364 GW ISSN 0026-9301
...ONATSSCHRIFT FUER KRIMINOLOGIE UND **STRAFRECHTSREFORM**. 1917. bi-m. DM.142 (effective 1996). (Gesellschaft fuer die Gesamte Kriminologie) Carl Heymanns Verlag KG, Luxemburgerstr. 449, 50939 Cologne, Germany. TEL 49-221-94373-0. FAX 49-221-94373901. adv.; bk.rev.; charts; index. circ. 950. (reprint service avail. from KTO,SCH) **Indexed:** Abstr.Crim.& Pen., Crim.Just.Abstr., IBR, P.A.I.S.For.Lang.Ind. **Document type:** bulletin.
—BLDSC (5906.430000); SWETS.
Formerly: Aschaffenburg'she Monatsschrift.

364 US ISSN 1046-3070
KF1030.R3
MONEY LAUNDERING ALERT. 1989. m. $345 (foreign $425) (effective 1996 & 1997). Alert Global Media, Inc., Box 11390, Miami, FL 33101. TEL 305-530-0500; 800-232-3652. FAX 305-530-9434. URL: http://www.moneylaundering.com. Ed. Miklas Korba; Pub. Charles A. Intriago. R&P contact: Deborah Pellard. adv.; circ. 1,475 (paid). (looseleaf format; back issues avail.; reprint service avail.) **Document type:** newsletter.
●Also available online. Vendor(s): Data-Star, Dow Jones News Retrieval, Information Access Co., Knight-Ridder Information, Inc., Lexis-Nexis.
—CCC.
Description: Covers all pertinent enforcement actions, regulatory changes, statutory amendments, criminal and civil cases, and international developments in the field of money laundering, asset forfeiture and related fields.

MONOGRAFIEEN STRAFRECHT. see *LAW — Criminal Law*

363.2 AG ISSN 0030-7955
MUNDO POLICIAL.* Variant title: P F A Revista. 1969. bi-m. Arg.$18188($90) (Policia Federal Argentina) Editorial Policial, Lavalle 1280, 1048 Buenos Aires, Argentina. Eds. Juana Maissonave, Miguel A. Pinella. adv.; bk.rev.; abstr.; bibl.; charts; illus.
Description: Deals with law enforcement and administration.

364.6 US
N A A W S GRAPEVINE NEWSLETTER. q. $25. (North American Association of Wardens and Superintendents) Central Michigan Printers, 221 W. Main St., Ionia, MI 48846. TEL 616-527-2500. Ed. Pam Whitman. bk.rev.; charts; stat.; tr.lit. circ. 4,500.
Description: Covers issues of current interest to wardens and superintendents of prisons.

364.3 361.6 UK
N A C R O ANNUAL REPORT. a. free. National Association for the Care and Resettlement of Offenders, 169 Clapham Rd., London SW9 0PU, England. TEL 44-171-582-6500. FAX 44-171-735-4666. **Document type:** corporate report.

364.6 UK
N A C R O CRIMINAL JUSTICE DIGEST. q. £12 to non-members; members £6 (effective 1996). National Association for the Care and Resettlement of Offenders, 169 Clapham Rd., London SW9 0PU, England. TEL 44-171-582-6500. FAX 44-171-735-4666. **Document type:** bulletin.

364.3 361.6 UK
N A C R O NEWS. q. National Association for the Care and Resettlement of Offenders, 169 Clapham Rd., London SW9 0PU, England. TEL 44-171-582-6500. FAX 44-171-735-4666. **Document type:** newsletter.

364.3 UK
N A C R O RACE UNIT NEWSLETTER. q. free. National Association for the Care and Resettlement of Offenders, 169 Clapham Rd., London SW9 0PU, England. TEL 44-171-582-6500. FAX 44-171-735-4666. **Document type:** newsletter.

N A C R O YOUTH CRIME SECTION. (National Association for the Care and Resettlement of Offenders) see *CHILDREN AND YOUTH — About*

363.2 UK
N A P O NEWS. 1965. m. membership. National Association of Probation Officers, 3-4 Chivalry Rd., Battersea, London SW11 1HT, England. FAX 44-171-223-3503. Ed. Harry Fletcher. adv.; bk.rev. circ. 7,500. **Document type:** newsletter.
Formerly: N A P O Newsletter.
Description: For law enforcement and probation administration, prison, and criminal justice personnel.

365 UK ISSN 0306-3313
N A P V NEWSLETTER. s-a. £1.50 (free to members). National Association of Prison Visitors, Fleur Field, Kingsdale Rd., Berkhamsted, Herts HP4 3BS, England. FAX 01442-875785. Ed. Carol Green. bk.rev. circ. 1,400. **Document type:** newsletter.

N R F PUBLIKATIES. (Nederlandse Federatie van Reclasseringsinstellingen) see *LAW — Criminal Law*

N V B B MAGAZINE - BRAND- EN DIEFSTALBEVEILIGING. (Nationale Vereniging voor Beveiliging tegen Brand en Binnendringing) see *FIRE PREVENTION*

NARC OFFICER. see *LAW*

364 IT
NARCOMAFIE. 1993. m. L.25000 (foreign L.55000) (effective 1995). Edizioni Gruppo Abele, Via Giolitti 21, 10123 Turin, Italy. TEL 39-11-8142745. FAX 39-11-8395577. Ed. Luigi Ciotti. (tabloid format)

340 US ISSN 1079-1582
NARCOTICS ENFORCEMENT & PREVENTION DIGEST. 1971. w. (51/yr.). $345 (Canada $355) (includes q. Calendar of Events) (effective 1998). Washington Crime News Services, 3918 Prosperity Ave., Ste. 318, Fairfax, VA 22031-3334. TEL 703-573-1600; 800-422-9267. FAX 703-573-1604. Ed. Robert H. Feldkamp; Pub. Richard J. O'Connell. bk.rev. (looseleaf format; also avail. in microform from UMI; reprint service avail. from UMI) **Indexed:** CJPI. **Document type:** newsletter.
—UMI.
Former titles (until 1995): Narcotics Demand Reduction Digest (ISSN 1043-8572); (until 1989): Narcotics Control Digest (ISSN 0889-5708)
Description: Covers various law-enforcement topics and news in the U.S. and throughout the world. Includes job listings.

350.765 US ISSN 8755-8289
KF3890.A59
NARCOTICS LAW BULLETIN. 1974. m. $59. Quinlan Publishing Co., Inc., 23 Drydock Ave., Boston, MA 02210-2387. TEL 617-542-0048; 800-229-2084. FAX 617-345-9646. index. (looseleaf format; also avail. in microform from UMI; reprint service avail. from UMI) **Indexed:** CJPI. **Document type:** newsletter.
—UMI. **CCC**.
Description: Summaries of current cases concerning narcotics, for non-lawyer law enforcement personnel.

364 US
NATIONAL ASSOCIATION OF DOCUMENT EXAMINERS. COMMUNIQUE. bi-m. $15. National Association of Document Examiners, Inc., Box 324, Joppa, MD 21085. TEL 410-679-8257. Ed. Katherine M. Koppenhaver. R&P contact: Katherine M. Koppenhaver. adv. contact: Katherine M. Koppenhaver. **Document type:** newsletter.

340 US ISSN 8755-1020
NATIONAL ASSOCIATION OF DOCUMENT EXAMINERS. JOURNAL. 1980. 3/yr. $50. National Association of Document Examiners, Inc., Box 324, Joppa, MD 21085. TEL 410-679-8257. Ed. Katherine M. Koppenhaver. R&P contact: Katherine M. Koppenhaver. bk.rev.; charts; illus. circ. 130. (back issues avail.)

364.36 371.93 US
NATIONAL ASSOCIATION OF JUVENILE CORRECTION AGENCIES. PROCEEDINGS. 1904. a. $20 to non-members; libraries $5. National Association of Juvenile Correction Agencies, 55 Albin Rd., Bow, NH 03304-3703. TEL 603-224-9749. E-mail: najcajohn@aol.com. Ed. John J. Sheridan. R&P contact: John J. Sheridan. adv. contact: John J. Sheridan. circ. 1,000. **Document type:** proceedings.
Formerly (until 1980): National Association of Training Schools and Juvenile Agencies. Proceedings (ISSN 0077-3476)

363.2 305.896073 US
NATIONAL BLACK - POLICE ASSOCIATION. NEWSLETTER. 1985. a. $20. National Black - Police Association, 3251 Mt. Pleasant St., N.W., Washington, DC 20010-2103. TEL 202-986-2070. FAX 202-987-0410. Ed. Fran Lassiter; Pub. Ronald E. Hampton. R&P contact: Fran Lassiter. adv. contact: Fran Lassiter. index. circ. 2,500. (tabloid format) **Document type:** newsletter.

C

CRIMINOLOGY AND LAW ENFORCEMENT

364 US ISSN 1042-5810
KF5399.A59
NATIONAL BULLETIN ON POLICE MISCONDUCT. 1982. m. $60 (effective 1993). Quinlan Publishing Co., Inc., 23 Drydock Ave., Boston, MA 02210-2387. TEL 617-542-0048; 800-229-2084. FAX 617-345-9646. index. (looseleaf format; back issues avail.) **Document type:** newsletter. —UMI. **CCC.**
 Description: Covers legal aspects of police misconduct and challenges to law enforcement personnel on such issues as wrongful death, civil rights, immunity, confessions, false arrest, brutality, use of force, and entrapment.

364.36 US ISSN 0163-2973
KF9772.3
NATIONAL CENTER FOR JUVENILE JUSTICE. ANNUAL REPORT. 1974. a. National Center for Juvenile Justice, 710 Fifth Ave., Pittsburgh, PA 15219. TEL 412-227-6950. FAX 412-227-6955. Dir. E. Hunter Hurst, III. illus.; stat. **Document type:** corporate report.
 Description: Presents an overview of the research activities and projects of the center.

364 US
NATIONAL COUNCIL ON CRIME AND DELINQUENCY. JUVENILE CUSTODY TRENDS. Cover title: Juvenile Court Trends. irreg. U.S. Department of Justice, National Council on Crime and Delinquency, Constitution Ave. & 10th St., N.W., Washington, DC 20530. TEL 202-739-0411. (Subscr. to: Superintendent of Documents, U.S. Government Printing Office, Box 317954, Pittsburgh, PA 15250-7954. TEL 202-512-1800. FAX 202-512-2250) stat. **Document type:** government publication.

364 US
NATIONAL COUNCIL ON CRIME AND DELINQUENCY. JUVENILES TAKEN INTO CUSTODY: FISCAL YEAR REPORT. Cover title: Juveniles Taken into Custody: Fiscal Year Report. irreg. U.S. Department of Justice, National Council on Crime and Delinquency, 633 Indiana Ave., N.W., Washington, DC 20531. TEL 202-739-0411. (Subscr. to: Superintendent of Documents, U.S. Government Printing Office, Box 317954, Pittsburgh, PA 15250-7954. TEL 202-512-1800. FAX 202-512-2250) **Document type:** government publication.

365 US ISSN 1066-5595
HV8130
NATIONAL DIRECTORY OF LAW ENFORCEMENT ADMINISTRATORS AND CORRECTIONAL INSTITUTIONS. 1964. a. $75. National Police Chiefs & Sheriffs Information Bureau, Box 365, Stevens Point, WI 54481. TEL 800-647-7579. FAX 715-345-7288. Ed. Steve Cywinski. adv. circ. 10,000. **Document type:** directory.
 ●Also available online. Vendor(s): Lexis-Nexis.
 Formerly: National Directory of Law Enforcement Administrators and Correctional Agencies.

364 US
NATIONAL F O P JOURNAL. 1915. q. $10. National Fraternal Order of Police, c/o Grand Lodge F O P, 1410 Donelson Pke., A17, Nashville, TN 37217-2933. TEL 615-399-0900. FAX 615-399-0400. Ed. Jerry Atnip. adv. contact: Lynne S. Martin. **Document type:** trade publication.

NATIONAL FIRE AND ARSON REPORT. see FIRE PREVENTION

364 US
NATIONAL INSTITUTE OF JUSTICE. SPONSORED RESEARCH PROGRAMS. a. U.S. Department of Justice, National Institute of Justice, 633 Indiana Ave., N.W., 11th Fl., Washington, DC 20531.

364 US ISSN 1067-7453
Z5703.4.C73
NATIONAL INSTITUTE OF JUSTICE JOURNAL; a selective notification of information program of the National Institute of Justice. 1972. q. free. U.S. Department of Justice, National Institute of Justice, National Criminal Justice Reference Service, Box 6000, Rockville, MD 20849-6000. TEL 301-251-5500; 800-851-3420. FAX 301-251-5212. circ. 80,000. **Indexed:** Crim.Just.Abstr.
 Supersedes in part (in 1992): National Institute of Justice Reports (ISSN 1067-8573); Which was formerly (until 1991): N I J Reports (ISSN 1067-8581); (until 1983): S N I: Selective Notification of Information (ISSN 0739-8107)

365 US ISSN 0192-8228
HV9463
NATIONAL JAIL AND ADULT DETENTION DIRECTORY. triennial. $70 to non-members; members $56. American Correctional Association, 4380 Forbes Blvd., Lanham, MD 20706-4322. TEL 301-918-1800. Ed. Gabriella Daley. R&P contact: Gabriella Daley. adv. contact: Marge Restivo. circ. 4,000. (also avail. in microfiche from CIS) **Indexed:** SRI. **Document type:** directory.

364 US ISSN 1041-3022
NATIONAL MISSING PERSONS REPORT. 1980. 3/yr. free to qualified personnel. Search Reports, Inc., 345 Boulevard, Hasbrouck Heights, NJ 07604. TEL 201-288-4445. FAX 201-288-8055. Pub. Charles A. Sutherland. R&P contact: Charles A. Sutherland. bk.rev.; circ. 45,000 (controlled). **Document type:** bulletin.
 Description: Provides information to law enforcement personnel about missing persons of all ages, including unidentified bodies.

NATIONAL ORGANIZATION FOR VICTIM ASSISTANCE NEWSLETTER. see SOCIAL SERVICES AND WELFARE

NATIONAL P A L UPDATE. see CHILDREN AND YOUTH — For

363.2 US ISSN 1072-6551
HV7551
NATIONAL POLICE REVIEW.* 1962. 4/yr. $39 (foreign $74). National Police Officers Association, 7811 Old Tree Run, Louisville, KY 40222-4694. TEL 502-425-9215; 800-457-6762. Ed. John R. Moore. adv.; bk.rev.; charts; illus.; circ. 22,500 (controlled). (also avail. in microform from UMI; reprint service avail. from UMI) **Indexed:** Abstr.Crim.& Pen., CJPI. **Document type:** newsletter. —UMI.
 Former titles (until 1992): Enforcement Journal (ISSN 0042-2347); (until 1971): Valor Magazine.
 Description: Reports on policing methods and administration.

364 US
NATIONAL PRETRIAL REPORTING PROGRAM (YEAR). (Subseries of: National Crime Victimization Survey Report) 1988. biennial. free. U.S. Department of Justice, Bureau of Justice Statistics, 633 Indiana Ave., N.W., 11th Fl., Washington, DC 20531. (Orders to: Superintendent of Documents, U.S. Government Printing Office, Box 371954, Pittsburgh, PA 15250-7954. TEL 202-512-1800. FAX 202-512-2250) stat. circ. 17,000. (also avail. in microfiche) **Document type:** government publication.

365 US ISSN 1076-769X
NATIONAL PRISON PROJECT JOURNAL. 1984. q. $30. American Civil Liberties Union Foundation, Inc., National Prison Project, 1875 Connecticut Ave., N.W., Ste. 410, Washington, DC 20009. TEL 202-234-4830. FAX 202-234-4890. Ed. Jenni Gainsborough. R&P contact: Jenni Gainsborough. adv.; bk.rev. circ. 2,000. (also avail. in microform; back issues avail.) **Indexed:** CJPI. **Document type:** newsletter. —UMI.
 Formerly: American Civil Liberties Union Foundation. National Prison Project. Journal (ISSN 0748-2655)
 Description: Information on prison issues, prisoner rights, litigation, and women in prison.

365 US
NATIONAL PRISON PROJECT STATUS REPORT. a. $5. American Civil Liberties Union Foundation, Inc., National Prison Project, 1875 Connecticut Ave., N.W., Ste. 410, Washington, DC 20009. TEL 202-234-4830. FAX 202-234-4890. Ed. Jenni Gainsborough. R&P contact: Jenni Gainsborough. **Document type:** academic/scholarly publication.
 Description: Lists states in which there are existing court decrees, or pending litigation, involving the entire state prison system or the major institutions within each state.

364 UA ISSN 0028-0054
NATIONAL REVIEW OF CRIMINAL SCIENCES. (Text in Arabic and English) 1957. 3/yr. $10. National Center for Social and Criminological Research, Zamalek P.O., Cairo, Egypt. Ed. Dr. Ahmed M. Khalifa. bk.rev.; charts; illus.

NATIONAL REVIEW OF SOCIAL SCIENCES. see SOCIAL SCIENCES: COMPREHENSIVE WORKS

365 NE ISSN 0077-6815
NETHERLANDS. CENTRAAL BUREAU VOOR DE STATISTIEK. GEVANGENISSTATISTIEK/NETHERLANDS. CENTRAL BUREAU OF STATISTICS. STATISTICS OF PRISONS. (Text in Dutch and English) 1950. a. fl.22.50. Centraal Bureau voor de Statistiek, Prinses Beatrixlaan 428, Voorburg, Netherlands. (Orders to: SDU - Publishers, Christoffel Plantijnstraat 2, Postbus 20014, 2500 EA The Hague, Netherlands) **Document type:** government publication.

364 GW
NEUE KRIMINOLOGISCHE SCHRIFTENREIHE. 1961. irreg. price varies. (Neue Kriminologische Gesellschaft) Kriminalistik Verlag Huethig GmbH, Im Weiher 10, 69121 Heidelberg, Germany. TEL 49-6221-489416. FAX 49-6221-489624. Eds. Christoph Mayerhofer, Joerg-Martin Jehle. adv. **Document type:** monographic series.
 Formerly: Kriminologische Schriftenreihe.

363.2 GW ISSN 0028-3681
NEUES POLIZEIARCHIV; ein Nachschlagewerk in Monatsheften. 1952. m. DM.11.50 per no. Richard Boorberg Verlag (Stuttgart), Scharrstr. 2, 70563 Stuttgart, Germany. TEL 0711-7385-0. Ed. Hans-Joern Bury. adv.; bk.rev. **Document type:** bulletin.
 —CCC.

NEW ENGLAND JOURNAL ON CRIMINAL AND CIVIL CONFINEMENT. see LAW

364 US
NEW JERSEY LAW ENFORCEMENT HANDBOOK. 1988. a. $44.95 (effective Jan. 1996). Gould Publications, 1333 N. U.S. Hwy. 17-92, Longwood, FL 32750-3724. TEL 407-695-9500. FAX 607-695-2906. Ed. Larry E. Holtz. adv.; bk.rev. (also avail. in looseleaf format)
 Description: Dissects and analyzes court decisions for NJ, with question and answer format covering many topics.

NEW LIFE (LONDON, 1971); prison service chaplaincy review. see RELIGIONS AND THEOLOGY

364 AT
NEW SOUTH WALES. ATTORNEY GENERAL'S DEPARTMENT. BUREAU OF CRIME STATISTICS AND RESEARCH. RESEARCH STUDIES. 1982. irreg. Attorney General's Department, Bureau of Crime Statistics and Research, Goodsell Bldg., 8-12 Chifley Square, Sydney, N.S.W. 2001, Australia. **Document type:** academic/scholarly publication.
 Formerly: New South Wales. Attorney-General Justice Department. Bureau of Crime Statistics and Research. Research Report.

364.4 US
NEW SPIRIT. 1981. q. $25. National Association of Town Watch, Inc., 7 Wynnewood Rd., Ste. 215, Box 303, Wynnewood, PA 19096. TEL 610-649-7055. FAX 610-649-5456. (Sponsor: America's Night Out Against Crime) Ed. Matt Peskin. adv.; bk.rev. circ. 8,000. (tabloid format) **Document type:** newsletter.

NEW YORK (CITY). DEPARTMENT OF JUVENILE JUSTICE. ANNUAL REPORT. see LAW — Family And Matrimonial Law

364 US
NEW YORK (CITY). OFFICE OF MIDTOWN ENFORCEMENT ANNUAL REPORT. a. Office of Midtown Enforcement, 330 W. 42nd St., 26th Fl., New York, NY 10036. TEL 212-971-6865. **Document type:** government publication.

364 US
NEW YORK (STATE). CRIME VICTIMS BOARD. REPORT. (Subseries of: New York (State) Legislature. Legislative Document) 1967. a., latest for years 1993-1993. free. Crime Victims Board, Counsel's Office, 845 Central Ave., Rm. 107, Albany, NY 12206-1588. TEL 578-457-8066. FAX 578-457-8658. R&P contact: Robert A. Mayhew. circ. 2,000 (controlled). **Document type:** government publication.
 Formerly (until 1982): New York (State) Crime Victims Compensation Board. Report (ISSN 0077-9148)

CRIMINOLOGY AND LAW ENFORCEMENT

353.9   US   ISSN 0095-4047
HV7282
NEW YORK (STATE). DIVISION OF CRIMINAL JUSTICE SERVICES. ANNUAL REPORT. Key Title: Annual Report - State of New York, Division of Criminal Justice Services. 1973. a. Division of Criminal Justice Services, Executive Park Tower, Stuyvesant Plaza, Albany, NY 12203. Ed.Bd. circ. 200.

NEW YORK (STATE). DIVISION OF CRIMINAL JUSTICE SERVICES. FELONY PROCESSING QUARTERLY REPORT. see *LAW — Criminal Law*

364   US
NEW YORK (STATE). DIVISION OF CRIMINAL SERVICES. OFFICE OF JUSTICE SYSTEMS ANALYSIS. CRIMINAL JUSTICE INDICATORS BULLETIN. 1987. irreg., latest 1992. Division of Criminal Justice Services, Office of Justice Systems Analysis, Bureau of Statistical Services, Executive Park Tower, Stuyvesant Plaza, Albany, NY 12203. TEL 518-457-8381. **Document type:** government publication, bulletin.
  Formerly (until 1992): New York (State). Division of Criminal Services. Office of Justice Systems Analysis. Bulletin.

363.2   US
HV7551
THE NEW YORK STATE TROOPER. 1963. q. free to qualified personnel. State Police, Public Security Bldg., State Campus, Albany, NY 12226. FAX 518-485-7818. Ed. Jon A. Lupo. illus.; circ. 14,000 (controlled). **Document type:** government publication.
  Formerly: Trooper (ISSN 0564-3287)

363.2   US
NEW YORK'S FINEST. 1980. bi-m. membership only. Patrolmen's Benevolent Association of the City of New York, Inc., 40 Fulton St., New York, NY 10038. TEL 212-233-5531. FAX 212-233-3952. Ed. Joe Mancini. illus. circ. 32,000.

364   NE   ISSN 0925-2711
NIEUWSBRIEF POLITIE. 1990. bi-w. Samsom H.D. Tjeenk Willink B.V. (Subsidiary of: Wolters Kluwer N.V.), Postbus 316, 2400 AH Alphen aan den Rijn, Netherlands. TEL 31-1720-66822. FAX 31-1720-66639. **Document type:** newsletter.

363.2 345   SW   ISSN 1100-522X
NORDISK KRIMINALPOLIS; organ foer kriminalpolissamarbetet i Nordiska kriminalpolisunionen. 1976. s-a. SEK 10 per no. (effective 1995). Nordiska Kriminalpolisunionen (NKU), Svenska Sektionen, c/o Stockholms Kriminalpolisfoerening, P.O. Box 12510, S-102 29 Stockholm, Sweden. TEL 46-8-769-40-51. FAX 46-8-653-47-28. (Subscr. to: Goeteborgs Kriminalpolisfoerening, P.O. Box 429, S-401 26, Goeteborg, Sweden) Ed. Christer H. Sjoeblom. adv. circ. 5,000. **Document type:** newsletter.

364.072 345.48   IC   ISSN 0805-5033
NORDISK KRIMINOLOGI; nyhedsbrev. (Text in Scandinavian languages) 1975. 3/yr. free. Nordisk Samarbejdsraad for Kriminologi - Scandinavian Research Council for Criminology, University of Iceland, IS-101 Reykjavik, Iceland. TEL 354-525-43-30. FAX 354-525-49-47. E-mail: elinkon@thi.hi.is. Ed. Elin Konradsdottir. adv. circ. 1,200. **Document type:** newsletter.
  Formerly (until 1992): Nordisk Kriminologi. Nyhetsbrev (ISSN 0349-1730)
  Description: Provides information on the activities of the Council, national reports of issues of criminological interest, abstracts of Nordic publications in the field of criminology and free advertisements of Nordic and international criminological conferences.

363.2   FR   ISSN 0753-4000
NOUVEAU DETECTIVE. 1981. w. 525 F. Editions Nuit et Jour, 9 rue Christiani, 75018 Paris, France. TEL 49-25-17-17. adv. circ. 300,000.
  Formerly: Qui? Police.

364   IT   ISSN 0392-0100
HV7748
NUOVA POLIZIA E RIFORMA DELLO STATO.* 1977. m. L.50000($77) Editoriale Nuova Polizia Srl., Via Chinotto 16, 00195 Rome, Italy. TEL 06-388910. FAX 06-3728091. Ed. Franco Fedeli. adv. circ. 60,000.

364 343   US
OHIO CRIMINAL LAW HANDBOOK. a., 17th ed. $31.95. Anderson Publishing Co., 2035 Reading Rd., Cincinnati, OH 45202. TEL 513-421-4142; 800-543-0883. FAX 513-562-8116. **Document type:** consumer publication.

364   ISSN 0190-2571
HV7231
ON THE LINE (LAUREL). 1977. bi-m. $25 to non-members. American Correctional Association, 4380 Forbes Blvd., Lanham, MD 20706-4322. TEL 301-918-1800. Ed. Gabrielle deGroot. circ. 20,000. **Document type:** newsletter.

ONDERZOEK EN BELEID. see *LAW — Criminal Law*

364   US   ISSN 0889-5716
HV6446
ORGANIZED CRIME DIGEST; an independent news summary of organized crime activities. 1980. bi-w. $295 (Canada $301) (includes q. Calendar of Events) (effective 1998). Washington Crime News Services, 3918 Prosperity Ave., Ste. 318, Fairfax, VA 22031-3334. TEL 703-573-1600; 800-422-9267. FAX 703-573-1604. Ed. Betty B. Bosarge; Pub. Richard J. O'Connell. (looseleaf format; also avail. in microform from UMI; reprint service avail. from UMI) Indexed: CJPI. **Document type:** newsletter.
  —UMI.
  Description: Covers issues in organized crime in the U.S. and throughout the world.

OUNCE OF PREVENTION; survey of security & loss prevention in the retail industry. see *BUSINESS AND ECONOMICS — Marketing And Purchasing*

363.2   RH   ISSN 0030-7289
HV8272.A2
OUTPOST. 1911. bi-m. Z.$52 (South Africa R.30; elsewhere £15) (effective 1997). Zimbabwe Republic Police, P.O. Box HG 106, Highlands, Harare, Zimbabwe. TEL 263-4-724571. Ed. Wayne Bvudzijena. adv.; bk.rev.; illus. circ. 18,900. **Document type:** trade publication.
  Description: Covers law enforcement and administration.

365   US   ISSN 1077-8209
HV7231   CODEN: OVTIFJ
OVERCROWDED TIMES; solving the prison problem. 1990. bi-m. $39 to individuals; institutions $75. Castine Research Corporation, Box 110, Castine, ME 04421. TEL 207-326-9521. FAX 207-326-9528. Ed. Michael Tonry.

363.5   US
P C N Y STATE REPORT. 4/yr. $20. Police Conference of New York, Inc., 112 State St., Ste. 1120, Albany, NY 12207. Ed. Edward W. Guzdek. illus. circ. 24,000. **Document type:** corporate report.

364   GW   ISSN 0720-6283
P F A SCHRIFTENREIHE. irreg. (3-4/yr.) DM.54 (foreign DM.57) (effective 1996). (Polizei-Fuehrungsakademie) Schmidt-Roemhild Verlag, Mengstr. 16, 23552 Luebeck, Germany. TEL 49-451-703101. FAX 49-451-7031253. **Document type:** monographic series.

P F I WORLD REPORT. (Prison Fellowship International) see *RELIGIONS AND THEOLOGY*

364   US
P I MAGAZINE; America's private investigation journal. 1988. q. $24. Bob Mackowiak, Ed. & Pub., 755 Bronx, Toledo, OH 43609. TEL 419-382-0967. FAX 419-382-0967. E-mail: pimag1@aol.com; URL: http://www.pimall.com. adv. contact: Bob Mackowiak. bk.rev.; illus. circ. 4,000. (back issues avail.) **Document type:** trade publication.
  Description: Contains stories of real investigators' unsolved cases, investigative techniques, personality profiles and more.

PANOPTICON; tijdschrift voor strafrecht, criminologie en forensisch welzijnswerk. see *LAW — Criminal Law*

PARKER'S CALIFORNIA PENAL CODE. see *LAW*

363   UK
PATROL. m. Sussex Police HQ, Public Relations Office, Mailing House, Lewes, E. Sussex BN7 2DZ, England. TEL 44-1273-475432. FAX 44-1273-404280. Ed. Jill Pedersen. circ. 10,000. **Document type:** bulletin.

364   US   ISSN 0091-4118
HV7288
PENNSYLVANIA. CRIME COMMISSION. REPORT.* 1970. a. free. Crime Commission, 1800 Elmerton Ave., 3rd Fl., Harrisburg, PA 17110-9718. TEL 215-834-1164. FAX 215-834-0737. circ. 40,000 (controlled). **Document type:** government publication.

363.2   US   ISSN 0031-4404
PENNSYLVANIA CHIEFS OF POLICE ASSOCIATION BULLETIN. 1931. q. $50. Pennsylvania Chiefs of Police Association, Public Relations Committee, 2941 N. Front St., Harrisburg, PA 17110. TEL 717-236-1059. Ed. Amy Corl. adv.; bk.rev.; bibl.; charts; illus.; stat. circ. 1,300. Indexed: P.A.I.S. **Document type:** bulletin.
  Description: News and features of interest to members of the association.

345.748   US   ISSN 0098-7174
KFP575.A59
PENNSYLVANIA POLICE CRIMINAL LAW BULLETIN. 1972. m. $32 (effective 1995 & 1996). Stanley Cohen, Ed. & Pub., 2579 Warren Rd., Indiana, PA 15701. index. circ. 650. (looseleaf format; back issues avail.) **Document type:** bulletin.

364 350   RM   ISSN 1220-6792
PENTRU PATRIE. 1949. m. 1000 lei. Ministerul Interior, Str. Mihai Voda 17, sector 5, 70622 Bucharest, Rumania. TEL 40-16138202. FAX 40-12121390. TELEX 88810 ZZRPP R. Ed. Nicolae Rotaru; Pub. Jon Anghel Manastire. illus. circ. 200,000. **Document type:** government publication.
  Description: Presents the activities of the Ministry: police, fire brigades, boundary police, passport services, frontier guards, national archives. Publishes criminal laws and defends human rights.

364
PHYSICAL SURVEILLANCE TRAINING MANUAL. 1981. a. $20. (National Association of Investigative Specialists) Thomas Publishing (Austin), Box 33244, Austin, TX 78764. TEL 512-832-0355. circ. 2,500.

363.2   UK   ISSN 0032-2555
POLICE. 1968. m. £15. Police Federation of England and Wales, 15-17 Langley Rd., Surbiton, Surrey KT6 6LP, England. TEL 44-181-399-2224. FAX 44-181-390-2249. (Subscr. to: Avon Direct Mail, Unit 12-14, Old Mill Rd., Portishead, Bristol BS20 9EG, England) Ed. Stewart Goodwin. R&P contact: Stewart Goodwin. adv. contact: David Pughe. bk.rev.; charts; illus. circ. 41,000. Indexed: Abstr.Crim.& Pen. **Document type:** trade publication.
  —BLDSC (6543.202000).
  Description: Gives officers the latest information on current developments in professional matters and on changes to their pay and conditions of service.

363.2   US   ISSN 0893-8989
HV7936.E7
POLICE; the law officer's magazine. 1976. m. $21395 (foreign $38.95) (effective 1997). Bobit Publishing Company, 2512 Artesia Blvd., Redondo Beach, CA 92278. TEL 310-376-8788. FAX 310-798-4598. E-mail: msutton@bobit.com. (Subscr. to: Box 1068, Skokie, IL 60076) Ed. Dennis Hall; Pub. Maurice Sutton. R&P contact: Maurice Sutton. adv. contact: Janet Pomerantz. circ. 52,000. **Document type:** trade publication.
  —UMI.
  Formerly: Police Product News (ISSN 0164-5196)
  Description: Trade journal for police officers.

363.2   UK   ISSN 0477-2008
POLICE & CONSTABULARY ALMANAC; official register. 1861. a. £24($42) Court & Judicial Publishing Co. Ltd., Box 39, Henley-on-Thames, Oxon. RG9 5UA, England. (Co-publisher: R. Hazell & Co.) Ed. C.G.A. Parker. adv.; index. **Document type:** directory.
  —BLDSC (6543.210000).
  Description: Lists all U.K. police forces and organizations, along with their senior personnel.

345   US   ISSN 0092-8933
HV8138
POLICE AND LAW ENFORCEMENT. 1973. a. $57.50. A M S Press, Inc., 56 E. 13th St., New York, NY 10003. TEL 212-777-4700. FAX 212-995-5413. Eds. Robert J. Homant, Daniel B. Kennedy. bibl.; stat.; index. (back issues avail.)
  Description: Annual collection of articles covering major facets of police work and law enforcement in the United States.

CRIMINOLOGY AND LAW ENFORCEMENT

363.2 US ISSN 1070-8111
POLICE AND SECURITY NEWS. 1984. bi-m. $15 (foreign $29) (effective Mar. 1997). Days Communications Inc., 1690 Quarry Rd., Box 330, Kulpsville, PA 19443. TEL 215-362-2233. FAX 215-368-9955. Ed. James Devery; Pub. David Yaw. R&P contact: Al Menear. adv. contact: Al Menear. circ. 20,960 (controlled). (tabloid format; back issues avail.) **Document type:** trade publication.
 Description: Information, products and training directed to middle and upper administration personnel in the law enforcement and security fields.

POLICE AVIATION HANDBOOK. see *TRANSPORTATION — Air Transport*

363 UK
POLICE BEAT. 11/yr. Royal Ulster Constabulary Police Federation for Northern Ireland, Garnerville, Belfast BT4 2NX, Northern Ireland. TEL 0232-760831. Ed. D. Rogers. circ. 5,000. **Document type:** trade publication.

636.2 371.42 US ISSN 8756-355X
HV8143
POLICE CAREER DIGEST. 1984. bi-m. $45. Gordon Co., Box 7772, Winter Haven, FL 33883. TEL 941-293-1159. FAX 941-294-6392. Pub. Jackye Bundschu. adv./ B&W page $300; 7 1/2 x 9 3/4; adv. contact: Pat Fisher. circ. 5,430. **Document type:** consumer publication, trade publication.

364 US ISSN 0032-2571
POLICE CHIEF;* professional voice of law enforcement. 1934. m. $25. International Association of Chiefs of Police, Inc., Ste. 200, 515 N. Washington St., Ste. 400, Alexandria, VA 22314-2340. TEL 703-243-6500. (Subscr. to: Box 90976, Washington, DC 20090-0976) Ed. Charles E. Higginbotham. film rev.; index. circ. 22,000. (also avail. in microfilm from UMI; back issues avail.; reprint service avail. from UMI) **Indexed:** Abstr.Crim.& Pen., CJPI, Crim.Just.Abstr., Curr.Cont., HRIS, P.A.I.S., Risk Abstr., Sage Pub.Admin.Abstr., Soc.Sci.Ind. (until 1994), SSCI.
 —BLDSC (6543.220000); KR SourceOne; UMI; UnCover.

POLICE, CRIMES AND OFFENSES AND MOTOR VEHICLE LAWS OF VIRGINIA. see *LAW — Criminal Law*

331 364 US
POLICE DEPARTMENT DISCIPLINARY LAW BULLETIN. 1992. m. $59. Quinlan Publishing Co., Inc., 23 Drydock Ave., Boston, MA 02210-2387. TEL 617-542-0048; 800-229-2084. FAX 617-345-9646. index. (looseleaf format; back issues avail.) **Document type:** newsletter.
 Description: Discusses all aspects of disciplinary issues facing U.S. police departments, including off-duty misconduct, insubordination, sexual harassment, falsification of reports, drug testing and more.

363.2 UK ISSN 0032-258X
HV7551
POLICE JOURNAL; a quarterly review for the police forces of the Commonwealth and English-speaking world. 1928. q. £52.80 (effective 1997). Barry Rose Law Periodicals, Little London, Chichester, W. Sussex PO19 1PG, England. TEL 44-1243-787841. FAX 44-1243-779278. Ed. R.W. Stone. R&P contact: Jean Harbut. adv. contact: Dora Curtis. bk.rev.; illus.; index, cum.index. (back issues avail.) **Indexed:** Abstr.Crim.& Pen., ASSIA, CJPI, Crim.Just.Abstr., Euro.LJI, Excerp.Med., HRIS, LJI, Pub.Admin.Abstr. **Document type:** academic/scholarly publication.
 —BLDSC (6543.250000); CISTI; UnCover.
 Description: Covers crime prevention and detection, public order, accident control, staff training, race relations, modern technology, psychology of crime and criminals, and terrorism.

363.2 AT ISSN 0032-2598
POLICE LIFE. 1955. 10/yr. free. Victoria Police, 637 Flinders St., Melbourne, Vic. 3005, Australia. TEL 61-3-92475979. FAX 61-3-92475982. Ed. Marilyn Miller. bk.rev.; illus.; index. circ. 13,000. **Document type:** government publication.

364 US ISSN 0164-8365
POLICE MARKSMAN. bi-m. Police Marksman Association, 6204 Hickory Hill Ct., Montgomery, AL 36117. TEL 334-271-2010. Ed. Darlene Hunter; Pub. Charles Dees. **Document type:** trade publication.

363.2 796.8 CN ISSN 1198-8398
POLICE MARTIAL ARTS ASSOCIATION NEWS. 1994. bi-m. Can.$20($15) Police Martial Arts Association, P.O. Box 7303, Sub 12, Riverview, NB E1B 4T9, Canada. TEL 506-387-5126. FAX 506-387-5126. Eds. Doug Devlin, Foster MacLeod. adv.; circ. 1,000 (controlled). (looseleaf format; back issues avail.) **Document type:** newsletter.
 Description: Covers police and martial arts issues for a law enforcement readership base. Studies use of force research, specialized training and procedures, confrontational analysis, officer safety and protection.

342 US ISSN 0738-0623
KF4742
POLICE MISCONDUCT AND CIVIL RIGHTS LAW REPORT. 1983. bi-m. $135. (National Lawyers Guild, Civil Liberties Committee) Clark - Boardman - Callaghan, 375 Hudson St., New York, NY 10014. TEL 212-929-7500; 800-422-2101. FAX 212-924-0460. index. (looseleaf format; back issues avail.)
 Description: Contains articles on the most current issues in police misconduct and civil rights litigation.

363.2 FR ISSN 0988-9760
POLICE MUTUALITE.* 1970. m. 6 F. Mutuelle Generale de la Police Francaise, 8 rue Thomas Edison, 94027 Creteil Cedex, France. adv. circ. 83,000.
 Formerly (until 1988): Mutalite Police (ISSN 0988-9779)

350.74 FR ISSN 0048-4695
POLICE NATIONALE.* no.7, 1972. m. 15 F. Syndicat des Grades de la Police Nationale, 11 rue des Ursins, 75004 Paris, France. Ed. M. Digard.

363.2 GH
POLICE NEWS. m. Police Headquarters, Accra, Ghana. Ed. S.S. Appiah. circ. 20,000.

363.2 FR
POLICE NOUVELLE. 6/yr. Syndicat National Autonome des Policiers en Civil, 21 square St. Charles, 75012 Paris, France. TEL 44-67-83-30. FAX 44-67-83-66. Ed. C. Morel. circ. 16,000.

331 364 US ISSN 0887-8285
KF5398.P6
POLICE OFFICER GRIEVANCES BULLETIN. 1982. m. $60 (effective 1993). Quinlan Publishing Co., Inc., 23 Drydock Ave., Boston, MA 02210-2387. TEL 617-542-0048; 800-229-2084. FAX 617-345-9646. index. (looseleaf format; back issues avail.) **Document type:** newsletter.
 —UMI. **CCC**.
 Description: Discusses decisions and legal issues relating to grievances and police labor issues such as hiring, firing, arbitration, notice and hearing procedures, for police and police-related employees.

363.2 US ISSN 1062-5216
POLICE OFFICERS JOURNAL. 1957. 4/yr. membership only. (Police Officers Labor Council) Dale Corporation, 22150 W. Nine Mile Rd., Southfield, MI 48034-6007. TEL 248-204-2244. FAX 248-204-2240. Ed. Barbara Logan. adv.: page $925. bk.rev.; charts; illus.; circ. 5,000 (controlled). **Document type:** trade publication.
 —UMI.
 Formerly (until 1992): Peace Officer (ISSN 0031-3556)

363.2 UK ISSN 0309-1414
HV7551
POLICE REVIEW. 1893. w. £61.20 (effective 1997). Police Review Publishing Co., Celcon House, 5th Fl., 289-293 High Holborn, London WC1V 7HU, England. TEL 44-171-440-4700. FAX 44-171-405-7163. Ed. Gary Mason; Pub. Fabiana Angelini. R&P contact: Sergio De Oliveira. adv. contact: Alice Codrington. bk.rev.; charts; illus.; tr.lit.; index; circ. 25,000 (paid). **Indexed:** Abstr.Crim.& Pen., ASSIA, C.L.I., HRIS, Leg.Per., Soc.Sci.Ind. **Document type:** trade publication.
 —BLDSC (6543.262000).

363.2 US
POLICE TIMES. 1964. q. membership. American Federation of Police, 3801 Biscayne Blvd., Miami 33137. TEL 305-573-0070. FAX 305-573-98 E-mail: policeinfo@aphf.org. Ed. Jim Gordon. adv bk.rev.; charts; illus. circ. 50,000. **Document type** trade publication.
 —UMI.
 Former titles: Police Times and Police Comman Police Times (ISSN 0032-2601)

363.2 SP ISSN 0213-4012
POLICIA. 1984. m. 2000 ptas. to non-members (foreign 3200 ptas.) (effective 1997). Direccion General de Policia, Instituto de Estudios de Polici Seccion de Documentacion y Publicaciones, Calle Rafael Calvo, 33, 3a pl., 28010 Madrid, Spain. TEL 34-1-4351720. Ed.Bd. adv.; bk.rev.; charts; illus. circ. 19,000.
 Formed by the merger of (1962-1984): Policia Espanola (ISSN 0048-4709); (1961-1984): Pol Nacional (ISSN 0210-5896); Which was formerly (until 1978): Policia Armada (ISSN 0210-590X)

363.2 UK ISSN 1363-951X
HV7551
POLICING; an international journal of police strategie and management. 1978. q. £189($299) (foreig Aus.$369) (effective 1998). M C B University Pr Ltd., 60-62 Toller Ln., Bradford, W. Yorks BD8 9B England. TEL 44-1274-777700.
 FAX 44-1274-785200. URL: http://www.mcb.co (Subscr. in N. America to: Box 10812, Birmingha AL 35201-0812. TEL 800-633-4931) Eds. Lawrence F. Travis, III, Geoffrey Alpert. adv.; bk.re index. (also avail. in microfilm from UMI; back iss avail.) **Indexed:** Abstr.Crim.& Pen., CJPI, Crim.Just.Abstr., P.A.I.S. **Document type:** academic/scholarly publication.
 —BLDSC (6543.283900); UMI; UnCover. **CCC**.
 Formerly (until 1997): Police Studies (ISSN 0141-2949); Incorporates (1981-1997): Americ Journal of Police (ISSN 0735-8547)
 Description: Devoted to the craft, science and practice of police work for senior police officers, government officials, university teachers, instructo students and research workers.

363.2 301 NE ISSN 1043-9463
HV7551 CODEN: POSOER
POLICING AND SOCIETY; an international journal of research & policy. 1991. 4/yr. (in 1 vol., 4 nos./vol.). $96 (effective 1998). Gordon and Brea - Harwood Academic, Amsteldisk 166, 1st Fl., 10 LH Amsterdam, Netherlands. (Subscr. to: International Publishers Distributor, Box 32160, Newark, NJ 07102. TEL 800-545-8398. FAX 215-750-6343) Eds. Robert Reiner, Rod Morgan. (also avail. in microform) **Indexed:** Abstr.Crim.& Crim.Just.Abstr.
 —BLDSC (6543.284300). **CCC**.
 Description: Concerns itself with the political economy of policing.
 Refereed Serial

363.2 UK ISSN 1355-4557
POLICING TODAY. 1984. q. £40 (E.U. £45; rest of world £60) (effective 1997). Police Review Publishing Co., Celcon House, 5th Fl., 289-293 H Holborn, London WC1V 7HU, England. TEL 44-171-440-4700. FAX 44-171-405-7163. Ed. Sean Howe; Pub. Fabiana Angelini. R&P contac Sergio De Oliveira. adv. contact: Alice Codrington. circ. 1,300 (paid). **Indexed:** Abstr.Crim.& Pen., Crim.Just.Abstr., Euro.LJI, LJI. **Document type:** trade publication.
 —BLDSC (6543.287000); SWETS.

363.2 378 PL ISSN 1230-9273
POLICYJNY BIULETYN SZKOLENIOWY. 1993. q. Wydawnictwo Wyzszej Szkoly Policyjnej, Ul. K. Swierczewskiego 111, 12-101 Szczytno, Polnad. TEL 43221. FAX 42610. **Document type:** academic/scholarly publication, bulletin.
 Description: Covers police education and law.

363.2 FI ISSN 0048-4725
POLIISIMIES. 1930. m. Fmk.100. Asemamiehenkatu 00520 Helsinki, Finland. Ed. Seppo Yrjoenen. adv. bk.rev.; charts; illus.; stat.

363.2 SW ISSN 0345-9454
POLISTIDNINGEN. 1904. 10/yr. SEK 75 (effective 1991). Svenska Polisfoerbundet, P.O. Box 12219, S-102 25 Stockholm, Sweden.
 Formerly (until 1941): Svensk Polistidning.

CRIMINOLOGY AND LAW ENFORCEMENT

363.2   NE   ISSN 0925-0980
POLITIE MAGAZINE; maandblad voor de nederlandse politie. 1957. 10/yr. fl.52. Vuga Uitgeverij B.V., Postbus 16400, 2500 BK The Hague, Netherlands. TEL 31-70-3614011. FAX 31-70-3625468. Ed. Bert Huizing. adv.; B&W page fl.1190, color page fl.3075; trim 210 x 297. bk.rev. circ. 5,000. (reprint service avail.) **Document type:** trade publication.
—SWETS.
    Former titles (until 1992): Rijkspolitie Magazine (ISSN 0921-6200); (until 1972): Korpsblad Rijkspolitie (ISSN 0023-4117)
    Description: News, features and information of interest to employees of the Dutch police force.

363.2 331.88   NO   ISSN 0332-883X
POLITIEMBETSMENNENES BLAD. 1926. m. (10/yr.). NOK 140. Politiembetsmennenes Landsforening, Trondheim Politikammer, 7000 Trondheim, Norway. Ed. Harald Ellefsen. adv.; bk.rev. circ. 500.

363.209489   DK   ISSN 0108-3376
HV7766
POLITIETS AARSBERETNING. (Text in Danish, English) 1948. a. free. Rigspolitichefen, Afdeling E - National Police Commissioner, Anker Heegaards Gade 3, 3, DK-1780 Copenhagen V, Denmark. TEL 45-33-14-88-88. FAX 45-33-91-22-78. Ed. Ki. Jens Bang. R&P contact: Jens Bang. circ. 6,100. **Document type:** government publication.
    Description: Presents the annual report of the Chief of State Police.

363.2   DK   ISSN 0107-3893
POLITIHISTORISK SELSKAB. AARSSKRIFT. 1981. a. DKK 80. Polithistorisk Selskab - Danish Police Historical Society, Polititorvet 14, DK-1780 Copenhagen V, Denmark. FAX 45-31-39-69-36. Ed. Flemming Steen Munch. illus. circ. 3,500.

363.2   GW   ISSN 0032-3519
DIE POLIZEI; Zentralorgan fuer das Sicherheits- und Ordnungswesen. 1908. m. DM.136 (effective 1996). Carl Heymanns Verlag KG, Luxemburgerstr. 449, 50939 Cologne, Germany. TEL 49-221-94373-0. FAX 49-221-94373901. Ed. O. Wenzky. adv.; bk.rev.; illus.; stat.; index. circ. 1,800. **Indexed:** Abstr.Crim.& Pen., Crim.Just.Abstr., IBR. **Document type:** monographic series.
—BLDSC (6544.165000).

364   AU
POLIZEI AKTUELL. q. Verein zur Foerderung des Klubs der Exekutive, Postgasse 9-1, A-1010 Vienna, Austria. TEL 01-513245. circ. 20,000.

363.2   GW
POLIZEI-HEUTE; Fuehrung - Technik - Ausbildung. 1971. bi-m. DM.54 (foreign DM.63). Richard Boorberg Verlag (Stuttgart), Scharrstr. 2, 70563 Stuttgart, Germany. TEL 0711-73850. FAX 0711-735244. Ed. Helmut Brueckmann; Pub. Erhard Denninger. adv.; B&W page DM.2500, color page DM.4300; trim 171 x 262; adv. contact: Helmut Brueckmann. bk.rev.; index. circ. 2,400. (back issues avail.) **Document type:** trade publication.
    Formerly (until 1994): Bereitschaftspolizei-Heute (ISSN 0723-6123)

363.2   GW   ISSN 0032-3527
DIE POLIZEI IM LANDE BERLIN. 1969. m. (Gewerkschaft Oeffentliche Dienste, Transport und Verkehr, Hauptabteilung Polizei) Verlagsanstalt Courier GmbH, Hauptvorstand, Kronprinzstr. 24, 70173 Stuttgart, Germany. Ed. Werner Beecken. adv.; charts; illus.; tr.lit.

363.2   GW   ISSN 0177-4573
POLIZEI INFO POLIZEIFORUM; unabhaengige Fachzeitschrift fuer den Polizeibeamten. m. DM.30. Verlagsgesellschaft fuer Polizeipublikationen mbH, Boekenbarg 2, 19067 Ahrensboek, Germany. TEL 04525-2528. Eds. Klaus-Peter Schuhmacher, Ehrenfried Kuehlewind. adv.

363.2   GW   ISSN 0722-5962
POLIZEIVERKEHR UND TECHNIK; Fachzeitschriften fuer Verkehrs- und Polizeitechnik. 1956. m. DM.61.40 (foreign DM.68.40) (effective 1997). Schmidt-Roemhild Verlag, Mengstr. 16, 23552 Luebeck, Germany. TEL 49-451-703101. FAX 49-451-7031253. Ed. Eugen Sauer. adv.; bk.rev.; illus.; index. circ. 10,000. **Document type:** trade publication.
—BLDSC (6544.171000).
    Formerly: Polizei Technik Verkehr (ISSN 0032-3535)

363.2   IT   ISSN 0032-356X
POLIZIA MODERNA; periodico mensile illustrato. 1948. m. L.28000. Fondo Assistenza del Personale della Pubblica Sicurezza, Piazza del Viminale, 00184 Rome, Italy. TEL 39-6-46671. FAX 39-6-4456903. E-mail: poliziamoderna@email.telpress.it; URL: http://www.polizia.telpress.it. (Editorial addr.: Via del Castro Pretorio, 5-00185 Roma, Italy) Ed. Massimo Occello. adv.; page L.4000000. bk.rev.; illus.; charts. circ. 45,000.
    ●Also available online.

080 362.127   US   ISSN 0197-7024
HV8078.A1
POLYGRAPH. 1972. q. $40 (foreign $50). American Polygraph Association, Box 8037, Chattanooga, TN 37414-0037. TEL 410-647-4581. Ed. Norman Ansley. R&P contact: Norman Ansley. adv.; bk.rev.; charts; index. circ. 3,500. (also avail. in microfilm from UMI; reprint service avail. from UMI) **Indexed:** Abstr.Crim.& Pen., Art & Archaeol.Tech.Abstr., Crim.Just.Abstr., Paper & Bd.Abstr. **Document type:** academic/scholarly publication.
    Supersedes: American Polygraph Association. Journal (ISSN 0003-0562)
    Description: Discusses forensic psychophysiology, polygraph operations, research, history, psychology, physiology, instrumentation, law notes, abstracts, and training.

POMPE REEKS. see LAW — Criminal Law

364 364.4   US   ISSN 0193-4015
KF9632.A15
THE PRETRIAL REPORTER. 1977. bi-m. $48. Pretrial Services Resource Center, 1325 G St., N.W., Ste. 770, Washington, DC 20005. TEL 202-638-3080. FAX 202-347-0493. E-mail: pretrial@gslink.com; URL: http://www.gslink.com/~pretrial. Ed. Jolanta Juszkiewicz; Pub. D. Alan Henry. R&P contact: Jolanta Juszkiewicz. bk.rev. circ. 500. (back issues avail.) **Document type:** newsletter.
    Description: Examines pretrial issues and jail crowding on a national basis, including legislation, program practices, research and case law. Serves as a resource for jobs, conferences and publications.

365   EI   ISSN 0254-5233
HV9638
PRISON INFORMATION BULLETIN. (Text in English, French) 1983. 2/yr. $4. (Council of Europe, Directorate of Legal Affairs) Council of Europe Publishing, F-67075 Strasbourg Cedex, France. TEL 33-3-88412263. FAX 33-3-88412780. TELEX 870 943 F. (Dist. in U.S. by: Manhattan Publishing Co., 468 Albany Post Rd., Croton-on-Hudson, NY 10520. FAX 914-271-5856) Ed. Marguerite-Sophie Eckert. charts. **Indexed:** Abstr.Crim.& Pen.

365   US   ISSN 0032-8855
HV7231
THE PRISON JOURNAL. 1845. q. $118 to institutions (effective Sep. 1996). (Pennsylvania Prison Society) Sage Publications, Inc., 2455 Teller Rd., Thousand Oaks, CA 91320. TEL 805-499-0721. FAX 805-499-0871. E-mail: libraries@sagepub.com; URL: http://www.sagepub.com. (Overseas subscr. to: Sage Publications Ltd., 6 Bonhill St., London EC2A 4PU, England; Sage Publications India Pvt. Ltd., P.O. Box 4215, New Delhi 110 048, India) Ed. Alan T. Harland. adv. contact: Margaret Travers. bk.rev.; illus.; index. circ. 1,000. (also avail. in microform from UMI; back issues avail.; reprint service avail.) **Indexed:** Abstr.Crim.& Pen., Alt.Press Ind., Chic.Per.Ind., Crim.Just.Abstr., Curr.Cont., Fam.Ind., P.A.I.S., SSCI, Viol.& Abuse Abstr. **Document type:** academic/scholarly publication.
    ●Also available online. Vendor(s): Information Access Co.
—BLDSC (6617.058000); SWETS; UMI. CCC.
    Description: Devoted to the advancement of theory, research, policy, and practice in the areas of adult and juvenile incarceration and all related aspects of the more broadly defined field of correctional alternatives and penal sanctions.
    Refereed Serial

PRISON LEGAL NEWS; working to extend democracy to all. see LAW

051   US   ISSN 1065-0709
HV9471
PRISON LIFE MAGAZINE.* 1992. bi-m. $19.95 (Canada $35; elsewhere $47); newsstand price: $3.95 (in Canada Can.$5.95). Prison Life Magazine, 1436 W. Gray St., Ste. 531, Houston, TX 77019-4946. TEL 800-207-2659. FAX 713-840-0428. E-mail: prisnlife@aol.com. (Editorial addr.: 505 Eighth Ave., 14th Fl., New York, NY 10018-6505. TEL 212-967-9760. FAX 212-967-7101) Ed. Richard Stratton. adv. contact: Richard DiAntone. **Document type:** consumer publication.
    Description: Advocacy coverage of issues affecting prisoners and their families.

364   US   ISSN 1072-1037
PRISON MIRROR; The Prison Mirror. 1887. bi-m. $5 to prison inmates; others $15 (foreign $27). Minnesota Correctional Facility, Box 55, Stillwater, MN 55082-0055. TEL 612-779-2809. FAX 612-779-2788. Eds. James Reed, Gerard Koel. bk.rev. circ. 3,400. (tabloid format; reprint service avail. from UMI) **Document type:** newspaper.
    Description: Oldest continuously published prison newspaper in the United States.

365.97   CN   ISSN 1191-9434
PRISON NEWS SERVICE. bi-m. Can.$10 to individuals; institutions Can.$25. P S C Publishers, 145 Kings St., W., Ste. 601, Toronto, ON M5H 1J8, Canada. E-mail: sage!pns@noc.tor.hookup.net. (Subscr. to: Box 5052, Sta. A, Toronto, ON M5W 1W4, Canada) (tabloid format) **Indexed:** Alt.Press Ind. **Document type:** newspaper.
    Description: Publishes first-hand news, letters, and commentary on prisoners' human and civil rights.

365   UK
PRISON REFORM TRUST. ANNUAL LECTURE. a. Prison Reform Trust, 15 Northburgh St., London EC1V OAH, England. TEL 44-171-251-5070. FAX 44-171-251-5076. **Document type:** bulletin.

365   UK   ISSN 0953-4377
PRISON REPORT. 1988. q. £20 (Europe £25; rest of world £30) to individuals; institutions £30 (Europe £35; rest of world £40) (effective 1997). Prison Reform Trust, 15 Northburgh St., London EC1V OAH, England. TEL 44-171-251-5070. FAX 44-171-251-5076. Ed. Stephen Shaw. R&P contact: Diana Ruthven. adv. contact: Diana Ruthven. bk.rev. circ. 2,000. **Document type:** newsletter.

CRIMINOLOGY AND LAW ENFORCEMENT

365   UK   ISSN 0300-3558
HV7231
PRISON SERVICE JOURNAL. 1960; N.S. 1971. q. £2 (foreign £2.50) (effective 1997 & 1998). H M Prison Service College, Newbold Rd., Rugby, Warwickshire CV23 OTN, England. TEL 44-1759-372447. FAX 44-1759-371206. Ed. Tim Newell. R&P contact: Anita Bentley. adv. contact: Anita Bentley. bk.rev.; illus.; circ. 7,000 (controlled). (also avail. in microform from UMI) **Indexed:** Abstr.Crim.& Pen., ASSIA, CJPI, Euro.LJI, LJI. **Document type:** academic/scholarly publication, government publication.
—BLDSC (6617.059000); UMI; UnCover. **CCC.**

364   UK   ISSN 0264-1461
PRISON SERVICE NEWS. 1982. m. £12. H.M. Prison Service, Rm. 302, Cleland House, Page St., London SW1P 4LN, England. TEL 44-171-217-6575. FAX 44-171-828-8692. Ed. Philip Wisdom. R&P contact: Philip Wisdom. adv. contact: T.G. Scott. bk.rev.; circ. 30,000 (controlled). pp./issue: 24. (back issues avail.) **Document type:** government publication.
Description: Contains news and features of interest to staff of Her Majesty's Prison Service personnel and their families.

364   323.4   US
PRISONERS AND THE LAW. 1985. 3 base vols. (plus s-a. updates). $495. Clark - Boardman - Callaghan, 375 Hudson St., New York, NY 10014. TEL 212-929-7500; 800-422-2101. FAX 212-924-0460. Ed. Ira P. Robbins.
Description: Covers critical issues involving prisoners' rights.

365   323.4   US
PRISONERS' ASSISTANCE DIRECTORY. irreg., 11th ed., 1996. $30. American Civil Liberties Union Foundation, c/o, National Prison Project, 1875 Connecticut Ave., N.W., Ste. 410, Washington, DC 20009. TEL 202-234-4830. FAX 202-234-4890. Ed. Jenni Gainsborough. **Document type:** directory.
Description: Identifies and describes national, state and local organizations and agencies that provide legal, library, AIDS, family support, and ex-offender aid and assistance to prisoners.

364   US
PRISONERS IN (YEAR). (Subseries of: National Crime Victimization Survey Report) 1971. a. free. U.S. Department of Justice, Bureau of Justice Statistics, 633 Indiana Ave., N.W., 11th Fl., Washington, DC 20531. (Orders to: Superintendent of Documents, U.S. Government Printing Office, Box 371954, Pittsburgh, PA 15250-7954. TEL 202-512-1800. FAX 202-512-2250) stat. circ. 15,000. **Document type:** government publication.

364   US
PRIVATE INVESTIGATOR'S CONNECTION. bi-m. $85. (National Association of Investigative Specialists) Thomas Publishing (Austin), Box 33244, Austin, TX 78764. TEL 512-832-0355. circ. 1,000. (back issues avail.)
Formerly: Tracer.
Description: News for private investigative personnel.

364   US
THE PRO-GRAM. m. Federal Criminal Investigators Association, 2200 Wilson Blvd., Ste. 102-219, Arlington, VA 22201-3324. TEL 512-229-5601. **Document type:** newsletter.

365   US   ISSN 0732-0965
HV9304
PROBATION AND PAROLE DIRECTORY. triennial. $60 to non-members; members $48. American Correctional Association, 4380 Forbes Blvd., Lanham, MD 20706-4322. TEL 301-918-1800. Ed. Glenda Beal. R&P contact: Gabriella Daley. adv. contact: Marge Restivo. (also avail. in microfiche from CIS) **Document type:** directory.

PROBATION AND PAROLE LAW REPORTS. see LAW — Judicial Systems

365   UK   ISSN 0264-5505
PROBATION JOURNAL. 1913. q. £8. National Association of Probation Officers, 3-4 Chivalry Rd., Battersea, London SW11 1HT, England. TEL 44-171-223-4887. Ed. Nigel Stone. adv.; bk.rev. circ. 7,200. **Indexed:** Abstr.Crim.& Pen., Adol.Ment.Hlth.Abstr., ASSIA, Crim.Just.Abstr., Euro.LJI, LJI. **Document type:** academic/scholarly publication.
—BLDSC (6617.243000); SWETS.
Formerly: Probation (ISSN 0048-539X)

364   AT
PROBATION OFFICER. 1960. q. Aus.$10. Probation Officers and Volunteers in Corrections Inc., G.P.O. Box 634E, Melbourne, Vic. 3001, Australia. TEL 61-3-4160408. FAX 61-3-4162362. Ed. Cleaone Sandford. bk.rev. circ. 1,000. **Indexed:** Abstr.Crim.& Pen.
Description: Support magazine for volunteers in Community Corrections.

364   NE   ISSN 0165-0076
PROCES; maandblad voor berechting en reclassering. m. fl.115. Barneveldse Drukkerij en Uitgeverij B.V., P.O. Box 67, 3770 AB Barneveld, Netherlands. TEL 31-3420-94911. FAX 31-3420-13141. (Editorial addr.: Zilvermeeuwhof 1, 5672 ED Nuenen, Netherlands. TEL 31-40-833856) Ed. K. de Graaf. adv. circ. 500. **Indexed:** Abstr.Crim.& Pen., Int.Polit.Sci.Abstr.
—SWETS.
Description: Penal law enforcement and probation.

PROFESSIONAL TRAINING SERIES. see POLITICAL SCIENCE — Civil Rights

364   US
PROSECUTOR'S BRIEF. 1975. q. $25. California District Attorneys Association, 731 K St., Ste. 300, Sacramento, CA 95814-3402. TEL 916-443-2017. FAX 916-443-0540. R&P contact: Cat Karnezis. adv.; bk.rev.; cum.index every 10 yrs. circ. 4,600. (back issues avail.)
Description: Covers issues that affect California prosecutors.

PROTECTING CHILDREN. see SOCIAL SERVICES AND WELFARE

364   GW   ISSN 0256-4319
PROTECTOR. 1973. 9/yr. DM.180 (effective 1997). I G T Informationsgesellschaft Technik GmbH, Albert-Schweitzer-Str. 64, 81735 Munich, Germany. TEL 49-89-67099326. FAX 49-89-6376708. Ed. Lothar Zobel; Pub. Lothar Zobel. adv.: B&W page DM.3245; trim 175 x 265; adv. contact: Michaela Richter. illus.; tr.lit. circ. 6,700. **Document type:** bulletin.

363.2   378   PL   ISSN 0867-5708
PRZEGLAD POLICYJNY. (Text in Polish; summaries in English, German) 1991. q. Wydawnictwo Wyzszej Szkoly Policyjnej, Ul. K. Swierczewskiego 111, 12-101 Szczytno, Poland. TEL 43221. FAX 42610. **Document type:** academic/scholarly publication.
Description: Covers police education, police history, police law, and criminology.

PSYCHOLOGY, CRIME AND LAW. see PSYCHOLOGY

364   US   ISSN 1094-4613
PUBLIC SAFETY PERSONNEL UPDATE. m. $95. Nyper Publications, Box 662, Latham, NY 12110. TEL 518-786-1654. FAX 518-456-8582. URL: http://www.nyper.com. Ed. Harvey Randall. (back issues avail.) **Document type:** newsletter.
Formerly: Law Enforcement Personnel Notes (ISSN 1071-7412)
Description: Discusses legal developments concerning police and corrections personnel.

PUNGOLO; periodico dei giovani. see CHILDREN AND YOUTH — For

365   US
QUESTION MARK. 1973. m. $8. (Massachusetts Correctional Institution, Norfolk Resident Council) Norfolk Inmate Council Publishing, Box 43, Norfolk, MA 02056-0043. TEL 617-668-0800. FAX 617-727-1480. Ed. Ralph Carey. adv.; bk.rev. circ. 1,500. (tabloid format)
Formerly: Colony (ISSN 0045-740X)

363.2   CN   ISSN 0033-6858
R C M P QUARTERLY/G R C REVUE TRIMESTRIELLE. (Editions in English and French) 1933. q. Can.$5. Royal Canadian Mounted Police, Ottawa, Ont. K1A 0R2, Canada. TEL 613-998-6317. Ed. Sgt. P.T. Hughes. bk.rev.; illus. circ. 22,500. **Indexed:** Abstr.Crim.& Pen.

R P U PAPERS. see PUBLIC ADMINISTRATION

362.7   UK
RAINER FOUNDATION. ANNUAL REPORT. 1876. a. free. Rainer Foundation, 89 Blackheath Hill, London SE10 8TJ, England. Ed. J. Longley. circ. 5,000. **Document type:** corporate report.
Formerly: London Police Court Mission. Annual Report.

364   IT
RASSEGNA ITALIANA DI CRIMINOLOGIA. 1990. q. Lit.90000 (foreign Lit.135000) (effective 1997). Casa Editrice Dott. A. Giuffre, Via Busto Arsizio 40, 20151 Milan, Italy. TEL 39-2-38089200. FAX 39-2-38009582. Ed. G. Canepa. **Indexed:** Crim.Just.Abstr.

364   IT   ISSN 0392-7156
RASSEGNA PENITENZIARIA E CRIMINOLOGICA. (Text in Italian; summaries in English, French, German) 1931. 3/yr. L.50000 (foreign L.78000) (effective 1995). Ministero di Grazia e Giustizia, Dipartimento dell'Amministrazione Penitenziaria, Via Silvestri 252 00164 Rome, Italy. TEL 39-6-66156221. FAX 39-6-66161736. (Subscr. to: Istituto Poligrafico e Zecca dello Stato, 10 Piazza Verdi, 00198 Rome, Italy. TEL 39-6-85081. FAX 39-6-85082517) Ed. Marcello Marinari. adv.; bk.rev.; abstr.; bibl.; charts; index. circ. 2,500. **Document type:** academic/scholarly publication, government publication.
Formed by the 1978 merger of: Quaderni di Criminologia Clinica (ISSN 0033-4928); Rassegna di Studi Penitenziari (ISSN 0033-9628); Which was formerly (until 1951): Rivista di Diritto Penitenziario
Description: Collection of juridical, penitentiary, psychological and pedagogical writings with regard to life of the prisoner, his treatment and insertion in society.

REAL CRIME BOOK DIGEST. see PUBLISHING AND BOOK TRADE

364   SZ   ISSN 0034-138X
RECHTSPRECHUNG IN STRAFSACHEN. (Text in French and German) q. 44 SFr. (foreign 48 SFr.) (effective 1997). (Schweizerische Kriminalistische Gesellschaft) Staempfli AG, Hallerstr. 7-9, CH-3012 Bern, Switzerland. TEL 41-31-3006666. FAX 41-31-3006699. circ. 2,400. **Document type:** bulletin.
—CCC.

RED FEMINISTA LATINOAMERICANA Y DEL CARIBE CONTRA LA VIOLENCIA DOMESTICA Y SEXUAL. BOLETIN. see WOMEN'S STUDIES

REGENCY INTERNATIONAL DIRECTORY; of private investigators, process servers, private detectives & debt collecting agencies. see BUSINESS AND ECONOMICS — Trade And Industrial Directories

364   365   AT   ISSN 0157-3470
RELEASE. 1969. q. Aus.$10 (foreign Aus.$25). Offenders Aid & Rehabilitation Services of South Australia Inc., 234 Sturt St., Adelaide, S.A. 5000, Australia. TEL 61-8-82124911. FAX 61-8-2125344. Ed. Leigh Garrett. R&P contact Alex Soria. adv.; bk.rev.; illus. circ. 3,500. **Document type:** newsletter.

363.2   CC
RENMIN JINGCHA/PEOPLE'S POLICE. (Text in Chinese) m. Shanghai Shi Gong'an Ju, 21 Shaoxing Lu, Shanghai 200020, People's Republic of China. TEL 4373247. Ed. Zhou Guangwen.

365   MF
REPORT ON THE TREATMENT OF OFFENDERS IN MAURITIUS; PART 1: PRISONS SERVICE. (Text in English) a. Government Printing Office, Elizabeth II Ave., Port Louis, Mauritius. (Subscr. to: Government Printing Office, La Tour Koenig, Pointe aux Sables, Port Louis, Mauritius. TEL 230-2345294. FAX 230-2084011) **Document type:** government publication.

CRIMINOLOGY AND LAW ENFORCEMENT

364 — MF
REPORT ON THE TREATMENT OF OFFENDERS IN MAURITIUS; PART 2: PROBATION SERVICE. (Text in English) a. Government Printing Office, Elizabeth II Ave., Port Louis, Mauritius. (Subscr. to: Government Printing Office, La Tour Koenig, Pointe aux Sables, Port Louis, Mauritius. TEL 230-2345294. FAX 230-2084011) **Document type:** government publication.

364 — US — ISSN 1042-4636
RESEARCH AND BIBLIOGRAPHICAL GUIDES IN CRIMINAL JUSTICE. 1989. irreg. price varies. Greenwood Press, Inc. (Subsidiary of: Greenwood Publishing Group Inc.), 88 Post Rd. W., Box 5007, Westport, CT 06881-5007. TEL 203-226-3571. FAX 203-222-1502. **Document type:** monographic series.

364 — US
RESEARCH IN CRIMINOLOGY. 1986. irreg. price varies. Springer-Verlag, 175 Fifth Ave., New York, NY 10010. TEL 212-460-1500. FAX 212-473-6272. (Also: Berlin, Heidelberg, Tokyo and Vienna) (reprint service avail. from ISI)

364 — XV — ISSN 0034-690X
REVIJA ZA KRIMINALISTIKO IN KRIMINOLOGIJO. (Text in Slovenian; summaries in English) 1950. q. $30 to individuals; institutions $40 (effective 1995). Ministerstvo za Notranje Zadeve Republike Slovenije, Stefanova 2, 61000 Ljubljana, Slovenia. TEL 386-61-1251400. FAX 388-61-214330. Eds. Anton Dvorsek, Darko Maver. bk.rev.; abstr.; bibl.; charts; stat.; index. circ. 620. **Indexed:** Abstr.Crim.& Pen., Crim.Just.Abstr.
Description: Examines juvenile delinquency, criminal justice, juvenile justice, social work, and forensic sciences.

365 — AG — ISSN 0325-9501
K19
REVISTA ARGENTINA DE CIENCIAS PENALES. 1975. Editorial Plus Ultra, Callao 575, 1022 Buenos Aires, Argentina. Ed. Ricardo Levene.

636.2 — SP
REVISTA CIENCIA POLICIAL. bi-m. 2400 ptas. to non-members (foreign 3000 ptas.) (effective 1997). Direccion General de la Policia, Instituto de Estudios de la Policia, Seccion de Documentacion y Publicaciones, C. Rafael Calvo, 33, 3a pl., 28010 Madrid, Spain. TEL 34-1-4351720. **Document type:** government publication.
Description: Provides technical information on police subjects.

364 — CL — ISSN 0716-792X
REVISTA DE CIENCIAS PENALES.* vol.30, 1971. s-a. Instituto de Ciencias Penales, Huerfanos 1147, Oficina 546, Santiago de Chile, Chile. Ed. Juan Bustos. bk.rev.; bibl.

364 — CK — ISSN 0121-0483
K4
REVISTA DE DERECHO PENAL Y CRIMINOLOGIA. 1977. 3/yr. Col.5000 per no. (effective Jan. 1993). Universidad Externado do Colombia, Instituto de Ciencias Penales y Criminologia, Apdo. Aereo 034141, Calle 12, No. 0-46 Este, Bogota, Colombia. TEL 341-2610. FAX 2843769. Ed. Efrain Lizcano C. adv.

365 — SP — ISSN 0210-6035
REVISTA DE ESTUDIOS PENITENCIARIOS. N.S. 1986. s-a. 760 ptas. per no. (foreign 942 ptas.) (effective 1996). Ministerio de Justicia e Interior, Centro de Publicaciones, Secretaria General Tecnica, Gran Via, 76-8, 28013 Madrid, Spain. TEL 547-54-22. FAX 559-29-48. **Document type:** government publication.
—CINDOC.

363.2 — SP
REVISTA INTERNACIONAL DE POLICIA CRIMINAL. 1954. bi-m. 1442 ptas. (foreign 1731 ptas.) (effective 1996). Direccion General de la Policia, Instituto de Estudios de la Policia, C. Rafael Calvo, 33, 3a pl., 28071 Madrid, Spain. TEL 34-1-3223329. **Document type:** government publication.

REVUE DE DROIT PENAL ET DE CRIMINOLOGIE. see *LAW — Criminal Law*

363.2 — FR — ISSN 0035-1237
HV7551
REVUE DE LA POLICE NATIONALE. 1957. q. free. Ministere de l'Interieur, Service d'Information et de Relations Publiques, Place Beauveau, 75800 Paris, France. TEL 45-22-90-90. Ed. Michel Hainque. bk.rev.; abstr.; bibl.; charts; illus.; stat.

364 365 — FR — ISSN 0035-1733
K21
REVUE DE SCIENCE CRIMINELLE ET DE DROIT PENAL COMPARE. 1936. q. 610 F. (foreign 750 F.) (effective 1996). (Universite de Paris II - Universite de Droit, d'Economie et des Sciences Sociales, Institut de Droit Compare) Editions Sirey, 11 rue Soufflot, 75240 Paris Cedex 05, France. TEL 40-51-54-54. FAX 45-87-37-48. TELEX 206 446 F. (Subscr. to: Diffusion Dalloz, 35 rue Tournefort, 75240 Paris Cedex 05, France. TEL 40-51-54-35) bk.rev.; abstr.; bibl.; tr.lit.; index. (reprint service avail. from SCH) **Indexed:** Abstr.Crim.& Pen., Crim.Just.Abstr., ELLIS, IBR. **Document type:** academic/scholarly publication.
—BLDSC (7947.600000); SWETS. **CCC.**

364 — SZ
REVUE I P A. 6/yr. International Police Association, Chemin de l'Epine, CH-1055 Froideville, Switzerland. TEL 021-8812627. Ed. Maurice Gehri. circ. 8,000.

364 — SZ — ISSN 0035-3329
HV6002
REVUE INTERNATIONALE DE CRIMINOLOGIE ET DE POLICE TECHNIQUE. 1947. q. 120 SFr. Marcel Meichtry Editions, Chemin de la Caroline 26, CH-1213 Petit-Lancy, Switzerland. TEL 41-22-8798820. FAX 41-22-8798825. E-mail: revue_polytech@mail.dotcom.fr. Ed. Michel Giannoni. R&P contact: Michel Giannoni. adv. contact: Andre Almy. bk.rev.; bibl.; charts; illus.; index, cum.index: 1947-1961; circ. 1,500 (controlled). (reprint service avail. from SCH) **Indexed:** Abstr.Crim.& Pen., Chem.Abstr., Crim.Just.Abstr., Psychol.Abstr. (1983-). **Document type:** trade publication.
—BLDSC (7924.570000); SWETS. **CCC.**
Formerly (until 1953): Revue de Criminologie et de Police Technique.

363.2 — FR — ISSN 0035-3396
REVUE INTERNATIONALE DE POLICE CRIMINELLE. English edition: International Criminal Police Review (ISSN 0367-729X); Spanish edition: Revista Internacional de Policia Criminal (ISSN 0255-4321); Arabic edition: Al-Majallah al-Duwaliyyah lil-Shurtah al-Jina'iyyah (ISSN 0255-2752) (Editions in Arabic, English, French, Spanish) 1946. 6/yr. 180 F. (effective 1997). International Criminal Police Organization (Interpol), Secretariat General - Organisation Internationale de Police Criminelle (Interpol), 200 quai Charles de Gaulle, 69006 Lyon, France. TEL 33-4-72447000. FAX 33-4-72447163. TELEX OIPC 301987F. Ed. R.E. Kendall. R&P contact: V. Razafindranaly. TEL 33-4-72447255. bk.rev.; bibl.; charts; illus. circ. 7,000. **Indexed:** Crim.Just.Abstr., Pt.de Rep. **Document type:** academic/scholarly publication.
Refereed Serial

REVUE PENITENTIAIRE ET DE DROIT PENAL. see *LAW*

363.24 614.19 — UK — ISSN 0951-645X
RIDGE DETAIL IN NATURE. 1979. a. $5. Fingerprint Society, Merseyside Police, Fingerprint Bureau, Canning Pl., Liverpool L1 8JX, England. (Subscr. to: The Fingerprint Society, Vivienne Galloway, 5 Slate Close, Glenfield, Leics. LE3 8QQ, England) Ed. John Berry. circ. 100. **Document type:** trade publication.

363.2 — IT — ISSN 0035-6476
RIVISTA DI POLIZIA; rassegna di dottrina tecnica e legislazione. 1947. m. L.15000. Via Mazzocchi 175, Santa Maria Capua Vetere (Caserta), Italy. bk.rev.; abstr.

363.2 — IT — ISSN 0394-834X
RIVISTA GIURIDICA DI POLIZIA LOCALE; bimestrale di dottrina, giurisprudenza e legislazione. 1984. bi-m. L.180000 (effective 1994). Maggioli Editore, Viale Vespucci 12-n, Casella Postale 290, 47037 Rimini, Italy. TEL 0541-626777. FAX 0541-622020. Ed.Bd. adv.: B&W page L.1200000, color page L.1950000; trim 115 x 195.

365 — US
ROCKETEER.* 1976. m. free. Missouri Training Center for Men, Box 7, Moberly, MO 65270. TEL 816-263-3778. Ed. Bill Caudel. circ. 2,700 (controlled). (tabloid format)
Former titles: Inmate Free Press; Rocketeer (ISSN 0035-7502)

364 — NE — ISSN 0920-5128
S E C; tijdschrift over samenleving en criminaliteitspreventie. 1986. bi-m. free. Ministerie van Justitie, Postbus 20301, 2500 EH The Hague, Netherlands. TEL 31-70-3706740. FAX 31-70-3707916. (Dist. by: S D U Uitgeverij, Postbus 20014, 2500 EA The Hague, Netherlands. TEL 31-70-3789538. FAX 31-70-3838151) bk.rev.; bibl.; illus.; index. (back issues avail.) **Document type:** government publication.
Description: Contains articles about crime prevention, including residential burglary, designed to inform about and stimulate crime prevention projects.

364.4 — US — ISSN 1062-2365
S.W.A.T. MAGAZINE.* (Special Weapons and Tactics); the magazine for prepared Americans. 1982. 9/yr. $26.95 (foreign $36.95). Larry Flynt Publications, Inc., 8484 Wilshire Blvd., Ste. 900, Beverly Hills, CA 90211-3227. TEL 310-858-7100. FAX 310-274-7985. Ed. Denny Hansen. adv.; bk.rev. circ. 80,500.
Description: Covers weapons and police equipment for special tactical duty use.

343 — US
SAGE CRIMINAL JUSTICE SYSTEMS SERIES. 1972. irreg., Jul. 1993. $21.95 (hardcover edition $46) (effective 1996). Sage Publications, Inc., 2455 Teller Rd., Thousand Oaks, CA 91320. TEL 805-499-0721. FAX 805-499-0871. E-mail: libraries@sagepub.com; URL: http://www.sagepub.com. (Overseas subscr. to: Sage Publications Ltd., 6 Bonhill St., London EC2A 4PU, England; Sage Publications India Pvt. Ltd., P.O. Box 4215, New Delhi 110 048, India) Ed.Bd. (back issues avail.) **Document type:** monographic series.

364 — NE — ISSN 0925-0530
SANCTIES; tijdschrift over straffen en maatregelen. 1980. bi-m. fl.150 (effective 1996). Gouda Quint B.V. (Subsidiary of: Wolters Kluwer N.V.), Postbus 1148, 6801 MK Arnhem, Netherlands. (Dist. by: Libresso Distribution Centre, P.O. Box 23, 7400 GA Deventer, Netherlands. TEL 31-570-633155. FAX 31-570-633834) **Document type:** academic/scholarly publication.
Formerly (until 1990): Penitentiaire Informatie (ISSN 0166-610X)
Description: Publishes scholarly studies on issues and developments in criminal law, and documentary information on penal law enforcement, including case law and circulars.

364 — CN — ISSN 0316-4209
SCARLET & GOLD. 1919. a. Can.$10. (Veterans of Royal Canadian Mounted Police, Vancouver Division) Scarlet & Gold Enterprises, 1215 Alder Bay Walk, Vancouver, BC V6H 3T6, Canada. TEL 604-738-4423. Ed. J. Murphy. adv.; bk.rev. circ. 2,500. (back issues avail.) **Document type:** bulletin.
Description: Articles about the mounted police, written mainly by veterans.

365 — SZ — ISSN 0036-7893
SCHWEIZERISCHE ZEITSCHRIFT FUER STRAFRECHT/REVUE PENALE SUISSE/RIVISTA PENALE SVIZZERA. (Text in French, German, Italian) 1888. q. 108 SFr. Staempfli AG, Hallerstr. 7-9, CH-3012 Bern, Switzerland. TEL 41-31-3006666. FAX 41-31-3006699. Eds. Niklaus Schmid, Jean Gauthier. adv.; bk.rev.; bibl.; index. circ. 1,300. **Indexed:** Abstr.Crim.& Pen. **Document type:** bulletin.
—SWETS. **CCC.**

CRIMINOLOGY AND LAW ENFORCEMENT

343   US   ISSN 0037-0193
KF9630.A59
SEARCH AND SEIZURE BULLETIN. 1964. m. $62. Quinlan Publishing Co., Inc., 23 Drydock Ave., 2nd Fl., Boston, MA 02210-2387. TEL 617-542-0048; 800-229-2084. FAX 617-345-9646. cum.index. (looseleaf format; also avail. in microform from UMI; back issues avail.; reprint service avail. from UMI) **Indexed:** CJPI. **Document type:** newsletter.
—UMI. **CCC.**
   Description: Summarizes current cases involving search and seizure. For non-lawyer law enforcement personnel.

SECURE SIGNALS. see COMMUNICATIONS — Television And Cable

364.4   UK
SECURITECH; the international guide to security equipment. (Text in English, French, Italian, Spanish) 1972. a. £64.90 (overseas $103.85) (effective 1997). Argus Business Media Ltd. (Subsidiary of: D M G Exhibitions Group Ltd.), Queensway House, 2 Queensway, Redhill, Surrey RH1 1QS, England. TEL 44-1737-768611. FAX 44-1737-761685. circ. 8,000. **Document type:** directory.
   Former titles: Securitech Europe; Securitech (ISSN 0307-7780)
   Description: Lists equipment and services for the security industry.

SECURITY INTELLIGENCE. see POLITICAL SCIENCE

365   BL
SERIE ESTUDOS PENITENCIARIOS. irreg. Cortez e Moraes Ltda., Rua Ministro Godoy 1002, 05015 Sao Paulo, Brazil. bibl.

363.2   SA   ISSN 1015-2385
SERVAMUS. (Text in Dutch and English) 1907. m. R.59.64. (South African Police Service) S A R P Uitgewers, Postbus 828, Pretoria 0001, South Africa. TEL 27-12-3220557. Ed. David J. Pieterse. R&P contact: Johan Heijer. adv. contact: Sporie Raklame. bk.rev.; illus. circ. 60,000. **Document type:** trade publication.
   Former titles (until Apr. 1979): S A P Magazine; S A R P (ISSN 0036-4819); (until 1964): Justitie; (until 1961): Nongqai.
   Refereed Serial

SHARING TIMES. see SOCIOLOGY

364   US
SHEPARD'S EXPERT AND SCIENTIFIC EVIDENCE QUARTERLY. (Part of the Evidence Series) 1994. q. $195. Shepard's - McGraw-Hill, Inc., Box 35300, Colorado Springs, CO 80935-3530. TEL 800-525-2474. Ed.Bd. (back issues avail.) **Document type:** trade publication.

364   US   ISSN 0192-0634
HV8145.W2
SHERIFF & POLICE REPORTER.* 1938. q. $15. 1506 Brigman Ave., No. A, Jefferson, IN 47130-4710. Ed. Patrick Murphy. adv.; bk.rev. circ. 5,000. **Document type:** trade publication.

363.2   US   ISSN 1070-8170
HV7551
SHERIFF MAGAZINE. 1948. bi-m. $25 to non-members (effective 1996). National Sheriffs' Association, 1450 Duke St., Alexandria, VA 22314-3490. TEL 703-836-7827. FAX 703-683-6541. Ed. Suzanne Kitts. R&P contact: Suzanne Kitts. adv. contact: David Strigel. charts; illus.; stat.; index. circ. 22,000. **Indexed:** CJPI, Crim.Just.Abstr. **Document type:** trade publication.
—UMI; UnCover.
   Formerly (until 1991): National Sheriff (ISSN 0028-016X)

363.2   TS
AL-SHURTI/POLICEMAN. (Supplement avail.: Al-Shurti al-Saghir - Young Policeman) (Text in Arabic) 1989. m. exchange basis. General Administration for Sharjah Police, Public Relations Department, P.O. Box 29, Sharjah, United Arab Emirates. TEL 541664. FAX 541595. TELEX 69611 SHURTAH EM. circ. 2,000.
   Description: Covers local police affairs.

364   IT
SICUREZZA E TERRITORIO; per una politica di prevenzione della criminalita. bi-m. L.10000 per no. Societa Editorial L' Angelo Azzurro, Via Barberia 4, 40123 Bologna, Italy. TEL 051-291234.

363.2   US   ISSN 0037-5012
SIGNAL 8-2. 1958. s-a. Port Authority of New York and New Jersey, Police Division, J.S.T.C., One Path Plaza, Jersey City, NJ 07306. TEL 201-963-7111. Ed. Sgt. Paul Magda. illus.; stat.

364   II   ISSN 0037-7716
HV9397   CODEN: SDEFDL
SOCIAL DEFENCE; a quarterly review of policies and practices in the field of prevention of crime and treatment of offenders. (Text in English) 1961. q. Rs.60($31.60) Government of India, Department of Publications, Civil Lines, Delhi 110 054, India. Ed. Hira Singh. adv.; bk.rev.; bibl.; stat. circ. 500. **Indexed:** Crim.Just.Abstr., Psychol.Abstr. **Document type:** government publication.
—BLDSC (8318.077000).

SOCIAL JUSTICE; a journal of crime, conflict and world order. see POLITICAL SCIENCE — International Relations

SOCIAL PATHOLOGY; a journal of reviews. see SOCIOLOGY

364.12   US   ISSN 0038-0008
SOCIETY OF PROFESSIONAL INVESTIGATORS. BULLETIN.* 1956. a. free to qualified personnel. Society of Professional Investigators, 85-04 Queens Midtown Expy., Elmhurst, NY 11373. TEL 718-335-3257. bk.rev. circ. 1,000. (processed) **Indexed:** Abstr.Crim.& Pen.

STATE CAPITALS. FAMILY RELATIONS. see PUBLIC ADMINISTRATION

364   US   ISSN 0090-3221
HV7277
STATE OF NEBRASKA UNIFORM CRIME REPORT. Cover title: Crime in Nebraska. 1972. a. free. Commission on Law Enforcement and Criminal Justice, Box 94946, Lincoln, NE 68509. Ed. Marilyn Keelan. charts; stat. circ. 1,500. **Document type:** government publication.

363.2   US   ISSN 0192-4222
STATE PEACE OFFICERS JOURNAL. q. $10 (free to qualified personnel). North American Publishing Company, Box 130155, Houston, TX 77219-0155. TEL 713-526-6425. Ed. Lois Pilant. circ. 20,000. (controlled). **Document type:** trade publication.
   Description: Covers a variety of administrative and technical topics of interest to law enforcement officers, corrections and criminal justice personnel.

STRAFVERTEIDIGER. see LAW

363.2   GW   ISSN 0585-4202
STREIFE. m. (Innenministerium fuer Beschaeftige der Polizei in N R W) Vereinigte Verlagsanstalten GmbH, Hoeherweg 278, 40231 Duesseldorf, Germany. TEL 49-211-7357-0. FAX 49-211-7357223. circ. 24,000. **Document type:** bulletin.

364.4 345.85   NO
STUDIES ON CRIME AND CRIME PREVENTION. (Text in English) 1980. biennial. free. (Brottsfoerebyggande Raadet - National Swedish Council for Crime Prevention) Scandinavian University Press, P.O. Box 2959, N-0608 Oslo, Norway. E-mail: mail@scup.no; URL: http://www.scup.no. (US addr.: 875 Massachusetts Ave., Ste. 84, Cambridge, MA 02139. TEL 617-497-6515. FAX 617-354-6875) Ed. Artur Solarz.
   Formerly: National Council for Crime Prevention. Information Bulletin (ISSN 0281-336X)

364 345   NO   ISSN 1102-3937
STUDIES ON CRIME AND CRIME PREVENTION; bi-annual review. (Text in English) 1991. 2/yr. NOK 475 in Nordic countries; elsewhere $81 (effective 1997). (National Council for Crime Prevention (BRAA)) Scandinavian University Press, P.O. Box 2959 Toeyen, N-0608 Oslo, Norway. TEL 47-22-57-54-00. FAX 47-22-57-53-53. E-mail: subscription@scup.no; URL: http://www.scup.no. (US addr.: 875 Massachusetts Ave., Ste. 84, Cambridge, MA 02139. TEL 617-497-6515. FAX 617-354-6875) Eds. Artur Solarz, Viveka Engwall. **Indexed:** Abstr.Crim.& Pen., Crim.Just.Abstr., Psychol.Abstr. (1992-). **Document type:** academic/scholarly publication.
—BLDSC (8490.313500). **CCC.**
   Description: Deals with etiological and phenomenological aspects of both traditional and modern forms of crime, as well as with new ideas on crime prevention.

363.2   US   ISSN 1084-7316
SUBJECT TO DEBATE. 1987. m. $35 (effective 1994). Police Executive Research Forum, 1120 Connecticut Ave., N.W., Ste. 930, Washington, DC 20036. TEL 202-466-7820. FAX 202-466-7826. E-mail: ep-perf@intr.net; URL: http://www.policeforum.org. Ed. Ellen Painter. R&P contact: Ellen Painter. adv. contact: Ellen Painter. bk.rev. circ. 1,400. (back issues avail.) **Document type:** newsletter.
   Description: Informs police chiefs, municipal officials, criminal justice experts, community groups, and legislators about advances and issues in policing, public safety, and crime prevention.

363.2   PN
SUCESOS. w. newsstand price: $.25. Corporacion Universal de Informacion S.A., Urb. Obarrio, Calle 58, Ed. El Siglo, Apto. W, Panama 4, Panama. TEL 507-269-3311. FAX 507-2696954. Ed. Roberto Rodriguez. circ. 18,000 (paid). **Document type:** newspaper.
   Description: Sensationalist paper of police cases.

364   AT
SUMMARY JUSTICE S.A. 1983; N.S. 1993. 6/yr. Aus.$325 with updates. L B C Information Services, 50 Waterloo Rd., N. Ryde, N.S.W. 2113, Australia. TEL 61-2-99366444. FAX 61-2-98889706. TELEX ASBOOK 27995. (looseleaf format)
   Description: Provides South Australian practitioner with a comprehensive guide to the practice and procedure of the criminal jurisdiction of the Magistrates Courts.

SURVEILLANT; acquisitions and commentary for intelligence and security professionals. see POLITICAL SCIENCE — International Relations

363.2 340   SW   ISSN 1101-6817
SVENSKA NARKOTIKAPOLISFOERENINGEN. PUBLIKATION. Key Title: Publikation foer Svenska Narkotikapolisfoereningen. Variant title: Svenska Narkotikapolisfoereningens Tidning. 1988. q. SEK 50 membership (effective 1990). Svenska Narkotikapolisfoereningen (SNPF), P.O. Box 429, S-401 26 Goeteborg, Sweden.

364.4   US   ISSN 1041-8474
HV6431
T V I REPORT. (Terrorism Violence Insurgency); comprehensively reporting terrorism, violence, insurgency worldwide. 1979. q. $85 (foreign $110). T V I, Inc., Box 849, Klamath Falls, OR 97601. TEL 213-276-3378. Ed. Brian Michael Jenkins. bk.rev.; bibl.; charts; stat.; index. circ. 900.
—BLDSC (9076.727500).
   Formerly (until vol.6): T V I Journal.

364   US
TAKING SIDES: CLASHING VIEWS ON CONTROVERSIAL ISSUES IN CRIME AND CRIMINOLOGY. 1989. irreg., 2nd ed., 1991. $13.95. Dushkin Publishing Group Sluice Dock, Guilford, CT 06437-9989. TEL 203-453-4351. FAX 203-453-6000. Ed. Richard C. Monk; Pub. Mimi Egan. illus. **Document type:** academic/scholarly publication.

363.2   II   ISSN 0039-9329
TAMIL NADU POLICE JOURNAL. (Text in English) vol.3 1969. q. Rs.24. North Arcot Police Department, Police Training College, Vellore, North Arcot District Tamil Nadu, India. Ed. J. Vasudeva Bhat. adv.; bk.rev.; charts; illus.; stat. circ. 2,500.

364   GW   ISSN 0082-1934
TASCHENBUCH FUER KRIMINALISTEN. 1951. a. DM.23.50. Verlag Deutsche Polizeiliteratur GmbH, Forststr. 3a, 40721 Hilden, Germany. Ed. Manfred Teufel. adv.; bk.rev. circ. 1,000.

363.2   US   ISSN 1059-5082
TENNESSEE LAW ENFORCEMENT BULLETIN. 1977. bi-m. $85. M. Lee Smith Publishers LLC, 5201 Virginia Way, Box 5094, Brentwood, TN 67024-5094. TEL 615-373-7517; 800-274-6774. FAX 615-373-5183. Ed. Bill Parker; Pub. M. Lee Smith. index. **Document type:** bulletin.
   Description: Summarizes Tennessee legal developments of concern to law enforcement officials.

CRIMINOLOGY AND LAW ENFORCEMENT

363.2 US ISSN 0040-327X
TENNESSEE LAW ENFORCEMENT JOURNAL. 1955. q. $3. Tennessee Law Enforcement Officers Association, c/o Lt. J.P. Ruff, Box 139, Ellendale, TN 38029-0139. FAX 612-541-0435. Ed. Gail Van Horn. adv.; bk.rev.; charts; illus.; stat.; circ. 3,000 (controlled). **Document type:** trade publication.

364 US ISSN 0278-663X
HV6431
TERRORISM (MINNEAPOLIS). 1982. q. $45 (effective 1997 & 1998). J.L. Scherer, Ed. & Pub., 4900 18th Ave. S., Minneapolis, MN 55417. TEL 612-722-2947. stat. **Indexed:** Crim.Just.Abstr., Lang.& Lang.Behav.Abstr., PROMT. **Document type:** trade publication.
 Formerly (until 1986): Terrorism: An Annual Survey.
 Description: Contains information and statistics on terrorism. Includes special surveys and reports on terrorism and biographies.

TERRORISM AND POLITICAL VIOLENCE. see POLITICAL SCIENCE — International Relations

364.6 US ISSN 0095-1900
HV9274
TEXAS. DEPARTMENT OF CORRECTIONS. RESEARCH AND DEVELOPMENT DIVISION. RESEARCH REPORT. Key Title: Research Report - Texas Department of Corrections; Treatment Directorate, Research and Development Division. 1971. irreg., no.27, 1975. Department of Corrections, Research and Development Division, Huntsville, TX 77348. TEL 713-295-6371.

365 US
TEXAS JOURNAL OF CORRECTIONS. bi-m. $50 to non-members. Texas Corrections Association, 1033 La Posada Dr., Ste. 220, Austin, TX 78752-3880. TEL 512-454-8626. FAX 512-454-3036. E-mail: dseago@assnmgmt.com. Ed. Donna Seago. adv.: page $300. bk.rev. circ. 1,300. **Document type:** newsletter.

363.2 US ISSN 0040-442X
TEXAS LAWMAN; dedicated to all Texas peace officers. 1930. q. membership. Sheriffs' Association of Texas, Box 4488, Austin, TX 78765. TEL 512-445-5888. FAX 512-445-0228. Ed. Dolores Shirley. adv.; bk.rev.; illus. circ. 30,000.

364 UK ISSN 1362-4806
THEORETICAL CRIMINOLOGY. 1997. q. £32($51) to individuals; institutions £115($184) (effective 1998). Sage Publications Ltd., 6 Bonhill St., London EC2A 4PU, England. TEL 44-171-374-0645. FAX 44-171-374-8741. E-mail: market@sagepub.co.uk; URL: http://www.sagepub.co.uk/. Eds. Piers Beirne, Colin Sumner. adv. contact: Bernie Folan. bk.rev. **Document type:** academic/scholarly publication.
 —BLDSC (8814.556500).
 Description: Concerned with theories, concepts, narratives and myths of crime, criminal behavior, social deviance, criminal law, morality, justice and social regulation.

364 SW ISSN 0040-6821
TIDSKRIFT FOER KRIMINALVAARD. 1946. q. SEK 75 (effective 1996). Svenska Faangvaardssaellskapet, P.O. Box 236, S-101 24 Stockholm, Sweden. Ed.Bd. bk.rev.; bibl. circ. 1,200.

364 NE ISSN 0165-182X
HV6005
TIJDSCHRIFT VOOR CRIMINOLOGIE. 1959. q. fl.114 to individuals; institutions fl.168 (effective 1996). Gouda Quint B.V. (Subsidiary of: Wolters Kluwer N.V.), Postbus 1148, 6801 MK Arnhem, Netherlands. (Dist. by: Libresso Distribution Centre, P.O. Box 23, 7400 GA Deventer, Netherlands. TEL 31-570-633155. FAX 31-570-633834) Ed.Bd. adv.; bk.rev.; abstr.; charts; illus.; index; circ. 600 (controlled). **Indexed:** Abstr.Crim.& Pen., Excerp.Med. **Document type:** academic/scholarly publication. —SWETS.
 Formerly: Nederlands Tijdschrift voor Criminologie (ISSN 0028-2154)
 Description: Studies and abstracts on criminology.

363.2 NE ISSN 0165-0122
HET TIJDSCHRIFT VOOR DE POLITIE. vol.35, 1973. 10/yr. fl.119. Vuga Uitgeverij B.V., Postbus 16400, 2500 BK The Hague, Netherlands. TEL 31-70-3614011. FAX 31-70-36254688. Ed. N.H.E.V. Helten. adv.: B&W page fl.1245, color page fl.3130; trim 210 x 297. bk.rev.; charts; illus.; abstr. **Indexed:** Abstr.Crim.& Pen. **Document type:** trade publication.
 —BLDSC (8844.010000); SWETS.
 Description: Information on police science.

364.36 US ISSN 0733-6551
HV9104
TODAY'S DELINQUENT. 1982. a. $12. National Center for Juvenile Justice, 710 Fifth Ave., Pittsburgh, PA 15219. TEL 412-227-6950. Ed. Hunter Hurst. charts; stat. circ. 200.

364.4 US
TODAY'S POLICEMAN. 1960. q. $9. Towerhigh Publications Inc., Box 875108, Los Angeles, CA 90087. TEL 310-795-4010. Ed. Jayney Mack. adv. circ. 15,400. (tabloid format) **Document type:** trade publication.
 Description: Covers police work, crime prevention, the public and law enforcement.

364.33 US
TODAY'S YOUTH: AMERICA'S FUTURE; a periodic information brief. irreg. National Center for Juvenile Justice, 710 Fifth Ave., Pittsburgh, PA 15219-3000. TEL 412-227-6950. FAX 412-227-6955. charts; stat. **Document type:** bulletin.
 Description: Alerts readers to issues in juvenile justice and criminology.

364 US
TRACKING OFFENDERS (YEAR). (Subseries of: National Crime Victimization Survey Report) 1983. a. free. U.S. Department of Justice, Bureau of Justice Statistics, 633 Indiana Ave., N.W., 11th Fl., Washington, DC 20531. (Orders to: Superintendent of Documents, U.S. Government Printing Office, Box 371954, Pittsburgh, PA 15250-7954. TEL 202-512-1800. FAX 202-512-2250) circ. 17,000. (also avail. in microfiche) **Document type:** government publication.

344 US ISSN 0893-3030
KF2226.A3
TRAFFIC LAW REPORTS. 1987. m. $140.95 in U.S. and Canada; elsewhere $171 (effective 1997). Knehans-Miller Publications, Box 88, Warrenburg, MO 64093-0088. TEL 816-429-1102. Ed. Dane C. Miller; Pub. Jaclyn Miller. m. index, sep. a. cum.index. (looseleaf format) **Document type:** trade publication.
 Description: In-depth summaries, often with verbatim excerpts, and thorough subject and jurisdictional indexing of all federal and state appellate court decisions dealing with all aspects of traffic enforcement and administration.

TRANSNATIONAL ORGANIZED CRIME. see POLITICAL SCIENCE — International Relations

364 AT ISSN 0817-8542
TRENDS AND ISSUES IN CRIME AND CRIMINAL JUSTICE. 1986. 15/yr. Aus.$60. Australian Institute of Criminology, G.P.O. Box 2944, Canberra, A.C.T. 2601, Australia. TEL 61-6-2609256. FAX 61-6-2609260. E-mail: aicpress@aic.gov.au. Ed. Adam Graycar. **Document type:** monographic series.
 Incorporates part of (1990-1992): Homicides in Australia (ISSN 1038-6912)

364 US ISSN 1056-4160
HV6771.U6
TRENDS IN MONEY LAUNDERING.* irreg. Financial Crimes Enforcement Network, 207 Chain Bridge Rd., Vienna, VA 22182. TEL 703-516-0591.

364 US ISSN 1084-4791
HV6441
▼**TRENDS IN ORGANIZED CRIME.** 1995. q. $60 to individuals (foreign $92); institutions $120 (foreign $152) (effective 1997). (National Strategy Information Center) Transaction Publishers, Transaction Periodicals Consortium, Department 3092, Rutgers University, New Brunswick, NJ 08903. TEL 908-445-2280. FAX 908-445-3138. Ed.Bd. adv.: page $200; 5 1/4 x 8 1/2. circ. 300. (back issues avail.) **Document type:** academic/scholarly publication.
 Description: Provides information and analysis about international efforts to anticipate the development of organized crime activities and to devise strategies to counter them.

363.2 US
TRUE POLICE CASES.* bi-m. Globe Communications Corp. (New York), 3 E. 54th St., 15th Fl., New York, NY 10022-3108. TEL 800-472-7744. Ed. Dominick A. Merle.

364 US ISSN 0732-6688
HV8074
U S IDENTIFICATION MANUAL. 1976. base vol. (plus q. updates). $149 for base vol.; updates $72.50. Drivers License Guide Company, 1492 Oddstad Dr., Redwood City, CA 94063. TEL 415-369-4849.
 Description: Covers all classes of licenses and special licenses. Contains full front and back description, expiration, restrictions and license number coding.

364 US ISSN 0082-7592
HV6787
UNIFORM CRIME REPORTS FOR THE UNITED STATES. Cover title: Crime in the United States. Title varies: Uniform Crime Reports. a. (plus s-a. updates). price varies. U.S. Federal Bureau of Investigation, Uniform Crime Reporting Section, 1000 Custer Hollow Rd., Clarksburg, WV 26306. TEL 304-625-4995. (Dist. by: U.S. Government Printing Office, Superintendent of documents, Box 371954, Pittsburgh, PA 15250-7954. TEL 202-512-1800) **Document type:** government publication.
 —BLDSC (9090.666500); UMI.

364 UN ISSN 0082-8025
UNITED NATIONS CONGRESS ON THE PREVENTION OF CRIME AND THE TREATMENT OF OFFENDERS. REPORT. 1956. irreg. price varies. United Nations Publications, Sales and Marketing Section, Room DC2-0853, New York, NY 10017. TEL 212-963-8302; 800-253-9646. FAX 212-963-3489. E-mail: publications@un.org; URL: http://www.un.org/publications. (Or: Distribution and Sales Section, CH-1211 Geneva 10, Switzerland) (also avail. in microfiche)

364 UN ISSN 1020-1548
HV6024.5 CODEN: ISREFC
UNITED NATIONS INTERREGIONAL CRIME AND JUSTICE RESEARCH INSTITUTE. ISSUES AND REPORTS SERIES/INSTITUTE INTERREGIONAL DE RECHERCHE DES NATIONS UNIES SUR LA CRIMINALITE ET LA JUSTICE. THEMES ET RAPPORTS SERIE. (Text in English, French) 1994. irreg., latest no.5. free. United Nations Interregional Crime and Justice Research Institute - Institute Interregional de Recherche des Nations Unies sur la Criminalite et la Justice, Via Giulia 52, 00186 Rome, Italy. TEL 06-6877437. FAX 06-6892638. E-mail: unicri.org@agora.stm.it. **Document type:** monographic series, academic/scholarly publication.
 Description: Explores criminal justice issues throughout the world.

364 UN
UNITED NATIONS INTERREGIONAL CRIME AND JUSTICE RESEARCH INSTITUTE. PUBLICATION. 1969. irreg., latest no.55. United Nations Interregional Crime and Justice Research Institute - Institut Interregional de Recherche des Nations Unies sur la Criminalite et la Justice, Via Giulia 52, 00186 Rome, Italy. TEL 06-6877437. FAX 06-6892638. E-mail: unicri.org@agora.stm.it. circ. 2,000. **Document type:** monographic series.
 Formerly: United Nations Social Defence Research Institute. Publication.

CRIMINOLOGY AND LAW ENFORCEMENT

364.164 US ISSN 0273-5032
HV6635
U.S. BUREAU OF ALCOHOL, TOBACCO AND FIREARMS. EXPLOSIVES INCIDENTS; annual report. 1977. a. U.S. Bureau of Alcohol, Tobacco & Firearms, 12th & Pennsylvania Ave., N.W., Washington, DC 20224. TEL 202-566-7777.

364 US
U.S. DEPARTMENT OF JUSTICE. OFFICE OF JUVENILE JUSTICE AND DELINQUENCY PREVENTION. ANNUAL REPORT. a. U.S. Department of Justice, Office of Juvenile Justice and Delinquency Prevention, 633 Indiana Ave., N.W., Washington, DC 20531. TEL 202-307-5911. (Subscr. to: Superintendent of Documents, U.S. Government Printing Office, Box 317954, Pittsburgh, PA 15250-7954. TEL 202-512-1800. FAX 202-512-2250) **Document type**: government publication.

364.1 US
HV8059
U.S. FEDERAL BUREAU OF INVESTIGATION. (YEAR) BOMBING INCIDENTS. 1970. a. U.S. Federal Bureau of Investigation, Explosives Unit, Bomb Data Center, 935 Pennsylvania Ave., N.W., Washington, DC 20535-0001. TEL 202-324-3000. **Document type**: government publication.
 Supersedes (in 1994): U.S. Federal Bureau of Investigation. Bomb Summary (ISSN 0360-3245)
 Description: Compiles bombings in the U.S. over the past year.

353 US ISSN 0272-8974
HV7245
U.S. URBAN INITIATIVES ANTI-CRIME PROGRAM. ANNUAL REPORT TO CONGRESS. Key Title: Annual Report to Congress - Urban Initiatives Anti-Crime Program. 1980. a. U.S. Department of Housing and Urban Development, Urban Initiatives Anti-Crime Program, 451 Seventh St., S.W., Washington, DC 20410. TEL 202-655-4000. (Subscr. to: HUD User, Box 280, Germantown, MD 20874-0280. TEL 800-245-2691) **Document type**: government publication.

364 VE ISSN 0507-570X
UNIVERSIDAD CENTRAL DE VENEZUELA. INSTITUTO DE CIENCIAS PENALES Y CRIMINOLOGICAS. ANUARIO. 1967. irreg., no.5, 1977. price varies. Universidad Central de Venezuela, Facultad de Ciencias Juridicas y Politicas, Instituto de Ciencias Penales y Criminologicas, Caracas, Venezuela. Ed. Tulio Chiossone. bk.rev.; bibl.; charts.

364 CN ISSN 0824-5134
UNIVERSITY OF ALBERTA. CENTRE FOR CRIMINOLOGICAL RESEARCH. DISCUSSION PAPERS. 1983. irreg. free. University of Alberta, Department of Sociology, Centre for Criminological Research, Edmonton, AB T6G 2H4, Canada. TEL 403-492-3322. FAX 403-492-7196. circ. 150 (controlled). (also avail. in microfiche from MML)
 Description: Monographs by scholars in criminology and related fields.

364 UK
UNIVERSITY OF CAMBRIDGE. INSTITUTE OF CRIMINOLOGY. OCCASIONAL PAPERS. 1974. irreg., no.20, 1995. £10.50. University of Cambridge, Institute of Criminology, 7 West Rd., Cambridge CB3 9DT, England. TEL 44-1223-335362. FAX 44-1223-335356. (back issues avail.) **Document type**: academic/scholarly publication.

365 360 AT ISSN 1039-9216
V A C R O REPORTER. 1977. 3/yr. Aus.$20. Victorian Association for the Care and Resettlement of Offenders, P.O. Box 14093, Melbourne Mail Centre, Vic. 8001, Australia. TEL 61-3-93298865. FAX 61-3-93298852. Ed. Judith Lazarus. adv.; bk.rev. circ. 2,000. (back issues avail.) **Document type**: academic/scholarly publication.
 Formerly (until Aug. 1992): Bridge.

VANDALISME, CRIMINALITEIT EN VOLKSHUISVESTING. see HOUSING AND URBAN PLANNING

VERKEERSKNOOPPUNT; tijdschrift voor verkeersvraagstukken. see TRANSPORTATION — Roads And Traffic

364 US ISSN 0361-5170
HV6250
VICTIMOLOGY; an international journal. 1976. irreg., vols.11-13, 1996. $115 (effective 1996). (National Institute of Victimology) Victimology, Inc., 2333 N. Vernon St., Arlington, VA 22207. TEL 703-528-3387. Ed. Emilio C. Viano. adv.; bk.rev. circ. 2,000. (back issues avail.) **Indexed**: Abstr.Crim.& Pen., Adol.Ment.Hlth.Abstr., C.L.I., Chicago Psychoanal.Lit.Ind., CJPI, Crim.Just.Abstr., Hlth.Ind., IBR, L.R.I., Leg.Cont., Mid.East: Abstr.& Ind., Past.Care & Couns.Abstr., Psychol.Abstr., Sociol.Abstr., Stud.Wom.Abstr., Viol.& Abuse Abstr. **Document type**: academic/scholarly publication.
 —KR SourceOne; SWETS. **CCC**.

VICTIMS OF VIOLENCE NEWSLETTER. see LAW — Criminal Law

363.2 IT ISSN 0394-8285
VIGILE URBANO; rivista mensile di polizia municipale. 1974. m. (11/yr.) L.70000 to individuals; institutions L.140000 (effective 1994). Maggioli Editore, Viale Vespucci 12-n, Casella Postale 290, 47037 Rimini, Italy. TEL 0541-626777. FAX 0541-622020. adv.: B&W page L.1300000, color page L.2000000; trim 115 x 195. bk.rev. circ. 6,726.
 ●Also available on CD-ROM.

VIOLENCE AND VICTIMS. see SOCIOLOGY

636.2 IT
VOCE DEI VIGILI URBANI. 12/yr. Viale Tunisia 41, 20124 Milan, Italy. TEL 2-65-70-848. FAX 2-65-72-329. Ed. Luigi Gambino. circ. 92,000.

VOICE FOR THE DEFENSE. see LAW

364 US
W A D E EXCHANGE. 1970. m. World Association of Document Examiners, 111 N. Canal St., Chicago, IL 60606. TEL 312-930-9446. E-mail: wade4@earthlink.net. Ed. Lew Osborne. bk.rev. circ. 2,000. **Document type**: trade publication.
 Description: Presents news of developments affecting professionals in the field of questioned document examination, including national and regional association activities.

364 US
W A D E JOURNAL. 1970. q. World Association of Document Examiners, 111 N. Canal St., Chicago, IL 60606-7206. TEL 312-930-9446. E-mail: wade4@earthlink.net. Ed. Corrine Lamb. **Document type**: trade publication.
 Description: Presents scientific studies in the field of questioned document examination.

364 GW ISSN 0179-0927
HV8290
W & S - WIRTSCHAFTSSCHUTZ UND SICHERHEITSTECHNIK; Zeitschrift fuer das Sicherheitswesen in der Wirtschaft. 10/yr. DM.259 (foreign DM.274) (effective 1997). Huethig GmbH, Postfach 102869, 69018 Heidelberg, Germany. TEL 49-6221-489411. FAX 49-6221-489323. URL: http://www.huethig.de. Ed. Holger Best. adv. contact: Isabel Pfisterer. index. circ. 8,000. **Indexed**: PROMT. **Document type**: trade publication.
 —**CCC**.
 Formerly (until 1985): Wirtschaftsschutz und Sicherheitstechnik (ISSN 0173-3303); Which was formed by the merger of: Sicherheitstechnik; Wirtschaftsschutz (ISSN 0171-9262)

364 332.1 GW ISSN 0177-5251
W I K. 1979. bi-m. DM.189 (foreign DM.215) (effective 1996). SecuMedia Verlags GmbH, Gaulsheimerstr. 17, 55218 Ingelheim-Sporkenheim, Germany. TEL 49-6725-9304-0. FAX 49-6725-5994. adv.; bk.rev.; index. circ. 5,800. (back issues avail.) **Document type**: trade publication.
 —**CCC**.

363.2 614.86 US
WASHINGTON (STATE) PATROL. ANNUAL REPORT. a. free. State Patrol, Research & Development, General Administration Bldg., Box 42607, Olympia, WA 98504-2607. TEL 206-753-4453. FAX 206-753-2492. **Document type**: government publication.

WASHINGTON CRIME NEWS SERVICES CALENDAR OF EVENTS; seminars, workshops, conferences, etc. see MEETINGS AND CONGRESSES

364 US
WASHINGTON DIGEST. q. National Association of Criminal Defense Lawyers, 1627 K St., N.W, 12th Fl., Washington, DC 20006. TEL 202-872-8688. FAX 202-331-8269.

363.2 614.86 US ISSN 0883-5799
WASHINGTON TROOPER. 1981. q. $9.97. (Washington State Patrol Troopers Association) Mercury Services Inc., Box 1523, Longview, WA 98632-0144. TEL 206-577-8598. (Subscr. to: Bob Wheeler, WSPTA, Box 916, Kelso, WA 98626) Ed. Bruce D. Grimm. adv.; bk.rev. circ. 5,000. (back issues avail.)

WAYNE STATE UNIVERSITY LAW SCHOOL. COMPARATIVE CRIMINAL LAW PROJECT. PUBLICATIONS SERIES. see LAW — Criminal Law

364 US ISSN 0891-6721
KF9350.A15
WHITE-COLLAR CRIME REPORTER; information and analyses concerning white-collar practice. 1987. 10/yr. $525. Andrews Publications, 175 Strafford Ave., Bldg. 4, Ste. 140, Wayne, PA 19087. TEL 610-225-0510; 800-345-1101. FAX 610-225-0501. Ed. Jason Schossler; Pub. John Backe Jr. R&P contact: Robert Maroldo. adv. contact: Melissa Webber. bibl.; stat. (looseleaf format; back issues avail.) **Document type**: newsletter.
 Description: Each issue covers one topic in depth, with interviews and relevant news items involving white-collar crime.

363.2 JA
WHITE PAPER ON POLICE (YEAR). (Text in English) a. 1550 Yen. (National Police Agency) Japan Times Ltd., 4-5-4 Shibaura, Minato-ku, Tokyo 108, Japan. TEL 03-3453-2013. FAX 03-3453-8023. **Document type**: government publication.
 Description: Covers international safety, the general crime situation and investigative activities, police activities for residents in regional communities, prevention of juvenile delinquency, environmental safety and cleanliness, traffic safety, public security, disasters and accidents, and support for police activities.

WHITECHAPEL JOURNAL. see LITERATURE — Science Fiction, Fantasy, Horror

363.2 UK
▼**THE WIRE (GLASGOW)**. 1996. bi-m. free. Strathclyde Police, 173 Pitt St., Glasgow G2 4JS, Scotland. TEL 44-141-532-2659. FAX 44-141-532-2562. Ed. Valerie Chisholm-White. **Document type**: newsletter.
 Description: Contains topical policing issues and news from around the Force.

364 US
WISCONSIN SHERIFF AND DEPUTY. 1949. q. $5. Wisconsin Sheriffs and Deputy Sheriffs Association, Box 145, Chippewa Falls, WI 54724. TEL 715-723-7173. Ed. James I. Cardinal. adv.; bk.rev.; charts; illus. circ. 3,000.

363.2 US ISSN 0890-5894
WOMENPOLICE. 1987. q. $25. R.R. 1, Box 149, Deer Isle, ME 04627. TEL 207-348-6976. FAX 207-348-6171. E-mail: jeanet6877@aol.com. Ed. Jeanette Taylor. adv.: B&W page $823; trim 7 1/4 x 9 1/2; adv. contact: Jeanette Taylor. bk.rev.; software rev, video rev, tr.lit.; circ. 3,500 (controlled). (back issues avail.) **Document type**: trade publication.
 Description: Promotes the professional development of women police officers and the utilization of women police officers internationally.

WORLDWIDE MILITARY AND POLICE AWARD. see MILITARY

WOUND BALLISTICS REVIEW. see MEDICAL SCIENCES — Forensic Sciences

WUJING YIXUE. see MEDICAL SCIENCES

YOUTH AND POLICY. see CHILDREN AND YOUTH — About

ZAKBOEK VOOR DE HULPOFFIZIER VAN JUSTITIE. see LAW — Criminal Law

CRIMINOLOGY AND LAW ENFORCEMENT — ABSTRACTING, BIBLIOGRAPHIES, STATISTICS

365   ZA   ISSN 0084-4659
ZAMBIA. PRISONS DEPARTMENT. REPORT. 1964. a. K.250. Zambia Government Printing Department, P.O. Box 30136, Lusaka, Zambia. **Document type:** government publication.

364   GW   ISSN 0342-3514
ZEITSCHRIFT FUER STRAFVOLLZUG UND STRAFFAELLIGENHILFE. 1954. 6/yr. DM.39 (foreign DM.39.80) (effective 1996). Gesellschaft fuer Fortbildung der Strafvollzugsbediensteten e.V., Steinstr. 21, 74072 Heilbronn, Germany. TEL 49-511-1209231. Ed. Heinz Mueller-Dietz. R&P contact: Winfried Hartmann. adv. contact: Klaus-Dieter Janke. bk.rev.; index. circ. 2,550. (back issues avail.) **Indexed:** Abstr.Crim.& Pen., IBR. **Document type:** bulletin.

ZERO HOUR; where culture meets crime. see *LITERARY AND POLITICAL REVIEWS*

364   US   ISSN 1040-7316
9-1-1 MAGAZINE. 1988. bi-m. $24. Official Publications, Inc., Box 11788, Santa Ana, CA 92711-1788. TEL 714-544-7776. FAX 714-838-9233. E-mail: magazn911@aol.com; URL: http://9-1-1magazine.com. Ed. Randall Larson; Pub. James E. Voelkl. adv.; B&W page $1705; trim 8 3/8 x 10 7/8; adv. contact: B. Underwood. bk.rev. circ. 18,100. **Document type:** trade publication. **Description:** Technical and informational magazine for senior personnel in public safety communications and response, including news of technical conferences, product evaluations and field reports.
Refereed Serial

CRIMINOLOGY AND LAW ENFORCEMENT — Abstracting, Bibliographies, Statistics

362.8   US
BUREAU OF JUSTICE STATISTICS REPORTS. JUSTICE EXPENDITURE AND EMPLOYMENT. 1969. irreg. free. U.S. Department of Justice, Bureau of Justice Statistics, 633 Indiana Ave., N.W., 11th Fl., Washington, DC 20531. (Orders to: Bureau of Justice Statistics Clearinghouse, Box 179, Dept. BJS C-1, Annapolis Junction, MD 20707-0179. TEL 800-732-3277. FAX 412-792-4358) circ. 8,800. **Document type:** government publication. **Former titles:** Justice Expenditure and Employment Data in the U.S; Expenditure and Employment Data for the Criminal Justice Systems (ISSN 0149-0478)

364.9   US
CALIFORNIA. BUREAU OF CRIMINAL STATISTICS AND SPECIAL SERVICES. CRIMINAL JUSTICE PROFILE; STATEWIDE. a. Department of Justice, Division of Law Enforcement, Bureau of Criminal Statistics and Special Services, Box 13427, Sacramento, CA 95813. TEL 916-739-2222. **Indexed:** SRI. **Formerly:** California. Bureau of Criminal Statistics. Criminal Justice Profile; Statewide.

362.8   US   ISSN 0191-3220
HV8699.U5
CAPITAL PUNISHMENT (YEAR). (Subseries of: Bureau of Justice Statistics Reports. Corrections) 1971. a. free. U.S. Department of Justice, Bureau of Justice Statistics, 633 Indiana Ave., N.W., 11th Fl., Washington, DC 20531. (Subscr. to: Bureau of Justice Statistics Clearinghouse, Box 179, Dept. BJS C-1, Annapolis Junction, MD 20701-0179. TEL 800-732-3277. FAX 410-792-4358) circ. 15,000. **Document type:** government publication. **Description:** Describes capital punishment court cases throughout the nation for year; also studies state statutory provisions relating to the death penalty and provides demographic statistics of death row inmates.

364   UK   ISSN 0967-5159
KD7122.5.A13
CHARTERED INSTITUTE OF PUBLIC FINANCE AND ACCOUNTANCY. ADMINISTRATION OF JUSTICE. ESTIMATES & ACTUALS. 1983. a. £55. Chartered Institute of Public Finance and Accountancy, Statistical Information Service, 3 Robert St., London WC2N 6BH, England. TEL 44-171-543-5600. FAX 44-171-543-5700. (back issues avail.) **Formerly** (until 1992): Chartered Institute of Public Finance and Accountancy. Administration of Justice. Estimates (ISSN 0264-6552)

362.2   UK
CHARTERED INSTITUTE OF PUBLIC FINANCE AND ACCOUNTANCY. POLICE STATISTICS. ACTUALS AND ESTIMATES. 1949-1989; resumed 199? a. £105. Chartered Institute of Public Finance and Accountancy, Statistical Information Service, 3 Robert St., London WC2N 6BH, England. TEL 44-171-543-5600. FAX 44-171-543-5700. (back issues avail.)
—BLDSC (6543.263500).
Formed by the merger of: Chartered Institute of Public Finance and Accountancy. Police Statistics. Actuals (ISSN 0144-9915) & Chartered Institute of Public Finance and Accountancy. Police Statistics. Estimates (ISSN 0144-9885)

CHARTERED INSTITUTE OF PUBLIC FINANCE AND ACCOUNTANCY. PROBATION. ESTIMATES & ACTUALS. see *SOCIAL SERVICES AND WELFARE — Abstracting, Bibliographies, Statistics*

364 317   US   ISSN 1081-6453
HV6787
▼**CITY CRIME RANKINGS**; crime in metropolitan America. 1995. a. $37.95 (effective 1997). Morgan Quitno Corporation, Box 1656, Lawrence, KS 66044-8656. TEL 913-841-3534; 800-457-0742. FAX 913-841-3568. URL: http://www.morganquitno.com. Eds. Scott Morgan, Kathleen O'Leary. (also avail. in diskette format) **Document type:** bulletin. **Description:** Provides detailed comparative crime statistics on cities with more than 75,000 inhabitants and all metro areas.

364.36   US
CRIME AND DELINQUENCY IN CALIFORNIA. 1965. a. free. Department of Justice, Bureau of Criminal Statistics and Special Services, Box 13427, Sacramento, CA 95813. TEL 916-227-3509. **Indexed:** SRI. **Formerly:** California. Bureau of Criminal Statistics. Crime and Delinquency; Incorporates: Adult Criminal Detention Reference Tables (ISSN 0092-2080); Adult Probation Program Report; Which was formerly: Adult Probation Reference Report; Adult Prosecution; Crimes and Arrests; Juvenile Probation; Reference Tables Adult and Juvenile Probation (ISSN 0094-7717).

364.973021   US   ISSN 1077-4408
HV6787
CRIME STATE RANKINGS; crime in the 50 United States. 1994. a. $49.95 (effective 1997). Morgan Quitno Corporation, Box 1656, Lawrence, KS 66044. TEL 913-841-3534; 800-457-0742. FAX 913-841-3568. URL: http://www.morganquitno.com. Eds. Scott Morgan, Kathleen O'Leary. R&P contact: Scott Morgan. stat. (diskette format) **Description:** Provides detailed, comparative statistical information on crime and law enforcement in more than 512 categories, for each of the 50 states.

364 016   US   ISSN 0146-9177
HV6001
CRIMINAL JUSTICE ABSTRACTS. 1968. q. $165 (foreign $180). Willow Tree Press, Inc., 124 Willow Tree Rd., Monsey, NY 10952. TEL 914-354-9139. FAX 914-362-8376. Ed. Richard Allinson; Pub. Richard Allinson. adv.; abstr.; bibl.; index, cum.index. circ. 1,000. (also avail. in microfilm from PMC,WSH; microform from UMI,WSH; microfiche from WSH; reprint service avail. from KTO,WSH) **Indexed:** Abstr.Crim.& Pen., C.L.I., CJPI, Crim.Just.Abstr., Leg.Per. **Document type:** academic/scholarly publication, abstracting/indexing.
●Also available online. Vendor(s): West Group. Also available on CD-ROM. Producer(s): SilverPlatter Information, Inc.
—BLDSC (3487.347500); UMI.
Former titles: Abstracts on Crime and Juvenile Delinquency; Crime and Delinquency Literature (ISSN 0037-1327); Formed by the merger of: Information Review on Crime and Delinquency; Selected Highlights of Crime and Delinquency.
Description: Summarizes worldwide criminal justice literature from all disciplines, especially the social sciences, law and public administration.

364 016   US   ISSN 0145-5818
Z5118.C9
CRIMINAL JUSTICE PERIODICAL INDEX. 1975. 3/yr. (base vol. plus s-a. update). U M I (Subsidiary of: Bell & Howell Company), 300 N. Zeeb Rd., Ann Arbor, MI 48106. TEL 313-761-4700; 800-521-0600. FAX 800-864-0019. bk.rev. (back issues avail.)
●Also available online. Vendor(s): Knight-Ridder Information, Inc. (File no. 171).
—BLDSC (3487.350800); UMI.

362.8   US   ISSN 0095-5833
HV7245
CRIMINAL VICTIMIZATION IN THE UNITED STATES. (Subseries of: National Crime Victimization Survey Report) 1973. a. free. U.S. Department of Justice, Bureau of Justice Statistics, 633 Indiana Ave., N.W., 11th Fl., Washington, DC 20531. (Orders to: Bureau of Justice Statistics Clearinghouse, Box 179, Dept. BJS C-1, Annapolis Junction, MD 20701-0179. TEL 800-732-3277. FAX 410-792-4358) stat. circ. 17,000. (also avail. in microfiche; back issues avail.) **Document type:** government publication.

364 614.19   US
CRIMINALIST'S SOURCE BOOK.* a. $25. International Reference Organization in Forensic Medicine & Sciences, c/o Wm. G. Eckert, Ed., 1877 Claudia Ave., Simi Valley, CA 93065-3642. TEL 316-685-7612.

364 016   NE   ISSN 0928-8759
HV6001
CRIMINOLOGY, PENOLOGY & POLICE SCIENCE ABSTRACTS. 1961. bi-m. $540 (effective 1996). (Criminologica Foundation) Kugler Publications B.V., P.O. Box 11188, 1001 GD Amsterdam, Netherlands. TEL 31-20-6278070. FAX 31-20-6380524. Eds. J.J.M. van Dijk, Mrs. K. van Leeuwen. (back issues avail.) **Document type:** abstracting/indexing.
—BLDSC (3487.375400).
Formed by the merger of: Police Science Abstracts (ISSN 0166-6282); Which was formerly: Abstracts on Police Science (ISSN 0301-0112) & Criminology and Penology Abstracts (ISSN 0166-6231); Former titles: Abstracts on Criminology and Penology; Excerpta Criminologica (ISSN 0001-3684)
Description: An international abstracting service covering the etiology of crime and juvenile delinquency, the control and treatment of offenders, criminal procedure, the administration of justice, and forensic and police sciences, including forensic medicine.

364   CN   ISSN 1205-8629
JC578
CRITICAL CRIMINOLOGY; international journal. 1989. s-a. $20 to individuals; institutions $30 (effective 1997). (American Society of Criminology, Division of Critical Criminology) Collective Press, 185-9040 Blundell Rd., Ste. 361, Richmond, BC V6Y 1K3, Canada. TEL 604-869-8270. FAX 604-869-7620. E-mail: bdspm@aol.com. Ed. Brian MacLean. R&P contact: Brian MacLean. adv. contact: Brian MacLean. circ. 300. **Indexed:** Crim.Just.Abstr. **Document type:** academic/scholarly publication, abstracting/indexing.
—BLDSC (3487.451740).
Formerly: Journal of Human Justice (ISSN 0847-2971)
Description: Offers a forum for progressive analyses of economic, gender, legal and political relations as they pertain to studies of social justice worldwide.
Refereed Serial

364 314   CY   ISSN 0253-8695
HV8485.C93
CYPRUS. DEPARTMENT OF STATISTICS AND RESEARCH. CRIMINAL STATISTICS. (Text in English, Greek) 1974. a. £C4. Ministry of Finance, Department of Statistics and Research, 13 Lord Byron Ave., Nicosia, Cyprus. TEL 357-2-302349. FAX 357-2-456712. **Document type:** government publication. **Description:** Gives police, judicial, and prison statistics.

364.9489   DK   ISSN 0070-3540
HV7023
DENMARK. DANMARKS STATISTIK. KRIMINALSTATISTIK (YEAR)/CRIMINAL STATISTICS. 1933. a. DKK 164.80 (effective 1997). Danmarks Statistik, Sejroegade 11, DK-2100 Copenhagen OE, Denmark. TEL 45-39-17-39-17. FAX 45-31-18-48-01. TELEX 16236. **Document type:** government publication.

CRIMINOLOGY AND LAW ENFORCEMENT — ABSTRACTING, BIBLIOGRAPHIES, STATISTICS

364 318   **CK**
ESTADISTICA DE CRIMINALIDAD. 1963. a. Policia Nacional, Carrera 15, No. 10-41, Bogota, Colombia. illus.; stat.
   Formerly (until 1973): Criminalidad.

363.2   **CL**
ESTADISTICAS POLICIALES. CARABINEROS DE CHILE. 1977. a. Ch.$2000 (US $13.50; elsewhere $14.20) (effective 1995). Instituto Nacional de Estadisticas, Av. Bulnes 418, Casilla 498, Correo 3 Santiago, Chile. TEL 56-2-6991441. FAX 56-2-6712169.

363.2   **CL**
ESTADISTICAS POLICIALES. POLICIA DE INVESTIGACIONES DE CHILE. 1983. a. Ch.$2000 (US $13.50; elsewhere $15.90) (effective 1995). Instituto Nacional de Estadisticas, Av. Bulnes 418, Casilla 498, Correo 3 Santiago, Chile. TEL 56-2-6991441. FAX 56-2-6712169.

364   **US**
HV9278
FELONY SENTENCES IN STATE COURTS. 1989. biennial. free. U.S. Department of Justice, Bureau of Justice Statistics, 633 Indiana Ave., N.W., 11th Fl., Washington, DC 20531. (Orders to: Superintendent of Documents, U.S. Government Printing Office, Box 371954, Pittsburgh, PA 15250-7954. TEL 202-512-1800. FAX 202-512-2250) stat. circ. 13,300. (back issues avail.) Document type: government publication.
   Description: Provides statistics on felony arrests in the U.S. and data on outcomes of arrests.

364   **FI**   ISSN 0784-882X
HA1448
FINLAND. TILASTOKESKUS. POLIISIN TIETOON TULLUT RIKOLLISUUS/FINLAND. STATISTIKCENTRALEN. BROTTSLIGHET SOM KOMMIT TILL POLISENS KAENNEDOM/FINLAND. CENTRAL STATISTICAL OFFICE. CRIMINALITY KNOWN TO THE POLICE. (Text in English, Finnish and Swedish) 1928. a. FIM 90. Tilastokeskus, P.O. Box 2B, SF-00022 Tilastokeskus, Finland. Document type: government publication.
   Formerly: Finland. Tilastokeskus. Rikollisuus. Poliisin Tietoon Tullut Rikollisuus (ISSN 0355-2160)

364   **GW**   ISSN 0431-5480
GERMANY. BUNDESKRIMINALAMT. POLIZEILICHE KRIMINALSTATISTIK (YEAR). (Text in German; summaries in English) 1953. a. Bundeskriminalamt, KI-12, 65173 Wiesbaden, Germany. TEL 49-611-556834. FAX 49-611-556804. TELEX 4186867-BKA-D. Ed. Uwe Doermann. circ. 3,200. Document type: government publication.
   Description: Crime statistics of the police in Germany.

364   **GR**   ISSN 0256-3665
GREECE. NATIONAL STATISTICAL SERVICE. STATISTICS ON CIVIL, CRIMINAL AND REFORMATORY JUSTICE. (Text in Greek) 1962. a. $16. National Statistical Service of Greece, Statistical Information and Publications Division - Ethniki Statistiki Yperesia tes Ellados, 14-16 Lykourgou, 101-66 Athens, Greece. TEL 30-1-3244-748. FAX 30-1-3241-102. TELEX 216734 ESYE GR. (back issues avail.) Document type: government publication.
   Formerly (until 1961): Greece. National Statistical Service. Criminal Justice Statistics.

HOMICIDE IN CALIFORNIA. see CRIMINOLOGY AND LAW ENFORCEMENT

364   **IE**
IRELAND. REPORT ON CRIME. a. Stationery Office, Dublin, Ireland. TEL 353-1-6613111. FAX 353-1-4752760. Document type: government publication.

364   **IS**   ISSN 0075-1006
ISRAEL. CENTRAL BUREAU OF STATISTICS. CRIMINAL STATISTICS. (Text in English and Hebrew) 1948. irreg., latest 1992. price varies. Central Bureau of Statistics, P.O. Box 13015, Jerusalem 91130, Israel. TEL 972-2-6553400. FAX 972-2-6553325. Document type: government publication.

362.8   **IS**   ISSN 0333-7634
ISRAEL. CENTRAL BUREAU OF STATISTICS. VICTIMIZATION SURVEY. (Text in English, Hebrew) 1981. irreg., latest 1990. Central Bureau of Statistics, P.O. Box 13015, Jerusalem 91130, Israel. TEL 972-2-6553400. FAX 972-2-6553325. Document type: government publication.

340 364 016   **NE**   ISSN 0167-5850
JUSTITIELE VERKENNINGEN. 1956. 9/yr. fl.100 (effective 1996). (Ministerie van Justitie, Wetenschappelijk Onderzoek- en Documentatiecentrum - Ministry of Justice, Research and Documentation Centre) Gouda Quint B.V. (Subsidiary of: Wolters Kluwer N.V.), Postbus 1148, 6801 MK Arnhem, Netherlands. (Dist. by: Libresso Distribution Centre, P.O. Box 23, 7400 GA Deventer, Netherlands. TEL 31-570-633155. FAX 31-570-633834) Ed.Bd. abstr.; index. circ. 3,500. Indexed: Abstr.Crim.& Pen., Crim.Just.Abstr., Key to Econ.Sci.
—SWETS.
   Formerly (until 1975): Documentatieblad (ISSN 0012-4532)
   Description: Short studies on criminology and abstracts of books and journals in the field.

364   **US**
LAW ENFORCEMENT MANAGEMENT AND ADMINISTRATIVE STATISTICS (YEAR). 1987. triennial. free. U.S. Department of Justice, Bureau of Justice Statistics, 633 Indiana Ave., N.W., 11th Fl., Washington, DC 20531. (Orders to: Superintendent of Documents, U.S. Government Printing Office, Box 371954, Pittsburgh, PA 15250-7954. TEL 202-512-1800. FAX 202-512-2250) stat. circ. 17,000. (also avail. in microfiche) Document type: government publication.

364.6   **US**   ISSN 0364-5754
N C J R S DOCUMENT RETRIEVAL INDEX. Cover title: National Institute of Justice - N C J R S Document Retrieval Index (D R I) - Cumulative. 1972. a. price varies. U.S. National Institute of Justice, National Criminal Justice Reference Service, Box 6000, Department F, Rockville, MD 20849-6000. TEL 301-251-5500; 800-851-3420. FAX 301-251-5212. Document type: bibliography.
●Also available online. Vendor(s): Knight-Ridder Information, Inc.
Also available on CD-ROM.
   Former titles: U.S. Department of Justice. National Institute of Justice. Document Retrieval Index; U.S. Law Enforcement Assistance Administration. Document Retrieval Index.

364   **US**
NATIONAL JUDICIAL REPORTING PROGRAM. 1984. biennial. free. U.S. Department of Justice, Bureau of Justice Statistics, 633 Indiana Ave., N.W., 11th Fl., Washington, DC 20531. (Orders to: Superintendent of Documents, U.S. Government Printing Office, Box 371954, Pittsburgh, PA 15250-7954. TEL 202-512-1800. FAX 202-512-2250) Ed. Patricia Langan. circ. 13,000. (also avail. in microfiche) Document type: government publication.
   Formerly (until 1992): Prosecution of Felony Arrests (Year).
   Description: Provides statistics on felony arrests in 28 jurisdictions with qualitative data on arrest decisions.

346.36   **US**
NATIONAL JUVENILE DETENTION DIRECTORY. 1991. triennial. $50 to non-members; members $40. American Correctional Association, 4380 Forbes Blvd., Lanham, MD 20706-4322. TEL 301-918-1800. R&P contact: Gabriella Daley. adv. contact: Marge Restivo. (also avail. in microfiche from CIS) Document type: directory.

353.9   **US**   ISSN 0094-1247
HV7571.N25
NEBRASKA. STATE PATROL. ANNUAL REPORT. Key Title: Annual Report - Nebraska State Patrol. 1971? a. free. State Patrol, State House, Box 94907, Lincoln, NE 68509. TEL 402-471-4545. circ. 75. Document type: government publication.

364   **NE**   ISSN 0168-9029
NETHERLANDS. CENTRAAL BUREAU VOOR DE STATISTIEK. CRIMINALITEIT STRAFRECHTSPLEGING. (Text in Dutch and English) 1950. a. fl.22.50. Centraal Bureau voor de Statistiek, Prinses Beatrixlaan 428, 2270 AZ Voorburg, Netherlands. TEL 070-694341. (Subscr. to: SDU - Publishers, Christoffel Plantijnstraat, The Hague, Netherlands) Document type: government publication.
   Supersedes in part (in 1983): Netherlands. Centraal Bureau voor de Statistiek. Juristiele Statistiek. Judicial Statistics (ISSN 0168-4531); Which was formerly: Netherlands. Centraal Bureau voor de Statistiek. Justitiele Statistiek en Faillissements Statistiek.

364   **GW**   ISSN 0938-0590
NEUE KRIMINOLOGISCHE LITERATUR/NEW CRIMINOLOGICAL LITERATURE/NOUVELLE LITTERATURE CRIMINOLOGIQUE/NUEVA LITERATURA CRIMINOLOGICA. 1981. irreg. Universitaetsbibliothek Tuebingen, Schwerpunkt Kriminologie, Postfach 2620, 72016 Tuebingen, Germany. Document type: monographic series.
   Formerly (until 1990): Neuerwerbungen Kriminologie (ISSN 0720-3780)

345   **NO**   ISSN 0333-3914
HA1501
NORWAY. STATISTISK SENTRALBYRAA. KRIMINALSTATISTIKK/STATISTICS NORWAY. CRIMINAL STATISTICS. (Subseries of: Norges Offisielle Statistikk) (Text in English and Norwegian) 1955. a. NOK 80 (effective 1997). Statistisk Sentralbyraa, P.O. Box 8131 Dep., N-0033 Oslo, Norway. TEL 47-22-864500. FAX 47-22-864976. circ. 1,100. Document type: government publication.

365 310   **US**   ISSN 0031-4366
PENNSYLVANIA. BOARD OF PROBATION AND PAROLE. MONTHLY STATISTICAL REPORT. 1942. m. free. Board of Probation and Parole, Management Information Division, Box 1661, Harrisburg, PA 17110. TEL 717-787-5988. stat. circ. 205. (processed) Document type: government publication.
   Incorporates: Pennsylvania. Board of Probation and Parole. Quarterly Statistical Report (ISSN 0031-4374)

364   **GW**   ISSN 0171-2802
POLIZEILICHE KRIMINALSTATISTIK N - W. 1958. a. free. Landeskriminalamt Nordrhein-Westfalen, Voelklingerstr. 49, 40221 Duesseldorf, Germany. TEL 0211-9396038. FAX 0211-9396941. Document type: government publication.
   Description: Information and statistics on crime in the Nordrhein-Westphalia district of Germany.

364   **GW**   ISSN 0171-2721
HV7349.S38
POLIZEILICHE KRIMINALSTATISTIK NIEDERSACHSEN MIT INFORMATIONEN AUS DEM LANDESKRIMINALAMT. 1971. a. free. Landeskriminalamt Niedersachsen, Schuetzenstr. 25, 30161 Hannover, Germany. TEL 49-511-330-0. FAX 49-511-3301250. circ. 300. (back issues avail.) Document type: government publication.

362.8   **US**
PROBATION AND PAROLE (YEAR). (Subseries of: Uniform Parole Reports) 1976. a. free. U.S. Department of Justice, Bureau of Justice Statistics, 633 Indiana Ave., N.W., 11th Fl., Washington, DC 20531. (Subscr. to: Bureau of Justice Statistics Clearinghouse, Box 179, Dept. BJS C-1, Annapolis Junction, MD 20701-0179. TEL 800-732-3277. FAX 410-792-4358) circ. 25,000. Document type: government publication.
   Formerly: Parole in the United States.
   Description: Compiles statistics on the number of entries and exits of adults under probation or parole supervision for each state, including the District of Columbia. Also describes programs of adult and juvenile agencies nationwide and provides a demographic summary.

364   **UK**   ISSN 1350-441X
SCOTTISH OFFICE. STATISTICAL BULLETIN. CRIMINAL JUSTICE SERIES. 1990. irreg. £2. Scottish Office, New St. Andrew's House, Rm. 1-44, Edinburgh EH1 3TG, Scotland. TEL 0131-244-4806. Document type: government publication.
—BLDSC (8447.679402).

CRIMINOLOGY AND LAW ENFORCEMENT — Security

362.8 US ISSN 0360-3431
HV7245
SOURCEBOOK OF CRIMINAL JUSTICE STATISTICS. 1973. a. price varies. U.S. Department of Justice, Bureau of Justice Statistics, 633 Indiana Ave., N.W., 11th Fl., Washington, DC 20531. (Subscr. to: Bernan, 4611-F Assembly Dr., Lanham, MD 20706-4391. TEL 800-274-4447. FAX 301-459-0056; Or: Bureau of Justice Statistics Clearinghouse, Box 179, Dept. GJS C-1, Annapolis Junction, MD 20701-0179. TEL 800-732-3277. FAX 410-792-4358) bibl.; charts. circ. 22,000. **Document type:** government publication.
Description: Presents a wide variety of criminal justice data on characteristics of the criminal justice system, public attitudes toward crime and enforcement, the nature and distribution of known offenses, demographics of persons arrested, and judicial processing of defendants.

364 US ISSN 0360-9146
HV6793.M5
UNIFORM CRIME REPORT FOR THE STATE OF MICHIGAN. 1973. a. Department of State Police, 714 S. Harrison Rd., East Lansing, MI 48823. TEL 517-332-2521. illus. (also avail. in microfiche from CIS) **Indexed:** SRI.
Continues: Michigan Law Enforcement Officials Report on Crime.

362.8 US
U.S. DEPARTMENT OF JUSTICE. BUREAU OF JUSTICE STATISTICS. CRIME AND JUSTICE DATA. a.? Inter-University Consortium for Political and Social Research, National Archive of Criminal Justice Data, Box 1248, Ann Arbor, MI 48106-1248. TEL 313-764-2570; 800-999-0960. FAX 313-764-8041. E-mail: netmail@icpsr.umich.edu. (Orders to: Justice Statistics Clearinghouse, National Criminal Justice Reference Service, Box 6000, Rockville, MD 20850. TEL 800-732-3277; Alt. addr.: Bureau of Justice Statistics, U.S. Department of Justice, 633 Indiana Ave., N.W., Washington, DC 20531)
●Available only on CD-ROM.
Description: Provides a statistical overview of criminal law enforcement and prison populations.

364 015 CN ISSN 0701-0524
UNIVERSITY OF TORONTO. CENTRE OF CRIMINOLOGY LIBRARY. ACQUISITIONS LIST. 1975-1995 (no. 2). 2/yr. Can.$13. University of Toronto, Center of Criminology Library, 130 St. George St., Rm. 8001, Toronto, ON M5S 1A5, Canada. TEL 416-978-7068. FAX 416-978-4195. bibl. circ. 100.

365 US
WISCONSIN. DIVISION OF CORRECTIONS. OFFICE OF INFORMATION MANAGEMENT. ADMISSIONS TO JUVENILE INSTITUTIONS. (Subseries of: Statistical Bulletin) 1972. a. Division of Corrections, Office of Information Management, Box 7925, Madison, WI 53707. TEL 608-266-2471. stat. (processed)

365 US
WISCONSIN. DIVISION OF CORRECTIONS. OFFICE OF INFORMATION MANAGEMENT. RELEASES FROM JUVENILE INSTITUTIONS. Title varies slightly. (Statistical Bulletin C-52) 1972. a. Division of Corrections, Office of Information Management, Box 7925, Madison, WI 53707. TEL 608-266-2471. stat. (processed)
Formerly: Wisconsin. Division of Corrections. Bureau of Planning, Development and Research. Releases from Juvenile Institutions (ISSN 0362-7470).

364 US
WISCONSIN CRIME AND ARRESTS (YEAR). 1969. a. free. Office of Justice Assistance, Statistical Analysis Center, 222 State St., 2nd Fl., Madison, WI 53702. TEL 608-266-7644. FAX 608-266-6676. Ed. Thomas G. Eversen. index. circ. 800. (tabloid format) **Indexed:** SRI. **Document type:** government publication.
Description: Provides crime and arrest statistics for Wisconsin and each law enforcement agency in the state. Contains current statistics and depicts five- and ten-year trends.

CRIMINOLOGY AND LAW ENFORCEMENT — Security

see also Computers–Computer Security

363.22 690 US
ACCESS CONTROL & SECURITY INTEGRATION; perimeter access to internal control. 1957. m. (plus a. Buyer's Guide). $54 (foreign $120). Intertec Publishing Corp. (Atlanta), 6151 Powers Ferry Rd., N.W., Atlanta, GA 30339-2491. TEL 707-955-2500. FAX 707-955-0400. Ed. Nick Vance. adv.; charts; illus.; tr.lit.; index. circ. 27,170. (tabloid format; also avail. in microform; reprint service avail. from UMI) **Document type:** trade publication.
—UMI. **CCC.**
Former titles: Access Control (ISSN 1042-2617); (until 1988): Access Control - Fence Industry (ISSN 0894-6639); (until 1987): Fence Industry - Access Control (ISSN 0885-8411); Fence Industry Trade News (ISSN 0014-9977).
Description: Edited for access control dealers and installers, security managers, architects and specifiers. Includes installation case histories, product overviews, consultants' articles and trade literature covering access control and fencing equipment, and alarm and sensor systems.

365.64 BA
AFAQ AMNIYA/SECURITY OUTLOOK. (Text in Arabic) 1983. m. Ministry of the Interior, P.O. Box 13, Police Fort Compound, Manama, Bahrain. TEL 254021. TELEX 8333.

621.389 FR ISSN 0290-0106
ALARMES - PROTECTION - SECURITE. bi-m. 540 F. 22-24 rue du President Wilson, 99539 Levallois Perret Cedex, France. TEL 47-56-50-00. FAX 47-56-90-49. TELEX 250 303. Ed. Jean Macon. adv. contact: Jean-Francois Sol Dourdin. circ. 6,000. **Document type:** trade publication.
Formerly: Alarmes Protection Vol (ISSN 0240-8155)

365.64 TS
AL-AMN/SECURITY. (Text in Arabic) 1975. m. General Directorate of Police, Public Relations, P.O. Box 1493, Dubai, United Arab Emirates. TEL 291279. FAX 662219. circ. 1,000.

365.64 CC ISSN 0259-059X
ASIAN SECURITY & SAFETY JOURNAL. 1984. 6/yr. $28 in Hong Kong, Taiwan & P.R.China; elsewhere $35. Elgin Consultants Ltd., Crawford Tower, 18th Fl., Ste. B, No. 99 Jervois St., Sheungwan, Hong Kong, People's Republic of China. TEL 852-815-1680. FAX 852-815-1706. Ed. David Slough. bk.rev. circ. 12,000.
Description: Introduces new security, fire protection and industrial safety products and services and provides professional advice to installers, practitioners, and endusers.

365.34 338.025 CC
▼**ASIAN SOURCES SECURITY PRODUCTS.** (Text in English) 1995. m. $60. Asian Sources Media Group, G.P.O. Box 12367, Hong Kong, People's Republic of China. TEL 852-2555-4777. E-mail: asmgroup@singnet.com.sg. (Subscr. to: Wordright Enterprises Inc., Box 3062, Evanston, IL 60204-3062. TEL 708-475-1900) Ed. Spenser Au. **Indexed:** HongKongiana. **Document type:** trade publication.
Description: Covers home, auto and personal security products.

AUERBACH DATA SECURITY MANAGEMENT. see COMPUTERS — Computer Security

BAILRIGG MEMORANDA. see POLITICAL SCIENCE — International Relations

BAILRIGG PAPERS ON INTERNATIONAL SECURITY. see POLITICAL SCIENCE — International Relations

364 US ISSN 0162-7457
BANK SECURITY REPORT. 1972. m. Warren, Gorham & Lamont, 395 Hudson St., New York, NY 10014. TEL 212-367-3006. FAX 212-367-6718. (Subscr. to: The Park Square Bldg., 31 St. James Ave., Boston, MA 02116-4112. TEL 800-950-1207) Ed. Richard F. Cross. (looseleaf format; also avail. in microform from UMI) **Document type:** newsletter.
—UMI. **CCC.**
Formerly (until 1993): Bank Technology Report.
Description: Informs security operations officers of the latest developments and newest strategies in both physical and computer security.

363 NE ISSN 0926-7859
BEVEILIGING; onafhankelijk vakblad voor de beveiligingsector. vol.4, 1991. 11/yr. fl.192.50 (foreign fl.340). Keesing Bedrijsinformatie, P.O. Box 1118, 1000 BC Amsterdam, Netherlands. TEL 31-30-5641111. FAX 31-30-5641271. circ. 5,069. **Document type:** trade publication.
—SWETS.

BRITAIN'S GUARDING INDUSTRY. see BUSINESS AND ECONOMICS — Trade And Industrial Directories

364.4 CN
C A N A S A NEWSLETTER. q. free to members. Canadian Alarm & Security Association, B.C. Chapter, 409 Granville St., Ste. 523, Vancouver, BC V6C 1T1, Canada. TEL 604-669-3177. FAX 604-669-5343. Ed. Norm Cheesman. R&P contact: Shayla Gunter. adv. contact: Shayla Gunter. **Document type:** newsletter.
Formerly: C A N A S A British Columbia Chapter Bulletin.
Description: Provides information on the latest technologies, products and legislation in the electronic security industry and chapter news.

364.4 CN
C A N A S A QUEBEC CHAPTER BULLETIN. bi-m. free to members. Canadian Alarm & Security Association, Quebec Office, 210 Blvd. Montarville, Ste. 3006, Boucherville PQ J4B 6T3, Canada. TEL 514-990-2349. FAX 514-641-3145. Ed. Louise Marcoux. **Document type:** newsletter.
Description: Information on the latest technologies, products and legislation in the electronic security industry.

365.34 330 GW ISSN 0933-0186
C D SICHERHEITS-MANAGEMENT. (Criminal Digest) 1976. bi-m. DM.66 (foreign DM.73). Richard Boorberg Verlag (Stuttgart), Scharnstr. 2, 70563 Stuttgart, Germany. TEL 0711-73850. FAX 0711-7352244. Ed. Helmut Brueckmann. adv.: B&W page DM.3150, color page DM.5550; trim 125 x 180; adv. contact: Helmut Brueckmann. bk.rev.; circ. 14,000. (back issues avail.) **Document type:** trade publication.
Formerly (until 1994): Criminal Digest.

364 327 FR ISSN 1150-1634
CAHIERS DE LA SECURITE INTERIEURE. 4/yr. 370 F. (Europe 380 F.; elsewhere 425 F.) (effective 1997). (Institut des Hautes Etudes de la Securite Interieure) Documentation Francaise, 29-31 quai Voltaire, 75344 Paris Cedex 07, France. TEL 33-1-40157000. FAX 33-1-40157230. TELEX 215 666 DOCFRAN. (Subscr. to: 124 rue Henri Barbusse, 93308 Aubervilliers Cedex, France. TEL 33-1-48395600. FAX 33-1-48395601) (also avail. in microfiche from DFR) **Indexed:** Abstr.Crim.& Pen., Crim.Just.Abstr. **Document type:** government publication.
Description: Seeks a better understanding of security problems.

365.64 US ISSN 1054-3821
HV8291.U6
CAMPUS CRIME. 1991. m. $240. Business Publishers, Inc., 951 Pershing Dr., Silver Spring, MD 20910-4464. TEL 301-587-6300. FAX 301-585-9075. Ed. Anthony R. Cooke. (looseleaf format; back issues avail.) **Document type:** newsletter.
●Also available online. Vendor(s): NewsNet.
—**CCC.**
Description: Advice for university security officers and university officials on reducing incidents of crime on campus. Tracks federal crime reporting legislation.

CRIMINOLOGY AND LAW ENFORCEMENT — SECURITY

364.4 US ISSN 1055-4319
LB2866
CAMPUS SECURITY REPORT. m. $199 (foreign $224). Rusting Publications, 402 Main St., Box 190, Port Washington, NY 11050. TEL 516-883-1440. FAX 516-883-1683. Ed. Susan Krivin; Pub. Robert Rusting. adv. contact: Jill Hillje. **Document type:** newsletter.

364.4 CN ISSN 0709-3403
CANADIAN SECURITY; journal of protection and communications. 1979. 7/yr. Can.$30 (US Can.$35; elsewhere Can.$40) (effective 1997 & 1998). Security Publishing Limited, 46 Crockford Blvd., Scarborough, ON M1R 3C3, Canada. TEL 416-755-4343. FAX 416-755-7487. Ed. Robert Robinson; Pub. Maureen Percival. R&P contact: Maureen Percival. adv. contact: Maureen Percival. bk.rev. circ. 15,000. **Document type:** trade publication.
  Description: For Canadian protection and communications professionals.

364 US ISSN 0884-5409
HV7936.E7
CARNAHAN CONFERENCE ON SECURITY TECHNOLOGY. PROCEEDINGS. 1968. a. $22.50. (University of Kentucky, College of Engineering) O E S Publications, Office of Engineering Services, University of Kentucky, Lexington, KY 40506-0046. TEL 606-257-3343. FAX 606-257-3342. Eds. R. William DeVore. circ. 500. (back issues avail.) **Document type:** proceedings.
  Former titles: Conference on Crime Countermeasures and Security. Proceedings (ISSN 0737-1160); Carnahan Conference on Security Technology. Proceedings (ISSN 0731-7875); Carnahan Conference on Electronic Crime Countermeasures. Proceedings.

364.5 SZ
CERBERUS SECURITY. (Editions in English, French, and German) 1975. 2-3/yr. free. Cerberus Ltd., CH-8708 Maennedorf, Switzerland. TEL 01-922-6239. FAX 01-922-6450. TELEX 875528-CSM-CH. adv. contact: Franz Poltera. bk.rev.; illus. circ. 9,000. **Document type:** bulletin.

CHIEFS OF STATE AND CABINET MEMBERS OF FOREIGN GOVERNMENTS. see POLITICAL SCIENCE — International Relations

COMPENSATION IN THE SECURITY - LOSS PREVENTION FIELD. see BUSINESS AND ECONOMICS — Labor And Industrial Relations

COMPUTER FRAUD & SECURITY. see COMPUTERS — Computer Security

COMPUTER SECURITY JOURNAL. see COMPUTERS — Computer Security

COMPUTERS & SECURITY; the international journal devoted to the study of the technical and financial aspects of computer security. see COMPUTERS — Computer Security

COMPUTING & COMMUNICATIONS: LAW & PROTECTION REPORT. see COMPUTERS — Computer Security

636.22 346 US ISSN 0897-4101
KF9351.A15
CORPORATE CRIME REPORTER. 1987. 48/yr. $795. American Communications & Publishing Co., Inc., Box 18384, Washington, DC 20036. TEL 202-429-6928. Ed. Russel Mokhiber. index. (looseleaf format; back issues avail.) **Document type:** newsletter.

364.4 SP
CUADERNOS DE SEGURIDAD. 1988. 11/yr. 10500 ptas. (foreign 16500 ptas.) (effective 1997). Estudios Tecnicos, S.A., Avda. Industria, 32, Edif. 2, 28108 Alcobendas (Madrid), Spain. TEL 34-1-6615189. FAX 34-1-6616884. Ed. Manuel S. Gomez-Merelo. R&P contact: Manuel S. Gomez-Merelo. adv. contact: B&W page 150500 ptas.; color page 197000 ptas.; 210 x 280; adv. contact: Adolfo Castano Megia. bk.rev.; circ. 3,833 (controlled). **Document type:** monographic series.

D I S A M JOURNAL. (Defense Institute of Security Assistance Management) see POLITICAL SCIENCE — International Relations

DATA SECURITY LETTER. see COMPUTERS — Computer Security

DATA SECURITY MANUAL; guidelines and procedures for data protection. see COMPUTERS — Computer Security

DATAPRO REPORTS ON INFORMATION SECURITY. see COMPUTERS — Electronic Data Processing

365.34 GW ISSN 0941-4460
DETEKTIV-KURIER. 1988. q. DM.41 (effective 1997). Zentralstelle fuer die Ausbildung im Detektivgewerbe, Zur Boeckelt 20, 47608 Geldern, Germany. TEL 49-2831-1095. FAX 49-2831-1097. (Dist. by: SPS, Karl-Mand-Str. 2, 56070 Koblenz, Germany. TEL 49-261-807060. FAX 49-261-8070654) Ed. Manfred Kocks; Pub. Manfred Kocks. adv.: B&W page DM.2100, color page DM.3150; trim 180 x 250; adv. contact: Joerg Klausewitz. bk.rev.; circ. 6,000 (paid). (back issues avail.) **Document type:** trade publication.
  Refereed Serial

621.3 SA
▼**ELECTRONIC SECURITY SYSTEMS BUYER'S GUIDE.** 1997. a. Technews (Pty) Ltd., P.O. Box 626, Kloof 3640, South Africa. TEL 27-31-7640386. FAX 27-31-7640386. E-mail: technews@iafrica.com. adv. **Document type:** trade publication.

621.3 SA
▼**ELECTRONIC SECURITY SYSTEMS SOUTH AFRICA.** 1996. bi-m. Technews (Pty) Ltd., P.O. Box 626, Kloof 3640, South Africa. TEL 27-31-7640593. FAX 27-31-7640386. E-mail: technews@iafrica.com. Ed. Darren Smith. adv. contact: Viv Dorrington. illus. circ. 7,000. **Document type:** trade publication.
  Description: Addresses professional and business personnel concerned with the design, installation, operation and end use of high-tech electronic security devices.

365 FR
ERGONOMIE, HYGIENE ET SECURITE. 4/yr. Editions d' Ergonomie, 48 rue Raphael, B.P. 138, 13267 Marseille Cedex 08, France. TEL 91-22-17-25. FAX 91-71-00-10. Ed. Charles-P. Bernard. circ. 9,500.

364.4 IT ISSN 0394-8625
ESSECOME. 1981. m. (11/yr.). L.110000($75) (effective 1997). E D I S, s.r.l., Via Emilia Ponente 20-4, 40133 Bologna, Italy. TEL 39-51-382606. FAX 39-51-380605. Ed. Andrea Sandrolini. adv. contact: Carolina Pattuelli. bk.rev. circ. 10,800. **Document type:** trade publication.
  Formerly: Selezione Sicurezze.

364.4 IT
ESSECOME INTERNATIONAL. (Text in English) 6/yr. L.210000($145) (effective 1997). E D I S, s.r.l., Via Emilia Ponente 20-4, 40133 Bologna, Italy. TEL 39-51-382606. FAX 39-51-380605. Ed. Fabrizia Montanari. adv. contact: Carolina Pattuelli. circ. 6,800. **Document type:** trade publication.

365.64 IT
FORCESICUREZZA. (Includes a. directory: La Sicurezza in Italia) 1986. m. $107 (effective 1995). Publi & Consult S.p.A., Via Tagliamento, 29, 00198 Rome, Italy. TEL 39-6-8543267. FAX 39-6-85350021. adv.: B&W page $2040, color page $3250; trim 185 x 275; adv. contact: Claudia Severini. **Document type:** trade publication.
  Formerly: Force (ISSN 1120-1673)
  Description: Covers the security industry and technology and operational aspects of crime fighting.

364.4 SP ISSN 1130-9148
FORMACION DE SEGURIDAD. 1988. 4/yr. D. Ramon de la Cruz 68, 6o, 28001 Madrid, Spain. TEL 1-40-296-19. FAX 1-401-88-74. Ed. Francisco J.B. Marti. circ. 12,000.

365.64 323.4 US ISSN 1053-4962
FULL DISCLOSURE;* for truth, justice, and the American way. 1983. bi-m. $29.95 (effective Jan. 1993). Box 1533, Oil City, PA 16301-5533. TEL 616-897-7222. Ed. Glen L. Roberts. adv.; charts; illus.; stat. (tabloid format)

638.5 669 IT
GIORNALE DEL FABBRO E DEL SERRAMENTISTA. 12/yr. Via Toce 4, Varese, Italy. TEL 332-224-068. FAX 332-212-312. Ed. Franco Diari. circ. 8,000.

365.64 CC
GONG'AN YANJIU/PUBLIC SECURITY STUDY. (Text in Chinese) bi-m. P.O. Box 3052, Beijing 100051, People's Republic of China. TEL 5128871. Ed. Wang Zhimin.

364.4 658.3 US
GUIDE TO BACKGROUND INVESTIGATIONS. 1987. biennial. $129.50. Transportation Information Services Inc. (T I S I), 4110 S. 100th East Ave., Tulsa, OK 74146. TEL 918-664-9074; 800-247-8713. Kim Schauer. R&P contact: Kim Schauer. adv. contact: Paula Lee. (also avail. in diskette format) **Document type:** directory.
  Description: Lists sources for obtaining public records to use in background searches.

364.4 US ISSN 0745-1148
HOSPITAL SECURITY AND SAFETY MANAGEMENT. 1980. m. $199 (foreign $224). Rusting Publications, 402 Main St., Box 190, Port Washington, NY 11050. TEL 516-883-1440. FAX 516-883-1683. Ed. Susan Krivin; Pub. Robert Rusting. circ. 1,200. (back issues avail.) **Document type:** newsletter.

HOTEL - MOTEL SECURITY AND SAFETY MANAGEMENT; a newsletter of loss prevention, crime prevention, and accident prevention. see HOTELS AND RESTAURANTS

363.22 SZ ISSN 0257-2435
HOTEL SECURITY WORLDWIDE MAGAZINE. (Text in French) 1987. s-a. Marcel Meichtry Editions, Chemi de la Caroline 26, CH-1213 Petit-Lancy, Switzerland. TEL 41-22-8798820. FAX 41-22-8798825. E-mail: revue__polytech@mail.dotcom.fr. Ed. Michel Giannoni. R&P contact: Michel Giannoni. adv. contact: Andre Almy. circ. 10,000. **Document type:** trade publication.

I E E E SYMPOSIUM ON RESEARCH IN SECURITY AND PRIVACY. PROCEEDINGS. see COMPUTERS — Computer Security

I S AUDIT & CONTROL JOURNAL. (Information Systems see COMPUTERS — Electronic Data Processing

051 US
I S P NEWS. (InfoSecurity Product) 1990. bi-m. $36. I S Training Institute Press, Inc., 498 Concord St., Framingham, MA 01701. TEL 508-879-7999. Ed. Russell Kan. circ. 25,000 (controlled). (tabloid format)
  Description: Provides a broad description of information security issues, technologies, services, products and their applications for MIS, information security and EDP audit professionals.

INSTELEC. see COMMUNICATIONS

364.4 US
INTELLIGENCE PROFESSION SERIES. irreg. $11.95 per no. Association of Former Intelligence Officers, 672 Whittier Ave., Ste. 303A, McLean, VA 22101. TEL 707-790-0320. **Document type:** monographic series.

365.64 US ISSN 1047-8779
HV6431
INTERNATIONAL COUNTERTERRORISM & SECURITY. 1990. q. $65 (foreign $85) (effective 1998). Counterterrorism & Security, Inc., Box 10265, Arlington, VA 22210. TEL 703-243-0993. FAX 703-243-1197. URL: http://www.securitynet.net. Ed. Steven J. Fustero; Pub. Steven J. Fustero. R&P contact: Steven J. Fustero. adv. contact: Phil Friedman. bk.rev. circ. 10,000. **Document type:** newsletter, consumer publication.
  ●Also available online. Vendor(s): NewsNet.
  Formerly (until 1991): Counterterrorism and Security.
  Description: Provides analysis, interviews, reports and information in the world of terrorism.

INTERNATIONAL JOURNAL OF INTELLIGENCE AND COUNTERINTELLIGENCE. see POLITICAL SCIENCE

365 UK ISSN 1359-1886
▼**INTERNATIONAL JOURNAL OF RISK, SECURITY AND CRIME PREVENTION.** 1996. q. £130 (overseas £145) (effective 1996). Perpetuity Press, P.O. Box 376, Leicester LE2 3ZZ, England. TEL 44-116-270-4186. FAX 44-116-270-7742. **Document type:** bulletin.
  —BLDSC (4542.538300).

CRIMINOLOGY AND LAW ENFORCEMENT — SECURITY

364 UK ISSN 0141-8017
INTERNATIONAL SECURITY REVIEW. (Text in English, French, German, Spanish) 1978. bi-m. £73.80 (foreign £89.20) (effective 1997). Argus Business Media Ltd. (Subsidiary of: D M G Exhibitions Group Ltd.), Queensway House, 2 Queensway, Redhill, Surrey RH1 1QS, England. TEL 44-1737-768611. FAX 44-1737-761685. Ed. T. Slinn. **Indexed:** Amer.Bibl.Slavic & E.Eur.Stud, DM & T. **Document type:** trade publication.
—BLDSC (4548.897000); SWETS.
  Incorporates (in 1991): Security Times (ISSN 0265-6442)
  Description: Serves the commercial and industrial security market.

INTERNATIONALES WAFFEN-MAGAZIN. see *SPORTS AND GAMES*

364.4 UK ISSN 0963-0058
INTERSEC. 1991. 10/yr. £59 (U.S. & Canada $120; rest of world £79) (effective 1997). Three Bridges Publishing Ltd., Bridge House, Aviary Rd., Woking, Surrey GU22 8TH, England. TEL 44-1932-340418. FAX 44-1932-340419. Ed. Brian Cruickshank. R&P contact: Brian Cruickshank. adv.: B&W page $3205, color page $4935; trim 8 1/4 x 11 3/4; adv. contact: Anne Heasman. circ. 12,965. **Document type:** trade publication.

365.64 US ISSN 0743-3077
INTRIGUE. 1983. s-m. $290. Ted Michaels, Ed. & Pub., Box 68, Woodbridge, NJ 07095-0068. adv.

364.4 613 IE
IRISH SECURITY NEWS. 3/yr. Security Media, P.O. Box 1822, Baldoyle, Dublin, Ireland. TEL 391115. FAX 735934. Ed. Fionnuala Tattersall. circ. 3,000.

365.34 UK
JANE'S POLICE AND SECURITY EQUIPMENT. 1988. a. £215 (effective 1997). Jane's Information Group, Sentinel House, 163 Brighton Rd., Coulsdon, Surrey CR5 2NH, England. TEL 44-181-700-3700. FAX 44-181-700-3788. TELEX 916907-JANES-G. E-mail: info@janes.co.uk; URL: http://www.janes.com/janes.html. (Orders in U.S. and Canada to: Dept. DSM, 1340 Braddock Pl., Ste. 300, Box 1436, Alexandria, VA 22314-1651. TEL 703-683-3700. FAX 703-836-0029) Ed. Charles Heyman. **Document type:** trade publication.
●Also available on CD-ROM.
  Former titles: Jane's Security & Counter-Insurgency Equipment; Jane's Security and Co-In Equipment (ISSN 0966-3681); (until 1991): Jane's Security and Co-In (ISSN 0954-3783)
  Description: Over 2,000 items of security equipment for police, military, and security organizations.

JOURNAL OF HEALTHCARE PROTECTION MANAGEMENT. see *HOSPITALS*

363.2 US ISSN 0195-9425
HV8290
JOURNAL OF SECURITY ADMINISTRATION. 1978. s-a. $25 (foreign $45) to individuals; institutions $40 (foreign $60) (effective 1994). (Western Illinois University) B L S S, Inc., Box 164509, Miami, FL 33116-4509. TEL 305-254-7006. FAX 305-254-9662. (Co-sponsor: Academy of Security Educators and Trainers) Ed. Norman R. Bottom. R&P contact: Norman Bottom. adv.; bk.rev. circ. 2,500. (also avail. in microform from UMI; back issues avail.; reprint service avail. from UMI) **Indexed:** CJPI, Crim.Just.Abstr. **Document type:** academic/scholarly publication.
—UMI; UnCover.
  Formerly: Journal of Security Administration and Private Police.
  Description: Covers business administration, criminal justice, law, psychology, public administration, and sociology topics related to the field of security administration.
  Refereed Serial

365 UK
KEY NOTE MARKET REPORT: PRISON SERVICES. Variant title: Prison Services. 1994. irreg. £205. Key Note Ltd., Field House, 72 Oldfield Rd., Hampton, Middlesex TW12 2HQ, England. TEL 44-181-783-0755. FAX 44-181-783-0049. **Document type:** trade publication.
●Also available online.
Also available on CD-ROM.
  Formerly: Key Note Report: Prison Services (ISSN 1355-0063)

365 UK
KEY NOTE MARKET REPORT: SECURITY. Variant title: Security. irreg., no.7, 1991. £185. Key Note Ltd., Field House, 72 Oldfield Rd., Hampton, Middlesex TW12 2HQ, England. TEL 44-181-783-0755. FAX 44-181-783-1940. **Document type:** trade publication.

KEY NOTE MARKET REPORT: VEHICLE SECURITY. see *TRANSPORTATION — Automobiles*

365.64 UK ISSN 1356-613X
KEY NOTE MARKET REVIEW: U K SECURITY MARKET. Variant title: U K Security Market. 1992. irreg., no.4, 1995. £410. Key Note Ltd., Field House, 72 Oldfield Rd., Hampton, Middlesex TW12 2HQ, England. TEL 44-181-783-0755. FAX 44-181-783-0049. **Document type:** trade publication.
●Also available online.
Also available on CD-ROM.

365.64 US ISSN 0277-0792
KEYNOTES (DALLAS). 1957. m. $15 membership only. Associated Locksmiths of America, Inc., 3003 Live Oak St., Dallas, TX 75204. TEL 214-827-1701. FAX 214-827-1810. Ed. Anne McDonald Davis. adv. contact: Frances Rushing. tr.lit. circ. 17,000. (reprint service avail.) **Document type:** trade publication.

LIBRARY & ARCHIVAL SECURITY. see *LIBRARY AND INFORMATION SCIENCES*

364.4 US
LIPMAN REPORT. m. $60. Guardsmark, Inc., Box 444, Memphis, TN 38101. TEL 901-522-6092. FAX 901-522-6013. Ed. Ira A. Lipman. **Document type:** newsletter.

683.029 US
TS519
LOCKSMITH LEDGER - INTERNATIONAL DIRECTORY. 1939. a. $28 (effective 1997). Locksmith Publishing Corp., 850 Busse Hwy., Park Ridge, IL 60068-5980. FAX 847-692-4604. Ed. Gale Johnson. adv. contact: Nancy L. Campanale. circ. 25,000. (reprint service avail. from UMI) **Document type:** directory.
  Former titles: Locksmith Ledger - International Directory; Locksmith Ledger - Security Guide and Directory.

LOSS PREVENTION LETTER FOR SUPERMARKET EXECUTIVES. see *FOOD AND FOOD INDUSTRIES — Grocery Trade*

MERCADO PREVISOR. see *INSURANCE*

363.22 US ISSN 0882-9667
N S I ADVISORY. 1985. m. $324. National Security Institute, 57 E. Main St., No. 217, Westborough, MA 01581-1464. TEL 508-366-5800. FAX 508-898-0132. Ed. David A. Marston. **Document type:** newsletter.
  Description: Provides news, analysis, and commentary on national security issues of concern to government and industry security directors.

NATIONAL ENVIRONMENTAL ENFORCEMENT JOURNAL. see *ENVIRONMENTAL STUDIES*

365.64 US ISSN 0364-3719
TS519.N3
NATIONAL LOCKSMITH. 1929. m. $30. National Publishing Co., 1533 Burgundy Pkwy., Streamwood, IL 60107. TEL 708-837-2044. Ed. Marc Goldberg.
  Description: Focuses on security and locksmithing.

364 UK
THE NATIONAL SAFETY AND SECURITY YEARBOOK (YEAR). 1994. a. £25 (diskette ed. £150). Commerce Publications, Commerce Business Directories, Station House, Station Rd., Newport Pagnell, Milton Keynes, Bucks. MK16 0AG, England. TEL 01908-614477. FAX 01908-217425. Ed. Karen Pickwick; Pub. Maria Luisi. (also avail. in diskette format) **Document type:** directory.
  Description: Lists manufacturers and services of safety and security systems.

NATIONAL SECURITY REVIEW. see *POLITICAL SCIENCE*

364.4 US ISSN 1052-9985
TL175
PARKING SECURITY REPORT. m. $199 (foreign $224). Rusting Publications, 402 Main St., Box 190, Port Washington, NY 11050. TEL 516-883-1440. FAX 516-883-1683. Ed. Susan Krivin; Pub. Robert Rusting. **Document type:** newsletter.

364.4 US
PERISCOPE (MCLEAN). q. membership. Association of Former Intelligence Officers, 6723 Whittier Ave., Ste. 303A, McLean, VA 22101. TEL 703-790-0320. **Document type:** newsletter.

364.4 UK ISSN 1355-6479
POLICE AND GOVERNMENT SECURITY TECHNOLOGY. 1994. q. Ballantyne Ross Ltd., 12-14 Tiller Rd., Docklands, London E14 8PX, England. TEL 44-171-363-0350. FAX 44-171-363-0354. Ed. Michael Tanner. **Document type:** trade publication.
—BLDSC (6543.210500).

364.4 UK ISSN 1359-7523
▼**POLICE SCIENCE & TECHNOLOGY REVIEW.** 1995. q. £45 (Europe £49; elsewhere £57) (effective 1996). Police Review Publishing Co. Ltd., 100 Avenue Rd., Swiss Cottage, London NW3 3PG, England. TEL 44-171-393-7600. FAX 44-171-393-7471. Ed. Gary Mason; Pub. Fabiana Angelini. adv. contact: Melvyn Broad. **Document type:** trade publication.
—BLDSC (6543.262820).

365 UK
PRISON SERVICE MAGAZINE. q. National Press Publishers, Peel House, 5 Balfour Rd., Weybridge, Surrey KT13 8HE, England. TEL 44-1932-859155. FAX 44-1932-859661. Ed. Chris Locke. circ. 10,000. **Document type:** trade publication.

PRIVACY AND SECURITY 2001. see *LAW*

364 343 US ISSN 0738-6958
KF5399.5.P7
PRIVATE SECURITY CASE LAW REPORTER; the security professional's digest of state & federal court decisions. 1982. 10/yr. $347 (Canada $377; elsewhere $402) (effective Oct. 1996). Strafford Publications, Inc., Specialized Information Services, 590 Dutch Valley Rd., N.E., Drawer 13729, Atlanta, GA 30324-0729. TEL 404-881-1141. FAX 404-881-0074. E-mail: custserv@straffordpub.com. Ed. Jennifer F. Vaughan; Pub. Richard M. Ossoff. index, cum.index: 1982-1991. (looseleaf format; back issues avail.) **Document type:** newsletter.
  Description: Covers a wide range of judicial decisions on all areas of interest to private security managers in all industries.

364.4 US
PROTECTION NEWS. 1980. 3/yr. Can.$18. International Foundation for Protection Officers, Bellingham Business Park, 4200 Meridian, Ste. 200, Bellingham, WA 98226. TEL 360-733-1571. FAX 360-671-4329. Ed. Sandi J. Davies. adv. circ. 10,000. **Document type:** newsletter, trade publication.
  Former titles: Protection Officer News (ISSN 0823-9304); (until 1984): Professional Protection Magazine; (until 1981): Protection Canada.

364.4 US ISSN 0740-137X
CODEN: PABUEW
PROTECTION OF ASSETS BULLETIN. 1974. m. $397 to qualified personnel. Merritt Publishing, P.O. Box 955, Santa Monica, CA 90406. TEL 310-450-7234. FAX 310-396-4563. Ed. Timothy J. Walsh. bk.rev.; index. circ. 3,500. (looseleaf format) **Document type:** newsletter.
—CASDDS.

RECHERCHE - TRANSPORTS - SECURITE. see *TRANSPORTATION*

S I G S A C REVIEW. (Special Interest Group for Security Audit Control) see *COMPUTERS — Computer Security*

CRIMINOLOGY AND LAW ENFORCEMENT — SECURITY

683   US   ISSN 0889-9010
SAFE & VAULT TECHNOLOGY. (Former name of issuing body: Safeman, Inc.) 1983. m. $96 (Canada $109; overseas $136). Safe & Vault Technicians Association, 3003 Live Oak St., Dallas, TX 75204-6189. TEL 214-827-7233. FAX 214-827-1810. Ed. Wendy Lucas. R&P contact: Charles Gibson. adv. contact: Anelia M. Banda. bk.rev.; tr.lit.; circ. 2,500 (paid). **Document type:** trade publication.
    Formerly (until 1986): Professional Locksmithing.
    Description: Directed exclusively to the safe, vault and physical security fields.
    Refereed Serial

364.4   US   ISSN 1060-426X
LB3013.3
SCHOOL SECURITY REPORT. m. $199 (foreign $224). Rusting Publications, 402 Main St., Box 190, Port Washington, NY 11050. TEL 516-883-1440. FAX 516-883-1683. Ed. Susan Krivin; Pub. Robert Rusting. **Document type:** newsletter.

363.22   GW   ISSN 0937-2555
SCHUTZ AKTUELL; magazin fuer sicherheit. 1986. q. DM.30. Thome Verlag GmbH, Goethestr. 21, 80336 Munich, Germany. TEL 089-591964. FAX 089-553079. Ed. Angela-Christiane Grond. adv. contact: Doris Tegethoff. bk.rev. adv. circ. 6,500. (back issues avail.) **Document type:** consumer publication.
    Formerly: Katastrophenschutz Aktuell (ISSN 0930-1240)

SCIENCE AND GLOBAL SECURITY; the technical basis for arms control and environmental policy initiatives. see *SCIENCES: COMPREHENSIVE WORKS*

365   UK   ISSN 0950-2254
SCOTTISH PRISON SERVICE. OCCASIONAL PAPER. irreg. £10. Scottish Prison Service, Prisons Research Branch, Calton House, Rm. 306, 5 Redheughs Rigg, Edinburgh EH12 9HW, Scotland. **Document type:** monographic series.

658   JA
SECOM ANNUAL REPORT (YEAR). (Text in English) a. free. Secom Co., Ltd., Management Control Division, Shinjuku Nomura Bldg., 26-2 Nishi Shinjuku 1-chome, Shinjuku-ku, Tokyo 163-05, Japan. TEL 03-3348-7511. FAX 03-3348-1799. TELEX 0232-4982-3. charts; stat.; illus. **Document type:** corporate report.

363.22   SZ
SECUR FLASH. 6/yr. Verlag Binkert AG, CH-4335 Laufenburg, Switzerland. TEL 41-64-697272. FAX 41-64-697333. Ed. Daniel Boehler. adv.: B&W page 2395 SFr., color page 3430 SFr.; trim 185 x 266; adv. contact: Markus Wuersch. circ. 8,860. **Document type:** trade publication.

SECURE COMPUTING; the international journal of computer security. see *COMPUTERS — Computer Security*

365.64   FR   ISSN 1244-5053
T55.A1   CODEN: RTFEAJ
SECURITE. 1883. 9/yr. 560 F. (foreign 630 F.). Societe Alpine de Publications, 7 chemin des Gordes, 38100 Grenoble, France. adv.; bk.rev.; bibl.; charts; illus.; stat.; tr.lit.; index. circ. 6,500. **Indexed:** C.I.S. Abstr.
    —CASDDS; CISTI.
    Formed by the 1993 merger of: R G S Revue Generale de Securite (ISSN 0242-6277); Which was formed by the merger of (1969-1980): Revue Technique de Feu (ISSN 0048-8194); (1980-1980): Revue de la Protection des Hommes et des Biens (ISSN 0240-9747); (1985-1992): Preventique (ISSN 0766-5687); Which was formerly (until 1985): Revue de la Securite (ISSN 0035-1261); And (until 1965): Protection, Securite, Hygiene du Travail.
    Description: Information on present-day and future security systems and how to obtain them.

621.389   FR   ISSN 1151-4787
SECURITE ECHOS. 21/yr. Editions du Gaillard, 29 rue de la Fontaine-au-Roi, 75011 Paris, France. TEL 43-38-99-77. circ. 5,000.

365 658.478   US   ISSN 0890-8826
HV8290   CODEN: SECUEU
SECURITY; the magazine for buyers of security products, systems and service. 1964. 12/yr. $79.90 (Canada $109.90; Mexico $99.90; elsewhere $149.95). Cahners Publishing Company (Des Plaines), Division of Reed Elsevier Inc., 1350 E. Touhy Ave., Box 5080, Des Plaines, IL 60018-5080. TEL 847-390-2078. FAX 847-635-9950. URL: http://www.secmag.com. (Subscr. to: 8773 Ridgeline Blvd., Highlands Ranch, CO 80126-2329. TEL 800-662-7776) Ed. Bill Zalud; Pub. Rick Schwer. R&P contact: Bill Zalud. adv. contact: Jo Anderson. charts; illus.; tr.lit.; index. circ. 40,400. (also avail. in microform from UMI; microfiche from CIS; reprint service avail. from UMI) **Indexed:** ABI Inform., CJPI, Comput.Lit.Ind., Crim.Just.Abstr., INSPEC (1987-), SRI. **Document type:** trade publication.
    —BLDSC (8217.143000); AskIEEE; KR SourceOne; SWETS; UMI. **CCC.**
    Formerly (until 1986): Security World (ISSN 0037-0703)
    Description: For buyers and specifiers of security products, systems and services in corporate, institutional, financial, retail, and government settings. Finely focused articles update readers on the latest technology available in categories including access control, CCTV, fire protection, identification, integrated systems, monitoring, and hardware.

364.4 345   US   ISSN 0741-482X
KF5399.5.P7
SECURITY AND SPECIAL POLICE LEGAL UPDATE. 1983. m. $188 (effective Sep. 1997). Americans for Effective Law Enforcement, Inc., 5519 N. Cumberland Ave., Ste. 1008, Chicago, IL 60656-1471. TEL 773-763-2800. FAX 773-763-3225. E-mail: aele@aol.com. Ed. B.J. Farber. index, cum.index: 1983-1993. circ. 500. (looseleaf format) **Document type:** newsletter.
    Description: Covers cases that impact upon professionals in the private security field.

364.5 614.84   AT   ISSN 0728-3725
SECURITY AUSTRALIA. m. Aus.$80($125) (effective 1996). Reed Business Publishing Pty. Ltd. (Subsidiary of: Reed International PLC), P.O. Box 5487, W. Chatswood, N.S.W. 2057, Australia. TEL 61-2-372-5222. FAX 61-2-419-7399. Ed. Janet De Silva. circ. 4,300.
    Description: Provides news and information on commercial, industrial and domestic security.

365   US   ISSN 1071-0833
SECURITY CONCEPTS. 1993. m. Terra Publishing, Inc., R.D. 1, Box 142, Center St. Ext., Salamanca, NY 14779. TEL 716-945-3488. FAX 716-945-5238. (Alt. addr.: Terra Publishing, Inc., Box 460, Salamanca, NY 14779) Ed. Sandra Jackson. R&P contact: Tim Jackson. adv. contact: Linda Robinson. circ. 21,000 (controlled). **Document type:** newspaper.
    Description: Aimed at corporate security directors and safety managers.

365.34   II
SECURITY CONTROLS. (Text in English) 1986. m. B-14, Deepali, 92 Nehru Place, New Delhi 110 019, India. Pub. V.K.Sharma. adv.: B&W page Rs.2500, color page Rs.5500; trim 205 x 265; adv. contact: Meenu Kanwar.

SECURITY DEALER. see *BUSINESS AND ECONOMICS — Office Equipment And Services*

364   US   ISSN 1079-1590
HV6769
SECURITY DIRECTOR'S DIGEST. 1987. w. (51/yr.). $345 (Canada $355) (includes q. Calendar of Events) (effective 1998). Washington Crime News Services, 3918 Prosperity Ave., Ste. 318, Fairfax, VA 22031-3334. TEL 703-573-1600; 800-422-9267. FAX 703-573-1604. Ed. Betty B. Bosarge; Pub. Richard J. O'Connell. bk.rev. (looseleaf format; also avail. in microform from UMI; reprint service avail. from UMI) **Indexed:** CJPI. **Document type:** newsletter.
    —UMI.
    Formerly (until 1995): Corporate Security Digest (ISSN 0894-3826); Which was formed by the merger of (1970-1987): Security Systems Digest (ISSN 0037-069X); (1982-1987): Computer Crime Digest (ISSN 0889-5694)
    Description: Covers issues in the face of terrorism throughout the world.

SECURITY DISTRIBUTING & MARKETING. see *BUSINESS AND ECONOMICS — Marketing And Purchasing*

364.4   UK   ISSN 0049-0024
SECURITY GAZETTE.* 1958. m. £23. A G B Publications Ltd., c/o E M A P Business Communications Ltd., Maclaren House, 19 Scarbrook Rd., Croydon CR9 1QH, England. TEL 44-181-868-4499. FAX 44-181-429-3117. TELEX 926726. Ed. Perry Casi. adv.; bk.rev.; illus.; tr.lit.; index. circ. 3,764. (also avail. in microform from UMI; reprint service avail. from UMI) **Indexed:** Abstr.Crim.& Pen., CJPI. **Document type:** trade publication.
    —BLDSC (8217.200000); SWETS; UMI. **CCC.**
    Incorporates: Crime and Fire Prevention (ISSN 0071-5387)
    Description: Provides information for security executives in industry and commerce.

364.4 338.4768   UK   ISSN 0955-3592
SECURITY INDUSTRY. 1989. m. £30 (Europe £40.40; overseas £50) (effective 1997). S P L, Berwick House, 8-10 Knoll Rise, Orpington, Kent BR6 0PS, England. TEL 44-1689-874025. FAX 44-1689-896847. Ed. Stephen Ulph; Pub. John Beese. R&P contact: John Beese. adv.: B&W page £1540, color page £2545; trim 297 x 210; adv. contact: Karen Hollebone. circ. 6,000. **Document type:** trade publication.
    Description: Investigative news and comprehensive coverage of U.K. private security industry.

SECURITY INDUSTRY BUYERS GUIDE. see *BUSINESS AND ECONOMICS — Trade And Industrial Directories*

364 658   IE   ISSN 0955-1662
HV8290   CODEN: SJOUEN
SECURITY JOURNAL. 1989. bi-m. fl.739($425) (effective 1998). (A S I S Foundation) Elsevier Science Ireland Ltd., P.O. Box 85, Limerick, Ireland. TEL 353-61-471944. FAX 353-61-472144. (Subscr. to: Elsevier Science, Regional Sales Office, P.O. Box 211, 1000 AE Amsterdam, Netherlands. TEL 31-20-4853757. FAX 31-20-4853432; Subscr. in the Americas to: Elsevier Science, Regional Sales Office, Box 945, New York, NY 10159-0945. TEL 212-633-3730. FAX 212-633-3680; Subscr. in Australasia and the Far East to: Elsevier Science (Singapore) Pte Ltd, No.1 Temasek Ave., No.17-01 Millenia Tower, Singapore 039192, Singapore. TEL 65-434-3727. FAX 65-337-2230) Ed. Robert D. McCrie. R&P contact: Annette Moloney. (also avail. in microform from UMI; back issues avail.) **Indexed:** Abstr.Crim.& Pen., Crim.Just.Abstr., INSPEC (1991-). **Document type:** academic/scholarly publication.
    —BLDSC (8217.206500); AskIEEE; KR SourceOne; UMI. **CCC.**
    Description: Provides a forum for research and findings in industrial, commercial, institutional and governmental security. Covers such topics as management, operations, crime prevention and technology as they relate to security.
    Refereed Serial

364.4   US   ISSN 0889-0625
SECURITY LAW NEWSLETTER. 1981. m. $297 to individuals; academic institutions $125 (effective 1998). 2125 Bancroft Pl., N.W., Washington, DC 20008-4019. TEL 202-337-2700. FAX 202-337-8324. Ed. Lawrence W. Sherman; Pub. Carol Bridgeforth. **Document type:** newsletter.

381   US   ISSN 0363-4922
    CODEN: SECLD2
SECURITY LETTER. 1970. s-m. $187 in U.S. and Canada; elsewhere $217 (effective 1997). Robert D. McCrie, Ed. & Pub., 166 E. 96th St., New York, NY 10128. TEL 212-348-1553. FAX 212-534-2957. bk.rev.; stat.; index. (processed; also avail. in microform from UMI; reprint service avail. from UMI) **Indexed:** CJPI. **Document type:** newsletter.
    —CASDDS; UMI.
    Description: Covers all aspects of corporate, institutional, and governmental security.

364 HD9999.S453 US ISSN 0736-0401
SECURITY LETTER SOURCE BOOK. 1983. biennial. $75. (Security Letter) Robert D. McCrie, Ed. & Pub., 166 E. 96th St., New York, NY 10128. TEL 212-348-1553. FAX 212-534-2957. E-mail: rmccrie@cuny.campus.mci.net. adv. circ. 3,000. **Document type:** directory.
Description: Directory of leading security consultants, services, systems, and products. Provides information on training, standards, reference materials and industry compensation.

SECURITY MANAGEMENT. see *BUSINESS AND ECONOMICS — Management*

345 US ISSN 1062-1628
SECURITY MANAGEMENT BULLETIN; protecting people, property & assets. 1972. s-m. $137.88. Bureau of Business Practice, 24 Rope Ferry Rd., Waterford, CT 06386. TEL 860-442-4365. FAX 860-437-3555. URL: http://www.bbpnews.com. Ed. Alex Vaughn; Pub. Peter Garabedian. R&P contact: Debra Ferraro. illus. **Document type:** newsletter.
Former titles: Security Management - Protecting Property, People and Assets (ISSN 0745-6093) & Security Management - Plant and Property Protection.
Description: Provides tips and pointers to help managers protect their assets and stymie losses of all kinds.

363.22 UK ISSN 0960-2895
SECURITY MANAGEMENT TODAY. 1990. m. £48 (foreign £68). Blenheim, Blenheim House, 630 Chiswick High Rd., London W4 5BG, England. TEL 44-181-742-2828. FAX 44-181-742-0387. (Subscr. to: Turpin Distribution Services, Tower House, Sovereign Park, Market Harborough, Leics. LE16 9EF, England. TEL 44-1858-468888) Ed. Perry Cass; Pub. Jane Risby-Rose. adv.: B&W page £1610, color page £2260; trim 297 x 224; adv. contact: Paul Sweeney. bk.rev.; tr.lit. circ. 9,674. (back issues avail.) **Document type:** trade publication.
Description: Deals with all aspects of security affecting business. Aimed primarily at chiefs of security in all sectors of business and commerce.

365.64 US ISSN 1059-8294
SECURITY NEWS (SALAMANCA). 1990. m. Terra Publishing, Inc., R.D. 1, Box 142, Center St. Ext., Salamanca, NY 14779. TEL 716-945-3488. FAX 716-945-5238. (Alt addr.: Terra Publishing, Inc., Box 460, Salamanca, NY 14779) Ed. Sandra Jackson. R&P contact: Tim Jackson. adv. contact: Jack Sword. bk.rev.; circ. 21,000 (controlled). **Document type:** trade publication.
Description: Contains material of interest to commercial and residential security dealers and installers.

364.4 CN
SECURITY PULSE. 1995. 4/yr. membership. Canadian Alarm & Security Association - Association Canadienne de l'Alarme et de la Securite, 610 Alden Rd., Ste. 201, Markham, ON L3R 9Z1, Canada. TEL 905-513-0622. FAX 905-513-0624. E-mail: staff@canasa.org; URL: http://www.canasa.org. Ed. Shayla Gunter. adv.; stat.; circ. 1,500 (controlled). **Document type:** newsletter.
Formerly: C A N A S A National Magazine.
Description: Highlights relevant, topical issues for daily business practices in the alarm industry, including installation techniques, home automation, taxes, accounting, false dispatches, and general management and CANASA chapter updates.

364.4 338.4768 UK ISSN 0266-318X
SECURITY RETAILER. 1984. bi-m. £15 (foreign £18.60) (effective 1997). (Builder Group Ltd.) S P L, Berwick House, 8-10 Knoll Rise, Orpington, Kent BR6 0PS, England. TEL 44-1689-874025. FAX 44-1689-896847. Ed. Tom Reeve; Pub. John Beese. R&P contact: John Beese. adv.: page £1850; trim 297 x 210; adv. contact: Jane Morris. circ. 5,000. (back issues avail.) **Document type:** trade publication.

SECURITY SALES; technology for security installation and service. see *BUILDING AND CONSTRUCTION — Hardware*

364.4 UK
SECURITY SPECIFIER. 1984. 6/yr. £24. Portland Europe Ltd., 32 Portland St., Cheltenham, Glos. GL52 2PB, England. TEL 44-1242-583222. FAX 44-1242-222331. Ed. D.G. Constantine. adv. contact: Christopher Musk. circ. 14,803. **Document type:** trade publication.

363.35 UK ISSN 0306-6118
SECURITY SURVEYOR. 1970. bi-m. £30 (foreign £36) (effective 1998). (Association of Burglary Insurance Surveyors) Paramount Publishing Ltd., 17-21 Shenley Rd., Borehamwood, Herts. WD6 1RT, England. TEL 44-181-207-5599. FAX 44-181-207-2598. Ed. Ian Drury. R&P contact: Ian Drury. adv. contact: John McDowell. bk.rev.; charts; illus.; index. circ. 4,800. **Document type:** bulletin.
—BLDSC (8217.230000).

363.22 US ISSN 1069-1804
SECURITY TECHNOLOGY & DESIGN. 1991. 10/yr. $38 (effective 1997). Locksmith Publishing Corp., 850 Busse Hwy., Park Ridge, IL 60068. TEL 847-692-5940. FAX 847-692-4604. E-mail: securitytech@simon-net.com. Ed. Steven Lasky. adv.: B&W page $3065, color page $4060; trim 8 1/8 x 10 7/8. circ. 28,500 (controlled). **Document type:** trade publication.
Description: Devoted to sophisticated integrated systems, including their applications and technical aspects.

364.4 SA
SECURITY TODAY. 1993. m. R.75. Phase 4, P.O. Box 5328, Halfway House 1685, South Africa. Ed. Bryan Rudolph. adv. contact: Joan Nuttall. illus. **Document type:** trade publication.

364.4 BL
SEGURIDAD/SECURITY.* (Text in English, Spanish) bi-m. International Security Association, Rua Almirante Baltazar no. 349, Sao Cristovao 20941, Brazil.

364.4 SP ISSN 0210-8747
SEGURITECNICA. 1980? m. Muntaner 117, 08036 Barcelona, Spain. TEL 3-253-60-90. FAX 3-401-88-74. Ed. Jose A. Loren. circ. 25,000. **Document type:** trade publication.

365.34 330 GW
SICHERHEITS-BESCHAFFUNGSDIENST; aktuelle Produkte und Dienstleistungen fuer Sicherheit in der Wirtschaft. 1987. bi-m. Richard Boorberg Verlag (Stuttgart), Scharrstr. 2, 70563 Stuttgart, Germany. TEL 0711-73850. FAX 0711-7352244. Ed. Ilse Weisenstein. adv.: B&W page DM.3530, color page DM.5630; trim 186 x 280; adv. contact: Ilse Weisenstein. circ. 15,000. (back issues avail.) **Document type:** consumer publication.

363.22 GW ISSN 0944-7520
SICHERHEITS-MARKT. 1993. m. DM.108 (effective 1997). Verlag Siegfried Rohn GmbH & Co. KG, Stolberger Str. 84, 50933 Cologne, Germany. TEL 49-221-54974. FAX 49-221-5497278. Ed. Clarissa Cordroch. adv.: B&W page DM.3675, color page DM.6555; trim 185 x 270; adv. contact: Jenny Jones-Steinkamp. circ. 6,800. **Document type:** trade publication.

364.4 IT
SICUREZZA; componenti, sistemi, tecnologie, normative, mercato, gestione. 1978. m. (11/yr.). L.130000 (effective 1997). Gruppo Editoriale J C E, Via Ferri 6, 20092 Cinisello Balsamo (MI), Italy. TEL 39-2-660251. FAX 39-2-6127620. E-mail: info@jce.it; URL: http://www.jce.it. Ed. Bruno Carlucci. adv.: B&W page L.1990000, color page L.3190000; trim 210 x 280. circ. 7,000.
Formerly: Sicurezza e Prevenzione (ISSN 0392-9000)
Description: Provides information on systems and equipment to crime prevention.

643.16 368.8 SW ISSN 0283-5452
SKYDD & SAEKERHET/SAFETY AND SECURITY. 1986. 10/yr. SEK 320 (effective 1997). Svenska Stoeldskyddsfoereningen - Swedish Theft Prevention Association, S-115 87 Stockholm, Sweden. TEL 46-8-783-7450. FAX 46-8-663-9652. Ed. Georg Hahne. adv.: B&W page SEK 14900, color page SEK 20700; trim 185 x 265; adv. contact: Ove Petre. circ. 30,000. **Document type:** newspaper.
Incorporates: Stoeldskydd; Supersedes in part: Brandfoersvar.
Refereed Serial

365 FI ISSN 0782-7571
TURVALLISUUS. 1984. 6/yr. FIM 195. Helsinki Media Company Oy, Special Magazines, P.O. Box 2, FIN-00040 Helsinki Media, Finland. TEL 358-0-1205911. FAX 358-0-1205959. Ed. Reino Lantto. adv. contact: Mia Kemppi. **Document type:** trade publication.

364 364 US ISSN 1062-3450
JK468.I6
UNCLASSIFIED. 1989. q. $20 (foreign $35). Association of National Security Alumni, 1909 Martin Luther King Jr. Pkwy., Des Moines, IA 50314-1534. TEL 515-283-2115. FAX 515-278-4023. E-mail: 73623.2551@compuserve.com; URL: http://ourworld.compuserve.com/homepages/verne__lyon. Ed. Verne Lyon; Pub. Verne Lyon. R&P contact: Verne Lyon. bk.rev.; illus.; circ. 1,400. circ. 700 (paid). Indexed: Alt.Press Ind. **Document type:** newsletter.
Description: Covers political and national security.

VYZOV. see *POLITICAL SCIENCE — Civil Rights*

364.1 US
THE WHITE PAPER. 1987. bi-m. $36 to non-members in N. America; elsewhere $56. Association of Certified Fraud Examiners, 716 West Ave., Austin, TX 78701. TEL 512-478-9070; 800-245-3321. FAX 512-478-9297. Ed. Dick Carozza; Pub. Kathie Green. R&P contact: Dick Carozza. adv. contact: Glenn Garrett. circ. 14,000 (controlled). **Document type:** trade publication.
Description: Presents technical articles on a variety of issues related to the detection and deterrence of white-collar crime. Includes case studies of actual fraud schemes, columns, departments, and news articles on fraud to increase the knowledge of auditing and security practitioners.

CROP PRODUCTION AND SOIL

see *Agriculture–Crop Production and Soil*

CRYSTALLOGRAPHY

see *Chemistry–Crystallography*

CYBERNETICS

see *Computers–Cybernetics*

CYTOLOGY AND HISTOLOGY

see *Biology–Cytology and Histology*

DAIRYING AND DAIRY PRODUCTS

see *Agriculture–Dairying and Dairy Products*

DANCE

see also *Music; Theater*

A D T A NEWSLETTER. (American Dance Therapy Association) see *MEDICAL SCIENCES — Physical Medicine And Rehabilitation*

A I C F NEWSLETTER. (America-Israel Cultural Foundation) see *ART*

793.33 617.1 US
ABILITY BALLROOM DANCE JOURNAL.* q. $25. World Dance and Dance Sport Council, 301 W. 55th. St., Ste. 4, New York, NY 10019-4532. Ed. Richard Diaz.
Description: Covers news, interviews, sports medicine and health products.

DANCE

792.8
GV1587
NE ISSN 1053-4261
CODEN: ADLAEE
ADVANCED LABANOTATION. 1991. irreg. $89 (effective 1998). Gordon and Breach - Harwood Academic, Amsteldisk 166, 1st Fl., 1079 LH Amsterdam, Netherlands. (Subscr. to: International Publishers Distributor, Box 32160, Newark, NJ 07102. TEL 800-545-8398. FAX 215-750-6343) Ed. Ann Hutchinson Guest. (also avail. in microform) **Document type:** monographic series.
—CCC.
  Description: Examines the symbols, rules and current usage of the movement notation system which has been in popular use since the 1920s.
  Refereed Serial

AEROBIC BEAT. see *PHYSICAL FITNESS AND HYGIENE*

793.3 **US** ISSN 1061-8155
AMATEUR DANCERS. 1979. bi-m. $23 (effective 1997). United States Amateur Ballroom Dancers Association, Inc., 1427 Gibsonwood Rd., Baltimore, MD 21228. TEL 410-747-7855. FAX 410-747-7955. E-mail: ecb@world.std.com; URL: http://world.std.com/~usabdant/. Ed. Robert Jacob Meyer; Pub. Robert Jacob Meyer. R&P contact: Robert Jacob Meyer. adv.: page $840. bk.rev.; circ. 300 (paid); 13,667 (controlled). **Document type:** newsletter.
  Description: Covers national and international news on ballroom dancing, competition calendar and results, professional pointers, articles, opinions and reports.

793.31 **US**
AMERICAN DANCE CIRCLE. 1979. q. $25 membership (effective 1997). Lloyd Shaw Foundation, 622 Mt. Evans Rd., Golden, CO 80401. TEL 816-587-4337. Ed. Diane Ortner. adv.; bk.rev. circ. 500. **Document type:** newsletter.
  Description: Presents articles on American folk dance and dance events, covering dance descriptions.

793 **US**
AMERICAN DANCE GUILD QUARTERLY. 1955. q. membership. American Dance Guild, 31 W. 21st St., 3rd Fl., New York, NY 10010. TEL 212-932-2789. Ed. Marilynn Danitz. adv. contact: Marilynn Danitz. bk.rev.; bibl. circ. 400. (processed; back issues avail.) **Document type:** newsletter.
  Formerly: American Dance Guild Newsletter (ISSN 0300-7448)
  Description: Covers issues of concern in th field, reviews and member news.

AMERICAN DANCE THERAPY ASSOCIATION. (NO.) ANNUAL CONFERENCE PROCEEDINGS. see *MEDICAL SCIENCES — Physical Medicine And Rehabilitation*

792 **US** ISSN 0146-3721
RC489.D3
AMERICAN JOURNAL OF DANCE THERAPY. 1968. s-a. $150 (foreign $175) (effective 1998). (American Dance Therapy Association) Human Sciences Press, Inc. (Subsidiary of: Plenum Publishing Corp.), 233 Spring St., New York, NY 10013-1578. TEL 212-620-8000. FAX 212-463-0742. TELEX 23-421139. Ed.Bd. adv.; bk.rev.; abstr.; bibl. (back issues avail.) Indexed: Arts & Hum.Cit.Ind., ASCA, Curr.Cont., Excerp.Med., Fam.Ind., Psychol.Abstr. (1977-), SSCI. **Document type:** academic/scholarly publication.
  —BLDSC (0824.220000); Genuine Article; UMI; UnCover. CCC.
  Supersedes: American Dance Therapy Association. Monograph.
  Description: Covers clinical use of dance therapy, theoretical considerations which provide a framework for dance therapy intervention, and research in dance therapy.
  Refereed Serial

793.31 **US**
AMERICAN MORRIS NEWSLETTER. 1976. 3/yr. $10. 2371 Virginia, Ste. 1, Berkeley, CA 94709. TEL 510-644-2706. Ed.Bd. adv.; bk.rev. circ. 400.
  Description: Current issues and historical background of English ritual dances known as Morris Dancing.

793.34 **US** ISSN 0091-3383
GV1763
AMERICAN SQUAREDANCE; square dance and round dance. 1945. m. $20 (Canada $23; elsewhere $32). (Sanborn Enterprises) Jon Sanborn, Ed. & Pub., 661 Middlefield Rd., Salinas, CA 93906-1004. TEL 408-443-0761. FAX 408-443-6402. adv.; bk.rev.; bibl.; illus.; index. circ. 20,000. (also avail. in microform from UMI) **Document type:** consumer publication.
  —UMI.
  Formerly: Square Dance (ISSN 0038-8734)
  Description: Covers all aspects of square dancing worldwide.

ANNUAIRE MUSIQUE ET DANSE. see *MUSIC*

790 **US** ISSN 0148-5865
GV1703.N36
ARABESQUE; a magazine of international dance. 1975. q. $25 to individuals; institutions $36 (effective 1996). Ibrahim Farrah, Inc., One Sherman Sq., Ste. 22F, New York, NY 10023. TEL 212-595-1677. Ed. Nina Costanza. adv.; bk.rev.; illus. circ. 6,000. **Document type:** academic/scholarly publication.
  —BLDSC (1583.306000); UnCover.
  Description: Covers Middle Eastern dance and music; examines the dance's roots, and the essence behind its beauty. Researches various topics suggested by danse orientale.

793.31 781.7 **US**
ARKANSAS COUNTRY DANCER. 1980. q. $7.50. Arkansas Country Dance Society, 31 Hampshire Circle, Little Rock, AR 72212. TEL 501-224-3486. Ed. Neil Kelley. circ. 175. **Document type:** newsletter.
  Description: Provides news about the society, including information about traditional Arkansas, American, English, Irish dance and music.

ARTS MANAGEMENT. see *THEATER*

ARTS MANAGEMENT WEEKLY. see *BUSINESS AND ECONOMICS — Management*

ARTS NEWS. see *ART*

ARTSBOARD. see *THEATER*

793 **US** ISSN 0882-3472
GV1580
ATTITUDE; the dancers' magazine. 1982. q. $20 (foreign $40); newsstand price: $6. Dance Giant Steps, Inc., 1040 Park Pl., Ste. C-5, Brooklyn, NY 11213-1946. TEL 718-773-3046. FAX 908-245-3373. Eds. Bernadine Jennings, Arthur T. Wilson. R&P contact: Bernadine Jennings. adv. contact: B. Jennings. bk.rev. circ. 2,500. **Document type:** trade publication, consumer publication.
  —UnCover.
  Description: Artist initiated trade journal and audience development tool that fosters cultural pluralism by documenting the diverse artists of New York State. Includes features, reviews and research news.

792.8 **AT** ISSN 0818-6022
AUSTRALIAN BALLET NEWS. 1986. 3/yr. free to patrons. Australian Ballet Foundation, 2 Kavanagh St., Southbank, Vic. 3006, Australia. TEL 61-3-96848600. FAX 61-3-96867081. URL: http://www.vicnet.net.au/vicnet/ballet. Ed. Debra Howlett. R&P contact: Debra Howlett. circ. 28,000 (controlled). **Document type:** newsletter.
  Refereed Serial

792.62 **IT**
BALLANDO; la rivista per chi ama la danza. bi-m. L.70000 in Europe L.100000; elsewhere L.150000. Editoriale Pantheon s.r.l., Via Lattanzio, 47, 00136 Rome, Italy. TEL 39-6-7293291. (Dist. by: Societa Parrini s.r.l., P.zza Colonna, 61 00186 Rome, Italy. TEL 39-6-6840731) Ed. Enrico Catiglione.

792.8 **CN** ISSN 0045-1347
BALLET-HOO. 1969. q. $10 membership. Royal Winnipeg Ballet, Communications Department, 380 Graham Ave., Winnipeg, MB R3C 4K2, Canada. TEL 204-956-0183. FAX 204-943-1994. Ed. Arlette Anderson. adv. contact: Arlette Anderson. circ. 53,000 (controlled).
  Description: Contains news about the Royal Winnipeg Ballet, its various activities, artists and performances.

792.8 **JA**
BALLET NO HON/BOOK ON BALLET. (Text in Japanese) q. 1750 Yen. Ongaku No Tomo Sha Corp., Kagurazaka 6-30, Shinjuku-ku, Tokyo 162, Japan. TEL 81-3-3235-2111. FAX 81-3-3235-2129. Ed. Natsuo Tsukatanl; Pub. Jun Meguro. R&P contact: Kazuyuki Nabeshima. adv.: B&W page 288000 Yen, color page 552000 Yen; trim 277 x 210; adv. contact: Hiroshi Asakawa. circ. 100,000. **Document type:** trade publication.
  Description: Covers ballet scenes in Japan and abroad.

792.8 **US** ISSN 0522-0653
GV1787
BALLET REVIEW. 1965. q. $23 to individuals (foreign $31); institutions $42 (foreign $50) (effective 1997). Dance Research Foundation, Inc., 37 W. 12th St., 7J, New York, NY 10011. TEL 212-924-5183. FAX 212-924-2176. Ed. Francis Mason. R&P contact: Francis Mason. adv.: page $375; trim 6 x 9 1/8; adv. contact: Marvin Hoshino. bk.rev.; charts; illus.; circ. 2,500 (paid). (also avail. in microform from UMI) Indexed: Arts & Hum.Cit.Ind., ASCA, Curr.Cont., Hum.Ind., Mid.East: Abstr.& Ind. **Document type:** academic/scholarly publication.
  —BLDSC (1861.029000); Genuine Article; KR SourceOne; UnCover. CCC.
  Description: Devoted to critical and scholarly writing about all aspects of theatrical dance.

792.8 **FR** ISSN 1166-5025
BALLET 2000. bi-m. 220 F. (foreign 280 F.) for 10 nos. Editions Ballet 2000, 37, bd. Dubouchage, 0600 Nice, France. Ed. Alfio Agostini. adv. contact: Antoms de Freitas. **Document type:** newspaper.

792.8 **GW**
GV1787
BALLETT INTERNATIONAL - TANZ AKTUELL. (Text in English, German) 1978. m. Friedrich Kulturzeitschriftenverlag, Luetzowplatz 7, 10785 Berlin, Germany. TEL 49-30-254495-0. FAX 49-30-25449524. Ed. Rolf Garske. adv.; bk.rev.; illus. circ. 12,000. (back issues avail.) Indexed: Arts & Hum.Cit.Ind., ASCA, Curr.Cont., SSC **Document type:** trade publication.
  —BLDSC (1861.029280); Genuine Article.
  Formed by the 1994 merger of: Tanz Aktuell (ISSN 0933-0585) & Ballett International (ISSN 0722-6268); Which incorporated (in 1991): Tanz International (ISSN 0937-8286); Which incorporated (in 1989): Tanz (ISSN 0138-1482); Formerly (until 1982): Ballett Info (ISSN 0171-7995).

792.8 **IT** ISSN 1123-7813
BALLETTO OGGI; attualita e cultura di danza. 1980. bi-m. L.49000 (foreign L.70000) for 10 nos. Editions Ballet 2000, Alzaia Naviglio Grande 46, 20144 Milan, Italy. TEL 2-58-111192. FAX 2-58-111238. (French addr.: 37 Bd. Dubouchage, 0600 Nice, France) Ed. Alfio Agostini. adv.; bk.rev. circ. 20,000. (back issues avail.) **Document type:** newspaper.
  Description: Covers national and international dance and dance culture.

793.33 **US** ISSN 1061-8147
BALLROOM DANCE COMPETITION CALENDAR. 6/yr. $ 6708-G Lee Highway, Arlington, VA 22205. TEL 703-534-4947. FAX 703-535-2222. Ed. Peter L. Collins; Pub. Peter L. Collins. R&P contact: Peter L. Collins. adv. contact: Peter L. Collins. **Document type:** directory.
  Description: Comprehensive listing of U.S., Canada and international ballroom dance competitions and non-competitive events, including dates, addresses, phone numbers and deadlines.

793.33 **US**
BALLROOM DANCER'S RAG. 10/yr. $13.75. 1448 Montego Dr., San Jose, CA 95120-5105. TEL 408-268-6042. Ed. Richard Wilson. **Document type:** newsletter.
  Description: Covers dance scene in San Francisco area.

793.33 **UK** ISSN 0005-4380
BALLROOM DANCING TIMES. 1956. m. £15.50 (foreign £17 ($34)) (effective 1997). Dancing Times Ltd., Clerkenwell House, 45-47 Clerkenwell Green, London EC1R 0EB, England. TEL 44-171-250-3006. FAX 44-171-253-6679. Ed. Mary Clarke. dance rev.; rec.rev.; illus. (back issues avail.) **Document type:** consumer publication.

793.33 792.809   US   ISSN 1072-5156
THE BALLROOM REVIEW; a guide to dance news and events. 1991. 5-7/yr. $27 (effective 1997). T B R Communications, Ltd., 60 Gramercy Park N., New York, NY 10010. TEL 212-673-3442. FAX 212-673-3442. E-mail: balrmevus@aol.com. Ed. Nicholas M. Ullo; Pub. Nicholas M. Ullo. R&P contact: Nicholas M. Ullo. TEL 212-673-3442. adv.: B&W page $840; trim 7 1/2 x 10; adv. contact: Nicholas M. Ullo. bk.rev.; dance rev.; film rev.; play rev. circ. 3,000. (back issues avail.) **Document type:** newsletter, trade publication, bulletin.
 Description: Features selective listings of ballroom dance events and news items. Carries feature articles on the history of dance and dance music (ballroom and modern) and on people who have contributed to the field of dance.

BETRIFFT SPORT. see *PHYSICAL FITNESS AND HYGIENE*

BOLETIN DE MUSICA Y DANZA. see *MUSIC*

793.31   US   ISSN 0274-6034
BOW & SWING. 1951. m. $12 (foreign $14) (effective 1997 & 1998). (Florida Callers Association, Inc.) Atek - Gramac, Inc., 34 E. Main St., Apopka, FL 32703. TEL 305-886-7151. FAX 407-886-8464. Ed. Randy Boyd. R&P contact: Bill Boyd. adv. contact: Bill Boyd. circ. 2,500. **Document type:** trade publication.
 Description: Contains information and news on square and round dancing.

BRITISH PERFORMING ARTS YEARBOOK. see *THEATER*

CANA NEWS. (Christians in the Arts Networking, Inc.) see *ART*

793.3   US   ISSN 1069-7241
C D R NEWSLETTER. 1983. s-a. $20 to individuals; organizations $40. Cross-Cultural Dance Resources, Inc., 518 S. Agassiz, Flagstaff, AZ 86001-5711. TEL 602-774-8108. Ed. Joann Kealiinohomoku. circ. 500. (looseleaf format; back issues avail.) **Document type:** newsletter.
 Description: To learn about culture through studying movement - dance.

793.3   US
C T NEWSLETTER. (Choreographers Theatre) irreg. $10. 94 Chambers St., 3rd Fl., New York, NY 10007. TEL 212-925-3721.

792.8   US   ISSN 0734-4856
C O R D NEWSLETTER. 1981. s-a. $60 to individuals (outside N. America $72); institutions $72 (outside N. America $84); students $30 (outside N. America $42) (includes Dance Research Journal) (membership only) (effective 1996). Congress on Research in Dance, Department of Dance, State University of New York, College at Brockport, Brockport, NY 14420-2939. TEL 716-395-2590. FAX 716-395-5413. Ed. Linda James. R&P contact: Kista Tucker. circ. 850. (reprint service avail. from ISI) **Document type:** newsletter.
 Description: Features news, activities, inquiries, and brief articles on dance and related areas.

793.33   US
C A B D A NEWSLETTER. m. Connecticut American Ballroom Dance Association, 3 Bright Hill Dr., Clinton, CT 06413. Ed. Sandra Trahan. **Document type:** newsletter.

792.8   US
CAJUN NEWS. every 5 wks. 19 Purcell Dr., Danbury, CT 06810. Ed. Nancy Weston.

CANADA'S CULTURE, HERITAGE AND IDENTITY: A STATISTICAL PERSPECTIVE/LE CANADA, SA CULTURE, SON PATRIMOINE ET SON IDENTITE: PERSPECTIVE STATISTIQUE. see *PUBLIC ADMINISTRATION — Abstracting, Bibliographies, Statistics*

793.3   IT
CHOREGRAPHIE; studi e ricerche sulla danza. (Text in Italian; abstracts in English) 1993. s-a. L.40000 (Europe L.52000; America L.55000) (effective 1996). (National Research Council) DiGiacomo Editore, Via Oglio 5, 00198 Rome, Italy. TEL 39-6-7804838. FAX 39-6-85352222. Ed. Flavia Pappacena. bk.rev. circ. 1,000. **Indexed:** RILM. **Document type:** academic/scholarly publication.
 Description: Dedicated to updating information on technical-cultural developments and new research in the various specializations within the art of dance.

792.8   NE   ISSN 0891-6381
GV1580   CODEN: CHDAEO
CHOREOGRAPHY AND DANCE; an international journal. 1988. 4/yr. $80 (effective 1998). Gordon and Breach - Harwood Academic, Amsteldisk 166, 1st Fl., 1079 LH Amsterdam, Netherlands. (Subscr. to: International Publishers Distributor, Box 32160, Newark, NJ 07102. TEL 800-545-8398. FAX 215-750-6343) Ed. Robert P. Cohan. (also avail. in microform) **Document type:** academic/scholarly publication.
 —UnCover. **CCC.**
 Description: Concerned with the ballet and related forms of dance performed on stage, including the techniques whereby choreographers are trained. Covers historical and social influences on dance. *Refereed Serial*

793.31   US
CINCINNATI FOLK LIFE. m. $20. Cincinnati Folk Life, Box 9008, Cincinnati, OH 45209-9998. TEL 513-533-4822. E-mail: cfl@fuse.net. circ. 300. **Document type:** newsletter.

793.33   AG   ISSN 0328-0403
CLUB DE TANGO. 1993. bi-m. Parana 123, 5o piso, Of. 114, 1017 Buenos Aires C.F., Argentina. TEL 54-1-3727251. FAX 54-1-3727251. Ed. Oscar B. Himschoot.

CONSORTIUM FOR DRAMA & MEDIA IN HIGHER EDUCATION. NEWSLETTER. see *THEATER*

790   US   ISSN 0198-9634
GV1580
CONTACT QUARTERLY; a vehicle for moving ideas. 1975. 2/yr. $14 to individuals (Europe & S. America $20; elsewhere $22); institutions $25 (Europe & S. America $28; elsewhere $30). Contact Collaborations, Inc., Box 603, Northampton, MA 01061. TEL 413-586-1181. Eds. Nancy Stark Smith, Lisa Nelson. bk.rev.; charts; illus.; cum.index. circ. 2,400. (back issues avail.) **Document type:** academic/scholarly publication, newsletter.
 —UnCover.
 Description: Journal of contemporary dance, improvisation and performance. Offers views on the craft of movement expression through articles, interviews, poetry, photos and graphics.

CONTRIBUTIONS TO THE STUDY OF MUSIC AND DANCE. see *MUSIC*

CORADDI. see *ART*

793.34 780   US   ISSN 0070-1262
GV1580
COUNTRY DANCE AND SONG. 1968. a. $5. Country Dance & Song Society, Inc., 17 New South St., Northampton, MA 01060-4012. TEL 413-584-9913. Ed. David Sloane. bk.rev. circ. 3,000. **Indexed:** MLA Intl.Bibl., Music Ind.
 Formerly: Country Dancer.

793.31   US   ISSN 1070-8251
GV1763
COUNTRY DANCE & SONG SOCIETY NEWS. bi-m. $15. Country Dance & Song Society, Inc., 17 New South St., Northampton, MA 01060-4012. TEL 413-584-9913. FAX 413-585-8728. E-mail: 71232.2526@compuserve.com. Ed. Caroline Batson. adv.; bk.rev. circ. 3,500.

793   US   ISSN 1083-3307
COUNTRY DANCE LINES. 1984. m. $20 (Canada & Mexico $50; Europe $60; elsewhere $80). Drawer 139, Woodacre, CA 94973-0139. TEL 415-488-0154. FAX 415-488-4671. Ed. Michael Hunt. R&P contact: Michael Hunt. adv. contact: Rhys McCume. bk.rev. circ. 10,000.

793.34   CN   ISSN 0319-8561
CROSS TRAIL NEWS. vol.25, 1977. 5/yr. Vancouver Island Western Square Dance Association, 244 Fenton Rd., Victoria, B.C. V9B 1C1, Canada. adv.

792.8   CU   ISSN 0864-1307
CUBA EN EL BALLET. 4/yr. $10 in N. America; S. America $12; elsewhere $17. (Ministerio de Cultura, Ballet Nacional de Cuba) Ediciones Cubanas, Obispo No. 527, Apdo. 605, Havana, Cuba. illus. **Indexed:** IBR.
 Description: Presents articles and commentaries on the national and international activities of the National Ballet of Cuba, including theoretical papers on ballet and related topics, plus news and information.

THE DAILY CLOG. see *FOLKLORE*

793.33   US
DANCE ACTION INTERNATIONAL.* 8/yr. $40. Box 4918, Laguna Beach, CA 92652-4918. Ed. Cay Cannon.
 Description: Contains color action photos and specialty columns with emphasis on California.

792   UK   ISSN 0011-5983
GV1580
DANCE & DANCERS.* m. £28. 214 Panther House, 38 Mount Pleasant, London WC1X 0AP, England. adv.; illus. **Indexed:** Arts & Hum.Cit.Ind., ASCA, Curr.Cont.
 —BLDSC (3518.223000); Genuine Article; SWETS; UnCover. **CCC.**
 Description: Aimed at ballet enthusiasts and dancers.

793 780   US   ISSN 1062-4066
DANCE AND MUSIC SERIES. 1987. irreg., no.9, 1997. Pendragon Press, 41 Ferry Rd., Stuyvesant, NY 12173-9720. TEL 518-828-3008. FAX 518-828-2368. E-mail: penpress@capital.net; URL: http://www.bmtsinc.com/pdragon. Ed. Wendy Hilton. **Document type:** monographic series.

790   US
DANCE AND THE ARTS. 1983. bi-m. $18 (Canada $30; Europe $36; Asia $48) (effective 1997). Dance Pages, Inc., Box 916, Ansonia Sta., New York, NY 10023. TEL 212-362-8160. FAX 212-362-8118. Ed. Donna Gianell; Pubs. Kenneth Romo, Donna Gianell. R&P contact: Kenneth Romo. adv. contact: Kenneth Romo. **Document type:** consumer publication.
 —UnCover.
 Former titles (until 1995): Dance Pages Magazine (ISSN 1064-6183); (until 1989): Dance Pages (ISSN 0882-5211)
 Description: Provides articles on all aspects of dance, with a dual emphasis on teaching and performance. Features include profiles of dancers and dance companies, reviews of musicals, and a calendar of events for both New York and the rest of the dance world. Includes information on dance schools and instructors.

793.3   AT   ISSN 0159-6330
DANCE AUSTRALIA. 1980. bi-m. Aus.$33 (foreign Aus.$92) (effective Aus. 1996). Yaffa Publishing Group, 17-21 Bellevue St., Surry Hills, N.S.W. 2010, Australia. TEL 61-2-92812333. FAX 61-2-92812750. E-mail: yaffa@yaffa.com.au. Ed. Karen Van Ulzen; Pub. Michael Merrick. adv.: B&W page Aus.$1720, color Aus.$2645; trim 273 x 210; adv. contact: Ann Nelson. bk.rev. circ. 5,999. **Indexed:** Gdlns. **Document type:** consumer publication.
 —BLDSC (3518.223200); UnCover.
 Description: Devoted to dance both as artistic expression and recreational activity.

792.8   US
DANCE BEAT. 12/yr. $30. 12265 S. Dixie Hwy., Ste. 909, Miami, FL 33156. TEL 305-251-6477. FAX 305-665-0828. Ed. Keith Todd.
 Description: Covers news from the governing bodies, both here and world-wide, plus informative articles on all aspects of dancesport.

793.3   US   ISSN 0271-9940
DANCE BOOK FORUM.* 1980. q. $6. Dance Institute International, c/o Zuck, Box 105, New York, NY 10024-0105. Ed. Maria-Ann Bryant. bk.rev.; bibl.; illus.; tr.lit. circ. 15,000.

790   US   ISSN 0147-2526
GV1580   CODEN: DCHRD2
DANCE CHRONICLE; studies in dance & the related arts. 1978. 3/yr. $415 (foreign $426.25) (effective 1998). Marcel Dekker Journals, 270 Madison Ave., New York, NY 10016. TEL 212-696-9000. FAX 212-685-4540. TELEX 421419. (Subscr. to: Box 5017, Monticello, NY 12701) Eds. George Dorris, Jack Anderson. illus. (also avail. in microform from RPI) **Indexed:** Amer.Bibl.Slavic & E.Eur.Stud, Arts & Hum.Cit.Ind., ASCA, Curr.Cont., Hum.Ind., Music Ind., Phys.Ed.Ind. **Document type:** academic/scholarly publication.
 —BLDSC (3518.224000); Genuine Article; KR SourceOne; UMI; UnCover. **CCC.**

792.8   US
DANCE CORRAL. m. $12 (Canada $25; elsewhere $30). Box 27, Berrien Springs, MI 49103. TEL 616-473-3261. Ed. Dennis Waite.
 Description: Covers country dancers and dances.

DANCE

793.3 US
DANCE CRITICS ASSOCIATION. NEWSLETTER. 1978. q. $40 membership (overseas $47). Dance Critics Association, Box 1882, Old Chelsea Sta., New York, NY 10011. TEL 212-343-3584. Ed. Rita Felciano. bk.rev.; illus.; tr.lit. (looseleaf format) **Document type:** newsletter.
Description: Contains articles on the writing of dance criticism. Also covers job opportunities, and news of conventions and seminars.
Refereed Serial

900 US ISSN 0894-4849
GV1580
DANCE: CURRENT SELECTED RESEARCH. 1988. a. $37.50. (National Dance Foundation) A M S Press, Inc., 56 E. 13th St., New York, NY 10003. TEL 212-777-4700. FAX 212-995-5413. Eds. Lynette Y. Overby, James H. Humphrey. bk.rev.; index.
—BLDSC (3518.221700).
Description: Review articles and essays on experimental, historical, philosophical and anthropological aspects of dance.

793.3 US ISSN 0070-2676
DANCE DIRECTORY (YEAR); programs of professional preparation in American colleges and universities. irreg., 15th ed., 1992. $14.95 per no. American Alliance for Health, Physical Education, Recreation, and Dance, 1900 Association Dr., Reston, VA 22091-1502. TEL 703-476-3400; 800-321-0789. FAX 703-436-9527. (Orders to: Hapard, Box 385, Oxon Hill, MD 20750-0385. TEL 800-321-0789) circ. 2,000,000. (reprint service avail. from ISI,UMI) **Indexed:** ERIC. **Document type:** directory.
Description: Offers a guide to programs in professional dance at U.S. colleges and universities. The 1997 edition will also include secondary schools.

792.8 US
DANCE DIRECTORY OF BALLET COMPANIES. AMERICAN EDITION. 1994. a. $39.95. Dance Directory, Box 904, New York, NY 10023. TEL 212-535-3757. FAX 212-535-3757. E-mail: dancedir@aol.com. **Document type:** directory.

792.8 US
DANCE DIRECTORY OF BALLET COMPANIES. EUROPEAN EDITION. 1994. a. $39.95. Dance Directory, Box 904, New York, NY 10023. TEL 212-535-3757. FAX 212-535-3757. E-mail: dancedir@aol.com. Pub. Faith Shaw Petrides.

793.3 UK
DANCE EAST. 3/yr. B C Publications, 16C Market Pl., Diss, Norfolk IP22 3AB, England. TEL 44-1379-644200. FAX 44-1379-650480. Ed. Emma Jackson. adv.; circ. 2,500. (tabloid format; back issues avail.) **Document type:** consumer publication.

793.33 JA
DANCE FAN; monthly ballroom dancing magazine. (Text in Japanese) m. 700 Yen per no. Byakuya Shobou, 3-29-3 Takada, Toshima-ku, Tokyo 171, Japan. TEL 81-3-5950-3561. FAX 81-3-5950-4905.

792.8 UK ISSN 0306-0128
DANCE GAZETTE. 1930. 3/yr. membership. Royal Academy of Dancing, 36 Battersea Sq., London SW11 3RA, England. TEL 44-171-223-0091. FAX 44-171-924-3129. (U.S. orders to: 15 Franklin Pl., Rutherford, NJ 07070) Ed. Sally Anne Lowe; Pub. David Watchman. R&P contact: Sally Anne Lowe. adv.: B&W page £490, color page £850; trim 270 x 181; adv. contact: Julia Bennett. bk.rev. circ. 20,000. (also avail. in microform from UMI; reprint service avail. from UMI) **Document type:** newsletter.

792.8 US
DANCE GYPSY. 1990. 12/yr. $12 (effective 1996). 57 Sleepy Hollow Rd., Essex Junction, VT 05452-2721. TEL 802-899-2378. FAX 802-899-1394. Ed. Valerie Medve. bk.rev.; rec.rev.; circ. 600 (paid). **Document type:** newsletter.
Description: Covers contra, square, swing, ballroom and international folk dances in Vermont, Massachusetts, New Hampshire, and New York area.

792.8 CN ISSN 1189-9816
GV1580
DANCE INTERNATIONAL. 1984. q. Can.$19.26 (effective 1997). Vancouver Ballet Society, 1415 Barclay St., Vancouver, BC V6G 1J6, Canada. TEL 604-681-1525. FAX 604-681-7732. Ed. Maureen Riches. R&P contact: Maureen Riches. adv.: B&W page Can.$900, color page Can.$1325; trim 8 1/4 x 11 3/4; adv. contact: Maureen Riches. bk.rev.; dance rev.; illus. circ. 4,000. (processed; also avail. in microfiche; back issues avail.) **Indexed:** Can.B.P.I. **Document type:** trade publication.
Former titles (until 1993): Vandance International (ISSN 1189-9808); (until 1992): Vandance (ISSN 0705-8063); (until 1977): Vancouver Ballet Society. Newsletter (ISSN 0703-1335); Ballet - Who (ISSN 0005-4348)
Description: Provides national and international dance coverage.
Refereed Serial

793.3 US ISSN 0011-6009
GV1580
DANCE MAGAZINE. 1926. m. $34.95; newsstand price: $3.95. Dance Magazine, Inc., 33 W. 60th St., New York, NY 10023. TEL 212-245-9050. FAX 212-956-6487. E-mail: dancemag@wairus.com. (Subscr. to: Box 5068, Brentwood, TN 37024-9725) Ed. Richard Philp. adv.: B&W page $3200, color page $4965; trim 8 1/4 X 10 3/4. bk.rev.; film rev.; play rev.; illus.; index. (also avail. in microform from UMI) **Indexed:** Acad.Ind., Amer.Bibl.Slavic & E.Eur.Stud., Arts & Hum.Cit.Ind., ASCA, Biog.Ind., Bk.Rev.Ind. (1967-), Child.Bk.Rev.Ind. (1967-), Curr.Cont., Film Lit.Ind. (1973-), Hum.Ind., Ind.Bk.Rev.Hum., Mag.Ind., Media Rev.Dig., Mid.East: Abstr.& Ind., Phys.Ed.Ind., R.G.Abstr., Sports Per.Ind., SSCI. **Document type:** trade publication.
●Also available online. Vendor(s): Information Access Co., UMI.
—BLDSC (3518.227500); Genuine Article; KR SourceOne; SWETS; UMI; UnCover.
Description: International listing of dance performances, workshops, courses, festivals, and tours.

792.8 378.0025 US ISSN 0193-1202
GV1623
DANCE MAGAZINE COLLEGE GUIDE; a directory to dance in North American colleges and universities. biennial. $17.95. Dance Magazine, Inc., 33 W. 60th St., New York, NY 10023. TEL 212-245-9050. FAX 212-956-6487. E-mail: dancemag@wairus.com. Ed. Allen McCormack. adv.; illus. **Document type:** directory.
Formerly: Dance Magazine Directory of College and University Dance.

DANCE MEDICINE-HEALTH NEWSLETTER. see *MEDICAL SCIENCES — Physical Medicine And Rehabilitation*

DANCE MUSIC AUTHORITY. see *MUSIC*

DANCE MUSIC MAGAZINE. see *MUSIC*

793.3 NZ ISSN 0112-4951
DANCE NEWS. 1977. 2/yr. NZ.$20. Royal New Zealand Ballet, P.O. Box 10-786, The Terrace, Wellington, New Zealand. TEL 64-4-499-1107. FAX 64-4-499-0773. Ed. Barbara Hyde. adv.; bk.rev.; illus. circ. 3,000. (back issues avail.) **Document type:** newsletter.
—CCC.
Formerly (until 1988): Pointe.
Description: A newsletter detailing ballet and dance tours and productions in New Zealand including profiles on dancers and information of interest to dancers, teachers and patrons.

793.3 IE ISSN 0790-5203
DANCE NEWS IRELAND. 1985. q. I£7. Dance Council of Ireland, 65 Fitzwilliam Sq., Dublin 2, Ireland. TEL 01-6762677. FAX 01-6610395. (Dist. by: Easons, P.O. Box 810, Dublin 1, Ireland. TEL 01-8788644) Ed. Michael Seaver. adv.; bk.rev. circ. 1,000. (back issues avail.) **Document type:** newsletter.
Description: Features national and international dance-related issues.

793.3 UK ISSN 0966-6346
DANCE NOW. 1992. q. £15 (foreign £17.50). Dance Books Ltd., 15 Cecil Ct., London WC2N 4EZ, England. TEL 44-171-836-2314. FAX 44-171-497-0473. E-mail: dances@dircon.co.uk. Eds. David Leonard, Sanjoy Roy; Pubs. David Leonard, John O'Brien. adv. contact: Susan Philo. circ. 5,000 (paid). **Document type:** bulletin.

793.3 US
DANCE ON CAMERA NEWS. 1967. bi-m. $25 membership; foreign $35. Dance Films Association, Inc., 31 W. 21st St., 3rd Fl., New York, NY 10010. TEL 212-727-0764. FAX 212-675-9657. Ed. Deirdre Towers. bk.rev. circ. 200. **Document type:** newsletter.
Former titles: Dance Films Association. Bulletin (ISSN 0270-8981); Dance Films Association Newsletter (ISSN 0011-5991); Dance Films Association and Dance Society Newsletter (ISSN 0011-5991); Dance Films Newsletter.

793 UK ISSN 0264-2875
GV1580
DANCE RESEARCH. 1984. s-a. £46 (foreign $83) (effective 1998). (Society for Dance Research) Oxford University Press, Academic Division, Great Clarendon St., Oxford OX2 6DP, England. TEL 44-1865-267907. FAX 44-1865-267485. TELEX 837330-OXPRES-G. URL: http://www.oup.co.uk/journals. (U.S. subscr. to: Oxford University Press Inc., 2001 Evans Rd., Cary, NC 27513. TEL 800-852-7323. FAX 919-677-1714) Ed. Richard Ralph; Pub. Nina Curtis. R&P contact: Joolz Longley. adv. contact: Jane Parker. bk.rev.; circ. 650 (controlled). (back issues avail.) **Document type:** academic/scholarly publication.
—BLDSC (3518.233800); UMI; UnCover. **CCC**.
Description: Contains academic and scholarly articles on all forms of dance ranging from the history of European theatre to dance anthropology and Renaissance spectacle.

793.3 US ISSN 0149-7677
GV1580
DANCE RESEARCH JOURNAL. 1969. s-a. $60 to individuals (outside N. America $72); institutions $72 (outside N. America $84); students $30 (outside N. America $42) (includes C O R D Newsletter) (effective 1996). Congress on Research in Dance, Department of Dance, State University of New York, College at Brockport, Brockport, NY 14420-2939. TEL 716-395-2590. FAX 716-395-5413. Ed. Lynn Matluck Brooks. R&P contact: Kista Tucker. adv.; bk.rev.; film rev.; abstr.; bibl.; charts; illus. (reprint service avail. from ISI) **Indexed:** Arts & Hum.Cit.Ind., ASCA, Bk.Rev.Ind. (1986-), Child.Bk.Rev.Ind. (1986-), Curr.Cont., Hum.Ind., Phys.Ed.Ind., RILM. **Document type:** academic/scholarly publication.
—KR SourceOne; UnCover.
Formerly: C O R D News (ISSN 0588-7356)
Description: Contains recent doctoral dissertation research information, articles on dance and related areas.

790 UK
THE DANCE TEACHER. 1952. m. £37.50 to non-members (outside Europe £55) (effective 1996). International Dance Teachers' Association, International House, 76 Bennett Rd., Brighton BN2 5JL, England. TEL 44-1273-685652. FAX 44-1273-674388. E-mail: idta@fastnet.co.uk. Ed. Jay Dearling. R&P contact: Jay Dearling. adv.: page £157.50; 185 x 130; adv. contact: Elaine Bailey. bk.rev.; illus. circ. 6,000. **Document type:** trade publication.
Description: Contains information on area meetings and dance, with reviews, letters and photographs.

793 370 US ISSN 0199-1795
GV1580
DANCE TEACHER NOW; the practical magazine of dance. 1979. 10/yr. $29.95 (Canada & Mexico $38: foreign $48). S M W Communications, Inc., Beacon Bldg., 3101 Poplarwood Ct., No. 310, Raleigh, NC 27604-1010. TEL 919-972-7888. FAX 919-872-6888. E-mail: dancenow@aol.com; URL: http://www.enews.com/magazines/dance. (Subscr. to: Box 41204, Raleigh, NC27629) Ed. K.C. Patrick; Pub. Susan Wershing. R&P contact: Diane Despopoulos. adv. contact: Lori Vizza. bk.rev.; tr.lit. circ. 7,000. **Indexed:** Phys.Ed.Ind. **Document type:** trade publication.
—BLDSC (3518.245000); UnCover.

792.8 UK ISSN 0264-9160
GV1645
DANCE THEATRE JOURNAL. 1982. 3/yr. £10 (foreign £14) to individuals; institutions £12 (foreign £17) (effective 1997). Laban Centre for Movement and Dance, Laurie Grove, New Cross, London SE14 6NH, England. TEL 44-181-692-4070. FAX 44-181-694-8749. (Subscr. in UK to: Dance Theatre Journal, Freepost, London SE14 6BR, England. TEL 44-181-694-9620) Ed. Ann Nugent. R&P contact: Nick Bodger. adv. B&W page £445, color page £590; trim 272 x 185; adv. contact: Brian Shilling. bk.rev. circ. 3,000. (back issues avail.) **Indexed:** Arts & Hum.Cit.Ind., ASCA, Curr.Cont. **Document type:** academic/scholarly publication.
—BLDSC (3518.248000); Genuine Article; UnCover.
 Formerly (until 1983): Labanews.
 Description: For dance professionals, students and those who take an informed interest in dance. Covers ballet, contemporary, new and non-Western dance. Includes national dance listings, tours, workshops.

793.33 US
▼**DANCE VISION U S A IN THE NEWS.*** 1995. q. free. Dance Vision U S A, 4270 Cameron St., Ste. 3A, Las Vegas, NV 89103-3718. TEL 800-851-2813. FAX 310-533-8635. Ed. Wayne Eng. dance rev.; rec.rev.; illus. circ. 7,000. **Document type:** trade publication, consumer publication.

792.8 US
DANCE WEEK. 1976. 52/yr. $33 (Canada $40). Box 55, McLean, VA 22101. TEL 703-450-7760. FAX 301-320-4150. E-mail: telemarit96@aol.com. Ed. Richard Mason; Pub. Richard S. Mason. adv. contact: Richard S. Mason. music rev.; circ. 600 (paid). **Document type:** newsletter.
 Description: Provides up-to-date information on ballroom dance events, people, and competitions.

793.33 US
DANCERS' DATELINE. 1992. m. $12. Box 346, Random Lake, WI 53075-0346. TEL 414-893-0908. FAX 414-994-4817. Ed. Rod Hagan. R&P contact: Gary Feider. adv. contact: Rod Hagan. bk.rev.; circ. 750 (paid). **Document type:** newsletter.
 Description: Contains information about ballroom dances, showcases and competitions in Southern Wisconsin.

793.32 322.4 US
DANCERS FOR DISARMAMENT NEWSLETTER.* 4/yr. c/o Judy Trupin, 124 E. 84th St., New York, NY 10028.

793.3 UK ISSN 0011-605X
DANCING TIMES. 1910. m. £26.50 (foreign £32 ($64)) (effective Jan. 1997). Dancing Times Ltd., Clerkenwell House, 45-47 Clerkenwell Green, London EC1R 0EB, England. TEL 44-171-250-3006. FAX 44-171-253-6679. Ed. Mary Clarke. adv.; bk.rev.; illus. circ. 12,000. (back issues avail.) **Indexed:** Arts & Hum.Cit.Ind., ASCA, Curr.Cont. **Document type:** consumer publication.
—BLDSC (3518.300000); UnCover.
 Description: Provides international coverage of theater dance with special reference to dance medicine and teaching.

793.33 780 US ISSN 1053-5454
DANCING U S A. 1983. bi-m. $21.97 in U.S.; Canada and Mexico $38.97; elsewhere $50.97 (effective 1997). Dot Publications, Inc., 10600 University Ave., N.W., Minneapolis, MN 55448-6166. TEL 612-757-4414. FAX 612-757-6605. Ed. Patti Johnson; Pub. LeAnn Bamford. R&P contact: Patti Johnson. adv.: B&W page $1236, color page $1626; trim 8 3/8 x 10 1/2. bk.rev.; music rev. circ. 20,000. **Document type:** consumer publication.
 Formerly (until 1989): Ballroom Dancing Across the U S A.
 Description: Contains ballroom Latin and swing dance techniques and tips, inspiring stories, history of dance and big bands, as well as source for how-to videos, music, dancing shoes, big bands and dance styles.

793.33 UK
DANCING YEAR BOOK. 1958. a. £10.50 to non-members (effective 1996). International Dance Teachers Association, International House, 76 Bennett Rd., Brighton BN2 5JL, England. TEL 44-1273-685652. FAX 44-1273-674388. E-mail: idta@fastnet.co.uk. Ed. Jay Dearling. R&P contact: Jay Dearling. adv. contact: Elaine Bailey. bibl.; index, cum.index. circ. 4,000. **Document type:** trade publication.
 Formerly: Ballroom Dancing Year Book (ISSN 0404-6919)
 Description: Reference to dance organizations, dancing press, ballroom, and theater festivals.

792 US ISSN 0745-3949
DANCSCENE.* 6/yr. Koine Publishing Co., c/o Suzanna Penn, 87 Glen Rd., Apt. 9, Brookline, MA 02146-7762. TEL 214-750-0275.

792.8 793.3 NE ISSN 0168-0137
DANS. 1982. m. fl.70 (foreign fl.90). Landelijk Centrum voor Amateurdans, Postbus 452, 3500 AL Utrecht, Netherlands. TEL 31-30-2334255. FAX 31-30-2332721. E-mail: dans_lca@knoware.nl. Ed. Willemijn in 't Veld. adv.; bk.rev. circ. 1,500.
—SWETS.

793.319489 DK ISSN 0107-685X
DANSK DANSEHISTORISK ARKIV. MEDDELELSER; dansearkivets aarsskrift. (Text in Danish; summaries in English) 1981. a. DKK 100 (effective 1997). Dansk Dansehistorisk Arkiv, Musikvidenskabeligt Institut, Klerkegade 2, DK-1308 Copenhagen K, Denmark. Ed. Henning Urup. illus. **Document type:** academic/scholarly publication.

792.8 793.3 SW ISSN 1102-0814
DANSTIDNINGEN. 1991. bi-m. SEK 150 ; in Sweden; other Nordic countries SEK 200; elsewhere SEK 250 (effective 1997). Danstidningen i Stockholm Ekonomisk Foerening, P.O. Box 9237, Bergsundsgatan 6, S-102 73 Stockholm, Sweden. TEL 46-8-658-38-18. FAX 46-8-669-01-11. Ann-Marie Wrange. adv.: color page SEK 8000. bk.rev. circ. 3,000. (back issues avail.) **Document type:** trade publication.
 Description: Contains articles and news about all forms of dance; training, competitions and performances in Denmark, Finland, Iceland, Norway and Sweden.
 Refereed Serial

792.8 MX
DANZARIA; danza viva de Iberoamerica. m. (10/yr.). Mex.$80. Vista Hermosa 65, Col. Portales, 03300 Mexico DF, Mexico. TEL 525-6744595. FAX 525-6588639. Ed. Roberto Aguilar.
 Description: Documents, presents and supports national and Latin American dance movements.

DENVER ARTS CENTER PROGRAMS. see *THEATER*

DEUTSCHES MUSIKLEBEN (YEAR). see *MUSIC*

793.3 US ISSN 0363-972X
GV1623
DIRECTORY OF DANCE COMPANIES.* a. (National Endowment for the Arts) Charles Reinhart Management, Inc., 1697 Broadway, Ste. 1201, New York, NY 10019-5904.

780 IT
DISCO & DANCING.* 1986. m. L.60000 (foreign L.170000). (Sindacato Italiano Locali da Ballo) Mielle s.r.l., Via E. Romagnoli 1, 20146 Milan, Italy. TEL 39-2-47710636. FAX 39-2-47710065. Ed. Giuseppe Bonazzoli. circ. 14,000.

793.3 AG ISSN 0329-093X
DOCUMENTOS E INVESTIGACIONES SOBRE LA HISTORIA DEL TANGO. 1994. a. $12. Instituto de Investigaciones del Tango, Carabelas 344, Piso 5, 1009 Buenos Aires, Argentina. TEL 54-1-3299217. FAX 54-1-2365521. E-mail: gomezq@mbox.servicenet.com.ar. Ed. Marisa Donadio. R&P contact: Marisa Donadio. circ. 1,000. **Document type:** monographic series.
 Description: Covers all aspects of tango and related fields. Lists places to dance tango, instruments, singers and old tango orchestras in Buenos Aires.

DUE SOUTH; the biggest guide to what's on in the South. see *ARTS AND HANDICRAFTS*

792.8 US ISSN 1048-9894
EMERALD CITY DANCE NEWS. 1984. m. $15 (foreign $35) (effective 1997). 16755 Wallingford N., Seattle, WA 98133. TEL 206-542-1639. FAX 206-542-1639. E-mail: ecdnj@aol.com. Ed. Joan Adams. circ. 350. **Document type:** newsletter.

ENGLISH DANCE AND SONG. see *MUSIC*

ENTR'ACTE; muziek journal. see *MUSIC*

793.3 SZ
FESTIVALMAGAZIN. 1988. a. free. Verein Berner Tanztage, Postfach 317, CH-3000 Bern 14, Switzerland. TEL 41-31-3760303. FAX 41-31-3710333. E-mail: bernertanztage@access.ch; URL: http://www.access.ch/whoiswho/bernertanztage.html. Ed. Claudia Rosiny. adv. contact: Reto Clavadetscher. circ. 10,000. (back issues avail.) **Document type:** bulletin.

781.626 793.319 SW
▼**FLAMENCOTIDNINGEN DUENDE.** 1996. q. SEK 120 membership. Goeteborgs Flamencofoerening, c/o Arbaeus, Loevskogsgatan 2 C, S-413 20 Goeteborg, Sweden. TEL 46-31-16-04-88. E-mail: elli.arbaeus@mailbox.swipnet.se.
 Description: Deals with flamenco as dance, music, culture and living art form.

793.31 US ISSN 0163-528X
FOLK DANCE DIRECTORY. a. $0.60. Folk Dance Association, Box 500, Midwestern Station, Brooklyn, NY 11230. TEL 718-434-2304.

793.31 398.2 US ISSN 1081-2695
FOLK DANCE PHONE BOOK AND GROUP DIRECTORY (YEAR); a demographic study of recreational and international folk dancing. 1993. a. $15 (effective 1996-1997). Society of Folk Dance Historians, 2100 Rio Grande, Austin, TX 78705-5513. TEL 512-478-9676. FAX 512-478-8900. E-mail: ron@ccwf.cc.utexas.edu. Ed. Ron Houston; Pub. Ron Houston. R&P contact: Ron Houston. adv.: page $150. circ. 500. **Document type:** directory, monographic series.

793.31 398.2 US ISSN 1081-7654
FOLK DANCE PROBLEM SOLVER. 1987. a. $15 (effective 1997). Society of Folk Dance Historians, 2100 Rio Grande, Austin, TX 78705-5513. TEL 512-478-9676. FAX 512-478-8900. E-mail: ron@ccwf.cc.utexas.edu. Ed. Ron Houston; Pub. Ron Houston. circ. 350. **Document type:** academic/scholarly publication, monographic series.
 Description: Descriptions, histories, backgrounds, lyrics, anecdotes, essays, poetry, scores, and illustrations about international folk dances.

793.31 UK
FOLK DIRECTORY. 1977? a. £5.95 to non-members; members £4.95. English Folk Dance and Song Society, Cecil Sharp House, 2 Regents Park Rd., London NW1 7AY, England. Ed. Hilary Warburton. **Document type:** directory.

FOLK MUSIC JOURNAL. see *MUSIC*

FOLK NORTH-WEST. see *MUSIC*

793.33 US
FOOTNOTES (LONDONDERRY). bi-m.? New Hampshire American Ballroom Dance Association, 13 Merlin Place, Londonderry, NH 03053. Ed. Bill Cahill. **Document type:** newsletter.

793.31 US
FORWARD AND BACK. 1979. irreg. $1 per no. Jacob Bloom, Ed. & Pub., 34 Andrew St., Newton, MA 02161. circ. 100.

793.3 US
FRIENDS LINE. s-a. membership. Paul Taylor Dance Company, 552 Broadway, New York, NY 10012. TEL 212-431-5562. FAX 212-966-5673. **Document type:** newsletter.

793.33 US
FRIENDS OF BALLROOM DANCING NEWSLETTER. bi-m.? 253 E. Main Rd., Portsmouth, RI 02871. Ed. Skip Jones. **Document type:** newsletter.

DANCE

792.8 780.904   IT   ISSN 0017-0232
GIORNALE DELLO SPETTACOLO. 1945. w. L.90000 (Europa L.110000; elsewhere L.170000). Gestioni Editoriali A G I S, Via di Villa Patrizi 10, 00161 Rome, Italy. TEL 39-6-4402704. FAX 39-6-4404257. Ed. Luigi Filippi. adv.; film rev.; charts; stat.; circ. 13,000 (controlled). (looseleaf format) **Document type:** newspaper.

LE GRAND HUIT. see *THEATER*

DER HEIMATPFLEGER; Zeitschrift fuer Volkstanz, Volksmusik, Brauchtum und Heimatpflege. see *FOLKLORE*

793.31 781.7   SW   ISSN 0346-9018
HEMBYGDEN. 1921. 5/yr. SEK 55 (effective 1996). Svenska Ungdomsringen foer Bygdekultur, P.O. Box 34056, S-100 26 Stockholm, Sweden. TEL 46-8-695-00-15. FAX 46-8-695-00-22. Ed. Boel Henckel. adv.; bk.rev.; illus. circ. 35,000.
Formerly (until 1923): Folkdansringen.
Description: Folkdance and folk music.

793.31   US   ISSN 0741-9384
HORA.* 1968. 2/yr. $3. American Zionist Youth Foundation, Israel Folk Dance Institute, 110 E. 59th St., New York, NY 10022. TEL 212-318-6123. Ed. Ruth Goodman. charts; illus.
Description: Review of Israeli Jewish folk dance news.

793.3   US   ISSN 1063-8520
GV1580
IMPULSE: THE INTERNATIONAL JOURNAL OF DANCE SCIENCE. Short title: Impulse (Champaign). 1993. q. $40 to individuals (foreign $44); institutions $90 (foreign $94); students $24 (foreign $28). Human Kinetics Publishers, Inc., Box 5076, Champaign, IL 61825-5076. TEL 217-351-5076. FAX 217-351-2674. Ed. Luke Kahlich. adv.; abstr.; bibl.; charts; stat. circ. 200. **Indexed:** RILM. **Document type:** academic/scholarly publication.
—CCC.
Description: Contains articles on all aspects of dance science, medicine, and education.

INDIAN MUSICOLOGICAL SOCIETY. JOURNAL. see *MUSIC*

IRISH MUSIC AND DANCE ASSOCIATION NEWSLETTER. see *MUSIC*

793.31   IS
ISRAEL DANCE QUARTERLY. 1993. q. $37 overseas (effective 1995). Zoom Hafakot, 39 Shoham St., Haifa 34679, Israel. TEL 972-4-8344051. FAX 972-4-8344051. Eds. Giora Manor. adv.; bk.rev.; illus.; cum.index: 1975-1985. circ. 2,000. **Document type:** newspaper.
Supersedes (1975-1989): Israel Dance (Annual) (ISSN 0334-2301)
Description: News of dance activities in Israel.

792.8   US
JITTERBUG;* the premiere swing dance publication. 4/yr. $25. P.O. Box 4918, Laguana Beach, CA 92652-4918. TEL 714-494-5086. Ed. Catherine E. Cannon.
Description: Covers star biographies, swing history, competition reviews, coming events, and music and video listings.

JUILLIARD JOURNAL; monthly newspaper. see *MUSIC*

793   II   ISSN 0047-3103
PN1582.I4
KALAKALPAM. (Text in English) 1966. s-a. Rs.2. Karyalaya Natya Kala Kendram Institute, 30-A Paddapukur Rd., Calcutta 320, India. Ed. Ammini S. Menon. adv.; illus.

790 613.7   US   ISSN 1058-7438
RC1220.D35
KINESIOLOGY AND MEDICINE FOR DANCE.* 1977-1983; resumed 1984. s-a. $30 to individuals; institutions $62.50. A Cappella Books, Inc., 814 N. Franklin St., Chicago, IL 60610-3109. TEL 609-737-6525. FAX 609-737-3787. Eds. Robin Chmelar, Diana Clanin. adv.: B&W page $330. bk.rev.; video rev.; abstr.; bibl.; charts; illus. circ. 550. (also avail. in microform from RPI; back issues avail.) **Indexed:** Phys.Ed.Ind., Sportsearch (1990-). **Document type:** academic/scholarly publication.
—BLDSC (5096.020500); UnCover.
Former titles: Kinesiology for Dance; Kinesiology for Dance Newsletter (ISSN 0731-2504); Kinesiology for Dance.
Description: Articles on different aspects of dance medicine, emphasizing practical applications for dancers, teachers and doctors. Also lists conferences and workshops.

792.8   SP
KOS. 6/yr. 1500 ptas. Associacio de Ballarins i Coreografs Professionals de Catalunya, Via Laietana, 52, 08003 Barcelona, Spain. TEL 34-3-2682473. FAX 34-3-2680680. adv. contact: Elisa Huertas.

793.3   NE   ISSN 0888-1286
LANGUAGE OF DANCE. 1987. irreg., latest vol.6. price varies. Gordon and Breach - Harwood Academic, Amsteldisk 166, 1st Fl., 1079 LH Amsterdam, Netherlands. (Subscr. to: International Publishers Distributor, Box 32160, Newark, NJ 07102. TEL 800-545-8398. FAX 215-750-6343) Ed. A. Hutchinson Guest. **Document type:** monographic series.
Refereed Serial

793.31   AT   ISSN 0726-626X
LEAPING; magazine of Christian dance fellowship of Australia. 1978. q. Aus.$25 membership. Christian Dance Fellowship of Australia, P.O. Box 210, Broadway, N.S.W. 2007, Australia. TEL 61-2-92811219. FAX 61-2-96984223. Ed. Lucy Jarasius. adv.; bk.rev.; circ. 400. (back issues avail.) **Document type:** newsletter.

790   US   ISSN 0024-1253
GV1580
LET'S DANCE. 1949. m. (10/yr.). $15 (foreign $20) (effective 1997 & 1998). Folk Dance Federation of California, Inc., Box 1282, Alameda, CA 94501-0135. TEL 510-814-9282. Ed. Genevieve Pereira. adv.: B&W page $80; 7 1/2 x 10. circ. 500.
—UnCover.
Description: Covers the where, when, how and who of international folk dance.

793.34   UK   ISSN 0301-8881
GV1763
LET'S SQUARE DANCE. 1953. m. £2.70. British Association of American Square Dance Clubs, 32 Great Whyte Ramsey, Huntington, Cambs PE17 1HA, England. (Subscr. to: Mr. S. Nye, 4 Devonshire Gardens, Winchmore Hill, London N21 2AL, England) Ed. D. White. adv. circ. 1,000.

MAILOUT; arts work with people. see *ART*

MARCAN HANDBOOK OF ARTS ORGANISATIONS. see *ART*

793.33   US
MASS A B D A NEWSLETTER.* bi-m. Massachusetts American Ballroom Dance Association, 9 Isabelle Cir., Rowley, MA 01969-2517. Ed. Laurie Gienapp. **Document type:** newsletter.

MEDICAL PROBLEMS OF PERFORMING ARTISTS. see *MEDICAL SCIENCES*

791 956   US   ISSN 1041-7591
MIDDLE EASTERN DANCER MAGAZINE. 1979. m. $24 (Canada and Mexico $34; elsewhere $44). Mideastern Connection, Inc., Box 181572, Casselberry, FL 32718-1572. TEL 407-831-3402. FAX 407-869-0830. Ed. Karen Kuzsel. adv.: B&W page $195. bk.rev.; film rev.; play rev.; illus.; tr.lit. circ. 2,500. (back issues avail.)
Formerly: Southern Dancer.
Description: Covers dance and culture of the Middle East for performers and enthusiasts; news and reviews.

792.8   US
MINNESOTA DANCE NEWSLETTER. 1979. bi-m. $15. Minnesota Dance Alliance, 528 Hennepin Ave., Ste. 600, Minneapolis, MN 55403. TEL 612-340-1900. FAX 612-340-9919. Ed. Mykl Roventine. adv. contact: Mykl Roventine. bk.rev. circ. 1,600. **Document type:** newsletter.
Formerly: M I C A Newsletter.

793.31   US   ISSN 0163-5271
MIXED PICKLES; the magazine of folk dance, folk lore, and related folk arts. 1976. m. (Oct.-July). $5. Folk Dance Association, Box 500, Midwood Station, Brooklyn, NY 11230. TEL 718-434-2304. Ed. Raymond La Barbara. adv.; illus. (tabloid format)

792.8   JA
MONTHLY DANCE VIEW; monthly magazine for dance life. (Text in Japanese) m. 700 Yen per no. Modan Shuppan, 3-2-1 Ueno, Taitoh-ku, Tokyo 110, Japan. TEL 81-3-5818-5655.

792.8   UK
MOVEMENT AND DANCE QUARTERLY. 1948. q. £12.50 (foreign £15) (effective 1997). Laban Guild, 3 Layton Ln., Shaftsbury, Dorset SP7 8EY, England. TEL 44-1747-54634. FAX 44-15047-68433. Ed. Lydia Everitt. R&P contact: Lydia Everitt. adv. contact: Ann Ward. bk.rev. circ. 1,000. **Document type:** academic/scholarly publication, newsletter.
Former titles (until 1992): Movement and Dance; (until Jan. 1982): Laban Art of Movement Guild Magazine.
Description: Explores dance and movement based upon Laban's principles and analysis of human movement as applied to theatre, therapy, recreational dance, management consultancy, education, and choreography.

793.33 780   US   ISSN 1072-8481
MUSIC & DANCE NEWS.* 1972. bi-m. $12. (Minnesota Ballroom Operators Association) Von Meyer Publishing, Box 324, St. Joseph, MN 56374-0324. TEL 612-352-2261. FAX 612-352-2261. Ed. Janelle Von Pinnon; Pub. Janelle Von Pinnon. R&P contact: Janelle Von Pinnon. adv. contact: Janelle Von Pinnon. rec.rev. circ. 20,000. (tabloid format) **Document type:** newspaper.
Formerly (until Sep. 1992): Entertainment Bits (ISSN 0192-8430)
Description: News, articles, announcements, and reviews on ballroom, polka, country and 50's dancing in the Midwest.

MUSIK & THEATER; die aktuelle Kulturzeitschrift. see *MUSIC*

793.34 796.54   US   ISSN 0195-0150
N S D C A TIMES. 1969. q. $15 membership. National Square Dance Campers Association, P.O. Box 18, Lower Waterford, VT 05848-0018. TEL 802-748-9478. FAX 802-748-4742. E-mail: jbc___nsdca___times@juno.com. Ed. Jim Connelly; Pub. Jim Connelly. adv.: page $125; 6 7/8 x 9 1/2 circ. 5,000 (controlled). **Document type:** newsletter.

N Y C - ON STAGE. see *THEATER*

NATIONAL FOUNDATION FOR ADVANCEMENT IN THE ARTS. ANNUAL REPORT. see *ART*

793.34   US   ISSN 0746-3685
NATIONAL SQUARES; a national square dance magazine. 1977. q. $6. National Square Dance Convention, 6768 S. East St., No.2, Indianapolis, IN 46227. TEL 317-787-7864. Eds. Floyd and Clare Lively. adv. circ. 3,000.
Description: Covers past and future conventions and other activities of the Convention.

NATYA. see *THEATER*

792.8   US   ISSN 1040-8908
THE NEW DANCE REVIEW. 1987. q. $20 (foreign $40). Anita Finkel, Ed. & Pub., 32 W. 82nd St., Apt. 2F, New York, NY 10024. bk.rev. circ. 600. **Document type:** consumer publication.
—UnCover.
Description: International coverage of dance, including list of events.

NEW YORK CASTING - SURVIVAL GUIDE. see *THEATER*

DANCE

792.8 US
NEW YORK CITY BALLET NEWS. 1977. 3/yr. membership. New York City Ballet Guild, New York City Ballet, Inc., New York State Theater, 20 Lincoln Center, New York, NY 10023. TEL 212-870-5677. FAX 212-870-4244. Ed. Carol Landers. circ. 6,000 (controlled). **Document type:** newsletter.
Description: Features articles, news and updates on the company, its dancers, and people and events which influence the world of ballet. Includes dancer profiles and notices of events.

793.33 US
NEXT GENERATION NEWSLETTER. 1989. q. $25 membership. Next Generation Swing Dance Club, 236 W. Portal Ave., Ste. 329, San Francisco, CA 94127-0901. TEL 415-979-4456. adv. **Document type:** newsletter.

793.34 US ISSN 1044-2928
THE NORTHEAST SQUARE DANCER MAGAZINE.* 1951. m. $10. New England Caller, Inc., 2905 Scenic Dr., Marion, OH 43302-8386. TEL 617-452-3222. Ed. Raymond Aubut. adv.; bk.rev. circ. 5,000. **Document type:** consumer publication.
Formerly: New England Square Dance Caller (ISSN 0028-4920)

792.8 BE ISSN 0778-9580
NOUVELLES DE DANSE. (Text in French) 1990. q. 2250 BEF($80) (effective Oct. 1994). Contredanse, 46 rue de Flandres, 1000 Brussels, Belgium. TEL 32-2-5020327. FAX 32-2-5138739. Ed. Patricia Kuypers; Pub. Patricia Kuypers. adv.; bk.rev.; bibl.; illus. (back issues avail.)
Description: Covers dance as a performing art. Publishes articles on specific topics in dance, interviews, news and information on performances, festivals, workshops.

792.8 US
PARTY PLATTER. 1988. q. 229 Coolidge Ave., Apt. 304, Watertown, MA 02172-1554. TEL 617-923-8211. E-mail: aatheling@aol.com. Ed. Anne Atheling. R&P contact: Anne Atheling. **Document type:** newsletter.
Description: Covers news on ballroom dancing in New England.

PERFORMANCE RESEARCH. see THEATER

792.8 CN ISSN 1193-3968
PERFORMER. (Text in English) 1955. 3/yr. free to members. National Ballet of Canada, 470 Queens Quay W., Toronto, ON M5V 3KA, Canada. TEL 416-345-9686. FAX 416-345-8323. E-mail: info@national.ballet.ca. Ed. Julia Drake. bk.rev.; circ. 14,000 (controlled). (back issues avail.) **Document type:** newsletter.
Former titles (until Oct. 1991): Front Page News; National Ballet News.

PERFORMING ARTS AND ENTERTAINMENT IN CANADA. see THEATER

792 US
PERFORMING ARTS BUYERS GUIDE: FOOTNOTES. 1974. q. $2 (foreign $5). Stagestep, 2000 Hamilton St., Ste. C200, Philadelphia, PA 19130. TEL 215-636-9000. FAX 800-877-3342. E-mail: stagestep@juno.com. Ed. Virginia Villion; Pub. Randy Swartz. adv. contact: Barbara Solot. bk.rev.; tr.lit.; circ. 300,000 (controlled). (back issues avail.) **Document type:** catalog.
Incorporates: Buyers Guide: Footnotes; Footnotes (Philadelphia).

792.8 NE ISSN 1026-0927
PERFORMING ARTS INTERNATIONAL; an international journal. 1997. q? $80 (effective 1998). Gordon and Breach - Harwood Academic, Amsteldisk 166, 1st Fl., 1079 LH Amsterdam, Netherlands. (Subscr. to: International Publishers Distributor, Box 32160, Newark, NJ 07102. TEL 800-545-8398. FAX 215-750-6343) pp./issue: 350.

PLACE DES ARTS. MAGAZINE. see THEATER

793.33 US
POTOMAC BALLROOM NEWS. 1986. m. $15. Box 55, McLean, VA 22101. TEL 703-450-7760. FAX 301-320-4150. E-mail: telemarkt96@aol.com. Ed. Richard Mason; Pub. Richard Mason. R&P contact: Richard Mason. TEL 301-320-4150. adv. contact: Richard Mason. bk.rev.; music rev. circ. 100. **Document type:** newsletter.
Description: Lists local ballroom dancing news and events for Maryland, Washington DC, and Virginia.

793.3 FR ISSN 0183-3189
POUR LA DANSE;* chaussons et petits rats. no.31, 1975. bi-m. 190 F. Societe Rivanova, 51 rue de Belleville, 75019 Paris, France. Ed. Annie Bozzini. adv.; bk.rev.; charts; illus.

793 780 792 CN
PRELUDE. (Text in English, French) 1969. 5/yr. free. (National Arts Centre, Marketing Department) Capital Publishers, 400 Cumberland St., Ottawa, ON K1N 8X3, Canada. TEL 613-241-7888. FAX 613-241-3112. Ed. Jennifer Millar. adv. contact: Dianne Wing. circ. 56,000. **Document type:** bulletin.
Former titles: N A C Calendar of Events; Ovation; National Arts Centre. Calendar of Events (ISSN 0033-1023); Supersedes: Prologue.

793.33 US
R I A B D A NEWSLETTER. bi-m. Rhode Island American Ballroom Dance Association, 25 Zipporah St., North Providence, RI 02911. Ed. Gall Stone. **Document type:** newsletter.

REALTIME. see THEATER

792.8 FR ISSN 0752-5729
GV1580
RECHERCHE EN DANSE. 1982. a. 76 F. Librairie Bonaparte, 31 rue Bonaparte, 75006 Paris, France. TEL 33-1-43269756. FAX 33-1-43294465. adv.; bk.rev. circ. 2,000.
Description: Articles on the history of dance, dance and psychology, dance and mysticism, dance and poetry.

792.8 UK
ROYAL ACADEMY OF DANCING. ANNUAL REPORT. a. membership. Royal Academy of Dancing, 36 Battersea Sq., London SW11 3RA, England. TEL 44-171-223-0091. FAX 44-171-924-3129. Pub. David Watchman. **Document type:** corporate report.

793.31 UK
ROYAL SCOTTISH COUNTRY DANCE SOCIETY BULLETIN. 1924. a. membership. 12 Coates Crescent, Edinburgh EH3 7AF, Scotland. TEL 44-131-225-3854. FAX 44-131-225-7783. adv. circ. 24,500. **Document type:** newsletter.

793.31 993.33 XO ISSN 0231-7214
RYTMUS. 1969. m. $31. (Cultural Institute) Obzor, Spitalska 35, 815 85 Bratislava, Slovakia. **Indexed:** RILM.

793 US
S O S CAREFREE TIMES. (Society of Stranders) 2/yr. $12. Association of Carolina Shag Clubs, Box 4688, Columbia, SC 29204. Ed. Phil Sawyer.
Description: Covers about 90 Shag clubs in Southeast U.S.

793.31 200 US ISSN 1043-5328
SACRED DANCE GUILD JOURNAL. 1958. 3/yr. $28 membership (Canada $31; overseas $37). Sacred Dance Guild, 201 Hewitt, Carbondale, IL 62901. TEL 618-457-8603. (Subscr. to: 762 Olive St., Denver, CO) Ed. Toni Intravaia; Pub. Toni Intravaia. R&P contact: Toni Intravaia. adv. contact: Toni Intravaia. bk.rev. circ. 600. **Document type:** academic/scholarly publication.
Description: Contains chapter and membership news to network information. Also shares insights in the field of sacred dance.

SANGEET NATAK; journal of Indian music, dance, theatre. see MUSIC

793.31 398.2 US
SOCIETY OF FOLK DANCE HISTORIANS. REPORT TO MEMBERS. 1990. a. $15 (effective 1997). Society of Folk Dance Historians, 2100 Rio Grande, Austin, TX 78705-5513. TEL 512-478-9676. FAX 512-478-8900. E-mail: ron@ccwf.cc.utexas.edu. Ed. Ron Houston; Pub. Ron Houston. bk.rev. circ. 350. **Document type:** newsletter.

SPILLEROM; tidsskrift for scenekunst. see THEATER

SRUTI; India's premier music and dance magazine. see MUSIC

793.3 780 US ISSN 0896-3193
GV1580
STERN'S PERFORMING ARTS DIRECTORY; catalogue of classical music and dance artists and attractions, programs, resources and services. 1967. a. $65. Dance Magazine, Inc., 33 W. 60th St., New York, NY 10023. TEL 212-245-8937. FAX 212-956-6487. E-mail: dancemag@mairus.com. Ed. Allen McCormack; Pub. Robert D. Stern. adv. contact: Barbara Kaplan. index. circ. 10,000. **Indexed:** Mag.Ind. **Document type:** directory, trade publication.
Former titles: Dance Magazine Annual Performing Arts Directory; Dance Magazine Annual (ISSN 0070-2684)

STRINGS AND SQUARES; bladet for traditionel amerikansk musik og dans i Danmark. see MUSIC

793.3 US ISSN 1043-7592
GV1601
STUDIES IN DANCE HISTORY.* 1989. s-a. $30 to individuals; institutions $62.50. (Society of Dance History Scholars) A Cappella Books, Inc., 106 W. Franklin Ave., 814 N. Franklin St., Chicago, IL 60610-3109. TEL 609-737-6525. FAX 609-737-3787. Ed. Lynn Garafola. adv.: page $300; adv. contact: Susan F. Binding. illus. circ. 650. (also avail. in microform from RPI) **Indexed:** Amer.Hist.& Life (1992-), Hist.Abstr. (1992-). **Document type:** academic/scholarly publication, monographic series.
—UnCover.
Description: Covers the history of dance and related disciplines.
Refereed Serial

793.3 XR ISSN 0039-937X
TANECNI LISTY.* 1963. 10/yr. 30 Kc.($31.40) Divadelni Ustav, Celetna 17, 110 00 Prague 1, Czech Republic. Ed. Marie Kmochova. adv.; bk.rev. circ. 4,000.

793 796.41 SZ
TANZ UND GYMNASTIK. (Text in German and French) 1944. q. 35 SFr. (foreign 40 SFr.). Schweizerischer Berufsverband fuer Tanz und Gymnastik - Association of Swiss Professionals in Dance and Movement, c/o Marianne Forster, Ed., Mittlere Str. 4, CH-4056 Basel, Switzerland. TEL 41-61-2611662. FAX 41-61-2611604. adv. contact: Hans Ritmeyer. bk.rev.; illus. circ. 1,100. **Document type:** bulletin.
Description: Focuses on ballet and modern dance. Includes coming events, courses, workshops, auditions, book information and reviews.

793.3 GW ISSN 0724-1062
TANZEN. 1983. q. DM.32. Deutscher Bundesverband Tanz e.V., Kueppelstein 34, 42897 Remscheid, Germany. TEL 02191-794241. Ed. Klaus Kramer. circ. 2,200. (back issues avail.; reprint service avail.)

793.3 GW ISSN 0940-1008
TANZFORSCHUNG. 1991. a. (Gesellschaft fuer Tanzforschung e.V.) Florian Noetzel Verlag, Heinrichshofen Buecher, Valoisstr. 11, 26382 Wilhelmshaven, Germany. **Document type:** academic/scholarly publication.

TEEN STAR ZINE; a newsletter for 10-18 year olds who love the performing arts. see CHILDREN AND YOUTH — For

THEATER HEUTE. see THEATER

DANCE — ABSTRACTING, BIBLIOGRAPHIES, STATISTICS

793.31   US   ISSN 0884-3198
GV1580
U C L A JOURNAL OF DANCE ETHNOLOGY. 1977. a. $15. University of California at Los Angeles, Department of Dance, Dance Bldg. 124, Los Angeles, CA 90095-1608. TEL 310-825-3951. FAX 310-825-7507. Ed. Yvonne Cootz. bk.rev. circ. 250. **Indexed:** Anthropol.Lit. **Document type:** academic/scholarly publication.
—BLDSC (9079.632800); UnCover.
   Formerly (until vol.9, 1985): Association of Graduate Dance Ethnologists U C L A Journal (ISSN 0273-2068)
   Refereed Serial

UNGA ATALANTE. see *THEATER*

VICE; art and entertainment magazine. see *ART*

VOLKSDANS. see *FOLKLORE*

W P A S MUSELETTER. (Washington Performing Arts Society) see *MUSIC*

793 792   GW
DIE WERKSTATT. 1977. s-a. Die Werkstatt e.V., Boernestr. 10, 40211 Duesseldorf, Germany. TEL 0211-360391. FAX 0211-3613816. Ed. Thomas Hinrichsen. adv.; bk.rev. circ. 20,000. (back issues avail.)

793.31   US
WOODS HOLE FOLK MUSIC SOCIETY NEWSLETTER. 1975. irreg., vol.2, 1991. free to qualified members. Woods Hole Folk Music Society, 174 Lakeshore Dr., East Falmouth, MA 02536. TEL 508-540-0320. illus. circ. 600. (back issues avail.) **Document type:** newsletter.
   Description: Presents folk performers of the society, local folk festivals, club business, and local folk radio.

793.3   CC   ISSN 0512-4204
WUDAO/DANCING. (Text in Chinese) 1958. bi-m. $26.60. Zhongguo Wudaojia Xiehui - China Dancers' Association, Wenlian Dalou, 16th Floor, 10 Nongzhanguan Nanli, Beijing 100026, People's Republic of China. TEL 5003414. (Dist. in US by: China Books & Periodicals, Inc., 2929 24th St., San Francisco, CA 94110. TEL 415-282-2994)

793.3   US
WUDAO LUNCONG/FORUM OF DANCING. (Text in Chinese) s-a. $12. China Books & Periodicals, Inc., 2929 24th St., San Francisco, CA 94110. TEL 415-282-2994. FAX 415-282-0994.

793   CC   ISSN 1003-3777
WUDAO YISHU/ART OF DANCING. (Text in Chinese) q. Zhongguo Yishu Yanjiuyuan - Chinese Academy of Arts, 17 Qianhai Xijie, Beijing 100009, People's Republic of China. TEL 651128. Ed. Zi Huajun.

YINYUE, WUDAO YANJIU/STUDIES ON MUSIC AND DANCE. see *MUSIC*

2029 MAGAZIN. see *PHOTOGRAPHY*

DANCE — Abstracting, Bibliographies, Statistics

792.8 793.3   US   ISSN 0889-8847
ATTITUDES AND ARABESQUES. 1980. m. $25 to individuals (Canada & Mexico $35); institutions in N. America $35; elsewhere $40. Mid-Peninsula Dance Guild, Cultural Center, 1313 Newell Rd., Palo Alto, CA 94303. TEL 415-962-1642. E-mail: jogil415@aol.com. (Edit. addr.: 150 Claremont Ave., No.2C, New York, NY 10027. TEL 212-662-6515) Ed. Leslie Getz. R&P contact: Leslie Getz. bk.rev. circ. 248. **Indexed:** Sportsearch (1981-). **Document type:** bibliography.
   Description: Bibliographic guide to English language dance periodicals and publications.

792 016   US   ISSN 0360-2737
Z7514.D2
BIBLIOGRAPHIC GUIDE TO DANCE. (Supplement to: New York Public Library. Performing Arts Research Center. Dictionary Catalog of the Dance Collection) 1975. a. $585 (effective 1997). G.K. Hall & Co., MacMillan Library Reference USA, Box 159, Thorndike, ME 04986. TEL 212-654-8452; 800-223-6121. FAX 207-948-2863. URL: http://www.mir.com/thorndike. (Subscr. to: Simon & Schuster, Library Reference Order Processing, 200 Old Tappan Rd., Old Tappan, NJ 07675. TEL 800-223-2336) **Document type:** bibliography, abstracting/indexing.
   Description: Covers all aspects of dance and every type of dance.

BIBLIOGRAPHIES AND INDEXES IN THE PERFORMING ARTS. see *THEATER — Abstracting, Bibliographies, Statistics*

BIO-BIBLIOGRAPHIES IN THE PERFORMING ARTS. see *THEATER — Abstracting, Bibliographies, Statistics*

793.3 011   US   ISSN 1059-0382
Z7514.D2
DANCE RESEARCH. 1989. biennial. $15. International Council for Traditional Music Study Group on Ethnochoreology, Dept. of Dance, Dance Bldg., University of California, Los Angeles, CA 90095-1608. TEL 310-825-3951. FAX 310-825-7507. (Co-sponsor: Study Group on Ethnochoreology) Ed. Elsie Ivancich Dunin. **Document type:** bibliography.

793   US   ISSN 1058-6350
Z7514.D2
INDEX TO DANCE PERIODICALS. 1991. a. $215 (effective 1997). G.K. Hall & Co., MacMillan Library Reference USA, Box 159, Thorndike, ME 04986. TEL 212-654-8452; 800-223-6121. FAX 207-948-2863. URL: http://www.mir.com/thorndike. (Subscr. to: Simon & Schuster, Library Reference Order Processing, 200 Old Tappan Rd., Old Tappan, NJ 07675. TEL 800-223-2336) **Document type:** abstracting/indexing.
   Description: Indexes articles, reviews, essays, biographical articles, and obituaries from approximately 30 periodicals published in U.S., Canada, England, France, Germany, Italy, Spain and other countries.

MUSIC AND DANCE PERIODICALS; an international directory and guide book. see *MUSIC — Abstracting, Bibliographies, Statistics*

DATA BASE MANAGEMENT

see *Computers–Data Base Management*

DATA COMMUNICATIONS AND DATA TRANSMISSION SYSTEMS

see *Computers–Data Communications and Data Transmission Systems*

DENTISTRY

see *Medical Sciences–Dentistry*

DERMATOLOGY AND VENEREOLOGY

see *Medical Sciences–Dermatology and Venereology*

DOMESTIC COMMERCE

see *Business and Economics–Domestic Commerce*

DRUG ABUSE AND ALCOHOLISM

see also *Pharmacy and Pharmacology*

616.86   US
A D A M H A NEWS. 1976. bi-m. $6. U.S. Department of Health and Human Services, Alcohol, Drug Abuse, and Mental Health Administration, Parklawn Bldg., Rm. 13C-05, 5600 Fishers Ln., Rockville, MD 20857. TEL 301-443-0746. FAX 301-443-9050. Eds. Deborah Goodman, Bernardine A. Moore. circ. 12,000. **Indexed:** Ind.U.S.Gov.Per., Med.Care Rev., MEDOC.

A N S A JOURNAL. (Association of Nurses in Substance Abuse) see *MEDICAL SCIENCES — Nurses And Nursing*

616.86   US
A S A M NEWS. 1985. bi-m. $25 to non-members; members free. American Society of Addiction Medicine, 4601 N. Park Ave., Ste. U101, Chevy Chase, MD 20815-4519. TEL 202-244-8948. FAX 202-537-7252. Ed. Lucy Barry Robe. adv. contact: Lucy Robe. circ. 3,000. **Document type:** newsletter.
   Formerly: American Medical Society on Alcoholism and Other Drug Dependencies. Newsletter (ISSN 0889-9215)
   Description: Covers health care reform; current events related to alcohol, tobacco, and other addicting drugs; association news.

616.86   SZ   ISSN 1420-2999
ABHAENGIGKEITEN. 1995. 4/yr. 45 SFr. Schweizerische Fachstelle fuer Alkohol- und andere Drogenprobleme, Postfach 870, CH-101 Lausanne, Switzerland. TEL 41-21-3202921. FAX 41-21-3231930. Ed. Regina Burri. adv.; bk.rev.; abstr.; bibl. circ. 1,100. **Document type:** bulletin.
   Formed by the merger of (1977-1995): Drogalkohol (ISSN 0250-6815); (1932-1995): Suchtprobleme und Sozialarbeit (ISSN 1420-3065), Which was formerly (until 1980): Fuersorger (ISSN 0016-3139)
   Description: Provides experts and other interested people with results of the latest research and information on the treatment of alcoholism and other addictions.

616.86 157.63   SW   ISSN 0345-0406
ACCENT. 1879. 20/yr. SEK 175 (effective 1997). I C G T - N T O , U N F, Birger Jarlsgatan 25, Box 174 S-111 87 Stockholm, Sweden. TEL 46-8-789-49-50. FAX 46-8-20-43-54. Ed. Kjell-Ove Oscarsson. adv.; bk.rev.; circ. 50,271 (controlled).
   Formerly (until 1974): Accent, Unga Tankar.

DRUG ABUSE AND ALCOHOLISM

616.86   UK   ISSN 0965-2140
HV5800   CODEN: ADICE5
ADDICTION. Online edition (UK ISSN 1360-0443) 1884. m. £194($356) to individuals; institutions £564 ($986) (effective 1997). (Society for the Study of Addiction) Carfax Publishing Co., P.O. Box 25, Abingdon, Oxon. OX14 3UE, England. TEL 44-1235-401000. FAX 44-1235-401550. E-mail: enquiries@carfax.co.uk. (Subscr. in N. America to: Carfax Publishing Co., 875-81 Massachusetts Ave., Cambridge, MA 02139) Ed. Griffith Edwards. adv.; bk.rev.; charts; illus.; stat.; index. (also avail. in microfiche; back issues avail.) **Indexed:** Abstr.Crim.& Pen., Abstr.Hyg., Adol.Ment.Hlth.Abstr., Arts & Hum.Cit.Ind., ASCA, ASSIA, Biol.Abstr., Chem.Abstr., Crim.Just.Abstr., Curr.Adv.Ecol.Sci., Curr.Cont., Excerp.Med., Fam.Ind., I.P.A., IMFL, Ind.Med., Ind.Sci.Rev., Mid.East: Abstr.& Ind., Mult.Ed.Abstr., NRN, Nutr.Abstr., Psychol.Abstr. (1971-), Risk Abstr., Sci.Cit.Ind., Sp.Ed.Needs Abstr., SSCI, Stud.Wom.Abstr., THA, Trop.Dis.Bull. **Document type:** academic/scholarly publication.
●Also available online.
—BLDSC (0678.548000); ADONIS; EMDOCS; Genuine Article; KNAW; KR SourceOne; SWETS; UMI; UnCover. **CCC.**
    Former titles (until 1993): British Journal of Addiction (ISSN 0952-0481); (until 1980): British Journal of Addiction to Alcohol and Other Drugs (ISSN 0007-0890); (until 1947): British Journal of Inebriety (ISSN 0366-0796)
Refereed Serial

616.86   UK   ISSN 0968-7610
ADDICTION ABSTRACTS. 1994. q. £88($158) to individuals; institutions £178 ($318) (effective 1997). Carfax Publishing Co., P.O. Box 25, Abingdon, Oxon. OX14 3UE, England. TEL 44-1235-401000. FAX 44-1235-401550. E-mail: enquiries@carfax.co.uk. (Subscr. in N. America to: Carfax Publishing Co., 875-81 Massachusetts Ave., Cambridge, MA 02139) Ed. Mike Gossop. adv.; index. (also avail. in microfiche) **Document type:** abstracting/indexing.
—UMI. **CCC.**

616.86   UK   ISSN 1355-6215
                    CODEN: ADBIFN
▼**ADDICTION BIOLOGY.** 1996. q. £98($148) to individuals; institutions £198 ($298) (effective 1997). Carfax Publishing Co., P.O. Box 25, Abingdon, Oxon. OX14 3UE, England. TEL 44-1235-401000. FAX 44-1235-401550. E-mail: enquiries@carfax.co.uk. (N. American subscr. to: Carfax Publishing Co., 875-81 Massachusetts Ave., Cambridge, MA 02139) **Document type:** academic/scholarly publication.
—BLDSC (0678.557000); CASDDS; Genuine Article. **CCC.**

616.863   UK   ISSN 1351-8151
▶**ADDICTION COUNSELLING WORLD.** 1989. bi-m. £24 (U.S. £30) (effective 1996 & 1997). Addiction Recovery Foundation, 122A Wilton Rd., London SW1V 1JZ, England. TEL 44-171-233-5333. FAX 44-171-233-8123. E-mail: acw@easynet.co.uk. Ed. Deirdre Boyd. adv. contact: David Leonard. bk.rev. circ. 5,000. **Document type:** trade publication.
    Description: Reports on approaches to treatment, controversial issues, news and developments in drug and alcohol rehabilitation, and addictive behavior and related issues.

616.86   NE   ISSN 1058-6989
                    CODEN: AREREQ
▶**ADDICTION RESEARCH.** 1993. bi-m. $118 (effective 1998). Gordon and Breach - Harwood Academic, Amsteldisk 166, 1st Fl., 1079 LH Amsterdam, Netherlands. (Subscr. to: International Publishers Distributor, Box 32160, Newark, NJ 07102. TEL 800-545-8398. FAX 215-750-6343) (also avail. in microform) **Indexed:** ASCA, Crim.Just.Abstr., Curr.Cont., Fam.Ind.
—BLDSC (0678.590000). **CCC.**

616.86   CN   ISSN 0044-6203
ADDICTION RESEARCH FOUNDATION. JOURNAL; addictions news for professionals. French edition: Fondation de la Recherche sur la Toxicomanie. Journal (ISSN 1201-2572) 1972. 6/yr. Can.$19 (foreign Can.$36). Addiction Research Foundation of Ontario, Subscription - Marketing Department, 33 Russell St., Toronto, ON M5S 2S1, Canada. TEL 416-595-6059. FAX 416-593-4694. E-mail: adubey@arf.org; URL: http://www.intropage.html. Ed. Anita Dubey. adv. contact: Linda O'Meara. bk.rev.; abstr.; index. circ. 10,700. (tabloid format; also avail. in microfiche; back issues avail.) **Indexed:** Can.B.P.I. **Document type:** government publication, trade publication.
●Also available online.
—BLDSC (4676.200000). **CCC.**
    Description: Covers the latest developments in the alcohol and drug field in North America.

616.86 157.63   CN
ADDICTION RESEARCH FOUNDATION OF ONTARIO. ANNUAL REPORT. 1951. a. free. Addiction Research Foundation of Ontario, Subscription - Public Affairs Department, 33 Russell St., Toronto, ON M5S 2S1, Canada. TEL 416-595-6054. FAX 416-595-6881. URL: http://www.mktg@arf.org. circ. 2,000 (controlled). **Document type:** government publication.
—CISTI.
    Formerly: Alcoholism and Drug Addiction Research Foundation. Annual Report (ISSN 0065-6119)

616.86   UK   ISSN 0306-4603
RC565
ADDICTIVE BEHAVIORS; an international journal. 1976. bi-m. fl.1218($700) (effective 1998). Elsevier Science Ltd., Pergamon, P.O. Box 800, Kidlington, Oxford OX5 1DX, England. TEL 44-1865-843000. FAX 44-1865-843010. E-mail: nlinfo-f@elsevier.nl; usinfo-f@elsevier.com; forinfo-kyf04035@niftyserve.or.jp; URL: http://www.elsevier.nl/. (Subscr. to: Elsevier Science, Regional Sales Office, P.O. Box 211, 1000 AE Amsterdam, Netherlands. TEL 31-20-4853757. FAX 31-20-4853432; Subscr. in the Americas to: Elsevier Science, Regional Sales Office, Box 945, New York, NY 10159-0945. TEL 212-633-3730. FAX 212-633-3680; Subscr. in Australasia and the Far East to: Elsevier Science (Singapore) Pte Ltd, No.1 Temasek Ave., No.17-01 Millenia Tower, Singapore 039192, Singapore. TEL 65-434-3727. FAX 65-337-2230) Ed. Peter M. Miller. adv.; bk.rev.; charts; illus.; index. circ. 1,200. (also avail. in microform from UMI) **Indexed:** Abstr.Crim.& Pen., Adol.Ment.Hlth.Abstr., ASCA, Behav.Med.Abstr., Bibl.Ind., Biol.Abstr., Curr.Adv.Ecol.Sci., Curr.Cont., Excerp.Med., Fam.Ind., High.Educ.Abstr., HRIS, Ind.Med., Mid.East: Abstr.& Ind., Nutr.Abstr., Psychol.Abstr. (1976-), Risk Abstr., Soc.Sci.Ind. (1994-), SSCI. **Document type:** academic/scholarly publication.
—BLDSC (0678.750000); CISTI; EMDOCS; Genuine Article; KNAW; KR SourceOne; SWETS; UMI; UnCover. **CCC.**
    Incorporates (1990-1994): Annual Review of Addictions Research and Treatment (ISSN 0955-663X)
    Description: Publishes original research and theoretical papers in the area of substance abuse, with particular emphasis on alcohol and drug abuse, smoking and problems associated with eating.
Refereed Serial

616.8   SP   ISSN 0214-4840
ADICCIONES. 1989. q. 4700 ptas.($45) (effective 1996) 5000 ptas.($47) (effective 1997). Socidrogalcohol, C. Rambla 15, 2a 3a, 07003 Palma de Mallorca, Spain. TEL 34-71-727434. FAX 34-71-718073. Ed. Amador Calafat. adv.; bk.rev. circ. 2,000. **Indexed:** Excerp.Med. (1994-). **Document type:** academic/scholarly publication.
—CINDOC; EMDOCS.
    Description: Journal on drug issues for Spanish-speaking audience.
Refereed Serial

616.8   UK   ISSN 0272-1740
RC563
ADVANCES IN SUBSTANCE ABUSE: BEHAVIORAL AND BIOLOGICAL RESEARCH. (Supplement avail.: Control Issues in Alcohol Abuse Prevention) 1980. irreg., vol.4, 1991. $88. Jessica Kingsley Publishers, 116 Pentonville Rd., London N1 9JB, England. TEL 44-171-833-2307. FAX 44-171-837-2917. E-mail: post@jkp.com; URL: http://www.jkp.com. (Dist. in U.S. by: Taylor & Francis, 1900 Frost Rd., Ste. 101, Bristol PA 19007-1598. TEL 215-785-5800. FAX 215-785-5515) Ed. Nancy K. Mello. **Indexed:** Psychol.Abstr. **Document type:** academic/scholarly publication.
—CISTI. **CCC.**
    Description: Reviews recent advances in behavioral and biological research on a variety of addictive behaviors; also traces the development of ideas and concepts about addictive disorders.
Refereed Serial

AKTION JUGENDSCHUTZ. INFORMATIONEN. see CHILDREN AND YOUTH — About

616.861   US   ISSN 1054-1446
AL-ANON SPEAKS OUT; a community resource for professionals. (Text in English, Spanish) 1978. s-a. free. (Al-Anon Family Group Headquarters, Inc., Public Outreach Department) A F G, Inc., 1600 Corporate Landing Pkwy., Virginia Beach, VA 23454-5617. TEL 757-563-1600. FAX 757-563-1655. circ. 9,000. **Document type:** newsletter.
    Description: Informs members of the helping professions about the help available to the families and friends of alcoholics through Al-Anon - Alateen program.

353.9   US
HV5297.A4
ALASKA. DEPARTMENT OF HEALTH AND SOCIAL SERVICES. DIVISION OF ALCOHOLISM AND DRUG ABUSE. REPORT. a. free. Department of Health and Social Services, Division of Alcoholism and Drug Abuse, Box 110607, Juneau, AK 99811-0607. TEL 907-465-2071. FAX 907-465-2185. illus.
    Formerly: Alaska. Department of Health and Social Services. Office of Alcoholism. Report (ISSN 0095-3318)

616.861 362.292   CN   ISSN 0840-7819
ALBERTA ALCOHOL AND DRUG ABUSE COMMISSION. ANNUAL REPORT. 1970. a. Alberta Alcohol and Drug Abuse Commission, Production & Distribution, Pacific Plaza Bldg., 2nd Fl., 10909 Jasper Ave., Edmonton, AB T5J 3M9, Canada. TEL 403-427-7319. FAX 403-422-5237. Ed. Lisa Austin. R&P contact: Lisa Austin. adv. contact: Grace Whitehouse. circ. 1,200. **Document type:** government publication, corporate report.
    Formerly: Alberta. Alcoholism and Drug Abuse Commission. Annual Report (ISSN 0319-423X)
    Description: Provides a concise program, financial and statistical summary of AADAC's activities.

616.861   US   ISSN 0272-9814
HV5001
ALCOHOL (BOCA RATON). (Subseries of: S I R S Social Issues Series (ISSN 0740-3127)) 1972. a. price varies; a. supplement $19. Social Issues Resources Series, Box 2348, Boca Raton, FL 33427-2348. TEL 561-994-0079; 800-232-SIRS. FAX 561-994-4704. E-mail: custserve@sirs.com; URL: http://www.sirs.com. Ed. Trudy Collins; Pub. Eleanor Goldstein. R&P contact: Bonnie Milnes. (looseleaf format; back issues avail.) **Document type:** academic/scholarly publication.
    Description: Reprints articles that explore the effects of alcoholism on society.

DRUG ABUSE AND ALCOHOLISM

616.861   US   ISSN 0741-8329
QP801   CODEN: ALCOEX
ALCOHOL (NEW YORK); an international biomedical journal. 1984. 8/yr. fl.1716($986) (effective 1998). Elsevier Science Inc., Box 945, New York, NY 10159-0945. TEL 212-633-3730. FAX 212-633-3680. E-mail: nlinfo-f@elsevier.nl; usinfo-f@elsevier.com; forinfo-kyf04035@niftyserve.or.jp; URL: http://www.elsevier.nl/. (Subscr. outside the Americas to: Elsevier Science, Regional Sales Office, P.O. Box 211, 1000 AE Amsterdam, Netherlands. TEL 31-20-4853757. FAX 31-20-4853432; Subscr. in Australasia and the Far East to: Elsevier Science (Singapore) Pte Ltd, No.1 Temasek Ave., No.17-01 Millenia Tower, Singapore 039192, Singapore. TEL 65-434-3727. FAX 65-337-2230; Subscr. in Japan to: Elsevier Science Japan, 9-15 Higashi-Azabu 1-chome, Minato-ku, Tokyo 106, Japan. TEL 81-3-5561-5033. FAX 81-3-5561-5047) Ed. Robert D. Myers. adv.; illus.; index. circ. 1,500. (also avail. in microform from UMI; reprint service avail.) **Indexed:** Biol.Abstr., Chem.Abstr., Curr.Adv.Ecol.Sci., Curr.Cont., Excerp.Med., Ind.Med., Ind.Sci.Rev., INIS Atomind., Neurosci.Cit.Ind., NRN, Psychol.Abstr. (1984-). **Document type:** academic/scholarly publication. —BLDSC (0786.754600); CASDDS; CISTI; EMDOCS; Genuine Article; KNAW; SWETS; UMI; UnCover. **CCC.**
Incorporates: Alcohol and Drug Research; Former titles (until 1986): Substance and Alcohol Actions - Misuse (ISSN 0191-8877); Substance and Alcohol Misuse.
Description: Publishes original research articles and reviews on biomedical aspects of alcohol abuse and alcoholism.
Refereed Serial

616.861   UK   ISSN 0735-0414
HV5441   CODEN: ALALDD
ALCOHOL & ALCOHOLISM. 1963. bi-m. £285 (foreign $440) (effective 1998). (Medical Council on Alcoholism) Oxford University Press, Academic Division, Great Clarendon St., Oxford OX2 6DP, England. TEL 44-1865-267907. FAX 44-1865-267485. E-mail: jnl.info@oup.co.uk; URL: http://www.oup.co.uk/journals. (U.S. subscr. to: Oxford University Press, Inc., 2001 Evans Rd., Cary, NC 27513. TEL 800-852-7323. FAX 919-677-1714) (Co-sponsor: European Society for Biomedical Research on Alcoholism) Ed. Abdulla Badawy; Pub. Steven Johnson. R&P contact: Joolz Longley. adv.; bk.rev.; charts; stat.; index. circ. 1,000. (also avail. in microfilm from UMI; back issues avail.; reprint service avail. from UMI) **Indexed:** Abstr.Crim.& Pen., Abstr.Hyg., ASCA, ASSIA, Biol.Abstr., Chem.Abstr., Curr.Adv.Ecol.Sci., Curr.Cont., Excerp.Med., Ind.Med., Ind.Sci.Rev., Lang.& Lang.Behav.Abstr., Neurosci.Cit.Ind., NRN, Nutr.Abstr., Psychol.Abstr. (1983-), Sci.Cit.Ind., SSCI, THA, Trop.Dis.Bull. **Document type:** academic/scholarly publication. —BLDSC (0786.754800); CASDDS; CISTI; EMDOCS; Genuine Article; KNAW; SWETS; UMI; UnCover. **CCC.**
Former titles (until 1983): British Journal of Alcohol and Alcoholism (ISSN 0309-1635); (until 1976): Journal of Alcoholism: Bulletin of Alcoholism (ISSN 0021-8685)
Description: Publishes research from all clinical disciplines of medicine, the basic medical sciences, psychology, sociology, and epidemiology.
Refereed Serial

616.861 157.61   US   ISSN 0090-838X
HV5285   CODEN: AHRWDZ
ALCOHOL HEALTH & RESEARCH WORLD. 1975. q. $18 (foreign $22.50) (effective 1997). U.S. National Institute on Alcohol Abuse and Alcoholism, 6000 Executive Blvd., Bethesda, MD 20892-7003. TEL 301-443-3860. FAX 301-480-1726. URL: http://www.niaace.nih.gov. (Subscr. to: Superintendent of Documents, U.S. Government Printing Office, Box 371954, Pittsburgh, PA 15250-7954. TEL 202-512-1800. FAX 202-512-2250; Back issues avail. from: National Technical Information Service, 5285 Port Royal Rd., Springfield, VA 22161. TEL 703-487-4650. FAX 703-321-8547) Ed. Dianne M. Welsh. R&P contact: Barbara Vann. TEL 202-842-7600. bibl.; charts; illus.; circ. 3,700 (paid). (back issues avail.) **Indexed:** Adol.Ment.Hlth.Abstr., Amer.Stat.Ind. (1973-), ASCA, Chem.Abstr., Curr.Cont., Fam.Ind., Hlth.Ind., HRIS, Ind.U.S.Gov.Per., MEDOC, Mid East: Abstr.& Ind., NRN, Psychol.Abstr. (1985-), Soc.Sci.Ind (1994-), Soc.Work Res.& Abstr. **Document type:** government publication, academic/scholarly publication.
●Also available online. Vendor(s): Information Access Co., UMI.
—BLDSC (0786.775000); CASDDS; Genuine Article; KR SourceOne; SWETS; UMI; UnCover.
Description: Presents current research findings and contains articles on the effects, prevention and treatment of alcoholism.
Refereed Serial

ALCOHOL ISSUES INSIGHTS. see *BEVERAGES*

616.86   CI   ISSN 0002-502X
   CODEN: ALCMAN
ALCOHOLISM; journal on alcoholism and related addictions. (Includes monograph supplements) (Text in English; summaries in Croatian, English) 1965. s-a. $20. Centar za Proucavanje i Suzbijanje Alkoholizma i Drugih Ovisnosti - Centre for Study and Control of Alcoholism and Other Addictions, Vinogradska 29, 41000 Zagreb, Croatia. (Co-sponsor: International Council on Alcoholism and Addictions) Ed. Dr. Vladimir Hudolin. adv.; bk.rev.; charts; illus.; stat.; index. circ. 1,000. (reprint service avail. from UMI) **Indexed:** ASCA, Biol.Abstr., CHNI, Excerp.Med., Fam.Ind., NRN, Trop.Dis.Bull.
—KNAW; SWETS; UMI.

616.863   US   ISSN 1042-1394
ALCOHOLISM & DRUG ABUSE WEEKLY; news for policy and program decision-makers. 1986. w. (48/yr.). $549 (Canada $569; elsewhere $589) (effective 1997). Manisses Communications Group, Inc., Box 9758, Providence, RI 02940-9758. TEL 401-831-6020; 800-333-7771. FAX 401-861-6370. E-mail: manissesCS@manisses.com; URL: http://www.manisses.com. Eds. Gary A. Enos, Melissa DeMeo; Pub. Fraser A. Lang. **Document type:** newsletter.
●Also available online. Vendor(s): Data-Star, Information Access Co., Knight-Ridder Information, Inc., Ovid Technologies, Inc.
—**CCC.**
Incorporates (in 1991): Addictions Program Management; Formerly (until 1988): Drug Abuse Report (ISSN 0889-7050)
Description: Covers public policy and economic issues for addiction professionals in the public, private and non-profit sectors.

616.861   US   ISSN 1076-2507
ALCOHOLISM BRIEFS. 1986. q. $8.95. Del Mar Publications, 1165 Elmwood Pl., Deerfield, IL 60015. TEL 847-945-1790. Ed. Bob Aitchison. R&P contact: Bob Aitchison. circ. 650. **Document type:** newsletter.
Description: National digest to provide a clearing house and exchange for concise news and information on alcoholism and related subjects.

616.861   US   ISSN 0145-6008
RC565   CODEN: ACRSDM
ALCOHOLISM: CLINICAL AND EXPERIMENTAL RESEARCH. 1977. bi-m. $215 to individuals (foreign $260); institutions $415 (foreign $470) (effective 1998). (Research Society on Alcoholism) Williams & Wilkins (Subsidiary of: Waverly International), 351 W. Camden St., Baltimore, MD 21201-2436. TEL 410-528-4068; 800-222-3790. FAX 410-528-4452. E-mail: djones@wwilkins.com; URL: http://www.wwilkins.com. (Co-sponsor: International Society for Biomedical Research on Alcoholism) Ed. Dr. Marcus A. Rothschild. adv. contact: David Jones. circ. 1,740. (also avail. in microfilm from WWS; back issues avail.) **Indexed:** Abstr.Hyg., Adol.Ment.Hlth.Abstr., Behav.Med.Abstr., CINAHL, Curr.Adv.Ecol.Sci., Curr.Cont., Excerp.Med., Ind.Med., Ind.Sci.Rev., Neurosci.Cit.Ind., Nutr.Abstr., Pig News & Info., Psychol.Abstr. (1981-), Risk Abstr., Sci.Cit.Ind., SSCI, THA. **Document type:** academic/scholarly publication.
—BLDSC (0786.789300); CASDDS; CISTI; EMDOCS; Genuine Article; KNAW; SWETS; UnCover. **CCC.**
Description: Presents original clinical and research studies on alcoholism, alcohol-induced syndromes and resultant organ damage.
Refereed Serial

362.2 616.8   US   ISSN 0093-3279
HV5001
ALCOHOLISM DIGEST ANNUAL.* 1973. a. Information Planning Associates, Inc., 5205 Leesburg Pike, Falls Church, VA 22041. TEL 202-820-6100. illus.

616.861   US   ISSN 0734-7324
ALCOHOLISM TREATMENT QUARTERLY; the practitioner's quarterly for individual, group, and family therapy. 1984. q. $60 to individuals (Canada $78; elsewhere $84); institutions $120 (Canada $156; elsewhere $168); libraries $320 (Canada $416; elsewhere $448) (effective 1997-1998). Haworth Press, Inc., 10 Alice St., Binghamton, NY 13904. TEL 607-722-5857; 800-342-9676. FAX 607-722-6362. E-mail: getinfo@haworth.com; URL: http://www.haworth.com. Ed. Thomas McGovern; Pub. Bill Cohen. R&P contact: Ruthann Heath. adv.: B&W page $300; trim 4 3/8 x 7 1/8; adv. contact: Jackie Blakeslee. bk.rev.; abstr.; bibl. circ. 474. (also avail. in microfiche from UMI; microform from HAW; reprint service avail. from HAW) **Indexed:** A.D.& D., Abstr.Anthropol., Abstr.Crim.& Pen., Crim.Just.Abstr., Excerp.Med., IMFL, Ind.Per.Art.Relat.Law, Past.Care & Couns.Abstr., Psychol.Abstr. (1984-), Rehabil.Lit., Soc.Work Res.& Abstr., Stud.Wom.Abstr., THA. **Document type:** trade publication.
—BLDSC (0786.797000); EMDOCS; Haworth; KNAW; SWETS; UnCover.
Formerly: Alcoholism Counseling and Treatment.
Description: Geared toward the needs of clinicians who work with alcoholic clients and their families.
Refereed Serial

616.861 362.29
344   IT   ISSN 0394-9826
ALCOLOGIA; European journal of alcohol studies. (Text in English) 1989. q. Lit.80000($60) (effective 1997). Editrice Compositori s.r.l., Via Stalingrado 97-2, 40128 Bologna, Italy. TEL 39-51-327811. FAX 39-51-327877. E-mail: 1865@compositori.it; URL: http://www.compositori.it. Ed. Giovanni Gasbarrini. R&P contact: Emanuela Amati. adv.: color page Lit.9000000; adv. contact: Stefano Melloni. circ. 1,100. **Indexed:** Excerp.Med. (1996-). **Document type:** academic/scholarly publication.
—BLDSC (0786.797300); EMDOCS.
Description: Publishes articles on all aspects of man's use and misuse of ethyl alcohol. Aims to provide a forum for European societies with alcohol problems.

616.8   FR   ISSN 0002-5054
ALCOOL OU SANTE. 1951. q. 80 F. (foreign 105 F.) (effective 1997). Association Nationale de Prevention de l'Alcoolisme, 20 rue St. Fiacre, 75002 Paris, France. TEL 33-1-42335104. FAX 33-1-45081702. Ed. Patrick Elineau. R&P contact: Elisabeth Francois. adv.; bk.rev.; abstr.; bibl. charts; illus.; index. circ. 7,000. **Document type:** consumer publication.
Description: Covers the different aspects of alcoholism such as prevention, trafficking, general news.

616.86   FR   ISSN 1142-1983
ALCOOLOGIE. (Text in French, summaries in English) 1978. q. 430 F. to individuals (foreign 530 F.); institutions 570 F. (foreign 670 F.) (effective 1998). (Societe Francaise d'Alcoologie) Princeps Editions, 64 av. Charles de Gaulle, 92130 Issy-les-Moulineaux, France. TEL 33-1-46382414. FAX 33-1-40957215. Ed. J.D. Favre.
—BLDSC (0786.801500).
Description: Transdisciplinary approach of alcoholism with interest in other addictions.

616.86 362.42   US
ALERT (TRENTON); news on alcoholism and drug addiction services for persons who are hard of hearing. 1989. s-a. free. Signs of Sobriety, Inc., 865 Lower Ferry Rd., Ste. B-9, Ewing, NJ 08628. TEL 609-882-7677. E-mail: SOSNJ@juno.com. Ed. Steven Shevlin. R&P contact: Heather Bird. adv. contact: Heather Bird. circ. 2,000. (back issues avail.) **Document type:** newsletter.
Description: Disseminates local and national news on alcohol and drug use among persons who are deaf or hard of hearing. Contains information on service providers.

616.86   SW   ISSN 0345-0732
ALKOHOL OCH NARKOTIKA/ALCOHOL AND OTHER DRUGS; CAN:s tidskrift. (Text in Swedish; summaries in English) 1906. 6/yr. SEK 225 (effective 1997). Centralfoerbundet foer Alkohol- och Narkotikaupplysning, Olof Palmes gata 17, Box 70412, S-107 25 Stockholm, Sweden. TEL 46-8-412-46-00. FAX 46-8-10-46-41. Ed. Staffan Hasselgren. adv.; bk.rev.; bibl.; illus.; stat.; index, cum.index. circ. 6,000. **Document type:** newspaper.
Incorporates (in 1989): Forskningsnytt; Formerly (until 1973): Alkoholfraagen (ISSN 0002-5518); Which was formed by the 1956 merger of: Tidskrift foer Systembolagen; Tirfing.

616.8   SW   ISSN 0002-550X
ALKOHOLDEBATT. 1954. q. SEK 50. Riksfoerbundet Mot Alkohol- och Narkotikamissbruk, Box 17136, S-104 62 Stockholm, Sweden. Ed. Ethel Floren-Winther. adv.; bk.rev.; illus. circ. 6,000. (also avail. in microfilm from UMI)
—UMI.

616.863   US   ISSN 0095-2990
HV5800   CODEN: AJDABD
AMERICAN JOURNAL OF DRUG AND ALCOHOL ABUSE. 1974. q. $595 (foreign $610) (effective 1998). Marcel Dekker Journals, 270 Madison Ave., New York, NY 10016. TEL 212-696-9000. FAX 212-685-4540. TELEX 421419. (Subscr. to: Marcel Dekker Journals, Box 5017, Monticello, NY 12701) Ed. E. Kaufman. R&P contact: Julia Mulligan. adv. contact: Lourdes Barroso. bibl.; charts; illus. (also avail. in microfilm from RPI) **Indexed:** Adol.Ment.Hlth.Abstr., ASCA, Behav.Med.Abstr., Biol.Abstr., Curr.Adv.Ecol.Sci., Curr.Cont., Curr.Lit.Fam.Plan., Excerp.Med., Fam.Ind., Gen.Sci.Ind., HRIS, I.P.A., Ind.Med., Mid.East: Abstr.& Ind., NRN, Psychol.Abstr. (1976-), Soc.Sci.Ind. (1994-), Soc.Work Res.& Abstr., SSCI, THA. **Document type:** academic/scholarly publication.
●Also available online. Vendor(s): Information Access Co.
—BLDSC (0824.320000); CASDDS; CISTI; EMDOCS; Genuine Article; KNAW; KR SourceOne; SWETS; UMI; UnCover. **CCC.**
Refereed Serial

616.8   US   ISSN 1055-0496
RC563   CODEN: AJADEA
AMERICAN JOURNAL ON ADDICTIONS. 1992. q. $135 (foreign $150) (effective 1997). (American Academy of Psychiatrists in Alcoholism and Addictions) American Psychiatric Press, Inc., Journals Division, 1400 K St., N.W., Ste. 1101, Washington, DC 20005. TEL 202-682-6340. FAX 202-682-6341. (UK addr.: 17 Belgrave Sq., London SW1X 8PG, England) Ed. Dr. Sheldon F. Miller. R&P contact: John McDuffie. adv. contact: Deana Roderick. bk.rev.; abstr.; bibl.; charts; illus.; stat.; index. circ. 1,300. (also avail. in microform from UMI) **Indexed:** ASCA, Curr.Cont., Excerp.Med. (1994-), Psychol.Abstr. (1992-). **Document type:** consumer publication, academic/scholarly publication.
—BLDSC (0820.947000); EMDOCS; Genuine Article; KNAW; UMI; UnCover. **CCC.**
Description: Presents original research related to the assessment and treatment of addictive disorders.

362.29 616.863   SW   ISSN 0280-512X
ANHOERIG.* 1981. bi-m. Riksfoerbundet Foeraeldrafoereningen mod Narkotika, Pipersgatan 27, S-112 28 Stockholm, Sweden.

ANNUAL EDITIONS: DRUGS, SOCIETY & BEHAVIOR. see *SOCIOLOGY*

362.29 616.863   SW   ISSN 0281-577X
ANONYMA ALKOHOLISTER - A A -BULLETIN. 1965-1980; resumed 1982. bi-m. SEK 120 (effective 1994). Anonyma Alkoholister (AA), P.O. Box 16387, S-103 27 Stockholm, Sweden. TEL 47-8-642-26-09. FAX 47-8-714-82-24. circ. 1,500. **Document type:** bulletin.

616.861   JA   ISSN 0910-495X
ARUKORU IRYO KENKYU/JAPANESE STUDIES ON ALCOHOLISM TREATMENT. (Text in Japanese) 1984. q. 1880 Yen. (Shiheki Mondai Rinsho Kenkyujo - Clinical Institute on Addiction Problems) Seiwa Shoten Co., Ltd., 2-5, Kamitakaido 1-chome, Suginmi-ku, Tokyo 168, Japan.

616.861   JA   ISSN 0389-4118
RC565   CODEN: AKYIDF
ARUKORU KENKYU TO YAKUBUTSU IZON/JAPANESE JOURNAL OF ALCOHOL STUDIES AND DRUG DEPENDENCE. (Text in English, Japanese) 1966. q. Nihon Arukoru Igakkai - Japanese Medical Society of Alcohol Studies, c/o Kyoto Furitsu Ika Daigaku Hoigaku Kyoshitsu, 465 Kajiicho, Hirokoji Agaru, Kawaramachi Dori, Kamigyo-ku, Kyoto 602, Japan. Ed.Bd. adv.; bk.rev.; abstr.; bibl.; charts; illus.; index. circ. 1,000. **Indexed:** Biol.Abstr., Chem.Abstr., Excerp.Med., Ind.Med. **Document type:** academic/scholarly publication.
—BLDSC (4650.783000); CASDDS; EMDOCS.
Formerly (until 1981): Arukoru Kenkyu - Japanese Journal of Studies on Alcohol (ISSN 0021-5244)

616.861   AT   ISSN 0726-4607
AUSTRA-LINK. 1981. m. Aus.$10 (foreign Aus.$15). Al-Anon Family Groups (Australia) Pty. Ltd., G.P.O. Box 1002 H, Melbourne, Vic. 3001, Australia. TEL 61-3-96298327. Ed. Mary Richards. circ. 1,500. **Document type:** newsletter.
Description: Recovering from effects of living with someone else's alcoholism, using the Al-Anon program.
Refereed Serial

178   AT
AUTUMN SCHOOL OF STUDIES ON ALCOHOL & DRUGS. PROCEEDINGS OF SEMINARS. 1966. a. Aus.$18. St. Vincent Hospital, Department of Drug and Alcohol Studies, Victoria Parade, Fitzroy, Vic. 3065, Australia. TEL 61-3-288-2627. FAX 61-3-288-2642. TELEX SVHOSM AA 32229. Ed.Bd. circ. 250. (back issues avail.) **Document type:** proceedings.

B I M S. (Blaukreuz Information - Meinungen - Szene) see *RELIGIONS AND THEOLOGY — Protestant*

BACK STREET HEROES. see *TRANSPORTATION — Automobiles*

616.86   US   ISSN 1075-6701
HV5285
BEHAVIORAL HEALTH MANAGEMENT. 1980. bi-m. $60 (Canada and Mexico $70; elsewhere $75) (effective 1997). Medquest Communications Inc., 629 Euclid Ave., Ste. 500, Cleveland, OH 44114-3003. TEL 216-522-9700. FAX 216-522-9707. Ed. Richard L. Peck; Pub. John H. Whaley III. adv.; bk.rev. circ. 23,000. **Indexed:** Hlth.Ind., Soc.Sci.Ind. (1994-).
●Also available online. Vendor(s): Information Access Co., UMI.
—KR SourceOne; UMI; UnCover. **CCC.**
Former titles (until 1994): Addiction and Recovery (ISSN 1052-4614); (until 1989): Alcoholism and Addiction and Recovery Life (ISSN 1053-3923); (until 1988): Alcoholism and Addiction (ISSN 0899-8043); (until 1987): Alcoholism and Addiction Magazine (ISSN 0884-1403); (until 1985): Alcoholism (ISSN 0275-9519)
Description: Addresses the problems of providing cost-effective mental health and substance abuse treatment in an environment of managed care.

362.1068 616.891   US   ISSN 1089-2559
BEHAVIORAL HEALTH TREATMENT. m. $199 in U.S.; Canada $209; elsewhere $219 (effective 1997). Manisses Communications Group, Inc., Box 9758, Providence, RI 02940-9758. TEL 401-831-6020; 800-333-7771. FAX 401-861-6370. E-mail: manissesCS@manisses.com; URL: http://www.manisses.com. Ed. Lu Cribari; Pub. Fraser A. Lang.
●Also available online. Vendor(s): Information Access Co.
—**CCC.**
Formed by the merger of (1985-1996): Addiction Letter (ISSN 8756-405X); (1992-1996): Psychotherapy Letter (ISSN 1062-9475); Which was formed by the merger of (1989-1992): Brown University Family Therapy Letter (ISSN 1045-5051); Which was formerly (1986-1989): Family Therapy Today (ISSN 0887-9109); (1989-1992): Psychotherapy Today (ISSN 1047-9848)
Description: News and analysis on the delivery, funding and management of behavioral health treatment services.

362.29 616.863   SW   ISSN 0345-1577
BLAA BANDET; Blaabandsroerelsens tidning. 1883. m. SEK 75 (effective 1997). Blaa Bandet, P.O. Box 1233, S-701 12 Oerebro, Sweden. TEL 46-19-130575. FAX 46-19-121136. Ed. Per-Olof Svensson. **Document type:** newsletter.

362.29 616.863   SW   ISSN 0345-1585
BLAA KORSET; informationsblad. 1969. q. SEK 30 (effective 1990). Blaa Korset, Soergaarden, S-731 92 Koeping, Sweden.

178   NE   ISSN 0921-3996
BLAUWE WEGWIJZER. 1963. bi-m. fl.10. Christelijke Beweging voor Drankbestrijding, Groningensingel 677, 6835 GA Arnhem, Netherlands. TEL 31-26-3217889. Ed. H. Ploeger. adv.; bk.rev.; illus.; stat. circ. 3,400. (looseleaf format) **Document type:** consumer publication.
Formerly: Blauwe Kruis (ISSN 0006-4653)

616.86 344   GW   ISSN 0006-5250
                            CODEN: BLALAL
BLUTALKOHOL; wissenschaftliche Zeitschrift fuer die medizinische und juristische Praxis. 1961. q. DM.80. Bund gegen Alkohol im Strassenverkehr e.V., Alsterchausee 17, 20149 Hamburg, Germany. Ed. Dr. J. Gerchow. adv.; bk.rev.; bibl.; charts; s-a. index, cum.index: 1961-62. circ. 3,200. **Indexed:** Abstr.Crim.& Pen., Biol.Abstr., Chem.Abstr., Excerp.Med. **Document type:** academic/scholarly publication.
—CASDDS; KNAW. **CCC.**

178 364   UN   ISSN 0392-3126
BOLLETTINO PER LE FARMACODIPENDENZE E L'ALCOOLISMO. 1991. q. free. (Ministero della Sanita, Settore Tossicodipendenze e Patologie, IT) United Nations Interregional Crime and Justice Research Institute, Via Giulia 52, 00186 Rome, Italy. TEL 39-6-6877437. FAX 39-6-6892638. E-mail: unicri.org@agora.stm.it. Ed. Dr. Carlo Vetere. bk.rev. circ. 7,000. **Document type:** bulletin, government publication.

616.861   US   ISSN 0362-2584
HV5275
BOX 1980;* the international monthly journal of Alcoholics Anonymous. 1974. m. $10 (foreign $12). Alcoholics Anonymous Grapevine, Inc., Box 1980, Grand Central Sta., New York, NY 10063-1980. TEL 212-870-3400.

616.863   US   ISSN 1040-6328
RC563
BROWN UNIVERSITY DIGEST OF ADDICTION THEORY & APPLICATION. Variant title: D A T A m. $197 (Canada $217; elsewhere $217) (effective 1997). Manisses Communications Group, Inc., Box 9758, Providence, RI 02940-9758. TEL 401-831-6020; 800-333-7771. FAX 401-861-6370. E-mail: manissesCS@manisses.com; URL: http://www.manisses.com. Ed. Dr. David C. Lewis; Pub. Fraser A. Lang. **Document type:** newsletter, abstracting/indexing.
●Also available online. Vendor(s): Information Access Co.
—**CCC.**
Incorporates (in 1991): Addictions Alert (ISSN 0887-8145)
Description: Contains a digest of articles that have appeared in leading medical and professional journals concerning addiction.

DRUG ABUSE AND ALCOHOLISM

BROWN UNIVERSITY LONG-TERM CARE QUALITY ADVISOR. see *HOSPITALS*

615.1   UN   ISSN 0007-523X
HV5800   CODEN: BNUNA5
BULLETIN ON NARCOTICS. Arabic edition: Nashrat al-Mukhaddirat (ISSN 0256-9000); Chinese edition: Mazuipin Gongbao (ISSN 0251-8694); French edition: Bulletin des Stupefiants (ISSN 0251-3706); Russian edition: Byulleten' po Narkoticheskim Sredstvam (ISSN 0251-7094); Spanish edition: Boletin de Estupefacientes (ISSN 0251-7086) 1949. q. $10 per issue. United Nations Publications, Sales and Marketing Section, Room DC2-0853, New York, NY 10017. TEL 212-963-8302; 800-253-9646. FAX 212-963-3489. E-mail: publications@un.org; URL: http://www.un.org/publications. (Or Distribution and Sales Section, Palais des Nations, CH-1211 Geneva 10, Switzerland) bibl.; charts; illus.; index. (also avail. in microform from UMI,PMC; reprint service avail. from UMI) **Indexed:** Abstr.Crim.& Pen., Abstr.Hyg., Adol.Ment.Hlth.Abstr., ASSIA, Biol.Abstr., Biotech.Abstr., Chem.Abstr., Crim.Just.Abstr., Curr.Cont., Excerp.Med., HRIS, I.P.A., IIS, Ind.Med., Ind.Sci.Rev., P.A.I.S., Psychol.Abstr., Soc.Sci.Ind., SSCI, Trop.Dis.Bull.
● Also available online.
—BLDSC (2881.430000); CASDDS; Linda Hall; SWETS; UMI; UnCover. CCC.
Formerly: Bulletin of Narcotic Drugs.
Description: Provides current information on all aspects of national and international drug control.

616.86   US
C S A P PREVENTION MONOGRAPH. irreg., no.14, 1993. National Clearinghouse for Alcohol and Drug Information, Center for Substance Abuse Prevention, Box 2345, Rockville, MD 20847-2345. TEL 800-729-6686. FAX 301-468-6433. E-mail: info@prevline.health.org; URL: http://www.health.org. **Document type:** government publication, monographic series.

616.861   CN   ISSN 0045-799X
CONCERNS. 1902. q. Can.$25 membership. Concerns Canada, 4500 Sheppard Ave., E., Ste. 112H, Agincourt, ON M1S 3R6, Canada. TEL 416-293-3400. FAX 416-293-1142. Ed. Karl N. Burden. bk.rev.; illus. circ. 16,000. **Indexed:** Abstr.Bk.Rev.Curr.Leg.Per. **Document type:** newsletter.
Formerly: Advocate (Scarborough).
Description: Informs members of issues and programs involving the organization, its Board and staff.

362.2   US   ISSN 0091-4509
HV5800
CONTEMPORARY DRUG PROBLEMS. 1971. q. $45 to individuals in U.S. & Canada; elsewhere $48 (effective 1997). Federal Legal Publications, Inc., 157 Chambers St., New York, NY 10007. TEL 212-619-4949. Ed. Robin Room. adv.; bk.rev. circ. 1,800. (also avail. in microform from UMI; back issues avail.; reprint service avail. from UMI,WSH) **Indexed:** Abstr.Crim.& Pen., Adol.Ment.Hlth.Abstr., C.L.I., Crim.Just.Abstr., Curr.Cont., Excerp.Med., Hlth.Ind., I.P.A., Ind.Per.Art.Relat.Law, L.R.I., Leg.Per., Mid.East: Abstr.& Ind., Psychol.Abstr., Sage Pub.Admin.Abstr., Soc.Sci.Ind., SSCI. **Document type:** trade publication.
—BLDSC (3425.179000); KR SourceOne; SWETS; UnCover.

616.863   US
CONTROLLED SUBSTANCES HANDBOOK. 1972. a. (plus q. updates). $248. Government Information Services, 4301 Fairfax Dr., Ste. 875, Arlington, VA 22203-1627. TEL 703-528-1000. FAX 703-528-6060. Ed. Ken Baumgartner. (looseleaf format)
Description: Comprehensive guide to current Drug Enforcement Administration requirements for manufacturing, storing, securing, shipping and distributing controlled substances.

COUNCIL FOR TOBACCO RESEARCH, U S A REPORT. see *TOBACCO*

616.86   US   ISSN 1047-7314
HV5279
THE COUNSELOR (ARLINGTON). 1983. bi-m. $42. National Association of Alcoholism and Drug Abuse Counselors, 1911 Fort Myer Dr., Ste. 900, Arlington, VA 22209-1603. TEL 703-741-7686. FAX 703-741-7648. Ed. Joanne Kaldy. R&P contact: Elsie Smith. adv. circ. 18,000.
Description: Provides information on current research and treatment.
Refereed Serial

616.863   IT   ISSN 1121-0311
DELFINO. 1976. bi-m. L.30000 (foreign L.55000) (effective 1994). Centro Italiano di Solidarieta, Via Attiliu Ambrosini 129, 00147 Rome, Italy. TEL 39-6-541951. FAX 6-5407306. E-mail: ceis@inroma.roma.it. (Subscr. to: Centro Italiano di Solidarieta, Piazza Benedetto Cairoli 118, 00186 Rome, Italy) Ed. Enzo Caffarelli. adv. contact: Simona Cordeschi. bk.rev.; film rev.; index.
Description: Focuses its attention on the drug addict, includes interviews, looks at personal experiences of the drug addict, family and friends. Also looks at other addictions such as alcoholism, smoking and other forms of drugs.

616.86 800   US   ISSN 1044-4149
DIONYSOS. 1989-1994; resumed 1995. 3/yr. $5 to individuals in U.S. and Canada (elsewhere $8); institutions in U.S. and Canada $8 (elsewhere $11) (effective 1997). Seattle University, Addiction Studies Program, Broadway and Madison, Seattle, WA 98122-4490. TEL 206-296-5350. FAX 206-296-5997. E-mail: jimharb@seattleu.edu. Ed. Dr. James Harbaugh. R&P contact: James Harbaugh. bk.rev.; circ. 150 (paid). **Indexed:** MLA Intl.Bibl. **Document type:** academic/scholarly publication.
Former titles: Addiction; Intoxication.
Description: Contains news notes and articles dealing with the cultural and aesthetic side of intoxication. Covers both the creative and destructive role of drinking and drug use in the lives and works of writers and artists.
Refereed Serial

616.863   NE   ISSN 1381-1959
DR. USE GOOD; health information for drug users. 1986. q. fl.40($25) Foundation Gezondheidsinformatie Druggebruikers, Postbus 11493, 1001 GL Amsterdam, Netherlands. TEL 31-20-5702355. FAX 31-20-6267249. Ed. Janhuib Blans. circ. 8,000. **Document type:** newspaper.
Description: Journalistic approach to health matters and lifestyles for hard drug users in line with the harm reduction concept in the Netherlands.

616.86   SW   ISSN 1101-7015
DROGFRITT LIV; folkets tidn. 1922. 6/yr. SEK 95. Kristna Samfundens Nykterhetsroerelse - DKSN, P.O. Box 1769, 111 87 Stockholm, Sweden. TEL 46-8-453-68-50. FAX 46-8-453-68-60. Ed. Bengt Taranger. adv.; bk.rev.; illus. circ. 10,000. **Document type:** newspaper.
Formerly (until vol.5, 1989): Folkets Vael (ISSN 0015-5861)

616.863   SW   ISSN 0283-8117
RC563
DRUG ABUSE; current research on alcohol and drug dependence. (Text in English) 1980. q. SEK 175 (effective 1996). Swedish Council for Information on Alcohol and other Drugs (CAN), Documentation Center - Centralfoerbundet foer Alkohol- och Narkotikaupplysning (CAN), P.O. Box 27302, S-102 54 Stockholm, Sweden. FAX 46-8-661-64-84. E-mail: biblioteket@can.se. Ed. Eva Reqvard. circ. 900. **Document type:** abstracting/indexing.
● Also available online.
Also available on CD-ROM.
Refereed Serial

616.86   US   ISSN 0160-0028
CODEN: DAAND4
DRUG ABUSE AND ALCOHOLISM NEWSLETTER. 1971. bi-m. free. Vista Hill Foundation, 2355 Northside Dr., San Diego, CA 92108-2705. TEL 619-563-1770. Ed. Dr. Marc A. Schuckit. circ. 32,500. (tabloid format; also avail. in microform from UMI; reprint service avail. from UMI; back issues avail.) **Indexed:** Psychol.Abstr. **Document type:** newsletter.
—UMI.

616.863 158.8   US   ISSN 0739-6562
HV5825
DRUG ABUSE UPDATE. 1982. q. $30 (foreign $40). National Families in Action, 2296 Henderson Mill Rd., Ste. 300, Atlanta, GA 30345. TEL 770-934-6364. FAX 770-934-7137. URL: http://www.emory.edu/NFIA/. Ed. Paula Kemp. bk.rev.; video rev.; abstr.; charts; stat.; index. circ. 10,000. (back issues avail.)

616.86   US   ISSN 1067-814X
DRUG, ALCOHOL, AND OTHER ADDICTIONS. 1989. irreg. Oryx Press, 4041 N. Central Ave., No. 700, Phoenix, AZ 85012-3397. TEL 602-265-2651. FAX 602-265-6250. E-mail: info@oryxpress.com; URL: http://www.oryxpress.com/. Ed. Jennifer Ashley. (also avail. in magnetic tape) **Document type:** directory.

616.86 157.6   IE   ISSN 0376-8716
RC566.A1   CODEN: DADEDV
DRUG AND ALCOHOL DEPENDENCE; an international journal on biomedical and psychosocial approaches. 1975. m. fl.2126($1222) (effective 1998). (International Council on Alcohol and Addictions) Elsevier Science Ireland Ltd., P.O. Box 85, Limerick, Ireland. TEL 353-61-471944. FAX 353-61-472144. (Subscr. to: Elsevier Science, Regional Sales Office, P.O. Box 211, 1000 AE Amsterdam, Netherlands. TEL 31-20-4853757. FAX 31-20-4853432; Subscr. in the Americas to: Elsevier Science, Regional Sales Office, Box 945, New York, NY 10159-0945. TEL 74B-633-3730. FAX 212-633-3680; Subscr. in Australasia and the Far East to: Elsevier Science (Singapore) Pte Ltd, No.1 Temasek Ave., No.17-01 Millenia Tower, Singapore 039192, Singapore. TEL 65-434-3727. FAX 212-633-3990) (Co-sponsor: College on Problems of Drug Dependence) Ed. C.-E. P.D. Johanson. R&P contact: Annette Moloney. bk.rev (also avail. in microform from UMI) **Indexed:** Abstr.Crim.& Pen., Adol.Ment.Hlth.Abstr., ASCA, ASSIA, Biol.Abstr., Bull.Signal., Chem.Abstr., Chic.Per.Ind., Community Ment.Health Rev., Crim.Just.Abstr., Curr.Adv.Ecol.Sci., Curr.Cont., Dairy Sci.Abstr., Excerp.Med., HRIS, I.P.A., Ind.Med., Ind.Sci.Rev., Mid.East: Abstr.& Ind., Neurosci.Cit.Ind., Psychol.Abstr. (1975-), Sci.Cit.Ind., Sociol.Abstr., SSCI, THA. **Document type:** academic/scholarly publication.
—BLDSC (3627.890000); ADONIS; CASDDS; CIST; EMDOCS; Genuine Article; KNAW; SWETS; UnCover. CCC.
Description: For workers in the fields of biomedical as well as clinical, epidemiological, psychosocial, socio-cultural, educational and medico-legal research.
Refereed Serial

178   UK   ISSN 0959-5236
DRUG AND ALCOHOL REVIEW. 1982. q. £76 to individuals; institutions £212 (effective 1996). (Australian Medical and Professional Society on Alcohol and Drug Related Problems, AT) Carfax Publishing Co., P.O. Box 25, Abingdon, Oxon. OX14 3UE, England. TEL 44-1235-401000. FAX 44-1235-401550. E-mail: enquiries@carfax.co.uk. (Subscr. in N. America to: Carfax Publishing Co 875-81 Massachusetts Ave., Cambridge, MA 02139) Ed. John B. Saunders. bk.rev.; index. (back issues avail.) **Indexed:** ASCA, Curr.Cont., Mult.Ed.Abstr., Psychol.Abstr. (1994-), Stud.Wom.Abstr. **Document type:** academic/scholarly publication.
—BLDSC (3627.895000); Genuine Article; KNAW; UMI; UnCover. CCC.
Former titles (until Jan. 1990): Australian Drug and Alcohol Review; Australian Alcohol - Drug Review (ISSN 0726-4550)
Description: Reviews the clinical, biomedical, psychological and sociological aspects of alcohol, tobacco, and drug use.
Refereed Serial

616.86 353   US   ISSN 1076-1519
DRUG AND CRIME PREVENTION FUNDING NEWS. 199? w. (50/yr.). $289. Government Information Services, 4301 Fairfax Dr., Ste. 875, Arlington, VA 22203-1627. TEL 703-528-1000. FAX 703-528-6060. Ed. Erika Fitzpatrick.
Formerly (until 1994): Anti-Drug Funding Alert (ISSN 1060-4707)
Description: Covers developments affecting federal aid for anti-drug programs and for law enforcement

DRUG DETECTION REPORT. see *BUSINESS AND ECONOMICS — Personnel Management*

DRUG INDUCED DISORDERS. see *PHARMACY AND PHARMACOLOGY*

616.863 340   US   ISSN 0734-6166
KF3890.A15
DRUG LAW REPORT. 1983. bi-m. $175. (National Organization for Reform of Marijuana Laws) Clark - Boardman - Callaghan, 375 Hudson St., New York, NY 10014. TEL 212-929-7500; 800-422-2101. FAX 212-924-0460. Ed. Kevin B. Zeese. bk.rev. (looseleaf format; back issues avail.) **Document type:** newsletter.
—CCC.
Formerly: Drug Law Journal.

THE DRUG LIBRARY. see *CHILDREN AND YOUTH — For*

616.863 157.63   UK   ISSN 0305-4349
DRUGLINK. 1976. bi-m. £36 (foreign £45). Institute for the Study of Drug Dependence, Waterbridge House, 32-36 Loman St., London SE1 0EE, England. TEL 44-171-928-1211. FAX 44-171-928-1771. E-mail: services@isdd.co.uk; URL: http://www.isdd.co.uk. Ed. Oswin Baker. adv.: page £220; 264 x 181. bk.rev.; bibl. circ. 2,300. (back issues avail.) **Document type:** bulletin.
Description: Examines the abuse and misuse of drugs.

616.86   US   ISSN 0273-2505
HV5825
DRUGS. (Subseries of: S I R S Social Issues (0740-3127)) 1970. a. price varies; a. supplement $19. Social Issues Resources Series, Box 2348, Boca Raton, FL 33427-2348. TEL 561-994-0079; 800-232-SIRS. FAX 561-994-4704. E-mail: custserve@sirs.com; URL: http://www.sirs.com. Ed. Trudy Collins; Pub. Eleanor Goldstein. R&P contact: Bonnie Milnes. (looseleaf format; back issues avail.) **Document type:** academic/scholarly publication.
Description: Reprints articles that explore the history of drug use and how it affects society.

616.863   US   ISSN 0744-2823
HV5825
DRUGS & DRUG ABUSE EDUCATION. NEWSLETTER. 1969. m. $79. Editorial Resources, Inc., Box 21133, Washington, DC 20009. TEL 206-322-8387. (Subscr. to: Box 20754, Seattle, WA 98102) Ed. David L. Howell. bk.rev.; charts.
Incorporates: Alcoholism and Alcohol Education (ISSN 0044-7226); Formerly: Washington Drug Review (ISSN 0146-728X)
Description: Covers treatment, prevention education, congressional and agency developments, and state and local programs.

616.863   US   ISSN 8756-8233
HV5800   CODEN: DRSOEI
DRUGS & SOCIETY; a journal of contemporary issues. 1986. q. $42 to individuals (Canada $54.60; elsewhere $58.80); institutions $90 (Canada $117; elsewhere $126); libraries $175 (Canada $227.50; elsewhere $245) (effective 1996-1997). Haworth Press, Inc., 10 Alice St., Binghamton, NY 13904. TEL 607-722-5857; 800-342-9676. FAX 607-722-6362. E-mail: getinfo@haworth.com; URL: http://www.haworth.com. Ed. Bernard Segal; Pub. Bill Cohen. R&P contact: Ruthann Heath. adv.: B&W page $300; trim 4 3/8 x 7 1/8; adv. contact: Jackie Blakeslee. bk.rev. circ. 256. (also avail. in microfiche from UMI; microform from HAW; reprint service avail. from HAW) **Indexed:** Abstr.Anthropol., Excerp.Med., I.P.A., IMFL, Int.Polit.Sci.Abstr., Psychol.Abstr. (1986-), Soc.Work Res.& Abstr. **Document type:** academic/scholarly publication.
—BLDSC (3629.652000); EMDOCS; Haworth; UnCover.
Description: Provides current information pertaining to the field of substance abuse. Directed toward researchers, professionals, and practitioners in substance abuse related fields and to students seeking to enter the field.
Refereed Serial

616.86   UK   ISSN 0968-7637
CODEN: DEPPEH
DRUGS: EDUCATION, PREVENTION & POLICY. 1994. 3/yr. £46($74) to individuals; institutions £172 ($274) (effective 1997). Carfax Publishing Co., P.O. Box 25, Abingdon, Oxon. OX14 3UE, England. TEL 44-1235-401000. FAX 44-1235-401550. E-mail: enquiries@carfax.co.uk. (N. American subscr. to: Carfax Publishing Co., 875-81 Massachusetts Ave., Cambridge, MA 02139) Ed. Stuart Ware. adv.; bk.rev.; index. (also avail. in microfiche) **Indexed:** ASCA, Br.Educ.Ind., Curr.Cont., Mult.Ed.Abstr. **Document type:** academic/scholarly publication.
—BLDSC (3629.818000); Genuine Article; UMI.
CCC.
Description: Publishes multidisciplinary papers on the prevention of substance abuse and related problems. Provides a forum for those concerned with education and prevention policy and its application in the community, and promotes dialogue with those affected by such applications and community practice.
Refereed Serial

616.86   US   ISSN 0273-8910
HF5549.5.E42   CODEN: EAPDEW
E A P DIGEST. (Employee Assistance Programs) 1980. bi-m. $36 (Canada $45; elsewhere $55) (effective 1997). Performance Resource Press, Inc., 1270 Rankin Dr., Ste. F, Troy, MI 48083-2843. TEL 810-588-7733. FAX 810-588-6633. Ed. Brent Chartier. adv.; bk.rev. circ. 10,000. **Indexed:** Soc.Work Res.& Abstr. **Document type:** trade publication.
—UnCover.

EMPLOYEE ASSISTANCE QUARTERLY. see *BUSINESS AND ECONOMICS — Personnel Management*

362.29 616.86   SZ   ISSN 1022-6877
CODEN: EADREE
▼**EUROPEAN ADDICTION RESEARCH**. (Text in English) 1995. q. 123.90 SFr.($94.90) to individuals; institutions 354 SFr.($271) (effective 1998). S. Karger AG, Allschwilerstr. 10, P.O. Box, CH-4009 Basel, Switzerland. TEL 41-61-3061111. FAX 41-61-3061234. E-mail: karger@karger.ch; URL: http://www.karger.ch. Eds. M. Krausz, A. Uchtenhagen. **Indexed:** Excerp.Med. (1996-). **Document type:** academic/scholarly publication.
—BLDSC (3829.482945); CISTI; EMDOCS; KNAW; SWETS.
Description: International forum for the exchange of interdisciplinary information and expert opinions on all aspects of addiction research.

616.863   GW
FAMILIEN-KALENDER. 1902. a. DM.6.50. Blaukreuz Verlag, Freiligrathstr. 27, 42289 Wuppertal, Germany. Ed. Alexander Schubert. bk.rev. circ. 21,500. (back issues avail.) **Document type:** bulletin.

FAMILY THERAPY NETWORKER. see *PSYCHOLOGY*

THE FARNATCHI SERIES. see *EDUCATION — Teaching Methods And Curriculum*

051   US   ISSN 0194-8121
THE FORUM (VIRGINIA BEACH). 1978. m. $9 (Braille ed. & large print ed. $100). (Al-Anon Family Group Headquarters, Inc., Communications Department) A F G, Inc., 1600 Corporate Landing Pkwy., Virginia Beach, VA 23454-5617. TEL 757-563-1600. FAX 757-563-1655. (Large print and Braille editions avail. from: Volunteer Braille Services, c/o Victor Hemphill, 2745 Limore Ln., Hisleett, MI 48440-8251. TEL 517-339-9872) index. circ. 40,000. (also avail. in Braille; large print edition in 22 pt.; back issues avail.)
Description: Family members and friends of alcoholics relate personal experiences regarding Twelve Step program of recovery.

178   CN
FORWARD. 1894. m. Can.$2($2.25) (Grand Division Sons of Temperance of Nova Scotia) David Allbon & Co. Ltd., Box 1090, Windsor, N.S. B0N 2T0, Canada. TEL 902-798-2456. Ed. Annie L. Bird. adv.; illus. circ. 600. (tabloid format)

FREIE FAHRT/ROUTE LIBRE. see *PUBLIC HEALTH AND SAFETY*

DRUG ABUSE AND ALCOHOLISM   2301

616.861   GW   ISSN 0342-4685
FUEREINANDER. 1971. 2/m. DM.21.60. (Blaues Kreuz in Deutschland e.V.) Blaukreuz Verlag, Freiligrathstr. 27, 42289 Wuppertal, Germany. Ed. Alexander Schubert. circ. 8,500. **Document type:** bulletin.

616.863   US   ISSN 1056-9340
HV5825.
GUIDE TO FEDERAL FUNDING FOR ANTI-DRUG PROGRAMS. 1990. a. $191. Government Information Services, 4301 Fairfax Dr., Ste. 875, Arlington, VA 22203-1627. TEL 703-528-1000. FAX 703-528-6060. Ed.Bd. (looseleaf format)
Description: Describes federal anti-drug and anti-alcohol abuse grant programs. Includes drug prevention, education, treatment and domestic law enforcement programs.

616.86   US
GUILFORD SUBSTANCE ABUSE SERIES. irreg. (approx. 2/yr.). Guilford Publications, Inc., 72 Spring St., New York, NY 10012. TEL 212-431-9800; 800-365-7006. FAX 212-966-6708. E-mail: info@guilford.com. Eds. Howard T. Blane, Thomas R. Kosten. **Document type:** monographic series.
Description: Provides therapies and theories that can be used to treat and understand people with alcohol and drug problems and their families.

362.29   SW   ISSN 1100-4312
HASSELA SOLIDARITET; en tidning fraan Hasselaroerelsen. 1985. q. SEK 100 (effective 1991). Foerbundet Hassela Solidaritet, P.O. Box 5031, S-103 69 Stockholm, Sweden.

616.86   US
HAZELDEN VOICE; news and opinion for recovering people and professionals. 1990. 2/yr. free. Hazelden Foundation, Box 11, Center City, MN 55012-0011. TEL 612-213-4455. FAX 612-257-1055. Ed. Marty Duda. R&P contact: Marty Duda. bk.rev.; circ. 60,000 (controlled). **Document type:** newsletter.
Formerly (until 1996): Hazelden News and Professional Update.
Description: Covers a broad range of issues for professionals in the chemical health field and for those in recovery from chemical dependency and other related addictive behaviors.

178   UK
THE HERALD (BRISTOL). 1836. 2/yr. free. Western Alcohol and Drugs Education Society, 6 Gloucester St., Upper Eastville, Bristol BS5 6QE, England. TEL 0272-512187. Ed. Raymond Foster. circ. 3,500. **Document type:** bulletin.
Formerly: Western Temperance Herald (ISSN 0049-7517)
Description: Facts, views, comments from Christian viewpoint, on the alcohol-drug scene.

HIGHLIFE; tijdschrift voor levensgenieters. see *LITERARY AND POLITICAL REVIEWS*

HOLY SMOKE; for people who need good medicine. see *ALTERNATIVE MEDICINE*

362.2   CC
HONG KONG NARCOTICS REPORT. 1965. a. free to qualified personnel. Action Committee Against Narcotics, c/o Narcotics Division, Government Secretariat, Queensway Government Offices, High Block, 66 Queensway, Hong Kong, People's Republic of China. FAX 852-2521-7761. illus. circ. 10,000.
Former titles: Action Committee Against Narcotics. Annual Report; Narcotics Progress Report.

178   SZ
I C A A. PUBLICATIONS. (Text in English) 1982. irreg. price varies. International Congress on Alcohol and Addictions, Case Postale 189, CH-1001 Lausanne, Switzerland. TEL 41-21-3209865. FAX 41-21-3209817. E-mail: icaa@pingnet.ch; URL: http://www.icaa.ch. **Document type:** monographic series.
Description: Discusses innovations in treatment, education and control of substance abuse.

613.81   SZ   ISSN 1012-8360
I C A A NEWS. 1973. q. 45 SFr.($40) International Council on Alcohol and Addictions, Case Postale 189, CH-1001 Lausanne, Switzerland. TEL 41-21-3209865. FAX 41-21-3209817. E-mail: icaa@pingnet.ch; URL: http://www.icaa.ch. **Document type:** newsletter.

DRUG ABUSE AND ALCOHOLISM

IMPAIRED DRIVING & BREATHALYZER LAW. see *LAW*

613.81   SZ
INTERNATIONAL CONGRESS ON ALCOHOLISM AND DRUG DEPENDENCE. PROCEEDINGS. triennial, 36th, 1992, Glasgow. 175 SFr. International Council on Alcohol and Addictions, Case Postale 189, CH-1001 Lausanne, Switzerland. TEL 41-21-3209865. FAX 41-21-3209817. E-mail: icaa@pingnet.ch; URL: http://www.icaa.ch. **Document type:** proceedings.
    Former titles: International Congress on Alcoholism and Addictions. Proceedings; International Congress on Alcohol and Alcoholism. Proceedings.

INTERNATIONAL DRUG REPORT. see *CRIMINOLOGY AND LAW ENFORCEMENT*

613.81   SZ
HV5801   CODEN: PIIDD3
INTERNATIONAL INSTITUTE ON THE PREVENTION AND TREATMENT OF DEPENDENCIES. SELECTED PAPERS. 1970. irreg. International Council on Alcohol and Addictions, Case Postale 189, CH-1001 Lausanne, Switzerland. TEL 41-21-3209865. FAX 41-21-3209817. E-mail: icaa@pingnet.ch; URL: http://www.icaa.ch. circ. 1,000. **Indexed:** Chem.Abstr. **Document type:** monographic series.
—CASDDS.
    Former titles (until 1996): International Institutes on the Prevention and Treatment of Addictions. Selected Papers (ISSN 0254-2536); International Institute on the Prevention and Treatment of Drug Dependence. Selected Papers.

616.86   UK   ISSN 0955-3959
HV5800   CODEN: IJDPED
INTERNATIONAL JOURNAL OF DRUG POLICY. 1989. q. £49 to individuals; institutions £99 (effective 1997). Whurr Publishers Ltd., 19b Compton Terrace, London N1 2UN, England. TEL 44-171-359-5979. FAX 44-171-226-5290. (Subscr. to: Turpin Distribution Services Ltd., Blackhorse Rd., Letchworth, Herts. SG6 1HN, England. TEL 44-1462-672555. FAX 44-1462-480947; Subscr. in N. America to: Whurr Publishers Ltd., Box 1897, Lawrence, KS 66044-8897. TEL 913-843-1221. FAX 913-843-1274) Ed. Pat O'Hare. adv.: page £225; adv. contact: Maggy Park. bk.rev. circ. 400. **Indexed:** Abstr.Crim.& Pen., Crim.Just.Abstr., I.P.A. **Document type:** academic/scholarly publication.
—BLDSC (4542.188500); KNAW.
Refereed Serial

INTERNATIONAL NARCOTIC ENFORCEMENT OFFICERS ASSOCIATION DIRECTORY. see *CRIMINOLOGY AND LAW ENFORCEMENT*

INTERNATIONAL NARCOTICS CONTROL BOARD. REPORT FOR (YEAR). see *PHARMACY AND PHARMACOLOGY*

616.86   SZ
INTERNATIONALES SYMPOSIUM GEGEN DROGEN IN DER SCHWEIZ. 1991. irreg. Verein zur Foerderung der Psychologischen Menschenkenntnis, Susenbergstr. 53, CH-8044 Zurich, Switzerland. **Document type:** proceedings.

362.2   US
IOWA SUBSTANCE ABUSE REPORT (YEAR). 1973. a. free. Department of Public Health, Division of Substance Abuse, Lucas State Office Bldg., 321 E. 12th St., Des Moines, IA 50319. TEL 515-281-3641. FAX 515-281-4535. circ. 1,000. **Document type:** government publication.
    Former titles: Iowa Comprehensive State Plan for Substance Abuse (Year); Iowa Comprehensive State Plan for Substance Abuse Prevention: Annual Performance Report; (until 1980): Iowa Comprehensive State Plan for Drug Abuse Prevention: Annual Performance Report (ISSN 0363-4507)

616.8   GW   ISSN 0940-4910
JAHRBUCH SUCHT. 1958. a. DM.22. (Deutsche Hauptstelle gegen die Suchtgefahren) Neuland Verlagsgesellschaft mbH, Markt 24-26, 21502 Geesthacht, Germany. TEL 49-4152-81342. FAX 49-4152-81343. Ed.Bd. adv. circ. 9,000. **Document type:** academic/scholarly publication.
    Former titles: Jahrbuch zur Frage der Suchtgefahren (ISSN 0170-7337); Jahrbuch zur Alkohol- und Tabakfrage (ISSN 0075-2827)

362.29   SW   ISSN 0348-1565
JEPPE. 1974. bi-m. SEK 75 membership (effective 1990). Alkoholproblematikers Riksorganisation (ALRO), P.O. Box 17009, S-104 62 Stockholm, Sweden.

JOURNAL OF ADDICTIONS NURSING. see *MEDICAL SCIENCES — Nurses And Nursing*

616.86   US   ISSN 1055-0887
HV5800   CODEN: JADDER
JOURNAL OF ADDICTIVE DISEASES. 1981. q. $50 to individuals (Canada $65; elsewhere $70); institutions $90 (Canada $117; elsewhere $126); libraries $375 (Canada $487.50; elsewhere $525) (effective 1997-1998). (American Society of Addiction Medicine) Haworth Press, Inc., 10 Alice St., Binghamton, NY 13904. TEL 607-722-5857; 800-342-9676. FAX 607-722-6362. E-mail: getinfo@haworth.com; URL: http://www.haworth.com. Ed. Dr. Barry Stimmel; Pub. Bill Cohen. R&P contact: Ruthann Heath. adv.: B&W page $300; trim 4 3/8 x 7 1/8; adv. contact: Jackie Blakeslee. bk.rev.; bibl. circ. 3,506. (also avail. in microfiche from UMI; microform from HAW; back issues avail.; reprint service avail. from HAW) **Indexed:** Abstr.Anthropol., Abstr.Crim.& Pen., Adol.Ment.Hlth.Abstr., ASCA, Biol.Abstr., Chem.Abstr., Child Devel.Abstr., CJPI, Crim.Just.Abstr., Curr.Adv.Ecol.Sci., Curr.Cont., Excerp.Med., Fam.Ind., I.P.A., IMFL, Ind.Med., Past.Care & Couns.Abstr., Psychol.Abstr. (1981-), Ref.Zh., Saf.Sci.Abstr., Soc.Work Res.& Abstr., Sociol.Abstr., Stud.Wom.Abstr., THA. **Document type:** academic/scholarly publication.
—BLDSC (4918.934050); CASDDS; CISTI; EMDOCS; Genuine Article; Haworth; KNAW; SWETS; UnCover.
    Formerly (until 1991): Advances in Alcohol and Substance Abuse (ISSN 0270-3106); Supersedes (1977-1981): Drug Abuse and Alcoholism Review (ISSN 0149-5968)
    Description: Covers current topics in alcoholism and substance abuse field and devotes an entire issue to each topic.
Refereed Serial

616.86   US   ISSN 0090-1482
HV5128.U5   CODEN: JADEDT
JOURNAL OF ALCOHOL AND DRUG EDUCATION. Short title: J.A.D.E. 1955. 3/yr. $45 to non-members; foreign $55 (effective 1997). American Alcohol and Drug Information Foundation (Lansing), c/o M I C A P, Box 10212, Lansing, MI 48901. TEL 517-484-2636. FAX 517-484-0444. Eds. Richard D. Stacy, David E. Corbin. R&P contact: Kenton L. Owens. (also avail. in microform from UMI; reprint service avail. from UMI) **Indexed:** Adol.Ment.Hlth.Abstr., ASCA, C.I.J.E., Cont.Pg.Educ., Crim.Just.Abstr., Curr.Cont., Educ.Ind., Fam.Ind., High.Educ.Abstr., HRIS, Mult.Ed.Abstr., Psychol.Abstr. (1972-), Risk Abstr., Sp.Ed.Needs Abstr., SSCI, Tech.Educ.Abstr. **Document type:** academic/scholarly publication.
—BLDSC (4926.720000); Genuine Article; KR SourceOne; SWETS; UMI; UnCover.
    Formerly: Journal of Alcohol Education (ISSN 0021-8677)
    Description: Serves as a forum for various educational philosophies and differing points of view in regard to alcohol and drugs. Reports teacher experience and experiments and provides a reference for actual teaching materials, factual guide for prevention, techniques and procedures.
Refereed Serial

616.863   US   ISSN 0885-4734
RC563
JOURNAL OF CHEMICAL DEPENDENCY TREATMENT. 1987. s-a. $36 to individuals (Canada $46.80; elsewhere $50.40); institutions $90 (Canada $117; elsewhere $126); libraries $175 (Canada $227.50; elsewhere $245) (effective 1997-1998). Haworth Press, Inc., 10 Alice St., Binghamton, NY 13904. TEL 607-722-5857; 800-342-9676. FAX 607-722-6362. E-mail: getinfo@haworth.com; URL: http://www.haworth.com. Ed. Dana Finnegan; Pub. Bill Cohen. R&P contact: Ruthann Heath. adv.: B&W page $300; trim 4 3/8 x 7 1/8; adv. contact: Jackie Blakeslee. circ. 726. (also avail. in microfiche from UMI; microform from HAW; back issues avail.; reprint service avail. from HAW) **Indexed:** Crim.Just.Abstr., IMFL, Psychol.Abstr., Soc.Work Res.& Abstr., THA. **Document type:** academic/scholarly publication.
—BLDSC (4955.900000); Haworth; KNAW; SWETS.
    Description: For professionals providing direct clinical services. Each issue examines a specific chemical dependency problem. Stresses clinical techniques and methods but integrates theory and research.
Refereed Serial

616.863   US   ISSN 1067-828X
RJ506.D78   CODEN: JCAAFI
JOURNAL OF CHILD & ADOLESCENT SUBSTANCE ABUSE. 1989. q. $36 to individuals (Canada $46.80; elsewhere $50.40); institutions $75 (Canada $97.50; elsewhere $105); libraries $145 (Canada $188.50; elsewhere $203) (effective 1996-1997). Haworth Press, Inc., 10 Alice St., Binghamton, NY 13904. TEL 607-722-5857; 800-342-9676. FAX 607-722-6362. E-mail: getinfo@haworth.com; URL: http://www.haworth.com. Eds. Frank de Piano, Vincent B. Van Hasselt; Pub. Bill Cohen. R&P contact: Ruthann Heath. adv.: B&W page $300; trim 4 3/8 x 7 1/8; adv. contact: Jackie Blakeslee. bk.rev. (also avail. in microfiche from UMI; microform from HAW; reprint service avail. from HAW) **Indexed:** ASCA, C.I.J.E., Chem.Abstr., Curr.Cont., Except.Child.Educ.Abstr., Fam.Ind., IMFL, Ind.Med., Psychol.Abstr. (1991-), Soc.Work Res.& Abstr., Sp.Ed.Needs Abstr., THA. **Document type:** academic/scholarly publication.
—BLDSC (4957.425300); Genuine Article; Haworth; KNAW.
    Formerly: Journal of Adolescent Chemical Dependency (ISSN 0896-7768)
    Description: Provides realistic and usable strategies in a clear and concise manner for the chemically dependent adolescent and his or her family.
Refereed Serial

362.293   US   ISSN 0047-2379
HV5808   CODEN: JDGEBT
JOURNAL OF DRUG EDUCATION. 1970. q. $136 (effective 1997). Baywood Publishing Co., Inc., 26 Austin Ave., Box 337, Amityville, NY 11701. TEL 516-691-1270. FAX 516-691-1770. E-mail: baywood@baywood.com; URL: http://baywood.com. Ed. Dr. Seymour Eiseman. R&P contact: Julie Krempa. adv. contact: Lorna Roher. bk.rev.; abstr.; charts; illus. (back issues avail.) **Indexed:** Abstr.Anthropol., Adol.Ment.Hlth.Abstr., ASCA, Biol.Abstr., C.I.J.E., Cont.Pg.Educ., Crim.Just.Abstr., Curr.Cont., Educ.Ind., Educ.Tech.Abstr., Excerp.Med., Fam.Ind., I.P.A., Ind.Med., Mid.East: Abstr.& Ind., Mult.Ed.Abstr., Psychol.Abstr. (1971-), Risk Abstr., Sp.Ed.Needs Abstr., SSCI, Stud.Wom.Abstr., Tech.Educ.Abstr. **Document type:** academic/scholarly publication.
●Also available online.
—BLDSC (4970.550000); CISTI; EMDOCS; KNAW; KR SourceOne; SWETS; UnCover. CCC.
    Description: Contains current, authoritative and practical articles on the latest developments in preventive practices, and issues and trends in drug education and addiction management.
Refereed Serial

DRUG ABUSE AND ALCOHOLISM

616.86 US ISSN 0022-0426
HV5800 CODEN: JDGIA6
JOURNAL OF DRUG ISSUES. 1971. q. $80 (foreign $90) (effective 1996). Journal of Drug Issues Inc., Box 4021, Leon Sta., Tallahassee, FL 32315. TEL 904-668-6669. Ed. Richard L. Rachin. adv.; bk.rev.; bibl.; charts; index, cum.index. circ. 1,000. (also avail. in microfilm from UMI; reprint service avail. from RRI,UMI,WSH) **Indexed:** Abstr.Crim.& Pen., Abstr.Soc.Work., Adol.Ment.Hlth.Abstr., ASCA, ASSIA, Behav.Abstr., Biol.Abstr., C.L.I., Crim.Just.Abstr., Curr.Cont., Excerp.Med., I.P.A., IMFL, Ind.Per.Art.Relat.Law, Leg.Per., Mid.East: Abstr.& Ind., Psychol.Abstr. (1972-), Soc.Sci.Ind., Soc.Work Res.& Abstr., SSCI, THA. **Document type:** academic/scholarly publication.
●Also available online.
—BLDSC (4970.570000); Genuine Article; KNAW; KR SourceOne; SWETS; UMI; UnCover. **CCC.**
Description: Critical commentary on a wide range of drug policy issues.
Refereed Serial

616.863 US ISSN 1091-1332
RC568.M4
▼**JOURNAL OF MAINTENANCE IN THE ADDICTIONS**; innovations in research, theory, & practice. 1996. q. $36 to individuals (Canada $46.80; elsewhere $50.40); institutions $48 (Canada $62.40; elsewhere $67.20); libraries $60 (Canada $78; elsewhere $84) (effective 1997-1998). Haworth Press, Inc., 10 Alice St., Binghamton, NY 13904. TEL 607-722-5857; 800-342-9676. FAX 607-722-6362. E-mail: getinfo@haworth.com; URL: http://www.haworth.com. Ed. Dr. J. Thomas Payte; Pub. Bill Cohen. R&P contact: Ruthann Heath. adv.: B&W page $300; trim 4 3/8 x 7 1/8; adv. contact: Jackie Blakeslee. (also avail. in microfiche from UMI; microform from HAW; reprint service avail. from HAW) **Document type:** academic/scholarly publication.
—Haworth.
Description: Provides cutting-edge articles that assist in the understanding of clinical management at the most practical level.
Refereed Serial

JOURNAL OF MENTAL HEALTH ADMINISTRATION. see *PUBLIC HEALTH AND SAFETY*

JOURNAL OF MINISTRY IN ADDICTION & RECOVERY. see *RELIGIONS AND THEOLOGY*

301 616.8 615 US ISSN 0279-1072
BF207 CODEN: JPDRD3
JOURNAL OF PSYCHOACTIVE DRUGS; a multidisciplinary forum. 1967. q. $90 to individuals; institutions $160. Haight-Ashbury Publications, 612 Clayton St., San Francisco, CA 94117. TEL 415-565-1904. FAX 415-864-6162. URL: http://www.hooked.net/users/hafei/. Ed. Richard B. Seymour. adv.; bk.rev.; charts; illus.; stat. circ. 7,023. (also avail. in microform from UMI; reprint service avail. from ISI,UMI) **Indexed:** Adol.Ment.Hlth.Abstr., ASCA, Biol.Abstr., Chem.Abstr., Crim.Just.Abstr., Curr.Cont., Excerp.Med., Fam.Ind., HRIS, IMFL, Ind.Med., Psychol.Abstr. (1971-), Soc.Sci.Ind., SSCI, THA. **Document type:** academic/scholarly publication.
—BLDSC (5043.263000); CASDDS; CISTI; EMDOCS; Genuine Article; KNAW; SWETS; UMI; UnCover.
Formerly (until vol.13, 1981): Journal of Psychedelic Drugs (ISSN 0022-393X)
Description: Focuses on human use and abuse of alcohol and other drugs, as well as related issues, such as treatment modalities, AIDS, and dual diagnosis.
Refereed Serial

JOURNAL OF PUBLIC HEALTH POLICY. see *PUBLIC HEALTH AND SAFETY*

JOURNAL OF SOCIAL WORK PRACTICE. see *SOCIAL SERVICES AND WELFARE*

616.861 016 US ISSN 0096-882X
RC565 CODEN: JSALDP
JOURNAL OF STUDIES ON ALCOHOL. (Supplements avail.) 1940. bi-m. $140 to individuals (foreign $155); institutions $175 (foreign $190) (effective 1998). (Rutgers Center of Alcohol Studies) Alcohol Research Documentation, Inc., c/o Charles Rouse, Bus. Admin., Box 969, Piscataway, NJ 08855. TEL 908-445-2190. Ed. Marc A. Schuckit. R&P contact: Pat Castellano. TEL 732-445-3510. adv. contact: Lisheg Xu. bk.rev.; abstr.; bibl.; charts; illus.; index. circ. 2,700. (also avail. in microform from UMI; back issues avail.) **Indexed:** Abstr.Crim.& Pen., Abstr.Soc.Work., Adol.Ment.Hlth.Abstr., Amer.Hist.& Life, ASCA, ASSIA, Behav.Med.Abstr., Biol.Abstr., Bull.Signal., C.I.S. Abstr., Chem.Abstr., Crim.Just.Abstr., Curr.Adv.Ecol.Sci., Curr.Cont., Dent.Ind., Dok.Arbeitsmed., Excerp.Med., Fam.Ind., High.Educ.Abstr., Hist.Abstr., HRIS, HRIS, Ind.Med., Ind.Sci.Rev., Int.Nurs.Ind., Lang.& Lang.Behav.Abstr., Mid.East: Abstr.& Ind., Neurosci.Cit.Ind., Nurs.Res.Abstr., Nutr.Abstr., P.A.I.S., Psychol.Abstr. (1940-), Psychopharmacol.Abstr., Ref.Zh., Risk Abstr., Sci.Cit.Ind., Soc.Sci.Ind., Soc.Work Res.& Abstr., Sociol.Abstr., SSCI, THA, VITIS. **Document type:** academic/scholarly publication.
—BLDSC (5066.895000); CASDDS; Genuine Article; KNAW; KR SourceOne; SWETS; UMI; UnCover. **CCC.**
Formerly (until 1974): Quarterly Journal of Studies on Alcohol (ISSN 0033-5649)
Description: Contributes to knowledge about alcohol, its use, misuse and its biomedical, behavioral and sociocultural effects.

616.861 US ISSN 0363-468X
JOURNAL OF STUDIES ON ALCOHOL. SUPPLEMENT. 1961. irreg. $140 (foreign $155) to individuals; institutions $175 (foreign $190) (effective 1998). (Rutgers Center of Alcohol Studies) Alcohol Research Documentation, Inc., Box 969, Piscataway, NJ 08855. TEL 732-445-3510. FAX 732-445-3500. Ed. Dr. Marc A. Schuckit. R&P contact: Pat Castellano. TEL 908-445-3510. adv. contact: Lisheg Xu. index; circ. 2,300 (paid). (also avail. in microfilm from UMI) **Indexed:** Abstr.Crim.& Pen., Biol.Abstr., Bull.Signal., C.I.S. Abstr., Chem.Abstr., Crim.Just.Abstr., Curr.Cont., Excerp.Med., Hist.Abstr., Ind.Med., P.A.I.S., Psychol.Abstr., Psychopharmacol.Abstr., Ref.Zh., Soc.Work Res.& Abstr., Sociol.Abstr., SSCI. **Document type:** academic/scholarly publication.
—BLDSC (5066.896000); KNAW; UMI. **CCC.**
Formerly (until 1975): Quarterly Journal of Studies on Alcohol. Supplement (ISSN 0079-8312)
Description: Reports research on alcohol-related problems.
Refereed Serial

616.86 US ISSN 0899-3289
RC563 CODEN: JSABEU
JOURNAL OF SUBSTANCE ABUSE. 1988. q. $45 to individuals; institutions $140 (effective 1996). Ablex Publishing Corporation, Box 5297, Greenwich, CT 06831-0504. TEL 203-661-7602. FAX 203-661-0792. E-mail: ted_nirenberg@brown.edu. Ed. Ted D. Nirenberg. index. circ. 350. **Indexed:** Excerp.Med. (1995-), IMFL, Ind.Med. (1992-), Mult.Ed.Abstr., Psychol.Abstr. (1989-), Soc.Work Res.& Abstr., Stud.Wom.Abstr., THA. **Document type:** academic/scholarly publication.
—BLDSC (5066.931000); Genuine Article; KNAW; SWETS. **CCC.**

363 US ISSN 0740-5472
RC563 CODEN: JSATEG
JOURNAL OF SUBSTANCE ABUSE TREATMENT. 1984. bi-m. fl.677($389) (effective 1998). (North Shore University Hospital) Elsevier Science Inc., Box 945, New York, NY 10159-0945. TEL 212-633-3730. FAX 212-633-3680. E-mail: nlinfo-f@elsevier.nl; usinfo-f@elsevier.com; forinfo-kyf04035@niftyserve.or.jp; URL: http://www.elsevier.nl/. (Subscr. outside the Americas to: Elsevier Science, Regional Sales Office, P.O. Box 211, 1000 AE Amsterdam, Netherlands. TEL 31-20-4853757. FAX 31-20-4853432; Subscr. in Australasia and the Far East to: Elsevier Science (Singapore) Pte Ltd, No.1 Temasek Ave., No.17-01 Millenia Tower, Singapore 039192, Singapore. TEL 65-434-3727. FAX 65-337-2230; Subscr. in Japan to: Elsevier Science Japan, 9-15 Higashi-Azabu 1-chome, Minato-ku, Tokyo 106, Japan. TEL 81-3-5561-5033. FAX 81-3-5561-5047) Eds. John Imhof, Robert Hirsch. adv.; bk.rev.; index. (also avail. in microfilm from UMI; back issues avail.) **Indexed:** ASCA, Curr.Adv.Ecol.Sci., Curr.Cont., Fam.Ind., Psychol.Abstr. (1984-), Sociol.Abstr., SSCI, THA. **Document type:** academic/scholarly publication.
—BLDSC (5066.932000); EMDOCS; Genuine Article; KNAW; UMI; UnCover. **CCC.**
Refereed Serial

616.8 610.73 UK ISSN 1357-5007
CODEN: JSMIFA
▼**JOURNAL OF SUBSTANCE MISUSE**; for nursing, health and social care. 1996. q. £35($56) to individuals; institutions £120 ($190) (effective 1998). Churchill Livingstone (Subsidiary of: Pearson Professional), Robert Stevenson House, 1-3 Baxter's Pl., Leith Walk, Edinburgh EH1 3AF, Scotland. TEL 44-131-556-2424. FAX 44-131-535-1704. URL: http://www.churchillmed.com. (Subscr. to: Pearson Professional Ltd., P.O. Box 77, Fourth Ave., Harlow, Essex CM19 5BQ, England. TEL 44-1279-623924. FAX 44-1279-639609; US subscr. to: Churchill Livingstone, Box 3217, Secaucus, NJ 07096-3217. TEL 800-553-5426. FAX 201-319-9659) Ed. David B. Cooper. adv. contact: David Dunnachie. (back issues avail.) **Indexed:** ASSIA, CINAHL. **Document type:** academic/scholarly publication.
—BLDSC (5066.932500); EMDOCS.
Refereed Serial

615.9 US ISSN 0731-3810
RA1190 CODEN: JTCTDW
JOURNAL OF TOXICOLOGY. CLINICAL TOXICOLOGY. 1968. 7/yr. $1295 (foreign $1321.25) (effective 1998). (American Academy of Clinical Toxicology) Marcel Dekker Journals, 270 Madison Ave., New York, NY 10016. TEL 212-696-9000. FAX 212-685-4540. TELEX 421419. E-mail: eperez@dekker.com; URL: http://www.dekker.com. (Subscr. to: Box 5017, Monticello, NY 12701) (Co-sponsor: European Association of Poison Centres and Clinical Toxicologoists) Ed. Carol R. Angle. adv. contact: Lourdes Barroso. cols./p.: 00000292. (also avail. in microform from RPI) **Indexed:** Abstr.Hyg., AIM, ASCA, Biol.Abstr., Biol.Dig., Biotech.Abstr., C.I.S.Abstr., Chem.Abstr., Curr.Adv.Ecol.Sci., Curr.Cont., Dairy Sci.Abstr., Dent.Ind., Energy Rev., Environ.Abstr., Environ.Per.Bibl. (1991-1994), Excerp.Med., I.P.A., Ind.Med., Ind.Sci.Rev., Ind.Vet., INIS Atomind., JAMA, Lab.Haz.Bull., Med.Abstr., Nutr.Abstr., Rev.Plant Path., Risk Abstr., Sci.Cit.Ind., Sport Fish.Abstr., THA, Trop.Dis.Bull., Vet.Bull., Weed Abstr., Wild.Rev. **Document type:** academic/scholarly publication.
●Also available online.
—BLDSC (5069.736000); ADONIS; CASDDS; CISTI; EMDOCS; Genuine Article; KNAW; Linda Hall; SWETS; UMI; UnCover. **CCC.**
Supersedes (in 1981): Clinical Toxicology (ISSN 0009-9309)
Description: Correlates the various disciplines that deal directly with and contribute to the practical aspects of poisoning per se.
Refereed Serial

362.29 SW ISSN 0345-7478
LAENK-NYTT. 1951. m. SEK 70 (effective 1990). Fria Saellskapen Laenkerna, Laenk-nytt, P.O. Box 6056, S-400 60 Goeteborg, Sweden.

DRUG ABUSE AND ALCOHOLISM

616.863   US   ISSN 0024-435X
HV5285
LISTEN; journal of better living. (Supplement avail.: Teaching Guide) 1947. m. $18.97 (supplement $6.97). Health Connection, 55 W. Oak Ridge Dr., Hagerstown, MD 21740. TEL 301-745-3888. FAX 301-790-9734. Ed. Lincoln Steed. illus.; index. circ. 40,000. (also avail. in microform from UMI) **Indexed:** CCR.
—UMI.

MANAGED BEHAVIORAL HEALTH NEWS. see *INSURANCE*

616.8   340   UN   ISSN 1010-9595
HD9665.3
MANUFACTURE OF NARCOTIC DRUGS AND PSYCHOTROPIC SUBSTANCES UNDER INTERNATIONAL CONTROL. (Text in English, French, Spanish) 1948. a. (United Nations Commission on Narcotic Drugs) United Nations Publications, Sales and Marketing Section, Room DC2-0853, New York, NY 10017. TEL 212-963-8302; 800-253-9646. FAX 212-963-3489. E-mail: publications@un.org; URL: http://www.un.org/publications.
     Formed by the 1987 merger of: Manufacture of Narcotic Drugs and Psychotropic Substances (ISSN 0251-6713); Fabrication de Stupefiants et de Substances Psychotropes (ISSN 0251-673X); Fabricacion de Estupefacientes y Sustancias Sicotropicas (ISSN 0251-6721)

616.861   US   ISSN 0891-8651
MONDAY MORNING REPORT. 1977. s-m. $30 (foreign $40) (effective 1997 & 1998). Alcohol Research Information Service, 1106 E. Oakland Ave., Lansing, MI 48906. TEL 517-485-9900. FAX 517-485-1928. Ed. Robert Hammond. R&P contact: Robert Hammond. circ. 1,000. **Document type:** newsletter.
     Description: Covers significant issues, events, and opinions in the alcohol problems field.

MONITORING THE FUTURE; questionnaire responses from the nation's high school seniors. see *EDUCATION*

362.2   US
MONTANA COMPREHENSIVE CHEMICAL DEPENDENCY PLAN. 1972. a. Department of Corrections and Human Services, 1539 11th Ave., Helena, MT 59620. TEL 406-449-3930. circ. 100. **Document type:** government publication.
     Formerly: Montana State Plan for Alcohol Abuse and Alcoholism Prevention, Treatment and Rehabilitation (ISSN 0090-3809)

306   362.29   616.89   SW   ISSN 0280-3348
MOTDRAG; Accent. 1980. bi-m. SEK 70 (effective 1990). U N F - Ungdomens Nykterhetsfoerbund, P.O. Box 1747, S-111 87 Stockholm, Sweden. TEL 46-8-789-49-50. FAX 46-8-20-43-54. Ed. Helena Karlsson.
     Incorporates (in 1988): Accent Ung; Former titles (until 1982): Motdrag foer Drogfrihet; (until 1981): Klartext om Droger (ISSN 0349-408X)

362   US   ISSN 1046-5421
THE N A WAY MAGAZINE. 1982. m. $15 (Canada $20). Narcotics Anonymous, World Service Office, Box 9999, Van Nuys, CA 91409. TEL 818-773-9999. FAX 818-700-0700. Ed. Cynthia Tooredman. illus. circ. 10,000. (back issues avail.)
     Formerly (until 1988): N.A. Way (ISSN 0896-9116)
     Description: Covers drug addiction, the N A recovery fellowship and more.

N C A A DRUG TESTING PROGRAM. (National Collegiate Athletic Association) see *SPORTS AND GAMES*

616.863   US   ISSN 0048-0673
N C I CATALYST; interfaith action on alcohol and other drug problems. 1967. s-a. $15. North Conway Institute, Inc., 168 Mount Vernon St., West Newton, MA 02165-2517. TEL 617-742-0424. Ed. Priscilla Martin. bk.rev.; bibl.; illus. circ. 2,500. **Document type:** newsletter.

616.861   US   ISSN 0147-0515
N I A A A - R U C A S ALCOHOLISM TREATMENT SERIES. (National Institute on Alcohol Abuse and Alcoholism - Rutgers University Center of Alcohol Studies) 1978. irreg. price varies. Rutgers Center of Alcohol Studies, Publications Division, c/o Charles Rouse, Bus. Admin., Box 969, Piscataway, NJ 08855. TEL 908-445-2190. Ed. Marc Schuckit. index. **Indexed:** Psychol.Abstr. **Document type:** monographic series.
     Formerly: N.I.A.A.A. - R.U.C.A.S. Alcoholism Treatment Monographs.

616.863   616.863   US   ISSN 1046-9516
                           CODEN: MIDAD
N I D A RESEARCH MONOGRAPH. 1975. irreg., no.121, 1992. free. U.S. National Institute on Drug Abuse, 5600 Fishers Lane, Rockville, MD 20857. TEL 301-443-6245. bibl.; charts. circ. 3,000. (also avail. in microfiche; back issues avail.) **Indexed:** Chem.Abstr., Curr.Cont., Excerp.Med., Ind.Med., Psychol.Abstr., Psychopharmacol.Abstr.
—CASDDS; CISTI; EMDOCS; KNAW.
     Formerly (until 1976): U.S. National Institute on Drug Abuse. Research Monograph Series (ISSN 0361-8595)

NARC OFFICER. see *LAW*

362.29   616.863   SW   ISSN 0281-3629
NARCONON-NYTT. 1977-1978; resumed 1982. q. SEK 100 (effective 1990). Riksorganisationen Narconon i Sverige (RONS), P.O. Box 3081, S-143 03 Vaarby, Sweden. Ed. Haakan Larsson. **Document type:** newspaper.

616.86   US   ISSN 0094-3991
HV5800
NARCOTICS AND DRUG ABUSE A TO Z. 1971. base vol. (plus q. supplements). $90. Croner Publications, Inc., 10951 Sorrento Valley Rd., Ste. 1-D, San Diego, CA 92121-1613. TEL 619-546-1894; 800-441-4033. FAX 619-546-1955. bibl. (looseleaf format) **Document type:** directory.
     Description: Lists narcotics and drugs and treatment centers arranged by state.

NARCOTICS LAW BULLETIN. see *CRIMINOLOGY AND LAW ENFORCEMENT*

362.29   SW   ISSN 0347-4836
NARKOTIKAFRAAGAN. 1971-1972; resumed 1976. bi-m. SEK 125 (effective 1997). R N S - Riksfoerbundet Narkotikafritt Samhaelle - National Association for a Drug Free Society, Ragvaldsgatan 14, 2tr, S-118 46 Stockholm, Sweden. TEL 46-8-643-04-67. FAX 46-8-643-04-98. Ed. Pelle Olsson. adv. contact: Ulla Soederberg. bk.rev.; circ. 19,000 (paid).
     Description: Focuses on drug problem and the drug policy in Sweden as well as international drug problems and treatment.

616.861   616.863   US
NATIONAL DIRECTORY OF DRUG ABUSE AND ALCOHOLISM TREATMENT AND PREVENTION PROGRAMS. 1979. a. free. U.S. Substance Abuse and Mental Health Services Administration, Office of Applied Studies, 5600 Fishers Ln., Rm. 16-105, Rockville, MD 20857. TEL 301-443-7934. FAX 301-443-9847. circ. 12,500. **Document type:** government publication, directory.

NERVNI I PSIKHICHNI ZABOLIAVANIIA. see *MEDICAL SCIENCES — Psychiatry And Neurology*

178   GW
NEUES VON SYNANON; der nuechterne Weg. q. free. Synanon e.V., Herzbergstr. 84, 10365 Berlin, Germany. TEL 49-30-55000-0. FAX 49-30-55000220. Ed. Erich Mayer. R&P contact: Erich Mayer. circ. 50,000. (back issues avail.) **Document type:** bulletin.
     Description: News and information from Synanon, a self-help group of former drug addicts and alcoholics.

616.861   US   ISSN 1068-302X
NEWSLETTER FROM DICK B. ON THE SPIRITUAL ROOTS OF ALCOHOLICS ANONYMOUS. 1992. bi-m. free. Good Book Publishing Co., Box 959, Kihei, HI 96753-0959. TEL 808-874-4876. FAX 808-874-4876. E-mail: dickb@dickb.com; URL: http://www.dickb.com. Ed. Richard G. Burns. bk.rev.; bibl.; index; circ. 800 (controlled). (looseleaf format; back issues avail.) **Document type:** newsletter.
     Description: Reports and reviews current research and writings on the spiritual history and successes of early A.A.

362.29   616.86   344   SW   ISSN 1102-9021
OBEROENDE. 1969. q. SEK 145 (effective 1997). R F H L - Riksfoerbundet foer Hjaelp aat Laekemedelsmissbrukare, P.O. Box 23076, S-104 35 Stockholm, Sweden. TEL 46-8-34-15-65.
     Former titles (until 1992): Slaa Tillbaka (ISSN 0349-2958); (until 1980): RFHL Kontakt (ISSN 0345-9993)

616.863   US
P R I D E QUARTERLY NEWSLETTER. q. (National Parents' Resource Institute for Drug Education, Inc.) Standard Press, 1210 Menlo Dr., Atlanta, GA 30318. TEL 404-351-6780. (Subscr. to: PRIDE, The Hurt Bldg., Ste. 210, 50 Hurt Plaza, Atlanta, GA 30303) Ed. Doug Hall. bk.rev.
     Description: Covers activities of PRIDE and information concerning drug education and prevention.

PATIENTENPOST. see *CHILDREN AND YOUTH — For*

616.863   615.19   US   ISSN 0278-6850
PHARMALERT. 1969. q. $8.50. University of Maryland, School of Pharmacy, Office of Substance Abuse Studies, Baltimore, MD 21201. FAX 301-328-7184. Ed. Trent Tschirgi. bibl.; illus.; stat. circ. 27,000. (tabloid format; back issues avail.) **Document type:** newsletter.

178   IE
PIONEER. 1948. m. I£10.50 (U.K. £11; elsewhere I£19) (effective 1997). Pioneer Total Abstinence Association, 27 Upper Sherrard St., Dublin 1, Ireland. TEL 353-1-8749464.
FAX 353-1-8748485. Ed. Maureen Manning. adv.: B&W page I£600, color page I£780; trim 297 x 210. bk.rev.; charts; illus. circ. 16,665. **Document type:** newsletter.
     Former titles: New Pioneer (ISSN 0332-1827); (until vol.33, Sep. 1980): Pioneer (ISSN 0031-997X)

PIPE CLUB; Magazin fuer Tabakgeniesser. see *TOBACCO*

616.86   BO
PREVENCION. irreg. free. Direccion Nacional de Prevencion Integral de Drogodependencias y Salud Mental, Av. 20 de Octubre 1819, Casilla 7194, La Paz, Bolivia. TEL 591-2-328390. Ed. Franklin Alcaraz del Castillo. R&P contact: Franklin Alcaraz del Castillo. **Document type:** monographic series.

616.86   US   ISSN 1040-9882
HV5285
PREVENTION PIPELINE; an alcohol and drug awareness service. Variant title: C S A P Prevention Pipeline. 1982. bi-m. $28 (foreign $32) (effective 1998). National Clearinghouse for Alcohol and Drug Information, Center for Substance Abuse Prevention, Box 2345, Rockville, MD 20847-2345. TEL 800-729-6686. FAX 301-468-6433. E-mail: info@prevline.health.org; URL: http://www.health. org. Ed. Barbara Ryan. circ. 3,200 (paid). **Document type:** government publication.
     Formerly (until 1987): Alcohol Awareness Service
     Description: Intended to stimulate an exchange of information and experiences among specialists in the field of drug and alcohol abuse prevention, focusing on the announcement of programmatic resources and selected scientific and technical literature, upcoming conferences, and news from the field.

DRUG ABUSE AND ALCOHOLISM

362.292   PL   ISSN 0032-9495
OBLEMY ALKOHOLIZMU. (Text in Polish; summaries in English) 1953. m. 60000 Zl. Polska Liga "Trzezwosc", Ul. Kopernika 36-40, 00-924 Warsaw, Poland. TEL 48-22-6358620. Ed. Jan Brodzki. bk.rev.; abstr. circ. 34,080. (back issues avail.)
—BLDSC (6617.945500).
   Supersedes in part (in 1976): Problemy Alkoholizmu, Zdrowie i Trzezwosc (ISSN 0137-3889); Which was formed by the merger of (1957-1975): Zdrowie i Trzezwosc (ISSN 0867-3632); (1966-1975): Problemy Alkoholizmu (ISSN 0239-4308); Which was formerly (1953-1965): Walka z Alkoholizmem (ISSN 0509-5948).

OFESSIONAL COUNSELOR MAGAZINE; serving the mental health and addictions fields. see *PSYCHOLOGY*

616.86   NE   ISSN 0921-8742
OGRESS IN ALCOHOL RESEARCH. (Text in English) 1985. irreg., vol.2, 1990. price varies. V S P, P.O. Box 346, 3700 AH Zeist, Netherlands. TEL 31-30-6925790. FAX 31-30-6932081. E-mail: 100341.2372@compuserve.com. (Dist. in U.S. and Canada by: Books International Inc., Box 605, Herndon, VA 22070. TEL 703-661-1500. FAX 703-661-1501) Ed. H. Ollat. (back issues avail.) **Document type:** monographic series.
—BLDSC (6865.902500); KNAW.

616.86   CN   ISSN 0229-2947
OJECTION (TORONTO); an audio-visual review service. 1971. bi-m. Can.$18 (foreign Can.$23). Addiction Research Foundation of Ontario, Marketing Department, 33 Russell St., Toronto, ON M5S 2S1, Canada. TEL 416-595-6059; 800-661-1111. FAX 416-593-4694. Ed. Debbie Monkman. film rev. circ. 750. (looseleaf format)

616.861   XO   ISSN 0862-0350
OTIALKOHOLICKY OBZOR. (Text in Czech or Slovak; summaries in English, German, Russian) 1966. bi-m. $27. (Ministry of Health Care of the Slovak Republic) Obzor, Spitalska 35, 815 85 Bratislava, Slovakia. (Co-sponsor: Institute of Further Education of Physicians and Pharmacists)

616.86   US   ISSN 0893-164X
RC563   CODEN: PABEEI
YCHOLOGY OF ADDICTIVE BEHAVIORS. 1987. 4/yr. $58 to non-members (foreign $73); members $47 (foreign $55); institutions $70 (foreign $100) (effective 1997). American Psychological Association, 750 First St., N.E., Washington, DC 20002-4242. TEL 202-336-5600; 800-374-3721. FAX 202-336-5568. E-mail: subscriptions@apa.org; URL: http://www.apa.org/journals/adb.html. Ed. Susan J. Curry. adv. contact: Jodi Ashcraft. bk.rev. circ. 725. (back issues avail.) **Indexed:** ASCA, Curr.Cont., Excerp.Med. (1995-), Fam.Ind., Psychol.Abstr. (1981-), Soc.Work Res.& Abstr. **Document type:** academic/scholarly publication.
—BLDSC (6946.535315); Genuine Article; UnCover. **CCC.**
   Former titles (until 1987): Society of Psychologists in Addictive Behaviors. Bulletin; Society of Psychologists in Substance Abuse. Bulletin.
   Description: Covers alcoholism, drug abuse, eating disorders, smoking and nicotine addiction, and other compulsive behaviors such as gambling.
   Refereed Serial

BLIC HEALTH REVIEWS; an international quarterly. see *PUBLIC HEALTH AND SAFETY*

AL TALK. see *CHILDREN AND YOUTH — For*

616.863   US   ISSN 0738-422X
HV5001   CODEN: RDALE9
CENT DEVELOPMENTS IN ALCOHOLISM. irreg., vol.13, 1997. price varies. (American Medical Society on Alcoholism) Plenum Publishing Corp., 233 Spring St., New York, NY 10013-1578. TEL 212-620-8000. FAX 212-463-0742. TELEX 23-421139. E-mail: books@plenum.com. (Co-sponsor: Research Society on Alcoholism) Ed. Marc Galanter. **Indexed:** Dent.Ind., Ind.Med., Psychol.Abstr. **Document type:** monographic series.
—BLDSC (7304.104500); CASDDS; KNAW. **CCC.**
   Refereed Serial

616.86   US   ISSN 1061-7191
RECOVERY TODAY; the newsmagazine for today's recovering community. 1990. m. $15. Recovery Today, 1313 S. Military Tr., Ste. 314, Deerfield Beach, FL 33442. TEL 407-488-6362. Ed. Kathleen Low. circ. 30,000. (tabloid format)
   Description: Focuses on recovery from alcoholism, drug addiction and eating disorders. Promotes personal growth.

362.29   SA   ISSN 0034-3471
REGMAKER. (Text in Afrikaans, English) 1968. bi-m. R.3.60 per no. Alcoholics Anonymous South Africa, General Service Office of Alcoholics Anonymous, Box 23005, Joubert Park, Johannesburg, South Africa. Ed. Eddie McGinn. circ. 1,700.

616.861   US
REPORT ON ALCOHOL, DRUGS, AND DISABILITY. 1992. q. free. National Association on Alcohol, Drugs, and Disability, 2165 Bunker Hill Dr., San Mateo, CA 94402. TEL 415-578-8047. Ed. John de Miranda. bk.rev. circ. 1,500. (also avail. in audio cassette) **Document type:** newsletter.
   Description: Includes a calendar of events and activities, legislative updates, successful program descriptions, editorial opinion, leadership profiles, and networking opportunities.

616.8   US   ISSN 0093-9714
RC565   CODEN: RAALBJ
RESEARCH ADVANCES IN ALCOHOL & DRUG PROBLEMS. 1974. irreg., vol.11, 1994. price varies. Plenum Publishing Corp., 233 Spring St., New York, NY 10013-1578. TEL 212-620-8000.
FAX 212-463-0742. TELEX 23-421139. E-mail: books@plenum.com. Ed. Yedy Israel. **Indexed:** ASCA, Biol.Abstr. **Document type:** monographic series.
—BLDSC (7714.375000); CISTI; KNAW. **CCC.**
   Refereed Serial

RESEARCH COMMUNICATIONS IN ALCOHOL & SUBSTANCES OF ABUSE. see *PHARMACY AND PHARMACOLOGY*

362.29   GW   ISSN 0048-7430
RETTUNG. 1906. w. DM.21.60. (Blaues Kreuz in Deutschland e.V.) Blaukreuz Verlag, Freiligrathstr. 27, 42289 Wuppertal, Germany. Ed. Alexander Schubert. bk.rev.; abstr.; illus.; stat. circ. 8,600. (reprint service avail. from KTO) **Document type:** bulletin.
—**CCC.**

616.861   AT
REVIVER. 1954. m. Aus.$24. Alcoholics Anonymous Central Service Office, 127 Edwin St., Croydon, N.S.W. 2132, Australia. TEL 61-2-97991199. FAX 61-2-9716754. circ. 2,500 (paid). **Document type:** consumer publication, directory.
   Refereed Serial

616.8   US
RUTGERS CENTER OF ALCOHOL STUDIES. MONOGRAPH. 1958. irreg., no.14, 1981. price varies. Rutgers Center of Alcohol Studies, Publications Division, c/o Charles Rouse, Bus. Admin., Box 969, Piscataway, NJ 08855. TEL 908-445-2190. Ed. Marc Schuckit. index. **Indexed:** Biol.Abstr. **Document type:** monographic series.
   Formerly: Rutgers University. Center of Alcohol Studies. Monograph (ISSN 0080-4983)

S A L I S DIRECTORY. (Substance Abuse Librarians and Information Specialists) see *LIBRARY AND INFORMATION SCIENCES*

S A L I S NEWS. (Substance Abuse Librarians and Information Specialists) see *LIBRARY AND INFORMATION SCIENCES*

616.861   US
S A M H S A NEWS. bi-m. $9.50 (foreign $11.90) (effective 1995). U.S. Substance Abuse and Mental Health Services Administration, Office of Applied Studies, 5600 Fishers Ln., Rm. 16-105, Rockville, MD 20857. TEL 301-443-7934.
FAX 301-443-9847. (Subscr. to: Superintendent of Documents, U.S. Government Printing Office, Box 371954, Pittsburgh, PA 15250-7954. TEL 202-512-1800. FAX 202-512-2250) (back issues avail.) **Document type:** newsletter, government publication.
   Description: Publishes articles on agency-related issues, such as AIDS, alcoholism, drug abuse, and general mental health. Publicizes agency events.

354   CN   ISSN 1185-295X
HV5283.C32
SASKATCHEWAN. ALCOHOL AND DRUG ABUSE COMMISSION. ANNUAL REPORT. 1969. a. free. Saskatchewan Alcohol and Drug Abuse Commission, Prevention and Training Division, 1942 Hamilton St., Regina, SK S4P 3V7, Canada. TEL 306-787-4085. FAX 306-787-9000. illus.; stat. circ. 1,000.
   Former titles (until 1986): Saskatchewan Alcoholism Commission. Annual Report (ISSN 0825-7795); Alcoholism Commission of Saskatchewan. Annual Report (ISSN 0381-2278)

SCHOOL INTERVENTION REPORT. see *CHILDREN AND YOUTH — About*

SMOKE; cigars, pipes and life's other burning desires. see *GENERAL INTEREST PERIODICALS — United States*

SMOKING AND HEALTH NEWSLETTER. see *PHYSICAL FITNESS AND HYGIENE*

616.86   US   ISSN 1059-6259
SOBER TIMES;* the recovery magazine. 1987. bi-m. $16.50 (foreign $39). Box 13013, Mill Creek, WA 98082-1013. Ed. Cliff Creager; Pub. Jerauld D. Miller. adv. contact: Joe Wooley. bk.rev.; circ. 80,000. **Document type:** consumer publication.
   Description: Focuses on ways to maintain happy, healthy lives, free of substance abuse and compulsive behavior.

362.292   US   ISSN 1071-4111
SOBERING THOUGHTS. 1976. m. $18. Women for Sobriety, Inc., Box 618, Quakertown, PA 18951. TEL 610-536-8026. Ed. Dr. Jean Kirkpatrick. bk.rev.; index. circ. 5,000. (back issues avail.) **Document type:** newsletter.
   Formerly: Women for Sobriety. Newsletter.
   Description: For women who are recovering alcoholics. Contains personal reminiscences, inspirational articles, poetry, and news of self-help groups worldwide.

616.86   CN   ISSN 0845-924X
HD9390.C23
SOCIETE DES ALCOOLS DU QUEBEC. RAPPORT ANNUEL. (Vols. for 1967/68-1969/70 issued by the Board under its French form of name: Regie des Alcools du Quebec) 1971. a. free. Societe des Alcools du Quebec, 905 DeLorimier, Montreal, PQ H2K 3V9, Canada. TEL 514-873-7225. E-mail: info@saq.qc.ca; URL: http://www.saq.com. Ed. Josee Rondeau. R&P contact: Josee Rondeau. adv. contact: Sonia Gagnon. **Document type:** government publication, corporate report.
   Former titles (until 1985): Societe des Alcools du Quebec. Rapport d'Activite (ISSN 0715-8254); (until 1982): Societe des Alcools du Quebec. Rapport Annuel (ISSN 0715-884X); Which has English editions (1972-1974): Quebec Liquor Corporation. Annual Report (ISSN 0715-8858); (1962-1971): Quebec (Province). Liquor Board. Annual Report (ISSN 0481-2875)

616   US   ISSN 0898-6002
HV5285
STATE RESOURCES AND SERVICES FOR ALCOHOL AND DRUG ABUSE PROBLEMS. irreg. Alcohol, Drug Abuse, and Mental Health Administration, 5600 Fisheries Ln., Rockwall II Bldg., Rockville, MD 20857.

616.86   US
STATE SUBSTANCE ABUSE QUARTERLY. 1971. q. $80 to individuals; institutions $100 (effective 1997). National Association of State Alcohol and Drug Abuse Directors, 808 17th St., N.W., Ste. 410, Washington, DC 20006. TEL 202-293-0090. FAX 202-293-1250. E-mail: dcoffice@nasadad.org. Eds. Stephanie McGencey, Kathleen Sheehan. circ. 600 (paid). (back issues avail.) **Document type:** newsletter.
   Incorporates: National Prevention Network News; Former titles: Public Policy Quarterly; Alcohol and Drug Abuse Public Policy Quarterly; Alcohol and Drug Abuse Report (ISSN 0270-2770)
   Description: Includes news of legislation and national reports and studies.

DRUG ABUSE AND ALCOHOLISM

616.86   NO   ISSN 0333-144X
STOFFMISBRUK. (Text in Norwegian) 1980. 6/yr. NOK 450 in Nordic countries; elsewhere $90 (effective 1997). Scandinavian University Press, P.O. Box 2959 Toeyen, N-0608 Oslo, Norway. TEL 47-22-57-54-00. FAX 47-22-57-53-53. E-mail: mail@scup.no; URL: http://www.scup.no. (US addr.: 875 Massachusetts Ave., Ste. 84, Cambridge, MA 02139. TEL 617-497-6515. FAX 617-354-6875) Ed. Martin Blindheim. adv.; bk.rev. circ. 5,000. **Document type:** academic/scholarly publication.
—CCC.
   Description: Presents information and debate on drug problems in Norway and internationally.

STRAIGHT TALK (PLEASANTVILLE); a magazine for teens. see *CHILDREN AND YOUTH — For*

616.863   US   ISSN 0735-6544
RM301.15
STREET PHARMACOLOGIST. 1978. 4/yr. $25. Up Front, Inc., 5701 Biscayne Blvd., Ste. 602, Miami, FL 33137. TEL 305-757-2566. FAX 305-758-4676. Ed. James N. Hall. bk.rev.; film rev.; bibl.; charts; illus.; stat.; index, cum.index: 1978-1983. circ. 1,500. (back issues avail.)
   Description: Discusses substance abuse trends and other drug-related issues.

STREETWIZE COMICS; youth rights comics. see *CHILDREN AND YOUTH — For*

616.86   US   ISSN 1042-6388
STUDENT ASSISTANCE JOURNAL. 1988. 5/yr. $34 (Canada $43; elsewhere $52) (effective 1997). Performance Resource Press, Inc., 1270 Rankin Dr., Ste. F, Troy, MI 48083-2843. TEL 810-588-7733. FAX 810-588-6633. Ed. Gerri Andrews. film rev.; tr.lit. circ. 10,000. (back issues avail.) **Indexed:** Soc.Work Res.& Abstr. **Document type:** trade publication.
   Description: Looks at the various personal problems of students and how they affect their behavior at school. Emphasis is on drug abuse and alcoholism.

616.863   US   ISSN 0889-7077
SUBSTANCE ABUSE. 1984. q. $225 (foreign $265) (effective 1998). (Association for Medical Education and Research in Substance Abuse) Plenum Publishing Corp., 233 Spring St., New York, NY 10013-1578. TEL 212-620-8000. FAX 212-463-0742. (Editorial addr.: c/o Center for Alcohol & Addiction Studies, Brown University, Box G-BH, Providence, RI 02912) Ed. Marc Galanten. bk.rev. circ. 600. **Document type:** academic/scholarly publication.
—UnCover.
   Description: International, interdisciplinary forum for the publication of original empirical research papers and reviews in the field of addiction and substance abuse. Topics covered include clinical and preclinical research, education, health-service delivery, and policy.
Refereed Serial

362.293   US   ISSN 1076-979X
SUBSTANCE ABUSE LETTER; an independent report on prevention and treatment issues. s-m. $195. Pace Publications, 443 Park Ave. S., New York, NY 10016. TEL 212-685-5450. FAX 212-679-4701. Ed. Molly Parrish. (looseleaf format) **Document type:** newsletter.

616.863   US   ISSN 1040-4163
SUBSTANCE ABUSE REPORT; twice-monthly newsletter covering all aspects of drug abuse: its prevention, detection and treatment. 1970. s-m. $275. Business Research Publications, Inc., 65 Bleecker St., 5th FL., New York, NY 10012-2450. TEL 212-673-4700. FAX 212-475-1790. Ed. Alison Knopf. bk.rev. **Document type:** trade publication. ●Also available online. Vendor(s): Information Access Co.
   Former titles: Addiction and Substance Abuse Report (ISSN 0160-967X); Addiction and Drug Abuse Report (ISSN 0001-8074)
   Description: Analyzes developments in the field of substance abuse treatment. Contains news and information on treatment programs, medical research and laboratory breakthroughs written for a professional audience.

616.86 157.6   US   ISSN 1082-6084
RC566.A1   CODEN: SUMIFL
SUBSTANCE USE AND MISUSE. 1966. 14/yr. $1675 (foreign $1727.50) (effective 1998). Marcel Dekker Journals, 270 Madison Ave., New York, NY 10016. TEL 212-696-9000. FAX 212-685-4540. TELEX 421419. (Subscr. to: Box 5017, Monticello, NY 12701. TEL 800-228-1160) Ed. Stanley Einstein. adv. contact: Lourdes Barroso. charts. circ. 700. (also avail. in microform) **Indexed:** Abstr.Crim.& Pen., Adol.Ment.Hlth.Abstr., ASCA, ASSIA, Biol.Abstr., Chem.Abstr., Crim.Just.Abstr., Curr.Cont., Excerp.Med., Fam.Ind., I.P.A., Ind.Med., Ind.Sci.Rev., Mid.East: Abstr.& Ind., Psychol.Abstr. (1971-), Risk Abstr., Sci.Cit.Ind., Soc.Work Res.& Abstr., SSCI. **Document type:** academic/scholarly publication.
—BLDSC (8503.493000); ADONIS; CISTI; EMDOCS; Genuine Article; KNAW; SWETS; UMI; UnCover. **CCC**.
   Formerly (until vol.31, 1996): International Journal of the Addictions (ISSN 0020-773X)
Refereed Serial

616.861   GW   ISSN 0939-5911
SUCHT. 1955. bi-m. DM.132 (foreign DM.174) (effective 1997). (Deutsche Hauptstelle Gegen die Suchtgefahren) Neuland Verlagsgesellschaft mbH, Markt 24-26, 21502 Geesthacht, Germany. TEL 49-4152-81342. FAX 49-4152-81343. Ed. Rolf Huellinghorst. R&P contact: Jens Burmester. adv. contact: Jens Burmester. bk.rev.; index. circ. 3,000. **Indexed:** Excerp.Med. **Document type:** academic/scholarly publication.
—BLDSC (8505.640000); EMDOCS; KNAW; SWETS. **CCC**.
   Formerly (until 1991): Suchtgefahren (ISSN 0491-421X)
Refereed Serial

178   GW   ISSN 0930-8350
SUCHTREPORT. 6/yr. DM.54 (Europe DM.60; elsewhere DM.64). Synanon e.V., Herzbergstr. 84, 10365 Berlin, Germany. TEL 49-30-55000-0. FAX 49-30-55000220. Ed. Andrea Schirz. R&P contact: Andrea Schirz. adv. contact: Andrea Schirz. **Document type:** bulletin.

TABAC ET SANTE; tabagisme. see *PHYSICAL FITNESS AND HYGIENE*

616.863   US
TAKING SIDES: CLASHING VIEWS ON CONTROVERSIAL ISSUES IN DRUGS AND SOCIETY. 1993. irreg. $13.95. Dushkin Publishing Group, Sluice Dock, Guilford, CT 06437-9989. TEL 203-453-4351. Ed. Raymond Goldberg; Pub. Mimi Egan. illus. **Document type:** academic/scholarly publication.

616.86   NE   ISSN 0378-2778
RC566.A1
TIJDSCHRIFT VOOR ALCOHOL, DRUGS EN ANDERE PSYCHOTROPE STOFFEN. (Text in Dutch; summaries in Dutch and English) 1975. 4/yr. fl.100 (students fl.85). Stichting T A D P, P.O. Box 725, 3500 AS Utrecht. Ed.Bd. adv.; bk.rev. circ. 1,500. (back issues avail.) **Indexed:** Abstr.Crim.& Pen., Psychol.Abstr. (1984-). **Document type:** academic/scholarly publication.
—BLDSC (8837.860000); EMDOCS; KNAW; SWETS.

615.9   AG   ISSN 0325-3961
TOXICOMANIAS. 1974. 3/yr. Paraguay 2155, Buenos Aires, Argentina.

616.863   US
TWELVE STEP RAG. 1972. bi-m. $4.50 (effective 1996). Families Anonymous, Inc., Box 3475, Culver City, CA 90231-3475. TEL 310-313-5800; 800-736-9805. FAX 310-313-6841. E-mail: famanon@earthlink.net; URL: http://home.earthlink.net/~famanon/index.html. circ. 3,500. **Document type:** newsletter, catalog, directory.
   Description: For families and friends affected by someone else's use of drugs and alcohol or related behavioral problems.
Refereed Serial

178   UK   ISSN 0969-2029
U K ALCOHOL ALERT. 1854. q. £15 (foreign £18). United Kingdom Temperance Alliance Ltd., Alliance House, 12 Caxton St., London SW1H 0QS, England. TEL 44-171-222-5880. FAX 44-171-799-2510. Ed. D. Rutherford. adv.; bk.rev.; abstr.; charts; illus.; stat. circ. 5,000. **Document type:** newsletter.
—BLDSC (9082.651270).
   Formerly: United Kingdom Temperance Alliance. Alliance News (ISSN 0309-3115)
   Description: Presents news articles, briefs, and commentary on government policies and social activities directed against drug, alcohol, and tobacco use and abuse.

178   US   ISSN 0041-7033
UNION SIGNAL. 1875. q. $8. National Woman's Christian Temperance Union, 1730 Chicago Ave., Evanston, IL 60201. TEL 847-864-1396. Ed. Sarah F. Ward. R&P contact: Michael C. Vitucci. adv. contact: Michael C. Vitucci. illus.; circ. 10,000 (controlled). (also avail. in microform from UMI)

613.83   UN   ISSN 0085-7491
UNITED NATIONS. DIVISION OF NARCOTIC DRUGS. INFORMATION LETTER. (Editions in Arabic, English, French, and Spanish) 1971. bi-m. free. United Nations, Division of Narcotic Drugs, Vienna International Centre, P.O. Box 500, A-1400 Vienna, Austria. Ed. L. Manueco Jenkins. bk.rev. circ. 12,000.

616.863 610   US   ISSN 0098-311X
RA1242.T6
U.S. SURGEON GENERAL. REPORT. (Includes sub-series: Health Benefits of Smoking Cessation; Health Consequences of Involuntary Smoking; Health Consequences of Smoking; Health Consequences of Smoking for Women; Preventing Tobacco Use Among Young People; Reducing the Health Consequences of Smoking; Smoking and Health in the Americas) 1964. a. free. U.S. Centers for Disease Control, National Center for Chronic Disease Prevention and Health Promotion, Office on Smoking and Health, 4770 Buford Hwy., N.E., MS K-50, Atlanta, GA 30341-3724. TEL 404-488-5705; 800-CDC-1311. FAX 404-488-5939. (Orders to: Superintendent of Documents, U.S. Government Printing Office, Box 371954, Pittsburgh, PA 15250-7954. TEL 202-512-1800. FAX 202-512-2250; Alt. addr.: U.S. Centers for Disease Control, MS K-12, 1600 Clifton Rd., N.E., Atlanta, GA 30333) bibl.; charts; illus.; stat.; index, cum.index: 1964-1982; circ. controlled. **Document type:** consumer publication, government publication.
—CISTI.
   Description: Addresses the prevention and cessation of tobacco use and the protection of nonsmokers.

178   NE   ISSN 0028-999X
VERANTWOORD LEVENSVERKEER. 1945. q. fl.10. Sobrietas, Postbus 262, 5550 AG Valkenswaard, Netherlands. adv.; bk.rev. circ. 2,000. (looseleaf format)
   Formerly: Mededelingenblad van Sobrietas.

VICTORY SCARS; through the eyes of recovering women. see *WOMEN'S INTERESTS*

178   UK   ISSN 0043-4973
THE WHITE RIBBON. 1896. q. £2. The White Ribbon Association, Rosalind Carlisle House, 23 Dawson Place, London W2 4TH, England. TEL 44-171-229-0804. Ed. Maureen Long. R&P contact: Maureen Long. adv.; bk.rev.; illus. circ. 1,000. **Document type:** newsletter.

178   US   ISSN 0043-4965
WHITE RIBBON BULLETIN. 1883. q. $4 (foreign $7) (effective 1997). (World's Woman's Christian Temperance Union) M & D Printing Co., R.I. Box 43 Lowpoint, IL 61545. TEL 309-443-5275. FAX 309-364-3355. Ed. Mrs. Melvin Christ. bk.rev circ. 4,250. **Document type:** newsletter.
Refereed Serial

616.8   US   ISSN 0043-5937
WINNER (HAGERSTOWN). 1957. m. (during school term). $8.97. Health Connection, 55 W. Oak Ridge Dr., Hagerstown, MD 21740. TEL 301-745-3888. Ed. Lincoln Steed. charts; illus. circ. 35,000.

DRUG ABUSE AND ALCOHOLISM — Abstracting, Bibliographies, Statistics

616.863 362.29 US
HV4997
WORKPLACE SUBSTANCE ABUSE ADVISOR. 1986. bi-w. $377 (foreign $399) (effective 1997). L R P Publications, 747 Dresher Rd., Box 908, Horsham, PA 19044-0980. TEL 215-784-0941; 800-341-7874. FAX 215-784-9639. URL: http://www.lrp.com. Ed. Karin Lillis. index. (back issues avail.) **Document type:** newsletter.
●Also available online. Vendor(s): Human Resources Information Network (CDD, HDD).
—CCC.
Formerly (until 1996): National Report on Substance Abuse (ISSN 0891-5709)
Description: Reviews federal, state, local laws and regulations involving alcohol and drug use, testing policies, EAP's, court decisions, and drug enforcement budgets.

178 360 US
WORLD'S WOMAN'S CHRISTIAN TEMPERANCE UNION. TRIENNIAL REPORT. 1891. triennial. $5. World's Woman's Christian Temperance Union, HCR 3, Box 155, Wannaska, MN 56761. Ed. Pearl Loe. bk.rev.; index. circ. 600.
Formerly: World's Woman's Christian Temperance Union. Convention Report (ISSN 0084-2540)

616.86 PL ISSN 0513-8809
ZDROWIE I TRZEZWOSC.* 1976. m. 180000 Zl. Polska Liga "Trzezwosc", Ul. Kopernika 36-40, 00-924 Warsaw, Poland. TEL 48-22-6358620. Ed. Henryk Babendich. circ. 70,000. (back issues avail.)
Supersedes in part (in 1976): Problemy Alkoholizmu, Zdrowie i Trzezwosc (ISSN 0137-3889); Which was formed by the merger of (1957-1975): Zdrowie i Trzezwosc (ISSN 0867-3632); (1966-1975): Problemy Alkoholizmu (ISSN 0239-4308); Which was formerly (1953-1965): Walka z Alkoholizmem (ISSN 0509-5948).

DRUG ABUSE AND ALCOHOLISM — Abstracting, Bibliographies, Statistics

616.861 157.61
016 US ISSN 0161-1267
BOTTOM LINE (LANSING); on alcohol in society. (Former name of issuing body: American Business Men's Research Foundation) 1974. q. $20 (foreign $30) (effective 1997 & 1998). Alcohol Research Information Service, 1106 E. Oakland Ave., Lansing, MI 48906. TEL 517-485-9900. FAX 517-485-1928. Ed. Robert Hammond. R&P contact: Robert Hammond. bk.rev. circ. 5,000. **Document type:** academic/scholarly publication.
Formed by the 1977 merger of: Alcohol Abstracts; Report on Alcohol (ISSN 0002-7774); Viewpoint.
Description: Deals with research, issues, events and opinions relating to public policy in the field of alcohol problems, with special emphasis on prevention.

DRUG FILE UPDATE; a current awareness index to publications on drugs and doping in sport. see *SPORTS AND GAMES — Abstracting, Bibliographies, Statistics*

OOM. see *CHILDREN AND YOUTH — For*

016 613.83 NE ISSN 0925-5958
CODEN: DRDPA
EXCERPTA MEDICA. SECTION 40: DRUG DEPENDENCE, ALCOHOL ABUSE AND ALCOHOLISM. 1973. bi-m. fl.1595($917) (effective 1998). Elsevier Science B.V., P.O. Box 211, 1000 AE Amsterdam, Netherlands. TEL 31-20-4853757. FAX 31-20-4853432. TELEX 18582 ESPA NL. E-mail: nlinfo-f@elsevier.nl; URL: http://www.elsevier.nl/. (Subscr. in the Americas to: Elsevier Science, Regional Sales Office, Box 945, New York, NY 10159-0945. TEL 212-633-3730. FAX 212-633-3680; Subscr. in Australasia and the Far East to: Elsevier Science (Singapore) Pte Ltd, No.1 Temasek Ave., No.17-01 Millenia Tower, Singapore 039192, Singapore. TEL 65-434-3727. FAX 65-337-2230; Subscr. in Japan to: Elsevier Science Japan, 9-15 Higashi-Azabu 1-chome, Minato-ku Tokyo 106, Japan. TEL 81-3-5561-5033. FAX 81-3-5561-5047) Ed.Bd. adv.; index, cum.index. **Document type:** abstracting/indexing.
●Also available online. Vendor(s): DIMDI, Data-Star, JICST, Knight-Ridder Information, Inc., Ovid Technologies, Inc.
Also available on CD-ROM. Producer(s): SilverPlatter Information, Inc.
—BLDSC (3835.828920); CISTI; Linda Hall. **CCC.**
Formerly: Excerpta Medica. Section 40: Drug Dependence (ISSN 0304-4041)
Description: Covers all aspects of the abuse of drugs, alcohol and organic solvents and includes material relating to experimental pharmacology of addiction.

616.861 016 US ISSN 0074-204X
INTERNATIONAL BIBLIOGRAPHY OF STUDIES ON ALCOHOL. 1966. irreg. price varies. Rutgers Center of Alcohol Studies, Publications Division, c/o Charles Rouse, Bus. Admin., Box 969, Piscataway, NJ 08855. TEL 908-445-2190. Ed. Marc Schuckit. index. **Document type:** bibliography.

INTERNATIONAL NARCOTICS CONTROL BOARD. PSYCHOTROPIC SUBSTANCES; assessments of medical and scientific requirements for substances in schedules II, III and IV. Requirements of import authorization for substances in schedules III and IV. see *PHARMACY AND PHARMACOLOGY — Abstracting, Bibliographies, Statistics*

616.86 011 GW ISSN 0932-4240
SUCHTINFORMATION. (Text in English or German) 1987. irreg. DM.13 per no. Landesinstitut fuer den Oeffentlichen Gesundheitsdienst des Landes Nordrhein-Westfalen, Westerfeldstr. 35-37, 33611 Bielefeld, Germany. TEL 49-521-8007265. FAX 49-521-8007297. (Subscr. to: Postfach 201012, 33548 Bielefeld, Germany) **Document type:** abstracting/indexing.